BOOKS IN PRINT SUPPLEMENT
1982-1983

Senior staff of the Department of Bibliography includes:
Andrew H. Uszak, Senior Vice President, Data Services/Systems;
Peter Simon, Database Manager;
R. Dean Hollister, Ernest Lee, Brenda Sutton, Emilia Tomaszewski,
Senior Product Managers;
Anne Wilson, Project Manager;
Beverley McDonough, Quality Control Editor;
Andrew Grabois, Michael Olenick, Rebecca Olmo,
Editorial Coordinators;
Jacqueline Artis, Paul Deland, Basmattie Gravesande,
Brian Leonard, Malcolm MacDermott, Kelly McNeill,
Constance Mariner, Jane Marlowe, Helen Murray,
Hyacinth Myers, Beverly Palacio,
Brian Phair, John Rush, Joanne Schwendner, Maria Sillitti,
John Thompson, Frances Walsh, and Sonja Wright,
Assistant Editors.

Michael B. Howell, Manager, Systems Planning.

BOOKS IN PRINT SUPPLEMENT 1982-1983

Volume 1

Authors
Subjects

R. R. BOWKER COMPANY
New York & London

Published by R. R. Bowker Company (a Xerox Publishing Company)
1180 Avenue of the Americas, New York, N.Y. 10036

International Standard Book Number set: 0-8352-1664-0
Vol. 1—0-8352-1665-9
Vol. 2—0-8352-1666-7
International Standard Serial Number 0000-0310
Library of Congress Catalog Card Number 4-12648

Printed and Bound in the United States of America

DATA BASES and PUBLICATIONS of the Department of Bibliography

BIPS DATA BASE

Books in Print Supplement 1982-1983 was produced from the BIPS Data Base of the R. R. Bowker Company. This data base is used to produce a complete, complementary line of bibliographic publications that give booksellers, librarians, publishers, and all other book, on-line, and microfiche users access to the latest bibliographic and ordering information. Following is a description of this data base and its publications.

The bibliographic data base was begun in 1948 primarily as a listing of titles included in Bowker's *Publishers' Trade List Annual (PTLA)*. The computerization of this data base during the late nineteen-sixties using the Bibliographic Information Publication System (BIPS) made it possible for Bowker to expand the amount of information included in the bibliographic entries and to increase the number of essential tools of the trade we produced.

During the early nineteen-seventies the data base was greatly expanded to include information from additional publishers whose titles were not included in *PTLA*. Since that time, the data base has been composed of and compiled from information received on an on-going basis directly from publishers. Prior to each publication from the data base, publishers review and correct their entries, providing current price, availability, and ordering information and update their list with recently published and forthcoming titles.

The data base includes scholarly, popular, adult, juvenile, reprint, and all other types of books covering all subjects provided they are published or exclusively distributed in the United States and are available to the trade or to the general public for single or multiple copy purchase. All editions and bindings are included: hardcover, paperbound, library binding, perfect binding, boards, spiral binding, text editions, teachers' editions, and workbooks.

Bibles as such are excluded, although commentaries, histories, and versions other than the standard English are extensively covered. Free books, books priced at less than 25 cents, unbound materials, pamphlets, periodicals, serials, government publications, puzzles, calendars, maps, microforms, audio-visual materials, and most books available only to members of a particular organization, subscription-only titles or those sold only to schools are omitted. Spanish language books published outside of the United States are not included, but are covered in *Libros En Venta*.

Bibliographic entries contain the following information when available: author, co-author, editor, co-editor, translator, co-translator, title, original title, number of volumes, volume number, edition, whether or not reprinted, Library of Congress number, subject information, series information, language if other than English, whether or not illustrated, page numbers, grade range, date of publication, type of binding if other than cloth over boards, price, ISBN, imprint, publisher, and distributor, if other than the publisher.

In addition to the various publications described below, the full BIPS data base is available for use through online services and microfiche. In these media, two years of out-of-print information are included as well.

Other data bases of the Data Services Division include: the Department of Bibliography's Textbook Data Base, Publishers' Authority Data Base, Associations Publications Data Base, Law Books Data Base, and the Serials Bibliography Department's Bowker Serial Bibliography Data Base.

Data Services Division's other publications include: *American Book Publishing Record, American Book Publishing Record Cumulative, 1876-1949, American Book Publishing Record Cumulative, 1950-1977, Art Books, 1950-1979, Associations' Publications in Print, Health Science Books, 1876-1982, Irregular Serials and Annuals, Law Books 1876-1981, Performing Arts Books 1876-1981, Pure and Applied Science Books, 1876-1982, Ulrich's International Periodicals Directory, Weekly Record*, and *World Museum Publications*.

DESCRIPTION OF PUBLICATIONS

Books In Print

An annual publication listing all in-print and forthcoming titles from more than 13,900 publishers.

Indexes: *Author/Title/New Publishers & Distributors/Key to Publishers' & Distributors' Abbreviations/ Directory of U.S. Publishers & Distributors*

Subject Guide to Books In Print

A companion volume to *Books In Print,* this annual lists all in-print and forthcoming titles except fiction, literature, poetry, and drama by one author, under approximately 61,700 Library of Congress (LC) subject headings.

Indexes: *Subject/Key to Publishers' & Distributors' Abbreviations*

Publishers, Distributors and Wholesalers in the United States

The main index of this publication contains the full name with editorial and ordering addresses for some 39,000 publishers currently listed in Bowker's Publisher Authority Data Base and active in the United States. In addition, an ISBN index supplies the ISBN prefixes, a Key to Publishers' Abbreviations Index supplies the publishers' abbreviations from *Books in Print,* and a Wholesalers Index supplies the full name and addresses for United States Wholesalers. This directory is a useful companion tool to users of *Books in Print* as it increases the number of people who can use it simultaneously, and to librarians, booksellers, and others who need a comprehensive and up-to-date directory of U.S. publishing companies.

Indexes: *Publisher Name/BIP Abbreviation/ ISBN Prefix/Wholesalers*

Books In Print Supplement

An annual publication which updates *Books In Print* by listing all entries which have changes or additions to price, date of publication, ISBN, LC card number, or availability. Expands *Books In Print* by listing backlist titles new to the data base and titles published since January or forthcoming through July. Expands *Subject Guide To Books In Print* by listing all new and forthcoming titles under LC subject headings.

Indexes: *Author/Title/Subject/Key to Publishers' & Distributors' Abbreviations*

Books In Series In the United States

A publication listing in-print *and* out-of-print titles in popular, scholarly, and professional series.

Indexes: *Series Heading/Series/Author/ Title/Subject Index to Series/ Directory of Publishers' & Distributors'*

Forthcoming Books

A bi-monthly cumulative publication listing forthcoming titles and titles published since July. Beginning with the November 1977 issue, an asterisk indicates titles new to the data base since the last issue. Beginning with the May 1981 issue, a separate index was added of publishers new to the database since the last issue.

Indexes: *Author/Title/New Publishers & Distributors/Key to Publishers' & Distributors' Abbreviations*

Subject Guide To Forthcoming Books

A bi-monthly companion to *Forthcoming Books* covering the coming five-month season. Each issue overlaps and updates its predecessor. Adult and juvenile titles are listed under LC subject headings, as well as under additional headings created for literature, drama, and poetry by one author and for children's literature. In addition to their listing in the subject section, all titles for the juvenile market are listed by author in a separate section. Beginning with the July 1977 issue an asterisk indicates titles new to the data base since the last issue. Beginning with the May 1981 issue, a separate index was added of publishers new to the data base since the last issue.

Indexes: *Subject/Juvenile Books/New Publishers & Distributors/Key to Publishers' & Distributors' Abbreviations*

Paperbound Books In Print

A semi-annual* publication listing all in-print and forthcoming paper trade and paper text editions. Entries are listed under approximately 420 subject headings.

Indexes: *Author/Title/Subject/Key to Publishers' & Distributors' Abbreviations*

*semi-annual beginning 1978.

Children's Books In Print

An annual publication listing all books written for children or on the subject of children's literature. Grade or reading levels, where available, are indicated.

Indexes: *Author/Title/Illustrator/Key to Publishers' & Distributors' Abbreviations*

Subject Guide To Children's Books In Print

A companion to *Children's Books In Print* this annual lists fiction and non-fiction titles under appropriate Sears or LC subject headings.

Indexes: *Subject/Key to Publishers' & Distributors' Abbreviations*

Scientific And Technical Books And Serials In Print*

An annual subject selection of entries on science and technology *and* a selection of the same subject areas from the Bowker Serials Bibliography Data Base.

Indexes: *Book Section: Subject/Author/ Title/Key to Publishers' & Distributors' Abbreviations*
Serial Section: Subject/Title

*beginning with the 1978 editon. Prior editions (1972, 1973, 1974) were titled *Scientific And Technical Books In Print* and did not include serial publications.

Medical Books And Serials In Print*

An annual subject selection of entries on medicine, psychiatry, dentistry, nursing, and allied areas of the health field *and* a selection of the same subject areas from the Bowker Serials Bibliography Data Base.

Indexes: *Book Section: Subject/Author/ Title/Key to Publishers' & Distributors' Abbreviations*
Serial Section: Subject/Title

*beginning with the 1978 edition. Prior editions (1972-1977) were titled *Bowker's Medical Books In Print* and did not include serial publications.

Business and Economics Books And Serials In Print*

A subject selection of entries in the areas of economics, industry, finance, management, industrial psychology, vocational guidance, and other business-related topics *and* a selection of the same subject areas from the Bowker Serials Bibliography Data Base.

Indexes: *Book Section: Subject/Author/ Title/Key to Publishers' & Distributors' Abbreviations*
Serial Section: Subject/Title

*beginning with the 1981 edition. The 1973 and 1974 editions were titled *Business Books In Print* and did not include serial publications. The 1977 edition and its 1978 supplement were titled Business Books and Serials in Print.

Religious Books And Serials In Print

A subject selection of all entries on the world's religions and on allied religious and moral topics *and* a selection of the same subject areas from the Bowker Serials Bibliography Data Base. A Subject Area Directory provides access by broad areas to the subjects included. A Sacred Works Index provides a listing of the sacred books of the world's religions available in the U.S.

Indexes: *Book Section: Subject/Author/ Title/Key to Publishers' & Distributors' Abbreviations*
Subject Area Directory/
Sacred Works Index
Serial Section: Subject/Title

Large Type Books In Print

An annual* publication listing all books which are produced in 14 point or larger type and intended for the visually handicapped. This volume is printed in 18 point type.

Indexes: *Subject/Textbook/Title/Author/ Key to Publishers' & Distributors' Abbreviations*

*Annual beginning with 1982 edition. Previous editions were issued in 1970, 1976, 1978, and 1980.

OTHER DATA BASES

TEXTBOOK DATA BASE

The Textbook Data Base was separated from the BIPS Data Base and expanded beyond the BIPS scope in 1973. Included are book and non-book materials for kindergarten through the first year of college as well as pedagogical material available and related to the educational world but not marketed to nor always available to the trade. The data base includes all editions and bindings (hardcover, paperbound, boards, spiral binding, reprints) as well as kits, maps, audio-visual materials and other teaching aids. Bibliographic entries contain the same elements as on the BIPS Data Base.

PUBLICATIONS:

El-Hi Textbooks In Print

An annual publication listing in-print and forthcoming titles.

Indexes: *Subject/Title/Author/Series/ Key to Publishers' & Distributors' Abbreviations*

PUBLISHERS' AUTHORITY DATA BASE

PUBLICATIONS:

Key to Publishers' and Distributors' Abbreviations

Provides the abbreviation, full name, ordering address, and ISBN prefix for all publishers and distributors whose bibliographic entries appear in the publication being indexed.

Directory of United States' Publishers, Distributors and Wholesalers

A listing of full name, editorial address, telephone number, and ISBN prefix for all active U.S. publishers, distributors and wholesalers currently on record in the files of the Department of Bibliography.

BOWKER SERIALS BIBLIOGRAPHY DATA BASE

This Data Base contains up-to-date information on 114,000 serial titles published by 63,000 serial publishers and corporate authors around the world. Maintained by the Bowker Serials Bibliography Department.

PUBLICATIONS:

Ulrich's International Periodicals Directory (biennial); **Irregular Serials and Annuals** (biennial); **Ulrich's Quarterly,** a supplement to **Ulrich's** and **Irregular Serials; Sources of Serials,** an international directory of serial publishers and corporate authors and their titles by country.

ISBN
INTERNATIONAL STANDARD BOOK NUMBER

The 1982-1983 BOOKS IN PRINT SUPPLEMENT lists each title or edition of a title with an ISBN. All publishers were notified and requested to submit a valid ISBN for their titles.

During the past decade, the majority of the publishers complied with the requirements of the standard and implemented the ISBN. At present, approximately 97% of all new titles and all new editions are submitted for listing with a valid ISBN.

To fulfill the responsibility of accomplishing total book numbering, the ISBN Agency allocated the ISBN prefixes 0-685 and 0-686 to number the titles in the BOOKS IN PRINT database without an ISBN. Titles not having an ISBN at the closing date of this publication were assigned an ISBN with one of these prefixes by the International Standard Book Numbering Agency.

Titles numbered within the prefixes 0-685 and 0-686 are:

— Publishers who did not assign ISBN to their titles.

— Distributors with titles published and imported from countries not in the ISBN system, or not receiving the ISBN from the originating publisher.

— Errors from transposition and transcription which occurred in transmitting the ISBN to the BOOKS IN PRINT database.

All the ISBN listed in BOOKS IN PRINT SUPPLEMENT are validated by using the check digit control, and only valid ISBN are listed in the BIP database.

All publishers participating in the ISBN system having titles numbered within the prefixes 0-685 and 0-686 will receive a computer printout, requesting them to submit the correct ISBN.

Publishers not participating in the ISBN system may request from the ISBN Agency the assignment of an ISBN Publisher Prefix, and start numbering their titles.

By having an ISBN for each title and edition of a title, order fulfillment and inventory control systems will be able to operate more efficiently and economically. The ISBN Agency will produce and publish an ISBN Index on microfiche. Users encountering an ISBN in the range of 0-685 and 0-686 who are unable to identify the title in their file, will be able to refer to the ISBN microfiche Index. Each ISBN in the Index will have the information on title, author and publisher, or a cross reference to another ISBN. When publishing rights are sold and the title is published under the new imprint with a separate ISBN, the ISBN Index will carry a cross reference from the previous ISBN to the new one.

The Book Industry System Advisory Committee (BISAC) developed a standard format for data transmission, and many companies are already accepting orders transmitted on magnetic tape using the ISBN. Another standard format by BISAC for title updating is under development.

The ISBN Agency and the Data Services Division of the Bowker Company wish to express their appreciation to all publishers who collaborated in making the ISBN system the standard of the publishing industry.

For additional information related to the ISBN total numbering, please refer to Emery Koltay, Director of the ISBN Agency, R. R. Bowker Co.

How to Use
BOOKS IN PRINT SUPPLEMENT
1982–1983

Books in Print Supplement 1982-1983, the eleventh edition of an annual publication, is issued six months after the publication of *Books in Print 1982-1983* to update the information that appeared therein. It includes approximately 125,650 titles with price or other major changes, 25,200 titles which have gone out of print, and 37,500 titles received since *Books in Print 1982-1983*.

The Supplement includes author and title indexes. The subject index lists titles new to the data base since *Subject Guide to Books in Print 1982-1983*. A listing of the publishers represented plus any others which have indicated changes of name or address since *Books in Print* is also included.

Like *Books in Print,* the *Supplement* was produced from records stored on magnetic tape, edited by computer programs, and set in type by computer-controlled photocomposition.

AUTHOR AND TITLE INDEXES

Each of these indexes includes a single alphabetical listing of all corrected titles, those which have gone out of print or are out of stock indefinitely, those which were cancelled or postponed, and new titles. The notations "o.p." or "o.s.i." following the price information, indicate that the book is either out of print or out of stock indefinitely. All titles with price or other major changes and new titles which appear in the *March, 1983* issue of *Forthcoming Books* are also included.

ALPHABETICAL ARRANGEMENT OF AUTHOR AND TITLE INDEXES

Within each index entries are filed alphabetically by word, with the following exceptions:

Initial articles of titles in English, French, German, Italian, and Spanish are deleted from the title index.

M', Mc and *Mac* are filed as if they were *Mac* and are interfiled with other names beginning with *Mac;* for example, Macan, McAnally, Macardle, McAree, McArthur, Macarthur, M'Aulay, Macaulay, McAuley. Within a specific name grouping *Mc* and *Mac* are interfiled according to the given name of the author; for example, Macdonald, Agnes; McDonald, Annie L.; MacDonald, Austin F.; Macdonald, Betty. Compound names are listed under the first part of the name, and cross-references appear under the last part of the name.

Entries beginning with initial letters (whether authors' given names or titles) are filed first, e.g., Smith, H.C., comes before Smith, Harold A.; B E A M A Directory comes before Baal, Babylon.

Numerals, including year dates, are written out in most cases and filed alphabetically:

Seven years in Tibet
Seventeen
Seventeen famous operas
Seventeen-Fifteen to the present
Seventeen party book
Seventeen reader
Seventeenth century

U.S., UN, Dr., Mr., and St. are filed as though they were spelled out.

SPECIAL NOTE ON HOW TO FIND AN AUTHOR'S COMPLETE LISTING

In sorting author listings by computer it is not possible to group the entire listing for an author together unless a standard spelling and format for each name is used. If an author's name is given in various forms by the contributing publishers, his listings in the author index may be divided into several groups.

Variant forms of an author's first and middle names may not be adjacent in the filing sequence, as in Aiken, Conrad and Aiken, Conrad P. or Jung, C.G. and Jung, Carl G. For most surnames, variant forms of entry will fall close together, but for the most common surnames (Smith, Brown, etc.) it is suggested you check specifically for all variant forms of first and middle names.

Foreign names which may or may not be given with a prefix will not be adjacent in the filing sequence, such as: Balzac and de Balzac and Goethe or von Goethe. German names with umlauts may appear in two alphabets because of the varying treatment of the umlauted vowel: Müller, F. Max or Mueller, F. Max. Acronyms for names of corporate authors may appear in two or more groups of listings if one form is presented with no space between initials—UNESCO, and another with spaces, U N E S C O.

You will find cross-references to the variant forms of an author's name wherever we anticipated that his listings might not be filed together.

INFORMATION INCLUDED IN AUTHOR, TITLE, AND SUBJECT ENTRIES

Entries in all indexes include the following bibliographic information, when available: author, co-author, editor, co-editor, translator, co-translator, title, number of volumes, edition, Library of Congress number, series information, language if other than English, whether or not illustrated, grade range, year of publication, type of binding if other than cloth over boards, price, International Standard Book Number, publisher's order number, imprint and publisher. When an entry includes the prices for both the hardcover and paperback editions, the publication date within the entry refers to the hardcover binding; however, when the paperback binding is the only one included in the entry, the publication date is the paperback publication date. (Information on the International Standard Book Numbering System developing in the United States and other English-speaking countries is available from R.R. Bowker Company.)

GENERAL EDITORIAL POLICIES

In order to insure that the essential information in these listings is uniform, complete, and easy to find, the following editorial policies have been maintained:

When two authors or editors are responsible for a book, full bibliographic information is included in the author entry for the author or editor named first, and a cross-reference directs the user from the second author or editor to the primary entry; e.g., Wilson, Robert E., jt. auth. see Fensch, E.A. If more than two authors or editors are responsible for a certain publication, only the name of the first is given followed by *et al.*

Titles of single volumes as part of a set are given if the volumes are sold singly. Cross-references from single volume titles to set title are included whenever the former are distinctive. Some series are also listed in the title index.

Although the *Supplement* is designed to provide accurate, updated price and out-of-print information until the publication of *Books in Print 1983-1984*, a certain amount of additional price changes will occur and a certain number of titles will become unavailable in the interim.

A Bowker tool for keeping up with new titles is *Forthcoming Books,* a separate bimonthly publication which provides author-title indexes to all books due to appear in the coming 5 month period. In addition, it cumulates all books that have appeared since July 1982. Yearly subscriptions are available at $67.50U.S.A., single copies for $15.00 U.S.A.

All prices are subject to change without notice. Most prices are list prices. Lack of uniformity by the participating publishers prohibits indicating trade discounts. A lowercase "a" follows some of the trade edition prices and indicates that a specially priced library edition is available; "t" indicates a tentative price; "g" a guaranteed binding on a juvenile title; and "x" a short discount—20% or less. PLB indicates a publishers' library binding. YA indicates that a title may be used for young adults.

An "i" following the price indicates an invoice price. Specific policies for such titles should be obtained from the individual publishers.

Publishers' names, in most instances, are abbreviated. A key to the abbreviations together with the complete addresses of the various publishing firms will be found in the Key to Publishers' Abbreviations.

SUBJECT INDEX

The subject index supplements *Subject Guide to Books in Print 1982-1983* by listing titles published or announced for publication prior to July 1983 which did not appear in *Subject Guide to Books in Print 1982-1983*. It follows the headings assigned by the Library of Congress. Some books have been assigned a single heading, some two, three or more headings, and therefore some books appear two, three or more times in the subject index. Wherever official LC classification was unavailable, generally because the publication date was too recent or is in the future, provisional headings were assigned.

Headings and cross-references have been updated to conform with the latest supplement to the Ninth Edition of *Library of Congress Subject Headings* although many subheadings have been consolidated where they seem too cumbersome for the needs of the *Subject Guide to Books in Print* and this *Supplement,* and a few were changed when the needs of these books seemed to diverge from LC practice.

Where the Library of Congress does not assign subject headings to cataloged books, they are usually omitted from this subject listing. For example:

Fiction is omitted except where a work's background (biographical, historical, etc.) seemed extensive and authentic enough to warrant mention. However, collections of works of fiction may be included, and of course, criticism.

Poetry and drama are omitted, at least as regards works by a single author best sought in *Books in Print* or the Author Index of the *Supplement*. However, collections and criticism are included.

Juvenile fiction, like adult fiction, is usually omitted, though juvenile nonfiction (at least above the picture-book level) is represented. In some cases, juvenile titles have been set apart under a heading such as AERONAUTICS—JUVENILE LITERATURE. In other cases, juvenile titles are listed with adult books and are identified by grade range.

Bibles as such are omitted, though commentaries, histories, and versions other than the standard English are extensively covered.

Books priced at less than 25 cents are not listed.

Subject headings are arranged alphabetically:

ACCOUNTING
ACETYLENE
ACTING
ACTINOMYCETES
ADAMS, HENRY, 1838–1918
ADHESIVES

Many of the main entries are broken down still further:

ACCOUNTING
ACCOUNTING—DICTIONARIES
ACCOUNTING—EXAMINATIONS, QUESTIONS
ACCOUNTING—LAW
ACCOUNTING—PROBLEMS, EXERCISES

There are also many cross-references:

ACCOUNTING
see also Auditing; Bookkeeping; Business Losses; Business Mathematics; Cost Accounting; Depreciation; Financial Statements; Income Accounting; Inventories; Liquidation; Machine Accounting; Productivity Accounting; Tax Accounting

ACCOUNTING—FORMS, BLANKS, etc.
see Business—Forms, Blanks, etc.

ACCOUNTS, COLLECTING of
see Collecting of Accounts.

Headings, patterned after those used in the card catalog in the Library of Congress, are explicit rather than general. Thus books on cost accounting are under COST ACCOUNTING, not under ACCOUNTING. Books on actors are under ACTORS and ACTRESSES, not under THEATER.

Similarly, look first under PLASTICS rather than CHEMISTRY, or under ACRYLATES rather than PLASTICS.

In looking for books on painting, search past the main entry to the various subheadings:

PAINTING
PAINTING—DICTIONARIES
PAINTING—EARLY WORKS TO 1800
PAINTING—HISTORY
PAINTING—STUDY AND TEACHING
PAINTING—TECHNIQUE
PAINTING, AMERICAN
PAINTING, INDUSTRIAL
PAINTINGS

Note the sequence of the above cited headings and subheadings. The editors of the *Subject Guide* took as a guideline the *Filing Rules for the Dictionary Catalogs of the Library of Congress,* as prepared by the Processing Department of the Library of Congress.

Other typical examples of the sequences used are:

ART
ART—HISTORY
ART, AMERICAN
ART OBJECTS
ART OBJECTS—COLLECTORS AND COLLECTING
BIBLE—COMMENTARIES
BIBLE—COMMENTARIES—N.T.
BIBLE—COMMENTARIES—N.T. GOSPELS
GREAT BRITAIN
GREAT BRITAIN—HISTORY
GREAT BRITAIN—PARLIAMENT
GREAT BRITAIN—PARLIAMENT—HOUSE OF COMMONS

Although a constant effort is made to maintain consistency and to avoid splitting entries on a given subject among several headings, a certain amount is inevitable. The Library of Congress updates its subject headings constantly but cannot make such updating retroactive to cards and catalogs previously issued. For example, LC is now subdividing the heading EVOLUTION according to the subject matter of the material processed, e.g., HUMAN EVOLUTION; PLANTS — EVOLUTION. If old entries which belong in more precise subdivisions did not indicate by their titles where they should be listed, they were left under the main entry.

The editor's first principle is to list books where the user will be most likely to look for them with as many references as seem necessary. If an official heading is one under which the lay user might not think to look, additional popular cross-references have been added.

Each entry is filed alphabetically by author, or title when there is no author cited, under the appropriate subject. Filing rules are the same used in the author and title indexes.

KEY TO PUBLISHERS' AND DISTRIBUTORS' ABBREVIATIONS

Publishers' and distributors' names, in most instances, are abbreviated. A key to these abbreviations will be found in the *Key to Publishers' & Distributors' Abbreviations* at the end of this *Supplement*.

Entries in this "Key" are arranged alphabetically by the abbreviations used in the bibliographic entries. The full name, ISBN prefix, editorial address, telephone number, ordering address (if different from the editorial address), and imprints follow the abbreviation. SAN (Standard Address Number) is a unique identification code for each address of each organization in or served by the book industry.

For example:

> **Bowker,** (Bowker, R.R., Co., 0-8352),
> A Xerox Publishing Co., 1180 Ave. of
> the Americas, New York, NY 10036
> Tel 212-764-5100 (SAN 214-1191);
> Orders to: P.O. Box 1807, Ann Arbor, MI 48106
> (SAN 214-1205).

If an entry contains a "Pub. by" note after the price, the title should be ordered from the company whose abbreviation appears at the end of the entry. For example, an entry for a book published by Melbourne U Pr., but distributed by International Scholarly Book Services, Inc., will convey this information in the form "Pub. by Melbourne U Pr." after the price with "Intl Schol Bk Serv." at the end of the entry.

The R.R. Bowker Company has used its best efforts in collecting and preparing material for inclusion in *Books in Print Supplement 1982-1983* but does not assume, and hereby disclaims, any liability to any party for any loss or damage caused by errors or omissions in *Books in Print Supplement 1982-1983* whether such errors or omissions result from negligence, accident, or any other cause.

KEY TO ABBREVIATIONS

a	after price, specially priced library edition available
abr.	abridged
adpt.	adapted
Amer.	American
annot.	annotation(s), annotated
ans.	answer(s)
app.	appendix
approx.	approximately
assn.	association
auth.	author
bd.	bound
bdg.	binding
bds.	boards
bibl(s).	bibliography (ies)
bk(s).	book, books
bklet(s)	booklets
Bro.	Brother
coll.	college
comm.	commission, committee
co.	company
cond.	condensed
comp(s).	compiler(s)
corp.	corporation
dept.	department
diag(s).	diagram(s)
dir.	director
dist.	distributed
Div.	Division
doz.	dozen
ea.	each
ed.	editor, edited, edition
eds.	editions, editors
educ.	education
elem.	elementary
ency.	encyclopedia
Eng.	English
enl.	enlarged
exp.	expurgated
fac.	facsimile
fasc.	fascicule
fict.	fiction
fig(s).	figure(s)
for.	foreign
Fr.	French
frwd.	foreword
g	after price, guaranteed juvenile binding
gen.	general
Ger.	German
Gr.	Greek
gr.	grade, grades
hdbk.	handbook
Heb.	Hebrew
i	invoice price—see publisher for specific pricing policies
i.t.a.	initial teaching alphabet
Illus.	illustrated, illustration(s), illustrator(s)
in prep.	in preparation
incl.	includes, including
inst.	institute
intro.	introduction
It.	Italian
Jr.	Junior
jt. auth.	joint author
jt. ed.	joint editor

k	kindergarten audience level
l.p.	long playing
ltd. ed.	limited edition
lab.	laboratory
lang(s).	language(s)
Lat.	Latin
lea.	leather
lib.	library
lit.	literature, literary
math.	mathematics
mod.	modern
mor.	morocco
MS, MSS	manuscript, manuscripts
natl.	national
no., nos.	number, numbers
o.p.	out of print
orig.	original text, not a reprint
O.S.I.	out of stock indefinitely
pap.	paper
photos	photographs, photographer
PLB	publisher's library binding
Pol.	Polish
pop. ed.	popular edition
Port.	Portuguese
prep.	preparation
probs.	problems
prog. bk.	programmed book
ps	preschool audience level
pseud.	pseudonym
pt(s).	part, parts
pub.	published, publisher, publishing
pubn.	publication
ref(s).	reference(s)
repr.	reprint
reprod(s).	reproduction(s)
rev.	revised
rpm.	revolution per minute (phono records)
Rus.	Russian
s.p.	school price
scp	single copy Direct to the Consumer Price
sec.	section
sel.	selected
ser.	series
Soc.	Society
sols.	solutions
Span.	Spanish
Sr. (after given name)	Senior
Sr. (before given name)	Sister
St.	Saint
subs.	subsidiary
subsc.	subscription
suppl.	supplement
t	after price, tentative price
tech.	technical
text ed.	text edition
tr.	translator, translated, translation
univ.	university
vol(s).	volume, volumes
wkbk.	workbook
x	after price, short discount (20% or less)
YA	young adult audience level
yrbk.	yearbook

AUTHOR INDEX

A

AAA College Editors, ed. Clip Art, Book 4. 1978. pap. 14.95x (ISBN 0-8134-2039-3, 2039). Interstate.
Aaberson, Max, ed. see Carter, Lark, et al.
Aabert, Geoffry F. After the Crash: How to Survive & Prosper During the Depression of the 1980's. 1980. pap. 3.95 (ISBN 0-451-11869-3, AE1869, Sig). NAL.
AACP. AACP Roster of Teachers in Colleges of Pharmacy: Annual. 15.00 (ISBN 0-937526-00-2). Am Assn Coll Pharm.
--Doctoral Roster. annual 3.00 o.p. (ISBN 0-937526-03-7). Am Assn Coll Pharm.
AACP Section of Librarians. Standards & Planning Guide for Pharmacy Library Service, 1975. 90p. 1975. 5.00 o.p. (ISBN 0-937526-09-6). Am Assn Coll Pharm.
AAG Consulting Panel, 1974. Self-Study Data Forms. pap. 1.00 o.p. (ISBN 0-89291-142-5). Assn Am Geographers.
AAG Consulting Services Panel. Suggestions for Self-Evaluation of Geography Programs with Self-Study Data Forms. 1974. pap. 2.00 (ISBN 0-89291-141-7). Assn Am Geographers.
Aagaard-Mogensen, Lars, ed. Culture & Art: An Anthology. 1976. pap. 7.95x (ISBN 0-391-00539-1). Humanities.
Aagre, Scott & Martin, Lance. Calligraphy & Related Ornamentation. (Illus.). 96p. (Orig.). 1982. pap. 5.95. Lighthouse Hill Pub.
AAHPER Convention, Seattle, 1977. Abstracts of Research Papers. 1977. pap. 3.00x o.p. (ISBN 0-685-81938-8, 248-25978). AAHPERD.
AAHPER National Convention, Milwaukee. Abstracts of Research Papers. 1976. 3.00x o.p. (ISBN 0-685-67036-8, 248-25808). AAHPERD.
Aaker, David A. Multivariate Analysis in Marketing. 2nd ed. 1980. pap. text ed. 17.50x (ISBN 0-89426-029-4). Scientific Pr.
Aaker, David A. & Day, George S. Marketing Research: Private & Public Sector Decisions. LC 79-18532. (Marketing Ser.). 628p. 1980. text ed. 26.95 (ISBN 0-471-00059-0). Wiley.
Aaker, David A. & Day, George S., eds. Consumerism: Search for the Consumer Interest. 4th ed. LC 77-83163. (Illus.). 1982. 20.95 (ISBN 0-02-900050-5); pap. text ed. 12.95 (ISBN 0-02-900040-8). Free Pr.
Aalen, F. H. Man & the Landscape in Ireland. 1978. 29.50 (ISBN 0-12-041350-7). Acad Pr.
Aaltio, M. Finnish for Foreigners, 3 vols. Set. pap. 40.00 (ISBN 0-686-66991-6). Vol. 1 (ISBN 9-5110-0397-6). Vol. 2 (ISBN 9-5110-1483-8). Vol. 3 (ISBN 9-5110-1919-8). Vol. 4 Oral Drills. pap. 10.00 (ISBN 9-5110-1231-2). Heinman.
Aaltio, M-H. Finnish for Foreigners: Pt 2, Lessons 27 to 40. 8th rev. ed. (Illus.). 192p. 1976. pap. text ed. 20.00x (ISBN 951-1-01483-8, F 562). Vanous.
Aaltio, M. J. Finnish for Foreigners, Pt. 1: Lessons 1-25. 10th ed. (Illus.). 254p. 1978. pap. text ed. 20.00x (ISBN 951-1-00397-6, F561); cassette a, cassettes b-e, 100.00x 45.00x (ISBN 0-686-66923-1). Vanous.
Aaltio, Maija-Hellikki. Finnish for Foreigners, 2 vols. Date not set. Vol. 1. includes 5 cassettes 85.00x (ISBN 0-88432-093-6, FN01); Vol. II. includes 4 cassettes 60.00x (ISBN 0-88432-094-4, FN10). J Norton Pubs.
--Korva Tarkkana. 102p. Date not set. includes 1 cassette 25.00x (ISBN 0-88432-095-2, FN20). J Norton Pubs.
Aan-Ta-T'Loot & Pack, Raymond. Tlingit Designs & Carving Manual. LC 78-11887. (Illus.). 1978. 7.95 (ISBN 0-87564-862-2); pap. 6.95 o.s.i. (ISBN 0-87564-861-4). Superior Pub.
Aardema, Verna. Bringing the Rain to Kapiti Plain. (Illus.). 32p. (ps-2). 1983. pap. 3.95 (ISBN 0-8037-0904-8, 0383-120). Dial Bks Young.
--Tales from the Story Hat. (Illus.). (gr. 3-5). 1960. PLB 4.99 (ISBN 0-698-30348-2, Coward). Putnam Pub Group.
--What's So Funny, Ketu? LC 82-70195. (Illus.). 32p. (ps-2). 1982. 9.95 (ISBN 0-8037-9364-2); PLB 9.89 (ISBN 0-8037-9370-7). Dial.
Aaron, Benjamin, ed. Reference Supplement: Labor Relations & Social Problems - A Course Book, Unit R. 5th ed. 216p. 1981. pap. text ed. 4.00 o.p. (ISBN 0-87179-345-8). BNA.
Aaron, Benjamin see Labor Law Group.
Aaron, Chester. Duchess. LC 81-47755. 192p. (YA) (gr. 7 up). 1982. 10.10i (ISBN 0-397-31947-9, JBL-J); PLB 10.89g (ISBN 0-397-31948-7). Har-Row.
Aaron, Henry J. Economic Effects of Social Security. (Studies of Government Finance). 100p. 1982. 12.95 (ISBN 0-8157-0030-X, 82-73654); pap. 5.95 (ISBN 0-8157-0029-6). Brookings.
--Politics & the Professors: The Great Society in Perspective. LC 77-91809. (Studies in Social Economics). 1978. 17.95 (ISBN 0-8157-0026-1); pap. 6.95 (ISBN 0-8157-0025-3). Brookings.
--Shelter & Subsidies: Who Benefits from Federal Housing Policies? (Studies in Social Economics). 200p. 1972. 15.95 (ISBN 0-8157-0018-0); pap. 5.95 (ISBN 0-8157-0017-2). Brookings.
--Who Pays the Property Tax? A New View. (Studies of Government Finance). 1975. 14.95 (ISBN 0-8157-0022-9); pap. 5.95 (ISBN 0-8157-0021-0). Brookings.
--Why Is Welfare So Hard to Reform? (Studies in Social Economics). 71p. 1973. pap. 4.95 (ISBN 0-8157-0019-9). Brookings.
Aaron, Henry J., ed. Inflation & the Income Tax. LC 76-28669. (Studies of Government Finance). 1976. 23.95 (ISBN 0-8157-0024-5); pap. 9.95 (ISBN 0-8157-0023-7). Brookings.
--The Value-Added Tax: Lessons from Europe. LC 81-38475. (Studies of Government Finance). 120p. 1981. 12.95 (ISBN 0-8157-0028-8); pap. 5.95 (ISBN 0-8157-0027-X). Brookings.
Aaron, Henry J. & Boskin, Michael J., eds. The Economics of Taxation. (Studies of Government Finance). 1980. 22.95 (ISBN 0-8157-0014-8); pap. 9.95 (ISBN 0-8157-0013-X). Brookings.
Aaron, Henry J. & Pechman, Joseph A., eds. How Taxes Affect Economic Behavior. LC 81-1040. (Studies of Government Finance). 454p. 1981. 29.95 (ISBN 0-8157-0012-1); pap. 12.95 (ISBN 0-8157-0011-3). Brookings.
Aaron, Howard. What the Worms Ignore the Birds Are Wild About. 1979. 4.00 (ISBN 0-918116-15-5). Jawbone Pr.
Aaron, James, jt. auth. see Strasser, Maryland K.
Aaron, James E. & Strasser, Marland K. Driver & Traffic Safety Education. 2nd ed. 1977. 22.95 (ISBN 0-02-300010-4, 30001). Macmillan.
--Driving Task Instruction: Dual Control, Simulation, & Multiple-Car. 1974. pap. 17.95x (ISBN 0-02-300040-6, 30004). Macmillan.
Aaron, James E., et al. First Aid Emergency Care: Prevention & Protection of Injuries. 2nd ed. 1979. pap. text ed. 14.95x (ISBN 0-02-300060-0). Macmillan.
Aaron, Jan. Plantworks: Indoor Gardening Made Easy. LC 74-21357. 208p. 1983. 14.95 (ISBN 0-8303-0146-1). Fleet.
Aaron, Jan & Salom, Georgine S. The Art of Mexican Cooking. 1982. pap. 2.95 (ISBN 0-451-11433-7, AE1433, Sig). NAL.
Aaron, Raymond. Industrial Society. LC 66-18887. 1968. pap. 1.95 o.p. (ISBN 0-671-20804-7, Touchstone Bks). S&S.
Aaron, Shirley L. & Scales, Part R., eds. School Library Media Annual, 1983, Vol. 1. 350p. 1983. lib. bdg. 23.50 (ISBN 0-87287-353-6). Libs Unl.
Aaronovitch, S. & Smith, R. The Political Economy of British Capitalism: A Marxist Analysis. 416p. 1982. 17.00 (ISBN 0-07-084121-7). McGraw.
Aaronovitch, Sam. The Ruling Class: A Study of British Finance Capital. LC 78-23485. 1979. Repr. of 1961 ed. lib. bdg. 20.50x (ISBN 0-313-20764-X, AARC). Greenwood.
Aarons, Howell, jt. auth. see Schweitzer, Burton L.
Aarons, Trudy & Koelsch, Francine. One Hundred & One Language Arts Activities. (Illus.). 1979. pap. text ed. 11.95 (ISBN 0-88450-795-5, 3053-B). Communication Skill.
--One Hundred One Math Activities. 118p. 1981. pap. text ed. 11.95 (ISBN 0-88450-740-8, 2065-B). Communication Skill.
--One Hundred One Reading Activities. 125p. (ps-4). 1982. pap. text ed. 11.95 (ISBN 0-88450-833-1). Communication Skill.
Aaronson, Doris & Rieber, Robert W., eds. Developmental Psycholinguistics & Communication Disorders, Vol. 263. (Annals of the New York Academy of Sciences). 287p. 1975. 22.00x (ISBN 0-89072-016-9). NY Acad Sci.
Aasen, Andreas. The Life of a Bastard. LC 76-66203. 169p. pap. 4.50 (ISBN 0-9603056-1-0). Aasen.
Aaseng, Nate. Baseball: You Are the Manager. LC 82-268. (You Are the Coach Ser.). (Illus.). 104p. (gr. 4up). 1983. PLB 8.95g (ISBN 0-8225-1552-0). Lerner Pubns.
--Baseball's Hottest Hitters. (Sports Heroes Library). (Illus.). 80p. (gr. 4up). 1983. PLB 7.95g (ISBN 0-8225-1331-5). Lerner Pubns.
--Baseball's Power Hitters. (Sports Heroes Library). (Illus.). 80p. (gr. 4up). 1983. PLB 7.95g (ISBN 0-8225-1332-3). Lerner Pubns.
--Basketball: You Are the Coach. LC 82-17261. (You Are the Coach Ser.). (Illus.). 104p. (gr. 4up). 1983. PLB 8.95g (ISBN 0-8225-1553-9). Lerner Pubns.
--Basketball's Playmakers. (Sports Heroes Library). (Illus.). 80p. (gr. 4up). 1983. PLB 7.95g (ISBN 0-8225-1330-7). Lerner Pubns.
--Basketball's Sharpshooters. (Sports Heroes Library). (Illus.). 80p. (gr. 4up). 1983. PLB 7.95g (ISBN 0-8225-1329-3). Lerner Pubns.
--Football: You Are the Coach. LC 82-269. (You Are the Coach Ser.). (Illus.). 104p. (gr. 4up). 1983. PLB 8.95g (ISBN 0-8225-1551-2). Lerner Pubns.
--Hockey: You Are the Coach. LC 82-17170. (You Are the Coach Ser.). (Illus.). 104p. (gr. 4up). 1983. PLB 8.95g (ISBN 0-8225-1554-7). Lerner Pubns.
--I'm Searching, Lord, but I Need Your Light. LC 82-72644. 112p. (gr. 3-6). 1983. pap. 3.50 (ISBN 0-8066-1950-3, 10-3203). Augsburg.
--Supersubs of Pro Sports. (Sports Heroes Library). (Illus.). 80p. (gr. 4up). 1983. PLB 7.95g (ISBN 0-8225-1328-5). Lerner Pubns.
Aaseng, Nathan. Baseball's Brilliant Managers. LC 81-13643. (Sports Heroes Library). (Illus.). 80p. (gr. 4 up). 1982. PLB 6.95g (ISBN 0-8225-1071-5). Lerner Pubns.
--Comeback Stars of Pro Sports. (Sports Heroes Library). (Illus.). 80p. (gr. 4up). 1983. PLB 7.95g (ISBN 0-8225-1327-7). Lerner Pubns.
--Football's Crushing Blockers. LC 81-13681. (Sports Heroes Library). (Illus.). 80p. (gr. 6 up). 1982. PLB 7.95g (ISBN 0-8225-1074-X). Lerner Pubns.
--Football's Super Bowl Champions: I-VIII. LC 81-13659. (Sports Heroes Library). (Illus.). 80p. (gr. 4 up). 1982. PLB 7.95g (ISBN 0-8225-1072-3). Lerner Pubns.
--Football's Super Bowl Champions: IX-XVI. LC 82-10099. (Sports Heroes Library). (Illus.). 72p. (gr. 4 up). 1982. lib. bdg. 7.95g (ISBN 0-8225-1333-1). Lerner Pubns.

--Memorable World Series Moments. LC 81-13725. (Sports Heroes Library). (Illus.). 80p. (gr. 4 up). 1982. PLB 7.95g (ISBN 0-8225-1073-1). Lerner Pubns.

--Pete Rose. LC 79-27377. (The Achievers Ser.). (Illus.). (gr. 4-9). 1981. PLB 5.95g (ISBN 0-8225-0480-4). Lerner Pubns.

--Superstars Stopped Short. LC 81-12431. (Sports Heroes Library). (Illus.). 80p. (gr. 4 up). 1982. PLB 7.95g (ISBN 0-8225-1326-9). Lerner Pubns.

--World-Class Marathoners. LC 81-13660. (Sports Heroes Library). (Illus.). 80p. (gr. 4 up). 1982. PLB 7.95g (ISBN 0-8225-1325-0). Lerner Pubns.

Aasheim, Ashley. A Stillness at Sea. 368p. (Orig.). 1983. pap. 3.50 (ISBN 0-440-08250-1, Emerald). Dell.

AASL & AECT Program Standards Committees. Media Programs: District & School. LC 74-32316. 128p. 1975. pap. 4.95 (ISBN 0-89240-016-1, 908). Assn Ed Comm Tech.

AASL School Media Centers. Instructional Design & the Library Media Specialist. (Focus on Trends & Issues Ser.: No. 5). 44p. (Orig.). 1979. pap. text ed. 5.00 (ISBN 0-8389-3234-7). ALA.

Abad, Gemino H. A Formal Approach to Lyric Poetry. 1978. text ed. 20.00x (ISBN 0-8248-0632-8); pap. text ed. 16.00x (ISBN 0-8248-0643-3). UH Pr.

--In Another Light: Poems & Essays. 1976. text ed. 12.00x (ISBN 0-8248-0471-6). UH Pr.

Abadan-Unat, Nermin. Women in Turkish Society. (Social, Economic & Political Studies of the Middle East Ser.: Vol. 30). (Illus.). xii, 338p. 1982. pap. write for info. (ISBN 90-04-06346-3). E J Brill.

Abadi, Jacob. Britain's Withdrawal from the Middle East: The Economic & Strategic Imperatives (1947-1971) (Leaders, Politics, & Social Change in the Islamic World: No. 4). 275p. 1983. 26.00 (ISBN 0-940670-19-4). Kingston Pr.

Abadinsky, Howard. Probation & Parole: Theory & Practice. 2nd ed. (Illus.). 480p. 1982. 20.95 o.p. (ISBN 0-13-715979-X). P-H.

--Social Service in Criminal Justice: Theory & Practice. (Criminal Justice Ser.). (Illus.). 1979. ref. ed. 19.95 (ISBN 0-13-818344-9). P-H.

Abagnale, Frank M., Jr. Catch Me If You Can. LC 79-91619. 1980. 10.00 (ISBN 0-448-16538-4, G&D). Putnam Pub Group.

Abailard, P. Sic et Non: A Critical Edition, 7 fascicles. Boyer, Blanche & McKeon, Richard, eds. Incl. Fascicle 1. o.s.i. (ISBN 0-226-00058-3);;; Fascicle 4. O.S.I. (ISBN 0-226-00061-3); Fascicle 5. O.S.I. (ISBN 0-226-00062-1);;. LC 74-7567. 1978. pap. text ed. 16.00x ea; fascicles 1-7 complete in one clothbound vol. 110.00 (ISBN 0-226-00066-4). U of Chicago Pr.

Abajian, James T., compiled by. Blacks & Their Contributions to the American West: A Bibliography & Union List of Library Holdings Through 1970. 483p. 1974. lib. bdg. 37.00 (ISBN 0-8161-1139-1, Hall Reference). G K Hall.

Abakanowicz, Magdalena, jt. auth. see Reichardt, Jasia.

Abarbanel, Jerome. Redefining the Environment. (Key Issues Ser.: No. 9). 40p. 1972. pap. 2.00 (ISBN 0-87546-200-6). ILR Pr.

Abata, Russell M., jt. auth. see Weir, William.

Abate, Susan & Lucia, Nancy. Consumer Power: Classroom Resources for Consumer Education. 1983. pap. text ed. 14.95 (ISBN 0-673-16594-9). Scott F.

Abauzit, Firmin. Discours Historique sur l'Apocalypse. (Holbach & His Friends Ser). 104p. (Fr.). 1974. Repr. of 1770 ed. lib. bdg. 36.00x o.p. (ISBN 0-8287-0002-8, 1507). Clearwater Pub.

Abba, Giuseppe C. The Diary of One of Garibaldi's Thousand. Vincent, E. R., tr. from Ital. LC 80-24181. (Oxford Library of Italian Classics). (Illus.). xxi, 166p. 1981. Repr. of 1962 ed. lib. bdg. 20.75x (ISBN 0-313-22446-3, ABDO). Greenwood.

Abbas, B. M. The Ganges Water Dispute. 160p. 1982. text ed. 27.50x (ISBN 0-7069-2080-5, Pub. by Vikas India). Advent NY.

Abbas, S. A., jt. auth. see Brecher, Irving.

Abbasi, Abdul S. Echocardiographic Interpretation. (Illus.). 564p. 1981. 49.75x (ISBN 0-398-04153-9). C C Thomas.

Abbate, Marcia & LaChappelle, Nancy. Pictures, Please! A Language Supplement. (Illus.). 1979. looseleaf 39.00 (ISBN 0-88450-773-4, 3092-B). Communication Skill.

Abbazia, Patrick. John Paul Jones, America's First Naval Hero. Rahmas, D. Steve, ed. (Outstanding Personalities Ser: No. 86). 1976. lib. bdg. 2.95 incl. catalog cards (ISBN 0-87157-586-8); pap. 1.95 vinyl laminated covers (ISBN 0-87157-086-6). SamHar Pr.

--Mr. Roosevelt's Navy: The Private War of the U. S. Atlantic Fleet 1939-1942. LC 74-31739. (Illus.). 480p. 1975. 18.50 o.p. (ISBN 0-87021-395-4). Naval Inst Pr.

--Nathanael Greene, Commander of the American Continental Army in the South. Rahmas, Steve, ed. (Outstanding Personalities Ser.: No. 87). 1976. lib. bdg. 2.95 incl. catalog cards (ISBN 0-87157-587-6); pap. 1.95 vinyl laminated covers (ISBN 0-87157-087-4). SamHar Pr.

Abbe, George. Funeral. 4.95 o.p. (ISBN 0-912292-03-2). The Smith.

Abbe, Kathryn M., jt. auth. see Gill, Frances M.

Abbensetts, Michael. Sweet Talk. 1981. pap. 6.95 o.p. (ISBN 0-413-31470-7, Pub. by Eyre Methuen). Methuen Inc.

Abbett, R. W. American Civil Engineering Practice, Vol. 3. 1957. 62.95 o.s.i. (ISBN 0-471-00132-5). Wiley.

--Engineering Contracts & Specifications. 4th ed. LC 63-14072. 461p. 1963. 33.95x (ISBN 0-471-00035-3, Pub. by Wiley-Interscience). Wiley.

Abbey, Augustus. Technological Innovation: The R & D Work Environment. Dufey, Gunter, ed. LC 82-4883. (Research for Business Decisions Ser.: No. 49). 140p. 1982. 39.95 (ISBN 0-8357-1335-0, Pub. by UMI Res Pr). Univ Microfilms.

Abbey, Edward. Abbey's Road: Take the Other. 1979. 9.95 o.p. (ISBN 0-525-05006-X, 0655-20); pap. 6.95 (ISBN 0-525-03001-8). Dutton.

--Cactus Country. LC 72-91599. (American Wilderness Ser.). (Illus.). (gr. 6 up). 1973. PLB 15.96 (ISBN 0-8094-1169-5, Pub. by Time-Life). Silver.

--Good News. 256p. 1980. 11.95 (ISBN 0-525-11583-8); pap. 6.95 (ISBN 0-525-03467-6, 0674-210). Dutton.

--The Journey Home: Some Words in Defense of the American West. 1977. 10.95 o.p. (ISBN 0-525-13753-X); pap. 6.75 (ISBN 0-525-03700-4, 0655-200). Dutton.

--The Monkey Wrench Gang. 400p. 1983. pap. 3.95 (ISBN 0-380-00741-X, 6254474). Avon.

Abbey, Edward, jt. auth. see Muench, David.

Abbey, Lester. A History of Music for Those Who Don't Want to Know Too Much About Music History. LC 80-124026. (Illus.). 278p. 1982. 9.00 o.p. (ISBN 0-939400-01-4); pap. 5.00 (ISBN 0-939400-03-0). RWS Bks.

Abbey, Lynn. The Guardians. 1982. pap. 2.95 (ISBN 0-441-30589-X, Pub. by Ace Science Fiction). Ace Bks.

Abbey, Merrill R. Communication in Pulpit & Parish. LC 72-14329. 1980. pap. 8.50 (ISBN 0-664-24312-6). Westminster.

Abbey, Merrill R. & Edwards, O. C. Epiphany. LC 74-76935. (Proclamation 1: Aids for Interpreting the Lessons of the Church Year, Ser. A: Ser. A). 64p. (Orig.). 1974. pap. 2.50 (ISBN 0-8006-4062-4, 1-4062). Fortress.

Abbey, Staten. Book of Hillman Minx & Hunter. (Illus.). pap. 5.00x (ISBN 0-273-40039-8, SpS). Sportshelf.

--Book of the Rover. pap. 5.00x (ISBN 0-392-05798-0, SpS). Sportshelf.

--Book of the Triumph Two Thousand. pap. 5.00x (ISBN 0-392-05803-0, SpS). Sportshelf.

--Motorist Afloat. 14.50x (ISBN 0-392-01623-0, SpS). Sportshelf.

Abbey, Staton. Book of B.M.C. Eleven Hundred. pap. 5.00x (ISBN 0-392-02285-0, SpS). Sportshelf.

--Book of B.M.C. Minis. pap. 5.00x (ISBN 0-392-02299-0, SpS). Sportshelf.

--Book of Vauxhall Viva & Bedford Beagle. (Illus.). pap. 5.00x (ISBN 0-392-02366-0, SpS). Sportshelf.

Abbey-Harris, Nancy & Bignell, Steven. Family Life Education: Parent Involvement Handbook. 100p. (Orig.). 1983. pap. 12.00 (ISBN 0-941816-07-9). Network Pubns.

Abbot, David W. & Rogowsky, Edward T. Political Parties. 1978. 14.95 (ISBN 0-395-30780-5). HM.

Abbot, Marie Richmond see Richmond-Abbot, Marie.

Abbot, Rose Marie. Bride of Vengeance. (Candlelight Romance Ser.). (Orig.). 1981. pap. 1.50 o.s.i. (ISBN 0-440-10819-5). Dell.

Abbot, W. W. The Colonial Origins of the United States, 1607-1763. LC 74-28127. (American Republic Ser). 160p. 1975. pap. text ed. 11.50 (ISBN 0-471-00140-6). Wiley.

Abbot, William W., ed. The Papers of George Washington, Vols. 1 & 2. LC 81-16307. (Colonial Ser. I). (Illus.). 1983. 25.00 ea. Vol. 1 (ISBN 0-8139-0912-0). Vol. 2 (ISBN 0-8139-0923-6). U Pr of Va.

Abbott, jt. auth. see Lunneborg.

Abbott, Agatin T., jt. auth. see Macdonald, Gordon A.

Abbott, Berenice. New York in the Thirties. LC 73-77375. Orig. Title: Changing New York. (Illus.). 112p. 1973. Repr. of 1939 ed. 6.00 (ISBN 0-486-22967-X). Dover.

--The World of Atget. LC 79-13747. (Illus.). 1979. 10.95 (ISBN 0-399-50391-9, Perige). Putnam Pub Group.

Abbott, C. B., jt. auth. see Lerner, Elaine.

Abbott, Carl. The New Urban America: Growth & Politics in Sunbelt Cities. LC 80-22848. ix, 317p. 1981. 19.95x (ISBN 0-8078-1464-4); pap. 7.95 (ISBN 0-8078-4079-3). U of NC Pr.

Abbott, Carl, et al. Colorado: A History of the Centennial State. 1982. 17.50x (ISBN 0-87081-130-4); pap. 11.95 (ISBN 0-87081-128-2); pap. text ed. 8.95x (ISBN 0-87081-129-0). Colo Assoc.

Abbott, Daniel J., jt. auth. see Clinard, Marshall B.

Abbott, David. Basic Notes on Advanced Level Chemistry. pap. 6.50x (ISBN 0-392-08409-0, SpS). Sportshelf.

Abbott, David, ed. The Biographical Encyclopedias of Sciences: The Biologists. 1982. 30.00x (ISBN 0-584-10853-2, Pub. by Muller Ltd). State Mutual Bk.

--The Biographical Encyclopedias of Science: The Chemists. 1982. 30.00x (ISBN 0-584-10854-0, Pub. by Muller Ltd). State Mutual Bk.

Abbott, Edwin A. Flatland. (Illus.). 128p. 1982. 9.95 (ISBN 0-87523-199-3). Emerson.

--Flatland. (Illus.). 144p. 1983. pap. 3.80i (ISBN 0-06-463573-2, EH 573). B&N NY.

--Flatland: A Romance of Many Dimensions. 5th rev. ed. 1963. pap. 3.80i (ISBN 0-06-463210-5, EH 210, EH). B&N NY.

Abbott, Evelyn. Pericles & the Golden Age of Athens. 379p. 1982. Repr. of 1891 ed. lib. bdg. 50.00 (ISBN 0-89984-014-0). Century Bookbindery.

Abbott, Frank F. A History & Description of Roman Political Institutions. 3rd ed. LC 63-10766. 451p. (gr. 7 up). 1910. 10.00x (ISBN 0-8196-0117-9). Biblo.

--Society & Politics in Ancient Rome: Essays & Sketches. LC 63-10767. 267p. (gr. 7 up). 1909. 10.00x (ISBN 0-8196-0118-7). Biblo.

Abbott, G. Ghosts of the Tower of London. (Illus.). 85p. pap. 4.95 (ISBN 0-434-00595-9, Pub. by Heinemann). David & Charles.

--Great Escapes from the Tower of London. (Illus.). 128p. 1982. 6.50 (Pub. by W Heinemann). David & Charles.

Abbott, George C. International Indebtedness & the Developing Countries. LC 79-5070. 1979. 30.00 (ISBN 0-87332-149-9). M E Sharpe.

Abbott, Grace. The Immigrant & the Community. LC 70-145468. (The American Immigration Library). xii, 303p. 1971. Repr. of 1917 ed. lib. bdg. 16.50x (ISBN 0-89198-000-8). Ozer.

Abbott, Grace, jt. auth. see Hockett, Betty.

Abbott, Ira H. & Von Doenhoff, Albert E. Theory of Wing Sections: Including a Summary of Airfoil Data. (Illus.). 1949. pap. 9.00 (ISBN 0-486-60586-8). Dover.

Abbott, J. C. Marketing Fruit & Vegetables. 2nd rev. ed. (FAO Marketing Guides, No. 2; FAO Plant Production & Protection Papers: No. 6). 1978. pap. 12.25 (ISBN 0-686-92991-8, F271, FAO). Unipub.

Abbott, J. C., jt. auth. see Stewart, G. F.

Abbott, Jacob. The Franconia Stories, 10 vols. in 2. LC 75-32164. (Classics of Children's Literature, 1621-1932: Vol. 28). (Illus.). 1976. Repr. of 1853 ed. Set. PLB 60.00 o.s.i. (ISBN 0-8240-2277-7); PLB 38.00 ea. o.s.i. Garland Pub.

Abbott, James H., tr. see Zea, Leopoldo.

Abbott, Jean, et al. Protocols for Prehospital Emergency Medical Care. (Illus.). 216p. 1980. softcover 12.95 (ISBN 0-683-00043-8). Williams & Wilkins.

Abbott, Joe. On-Line Programming: A Management Guide. 110p. (Orig.). 1981. pap. 20.00x (ISBN 0-85012-295-3). Intl Pubns Serv.

Abbott, John, jt. auth. see Prillaman, Douglas.

Abbott, John L. John Hawkesworth, Eighteenth-Century Man of Letters. 316p. 1982. text ed. 22.50 (ISBN 0-299-08610-0). U of Wis Pr.

Abbott, John S. History of Joseph Bonaparte: King of Naples & Italy. 391p. Repr. of 1869 ed. lib. bdg. 30.00 (ISBN 0-686-82064-9). Darby Bks.

Abbott, Katharine M. Old Paths & Legends of the New England Border: Connecticut, Deerfield, Berkshire. LC 72-75227. 1970. Repr. of 1907 ed. 34.00x (ISBN 0-8103-3562-X). Gale.

Abbott, Katherine M. Old Paths & Legends of New England: Saunterings Over Historic Roads with Glimpses of Picturesque Fields & Old Homesteads in Massachusetts, Rhode Island & New Hampshire. LC 76-75228. Repr. of 1903 ed. 34.00x (ISBN 0-8103-3564-6). Gale.

Abbott, Kenneth M., et al. Index Verborum in Ciceronis Rhetorica: Necnon Incerti Auctoris Libros Ad Herennium. LC 64-19115. 1964. 75.00 o.p. (ISBN 0-252-72481-X). U of Ill Pr.

Abbott, M. B. Computational Hydraulics: Elements of the Theory of Free Surface Flows. (Water Resources Engineering Ser.). 324p. 1979. text ed. 60.50 (ISBN 0-273-01140-5). Pitman Pub MA.

Abbott, M. B. & Cunge, J. A. Engineering Applications of Computational Hydraulics. (Water Resources Engineering Ser.). 288p. 1982. pap. text ed. 60.50 (ISBN 0-273-08512-3). Pitman Pub MA.

Abbott, M. M. & VanNess, H. C. Thermodynamics. (Schaum Outline Ser). 1972. pap. 8.95 (ISBN 0-07-000040-9, SP). McGraw.

Abbott, M. M., jt. auth. see Van Ness, H. C.

Abbott, Philip. The Shotgun Behind the Door: Liberalism & the Problem of Political Obligation. LC 74-84590. 212p. 1975. 12.50x o.p. (ISBN 0-8203-0359-3). U of Ga Pr.

Abbott, R. Tucker, jt. auth. see Wagner, R. J.

Abbott, R. Tucker, jt. auth. see Warmke, Germaine L.

Abbott, Roger H., tr. see Nachtigall, Werner.

Abbott, Sally A. Esther: A Melodrama in three Acts. (Orig.). Date not set. pap. 1.50 (ISBN 0-937172-45-6). JLJ Pubs. Postponed.

Abbott, Sheldon. Automotive Brakes: Text-Lab Manual. 1st ed. 1977. pap. 12.76 (ISBN 0-02-810150-2); tchrs manual 2.40 (ISBN 0-02-810160-X). Glencoe.

Abbott, Sheldon L. Automotive Power Trains. LC 77-73274. 256p. 1978. pap. text ed. 12.76 (ISBN 0-02-810130-8); instrs'. manual 2.40 (ISBN 0-02-810140-5). Glencoe.

--Automotive Transmissions. 320p. 1980. pap. text ed. 12.76 (ISBN 0-02-810170-7); instr. manual 2.40 (ISBN 0-02-810180-4). Glencoe.

Abbott, Sheldon L. & Hinerman, Ivan D. Automotive Suspension & Steering. LC 74-25602. 377p. 1982. pap. text ed. 13.56 (ISBN 0-02-810350-5); instrs'. manual 2.40 (ISBN 0-02-810360-2). Glencoe.

Abbott, Shirley. Womenfolks: Growing up Down South. LC 82-16880. 224p. 1983. 13.95 (ISBN 0-89919-156-8). Ticknor & Fields.

Abbott, T. K. Ephesians & Colossians. LC 40-15742. (International Critical Commentary Ser.). 392p. Repr. of 1979 ed. text ed. 21.00x o.p. (ISBN 0-567-05030-0). Attic Pr.

Abbott, Tucker & Dance, Peter. Compendium of Seashells: A Color Guide to More than Four Thousand of the World's Marine Shells. (Illus.). 400p. 1983. 50.00 (ISBN 0-525-93269-0). Dutton.

Abbott, W. M., et al. The Bible Reader: An Interfaith Interpretation. 1969. 6.95 o.p. (ISBN 0-02-800010-2). Glencoe.

Abbott, Waldo M. & Rider, R. L. Handbook of Broadcasting. 4th ed. (Illus.). 1957. 29.00 (ISBN 0-07-000028-X, C). McGraw.

Abbott, Walter. Foundations of Modern Sociology: Study Guide & Workbook. 3rd ed. 224p. 1982. pap. 8.95 (ISBN 0-13-330431-0). P-H.

Abbott, Wilbur C. Bibliography of Oliver Cromwell. LC 29-21262. Repr. of 1929 ed. 28.00 (ISBN 0-527-00110-4). Kraus Repr.

--Conflicts With Oblivion. 1924. text ed. 14.50x (ISBN 0-686-83509-3). Elliots Bks.

Abbott-Smith, G. A Manual Greek Lexicon of the New Testament. 3rd ed. 528p. 1977. text ed. 20.95 o.p. (ISBN 0-567-01001-5). Attic Pr.

Abbs, B., et al. Strategies. (English As a Second Language Bk.). (Illus.). 1976. pap. text ed. 7.00x (ISBN 0-582-51872-5). skyhigh cassette songsheet 15.50 (ISBN 0-582-56948-6); skyhigh record & songsheet 14.00 (ISBN 0-686-31668-1). Longman.

Abbs, Peter. English Within the Arts. 148p. (Orig.). 1983. pap. 8.50 (ISBN 0-89874-599-3). Krieger.

Abbs, Peter, ed. Autobiography in Education. 1974. text ed. 12.95x o.p. (ISBN 0-435-80011-6); pap. text ed. 4.50x o.p. (ISBN 0-435-80012-4). Heinemann Ed.

ABC-Clio Staff. Political & Social Science Journals: A Handbook for Writers & Reviewers. LC 82-18455. (Clio Guides to Publishing Opportunities: No. 2). 250p. 1983. lib. bdg. 24.85 (ISBN 0-87436-026-9); pap. 12.85 (ISBN 0-87436-037-4). ABC Clio.

Abcarian, Gilbert & Soule, John W. Social Psychology & Political Behavior. LC 79-138967. 1971. pap. 6.95x (ISBN 0-675-09261-2). Merrill.

Abcarian, Richard & Klotz, Marvin, eds. The Experience of Fiction. LC 74-23048. (Illus.). 500p. 1975. pap. text ed. 11.95 (ISBN 0-312-27615-X); inst. manual avail. (ISBN 0-312-27650-8). St Martin.

--Literature: The Human Experience. 3rd ed. LC 81-51834. 1260p. 1982. pap. text ed. 14.95 (ISBN 0-312-48795-9); Instr's. manual avail. St Martin.

Abdallah. Abdallah Dictionary of International Relations & Conference Terminology in English-Arabic. 1982. 40.00x (ISBN 0-86685-289-1). Intl Bk Ctr.

Abdallah, Maureen S. Middle East. LC 80-53900. (Countries Ser.). PLB 12.68 (ISBN 0-382-06417-8). Silver.

Abd al-Rahman al Jami. The Precious Pearl: Al-Durrah Al-Fakhirah. Heer, Nicholas L., tr. from Arabic. LC 78-126071. 1979. 34.50x (ISBN 0-87395-379-7). State U NY Pr.

Abdeen, Adnan. English-Arabic Dictionary for Accounting & Finance. LC 79-41213. 1981. 23.95x (ISBN 0-471-27673-1, Pub. by Wiley-Interscience). Wiley.

Abdelali, Benharbit, jt. auth. see Al-Moajil, Abdullah H.

Abdel-Fadil, M. Development, Income Distribution & Social Change in Rural Egypt 1952-1970. LC 75-17114. (Department of Applied Economics, Occasional Papers Ser.: No. 45). 1976. pap. 16.95x (ISBN 0-521-29019-8). Cambridge U Pr.

--The Political Economy of Nasserism. LC 80-49995. (Cambridge Department of Applied Economics, Occasional Papers: No. 52). (Illus.). 140p. 1980. 29.95 (ISBN 0-521-22313-X); pap. 16.95 (ISBN 0-521-29446-0). Cambridge U Pr.

Abdel-khalik, A. Rashad, ed. Internal Control & the Impact of the Foreign Corrupt Practices Act. LC 82-17480. (Accounting Ser.-University of Florida: No. 12). (Illus.). 240p. 1982. pap. 8.00 (ISBN 0-8130-0730-5). U Presses Fla.

Abdelkofi, Mohamed. One Hundred Arabic Proverbs from Libya. 9.50x (ISBN 0-392-14274-0, ABC). Sportshelf.

Abdella, Fay G. & Levine, Eugene. Better Patient Care Through Nursing Research. 2nd ed. 1978. 28.95x (ISBN 0-02-300110-0). Macmillan.

Abdel-Malek, A., jt. auth. see Pecufflic, M.

Abdel-Malek, Anouar. Civilizations & Social Theory: Social Dialectics. Gonzalez, M., tr. from Fr. LC 80-25061. 207p. 1981. 34.50x (ISBN 0-87395-500-5); pap. 12.95x (ISBN 0-87395-502-1). State U NY Pr.

--Nation & Revolution: Social Dialectics. Gonzalez, M., tr. from Fr. LC 80-25061. 217p. 1981. 34.50x (ISBN 0-87395-501-3); pap. 12.95x (ISBN 0-686-72181-0). State U NY Pr.

Abdel-Massih, Ernest. The Life & Miracles of Pope Kirillos VI. 139p. (Orig.). 1982. pap. text ed. 3.00 (ISBN 0-932098-20-7). St Mark Coptic Orthodox.

Abdel-Massih, Ernest T. A Course in Moroccan Arabic. LC 72-24740. 1970. pap. text ed. 6.00 o.p. (ISBN 0-932098-03-7). Ctr for NE & North African Stud.
--An Introduction to Moroccan Arabic. rev. ed. LC 74-154239. 1982. pap. text ed. 8.00x (ISBN 0-932098-07-X). Ctr for NE & North African Stud.
--The Life & Miracles of Pope Kirillos VI. 1982. pap. text ed. 3.00 (ISBN 0-686-84212-X). Ctr for NE & North African Stud.
--Tamazight Verb Stucture: A Generative Approach. LC 72-633892. (African Ser: Vol. 2). (Orig.). 1968. pap. text ed. 9.00x o.p. (ISBN 0-87750-160-2). Res Ctr Lang Semiotic.
Abdel-Monem, Mahmoud M. & Henkel, James G. Essentials of Drug Product Quality: Concepts & Methodology. LC 77-27069. (Illus.). 1978. text ed. 19.95 o.p. (ISBN 0-8016-0031-6). Mosby.
Abd-El-Wahed. Refrigeration & Conditioning Dictionary. 395p. (Eng. Fr. Ger. & Arabic.). 1979. 45.00 (ISBN 0-686-97399-2, M-9756). French & Eur.
Abd-El-Wahed, A. M. Iron & Steel Industry Dictionary. 441p. (Eng., Fr., Ger. & Arabic.). 1974. 45.00 (ISBN 0-686-92487-8, M-9760). French & Eur.
Abdi, Ali Issa. Commercial Banks & Economic Development: The Experience of Eastern Africa. LC 77-12813. (Praeger Special Studies). 160p. 1978. 23.95 o.p. (ISBN 0-03-023031-4). Praeger.
Abdillah Ahmed Wied. Out of the Somali World. 1983. price not set (ISBN 0-914110-13-6). Blyden Pr.
Abdu'l-Baha. A Traveler's Narrative: Written to Illustrate the Episode of the Bab. rev. ed. Browne, Edward G., tr. from Persian. LC 79-19025. 1980. 11.95 (ISBN 0-87743-134-5, 106-027); pap. 5.95 (ISBN 0-686-96668-6, 106-028). Baha'i.
Abdu'l-Baha, jt. auth. see Bahau'lah.
Abdu'l-Baha, jt. auth. see Baha'u'llah, The Bab.
Abdulla, Ummi. Malabar Muslim Cookery. 112p. 1981. pap. text ed. 4.25x (ISBN 0-86131-241-4, Pub. by Orient Ltd India). Apt Bks.
Abdullah, M., jt. auth. see Kuffel.
Abdullah, M. Mansur. Permata-Permata Di Lumpur. (Karyawan Malaysia Ser.). (Malay.). 1979. pap. text ed. 3.25x o.p. (ISBN 0-686-60458-X, 00354). Heinemann Ed.
Abdullah, Yahya Taher. The Mountain of Green Tea. 130p. 1983. 15.00X (ISBN 0-89410-353-9); pap. 5.00X (ISBN 0-89410-352-0). Three Continents.
Abdulrazak, Fawzi. Arabic Historical Writing, Nineteen Seventy-Five-Nineteen Seventy-Six: An Annotated Bibliography of Books in History from All Parts of the Arab World. 228p. 1979. pap. 27.00 o.p. (ISBN 0-7201-0836-5, Pub. by Mansell England). Wilson.
Abe, E. Hopf Algebras. LC 79-50912. (Cambridge Tracts in Mathematics Ser.: No. 74). 1980. 42.50 (ISBN 0-521-22240-0). Cambridge U Pr.
Abe, Kobo. The Box Man. Saunders, E. D., tr. (The Perigee Japanese Library). (Illus.). 192p. 1981. pap. 4.95 (ISBN 0-399-50485-0, Perige). Putnam Pub Group.
--The Face of Another. Saunders, E. D., tr. (The Perigee Japanese Library). 256p. 1981. pap. 4.95 (ISBN 0-399-50484-2, Perige). Putnam Pub Group.
--Friends. Keene, Donald, tr. from Japanese. (Orig.). 1969. pap. 2.45 o.s.i. (ISBN 0-394-17312-0, E487, Ever). Grove.
--Inter Ice Age Four. Saunders, E. Dale, tr. from Jap. (Perigee Japanese Library). 240p. 1981. pap. 4.95 (ISBN 0-399-50519-9, Perige). Putnam Pub Group.
--The Ruined Map. Sanders, E. Dale, tr. (The Perigee Japanese Library). (Illus.). 320p. 1981. pap. 5.95 (ISBN 0-399-50470-2, Perige). Putnam Pub Group.
--The Secret Rendezvous. Carpenter, Juliet W., tr. (The Perigee Japanese Library). 192p. 1981. pap. 4.95 (ISBN 0-399-50501-6, Perige). Putnam Pub Group.
Abecassis De Laredo, E., ed. see Latin School of Physics, 14th Caracas, Venezuela July 10-28, 1972.
A Beckett, Arthur W. A Becketts of Punch. LC 69-17341. 1969. Repr. of 1903 ed. 34.00x (ISBN 0-8103-3518-2). Gale.
Abegglen, James C. The Japanese Factory. rev. ed. LC 80-52878. 200p. 1983. pap. 6.25 (ISBN 0-8048-1372-8). C E Tuttle.
Abegglen, James C., et al. U. S. - Japan Economic Relations: A Symposium on Critical Issues. LC 80-620017. (Research Papers & Policy Studies: No. 1). 68p. 1980. pap. 5.00x (ISBN 0-912966-25-4). IEAS.
Abehsera, Michael, compiled by see Muramoto, Naboru.
Abel, et al. Poetic Humor. new ed. Jensen, Sheila R., ed. LC 77-93188. (Illus.). 36p. 1978. pap. 3.00 (ISBN 0-932044-06-9). M O Pub Co.
Abel, Alan. Don't Get Mad...Get Even! A Manual for Retaliation. (Illus.). 1983. 10.95 (ISBN 0-393-01614-5); pap. 4.95 (ISBN 0-393-30118-4). Norton.
Abel, Andrew, ed. see Modigliani, Franco.
Abel, Andrew B. Investment & the Value of Capital. LC 78-75063. (Outstanding Dissertations in Economics Ser.). 1979. lib. bdg. 22.00 o.s.i. (ISBN 0-8240-4139-9). Garland Pub.
Abel, Bob. The Beer Book. (Illus.). 96p. 1981. ring bd. 12.95 (ISBN 0-8256-3236-6, Quick Fox); 13 copy prepack 155.40 (ISBN 0-8256-3258-7). Putnam Pub Group.
Abel, Charles, jt. auth. see Falk, Edwin A.
Abel, E. L. Marihuana: The First Twelve Thousand Years. 1982. pap. 6.95 (ISBN 0-07-000047-6). McGraw.
Abel, E. W. & Stone, F. G. Organometallic Chemistry, Vol. 9. 557p. 1982. 290.00x (ISBN 0-85186-571-2, Pub. by Royal Soc Chem England). State Mutual Bk.
Abel, Elie, ed. What's News: The Media in American Society. LC 81-81414. 296p. (Orig.). 1981. text ed. 18.95 (ISBN 0-87855-448-3); pap. text ed. 7.95 (ISBN 0-917616-41-3). ICS Pr.
--What's News: The Media in American Society. 300p. 1981. 18.95 (ISBN 0-87855-448-3); pap. 7.95. Transaction Bks.
Abel, Elizabeth. Writing & Sexual Difference. LC 82-11131. (Phoenix Ser.). 312p. 1983. pap. 7.95 (ISBN 0-226-00076-1). U OF CHICAGO PR.
Abel, Elizabeth & Hirsch, Marianne, eds. The Voyage IN: Fictions of Female Development. LC 82-40473. 340p. 1983. text ed. 25.00x (ISBN 0-87451-250-6); pap. 12.50 (ISBN 0-87451-251-4). U Pr of New Eng.
Abel, Ernest L. Drugs & Behavior: A Primer in Neuropsychopharmacology. LC 80-11313. 240p. 1982. Repr. of 1974 ed. lib. bdg. 16.50 (ISBN 0-89874-137-8). Krieger.
--Drugs & Behavior: A Primer in Neuropsychopharmacology. LC 74-8969. 240p. 1974. 19.95 o.p. (ISBN 0-471-00155-4, Pub. by Wiley-Interscience). Wiley.
--Smoking & Reproduction: A Comprehensive Bibliography. LC 82-15660. 178p. 1982. lib. bdg. 35.00 (ISBN 0-313-23663-1, ASR/). Greenwood.
Abel, Ernest L. & Buckley, Barbara E. The Handwriting on the Wall: Toward a Sociology & Psychology of Graffiti. LC 76-50408. (Contributions in Sociology: No. 27). 1977. lib. bdg. 22.50x (ISBN 0-8371-9475-X, AVJ/). Greenwood.
Abel, Ernest L., compiled by. Alcohol & Reproduction. LC 82-6202. xviii, 235p. 1982. lib. bdg. 29.95 (ISBN 0-313-23474-4, AAR/). Greenwood.
--A Comprehensive Guide to the Cannabis Literature. LC 78-20014. 1979. lib. bdg. 45.50 (ISBN 0-313-20721-6, ACG/). Greenwood.
Abel, Martin S. Occult Traumatic Lesions of the Cervical & Thoraco-Lumbar Vertebrae. 2nd ed. 386p. 1983. 42.50 (ISBN 0-87527-312-2). Green.
--Occult Traumatic Lesions of the Cervical Vertebrae. LC 76-107200. (Illus.). 156p. 1971. 15.00 (ISBN 0-87527-000-X). Green.
Abel, Peter. Programming Assembler Language. (Illus.). 1979. text ed. 22.95 (ISBN 0-8359-5658-X); instrs'. manual avail. (ISBN 0-8359-5659-8). Reston.
--Structured PL-One & PL: A Problem Solving Approach. 1981. text ed. 22.95 (ISBN 0-8359-7120-1); pap. text ed. 16.95 (ISBN 0-8359-7119-8); instr's. manual avail. (ISBN 0-8359-7121-X). Reston.
Abel, Reuben E., ed. Humanistic Pragmatism: The Philosophy of F. C. S. Schiller. (Orig.). 1966. pap. text ed. 6.95 (ISBN 0-02-900120-X). Free Pr.
Abel, Richard, ed. The Politics of Informal Justice: Vol. 2, Comparative Studies. LC 81-14920. (Studies on Law & Social Control Ser.). 1981. 29.50 (ISBN 0-12-041502-X). Acad Pr.
Abel, Wilhelm. Agricultural Fluctuations in Europe: From the Thirteenth to the Twentieth Centuries. Ordish, Olive, tr. LC 80-5072. 1980. 42.50 (ISBN 0-312-01465-1). St Martin.
Abele, Lawrence, jt. ed. see Bliss, Dorothy.
Abeles, P W. & Bardham Roy, B K. Prestressed Concrete Designer's Handbook. 3rd ed. (Illus.). 550p. 1981. lib. bdg. 60.00x (ISBN 0-7210-1232-9, Pub. by Viewpoint); pap. text ed. 42.50x (ISBN 0-7210-1227-2, Pub. by Viewpoint). Scholium Intl.
Abeles, Ronald P., jt. ed. see Riley, Matilda W.
Abell, George & Singer, Barry. Science & the Paranormal. (Illus.). 432p. 1983. pap. 8.95 (ISBN 0-686-83708-8, ScribT). Scribner.
Abell, J. M. & Sengel, E. W., eds. Petroleum Production Technology. 1981. 36.00 (ISBN 0-89931-027-3). Inst Energy.
Abell, Millicent, ed. Collective Bargaining in Higher Education. (ACRL Publications in Librarianship Ser.: No. 38). 170p. 1977. pap. 8.00 o.p. (ISBN 0-8389-3189-8). ALA.
Abell, Peter. Model Building in Sociology. LC 74-163325. (Basic Ideas in the Human Sciences Ser). (Illus.). 1971. 12.00x o.p. (ISBN 0-8052-3413-6). Schocken.
Abell, Troy D. Better Felt Than Said. LC 81-86285. 206p. 1982. 18.00 (ISBN 0-918954-35-5). Markham Pr Fund.
Abell, Vivian & Farlie, Barbara L. Flower Craft. 192p. 1982. pap. 10.95 (ISBN 0-686-97308-9). Bobbs.
Abell, Vivian, jt. auth. see Farlie, Barbara.
Abell, Walter. Representation & Form. LC 79-138573. (Illus.). 1971. Repr. of 1936 ed. lib. bdg. 18.50x (ISBN 0-8371-5772-2, ABRF). Greenwood.
Abella, Irving & Millar, David, eds. The Canadian Worker in the Twentieth Century. 1978. pap. 9.95x (ISBN 0-19-540250-2). Oxford U Pr.
Abella, Irving M. Nationalism, Communism & Canadian Labour: The CIO, the Communist Party, & the Canadian Congress of Labour, 1935-56. LC 72-80712. 304p. 1973. pap. 7.50 o.p. (ISBN 0-8020-6150-8). U of Toronto Pr.
Abells, Chana. The Children-We Remember. LC 82-23377. (Illus.). 48p. (gr. 1-6). 1983. 6.95 (ISBN 0-930494-20-2); pap. 7.95 (ISBN 0-930494-21-0). Kar Ben.
Abelman, Paul. Tests: Maximum Characters in Any Play-5. 1981. pap. 5.95 (ISBN 0-413-31570-3). Methuen Inc.
Abeloff, Diane. Medical Art: Graphics for Use. (Illus.). 264p. 1982. spiral 65.00 (ISBN 0-683-00033-0). Williams & Wilkins.
Abelow, Dan. Total Sex. LC 76-27127. (Illus.). 96p. 1981. pap. 6.95 (ISBN 0-448-12851-9, G&D). Putnam Pub Group.
Abels. Painting: Materials & Methods. (The Grosset Art Instruction Ser.: No. 28). (Illus.). 48p. 1982. pap. 2.95 (ISBN 0-448-00537-9, G&D). Putnam Pub Group.
Abels, Harriette S. A Forgotten World. Schroeder, Howard, ed. LC 79-4633. (Galaxy I Ser.). (Illus.). (gr. 3-5). 1979. PLB 6.95 (ISBN 0-89686-032-9); pap. 3.50 (ISBN 0-89686-041-8). Crestwood Hse.
--Future Business. Schroeder, Howard, ed. LC 80-14859. (Our Future World Ser.). (Illus.). 48p. (gr. 6-9). 1980. PLB 7.95 (ISBN 0-89686-081-7); pap. text ed. 3.95 (ISBN 0-89686-090-6). Crestwood Hse.
--Future Communication. Schroeder, Howard, ed. LC 80-16529. (Our Future World Ser.). (Illus.). 48p. (gr. 6-9). 1980. PLB 7.95 (ISBN 0-89686-084-1); pap. text ed. 3.95 (ISBN 0-89686-093-0). Crestwood Hse.
--Future Family. Schroeder, Howard, ed. LC 80-16400. (Our Future World Ser.). (Illus.). 48p. (gr. 6-9). 1980. PLB 7.95 (ISBN 0-89686-085-X); pap. text ed. 3.95 (ISBN 0-89686-094-9). Crestwood Hse.
--Future Food. Schroeder, Howard, ed. LC 80-14823. (Our Future World Ser.). (Illus.). 48p. (Orig.). (gr. 6-9). 1980. PLB 7.95 (ISBN 0-89686-083-3); pap. text ed. 3.95 (ISBN 0-89686-092-2). Crestwood Hse.
--Future Government. Schroeder, Howard, ed. LC 80-14940. (Our Future World Ser.). (Illus.). 48p. (gr. 4 up). PLB 7.95 (ISBN 0-89686-082-5); pap. 3.95 (ISBN 0-89686-091-4). Crestwood Hse.
--Future Science. Schroeder, Howard, ed. LC 80-19412. (Our Future World Ser.). (Illus.). 48p. (Orig.). (gr. 6-9). 1980. PLB 7.95 (ISBN 0-89686-080-9); pap. 3.95 (ISBN 0-89686-089-2). Crestwood Hse.
--Future Space. Schroeder, Howard, ed. LC 80-16457. (Our Future World Ser.). (Illus.). 48p. (Orig.). (gr. 4 up). PLB 7.95 (ISBN 0-89686-087-6); pap. 3.95 (ISBN 0-89686-096-5). Crestwood Hse.
--Future Travel. Schroeder, Howard, ed. (Our Future World Ser.). (Illus.). 48p. (gr. 6-9). 1980. PLB 7.95 (ISBN 0-89686-088-4); pap. 3.95 (ISBN 0-89686-097-3). Crestwood Hse.
--The Green Invasion. Schroeder, Howard, ed. LC 79-4639. (Galaxy I Ser.). (Illus.). (gr. 3-5). 1979. PLB 6.95 (ISBN 0-89686-030-2); pap. 3.50 (ISBN 0-89686-039-6). Crestwood Hse.
--Medical Emergency. Schroeder, Howard, ed. LC 79-9823. (Galaxy I Ser.). (Illus.). (gr. 3-5). 1979. PLB 6.95 (ISBN 0-89686-029-9); pap. 3.50 (ISBN 0-89686-038-8). Crestwood Hse.
--Meteor from the Moon. Schroeder, Howard, ed. LC 79-4650. (Galaxy I Ser.). (Illus.). (gr. 3-5). 1979. PLB 6.95 (ISBN 0-89686-025-6); pap. 3.50 (ISBN 0-89686-034-5). Crestwood Hse.
--Mystery on Mars. Schroeder, Howard, ed. LC 79-9923. (Galaxy I Ser.). (Illus.). (gr. 3-5). 1979. PLB 6.95 (ISBN 0-89686-024-8); pap. 3.50 (ISBN 0-89686-033-7). Crestwood Hse.
--Planet of Ice. Schroeder, Howard, ed. LC 79-9920. (Galaxy I Ser.). (Illus.). (gr. 3-5). 1979. PLB 6.95 (ISBN 0-89686-026-4); pap. 3.50 (ISBN 0-89686-035-3). Crestwood Hse.
--September Storm. LC 80-28430. (Prime Time Adventures Ser.). (Illus.). 64p. (gr. 4 up). 1981. PLB 8.65 (ISBN 0-516-02110-9). Childrens.
--The Silent Invaders. Schroeder, Howard, ed. LC 79-4644. (Galaxy I Ser.). (Illus.). (gr. 3-5). 1979. PLB 6.95 (ISBN 0-89686-031-0); pap. 3.50 (ISBN 0-89686-040-X). Crestwood Hse.
--Strangers on NMA-6. Schroeder, Howard, ed. LC 79-4627. (Galaxy I Ser.). (Illus.). (gr. 3-5). 1979. PLB 6.95 (ISBN 0-89686-027-2); pap. 3.50 (ISBN 0-89686-036-1). Crestwood Hse.
--Unwanted Visitors. Schroeder, Howard, ed. LC 79-9922. (Galaxy I Ser.). (Illus.). (gr. 3-5). 1979. PLB 6.95 (ISBN 0-89686-028-0); pap. 3.50 (ISBN 0-89686-037-X). Crestwood Hse.
Abels, Harriette Sheffer. Follow Me, Love. (YA) 1978. 6.95 (ISBN 0-685-05586-8, Avalon). Bouregy.
Abels, Linda F., et al. Critical Care Nursing: Process & Practice. (Illus.). 825p. 1983. pap. text ed. 25.95 (ISBN 0-8016-0083-9). Mosby.
Abels, Paul & Murphy, Michael J. Administration in the Human Services: A Normative Systems Approach. (P-H Ser. in Social Work). (Illus.). 256p. 1981. text ed. 21.95 (ISBN 0-13-005850-5). P-H.
Abel-Smith, Brian. Value for Money in Health Services. 1976. pap. text ed. 11.00x (ISBN 0-435-82006-0). Heinemann Ed.
Abel-Smith, Brian, et al. Legal Problems & the Citizen. 1973. text ed. 26.00x o.p. (ISBN 0-435-82865-7). Heinemann Ed.
Abelson, H. Logo for the Apple II. 1982. 14.95 (ISBN 0-07-000426-9). McGraw.
Abelson, Harold & DiSessa, Andrea. Turtle Geometry: The Computer As a Medium for Exploring Mathematics. (Illus.). 416p. 1981. text ed. 22.50x (ISBN 0-262-01063-1). MIT Pr.
Abelson, Philip H., ed. Food: Politics, Economics, Nutrition & Research. 1976. 22.50 (ISBN 0-12-041652-2); pap. 9.50 (ISBN 0-12-041653-0). Acad Pr.
Abelson, Raziel. Persons: A Study in Philosophical Psychology. LC 76-19225. 1977. 22.50x (ISBN 0-312-60235-9). St Martin.
Abelson, Robert, jt. auth. see Schank, Roger.
Aben, Hillar. Integrated Photoelasticity. (Illus.). 1979. 42.50x (ISBN 0-07-000043-3). McGraw.
Aberbach, Joel D. & Putnam, Robert D. Bureaucrats & Politicians in Western Democracies. 324p. 1982. pap. text ed. 9.95x (ISBN 0-674-08627-9). Harvard U Pr.
Abercrombie, A. Vaughn. His Everlasting Words. 80p. 7.95 (ISBN 0-89962-326-3). Todd & Honeywell.
Abercrombie, Barbara. Good Riddance. LC 78-20197. 1979. 11.49 (ISBN 0-06-010021-4, HarpT). Harrow.
Abercrombie, Lascelles. Principles of Literary Criticism. LC 78-21288. 1979. Repr. of 1932 ed. lib. bdg. 17.50x (ISBN 0-313-20025-4, ABPL). Greenwood.
Abercrombie, M. & Brachet, J., eds. Advances in Morphogenesis, 10 vols. Incl. Vol. 1. 1961 (ISBN 0-12-028601-7); Vol. 2. 1963 (ISBN 0-12-028602-5); Vol. 3. 1964. (ISBN 0-12-028603-3); Vol. 4. 1965 (ISBN 0-12-028604-1); Vol. 5. 1966 (ISBN 0-12-028605-X); Vol. 6. 1967 (ISBN 0-12-028606-8); Vol. 7. King, T. J., ed. 1968 (ISBN 0-12-028607-6); Vol. 8. King, T. J., ed. 1970 (ISBN 0-12-028608-4); Vol. 9. King, T. J., ed. 1971 (ISBN 0-12-028609-2); Vol. 10. 1973 (ISBN 0-12-028610-6). 55.00 ea. Acad Pr.
Abercrombie, V. T. & Gaylord, Louise. Catering to Houston. LC 80-70604. 1981. 9.95. Brown Rabbit.
Aberg, F. A., ed. Medieval Moated Sites. (CBA Research Report Ser.: No. 17). 91p. 1978. pap. text ed. 17.95x (ISBN 0-900312-58-0, Pub. by Coun Brit Archaeology). Humanities.
Aberle, D. F., jt. auth. see Dyen, D.
Abernathey, William J. & Clark, Kim B. Industrial Renaissance: Producing a Competitive Future in America. 1983. 19.00 (ISBN 0-465-03254-0). Basic.
Abernathy, Billy, jt. auth. see Jones, LeRoi.
Abernathy, David & Perrin, Norman. Understanding the Teaching of Jesus. 288p. (Orig.). 1983. pap. 13.95 (ISBN 0-8164-2438-1). Seabury.
Abernathy, Estelle K. Pumpkin Corner. (Illus.). 160p. 1979. pap. 5.00 (ISBN 0-9608428-2-9). Straw Patch.
Abernathy, Steve. Learning Safety First. (Science Ser.). 24p. (gr. 5-9). 1977. wkbk. 5.00 (ISBN 0-8209-0158-X, S-20). ESP.
Abernathy, William J., jt. auth. see Ginsburg, Douglas H.
Abernethy, Francis E., ed. Legendary Ladies of Texas. LC 80-68402. (Publications of the Texas Folklore Society No. 43 in Cooperation with the Texas Foundation for Women's Resources Women in Texas History Project). (Illus.). 236p. (Orig.). 1981. o.p 24.95 (ISBN 0-935014-01-2); pap. 12.95 (ISBN 0-935014-02-0). E-Heart Pr.
Abernethy, George L. & Langford, Thomas A., eds. Philosophy of Religion: A Book of Readings. 2nd ed. 1968. 21.95x (ISBN 0-02-300150-X, 30015). Macmillan.
Abernethy, Virginia, ed. Frontiers in Medical Ethics: Applications in a Medical Setting. LC 79-26566. 216p. 1980. prof ref 25.00x (ISBN 0-88410-710-8). Ballinger Pub.
Abert, Geoffrey. After the Crash. rev. ed. 1982. pap. 3.95 (ISBN 0-451-11869-3, AE1869, Sig). NAL.
Aberth, Oliver. Computable Analysis. new ed. (Illus.). 208p. 1980. text ed. 37.50 (ISBN 0-07-000079-4, C). McGraw.
Abhishiktananda. Prayer. LC 73-600. 1973. pap. 3.95 (ISBN 0-664-24973-6). Westminster.
Abian, Alexander. Linear Associative Algebras. 1972. text ed. 23.00 (ISBN 0-08-016564-8). Pergamon.
Abidin, Richard R. Parenting Skills: Workbook & Trainer's Manual. 2nd ed. LC 81-13314. 84p. 1982. 8.95 (ISBN 0-89885-118-1); lab manual 155 16.95 (ISBN 0-89885-117-3); Set. 19.95 (ISBN 0-89885-119-X). Human Sci Pr.
Abiko, Yasushi, jt. ed. see Winbury, Martin.
Abildness, Abby J. Biofeedback Strategies. (Illus.). 160p. (Orig.). 1982. pap. text ed. 24.00 (ISBN 0-910317-09-7). Am Occup Therapy.
Abish, Walter. How German Is It. 195p. 1982. text ed. 14.75x (ISBN 0-85635-396-5, Pub. by Carcanet Pr England). Humanities.
Abish, Walter, et al see Messerli, Douglas.
Able-Peterson, Trudee. Children of the Evening. 264p. 1981. 12.95 (ISBN 0-399-12631-7). Putnam Pub Group.

Abler, Ronald, et al. Spatial Organization: The Geographer's View of the World. LC 71-123081. (Geography Ser). (Illus.). 1971. text ed. 30.95 (ISBN 0-13-824086-8). P-H.
--The Twin Cities of St. Paul & Minneapolis. LC 76-4801. (Contemporary Metropolitan Analysis Ser.). (Illus.). 1976. pap. 8.95x prof ref (ISBN 0-88410-434-6). Ballinger Pub.
Abler, Tom, et al, eds. Canadian Indian Bibliography Nineteen Sixty to Nineteen Seventy. LC 73-85083. 1974. 50.00x o.p. (ISBN 0-8020-2092-5). U of Toronto Pr.
Ables, Billie S., jt. auth. see Confer, William N.
Ablin, Fred, ed. Contemporary Soviet Education: A Collection of Readings from Soviet Journals. LC 68-14428. 1969. 22.50 (ISBN 0-87332-022-0). M E Sharpe.
Ablin, Richard J. Immunobiology of the Prostate. 320p. 1983. 27.50 (ISBN 0-87527-178-2). Green.
Ablon, Leon, et al. Series in Mathematics Modules, 5 modules. 1981. softbound 5.95 ea. Module 1 (ISBN 0-8053-0131-3). Module 2 (ISBN 0-8053-0132-1). Module 3 (ISBN 0-8053-0133-X). Module 4 (ISBN 0-8053-0134-8). Module 5 (ISBN 0-8053-0135-6). Benjamin-Cummings.
--The Steps in Mathematics Modules One Thru Five. 1981. pap. 21.95 (ISBN 0-8053-0140-2). Benjamin-Cummings.
Abo, Takaji, et al. Marshallese-English Dictionary. LC 76-26156. (PALI Language Texts-Micronesia). 624p. 1976. pap. text ed. 12.50x (ISBN 0-8248-0457-0). UH Pr.
Abodaher, David. Iacocca. (Illus.). 288p. 1982. 14.75 (ISBN 0-02-500120-5). Macmillan.
Abodaher, David J. Mag Wheels & Racing Stripes. LC 72-1828. (Illus.). 160p. (gr. 7 up). 1973. PLB 6.29 o.p. (ISBN 0-671-32557-4). Messner.
--The Speedmakers: Great Race Drivers. LC 78-27649. (Illus.). 192p. (gr. 7 up). 1979. PLB 7.79 o.p. (ISBN 0-685-99808-8). Messner.
Abolfathi, Farid, et al. The OPEC Market to Nineteen Eighty-Five. LC 76-44612. (Illus.). 1977. 25.95x o.p. (ISBN 0-669-01102-9). Lexington Bks.
Abouchar, Alan. Transportation Economics & Public Policy: With Urban Extensions. LC 76-51828. 1977. 32.95x o.p. (ISBN 0-471-02101-6, Pub. by Wiley-Interscience). Ronald Pr.
--Transportation Economics & Public Policy: With Urban Extensions. LC 82-17081. 344p. 1983. Repr. of 1977 ed. lib. bdg. price not set (ISBN 0-89874-563-2). Krieger.
Aboud, Antone, jt. auth. see Sterrett, Grace.
Aboud, Grace. Hiring & Training the Disadvantaged for Public Employment. (Key Issues Ser.: No. 11). 60p. 1973. pap. 2.00 (ISBN 0-87546-202-2). ILR Pr.
Aboud, Grace S. & Doherty, Robert E. Practices & Procedures Under the Taylor Law: A Practical Guide in Narrative Form. 84p. 1974. pap. 2.00 (ISBN 0-87546-203-0). ILR Pr.
Aboulafia, Mitchell. The Self-Winding Circle: A Study of Hegel's System. 1982. 14.75 (ISBN 0-87527-307-6). Green.
Abouleish. Pain Control in Obstetrics. 2nd ed. (Illus.). 277p. 1977. text ed. 39.50 o.p. (ISBN 0-397-50376-8, Lippincott Medical). Lippincott.
Abouleish, Ezzat. Pain Control in Obstetrics. LC 77-13971. 1977. 39.50i (ISBN 0-397-50376-8). Har-Row.
Abou-Rass, Marwan, jt. ed. see Frank, Alfred L.
Abraham, A. J. Lebanon at Mid-Century: Maronite-Druze Relations in Lebanon 1840-1860; a Prelude to Arab Nationalism. LC 80-6253. 156p. 1981. lib. bdg. 19.75 (ISBN 0-8191-1536-3); pap. text ed. 9.25 (ISBN 0-8191-1537-1). U Pr of Amer.
Abraham, Claude. Jean Racine. (World Authors Ser.). 1977. lib. bdg. 12.95 (ISBN 0-8057-6295-7, Twayne). G K Hall.
--Pierre Corneille. (World Authors Ser.). lib. bdg. 12.95 (ISBN 0-8057-2244-0, Twayne). G K Hall.
--Tristan L'Hermite. (World Authors Ser.). 1980. lib. bdg. 15.95 (ISBN 0-8057-6411-9, Twayne). G K Hall.
Abraham, Claude, et al, eds. Le Theatre Complet De Tristan l'Hermite. LC 73-7453. 859p. 1975. 27.50 (ISBN 0-8173-8600-9). U of Ala Pr.
Abraham, Fern-Rae. Tin Craft. (Illus.). 48p. (Orig.). 1975. pap. 5.00 (ISBN 0-913270-05-9). Sunstone Pr.
Abraham, George. Green Thumb Book of Fruit & Vegetable Gardening. LC 78-85000. (Illus.). 384p. 1981. 11.95 (ISBN 0-13-365189-4); pap. 6.95 (ISBN 0-13-365064-2). P-H.
Abraham, Gerald. The Concise Oxford History of Music. (Illus.). 1980. 42.50 (ISBN 0-19-311319-8). Oxford U Pr.
Abraham, Gerald, ed. The History of Music in Sound, Vols. 1-3. Incl. Vol. 1. Ancient & Oriental Music. Wellesz, Egon, ed. (Illus.). 1957 (ISBN 0-19-323100-X); Vol. 2. Early Medieval Music up to 1300. Hughes, Dom A., ed. 1953 (ISBN 0-19-323101-8); Vol. 3. Ars Nova & the Renaissance, - C. 1300-1540. Westrup, J. A., ed. 70p. 1954 (ISBN 0-19-323102-6). 6.00 ea. Oxford U Pr.
--The Music of Sibelius. LC 74-23413. (Music Ser.). 218p. 1975. Repr. of 1947 ed. lib. bdg. 25.00 (ISBN 0-306-70716-0). Da Capo.
--The New Oxford History of Music, Vol. VIII: The Age of Beethoven, 1790-1830. (Illus.). 778p. 1983. 49.95 (ISBN 0-19-316308-X). Oxford U Pr.
Abraham, Gerald see Abraham, Gerald, et al.
Abraham, Gerald, et al, eds. New Oxford History of Music. Incl. Vol. 1. Ancient & Oriental Music. Wellesz, Egon, ed. (15 plates). 1957. 49.95x (ISBN 0-19-316301-2); Vol. 2. Early Medieval Music up to 1300. Hughes, Dom Anselm, ed. 1954. 49.95 (ISBN 0-19-316302-0); Vol 3. Ars Nova & the Renaissance, 1300-1540. Hughes, Dom Anselm & Abraham, Gerald, eds. 1960. 49.95 (ISBN 0-19-316303-9); Vol. 4. The Age of Humanism, 1540-1630. Abraham, Gerald, ed. (Illus.). 1968. 44.00x (ISBN 0-19-316304-7); Vol. 7. The Age of Enlightenment, 1745-1790. Wellesz, Egon & Sternfeld, Frederick, eds. (Illus.). 1973. 49.95 (ISBN 0-19-316307-1); Vol. 10. Modern Age, 1890-1960. Cooper, Martin, ed. 1974. 49.95x (ISBN 0-19-316310-1). Oxford U Pr.
Abraham, Gerald E. Chopin's Musical Style. LC 79-25521. xii, 116p. 1980. Repr. of 1939 ed. lib. bdg. 16.25x (ISBN 0-313-22251-7, ABCM). Greenwood.
Abraham, Henry J. The Judicial Process: An Introductory Analysis of the United States, England, & France. 4th ed. 1980. text ed. 19.95x (ISBN 0-19-502612-8); pap. text ed. 10.95x (ISBN 0-19-502613-6). Oxford U Pr.
--Justices & Presidents: A Political History of Appointments to the Supreme Court. 1974. 19.95x (ISBN 0-19-501786-2). Oxford U Pr.
Abraham, Horst. Skiing Right. LC 82-8105. (Illus.). 237p. 1983. pap. 12.95 (ISBN 0-933472-74-9). Johnson Bks.
Abraham, Horst & Psia. Skiing Right. LC 81-43737. (Illus.). 224p. 1982. cancelled (ISBN 0-385-17912-X). Doubleday.
--Skiing Right. LC 81-43737. (Illus.). 224p. 1982. pap. cancelled (ISBN 0-385-17913-8, Dolp). Doubleday.
Abraham, Kurt B. Psychological Types & the Seven Rays, Vol. 1. LC 82-81863. 163p. (Orig.). 1983. pap. 8.95 (ISBN 0-9609002-0-9). Lampus Pr.
Abraham, M. Francis. Perspectives on Modernization: Toward a General Theory of Third World Development. LC 79-6811. 262p. 1980. pap. text ed. 11.75 (ISBN 0-8191-0961-4). U Pr of Amer.
Abraham, Paul & Mackey, Joan. Contact U.S.A. An ESL Reading & Vocabulary Textbook. 200p. 1982. pap. text ed. 10.95 (ISBN 0-13-169599-1). P-H.
Abraham, R. J. & Loftus, P. Proton & Carbon-13 Nmr Spectroscopy, an Integrated Approach. 1978. 24.95 (ISBN 0-471-25576-9, Wiley Heyden). Wiley.
Abraham, Ralph & Shaw, Chris. Dynamics, the Geometry of Behavior. LC 81-71616. (Visual Mathematics Ser.). (Illus.). 240p. 1982. pap. text ed. 29.00x (ISBN 0-942344-01-4). Pt. 1, Periodic Behavior. Pts. 2 & 3 Future. Aerial Pr.
--Dynamics: The Geometry of Behavior: Pt. 2, Stable & Chaotic Behavior. (Visual Mathematics Ser.). 1983. price not set. Aerial Pr.
Abraham, Robert M. Easy to Do Entertainments & Diversions with Cards, Strings, Coins, Paper & Matches. Orig. Title: Winter Nights Entertainments. 1933. pap. 2.95 (ISBN 0-486-20921-0). Dover.
--Tricks & Amusements. Orig. Title: Diversions & Pastimes with Cards, Strings, Coins, Paper & Matches. (Illus.). 1933. pap. 2.50 (ISBN 0-486-21127-4). Dover.
Abraham, Roberta G. Structure & Meaning. LC 78-23493. 1979. pap. text ed. 8.95 (ISBN 0-88377-126-8). Newbury Hse.
Abraham, Roger D. & Troike, Rudolph D., eds. Language & Cultural Diversity in American Education. 384p. 1972. pap. text ed. 12.95 (ISBN 0-13-522888-3). P-H.
Abraham, Samuel V. Real Estate Dictionary & Reference Guide. McFadden, S. Michele & Wilson-Fulkerson, Roberta, eds. LC 79-9761. 1983. pap. text ed. 6.95x (ISBN 0-89262-059-5). Career Pub.
Abraham, Sidney, jt. auth. see Carroll, Margaret D.
Abraham, Stanley C. The Public Accounting Profession. LC 77-7804. (Illus.). 320p. 1978. 23.95 (ISBN 0-669-01606-3). Lexington Bks.
Abraham, W. E. Mind of Africa. LC 63-9733. (Nature of Human Society). 1963. pap. 3.95 (ISBN 0-226-00086-9, P233, Phoen). U of Chicago Pr.
Abraham, Werner. On the Formal Syntax of the West-Germania: Papers from the "Third Groninger Grammar Talks," Groningen, January 1981. 200p. 1983. 20.00 (ISBN 90-272-2723-3). Benjamins North Am.
Abraham, William J. Divine Revelation & the Limits of Historical Criticism. 232p. 1982. 24.95x (ISBN 0-19-826665-0). Oxford U Pr.
Abraham-Frois, Gilbert & Berrebi, E. Theory of Value, Prices & Accumulation: Two Mathematical Integrations of Marx, Von Neumann & Straffa. Kregel-Javaux, M. P., tr. LC 78-16277. (Illus., Fr.). 1979. 34.50 (ISBN 0-521-22385-7). Cambridge U Pr.
Abrahams, et al. An Introduction to BASIC Programming for Small Computers. 96p. 1983. text ed. 5.96x (ISBN 0-7715-0790-9); tchr's manual 5.96x (ISBN 0-7715-0791-7). Forkner.
Abrahams, Harold J. Heroic Efforts at Meteor Crater, Arizona: Selected Correspondence Between Daniel Moreau Barringer & Elihu Thomson. LC 78-75170. 480p. 1983. 35.00 (ISBN 0-8386-2399-9). Fairleigh Dickinson.
Abrahams, Harold J. & Savin, Marion B., eds. Selections from the Scientific Correspondence of Elihu Thomson. 1971. 27.50x (ISBN 0-262-01034-8). MIT Pr.
Abrahams, Peter. Mine Boy. 1970. pap. 1.95 o.p. (ISBN 0-02-048050-4, Collier). Macmillan.
Abrahams, R. G. The Nyamwezi Today: A Tanzanian People in the Seventies. LC 80-41012. (Changing Cultures Ser.). (Illus.). 176p. 1981. 32.50 (ISBN 0-521-22694-5); pap. 10.95 (ISBN 0-521-29619-6). Cambridge U Pr.
--Political Organization of Unyamwezi. (Cambridge Studies in Social Anthropology: No. 1). (Illus.). 1967. 27.50 (ISBN 0-521-04001-9). Cambridge U Pr.
Abrahams, Roger D. Deep the Water, Shallow the Shore: Three Essays on Shantying in the West Indies. (AFS Monographs: No. 60). (Illus.). 139p. 1974. text ed. 10.95x o.p. (ISBN 0-292-71502-1). U of Tex Pr.
--Talking Black. LC 76-77. (Sociolinguistics Ser.). 1976. pap. text ed. 8.95 o.p. (ISBN 0-88377-039-3). Newbury Hse.
Abrahams, Roger D., ed. Jump-Rope Rhymes: A Dictionary. (AFS Bibliographical & Special Ser.: Vol. 20). 252p. 1969. 12.50x o.p. (ISBN 0-292-78400-7). U of Tex Pr.
Abrahams, Roger D. & Szwed, John F., eds. After Africa: Extracts from British Travel Accounts & Journals of the Seventeenth, Eighteenth, & Nineteenth Centuries Concerning the Slaves, Their Manners, & Customs in the British West Indies. LC 82-20110. 480p. 1983. text ed. 45.00x (ISBN 0-300-02748-6); pap. text ed. 12.95x (ISBN 0-300-03030-4). Yale U Pr.
Abrahams, S. C., ed. Accuracy in X-Ray Intensity Measurements. pap. 3.50 (ISBN 0-686-60372-9). Polycrystal Bk Serv.
Abrahams, William, ed. Prize Stories of the Seventies from O. Henry Awards. LC 80-22790. 408p. 1981. 12.95 (ISBN 0-385-17158-7). Doubleday.
--Prize Stories 1983: The O. Henry Awards. 360p. 1983. 16.95 (ISBN 0-385-18115-9). Doubleday.
Abrahamsen, D. Child Language: An Interdisciplinary Guide to Theory & Research. 256p. 1977. pap. text ed. 24.50 (ISBN 0-8391-1128-2). Univ Park.
Abrahamsen, David. Crime & the Human Mind. LC 69-14906. (Criminology, Law Enforcement, & Social Problems Ser.: No. 43). 1969. Repr. of 1944 ed. 15.00x (ISBN 0-87585-043-X). Patterson Smith.
--Who Are the Guilty? A Study of Education & Crime. LC 70-143306. 340p. 1972. Repr. of 1952 ed. lib. bdg. 20.75x (ISBN 0-8371-5807-9, ABWG). Greenwood.
Abrahamsen, M. A. Cooperative Business Enterprise. 1976. 29.95 (ISBN 0-07-000151-0, C). McGraw.
Abrahamsen, Samuel. Say It in Norwegian. (Orig.). 1957. pap. 1.95 (ISBN 0-486-20814-1). Dover.
Abrahamson, M. Functionalism. LC 77-6828. 1978. pap. 11.95 ref. (ISBN 0-13-331900-8). P-H.
Abrahamson, Mark. Social Research Methods. (Illus.). 400p. 1983. 21.95 (ISBN 0-13-818088-1). P-H.
--Urban Sociology. 2nd ed. (Ser. in Sociology). (Illus.). 1980. text ed. 22.95 (ISBN 0-13-939587-3). P-H.
Abrahamson, Royce L., jt. auth. see Pickle, Hal B.
Abrahamsson, Bernhard J., ed. Conservation & the Changing Direction of Economic Growth. LC 77-28753. (Westview Special Studies in Natural Resources & Energy Management Ser.). 1978. lib. bdg. 23.25 o.p. (ISBN 0-89158-413-7). Westview.
Abrahamsson, Sixten, jt. auth. see McLafferty, Fred W.
Abrahms, Eliot, jt. auth. see Ellis, Albert.
Abrahms, Eliot R., jt. auth. see Ellis, Albert.
Abrahms, Sally. Children in the Crossfire: The Tragedy of Parental Kidnapping. LC 82-73030. 320p. 1983. 12.95 (ISBN 0-689-11339-0). Atheneum.
Abrahson, R. L., jt. auth. see Pickle, H. B.
Abramovitch, R. A., ed. Reactive Intermediates, Vol. 3. 615p. 1982. 59.50x (ISBN 0-306-40970-4, Plenum Pr). Plenum Pub.
Abramowitz, Milton & Stegun, Irene A., eds. Handbook of Mathematical Functions with Formulas, Graphs & Mathematical Tables. (Illus.). 1964. pap. 17.95 (ISBN 0-486-61272-4). Dover.
Abrams, jt. ed. see Reinhoff.
Abrams, Alan E., ed. Journalist Biographies Master Index. 1st ed. LC 77-9144. (Gale Biographical Index Ser.: No. 4). 1979. 70.00x (ISBN 0-8103-1086-4). Gale.
Abrams, Anne C. Clinical Drug Therapy: Rationales for Nursing Practice. (Illus.). 600p. 1983. text ed. write for info. (ISBN 0-397-54336-0, Lippincott Medical). Lippincott.
Abrams, Carl, jt. auth. see Monroe, Manus.
Abrams, Don. The Profit-Taker: The Proven Rapid Money-Maker in Good & Bad Markets. LC 79-22695. 124p. 1980. 12.95 (ISBN 0-471-06228-6, Pub. by Wiley-Interscience). Wiley.
Abrams, Herbert L. Abrams Angiography: Vascular & Interventional Radiology, 3 vols. 2nd ed. 1983. Vol. 1. text ed. (ISBN 0-316-00466-9); Vol. 2. text ed. (ISBN 0-316-00467-7); Vol. 3. text ed. (ISBN 0-316-00468-5); text ed. 275.00 set. Little.
--Coronary Arteriography. 1982. text ed. write for info. (ISBN 0-316-00469-3). Little.
Abrams, Jerome S. A Concise Handbook for the Care of Patients with Abdominal Stomas. (Illus.). 164p. 1982. cancelled (ISBN 0-88416-292-3). Wright-PSG.
Abrams, Kathleen, jt. auth. see Abrams, Lawrence.
Abrams, Lawrence & Abrams, Kathleen. Salvaging Old Barns & Houses: Tear it Down & Save Their Places. LC 82-19330. (Illus.). 128p. (Orig.). 1983. pap. 7.95 (ISBN 0-8069-7666-7). Sterling.
Abrams, LeRoy. Illustrated Flora of the Pacific States, 4 vols. Incl. Vol. 1. Ferns to Birthworts, 4 vol.set. xi, 557p. 1923. 35.00x (ISBN 0-8047-0003-6); Vol. 2. Buckwheats to Kramerias. viii, 635p. 1944. 30.00x (ISBN 0-8047-0004-4); Vol. 3. Geraniums to Figworts. viii, 866p. 1951. 40.00x (ISBN 0-8047-0005-2); Vol. 4. Bignonias to Sunflowers. Ferris, Roxana S. v, 732p. (Contains index to vols. 1-4). 1960. 35.00x (ISBN 0-8047-0006-0). (Illus.). 140.00 set (ISBN 0-8047-1100-3). Stanford U Pr.
Abrams, Linsey. Charting by the Stars. 1979. pap. 9.95 o.p. (ISBN 0-517-53898-9, Harmony). Crown.
Abrams, M. H., ed. English Romantic Poets: Modern Essays in Criticism. 2nd ed. 1975. pap. 9.95 (ISBN 0-19-501946-6, 35, GB). Oxford U Pr.
Abrams, M. H., et al, eds. The Norton Anthology of English Literature, 2 vols. 4th ed. (Illus.). 1979. text ed. 19.95x (ISBN 0-393-95039-5); Vol. II. text ed. 19.95x (ISBN 0-393-95043-3); Vol. I. pap. text ed. 17.95x (ISBN 0-393-95048-4); Vol II. pap. text ed. 17.95x (ISBN 0-685-94872-2). Vol. II (ISBN 0-393-95051-4). Norton.
--Norton Anthology of English Literature: Third Major Authors Edition. 1975. text ed. 19.95x (ISBN 0-393-09298-4); pap. text ed. 17.95x (ISBN 0-393-09299-2). Norton.
Abrams, Marshall D. & Stein, Philip G. Computer Hardware & Software: An Interdisciplinary Introduction. LC 72-3455. 1973. text ed. 25.95 (ISBN 0-201-00019-9). A-W.
Abrams, Meyer H. Mirror & the Lamp: Romantic Theory & the Critical Tradition. pap. 8.95 (ISBN 0-19-501471-5, 360, GB). Oxford U Pr.
Abrams, Natalie & Buckner, Michael D. Medical Ethics: A Clinical Textbook & Reference for the Health Care Professions. 848p. 1982. text ed. 45.00 (ISBN 0-262-01068-2, Pub. by Bradford); pap. text ed. 25.00 (ISBN 0-262-51024-3). MIT Pr.
Abrams, P. & McCulloch, A. Communes, Sociology & Society. LC 75-40985. (Themes in the Social Sciences Ser.: No. 3). 200p. 1976. 32.50 (ISBN 0-521-21188-3); pap. 9.95x (ISBN 0-521-29067-8). Cambridge U Pr.
Abrams, P. & Wrigley, E. A., eds. Towns in Societies. LC 77-82481. (Past & Present Publications). 1978. 37.50 (ISBN 0-521-21826-8); pap. 13.95 (ISBN 0-521-29594-7). Cambridge U Pr.
Abrams, P., et al, eds. Practice & Progress: British Sociology 1950-1980. 240p. 1981. text ed. 28.50x (ISBN 0-04-301131-4); pap. text ed. 12.50x (ISBN 0-04-301132-2). Allen Unwin.
Abrams, P. H. Urodynamics. (Clinical Practice in Urology Ser.). (Illus.). 240p. 1983. 44.00 (ISBN 0-387-11903-5). Springer-Verlag.
Abrams, Philip. Historical Sociology. 1983. text ed. 29.95x (ISBN 0-8014-1578-0); pap. 11.95x (ISBN 0-8014-9243-2). Cornell U Pr.
--Origins of British Sociology: Eighteen Thirty-Four to Nineteen Fourteen: An Essay with Selected Papers. LC 68-54221. (Heritage of Sociology Ser). 472p. 1969. 15.00x o.s.i. (ISBN 0-226-00170-9); pap. 3.25 (ISBN 0-226-00171-7). U of Chicago Pr.
Abrams, Philip, ed. see Locke, John.
Abrams, Richard. F-Four-U Corsair at War. LC 78-311995. (Illus.). 1977. 17.50x o.p. (ISBN 0-7110-0766-7). Intl Pubns Serv.
Abrams, Richard I. & Hutchinson, Warner A. An Illustrated Life of Jesus: From The National Gallery of Art Collection. LC 81-17575. (Illus.). 1982. 40.00 (ISBN 0-687-01356-9); deluxe ed. 60.00 (ISBN 0-687-01358-5); ltd. ed. 300.00 (ISBN 0-687-01357-7). Abingdon.
Abrams, Richard M. The Burdens of Progress, 1900-1929. 1978. pap. text ed. 11.95x (ISBN 0-673-05778-X). Scott F.
Abrams, Richard M., ed. Issues of the Populist & Progressive Eras, 1892-1912. LC 76-625503. (Documentary History of the United States Ser.). 1970. 19.95x (ISBN 0-87249-164-1). U of SC Pr.
Abrams, Robert. Foundations of Political Analysis: An Introduction to the Theory of Collective Choice. LC 79-20850. 1980. 24.00x (ISBN 0-231-04480-1); pap. 12.50 (ISBN 0-686-82881-X). Columbia U Pr.
Abrams, Robert E. & Canemaker, John. Treasures of Disney Animation Art. LC 82-72998. (Illus.). 320p. 1982. 85.00 (ISBN 0-89659-315-0). Abbeville Pr.
Abrams, Stanley. Polygraph Handbook for Attorneys. LC 77-6074. (Illus.). 1977. 23.95 (ISBN 0-669-01598-9). Lexington Bks.
Abrams, Stanley D. How to Win the Zoning Game. 1978. with 1982 suppl. 35.00 (ISBN 0-87215-203-0); 1982 Suppl. 15.00 (ISBN 0-87215-574-9). Michie-Bobbs.
Abramson, Alan J., jt. auth. see Salamon, Lester M.
Abramson, David H., jt. auth. see Sagerman, Robert H.

Abramson, Edwin & Ostroy, Sanford E., eds. Molecular Processes in Vision. LC 80-29543. (Benchmark Papers in Biochemistry: Vol. 3). 448p. 1981. 55.00 (ISBN 0-87933-372-3). Hutchinson Ross.

Abramson, Glenda. Modern Hebrew Drama. LC 79-16608. (Illus.). 1979. 26.00x (ISBN 0-312-53988-6). St Martin.

Abramson, J. H. & Peritz, E. Calculator Programs for the Health Sciences. (Illus.). 326p. 1983. text ed. 37.50x (ISBN 0-19-503187-3); pap. text ed. 18.95x (ISBN 0-19-503188-1). Oxford U Pr.

Abramson, J. H., ed. see Emanuel, N. M. & Evseenko, D. S.

Abramson, Joan. Practical Application of the Gas Laws to Pulmonary Physiology. 97p. (Orig.). 1981. pap. text ed. 5.95 (ISBN 0-89787-107-3). Gorsuch Scarisbrick.

Abramson, Leslie W. Criminal Detainers. LC 79-11947. (Illus.). 224p. 1979. prof ref 19.50x (ISBN 0-88410-801-5). Ballinger Pub.

Abramson, N. & Kuo, F., eds. Computer-Communications Networks. 1973. 39.95 (ISBN 0-13-165431-4). P-H.

Abramson, Norman. Information Theory & Coding. (Electronic Sciences Ser). 1963. 39.95 (ISBN 0-07-000145-6, C). McGraw.

Abramson, Paul, jt. auth. see Murray, Joan.

Abramson, Paul R. & Aldrich, John H. Change & Continuity in the Nineteen Eighty Elections. LC 82-1359. 279p. 1982. pap. 9.25 (ISBN 0-87187-221-8). Congr Quarterly.

Abramson, Robert. An Integrated Approach to Organization Development & Performance Improvement Planning. LC 78-70028. (Library of Management for Development). 92p. (Orig.). 1978. pap. 4.95x (ISBN 0-931816-26-2). Kumarian Pr.

Abranson, Erik. Ships & Seafarers. LC 80-50953. (Adventures in History Ser.). PLB 12.68 (ISBN 0-382-06382-1). Silver.

Abrashi. Snow White & Seven Dwarfs. (Illus.). pap. 2.50x Arabic o.p. (ISBN 0-86685-268-9). Intl Bk Ctr.

Abrashkin, R., jt. auth. see Williams, Jay.

Abrashkin, Raymond, jt. auth. see Williams, Jay.

Abrashkin, William, jt. auth. see Williams, Jay.

Abravanel, Eliott D. & King, Elizabeth A. Dr. Abravanel's Body Type Diet & Lifetime Nutrition Plan. (Illus.). 256p. 1983. 12.95 (ISBN 0-553-05036-2). Bantam.

Abrecht, Paul, ed. Faith & Science in an Unjust World, Vol. 2: Reports & Recommendations. LC 80-81141. 224p. 1980. pap. 6.95 o.p. (ISBN 0-8006-1391-0, 1-1391). Fortress.

Abreu, Beatriz. Physical Disabilities Manual. 380p. 1981. text ed. 35.00 (ISBN 0-89004-505-4). Raven.

Abreu, Maria I. & Rameh, Clea. Portugues Contemporaneo, 2 vols. Incl. Vol. 1. 256p. pap. 7.25 (ISBN 0-87840-026-5); 11 cassettes 65.00 (ISBN 0-87840-048-6); 22 reel-to-reel tapes 120.00 (ISBN 0-87840-075-3); Vol. 2. 346p. pap. 7.95 (ISBN 0-87840-025-7); 10 cassettes 65.00 (ISBN 0-87840-049-4); 20 tapes 120.00 (ISBN 0-87840-076-1). LC 66-25520. 1971. Georgetown U Pr.

Abreu, Rosendo. The Cambridge Program for the GED Social Studies Test. (GED Preparation Ser.). (Illus.). 272p. (Orig.). 1981. pap. text ed. 5.87 (ISBN 0-8428-9388-1); Cambridge Exercise Book for the Social Studies Test. wkbk. 3.33 (ISBN 0-8428-9394-6). Cambridge Bk.

Abriel, Vera. Too Near the Flame. LC 82-61844. 222p. (Orig.). 1983. pap. 1.75 (ISBN 0-943654-00-9). New Paradise Bks.

--The Woman's Total Reshape Program: Have the Figure You Always Wanted. (Illus.). 256p. 1981. 12.95 o.p. (ISBN 0-525-93148-1). Dutton.

Abrikosov, A. A., et al. Quantum Field Theoretical Methods in Statistical Physics. (Vol. 4). 1965. text ed. inquire for price o.p. (ISBN 0-08-010406-1); pap. text ed. 8.75 o.p. (ISBN 0-08-013470-X). Pergamon.

Abroms, Israel F., jt. auth. see Scheiner, Albert P.

Abruscato, Joe & Hassard, Jack. The Earthpeople Activity Book: People, Places, Pleasures & Other Delights. LC 78-7602. (Illus.). 1978. 13.95 (ISBN 0-673-16359-8); pap. 11.95 (ISBN 0-673-16360-1). Scott F.

Absalom, R. N. Comprehension of Spoken Italian. LC 76-21015. 1978. limp bdg. 4.95x (ISBN 0-521-29115-1). Cambridge U Pr.

--Passages for Translation from Italian. 1967. pap. 7.95x (ISBN 0-521-09431-3, 431). Cambridge U Pr.

Absar, Ilyas, jt. auth. see Van Wazer, John R.

Abse, Dannie. Collected Poems. LC 76-21049. (Pitt Poetry Ser.). 1977. pap. 4.95 (ISBN 0-685-75151-1). U of Pittsburgh Pr.

--Dannie Abse. (Pocket Poet Ser.). 1963. pap. 1.25 (ISBN 0-8023-9036-6). Dufour.

Abse, Dannie, ed. Modern European Verse. (Pocket Poet Ser.). 1964. pap. 1.25 (ISBN 0-8023-9037-4). Dufour.

Abt, Lawrence E., jt. auth. see Rosner, Stanley.

Abu, Salim M., jt. auth. see O'Fahey, R. S.

Abu-Ala, Maududi. Birth Control. pap. 3.75 (ISBN 0-686-18437-8). Kazi Pubns.

Abu-Jaber, Faiz S. American-Arab Relations from Wilson to Nixon. LC 78-65853. 1979. pap. 11.50 (ISBN 0-8191-0680-1). U Pr of Amer.

--Middle East Issues. 200p. 1977. pap. text ed. 8.00 (ISBN 0-8191-0044-7). U Pr of Amer.

Abulafia, Abraham Ben Samuel. The Path of Names. Finkel, Bruria & Hirschman, Jack, trs. LC 75-22792. pap. 4.00 o.p. (ISBN 0-686-17261-2). Tree Bks.

Abulafia, D. The Two Italies. LC 76-11069. (Cambridge Studies in Medieval Life & Thought Ser.: No. 9). (Illus.). 1977. 54.50 (ISBN 0-521-21211-1). Cambridge U Pr.

Abu-Lughod, Ibrahim, ed. Palestinian Rights: Affirmation & Denial. 225p. 1982. 17.95 (ISBN 0-914456-22-9); pap. 7.95 (ISBN 0-914456-23-7). Medina Pr.

Abu-Lughod, Janet & Hay, Richard, eds. Third World Urbanization. LC 76-53367. (Illus.). 1977. text ed. 14.95x (ISBN 0-685-76992-5); pap. text ed. 7.95x (ISBN 0-88425-005-9). Maaroufa Pr.

Abun-Nasr, J. M. A History of the Maghrib. 2nd ed. LC 74-25653. (Illus.). 432p. 1975. 54.50 (ISBN 0-521-20703-7); pap. 16.95x (ISBN 0-521-09927-7). Cambridge U Pr.

Aby, Carroll D. & Vaughn, Donald E., Jr., eds. Investment Classics. LC 78-27774. 1979. pap. text ed. 17.95x (ISBN 0-673-16174-9). Scott F.

Aby, Carroll, Jr. & Vaughn, Donald E. Financial Management Classics. LC 79-10710. (Illus.). 1979. pap. text ed. 17.95x (ISBN 0-673-16168-4). Scott F.

Abzug, Robert H. Passionate Liberator: Theodore Dwight Weld & the Dilemma of Reform. LC 80-11819. (Illus.). 384p. 1980. 24.50x (ISBN 0-19-502771-X). Oxford U Pr.

--Passionate Liberator: Theodore Dwight Weld & the Dilemma of Reform. 384p. 1982. pap. 6.95 (ISBN 0-19-503061-3, GB 683, GB). Oxford U Pr.

Academic Committee on Soviet Jewry & the Anti-Defamation League. Perspectives on Soviet Jewry. 150p. pap. 2.50 (ISBN 0-686-95144-1). ADL.

Academy Forum National Academy of Sciences. Energy: Future Alternatives & Risks. LC 74-13084. 202p. 1974. prof ref 18.50x (ISBN 0-88410-025-1). Ballinger Pub.

Academy of Motion Picture Arts & Sciences. Annual Index to Motion Picture Credits, 1981. LC 79-644761. (Annual Index to Motion Picture Credits Ser.). 469p. 1982. lib. bdg. 150.00 (ISBN 0-686-97993-1). Greenwood.

Academy of Motion Picture Arts & Science. Annual Index to Motion Picture Credits, 1981. LC 79-644761. 469p. 1982. lib. bdg. 150.00 (ISBN 0-686-82498-9, AN81). Greenwood.

Academy of Natural Sciences of Philadelphia. Catalog of the Library of the Academy of Natural Sciences of Philadelphia, 16 vols. 1972. Set. lib. bdg. 1530.00 (ISBN 0-8161-0946-X, Hall Library). G K Hall.

Academy of Political Science. The Soviet Union Since Khrushchev: New Trends & Old Problems. LC 65-23730. Repr. of 1965 ed. 12.00 o.s.i. (ISBN 0-527-00301-8). Kraus Repr.

Acarnley, P. P. Stepping Motors: A Guide to Modern Theory & Practice. (IEE Control Engineering Ser.: No. 19). 160p. 1982. casebound 41.00 (ISBN 0-906048-83-4); pap. 25.00 (ISBN 0-906048-75-3). Inst Elect Eng.

Accardo. Pediatrician & the Developmentally Delayed Child. 256p. 1978. text ed. 19.95 (ISBN 0-8391-1331-5). Univ Park.

Accardo, Pasquale J. Failure to Thrive in Infancy & Early Childhood: A Multidisciplinary Team Approach. 432p. 1981. text ed. 29.95 (ISBN 0-8391-1678-0). Univ Park.

Acconci, Vito. Kay Price & Stella Pajunas: Work for a Poetry Context 1967-1969. LC 77-77011. 1982. pap. text ed. 10.95 o.p. (ISBN 0-915570-08-4). Oolp Pr.

Accurso, Frank. Machine Trades Projects & Procedures: Standard & Metric. LC 77-8691. 1978. pap. text ed. 11.50 o.p. (ISBN 0-672-97101-1); tchr's manual o.p. 3.33 o.p. (ISBN 0-672-97155-0). Bobbs.

ACES Commission on Sex Equity. For Women & Men: Sex Equality in Counselor Education & Supervision. 91p. 3.75 (ISBN 0-686-36421-X, 72180). Am Personnel.

Acevedo, Eloy. The Answer to the Riddle of the Universe. 1982. 8.95 (ISBN 0-533-05343-9). Vantage.

Aceves, Joseph, et al, eds. Economic Transformation & Steady-State Values: Essays in the Ethnography of Spain. (Publications in Anthropology Ser: No. 2). 1976. pap. 4.00 o.p. (ISBN 0-930146-09-3). Queens Coll Pr.

Aceves, Joseph B. & King, H. Gill. Cultural Anthropology. 1978. pap. text ed. 14.95x o.p. (ISBN 0-673-15305-3); study guide 5.95x o.p. (ISBN 0-673-15292-8). Scott F.

--Introductory Anthropology. 1979. text ed. 17.95x o.p. (ISBN 0-673-15303-7). Scott F.

Acha, Eduardo de see De Acha, Eduardo.

Acharya, Shankar N. Incentives for Resource Allocation: A Case Study of Sudan. (Working Paper: No. 367). iii, 113p. 1979. 5.00 (ISBN 0-686-36088-5, WP-367). World Bank.

Achebe, Chinua. Arrow of God. LC 75-79409. 1969. pap. 4.95 o.p. (ISBN 0-385-01480-5, A698, Anch). Doubleday.

--Arrow of God. (Anchor Literary Library). 1982. pap. 4.95 (ISBN 0-686-42700-9, Anch). Doubleday.

--Things Fall Apart. (African Writers Ser.). pap. 3.00x (ISBN 0-435-90001-3). Heinemann Ed.

--Things Fall Apart. Dabey, John, ed. (Guided Readers Ser.). (Orig.). 1981. pap. text ed. 2.00x o.p. (ISBN 0-435-27010-9). Heinemann Ed.

Achebe, Chinua & Iroaganachi, John. How the Leopard Got His Claws. LC 72-93382. (Illus.). 32p. (gr. 6 up). 1973. 5.95 (ISBN 0-89388-056-6). Okpaku Communications.

Achelis, Elisabeth. World Calendar: Addresses & Occasional Papers Chronologically Arranged on the Progress of Calendar Reform Since 1930. LC 73-102214. Repr. of 1937 ed. 34.00x (ISBN 0-8103-3784-3). Gale.

ACHEMA Symposium, 1970, Frankfurt. Wastes: Solids, Liquids & Gases. Wulfinghoff, M., tr. 1974. 39.50 o.p. (ISBN 0-8206-0243-4). Chem Pub.

Achen, Christopher H. Interpreting & Using Regression. LC 82-42675. (Quantitative Applications in the Social Sciences Ser.: No. 29). 88p. 1982. pap. 4.50 (ISBN 0-8039-1915-8). Sage.

Achenbach, J. D. Wave Propagation in Elastic Solids. (Applied Mathematics & Mechanics Ser.: Vol. 16). 400p. 1973. 76.75 (ISBN 0-444-10465-8, North-Holland); pap. 36.25 (ISBN 0-444-10840-8). Elsevier.

Achenbach, Thomas M. Developmental Psychopathology. 2nd ed. LC 82-2838. 770p. 1982. text ed. 27.95x (ISBN 0-471-05536-0). Wiley.

--Developmental Psychopathology. (Illus.). 725p. 1974. 27.50x (ISBN 0-471-06889-6). Wiley.

Acheson, Dean & Smith, Mike. How to Increase Productivity. (The Common Sense Management Ser.). (Illus.). 128p. (Orig., also avail. in Spanish, French, German, & Norwegian). 1981. pap. text ed. 19.95 spiral wire (ISBN 0-942966-01-5); avail. as a kit with cassettes, binders, posters, pads of forms, etc 129.95 (ISBN 0-686-36409-0). Hanover Pr.

Acheson, E. D., ed. Medicine: An Outline for the Intending Student. (Outlines Ser). 1970. cased 14.00 o.p. (ISBN 0-7100-6866-2); pap. 7.95x o.p. (ISBN 0-7100-6867-0). Routledge & Kegan.

Acheson, E. J., jt. auth. see Hutchinson, E. C.

Acheson, H. M. Acridines: Chemistry of Heterocyclic Compounds. 2nd ed. 878p. 1973. 226.50x o.s.i. (ISBN 0-471-37753-8, Pub. by Wiley-Interscience). Wiley.

Acheson, Roy M. & Aird, Lesley A., eds. Seminars in Community Medicine: Sociology, Vol. I. (Seminars in Community Medicine). (Illus.). 192p. 1976. pap. text ed. 8.75x o.p. (ISBN 0-19-261120-8). Oxford U Pr.

Acheson, Sam H. Thirty-Five Thousand Days in Texas: A History of the Dallas News & Its Forbears. LC 72-136510. (Illus.). xi, 337p. Repr. of 1938 ed. lib. bdg. 18.25x (ISBN 0-8371-5428-6, ACTD). Greenwood.

Achinstein, Peter. The Nature of Explanation. (Illus.). 320p. 1983. 27.50 (ISBN 0-19-503215-2). Oxford U Pr.

Achison, Dean & Smith, Mike. How to Analyze a Business & Determine a Management Strategy. (The Common Sense Management Ser.). (Illus.). 192p. (Orig.). 1983. pap. text ed. 44.95 spiral wire (ISBN 0-942966-02-3); six cassette kits & working terms for full system of analysis 249.95 (ISBN 0-686-36406-6). Hanover Pr.

Acht, R. J. van, et al. Historische Blaasinstrumenten (Exhibition Catalogue of Woodwind Instruments) Catalogus Tentoonstelling Kasteel Ehrenstein, Kerkrade 1974. (Collectie Haags Gemeente - Museum Ser.). 15.00 o.s.i. (ISBN 90-6027-143-2, Pub. by Frits Knuf Netherlands). Pendragon NY.

Acht, R. Van see Scheurwater, W. & Van Acht, R.

Achtemeier, Elizabeth. The Old Testament & the Proclamation of the Gospel. LC 73-7863. 1980. pap. 5.95 (ISBN 0-664-24287-1). Westminster.

Achtemeier, Paul J., ed. Society of Biblical Literature 1980: Seminar Papers. (SBL Seminar Papers). 6.00 o.p. (ISBN 0-686-96230-3, 06 09 19). Scholars Pr CA.

Achtemeier, Paul J., ed. see Williamson, Lamar, Jr.

Achtenberg, Anya. I Know What the Small Girl Knew. LC 82-81350. 72p. 1983. pap. 4.00 (ISBN 0-930100-11-5). Holy Cow.

Achterberg, Jeanne & Lawlis, G. Frank. Imagery of Cancer(Image-Ca) An Evaluation Tool for the Process of Disease. LC 77-90181. 9.75 (ISBN 0-918296-10-2). Inst Personality & Ability.

Achtermier, William O. Rhode Island Arms Makers & Gunsmiths: 1643-1883. LC 80-84583. (Illus.). 108p. 1980. 16.50 (ISBN 0-917218-15-9). Mowbray Co.

Ackart, Robert. Cooking in a Casserole. LC 73-6900. (Illus.). 334p. 1981. pap. 5.95 (ISBN 0-448-12252-9, G&D). Putnam Pub Group.

--The Frugal Fish: Three Hundred Delicious Recipes for All Seasons. 320p. 1983. 16.45i (ISBN 0-316-00646-7); pap. 10.45 lexitone (ISBN 0-316-00645-9). Little.

--The Hundred Menu Chicken Cookbook. LC 77-183034. (Illus.). 164p. 1981. pap. 4.95 (ISBN 0-448-01735-0, G&D). Putnam Pub Group.

Ackenhusen-Johns, A. & Nixon, D. W., eds. Marine Affairs Journal, No. 7. (Marine Bulletin Ser.: No. 46). 100p. 1981. 1.00 o.p. (ISBN 0-686-36977-7, P904). URI Mas.

Acker, D. Animal Science & Industry. 2nd ed. 1971. text ed. 25.95 (ISBN 0-13-037655-8). P-H.

Acker, Duane. Animal Science & Industry. (Illus.). 720p. 1983. 27.95 (ISBN 0-13-037416-4). P-H.

Acker, Kathy & Cherches, Peter. Diana's Third Almanac. Ahern, Tom, ed. Waldrop, Keith, tr. 96p. (Orig.). 1982. pap. 4.95 (ISBN 0-933442-06-8). Dianas Bimonthly.

Acker, Louis S., jt. auth. see Sakoian, Frances.

Ackerley, J. My Dog, Tulip. LC 65-24027. 7.95 (ISBN 0-8303-0056-2). Fleet.

Ackerly, Salley M., jt. auth. see Riekes, Linda.

Ackerman. The Pathology of Malignant Melanoma. LC 81-8393. (Monographs in Dermatopathology, Vol. 1). 406p. 1981. 62.50x (ISBN 0-89352-132-9). Masson Pub.

Ackerman, A. Bernard. Your Skin Is Showing. 32p. (gr. 1 up). 1979. text ed. 7.00 (ISBN 0-89352-082-9). Masson Pub.

Ackerman, A. Bernard & Ragaz, Anna. Lives of Lesions. 352p. 1983. write for info. (ISBN 0-89352-095-0). Masson Pub.

Ackerman, Bruce A. Social Justice in the Liberal State. LC 80-12618. 408p. 1980. 27.50x (ISBN 0-300-02439-8, Y-401); pap. 8.95x (ISBN 0-300-02757-5). Yale U Pr.

Ackerman, Bruce A. & Hassler, William T. Clean Coal - Dirty Air. LC 80-1089. (Illus.). 175p. 1981. 22.50x (ISBN 0-300-02628-5); pap. 5.95x (ISBN 0-300-02643-9). Yale U Pr.

Ackerman, Carolyn. Cooking with Kids. 76p. 1982. pap. 5.50 (ISBN 0-87659-104-7). Gryphon Hse.

Ackerman, D. G., et al. Destruction & Disposal of PCB'S by Thermal & Non-Thermal Methods. LC 82-22312. (Pollution Technology Review: No. 97). (Illus.). 417p. 1983. 48.00 (ISBN 0-8155-0934-0). Noyes.

Ackerman, Diane L. Getting Rich: A Smart Woman's Guide to Successful Money Management. 1982. pap. 3.95 (ISBN 0-553-22672-X). Bantam.

Ackerman, Eugene, et al. Biophysical Science. 2nd ed. (Illus.). 1979. ref. ed. 29.95 (ISBN 0-13-076901-0). P-H.

Ackerman, Forrest J. Mr. Monster's the Beauties & the Beasts. Stine, Hank, ed. (Illus.). 206p. (Orig.). 1983. pap. 12.95 (ISBN 0-89865-289-8). Donning Co.

Ackerman, G. Adolph, jt. auth. see Wismar, Beth L.

Ackerman, Gerald M., jt. auth. see Zafran, Eric.

Ackerman, J. Mark. Operant Conditioning Techniques for the Classroom Teacher. 1972. pap. 8.95x (ISBN 0-673-07664-4). Scott F.

Ackerman, Lauren & Spjut, Harlin, eds. Bones & Joints. (International Academy of Pathology Monograph: No. 17). 368p. 1976. 31.00 o.p. (ISBN 0-683-00039-X). Williams & Wilkins.

Ackerman, Marian. Saints & Sinners. LC 79-90323. (Illus.). 1979. 4.50 o.p. (ISBN 0-932906-07-9); pap. 2.75 o.p. (ISBN 0-932906-06-0). Pan-Am Publishing Co.

Ackerman, Nancy, jt. auth. see Rundback, Betty.

Ackerman, Nathan W. Psychodynamics of Family Life: Diagnosis & Treatment of Family Relationships. LC 58-13043. 1972. pap. 7.95x (ISBN 0-465-09503-8, TB5004). Basic.

Ackerman, Paul & Kappelman, Murray. Signals: What Your Child Is Really Telling You. 1980. pap. 3.95 (ISBN 0-451-12186-4, AE2186, Sig). NAL.

Ackerman, Robert W. Backgrounds to Medieval English Literature. (Orig.). 1967. 6.00 (ISBN 0-394-30627-9, RanC). Random.

Ackerman, Robert W. & Dahood, Roger G., eds. Ancrene Riwle: Introduction & Part One-A Critical Edition. 1982. write for info. (ISBN 0-86698-055-5). Medieval & Renaissance NY.

Ackerman, Winona B. & Lohnes, Paul R. Research Methods for Nurses. (Illus.). 304p. 1981. text ed. 23.50x (ISBN 0-07-000182-0, HP). McGraw.

Ackermann, A. S. Popular Fallacies, a Book of Common Errors: Explained & Corrected with Copious References to Authorities. 4th ed. LC 79-121184. 1970. Repr. of 1950 ed. 63.00 (ISBN 0-8103-3295-7). Gale.

Ackermann, Paul K., ed. see Durrenmatt, Friedrich.

Ackermann, Paul K., ed. see Frisch, Max.

Ackermann, Rudolph. Ackermann's Costume Plates: Women's Fashions in England, 1818-1828. Blum, Stella, ed. (Illus.). 1979. pap. 5.00 (ISBN 0-486-23690-0). Dover.

Ackermann, W., jt. auth. see Hilbert, David.

Ackermann, William C., et al, eds. Man-Made Lakes: Their Problems & Environmental Effects. LC 73-86486. (Geophysical Monograph Ser.: Vol. 17). (Illus.). 1973. 35.00 (ISBN 0-87590-017-8). Am Geophysical.

Ackers, P., et al. Weirs & Fumes for Flow Measurement. 327p. 1978. 79.95x (ISBN 0-471-99637-8, Pub. by Wiley-Interscience). Wiley.

Ackerson, et al. Gateways to Science. 4th ed. 1982. write for info. laboratory bks. McGraw.

Ackins, Ralph. Energy Machines. LC 79-27714. (Machine World Ser.). (Illus.). (gr. 2-4). 1980. PLB 13.85 (ISBN 0-8172-1336-8). Raintree Pubs.

Ackland, Donald F. Broadman Comments, July-September, 1983. (Orig.). 1983. pap. 2.35 (ISBN 0-8054-1479-7). Broadman.

--Broadman Comments, October-December, 1983. 1983. pap. 2.35 (ISBN 0-8054-1480-0). Broadman.

--Day by Day with John. LC 81-67374. 1982. pap. 4.50 (ISBN 0-8054-5187-0). Broadman.

Ackland, Donald F., et al. Broadman Comments, 1982-83. LC 45-437. 1982. pap. 4.95 (ISBN 0-8054-1468-1). Broadman.

--Broadman Comments, 1983-1984. (Orig.). 1983. pap. 5.50 (ISBN 0-8054-1481-9). Broadman.

Ackland, John W. Girls in Care. 166p. 1982. text ed. 27.50x (ISBN 0-566-00511-5). Gower Pub Ltd.

Ackley, Clifford. Photographs from the Museum Collection. (MFA Bulletin: Vol. 80). (Illus.). 80p. 1983. pap. 4.95 (ISBN 0-686-83421-6). Mus Fine Arts Boston.

--Private Realities: Recent American Photography. LC 73-90126. (Illus.). 1974. 17.50 o.p. (ISBN 0-87846-077-2, Pub. by Boston Museum of Fine Arts); pap. 8.95 o.p. (ISBN 0-87846-089-6, Pub. by Boston Museum of Fine Arts). NYGS.

Ackley, Clifford S. Exposures: Photographs from the Museum Collection. (MFA Bulletin: Vol. 80). (Illus.). 80p. 1983. pap. 4.95 (ISBN 0-87846-229-5). Mus Fine Arts Boston.

Ackley, Gardner. Macroeconomic Theory & Policy. (Illus.). 1978. text ed. 25.95 o.s.i. (ISBN 0-02-300290-5). Macmillan.

Ackoff, R. L. Concept of Corporate Planning. LC 74-100318. 158p. 1969. 19.95 (ISBN 0-471-00290-9, Pub. by Wiley-Interscience). Wiley.

--Progress in Operations Research. LC 61-10415. (Operations Research Ser.: Vol. 1). 1961. 35.95 o.p. (ISBN 0-471-00330-1, Pub. by Wiley-Interscience). Wiley.

--Scientific Method: Optimizing Applied Research Decisions. LC 62-10914. 464p. 1962. 32.95x (ISBN 0-471-00297-6). Wiley.

Ackoff, R. L. & Rivett, Patrick. Manager's Guide to Operations Research. LC 63-14115. (Managers Guide Ser.). 107p. 1963. 22.95 o.p. (ISBN 0-471-00335-2, Pub. by Wiley-Interscience). Wiley.

Ackoff, Russell L. The Art of Problem Solving: Accompanied by Ackoff's Fables. LC 78-5627. 214p. 1978. 19.95 (ISBN 0-471-04289-7, Pub. by Wiley-Interscience). Wiley.

--Creating the Corporate Future: Plan or Be Planned for. LC 80-28005. 297p. 1981. 18.95 (ISBN 0-471-09009-3). Wiley.

--Redesigning the Future: A Systems Approach to Societal Problems. LC 74-10627. 320p. 1974. 22.95 (ISBN 0-471-00296-8, Pub. by Wiley-Interscience). Wiley.

Ackrill, J. L. Aristotle's Ethics. text ed. 15.00x o.p. (ISBN 0-391-00281-3). Humanities.

Ackroyd, Peter. The Great Fire of London. 192p. 1982. 16.95 (ISBN 0-241-10704-0, Pub. by Hamish Hamilton England). David & Charles.

Ackroyd, Peter R. Exile & Restoration: A Study of Hebrew Thought of the Sixth Century B. C. LC 68-27689. (Old Testament Library). 1968. 14.95 (ISBN 0-664-20843-6). Westminster.

--Israel under Babylon & Persia. (New Clarendon Bible Ser.). 1970. pap. 14.95x (ISBN 0-19-836917-4). Oxford U Pr.

Ackroyd, Peter R. & Lindars, Barnabas, eds. Words & Meanings: Essays Presented to David Winton Thomas. LC 68-29649. 1968. 39.50 (ISBN 0-521-07270-0). Cambridge U Pr.

Ackroyd, Petr R. Chronicles One & Two, Ezra, Nehemiah. (Student Christian Movement Press - Torch Bible Ser.). (Orig.). 1973. pap. 7.95x (ISBN 0-19-520292-9). Oxford U Pr.

Ackroyd, Ted J., ed. Health & Medical Economics: A Guide to Information Sources. LC 73-17567. (Economics Information Guide Ser.: Vol. 7). 1977. 42.00 (ISBN 0-8103-1390-1). Gale.

Acland, C. H. D. The Country Life Picture Book of the Lake District. (Illus.). 1983. 19.95 (ISBN 0-393-01733-8, Country Life). Norton.

Acland, Robert D. Microsurgery Practice Manual. LC 79-17533. (Illus.). 1979. pap. text ed. 19.95 (ISBN 0-8016-0076-6). Mosby.

ACLD. ACLD Pantry Cookbook. 300p. 1982. 10.45 (ISBN 0-686-36324-8, Dist. by ACLD). Rahija.

ACMRR Working Party on FAO Regional Fisheries Councils & Commissions. Report: Supplement Two to the Report of the Fifth Session of the Advisory Committee on Marine Resources Research, Rome, 1968. (FAO Fisheries Report: No. 56, Suppl. 2). 29p. 1968. pap. 7.50 (ISBN 0-686-92754-0, F1671, FAO). Unipub.

Acoca, Miguel, tr. see Timerman, Jacobo.

Acocella, Joan, jt. auth. see Bootzin, Richard R.

Aconcio, Giacomo. Darkness Discovered (Satans Stratagems) LC 78-9490. 1978. Repr. of 1651 ed. 35.00x (ISBN 0-8201-1313-1). Schol Facsimiles.

Acosta, Antonio A. & Calvo, Zoraida. Matematicas: Preparacion Para el Examen el Espanol De Equivalencia De la Escuela Superior. rev. ed. LC 80-25182. 272p. (Orig.). 1982. pap. 6.95 (ISBN 0-668-04821-2, 4821-2). Arco.

Acquaviva, Sabino & Santuccio, Mario. Social Structure in Italy: Crisis of a System. LC 76-13602. 272p. 1976. 36.25 o.p. (ISBN 0-89158-615-6). Westview.

Acri, Michael J., jt. auth. see Miller, Albert J.

ACSM-ASP Fall Convention, Sept. 1982. Technical Papers. pap. 12.50 (ISBN 0-937294-39-X). ASP.

Action for Children's Television, Inc., jt. ed. see Harmonay, Maureen.

Acton, E. Alexander Herzen & the Role of the Intellectual Revolutionary. LC 78-56747. 1979. 27.95 (ISBN 0-521-22166-8). Cambridge U Pr.

Acton, H. B., ed. Philosophy of Punishment: A Collection of Papers. LC 73-97179. 1970. 17.95 o.p. (ISBN 0-312-60690-7). St Martin.

Acton, Harold. The Soul's Gymnasium. 165p. 1982. 16.95 (ISBN 0-241-10740-7, Pub. by Hamish Hamilton England). David & Charles.

Acuna, Victor E., jt. auth. see Riley, Eugene W.

Ad Hoc Consultation on Codes of Practice for Fish & Fishery Products, 2nd, Rome, 1969. Report. (FAO Fisheries Reports: No. 73). 6p. 1969. pap. 7.50 (ISBN 0-686-93029-0, F1680, FAO). Unipub.

A.D. Little, Inc. Federal Funding of Civilian Research & Development: A Report to the Experimental Technology Incentives Program, U. S. Dept. of Commerce. Michaelis, Michael, ed. LC 76-43308. 1977. lib. bdg. 38.50 o.p. (ISBN 0-89158-205-3). Westview.

Ada, Alama F., tr. see Rohmer, Harriet.

Ada, Alma F., jt. auth. see Perl, Lila.

Ada, Alma F., tr. see Blume, Judy.

Ada, G. L., jt. auth. see Nossal, G. J.

Adachi, Geraldine, ed. see Demura, Fumio & Ivan, Dan.

Adachi, M., et al. Sphingolipidoses & Allied Disorders, Vol. 1. Horrobin, D. F., ed. (Annual Research Reviews). 1979. 26.00 (ISBN 0-88831-055-2). Eden Pr.

Adair, Casey & Adair, Nancy. Word Is Out. 1978. 7.95 o.s.i. (ISBN 0-440-59709-9, Delta). Dell.

Adair, D., jt. auth. see Hamilton, W. H.

Adair, Dennis & Rosenstock, Janet. Bitter Shield. 288p. (Orig.). 1983. pap. 2.95 (ISBN 0-380-79053-X, 79053). Avon.

--The Fire, the Sword & the Devil. 382p. 1982. 14.95 (ISBN 0-920510-44-2, Pub. by Personal Lib). Dodd.

--Wildfires: The Story of Canada, Bk. IV. 336p. 3.50 (ISBN 0-380-82313-6). Avon.

Adair, Ian, jt. auth. see Amery, Heather.

Adair, J. & Blitt. Training for Series (Trilogy) 1978. text ed. 19.50x ea. (ISBN 0-685-96474-4); No. 1. (ISBN 0-566-02110-2); No. 2. (ISBN 0-566-02111-0); No. 3. (ISBN 0-566-02112-9). Gower Pub Ltd.

Adair, James. History of the American Indians. (American Studies). Repr. of 1775 ed. 40.00 (ISBN 0-384-00305-2). Johnson Repr.

Adair, James R. & Miller, Ted. Escape from Darkness. 156p. 1982. pap. 4.95 (ISBN 0-88207-318-4). Victor Bks.

Adair, John. Action Centered Leadership. 1979. text ed. 31.00x (ISBN 0-566-02143-9). Gower Pub Ltd.

--Cheriton, Sixteen Forty-Four. 1980. 24.00x o.p. (ISBN 0-900093-19-6, Pub. by Roundwood). State Mutual Bk.

--Management & Morality: The Problems & Opportunities of Social Capitalism. 196p. 1980. text ed. 28.25x (ISBN 0-566-02241-9). Gower Pub Ltd.

--Royal Palaces of Britain. 192p. 1981. 19.95 (ISBN 0-517-54554-3, C N Potter Bks). Crown.

Adair, John, jt. auth. see Young, Peter.

Adair, Nancy, jt. auth. see Adair, Casey.

Adair, Robert. Concepts in Physics. 1969. 21.00 (ISBN 0-12-044050-4); guide 5.00 tchr's. (ISBN 0-12-044056-3). Acad Pr.

Adal. The Evidence of Things Not Seen. LC 74-31350. (Photography Ser.). (Illus.). 1975. 19.50 (ISBN 0-306-70722-5); pap. 7.95 (ISBN 0-306-80013-6). Da Capo.

Adam, A. M., ed. see Plato.

Adam, Addie. Maggie Cameron, Cruise Nurse. (YA) 1978. 6.95 (ISBN 0-685-05591-4, Avalon). Bouregy.

Adam, Adolf. The Liturgical Year: Its History & Its Meaning After the Reform of the Liturgy. O'Connell, Matthew J., tr. from Ger. 1981. pap. 14.95 (ISBN 0-916134-47-4). Pueblo Pub Co.

Adam, Alan, jt. auth. see Dunlop, Stewart.

Adam, Ben. Astrologia-Una Antigua Conspiracion. 128p. Date not set. 1.75 (ISBN 0-88113-007-9). Edit Betania.

Adam, H., ed. Transactions: International Vacuum Congress - 3rd - Stuttgart - 1965, Vol. 2, 3 Pts. 1967. text ed. 49.00 (ISBN 0-08-012127-6). Pergamon.

Adam, Henry S., jt. auth. see Hoppin, Martha J.

Adam, J. G., jt. auth. see Balian, R.

Adam, J. H., ed. Longman Dictionary of Business English. 528p. 1982. 15.95 (ISBN 0-582-55558-2). Longman.

Adam, James, ed. see Plato.

Adam, Kirstine, jt. auth. see Oswald, Ian.

Adam, Michael. Womankind: A Celebration. LC 78-20623. (Illus.). 1979. pap. 5.95i o.p. (ISBN 0-06-090675-8, CN-675, CN). Har-Row.

Adam, Ruth. What Shaw Really Said. LC 66-24901. (What They Really Said Ser). 1967. 6.00x o.p. (ISBN 0-8052-3288-5). Schocken.

--Woman's Place Nineteen Ten to Nineteen Seventy-Five. (Illus.). 1977. 8.95 o.s.i. (ISBN 0-393-05622-8). Norton.

Adam, Waldemar & Cilento, G., eds. Chemical & Biological Generation of Excited States. 1982. 59.50 (ISBN 0-12-044080-6). Acad Pr.

Adamec, Cannie S., ed. Sex Roles: Origins, Influences & Implications for Women. 1980. 17.95 (ISBN 0-920792-00-6). Eden Pr.

Adami, Marie. Fanny Keats. 1938. 39.50x (ISBN 0-686-51385-1). Elliots Bks.

Adamic, Louis. My America: 1928-1938. LC 76-2050. (FDR & the Era of the New Deal). 1976. Repr. of 1938 ed. lib. bdg. 59.50 (ISBN 0-306-70801-9). Da Capo.

Adams. Atlas of the World in the Middle Ages. (Illus.). 1981. 11.90 o.p. (ISBN 0-531-09179-1). Watts.

--Italy at War. LC 82-3182. (World War II Ser.). PLB 19.92 (ISBN 0-8094-3449-0). Silver.

Adams, jt. auth. see Smellie.

Adams, A. & Schots, C. Biochemical & Biological Applications of Isotachophoresis: Proceedings of the 1st International Symposium, Baconfoy, May 1979. (Analytical Chemistry Symposia Ser.: Vol. 5). 1980. 64.00 (ISBN 0-444-41891-1). Elsevier.

Adams, A. Dana, ed. Four Thousand Questions & Answers on the Bible. 1983. 3.95 (ISBN 0-8054-1148-8); pap. 1.95 (ISBN 0-8054-1149-6). Broadman.

Adams, Abigail. New Letters of Abigail Adams, 1788-1801. Mitchell, Stewart, ed. LC 73-13398. (Illus.). 281p. 1973. Repr. of 1947 ed. lib. bdg. 20.25x (ISBN 0-8371-7055-9, ADNL). Greenwood.

Adams, Adrienne. Christmas Party. LC 78-16230. 1982p. 1982. pap. 2.95 (ISBN 0-689-70747-9, A-123, Aladdin). Atheneum.

Adams, Adrienne, illus. The Ugly Duckling. LC 65-21364. (Illus.). 1982. pap. 2.95 (ISBN 0-689-70748-7, A-123, Aladdin). Atheneum.

Adams, Alexander B. The Disputed Lands. 480p. 1981. 17.95 (ISBN 0-399-12530-2). Putnam Pub Group.

--Sunlight & Storm: The Great American Plains. (Illus.). 1977. 22.50 o.p. (ISBN 0-399-11563-3). Putnam Pub Group.

Adams, Alexander B., ed. see Thoreau, Henry D.

Adams, Alice. Careless Love. pap. 1.95 o.p. (ISBN 0-451-08658-9, J8658, Sig). NAL.

--To See You Again. (Contemporary American Fiction Ser.). 1983. pap. 5.95 (ISBN 0-14-006483-4). Penguin.

Adams, Andy. Log of a Cowboy. (Classics of the Old West Ser.). PLB 17.28 (ISBN 0-8094-3979-4). Silver.

Adams, Anna. The Ratio of One to a Stone. 25p. (Orig.). 1982. pap. 4.50 (ISBN 0-910829-02-0). First East.

Adams, Anne & Bebensee, Elisabeth L. Success in Reading & Writing: Grade 6. 1983. text ed. 15.95 (ISBN 0-673-16586-8). Scott F.

Adams, Anne H. Success in Reading & Writing: Grade 3. 1980. text ed. 13.95x (ISBN 0-673-16436-5). Scott F.

Adams, Ansel. Polaroid Land Photography. LC 78-7069. 1978. 18.95 (ISBN 0-8212-0729-6, 712744). NYGS.

--The Print. LC 76-50536. (Basic Photo Ser.). (Illus.). 1977. 11.95 o.p. (ISBN 0-8212-0718-0, 719315). NYGS.

--Yosemite & the Range of Light. LC 78-72074. (Illus.). 1979. 100.00 (ISBN 0-8212-0750-4, 969605); pap. 19.95 (ISBN 0-8212-1523-X). NYGS.

Adams, Ansel, photos by. Ansel Adams: Images Nineteen Twenty-Three to Nineteen Seventy-Four. LC 74-78740. (Illus.). 125.00 (ISBN 0-8212-1132-3). NYGS.

Adams, Ansel, et al. Death Valley. (Illus.). 1954. 8.95 (ISBN 0-8212-0724-5, 178012); pap. 8.95 (ISBN 0-8212-0725-3, 178004). NYGS.

Adams, Arthur E., ed. Russian Revolution & Bolshevik Victory: Causes & Processes. 2nd ed. (Problems in European Civilization Ser.). (Orig.). 1972. pap. text ed. 5.50 (ISBN 0-669-81745-7). Heath.

Adams, Arthur G. The Hudson: A Guidebook to the River. LC 79-14846. (Illus.). 424p. 1981. 19.95 (ISBN 0-87395-406-8). State U NY Pr.

Adams, Arthur M. Effective Leadership for Today's Church. LC 77-27547. 1978. softcover 6.95 (ISBN 0-664-24196-4). Westminster.

Adams, B. Ballistic Missile Defense. 1971. 25.00 (ISBN 0-444-00111-5). Elsevier.

Adams, Bernard. London Illustrated, 1604-1851: A Survey & Index of Topographical Books & Their Plates. (Illus.). 492p. 1983. lib. bdg. 110.00x (ISBN 0-85365-734-3, Pub. by Lib Assn England). Oryx Pr.

Adams, Bert N. The Family: A Sociological Interpretation. 3rd ed. LC 81-80805. 530p. 1980. text ed. 22.95 (ISBN 0-395-30555-1); instr's manual 2.95 (ISBN 0-395-30556-X). HM.

Adams, Bob, tr. see Maston, T. B.

Adams, Brooks. The New Empire. LC 79-67060. (Social Science Classics Ser.). 243p. 1983. text ed. cancelled (ISBN 0-87855-315-0); pap. 5.95 cancelled (ISBN 0-87855-691-5). Transaction Bks.

Adams, Bruce & Kavanaugh-Baran, Kathryn. Promise & Performance: Carter Builds a New Administration. LC 78-24790. 224p. 1979. 21.95x o.p. (ISBN 0-669-02817-7). Lexington Bks.

Adams, C. D. Flowering Plants of Jamaica. 848p. 1972. 41.50 (ISBN 0-565-00841-2, Pub. by Brit Mus Nat Hist England). Sabbot-Natural Hist Bks.

Adams, C. K. A Beginner's Guide to Computers & Microprocessors--with Projects. (Illus.). (gr. 10 up). 1978. 10.95 o.p. (ISBN 0-8306-9890-6); pap. 8.95 (ISBN 0-8306-1015-4, 1015). TAB Bks.

Adams, Candice. Diamond of Desire. (Orig.). 1983. pap. 2.95 (ISBN 0-440-01990-7). Dell.

--Going Places. (Love & Life Romance Ser.). (Orig.). 1982. pap. write for info. (ISBN 0-345-30525-6). Ballantine.

Adams, Carol. Ordinary Lives: A Hundred Years Ago. 230p. 1983. pap. 8.95 (ISBN 0-86068-239-0, Virago Pr). Merrimack Bk Serv.

Adams, Carol & Laurikietis, Rae. The Gender Trap: A Closer Look at Sex Roles, Bk. 1: Education & Work. Sellers, Jill, ed. (Illus.). 1977. lib. bdg. 9.95 o.p. (ISBN 0-915864-30-4); pap. 4.95 (ISBN 0-915864-09-6). Academy Chi Ltd.

Adams, Carolyn E. & Bogle, Irma. Study Guide & Review of Practical-Vocational Nursing. (Illus.). 464p. 1982. pap. text ed. 12.75 (ISBN 0-397-54347-6, Lippincott Nursing). Lippincott.

Adams, Charles C. Middletown Upper Houses. 900p. 1983. 60.00 (ISBN 0-914016-95-4). Phoenix Pub.

Adams, Charles F. The Antinomian Controversy. LC 74-164507. 1976. Repr. of 1892 ed. lib. bdg. 25.00 (ISBN 0-306-70290-8). Da Capo.

--Charles Francis Adams, 1835-1915: An Autobiography. LC 73-10847. (Illus.). 224p. 1973. Repr. of 1916 ed. lib. bdg. 14.00x o.p. (ISBN 0-8371-7037-0, ADAU). Greenwood.

--Richard Henry Dana, 2 Vols. LC 67-23883. 1968. Repr. of 1890 ed. 37.00 (ISBN 0-8103-3038-5). Gale.

Adams, Charles F., jt. auth. see Nathan, Richard P.

Adams, Charles L., ed. see Evans-Wentz, W. Y.

Adams, Charlotte. The ABC's of Cooking. LC 82-45139. (Illus.). 256p. 1983. 12.95 (ISBN 0-385-18512-X). Doubleday.

Adams, Chuck. Digest Book of Duck & Goose Hunting. 96p. pap. 2.95 (ISBN 0-686-81356-1). DBI.

--Using & Programming the 6809. 240p. 1983. pap. 15.95 (ISBN 0-918398-16-9). Dilithium Pr.

Adams, D. K., jt. auth. see Thut, I. N.

Adams, D. M. Inorganic Solids: An Introduction to Concepts in Solid State Structural Chemistry. LC 73-16863. 352p. 1974. pap. 23.95x (ISBN 0-471-00471-5, Pub. by Wiley-Interscience). Wiley.

Adams, Daniel. Brothers & Enemies. 384p. 1982. pap. 3.50 (ISBN 0-515-05854-8). Jove Pubns.

Adams, Dickinson W., ed. Jefferson's Extracts from the Gospels: "The Philosophy of Jesus" & "The Life & Morals of Jesus". LC 82-61371. (The Papers of Thomas Jefferson, Second Ser.). 384p. 1983. 30.00x (ISBN 0-691-04699-9). Princeton U Pr.

Adams, Doris G. Iraq's People & Resources. LC 80-19079. (University of California Publications in Economics Ser.: Vol. XVIII). (Illus.). viii, 160p. 1980. Repr. of 1958 ed. lib. bdg. 20.75x (ISBN 0-313-22759-4, ADIP). Greenwood.

Adams, Dorothy & Kurtz, Margaret. The Legal Secretary: Terminology & Transcription. (Illus.). 1980. text ed. 18.55t (ISBN 0-07-000330-0, G); legal typing practice. 8.65 (ISBN 0-07-000336-X); student transcript 5.60 (ISBN 0-07-000337-8). McGraw.

--Technical Secretary: Terminology & Transcription. (Diamond Jubilee Ser.). 1967. 21.50 (ISBN 0-07-000320-3, G); instructor's manual & key 7.00 (ISBN 0-07-000322-X); wkbk. 8.25 (ISBN 0-07-000321-1); tapes 325.00 (ISBN 0-07-088980-5). McGraw.

Adams, Doug. Involving the People in Dancing Worship: Historic & Contemporary Patterns. 1975. 2.00 (ISBN 0-941500-11-X). Sharing Co.

Adams, Douglas. The Hitchhiker's Guide to the Galaxy. 224p. 1980. 8.95 (ISBN 0-517-54209-9, Harmony); 10-copy pre-pack 89.50 (ISBN 0-517-54230-7). Crown.

--Hitchhiker's Guide to the Galaxy. 1981. pap. 2.95 (ISBN 0-671-43241-9). PB.

--The Restaurant at the End of the Universe. 256p. 1982. 9.95 (ISBN 0-517-54535-7, Harmony). Crown.

Adams, E. M., ed. The Idea of America: A Reassessment of the American Experiment. LC 77-2720. 272p. 1977. prof ref 17.50x (ISBN 0-88410-361-7). Ballinger Pub.

Adams, Edith. The Noisy Book Starring Yakety Yak. LC 82-50431. (Sweet Pickles Mini-Storybooks). (Illus.). 32p. (ps-4). 1983. pap. 1.25 (ISBN 0-394-85544-2). Random.

Adams, Edward L., Jr. Career Advancement Guide. 1975. 29.95 (ISBN 0-07-000275-4, P&RB). McGraw.

Adams, Elaine P., jt. ed. see Lukenbill, W. Bernard.

Adams, Elbridge. Joseph Conrad: The Man. LC 72-2130. (Studies in Conrad, No. 8). 1972. Repr. of 1925 ed. lib. bdg. 28.95 (ISBN 0-8383-1487-2). Haskell.

Adams, Elizabeth B., ed. Management of Information Technology - Case Studies. 1975. pap. text ed. 11.95x o.p. (ISBN 0-442-80286-2). Van Nos Reinhold.

Adams, Ellen. The Scaredy Book Starring Worried Walrus. LC 82-50426. (Sweet Pickles Mini-Storybooks). (Illus.). 32p. (ps-4). 1983. pap. 1.25 (ISBN 0-394-85542-6). Random.

Adams, Ephraim D. Great Britain & the American Civil War, 2 vols. Set. 20.00 (ISBN 0-8446-1005-4). Peter Smith.

Adams, F. Gerald & Behrman, Jere R. Commodity Exports & Economic Development: The Commodity Problem & Policies in Developing Countries. LC 81-47961. (The Wharton Econometric Studies Ser.). 352p. 1982. 26.95x (ISBN 0-669-05145-4). Lexington Bks.

Adams, F. Gerald & Klein, Lawrence R., eds. Industrial Policies for Growth & Competitiveness: An Economic Perspective. LC 82-48557. (Wharton Econometric Studies). 1983. write for Info. (ISBN 0-669-05412-7). Lexington Bks.

Adams, F. Gerard & Behrman, Jere R. Econometric Modeling of World Commodity Policy. LC 77-18596. (The Wharton Econometric Studies Ser.: No. 2). (Illus.). 240p. 1978. 22.95x (ISBN 0-669-02111-3). Lexington Bks.

--Econometric Models of World Agricultural Commodity Markets: Cocoa, Coffee, Tea, Wool, Cotton, Sugar, Wheat, Rice. LC 76-3624. 128p. 1976. prof ref 20.00 (ISBN 0-88410-290-4). Ballinger Pub.

Adams, F. Gerard & Glickman, Norman. Modeling the Multiregional Economic System: Perspectives for the Eighties. LC 79-48005. (Wharton Econometric Ser.). 320p. 1980. 26.95x (ISBN 0-669-03627-7). Lexington Bks.

Adams, F. Gerard & Klein, Sonia, eds. Stabilizing World Commodity Markets. LC 77-7805. (The Wharton Econometric Studies Ser.: No. 1). 368p. 1978. 26.95x (ISBN 0-669-01622-5). Lexington Bks.

Adams, Florence. Mushy Eggs. (Illus.). 32p. (gr. k-3). 1973. PLB 5.29 o.p. (ISBN 0-399-60854-0). Putnam Pub Group.

Adams, Forrest H. & Emmanouilides, George C. Moss' Heart Disease in Infants, Children, & Adolescents. 3rd ed. 800p. 1983. lib. bdg. write for info (ISBN 0-683-00051-9). Williams & Wilkins.

Adams, Frank O. Sindon: A Layman's Guide to the Shroud of Turin. DeSalvo, John A., ed. LC 82-90138. (Illus.). 1982. 12.50 (ISBN 0-86700-008-2, Synergy Bks); pap. 7.50 (ISBN 0-86700-009-0). P Walsh Pr.

Adams, Fred T. Way to Modern Man: An Introduction to Human Evolution. LC 68-28011. (Illus.). 1968. text ed. 11.00 (ISBN 0-8077-1001-6); pap. text ed. 7.00 (ISBN 0-8077-1003-2). Tchrs Coll.

Adams, G. Donald. Museum Public Relations. (AASLH Management Ser.: Vol. 2). Date not set. text ed. price not set (ISBN 0-910050-65-1). AASLH.

Adams, G. Rollie & Christian, Ralph J. Nashville: A Pictorial History. LC 80-20196. (Illus.). 1980. 13.95 (ISBN 0-89865-013-5). Donning Co.

Adams, Gary, jt. auth. see Sternberg, Les.

Adams, George. The Lemniscatory Ruled Surface in Space & Counterspace. Eberhart, Stephen, tr. from Ger. & Eng. (Illus.). 83p. 1979. pap. 9.95 (ISBN 0-686-43395-5, Pub. by Steinerbooks). Anthroposophic.

Adams, George & Whicher, Olive. The Plant Between Sun & Earth. LC 82-50276. (Illus.). 224p. (Orig.). 1982. pap. 12.95 (ISBN 0-394-71231-5). Shambhala Pubns.

Adams, George, tr. see Steiner, Rudolf.

Adams, George F., ed. Planation Surfaces: Peneplains, Pediplains, Etchplains. LC 75-12942. (Benchmark Papers in Geology Ser: Vol. 22). 1975. 59.50 (ISBN 0-12-786020-7). Acad Pr.

Adams, George L., jt. auth. see Moffic, H. Steven.

Adams, George L., et al. Boies's Fundamentals of Otolaryngology: A Textbook of Ear, Nose & Throat Diseases. 5th ed. LC 75-44601. (Illus.). 1978. text ed. 32.00 (ISBN 0-7216-1035-8). Saunders.

Adams, George R., jt. ed. see Gardner, James B.

Adams, Gerald R. & Gullotta, Thomas. Adolescent Life Experiences. LC 82-20748. (Psychology Ser.). 600p. 1983. text ed. 20.95 (ISBN 0-534-01242-6). Brooks-Cole.

Adams, Gleason R., jt. tr. see Latortue, Regine.

Adams, H. M. Catalogue of Books Printed on the Continent of Europe, 2 Vols. 1967. Set. 375.00 (ISBN 0-521-06951-3). Cambridge U Pr.

Adams, Harry B. Project Nineteen Eighty-Two. (Illus.). 142p. 1982. pap. 6.95 (ISBN 0-686-36288-8). Avcom Intl.

--Propjet Eighty-Two. (Illus.). 142p. 1982. pap. 6.95 (ISBN 0-686-97327-5, Pub. by AvCom Intl). Aviation.

Adams, Hazard. Philosophy of the Literary Symbolic. 1982. write for info. (ISBN 0-8130-0743-7). U Presses Fla.

Adams, Henry. The Education of Henry Adams. Samuels, Ernest, ed. (Riverside Edition Ser.). 600p. 1973. pap. 6.75 (ISBN 0-395-16620-9, RivEd). HM.

--The Education of Henry Adams. LC 19-7386. 529p. 1975. Repr. of 1918 ed. 14.95 (ISBN 0-910220-74-3). Berg.

--The Education of Henry Adams. 8.95 (ISBN 0-395-08352-4, SenEd). HM.

--Esther. Spiller, Robert, ed. LC 38-18393. 1976. Repr. lib. bdg. 39.00x (ISBN 0-8201-1187-2). Schol Facsimiles.

--The Letters of Henry Adams, Volumes 1-3: 1858-1892. Levenson, J. C. & Samuels, Ernest, eds. (Illus.). 2000p. 1983. Set. text ed. 100.00x (ISBN 0-674-52685-6, Belknap Pr). Harvard U Pr.

--The Life of George Cabot Lodge. LC 78-16619. 1978. Repr. of 1911 ed. 30.00x (ISBN 0-8201-1316-6). Schol Facsimiles.

--Mont Saint Michel & Chartres. LC 36-27246. 1978. 14.95 (ISBN 0-910220-94-8). Berg.

--Mont-Saint-Michel & Chartres. (Illus.). 300p. 1980. 20.00 o.p. (ISBN 0-399-12498-5). Putnam Pub Group.

--The United States in Eighteen Hundred. (YA) 1955. pap. 2.95x (ISBN 0-8014-9014-6). Cornell U Pr.

Adams, Henry H. Harry Hopkins: A Biography. LC 76-48985. (Illus.). (YA) 1977. 15.00 o.p. (ISBN 0-399-11833-0). Putnam Pub Group.

Adams, Henry M. Prussian-American Relations, Seventeen Seventy-Five to Eighteen Seventy-One. LC 79-25884. 135p. 1980. Repr. of 1960 ed. lib. bdg. 17.75x (ISBN 0-313-22270-3, ADPA). Greenwood.

Adams, Herbert B. Historical Scholarship in the United States, 1876-1901. Holt, W. Stull, ed. LC 71-113060. 314p. Repr. of 1938 ed. lib. bdg. 14.25x o.p. (ISBN 0-8371-4695-X, ADHS). Greenwood.

Adams, Herbert F., jt. auth. see Cooke, Nelson M.

Adams, Herbert R., jt. auth. see Glatthorn, Allan A.

Adams, J. Arthritis & Back Pain. 1975. 14.95 (ISBN 0-8391-0576-2). Univ Park.

Adams, J. A. & Rogers, D. F. Computer Aided Analysis in Heat Transfer. 1973. 25.95 o.p. (ISBN 0-07-000285-1, C); solutions manual 4.00 o.p. (ISBN 0-07-000286-X). McGraw.

Adams, J. Alan, jt. auth. see Rogers, David F.

Adams, J. Donald. Copey of Harvard: A Biography of Charles Townsend Copeland. LC 72-6191. (Illus.). 306p. 1973. Repr. of 1960 ed. lib. bdg. 17.25x (ISBN 0-8371-6465-6, ADCO). Greenwood.

Adams, J. Edison, jt. auth. see Greulach, Victor A.

Adams, J. Frank. Lectures on Lie Groups. LC 82-51014. (Midway Reprints Ser.). 168p. 1983. pap. text ed. 10.00x (ISBN 0-226-00530-5). U of Chicago Pr.

Adams, J. H. & Murray, Margaret F. Atlas of Post-Mortem Techniques in Neuropathology. LC 82-4313. (Illus.). 120p. 1982. 29.95 (ISBN 0-521-24121-9). Cambridge U Pr.

Adams, J. M., jt. auth. see Stadt, R.

Adams, J. Mack & Haden, Douglas H. Social Effects of Computer Use & Misuse. LC 76-10698. 326p. 1976. text ed. 22.95 (ISBN 0-471-00463-4). Wiley.

Adams, J. McKee, jt. ed. see Callaway, Joseph A.

Adams, J. Michael. Career Change: A Planning Book. (Illus.). 208p. 1983. pap. text ed. 7.95 (ISBN 0-07-000401-3, G). McGraw.

Adams, J. Michael, jt. auth. see Kagy, Frederick D.

Adams, J. R. Degree of Difference. 1979. cancelled o.s.i. (ISBN 0-686-15538-6); pap. cancelled o.s.i. (ISBN 0-686-15539-4). Writers West.

Adams, J. T. The Complete Home Electrical Wiring Handbook. LC 78-21969. (Illus.). 1979. lib. bdg. 12.95 o.p. (ISBN 0-668-04525-6). Arco.

--The Homeowner's Guide to Paint & Painting. LC 81-19149. (Illus.). 320p. 1982. lib. bdg. 16.95 (ISBN 0-668-05124-8). Arco.

Adams, Jack A. Human Memory. (Psychology Ser). 1967. 24.95 o.p. (ISBN 0-07-000307-6, C). McGraw.

Adams, James. Autopsy. (Illus.). 1976. 35.00 o.p. (ISBN 0-8151-0079-5). Year Bk Med.

Adams, James E. Electrical Principles & Practices. 2nd ed. 1973. text ed. 23.95 (ISBN 0-07-000281-9, G); ans. key 1.50 (ISBN 0-07-000282-7). McGraw.

Adams, James L. Paul Tillich's Philosophy of Culture, Science & Religion. LC 81-43775. 320p. 1982. lib. bdg. 23.25 (ISBN 0-8191-2221-1); pap. text ed. 12.25 (ISBN 0-8191-2222-X). U Pr of Amer.

Adams, James L., tr. see Tillich, Paul.

Adams, James M. Data Processing: An Introduction. LC 81-66793. (Data Processing Ser.). (Illus.). 253p. 1982. text ed. 10.20 (ISBN 0-686-96702-X); tchr's. guide 4.75 (ISBN 0-8273-1617-8). Delmar.

Adams, James T. The Adams Family. LC 73-21487. (Illus.). 364p. 1974. Repr. of 1930 ed. lib. bdg. 20.50x (ISBN 0-8371-6427-3, ADAF). Greenwood.

--The Adams Family. 1976. pap. 1.95 o.p. (ISBN 0-451-06853-X, J6853, Sig). NAL.

--Henry Adams. LC 70-109703. (Illus.). 246p. Repr. of 1933 ed. lib. bdg. 15.00 o.p. (ISBN 0-8371-4194-X, ADHA). Greenwood.

Adams, Jan S. Citizen Inspectors in the Soviet Union: The Peoples Control Committee. LC 77-83460. 254p. 1978. 29.95 (ISBN 0-03-023201-5). Praeger.

Adams, Jane. Sex & the Single Parent. LC 77-13394. 1978. 8.95 o.p. (ISBN 0-698-10879-5, Coward). Putnam Pub Group.

--Tradeoffs. Golbitz, Pat, ed. 372p. 1983. 14.95 (ISBN 0-688-01366-X). Morrow.

Adams, Jane I. Are You Ready for More on the Dulcimore? 84p. 1982. pap. 8.95 (ISBN 0-941126-04-8). Meadowlark.

Adams, Janet. Decorative Folding Screens. LC 82-70178. (Illus.). 208p. 1982. 30.00 (ISBN 0-670-26287-0, Studio). Viking Pr.

Adams, Jay E. Christian Living in the Home. 1974. pap. 2.95 (ISBN 0-8010-0052-1). Baker Bk.

--Journal of Pastoral Practice, Vol. II, No. I. pap. 4.00 o.p. (ISBN 0-8010-0137-4). Baker Bk.

--Journal of Pastoral Practice, Vol. V, No.1. 1981. pap. 5.00 (ISBN 0-8010-0178-1). Baker Bk.

--Journal of Pastoral Practice, Vol. V, No. 2. 1981. pap. 5.00 (ISBN 0-8010-0183-8). Baker Bk.

--Journal of Pastoral Practice, Vol. V, No 3. 1982. pap. 5.00 (ISBN 0-8010-0186-2). Baker Bk.

--Preaching with Purpose. 1983. pap. 5.95 (ISBN 0-87552-078-2). Presby & Reformed.

--Ready to Restore. (Orig.). 1981. pap. 3.50 (ISBN 0-8010-0171-4). Baker Bk.

--Update on Christian Counseling, Vol. 1. pap. 3.50 (ISBN 0-8010-0153-6). Baker Bk.

--Use of Scripture in Counseling. (Direction Bks). 1976. pap. 2.95 (ISBN 0-8010-0099-8). Baker Bk.

Adams, Jennifer A. The Solar Church. Hoffman, Douglas R., ed. 288p. (Orig.). 1982. pap. 9.95 (ISBN 0-8298-0482-X). Pilgrim NY.

Adams, Jerry L., jt. auth. see Shipman, James T.

Adams, Joan & Whitridge, Jackie. ESCORTGUIDE. 2nd ed. 207p. 1982. pap. 6.95 (ISBN 0-9607818-0-3). Escortguide.

Adams, Joey. Strictly for Laughs. 176p. 1982. pap. 1.95 o.p. (ISBN 0-523-41828-0). Pinnacle Bks.

Adams, John. Discourses on Davila. LC 70-87665. (American Constitutional & Legal History Ser.). 260p. 1973. Repr. of 1805 ed. lib. bdg. 32.50 (ISBN 0-306-71761-1). Da Capo.

--Drowned Valley: The Piscataqua River Basin. LC 75-40868. (Illus.). 294p. 1976. 29.95 (ISBN 0-87451-123-2). U Pr of New Eng.

--The Lenten Psalms. (Short Course Ser.). 124p. Repr. of 1912 ed. text ed. 3.95 o.p. (ISBN 0-567-08304-7). Attic Pr.

--Teach Your Child Soccer. (Teach Your Child Ser). (Illus.). 1978. pap. 4.95 o.p. (ISBN 0-86019-021-8). Transatlantic.

Adams, John & Iqbal, Sabiha. Exports, Politics, & Economic Development: Pakistan, 1970-1982. (Replica Edition Ser.). 185p. 1983. softcover 18.50x (ISBN 0-86531-959-6). Westview.

Adams, John, et al. Transition: Understanding & Managing Personal Change. LC 77-5833. 1977. text ed. 18.50x o.p. (ISBN 0-916672-97-2). Allanheld.

Adams, John A. A Defense of the Constitutions of Government of the United States of America, 3 Vols. LC 69-11328. (American Constitutional & Legal History Ser). 1971. Repr. of 1788 ed. Set. lib. bdg. 165.00 (ISBN 0-306-71176-1). Da Capo.

Adams, John D. Understanding & Managing Stress: A Facilitator's Guide. LC 80-50474. 38p. 1980. pap. 45.00 pkg. with readings & workbook (ISBN 0-88390-157-9). Univ Assocs.

--Understanding & Managing Stress: A Workbook in Changing Life Styles. LC 80-50474. 102p. 1980. pap. 10.00 (ISBN 0-88390-157-9). Univ Assocs.

Adams, John D., ed. Understanding & Managing Stress: A Book of Readings. LC 80-50474. 217p. 1980. pap. 15.95 (ISBN 0-88390-158-7). Univ Assocs.

Adams, John F. Algebraic Topology: A Student's Guide. LC 75-163178. (London Mathematical Lecture Note Ser.: No. 4). (Illus.). 1972. 25.95x (ISBN 0-521-08076-2). Cambridge U Pr.

Adams, John G. Without Precedent. (Illus.). 1983. 17.50 (ISBN 0-393-01616-1). Norton.

Adams, John L. Musicians' Autobiographies: An Annotated Bibliography of Writings Available in English 1800 to 1980. 128p. 1982. lib. bdg. 24.95x (ISBN 0-89950-049-8). McFarland & Co.

Adams, John P. John P. Adams' Third Bottle Book. LC 72-80183. (Illus.). 128p. 1972. pap. 5.95 (ISBN 0-912274-19-0). Backcountry Pubns.

Adams, John R. Edward Everett Hale. (United States Authors Ser.). 1977. lib. bdg. 11.95 (ISBN 0-8057-7186-7, Twayne). G K Hall.

--Harriet Beecher Stowe. (United States Authors Ser.). 1963. lib. bdg. 10.95 (ISBN 0-8057-0700-X, Twayne). G K Hall.

Adams, John S., ed. Contemporary Metropolitan America, Part I: Cities of the Nation's Historic Metropolitan Core. (Comparative Metropolitan Analysis Project Ser). (Illus.). 1976. prof ref 26.00x (ISBN 0-88410-467-2). Ballinger Pub.

--Contemporary Metropolitan America, Part 2: Nineteenth Century Ports. (Comparative Metropolitan Analysis Project Ser.). (Illus.). 336p. 1976. prof ref 25.00x (ISBN 0-88410-464-8). Ballinger Pub.

--Contemporary Metropolitan America, Part 3: Nineteenth Century Inland Centers & Ports. (Comparative Metropolitan Analysis Project Ser.). (Illus.). 528p. 1976. prof ref 33.50x (ISBN 0-88410-465-6). Ballinger Pub.

--Contemporary Metropolitan America, Part 4: Twentieth Century Cities. (Comparative Metropolitan Analysis Project Ser.). (Illus.). 368p. 1976. prof ref 23.50x (ISBN 0-88410-466-4). Ballinger Pub.

--Contemporary Metropolitan America: Twenty Geographical Vignettes. LC 76-56167. (Comparative Metropolitan Analysis Project Ser). 1976. Set. prof ref 100.00x (ISBN 0-88410-425-7). Ballinger Pub.

Adams, John S., ed. see Marshall, John.

Adams, Judith. Against the Gates of Hell. 152p. pap. 2.50 (ISBN 0-87509-232-2). Chr Pubns.

Adams, Judith-Anne & Dwyer, Margaret A. English for Academic Uses: A Writing Workbook. (Illus.). 208p. 1982. pap. text ed. 10.95 (ISBN 0-13-279653-8). P-H.

Adams, K. M. The First Australians: Prehistory, Eighteen-Ten. 16.95x (ISBN 0-392-02965-0, ABC). Sportshelf.

Adams, Kathleen J., jt. ed. see Hareven, Tamara K.

Adams, Kenneth, jt. ed. see Wesson, Donald R.

Adams, L. & Llanas, A. Read It Right It: Materials for Elementary Reading Comprehension. (Materials for Language Practice Ser.). (Illus.). 96p. 1983. pap. 4.95 (ISBN 0-08-029435-9). Pergamon.

Adams, L. D. The Wines of America. 2nd ed. 1978. 16.95 (ISBN 0-07-000318-1). McGraw.

Adams, Lane. How Come It's Taking Me So Long to Get Better? 1975. pap. 4.95 (ISBN 0-8423-1507-1). Tyndale.

Adams, Larry L. Walter Lippmann. (World Leaders Ser.). 1977. lib. bdg. 12.95 (ISBN 0-8057-7709-1, Twayne). G K Hall.

Adams, Laura. Existential Battles: The Growth of Norman Mailer. LC 74-27710. viii, 192p. 1976. 12.95x (ISBN 0-8214-0182-3, 82-81818); pap. 5.25 (ISBN 0-8214-0401-6, 82-818126). Ohio U Pr.

Adams, Laurie & Coudert, Allison. Alice & the Boa Constrictor. LC 82-15769. (Illus.). 96p. (gr. 3-6). 1983. 8.95. HM.

Adams, Laurie & Volpe, Robert. Art Cop. LC 74-15238. (Illus.). 250p. 1974. 8.95 o.p. (ISBN 0-396-07020-5). Dodd.

Adams, Leonard P. Public Employment Service in Transition, 1933-1968: Evolution of a Placement Service into a Manpower Agency. LC 68-66941. (Cornell Studies in Industrial & Labor Relations: No. 16). 264p. 1969. pap. 3.50 (ISBN 0-87546-037-2); pap. 6.50 special hard bdg. (ISBN 0-87546-274-X). ILR Pr.

Adams, Les & Rainey, Buck. Shoot-Em-Ups: The Complete Reference Guide to Westerns of the Sound Era. (Illus.). 1978. 30.00 o.p. (ISBN 0-87000-393-3, Arlington Hse). Crown.

Adams, M. Ian. Three Authors of Alienation: Bombal, Onetti, Carpentier. LC 74-32397. (Latin American Monographs Ser.: No. 36). 140p. 1975. 10.00x o.p. (ISBN 0-292-78009-5). U of Tex Pr.

Adams, M. J. An Introduction to Optical Waveguides. LC 80-42059. 384p. 1981. 51.95x (ISBN 0-471-27969-2, Pub. by Wiley Interscience). Wiley.

Adams, Marilyn M., tr. see William Of Ockham.

Adams, Martin R. Studies in the Literary Backgrounds of English Radicalism, with Special Reference to the French Revolution. LC 68-28591. (Illus.). 1968. Repr. of 1947 ed. lib. bdg. 20.50x (ISBN 0-8371-0000-3, ADSL). Greenwood.

Adams, Mary, ed. see Ferrari, Guy.

Adams, Mary, tr. see Steiner, Rudolf.

Adams, Maurice see Godwin, E. W.

Adams, Monni. Designs for Living: Symbolic Communication in African Art. (Illus.). 150p. 1982. pap. text ed. 12.00x (ISBN 0-674-19969-3). Carpenter Ctr.

Adams, Neal. Well Control Problems & Solutions. 683p. 1980. 59.95x (ISBN 0-87814-124-3). Pennwell Book Division.

--Workover Well Control. 320p. 1981. 42.95x (ISBN 0-87814-142-1). Pennwell Book Division.

Adams, Norman & Singer, Joe. Drawing Animals. (Illus.). 1979. 19.95 (ISBN 0-8230-1361-8). Watson-Guptill.

Adams, O. Eugene, Jr., jt. auth. see Black, Paul H.

Adams, Oscar F. Dictionary of American Authors. 5th ed. LC 68-2175. 1969. Repr. of 1904 ed. 42.00 (ISBN 0-8103-3148-9). Gale.

Adams, P., illus. The Child's Play Museum. (Illus.). 1977. 5.50 (ISBN 0-85953-094-9, Pub. by Childs's Play England). Playspaces.

Adams, Pam. Mrs. Honey's Hat. (Illus.). 24p. 1980. 5.50 (ISBN 0-85953-099-X, Pub. by Child's Play England). Playspaces.

Adams, Pam, illus. Angels. (Pre-Reading Ser.). (Illus.). 24p. (Orig.). 1974. 4.50 (ISBN 0-85953-034-5, Pub. by Child's Play England). Playspaces.

--The Best Things. (Pre-Reading Ser.). 24p. 1974. 4.50 (ISBN 0-85953-031-0, Pub. by Child's England). Playspaces.

--Day Dreams. (Imagination Ser.). (Illus.). 32p. (Orig.). 1978. 5.50 (ISBN 0-85953-105-8, Pub. by Child's Play England); pap. 4.00 (ISBN 0-85953-082-5). Playspaces.

--The Gingerbread Man. (Illus.). 24p. 1981. 5.50 (ISBN 0-85953-107-4, Pub. by Child's Play England). Playspaces.

--The House That Jack Built. (Books with Holes Ser.). (Illus.). 16p. 1978. 8.00 (ISBN 0-85953-076-0, Pub. by Child's Play England). Playspaces.

--How Many? (Motivation Ser.). (Illus.). 16p. (Orig.). 1975. pap. 2.00 (ISBN 0-85953-045-0, Pub. by Child's Play England). Playspaces.

--I-Spy ABC. (Books with Holes Ser.). (Illus.). 16p. 1978. 8.00 (ISBN 0-85953-066-3, Pub. by Child's Play England). Playspaces.

--If I Weren't Me. (Illus.). 24p. 1981. 5.50 (ISBN 0-85953-108-2, Pub. by Child's Play England). Playspaces.

--Magic. (Imagination Ser.). (Illus.). 32p. (Orig.). 1978. 5.50 (ISBN 0-85953-104-X, Pub. by Child's Play England); pap. 4.00 (ISBN 0-85953-081-7). Playspaces.

--Oh, Soldier! Soldier! (Books with Holes Ser.). (Illus.). 16p. 1978. 8.00 (ISBN 0-85953-093-0, Pub. by Child's Play England). Playspaces.

--Old MacDonald. (Books with Holes Ser.). (Illus.). 16p. 1978. 8.00 (ISBN 0-85953-054-X, Pub. by Child's Play England). Playspaces.
--Old Macdonald Had a Farm. (Books with Holes Ser.). (Illus., Orig.). 1975. pap. 5.00 (ISBN 0-85953-053-1, Pub. by Child's Play England). Playspaces.
--On Soldier, Soldier Wont You Marry Me. (Books with Holes Ser.). (Illus.). 16p. 1978. pap. 5.00 (ISBN 0-85953-092-2, Pub. by Childs Play England). Playspaces.
--Shopping Day. (Pre-Reading Ser.). (Illus.). 24p. 1974. 4.50 (ISBN 0-85953-033-7, Pub. by Child's Play England). Playspaces.
--There Was an Old Lady. (Books with Holes). (Illus.). 16p. 1975. 8.00 (ISBN 0-85953-021-3, Pub. by Child's Play England). Playspaces.
--There Was an Old Lady Who Swallowed a Fly. (Books with Holes Ser.). (Illus.). 16p. 1973. pap. 5.00 (ISBN 0-85953-018-3, Pub. by Child's Play England). Playspaces.
--There Were Ten in the Bed. (Illus.). 24p. 1979. 5.50 (ISBN 0-85953-095-7, Pub. by Childs's Play England). Playspaces.
--This Old Man. (Books with Holes Ser.). (Illus.). 16p. (Orig.). pap. 5.00 (ISBN 0-85953-026-4, Pub. by Childs Play England). Playspaces.
--This Old Man. (Books with Holes). (Illus.). 16p. 8.00 (ISBN 0-85953-027-2, Pub. by Child's Play England). Playspaces.
--The Zoo. (Pre-Reading Ser.). (Illus.). 24p. 1974. 4.50 (ISBN 0-85953-032-9, Pub. by Child's Play England). Playspaces.
Adams, Pam & Jones, Ceri, illus. A Book of Ghosts. (Imagination Ser.). (Illus.). 32p. (Orig.). 1974. 5.50 (ISBN 0-85953-073-6, Pub. by Child's Play England); pap. 4.00 (ISBN 0-85953-028-0). Playspaces.
Adams, Patricia & Johnson, Vicki. Wild Animal Care & Rehabilitation Manual. rev. ed. (Illus.). 136p. 1982. pap. text ed. 9.50 (ISBN 0-939294-04-4). Beech Leaf.
Adams, Patsy. Ceramica Culina. (Comunidades y Culturas Peruanas: No. 7). 1976. 1.65x (ISBN 0-88312-742-3); microfiche 3.75 (ISBN 0-88312-339-8). Summer Inst Ling.
--La Musica Culina y la Educacion Informal. (Comunidades y Culturas Peruanas: No. 10). 5p. 1976. pap. 0.75x (ISBN 0-88312-789-X); microfiche 1.50 (ISBN 0-88312-331-2). Summer Inst Ling.
Adams, Paul. The Complete Legal Guide for Your Small Business. LC 81-11445. (Small Business Management Ser.). 218p. 1982. 19.95 (ISBN 0-471-09436-6). Ronald Pr.
--Obsessive Children: A Sociopsychiatric Study. LC 73-78725. 1973. pap. 8.95 o.p. (ISBN 0-87630-204-5). Brunner Mazel.
Adams, Pauline & Thornton, Emma S. A Populist Assault: Sarah E. Van de Vort Emery on American Democracy 1862-1895. LC 82-60665. (Illus.). 146p. 1982. 13.95 (ISBN 0-87972-203-7); pap. 6.95 (ISBN 0-87972-204-5). Bowling Green Univ.
Adams, Phyllis, et al. Stop the Bed. (Double Scoop Ser.). (Illus.). 32p. (gr. k-3). 1982. PLB 4.95 (ISBN 0-695-41644-8, Dist. by Caroline Hse); pap. 2.25 (ISBN 0-695-31644-3). Follett.
Adams, Phylliss, et al. Pippin at the Gym. (Double Scoop Ser.). (Illus.). 32p. (gr. k-3). 1983. PLB 4.95 (ISBN 0-695-41681-2, Dist. by Caroline Hse); pap. 2.25 (ISBN 0-695-31681-8). Follett.
--Pippin Cleans Up. (Double Scoop Ser.). (Illus.). 32p. (gr. k-3). 1983. PLB 4.95 (ISBN 0-695-41680-4, Dist. by Caroline Hse); pap. 2.25 (ISBN 0-695-31680-X). Follett.
--Pippin Eats Out. (Double Scoop Ser.). (Illus.). 32p. (gr. k-3). 1983. PLB 4.95 (ISBN 0-695-41679-0, Dist. by Caroline Hse); pap. 2.25 (ISBN 0-695-31679-6). Follett.
--Pippin Goes to Work. (Double Scoop Ser.). (Illus.). 32p. (gr. k-3). 1983. PLB 4.95 (ISBN 0-695-41678-2, Dist. by Caroline Hse); pap. 2.25 (ISBN 0-695-31678-8). Follett.
--Pippin Learns a Lot. (Double Scoop Ser.). (Illus.). 32p. (gr. k-3). 1983. PLB 4.95 (ISBN 0-695-41677-4, Dist. by Caroline Hse); pap. 2.25 (ISBN 0-695-31677-X). Follett.
--Pippin's Lucky Penny. (Double Scoop Ser.). (Illus.). 32p. (gr. k-3). 1983. PLB 4.95 (ISBN 0-695-41682-0, Dist. by Caroline Hse); pap. 2.25 (ISBN 0-695-31682-6). Follett.
Adams, R., jt. auth. see Christ, F.
Adams, R. D. & Lyon, G. Neurology of Hereditary Metabolic Diseases of C hildren. 1981. 49.50 (ISBN 0-07-000318-1). McGraw.
Adams, R. D. & Victor, M. Principles of Neurology. 2nd ed. 1981. 47.00 (ISBN 0-07-000294-0). McGraw.
Adams, R. L. Cell Culture for Biochemists. (Laboratory Techniques in Biochemistry & Molecular Biology Ser.: Vol. 8, No. 1). 1980. pap. 27.00 (ISBN 0-444-80199-5). Elsevier.
Adams, Ramon F. A Fitting Death for Billy the Kid. LC 60-5112. (Illus.). 310p. 1982. 16.95 (ISBN 0-8061-0458-9); pap. 7.95 (ISBN 0-8061-1764-8). U of Okla Pr.
--More Burs Under the Saddle: Books & Histories of the West. LC 77-18606. 1979. 16.95 (ISBN 0-8061-1469-X). U of Okla Pr.
Adams, Ramon F., ed. see Wolfenstine, Manfred R.
Adams, Raymond D., jt. auth. see Isselbacher, Kurt J.
Adams, Raymond D., jt. auth. see Petersdorf, Robert G.
Adams, Raymond J., Jr. Avian Research at the Kalamazoo Nature Center 1970 to 1978. (Illus.). 86p. 1982. pap. 5.00 (ISBN 0-939294-11-7). Beech Leaf.
Adams, Rex. Miracle Medicine Foods. LC 77-6245. 1977. pap. 4.95 (ISBN 0-13-585463-6, Reward). P-H.
Adams, Richard. Our Amazing Sun. LC 82-17419. (Question & Answer Bks.). (Illus.). 32p. (gr. 3-6). 1983. PLB 8.59 (ISBN 0-89375-890-6); pap. text ed. 1.95 (ISBN 0-89375-891-4). Troll Assocs.
--Our Wonderful Solar System. LC 82-17413. (Question & Answer Bks.). (Illus.). 32p. (gr. 3-6). 1983. PLB 8.59 (ISBN 0-89375-872-8); pap. text ed. 1.95 (ISBN 0-89375-873-6). Troll Assocs.
--Shardik. (YA) 1976. pap. 4.95 (ISBN 0-380-00516-6, 62554-7). Avon.
--Watership Down. 1975. pap. 4.95 (ISBN 0-380-00428-3, 614995). Avon.
Adams, Richard & Lockley, Ronald. Voyage Through the Antarctic. LC 82-48484. (Illus.). 160p. 1982. 13.95 (ISBN 0-394-52858-1). Knopf.
Adams, Richard N. Cultural Surveys of Panama, Nicaragua, Guatemala, El Salvador, Honduras. LC 76-41776. 1976. Repr. of 1957 ed. 35.00 o.p. (ISBN 0-87917-056-5). Ethridge.
--Paradoxical Harvest: Energy & Explanation in British History, 1870-1914. LC 81-21631. (ASA Rose Monograph). (Illus.). 160p. 1982. 27.50 (ISBN 0-521-24637-7); pap. 8.95 (ISBN 0-521-28866-5). Cambridge U Pr.
Adams, Robert. Bili the Axe. 185p. 1983. pap. 2.50 (Sig). NAL.
--Castaways in Time. Freas, Polly & Freas, Kelly, eds. LC 79-11600. (Illus.). 1980. pap. 5.95 (ISBN 0-915442-96-5, Starblaze). Donning Co.
--Castaways in Time. 1982. pap. 2.50 (ISBN 0-451-12257-7, AE2257, Sig). NAL.
--A Cat of Silvery Hue: Horseclaus IV. (Orig.). 1979. pap. 2.25 (ISBN 0-451-11579-1, AE1579, Sig). NAL.
--The Death of a Legend. (Horseclans Ser.: No. 8). 1981. pap. 2.75 (ISBN 0-451-12324-7, AE2324, Sig). NAL.
--Denver: A Photographic Survey of the Metropolitan Area. LC 76-44035. (Illus.). 1977. pap. 5.95 (ISBN 0-87081-102-9). Colo Assoc.
--Horseclan, No. 9: The Witch Goddess. 1982. pap. 2.75 (ISBN 0-451-11792-1, AE1792, Sig). NAL.
--Horseclans, No. 1: The Coming of the Horseclans. 1982. pap. 2.50 (ISBN 0-451-11652-6, AE1652, Sig). NAL.
--Horseclans Odyssey. (Orig.). 1981. pap. 2.75 (ISBN 0-451-09744-0, E9744, Sig). NAL.
--The Patrimony (a Horsclans Novel) (Orig.). 1980. pap. 2.50 (ISBN 0-451-11815-4, AE1815, Sig). NAL.
--Revenge of the Horseclans. 1982. pap. 2.50 (ISBN 0-451-11431-0, AE1431, Sig). NAL.
--The Savage Mountains: A Horseclans Science Fiction Novel. (Orig.). 1980. pap. 2.50 (ISBN 0-451-12316-6, AE2316, Sig). NAL.
--Selections from the Strauss Photography Collection. LC 82-71437. 40p. (Orig.). 1982. pap. 7.95 (ISBN 0-914738-29-1). Denver Art Mus.
--The Witch Goddess. (Horseclans Ser.: No. 9). 1982. pap. 2.50 (ISBN 0-451-11792-1, AE1792, Sig). NAL.
Adams, Robert, ed. The New Times Network: Groups & Centres for Personal Growth. 192p. 1983. pap. 8.95 (ISBN 0-7100-9355-1). Routledge & Kegan.
Adams, Robert, et al. Dry Lands: Man & Plants. LC 78-65219. 1979. 30.00x (ISBN 0-312-22042-1). St Martin.
Adams, Robert E. Encuentro Con Jesus. (Illus.). 1977. pap. 1.50 (ISBN 0-311-04657-6). Casa Bautista.
Adams, Robert H. White Churches of the Plains: Examples from Colorado. LC 70-119708. (Illus.). 1970. 7.95 o.p. (ISBN 0-87081-000-6). Colo Assoc.
Adams, Robert L. Boston Job Bank. expanded ed. (Job Bank Ser.). 168p. 1980. pap. 5.95 o.p. (ISBN 0-937860-01-8). Adams Inc MA.
Adams, Robert L., ed. Greater Washington Job. 300p. (Orig.). 1983. pap. 9.95 (ISBN 0-937860-10-7). Adams Inc MA.
Adams, Robert L., et al, eds. The Boston Job Bank: A Comprehensive Guide to Major Employers Throughout Greater Boston. 2nd ed. (Job Bank Ser.). 300p. 1983. pap. 9.95 (ISBN 0-937860-18-2). Adams Inc MA.
--Greater Atlanta Job Bank: A Comprehensive Guide to Major Employers Throughout Greater Atlanta. (Job Bank Ser.). 250p. (Orig.). 1983. pap. 9.95 (ISBN 0-937860-17-4). Adams Inc MA.
Adams, Robert M. After Joyce: Studies in Fiction After Ulysses. 1977. 17.50x (ISBN 0-19-502168-1). Oxford U Pr.
--Decadent Societies. LC 82-73710. 208p. 1983. 15.00 (ISBN 0-86547-103-7). N Point Pr.
--Occupational Skin Disease. 1982. 69.50 (790026). Grune.
--Proteus: His Lies, His Truth. 192p. 1973. 7.95x o.p. (ISBN 0-393-04353-3). Norton.
Adams, Robert M., ed. see Berkeley, George.
Adams, Robert M., tr. & intro. by see Villiers de l'Isle Adam.
Adams, Roger, ed. Organic Reactions, Vol. 1. LC 42-20265. 400p. 1978. Repr. of 1942 ed. 29.50 (ISBN 0-88275-729-6). Krieger.
--Organic Reactions, Vol. 2. LC 42-20265. 470p. 1981. Repr. of 1944 ed. 29.50 (ISBN 0-89874-375-3). Krieger.
--Organic Reactions, Vol. 3. LC 42-20265. 468p. 1975. Repr. of 1946 ed. 29.50 (ISBN 0-88275-875-6). Krieger.
--Organic Reactions, Vol. 4. LC 42-20265. 438p. 1979. Repr. of 1948 ed. 29.50 (ISBN 0-88275-780-6). Krieger.
--Organic Reactions, Vol. 5. LC 42-20265. 454p. 1977. Repr. of 1949 ed. 29.50 (ISBN 0-88275-249-9). Krieger.
--Organic Reactions, Vol. 6. LC 42-20265. 526p. 1975. Repr. of 1951 ed. 29.50 (ISBN 0-88275-876-4). Krieger.
--Organic Reactions, Vol. 7. LC 42-20265. 448p. 1975. Repr. of 1953 ed. 29.50 (ISBN 0-88275-877-2). Krieger.
--Organic Reactions, Vol. 8. LC 42-20265. 446p. 1975. Repr. of 1954 ed. 29.50 (ISBN 0-88275-878-0). Krieger.
--Organic Reactions, Vol. 9. LC 42-20265. 476p. 1975. Repr. of 1957 ed. 29.50 (ISBN 0-88275-879-9). Krieger.
--Organic Reactions, Vol. 10. LC 42-20265. 572p. 1975. Repr. of 1959 ed. 29.50 (ISBN 0-88275-880-2). Krieger.
Adams, Roger, et al. Laboratory Experiments in Organic Chemistry. 7th ed. 1979. text ed. 24.95 (ISBN 0-02-300590-4); instrs'. manual avail. Macmillan.
Adams, Romanzo. Interracial Marriage in Hawaii: A Study of Mutually Conditioned Processes of Acculturation & Amalgamation. LC 69-14907. (Criminology, Law Enforcement, & Social Problems Ser.: No. 65). (Illus.). 1969. Repr. of 1937 ed. 12.50x (ISBN 0-87585-065-0). Patterson Smith.
Adams, Ronald C., et al. Games, Sports & Excercises for the Physically Handicapped. 3rd. ed. LC 81-7288. (Illus.). 430p. 1982. pap. 28.50 (ISBN 0-8121-0785-3). Lea & Febiger.
Adams, Roy. The Sanctuary Doctrine: Three Approaches in the Seventh-day Adventist Church. (Andrews University Seminary Doctoral Dissertation Ser.). viii, 327p. (Orig.). 1981. pap. 8.95 (ISBN 0-943872-33-2). Andrews Univ Pr.
Adams, Russell. King C. Gillette: The Man & His Wonderful Shaving Device. LC 78-15749. 1978. 10.00 o.p. (ISBN 0-316-00937-7). Little.
Adams, Russell E., jt. ed. see Lucas, Jay P.
Adams, Russell L. Great Negroes, Past & Present. 3rd rev. ed. Ross, David P., Jr., ed. LC 72-87924. (Orig.). 1976. 14.95 (ISBN 0-910030-07-3); pap. text ed. 9.95 (ISBN 0-910030-08-1); 9 portfolios of display prints 12.95 ea. Afro-Am.
Adams, Ruth. The Complete Home Guide to All the Vitamins. 432p. 1972. pap. 3.25 (ISBN 0-915962-05-5). Larchmont Bks.
Adams, Ruth & Murray, Frank. Megavitamin Therapy. 277p. (Orig.). 1973. pap. 3.25 (ISBN 0-915962-03-9). Larchmont Bks.
Adams, St. Claire, jt. ed. see Morris, Joseph.
Adams, Sallie & Orgel, Michael. Through the Mental Health Maze: A Consumer's Guide to Finding a Psychotherapist. 78p. 1982. 3.25 (ISBN 0-686-96298-2). Pub Citizen Health.
Adams, Sam, et al. Teaching Mathematics: With Emphasis on the Diagnostic Approach. (Illus.). 1977. pap. text ed. 15.50 scp o.p. (ISBN 0-06-040164-8, HarpC). Har-Row.
Adams, Stephen. R. Murray Schafer. (Canadian Composers Ser.). 248p. 1983. 27.50x (ISBN 0-8020-5571-0). U of Toronto Pr.
Adams, T. Police Patrol: Tactics & Techniques. LC 71-138484. (Essential of Law Enforcements Ser). 1971. ref. ed. 21.95 (ISBN 0-13-684662-9). P-H.
Adams, Thomas. Lore Power is "Man" Power. 64p. 1981. pap. write for info. (ISBN 0-9609242-0-5). T Adams.
Adams, Thomas F. Introduction to the Administration of Criminal Justice: An Overview of the Justice System & Its Components. 2nd ed. (Ser. in Criminal Justice). (Illus.). 1980. text ed. 20.95 (ISBN 0-13-477794-8). P-H.
--Law Enforcement: An Introduction to the Police Role in the Criminal Justice System. 2nd ed. (Illus.). 1973. ref. ed. 21.95 (ISBN 0-13-526301-8). P-H.
Adams, Tom, jt. auth. see Symons, Julian.
Adams, V. Dean, ed. Aquatic Resources Management of the Colorado River Ecosystem. Lamarra, Vincent A. LC 82-72349. 400p. 1983. 29.95 (ISBN 0-686-84637-0). Ann Arbor Science.
Adams, W. Fundamentals of Mathematics for Business, Social, & Life Sciences. 1979. 25.95 (ISBN 0-13-341073-0). P-H.
Adams, W. & Goldstein, L. Introduction to Number Theory. 1976. text ed. 22.95 (ISBN 0-13-491282-9). P-H.
Adams, W. J. Calculus for Business & Social Science. LC 74-5524. 250p. 1975. text ed. 23.50 (ISBN 0-471-00988-1). Wiley.
Adams, W. Lindsay & Borza, Eugene N., eds. Philip II: Alexander the Great & the Macedonian Heritage. LC 81-43664. (Illus.). 318p. (Orig.). 1982. PLB 25.25 (ISBN 0-8191-2447-8); pap. text ed. 13.50 (ISBN 0-8191-2448-6). U Pr of Amer.
Adams, W. Royce. Increasing Reading Speed. 2nd ed. 1982. text ed. 12.95 (ISBN 0-02-300340-5). Macmillan.
--Reading Skills: A Guide for Better Reading. LC 73-21849. (Self-Teaching Guides Ser). 245p. 1974. 6.95 (ISBN 0-471-00780-3). Wiley.
Adams, W. Royce, Jr., jt. auth. see Carman, Robert A.
Adams, Walter. The Structure of American Industry. 6th ed. 1982. text ed. 15.95 (ISBN 0-02-300800-8). Macmillan.
Adams, Walter, et al. Tariffs, Quotas, & Trade: The Politics of Protectionism. LC 78-66267. 330p. 1979. pap. text ed. 7.95 (ISBN 0-917616-34-0). ICS Pr.
Adams, William & Schreibman, Fay, eds. Television Network News: Issues in Content Research. LC 78-64489. 1978. 6.50 (ISBN 0-932768-00-8). CTS-GWU.
Adams, William, ed. see Momaday.
Adams, William, et al, eds. Asian-American Authors. (Multi-Ethnic Literature Ser.). pap. 6.08 o.p. (ISBN 0-395-24039-5); instr's. guide 6.08 o.p. (ISBN 0-395-24042-5). HM.
Adams, William B. Handbook of Motion Picture Production. LC 76-51818. (Wiley Ser. on Human Communication). 352p. 1977. 33.95x (ISBN 0-471-00459-6, Pub. by Wiley-Interscience). Wiley.
Adams, William C. Television Coverage of the Middle East. (Communications & Information Sciences Ser.). 176p. 1981. text ed. 17.50x (ISBN 0-89391-083-X). Ablex Pub.
Adams, William C., ed. Television Coverage of International Affairs. (The Communication & Information Science Ser.). 1982. 23.50 (ISBN 0-89391-103-8). Ablex Pub.
--Television Coverage of the Nineteen Eighty Presidential Campaign. (Communication & Information Science Ser.). 1983. 21.50 (ISBN 0-89391-104-6). Ablex Pub.
Adams, William C., et al. Foundations of Physical Activity. 1968. pap. 5.80x (ISBN 0-87563-006-5). Stipes.
Adams, William D. Dictionary of English Literature. LC 66-25162. 1966. Repr. of 1880 ed. 55.00 (ISBN 0-8103-0150-4). Gale.
Adams, William D., ed. English Epigrams. LC 74-77039. 1974. Repr. of 1878 ed. 37.00 (ISBN 0-8103-3700-2). Gale.
Adams, William H. D. Curiosities of Superstition. LC 76-155434. 1971. 37.00 o.p. (ISBN 0-8103-3383-X). Gale.
--Witch, Warlock, & Magician. LC 73-5621. 1971. Repr. of 1889 ed. 54.00 (ISBN 0-8103-3619-7). Gale.
Adams, William J. Finite Mathematics: For Business & Social Science. LC 73-84448. 354p. 1980. Repr. of 1974 ed. 14.50 o.p. (ISBN 0-536-00986-4). Krieger.
--Finite Mathmatics for Business & Social Science. LC 73-84448. 1974. text ed. 19.95 o.s.i. (ISBN 0-471-00986-5); study guide 8.50x o.s.i. (ISBN 0-471-00987-3). Wiley.
Adams, William M., ed. Tsunamis in the Pacific Ocean. 1970. 25.00x (ISBN 0-8248-0095-8, Eastwest Ctr). UH Pr.
Adamski, George. Inside the Spaceships: UFO Experiences of George Adamski 1952-1955. LC 80-80385. (Illus.). 296p. Date not set. pap. 9.95 (ISBN 0-942176-01-4). GAF Intl.
Adamson, Arthur. A Textbook of Physical Chemistry. 2nd ed. 953p. 1979. 25.00 (ISBN 0-12-044260-4); solutions manual 2.50 (ISBN 0-12-044265-5). Acad Pr.
Adamson, Arthur W. Physical Chemistry of Surfaces. 3rd ed. LC 76-13885. 736p. 1976. 39.95x o.p. (ISBN 0-471-00794-3, Pub. by Wiley-Interscience). Wiley.
--Understanding Physical Chemistry. 3rd ed. 1980. 13.95 (ISBN 0-8053-0128-3). Benjamin Cummings.
Adamson, Arthur W. & Fleischauer, Paul D. Concepts of Inorganic Photochemistry. LC 74-30198. 439p. 1975. 38.95 o.s.i. (ISBN 0-471-00795-1, Pub. by Wiley-Interscience). Wiley.
Adamson, Authur W. & Fleischauer, Paul, eds. Concepts of Inorganic Photochemistry. LC 74-30198. 456p. 1975. Repr. 33.95 o.p. (ISBN 0-471-00795-1). Krieger.
Adamson, Donald see Bates, Martin & Dudley-Evans, Tony.
Adamson, Douglas. Charles Bear & the Mystery of the Forest. LC 77-2805. (Illus.). (gr. 1 up). 1977. 6.95 o.p. (ISBN 0-395-25841-3). HM.
Adamson, Elizabeth C. Mind Your Manners. (gr. 1-3). 1981. 4.95 (ISBN 0-86653-014-2, GA 243). Good Apple.
Adamson, George. Widdecombe Fair. (Illus.). 32p. (ps-5). 1966. 6.50 o.p. (ISBN 0-571-06559-7). Faber & Faber.
Adamson, Iain T. An Introduction to Field Theory. 2nd ed. LC 82-1164. 192p. 1982. 19.95 (ISBN 0-521-24388-2); pap. 9.95 (ISBN 0-521-28658-1). Cambridge U Pr.
Adamson, Ian, jt. auth. see Morse, Peter.

Adamson, J. H. & Folland, H. F. Shepherd of the Ocean: Sir Walter Raleigh & His Times. LC 69-17747. (Illus.). 1969. 14.95 (ISBN 0-87645-018-4). Gambit.
--Sir Harry Vane: His Life & Times, 1613-1662. LC 72-94005. (Illus.). 540p. 1973. 14.95 (ISBN 0-87645-064-8). Gambit.
Adamson, Jane. Othello As Tragedy: Some Problems of Judgement & Feeling. LC 79-41437. 230p. 1980. 37.50 (ISBN 0-521-22368-7); pap. 11.95 (ISBN 0-521-29760-5). Cambridge U Pr.
Adamson, Joe. Groucho, Harpo, Chico & Sometimes Zeppo: A Celebration of the Marx Brothers. (Illus.). 1983. pap. 3.95 (ISBN 0-671-47072-8, Touchstone Bks). S&S.
Adamson, Wendy, jt. auth. see Gadler, Steve.
Adamson, Wendy W. Saving Lake Superior. LC 74-17351. (Story of Environmental Action Ser.). (Illus.). (gr. 7 up). 1974. PLB 8.95 (ISBN 0-87518-083-3). Dillon.
--Who Owns a River? LC 76-53011. (Story of Environmental Action Ser.). (Illus.). (gr. 7 up). 1977. PLB 8.95 o.p. (ISBN 0-87518-140-6). Dillon.
Adams-Webber, J. R. Personal Construct Theory: Concepts & Applications. 239p. 1979. 37.95x (ISBN 0-471-99669-6, Pub. by Wiley-Interscience). Wiley.
Adamthwaite, Anthony. The Lost Peace: International Relations in Europe 1918-1939. 250p. 1981. 25.00 (ISBN 0-312-49882-9). St Martin.
Adanson, M. Familles des Plantes, 2 vols. in 1. (Illus.). 1966. Repr. of 1763 ed. 80.00 (ISBN 3-7682-0345-X). Lubrecht & Cramer.
Adanson, Michel. Histoire Naturelle du Senegal. (Bibliotheque Africaine Ser.). 196p. (Fr.). 1974. Repr. of 1757 ed. lib. bdg. 56.00x o.p. (ISBN 0-8287-0005-2, 73-2137). Clearwater Pub.
Adashko, J. George, tr. see Basov, N. G.
Adcock, Doon, jt. auth. see Segal, Marilyn.
Adcock, Fleur. The Inner Harbour. 1983. pap. 8.95 (ISBN 0-19-211888-9). Oxford U Pr.
Adcock, Fleur, ed. Contemporary New Zealand Poetry: An Anthology. 160p. 1983. pap. 14.95 (ISBN 0-19-558092-3). Oxford U Pr.
Addams, Charles. Creature Comforts: A New Collection of Classic Cartoons. (Illus.). 1981. 12.95 o.s.i. (ISBN 0-671-43835-2). S&S.
Addams, Chas. Chas Addams' Favorite Haunts. 1976. 8.95 o.p. (ISBN 0-671-22429-8). S&S.
Addams, Jane. Newer Ideals of Peace. LC 71-137523. (Peace Movement in America Ser). xviii, 243p. 1972. Repr. of 1907 ed. lib. bdg. 16.95x (ISBN 0-89198-050-4). Ozer.
--Peace & Bread in Time of War. LC 75-137524. (Peace Movement in America Ser). 269p. 1972. Repr. of 1922 ed. lib. bdg. 16.95x (ISBN 0-89198-051-2). Ozer.
--Twenty Years at Hull-House. pap. 2.50 (ISBN 0-451-51564-1, CE1564, Sig Classics). NAL.
Addams, Jane, et al. Philanthropy & Social Progress: Seven Essays. LC 75-108221. (Criminology, Law Enforcement, & Social Problems Ser.: No. 104). (Index added). 1970. Repr. of 1893 ed. 10.00x (ISBN 0-87585-104-5). Patterson Smith.
--Women at the Hague: The International Congress of Women & Its Results. LC 73-147452. (Library of War & Peace; Peace Leaders: Biographies & Memoirs). lib. bdg. 38.00 o.s.i. (ISBN 0-8240-0246-6). Garland Pub.
Addanki, Sam & Kindrick, Shirley A. Renewed Health for Diabetics & Obese People. Brennan, R. O., ed. (Orig.). 1982. pap. 3.50 (ISBN 0-9609896-0-9). Nu-Diet.
Addeo, Edmond G., jt. auth. see Wiederanders, Rex E.
Addington, A. C. The Royal House of Stuart, 3 vols. 1064p. 1982. 220.00x set (ISBN 0-686-94087-3, Pub. by C Skilton Scotland). State Mutual Bk.
Addink, A. D. & Spronk, N., eds. Exogenous & Endogenous Influences on Metabolic & Neural Control, Vol. 1, Invited Lectures: Proceedings of the Third Congress of the European Society for Comparative Physiology & Biochemistry, August 31-September 3, 1981, Noorwijkerhout Netherlands. (Illus.). 432p. 1982. 75.00 (ISBN 0-08-027986-4). Pergamon.
--Exogenous & Endogenous Influences on Metabolic & Neural Control, Vol. 2, Abstracts: Proceedings ot the Third Congress of the European Society for Compara07394366xxxlogy & Biochemistry, August 31-September 3, 1981, Noorwijkerhout,Netherlands. (Illus.). 260p. 1982. 50.00 (ISBN 0-08-028845-6). Pergamon.
Addis, Ann B., jt. auth. see Levin, Harry.
Addis, Patricia K. Through a Woman's I: An Annotated Bibliography of American Women's Autobiographical Writings, 1946-1976. LC 82-10813. 621p. 1983. 37.50 (ISBN 0-8108-1588-5). Scarecrow.
Addison, A. W. & Cullen, W. R. Biological Aspects of Inorganic Chemistry. 410p. Repr. of 1977 ed. text ed. 35.00 (ISBN 0-471-02147-4). Krieger.
Addison, A. W., et al, eds. Biological Aspects of Inorganic Chemistry. LC 76-44225. 410p. 1977. 39.50 o.s.i. (ISBN 0-471-02147-4, Pub. by Wiley-Interscience). Wiley.
Addison, Daniel D. Lucy Larcom: Life, Letters & Diary. LC 75-99065. (Library of Lives & Letters). 1970. Repr. of 1894 ed. 34.00 (ISBN 0-8103-3611-1). Gale.
Addison, John & Siebert, W. S. The Market for Labor: An Analytical Treatment. LC 78-10976. (Illus.). 1979. 27.50x (ISBN 0-673-16175-7). Scott F.
Addison, John, et al. Suleyman & the Ottoman Empire. Yapp, Malcolm & Killingray, Margaret, eds. (Illus.). (gr. 10). 1980. lib. bdg. 6.95 (ISBN 0-89908-038-3); pap. text ed. 2.25 (ISBN 0-89908-013-8). Greenhaven.
--Traditional Africa. Yapp, Malcolm, et al, eds. (World History Ser.). (Illus.). 32p. (gr. 10). 1980. lib. bdg. 6.95 (ISBN 0-89908-034-0); pap. text ed. 2.25 (ISBN 0-89908-009-X). Greenhaven.
Addison, Joseph. Addison: The Freeholder. Leheny, James, ed. 52.00x (ISBN 0-19-812494-5). Oxford U Pr.
Addison, William. Worthy Doctor Fuller. LC 71-106707. Repr. of 1951 ed. lib. bdg. 16.75x (ISBN 0-8371-3437-4, ADDF). Greenwood.
Addiss, Stephen. Samurai Painters. LC 82-48781. (Great Japanese Art Ser.). (Illus.). 48p. 1982. 18.95 (ISBN 0-87011-563-4). Kodansha.
Addkison, Roy & Sellick, Douglas. Running Dry: How to Conserve Water Indoors & Out. LC 81-40347. (Illus.). 120p. 1982. 16.95 (ISBN 0-8128-2836-4); pap. 9.95 (ISBN 0-8128-6136-1). Stein & Day.
Addlestone, David F., et al. The Rights of Veterans. 1978. pap. 2.50 o.p. (ISBN 0-380-01838-1, 77008, Discus). Avon.
Addy, John & Reeves, Marjorie. A Coal & Iron Community in the Industrial Revolution. (Then & There Ser.). (Illus.). 108p. (Orig.). (gr. 7-12). 1980. pap. text ed. 3.10 (ISBN 0-582-20456-9). Longman.
Addy, P. N. Anglo-Tibetan Relations Eighteen Ninety-Nine to Nineteen Forty-Seven. (Illus.). 1979. pap. text ed. 10.25x o.p. (ISBN 0-391-01125-1). Humanities.
Ade, George. The Old-Time Saloon: Not Wet-Not Dry, Just History. LC 77-181797. (Illus.). xii, 176p. 1975. Repr. of 1931 ed. 34.00 (ISBN 0-8103-4076-3). Gale.
Adebayo, Augustus. Principles & Practice of Public Administration in Nigeria. LC 80-41173. 192p. 1981. 27.00 o.p. (ISBN 0-471-27897-1, Pub. by Wiley-Interscience); pap. 13.50 o.p. (ISBN 0-471-27898-X). Wiley.
Adell, Judith & Klein, Hilary D., eds. A Guide to Non-Sexist Children's Books. LC 75-34396. 1976. 11.95 (ISBN 0-915864-01-0); pap. 4.95 (ISBN 0-915864-02-9). Academy Chi Ltd.
Adelman, Benjamin & Adelman, Saul J. Bound for the Stars: An Enthusiastic Look at the Opportunities & Challenges Space Exploration Offers. (Illus.). 368p. 1981. text ed. 17.95 (ISBN 0-13-080390-1, Spec); pap. text ed. 8.95 (ISBN 0-13-080382-0). P-H.
Adelman, Harvey, jt. auth. see Sanford, Edward.
Adelman, Howard S. & Taylor, Linda. Learning Disabilities in Perspective. 1982. text ed. 21.95x (ISBN 0-673-15398-3). Scott F.
Adelman, Jonathan R. The Revolutionary Armies: The Historical Development of the Soviet & the Chinese People's Liberation Armies. LC 79-7728. (Contributions in Political Science: No. 38). (Illus.). 1980. lib. bdg. 25.00 (ISBN 0-313-22026-3, ADR/). Greenwood.
Adelman, Jonathan R., ed. Communist Armies in Politics: Their Origins & Development. (Special Studies in Military Affairs). 300p. 1982. lib. bdg. 25.00 (ISBN 0-89158-880-9). Westview.
--Terror & Communist Politics: The Role of the Secret Police in Communist States. (Special Study). 300p. 1983. lib. bdg. 25.00 (ISBN 0-86531-293-1). Westview.
Adelman, M. A. & Kaufman, G. A. Energy Resources in an Uncertain Future: Coal, Gas, Oil & Uranium Supply Forecasting. 1983. prof ref 35.00x (ISBN 0-88410-644-6). Ballinger Pub.
Adelman, Mara B., jt. auth. see Levine, Deena.
Adelman, Morris, et al. No Time to Confuse. LC 75-10230. 1975. pap. 4.95 o.p. (ISBN 0-917616-01-4). ICS Pr.
Adelman, Paul. Gladstone, Disraeli & Later Victorian Politics. 1970. pap. text ed. 5.95x (ISBN 0-582-31409-7). Longman.
--The Rise of the Labour Party, 1880-1945. 1972. pap. text ed. 5.95x (ISBN 0-582-31427-5). Longman.
Adelman, Saul J., jt. auth. see Adelman, Benjamin.
Adelmann, F. J. Contemporary Chinese Philosophy. 1983. lib. bdg. 32.50 (ISBN 90-247-3057-0, Pub. by Martinus Nijhoff Netherlands). Kluwer Boston.
Adelmann, Nora E. Directory of Life Care Communities: A Guide to Retirement Communities for Independent Living. LC 81-11626. 256p. 1981. 20.00 (ISBN 0-8242-0663-0). Wilson.
Adelsberg, Sandra, jt. ed. see Hamelsdorf, Ora.
Adelson, Joseph, ed. Handbook of Adolescent Psychology. LC 79-21927. (Wiley Ser. on Personality Processes). 624p. 1980. 42.95x (ISBN 0-471-03793-1, Pub. by Wiley-Interscience). Wiley.
Adelson, Leone & Moore, Lillian. Mr. Twitmeyer & the Poodle. (gr. 3-5). 1979. pap. 0.95 o.p. (ISBN 0-440-47298-9, YB). Dell.
Adelson, Lester. The Pathology of Homicide: A Vade Mecum for Pathologist, Prosecutor & Defense Counsel. (Illus.). 992p. 1974. 67.50x (ISBN 0-398-03000-6). C C Thomas.
Adelstein, James, et al, eds. see Brill, Bertrand.
Adelstein, Michael E. & Pival, Jean G. The Reading Commitment. 2nd ed. 390p. 1982. pap. text ed. 10.95 (ISBN 0-15-575572-2, HC); instr's. manual 4.95 (ISBN 0-15-575573-0). HarBraceJ.
--The Writing Commitment. 2nd ed. 536p. 1980. text ed. 13.95 (ISBN 0-15-597851-9, HC); instructor's manual 1.95 (ISBN 0-15-597852-7). HarBraceJ.
Adelung, J. Mithridates, oder allgemeine Sprachenkunde, 6 vols. (Linguistics 13th-18th Centuries Ser.). (Fr.). 1974. Repr. of 1806 ed. Set. lib. bdg. 815.50x, order nos. 71-5019 to 71-5024 o.p. (ISBN 0-8287-0006-0). Clearwater Pub.
Aden, John M. Pope's Once & Future Kings: Satire & Politics in the Early Career. LC 78-16618. 1978. 16.50x (ISBN 0-87049-252-7). U of Tenn Pr.
Adenauer, Konrad. Konrad Adenauer: Memoirs 1945-1953. Ruhm von Oppen, Beate, tr. from German. LC 65-26906. (Illus.). 478p. 1966. 35.00 (ISBN 0-89526-651-2). Regnery-Gateway.
Adeney, Walter D. The Books of Ezra & Nehemiah. 1980. 13.00 (ISBN 0-86524-050-7, 7004). Klock & Klock.
Ader, Paul. How to Make a Million at the Track. LC 77-91196. 1978. pap. 8.95 (ISBN 0-8092-7531-7). Contemp Bks.
Ader-Brin, Dianne, ed. see Ingebritsen, Karl J.
Aderman, Ralph M. & Kleinfield, Herbert L., eds. Letters of Washington Irving: Vol. III, 1839-1846. (Critical Editions Program). 1982. lib. bdg. 50.00 (ISBN 0-8057-8524-8, Twayne). G K Hall.
--Letters of Washington Irving: Vol. IV, 1847-1859. (Critical Editions Program). 1982. lib. bdg. 45.00 (ISBN 0-8057-8525-6, Twayne). G K Hall.
Aderman, Ralph M., et al, eds. The Complete Works of Washington Irving: Letters, 1802-1823. (Critical Editions Program). 1978. lib. bdg. 30.00 (ISBN 0-8057-8522-1, Twayne). G K Hall.
Adermanm, Ralph M., et al, eds. Letters: Volume II, 1823-1838. (Critical Editions Program Ser.). 1979. 35.00 (ISBN 0-8057-8523-X, Twayne). G K Hall.
Aders, Gebhard. History of the German Night Fighter Force 1917-1945. (Illus.). 360p. 1980. 19.95 (ISBN 0-86720-581-4). Sci Bks Intl.
Aderton, Mimi & Liss, Douglas. The Book of Gross. (Illus.). 96p. (Orig.). 1983. pap. 3.95 (ISBN 0-8065-0838-8). Citadel Pr.
Ades, Dawn. Dali & Surrealism. LC 82-47545. (Icon Editions). (Illus.). 224p. 1982. 19.18i (ISBN 0-06-430295-4, HarpT); pap. 9.95i (ISBN 0-06-430119-2, IN-119). Har-Row.
Adesanya, M. O. & Oloyede, E. O. Business Law in Nigeria. LC 77-188223. 320p. 1972. 38.50x (ISBN 0-8419-0115-5, Africana). Holmes & Meier.
Adey, Margaret, et al. Galeria Hispanica. 3rd ed. (Illus.). 1979. 23.00 (ISBN 0-07-000361-0, W); tchr's. guide 3.36 (ISBN 0-07-000362-9); tests 61.32 (ISBN 0-07-000363-7); tapes 327.72 (ISBN 0-07-098595-2). McGraw.
Adgey, A. J. Acute Phase of Ischemic Heart Disease & Myocardial Infarction. 1982. text ed. 49.50 (ISBN 90-247-2675-1, Pub. by Martinus Nijhoff Netherlands). Kluwer Boston.
Adhikarya, R. Broadcasting in Peninsular Malaysia. (Case Studies on Broadcasting Systems). 1977. pap. 15.95 (ISBN 0-7100-8530-3). Routledge & Kegan.
Adian, S. T. Word Problems II. (Studies in Logic: Vol. 95). 1980. 85.00 (ISBN 0-444-85343-X). Elsevier.
Adib, Kanafani. Transportation Demand Analysis. (Illus.). 352p. 1983. text ed. 34.50x (ISBN 0-07-033271-1, C). McGraw.
Adidevananda, Swami, tr. see Srinivasadasa.
Adie, R. & Poitras, G. Latin America: The Politics of Immobility. 1974. pap. 12.95 (ISBN 0-13-524272-X). P-H.
Adie, R., ed. Antarctic Geology. 1965. 97.75 (ISBN 0-444-10131-4). Elsevier.
Adiercretz, R., et al, eds. Endocrinological Cancer: Ovarian Function & Disease. (International Congress Ser.: No. 515). 1981. 81.00 (ISBN 0-444-90149-3). Elsevier.
Adinolfi, L. Common Stock Sense. (Finite Math Text Ser.). write for info. (ISBN 0-685-84481-1). J W Wills.
Adirondack Mountain Club. Guide to Adirondack Trails: High Peak Region. 10th ed. LC 80-15403. (Illus.). 304p. 1980. pap. 9.00 (ISBN 0-935272-11-9). ADK Mtn Club.
Adiyodi, K. G. & Adiyodi, Rita G. Reproductive Biology of Invertebrates, Vol. 1: Oogenesis, Oviposition & Oosorption. 500p. 1983. write for info. (ISBN 0-471-10128-1, Pub. by Wiley-Interscience). Wiley.
Adiyodi, Rita G., jt. auth. see Adiyodi, K. G.
Adkins, Arthur W. Merit & Responsibility: A Study in Greek Values. (Midway Reprint Ser). 396p. 1975. pap. text ed. 15.00x (ISBN 0-226-00728-6). U of Chicago Pr.
Adkins, B. & Harley, R. G. The General Theory of Alternating Current Machines: Application to Practical Problems Sl. 1978. pap. 17.95x (ISBN 0-412-15560-5, Pub. by Chapman & Hall). Methuen Inc.
Adkins, Dorothy C. Test Construction: Development & Interpretation of Achievement Tests. 2nd ed. LC 73-89607. 1974. pap. 8.95 (ISBN 0-675-08845-3). Merrill.
Adkins, Hal. The Directory of Homebuilt Ultra Light Aircraft. (Illus.). 106p. (Orig.). 1982. pap. 10.00 (ISBN 0-910907-00-5). Haljan Pubns.
Adkins, J. S., jt. auth. see Bodwell, C. E.
Adkins, Jan. Art & Industry of Sandcastles. (gr. k up). 1982. 7.95 (ISBN 0-8027-0336-4); pap. 4.95 (ISBN 0-8027-7205-6). Walker & Co.
--The Art & Ingenuity of the Woodstove. LC 78-57414. (Illus.). 1978. 12.95 o.p. (ISBN 0-89696-012-9, An Everest House Book). Dodd.
--Art & Ingenuity of the Woodstove. 1980. pap. 7.95 o.p. (ISBN 0-89696-096-X, An Everest House Book). Dodd.
--How a House Happens. (Illus.). 30p. 1983. pap. 3.95 (ISBN 0-8027-7206-4). Walker & Co.
--A Storm Without Rain. LC 82-20342. 192p. (gr. 7 up). 1983. 12.45i (ISBN 0-316-01084-7). Little.
Adkins, John. Equilibrium Thermodynamics. 2nd ed. (European Physics Ser). 304p. 1975. pap. text ed. 11.95 o.p. (ISBN 0-07-084057-1, C). McGraw.
Adkinson, A. Wyle & Fry, N., eds. The House of Horror: The Story of Hammer Films. LC 74-146693. 1974. 6.95 (ISBN 0-89388-163-5). Okpaku Communications.
Adkinson, B. W. Two Centuries of Federal Information. LC 78-7294. (Publications in the Information Science Ser.). 235p. 1978. 43.50 (ISBN 0-87933-269-7). Hutchinson Ross.
Adkinson, Burton W. Heller Report Revisited. 1971. 15.00 (ISBN 0-942308-00-X). NFAIS.
Adlam, Brian H. The Book of Dorchester. 1981. 39.50x o.p. (ISBN 0-86023-141-0, Pub. by Barracuda England). State Mutual Bk.
Adland, Mark. The Greenlander. 1982. pap. 2.95 o.p. (ISBN 0-425-05196-X). Berkley Pub.
Adlard, John, ed. Fruit of That Forbidden Tree: Restoration Poems, Songs & Jests on the Subject of Sensual Love. (Fyfield Ser.). 1980. 7.95 o.p. (ISBN 0-85635-146-6, Pub. by Carcanet New Pr England); pap. 4.95 o.p. (ISBN 0-85635-147-4). Humanities.
Adlard, John, ed. see Wilmot, John.
Adler, Alan D., ed. Biological Role of Porphyrins & Related Structures. (Annals of the New York Academy of Sciences: Vol. 244). 694p. 1975. 60.00x (ISBN 0-89072-758-9). NY Acad Sci.
Adler, Alexandra. Guiding Human Misfits. new & rev. ed. LC 49-8697. Repr. of 1948 ed. 11.00 o.s.i. (ISBN 0-527-00590-8). Kraus Repr.
Adler, Alfred. Individual Psychology of Alfred Adler: A Systematic Presentation in Selections from His Writings. Ansbacher, Heinz L. & Ansbacher, Rowena R., eds. LC 55-6679. 1956. 17.95x o.s.i. (ISBN 0-465-03239-7). Basic.
--The Pattern of Life. 2nd ed. LC 81-71160. pap. 10.00x (ISBN 0-918560-28-4). A Adler Inst.
--Souvenirs Fresh & Rancid. 224p. 1982. 14.95 (ISBN 0-394-53218-X). Grove.
--Souvenirs Fresh & Rancid. 224p. 1982. pap. 5.95 (ISBN 0-394-62467-X, Ever). Grove.
Adler, Allan & Halperin, Morton H., eds. The Litigation Under the Federal Freedom of Information Act & Privacy Act, 1983 Edition. LC 82-72706. 350p. 1982. pap. 30.00 (ISBN 0-86566-025-5). Ctr Natl Security.
Adler, Bill. The Divorce Personality. cancelled. Green Hill.
--Firsts-Facts & Feats. new ed. (Illus.). 128p. (gr. 4-8). 1975. 4.95 o.p. (ISBN 0-448-11950-1, G&D). Putnam Pub Group.
--Inside Publishing. LC 81-17978. 1982. 12.95 o.p. (ISBN 0-672-52680-8). Bobbs.
--The Runner's Liar's Diary. (Orig.). 1979. pap. 2.50 (ISBN 0-448-16462-0, G&D). Putnam Pub Group.
--Sports Question & Answer Book. LC 77-85636. (Illus.). (gr. 4 up). 1978. pap. 1.95 (ISBN 0-448-14295-3, G&D). Putnam Pub Group.
--Still More Letters from Camp. 1973. pap. 1.25 (ISBN 0-451-08946-4, Y8946, Sig). NAL.
Adler, Bill & King, Norman. All in the First Family. 256p. 1982. 13.95 (ISBN 0-399-12682-1). Putnam Pub Group.
Adler, Bill, jt. auth. see Chaffee, Suzy.
Adler, Bill, jt. auth. see George, Phyllis.
Adler, Bill, jt. auth. see Myerson, Bess.
Adler, Bill, ed. Kids' Letters to President Carter. LC 77-87789. (Illus.). 1978. 7.95 (ISBN 0-448-14569-3, G&D); pap. 4.95 (ISBN 0-448-14651-7, Today Press). Putnam Pub Group.
--Wit & Wisdom of Billy Graham. LC 80-65430. 256p. 1981. pap. cancelled o.p. (ISBN 0-915684-61-6). Christian Herald.
Adler, C. S. Down by the River. (gr. 7up). 1981. 9.95 (ISBN 0-698-20532-4, Coward). Putnam Pub Group.
--Get Lost, Little Brother. 144p. (gr. 4-7). 1983. 9.95 (ISBN 0-89919-154-1, Clarion). HM.
--The Once in a While Hero. 112p. 1982. 8.95 (ISBN 0-698-20553-7, Coward). Putnam Pub Group.
--Shelter on Blue Barns Road. 1982. pap. 1.75 (ISBN 0-451-11438-8, Sig Vista). NAL.
--The Silver Coach. LC 79-10430. (gr. 4-7). 1979. 7.95 (ISBN 0-698-20504-9, Coward). Putnam Pub Group.
--Some Other Summer. LC 82-7161. 132p. (gr. 5-9). 1982. 9.95 (ISBN 0-02-700290-X). Macmillan.

Adler, Claire F. Modern Geometry. 2nd ed. 1967. text ed. 21.95 (ISBN 0-07-000421-8, C); teachers' manual 3.95 (ISBN 0-07-000419-6). McGraw.

Adler, Cy A. Ecological Fantasies. 352p. 1974. pap. 2.95 o.s.i. (ISBN 0-440-53209-4, Delta). Dell.

Adler, David. All About the Moon. LC 82-17422. (Question & Answer Bks.). (Illus.). 32p. (gr. 3-6). 1983. PLB 8.59 (ISBN 0-89375-886-8); pap. text ed. 1.95 (ISBN 0-89375-887-6). Troll Assocs.

--Amazing Magnets. LC 82-17377. (Question & Answer Bks.). (Illus.). 32p. (gr. 3-6). 1983. PLB 8.59 (ISBN 0-89375-894-9); pap. text ed. 1.95 (ISBN 0-89375-895-7). Troll Assocs.

--Bunny Rabbit Rebus. LC 82-45574. (Illus.). 40p. (gr. 1-4). 1983. 7.64i (ISBN 0-690-04196-9, TYC-J); PLB 7.89g (ISBN 0-690-04197-7). Har-Row.

--Our Amazing Ocean. LC 82-17373. (Question & Answer Bks.). (Illus.). 32p. (gr. 3-6). 1983. PLB 8.59 (ISBN 0-89375-882-5); pap. text ed. 1.95 (ISBN 0-89375-883-3). Troll Assocs.

--Wonders of Energy. LC 82-20042. (Question & Answer Bks.). (Illus.). 32p. (gr. 3-6). 1983. PLB 8.59 (ISBN 0-89375-884-1); pap. text ed. 1.95 (ISBN 0-89375-885-X). Troll Assocs.

--World of Weather. LC 82-17398. (Question & Answer Bks.). (Illus.). 32p. (gr. 3-6). 1983. PLB 8.59 (ISBN 0-89375-870-1); pap. text ed. 1.95 (ISBN 0-89375-871-X). Troll Assocs.

Adler, David A. Base Five. LC 74-18325. (Young Math Ser.). (Illus.). (gr. k-3). 1975. 10.53i (ISBN 0-690-00668-3, TYC-J); PLB 9.89 (ISBN 0-690-00669-1). Har-Row.

--Calculator Fun. LC 81-233. (Easy-Read Activity Bks.). (Illus.). 32p. (gr. 1-3). 1981. PLB 8.90 (ISBN 0-531-04306-1). Watts.

--Cam Jansen & the Mystery of the Circus Clown. (Cam Jansen Mystery Adventure Ser.). (Illus.). 64p. (gr. 1-6). 1983. 8.50 (ISBN 0-670-20036-0). Viking Pr.

--Cam Jansen & the Mystery of the Missing Dinosaur Bones. (Illus.). (gr. 1-4). 1983. pap. 1.75 (ISBN 0-440-41199-8, YB). Dell.

--Cam Jansen & the Mystery of the Television Dog. (Illus.). (gr. 1-4). 1983. pap. 1.75 (ISBN 0-440-41196-3, YB). Dell.

--The Carsick Zebra & Other Animal Riddles. LC 82-48750. (Illus.). 64p. (gr. 1-4). 1983. reinforced binding 8.95 (ISBN 0-8234-0479-X). Holiday.

--Finger Spelling Fun. LC 80-11411. (gr. 1-3). 1980. PLB 8.90 (ISBN 0-531-04140-9). Watts.

--Hyperspace! Facts & Fun from All Over the Universe. LC 81-70404. (Illus.). 80p. (gr. 3-7). 1982. 10.95 (ISBN 0-670-38908-0); pap. 4.95 (ISBN 0-670-05117-9). Viking Pr.

--My Dog & the Key Mystery. LC 82-2790. (Easy-Read Storybook Ser.). (Illus.). (gr. k-3). 1982. 3.95 (ISBN 0-531-03555-7); PLB 8.60 (ISBN 0-531-04449-1). Watts.

--A Picture Book of Hanukkah. LC 82-2942. (Illus.). 32p. (ps-3). 1982. Reinforced bdg. 9.95 (ISBN 0-8234-0458-7). Holiday.

--A Picture Book of Jewish Holidays. LC 81-2765. (Illus.). 32p. (gr. k-3). 1981. PLB 9.95 (ISBN 0-8234-0396-3). Holiday.

--Redwoods Are the Tallest Trees in the World. LC 77-4713. (A Let's-Read-and-Find-Out Science Bk). (Illus.). (gr. k-3). 1978. PLB 11.89 (ISBN 0-690-01368-X, TYC-J). Har-Row.

--Roman Numerals. LC 77-2270. (Young Math Ser.). (Illus.). (gr. 1-4). 1977. PLB 10.89 (ISBN 0-690-01302-7, TYC-J). Har-Row.

--Three-D, Two-D, One-D. LC 74-5156. (Young Math Ser.). (Illus.). 40p. (gr. k-3). 1974. 10.53i (ISBN 0-690-00456-7, TYC-J); 10.89 (ISBN 0-690-00543-1). Har-Row.

Adler, Denise. Five Women. 1980. pap. 2.50 (ISBN 0-8423-0874-1). Tyndale.

--Jonah. 1980. pap. 1.95 (ISBN 0-8423-1948-4). Tyndale.

Adler, Denise R. Morning Star. 1977. pap. write for info o.s.i. (ISBN 0-515-09666-0). Jove Pubns.

Adler, Diane & Shoemaker, Norma J., eds. AACN Organization & Management of Critical Care Facilities. LC 78-31498. (Illus.). 1979. text ed. 18.95 (ISBN 0-8016-0130-4). Mosby.

Adler, Elkan N. About Hebrew Manuscripts. LC 78-136769. (Illus.). 1971. Repr. of 1905 ed. 14.50 (ISBN 0-87203-025-3). Hermon.

Adler, Freda & Simon, Rita J. The Criminology of Deviant Women. LC 78-69555. (Illus.). 1979. pap. text ed. 12.50 (ISBN 0-395-26719-6). HM.

Adler, G., ed. see Fifth International Symposium on Organic Solid State Chemistry, Brandeis Univ., June 1978.

Adler, George L., jt. ed. see Nanda, Ravinder.

Adler, Gerhard. Studies in Analytical Psychology. LC 68-28585. (Illus.). 1968. Repr. of 1948 ed. lib. bdg. 18.50x (ISBN 0-8371-0001-1, ADAP). Greenwood.

Adler, Helmut E. Fish Behavior: Why Fish Do What They Do. (Illus.). 271p. 1975. 29.95 (ISBN 0-87666-162-2, PS-734). TFH Pubns.

Adler, Irene. I Remember Jimmy: The Life & Times of Jimmy Durante. (Illus.). 192p. (Orig.). 1980. 19.95 o.p. (ISBN 0-87000-483-2, Arlington Hse); pap. 8.95 o.p. (ISBN 0-87000-490-5). Crown.

--Peter Frampton. 1979. pap. 4.95 (ISBN 0-8256-3933-6, Quick Fox). Putnam Pub Group.

Adler, Irving. Hot & Cold. rev. ed. LC 74-9357. (Illus.). 1975. PLB 10.89 (ISBN 0-381-99990-4, A34461, JD-J). Har-Row.

--How Life Began. rev. ed. LC 76-16161. (Illus.). (gr. 7 up). 1977. 10.53i (ISBN 0-381-99603-4, JD-J). Har-Row.

--Magic House of Numbers. LC 73-19471. (Illus.). 144p. (gr. 5-9). 1974. PLB 10.89 (ISBN 0-381-99986-6, JD-J). Har-Row.

--Petroleum: Gas, Oil, & Asphalt. LC 78-2431. (Reason Why Ser.). (Illus.). (gr. 3-6). 1975. PLB 10.89 (ISBN 0-381-99624-7, JD-J). Har-Row.

--The Stars: Decoding Their Messages. rev. ed. LC 77-27665. (Illus.). 128p. (gr. 5-12). 1980. 9.57i (ISBN 0-690-03993-X, TYC-J); PLB 9.89i (ISBN 0-690-03994-8). T Y Crowell.

--Sun & Its Family. rev. ed. LC 68-57377. (Illus.). (gr. 5-9). 1969. PLB 10.89 (ISBN 0-381-99983-1, A76000, JD-J). Har-Row.

Adler, Irving & Adler, Peggy. Adler Book of Puzzles & Riddles: Or, Sam Loyd Up-To-Date. LC 62-14898. (Illus.). (gr. 3-6). 1962. PLB 10.89 (ISBN 0-381-99977-7, A00800, JD-J). Har-Row.

Adler, Irving & Adler, Ruth. Calendar. LC 67-23865. (Reason Why Ser). (Illus.). (gr. 3-6). 1967. PLB 9.89 (ISBN 0-381-99975-0, A11200, JD-J). Har-Row.

--Houses. LC 64-20708. (Reason Why Ser). (Illus.). (gr. 3-6). 1965. PLB 9.89 (ISBN 0-381-99967-X, A35060, JD-J). Har-Row.

--Taste, Touch & Smell. LC 66-11448. (Reason Why Ser). (Illus.). (gr. 3-6). 1966. PLB 10.89 (ISBN 0-381-99953-X, A76400, JD-J). Har-Row.

Adler, Irving, jt. auth. see Adler, Peggy.

Adler, Isidore. X-Ray Emission Spectrography in Geology. (Methods in Geochemistry & Geophysics: Vol. 4). 1966. 59.75 (ISBN 0-444-40004-4). Elsevier.

Adler, J. A. Elsevier's Dictionary of Criminal Science. (Eng., Fr., Span., Ital., Port., Dutch, Swedish, & Ger., Polyglot). 1960. 127.75 (ISBN 0-444-40003-6). Elsevier.

Adler, Jack. A Consumer's Guide to Travel. LC 82-22195. 240p. (Orig.). 1983. pap. 8.95 (ISBN 0-88496-194-X). Capra Pr.

--Fundamentals of Group Child Care: A Textbook & Instructional Guide for Child Care Workers. 376p. 1981. text ed. 26.00x (ISBN 0-88410-198-3). Ballinger Pub.

Adler, Jacob. Claus Spreckels: The Sugar King in Hawaii. (Illus.). 1966. 9.00 o.p. (ISBN 0-87022-007-1). UH Pr.

Adler, Jacob & Barrett, Gwynn W. The Diaries of Walter Murray Gibson, 1886-1887. LC 75-188977. (Illus.). 200p. 1973. 14.00 (ISBN 0-8248-0211-X). UH Pr.

Adler, Jacob, ed. see Liholiho, Alexander.

Adler, James B., ed. ASI: Annual & Retrospective Edition, 2 vols. LC 73-82599. Set. 490.00 (ISBN 0-912380-16-0). Cong Info.

--CIS Index: 1977 Annual, 2 vols. LC 79-158879. 1978. 260.00 set (ISBN 0-912380-50-0); Index Vol. (ISBN 0-912380-51-9); Abstract Vol. (ISBN 0-912380-52-7). Cong Info.

--CIS Index 1979 Annual, 2 vols. LC 79-158879. lib. bdg. 300.00 (ISBN 0-912380-73-X). Cong Info.

Adler, James R., jt. auth. see Delaney, Patrick R.

Adler, John H., jt. auth. see Wallich, Henry C.

Adler, Joseph & Doherty, Robert E., eds. Employment Security in the Public Sector: A Symposium. 68p. 1974. pap. 2.00 (ISBN 0-87546-204-9). ILR Pr.

Adler, K. The Art of Accompanying & Coaching. LC 79-147128. (Music Ser.). 260p. 1971. lib. bdg. 29.50 (ISBN 0-306-70360-2); pap. 7.95 (ISBN 0-306-80027-6). Da Capo.

Adler, Lenore L. This Is the Dachshund. 3rd ed. 1966. 12.95 (ISBN 0-87666-278-5, PS637). TFH Pubns.

Adler, Leonore L. Cross-Cultural Research at Issue. 1982. 37.50 (ISBN 0-12-044280-9). Acad Pr.

Adler, Leonore L., ed. Issues in Cross-Cultural Research. (Annals of the New York Academy of Sciences: Vol. 285). 1977. 22.00x (ISBN 0-89072-031-2). NY Acad Sci.

Adler, M. W., et al, eds. Factors Affecting the Action of Narcotics. LC 78-2999. (Monographs of the Mario Negri Institute for Pharmacological Research). 796p. 1978. 54.00 (ISBN 0-89004-272-1). Raven.

Adler, Michael & Asquith, Stewart, eds. Discretion & Welfare. (Studies in Social Policy & Welfare). 269p. 1981. text ed. 30.00x (ISBN 0-435-82009-5). Heinemann Ed.

Adler, Morris. The World of the Talmud. 2nd ed. LC 63-18390. 1963. pap. 4.95 (ISBN 0-8052-0058-4). Schocken.

Adler, Mortimer. Some Questions About Language. LC 75-1221. 203p. 1976. 16.00 (ISBN 0-87548-320-8). Open Court.

Adler, Mortimer, ed. Annals of America: Fourteen Ninety-Three to Nineteen Seventy-Three, 23 vols. (Illus.). (YA) (gr. 10 up). 1976. Set. 389.00 (ISBN 0-87827-199-6). Ency Brit Ed.

Adler, Mortimer, jt. ed. see Hutchins, Robert M.

Adler, Mortimer J. How to Speak-How to Listen: A Guide to Pleasurable & Profitable Conversation. (Illus.). 288p. 1983. 12.95 (ISBN 0-02-500570-7). Macmillan.

--Philosopher at Large: An Intellectual Autobiography. LC 77-1383. 1977. 16.95 (ISBN 0-02-500490-5, 50049). Macmillan.

--Saint Thomas & the Gentiles. 1938. 7.95 (ISBN 0-87462-102-X). Marquette.

--Six Great Ideas. 243p. 1981. 12.95 (ISBN 0-02-500560-X). Macmillan.

Adler, Mortimer J. & Van Doren, Charles. How to Read a Book. rev. ed. 1972. 15.95 o.p. (ISBN 0-671-21280-X, Touchstone Bks); pap. 7.95 (ISBN 0-671-21209-5, Touchstone Bks). S&S.

Adler, Mortimer J., jt. auth. see Michael, Jerome.

Adler, Peggy. Second Adler Book of Puzzles & Riddles. LC 63-15912. (Illus.). (gr. 3-6). 1963. PLB 10.89 (ISBN 0-381-99946-7, A68801, JD-J). Har-Row.

Adler, Peggy & Adler, Irving. Math Puzzles. LC 78-2833. (Illus.). (gr. 4-6). 1978. PLB 7.90 s&l (ISBN 0-531-02216-1). Watts.

Adler, Peggy, jt. auth. see Adler, Irving.

Adler, R. Introduction to General Relativity. 2nd ed. 1975. 39.95 (ISBN 0-07-000423-4). McGraw.

--Vertical Transportation for Buildings. 1970. 35.00 (ISBN 0-444-00072-0). Elsevier.

Adler, Richard. All in the Family: A Critical Appraisal. LC 79-89505. (Illus.). 384p. 1979. 34.50 (ISBN 0-03-053996-X). Praeger.

Adler, Richard B., et al. Introduction to Semiconductor Physics. (S. E. E. C. Ser.). (Illus.). 247p. 1964. pap. 20.95x (ISBN 0-471-00887-7). Wiley.

Adler, Richard P. The Effects of Television Advertising on Children: Review & Recommendations. LC 78-24714. 352p. 1980. 32.95x (ISBN 0-669-02814-2). Lexington Bks.

Adler, Robert J. The Geometry of Random Fields. LC 80-40842. (Probability & Mathematical Statistics Ser.). 304p. 1981. 52.95x (ISBN 0-471-27844-0, Pub. by Wiley-Interscience). Wiley.

Adler, Roy D. Marketing & Society: Cases & Commentaries. (Illus.). 528p. 1981. text ed. 17.95 (ISBN 0-13-557074-3). P-H.

Adler, Ruth, jt. auth. see Adler, Irving.

Adler, Samuel. The Study of Orchestration. 400p. 1982. text ed. 19.95 (ISBN 0-393-95188-X); wkbk 7.95 (ISBN 0-393-95213-4); write for info. tapes (ISBN 0-393-95217-7). Norton.

Adler, Sebastian J., frwd. by see Tigerman, Stanley & Lewin, Susan Grant.

Adler, Stephen. International Migration & Dependence. 250p. 1980. text ed. 28.00x (ISBN 0-566-00202-7). Gower Pub Ltd.

Adler, Thomas P. Robert Anderson. (United States Authors Ser). 1978. lib. bdg. 13.95 (ISBN 0-8057-7204-9, Twayne). G K Hall.

Adler, Warren. Banquet Before Dawn. LC 75-31651. 256p. 1976. 7.95 o.p. (ISBN 0-399-11642-7). Putnam Pub Group.

--Blood Ties. LC 78-10738. 1979. 10.95 o.p. (ISBN 0-399-12309-1). Putnam Pub Group.

--The Casanova Embrace. LC 77-18423. 1978. 9.95 o.p. (ISBN 0-399-12107-2). Putnam Pub Group.

--The Henderson Equation. LC 76-13040. 1976. 8.95 o.p. (ISBN 0-399-11755-5). Putnam Pub Group.

--The Trans-Siberian Express. 1977. 9.95 o.p. (ISBN 0-399-11895-0). Putnam Pub Group.

Adler, Winston, ed. see Fitch, Asa.

Adler-Karlsson, Gunnar, jt. auth. see Wriggins, W. Howard.

Adloff, Richard, jt. auth. see Thompson, Virginia.

Adlr, David A. Cam Jansen & the Mystery of the Dinosaur Bones. (Cam Jansen Adventure Ser.). (Illus.). 64p. (gr. 2-5). 1981. 7.95 (ISBN 0-670-20040-9). Viking Pr.

Admon, K., jt. auth. see Goldschmidt, Y.

Adney, Edwin T. & Chapelle, Howard I. The Bark Canoes & Skin Boats of North America. 2nd ed. (Illus.). 260p. 1983. Repr. of 1964 ed. text ed. 19.95 (ISBN 0-87474-204-8). Smithsonian.

Adock, Francis & Mosley, D. J. Diplomacy in Ancient Greece. LC 74-30066. 275p. 1975. text ed. 22.50x o.p. (ISBN 0-312-21105-8). St Martin.

Adoff, Arnold. All the Colors of the Race. (gr. 5 up). 1982. 9.00 (ISBN 0-688-00879-8); PLB 8.59 (ISBN 0-688-00880-1). Lothrop.

--Black Is Brown Is Tan. LC 73-9855. (Illus.). 32p. (ps-3). 1973. PLB 10.89 (ISBN 0-06-020084-7, HarpJ). Har-Row.

--Celebrations. (gr. 3-6). PLB 5.31 (ISBN 0-695-40699-X, Dist. by Caroline Hse). Follett.

--I Am the Running Girl. LC 78-14083. (Illus.). 48p. (gr. 2-7). 1979. 8.61i (ISBN 0-06-020094-4, HarpJ); PLB 10.89 (ISBN 0-06-020095-2). Har-Row.

--Make a Circle Keep Us in: Poems for a Good Day. LC 74-22162. (Illus.). 32p. (ps-3). 1975. 5.95 o.s.i. (ISBN 0-440-05908-9); PLB 5.47 o.s.i. (ISBN 0-440-05909-7). Delacorte.

--Tornado! Poems. LC 76-47241. (Illus.). (gr. 1-3). 1977. 7.95 o.s.i. (ISBN 0-440-08964-6); PLB 7.45 o.s.i. (ISBN 0-440-08965-4). Delacorte.

--Under the Early Morning Trees. LC 78-5561. (Illus.). (gr. 4-9). 1978. 7.50 o.p. (ISBN 0-525-41860-1). Dutton.

--Where Wild Willie. LC 76-21390. (Illus.). (ps-3). 1978. PLB 6.95 o.p. (ISBN 0-06-020092-8, HarpJ); PLB 10.89 (ISBN 0-06-020093-6). Har-Row.

Adoff, Arnold, ed. I Am the Darker Brother: An Anthology of Modern Poems by Black Americans. (gr. 6 up). 1970. pap. 3.95 (ISBN 0-02-041120-0, Collier). Macmillan.

Adomeit, Hannes, ed. Foreign Policy Making in Communist Countries. LC 78-70493. 172p. 1979. 26.95 o.p. (ISBN 0-03-046201-0). Praeger.

Adomian, George, ed. Stochastic Systems: Monograph. (Mathematics in Science & Engineering Ser.). 345p. 1983. price not set (ISBN 0-12-044370-8). Acad Pr.

Adorjan, Carol. Jonathan Bloom's Room. LC 78-186883. (A Lead-off Bk). (Illus.). 32p. (gr. k-3). 1972. 3.99 (ISBN 0-87955-102-X); PLB 2.99 (ISBN 0-87955-702-8). O'Hara.

Adorjan, Carol M. Someone I Know. Keyser, Corinne, tr. LC 68-23664. (Early Bird Books Ser.). (Illus.). (ps-1). 1968. PLB 3.99 o.p. (ISBN 0-394-91636-0, BYR). Random.

Adorno, T. W. Aesthetic Theory. Lenhardt, G., tr. from Ger. (The International Library of Phenomenology & Moral Sciences). 480p. 1983. 39.95 (ISBN 0-7100-9204-0). Routledge & Kegan.

Adorno, Theodor. Against Epistemology: Studies in Husserl & the Phenomenological Antimonies. Domingo, Willis, tr. from Ger. (Studies in Contemporary German Social Thought). 256p. 1983. 27.50x (ISBN 0-262-01073-9). MIT Pr.

--Minima Moralia: Reflections from Damaged Life. Jephcott, E. F., tr. from Ger. 1978. 11.95 o.p. (ISBN 0-902308-95-5, Pub by NLB). Schocken.

Adorno, Theodor W. Prisms. Weber, Samuel & Weber, Shierry, trs. from Ger. 272p. 1983. pap. 6.95x (ISBN 0-262-51025-1). MIT Pr.

Adouse, J., jt. auth. see Balian, R.

Adriaansz, Willem. Introduction to Shamisen Kumiuta: History, Analysis & Anthology. (Source Materials & Studies in Ethnomusicology Ser.: Vol. 10). 1978. 47.50 o.s.i. (ISBN 90-6027-149-1, Pub. by Frits Knuf Netherlands); wrappers 35.00 o.s.i. (ISBN 0-686-30875-1, Pub. by Frits Knuf Netherlands). Pendragon NY.

Adriaenssen, Emanuel. Pratum Musicum Longe Amoenissimum. xvi, 180p. Repr. of 1976 ed. 67.50 o.s.i. (ISBN 90-6027-157-2, Pub. by Frits Knuf Netherlands); wrappers 52.50 o.s.i. (ISBN 90-6027-155-6). Pendragon NY.

Adrian. CM: The Construction Management Process. (Illus.). 368p. 1981. text ed. 22.95 (ISBN 0-8359-0829-1). Reston.

Adrian, Ann & Dennis, Judith. The Herbal Tea Book. 1981. pap. 2.25 o.s.i. (ISBN 0-87904-040-8). Lust.

Adrian, C. R. & Press, C. Governing Urban America. 5th ed. 1977. 26.50 (ISBN 0-07-000446-3). McGraw.

Adrian, Charles R. Governing Our Fifty States & Their Communities. rev. 3rd ed. (Foundations of American Government). (Illus.). 160p. 1972. text ed. 9.95 o.p. (ISBN 0-07-000439-0, C). McGraw.

--Governing Our Fifty States & Their Communities. 4th ed. LC 77-11933. (Illus.). 1978. pap. text ed. 14.95 (ISBN 0-07-000453-6, C). McGraw.

--State & Local Governments. 4th ed. 1976. 27.50 (ISBN 0-07-000450-1, C). McGraw.

Adrian, Charles R. & Press, Charles. American Politics Reappraised: The Enchantment of Camelot Dispelled. (Illus.). 336p. 1974. 16.50 (ISBN 0-07-000441-2, C). McGraw.

Adrian, Charles R., jt. auth. see Griffith, Ernest S.

Adrian, Cheri, jt. ed. see Barber, Joseph.

Adrian, James. Construction Accounting. (Illus.). 1979. text ed. 23.95 (ISBN 0-8359-0911-5). Reston.

Adrian, Mary. North American Bighorn Sheep. (Illus.). (gr. 2-5). 1966. 5.95g o.s.i. (ISBN 0-8038-5008-5). Hastings.

--Secret Neighbors: Wildlife in a City Lot. (Illus.). (gr. 2-5). 1972. 6.95g o.s.i. (ISBN 0-8038-6708-5). Hastings.

--Wildlife in the Antarctic. LC 78-7256. (Illus.). 64p. (gr. 3-5). 1978. PLB 6.97 o.p. (ISBN 0-671-32946-4). Messner.

--Wildlife on the African Grasslands. LC 79-994. (Illus.). 64p. (gr. 4 up). 1979. PLB 6.97 o.p. (ISBN 0-671-32999-5). Messner.

Adrian, R. H., et al, eds. Reviews of Physiology, Biochemistry & Pharmacology, Vol. 96. (Illus.). 194p. 1983. 39.00 (ISBN 0-387-11849-7). Springer-Verlag.

--Reviews of Physiology, Biochemistry, & Pharmacology, Vol. 97. (Illus.). 180p. 1983. 35.50 (ISBN 0-387-12135-8). Springer-Verlag.

Adriani, John. Drugs: The Drug Industry & Prices. LC 70-176187. 192p. 1983. 10.50 (ISBN 0-87527-196-0). Green.

--Labat's Regional Anesthesia: Techniques & Clinical Applications. 4th ed. (Modern Concepts of Medicine Ser.). (Illus.). 600p. 1983. 58.75x (ISBN 0-87527-187-1). Green.

Adriani, John & Eaton, Allen. The Law & Health Professionals: Fundamentals of the Law & Malpractice. 192p. 1983. 10.50x (ISBN 0-87527-189-8). Green.

Adriano, Domy C. & Brisbin, I. Lehr, eds. Environmental Chemistry & Cycling Processes: Proceedings. LC 78-6603. (DOE Symposium Ser.). 943p. 1978. pap. 31.50 (ISBN 0-87079-302-0, CONF-760429); microfiche 4.50 (ISBN 0-87079-199-0, CONF-760429). DOE.

Adrianov, O. S. & Mering, T. A. Atlas of the Canine Brain. Ignatieff, E., tr. LC 64-63010. (Illus.). 349p. 1964. 35.00x (ISBN 0-916182-01-0). NPP Bks.

Adrienne. Fast French. 1983. 15.50 (ISBN 0-393-01705-2); pap. 6.95 (ISBN 0-393-30105-2). Norton.

--French in Thirty-Two Lessons. (Gimmick Ser.). 1979. 10.95 (ISBN 0-393-04520-X); pap. 6.95 (ISBN 0-393-04531-5). Norton.

--El Gimmick, Espanol Hablado. 1977. 9.95 (ISBN 0-393-04444-0); pap. 5.95 (ISBN 0-393-04477-7). Norton.

--Le Gimmick, Francais Parle. 1977. 9.95 (ISBN 0-393-04438-6); pap. 5.95 (ISBN 0-393-04474-2). Norton.

--Italian in Thirty-Two Lessons. 1983. 12.95 (ISBN 0-393-01617-X); pap. 6.95 (ISBN 0-393-30053-6). Norton.

--Spanish in Thirty Two Lessons. (Gimmick Ser.). 1980. 14.95 (ISBN 0-393-01311-1); pap. 5.95 (ISBN 0-393-00979-3). Norton.

Adrion. Art of Magic. Date not set. pap. 3.95 (ISBN 0-8120-2086-3). Barron. Postponed.

Adshead, S. A. The End of the Chinese Empire 1894-1924. (History Monographs). 1974. pap. text ed. 4.50x o.p. (ISBN 0-435-31030-5). Heinemann Ed.

Adside, Joseph W. Attitudes in Sub-Communities. 1983. 6.95 (ISBN 0-8062-2133-X). Carlton.

Advaita Ashrama Staff, compiled by. Life of Sri Ramakrishna. 8.95 (ISBN 0-87481-077-9). Vedanta Pr.

Advanced Sales Reference Service Editorial Staff. Tax Facts on Life Insurance. 1982 ed. 470p. 1982. pap. 6.00 (ISBN 0-87218-414-5). Natl Underwriter.

Advisory Commission on Forestry Education, 9th Session, Jakarta, 1978. Report. (Forestry Ser.: No. 48). 139p. 1979. pap. 9.50 (ISBN 0-686-93009-6, F1848, FAO). Unipub.

Advisory Committee of Experts on Marine Resources Research, 9th Session, Rome, 1978. Report, Supplement 1: Selected Working Papers Submitted to the 9th Session of ACMRR. (FAO Fisheries Reports: No. 206, Suppl. 1). 36p. 1978. pap. 7.50 (ISBN 0-686-93092-4, FAO). Unipub.

Advisory Committee on Marine Resources Research, 7th Session, Rome, 1973. Report. (FAO Fisheries Reports: No. 142). 49p. 1974. pap. 7.50 (ISBN 0-686-93972-7, F788, FAO). Unipub.

Advisory Committee on Marine Resources Research, Working Party on Biological Accumulators, 2nd Session, Rome, 1975. Report. (FAO Fisheries Reports: No. 165). 9p. 1975. pap. 7.50 (ISBN 0-686-93986-7, F165, FAO). Unipub.

Advisory Committee on Marine Resources Research, 8th Session, Sesimbra, Portugal, 1975. Report. (FAO Fisheries Reports: No. 171). 24p. 1975. pap. 7.50 (ISBN 0-686-93988-3, F819, FAO). Unipub.

Advisory Committee on Marine Resources Research Working Party on Marine Mammals. Report. (FAO Fisheries Reports: No. 194). 52p. 1977. pap. 7.50 (ISBN 0-686-93996-4, F1313, FAO). Unipub.

Advisory Committee on Marine Resources Research, Working Party on biological Accumulators, 1st Session. Report. 18p. 1975. pap. 7.50 (ISBN 0-686-94403-8, F803, FAO). Unipub.

Advisory Committee on Marine Resources Research, 7th Session, Rome, 1973. Report, Supplement 1: The Scientific Advisory Function in International Fishery Management & Development Bodies. (FAO Fisheries Reports: No. 142, Suppl. 1). 14p. 1974. pap. 7.50 (ISBN 0-686-93096-7, F787, FAO). Unipub.

Aebi, H., et al, eds. Einfuehrung in die Praktische Biochemie. 3rd ed. xii, 462p. 1982. pap. 45.00 (ISBN 3-8055-3448-5). S Karger.

AEC Technical Information Center see Kline, A. Burt, Jr.

AECT Intellectual Freedom Commitee. Media, the Learner & Intellectual Freedom: A Handbook. (Orig.). 1979. pap. 8.95 (ISBN 0-89240-034-X). Assn Ed Comm Tech.

AECT, Program Standards Committee Task Force. College Learning Resources Programs: A Book of Readings. 1977. pap. 6.95 (ISBN 0-89240-005-6). Assn Ed Comm Tech.

Aegerter, Ernest E. & Kilpatrick, John A., Jr. Orthopedic Diseases: Physiology, Pathology, Radiology. 4th ed. LC 74-4551. (Illus.). 791p. 1975. text ed. 45.00 (ISBN 0-7216-1062-5). Saunders.

AElfric. AElfric's Catholic Homilies: The Second Series Text. Godden, Malcolm, ed. (Early English Text Soc., Supplementary Ser.: No. 5). (Illus.). 480p. 1979. text ed. 54.00x (ISBN 0-19-722405-9). Oxford U Pr.

Aero, Rita. The Complete Book of Longevity. 1980. 16.95 o.p. (ISBN 0-686-61759-2). Putnam Pub Group.

--The Complete Book of Longevity. (Illus.). 1979. 16.95 o.p. (ISBN 0-399-12363-6); pap. 10.95 o.p. (ISBN 0-399-50401-X, Perigee). Putnam Pub Group.

Aero, Rita & Weiner, Elliot. The Mind Test. LC 81-2341. (Illus.). 192p. (Orig.). 1981. pap. 9.95 (ISBN 0-688-00401-6). Quill NY.

Aeschylus. Aeschylus One: Oresteia, Agamemnon, the Libation Bearers, the Eumenides. Lattimore, Richmond, tr. & intro. by. LC 53-9655. 171p. 1953. pap. text ed. 4.95 (ISBN 0-226-30778-6, P306, Phoen). U of Chicago Pr.

--Persae. Sidgwick, A., ed. 1903. 9.95x o.p. (ISBN 0-19-831802-2). Oxford U Pr.

--Prometheus Bound. Anderson, Warren D., tr. (Orig.). 1963. pap. 3.50 (ISBN 0-672-60357-8, LLA143). Bobbs.

Aeschylus & Johnston, Robert A. Oresteia by Aeschylus. acting ed. 1955. 3.95 o.p. (ISBN 0-8158-0120-3). Chris Mass.

Aeschylus & Sophocles. An Anthology of Greek Tragedy. Cook, Albert & Dolin, Edwin, eds. Sylvester, William & Sugg, Alfred, trs. (Dunquin Series: No. 15). (Illus.). 445p. 1983. pap. 14.50 (ISBN 0-88214-215-1). Spring Pubns.

Aeschylus see Hadas, Moses.

Aeseng, Nate. Batting Ninth for the Braves. (Pennypincher Bks.). 132p. (Orig.). (gr. 3-6). 1982. pap. 1.75 (ISBN 0-89191-708-X). Cook.

Aesop. Aesop's Fables. (Illus.). (gr. 4-6). 1947-63. Illustrated Junior Library. illus. jr. lib. o.p. 5.95 (ISBN 0-448-05803-0, G&D); deluxe ed. 7.95 (ISBN 0-448-06003-5); Companion Library. companion lib. 2.95 (ISBN 0-448-05453-1); pap. ed (IJL) 4.95 (ISBN 0-686-76870-1). Putnam Pub Group.

--Aesop's Fables. LC 80-26265. (Illus.). 1981. 12.95 (ISBN 0-670-10643-7). Viking Pr.

--Fables of Aesop. Handford, S. A., tr. (Classics Ser.). (Orig.). 1964. pap. 3.95 (ISBN 0-14-044043-7). Penguin.

--The Lion & the Mouse. LC 79-1863. (Illus.). (gr. 1-3). 1980. 7.95a o.p. (ISBN 0-385-15462-3); PLB (ISBN 0-385-15463-1). Doubleday.

Aesopus. The Book of Subtyl Histories & Fables of Esope. Bd. with The Siege of Rhodes. Caoursin, Guillaume. LC 76-14086. 1975. Repr. of 1484 ed. 39.00x (ISBN 0-8201-1154-6). Schol Facsimilies.

Afanasiev, A. N. Ivan Korovavich: The Son of the Cow. (Illus.). 1982. 11.95 (ISBN 0-903540-57-6, Pub. by Floris Books). St George Bk Serv.

Af Enehjelm, Curt. Cages & Aviaries. Friese, U. Erich, tr. from Ger. Orig. Title: Kafige und Volieren. (Illus.). 160p. 1981. 9.95 (ISBN 0-87666-840-6, H-1039). TFH Pubns.

Afflerbach, Lois & Franck, Marga, eds. The Emerging Field of Sociobibliography: The Collected Essays of Ilse Bry. LC 76-28644. (Contributions in Librarianship & Information Science: No. 19). 1977. lib. bdg. 29.95 (ISBN 0-8371-9289-7, BRB/). Greenwood.

Affre, Jean, ed. see Moreau, Jean-Francois & Mazzara, Laure.

Affron, Charles. Cinema & Sentiment. LC 82-2687. 1982. lib. bdg. 20.00x (ISBN 0-226-00820-7). U of Chicago Pr.

Afgan, N. H. & Schlunder, E. U. Heat Exchangers: Design & Theory. (Illus.). 928p. 1974. 72.50 (ISBN 0-07-000460-9, P&RB). McGraw.

Afgan, N. H., jt. ed. see DeVries, D. A.

Afifi, A. A. & Azen, Stanley P. Statistical Analysis: A Computer Oriented Approach. 2nd ed. 1979. 16.00 (ISBN 0-12-044460-7). Acad Pr.

AFIPS Taxonomy Committee & Ashenhurst, Robert L. Taxonomy of Computer Science & Engineering. LC 79-57474. ix, 462p. 1980. 40.25 (ISBN 0-88283-008-2). AFIPS Pr.

Aflaki. The Whirling Ecstasy. Huart, C., tr. (Illus.). 30p. (Orig.). 1973. pap. 1.95 (ISBN 0-915424-02-9, Prophecy Pressworks). Sufi Islamia-Prophecy.

Aflalo, F. G., jt. ed. see Peek, Hedley.

Afrasiabe, A. Ali, jt. auth. see Valenta, Lubomir.

Afriat, S. N. The Price Index. LC 77-2134. (Illus.). 1978. 32.50 (ISBN 0-521-21665-6). Cambridge U Pr.

Africa, Thomas W. Ancient World. (Illus., Orig.). 1969. pap. text ed. 16.95 (ISBN 0-395-04095-7). HM.

--The Immense Majesty: A History of Rome & the Roman Empire. LC 73-14536. 1974. 23.95x (ISBN 0-88295-700-7). Harlan Davidson.

African Bibliographic Center. A Short Guide to the Study of Ethiopia: A General Bibliography. Hidaru, Alula & Rahmato, Dessalegn, eds. LC 76-27128. (Special Bibliographic Ser.: New Ser.: No. 2). 192p. 1976. lib. bdg. 27.50x (ISBN 0-8371-9284-6, HE/A02). Greenwood.

Africano, Lillian. Something Old, Something New. 384p. 3.50 (ISBN 0-515-05865-3). Jove Pubns.

Afshar, F., et al. Stereotaxic Atlas of the Human Brainstem & Cerebellar Nuclei: A Variability Study. LC 76-5676. 256p. 1978. 172.00 (ISBN 0-89004-132-6). Raven.

Aftel, Mandy. Death of a Rolling Stone: The Brian Jones Story. (Illus.). 192p. (Orig.). 1982. pap. 8.95 (ISBN 0-933328-37-0). Delilah Bks.

Afterman, Alan B. Accounting & Auditing Disclosure Manual 1983. 1983. 56.00 (ISBN 0-88262-806-2). Warren.

Afzal-Ur-Rehman. Economic Doctrines of Islam, 3. 22.50 (ISBN 0-686-18354-1). Kazi Pubns.

Agar, A. W., et al. Principles & Practice of Electron Microscope Operation. (Practical Methods in Electron Microscopy: Vol. 2). 1974. pap. 27.75 (ISBN 0-444-10645-6, North-Holland). Elsevier.

Agar, Herbert. People's Choice. LC 33-19369. (Illus.). 1969. Repr. of 1933 ed. 15.95 (ISBN 0-910220-01-8). Berg.

Agar, Herbert & Tate, Allen, eds. Who Owns America? A New Declaration of Independence. LC 82-24752. 352p. 1983. pap. text ed. 12.75 (ISBN 0-8191-2767-1). U Pr of Amer.

Agarival. Bacterial Endotoxins & Host Response. 1981. 78.50 (ISBN 0-444-80301-7). Elsevier.

Agarwal, B. D. & Broutman, Lawrence J. Analysis & Performance of Fiber Composites. (Society of Plastics Engineers Monograph). 1980. 34.95x (ISBN 0-471-05928-5, Pub. by Wiley-Interscience). Wiley.

Agarwal, M. K., ed. Antihormones. 1979. 78.50 (ISBN 0-444-80119-7, Biomedical Pr). Elsevier.

--Multiple Molecular Forms of Steroid Hormone Receptors. (Developments in Endocrinology: Vol. 1). 1977. 50.75 (ISBN 0-444-80010-7, Biomedical Pr). Elsevier.

--Streptozotocin: Fundamentals & Therapy. 1981. 90.00 (ISBN 0-444-80302-5). Elsevier.

Agarwal, Manmoohan. Paraguay: Economic Memorandum. v, 178p. 1979. pap. 15.00 (ISBN 0-686-36113-X, RC-7906). World Bank.

Agarwal, N. R. Soil Fertility in India. 1967. 8.50x o.p. (ISBN 0-210-22639-0). Asia.

Agarwal, R. S. Prevention of Crime. 1977. text ed. 7.25x (ISBN 0-391-01013-1). Humanities.

Agarwal, S. C. John Keats: Selected Poems. viii, 346p. 1982. text ed. 35.00 (ISBN 0-7069-1761-8, Pub. by Vikas India). Advent NY.

Agarwal, V. P. & Sharma, V. K., eds. Progress of Plant Ecology in India, Vol. 4. 167p. 1980. 10.00 (ISBN 0-686-82969-7, Pub. by Messers Today & Tomorrows India). Scholarly Pubns.

Agarwala, Amar N. & Singh, S. P., eds. Economics of Underdevelopment: A Series of Articles & Papers. 1963. pap. 7.95x (ISBN 0-19-560674-4). Oxford U Pr.

Agarwala, P. N. The New International Economic Order. (Pergamon Studies on the New International Economic Order). 350p. 1983. 35.00 (ISBN 0-08-028823-5). Pergamon.

Agarwala, S. N., ed. see Seminar on Population Growth & India's Economic Development.

Agassi, Judith B. Comparing the Work Attitudes of Women & Men. LC 81-47552. 368p. 1982. 36.95 (ISBN 0-669-04657-4). Lexington Bks.

Agassi, Judity B. Women on the Job: The Attitudes of Women to Their Work. LC 78-24789. (Illus.). 272p. 1979. 27.95x (ISBN 0-669-02815-0). Lexington Bks.

Agcaoili, T. D., ed. Philippine Writing: An Anthology. LC 76-98742. 1971. Repr. of 1953 ed. lib. bdg. 17.75x (ISBN 0-8371-3063-8, AGPW). Greenwood.

Agee, Anne & Kline, Gary. The Basic Writer's Book. (Illus.). 384p. 1981. text ed. 13.95 (ISBN 0-13-069476-2). P-H.

Agee, E. M. & Assai, T., eds. Cloud Dynamics. 1982. 49.50 (ISBN 90-277-1458-4, Pub. by Reidel Holland). Kluwer Boston.

Agee, James. Agee on Film, 2 vols. 1969. pap. 4.95 ea. o.p. (G&D); Vol. 1. pap. (ISBN 0-448-00236-1); Vol. 2. pap. (ISBN 0-448-00237-X). Putnam Pub Group.

--The Collected Short Prose of James Agee. LC 68-29549. 1978. Repr. of 1962 ed. 14.95 (ISBN 0-910220-92-1). Berg.

Agee, James & Phelps, Robert. Letters of James Agee to Father Flye. 2nd ed. LC 76-146717. 1978. Repr. 14.95 (ISBN 0-910220-91-3). Berg.

Agee, Jonis. Mercury. 1982. signed o. p. 30.00 (ISBN 0-915124-53-X); pap. 7.50 (ISBN 0-915124-50-5). Toothpaste.

--Two Poems. (Orig.). 1981. pap. 6.00 (ISBN 0-915316-97-8). Pentagram.

Agee, Philip & Wolf, Louis. Dirty Work II: The CIA in Africa. 1980. 20.00 o.p. (ISBN 0-8184-0294-6). Lyle Stuart.

--Dirty Work: The CIA in Western Europe. 1978. 24.95 o.p. (ISBN 0-8184-0268-7). Lyle Stuart.

Agee, Roy. Effective Study Habits. McFadden, S. Michele, ed. 1981. 0.50 ea. (ISBN 0-89262-026-9); pak of 30 14.50. Career Pub.

Agee, Vicki L. Treatment of the Violent Incorrigible Adolescent. LC 78-24653. (Illus.). 192p. 1979. 19.95x (ISBN 0-669-02811-8). Lexington Bks.

Agee, Warren K., et al. Introduction to Mass Communications. 7th ed. 498p. 1982. pap. text ed. 15.00 scp (ISBN 0-06-040175-3, HarpC); instr's. manual avail. (ISBN 0-06-360178-8). Har-Row.

--Reporting & Writing the News. 384p. 1983. pap. text ed. 12.50 scp (ISBN 0-06-040173-7, HarpC); instr's. manual avail. (ISBN 0-06-365516-0); test bank avail. Har-Row.

Agel, Jerome B. American at Random - Q. & A. 1983. 6.95 (ISBN 0-87795-455-0, Pub. by Priam). Arbor Hse.

Ageloff, Roy & Mojena, Richard. Applied Basic Programming. 464p. 1980. pap. text ed. 18.95x (ISBN 0-534-00808-9). Wadsworth Pub.

Agenbroad, Larry D. The Hudson-Meng Site: An Alberta Bison Kill in the Nebraska High Plains. LC 78-57606. (Illus.). 1978. pap. text ed. 11.25 (ISBN 0-8191-0530-9). U Pr of Amer.

Agenjo, C. Enciclopedia de la Inspeccion Veterinaria y Analisis de los Alimentos. 1300p. (Span.). 1980. 170.00 (ISBN 0-686-97333-X, S-37346). French & Eur.

Ager, D. V. & Brook, M. Europe from Crust to Core. LC 76-40096. 202p. 1977. 49.95x o.s.i. (ISBN 0-471-99420-0, Pub. by Wiley-Interscience). Wiley.

Ager, Derek V. Principles of Paleoecology. (International Earth & Planetary Sciences Ser.). 1963. 31.50 o.p. (ISBN 0-07-000535-4, C). McGraw.

Ager, Trygve M., tr. see Rolvaag, O. E.

Ager, Trygve M., tr. see Rolvaag, Ole E.

Agersnap, Harald, et al see Ralov, Kirsten.

Aggarwal, J. K. & Vidyasagar, M., eds. Nonlinear Systems: Stability Analysis. (Benchmark Papers in Electrical Engineering & Computer Science: Vol. 16). 1977. 58.50 (ISBN 0-12-786035-5). Acad Pr.

Aggarwal, J. K., jt. ed. see Arya, V. K.

Aggarwal, J. K., et al, eds. Computer Methods in Image Analysis. LC 76-50335. (IEEE Press Selected Reprint Ser.). 466p. 1977. 35.95 o.p. (ISBN 0-471-03112-7); pap. 28.95x o.p. (ISBN 0-471-03113-5, Pub. by Wiley-Interscience). Wiley.

--Computer Methods in Image Analysis. LC 76-50335. 1977. 21.95 (ISBN 0-87942-090-1). Inst Electrical.

Aggarwal, Raj. International Business Finance. 1983. 17.95 (ISBN 0-03-047191-5). Praeger.

Agger, Ben, ed. Western Marxism: An Introduction. LC 78-21654. 1979. text ed. 17.95x (ISBN 0-673-16277-X). Scott F.

Agger, Jens P., ed. see Eisner, Will.

Agger, Lee. Women of Maine. (Illus.). 250p. 1982. pap. 10.95 (ISBN 0-930096-21-5). G Gannett.

Agger, Simona G. Urban Self-Management: Planning for a New Society. LC 78-73223. Orig. Title: L'autogesione Urbana. 1979. 22.50 (ISBN 0-87332-125-1). M E Sharpe.

Aginsky, Bernard W. Kinship Systems & the Forms of Marriage. LC 36-6759. (AAA. M Ser.: No. 45). 1935. pap. 12.00 (ISBN 0-527-00544-4). Kraus Repr.

Agius, Pauline. British Furniture: 1880-1915. (Illus.). 195p. 1977. 39.50 o.p. (ISBN 0-902028-76-6). Antique Collect.

Agle, Nan H. Princess Mary of Maryland. LC 70-12561. (Illus.). viii, 109p. 1967. Repr. 30.00x (ISBN 0-8103-5029-7). Gale.

Aglietta, Michel. A Theory of Capitalist Regulation: The U. S. Experience. 1979. 24.50 (ISBN 0-8052-7066-3, Pub. by NLB). Schocken.

Aglow Staff Editors. Aglow Prayer Diary. 421p. 1982. 9.95 (ISBN 0-930756-70-3). Womens Aglow.

Agmon, Samuel. Lectures on Exponential Decay of Solutions of Second-Order Elliptic Equations. LC 82-14978. (Mathematical Notes Ser.: No. 29). 118p. 1983. 10.50 (ISBN 0-691-08318-5). Princeton U Pr.

Agmon, Tamir & Kindleberger, Charles P., eds. Multinationals from Small Countries. 1977. 22.00x (ISBN 0-262-01050-X). MIT Pr.

Agner, Dwight. Father Catich's Visit with Bill Dwiggins. 16p. 1982. pap. 12.50 (ISBN 0-912960-14-0). Nightowl.

Agnew, H. W., jt. auth. see Breithaupt, S.

Agnew, James B. Eggnog Riot: The Christmas Mutiny at West Point. LC 78-21641. (Illus.). 1979. 12.95 o.p. (ISBN 0-89141-036-8). Presidio Pr.

Agnew, Jeanne & Knapp, Robert C. Linear Algebra with Applications. 2nd ed. LC 82-20752. (Mathematics Ser.). 400p. text ed. 22.95 (ISBN 0-534-01364-3). Brooks-Cole.

Agnew, Jeremy. Exploring the Colorado High Country. LC 77-77959. (Illus.). 1977. pap. 4.95 (ISBN 0-918944-00-7). Wildwood.

Agnew, Joseph. Life's Christ Places. 206p. 1911. 3.95 o.p. (ISBN 0-567-02008-8). Attic Pr.

Agnew, Swanzie & Stubbs, Michael, eds. Malawi in Maps. LC 74-654433. (Graphic Perspectives of Developing Countries Ser). (Illus.). 141p. 1972. text ed. 35.50x (ISBN 0-8419-0127-9, Africana). Holmes & Meier.

Agnihotri, O. P. & Gupta, B. K. Solar Selective Surfaces. LC 80-17392. (Wiley Alternate Energy Ser.). 250p. 1981. 39.95x (ISBN 0-471-06035-6, Pub. by Wiley-Interscience). Wiley.

Agnihotri, S. N. Sanskrit Without Tears. new ed. LC 78-112033. 1978. pap. 2.95 (ISBN 0-89389-045-6). Himalayan Intl Inst.

Agnoli, A., jt. ed. see Muller, E. E.

Agnon, S. Y. The Bridal Canopy. Lask, I. M., tr. from Hebrew. LC 67-19455. 300p. 1967. pap. 8.95 (ISBN 0-8052-0182-3). Schocken.

Agnon, Y. Days of Awe: A Treasury of Tradition, Legends & Learned Commentaries Concerning Rosh Hashanah, Yom Kippur & the Days Between. LC 48-8316. 1965. 7.50x o.p. (ISBN 0-8052-3049-1); pap. 5.95 (ISBN 0-8052-0100-9). Schocken.

--Twenty-One Stories. Glatzer, Nahum N., ed. LC 71-108902. 1971. 10.00x (ISBN 0-8052-3350-4); pap. 5.95 (ISBN 0-8052-0313-3). Schocken.

--Two Tales. Incl. Betrothed; Edo & Enam. LC 65-25414. 1966. 4.95x (ISBN 0-8052-3271-0). Schocken.

Agonito, Rosemary, ed. History of Ideas on Woman: A Source Book. LC 77-5061. 1977. 12.95 o.p. (ISBN 0-399-11964-7); pap. 5.95 (ISBN 0-399-50379-X, Perigee). Putnam Pub Group.

Agopian, Michael W. Parental Child-Stealing. LC 80-8591. (Illus.). 176p. 1981. 18.95x (ISBN 0-669-04152-1). Lexington Bks.

Agostinelli, Maria E. On Wings of Love: The United Nations Declaration of the Rights of the Child. LC 78-10318. (Illus.). 32p. (ps-3). 1981. 8.95 o.p. (ISBN 0-399-20765-1, Philomel); PLB 8.99 o.p. (ISBN 0-399-61168-1). Putnam Pub Group.

Agostini, Beatrice, tr. see McConkey, James H.

Agpalo, Remigio E. Pandanggo-Sa-Ilaw: The Politics of Occidental Mindoro. LC 71-631241. (Papers in International Studies: Southeast Asia: No. 9). (Illus.). 32p. 1969. pap. 3.00 o.p. (ISBN 0-89680-004-0, Ohio U Ctr Intl). Ohio U Pr.

Agran, Larry. The Cancer Connection. LC 78-21356. 1979. pap. 8.95 o.p. St Martin.

Agranoff, B. W., jt. auth. see Tsukada, Y.

Agranoff, Robert, ed. Human Services on a Limited Budget. (Practical Management Ser.). (Illus.). 224p. (Orig.). 1983. pap. 19.50 (ISBN 0-87326-038-4). Intl City Mgt.

Agranovich, V. M. & Mills, D. L., eds. Surface Polaritons: Electromagnetic Waves of Surfaces & Interfaces. (Modern Problems in Solid State Physics Ser.: Vol. 1). 704p. 1982. 147.00 (ISBN 0-444-86165-3). Elsevier.

Agranovitch, V. M. & Galanin, M. D. Electronic Excitation Energy Transfer in Condensed Matter. 1982. 95.75 (ISBN 0-444-86335-4). Elsevier.

Agrawal, A. N. Indian Economy: Problems of Development & Planning. 8th ed. 860p. 1983. text ed. 45.00x (ISBN 0-7069-1898-3, Pub. by Vikas India). Advent NY.

Agrawal, A. N. & Lal, Kundan. Economic Planning. 2nd rev. ed. xiii, 492p. 1981. text ed. 25.00x o. p. (ISBN 0-7069-1256-X, Pub. by Vikas India); pap. 13.95x (ISBN 0-7069-1542-9). Advent NY.

Agrawal, D. & Chakravarti, D., eds. Essays in Indian Protohistory. 1980. text ed. 44.00x (ISBN 0-391-01866-3). Humanities.

Agrawal, H. N. A Portrait of Nationalized Banks. 334p. 1980. text ed. 19.00x (ISBN 0-391-02130-3). Humanities.

Agrawal, R. C. & Heady, Earl O. Operations Research Methods for Agricultural Decisions. (Illus.). 1972. 12.50x (ISBN 0-8138-1200-3). Iowa St U Pr.

Agrawal, R. P., jt. auth. see Misra, A.

Agrawala, Ashok K. Machine Recognition of Patterns. LC 76-53069. (IEEE Press Selected Reprint Ser.). 463p. 1977. 43.95 (ISBN 0-471-03014-7); pap. 28.95x o.p. (ISBN 0-471-03015-5, Pub. by Wiley-Interscience). Wiley.

Agrawala, Ashok K., ed. Machine Recognition of Patterns. LC 76-53069. 1977. 43.95 (ISBN 0-87942-091-X). Inst Electrical.

Agress, Clarence. Energetics. 1978. 2.95 o.p. (ISBN 0-448-14309-7, G&D). Putnam Pub Group.

Agress, Clarence M. The Interval Training Book. LC 77-94844. 1980. pap. 5.95 o.p. (ISBN 0-448-16547-3, G&D). Putnam Pub Group.

Agricultural Board. Body Composition in Animals & Man. 1968. pap. 15.25 (ISBN 0-309-01598-7). Natl Acad Pr.

--Soils of the Humid Tropics. LC 78-189475. (Illus.). 224p. 1972. pap. 9.25 o.p. (ISBN 0-309-01948-6). Natl Acad Pr.

Agricultural Communicators in Education. Communications Handbook. 4th ed. (Illus.). 1983. pap. text ed. 14.95x (ISBN 0-8134-2226-4, 2226). Interstate.

Agrin, Alice R., jt. ed. see Briggs, Anne K.

Agrios, George N. Plant Pathology. 2nd ed. 1978. 23.25 (ISBN 0-12-044560-3). Acad Pr.

Agrippa, Cornelius. The Ladies' Oracle. 1982. pap. 5.95 (ISBN 0-374-18263-9). FS&G.

Agris, Paul F. The Modified Nucleosides of Transfer RNA, II: A Laboratory Manual of Genetic Analysis, Identification, & Sequence Determination. LC 80-81197. 220p. 1983. 32.00 (ISBN 0-8451-0207-9). A R Liss.

Aguayo, A. G. & Karpati, G., eds. Current Topics in Nerve & Muscle Research. LC 79-13037. (International Congress Ser.: No. 455). 328p. 1979. 66.50 (ISBN 0-444-90057-8, North Holland). Elsevier.

Aguf, I. A., jt. auth. see Dasoyan, K. A.

Aguiar, Neuma, ed. The Structure of Brazilian Development. LC 78-55936. 258p. 1979. 14.95 (ISBN 0-87855-138-7). Transaction Bks.

Aguilar, Luis. Marxism in Latin America. 1967. pap. text ed. 4.50x (ISBN 0-394-30002-5). Phila Bk Co.

Aguilar, Luis E., ed. & intro. by. Marxism in Latin America. rev. 2nd ed. LC 77-81331. 426p. 1978. 24.95 (ISBN 0-87722-106-5); pap. 9.95 (ISBN 0-87722-108-1). Temple U Pr.

Aguilar, Rodolfo J. Systems Analysis & Design in Engineering, Architecture, Construction, & Planning. (Civil Engineering & Engineering Mechanics Ser). (Illus.). 448p. 1973. ref. ed. 31.95 (ISBN 0-13-881458-9). P-H.

Aguilera, Donna & Messick, Janice. Crises Intervention: Theory & Methodology. 4th ed. LC 81-9470. (Illus.). 194p. 1981. pap. text ed. 13.95 (ISBN 0-8016-0087-1). Mosby.

Aguilera, Donna C. Review of Psychiatric Nursing. LC 76-40460. 1977. pap. text ed. 8.50 o.p. (ISBN 0-8016-0090-1). Mosby.

Aguilera, Donna C. & Messick, Janice M. Crisis Intervention: Therapy for Psychological Emergencies. (Mosby Medical Library). 1982. pap. 7.95 (ISBN 0-452-25369-1, Plume). NAL.

--Crisis Intervention: Therapy for Psychological Emergencies. LC 81-9470. (Medical Library). 146p. 1982. pap. 6.95 (ISBN 0-686-84855-1, 0086-3). Mosby.

Aguilera, Francisco E. Santa Eulalia's People: Ritual Structure & Process in an Andalucian Multicommunity. (American Ethnological Society Ser.). (Illus.). 1978. text ed. 23.95 (ISBN 0-8299-0164-7). West Pub.

Aguilera, Robert. Naturally Fractured Reservoirs. 703p. 1980. 63.95x (ISBN 0-87814-122-7). Pennwell Pub.

Aguilera-Hellweg, Max, jt. ed. see Barasch, Marc.

Aguirre, Angela M. Vida y Critica Literaria De Enrique Pineyro. LC 81-51622. (Senda De Estudios y Ensayos). 274p. (Orig., Span.). 1981. pap. 11.95 (ISBN 0-918454-26-3). Senda Nueva.

Agulhon, Maurice. The Republic in the Village: The People of the War from the French Revolution to the Second Republic. Lloyd, Janet, tr. LC 81-17095. (Past & Present Publications). (Illus.). 438p. 1982. 44.50 (ISBN 0-521-23693-2). Cambridge U Pr.

Aguolu, Christian C. Ghana in the Humanities & Social Sciences, 1900-71: A Bibliography. LC 73-9519. 1973. 18.00 o.p. (ISBN 0-8108-0635-5). Scarecrow.

Agusiobo, Obiora N., jt. auth. see Olaitan, Samson O.

Agustin, Ruiz V. Arpa Sagrada. 1979. pap. 2.50 (ISBN 0-311-08751-5). Casa Bautista.

Agwani, M. S. Politics in the Gulf. 1978. text ed. 14.75x (ISBN 0-7069-0589-X). Humanities.

Agyeman-Badu, Yaw & Osei-Hwedie, Kwaku. The Political Economy of Instability: Colonial Legacy, Inequality & Political Instability in Ghana. Raymond, Walter J., ed. LC 82-71488. (Illus.). 68p. (Orig.). 1982. pap. 2.50x o.p. (ISBN 0-931494-18-4). Brunswick Pub.

AHA Clearinghouse for Hospital Management Engineering. Health Facility Design Using Quantitative Techniques: A Collection of Case Studies. 148p. 1982. pap. 18.75 (ISBN 0-87258-397-X, AHA-043170). Am Hospital.

AHA Clearinghouse for Hospital Management Engineering, compiled by. In-House Training Programs on Quantitative Techniques: A Collection of Case Studies. LC 82-11654. 148p. 1982. pap. text ed. 18.75 (ISBN 0-87258-369-4, AHA-133200). Am Hospital.

AHA Clearinghouse for Hospital Management Engineering, ed. Medical Staffing Based on Patient Classification: An Examination of Cases Studies. 176p. 1983. pap. 18.75 (ISBN 0-87258-384-8). Am Hospital.

Aharoni, Yair. Markets, Planning & Development: The Private & Public Sectors in Economic Development. LC 77-8200. 364p. 1977. prof ref 29.50x (ISBN 0-88410-659-4). Ballinger Pub.

Aharoni, Yair & Baden, Clifford. Business in the International Environment. LC 76-55003. 1978. lib. bdg. 30.00x o.p. (ISBN 0-89158-723-3). Westview.

Aharoni, Yair, jt. ed. see Vernon, Raymond.

Aharoni, Yohanan & Avi-Yonah, Michael. Macmillan Atlas. 1968. 14.95 o.s.i. (ISBN 0-02-500600-2). Macmillan.

Aharoni, Yohanon & Avi-Yonah, Michael. The Macmillan Bible Atlas. rev. ed. LC 77-4313. (Illus.). 1977. 25.95 (ISBN 0-02-500590-1). Macmillan.

Ahearn, Barry. Zukofsky's "A". An Introduction. LC 81-13000. 250p. 1983. 19.95 (ISBN 0-520-04378-2). U of Cal Pr.

Ahearn, Harry J. Ghetto Fire Fighter. 1977. 5.95 o.p. (ISBN 0-533-02447-1). Vantage.

Ahern, Barnabas. Men of Prayer, Men of Action: Christian Spirituality Today. 1971. 3.50 o.p. (ISBN 0-02-800050-1). Glencoe.

Ahern, C., jt. auth. see Hettich, M.

Ahern, Colleen, ed. see Budy, Andrea H.

Ahern, Colleen, ed. see Dragone, Carol.

Ahern, Colleen, ed. see Sandy, Stephen.

Ahern, Dee Dee. Money Signals. Date not set. 10.95 o.p. (ISBN 0-399-12253-2). Putnam Pub Group.

Ahern, Denise. Bread & the Wine, No. Sixteen. (Arch Bk.). (Illus.). 1979. 0.89 (ISBN 0-570-06127-X, 59-1245). Concordia.

Ahern, Emily M. & Gates, Hill, eds. The Anthropology of Taiwanese Society. LC 79-64212. xvi, 491p. 1981. 30.00x (ISBN 0-8047-1043-0). Stanford U Pr.

Ahern, Jerry. The Survivalist, No. 1: Total War. (Orig.). 1981. pap. 2.25 (ISBN 0-89083-768-6). Zebra.

--The Survivalist, No. 2: The Nightmare Begins. (Orig.). 1981. pap. 2.50 (ISBN 0-89083-810-0). Zebra.

--The Survivalist, No. 3: The Quest. (Illus.). 1981. pap. 2.50 (ISBN 0-89083-851-8). Zebra.

--The Survivalist, No. 4: The Doomsayer. (Orig.). 1981. pap. 2.50 (ISBN 0-89083-893-3). Zebra.

--The Survivalist, No. 5: The Web. 1983. pap. 2.50 (ISBN 0-8217-1145-8). Zebra.

Ahern, John E. The Exergy Method of Energy Systems Analysis. LC 79-24500. 295p. 1980. 34.95x (ISBN 0-471-05494-1, Pub. by Wiley-Interscience). Wiley.

Ahern, John F. & Lucas, Nanci D. Ideas: A Handbook for Elementary Social Studies. 256p. 1975. pap. text ed. 10.50 scp o.p. (ISBN 0-06-040168-0, HarpC). Har-Row.

Ahern, Mary, jt. auth. see Malerstein, Abraham J.

Ahern, Tom. Superbounce. (Burning Deck Poetry Ser.). 28p. 1983. pap. 3.00 (ISBN 0-930901-12-6). Burning Deck.

Ahern, Tom, ed. see Acker, Kathy & Cherches, Peter.

Ahern, William, Jr. Oil & the Outer Coastal Shelf: The Georges Bank Case. LC 73-12300. 160p. 1973. text ed. 18.50 o.p. (ISBN 0-88410-303-X). Ballinger Pub.

Aherne, Brian. A Dreadful Man. 1979. 9.95 o.s.i. (ISBN 0-671-24797-2). S&S.

Aherne, William & Dunnill, Michael. Morphometry. 176p. 1982. text ed. 49.50 (ISBN 0-7131-4403-3). E Arnold.

Aherne, William A. An Introduction to Cell Population Kinetics. 96p. 1979. pap. text ed. 14.95 (ISBN 0-8391-1320-X). Univ Park.

Ahier, John & Flude, Michael, eds. Contemporary Education Policy. 304p. 1983. pap. text ed. 19.50x (ISBN 0-7099-0512-2, Pub. by Croom Helm Ltd England). Biblio Dist.

Ahituv, Niv & Neumann, Seev. Principles of Information Systems for Management. 544p. 1982. text ed. write for info. (ISBN 0-697-08154-0); solutions manual avail. (ISBN 0-697-08155-9). Wm C Brown.

Ahl, David, ed. More Basic Computer Games. LC 78-74958. (Illus.). 1979. pap. 7.95 (ISBN 0-916688-09-7). Creative Comp.

Ahl, David H. Computers in Mathematics: A Sourcebook of Ideas. LC 79-57487. (Illus.). 214p. 1979. pap. 15.95 (ISBN 0-916688-16-X). Creative Comp.

Ahl, David H., ed. The Colossal Computer Cartoon Book. LC 77-71269. (Illus.). 120p. 1977. pap. 5.95 (ISBN 0-916688-06-2). Creative Comp.

--Computers in Science & Social Studies. 192p. 1983. pap. 14.95 (ISBN 0-916688-44-5). Creative Comp.

--More Basic Computer Games: TRS-80. LC 78-50028. (Illus.). 196p. (Orig.). 1980. pap. 7.95 (ISBN 0-916688-19-4). Creative Comp.

Ahlberg, Allan. Master Salt the Sailor's Son. (Wacky Families Ser.). (Illus.). 32p. (gr. k-3). 1982. 2.95 (ISBN 0-307-31708-0, 11708, Golden Pr); PLB 7.62 (ISBN 0-307-61708-4). Western Pub.

--Miss Brick the Builder's Baby. (Wacky Families Ser.). (Illus.). 32p. (gr. k-3). 1982. 2.95 (ISBN 0-307-31702-1, 11702, Golden Pr); PLB 7.62 (ISBN 0-307-61702-5). Western Pub.

--Mr. Biff the Boxer. (Wacky Families Ser.). (Illus.). 32p. (gr. k-3). 1982. 2.95 (ISBN 0-307-31701-3, 11701, Golden Pr); PLB 7.62 (ISBN 0-307-61701-7). Western Pub.

--Mr. Buzz the Beeman. (Wacky Families Ser.). (Illus.). 32p. (gr. k-3). 1982. 2.95 (ISBN 0-307-31703-X, 11703, Golden Pr); PLB 7.62 (ISBN 0-307-61703-3). Western Pub.

--Mrs. Lather's Laundry. (Wacky Families Ser.). (Illus.). 32p. (gr. k-3). 1982. 2.95 (ISBN 0-307-31705-6, 11705, Golden Pr); PLB 7.62 (ISBN 0-307-61705-X). Western Pub.

--Mrs. Plug the Plumber. (Wacky Families Ser.). (Illus.). 32p. (gr. k-3). 1982. 2.95 (ISBN 0-307-31706-4, 11706, Golden Pr); PLB 7.62 (ISBN 0-307-61706-8). Western Pub.

Ahlberg, Allan, jt. auth. see Ahlberg, Janet.

Ahlberg, Janet & Ahlberg, Allan. The Baby's Catalogue. LC 82-9928. (Illus.). 32p. (gr. k up). 1983. 10.00i (ISBN 0-316-02037-0, Pub. by Atlantic Monthly Pr.). Little.

--Each Peach Pear Plum: An I-Spy Story. LC 79-16726. (Illus.). (gr. k-3). 1979. 9.95 (ISBN 0-670-28705-9). Viking Pr.

--The Ha Ha Bonk Book. (Illus.). (gr. 3-7). 1982. pap. 2.50 (ISBN 0-14-031412-1, Puffin). Penguin.

--The Old Joke Book. (Illus.). (gr. 3 up). 1977. 6.95 (ISBN 0-670-52273-2). Viking Pr.

Ahlem, Lloyd. Help for Families of the Mentally Ill. (Trauma Bks.: Ser. 2). 1983. pap. 2.50 (ISBN 0-570-08257-9). Concordia.

Ahlers, Arvel & Amphoto Editorial Board. Where & How to Sell Your Photography. 9th ed. (Illus.). 1979. 14.95 o.p. (ISBN 0-8174-2494-6, Amphoto); pap. 9.95 (ISBN 0-8174-2166-1). Watson-Guptill.

Ahlers, Arvel W. Where & How to Sell Your Photographs. 8th ed. (Illus.). 1977. 14.95 o.p. (ISBN 0-8174-2424-5, Amphoto); pap. 9.95 o.p. (ISBN 0-8174-2108-4). Watson-Guptill.

Ahlers, David M. A New Look at Portfolio Management. Altman, Edward I. & Walter, Ingo, eds. LC 76-10448. (Contemporary Studies in Economic & Financial Analysis: Vol. 5). 1977. lib. bdg. 36.50 (ISBN 0-89232-012-5). Jai Pr.

Ahlfors, Lars. Complex Analysis. 3rd ed. (Illus.). 1979. text ed. 28.00 (ISBN 0-07-000657-1, C). McGraw.

--Conformal Invariants. (Higher Mathematics Ser.). (Illus.). 168p. 1973. 27.50 (ISBN 0-07-000659-8, C). McGraw.

Ahlfors, Lars V. Lars Valerian Ahlfors: Collected Papers, 2 Vols. 544p. 1982. text ed. 55.00X ea. Vol. 1 (ISBN 3-7643-3075-9). Vol. 2 (ISBN 3-7643-3076-7). Set. text ed. 110.00x (ISBN 3-7643-3077-5). Birkhauser.

Ahlqvist, Anders, ed. Papers from the Fifth International Conference on Historical Linguistics, Galway, April 6-10, 1981. (Current Issues in Linguistic Theory Ser.: 21). 450p. 1983. 44.00 (ISBN 90-272-3514-7). Benjamins North Am.

Ahlstrand, Alan & Wauson, Sydnie A. Datsun 280ZX 1979-1981 Includes Turbo Shop Manual. (Illus.). 314p. 1982. pap. 11.95 (ISBN 0-89287-346-9). Clymer Pubns.

Ahlstrom, G. W. Royal Administration & National Religion in Ancient Palestine. (Studies in the History of Ancient Near East Ser.: Vol. 1). xiv, 112p. 1982. pap. write for info. (ISBN 90-04-06562-8). E J Brill.

Ahlstrom, Mark. The Foxes. Schroeder, Howard, ed. (Wildlife Habits & Habitat Ser.). (Illus.). 48p. (gr. 4-5). 1983. lib. bdg. 8.95 (ISBN 0-89686-220-8). Crestwood Hse.

--The Whitetail. Schroeder, Howard, ed. (Wildlife Habits & Habitat Ser.). (Illus.). 48p. (gr. 4-5). 1983. lib. bdg. 8.95 (ISBN 0-89686-224-0). Crestwood Hse.

Ahlstrom, Sydney E. & Carey, Jonathan S., eds. An American Reformation: A Documentary History of Unitarian Christianity. 1983. 29.95 (ISBN 0-8195-5080-9). Wesleyan U Pr.

Ahluwalia, Jasbir Singh. Marxism & Contempory Reality. 60p. 1973. lib. bdg. 6.25x (ISBN 0-210-40548-1). Asia.

Ahmad, Akhtaruddin. Nationalism or Islam: Indo-Pakistan Episode. LC 80-52050. 338p. 1982. 10.95 (ISBN 0-533-04737-4). Vantage.

Ahmad, Enayat. Coastal Geomorphology of India. (Illus.). 222p. 1973. text ed. 8.50x (ISBN 0-391-00632-0). Humanities.

--Soil Erosion in India. 102p. 1973. 5.00x o.p. (ISBN 0-210-22247-6). Asia.

Ahmad, Fazal, et al, eds. Miami Winter Symposium: Vol. 19: From Gene to Protein: Translation into Biotechnology (Symposium) (Serial Publication). 1982. 45.00 (ISBN 0-12-045560-9). Acad Pr.

Ahmad, Feroz. The Turkish Experiment in Democracy: 1950 to 1975. LC 76-25499. 1977. lib. bdg. 40.00 o.p. (ISBN 0-89158-629-6). Westview.

Ahmad, Ghazi. Sayings of Muhammad. pap. 2.00 (ISBN 0-686-18342-8). Kazi Pubns.

Ahmad, H. M. Invitation to Ahmadiyyat. 1980. 32.95x (ISBN 0-7100-0119-3). Routledge & Kegan.

Ahmad, Imtiaz. Muslim Political Behaviour: A Study of the Muslim Stratagem in Indian Electoral Politics. Date not set. 14.00x (ISBN 0-88386-756-7). South Asia Bks. Postponed.

Ahmad, Imtiaz, ed. Modernization & Social Change Among Muslims in India. 1983. 17.50x (ISBN 0-88386-892-X). South Asia Bks.

--Ritual & Religion among Muslims in India. 1982. 20.00x (ISBN 0-8364-0852-7, Pub. by Manohar India). South Asia Bks.

Ahmad, Jalal Al-e. Gharbzadegi: Weststruckness. Green, John & Alizadeh, Ahmad, trs. from Persian. LC 82-61280. (Illus.). 204p. (Orig.). 1982. text ed. 16.95 (ISBN 0-939214-08-3); pap. text ed. 9.95 (ISBN 0-939214-07-5). Mazda Pubs.

Ahmad, Jaleel. Import Substitution, Trade & Development, Vol. 11. Altman, Edward I. & Walter, Ingo, eds. LC 76-52015. (Contemporary Studies in Economic & Financial Analysis). (Orig.). 1977. lib. bdg. 32.00 (ISBN 0-89232-055-9). Jai Pr.

Ahmad, M. Saiyid Ahmad Shahid. pap. 12.50 (ISBN 0-686-18311-8). Kazi Pubns.

Ahmad, R. Fundamentals of Mechanics. 4.50x o.p. (ISBN 0-210-31233-5). Asia.

Ahmad, Sami, ed. Herbivorous Insects: Host-Seeking Behavior & Mechanisms. LC 82-20717. Date not set. price not set (ISBN 0-12-045580-3). Acad Pr.

Ahmad, Shahnon. Selesai Sudah. (Karyawan Malaysia Ser.). (Malay.). 1979. pap. text ed. 3.25x o.p. (ISBN 0-686-60467-9, 00352). Heinemann Ed.

--Seluang Menodak Baung. (Karyawan Malaysia Ser.). (Malay.). 1979. pap. text ed. 5.50x o.p. (ISBN 0-686-60468-7, 00355). Heinemann Ed.

Ahmad, Sultan. Approaches to Purchasing Power Parity & Real Product Comparisons Using Shortcuts & Reduced Information. (Working Paper: No. 418). ii, 60p. 1980. 3.00 (ISBN 0-686-36083-4, WP-0418). World Bank.

Ahmann, Mathew, ed. see National Conference on Religion & Race.

Ahmann, Mathew H. New Negro. LC 73-77031. 1969. Repr. of 1961 ed. 9.00x (ISBN 0-8196-0232-9). Biblo.

Ahmed, A. Karim, jt. auth. see Perera, Frederica P.

Ahmed, A. Karim, jt. ed. see Norris, Ruth.

Ahmed, Aziz. Gleanings from the Glorious Quran. 1981. pap. 12.95x (ISBN 0-19-577280-6). Oxford U Pr.

Ahmed, H. & Spreadbury, P. J. Electronics for Engineers. LC 72-93138. (Illus.). 280p. (Orig.). 1973. 37.50 (ISBN 0-521-20114-4); pap. 13.95x (ISBN 0-521-09789-4). Cambridge U Pr.

Ahmed, H. & Nixon, W. C., eds. Microcircuit Engineering. LC 79-8907. (Illus.). 1980. 49.50 (ISBN 0-521-23118-3). Cambridge U Pr.

Ahmed, K. The Religion of Islam. pap. 1.00 (ISBN 0-686-18481-5). Kazi Pubns.

Ahmed, M. Economics of Islam. 6.95 (ISBN 0-686-18350-9). Kazi Pubns.

--Polypropylene Fibers: Science & Technology. (Textile Science & Technology Ser.: Vol. 5). 766p. 1982. 127.75 (ISBN 0-444-42090-8). Elsevier.

Ahmed, Manzooruddin, ed. Pakistan: Contemporary Politics, Economy, Society. LC 79-51941. 1980. 19.95 (ISBN 0-89089-126-5). Carolina Acad Pr.

Ahmed, N. & Rao, K. R. Orthogonal Transforms for Digital Signal Processing. LC 73-18912. (Illus.). 280p. 1975. text ed. 30.70 o.p. (ISBN 0-387-06556-3). Springer-Verlag.

Ahmed, Nasir & Natarajan, T. Discrete Time Systems & Signals. 1983. text ed. 25.95 (ISBN 0-8359-1375-9); solution manual incl. Reston.

Ahmed, Nasir, jt. auth. see Unger, E. A.

Ahmed, Osman S. The Potential Effects of Income Redistribution on Selected Growth Constraints: A Case Study of Kenya. LC 80-6093. (Illus.). 368p. (Orig.). 1982. lib. bdg. 25.50 (ISBN 0-8191-2112-6); pap. text ed. 14.00 (ISBN 0-8191-2113-4). U Pr of Amer.

Ahmed, P. Living & Dying with Cancer. (Coping with Medical Issues Ser.: Vol. 1). 1981. 36.95 (ISBN 0-444-00575-7). Elsevier.

Ahmed, Rafiuddin. The Bengal Muslims, Eighteen Seventy-One to Nineteen Six: A Quest for Identity. (Illus.). 1981. 29.95x (ISBN 0-19-561260-4). Oxford U Pr.

Ahmed, S. Basheer. Nuclear Fuel & Energy Policy. LC 78-19673. 1979. 19.95x o.p. (ISBN 0-669-02714-6). Lexington Bks.

Ahmed, Said B. The Swahili Chronicle of Ngazija. Harries, Lyndon, ed. (African Humanities Ser.). (Illus.). 136p. (Orig.). 1977. pap. text ed. 5.00 (ISBN 0-941934-20-9). Ind U Afro-Amer Arts.

Ahmed, Shemsu-D-Din, ed. Legends of the Sufis. 1977. pap. 4.95 (ISBN 0-7229-5050-0). Theos Pub Hse.

Ahmed, Yusef & O'Sullivan, Patrick. Road Investment Programming for Developing Countries: An Indonesian Example. 214p. 1976. pap. 5.00 (ISBN 0-686-94039-3, Trans). Northwestern U Pr.

Ahmed ibn Fartua. History of the First Twelve Years of the Reign of Mai Idris Alooma of Burnu (1571-1583) Palmer, H. R., tr. 121p. 1970. Repr. of 1926 ed. 30.00x (ISBN 0-7146-1709-1, F Cass Co). Biblio Dist.

Ahm Kim, Esther. If I Perish. LC 76-49627. (Illus.). 1977. 6.95 (ISBN 0-8024-4001-0); pap. 3.95 (ISBN 0-8024-4003-7). Moody.

Ah Nan, jt. ed. see Ah Xin.

Ahnert, Gerald T. Retracing the Butterfield Overland Trail Through Arizona. LC 73-83025. (Illus.). 112p. 12.00 (ISBN 0-87026-030-8). Westernlore.

Aho, Alfred & Hopcroft, John. The Design & Analysis of Computer Algorithms. 480p. 1974. text ed. 27.95 (ISBN 0-201-00029-6). A-W.

Aho, Alfred V. & Ullman, Jeffrey D. Theory of Parsing, Translation, & Compiling, Vol. 2 Compiling. (Illus.). 471p. 1973. ref. ed. 32.95 (ISBN 0-13-914564-8). P-H.

--Theory of Parsing, Translation & Compiling: Vol. 1, Parsing. (Illus.). 592p. 1972. ref. ed. 34.95 (ISBN 0-13-914556-7). P-H.

Aho, Gernard. The Lively Skeleton. (Preacher's Workshop Ser.). 48p. 1977. pap. 2.50 (ISBN 0-570-07403-7, 12-2675). Concordia.

Aholi, Paul. Pathologie du Pancreas et Malnutrition Proteique En Zone Intertropicale. (Black Africa Ser.). 65p. (Fr.). 1974. Repr. of 1970 ed. lib. bdg. 27.50x o.p. (ISBN 0-8287-0010-9, 71-2020). Clearwater Pub.

Ahr, Albert H. Democracy at Its Best: America's Hope - the People's Branch of Government. 1979. 5.00 o.p. (ISBN 0-682-49401-1). Exposition.

Ahrens, Christa, tr. see Kubler, Rolf.

Ahrens, Christa, tr. see Raethel, Heinz-Sigurd.

Ahrens, Christa, tr. see Thies, Dagmar.

Ahrens, Christa, tr. see Vierke, Jorg.

Ahrens, Donald C. Meteorology Today. (Illus.). 528p. 1982. text ed. 24.95 (ISBN 0-314-63147-X). West Pub.

Ahrens, Herman C., Jr. Life with Your Parents. 24p. 1983. pap. 1.25 (ISBN 0-8298-0667-9). Pilgrim NY.

Ahrens, Herman, Jr. Feeling Good About Yourself. 24p. (Orig.). 1983. pap. 1.25 (ISBN 0-8298-0644-X). Pilgrim NY.

Ahrens, L. H. Ionization Potentials: Some Variations, Implications & Applications. (Illus.). 100p. 1983. 30.00 (ISBN 0-08-025274-5). Pergamon.

Ahrens, Richard A. Nutrition for Health. 1970. pap. 6.95x o.p. (ISBN 0-534-00675-2). Wadsworth Pub.

Ahsen, Akhter & Dolan, A. T., eds. Handbook of Imagery Research & Practice. 400p. (Orig.). 1983. pap. price not set (ISBN 0-913412-19-8). Brandon Hse.

Ahstrom, James P., Jr. Current Practice in Orthopaedic Surgery, Vol. 8. LC 63-18841. (Illus.). 1979. text ed. 35.50 o.p. (ISBN 0-8016-0089-8). Mosby.

Ahuja, Elizabeth M., jt. auth. see Roberts, Jean.

Ahuja, H. N. Construction Performance Control by Networks. LC 76-4774. (Construction Management & Engineering Ser.). 688p. 1976. 58.50x (ISBN 0-471-00960-1, Pub. by Wiley-Interscience). Wiley.

--Successful Construction Cost Control. LC 80-10156. (Construction Management & Engineering Ser.). 388p. 1980. 44.95x (ISBN 0-471-05378-3, Pub. by Wiley-Interscience). Wiley.

Ahuja, Hira N. & Walsh, Michael A. Successful Methodsin Cost Engineering. (Construction Management & Engineering Ser.). 425p. 1983. 44.95 (ISBN 0-471-86435-8, Pub. by Wiley Interscience). Wiley.

Ahuja, Narendra & Schachter, Bruce J. Pattern Models. 336p. 1983. 39.95 (ISBN 0-471-86194-4, Pub. by Wiley-Interscience). Wiley.

Ahuja, V. Design & Analysis of Computer Communication Networks. 1982. 32.95x (ISBN 0-07-000697-0). McGraw.

Ahumada, Rodolfo. A History of Western Ontology from Thales to Heidegger. LC 78-60794. 1978. pap. text ed. 11.00 (ISBN 0-8191-0507-4). U Pr of Amer.

Ah Xin & Ah Nan, eds. Trapped at White Tiger Sanctum. (Illus.). 114p. 1982. pap. 4.95 (ISBN 0-8351-1110-5). China Bks.

Ai. Killing Floor. Date not set. 7.95 o.s.i. (ISBN 0-395-27593-8); pap. 3.95 o.s.i. (ISBN 0-395-27590-3). HM.

AIA Journal. New American Architecture. (Illus.). 1979. 9.95 (ISBN 0-07-000701-2, P&RB). McGraw.

AIA Research Corporation. Solar Dwelling Design Concepts. 146p. 1981. pap. 9.95x (ISBN 0-930978-24-2). Solar Energy Info.

Aichele, George, Jr. Theology As Comedy: Critical & Theoretical Implications. LC 80-5384. 161p. 1980. lib. bdg. 19.00 (ISBN 0-8191-1082-5); pap. text ed. 9.50 (ISBN 0-8191-1083-3). U Pr of Amer.

Aichinger, Ilse. Selected Poetry & Prose. Chappel, Allen H., tr. from Ger. 144p. 1983. 15.00 (ISBN 0-937406-25-2); pap. 6.50 (ISBN 0-937406-24-4); price not set Limited Edition (ISBN 0-937406-26-0). Logbridge-Rhodes.

Aichinger, Peter. Earle Birney. (World Authors Ser.). 1979. lib. bdg. 14.95 (ISBN 0-8057-6380-5, Twayne). G K Hall.

Aid, Frances M. Semantic Structures in Spanish: A Proposal for Instructional Materials. LC 72-96297. 146p. 1973. pap. 4.95 (ISBN 0-87840-031-1). Georgetown U Pr.

Aidala, Joseph B. & Katz, Leon. Transients in Electric Circuits. (Illus.). 1980. text ed. 24.95 (ISBN 0-13-929943-2). P-H.

Aidley, D. J. The Physiology of Excitable Cells. 2nd ed. LC 77-87375. (Illus.). 1979. 75.00 (ISBN 0-521-21913-2); pap. 21.95x (ISBN 0-521-29308-1). Cambridge U Pr.

Aidoo, Ama A. Anowa. (Sun-Lit Ser.). 64p. 1980. 9.00x o.s.i. (ISBN 0-89410-087-4); pap. 5.00x o.s.i. (ISBN 0-89410-088-2). Three Continents.

Aiello, David. Man on a String. LC 80-20345. 1983. pap. 10.95 (ISBN 0-87949-193-0). Ashley Bks.

Aiello, Janette. Cats & Kittens Iron-on Transfer Patterns. (Illus., Orig.). 1983. pap. 2.25 (ISBN 0-486-24461-X). Dover.

Aiello, Joseph A & Moore, Charles A. The College Writing Book. 1979. pap. text ed. 12.00 (ISBN 0-8403-1954-1, 40195401). Kendall-Hunt.

Aiello, Leslie. Discovering the Origins of Man. 1982. write for info. (ISBN 0-86706-027-1). Time-Life.

Aiello, Roger, jt. auth. see Sherrill, Chris.

Aigner, D. J. & Goldberger, A. S., eds. Latent Variables in Socio-Economic Models. (Contributions to Economic Analysis: Vol. 103). 1977. 76.75 (ISBN 0-7204-0526-2, North-Holland). Elsevier.

Aigner, Hal, ed. see Galloway, Russell.

Aihara, Cornellia, intro. by. The Do of Cooking. 230p. 1982. pap. 19.95 (ISBN 0-918860-39-3). G Ohsawa.

Aihara, Herman, ed. see Ohsawa, George.

Aikawa, Jerry K & Pinfield, Edward R. Computerizing a Clinical Laboratory. (Illus.). 112p. 1973. 12.75x o.p. (ISBN 0-398-02847-8). C C Thomas.

Aiken, B. The Waiter-Waitress Manual. 1976. 8.84 (ISBN 0-07-000742-X, G); tchr's manual & key 4.95 (ISBN 0-07-000744-6). McGraw.

Aiken, Conrad. Selected Poems. LC 82-3234. 288p. 1982. pap. 9.95 (ISBN 0-8052-0718-X). Schocken.

Aiken, Conrad, ed. Anthology of American Poetry. 1931. pap. 3.95 o.s.i. (ISBN 0-394-60101-7). Modern Lib.

--Twentieth Century American Poetry. 1963. 3.95 o.s.i. (ISBN 0-394-60127-0, M127). Modern Lib.

Aiken, Conrad P. Scepticisms, Notes On Contemporary Poetry. Repr. of 1919 ed. 18.00 (ISBN 0-384-00525-X). Johnson Repr.

--Selected Poems. 1961. 19.95 (ISBN 0-19-500470-1). Oxford U Pr.

--Ushant: An Essay. 1971. 25.00x (ISBN 0-19-501452-9). Oxford U Pr.

Aiken, D. W. & Fuller, K. J. Living Volute of Africa. 1970. pap. 3.50 (ISBN 0-913792-01-2). Shell Cab.

Aiken, Henry D., ed. Age of Ideology: The Nineteenth Century Philosophers. (Orig.). pap. 2.95 (ISBN 0-451-62063-1, ME2063, Ment). NAL.

Aiken, Joan. Arabel & Mortimer. (gr. k-6). 1983. pap. 2.25 (ISBN 0-440-40253-0, YB). Dell.

--Arabel's Raven. LC 73-81120. 128p. (gr. 4-7). 1974. 9.95a o.p. (ISBN 0-385-07493-X); 9.95a (ISBN 0-385-08675-X). Doubleday.

--The Five-Minute Marriage. 1979. pap. 1.75 o.p. (ISBN 0-446-84682-1). Warner Bks.

--Foul Matter. LC 82-43536. 264p. 1983. 14.95 (ISBN 0-385-18371-2). Doubleday.

--The Girl from Paris. (General Ser.). 1983. lib. bdg. 17.50 (ISBN 0-8161-3497-9, Large Print Bks). G K Hall.

--Go Saddle the Sea. LC 77-76958. (gr. 6-9). 1977. PLB 8.95 o.p. (ISBN 0-385-13226-3). Doubleday.

--Not What You Expected. LC 73-81121. 288p. 1974. 5.95 o.p. (ISBN 0-385-07518-9). Doubleday.

--The Way to Write for Children. 112p. 1983. 10.95 (ISBN 0-312-85839-6); pap. 4.95 (ISBN 0-312-85840-X). St Martin.

Aiken, Linda, ed. Health Policy & Nursing Practice. (Illus.). 308p. 1980. pap. text ed. 12.50 (ISBN 0-07-000745-4, HP). McGraw.

Aiken, Michael, jt. auth. see Zey-Ferrell, Mary.

Aiken, S. R. & Leigh, C. H. Development & Environment in Peninsular Malaysia. 1982. 34.50 (ISBN 0-07-099204-5). McGraw.

Aiken, William & LaFollette, Hugh. World Hunger & Moral Obligation. 224p. 1977. text ed. 12.95 (ISBN 0-13-967968-5); pap. text ed. 11.95 (ISBN 0-13-967950-2). P-H.

Aiken, Wm. A. Conduct of the Earl of Nottingham: 1689-1694. (Yale Historical Pubs., Manuscripts & Edited Texts: No. XVII). 1941. 57.50x (ISBN 0-685-69786-X). Elliots Bks.

Aikens, C. Melvin. Fremont-Promontory-Plains Relationships in Northern Utah. (University of Utah Anthropological Papers: No. 82). 112p. 1966. pap. 10.00x (ISBN 0-87480-213-X). U of Utah Pr.

Aikin, Judith P. German Baroque Drama. (World Authors Ser.). 1982. lib. bdg. 17.95 (ISBN 0-8057-6477-1, Twayne). G K Hall.

Aikins, Carrol, tr. see Grimm, George.

Aikman, Lonnelle. Nous le Peuple. 1982. pap. 3.00 (ISBN 0-916200-01-9). US Capitol Hist Soc.

--We, the People. LC 81-52034. text ed. 3.50 (ISBN 0-916200-00-0); pap. 2.00 (ISBN 0-916200-14-0). US Capitol Hist Soc.

--Wir, das Volk. Vidal, Paul, tr. (Illus.). 144p. (Ger.). 1982. pap. 3.00 o.p. (ISBN 0-916200-02-7). US Capitol Hist Soc.

Ailor, William H. Atmospheric Corrosion. LC 82-2059. (Corrosion Monograph). 1056p. 1982. 150.00 (ISBN 0-471-86558-3, Pub. by Wiley-Interscience). Wiley.

Ailor, William H., Jr., ed. Handbook on Corrosion Testing & Evaluation. LC 74-162423. (Corrosion Monograph Ser.). 873p. 1971. 84.00x (ISBN 0-471-00985-7, Pub. by Wiley-Interscience). Wiley.

Ainger, Alfred. Charles Lamb. 226p. 1982. Repr. of 1888 ed. lib. bdg. 25.00 (ISBN 0-686-94632-4). Century Bookbindery.

--Crabbe. LC 72-78107. (Library of Lives & Letters). 1970. Repr. of 1903 ed. 30.00 o.p. (ISBN 0-8103-3600-6). Gale.

Ainley, David G. & LeResche, Robert E. Breeding Biology of the Adelie Penguin. LC 82-17573. (Illus.). 198p. 1983. text ed. 30.00x (ISBN 0-520-04838-5). U of Cal Pr.

Ainley, Stephen. Mathematical Puzzles. 168p. 1983. 12.95 (ISBN 0-13-561845-2); pap. 4.95 (ISBN 0-13-561837-1). P-H.

--Mathemtical Puzzles. 156p. 1982. 30.00x (ISBN 0-7135-1327-6, Pub. by Bell & Hyman England). State Mutual Bk.

Ainscow, Mel & Tweddle, David A. Preventing Classroom Failure: An Objectives Approach. LC 78-31618. 205p. 1979. 27.00x (ISBN 0-471-27564-6, Pub. by Wiley-Interscience). Wiley.

Ainsfeld, Evelyn R., jt. ed. see Ainsfeld, Michael H.

Ainsfeld, Michael H. & Ainsfeld, Evelyn R., eds. International Device GMP's. 200p. 1981. text ed. 165.00 (ISBN 0-935184-01-5). Interpharm.

Ainslie, Douglas, tr. see Croce, Benedetto.

Ainslie, Tom. Ainslie on Jockeys. rev. ed. LC 74-32023. 160p. 1975. 9.95 o.p. (ISBN 0-671-22068-3). S&S.

--Ainslie's Complete Hoyle. LC 74-32023. 544p. 1975. 15.95 (ISBN 0-671-21967-7); pap. 7.95 o.p. (ISBN 0-671-24779-4). S&S.

--How to Gamble in a Casino: The Most Fun at the Least Risk. LC 78-31610. (Tome Ainslie-Winner's Circle Bk). (Illus.). 1979. 10.95 (ISBN 0-688-03460-8). Morrow.

Ainslie, Tom & Ledbetter, Bonnie. The Body Language of Horses: Revealing the Nature of Equine Needs, Wishes & Emotions & How Horses Communicate Them--for Owners, Breeders, Trainers, Riders & All Other Horse Lovers--Including Handicappers. LC 79-26995. (Illus.). 224p. 1980. 12.95 (ISBN 0-688-03620-1). Morrow.

Ainsworth, Fay, ed. see Waltz, Julie.

Ainsworth, G. C. Introduction to the History of Mycology. LC 75-21036. (Illus.). 350p. 1976. 52.50 (ISBN 0-521-21013-5). Cambridge U Pr.

--Introduction to the History of Plant Pathology. LC 80-40476. 220p. 1981. 64.50 (ISBN 0-521-23032-2). Cambridge U Pr.

Ainsworth, Geoffrey C. & Sussman, A. S., eds. Fungi: An Advanced Treatise, 4 vols. LC 65-15769. Vol. 1, 1965. 82.50 (ISBN 0-12-045601-X); Vol. 2, 1966. 82.50 (ISBN 0-12-045602-8); Vol. 3, 1968. 82.50 (ISBN 0-12-045603-6); Vol. 4A, 1973. 69.00 (ISBN 0-12-045604-4); Vol. 4B, 1973. 65.00 (ISBN 0-12-045644-3); Set. 280.50 (ISBN 0-685-05128-5). Acad Pr.

Ainsworth, Ralph M. Basic Principles of Successful Commodity Futures Speculation. (Illus.). 174p. 1983. 117.45 (ISBN 0-86654-069-5). Inst Econ Finan.

Ainsworth, Robert G. Sports in the Nation's Capital: A Pictorial History of Sports in Washington, D. C., & Surrounding Virginia & Maryland Communities. LC 78-11504. 1978. pap. 12.95 o.p. (ISBN 0-915442-66-3). Donning Co.

Ainsworth, Ruth. The Phantom Carousel. (Illus.). (ps-5). 1978. PLB 7.98 (ISBN 0-695-40875-5). Follett.

--The Phantom Cyclist & Other Ghost Stories. 160p. (gr. 3-6). 1974. PLB 5.97 (ISBN 0-695-40461-X). Follett.

Ainsworth, Stanley. Positive Emotional Power: How to Manage Your Feelings. (Illus.). 256p. 1981. 12.95 (ISBN 0-13-687616-1); pap. 6.95 (ISBN 0-13-687608-0). P-H.

Ainsworth, Thomas. Live or Die. 192p. 1983. 14.95 (ISBN 0-02-500640-1). Macmillan.

Ainsztein, Reuben. Warsaw Ghetto Revolt. LC 78-71295. (Illus.). 1979. pap. 4.95 (ISBN 0-8052-5007-7, Pub. by Holocaust Library). Schocken.

--The Warsaw Ghetto Revolt. (Illus.). 248p. pap. 4.95 (ISBN 0-686-95102-6). ADL.

Ainworth, Maryan W. & Brealy, John. Art & Autoradiography: Insights Into the Genesis pf Paintings of Rembrandt, Van Dyck, & Vermeer. Wasserman, Rosanne, ed. (Illus.). 112p. 1982. 35.00 (ISBN 0-87099-285-6); pap. 19.50 (ISBN 0-87099-286-4). Metro Mus Art.

AIP Conference, 84th, APS-AISI, Lehigh University, 1981. Physics in the Steel Industry: Proceedings. Schwerer, Fred C., ed. LC 82-72033. 409p. 1982. lib. bdg. 36.00 (ISBN 0-88318-183-5). Am Inst Physics.

AIP Conference, 85th, Madison, Wisconsin, 1982. Proton-Antiproton Collider Physics: Proceedings. Barger, V., et al, eds. LC 82-72141. 676p. 1982. lib. bdg. 42.00 (ISBN 0-88318-184-3). AM Inst Physics.

AIP Conference, 86th, Adelaide, Australia, 1982. Momentum Wave Functions: Proceedings. Weigold, Erich, ed. LC 82-72375. 345p. 1982. lib. bdg. 34.00 (ISBN 0-88318-185-1). Am Inst Physics.

AIP Conference, 87th, Fermilab School, 1981. Physics of High Energy Particle Accelerators: Proceedings. Carrigan, R. A., et al, eds. LC 82-72421. 960p. 1982. lib. bdg. 48.00 (ISBN 0-88318-186-X). Am Inst Physics.

AIP Conference, 88th, La Jolla Institute, 1981. Mathematical Methods in Hydrodynamics & Integrability in Dynamical Systems: Proceedings. Tabor, Michael & Treves, Yvain M., eds. LC 82-72462. 352p. 1982. lib. bdg. 34.00 (ISBN 0-88318-187-8). Am Inst Physics.

AIP Conference, 89th, Argonne National Laboratory, 1981. Neutron Scattering: Proceedings. Faber, John, Jr., ed. LC 82-73094. 397p. 1982. lib. bdg. 35.50 (ISBN 0-88318-188-6). Am Inst Physics.

AIP Conference, 90th, Boulder, 1982. Laser Techniques for Extreme Ultraviolet Spectroscopy: Proceedings. McIlrath, T. J. & Freeman, R. R., eds. LC 82-73205. 497p. 1982. lib. bdg. 37.00 (ISBN 0-88318-189-4). Am Inst Physics.

AIP Conference, 91st, Los Alamos, 1982. Laser Acceleration of Particles: Proceedings. Channell, Paul J., ed. LC 82-73361. 276p. 1982. lib. bdg. 32.00 (ISBN 0-88318-190-8). Am Inst Physics.

Air Force Cambridge Research Laboratories - Boston College - 1967. Physics of the Magnetosphere: Proceedings. Carovillano, R. L., et al, eds. (Astrophysics & Space Science Library: Vol. 10). (Illus.). 1969. 44.00 o.p. (ISBN 0-387-91023-9). Springer-Verlag.

Air Transportation Research International Forum, San Francisco, CA May 9, 1977. The Next Commericial Jet Transport - The Need, Economics, Technology & Financing: Proceedings. 123p. 1977. pap. 5.00 (ISBN 0-686-94049-0, Trans). Northwestern U Pr.

Aird, Catherine. Last Respects. LC 82-45344. (Crime Club Ser.). 192p. 1982. 11.95 (ISBN 0-385-18256-2). Doubleday.

--Some Die Eloquent. LC 79-8046. (Crime Club Ser.). 1980. 10.95 o.p. (ISBN 0-385-15747-9). Doubleday.

Aird, Lesley A., jt. ed. see Acheson, Roy M.

Aires, C., jt. auth. see Michalson, D.

Airhart, Arnold E. Beacon Bible Expositions: Vol. 5, Acts. Greathouse, William M. & Taylor, Willard H., eds. (Beacon Bible Exposition Ser.). 1977. 6.95 (ISBN 0-8341-0316-8). Beacon Hill.

Airlife Publishing Ltd., ed. Pooley's Flight Guide: United Kingdom & Ireland. 400p. 1982. 59.00x (ISBN 0-902037-07-2, Pub. by Airlife England). State Mutual Bk.

Airola, Paavo. Every Woman's Book. 1979. 17.95x (ISBN 0-686-36345-0); pap. 12.95x (ISBN 0-686-37289-1). Cancer Control Soc.

--How to Keep Slim, Healthy & Young with Juice Fasting. 1971. 3.25x (ISBN 0-686-32624-5). Cancer Control Soc.

--Rejuvenation Secrets from Around the World - That "Work". 1974. 3.95 (ISBN 0-932090-09-5). Health Plus.

--Stop Hair Loss. 2.00x (ISBN 0-686-36364-7). Cancer Control Soc.

--Swedish Beauty Secrets. 1971. 1.50x (ISBN 0-686-36365-5). Cancer Control Soc.

--Worldwide Secrets for Staying Young. 206p. 1982. 6.95 (ISBN 0-932090-12-5). Health Plus.

Airola, Paavo O. There Is a Cure For Arthritis. 1982. pap. 4.95 o.p. (ISBN 0-13-914671-7, Reward). P-H.

Aissen, Judith. The Syntax of Causative Constructions. Hankamer, Jorge, ed. LC 78-66533. (Outstanding Dissertations in Linguistics Ser.). 1979. lib. bdg. 27.50 o.s.i. (ISBN 0-8240-9690-8). Garland Pub.

Aitchison, G. D. Moisture Equilibria & Moisture Changes in Soils Beneath Covered Areas. 1982. 59.00x (ISBN 0-686-97906-0, Pub. by CSIRO Australia). State Mutual Bk.

Aitchison, I. J. & Hey, A. J. Gauge Theories in Particle Physics. 332p. 1982. 50.00x o.p. (ISBN 0-85274-534-6, Pub. by A Hilger). State Mutual Bk.

Aitchison, Ian J. An Informal Introduction to Gauge Field Theories. LC 81-21753. (Illus.). 150p. 1982. 22.50 (ISBN 0-521-24540-0). Cambridge U Pr.

Aitchison, J. & Dunsmore, I. R. Statistical Prediction Analysis. (Illus.). 284p. 1980. pap. 17.95x (ISBN 0-521-29858-X). Cambridge U Pr.

--Statistical Prediction Analysis. LC 74-25649. (Illus.). 276p. 1975. 49.50 (ISBN 0-521-20692-8). Cambridge U Pr.

Aitchison, Jean. The Articulate Mammal: An Introduction to Psycholinguistics. (Illus.). 1978. pap. 4.95 (ISBN 0-07-000736-5, SP). McGraw.

Aitchison, John. Choice Against Chance: An Introduction to Statistical Decision Theory. LC 70-109505. (Business & Economics Ser). 1970. text ed. 25.95 (ISBN 0-201-00141-1). A-W.

Aitchison, John & Brown, J. A. Lognormal Distribution. (Cambridge Department of Applied Economic Monographs: No. 5). 1957. 32.50 (ISBN 0-521-04011-6). Cambridge U Pr.

Aitchison, June. The Articulate Mammal. 2nd., rev., & enl. ed. LC 82-49138. (Illus.). 288p. 1983. text ed. 15.50x (ISBN 0-87663-422-6). Universe.

Aitchison, Robert, jt. auth. see Eimers, Robert.

Aitchison, Stewart. A Naturalist's San Juan River Guide. (Illus.). 100p. (Orig.). 1983. pap. 8.95 (ISBN 0-87108-626-3). Pruett.

Aitio, Antero, et al, eds. Biological Monitoring & Surveillance of Workers Exposed to Chemicals. LC 82-2946. (Illus.). 432p. 1983. text ed. 45.00 (ISBN 0-89116-253-4) Hemisphere Pub.

Aitken, A. J., et al, eds. A Dictionary of the Older Scottish Tongue: From the Twelfth Century to the End of the Seventeeth, Part XXIX. 1977. lib. bdg. 16.00x o.p. (ISBN 0-226-11720-0). U of Chicago Pr.

Aitken, Alexander C. Determinants & Matrices. LC 82-24168. (University Mathematical Texts Ser.). 144p. 1983. Repr. of 1956 ed. lib. bdg. 27.50x (ISBN 0-313-23294-6, AIDE). Greenwood.

Aitken, Amy. Kate & Mona in the Jungle. LC 80-15110. (Illus.). 32p. (ps-2). 1981. 9.95 (ISBN 0-02-700320-5). Bradbury Pr.

--Ruby! LC 78-21283. (Illus.). 32p. (ps-2). 1979. 9.95 (ISBN 0-02-700330-2). Bradbury Pr.

--Ruby, the Red Knight. LC 82-9590. (Illus.). 32p. (ps-2). Date not set. 10.95 (ISBN 0-87888-208-1). Bradbury Pr.

Aitken, Eleanor, ed. see Tolstoy, Leo.

Aitken, George A. Life of Richard Steele, 2 Vols. LC 68-30994. (Illus.). 1968. Repr. of 1889 ed. Set. lib. bdg. 29.00x o.p. (ISBN 0-8371-0002-X, AIRS). Greenwood.

Aitken, Gloria S., ed. see Stone, Hannah & Stone, Abraham.

Aitken, Hugh G. Syntony & Spark - the Origins of Radio Technology. LC 75-34247. (Science, Culture & Society Ser.). 347p. 1976. 28.50 o.p. (ISBN 0-471-01816-3, Pub. by Wiley-Interscience). Wiley.

Aitken, J. B. Automatic Weaving. 7.50 o.s.i. (ISBN 0-87245-000-7). Textile Bk.

Aitken, Michael, jt. ed. see Gaffikin, Michael.

Aitken, W. R., ed. Scottish Literature in English & Scots: A Guide to Information Sources. LC 73-16971. (American Literature, English Literature, & World Literature in English Ser.: Vol. 37). 400p. 1982. 42.00x (ISBN 0-8103-1249-2). Gale.

Aitkin, D. Stability & Change in Australian Politics. new ed. 400p. (Orig.). 1982. pap. text ed. 25.95 (ISBN 0-7081-0022-8, 1241, Pub. by ANUP Australia). Bks Australia.

Aitkin, Don. Stability & Change in Australian Politics. LC 76-56692. 1977. 25.00x (ISBN 0-312-75478-7). St Martin.

Aiton, E. Vortex Theory of Planetary Motions. 1972. 21.00 (ISBN 0-444-19595-5). Elsevier.

Ajami, Fouad. The Arab Predicament: Arab Political Thought & Practice Since 1967. LC 80-27457. 250p. 1982. 24.95 (ISBN 0-521-23914-1); pap. 8.95 (ISBN 0-521-27063-4). Cambridge U Pr.

Ajami, Riad A. Arab Response to Multinationals. LC 79-16048. (Int'l Bus. Ser.). 160p. 1979. 22.50 o.p. (ISBN 0-03-048436-7). Praeger.

Ajayi, S. S., jt. ed. see Halstead, L. B.

Ajdukiewicz, K. Problems & Theories of Philosophy. Quinton, A. & Skolimowski, H., trs. from Polish. LC 72-97878. 160p. 1973. 23.95 (ISBN 0-521-20219-1); pap. 7.50x (ISBN 0-521-09993-5). Cambridge U Pr.

Ajiboye, Goke. Abiku. Date not set. 8.95 (ISBN 0-533-05110-X). Vantage.

Ajmone-Marsan, C., jt. ed. see Pompeiano, O.

Ajmone-Marsan, Cosimo & Matthies, H., eds. Neuronal Plasticity & Memory Formation. (International Brain Research Organization Monograph: Vol. 9). 682p. 1982. text ed. 71.50 (ISBN 0-89004-681-6). Raven.

Ajmone-Marson, Cosimo, et al, eds. Neuropeptides & Neural Transmission. (International Brain Research Organization (IBRO) Monograph: Vol. 7). 412p. 1980. text ed. 50.00 (ISBN 0-89004-501-1). Raven.

A Juriaguerra, J. de see De Ajuriaguerra, J.

Ajzen, Icek, jt. auth. see Fishbein, Martin.

Akabas, Sheila H. & Kurzman, Paul. Work, Workers, & Work Organizations: A View from Social Work. 272p. 1982. 20.95 (ISBN 0-13-965335-X). P-H.

Akademia Nauk USSR. Pacific: Russian Scientific Investigations. LC 68-55176. Repr. of 1926 ed. lib. bdg. 20.25x (ISBN 0-8371-0282-0, AKTP). Greenwood.

Akao, Nobutoshi, ed. Japan's Economic Security. LC 82-10257. 1982. 27.50x (ISBN 0-312-44064-2). St Martin.

Akasaka, T., jt. ed. see Kawata, K.

Akbar, Ahmed. Religion & Politics in Muslim Society: Order & Conflict in Pakistan. LC 82-14774. (Illus.). 225p. Date not set. price not set (ISBN 0-521-24635-0). Cambridge U Pr.

Akcasu, Ziya, et al. Mathematical Methods in Nuclear Reactor Dynamics. (Nuclear Science & Technology Ser.: Vol. 7). 1971. 76.50 o.s.i. (ISBN 0-12-047150-7). Acad Pr.

Ake, Claude. Revolutionary Pressures in Africa. 112p. 1978. 19.95 (ISBN 0-905762-14-2, Pub. by Zed Pr England); pap. 8.95 (ISBN 0-686-71681-7, Pub by Zed Pr England). Lawrence Hill.

A'Kempis, Thomas. Imitation of Christ. LC 79-27467. 1980. 8.95 (ISBN 0-8024-4004-5); pap. 2.95 (ISBN 0-8024-0024-8). Moody.

--The Imitation of Christ. LC 82-80472. (Treasures from the Spiritual Classics Ser.). 64p. 1982. pap. 2.95 (ISBN 0-8192-1307-1). Morehouse.

--The Imitation of Christ: Paraphrased. 304p. 1982. pap. 9.95 (ISBN 0-8010-0184-6). Baker Bk.

A Kempis, Thomas see Thomas A Kempis.

Aken, A. Van see Van Aken, A.

Akens, David S., jt. auth. see Shea, John J.

Akens, Helen M., jt. auth. see Brown, Virginia P.

Akers, Alan B. Golden Scorpio. (Science Fiction Ser.). (Orig.). 1978. pap. 1.50 o.p. (ISBN 0-87997-424-9, UW1424). DAW Bks.

Akers, Glenn A. Phonological Variation in the Jamaican Continuum. 158p. 1981. pap. 8.50 o.p. (ISBN 0-89720-038-1). Karoma.

Akers, Herbert. Modern Mailroom Management. (Illus.). 1979. 24.95 (ISBN 0-07-000760-8, P&RB). McGraw.

Akers, Lane, ed. see Charles, C. M.

Akers, Michael J., jt. auth. see Avis, Kenneth E.

Akers, Ronald L. & Hawkins, Richard. Law & Control in Society. LC 74-22213. (Sociology Ser.). 384p. 1975. 22.95 (ISBN 0-13-526095-7). P-H.

Akert, K. & Waser, P., eds. Mechanisms of Synaptic Transmission. (Progress in Brain Research: Vol. 31). 1969. 91.00 (ISBN 0-444-40777-4). Elsevier.

Akesson, N. B. & Yates, W. E. The Use of Aircraft for Mosquito Control, Oct. 1982. 96p. 10.00 (ISBN 0-686-84357-6). Am Mosquito.

Akey, Denise, ed. Encyclopedia of Associations: Vol. 1, National Organizations of the United States. 16th ed. 1500p. 1981. 140.00 o.p. (ISBN 0-8103-0144-X). Gale.

--Encyclopedia of Associations: Vol. 1, National Organization of the U. S, 2 Vols. 17th ed. 1700p. 1982. 155.00x (ISBN 0-8103-0147-4). Gale.

--Encyclopedia of Associations: Vol. 2, Geographic & Executive Index. 16th ed. 900p. 1981. 125.00 o.p. (ISBN 0-8103-0145-8). Gale.

--Encyclopedia of Associations: Vol. 2, Geographic & Executive Indexes. 17th ed. 1000p. 1982. 140.00x (ISBN 0-8103-0148-2). Gale.

--Encyclopedia of Associations: Vol. 3, New Associations & Projects. 16th ed. 1981. 140.00 o.p. (ISBN 0-8103-0146-6). Gale.

--Encyclopedia of Associations: Vol. 3-New Associations & Projects. 17th ed. 1982. pap. 155.00 (ISBN 0-8103-0130-X). Gale.

Akhand, Dorothea G. Student's Workbook of Grammar Exercises. (Pitt Series in English as a Second Language). 100p. (Orig.). 1976. pap. 4.95 (ISBN 0-8229-8206-4, Pub. by U Ctr Intl St). U of Pittsburgh Pr.

Akhapkin, Yuri. First Decrees of Soviet Power. 1970 ed. 186p. 16.00 (ISBN 0-686-37391-X). Beekman Pubs.

Akhavi, Shahrough. Religion & Politics in Contemporary Iran. LC 79-22084. 1980. 39.50x (ISBN 0-87395-408-4); pap. 10.95x (ISBN 0-87395-456-4). State U NY Pr.

Akheizer, N. I. Theory of Linear Operators in Hilbert Space, Vol. 1. Everitt, N., ed. Dawson, E. R., tr. (Monographs & Studies: No. 9). 320p. 1980. text ed. 87.95 (ISBN 0-273-08495-X). Pitman Pub MA.

Akheizer, N. I. & Glazman, I. M. Theory of Linear Operators in Hilbert Space, Vol. 2. Everitt, N., ed. Dawson, E. R., tr. (Monographs & Studies: No. 10). 280p. 1980. text ed. 79.95 (ISBN 0-273-08496-8). Pitman Pub MA.

Akhilananda, Swami. Hindu Psychology: Its Meaning for the West. pap. 7.00 (ISBN 0-8283-1353-9). Branden.

--Hindu Psychology: Its Meaning for the West. 1971. Repr. of 1948 ed. 21.95 (ISBN 0-7100-1006-0). Routledge & Kegan.

--Hindu View of Christ. pap. 7.00 (ISBN 0-8283-1355-5). Branden.

--Hindu View of Christ. 2nd ed. LC 75-4134. (God Ser.: No. 152). (Illus.). 291p. 1981. 8.50 (ISBN 0-89007-152-7). C Stark.

--Mental Health & Hindu Psychology. pap. 7.00 (ISBN 0-8283-1354-7). Branden.

--Modern Problems & Religion. pap. 7.00 (ISBN 0-8283-1146-3). Branden.

--Spiritual Practices. new ed. LC 78-175140. 125p. 1972. 12.00 (ISBN 0-8283-1350-4). Branden.

--Spiritual Practices: Memorial Edition with Reminiscences by His Friends. Stark, Alice M. & Stark, Claude A., eds. LC 74-76003. (God Ser.). (Illus.). 225p. 1974. 10.00 (ISBN 0-89007-001-6); pap. 5.00 (ISBN 0-89007-104-7). C Stark.

Akhmanova, O. S. & Wilson, E. English-Russian Dictionary. 639p. (Rus. & Eng.). 1979. 9.95 (ISBN 0-686-97370-4). French & Eur.

Akhmatova, Anna. Poems. Coffin, Lyn, tr. from Rus. 1983. 15.50 (ISBN 0-393-01567-X); pap. 5.95 (ISBN 0-393-30014-5). Norton.

--Requiem & Poem Without a Hero. Thomas, D. M., tr. from Rus. LC 76-7252. 78p. 1976. 10.00x (ISBN 0-8214-0350-8, 82-82402); pap. 5.50 (ISBN 0-8214-0357-5, 82-82410). Ohio U Pr.

--Way of All the Earth. Thomas, D. M., tr. from Rus. LC 79-1953. 96p. 1980. 11.95x (ISBN 0-8214-0429-6, 82-83186); pap. 6.95 (ISBN 0-8214-0430-X, 82-83194). Ohio U Pr.

Akhtar, S. Health Care in the People's Republic of China: A Bibliography with Abstracts. 182p. 1975. pap. 15.00 (ISBN 0-88936-044-8, IDRC38, IDRC). Unipub.

Akiba, K. Bond Switch at Hypervalent Sulfur in Thiathiophtene Analogous Systems. (Sulfur Reports Ser.). 29p. Date not set. write for info. flexicover (ISBN 3-7186-0037-4). Harwood Academic.

Akilov, G. P., jt. auth. see Kantorovich, L. V.

Akimoto, H., ed. see Epilepsy International Symposium, 13th., et al.

Akimoto, S. & Manghnani, M. H. High Pressure Research in Geophysics. 1982. 113.00 (ISBN 90-277-1439-8, Pub. by Reidel Holland). Kluwer Boston.

Akin, J. E. Application & Implementation of Finite Element Methods. (Computational Mathematics & Applications Ser.). 1982. 55.50 (ISBN 0-12-047650-9). Acad Pr.

Akin, Omar, ed. Representation & Architecture. 300p. 1981. pap. 19.50 o.p. (ISBN 0-8408-0506-3). Carrollton Pr.

Akiner, Shirin. Islamic Peoples of the Soviet Union. (Illus.). 400p. 1983. 35.00 (ISBN 0-7103-0025-5, Kegan Paul). Routledge & Kegan.

Akins, W. R. & Nurnberg, H. George. How to Meditate Without Attending a TM Class. 136p. 1976. 6.95 o.p. (ISBN 0-517-52636-0). Crown.

Akins, William R. ESP: Your Psychic Powers & How to Test Them. LC 79-23929. (gr. 4 up). 1980. PLB 8.90 (ISBN 0-531-02947-6). Watts.

Akinsanya, Adeoye A. The Exploration of Multinational Property in the Third World: Finance Trade & Investment. (Int'l Business Ser.). 400p. 1980. 35.95 (ISBN 0-03-055811-5). Praeger.

Aklonis, John J. & MacKnight, William J. Introduction to Polymer Viscoelasticity. 2nd ed. 275p. 1983. 37.50 (ISBN 0-471-86729-2, Pub. by Wiley Interscience). Wiley.

Aklonis, John J., et al, eds. Introduction to Polymer Viscoelasticity. LC 72-473. 256p. 1972. 34.95x (ISBN 0-471-01860-0, Pub. by Wiley-Interscience). Wiley.

Akmajian, Adrian. Aspects of the Grammar of Focus in English. Hankamer, Jorge, ed. LC 78-66534. (Outstanding Dissertations in Linguistics Ser.). 1979. lib. bdg. 37.50 o.s.i. (ISBN 0-8240-9691-6). Garland Pub.

Akmajian, Adrian & Heny, Frank W. An Introduction to the Principles of Transformational Syntax. LC 74-3054. 544p. 1975. 20.00x (ISBN 0-262-01043-7); pap. 11.00x (ISBN 0-262-51022-7). MIT Pr.

Akmajian, Adrian, et al. Linguistics: An Introduction to Language & Communication. (Illus.). 1979. text ed. 24.50x (ISBN 0-262-01058-5); pap. 10.95x (ISBN 0-262-51019-7). MIT Pr.

Akoak, J., ed. Management of Distributed Data Processing: Proceedings of the International Conference, Paris, France, June 23-26, 1982. 294p. 1982. 40.50 (ISBN 0-444-86458-X, North Holland). Elsevier.

Akpan, Moses E. Nigerian Politics: A Search for National Unity & Stability. 170p. 1977. pap. text ed. 9.50 (ISBN 0-8191-0104-4). U Pr of Amer.

Akrasanee, Narongchai, et al, eds. Trade & Employment in Asia & the Pacific. 1977. pap. text ed. 12.00x (ISBN 0-8248-0573-9). UH Pr.

Aks, Patricia. No More Candy. 176p. (gr. 5 up). 1982. pap. 1.95 (ISBN 0-448-16987-8, Pub. by Tempo). Ace Bks.

Aksehov, Vasilii. Azistofaniana Slyagushkami: Azistophaniana & the Frogs. (Illus.). 384p. (Rus.). 1981. text ed. 20.00 (ISBN 0-938920-06-5); pap. 11.50 (ISBN 0-938920-07-3). Hermitage MI.

Aksen, Gerald, jt. ed. see Levin, Noel A.

Aksenov, Arthur, tr. see Dubovik, Alexander.

Aksyonov, Vasily & Yerofeyev, Viktor, eds. Metropol: A Literary Almanac. 1983. 24.95 (ISBN 0-393-01438-X). Norton.

Akutagawa, Ryunosuke. Hell Screen & Other Stories. Norman, W. H., tr. LC 78-98800. Repr. of 1948 ed. lib. bdg. 19.25x (ISBN 0-8371-3017-4, AKHS). Greenwood.

Akuts, Timias, et alcompiled by. Historia Aguaruna, 3 vols. (Comunidades y Culturas Peruanas Ser.: No. 16). 1979. Set. pap. 15.20 (ISBN 0-88312-773-3); Tomo I, 235p. 3.60; Tomo II, 8.00; Tomo III. 3.60. Summer Inst Ling.

Akyuz, O., jt. auth. see Odabasi, Halis.

Al-Anon Family Group Headquarters. Al-Anon's Twelve Steps & Twelve Traditions. LC 80-28087. 140p. 5.00 (ISBN 0-910034-24-9). Al-Anon.

Al-Anon Family Group Headquarters, Inc. Al-Anon's Favorite Forum Editorials. LC 79-126349. 1978. 5.75 o.p. (ISBN 0-910034-22-2). Al-Anon.

--Alateen: Hope for Children of Alcoholics. rev. ed. LC 73-82710. 1973. 4.00 (ISBN 0-910034-20-6). Al-Anon.

Ala-Cla-La. AACR2 Revisions. LC 82-13719. 24p. 1982. pap. text ed. 2.50 (ISBN 0-686-37952-7). ALA.

Alabaster, J. S. Biological Monitoring of Inland Fisheries. 1977. 59.50 o.s.i. (ISBN 0-85334-719-0). Elsevier.

Alabaster, J. S., jt. ed. see Lloyd, Richard.

Alacevic, M., ed. Progress in Environmental Mutagenesis. (Developments in Toxicology & Environmental Science Ser.: Vol. 7). 1980. 58.50 (ISBN 0-444-80241-X). Elsevier.

Aladjalowa, Nina. Slow Electrical Processes in the Brain. (Progress in Brain Research: Vol. 7). 1964. 63.00 (ISBN 0-444-40007-9). Elsevier.

Aladjem, Silvio & Brown, Audrey K., eds. Perinatal Intensive Care. LC 76-57754. (Illus.). 1977. 39.50 o.p. (ISBN 0-8016-0105-3). Mosby.

Aladjem, Silvio, et al. Clinical Perinatology. 2nd ed. LC 79-24340. (Illus.). 1979. text ed. 54.50 o.p. (ISBN 0-8016-0103-7). Mosby.

Alagille, Daniel & Odievre, Michel. Liver & Biliary Tract Disease in Children. LC 79-12354. 364p. 1979. 66.50 (ISBN 0-471-05256-6, Pub. by Wiley-Medical). Wiley.

Al-Ahmad, Jalal. Plagued by the West: Gharbzadegi. Sprachman, Paul, tr. LC 81-18168. (Modern Persian Literature Ser.). 1983. 25.00x (ISBN 0-88206-047-3). Caravan Bks.

Alaia, Cheri, jt. auth. see Rafter, Rosalie.

Alain, Hermano, jt. auth. see Leon, H.

Alain-Fournier, Henri. Wanderer. Date not set. pap. 2.75 (ISBN 0-451-51571-4, CE1571, Sig Classics). NAL.

Alam. Handbook of Gasoline Automobiles, 2 vols. Vol. 1, 1904-1906. pap. 5.00 (ISBN 0-486-22440-6); Vol. 3, 1925-1926. pap. 7.00 (ISBN 0-486-22690-5). Dover.

Alam, M. S., jt. ed. see Panvini, R. S.

Alan Sloan, Inc., jt. auth. see Sea World Press.

Aland, K., ed. Greek-English New Testament. 26th ed. 1981. 11.50 (ISBN 3-438-05408-6, 56495). Am Bible.

--Synopsis of the Four Gospels. 1983. 5.95 (ISBN 0-8267-0500-6, 08564). Am Bible.

Alanne, V. S. Finnish Dictionary: Suomalais-Englantilainen, Vol. 1. 3rd ed. 1980. 80.00x (ISBN 9-5100-1069-3, F563). Vanous.

Al-Ansary, Rahman. Qaryat Al-Fau: A Portrait of Pre-Islamic Civilization in Saudi Arabia. LC 81-21329. 1982. 35.00 (ISBN 0-312-65742-0). St Martin.

Alarcon, Arthur L., jt. auth. see Fricke, Charles W.

Alarcon, Arthur L., ed. see Fricke, Charles W.

Alarcon, P. A. El Sombrero De Tres Picos. 2nd ed. 321p. 1965. 11.95 o.p. (ISBN 0-471-00004-3). Wiley.

Alas, Leopoldo. La Regenta. 1983. pap. 5.95 (ISBN 0-14-044346-0). Penguin.

Alaska Geographic, ed. A Photographic Geography of Alaska. (Alaska Geographic Ser.: Vol. 7, No. 2). (Illus.). 192p. (Orig.). 1980. pap. 14.95 o.s.i. (ISBN 0-88240-142-4). Alaska Northwest.

Alaska Geographic, jt. ed. see Alaska Magazine Staff.

Alaska Geographic Staff. Bristol Bay Basin. LC 72-92087. (Alaska Geographic: Vol. 5, No. 3). (Illus.). 1978. pap. 9.95 album style o.p. (ISBN 0-88240-113-0). Alaska Northwest.

Alaska Geographic Staff, ed. Island of the Seals: The Pribilofs. (Alaska Geographic Ser.: Vol. 9 No. 3). (Illus., Orig.). 1982. pap. 9.95 (ISBN 0-88240-169-6). Alaska Northwest.

--Sitka & Its Ocean-Island World. (Alaska Geographic Ser.: Vol. 9 No. 2). (Illus., Orig.). 1982. pap. 8.95 (ISBN 0-88240-169-6). Alaska Northwest.

Alaska Magazine, ed. The Alaska Almanac: Facts About Alaska. 6th ed. 180p. 1982. pap. 4.95 o.p. (ISBN 0-88240-163-7). Alaska Northwest.

--The Alaska Almanac: Facts about Alaska. 7th ed. (Illus.). 186p. 1983. pap. 4.95 (ISBN 0-88240-240-4). Alaska Northwest.

--Alaska Wild Berry Guide & Cookbook. (Illus.). 216p. 1983. pap. 13.95 (ISBN 0-88240-229-3). Alaska Northwest.

--Bits & Pieces of Alaskan History: Vol. II: 1960-1974. (Illus.). pap. 14.95 (ISBN 0-88240-228-5). Alaska Northwest.

Alaska Magazine Publishers & Tolan, Fred, eds. Alaska Shippers Guide, Vol. 2. 2nd ed. 224p. 1981. pap. 9.95 o.p. (ISBN 0-88240-166-1). Alaska Northwest.

Alaska Magazine Staff & Alaska Geographic, eds. Introduction to Alaska. (Illus.). 64p. 1983. pap. 4.95 (ISBN 0-88240-230-7). Alaska Northwest.

Alaska Scinece Conference, 20th, University of Alaska, 1969. Change in Alaska: People, Petroleum & Politics: Papers. Rogers, George W., ed. LC 75-11734. (Illus.). 213p. 9.95 (ISBN 0-686-32525-7). U of Alaska Pr.

Alaska Travel Publications Editors. Exploring Alaska's Mount McKinley National Park. 2nd ed. LC 76-4404. (Illus.). 1976. 11.00 o.p. (ISBN 0-914164-04-X). Alaska Travel.

Alastair, McKinnon. Kierkegaard: Resources & Results. 250p. 1982. text ed. 17.50x (ISBN 0-88920-126-9, Pub. by Wilfrid Laurier U Pr). Humanities.

Alateen Staff. Alateen: Hope for Children of Alcoholics. 3.75 o.p. (ISBN 0-686-92121-6). Hazelden.

Alatis, James E. & Tucker, Richard, eds. Georgetown University Round Table on Languages & Linguistics: Language in Public Life. LC 58-31607. (Georgetown Univ. Round Table Ser., 1979). 310p. (GURT 1979). 1980. pap. 7.75 (ISBN 0-87840-112-1). Georgetown U Pr.

Alatis, James E., et al, eds. The Second Language Classroom: Directions for the 1980's. Altman, Howard B. & Alatis, Penelope M. (Illus.). 1981. text ed. 14.95x (ISBN 0-19-502928-3); pap. text ed. 8.95x (ISBN 0-19-502929-1). Oxford U Pr.

Alatis, Penelope M. see Alatis, James E., et al.

Alavi, Hamza, jt. ed. see Shanin, Teodor.

Alavi, Hamza, et al. Capitalism & Colonial Production. (Illus.). 208p. 1982. 28.00x (ISBN 0-7099-0634-X, Pub. by Croom Helm Ltd England). Biblio Dist.

Alazard, Jean. The Florentine Portrait. Whelpton, Barbara, tr. LC 68-26731. (Illus.). 1968. 10.00x o.p. (ISBN 0-8052-3074-2). Schocken.

Alba. Alba's Medical Technology Board Examination Review, Vol. I. 9th ed. (Illus.). 1980. pap. text ed. 25.00 (ISBN 0-910224-05-6). Berkeley Sci.

--Alba's Medical Technology Board Examination Review, Vol. II. 5th ed. LC 72-172446. (Illus.). 1981. pap. text ed. 22.00 (ISBN 0-910224-06-4). Berkeley Sci.

Alba, Esther S. Teatro cubano: Tres obras de Jose Antonio Ramos. (Caliban Rex, El Traidor y La recurva) LC 81084199. 160p. (Orig., Span.). 1983. pap. 11.95 (ISBN 0-918454-30-1). Senda Nueva.

Alba, Francisco. The Population of Mexico: Trends, Issues, & Policies. LC 81-1432. 150p. 1981. 24.95 (ISBN 0-87855-359-2). Transaction Bks.

Alba, Victor. The Communist Party in Spain. Smith, Vincent G., tr. from Span. 500p. 1983. 39.95 (ISBN 0-87855-464-5). Transaction Bks.

--Peru. 1977. lib. bdg. 25.00 o.p. (ISBN 0-89158-111-1). Westview.

Alba-Buffill, Elio. Los Estudios Cervantinos de Enrique Jose Varona. LC 78-73618. (Senda De Estudios y Ensayos Ser.). (Orig., Span.). 1979. pap. 9.95 (ISBN 0-918454-11-5). Senda Nueva.

Alba-Buffill, Elio & Feito, Francisco E. Indice de El Pensamiento: Cuba, 1879-1880. LC 77-75370. (Senda Bibliografica). (Orig., Span.). 1977. pap. 4.95 (ISBN 0-918454-00-X). Senda Nueva.

Albaiges, J., ed. see Second International Congress on Analytical Techniques in Environmental Chemistry.

Alban, Laureano. Autumn's Legacy. Fornoff, Frederick, tr. from Span. LC 82-6455. xiv, 77p. 1982. lib. bdg. 18.95x (ISBN 0-8214-0667-1, 82-84358); pap. 10.95 (ISBN 0-8214-0696-5, 82-84655). Ohio U Pr.

Albanese, Catherine. Sons of the Fathers: The Civil Religion of the American Revolution. LC 76-17712. 288p. 1976. 24.95 (ISBN 0-87722-073-5). Temple U Pr.

Albanese, Catherine L. America: Religions & Religion. LC 80-21031. (The Wadsworth Series in Religion Studies). 389p. 1981. pap. 13.95x (ISBN 0-534-00928-X). Wadsworth Pub.

--Corresponding Motion: Transcendental Religion & the New America. LC 77-70329. 234p. 1977. 27.95 (ISBN 0-87722-098-0). Temple U Pr.

Albanese, Jay S., et al. Is Probation Working? A Guide for Managers & Methodologists. LC 80-6311. 190p. 1981. lib. bdg. 20.00 (ISBN 0-8191-1507-X); pap. text ed. 9.50 (ISBN 0-8191-1508-8). U Pr of Amer.

Albanese, Joseph. The Nurses' Drug Reference. 2nd ed. (Illus.). 1184p. 1981. 28.50x (ISBN 0-07-000767-5); pap. 21.50 (ISBN 0-07-000768-3). McGraw.

Albanese, Joseph & Bond, Thomas. Drug Interactions: Basic Principles & Clinical Problems. (Illus.). 1978. pap. text ed. 12.95 (ISBN 0-07-000940-6, HP). McGraw.

Al-Banna, Hasan, jt. auth. see Wendell, Hasan.

Albano, Charles. TA on the Job. 1976. pap. 1.50i o.p. (ISBN 0-06-080385-1, P385, PL). Har-Row.

Albans, Suzanne St. see St. Albans, Suzanne.

Albanse, Robert & Van Fleet, David. Organizational Behavior. 640p. 1983. 25.95 (ISBN 0-03-050736-7). Dryden Pr.

Albany County Sessions. Minutes of the Commissioners for Detecting & Defeating Conspiracies in the State of New York, 3 vols. in 2. Paltsits, Victor H., ed. LC 72-1835. (Era of the American Revolution Ser.). (Illus.). 1972. Repr. of 1909 ed. Set. lib. bdg. 125.00 (ISBN 0-306-70504-4). Da Capo.

Albany, Eric A., ed. see Nuffield Foundation.

Albarracin-Sarmiento, Carlos. Estructura del 'Martin Fierro' (Purdue University Monographs in Romance Languages: No. 9). xx, 230p. (Span.). 1982. 36.00 (ISBN 90-272-1719-X). Benjamins North Am.

Al-Bashir, Faisal S. A Structural Econometric Model of the Saudi Arabian Economy: 1960-1970. LC 77-441. 1977. 36.50x o.p. (ISBN 0-471-02177-6). Ronald Pr.

Al-Bashir, Faisal Safooq. A Structural Econometric Model of the Saudi Arabian Economy: Nineteen Sixty to Nineteen Seventy. LC 77-441. 144p. Repr. of 1977 ed. text ed. 36.50 (ISBN 0-471-02177-6). Krieger.

Al-Bashir, P. S. A Structural Econometric Model of the Saudi Arabian Economy. 134p. 1977. 36.50 o.p. (ISBN 0-471-02177-6, Pub. by Wiley-Interscience). Wiley.

Albaum, Charlet. Ojo de Dios: Eye of God. (Illus.). 96p. (Orig.). 1972. pap. 2.50 (ISBN 0-448-01149-2, G&D). Putnam Pub Group.

Albee, Edward. The American Dream. 1961. pap. 3.75 o.s.i. (ISBN 0-698-10013-1, Coward). Putnam Pub Group.

--American Dream & Zoo Story. pap. 1.95 (ISBN 0-451-11235-0, AJ1235, Sig). NAL.

--The Plays, Vol. 4: Everything In The Garden, Malcolm, The Ballad Of The Sad Cafe. LC 81-3616. 512p. 1982. pap. 10.95 (ISBN 0-689-70616-2). Atheneum.

--Sandbox. Bd. with Death of Bessie Smith. 1964. pap. 2.50 (ISBN 0-451-11295-4, AE1295, Sig). NAL.

--Selected Plays. 1981. pap. 6.95 o.s.i. (ISBN 0-698-11092-7, Coward). Putnam Pub Group.

--The Zoo Story. Bd. with The Death of Bessie Smith; The Sandbox. 1960. pap. 3.25 o.s.i. (ISBN 0-698-10418-8, Coward). Putnam Pub Group.

Albee, Edward see Strasberg, Lee.

Albee, Edward, intro. by. Louise Nevelson: Atmospheres & Environments. (Illus.). 192p. 1980. 35.00 (ISBN 0-517-54054-1, C N Potter Bks). Crown.

Albee, Edward A. Delicate Balance. LC 66-28773. 1966. 5.00 o.p. (ISBN 0-689-10005-1). Atheneum.

--Everything in the Garden. LC 68-16862. 1968. 5.95 o.p. (ISBN 0-689-10002-7). Atheneum.

Albee, George & Gordon, Sol, eds. Promoting Sexual Responsibility & Preventing Sexual Problems. (Primary Prevention of Psychopathology Ser.: No. 7). (Illus.). 600p. 1983. text ed. 35.00x (ISBN 0-87451-248-4). U Pr of New Eng.

Albee, George W. & Joffe, Justin M., eds. The Issues: An Overview of Primary Prevention. LC 76-53992. (Primary Prevention of Psychopathology Ser.: Vol. 1). (Illus.). 440p. 1977. text ed. 27.50x (ISBN 0-87451-135-6). U Pr of New Eng.

Albee, George W., jt. ed. see Joffe, Justin M.

Albe-Fessard, Denise, ed. see World Congress on Pain, 1st, Florence, 1975.

Albegov. Regional Development Modelling Theory & Practice. (Studies in Regional Science: Vol. 8). 1982. 53.25 (ISBN 0-444-86473-3). Elsevier.

Alber, Charles A., tr. see Semanov, V. I.

Alberger, Particia L., ed. Winning Techniques for Athletic Fund Raising. 97p. 1981. 14.50 (ISBN 0-89964-188-1). CASE.

Alberger, Patricia L., ed. How to Work Effectively with Alumni Boards. 81p. (Orig.). 1981. 14.50 (ISBN 0-89964-182-2). CASE.

Albergotti, J. Clifton. Mighty Is the Charm: Lectures on Science, Literature, & the Arts. LC 81-40158. (Illus.). 248p. (Orig.). 1982. lib. bdg. 23.00 (ISBN 0-8191-2207-6); pap. text ed. 10.75 (ISBN 0-8191-2208-4). U Pr of Amer.

Albers, Henry H. Management: The Basic Concepts. 2nd ed. LC 80-12568. 336p. 1982. lib. bdg. 17.50 (ISBN 0-89874-312-5). Krieger.

--Principles of Management: A Modern Approach. 4th ed. LC 73-12217. (Management & Administration Ser.). 560p. 1974. text ed. 24.95 o.p. (ISBN 0-471-01916-X); tchrs'. manual 7.95 o.p. (ISBN 0-471-01915-1). Wiley.

Albers, Henry H. & Schoer, Lowell A. Programmed Organization & Management Principles. LC 77-3561. 128p. 1977. pap. 5.95 (ISBN 0-88275-555-2). Krieger.

Albers, Josef & Bucher, Francois. Despite Straight Lines. rev. ed. 1977. 12.00 o.p. (ISBN 0-262-01049-6); deluxe ed. 22.00 (ISBN 0-262-01052-6); pap. 6.95 (ISBN 0-262-51015-4). MIT Pr.

Albers, Patricia & Medicine, Beatrice. The Hidden Half: Studies of Plains Indian Women. LC 82-23906. 286p. (Orig.). 1983. lib. bdg. 22.50 (ISBN 0-8191-2956-9); pap. text ed. 11.75 (ISBN 0-8191-2957-7). U Pr of Amer.

Albers, Vernon M. Acoustical Society of America Suggested Experiments for Laboratory Courses in Acoustics & Vibrations. 2nd ed. LC 75-165357. 175p. 1973. text ed. 16.95x (ISBN 0-271-01104-1). Pa St U Pr.

Albers, Vernon M., ed. Underwater Sound. LC 72-79141. (Benchmark Papers in Acoustics: Vol. 1). 468p. 1972. text ed. 55.00 (ISBN 0-87933-006-6). Hutchinson Ross.

Albert, A. Adrian. Fundamental Concepts of Higher Algebra. LC 81-2528. 1981. 4.95 (ISBN 0-936428-04-X). Polygonal Pub.

Albert, A. Adrian, ed. see Dickson, Leonard E.

Albert, Adelin, jt. ed. see Heusghem, Camille.

Albert, Adrien. Selective Toxicity: The Physico-Chemical Basis of Therapy. 6th ed. LC 78-15491. 676p. 1981. 39.95 (ISBN 0-412-15650-4, 6005, Pub by Chapman & Hall England); pap. 21.95x (ISBN 0-412-23650-8, 6562). Methuen Inc.

--The Selectivity of Drugs. (Outline Studies in Biology Ser.). 1975. pap. 6.50x (ISBN 0-412-13090-4, Pub. by Chapman & Hall). Methuen Inc.

Albert, Bill. South America & the World Economy from Independence to 1930. (Studies in Economic & Social History). 88p. 1983. pap. text ed. 6.25x (ISBN 0-333-34223-2, 41241, Pub. by Macmillan England). Humanities.

Albert, Burton. Clubs for Kids. 144p. (Orig.). 1983. pap. price not set (ISBN 0-345-30292-3). Ballantine.

Albert, Burton, Jr. Codes for Kids. Grant, Neil, rev. by. (Illus.). (gr. 3-7). 1982. pap. 2.50 (ISBN 0-14-031367-2, Puffin). Penguin.

Albert, Daniel, jt. auth. see Dueker, David.

Albert, Donna. Beautiful American Marine. LC 82-90348. (Illus., Orig.). 1982. pap. 5.95 (ISBN 0-9608924-0-0). DJA Writ Circle.

Albert, Ernest, jt. ed. see Gautherie, Michel.

Albert, Ethel, et al. Great Traditions in Ethics: An Introduction. 4th ed. 1980. pap. 9.95x (ISBN 0-442-26255-8); study guide by Franco Bell 3.95 (ISBN 0-442-20564-3). Van Nos Reinhold.

Albert, Gail. Matters of Chance. 256p. 1982. 14.95 (ISBN 0-399-12747-X). Putnam Pub Group.

Albert, Harry D., ed. see Stone, Michael H. & Forest, David.

Albert, Kenneth J. Handbook of Business Problem Solving. LC 79-18680. (Illus.). 1980. 35.95 (ISBN 0-07-000752-7). McGraw.

--How to Be Your Own Management Consultant. (Illus.). 1978. 21.00 (ISBN 0-07-000751-9, P&RB). McGraw.

--How to Pick the Right Small Business Opportunity. 252p. 1980. pap. 5.95 (ISBN 0-07-000952-X, SP). McGraw.

--How to Pick the Right Small Business Opportunity: The Key to Success in Your Own Business. (Illus.). 1977. 19.95 (ISBN 0-07-000947-3, P&RB). McGraw.

--How to Solve Business Problems: The Consultant's Approach to Business Problem Solving. LC 82-14956. 224p. 1983. pap. 9.95 (ISBN 0-07-000753-5, P&RB). McGraw.

--Straight Talk About Small Business. (Illus.). 256p. 1980. 16.95 (ISBN 0-07-000949-X, P&RB). McGraw.

--The Strategic Management Handbook. (Illus.). 544p. 1982. 49.95 (ISBN 0-07-000954-6, P&RB). McGraw.

Albert, Linda. Linda Albert's Advice for Coping with Kids. Harris, Diane F., ed. 168p. 1982. 10.95 (ISBN 0-525-93262-3, 01063-320). Dutton.

Albert, Louise. But I'm Ready to Go. LC 76-9949. 240p. (gr. 6-8). 1976. 9.95 (ISBN 0-02-700310-8). Bradbury Pr.

Albert, M., ed. Allergology. (International Congress Ser.: No. 42). (Abstracts - 4th Congress). 1961. 15.50 (ISBN 90-219-1037-3, Excerpta Medica). Elsevier.

Albert, Martin L., jt. auth. see Hecaen, Henri.

Albert, Martin L., jt. auth. see Obler, Loraine K.

Albert, Marv & Bock, Hal. Yesss! Marv Albert on Sportscasting. (Illus., Orig.). 1979. pap. 1.95 o.p. (ISBN 0-451-08891-3, J8891, Sig). NAL.

Albert, Marvin H. Hidden Lives. 1981. 12.95 o.s.i. (ISBN 0-440-03586-4, Sey Lawr). Delacorte.

Albert, Michael & Dellinger, Dave, eds. Mobilizing for Survival. 300p. 1983. 20.00 (ISBN 0-89608-176-1); pap. 7.50 (ISBN 0-89608-175-3). South End Pr.

Albert, Peter J., jt. ed. see Hoffman, Ronald.

Albert, R. S., ed. Genius & Eminence: The Social Psychology of Creativity & Exceptional Achievement. (International Series in Experimental Social Psychology). 300p. 1983. 35.00 (ISBN 0-08-028105-2). Pergamon.

Albert, Renaud S., ed. A Tour de Role. (Neuf Pieces en un Acte Ser.). 204p. (Fr.). (gr. 7-12). 1980. pap. 4.00x (ISBN 0-911409-11-4). Natl Mat Dev.

Albert, Salich, jt. auth. see Harrison, Sheldon P.

Albert, Solomon N. Blood Volume & Extracellular Fluid Volume. 2nd ed. (Illus.). 336p. 1971. photocopy e. spiral 33.75x (ISBN 0-398-02193-7). C C Thomas.

Albert, William. Turnpike Road System, 1663-1840. LC 78-163062. (Illus.). 1972. 39.50 (ISBN 0-521-08221-8). Cambridge U Pr.

Albertazzie, Ralph & TerHorst, Jerald F. The Flying White House: The Story of Air Force One. LC 78-25556. (Illus.). 1979. 11.95 o.p. (ISBN 0-698-10930-9, Coward). Putnam Pub Group.

Alberti, G., jt. auth. see Whyte, W.

Alberti, Leon B. De Re Aedificatoria. (Documents of Art & Architectural History Ser. 2: Vol. 1). 420p. (Latin.). 1981. Repr. of 1485 ed. 45.00x (ISBN 0-89371-201-9). Broude Intl Edns.

Alberti, Leone B. On Painting. Spencer, John R., tr. from Ital. LC 76-22485. (Illus.). 141p. 1976. Repr. of 1966 ed. lib. bdg. 20.00 (ISBN 0-8371-8974-8, ALOP). Greenwood.

Alberti, P. W., ed. Personal Hearing Protection in Industry. 624p. 1982. text ed. 63.50 (ISBN 0-89004-698-0). Raven.

Alberti, Rafael. Concerning the Angels. LC 82-70373. (Poetry in Europe Ser.: No. 2). 1967. 6.50 (ISBN 0-8040-0055-7). Swallow.

--The Lost Grove: Autobiography of a Spanish Poet in Exile. Berns, Gabriel, ed. & tr. LC 74-79760. 1977. 17.50x (ISBN 0-520-02786-8); pap. 5.95 (ISBN 0-520-04265-4, CAL464). U of Cal Pr.

Alberti, Robert E. & Emmons, Michael L. Your Perfect Right. 5.95 o.p. (ISBN 0-686-92425-8, 6720). Hazelden.

Alberti, Robert E., ed. Assertiveness: Innovations, Applications, Issues. LC 77-5774. 1977. 12.95 o.s.i. (ISBN 0-915166-38-0). Impact Pubs Cal.

Albertini, ed. Radioimmunoassay. (International Congress Ser.: Vol. 528). 1981. 61.00 (ISBN 0-444-90173-6). Elsevier.

Albertini, A. & Ekins, R. P., eds. Free Hormones in Blood: Proceedings of the Advanced Course on Free Hormone Assays & Neuropeptides, Venice, Italy, June 15-17, 1982. (Symposia of the Giovanni Lorenzini Foundation Ser.: Vol. 14). 392p. 1982. 70.25 (ISBN 0-444-80463-3, Biomedical Pr). Elsevier.

Albertini, A. & Elkins, R., eds. Monoclonal Antibodies & Developments in Immunoassay. (Symposia of the Giovanni Lorenzini Founadtion Ser.: Vol. 11). 1981. 68.00 (ISBN 0-444-80373-4). Elsevier.

Albertini, A., et al, eds. Radioimmunoassay of Drugs & Hormones in Cardiovascular Medicine. 364p. 1979. 65.00 (ISBN 0-444-80176-6, North Holland). Elsevier.

Albertini, A., jt. ed. see Godfraind, T.

Alberto, Paul & Troutman, Anne. Applied Behavior Analysis for Teachers. 448p. 1982. pap. text ed. 18.50 (ISBN 0-675-09840-8). Additional Supplements May Be Obtained From Publisher. Merrill.

Alberts, A. The Islands. Beekman, E. M., ed. Koning, Hans, tr. from Dutch. LC 82-21882. (Library of the Indies Ser.). Orig. Title: De Eilanden. 172p. 1983. lib. bdg. 12.00x (ISBN 0-87023-385-8). U of Mass Pr.

Alberts, Bruce & Bray, Dennis. Molecular Biology of the Cell. LC 82-15692. 1250p. 1983. lib. bdg. 29.95 (ISBN 0-8240-7282-0). Garland Pub.

Alberts, Cecil D. Daterdata. 9.95 o.p. (ISBN 0-915048-03-5). Spin-a-Test Pub.

--Game Power for Phonics, Computerized. 1981. 28.50 (ISBN 0-686-84762-8). Spin-A-Test Pub.

--Game Power for Phonics Professional Kit. (Illus.). 1978. 40.00 (ISBN 0-915048-02-7). Spin-a-Test Pub.

Albertson, Dean. Roosevelt's Farmer: Claude R. Wickard in the New Deal. LC 74-23430. (Fdr & the Era of the New Deal Ser.). 1975. Repr. of 1961 ed. lib. bdg. 49.50 (ISBN 0-306-70702-0). Da Capo.

Albertson, Dorothy. RPM Unlimited: A Business Machines Practice Set. 2nd ed. (Illus.). (gr. 9-12). 1980. 8.84 (ISBN 0-07-000955-4, G); tchrs. manual & key 5.10 (ISBN 0-07-000956-2). McGraw.

Albertson, Dorothy L. Business Machine Practice Set. (Illus.). 192p. (gr. 10-12). 1974. text ed. 7.36 o.p. (ISBN 0-07-000950-3, G); tchr's manual & key 5.10 o.p. (ISBN 0-07-000951-1). McGraw.

Albertson, Maurice L., et al. Fluid Mechanics for Engineers. 1960. text ed. 31.95 (ISBN 0-13-322578-X). P-H.

Albertus Magnus. The Book of Secrets of Albertus Magnus of the Virtues of Herbs, Stones & Certain Beasts; Also, a Book of the Marvels of the World. Best, Michael R. & Best, Michael R., eds. (Illus.). 1974. pap. 6.95 (ISBN 0-19-519786-0, GB421, GB). Oxford U Pr.

Alberty, H. B., ed. see John Dewey Society.

Alberty, Robert A. Physical Chemistry. 6th ed. 832p. 1983. text ed. 29.95 (ISBN 0-471-09284-3); solutions manual avail. (ISBN 0-471-87208-3). Wiley.

Alberty, Robert A. & Daniels, Farrington. Physical Chemistry. 5th ed. LC 78-14876. 692p. 1979. text ed. 28.95 (ISBN 0-471-02222-5); solutions manual 10.95 (ISBN 0-471-04749-X). Wiley.

--Physical Chemistry SI Version. LC 78-14876. 692p. 1980. text ed. 28.95 (ISBN 0-471-05716-9); solutions manual 12.95 (ISBN 0-471-06376-2). Wiley.

Albeverio, S., et al, eds. Stochastic Processes in Quantum Theory & Statistical Physics: Proceedings, Marseille, France, 1981. (Lecture Notes in Physics Ser.: Vol. 173). 337p. 1983. pap. 17.00 (ISBN 0-387-11956-6). Springer-Verlag.

Albietz, Carol, jt. ed. see Rolih, Susan.

Albin, Francis M. Consumer Economics & Personal Money Management. (Illus.). 496p. 1982. 20.95 (ISBN 0-13-169490-1). P-H.

Albin, Mel, et al, eds. New Directions in Psychohistory: The Adelphi Papers in Honor of Erik H. Erikson. LC 78-4410. 240p. 1980. 27.95x (ISBN 0-669-02350-7). Lexington Bks.

Albion, Mark S. Advertising's Hidden Effects: Manufacturer's Advertising & Retail Pricing. (Illus.). 314p. 1983. 22.95 (ISBN 0-86569-111-8). Auburn Hse.

Albion, Mark S. & Farris, Paul. Advertising Controversy: Evidence on the Economic Effects of Advertising. LC 80-24645. 256p. 1981. 21.95 (ISBN 0-86569-057-X). Auburn Hse.

Albion, Robert G. Five Centuries of Famous Ships: From the Santa Maria to the Glomar Explorer. LC 77-4904. (Illus.). 1978. 26.95 (ISBN 0-07-000953-8, P&RB). McGraw.

Albis, Abelardo S. The Bell Ringer & Other Stories. 103p. (Orig.). 1982. pap. 4.75 (ISBN 0-686-37572-6, Pub. by New Day Philippines). Cellar.

Albisetti, James C. Secondary School Reform in Imperial Germany. LC 82-12223. 392p. 1983. 35.00x (ISBN 0-691-05373-1). Princeton U Pr.

Albone, D. J. & Payne, K. W. The Determination of Microgram Quantities of Sulphur & Other Elements in Rainwater by X-Ray Fluorescence Spectrometry. 1978. 1981. 40.00x (ISBN 0-686-97056-X, Pub. by W Spring England). State Mutual Bk.

Albracht, James & Kurtz, Ray. Introduction to AG Metrics. text ed. 16.75x (ISBN 0-8134-1999-9). Interstate.

Albran, Kehlog. The Profit. 108p. (Orig.). 1973. pap. 2.95 (ISBN 0-8431-0260-8). Price Stern.

Albrand, Martha. A Taste of Terror. LC 77-3446. 1977. 7.95 o.p. (ISBN 0-399-11965-5). Putnam Pub Group.

Albrecht, Adalbert, tr. see Aschaffenburg, Gustav.

Albrecht, Bob L., et al. Atari Basic. LC 79-12513. (Self-Teaching Guides). 333p. 1979. pap. text ed. 8.95 (ISBN 0-471-06496-3). Wiley.

Albrecht, F. O. The Anatomy of the Red Locust (Nomadacris Septemfasciate Serville) 1956. 35.00x (ISBN 0-85135-067-4, Pub. by Centre Overseas Research). State Mutual Bk.

Albrecht, Gary L. & Higgins, Paul C. Health, Illness & Medicine: A Reader in Medical Sociology. 1979. 18.50 (ISBN 0-395-30557-8). HM.

Albrecht, J. & Collatz, L., eds. Numerical Treatment of Free Boundary Value Problems. (International Series of Numerical Mathematics: Vol. 58). 350p. 1982. text ed. 35.00x (ISBN 3-7643-1277-7). Birkhauser.

Albrecht, K. Learn to Improve Your Thinking Skills. 1980. 14.95 o.p. (ISBN 0-13-136325-5, Spec); pap. 6.95 o.p. (ISBN 0-13-136317-4). P-H.

Albrecht, Karl. Organization Development: A Total Systems Approach to Positive Change in Any Business Organization. 288p. 1983. 18.95 (ISBN 0-13-641696-9). P-H.

--Stress & the Manager: Making It Work for You. (Illus.). 1979. 14.95 o.p. (ISBN 0-13-852681-8, Spec); pap. 6.95 (ISBN 0-13-852673-7). P-H.

--Successful Management by Objectives: An Action Manual. LC 77-14971. (Illus.). 1978. 14.95 (ISBN 0-13-863266-9, Spec); pap. 6.95 (ISBN 0-13-863258-8, Spec). P-H.

Albrecht, Karl G., jt. auth. see Boshear, Walton C.

Albrecht, M. E. Printed Fabrics of Mulhouse & Alsace, 1750-1800. 33.50x (ISBN 0-87245-001-5). Textile Bk.

--Printed Fabrics of Mulhouse & Alsace, 1801-1850. 33.50x (ISBN 0-87245-002-3). Textile Bk.

Albrecht, Mark. Reincarnation: A Christian Appraisal. 96p. (Orig.). 1982. pap. 4.95 (ISBN 0-87784-378-3). Inter-Varsity.

Albrecht, Maryann, jt. auth. see Hall, Francine.

Albrecht, P., jt. ed. see Birch, C.

Albrecht, R. L., et al. Basic for Home Computers. LC 78-9010. (Self-Teaching Guides). 336p. 1978. 9.50x (ISBN 0-471-03204-2). Wiley.

Albrecht, R. M., jt. ed. see Johari, Om.

Albrecht, Robert C., ed. World of Short Fiction. LC 69-11841. 1970. pap. text ed. 10.95 (ISBN 0-02-900335-0). Free Pr.

Albrecht, Robert L., et al. Basic. 2nd ed. LC 77-14998. (Self-Teaching Guide Ser.). 325p. 1978. pap. text ed. 9.95 (ISBN 0-471-03500-9). Wiley.

Albrecht, William P., Jr. Economics. 3rd ed. (Illus.). 768p. 1983. text ed. 25.95 (ISBN 0-13-224345-8); study guide & wkbk. 9.95 (ISBN 0-13-224360-1). P-H.

Albrecht-Carrie, Rene. Adolphe Thiers. (World Leaders Ser.). 1977. lib. bdg. 13.95 (ISBN 0-8057-7717-2, Twayne). G K Hall.

Albrektsson, T., jt. auth. see Lee, A. J.

Albricus. Allegoriae Poeticae, Repr. Of 1520 Ed. Incl. Theologia Mythologica. Pictorius, Georg. Repr. of 1532 ed; Apotheoseos Tam Exterarum Gentium Quam Romanorum Deorum. Pictorius, Georg. Repr. of 1558 ed. LC 75-27845. (Renaissance & the Gods Ser.: Vol. 4). (Illus.). 1976. lib. bdg. 73.00 o.s.i. (ISBN 0-8240-2053-7). Garland Pub.

Albright, Arnita, jt. auth. see Albright, Hardie.

Albright, Bets P., jt. auth. see Albright, Peter.

Albright, David E. Communism & Political Systems in Western Europe. (Westview Special Studies in West European Politics & Society). 1979. lib. bdg. 32.50 (ISBN 0-89158-308-4). Westview.

Albright, Hardie & Albright, Arnita. Acting: The Creative Process. 3rd ed. 432p. 1980. pap. text ed. 17.95x (ISBN 0-534-00744-9). Wadsworth Pub.

Albright-Knox Art Gallery & Nash, Steven A. Painting & Sculpture from Antiquity to Nineteen Forty-Two. LC 77-79651. (Illus.). 1979. 35.00 (ISBN 0-8478-0146-2); pap. 18.95 (ISBN 0-914782-17-7). Buffalo Acad.

Albright, Lyle, et al. Pyrolysis: Theory & Industrial Practice. 446p. 1983. 65.00 (ISBN 0-12-048880-9). Acad Pr.

Albright, Lyle F. Processes for Major Addition-Type Plastics & Their Monomers. rev. ed. LC 80-12568. 396p. 1983. Repr. of 1974 ed. lib. bdg. write for info. (ISBN 0-89874-074-6). Krieger.

--Processes for Major Addition-Type Plastics & Their Monomers. (Illus.). 388p. 1974. 34.50 o.p. (ISBN 0-07-000965-1, P&RB). McGraw.

Albright, Nancy. Do Tell! Holiday Draw & Tell Stories. (Draw & Tell Stories). (gr. 1-7). 1981. 4.50 (ISBN 0-686-38119-X). Moonlight FL.

--Natural Foods Epicure: The No Salt, No Sugar, No Artificial Ingredients, All Natural Foods Cookbook. Gerras, Charles, ed. (Orig.). 1983. pap. 10.95 (ISBN 0-87857-468-9, 03-545-1). Rodale Pr Inc.

Albright, Nancy, illus. I Know an Old Lady Who Swallowed a Fly. (Flannel Board Ser.). (Illus.). Date not set. price not set. Moonlight FL.

Albright, Peter & Albright, Bets P. Body, Mind & Spirit. 2nd ed. LC 80-12671. (Illus.). 320p. 1981. pap. 9.95 o.p. (ISBN 0-8289-0386-7); 12.95 o.p. (ISBN 0-8289-0385-9). Greene.

Albright, Priscilla, jt. auth. see Albright, Rod.

Albright, Rod & Albright, Priscilla. Walks in the Great Smokies. LC 79-4898. (Illus.). 192p. 1979. pap. 7.95 (ISBN 0-914788-14-0). East Woods.

Albright, Thomas & Butterfield, Jan. Oliver Jackson. LC 82-61511. (Illus.). 32p. (Orig.). 1982. pap. 10.00 (ISBN 0-932216-10-2). Seattle Art.

Albright, William F. The Vocalization of the Egyptian Syllabic Orthography. 1934. pap. 10.00 (ISBN 0-685-13730-9). Kraus Repr.

Albright, William F. & Mann, C. S., eds. Matthew. LC 77-150875. (Anchor Bible Ser.: Vol. 26). 1971. 18.00 (ISBN 0-385-08658-X, Anchor Pr). Doubleday.

Album, Manual. Dentistry for the Handicapped Patient. (Masson Monographs in Dentistry: Vol. 4). (Illus.). 220p. 1983. lib. bdg. write for info (ISBN 0-89352-170-1). Masson Pub.

Alburger, Mary A. Scottish Fiddlers & Their Music. (Illus.). 224p. 1983. 37.50 (ISBN 0-575-03174-3, Pub. by Gollancz England). David & Charles.

Albus, J. S., ed. Information Control Problems in Manufacturing Technology 1982: Proceedings of the 4th IFAC-IFIP Symposium, National Bureau of Standards, Maryland, USA, 26-28 October 1982. (IFAC Proceedings Ser.). 199p. 1983. 50.00 (ISBN 0-08-029946-6). Pergamon.

Alcamo, I. Edward. Microbiology. (Biology Ser.). (Illus.). 600p. Date not set. text ed. 24.95 (ISBN 0-201-10068-1); Instrs' Manual avail. (ISBN 0-201-10069-X); Study Guide avail. (ISBN 0-201-11180-2); Labortory Manual avail. (ISBN 0-201-11181-0); Transparencies avail. (ISBN 0-201-11182-9). A-W.

Alcantara, Ruben R. Sakada: Filipino Adaptation in Hawaii. LC 80-5858. 202p. (Orig.). 1981. lib. bdg. 20.00 (ISBN 0-8191-1578-9); pap. text ed. 9.75 (ISBN 0-8191-1579-7). U Pr of Amer.

Alcantara, Ruben R. & Alconcel, Nancy S. The Filipinos in Hawaii: An Annotated Bibliography. LC 77-84531. (Hawaii Bibliographies Ser: No. 6). 1977. pap. text ed. 6.00x (ISBN 0-8248-0612-3). UH Pr.

Alcantud, Adela. Diccionario Bilingue De Psicologia. LC 78-50649. (Senda Lexicografica Ser.). 1978. pap. 7.95 (ISBN 0-918454-05-0). Senda Nueva.

Al-Chalabi, Fadhil J. OPEC & the International Oil Industry: A Changing Structure. (Illus.). 176p. 1980. pap. 9.95 (ISBN 0-19-877155-X). Oxford U Pr.

Alchian, Armen A. & Allen, William R. Exchange & Production: Theory in Use. 2nd ed. 1977. pap. 18.95x (ISBN 0-534-00493-8). Wadsworth Pub.

--University Economics: Elements of Inquiry. 3rd ed. 1971. 24.95x (ISBN 0-534-00030-4); study guide 6.95x (ISBN 0-534-00184-X). Wadsworth Pub.

Alchin, Carrie A. Ear Training for Teacher & Pupil. LC 74-27326. 152p. 1982. Repr. of 1904 ed. 19.00 (ISBN 0-404-12852-1). AMS Pr.

Alcocer, Pablo H., jt. auth. see Burns, Donald.

Alcock, A. Materials for a Carcenological Fauna of India: 1895-1900, 6pts. in 1. 1968. 80.00 (ISBN 3-7682-0544-4). Lubrecht & Cramer.

Alcock, Antony E., et al, eds. The Future of Cultural Minorities. LC 78-13725. 1979. 19.95x o.p. (ISBN 0-312-31470-1). St Martin.

Alcock, C. B., ed. Electromotive Force Measurements in High-Temperature Systems. 227p. 1968. 28.75 (ISBN 0-686-38299-4). IMM North Am.

Alcock, L. Arthur's Britain: History & Archaeology AD 367-634. 1972. 19.95 o.p. (ISBN 0-312-05530-7). St Martin.

Alcock, N. W. Cruck Construction: An Introduction & Catalogue. (CBA Research Reports Ser.: No. 42). 180p. 1981. pap. text ed. 24.00x (ISBN 0-906780-11-X, Pub. by Coun Brit Archaeology). Humanities.

Alcock, N. W., ed. Warwickshire Grazier & London Skinner, 1532 to 1555: The Account Book of Peter Temple & Thomas Heritage. (Records of Social & Economic History Ser.). (Illus.). 1982. 94.00x (ISBN 0-19-726008-X). Oxford U Pr.

Alcock, Randal H. Botanical Names for English Readers. LC 73-174935. xviii, 236p. 1971. Repr. of 1876 ed. 34.00 (ISBN 0-8103-3823-8). Gale.

Alcock, Sheila. Puppies & Dogs. LC 80-52201. (Whizz Kids Ser.). 8.00 (ISBN 0-382-06457-7). Silver.

Alcock, Vivien. The Stonewalkers. LC 82-13956. 192p. (gr. 5-8). 1983. 12.95 (ISBN 0-440-08321-4). Delacorte.

Alconcel, Nancy S., jt. auth. see Alcantara, Ruben R.

Alcorn, George T., jt. ed. see Jordan, James M.

Alcorn, John, jt. auth. see Hine, Al.

Alcorn, Pat. Success & Survival in the Family Owned Business. 256p. 1982. 19.95 (ISBN 0-07-000961-9). McGraw.

Alcott, Edward, ed. A Great Treasury of Christian Spirituality. LC 78-59319. 1978. 8.95 (ISBN 0-89310-039-0); pap. 4.95 o.p. (ISBN 0-89310-040-4). Carillon Bks.

Alcott, L. M. Little Men. (Deluxe Illustrated Classics Ser.). 1977. 4.50 (ISBN 0-307-12220-4, Golden Pr). Western Pub.

--Little Women. (Deluxe Illustrated Classics Ser.). 1977. 4.50 (ISBN 0-307-12213-1, Golden Pr). Western Pub.

Alcott, Louisa M. Eight Cousins. (Louisa May Alcott Library). (gr. 5-9). 1971. Repr. 4.95 (ISBN 0-448-02359-8, G&D). Putnam Pub Group.

--Eight Cousins. 1977. 4.50 (ISBN 0-307-12224-7, Golden Pr). Western Pub.

--Flower Fables. LC 77-89715. (Children's Literature Reprint Ser.). (Illus.). (gr. 4-6). 1977. Repr. of 1894 ed. cancelled 17.50x o.p. (ISBN 0-8486-0212-9). Core Collection.

--Garland for Girls. (Louisa May Alcott Library). (gr. 5-9). 1971. Repr. 4.95 (ISBN 0-448-02360-1, G&D). Putnam Pub Group.

--Good Wives. (Childrens Illustrated Classics Ser). (Illus.). 303p. 1974. Repr. of 1953 ed. 11.95x (ISBN 0-460-05019-2, Pub. by J. M. Dent England). Biblio Dist.

--Good Wives. 1983. pap. 2.25 (ISBN 0-14-035009-8, Puffin). Penguin.

--Jack & Jill. (Louisa May Alcott Library). (gr. 5-9). 1971. Repr. 4.95 (ISBN 0-448-02361-X, G&D). Putnam Pub Group.

--Jack & Jill. (gr. 5 up). 1879. 10.95 (ISBN 0-316-03092-9). Little.

--Jo's Boys. (Illustrated Junior Library). (gr. 4-6). 1949. 5.95 (ISBN 0-448-05813-8, G&D); deluxe ed. 8.95 (ISBN 0-448-06013-2). Putnam Pub Group.

--Little Men. (Childrens Illustrated Classics Ser). (Illus.). 200p. 1983. Repr. of 1957 ed. text ed. 11.45 o.p. (ISBN 0-460-05038-9, Pub. by J. M. Dent England). Biblio Dist.

--Little Men. (Louisa May Alcott Library). (gr. 4-6). 4.95 (ISBN 0-448-02363-6, G&D). Putnam Pub Group.

--Little Men. (Illus.). (gr. 4-6). Illustrated Junior Library. 5.95 (ISBN 0-448-05818-9, G&D); deluxe ed. 8.95 (ISBN 0-448-06018-3); Campion Library. 2.95 (ISBN 0-448-05465-5). Putnam Pub Group.

--Little Women. (Classics Ser). (gr. 6 up). pap. 2.50 (ISBN 0-8049-0106-6, CL-106). Airmont.

--Little Women. 1978. pap. text ed. 1.95x (ISBN 0-460-01248-7, Evman). Biblio Dist.

--Little Women. (Childrens Illustrated Classics Ser). (Illus.). 314p. 1977. Repr. of 1948 ed. 11.95x (ISBN 0-460-05002-8, Pub. by J. M. Dent England). Biblio Dist.

--Little Women. (Louisa May Alcott Library). (gr. 4-6). 1947. 4.95 (ISBN 0-448-02364-4, G&D). Putnam Pub Group.

--Little Women. (Illus.). (gr. 4-6). 1947. Illustrated Junior Library. pap. 5.95 (ISBN 0-448-11019-9, G&D); deluxe ed. 8.95 (ISBN 0-448-06019-1); Companion Library 3.95 (ISBN 0-448-05466-3). Putnam Pub Group.

--Little Women. (gr. 4-8). 1954. pap. 2.50 (ISBN 0-14-035008-X, Puffin). Penguin.

--Little Women. LC 78-2919. (Raintree's Illustrated Classics). (Illus.). (gr. 5-8). 1978. PLB 13.30 (ISBN 0-8172-1135-7). Raintree Pubs.

--Little Women. Barish, Wendy, ed. (Illus.). 576p. 1982. 14.95 (ISBN 0-671-44447-6). Wanderer Bks.

--Little Women. (Classics Ser.). (Illus.). 576p. (gr. 3 up). 1982. lib. bdg. 14.79 (ISBN 0-671-45651-2). Messner.

--Little Women. 1983. pap. 2.50 (ISBN 0-14-035008-X, Puffin). Penguin.

--Little Women. 1981. pap. 5.95 (ISBN 0-686-38903-4, Mod LibC). Modern Lib.

--Little Women (Centennial Edition) (Illus.). 1968. 13.95 (ISBN 0-316-03090-2). Little.

--Little Women, Tasha Tudor. LC 75-82776. (Illus.). (gr. 5 up). 1969. 15.00 (ISBN 0-529-00529-8, Philomel). Putnam Pub Group.

--Old-Fashioned Girl. (Louisa May Alcott Library). (gr. 5-9). 1971. Repr. 4.95 (ISBN 0-448-02365-2, G&D). Putnam Pub Group.

--Old-Fashioned Girl. (Illus.). (gr. 7 up). 1869. 10.95 (ISBN 0-316-03096-1). Little.

--Rose in Bloom. (Louisa May Alcott Library). (gr. 5-9). 1971. Repr. 4.95 (ISBN 0-448-02366-0, G&D). Putnam Pub Group.

--Under the Lilacs. (Louisa May Alcott Library). (gr. 5-9). 1971. Repr. 4.95 o.p. (ISBN 0-448-02367-9, G&D). Putnam Pub Group.

Alcott, Louisa M see Swan, D. K.

Alcott, Louisa May. Little Men. (The Illustrated Junior Library). (Illus.). 384p. 1982. pap. 5.95 (ISBN 0-448-11018-0, G&D). Putnam Pub Group.

Alcyone, pseud. At the Feet of the Master. 1967. 4.50 (ISBN 0-8356-0098-X). Theos Pub Hse.

Ald, Roy. Jogging, Aerobics & Diet. Orig. Title: The Aerobic Joggers' Guide & Diet Plan. 192p. 1973. pap. 2.50 (ISBN 0-451-11977-0, AE1977, Sig). NAL.

Alda, Arlene. Sonya's Mommy Works. Klimo, Kate, ed. (Illus.). 48p. (ps-3). 1982. 7.95 (ISBN 0-671-45157-X, Little Simon). S&S.

Al-Daffa, A. A. A Brief Exposition of Arabic & Islamic Scientific Heritage: Arabic Edition. 1979. pap. text ed. 12.00 (ISBN 0-471-05348-1). Wiley.

--Great Arab & Muslim Mathematicians: Arabic Edition. 296p. 1978. 13.25 o.p. (ISBN 0-471-04611-6); pap. 8.80 o.p. (ISBN 0-471-06327-4). Wiley.

--Modern Mathematics & Intellect: Arabic Edition. 1979. pap. text ed. 5.50 (ISBN 0-471-05139-X). Wiley.

Al-Daffa, Ali A. The Muslim Contribution to Mathematics. 1977. text ed. 23.00x (ISBN 0-391-00714-9). Humanities.

Aldag, Ramon & Brief, Arthur. Managing Organizational Behavior. (Illus.). 510p. 1980. text ed. 22.95 (ISBN 0-8299-0306-2). West Pub.

Aldag, Ramon J. & Brief, Arthur P. Task Design & Employee Motivation. 1979. pap. text ed. 10.95x (ISBN 0-673-15146-8). Scott F.

Aldam, Diana, et al, eds. Ideology & Consciousness Autumn 1978, No. 4. pap. text ed. 3.25x (ISBN 0-391-01214-2). Humanities.

Aldan, Daisy. The Art & Craft of Poetry. LC 80-27694. 128p. 1981. 8.95 (ISBN 0-88427-047-5). North River.

Aldanov, Mark. Nightmare & Dawn. Carmichael, Joel, tr. LC 73-21489. 343p. 1974. Repr. of 1957 ed. lib. bdg. 18.75x (ISBN 0-8371-6406-0, ALND). Greenwood.

Aldcroft, D., jt. ed. see Slaven, A.

Aldcroft, Derek & Fearon, Peter. Economic Growth in Twentieth Century Britain. 1970. 9.50x (ISBN 0-333-10041-7); pap. text ed. 4.75x (ISBN 0-333-10595-8). Humanities.

Aldcroft, Derek H. From Versailles to Wall Street: The International Economy in the 1920's. LC 76-40824. (History of the World Economy in the 20th Century Ser.: Vol. 3). 1977. 32.00x (ISBN 0-520-03336-1); pap. 8.95 (ISBN 0-520-04506-8, CAL531). U of Cal Pr.

Aldcroft, Derek H. & Fearon, Peter, eds. British Economic Fluctuations: Seventeen-Ninety to Nineteen Thirty-Nine. LC 77-178900. 1972. text ed. 25.00 (ISBN 0-312-10045-0). St Martin.

Aldecoa, Ignacio. Cuentos. (Easy Readers). (Illus.). 1976. pap. text ed. 3.95 (ISBN 0-88436-283-3). EMC.

Alden, Dauril. Royal Government in Colonial Brazil: With Special Reference to the Administration of the Marquis of Lavradio, Viceroy, 1769-1779. LC 68-26064. (Illus.). 1968. 46.50x (ISBN 0-520-00008-0). U of Cal Pr.

Alden, Dauril, ed. Colonial Roots of Modern Brazil: Papers of the Newberry Library Conference. LC 78-174458. 1973. 34.50x (ISBN 0-520-02140-1). U of Cal Pr.

Alden, Douglas W., et al, eds. French Twenty Bibliography: Critical & Biographical References for the Study of French Literature Since 1885, Nos. 1-32. Incl. Nos. 1-9. 1949-1957. pap. 4.00x ea.; No. 1. 1949. pap. (ISBN 0-933444-02-8); No. 2, 1950. pap. (ISBN 0-933444-03-6); No. 3. 1951. pap. (ISBN 0-933444-04-4); No. 4. 1952. pap. (ISBN 0-933444-05-2); No. 5. 1953. pap. (ISBN 0-933444-06-0); No. 6. 1954. pap. (ISBN 0-933444-07-9); No. 7. 1955. pap. (ISBN 0-933444-08-7); No. 8. 1956. pap. (ISBN 0-933444-09-5); No. 9. 1957. pap. (ISBN 0-933444-10-9); No. 10. 1958. Incl. Index To Nos. 1-10. pap. 7.00x (ISBN 0-933444-11-7); Nos. 11-16. pap. 6.00x ea.; No. 11. 1959. pap. (ISBN 0-933444-12-5); No. 12. 1960. pap. (ISBN 0-933444-13-3); No. 13. 1961. pap. (ISBN 0-933444-14-1); No. 14. 1962. pap. (ISBN 0-933444-15-X); No. 15. 1963. pap. (ISBN 0-933444-16-8); No. 16. 1964. pap. (ISBN 0-933444-17-6); Nos. 17-20. pap. 12.00x ea.; No. 17. 1965. pap. (ISBN 0-933444-18-4); No. 18. 1966. pap. (ISBN 0-933444-19-2); No. 19. **1967. pap. (ISBN 0-933444-20-6); No. 20. 1968. pap. (ISBN 0-933444-21-4); General Index to Nos. 11-20. Tussing, Ruth-Elaine, et al, eds. 1969. pap. 15.00x (ISBN 0-933444-22-2); No. 21. 1969. pap. 12.00x (ISBN 0-933444-23-0); Nos. 22-24. pap. 18.00x ea.; No. 22. 1970. pap. (ISBN 0-933444-24-9); No. 23. 1971. pap. (ISBN 0-933444-25-7); No. 24. 1972. pap. (ISBN 0-933444-26-5); No. 25. 1973. pap. 24.00x (ISBN 0-933444-27-3); Index to Nos. 21-25. Tussing, Ruth-Elaine, ed. 1974. pap. 26.00x (ISBN 0-933444-28-1); Nos. 26-27. pap. 30.00x ea.; No. 26. 1974. pap. (ISBN 0-933444-29-X); No. 27. 1975. pap. (ISBN 0-933444-30-3); No. 28, 1976. pap. 36.00x (ISBN 0-933444-31-1); No. 29, 1977. pap. 42.00x (ISBN 0-933444-33-8); No. 30, 1978. pap. 42.00x (ISBN 0-933444-34-6); No. 31, 1979. pap. 42.00 (ISBN 0-933444-36-2); No. 32, 1980. pap. 42.00x (ISBN 0-933444-37-0); Index to Nos. 26-30. 1981. pap. 34.00x (ISBN 0-933444-38-9); No. 33. 1981. pap. 48.00 (ISBN 0-933444-40-0). (Orig., Nos. 1-20, IC 49-3084; nos. 21-33, LC 77-648803. Nos. 1-20 originally published as French Seven Bibliography). 1949-81. Set. pap. 490.00x (ISBN 0-933444-01-X). French Inst.**

Alden, John & Landis, Dennis C. European Americana: A Chronological Guide to Works Printed in Europe Relating to the Americas, 1493-1776, 8 vols. 954p. 1982. Vol. 2, 1601-1650. 85.00 (ISBN 0-918414-09-1). Readex Bks.

Alden, John R. American Revolution, Seventeen Seventy Five to Seventeen Eighty-Three. LC 53-11826. (New American Nation Ser). 1954. 21.10i (ISBN 0-06-010045-1, HarpT). Har-Row.

--American Revolution: Seventeen Seventy-Five to Seventeen Eighty-Three. (New American Nation Ser.). (Illus.). pap. 7.95xi (ISBN 0-06-133011-6, TB3011, Torch). Har-Row.

--General Gage in America. LC 77-90459. Repr. of 1948 ed. lib. bdg. 15.00 o.p. (ISBN 0-8371-2264-3, ALGG). Greenwood.

Alden, Laura. Sorry. LC 82-9660. (What Does it Mean? Ser.). (Illus.). 32p. (gr. 1-2). 1982. PLB 4.95 (ISBN 0-89565-236-6, 4897, Pub. by Childs World). Standard Pub.

Alden, Maureen J. Bronze Age Population in the Argolid from the Evidence of Mycenaean Tombs. (Studies in Mediterranean Archaeology Ser.: NO. 15). 436p. 1981. pap. text ed. 48.00x (ISBN 91-86098-00-4, Pub. by Astroms Sweden). Humanities.

Alden, Robert & Alden, Sunny. Lover's Coupon Book. (Illus.). 76p. 1983. pap. 4.95 (ISBN 0-911829-06-7). Sunfish Prods.

Alden, Robert L. Psalms: Songs of Discipleship, 3 vols. (Everyman's Bible Commentary Ser.). 1975. pap. 4.50 ea. Vol. 1 (ISBN 0-8024-2018-4). Vol. 2 (ISBN 0-8024-2019-2). Vol. 3 (ISBN 0-8024-2020-6). Moody.

Alden, Sunny, jt. auth. see Alden, Robert.

Aldenhoff, J. B., jt. ed. see Lux, H. D.

Alder, Alfred A. My Computer & I Make Money. 250p. 1983. pap. 13.95 (ISBN 0-88056-105-X). Dilithium Pr.

Alder, Jim. Guide to Service Selection & Integration in Low Rise Buildings. (Illus.). 160p. 1983. pap. 24.95 (ISBN 0-89397-153-7). Nichols Pub.

Alder, R. W., et al. Mechanisms in Organic Chemistry. LC 72-147196. 378p. 1975. 33.95x (ISBN 0-471-02050-8, Pub. by Wiley-Interscience). Wiley.

Alderfer, Clayton, jt. auth. see Cooper, Cary L.

Alderfer, Clayton P. & Cooper, Cary L. Advances in Experimental Social Processes, Vol. 2. 329p. 1980. 53.95x (ISBN 0-471-27623-5, Pub. by Wiley-Interscience). Wiley.

Alderman, Clifford L. Devil's Shadow: The Story of Witchcraft in Massachusetts. LC 67-10629. (Illus.). 192p. (gr. 7 up). 1967. PLB 4.79 o.p. (ISBN 0-671-32483-7). Messner.

Alderman, Geoffrey. British Elections. 1978. 14.95 (ISBN 0-7134-0195-8, Pub. by Batsford England); pap. 14.95 (ISBN 0-7134-0196-6). David & Charles.

Alderman, Harold G. Nietzsche's Gift. LC 76-25612. xvi, 184p. 1977. 15.00x (ISBN 0-8214-0231-5, 82-82329); pap. 6.95x (ISBN 0-8214-0385-0, 82-82337). Ohio U Pr.

Alderman, Robert. How to Make More Money at Interior Design. 192p. 1982. 18.95 (ISBN 0-442-20876-6). Inter Design.

Alderson, jt. ed. see Maunder, W. F.

Alderson, Brian, compiled by. Cakes & Custards: Children's Rhymes. LC 75-24523. (Illus.). 176p. 1975. PLB 11.28 (ISBN 0-688-32050-3). Morrow.

Alderson, Frederick. Bicycles. (Illus.). 64p. (gr. 7 up). 1975. 6.50 o.s.i. (ISBN 0-7136-1464-1). Transatlantic.

Alderson, Michael, ed. The Prevention of Cancer. (Management of Malignant Disease Ser.: No. 4). 304p. 1982. text ed. 49.50 (ISBN 0-7131-4401-7). E Arnold.

Alderson, Nannie T. & Smith, Helena H. Bride Goes West. LC 42-12918. (Illus.). viii, 273p. 1969. pap. 5.95 (ISBN 0-8032-5001-0, BB389, Bison). U of Nebr Pr.

Alderson, R. H., ed. Design of the Electron Microscope Laboratory. (Practical Methods in Electron Microscopy Ser.: Vol. 4). 1975. pap. 13.75 (ISBN 0-444-10816-5, North-Holland). Elsevier.

Alderson, William T. & Low, Shirley P. Interpretation of Historic Sites. LC 75-33292. (Illus.). 1976. pap. 8.50 (ISBN 0-910050-19-8). AASLH.

Alderton, David. Looking After Cage Birds. LC 82-11598. (Illus.). 96p. 1983. 11.95 (ISBN 0-668-05707-6, 5707). Arco.

Alderton, Patrick M. Sea Transport: Operation & Economics. 2nd ed. (Illus.). 1980. 22.50 (ISBN 0-900335-63-7). Heinman.

Alding, Peter. A Man Condemned. 176p. 1983. pap. 2.95 (ISBN 0-8027-3018-3). Walker & Co.

--Murder is Suspected. 184p. 1983. pap. 2.95 (ISBN 0-8027-3017-5). Walker & Co.

Aldington, Richard. A Passionate Prodigality: Letters to Alan Bird from Richard Aldington, 1949-1962. Benkovitz, Miriam J., ed. LC 75-23105. (Illus.). 376p. 1975. 20.00 (ISBN 0-87104-259-2). NY Pub Lib.

Aldington, Richard & Weintraub, eds. The Portable Oscar Wilde. rev. ed. LC 80-39827. 1981. 14.95 (ISBN 0-670-76743-3). Viking Pr.

Aldis, Dorothy. All Together: A Child's Treasury of Verse. (Illus.). (gr. 1-4). 1952. 7.95 o.p. (ISBN 0-399-20006-1). Putnam Pub Group.

--Favorite Poems of Dorothy Aldis. (Illus.). (gr. 1-5). 1970. PLB 3.97 o.p. (ISBN 0-399-60164-3). Putnam Pub Group.

Aldis, Mary. Plays for Small Stages. LC 76-40384. (One-Act Plays in Reprint Ser.). 1976. Repr. of 1912 ed. 15.00x o.p. (ISBN 0-8486-2000-3). Core Collection.

Aldiss, Brian. Billion Year Spree: The True History of Science Fiction. LC 74-9868. 1974. pap. 3.95 (ISBN 0-8052-0450-4). Schocken.

--Brothers of the Head. (Illus.). 1977. pap. 7.95 o.p. (ISBN 0-8467-0386-6, Pub. by Two Continents). Hippocrene Bks.

--Dark Light Years. pap. 1.50 o.p. (ISBN 0-451-08582-5, W8582, Sig). NAL.

--Long Afternoon of Earth. pap. 1.75 o.p. (ISBN 0-451-08575-2, E8575, Sig). NAL.

--New Arrivals, Old Encounters. LC 79-2642. 1980. 11.49i (ISBN 0-06-010055-9, HarpT). Har-Row.

--Starswarm. 160p. (RL 9). Date not set. pap. 1.25 o.p. (ISBN 0-451-06883-1, Y6883, Sig). NAL.

--Who Can Replace a Man? (RL 7). pap. 1.25 o.p. (ISBN 0-451-07083-6, Y7083, Sig). NAL.

Aldiss, Brian, ed. New Arrivals, Old Encounters: Twelve Stories. LC 79-2642. 224p. 1979. 15.00. Ultramarine Pub.

Aldiss, Brian W. Galaxies Like Grains of Sand. (Science Fiction Ser.). 1977. Repr. of 1976 ed. lib. bdg. 9.95 o.p. (ISBN 0-8398-2376-2, Gregg). G K Hall.

--Hothouse. (Science Fiction Ser.). 272p. 1976. Repr. of 1962 ed. lib. bdg. 12.50 (ISBN 0-8398-2325-8, Gregg). G K Hall.

--The Saliva Tree. 1981. lib. bdg. 16.95 (ISBN 0-8398-2566-8, Gregg). G K Hall.

--Starswarm. (Science Fiction Ser.). 1978. lib. bdg. 9.95 (ISBN 0-8398-2408-4, Gregg). G K Hall.

Aldiss, Brian W. & Harrison, Harry. Decade of the Nineteen Forties. 1980. pap. 3.95 o.p. (ISBN 0-312-18986-9). St Martin.

Aldiss, Bryan, intro. by. Science-Fiction Art: The Fantasies of Science Fiction. (Illus.). 128p. 1975. pap. 9.95 o.p. (ISBN 0-517-52432-5). Crown.

Aldous, Joan. Family Careers: Developmental Change in Families. LC 77-15043. 358p. 1978. text ed. 21.95 (ISBN 0-471-02046-X). Wiley.

--Her & His Paychecks: Life in Dual Earner Families. (Sage Focus Editions). (Illus.). 232p. 1982. 22.00 (ISBN 0-8039-1882-8); pap. 10.95 (ISBN 0-8039-1883-6). Sage.

--Two Paychecks: Life in Dual Earner Families. (Sage Focus Editions). (Illus.). 232p. 1982. 22.00 (ISBN 0-8039-1882-8); pap. 10.95 (ISBN 0-8039-1883-6). Sage.

Aldous, Tony. Illustrated London News Book of London's Villages. 1981. 29.95 (ISBN 0-436-01150-6, Pub. by Secker & Warburg); pap. 12.50 (ISBN 0-436-01151-4). David & Charles.

Aldous, W. H., jt. auth. see Dix, C. H.

Aldred, Cyril. Egypt to the End of the Old Kingdom. (Illus.). (gr. 9-12). 1965. pap. 4.95 o.p. (ISBN 0-07-000995-3, SP). McGraw.

Aldred, Jennifer & Wilkes, John, eds. A Fractured Federation. 128p. 1983. text ed. 19.95 (ISBN 0-86861-109-3). Allen Unwin.

Aldred, William H., jt. auth. see Jones, Fred R.

Aldrich, Dot & Aldrich, Genevieve. Creating with Cattails, Cones & Pods. LC 68-8521. (Illus.). 1971. 6.95 (ISBN 0-686-76844-2). Hearthside.

Aldrich, Ella V. Using Books & Libraries. 5th ed. (gr. 9-12). 1967. pap. 8.95 (ISBN 0-13-939223-8). P-H.

Aldrich, Genevieve, jt. auth. see Aldrich, Dot.

Aldrich, Henry. Cell Biology of Physarum & Didymium, Vol. 2. (Cell Biology Ser.). 1982. 44.50 (ISBN 0-12-049602-X). Acad Pr.

Aldrich, John H., jt. auth. see Abramson, Paul R.

Aldrich, Jonathan. Croquet Lover at the Dinner Table. LC 76-45630. 64p. 1977. 7.95 (ISBN 0-8262-0205-5). U of Mo Pr.

Aldrich, Joseph C. Life-Style Evangelism: Study Guide. 1983. pap. price not set (ISBN 0-88070-020-3). Multnomah.

Aldrich, Lawson. The Cheechako: Facts, Fables & Recipes. LC 82-72999. 192p. 1982. pap. 7.95 (ISBN 0-89272-156-1). Down East.

Aldrich, Pearl. The Impact of Mass Media. LC 75-1012. 192p. (gr. 10-12). 1975. pap. text ed. 6.50x (ISBN 0-8104-6000-9). Boynton Cook Pubs.

Aldrich, Putnam. Ornamentation in J. S. Bach's Organ Works. LC 78-17258. (Music Reprint Ser.). (Illus.). 1978. Repr. of 1950 ed. lib. bdg. 18.50 (ISBN 0-306-77590-5). Da Capo.

Aldrich, Ruth I. John Galt. (English Authors Ser.). 1978. lib. bdg. 14.95 (ISBN 0-8057-6657-X, Twayne). G K Hall.

Aldrich, Virgil. Philosophy of Art. (Illus.). 1963. pap. 9.95 ref. ed. (ISBN 0-13-663765-5). P-H.

Aldridge, A. Owen, ed. The Ibero-American Enlightenment: A Collection of Essays. LC 78-126520. 1971. 19.95 o.p. (ISBN 0-252-00122-2). U of Ill Pr.

Aldridge, Adele. Notpoems. LC 72-23824. 1976. pap. 5.95 o.p. (ISBN 0-915600-01-3, 0753-5). Swallow.

Aldridge, Alan & Ryder, George E. The Peacock Party. (Illus.). 1979. 7.95 o.p. (ISBN 0-670-54549-X, Studio). Viking Pr.

Aldridge, Alfred O. Franklin & His French Contemporaries. LC 76-21244. 260p. 1976. Repr. of 1957 ed. lib. bdg. 18.50x o.p. (ISBN 0-8371-9007-X, ALFF). Greenwood.

Aldridge, Bill G., compiled by. Science & Engineering Technician Curriculum. 1976. Set. 75.00. Natl Sci Tchrs.

Aldridge, D. C., jt. auth. see Turner, W. B.

Aldridge, James. The Broken Saddle. (Julia MacRae Ser.). 128p. (gr. 5 up). 1983. 8.95 (ISBN 0-531-04579-X, MacRae). Watts.

--Goodbye Un-America. LC 79-1029. 1979. 8.95 o.p. (ISBN 0-316-03114-3). Little.

Aldridge, John W. The American Novel & the Way We Live Now. 192p. 1983. 16.95 (ISBN 0-19-503198-9). Oxford U Pr.

Aldridge, John W., ed. Critiques & Essays on Modern Fiction, Nineteen Twenty to Nineteen Fifty-One: Representing the Achievement of Modern American & British Critics. 1952. text ed. 20.95x (ISBN 0-673-15650-8). Scott F.

Aldridge, M. V. English Quantifiers: A Study of Quantifying Expressions in Linguistic Science & Modern English Usage. 70.00x o.p. (ISBN 0-686-75546-4, Pub. by Avebury Pub England). State Mutual Bk.

Aldridge, Martha. Beyond Management. 180p. 1982. pap. 6.95 (ISBN 0-87414-025-0). U of Iowa Sch Soc Wk.

Aldridge, Robert C. First Strike. (Illus.). 300p. 1982. 20.00 (ISBN 0-89608-154-0); pap. 7.50 (ISBN 0-89608-155-9). South End Pr.

Aldridge, Sarah. Cytherea's Breath. 1982. 6.95 (ISBN 0-930044-02-9). Naiad Pr.

--The Latecomer. 1982. 5.00 (ISBN 0-930044-00-2). Naiad Pr.

Aldyne, Nathan. Vermilion. 1980. pap. 2.75 (ISBN 0-380-76596-9, 81570-2). Avon.

Aldyne, Nathen. Cobalt. 224p. 1982. pap. 2.75 (ISBN 0-380-81117-0, 81117-0). Avon.

Aledort, L. M., et al. Outpatient Medicine. LC 78-51280. 335p. 1979. text ed. 11.50 (ISBN 0-89004-354-X). Raven.

Alee, John G., ed. Webster's Dictionary for Everyday Use. pap. 2.50 o.p. (ISBN 0-06-463330-6, EH 330, EH). B&N NY.

Alefeld, F. Landwirtschaftliche Flora. 1966. Repr. of 1866 ed. lib. bdg. 48.80x (ISBN 3-87429-001-8). Lubrecht & Cramer.

Alefeld, Gotz & Herzberger, Jurgen. Introduction to Interval Computations. Rockne, Jon, tr. from Ger. (Computer Science & Applied Mathematics Ser.). Date not set. price not set (ISBN 0-12-049820-0). Acad Pr.

Alegria, Claribel. Flowers from the Volcano. Forche, Carolyn, tr. from Span. LC 82-70893. (Pitt Poetry Ser.). 101p. 1982. 12.95 (ISBN 0-8229-3469-8); pap. 5.95 (ISBN 0-8229-5344-7). U of Pittsburgh Pr.

Alegria, Fernando. The Chilean Spring Discoveries. Miller, Yvette, ed. Fredman, Stephen, tr. from Span. 160p. (Orig.). 1980. pap. 7.95 (ISBN 0-935480-00-5). Lat Am Lit Rev Pr.

Alegria, Fernando, et al, eds. Chilean Writers in Exile. Dagnino, Alfonso G. & Delano, Poli. LC 81-12567. (Crossing Press Translation Ser.). (Illus.). 224p. 1981. 16.95 (ISBN 0-89594-059-0); pap. 7.95 (ISBN 0-89594-060-4). Crossing Pr.

Aleichem, Sholom. The Adventures of Menahem-Mendl. LC 79-13506. 1979. pap. 4.95 (ISBN 0-399-50396-X, Perige). Putnam Pub Group.

--Inside Kasrilevke. LC 65-14829. (Illus.). 1968. 9.95x (ISBN 0-8052-3113-7); pap. 4.95 (ISBN 0-8052-0173-4). Schocken.

--Marienbad. Shevin, Aliza, tr. 192p. 1982. 13.95 (ISBN 0-399-12732-1). Putnam Pub Group.

--Old Country Tales. LC 79-13846. 1979. pap. 4.95 (ISBN 0-399-50394-3, Perige). Putnam Pub Group.

--Some Laughter, Some Tears. LC 79-13849. 1979. pap. 4.95 (ISBN 0-399-50395-1, Perige). Putnam Pub Group.

--Tevye's Daughters. 1959. 2.98 o.p. (ISBN 0-517-03053-5). Crown.

Aleixandre, Vicente. A Bird of Paper: Poems of Vicente Aleixandre. Barnstone, Willis & Garrison, David, trs. (International Poetry Ser.: Vol. 6). viii, 75p. (Span.). 1982. lib. bdg. 16.95x (ISBN 0-8214-0661-2, 82-84317); pap. 10.95 (ISBN 0-8214-0662-0, 82-84325). Ohio U Pr.

--A Longing for the Light: Selected Poems. Hyde, Lewis, ed. LC 78-2113. (Span. & Eng.). 1979. 13.45i (ISBN 0-06-010059-1, HarpT). Har-Row.

Alejandro, Carlos F. Diaz see Bacha, Edmar L. & Diaz Alejandro, Carlos F.

Alejandro, Reynaldo. The Philippine Cookbook. (Illus.). 288p. 1983. 17.95 (ISBN 0-698-11174-5, Coward). Putnam Pub Group.

Alejandro, Rufino, jt. ed. see Wolfenden, Elmer, Jr.

Aleksandrova, V. D. The Arctic & Antarctic. Love, Doris, tr. from Russ. LC 79-41600. (Illus.). 200p. 1980. 37.50 (ISBN 0-521-23119-1). Cambridge U Pr.

Aleksin, Anatoli. Alik the Detective. Carey, Bonnie, tr. from Russ. (gr. 7-9). 1977. 9.95 (ISBN 0-688-22117-3); PLB 9.55 (ISBN 0-688-32117-8). Morrow.

Aleksova, Blaga, jt. ed. see Wiseman, James.

Aleman Valdes, Miguel. Miguel Aleman contesta. LC 75-720022. (Mexico Ser.: No. 4). 66p. (Text in Spanish). 1976. pap. 2.95x (ISBN 0-292-75024-2). U of Tex Pr.

Alembert, Jean Le Rond. Histoire De L'academie De Berlin, Excerpts. Repr. of 1746 ed. 52.00 o.p. (ISBN 0-8287-0011-7). Clearwater Pub.

--Opuscules Mathematiques. Repr. of 1761 ed. 906.00 o.p. (ISBN 0-8287-0012-5). Clearwater Pub.

--Reflexions Sur la Cause Generale Des Vents. Repr. of 1747 ed. 103.00 o.p. (ISBN 0-8287-0013-3). Clearwater Pub.

Aleramo, Sibilla. A Woman. Delmar, Rosalind, tr. from Ital. 255p. 1983. pap. 5.95 (ISBN 0-520-04949-7, CAL 620). U of Cal Pr.

Alerich, Walter N. Electric Motor Control. 3rd ed. (Electric Trades Ser.). (Illus.). 272p. 1983. pap. text ed. 6.40 (ISBN 0-8273-1365-9); write for info instructor's guide (ISBN 0-8273-1366-7); lab manual avail. (ISBN 0-8273-1369-1). Delmar.

--Electricity Four: AC Motors, Controls, Alternators. LC 79-93325. (Electrical Trades Ser.). 215p. 1981. pap. 9.60 (ISBN 0-8273-1363-2); instructor's guide 2.75 (ISBN 0-8273-1364-0). Delmar.

--Electricity Three: DC Motors & Generators, Controls, Transformers. LC 79-93324. (Electrical Trades Ser.). 224p. 1981. pap. 9.60 (ISBN 0-8273-1361-6); instructor's guide 2.75 (ISBN 0-8273-1362-4). Delmar.

Alers, Benjamin. Your America - My America. 1978. 4.95 o.p. (ISBN 0-533-03046-3). Vantage.

Alesi, Gladys. How to Prepare for the U. S. Citizenship Test. 1982. pap. 6.95 (ISBN 0-8120-2525-3). Barron.

Al-Esman, Mashef, ed. Quran. (Arabic.). 20.00x (ISBN 0-86685-135-6). Intl Bk Ctr.

Al-Esmani, Abed. Batal Al Abtal: Novel in Arabic. pap. 6.00x (ISBN 0-86685-139-9). Intl Bk Ctr.

Aletti, Ann & Brinkley, Jeanne. Altering Ready-to-Wear Fashions. (gr. 10-12). 1976. text ed. 19.32 (ISBN 0-87002-083-8); avail. tchr's guide 1.28 (ISBN 0-87002-110-9). Bennett IL.

Alex, Ben, jt. auth. see Alex, Marlee.

Alex, Marlee & Alex, Ben. Grandpa & Me. 44p. (Orig.). (gr. k-2). 1983. 7.95 (ISBN 0-87123-257-X). Bethany Hse.

--I Love You. 60p. 1983. 10.95 (ISBN 0-87123-262-6). Bethany Hse.

Alex, Nicholas. New York Cops Talk Back: A Study of a Beleaguered Minority. LC 76-1852. 225p. 1976. 21.95 o.p. (ISBN 0-471-02055-9, Pub. by Wiley-Interscience). Wiley.

Alex, William, ed. see Miliutin, Nikolai A.

Alexader Hamilton Institute, Inc. Administracion Por Objectivos: Sistema Moderno Para Lograr Resultados. Jenks, James M., ed. (Illus.). 71p. (Orig., Span.). 1978. pap. 54.40 (ISBN 0-86604-033-1). Hamilton Inst.

Alexander. International Violence. 256p. 1982. 24.95 (ISBN 0-03-061922-X). Praeger.

Alexander, A. G. Sugarcane Physiology. 1973. 121.50 (ISBN 0-444-41016-3). Elsevier.

Alexander, A. L., compiled by. Poems That Touch the Heart. rev. & enl. ed. LC 56-11498. 1956. 12.95 (ISBN 0-385-04401-1). Doubleday.

Alexander, Alan. Politics of Local Government in the United Kingdom. LC 81-20872. 1982. pap. 50.00 cancelled (ISBN 0-582-29541-6). Longman.

Alexander, Ann, jt. auth. see Dodson, Fitzhugh.

Alexander, Anne. ABC of Cars & Trucks. (ps-k). 1971. 8.95a (ISBN 0-385-07576-6); PLB (ISBN 0-385-07720-3); pap. 1.95 (ISBN 0-385-01061-3). Doubleday.

Alexander, Arch. The Joy of Golf. 341p. 1982. write for info. (ISBN 0-941760-00-6). Pendulum Bks.

Alexander, C. P. The Crane Flies of California. (Bulletin of the California Insect Survey: Vol. 8). 1967. pap. 12.50x (ISBN 0-520-09033-0). U of Cal Pr.

Alexander, Christine, ed. Bibliography of the Manuscripts of Charlotte Bronte. 1983. 45.00X (ISBN 0-930466-56-X). Meckler Pub.

Alexander, Christopher. The Production of Houses. (Illus.). 1983. 30.00 (ISBN 0-19-503223-3). Oxford U Pr.

Alexander, Curtis. Doc Ben Speaks Out. (Monograph: No. 1). 52p. 1982. pap. 2.95 (ISBN 0-938818-04-X, Pub by Alkebulan Hist Res Soc). ECA Assoc.

Alexander, D. A., jt. ed. see Haldane, J. D.

Alexander, Dale. Arthritis & Common Sense. 5.95x (ISBN 0-686-29829-2). Cancer Control Soc.

--Common Cold & Common Sense. 1971. 8.95x o.p. (ISBN 0-686-36343-4). Cancer Control Soc.

--Dry Skin & Common Sense. 8.25x (ISBN 0-911638-05-9). Cancer Control Soc.

--Good Health & Common Sense. 9.95x (ISBN 0-911638-03-2). Cancer Control Soc.

Alexander, Daniel E. & Messer, Andrew C. FORTRAN Four Pocket Handbook. 96p. (Orig.). 1972. pap. 4.95 (ISBN 0-07-001015-3, SP). McGraw.

Alexander, David & Alexander, Patricia. Eerdmans' Handbook to the Bible. 1973. 24.95 (ISBN 0-8028-3436-1). Eerdmans.

Alexander, David G. Atlantic Canada & Confederation: Essays in Canadian Political Economy. 160p. 1983. 20.00x (ISBN 0-8020-2487-4); pap. 6.00 (ISBN 0-8020-6512-0). U of Toronto Pr.

Alexander, David M. The Chocolate Spy. LC 78-3579. 1978. 8.95 o.p. (ISBN 0-698-10909-0, Coward). Putnam Pub Group.

Alexander, Donald C. Arkansas Plantation, 1920-1942. 1943. text ed. 32.50x (ISBN 0-686-83477-1). Elliots Bks.

Alexander, Douglas G., jt. auth. see Alexander, Gordon.

Alexander, E. Curtis. Adam Clayton Powell, Jr. A Black Power Political Educator. LC 81-69171. (African American Educator Ser.: Vol. II). (Illus.). 120p. (Orig.). 1982. pap. 6.95 (ISBN 0-938818-03-1). ECA Assoc.

Alexander, Edward. Isaac Bashevis Singer. (World Authors Ser.). 1980. lib. bdg. 11.95 (ISBN 0-8057-6424-0, Twayne). G K Hall.

--John Morley. (English Authors Ser.: No. 147). lib. bdg. 13.95 o.p. (ISBN 0-8057-1404-9, Twayne). G K Hall.

Alexander, Edward P. Museum Masters. Date not set. text ed. price not set (ISBN 0-910050-68-6). AASLH.

--Museums in Motion. LC 78-1189. 1978. 17.50 (ISBN 0-910050-39-2); pap. 12.50 (ISBN 0-910050-35-X). AASLH.

Alexander, Edwin P. Civil War Railroads & Models. (Illus.). 1977. 15.00 o.p. (ISBN 0-517-53073-2, C N Potter Bks). Crown.

Alexander, F. Matthias. The Resurrection of the Body. 256p. 1974. pap. 4.95 o.s.i. (ISBN 0-440-57374-2, Delta). Dell.

Alexander, Frank. I'm in Love with a Mannequin. LC 76-8767. 1976. pap. 1.95 (ISBN 0-916956-00-8). Kokono.

Alexander, Frank, ed. see Hall, Tom.

Alexander, Franz & Healy, William. Roots of Crime: Psychoanalytic Studies. LC 69-14908. (Criminology, Law Enforcement, & Social Problems Ser.: No. 68). 1969. Repr. of 1935 ed. 15.00x (ISBN 0-87585-068-5). Patterson Smith.

Alexander, G. M. The Prelude to the Truman Doctrine: British Policy in Greece, 1944-47. 1982. 46.00x (ISBN 0-19-822653-5). Oxford U Pr.

Alexander, George L., jt. auth. see Gordon, Craig A.

Alexander, George M. The Handbook of Biblical Personalities. 320p. 1981. pap. 6.95 (ISBN 0-8164-2316-4). Seabury.

Alexander, Gordon & Alexander, Douglas G. Biology. 9th ed. LC 77-118098. (Illus.). 1970. pap. 5.95 (ISBN 0-06-460004-1, CO 4, COS). B&N NY.

Alexander, H. G., ed. see Leibniz.

Alexander Hamilton Institute, Inc. Administracao Por Objectivos: Sistema Moderno Para Obter Resultados. Jenks, James M., ed. (Illus.). 68p. (Orig., Portuguese.). 1978. pap. 56.15 (ISBN 0-86604-034-X). Hamilton Inst.

--El Analisis del Rendimiento de los Vendedores. Jenks, James M., ed. (Illus.). 78p. (Orig., Span.). 1977. pap. 72.60 (ISBN 0-86604-019-6). Hamilton Inst.

--Como Aumentar a Productividade. Jenks, James M., ed. (Illus.). 69p. (Portuguese.). 1979. pap. 60.00 (ISBN 0-86604-025-0). Hamilton Inst.

--Como Aumentar la Productividad. Jenks, James M., ed. (Illus.). 77p. (Orig., Span.). 1977. pap. 53.40 (ISBN 0-86604-024-2). Hamilton Inst.

--Como los Ejecutivos Toman Decisiones. Jenks, James M., ed. (Illus.). 79p. (Orig., Span.). 1976. pap. 49.50 (ISBN 0-86604-006-4). Hamilton Inst.

--Como Motivar a Su Equipo De Ventas. Jenks, James M., ed. 103p. (Orig., Span.). 1977. pap. 59.10 (ISBN 0-86604-017-X, A843698). Hamilton Inst.

--Las Dotes De Supervision y Su Perfeccionamiento. Jenks, James M., ed. (Illus.). 91p. (Orig., Span.). 1977. pap. 54.10 (ISBN 0-86604-029-3, A896533). Hamilton Inst.

--El Ejecutivo Bajo Stress. Jenks, James M., ed. (Illus.). 72p. (Orig., Span.). 1976. pap. 50.50x (ISBN 0-86604-008-0, A783158). Hamilton Inst.

--La Elaboracion Electronica De Datos: Guia Del Ejecutivo. Jenks, James M., ed. (Illus.). 98p. (Orig., Span.). 1977. pap. 55.00 (ISBN 0-86604-076-5, A927396). Hamilton Inst.

--Executive's Guide to Electronic Data Processing. Jenks, James M., ed. (Illus.). 98p. (Orig.). 1977. pap. 54.75 (ISBN 0-86604-075-7, A907657). Hamilton Inst.

--Executivo Sob Tensao. Jenks, James M., ed. (Illus.). 71p. (Orig., Portuguese.). 1978. pap. 52.50 (ISBN 0-86604-009-9). Hamilton Inst.

--How Executives Make Decisions. Jenks, James M., ed. (Illus.). 79p. (Orig.). 1976. pap. 49.25 (ISBN 0-86604-005-6, A783159). Hamilton Inst.

--How to Increase Productivity. Jenks, James M., ed. (Illus.). 69p. (Orig.). 1977. pap. 53.25 (ISBN 0-86604-023-4, A866692). Hamilton Inst.

--How to Motivate Your Sales Force. 96p. (Orig.). 1977. pap. 58.85 (ISBN 0-86604-016-1, A829658). Hamilton Inst.

--Improving Supervisory Skills. Jenks, James M., ed. (Illus.). 96p. (Orig.). 1977. pap. 53.75 (ISBN 0-86604-028-5, A896534). Hamilton Inst.

--Management by Objectives: A Modern System for Getting Results. Jenks, James M., ed. (Illus.). 66p. (Orig.). 1978. pap. 54.15 (ISBN 0-86604-032-3). Hamilton Inst.

--Manual De Practica De Credito y Cobranzas. Jenks, James M., ed. (Illus.). 93p. (Orig., Span.). 1977. pap. 53.00 (ISBN 0-86604-013-7, A833209). Hamilton Inst.

--Manual De Practica Moderna De Compras. Jenks, James M., ed. (Illus.). 88p. (Orig., Span.). 1977. pap. 59.00 (ISBN 0-86604-021-8, A872197). Hamilton Inst.

--Manual De Practica Moderna De Comprias. Jenks, James M., ed. (Illus.). 84p. (Orig., Portugese.). 1978. pap. 59.75 (ISBN 0-86604-022-6, TX150-973). Hamilton Inst.

--Manual De Practicas De Credito E Cobrancas. Jenks, James M., ed. (Illus.). 90p. (Orig., Portuguese.). 1978. pap. 56.25 (ISBN 0-86604-014-5, TX70-795). Hamilton Inst.

--Manual De Practicas Orcamentaries Modernas. Jenks, James M., ed. (Illus.). 84p. (Orig., Portuguese.). 1978. pap. 60.25 (ISBN 0-86604-002-1, TX-15-336). Hamilton Inst.

--Manual De Practica Presupuestaria Moderna. Jenks, James M., ed. (Illus.). 90p. (Orig., Span.). 1976. pap. 58.60 (ISBN 0-86604-001-3, A783161). Hamilton Inst.

--The Manual of Modern Budgetary Practices. Jenks, James M., ed. (Illus.). 85p. (Orig.). 1976. pap. 58.35 (ISBN 0-86604-000-5, A783160). Hamilton Inst.

--The Manual of Modern Credit & Collection Practices. (Illus.). 83p. (Orig.). 1976. pap. 52.75 (ISBN 0-86604-012-9, A811915). Hamilton Inst.

--Manual of Modern Purchasing Practices. Jenks, James M., ed. (Illus.). 83p. (Orig.). 1977. pap. 58.75 (ISBN 0-86604-020-X, A866693). Hamilton Inst.

--Measuring Morale: Key to Increased Productivity. (Illus.). 53p. (Orig.). 1976. pap. 54.25x (ISBN 0-86604-010-2, A806007). Hamilton Inst.

--La Medicion De la Moral: Clave Para Aumentar la Productividad. Jenks, James M., ed. (Illus.). 50p. (Orig., Span.). 1976. pap. 54.60 (ISBN 0-86604-011-0, A811102). Hamilton Inst.

--Performance Appraisal for Salesmen. Jenks, James M., ed. (Illus.). 68p. (Orig.). 1977. pap. 72.25 (ISBN 0-86604-018-8, A840845). Hamilton Inst.

--Practicas Modernas De Reduccionde Costos. Jenks, James M., ed. (Illus.). 83p. (Orig., Span.). 1977. pap. 53.70 (ISBN 0-86604-027-7, A893317). Hamilton Inst.

Alexander, Harold H. Design: Criteria for Decisions. (Illus.). 640p. 1976. text ed. 24.95x (ISBN 0-02-301660-4, 30166). Macmillan.

Alexander, Herbert. Financing Politics: Money, Elections & Political Reform. 2nd ed. O'Connor, Ann & Woy, Jean, eds. LC 80-10844. (Politics & Public Policy Ser.). 210p. 1980. pap. 8.50 (ISBN 0-87187-182-3). Congr Quarterly.

--Financing the Nineteen Seventy-Six Election. Woy, Jean, ed. LC 79-9099. 896p. 1979. 35.00 (ISBN 0-87187-180-7). Congr Quarterly.

Alexander, Herbert E. Parties, Pacs & Political Finance Reform: How & Why has Election Financing Reform Gone Awry? What to do About it? (Vital Issues Ser.: Vol. XXXII, No. 1). 0.80 (ISBN 0-686-84152-2). Ctr Info Am.

Alexander, Herbert E. & Haggerty, Brian A. The Federal Election Campaign Act: After a Decade of Political Reform. LC 81-17113. 135p. 1981. pap. 5.00 (ISBN 0-87436-173-7). ABC-Clio.

--Financing the Nineteen-Eighty Election. LC 82-48863. 1983. price not set (ISBN 0-669-06375-4). Lexington Bks.

--Political Reform in California: How Has it Worked? LC 80-22201. 71p. 1980. pap. 3.00 (ISBN 0-87436-174-5, 80-22201). ABC-Clio.

Alexander, Herbert E. & Lambert, Richard D., eds. Political Finance: Reform & Reality. LC 75-45503. (Annals Ser.: No. 425). 250p. 1976. 15.00 (ISBN 0-87761-200-5); pap. 7.95 (ISBN 0-87761-201-3). Am Acad Pol Soc Sci.

Alexander, Holmes. Equivocal Men: Tales of the Establishment. LC 64-25260. 1964. 7.00 (ISBN 0-88279-205-9). Western Islands.

--How to Read the Federalist. 1961. pap. 2.00 (ISBN 0-88279-124-9). Western Islands.

--To Covet Honor. LC 77-75276. 1977. 12.00 (ISBN 0-88279-232-6). Western Islands.

Alexander Institute, Inc. The Executive Under Stress. Jenks, Jamess M., ed. (Illus.). 71p. (Orig.). 1976. pap. 50.25x (ISBN 0-86604-007-2, A783157). Hamilton Inst.

--Modern Cost Reduction Practices. Jenks, James M., ed. (Illus.). 83p. (Orig.). 1977. pap. 53.45 (ISBN 0-86604-026-9, A889458). Hamilton Inst.

Alexander, J. A. Acts of the Apostles, 2 vols. in 1. (Banner of Truth Geneva Series Commentaries). 1980. 21.95 (ISBN 0-85151-309-3). Banner of Truth.

Alexander, J. Estill, et al. Teaching Reading. 1979. text ed. 18.95 (ISBN 0-316-03129-1); tchr's ed. avail. (ISBN 0-316-03130-5). Little.

Alexander, J. H. Marmion: Studies in Interpretation & Composition. (Salzburg-Romantic Reassessment Ser.: No. 30). 257p. 1981. pap. text ed. 25.00x (ISBN 0-391-02768-9, 40662, Pub. by Salzburg Austria). Humanities.

Alexander, J. J. A History of Manuscripts Illuminated in the British Isles: Insular Manuscripts Sixth to Ninth Century, Vol. 1. (Illus.). 1978. 74.00x (ISBN 0-19-921008-X). Oxford U Pr.

Alexander, J. J., jt. auth. see Pacht, Otto.

Alexander, J. M. Strength of Materials: Fundamentals, Vol. 1. LC 80-42009. (Mechanical Engineering Ser.). 267p. 1981. 84.95 o.p. (ISBN 0-470-27119-1). Halsted Pr.

Alexander, J. M., jt. auth. see Ford, High.

Alexander, J. W. Plan Para Memorizar las Escrituras. Orig. Title: Fire in My Bones. 1981. Repr. of 1979 ed. 1.75 (ISBN 0-311-03660-0). Casa Bautista.

Alexander, Jack, ed. The Book of the Secrets of Enoch. (Illus.). 93p. 1972. 5.50 (ISBN 0-914732-04-8). Bro Life Inc.

Alexander, James & Parsons, Bruce V. Functional Family Therapy. LC 81-17058. (Counseling Ser.). 233p. 1982. text ed. 10.95 (ISBN 0-8185-0485-4). Brooks-Cole.

Alexander, James A. A Brief Narrative of the Case & Trial of John Peter Zenger, Printer of the New York Weekly. 2nd ed. (Belknap Ser.). (Illus.). 953p. 1969. 15.00 (ISBN 0-674-37501-7). Harvard U Pr.

Alexander, James W. Medieval World. LC 78-67276. 1979. pap. text ed. 3.25x (ISBN 0-88273-320-6). Forum Pr IL.

Alexander, Jeffrey A. Nursing Unit Organization: Its Effects on Staff Professionalism. Kalisch, Philip & Kalisch, Beatrice, eds. LC 82-13485. (Studies in Nursing Management: No. 4). 151p. 1982. 34.95 (ISBN 0-8357-1369-5, Pub. by UMI Res Pr). Univ Microfilms.

Alexander, Jeffrey C. Theoretical Logic in Sociology: The Antinomies of Classical Thought: Marx & Durkheim, Vol. 2. LC 82-40096. 560p. 1982. 35.00x (ISBN 0-520-04481-9). U of Cal Pr.

--Theoretical Logic in Sociology, Vol. 3: The Classical Attempt at Theoretical Synthesis: Max Weber. LC 75-17305. 224p. 1983. text ed. 25.00x (ISBN 0-520-04482-7). U of Cal Pr.

Alexander, Jerome & Elins, Roberta. Be Your Own Makeup Artist: Jerome Alexander's Complete Makeup Workshop. LC 82-48107. (Illus.). 128p. 1983. 14.95 (ISBN 0-06-015088-2, HarpT). Har-Row.

Alexander, John J. & Steffel, Margaret J. Chemistry in the Laboratory. 374p. 1976. pap. text ed. 12.95 (ISBN 0-15-506466-5, HC); instructor's manual 1.00 (ISBN 0-15-506469-X). HarBraceJ.

Alexander, John W. & Gibson, L. Economic Geography. 2nd ed. 1979. 29.95 (ISBN 0-13-225151-5). P-H.

Alexander, Joseph. Commentary on the Acts of the Apostles. 1979. 27.50 (ISBN 0-86524-025-6, 4401). Klock & Klock.

--Commentary on the Gospel of Mark. 1980. 16.75 (ISBN 0-86524-018-3, 4101). Klock & Klock.

Alexander, Joseph A. Isaiah, 2 Vols. 1981. Set. lib. bdg. 29.95 (ISBN 0-86524-072-8, 2302). Klock & Klock.

Alexander, Joy, tr. see Nikkyo, Niwano.

Alexander, Karen. Palaces of Desire. LC 78-614. 1978. 9.95 o.p. (ISBN 0-698-10885-X, Coward). Putnam Pub Group.

Alexander, Karl. A Private Investigation. 1980. 10.95 o.s.i. (ISBN 0-440-06834-7). Delacorte.

Alexander, Kate. Fields of Battle. 1982. pap. 3.50 (ISBN 0-451-11611-9, AE1611, Sig). NAL.

--Friends & Enemies. 304p. 1983. 12.95 (ISBN 0-312-30545-1). St Martin.

Alexander, L. G. Developing Skills: Student's Book. (New Concept English Ser.). (Illus.). 145p. 1964. pap. 5.75 (ISBN 0-582-52331-1); drills tapescript 2.50 (ISBN 0-582-52344-3); suppl. written exercises 2.25 (ISBN 0-582-52336-2). Longman.

--For & Against. (English As a Second Language Bk.). 1975. pap. text ed. 3.75x (ISBN 0-582-52306-0). Longman.

--New Concept English, 4 pts. Incl. First Things First: An Integrated Course for Beginners. pap. text ed. 5.75x student bk. complete (ISBN 0-582-52329-X); pap. text ed. 3.75x student bk. pt. 1 (ISBN 0-582-52345-1); pap. text ed. 3.75x student bk. pt. 2 (ISBN 0-582-52346-X); tchr's bk. 11.95x (ISBN 0-582-52333-8); drills tapescript 2.75x (ISBN 0-582-52342-7); suppl. written exercises 2.50x (ISBN 0-582-52474-1). (English As a Second Language Bk.). 1967. Longman.

--Question & Answer: Graded Oral Comprehension. new ed. (English As a Second Language Bk.). 1977. pap. text ed. 4.75x (ISBN 0-582-55206-0). Longman.

Alexander, L. G. & Cornelius, E. T., Jr. COMP: Exercises in Comprehension & Composition. (English As a Second Language Bk.). (Illus.). 1978. pap. text ed. 3.55x (ISBN 0-582-79703-9). Longman.

Alexander, L. G see Allen, W. S.

Alexander, L. G., ed. Longman Integrated Comprehension & Composition Series, 6 stages, Wave 1. Incl. Stage 1. Round the World. (Nonfiction). pap. 1.90x (ISBN 0-582-52295-1); Stage 3. Strange but True. (Nonfiction). pap. 2.10x (ISBN 0-582-52299-4); Stage 4. Spare Time. (Nonfiction). pap. 2.10x (ISBN 0-582-52289-7); Stage 4. The Search. (Fiction). pap. 2.10x (ISBN 0-582-52288-9); Stage 5. Flight. (Nonfiction). pap. 2.25x (ISBN 0-582-52291-9); Stage 6. People at Work. (Nonfiction). pap. 2.30x (ISBN 0-582-52293-5). (English As a Second Language Bk.). 1971-81. Longman.

--Longman Integrated Comprehension & Composition Series, 6 stages, Wave 2. Incl. Stage 1. All in a Year. (Nonfiction). pap. 1.75 (ISBN 0-582-55330-X); Stage 1. It's in the Bag. (Fiction). pap. 1.90x (ISBN 0-582-55326-1); Stage 2. Mysteries. (Nonfiction). pap. 1.90x (ISBN 0-582-55331-8); Stage 2. Egyptian Cat. (Fiction). pap. 1.90x (ISBN 0-582-55327-X); Stage 3. Energy. (Nonfiction). pap. 2.10x (ISBN 0-582-55332-6); Stage 3. A Week by the Sea. (Fiction). pap. 2.00x (ISBN 0-582-55328-8); Stage 4. Food Matters. (Nonfiction). pap. 2.10x (ISBN 0-582-55333-4); Stage 4. Nobody Sings Like Ted. (Fiction). pap. 2.00x (ISBN 0-582-55329-6); Stage 5. Cities. (Nonfiction). pap. 2.30x (ISBN 0-582-55336-9); Stage 5. Untitled. (Fiction). pap. price not set (ISBN 0-582-55334-2); Stage 6. Animal Behavior. (Nonfiction). pap. 2.30x (ISBN 0-582-55337-7); Stage 6. Untitled. (Fiction). pap. price not set (ISBN 0-582-55335-0). (English As a Second Language Bk.). 1971-81. write for info. tchr's bk. & key. Longman.

Alexander, L. G., et al. Take a Stand: Discussion Topics for Intermediate Adult Students. (English As a Second Language Bk.). (Illus.). 1978. pap. text ed. 2.95x (ISBN 0-582-79721-7); cassettes 9.95x (ISBN 0-582-79722-5). Longman.

Alexander, Laurence A., ed. How to Achieve Downtown Action in the 80's: Realistic Private & Public Implementation Techniques. LC 82-71571. 120p. 1982. pap. 45.00 (ISBN 0-915910-19-5). Downtown Res.

Alexander, Leroy E., jt. auth. see Klug, Harold P.

Alexander, Lloyd. The High King. (YA) (gr. 7-12). 1980. pap. 2.50 (ISBN 0-440-93574-1, LFL). Dell.

--The Krestel. 256p. (gr. 5 up). 1982. 10.95 (ISBN 0-525-45110-2, 01063-320). Dutton.

--Marvelous Misadventures of Sebastian. LC 70-166879. (gr. 4 up). 1970. 14.95 (ISBN 0-525-34739-9, 01451-440); pap. 1.95 o.p. (ISBN 0-525-45009-2). Dutton.

--Westmark. LC 80-22242. (gr. 5 up). 1981. 10.95 (ISBN 0-525-42335-4, 01063-320). Dutton.

Alexander, Lloyd, tr. see Sartre, Jean-Paul.

Alexander, Lynn, ed. see Atwood, Evangeline.

Alexander, Lynn, ed. see MacArthur, William J.

Alexander, Marc. Phantom Britain. (Illus.). 256p. 1976. 15.00 o.p. (ISBN 0-584-10210-0). Transatlantic.

Alexander, Margaret Y. The River Knows My Name. 224p. (Orig.). 1981. pap. 2.25 o.p. (ISBN 0-523-41460-9). Pinnacle Bks.

Alexander, Marguerite. Kirsty's Secrets: A Yearly Round of Scottish Fare. LC 58-59766. (Illus.). 1958. 4.95 o.p. (ISBN 0-910244-14-6). Blair.

Alexander, Martha. How My Library Grew, By Dinah. (Illus.). 32p. 1983. 12.00 (ISBN 0-8242-0679-7). Wilson.

--I'll Protect You from the Jungle Beasts. LC 73-6015. (Illus.). 32p. (ps-2). 1973. 8.95 (ISBN 0-8037-4308-4); PLB 8.89 (ISBN 0-8037-4309-2). Dial Bks Young.

--Maybe a Monster. LC 68-28732. (Illus.). 32p. (ps-2). 1968. PLB 7.95 (ISBN 0-8037-5508-2); PLB 7.89 (ISBN 0-8037-5513-9). Dial Bks Young.

--Move Over, Twerp. (Pied Piper Bks.). (Illus.). 32p. (gr. k-3). 1982. pap. 3.25 (ISBN 0-8037-5814-6). Dial.

--Pigs Say Oink. (Illus.). 32p. (ps-3). 1981. PLB 4.99 (ISBN 0-394-93838-0); pap. 1.50 (ISBN 0-394-83838-6). Random.

Alexander, Martin. Introduction to Soil Microbiology. 2nd ed. LC 77-1319. 467p. 1977. text ed. 28.95 (ISBN 0-471-02179-2); arabic translation avail. Wiley.

Alexander, Mary M. & Brown, Marie S. Pediatric History Taking & Physical Diagnosis for Nurses. 2nd ed. (Illus.). 1979. text ed. 24.95 (ISBN 0-07-001019-6, HP); pap. text ed. 9.95 (ISBN 0-07-001018-8). McGraw.

Alexander, Michael. The Poetic Achievement of Ezra Pound. LC 78-59449. 1979. 26.50x (ISBN 0-520-03739-1); pap. 6.95 (ISBN 0-520-04507-6). U of Cal Pr.

Alexander, Michael, intro. by. Celestial Visitations: The Art of Gilbert Williams. (Illus.). 96p. 15.95 o.p. (ISBN 0-517-53899-7, Harmony); pap. 8.95 o.p. (ISBN 0-517-53900-4, Harmony). Crown.

Alexander, Milton J. Information Systems Analysis: Theory & Application. LC 73-89599. (Illus.). 432p. 1974. text ed. 22.95 (ISBN 0-574-19100-3, 13-2100); instr's guide avail. (ISBN 0-574-19101-1, 13-2101). SRA.

Alexander, Morris. Israel & Me. LC 76-40091. 1977. 10.00 o.p. (ISBN 0-8467-0265-7, Pub. by Two Continents). Hippocrene Bks.

Alexander, Nigel. Poison, Play & Duel: A Study in "Hamlet". LC 79-130871. (Illus.). xii, 212p. 1971. 14.50x o.p. (ISBN 0-8032-0772-7). U of Nebr Pr.

Alexander, Pat. Eerdmans' Atlas of the Bible with A-Z Guide to Places. (Illus.). 68p. 1983. 7.95 (ISBN 0-8028-3583-X). Eerdmans.

Alexander, Patricia, jt. auth. see Alexander, David.

Alexander, Paul J. Ancient World: To A.D. 300. 2nd ed. (Orig.). 1968. pap. text ed. 13.95x (ISBN 0-02-301650-7, 30165). Macmillan.

Alexander, R. M. Biomechanics. 1975. pap. 6.50x (ISBN 0-412-13080-7, Pub. by Chapman & Hall). Methuen Inc.

Alexander, R. McNeill. The Chordates. 2nd. ed. (Illus.). 500p. 1981. text ed. 69.50 (ISBN 0-521-23658-4); pap. text ed. 21.95 (ISBN 0-521-28141-5). Cambridge U Pr.

--The Invertebrates. LC 78-6275. (Illus.). 1979. 75.00 (ISBN 0-521-22120-X); pap. 21.95x (ISBN 0-521-29361-8). Cambridge U Pr.

--Optima for Animals. 120p. 1982. pap. text ed. 13.95 (ISBN 0-7131-2843-7). E Arnold.

Alexander, R. McNeill & Goldspink, G., eds. Mechanics & Energetics of Animal Locomotion. LC 77-6737. 346p. 1977. 47.00x (ISBN 0-412-13630-9, Pub. by Chapman & Hall). Methuen Inc.

Alexander, Ralph. Ezekiel. (Everyman's Bible Commentary Ser). 160p. (Orig.). 1976. pap. 4.50 (ISBN 0-8024-2026-5). Moody.

Alexander, Richard D. Darwinism & Human Affairs. LC 78-65829. (Jessie & John Danz Lecture Ser.). (Illus.). 342p. 1980. 14.95 (ISBN 0-295-95641-0); pap. 9.95 (ISBN 0-295-95901-0). U of Wash Pr.

Alexander, Robert J. Bolivia: Past, Present, & Future of Its Politics. Wesson, Robert, ed. (Politics in Latin America Ser.). 184p. 1982. 22.95 (ISBN 0-03-061762-6). Praeger.

--Bolivian National Revolution. LC 73-20876. (Illus.). 302p. 1974. Repr. of 1958 ed. lib. bdg. 20.00x (ISBN 0-8371-5730-7, ALBN). Greenwood.

--Romulo Betancourt & the Transformation of Venezuela. LC 81-14684. 600p. 1982. 19.95 (ISBN 0-87855-450-5). Transaction Bks.

--The Tragedy of Chile. LC 77-91101. (Contributions in Political Science: No. 8). 1978. lib. bdg. 35.00x (ISBN 0-313-20034-3, ATC/). Greenwood.

Alexander, Robert J., ed. Political Parties of the Americas: Canada, Latin America, & the West Indies. LC 81-6952. (The Greenwood Historical Encyclopedia of the World's Political Parties). (Illus.). 736p. 1982. lib. bdg. 65.00x (ISBN 0-313-21474-3, APA/). Greenwood.

Alexander, Roy, jt. auth. see Roth, Charles B.

Alexander, Samuel. Philosophical & Literary Pieces. LC 74-98207. Repr. of 1939 ed. lib. bdg. 18.50x (ISBN 0-8371-3241-X, ALPL). Greenwood.

Alexander, Shana. Very Much a Lady: The Untold Story of Jean Harris & Dr. Herman Tarnower. 1983. 17.50 (ISBN 0-316-03125-9). Little.

Alexander, Sidney. The Hand of Michaelangelo. LC 77-154999. 693p. 1977. pap. 10.95x (ISBN 0-8214-0235-8, 82-82378). Ohio U Pr.

--Lions & Foxes: Men & Ideas of the Italian Renaissance. LC 77-92250. (Illus.). xi, 375p. 1978. 20.00x (ISBN 0-8214-0404-0, 82-82956); pap. text ed. 9.00x (ISBN 0-8214-0394-X, 82-82964). Ohio U Pr.

--Marc Chagall: A Biography. LC 77-16526. (Illus.). 1978. 14.95 o.p. (ISBN 0-399-11894-2). Putnam Pub Group.

--Michelangelo the Florentine. LC 65-25109. 464p. 1965. pap. 9.50 (ISBN 0-8214-0236-6, 82-82386). Ohio U Pr.

Alexander, Stan & Broussard, Sharon. An Analysis of the 1973 Atlanta Elections. 1973. 3.00 (ISBN 0-686-38001-0). Voter Ed Proj.

Alexander, Stella. Church & State in Yugoslavia Since Nineteen Forty-Five. LC 77-88668. (Soviet & East European Studies). 1979. 47.50 (ISBN 0-521-21942-6). Cambridge U Pr.

Alexander, Sue. Finding Your First Job. LC 79-26487. (Illus.). (gr. 9 up). 1980. 8.95 (ISBN 0-525-29725-1, 0869-260, Skinny Bk); pap. 2.50 (ISBN 0-525-45049-1, Skinny Bk). Dutton.

--Nadia the Willful. LC 82-12602. (Illus.). 48p. (gr. k-3). 1983. 10.95 (ISBN 0-394-85265-6); PLB 10.99 (ISBN 0-394-95265-0). Pantheon.

Alexander, Thea. Macro Study Series. Incl. How to Develop Your Macro Awareness; How to Live a Macro Lifestyle; How to Interpret Your Dreams from a Macro View; The Prophetess: Conversations with Rana; Simulataneous Time: Your Parallel Lives, Twin Souls, & Soul Mates; How to Do Personal Evolution Tutoring; The Macro Study Guide & Workbook. 28.00 set (ISBN 0-913080-12-8). Macro Bks.

--Twenty-One Fifty A.D. 281p. (Orig.). 1971. pap. 4.25 (ISBN 0-913080-03-9). Macro Bks.

Alexander, Thomas B. Thomas A. R. Nelson of East Tennessee. (Illus.). 200p. 1956. 14.50x (ISBN 0-87402-007-7). U of Tenn Pr.

Alexander, Vicente. World Alone. Hyde, Lewis & Unger, David, trs. (Illus.). 76p. 1982. 17.50x (ISBN 0-915778-41-6); deluxe ed. 125.00x (ISBN 0-686-96847-6). Penmaen Pr.

Alexander, Wilfrid B. Birds of the Ocean. (Putnam's Nature Field Bks.). (Illus.). 1963. 6.95 o.p. (ISBN 0-399-10089-X). Putnam Pub Group.

Alexander, Yonah & Nanes, Allan. The United States & Iran: A Documentary History. 524p. Date not set. lib. bdg. 24.00 (ISBN 0-89093-378-2, Aletheia Bks); pap. 8.00 (ISBN 0-686-96909-X, Aletheia Bks). U Pubns Amer.

Alexander, Yonah & Friedlander, Robert A., eds. Self-Determination: National, Regional, & Global Dimensions. (Special Studies in National & International Terrorism). 1980. lib. bdg. 32.50 (ISBN 0-89158-090-5). Westview.

Alexander, Yonah & Myers, Kenneth, eds. Terrorism in Europe. LC 81-21306. 230p. 1982. 25.00x (ISBN 0-312-79250-6). St Martin.

Alexander, Yonah, jt. ed. see Freedman, Lawrence Z.

Alexander, Yonah, et al, eds. Terrorism: Theory & Practice. (Westview Special Studies in National & International Terrorism). 200p. 1979. lib. bdg. 27.50 (ISBN 0-89158-089-1); pap. text ed. 12.00 (ISBN 0-86531-041-6). Westview.

Alexander, Ziggi, ed. see Seacole, Mary.

Alexanderescu, Sorin, ed. Transformational Grammar & the Rumanian Language. (PDR Press Publications on Rumanian Ser.: No. 1). 1977. pap. text ed. 9.25x o.p. (ISBN 90-316-0144-6). Humanities.

Alexanderson, Gerald L., jt. auth. see Hillman, Abraham P.

Alexandersson, G. The Baltic Straits. 1982. lib. bdg. 32.50 (ISBN 90-247-2595-X, Pub. by Martinus Nijhoff Netherlands). Kluwer Boston.

Alexandersson, Gunnar. Geography of Manufacturing. 1967. pap. 11.95 ref. ed. (ISBN 0-13-351262-2). P-H.

Alexander-Williams, J. Large Intestine. new ed. (BIMR Gastroenterolgy Ser.: vol. 3). 1983. text ed. price not set (ISBN 0-407-02289-9). Butterworth.

Alexandrian, Sarane. Seurat. (QLP Ser.). (Illus.). 96p. 1980. 7.95 (ISBN 0-517-54106-8). Crown.

Alexandridis, Nikitas. Microprocessor Systems Architecture & Engineering. 1983. text ed. p.n.s. (ISBN 0-914894-66-8). Computer Sci.

Alexandroff, Paul S. & Hopf, H. Topologie. LC 65-21833. (Ger.). 19.50 (ISBN 0-8284-0197-7). Chelsea Pub.

Alexandrov, Eugene, ed. Geological Bulletins, 5 bks. Incl. No. 1. Metallogenic Provinces & Metallogenic Epochs. Bilibin, Yu. A. 1968. pap. 1.00 o.p. (ISBN 0-930146-00-X); No. 2. Distribution & Preservation of Pollen in Sediments in the Western Part of the Pacific Ocean. Koreneva, Ye. V. 1968. pap. 1.00 o.p. (ISBN 0-930146-01-8); No. 3. Symposium on the New York City Group of Formations. 1969. pap. 3.00 o.p. (ISBN 0-930146-02-6); No. 4. Essays on Metallogeny. Smirnov, V. I., ed. 1971. pap. 2.00 o.p. (ISBN 0-930146-03-4); No. 5. Transactions of the Fifth Caribbean Geological Conference. Mattson, Peter H., ed. 1971. pap. 5.00 o.p. (ISBN 0-930146-04-2). pap. Queens Coll Pr.

Alexandrowicz, Harry. Six Hundred Ninety-Nine Ways to Improve the Performance of Your Car. LC 79-93251. (Illus.). 192p. 1980. 14.95 (ISBN 0-8069-5550-3); lib. bdg. 17.79 (ISBN 0-8069-5551-1); pap. 7.95 (ISBN 0-8069-8900-9). Sterling.

Alexie, Angela. The Velvet Thorn. 320p. (Orig.). 1982. pap. 2.95 (ISBN 0-449-14502-6, GM). Fawcett.

Alexis, Marcus & Wilson, C. Organizational Decision Making. 1967. text ed. 19.95 o.p. (ISBN 0-13-641043-X). P-H.

Alexis de Saint Lo. Relation du Voyage du Cape Vert. (Bibliotheque Africaine Ser.). 240p. (Fr.). 1974. Repr. of 1637 ed. lib. bdg. 66.00x o.p. (ISBN 0-8287-0015-X, 72-2161). Clearwater Pub.

Alexopoulos, Constantine J. & Bold, Harold C. Algae & Fungi. 1967. pap. 12.95x (ISBN 0-02-301700-7, 30170). Macmillan.

Alfano, Genrose J. All-RN Nursing Staff. LC 81-80201. 133p. 1980. pap. text ed. 16.95 (ISBN 0-913654-68-X). Aspen Systems.

Alfaro, Juan. Preguntas y Respuestas sobre la Biblia. 64p. (Spanish.). 1982. pap. 1.50 (ISBN 0-89243-162-8). Liguori Pubns.

Alfaruqi, Ismael R., jt. auth. see Chan, Wing T.

Al Faruqi, Lois I., ed. An Annotated Glossary of Arabic Musical Terms. LC 81-4129. 536p. 1981. lib. bdg. 55.00x (ISBN 0-313-20554-X, AFM/). Greenwood.

Alfassa, Mira. Conversations: The Mother. 1973. pap. 1.75 o.p. (ISBN 0-89071-246-8). Matagiri.

--Health & Healing in Yoga. 305p. 1979. 7.50 (ISBN 0-89071-284-0, Pub. by Sri Aurobindo Ashram India); pap. 6.00 (ISBN 0-89071-283-2). Matagiri.

Al-Fawaris, Abu. The Political Doctrine of the Isma'ilis. Makarim, Sami N., ed. LC 77-16600. 1977. 25.00x (ISBN 0-88206-016-3). Caravan Bks.

Alfeld, Louis & Graham, Alan K. Introduction to Urban Dynamics. LC 76-19725. 1976. 30.00x (ISBN 0-262-01054-2). MIT Pr.

Alfoldy, Geza. Noricum. Birley, Anthony, tr. from Ger. (The Provinces of the Roman Empire Ser.). (Illus.). 406p. 1974. 47.50x o.p. (ISBN 0-7100-7372-0). Routledge & Kegan.

Alfonsi, Petrus. The Disciplina Clericalis of Petrus Alfonsi. Hermes, Eberhard, ed. Quarrie, P. R., tr. LC 73-94434. (Islamic World Ser.). 250p. 1977. 28.50x (ISBN 0-520-02704-3). U of Cal Pr.

Alfonso, Anthony. Japanese--Book One, Bk. 1. (Illus.). (gr. 3-7). 1976. pap. 10.00x o.p. (ISBN 0-8048-1233-0). C E Tuttle.

Alfonso, Felipe B., jt. ed. see Korten, David C.

Alfonso, John B. Reflections of My Soul on Paper. LC 78-52077. 1979. 4.50 o.p. (ISBN 0-533-03588-0). Vantage.

Alfonso Tenth. El Sabio. Libro De las Cruzes. 1961. deluxe 20.00x (ISBN 0-686-28301-5); pap. 10.00x (ISBN 0-686-28302-3). Hispanic Seminary.

Alfonso X. General Estoria, 2 Vols, Part II. 1961. 35.00 (ISBN 0-942260-01-5); deluxe ed. 100.00 (ISBN 0-942260-02-3). Hispanic Seminary.

--Lapidario & Libro de las formas & Magenes. Winget, Lynn W. & Diman, Roderic C., eds. xix, 202p. 1980. 20.00 (ISBN 0-942260-12-0). Hispanic Seminary.

--Libros de las cruzes. Kasten, L. A. & Kiddle, L. B., eds. 173p. 1961. pap. 10.00; deluxe ed. 20.00. Hispanic Seminary.

Alford, Betty B. & Bogle, Margaret L. Nutrition During the Life Cycle. 384p. 1982. 24.95 (ISBN 0-13-627810-8). P-H.

Alford, Dean H. The Book of Genesis & Part of the Book of Exodus. 1979. 12.50 (ISBN 0-86524-001-9, 7002). Klock & Klock.

Alford, Henry A. Alford's Greek Testament, 4 vols. 1980. Repr. 75.00 o.p. (ISBN 0-8010-0158-7). Baker Bk.

Alford, M. Needlework As Art. (Illus.). 620p. 1975. Repr. of 1886 ed. 25.95x o.p. (ISBN 0-8464-0669-1). Beekman Pubs.

Alford, Robert L. Tips on Testing: Strategies for Test-Taking. LC 79-88269. 1979. pap. text ed. 7.00 (ISBN 0-8191-0770-0). U Pr of Amer.

Alford, Terry W. Facility Planning, Design, & Construction of Rural Health Centers. LC 78-31993. (Rural Health Center Ser.). (Illus.). 256p. 1979. prof ref 25.00x (ISBN 0-88410-539-3); pap. 13.50x (ISBN 0-88410-545-8). Ballinger Pub.

Alfred, ed. Four Medieval Epics. 1963. 5.95 o.s.i. (ISBN 0-394-60787-2, G87). Modern Lib.

Alfred, Richard L., ed. Institutional Impacts on Campus, Community, & Business Constituencies. LC 81-48566. 1982. 7.95x (ISBN 0-87589-884-X, CC-38). Jossey-Bass.

Alfrey, T., Jr. Mechanical Behavior of High Polymers, Vol. 6. 1948. 19.50 (ISBN 0-470-39040-9). Krieger.

Algar, Hamid. Mirza Malkum Khan: A Biographical Essay in 19th Century Iranian Modernism. LC 78-187750. 1973. 39.75x (ISBN 0-520-02217-3). U of Cal Pr.

--Religion & State in Iran, Seventeen Eighty-Five to Nineteen Six: The Role of the 'Ulama in the Qajar Period. LC 72-79959. (Near Eastern Center, UCLA; Ca. Library Reprint Ser.: No. 106). 1980. 28.50x (ISBN 0-520-04100-3). U of Cal Pr.

Algar, Hamid, jt. ed. see Khouri, Mounah A.

Algar, Hamid, tr. see Khouri, Mounah A. & Algar, Hamid.

Algar, Hamid, tr. see Razi, Najm A.

Algeo, John. Exercises in Contemporary English. 217p. (Orig.). 1974. pap. text ed. 9.95 (ISBN 0-15-512931-7, HC); instructor's key 1.00 (ISBN 0-15-512932-5). HarBraceJ.

--Problems in the Origins & Development of the English Language. 3rd ed. 288p. (Orig.). 1982. pap. text ed. 11.95 (ISBN 0-15-567609-1, HC); ans. key 1.00 (ISBN 0-15-567605-9, HC). HarBraceJ.

Alger, Horatio. Phil the Fiddler. 1971. Fasc. 6.95 o.s.i. (ISBN 0-87874-004-X, Nautilus). Galloway.

Alger, Horatio, Jr. Grand'ther Baldwin's Thanksgiving with Other Ballads & Poems. 125p. 1978. Repr. of 1875 ed. 16.50 (ISBN 0-686-35750-7). G K Westgard.

--Hugo, the Deformed. (Illus.). 84p. 1978. 19.50 (ISBN 0-686-37019-8). G K Westgard.

--The New Schoolma'am: A Summer in North Sparta. 140p. 1976. Repr. of 1877 ed. 18.75 (ISBN 0-686-37020-1). G K Westgard.

--Nothing to Do: A Tilt at Our Best Society. (Illus.). 45p. 1978. Repr. of 1857 ed. 15.00 (ISBN 0-686-37021-X). G K Westgard.

--Number 91: The Adventures of A New York Telegraph Boy. (Illus.). 205p. 1977. Repr. of 1889 ed. 19.50 (ISBN 0-686-37022-8). G K Westgard.

--Struggling Upward. 1971. Fasc. 6.95 o.s.i. (ISBN 0-87874-005-8, Nautilus). Galloway.

--Timothy Crump's Ward: The New Years Loan & What Became of It. 188p. 1977. Repr. of 1866 ed. 24.00 (ISBN 0-686-37023-6). G K Westgard.

Alger, Philip L. Induction Machines: Behavior & Uses. 2nd ed. 526p. 1970. 81.00x (ISBN 0-677-02390-1). Gordon.

--Mathematics for Science & Engineering. 2nd ed. LC 69-11937. (Illus.). 1969. 19.50 o.p. (ISBN 0-07-001050-1, P&RB). McGraw.

--Mathematics for Science & Engineering. LC 82-10029. 384p. 1983. Repr. of 1957 ed. lib. bdg. write for info. (ISBN 0-89874-519-5). Krieger.

Alger, Philip L., ed. see Steinmetz, Charles P.

Alger, Ralph K. Basic Skills in Grammar, 2 Bks. (Illus.). pap. text ed. 4.00 ea.; Bk. 1. pap. text ed. (ISBN 0-8428-0004-2); Bk. 2. pap. text ed. (ISBN 0-8428-0005-0); Bk. 1. keys 1.47 (ISBN 0-8428-0031-X); Bk. 2. keys 2.00 (ISBN 0-8428-0032-8). Cambridge Bk.

Al-Ghazali. On the Duties of Brotherhood. 6.95 (ISBN 0-686-83895-5). Kazi Pubns.

Al-Ghazali, tr. see McCarthy, Richard J.

Algier, Ann S., ed. Improving Reading & Study Skills. LC 81-48565. 1982. 7.95x (ISBN 0-87589-880-7, CLA-8). Jossey-Bass.

Algosaibi, Ghazi. Arabian Essays. 120p. 1982. 18.00 (ISBN 0-7103-0019-0, Kegan Paul). Routledge & Kegan.

Algosaibi, Ghazi A. From the Orient & the Desert. 1977. deluxe ed. 15.00 (ISBN 0-85362-165-9, Oriel). Routledge & Kegan.

Algozzine, Robert. Problem Behavior Management: Educator's Resource Service. LC 82-1663. 350p. 1982. text ed. 79.00 looseleaf (ISBN 0-89443-678-3). Aspen Systems.

Algozzine, Robert, jt. auth. see Ysselyke, James E.

Algren, N. Chicago: City on the Make. 128p. 1983. pap. 5.95 (ISBN 0-07-001012-9, GB). McGraw.

Algren, Nelson. A Walk on the Wild Side. 1977. pap. 2.50 o.p. (ISBN 0-14-003565-6). Penguin.

Alhadeff, David A. Microeconomics & Human Behavior: Toward a New Synthesis of Economics & Psychology. LC 81-3356. (Illus.). 264p. 1982. 24.50x (ISBN 0-520-04353-7). U of Cal Pr.

Al-Hakim, Tawfiq. Plays, Prefaces & Postscripts of Tawfiq Al-Hakim: Theater of Society, Vol. 2. Hutchins, William M., tr. LC 80-80887. (Orig.). 1983. 25.00 (ISBN 0-89410-280-X); pap. 8.00 (ISBN 0-89410-147-1). Three Continents.

Alhamsi, Ahmed & Wangara, Harun K., eds. Black Arts: An Anthology of Black Creations. 1969. pap. 3.50 o.p. (ISBN 0-685-07539-7). Broadside.

Al-Hibri, A. Women & Islam. 106p. 1982. 17.80 (ISBN 0-08-027928-7). Pergamon.

Al-Hibri, Azizah. Deontic Logic: A Comprehensive Appraisal & a View Proposal. LC 78-66422. 1978. pap. text ed. 9.75 (ISBN 0-8191-0303-9). U Pr of Amer.

Al-Husayn al-Sulami, Ibn. The Book of Sufi Chivalry: Lessons to a Son of the Moment (Futuwwah) Bayrak, Tosun, tr. from Arabic. 192p. 1983. 10.95 (ISBN 0-89281-031-9). Inner Tradit.

Al-Husry, Khaldun S. Origins of Modern Arab Political Thought. LC 80-11794. Repr. of 1966 ed. 25.00x (ISBN 0-88206-037-6). Caravan Bks.

Ali, jt. auth. see Stanton.

Ali, Abdullah Y. The Meaning of the Glorious Qur'an, 2 Vols. Ali, Abdullah Y., tr. 10.00 set (ISBN 0-686-37146-1). New World Press NY.

Ali, Amjad, jt. ed. see Fordham, Ernest W.

Ali, B. Hajjat-ul-Wada: Last Sermon. 1981. 1.25 (ISBN 0-686-97858-7). Kazi Pubns.

Ali, Majid & Fayemi, A. Olusegun. The Pathology of Maintenance Hemodialysis. (Illus.). 424p. 1982. 39.75x (ISBN 0-398-04588-7). C C Thomas.

Ali, Majid, et al. Visa Qualifying Examination Review, Vol. 1: Basic Sciences. LC 78-61617. 1978. pap. 15.50 (ISBN 0-87488-124-2). Med Exam.

Ali, S. Teach Yourself Arabic. 7.00 (ISBN 0-686-83575-1). Kazi Pubns.

Ali, Salim & Ripley, Dillon. Compact Edition of the Handbook of the Birds of India & Pakistan, Together with Those of Bangladesh, Nepal, Bhutan & Sri Lanka. (Illus.). 1981. 96.95x (ISBN 0-19-561245-0). Oxford U Pr.

Ali, Salim & Ripley, S. Dillon. Handbook of the Birds of India & Pakistan: Together with Those of Nepal, Sikkim, Bhutan, & Ceylon, 7 vols. Incl. Vol. 2. Megapodes to Crab Plover. 362p. 1969. 20.00 o.p. (ISBN 0-19-635262-2); Vol. 3. Stone Curlews to Owls. 2nd ed. 1981. 33.00x (ISBN 0-19-561302-3); Vol. 4. Frogmouths to Pittas. 1970. 23.75x (ISBN 0-19-635275-4); Vol. 5. Larks to the Grey Hypocolius. 292p. 1972. 29.50x (ISBN 0-19-560166-1); Vol. 6. Cuckoo-Shrikes to Babaxes. 1971. 23.50x (ISBN 0-19-560101-7); Vol. 7. Laughing Thrushes to the Mangrove Whistler. 1972. 29.50x (ISBN 0-19-560263-3); Vol. 8. Warblers to Redstarts. 294p. 1973. 29.50x (ISBN 0-19-560291-9); Vol. 9. Robins to Wagtails. 322p. 1973. 29.50x (ISBN 0-19-560349-4); Vol. 10. Flowerpackers to Buntings. 1974. 29.50 (ISBN 0-19-560385-0). (Illus.). Oxford U Pr.

Ali, Shanti S. & Ramchandani, R. R., eds. India & the Western Indian Ocean States: Towards Regional Cooperation in Development. 310p. 1981. 27.50x (ISBN 0-940500-85-X, Pub by Allied Pubs India). Asia Bk Corp.

Ali, Syed A. & Arif, Abu A. Labor Migration from Bangladesh to the Middle East. (Working Paper: No. 454). 396p. 1981. 5.00 (ISBN 0-686-36046-X, WP-0454). World Bank.

Ali, Yousuf. The Holy Quran with Arabic Text Commentary & Translation. 19.95 (ISBN 0-686-18528-5). Kazi Pubns.

--An Interpretation of the Holy Quran with Arabic Text. 12.95 (ISBN 0-686-18338-X). Kazi Pubns.

Aliaga, Barbara. Learn to Type: Completely New, Easy Method for Beginners. (Illus.). 77p. 1981. pap. 6.50 (ISBN 0-88908-088-7). Self Counsel Pr.

Ali Ahmed Said, see Said, Ali A., pseud.

Aliandro, H. Dicionario Ingles-Portugues. 402p. (Eng. & Port.). 1980. pap. 6.95 (ISBN 0-686-97638-X, M-9215). French & Eur.

--Dicionario Portugues-Ingles. 311p. (Port. & Eng.). 1980. pap. 6.95 (ISBN 0-686-97641-X, M-9216). French & Eur.

Aliano, Richard A. American Defense Policy from Eisenhower to Kennedy: The Politics of Changing Military Requirements, 1957-1961. LC 74-27709. xi, 309p. 1975. 18.50x (ISBN 0-8214-0181-5, 82-81792). Ohio U Pr.

--American Defense Policy from Eisenhower to Kennedy: The Politics of Changing Military Requirements, 1957-1961. LC 74-27709. xi, 309p. 1978. pap. 8.95x (ISBN 0-8214-0406-7, 82-81800). Ohio U Pr.

--The Crime of World Power: Politics Without Government in the International System. LC 77-25866. 1978. 15.00 (ISBN 0-399-12027-0). Putnam Pub Group.

Alibegasvili, Gaiane, jt. auth. see Weitzmann, Kurt.

Aliber, Robert Z. The International Money Game. 3rd, expanded ed. LC 78-73770. 1979. 7.95 (ISBN 0-465-03375-X); pap. 6.95x (ISBN 0-465-03376-8). Basic.

--The International Money Game. 4th, rev. ed. 350p. 1983. 15.00 (ISBN 0-465-03377-6); pap. 8.95 (ISBN 0-465-03379-2). Basic.

--Your Money & Your Life: A Lifetime Approach to Money Management. 1982. 15.95 (ISBN 0-465-09340-X). Basic.

Aliber, Robert Z., ed. The Political Economy of Monetary Reform. LC 76-26692. 320p. Date not set. 21.00 (ISBN 0-87663-810-8). Allanheld & Schram.

Aliboni, Roberto, ed. Arab Industrialization & Economic Integration. LC 78-10632. 1979. 26.00 (ISBN 0-312-04702-9). St Martin.

Alibrandi, Tom. Custody. (Orig.). 1979. pap. 2.95 (ISBN 0-523-41871-X). Pinnacle Bks.

--Killshot. 1979. pap. 2.25 o.p. (ISBN 0-523-40375-5). Pinnacle Bks.

Alice. The Story of the Little Round Man. LC 79-63277. (Illus.). (ps-1). 1979. 6.95g o.p. (ISBN 0-7232-2185-5). Warne.

Aliesan, Jody. As If It Will Matter. LC 78-63399. 60p. (Orig.). 1978. 15.00 o.p. (ISBN 0-931188-04-0); pap. 4.00 (ISBN 0-931188-03-2). Seal Pr WA.

Aliesan, Jody & Jacques, Hylah. How to Wake from This? 50p. 1983. price not set (ISBN 0-931188-17-2). Seal Pr WA.

Aliev, M. R., jt. auth. see Papousek, D.

Aligarh Muslim University, ed. Changing Concept of the Universe. 1964. 4.75x o.p. (ISBN 0-210-26974-X). Asia.

Aliger, Margarita, et al. Three Russian Poets. Feinstein, Elaine, tr. from Rus. (Translation Ser.). 1979. pap. 4.95 o.p. (ISBN 0-85635-227-6, Pub. by Carcanet New Pr England). Humanities.

Alighiere, Dante. Paradiso. Ciardi, John, tr. 1970. pap. 3.50 (ISBN 0-451-62169-7, ME2169, Ment). NAL.

Alighieri, Dante. The Inferno. Mandelbaum, Allen, tr. from Italian. (Bantam Classics Ser.). (Illus.). 350p. (gr. 9-12). 1982. pap. 2.50 (ISBN 0-553-21069-6). Bantam.

Ali ibn Isma'il, A. H., et al. Al ibanah 'an usul addiyanah. Klein, W. C., tr. (American Oriental Ser.: Vol. 19). 1940. pap. 20.00 (ISBN 0-527-02693-X). Kraus Repr.

Ali-Khaklifa Al-Kuwari. Oil Revenues in the Gulf Emirates. LC 78-7358. (Illus.). 1978. lib. bdg. 46.25 (ISBN 0-89158-831-0). Westview.

Aliki. Corn Is Maize: The Gift of the Indians. LC 75-6928. (A Let's-Read-&-Find-Out Science Bk). (Illus.). 40p. (gr. k-3). 1976. PLB 10.89 (ISBN 0-690-00975-5, TYC-J); pap. 3.95 (ISBN 0-690-04203-5, TYC-J). Har-Row.

--Digging up Dinosaurs. LC 80-2250. (A Let's Read & Find Out Science Bk.). (Illus.). 40p. (gr. k-3). 1981. 10.53i (ISBN 0-690-04098-9, TYC-J); PLB 10.89 (ISBN 0-690-04099-7). Har-Row.

--Fossils Tell of Long Ago. LC 78-170999. (A Let's-Read-&-Find-Out Science Bk). (Illus.). 40p. (gr. k-3). 1972. PLB 10.89 (ISBN 0-690-31379-9, TYC-J). Har-Row.

--Hush Little Baby. (Illus.). (ps-1). 1968. PLB 8.95x (ISBN 0-13-448167-4); pap. 3.95 (ISBN 0-13-448175-5). P-H.

--The Long Lost Coelacanth & Other Living Fossils. LC 72-83773. (A Let's-Read-&-Find-Out Science Bk.). (Illus.). 40p. (gr. k-3). 1973. 7.95i o.p. (ISBN 0-690-50478-0, TYC-J). Har-Row.

--My Five Senses. LC 62-7150. (A Let's-Read-&-Find-Out Science Bk). (Illus.). (gr. k-3). 1962. PLB 10.89 (ISBN 0-690-56763-4, TYC-J). Har-Row.

--My Hands. LC 62-12810. (A Let's-Read-&-Find-Out Science Bk). (Illus.). (gr. k-3). 1962. PLB 10.89 (ISBN 0-690-56834-7, TYC-J). Har-Row.

--My Visit to the Dinosaurs. LC 70-78255. (A Let's-Read-&-Find-Out Science Bk). (Illus.). (gr. k-3). 1969. bds. 6.95 o.p. (ISBN 0-690-57401-0, TYC-J); PLB 10.89 (ISBN 0-690-57402-9, TYC-J); pap. 2.95 (ISBN 0-690-57403-7, TYC-J). Har-Row.

--New Year's Day. LC 67-10069. (Holiday Ser.). (Illus.). (gr. 1-3). 1967. 7.95i o.p. (ISBN 0-690-58182-3, TYC-J). Har-Row.

--Story of Johnny Appleseed. (Illus.). (ps-2). 1963. lib. bdg. 6.95 (ISBN 0-13-850800-3); pap. 2.50 (ISBN 0-13-850818-6). P-H.

--We Are Best Friends. (gr. 1-4). 1982. 9.00 (ISBN 0-688-00822-4); PLB 8.59 (ISBN 0-688-00823-2). Greenwillow.

--Wild & Woolly Mammoths. LC 76-18082. (A Let's-Read-&-Find-Out Science Bk.). (Illus.). (gr. k-3). 1977. PLB 10.89 (ISBN 0-690-01276-4, TYC-J). Har-Row.

Ali Majid, et al. Pathology Review. 7th ed. (Medical Exam Review Ser.). 1980. pap. 11.95 (ISBN 0-87488-204-4). Med Exam.

Ali-Nadawi, Abul H. Prophet's Stories. Quinlan, Hamid, ed. El-Helbawy, Kamal, tr. from Arabic. LC 82-70453. (Illus.). 200p. (Orig.). 1982. pap. 5.00 (ISBN 0-89259-038-6). Am Trust Pubns.

Alinder, James. The Contact Print, Nineteen Forty-Six to Nineteen Eighty-Two. LC 82-83985. (Untitled Thirty Ser.). (Illus.). 52p. 1982. pap. 15.00 (ISBN 0-933286-32-5). Friends Photography.

Alinder, James, ed. see DeCarava, Roy.

Alinder, James, ed. see Featherstone, David.

Alinder, James, ed. see Morris, Wright.

Alinder, James, ed. see Nixon, Nicholas.

Alireza, Marianne. At the Drop of a Veil. 1971. 12.95 (ISBN 0-395-12090-X). HM.

Alisin, V. V., jt. ed. see Kragelsky, I. V.

Alison, Robert M. Breeding Biology & Behavior of the Oldsquaw (Clangula hyemalis L.) 52p. 1975. 3.50 (ISBN 0-943610-18-4). Am Ornithologists.

Al-Issa, Ihsan. The Psychopathology of Women. (Illus.). 1979. 15.95 (ISBN 0-13-736827-5, Spec); pap. 7.95 (ISBN 0-13-736819-4). P-H.

Al-Issa, Ihsan, ed. Gender & Psychopathology. (Personality & Psychopathology Ser.). 355p. 1982. 32.50 (ISBN 0-12-050350-6). Acad Pr.

Alitto, Guy S. The Last Confucian: Liang Shu-Ming & the Chinese Dilemma of Modernity. LC 75-27920. (Center for Chinese Studies, U. C. Berkeley). 1979. 27.50x (ISBN 0-520-03123-7). U of Cal Pr.

Alizadeh, Ahmad, tr. see Ahmad, Jalal Al-e.

Al-Jarrahi, Abdussamad, ed. see Badawi, Gamal.

Al-Jarrahi, Abdussamad, tr. see Boisard, Marcel.

Aljian, George W. Purchasing Handbook. 3rd ed. 1152p. 1973. 59.95 (ISBN 0-07-001068-4, P&RB). McGraw.

Alkema, Chester J. Alkema's Complete Guide to Creative Art for Young People. LC 70-167654. (Illus.). 1971. 16.95 (ISBN 0-8069-5188-5); PLB 19.99 (ISBN 0-8069-5189-3). Sterling.

--Mask-Making. LC 80-54343. (Illus.). 96p. 9.95 (ISBN 0-8069-7038-3); lib. bdg. 12.49 (ISBN 0-8069-7039-1). Sterling.

--Puppet-Making. LC 72-167668. (Little Craft Book Ser.). (Illus.). (gr. 4 up). 1971. 6.95 (ISBN 0-8069-5174-5); PLB 8.99 (ISBN 0-8069-5175-3). Sterling.

Alkemade, Cornelis T. & Herrmann, Roland. Fundamentals of Analytical Flame Spectroscopy. LC 79-4376. 442p. 1979. 99.95 (ISBN 0-470-26710-0). Halsted Pr.

Alken & Sokeland. Urology. 1982. 17.95 (ISBN 0-8151-0108-2). Year Bk Med.

Alker, Hayward R. Dialectical Logics for the Political Sciences. (Ponzan Studies: No. 7). 96p. 1982. pap. text ed. 11.50x (ISBN 90-6203-684-8, Pub. by Rodopi Holland). Humanities.

Al-Khalesi, Yasin M. The Court of the Palms: A Functional Interpretation of the Mari Palace. LC 77-94987. (Bibliotheca Mesopotamica Ser.: Vol. 8). (Illus.). viii, 90p. 1978. 19.00x (ISBN 0-89003-029-4); pap. 14.50x (ISBN 0-89003-030-8). Undena Pubns.

Alkin, Glyn. TV Sound Operations. (Media Manual Ser.). (Illus.). 1975. pap. 10.95 o.s.i. (ISBN 0-240-50865-3). Focal Pr.

Alkin, Marvin C., et al. Conducting Evaluations: Three Perspectives. LC 80-52791. 60p. (Orig.). 1980. pap. 2.95 (ISBN 0-87954-051-6). Foundation Ctr.

Al-Kindi. Medical Formulary or Aqrabadhin of al-Kindi. Levey, Martin, tr. (Medieval Science Pubns., No. 7). 424p. 1966. 32.50x (ISBN 0-299-03600-6). U of Wis Pr.

Alkins, Arthur C. Fundamentals of Data Processing. (Plaid Ser.). 200p. 1983. pap. 8.95 (ISBN 0-87094-389-8). Dow Jones-Irwin.

Alkire, Leland G., Jr., ed. Periodical Title Abbreviations: Vol. 1, by Abbreviation. 3rd ed. 700p. 1981. 94.00 (ISBN 0-8103-0337-X). Gale.

--Periodical Title Abbreviations: Vol. 2, By Title. 3rd ed. LC 81-2677. 700p. 1981. 105.00 (ISBN 0-8103-0338-8). Gale.

Alkire, William. Coral Islanders. Goldschmidt, Walter, ed. LC 77-90673. (World of Man Ser.). (Illus.). 1978. text ed. 13.95x (ISBN 0-88295-618-3); pap. text ed. 7.95x (ISBN 0-88295-619-1). Harlan Davidson.

All India Sociological Conference. Sociology, Social Research, & Social Problems in India. Saksena, R. N., ed. LC 77-27251. 1978. Repr. of 1961 ed. lib. bdg. 19.00x (ISBN 0-8371-7893-2, SSRP). Greenwood.

Allaby, M. World Food Resources: Actual & Potential. 1977. 33.00 (ISBN 0-85334-731-X, Pub. by Applied Sci England). Elsevier.

Allaby, Michael & Lovelock, James. Great Extinction. LC 81-43613. 192p. 1983. 13.95 (ISBN 0-385-18011-X). Doubleday.

Allain, Marie-Francoise. The Other Man: Conversations with Graham Greene. 1983. price not set (ISBN 0-671-44767-X). S&S.

Allain, Mathe & Ancelet, Barry, eds. Litterature Francais de la Louisiana. (Anthologie Ser.). (Illus.). 360p. (Fr.). (gr. 10 up). 1981. pap. text ed. 7.00x (ISBN 0-911409-34-3). Natl Mat Dev.

Allaire, Barbara & McNeil, Robert. Teaching Patient Relations in Hospitals: The Hows & Whys. LC 82-22765. (Illus.). 200p. 1983. 75.00 (ISBN 0-87258-377-5, AHA-049150). Am Hospital.

Allaire, Pierre. Bird Species on Mined Lands. (Illus.). 72p. (Orig.). 1982. pap. text ed. 10.00 (ISBN 0-86607-010-9). Inst Mining & Minerals.

Allal, M. & Chuta, E. Cottage Industries & Handicrafts: Some Guidelines for Employment Promotion. 200p. 11.40 (ISBN 92-2-103029-6). Intl Labour Office.

Allan, Cecil J. Nineteen Forty-Eight British Railway Locomotives, Comb. Vol. 10.00x (ISBN 0-686-97953-2, SpS). Sportshelf.

--Swiss Travel Wonderland. 29.50x (ISBN 0-7110-0296-7, SpS). Sportshelf.

Allan, Duncan. Outlines of Animal Immunobiology. 160p. 1980. pap. 24.00 o.p. (ISBN 0-8121-0724-1). Lea & Febiger.

Allan, J. A., ed. Libya Since Independence: Economic & Social Development. LC 82-42564. 1982. 22.50x (ISBN 0-312-48363-5). St Martin.

Allan, J. W. Persian Metal Technology 700-1300 A.D. 208p. 1979. 79.00x (ISBN 0-686-97689-4, Pub. by Ashmolean Mus Oxford). State Mutual Bk.

Allan, John J., 3rd. CAD Systems: Proceedings of the IFIP Working Conference on Computer Aided Design Systems. 1976. 59.75 (ISBN 0-7204-0472-X, North-Holland). Elsevier.

Allan, Mabel E. The Horns of Danger. 192p. (gr. 7 up). 1981. 7.95 (ISBN 0-396-07987-3). Dodd.

--A Lovely Tomorrow. LC 79-6642. (gr. 7 up). 1980. 7.95 (ISBN 0-396-07813-3). Dodd.

Allan, Mea. William Robinson: 1838-1935. (Illus.). 288p. 1983. 19.95 (ISBN 0-571-11865-8). Faber & Faber.

Allan, Peta & Jolley, Moya. Nursing, Midwifery & Health Visiting since 1900. 316p. 1982. 18.95 (ISBN 0-686-83081-4); pap. 10.95 (ISBN 0-571-11840-2). Faber & Faber.

Allan, Pierre. Crisis Bargaining & the Arms Race: A Theoretical Model. (Peace Science Studies). 184p. 1983. prof ref 22.50x (ISBN 0-88410-911-9). Ballinger Pub.

Allan, Richard G., jt. auth. see Royer, James M.

Allan, Richard G., et al. U. S. History - Two, 5 vols. Incl. Vol. 1: Modern America Takes Shape. 242p (ISBN 0-86624-005-5, UU4); Vol. 2: Imperialism to Progressivism. 192p (ISBN 0-86624-006-3, UU5); Vol. 3: War, Prosperity & Depression. 180p (ISBN 0-86624-007-1, UU6); Vol. 4: The Roosevelt Years of Depression & War. 184p (ISBN 0-86624-008-X, UU7); Vol. 5: The Cold War Years. 244p (ISBN 0-86624-009-8, UU8); Teacher's Guide. avail. (UV9); End of Unit Test. avail. (UV0). (Illus.). 1981. pap. text ed. 5.95 ea. Bilingual Ed Serv.

Allan, Ted, ed. see Shaw, Arnold.

Allan, Thomas D. Satellite Microwave Remote Sensing. (Marine Science Ser.). 450p. 1983. 110.00 (ISBN 0-470-27397-6). Halsted Pr.

Allan, W. J. Power & Sail: A Complete Guide to Yachting & Boating in New Zealand. (Illus.). 228p. 1975. pap. 9.95 (ISBN 0-686-42804-8, Pub. by Heinemann Pubs New Zealand). Intl Schol Bk Serv.

Alland, Alexander. To Be Human: An Introduction to Cultural Anthropology. LC 80-17252. 388p. 1981. text ed. 16.95 (ISBN 0-471-06213-8). Wiley.

Alland, Alexander, Jr. To Be Human: An Introduction to Anthropology. LC 79-19497. 657p. 1980. text ed. 20.95 (ISBN 0-471-01747-7); tchrs' ed 7.00 (ISBN 0-471-06054-2). Wiley.

Alland, Guy, et al. Know-How: A Fix-It Book for the Clumsy but Pure of Heart. (Illus.). 1975. 12.50 o.p. (ISBN 0-316-03140-2); pap. 6.95 o.p. (ISBN 0-316-03141-0). Little.

Allard, Harry. I Will Not Go to Market Today. LC 78-72474. (Illus.). (ps-2). 1979. 8.95 (ISBN 0-8037-4019-0); PLB 8.89 (ISBN 0-8037-4020-4). Dial.

--Miss Nelson is Back. (Illus.). (gr. k-3). 1982. PLB 8.95 (ISBN 0-395-32956-6); 8.70. HM.

Allard, Harry & Marshall, James. Miss Nelson Is Missing! (Illus.). (gr. k-3). 1977. reinforced bdg. 9.95 (ISBN 0-395-25296-2). HM.

--The Stupids Step Out. (Illus.). (gr. k-3). 1977. pap. 2.95 (ISBN 0-395-25377-2). HM.

Allard, Harry, tr. see Waechter, Friedrich K.

Allard, Robert W. Principles of Plant Breeding. LC 60-14240. 485p. 1960. 27.95x (ISBN 0-471-02310-8). Wiley.

Allard, Sven. Russia & the Austrian State Treaty: A Case Study of Soviet Policy in Europe. LC 68-8176. 1970. 19.75x (ISBN 0-271-00083-X). Pa St U Pr.

Allard, William A. Vanishing Breed: Photographs of the Cowboy & the West. LC 82-60768. 1982. 34.95 (ISBN 0-8212-1505-1); Deluxe ed. 125.00 (ISBN 0-8212-1524-8). NYGS.

Allardt, Erik & Andre, Nils, eds. Nordic Democracy. Friis, Erik J., et al. Valen, Henry & Wendt, Frantz, trs. from Danish, Swedish, Norwegian, Icelandic & Finish. (Illus.). 780p. 1981. 32.95X (ISBN 87-7429-040-1). Nordic Bks.

Allardt, Linda. The Names of the Survivors. LC 79-25878. 49p. 1979. 4.00 (ISBN 0-87886-108-4). Ithaca Hse.

Allardt, Linda see Emerson, Ralph W.

Allardyce, Paula. Miss Philadelphia Smith. 1977. 7.95 o.p. (ISBN 0-698-10811-6, Coward). Putnam Pub Group.

Allasio, John. Practice RCT Math Exam, No. 12. (gr. 9-12). 1982. of 20 5.50 set (ISBN 0-937820-44-X). Westsea Pub.

Allasio, John, et al. Practice RCT Math Exam, No. 10. (gr. 9-12). of 20 5.50 set (ISBN 0-937820-40-7). Westsea Pub.

--Practice RCT Math Exam, No. 11. (gr. 9-12). 1982. of 20 5.50 set (ISBN 0-937820-42-3). Westsea Pub.

Allason, Julian, jt. auth. see Bradbeer, Robin.

Allaud, Louis & Martin, Maurice H. Schlumberger, The History of a Technique. LC 77-23566. 333p. 1977. 49.95x (ISBN 0-471-01667-5, Pub. by Wiley-Interscience). Wiley.

Al-Layla, M. Anis, et al. Water Supply Engineering Design. LC 76-46026. 1977. 39.95 (ISBN 0-250-40147-9). Ann Arbor Science.

Allbritton, Cliff. How to Get Married: And Stay That Way. LC 82-71219. (Orig.). 1983. pap. 4.95 (ISBN 0-8054-5653-8). Broadman.

Allchin, A. M. The Kingdom of Love & Knowledge: The Encounter Between Orthodoxy & the West. 224p. (Orig.). 1982. 14.95 (ISBN 0-8164-0532-8). Seabury.

Allchin, Bridget & Allchin, Raymond. The Rise of Civilization in India & Pakistan. LC 82-1262. (World Archaeology Ser.). (Illus.). 352p. 1982. 49.50 (ISBN 0-521-24244-4); pap. 14.95 (ISBN 0-521-28550-X). Cambridge U Pr.

Allchin, Raymond, jt. auth. see Allchin, Bridget.

Allcock, John B., ed. see Durkheim, Emile.

Allday, Elizabeth. Stefan Zweig: A Critical Biography. LC 74-190753. 1972. 13.50 (ISBN 0-87955-301-4). O'Hara.

Allegre, C. J. & Hart, S. R., eds. Trace Elements in Igneous Petrology. (Developments in Petrology: Vol. 5). 1978. Repr. 64.00 (ISBN 0-444-41658-7). Elsevier.

Alleine, Joseph. Alarm. 1978. pap. 2.95 (ISBN 0-85151-081-7). Banner of Truth.

Alleman, Herman C. Prayers for Boys. LC 66-14195. (gr. 4-9). pap. 3.95 (ISBN 0-8407-5241-5). Nelson.

Alleman, James E., ed. see Mid-Atlantic Conference.

Allen. Degradation & Stabilisation of Polyolefins. Date not set. price not set (ISBN 0-85334-194-X, Pub. by Applied Sci England). Elsevier.

--Secrets of Good Digestion. LC 82-694. (Library of Health). lib. bdg. 18.60 (ISBN 0-686-79855-4). Silver.

--Sewing & Knitting. (Beginner's Guides Ser.). (gr. 4-9). 1979. 5.95 (ISBN 0-86020-408-1, Usborne-Hayes); PLB 8.95 (ISBN 0-88110-035-8); pap. 2.95 (ISBN 0-86020-311-5). EDC.

Allen, jt. auth. see Bark.

Allen, jt. auth. see Booz.

Allen, A. & Eberly, J. H. Optical Resonance & Two-Level Atoms. LC 74-18023. (Interscience Monographs & Texts in Physics & Astronomy: No. 28). 224p. 1975. 45.95 (ISBN 0-471-02327-2, Pub. by Wiley-Interscience). Wiley.

Allen, A. H. An Introduction to Prestressed Concrete. (Educational Ser.). (Illus.). 1978. pap. 16.50x (ISBN 0-7210-1090-3). Scholium Intl.

Allen, Anne S. Introduction to Health Professions. 3rd ed. LC 79-26136. (Illus.). 1980. pap. text ed. 13.95 (ISBN 0-8016-0113-4). Mosby.

Allen, Arthur C. The Kidney: Medical & Surgical Diseases. 2nd ed. LC 61-17894. (Illus.). 1962. 129.50 o.p. (ISBN 0-8089-0008-0). Grune.

--The Skin. 2nd ed. LC 66-20173. (Illus.). 1966. 138.50 o.p. (ISBN 0-8089-0009-9). Grune.

Allen, Barbara A., jt. ed. see Allen, James.

Allen, Barbie. Barbie Allen's Dance Exercise. (Illus.). 128p. (Orig.). 1982. pap. 9.95 (ISBN 0-920510-65-5, Pub. by Personal Lib). Dodd.

Allen, Barry. Sports Illustrated Skin Diving & Snorkeling. LC 72-14150. 1973. 5.95 o.p. (ISBN 0-397-00969-0); pap. 2.95i (ISBN 0-397-00970-4, LP79). Har-Row.

Allen, C. F. Six-Membered Heterocyclic Nitrogen Compounds with Three Condensed Rings, Vol. 12. 646p. 1958. 83.50 o.p. (ISBN 0-470-37851-4, Pub. by Wiley-Interscience). Wiley.

Allen, C. Frank. Railroad Curves & Earthwork (with Tables) 7th ed. 1947. 43.50 (ISBN 0-07-001090-0, C). McGraw.

Allen, C. G. A Short Economic History of Modern Japan. 272p. 1980. 25.00 (ISBN 0-312-71771-7). St Martin.

Allen, Carl, jt. auth. see Allen, Marjorie.

Allen, Carleton K. Law in the Making. 7th ed. 1964. pap. 19.95x (ISBN 0-19-881029-6, OPB29). Oxford U Pr.

Allen, Carlos. Guia De Estudios Sobre Estudios En el Nuevo Testamento. (Illus.). 96p. 1981. pap. 3.50 (ISBN 0-311-43502-5). Casa Bautista.

Allen, Celine & Bartow, Maxine, eds. The Book of Catholic Names & Numbers. LC 79-54375. 168p. (Orig.). 1980. 9.95 o.p. (ISBN 0-89958-000-9, Pub. by Cath Heritage Pr). Winston Pr.

Allen, Charles. Raj: A Scrapbook of British India 1877-1947. LC 77-9126. (Illus.). 1978. 12.95 o.p. (ISBN 0-312-66307-2). St Martin.

Allen, Charles E., jt. auth. see Harman, Thomas L.

Allen, Charles L. All Things Are Possible Through Prayer. 1982. pap. 2.25 (ISBN 0-515-06492-0, PV072). Jove Pubns.

--All Things Are Possible Through Prayer. 7.95 (ISBN 0-8007-0007-4); pap. 2.25 (ISBN 0-8007-8000-0, Spire Bks). Revell.

--The Charles L. Allen Collector's Library. cancelled 44.95 (ISBN 0-8007-1330-3). Revell.

--Charles L. Allen Treasury. Wallis, Charles L., ed. 192p. 1970. 9.95 (ISBN 0-8007-0398-7). Revell.

--God's Psychiatry. 160p. 8.95 (ISBN 0-8007-0113-5); pap. 2.50 (ISBN 0-8007-8015-9, Spire Bks); pap. 4.95 (ISBN 0-8007-5010-1, Power Bks). Revell.

--In Quest of God's Power. 1952. pap. 3.95 o.p. (ISBN 0-8007-5020-9, Power Bks). Revell.

--Joyful Living in the Fourth Dimension. 160p. 1983. 8.95 (ISBN 0-8007-1351-6). Revell.

--Life More Abundant. 1976. pap. 2.25 (ISBN 0-515-06412-2). Jove Pubns.

--The Miracle of the Holy Spirit. 64p. 1974. 6.95 (ISBN 0-8007-0688-9). Revell.

--La Siquiatria de Dios. 176p. Date not set. 2.50 (ISBN 0-88113-280-2). Edit Betania.

--What I Have Lived by: An Autobiography. 160p. 1976. 5.95 o.p. (ISBN 0-8007-0805-9); ltd. gift ed 9.95 (ISBN 0-8007-0806-7). Revell.

Allen, Charles L. & Rice, Helen S. When You Lose a Loved One-Life is Forever. 1979. pap. 4.95 (ISBN 0-8007-5031-4, Power Bks). Revell.

Allen, Charlotte V. Acts of Kindness. 1979. pap. 1.95 o.p. (ISBN 0-451-08690-2, J8690, Sig). NAL.

--Intimate Friends. LC 82-12964. 300p. 1983. 14.95 (ISBN 0-525-24161-2, 01451-440). Dutton.

--The Marmalade Man. 1981. 14.50 o.p. (ISBN 0-525-15294-6, 01408-420). Dutton.

--Promises. (Orig.). 1982. pap. 3.50 (ISBN 0-425-06167-1). Berkley Pub.

Allen, Charotte V. Gifts of Love. (Orig.). 1978. pap. 1.95 o.p. (ISBN 0-451-08388-1, J8388, Sig). NAL.

Allen, Chris & Williams, Gavin, eds. Sub-Saharan Africa. LC 81-84744. (Sociology of "Developing Societies" Ser.). 240p. 1982. 18.00 (ISBN 0-85345-597-X, CL597X); pap. 8.00 (ISBN 0-85345-598-8, PB5998). Monthly Rev.

Allen, Christopher & Johnson, R. W., eds. African Perspectives. LC 78-128497. (Illus.). 1971. 39.50 (ISBN 0-521-07948-9). Cambridge U Pr.

Allen, Clarence, jt. auth. see Allen, Roach V.

Allen, Connie J., jt. auth. see Allen, Gerald R.

Allen, D. E., jt. auth. see Reekie, W. D.

Allen, David, et al, eds. Whole-Person Medicine. LC 79-2807. 1980. pap. 8.95 o.p. (ISBN 0-87784-815-7). Inter-Varsity.

Allen, David B., jt. auth. see Getz, William L.

Allen, David G. In English Ways: The Movement of Societies & the Transferal of English Local Law & Custom to Massachusetts Bay in the Seventeenth Century. 1982. pap. 7.95x (ISBN 0-393-95238-X). Norton.

Allen, Dell. Elements of Meat Processing. 1980. text ed. 16.95 (ISBN 0-8359-1662-6); instrs' manual avail. Reston.

Allen, Delmas J., jt. auth. see Pansky, Ben.

Allen, Devere. The Fight for Peace. LC 79-137525. (Peace Movement in America Ser). xi, 740p. 1972. Repr. of 1930 ed. lib. bdg. 37.95x (ISBN 0-89198-052-0). Ozer.

Allen, Devere, ed. Pacifism in the Modern World. LC 72-137526. (Peace Movement in America Ser). xviii, 278p. 1972. Repr. of 1929 ed. lib. bdg. 18.95x (ISBN 0-89198-053-9). Ozer.

Allen, Diogenes. Between Two Worlds: A Guide for Those Beginning to Be Religious. LC 76-12395. 1977. pap. 5.25 (ISBN 0-8042-1168-X). John Knox.

--Three Outsiders: Pascal, Kierkegaard, Simon Weil. 120p. (Orig.). 1983. pap. 6.00 (ISBN 0-936384-08-5). Cowley Pubns.

Allen, Don, ed. The World of Film & Filmmakers: A Visual History. (Illus.). 1979. 19.95 o.p. (ISBN 0-517-53662-5). Crown.

Allen, Don C., ed. The Moment of Poetry. LC 80-17079. (The Percy Graeme Turnbull Memorial Lectures on Poetry, 1961). 135p. 1980. Repr. of 1962 ed. lib. bdg. 19.25x (ISBN 0-313-22406-4, ALMP). Greenwood.

Allen, Donald, ed. see Kerouac, Jack.

Allen, Donald M., ed. see Lorca, Federico Garcia.

Allen, Donna. Fringe Benefits: Wages or Social Obligation? LC 75-627371. (Cornell Studies in Industrial & Labor Relations: No. 13). 288p. 1969. pap. 4.00 (ISBN 0-87546-006-2); pap. 7.00 special hard bdg. o.s.i. (ISBN 0-87546-265-0). ILR Pr.

Allen, Doris V., jt. auth. see Bliss, Lynn S.

Allen, Dorothy H. & Country Beautiful Magazine Editors. The Story of Animals. (World Is Nature Ser.). (Illus.). (gr. 3-6). 1973. PLB 5.69 o.p. (ISBN 0-399-60815-X). Putnam Pub Group.

Allen, Dorothy H. & Country Beautiful Editors. The Story of Soil. (World Is Nature Ser.). (Illus.). (gr. 3-6). 1971. PLB 5.69 o.p. (ISBN 0-399-60612-2). Putnam Pub Group.

Allen, Dorothy H. & Country Beautiful Magazine Editors. The Story of Trees. (World Is Nature Ser.). (Illus.). (gr. 3-6). 1974. PLB 5.69 o.p. (ISBN 0-399-60796-X). Putnam Pub Group.

Allen, Douglas & Allen, Douglas, Jr. N. C. Wyeth. 1972. 29.95 o.p. (ISBN 0-517-50054-X). Crown.

Allen, Durward L. Life of Prairies & Plains. (Our Living World of Nature Ser). 1967. 14.95 (ISBN 0-07-001099-4, P&RB); by subscription 3.95 (ISBN 0-07-046005-1). McGraw.

Allen, Dwight W., et al, eds. The Teacher's Handbook. 1971. 21.95x (ISBN 0-673-05880-8). Scott F.

Allen, E. M. Lafayette's Second Expedition to Virginia in 1781. 1891. 3.50 (ISBN 0-686-36851-7). Md Hist.

Allen, E. W. Essentials of Ophthalmic Optics. (Illus.). 1979. pap. text ed. 8.95x (ISBN 0-19-261173-9). Oxford U Pr.

Allen, E. Waterhouse. How to Execute an Agency. LC 79-53977. (Illus., Orig.). 1980. pap. 3.95 (ISBN 0-9603338-1-9). Bark-Back.

Allen, Edith B. One Hundred Bible Games. (Paperback Program Ser). (YA) 1968. pap. 3.50 (ISBN 0-8010-0033-5). Baker Bk.

Allen, Edward & Goldberg, Gale. Teach Yourself to Build. (Illus.). 1979. pap. text ed. 5.95x (ISBN 0-262-51020-0); student ed. looseleaf 5.95x (ISBN 0-262-51021-9). MIT Pr.

Allen, Edward B. Early American Wall Paintings, 1710-1850. LC 77-77694. (Library of American Art Ser.). 1971. Repr. of 1926 ed. lib. bdg. 29.50 (ISBN 0-306-71332-2). Da Capo.

Allen, Edward B., ed. The Responsive House. LC 74-23518. 320p. 1974. 25.00x (ISBN 0-262-01040-2); pap. 9.95x (ISBN 0-262-51012-X). MIT Pr.

Allen, Edward L. Energy & Economic Growth in the United States. 1979. text ed. 27.50x (ISBN 0-262-01062-3). MIT Pr.

Allen, Edward S. Six-Place Tables. 7th ed. 1947. 9.95 o.p. (ISBN 0-07-057751-X, P&RB). McGraw.

Allen, Elizabeth C. Mother, Can you Hear Me? 1983. 13.95 (ISBN 0-89696-194-X). Dodd.

Allen, Ethan. Baseball Play & Strategy. 3rd ed. LC 81-17177. 456p. 1982. lib. bdg. 26.50 (ISBN 0-89874-450-4). Krieger.

--Baseball Play & Strategy. 2nd ed. LC 69-14668. (Illus.). 445p. 1969. 17.95 o.p. (ISBN 0-8260-0305-2). Wiley.

Allen, Everett S. The Black Ships: Rumrunners of Prohibition. 1979. 12.95 (ISBN 0-316-03258-1). Little.

--Martha's Vineyard: An Elegy. 1982. 15.95 (ISBN 0-316-03257-3). Little.

Allen, Fay W. Waldo Emerson. (Illus.). 782p. 1982. pap. 10.95 (ISBN 0-14-006278-5). Penguin.

Allen, Frances C. Little Hippo. LC 75-129236. (Illus.). (gr. k-1). 1971. PLB 4.29 o.p. (ISBN 0-399-60420-0). Putnam Pub Group.

--Little Mouse's Wonderful Journey. (Arch Bks: Set 9). (Illus.). 32p. (ps-4). 1972. pap. 0.89 (ISBN 0-570-06069-9, 59-1187). Concordia.

Allen, Frank Kenyon, et al. Golfer's Bible. LC 68-11788. 1968. pap. 4.50 (ISBN 0-385-01402-3). Doubleday.

Allen, Frederick L. The Big Change: America Transforms Itself, 1900-1950. LC 82-18395. xii, 308p. 1983. Repr. of 1952 ed. lib. bdg. 35.00x (ISBN 0-313-23791-3, ALBC). Greenwood.

--Big Change, America Transforms Itself, Nineteen Hundred - Nineteen Fifty. 1969. pap. 2.95i (ISBN 0-06-080150-6, P150, PL). Har-Row.

--Only Yesterday. pap. 3.71i (ISBN 0-06-080004-6, P4, PL). Har-Row.

--Since Yesterday. 1972. pap. 2.95i (ISBN 0-06-080256-1, P256, PL). Har-Row.

Allen, G., ed. Sequencing of Proteins & Peptides. (Laboratory Techniques in Biochemistry & Molecular Biology Ser.: Vol. 9). 1981. pap. 28.50 (ISBN 0-444-80254-1). Elsevier.

Allen, G. C. British Industry & Economic Policy. 220p. 1979. text ed. 29.75 (ISBN 0-8419-5048-2). Holmes & Meier.

Allen, G. D. & Chui, Charles K. Elements of Calculus. LC 82-12874. (Mathematics Ser.). 512p. 1983. text ed. 24.95 (ISBN 0-534-01188-8). Brooks-Cole.

Allen, G. E. Life & Science in the Twentieth Century. LC 77-83985. (History of Science Ser.). (Illus.). 1978. 29.95 (ISBN 0-521-21864-0); pap. 9.95x (ISBN 0-521-29296-4). Cambridge U Pr.

Allen, G. F. Taoist Words of Wisdom Diary. (Illus.). 196p. Date not set. 5.00 (ISBN 0-7224-0198-1). Robinson & Watkins.

Allen, G. Freeman. Luxury Trains of the World. (Illus.). 1979. 14.95 (ISBN 0-89696-035-8, An Everest House Book). Dodd.

Allen, G. R. A Field Guide to Inland Fishes of Western Australia. (Illus.). 92p. 1982. pap. 15.00 (ISBN 0-7244-8409-4, Pub. by U of West Austral Pr). Intl Schol Bk Serv.

Allen, G. R. & Cross, N. J. Rainbowfishes of Australia & Papua New Guinea. (Illus.). 160p. 1982. 19.95 (ISBN 0-87666-547-4, H-1047). TFH Pubns.

Allen, Garland A., jt. auth. see Baker, Jeffrey J.

Allen, Garland E., jt. auth. see Baker, Jeffrey J. W.

Allen, Gary. Jimmy Carter-Jimmy Carter. LC 76-27187. (Orig.). 1976. pap. 1.50 (ISBN 0-89245-006-1). Seventy Six.

--The Kissinger: The Secret Side of the Secretary of State. LC 76-14012. (Orig.). 1976. pap. 1.75 (ISBN 0-685-65508-3). Seventy-Six.

--The Rockefeller File. LC 75-39136. (Orig.). 1976. pap. 2.95 (ISBN 0-89245-001-0). Seventy Six.

--Tax Target: Washington. new ed. 1979. 8.95 (ISBN 0-89245-015-0); pap. 2.95 (ISBN 0-89245-014-2). Seventy-Six.

Allen, Gay W. Studies in Leaves of Grass. LC 74-170214. 1972. pap. text ed. 2.50x o.p. (ISBN 0-675-09174-8). Merrill.

Allen, Gay W. & Clark, Harry H., eds. Literary Criticism: Pope to Croce. LC 61-12267. (Waynebooks Ser: No. 2). 1962. 15.95 (ISBN 0-8143-1157-1); pap. 8.95 (ISBN 0-8143-1158-X). Wayne St U Pr.

Allen, Gay Wilson. The Solitary Singer: A Critical Biography of Walt Whitman. LC 67-23414. 1967. 25.00x o.p. (ISBN 0-8147-0006-3). NYU Pr.

Allen, Gayle & Allen, Robert F. The Complete Recreational Vehicle Cookbook: For Campers, Motor Homes, RV's, & Vans. LC 76-54176. (Orig.). 1977. pap. 4.95 o.p. (ISBN 0-89087-174-4). Celestial Arts.

--Three Worlds Cookbook. LC 75-19542. (Illus.). 192p. 1975. 7.95 o.p. (ISBN 0-87983-096-4). Keats.

Allen, Gene P., jt. ed. see Wright, Nancy D.

Allen, George. The Agile Administrator. LC 79-65136. (Illus.). 136p. 1979. 12.95 (ISBN 0-933554-13-3); pap. 9.95 (ISBN 0-933554-12-5). Tempe Pubs.

--Life of Philidor: Musician & Chess-Player. LC 70-139198. (Music Ser). 1971. Repr. of 1863 ed. 22.50 (ISBN 0-306-70075-1). Da Capo.

Allen, George & Ritger, Dick. Encyclopedia of Bowling Instruction, 3 vols. 1982. Set. write for info. (ISBN 0-933554-14-1). Tempe Pubs.

Allen, George R. The Graduate Students' Guide to Theses & Dissertations: A Practical Manual for Writing & Research. LC 73-3774. (Higher Education Ser.). 256p. 1973. 12.95x (ISBN 0-87589-182-9). Jossey-Bass.

Allen, Gerald. Anemone Fishes. new ed. 24.95 (ISBN 0-87666-001-4, H-942). TFH Pubns.

--Charles Moore. (Illus.). 128p. 1980. 19.95 (ISBN 0-8230-7375-0, Whitney Lib). Watson-Guptill.

Allen, Gerald, jt. auth. see Moore, Charles.

Allen, Gerald D. Dental Anesthesia & Analgesia: Local & General. 2nd ed. 460p. 1979. 28.95 o.p. (ISBN 0-683-00067-5). Williams & Wilkins.

Allen, Gerald R. Butterfly & Angelfishes of the World: Vol. 2, Atlantic Ocean, Caribbean Sea, Red Sea, Indo-Pacific. LC 78-17351. 352p. 1980. 39.95 (ISBN 0-471-05618-9, Pub. by Wiley-Interscience). Wiley.

--Cockatiel Handbook. 14.95 (ISBN 0-87666-956-9, PS-741). TFH Pubns.

--Damselfishes. (Illus.). 240p. 1975. 19.95 (ISBN 0-87666-034-0, H-950). TFH Pubns.

Allen, Gerald R. & Allen, Connie J. All About Cockatiels. (Illus.). 1977. 7.95 (ISBN 0-87666-757-4, PS746). TFH Pubns.

Allen, Gertrude E. Everyday Insects. (Illus.). (gr. k-3). 1963. reinforced bdg. 5.95 o.p. (ISBN 0-395-17891-6). HM.

Allen, Glover M. Extinct & Vanishing Mammals of the Western Hemisphere: With the Marine Species of All Oceans. LC 72-85661. xv, 620p. 1973. Repr. of 1942 ed. lib. bdg. 28.50x (ISBN 0-8154-0433-6). Cooper Sq.

Allen, Grant. Physiological Aesthetics. Fletcher, Ian & Stokes, John, eds. LC 76-20038. (Decadent Consciousness Ser.: Vol. 3). 1977. Repr. of 1877 ed. lib. bdg. 38.00 o.s.i. (ISBN 0-8240-2752-3). Garland Pub.

Allen, H. B. & Campbell, R. N. Teaching English as a Second Language: A Book of Readings. 2nd ed. 1975. pap. 6.50 (ISBN 0-07-001072-2). McGraw.

Allen, H. C. & Hill, C. P., eds. British Essays in American History. LC 82-20916. x, 350p. 1983. Repr. of 1957 ed. lib. bdg. 39.75x (ISBN 0-313-23789-1, ALBE). Greenwood.

Allen, H. C. & Thompson, Roger, eds. Contrast & Connection: Bicentennial Essays in Anglo-American History. LC 76-7095. x, 373p. 1976. 20.00x (ISBN 0-8214-0355-9, 82-82485). Ohio U Pr.

Allen, H. C., Jr. & Cross, P. C. Molecular Vib-Rotors: Theory & Interpretation of High Resolution Infrared Spectra. LC 63-11426. 324p. 1963. text ed. 22.50 (ISBN 0-686-86259-7, Pub. by Wiley). Krieger.

Allen, H. G. & Bulson, P. S. Background to Buckling. (Illus.). 1980. text ed. 49.50x (ISBN 0-07-084100-4). McGraw.

Allen, Harold B. The Linguistic Atlas of the Upper Midwest, 3 vols. Vol. 1, 425 p., 1973. 32.00 (ISBN 0-8166-0686-2); Vol. 2, 92 p., 1975. 32.00 (ISBN 0-8166-0756-7); Vol. 3, 362p., 1976. 32.00 (ISBN 0-686-97793-9). Gale.

--Linguistics & English Linguistics. 2nd ed. LC 75-42974. (Goldentree Bibliographies in Language & Literature Ser.). 1977. pap. text ed. 16.95x (ISBN 0-88295-558-6). Harlan Davidson.

Allen, Hazel O. & Murrell, John, eds. Nurse Training. 224p. 1978. 30.00x (ISBN 0-7121-1405-X, Pub. by Macdonald & Evans). State Mutual Bk.

Allen, Helena G. The Betrayal of Liliukalani: Last Queen of Hawaii, 1838-1917. LC 82-71912. (Illus.). 420p. 1983. 19.95 (ISBN 0-87062-144-0). A H Arthur.

Allen, Henry E. Turkish Transformation: A Study in Social & Religious Development. LC 68-57588. (Illus.). 1968. Repr. of 1935 ed. lib. bdg. 18.75x (ISBN 0-8371-0284-7, ALTT). Greenwood.

Allen, Hervey. Anthony Adverse, Pt. 1: The Roots of the Tree. 1978. pap. 2.50 o.p. (ISBN 0-446-81439-3). Warner Bks.

Allen, Horace T., Jr. A Handbook for the Lectionary. LC 80-19735. pap. 8.95 (ISBN 0-664-24347-9). Geneva Divinity.

--A Handbook for the Lectionary. LC 80-19735. 1980. softcover 8.95 (ISBN 0-664-24347-9, Pub. by Geneva Pr. Pub.). Westminster.

Allen, Ira. Natural & Political History of the State of Vermont. LC 69-19611. 1969. Repr. 7.50 o.p. (ISBN 0-8048-0419-2). C E Tuttle.

Allen, Irving L. The Language of Ethnic Conflict. 168p. 1983. 20.00x (ISBN 0-231-05556-0); pap. 9.50x (ISBN 0-231-05557-9). Columbia U Pr.

Allen, Irving L., ed. New Towns & the Suburban Dream. (Interdisciplinary Urban Ser). 1976. 24.00 (ISBN 0-8046-9161-4, Natl U); pap. 9.95 (ISBN 0-8046-9165-7). Kennikat.

Allen, J. A. Preliminary List of Works & Papers Relating to the Mammalian Orders Cete & Sirenia. 562p. 1981. 50.00x (ISBN 0-686-97097-7, Pub. by Corner Place England). State Mutual Bk.

Allen, J. Dev, jt. auth. see Wright, Leigh R.

Allen, J. P. & Widdowson, H. G. English in Physical Science. (English in Focus Ser). (Illus.). 1974. Student's Edition. pap. 9.95x (ISBN 0-19-437510-2); Tchr's Edition. 12.00x (ISBN 0-19-437504-8). Oxford U Pr.

Allen, J. R. Sedimentary Structures, 2 Pts. (Developments in Sedimentology Ser.: Vol. 30). 594p. 1982. Pt. A. 104.25 (ISBN 0-444-41935-7); Pt. B. 110.75 (ISBN 0-444-41945-4). Elsevier.

Allen, J. S., ed. see Lenin, Vladimir I.

Allen, James. All These Things Added. 192p. 6.50 (ISBN 0-686-38209-9). Sun Bks.

--As a Man Thinketh. 1959. 2.95 (ISBN 0-448-01631-1, G&D). Putnam Pub Group.

--As a Man Thinketh. 88p. 3.50 (ISBN 0-686-38211-0). Sun Bks.

--The Life Triumphant. 112p. 4.50 (ISBN 0-686-38224-2). Sun Bks.

--Morning & Evening Thoughts. 80p. 3.50 (ISBN 0-686-38228-5). Sun Bks.

Allen, James & Allen, Barbara A., eds. Psychiatry. 7th ed. (Medical Examination Review Book: Vol 7). 1982. 11.95 (ISBN 0-87488-107-2). Med Exam.

Allen, James, et al. Inspiration Three, Vol. 1: Three Famous Classics in One Book. LC 73-80032. (Pivot Family Reader Ser.). 128p. 1973. pap. 1.75 o.p. (ISBN 0-87983-041-7). Keats.

Allen, James A. Studies in Innovation in the Steel & Chemical Industries. LC 68-583. 246p. 1967. lib. bdg. 22.50x (ISBN 0-678-06790-2). Kelley.

Allen, James A. Van see Van Allen, James A.

Allen, James C. & Beam, Thomas R. Infectious Disease for the House Officer. (House Officer Ser.). (Illus.). 196p. 1982. pap. 10.95 (ISBN 0-683-00069-1). Williams & Wilkins.

Allen, James L. The Choir Invisible. 361p. 1982. lib. bdg. 25.00 (ISBN 0-686-81830-X). Darby Bks.

--Yeats's Epitaph: A Key to Symbolic Unity in His Life & Work. LC 80-5848. 282p. (Orig.). 1982. lib. bdg. 24.00 (ISBN 0-8191-2592-X); pap. text ed. 11.50 (ISBN 0-8191-2593-8). U Pr of Amer.

Allen, James T. First Year of Greek. rev. ed. 1931. text ed. 19.95x (ISBN 0-02-301750-3). Macmillan.

Allen, Jana & Gin, Margaret. Innards & Other Variety Meats. LC 73-91942. (Illus.). 144p. 1974. 7.95 o.s.i. (ISBN 0-912238-49-6); pap. 4.95 o.p. (ISBN 0-912238-48-8). One Hund One Prods.

Allen, Jane A., ed. see Day, Holliday D.

Allen, Janet. Exciting Things to Do with Color. LC 76-39906. (gr. 3 up). 1977. 4.95 (ISBN 0-397-31742-5, JBL-J). Har-Row.

Allen, Janice, jt. auth. see Allen, Jerry.

Allen, Jean & Mix, Emily S. Build a Better- & Slimmer-You. 1977. 8.95 o.p. (ISBN 0-87000-369-0, Arlington Hse). Crown.

Allen, Jeffrey. Bonzini! The Tattooed Man. 48p. (gr. 1-4). 1976. 5.95 o.p. (ISBN 0-316-03427-4). Little.

--The Secret Life of Mr. Weird. (Illus.). 32p. 1982. 8.95 (ISBN 0-316-03428-2). Little.

--You're Hired! How to Turn an Interview into a Job Offer. 1983. price not set (ISBN 0-671-47173-2). S&S.

Allen, Jerry & Allen, Janice. Halia Language Course. 68p. 1965. pap. 1.00x (ISBN 0-88312-771-7); 1.50 (ISBN 0-88312-393-2). Summer Inst Ling.

Allen, Jerry, ed. see Conrad, Joseph.

Allen, Jim & Curnow, Wystan. New Art: Some Recent New Zealand Sculpture & Past Object Art. (Illus.). 1976. 9.95 (ISBN 0-686-38948-4, Pub. by Heinemann Pub New Zealand). Intl Schol Bk Serv.

Allen, Joan, illus. Baby Animal Dress-up Book. (Platt & Munk Peggy Dress-up Bks). (Illus.). 10p. (ps). Date not set. price not set cloth (ISBN 0-448-40025-1, G&D). Putnam Pub Group.

Allen, Joe & Lientz, Bennett. Effective Business Communication: A Practical Guide. LC 78-32083. 1979. text ed. 23.50x (ISBN 0-673-16081-5). Scott F.

Allen, John. Assault with a Deadly Weapon: The Autobiography of a Street Criminal. Kelly, Dianne H. & Heyma, K., eds. 1978. pap. 4.95 (ISBN 0-07-001073-0, SP). McGraw.

--Drama in Schools. 1979. text ed. 19.50x o.p. (ISBN 0-435-18031-2). Heinemann Ed.

Allen, John & Hammond, Paul. The Magnificent Gateway: A Geology of the Columbia River Gorge. LC 79-2714. (Illus.). 1979. pap. 8.50 (ISBN 0-917304-10-1). Timber.

Allen, John A. Lean Divider. LC 68-26742. 1968. 4.00 o.p. (ISBN 0-8233-0002-1). Golden Quill.

Allen, John E. Early Aircraft. LC 78-64653. (Fact Finders Ser.). (Illus.). 1979. PLB 8.00 (ISBN 0-382-06244-2). Silver.

Allen, John R. Physical Geology. (Introducing Geology Ser.). 1975. pap. text ed. 11.95 (ISBN 0-04-550022-3). Allen Unwin.

--Physical Processes of Sedimentation: An Introduction. (Earth Science Ser.). (Illus.). 1970. pap. text ed. 11.95x (ISBN 0-04-551014-8). Allen Unwin.

Allen, Jonathan. A Bad Case of Animal Nonsense. LC 81-47137. (Illus.). (ps up). 1981. 8.95 (ISBN 0-87923-398-2). Godine.

Allen, Judy. Exciting Things to Do with Nature Materials. LC 76-39960. (gr. 3 up). 1977. 4.95 (ISBN 0-397-31743-3, JBL-J). Har-Row.

Allen, June, tr. see Garin, Eugenio.

Allen, K. Eileen. Mainstreaming in Early Childhood Education. LC 78-74838. (Early Childhood Education Ser.). (Illus.). 260p. (Orig.). 1980. pap. text ed. 11.00 (ISBN 0-8273-1692-5); instructor's guide 3.25 (ISBN 0-8273-1693-3). Delmar.

Allen, K. Eileen & Goetz, Elizabeth M. Early Childhood Education: Special Problems, Special Solutions. LC 82-4029. 349p. 1982. 26.95 (ISBN 0-89443-657-0). Aspen Systems.

Allen, K. W., ed. Adhesion, Vols. 1-5. 1977-81. Vol. 1. 45.00 (ISBN 0-85334-735-2, Pub. by Applied Sci England); Vol. 2. 41.00 (ISBN 0-85334-743-3); Vol. 3. 41.00 (ISBN 0-85334-808-1); Vol. 4. 43.00 (ISBN 0-85334-861-8); Vol. 5. 65.75 (ISBN 0-85334-929-0). Elsevier.

--Adhesion, Vol. 6. (Illus.). x, 210p. 1982. 72.50x (ISBN 0-85334-106-0, Pub. by Applied Sci England). Elsevier.

--Adhesion, Vol. 6. Date not set. 65.75 (ISBN 0-85334-106-0, Pub. by Applied Sci England). Elsevier.

--Adhesion, Vol. 7. Date not set. price not set (ISBN 0-85334-195-8, Pub. by Applied Sci England). Elsevier.

Allen, Keith, jt. ed. see Stavrakas, Nick.

Allen, Kerry K. Volunteering: Rediscovering Our Greatest Natural Resource. (Vital Issues Ser.: Vol. XXXI, No. 7). 0.80 (ISBN 0-686-84145-X). Ctr Info Am.

Allen, Kevin, ed. Balanced National Growth. LC 78-13820. 352p. 1979. 25.95x (ISBN 0-669-02668-9). Lexington Bks.

Allen, L. A. Making Managerial Planning More Effective. 320p. 1982. 27.50 (ISBN 0-07-001078-1). McGraw.

Allen, L. David. Herbert's Dune & Other Works Notes. 101p. 1975. pap. text ed. 2.95 (ISBN 0-8220-0419-4). Cliffs.

Allen, Laura J. Rollo & Tweedy & the Case of the Missing Cheese. LC 82-47731. (Illus.). 48p. (gr. k-3). 1983. 10.53i (ISBN 0-06-020096-0, HarpJ); PLB 10.89g (ISBN 0-06-020097-9). Har-Row.

Allen, Lee. Dizzy Dean: His Story in Baseball. (Putnam Sports Shelf). (Illus.). (gr. 5 up). 1967. PLB 5.49 o.p. (ISBN 0-399-60128-7). Putnam Pub Group.

Allen, Linda. Lionel & the Spy Next Door. LC 79-23275. (Illus.). 96p. (gr. 4-6). 1980. 8.75 (ISBN 0-688-22225-0); PLB 8.40 (ISBN 0-688-32225-5). Morrow.

--Mr. Simkin's Grandma. LC 78-20917. (Illus.). 32p. (gr. k-3). 1979. 8.75 (ISBN 0-688-22191-2); PLB 8.40 (ISBN 0-688-32191-7). Morrow.

--Mrs. Simkin's Bed. LC 80-12262. (Illus.). 32p. (gr. k-3). 1980. 8.75 (ISBN 0-688-22233-1); PLB 8.40 (ISBN 0-688-32233-6). Morrow.

Allen, Loring. Venezuelan Economic Development: A Politico-Economic Analysis. Altman, Edward I. & Walter, Ingo, eds. LC 76-10395. (Contemporary Studies in Economic & Financial Analysis: Vol. 7). 1977. lib. bdg. 36.50 (ISBN 0-89232-011-7). Jai Pr.

Allen, Louis A. Management Profession. (Management Ser.). 1964. 27.95 (ISBN 0-07-001375-6, P&RB). McGraw.

--Professional Management. 256p. 1973. 26.50 (ISBN 0-07-001110-9, P&RB). McGraw.

Allen, Louis L. Starting & Succeeding in Your Own Small Business. 1967. 7.95 o.p. (ISBN 0-448-01177-8, G&D). Putnam Pub Group.

--Starting & Succeeding in Your Own Small Business. 1978. pap. 4.95 (ISBN 0-448-14583-9, G&D). Putnam Pub Group.

Allen, Loyd V., Jr. Drug Abuse: What Can We Do? LC 79-92950. 144p. (Orig.). 1981. pap. text ed. 2.50 o.p. (ISBN 0-8307-0744-1, 5016702). Regal.

Allen, M. W. & Noffsinger, Ella M. A Revision of the Marine Nematodes of the Superfamily Draconematoidea Filipjev 1918. (Publications in Zoology Ser.: Vol. 109). 1978. 13.00x (ISBN 0-520-09583-9). U of Cal Pr.

Allen, Marcus. Astrology for the New Age: An Intuitive Approach. LC 79-10433. 129p. 1979. pap. 5.95 (ISBN 0-931432-03-0). Whatever Pub.

Allen, Margaret V. The Achievement of Margaret Fuller. LC 79-1732. 1979. 16.95x (ISBN 0-271-00215-8). Pa St U Pr.

Allen, Marjorie & Allen, Carl. Farley, Are You for Real? LC 76-15628. (Break-of-Day Books). (Illus.). (gr. k-3). 1976. PLB 6.99 o.p. (ISBN 0-698-30633-3, Coward). Putnam Pub Group.

--The Marble Cake Cat. (Illus.). (gr. 3-5). 1977. 5.95 o.p. (ISBN 0-698-20401-8, Coward). Putnam Pub Group.

Allen, Marjorie N. One, Two, Three---Ah-Choo! (Illus.). 64p. (gr. 3-5). 1980. PLB 6.99 (ISBN 0-698-30718-6, Coward). Putnam Pub Group.

Allen, Marshall B., Jr., ed. see Symposium on the Pituitary, Medical College of Georgia, Augusta, Georgia, May 20-22, 1976.

Allen, Mary. Animals in American Literature. LC 82-17369. (Illus.). 218p. 1983. 14.95 (ISBN 0-252-00975-4). U of Ill Pr.

Allen, Mary J. & Yen, Wendy M. Introduction to Measurement Theory. LC 78-25821. 1979. text ed. 22.95 (ISBN 0-8185-0283-5). Brooks-Cole.

Allen, Mary M., ed. see International Science & Technology, Inc.

Allen, Maury. Baseball's One Hundred: A Personal Ranking of the Best Players in Baseball History. (Illus.). 336p. 1981. 14.95 (ISBN 0-89104-208-3, A & W Visual Library); pap. 7.95 (ISBN 0-89104-200-8, A & W Visual Library). A & W Pubs.

--Big-Time Baseball. (Illus.). 288p. (Orig.). 1978. pap. 6.95 o.s.i. (ISBN 0-89104-222-9, A & W Visual Library). A & W Pubs.

--Mr. October. 1982. pap. 2.50 (ISBN 0-451-11420-5, AE1420, Sig). NAL.

Allen, Michael & Mokherjee, Sal. Women in India & Nepal. 1982. pap. 24.00 (ISBN 0-908070-07-1, Pub. by Australia Nat Univ). South Asia Bks.

Allen, Michael J., ed. see Shakespeare, William.

Allen, Milton H. Why Do Good People Suffer? 1983. pap. 4.95 (ISBN 0-8054-5208-7). Broadman.

Allen, N. S. Photochemistry of Dyed & Pigmented Polymers. 1980. 51.25 (ISBN 0-85334-898-7, Pub. by Applied Sci England). Elsevier.

Allen, N. S., jt. auth. see McKellar, J. F.

Allen, N. S., ed. Developments in Polymer Photochemistry, Vols. 1-3. 1980-82. Vol. 1. 69.75 (ISBN 0-85334-911-8, Pub. by Applied Sci England); Vol. 2. 82.00 (ISBN 0-85334-936-3); Vol. 3. 69.75 (ISBN 0-85334-978-9). Elsevier.

Allen, O. Wildflower Gardening. LC 77-73630. (Encyclopedia of Gardening Ser.). (Illus.). (gr. 6 up). 1977. PLB 17.28 (ISBN 0-8094-2555-6, Pub. by Time-Life). Silver.

Allen, Oliver. Atmosphere. (Planet Earth Ser.). 1983. lib. bdg. 19.92 (ISBN 0-8094-4337-6, Pub. by Time-Life). Silver.

Allen, Oliver E. The Airline Builders. LC 80-15249. (Epic of Flight Ser.). PLB 19.96 (ISBN 0-8094-3284-6). Silver.

--Building Sound Bones & Muscles. LC 81-18208. (Library of Health). PLB 18.60 (ISBN 0-8094-3787-2). Silver.

--The Pacific Navigators. LC 80-13963. (Seafarers Ser.). PLB 19.92 (ISBN 0-8094-2686-2). Silver.

--The Windjammers. LC 78-10819. (The Seafarers Ser.). (Illus.). 1979. lib. bdg. 19.92 (ISBN 0-8094-2704-4). Silver.

Allen, Oliver E., jt. auth. see Crockett, James U.

Allen, P. The Cambridge Apostles. LC 77-82482. (Illus.). 1979. 42.50 (ISBN 0-521-21803-9). Cambridge U Pr.

--The Practice of Exporting. 240p. 1977. 29.00x (ISBN 0-7121-1658-3, Pub. by Macdonald & Evans). State Mutual Bk.

Allen, P. S. The Romanesque Lyric: Studies in Its Background & Development from Petronius to the Cambridge Songs. 1969. Repr. of 1928 ed. text ed. 10.00x o.p. (ISBN 0-391-02040-4). Humanities.

Allen, P. S., ed. Selections from,...Principally from his Epistles. 1982. 20.00 (ISBN 0-89241-361-1); pap. 11.50 (ISBN 0-89241-116-3). Caratzas Bros.

Allen, Pamela. Mr. Archimedes' Bath. 1980. 10.75 (ISBN 0-688-41919-4); lib. bdg. 10.32 (ISBN 0-688-51919-9). Lothrop.

Allen, Paul. A History of the American Revolution, 2 vols. LC 72-10761. (American Revolutionary Ser.). Repr. of 1822 ed. Vol. 1. lib. bdg. 36.00x (ISBN 0-8290-0369-X); Vol. 2. lib. bdg. 28.00x (ISBN 0-686-96756-9); Set. lib. bdg. 59.00x (ISBN 0-8290-0370-3). Irvington.

--The Life of Charles Brockden Brown. LC 75-25800. 424p. 1975. lib. bdg. 48.00x (ISBN 0-8201-1160-0). Schol Facsimiles.

Allen, Paul M. Vladimir Soloviev: Russian Mystic. LC 72-81592. (Spiritual Science Library). (Illus.). 544p. 1978. 17.00 (ISBN 0-89345-032-4, Steinerbks); pap. 11.00 (ISBN 0-89345-213-0). Garber Comm.

Allen, Paul M., ed. A Christian Rosenkreutz Anthology. 2nd, rev. ed. LC 68-13130. (Illus.). 640p. 1981. Repr. of 1968 ed. 40.00 (ISBN 0-89345-009-X, Spiritual Sci Lib). Garber Comm.

Allen, Paul M., ed. see Steiner, Rudolf.

Allen, Paul M., ed. see Steiner, Rudolf, et al.

Allen, Paul M., ed. see Steiner, Rudolf.

Allen, Paula G., ed. Studies in American Indian Literature: Critical Essays & Course Designs. LC 82-12516. (MLA Commission on the Literatures & Languages of America Ser.). 384p. 1983. 22.50x (ISBN 0-87352-354-7); pap. 12.50x (ISBN 0-87352-355-5). Modern Lang.

Allen, Philip, jt. auth. see Huelsman, Lawrence P.

Allen, Philip W. Tumors & Proliferations of Adipose Tissue: A Clinicopathologic Approach. LC 80-28916. (Masson Monographs in Diagnostic Pathology: Vol. 1). 200p. 1981. text ed. 43.50x (ISBN 0-89352-057-8). Masson Pub.

Allen, Polly R. & Kenen, Peter B. Asset Markets & Exchange Rates: Modeling an Open Economy. LC 79-16874. 352p. Date not set. pap. 17.95 (ISBN 0-521-27406-0). Cambridge U Pr.

--Asset Markets, Exchange Rates, & Economic Integration. LC 79-16874. (Illus.). 1980. 59.50 (ISBN 0-521-22982-0). Cambridge U Pr.

Allen, R. C. World Best Bits of Wisdom. 1977. 7.95 (ISBN 0-910228-08-6); pap. 4.95 (ISBN 0-910228-09-4). Best Bks.

Allen, R. E. The Attalid Kingdom: A Constitutional History. (Illus.). 288p. 1982. text ed. 45.00x (ISBN 0-19-814845-3). Oxford U Pr.

--Plato's Euthyphro & the Earlier Theory of Forms. (International Library of Philosophy & Scientific Method). 1970. text ed. 17.50x (ISBN 0-391-00055-1). Humanities.

--Plato's Parmenides: Translation & Analysis. LC 82-7051. 320p. 1983. 25.00x (ISBN 0-8166-1070-3). U of Minn Pr.

Allen, R. Earl. Good Morning, Lord: Devotionals for Times of Sorrow. (Good Morning, Lord Ser.). 96p. 1983. 4.95 (ISBN 0-8010-0191-9). Baker Bk.

Allen, R. J. & Lientz, Bennett P. Systems in Action. LC 77-16546. 1979. text ed. 18.95x (ISBN 0-673-16149-8); pap. text ed. 15.50x (ISBN 0-673-16150-1). Scott F.

Allen, Reginald E., ed. Studies in Plato's Metaphysics. (International Library of Philosophy & Scientific Method). 1968. text ed. 46.25x (ISBN 0-7100-3626-4). Humanities.

Allen, Rex W. & Von Karolyi, Ilona. Hospital Planning Handbook. LC 75-30599. 272p. 1976. text ed. 32.50x (ISBN 0-471-02319-1, Pub. by Wiley-Interscience). Wiley.

Allen, Richard. Imperialism & Nationalism in the Fertile Crescent: Sources & Prospects of the Arab-Israeli Conflict. (Illus.). 1974. 25.00x (ISBN 0-19-501782-X). Oxford U Pr.

--The Life Experience & Gospel Labors of The Rt. Rev. Richard Allen. 96p. (Orig.). 1983. pap. 3.95 (ISBN 0-687-21844-6). Abingdon.

Allen, Richard B., ed. Atlantic Fishermans Handbook. (Illus.). 482p. (Orig.). 1982. pap. 12.95 (ISBN 0-9608932-0-2). Fisheries Comm.

Allen, Richard C., Jr., jt. auth. see Sanchez, David A.

Allen, Richard E., tr. see Konrad, George & Szelenyi, Ivan.

Allen, Richard G., et al. American Government, 3 vols. Incl. Vol. 1. Origins of American Government & Citizenship: Political Parties & Elections. 156p (ISBN 0-86624-035-7, US0); Vol. 2. The Birth of Our Nation-Congress & the Laws-The President & His Cabinet. 256p (ISBN 0-86624-036-5, US1); Vol. 3. The Courts & Liberty: The World at Our Doorstep. 174p (ISBN 0-86624-037-3, US2). (Illus.). 1981. pap. text ed. write for info.; write for info. tchr's guide (US3); write for info. end-of-unit test (US4). Bilingual Ed Serv.

--U. S. History - One, 4 vols. Incl. Vol. 1: America Its Discovery, Independence & Early Problems. 290p (ISBN 0-86624-001-2, UT1); Vol. 2: Strengthening the New Nation. 270p (ISBN 0-86624-002-0, UT2); Vol. 3: The Republic Expands. 192p (ISBN 0-86624-003-9, UT3); Vol. 4: Expansion, Destruction & Reconstruction. 156p (ISBN 0-86624-004-7, UT4); Teacher's Guide. avail. (UT5); End of Unit Test. avail. (UT6). (Illus.). 1981. pap. text ed. 5.95 ea. Bilingual Ed Serv.

Allen, Richard J., jt. ed. see Jacobs, Frederic.

Allen, Richard P., jt. auth. see Safer, Daniel J.

Allen, Richard S. Covered Bridges of the Northeast. (Illus.). 128p. 1983. pap. 9.95 (ISBN 0-8289-0439-1). Greene.

Allen, Richard V., jt. auth. see Lee, Dorris M.

Allen, Roach V. Language Experiences in Communication. LC 75-31011. (Illus.). 512p. 1976. text ed. 22.95 (ISBN 0-395-18624-2); instr's. manual 1.50 (ISBN 0-395-18798-2). HM.

Allen, Roach V. & Allen, Clarence. Language Experience Activities. 2nd ed. (Illus.). 384p. 1982. pap. 13.95 (ISBN 0-395-31802-5). HM.

Allen, Robert. Blues & Ballads. 103p. 1974. 3.95 (ISBN 0-87886-047-9). Ithaca Hse.

--A Child's Book of Animals. (Illus.). 64p. (ps-1). 1981. 3.95 (ISBN 0-448-41056-7, G&D). Putnam Pub Group.

--One-Two-Three: First Counting Book. (Illus.). 72p. (ps-1). 1981. 3.95 (ISBN 0-448-41055-9, G&D). Putnam Pub Group.

--Reluctant Reformers: The Impact of Racism on American Social Reform Movements. LC 73-85495. 1974. 8.95 (ISBN 0-88258-002-7); pap. 6.95 (ISBN 0-88258-026-4). Howard U Pr.

--Valhalla at the OK. 53p. 1971. 2.95 o.p. (ISBN 0-87886-007-X). Ithaca Hse.

Allen, Robert D. & Wolfe, Thomas E. The Allen & Wolfe Illustrated Dictionary of Real Estate. LC 82-13445. (Real Estate for Professional Practitioners). 266p. 1983. 24.95 (ISBN 0-471-09415-3, Pub. by Wiley-Interscience). Wiley.

--Real Estate Almanac. LC 80-12417. (Real Estate for Professional Practitioners Ser.). 472p. 1980. pap. 22.95 (ISBN 0-471-05854-8). Wiley.

Allen, Robert E. & Keaveny, Timothy J. Contemporary Labor Relations. 672p. 1983. text ed. 24.95 (ISBN 0-686-82182-3). A-W.

Allen, Robert F. & Kraft, Carlotte. Beat the System! A Way to Create More Human Environments. (Illus.). 1980. 21.95 o.p. (ISBN 0-07-001080-3). McGraw.

Allen, Robert F. & Kraft, Charlotte. The Organizational Unconscious: How to Create the Organizational Environment. (Illus.). 229p. 1982. 14.95 (ISBN 0-13-641381-1); pap. 6.95 (ISBN 0-13-641373-0). P-H.

Allen, Robert F., jt. auth. see Allen, Gayle.

Allen, Robert G. Creating Wealth Through Real Estate. 1983. 14.50 (ISBN 0-671-44281-3). S&S.

--Nothing Down. 1980. 16.50 (ISBN 0-671-24748-4). S&S.

Allen, Robert L. Black Awakening in Capitalist America: An Analytic History. LC 69-20059. pap. 5.50 (ISBN 0-385-07718-1, Anch). Doubleday.

Allen, Robert S., jt. auth. see Pearson, Drew.

Allen, Robert T. The Violin. (Illus.). (gr. 3-6). 1977. pap. 7.95 (ISBN 0-07-082620-X, GB). McGraw.

Allen, Robert V., tr. see Gohdes, Clarence & Libman, Valentina A.

Allen, Robert W. & Porter, Lyman W. Organizational Influence Processes. 1983. pap. text ed. 15.95x (ISBN 0-673-15318-5). Scott F.

Allen, Rodger van see Van Allen, Rodger.

Allen, Rodney F., et al, eds. The Works of Thy Hands. LC 72-95647. (Illus.). 89p. (Orig.). 1973. pap. 3.25 (ISBN 0-88489-051-1). St Marys.

Allen, Roger, jt. ed. see Ringold, Fran.

Allen, Roland. The Spontaneous Expansion of the Church. 1962. pap. 4.95 (ISBN 0-8028-1002-0). Eerdmans.

Allen, Ronald B. When Song is New. 1983. 5.95 (ISBN 0-8407-5825-1). Nelson.

Allen, Ronald B., et al. Worship: Rediscovering the Missing Jewel. LC 82-2198. (Critical Concern Ser.). 180p. 1982. 9.95 (ISBN 0-930014-86-3). Multnomah.

Allen, Ronald J. Our Eyes Can Be Opened: Preaching the Miracle Stories of the Synoptic Gospels Today. LC 81-43679. 146p. 1983. pap. text ed. 8.25 (ISBN 0-8191-2671-3). U Pr of Amer.

Allen, Roy F. German Expressionist Poetry. (World Authors Ser.). 1979. lib. bdg. 14.50 (ISBN 0-8057-6386-4, Twayne). G K Hall.

--Literary Life in German Expressionism & the Berlin Circles. Foster, Stephen, ed. LC 82-4762. (Studies in Fine Arts: The Avant-Garde: No. 25). 1983. write for info (ISBN 0-8357-1315-6, UMI Res Pr). Univ Microfilms.

Allen, Ruth. East Texas Lumber Workers: An Economic & Social Picture, 1870-1950. (Illus.). 249p. 1961. 12.50x o.p. (ISBN 0-292-73219-8). U of Tex Pr.

--What's the Matter with Christy? 110p. (Orig.). 1982. pap. 3.95 (ISBN 0-87123-629-X, 210629). Bethany Hse.

Allen, S. Manager's Guide to Audiovisuals. 1972. pap. 4.50 (ISBN 0-07-001093-5). McGraw.

Allen, Sarah. A Cleaner World. (Cambridge Dinosaur Information Ser.). (Illus.). 26p. (gr. 7-10). 1983. pap. 1.50 (ISBN 0-521-27200-9). Cambridge U Pr.

Allen, Sheila. New Minorities, Old Conflicts: Asian & West Indian Migrants in Britain. 1971. pap. text ed. 3.95x (ISBN 0-394-31477-8). Phila Bk Co.

Allen, Shirley W. & Leonard, J. W. Conserving Natural Resources. 3rd ed. 1966. 17.50 o.p. (ISBN 0-07-001081-1, C). McGraw.

Allen, Stephen A., 3rd, jt. auth. see Lorsch, Jay W.

Allen, Steve. Meeting of Minds. 1978. 10.00 o.p. (ISBN 0-517-53383-9). Crown.

--Meeting of Minds: Second Series. (Illus.). 1979. 10.00 o.p. (ISBN 0-517-53894-6). Crown.

--Meeting of Minds: Third Series. (Meeting of Minds Ser.). 288p. 1980. 10.95 o.p. (ISBN 0-517-54220-X). Crown.

Allen, T. Particle Size Measurement. 3rd ed. (Powder Technology Ser.). 1981. 58.00x (ISBN 0-412-15410-2, Pub. by Chapman & Hall). Methuen Inc.

Allen, T., jt. auth. see Stanley-Wood, N.

Allen, T. D. Writing to Create Ourselves: New Approaches for Teachers, Students, & Writers. 225p. 1982. 16.95 (ISBN 0-8061-1768-0). U of Okla Pr.

Allen, T. D., jt. auth. see Autry, Gloria D.

Allen, T. Earl, jt. auth. see Miller, David K.

Allen, T. O. & Roberts, Alan P. Production Operations, Vol. 1. 225p. 1978. 47.50x. Pennwell Book Division.

Allen, T. O. & Roberts, Allen P. Production Operations, Vol. 2. 231p. 1978. 47.50x. Pennwell Book Division.

Allen, Thomas. Ship of Gold. LC 81-48027. 256p. 1982. write for info. o.p. (ISBN 0-06-038017-9, HarpT). Har-Row.

Allen, Thomas B., et al. America's Wildlife Sampler. LC 82-60674. (Illus.). 208p. 1983. 14.95 o.p. (ISBN 0-912186-45-3). Natl Wildlife.

Allen, Thomas J. Managing the Flow of Technology. 1977. text ed. 27.50x (ISBN 0-262-01048-8). MIT Pr.

Allen, Thomas L. & Keefer, Raymond M. Chemistry: Experiment & Theory. 2nd ed. 742p. 1982. text ed. 30.50 scp (ISBN 0-06-040209-1, HarpC); sol. manual scp 5.95 (ISBN 0-06-040211-3); instr's. manual avail. (ISBN 0-06-360203-2). Har-Row.

Allen, Thomas W. The ASEAN Report, 2 vols. Wain, Barry, ed. Incl. Vol. 1. A Comparative Assessment of the ASEAN Countries; Vol. 2. The Evolution & Programs of ASEAN: The Asian Wall Street Journal. LC 80-110683. (Illus.). 414p. 1980. Set. pap. 125.00 (ISBN 0-295-95740-9, 80-110683). U of Wash Pr.

Allen, Vera, ed. see Larsen, Phyllis.

Allen, Virginia F. Inside English. Date not set. pap. text ed. 7.95 (ISBN 0-88345-491-2, 21181). Regents Pub.

--Techniques in Teaching Vocabulary. (Illus.). 128p. (Orig.). 1983. pap. 3.95x (ISBN 0-19-503231-4). Oxford U Pr.

Allen, Virginia M. The Femme Fatale: Erotic & Fatal Muse. 300p. 1983. 25.00X (ISBN 0-87875-267-6). Whitston Pub.

Allen, W. C. St. Matthew. 3rd ed. (International Critical Commentary Ser.). 456p. Repr. of 1907 ed. text ed. 21.00x o.p. (ISBN 0-686-70891-1). Attic Pr.

Allen, W. S. Vox Latina. 2nd ed. LC 78-1153. (Illus.). 1978. 19.95 (ISBN 0-521-22049-1). Cambridge U Pr.

Allen, W. S., ed. Longman Structural Readers, 14 bks, Stage 1. Incl. The Battle of Newton Road. Dunklin, L (ISBN 0-582-53710-X); Car Theives. Alexander, L. G (ISBN 0-582-53705-3); Detectives from Scotland Yard. Cox, Alwyn (ISBN 0-582-53704-5); The Flying Spy. Cox, Alwyn (ISBN 0-582-53709-6); Green Island. Eyre, A. G (ISBN 0-582-53703-7); The Houe Near the Sea. Musman, R (ISBN 0-582-53707-X); Kate & the Clock. Dunkling, L (ISBN 0-582-53708-8); King Henry. Shakespeare, William (ISBN 0-582-53702-9); Mr. Punch. Alexander, L. G (ISBN 0-582-53706-1); The Mystery of the Loch Ness Monster. Dunkling, Leslie (ISBN 0-582-52514-4); Operation Janus. Alexander, L. G (ISBN 0-582-53713-4); Pele: King of Football. Machin, Noel (ISBN 0-582-52674-4); The Prisoners. Byrne, Donn (ISBN 0-582-53701-0); Scoops: Especially for Young Readers. see sep. entry; Seven Sketches. Dunkling, Leslie (ISBN 0-582-52515-2); Sherlock Holmes & the Dancing Men. Conan Doyle, Arthur (ISBN 0-582-53677-4); The Storm. Musman, Richard **(ISBN 0-582-53679-0); The Sheriff. O'Neill, Robert (ISBN 0-582-52518-7). (English As a Second Language Bk.). (Basic vocabulary about 300 words). 1965-81. pap. 1.40x ea.; cassettes avail. Longman.**

--Longman Structural Readers, 12 bks, Stage 2. Incl. April Fool's Day. Alexander, L. G (ISBN 0-582-53719-3); The Boy & the Donkey. Turvey, Celia (ISBN 0-582-53723-1); Don Quixote & Sancho Panza. Cervantes (ISBN 0-582-53718-5); Elvis Presley: King of Rock'n'Roll. Harmer, J (ISBN 0-582-53041-5); The Face on the Screen & Other Stories. Victor, Paul (ISBN 0-582-53676-6); Girl Against the Jungle. Vincent, Monica (ISBN 0-582-53729-0). cassette 7.00x (ISBN 0-582-52679-5); Hamad the Diver: A Tale As Told by His Grandson (ISBN 0-582-53720-7); In the Beginning. Christopher, John (ISBN 0-582-53726-6); Island of the Volcanoes. Byrne, Donn (ISBN 0-582-53715-0); K's First Case. Alexander, L. G (ISBN 0-582-53730-4). cassette 7.00x (ISBN 0-582-79051-4); The Lost Love & Other Stories (ISBN 0-582-53690-1); My Dear Aunt & Morning in London. Byrne, Donn (ISBN 0-582-53725-8); On the Road. Byrne, Donn (ISBN 0-582-53716-9); Pop Festival. Serraillier, Ian (ISBN 0-582-53714-2); Professor Boffin's Unbrella. Alexander, L. G (ISBN 0-582-53724-X); Rockstars (ISBN 0-582-52701-5); Some Adventures of Don Quixote. Cervantes (ISBN 0-582-53717-7); The Stone Mother & Child. Heaton, J. B (ISBN 0-582-53722-3); Worth a Fortune. Alexander, L. G (ISBN 0-582-53721-5). (English As a Second Language Bk.). (Basic vocabulary about 500 words). 1965-81. pap. 1.55x ea. Longman.

--Longman Structural Readers, 17 bks, Stage 3. Incl. Clint Magee. Alexander, L. G (ISBN 0-582-53682-0); Stage 4. Computers (ISBN 0-582-53334-1); Dangerous Game. Harris, William (ISBN 0-582-53681-2); David & Marianne. Dent, John (ISBN 0-582-53742-8); David Cofferfield. Dickens, Charles (ISBN 0-582-53734-7); Everest the Hard Way. Bonington, Chris & Grant, Neville. (ISBN 0-582-52337-0); Galileo. Eyre, A. G (ISBN 0-582-53738-X); Good Morning, Mexico! Alexander, L. G (ISBN 0-582-53817-3); How Life Began. Jones, Lewis (ISBN 0-582-53812-2); Inspector Thackeray Calls. James, Kenneth & Mullen, Lloyd. (ISBN 0-582-53745-2); The Last Experiment. Jones, Lewis (ISBN 0-582-53824-6); Operation Mastermind. Alexander, L. G (ISBN 0-582-53741-X); Round the World in Eighty Days. Verne, Jules (ISBN 0-582-53731-2); SOS in Space. Jones, Lewis (ISBN 0-582-53810-6); Stunt! Jones, Lewis (ISBN 0-582-53680-4); The Spy & Other Stories. Victor, Paul (ISBN 0-582-52548-9); Survive the Savage Sea. Robertson, Douglas & Kingsbury, Ray. (ISBN 0-582-52548-9); Tales from Arab History (ISBN 0-582-53733-9); The World Under the Sea. Wright, Andrew & Buckby, M. (ISBN 0-582-53728-2). (English As a Second Language Bk.). (Basic vocabulary about 750 words). 1965-81. pap. 1.65x ea. Longman.

--Longman Structural Readers, 18 bks, Stage 4. Incl. The Angry Valley. Grimshaw, Nigel (ISBN 0-582-53753-3); Desiree, Wife of Marshall Bernadotte. Selinko, Annemarie (ISBN 0-582-53759-2); Doomwatch: The World in Danger. Pedler, K. & Davis, G. (ISBN 0-582-53823-8); Eight Ghost Stories. Burton, S. H (ISBN 0-582-54078-X); The Energy Crisis. Walsh, Gordon (ISBN 0-582-53834-3); Fair Play! Sport, Money & Success in the World Today. McLean, Alan (ISBN 0-582-52516-0); The Forger. O'Neill, Robert (ISBN 0-582-53795-9); I Can Jump Puddles. Marshall, Alan (ISBN 0-582-53672-3); Island of the Blue Dolphins. O'Dell, Scott (ISBN 0-582-53819-X); Me, Myself & I: Seven Science Fiction Stories (ISBN 0-582-53844-0); Nothing to Fear & Other Stories. Hartley, L. P., et al. (ISBN 0-582-53109-8); Oil. Wymer, N (ISBN 0-582-53755-X); The Prisoner of Zenda. Hope, Anthony (ISBN 0-582-53746-0); Race to the South Pole. Jones, Lewis & Brett, Bernard. (ISBN 0-582-53848-3); A Scandal in Bohemia & Other Stories. Conan Doyle, Arthur (ISBN 0-582-53850-5); Silas Marner. Eliot, George (ISBN 0-582-53751-7); Stories from the Arab World. Fariz, Husni (ISBN 0-582-53747-9); Water. Jones, Lewis (ISBN 0-582-53684-7); What's Happening in Medicine. Dent, John (ISBN 0-582-53821-1); The White Mountains. Christopher, John (ISBN 0-582-53758-4). (English As a Second Language Bk.). (Basic vocabulary about 1100 words). 1965-81. pap. 1.75x ea. Longman.

--Longman Structural Readers, 9 bks, Stage 5. Incl. The Adventures of Tom Sawyer. Twain, Mark (ISBN 0-582-53761-4); Animals Dangerous to Man. Musman, R (ISBN 0-582-53768-1); Desiree, Queen of Sweden. Selinko, Annemarie (ISBN 0-582-53773-8); Hard Times. Dickens, Charles (ISBN 0-582-53831-9); Inspector Thackeray Investigates. James, Kenneth & Mullen, Lloyd. (ISBN 0-582-53774-6); Kidnapped. Stevenson, Robert L (ISBN 0-582-53762-2); Man & Modern Science. Wymer, N (ISBN 0-582-53764-9); Mogul. Eliot, John (ISBN 0-582-53771-1); Stranger Things Have Happened & It's Not Right, Is It? Bennett, Susan (ISBN 0-582-53769-X); The Valentine Generation & Other Stories. Updike, John, et al. (ISBN 0-582-53108-X); Winds of Change: Modern Short Stories from Black Africa (ISBN 0-582-53765-7); Your Choice? A Self-Defense Guide to Advertising. Williams, Alma (ISBN 0-582-53849-1). (English As a Second Language Bk.). (Basic vocabulary about 1500 words). 1965-81. pap. 1.95x ea. Longman.

--Longman Structural Readers, 4 bks, Stage 6. Incl. Arctic Oil Strike. Musman, R (ISBN 0-582-53794-0); The Go-Between. Hartley, L. P (ISBN 0-582-53783-5); The Kon-Tiki Expedition. Heyerdahl, Thor (ISBN 0-582-53776-2); Modern Short Stories (ISBN 0-582-53777-0). (English As a Second Language Bk.). (Basic vocabulary about 1800 words). 1965-81. pap. 2.10x ea. Longman.

--Longman Structural Readers: Stage 1, Scoops, 5 bks. Incl. The Ghost of Granby Hall (ISBN 0-582-53039-3); The Gold Divers (ISBN 0-582-53040-7); Jane Saves the Jet (ISBN 0-582-53036-9); A Lucky Escape (ISBN 0-582-53038-5); Oil Rig in Danger (ISBN 0-582-53037-7). (English As a Second Language Bk.). 1965-81. pap. 1.55x ea.; cassette 8.00x (ISBN 0-582-53113-6); handbk. o.p. 1.75x (ISBN 0-582-53699-5). Longman.

Allen, W. Stannard. Living English Structure. rev. ed. (English As a Second Language Bk.). 338p. 1947. pap. text ed. 6.60x (ISBN 0-582-52506-3); key 1.95 (ISBN 0-582-55204-4). Longman.

Allen, Walter. The Short Story in English. 1981. 25.00x (ISBN 0-19-812666-2). Oxford U Pr.

Allen, Walter C., ed. Studies in Jazz Discography: No. 1. LC 78-5037. 1978. Repr. of 1971 ed. lib. bdg. 19.75x (ISBN 0-313-20407-1, ALJD). Greenwood.

Allen, Walter P. Easy Crossword Puzzles for People Learning English. 1956. pap. 2.50 (ISBN 0-87789-026-9). Eng Language.

--More Easy Crossword Puzzles for People Learning English. 1970. pap. 2.50 (ISBN 0-87789-031-5). Eng Language.

Allen, Warren D. Our Marching Civilization. LC 77-25408. (Music Reprint Ser.). 1978. Repr. of 1943 ed. lib. bdg. 19.95 (ISBN 0-306-77568-9). Da Capo.

Allen, William. Halfmoons & Dwarf Parrots. pap. 7.95 (ISBN 0-87666-424-9, PS647). TFH Pubns.

Allen, William C. The Annals of Haywood County, North Carolina: Historical, Sociological, & Genealogical. LC 77-24593. (Illus.). 1977. Repr. of 1935 ed. 36.50 (ISBN 0-87152-251-9). Reprint.

Allen, William H., Jr. Budgerigars. (Orig.). pap. 2.95 (ISBN 0-87666-415-X, M502). TFH Pubns.

--How to Raise & Train Pigeons. LC 58-7602. (Illus.). 160p. (gr. 10 up). 1972. 13.95 (ISBN 0-8069-3706-8); PLB 16.79 (ISBN 0-8069-3707-6). Sterling.

--How to Raise & Train Pigeons. LC 58-7602. (Illus.). 160p. 1982. pap. 8.95 (ISBN 0-8069-7652-7). Sterling.

Allen, William J. Sexuality Summary. LC 76-47357. 160p. (Orig.). 1977. pap. 1.75 o.p. (ISBN 0-8189-1141-7, Pub. by Alba Bks). Alba.

Allen, William R. & Bragaw, Louis K. Social Forces & the Manager: Readings & Cases. LC 81-10402. (Series in Management). 502p. 1982. pap. text ed. 19.95 (ISBN 0-471-08611-8); tchrs'. ed. (ISBN 0-471-08933-8). Wiley.

Allen, William R., jt. auth. see Alchian, Armen A.

Allen, Woody. Getting Even. 128p. Date not set. pap. 2.95 (ISBN 0-394-72640-5, V-640, Vin). Random.

--Without Feathers. 224p. 1983. pap. 2.95 (ISBN 0-345-30128-5). Ballantine.

Allenbright, J. P. The Ten-Dollar Wildcat. 1980. 14.95 o.p. (ISBN 0-87000-475-1, Arlington Hse). Crown.

Allen-Browne, Patricia, ed. see Fritz, Jack.

Allenby, R. B. Rings, Fields & Groups. 304p. 1983. pap. text ed. 27.50 (ISBN 0-7131-3476-3). E Arnold.

Allendoerfer, Carl B. & Oakley, Cletus O. Fundamentals of Freshman Mathematics. 3rd ed. (Illus.). 1972. text ed. 27.50 (ISBN 0-07-001366-7, C); instructor's manual 9.95 (ISBN 0-07-001367-5). McGraw.

--Principles of Mathematics. 3rd ed. LC 69-12258. (Illus.). 1969. text ed. 25.00 o.p. (ISBN 0-07-001390-X, C). McGraw.

Allendoerfer, Carl B., et al. Elementary Functions. 1976. text ed. 19.95 (ISBN 0-07-001371-3, C); instructor's manual 9.95 (ISBN 0-07-001374-8). McGraw.

Allendorf, Katherine. Applique. LC 72-13333. (Early Craft Bks.). (Illus.). 36p. (gr. 1-4). 1973. PLB 3.95g (ISBN 0-8225-0851-6). Lerner Pubns.

Allendorfer, Carl B. Principles of Arithmetic & Geometry: For Elementary Teachers. 1971. text ed. 24.95x (ISBN 0-02-301860-7, 30186). Macmillan.

Allen-Shore, Lena. Ten Steps in the Land of Life. LC 82-61165. 1983. 13.95 (ISBN 0-88400-088-5); pap. 6.95 (ISBN 0-88400-089-3). Shengold.

Allen-Shore, Lena, jt. auth. see Herzig, Jakub.

Allensworth, Carl, et al. The Complete Play Production Handbook. LC 73-14814. (Illus.). 366p. 1973. 2.95i o.p. (ISBN 0-690-20752-2). T Y Crowell.

--The Complete Play Production Handbook Revised & Updated. LC 81-48151. (Illus.). 384p. 1982. 14.38 (ISBN 0-06-015000-9, HarpT); pap. 6.68i (ISBN 0-06-463558-9). Har-Row.

Allensworth, Don T., jt. auth. see Linowes, R. Robert.

Allerton, D. J. Valency & the English Verb. 1982. 23.00 (ISBN 0-12-052980-7). Acad Pr.

Allerton, D. J., et al, eds. Function & Context in Linguistics Analysis. LC 78-11603. 1979. 29.95 (ISBN 0-521-22429-2). Cambridge U Pr.

Alles, jt. auth. see Florio, A. E.

Alles, Wesley F., jt. auth. see Eddy, James M.

Alley, Brian & Cargill, Jennifer S. Keeping Track of What You Spend: The Librarian's Guide to Simple Bookkeeping. 108p. 1982. pap. 25.00x (ISBN 0-912700-79-3). Oryx Pr.

Alley, Charles L. & Atwood, Kenneth W. Electronic Engineering. 3rd ed. LC 72-8520. 838p. 1973. text ed. 35.95x (ISBN 0-471-02450-3). Wiley.

Alley, Louis E., jt. ed. see Horkheimer, Foley A.

Alley, Rewi, tr. Folk Poems From China's Minority. (Illus.). 147p. 1982. 5.95 (ISBN 0-8351-1104-0); pap. 4.95 (ISBN 0-8351-1105-9). China Bks.

Alley, Robert. Still of the Night. 224p. (Orig.). 1982. pap. 2.50. Ballantine.

Alley, Roderic. New Zealand & the Pacific. (Replica Edition). (Illus.). 300p. 1982. soft cover 21.50 (ISBN 0-86531-929-4). Westview.

Alleyne, Reginald H., Jr. see Grodin, Joseph R., et al.

Allgeier, Elizabeth & McCormick, Naomi, eds. Changing Boundaries: Gender Roles & Sexual Behavior. LC 82-60885. 347p. 1982. pap. 10.95 (ISBN 0-87484-536-X). Mayfield Pub.

Allgood, J. H., et al. Mexico: The Fertilizer Industry. (Technical Bulletin Ser.: T-16). (Illus.). 61p. (Orig.). 1979. pap. 4.00 (ISBN 0-88090-015-6). Intl Fertilizer.

Allgower, M. & Perren, S. M. Internal Fixation: Basic Principles, Modern Means, Biomechanics. (Illus.). 1976. with slides 160.00 o.p. (ISBN 0-387-92106-0). Springer-Verlag.

Alliance of Guardian Angels, Inc., jt. auth. see Sliwa, Curtis.

Alliband, Terry. Voluntary Agencies in Rural Community Development. (Library of Management for Development). 128p. 1983. pap. write for info. (ISBN 0-931816-28-9). Kumarian Pr.

Allibone, S. Austin. Critical Dictionary of English Literature & British & American Authors, 3 Vols. LC 67-295. 1965. Repr. of 1872 ed. Set. 191.00x (ISBN 0-8103-3017-2). Gale.

Allibone, Samuel A. Prose Quotations from Socrates to Macauley. LC 68-30642. 764p. 1973. Repr. of 1876 ed. 37.00 (ISBN 0-8103-3181-0). Gale.

Allighieri, Dante. De Vulgari Eloquentia, Sive Idiomate. (Linguistics 13th-18th Centuries Ser.). 212p. (Fr.). 1974. Repr. of 1878 ed. lib. bdg. 60.00x o.p. (ISBN 0-8287-0248-9, 5002). Clearwater Pub.

Alliluyeva, Svetlana. Twenty Letters to a Friend. McMillan, Priscilla J., tr. 1967. 11.49i (ISBN 0-06-010099-0, HarpT). Har-Row.

Allin, John. John Allin's Circus Life. (ps-5). 1983. 9.95 (ISBN 0-686-38880-1, Pub. by Michael Joseph). Merrimack Bk Serv.

Allin, Trevor B. Grammer of Resigaro, 3 vols. 1976. pap. 6.50x o.s.i. (ISBN 0-88312-768-7); microfiche 5.25x (ISBN 0-88312-349-5). Summer Inst Ling.

Alling, N. L. Real Elliptic Curves. (North-Holland Mathematics Studies: Vol. 54). 1981. 42.75 (ISBN 0-444-86233-1, North-Holland). Elsevier.

Allinger, N. L., jt. ed. see Eliel, E. L.

Allinger, Norman, et al. Topics in Stereochemistry, Vol. 13. LC 61-13943. 489p. 1982. 85.00 (ISBN 0-471-05680-4, Pub. by Wiley-Interscience). Wiley.

Allinger, Norman L. & Eliel, Ernest L. Topics in Stereochemistry, Vol. 9. 399p. 1976. 59.50 o.p. (ISBN 0-471-02472-4, Pub. by Wiley-Interscience). Wiley.

Allinger, Norman L., jt. auth. see Eliel, Ernest L.

Allinger, Norman L. & Eliel, Ernest L., eds. Topics in Stereochemistry. LC 67-13943. Vol. 9, 1976. 72.00 (ISBN 0-471-02472-4, Pub. by Wiley-Interscience); Vol. 11, 1979. 62.00 (ISBN 0-471-05445-3). Wiley.

Allinger, Norman L., et al. Organic Chemistry. 2nd ed. LC 75-18431. 1976. 32.95x (ISBN 0-87901-050-9). Worth.

Allingham, Margery. The Margery Allingham Omnibus. Incl. Mystery Mile; The Crime at Black Dudley; Look to the Lady. 592p. 1983. pap. 7.95 (ISBN 0-14-006058-8). Penguin.

--Police at the Funeral. 1949. pap. 2.50 o.p. (ISBN 0-14-000219-7). Penguin.

Allington, Richard & Strange, Michael. Learning Through Reading in the Content Areas. 1980. pap. text ed. 9.95 (ISBN 0-669-01375-7). Heath.

Allington, Richard L. & Krull, Kathleen. Letters. New ed. Krull, Kathleen, ed. (Beginning to Learn About Ser.). (Illus.). 32p. (gr. 1-2). 1983. PLB 13.30 (ISBN 0-8172-1384-8). Raintree Pubs.

--Measuring. Krull, Kathleen, ed. (Beginning to Learn About Ser.). (Illus.). 32p. (gr. 1-2). 1983. PLB 13.30 (ISBN 0-8172-1389-9). Raintree Pubs.

--Reading. LC 80-16547. (Beginning to Learn About Ser.). (Illus.). 32p. (ps-2). 1980. PLB 13.30 (ISBN 0-8172-1322-8). Raintree Pubs.

--Science. Krull, Kathleen, ed. (Beginning to Learn About Ser.). (Illus.). 32p. (gr. 1-2). 1983. PLB 13.30 (ISBN 0-8172-1387-2). Raintree Pubs.

--Stories. Krull, Kathleen, ed. (Beginning to Learn About Ser.). (Illus.). 32p. (gr. 1-2). 1983. PLB 13.30 (ISBN 0-8172-1386-4). Raintree Pubs.

--Talking. LC 80-17021. (Beginning to Learn About Ser.). (Illus.). 32p. (ps-2). 1980. PLB 13.30 (ISBN 0-8172-1320-1). Raintree Pubs.

--Thinking. LC 80-15390. (Beginning to Learn About Ser.). (Illus.). 32p. (ps-2). 1980. PLB 13.30 (ISBN 0-8172-1319-8). Raintree Pubs.

--Time. Krull, Kathleen, ed. (Beginning to Learn about Ser.). (Illus.). 32p. (gr. 1-2). 1983. PLB 13.30 (ISBN 0-8172-1388-0). Raintree Pubs.

--Words. Krull, Kathleen, ed. (Beginning to Learn About Ser.). (Illus.). 32p. (gr. 1-2). 1983. PLB 13.30 (ISBN 0-8172-1385-6). Raintree Pubs.

--Writing. LC 80-15334. (Beginning to Learn About Ser.). (Illus.). 32p. (ps-2). 1980. PLB 13.30 (ISBN 0-8172-1321-X). Raintree Pubs.

Allinson, Alfred, tr. see Maeterlinck, M.

Allinson, Beverley. Mitzi's Magic Garden. LC 77-155567. (Venture Ser). (Illus.). (gr. 1). 1971. PLB 6.69 (ISBN 0-8116-6702-2). Garrard.

Allinson, Gary D. Japanese Urbanism: Industry & Politics in Kariya, 1872-1972. LC 74-84141. (Center for Japanese & Korean Studies, U. C. Berkeley). 296p. 1975. 36.50x (ISBN 0-520-02842-2). U of Cal Pr.

--Suburban Tokyo: A Comparative Study in Politics & Social Change. LC 78-62852. (Center for Japanese & Korean Studies, U. C. Berkeley). 1979. 31.00x (ISBN 0-520-03768-5). U of Cal Pr.

Allis, Jeannette B. West Indian Literature: An Index to Criticism, 1930-1975. (Reference Bks.). 1981. lib. bdg. 32.00 (ISBN 0-8161-8266-3, Hall Reference). G K Hall.

Allison, A. C., jt. auth. see Gregoriadis, G.

Allison, Alexander W., et al. Masterpieces of the Drama. 4th ed. 1978. pap. text ed. 15.95x (ISBN 0-02-301910-7). Macmillan.

Allison, C. Fitzsimons. Guilt, Anger, & God. 1972. pap. 5.95 (ISBN 0-8164-2091-2). Seabury.
Allison, C. Fitzsimons & Kelber, Werner H. Epiphany. LC 74-24900. (Proclamation 1: Aids for Interpreting the Lessons of the Church Year). 64p. 1974. pap. 2.50 (ISBN 0-8006-4072-1, 1-4072). Fortress.
Allison, David, ed. The New Nietzsche: Contemporary Styles of Interpretation. 1977. pap. 3.95 o.s.i. (ISBN 0-440-55876-X, Delta). Dell.
Allison, Donald, jt. auth. see Lewis, Hunter.
Allison, Donald, jt. auth. see Perrott, Ronald.
Allison, E. M. Through the Valley of Death. (Crime Club Ser.). 192p. 1983. 11.95 (ISBN 0-385-18462-X). Doubleday.
Allison, Ellyn, ed. see Fahy, Everett.
Allison, Gary D., ed. The Western Water Law. 1982. 48.00 (ISBN 0-89419-202-7). Inst Energy.
Allison, Henry E. Benedict De Spinoza. LC 75-2059. (World Authors Ser.). 1975. lib. bdg. 14.95 (ISBN 0-8057-2853-8, Twayne). G K Hall.
Allison, Ira S. & Palmer, Donald F. Geology: The Science of a Changing Earth. 7th ed. (Illus.). 1980. text ed. 28.95x (ISBN 0-07-001123-0); pap. text ed. 22.50x (ISBN 0-07-001121-4). McGraw.
Allison, Ira S., et al. Geology: The Science of a Changing Earth. 6th ed. (Illus.). 448p. 1974. text ed. 18.95 (ISBN 0-07-001118-4, C); pap. text ed. 18.95 (ISBN 0-07-001119-2); instructor's manual 10.00 (ISBN 0-07-001120-6). McGraw.
Allison, J. M., ed. Concerning the Education of a Prince: Correspondence of the Princess of Nassau-Saarbruck 13 June - 15 November 1758. 1941. 29.50x (ISBN 0-686-51358-4). Elliots Bks.
Allison, J. P., ed. Criteria for Quality of Petroleum Products. (Illus.). xii, 286p. 1973. 39.00 (ISBN 0-85334-469-8, Pub. by Applied Sci England). Elsevier.
Allison, John M. Lamoignon de Malesherbes: Defender & Reformer of the French Monarchy, 1721-1794. 1938. text ed. 42.50x (ISBN 0-686-83605-7). Elliots Bks.
Allison, Linda. The Reasons for Seasons: The Great Cosmic Megagalactic Trip Without Moving from Your Chair. (A Brown Paper School Book). (Illus.). 128p. (gr. 4 up). 1975. 9.95 (ISBN 0-316-03439-8); pap. 5.95 (ISBN 0-316-03440-1). Little.
Allison, R. Bruce. Tree Walks: Milwaukee County. (Illus.). 56p. 1982. pap. 5.95 (ISBN 0-913370-13-4). Wisconsin Bks.
Allison, R. Bruce & Durbin, Elizabeth. Wisconsin's Famous & Historic Trees. (Illus.). 120p. pap. 14.95 (ISBN 0-913370-14-2). Wisconsin Bks.
Allison, R. G., jt. auth. see Feeney, Robert E.
Allison, W. H. Inventory of Unpublished Material for American Religion History in Protestant Church Archives & Other Repositories. 1910. pap. 23.00 (ISBN 0-527-00683-1). Kraus Repr.
Allison-Booth, William. Devils Island: Revelations of the French Penal Settlements in Guiana. LC 71-162504. (Illus.). 1971. Repr. of 1931 ed. 34.00 (ISBN 0-8103-3761-4). Gale.
Allman, Ethel. Moments. 64p. 1983. 5.95 (ISBN 0-89962-328-X). Todd & Honeywell.
Allman, Fred L., jt. auth. see Ryan, Allan J.
Allman, Fred L., Jr. The Knee in Sports. Darden, Ellington, ed. LC 77-76075. (Physical Fitness & Sports Medicine Ser). (Illus.). pap. cancelled o.s.i. (ISBN 0-89305-013-X). Anna Pub.
Allman, James, ed. Women's Status & Fertility in the Muslim World. LC 78-5897. 1978. 43.95 o.p. (ISBN 0-03-042926-9). Praeger.
Allman, Marie Von see Nemiro, Beverly & Von Allman, Marie.
Allman, Ruth. Alaska Sourdough: The Real Stuff by a Real Alaskan. LC 76-13604. 1976. pap. 6.95 (ISBN 0-88240-085-1). Alaska Northwest.
Allman, S. A., et al. Curriculum Development: A Reflection of Programmatic Trends. (Illus.). 231p. (Orig.). 1980. pap. text ed. 9.95x (ISBN 0-89641-049-8). American Pr.
Allman, S. Andean & Kopp, O. W. Environmental Education: A Promise for the Future. 196p. 1981. pap. text ed. 8.95x (ISBN 0-89641-085-4). American Pr.
Allmand. War, Literature, & Politics in the Late Middle Ages. 216p. 1982. 50.00x (ISBN 0-85323-273-3, Pub. by Liverpool Univ England). State Mutual Bk.
Allmand, C. T. & Armstrong, C. A., eds. English Suits Before the Parlement of Paris,1420-1436, Vol. 26. (Camden Fourth Ser.). 336p. 1982. text ed. 25.00x (ISBN 0-86193-095-9, Pub. by Boydell & Brewer). Biblio Dist.
Allon, Dafna, et al, trs. see Ringelblum, Emmanuel.
Allosso, Michael. Your Career in Theater, Radio, Television or Filmmaking. LC 77-14145. (Career Guidance Ser.). (YA) 1978. lib. bdg. 7.95 (ISBN 0-668-04438-1); pap. 4.50 (ISBN 0-668-04445-4). Arco.
Allott. Essays on Shelley. 304p. 1982. 60.00x (ISBN 0-85323-294-6, Pub. by Liverpool Univ England). State Mutual Bk.
Allott, Antony N. Essays in African Law, with Special Reference to the Law of Ghana. LC 74-30925. 323p. 1975. Repr. of 1960 ed. lib. bdg. 19.00x (ISBN 0-8371-7885-1, ALAL). Greenwood.
Allott, Kenneth, ed. Writers & Their Background: Matthew Arnold. LC 75-15339. (Writers & Their Background Ser.). xxvi, 353p. 1976. 18.00x (ISBN 0-8214-0197-1, 82-82022); pap. 7.50x (ISBN 0-8214-0198-X, 82-82030). Ohio U Pr.
Alloway, David N., jt. ed. see Cordasco, Francesco.
Alloway, Lawrence. American Pop Art. LC 73-22532. (Illus.). 160p. 1974. 9.95 o.s.i. (ISBN 0-02-627700-X); pap. 5.95 o.p. (ISBN 0-685-40223-1). Macmillan.
--Roy Lichtenstein. (Modern Masters Ser.). (Illus.). 128p. 1983. 24.95 (ISBN 0-89659-330-4); pap. 16.95 (ISBN 0-89659-331-2). Abbeville Pr.
--Topics in American Art Since 1945. (Illus.). 320p. 1975. text ed. 12.95x (ISBN 0-393-04401-7); pap. text ed. 6.95x (ISBN 0-393-09237-2). Norton.
Alloway, Lawrence & MacNaughton, Mary D. Adolph Gottlieb: A Retrospective. LC 81-65351. (Illus.). 175p. 1982. 40.00 o.p. (ISBN 0-8390-0288-2). Allanheld & Schram.
Allport, D. C. Block Copolymers. Date not set. price not set (ISBN 0-85334-557-0). Elsevier.
Allport, Floyd H. Institutional Behaviour: Essays. LC 71-90460. Repr. of 1933 ed. lib. bdg. 20.75x (ISBN 0-8371-2145-0, ALIB). Greenwood.
Allport, Gordon. Letters from Jenny. LC 65-18327. (Illus., Orig.). 1965. pap. 2.95 (ISBN 0-15-650700-5, Harv). HarBraceJ.
Allport, Gordon W. The Nature of Prejudice. 496p. pap. 5.95 (ISBN 0-686-95007-0). ADL.
--Study of Values. 3rd ed. test booklets 15.40 (ISBN 0-686-84785-7); instrs' manual 2.48 (ISBN 0-686-84786-5). HM.
--Use of Personal Documents in Psychological Science. LC 42-14430. (Social Science Research Council: Bulletin 49). 1942. pap. 4.50 o.s.i. (ISBN 0-527-03280-8). Kraus Repr.
Allport, J. A. & Stewart, C. M. Economics. 2nd ed. LC 77-28479. 1978. 19.95 (ISBN 0-521-22013-0); pap. 15.50x o.p. (ISBN 0-686-31688-6). Cambridge U Pr.
Allred, Mary. The Move to a New House. (gr. k-3). 1979. 4.95 (ISBN 0-8054-4252-9). Broadman.
Allred, Tamera S. From Deadlines to Diapers: A Career Guide for Successful Homemaking. 174p. 1982. pap. 6.95 (ISBN 0-936860-10-3). Liberty Pr.
Allsen, Philip E. & Witbeck, Alan R. Racquetball. 4th ed. (Exploring Sports Ser.). 92p. 1983. pap. write for info. (ISBN 0-697-09963-6). Wm C Brown.
Allsop, D. F. Pressure Diecasting: The Technology of the Casting & the Die, Pt. 2. (Materials Engineering Practice Ser.). (Illus.). 200p. 1983. 27.50 (ISBN 0-08-027615-6); pap. 13.00 (ISBN 0-08-027614-8). Pergamon.
Allsop, R. T. & Healey, J. A. Chemical Analysis, Chromatography, & Ion Exchange. 1974. pap. text ed. 4.00x o.p. (ISBN 0-435-65954-5); tchr's guide 5.00x o.p. (ISBN 0-435-65955-3). Heinemann Ed.
Allsopp, Bruce. A Modern Theory of Architecture. (Illus.). 112p. (Orig.). 1981. pap. 7.95 (ISBN 0-7100-0950-X). Routledge & Kegan.
Allston, Washington. Lectures on Art, & Poems, 1850, & Monaldi, 1841. LC 67-10124. 1967. 60.00x (ISBN 0-8201-1001-9). Schol Facsimiles.
--Lectures on Art-Poems. LC 75-171379. (Library of American Art Ser.). 1972. Repr. of 1892 ed. lib. bdg. 39.50 (ISBN 0-306-70414-5). Da Capo.
Allsup, Carl. The American G.I. Forum: Origins & Evolution. (Mexican American Monographs: No. 6). 222p. (Orig.). 1982. pap. 8.95x (ISBN 0-292-70362-7). U of Tex Pr.
Allswang, John M. The New Deal & American Politics: A Study in Political Change. LC 78-5733. (Critical Episodes in American Politics Ser.). 155p. 1978. pap. text ed. 11.50x (ISBN 0-471-02516-X). Wiley.
Allswede, Jerry L., jt. ed. see Heiser, Edward J.
Allum, J. A. Photogeology & Regional Mapping. 1966. 23.00 (ISBN 0-08-012033-4); pap. 9.95 (ISBN 0-08-012032-6). Pergamon.
Allum, P. A. Politics & Society in Post-War Naples, 1945-1970. LC 75-174259. (Illus.). 1971. 54.50x (ISBN 0-521-08424-5). Cambridge U Pr.
Allums, John, jt. auth. see Saye, Albert.
Alluri, F. M., jt. auth. see Lawani, S. M.
Allwood, J., et al, eds. Logic in Linguistics. LC 76-46855. (Cambridge Textbooks in Linguistics Ser.). (Illus.). 1977. 32.50 (ISBN 0-521-21496-3); pap. 10.95 (ISBN 0-521-29174-7). Cambridge U Pr.
Allwood, Martin S. & Wilhelmsen, Inga. Basic Swedish Word List. LC 47-26851. (Swedish Language Textbooks). 1947. pap. 0.75x o.p. (ISBN 0-8006-1081-4, 1-1081). Fortress.
Allworth, Edward. Central Asian Publishing & the Rise of Nationalism: An Essay & a List of Publications in the New York Public Library. LC 65-28277. 1965. pap. 7.00 o.p. (ISBN 0-87104-040-9). NY Pub Lib.
--Soviet Asia: Bibliographies. LC 73-9061. (Illus.). 756p. 1976. 58.95 o.p. (ISBN 0-275-07540-0). Praeger.
Allworth, Edward, ed. Ethnic Russia in the U. S. S. R. The Dilemma of Dominance. LC 79-22959. (Pergamon Policy Studies Ser.). 270p. 1980. 40.00 (ISBN 0-08-023700-2). Pergamon.
--Nationality Group Survival in Multi-Ethnic States: Shifting Support Patterns in the Soviet Baltic Region. LC 77-4952. 1977. 34.95 o.p. (ISBN 0-275-24040-1). Praeger.
Allyn, Charles, ed. see Allyn, Rube.
Allyn, Jennifer. Forgiveness. (Love & Life Romance Ser.). 176p. (Orig.). 1983. pap. 1.75 (ISBN 0-345-31082-9). Ballantine.
Allyn, Rube. Dictionary of Reptiles & Amphibians. (Orig.). pap. 2.95 o.p. (ISBN 0-8200-0301-8). Great Outdoors.
--Florida Fishes. Allyn, Charles, ed. LC 74-14516. (Illus., Orig.). 1969. pap. 2.95 (ISBN 0-8200-0108-2). Great Outdoors.
Allyn, Steve. Heave To! You'll Drown Yourselves! (Illus.). 1982. pap. 6.50 (ISBN 0-8323-0410-7). Binford.
Allyne, Kerry. Spring Fever. (Harlequin Romances Ser.). 192p. 1983. pap. 1.50 (ISBN 0-373-02527-0). Harlequin Bks.
Allyson, June & Leighton, Frances S. June Allyson. (Illus.). 320p. 1982. 14.95 (ISBN 0-399-12726-7). Putnam Pub Group.
Almagor, Uri, jt. ed. see Baxter, P. T.
Almaney, A. J. & Alwan, A. J. Communicating with the Arabs: A Handbook for the Business Executive. LC 81-70668. (Illus.). 296p. 1982. pap. 15.00x (ISBN 0-917974-81-6). Waveland Pr.
Almansi, Guido. Writer As Liar. 1975. 22.50x (ISBN 0-7100-8147-2). Routledge & Kegan.
Almanza, Francisco G., tr. see Baker, R. A.
Al-Marayati, Abid A., ed. International Relations of the Middle East & North Africa. 400p. 1983. text ed. 22.50x (ISBN 0-87073-824-0). Schenkman.
Al-Mawrid & Ba'Albaki, Munir. English-Arabic Dictionary. 1980. 48.00x o.p. (ISBN 0-86685-059-7). Intl Bk Ctr.
Almeda, Frank, Jr. Systematics of the Genus Monochaetum (Melastomataceae) in Mexico & Central America. (U. C. Publications in Botany Ser.: Vol. 75). 1978. 15.50x (ISBN 0-520-09587-1). U of Cal Pr.
Almeder, Robert, ed. Praxis & Reason: Studies in the Philosophy of Nicholas Rescher. LC 81-43602. (Nicholas Rescher Ser.). 276p. (Orig.). 1982. lib. bdg. 25.25 (ISBN 0-8191-2648-9); pap. text ed. 12.25 (ISBN 0-8191-2649-7). U Pr of Amer.
Almeder, Robert, jt. ed. see Humber, James H.
Almeder, Robert, jt. ed. see Smoeyenbos, Milton.
Almedingen, E. M. A Candle at Dusk. LC 69-14972. (gr. 7 up). 1969. 3.75 o.p. (ISBN 0-374-31056-4). FS&G.
--Ellen. LC 76-125150. (gr. 7 up). 1970. 4.50 o.p. (ISBN 0-374-32105-1). FS&G.
Almeida, Bira. Capoeira: A Brazilian Art Form. 2nd ed. (Illus.). 152p. 1982. pap. 7.95 (ISBN 0-938190-09-1). North Atlantic.
Almeida, Elza M., jt. auth. see Chapman, A. H.
Almeida, Jose, et al. Descubrir y Crear. 2nd ed. (Illus.). 430p. (Span.). 1981. text ed. 24.50 scp (ISBN 0-06-040224-5, HarpC); scp tape manual 8.95 (ISBN 0-06-044563-7); inst manual avail. (ISBN 0-06-360251-2); scp tapes 250.00 (ISBN 0-06-047497-1). Har-Row.
Almeida, Laurindo. Guitar Tutor. 8.95 (ISBN 0-910468-03-6). Criterion Mus.
Almeida, Onesimo T., ed. see Joao Teixeira de Medeiros.
Almendros, Nestor. A Man with a Camera. Belash, Rachel P., tr. from French. Truffaut, Francois, pref. by. (Illus.). 280p. 1982. 14.50 (ISBN 0-374-20172-2). FS&G.
Almers, Ambrose J. How to Build by Yourself Scientifically the Log Cabin of Your Dreams. (Illus.). 187p. 1982. 125.55 (ISBN 0-86650-029-4). Gloucester Art.
Al-Moajil, Abdullah H. & Abdelali, Benharbit. Basic Mathematics: A Pre-Calculus Course for Science & Engineering. LC 80-41685. 480p. 1982. 35.00x (ISBN 0-471-27941-2, Pub. by Wiley Interscience); pap. 12.95 (ISBN 0-471-27942-0). Wiley.
Almogi, Yosef. Total Commitment. LC 81-70146. (Illus.). 320p. 1982. 20.00 (ISBN 0-8453-4749-7). Cornwall Bks.
Almon, John, ed. A Collection of Papers Relative to the Dispute Between Great Britain & America, 1764-1775. LC 70-146277. (Era of the American Revolution Ser). 1971. Repr. of 1777 ed. lib. bdg. 39.50 (ISBN 0-306-70127-8). Da Capo.
Almond, Gabriel & Verba, Sidney. Civic Culture Study, 1959-1960. 1974. codebook write for info. (ISBN 0-89138-065-5). ICPSR.
Almond, Gabriel, jt. ed. see Smelser, Neil J.
Almond, Gabriel, et al. Freedom & Development. 4.75x o.p. (ISBN 0-210-22595-5). Asia.
Almond, Gabriel A. & Powell, G. Bingham, Jr. Comparative Politics: Systems, Process, & Policy. 2nd ed. (The Little, Brown Series in Comparative Politics). 1978. pap. text ed. 12.95 (ISBN 0-316-03498-3). Little.
Almond, Gabriel A. & Verba, Sidney. The Civic Culture: Political Attitudes & Democracy in Five Nations. (The Little, Brown Series in Comparative Politics). 379p. 1965. pap. text ed. 11.95 (ISBN 0-316-03493-2). Little.
Almond, Gabriel A. & Verba, Sidney, eds. The Civic Culture Revisited. 421p. 1980. pap. text ed. 11.95 (ISBN 0-316-03490-8). Little.
Almond, Joseph P., Sr. Plumbers' Handbook. 6th ed. LC 82-1342. 1982. 9.95 (ISBN 0-672-23370-3). Bobbs.
Almozning, Albert. Hand Shadows for Classroom & Home Activities. (Illus.). 92p. 1982. 12.95 (ISBN 0-87396-096-3). Stravon.
Almquist, Alan J., jt. auth. see Heizer, Robert F.
Almquist, Elizabeth M. Minorities, Gender & Work. LC 77-4537. 1979. 22.95x (ISBN 0-669-01488-5). Lexington Bks.
Almroth, B., jt. auth. see Brush, Don O.
Al-Mufid, Shaykh. Kitab Al-Irshad. Howard, I. K., tr. from Arabic. 606p. Date not set. 15.00 (ISBN 0-940368-12-9); pap. 7.95 (ISBN 0-940368-11-0). Tahrike Tarsile Quran.
Almy, Millie. Early Childhood Educator at Work. 276p. 1975. text ed. 14.00 (ISBN 0-07-001126-5, C); pap. text ed. 3.25 (ISBN 0-07-001125-7). McGraw.
Almy, Millie & Genishi, Celia. Ways of Studying Children: An Observational Manual for Early Childhood Teachers. 2nd ed. LC 79-13881. 1979. pap. text ed. 9.50x (ISBN 0-8077-2551-X). Tchrs Coll.
Almy, Millie, et al. Logical Thinking in Second Grade. LC 73-117980. (Illus.). 1970. pap. text ed. 6.95x (ISBN 0-8077-1016-4). Tchrs Coll.
--Young Children's Thinking: Studies of Some Aspects of Piaget's Theory. LC 66-16091. (Illus., Orig.). 1966. pap. text ed. 5.75x (ISBN 0-8077-1017-2). Tchrs Coll.
Almy, Richard R., et al. Improving Real Property Assessment: A Reference Manual. LC 78-70575. 1978. 25.00 (ISBN 0-88329-010-3). Intl Assess.
Alo, R. A. & Shapiro, H. L. Normal Topological Spaces. LC 73-79304. (Tracts in Mathematics Ser.: No. 65). (Illus.). 250p. 1974. 47.50 (ISBN 0-521-20271-X). Cambridge U Pr.
Alocroff, Derek. European Economy: Nineteen Fourteen to Nineteen Seventy. LC 77-9232. 1978. 17.95x o.p. (ISBN 0-312-27062-3). St Martin.
Aloia, Roland. Membrane Fluidity in Biology: Concepts of Membrane Structure, Vol. 2. LC 82-11535. 336p. 1982. write for info. (ISBN 0-12-053002-3). Acad Pr.
Aloia, Roland C., ed. Membrane Fluidity in Biology: Vol. 1: Concepts of Membrane Structure. 1982. 43.00 (ISBN 0-12-053001-5). Acad Pr.
Alonso, J. R. Simple, a Software Handbook of Statistical Techniques. 1978. pap. text ed. 11.95 o.p. (ISBN 0-88408-100-1). Sterling Swift.
Alonso, Lou, ed. see Raynor, Sherry & Drouillard, Richard.
Alonso, Nina. This Body. LC 70-168711. (Orig.). 1971. pap. 5.95 (ISBN 0-87923-043-6). Godine.
Alonso, William, jt. ed. see Friedmann, John.
Alotta, Robert I. Stop the Evil. LC 78-10425. (Illus.). 1978. 10.00 o.p. (ISBN 0-89141-018-X). Presidio Pr.
--Street Names of Philadelphia. LC 75-14689. 158p. 1975. 10.95 (ISBN 0-87722-046-8). Temple U Pr.
Aloysius. Piff, Paff, Peuff: Diary of a Young Male Schizophrenic. 1978. 7.50 o.p. (ISBN 0-533-03582-1). Vantage.
Alpatov, M. V., compiled by. Early Russian Icon Painting. Johnstone, N., tr. (Illus.). 332p. 1979. 47.50 (ISBN 0-89893-030-8). CDP.
Alpatov, M. V., intro. by. Frescoes of the Church of the Assumption at Volotovo. Friedman, V. S., tr. 1980. 25.00 (ISBN 0-89893-040-5). CDP.
Alpatov, Mikhail V. Geschichte der Altrussischen Kunst. (Illus., Ger.). Repr. 60.00 (ISBN 0-384-00910-7). Johnson Repr.
Alpaugh, Patricia & Haney, Margaret. Counseling the Older Adult. Date not set. 9.95 (ISBN 0-686-94882-3). Hollander Co.
Alpenvereins Buchereio, Munich. Kataloge der Alpenvereins Bucherei: Catalogs of the Alpine Association Library, 2 pts. Incl. Pt. 1. Autorenkatalog,Author Catalog, 3 vols. 285.00 (ISBN 0-8161-0849-8); Pt. 2. Sachkatalog,Subject Catalog, 3 vols. 285.00 (ISBN 0-8161-0101-9). 1970 (Hall Library). G K Hall.
Alper, B. S. Prisons Inside Out: Alternatives in Correctional Reform. LC 74-2268. 1975. text ed. 16.50 (ISBN 0-88410-200-9); pap. 10.95x prof ref (ISBN 0-88410-211-4). Ballinger Pub.
Alper, Benedict S. & Nichols, Lawrence T. Beyond the Courtroom: Community Justice & Programs in Conflict Resolution. LC 78-20376. 320p. 1981. 25.95x (ISBN 0-669-02724-3). Lexington Bks.
Alper, T. Cellular Radiobiology. LC 78-68331. (Illus.). 1979. 52.50 (ISBN 0-521-22411-X); pap. 16.95x (ISBN 0-521-29479-7). Cambridge U Pr.
Alperin, David S., ed. see Interstate Bureau of Regulations.
Alperin, Kenneth & Grover, Margaret. Tracheostomy Care Manual. 28p. 4.95 (ISBN 0-86577-071-9). Thieme-Stratton.
Alperin, Melvin, jt. auth. see Alperin, Stanley.
Alperin, Melvin S., jt. ed. see Alperin, Stanley.
Alperin, Stanley. Careers in Nursing. 208p. 1981. prof. ref 15.00x (ISBN 0-88410-731-0). Ballinger Pub.
Alperin, Stanley & Alperin, Melvin. One Hundred Twenty Careers in the Health Care Field. LC 79-53587. 320p. 1980. prof ref 27.50x (ISBN 0-88410-709-4). Ballinger Pub.
Alperin, Stanley, ed. The Federal Hospital Phone Book: 1983-84. pap. 24.95 (ISBN 0-916524-19-1). US Direct Serv.
--The Hospital Phone: 1983-84. pap. 29.95 (ISBN 0-916524-18-3). US Direct Serv.
Alperin, Stanley & Alperin, Melvin S., eds. Directory of Medical Schools Worldwide. 2nd ed. LC 77-93356. 1980. text ed. 19.95 o.p. (ISBN 0-916524-15-9). US Direct Serv.

Alpern, Andrew. Apartments for the Affluent: A Historical Survey of Buildings in New York. (Illus.). 1975. 44.50 o.p. (ISBN 0-07-001372-1, P&RB). McGraw.

Alpern, Gerald D. & Boll, Thomas J., eds. Education & Care of Moderately & Severely Retarded Children. LC 71-170090. (Orig.). 1971. pap. text ed. 9.00x o.p. (ISBN 0-87562-030-2). Spec Child.

Alperovitch, A., et al, eds. Evaluation of Efficacy of Medical Action. 536p. 1980. 72.50 (ISBN 0-444-85379-0). Elsevier.

Alpers, Edward A. Ivory & Slaves in East Central Africa: Changing Patterns of International Trade to the Later Nineteenth Century. LC 73-93046. (Illus.). 1974. 33.00x (ISBN 0-520-02689-6). U of Cal Pr.

Alpers, Edward A. & Fontaine, Pierre-Michel, eds. Walter Rodney, Revolutionary & Scholar: A Tribute. LC 82-4509. (CAAS Special Publications Ser.). (Illus.). 200p. (Orig.). 1983. 17.95x (ISBN 0-934934-09-6); pap. 10.95x (ISBN 0-934934-08-8). Ctr Afro-Am Stud.

Alpers, Paul. The Singer of the Eclogues: A Study of Virgilian Pastoral. LC 77-93465. 1979. 24.50x (ISBN 0-520-03651-4). U of Cal Pr.

Alpers, Paul J. Poetry "The Facerie Queene". LC 80-50217. 432p. 1983. pap. 10.00 (ISBN 0-8262-0383-3); 25.00. U of MO Pr.

Alpers, Svetlana. The Art of Describing Dutch Art in the Seventeenth Century. LC 82-13468. (Illus.). 1983. 37.50 (ISBN 0-226-01512-2). U of Chicago Pr.

Alpert, Barry, ed. see Davie, Donald.

Alpert, Carl. Technion: The Story of Israel's Institute of Technology. LC 82-11556. (Illus.). 439p. 1983. 25.00x (ISBN 0-87203-102-0). Hermon.

Alpert, Elliot, jt. ed. see Hirai, Hidematsu.

Alpert, Geoffrey P. Legal Rights of Prisoners: An Analysis of Legal Aid. LC 78-4343. (Illus.). 192p. 1978. 21.95 (ISBN 0-669-02347-7). Lexington Bks.

Alpert, George & Leogrande, Ernest. A Second Chance to Live: The Suicide Syndrome. LC 75-20452. (Photography Ser.). (Illus.). 90p. 1976. lib. bdg. 17.50 (ISBN 0-306-70751-9); pap. 6.95 (ISBN 0-306-80023-3). Da Capo.

Alpert, Jane. Growing up Underground. LC 82-62184. 372p. 1983. Repr. pap. 6.95 (ISBN 0-688-01396-1). Quill NY.

Alpert, Judith, et al. Psychological Consultation in Educational Settings: A Casebook for Working with Administrators, Teachers, Students, & Community. LC 82-8995. (Social & Behavioral Science Ser.). 1982. text ed. 18.95x (ISBN 0-87589-528-X). Jossey Bass.

Alpert, Judith L. & Meyers, Joel. Training in Consultation: Perspectives from Mental Health, Behavioral & Organizational Consultation. (Illus.). 252p. 1983. 21.50x (ISBN 0-398-04801-0). C C Thomas.

Alpert, Leo M. Florida Automobile Accident Law. 2nd ed. 1967. 35.00 o.p. (ISBN 0-87215-078-X). Michie-Bobbs.

Alpert, Nathaniel M., jt. ed. see Bacharach, Stephen L.

Alpert, Norman R., ed. Myocardial Hypertrophy & Failure. (Perspectives in Cardiovascular Research Ser.: Vol. 7). 640p. 1982. text ed. write for info. (ISBN 0-89004-743-X). Raven.

Alpert, Richard & Cohen, Sidney. LSD. pap. 2.95 o.p. (ISBN 0-452-25703-4, Z5703, Plume). NAL.

Alpert, Stuart W., jt. auth. see Taylor, Delores A.

Alphonso-Karkala, John B. Jawaharlal Nehru. (World Authors Ser.). 1975. lib. bdg. 13.95 (ISBN 0-8057-2649-7, Twayne). G K Hall.

Alpiner, Jerome G. Handbook of Adult Rehabilitative Audiology. 2nd ed. (Illus.). 376p. 1982. lib. bdg. 33.00 (ISBN 0-683-00076-4). Williams & Wilkins.

Al-Qirqisani, Ya'Qub. Kitab Al-Anwar Wal-Maraoib: Code of Karaite Law, 3 vols. Incl. Vol. 1. First Discourse - Historical Introduction; Second Discourse - Philosophical & Theological Principles of JurisPrudence; Vol. 2. Third Discourse - Criticism of Sectarian Doctrines; Fourth Discourse - Methods of Construction & Interpretation of Law; Vol. 3. Fifth Discourse - Circumcion - Sabbath; Sixth Discourse - Civil & Criminal Law Liturgy. pap. 37.50 ea.; Set. pap. 125.00x (ISBN 0-686-52167-6). Elliots Bks.

Al-Rashid, Rashid A. Pediatric Cancer Chemotherapy. (Medical Outline Ser.). 1979. 33.00 (ISBN 0-87488-685-6); pap. 24.00 (ISBN 0-87488-663-5). Med Exam.

Alroy, Gil C. Behind the Middle East Conflict: The Real Impasse Between Arab & Jew. LC 75-7558. 224p. 1975. 9.95 o.p. (ISBN 0-399-11525-0). Putnam Pub Group.

Al-Sayyid-Marsot, Afaf L. Egypt's Liberal Experiment, 1922-1936. LC 75-22659. 1977. 31.50x (ISBN 0-520-03109-1). U of Cal Pr.

Alsberg, P. In Quest of Man. 1970. text ed. inquire for price o.p. (ISBN 0-08-015680-0). Pergamon.

Alsburg, Chris Van see Van Alsburg, Chris.

Alsen, Eberhard. Salinger's Glass Stories As A Composite Novel. LC 82-50411. 300p. 1983. 22.50X (ISBN 0-87875-243-9). Whitston Pub.

Alsmeyer, D. & Atkins, A. G., eds. Guide to Science & Technology in the Asia Pacific Area. 540p. 145.00x (ISBN 0-686-75638-X, Pub. by Longman). Gale.

Alsop, John R. An Index to Bauer Arndt, Gingrich Greek Lexicon. 2nd ed. Date not set. 11.95 (ISBN 0-310-44031-9). Zondervan.

Alsop, Joseph. FDR. large type ed. LC 82-5870. (Illus.). 303p. 1982. Repr. of 1982 ed. 11.95 (ISBN 0-89621-369-2). Thorndike Pr.

--FDR: A Centenary Remembrance 1882-1945. (Illus.). 1982. pap. 3.50 (ISBN 0-671-45891-4). WSP.

--The Rare Art Traditions: A History of Art Collecting & Its Linked Phenomena. LC 81-47218. (Illus.). 464p. 1982. 57.64i (ISBN 0-06-010091-5, HarpT). Har-Row.

Alsop, Joseph & Catledge, Turner. The One Hundred Sixty-Eight Days. LC 72-2362. (American Constitutional & Legal History Ser). 324p. 1973. Repr. of 1938 ed. lib. bdg. 39.50 (ISBN 0-306-70481-1). Da Capo.

Alsop, Stewart. Stay of Execution: A Sort of Memoir. LC 73-13691. 1973. 12.45i (ISBN 0-397-00897-X). Har-Row.

Alston, Eugenia. Come Visit a Prairie Dog Town. LC 75-37005. (Let Me Read Ser.). (Illus.). 64p. (gr. 1-5). 1976. 4.95 (ISBN 0-15-219482-7, HJ); pap. 1.95 (ISBN 0-15-219481-9, VoyB). HarBraceJ.

--Growing up Chimpanzee. LC 74-12307. (Illus.). 32p. (gr. 1-4). 1975. 10.53i (ISBN 0-690-00015-4, TYC-J); PLB 7.89 o.p. (ISBN 0-690-00564-4). Har-Row.

Alston, Frances K., ed. Caring for Other People's Children. (Illus.). 1983. text ed. write for info (16624). Univ Park.

Alston, Pat, ed. see Fong, Leo T.

Alston, Richard M. The Individual vs. the Public Interest: Political Idiology & National Forest Policy. (Replica Edition Ser.). 200p. 1982. softcover 20.00x (ISBN 0-86531-950-2). Westview.

Alston, William P. Philosophy of Language. (Orig.). 1964. pap. 9.95x ref. ed. (ISBN 0-13-663799-X). P-H.

Alstrom, Torgny, jt. ed. see Grasbeck, Ralph.

Alstyne, Richard W. Van see Van Alstyne, Richard W.

Alswang, Hope, jt. auth. see Peirce, Donald.

Alt, A. Tilo. Theodor Storm. (World Authors Ser.). 1971. lib. bdg. 15.95 (ISBN 0-8057-2865-1, Twayne). G K Hall.

Alt, David & Hyndman, Donald. Roadside Geology of Northern California. LC 74-81834. (Roadside Geology Ser.). (Illus.). 244p. 1975. pap. 8.95 (ISBN 0-87842-055-X). Mountain Pr.

--Roadside Geology of Oregon. LC 77-2581. (Roadside Geology Ser.). (Illus.). 268p. 1978. pap. 9.95 (ISBN 0-87842-063-0). Mountain Pr.

Alt, Edith, jt. auth. see Alt, Herschel.

Alt, Herschel & Alt, Edith. Russia's Children: A First Report on Child Welfare in the Soviet Union. LC 75-18353. 240p. 1975. Repr. of 1959 ed. lib. bdg. 15.50x (ISBN 0-8371-8330-8, ALRC). Greenwood.

Alt, James E. The Politics of Economic Decline. LC 78-67295. 1979. 32.50 (ISBN 0-521-22327-X). Cambridge U Pr.

Alt, James E., jt. ed. see Herman, Valentine.

Alt, M. B., jt. auth. see Miles, R. S.

Alta. I Am Not a Practicing Angel. LC 74-32443. 80p. 1975. 12.95 (ISBN 0-912278-54-4); pap. 3.95 (ISBN 0-912278-55-2). Crossing Pr.

--The Shameless Hussy: Selected Prose & Poetry. LC 80-15551. (The Crossing Press Feminist Ser.). 1980. 14.95 (ISBN 0-89594-035-3); pap. 6.95 (ISBN 0-89594-036-1). Crossing Pr.

Al-Tabataba'I, Muhammed H. Shi'ite Islam. Nasr, Seyyed H., tr. LC 74-8289. 1979. 34.50x (ISBN 0-87395-272-3); pap. 10.95x (ISBN 0-87395-390-8); microfiche o.p. 18.50 (ISBN 0-87395-273-1). State U NY Pr.

Altabe, Joan. Fantasy: A Cartoon Novella. 94p. (Orig.). 1982. pap. 9.95 (ISBN 0-931494-36-2). Brunswick Pub.

Al-Tajir, Mahdi A. Baharnah Dialect of Arabic: A Study in Language & Linguistic Origin. (Library of Arab Linguistics). 188p. 1983. 50.00 (ISBN 0-7103-0024-7). Routledge & Kegan.

Altbach, Edith H. Woman in America. 1972. pap. text ed. 3.95x o.p. (ISBN 0-669-63453-0). Heath.

Altbach, Philip G. Student Politics in Bombay. 10.00x (ISBN 0-210-22204-2). Asia.

Altbach, Philip G. & Lambert, Richard D., eds. The Academic Profession. LC 80-65242. (Annals of the American Academy of Political & Social Science: No. 448). 1980. 15.00 (ISBN 0-87761-248-X); pap. 7.95 (ISBN 0-87761-249-8). Am Acad Pol Soc Sci.

Altbach, Philip G. & Laufer, Robert, eds. Students Protest. LC 72-160738. (Annals Ser: No. 395). 1971. pap. 7.95 (ISBN 0-87761-138-6). Am Acad Pol Soc Sci.

Altbach, Philip G., ed. see Eisemon, Thomas O.

Altbach, Phillip G., et al. Comparative Education. 1982. text ed. 24.95x (ISBN 0-02-301920-4). Macmillan.

Altenbach, J. Scott. Locomotor Morphology of the Vampire Bat, Desmodus Rotundus. (ASM Special Publication Ser.: No. 6). (Illus.). vi, 137p. 1979. 12.00 (ISBN 0-943612-05-5). Am Soc Mammalogists.

Altenberg, G. A. & Ubaldi, V. Dizionario Italiano-Tedesco, Tedesco-Italian. 395p. (Ger. & Ital.). 1979. leatherette 5.95 (ISBN 0-686-97349-6, M-9176). French & Eur.

Altenbernd, Lynn. Anthology: An Introduction to Literature. 1977. 15.95x (ISBN 0-02-301960-3, 30196). Macmillan.

Altenbernd, Lynn & Lewis, Leslie L. Handbook for the Study of Drama. rev. ed. (Orig.). 1966. pap. text ed. 6.95x (ISBN 0-02-301940-9, 30194). Macmillan.

--Handbook for the Study of Poetry. rev. ed. (Orig.). 1966. pap. text ed. 6.95x (ISBN 0-02-301930-1, 30193). Macmillan.

--Introduction to Literature: Poems. 3rd ed. 800p. 1975. pap. text ed. 12.95x (ISBN 0-02-302060-1, 30206). Macmillan.

--Introduction to Literature: Stories. 3rd ed. 1980. pap. 12.95x (ISBN 0-02-302070-9). Macmillan.

Altenstetter, Christa & Bjorkman, James W. Federal-State Health Policies & Impacts: The Politics of Implementation. LC 78-62173. (Illus.). 1978. pap. text ed. 8.25 (ISBN 0-8191-0503-1). U Pr of Amer.

Alter, Aaron A., et al. Medical Technology Examination Review Book, Vol. 1. 4th ed. 1977. spiral bdg. 12.75 (ISBN 0-87488-451-9). Med Exam.

--Medical Technology Examination Review Book, Vol. 2. 4th ed. 1978. spiral bdg. 12.75 (ISBN 0-87488-452-7). Med Exam.

Alter, Dinsmore, et al. Pictorial Astronomy. 5th ed. LC 81-47878. (Illus.). 384p. 1983. 19.18i (ISBN 0-06-181019-3, HarpT). Har-Row.

--Pictorial Astronomy. 4th, rev. ed. LC 73-15577. (Illus.). 352p. 1973. 14.95i (ISBN 0-690-00095-2). T Y Crowell.

Alter, Eric. The Dukes of Hazzard: Gone Racin' 224p. Date not set. pap. 2.50 (ISBN 0-446-30324-0). Warner Bks.

Alter, G., tr. see Ulehla, Ivan, et al.

Alter, J. Cecil. Early Utah Journalism. LC 79-98803. Repr. of 1938 ed. lib. bdg. 17.75x (ISBN 0-8371-3065-4, ALUJ). Greenwood.

Alter, JoAnne. A Part-Time Career for Full-Time You. (Illus.). 320p. 1982. 15.95 o.s.i. (ISBN 0-395-31284-1); pap. 8.95 (ISBN 0-395-31868-8). HM.

Alter, Joseph D. Life After Fifty. (Illus.). 144p. 1983. 12.50 (ISBN 0-89313-060-5). G F Stickley.

Alter, Judy. After Pa Was Shot. (gr. 7-9). 1978. PLB 9.36 (ISBN 0-688-32136-4). Morrow.

Alter, Robert. The Art of Biblical Narrative. LC 80-68958. 208p. 1981. 14.50 (ISBN 0-465-00424-5). Basic.

--Partial Magic: The Novel As Self-Conscious Genre. LC 74-77725. 1975. 24.00x (ISBN 0-520-02755-8); pap. 3.95 (ISBN 0-520-03732-4). U of Cal Pr.

Alter, Robert, ed. Modern Hebrew Literature. LC 75-9928. (Library of Jewish Studies). 384p. 1975. pap. text ed. 9.95x (ISBN 0-87441-235-8). Behrman.

Alter, Robert E. High Spy. (Illus.). (gr. 5 up). 1967. PLB 5.29 o.p. (ISBN 0-399-60260-7). Putnam Pub Group.

Alter, Robert M. The No-Nibbling Book: One Hundred Twenty-Eight Things to Do at the Refrigerator Door So You Won't Open It. 144p. 1981. 9.95 o.p. (ISBN 0-399-12581-7). Putnam Pub Group.

Alter, Steven L. Decision Support Systems-Current Practice & Continuing Challenges: Current Practice & Continuing Challenges. LC 78-67960. 1979. text ed. 24.95 (ISBN 0-201-00193-4). A-W

Altfeld, E. Milton. The Jews' Struggle for Religious & Civil Liberty in Maryland. LC 78-99859. (Civil Liberties in American History Ser). 1970. Repr. of 1924 ed. lib. bdg. 29.50 (ISBN 0-306-71859-6). Da Capo.

Altfest, Karen C. Robert Owen. (World Leaders Ser.). 1977. lib. bdg. 12.95 (ISBN 0-8057-7711-3, Twayne). G K Hall.

Alth, Charlotte, jt. auth. see Alth, Max.

Alth, Max. Do-It-Yourself Plumbing. LC 74-27320. (A Popular Science Bk.). (Illus.). 316p. 1975. 14.37i (ISBN 0-06-010122-9, HarpT). Har-Row.

--Do-It-Yourself Roofing & Siding. LC 76-56515. (Illus.). 1978. pap. 4.95 o.p. (ISBN 0-8015-2151-3, Hawthorn). Dutton.

--The Handbook of Do-It Yourself Materials. (Illus.). 320p. 1983. 18.95 (ISBN 0-517-54366-4). Crown.

--How to Farm Your Backyard the Mulch Organic Way. (Illus.). 1977. 3.25 (ISBN 0-07-001128-1, P&RB). McGraw.

--Motorcycles & Motorcycling. (First Bks.). (Illus.). (gr. 4 up). 1979. PLB 8.90 s&l (ISBN 0-531-02945-X). Watts.

Alth, Max & Alth, Charlotte. Making Plastic Pipe Furniture. 224p. 1981. 17.95 (ISBN 0-89696-087-0, An Everest House Book); pap. 10.95 (ISBN 0-89696-133-8). Dodd.

Alth, Max And Charlotte. Disastrous Hurricanes & Tornadoes. LC 81-7544. (First Bks.). (Illus.). 72p. (gr. 4 up). 1981. lib. bdg. 8.90 (ISBN 0-531-04327-4). Watts.

Al Tha'alibi. Dhikra al Babbaga. Wormhoudt, Arthur, tr. (Arab Translation Ser.: No. 24). 1976. pap. 6.50x (ISBN 0-916358-74-7). Wormhoudt.

Althaus, Paul. The Ethics of Martin Luther. Schultz, Robert C., tr. from Ger. LC 72-164552. 192p. 1972. 7.95 (ISBN 0-8006-1709-6, 1-47). Fortress.

--Fact & Faith in the Kerygma of Today. Cairas, David, tr. 89p. 1978. Repr. of 1959 ed. lib. bdg. 15.50x (ISBN 0-313-20446-2, ALFA). Greenwood.

Althea. Bridges. (Cambridge Dinosaur Wingate Ser.). (Illus.). 32p. (gr. 10-12). 1983. pap. 1.95 (ISBN 0-521-27170-3). Cambridge U Pr.

--Building a House. (Cambridge Dinosaur Information Ser.). (Illus.). 26p. (gr. 7-10). 1983. pap. 1.50 (ISBN 0-521-27152-5). Cambridge U Pr.

--Going on a Train. (Cambridge Dinosaur Information Ser.). (Illus.). 26p. 1983. pap. 1.50 (ISBN 0-521-27150-9). Cambridge U Pr.

--How Life Began. (Cambridge Dinosaur Information Ser.). (Illus.). 26p. (gr. 7-10). 1983. pap. 1.50 (ISBN 0-521-27167-3). Cambridge U Pr.

--Jeremy Mouse & Cat. (Illus.). 1979. pap. 1.60 o.p. (ISBN 0-85122-201-3, Pub. by Dinosaur Pubns); in 5-pack avail. o.p. Merrimack Bk Serv.

--Life in a Castle. (Cambridge Dinosaur Wingate Ser.). (Illus.). 32p. (gr. 10-12). 1983. pap. 1.95 (ISBN 0-521-27169-X). Cambridge U Pr.

--Machines on a Farm. (Cambridge Dinosaur Information Ser.). (Illus.). 26p. (gr. 7-10). 1983. pap. 1.50 (ISBN 0-521-27156-8). Cambridge U Pr.

--Making a Book. (Cambridge Dinosaur Information Ser.). (Illus.). 26p. (gr. 7-10). 1983. pap. 1.50 (ISBN 0-521-27159-2). Cambridge U Pr.

--Man Flies On. (Cambridge Dinosaur Wingate Ser.). (Illus.). 32p. (gr. 10-12). 1983. pap. 1.95 (ISBN 0-521-27173-8). Cambridge U Pr.

--Man in the Sky. (Cambridge Dinosaur Wingate Ser.). (Illus.). 32p. (gr. 10-12). 1983. pap. 1.95 (ISBN 0-521-27172-X). Cambridge U Pr.

--The School Fair. (Cambridge Dinosaur Information Ser.). (Illus.). 26p. (gr. 7-10). 1983. pap. 1.50 (ISBN 0-521-27166-5). Cambridge U Pr.

--Signposts of the Sea. (Cambridge Dinosaur Wingate Ser.). (Illus.). 32p. (gr. 10-12). 1983. pap. 1.95 (ISBN 0-521-27171-1). Cambridge U Pr.

--Visiting a Museum. (Cambridge Dinosaur Information Ser.). 26p. (gr. 7-10). 1983. pap. 1.50 (ISBN 0-521-27160-6). Cambridge U Pr.

Alther, Lisa. Kinflicks. 1977. pap. 3.95 (ISBN 0-451-11985-1, AE1985, Sig). NAL.

--Original Sins. 1982. pap. 3.95 (ISBN 0-451-11448-5, AE1448, Sig). NAL.

Altherr, Thomas L. American Sexual Dilemma. 1984. text ed. price not set (ISBN 0-89874-609-4). Krieger.

Althoff, Karl F. The Magna Charta of the Christian Church. Grimm, Werner, tr. from Ger. 19p. 1982. pap. 3.00 (ISBN 0-919924-15-8, Pub. by Steiner Book Centre Canada). Anthroposophic.

Althouse, Andrew, et al. Modern Refrigeration & Air Conditioning. LC 81-20002. (Illus.). 1004p. 1982. text ed. 24.00 (ISBN 0-87006-340-5); lab manual 5.28 (ISBN 0-87006-422-3). Goodheart.

--Modern Welding. LC 79-15573. (Illus.). 752p. text ed. 17.60 (ISBN 0-87006-279-4). Goodheart.

Althouse, Rosemary. The Young Child: Learning with Understanding. LC 81-4600. 1981. text ed. 17.95x (ISBN 0-8077-2658-3). Tchrs Coll.

Althusser, Louis. For Marx. Brewster, Ben, tr. from Ger. 1979. pap. 9.50 (ISBN 0-8052-7018-3, Pub. by Verso). Schocken.

--Politics & History: Montesquieu, Rousseau, Hegel, Marx. 1978. pap. 7.95 (ISBN 0-8052-7136-8, Pub by NLB). Schocken.

Althusser, Louis & Balibar, Etienne. Reading Capital. 1979. pap. 10.25 (ISBN 0-8052-7016-7, Pub by NLB). Schocken.

Altick, Richard D. English Common Reader: A Social History of the Mass Reading Public, 1800-1900. LC 57-6975. (Midway Reprints Ser.). 1983. pap. 8.50x o.s.i. (ISBN 0-226-01539-4); write for info (ISBN 0-226-01540-8). U of Chicago Pr.

Altick, Richard D. & Wright, Andrew. Selective Bibliography for the Study of English & American Literature. 6th ed. 1978. pap. text ed. 9.95 (ISBN 0-02-302110-1). Macmillan.

Altieri, Charles F. Modern Poetry. LC 76-4656. (Goldentree Bibliographies in Language & Literature). 1980. text ed. 22.50x (ISBN 0-88295-566-7); pap. text ed. 13.95 (ISBN 0-88295-550-0). Harlan Davidson.

Altimir, Oscar. The Extent of Poverty in Latin American. rev. ed. LC 82-8533. (World Bank Staff Working Papers: No. 522). (Orig.). 1982. pap. text ed. 3.00 (ISBN 0-8213-0012-1). World Bank.

Alting, J. H., jt. auth. see Buning, W. De Cock.

Alting von Geuseau, Frans A., ed. Allies in a Turbulent World: Challenges to U. S. & Eastern European Cooperation. LC 82-47776. (Illus.). 192p. 1982. 24.95x (ISBN 0-669-05581-6). Lexington Bks.

Altizer, Thomas J. The Descent into Hell: A Study of the Radical Reversal of the Christain Consciousness. 222p. 1979. pap. 6.95 (ISBN 0-8164-1194-8). Seabury.

Altizer, Thomas J., jt. ed. see Griffin, David R.

Altman, Dennis. Homosexual: Oppression & Liberation. 1973. pap. 1.95 o.p. (ISBN 0-380-01256-1, 27425, Discus). Avon.

--The Homosexualization of America. LC 82-73959. 256p. 1983. pap. 9.13 (ISBN 0-8070-4143-2, BP-654). Beacon Pr.

--Rehearsals for Change. 215p. 1982. pap. 6.95 (ISBN 0-686-97017-9, Pub by Fontana-Collins). Intl Schol Bk Serv.

Altman, Edward I. Corporate Financial Distress: A Complete Guide to Predicting, Avoiding & Dealing with Bankruptcy. (Professional Banking & Finance Ser.). 285p. 1982. 29.95 (ISBN 0-471-08707-6, Pub. by Wiley-Interscience). Wiley.
--Financial Handbook. 5th ed. LC 81-10473. 1344p. 1981. 55.00x (ISBN 0-471-07727-5, Pub. by Ronald Pr). Wiley.
Altman, Edward I. & Sametz, Arnold W. Financial Crises: Institutions & Markets in a Fragile Environment. LC 77-2308. 336p. 1977. 44.95x (ISBN 0-471-02685-9). Ronald Pr.
Altman, Edward I., ed. see Ahlers, David M.
Altman, Edward I., ed. see Ahmad, Jaleel.
Altman, Edward I., ed. see Allen, Loring.
Altman, Edward I., ed. see Altman, Edward I., et al.
Altman, Edward I., ed. see Balbkins, Nicholas.
Altman, Edward I., ed. see Bierwag, G. O.
Altman, Edward I., ed. see Bloch, Ernest & Schwartz, Robert A.
Altman, Edward I., ed. see Dreyer, Jacob S.
Altman, Edward I., ed. see Fewings, David R.
Altman, Edward I., ed. see Ghatak, Subrata.
Altman, Edward I., ed. see Gladwin, Thomas N.
Altman, Edward I., ed. see Hallwood, Paul.
Altman, Edward I., ed. see Hunt, Lacy H.
Altman, Edward I., ed. see Kaufman, George G.
Altman, Edward I., ed. see Kobrin, Stephen J.
Altman, Edward I., ed. see Levich, Richard M.
Altman, Edward I., ed. see Newfarmer, Richard.
Altman, Edward I., ed. see Oh, John.
Altman, Edward I., ed. see Oldfield, George S., Jr.
Altman, Edward I., ed. see Parry, Thomas G.
Altman, Edward I., ed. see Pastre, Oliver.
Altman, Edward I., ed. see Ramsey, James B.
Altman, Edward I., ed. see Roxburgh, Nigel.
Altman, Edward I., ed. see Sciberras, Edmond.
Altman, Edward I., ed. see Siebert, Horst, et al.
Altman, Edward I., ed. see Sinkey, Joseph F., Jr.
Altman, Edward I., ed. see Stapleton, Richard.
Altman, Edward I., ed. see Thompson, John K.
Altman, Edward I., ed. see Uri, Noel D.
Altman, Edward I., et al. Application of Classification Techniques in Business, Banking & Finance, Vol. 3. Walter, Ingo & Altman, Edward I., eds. LC 76-5759. (Contemporary Studies in Economic & Financial Analysis). 325p. 1981. lib. bdg. 47.50 (ISBN 0-89232-004-4). Jai Pr.
Altman, Edward V., ed. see Walker, William B.
Altman, Ellen & Plate, Kenneth. Problems in Library Supervision. (The Libraries & Infromation Sciences Ser.). Date not set. price not set (ISBN 0-89391-111-9). Ablex Pub.
Altman, Howard B. see Alatis, James E., et al.
Altman, Howard B., ed. see PIE Seminar,Papers, Oxford, April 1979.
Altman, Irwin & Chemers, Martin M. Culture & Environment. LC 79-17384. 1979. pap. text ed. 13.95 (ISBN 0-8185-0348-3). Brooks-Cole.
Altman, J. C. & Nieuwenhuysen, J. P. The Economic Status of Australian Aborigines. LC 78-14917. 1979. 42.50 (ISBN 0-521-22421-7). Cambridge U Pr.
Altman, Joel B. The Tudor Play of Mind: Rhetorical Inquiry & the Development of Elizabethan Drama. LC 76-52022. 1978. 33.00x (ISBN 0-520-03427-9). U of Cal Pr.
Altman, Kurt I. Radiation Biochemistry, 2 vols. Incl. Vol. 1. Cells. Okada, Shigefumi (ISBN 0-12-054501-2); Vol. 2. Tissues & Body Fluids. Altman, Kurt I. & Gerber, Georg B. (ISBN 0-12-054502-0). 1970. 60.00 ea. (ISBN 0-685-23199-2); Set. 99.00 (ISBN 0-685-23200-X). Acad Pr.
Altman, Laurence, ed. see Electronics Magazine.
Altman, M. Dicionario Tecnico Contabil: Portugues-Ingles, Ingles-Portugues. 126p. (Port. & Eng.). 1980. pap. 9.95 (ISBN 0-686-97637-1, M-9355). French & Eur.
Altman, Margery. Jaws2-Shark Tales. Duenewald, Doris, ed. LC 78-58462. (Inkpot Books Ser.). (Illus.). (gr. 3-7). 1978. pap. 0.95 o.s.i. (ISBN 0-448-16337-3, G&D). Putnam Pub Group.
--Jaws2-Sharks: All That's Good & Bad About Them. Duenewald, Doris, ed. LC 78-58461. (Inkpot Ser.). (Illus.). (gr. 3-7). 1978. pap. 0.95 o.s.i. (ISBN 0-448-16336-5, G&D). Putnam Pub Group.
Altman, Michael L. Standards Relating to Juvenile Records & Information Systems. LC 77-3228. (IJA-ABA Juvenile Justice Standards Project Ser.). 208p. 1980. prof ref 20.00x (ISBN 0-88410-247-5); pap. 10.00x (ISBN 0-88410-819-8). Ballinger Pub.
Altman, Ralph. Availability for Work: A Study in Unemployment Compensation. LC 68-8935. (Illus.). 1968. Repr. of 1950 ed. lib. bdg. 19.00x (ISBN 0-8371-0004-6, ALAW). Greenwood.
Altman, Sidney, ed. Transfer RNA. (MIT Press Cell Monograph Ser.: No. 2). 1978. text ed. 40.00x (ISBN 0-262-01056-9). MIT Pr.
Altman, Stuart & Sapolsky, Harvey M., eds. Federal Health Programs: Improving the Health-Care System? LC 79-48059. (The University Health Policy Consortium Ser.). 272p. 1981. 13.95x (ISBN 0-669-06371-1). Lexington Bks.
Altman, Stuart A. Social Communication Among the Primates. LC 65-25120. (Midway Reprints Ser.). (Illus.). xiv, 392p. 1982. pap. text ed. 14.00x (ISBN 0-226-01597-1). U of Chicago Pr.
Altmann, Alexander. Essays in Jewish Intellectual History. LC 80-54471. 336p. 1981. text ed. 27.50x (ISBN 0-87451-192-5). U Pr of New Eng.
--Moses Mendelssohn: A Biographical Study. LC 72-12430. 961p. 1973. 27.50 o.p. (ISBN 0-8173-6860-4). U of Ala Pr.
Altmann, Stuart A., ed. Social Communication Among Primates. LC 65-25120. (Illus.). 1967. 8.50x o.s.i. (ISBN 0-226-01599-8). U of Chicago Pr.
Altobello, Pat & Pierce, Deirdre. The Food Lover's Book of Lists; or the Book Lover's List of Food. (Illus., Orig.). 1979. pap. 4.95 o.p. (ISBN 0-452-25201-6, Z5201, Plume). NAL.
Altomara, Rita E. Hollywood on the Palisades: A Filmography of Silent Feaures Made in Fort Lee, New Jersey 1903-1927. 120p. 1983. lib. bdg. 20.00 (ISBN 0-8240-9225-2). Garland Pub.
Alton, Thad P. Polish Postwar Economy. LC 74-5780. (Studies of the Russian Institute, Columbia University). 330p. 1974. Repr. of 1955 ed. lib. bdg. 20.00x (ISBN 0-8371-7502-X, ALLP). Greenwood.
Alton, W. G. Hats Galore. (Make & Play Ser.). (Illus.). 48p. (gr. k-6). 1976. pap. 1.50 o.p. (ISBN 0-263-05936-7). Transatlantic.
Altounyan, Taqui. In Aleppo Once. (Illus.). 1971. 9.50 o.p. (ISBN 0-7195-1922-5). Transatlantic.
Altschiller, Donald. Transportation in America. (The Reference Shelf Ser.: Vol. 54, No. 3). 204p. 1982. text ed. 6.25 (ISBN 0-8242-0667-3). Wilson.
Altschul, Aaron M., jt. ed. see Scrimshaw, Nevin S.
Altschule, Mark D., ed. Frontiers of Pineal Physiology. 1974. 30.00x (ISBN 0-262-01041-0). MIT Pr.
Altschuler, Glenn C. & Saltzgaber, Jan M. Revivalism, Social Conscience, & Community in the Burned-Over District: The Trial of Rhoda Bement. (Illus.). 184p. 1983. 22.50x (ISBN 0-8014-1541-1); pap. 7.95x (ISBN 0-8014-9246-7). Cornell U Pr.
Altshuler, Alan, ed. Current Issues in Transportation Policies. LC 78-19631. (Policy Studies Organization Ser.). (Illus.). 224p. 1979. 22.95x (ISBN 0-669-02623-9). Lexington Bks.
--Transportation & Communication Policy. new ed. 1977. pap. 6.00 (ISBN 0-918592-22-4). Policy Studies.
Altshuler, Alan A., et al. The Urban Transportation System: Politics & Policy Innovation. 1979. text ed. 38.50x (ISBN 0-262-01055-0); pap. 12.50x (ISBN 0-262-51023-5). MIT Pr.
Altshuler, Constance W. Starting with Defiance: Nineteenth Century Arizona Military Posts. (Historical Monograph: No. 7). (Illus.). 88p. 1982. 10.00 (ISBN 0-910037-19-1); pap. 6.00 (ISBN 0-910037-20-5). AZ Hist Soc.
Altshuler, Thelma, jt. auth. see Janaro, Richard P.
Altstein, Howard, jt. auth. see Simon, Rita J.
Altura, B. M., jt. auth. see Kaley, G.
Altura, B. M. & Altura, Bella T., eds. Dietary Minerals & Cardiovascular Disease. (Journal: Magnesium: Vol. 1, No. 3-6). (Illus.). 140p. 1983. pap. write for info. (ISBN 3-8055-3682-8). S Karger.
Altura, Bella T., jt. ed. see Altura, B. M.
Altura, Burton M. & Saba, Thomas M., eds. Pathophysiology of the Reticuloendothelial System. 248p. 1981. text ed. 26.50 (ISBN 0-89004-441-4). Raven.
Aluko, T. M. Wrong Ones in the Dock. (African Writers Ser.: No. 242). 195p. 1982. pap. text ed. 6.00x (ISBN 0-435-90242-3). Heinemann Ed.
Alvardo, Arturo R. Cronica De Aztlan. LC 73-87742. (Illus.). 1977. pap. 6.00 (ISBN 0-88412-107-0). Tonatiuh-Quinto Sol Intl.
Alvarenga, Beatriz. Fisica General. 2nd ed. 1024p. (Span.). 1983. pap. text ed. write for info (ISBN 0-06-310016-9, Pub. by HarLA Mexico). Har-Row.
Alvarez, Charles & Fleckles, David. Introduction to Electron Devices. 2nd ed. (Illus.). 416p. 1974. text ed. 23.95 (ISBN 0-07-001405-1, G); instructor's manual 1.95 (ISBN 0-07-001406-X). McGraw.
Alvarez, Francois. Historiale Description de l'Ethiopie. (Bibliotheque Africaine Ser.). 715p. (Fr.). 1974. Repr. of 1558 ed. lib. bdg. 171.00x o.p. (ISBN 0-8287-0016-8, 72-2127). Clearwater Pub.
Alvarez, Joseph A. Vice-Presidents of Destiny. (Illus.). (gr. 6 up). 1969. PLB 5.89 o.p. (ISBN 0-399-60653-X). Putnam Pub Group.
Alvarez, Max J. Index to Motion Pictures Reviewed by Variety, 1907-1980. LC 81-23236. 520p. 1982. 32.50 (ISBN 0-8108-1515-X). Scarecrow.
Alvarez, Peter G. Visions Unknown. Date not set. pap. cancelled (ISBN 0-89293-054-3). Beta Bk.
Alvarez, Ramon, tr. see Gaunt, Leonard.
Alvarez, Russell R De see De Alvarez, Russell R.
Alvarez-Altman, Grace, jt. ed. see Woods, Richard D.
Alvarez-Borland, Isabel. Discontinuidad y Ruptura en Guillermo Cabrera Infante. LC 82-84325. 144p. 1983. pap. text ed. 9.95 (ISBN 0-935318-09-7). Edins Hispamerica.
Alvarez-Detrell, Tamara & Paulson, Michael G., eds. The Gambling Mania on & off the Stage in Pre-Revolutionary France. LC 81-43819. 192p. (Orig.). 1982. lib. bdg. 21.25 (ISBN 0-8191-2586-5); pap. text ed. 10.00 (ISBN 0-8191-2587-3). U Pr of Amer.
Alvarez-Mena, Sergio C., jt. auth. see Frank, Martin J.
Alvarino, Angeles. Siphonophores of the Pacific, with a Review of the World Distribution. (Bulletin of the Scripps Institution of Oceanography: Vol. 16). pap. 10.50x (ISBN 0-520-09321-6). U of Cal Pr.
Alves, A. Pereira. Triunfa En la Vida. (Illus.). 128p. 1977. pap. 2.25 (ISBN 0-311-46033-X). Casa Bautista.
Alves, Robert. Sketches of a History of Literature. LC 67-18714. 1967. Repr. of 1794 ed. 35.00x (ISBN 0-8201-1002-7). Schol Facsimiles.
Alvey, C. George, jt. auth. see Rosenberg, R. Robert.
Alvey, R. Gerald. Dulcimer Maker: The Craft of Homer Ledford. LC 82-40463. (Illus.). 1983. price not set (ISBN 0-8131-1447-0). U Pr of Ky.
Alvin, K. L., jt. auth. see Cutler, E. F.
Alvisi, C. & Hill, C. R. Investigative Ultrasonlogy Two: Clinical Advances. 256p. 1981. text ed. 35.95 (ISBN 0-272-79576-3). Pitman Pub MA.
Alvord, David W., jt. auth. see Wass, Stan.
Alwan, A. J., jt. auth. see Almaney, A. J.
Alwin, John A. Eastern Montana: A Portrait of the Land & its People. (Montana Geographic Ser.: No. 2). (Illus.). 128p. 1982. pap. 12.95 (ISBN 0-938314-02-5). MT Mag.
Alwin, Robert H. & Hackworth, Robert D. Algebra Programmed, Pt. 2. 2nd ed. (Illus.). 1978. pap. text ed. 16.95 (ISBN 0-13-022020-5). P-H.
--Algebra Programmed, Pt. 1. 2nd ed. (Illus.). 1978. pap. text ed. 16.95 (ISBN 0-13-022038-8). P-H.
Alwin, Robert H., et al. Algebra Text: Intermediate. (Illus.). 1974. pap. 19.95 ref. ed. (ISBN 0-13-022400-6). P-H.
--Algebra Text: Elementary. (Illus.). 424p. 1974. pap. 19.95x ref. ed. (ISBN 0-13-022293-3). P-H.
Alwine, Nevin S., ed. Readings for Foundation of Education. 121p. 1969. pap. text ed. 9.95x (ISBN 0-8290-1310-5). Irvington.
Alworth, E. Paul. Will Rogers. (U. S. Authors Ser.: No. 236). 1974. lib. bdg. 10.95 o.p. (ISBN 0-8057-0634-8, Twayne). G K Hall.
Aly, Osman M., jt. auth. see Faust, Samuel D.
Aly, Raza & Shinefield, Henry R. Bacterial Interference. 192p. 1982. 60.00 (ISBN 0-8493-6285-7). CRC Pr.
Alyeshmreni, Mansoor, tr. see Bahar, Mehrdad.
Alyn, Irene B., jt. auth. see Gillies, Dee Ann.
Alyson Pubns. Staff. The Gay Almanac. 150p. (Orig.). 1983. pap. text ed. write for info (ISBN 0-932870-19-8). Alyson Pubns.
Am-Fem Company. International Directory of Amateur Female Fighting. 1983. pap. 20.00 (ISBN 0-686-32796-9). AM FEM Co.
AMA. AMA Drug Evaluations. 4th ed. LC 76-9254. 1470p. 1980. 83.00 (ISBN 0-471-08125-6, Pub. by Wiley-Med). Wiley.
Amacher, P., jt. ed. see Gardner, L. I.
Amacher, Richard E. American Political Writers: 1588-1800. (United States Authors Ser.). 1979. 13.94 (ISBN 0-8057-7217-0, Twayne). G K Hall.
--Edward Albee. (United States Authors Ser.). 1968. lib. bdg. 11.95 (ISBN 0-8057-0011-0, Twayne). G K Hall.
--Edward Albee. Rev. ed. (United States Author Ser.). 1982. lib. bdg. 12.95 (ISBN 0-8057-7349-5, Twayne). G K Hall.
Amacker, Robert, ed. see Lo, Benjamin P., et al.
Amada, Gerald. A Guide to Psychothearpy. LC 82-21918. (Illus.). 128p. (Orig.). 1983. lib. bdg. 19.25 (ISBN 0-8191-2928-3); pap. text ed. 8.25 (ISBN 0-8191-2929-1). U Pr of Amer.
--Mental Health & Authoritarianism on the College Campus. LC 79-66480. 1979. pap. text ed. 13.50 (ISBN 0-8191-0831-6). U Pr of Amer.
Amadeo, et al. Oasis. new ed. Jensen, Sheila R., ed. LC 78-52075. (Illus.). 1978. pap. 3.00 (ISBN 0-932044-12-3). M O Pub Co.
Amadi, Elechi. Ethics in Nigerian Culture. 128p. (Orig.). 1982. pap. text ed. 7.50 (ISBN 0-435-89030-1). Heinemann Ed.
Amador, Luis V. Brain Tumors in the Young. (Illus.). 736p. 1983. 95.00x (ISBN 0-398-04697-2). C C Thomas.
Amaldas, Brahmachari. Yoga & Contemplation. 146p. 1981. 10.00x p.p. (ISBN 0-232-51530-1, Pub. by Darton-Longman-Todd England). State Mutual Bk.
Aman, Reinhold, ed. Do It! 60p. 1982. pap. 3.50 (ISBN 0-916500-09-8). Maledicta.
--Maledicta Nineteen Eighty-Two: International Journal of Verbal Aggression, Vol. 6, Nos. 1 & 2. (Illus.). 360p. 1982. pap. 23.50 (ISBN 0-916500-26-8). Maledicta.
Aman, Reinhold, ed. see Raeithel, Gert.
Aman, Reinhold A., ed. see Morse, A. Reynolds.
Amandola, Sal, et al. Perspective for the Artist. (Illus.). 64p. (Orig.). 1983. pap. 4.95 (Pentalic). Taplinger.
Amann, Barbara, jt. auth. see Amann, Dick.
Amann, Dick. Airplanes, Airports & Noise Pollution. 1981. 49.95x o.p. (ISBN 0-917194-11-X). Prog Studies.
--Airports: Today's Small Field, Tomorrow's Neighborhood Nightmare. 1981. 45.00 o.p. (ISBN 0-917194-05-5). Prog Studies.
Amann, Dick & Amann, Barbara. Caribbean Trip Planner: A New Looseleaf Guide to the Caribbean. (Illus.). 1981. looseleaf 19.95 o.p. (ISBN 0-917194-04-7). Prog Studies.
Amann, Dick & Smith, Dick. Forgotten Women of Computer History. Whitson, Dick, ed. (Illus.). 1978. pap. 8.95 (ISBN 0-917194-09-8). Prog Studies.
Amann, H., et al, eds. Applications of Nonlinear Analysis in the Physical Sciences. LC 80-21067. (Surveys & References Ser.: No. 6). 352p. 1981. text ed. 76.95 (ISBN 0-273-08501-8). Pitman Pub MA.
Amant, Kristi, ed. see Arrants, Cheryl & Asbjornsen, Jan.
Amanuddin, Syed. World Poetry in English: Essays & Interviews. 179p. 1981. text ed. 12.75x (ISBN 0-391-02790-5, 41054, Pub. by Sterling India). Humanities.
Amara, Roy C. & Lipinski, Andrew J. Business Planning for an Uncertain Future: Scenarios & Strategies. (PPS on Business & Economics Ser.). 200p. 1983. 25.00 (ISBN 0-08-027545-1). Pergamon.
--Business Planning for an Uncertain Future: Scenarios & Strategies. 250p. 25.00 (ISBN 0-686-84789-X). Work in Amer.
Amaral, David. Lusophone African Liberators: The University Years. (Graduate Student Paper Competition Ser.). 20p. (Orig.). 1979. pap. text ed. 2.00 (ISBN 0-941934-27-6). Ind U Afro-Amer Arts.
Amarasinghe, Upali. Dryden & Pope in the Early 19th Century. 1962. 44.50 (ISBN 0-521-04026-4). Cambridge U Pr.
Amari, S. & Arbib, M. A., eds. Competition & Cooperation in Neural Nets, Kyoto, Japan, 1982: Proceedings. (Lecture Notes in Biomathematics: Vol. 45). 441p. 1982. pap. 26.00 (ISBN 0-387-11574-9). Springer-Verlag.
Amarshu, Azeem, et al. Development & Dependency: The Political Economy of Papua New Guinea. (Illus.). 1979. text ed. 32.50x (ISBN 0-19-550582-4). Oxford U Pr.
Amastae, Jon & Elias-Olivares, Lucia, eds. Spanish in the United States: Sociolinguistic Aspects. LC 81-15437. (Illus.). 448p. 1982. 49.50 (ISBN 0-521-24448-X); pap. 18.95 (ISBN 0-521-28689-1). Cambridge U Pr.
Amateur Hockey Association of the U. S. Hockey Coaching. (Illus.). 248p. 1982. 29.95 (ISBN 0-684-17457-X, ScribT). Scribner.
Amato, Antony & Edwards, Katherine. Affair. LC 77-20490. 1978. 7.95 o.p. (ISBN 0-399-12106-4). Putnam Pub Group.
Amato, Joseph A. Ethics: Living or Dead? Themes in Contemporary Values. 1982. 10.50 (ISBN 0-916620-62-X). Portals Pr.
Amato, P. R., jt. auth. see Smithson, M.
Amatuzzi, Joseph R. Television & the School. LC 82-60522. 125p. 1983. pap. 14.95 (ISBN 0-88247-676-9). R & E Res Assoc.
Amazigo, John C. Advanced Calculus & Its Applications to the Engineering & Physical Sciences. LC 80-283. 407p. 1980. text ed. 26.95x (ISBN 0-471-04934-4). Wiley.
Amazing Randi & Sugar, Bert R. Houdini: His Life & Art. Torgoff, Martin, ed. (Illus.). 192p. 1976. 5.95 o.p. (ISBN 0-448-12546-3, G&D); pap. 6.95 o.p. (ISBN 0-448-12552-8, Today Press). Putnam Pub Group.
Ambartzumian, R. V. Combinatorial Integral Geometry. LC 81-14773. (Probability & Mathematical Statistics). 220p. 1982. 45.00 (ISBN 0-471-27977-3, Pub. by Wiley-Interscience). Wiley.
Ambasz, Emilio. The Architecture of Luis Barragan. LC 74-21724. (Illus.). 1976. 27.50 (ISBN 0-87070-234-3); pap. 15.95 (ISBN 0-87070-233-5). Museum Mod Art.
Amber, John T. Gun Digest Treasury. 5th ed. (DBI Ser.). 1977. pap. 7.95 o.s.i. (ISBN 0-695-80841-9). Follett.
--Gun Digest, 1979. 33rd ed. 1978. pap. 9.95 o.s.i. (ISBN 0-685-48913-2). Follett.
Amber, John T., ed. see Clayton, Joseph D.
Amber, Reuben. Color Therapy. pap. 8.95 (ISBN 0-686-36340-X). Aurora Press.
Amberg, George. Ballet in America. (Series in Dance). (Illus.). xv, 244p. 1983. Repr. of 1949 ed. lib. bdg. 39.50 (ISBN 0-306-76154-8). Da Capo.
Amberger, E., jt. auth. see Wiberg, E.
Amberson, Max, ed. see Peterson, Paul, et al.
Amberson, Max L., ed. see Bishop, Douglas D.
Amberson, Max L., ed. see Lee, Jasper S.
Amberson, Max L., ed. see Shinn, Glen C. & Weston, Curtis.
Amberson, Max L., ed. see Stewart, Robert.
Amberson, Rosanne. Raising Your Cat. LC 79-93393. (Illus.). 1969. 7.95 o.p. (ISBN 0-517-50752-8). Crown.
Ambirajan, S. Classical Political Economy & British Policy in India. LC 76-21020. (South Asian Studies: No. 21). (Illus.). 1978. 47.50 (ISBN 0-521-21415-7). Cambridge U Pr.
Ambler, C. H., jt. auth. see Summers, Festus P.
Ambler, Charles H. History of Transportation in the Ohio Valley. LC 72-98804. Repr. of 1932 ed. lib. bdg. 20.25x (ISBN 0-8371-2905-2, AMTO). Greenwood.
Ambler, Charles H., ed. Correspondence of Robert M. T. Hunter, 1826-1876. LC 76-75307. (American Scene Ser). 1971. Repr. of 1918 ed. lib. bdg. 49.50 (ISBN 0-306-71257-1). Da Capo.
Ambler, Eric. Doctor Frigo. LC 81-70068. 1982. pap. 7.95 (ISBN 0-689-70617-0). Atheneum.
--To Catch a Spy. pap. 0.95 o.p. (ISBN 0-451-05750-3, Q5750, Sig). NAL.

Ambraseys, N. N. & Melville, C. P. A History of Persian Earthquakes. LC 81-15540. (Cambridge Earth Science Ser.). (Illus.). 400p. 1982. 62.50 (ISBN 0-521-24112-X). Cambridge U Pr.

Ambrecht, Biliana C. Politicizing the Poor: The Legacy of the War on Poverty in a Mexican American Community. LC 74-31501. 1976. 32.95 o.p. (ISBN 0-275-05900-6). Praeger.

Ambrester, Marcus L. & Julian, Faye D. Speech Communication Reader. 217p. (Orig.). 1983. pap. text ed. 8.95x (ISBN 0-88133-013-2). Waveland Pr.

Ambros, Arne, ed. Damascus Arabic. LC 74-21134. (Afroasiatic Dialects: Vol. 3). 123p. 1977. pap. 14.95x o.p. (ISBN 0-89003-009-X). Undena Pubns.

Ambrose, Alice & Lazerowitz, Morris, eds. Ludwig Wittgenstein: Philosophy & Language. (Muirhead Library of Philosophy). 1972. text ed. 39.00x (ISBN 0-391-00190-6). Humanities.

Ambrose, Andrew, ed. Jane's Merchant Shipping Review. (Jane's Reviews Ser.). 150p. 1983. 17.95 (ISBN 0-686-84473-4). Sci Bks Intl.

Ambrose, David R., jt. auth. see Willet, Shelagh M.

Ambrose, E. J. Nature & Origin of the Biological World. 190p. 1982. 49.95X (ISBN 0-470-27513-8); pap. 22.95X (ISBN 0-470-27514-6). Halsted Pr.

Ambrose, E. J. & Roe, F. J. C., eds. The Biology of Cancer. 2nd rev. ed. LC 74-26860. 315p. 1975. 69.95 (ISBN 0-470-02527-1). Halsted Pr.

Ambrose, E. R. Heat Pumps & Electric Heating: Residential, Commercial, Industrial Year-Round Air Conditioning. LC 65-27664. 205p. 1966. 29.95x o.p. (ISBN 0-471-02530-5, Pub. by Wiley-Interscience). Wiley.

Ambrose, James. Building Structures Primer. 2nd ed. LC 81-4336. 136p. 1981. 24.95 (ISBN 0-471-08678-9, Pub. by Wiley-Interscience). Wiley.

--Simplified Design of Building Foundations. LC 80-39880. 338p. 1981. 25.50x (ISBN 0-471-06267-7, Pub. by Wiley-Interscience). Wiley.

--Simplified Design of Building Structures. LC 79-413. 268p. 1979. 26.50 (ISBN 0-471-04721-X, Pub. by Wiley-Interscience). Wiley.

Ambrose, James & Vergun, Dimitry. Simplified Building Design for Wind & Earthquake Forces. LC 79-26660. 142p. 1980. 26.95x (ISBN 0-471-05013-X, Pub. by Wiley-Interscience). Wiley.

Ambrose, James, jt. auth. see Parker, Harry.

Ambrose, Peter & Harper, John. Surviving Divorce: Fathers & the Child. 226p. 1983. text ed. 24.95x (ISBN 0-86598-122-1). Rowman.

Ambrose, Peter, ed. Analytical Human Geography. 1970. text ed. 20.00 (ISBN 0-444-19726-5). Elsevier.

Ambrose, Stephen E. Rise to Globalism: American Foreign Policy, 1938-1980. rev. ed. 1980. pap. 5.95 (ISBN 0-14-021247-7, Pelican). Penguin.

Ambrose, William G. College Algebra. (Illus.). 320p. 1976. text ed. 22.95 (ISBN 0-02-302520-4, 30252). Macmillan.

--College Algebra & Trigonometry. 1977. pap. text ed. 24.95x (ISBN 0-02-302500-X, 30250). Macmillan.

Ambrose-Grillet, Jeanne. Glossary of Transformational Grammar. LC 78-1819. 1978. pap. text ed. 10.95 (ISBN 0-88377-099-7). Newbury Hse.

Ambrosi, Hans. Where the Great German Wines Grow. Pringle, Thom & Hamilton, Gavin, trs. (Illus.). 248p. 1976. 12.95 (ISBN 0-8038-8070-7). Hastings.

Ambrozy, Andras. Electronic Noise. (Series in Electrical Engineering). (Illus.). 284p. 1982. text ed. 34.00x (ISBN 0-07-001124-9, C). McGraw.

Ambrus, Victor G. Blackbeard the Pirate. (Illus.). 32p. (gr. 2-9). 1983. bds. 9.95 (ISBN 0-19-279771-9, Pub by Oxford U Pr Childrens). Merrimack Bk Serv.

--Dracula: Everything you Always Wanted to Know, but were too Afraid to Ask. (Illus.). 32p. 1982. 9.95 (ISBN 0-686-37794-X, Pub. by Oxford U Pr Childrens). Merrimack Bk Serv.

--Dracula: Everything You Always Wanted to Know But Were Too Afraid to Ask. (Illus.). 32p. (gr. 2-9). 1983. pap. 4.95 (ISBN 0-19-272121-6, Pub by Oxford U Pr Childrens). Merrimack Bk Serv.

--Dracula's Bedtime Storybook: Tales to Keep you Awake at Night. (Illus.). 32p. 1982. 9.95 (ISBN 0-19-279762-X, Pub. by Oxford U Pr Childrens); pap. 4.95 (ISBN 0-19-272130-5). Merrimack Bk Serv.

--Under the Double Eagle. (Illus.). 48p. 1982. 10.95 (ISBN 0-19-279737-9, Pub. by Oxford U Pr Childrens). Merrimack Bk Serv.

--The Valiant Little Tailor. (Illus.). 24p. (ps-3). 1980. 11.95 (ISBN 0-19-279727-1). Oxford U Pr.

Ambuter, Carolyn. Open Canvas. LC 82-60066. (Illus.). 320p. 1982. 22.50 (ISBN 0-89480-170-8); pap. 14.95 (ISBN 0-89480-171-6). Workman Pub.

Ambuter, Jeanne, jt. auth. see Crandall, Dorothy.

Amchin, Jess & Leflar, Robert B. The Hazards of Intra-Ocular Lenses. 81p. 1982. 5.00 (ISBN 0-686-96345-8). Pub Citizen Health.

Amdur, Neil, jt. auth. see Ashe, Arthur.

Amdursky, Robert S., ed. Basics for Municipal Bond Lawyers: Course Handbook. LC 80-82474. (Corporate Law & Practice Course Handbook Series, 1979-1980). 887p. 1980. pap. 30.00 (ISBN 0-686-69164-4, B4-6551). PLI.

Amedeo, Douglas & Golledge, Reginald G. Introduction to Scientific Reasoning in Geography. LC 75-1411. 431p. 1975. text ed. 34.95x (ISBN 0-471-02537-2). Wiley.

Amelar, Richard D., et al. Male Infertility. LC 76-50145. (Illus.). 258p. 1977. text ed. 27.00 (ISBN 0-7216-1214-8). Saunders.

Amelinckx, S., et al. Diffraction & Imaging Techniques in Material Science, 2 vols. 2nd rev. ed. 1978. Set. 127.75 (ISBN 0-444-85130-5, North-Holland); Vol. 1: Electron Microscopy. 72.50 (ISBN 0-444-85128-3); Vol. 2: Imaging & Diffraction Techniques. 72.50 (ISBN 0-444-85129-1). Elsevier.

Amen, Carol V. Love Goes 'Round the Circle. (Better Living Ser.). pap. 0.95 (ISBN 0-8280-1268-7). Review & Herald.

Amenta, Peter S. Histology & Embryology Review. LC 82-11322. (Illus.). 172p. 1983. pap. text ed. 10.00 (ISBN 0-668-05486-7, 5486). Arco.

America Pulpwood Association. Chain Saw Manual. 118p. 1980. pap. text ed. 5.95x (ISBN 0-8134-2133-0). Interstate.

America, R. & Anderson, B. Moving Ahead: Black Managers in American Business. 1978. 21.95 (ISBN 0-07-001355-1). McGraw.

American Academy for Jewish Research. Louis Ginzberg Jubilee Volume, on the Occasion of His 70th Birthday, 2 Vols. (Eng-Heb). 1945. Set. pap. 28.00 o.s.i. (ISBN 0-527-02359-0). Kraus Repr.

--Rashi Anniversary Volume. 1941. 14.00 o.s.i. (ISBN 0-527-01135-5). Kraus Repr.

American Academy of Orthopaedic Surgeons. American Academy of Orthopaedic Surgeons: Instructional Course Lectures, Vols. 21-29. Incl. Vol. 21. 1972. 49.50 o.p. (ISBN 0-8016-0010-3); Vol. 22. 1973. 49.50 o.p. (ISBN 0-8016-0011-1); Vol. 23. 1974. 49.50 o.p. (ISBN 0-8016-0012-X); Vol. 24. 328p. 1975. 49.50 o.p. (ISBN 0-8016-0013-8); Vol. 25. 1976. 49.50 o.p. (ISBN 0-8016-0014-6); Vol. 26. 1977. 49.50 (ISBN 0-8016-0022-7); Vol. 27. 1978. 49.50 (ISBN 0-8016-0023-5); Vol. 28. 1979. 49.50 (ISBN 0-8016-0032-4); Vol. 29. 156p. 1980. 44.50 (ISBN 0-8016-0047-2). LC 43-17054. Mosby.

--The Foot & Leg in Running Sports: Symposium. LC 82-8188. (Illus.). 188p. 1982. text ed. 39.50 (ISBN 0-8016-0054-5). Mosby.

--Symposium on the Athlete's Knee: Surgical Repair & Reconstruction. LC 80-19414. (Illus.). 218p. 1980. text ed. 52.50 (ISBN 0-8016-0077-4). Mosby.

--Symposium on the Foot & Ankle. Kiene, Richard H. & Johnson, Kenneth A., eds. (Illus.). 240p. 1983. text ed. 47.50 (ISBN 0-8016-0133-9). Mosby.

--Symposium on Trauma to the Leg & Its Sequelae. LC 81-11104. (Illus.). 388p. 1981. text ed. 59.50 (ISBN 0-8016-0081-2). Mosby.

American Academy of Orthopedic Surgeons. Instructional Course Lectures, Vol. XXXI. LC 43-10754. (Illus.). 282p. 1982. text ed. 44.50 (ISBN 0-8016-0062-6). Mosby.

American Academy of Political & Social Science, 79th. Adjusting to Scarcity: Proceedings. Lambert, Richard D. & Wolfgang, Marvin E., eds. LC 74-29624. (Annals Ser.: No. 420). 250p. 1975. pap. 7.95 (ISBN 0-87761-191-2). Am Acad Pol Soc Sci.

American Academy of Political & Social Science, Annual Meeting, 83rd. The Environment & the Quality of Life: A World View: Proceedings. Wolfgang, Marvin E. & Ginsberg, Ralph B., eds. LC 79-50266. (Annals: No. 444). 1979. 15.00 (ISBN 0-87761-240-4); pap. 7.95 (ISBN 0-87761-241-2). Am Acad Pol Soc Sci.

American Academy of Political & Social Science Annual Meeting, 82nd. Planning for the Elderly: Proceedings. Wolfgang, Marvin E. & Lambert, Richard D., eds. LC 78-56921. (Annals: No. 438). 1978. 7.50 o.p. (ISBN 0-87761-228-5); pap. 6.00 o.p. (ISBN 0-87761-229-3). Am Acad Pol Soc Sci.

American Academy of Political & Social Science, 78th. U. S. A.-U. S. S. R.: Agenda for Communication: Proceedings. Wolfgang, Marvin E. & Lambert, Richard D., eds. LC 74-80143. (Annals Ser.: No. 414). 300p. (Orig.). 1974. pap. 7.95 (ISBN 0-87761-179-3). Am Acad Pol Soc Sci.

American Alliance for Health, Phsyical Education & Recreation. Athletics in Education. 1963. pap. 1.50x o.p. (ISBN 0-685-05081-5, 241-07448). AAHPERD.

American Alliance for Health, Physical Education & Recreation. Abstracts of Research Papers, 1971. pap. 2.00x o.p. (ISBN 0-685-31260-7). AAHPERD.

--Abstracts of Research Papers, 1972. pap. 2.00x o.p. (ISBN 0-685-42021-3, 248-25306). AAHPERD.

--Abstracts of Research Papers, 1973. pap. 2.50 o.p. (ISBN 0-685-42022-1, 248-25436). AAHPERD.

--Abstracts of Research Papers, 1975. 1975. pap. 2.75x o.p. (ISBN 0-685-52989-4, 248-25696). AAHPERD.

--Administration of Athletics in Colleges & Universities. 1971. pap. 9.50x o.p. (ISBN 0-685-42435-9, 241-06734). AAHPERD.

American Alliance for Health, Physical Health, & Recreation. Annotated Bibliography on Perceptual-Motor Development. 1972. pap. 5.25 (ISBN 0-88314-016-0, 245-25412). AAHPERD.

American Alliance for Health, Physical Education, Recreation & Dance. Annotated Research, Bibliography in Physical Education Recreation & Psychomotor Function of Mentally Retarded Persons. 296p. 1975. pap. 8.95 (ISBN 0-88314-017-9, 245-25764). AAHPERD.

American Alliance for Health, Physical Education & Recreation. Annual Safety Education Review, 1972. pap. 1.75 o.p. (ISBN 0-685-42025-6, 244-25410). AAHPERD.

--Archery Selected Articles, 1971. pap. 0.60 o.p. (ISBN 0-685-42003-5, 243-25160). AAHPERD.

--Basketball Guide 1982-83. (NAGWS Sports Guides Ser.). pap. 3.75 (ISBN 0-88314-080-2). AAHPERD.

--Basketball Rules 1982-83. pap. 3.75 (ISBN 0-88314-156-6). AAHPERD.

--Best of Challenge, 3 vols. Incl. Vol. 1. Articles from the Dec. 1965 Through May-June 1970 Issues (ISBN 0-88314-032-2, 245-25124); Vol. 2. Articles from the Sep.-Oct. 1970 Through May-June 1973 Issues (ISBN 0-88314-033-0, 245-25562); Vol. 3. Articles from Sept. 73-May 76 (ISBN 0-88314-034-9). pap. 4.95x ea. AAHPERD.

--Bibliography of Research Involving Female Subjects. 1975. 3.00x o.p. (ISBN 0-685-58286-8, 243-25714). AAHPERD.

--Certification of High School Coaches. 1971. pap. 2.25x o.p. (ISBN 0-685-42436-7, 241-25138). AAHPERD.

--Children's Dance. rev. ed. 1981. pap. 8.95x (ISBN 0-88314-041-1, 243-25446). AAHPERD.

--College Physical Education: The General Program. 1973. pap. 1.95x o.p. (ISBN 0-685-42011-6, 245-25524). AAHPERD.

--Completed Research in Health, Physical Education, & Recreation, Vol. 13. 1971. pap. 3.50x o.p. (ISBN 0-685-42448-0, 248-25144). AAHPERD.

--Completed Research in Health, Physical Education, & Recreation, Vol. 15. 1973. pap. 4.25x o.p. (ISBN 0-685-42024-8, 248-25462). AAHPERD.

--Completed Research in Health, Physical Education, & Recreation, Vol. 16. 1974. 8.95x o.p. (ISBN 0-685-42023-X, 248-25686). AAHPERD.

--Crowd Control for High School Athletics. 1970. pap. 0.60x o.p. (ISBN 0-685-42437-5, 241-25120). AAHPERD.

--Dance Facilities. 1972. pap. 1.50x o.p. (ISBN 0-685-42439-1, 240-25242). AAHPERD.

--Drugs & the Coach. rev. ed. 1977. pap. 4.95 (ISBN 0-88314-062-4, 241-25948). AAHPERD.

--Evaluating the High School Athletic Program. 1973. pap. 3.50x (ISBN 0-88314-068-3, 241-25530). AAHPERD.

--Field Hockey Guide 1982-84. (NAGWS Sports Guides Ser.). pap. 3.75 (ISBN 0-88314-083-7, 243-26186). AAHPERD.

American Alliance for Health, Physical Education, & Recreation. Field Hockey-Lacrosse Selected Articles. 1974. pap. 0.60x o.p. (ISBN 0-685-05087-4, 243-25538). AAHPERD.

American Alliance for Health, Physical Education & Recreation. Flag Football-Speedball Guide 1982-84. (NAGWS Sports Guides Ser.). (Illus.). pap. 3.75 (ISBN 0-88314-084-5). AAHPERD.

--Focus on Dance: Dance Therapy, Vol. 7. 80p. 1974. pap. 8.25 (ISBN 0-685-42001-9, 243-25570). AAHPERD.

--Gymnastics Guide 1982-84. (NAGWS Sports Guides Ser.). plastic bdg. 6.95 (ISBN 0-88314-085-3). AAHPERD.

--Health Education. 252p. 1975. pap. 12.50 (ISBN 0-88314-097-7, 244-25732). AAHPERD.

--Intramural Portfolio. 1978. pap. 6.95 (ISBN 0-88314-108-6, 245-26220). AAHPERD.

--Introduction to School Nursing Curriculum. 1973. pap. 3.75x o.p. (ISBN 0-685-42008-6, 244-25470). AAHPERD.

--Kinesiology, Four. 1974. pap. 2.25x o.p. (ISBN 0-685-42012-4, 245-25548). AAHPERD.

--Kinesiology, Three. 1973. pap. 2.25x o.p. (ISBN 0-685-42013-2, 245-25440). AAHPERD.

--League Constitution & by-Laws for Girl's Interscholastic Sports - a Suggested Guide. 1975. 3.75x o.p. (ISBN 0-685-57477-6, 243-25766). AAHPERD.

--Learning About Alcohol: A Resource Book for Teachers. 1974. pap. 4.00x o.p. (ISBN 0-685-42007-8, 244-25564). AAHPERD.

--Materials on the Creative Arts: For Persons with Handicapping Conditions. 1977. 4.00x o.p. (ISBN 0-685-58289-2, 245-26002). AAHPERD.

--Movement Activities for Places & Spaces. 48p. 1978. pap. 4.95 (ISBN 0-88314-133-7, 245-25996). AAHPERD.

--NAGWS Research Reports, Vol. 2. 1973. pap. 2.25x o.p. (ISBN 0-685-42005-1, 243-25472). AAHPERD.

--Physical Education & Recreation for the Visually Handicapped. 1973. pap. 3.75x o.p. (ISBN 0-685-42010-8, 245-25416). AAHPERD.

--Physical Education Around the World: Monograph No. 2-6. pap. 3.00x ea. o.p. AAHPERD.

--Preparing Teachers for a Changing Society. 1970. pap. 1.25 o.p. (ISBN 0-685-42446-4, 240-25100). AAHPERD.

--Preparing the Elementary Specialist. 1973. 3.50x o.p. (ISBN 0-685-42014-0, 245-25448). AAHPERD.

--Professional Preparation in Aquatics Education: Curriculum Guidelines. 1974. pap. 5.50 o.p. (ISBN 0-685-41997-5, 240-25554). AAHPERD.

--Professional Preparation in Dance, Physical Education, Recreation Education, Safety Education, & School Health Education. 208p. 1974. pap. 4.95 (ISBN 0-88314-144-2, 240-25556). AAHPERD.

--Professional Preparation in Physical Education & Coaching. 1974. pap. 1.25x o.p. (ISBN 0-685-42018-3, 245-25574). AAHPERD.

--Professional Preparation in Safety Education & School Health Education. 1974. pap. 1.25x o.p. (ISBN 0-685-42019-1, 244-25572). AAHPERD.

--Proficiency Testing in Physical Education. 1974. pap. 3.75x o.p. (ISBN 0-685-42015-9, 245-25558). AAHPERD.

American Alliance for Health, Physical Educatiion & Recreation, National Convention, 1978. Research Consortium Abstracts, 3 bks, Vol. 1. Incl. Bk. 1. Teaching Behavior & Sport History. pap. 3.00 o.p. (ISBN 0-685-33323-X, 248-26232); Bk. 2. Sport, Health & Dance. pap. 2.50 o.p. (ISBN 0-685-33324-8, 248-26234); Bk. 3. Movement Studies. pap. 2.00 o.p. (ISBN 0-685-33325-6, 248-26236). 1978. pap. AAHPERD.

American Alliance for Health, Physical Education & Recreation. Research in Dance, Vol. 2. 1973. pap. 3.50x o.p. (ISBN 0-685-42002-7, 243-25404). AAHPERD.

--Safety in Aquatic Activities. (Sports Safety Monograph: No. 5). 1978. pap. 3.95x (ISBN 0-88314-163-9, 244-26224). AAHPERD.

--Safety in Individual & Dual Sports. (Sports Safety Monograph Ser.: No. 4). 1978. pap. 3.95 (ISBN 0-88314-164-7, 244-26222). AAHPERD.

--Selected Problems in Sports Safety. 1975. 4.50x o.p. (ISBN 0-685-57474-1, 244-25776). AAHPERD.

--Special Olympics Instructional Manual: From Beginners to Champions. 128p. 1972. pap. 6.25 (ISBN 0-88314-173-6, 245-25322). AAHPERD.

American Alliance for Health, Physical Education, & Recreation. Sports Skill Test Manuals for Ages 10-18, 8 bks. Incl. Bk. 1. Archery (Boys & Girls (ISBN 0-88314-178-7, 242-07328); Bk. 2. Basketball (Boys) o.p. (242-07698); Bk. 3. Basketball (Girls (ISBN 0-88314-179-5, 242-07736); Bk. 4. Football (Boys (ISBN 0-88314-180-9, 242-07644); Bk. 5. Softball (Boys (ISBN 0-88314-181-7); Bk. 6. Softball (Girls) o.p. (242-07734); Bk. 7. Volleyball (Boys & Girls (ISBN 0-88314-182-5, 242-07946). pap. 3.95 ea. AAHPERD.

American Alliance for Health, Physical Education & Recreation. State Requirements in Physical Education for Teachers & Students. 1973. pap. 3.25x o.p. (ISBN 0-685-42016-7, 240-25550). AAHPERD.

--Swimnastics is Fun, Vol. 1. 1975. 6.95 (ISBN 0-88314-185-X, 246-25756). AAHPERD.

--Teaching Safety in the Elementary School. 1972. pap. 1.95 (ISBN 0-88314-188-4, 244-25384). AAHPERD.

--Tennis Group Instruction. rev. ed. 1972. pap. 3.75x o.p. (ISBN 0-685-42445-6, 241-07558). AAHPERD.

--Utilization of Disadvantaged Workers in Public Park & Recreation Services. 1974. pap. 4.50x o.p. (ISBN 0-685-42020-5, 246-25566). AAHPERD.

--Volleyball Guide 1982-83. (NAGWS Sports Guides Ser.). pap. 3.75 (ISBN 0-88314-092-6). AAHPERD.

--Volleyball Rules 1982-83. pap. 1.50 (ISBN 0-88314-161-2). AAHPERD.

--Volleyball Scorebook. pap. 2.95 (ISBN 0-88314-169-8). AAHPERD.

--What Recreation Research Says to the Recreation Practitioner. 1975. 6.50x (ISBN 0-685-58287-6, 246-25728). AAHPERD.

American Alliance for Health, Physical Education, & Recreation. What Research Tells the Coach About Distance Running. 1968. pap. 3.50x (ISBN 0-88314-205-8, 241-07944). AAHPERD.

American Alliance for Health, Physical Education & Recreation. What Research Tells the Coach About Football. 1973. 3.50 (ISBN 0-88314-206-6, 241-25476). AAHPERD.

--What Research Tells the Coach about Swimming. 1967. pap. 2.95x (ISBN 0-88314-209-0). AAHPERD.

--Women's Athletics: Coping with Controversy. 1974. pap. 4.50x o.p. (ISBN 0-685-42006-X, 243-25508). AAHPERD.

American Antiquarian Society. Catalogue of the Manuscript Collections of the American Antiquarian Society. 1979. lib. bdg. 375.00 (ISBN 0-8161-0258-9, Hall Library). G K Hall.

American Artist Magazine, ed. The American Artist Diary Nineteen Eighty-One. (Illus.). 232p. 1980. 12.95 o.p. (ISBN 0-8230-0208-X). Watson-Guptill.

American Association for Artifical Intelligence. National Conference on Artificial Intelligence: Proceedings. 456p. (Orig.). 1982. pap. text ed. 25.00x (ISBN 0-86576-043-8). W Kaufmann.

American Association for Gifted Children. On Being Gifted. LC 78-58622. 1979. 8.95 o.p. (ISBN 0-8027-0616-9); pap. 7.95 (ISBN 0-8027-7138-6). Walker & Co.

American Association for Health, Physical Education & Recreation. Professional Preparation Directory for Elementary School Physical Education. 56p. 1978. pap. 3.00 (ISBN 0-88314-143-4, 245-26334). AAHPERD.

American Association for State & Local History. Directory of Historical Societies & Agencies in the United States & Canada. 12th ed. Craig, Tracey L., ed. LC 56-4164. (Illus.). 1982. pap. 35.00x (ISBN 0-910050-58-9). AASLH.

American Association of Critical Care Nurses. Core Curriculum for Critical Care Nurses. Borg, Nan, ed. 400p. 1981. soft cover 19.95 (ISBN 0-7216-1215-6). Saunders.

American Association of Critical-Care Nurses. Critical Care Nursing of Children & Adolescents. Oakes, Annalee, ed. (Illus.). 750p. 1981. pap. 16.50 (ISBN 0-7216-1003-X). Saunders.

American Association of Critical Care Nurses. Standards of Nursing Care of the Critically Ill. (Illus.). 368p. 1980. pap. text ed. 14.95 (ISBN 0-8359-7061-2). Reston.

American Association of Directors of Psychiatric Residency Training & American Medical Student Association. Directory of Psychiatry Residency Training Programs. 610p. 1982. pap. 15.00x (ISBN 0-89042-701-1). Am Psychiatric.

American Association Of Hospital Consultants. Functional Planning of General Hospitals. Mills, Alden, ed. (Illus.). 1969. 30.00 o.p. (ISBN 0-07-001273-3, HP). McGraw.

American Association of Law Libraries. Providing Legal Services for Prisoners: A Tool for Correctional Administrators. Rev. ed. Orig. Title: Guidelines for Legal Reference Service. 104p. Date not set. pap. 10.00 (ISBN 0-942974-02-6). Am Correctional.

American Association of Retired Persons, jt. auth. see National Retired Teachers Association.

American Association of School Administrators. The Administrative Leadership Team. (Superintendent Career Development Ser.). 3.50 (ISBN 0-686-36524-0, 021-00820). Am Assn Sch Admin.

--Champions of Children. 4.95 (ISBN 0-686-36533-X, 021-00324). Am Assn Sch Admin.

--Community Education: Managing for Success. 9.95 (ISBN 0-686-36532-1, 021-00202). Am Assn Sch Admin.

--Compensating the Superintendent: Full Report. 15.00 (ISBN 0-686-36526-7, 021-00825). Am Assn Sch Admin.

--Compensating the Superintendent: Summary Report. (Superintendent Career Development Ser.). 3.50 (ISBN 0-686-36523-2, 021-00819). Am Assn Sch Admin.

--Educational Management Tools for the Practicing School Administrator. 5.00 (ISBN 0-686-36529-1, 021-00337). Am Assn Sch Admin.

--Evaluating the Superintendent. (Superintendent Career Development Ser.). 3.50 (ISBN 0-686-36525-9, 021-00821). Am Assn Sch Admin.

American Association of School Administrators, ed. Nineteen-Eighty AASA Convention Reporter. 5.00 (ISBN 0-686-36534-8). Am Assn Sch Admin.

American Association of School Administrators. Regionalism: Past, Present, & Future, Bk. 10. (Executive Handbook Ser.). 2.50 (ISBN 0-686-36528-3, 021-00352). Am Assn Sch Admin.

--School Building Slide Program. 35.00 (ISBN 0-686-36531-3, 021-00770). Am Assn Sch Admin.

--Selecting a Superintendent. (Superintendent Career Development Ser.). 3.50 (ISBN 0-686-36521-6, 021-00817). Am Assn Sch Admin.

--Sex Equality in Schools, Bk. 5. (Executive Handbook Ser.). 1.00 (ISBN 0-686-36527-5, 021-00438). Am Assn Sch Admin.

--Special Education in Transition. 4.95 (ISBN 0-686-36530-5, 021-00323). Am Assn Sch Admin.

--The Superintendent's Contract. (Superintendent Career Development Ser.). 3.50 (ISBN 0-686-36522-4, 021-00818). Am Assn Sch Admin.

American Association of School Librarians. Certification Model for Professional School Media Personnel. 40p. 1976. pap. 4.00 (ISBN 0-8389-3179-0). ALA.

American Astroanalysis Institute. Astro-Analysis Sun Signs Horoscopes. 7.95 o.p. (ISBN 0-448-14364-X, G&D). Putnam Pub Group.

American AstroAnalysts Institute. Astroanalysis. Incl. Aries. pap. (ISBN 0-448-12556-0); Taurus. pap. (ISBN 0-448-12557-9); Gemini. pap. (ISBN 0-448-12558-7); Cancer. pap. (ISBN 0-448-12559-5); Leo. pap. (ISBN 0-448-12560-9); Virgo. pap. (ISBN 0-448-12561-7); Libra. pap. (ISBN 0-448-12562-5); Scorpio. pap. (ISBN 0-448-12563-3); Sagittarius. pap. (ISBN 0-448-12564-1); Capricorn. pap. (ISBN 0-448-12565-X); Aquarius. pap. (ISBN 0-448-12566-8); Pisces. pap. (ISBN 0-448-12567-6). 360p. 1977. pap. 8.95 ea. (G&D). Putnam Pub Group.

American Automobile Association. Sportsmanlike Driving. 7th ed. 1975. text ed. 15.24 (ISBN 0-07-001292-X, W); pap. text ed. 9.88 (ISBN 0-07-001298-9); tchr's ed. 17.76 (ISBN 0-07-001293-8); wkbk. 5.12 (ISBN 0-07-001296-2). McGraw.

--Sportsmanlike Driving. 6th ed. Monward, Richard, ed. (gr. 9-12). 1970. text ed. 12.24 o.p. (ISBN 0-07-001285-7, W); tchrs' handbk. 14.44 o.p. (ISBN 0-07-001289-X). McGraw.

--Sportsmanlike Driving. rev. ed. Cranford, Carolyn E., ed. (Illus.). (gr. 10-12). 1979. text ed. 11.96 (ISBN 0-07-001330-6, W); pap. text ed. 9.12 (ISBN 0-07-001331-4); tchr's ed. 16.40 (ISBN 0-07-001332-2). McGraw.

--Teaching Driver & Traffic Safety Education. 1965. 34.95 (ISBN 0-07-001275-X, C); manual 15.00instructor's (ISBN 0-07-001276-8). McGraw.

American Bar Association. ABA: Legal Status of Prisoners. 1982. pap. write for info. (ISBN 0-316-03720-6). Little.

--ABA Standards for Criminal Justice, 4 vols. LC 79-91936. 1980. Set. 215.00 (ISBN 0-316-03709-5); 55.00 ea.; 1982 supplement 32.00 (ISBN 0-316-00093-0). Little.

American Bar Association, jt. auth. see Committee on Jury Standards.

American Bar Association, Committee on International Labor Law Section of Labor Relations Law. The Labor Relations Law of Canada. LC 77-23122. 258p. 1977. 17.50 (ISBN 0-87179-247-8). BNA.

American Book Collector Staff. Directory of Specialized American Bookdealers 1981-1982. 256p. 1981. lib. bdg. 19.95 (ISBN 0-668-05203-1). Arco.

American Camping Association Publicaions Committee, ed. Sing. 1978. pap. 1.50 (ISBN 0-87603-037-1, SO 01). Am Camping.

American Cancer Society. Show Me Missouri Four Seasons Cookbook, 1982. 192p. 1982. pap. 6.00 (ISBN 0-686-31483-2). Am Cancer MO.

--Show Me Missouri Four Seasons Cookbook, 1983. 1983. pap. 6.00 (ISBN 0-686-43081-6). Am Cancer MO.

American Chain Association, compiled by. Chains for Power Transmission & Materials Handling: Design & Applications Handbook. (Mechanical Engineering Ser.: Vol. 18). (Illus.). 368p. 1982. 35.00 (ISBN 0-8247-1701-5). Dekker.

American Chamber of Commerce in Hong Kong. Doing Business in Today's Hong Kong. 1980. 15.00 (ISBN 0-686-32786-1). A M Newman.

American Chamber of Commerce in Japan. Exporting to Japan. 1982. 10.00 (ISBN 0-686-37954-3). A M Newman.

American Civil Liberties Union, jt. auth. see Robertson, John A.

American College. Test Wiseness: Test Taking Skills for Adults. (Illus.). 1978. pap. 8.95 (ISBN 0-07-001438-8, C). McGraw.

American College of Emergency Physicians. Emergency Department Organization & Management. 2nd ed. Jenkins, A. L. & Van De Leuv, John H., eds. LC 78-13594. (Illus.). 1978. text ed. 29.50 o.p. (ISBN 0-8016-0122-3). Mosby.

American College of Sports Medicine. Exercise & Aging: The Scientific Basis. Serfass, Robert C. & Smith, Everett L., eds. LC 80-24700. (Illus.). 191p. 1981. text ed. 16.95x (ISBN 0-89490-042-0). Enslow Pubs.

American College of Surgeons. Early Care of the Injured Patient. 2nd ed. LC 76-8566. (Illus.). 1976. text ed. 19.00 o.p. (ISBN 0-7216-1161-3). Saunders.

American College of Surgeons Committee on Pre & Postoperative Care. Manual of Preoperative & Postoperative Care. 2nd ed. Kinney, John M., et al, eds. LC 75-158397. (Illus.). 1971. 19.95 o.p. (ISBN 0-7216-5440-1). Saunders.

American College Testing Program. College Planning - Search Book. 6th ed. LC 75-28517. (Illus., Orig.). (gr. 9-12). pap. text ed. 6.00 o.p. (ISBN 0-937734-00-4). Am Coll Testing.

American Consulting Engineers Council. Consulting Engineering Practice Manual. Cohen, Stanley, ed. (Illus.). 192p. 1981. 27.50 (ISBN 0-07-001352-7, P&RB). McGraw.

American Correctional Association. Correctional Career Logbook. 52p. (Orig.). Date not set. pap. 4.50 (ISBN 0-942974-01-8). Am Correctional.

--Correctional Law: An Updated Bibliography of Selected Books & Articles. Rev. ed. 44p. Date not set. pap. 4.00 (ISBN 0-942974-15-8). Am Correctional.

--Correctional Personnel Compensation & Benefits. Rev. ed. 36p. Date not set. pap. 5.00 (ISBN 0-942974-06-9). Am Correctional.

--Directory of Juvenile & Adult: Correctional Departments, Institutions, Agencies & Paroling Authorities. Rev. ed. 400p. Date not set. pap. 25.00 (ISBN 0-942974-03-4). Am Correctional.

--Korrectional Kartoon for the Captive Audience. (Illus.). 32p. (Orig.). Date not set. pap. 4.00 (ISBN 0-942974-00-X). Am Correctional.

--Legal Responsibility & Authority of Correctional Officers. Rev. ed. 64p. Date not set. pap. 3.50 (ISBN 0-942974-11-5). Am Correctional.

--Proceedings: One Hundred & Eleventh Annual Congress of Correction of the American Correctional Association. 192p. (Orig.). Date not set. pap. 10.00 (ISBN 0-942974-09-3). Am Correctional.

American Correctional Association Staff. An Administrator's Guide to Conditions of Confinement Litigation. 22p. (Orig.). 1979. text ed. 3.50 (ISBN 0-942974-12-3). Am Correctional.

--Classification. (Series 1: No. 4). 83p. (Orig.). 1981. pap. 5.00 (ISBN 0-942974-21-2). Am Correctional.

--Classification as a Management Tool: Theories & Models for Decision-Makers. 155p. (Orig.). 1981. pap. 9.00 (ISBN 0-942974-40-9). Am Correctional.

--Community Corrections. (Series 1: No. 5). 79p. (Orig.). 1981. pap. 5.00 (ISBN 0-942974-20-4). Am Correctional.

--Correctional Management. 40p. (Orig.). 1981. pap. 5.00 (ISBN 0-686-37661-7). Am Correctional.

--Corrections & Public Awareness. (Series 2: No. 1). 25p. (Orig.). 1981. pap. 3.50 (ISBN 0-942974-22-0). Am Correctional.

--Guidelines for Adult Parole Authorities-Adult Probation & Parole Field Services. 281p. (Orig.). 1981. pap. 15.00 (ISBN 0-942974-33-6). Am Correctional.

--Guidelines for the Development of Policies & Procedures-Adult Community Residential Services. 220p. (Orig.). 1981. pap. 15.00 (ISBN 0-942974-32-8). Am Correctional.

--Guidelines for the Development of Policies & Procedures-Adult Correctional Institutions. 500p. (Orig.). 1981. pap. 20.00 (ISBN 0-942974-30-1). Am Correctional.

--Issues in Juvenile Corrections. (Series 2: No. 2). 29p. (Orig.). 1981. pap. 3.50 (ISBN 0-942974-24-7). Am Correctional.

--Jails. (Series 1: No. 3). 29p. (Orig.). 1981. pap. 3.50 (ISBN 0-942974-19-0). Am Correctional.

--Model Correctional Rules & Regulations. rev. ed. 50p. 1979. pap. 4.50 (ISBN 0-942974-13-1). Am Correctional.

--National Jail & Adult Detention Directory. rev. ed. 325p. 1980. pap. 25.00 (ISBN 0-942974-04-2). Am Correctional.

--Probation & Parole Directory. 480p. (Orig.). 1981. pap. 25.00 (ISBN 0-942974-05-0). Am Correctional.

--Riots & Disturbances in Correctional Institutions. rev. ed. 56p. 1981. pap. 8.00 (ISBN 0-942974-07-7). Am Correctional.

--Standards for Adult Community Residential Services. 2nd ed. 65p. 1980. pap. 7.50 (ISBN 0-942974-27-1). Am Correctional.

--Standards for Adult Correctional Institutions. 2nd ed. 163p. 1981. pap. 10.00 (ISBN 0-942974-25-5). Am Correctional.

--Standards for Adult Local Detention Facilities. 2nd ed. 142p. 1981. pap. 10.00 (ISBN 0-942974-26-3). Am Correctional.

--Standards for Adult Parole Authorities. 2nd ed. 53p. 1980. pap. 7.50 (ISBN 0-942974-28-X). Am Correctional.

--Standards for Adult Probation & Parole Field Services. 2nd ed. 65p. 1981. pap. 7.50 (ISBN 0-942974-29-8). Am Correctional.

--Standards for Correctional Industries. 32p. (Orig.). 1981. pap. 5.00 (ISBN 0-942974-39-5). Am Correctional.

--Standards for Juvenile Community Residential Services. 52p. (Orig.). 1978. pap. 7.50 (ISBN 0-942974-37-9). Am Correctional.

--Standards for Juvenile Detention Facilities & Services. 94p. (Orig.). 1979. pap. 10.00 (ISBN 0-942974-34-4). Am Correctional.

--Standards for Juvenile Probation & Aftercare Services. 62p. (Orig.). 1979. pap. 7.50 (ISBN 0-942974-36-0). Am Correctional.

--Standards for Juvenile Training Schools & Services. 109p. (Orig.). 1979. pap. 10.00 (ISBN 0-942974-35-2). Am Correctional.

--Standards for the Administration of Correctional Agencies. 42p. (Orig.). 1979. pap. 5.00 (ISBN 0-942974-38-7). Am Correctional.

--The Status of Probation & Parole. (Series 2: No. 3). 30p. (Orig.). 1981. pap. 3.50 (ISBN 0-942974-23-9). Am Correctional.

--Women in Corrections. (Series 1: No. 1). 85p. (Orig.). 1981. pap. 5.00 (ISBN 0-942974-17-4). Am Correctional.

American Council on Education. Youth & the Future: A General Report of the American Youth Commission. LC 73-7694. 296p. 1973. Repr. of 1942 ed. lib. bdg. 17.75x (ISBN 0-8371-6937-2, YOFU). Greenwood.

American Craft Council. Glass: A Bibliography. rev. ed. 14p. 1978. 3.70 o.p. (ISBN 0-88321-027-4). Am Craft.

American Dental Association - Bureau of Library & Indexing Service. Index to Dental Literature. 1981. annual cumulative 100.00 (ISBN 0-934510-11-3); quarterly cumulative 125.00 (ISBN 0-686-77270-9). Am Dental.

American Dental Association-Council on Dental Therapeutics. Accepted Dental Therapeutics. 39th ed. 1982. 15.00 (ISBN 0-934510-10-5). Am Dental.

American Dietetic Association. Abstracts 1982: Sixty-Fifth Annual Meeting of The American Dietetic Association in San Antonio, Texas. 240p. 1982. pap. 8.50 (ISBN 0-88091-007-0). Am Dietetic Assn.

--Handbook of Clinical Dietetics. LC 80-11317. 480p. 1981. text ed. 25.00x (ISBN 0-300-02256-5). Yale U Pr.

American Economic Association & Royal Economic Society. Surveys of Economic Theory, 3 vols. Robinson, E. A., ed. Incl. Vol. 1. Money, Interest & Welfare. (Illus.). 222p. 1965 (ISBN 0-312-77805-8); Vol. 2. Growth & Development. (Illus.). 272p. 1965. o.p. (ISBN 0-312-77840-6); Vol. 3. Resource Allocation. 224p. 1966 (ISBN 0-312-77875-9). 15.95 ea. St Martin.

American Ethnological Society. American Indian Intellectuals: 1976 Proceedings. Liberty, Margot, ed. (Illus.). 1978. pap. text ed. 16.95 (ISBN 0-8299-0223-6). West Pub.

--Forms of Play of Native North Americans: Proceedings. Norbeck, Edward & Ferrer, Claire R., eds. (Illus.). 1979. pap. text ed. 16.95 (ISBN 0-8299-0262-7). West Pub.

American Ethnological Society & Bennett, John W. The New Ethnicity, Perspectives from Ethnology: Proceedings. (AES Ser). 1975. pap. text ed. 16.95 (ISBN 0-8299-0032-2). West Pub.

American Ethnological Society, et al. Material Culture: Styles, Organization & Dynamics of Technology. 1978. pap. text ed. 16.95 (ISBN 0-8299-0138-8). West Pub.

American Ethnological Society, 1974. American Anthropology, the Early Years: Proceedings. Murra, John V., ed. (AES Ser). (Illus.). 235p. 1976. pap. text ed. 16.95 (ISBN 0-8299-0097-7). West Pub.

American Express. The American Express International Traveler's Pocket Dictionary & Phrase Books. Incl. French (ISBN 0-671-43484-5); German (ISBN 0-671-44658-4); Italian (ISBN 0-671-47031-0); Spanish (ISBN 0-671-47028-0). 1983. price not set. S&S.

American Fabrics Magazine. Encyclopedia of Textiles. 59.00x (ISBN 0-87245-507-6). Textile Bk.

American Folklife Center. Ethnic Recordings in America: A Neglected Heritage. LC 80-607133. (Studies in American Folklife: No. 1). (Illus.). xiii, 269p. 1982. 13.00 (ISBN 0-8444-0339-3). Lib Congress.

American Foundation for the Blind (New York) Dictionary Catalog of the M. C. Migel Memorial Library, 2 Vols. 1966. Set. lib. bdg. 150.00 (ISBN 0-8161-0705-X, Hall Library). G K Hall.

American Friends Service Committee. A Compassionate Peace: A Future for the Middle East. 1981. 6.95 (ISBN 0-686-95355-X). Am Fr Serv Comm.

--A Compassionate Peace: A Future for the Troubled Middle East. (Illus.). 236p. 1982. 13.95 (ISBN 0-8090-3575-8); pap. 6.95 (ISBN 0-8090-1399-1). Hill & Wang.

American Geographical Society Library New York. Author, Title, Subject & Geographic Catalogs of the Glaciology Collection, Department of Exploration & Field Research, 3 vols. 1971. Set. 285.00 (ISBN 0-8161-0922-2, Hall Library). G K Hall.

--Research Catalogue of the American Geographical Society, 15 Vols. (Illus.). 1962. Set. 1395.00 (ISBN 0-8161-0628-2, Hall Library). G K Hall.

American Geographical Society Library-New York. Research Catalogue of the American Geographical Society: First Supplement, 2 pts. Incl. Pt. 1. Regional Catalogue, 2 vols. 1972. lib. bdg. 250.00 (ISBN 0-8161-0999-0); Pt. 2. Topical Catalogue, 2 vols. 1974. lib. bdg. 255.00 (ISBN 0-8161-1083-2). Hall Library). G K Hall.

American Geographical Society, Map Department, New York. Index to Maps in Books & Periodicals, First Supplement. 1971. lib. bdg. 105.00 (ISBN 0-8161-0806-4, Hall Library). G K Hall.

--Index to Maps in Books & Periodicals, 10 vols. 1968. Set. lib. bdg. 950.00 (ISBN 0-8161-0753-X, Hall Library). G K Hall.

--Index to Maps in Books & Periodicals, Second Suppl. 1976. lib. bdg. 105.00 (ISBN 0-8161-0995-8, Hall Library). G K Hall.

American Geological Institute. Dictionary of Geological Terms. rev. ed. LC 73-9004. 600p. 1976. pap. 6.95 (ISBN 0-385-08452-8, Anch). Doubleday.

American Health Research Institute. Computers in Medicine: Current Medical Subject Analysis & Research Directory with Bibliography. Bartone, J. C., et al, eds. LC 81-71809. 120p. 1982. 29.95 (ISBN 0-941864-32-4); pap. 21.95 (ISBN 0-941864-33-2). ABBE Pubs Assn.

--Depression: Medical Subject Analysis & Research Directory with Bibliography. Bartone, J. C., et al, eds. LC 81-71808. 133p. 1982. 29.95 (ISBN 0-941864-30-8); pap. 21.95 (ISBN 0-941864-31-6). ABBE Pubs Assn.

--Marriage & Marital Therapy: Current Medical Subject Analysis & Research Directory with Bibliography. Bartone, J. C., et al, eds. LC 81-71811. 120p. 1983. 29.95 (ISBN 0-941864-78-2); pap. 21.95 (ISBN 0-941864-79-0). ABBE Pubs Assn.

--Medical Subject Analysis of a Selected Bibliography Concerning General Counseling. Bartone, J. C., ed. LC 81-71268. 266p. 1982. 39.95 (ISBN 0-941864-18-9); pap. 29.95 (ISBN 0-941864-19-7). ABBE Pubs Assn.

--Subject Analysis of Medical Bibliography Relevant to Forensic Psychiatry. Bartone, J. C., ed. LC 8-7269. 110p. 1982. 29.95 (ISBN 0-941864-20-0); pap. 21.95 (ISBN 0-941864-21-9). ABBE Pubs Assn.

American Health Research Institute Ltd. Academic Malpractice: Medical & Psychological Mismanagement in American Education. Bartone, J. C., ed. LC 81-70672. 120p. 1983. 29.95 (ISBN 0-941864-02-2); pap. 19.95 (ISBN 0-941864-05-7). ABBE Pubs Assn.

American Health Research Institute, Ltd. Accident Prevention & Injury Control: A Medical & Behavioral Subject Analysis & Research Index with Bibliography. Bartone, John C., ed. 120p. 1983. 29.95 (ISBN 0-88164-030-1); pap. 21.95 (ISBN 0-88164-031-X). ABBE Pubs Assn.

--Accidents in Occupations & Industry: A Medical Subject Analysis & Research Index with Bibliography. Bartone, John C., ed. 120p. 1983. 29.95 (ISBN 0-88164-012-3); pap. 21.95 (ISBN 0-88164-013-1). ABBE Pubs Assn.

--Aggression: A Psychological, Behavioral & Medical Subject Analysis with Research Index & Bibliography. Bartone, John C., ed. 120p. 1983. 29.95 (ISBN 0-88164-028-X); pap. 21.95 (ISBN 0-88164-029-8). ABBE Pubs Assn.

--Alcohol Drinking: A Medical Subject Analysis & Research Index with Bibliography. Bartone, John C., ed. 120p. 1983. 29.95 (ISBN 0-88164-010-7); pap. 21.95 (ISBN 0-88164-011-5). ABBE Pubs Assn.

--Anxiety: Medical Subject Analysis & Research Directory with Bibliography. Bartone, J. C., et al, eds. LC 81-71807. 120p. 1982. 29.95 (ISBN 0-941864-28-6); pap. 19.95 (ISBN 0-941864-29-4). ABBE Pubs Assn.

--Asbestos & Asbestosis: A Medical Subject Analysis & Research Index with Bibliography. Bartone, John C., ed. 120p. 1983. 29.95 (ISBN 0-941864-84-7); pap. 21.95 (ISBN 0-941864-85-5). ABBE Pubs Assn.

--Attitude & Attitudes: A Psychological & Medical Subject Analysis with Research Index & Bibliography. Bartone, John C., ed. 120p. 1983. 29.95 (ISBN 0-88164-026-3); pap. 21.95 (ISBN 0-88164-027-1). ABBE Pubs Assn.

--Brain Diseases: Medical Research Subject Directory of Etiology, Occurrence, & Diagnosis with Bibliography. Bartone, John C., ed. LC 82-72026. 120p. 1982. 29.95 (ISBN 0-941864-68-5); pap. 21.95 (ISBN 0-941864-69-3). ABBE Pubs Assn.

--Caffeine: A Medical & Scientific Subject Analysis & Research Index with Bibliography. Bartone, John C., ed. 120p. 1983. 29.95 (ISBN 0-941864-95-2); pap. 21.95 (ISBN 0-941864-94-4). ABBE Pubs Assn.

--Cannabis (Marijuana) & Cannabinoids: Medical Subject Research Directory with Bibliography. Bartone, John C., ed. LC 82-72018. 105p. 1982. 29.95 (ISBN 0-941864-52-9); pap. 21.95 (ISBN 0-941864-53-7). ABBE Pubs Assn.

--Cattle Diseases: Medical Research Subject Directory with Bibliography. Bartone, John C., ed. LC 82-72020. 120p. 1982. 29.95 (ISBN 0-941864-56-1); pap. 21.95 (ISBN 0-941864-57-X). ABBE Pubs Assn.

--Crime Research Index For, 1983: With Medical Subject Analysis & Bibliography. Bartone, John C., ed. 120p. 1983. 29.95 (ISBN 0-88164-036-0); pap. 21.95 (ISBN 0-88164-037-9). ABBE Pubs Assn.

--Criminal Psychology: A Medical Subject Analysis & Research Index with Bibliography. Bartone, John C., ed. 120p. 1983. 29.95 (ISBN 0-88164-024-7); pap. 21.95 (ISBN 0-88164-025-5). ABBE Pubs Assn.

--Developing Countries: Status & Progress by Medical Subject Analysis & Research Index with Bibliography. Bartone, John C., ed. 120p. 1983. 29.95 (ISBN 0-941864-93-6); pap. 21.95 (ISBN 0-941864-92-8). ABBE Pubs Assn.

--Diagnosis: General Survey with Medical Research Subject Directory & Bibliography. Bartone, John C., ed. LC 82-72023. 120p. 1982. 29.95 (ISBN 0-941864-62-6); pap. 21.95 (ISBN 0-941864-63-4). ABBE Pubs Assn.

--Diagnostic Errors in Medicine: International Survey with Medical Resea h Subject Index & Bibliography. Bartone, John C., ed. LC 82-72015. 115p. 1982. 29.95 (ISBN 0-941864-46-4); pap. 21.95 (ISBN 0-941864-47-2). ABBE Pubs Assn.

--Drug Addiction, Substance Abuse & Narcotic Dependence: A Medical Subject Analysis & Research Index With Bibliography. Bartone, John C., ed. 120p. 1983. 29.95 (ISBN 0-88164-006-9); pap. 21.95 (ISBN 0-88164-007-7). ABBE Pubs Assn.

--Drug Withdrawal Symptoms: A Medical Subject Analysis & Research Index with Bibliography. Bartone, John C., ed. 120p. 1983. 29.95 (ISBN 0-941864-88-X); pap. 21.95 (ISBN 0-941864-89-8). ABBE Pubs Assn.

--Family Practice: A Medical Subject Analysis & Research Index With Bibliography. Bartone, John C., ed. 120p. 1983. 29.95 (ISBN 0-88164-000-X); pap. 21.95 (ISBN 0-88164-001-8). ABBE Pubs Assn.

--Gunshot Wounds in Crime & Medicine: A Medical Subject Analysis & Research Index With Bibliography. Bartone, John C., ed. 120p. 1983. 29.95 (ISBN 0-941864-82-0); pap. 21.95 (ISBN 0-941864-83-9). ABBE Pubs Assn.

--Intelligence: International Survey with Research Subject Index & Bibliography. Bartone, John C., ed. LC 82-72014. 115p. 1982. 29.95 (ISBN 0-941864-44-8); pap. 21.95 (ISBN 0-941864-45-6). ABBE Pubs Assn.

--Intelligence Tests: General Survey with Research Subject Index & Bibliography. Bartone, John C., ed. LC 82-72024. 120p. 1982. 29.95 (ISBN 0-941864-64-2); pap. 21.95 (ISBN 0-941864-65-0). ABBE Pubs Assn.

American Health Research Institute Ltd. International Bibliography & Medical Subject Index of Crime Publications. Bartone, J. C., ed. LC 81-71266. 155p. 1982. 29.95 (ISBN 0-941864-14-6); pap. 19.95 (ISBN 0-941864-15-4). ABBE Pubs Assn.

American Health Research Institute, Ltd. Intractable Pain: International Survey with Medical Research Subject Index & Bibliography. Bartone, John C., ed. LC 82-72021. 120p. 1982. 29.95 (ISBN 0-941864-58-8); pap. 21.95 (ISBN 0-941864-59-6). ABBE Pubs Assn.

--Juvenile Delinquency: A Medical & Psychological Subject Analysis & Research Index With Bibliog. Bartone, John C., ed. 1983. 29.95 (ISBN 0-88164-002-6); pap. 21.95 (ISBN 0-88164-003-4). ABBE Pubs Assn.

American Health Research Institute Ltd. Medical & Psychological Subject Classification of Persuasive Communication Literature. Bartone, J. C., ed. LC 81-71264. 121p. 1982. 29.95 (ISBN 0-941864-10-3); pap. 21.95 (ISBN 0-941864-11-1). ABBE Pubs Assn.

American Health Research Institute, Ltd. Medical Emergencies: A Medical Subject Analysis & Research Index with Bibliography. Bartone, John C., ed. 120p. 1983. 29.95 (ISBN 0-88164-004-2); pap. 21.95 (ISBN 0-88164-005-0). ABBE Pubs Assn.

--Medical Jurisprudence & Criminal Law: A Medical Subject Analysis with Research Index & Bibliography. Bartone, John C., ed. 120p. 1983. 29.95 (ISBN 0-88164-008-5); pap. 21.95 (ISBN 0-88164-009-3). ABBE Pubs Assn.

American Health Research Institute Ltd. Medical Subject Research Directory & Bibliography of Iatrology, Iatrogenesis & Iatrogenic Diseases. Bartone, J. C., ed. LC 81-71263. 272p. 1982. 39.95 (ISBN 0-941864-08-1); pap. 29.95 (ISBN 0-941864-09-X). ABBE Pubs Assn.

--Medical Subject Research Directory of Medical Malpractice Exclusive of Iatrology. Bartone, J. C., ed. LC 81-71270. 132p. 1982. 29.95 (ISBN 0-941864-22-7); pap. 21.95 (ISBN 0-941864-23-5). ABBE Pubs Assn.

--Medical Subject Research Index of International Bibliography Concerning Cocaine. Bartone, J. C., ed. LC 81-71267. 198p. 1982. 34.95 (ISBN 0-941864-16-2); pap. 24.50 (ISBN 0-941864-17-0). ABBE Pubs Assn.

--Medical Subjects Directory & Bibliography for Psychosomatic Medicine. Bartone, J. C., ed. LC 81-71262. 120p. 1982. 29.95 (ISBN 0-941864-06-5); pap. 21.95 (ISBN 0-941864-07-3). ABBE Pubs Assn.

American Health Research Institute, Ltd. Mental Disorders: Medical Research Subject Directory on the Occurrence, Diagnosis, Etiology & Therapy with Bibliography. Bartone, John C., ed. LC 82-72019. 120p. 1982. 29.95 (ISBN 0-941864-54-5); pap. 21.95 (ISBN 0-941864-55-3). ABBE Pubs Assn.

--Occupational Diseases: International Survey with Medical Research Subject Directory & Bibliography. Bartone, John C., ed. LC 82-72017. 120p. 1982. 29.95 (ISBN 0-941864-50-2); pap. 21.95 (ISBN 0-941864-51-0). ABBE Pubs Assn.

--Occupational Medicine: International Survey with Medical Subject Directory & Bibliography. LC 82-72030. 120p. 1983. 29.95 (ISBN 0-941864-77-4); pap. 21.95 (ISBN 0-941864-76-6). ABBE Pubs Assn.

--Pain: Medical Subject Analysis & Research Index With Bibliography. Bartone, John C., ed. LC 82-72028. 120p. 1983. 29.95 (ISBN 0-941864-72-3); pap. 21.95 (ISBN 0-941864-73-1). ABBE Pubs Assn.

--Patients: A Medical Subject Analysis & Research Index With Bibliography. Bartone, John C., ed. LC 82-72029. 120p. 1983. 29.95 (ISBN 0-941864-74-X); pap. 21.95 (ISBN 0-941864-75-8). ABBE Pubs Assn.

--Preventive Medicine: Current Medical Subject Analysis & Research Directory with Bibliography. Bartone, John C., ed. LC 81-71811. 120p. 1982. 29.95 (ISBN 0-941864-36-7); pap. 21.95 (ISBN 0-941864-37-5). ABBE Pubs Assn.

--Psychological Tests: International Survey with Research Subject Index & Bibliography. Bartone, John C., ed. LC 82-72016. 120p. 1982. 29.95 (ISBN 0-941864-48-0); pap. 21.95 (ISBN 0-941864-49-9). ABBE Pubs Assn.

--Psychotherapy, Medical & Psychological Research Subject Index with Bibliography. Bartone, John C., ed. LC 82-72022. 120p. 1982. 29.95 (ISBN 0-941864-60-X); pap. 21.95 (ISBN 0-941864-61-8). ABBE Pubs Assn.

--Religion & Medicine: A Medical Subject Analysis & Research Index with Bibliography. Bartone, John C., ed. 120p. 1983. 29.95 (ISBN 0-88164-032-8); pap. 21.95 (ISBN 0-88164-033-6). ABBE Pubs Assn.

--Religion & Psychology: A Medical Subject Analysis & Research Index with Bibliography. Bartone, John C., ed. 120p. 1983. 29.95 (ISBN 0-88164-034-4); pap. 21.95 (ISBN 0-88164-035-2). ABBE Pubs Assn.

--Sex & Sex Behavior: A Medical Subject Analysis & Research Index with Bibliography. Bartone, John C., ed. 120p. 1983. 29.95 (ISBN 0-941864-96-0); pap. text ed. 21.95 (ISBN 0-941864-97-9). ABBE Pubs Assn.

--Social Security: A Medical Subject Analysis & Research Index with Bibliography. Bartone, John C., ed. 120p. 1983. 29.95 (ISBN 0-941864-86-3); pap. 21.95 (ISBN 0-941864-87-1). ABBE Pubs Assn.

--Space Flight & Aerospace Medicine: General Survey with Research Subject Directory & Bibliography. Bartone, John C., ed. LC 82-7225. 120p. 1982. 29.95 (ISBN 0-941864-66-9); pap. 21.95 (ISBN 0-941864-67-7). ABBE Pubs Assn.

--Sports Medicine: International Survey with Research Subject Index & Bibliography. Bartone, John C., ed. LC 82-72013. 120p. 1982. 29.95 (ISBN 0-941864-42-1); pap. 21.95 (ISBN 0-941864-43-X). ABBE Pubs Assn.

American Health Research Institute Ltd. Sudden Death: Medical Subject Analysis & Research Directory with Bibliography. Bartone, J. C., et al, eds. LC 81-71810. 120p. 1982. 29.95 (ISBN 0-941864-34-0); pap. 21.95 (ISBN 0-941864-35-9). ABBE Pubs Assn.

American Health Research Institute, Ltd. Traffic Accidents: A Medical Subject Analysis & Research Index with Bibliography. Bartone, John C., ed. 120p. 1983. 29.95 (ISBN 0-88164-016-6); pap. 21.95 (ISBN 0-88164-017-4). ABBE Pubs Assn.

--Violence-Psychological, Medical & Legal Aspects: A Subject Analysis & Research Index with Bibliography. Bartone, John C., ed. 120p. 1983. 29.95 (ISBN 0-88164-022-0); pap. 21.95 (ISBN 0-88164-023-9). ABBE Pubs Assn.

--Vitamins: A Medical Subject Analysis & Research Index With Bibliography. Bartone, John C., ed. LC 82-72027. 120p. 1983. 29.95 (ISBN 0-941864-70-7); pap. 21.95 (ISBN 0-941864-71-5). ABBE Pubs Assn.

--War: A Medical, Psychological & Scientific Subject Analysis with Research Index & Bibliography. Bartone, John C., ed. 120p. 1983. 29.95 (ISBN 0-941864-91-X); pap. 21.95 (ISBN 0-941864-90-1). ABBE Pubs Assn.

--Water Pollution by Chemical, Radioactive, Thermal, Softening & Extraneous Materials: A Medical Subject Analysis & Research Index with Bibliography. Bartone, John C., ed. 120p. 1983. 29.95 (ISBN 0-88164-018-2); pap. 21.95 (ISBN 0-88164-019-0). ABBE Pubs Assn.

--Women & Women's Rights: A Medical, Psychological & International Subject Survey with Research Index & Bibliography. Bartone, John C., ed. 120p. 1983. 29.95 (ISBN 0-941864-98-7); pap. 21.95 (ISBN 0-941864-99-5). ABBE Pubs Assn.

--World Health & the World Health Organization: A Medical Subject Analysis & Research Index with Bibliography. Bartone, John C., ed. 120p. 1983. 29.95 (ISBN 0-88164-020-4); pap. 21.95 (ISBN 0-88164-021-2). ABBE Pubs Assn.

--World Survey of Drug & Narcotic Control: A Medical Subject Analysis & Research Index with Bibliography. Bartone, John C., ed. 120p. 1983. 29.95 (ISBN 0-88164-014-X); pap. 21.95 (ISBN 0-88164-015-8). ABBE Pubs Assn.

American Home Editors. American Home Garden Book & Plant Encyclopedia. LC 63-19657. (Illus.). 512p. 1964. pap. 0.95 (ISBN 0-87131-035-X). M Evans.

American Home Food Staff, ed. The American Home All-Purpose Cookbook. LC 66-23272. 572p. 1978. pap. 7.95 (ISBN 0-87131-268-9). M Evans.

American Hospital Assn. Digest of Hospital Cost Containment Projects. 3rd ed. LC 79-27674. 132p. (Orig.). 1980. pap. 6.25 o.p. (ISBN 0-87258-299-X, 061124). Am Hospital.

American Hospital Association. American Hospital Association Guide to the Health Care Field. 584p. 1982. pap. 60.00 (ISBN 0-87258-363-5, AHA-010082). Am Hospital.

--Appropriateness Review of Health Care Services: Manual for Lawyers, Planners & Hospitals. LC 80-23209. 128p. 1980. pap. 18.75 (ISBN 0-87258-336-8, AHA-076148). Am Hospital.

--Auxiliary Gift & Coffee Shop Management. LC 76-26604. 152p. (Orig.). 1976. pap. 18.75 (ISBN 0-87258-155-1, AHA-019111). Am Hospital.

--Auxiliary: New Concepts, New Directions. LC 74-22174. 236p. (Orig.). 1974. pap. 24.50 (ISBN 0-87258-160-8, AHA-019110). Am Hospital.

--Basic Personnel Policies & Programs for a Health Care Institution: Guidelines for Development. LC 74-11014. 48p. 1974. pap. 8.75 (ISBN 0-87258-156-X, AHA-088175). Am Hospital.

--Budgeting Procedures for Hospitals. (Financial Management Ser.). (Illus.). 96p. 1971. pap. 8.25 o.p. (ISBN 0-87258-066-0, 061102). Am Hospital.

--Catalog of the Library of the American Hospital Association, Asa S. Bacon Memorial Chicago Library, 5 vols. 1976. Set. lib. bdg. 460.00 (ISBN 0-8161-1210-X, Hall Library). G K Hall.

--Cost Finding & Rate Setting for Hospitals. (Financial Management Ser.). (Illus.). 112p. 1968. pap. 15.00 o.p. (ISBN 0-87258-036-9, 061101). Am Hospital.

--Cumulative Index of Hospital Literature: 1965-1969. 864p. 1970. 125.00 (ISBN 0-87258-055-5, AHA-121003). Am Hospital.

--Cumulative Index of Hospital Literature: 1955-1959. Incl. 1955-1959. 460p. 1960. casebound 125.00 (ISBN 0-87258-329-5, AHA-121002); 1950-1954. 540p. 1955. 125.00 (ISBN 0-87258-328-7, AHA-121001). Am Hospital.

--Cumulative Index of Hospital Literature: 1970-1974. 1004p. 1976. casebound 125.00 (ISBN 0-87258-192-6, AHA-121004). Am Hospital.

--Cumulative Index of Hospital Literature: 1975-1977. 564p. 1979. casebound 125.00 (ISBN 0-87258-260-4, AHA-121005). Am Hospital.

--Directory of Architects for Health Facilities, 1981 Edition. LC 80-641180. 56p. 1981. pap. 19.50 (ISBN 0-87258-350-3, AHA-043160). Am Hospital.

--Directory of Multihospital Systems, 1981 Edition. (Illus.). 80p. (Orig.). 1981. pap. 37.50 (ISBN 0-87258-355-4, AHA-103145). Am Hospital.

--Directory of Shared Services Organizations for Health Care Institutions, 1981. 192p. (Orig.). 1981. 40.00 (ISBN 0-87258-354-6, AHA-103149). Am Hospital.

--Educational Programs in the Health Field. LC 79-24621. 48p. 1979. pap. 7.50 o.p. (ISBN 0-87258-283-3, 049121). Am Hospital.

--Estimated Useful Lives of Depreciable Hospital Assets. 1978. pap. 5.00 (ISBN 0-87258-247-7, AHA-061107). Am Hospital.

--The Extended Care Unit in a General Hospital: A Guide to Planning, Organization, & Management. rev. ed. LC 73-80342. (Illus.). 60p. 1973. pap. 7.50 o.p. (ISBN 0-87258-131-4, 130152). Am Hospital.

--Fire Safety Training in Health Care Institutions. LC 75-20295. (Illus.). 60p. 1975. pap. 10.00 (ISBN 0-87258-163-2, AHA-181147). Am Hospital.

--Guide for Preparation of Constitution & Bylaws for General Hospitals. rev. ed. LC 81-2788. 32p. 1981. 12.50 (ISBN 0-87258-123-3, AHA-118130). Am Hospital.

--The Hospital Admitting Department. LC 76-54284. (Illus.). 100p. (Orig.). 1977. pap. 13.75 (ISBN 0-87258-200-0, AHA-004155). Am Hospital.

--Hospital Computer Systems Planning: Preparation of Request for Proposal. LC 80-18002. 124p. 1980. 25.00 (ISBN 0-87258-295-7, AHA-040145). Am Hospital.

--Hospital Cost Containment Through Operations Management, 2 pts. (Illus.). 1980. Instructor's Manual. loose-leaf 37.50 o.p. (ISBN 0-87258-304-X, 061135,206 PAGES); Participant's Manual. loose-leaf 10.00 o.p. (ISBN 0-87258-305-8, 060036,061134, 264 PAGES). Am Hospital.

--Hospital Design Checklist. 48p. 1965. loose-leaf 10.00 (ISBN 0-87258-016-4, AHA-43110). Am Hospital.

--Hospital Housekeeping Handbook. Orig. Title: Housekeeping Manual for Health Care. (Illus.). 1980. 18.75 (ISBN 0-87258-273-6, AHA-085125). Am Hospital.

--Hospital Literature Index: 1978, Vol. 34. 350p. 125.00 (ISBN 0-87258-347-3, AHA-121340). Am Hospital.

--Hospital Literature Index: 1979, Vol. 35. Dunlap, Alice, et al, eds. 736p. 1980. 125.00 (ISBN 0-87258-346-5, AHA-121350). Am Hospital.

--Hospital Medical Records: Guidelines for Their Use & the Release of Medical Information. LC 70-188799. 70p. 1972. pap. 10.00 (ISBN 0-87258-087-3, AHA-148150). Am Hospital.

--Hospital Statistics: Data from the American Hospital Association Annual Survey, 1981. 240p. 1982. pap. text ed. 40.00 (ISBN 0-87258-364-3, AHA-082082). Am Hospital.

--Hospital Statistics: Data from the American Hospital Association 1980 Annual Survey. 256p. 1981. pap. 26.25 (ISBN 0-87258-312-0, AHA-082081). Am Hospital.

--Hospitals in the Nineteen Eighties: Nine Views. LC 77-11065. 240p. 1977. 23.25 o.p. (ISBN 0-87258-223-X, 001102). Am Hospital.

--ICD-9-CM Coding Handbook for Entry-Level Coders, with Answers. LC 79-18639. 348p. 1979. pap. text ed. 23.75 (ISBN 0-87258-264-7, AHA-148165). Am Hospital.

--Implementing Patient Education in the Hospital. LC 79-4292. (Illus.). 316p. 1979. pap. 34.25 (ISBN 0-87258-274-4, AHA-070188). Am Hospital.

--Improving Work Methods in Small Hospitals. LC 75-32509. (Illus.). 88p. 1975. pap. 12.50 (ISBN 0-87258-165-9, AHA-184125). Am Hospital.

--Internal Control, Internal Auditing, & Operations Auditing for Hospitals. LC 79-15042. (Financial Management Ser). (Illus.). 104p. 1979. pap. 18.75 (ISBN 0-87258-272-8, AHA-061108). Am Hospital.
--Interpreters' Services & the Role of Health Care Volunteers. LC 74-77268. (Illus.). 44p. (Orig.). 1974. pap. 8.75 (ISBN 0-87258-149-7, AHA-157135). Am Hospital.
--Introduction to Discharge Planning for Hospitals, 1982. LC 82-22644. 32p. 1982. pap. 9.50 (ISBN 0-87258-381-3, AHA-004160). Am Hospital.
--Managerial Cost Accounting for Hospitals. LC 79-29708. (Financial Management Ser.). (Illus.). 144p. 1980. 22.50 (ISBN 0-87258-296-5, AHA-061125). Am Hospital.
--Manual on Hospital Chaplaincy. 96p. 1970. pap. 8.75 (ISBN 0-87258-060-1, AHA-034115). Am Hospital.
--Medical Records Departments in Hospitals: Guide to Organization. 100p. 1972. pap. 11.25 (ISBN 0-87258-089-X, AHA-148158). Am Hospital.
--Medical Staff Cost Containment: Digest of Hospital Projects & Selected Bibliography. 72p. 1980. pap. 10.00 (ISBN 0-87258-314-7, AHA-145152). Am Hospital.
--Multihospital Arrangements: Public Policy Implications. Mason, Scott A., ed. LC 79-14654. (Illus.). 176p. (Orig.). 1979. pap. 11.50 o.p. (ISBN 0-87258-258-2, 103129). Am Hospital.
--Planning Hospital Health Promotion Services for Business & Industry. 140p. 1982. pap. 33.75 (ISBN 0-87258-378-3, AHA-070175). Am Hospital.
--A Portfolio of Architecture for Health. LC 77-23782. (Illus.). 168p. 1977. 22.00 (ISBN 0-87258-219-1, AHA-043130). Am Hospital.
--Readings in Hospital Risk Management. 64p. 1979. pap. 7.50 (ISBN 0-87258-284-1, AHA-178142). Am Hospital.
--Staff Manual for Teaching Patients about Chronic Obstructive Pulmonary Diseases. LC 82-6856. (Illus.). 456p. 1982. 47.50 (ISBN 0-87258-372-4, AHA-070120). Am Hospital.
--Taking Part in the Legislative Process: A Guide for the Hospital's Chief Executive Officer. LC 78-15750. 32p. 1978. pap. 6.25 (ISBN 0-87258-245-0, AHA-118527). Am Hospital.
--Technology Evaluation & Acquisition Methods (TEAM) for Hospitals. LC 79-21859. (Illus.). 212p. 1979. 200.00 (ISBN 0-87258-293-0, AHA-190688). Am Hospital.
--Volunteer in Long-Term Care. LC 68-3723. 60p. 1968. pap. 7.50 (ISBN 0-87258-043-1, AHA-202155). Am Hospital.
--The Volunteer Services Department in a Health Care Institution. LC 73-77522. 72p. 1973. pap. 8.75 (ISBN 0-87258-124-1, AHA-202165). Am Hospital.
--Who Cares About an Alcoholism Program in the General Hospital? 56p. 1972. pap. 6.25 (ISBN 0-87258-088-1, AHA-151045). Am Hospital.
American Hospital Association & National Safety Council. Safety Guide for Health Care Institutions. LC 72-81003. (Illus.). 248p. (Orig.). 1972. pap. 5.50 (ISBN 0-87258-106-3, AHA-181135). Am Hospital.
--Safety Guide for Health Care Institutions. (Illus.). 1983. write for info. (ISBN 0-87258-302-3, AHA-181136). Am Hospital.
American Hospital Association, et al. Sharing Responsibility for Patient Safety. 24p. 1979. 5.75 (ISBN 0-87258-248-5, AHA-178152). Am Hospital.
American Hospital Association Clearinghouse for Hospital Management Engineering, ed. Computer-Assisted Medical Record Systems: An Examination of Case Studies. 148p. 1982. pap. 18.75 (ISBN 0-87258-375-9, AHA-148200). Am Hospital.
American Hospital Association Staff. Capital Financing for Hospitals. LC 73-87100. (Financial Management Ser.). 60p. (Orig.). 1974. pap. 11.25 (ISBN 0-87258-139-X, AHA-03). Am Hospital.
American Indian Archaeological Institute, Inc. Ten Thousand Years of Indian Lifeways in Connecticut & Southern New England. 1983. pap. price not set (ISBN 0-936322-01-2). Am Indian Arch.
American Institute. AAI Policy Kit. 1981. 4.25 o.p. (ISBN 0-686-95947-7). IIA.
--Readings in Economics. 2nd ed. 1981. 10.00 o.p. (ISBN 0-686-95949-3). IIA.
--Readings in Management. 1981. 10.00 o.p. (ISBN 0-686-95941-8). IIA.
American Institute, ed. Reading in Economics. LC 81-66115. 189p. 1981. pap. 10.00 (ISBN 0-89463-028-8). Am Inst Property.
American Institute, ed. see Horn, Ronald C.
American Institute for Property & Liability Underwriters. Code of Professional Ethics. 1979. write for info. o.p. (CPCU 10). IIA.
--Readings in Economics. 1978. write for info. o.p. (CPCU 9). IIA.
American Institute of Accountants. Fiftieth Anniversary Celebration. LC 82-48350. (Accountancy in Transition Ser.). 568p. 1982. lib. bdg. 60.00 (ISBN 0-8240-5302-8). Garland Pub.
--Library Catalogue. LC 82-48337. (Accountancy in Transition Ser.). 242p. 1982. lib. bdg. 25.00 (ISBN 0-8240-5303-6). Garland Pub.
American Institute of Architects. AIA Metric Building & Construction Guide. Braybrooke, Susan, ed. LC 78-31997. 150p. 1980. 29.50x (ISBN 0-471-03812-1); pap. 19.50x (ISBN 0-471-03813-X, Pub. by Wiley-Interscience). Wiley.
--The Architect's Guide to Facility Programming. 304p. 1981. 39.95 (ISBN 0-07-001490-6, P&RB). McGraw.
--Architect's Handbook of Energy Practice: Active Solar Systems. (Illus.). 58p. 1982. pap. 18.00x (ISBN 0-913962-54-6). Am Inst Arch.
--Architect's Handbook of Energy Practice: Building Envelope. (Illus.). 42p. 1982. pap. 18.00x (ISBN 0-913962-51-1). Am Inst Arch.
--Architect's Handbook of Energy Practice: Climate & Site. (Illus.). 55p. 1982. pap. 18.00x (ISBN 0-913962-50-3). Am Inst Arch.
--Architect's Handbook of Energy Practice: Daylighting. (Illus.). 48p. 1982. pap. 18.00x (ISBN 0-913962-52-X). Am Inst Arch.
--Architect's Handbook of Energy Practice: HVAC Systems. (Illus.). 54p. 1982. pap. 18.00x (ISBN 0-913962-53-8). Am Inst Arch.
--Architect's Handbook of Energy Practice: Photovoltaics. (Illus.). 56p. 1982. pap. 18.00x (ISBN 0-913962-56-2). Am Inst Arch.
--Architect's Handbook of Energy Practice: Shading & Sun Control. (Illus.). 48p. 1982. pap. 18.00x (ISBN 0-913962-49-X). Am Inst Arch.
--Architect's Handbook of Energy Practice: Thermal Transfer Through the Envelope. (Illus.). 51p. 1982. pap. 18.00x (ISBN 0-913962-55-4). Am Inst Arch.
--Architect's Handbook of Professional Practice. looseleaf 60.00 (ISBN 0-913962-13-9); annual handbook supplement service 16.00 (ISBN 0-685-27662-7). Am Inst Arch.
--Compensation Guidelines for Architectural & Engineering Services. 2nd ed. LC 77-90943. 1977. pap. 20.00x (ISBN 0-913962-03-1). Am Inst Arch.
--Comprehensive Architectural Services: General Principles & Practice. 1965. 24.50 o.p. (ISBN 0-07-001487-6, P&RB). McGraw.
--Creative Control of Building Costs. 1967. 4.00 (ISBN 0-07-001488-4, P&RB). McGraw.
--Design Review Boards: A Guide for Communities. 1974. 7.75x (ISBN 0-913962-15-5). Am Inst Arch.
--Glossary of Construction Industry Terms. pap. 2.00 (ISBN 0-913962-18-X). Am Inst Arch.
American Institute of Architects & Griffin. Manual of Built-up Roof Systems. 1970. 36.50 (ISBN 0-07-001489-2, P&RB). McGraw.
American Institute of Architects, ed. The Sourcebook. 100p. 1981. 3 ring binder 25.00x (ISBN 0-913962-45-7). Am Inst Arch.
American Institute of Certified Public Accountants. Accountants' Index: 30th Supplement, 1981. 1982. 57.00 (ISBN 0-685-58296-5). Am Inst CPA.
--Accountants International Studies, 20 vols. 1968-78. pap. 76.50 set (ISBN 0-685-65553-9). Am Inst CPA.
--Accounting for Depreciable Assets. (Accounting Research Monograph: No.1). 1975. pap. 9.50 (ISBN 0-685-65408-7). Am Inst CPA.
--Accounting Trends & Techniques in Published Corporate Annual Reports. 36th ed. 1982. pap. 42.00 (ISBN 0-685-47687-1). Am Inst CPA.
--Audit & Accounting Guide: Audits of Employee Benefit Plans. 1983. write for info. Am Inst CPA.
--Auditing & EDP. 1983. write for info. Am Inst CPA.
--Behavior of Major Statistical Estimators in Sampling Accounting Populations. (Auditing Research Monograph: No. 2). 1975. pap. 11.50 (ISBN 0-685-65407-9). Am Inst CPA.
--Federal Taxation Division: Underreported Income Study. write for info. Am Inst CPA.
--Illustrations of Departures from the Auditor's Standard Report. (Financial Report Survey: No. 7). 1975. pap. 10.00 (ISBN 0-685-65410-9). Am Inst CPA.
--Illustrations of Interperiod Tax Allocation. (Financial Report Survey: No. 4). 1974. 10.00 (ISBN 0-685-47689-8). Am Inst CPA.
--Illustrations of Reporting Accounting Changes. (Financial Report Survey: No. 2). 1974. 8.00 o.p. (ISBN 0-685-41635-6). Am Inst CPA.
--Illustrations of Reporting the Results of Operations. (Financial Report Survey: No. 3). 1974. 9.50 (ISBN 0-685-47688-X). Am Inst CPA.
--Illustrations of the Disclosure of Related Party Transactions. (Financial Report Survey: No. 8). 1975. pap. 9.50 (ISBN 0-685-65409-5). Am Inst CPA.
--Illustrations of the Statement of Changes in Financial Position. (Financial Report Survey: No. 5). 1974. pap. 9.50 (ISBN 0-685-52588-0). Am Inst CPA.
--Illustrations of the Summary of Operations & Related Management Discussion & Analysis. (Financial Report Survey: No. 6). 1975. pap. 12.00 (ISBN 0-685-65411-7). Am Inst CPA.
--Industry Audit Guide: Audits of Banks. write for info. Am Inst CPA.
--International Accounting Standard Nineteen: Accounting for Retirement Benefits in the Financial Statements of Employers. 1983. write for info. Am Inst CPA.
--Management of an Accounting Practice Handbook, 3 vols. 1982. Set. 180.00 (ISBN 0-685-52589-9). Am Inst CPA.
--MAP Handbook: 1983. write for info. Am Inst CPA.
--Tax Practice Management. (Study in Federal Taxation: No. 4). 1974. 42.50 o.p. (ISBN 0-685-47690-1). Am Inst CPA.
--Tax Research Techniques. (Study in Federal Taxation: No. 5). 1976. 15.00 (ISBN 0-685-65552-0). Am Inst CPA.
--Taxation as a Professional Career. write for info. Am Inst CPA.
--Uniform CPA Examination: Questions & Unofficial Answers: Nov. 1982 supplement. 1983. write for info. Am Inst CPA.
American Institute of Decorators. Interior Design & Decoration: A Bibliography. LC 61-7059. 86p. 1961. 5.00 o.p. (ISBN 0-87104-254-1). NY Pub Lib.
American Institute of Maintenance. The Contract Cleaner Companion. LC 79-55158. 162p. 1982. pap. 34.95x (ISBN 0-9609052-0-0). Am Inst Maint.
--Floor Care Guide. 149p. 1982. pap. 5.95x (ISBN 0-9609052-1-9). Am Inst Maint.
--Handy Maintenance Tips. 80p. 1982. pap. 3.00 (ISBN 0-9609052-4-3). Am Inst Maint.
--Selection & Care of Cleaning Equipment. 86p. 1982. pap. 3.00 (ISBN 0-9609052-3-5). Am Inst Maint.
American Institute of Maintenance Ser. Carpet Selection & Care. 60p. 1982. pap. 3.00 (ISBN 0-9609052-2-7). Am Inst Maint.
American Institute of Physics. American Institute of Physics Handbook. 3rd ed. LC 71-109244. (Illus.). 2368p. 1972. 96.50 (ISBN 0-07-001485-X, P&RB). McGraw.
--Analytical Balance. (Physics of Technology Project Ser.). 1975. 7.95 (ISBN 0-07-001711-5, G). McGraw.
--Automobile Collisions. (Physics of Technology Project Ser). 64p. 1976. pap. text ed. 7.95 o.p. (ISBN 0-07-001726-3, G). McGraw.
--The Cloud Chamber. (Physics of Technology Project Ser). 1975. 7.95 (ISBN 0-07-001740-9, G). McGraw.
--The Geiger Counter. (Physics of Technology Project Ser.). 1975. 7.95 (ISBN 0-07-001739-5, G). McGraw.
--The Guitar. (Physics of Technology Project Ser.). (Illus.). 88p. 1975. pap. text ed. 7.95 (ISBN 0-07-001716-6, G). McGraw.
--Hydraulic Devices. (Physics of Technology Project Ser.). (Illus.). 64p. (Orig.). 1975. pap. text ed. 7.95 (ISBN 0-07-001724-7, G). McGraw.
--The Incandescent Lamp. (Physics of Technology Project Ser). 1975. 7.95 (ISBN 0-07-001717-4, G). McGraw.
--The Laser. (Physics of Technology Project Ser.). (Illus.). 64p. 1975. pap. text ed. 7.95 o.p. (ISBN 0-07-001713-1, G). McGraw.
--The Multimeter. (Physics of Technology Project Ser.). (Illus.). 64p. 1975. pap. text ed. 7.95 (ISBN 0-07-001728-X, G). McGraw.
--Photodetectors. (Physics of Technology Project Ser). (Illus.). 88p. 1976. pap. text ed. 7.95 (ISBN 0-07-001734-4, G). McGraw.
--The Power Transistor. (Physics of Technology Prroject Ser). 1975. 4.00 o.p. (ISBN 0-07-001729-8, G). McGraw.
--The Pressure Cooker. (Physics of Technology Project Ser.). 1975. 7.95 (ISBN 0-07-001730-1, G). McGraw.
--The Salenoid. (Physics of Technology Project Ser.). (Illus.). 64p. 1975. pap. text ed. 7.95 o.p. (ISBN 0-07-001723-9, G). McGraw.
--The Slide Projector. (Physics of Technology Project Ser.). 88p. 1976. pap. text ed. 7.95 (ISBN 0-07-001736-0, G). McGraw.
--The Spectrophotometer. (Physics of Technology Project Ser.). (Illus.). 80p. 1975. pap. text ed. 7.95 (ISBN 0-07-001731-X, G). McGraw.
--The Toaster. (Physics of Technology Project Ser). 1975. 7.95 (ISBN 0-07-001720-4, G). McGraw.
--The Transformer. (Physics of Technology Project Ser). (Illus.). 64p. 1976. pap. text ed. 7.95 (ISBN 0-07-001727-1, G). McGraw.
American Institute of Physics Staff. The Camera. (Physics of Technology Project Ser.). 1975. pap. 7.00 (ISBN 0-07-001712-3). McGraw.
American Institute of Timber Construction. Timber Construction Manual. 2nd ed. LC 73-11311. 816p. 1974. 32.95x (ISBN 0-471-02549-6, Pub. by Wiley-Interscience). Wiley.
American Jewish Archives, Cincinnati. Manuscript Catalog of the American Jewish Archives, 4 vols. 1971. Set. lib. bdg. 385.00 (ISBN 0-8161-0899-4, Hall Library). G K Hall.
--Manuscript Catalog of the American Jewish Archives, Cincinnati: First Supplement. 1978. lib. bdg. 100.00 (ISBN 0-8161-0934-6, Hall Library). G K Hall.
American Joint Committee on Cancer. Manual for Staging of Cancer. 2nd ed. Beahrs, Oliver H. & Myers, Max H., eds. (Illus.). 220p. 1983. pap. text ed. 17.50 (ISBN 0-686-42955-9, Lippincott Medical). Lippincott.
American Journal of Nursing, New York. Catalog of the Sophia F. Palmer Memorial Library of the American Journal of the Nursing Coompany, 2 vols. 1973. Set. lib. bdg. 180.00 (ISBN 0-8161-1066-2, Hall Library). G K Hall.
American Law Association. Medic Programs: District & School. 136p. Date not set. pap. text ed. 4.00 (ISBN 0-8389-3159-6). ALA.
American Law Institute. Restatement of the Law: Second Property, Donative Transfers, Vol. 1. Casner, A. James, ed. 552p. 1983. text ed. write for info. (ISBN 0-314-73635-2). Am Law Inst.
American Library Association. Librarian's Copyright Kit. 1977. pap. 7.00 o.p. (ISBN 0-8389-3209-6). ALA.
--Library Furniture & Equipment: Proceedings of a Three-Day Institute, June 14-16, 1962. LC 63-18322. 1963. pap. 5.00 o.p. (ISBN 0-8389-3044-1). ALA.
--Minimum Standards for Public Library Systems, 1966. LC 67-18362. 1967. pap. 3.00 o.p. (ISBN 0-8389-3049-2). ALA.
--Subject Index to Poetry for Children & Young People. Sell, Violet, compiled by. 1982. 99.99 (ISBN 0-8486-0013-4). Core Collection.
American Library Association, jt. auth. see Association of College & Research Libraries.
American Library Association. Book Catalogs Committee, RTSD. Guidelines for Book Catalogs. LC 77-1248. 1977. pap. text ed. 5.00 (ISBN 0-8389-3190-1). ALA.
American Library Association. Bookdealer-Library Relations Committee. Guidelines for Handling Library Orders for Microforms. LC 76-58322. 1977. 2.00 o.p. (ISBN 0-8389-3193-6). ALA.
American Library Association Centennial Celebration. Libraries & the Life of the Mind in America: Addresses. LC 77-3288. 1977. 10.00 (ISBN 0-8389-0238-3). ALA.
American Library Association - Children's Services Division. Notable Children's Books, 1940-1970. LC 77-641. 1977. pap. 4.00 (ISBN 0-8389-3182-0). ALA.
American Library Association, Library Administration Division, Personnel Administration Section. The Personnel Manual: An Outline for Libraries. LC 77-5539. 1977. pap. 5.00 (ISBN 0-8389-0239-1). ALA.
American Library Association. Reference & Subscription Books Reviews Committee. Reference & Subscription Book Reviews: 1976-1977. 1978. pap. text ed. 15.00 (ISBN 0-8389-3207-X). ALA.
American Library Association - Resources & Technical Services Division. International Subscription Agents. 4th ed. LC 77-2667. 1978. pap. 6.00 (ISBN 0-8389-0259-6). ALA.
American Library Association, Young Adult Services Division, Services Statement Development Committee. Directions for Library Service to Young Adults. 30p. 1978. pap. 4.00 (ISBN 0-8389-3204-5). ALA.
American Machinist. Metalforming: Modern Machines, Methods & Tooling for Engineers & Operating Personnel. 288p. 1982. text ed. 29.95x o.p. (ISBN 0-07-001546-5, C). McGraw.
American Machinist Magazine. Computers in Manufacturing. 300p. 1983. 33.95 (ISBN 0-07-001548-1, P&RB). McGraw.
--Tools of Our Trade. LC 82-7773. 1982. 33.95 (ISBN 0-07-001547-3, P&RB). McGraw.
American Machinist Magazine Staff. Metalcutting: Today's Techniques for Engineers & Shop Personnel. 1979. 24.50 (ISBN 0-07-001545-7). McGraw.
American Medical Association. American Medical Directory: Update to the 27th Edition. 814p. 1981. text ed. 75.00 o.p. (ISBN 0-88416-351-2). Wright-PSG.
--Manual on Alcoholism. 3.95 o.p. (ISBN 0-686-92204-2, 4284). Hazelden.
--Standard Nomenclature of Diseases & Operations. 5th ed. 1961. 28.00 o.p. (ISBN 0-07-001483-3, HP). McGraw.
American Medical Association, Division of Library & Archival Services. Index to Medical Socioeconomic Literature, 1962-1970, 4 vols. 1980. lib. bdg. 295.00 (ISBN 0-8161-0338-0, Hall Library). G K Hall.
American Medical Record Association. Glossary of Hospital Terms. 2nd rev. ed. 128p. 1974. 5.75 (ISBN 0-686-68577-6, 14911). Healthcare Fin Man Assn.
American Medical Student Association, jt. auth. see American Association of Directors of Psychiatric Residency Training.
American Meteorological Society - Boston. Cumulated Bibliography & Index to Meteorological & Geoastrophysical Abstracts: 1950-1969. 1972. Author Sequence, 5 Vols. 1340.00 (ISBN 0-685-01570-X, Hall Library). Dec. Class, 4 Vols (ISBN 0-8161-0183-3). G K Hall.
--Cumulated Bibliography & Index to Meteorological & Geoastrophysical Abstracts, 1950-1969: Author Sequence, 5 vols. 1972. 800.00 (ISBN 0-8161-0942-7, Hall Library). G K Hall.
American Micro Systems. Mos Integrated Circuits: Theory, Fabrication, Design & Systems Applications of MOS LSI. Penny, William M. & Lau, Lillian, eds. LC 79-1039. 454p. 1979. Repr. of 1972 ed. 27.50 (ISBN 0-88275-897-7). Krieger.

American Museum of Natural History, ed. Research Catalog of the Library of the American Museum of Natural History: Authors, 13 vols. 1977. lib. bdg. 1150.00 (ISBN 0-8161-0064-0, Hall Library). G K Hall.
American Museum of Natural History, New York. The New Catalog of the American Museum of Natural History. 1983. lib. bdg. 1300.00 (ISBN 0-8161-0274-0, Hall Library). G K Hall.
American National Red Cross. Adapted Aquatics: Swimming for Persons with Physical or Mental Impairments. LC 76-43131. 320p. 1977. pap. 3.95 o.p. (ISBN 0-385-12611-5). Doubleday.
--Advanced First Aid & Emergency Care. 2nd ed. LC 79-53479. (American Red Cross Bks.). (Illus.). 1980. pap. 3.50 o.p. (ISBN 0-385-15737-1). Doubleday.
--Canoeing. rev ed. LC 76-10517. 1977. pap. 5.50 o.p. (ISBN 0-385-08313-0). Doubleday.
--Family Health & Home Nursing. (Illus.). 1979. pap. 3.95 o.p. (ISBN 0-385-15281-7). Doubleday.
American National Standard Committee Z39 on Library & Information Sciences. American National Standard for Bibliographic References: Z39.29-1977. 16.00 (ISBN 0-686-10587-7). ANSI.
American National Standard Committee Z39 on Library Work & Information Sciences. American National Standard for Synoptics, Z39.34-1977. 6.00 (ISBN 0-686-02642-X). ANSI.
American National Standards Committee Z39 on Library Work & Information Sciences. American National Standard for Periodicals: Formats & Arrangement, Z39.1-1977. 6.00 (ISBN 0-686-02641-1). ANSI.
American National Standards Committee Z39 on Library Work & Information Sceinces. American National Standard for the Development of Identification Codes for Use by the Bibliographic Community: Z39.33-1977. 5.00 (ISBN 0-686-10588-5). ANSI.
American National Standards Institute, Standards Committee Z39 on Library Work & Information Sciences. American National Standard Abbreviation of Titles of Periodicals. rev ed. 1974. 5.00 (ISBN 0-686-01882-6, Z39.5). ANSI.
American National Standards Institute, Standards Committee Z39 on Library & Information Sciences. American National Standard Advertising of Micropublications. 1981. 5.00 (ISBN 0-686-15233-6, Z39.26). ANSI.
--American National Standard Basic Criteria for Indexes. 1974. 5.00 (ISBN 0-686-01881-8, Z39.4). ANSI.
--American National Standard Compiling Book Publishing Statistics, Z39.8. 1977. 5.00 (ISBN 0-686-01885-0). ANSI.
--American National Standard Compiling Newspaper & Periodical Publishing Statistics. 1979. 5.00 (ISBN 0-686-28240-X, Z39.39). ANSI.
--American National Standard Compiling U. S. Microform Publishing Statistics. 1979. 5.00 (ISBN 0-686-28241-8, Z39.40). ANSI.
American National Standards Institute, Standards Committee Z39 on Library Work, Documentation & Related Publishing Practices. American National Standard Criteria for Price Indexes for Library Materials, Z39.20. 1974. 5.00 (ISBN 0-686-15228-X). ANSI.
American National Standards Institute, Standards Committee Z39 on Library Work & Information Sciences. American National Standard Directories of Libraries & Information Centers. rev. ed. 1977. 5.00 (ISBN 0-686-01887-7, Z39.10). ANSI.
--American National Standard for Bibliographic Information Interchange on Magnetic Tape. 1979. 5.00 (ISBN 0-686-01880-X, Z39.2). ANSI.
--American National Standard for Book Numbering, Z39.21. 1980. 5.00 (ISBN 0-686-15229-8). ANSI.
--American National Standard for Book Spine Formats. 1979. 5.00 (ISBN 0-686-28242-6, Z39.41). ANSI.
--American National Standard for Describing Books in Advertisements, Catalogs, Promotional Materials, & Book Jackets. 1979. 5.00 (ISBN 0-686-01890-7, Z39.13). ANSI.
--American National Standard for the Preparation of Scientific Papers for Written or Oral Presentation, Z39.16. 1979. 6.00 (ISBN 0-686-05270-6). ANSI.
--American National Standard Format for Scientific & Technical Translations. 1976. 5.00 (ISBN 0-686-28237-X, Z39.31). ANSI.
American National Standards Institutes, Standards Committee Z39 on Library Work & Information Sciences. American National Standard Guidelines for Format & Production of Scientific & Technical Reports, Z39.18. 1974. 6.00 (ISBN 0-686-15226-3). ANSI.
American National Standards Institute, Standards Committee Z39 on Library Work & Information Sciences. American National Standard Guidelines for Thesaurus Structure, Construction & Use, Z39.19. 1980. 6.00 (ISBN 0-686-15227-1). ANSI.
--American National Standard International Standard Serial Numbering, Z39.9. 1979. 5.00 (ISBN 0-686-01886-9). ANSI.
American National Standards Institute, Standards Committee Z39 on Library Work, Documentation & Related Publishing Practices. American National Standard Library Statistics. rev. ed. 1974. 8.00 (ISBN 0-686-01884-2, Z39.7). ANSI.
American National Standards Institute, Standards Committee Z39 on Library Work & Informartion Sciences. American National Standard Proof Corrections, Z39.22. 1981. 7.00 (ISBN 0-686-15230-1). ANSI.
American National Standards Institute. Standards Committee Z39 on Library Work & Information Sciences. American National Standard Structure for the Identification of Countries of the World for Information Interchange, Z39.27. 1976. 3.00 (ISBN 0-686-16672-8). ANSI.
American National Standards Institute, Standards Committee Z39 on Library Work & Information Sciences. American National Standard System for Romanization of Hebrew. 1975. 6.00 (ISBN 0-686-15232-8, Z39.25). ANSI.
--American National Standard System for the Romanization of Arabic, Z39.12. rev. ed. 1978. 5.00 (ISBN 0-686-01889-3). ANSI.
--American National Standard System for the Romanization of Japanese. rev. ed. 1978. 5.00 (ISBN 0-686-01888-5, Z39.11). ANSI.
--American National Standard System for the Romanization of Lao, Khmer, & Pali, Z39.35. 1979. 6.00 (ISBN 0-686-28238-8). ANSI.
--American National Standard System for the Romanization of Slavic Cyrillic Characters, Z39.24. 1976. 5.00 (ISBN 0-686-16673-6). ANSI.
--American National Standard Technical Report Number, (STRN), Z39.23. 1974. 5.00 (ISBN 0-686-15231-X). ANSI.
--American National Standard Title Leaves of a Book. 1980. 5.00 (ISBN 0-686-01892-3, Z39.15). ANSI.
--American National Standard Trade Catalogs. rev. ed. 1977. 5.00 (ISBN 0-686-01883-4, Z39.6). ANSI.
American National Standards Institute, Standards Committee Z39 on Library Work, Documentation & Related Publishing Practices. American National Standard Writing Abstracts. 1979. 6.00 (ISBN 0-686-01891-5, Z39.14). ANSI.
American National Standards Institute, Z39 on Library Work & Information Sciences. American National Standards Identification Code for the Book Industry. 1980. 5.00 (ISBN 0-686-38030-4, Z39.43). ANSI.
American National Standards Institute Z39 on Library Work & Information Sciences. American National Standards Order Form for Single Titles of Library Materials in 3-Inch by 5-Inch Format. 1982. 6.00 (ISBN 0-686-38032-0, Z39.30). ANSI.
American National Standards Institute. American National Standards Serial Holdings Statement at the Summary Level. 1980. 7.00 (ISBN 0-686-38029-0, Z39.42). ANSI.
American National Standards Institute, Standards Committee Z39 on Library Work & Information Sciences. American National System for the Romanization of Armenian, Z39.37. 1979. 5.00 (ISBN 0-686-28239-6). ANSI.
American Neurological Assoc. Transactions: 1979, Vol. 104. Duvoisin, Roger, ed. LC 61-705. 1980. text ed. 34.50 o.p. (ISBN 0-8261-0479-7). Springer Pub.
American Neurological Association. Transactions of the ANA, Vol. 105, 1980. 1981. 49.00 (ISBN 0-8261-0480-0). Springer Pub.
American Numismatic Association. Official A.N.A. Grading Guide. (Whitman Coin Hobby Books). (Illus.). 1977. 6.95 (ISBN 0-307-09097-3). Western Pub.
American Numismatic Society. Dictionary & Auction Catalogues of the Library of the American Numismatic Society, New York, 7 Vols. 1962. Set. lib. bdg. write for info. (ISBN 0-685-11673-5, Hall Library); lib. bdg. 530.00 dictionary catalog, 6 vols. (ISBN 0-8161-0630-4); lib. bdg. 90.00 auction catalog, 1 vol. (ISBN 0-8161-0102-7). G K Hall.
American Numismatic Society, New York. Dictionary & Auction Catalogues of the Library of the American Numismatic Society: First Supplement 1962-67. 1967. lib. bdg. 105.00 (ISBN 0-8161-0788-2, Hall Library). G K Hall.
--Dictionary & Auction Catalogues of the Library of the American Numismatic Society, Second Supplement. 1973. lib. bdg. 105.00 (ISBN 0-8161-1058-1, Hall Library). G K Hall.
American Ornithologists' Union, jt. auth. see Owre, Oscar T.
American Ornithologists' Union, ed. see Mengel, Robert M.
American Ornithologists' Union, jt. ed. see Sibley, Charles G.
American Ornithologists' Union, ed. see Van Tets, Gerard F.
American Peptide Symposium, Fifth see Goodman, Murray & Meienhofer, Johannes.
American Personnel & Guidance Association & American Vocational Association, eds. Solving the Guidance Legislative Puzzle. 126p. 1978. 7.75 (ISBN 0-686-36434-1, 72296); nonmembers 8.75 (ISBN 0-686-37318-9). Am Personnel.
American Petroleum Institute. Manual of Petroleum Measurement Standards. LC 80-67080. (Chapter 11.1 -- Volume Correction Factors Ser.: Vol. I). (Illus.). 678p. 1980. write for info. o.p. (ISBN 0-89364-022-0). Am Petroleum.
--Manual of Petroleum Measurement Standards. LC 80-67080. (Chapter 11.1 -- Volume Correction Factors: Vol. III). (Illus.). 563p. 1980. write for info. o.p. (ISBN 0-89364-024-7). Am Petroleum.
--Two Energy Futures: A National Choice for the 80's. 2nd ed. LC 80-24004. (Illus.). 166p. 1982. pap. text ed. write for info. (ISBN 0-89364-037-9). Am Petroleum.
--Two Energy Futures: A National Choice for the 80's. LC 82-73749. (Illus.). 196p. 1982. pap. write for info. (ISBN 0-89364-048-4). Am Petroleum.
American Petroleum Institute Staff. Two Energy Futures: A National Choice for the Eighty's. rev. ed. LC 81-7926. (Illus.). 187p. 1981. pap. text ed. write for info. o.p. (ISBN 0-89364-041-7). Am Petroleum.
American Pharmaceutical Association. Computer Sources: A Practical Guide for Pharmacists. Casler, Robin E., ed. 1982. pap. text ed. 18.00 (ISBN 0-917330-38-2). Am Pharm Assn.
--Handbook of Nonprescription Drugs. 7th ed. 1982. text ed. 45.00 (ISBN 0-917330-40-4). Am Pharm Assn.
American Pharmaceutical Association Committee on Tableting Specifications. Tableting Specification Manual. rev. ed. (Illus.). 39p. 1981. pap. text ed. 42.00 (ISBN 0-917330-36-6). Am Pharm Assn.
American Philatelic Society. APS Stamp Finder. 66p. 1982. pap. 2.00 (ISBN 0-933580-10-X). Am Philatelic.
American Photographic Book Publishing Co. & Eastman Kodak Co. Encyclopedia of Practical Photography, 14 vols. 1978. Set. lib. bdg. 223.30 o.p. (ISBN 0-8174-3200-0, Amphoto); Set. 159.95 o.p. (ISBN 0-8174-3050-4). Watson-Guptill.
American Physical Therapy Assn. & Courseware, Inc. Competencies in Physical Therapy: An Analysis of Practice. 1979. looseleaf binder 34.50 (ISBN 0-89805-002-2). Am Phys Therapy Assn.
American Physical Therapy Association Section for Education. Clinical Education in Physical Therapy: Present Status - Future Needs. 1976. pap. 15.00 cancelled o.s.i. (ISBN 0-912452-05-6). Am Phys Therapy Assn.
--Clinical Education in the Health Professions: An Annotated Bibliography. 1976. pap. 5.00 cancelled o.s.i. (ISBN 0-912452-06-4). Am Phys Therapy Assn.
American Physical Therapy Association. Physical Therapy Administration & Management. 2nd ed. Hickok, Robert, ed. 225p. 1974. 21.00 o.p. (ISBN 0-683-03975-X). Williams & Wilkins.
American Physiological Society. Disturbances in Body Fluid Osmolality. Andreoli, T. E., et al, eds. 1977. 25.00 o.p. (ISBN 0-683-00207-4). Williams & Wilkins.
--Handbook of Physiology, Section 5: Adipose Tissue. Renold, Albert E. & Cahill, George F., Jr., eds. 1965. 28.00 o.p. (ISBN 0-683-07232-3). Williams & Wilkins.
--Handbook of Physiology: Section 6: The Alimentary Canal, 5 Vols. Code, Charles F & Heidel, Werner, eds. Incl. Vol. I. Control of Food & Water Intake. 486p. 22.00 (ISBN 0-683-01951-1); Vol. II. Secretion. 663p. 32.00 (ISBN 0-683-01952-X); Vol. III. Intestinal Absorbtion. 491p. 22.00 (ISBN 0-683-01953-8); Vol. IV. Motility. 785p. 38.50 (ISBN 0-683-01954-6); Bile; Digestion; Ruminal Physiology. 557p. 30.00 (ISBN 0-683-01955-4). 1967-68. Williams & Wilkins.
--Handbook of Physiology, Section 7: Endocrinology, 7 vols. Greep, Roy O. & Astwood, Edwin B., eds. Incl. Vol. I. Endocrine Pancreas. 731p. 1972. 45.00 (ISBN 0-683-03588-6); Vol. II. Reproductive System - Female Part 1. 666p. 1973. 44.50, Pt. 1, 25.00 Pt. 2 (ISBN 0-683-03564-9); Vol. III. Thyroid. 500p. 1974. 38.00 (ISBN 0-683-03566-5); Vol. IV. The Pituitary Gland & it's Neuroendocrine Control. 1974p. pts. 1 & 2 49.50 ea.; Vol. V. Male Reproductive System. 528p. 1975. 47.50 (ISBN 0-683-03567-3); Vol. VI. Adrenal Gland. 754p. 1975. 75.00 (ISBN 0-683-03570-3); Vol. 7. Parathyroid. 500p. 1976. 55.00 (ISBN 0-683-03571-1). Williams & Wilkins.
--Pulmonary Edema. Fishman, Alfred & Renkin, Eugene, eds. (Clinical Physiology Ser.). (Illus.). 1979. 30.00 o.p. (ISBN 0-683-03245-3). Williams & Wilkins.
American Psychiatric Association. American Psychiatric Association Biographical Directory, 1983. 1600p. 1983. 89.95x (ISBN 0-89042-182-X); pap. 69.95x (ISBN 0-89042-181-1). Am Psychiatric.
--Biofeedback: Task Force Report Nineteen. LC 80-66989. (Monographs). 119p. 1980. 11.00 (ISBN 0-89042-219-2, 42-219-2). Am Psychiatric.
--Continuing Medical Education Syllabus & Scientific Proceedings in Summary Form: 135th Annual Meeting, Toronto, Canada, May 1982. new ed. (Scientific Proceedings of the APA Ser.). 350p. 1979. pap. text ed. 15.00x (ISBN 0-89042-082-3, 153-9). Am Psychiatric.
--Diagnostic & Statistical Manual of Mental Disorders (DSM-III) LC 79-55868. (Illus.). 506p. 1980. Casebound. 29.95x (ISBN 0-89042-041-6, 42-041-6); pap. 23.95x (ISBN 0-89042-042-4, 42-042-4). Am Psychiatric.
--Electroconvulsive Therapy. LC 78-69521. (Task Force Report: No. 14). 200p. 1978. pap. 10.00x (ISBN 0-89042-214-1). Am Psychiatric.
--A Psychiatric Glossary. 5th ed. LC 79-55869. 152p. 1980. pap. 5.95x (ISBN 0-89042-005-X). Am Psychiatric.
--Psychosocial Aspects of Nuclear Developments, Task Force Report, Twenty. LC 82-71902. (Monographs). 96p. 1982. 12.00x (ISBN 0-89042-220-6, 42-220-6). Am Psychiatric.
--Quick Reference to the Diagnostic Criteria from (DSM-III) (Illus.). 267p. 1980. 12.00x (ISBN 0-89042-043-2, 42-043-2). Am Psychiatric.
--Tardive Dyskinesia, Task Force Report Eighteen. LC 80-65372. (Monographs). (Illus.). 1980. 11.00 (ISBN 0-89042-218-4, 42-218-4). Am Psychiatric.
American Psychiatric Association & Task Force on Community Residential Services. A Typology of Community Residential Services. LC 82-24467. (APA Task Force Report Ser.: No. 21). (Illus.). 64p. 1982. pap. 5.00x (ISBN 0-89042-221-4, 42-221-4). Am Psychiatric.
American Psychiatric Association Task Force. Professional Liability Insurance & Psychiatric Malpractice. LC 77-94900. (Task Force Report: No. 13). 92p. 1978. pap. 6.00x (ISBN 0-89042-213-3). Am Psychiatric.
American Psychiatric Association's Task Force on Psychohistory, ed. The Psychiatrist As Psychohistorian. (Task Force Reports: No. 11). 33p. 1976. 5.00 o.p. (ISBN 0-685-76790-6, P221-0). Am Psychiatric.
American Psychiatric Association's Task Force on Religion & Psychiatry, ed. Psychiatrists' Viewpoints on & Their Services to Religious Institutions & the Ministry. (Task Force Reports: No. 10). 49p. 1975. 5.00 o.p. (ISBN 0-685-77445-7, P220-0). Am Psychiatric.
American Psychological Association. Ethical Principles in the Conduct of Research with Human Participants. 1973. pap. 5.50x o.p. (ISBN 0-912704-48-9). Am Psychol.
--Publication Manual of the American Psychological Association. 2nd ed. LC 74-11314. 1974. pap. 10.00x o.p. (ISBN 0-912704-53-5). Am Psychol.
--Standards for Educational & Psychological Tests. LC 74-75734. 1974. pap. 6.00x (ISBN 0-912704-55-1). Am Psychol.
American Radio Relay League. A Course in Radio Fundamentals. LC 55-9760. 4.00 o.p. (ISBN 0-87259-755-5). Am Radio.
--Radio Amateur's License Manual. LC 37-8925. 1981. 4.00 o.p. (ISBN 0-87259-279-0). Am Radio.
--Radio Amateur's License Manual. LC 37-8925. 4.00 (ISBN 0-87259-281-2). Am Radio.
--Single Sideband for the Radio Amateur. LC 54-12271. 4.00 o.p. (ISBN 0-87259-505-6). Am Radio.
American Red Cross. Basic First Aid, 4 vols. (Illus.). Set. pap. 5.25 slipcased o.p. (ISBN 0-385-17211-7). Doubleday.
American Red Cross, ed. Lifesaving, Rescue & Water Safety. 240p. 1974. pap. 2.25 o.p. (ISBN 0-385-06349-0). Doubleday.
American Registry Of Pathology. Manual of Histologic Staining Methods of the Armed Forces Institute of Pathology. 3rd ed. (Illus.). 1968. 27.50 (ISBN 0-07-001507-4, HP). McGraw.
American Scandinavian Foundation. Index Nordicus: A Cumulative Index to English-Language Periodicals on Scandinavian Studies. 1980. lib. bdg. 80.00 (ISBN 0-8161-0080-2, Hall Library). G K Hall.
American School of Classical Studies at Athens. Catalogue of the Gennadius Library. American School of Classical Studies at Athens, 7 Vols. 1968. 665.00 (ISBN 0-8161-0707-6, Hall Library). G K Hall.
--Catalogue of the Gennadius Library. American School of Classical Studies at Athens, First Supplement. 1973. lib. bdg. 120.00 (ISBN 0-8161-0835-8, Hall Library). G K Hall.
--Catalogue of the Gennadius Library. American School of Classical Studies at Athenss, Second Supplement. 1981. lib. bdg. 160.00 (ISBN 0-8161-0011-X, Hall Library). G K Hall.
American School of Classical Studies at Athens Staff. Studies in Athenian Architecture, Sculpture & Topography. LC 81-14994. (Hesperia Ser.: Suppl. 20). 1982. 15.00x (ISBN 0-686-85626-0). Am Sch Athens.
American School of Needlework. The Great Afghan Book. Thomas, Mary, ed. LC 80-68389. (Illus.). 160p. 1981. 17.95 (ISBN 0-8069-5444-2, Columbia Hse). Sterling.
--Great Crochet Bazaar Book. LC 81-85030. (Illus.). 160p. 1982. 17.95 (ISBN 0-8069-5456-6); lib. bdg. 14.99 o.p. (ISBN 0-8069-5457-4). Sterling.
American Section of the International Solar Energy Society. Membership Directory, 1981-82. (Illus.). 1982. pap. text ed. 35.00x o.p. (ISBN 0-686-79760-4). Am Solar Energy.
American Society for Hospital Central Service Personnel. Ethylene Oxide Use in Hospitals: A Manual for Health Care Personnel. LC 82-13871. (Illus.). 176p. 1982. pap. 52.50 (ISBN 0-87258-371-6, AHA-031180). Am Hospital.

American Society for Hospital Engineering. Arrhythmia Monitoring Systems. LC 78-15938. 32p. (Orig.). 1978. pap. 5.00 o.p. (ISBN 0-87258-244-2, 090112). Am Hospital.
American Society for Hospital Engineering of the American Hospital Association. Controlling Waste Anesthetic Gases. (Illus.). 52p. 1980. 10.75 (ISBN 0-87258-307-4, AHA-181152). Am Hospital.
American Society for Hospital Engineering. Hospital Engineering Handbook. (Illus.). 348p. 1980. casebound 31.25 (ISBN 0-87258-311-2, AHA-055120). Am Hospital.
--Mass Spectrometer Respiratory Monitoring Systems. LC 79-26957. (Illus.). 56p. (Orig.). 1980. pap. 8.75 (ISBN 0-87258-279-5, 190126). Am Hospital.
American Society for Hospital Engineering of the American Hospital Association. Multiphasic Health Testing. LC 79-11129. (Illus.). 52p. 1979. pap. 7.00 (ISBN 0-87258-269-8, AHA-190118). Am Hospital.
American Society for Hospital Engineering & American Society for Hospital Purchasing & Materials Management. Silver Recovery for Hospitals. LC 80-19943. 36p. 1980. pap. 10.00 (ISBN 0-87258-331-7, AHA-172100). Am Hospital.
American Society for Hospital Food Service Administrators. Determination & Allocation of Food Service Costs. 24p. 1975. pap. 8.75 (ISBN 0-87258-316-3, AHA-046110). Am Hospital.
--Hospital Food Service Management Review. LC 80-11834. 80p. (Orig.). 1980. 12.50 (ISBN 0-87258-323-6, AHA-046160). Am Hospital.
American Society for Hospital Food Service Administrators of the American Hospital Association. Preparation of a Hospital Food Service Department Budget. LC 78-24399. 56p. 1978. pap. 9.50 (ISBN 0-87258-254-X, AHA-046140). Am Hospital.
American Society for Hospital Purchasing & Materials Management, jt. auth. see American Society for Hospital Engineering.
American Society for Information Science, jt. auth. see National Federation of Abstracting & Indexing Services.
American Society for Information Science, 44th, 1981. The Information Community: An Alliance for Progress: Proceedings. Lunin, Lois F., et al, eds. LC 64-8303. 401p. 1981. pap. 19.50 (ISBN 0-914236-85-7). Knowledge Indus.
American Society for Training & Development Inc. Quality of Work Life: Perspectives for Business & the Public Sector. Skrovan, Daniel J., ed. 208p. Date not set. text ed. 17.95 (ISBN 0-201-07755-8). A-W.
American Society for Training & Development. Training & Development Handbook: A Guide to Human Resource Development. 2nd ed. (Handbook Ser.). (Illus.). 1976. 49.95 (ISBN 0-07-013350-6, P&RB); assessment supplement 5.95 (ISBN 0-07-013352-2). McGraw.
American Society of Civil Engineers, jt. auth. see U. S. National Committee on Rock Mechanics, 15th, South Dakota School of Mines & Technology, Sept. 1973.
American Society of Civil Engineers, compiled By see ASCE Geotechnical Engineering Division Conference, Ann Arbor, June 1977.
American Society of Civil Engineers, compiled By see ASCE Irrigation & Drainage Division, July 1976.
American Society of Civil Engineers, compiled By see ASCE Technical Council on Computer Practices, June 1978.
American Society of Civil Engineers, compiled By see Coastal Engineering International Conference, 10th, Tokyo, Aug. 1966.
American Society of Civil Engineers, et al, eds. see Rock Mechanics International Society & the U. S. National Committee, 16th.
American Society of Civil Engineers, compiled By. Air Supported Structures. 104p. 1979. pap. text ed. 11.00 o.p. Am Soc Civil Eng.
--Analyses for Soil Structure Interaction Effects for Nuclear Power Plants. 1979. pap. text ed. 13.50 (ISBN 0-87262-183-9). Am Soc Civil Eng.
American Society of Civil Engineers. ASCE Combined Index, 1981. 212p. 1982. pap. text ed. 20.00 (ISBN 0-87262-314-9). Am Soc Civil Eng.
American Society of Civil Engineers, compiled by. ASCE Salary Survey 1981. LC 82-73522. 80p. 1982. pap. text ed. 12.00. Am Soc Civil Eng.
--Bicycle Transportation: A Civil Engineer's Notebook. LC 80-70171. 189p. 1980. pap. text ed. 15.50 (ISBN 0-87262-260-6). Am Soc Civil Eng.
American Society of Civil Engineers, ed. Classic Papers in Hydraulics. 672p. 1982. pap. text ed. 49.00 (ISBN 0-87262-310-6). Am Soc Civil Eng.
American Society of Civil Engineers, compiled By. Construction Cost Control. 108p. 1979. pap. text ed. 10.00 o.p. Am Soc Civil Eng.
--Current Geotechnical Practice in Mine Waste Disposal. 272p. 1979. pap. text ed. 19.25 o.p. (ISBN 0-87262-141-3). Am Soc Civil Eng.
--Design of Water Intake Stuctures for Fish Protection. LC 81-70988. 176p. 1982. pap. text ed. 18.50 (ISBN 0-87262-291-6). Am Soc Civil Eng.
--Engineering & Construction in Tropical & Residual Soils. LC 81-71563. 750p. 1982. pap. text ed. 49.50 (ISBN 0-87262-292-4). Am Soc Civil Eng.
--Engineering & Contracting Procedure for Foundations. (Manual & Report on Engineering Practice Ser.: No. 8). 1953. pap. text ed. 3.00 o.p. (ISBN 0-87262-204-5). Am Soc Civil Eng.
--Evaluation, Maintenance & Upgrading of Wood Structures. LC 82-72779. 440p. 1982. pap. text ed. 13.00 (ISBN 0-87262-317-3). Am Soc Civil Eng.
--Field Test Sections Save Cost in Tunnel Support. 64p. 1975. pap. text ed. 9.75 o.p. (ISBN 0-87262-161-8). Am Soc Civil Eng.
--Finite Element Analysis of Reinforced Concrete. LC 82-71691. 560p. 1982. pap. text ed. 39.00. Am Soc Civil Eng.
American Society of Civil Engineers & American Water Works Association, eds. Glossary: Water & Wastewater Control Engineering. LC 80-70933. 456p. 1981. text ed. 25.00 (ISBN 0-87262-262-2). Am Soc Civil Eng.
American Society of Civil Engineers & Water Pollution Control Federation. Gravity Sanitary Sewer Design & Construction. LC 81-69182. 288p. 1982. text ed. 20.00 (ISBN 0-87262-313-0). Am Soc Civil Eng.
American Society of Civil Engineers, compiled By. Ground Water Management. (Manual & Report on Engineering Practice: No. 40). 1972. pap. text ed. 16.00 (ISBN 0-87262-216-9). Am Soc Civil Eng.
--In Situ Measurement of Soil Properties. 1975. pap. text ed. 28.00 o.p. (ISBN 0-87262-156-1). Am Soc Civil Eng.
American Society of Civil Engineers & Klohn, Charles H., eds. Joint Usage of Utility & Transportation Coorridors. LC 81-68750. 128p. 1981. pap. text ed. 15.50 (ISBN 0-87262-277-0). Am Soc Civil Eng.
American Society of Civil Engineers, compiled by. Methods of Structural Analysis. 1120p. 1976. pap. text ed. 39.50 o.p. (ISBN 0-87262-163-4). Am Soc Civil Eng.
--Nuclear Facilities Siting. LC 82-73507. 64p. 1982. pap. text ed. 11.75 (ISBN 0-87262-344-0). Am Soc Civil Eng.
--Nuclear Waste Management. LC 82-73506. 52p. 1982. pap. text ed. 11.75 (ISBN 0-87262-343-2). Am Soc Civil Eng.
American Society of Civil Engineers & Desai, C. S., eds. Numerical Methods in Geomechanics. 1568p. 1976. pap. text ed. 52.00 o.p. (ISBN 0-87262-168-5). Am Soc Civil Eng.
American Society of Civil Engineers, compiled by. Performance of Earth & Earth-Supported Structures. 1972. pap. text ed. 75.00 o.p. (ISBN 0-87262-046-8). Am Soc Civil Eng.
--Pipeline Design for Hydrocarbon Gases & Liquids. 88p. 1975. pap. text ed. 9.25 (ISBN 0-87262-118-9). Am Soc Civil Eng.
--Placement & Improvement of Soils. 448p. 1971. text ed. 19.75 o.p. (ISBN 0-87262-031-X). Am Soc Civil Eng.
--Practical Highway Esthetics. 80p. 1977. pap. text ed. 17.50 o.p. (ISBN 0-87262-096-4). Am Soc Civil Eng.
--Pure & Wholesome. LC 81-70989. 184p. 1982. pap. text ed. 18.50 (ISBN 0-87262-290-8). Am Soc Civil Eng.
--Reducing Risk & Liability Through Better Specifications & Inspections. LC 82-70874. 168p. 1982. pap. text ed. 18.75 (ISBN 0-87262-301-7). Am Soc Civil Eng.
--Reinforced Concrete Floor Slabs-Research & Design. 224p. 1978. pap. text ed. 15.00 o.p. (ISBN 0-87262-136-7). Am Soc Civil Eng.
--Rivers Seventy-Six. 1824p. 1976. pap. text ed. 72.50 o.p. (ISBN 0-87262-164-2). Am Soc Civil Eng.
--Rock Engineering for Foundations & Slopes. 728p. 1976. pap. text ed. 27.50 o.p. (ISBN 0-87262-082-4). Am Soc Civil Eng.
--Safety & Reliability of Metal Structures. 464p. 1972. pap. text ed. 12.75 o.p. (ISBN 0-87262-042-5). Am Soc Civil Eng.
--Soil Improvement: History, Capability & Outlook. 192p. 1978. pap. text ed. 14.50 o.p. (ISBN 0-87262-126-X). Am Soc Civil Eng.
--Stability & Performance of Slopes & Embankments. 704p. 1969. text ed. 33.00 o.p. (ISBN 0-87262-016-6). Am Soc Civil Eng.
American Society of Civil Engineers & Cording, Edward J., eds. Stability of Rock Slopes. 1008p. 1972. text ed. 34.50 o.p. (ISBN 0-87262-047-6). Am Soc Civil Eng.
American Society of Civil Engineers, compiled by. Stability of Structures Under Static & Dynamic Loads. 836p. 1978. pap. text ed. 30.00 (ISBN 0-87262-095-6). Am Soc Civil Eng.
--Structural Failures-Modes, Causes, Responsibilities. 112p. 1973. pap. text ed. 5.00 o.p. (ISBN 0-87262-051-4). Am Soc Civil Eng.
--Terzaghi Lectures. 432p. 1974. pap. text ed. 25.00 o.p. (ISBN 0-87262-060-3). Am Soc Civil Eng.
--Transactions of the American Society of Civil Engineers, Vol. 146, 1981. 1056p. 1982. pap. text ed. 52.50 (ISBN 0-87262-309-2). Am Soc Civil Eng.
--Underground Rock Chambers. 608p. 1972. text ed. 29.50 o.p. (ISBN 0-87262-033-6). Am Soc Civil Eng.
--Use of Shotcrete for Underground Structural Support. 480p. 1974. pap. text ed. 24.00 o.p. (ISBN 0-87262-066-2). Am Soc Civil Eng.
--Water Management for Irrigation & Drainage. 640p. 1977. pap. text ed. 46.00 o.p. (ISBN 0-87262-097-2). Am Soc Civil Eng.
--Water Systems Nineteen Seventy-Nine. 240p. 1979. pap. text ed. 17.75 o.p. (ISBN 0-87262-143-X). Am Soc Civil Eng.
--Watershed Management. 792p. 1975. pap. text ed. 29.50 o.p. (ISBN 0-87262-122-7). Am Soc Civil Eng.
American Society of Hospital Attorneys. Federal Regulation: Hospital Attorney's Desk Reference. 244p. (Orig.). 1980. pap. 35.00 (ISBN 0-87258-321-X, AHA-124138). Am Hospital.
American Society Of Mechanical Engineers. ASME Handbook: Engineering Tables. 1956. 67.90 (ISBN 0-07-001516-3, P&RB). McGraw.
--ASME Handbook: Metals Engineering: Processes. 1958. 49.50 o.p. (ISBN 0-07-001514-7, P&RB). McGraw.
--ASME Handbook: Metals Properties. (Illus.). 1956. 49.50 o.p. (ISBN 0-07-001513-9, P&RB). McGraw.
American Society of Photogrammetry, ed. Eighth Biennial Workshop on Color Aerial Photography in the Plant Sciences & Related Fields. 167p. pap. 15.00 (ISBN 0-937294-34-9); pap. 20.00 nonmember (ISBN 0-686-95492-0). ASP.
American Society of Photogrammetry. Pecora 7: Symposium held in Sioux Falls, S.D. in October, 1981. 19.50 (ISBN 0-686-95487-4); nonmember 27.50 (ISBN 0-686-99511-2). ASP.
--Proceedings: Second Technology Exchange Week in Panama. 724p. 1982. 15.00 (ISBN 0-686-95483-1); nonmember 20.00 (ISBN 0-686-99510-4). ASP.
--Workshop for Automated Photogrammetry & Cartography of Highways & Transport Systems. 138p. 1981. 11.00 (ISBN 0-937294-33-0); nonmember 16.00 (ISBN 0-686-95489-0). ASP.
American Society Of Tool And Manufacturing Engineers. A S T M E Die Design Handbook. 2nd ed. Wilson, Frank W., ed. 1965. 61.50 o.p. (ISBN 0-07-001523-6, P&RB). McGraw.
American Society of Tool & Manufacturing Engineers. Fundamentals of Tool Design. (Illus.). 1962. text ed. 25.95 (ISBN 0-13-344861-4). P-H.
American Society Of Tool And Manufacturing Engineers. Handbook of Fixture Design. Wilson, Frank W., ed. 1962. 39.50 (ISBN 0-07-001527-9, P&RB). McGraw.
American Society Of Tool & Manufacturing Engineers. Manufacturing Planning & Estimating Handbook. Wilson, Frank W., ed. 1963. 49.50 o.p. (ISBN 0-07-001536-8, P&RB). McGraw.
American Solar Energy Society Staff. American Solar Energy Society Membership Directory 1982-83 & Guide to Programs. 120p. 1982. pap. text ed. 45.00x (ISBN 0-89553-049-X). Am Solar Energy.
American Sunbeam Staff. Weather Made to Whose Order? (Illus.). 56p. Date not set. self cover 2.00 (ISBN 0-918700-04-3). Duverus Pub. Postponed.
American Telephone & Telegraph Co. Engineering Economy: A Manager's Guide to Economic Decision Making. 3rd ed. 1977. 43.50 (ISBN 0-07-001530-9). McGraw.
American Vocational Association, jt. ed. see American Personnel & Guidance Association.
American Vocational Association, jt. ed. see National Vocational Guidance Association.
American Water Works Association. American National Standard for Gray-Iron & Ductile-Iron Fitting, 3 in. Through 48 in., for Water & Other Liquids: C110-A21, 10-77. rev. ed. (AWWA Standards). (Illus.). 66p. 1976. pap. text ed. 10.20 (ISBN 0-89867-112-4). Am Water Wks Assn.
--American National Standard for Thickness Design of Cast-Iron Pipe: C101-A21,1-67. rev. ed. (AWWA Standards). (Illus.). 88p. 1967. pap. text ed. 9.00 o.p. (ISBN 0-89867-107-8). Am Water Wks Assn.
--American National Standard for Vertical Turbine Pumps - Line Shaft & Submersible Types: E101-77. rev. ed. (AWWA Standards). (Illus.). 56p. 1977. pap. text ed. 9.60 (ISBN 0-89867-163-9). Am Water Wks Assn.
--Analyzing Organics in Drinking Water. (AWWA Handbooks Ser.). (Illus.). 120p. 1981. pap. text ed. 17.10 (ISBN 0-89867-256-2). Am Water Wks Assn.
--Annual Conference: Proceedings: 1975. (AWWA Handbooks - Proceedings). (Illus.). 1120p. 1975. pap. text ed. 26.40 (ISBN 0-89867-044-6). Am Water Wks Assn.
--Annual Conference: Proceedings: 1976, Vol. 1. (AWWA Handbooks - Proceedings). (Illus.). 592p. 1976. pap. text ed. 22.80 (ISBN 0-89867-046-2). Am Water Wks Assn.
--Annual Conference: Proceedings: 1976, Vol. 2. (AWWA Handbooks Ser.). (Illus.). 700p. 1976. pap. text ed. 22.80 (ISBN 0-89867-047-0). Am Water Wks Assn.
--Annual Conference: Proceedings: 1977, 2 pts. (AWWA Handbooks - Proceedings). (Illus.). 1400p. 1977. pap. text ed. 39.00 (ISBN 0-89867-052-7). Am Water Wks Assn.
--Annual Conference: Proceedings: 1978, 2 pts. (AWWA Handbooks - Proceedings). (Illus.). 1400p. 1978. pap. text ed. 48.00 (ISBN 0-89867-056-X). Am Water Wks Assn.
--Annual Conference: Proceedings, 1979. (AWWA Proceedings Handbook Ser.). (Illus.). 1200p. 1979. pap. text ed. 57.60 (ISBN 0-89867-229-5). Am Water Wks Assoc.
--Annual Conference Proceedings, 1980. (AWWA Proceedings Handbook Ser.). (Illus.). 1452p. 1980. pap. text ed. 57.60 (ISBN 0-89867-238-4). Am Water Wks Assn.
--Annual Conference: Proceedings: 1981, 2 pts. (AWWA Handbooks Ser.). (Illus.). 1310p. 1981. Set. pap. text ed. 62.40 (ISBN 0-89867-260-0). Am Water Wks Assn.
--Annual Conference, 1982: Proceedings, 2 pts. (AWWA Handbooks-Proceedings Ser.). (Illus.). 1310p. 1982. Set. pap. 68.60 (ISBN 0-89867-281-3). Am Water Wks Assn.
--Automation & Instrumentation - M2. (AWWA Manuals). (Illus.). 160p. 1977. pap. text ed. 19.20 (ISBN 0-89867-060-8). Am Water Wks Assn.
--AWWA Distribution System Symposium Nineteen Eighty: Proceedings: 1980. (AWWA Handbooks Proceedings Ser.). (Illus.). 179p. 1980. pap. text ed. 11.40 (ISBN 0-89867-235-X). Am Water Wks Assn.
--AWWA Standard for Deep Wells: A100-66. rev. ed. (AWWA Standards). (Illus.). 64p. 1966. pap. text ed. 9.60 (ISBN 0-89867-082-9). Am Water Wks Assn.
--AWWA Standard for the Selection of Asbestos-Cement Transmission & Feeder Main Pipe, Sizes 18 in. Through 42 in. C403-78. (AWWA Standards). (Illus.). 64p. 1978. pap. text ed. 9.60 (ISBN 0-89867-134-5). Am Water Wks Assn.
--AWWA Standard for Welded Steel Elevated Tanks, Standpipes & Reservoirs for Water Storage: D-100-79. rev. ed. (AWWA Standards). (Illus.). 72p. 1979. pap. text ed. 10.20 (ISBN 0-89867-160-4). Am Water Wks Assn.
--Basic Management Principles for Small Water Systems. (AWWA Handbooks-General Ser.). (Illus.). 132p. 1982. pap. 18.20 (ISBN 0-89867-280-5). Am Water Wks Assn.
--Basic Water Treatment Operator's Practices - M18. (AWWA Manuals). (Illus.). 136p. 1971. pap. text ed. 10.20 (ISBN 0-89867-076-4). Am Water Wks Assn.
--Challenges in Water Utility Management. (AWWA Handbooks Ser.). (Illus.). 90p. 1980. pap. text ed. 12.00 (ISBN 0-89867-239-2). Am Water Wks Assn.
--Coagulation & Filtration: Back to Basics. (AWWA Handbooks Ser.). (Illus.). 168p. 1981. pap. text ed. 13.80 (ISBN 0-89867-257-0). Am Water Wks Assn.
--Community Relations Newsletter Collection, May 1975-April 1977. (Community Relations Publications Ser.). 100p. 1977. pap. text ed. 10.00 o.p. (ISBN 0-89867-165-5). Am Water Wks Assn.
--Computer-Based Automation in Water Systems. (AWWA Handbooks-General Ser.). (Illus.). 104p. 1980. pap. text ed. 12.00 (ISBN 0-89867-230-9). Am Water Wks Assn.
--Concrete Pressure Pipe-M9: AWWA Manuals. (Illus.). 1979. pap. text ed. 16.20 (ISBN 0-89867-067-5). Am Water Wks Assn.
--Controlling Corrosion Within Water Systems. (AWWA Handbooks - Proceedings). (Illus.). 120p. 1978. pap. text ed. 9.60 (ISBN 0-89867-057-8). Am Water Wks Assn.
--Controlling Organics in Drinking Water: Proceedings. (AWWA Handbooks-Proceedings). (Illus.). 136p. 1979. pap. text ed. 10.20 (ISBN 0-89867-223-6). Am Water Wks Assn.
--Corrosion Control. (AWWA Handbooks-Proceedings Ser.). (Illus.). 70p. 1982. pap. 10.20 (ISBN 0-89867-283-X). Am Water Wks Assn.
--Corrosion Control by Deposition of CaCO3 Films Handbook. (AWWA Handbooks - General). (Illus.). 68p. 1978. pap. text ed. 9.60 (ISBN 0-89867-020-9). Am Water Wks Assn.
--Cross-Connections & Backflow Prevention Handbook. 2nd ed. (AWWA Handbooks - General). (Illus.). 64p. 1974. pap. text ed. 8.40 (ISBN 0-89867-250-3). Am Water Wks Assn.
--Design of Pilot Plant Studies. (AWWA Handbooks-Proceedings Ser.). (Illus.). 108p. 1982. pap. 11.40 (ISBN 0-89867-285-6). Am Water Wks Assn.
--Developing Water Rates. (AWWA Handbooks - Proceedings). (Illus.). 116p. 1973. pap. text ed. 7.20 (ISBN 0-89867-040-3). Am Water Wks Assn.
--Disinfection. (AWWA Handbooks - Proceedings). (Illus.). 224p. 1977. pap. text ed. 12.00 (ISBN 0-89867-053-5). Am Water Wks Assn.
--Distribution Systems: Actions & Innovations. (General Handbooks). (Illus.). 256p. 1980. pap. text ed. 24.00 (ISBN 0-89867-246-5). Am Water Wks Assn.
--Dual Distribution Systems. (AWWA Handbooks - Proceedings). (Illus.). 112p. 1976. pap. text ed. 7.20 (ISBN 0-89867-050-0). Am Water Wks Assn.
--Emergency Planning for Water Utility Management, M19. (AWWA Manuals). (Illus.). 102p. 1973. pap. text ed. 16.20 (ISBN 0-89867-077-2). Am Water Wks Assn.
--Energy & Water Use Forecasting. (AWWA Handbooks-General Ser.). (Illus.). 104p. 1980. pap. text ed. 12.00 (ISBN 0-89867-236-8). Am Water Wks Assn.

--Financial Planning & the Use of Financial Information for General Management Personnel. (AWWA Handbooks-Proceedings Ser.). (Illus.). 80p. 1982. pap. 10.20 (ISBN 0-89867-277-5). Am Water Wks Assn.
--Getting the Most from Your Well Supply. (AWWA Handbooks - Proceedings). (Illus.). 72p. 1972. pap. text ed. 4.80 (ISBN 0-89867-038-1). Am Water Wks Assn.
--Ground Water - M21. (AWWA Manuals). (Illus.). 142p. 1973. pap. text ed. 17.10 (ISBN 0-89867-079-9). Am Water Wks Assn.
--Guidelines for Selection of Instruments for the Small Laboratory - M15. (AWWA Manuals). (Illus.). 90p. 1978. pap. text ed. 13.80 (ISBN 0-89867-073-X). Am Water Wks Assn.
--Hazardous Materials Spills. (AWWA Handbooks - Proceedings). (Illus.). 72p. 1977. pap. text ed. 8.40 (ISBN 0-89867-054-3). Am Water Wks Assn.
--Index to Journal AWWA: Nineteen Fifty-Six to Nineteen Sixty-Five. (Journal Indexes Ser.). 133p. 1967. text ed. 12.00 (ISBN 0-89867-000-4). Am Water Wks Assn.
--Index to Journal AWWA: Nineteen Forty to Nineteen Fifty-Five. (Journal Indexes Ser.). 192p. 1956. text ed. 9.00 o.p. (ISBN 0-89867-001-2). Am Water Wks Assn.
--Index to Journal AWWA: Nineteen Sixty-Six - Nineteen Seventy-Five. (Journal Indexes Ser.). 200p. 1977. text ed. 19.20 (ISBN 0-89867-006-3). Am Water Wks Assn.
--Journal AWWA, 1980, Vol. 72. (Journal Bound Volumes Ser.). (Illus.). 788p. 1981. pap. 28.80 (ISBN 0-89867-253-8). Am Water Wks Assn.
--Journal AWWA, 1981. (Journal Bound Volumes Ser.). (Illus.). 104p. 1982. pap. text ed. 28.80 (ISBN 0-89867-269-4). Am Water Wks Assn.
--Managing Water Rates & Finances. (AWWA Handbooks-General Ser.). (Illus.). 208p. 1980. pap. text ed. 19.20 (ISBN 0-89867-228-7). Am Water Wks Assn.
--Minimizing & Recycling Water Plant Sludge. (AWWA Handbooks - Proceedings). (Illus.). 124p. 1973. pap. text ed. 7.20 (ISBN 0-89867-039-X). Am Water Wks Assn.
--Op Flow: Vol. 6, 1980. (Illus.). 104p. 1981. text ed. 19.20 (ISBN 0-89867-254-6). Am Water Wks Assn.
--Operator Certification Study Guide. (AWWA Handbooks Ser.: General). (Illus.). 104p. 1979. pap. 12.00 (ISBN 0-89867-227-9). Am Water Wks Assn.
--OpFlow, Vol. 1, 1975. (OpFlow Bound Volumes). (Illus.). 104p. 1976. text ed. 16.80 (ISBN 0-89867-007-1). Am Water Wks Assn.
--OpFlow, Vol. 2, 1976. (OpFlow Bound Volumes). (Illus.). 104p. 1977. text ed. 16.80 (ISBN 0-89867-009-8). Am Water Wks Assn.
--OpFlow, Vol. 3, 1977. (OpFlow Bound Volumes). (Illus.). 104p. 1978. text ed. 16.80 (ISBN 0-89867-010-1). Am Water Wks Assn.
--Opflow, Vol. 4, 1978. (OpFlow Bound Volumes). (Illus.). 104p. 1979. text ed. 16.80 (ISBN 0-89867-221-X). Am Water Wks Assn.
--Opflow, Vol. 5, 1979. (OpFlow Bound Volumes). (Illus.). 104p. 1980. text ed. 16.80 (ISBN 0-89867-233-3). Am Water Wks Assn.
--OpFlow, 1981, Vol. 7. (OpFlow Bound Volumes Ser.). (Illus.). 104p. 1982. pap. text ed. 19.20 (ISBN 0-89867-270-8). Am Water Wks Assn.
--Organic Contaminants in Drinking Water: Transport & Removal. (AWWA Handbooks Ser.). (Illus.). 132p. 1981. pap. text ed. 12.00 (ISBN 0-89867-259-7). Am Water Wks Assn.
--Polyelectrolytes: Aids to Better Water Quality. (AWWA Handbooks-Proceedings). (Illus.). 128p. 1972. pap. text ed. 6.00 (ISBN 0-89867-037-3). Am Water Wks Assn.
--Processing Water-Treatment-Plant Sludge. (AWWA Handbooks - General). (Illus.). 160p. 1974. pap. text ed. 10.80 (ISBN 0-89867-016-0). Am Water Wks Assn.
--The Quest for Pure Water, 2 pts. 2nd ed. (General References Ser.). (Illus.). 840p. 1981. Set. pap. text ed. 47.40 (ISBN 0-89867-249-X). Am Water Wks Assn.
--Reference Handbook: Basic Science Concepts & Applications. (General References Ser.). (Illus.). 756p. 1980. text ed. 24.00 (ISBN 0-89867-202-3). Am Water Wks Assn.
--River Water Quality Assessment. (AWWA Handbooks - Proceedings). (Illus.). 112p. 1976. pap. text ed. 7.20 (ISBN 0-89867-048-9). Am Water Wks Assn.
--Safe Water: A Factbook on the SDWA for Noncommunity Water Systems. (Illus.). 52p. 1980. pap. 1.80 (ISBN 0-89867-224-4). Am Water Wks Assn.
--Safety Practice for Water Utilities-M3. (AWWA Manuals). (Illus.). 128p. 1977. pap. text ed. 16.20 (ISBN 0-89867-061-6). Am Water Wks Assn.
--Simplified Procedures for Water Examination, Including Supplement on Instrumental Methods - M12. (AWWA Manuals). (Illus.). 190p. 1978. pap. text ed. 20.40 (ISBN 0-89867-070-5). Am Water Wks Assn.
--Sizing Water Services Lines & Meters - M22. (AWWA Manuals). (Illus.). 112p. 1975. pap. text ed. 16.20 (ISBN 0-89867-080-2). Am Water Wks Assn.
--Small Water System Problems. (AWWA Handbooks-Proceedings Ser.). (Illus.). 117p. 1981. pap. text ed. 12.00 (ISBN 0-89867-266-X). Am Water Wks Assn.
--Small Water System Solutions. (AWWA Handbooks-Proceedings Ser.). (Illus.). 80p. 1982. pap. text ed. 10.20 (ISBN 0-89867-282-1). Am Water Wks Assn.
--Spanish Translations of Selected 1976 Journal Articles. (AWWA Handbooks - General). (Illus.). 88p. 1977. pap. text ed. 12.00 (ISBN 0-89867-018-7). Am Water Wks Assn.
--Spillway Design Practice - M13. (AWWA Manuals). (Illus.). 104p. 1976. pap. text ed. 13.00 o.p. (ISBN 0-89867-071-3). Am Water Wks Assn.
--Steel Pipe: Design & Installation - M11. (AWWA Manuals). (Illus.). 260p. 1964. pap. text ed. 23.40 (ISBN 0-89867-069-1, M11). Am Water Wks Assn.
--Taste & Odor Control Experiences Handbook. (AWWA Handbooks-General Ser.). (Illus.). 118p. 1976. pap. text ed. 8.00 (ISBN 0-89867-011-X). Am Water Wks Assn.
--A Training Course in Water Distribution - M8. (AWWA Manuals). (Illus.). 168p. 1962. pap. text ed. 10.20 (ISBN 0-89867-066-7). Am Water Wks Assn.
--A Training Course in Water Utility Management - M5. rev. ed. (AWWA Manuals). (Illus.). 168p. 1980. pap. text ed. 16.80 (ISBN 0-89867-063-2). Am Water Wks Assn.
--Treatment Techniques for Controlling Trihalomethanes in Drinking Water. (AWWA Handbooks-General Ser.). (Illus.). 312p. 1982. pap. text ed. 16.80 (ISBN 0-89867-279-1). Am Water Wks Assn.
--Upgrading Existing Water Treatment Plants. (AWWA Handbooks - Proceedings). (Illus.). 272p. 1974. pap. text ed. 12.60 (ISBN 0-89867-042-X). Am Water Wks Assn.
--Upgrading Water Treatment Plants to Improve Water Quality. (Handbooks-Proceedings). (Illus.). 132p. 1980. pap. text ed. 12.00 (ISBN 0-89867-245-7). Am Water Wks Assn.
--Wate Utility Management Practices-M5. (AWWA Manuals Ser.). (Illus.). 1980. pap. text ed. 16.80 (ISBN 0-89867-063-2). Am Water Wks Assn.
--Water Chlorination Principles & Practices - M20. (AWWA Manuals). (Illus.). 92p. 1973. pap. text ed. 8.40 (ISBN 0-89867-078-0). Am Water Wks Assn.
--Water Conservation Strategies. (AAWA Handbks. - General Ser.). (Illus.). 108p. 1980. pap. text ed. 12.00 (ISBN 0-89867-240-6). Am Water Wks Assn.
--Water Customer Information. (AWWA Handbooks Proceedings Ser.). (Illus.). 56p. 1979. pap. text ed. 7.20 (ISBN 0-89867-222-8). Am Water Wks Assn.
--Water Disinfection with Ozone, Chloramines, or Chlorine Dioxide. (Handbooks-Proceedings Ser.). (Illus.). 224p. 1980. pap. text ed. 11.40 (ISBN 0-89867-244-9). Am Water Wks Assn.
--Water Distribution Operator Training Handbook. (AWWA Handbooks - General). (Illus.). 232p. 1976. pap. text ed. 14.40 (ISBN 0-89867-013-6). Am Water Wks Assn.
--Water Fluoridation Principles & Practices - M4. (AWWA Manuals). (Illus.). 120p. 1977. pap. text ed. 9.60 (ISBN 0-89867-062-4). Am Water Wks Assn.
--Water Meters: Selection, Installation, Testing, & Maintenance - M6. (AWWA Manuals). (Illus.). 112p. 1973. pap. text ed. 9.60 (ISBN 0-89867-064-0). Am Water Wks Assn.
--Water Plant Instrumentation & Automation. (AWWA Handbooks - Proceedings). (Illus.). 304p. 1976. pap. text ed. 14.40 (ISBN 0-89867-049-7). Am Water Wks Assn.
--Water Quality & Treatment: A Handbook for Public Water Supplies. 3rd ed. 1971. 44.50 (ISBN 0-07-001539-2, P&RB). McGraw.
--Water Quality & Treatment: A Handbook of Public Water Supplies. 3rd ed. (General References Ser.). (Illus.). 654p. 1971. text ed. 42.60 (ISBN 0-89867-005-5). Am Water Wks Assn.
--Water Quality Technology Conference - 1979: Advances in Laboratory Techniques for Quality Control. (AWWA Handbooks Proceedings Ser.). (Illus.). 350p. 1980. pap. text ed. 14.40 (ISBN 0-89867-231-7). Am Water Wks Assn.
--Water Quality Technology Conference: Nineteen Seventy-Six-the Water Laboratory-Key to Process & Quality Control. (AWWA Handbooks - Proceedings). (Illus.). 342p. 1977. pap. text ed. 12.00 (ISBN 0-89867-051-9). Am Water Wks Assn.
--Water Quality Technology Conference, 1981: Advances in Laboratory Techniques for Quality Control. (AWWA Handbooks-Proceedings Ser.). (Illus.). 1982. pap. text ed. 18.60 (ISBN 0-89867-267-8). Am Water Wks Assn.
--Water Quality Technology Conference, 1980: Advances in Laboratory Techniques for Quality Control. (AWWA Handbooks-Proceedings Ser.). (Illus.). 1981. pap. text ed. 18.00 (ISBN 0-89867-251-1). Am Water Wks Assn.
--Water Quality Technology Conference: 1975-Laboratory Tools for Safe Water. (AWWA Handbooks - Proceedings). (Illus.). 1976. pap. text ed. 12.00 (ISBN 0-89867-045-4). Am Water Wks Assn.
--Water Quality Technology Conference: 1973-Water Quality. (AWWA Handbooks - Proceedings). (Illus.). 272p. 1974. pap. text ed. 12.00 (ISBN 0-89867-041-1). Am Water Wks Assn.
--Water Quality Technology Conference: 1974-Water Quality. (AWWA Handbooks - Proceedings). (Illus.). 248p. 1975. pap. text ed. 12.00 (ISBN 0-89867-043-8). Am Water Wks Assn.
--Water Quality Technology Conference: 1977-Water Quality in the Distribution System. (AWWA Handbooks - Proceedings). (Illus.). 320p. 1978. pap. text ed. 12.00 (ISBN 0-89867-055-1). Am Water Wks Assn.
--Water Treatment Plant Design. (General References Ser.). (Illus.). 362p. 1969. text ed. 18.00 (ISBN 0-89867-004-7). Am Water Wks Assn.
--Water Treatment Waste Disposal. (AWWA Handbooks - Proceedings). (Illus.). 136p. 1978. pap. text ed. 10.20 (ISBN 0-89867-058-6). Am Water Wks Assn.
--Water Utility Accounting. 2nd ed. (General References Ser.). (Illus.). 288p. 1980. text ed. 33.60 (ISBN 0-89867-237-6). Am Water Wks Assn.
American Water Works Association, jt. ed. see American Society of Civil Engineers.
American Welding Society. American Welding Society Welding Terms & Definitions. 80p. 1980. 20.00 (ISBN 0-686-43366-1). Am Welding.
--Arc Welding Safety & Health. 1982. wkbk. 45.00 (ISBN 0-686-43376-9); instr's manual 17.50 (ISBN 0-686-43377-7); cassettes & slides 125.00 (ISBN 0-686-43378-5). Am Welding.
--Certification Manual for Welding Inspectors. 2nd ed. 60p. 1980. 35.00 (ISBN 0-686-51723-7). Am Welding.
--Copper & Copper Alloy Arc-Welding Electrodes: A5.6-76. 5.00 o.p. (ISBN 0-685-65968-2). Am Welding.
--Corrosion-Resisting Chromium & Chromium-Nickel Steel Welding Rods & Bare Electrodes: A5.9-77. 5.00 o.p. (ISBN 0-685-65970-4). Am Welding.
--Current Welding Processes. text ed. 12.00 (ISBN 0-685-65944-5); instr's manual 2.50 (ISBN 0-685-65945-3); slides 105.00 (ISBN 0-685-65946-1). Am Welding.
--Effects of Welding on Health, No. II: Evaluation of the Literature from Jan. 1978 to May 1979. 45p. 1981. 32.00 (ISBN 0-686-43369-6). Am Welding.
--The Facts About Fumes. 1976. 13.00 (ISBN 0-686-43387-4). Am Welding.
--Fatigue Fractures in Welded Contructions. 1967. 25.00. Am Welding.
--Filler Metal Comparison Charts: A5.0. LC 78-54738. 1980. pap. 32.00 (ISBN 0-87171-156-7). Am Welding.
--Flame Spraying of Ceramics: C2.13. 1970. 8.00 (ISBN 0-686-43373-4). Am Welding.
--Guide for Steel Hull Welding: D3.5. 1976. 8.00 (ISBN 0-686-43383-1). Am Welding.
--Guide for the Nondestructive Inspection of Welds: B1.0. 1977. 8.00 (ISBN 0-686-43386-6). Am Welding.
--Handbook on the Ultrasonic Examination of Welds. 1977. 28.00 (ISBN 0-686-43357-2). Am Welding.
--Introductory Welding Metallurgy. 1968. text ed. 12.00 (ISBN 0-685-65950-X); instr's manual 2.50 (ISBN 0-685-65951-8); slides 105.00 (ISBN 0-685-65952-6). Am Welding.
--Iron & Steel Gas-Welding Rods: A5.2-69. 3.50 o.p. (ISBN 0-685-65964-X). Am Welding.
--Local Heat Treatment of Welds in Piping & Tubing: D10.10. 1975. 8.00 (ISBN 0-686-43381-5). Am Welding.
--Metric Practice Guide for the Welding Industry: A1.1. 1980. 8.00 (ISBN 0-686-43367-X). Am Welding.
--Mild Steel Covered Arc-Welding Electrodes: A5.1-69. 3.50 o.p. (ISBN 0-685-65963-1). Am Welding.
--Mild Steel Electrodes for Flux Cored Arc Welding: A5.20-69. 3.50 o.p. (ISBN 0-685-65981-X). Am Welding.
--Mild Steel Electrodes for Gas Metal-Arc Welding: A5.18-69. 3.50 o.p. (ISBN 0-685-65979-8). Am Welding.
--Minimum Requirements for Training of Welders: E3.1. 1975. 8.00 (ISBN 0-686-43355-6). Am Welding.
--Modern Joining Processes. text ed. 12.00 (ISBN 0-685-65947-X); instr's manual 2.50 (ISBN 0-685-65948-8); slides 105.00 (ISBN 0-685-65949-6). Am Welding.
--Operator's Manual for Oxyfuel Gas Cutting: C4.2. 1978. 8.00 (ISBN 0-686-43371-8). Am Welding.
--Practices for Welding of Chromium-Molybdenum Steel Piping & Tubing: D10.8. 8.00 (ISBN 0-87171-153-2). Am Welding.
--Recommendations for Arc Welded Joints in Clad Steel Construction. 66p. 1969. 4.00 (ISBN 0-686-43359-9). Am Welding.
--Recommended Practices & Procedures for Welding Plain Carbon Steel Pipe: D10.12. 1979. 8.00 (ISBN 0-686-43365-3). Am Welding.
--Recommended Practices for Air Carbon-Arc Grouping & Cutting: C5.3. 1982. 8.00 (ISBN 0-686-43370-X). Am Welding.
--Recommended Practices for Application of Metallized Coatings to Protect Against Heat Corrosion: C2.3-54. 3.00 o.p. (ISBN 0-685-66007-9). Am Welding.
--Recommended Practices for Automotive Welding Design: D8.4. 1961. 8.00 (ISBN 0-686-43362-9). Am Welding.
--Recommended Practices for Electrogas Welding: C5.7. 1981. 8.00 (ISBN 0-686-43372-6). Am Welding.
--Recommended Practices for Gas Tungsten Arc Welding: C5.5. 1980. 8.00 (ISBN 0-686-43375-0). Am Welding.
--Recommended Practices for Resistance Welding Coated Low Carbon Steel: C1.3-70. 8.00 (ISBN 0-685-65994-1). Am Welding.
--Recommended Practices for Resistance Welding: C1.1-66. 10.00 (ISBN 0-685-65992-5). Am Welding.
--Recommended Practices for Stud Welding: C5.4. 1974. 8.00 (ISBN 0-686-43379-3). Am Welding.
--Recommended Safe Practices for Gas-Shielded Arc Welding: A6.1-66. 2.00 o.p. (ISBN 0-685-65985-2). Am Welding.
--Recommended Safe Practices for Plasma Arc Cutting: C5.2. 1973. 8.00 (ISBN 0-685-65986-0). Am Welding.
--Recommended Safe Practices for Thermal Spraying: C2.1. 1973. 8.00 (ISBN 0-686-43368-8). Am Welding.
--Resistance Welding: Theory & Use. 1956. 10.00 o.p. (ISBN 0-685-65995-X). Am Welding.
--Sheet Steel Structural Welding Code: D1.3. 1981. 15.00 (ISBN 0-686-43350-5). Am Welding.
--Specification for Cast Iron, Welding Rods & Covered Electrodes for Welding. 1982. 8.00 (ISBN 0-686-43349-1). Am Welding.
--Specification for Corrosion-Resisting Chromium & Chromium-Nickel Steel Covered Electrodes: A5.4-69. 1981. 2.50 (ISBN 0-685-65966-6). Am Welding.
--Specification for Magnesium-Alloy Welding Rods & Bare Electrodes: A5.19-69. 1976. 8.00 (ISBN 0-685-65980-1). Am Welding.
--Specification for Metal Cutting Machine Tool Weldments. (incl. 1975 Revision). 1971. 8.00 (ISBN 0-686-43353-X). Am Welding.
--Specification for Nickel & Nickel-Alloy Bare Welding Rods & Electrodes: A5.14-76. 1976. 8.00 (ISBN 0-685-65976-3). Am Welding.
--Specification for Nickel & Nickel-Alloy Covered Welding Electrodes: A5.11-76. 1976. 8.00 (ISBN 0-685-65973-9). Am Welding.
--Specification for Silver, Aluminum, Gold, Cobalt, Copper, Magnesium & Nickel Alloys Brazing Filler Metal. 1981. 8.00 (ISBN 0-686-43351-3). Am Welding.
--Specification for Steel, Carbon, Covered Arc Welding Electrodes: A5.1. 1981. 8.00 (ISBN 0-686-43345-9). Am Welding.
--Specification for Steel, Low-Alloy Covered Arc Welding Electrodes: A5.5. 1981. write for info. Am Welding.
--Specification for Steel, Low-Alloy Electrodes & Fluxes for Submerged Arc Welding: A5.23. 1980. 8.00 (ISBN 0-686-43380-7). Am Welding.
--Specification for Steel, Low-Alloy Filler Metals for Gas Shielded Arc Welding: A5.28. 1979. 8.00 (ISBN 0-686-43352-1). Am Welding.
--Specification for Steel, Low-Alloy Flux Cored Arc Welding Electrodes: A5.29. 1980. 8.00 (ISBN 0-686-43360-2). Am Welding.
--Specification for Steels, Consumables Used for Electroslag Welding of Carbon & High Strength Low Alloy: A5.25. 1978. 8.00 (ISBN 0-686-43354-8). Am Welding.
--Specification for Steels, Consumables Used for Electrogas Welding of Carbon & High Strength Low Alloy: A5.26. 1978. 8.00 (ISBN 0-686-43356-4). Am Welding.
--Specification for Surface Welding Rods & Electrodes. 1980. Composite. 8.00 (ISBN 0-686-43346-7, A5.21); Solid. 8.00 (ISBN 0-686-43347-5, A5.13). Am Welding.
--Specification for Titanium & Titanium-Alloy Bare Welding Rods & Electrodes: A5.16-70. 1970. 8.00 (ISBN 0-685-65978-X). Am Welding.
--Specification for Tungsten Arc-Welding Electrodes: A5.12. 1980. 8.00 (ISBN 0-685-65974-7). Am Welding.
--Specification for Welding Industrial & Mill Cranes. 1970. 8.00 (ISBN 0-686-43384-X). Am Welding.
--Specification for Welding of Presses & Press Components. 83p. 1980. 18.00 (ISBN 0-686-43385-8). Am Welding.
--Specification for Welding of Sheet Metal: D9.1. 1980. 15.00 (ISBN 0-686-43348-3). Am Welding.
--Specification for Zirconium & Zirconium Alloy Bare Welding Rods & Electrodes: A 5.24. 1979. 8.00 (ISBN 0-686-43343-2). Am Welding.
--Specifications for Aluminum & Aluminum-Alloy Bare Welding Rods & Bare Electrodes: A5.10. 1980. 8.00 (ISBN 0-685-65972-0). Am Welding.
--Specifications for Aluminum & Aluminum-Alloy Covered Arc-Welding Electrodes: A5.3. 1980. 8.00 (ISBN 0-685-65965-8). Am Welding.

--Specifications for Composite Surfacing Welding Rods & Electrodes: A5.21. 1980. 8.00 (ISBN 0-685-65982-8). Am Welding.
--Specifications for Copper & Copper-Alloy Gas Welding Rods: A5.27. 1978. 8.00 (ISBN 0-685-65969-0). Am Welding.
--Standard Methods for Mechanical Testing of Welds: B4.0. 1977. 10.00 (ISBN 0-685-65990-9). Am Welding.
--Standard Qualification Procedure. 12.00 o.p. (ISBN 0-685-65989-5). Am Welding.
--Surfacing Welding Rods & Electrodes: A5.13-70. 3.50 o.p. (ISBN 0-685-65975-5). Am Welding.
--Terms for Ultrasonic Testing in 11 Languages. 102p. 1967. 8.00 (ISBN 0-686-43363-7). Am Welding.
--The Welding Environment. new ed. LC 72-95119. (Illus.). 160p. (Orig.). 1973. pap. text ed. 28.00 (ISBN 0-87171-103-6). Am Welding.
--Welding Fume Control: A Demonstration Project. 65p. 1982. 20.00 (ISBN 0-686-43388-2). Am Welding.
--Welding Fume Control with Mechanical Ventilation. 1981. 8.00 (ISBN 0-686-43342-4). Am Welding.
--Welding Inspection. 222p. 1980. 25.00 (ISBN 0-685-65988-7, WI). Am Welding.
--Welding Inspection & Quality Assurance. text ed. 10.00 o.p. (ISBN 0-685-65953-4); instr's manual 2.50 o.p. (ISBN 0-685-65954-2); slides 105.00 o.p. (ISBN 0-685-65955-0). Am Welding.
--Welding Rods & Covered Electrodes for Welding Cast Iron: A5.15-69. 3.50 o.p. (ISBN 0-685-65977-1). Am Welding.

American Welding Society, ed. see International Thermal Spraying Conference, 8th.

American Welding Society, Arc Welding & Arc Cutting Committee. Recommended Practices for Plasma-Arc Welding, C5.1-73. LC 73-88838. (Illus.). 78p. (Orig.). 1973. pap. text ed. 8.00 (ISBN 0-87171-107-9). Am Welding.

American Welding Society Committee on Thermal Spraying. Nineteen-Year Report of Tests of Flame-Sprayed Coated Steels, C2.14-74. (Illus.). 40p. (Orig.). 1974. pap. text ed. 10.00 (ISBN 0-87171-111-7). Am Welding.

American Welding Society. Committee on Filler Metal. Specification for Carbon Steel Filler Metals for Gas Shielded Arc Welding: AWS A5.18. LC 79-50636. 1979. pap. 8.00 (ISBN 0-87171-173-7). Am Welding.

American Welding Society, Committee on Definitons, Symbols, Metric Practice. Symbols for Welding & Nondestructive Testing: A2.4-76. rev ed. (Illus.). 1976. pap. 6.00 o.p. (ISBN 0-87171-130-3). Am Welding.

American Welding Society, Inc. Arc Welding & Cutting Noise. LC 79-51314. (Illus.). 1979. pap. 20.00 (ISBN 0-87171-176-1). Am Welding.
--Recommended Practices for Welding Austenitic Chromium-Nickel Stainless Steel Piping & Tubing: AWS D10.4. LC 79-51316. (Illus.). 1979. pap. 6.00 (ISBN 0-87171-175-3). Am Welding.

American Welding Society, Standards Committee. Safety in Welding & Cutting: Z49.1-73. rev. 4th ed. (Illus.). 70p. (Orig.). 1973. pap. text ed. 15.00 (ISBN 0-87171-104-4). Am Welding.

American Welding Society, Technical Department. Welding Zinc-Coated Steels: D19.0-72. LC 72-91061. 140p. 1972. pap. text ed. 6.00 o.p. (ISBN 0-87171-102-8). Am Welding.

Amerine, M. A. & Ough, C. S. Methods for Analysis of Musts & Wines. LC 79-17791. 341p. 1980. 43.95x (ISBN 0-471-05077-6, Pub. by Wiley-Interscience). Wiley.

Amerine, Maynard A., jt. auth. see Stewart, George F.

Ameringer. Democracy in Costa Rica. 154p. 1982. 20.95 (ISBN 0-03-062158-5). Praeger.

Amerongen, C. Van see Bruggeling, Ir A.

Amersfoort, Hans Van see Van Amersfoort, Hans.

Amery & Hindley. Letters, Numbers, & Colors. (Younger Books Ser.). (gr. k-2). 1979. 5.95 (ISBN 0-686-36309-4, Usborne-Hayes). EDC.

Amery, Colin. National Theatre: An Architectural Guide. (Illus.). 1977. 10.00 o.p. (ISBN 0-85139-442-6, Pub. by Architectural Pr). Nichols Pub.

Amery, Heather. The Know How Book of Experiments. LC 78-17788. (Know How Books). (gr. 4-5). 1978. text ed. 7.95 (ISBN 0-88436-531-X). EMC.

Amery, Heather & Adair, Ian. The Know How Book of Jokes & Tricks. LC 78-14807. (Know How Books). (gr. 4-5). 1978. text ed. 7.95 (ISBN 0-88436-530-1). EMC.

Ames & Ilg. Your Three-Year Old: Friend or Enemy. 1980. pap. 5.95 (ISBN 0-440-59478-2, Delta). Dell.
--Your Two Year Old: Terrible or Tender. 1980. pap. 5.95 (ISBN 0-440-59477-4, Delta). Dell.

Ames, Agnes. Ames Ancestry-Europe to Maine. enl. ed. LC 79-91192. 210p. 1982. pap. 20.00 (ISBN 0-941216-05-5). Cay Bel.

Ames, Agnes H. Ames Ancestry: Europe to Maine. LC 79-91992. (Illus., Orig.). 1979. 20.00x o.p. (ISBN 0-9603714-1-9); pap. 15.00x (ISBN 0-9603714-2-7). Cay-Bel.

Ames, Amyas. Private Lives of Our Natural Neighbors. 1980. 15.00 (ISBN 0-8076-0960-9); pap. 8.95 (ISBN 0-8076-0961-7). Braziller.

Ames, Bernice. In Syllables of Stars. 1958. 2.50 o.p. (ISBN 0-8233-0004-8). Golden Quill.

Ames, Bruce, et al, eds. Banbury Report 5: Ethyl Chloride: A Potential Health Risk? LC 80-7677. (Banbury eport Ser.: Vol. 5). (Illus.). 350p. 1980. 45.00x (ISBN 0-87969-204-9). Cold Spring Harbor.

Ames, Delano. Corpse Diplomatique. LC 82-48239. 256p. 1983. pap. 2.84i (ISBN 0-06-080637-0, P 637, PL). Har-Row.
--For Old Crime's Sake. LC 82-47790. 256p. 1983. pap. 2.84i (ISBN 0-06-080629-X, P 629, PL). Har-Row.
--Murder, Maestro, Please. LC 82-47791. 224p. 1983. pap. 2.84i (ISBN 0-06-080630-3, P 630, PL). Har-Row.
--She Shall Have Murder. LC 82-48240. 272p. 1983. pap. 2.84i (ISBN 0-06-080638-9, P 638, PL). Har-Row.

Ames, Evelyn. Glimpse of Eden. LC 67-11908. 1977. 12.95 (ISBN 0-910220-80-8). Berg.

Ames, Felicia. The Bird You Care For. Date not set. pap. 1.75 (ISBN 0-451-07527-7, E7527, Sig). NAL.
--Cat You Care For: A Manual of Cat Care. (Illus., Orig.). 1968. pap. 1.75 o.p. (ISBN 0-451-07862-4, E7862, Sig). NAL.
--Dog You Care For. (Illus., Orig.). (RL 5). 1968. pap. 1.75 o.p. (ISBN 0-451-07860-8, E7860, Sig). NAL.

Ames, Francis. Callahan Goes South. 1977. lib. bdg. 10.95 o.p. (ISBN 0-8161-6457-6, Large Print Bks). G K Hall.

Ames, Gerald & Wyler, Rose. Spooky Tricks. LC 68-16822. (I Can Read Bks.). (Illus.). (gr. k-3). 1968. 6.95 o.p. (ISBN 0-06-026633-3, HarpJ); PLB 8.89g (ISBN 0-06-026634-1). Har-Row.

Ames, Herman V., ed. State Documents on Federal Relations. LC 78-77697. (American Constitutional & Legal History Ser). 1970. Repr. of 1900 ed. lib. bdg. 42.50 (ISBN 0-306-71335-7). Da Capo.

Ames, J. Systems Study of Odorous Industrial Processes, 1979. 1981. 75.00x (ISBN 0-686-97144-2, Pub. by W Spring England). State Mutual Bk.

Ames, John, jt. auth. see Richards, Renee.

Ames, Lee. Graff-a-Doodle Do. (Illus.). 96p. 1981. pap. 3.95 (ISBN 0-686-69181-4, G&D). Putnam Pub Group.

Ames, Lee & MacClain, George. Cosmic Doodle Doo. (Illus.). 96p. (gr. k-3). 1982. pap. 3.95 (ISBN 0-448-11981-1, G&D). Putnam Pub Group.

Ames, Lee J. Draw Draw Draw. LC 62-7025. (gr. 3-9). 8.95a (ISBN 0-385-12767-7); PLB (ISBN 0-385-03388-5). Doubleday.
--Draw Fifty Airplanes, Aircraft & Spacecraft. LC 76-51554. (gr. 1 up). 1977. 8.95a (ISBN 0-385-12235-7); PLB (ISBN 0-385-12236-5). Doubleday.
--Draw Fifty Animals. LC 73-13083. 64p. (gr. 3-7). 1974. 8.95a (ISBN 0-385-07712-2); PLB (ISBN 0-385-07726-2). Doubleday.
--Draw Fifty Boats, Ships, Trucks & Trains. LC 75-19011. 64p. (gr. 1 up). 1976. 8.95a (ISBN 0-385-08903-1); PLB (ISBN 0-385-08904-X). Doubleday.
--Draw Fifty Buildings & Other Structures. LC 79-7483. (Illus.). (gr. 2 up). 1980. 8.95a (ISBN 0-385-14400-8); PLB (ISBN 0-385-14401-6). Doubleday.
--Draw Fifty Dinosaurs & Other Prehistoric Animals. LC 76-7285. (gr. 1 up). 1977. 8.95a (ISBN 0-385-11134-7); PLB (ISBN 0-385-11135-5). Doubleday.
--Draw Fifty Dogs. LC 79-6853. (Illus.). 64p. (gr. 4-6). 1981. 8.95a (ISBN 0-385-15686-3); PLB (ISBN 0-385-15687-1). Doubleday.
--Draw Fifty Famous Cartoons. LC 78-1176. 1979. 8.95a (ISBN 0-385-13661-7); PLB (ISBN 0-385-13662-5). Doubleday.
--Draw Fifty Famous Faces. LC 77-15878. (gr. 1 up). 1978. 8.95a (ISBN 0-385-13217-4); PLB (ISBN 0-385-13218-2). Doubleday.
--Draw Fifty Monsters, Creeps, Superheroes, Demons, Dragons, Nerds, Dirts, Ghouls, Giants, Vampires, Zombies, & Other Curiosa. LC 80-3006. (Illus.). 64p. (gr. 1 up). 1983. 8.95a (ISBN 0-385-17637-6); PLB (ISBN 0-385-17638-4). Doubleday.
--Draw Fifty Vehicles. LC 77-94862. (gr. 1 up). 1978. pap. 3.50 (ISBN 0-385-14154-8). Doubleday.

Ames, Louise B. Your Three Year Old. 1976. 10.95 (ISBN 0-440-09883-1). Delacorte.
--Your Two Year Old. 1976. 10.95 (ISBN 0-440-09882-3). Delacorte.

Ames, Louise B. & Chase, Joan A. Don't Push Your Preschooler. rev. ed. LC 80-8192. 240p. 1981. 12.45i (ISBN 0-06-010083-4, HarpT). Har-Row.

Ames, Louise B. & Ilg, Frances L. Your Five Year Old. 1979. 10.95 (ISBN 0-440-09876-9). Delacorte.
--Your Five Year Old: Sunny & Serene. 1981. pap. 5.95 (ISBN 0-440-59494-4, Delta). Dell.
--Your Four Year Old. 1976. 10.95 (ISBN 0-440-09884-X). Delacorte.
--Your Six Year Old. 1979. 10.95 (ISBN 0-440-09877-7). Delacorte.

Ames, Louise B., jt. auth. see Ilg, Frances L.

Ames, Louise B., et al. The Gesell Institute's Child from One to Six: Evaluating the Behavior of the Pre-School Child. LC 79-1795. (Illus.). 1979. 13.41i (ISBN 0-06-010087-7, HarpT). Har-Row.
--Your One-Year-Old: The Fun-Loving, Fussy 12-to-24-Month Old. (Illus.). 1983. pap. 5.95 (Delta). Dell.

Ames, Margery E., jt. ed. see Nelson, Ted.

Ames, Marjorie. Miniature Macrame for Dollhouses. 1981. pap. 2.25 (ISBN 0-486-23960-8). Dover.

Ames, Mary E. Outcome Uncertain: Science & the Political Process. 1982. pap. 3.50 (ISBN 0-380-59535-4, 59535, Discus). Avon.

Ames, Michael D. & Wellsfry, Norval L. Small Business Management. (Illus.). 450p. 1983. text ed. 19.95 (ISBN 0-314-69631-8). West Pub.

Ames, Roger T. The Art of Rulership: A Study in Ancient Chinese Political Thought. LC 82-25917. 1983. 25.00x (ISBN 0-8248-0825-8). UH Pr.

Ames, Russell E., Jr., jt. ed. see Mankin, Don.

Ames, Seth, ed. Works of Fisher Ames, 2 Vols. LC 69-14409. (American Scene Ser). 1969. Repr. of 1854 ed. Set. lib. bdg. 89.50 (ISBN 0-306-71122-2). Da Capo.

Ames, Thomas E., jt. auth. see Saylor, William L.

Ames, William. The Marrow of Theology. Eusden, John D., ed. & tr. from Latin. Orig. Title: Medulla Theologiae. xiv, 354p. 1983. pap. 14.95 (ISBN 0-939464-14-4). Labyrinth Pr.

Ames, William, tr. see Ovsiannikov, L. V.

Ames-Lewis, Francis. Drawing in Early Renaissance Italy. LC 81-40434. (Illus.). 196p. 1981. 45.00x (ISBN 0-300-02551-3). Yale U Pr.
--Drawing in Early Renaissance Italy. pap. 14.95 (ISBN 0-686-42818-8, Y-447). Yale U Pr.
--Drawings in Early Renaissance Italy. LC 81-40434. (Illus.). 208p. 1983. pap. 14.95 (ISBN 0-300-02978-0, Y-447). Yale U Pr.

Amey, J., jt. auth. see Coveney, James.

Amey, Peter. Imperialism. Yapp, Malcolm, et al, eds. (World History Ser.). (Illus.). (gr. 10). 1980. Repr. of 1977 ed. lib. bdg. 6.95 (ISBN 0-89908-226-2); pap. text ed. 2.25 (ISBN 0-89908-201-7). Greenhaven.
--Pax Romana. Yapp, Malcolm, et al, eds. (World History Ser.). (Illus.). 32p. (gr. 10). 1980. Repr. of 1977 ed. lib. bdg. 6.95 (ISBN 0-89908-027-8); pap. text ed. 2.25 (ISBN 0-89908-002-2). Greenhaven.
--The Scientific Revolution. Yapp, Malcolm, et al, eds. (World History Ser.). (Illus.). (gr. 10). 1980. lib. bdg. 6.95 (ISBN 0-89908-132-0); pap. text ed. 2.25 (ISBN 0-89908-107-X). Greenhaven.

Amey, Peter, et al. Leonardo Da Vinci. Yapp, Malcolm, et al, eds. (World History Ser.). (Illus.). (gr. 10). 1980. lib. bdg. 6.95 (ISBN 0-89908-041-3); pap. text ed. 2.25 (ISBN 0-89908-016-2). Greenhaven.
--Luther, Erasmus & Loyola. Yapp, Malcolm, et al, eds. (World History Ser.). (Illus.). (gr. 10). 1980. lib. bdg. 6.95 (ISBN 0-89908-043-X); pap. text ed. 2.25 (ISBN 0-89908-018-9). Greenhaven.

Amherst Student. The Student Guide to Fellowships & Internships. 356p. 1980. 15.95 o.p. (ISBN 0-525-93155-4); pap. 7.95 o.p. (ISBN 0-525-93147-3). Dutton.

Amichai, Yehuda. Amen. LC 76-50164. 1977. 7.95 (ISBN 0-06-010090-7, HarpT); pap. 4.95i (ISBN 0-06-010089-3, TD-278, HarpT). Har-Row.
--Time. LC 78-66388. 1979. 10.53i (ISBN 0-06-010088-5, HarpT). Har-Row.

Amick, Daniel J. & Walberg, Herbert, eds. Introductory Multivariate Analysis (for Educational Psychological and Social Research) LC 74-30754. (Illus.). 275p. 1975. 20.75 o.p. (ISBN 0-8211-0013-0); text ed. 18.95 in ten or more copies o.p. (ISBN 0-685-52138-9). McCutchan.

Amick, Robert, jt. auth. see Brennecke, John.

Amick, Robert G., jt. auth. see Brennecke, John H.

Amick, Robert G., jt. auth. see Brennecke, John J.

Amidon, Eva V. Easy Quillery: Projects with Paper Coils & Scrolls. (Illus.). (gr. 3-8). 1977. 8.95 (ISBN 0-688-22130-0); PLB 8.59 (ISBN 0-688-32130-5). Morrow.

Amiel, J. J. Hawks. LC 79-10989. 1979. 11.95 o.p. (ISBN 0-399-12312-1). Putnam Pub Group.

Amiel, Leon. Homage to Chagall. (Twentieth Century Art Ser.). (Illus.). 1982. 24.95 (ISBN 0-8148-0725-9). L Amiel Pub.

Amiel, M. & Moreau, J. F., eds. Contrast Media in Radiology, Appraisal & Prospects, Lyon 1981: Proceedings. (Illus.). 370p. 1982. 31.20 (ISBN 0-387-11534-X). Springer-Verlag.

Amiel, S., ed. Nondestructive Activation Analysis: With Nuclear Reactors & Radioactive Neutron Sources. (Studies in Analytical Chemistry: Vol. 3). 1981. 72.50 (ISBN 0-444-41942-X). Elsevier.

Amiel-Tison, Claudine & Grenier, Albert. Neurologic Examination of the Infant & Newborn. Steichen, Jean J., tr. (Illus.). 160p. 1982. write for info. (ISBN 0-89352-164-7). Masson Pub.

Amigo, Eleanor & Neuffer, Mark. Beyond the Adirondacks: The Story of St. Regis Paper Company. LC 80-1798. (Contributions in Economics & Economic History: No. 35). (Illus.). xi, 219p. 1980. lib. bdg. 25.00x (ISBN 0-313-22735-7, AFN/). Greenwood.

Amin, Mohamed & Willetts, Duncan. Journey Through Pakistan. (Illus.). 256p. 1982. 39.95 (ISBN 0-370-30489-6, Pub. by Chatto-Bodley-Jonathan). Merrimack Bk Serv.

Amin, R. & Faruqee, F. Fertility & Its Regulation in Bangladesh. (Working Paper: No. 383). iv, 50p. 1980. 5.00 (ISBN 0-686-36196-2, WP-0383). World Bank.

Amin, Samir. The Arab Economy Today. Pallis, M., tr. from French. 128p. 1982. 25.00 (ISBN 0-86232-081-X, Pub. by Zed Pr England). Lawrence Hill.
--The Arab Nation: Nationalism & Class Struggle. 116p. 1978. 19.95 (ISBN 0-905762-22-3, Pub. by Zed Pr England); pap. 6.50 (ISBN 0-905762-23-1, Pub. by Zed Pr England). Lawrence Hill.
--Dynamics of Global Crises. Arrighi, Giovanni, et al, eds. LC 81-84739. 288p. 1982. 18.00 (ISBN 0-85345-605-4, CL6054); pap. 7.50 (ISBN 0-85345-606-2, PB6062). Monthly Rev.
--The Future of Maoism. Finkelstein, Norman, tr. from Fr. LC 82-48035. 128p. 1983. 12.00 (ISBN 0-85345-622-4, CL6224); pap. 6.50 (ISBN 0-85345-623-2, PB6232). Monthly Rev.
--Imperialism & Unequal Development. LC 77-7619. 1979. pap. 5.00 (ISBN 0-85345-499-X, PB-499X). Monthly Rev.
--Imperialism & Unequal Development. LC 77-7619. 1977. 12.95 (ISBN 0-85345-418-3, CL-4183). Monthly Rev.
--The Law of Value & Historical Materialism. LC 78-15210. 1978. 6.50 (ISBN 0-85345-470-1, CL-4701). Monthly Rev.

Amin, Samir, ed. Modern Migrations in Western Africa: Studies Presented & Discussed at the 11th Int'l African Seminar, Dakar, 4/1972. (International African Institute Ser.). 428p. 1974. 37.50x o.p. (ISBN 0-19-724193-X). Oxford U Pr.

Amin, Sayed H. International & Legal Problems of the Gulf. (Illus.). 235p. 1982. lib. bdg. 35.00 (ISBN 0-906559-05-7). Westview.

Aminzade, Ronald. Class, Politics, & Early Industrial Capitalism: A Study of Mid-Nineteenth-Century Toulouse, France. LC 80-28284. (European Social History Ser.). (Illus.). 230p. 1981. 34.50x (ISBN 0-87395-528-5); pap. 10.95x (ISBN 0-87395-529-3). State U NY Pr.

Amiri, Imanu see Harrison, Paul C.

Amir-Moez, Ali R. & Menzel, Donald H. Fun with Numbers: Lines & Angles. (Handbooks Ser.). (gr. 3-6). 1981. pap. 1.95 (ISBN 0-87534-179-9). Highlights.

Amirthanayagam, G. & Harrex, S. C., eds. Only Connect: Literary Perspectives East & West. 335p. 1981. pap. text ed. 19.95x (ISBN 0-7258-0197-2, Pub. by Flinders U Australia). Humanities.

Amirthanayagam, Guy. Asian & Western Writers in Dialogue. 224p. 1982. text ed. 25.25x (ISBN 0-333-27341-9, Pub. by Macmillan England). Humanities.

Amis, Martin. Invasion of the Space Invaders. 128p. 1982. pap. 9.95 (ISBN 0-89087-351-8). Celestial Arts.

Amissah, A. N. The Contribution of the Courts to Government: A West African View. 392p. 1981. text ed. 57.00x (ISBN 0-19-825356-7). Oxford U Pr.

Amit, Daniel A. Field Theory: The Renormalization Group & Critical Phenomena. (International Series in Pure & Applied Physics). (Illus.). 1978. text ed. 39.50 o.p. (ISBN 0-07-001575-9, C). McGraw.

Amit, Raphael, jt. ed. see Avriel, Mordecai.

Amitsur, S. A & Saltman, D. J., eds. Algebraists' Homage: Papers in Ring Theory & Related Topics. LC 82-18934. (Contemporary Mathematics Ser.: vol. 13). 30.00 (ISBN 0-8218-5013-X, CONM/13). Am Math.

Amjad, Rashid. Private Industrial Investment in Pakistan, 1960-1970. LC 81-17996. (Cambridge South Asian Studies: No. 26). 256p. 1983. 44.50 (ISBN 0-521-23261-9). Cambridge U Pr.

Amjad, Rashid, ed. The Development of Labou-Intensive Industry in ASEAN Countries. 337p. 1981. 15.00 (ISBN 92-2-102750-3); pap. 10.00 (ISBN 92-2-102751-1). Intl Labour Office.

Amkreutz, Johann, jt. ed. see Wilhelm, Carl.

Amling, Fred. Plaid for Principles of Investments. 1977. pap. 5.95 o.p. (ISBN 0-256-02003-5, 06-0815-02). Dow Jones-Irwin.

Amling, Frederick. Investments. 5th ed. (Illus.). 704p. 1984. 25.95 (ISBN 0-13-504324-7). P-H.
--Investments: An Introduction to Analysis & Management. 4th ed. (Illus.). 1978. ref. 24.95 (ISBN 0-13-504308-5). P-H.
--Principles of Investment. 3rd ed. (Plaid Ser.). 198p. 1983. pap. 12.95 (ISBN 0-87094-336-7). Dow Jones-Irwin.

Ammer, Christine. The A to Z of Women's Health: A Concise Encyclopedia. LC 82-9778. (Illus.). 512p. 1983. pap. 13.95 (ISBN 0-89696-173-7, An Everest House Book). Dodd.
--Harper's Dictionary of Music. LC 77-134280. (Illus.). 1972. 19.18i (ISBN 0-06-010113-X, HarpT). Har-Row.
--Harper's Dictionary of Music. (Illus.). 414p. 1973. pap. 5.50 (ISBN 0-06-463347-0, EH 347). B&N NY.
--Musician's Handbook of Foreign Terms. 1971. pap. 6.95 (ISBN 0-02-870100-3). Schirmer Bks.
--Unsung: A History of Women in American Music. LC 79-52324. (Contributions in Women's Studies: No. 14). 1980. lib. bdg. 29.95x (ISBN 0-313-22007-7, AMU/); pap. text ed. 7.95 (ISBN 0-313-22909-0, AMU). Greenwood.

Ammer, Christine & Sidley, Nathan T. The Common Sense Guide to Mental Health Care. 1982. cancelled (ISBN 0-86616-020-5); pap. 10.95 (ISBN 0-86616-019-1). Greene.

Ammer, Dean S. Manufacturing Management & Control. (Illus.). 1968. pap. 12.95 (ISBN 0-13-555839-5). P-H.

--Purchasing & Materials Management for Health Care Institutions. LC 74-11416. (Illus.). 1975. 18.95 (ISBN 0-669-95604-X). Lexington Bks.

Ammerman, Robert R., ed. Classics of Analytic Philosophy. 1964. 14.95 o.p. (ISBN 0-07-001580-5, C). McGraw.

Ammon, G. A. Soviet Navy in War & Peace. 160p. 1981. 5.80 (ISBN 0-8285-2223-5, Pub. by Progress Pubs USSR). Imported Pubns.

Ammons, A. R. Lake Effect Country: Poems. 1983. 15.50 (ISBN 0-393-01702-8); pap. 5.95 (ISBN 0-393-30104-4). Norton.

Amnesty International. The Amnesty International Report on Torture. 285p. 1975. 8.95 o.p. (ISBN 0-374-24937-7); pap. 4.95 o.p. (ISBN 0-374-51154-3). FS&G.

Amneus, Nils. Life's Riddle. 1975. pap. 5.25 (ISBN 0-913004-26-X). Point Loma Pub.

Amoia, Alba, jt. ed. see Stebbins, Richard P.

Amoia, Alba della Fazia. Edmond Rostand. (World Authors Ser.). 1978. lib. bdg. 15.95 (ISBN 0-8057-6260-4, Twayne). G K Hall.

--Jean Anouilh. (World Authors Ser.). lib. bdg. 12.95 (ISBN 0-8057-2048-0, Twayne). G K Hall.

Amon, Aline. Road Runners & Other Cuckoos. LC 78-6648. (Illus.). (gr. 5-9). 1978. 7.95 o.p. (ISBN 0-689-30646-6). Atheneum.

Amon, Frank. Othello, Macbeth, & King Lear: A Formal Approach. LC 78-58445. 1978. pap. text ed. 9.50 (ISBN 0-8191-0533-3). U Pr of Amer.

Amon, Von. Broken Dolls. LC 81-14943. 1983. 16.95 (ISBN 0-87949-183-3). Ashley Bks.

Amon-Ra, Juba. Flights into Time. LC 80-81579. (Illus.). 52p. (Orig.). 1980. 7.50 o.p. (ISBN 0-936874-01-5, JNP-01); pap. 4.50 o.p. (ISBN 0-936874-00-7, JNP-00); special ed. 15.00 o.p. (ISBN 0-936874-02-3, JNP-02). Joyful Noise.

Amore, Adelaide, ed. A Woman's Inner World: Selected Poetry & Prose of Anne Bradstreet. LC 82-40198. 152p. (Orig.). 1982. lib. bdg. 19.50 (ISBN 0-8191-2639-X); pap. text ed. 8.25 (ISBN 0-8191-2640-3). U Pr of Amer.

Amore, Roy C., ed. Developments in Buddhist Thought: Canadian Contributions to Buddhist Studies. 196p. 1979. pap. text ed. 7.00x (ISBN 0-919812-11-2, Pub. by Wilfrid Laurier U Pr Canada). Humanities.

Amoretti, Giovanni see Marchione, Margherita & Scalia, S. Eugene.

Amory, Hugh & Munby, A. N., eds. Sales Catalogues of Libraries of Eminent Persons: Poets & Men of Letters, Atterbury, Blair, Fielding, Goldsmith, Mallet & Lady Mary Wortley Montagu, Vol. 7. 256p. 1974. 20.00 o.p. (ISBN 0-7201-0366-5, Pub. by Mansell England). Wilson.

Amory, Martha B. The Domestic & Artistic Life of John Singleton Copley. LC 71-77698. (Library of American Art Ser). 1969. Repr. of 1882 ed. lib. bdg. 45.00 (ISBN 0-306-71336-5). Da Capo.

Amos, D. Fish Handling & Preservation at Sea: A Fisherman's Guide to Various Methods of Handling & Preserving Fish on Board Fishing Vessels. (Marine Bulletin Ser.: No. 45). 28p. 1981. 2.00 (ISBN 0-938412-23-X, P889). URI Mas.

--A Fisherman's Guide to Echo Soundings & Sonar Equipment: Acoustic Fish Detection Instruments. (Marine Bulletin Ser.: No. 41). 68p. 1980. 2.00 (ISBN 0-938412-30-2, P870). URI Mas.

--Single Vessel Midwater Trawling. (Marine Bulletin Ser.: No. 43). 30p. 1980. 2.00 (ISBN 0-938412-26-4, P872). URI Mas.

Amos, Dan. Soils & Its Uses. 1979. text ed. 15.95 (ISBN 0-8359-7038-8); instrs' manual avail. Reston.

Amos, John M. & Sarchet, Bernard R. Management for Engineers. (Series in Industrial Systems Engineering). (Illus.). 384p. 1981. text ed. 21.95 (ISBN 0-13-549402-8). P-H.

Amos, Martha T. Fanny Runs the Bass Lake Runaround. 48p. (gr. 1-6). 1983. 5.95 (ISBN 0-8059-2861-8). Dorrance.

Amos, S. W., ed. Radio, T V & Audio Technical Reference Book. (Illus.). 1172p. 1977. 129.95 (ISBN 0-408-00259-X). Focal Pr.

Amos, Sheldon. Political & Legal Remedies for War. 254p. 1982. Repr. of 1880 ed. lib. bdg. 24.00x (ISBN 0-8377-0213-5). Rothman.

Amos, W. B. & Duckett, J. G., eds. Prokaryotic & Euraryotic Flagella. LC 81-38467. (Society for Experimental Biology Symposia: No. 35). 450p. 1982. 79.50 (ISBN 0-521-24228-2). Cambridge U Pr.

Amos, William E. & Manella, Raymond L., eds. Delinquent Children in Juvenile Correctional Institutions: State Administered Reception & Diagnostic Centers. (Illus.). 176p. 1973. 14.75x (ISBN 0-398-00040-9). C C Thomas.

Amos, William E., jt. ed. see Newman, Charles L.

Amos, William H. Life of the Pond. (Our Living World of Nature Ser). 1967. 14.95 (ISBN 0-07-001586-4, P&RB); by subscription 3.95 (ISBN 0-07-046009-4). McGraw.

--Life of the Seashore. (Our Living World of Nature Ser.). (gr. 7 up). 1966. 14.95 (ISBN 0-07-001585-6, P&RB); subscription 12.95by (ISBN 0-07-046004-3). McGraw.

Amos, Winsom. Youth Poems. (Illus.). 24p. (Orig.). (gr. 6-12). 1982. pap. 1.75 (ISBN 0-932510-00-0). Soma Pr.

Amoss, Harold L., ed. see Western Resources Conference, 3rd, Colorado State University, 1961.

Amoss, Pamela T. & Harrell, Stevan, eds. Other Ways of Growing Old: Anthropological Perspectives. LC 79-66056. 1981. 18.50x (ISBN 0-8047-1072-4); pap. 7.95 (ISBN 0-8047-1153-4, SP 13). Stanford U Pr.

Amphoto & Eastman Kodak Staff, ed. Photo Topics & Techniques. (Illus.). 192p. 1980. 14.95 o.p. (ISBN 0-8174-5537-X, Amphoto). Watson-Guptill.

Amphoto Corporation. Thirty-Five Millimeter Photography Simplified. rev. ed. (Modern Photo Guides Ser). (Illus.). 96p. 1974. Repr. 7.95t (ISBN 0-13-918888-6, Spec). P-H.

Amphoto Editorial Board. Official Nikon Nikkormat Manual. 7th ed. (Illus.). 160p. 1975. 8.95 o.p. (ISBN 0-8174-0582-8, Amphoto). Watson-Guptill.

--Official Nikon Nikkormat Manual. 8th ed. (Illus.). 1979. 11.95 o.p. (ISBN 0-8174-2464-4, Amphoto). Watson-Guptill.

Amphoto Editorial Board, jt. auth. see Ahlers, Arvel.

Amphoux, Nancy, tr. see Deshimaru, Taisen.

Amram, David. Makers of Hebrew Books in Italy. 350p. Date not set. 60.00 (ISBN 0-87556-013-X). Saifer.

Amrine, Frederick, tr. see Steiner, Rudolf.

Amrine, Harold & Ritchey, John A. Manufacturing Organization & Management. 4th ed. (Illus.). 576p. 1982. 25.95 (ISBN 0-13-555748-8). P-H.

Amritananda Das. Foundations of Gandhian Economics. LC 79-17126. 1979. 14.95x o.p. (ISBN 0-312-30005-0). St Martin.

Amsbury, Wayne. Structured Basic & Beyond. (Illus.). 1980. pap. text ed. 14.95x (ISBN 0-914894-16-1). Computer Sci.

Amsden, Alice H., ed. The Economics of Women & Work. LC 80-15970. 1980. 18.95 o.p. (ISBN 0-312-23670-0); pap. 9.95 (ISBN 0-312-23671-9). St Martin.

Amsden, Thomas W. Stratigraphy & Paleontology of the Brownsport Formation (Silurian) of Western Tennessee. 1949. 65.00x (ISBN 0-686-50033-4). Elliots Bks.

AMSS. Some Aspects of the Economics of Zakah. Date not set. price not set (ISBN 0-89259-019-X). Am Trust Pubns.

Amstadter, Bertram L. Reliability Mathematics Fundamental Practical Procedures. 1971. 31.50 o.p. (ISBN 0-07-001598-8, P&RB). McGraw.

Amstead, B. H., et al. Manufacturing Processes. 7th ed. LC 78-16185. 739p. 1979. text ed. 41.95x (ISBN 0-471-03575-0); solutions manual avail. (ISBN 0-471-03679-X). Wiley.

Amstell, I. Joel. What You Should Know About Advertising. LC 69-19797. (Business Almanac Ser.: No. 17). (Illus.). 83p. 1969. 5.95 (ISBN 0-379-11217-5). Oceana.

Amsterdam, Ezra & Holmes, Ann. Take Care of Your Heart: The Complete Book of Heart Facts. (Illus., Orig.). Date not set. pap. 12.95 (ISBN 0-448-14589-8, G&D). Putnam Pub Group.

Amsterdam, Ezra A. & Holmes, Ann M. Take Care of Your Heart. (Illus.). 256p. 1983. 14.95 (ISBN 0-87196-731-6). Facts on File.

Amsterdamska, Olga, tr. see Karpinski, Jakub.

Amstrup, C. R., et al. Suggested Fertilizer: Related Policies for Government & International Agencies. (Technical Bulletin T-10). 67p. (Orig.). 1978. pap. 4.00 (ISBN 0-88090-009-1). Intl Fertilizer.

Amstutz, Beverly. Sprouts: A Diary for the Foster Child. (Illus.). 38p. (Orig.). (gr. k-7). 1982. pap. 2.50x (ISBN 0-937836-07-9). Precious Res.

--You Are Number One! (Illus.). 30p. (YA) (gr. 6-12). 1982. pap. 2.50x (ISBN 0-937836-08-7). Precious Res.

Amstutz, Mark R. Economics & Foreign Policy: A Guide to Information Sources. LC 74-11566. (Vol. 7). 1977. 42.00 (ISBN 0-8103-1321-9). Gale.

--An Introduction to Political Science: The Management of Conflict. 1982. pap. text ed. 14.50x (ISBN 0-673-16053-X). Scott F.

Amundson, Neal R. Mathematical Methods in Chemical Engineering: Matrices & Their Application. 1966. ref. ed. 31.95 (ISBN 0-13-561084-2). P-H.

Amur, G. S. Images & Impressions. 1980. text ed. 11.50x (ISBN 0-391-01917-1). Humanities.

Amuzegar, Jahangir. Comparative Economics: National Priorities, Policies, & Performance. 1981. text ed. 20.95 (ISBN 0-316-03801-6). Little.

Amy, William O. & Recob, James B. Human Nature in the Christian Tradition. LC 82-45049. 118p. (Orig.). 1982. lib. bdg. 19.50 (ISBN 0-8191-2512-1); pap. text ed. 8.25 (ISBN 0-8191-2513-X). U Pr of Amer.

Amyot, C. Grant. The Italian Communist Party. 1981. 26.00 (ISBN 0-312-43920-2). St Martin.

Amyx, James W., et al. Petroleum Reservoir Engineering Physical Properties. 1960. 38.95 (ISBN 0-07-001600-3, C). McGraw.

Amyx, Richard, rev. by see Grosswirth, Marvin.

Ana, Julio De Santa see De Santa Ana, Julio.

Anagnostakos, Nicholas P., jt. auth. see Tortora, Gerard J.

Anagnostopoulos, Athan, tr. see Kakavelakis, Demetris.

Anagnostopoulos, Athan, tr. see Nephele, Maria.

Anagnostou, C. Demetrius "On Style". A New Edition with Commentary. (London Studies in Classical Philology). 1980. pap. text ed. no price set (ISBN 0-391-01158-8). Humanities.

Analytical Chemistry in Energy Technology. Analytical Chemistry in Nuclear Technology: Proceedings of the 25th ORNL Conference. Lyon, W. S., ed. LC 81-70867. (Illus.). 402p. 1982. 29.95 (ISBN 0-250-40469-9). Ann Arbor Science.

Analytical Sciences Corp-Technical Staff. Applied Optimal Estimation. Gelb, Arthur, ed. LC 74-1604. (Illus.). 382p. 1974. pap. text ed. 12.50x (ISBN 0-262-57048-3). MIT Pr.

Ananaba, Wogu. The Trade Union Movement in Africa: Promise & Performance. 1979. 26.00x (ISBN 0-312-81221-3). St Martin.

Anand, J. P., jt. auth. see Namboodiri, P. K.

Anand, Kewal K. Indian Philosophy: The Concept of Karma. 396p. 1982. 34.95 (ISBN 0-940500-91-4, Pub by Bharatiya Vidya India). Asia Bk Corp.

Anand, Mulk R. Conversations in Bloomsbury. 128p. 1981. text ed. 8.75x o.p. (ISBN 0-391-02426-4). Humanities.

Anand, Mulk R., ed. The Kama Sutra of Vatsyayana. 1982. 175.00x (ISBN 0-85692-093-2, Pub. by J M Dent). State Mutual Bk.

Anand, R. P. & Quisumbing, Purificacion V., eds. ASEAN: Identity, Development & Culture. 441p. 1982. text ed. 17.50x (ISBN 0-8248-0810-X, Eastwest Ctr). UH Pr.

Anand, Shahla. Of Costliest Emblem: Paradise Lost & the Emblem Tradition. LC 78-59853. (Illus.). 1978. pap. text ed. 12.75 (ISBN 0-8191-0556-2). U Pr of Amer.

Ananda. Spiritual Practice. pap. 1.50 (ISBN 0-87481-155-4). Vedanta Pr.

Anandamurti, Shrii Shrii. Namami krsnasundaram - Salutations to Lord Krsna. 252p. 1981. pap. 4.00 (ISBN 0-686-95432-7). Ananda Marga.

Anandanagar. Caryacarya, Vol. I & II. Vol. I - 37 p. pap. 2.00 (ISBN 0-686-95445-9); Vol. II - 49 p. pap. 1.00 (ISBN 0-686-99507-4). Ananda Marga.

Anania, Michael. Color of Dust. LC 82-70324. (New Poetry Ser.: No. 40). 70p. 1970. 6.50 (ISBN 0-8040-0048-4); pap. 4.50 (ISBN 0-8040-0049-2). Swallow.

Anania, Michael, ed. New Poetry Anthology I. LC 82-71538. 111p. (Orig.). 1969. 7.95x (ISBN 0-8040-0224-X); pap. 4.95x (ISBN 0-8040-0225-8). Swallow.

Ananthanarayan, R. & Paniker, Jayaram. Textbook of Microbiology. 2nd ed. (Illus.). 618p. 1982. pap. text ed. 25.00x (ISBN 0-86131-293-7, Pub. by Orient Longman Ltd India). Apt Bks.

Anas, Alex, ed. Residential Location Markets & Urban Transportation: Economic Theory, Econometrics & Policy Analysis with Discrete Choice Models. 257p. 1982. 37.50 (ISBN 0-12-057920-0). Acad Pr.

Anastaplo, George. The Artist As Thinker: From Shakespeare to Joyce. LC 82-6502. 512p. 1983. lib. bdg. 32.95x (ISBN 0-8040-0416-1); pap. 14.95 (ISBN 0-8040-0417-X). Swallow.

--Human Being & Citizen: Essays on Virtue, Freedom & the Common Good. LC 82-73757. xiv, 332p. 1975. 16.95 (ISBN 0-8040-0677-6). Swallow.

--Human Being & Citizen: Essays on Virtue, Freedom & the Common Good. LC 82-73765. 1978. pap. 8.95 (ISBN 0-8040-0678-4). Swallow.

Anastas, Peter, jt. auth. see Parsons, Peter.

Anastasi, Anne. Differential Psychology. 3rd ed. (Illus.). 1958. text ed. 22.95 (ISBN 0-02-302800-9, 30280). Macmillan.

--Fields of Applied Psychology. 2nd ed. (Illus.). 1979. text ed. 25.95 (ISBN 0-07-001602-X, C); instructor's manual 8.95 (ISBN 0-07-001603-8). McGraw.

--Psychological Testing. 5th ed. 768p. 1982. text ed. 27.95 (ISBN 0-02-302960-9). Macmillan.

Anastasio, William T., ed. see Hall, Viviana C.

Anastasiou, C. J. Ascomycetes & Fungi Imperfecti from the Salton Sea. 1963. 6.40 (ISBN 3-7682-0210-0). Lubrecht & Cramer.

Anastasiow, Nicholas. Identifying the Developmentally Delayed Child. LC 81-21838. (Illus.). 200p. 1982. text ed. 24.95 (ISBN 0-8391-1729-9, 16497). Univ Park.

--Language & Reading Strategies for Poverty Children. (Illus.). 232p. 1982. pap. text ed. 16.95 (ISBN 0-8391-1709-4, 13471). Univ Park.

Anastassatos, Popi, tr. see Jackins, Harvey.

Anatol, Karl W., jt. auth. see Applbaum, Ronald L.

Anawalt, Patricia R. Indian Clothing Before Cortes: Mesoamerican Costumes from the Codices. LC 80-5942. (The Civilization of the American Indian Ser.: Vol. 156). (Illus.). 400p. 1981. 42.50 (ISBN 0-8061-1650-1). U of Okla Pr.

Anaya, Rudolfo A. Bless Me, Ultima. LC 75-29996. 249p. 1976. pap. 8.00 (ISBN 0-89229-002-1). Tonatiuh-Quinto Sol Intl.

--The Silence of the LLano. LC 75-50703. 1982. pap. 8.00 (ISBN 0-89229-009-9). Tonatiuh-Quinto Sol Intl.

Anbar, Ada. How to Choose a Nursery School: A Parents' Guide to Preschool Education. LC 81-16872. (Illus.). 1982. 12.95 (ISBN 0-87015-233-5). Pacific Bks.

Anbar, Michael. Textbook of Clinical Biophysics. Gardner, Alvin F., ed. (Allied Health Professions Monographs). 1983. price not set (ISBN 0-87527-316-5). Green.

Anbarlian, Harry. Spreadsheeting on the TRS-80 Color Computer. 320p. 1982. text ed. 22.95 (ISBN 0-07-001595-3, C). McGraw.

Anbele, H. & Niederheitmann, F. The Violin: It's History & Construction. Broadhouse, John, tr. from Ger. (Illus.). 172p. 1983. pap. 6.50 (ISBN 0-686-38402-4). Tanager Bks.

Anbian, Robert. Bohemian Airs & Other Kefs. LC 81-90581. (Literature Ser.: No. 1). (Illus.). 74p. (Orig.). 1982. pap. 6.00 (ISBN 0-941842-00-2). Night Horn Books.

Ancel, Marc. Social Defense: A Modern Approach to Criminal Problems. LC 66-11367. 1966. 6.95x o.p. (ISBN 0-8052-3240-0). Schocken.

Ancelet, Barry, jt. ed. see Allain, Mathe.

Ancelot, Francois. Six Mois en Russie. (Nineteenth Century Russia Ser.). 426p. (Fr.). 1974. Repr. of 1827 ed. lib. bdg. 86.00x o.p. (ISBN 0-8287-0018-4, R67). Clearwater Pub.

Ancey, G. Beoumi: Exploitation Manuelle de l'Enquete Demographique Resultats Partield. (Black Africa Ser.). 32p. (Fr.). 1974. Repr. of 1967 ed. 39.00x o.p. (ISBN 0-8287-0019-2, 71-2066). Clearwater Pub.

--Les Centres de Productivite de Bounda et de Saminirko. (Black Africa Ser.). 38p. (Fr.). 1974. Repr. of 1967 ed. lib. bdg. 22.00 o.p. (ISBN 0-8287-1339-1, 71-2041). Clearwater Pub.

--Dabalaua: Recensement Demographique, 2 vols. Incl. Vol. 1. Resultats Commentes. 124p (71-2063); Vol. 2. Tableaux de Base. 46p (71-2064). (Black Africa Ser.). (Fr.). 1974. Repr. of 1969 ed. Set. lib. bdg. 50.50x o.p. (ISBN 0-8287-0020-6). Clearwater Pub.

--Etude Comparative de Cinq Strates d'Exploitations de la Zone Rurale de Brobo: Evaluation 1961-1967. (Black Africa Ser.). 171p. (Fr.). 1974. Repr. of 1968 ed. lib. bdg. 51.00x o.p. (ISBN 0-8287-0021-4, 71-2044). Clearwater Pub.

--Etude de la Zone Rurale de Brobo. (Black Africa Ser.). 37p. (Fr.). 1974. Repr. of 1967 ed. lib. bdg. 14.00x o.p. (ISBN 0-8287-0022-2, 71-2047). Clearwater Pub.

--Exploitations Agricoles en Pays Diamala-Djimini. (Black Africa Ser.). 193p. (Fr.). 1974. Repr. of 1969 ed. lib. bdg. 56.00x o.p. (ISBN 0-8287-0023-0, 71-2042). Clearwater Pub.

--Notes sur les Zones de Developpement de Brobo et De Diabo. (Black Africa Ser.). 113p. (Fr.). 1974. Repr. of 1969 ed. lib. bdg. 38.00x o.p. (ISBN 0-8287-0024-9, 71-2045). Clearwater Pub.

--Les Notions d'Activities et d'Actifs a l'Interieur d'une Exploitation Agricole. (Black Africa Ser.). 22p. (Fr.). 1974. Repr. of 1968 ed. 23.00x o.p. (ISBN 0-8287-1391-X, 71-2070). Clearwater Pub.

--Sakasso: Exploitation Manuelle de l'Enquete Demographique. Resultats Partiels. (Black Africa Ser.). 22p. (Fr.). 1974. Repr. of 1967 ed. 23.00 o.p. (ISBN 0-8287-1416-9, 71-2065). Clearwater Pub.

--La Zone Rurale de Brobo Vue a travers Son Marche Hebdomadaire. (Black Africa Ser.). 195p. (Fr.). 1974. Repr. of 1967 ed. lib. bdg. 56.00x o.p. (ISBN 0-8287-0026-5, 71-2043). Clearwater Pub.

Ancheta, Celadonio A., ed. The Wainwright Papers: Historial Documents of World War II in the Philippines, Vols. 3 & 4. (Illus.). 217p. (Orig.). 1982. each 18.50x (ISBN 0-686-37568-8, Pub. by New Day Philippines); pap. 10.75 each (ISBN 0-686-37569-6). Cellar.

Anchor, Kenneth N. Intensive Behavior Therapy. cancelled professional ref. o.s.i. (ISBN 0-88410-729-9). Ballinger Pub.

Anchor, Robert. The Enlightenment Tradition. LC 78-62855. 1979. 17.95x (ISBN 0-520-03805-3); pap. 3.95 (ISBN 0-520-03784-7). U of Cal Pr.

--Modern Western Experience. (Illus.). 1978. pap. text ed. 14.95 o.p. (ISBN 0-13-599357-1). P-H.

Ancien Chanoine De Meaux. Voltaire et Son Genie. Repr. of 1817 ed. 30.00 o.p. (ISBN 0-8287-1432-0). Clearwater Pub.

Anckarsvard, Karin. Madcap Mystery. MacMillan, Annabelle, tr. from Swed. LC 62-8343. (gr. 4-7). 1970. pap. 2.75 (ISBN 0-15-655108-X, VoyB). HarBraceJ.

--Mysterious Schoolmaster. MacMillan, Annabelle, tr. LC 59-10170. (Illus.). (gr. 3-7). 6.50 o.p. (ISBN 0-15-256527-2, HJ). HarBraceJ.

--Mysterious Schoolmaster. MacMillan, Annabelle, tr. LC 59-10170. (Illus.). (gr. 3-7). 1965. pap. 2.95 (ISBN 0-15-663971-8, VoyB). HarBraceJ.

--Robber Ghost. MacMillan, Annabelle, tr. LC 61-6307. (Illus.). (gr. 3-7). 1961. 6.50 o.p. (ISBN 0-15-267804-2, HJ). HarBraceJ.

--Robber Ghost. MacMillan, Annabelle, tr. LC 61-6307. (Illus.). (gr. 4-6). 1968. pap. 3.95 (ISBN 0-15-678350-9, VoyB). HarBraceJ.

Ancona, George. And What Do You Do? A Book About People & Their Work. 48p. (gr. 6). 1976. 12.00 (ISBN 0-525-25605-9, 01165-350). Dutton.

--I Feel: A Picture Book of Emotions. (Illus.). (ps-1). 1977. 9.95 (ISBN 0-525-32525-5, 0966-290). Dutton.

--It's a Baby! LC 79-10453. (Illus.). (gr. k-3). 1979. 10.95 (ISBN 0-525-32598-0, 01064-310). Dutton.

--Team Work. LC 82-45579. (Illus.). 48p. (gr. 3-6). 1983. 10.53i (ISBN 0-690-04247-7, TYC-J); PLB 10.89g (ISBN 0-690-04248-5). Har-Row.

Anctil, Pierre. A Franco-American Bibliography: New England. 137p. 1979. pap. 5.25x (ISBN 0-911409-36-X). Natl Mat Dev.

Andaya, Barbara, jt. auth. see Andaya, Leonard.

Andaya, Barbara W. & Matheson, Virginia, trs. The Precious Gift. Orig. Title: Tuhft al-Nafis. (Illus.). 1982. 49.00x (ISBN 0-19-582507-1). Oxford U Pr.

Andaya, Leonard & Andaya, Barbara. A History of Malaysia. LC 82-42612. 372p. 1982. 30.00x (ISBN 0-312-38120-4). St Martin.

Andemicael, Berhanykun. The OAU & the UN: Relations Between the Organization of African Unity & the United Nations. LC 74-84658. 350p. 1976. text ed. 37.50x (ISBN 0-8419-0186-4, Africana). Holmes & Meier.

Andemicael, Berhanykun, ed. Regionalism & the U. N. System. LC 79-14018. 603p. 1979. lib. bdg. 54.00 (ISBN 0-379-00591-3). Oceana.

Anderegg, G., ed. see International Union of Pure & Applied Chemistry.

Anderegg, Michael A. William Wyler. (Filmmakers Ser.). 1979. lib. bdg. 12.95 (ISBN 0-8057-9268-6, Twayne). G K Hall.

Andereggen, Anton. Etude Philologique du Jugement Dernier (Lo Jutgamen General), Drame Provencal du XVe Siecle. Williman, Joseph P., ed. LC 82-80909. 386p. 1983. lib. bdg. 40.00 (ISBN 0-938942-02-6). Pacific Gallery.

Anderhalden, A., ed. Das Behinderte Kind. Roelli, H. J. (Paediatrische Fortbildungskurse fuer die Praxis: Vol. 56). (Illus.). vi, 110p. 1982. pap. 38.50 (ISBN 3-8055-3493-0). S Karger.

Anderheggen, George C. A Wish for Your Christmas. (Illus.). 13p. (Orig.). 1982. write for info. Bookling Pub.

Anderhub, Beth. Manual of Abdominal Ultrasonography. (Illus.). 1983. write for info. (ISBN 0-8391-1804-X, 18589). Univ Park.

Anders, Evelyn, jt. auth. see Becker, Esther R.

Anders, James E., Sr. Industrial Hydraulics Troubleshooting. (Illus.). 192p. 1983. 28.00 (ISBN 0-07-001592-9, P&RB). McGraw.

Anders, Karl. Murder to Order. (Illus.). 1967. 6.95 (ISBN 0-8159-6207-X). Devin.

Anders, Leslie. The Twenty-First Missouri: From Home Guard to Union Regiment. LC 75-64. (Contributions in Military History: No. 11). (Illus.). 1975. lib. bdg. 25.00x (ISBN 0-8371-7962-9, AVI/). Greenwood.

Anders, Nedda C. Applique Old & New, Including Patchwork & Embroidery. LC 75-19756. (Illus.). 128p. 1976. pap. 3.00 (ISBN 0-486-23246-8). Dover.

--Chafing Dish Specialties. LC 54-11633. 2.50 o.p. (ISBN 0-685-56521-1, 8208-0205). Hearthside.

Anders, Rebecca. Camping Out. LC 76-12059. (Early Craft Bks.). (Illus.). (gr. k-5). 1976. PLB 3.95g (ISBN 0-8225-0886-9). Lerner Pubns.

--Careers in a Library. LC 77-90159. (Early Career Bks.). (Illus.). (gr. 2-5). 1978. PLB 5.95g (ISBN 0-8225-0334-4). Lerner Pubns.

--A Look at Aging. LC 75-38467. (Awarness Bks.). (Illus.). 36p. (gr. 3-6). 1976. PLB 4.95g (ISBN 0-8225-1304-8). Lerner Pubns.

--A Look at Alcoholism. LC 77-12981. (Awareness Bks.). (Illus.). (gr. 3-6). 1977. PLB 4.95g (ISBN 0-8225-1311-0). Lerner Pubns.

--A Look at Death. LC 77-14182. (Awareness Bks.). (gr. 3-6). 1977. PLB 4.95g (ISBN 0-8225-1308-0). Lerner Pubns.

--A Look at Drug Abuse. LC 77-12982. (Awareness Bks.). (Illus.). (gr. 3-6). 1977. PLB 4.95g (ISBN 0-8225-1309-9). Lerner Pubns.

--A Look at Drug Abuse. 4.95 o.p. (ISBN 0-686-92247-6, 5014). Hazelden.

--A Look at Mental Retardation. LC 75-38466. (Lerner Awareness Bks.). (Illus.). 36p. (gr. 3-6). 1976. PLB 4.95g (ISBN 0-8225-1303-X). Lerner Pubns.

--A Look at Prejudice & Understanding. LC 75-38469. (Awareness Bks.). (Illus.). 36p. (gr. 3-6). 1976. PLB 4.95g (ISBN 0-8225-1306-4). Lerner Pubns.

--Making Musical Instruments. LC 74-33533. (Early Craft Bks.). (Illus.). 32p. (gr. 1-4). 1975. PLB 3.95g (ISBN 0-8225-0868-0). Lerner Pubns.

Andersdatter, Karla. The Rising of the Flesh. 96p. (Orig.). 1983. pap. 5.95 (ISBN 0-911051-00-7). Plain View.

Andersen, Anker. Budgeting for Data Processing. 45p. pap. 4.95 (ISBN 0-86641-089-9, 82141). Natl Assn Accts.

Andersen, Arlow W. The Norwegian-Americans. (The Immigrant Heritage of American Ser). 1975. lib. bdg. 12.95 (ISBN 0-8057-3249-7, Twayne). G K Hall.

Andersen, Benny. Selected Stories. 120p. 1983. pap. 6.00 (ISBN 0-915306-25-5). Curbstone.

Andersen, Blaine W. The Analysis & Design of Pneumatic Systems. LC 76-16767. 314p. 1976. Repr. of 1967 ed. text ed. 21.50 (ISBN 0-88275-435-1). Krieger.

Andersen, Charles J., jt. auth. see Lanier, Lyle H.

Andersen, Christian A., ed. Microprobe Analysis. LC 72-8837. 656p. 1973. 47.50 o.p. (ISBN 0-471-02835-5, Pub. by Wiley-Interscience). Wiley.

Andersen, Christopher P. The Book of People. (Illus.). 500p. 1981. 19.95 (ISBN 0-399-12617-1, Perige); pap. 9.95 (ISBN 0-399-50530-X). Putnam Pub Group.

Andersen, Clifton R. & Cateora, Philip R., eds. Marketing Insights: Selected Readings. 3rd ed. LC 74-82804. (Illus.). 561p. 1974. pap. 7.95x (ISBN 0-914872-01-X). Austin Pr.

Andersen, Dan W., ed. see Herrick, Virgil E.

Andersen, David, jt. auth. see Roberts, Nancy.

Andersen, E. B. Discrete Statistical Models with Social Science Applications. 383p. 1979. 55.50 (ISBN 0-444-85334-0, North Holland). Elsevier.

Andersen, Francis & Forbes, A. Dean. A Linguistic Concordance of Jeremiah: Hebrew Vocabulary & Idiom. Baird, J. Arthur & Freedman, David Noel, eds. (The Computer Bible Ser.: Vols. XIV & XIV-a). 1978. Vol. Xiv-a. vol. 47.50 ea. o.p. (ISBN 0-935106-07-3). Biblical Res Assocs.

Andersen, Gail, jt. auth. see Weinhold, Barry K.

Andersen, Georg & Dean, Edith. Interior Decorating. 192p. 1983. 12.95 (ISBN 0-87123-288-X). Bethany Hse.

Andersen, Gretchen. Creative Exploration in Crafts. (Illus.). 368p. 1976. 19.95 (ISBN 0-87909-169-X); pap. 9.95 o.p. (ISBN 0-87909-168-1). Reston.

Andersen, H. C. The Red Shoes. Bell, Anthea, tr. from Danish. LC 82-61836. (Picture Book Studio Ser.). 40p. 1983. 10.95 (ISBN 0-907234-26-7). Neugebauer Pr.

Andersen, Hans C. Andersen's Fairy Tales. (Illus.). (gr. 4-6). 1945. companion lib. 2.95 (ISBN 0-448-05455-8, G&D); Illus. Junior Lib. pap. 4.95 (ISBN 0-448-11005-9); deluxe ed. 8.95 (ISBN 0-448-06005-1). Putnam Pub Group.

--Fir Tree. LC 73-121800. (Illus.). (gr. 1-7). 1970. 10.89 (ISBN 0-06-020077-4, HarpJ); PLB 9.89 (ISBN 0-06-020078-2). Har-Row.

--Hans Andersen's Fairy Tales. (Childrens Illustrated Classics Ser). (Illus.). 253p. 1977. Repr. of 1958 ed. 9.00x o.p. (ISBN 0-460-05021-4, J M Dent England). Biblio Dist.

--Hans Clodhopper. LC 74-23674. (gr. k-3). 1975. 9.57i (ISBN 0-397-31614-3, JBL-J). Har-Row.

--L' Improvisation ou la Vie en Italie, 2 Vols. (Fr.). 1981. Repr. of 1847 ed. Set. lib. bdg. 240.00 (ISBN 0-8287-1704-4). Vol. 1, 310 Pgs (ISBN 0-8287-1705-2). Vol. 2, 298 Pgs (ISBN 0-8287-1706-0). Clearwater Pub.

--Nightingale. Le Gallienne, Eva, tr. LC 64-18574. (Illus.). (gr. 3 up). 1965. 8.95 (ISBN 0-06-023780-5, HarpJ); PLB 10.89 (ISBN 0-06-023781-3). Har-Row.

--The Red Shoes. (Illus.). pap. 10.95 o.p. (ISBN 0-914676-82-2, Star & Eleph Bks). Green Tiger Pr.

--The Snow Queen. Lewis, Naomi, adapted by. (Illus.). (ps-3). 1982. pap. 2.95 (ISBN 0-14-050294-7, Puffin). Penguin.

--Thumbeline. Winston, Richard & Winston, Clara, trs. from Danish. LC 80-13012. Orig. Title: Tommelise. (Illus.). 40p. (gr. k-3). 1980. 10.75 (ISBN 0-688-22235-8); PLB 10.32 (ISBN 0-688-32235-2). Morrow.

Andersen, Hans Christian. Eighty Fairy Tales. Keigwin, R. P., tr. LC 82-47882. 483p. 1982. 14.95 (ISBN 0-394-52523-X). Pantheon.

--The Princess & the Pea. Stevens, Janet, adapted by. & illus. LC 81-13395. (Illus.). 32p. (gr. k-2). 1982. Reinforced bdg. 10.95 (ISBN 0-8234-0442-0). Holiday.

Andersen, Hans O. & Koutnik, Paul G. Toward More Effective Science Instruction in Secondary Education. 1972. 17.95 (ISBN 0-02-303200-6, 30320). Macmillan.

Andersen, Ian. Turning the Tables on Las Vegas. 1978. pap. 2.95 (ISBN 0-394-72509-3, Vin). Random.

Andersen, Jorgen. The Witch on the Wall. (Illus.). 1978. 35.00x (ISBN 0-04-940052-5). Allen Unwin.

Andersen, Juel. Tofu Fantasies. 80p. (Orig.). 1982. pap. 4.95 (ISBN 0-916870-44-8). Creative Arts Bks.

Andersen, Kaj B. African Traditional Architecture. (Illus.). 1977. 24.00x (ISBN 0-19-572380-5). Oxford U Pr.

Andersen, Kenneth E. Introduction to Communication: Theory & Practice. LC 72-75433. 400p. 1972. text ed. 13.95 o.p. (ISBN 0-8465-0294-1). Benjamin-Cummings.

Andersen, Kurt, et al. Tools of Power. LC 80-5511. (Illus.). 160p. 1980. 8.95 o.p. (ISBN 0-670-72039-9). Viking Pr.

Andersen, Martin P., et al. Speaker & His Audience: Dynamic Interpersonal Communication. 2nd ed. (Auer Ser.). (Illus.). 1974. pap. text ed. 18.50 scp o.p. (ISBN 0-06-040261-X, HarpC); instr's manual avail. o.p. (ISBN 0-06-360273-3). Har-Row.

Andersen, Niels T. Sunrise Over Jordan: A Twenty-First Century College. LC 82-84248. 283p. 1982. 11.95 (ISBN 0-910213-01-1); pap. 6.95 (ISBN 0-910213-00-3). Jordan Pub.

Andersen, Paul. United States Five-Cent Pieces, 1792-1982. LC 82-90453. (Illus.). 54p. (Orig.). 1982. pap. 2.95 (ISBN 0-9604720-3-7). P Andersen.

Andersen, Peter. The Syntax of Texts & the Syntax of Actions. 1979. pap. text ed. cancelled o.p. (ISBN 90-316-0103-9). Humanities.

Andersen, Richard. For Grieving Friends. 32p. 1975. pap. 1.50 o.p. (ISBN 0-570-06985-8, 12-2607). Concordia.

--Muckaluck. 1980. 8.95 o.s.i. (ISBN 0-440-05577-6). Delacorte.

--William Goldman. (United States Authors Ser.: No. 326). 1979. lib. bdg. 10.95 o.p. (ISBN 0-8057-7259-6, Twayne). G K Hall.

Andersen, Richard & Deffner, Donald. For Example... 1978. pap. 7.95 (ISBN 0-570-03766-2, 12-2701). Concordia.

Andersen, Roger W., ed. New Dimensions in Second Language Acquisition Research. (Illus.). 280p. (Orig.). 1981. pap. text ed. 17.95 (ISBN 0-88377-180-2). Newbury Hse.

--Pidginization & Creolization & Language Acquisition. 320p. 1983. pap. text ed. 20.95 (ISBN 0-88377-266-3). Newbury Hse.

Andersen, Ronald, et al. Two Decades of Health Services: Social Survey Trends in Use & Expenditure. LC 76-14785. 416p. 1976. prof ref 25.00x (ISBN 0-88410-117-7). Ballinger Pub.

Andersen, Ronald, et al, eds. Equity in Health Services: Empirical Analyses in Social Policy. LC 75-22328. 1975. prof ref 22.00x (ISBN 0-88410-104-5). Ballinger Pub.

Andersen, Sigrid, jt. auth. see Clute, Robin.

Andersen, Svend E. & Holstein, Bjorn E. Ausbildung Im Gefangnis: Lebenshilfe Fur Gefangene der Skadhauge-Plan Im Danischen Strafvolizug. xi, 162p. (Ger.). 1982. write for info. P Lang Pubs.

Andersen, Uell S. Success Cybernetics. pap. 5.00 (ISBN 0-87980-155-7). Wilshire.

Andersen, Wayne. American Sculpture in Process: 1930-1970. LC 74-21498. (Illus.). 272p. 1975. 19.95 o.p. (ISBN 0-8212-0567-6, 036811). NYGS.

Andersen, Yvonne. Make Your Own Animated Movies. (Illus.). (gr. 4 up). 1970. 10.95 (ISBN 0-316-03940-3). Little.

Andersland, Orlando B. & Anderson, Duwayne, eds. Geotechnical Engineering for Cold Regions. (Illus.). 1978. text ed. 44.50x (ISBN 0-07-001615-1, C). McGraw.

Anderson. Adventures in the Biology Laboratory. 1978. 5.00 (ISBN 0-942788-03-6). Marginal Med.

--It's O. K. to Cry. LC 79-10137. (Handling Diffcult Times Ser.). (Illus.). 32p. (gr. 2-5). 1979. lib. bdg. 8.35 (ISBN 0-516-06431-2). Childrens.

--Modern Compressible Flow: With Historical Perspective. (Mechanical Engineering Ser.). 1982. 37.50 (ISBN 0-07-001654-2). McGraw.

--Sulphur in Biology. (Studies in Biology: No. 101). 1979. 8.95 (ISBN 0-8391-0251-8). Univ Park.

Anderson & Grant. Heard at the Nineteenth. (Illus.). 13.50x (ISBN 0-392-03209-0, SpS). Sportshelf.

Anderson & Sadler. Perspectives in Differentiation & Hypertrophy. 1982. 72.00 (ISBN 0-444-00696-6). Elsevier.

Anderson & Savary, Louis M. Passages. (Illus.). 224p. 1972. pap. 9.95i (ISBN 0-06-067065-7, RD 51, HarpR). Har-Row.

Anderson & Sobieski. Introduction to Microbiology. 2nd ed. LC 79-20560. 1980. pap. 22.95 (ISBN 0-8016-0206-8). Mosby.

Anderson, jt. auth. see Farmer.

Anderson, jt. auth. see Proctor.

Anderson, jt. auth. see Webster.

Anderson, A. Grant. New Zealand in Maps. (Graphic Perspectives of Developing Countries Ser.). 144p. 1977. 35.00x (ISBN 0-8419-0324-7). Holmes & Meier.

Anderson, A. J. Problems in Library Management. LC 81-8153. (Library Science Text Ser.). 282p. 1981. text ed. 27.00 (ISBN 0-87287-261-0); pap. text ed. 20.00 (ISBN 0-87287-264-5). Libs Unl.

Anderson, Alan H., Jr. The Drifting Continents. (Illus.). (gr. 7 up). 1971. PLB 5.49 o.p. (ISBN 0-399-60140-6). Putnam Pub Group.

Anderson, Andrew R. Alexander's Gate, Gog & Magog & the Inclosed Nations. 1932. 7.50 (ISBN 0-910956-07-3). Medieval Acad.

Anderson, Anker. Graphing Financial Information. 50p. pap. 4.95 (ISBN 0-86641-086-4, 82138). Natl Assn Accts.

Anderson, Ann K. I Gave God Time. 1982. 7.95 (ISBN 0-8423-1560-8). Tyndale.

Anderson, Ann M., jt. auth. see Saunders, Susan.

Anderson, Arthur J., et al. Beyond the Codices: The Nahua View of Colonial Mexico. LC 74-29801. (Latin American Studies Center: Vol. 27). 225p. 1976. 34.50x (ISBN 0-520-02974-7). U of Cal Pr.

Anderson, Arthur L. Divided We Stand: Institutional Religion As a Reflection of Pluralism & Integration in America. LC 78-61582. 1978. pap. text ed. 8.95 (ISBN 0-8403-1935-5). Kendall-Hunt.

Anderson, Ava V. The Manhunt Was a Biggie. (Illus.). 144p. 1983. 10.95 (ISBN 0-89962-327-1). Todd & Honeywell.

Anderson, B., jt. auth. see America, R.

Anderson, B. Ray. How to Save Fifty Percent or More on Your Income Tax - Legally. 256p. 1983. 14.95 (ISBN 0-02-501980-5). Macmillan.

Anderson, B. Robert. Professional Sales Management. (Illus.). 432p. 1981. text ed. 21.95 (ISBN 0-13-725879-8). P-H.

--Professional Selling. (Illus.). 400p. 1981. text ed. 18.95 (ISBN 0-13-725960-3). P-H.

Anderson, B. W. Gem Testing. 9th rev. ed. 1980. 34.95 (ISBN 0-408-00440-1). Butterworth.

Anderson, Barbara & Shapiro, Pamela. Obstetrics for the Nurse. LC 77-83424. 1979. pap. text ed. 13.00 (ISBN 0-8273-1330-6); instructor's guide 3.75 (ISBN 0-8273-1331-4). Delmar.

Anderson, Barbara G., jt. auth. see Foster, George M.

Anderson, Barrie, et al. The Menopause Book. Rose, Louisa, ed. LC 76-19757. 1980. pap. 5.95 (ISBN 0-8015-4995-7, Hawthorn). Dutton.

Anderson, Benedict & Kahin, Audrey, eds. Interpreting Indonesian Politics: Thirteen Contributions to the Debate, 1964-1981. (Interim Report Ser.). 180p. (Orig.). 1982. monograph 9.00 (ISBN 0-87763-028-3). Cornell Mod Indo.

Anderson, Benedict, tr. see Simatupang, T. B.

Anderson, Benny. The Pillows. 164p. 1983. 7.50 (ISBN 0-915306-37-9). Curbstone.

Anderson, Berhard W., jt. auth. see Noth, Martin.

Anderson, Bernhard W. Understanding the Old Testament. 3rd ed. 608p. 1975. 23.95 (ISBN 0-13-936153-7). P-H.

Anderson, Beryl. Creative Spinning, Weaving, & Plant-Dyeing. LC 72-4194. 1973. pap. 3.25 o.p. (ISBN 0-668-02703-7). Arco.

Anderson, Betty A., et al. The Childbearing Family, Vol. 1: Pregnancy & Family Health. 2nd ed. (Illus.). 1979. pap. text ed. 17.50 (ISBN 0-07-001683-6, HP). McGraw.

--The Childbearing Family, Vol. 2: Interruptions in Family Health During Pregnancy. 2nd ed. (Illus.). 1979. pap. text ed. 17.50 (ISBN 0-07-001684-4, HP). McGraw.

Anderson, Beverly, jt. auth. see McConnell, Adeline P.

Anderson, Bob. Stretching. Kahn, Lloyd, ed. LC 79-5567. (Illus.). 192p. (Orig.). 1980. pap. 7.95 (ISBN 0-394-73874-8). Shelter Pubns.

Anderson, Bob, jt. auth. see North, Gail.

Anderson, Brian & Moore, John B. Optimal Filtering. 1979. 34.00 (ISBN 0-13-638122-7). P-H.

Anderson, Bruce & Wells, Malcolm. Passive Solar Energy. 1981. pap. 10.95 (ISBN 0-931790-09-3). Brick Hse Pub.

--Passive Solar Energy: The Homeowners Guide to Natural Heating & Cooling. (Illus., Orig.). 1981. 23.95 (ISBN 0-471-88651-3, Pub. by Brick Hse Pub). Wiley.

Anderson, Bruce N. Solar Energy: Fundamentals in Building Design. LC 76-45467. (Illus.). 1977. 36.50 (ISBN 0-07-001751-4, P&RB). McGraw.

Anderson, Burton. Vino: The Wine & Winemakers of Italy. (Illus.). 416p. 1980. 19.95 (ISBN 0-316-03948-9, Pub. by Atlantic Monthly Pr). Little.

Anderson, C. Dixon. Spanish in Context: A Basic Course. (Illus.). 1978. text ed. 20.95 (ISBN 0-13-824235-6); pap. 9.50 student wkbk (ISBN 0-13-824243-7); tapes 225.00 (ISBN 0-686-77213-X). P-H.

Anderson, Carl & Fox, John. Hold Em Poker for Winners. 144p. (Orig.). 1982. pap. 6.95 (ISBN 0-89650-741-6). Gamblers.

Anderson, Carl L. & Creswell, William H., Jr. School Health Practice. 7th ed. LC 79-27664. (Illus.). 1980. text ed. 20.95 (ISBN 0-8016-0216-5). Mosby.

Anderson, Carl R. & Gannon, Martin J. Readings in Management: An Organizational Perspective. 1977. write for info. o.p. (CPCU 7). IIA.

Anderson, Carl R., jt. auth. see Paine, Frank T.

Anderson, Carol & Stewart, Susan. Mastering Resistance: A Practical Guide to Family Therapy. (Family Therapy Ser.). 251p. 1983. text ed. 20.00x (ISBN 0-89862-044-9, G36). Guilford Pr.

Anderson, Carol, jt. ed. see Luber, Raymond F.

Anderson, Cay M. Here Comes Jonathan. (Illus.). 36p. (ps-1). 1982. 3.95 (ISBN 0-941478-04-1). Paraclete Pr.

Anderson, Chaney & Pierce, R. C., Jr. Elementary Calculus for Business, Economics & Social Sciences. 1975. text ed. 23.50 (ISBN 0-395-18960-8); instr's. manual 2.05 (ISBN 0-395-18959-4). HM.

Anderson, Charles. Political Economy of Social Class. 384p. 1974. text ed. 22.95 (ISBN 0-13-685149-5). P-H.

Anderson, Charles & Travis, L. D. Psychology & the Liberal Consensus. 200p. 1982. text ed. 10.50x (ISBN 0-88920-127-7, 40911, Pub. by Wilfrid Laurier U Pr). Humanities.

Anderson, Charles L. Life & Letters of Vasco Nunez De Balboa. LC 70-100140. Repr. of 1941 ed. lib. bdg. 17.00x o.p. (ISBN 0-8371-3242-8, ANVB). Greenwood.

Anderson, Charles R. Emily Dickinson's Poetry: Stairway of Surprise. LC 82-15844. (Illus.). xvii, 334p. 1982. Repr. of 1963 ed. lib. bdg. 35.00x (ISBN 0-313-23733-6, ANED). Greenwood.

Anderson, Charles S., ed. see Bender, Harold S.

Anderson, Charles S., ed. see McNally, Robert E.

Anderson, Charles W. Political Economy of Modern Spain: Policy-Making in an Authoritarian System. LC 72-106036. (Illus.). 298p. 1970. 25.00 (ISBN 0-299-05611-2); pap. 9.95 (ISBN 0-299-05614-7). U of Wis Pr.

--Statecraft: An Introduction to Political Choice & Judgment. LC 76-22740. 318p. 1977. text ed. 18.95x o.p. (ISBN 0-471-02896-7). Wiley.

Anderson, Charles W., jt. auth. see Glade, William P., Jr.

Anderson, Cheryl A. Lettering Techniques. 3rd ed. (Bridges for Ideas Handbook Ser.). 1982. pap. text ed. 6.00x (ISBN 0-913648-06-X). U Tex Austin Film Lib.

Anderson, Chester. The Butterfly Kid. LC 77-4498. (Science Fiction Ser.). 1977. Repr. of 1967 ed. lib. bdg. 12.50 o.p. (ISBN 0-8398-2374-6, Gregg). G K Hall.

Anderson, Chris. The Name Game. 1979. pap. 2.50 o.s.i. (ISBN 0-515-04857-7). Jove Pubns.

Anderson, Claire, ed. see League of Woman Voters of New York State.

Anderson, Clarence W. Billy & Blaze. (Illus.). (gr. k-3). 1969. 9.95 (ISBN 0-02-701880-6); pap. 3.50. Macmillan.

--Blaze & the Forest Fire. (Illus.). (gr. k-3). 1969. 8.95 (ISBN 0-02-702080-0); pap. 3.95. Macmillan.

--Blaze Finds the Trail. (Illus.). (gr. 1-3). 1972. 4.50g (ISBN 0-02-703130-6); pap. 1.95. Macmillan.

Anderson, Curtis B., et al. Chemistry: Principles & Applications. 1973. text ed. 24.95x o.p. (ISBN 0-669-73833-6); instructors' manual free o.p. (ISBN 0-669-81919-0). Heath.

Anderson, D. Chris & Borkowski, John G. Experimental Psychology: Research Tactics & Their Applications. 1978. 20.95x (ISBN 0-673-07866-3). Scott F.

Anderson, D. Chris, jt. auth. see Borkowski, John G.

Anderson, D. D. Analyzing Time Series: Proceedings of the International Time Series Meeting, Guernsey, Oct. 1979. 1980. 76.75 (ISBN 0-444-85464-9). Elsevier.

Anderson, D. G. New Practice Readers, 7 Bks. 1978. Bks. A-E. pap. text ed. 5.44 ea.; Bks. F-G. pap. text ed. 5.84 ea.; tchr's manual 2.76 (ISBN 0-07-001901-0); ans. key set of 4 6.60 (ISBN 0-07-001900-2). McGraw.

Anderson, D. J., jt. ed. see Gillison, A. N.

Anderson, D. L. Embryology & Phylogeny in Annelids & Arthropods. LC 73-1019. 492p. 1973. 54.00 (ISBN 0-08-017069-2). Pergamon.

Anderson, Daniel, jt. ed. see Bryant, Jennings.

Anderson, Daniel A. Psychopathology of Denial. 1981. 3.95 (ISBN 0-89486-143-3). Hazelden.

Anderson, Daniel J. The Joys & Sorrows of Sobriety. 20p. (Orig.). 1977. pap. 1.95 (ISBN 0-89486-035-6). Hazelden.

--Perspectives on Treatment. 1981. 3.95 (ISBN 0-89486-133-6). Hazelden.

Anderson, Dave, et al. The Yankees: Nineteen Eighty-One Edition. 1981. 10.95 o.p. (ISBN 0-394-51902-7). Random.

--The Yankees: The Four Fabulous Eras of Baseball's Most Famous Team. rev. ed. (Illus.). 1980. 9.95 o.p. (ISBN 0-394-51133-6). Random.

Anderson, David & Holland, I. I., eds. Forest & Forestry. 3rd ed. (gr. 10-12). 1982. 18.00 (ISBN 0-8134-2169-1); text ed. 13.50x. Interstate.

Anderson, David, et al. Essentials of Management Science: Applications to Decision Making. (Illus.). 1978. text ed. 25.50 (ISBN 0-8299-0147-7); study guide 9.95 (ISBN 0-8299-0202-3); test bank avail. (ISBN 0-8299-0455-7); instrs.' manual avail. (ISBN 0-8299-0453-0); transparency masters avail. (ISBN 0-8299-0454-9). West Pub.

Anderson, David B. Woodrow Wilson. (World Leaders Ser.). 1978. lib. bdg. 12.95 (ISBN 0-8057-7705-9, Twayne). G K Hall.

--Woodrow Wilson. (World Leaders Ser.: No. 76). 1978. 12.95 o.p. (ISBN 0-8057-7705-9, Twayne). G K Hall.

Anderson, David D. Abraham Lincoln. (United States Authors Ser.). 1970. lib. bdg. 11.95 (ISBN 0-8057-0452-3, Twayne). G K Hall.

--Brand Whitlock. (United States Authors Ser.). 13.95 (ISBN 0-8057-0788-3, Twayne). G K Hall.

--Critical Essays on Sherwood Anderson. (Critical Essays on American Literature). 1981. 25.00 (ISBN 0-8161-8421-6, Twayne). G K Hall.

--Ignatius Donnelly. (United States Authors Ser.). 1980. lib. bdg. 13.95 (ISBN 0-8057-7303-7, Twayne). G K Hall.

--Louis Bromfield. (United States Authors Ser.). lib. bdg. 13.95 (ISBN 0-8057-0092-7, Twayne). G K Hall.

--Robert Ingersoll. (United States Authors Ser.). lib. bdg. 13.95 (ISBN 0-8057-0396-9, Twayne). G K Hall.

--William Jennings Bryan. (United States Authors Ser.). 1981. lib. bdg. 11.95 (ISBN 0-8057-7294-4, Twayne). G K Hall.

Anderson, David D., ed. Michigan: A State Anthology: Writings About the Great Lake State, 1641-1981, Selected from Diaries, Journals, Histories, Fiction, & Verse. (Literature of the States: Vol. 1). 1982. 35.00 (ISBN 0-8103-1620-X, Pub. by Bruccoli). Gale.

Anderson, David R. & Sweeney, Dennis J. Quantitative Methods for Business. 2nd ed. (Illus.). 656p. 1983. text ed. 26.95 (ISBN 0-314-69633-4); write for info. study guide (ISBN 0-314-71075-2); write for info. test bank (ISBN 0-314-71077-9); instrs.' manual avail. (ISBN 0-314-71076-0). West Pub.

Anderson, David R., et al. An Introduction to Management Science. 3rd ed. (Illus.). 700p. 1982. text ed. 27.95 (ISBN 0-314-63149-6). West Pub.

Anderson, Debra, jt. auth. see Aves, Diane K.

Anderson, Decima M. Computer Programming: Fortran Four. (Illus., Orig.). 1966. pap. 16.95 (ISBN 0-13-164822-5). P-H.

Anderson, Dennis. Small Industry in Developing Countries: A Discussion of Issues. LC 82-11130. (World Bank Staff Working Papers: No. 518). (Orig.). 1982. pap. 3.00 (ISBN 0-8213-0006-7). World Bank.

Anderson, Dennis & Khambata, Farida. Financing Small Scale Industry & Agriculture in Developing Countries: The Merits & Limitations of Commercial Policies. LC 82-8664. (World Bank Staff Working Papers: No. 519). (Orig.). 1982. pap. 3.00 (ISBN 0-8213-0007-5). World Bank.

--Small Enterprises & Development Policy in the Philippines: A Case Study. (Working Paper: No. 468). 239p. 1981. 5.00 (ISBN 0-686-36178-4, WP-0468). World Bank.

Anderson, Dennis & Leiserson, Mark. Rural Enterprise & Nonfarm Employment. (Working Paper). 87p. 1978. 5.00 (ISBN 0-686-36150-4, PP-7802). World Bank.

Anderson, Dennis C., jt. auth. see Claxton, John D.

Anderson, Donald K., Jr. John Ford. (English Authors Ser.). lib. bdg. 12.95 (ISBN 0-8057-1204-6, Twayne). G K Hall.

Anderson, Donald L. & Raun, Donald L. Information Analysis in Management Accounting. LC 77-14938. (Wiley Ser. in Accounting & Information Systems). 706p. 1978. pap. text ed. 30.95x (ISBN 0-471-02815-0). Wiley.

Anderson, Dorothy B. & McClean, Lenora J., eds. Identifying Suicide Potential. LC 78-140045. 112p. 1971. text ed. 16.95 (ISBN 0-87705-024-4). Human Sci Pr.

Anderson, Doug. Picture Puzzles for Armchair Detectives. LC 82-19344. (Illus.). 128p. (gr. 6 up). 1983. 9.95 (ISBN 0-8069-4670-9); PLB 9.99 (ISBN 0-8069-4671-7); pap. 3.95 (ISBN 0-8069-7718-3). Sterling.

Anderson, Douglas P. Diseases of Fishes, Book 4: Fish Immunology. Snieszko, S. F. & Axelrod, Herbert R., eds. (Illus.). 240p. 1974. pap. 19.95 (ISBN 0-87666-036-7, PS-209). Tfh Pubns.

Anderson, Douglas R. Testing the Field of Vision. LC 81-14045. (Illus.). 301p. 1982. text ed. 44.50 (ISBN 0-8016-0207-6). Mosby.

Anderson, Duwayne, jt. ed. see Andersland, Orlando B.

Anderson, E., jt. auth. see Lund, C.

Anderson, E., jt. auth. see Lund, Charles.

Anderson, E. P. & Ley, C. J. Projecting a Picture of Home Economics: Public Relations in Secondary Programs. 1982. 4.00 (ISBN 0-686-38743-0). Home Econ Educ.

Anderson, E. Ruth. Contemporary American Composers: A Biographical Dictionary. 2nd ed. 1982. lib. bdg. 60.00 (ISBN 0-8161-8223-X, Hall Reference). G K Hall.

--Contemporary American Composers: A Biographical Dictionary. 513p. 1976. lib. bdg. 50.00 (ISBN 0-8161-1117-0, Hall Reference). G K Hall.

Anderson, Edith H. & Reed, Suellen B. Innovative Approaches to Baccalaureate Programs in Nursing. 50p. 1979. 4.50 (ISBN 0-686-38271-4, 15-1804). Natl League Nurse.

Anderson, Edith H., et al, eds. Current Concepts in Clinical Nursing, Vol. 4. LC 67-30797. 1973. 15.50 o.p. (ISBN 0-8016-0178-9). Mosby.

Anderson, Edward C. Florida Territory in 1844: The Diary of Master Edward Clifford Anderson USN. Hoole, W. Stanley, ed. LC 76-16071. 1977. 9.35 (ISBN 0-8173-5111-6). U of Ala Pr.

Anderson, Edward E. Fundamentals of Solar Thermal Energy Conversion. LC 81-22852. 576p. Date not set. text ed. 29.95 (ISBN 0-201-00008-3). A-W.

Anderson, Edwin P. Home Workshop & Tool Handy Book. 2nd ed. LC 73-81504. 1973. 6.50 o.p. (ISBN 0-672-23208-1). Audel.

--Wiring Diagrams for Light & Power. 3rd ed. LC 75-7017. 1975. 6.95 o.p. (ISBN 0-672-23232-4). Audel.

Anderson, Edwin P. & Miller, Rex. Electric Motors. new ed. (Audel Ser.). 1983. 12.95 (ISBN 0-672-23376-2). Bobbs.

Anderson, Elijah. A Place on the Corner: Identity & Rank Among Black Streetcorner Men. LC 78-1879. (Studies of Urban Society). 1978. 18.00x (ISBN 0-226-01953-5); pap. 6.95 (ISBN 0-226-01954-3). U of Chicago Pr.

Anderson, Elizabeth L., ed. Newspaper Libraries in the U. S. & Canada: An SLA Directory. 2nd ed. LC 80-25188. 1980. 17.50 (ISBN 0-87111-265-5). SLA.

Anderson, Ella. Jo-Jo. 1975. pap. 1.50 (ISBN 0-87508-693-4). Chr Lit.

Anderson, Elliott, jt. ed. see Hayman, David.

Anderson, Emily A., ed. English Poetry, Nineteen Hundred to Nineteen Fifty: A Guide to Information Sources. (American Literature, English Literature & World Literatures in English Information Guide Ser.). 350p. 1982. 42.00 (ISBN 0-8103-1360-X). Gale.

Anderson, Enid. The Technique of Soft Toy Making. (Illus.). 144p. 1982. 19.95 (ISBN 0-7134-2391-9, Pub. by Batsford England). David & Charles.

Anderson, Eric, jt. auth. see Ingraham, F.

Anderson, Eric A. & Earle, George, eds. Design & Aesthetics in Wood. LC 75-171186. 1972. 34.50x (ISBN 0-87395-216-2). State U NY Pr.

Anderson, Ernest C. & Sullivan, Elizabeth M., eds. Impact of Energy Production on Human Health: An Evaluation of Means for Assessment, Proceedings. LC 76-22540. (ERDA Symposium Ser.). 152p. 1976. pap. 11.75 (ISBN 0-87079-032-3, CONF-751022); microfiche 4.50 (ISBN 0-87079-245-8, CONF-751022). DOE.

Anderson, Ethel. Song of Hager to the Patriarch Abraham. 8.50 (ISBN 0-392-04747-0, ABC). Sportshelf.

Anderson, Eugene, et al. Fundamentals of Social Work Research: A Guide for Students & Beginning Practitioners. 97p. 1978. softcover 3.75 o.p. (ISBN 0-932930-02-6). Pilgrimage Inc.

Anderson, Evelyn M., jt. ed. see Carney, Andrew L.

Anderson, Farris. Alfonso Sastre. (World Authors Ser.: No. 155). 15.95 o.p. (ISBN 0-8057-2802-3, Twayne). G K Hall.

Anderson, Fletcher & Hopkinson, Ann. Rivers of the Southwest: A Boater's Guide to the Rivers of Colorado, New Mexico, Utah, & Arizona. (Illus.). 200p. (Orig.). 1982. pap. 12.95 (ISBN 0-87108-607-7). Pruett.

Anderson, Frances E. Christopher Smart. (English Authors Ser.). 1974. lib. bdg. 14.95 (ISBN 0-8057-1502-9, Twayne). G K Hall.

Anderson, Frank. Orchids. (Abbeville Library of Art Ser.). (Illus.). 112p. 1981. pap. 4.95 o.p. (ISBN 0-89659-122-0). Abbeville Pr.

--Redoute Roses. (Library of Art Ser.). (Illus.). 112p. 1981. pap. 4.95 o.p. (ISBN 0-89659-096-8). Abbeville Pr.

Anderson, Frank J. Cultivated Flowers. LC 79-64989. (Abbeville Library of Art Ser.). (Illus.). 112p. (Orig.). 1981. pap. 4.95 o.p. (ISBN 0-89659-182-4). Abbeville Pr.

Anderson, Frank R. Quality Controlled Investing: Or How to Avoid the Pick & Pray Method. LC 78-7607. 160p. 1978. 27.95 (ISBN 0-471-04382-6, Pub. by Wiley-Interscience). Wiley.

Anderson, Fred, jt. auth. see Sahn, David J.

Anderson, Fred A. The Complete PFE Study Reference. 96p. (Orig.). 1983. pap. 15.95 (ISBN 0-939570-01-7). Skills Improvement.

--Scoring High on Medical & Health Sciences Exams. 24p. (Orig.). 1983. pap. 1.75 (ISBN 0-939570-02-5). Skills Improvement.

Anderson, Frederick, ed. & intro. by see Twain, Mark.

Anderson, Frederick, et al, eds. see Twain, Mark.

Anderson, Frederick I. Quad-Cities: Joined by a River. (Illus.). 262p. 1982. 24.95 (ISBN 0-910847-00-2). Lee Enterprises.

Anderson, Fulton H., ed. see Bacon, Francis.

Anderson, G. L., ed. Asian Literature in English: A Guide to Information Sources. (American, English Literature & World Literatures in English Information Guide Ser.: Vol. 31). 300p. 1981. 42.00 (ISBN 0-8103-1362-6). Gale.

Anderson, G. W. The History & Religion of Israel. (New Clarendon Bible Ser.). (Illus.). 1966. pap. 10.95x (ISBN 0-19-836915-8). Oxford U Pr.

Anderson, Gary & Watson, Nancy. Programmed Power Phonics: A Simplified Method of Word Identification. 1978. 7.95 (ISBN 0-8403-1882-0). Kendall-Hunt.

Anderson, Gaylene, ed. Primary Primer: Simplified Piano Duets for Young Latter-day Saints. (Illus.). 32p. (Orig.). 1982. pap. 3.95 (ISBN 0-941214-10-9). Signature Bks.

Anderson, Gene. Coring & Core Analysis Handbook. LC 74-33713. 200p. 1975. 31.95x (ISBN 0-87814-058-1). Pennwell Books Division.

--Coyote Space. (Kestrel Ser.: No. 6). 28p. 1983. pap. 3.00 (ISBN 0-914974-38-6). Holmgangers.

Anderson, George. The Digest Book of Physical Fitness. (Sports & Leisure Library). (Illus.). 1979. pap. 2.95 o.s.i. (ISBN 0-695-81284-X). Follett.

--Magic Digest. (DBI Bks). 1972. pap. 6.95 o.s.i. (ISBN 0-695-80339-5). Follett.

Anderson, George B. Physical Fitness Digest. (Illus.). 1979. pap. 7.95 o.s.i. (ISBN 0-695-81275-0). Follett.

Anderson, George K. Legend of the Wandering Jew. LC 65-14290. 503p. 35.00x (ISBN 0-87057-094-3, Pub. by Brown U Pr). U Pr of New Eng.

Anderson, George K. & Buckler, William E. The Literature of England: An Anthology & a History, 2 vols. 5th ed. 1968. 16.95x ea. o.p.; Vol.1. (ISBN 0-673-05663-5); Vol. 2. (ISBN 0-673-05698-8). Scott F.

--The Literature of England: Single Volume Edition. rev. ed. 1967. 24.50x (ISBN 0-673-05656-2). Scott F.

Anderson, George K. & Warnock, Robert. The World in Literature. 1967. pap. 10.95xea.; Bk. 2. pap. o.p. (ISBN 0-673-05652-X); Bk. 3. (ISBN 0-673-05653-8); Bk. 4. (ISBN 0-673-05654-6). Scott F.

--The World in Literature, 2 vols. rev. ed. 1967. 19.95x ea. Vol. 1 (ISBN 0-673-05636-8). Vol. 2 (ISBN 0-673-05637-6). Scott F.

Anderson, George K., et al. The Literature of England. 3rd ed. Incl. Vol. 1. From the Middle Ages Through the Eighteenth Century. pap. text ed. 13.50x (ISBN 0-673-15156-5); Vol. 2. From the Romantic Period to the Present. pap. text ed. 13.50x (ISBN 0-673-15157-3). 1979. text ed. 24.95x single vol. (ISBN 0-673-15155-7). Scott F.

Anderson, George L., ed. Issues & Conflicts: Studies in Twentieth Century American Diplomacy. LC 69-13802. Repr. of 1959 ed. lib. bdg. 20.25 o.p. (ISBN 0-8371-0285-5, ANIC). Greenwood.

Anderson, Gerald D. Fascists, Communists, & the National Government: Civil Liberties in Great Britain, 1931-1937. LC 82-10985. 256p. 1983. text ed. 20.00x (ISBN 0-8262-0388-4). U of Mo Pr.

Anderson, Gerald F., jt. auth. see Settgast, Edward E.

Anderson, Gerald H. & Stransky, Thomas F., eds. Christ's Lordship & Religious Pluralism. LC 80-25406. 256p. (Orig.). 1981. pap. 8.95 (ISBN 0-88344-088-1). Orbis Bks.

Anderson, Gordon T., ed. see Mitchell, Alice & Szerny, Carl.

Anderson, Gordon T., ed. see Salvaggio, Jerry L.

Anderson, Graham. Eros Sophistes: Ancient Novelists at Play. LC 81-16573. (American Philological Association American Classical Studies). 1981. pap. 12.75 (ISBN 0-89130-547-5, 40-01-09). Scholars Pr CA.

Anderson, H., jt. auth. see Flores, A.

Anderson, H. D. & Eells, Walter C. Alaska Natives: A Survey of Their Sociological & Educational Status. LC 73-12562. (Illus.). xvi, 472p. 1973. Repr. of 1935 ed. 48.00 o.s.i. (ISBN 0-527-02485-6). Kraus Repr.

Anderson, Hans C see Swan, D. K.

Anderson, Henry R. & Raiborn, Mitchell H. Basic Cost Accounting Concepts. LC 76-12017. (Illus.). 720p. 1977. text ed. 25.95 (ISBN 0-395-20646-4); instr's manual with solutions 10.50 (ISBN 0-395-20648-0); test bank 3.75 (ISBN 0-395-20649-9). HM.

Anderson, Hershel M., jt. auth. see Sommerfeld, Ray M.

Anderson Hospital. Neoplasms of the Skin & Malignant Melanoma. (Illus.). 1976. 49.50 o.p. (ISBN 0-8151-0213-5). Year Bk Med.

Anderson Hospital Staff. Cancer Patient Care at M. D. Anderson Hospital & Tumor Institute. (Illus.). 1976. 82.50 o.p. (ISBN 0-8151-0217-8). Year Bk Med.

Anderson, Howard, ed. see Lewis, Matthew.

Anderson, Howard J. Major Labor-Law Principles Established by the NLRB & the Courts: December 1964-December 1975. LC 73-93852. 188p. 1976. 15.00 o.p. (ISBN 0-686-85721-6). BNA.

--Primer of Labor Relations. 21st ed. 160p. 1980. pap. 12.00 (ISBN 0-87179-343-1). BNA.

Anderson, Howard J. & Levin-Epstein, Michael. Primer of Equal Employment Opportunity. 2nd ed. LC 82-4321. 126p. 1982. 12.00 (ISBN 0-87179-380-6). BNA.

Anderson, Howard J., ed. Major Employment-Law Principles Established by the EEOC, the OFCCP, & the Courts: December 1964-December 1980. 118p. 1981. pap. text ed. 22.00 (ISBN 0-87179-342-3). BNA.

Anderson, Howard R., ed. see Logan, Rayford W. & Cohen, Irving S.

Anderson, Howard R., jt. ed. see Wade, Richard C.

Anderson, Hugh, et al, eds. Education for the Seventies. 1970. pap. text ed. 2.50x o.p. (ISBN 0-435-80026-4). Heinemann Ed.

Anderson, I. G., ed. Councils, Committees & Boards: A Handbook of Advisory, Consultative, Executive & Similar Bodies in British Public Life. 4th ed. 500p. 1981. 125.00x (ISBN 0-686-71975-1, Pub. by CBD Research Ltd). Gale.

--Directory of European Associations: National Industrial, Trade & Professional Associations, Pt. One. 3rd ed. 500p. 1981. 210.00x (ISBN 0-900246-35-9, Pub. by Cbd Research Ltd.). Gale.

--Directory of European Associations: Part 2-National Learned, Scientific & Technical Societies. 2nd ed. LC 76-11697. 1979. 145.00x (ISBN 0-900246-29-4, Pub. by CBD Research). Gale.

Anderson, Ian. A First Course in Combinatorial Mathematics. (Illus.). 132p. 1979. pap. text ed. 9.95x (ISBN 0-19-859617-0). Oxford U Pr.

Anderson, Isaac, tr. see Christiansen, Sigurd.

Anderson, J. & Subbarao, K. A Graphical Method Based on Frequency Domain for Passive Building Energy Analysis. (Progress in Solar Energy Supplements SERI Ser.). 60p. 1983. pap. text ed. 9.00x (ISBN 0-89553-088-0). Am Solar Energy.

Anderson, J., jt. ed. see Pinclroll, F.

Anderson, J., ed. see World Conference on First Medical Informatics, Aug. 5-10, 1974.

Anderson, J. A., jt. auth. see Grahame, R.

Anderson, J. C., et al. Data & Formulae for Engineering Students. 2nd ed. 1969. text ed. 9.25 o.s.i. (ISBN 0-08-013989-2); pap. text ed. 3.50 (ISBN 0-08-013988-4). Pergamon.

Anderson, J. Edward. Transit Systems Theory. LC 77-11856. (Illus.). 1978. 25.95x o.p. (ISBN 0-669-01902-X). Lexington Bks.

Anderson, J. G. The Structure of Western Europe. 1978. text ed. 32.00 o.s.i. (ISBN 0-08-022045-2); pap. text ed. 14.00 (ISBN 0-08-022046-0). Pergamon.

Anderson, J. G. C. & Owen, T. R. Field Geology in Britain. 1983. 40.01 (ISBN 0-08-022054-1); pap. 19.21 (ISBN 0-08-022055-X). Pergamon.

Anderson, J. J., ed. Patience. (Old & Middle English Texts Ser.). (Illus.). 112p. 1977. Repr. of 1972 ed. 9.50x (ISBN 0-686-63946-4). B&N Imports.

Anderson, J. J., jt. ed. see Cawley, A. C.

Anderson, J. K. Ancient Greek Horsemanship. LC 61-6780. (Illus.). 1961. 39.75x (ISBN 0-520-00023-4). U of Cal Pr.

--Military Theory & Practice in the Age of Xenophon. LC 74-104010. 1970. 37.50x (ISBN 0-520-01564-9). U of Cal Pr.

Anderson, J. Kerby. Genetic Engineering (CEP) 1982. pap. 4.95 o.p. (ISBN 0-310-45051-9). Zondervan.

Anderson, J. R. Muir's Textbook of Pathology. 1120p. 1980. pap. text ed. 42.50 (ISBN 0-7131-4357-6). E Arnold.

Anderson, J. R. & Boudart, M., eds. Catalysis: Science & Technology, Vol. 3. (Illus.). 290p. 1982. 56.00 (ISBN 0-387-11634-6). Springer-Verlag.

Anderson, J. W. Best of Both Worlds-A Guide to Home-Based Careers. 188p. 1982. 10.95 (ISBN 0-686-84292-8, Pub. by Betterway Pubns). Berkshire Traveller.

Anderson, Jack & Boyd, James. Confessions of a Muckraker. 416p. 1980. pap. 2.95 o.s.i. (ISBN 0-345-26025-2). Ballantine.

Anderson, Jack & Pronzini, Bill. The Cambodia File. LC 80-5447. 456p. 1981. 13.95 o.p. (ISBN 0-385-14984-0). Doubleday.

Anderson, Jack W., jt. auth. see Neff, Jerry M.

Anderson, James. The Affair of the Blood-Stained Egg Cosy. 1978. pap. 2.95 (ISBN 0-380-01919-1, 638266). Avon.

--Diabetes. 288p. 1983. pap. 3.50 (ISBN 0-446-30593-6). Warner Bks.

Anderson, James & Tatro, Earl E. Shop Theory. 6th ed. (Illus.). 576p. (gr. 9-11). 1974. text ed. 21.10 (ISBN 0-07-001612-7, W). McGraw.

--Shop Theory. 5th ed. 1968. 12.80 o.p. (ISBN 0-07-001608-9, W). McGraw.

Anderson, James, ed. Economic Regulatory Policy. 1975. pap. 6.00 (ISBN 0-918592-12-7). Policy Studies.

Anderson, James A. Natural Theology: The Metaphysics of God. 1962. 3.95 o.p. (ISBN 0-02-810200-2). Glencoe.

Anderson, James D. & Jones, Ezra E. The Management of Ministry. LC 76-62942. 1978. 12.45i (ISBN 0-06-060235-X, HarpR). Har-Row.

Anderson, James D., jt. ed. see Franklin, Vincent P.

Anderson, James E. Economic Regulatory Policies. 241p. 1976. pap. 9.95 (ISBN 0-8093-0818-5). Lexington Bks.

--Grant's Atlas of Anatomy. 7th ed. (Illus.). 1978. 35.50 o.p. (ISBN 0-683-00209-0). Williams & Wilkins.

--Grant's Atlas of Anatomy. 8th ed. (Illus.). 640p. 1983. 35.00 (ISBN 0-683-00211-2). Williams & Wilkins.

Anderson, James F. Bond of Being: An Essay on Analogy & Existence. LC 77-91752. Repr. of 1949 ed. lib. bdg. 15.75x (ISBN 0-8371-2435-2, ANBB). Greenwood.

--Introduction to the Metaphysics of St. Thomas Aquinas. LC 53-6515. 1969. pap. 5.95 (ISBN 0-89526-970-8). Regnery-Gateway.

Anderson, James L. & Cohen, Martin. The Competitive Edge. 1982. pap. 3.95 (ISBN 0-553-20358-4). Bantam.

Anderson, James L., et al, eds. see Krakauer, Lewis J.

Anderson, Jaynie, ed. see Wind, Edgar.

Anderson, Jean. Jean Anderson Cooks: Her Kitchen Reference & Recipe Collection. LC 82-7884. (Illus.). 672p. 1982. 19.95 (ISBN 0-688-01325-2). Morrow.

Anderson, Jean, jt. auth. see Kasten, Lloyd.

Anderson, Jean, jt. auth. see Kimball, Yeffe.

Anderson, Jennifer. Cave Exploring. (Illus.). 128p. 1974. pap. 4.95 o.s.i. (ISBN 0-8096-1889-3, Assn Pr). Follett.

Anderson, Jerry D. Success Strategies for Investment Real Estate: The Professional's Guide to Better Service & Increased Commissions. Berlin, Helene, ed. LC 82-61402. (Illus.). 300p. (Orig.). 1982. pap. text ed. 17.95 (ISBN 0-913652-33-4, BK 153). Realtors Natl.

Anderson, Jervis. This Was Harlem: A Cultural Portrait, 1900-1950. (Illus.). 1982. 17.95 (ISBN 0-374-27623-4); pap. 8.95 (ISBN 0-374-51757-6). FS&G.

Anderson, Jessica. Tirra Lirra by the River. 1983. pap. 3.95 (ISBN 0-14-070085-4). Penguin.

Anderson, Joan W. The Best of Both Worlds: A Guide to Home-Based Careers. LC 82-4283. 188p. (Orig.). 1982. 10.95 (ISBN 0-932620-14-0); pap. 6.95 (ISBN 0-932620-13-2). Betterway Pubns.

--Dear World: Don't Spin So Fast, I'm Having Trouble Hanging On. LC 82-73131. 160p. 1982. pap. 4.95 (ISBN 0-87029-188-2, 20280-4). Abbey.

--Teen is a Four-Letter Word: A Survival Kit for Parents. LC 82-25114. 140p. 1983. pap. 5.95 (ISBN 0-932620-19-1). Betterway Pubns.

Anderson, Johannes E. Myths & Legends of the Polynesians. LC 69-13509. (Illus.). (gr. 9 up). 1969. Repr. of 1928 ed. 25.00 (ISBN 0-8048-0414-1). C E Tuttle.

Anderson, John. Reptilia & Batrachia. (Zoology of Egypt: No. 1). (Illus.). 1965. Repr. of 1898 ed. 120.00 (ISBN 3-7682-0240-2). Lubrecht & Cramer.

Anderson, John, ed. Language Form & Linguistic Variation: Papers Dedicated to Angus McIntosh. (Current Issues in Linguistic Theory Ser.: No. 15). 496p. 1982. 50.00 (ISBN 90-272-3506-6). Benjamins North Am.

Anderson, John, jt. auth. see Snapp, Allen.

Anderson, John A. Las Vegas Survival Guide. LC 81-71218. 200p. (Orig.). 1982. pap. 5.95 (ISBN 0-9607626-0-4). Anderson Comm.

Anderson, John D. & Kennan, Elizabeth T., trs. Bernard of Clairvaux: Consideration: Advice to a Pope. LC 75-27953. (Cistercian Fathers Ser.: No. 37). 1976. 5.00 (ISBN 0-87907-137-0). Cistercian Pubns.

Anderson, John D., Jr. Introduction to Flight: Its Engineering & History. (Illus.). 1978. text ed. 34.95 (ISBN 0-07-001637-2, C); solutions manual 7.95 (ISBN 0-07-001638-0). McGraw.

Anderson, John E., jt. auth. see Goodenough, Florence L.

Anderson, John G. Technical Shop Mathematics. 510p. 1974. 18.95 o.p. (ISBN 0-8311-1085-6); wkd.-out solutions 6.00 o.p. (ISBN 0-8311-1106-2). Indus Pr.

--Technical Shop Mathematics. 2nd ed. (Illus.). 500p. 1983. 20.95 (ISBN 0-8311-1145-3); Answer Manual avail. Indus Pr.

Anderson, John J., ed. Nutrition & Vegetarianism. (Illus.). 245p. (Orig.). 1982. pap. 18.95 (ISBN 0-938938-04-5). Health Sci Consort.

Anderson, John L. Death in the Greenhouse: A Colonel Peter Blair Mystery. 192p. 1983. 11.95 (ISBN 0-686-83853-X, ScribT). Scribner.

Anderson, John M. Grammar of Case: Towards a Localistic Theory. LC 71-145602. (Studies in Linguistics Ser: No. 4). (Illus.). 1971. 44.50 (ISBN 0-521-08035-5); pap. 13.95 (ISBN 0-521-29057-0). Cambridge U Pr.

Anderson, John M., ed. see Calhoun, John C.

Anderson, John M., et al, eds. Historical Linguistics, 2 vols. 1974. Set. 73.25 o.p. (ISBN 0-444-10668-5, North-Holland); Set. pap. 53.25 (ISBN 0-444-10675-8). Elsevier.

Anderson, John Q., ed. see Stone, Kate.

Anderson, John Q., et al, eds. Southwestern American Literature: A Bibliography. LC 82-75745. 445p. 1980. 30.00x (ISBN 0-8040-0683-0, SB). Swallow.

Anderson, John R. The Architecture of Cognition. (Cognitive Science Ser.: No. 5). (Illus.). 352p. 1983. text ed. 25.00x (ISBN 0-674-04425-8). Harvard U Pr.

--Death in the City: A Colonel Peter Blair Mystery. 192p. 1982. 10.95 (ISBN 0-684-17758-7, ScribT). Scribner.

Anderson, John W. Bioenergetics of Autotrophs & Heterotrophs. (Studies in Biology: No. 126). 64p. 1980. pap. text ed. 8.95 (ISBN 0-7131-2807-0). E Arnold.

Anderson, Jon. Death & Friends. LC 70-117469. (Pitt Poetry Ser). 1970. 9.95 (ISBN 0-8229-3202-4); pap. 4.50 o.p. (ISBN 0-8229-5217-3). U of Pittsburgh Pr.

--The Milky Way. LC 82-11491. (The American Poetry Ser.: Vol. 25). 125p. 1983. 14.95 (ISBN 0-88001-006-1). Ecco Pr.

Anderson, Jonathan, et al. Thesis & Assignment Writing. LC 72-132006. 135p. 1970. pap. 7.50 o.p. (ISBN 0-471-02899-1, Pub. by Wiley-Interscience). Wiley.

Anderson, Joseph. Social Work Methods & Processes. 320p. 1981. text ed. 18.95x (ISBN 0-534-00955-7). Wadsworth Pub.

Anderson, Judith H. The Growth of a Personal Voice: Piers Plowman & "the Faerie Queene". LC 75-43300. 1976. 22.50x o.p. (ISBN 0-300-02000-7). Yale U Pr.

Anderson, Justo C. Historia De los Bautistas Tomo I: Sus Bases y Principios. 1978. pap. 5.75 (ISBN 0-311-15036-5). Casa Bautista.

Anderson, Karen. Wartime Women: Sex Roles, Family Relations, & the Status of Women During World War II. LC 80-1703. (Contributions in Women's Studies Ser.: No. 20). 198p. 1981. lib. bdg. 25.00x (ISBN 0-313-20884-0, AWW/). Greenwood.

Anderson, Kathleen. Your Baby, Your Birth: A Guide to Alternatives. 300p. 1983. write for info. (ISBN 0-917982-14-2). Cougar Bks.

Anderson, Kay. To Be Who You Are. 1979. 4.95 o.p. (ISBN 0-533-03669-0). Vantage.

Anderson, Kay W. Don't Forget Me, Mommy! LC 81-85048. (Illus.). 118p. (Orig.). 1982. pap. 6.95 (ISBN 0-686-96973-1). Marin Pub.

Anderson, Ken. The Fish Cookbook. 1981. 8.95 o.p. (ISBN 0-916752-17-8). Caroline Hse.

--The Sterno Guide to the Outdoors. LC 77-71480. 1977. 5.95 (ISBN 0-916752-12-7). Dorison Hse.

Anderson, Ken, jt. auth. see Berger, Bill.

Anderson, Ken E., jt. auth. see Berger, Bill D.

Anderson, Kenneth. The Pocket Guide to Coffees & Teas. (Illus.). 144p. 1982. pap. 5.95 (ISBN 0-399-50600-4, Perige); pap. 59.50 10-copy counter prepack (ISBN 0-399-50630-6). Putnam Pub Group.

Anderson, Kenneth, ed. Expense Analysis: Condominiums, Cooperatives, & Planned Unit Developments. 1978. pap. 10.00 (ISBN 0-912104-33-3). Inst Real Estate.

--Income-Expense Analysis: Apartments. 1978. pap. 22.50 (ISBN 0-912104-32-5). Inst Real Estate.

--Income, Expense Analysis: Apartments. 1979. pap. 22.50 (ISBN 0-912104-39-2). Inst Real Estate.

--Income-Expense Analysis: Apartments Condominums & Cooperatives, 1977. 1977. pap. 17.50 (ISBN 0-912104-27-9). Inst Real Estate.

--Income-Expense Analysis: Suburban Office Buildings, 1977. 1977. pap. 7.50 (ISBN 0-912104-28-7). Inst Real Estate.

--Income-Expense Analysis: Suburban Office Buildings. 1978. pap. 10.00 (ISBN 0-912104-34-1). Inst Real Estate.

--Income, Expense Analysis: Suburban Office Buildings. 1979. lib. bdg. 15.00 (ISBN 0-912104-40-6). Inst Real Estate.

Anderson, Kenneth E. & Haugh, Oscar M. A Handbook for the Preparation of Research Reports & Theses. LC 78-61395. 1978. pap. text ed. 5.25 (ISBN 0-8191-0597-X). U Pr of Amer.

Anderson, Kenneth R. Lease Escalators & Other Pass-Through Clauses: 1983. 2nd rev. ed. 35p. 1983. pap. 13.50 (ISBN 0-912104-70-8). Inst Real Estate.

Anderson, Kenneth R., ed. Computer Applications in Property Management Accounting. 3rd ed. 56p. 1982. pap. 13.50x (ISBN 0-912104-66-X). Inst Real Estate.

Anderson, Kenneth R. & Golden, Dale, eds. Certified Property Manager Profile & Compensation Study. 3rd, rev. ed. 1983. pap. 13.50 (ISBN 0-912104-69-4). Inst Real Estate.

Anderson, Kenneth R. & Ruiz, Stacey L., eds. Expense Analysis: Condominiums, Cooperatives, & Planned Unit Developments. 136p. 1982. pap. 39.00 (ISBN 0-912104-63-5). Inst Real Estate.

--Income-Expense Analysis: Apartments. 224p. (Orig.). 1982. pap. 59.00 (ISBN 0-912104-64-3). Inst Real Estate.

--Income-Expense Analysis: Office Buildings. 200p. (Orig.). 1982. pap. 59.00 (ISBN 0-912104-65-1). Inst Real Estate.

Anderson, Kenneth R., ed. see Institute of Real Estate Management.

Anderson, Kent, ed. Television Fraud: The History & Implications of the Quiz Show Scandals. LC 77-94755. (Contributions in American Studies: No. 39). lib. bdg. 27.50x (ISBN 0-313-20321-0, ATF/). Greenwood.

Anderson, Kim E. & Scott, Ronald M. Fundamentals of Industrial Toxicology. LC 80-69428. (Illus.). 120p. 1981. text ed. 14.95 (ISBN 0-250-40378-1). Ann Arbor Science.

Anderson, L. O. How to Build a Wood-Frame House. Orig. Title: Wood-Frame House Construction. (Illus.). 233p. 1970. pap. 5.50 (ISBN 0-486-22954-8). Dover.

Anderson, L. O. & Zornig, Harold F. Build Your Own Low Cost Home. 200p. 1972. pap. 9.95 (ISBN 0-486-21525-3). Dover.

Anderson, L. O., et al. Wood Decks: Construction & Maintenance. LC 79-91405. (Illus.). 128p. 1980. pap. 6.95 (ISBN 0-8069-8794-4). Sterling.

Anderson, L. W. Light & Color. LC 77-27460. (Read About Science Ser.). (Illus.). (gr. k-3). 1978. PLB 13.30 (ISBN 0-8393-0077-8). Raintree Pubs.

Anderson, La Vere. Allan Pinkerton: First Private Eye. LC 77-182270. (Americans All Ser.). (Illus.). 96p. (gr. 3-6). 1972. PLB 7.12 (ISBN 0-8116-4575-4). Garrard.

Anderson, Larry E., ed. see Zimmerman, John H.

Anderson, Larry L. & Tillman, David A. Synthetic Fuels from Coal: Overview & Assessment. LC 79-17786. 158p. 1979. 30.00x (ISBN 0-471-01784-1, Pub. by Wiley-Interscience). Wiley.

Anderson, LaVere. Abe Lincoln & the River Robbers. LC 79-148089. (Regional American Stories Ser.). (Illus.). 64p. (gr. 3-6). 1971. PLB 6.69 (ISBN 0-8116-4251-8). Garrard.

--Allan Pinkerton. (gr. k-6). Date not set. pap. 1.50 (ISBN 0-440-40210-7, YB). Dell.

--Balto: Sled Dog of Alaska. LC 75-45464. (Famous Animal Stories). (Illus.). 48p. (gr. 2-5). 1976. PLB 6.89 (ISBN 0-8116-4859-1). Garrard.

--Mary McLeod Bethune: Teacher with a Dream. LC 75-25765. (Discovery Books Ser). (Illus.). 80p. (gr. 2-5). 1976. PLB 6.69 (ISBN 0-8116-6321-3). Garrard.

--Mary Todd Lincoln: President's Wife. LC 74-18303. (Discovery Ser). (Illus.). 80p. (gr. 2-5). 1975. PLB 6.69 (ISBN 0-8116-6316-7). Garrard.

--Saddles & Sabers: Black Men of the Old West. LC 74-18122. (Toward Freedom Ser.). (Illus.). (gr. 5-9). 1975. PLB 3.98 (ISBN 0-8116-4805-2). Garrard.

--Sitting Bull: Great Sioux Chief. LC 70-120462. (Indians Ser). (Illus.). (gr. 2-5). 1970. PLB 6.69 (ISBN 0-8116-6608-5). Garrard.

--Story of Johnny Appleseed. LC 73-17255. (American Folktales Ser.). (Illus.). (gr. 2-5). 1974. PLB 6.69 (ISBN 0-8116-4040-X). Garrard.

--Svea: The Dancing Moose. LC 77-13922. (Famous Animal Ser.). (Illus.). (gr. 3). 1978. PLB 6.89 (ISBN 0-8116-4862-1). Garrard.

--Tad Lincoln: Abe's Son. LC 70-151987. (Discovery Ser.). (Illus.). (gr. 2-5). 1971. PLB 6.69 (ISBN 0-8116-6307-8). Garrard.

Anderson, Lee. Economic Analysis for Fisheries Management Plans. LC 80-68820. 319p. 1981. text ed. 49.95 (ISBN 0-250-40389-7). Ann Arbor Science.

Anderson, Lee G. & Settle, Russell F. Benefit-Cost Analysis. LC 77-3108. (Illus.). 1977. 18.95x (ISBN 0-669-01465-6). Lexington Bks.

Anderson, Lee G., ed. Economic Impacts of Extended Fisheries Jurisdiction. LC 76-46025. 1977. 49.95 (ISBN 0-250-40146-0). Ann Arbor Science.

Anderson, Leonard. Electric Machines & Transformers. (Illus.). 336p. 1980. text ed. 22.95 (ISBN 0-8359-1615-4); instr's. manual free (ISBN 0-8359-1616-2). Reston.

Anderson, Leone C. Learning about Towers & Dungeons. LC 82-9639. (The Learning About Ser.). 48p. (gr. 2-6). 1982. PLB 9.25 (ISBN 0-516-06538-6). Childrens.

--The Wonderful Shrinking Shirt. Fay, Ann, ed. (Just for Fun Bks.). (Illus.). 32p. (gr. k-3). 1983. PLB 8.25 (ISBN 0-8075-9171-8). A Whitman.

Anderson, LeRoy O. Handbook of Home Remodeling & Improvement. 1978. 14.95 o.p. (ISBN 0-442-20343-8). Van Nos Reinhold.

Anderson, Lewis F., ed. see Pestalozzi, Johann H.

Anderson, Linda A., ed. see Whitlock, Ruth.

Anderson, Linnea, et al. Nutrition in Health & Disease. 17th ed. (Illus.). 794p. 1982. text ed. 25.00 (ISBN 0-397-54282-8, Lippincott Nursing). Lippincott.

Anderson, Lorin W., jt. auth. see Block, James H.

Anderson, Lorraine. Leathercraft. LC 74-33529. (Early Craft Bks). (Illus.). 32p. (gr. 1-4). 1975. PLB 3.95g (ISBN 0-8225-0872-9). Lerner Pubns.

Anderson, Luleen S. Sunday Came Early This Week. 140p. 1982. 14.95 (ISBN 0-87073-599-3); pap. 7.95 (ISBN 0-87073-575-6). Schenkman.

Anderson, Lydia. Death. LC 79-23683. (gr. 4 up). 1980. PLB 8.90 (ISBN 0-531-04107-7). Watts.

--Folk Dancing. LC 81-3071. (First Bks.). (gr. 4 up). 1981. PLB 8.90 (ISBN 0-531-04193-X). Watts.

--Immigration. (Impact Ser.). 96p. (gr. 7 up). 1981. lib. bdg. 8.90 (ISBN 0-531-04335-5). Watts.

--Nigeria Cameroon Central Africa. LC 80-23042. (First Bks.). (gr. 4 up). 1981. PLB 8.90 (ISBN 0-531-04276-6). Watts.

Anderson, M. Help for Families of a Depressed Person. (Trauma Bks.: Ser. 2). 1983. pap. 2.50 ea. (ISBN 0-570-08258-7); Set. pap. 9.15. Concordia.

--Numerology: The Secret Power of Numbers. (Paths to Inner Power Ser.). pap. 2.25 (ISBN 0-87728-356-7). Weiser.

Anderson, M. D. History & Imagery of British Churches. (Illus.). 291p. 1972. 24.00 o.p. (ISBN 0-7195-2232-3). Transatlantic.

Anderson, Mrs. M. D. Book Indexing. (Authors' & Printers' Guides Ser.: No. 8). 1971. 4.95 (ISBN 0-521-08202-1). Cambridge U Pr.

Anderson, M. S., ed. Great Powers & the Near East. (Documents of Modern History Ser). 1971. 17.95 o.p. (ISBN 0-312-34650-6). St Martin.

Anderson, Madelyn. Greenland: Island at the Top of the World. LC 82-46003. (Illus.). 128p. (gr. 5 up). 1983. PLB 9.95 (ISBN 0-396-08139-8). Dodd.

Anderson, Madelyn K. Oil on Troubled Waters: Cleaning up Oil Spills. LC 80-21139. (Illus.). 128p. 1983. 8.95 (ISBN 0-8149-0842-X). Vanguard.

Anderson, Madelyn K., ed. see Benagh, Jim.

Anderson, Madelyn K., ed. see Herda, D. J.

Anderson, Maggie. Years That Answer. LC 79-2610. 1980. 11.49i (ISBN 0-06-010146-6, HarpT); pap. 5.95i (ISBN 0-06-090760-6, CN 760). Har-Row.

Anderson, Malcolm. Frontier Regions in Western Europe. 144p. 1983. text ed. 30.00 (ISBN 0-7146-3217-1, Pub. by Frank Cass). Biblio Dist.

Anderson, Marc & Rubin, Alan. Adsorption of Inorganics at Solid-Liquid Interfaces. LC 77-85090. 1981. text ed. 39.95 (ISBN 0-250-40226-2). Ann Arbor Science.

Anderson, Margaret. Arabic Materials in English Translation: A Bibliography of Works from the Pre-Islamic Period to 1977 Arabic. 1980. lib. bdg. 22.50 (ISBN 0-8161-7954-9, Hall Reference). G K Hall.

--Momentos Fleices Con Dios. 192p. Date not set. 2.95 (ISBN 0-88113-312-4). Edit Betania.

--My Thirty Years' War, an Autobiography. LC 76-136511. (Illus.). 1971. Repr. of 1930 ed. lib. bdg. 15.50x (ISBN 0-8371-5429-4, ANTY). Greenwood.

--The Unknowable Gurdjieff. (Illus.). 212p. (Orig.). 1973. pap. 6.95 (ISBN 0-87728-219-6). Weiser.

Anderson, Margaret J. Exploring City Trees & the Need for Urban Forests. new ed. LC 75-20481. (Illus.). 112p. (gr. 4-6). 1976. PLB 7.50 (ISBN 0-07-001695-X, GB). McGraw.

--Exploring the Insect World. LC 73-17412. (Illus.). 160p. (gr. 5 up). 1974. PLB 6.95 o.p. (ISBN 0-07-001625-9, GB). McGraw.

--Your Aging Parents. 1979. pap. 3.95 o.p. (ISBN 0-570-03789-1, 12-2752). Concordia.

Anderson, Mark. The Broken Boat. LC 78-14534. 75p. 1978. 3.50 (ISBN 0-87886-104-1). Ithaca Hse.

Anderson, Mark A. The Homzas' Son. 1983. 8.95 (ISBN 0-533-05187-8). Vantage.

Anderson, Marlene & Brearley, Joan M. This Is the Saint Bernard. (Illus.). 1973. 17.95 (ISBN 0-87666-376-5, PS-698). TFH Pubns.

Anderson, Martha G. & Arnoldi, Mary Jo. Art in Achebe's: Things Fall Apart & Arrow of God. (Graduate Student Paper Competition Ser.: No. 1). (Illus., Orig.). 1978. pap. text ed. 2.00 (ISBN 0-941934-25-X). Ind U Afro-Amer Arts.

Anderson, Martin, ed. The Military Draft: Selected Readings on Conscription, No. 258. LC 81-84641. (Publication Ser.). 630p. 1982. 19.95x (ISBN 0-8179-7581-0). Hoover Inst Pr.

Anderson, Mary. The Rise & Fall of a Teen Age Wacko. 1982. pap. 1.95 (ISBN 0-553-20532-3). Bantam.

--That's Not My Style. LC 82-13772. 168p. (gr. 6 up). 1983. 10.95 (ISBN 0-689-30968-6). Atheneum.

Anderson, Mary D. History by the Highway. 7.25 o.p. (ISBN 0-685-20592-4). Transatlantic.

Anderson, Mary Jo & Hayes, Arlene S. Building Blocks to Concept Mastery: Workbook. 130p. (gr. k-7). 1982. wkbk 29.95 (ISBN 0-88450-834-X). Communication Skill.

Anderson, Matthew S. Eastern Question: Seventeen Seventy-Four to Nineteen Twenty-Three. (Illus.). 1966. 19.95 o.p. (ISBN 0-312-22505-9). St Martin.

--Eighteenth-Century Europe, 1713-1789. (Orig.). 1968. pap. 5.95x (ISBN 0-19-500285-7). Oxford U Pr.

Anderson, Maxwell. Dramatist in America: Letters of Maxwell Anderson 1912-1958. Avery, Laurence G., ed. LC 77-4491. (Illus.). lxxxiii, 366p. 1977. 26.00x (ISBN 0-8078-1309-5). U of NC Pr.

--Off Broadway: Essays About the Theatre. LC 75-77699. (Theater, Film, & the Performing Arts Ser.). 92p. 1971. Repr. of 1947 ed. lib. bdg. 19.50 (ISBN 0-306-71337-3). Da Capo.

Anderson, Michael. Approaches to the History of the Western Family: 1500-1914. (Studies in Economic & Social History). 96p. 1980. pap. text ed. 5.50x (ISBN 0-333-24065-0, Pub. by Macmillan England). Humanities.

--Family Structure in Nineteenth Century Lancashire. LC 79-164448. (Cambridge Studies in Sociology: No. 5). (Illus.). 1971. 32.50 (ISBN 0-521-08237-4). Cambridge U Pr.

Anderson, Michael Q. Quantitative Management Decisionmaking. LC 81-6132. 768p. 1981. pap. text ed. 25.95 (ISBN 0-8185-0435-8). Brooks-Cole.

Anderson, Miles H. Upper Extremities Orthotics. (Illus.). 476p. 1979. 42.50x (ISBN 0-398-00044-1). C C Thomas.

Anderson, Miles H., ed. A Manual of Lower Extremities Orthotics. (Illus.). 552p. 1978. 49.50x (ISBN 0-398-02217-8). C C Thomas.

Anderson, Miles H., et al. Manual of Above Knee Wood Socket Prosthetics. rev. ed. (Illus.). 296p. 1980. ed. 34.50xspiral (ISBN 0-398-04071-0). C C Thomas.

Anderson, Nels. Men on the Move. LC 74-7427. (FDR & the Era of the New Deal Ser.). xii, 357p. 1974. Repr. of 1940 ed. lib. bdg. 45.00 (ISBN 0-306-70588-5). Da Capo.

Anderson, Nels, ed. Urbanism & Urbanization. (International Studies in Sociology & Social Anthropology: No. 2). (Orig.). 1964. pap. text ed. 12.00x o.p. (ISBN 90-0401-047-5). Humanities.

Anderson, Norma J. Pediatric Nursing: A Self Study Guide. 3rd ed. LC 77-26632. (Illus.). 1978. pap. text ed. 11.50 o.p. (ISBN 0-8016-0195-9). Mosby.

Anderson, Norman. Methods of Information Integration Theory, Vol. 2. 1982. 39.50 (ISBN 0-12-058102-7). Acad Pr.

Anderson, Norman & Brown, Walter. Rescue: The Young American Medal for Bravery. (Illus.). 128p. (gr. 5 up). 1983. 10.95 (ISBN 0-8027-6487-8). Walker & Co.

Anderson, Norman & Rentz, George. The Kingdom of Saudi Arabia. (Illus.). 256p. 1983. 60.00 (ISBN 0-905743-28-8, Pub by Salem Hse Ltd). Merrimack Bk Serv.

Anderson, Norman D. Investigating Science in the Swimming Pool & Ocean. (Illus.). (gr. 4-6). 1978. 8.95 (ISBN 0-07-001634-8, GB). McGraw.

--Investigating Science Using Your Whole Body. LC 74-32077. (Illus.). 96p. (gr. 5-9). 1975. PLB 6.95 o.p. (ISBN 0-07-001630-5, GB). McGraw.

Anderson, Norman D. & Brown, Walter R. Fireworks! Pyrotechnics on Display. LC 82-45995. (Illus.). 96p. (gr. 4 up). 1983. PLB 8.95 (ISBN 0-396-08142-8). Dodd.

--Halley's Comet. (Illus.). 80p. (gr. 4 up). 1981. 8.95 (ISBN 0-396-07974-1). Dodd.

Anderson, Norman D., jt. auth. see Simpson, Ronald D.

Anderson, O. D. Time Series Analysis & Forecasting: The Box Jenkins Approach. 168p. 1975. pap. 15.95 o.p. (ISBN 0-686-15234-4). Butterworth.

--Time Series Analysis Theory & Practice, Vol. 2. Date not set. 47.00 (ISBN 0-444-86536-5). Elsevier.

Anderson, O. D. & Perryman, M. R. Applied Time Series Analysis. 1982. 68.00 (ISBN 0-444-86424-5). Elsevier.

Anderson, O. D., ed. Forecasting Public Utilities. 1980. 40.50 (ISBN 0-444-86046-0). Elsevier.

--Time Series. 1980. 64.00 (ISBN 0-444-85418-5). Elsevier.

Anderson, O. D. & Perryman, M. R., eds. Time Series Analysis: Proceedings. 1981. 93.00 (ISBN 0-444-86177-7). Elsevier.

Anderson, O. D., et al, eds. Time Series Analysis: Theory & Practice One. Proceedings Of International Conference, Valencia, Spain, June 22-26, 1981. 756p. 1982. 85.00 (ISBN 0-444-86337-0). Elsevier.

Anderson, O. Roger. The Experience of Science: A New Perspective for Laboratory Teaching. LC 75-37967. 1976. pap. text ed. 8.95x (ISBN 0-8077-2489-0). Tchrs Coll.

--Teaching Modern Ideas of Biology. Jacobson, Willard, ed. LC 73-185961. 276p. 1972. text ed. 12.95x (ISBN 0-8077-1027-X). Tchrs Coll.

Anderson, Odin & Weeks, Lewis. Sociology of Health Care: An Inquiry Anthology. (Illus.). 340p. 1983. pap. text ed. price not set (ISBN 0-914904-78-7). Health Admin Pr.

Anderson, Odin W. Blue Cross Since 1929: Accountability & the Public Trust. LC 74-32003. 128p. 1975. prof ref 15.00 (ISBN 0-88410-122-3). Ballinger Pub.

--Health Care: Can There Be Equity? the United States, Sweden, & England. LC 72-7449. 273p. 1972. 28.95x o.p. (ISBN 0-471-02760-X, Pub. by Wiley-Interscience). Wiley.

Anderson, Olive. Liberal State at War: English Politics & Economics During the Crimean War. 1967. 20.00 (ISBN 0-312-48265-5). St Martin.

Anderson, Paul. The Horn of Time. 1982. pap. 1.75 (ISBN 0-451-11393-4, AE1390, Sig). NAL.

--Mirkheim. 1977. 7.95 o.p. (ISBN 0-399-11868-3, Pub. by Berkley). Putnam Pub Group.

--The People of the Wind: The Day of Their Return. 1982. pap. 2.75 (ISBN 0-451-11849-9, AE1849, Sig). NAL.

--The Rebel Worlds. Bd. with A Knight of Ghosts & Shadows. 1982. pap. 2.95 (ISBN 0-451-11885-5, AE1885, Sig). NAL.

--There Will be Time. Bd. with The Dancer From Atlantis. 1982. pap. 2.75 (ISBN 0-451-11752-2, AE1752, Sig). NAL.

--Winter of the World. Bd. with The Queen of Air & Darkness. 1982. pap. 3.50 (ISBN 0-451-11940-1, AE1940, Sig). NAL.

Anderson, Paul & Brockmann, John, eds. New Essays in Technical & Scientific Communications: Theory, Research, & Practice. (Baywood Technical Communication Ser.: Vol. 2). 272p. (Orig.). 1983. pap. text ed. 18.00x (ISBN 0-89503-036-5). Baywood Pub.

Anderson, Paul, et al. Addison Wesley General Mathematics. (gr. 9-12). 1980. text ed. 16.20 (ISBN 0-201-03825-0, Sch Div); tchr's. manual 18.52 (ISBN 0-201-03826-9, Sch Div); tests d.m. 14.44 (ISBN 0-201-03829-3). A-W.

Anderson, Paul E. Tax Factors in Real Estate Operations. 6th ed. (Illus.). 1980. 39.95 o.p. (ISBN 0-13-884858-0, Busn). P-H.

Anderson, Paul L. With the Eagles. LC 57-9447. (Illus.). (gr. 7-11). 1929. 9.00x (ISBN 0-8196-0100-4). Biblo.

Anderson, Paul S. & Lapp, Diane. Language Skills in Elementary Education. 3rd ed. 1979. text ed. 23.95 (ISBN 0-02-303140-9). Macmillan.

Anderson, Pauline & Clifford, Susan B. Dental Radiology. rev. ed. LC 79-56352. (Dental Assisting Ser.). (Illus.). 152p. 1981. pap. text ed. 8.80 (ISBN 0-8273-1871-5); instructor's guide 2.00 (ISBN 0-8273-1872-3). Delmar.

Anderson, Peggy, jt. auth. see Skouson, Sandra.

Anderson, Penny. The Big Storm. LC 82-7433. (Illus.). 32p. (gr. 3-4). 1982. lib. bdg. 4.95 (ISBN 0-686-83150-0). Dandelion Hse.

--The Operation. LC 79-16202. (Handling Difficult Times Ser.). (Illus.). 32p. (gr. 2-5). 1979. lib. bdg. 8.35 (ISBN 0-516-06433-9). Childrens.

--A Pretty Good Team. LC 79-15928. (Handling Difficult Times Ser.). (Illus.). 32p. (gr. 2-5). 1979. lib. bdg. 8.35 (ISBN 0-516-06434-7). Childrens.

Anderson, Penny, tr. see Landry, Monica & Olivier, Julien.

Anderson, Penny S. Frustrated. LC 82-4492. (What Does it Mean? Ser.). (Illus.). 32p. (gr. 1-2). 1982. PLB 4.95 (ISBN 0-89565-237-4, 4896, Pub. by Childs World). Standard Pub.

Anderson, Perry. Considerations on Western Marxism. 1976. 13.50x (ISBN 0-8052-7014-0, Pub. by Verso); pap. 6.95 (ISBN 0-8052-7070-1, Pub. by NLB). Schocken.

--Lineages of the Absolutist State. 1979. 17.50x (ISBN 0-8052-7025-6); pap. 9.95 (ISBN 0-8052-7059-0, Pub. by Verso). Schocken.

--Passages from Antiquity to Feudalism. 1978. 12.50x (ISBN 0-8052-7024-8); pap. 7.75 (ISBN 0-8052-7024-8, Pub. by NLB). Schocken.

Anderson, Peter. Robert Stewart, Earl of Orkney, Lord of Shetland, 1533-1593. 222p. 1982. text ed. 31.50x (ISBN 0-85976-082-0, Pub. by John Donald Scotland). Humanities.

Anderson, Poul. Agent of the Terran Empire. 1979. lib. bdg. 12.50 (ISBN 0-8398-2528-5, Gregg). G K Hall.

--The Avatar. LC 78-7875. 1978. 10.95 o.p. (ISBN 0-399-12228-1, Pub. by Berkley). Putnam Pub Group.

--Beyond the Beyond. pap. 1.50 o.p. (ISBN 0-451-07760-1, W7760, Sig). NAL.

--Book of Poul Anderson. (Science Fiction Ser.). 1978. pap. 1.95 o.p. (ISBN 0-87997-347-1, UV1347). DAW Bks.

--The Broken Sword. (A Del Rey Bk.). 1977. pap. 1.50 o.s.i. (ISBN 0-394-25512-7). Ballantine.

--The Byworlder. 1978. lib. bdg. 9.95 (ISBN 0-8398-2432-7, Gregg). G K Hall.

--A Circus of Hells. (Science Fiction Ser.). 1979. lib. bdg. 12.50 (ISBN 0-8398-2524-2, Gregg). G K Hall.

--Dancer from Atlantis. pap. 1.50 o.p. (ISBN 0-451-07806-3, W7806, Sig). NAL.

--Dominic Flandry of Terra Series. (Science Fiction Ser.). 1979. 72.50 (ISBN 0-686-74230-3, Gregg). G K Hall.

--The Earth Book of Stormgate. 1979. pap. 2.25 o.p. (ISBN 0-425-04090-9). Berkley Pub.

--The Earth Book of Stormgate. 1978. 10.95 o.p. (ISBN 0-399-12144-7, Pub. by Berkley). Putnam Pub Group.

--The Earth Book of Stormgate. 448p. 1983. pap. 2.95 (ISBN 0-425-05933-2). Berkley Pub.

--Ensign Flandry. 1979. lib. bdg. 10.00 (ISBN 0-8398-2526-9, Gregg). G K Hall.

--Flandry of Terra. 1979. lib. bdg. 12.50 (ISBN 0-8398-2527-7, Gregg). G K Hall.

--The Guardians of Time. rev. ed. 256p. 1981. pap. 2.95 (ISBN 0-523-48579-4). Pinnacle Bks.

--The Horn of Time. 1978. lib. bdg. 9.95 (ISBN 0-8398-2428-9, Gregg). G K Hall.

--A Knight of Ghosts & Shadows. (Science Fiction Ser.). 1979. lib. bdg. 12.50 (ISBN 0-8398-2523-4, Gregg). G K Hall.

--The Long Way Home. 1978. lib. bdg. 9.95 (ISBN 0-8398-2431-9, Gregg). G K Hall.

--Mirkheim. 1979. pap. 1.75 o.p. (ISBN 0-425-04309-6). Berkley Pub.

--Mirkheim. (Polesotechnic League Ser.: No. 4). 224p. 1983. pap. 2.25 (ISBN 0-425-05863-8). Berkley Pub.

--New America. 288p. 1983. pap. 2.95 (ISBN 0-523-48553-0). Pinnacle Bks.

--The Night Face & Other Stories. (Science Fiction, Worlds of Poul Anderson Ser.). 1978. lib. bdg. 9.95 (ISBN 0-8398-2412-2, Gregg). G K Hall.

--Orbit Unlimited. 1978. lib. bdg. 9.95 (ISBN 0-8398-2430-0, Gregg). G K Hall.

--People of the Wind. lib. bdg. 9.50 o.p. (ISBN 0-8398-2353-3, Gregg). G K Hall.

--The Queen of Air & Darkness. 1978. lib. bdg. 9.95 (ISBN 0-8398-2433-5, Gregg). G K Hall.

--The Rebel Worlds. (Science Fiction Ser.). 1979. lib. bdg. 12.50 (ISBN 0-8398-2525-0, Gregg). G K Hall.

--Satan's World. (Polesotechnic League Ser.: No. 3). 224p. 1983. pap. 2.25 (ISBN 0-425-05851-4). Berkley Pub.

--Sign of the Raven. (The Last Viking Ser.: No. 3). (Orig.). 1981. pap. 2.50 (ISBN 0-686-96926-X). Zebra.

--Trader to the Stars. pap. 1.75 o.p. (ISBN 0-425-04304-5). Berkley Pub.

--Trader to the Stars. (Polesotechnic League Ser.: No. 2). 160p. 1983. pap. 2.25 (ISBN 0-425-05746-1). Berkley Pub.

--Two Worlds. 1978. lib. bdg. 9.95 (ISBN 0-8398-2429-7, Gregg). G K Hall.

--Vault of the Ages. 1979. lib. bdg. 9.50 (ISBN 0-8398-2521-8, Gregg). G K Hall.

--War of the Wing Men. 1976. Repr. of 1958 ed. lib. bdg. 9.95 (ISBN 0-8398-2326-6, Gregg). G K Hall.

--The Worlds of Poul Anderson. 1978. 60.00 (ISBN 0-686-74231-1, Gregg). G K Hall.

Anderson, Poul & Dickson, Gordon R. Star Prince Charlie. LC 74-21078. 192p. (gr. 6-8). 1975. 6.95 o.p. (ISBN 0-399-20443-1). Putnam Pub Group.

Anderson, Poul, jt. auth. see Eklund, Gordon.

Anderson, R. Individualizing Educational Materials for Special Children in the Mainstream. 416p. 1978. pap. 19.95 (ISBN 0-8391-1253-X). Univ Park.

Anderson, R., jt. auth. see Nibbelink, D.

Anderson, R., et al. The Administrative Secretary. 2nd ed. 1976. 21.90 (ISBN 0-07-001747-6, G). McGraw.

Anderson, R. B. Proving Programs Correct. 184p. 1979. 14.50 (ISBN 0-471-03395-2). Wiley.

Anderson, R. C. & May, R. M., eds. Population Biology of Infectious Diseases: Berlin 1982. (Dahlem Workshop Reports: Vol. 25). (Illus.). 320p. 1982. 18.00 (ISBN 0-387-11650-8). Springer-Verlag.

Anderson, R. C. & Osborn, J., eds. Learning to Read in American Schools. 384p. 1983. text ed. write for info. (ISBN 0-89859-219-4). L Erlbaum Assocs.

Anderson, R. G. Dictionary of Data Processing & Computer Terms. 112p. 1982. pap. text ed. 9.95x (ISBN 0-7121-0429-1). Intl Ideas.

--Management, Planning & Control. 400p. 1981. 35.00x (ISBN 0-7121-1277-4, Pub. by Macdonald & Evans). State Mutual Bk.

Anderson, R. M., et al, eds. Population Dynamics: (the Twentieth Symposium of the British Ecological Society) (British Ecological Society Symposia Ser.). 434p. 1980. 99.95x (ISBN 0-470-26816-6). Halsted Pr.

Anderson, R. R., jt. ed. see Whitby, W. M.

Anderson, R. T., et al. Reliability Analysis Methodology for Photovoltaic Energy Systems. (Progress in Solar Energy Ser.). 142p. 1983. pap. 13.50 (ISBN 0-89553-132-1). Am Solar Energy.

Anderson, Rachel. The Poacher's Son. (Illus.). 137p. 1983. text ed. 11.95 (ISBN 0-19-271468-6, Pub. by Oxford U Pr Childrens). Merrimack Bk Serv.

Anderson, Raymond L., jt. auth. see Maass, Arthur.

Anderson, Richard. Representation in the Juvenile Court. (Direct Editions Ser). (Orig.). 1978. pap. 12.95 (ISBN 0-7100-8578-8). Routledge & Kegan.

--Robert Coover. (United States Authors Ser.). 1981. lib. bdg. 12.95 (ISBN 0-8057-7330-4, Twayne). G K Hall.

--Your Keys to the Executive Suite. 32p. 1973. pap. 1.50 o.p. (ISBN 0-570-06981-5, 12-2558). Concordia.

Anderson, Richard E. & Kasl, Elizabeth. The Costs of Financing of Adult Education & Training. LC 81-47276. (Illus.). 352p. 1982. 31.95x (ISBN 0-669-04570-5). Lexington Bks.

Anderson, Richard J. & Hofman, Peter L. Alternative Energy Sources for the United States. 19p. pap. 2.50x (ISBN 0-87855-743-1). Transaction Bks.

Anderson, Richard L. Art in Primitive Societies. (Illus.). 1979. pap. 14.95 ref. ed. (ISBN 0-13-048108-4). P-H.

Anderson, Robert. Stress Power! How to Turn Tension into Energy. LC 78-8308. 248p. 1978. 26.95 (ISBN 0-686-86076-4) (ISBN 0-87705-328-6). Human Sci Pr.

Anderson, Robert, jt. auth. see Haast, William E.

Anderson, Robert see Strasberg, Lee.

Anderson, Robert H., jt. auth. see Shinebourne, Elliot A.

Anderson, Robert J. & Schrier, Robert W. Clinical Uses of Drugs in Patients with Kidney & Liver Disease. (Illus.). 368p. 1981. text ed. 37.50 (ISBN 0-7216-1239-3). Saunders.

Anderson, Robert J., jt. ed. see Lopez, Enrique Campos.

Anderson, Robert M. & Greer, John G., eds. Educating the Severely & Profoundly Retarded. (Illus.). 444p. 1976. pap. 12.95 (ISBN 0-8391-0945-8). Univ Park.

Anderson, Robert M., jt. auth. see Greer, John G.

Anderson, Robert T. Studies in Samaritan Manuscripts & Artifacts: The Chamberlain-Warren Collection. LC 78-52697. (American Schools of Oriental Research Monograph: Vol. 1). 99p. 1978. text ed. 8.00x (ISBN 0-89757-402-8, Am Sch Orient Res). Eisenbrauns.

Anderson, Rodney J. The External Audit. (Pitman Series in Finance & Accounting). 537p. 1977. text ed. 39.95 (ISBN 0-7730-4223-7). Pitman Pub MA.

Anderson, Rodney U., jt. auth. see Kessler, Robert.

Anderson, Roger C. Seventeenth Century Rigging 1600-1725. (Illus.). 146p. 1964. 10.00x (ISBN 0-85344-080-8). Intl Pubns Serv.

Anderson, Roger F. Forest & Shade Tree Entomology. LC 60-11714. 428p. 1960. 28.95x (ISBN 0-471-02739-1). Wiley.

Anderson, Ron & Atkins, Walter J., Jr. The Rest of Eighty. (Illus.). 1983. write for info. Green.

Anderson, Ronald T. Automating Your Agency Book. LC 82-60877. 288p. 1982. text ed. 16.35 (ISBN 0-87218-321-1). Natl Underwriter.

Anderson, Ronald T., jt. auth. see Hammes, Carol A.

Anderson, Roy R., jt. auth. see Seibert, Robert F.

Anderson, Ruth I., et al. Word Finder. 4th ed. (gr. 9-12). 1974. text ed. 4.50o.p. (ISBN 0-8224-3330-3); pap. 3.95 (ISBN 0-8224-3355-9). Pitman Learning.

Anderson, Ruth L. Mark of the Land. 320p. (Orig.). 1983. pap. 5.95x (ISBN 0-933892-15-2). Child Focus Co.

Anderson, S. D. & Woodhead, R. W. Project Manpower Management: Management Process in Construction Practice. LC 80-22090. 264p. 1981. 39.95x (ISBN 0-471-95979-0, Pub. by Wiley-Interscience). Wiley.

Anderson, Sandra V. & Bauwens, Eleanor E. Chronic Health Problems: Concepts & Application. LC 80-29482. (Illus.). 336p. 1981. pap. 16.95 (ISBN 0-8016-0199-1). Mosby.

Anderson, Scarvia B. & Coburn, Louisa V., eds. Academic Testing & the Consumer. LC 81-48587. 1982. 7.95x (ISBN 0-87589-929-3, TM-15). Jossey-Bass.

Anderson, Scott. Funniest Baseball Stories of the Century. rev. ed. (Laughter Library). (Orig.). 1979. pap. 1.75 (ISBN 0-8431-0539-9). Price Stern.

--Funniest Football Stories of the Century. (Laughter Library). (Orig.). 1979. pap. 1.75 (ISBN 0-8431-0538-0). Price Stern.

Anderson, Scott, jt. auth. see Burgum, Thomas.

Anderson, Sharon, et al. Statistical Methods for Comparative Studies: Techniques for Bias Reduction. LC 79-27220. (Wiley Series in Probability & Mathematical Statistics: Applied Probability & Statistics). 289p. 1980. 33.95x (ISBN 0-471-04838-0, Pub. by Wiley-Interscience). Wiley.

Anderson, Sheridan. Baron Von Mabel's Backpacking. (Illus.). 96p. (Orig.). 1980. pap. 4.95 (ISBN 0-89620-082-5). Rip Off.

Anderson, Sherwood. Letters. Jones, Howard M. & Rideout, Walter B., eds. LC 52-12649. Repr. of 1953 ed. 24.00 o.s.i. (ISBN 0-527-02500-3). Kraus Repr.

--Return to Winesburg: Selections from Four Years of Writing for a Country Newspaper. White, Ray L., ed. LC 67-23499. xiii, 223p. 1967. 17.00 (ISBN 0-686-37889-X). U of NC Pr.

--Winesburg, Ohio. 2nd ed. 1960. 15.00 o.p. (ISBN 0-670-77236-4). Viking Pr.

Anderson, Stanford, ed. On Streets. 1978. 55.00x (ISBN 0-262-01036-4). MIT Pr.

Anderson, Stanley F. & Hull, Raymond. Art of Making Wine. 1971. pap. 3.50 (ISBN 0-8015-0390-6, 0340-100, Hawthorn). Dutton.

Anderson, Stanley H., jt. auth. see Purdom, P. Walton.

Anderson, Sydney & Jones, J. Knox, Jr., eds. Recent Mammals of the World: A Synopsis of Families. (Illus.). 453p. 1967. 28.50x (ISBN 0-471-06763-6, Pub. by Wiley-Interscience). Wiley.

Anderson, T. & Randell, B., eds. Computing Systems Reliability. LC 78-75253. (Illus.). 1979. 47.50 (ISBN 0-521-22767-4). Cambridge U Pr.

Anderson, T. W. & Sclove, Stanley L. An Introduction to the Statistical Analysis of Data. LC 77-78890. (Illus.). 1978. text ed. 24.50 (ISBN 0-395-15045-0); solutions manual 1.00 (ISBN 0-395-15046-9). HM.

Anderson, T. W., et al. A Bibliography of Multivariate Statistical Analysis. LC 76-54249. 1977. Repr. of 1972 ed. lib. bdg. 36.50 (ISBN 0-88275-477-7). Krieger.

Anderson, Terry. Water Rights: Scarce Resource Allocation, Bureaucracy & the Environment. (Pacific Institute on Public Policy Research Ser.). 1983. prof ref 32.50 (ISBN 0-88410-389-7). Ballinger Pub.

Anderson, Theodore W. Introduction to Multivariate Statistical Analysis. LC 58-6068. (Probability & Mathematical Statistics Ser.). 374p. 1958. 36.95x (ISBN 0-471-02640-9). Wiley.

--Statistical Analysis of Time Series. LC 70-126222. (Probability & Mathematical Statistics Ser.). 704p. 1971. 44.95x (ISBN 0-471-02900-9). Wiley.

Anderson, Thomas D., jt. auth. see Norwine, Jim.

Anderson, Totten J., jt. auth. see Rodee, Carlton C.

Anderson, Troels & Atkins, Guy. Asger Jorn. LC 82-60792. (Illus.). 98p. 1982. pap. 9.00 (ISBN 0-89207-034-X). S R Guggenheim.

Anderson, V. Elving, et al, eds. The Genetic Basis of the Epilepsies. 396p. 1982. text ed. 53.50 (ISBN 0-89004-676-X). Raven.

Anderson, V. Elving, jt. ed. see Sheppard, John R.

Anderson, V. S. King of the Roses. 384p. 1983. 14.95 (ISBN 0-312-45512-7). St Martin.

Anderson, Valborg, ed. & tr. see Strindberg, August.

Anderson, Vincent P. Reaction to Religious Elements in the Poetry of Robert Browning: Introduction & Annotated Bibliography. LC 82-50407. 350p. 1983. 25.00X (ISBN 0-87875-221-8). Whitston Pub.

Anderson, Virgil A. Training the Speaking Voice. 3rd ed. (Illus.). 1977. text ed. 18.95x (ISBN 0-19-502150-9). Oxford U Pr.

Anderson, Virgil A. & Newby, Hayes. Improving the Child's Speech. 2nd ed. (Illus.). 375p. 1973. text ed. 14.95x (ISBN 0-19-501708-0). Oxford U Pr.

Anderson, Virgil L. & McLean, Robert A. Design of Experiments: A Realistic Approach. (Statistics, Textbks & Monographs: Vol. 5). 440p. 1974. 22.50 (ISBN 0-8247-6131-6). Dekker.

Anderson, W. A. D. & Kissane, John M. Pathology. 7th ed. LC 77-1052. (Illus.). 1977. 64.50 (ISBN 0-8016-0186-X). Mosby.

Anderson, W. French, et al, eds. Cooley's Anemia Symposium, 4th. LC 80-17575. (Annals of the New York Academy of Sciences: Vol. 344). 448p. 1980. 81.00x (ISBN 0-89766-076-5); pap. 79.00x (ISBN 0-89766-077-3). NY Acad Sci.

Anderson, W. H. National Income Theory & Its Price Theoretic Foundations. (Economic Handbook Ser.). (Illus.). 1979. text ed. 39.95x (ISBN 0-07-001670-4). McGraw.

Anderson, W. H. & Putallaz, Ann. Macroeconomics. (Illus.). 480p. 1983. pap. text ed. 16.95 (ISBN 0-13-542811-4). P-H.

Anderson, W. Thomas, Jr., et al. Multidimensional Marketing: Managerial, Societal & Philosophical. LC 75-13358. (Illus.). 323p. (Orig.). 1976. pap. text ed. 7.95x (ISBN 0-914872-06-0). Austin Pr.

Anderson, Wallace L. Edwin Arlington Robinson: A Critical Introduction. LC 67-5760. 1967. 11.00x o.p. (ISBN 0-674-24025-1). Harvard U Pr.

Anderson, Walter. A Place of Power: The American Episode in Human Evolution. LC 76-12809. 1976. text ed. 15.95 o.p. (ISBN 0-87620-080-3); pap. text ed. 14.50x (ISBN 0-673-16268-0). Scott F.

Anderson, Walter I. Robinson: The Pleasant History of an Unusual Cat. LC 82-10897. (Illus.). 72p. 1982. 9.95 (ISBN 0-87805-170-8). U Pr of Miss.

Anderson, Warren D. Ethos & Education in Greek Music: The Evidence of Poetry & Philosophy. LC 66-21328. 1966. 12.50x o.p. (ISBN 0-674-26900-4). Harvard U Pr.

Anderson, Warren D., tr. see Aeschylus.

Anderson, William. In His Light: A Path into Catholic Belief. 216p. 1979. pap. 4.95 (ISBN 0-697-01716-8). Wm C Brown.

--Journeying in His Light. 160p. 1982. wire coil 4.25 (ISBN 0-697-01858-X). Wm C Brown.

--The Strawberry: A World Bibliography Nineteen Twenty to Nineteen Sixty Six. LC 72-3866. 1969. 22.50 o.p. (ISBN 0-8108-0262-7). Scarecrow.

--The Wild Man from Sugar Creek: The Political Career of Eugene Talmadge. LC 74-82002. (Illus.). xviii, 268p. 1975. 22.50x (ISBN 0-8071-0088-9); pap. 7.95x (ISBN 0-8071-0170-2). La State U Pr.

Anderson, William C. BAT-Twenty-One: Based on the True Story of Lt. Col. Iceal E. Hambleton, USAF. LC 80-20648. 1980. 9.95 o.p. (ISBN 0-13-069500-9). P-H.

--Home Sweet Home Has Wheels; or Please Don't Tailgate the Real Estate. 1979. 9.95 o.p. (ISBN 0-517-53830-X). Crown.

Anderson, William G. Analysis of Teaching Physical Education. LC 79-20074. 1980. pap. 11.95 (ISBN 0-8016-0179-7). Mosby.

--The Price of Liberty: The Public Debt of the American Revolution. LC 82-17420. 1983. 20.00x (ISBN 0-8139-0975-9). U Pr of Va.

Anderson, William P. Aspects of the Theology of Karl Barth. LC 81-40163. 198p. (Orig.). 1981. lib. bdg. 20.50 (ISBN 0-8191-1748-X); pap. text ed. 11.00 (ISBN 0-8191-1749-8). U Pr of Amer.

Anderson, William R., ed. see McVaugh, Rogers.

Anderson, William S. & Puhvel, Jaan, eds. California Studies in Classical Antiquity, Vol. 12. LC 68-26906. (Illus.). 400p. 1981. 33.00x (ISBN 0-520-04055-4). U of Cal Pr.

Anderson, William T. The Story of the Ingalls. (Laura Ingalls Wilder Family Ser.). (Illus.). 40p. (Orig.). 1971. pap. text ed. 2.95 (ISBN 0-9610088-0-6). Anderson MI.

Anderson, Wood P. Weed Science: Principles. 1977. text ed. 30.95 (ISBN 0-8299-0084-5). West Pub.

--Weed Science: Principles. 2nd ed. (Illus.). 650p. 1983. text ed. 23.95 (ISBN 0-314-69632-6). West Pub.

Anderson-Imbert, Enrique & Kiddle, Lawrence B., eds. Veinte Cuentos Espanoles Del Siglo Veinte. (Orig., Span.). (gr. 10-12). 1961. pap. text ed. 12.95 (ISBN 0-13-941567-X). P-H.

--Veinte Cuentos Hispanoamericanos Del Siglo Veinte. (Orig., Span.). 1956. pap. 12.95 (ISBN 0-13-941575-0). P-H.

Anderson Sweeney, David R. & Williams, Thomas A. Introduction to Statistics: An Applications Approach. (Illus.). 750p. text ed. 25.95 (ISBN 0-8299-0361-5). West Pub.

Andersson, Ake E. & Holmberg, Ingvar, eds. Demographic, Economic & Social Interactions. LC 76-2042. 368p. 1977. prof ref 25.00x (ISBN 0-88410-045-6). Ballinger Pub.

Andersson, Bjorn. Science Teaching & the Development of Thinking. (Goteborg Studies in Educational Sciences: No. 20). (Illus.). 1976. pap. text ed. 18.25x (ISBN 91-7346-026-5). Humanities.

Andersson, Christiane & Talbot, Charles. From a Mighty Fortress: Prints, Drawings, & Books in the Age of Luther, 1483-1546. (Illus.). 300p. (Orig.). 1983. pap. 15.00 (ISBN 0-89558-091-8). Detroit Inst Arts.

Andersson, Stig. The Boy Who Made an Elephant. 32p. (gr. k-3). 2.95 o.p. (ISBN 0-89191-190-1, 27789). Cook.

--No Two Zebras Look Exactly Alike. (gr. k-3). 2.95 o.p. (ISBN 0-89191-189-8, 27797). Cook.

Andersson, Theodore, jt. ed. see Mackey, William F.

AnderTon, Johana G. Collector's Encyclopedia of Cloth Dolls. 1982. write for info (ISBN 0-87069-402-2). Wallace-Homestead.

--Twentieth Century Dolls. (Illus.). 29.95 (ISBN 0-87069-272-0). Wallace-Homestead.

Anderton, R., et al. A Dynamic Stratigraphy of the British Isles. (Illus.). 1979. text ed. 35.00x (ISBN 0-04-551027-X); pap. text ed. 22.95x (ISBN 0-04-551028-8). Allen Unwin.

Ando, W. Oxidation of Organo-Sulfur Compounds. (Sulfur Reports Ser.). 80p. 1981. flexicover 17.00 (ISBN 3-7186-0073-0). Harwood Academic.

--Photoxidation of Organosulfur Compounds. (Sulfur Reports Ser.). 80p. 1981. pap. 17.00 (ISBN 3-7186-0073-0). Harwood Academic.

Andolenko, S. Badges of Imperial Russia Including Military, Civil & Religious. Werlich, R., tr. (Illus.). 1983. lib. bdg. 36.00 (ISBN 0-685-00798-7). Quaker.

Andolfi, Maurizio & Angelo, Claude. Behind the Family Mask: Therapeutic Change in Rigid Family Systems. 184p. 1983. 17.50 (ISBN 0-87630-330-0). Brunner-Mazel.

Andor, Jozsef. Frame Semantics & the Typology of Actions. (Pragmatics & Beyond Ser.). 120p. 1983. pap. 14.00 (ISBN 90-272-2521-4). Benjamins North Am.

Andors, Phyllis. The Unfinished Liberation of Chinese Women, 1949-1980. LC 81-48323. 224p. 1983. 22.50x (ISBN 0-253-36022-6). Ind U Pr.

Andors, Stephen, ed. Workers & Workplaces in Revolutionary China. Mathews, Jay, et al, trs. LC 76-53710. (The China Book Project Ser.). 1977. 27.50 (ISBN 0-87332-094-8). M E Sharpe.

Andrade. Introduccion a la Ciencia Politica. 400p. (Span.). 1982. pap. text ed. write for info. (ISBN 0-06-310030-4, Pub. by HarLA Mexico). Har-Row.

Andrade, Carlos D. The Minus Sign. De Araujo, Virginia, ed. (Illus.). 160p. 1981. 17.50x (ISBN 0-933806-03-5). Black Swan CT.

Andrade, Edward N. Sir Isaac Newton. LC 79-15162. 140p. 1979. Repr. of 1958 ed. lib. bdg. 16.00x (ISBN 0-313-22022-0). Greenwood.

Andrade, Victor. My Missions for Revolutionary Bolivia 1944-1962. LC 76-6656. (Pitt Latin American Ser). 1976. 12.95 o.p. (ISBN 0-8229-3320-9). U of Pittsburgh Pr.

Andrae, Tor. Mohammed: The Man & His Faith. LC 60-5489. 1977. pap. text ed. 4.95xi o.p. (ISBN 0-06-130062-4, TB 62, Torch). Har-Row.

Andraeson, Tjalve & Schmidt. Engineering Graphic Modelling. (Illus.). 1979. 15.95 (ISBN 0-408-00305-7). Butterworth.

Andras, Szekely, intro. by. Mihaly Munkacsy. Beres, Zsuzsa, tr. (Illus.). 160p. 1981. 55.00 (ISBN 0-89893-168-1). CDP.

Andrasik, Frank, jt. ed. see Matson, Johnny L.

Andre, G. David, the Man After God's Own Heart. (Let's Discuss It Ser.). pap. 1.50 (ISBN 0-88172-134-4); pap. 15.00 o.p. Believers Bkshelf.

--Gideon, Samson & Other Judges of Israel. (Let's Discuss It Ser.). pap. 0.95 (ISBN 0-88172-132-8); pap. 9.50 o.p. Believers Bkshelf.

--Jeremiah, the Prophet. (Let's Discuss It Ser.). pap. 0.95 (ISBN 0-88172-135-2). Believers Bkshelf.

--Moses, the Man of God. (Let's Discuss It Ser.). pap. 0.95 (ISBN 0-88172-131-X); pap. 9.50 o.p. Believers Bkshelf.

Andre, Jean. The Sperm Cell. 1982. 71.75 (ISBN 90-247-2784-7, Pub. by Martinus Nijhoff Netherlands). Kluwer Boston.

Andre, Michael, ed. Unmuzzled Ox Anthology, No. 15. Barnes, Djuna, et al. (Illus.). pap. 4.95 (ISBN 0-686-28478-X). Unmuzzled Ox.

Andre, Michael, ed. see Wright, James, et al.

Andre, Michael, et al, eds. see Stafford, William.

Andre, Nevin, jt. auth. see Palmore, Phyllis.

Andre, Nils, jt. ed. see Allardt, Erik.

Andre, Rae. Homemakers: The Forgotten Workers. LC 80-21258. 320p. 1981. 15.00 (ISBN 0-226-01993-4); pap. 8.95 (ISBN 0-226-01994-2). U of Chicago Pr.

Andrea, Alfred J. & Schmokel, W. The Living Past: Western Historiographical Traditions. LC 81-20878. 314p. 1982. Repr. of 1975 ed. 16.50 (ISBN 0-89874-152-1). Krieger.

Andreas, Burton G. Experimental Psychology. 2nd ed. LC 78-171910. 608p. 1972. text ed. 29.95 (ISBN 0-471-02905-X). Wiley.

Andreas, Carol. Sex & Caste in America. 1971. 12.95 (ISBN 0-13-807420-8, Spec); pap. 2.95 (ISBN 0-13-807438-0). P-H.

Andreas, Evelyn, ed. Fairy Tales. (Silver Dollar Library Ser.). (Illus.). (gr. k-7). 1962. 1.50 o.p. (ISBN 0-448-00323-6, G&D). Putnam Pub Group.

Andreassi, John L. Psychophysiology: Human Behavior & Physiological Response. 1980. text ed. 19.95x (ISBN 0-19-502581-4); pap. text ed. 12.95x (ISBN 0-19-502582-2). Oxford U Pr.

Andreassi, Michael W. & MacRae, C. Duncan. Homeowner Income Tax Provisions & Metropolitan Housing Markets: A Simulation Study. LC 81-51624. 78p. 1981. pap. 9.00 (ISBN 0-87766-297-5, URI 29900). Urban Inst.

Andrecht, Venus C. The Outrageous Herb Lady: How to Make a Mint in Selling & Multi-Level Marketing. McWhorter, Margaret L., ed. LC 82-60388. 144p. (Orig.). 1982. pap. 6.95 (ISBN 0-9604342-2-4). Ransom Hill.

Andre De Ligneville, J. F. Entretiens de Zerbes, Roi de Lydie, et de Son Ministre sur la Situation des Affaires de Son Royaume. (Utopias in the Enlightenment Ser.). 111p. (Fr.). 1974. Repr. of 1788 ed. lib. bdg. 37.50x o.p. (ISBN 0-8287-0027-3, 007). Clearwater Pub.

Andree, R., et al. Computer Programming: Techniques, Analyses & Mathematics. 1973. ref. ed. 25.95 (ISBN 0-13-166082-9). P-H.

Andree, Richard V. Computer Programming & Related Mathematics. LC 66-25215. 284p. 1967. text ed. 16.00x (ISBN 0-471-02920-3, Pub. by Wiley). Krieger.

Andreichin, L., et al. How to Write Bulgarian. 454p. 1981. 25.00 (ISBN 0-686-97390-9, M-9832). French & Eur.

Andreichina, K., et al. Russian-Bulgarian Phraseological Dictionary. Vlasova, ed. 582p. (Rus. & Bulgarian.). 1980. 65.00 (ISBN 0-686-97416-6, M-9830). French & Eur.

Andreissen, David. The Star Seed. LC 81-5402. (Illus., Orig.). 1981. pap. 5.95 (ISBN 0-89865-021-6, Starblaze). Donning Co.

Andrejko, Dennis A., jt. auth. see Wright, David.

Andreoli, Anthony L. & Shuman, D. R. Guide to Unclaimed Property & Escheat Laws, 2 Vols. LC 82-71985. 2100p. 1982. Vol. I. 249.50 set (ISBN 0-943882-02-8); write for info. (ISBN 0-943882-00-1); Vol. II. write for info. (ISBN 0-943882-02-8). Commonwlth Pub.

Andreoli, Kathleen G. & Fowkes, Virginia K. Comprehensive Cardiac Care: A Text for Nurses, Physicians & Other Health Practitioners. 5th ed. (Illus.). 562p. 1983. pap. text ed. 18.95 (ISBN 0-8016-0265-3). Mosby.

Andreoli, T. E., et al, eds. see American Physiological Society.

Andreopoulos, Spyros, jt. auth. see Dong, Eugene.

Andres, P. G., et al. Basic Mathematics for Engineers. LC 55-8369. 776p. 1944. text ed. 32.95 (ISBN 0-471-02937-8). Wiley.

--Basic Mathematics for Science & Engineering. LC 55-8369. 846p. 1955. text ed. 33.95x (ISBN 0-471-02970-X). Wiley.

Andres, U. Magnetohydrodynamic & Magnetohydrostatic Methods of Mineral Separation. 224p. 1976. 49.95 o.p. (ISBN 0-470-15014-9). Halsted Pr.

Andresen, Gail & Weinhold, Barry. Connective Bargaining: Communicating About Sex. (Illus.). 224p. 1980. 13.95 o.p. (ISBN 0-13-167791-8, Spec); pap. 5.95 o.p. (ISBN 0-13-167783-7). P-H.

Andresen, P. H. The Human Blood Groups: Utilized in Disputed Paternity Cases & Criminal Proceedings. 132p. 1952. photocopy ed. spiral 12.75x (ISBN 0-398-04193-8). C C Thomas.

Andreski, Iris, ed. Old Wives' Tales: Life-Stories of African Women. LC 77-107613. (Sourcebooks in Negro History Ser). 1971. 8.00x o.p. (ISBN 0-8052-3342-3). Schocken.

Andreski, Stanislav. Social Sciences As Sorcery. LC 72-94178. (Griffin Paperback Ser). 1973. 7.95 o.p. (ISBN 0-685-31231-3); pap. 3.95 o.p. (ISBN 0-312-73500-6). St Martin.

Andreski, Stanislav, ed. & tr. Max Weber on Capitalism, Bureaucracy & Religion. (A Selection of Texts Ser.). 192p. 1983. text ed. 22.95x (ISBN 0-04-301147-0); pap. text ed. 7.95x (ISBN 0-04-301148-9). Allen Unwin.

Andress, Barbara L. Music in Early Childhood: Prepared by the National Commission on Instruction. 54p. 1973. 3.50 (ISBN 0-686-37917-9). Music Ed.

Andress, Lesley. Caper. 1980. 10.95 (ISBN 0-399-12403-9). Putnam Pub Group.

Andress, Michael. Model Railway Guide Two: Layout Planning. 1979. 7.95 (ISBN 0-85059-359-X). Aztex.

Andretti, Mario & Collins, Bob. What's It Like Out There. 5.95 o.p. (ISBN 0-8092-9672-1). Contemp Bks.

Andreu, Helene C. Jazz Dance: An Adult Beginner's Guide. 192p. 1983. 15.95 (ISBN 0-13-509968-4); pap. 7.95 (ISBN 0-13-509950-1). P-H.

Andrew, Brother, et al. God's Smuggler. 1968. pap. 2.25 (ISBN 0-451-09868-4, E9868, Sig). NAL.

Andrew, Chris O. & Hildebrand, Peter E. Planning & Conducting Applied Agricultural Research. 96p. 1982. lib. bdg. 12.00 (ISBN 0-86531-461-6); pap. text ed. 7.95 (ISBN 0-86531-460-8). Westview.

Andrew, Dudley. Andre Bazin. (Illus.). 1978. 17.95x (ISBN 0-19-502165-7). Oxford U Pr.

Andrew, Dudley & Andrew, Paul. Kenji Mizoguchi: A Guide to References & Resources. 336p. 1981. lib. bdg. 35.00 (ISBN 0-8161-8469-0, Hall Reference). G K Hall.

Andrew, H. E. Laye. The Arco Encyclopedia of Crafts. LC 78-2841. 1982. pap. 12.95 (ISBN 0-668-05609-6, 5609). Arco.

Andrew, J., ed. The Structural Analysis of Russian Narrative Fiction. 1981. 60.00x o.p. (ISBN 0-86127-205-6, Pub. by Avebury Pub England). State Mutual Bk.

Andrew, Jan. Divorce & the American Family. LC 77-17398. (gr. 7 up). 1978. PLB 8.90 (ISBN 0-531-01470-3). Watts.

Andrew, Joe. Russian Writers & Society in the Second Half of the Nineteenth Century. 140p. 1982. 50.00x (ISBN 0-333-25911-4, Pub. by Macmillan England). State Mutual Bk.

Andrew, Joe, tr. see Pike, Christopher.

Andrew, Kenneth. Hong Kong Detective. (Illus.). 15.00 (ISBN 0-392-03260-0, LTB). Sportshelf.

Andrew, Malcolm & Waldron, Ronald, eds. The Poems of the Pearl Manuscript. LC 78-64464. (York Medieval Texts, Second Ser.). 1979. 46.50x (ISBN 0-520-03794-4). U of Cal Pr.

--The Poems of the Pearl Manuscript: Pearl, Cleanness, Patience, Sir Gawain & the Green Knight. 382p. 1982. pap. 10.95x (ISBN 0-520-04631-5, CAMPUS 292). U of Cal Pr.

Andrew, Paul, jt. auth. see Andrew, Dudley.

Andrew, Warren. Comparative Hematology. LC 64-25851. (Illus.). 1965. 83.50 o.p. (ISBN 0-8089-0012-9). Grune.

Andrew, William G. & Williams, H. B. Applied Instrumentation in the Process Industries: A Survey, Vol. 1. 2nd ed. 407p. 1979. 43.95x (ISBN 0-87201-382-0). Gulf Pub.

--Applied Instrumentation in the Process Industries: Engineering Data & Resource Material, Vol. 3. 2nd ed. 520p. 1982. 43.95x (ISBN 0-87201-384-7). Gulf Pub.

--Applied Instrumentation in the Process Industries: Practical Guidelines, Vol. 2. 2nd ed. 312p. 1980. 43.95x (ISBN 0-87201-383-9). Gulf Pub.

--Engineering Data & Resource Material. 2nd ed. (Applied Instrumentation in the Process Industries: Vol. 3). 520p. 1982. 43.95x (ISBN 0-87201-384-7). Gulf Pub.

Andrewartha, H. G. & Birch, L. C. The Distribution & Abundance of Animals. LC 54-13016. (Illus.). xvi, 782p. 1974. pap. 8.95 o.s.i. (ISBN 0-226-02025-8, P576, Phoen). U of Chicago Pr.

--Selections from The Distribution & Abundance of Animals. LC 82-6948. (Illus.). 288p. 1982. lib. bdg. 25.00x (ISBN 0-226-02031-2); pap. 7.95 (ISBN 0-226-02032-0). U of Chicago Pr.

Andrews. Competition of Economic Theory. 1969. 14.95 o.p. (ISBN 0-312-15505-0). St Martin.

--Liver. (Studies in Biology: No. 105). 1979. 8.95 (ISBN 0-8391-0255-0). Univ Park.

Andrews & Houston. Adult Learners: A Research Study. 1981. 5.00 (ISBN 0-686-38071-1). Assn Tchr Ed.

Andrews, jt. auth. see Waterman.

Andrews, A. Australasian Tokens & Coins. 1982. Repr. of 1921 ed. lib. bdg. 35.00 (ISBN 0-942666-10-0). S J Durst.

Andrews, Allen. The Flying Machine: Its Evolution Through the Ages. LC 77-75933. (Illus.). 1977. 12.95 o.p. (ISBN 0-399-11967-1). Putnam Pub Group.

Andrews, B. G. Tales of the Convict System. 1975. 23.00x o.s.i. (ISBN 0-7022-0929-5); pap. 10.95x o.s.i. (ISBN 0-7022-0936-8). U of Queensland Pr.

Andrews, Barbara. This Bittersweet Love. (Candlelight Ecstasy Ser.: No. 127). (Orig.). 1983. pap. 1.95 (ISBN 0-440-18797-4). Dell.

Andrews, Barry. Price Warung (William Astley) (World Authors Ser.: No. 383). 1976. lib. bdg. 15.95 (ISBN 0-8057-6225-6, Twayne). G K Hall.

Andrews, Barry G. & Wilde, William H., eds. Australian Literature to Nineteen Hundred: A Guide to Information Sources. LC 74-11521. (American Literature, English Literature & World Literatures in English Information Guide Ser.: Vol. 22). 472p. 1980. 42.00x (ISBN 0-8103-1215-8). Gale.

Andrews, Bart. The Official TV Trivia Quiz Book. (Illus., Orig.). 1975. pap. 1.25 o.p. (ISBN 0-451-06363-5, Y6363, Sig). NAL.

--The Official TV Trivia Quiz Book, No. 2. (Illus., Orig.). 1976. pap. 1.50 (ISBN 0-451-08410-1, W8410, Sig). NAL.

--Official TV Trivia Quiz Book, No. 3. (Illus., Orig.). 1978. pap. 1.75 o.p. (ISBN 0-451-08401-2, E8401, Sig). NAL.

--Super Sixties Quiz Book. (Orig.). 1979. pap. 1.75 o.p. (ISBN 0-451-08829-8, E8829, Sig). NAL.

--Trekkie Quiz Book. pap. 1.95 (ISBN 0-451-11656-9, AJ1656, Sig). NAL.

Andrews, Bart & Davenport, Howard. From the Blob to Star Wars: The Science Fiction Movie Quiz Book. (Orig.). 1977. pap. 1.50 o.p. (ISBN 0-451-07948-5, W7948, Sig). NAL.

Andrews, Bart & Dunning, Brad. The Fabulous Fifties Quiz Book. (Illus.). 1978. pap. 1.50 o.p. (ISBN 0-451-08116-1, W8116, Sig). NAL.

Andrews, Bart & Zuper, Bernie. The Tolkien Quiz Book. (Orig.). 1979. pap. 1.75 o.p. (ISBN 0-451-08525-6, E8525, Sig). NAL.

Andrews, Bruce J., jt. auth. see Andrews, Keith L.

Andrews, C. M. Guide to the Materials for American History, to 1783 in the Public Record Office of Great Britain, 2 Vols. 1912-1914. Set. 56.00 (ISBN 0-527-00686-6). Kraus Repr.

Andrews, Carol. The Rosetta Stone. 32p. 1982. pap. 25.00x (ISBN 0-7141-0931-2, Pub. by Brit Mus Pubns England). State Mutual Bk.

Andrews, Charles M. Colonial Folkways. 1919. text ed. 8.50x (ISBN 0-686-83505-0). Elliots Bks.

--Fathers of New England. 1919. text ed. 8.50x (ISBN 0-686-83545-X). Elliots Bks.

Andrews, Clarence A. Chicago in Story: A Literary History of Chicago. (Illus.). 420p. 1982. 19.95. Midwest Heritage.

Andrews, Clarence A., ed. Clarence Andrews' Christmas in Iowa. LC 79-89445. (Illus.). 128p. 1979. 8.95 (ISBN 0-934582-00-9). Midwest Heritage.

--Growing up in Iowa. (Illus.). 1978. 8.95 (ISBN 0-8138-0801-4). Iowa St U Pr.

Andrews, Clarence A., ed. see Childs, Marquis & Engel, Paul.

Andrews, Colman. Best Restaurants Los Angeles. LC 82-8173. (Best Restaurants Ser.). (Illus.). 224p. (Orig.). 1982. pap. 4.95 (ISBN 0-89286-203-3). One Hund One Prods.

Andrews, Craig, jt. auth. see Benson, Carl.

Andrews, Daniel, tr. see Butikov, Georgy.

Andrews, Deborah C. & Blickle, Margaret D. Technical Writing: Principles & Forms. 2nd ed. 1982. text ed. 17.95 (ISBN 0-02-303470-X). Macmillan.

Andrews, Donald H. Introductory Physical Chemistry. LC 70-102457. 1970. text ed. 21.00 o.p. (ISBN 0-07-001788-3, C). McGraw.

Andrews, E. H., ed. Developments in Polymer Fracture, Vol. 1. 1982. 65.75 (ISBN 0-85334-819-7, Pub. by Applied Sci England). Elsevier.

Andrews, Edward D. Gift to Be Simple. (Illus.). 1940. pap. 3.50 (ISBN 0-486-20022-1). Dover.

Andrews, Edward D. & Andrews, Faith. Fruits of the Shaker Tree of Life: Memoirs of Fifty Years of Collecting & Research. LC 75-33901. 1975. 15.95 o.p. (ISBN 0-912944-31-5); pap. 8.95 o.p. (ISBN 0-912944-32-3). Berkshire Traveller.

--Visions of the Heavenly Sphere: A Study in Shaker Religious Art. LC 79-83652. (Illus.). 1969. 15.00 o.p. (ISBN 0-8139-0260-6, Winterthur Museum). U Pr of Va.

--Work & Workshop Among the Shakers. (Illus.). 224p. 1982. pap. 6.00 (ISBN 0-486-24382-6). Dover.

Andrews, Emma. The Films of: Sean Connery. (Illus.). 96p. 1982. pap. 3.95 (ISBN 0-8253-0111-4); pap. 94.80 Prepack of 24 titles write for additional title info. (ISBN 0-686-83063-6). Beaufort Bks NY.

Andrews, Eva L., jt. ed. see Frizzell-Smith, Dorothy B.

Andrews, F., ed. Scientific Productivity. LC 78-21978. (Illus.). 1979. 39.50 (ISBN 0-521-22586-8). Cambridge U Pr.

Andrews, F. David, ed. Lost Peoples of the Middle East: Documents on the Struggle for Survival & Independence of the Kurds, Assyrians, & other Minority Races of the Middle East. Ltd. 350 Copies 34.95. Documentary Pubns.

Andrews, F. Emerson. Numbers, Please. 2nd enlarged ed. LC 77-20492. 1977. pap. 5.95x (ISBN 0-8077-2545-5). Tchrs Coll.

--Philanthropic Giving. 318p. 1950. 9.95x (ISBN 0-87154-022-3). Russell Sage.

Andrews, Faith, jt. auth. see Andrews, Edward D.

Andrews, Felicia. Moonwitch. (Historical Romance Ser.). 1980. pap. 2.50 o.s.i. (ISBN 0-515-04781-3). Jove Pubns.

--Mountain Witch. pap. 2.75 (ISBN 0-515-05846-7). Jove Pubns.

--Riverrun. (Orig.). 1979. pap. 2.50 o.s.i. (ISBN 0-515-04545-4). Jove Pubns.

--Silver Huntress. 2.95 (ISBN 0-441-76609-9). Ace Bks.

Andrews, Frank C. Equilibrium Statistical Mechanics. 2nd ed. LC 74-17197. 255p. 1975. 24.95x (ISBN 0-471-03123-2, Pub. by Wiley-Interscience). Wiley.

--Thermodynamics: Principles & Applications. LC 77-150607. 288p. 1971. 21.95x o.p. (ISBN 0-471-03183-6, Pub. by Wiley-Interscience). Wiley.

Andrews, Frank M. & Messenger, Robert C. Multivariate Nominal Scale Analysis: A Report on a New Analysis Technique & a Computer Program. LC 72-629721. 114p. 1973. 12.00x (ISBN 0-87944-135-6); pap. 8.00x (ISBN 0-87944-134-8). Inst Soc Res.

Andrews, Frank M., jt. auth. see Pelz, Donald C.

Andrews, Frank M., et al. A Guide for Selecting Statistical Techniques for Analyzing Social Science Data. 2nd ed. LC 74-620117. 80p. 1981. pap. 8.00x (ISBN 0-87944-274-3). Inst Soc Res.

--Multiple Classification Analysis: A Report on a Computer Program for Multiple Regression Using Categorical Predictors. rev. ed. LC 73-620206. 116p. 1973. 12.00x (ISBN 0-87944-148-8); pap. 8.00x (ISBN 0-87944-055-4). Inst Soc Res.

Andrews, G. Reid. The Afro-Argentines of Buenos Aires, 1800-1900. LC 80-5105. 304p. 1980. 22.50 (ISBN 0-299-08290-3). U of Wis Pr.

Andrews, George E. Number Theory: The Theory of Partitions. LC 76-41770. (Encyclopedia of Mathematics & Its Applications: Vol. 2). (Illus.). 1976. text ed. 29.50 (ISBN 0-201-13501-9). A-W.

Andrews, George E., ed. Percy Alexander MacMahon: Collected Papers: Combinatorics, Vol. 1. LC 77-28962. (Mathematicians of Our Time Ser.). 1978. 85.00x (ISBN 0-262-13121-8). MIT Pr.

Andrews, Gould A., jt. ed. see Kniseley, Ralph M.

Andrews, Gould A., et al, eds. Radioactive Pharmaceuticals: Proceedings. LC 66-60068. (AEC Symposium Ser.). 702p. 1966. pap. 25.50 (ISBN 0-87079-325-X, CONF-651111); microfiche 4.50 (ISBN 0-87079-326-8, CONF-651111). DOE.

Andrews, Harry C. Computer Techniques in Image Processing. 1970. 36.50 (ISBN 0-12-058550-2). Acad Pr.

--Introduction to Mathematical Techniques in Pattern Recognition. LC 72-772. 242p. 1972. 27.50 o.p. (ISBN 0-471-03172-0). Wiley.

Andrews, Heber J. How to Prevent Bicycle Theft: Owner's Guide. (Illus.). 32p. 1982. pap. 2.50x (ISBN 0-9609596-0-2). Hands Off.

Andrews, Henry N., Jr. Studies in Paleobotany. LC 61-6768. (Illus.). 487p. 1961. 30.95x (ISBN 0-471-03168-2). Wiley.

Andrews, Hilda, tr. see Cortot, Alfred.

Andrews, Hilda, tr. see Walicki, Andrzei.

Andrews, J. Paul Sixth: A Critical Appraisal. 1970. 6.95 o.p. (ISBN 0-685-07657-1, 80003). Glencoe.

Andrews, J. A. Human Rights in Criminal Procedure. 1982. lib. bdg. 85.00 (ISBN 90-247-2552-6, Pub. by Martinus Nijhoff Netherlands). Kluwer Boston.

Andrews, J. Austin & Wardian, Jeanne. Introduction to Music Fundamentals. 4th ed. 1978. pap. text ed. 17.95 (ISBN 0-13-489575-4). P-H.

Andrews, J. G. & McLone, R. R., eds. Mathematical Modeling. 1976. 16.95 (ISBN 0-408-10601-8). Butterworth.

Andrews, Jack. The Edge of the Anvil. LC 77-15115. 1977. 12.95 o.p. (ISBN 0-87857-186-8); pap. 10.95 o.p. (ISBN 0-87857-195-7). Rodale Pr Inc.

Andrews, James R. Essentials of Public Communicaton. LC 78-18182. 217p. 1979. text ed. 18.95x (ISBN 0-673-15652-4). Scott F.

--The Practice of Rhetorical Criticism. 288p. 1983. text ed. 20.95 (ISBN 0-02-303490-4). Macmillan.

Andrews, Jeanne. All's Fair in Love. (Sweet Dreams Ser.: No. 41). 160p. 1982. pap. 1.95 (ISBN 0-553-22607-X). Bantam.

Andrews, Jim. Catamarans for Cruising. 2nd. ed. (Illus.). 224p. 1981. 14.00 o.p. (ISBN 0-370-10339-4); pap. 14.00 o.s.i. (ISBN 0-370-30382-2). Transatlantic.

Andrews, Jim, jt. auth. see Andrews, Judy.

Andrews, John. The Price Guide to Victorian Furniture. (Price Guide Ser.). (Illus.). 346p. 1973. 21.50 o.p. (ISBN 0-902028-18-9). Antique Collect.

Andrews, John, jt. auth. see Taylor, Jennifer.

Andrews, John B., jt. auth. see Commons, John R.

Andrews, John C. Such Are the Valiant. (Inflation Fighter Ser.). 160p. 1982. pap. cancelled o.s.i. (ISBN 0-8439-1122-0, Leisure Bks). Nordon Pubns.

Andrews, John T., ed. Glacial Isostasy. LC 73-12624. (Benchmark Papers in Geology: Vol. 10). 491p. 1974. text ed. 54.00 (ISBN 0-87933-051-1). Hutchinson Ross.

Andrews, John W. A. D. Twenty-One Hundred. LC 71-82113. (Illus.). 1969. 4.25 o.s.i. (ISBN 0-8283-1033-5). Branden.

--First Flight. 2.25 o.s.i. (ISBN 0-8283-1228-1). Branden.

--Hill Country North. 3.75 o.s.i. (ISBN 0-8283-1226-5). Branden.

--Prelude to Icaros. 1966. pap. 1.95 o.s.i. (ISBN 0-8283-1227-3). Branden.

--Triptych for the Atomic Age. 5.25 o.s.i. (ISBN 0-8283-1281-8). Branden.

Andrews, Joseph & Coffin, George. Win at Hearts. (Bridge & Other Card Games Ser.). (Illus.). 96p. (Orig.). pap. 2.95 (ISBN 0-486-24406-7). Dover.

Andrews, Judith, tr. see Butikov, Georgy.

Andrews, Judy & Andrews, Jim. Family Boating. (Illus.). 160p. 1983. 14.95 (ISBN 0-370-30407-1, Pub by The Bodley Head); pap. 7.95 (ISBN 0-370-30473-X). Merrimack Bk Serv.

Andrews, K. W. Physical Metallurgy: Techniques & Applications, 2 vols, No.2. LC 72-11309. 347p. 1973. Vol. 2. 39.95 o.p. (ISBN 0-470-03151-4). Halsted Pr.

Andrews, Keith L. & Andrews, Bruce J. Commuter Calisthenics: a Contemporary Fitness Program for Busy People. (Illus.). 110p. (Orig.). 1982. pap. 6.95 o.p. (ISBN 0-686-36919-X). Fitness Alt Pr.

Andrews, Kenneth. The Concept of Corporate Strategy. LC 75-153173. 1971. 21.95 o.p. (ISBN 0-87094-012-0). Dow Jones-Irwin.

Andrews, Kenneth R. Elizabethan Privateering 1583-1603. 1964. 39.50 (ISBN 0-521-04032-9). Cambridge U Pr.

Andrews, Larry C. Ordinary Differential Equations with Applications. 1982. text ed. 25.50x (ISBN 0-673-15800-4). Scott F.

Andrews, Lewis R. & Kelly, Reaney J. Maryland's Way: The Hammond-Harwood House Cook Book. (Illus.). 372p. 1963. 10.95 (ISBN 0-686-36725-1). Md Hist.

Andrews, Linda. Philosophy of Economics. (Foundations of Philosophy Ser.). (Illus.). 200p. 1981. pap. text ed. 10.95 (ISBN 0-13-663336-6). P-H.

Andrews, Lynn V. Medicine Woman. LC 81-47546. (Illus.). 288p. 1981. 12.98i (ISBN 0-06-250025-2, HarpR). Har-Row.

Andrews, M. E. About Her. (Opportunity Knocks Ser). 1968. text ed. 3.40 o.p. (ISBN 0-07-001772-7, G); tchr's. source bk. for series avail. o.p. (ISBN 0-07-001777-8). McGraw.

--About Him. (Opportunity Knocks Ser). 1968. text ed. 3.40 o.p. (ISBN 0-07-001773-5, G); tchr's. source bk. for series avail. o.p. (ISBN 0-07-001777-8). McGraw.

--Gregg Office Job Training Program, Classroom Installation. Incl. Mail Clerk. training manual 4.16 (ISBN 0-07-001811-1); resource material 5.60 (ISBN 0-07-001812-X); File Clerk. training manual 3.96 (ISBN 0-07-001813-8); resource material 5.60 (ISBN 0-07-001814-6); Payroll Clerk. training manual 4.16 (ISBN 0-07-001815-4); resource material 4.96 (ISBN 0-07-001816-2); Typist. training manual 4.16 (ISBN 0-07-001817-0); resource material 5.60 (ISBN 0-07-001818-9); Clerk Typist. training manual 4.16 (ISBN 0-07-001819-7); resource material 5.60 (ISBN 0-07-001820-0); Accounts Payable Clerk. training manual 4.16 (ISBN 0-07-001821-9); resource material 5.60 (ISBN 0-07-001822-7); Accounts Receivable Clerk. training manual 4.16 (ISBN 0-07-001823-5); resource material 5.60 (ISBN 0-07-001824-3); Order Clerk. training manual 4.16 (ISBN 0-07-001825-1); resource material 5.60 (ISBN 0-07-001826-X); Credit Clerk. training manual 4.16 (ISBN 0-07-001827-8); resource material 5.60 (ISBN 0-07-001828-6); Stock Control Clerk. training manual 4.16 (ISBN 0-07-001829-4); resource material 5.60 (ISBN 0-07-001830-8); Office Cashier. Andrews, M. E. training manual 4.16 (ISBN 0-07-001831-6); resource material 5.60 (ISBN 0-07-001832-4); Purchasing Clerk. training manual 4.16 (ISBN 0-07-001833-2); resource material 5.60 (ISBN 0-07-001834-0); Traffic Clerk. training manual 3.96 (ISBN 0-07-001835-9); resource material 5.60 (ISBN 0-07-001836-7); Personnel Clerk. training manual 4.16 (ISBN 0-07-001837-5); resource material 4.96 (ISBN 0-07-001838-3); Billing Clerk. Andrews, M. E. & Hodges. training manual 4.16 (ISBN 0-07-001839-1); resource material 5.60 (ISBN 0-07-001840-5). 1973. presentation pkg 317.55 (ISBN 0-07-079665-3, G); job selection guides 4.16 (ISBN 0-07-001841-3); supervisor's handbk. 12.30 (ISBN 0-07-001843-X); filing supplies 10.08 (ISBN 0-07-086301-6). McGraw.

--It's Up to You. (Opportunity Knocks Ser.). 1970. text ed. 5.52 o.p. (ISBN 0-07-001776-X, G); tchr's source bk. for series 5.00 o.p. (ISBN 0-07-001777-8). McGraw.

--You Said It. (Opportunity Knocks Ser). 1969. text ed. 5.52 o.p. (ISBN 0-07-001774-3, G); tchr's source bk. for series 5.00 o.p. (ISBN 0-07-001777-8). McGraw.

Andrews, M. E., jt. auth. see Mulkerne, D. D.

Andrews, M. E., jt. auth. see Mulkerne, D. J.

Andrews, Mark. Satan's Manor. 288p. 1982. pap. 3.25 o.s.i. (ISBN 0-8439-1175-1, Leisure Bks). Nordon Pubns.

Andrews, Michael. Programming Microprocessor Interface for Control & Instrumentation. (Illus.). 368p. 1982. 32.95 (ISBN 0-13-729996-6). P-H.

Andrews, Michael A. The Flight of the Condor: A Wildlife Exploration of the Andes. LC 81-48533. (Illus.). 158p. 1982. 22.50 (ISBN 0-316-03958-6). Little.

Andrews, Miriam. Fifty Poems. LC 70-135873. (Orig.). 1971. pap. 2.95 o.s.i. (ISBN 0-8283-1304-0). Branden.

Andrews, Ondre H., ed. see Huston, Harvey.

Andrews, Patrick. The Bent Star. 192p. (Orig.). 1982. pap. 2.25 o.p. (ISBN 0-505-51843-0). Tower Bks.

Andrews, Peter, ed. Christmas in Colonial & Early America. LC 75-27283. (Round the World Christmas Program Ser.). 1975. 7.95 o.p. (ISBN 0-7166-2001-4). World Bk.

--Christmas in Germany. LC 74-83569. (Round the World Christmas Program Ser.). (Illus.). 1974. 7.95 o.p. (ISBN 0-7166-2000-6). World Bk.

Andrews, Peter P. & Layhe, Robert, eds. Excavations on Black Mesa, Nineteen Eighty: A Descriptive Report. LC 82-72189. (Research Paper Ser.: No. 24). Date not set. price not set (ISBN 0-88104-003-7). S Ill U Pr.

Andrews, Richard N. Environmental Policy & Administrative Change: Implementation of the National Environmental Policy Act. LC 76-7265. (Illus.). 1976. 22.95x o.p. (ISBN 0-669-00682-3). Lexington Bks.

Andrews, Richard N., ed. Land in America. LC 77-14735. (Illus.). 1979. 21.95 o.p. (ISBN 0-669-01989-5). Lexington Bks.

Andrews, Robert & Ericson, E. E. Teaching Industrial Education: Princples & Practices. 1976. pap. text ed. 11.96 (ISBN 0-87002-079-X). Bennett IL.

Andrews, Roy C. All About Dinosaurs. (Allabout Ser.: No. 1). (Illus.). (gr. 4-6). 1953. 3.95 (ISBN 0-394-80201-2, BYR); PLB 5.39 o.p. (ISBN 0-394-90201-7). Random.

--Ends of the Earth. LC 78-164078. (Towers Bks). (Illus.). x, 355p. 1972. Repr. of 1929 ed. 34.00x (ISBN 0-8103-3923-4). Gale.

Andrews, Samuel J. Christianity & Anti-Christianity in Their Final Conflict. 1982. lib. bdg. 15.00 (ISBN 0-86524-084-1, 9804). Klock & Klock.

Andrews, Samuel J. & Gifford, E. H. Man & the Incarnation: The Study of Philippians 2 & Psalm 110. 1981. lib. bdg. 15.00 (ISBN 0-86524-078-7, 9510). Klock & Klock.

Andrews, Sheila. The No-Cooking Fruitarian Recipe Book. (Illus.). 1976. pap. 5.00 (ISBN 0-7225-0290-7). Newbury Bks.

Andrews, Sherry, jt. auth. see Roberts, Pattie.

Andrews, Spike. C. A. T. No. 1: Tower of Blood. (Men of Action Ser.). 224p. (Orig.). 1982. pap. 1.95 (ISBN 0-446-30182-5). Warner Bks.

--C.A.T. No. Three: Cult of the Damned. 224p. (Orig.). 1983. pap. 2.25 (ISBN 0-446-30183-3). Warner Bks.

--C.A.T., No. Two: Kidnap Hotel. (Men of Action Ser.). 224p. 1983. pap. 1.95 (ISBN 0-446-30185-X). Warner Bks.

Andrews, Suzanna, et al, eds. The World Environment Handbook: A Directory of Government Natural Resource Management Agencies in 144 Countries. 144p. (Orig.). 1982. pap. write for info. (ISBN 0-910499-00-4). World Env Ctr.

Andrews, Theodora, et al. Bibliography on Herbs, Herbal Remedies, Natural Foods, & Unconventional Treatment. LC 82-128. 344p. 1982. lib. bdg. 25.00 (ISBN 0-87287-288-2). Libs Unl.

Andrews, Timothy. The Mammoth Book of Jokes & Cartoons. (Mammoth Bks.). (Illus.). 512p. (Orig.). Date not set. pap. 8.95 (ISBN 0-89104-283-0, A & W Visual Library). A & W Pubs. Postponed.

Andrews, V. C. Flowers in the Attic. 1980. 12.95 o.s.i. (ISBN 0-671-41124-1). S&S.

--Flowers in the Attic. (Readers Request Ser.). 1983. lib. bdg. 18.95 (ISBN 0-8161-3429-4, Large Print Bks). G K Hall.

--If There Be Thorns. 1981. 14.95 o.s.i. (ISBN 0-671-43122-6). S&S.

--If There Be Thorns. (Readers Request Ser.). 1983. lib. bdg. 18.95 (ISBN 0-8161-3429-4, Large Print Bks). G K Hall.

--My Sweet Audrina. 1982. 14.50 (ISBN 0-686-81877-6). S&S.

--Petals on the Wind. (Readers Request Ser.). 1982. lib. bdg. 19.95 (ISBN 0-8161-3427-8, Large Print Bks). G K Hall.

Andrews, Wayne. Architecture in Chicago & Mid-America: A Photographic History. (Icon Editions). (Illus.). 206p. 1973. pap. 8.95i o.p. (ISBN 0-06-430043-9, IN-43, HarpT). Har-Row.

--Architecture in Michigan. Rev. & enlarged ed. (Illus.). 160p. 1982. 22.00x (ISBN 0-8143-1718-9); pap. 13.95 (ISBN 0-8143-1719-7). Wayne St U Pr.

Andrews, William. At the Sign of the Barber's Pole. LC 74-77164. 1969. Repr. of 1904 ed. 30.00x (ISBN 0-8103-3846-7). Gale.

--Basic Federal Income Taxation: 1981 Supplement. 1981. 25.00 o.p. (ISBN 0-316-04211-0). Little.

--Basic Federal Income Taxation, 1982 Supplement. 1982. pap. 7.95 o.p. (ISBN 0-316-04225-0). Little.

--Bygone England: Social Studies in Its Historic Byways & Highways. LC 67-23910. (Social History Reference Ser.). (Illus.). 1968. Repr. of 1892 ed. 30.00x (ISBN 0-8103-3246-9). Gale.

--Bygone Punishments. 2nd ed. LC 76-129326. (Criminology, Law Enforcement, & Social Problems Ser.: No. 160). (Illus.). Date not set. o. p. 7.50 (ISBN 0-87585-160-6). Patterson Smith.

--Doctor in History, Literature, Folklore. LC 74-99779. 1970. Repr. of 1896 ed. 34.00x (ISBN 0-8103-3595-6). Gale.

--England in the Days of Old. LC 68-21752. 1968. Repr. of 1897 ed. 34.00x (ISBN 0-8103-3545-X). Gale.

--Federal Income Taxation of Corporate Transactions, 1982 Supplement. 1982. pap. 7.95 o.p. (ISBN 0-316-04224-2). Little.

--The Lawyer, in History, Literature & Humour. 276p. 1982. Repr. of 1896 ed. lib. bdg. 27.50x (ISBN 0-8377-0211-9). Rothman.

--Legal Lore: Curiosities of Law & Lawyers. xii, 117p. 1982. Repr. of 1897 ed. lib. bdg. 22.50x (ISBN 0-686-81666-8). Rothman.

--Old Time Punishments. LC 78-124585. 1970. Repr. of 1890 ed. 30.00x (ISBN 0-8103-3841-6). Gale.

Andrews, William D. Basic Federal Income Taxation. 1979. text ed. 26.00 (ISBN 0-316-04213-7). Little.

--Federal Income Taxation of Corporate Transactions. 1979. text ed. 26.00 (ISBN 0-316-04212-9). Little.

Andrews, William D. & Surrey, Stanley S., eds. Proposals of the American Law Institute on Corporate Acquisitions & Dispositions & Reporter's Study on Corporate Distributions. LC 82-71580. (Federal Income Tax Project Ser.: Subchapter C). 551p. 1983. 65.00 (ISBN 0-686-82168-8, 5650). Am Law Inst.

Andrews, William G. Presidential Government in Gaullist France: A Study of Executive Legislative Relations, 1958-1974. 320p. 1982. 33.50x (ISBN 0-87395-604-4); pap. 10.95x (ISBN 0-87395-605-2). State U NY Pr.

Andrews-Rusiecka, Hilda, tr. see Walicki, Andrzej.

Andreyev, L. N. Silence. Goldberg, Isaac, ed. Lowe, W. H., tr. (International Pocket Library). pap. 3.00 (ISBN 0-686-77234-2). Branden.

Andreyev, Leonid see Goldberg, Isaac.

Andrian, G. W. Fondo y Forma: Literature, Language, Grammar Review. 1970. text ed. 15.95x (ISBN 0-02-303420-3). Macmillan.

Andrian, Gustave W. Modern Spanish Prose: An Introductory Reader with a Selection of Poetry. 3rd ed. 1977. pap. text ed. 13.95 (ISBN 0-02-303430-0). Macmillan.

Andrian, Gustave W. & Davies, Jane. Pret a Lire. 1980. pap. 11.95 (ISBN 0-02-303440-8). Macmillan.

Andrianov, K. A. Metalorganic Polymers. LC 64-66350. (Polymer Review Ser.: No. 8). 371p. 1965. 22.50 (ISBN 0-470-03185-9, Pub. by Wiley). Krieger.

Andric, I., et al, eds. Particle Physics 1980. 1981. 85.00 (ISBN 0-444-86174-2). Elsevier.

Andriole, Stephen J. Handbook of Problem Solving. (Illus.). 327p. 1983. text ed. 25.00 (ISBN 0-89433-186-8). Petrocelli.

Andriole, Stephen J., jt. ed. see Hopple, Gerald W.

Andrisani, Paul J., et al. Work Attitudes & Labor Market Experience: Evidence from the National Longitudinal Surveys. LC 78-2520. 1978. 28.95 o.p. (ISBN 0-03-041586-1). Praeger.

Andrist, Ralph K. Long Death. (Illus.). 1969. pap. 6.95 (ISBN 0-02-030290-8, Collier). Macmillan.

--Steamboats on the Mississippi. LC 62-10384. (American Heritage Junior Library). 154p. (YA) (gr. 7 up). 1962. PLB 14.89 o.p. (ISBN 0-06-020136-3, HarpJ). Har-Row.

Androgeus, John C., ed. The Lost Gospel of the Ages: Key to Immortality & Companion to the Holy Bible. (Illus.). 979p. 1978. pap. text ed. 95.00 (ISBN 0-9609802-3-7). Life Science.

Andronicos, Manolis. The Acropolis: The Monuments & the Museum. (Athenon Illustrated Guides Ser.). (Illus.). 80p. 1983. pap. 14.00 (ISBN 0-88332-310-9, 8245, Pub. by Ekdotike Athenon Greecee). Larousse.

--Delphi. (Athenon Illustrated Guides Ser.). (Illus.). 80p. 1983. pap. 8.00 (ISBN 0-88332-298-6, Pub. by Ekdotike Athenon Greece). Larousse.

--Herakleion Museum. (Athenon Illustrated Guides Ser.). (Illus.). 80p. 1983. pap. 8.00 (ISBN 0-686-43393-9, 8235, Pub. by Ekdotike Athenon Greece). Larousse.

--National Museum. (Athenon Illustrated Guides Ser.). (Illus.). 96p. 1983. pap. 8.00 (ISBN 0-88332-296-X, 8240, Pub. by Ekdotike Athenon Greece). Larousse.

--Olympia. (Athenon Illustrated Guides Ser.). (Illus.). 80p. 1983. pap. 8.00 (ISBN 0-88332-300-1, 8242, Pub. by Ekdotike Athenon Greece). Larousse.

--Vergina, the Prehistoric Necropolis & the Hellenistic Palace. (Studies in Mediterranean Archaeology Ser.: No. 13). (Illus.). 1964. pap. text ed. 4.75x (ISBN 91-85058-12-2). Humanities.

Andronov, Alexander, et al. Theory of Oscillators. (Illus.). 1966. text ed. inquire for price o.p. (ISBN 0-08-009981-5). Pergamon.

Andropov, Y. V. Speeches & Writings. (Leaders of the World Ser.). 192p. 1983. 25.00 (ISBN 0-08-028177-X). Pergamon.

Andros, Phil. Below the Belt & Other Stories by Phil Andros. LC 82-3141. 140p. (Orig.). 1982. pap. 6.50 (ISBN 0-912516-75-5). Grey Fox.

Andros, Phil, pseud. Stud. rev, abr. ed. 216p. 1982. pap. 6.95 (ISBN 0-932870-02-3). Alyson Pubns.

Andrulis, Richard S. Adult Assessment: A Source Book of Tests & Measures of Human Behavior. 340p. 1977. 16.00x (ISBN 0-398-03603-9). C C Thomas.

Andrus, Vera. Sea Dust. (Illus.). 1955. 5.00 o.p. (ISBN 0-87482-009-X). Wake-Brook.

Andry, Carl F. Jesus & the Four Gospels. LC 78-1128. 1978. pap. 5.95 o.s.i. (ISBN 0-932970-03-6). Prinit Pr.

--Paul & the Early Christians. LC 78-71822. 1978. pap. 6.95 o.s.i. (ISBN 0-932970-00-1). Prinit Pr.

--Paul & the Early Christians. LC 81-40766. (Illus.). 148p. (Orig.). 1982. lib. bdg. 19.75 (ISBN 0-8191-1935-0); pap. text ed. 9.00 (ISBN 0-8191-1936-9). U Pr of Amer.

--Problems in Early Christianity. LC 79-83545. 1979. pap. 6.95 o.s.i. (ISBN 0-932970-04-4). Prinit Pr.

--Syllabus for New Testament Study. LC 78-71491. 1978. pap. 6.95 o.s.i. (ISBN 0-932970-02-8). Prinit Pr.

Andrykovitch, George, jt. auth. see Stanley, Melissa.

Andrzejewski, tr. see Cawl, Farrax M.

Anell, Lars. Recession, the Western Economies & the Changing World Order. 181p. 1982. pap. 9.50 (ISBN 0-86187-243-6). F Pinter Pubs.

Anell, Lars & Nygren, Birgitta. The Developing Countries & the World Economic Order. LC 80-5094. 230p. 1980. 27.50 (ISBN 0-312-19658-X). St Martin.

Anenbruck, John. Voice of the Turtle. LC 75-75071. 1976. pap. 1.95 (ISBN 0-686-15471-1). Lions Head.

Anene, J. C. Southern Nigeria in Transition, Eighteen Eighty-Five - Nineteen Six. 1966. 34.50 (ISBN 0-521-04033-7). Cambridge U Pr.

Anesaki, Masharu. Nichiren: The Buddhist Prophet. 1916. 8.50 (ISBN 0-8446-1029-1). Peter Smith.

Ang, A. H. & Tang, W. H. Probability Concepts in Engineering Planning & Design, Vol. 1. LC 75-5892. 409p. 1975. text ed. 30.50x (ISBN 0-471-03200-X). Wiley.

--Probability Concepts in Engineering Planning & Design, Vol. 2. 1982. 15.95 (ISBN 0-471-03201-8). Wiley.

Angebert, Jean-Michel. The Occult & the Third Reich: The Mystical Origins of Nazism & the Search for the Holy Grail. (McGraw-Hill Paperbacks Ser.). 336p. 1975. pap. 3.95 o.p. (ISBN 0-07-001850-2, SP). McGraw.

Angel, Allen R. & Porter, Stuart R. Survey of Mathematics: With Applications. LC 80-19471. (Mathematics Ser.). (Illus.). 576p. 1981. text ed. 21.95 (ISBN 0-201-00045-8); study supplement 5.95 (ISBN 0-201-00046-6); instrs' manual 4.00 (ISBN 0-201-00044-X). A-W.

Angel, Gerry & Petronko, Diane. Developing the New Assertive Nurse. 1983. pap. text ed. 17.95 (ISBN 0-8261-3511-0). Springer Pub.

Angel, Heather. The Book of Nature Photography. LC 81-48106. 1982. 16.50 (ISBN 0-394-52467-5). Knopf.

--Life on the Seashore. LC 78-64656. (Fact Finders Ser.). (Illus.). 1979. PLB 8.00 (ISBN 0-382-06245-0). Silver.

Angel, J. Lawrence. The People of Lerna: Analysis of a Prehistoric Aegean Population. LC 73-139121. (Illus.). 160p. 1971. 19.95x (ISBN 0-87474-098-3). Smithsonian.

Angel, Juvenal L. & Dixson, Robert J. Tests & Drills in Spanish Grammar, 2 bks. (Orig., Span. & Eng., Lessons correlated to Conversacion en Espanol). (gr. 9 up). 1973. Bk. 1. pap. text ed. 3.25 (ISBN 0-88345-161-1, 18100); Bk. 2. pap. text ed. 3.25 (ISBN 0-88345-162-X, 18101). Regents Pub.

Angel, Marc D. La America. 240p. 1982. 15.95 (ISBN 0-8276-0205-7). Jewish Pubn.

Angel, S. & Hyman, G. M. Urban Fields. 180p. 1976. 16.50x (ISBN 0-85086-052-0, Pub. by Pion England). Methuen Inc.

Angel, Velma. Those Sinsational Soaps. Lee, Karen, ed. 120p. (Orig.). 1983. pap. 4.95 (ISBN 0-88005-003-9). Uplift Bks.

Angelakos, Diogenes J. & Everhart, Thomas E. Microwave Communications. LC 81-18556. 264p. 1983. Repr. of 1968 ed. text ed. 22.50 (ISBN 0-89874-395-8). Krieger.

--Microwave Communications. (Electrical & Electronic Eng. Ser). 1967. 26.95 o.p. (ISBN 0-07-001789-1, C). McGraw.

Angelella, Michael. Trail of Blood. 1981. pap. 1.95 o.p. (ISBN 0-451-09673-8, J9673, Sig). NAL.

Angeles, Peter, ed. Critiques of God. LC 76-43520. (Skeptic's Bookshelf Ser.). 371p. 1976. 13.95o.p. (ISBN 0-87975-077-4); pap. 9.95 (ISBN 0-87975-078-2). Prometheus Bks.

Angeles, Peter A. Introduction to Sentential Logic: A Workbook Approach. new ed. (Philosophy Ser.). 128p. 1976. pap. text ed. 9.95 (ISBN 0-675-08665-5). Merrill.

--The Problem of God: A Short Introduction. rev. ed. LC 73-85469. (Skeptic's Bookshelf Ser.). 156p. 1981. pap. text ed. 9.95 (ISBN 0-87975-216-5). Prometheus Bks.

Angelides, Sotirios, jt. auth. see Bardach, Eugene.

Angelini, ed. Muscular Dystrophy Research: Advances & New Trends. (International Congress Ser.: Vol. 527). 1981. 74.00 (ISBN 0-444-90168-X). Elsevier.

Angell, George. Winning in the Commodities Market: A Money-Making Guide to Commodity Futures Trading. LC 78-18129. (Illus.). 1979. 15.95 (ISBN 0-385-14208-0). Doubleday.

Angell, George W. & Kelley, Edward P., Jr. Handbook of Faculty Bargaining: Asserting Administrative Leadership for Institutional Progress by Preparing for Bargaining, Negotiating & Administering Contracts, & Improving the Bargaining Process. LC 76-50713. (Higher Education Ser.). 1977. text ed. 25.00x o.p. (ISBN 0-87589-320-1). Jossey-Bass.

Angell, George W., ed. Faculty & Teacher Bargaining: The Impact of Unions on Education. LC 80-8769. 1981. 18.95x (ISBN 0-669-04360-5). Lexington Bks.

Angell, Ian O. A Practical Introduction to Computer Graphics. LC 81-11361. (Computers & Their Applications Ser.). 143p. 1981. pap. 16.95x (ISBN 0-470-27251-1). Halsted Pr.

Angell, J. C., II. The Acute Abdomen for the Man on the Spot. 3rd ed. 116p. 1979. pap. text ed. 13.95 (ISBN 0-272-79519-4). Univ Park.

Angell, J. William & Helm, Robert M. Meaning & Value in Western Thought: A History of Ideas in Western Culture. LC 80-67174. (The Ancient Foundations Ser.: Vol. I). 434p. 1981. lib. bdg. 25.50 (ISBN 0-8191-1368-9); pap. text ed. 15.50 (ISBN 0-8191-1369-7). U Pr of Amer.

Angell, James. Roots & Wings. 80p. 1983. text ed. 6.95 (ISBN 0-687-36585-6). Abingdon.

Angell, James R. American Education. 1937. text ed. 19.50x (ISBN 0-686-83461-5). Elliots Bks.

--The Higher Patriotism. 1938. pap. 17.50x (ISBN 0-685-89756-7). Elliots Bks.

Angell, Joseph K. A Treatise on the Right of Property in Tide Waters & in the Soil & Shores Thereof. 1983. Repr. of 1826 ed. lib. bdg. 37.50x (ISBN 0-8377-0214-3). Rothman.

Angell, Judie. The Buffalo Nickel Blues Band. LC 81-18075. 160p. (gr. 5-7). 1982. 9.95 (ISBN 0-02-705580-9). Bradbury Pr.

--The Buffalo Nickels Blues Band. (YA) (gr. 7-12). 1983. pap. price not set (ISBN 0-440-90822-1, LFL). Dell.

--Dear Lola: Or How to Build Your Own Family: a Tale. LC 80-15111. 160p. (gr. 4-6). 1980. 9.95 (ISBN 0-02-705590-6). Bradbury Pr.

--In Summertime It's Tuffy. LC 76-57810. 240p. (gr. 4-6). 1977. 9.95 (ISBN 0-02-705500-0). Bradbury Pr.

--In Summertime, It's Tuffy. (YA) 1979. pap. 2.25 (ISBN 0-440-94051-6, LFL). Dell.

--Ronnie & Rosey. LC 77-75362. 296p. (gr. 6-8). 1977. 9.95 (ISBN 0-02-705790-9). Bradbury Pr.

--Ronnie & Rosey. (YA) 1979. pap. 2.25 (ISBN 0-440-97491-7, LFL). Dell.

--Secret Selves. LC 79-12710. 192p. (gr. 5-7). 1979. 9.95 (ISBN 0-02-705780-1). Bradbury Pr.

--Secret Selves. pap. 1.95 (ISBN 0-686-74494-2, LE). Dell.

--Suds. LC 82-22732. 224p. (gr. 5-8). 1983. 9.95 (ISBN 0-02-705570-1). Bradbury Pr.

--Tina Gogo. LC 77-16439. 208p. (gr. 4-6). 1978. 9.95 (ISBN 0-02-705770-4). Bradbury Pr.

--What's Best for You. LC 80-27425. 192p. (gr. 6-9). 1981. 9.95 (ISBN 0-02-705760-7). Bradbury Pr.

--What's Best for You? (YA) (gr. 6-9). 1983. pap. 2.25 (ISBN 0-440-98959-0, LFL). Dell.

--Word from Our Sponsor: Or My Friend Alfred. LC 78-25716. (gr. 3-6). 1979. 9.95 (ISBN 0-02-705750-X). Bradbury Pr.

Angell, Marcia, jt. auth. see Robbins, Stanley L.

Angell, Robert C. The Family Encounters the Depression. 1936. 11.50 (ISBN 0-8446-1030-5). Peter Smith.

--The Quest for World Order. LC 78-14248. (Michigan Faculty Ser.). (Illus.). 1979. pap. 6.95x (ISBN 0-472-06304-9). U of Mich Pr.

Angell, Roger. Five Seasons. 416p. 1983. pap. 3.95 (ISBN 0-446-31103-0). Warner Bks.

--Late Innings. 448p. 1983. pap. 3.95 (ISBN 0-345-30936-7). Ballantine.

--The Summer Game. pap. cancelled o.s.i. (ISBN 0-14-006192-4). Penguin.

Angell, Tony. Owls. LC 74-6005. (Illus.). 80p. 1974. pap. 9.95 (ISBN 0-295-95666-6); limited ed. 100.00 (ISBN 0-295-95415-9). U of Wash Pr.

Angell, Tony & Balcolm, Kenneth C., III. Marine Birds & Mammals of Puget Sound. LC 82-10946. (Puget Sound Bks.). (Illus.). 145p. (Orig.). 1982. pap. 14.50 (ISBN 0-295-95942-8, Pub. by Wash Sea Grant). U of Wash Pr.

Angell, Tony, jt. auth. see Orians, Gordon.

Angelo, Claude, jt. auth. see Andolfi, Maurizio.

Angelo, Domenico. The School of Fencing. (Illus.). 104p. 1982. Repr. 200.00 (ISBN 0-88254-718-6, Pub. by Edita SA); Half Leather 400.00 (ISBN 0-686-99271-7). Hippocrene Bks.

Angelo, Joseph. The Dictionary of Space Technology. 384p. 1982. 70.00x (ISBN 0-584-95011-X, Pub. by Muller Ltd). State Mutual Bk.

Angeloch, Robert. Basic Oil Painting Techniques. (Pitman Art Ser.: No. 37). 1970. pap. 2.50 (ISBN 0-448-00575-1, G&D). Putnam Pub Group.

Angeloglou, Christopher & Schofield, Jack, eds. Successful Nature Photography: How to Take Beautiful Pictures of the Living World. 240p. 1983. 24.95 (ISBN 0-8174-5925-1, Amphoto). Watson-Guptill.

Angelou, Maya. Gather Together in My Name. 1974. 12.50 (ISBN 0-394-48692-7). Random.

--The Heart of a Woman. LC 81-40232. 288p. 1981. 12.50 (ISBN 0-394-51273-1). Random.

--Heart of a Woman. 1983. pap. 3.50 (ISBN 0-553-22839-0). Bantam.

--I Know Why the Caged Bird Sings. 1970. 13.50 (ISBN 0-394-42986-9). Random.

Angelsen, Bjorn, jt. auth. see Hatle, Liv.

Angelucci, Enzo. Airplanes: From the Dawn of Light to the Present Day. LC 72-12755. (Illus.). 288p. 1973. 24.95 (ISBN 0-07-001807-3, GB). McGraw.

--World Encyclopedia of Civil Aircraft, from Leonardo da Vinci to the Present. LC 82-4642. (Illus.). 414p. 1982. 50.00 (ISBN 0-517-54724-4). Crown.

Angelucci, Enzo & Matricardi, Paolo. World Aircraft: Origins-World War I. LC 78-72304. (Color Illustrated Guides). (Illus.). 1979. pap. 7.95 o.p. (ISBN 0-528-88165-5). Rand.

--World Aircraft-1918-1935. LC 78-64533. (Color Illustrated Guides). (Illus.). 1979. pap. 7.95 o.p. (ISBN 0-528-88166-3). Rand.

Anger, Kathryn. Breakout. LC 79-55871. (Feminist Novels Ser.). 128p. (Orig.). 1977. pap. 4.95 (ISBN 0-935772-01-4). Diotima Bks.

--Lockout. LC 79-57121. (Feminist Novels Ser.). 100p. 1975. pap. 4.95 (ISBN 0-935772-02-2). Diotima Bks.

--Override. LC 79-57122. (Feminist Novels Ser.). 100p. 1976. pap. 4.95 (ISBN 0-935772-03-0). Diotima Bks.

--Pilgrimage. (Feminist Novels Ser.). 1982. write for info. Diotima Bks.

Anger, Kenneth. Hollywood Babylon. 1976. pap. 7.95 o.s.i. (ISBN 0-440-55325-3, Delta). Dell.

Anger, Per. With Raoul Wallenberg in Budapest: Memories of the War Years in Hungary. Paul, David M. & Paul, Margareta, trs. from Swedish. (Illus.). 192p. 8.95 (ISBN 0-686-95103-4); pap. 4.95 (ISBN 0-686-99464-7). ADL.

Angermeier, W. F. Die Evolution des Lernens. (Illus.). xii, 208p. 1983. 67.25 (ISBN 3-8055-3522-8). S Karger.

Angers, Marilynn M. & Angers, William P. Creating Your Own Career for Job Satisfaction. LC 82-61718. 170p. (Orig.). 1983. pap. 9.95 (ISBN 0-910793-00-X). Marlborough Pr.

Angers, William P., jt. auth. see Angers, Marilynn M.

Angevine, Jay B., Jr. & Cotman, Carl W. Principles of Neuroanatomy. (Illus.). 1981. 32.50x (ISBN 0-19-502885-6); pap. 17.95x (ISBN 0-19-502886-4). Oxford U Pr.

Anghileri, Leopold J. & Tuffet-Anghileri, Anne M., eds. The Role of Calcium in Biological Systems, Vol. I. 288p. 1982. 81.00 (ISBN 0-8493-6280-6). CRC Pr.

Angier, Bradford. At Home in the Woods: Living the Life of Thoreau Today. (Illus.). 1971. pap. 3.95 (ISBN 0-02-062120-5, Collier). Macmillan.

--How to Stay Alive in the Woods. Orig. Title: Living off the Country. 1962. pap. 3.95 (ISBN 0-02-028050-5, Collier). Macmillan.

Angier, Bradford & Angier, Vena. How to Build Your Home in the Woods. (Illus.). 11.50 (ISBN 0-911378-10-3). Sheridan.

Angier, Vena, jt. auth. see Angier, Bradford.

Angino, E. D. & Long, D. T., eds. Geochemistry of Bismuth. LC 78-24291. (Benchmark Papers in Geology: Vol. 49). 432p. 1979. 53.50 (ISBN 0-87933-234-4). Hutchinson Ross.

Angins, E. & Billings, K. Atomic Absorption Spectrometry in Geology. 2nd ed. 1973. 16.75 (ISBN 0-444-41036-8). Elsevier.

Angle, Burr, ed. see Banks, Michael.

Angle, Burr, ed. see Beckman, Bob.

Angle, Burr, ed. see Berliner, Donald L.

Angle, Burr, ed. see Paine, Sheperd.

Angle, Burr, ed. see Poling, Mitch.

Angle, Burr, ed. see Sarpolus, Dick.

Angle, Burr, ed. see Schroder, Jack E.

Angle, Burr, ed. see Staszak, E. R.

Angle, Burr, ed. see Willard, Ken.

Anglemeyer, Mary, ed. see International Institute for Environment & Development (I.I.E.D.).

Anglin, D. L., jt. auth. see Crouse, W. H.

Anglin, D. L., jt. auth. see Crouse, William H.

Anglin, Donald L., jt. auth. see Crouse, William H.

Anglin, Douglas G. & Shaw, Timothy M. Zambia's Foreign Policy: Studies in Diplomacy & Dependence. 1979. 35.00 (ISBN 0-89158-191-X). Westview.

Anglin, Douglas G., et al, eds. Conflict & Change in Southern Africa: Papers from a Scandinavian-Canadian Conference. LC 78-70693. 1978. pap. text ed. 11.50 (ISBN 0-8191-0647-X). U Pr of Amer.

Anglin, R. L., Jr., ed. Energy & the Man Built Environment. LC 81-67745. 728p. 1982. pap. text ed. 47.00 (ISBN 0-87262-297-5). Am Soc Civil Eng.

Anglund, Joan W. A Child's Book of Old Nursery Rhymes. LC 73-75429. (Illus.). 32p. (ps up). 1973. 3.95g o.p. (ISBN 0-689-30413-7, McElderry Bk). Atheneum.

--Cowboy & His Friend. LC 61-6110. (Illus.). (gr. k-2). 1976. pap. 1.95 (ISBN 0-15-622715-0, VoyB). HarBraceJ.

--Cup of Sun: A Book of Poems. LC 67-24870. (Illus.). 1967. 4.95 (ISBN 0-15-123390-X). HarBraceJ.

--A Gift of Love, 5 vols. (Illus.). 32p. 1980. Set. pap. 8.95 (ISBN 0-15-634741-5, VoyB). HarBraceJ.

--In a Pumpkin Shell. LC 60-10243. (Illus.). (ps-2). 1977. pap. 2.95 (ISBN 0-15-644425-9, VoyB). HarBraceJ.

--Nibble Nibble Mousekin: A Tale of Hansel & Gretel. LC 62-14422. (Illus.). (gr. k-3). 1977. pap. 1.95 o.p. (ISBN 0-15-665588-8, VoyB). HarBraceJ.

Angoff, Allan, ed. Public Relations for Libraries: Essays in Communications Techniques. LC 72-776. (Contributions in Librarianship & Information Science: No. 5). 1973. lib. bdg. 25.00x (ISBN 0-8371-6060-X, ANP/). Greenwood.
Angolia, John R. For Fuhrer & Fatherland: Military Awards of the Third Reich. 1978. 19.00 (ISBN 0-686-82440-7). Quaker.
--On the Field of Honor: A History of the Knight's Cross Bearers, Vol. 1. (Illus.). 288p. 1979. 17.95 (ISBN 0-912138-19-X). Bender Pub CA.
--On the Field of Honor: A History of the Knight's Cross Bearers, Vol. 2. (Illus.). 368p. 1981. 17.95 (ISBN 0-912138-21-1). Bender Pub CA.
Angreova, R., jt. auth. see Stamov, Stefan.
Angrist, Stanley W. Other Worlds, Other Beings. LC 70-171001. (Illus.). (gr. 6-9). 1973. 8.95i o.p. (ISBN 0-690-60205-7, TYC-J). Har-Row.
Angsburger, David. The Freedom of Forgiveness. 128p. 1973. pap. 2.95 (ISBN 0-8024-2875-4). Moody.
Angst, J., jt. auth. see Ernst, C.
Angulo, D. & Sanchez, A. E. Corpus of Spanish Drawings, 1400-1600, Vol. 1 & Vol. 2. (Illus.). 1975. Vol. 1 74.00x, (ISBN 0-19-921021-7); Vol. 2 74.00x, (ISBN 0-19-921022-5). Oxford U Pr.
Angus, Fay. How to Do Everything Right & Live to Regret It: Confessions of a Harried Housewife. LC 82-48425. 192p. 1983. 10.95 (ISBN 0-686-82600-0, HarpR). Har-Row.
Angus, H. T. Cast Iron: Physical & Engineering Properties. 542p. 1976. 105.00 (ISBN 0-408-70933-2). Butterworth.
Angus, T. C. The Control of Indoor Climate. 1968. inquire for price o.p. (ISBN 0-08-012729-0). Pergamon.
Angyal, Andras. Foundations for a Science of Personality. LC 42-3548. (The Commonwealth Fund Publications Ser.). (Illus.). 1941. 20.00x o.p. (ISBN 0-674-31200-7). Harvard U Pr.
Angyal, Andrew J. Loren Eiseley. (United States Authors Ser.). 182p. 1983. lib. bdg. 15.95 (ISBN 0-8057-7381-9, Twayne). G K Hall.
Anhui Medical School Hospital. Chinese Massage Therapy. Lee, Hor M. & Whincup, Gregory, trs. from Chinese. LC 82-42677. (Illus.). 192p. (Orig.). 1983. pap. 6.95 (ISBN 0-394-71423-7). Shambhala Pubns.
Anicar, Thom. Secret Sex: Male Erotic Fantasies. (Orig.). 1976. pap. 3.95 (ISBN 0-451-12306-9, AE2306, Sig). NAL.
Anikin, A. V. A Science in Its Youth. Cook, K. M., tr. from Rus. LC 78-31568. 389p. 1979. pap. 3.50 (ISBN 0-7178-0503-4). Intl Pub Co.
Anikouchine, William & Sternberg, Richard. The World Ocean. 2nd ed. (Illus.). 512p. 1981. 26.95 (ISBN 0-13-967778-X). P-H.
Animalu, Alex O. E. Intermediate Quantum Theory of Crystalline Solids. LC 76-16858. (Illus.). 1977. 33.95 (ISBN 0-13-470799-0). P-H.
Anisfeld, Evelyn R., jt. ed. see Anisfeld, Michael H.
Anisfeld, Michael H. & Anisfeld, Evelyn R., eds. International Drug GMP's. 2nd ed. 250p. 1983. text ed. 180.00 (ISBN 0-935184-02-3). Interpharm.
Anjaneyulu, M. S. Elements of Modern Pure Geometry. 6.50x o.p. (ISBN 0-210-26948-0). Asia.
Ank, John A., jt. auth. see Breyer, Donald E.
Ankeny, Nesmith C. Poker Strategy: Winning With Game Theory. (Illus.). 208p. 1982. pap. 4.95 (ISBN 0-399-50669-1, Perige). Putnam Pub Group.
Anker, Carol T. Teaching Exceptional Children: A Special Career. LC 78-19028. (Illus.). 224p. (gr. 7 up). 1978. PLB 8.29 o.p. (ISBN 0-671-32892-1). Messner.
Anker, Richard. Reproductive Behavior in Households of Rural Gujarat: Social, Economic & Community Factors. 152p. 1982. text ed. 13.00x (ISBN 0-391-02719-0, Pub. by Concept). Humanities.
Anker, Richard, et al, eds. Women's Roles & Population Trends in the Third World. 288p. 1981. 33.50x (ISBN 0-7099-0508-4, Pub. by Croom Helm Ltd England). Biblio Dist.
Ankerl, Guy C. Beyond Monopoly Capitalism & Monopoly Socialism: Distributive Justice in a Competitive Society. 108p. 1978. 13.25 (ISBN 0-87073-938-7); pap. 6.95 o.p. (ISBN 0-87073-939-5). Schenkman.
Ann Arbor Publishers Editorial Staff. Cursive Tracking. 32p. (gr. 2-8). 1973. 4.00 (ISBN 0-89039-015-0). Ann Arbor Pubs.
--Manuscript Writing, 2 levels. (Manuscript Writing Ser.). (gr. 1-3). 1978. Level one. 4.00 (ISBN 0-89039-235-8); Level two. 4.00 (ISBN 0-89039-212-9). Ann Arbor Pubs.
--Manuscript Writing: Words Book 1 & 2. (Manuscript Writing Words Ser.). (gr. 3-6). Book 1. 5.00 (ISBN 0-89039-214-5); Book 2. 5.00 (ISBN 0-89039-216-1). Ann Arbor Pubs.
--Symbol Discrimination Series: Books 1, 2, 3, 4, 5, & 6. (Symbol Discrimination Series). (Illus.). 16p. (gr. k-1). 1974. 2.00 ea.; Book 1. 2.00 (ISBN 0-89039-078-9); Book 2. 2.00 (ISBN 0-89039-079-7); Book 3. 2.00 (ISBN 0-89039-080-0); Book 4. 2.00 (ISBN 0-89039-081-9); Book 5. 2.00 (ISBN 0-89039-082-7); Book 6. 2.00 (ISBN 0-89039-083-5). Ann Arbor Pubs.
Anna, Timothy E. Spain & the Loss of America. LC 82-11118. xxiv, 333p. 1983. 26.50x (ISBN 0-8032-1014-0). U of Nebr Pr.
Annala, Hilja. Rhymes of the Valley. 5.95 (ISBN 0-8323-0176-0). Binford.
Annan, Bill & Hinchcliffe, Keith. Planning Policy Analysis & Public Spending: Theory & the Papua New Guinea Practice. 168p. 1982. text ed. 35.00x (ISBN 0-566-00496-8). Gower Pub Ltd.
Annan, David. Movie Fantastic: Beyond the Dream Machine. (Illus.). 128p. 1974. pap. 2.95 o.p. (ISBN 0-517-51813-9). Crown.
Annan, Ralph. The Spider-Men: A Science-Fantasy Short Novel. 1979. 5.95 o.p. (ISBN 0-533-03684-4). Vantage.
Annand, Douglass R., ed. The Wheelchair Traveler. rev. ed. 1979. pap. 205.00 (ISBN 0-686-36866-5). Annand Ent.
Annandale, Barbara. The Bonnet Laird's Daughter. 1977. 8.95 o.p. (ISBN 0-698-10781-0, Coward). Putnam Pub Group.
--The French Lady's Lover. LC 77-10786. 1978. 9.95 o.p. (ISBN 0-698-10880-9, Coward). Putnam Pub Group.
Annarino, A. Bowling: Individualized Instructional Program. 1973. pap. 5.95 o.p. (ISBN 0-13-080440-1). P-H.
Annas, George J. The Rights of Doctors, Nurses, & Allied Health Professionals. 416p. 1981. pap. 3.95 o.p. (ISBN 0-380-77859-9, 77859, Discus). Avon.
--The Rights of Hospital Patients. (An American Civil Liberties Handbook). 1975. pap. 2.50 o.p. (ISBN 0-380-00286-8, 53694, Discus). Avon.
Annas, George J., et al. Informed Consent to Human Experimentation: The Subject's Dilemma. LC 77-2266. 360p. 1977. prof ref 25.00x (ISBN 0-88410-147-9). Ballinger Pub.
--The Rights of Doctors, Nurses, & Allied Health Professionals. 400p. 1981. prof ref 27.50x (ISBN 0-88410-727-2). Ballinger Pub.
Anne, Lady. Cooking with Abstinence. 3.75 o.p. (ISBN 0-686-92310-3, 9500). Hazelden.
Annemann, Theodore. Practical Mental Logic. (Illus.). 310p. (Orig.). 1983. pap. 5.95 (ISBN 0-486-24426-1). Dover.
Annenberg, Maurice. Advertising: Three Thousand B. C. to Nineteen Hundred A.D. LC 77-75421. 1969. 20.00 o.s.i. (ISBN 0-916526-02-X). Maran Pub.
--Type Foundries of America & Their Catalogs. LC 73-94198. 1978. Repr. of 1975 ed. 30.00 o.s.i. (ISBN 0-916526-03-8). Maran Pub.
Annenkov, Iurii. Portray. 1977. 18.00x o.p. (ISBN 0-931554-00-4); pap. 9.00x o.p. (ISBN 0-931554-01-2). Strathcona.
Annesley, Mabel. As the Sight Is Bent. 14.50 (ISBN 0-392-02142-0, SpS). Sportshelf.
Annis, Linda F. Study Techniques. 150p. 1983. pap. text ed. write for info. (ISBN 0-697-06069-1). Wm C Brown.
Annis, Verle L. The Architecture of Antigua Guatemala, 1543-1773. (Illus.). 35.00x o.p. (ISBN 0-686-11833-2). R Reed.
Annixter, Jane & Annixter, Paul. Wapootin. (Illus.). 64p. (gr. 3-5). 1976. 4.95 o.p. (ISBN 0-698-20353-4, Coward). Putnam Pub Group.
--The Year of the She-Grizzly. LC 77-26724. (Illus.). (gr. 3-5). 1978. 5.95 o.p. (ISBN 0-698-20456-5, Coward). Putnam Pub Group.
Annixter, Paul, jt. auth. see Annixter, Jane.
Anno, J. N., jt. auth. see Walowit, J. A.
Anno, Mitsumasa. Anno's Animals. LC 79-11721. (Illus.). 1979. 9.95 (ISBN 0-529-05545-7, Philomel); PLB 9.99 (ISBN 0-529-05546-5). Putnam Pub Group.
--Anno's Britain. (Illus.). 48p. 1982. 10.95 (ISBN 0-399-20861-5, Philomel). Putnam Pub Group.
--Anno's Counting House. (Illus.). 48p. 1982. 12.95 (ISBN 0-399-20896-8, Philomel). Putnam Pub Group.
--Anno's Italy. LC 79-17649. (Illus.). 48p. 1980. 9.95 o.p. (ISBN 0-529-05559-7, Philomel); PLB 9.99 o.p. (ISBN 0-529-05560-0). Putnam Pub Group.
--Anno's Journey. LC 77-16336. (Illus.). 1978. 9.95 o.p. (ISBN 0-399-20762-7, Philomel); PLB 9.99 o.p. (ISBN 0-529-05419-1). Putnam Pub Group.
--Anno's Medieval World. LC 79-28367. 32p. (gr. 3 up). 1980. 12.95 (ISBN 0-399-20742-2, Philomel); PLB 12.99 (ISBN 0-399-61153-3). Putnam Pub Group.
--The King's Flower. LC 78-9596. (Illus.). 32p. (ps-3). 1979. 8.95 (ISBN 0-399-20764-3, Philomel); PLB 8.99 (ISBN 0-399-61167-3). Putnam Pub Group.
--The Unique World of Mitsumasa Anno: Selected Works 1968-1977. Morse, Samuel, tr. LC 80-12827. (Illus.). 64p. (gr. 7 up). 1980. 19.95 (ISBN 0-399-20743-0, Philomel). Putnam Pub Group.
Annual Clinical Conference on Cancer, 22nd. Immunotherapy of Human Cancer: Proceedings. M. D. Anderson Hospital & Tumor Institute, ed. LC 77-17701. (Illus.). 437p. 1978. 45.00 (ISBN 0-89004-263-2). Raven.
Annual Conference of Microbeam Analysis Society, 9th, 1974. Microbeam Analysis: Proceedings. (Illus.). 20.00 (ISBN 0-686-50179-9); 1975 (10th conf.) 20.00 (ISBN 0-686-50180-2); 1976 (11th conf.) 20.00 (ISBN 0-686-50181-0); 1978 (13th conf.) o. 20.00 (ISBN 0-686-50183-7); 1979 (14th conf.) 25.00 (ISBN 0-686-67766-8); 1980 (15th conf.) 25.00 (ISBN 0-01-466725-8); 1981 (16th conf.) 25.00 (ISBN 0-686-77264-4); 1982 (17th conf.) 42.50; 1983 (18th conf.) 35.00. San Francisco Pr.
Annual Legal Conference on the Representation of Aliens 1978-1981. In Defense of the Alien: Proceedings, 4 vols. in 1, Vols. 1-4. Fragomen, Austin L. & Tomasi, Lydio F., eds. (In Defense of the Alien Ser.). 144p. 1979. lib. bdg. 25.00x (ISBN 0-913256-41-2, Dist. by Ozer). Ctr Migration.
Annual Symposium of Basic Medical Sciences, 10th & Piper, Priscilla J. SRS-A & Leukotrienes: Proceedings. LC 80-41758. (Prostaglandis Research Studies Press Ser.). 282p. 1981. 44.95x (ISBN 0-471-27959-5, Pub. by Wiley-Interscience). Wiley.
Annual Symposium on Fundamental Cancer Research, No. 31. Carcinogens: Identification & Mechanisms of Action. Griffin, A. Clark & Shaw, Charles R., eds. LC 78-23366. 505p. 1979. text ed. 50.00 (ISBN 0-89004-286-1). Raven.
Annual Uranium Seminar, 3rd. Proceedings. LC 79-48044. (Illus.). 177p. 1980. pap. 20.00x (ISBN 0-89520-260-3). Soc Mining Eng.
Anobile, Richard. The Book of Fame. Date not set. pap. 7.95 (ISBN 0-449-90044-4, Columbine). Fawcett.
Anobile, Richard & Anobile, Ulla. Beyond Open Marriage. LC 78-58769. (Illus.). 1979. 12.50 o.s.i. (ISBN 0-89479-029-3). A & W Pubs.
Anobile, Richard, jt. auth. see Marx, Groucho.
Anobile, Richard J. Hooray for Captain Spaulding. (Illus.). 1975. pap. 5.95 o.p. (ISBN 0-380-00458-5, 25890). Avon.
--Outland: The Movie. (Illus., Orig.). 1981. pap. 9.95 cancelled o.s.i. (ISBN 0-446-97829-9). Warner Bks.
Anobile, Richard J., ed. Godfrey Daniels. (Illus.). 224p. 1975. 8.95 o.p. (ISBN 0-517-52034-6). Crown.
--The Official Rocky Horror Picture Show Movie Novel. LC 79-24556. 192p. 1980. pap. 6.95 o.s.i. (ISBN 0-89104-180-X, A & W Visual Library); 15.00 o.s.i. (ISBN 0-89104-186-9). A & W Pubs.
Anobile, Richard J., ed. see Fields, W. C.
Anobile, Ulla, jt. auth. see Anobile, Richard.
Anonym, Kenneth, pseud. Understanding the Recovering Alcoholic. LC 73-20859. 152p. 1974. pap. 1.25 o.p. (ISBN 0-8189-1116-6, Pub. by Alba Bks.). Alba.
Anonym, Kenneth. Understanding the Recovering Alcoholic. 1980. pap. 4.95 (ISBN 0-89486-103-4). Hazelden.
Anosike, Benji O. How to Adopt a Child Without a Lawyer for Less Than Fifty Dollars. LC 78-74123. 72p. (Orig.). 1978. pap. text ed. 7.95x (ISBN 0-932704-00-X). Do-It-Yourself Legal Pubs.
--How to Buy or Sell Your Own Home Without a Lawyer or Broker. 120p. (Orig.). 1981. pap. text ed. 8.95x (ISBN 0-932704-09-3). Do-It-Yourself Legal Pubs.
--How to Declare Your Personal Bankruptcy Without a Lawyer. LC 80-66445. 130p. 1981. pap. text ed. 8.95 (ISBN 0-932704-07-7). Do-It-Yourself Legal Pubs.
--How to Do Your Own Divorce Without a Lawyer. LC 80-65725. 82p. (Orig.). 1980. pap. text ed. 8.95x (ISBN 0-932704-01-8). Do-It-Yourself Legal Pubs.
--How to Draw Up Your Legal Separation, Cohabitation, or Property Settlement Agreement Without a Lawyer. LC 80-66443. 120p. (Orig.). 1981. pap. text ed. 9.95x (ISBN 0-932704-04-2). Do-It-Yourself Legal Pubs.
--How to Draw up Your Own Will Without a Lawyer: Why You Can't Afford to Live--or Die--Without One! LC 80-966444. 96p. (Orig.). 1980. pap. text ed. 6.95x (ISBN 0-932704-05-0). Do-It-Yourself Legal Pubs.
--How to File For "Chapter II" Bankruptcy Relief from Your Business Debts, with or without A Lawyer. 140p. 1983. pap. text ed. 11.95 (ISBN 0-932704-14-X). Do-It-Yourself Pubns.
--How to Form Your Own Profit-Non-Profit Corporation Without a Lawyer. LC 80-66215. 130p. (Orig.). 1980. pap. text ed. 8.95x (ISBN 0-932704-03-4). Do-It-Yourself Legal Pubs.
--How to Handle Probate & Settle an Estate Without a Lawyer. LC 80-66446. 120p. (Orig.). 1982. pap. text ed. 8.95x (ISBN 0-932704-08-5). Do-It-Yourself Legal Pubs.
--How to Legally Beat the Traffic Ticket Without a Lawyer. 90p. (Orig.). 1982. pap. text ed. 5.95x (ISBN 0-932704-12-3). Do-It-Yourself Legal Pubs.
--How to Legally Reduce Your Real Estate Taxes Without a Lawyer. 100p. (Orig.). 1982. pap. 8.95x (ISBN 0-932704-11-5). Do-It-Yourself Legal Pubs.
--How to Obtain Your U. S. Immigration Visa Without a Lawyer. 150p. 1981. pap. text ed. 9.95x (ISBN 0-932704-10-7). Do-It-Yourself Legal Pubs.
--How to Settle Your Own Auto Accident Claims Without a Lawyer. 120p. (Orig.). 1982. pap. 8.95 (ISBN 0-932704-13-1). Do-It-Yourself Legal Pubs.
--Win Your Legal Rights As a Tennant Without a Lawyer. LC 80-66213. (Illus., Orig.). 1980. pap. text ed. 7.95 (ISBN 0-932704-02-6). Do-It-Yourself Legal Pubs.
Anouilh, Jean. Becket. 1960. pap. 5.95 (ISBN 0-698-10031-X, Coward). Putnam Pub Group.
--Lark. Fry, Christopher, tr. 1956. 9.95x (ISBN 0-19-500393-4). Oxford U Pr.
Anouilh, Jean see Moon, Samuel.
Anozie, S. O. Christopher Okigbo: Creative Rhetoric. LC 77-182593. (Modern African Writers Ser). 225p. 1972. text ed. 19.50x (ISBN 0-8419-0086-8, Africana); pap. 9.95x (ISBN 0-8419-0117-1, Africana). Holmes & Meier.
Anrais, David. Man & the Zodiac. LC 74-16328. pap. 5.95 (ISBN 0-87728-014-2). Weiser.
Ansay, Tugrul. American-Turkish Private International Law. LC 66-17535. 105p. 1966. 15.00 (ISBN 0-379-11416-X). Oceana.
--Introduction to Turkish Law. 2nd ed. 255p. 1978. 22.00 (ISBN 0-379-20332-4). Oceana.
Ansbacher. Portraits. (Pitman Art Ser.: Vol. 23). pap. 1.95 o.p. (ISBN 0-448-00532-8, G&D). Putnam Pub Group.
Ansbacher, Heinz L., ed. see Adler, Alfred.
Ansbacher, Max G. How to Profit from the Coming Bull Market. 256p. 1981. 12.95 o.p. (ISBN 0-13-429381-9). P-H.
--Stock Futures: New Strategies for Profit. (Illus.). 192p. 1983. 15.95 (ISBN 0-8027-0733-5). Walker & Co.
Ansbacher, Rowena R., ed. see Adler, Alfred.
Ansberger, Carolyn & Green, Mary J. Here's How to Handle "L". 1980. 50.00 (ISBN 0-88450-709-2, 3059-B). Communication Bks.
Anscombe, G. E., ed. see Wittgenstein, Ludwig.
Anscombe, G. E., tr. see Wittgenstein, Ludwig.
Anscombe, G. E. M., ed. see Wittgenstein, Ludwig.
Anscombe, G. E M, tr. see Wittgenstein, Ludwig.
Ansel, Willits D. The Whaleboat: A Study of Design, Construction & Use. (Illus.). 147p. 1978. 12.50 o.p. (ISBN 0-913372-39-0); pap. 7.50 o.p. (ISBN 0-913372-40-4). Mystic Seaport.
Ansell, G. Radiology in Clinical Toxicology. Trapnell, D. H., ed. (Radiology in Clinical Diagnosis Ser: Vol. 1). 1974. 18.75 o.p. (ISBN 0-407-10000-8). Butterworth.
Ansell, M. F., ed. Rodd's Chemistry of Carbon Compounds, 2 pts. in 1, Suppl. Vol. 1 C & D. (Pt. A: Monocarbon Derivatives, Pt. 2: Dihydric Alcohols). 1973. 93.75 (ISBN 0-444-41072-4). Elsevier.
--Rodd's Chemistry of Carbon Compounds, 2 pts. in 1, Suppl. Vol. 1 A & B. (Pt. A: Hydrocarbons, Pt. B: Monohydric Alcohols). 1975. 72.50 (ISBN 0-444-40972-6). Elsevier.
--Rodd's Chemistry of Carbon Compounds, 3 pts. in 1, Suppl. Vol. 2 C-E. 1974. 76.75 (ISBN 0-444-41135-6). Elsevier.
--Rodd's Chemistry of Carbon Compounds, 2 pts. in 1, Suppl. Vol. 2 A & B. 1974. 93.75 (ISBN 0-444-41133-X). Elsevier.
--Rodd's Chemistry of Carbon Compounds, Suppl. Vols. 3B & C. 1981. 78.75 (ISBN 0-444-42017-7). Elsevier.
--Rodd's Chemistry of Carbon Compounds, Suppl. Vols. 3D, E & F. Date not set. 102.25 (ISBN 0-444-42088-6). Elsevier.
Anselm, St. Saint Anselm: Basic Writings. 2nd ed. Deane, Sidney N., tr. Incl. Proslogium; Monologium; On Behalf of the Fool. Gaunilon; Cur Deus Homo. LC 74-3309. 371p. 1974. 21.00 (ISBN 0-87548-108-6); pap. 8.50 (ISBN 0-87548-109-4). Open Court.
Anselme, Michel. Freedom & Morality: A Nonsubjective Moral Code. Wald, Susan, tr. from Fr. 1983. 15.00 (ISBN 0-8022-2414-8). Philos Lib.
Anselm of Canterbury. Why God Became Man & The Virgin Conception & Original Sin. Colleran, Joseph M., tr. from Latin. & intro. by. LC 71-77166. 256p. (Orig.). 1982. pap. text ed. 4.95x (ISBN 0-87343-025-5). Magi Bks.
Anshen, Frank. Statistics for Linguists. LC 78-7216. 1978. pap. text ed. 4.95 o.p. (ISBN 0-88377-113-6). Newbury Hse.
Anshen, Ruth N., ed. see Lovell, Bernard.
Anshen, Ruth N., ed. see Mead, Margaret.
Ansley, Delight. Good Ways. rev. ed. LC 59-14674. (Illus.). (gr. 7-11). 1959. 9.95 (ISBN 0-690-33757-4, TYC-J). Har-Row.
Ansley, Margene. Barter Update Directory. 100p. 1983. pap. text ed. 9.95 (ISBN 0-939476-53-3). Biblio Pr GA.
--The Thrift Book. LC 80-70871. Date not set. 19.95 (ISBN 0-939476-10-X); pap. text ed. 14.95 (ISBN 0-939476-09-6). Biblio Pr GA.
Ansoff. Understanding & Managing Strategic Change. 1982. 38.50 (ISBN 0-444-86405-9). Elsevier.
Ansoff, H. Igor. Corporate Strategy: An Analytic Approach to Business Policy for Growth & Expansion. 1965. 27.50 (ISBN 0-07-002111-2, P&RB). McGraw.
Ansoff, Igor, et al, eds. From Strategic Planning to Strategic Management. LC 74-20598. 259p. 1976. 44.95x (ISBN 0-471-03223-9, Pub. by Wiley-Interscience). Wiley.
Anson, Barry & Donaldson, James A. Surgical Anatomy of the Temporal Bone. 3rd ed. (Illus.). 500p. 1981. 75.00 (ISBN 0-7216-1292-X). Saunders.
Anson, Barry J. & McVay, Chester B. Surgical Anatomy, 2 vols. 5th ed. LC 78-92125. (Illus.). 1282p. 1971. 63.00 set o.p. (ISBN 0-7216-1294-6); Vol. 1. 33.00 o.p. (ISBN 0-7216-1295-4); Vol. 2. 30.00 o.p. (ISBN 0-7216-1296-2). Saunders.
Anson, Elva & Liden, Kathie. The Compleat Family Book. LC 79-18254. (Illus.). 1979. text ed. 8.95 (ISBN 0-8024-1594-6). Moody.

Anson, George. A Voyage Round the World in the Years MDCCXL, I, II, III, IV. Williams, Glyndur, intro. by. (Oxford English Memoirs & Travels Ser). (Illus.). 1974. text ed. 17.75x o.p. (ISBN 0-19-255402-6). Oxford U Pr.

Anson, Jay. Six Six Six. 286p. 1981. 12.95 o.s.i. (ISBN 0-671-25144-9). S&S.

Anson, Joan. Before the Trees Turn Gray. Perrin, Arnold, ed. 65p. (Orig.). 1981. pap. 4.95 (ISBN 0-939736-22-5). Wings ME.

Anson, M. C., ed. Advances in Protein Chemistry, Vol. 35. 396p. 1982. 47.50 (ISBN 0-12-034235-9); lib. ed. 62.00 (ISBN 0-12-034286-3); microfiche 33.50 (ISBN 0-12-034287-1). Acad Pr.

Anson, M. L., et al, eds. Advances in Protein Chemistry. Incl. Vol. 1. 1944. 61.00 (ISBN 0-12-034201-4); Vol. 2. Anson, M. L., et al, eds. 1944. 61.00 (ISBN 0-12-034202-2); Vols. 3-4. 1947-48. 67.50. Vol. 3 (ISBN 0-12-034203-0). Vol. 4 (ISBN 0-12-034204-9); Vol. 5. 1949. 61.00 (ISBN 0-12-034205-7); Vol. 6. 1951. 67.50 (ISBN 0-12-034206-5); Vol. 7. 1952. 61.00 (ISBN 0-12-034207-3); Vols. 8-9. 1953-54. 67.50. Vol. 8 (ISBN 0-12-034208-1). Vol.9 (ISBN 0-12-034209-X); Vol. 10. 1955. 61.00 (ISBN 0-12-034210-3); Vol. 11. 1956. 69.50 (ISBN 0-12-034211-1); Vol. 12. 1957. 69.50 (ISBN 0-12-034212-X); Vol. 13. 1958. 67.50 (ISBN 0-12-034213-8); Vol. 14. 1959. 67.50 (ISBN 0-12-034214-6); Vol. 15. 1961. 61.00 (ISBN 0-12-034215-4); Vol. 16. 1962. 67.50 (ISBN 0-12-034216-2); Vol. 17. 1963. 67.50 (ISBN 0-12-034217-0); Vol. 18. 1964. 67.50 (ISBN 0-12-034218-9); Vol. 19. 1964. 61.00 (ISBN 0-12-034219-7); Vol. 20. 1965. 61.00 (ISBN 0-12-034220-0); Vols. 21-22. 1966. 61.00 (ISBN 0-685-30514-7). Vol. 21 (ISBN 0-12-034221-9). **Vol. 22 (ISBN 0-12-034222-7); Vol. 23. 1968. 61.00 (ISBN 0-12-034223-5); Vol. 24. 1970. 67.50 (ISBN 0-12-034224-3); Vol. 25. 1971. 61.00 (ISBN 0-12-034225-1); Vol. 26. 1972. 61.00 (ISBN 0-12-034226-X); Vol. 27. 1973. 67.50 (ISBN 0-12-034227-8); Vol. 28. 1974. 64.50 (ISBN 0-12-034228-6); Vol. 31. 1977. 57.50 (ISBN 0-12-034231-6); lib ed. 72.50 (ISBN 0-12-034278-2); microfiche 43.50 (ISBN 0-686-66772-7). LC 44-8853. Vols 1-26. Acad Pr.**

Anson, Peter F. Fishing Boats & the Fisher Folk on the East Coast of Scotland. (Illus.). 320p. 1974. Repr. of 1930 ed. 12.95x o.p. (ISBN 0-460-04213-0, Pub. by J. M. Dent England). Biblio Dist.

Anson, Robert S. Gone Crazy & Back Again: The Rise & Fall of the Rolling Stone Generation. LC 80-5448. 384p. 1981. 14.95 o.p. (ISBN 0-385-13114-3). Doubleday.

--The Yellow River. LC 80-52503. (Rivers of the World Ser.). PLB 12.68 (ISBN 0-382-06371-6). Silver.

Anson, Ronald J., jt. auth. see Rist, Ray C.

Anson, W. S. Mottoes & Badges of Families, Regiments, Schools, Colleges, States, Towns, Livery Companies, Societies, Etc. LC 74-14502. 192p. 1975. Repr. of 1904 ed. 37.00x (ISBN 0-8103-4055-0). Gale.

Ansorge, R., et al, eds. Iterative Solution of Nonlinear Systems of Equations, Oberwolfach, FRG, 1982: Proceedings. (Lecture Notes in Mathematics: Vol. 953). 202p. 1983. pap. 12.00 (ISBN 0-387-11602-8). Springer-Verlag.

Anspaugh, David & Ezell, Gene. Teaching Today's Health. 512p. 1983. text ed. 18.95 (ISBN 0-675-20025-3). Additional supplements may be obtained from publisher. Merrill.

Anstey, Roger & Antippas, A. P. The Atlantic Slave Trade & British Abolition, 1760-1810. (Cambridge Commonwealth Ser). 472p. 1975. 22.50x o.p. (ISBN 0-391-00371-2). Humanities.

Anstruther, Gilbert. Look, Dad, They're Hanging Grandpa. (Illus.). 1969. 11.50 (ISBN 0-392-06966-0, AUS67-2366, ABC). Sportshelf.

Antaki, Charles & Brewin, Chris, eds. Attributions & Psychological Change: Application of Attributional Theories to Clinical & Educational Practice. LC 81-71575. (Illus.). 1982. 26.50 (ISBN 0-12-058780-7). Acad Pr.

Antal, Evelyn, ed. see Klingender, Francis D.

Antal, Frederick. Florentine Painting & Its Social Background. (Icon Editions). (Illus.). 576p. 1975. pap. 8.95i o.p. (ISBN 0-06-430067-6, IN-67, HarpT). Har-Row.

Antaloczy, Z. Electrocardiology, 1981: Proceedings of the 8th International Congress, Budapest, Hungary, Sept. 1-4, 1981. Preda, I., ed. (International Congress Ser.: No. 586). 1982. 107.00 (ISBN 0-444-90295-3). Elsevier.

Antczak, D. F., jt. auth. see Kristensen, F.

Antczak, Janice. Science Fiction: The Mythos of a New Romance. Hannigan, Jane Anne, ed. (Diversity & Direction in Children's Literature Ser.). 250p. Date not set. 17.95 (ISBN 0-918212-43-X). Neal-Schuman. Postponed.

Ante-Nicene Fathers. Writings of the Ante-Nicene Fathers, 10 vols. Roberts, A. & Donaldson, J., eds. 1951. Set. 169.50 (ISBN 0-8028-8097-5); Vols. 1-10. 16.95 ea. Eerdmans.

Antebi, Elizabeth. The Electronic Epoch. 280p. 1983. 49.50 (ISBN 0-442-28254-0). Van Nos Reinhold.

Antelava, H. G. Abbreviated Turkish-Russian Dictionary of New Words. 95p. (Turkish & Rus.). 1978. pap. 4.75 (ISBN 0-686-97387-9, M-9054). French & Eur.

Antelman, M. S. The Analytical Encyclopedia of Thermoplastic Materials. 1974. 91.00 (ISBN 0-471-26115-7, Pub. by Wiley Heyden). Wiley.

Antelminelli, F. Castracane Degli see Castracane Degli Antelminelli, F.

Antezana, Jorge Garcia see Garcia-Antezana, Jorge.

Antheil, George. Bad Boy of Music. (Illus.). 378p. 1981. lib. bdg. 35.00 (ISBN 0-306-76084-3). Da Capo.

Anthes, Richard, et al. The Atmosphere. 3rd ed. (Illus.). 384p. 1981. text ed. 25.95 (ISBN 0-675-08043-6). Additional supplements may be obtained from Publisher. Merrill.

Anthes, Richard A. Weather Around Us. (Physical Science Ser.). 1976. pap. text ed. 7.95 (ISBN 0-675-08635-3); Set Of 4. cassettes & filmstrips O.S.I. 135.00 (ISBN 0-675-08634-5). Merrill.

Anthes, Richard A., jt. auth. see Miller, Albert.

Anthes, Rudolf, et al. Mit Rahineh, 1955. (Museum Monographs). (Illus.). 93p. 1958. soft bound 8.00x (ISBN 0-934718-09-1). Univ Mus of U PA.

--Mit Rahineh, 1956. (Museum Monographs). (Illus.). 170p. 1965. soft bound 7.50x (ISBN 0-934718-19-9). Univ Mus of U PA.

Anthologia Graeca Selections. Poems from the Greek Anthology, in English Paraphrase. Fitts, Dudley, tr. LC 78-13574. 1978. Repr. of 1956 ed. lib. bdg. 20.50x (ISBN 0-313-21017-9, AGPG). Greenwood.

Anthony. Plaid for Management Accounting. 3rd ed. 1980. 5.95 (ISBN 0-256-01277-6, 01-0814-03). Dow Jones-Irwin.

Anthony, Alberta P., jt. auth. see Kahananui, Dorothy M.

Anthony, Ann. The Diary of a Mad Golf Wife or How to Begin. (Illus.). 96p. 1983. pap. 5.95 (ISBN 0-911433-02-3). HealthRight.

Anthony, Barry T., jt. auth. see Bontrager, Kenneth L.

Anthony, C. & Anthony, R. There Is a Safe Place to Hide. 1950. pap. 2.00 (ISBN 0-910140-01-4). Anthony.

Anthony, Carol K. Guide to the I Ching. 2nd ed. 184p. 1982. pap. 5.95 (ISBN 0-9603832-3-9). Anthony Pub Co.

Anthony, Catherine P. & Thibodeau, Gary A. Basic Concepts in Anatomy & Physiology: A Programmed Presentation. 4th ed. LC 79-19392. (Illus.). 1979. pap. text ed. 12.95 (ISBN 0-8016-0260-2). Mosby.

--Structure & Function of the Body. 6th ed. LC 79-24006. 1980. text ed. 14.95 (ISBN 0-8016-0273-4); pap. text ed. 12.95 (ISBN 0-8016-0287-4). Mosby.

--Textbook of Anatomy & Physiology. 10th ed. LC 78-11405. (Illus.). 1979. text ed. 24.95 (ISBN 0-8016-0255-6). Mosby.

--Textbook of Anatomy & Physiology. 11th ed. (Illus.). 876p. 1983. text ed. 28.95 (ISBN 0-8016-0289-0). Mosby.

Anthony, Courtney L., et al. Pediatric Cardiology. (Medical Outline Ser.). 1979. pap. 24.00 (ISBN 0-87488-607-4). Med Exam.

Anthony, D. W., tr. see Morishima, M.

Anthony, Douglas. Do it In Bed: An Exercise Program. LC 82-90978. (Illus.). 96p. 1983. pap. 5.95 (ISBN 0-911433-00-7). HealthRight.

Anthony, Douglass. Sports Motions: A Primer For Winning. (Illus.). 96p. (Orig.). 1983. pap. 5.95 (ISBN 0-911433-01-5). HealthRight.

Anthony, E. James & Chiland, Colette. The Child in His Family: Children in Turmoil, Tomorrow's Parents, Vol. 7. LC 82-8421. (Yearbook of the International Association of Child & Adolescent Psychiatry & Allied Professions Ser.). 328p. 1982. 34.95x (ISBN 0-471-86873-6, Pub. by Wiley-Interscience). Wiley.

Anthony, Earl & Taylor, Dawson. Winning Bowling. LC 77-75718. (Winning Ser.). (Illus.). 1977. 8.95 o.p. (ISBN 0-8092-7792-1); pap. 7.95 (ISBN 0-8092-7791-3). Contemp Bks.

Anthony, Evelyn. The Avenue of the Dead. 320p. 1982. 14.95 (ISBN 0-698-11124-9, Coward). Putnam Pub Group.

--Clandara. 1976. pap. 1.95 o.p. (ISBN 0-451-08064-5, J8064, Sig). NAL.

--The Defector. 1981. 12.95 (ISBN 0-698-11064-1, Coward). Putnam Pub Group.

--The Defector. 1982. pap. 3.50 (ISBN 0-451-11765-4, AE1765, Sig). NAL.

--The Janus Imperative. 1980. 10.95 (ISBN 0-698-11016-1, Coward). Putnam Pub Group.

--Mission to Malaspiga. LC 74-79687. 1974. 7.95 o.p. (ISBN 0-698-10608-3, Coward). Putnam Pub Group.

--The Persian Price. LC 75-10472. 288p. 1975. 8.95 o.p. (ISBN 0-698-10694-6, Coward). Putnam Pub Group.

--The Return. LC 78-19118. 1978. 9.95 (ISBN 0-698-10938-4, Coward). Putnam Pub Group.

--The Silver Falcon. 1977. 9.95 (ISBN 0-698-10755-1, Coward). Putnam Pub Group.

--Stranger at the Gates. LC 73-78736. 1978. 9.95 o.p. (ISBN 0-698-10946-5, Coward). Putnam Pub Group.

Anthony, Geraldine. Gwen Pharis Ringwood. (World Authors Ser.). 1981. lib. bdg. 15.95 (ISBN 0-8057-6444-5, Twayne). G K Hall.

Anthony, Geraldine S. C. John Coulter. (World Authors Ser.). 1976. lib. bdg. 15.95 (ISBN 0-8057-6240-X, Twayne). G K Hall.

Anthony, Ilid E. Roman London. (Young Archaeologist Ser). (Illus.). (gr. 6-8). 1972. PLB 4.49 o.p. (ISBN 0-399-60698-X). Putnam Pub Group.

Anthony, J. Garner. Hawaii Under Army Rule. 213p. 1975. pap. 3.95 (ISBN 0-8248-0377-9). UH Pr.

Anthony, James M., jt. auth. see Meller, Norman.

Anthony, Julie & Bollettieri, Nick. A Winning Combination. (Encore Edition Ser.). (Illus.). 272p. 1982. pap. 6.95 (ISBN 0-684-17637-8, ScribT); 4.95 (ISBN 0-684-17583-5). Scribner.

Anthony, Katherine. The Lambs: A Study of Pre-Victorian England. LC 72-7815. (Illus.). 256p. 1973. Repr. of 1948 ed. lib. bdg. 16.00x (ISBN 0-8371-6523-7, ANLA). Greenwood.

Anthony, Lillian S., ed. see Sieben, J. Kenneth.

Anthony, Luean E., jt. auth. see Taylor, Keith B.

Anthony, Michael J. & Tolliver, Robert E. Effective Sales Presentations Guidebook. 128p. 1983. text ed. 25.00 (ISBN 0-201-00007-5). A-W.

Anthony, Nina. Thunder Activity Book. Duenewald, Doris, ed. (Elephant Books Ser.). (Illus.). (gr. 1-7). 1978. pap. 1.25 o.s.i. (ISBN 0-448-16170-2, G&D). Putnam Pub Group.

Anthony, P. D. Ideology of Work. 1977. 25.00x (ISBN 0-422-74310-0, Pub. by Tavistock); pap. 9.95x o.p. (ISBN 0-422-76650-X). Methuen Inc.

Anthony, Patricia A. Animals Grow. LC 74-77759. (You Look at Life Ser.). (Illus.). (gr. k-2). 1970. PLB 4.49 o.p. (ISBN 0-399-60028-0). Putnam Pub Group.

Anthony, Piers. Centaur Isle. 304p. (Orig.). 1982. pap. 2.75 (ISBN 0-345-29770-9, Del Rey). Ballantine.

--Chaining the Lady. 1978. pap. 2.95 (ISBN 0-380-01779-2, 61614-9). Avon.

--Chthon. (Orig.). 1982. pap. 2.75 (ISBN 0-425-06260-0). Berkley Pub.

--God of Tarot. (Orig.). 1979. pap. 1.75 o.s.i. (ISBN 0-515-05134-9). Jove Pubns.

--Juxtapositions. 352p. 1983. pap. 2.95 (ISBN 0-345-28215-9, Del Rey). Ballantine.

--Macroscope. 1969. pap. 3.95 (ISBN 0-380-00209 4, 81992-9). Avon.

--Mute. 448p. 1981. pap. 3.50 (ISBN 0-380-82354-3, 77578). Avon.

--Night Mare. 320p. 1983. pap. 2.95 (ISBN 0-345-30456-X, Del Rey). Ballantine.

--Omnivore. 1978. pap. 2.95 (ISBN 0-380-00262-0, 82362-4). Avon.

--Ox. 1976. pap. 2.95 (ISBN 0-380-00461-5, 82370-5). Avon.

Anthony, R., jt. auth. see Anthony, C.

Anthony, Raymond G., jt. auth. see Holland, Charles D.

Anthony, Richard, et al. The New Religious Movements: Conversion, Coercion & Commitment. 352p. Date not set. 19.50 (ISBN 0-8245-0484-4); pap. 9.95 (ISBN 0-686-83096-2). Crossroad NY.

Anthony, Robert N. Accounting for the Cost of Interest. LC 75-12484. 128p. 1975. 19.95x (ISBN 0-669-00027-2). Lexington Bks.

Anthony, T. M. The Way Out. LC 82-72166. (Illus.). 141p. (Orig.). 1982. pap. 5.95 (ISBN 0-89305-042-3). Anna Pub.

Anthony, T. Robert. Nineteenth-Century Fairy Lamps. 1971. spiral bdg 4.95 o.p. (ISBN 0-517-51088-X). Crown.

Anthony, Vivian. Banks & Markets. 2nd ed. (Studies in the British Economy). 1974. pap. text ed. 6.50x o.p. (ISBN 0-435-84558-6). Heinemann Ed.

--Britain's Overseas Trade. 3rd ed. (Studies in British Economy). 1976. pap. text ed. 4.00x o.p. (ISBN 0-435-84566-7). Heinemann Ed.

Anthony, William. Bible Stories. LC 77-71655. (Illus., Orig.). pap. 5.00 (ISBN 0-912330-25-2, Dist. by Inland Bk). Jargon Soc.

Anthony, William A., ed. Rehabilitating the Person with A Psychiatric Disability: The State of the Art. 1980. 4.00 (ISBN 0-686-36379-5). Am Personnel.

Antieau, C. J., et al. Current Constitutional Issues: A Symposium. LC 77-153885. (Symposia on Law & Society Ser.). 1971. Repr. of 1967 ed. lib. bdg. 25.00 (ISBN 0-306-70154-5). Da Capo.

Antieau, Chester J. Constitutional Construction. LC 82-1250. 255p. 1982. lib. bdg. 30.00 (ISBN 0-379-20682-X). Oceana.

Antill, James M. & Woodhead, Ronald. Critical Path Methods in Construction Practice. 2nd ed. LC 79-121902. 414p. 1970. 40.95x o.p. (ISBN 0-471-03246-8, Pub. by Wiley-Interscience). Wiley.

Antill, James M. & Woodhead, Ronald W. Critical Path Methods in Construction Practice. 3rd. ed. LC 81-19713. 416p. 1982. 37.50x (ISBN 0-471-86612-1, Pub. by Wiley-Interscience). Wiley.

Antippas, A. P., jt. auth. see Anstey, Roger.

Antolini, Renzo, et al, eds. Transport in Biomembranes: Model Systems & Reconstitution. 288p. 1982. text ed. 32.00 (ISBN 0-89004-868-1). Raven.

Anton, Haberkamp De see Haensch, G.

Anton, Hector R., et al. Contemporary Issues in Cost & Managerial Accounting: A Discipline in Transition. 3rd ed. LC 77-74383. (Illus.). 1978. pap. text ed. 24.95 (ISBN 0-395-25435-3). HM.

Anton, Howard. Calculus with Analytic Geometry. brief edition ed. LC 81-50266. 854p. 1981. text ed. 25.50 (ISBN 0-471-09443-9). Wiley.

--Calculus with Analytic Geometry. LC 79-11469. 1980. 33.95 (ISBN 0-471-03248-4); solution manual 11.95 (ISBN 0-471-04498-9). Wiley.

--Elementary Linear Algebra. 3rd ed. 375p. 1981. text ed. 22.95 (ISBN 0-471-05338-4). Wiley.

Anton, Howard & Kolman, Bernard. Applied Finite Mathematics. 2nd ed. 558p. 1978. 19.95 o.p. (ISBN 0-12-059565-6); SBP 21.75 o.p. (ISBN 0-686-85502-7); instr's. manual 3.00 o.p. (ISBN 0-12-059564-8). Acad Pr.

--Applied Finite Mathematics with Calculus. 760p. 1978. 21.95 (ISBN 0-12-059560-5); SBP 24.00 (ISBN 0-686-96634-1); instrs'. manual 3.00 (ISBN 0-12-059567-2). Acad Pr.

Anton, Howard & Rorres, Chris. Applications of Linear Algebra. 2nd ed. 1979. pap. text ed. 13.95 (ISBN 0-471-05337-6); solutions 7.00 (ISBN 0-471-06030-5). Wiley.

Anton, Howard & Kolman, B., eds. Mathematics with Applications for the Management, Life & Social Sciences. 2nd ed. LC 81-66947. 851p. 1982. text ed. 20.00 (ISBN 0-12-059561-3). Acad Pr.

Anton, John P., ed. Naturalism & Historical Understanding: Essays on the Philosophy of John Herman Randall, Jr. LC 67-63753. 1967. 39.50x (ISBN 0-87395-021-6). State U NY Pr.

Anton, John P., ed. see Papanoutsos, Evangelos P.

Anton, John P., jt. ed. see Walton, Craig.

Anton, John P., tr. see Papanoutsos, Evangelos P.

Anton, Thomas. Occupational Safety & Health Management. 1979. text ed. 24.50 (ISBN 0-07-002106-6, C). McGraw.

Anton, Thomas J. Governing Greater Stockholm: A Study of Policy Development & System Change. LC 79-94447. (Institute of Governmental Studies, U. C. Berkeley, & Lane Studies in Regional Government). 1974. 32.50x (ISBN 0-520-02718-3). U of Cal Pr.

Antonacci, R. J. & Lockhart, B. B. Tennis for Young Champions. 192p. 1982. 9.95 (ISBN 0-07-002145-7). Mcgraw.

Antonacci, Robert J. & Barr, Jene. Football for Young Champions. 2nd ed. LC 75-10825. (Illus.). 160p. (gr. 4-6). 1976. PLB 9.95 (ISBN 0-07-002154-6, GB). McGraw.

--Physical Fitness for Young Champions. 2nd ed. (Illus.). 144p. (gr. 3-7). 1975. 9.95 (ISBN 0-07-002142-2, GB). McGraw.

--Track & Field for Young Champions. new ed. (Illus.). (gr. 3-6). 1974. 9.95 (ISBN 0-07-002136-8, GB). McGraw.

Antonaccio, Michael J., ed. Cardiovascular Pharmacology. LC 74-14469. 544p. 1977. 34.00 (ISBN 0-89004-063-X). Raven.

Antonescu, V., compiled by. Capture Reactions. (Bibliographical Ser.: No. 12). 136p. 1964. pap. write for info. o.p. (ISBN 92-0-134064-8, STI-PUB-21-12, IAEA). Unipub.

Antoni, Manfred. Arbeit Als Betriebswirtschaftlicher Grundbegriff. vii, 286p. (Ger.). 1982. write for info. (ISBN 3-8204-5798-4). P Lang Pubs.

Antoniades, John, ed. Uncommon Malignant Melanomas. LC 82-6610. (Masson Cancer Management Ser.). (Illus.). 391p. 1982. 65.00 (ISBN 0-89352-046-2). Masson Pub.

Antonini, Chiara S., jt. auth. see Mazzeo, Donatella.

Antonini, E. & Brunori, M. Hemoglobin & Myoglobin in Their Reactions with Ligands. (Frontiers of Biology Ser. Vol. 21). 1971. 74.50 (ISBN 0-444-10096-2, North-Holland). Elsevier.

Antoniou, Andreas. Digital Filters: Analysis & Design. (Electrical Engineering Ser.). (Illus.). 1979. text ed. 39.50 (ISBN 0-07-002117-1, C); solution manual 26.50 (ISBN 0-07-002118-X). McGraw.

Antoniou, J. Environmental Management: Planning for Traffic. 1972. 38.00 (ISBN 0-07-094222-6, P&RB). McGraw.

Antoniou, Jim. Greece. LC 75-44871. (Macdonald Countries). (Illus.). (gr. 6 up). 1976. PLB 12.68 (ISBN 0-382-06104-7, Pub. by Macdonald Ed.). Silver.

Antonovich, Michael. How to Use Your Apple II Computer. LC 80-70465. (WSI's How to Use Your Microcomputer Ser.). 300p. (gr. 10-12). 1982. cancelled 19.95 (ISBN 0-938862-02-2); pap. 13.95 (ISBN 0-938862-03-0). Weber Systems.

Antonovsky, Aaron. Health, Stress, & Coping: New Perspectives on Mental & Physical Well-Being. LC 79-83566. (Social & Behavioral Science Ser.). 1979. 18.95x (ISBN 0-87589-412-7). Jossey-Bass.

Antonovsky, Helen F., et al. Adolescent Sexuality: A Study of Attitudes & Behavior. LC 80-8337. 176p. 1980. 21.95x (ISBN 0-669-04030-4). Lexington Bks.

Antony, Arthur. Guide to Basic Information Sources in Chemistry. LC 79-330. (Information Resources Ser.). 219p. 1979. 22.95 (ISBN 0-470-26587-6). Halsted Pr.

Antony, Joseph. Geschichtliche Darstellung der Entstehung und Vervollkommnung der Orgel. (Bibliotheca Organologica: Vol. 26). 1971. Repr. of 1832 ed. wrappers 22.50 o.s.i. (ISBN 90-6027-239-0, Pub. by Frits Knuf Netherlands). Pendragon NY.

Antosik, et al. Theory of Distributions: The Sequential Approach. LC 73-78246. 296p. 1973. 66.00 (ISBN 0-444-41082-1). Elsevier.

Antreassian, Jack, tr. see Baronian, Hagop.

Antrei, Albert C., et al, eds. see Sanpete County Commission.

Antrim, William. Advertising. Dorr, Eugene L., ed. (Occupational Manuals & Projects in Marketing). (Illus.). (gr. 11-12). 1978. pap. text ed. 7.32 (ISBN 0-07-002114-7, G); tchr's. manual & key 4.56 (ISBN 0-07-002115-5). McGraw.

Anttila, Raimo, jt. auth. see Slagle, Uhlan.

Anttila, Raimo A. An Introduction to Historical & Comparative Linguistics. (Illus.). 415p. 1972. text ed. 28.95 (ISBN 0-02-303630-3, 30363). Macmillan.

Antwerp, Margaret A. Van see Van Antwerp, Margaret A.

Antwerp, Margaret A. Van see Van Antwerp, Margret A.

Antwi, Anthony K. Public Expenditures: The Impact of Distribution on Income-the Ghana Case. LC 78-63269. 1978. pap. text ed. 11.00 (ISBN 0-8191-0620-8). U Pr of Amer.

Anuman, Rajadhon Phraya. Life & Ritual in Old Siam: Three Studies of Thai Life & Customs. Gedney, William J., ed. LC 78-23833. (Illus.). 1979. Repr. of 1961 ed. lib. bdg. 20.75x (ISBN 0-313-21193-0, ARLF). Greenwood.

Anwar, Chairil. Complete Poetry & Prose of Chairil Anwar. Raffel, Burton, tr. LC 76-91201. (Bahasa indonesian & eng.). 1970. 27.00x (ISBN 0-87395-060-7); pap. 14.95x (ISBN 0-87395-061-5). State U NY Pr.

Anwar, Rebecca A., ed. Emergency Medicine Residencies. (Emergency Health Services Quarterly: Vol. 1, No. 1). 133p. 1981. pap. text ed. 15.00 (ISBN 0-917724-57-7, B57). Haworth Pr.

Anyan, Walter R. Adolescent Medicine in Primary Care. LC 78-16772. 387p. 1978. 30.00x (ISBN 0-471-03976-4, Pub. by Wiley Medical). Wiley.

Anyanwu, K. C. The American Experts & the Academic Market: A Comparative Study of Cultural Philosophy. 128p. 1983. 5.00 (ISBN 0-682-49976-5). Exposition.

Anylan, William G, jt. ed. see Yaggy, Duncan.

Anzaldua, Mike M., Jr. & Pierce, James A. First Steps Grammar & Guided Composition for Basic Writing Students. 200p. 1980. pap. text ed. 9.95x wkbk. (ISBN 0-89641-034-X). American Pr.

Anzalone, Joseph T., jt. auth. see Phillips, Celeste R.

Aoams, Charles J., III. Ghost Stories of Berks County (Pennsylvania) 215p. 1982. pap. 5.95 (ISBN 0-9610008-0-5). C J Adams.

Aoki, Haruo. Nez Perce Grammar. (California Library Reprint: No. 41). 1974. 28.50x (ISBN 0-520-02524-5). U of Cal Pr.

--Nez Perce Texts. LC 77-91776. (Publications in Linguistics: Vol. 90). 1979. 17.00x (ISBN 0-520-09593-6). U of Cal Pr.

Aoki, Hiroyuki. Shintaido, a New Art of Movement & Life Expression. Thompson, Michael & Ito, Haruyoshi, trs. from Japanese. LC 82-80496. (Illus.). 120p. 1982. pap. 8.95 (ISBN 0-942634-00-4). Shintaido.

Aoki, Hisako & Gantschev, Ivan. Santa's Favorite Story. (Picture Book Studio Ser.). (Illus.). 28p. 1982. 8.95 (ISBN 0-907234-16-X). Neugebauer Pr.

Aoki, Katsutada, jt. auth. see Shimizu, Akinao.

Aoki, Michiko Y. & Dardess, Margaret B., eds. As the Japanese See It: Past & Present. LC 81-11526. 324p. 1981. text ed. 17.50x (ISBN 0-8248-0759-6); pap. text ed. 7.95x (ISBN 0-8248-0760-X). UH Pr.

Aoki, T. & Urushnizaki, I., eds. Manipulation of Host Defence Mechanisms. (International Congress Ser.: Vol. 576). 1982. 51.25 (ISBN 0-444-90245-7). Elsevier.

Aoyagi, Akiko, jt. auth. see Shurtleff, William.

APA Commission on Psychotherapies. Psychotherapy Research: Methodological & Efficacy Issues. LC 82-8763. (Illus.). 280p. 1982. pap. 15.00x Report (ISBN 0-89042-101-3). Am Psychiatric.

APA Library. Psychiatry & Confidentiality: An Annotated Bibliography. Jones, Jean C., ed. 51p. 1974. pap. 5.00 o.p. (ISBN 0-685-65578-4, P215-0). Am Psychiatric.

APA Task Force on Nomenclature & Statistics. Desk Reference to the Diagnostic Criteria from (DSM-III) (Illus.). 300p. 1983. spiral bound 15.00 (ISBN 0-89042-046-7, 42-046-7). Am Psychiatric.

APA Task Force on Standards for Psychiatric Facilities for Children. Standards for Psychiatric Facilities Serving Children and Adolescents. 136p. 1971. 5.00 o.p. (ISBN 0-685-37536-6, P160-0). Am Psychiatric.

Apadeva. Mimansa Nyaya Prakasa. Edgerton, Franklin, tr. 1929. 75.00x (ISBN 0-685-69815-7). Elliots Bks.

Apar, Bruce. The Home Video Book. (Illus.). 144p. (Orig.). 1982. 14.90 (ISBN 0-8174-3990-0, Amphoto); pap. 8.95 (ISBN 0-8174-3991-9). Watson-Guptill.

Aparna, jt. ed. see Ravi Dass.

Apel, Willi. The History of Keyboard Music to 1700. Tischler, Hans, tr. LC 79-135015. 896p. 1972. 35.00x (ISBN 0-253-32795-4). Ind U Pr.

Apel, Willi & Daniel, Ralph T. Harvard Brief Dictionary of Music. LC 60-7986. (Illus.). 8.50 o.p. (ISBN 0-674-37350-2). Harvard U Pr.

Apeldoorn, G. Jan Van see Van Apeldoorn, G. Jan.

Apenszlak, Jacob, ed. The Black Book of Polish Jewry: An Account of the Martyrdom of Polish Jewry Under Nazi Occupation. xvi, 343p. 1982. Repr. of 1943 ed. 27.50x (ISBN 0-86527-340-5). Fertig.

Aperjis, Dimitri. The Oil Market in the Nineteen Eighties: OPEC Oil Policy & Economic Development. 240p. 1982. Professional Ref. 35.00x (ISBN 0-88410-903-8). Ballinger Pub.

Apfel, Necia H. The Moon & Its Exploration. (First Bks). (Illus.). 72p. (gr. 4 up). 1982. PLB 8.90 (ISBN 0-531-04385-1). Watts.

--Stars & Galaxies. (First Bks). (Illus.). 72p. (gr. 4 up). 1982. PLB 8.90 (ISBN 0-531-04389-4). Watts.

Apgar, Kathryn & Riley, Donald P. Life Education in the Workplace: How to Design, Lead & Market Employee Seminars. 184p. 1982. 17.95 (ISBN 0-87304-197-6). Family Serv.

Apicius. Cookery & Dining in Imperial Rome. Vehling, Joseph D., ed. & tr. from Latin. LC 77-89410. Orig. Title: Apicius De Re Coquinaria. 1977. pap. 6.00 (ISBN 0-486-23563-7). Dover.

APICS. Management Seminar: Proceedings. 104p. 1982. 6.00 (ISBN 0-935406-15-8). Am Prod & Inventory.

--Master Planning Seminar: Proceedings. 84p. 1982. 6.00 (ISBN 0-935406-13-1). Am Prod & Inventory.

--Planning & Control Seminar: Proceedings. 156p. 1982. 8.50 (ISBN 0-935406-14-X). Am Prod & Inventory.

APICS, ed. Capacity Planning & Control Reprints. 110p. 1975. pap. 10.50 (ISBN 0-935406-16-6). Am Prod Inventory.

APICS Annual Conference, 25th. Proceedings. LC 79-640341. 590p. 1982. 30.00 (ISBN 0-686-84381-9). Am Prod & Inventory.

APICS Bucks-Mont Cnapter. Material Requirements Planning Training Aid. 62p. 1979. 37.50 (ISBN 0-935406-10-7). Am Prod & Inventory.

APICS Cirriculum & Certification Program Council Committee, ed. Shop Floor Controls Reprints. 165p. 1973. 13.50 (ISBN 0-935406-17-4). Am Prod & Inventory.

APICS Curriculum & Certification Program Council Planning & Control Committee, ed. Capacity Planning & Control Reprints. 110p. 1975. 10.50 (ISBN 0-686-84380-0). Am Prod & Inventory.

APICS 24th Annual Conference, 1981. Proceedings. 458p. 1981. pap. 30.00 (ISBN 0-935406-05-0). Am Prod & Inventory.

Apilado, Vincent P. & Morehart, Thomas B. Personal Financial Management. (Illus.). 650p. 1980. text ed. 22.50 (ISBN 0-8299-0327-5); instrs.' manual avail. (ISBN 0-8299-0457-3); study guide 7.50 (ISBN 0-8299-0308-9). West Pub.

Apilado, Vincent P., et al. Cases in Financial Management. 2nd ed. (Illus.). 250p. 1981. pap. text ed. 12.50 (ISBN 0-314-63152-6). West Pub.

Apley, A. Graham. System of Orthopedics & Fractures. 5th ed. 1977. 56.95 o.p. (ISBN 0-407-40653-0). Butterworth.

Apley, Alan, jt. auth. see Smith, Roger.

Apley, J. Modern Trends in Pediatrics-4. 1974. 28.95 o.p. (ISBN 0-407-30803-2). Butterworth.

Apley, J., ed. see Mowat, A. P.

Apley, John, jt. auth. see Craig, Oman.

Apley, John, ed. see Hamilton, W.

Apley, John, ed. see Stone, Fred H.

Apley, M. J., ed. see Nixon.

Apling, A. J., et al. Air Pollution from Oxides of Nitrogen, Carbon Monoxide & Hydrocarbons, 1979. 1981. 59.00x (ISBN 0-686-97009-8, Pub. by W Spring England). State Mutual Bk.

--Air Pollution in Homes: Validation of Diffusion Tube Measurements of Nitrogen Dioxide, 1979. 1981. 40.00x (ISBN 0-686-97013-6, Pub. by W Spring England). State Mutual Bk.

Apollinaire, Guillaume. Alcools. Greet, Anne Hyde, tr. & annotations by. LC 65-20148. 1966. 21.00x o.p. (ISBN 0-520-00028-5); pap. 3.75 (ISBN 0-520-00029-3, CAL121). U of Cal Pr.

--Bestiary, or the Parade of Orpheus. Karmel, Pepe, tr. from Fr. LC 80-66191. (Illus.). 80p. 1980. pap. 5.95 (ISBN 0-87923-359-1); 12.95. Godine.

Apolonio, Umbro, ed. Miro. (Art Library Ser: Vol. 29). 1969. pap. 2.95 o.p. (ISBN 0-448-00478-X, G&D). Putnam Pub Group.

Aponte, Barbara B., tr. see Marques, Rene.

Apostel, L., ed. Religious Atheism? (Philosophy & Anthropology Ser.: Vol. 3). 180p. 1981. pap. text ed. 26.25x (ISBN 90-6439-272-2, Pub. by E. Story Belgium). Humanities.

Apostle, H. G. & Gerson, Lloyd P. Aristotle: Selected Works. LC 82-62715. 650p. (Orig.). 1983. text ed. 24.00x (ISBN 0-911589-00-7); pap. 12.00x (ISBN 0-911589-01-5). Peripatetic.

Apostle, Richard A. & Glock, Charles Y. The Anatomy of Racial Attitudes. LC 82-4867. 277p. 1983. 27.50x (ISBN 0-520-04719-2). U of Cal Pr.

Apostol, T. M. Calculus: Multi-Variable Calculus & Linear Algebra with Application, Vol. 2. 2nd ed. LC 67-14605. 673p. 1969. text ed. 34.95 (ISBN 0-471-00007-8); student solution avail. (ISBN 0-471-04498-9). Wiley.

--Calculus: One-Variable Calculus with an Introduction to Linear Algebra, Vol. 1. 2nd ed. LC 73-20899. 666p. 1967. text ed. 30.95x (ISBN 0-471-00005-1). Wiley.

Apostolon, Billy. Preach the Word. (Sermon Outline Ser.). 1978. pap. 2.25 (ISBN 0-8010-0039-4). Baker Bk.

Apotheker, Nan, tr. see Garaudy, Roger.

Appadurai, Arjun. Worship & Conflict Under Colonial Rule: A South India Case. (Cambridge South Asian Studies: No. 27). (Illus.). 282p. 1981. 42.50 (ISBN 0-521-23122-1). Cambridge U Pr.

Appasamy, Jaya. Tanjavur Painting of the Maratha Period. 121p. 1981. text ed. 42.00x (ISBN 0-391-02235-0, Pub. by Abhinav India). Humanities.

Appel, Alfred. Nabokov's Dark Cinema. (Illus.). 334p. 1974. 25.00x (ISBN 0-19-501834-6). Oxford U Pr.

Appel, Benjamin. The People Talk: American Voices from the Great Depression. 1982. pap. 7.95 (ISBN 0-671-43809-3, Touchstone Bks). S&S.

Appel, Ellen. Sand Art. 1976. 6.95 o.p. (ISBN 0-517-52475-9). Crown.

Appel, Gerald. Double Your Money Every Three Years. 1974. 25.00 o.s.i. (ISBN 0-685-49184-6). Windsor.

--Ninety-Nine Ways to Make Money in a Depression. rev. ed. (Illus.). 256p. 1981. 14.95 o.p. (ISBN 0-87000-501-4, Arlington Hse). Crown.

Appel, Jeanette, jt. auth. see Keller, Clifton.

Appel, L. Lexique des Fruits et Legumes. 133p. (Fr. & Eng.). Date not set. pap. 7.95 (ISBN 0-686-97410-7, M-9238). French & Eur.

Appel, Libby & Flachmann, Michael. Shakespeare's Lovers: A Text for Performance & Analysis. 1982. pap. 5.95x (ISBN 0-8093-1072-4). S Ill U Pr.

Appel, Louis. The Word's the Thing. 1977. pap. text ed. 11.75 o.p. (ISBN 0-8191-0359-4). U Pr of Amer.

Appel, Martin & Goldblatt, Burt. Baseball's Best: The Hall of Fame Gallery. (Illus.). 1977. 24.95 o.p. (ISBN 0-07-002144-9, P&RB). McGraw.

Appel, Martin, jt. auth. see Munson, Thurman.

Appel, Martin, compiled by. & compiled by. Batting Secrets of the Major Leaguers. LC 80-13709. (Illus.). 112p. (gr. 7 up). 1981. PLB 8.79 o.p. (ISBN 0-671-41315-5). Messner.

Appel, Odette, jt. auth. see Sobieszek, Robert.

Appel, Stanley. Current Neurology, Vol. 4. 624p. 1982. 50.00 (ISBN 0-471-09556-7, Pub. by Wiley Med). Wiley.

Appel, Stanley H., ed. Current Neurology, Vol. 3. LC 78-68042. (Current Ser.). (Illus.). 545p. 1981. text ed. 52.50 (ISBN 0-471-09501-X, Pub by Wiley Med). Wiley.

Appel, Willa. Cults in America. LC 82-15538. 228p. 1983. 15.95 (ISBN 0-03-054836-5). HR&W.

Appel, William. Water World. 224p. (Orig.). 1983. pap. 2.75 (ISBN 0-449-12537-8, GM). Fawcett.

Appelbaum, Arlene, ed. see Ilse, Sherokee.

Appelbaum, Judith & Evans, Nancy. How to Get Happily Published: A Complete & Candid Guide. LC 77-3737. 1978. 12.45i (ISBN 0-06-010141-5, HarpT). Har-Row.

Appelbaum, Richard P. Theories of Social Change. LC 81-80801. 1970. pap. text ed. 10.50 (ISBN 0-395-30558-6). HM.

Appelbaum, S., ed. see Wurts, Richard.

Appelbaum, Stanley, ed. & tr. from Ger. Simplicissimus: 180 Satirical Drawings from the Famous German Weekly. LC 74-79171. (Illus.). 192p. 1975. 10.00 (ISBN 0-486-23099-6); pap. 8.95 (ISBN 0-486-23098-8). Dover.

Appelbaum, Stanley, tr. see Braque, Georges.

Appelbaum, Stanley, tr. see Seurat, Georges.

Appelfeld, Aharon. The Age of Wonders. 1983. pap. 3.95 (ISBN 0-671-45858-2). WSP.

--Tzili: The Story of a Life. Bilu, Dalya, tr. 192p. 1983. 12.95 (ISBN 0-525-24187-6, 1258-370). Dutton.

Appelgate, Ray D., ed. Trolleys & Streetcars on American Picture Postcards. LC 78-64854. (Illus.). 1979. pap. 5.00 (ISBN 0-486-23749-4). Dover.

Appelhof, Mary. Workshop on the Role of Earthworms in the Stabilization of Organic Residues, Vol. 1. (Orig.). 1981. pap. 25.00. Beech Leaf.

--Worms Eat My Garbage. (Illus., Orig.). 1982. pap. 5.95 (ISBN 0-942256-03-4). Flower Pr.

Appell, G. N., ed. The Societies of Borneo: Explorations in the Theory of Cognatic Social Structure. 1976. pap. 4.00 (ISBN 0-686-36568-2). Am Anthro Assn.

Appell, Madeleine. One-Stitch Stitchery. LC 78-51063. (Little Craft Book). (Illus.). 1978. 5.95 o.p. (ISBN 0-8069-5384-5); lib. bdg. 6.69 o.p. (ISBN 0-8069-5385-3). Sterling.

Appell, Paul, et al. Theorie Des Fonctions Algebriques, Vol. 1. 3rd ed. LC 72-114210. 1977. text ed. 35.00 (ISBN 0-8284-0285-X). Chelsea Pub.

--Theorie Des Fonctions Algebriques et Leurs Integrales: Volume II. LC 72-114210. text ed. 30.00 (ISBN 0-8284-0299-X). Chelsea Pub.

Appelqvist, L. A. & Ohlson, R., eds. Rapeseed. 1973. 93.75 (ISBN 0-444-40892-4). Elsevier.

Appenzeller, O. Autonomic Nervous System. 3rd ed. 1982. 110.75 (ISBN 0-444-80392-0). Elsevier.

Appenzeller, Otto, jt. auth. see Raskin, Neil H.

Appenzeller, Otto & Atkinson, Ruth A., eds. Sports Medicine: Fitness, Training, Injuries. 2nd ed. 1983. pap. text ed. price not set (ISBN 0-8067-0132-3). Urban & S.

Apperson, George L. English Proverbs & Proverbial Phrases: A Historical Dictionary. LC 70-76017. 1969. Repr. of 1929 ed. 39.00 o.p. (ISBN 0-8103-3881-5). Gale.

Appert, B. Rapport sur l'Etat Actuel des Prisons, des Hospices des Ecoles, Etc. (Conditions of the 19th Century French Working Class Ser.). 168p. (Fr.). 1974. Repr. of 1824 ed. lib. bdg. 50.00x o.p. (ISBN 0-8287-0035-4, 1080). Clearwater Pub.

Appia, Adolpho. The Work of Living Art & Man is the Measure of All Things. 1962. 20.00x (ISBN 0-87024-305-5). U of Miami Pr.

Appiah, Peggy. The Pineapple Child & Other Tales from Ashanti. (Illus.). 176p. (gr. 2-7). Date not set. 7.95 (ISBN 0-233-95875-4). Andre Deutsch.

--A Smell of Onions. 84p. (Orig.). 1979. pap. 5.00 o.s.i. (ISBN 0-686-64550-2). Three Continents.

Appiah-Kubi, Kofi & Torres, Sergio, eds. African Theology En Route: Papers from the Pan-African Conference of Third World Theologians, December 17-23, 1977, Accra, Ghana. LC 78-10604. 184p. (Orig.). 1978. pap. 9.95 (ISBN 0-88344-010-5). Orbis Bks.

Appignanesi, Lisa. Femininity & the Creative Imagination: A Study of Henry James, Robert Musil, & Marcel Proust. 1973. text ed. 7.00x o.p. (ISBN 0-85478-382-2). Humanities.

Appignanesi, Lisa, tr. see Bielski, Nella.

Appisson, Barbara, jt. auth. see McQueen-Williams, Morvyth.

Applbaum, Ronald & Hart, Roderick. Fundamentals of Group Discussion. (MODCOM Modules in Speech Communication). 1976. pap. text ed. 2.75 (ISBN 0-574-22566-8, 13-5566). SRA.

Applbaum, Ronald & Hart, Roderick, eds. MODCOM Modules in Speech Communication, 22 modules. 1976. Individual Modules. pap. text ed. 2.75 o.s.i. (ISBN 0-686-68014-6); Set. pap. 55.00 o.s.i. (ISBN 0-574-22529-3, 13-5529). SRA.

Applbaum, Ronald, ed. see Baird.

Applbaum, Ronald, ed. see Campbell, John A.

Applbaum, Ronald, ed. see Chesebro & Hamsher.

Applbaum, Ronald, ed. see Colburn, William & Weinberg, Sanford.

Applbaum, Ronald, ed. see Doolittle.

Applbaum, Ronald, ed. see Eadie & Kline.

Applbaum, Ronald, ed. see Felsenthal, Norman.

Applbaum, Ronald, ed. see Frandsen & Benson.

Applbaum, Ronald, ed. see Leathers.

Applbaum, Ronald, ed. see Measell.

Applbaum, Ronald, ed. see Motley.

Applbaum, Ronald, ed. see Osborn.

Applbaum, Ronald, ed. see Robb.

Applbaum, Ronald, ed. see Smith.

Applbaum, Ronald, ed. see Swanson, Delia.

Applbaum, Ronald, et al. The Process of Group Communication. 2nd ed. LC 78-18501. 1979. text ed. 16.95 (ISBN 0-574-22710-5, 13-5710); instr's guide avail. (ISBN 0-574-22711-3, 13-5711). SRA.

Applbaum, Ronald L. & Anatol, Karl W. Effective Oral Communication in Business & the Professions. 352p. 1982. 17.95 (ISBN 0-686-97514-6); tchr's guide avail. (ISBN 0-574-22591-9). SRA.

Apple, J. M. Plant Layout & Materials Handling. 3rd ed. LC 77-75127. (Illus.). 600p. 1977. 27.95x (ISBN 0-471-07171-4). Wiley.

Apple, James M. Material Handling Systems Design. (Illus.). 656p. 1972. 42.50 (ISBN 0-471-06652-4, Pub. by Wiley-Interscience). Wiley.

Apple, Max. Three Stories. 1983. signed limited ed. 45.00 (ISBN 0-939722-11-9). Pressworks.

Apple, Michael & Weis, Lois, eds. Ideology & Practice in Schooling. 1983. write for info. (ISBN 0-87722-295-9). Temple U Pr.

Apple, Michael W. Ideology & Curriculum. (Routledge Education Bks.). 212p. 1980. pap. 7.95x (ISBN 0-7100-0686-1). Routledge & Kegan.

Apple, Michael W., jt. ed. see Haubrich, Vernon F.

Apple, Michael W., et al. Educational Evaluation: Analysis & Responsibility. LC 73-17611. 1974. 22.00 (ISBN 0-8211-0011-4); 10 or more copies 20.20 ea. (ISBN 0-685-42624-6). McCutchan.

Applebaum, Eleanor G. & Firestein, Stephen. A Genetic Counseling Casebook. LC 82-48605. 320p. 1983. price not set (ISBN 0-02-931300-7). Free Pr.

Applebaum, Louis, et al. Glossary of United States Patent Practice. LC 70-103702. (Eng, Fr & Ger.). 1969. 25.00 o.p. (ISBN 0-87632-037-X). Boardman.

Applebaum, Robert, jt. auth. see Seidl, Frederick.

Applebaum, Sada, jt. auth. see Applebaum, Samuel.

Applebaum, Samuel & Applebaum, Sada. Way They Play, Bk. 1. (Illus.). 380p. 1972. 12.95 (ISBN 0-87666-437-0, Z-1). Paganiniana Pubns.

--The Way They Play, Bk. 2. (Illus.). 384p. 1973. 12.95 (ISBN 0-87666-438-9, Z-4). Paganiniana Pubns.

--The Way They Play, Bk. 3. (Illus.). 320p. 1975. 12.95 (ISBN 0-87666-447-8, Z-7). Paganiniana Pubns.

--Way They Play, Bk. 4. (Illus.). 320p. 1975. 12.95 (ISBN 0-87666-448-6, Z-8). Paganiniana Pubns.

Applebaum, Samuel & Roth, Henry. The Way They Play, Bk. 5. (Illus.). 320p. 1978. 12.95 (ISBN 0-87666-449-4, Z-11). Paganiniana Pubns.

--Way They Play, Bk. 6. (Illus.). 352p. 1978. 12.95 (ISBN 0-87666-615-2, Z-29). Paganiniana Pubns.

--The Way They Play, Bk. 7. (Illus.). 288p. 1980. 12.95 (ISBN 0-87666-620-9, Z-33). Paganiniana Pubns.

--The Way They Play, Bk. 8. (Illus.). 288p. 1980. 12.95 (ISBN 0-87666-622-5, Z-34). Paganiniana Pubns.

--The Way They Play, Bk. 9. (Illus.). 285p. (gr. 9-12). 1981. 12.95 (ISBN 0-87666-586-5, Z-56). Paganiniana Pubns.
--The Way They Play, Bk. 10. (Illus.). 253p. (gr. 9-12). 1982. 12.95 (ISBN 0-87666-595-4, 2-65). Paganiniana Pubns.
Applebaum, Sharon, jt. auth. see Hirshmann, Linda.
Applebaum, Stan & Cox, Victoria. Going My Way? LC 76-8492. (Let Me Read Ser). (Illus.). (gr. k-3). 1976. pap. 1.65 (ISBN 0-15-231126-2, VoyB). HarBraceJ.
Applebaum, Steven H., jt. auth. see Certo, Samuel C.
Applebe, G. E., jt. auth. see Dale, J. R.
Appleberg, Marilyn, compiled by. The I Love New York Guide, 1981. (Illus.). 208p. 1981. pap. 4.95 (ISBN 0-02-097220-2, Collier). Macmillan.
Appleberg, Marilyn J. I Love Boston Guide. (Illus.). 160p. 1983. pap. 6.95 (ISBN 0-02-097300-4, Collier). Macmillan.
--I Love Chicago Guide. (Illus.). 160p. 1982. pap. 3.95 (ISBN 0-02-097190-7, Collier). Macmillan.
--I Love Washington Guide. (Illus.). 160p. 1982. pap. 4.95 (ISBN 0-02-097290-3, Collier). Macmillan.
Appleby. Famine in Tudor & Stuart England. 262p. 1982. 50.00x (ISBN 0-85323-014-5, Pub. by Liverpool Univ England). State Mutual Bk.
Appleby, David P. The Music of Brazil. (Illus.). 248p. 1983. text ed. 22.50x (ISBN 0-292-75068-4). U of Tex Pr.
Applegate, Margaret, jt. auth. see Ranzou, Marie-Louise.
Applegath, John. Working Free: Practical Alternatives to the 9 to 5 Job. pap. 6.95 (ISBN 0-686-84798-9). Am Mgmt.
Appleman, Philip, ed. Darwin. 2nd ed. (Norton Critical Edition). 1979. 24.95x (ISBN 0-393-01192-5); pap. 8.95x (ISBN 0-393-95009-3). Norton.
Appleman, Philip, ed. see Darwin, Charles.
Appleman, Phillip. Shame the Devil. Michaelman, Herbert, ed. 160p. 1981. 10.00 o.p. (ISBN 0-517-54286-2, Michelman Books). Crown.
Applequist, Douglas E., et al. Introduction to Organic Chemistry. 3rd ed. LC 81-14694. 384p. 1982. 24.95 (ISBN 0-471-05641-3); solutions 5.95 (ISBN 0-471-09416-1). Wiley.
Appleton & Cellar. Laser & Electrons Beam Interactions with Solids. (Materials Research Society Symposia Ser.: Vol. 4). 1982. 95.00 (ISBN 0-444-00693-1). Elsevier.
Appleton, Arthur. Mary Ann Cotton: Her Story & Trial. 154p. 1974. 9.50 o.p. (ISBN 0-7181-1184-2). Transatlantic.
Appleton, George A. The Louvre Complete Treatise in Charcoal Drawing with the Lessons by M. Allonge. (The Promotion of the Arts Library Bk.). (Illus.). 139p. 1983. Repr. of 1880 ed. 49.75 (ISBN 0-89901-098-9). Found Class Reprints.
Appleton, J. D. Labour Economics. 3rd ed. 250p. 1982. pap. text ed. 15.95 (ISBN 0-7121-2703-8). Intl Ideas.
Appleton, Jane & Appleton, William. How Not to Split up. 1979. pap. 2.95 (ISBN 0-425-06124-8). Berkley Pub.
Appleton, Jay H. The Experience of Landscape. LC 73-20899. 293p. 1975. 54.95x (ISBN 0-471-03256-5, Pub. by Wiley-Interscience). Wiley.
Appleton, Jon H. & Perera, Ronald C., eds. The Development & Practice of Electronic Music. LC 74-12478. (Illus.). 288p. 1975. 24.95 (ISBN 0-13-207605-5). P-H.
Appleton, Leroy. American Indian Design & Decoration. Orig. Title: Indian Art of the Americas. (Illus.). 1971. pap. 7.00 (ISBN 0-486-22704-9). Dover.
Appleton, Nicholas & Benevento, Nicole. Cultural Pluralism in Education: Theoretical Foundations. (Illus.). 288p. (Orig.). 1983. pap. text ed. 12.95 (ISBN 0-582-28233-0). Longman.
Appleton, Victor. Tom Swift: Ark Two. (Tom Swift Ser.: No. 7). (Illus.). 192p. (gr. 3-7). 1982. 8.95 (ISBN 0-671-43952-9); pap. 2.95 (ISBN 0-671-43953-7). Wanderer Bks.
--Tom Swift: Gateway to Doom. Barish, Wendy, ed. (Tom Swift Ser.). 192p. (gr. 8-10). 1983. 8.95 (ISBN 0-671-43956-1); pap. 3.50 (ISBN 0-671-43957-X). Wanderer Bks.
--Tom Swift: No. 8: Crater of Mystery. Barish, Wendy, ed. (Tom Swift Ser.). 192p. (gr. 3-7). 1983. pap. 2.95 (ISBN 0-671-43955-3). Wanderer Bks.
--Tom Swift: The Alien Probe. (Tom Swift Ser.: No. 3). 192p. (Orig.). (gr. 3-7). 1981. 8.95 (ISBN 0-671-42538-2); pap. 2.95 (ISBN 0-671-42578-1). Wanderer Bks.
--Tom Swift: The City in the Stars. (Tom Swift Ser.: No. 1). 192p. (Orig.). (gr. 3-7). 1981. 8.95 (ISBN 0-671-41120-9); pap. 2.95 (ISBN 0-671-41115-2). Wanderer Bks.
--Tom Swift: The Rescue Mission. (Tom Swift Ser.: No. 6). 192p. (gr. 3-7). 1981. 8.95 (ISBN 0-671-43370-9); pap. 2.95 (ISBN 0-671-43386-5). Wanderer Bks.
--Tom Swift: The Space Fortress. (Tom Swift Ser.: No. 5). 192p. (gr. 3-7). 1981. 8.95 (ISBN 0-671-43369-5); pap. 2.95 (ISBN 0-671-43385-7). Wanderer Bks.
--Tom Swift: The War in Outer Space. (Tom Swift Ser.: No. 4). 192p. (Orig.). (gr. 3-7). 1981. 8.95 (ISBN 0-671-42539-0); pap. 2.95 (ISBN 0-671-42579-X). Wanderer Bks.
Appleton, Victor, 2nd. Tom Swift Jr. & His Aquatromic Tracker. (Tom Swift Jr. Ser.: Vol. 23). (gr. 5-9). 1964. 2.95 o.p. (ISBN 0-448-09123-2, G&D). Putnam Pub Group.
--Tom Swift Jr. & His Flying Lab. (Tom Swift Jr. Ser.: Vol. 1). (gr. 5-9). 1954. 2.95 o.p. (ISBN 0-448-09101-1, G&D). Putnam Pub Group.
--Tom Swift Jr. & His Jetmarine. (Tom Swift Jr. Ser.: Vol. 2). (gr. 5-9). 1954. 2.95 o.p. (ISBN 0-448-09102-X, G&D). Putnam Pub Group.
--Tom Swift Jr. & His Polar-Ray Dynasphere. (Tom Swift Jr. Ser.: Vol. 25). (gr. 5-9). 1964. 2.95 o.p. (ISBN 0-448-09125-9, G&D). Putnam Pub Group.
--Tom Swift Jr. & His Rocket Ship. (Tom Swift Jr. Ser.: Vol. 3). (gr. 5-9). 1954. 2.95 o.p. (ISBN 0-448-09103-8, G&D). Putnam Pub Group.
--Tom Swift Jr. & the Captive Planetoid. (Tom Swift Jr. Ser.). 2.95 o.p. (ISBN 0-448-09129-1, G&D). Putnam Pub Group.
Appleton, William, jt. auth. see Appleton, Jane.
Applewhite, Barry. Feeling Good About Your Feelings. 120p. 1980. pap. 3.95 (ISBN 0-88207-792-9). Victor Bks.
Applewhite, Edgar J., jt. auth. see Fuller, R. Buckminster.
Applewhite, James. Following Gravity. LC 80-21578. 1980. 8.95x (ISBN 0-8139-0885-X). U Pr of Va.
--Forseeing the Journey: Poems. LC 82-17165. 64p. 1983. text ed. 13.95 (ISBN 0-8071-1079-5); pap. 5.95 (ISBN 0-8071-1080-9). La State U Pr.
Appleyard, Donald. Planning a Pluralist City: Conflicting Realities in Ciudad Guayana. LC 75-40026. 350p. 1976. text ed. 27.50x (ISBN 0-262-01044-5). MIT Pr.
Appleyard, Donald & Gerson, M. S. Livable Streets. 382p. 1982. 27.50 (ISBN 0-520-03689-1); pap. 14.95 (ISBN 0-520-04769-9). U of Cal Pr.
Appleyard, Donald, ed. Conservation of European Cities. (Illus.). 1979. 35.00x (ISBN 0-262-01057-7). MIT Pr.
Applied Psychology Research Unit. Human Factors in Telephony. 1961. pap. 20.00 (ISBN 0-686-37971-3). Info Gatekeepers.
Applied Science Publishers Ltd., ed. see World Petroleum Congress, 9th, Japan, 1975.
Approved Methods Committee. Approved Methods of the American Association of Cereal Chemists, 2 vols. rev. ed. 1000p. 1976. binder 110.00 (ISBN 0-913250-03-1). Am Assn Cereal Chem.
Apps, Jerold. Study Skills for Adults Returning to School. 2nd ed. 240p. 1982. 10.95x (ISBN 0-07-002165-1). McGraw.
--Study Skills for Adults Returning to School. (Illus.). 1978. pap. text ed. 5.95 o.p. (ISBN 0-07-002163-5, C). McGraw.
Apps, Jerold W. Problems in Continuing Education. 1979. text ed. 18.95 (ISBN 0-07-002159-7, C). McGraw.
ApRoberts, Ruth. The Moral Trollope. LC 75-141383. 203p. 1971. 12.95x (ISBN 0-8214-0089-4, 82-80935). Ohio U Pr.
Apsche, Jack see Axelrod, Saul.
Apsimon, John. The Total Synthesis of Natural Products, Vol. 4. LC 72-4075. (The Total Synthesis of Natural Products Ser.). 610p. 1981. 67.00x (ISBN 0-471-05460-7, Pub. by Wiley-Interscience). Wiley.
ApSimon, John W., ed. The Total Synthesis of Natural Products, 3 vols. LC 72-4075. 603p. 1973. Vol. 1. 59.00x (ISBN 0-471-03251-4); Vol. 2. 54.95x (ISBN 0-471-03252-2); Vol. 3. 54.95x (ISBN 0-471-02392-2, Pub. by Wiley-Interscience). Wiley.
Apsler, Alfred. From Witch Doctor to Biofeedback: The Story of Healing by Suggestion. LC 76-56425. 192p. (gr. 7 up). 1977. PLB 7.29 o.p. (ISBN 0-671-32832-8). Messner.
Apstein, C., jt. ed. see Brandt, K.
Apt, Patricia, ed. Higher Education & the Older Learner. (Special Issue of Alternative Higher Education Ser.). 72p. 1980. pap. 8.95 o.p. (ISBN 0-89885-063-0). Human Sci Pr.
Apte, Robert Z., jt. auth. see Friedlander, Walter A.
Apte, Stuart C. Stu Apte's Fishing in the Florida Keys & Flamingo. 3rd ed. (Illus.). 1982. pap. 4.95 (ISBN 0-89317-019-4). Windward Pub.
Apte, Y. S. Linear Multivariable Control Theory. 1982. write for info. (ISBN 0-07-451512-8). McGraw.
Apted, F. I., jt. ed. see Manson-Bahr, P. E.
Apter, David E. Introduction to Political Analysis. 1977. text ed. 19.95 (ISBN 0-316-04930-1). Little.
Apter, David E. & Goodman, Louis W., eds. Multinational Corporation & Social Change. LC 75-1989. 225p. 1976. text ed. 21.95 o.p. (ISBN 0-275-23020-1); pap. 13.95 o.p. (ISBN 0-275-64580-0). Praeger.
Apter, Evelyn. Pas de Vacanes pour le Commissaire. LC 82-9670. (Illus.). 40p. (Fr.). (gr. 7-12). 1982. pap. text ed. 1.95 (ISBN 0-88436-908-0, 40285); cassettes 12.00. EMC.
Apter, Michael, ed. The Experience of Motivation: The Theory of Psychological Reversals. LC 81-66676. 392p. 1982. 31.50 (ISBN 0-12-058920-6). Acad Pr.
Apter, Michael J. & Westby, George. The Computer in Psychology. LC 72-5711. 309p. 1973. 44.95x (ISBN 0-471-03260-3, Pub. by Wiley-Interscience). Wiley.
Aptheker, Bettina. Woman's Legacy: Essays on Race, Sex, & Class in American History. LC 81-23137. 192p. 1982. lib. bdg. 16.50x (ISBN 0-87023-364-5); pap. text ed. 7.95x (ISBN 0-87023-365-3). U of Mass Pr.
Aptheker, Bettina, et al. Kent State Ten Years After. Bills, Scott, ed. (Illus.). 88p. (Orig.). 1980. pap. 3.95 o.p. (ISBN 0-933522-04-5). Kent Popular.
Aptheker, Herbert. The Nature of Democracy, Freedom & Revolution. 2nd ed. LC 67-20076. 128p. (Orig.). 1981. pap. 1.95 (ISBN 0-7178-0137-3). Intl Pub Co.
--The Negro People in America. LC 46-8650. 1946. pap. 4.50 o.s.i. (ISBN 0-527-02770-7). Kraus Repr.
Aptheker, Herbert, ed. Writings in Periodicals Edited by W. E. B. Du Bois: Selections from "The Crisis". (The Completed Published Works of W. E. B. Du Bois). (Orig.). 1983. lib. bdg. 125.00 (ISBN 0-527-25351-0). Kraus Intl.
Apuleius, Lucius. The Most Delectable Jests from Lucius Apuleius' the Golden Ass. (Essential Library of the Great Philosophers Ser.). (Illus.). 125p. 1983. 49.75 (ISBN 0-89266-398-7). Am Classical Coll Pr.
Aqua Group. Tenders & Contracts for Building. 100p. 1982. pap. text ed. 14.50x (ISBN 0-246-11838-5, Pub. by Granada England). Renouf.
Aquila, Richard E. Rhyme or Reason: A Limerick History of Philosophy. LC 81-40013. 126p. (Orig.). 1981. lib. bdg. 12.25 (ISBN 0-8191-1562-2); pap. text ed. 5.25 (ISBN 0-8191-1563-0). U Pr of Amer.
Aquinas, Thomas see Thomas Aquinas, Saint.
Aqvist, Lennary. New Approachs to the Logical Theory of Interrogatives. 2nd ed. (Tuebinger Beitrage Zur Linguistik Ser.: No. 65). 184p. pap. 13.00 (ISBN 3-87808-065-4). Benjamins North Am.
Arac, Johnathan, et al, eds. The Yale Critics: Deconstruction in America. LC 83-1127. (Theory & History of Literature Ser.: Vol. 6). 288p. 1983. 29.50x (ISBN 0-8166-1201-3); pap. 12.95 (ISBN 0-8166-1206-4). U of Minn Pr.
Arad, Uzi B., et al. Sharing Global Resources. LC 78-13233. (Council on Foreign Relations 1980's Project). (Illus.). 1979. text ed. 14.95 (ISBN 0-07-002150-3, P&RB); pap. 6.95 (ISBN 0-07-002151-1). McGraw.
Arad, Yitzhak. The Partisan: From the Valley of Death to Mount Zion. LC 78-71299. 1979. 9.95 (ISBN 0-8052-5010-7, Pub. by Holocaust Library); pap. 4.95 (ISBN 0-8052-7005-1, Pub. by Holocaust Library). Schocken.
Aragon, George, jt. auth. see Viscione, Jerry.
Aragon, Louis & Cocteau, Jean. Conversations on the Dresden Gallery. Scarfe, Francis, tr. from Fr. LC 81-6640. (Illus.). 288p. 1983. text ed. 49.50x (ISBN 0-8419-0730-7). Holmes & Meier.
Aragon, Ray J. De see De Aragon, Ray J.
Aragones, Sergio. Mad As the Devil. (Illus.). 192p. (Orig.). 1975. pap. 1.95 (ISBN 0-446-30427-1). Warner Bks.
--Mad Menagerie. 192p. 1983. pap. 1.95 (ISBN 0-446-90900-9). Warner Bks.
--Mad's Sergio Aragones on Parade. (Illus.). 160p. (Orig.). 1979. pap. 5.95 (ISBN 0-446-37369-9). Warner Bks.
Arakawa, A., jt. auth. see Mesinger, F.
Arakawa, H., ed. Climates of Northern & Eastern Asia. (World Survey of Climatology: Vol. 8). 1970. 93.75 (ISBN 0-444-40704-9). Elsevier.
Arakawa, H., jt. ed. see Takahashi, K.
Arakin, V. D. English-Russian Dictionary. (Eng. & Rus.). 1980. leatherette 17.95 (ISBN 0-686-97371-2, M-9107). French & Eur.
Aram, Dorothy M. & Nation, James E. Child Language Disorders. LC 81-14063. (Illus.). 302p. 1982. text ed. 19.95 (ISBN 0-8016-0288-2). Mosby.
Aram, Dorothy M., jt. auth. see Nation, James E.
Aram, John D. Dilemmas of Administrative Behavior. 144p. 1976. Ref. Ed. 13.95 (ISBN 0-13-214247-3). P-H.
--Managing Business & Public Policy. (Pitman Series in Business Management & Organizational Behavior). 600p. 1982. text ed. 24.95 (ISBN 0-273-01656-3). Pitman Pub MA.
Arambulo, Primo & Steele, James H., eds. Handbook Series in Zoonoses, CRC, Section C: Parasitic Zoonoses, 3 Vols. Date not set. Vol. I. 86.00 (ISBN 0-8493-2916-7); Vol. II. 79.50 (ISBN 0-8493-2917-5); Vol. III. 86.00 (ISBN 0-8493-2918-3). CRC Pr. Postponed.
Arana, Alice see Knorre, Marty, et al.
Arana, Oswaldo see Knorre, Marty, et al.
Aranda, Charles. Dichos: Sayings & Proverbs from the Spanish. LC 77-78611. (Eng. & Span.). 1977. pap. 3.50 (ISBN 0-913270-47-4). Sunstone Pr.
Aranda, Francisco. Luis Bunuel: A Critical Biography. Robinson, David, ed. LC 76-7621. 1976. lib. bdg. 25.00 (ISBN 0-306-70754-3); pap. 6.95 (ISBN 0-306-80028-4). Da Capo.
Aranda, J. V., jt. ed. see Vert, P.
Arango, E. Ramon. The Spanish Political System: Franco's Legacy. LC 78-8979. (Westview Special Studies in West European Politics & Society). 1978. lib. bdg. 32.00 (ISBN 0-89158-177-4). Westview.
Aranson, Peter H. American Government: Strategy & Choice. 1981. text ed. 20.95 (ISBN 0-316-04940-9); tchr's ed. avail. (ISBN 0-316-04941-7). Little.
Aranson, Peter H., ed. see Law & Economics Center of Emory University.
Arant, Olive G., illus. Magic: The Cookbook of the Junior League of Birmingham. 2nd ed. LC 81-85953. (Illus.). 348p. 1982. 9.95 (ISBN 0-686-38454-7). Jr League Birm.
Araoz, Daniel L. Hypnosis & Sex Therapy. LC 82-4128. 200p. 1982. 19.50 (ISBN 0-87630-299-1). Brunner-Mazel.
Araoz, Daniel L. & Bleck, Robert T. Hypnosex: Sexual Joy Through Self-Hypnosis. 1983. 5.95 (ISBN 0-87795-466-6, Pub. by Priam). Arbor Hse.
Arasaki, Seibin & Arasaki, Teruko. Vegetables from the Sea. LC 79-91516. (Illus.). 176p. (Orig.). 1983. pap. 13.95 (ISBN 0-87040-475-X). Japan Pubns.
Arasaki, Teruko, jt. auth. see Arasaki, Seibin.
Araski, Seibin & Araski, Teruko. Vegetables from the Sea. LC 79-91516. (Illus.). 176p. (Orig.). 1982. pap. 13.95 (ISBN 0-87040-475-X). Kodansha.
Araski, Teruko, jt. auth. see Araski, Seibin.
Arato, Andrew, tr. see Konrad, George & Szelenyi, Ivan.
Arato, M. Linear Stochastic Systems with Constant Coefficients: A Statistical Approach. (Lecture Notes in Control & Information Sciences: Vol. 45). 309p. 1983. pap. 15.50 (ISBN 0-387-12090-4). Springer-Verlag.
Araujo, Aloisio & Gine, Evarist. The Central Limit Theorem for Real & Banach Valued Random Variables. (Series in Probability & Mathematical Statistics). 1980. 43.50x (ISBN 0-471-05304-X, Pub. by Wiley-Interscience). Wiley.
Araujo, Virginia De see Andrade, Carlos D.
Araullo, E. V., compiled by. Directory of Food Science & Technology in Southeast Asia. 267p. 1975. pap. 10.00 (ISBN 0-88936-027-8, IDRC23, IDRC). Unipub.
Araya, G., et al, eds. Las Constantes Esteticas de la 'Comedia' del Siglo de Oro. (Dialogos Hispanicos de Amsterdam: No. 2). 137p. 1981. pap. text ed. 17.25x (ISBN 90-6203-583-3, Pub. by Rodopi Holland). Humanities.
Arbatov, G. A. The Soviet Viewpoint. LC 82-2466. 1983. 14.95 (ISBN 0-396-08058-8). Dodd.
Arbeiter, Jean & Cirino, Linda. Permanent Addresses: A Guide to the Resting Places of Famous Americans. (Illus.). 256p. 1983. pap. 7.95 (ISBN 0-87131-402-9). M Evans.
Arber, A. The Gramineae: A Study of Cereal, Bamboo & Grass. (Illus.). 1973. Repr. of 1934 ed. 32.00 (ISBN 3-7682-0276-3). Lubrecht & Cramer.
--Monocotyledons: A Morphological Study. (Illus.). 1961. Repr. of 1925 ed. 32.00 (ISBN 3-7682-0074-4). Lubrecht & Cramer.
Arber, Agnes. Water Plants: Study of Aquatic Angiosperms. (Illus.). 1963. Repr. of 1920 ed. 32.00 (ISBN 3-7682-0157-0). Lubrecht & Cramer.
Arber, E., ed. The First Three English Books on America: 1511-1555 A.D. Eden, Richard, tr. & compiled by. LC 2-7703. Repr. of 1895 ed. 45.00 o.s.i. (ISBN 0-527-02900-9). Kraus Repr.
Arber, Edward, ed. English Garner, 12 Vols. Repr. of 1890 ed. write for info. o.p. Cooper Sq.
Arber, Edward, ed. see Earle, John.
Arber, EDward, ed. see Gascoigne, George.
Arber, Edward, ed. see Googe, Barnabe.
Arber, Edward, ed. see Latimer, Hugh.
Arber, Edward, ed. see Naunton, Robert.
Arber, Edward, ed. see Selden, John.
Arber, Edward, ed. see Udall, Nicholas.
Arber, EDward, ed. see Villiers, George.
Arber, Edward, tr. see Habington, William.
Arber, Edward, tr. see Howell, James.
Arberry, A. J., ed. Rubaiyat of Omar Khayyam. 1977. pap. 2.50x (ISBN 0-460-01996-1, Evman). Biblio Dist.
Arberry, A. J., tr. see Rumi, Jalal A.
Arberry, A. J., tr. see Rumi, Jalal Al-Din.
Arberry, Arthur. A Maltese Anthology. LC 75-8831. 200p. 1975. Repr. of 1960 ed. lib. bdg. 18.25x (ISBN 0-8371-8112-7, ARMA). Greenwood.
Arberry, Arthur J. The Doctrine of the Sufis. LC 76-58075. 1977. 32.50 (ISBN 0-521-21647-8); pap. 10.95 (ISBN 0-521-29218-2). Cambridge U Pr.
--Religion in the Middle East, 2 Vols. LC 68-21187. (Illus.). 1969. Set. 89.50 (ISBN 0-521-07400-2); 57.50 ea.; Vol. 1. (ISBN 0-521-20543-3); Vol. 2. (ISBN 0-521-20544-1). Cambridge U Pr.
Arbetman, Lee P. & Mcmahon, Edward T. New York State Supplement to Street Law: A Course in Practical Law. 2d ed. 75p. (gr. 9-12). 1983. pap. text ed. 4.95 (ISBN 0-314-73470-8). West Pub.
--Street Law: New York Supplement. 2nd ed. (Illus.). (gr. 9-12). 1982. write for info. (ISBN 0-314-72084-7). West Pub.
Arbetman, Lee P., et al. Street Law: A Course in Practical Law, with Florida Supplement. 2nd ed. (Illus.). 80p. pap. text ed. write for info. o.s.i. (ISBN 0-314-63413-4). West Pub.
Arbib, M. A., jt. ed. see Amari, S.
Arbib, M. A., et al. A Basis for Theoretical Computer Science. (Computer Science Texts & Monographs). (Illus.). 224p. 1981. 18.50 (ISBN 0-387-90573-1). Springer-Verlag.

Arbib, Michael. Computers & the Cybernetic Society. 494p. 1977. 17.00 (ISBN 0-12-059040-9); SBP 20.75; instrs' manual 3.50 (ISBN 0-12-059042-5); transparency masters 3.00 (ISBN 0-12-059045-X). Acad Pr.

--The Metaphorical Brain: An Introduction to Cybernetics As Artificial Intelligence & Brains Theory. LC 72-2490. (Illus.). 243p. 1972. 31.50x (ISBN 0-471-03249-2, Pub. by Wiley-Interscience). Wiley.

Arbib, Michael A., jt. auth. see Szentagothai, John.

Arbit Books, ed. Toledoteinu: Finding Your Own Roots. Tarachow, Mike, tr. (Illus.). 1978. pap. text ed. 2.50 (ISBN 0-930038-10-X). Arbit.

Arbit, Naomi & Turner, June. Pies & Pastries. (Illus.). 64p. pap. 3.25 (ISBN 0-8249-3011-8). Ideals.

Arbiter, N., jt. ed. see Somasundaran, P.

Arbiter, N. Nathaniel, ed. Milling Methods in the Americas. 625p. 1965. 125.00x (ISBN 0-677-10690-4). Gordon.

Arblay, Frances B. Fanny Burney & Her Friends: Select Passages from Her Diary & Other Writings. LC 75-76135. 1969. Repr. of 1890 ed. 30.00x (ISBN 0-8103-3896-3). Gale.

Arbois De Jubainville, Henri D' The Irish Mythological Cycle & Celtic Mythology. LC 70-112679. 1970. Repr. of 1903 ed. text ed. 10.00x o.p. (ISBN 0-87696-006-9). Humanities.

Arbona, Guillermo & Ramirez de Arellano, Annette B. Regionalization of Health Services: The Puerto Rican Experience. (Illus.). 1979. pap. text ed. 19.95x (ISBN 0-19-261222-0). Oxford U Pr.

Arbor, Jane. Handmaid to MDAS. (Harlequin Romances Ser.). 192p. 1983. pap. 1.75 (ISBN 0-373-02545-9). Harlequin Bks.

Arbor, Marilyn. Tools & Trades of America's Past: The Mercer Collection. 116p. 6.95 (ISBN 0-910302-12-X). Bucks Co Hist.

Arbuckle, Elisabeth S., ed. Harriet Martineau's Letters to Fanny Wedgwood. LC 81-50783. 368p. 1983. 29.50x (ISBN 0-8047-1146-1). Stanford U Pr.

Arbuckle, J. Gordon & Frick, G. William. Environmental Law Handbook. 7th ed. 450p. 1983. text ed. 39.50 (ISBN 0-86587-098-5). Gov Insts.

Arbuckle, J. Gordon, et al. Environmental Law Handbook. 6th rev. ed. LC 76-41637. 349p. 1979. 39.50 o.p. (ISBN 0-86587-076-4). Gov Insts.

Arbuckle, Robert D. John Nicholson, 1757-1800: Pennsylvania Speculator & Patriot. LC 74-3446. 1975. 22.50x (ISBN 0-271-01168-8). Pa St U Pr.

Arbur, Rosemarie. Leigh Brackett, Marion Zimmer Bradley, & Anne McCaffrey: A Primary & Secondary Bibliography. 300p. 1982. lib. bdg. 33.00 (Hall Reference). G K Hall.

Arbuthnot, Archibald. Memoirs of the Remarkable Life & Surprising Adventures of Miss Jenny Cameron: Philamours & Philamena; or, Genuine Memoirs of a Late Affecting Transaction, 1746. LC 74-26901. (Novel in England, 1700-1775 Ser). 1974. lib. bdg. 50.00 o.s.i. (ISBN 0-8240-1117-1). Garland Pub.

Arbuthnot, May H. & Root, Shelton L., Jr. Time for Poetry. 3rd ed. 1968. 16.50x (ISBN 0-673-05549-3). Scott F.

Arbuthnott, Hugh & Edwards, Geoffrey, eds. A Common Man's Guide to the Common Market. 1982. text ed. 26.00 (ISBN 0-8419-5053-9); pap. text ed. 14.50x (ISBN 0-8419-5054-7). Holmes & Meier.

Arbuthnott, J. P. & Beeley, J. A., eds. Isoelectric Focusing. 400p. 1976. 59.95 o.p. (ISBN 0-408-70659-7). Butterworth.

Arbuzou, Grigory, jt. auth. see Sarabyanov, Dmitry.

ARC-MRC Committee, ed. Food & Nutrition Research. 210p. 1975. pap. text ed. 55.50 (ISBN 0-444-99871-3). Elsevier.

Arca, Julie, jt. auth. see Waite, Mitch.

Arcana, Judith. Every Mother's Son. LC 82-12912. 336p. 1983. 16.95 (ISBN 0-385-15640-5, Anchor Pr). Doubleday.

Arcangeli, Gianfranco, jt. auth. see Nee, T. S.

Arcangeli, Gianfranco, jt. auth. see Popejoy, Bill.

Arcangeli, Gianfranco, ed. see Eareckson, Joni.

Arcangeli, Gianfranco, ed. see Foglio, Frank.

Arcangeli, Gianfranco, ed. see Keller, W. Philip.

Arcangeli, Gianfranco, ed. see Richardson, Don.

Arce, Hector. Gary Cooper: An Intimate Biography. 1980. 10.95 o.p. (ISBN 0-688-03604-X). Morrow.

--Groucho. 1980. pap. 6.95 o.s.i. (ISBN 0-686-63014-9, Perige). Putnam Pub Group.

--Groucho: The Authorized Biography. LC 78-16019. (Illus.). 1979. 14.95 (ISBN 0-399-12046-7); pap. 6.95 o.p. (ISBN 0-399-50455-9). Putnam Pub Group.

Arce, Hector, jt. auth. see Marx, Groucho.

Arceri, Gene, jt. auth. see Waterbury, Ruth.

Arch, E. L. Man with Three Eyes. (YA) 6.95 (ISBN 0-685-07446-3, Avalon). Bouregy.

Archambault, Reginald D., ed. Philosophical Analysis & Education. 1972. text ed. 9.50x o.p. (ISBN 0-7100-1021-4); pap. text ed. 3.75x o.p. (ISBN 0-391-00239-2). Humanities.

Archambeault, Betty J., jt. auth. see Archambeault, William G.

Archambeault, James, photos by. Kentucky. Clark, Thomas D. (Illus.). 160p. 1982. 32.50 (ISBN 0-912856-74-2). Graphic Arts Ctr.

Archambeault, William G. & Archambeault, Betty J. Correctional Supervisory Management: Principles of Organization, Policy & Law. (Prentice Hall Series in Criminal Justice). (Illus.). 448p. 1982. reference 22.95 (ISBN 0-13-178269-X). P-H.

Archbishop of York. Palmer's Bible Atlas (Facsimile Edition) 84p. 1982. 14.95 (ISBN 0-686-43010-7, Carta Maps & Guides Pub Isreal). Hippocrene Bks.

Archdeacon, Thomas J. Becoming American. LC 82-48691. 320p. 1983. 17.95 (ISBN 0-02-900830-1). Free Pr.

Archdiocese of Dubuque, R.C.I.A. Foundations of Christian Initiation. 96p. 1982. wire coil 7.95 (ISBN 0-697-01781-8). Wm C Brown.

Archdiocese of Newark. Growing in Faith with Your Child. Ivory, Thomas P., ed. 48p. (Orig.). pap. 2.50 (ISBN 0-697-01693-5). Wm C Brown.

Archdiocese of San Francisco. Great Misconceptions: People with Disabilities. 48p. 1982. saddle stitched 4.95 (ISBN 0-8403-2674-2). Kendall-Hunt.

Archer, Carol R. Computed Tomography of the Larynx. (Illus.). 200p. 1983. 37.50 (ISBN 0-87527-240-1). Green.

Archer, Charles. William Archer: Life, Works & Friendships. 1931. 47.50x (ISBN 0-685-89793-1). Elliots Bks.

Archer, Clive & Maxwell, Stephen. The Nordic Model. 1980. text ed. 27.75x (ISBN 0-566-00341-4). Gower Pub Ltd.

Archer, F. C. & Stewart, J. R. Model Office Practice Set. 2nd ed. 1975. text ed. 7.44 (ISBN 0-07-002306-9, G); tchr's manual & key 5.60 (ISBN 0-07-002307-7). McGraw.

Archer, F. C., et al. General Office Practice. 3rd ed. 1968. text ed. 13.76 o.p. (ISBN 0-07-002173-2, G); tchr's manual & key 9.55 o.p. (ISBN 0-07-002175-9); wkbk. 7.44 o.p. (ISBN 0-07-002174-0); tests 1.68 o.p. (ISBN 0-07-002169-4). McGraw.

--General Office Procedures. 4th ed. (Illus.). 512p. (gr. 9-12). 1975. text ed. 15.44 (ISBN 0-07-002161-9, G); tchr's. manual & key 9.55 (ISBN 0-07-002164-3); wkbk. 7.44 (ISBN 0-07-002162-7). McGraw.

--Office Cashiering Practice Set. 1969. text ed. 7.44 (ISBN 0-07-002167-8, G); tchr's manual & key 5.60 (ISBN 0-07-002166-X). McGraw.

--Stock Control Practice Set. 1969. text ed. 7.44 (ISBN 0-07-002176-7, G); tchr's manual & key 5.60 (ISBN 0-07-002177-5). McGraw.

--Accounts Payable Practice Set. 1969. text ed. 7.44 (ISBN 0-07-002196-1, G); tchr's manual & key 5.66 (ISBN 0-07-002203-8). McGraw.

--Accounts Receivable Practice Set. 1970. text ed. 7.44 (ISBN 0-07-002195-3, G); tchr's manual & key 5.60 (ISBN 0-07-002204-6). McGraw.

Archer, Gleason L. A Survey of Old Testament Introduction. LC 64-20988. 582p. 1973. 17.95 (ISBN 0-8024-8446-8). Moody.

Archer, Jeffrey. Kane & Abel. 540p. 1980. 13.95 o.s.i. (ISBN 0-671-25121-X). S&S.

--The Prodigal Daughter. (General Ser.). 1983. lib. bdg. 21.50 (ISBN 0-8161-3499-5, Large Print Bks). G K Hall.

--A Quiver Full of Arrows. 1982. 9.95 (ISBN 0-671-42602-8, Linden). S&S.

Archer, Jerome W. & Schwartz, A. Reader for Writers. 3rd ed. 1971. text ed. 19.95 (ISBN 0-07-002193-7, C). McGraw.

Archer, John. Animals under Stress. (Studies in Biology: No. 108). 64p. 1979. pap. text ed. 8.95 (ISBN 0-7131-2737-6). E Arnold.

--Liars Poker: A Winning Strat. (Gambler's Book Shelf Ser.). 64p. (Orig.). 1982. pap. 2.95 (ISBN 0-89650-793-9). Gamblers.

--Winning at Twenty-One. 1977. pap. 5.00 (ISBN 0-87980-328-2). Wilshire.

Archer, John C. & Taylor, Peter J. Section & Party: A Political Geography of American Presidential Elections from Andrew Jackson to Ronald Reagan. (Geographical Research Studies Press Ser.). 271p. 1981. 44.95x (ISBN 0-471-10014-5, Pub. by Res Stud Pr). Wiley.

Archer, Jules. Epidemic! The Story of the Disease Detectives. LC 76-46790. 1977. 5.95 o.p. (ISBN 0-15-225980-5, HJ). HarBraceJ.

--Hunger on Planet Earth. LC 76-3603. (Illus.). (gr. 8 up). 1977. 14.38i (ISBN 0-690-01126-1, TYC-J). Har-Row.

--Police State: Could It Happen Here? LC 76-58720. (gr. 12 up). 1977. 7.95 o.p. (ISBN 0-06-020153-3, HarpJ); PLB 12.87 (ISBN 0-06-020154-1). Har-Row.

--Washington vs. Main Street: The Struggle Between Federal & Local Power. LC 74-8623. (Illus.). 256p. (gr. 7 up). 1974. 12.45i (ISBN 0-690-00005-7, TYC-J). Har-Row.

--Watergate: America in Crisis. LC 74-5567. (Illus.). (gr. 7 up). 1975. 14.38i (ISBN 0-690-00616-0, TYC-J). Har-Row.

Archer, M. An Introduction to Canadian Business. 4th ed. 1982. write for info. McGraw.

Archer, Margaret, jt. auth. see Vaughan, Michalina.

Archer, Margaret S., jt. ed. see Giner, Salvador.

Archer, Margaret S., tr. see Sullerot, Evelyne.

Archer, Marion F., ed. Reading for Young People: The Upper Midwest. LC 81-10771. 142p. 1981. pap. 11.00 (ISBN 0-8389-0339-8). ALA.

Archer, Peggy. One of the Family. LC 82-82289. (Little Golden Bk.). (Illus.). 24p. 1983. 0.89 (ISBN 0-307-02082-7, Golden Pr). Western Pub.

Archer, R. K. & Jeffcott, L. B., eds. Comparative Clinical Haematology. 1977. 93.75x o.p. (ISBN 0-632-00289-1, Blackwell Scientific). Mosby.

Archer, Richard P. Concept Spelling's the Secrets of Spelling: Cassette-Workbook. (Concept Spelling Ser.). 30p. (gr. 5-12). 1982. Wkbk. 19.95 (ISBN 0-935276-07-6). Concept Spelling.

--Introduction to Concept Spelling Teacher's Guide. 48p. (Orig.). 1980. tchrs. guide 5.00 (ISBN 0-935276-02-5); 5.00 (ISBN 0-935276-01-7). Concept Spelling.

Archer, Richard P., ed. Concept Spelling Teacher's Manual. 132p. 1979. 50.00 (ISBN 0-935276-03-3). Concept Spelling.

Archer, Robert & Bouillon, Antoine. The South African Game: Sport & Racism. 368p. 1982. 25.00 (ISBN 0-86232-066-6, Pub. by Zed Pr England); pap. 9.95 (ISBN 0-86232-082-8, Pub. by Zed Pr England). Lawrence Hill.

Archer, S. H., et al. Financial Management: An Introduction. 724p. 1979. 33.95x (ISBN 0-471-02987-4); study guide 13.95 (ISBN 0-471-02988-2); tchrs. manual 5.00 (ISBN 0-471-02989-0). Wiley.

Archer, Stephen H. & D'Ambrosie, Charles A. Theory of Business Finance: A Book of Readings. 2nd ed. (Illus.). 1976. text ed. 25.95 (ISBN 0-02-303820-9). Macmillan.

Archer, Stephen H., jt. auth. see Francis, Clark.

Archer, Stephen M. How Theatre Happens. 2nd ed. 304p. 1983. text ed. 12.95 (ISBN 0-02-303750-4). Macmillan.

Archer, Stephen M., ed. American Actors & Actresses: A Guide to Information Sources. (Performing Arts Information Guide Ser.: Vol. 8). 350p. 1983. 42.00x (ISBN 0-8103-1495-9). Gale.

Archer, Stephen N. & D'Ambrosio, Charles A. The Theory of Business Finance: A Book of Readings. 3rd ed. 720p. 1983. pap. 23.95 (ISBN 0-02-304150-1). Macmillan.

Archer, Victor E., jt. ed. see Rom, William N.

Archetti, F. & Cugiani, M. Numerical Techniques for Stochastic Systems. 1980. 72.50 (ISBN 0-444-86000-2). Elsevier.

Archibald, Claudia J. Noise Control Directory, 1978-79. 1978. pap. text ed. 35.00x o.p. (ISBN 0-89671-012-2). Southeast Acoustics.

Archibald, David J. A Study of Mammalia & Geology Across the Cretaceous-Tertiary Boundary in Garfield County, Montana. (Publications in Geological Sciences: Vol. 122). 1982. pap. 32.00x (ISBN 0-520-09639-8). U of Cal Pr.

Archibald, Douglas. Yeats. (Irish Studies Ser.). 320p. 1983. 25.00 (ISBN 0-8156-2263-5). Syracuse U Pr.

Archibald, Jim, ed. see Schacht, Wilhelm.

Archibald, Joe. Backcourt Commando. (gr. 5 up). 1970. 6.25 (ISBN 0-8255-1350-2); PLB 6.47 (ISBN 0-8255-1351-0). Macrae.

--Centerfield Rival. 192p. (gr. 5 up). 1974. 6.95 (ISBN 0-8255-1434-7); PLB 6.47 (ISBN 0-8255-1435-5). Macrae.

--Fast Break Fury. LC 68-31144. (gr. 5 up). 1968. 6.25 (ISBN 0-8255-1372-3); PLB 5.97 (ISBN 0-8255-1373-1). Macrae.

--Long Pass. (gr. 4-6). 1966. PLB 6.47 (ISBN 0-8255-1396-0). Macrae.

--Payoff Pitch. (gr. 5up). 1971. 6.25 (ISBN 0-8255-1407-X); PLB 6.47 (ISBN 0-8255-1408-8). Macrae.

--Phantom Blitz. 192p. (gr. 5up). 1972. 6.25 (ISBN 0-8255-1428-2); PLB 6.47 (ISBN 0-8255-1429-0). Macrae.

--Powerback. LC 79-127425. (gr. 5 up). 1970. PLB 6.47 (ISBN 0-8255-1405-3). Macrae.

--Pro Coach. LC 75-87981. (gr. 5 up). 1969. 6.25 (ISBN 0-8255-1402-9); PLB 6.47 (ISBN 0-8255-1403-7). Macrae.

--Right Field Rookie. (gr. 7-10). 1967. PLB 6.47 (ISBN 0-8255-1411-8). Macrae.

--Right Field Runt. 192p. (gr. 5 up). 1972. 6.25 (ISBN 0-8255-1417-7); PLB 6.47 (ISBN 0-8255-1418-5). Macrae.

--Scrambler. (gr. 5 up). 1967. PLB 6.47 (ISBN 0-8255-1414-2). Macrae.

--Southpaw Speed. (gr. 7 up). 1966. PLB 6.47 (ISBN 0-8255-1416-9). Macrae.

--Three-Point Hero. 176p. (gr. 5 up). 1973. 6.25 (ISBN 0-8255-1432-0); PLB 6.47 (ISBN 0-8255-1433-9). Macrae.

--Two Time Rookie. LC 69-18899. (gr. 5 up). 1969. 6.25 (ISBN 0-8255-1445-2); PLB 6.47 (ISBN 0-8255-1446-0). Macrae.

Archibald, John & Darisse, Alan. A Guide to Multilingual Publishing. 10p. 1982. pap. 6.00 (ISBN 0-914548-36-0). Soc Tech Comm.

Archibald, Katherine. Wartime Shipyard: A Study in Social Disunity. LC 76-7621. (FDR & the Era of the New Deal Ser.). 1976. Repr. of 1947 ed. 27.50 (ISBN 0-306-70802-7). Da Capo.

Archibald, Peter W. Social Psychology As Political Economy. (McGraw-Hill Ryerson Series in Canadian Sociology). 1978. pap. text ed. 19.50 (ISBN 0-07-082347-2, C). McGraw.

Archibald, Russell D. Managing High-Technology Programs & Projects. LC 76-3789. 288p. 1976. 39.95x (ISBN 0-471-03308-1, Pub. by Wiley-Interscience). Wiley.

Archibald, Sandra O., jt. auth. see McCorkle, Chester O., Jr.

Archilla, Rogelio. Meditaciones Sobre el Padrenuestro. 96p. (Span.). 1982. pap. 5.50 (ISBN 0-311-40046-9, Edit Mundo). Casa Bautista.

Archimandrite Kallistos Ware, jt. tr. see Mother Mary.

Archirtectural Record, ed. see Wagner, Walter F., Jr.

Architectural Design Special Issue. British Architecture. (Illus.). 240p. 1983. pap. 29.95 (ISBN 0-312-10035-3). St Martin.

Architectural History Foundation, jt. auth. see Fondation Le Corbusier.

Architectural History Foundation, jt. auth. see Oliver, Richard.

Architectural History Foundation, jt. ed. see Fondation Le Corbusier.

Architectural Record. Great American Architect Series for the Architectural Record, Nos. 1-6. (Architecture & Decorative Art. Ser.). 1977. Repr. of 1899 ed. lib. bdg. 75.00 (ISBN 0-306-70797-7). Da Capo.

Architectural Record, ed. see Architectural Record Magazine.

Architectural Record Editors. Great Houses for View Sites, Beach Sites, Wood Sites, Meadows Sites, Small Sites, Sloping Sites, Steep Sites, Flat Sites. 1976. 27.95 o.p. (ISBN 0-07-002314-X, P&RB). McGraw.

--Office Building Design. 2nd ed. 1975. 39.50 o.p. (ISBN 0-07-002320-4, P&RB). McGraw.

Architectural Record Magazine. Affordable Houses Designed by Architects. (Illus.). 1979. 29.95 (ISBN 0-07-002341-7, P&RB). McGraw.

--Apartments, Townhouses & Condominiums. 2nd ed. 1975. 42.50 (ISBN 0-07-002321-2, P&RB). McGraw.

--Apartments, Townhouses & Condominiums. 3rd ed. (Architectural Record Ser.). (Illus.). 224p. 1981. 36.50 (ISBN 0-07-002356-5, P&RB). McGraw.

--Architecture Nineteen Seventy to Nineteen Eighty: A Decade of Change. Davern, Jeanne & Architectural Record, eds. (Architectural Record Book). (Illus.). 320p. 1980. 36.50 (ISBN 0-07-002352-2). McGraw.

--Behavioral Architecture. 1977. 19.50 o.p. (ISBN 0-07-027890-3, P&RB). McGraw.

--Building for Commerce & Industry. LC 7-1421. 1978. 34.50 (ISBN 0-07-002329-8, P&RB). McGraw.

--Contextual Architecture: Responding to Existing Styles. Ray, Keith, ed. (Architecture Ser.). (Illus.). 1981. 36.50 (ISBN 0-07-002332-8). McGraw.

--Energy-Efficient Buildings. Wagner, Walter F., Jr. & Architectural Record, eds. (Architectural Record Bk.). (Illus.). 256p. 1980. 32.50 (ISBN 0-07-002344-1). McGraw.

--Houses Architects Design for Themselves. 1974. 32.50 (ISBN 0-07-002214-3, P&RB). McGraw.

--Houses of the West. (Illus.). 1979. 34.50 (ISBN 0-07-002339-5, P&RB). McGraw.

--Institutional Buildings: Architecture of the Controlled Environment. (Illus.). 182p. 1980. 32.50 (ISBN 0-07-002343-3). McGraw.

--Interior Spaces Designed by Architects. 1974. 32.50 o.p. (ISBN 0-07-002220-8, P&RB). McGraw.

--Interior Spaces Designed by Architects. 2nd ed. (Architectural Record Ser.). (Illus.). 224p. 1981. 37.50 (ISBN 0-07-002354-9, P&RB). McGraw.

--Public, Municipal & Community Buildings. 1980. 34.50 (ISBN 0-07-002351-4). McGraw.

--Record Houses of 1978. 1978. 5.00 o.p. (ISBN 0-07-002328-X, P&RB). McGraw.

--Record Interiors. 1983. pap. write for info. (ISBN 0-07-002391-3). McGraw.

--Recycling Buildings: Renovations, Remodelings, & Reuses. LC 76-21329. 1977. 31.50 o.p. (ISBN 0-07-002335-2, P&RB). McGraw.

--Religious Buildings. 1980. 36.50 (ISBN 0-07-002342-5). McGraw.

--Techniques of Successful Practice for Architectural Engineering. 2nd ed. 1975. 29.50 o.p. (ISBN 0-07-002229-1, P&RB). McGraw.

--A Treasury of Contemporary Houses. (Illus.). 1978. 27.50 (ISBN 0-07-002330-1, P&RB). McGraw.

Architectural Record Magazine, jt. ed. see Fischer, Robert.

Architectural Record Magazine Staff. Building for the Arts. 1978. 42.50 (ISBN 0-07-002325-5). McGraw.

--Hospitals & Health Care Facilities. 1978. 41.95 (ISBN 0-07-002338-7). McGraw.

--Places for People: Hotel, Restaurants, Bars, Clubs, Community Recreation Facilities Camps, Parks, Plazas, Playgrounds. 1976. 36.50 (ISBN 0-07-002201-1). McGraw.

Architectural Record Magozine Staff. The Architectural Record Book of Vacation Houses. 2nd ed. 1977. 32.50 (ISBN 0-07-002337-9). McGraw.

Arco Editorial Board. Accountant-Auditor. 7th ed. (Orig.). 1972. pap. 8.00 o.p. (ISBN 0-668-00001-5). Arco.

--Auto Mechanic, Auto Serviceman. 4th ed. LC 66-29643. (Illus.). 1974. pap. 8.00 o.p. (ISBN 0-668-00514-9). Arco.

--Bookkeeper-Account Clerk. 5th ed. LC 75-46183. 1976. pap. 8.00 o.p. (ISBN 0-668-00035-X). Arco.

--Court Officer. 5th ed. LC 71-99892. 1974. lib. bdg. 7.50 o.p. (ISBN 0-668-01534-9); pap. 9.00 (ISBN 0-668-00519-X). Arco.

--Federal Aviation Regulations. LC 77-13330. (Illus.). 1978. pap. text ed. 5.00 o.p. (ISBN 0-668-04416-0). Arco.

--Mathematics, Simplified & Self Taught. 5th ed. LC 65-21203. (Orig.). 1968. pap. 5.95 o.p. (ISBN 0-668-00567-X); lib. bdg. 10.00 (ISBN 0-668-01399-0). Arco.

--Personnel Examiner - Junior Personnel Examiner. 2nd ed. LC 59-10038. (Orig.). 1969. lib. bdg. 8.50 o.p. (ISBN 0-668-02069-5); pap. 7.00 (ISBN 0-668-00648-X). Arco.

--Post Office Clerk-Carrier. 13th ed. LC 78-23985. 1979. pap. 6.00 o.p. (ISBN 0-668-04846-8, 4846-8). Arco.

--Probation & Parole Officer. 3rd ed. LC 76-55347. (Orig.). 1978. pap. 8.00 o.p. (ISBN 0-668-04203-6). Arco.

--Senior Clerk-Stenographer. 3rd ed. LC 73-85513. (Orig.). 1974. lib. bdg. 6.50 o.p. (ISBN 0-668-01798-8); pap. 9.00 (ISBN 0-668-01797-X). Arco.

--Stationary Engineer & Fireman. 5th ed. LC 66-25664. (Orig.). 1967. lib. bdg. 12.50 o.p. (ISBN 0-668-01702-3); pap. 9.00 (ISBN 0-668-00070-8). Arco.

--Storekeeper-Stockman, Senior Storekeeper. 3rd ed. LC 75-21510. 1976. pap. 8.00 o.p. (ISBN 0-668-01691-4). Arco.

--Supervising Clerk-Stenographer. 4th ed. LC 67-25272. 1977. lib. bdg. 9.00 o.p. (ISBN 0-668-01705-8); pap. 8.00 (ISBN 0-668-04309-1). Arco.

--Surface Line Dispatcher. 4th ed. LC 78-86828. 1974. pap. 6.00 o.p. (ISBN 0-668-00140-2). Arco.

--Welder. 2nd ed. LC 78-1061. (Illus.). 1978. pap. text ed. 8.00 o.p. (ISBN 0-668-01374-5, 78-1061). Arco.

Arctic Institute of North America, Montreal. Catalogue of the Library of the Arctic Institute of North America, First Supplement. 1971. Vol. 1. 115.00 (ISBN 0-8161-0830-7, Hall Library). G K Hall.

--Catalogue of the Library of the Arctic Institute of North America, Third Supplement. 1980. lib. bdg. 395.00 (ISBN 0-8161-1162-6, Hall Library). G K Hall.

--Catalogue of the Library of the Artic Institute of North America, Second Supplement, 2 vols. 1974. Set. 230.00 (ISBN 0-8161-1030-1, Hall Library). G K Hall.

Ard, B. & Ellis, A. Growth Through Reason: Verbatim Cases in Rational-Emotive Therapy. 8.95 (ISBN 0-686-36740-5); pap. 4.00 (ISBN 0-686-37351-0). Inst Rat Liv.

Ard, Ben N., Jr. Rational Sex Ethics. LC 78-62739. 1978. pap. text ed. 8.50 (ISBN 0-8191-0592-9). U Pr of Amer.

Ardagh, John. France in the 1980s. 672p. 1983. pap. 7.95 (ISBN 0-14-022409-2, Pelican). Penguin.

--France in the 1980's. 720p. 1983. 37.50 (ISBN 0-436-01747-4, Pub. by Secker & Warburg). David & Charles.

Ardell, Donald & James, John, eds. Author's Guide to Journals in the Health Field. LC 80-13403. (Author's Guide to Journals Ser.). 176p. 1980. 19.95 (ISBN 0-917724-09-7, B9). Haworth Pr.

Arden, Bruce W. An Introduction to Digital Computing. 1963. 22.95 (ISBN 0-685-77356-6, 0-201-00340). A-W.

Arden, Bruce W. & Astill, Kenneth N. Numerical Algorithms: Origins & Applications. LC 76-100853. 1970. 23.95 (ISBN 0-201-00336-8). A-W.

Arden, Bruce W., ed. What Can Be Automated? The Computer Science & Engineering Research Study (COSERS) 920p. 1980. text ed. 35.00x (ISBN 0-262-01060-7). MIT Pr.

Arden, Heather. Fools' Play. LC 78-73603. 1980. 39.95 (ISBN 0-521-22513-2). Cambridge U Pr.

Arden, John. Pearl. 80p. 1979. pap. 5.95 (ISBN 0-413-40100-6). Methuen Inc.

Arden, William. Alfred Hitchcock & the Three Investigators in the Mystery of the Dancing Devil. LC 76-8134. (Illus.). (gr. 4-7). 1976. 1.95 o.p. (ISBN 0-394-84862-4, BYR); PLB 5.39 o.p. (ISBN 0-394-93289-7). Random.

--Alfred Hitchcock & the Three Investigators in the Mystery of the Moaning Cave. Hitchcock, Alfred, ed. LC 68-23677. (Three Investigators Ser.: No. 10). (Illus.). (gr. 4-7). 1968. 2.95 o.p. (ISBN 0-394-81423-1, BYR); PLB 5.39 (ISBN 0-394-91423-6); pap. 1.95 o.p. (ISBN 0-394-83773-8). Random.

Ardery, Julia S., ed. see Garland, Jim.

Ardiff, Martha B. & Seaward, Eileen. Great Ideas. (Readers Ser.: Stage 4-Intermediate). (Orig.). 1980. pap. text ed. 3.95 (ISBN 0-88377-159-4). Newbury Hse.

Arditi, Luigi. My Reminiscences. LC 77-5500. (Music Reprint Ser.). (Illus.). 1977. Repr. of 1896 ed. lib. bdg. 32.50 (ISBN 0-306-77417-8). Da Capo.

Arditti, Joseph, ed. Orchid Biology: Reviews & Perspectives, I. LC 76-25648. (Illus.). 328p. 1977 42.50x (ISBN 0-8014-1040-1). Cornell U Pr.

--Orchid Biology: Reviews & Perspectives, II. LC 76-25648. (Illus.). 368p. 1982. 42.50x (ISBN 0-8014-1276-5). Cornell U Pr.

Arditti, M., jt. auth. see Cromwell, Leslie.

Arditty, H. J., jt. ed. see Ezekiel, S.

Ardizzone, Edward. Ardizzone's Hans Anderson. LC 78-18908. 1979. 10.95 (ISBN 0-689-50128-5, Pub. by McElderry Bk). Atheneum.

--Little Tim & Brave Sea. 1983. pap. 3.50 (ISBN 0-14-050175-4, Puffin). Penguin.

--Tim & Charlotte. (Illus.). (ps-3). 1979. Repr. of 1951 ed. 11.95 (ISBN 0-19-279562-7). Oxford U Pr.

--Tim & Charlotte. (Illus.). (ps-3). 1979. pap. 4.95 o.p. (ISBN 0-19-272118-6). Oxford U Pr.

--Tim & Ginger. (Illus.). (ps-3). 1981. pap. 4.95 o.p. (ISBN 0-19-272113-5). Oxford U Pr.

--Tim in Danger. (Illus.). (ps-3). 1980. pap. 3.95 o.p. (ISBN 0-19-272106-2). Oxford U Pr.

--Tim to the Lighthouse. (Illus.). (gr. 1-4). 1980. pap. 3.95 o.p. (ISBN 0-19-272107-0). Oxford U Pr.

--Tim's Friend Towser. (Illus.). 48p. (ps-3). 1981. pap. 4.95 o.p. (ISBN 0-19-272112-7). Oxford U Pr.

Ardizzone, Tony, et al, eds. Intro Twelve. LC 80-65855. 244p. (Orig.). 1981. pap. 7.95x o.p. (ISBN 0-936266-02-3). Assoc Writing Progs.

Ardley, Neil. Birds. LC 80-50961. (New Reference Library Ser.). PLB 11.96 (ISBN 0-382-06393-7). Silver.

--Man & Space. LC 80-52762. (New Reference Library Ser.). PLB 11.96 (ISBN 0-382-06387-2). Silver.

--Musical Instruments. LC 80-50427. (Fact Finders Ser.). PLB 8.00 (ISBN 0-382-06362-7). Silver.

Ardley, Neil & Ridpath, Iran. The Universe. LC 80-50338. (World of Knowledge Ser.). 16.72 (ISBN 0-382-06405-4). Silver.

Ardman, Harvey & Ardman, Perri. The Complete Apartment Guide: Everything You Should Know About Selecting & Utilizing Your Living Space. (Illus.). 320p. 1982. 19.95 (ISBN 0-02-500110-8, Collier); pap. 9.95 (ISBN 0-02-079020-1). Macmillan.

Ardman, Perri, jt. auth. see Ardman, Harvey.

Ardoin, Birthney, jt. auth. see Frair, John.

Ardrey, Robert. Social Contract. 1971. pap. 2.65 o.s.i. (ISBN 0-440-57896-5, Delta). Dell.

--Territorial Imperative. 1968. pap. 3.25 o.s.i. (ISBN 0-440-58619-4, Delta). Dell.

ARE Editorial Department. An Edgar Cayce Health Anthology. 198p. (Orig.). 1979. pap. 4.95 (ISBN 0-87604-119-5). ARE Pr.

Arecchi, F. T. & Schulz-Dubois, E. D., eds. Laser Handbook, 2 vols. LC 73-146191. 1973. Set. 213.00 (ISBN 0-444-10379-1, North-Holland). Elsevier.

Areeda, Philip & Turner, Donald. Antitrust Law: Vol. I & III Lawyer's Supplement. LC 77-15710. 300p. 1982. 45.00 (ISBN 0-316-05039-3). Little.

Areeda, Phillip. Antitrust Analysis. 3rd ed. LC 80-84032. 1418p. 1981. text ed. 27.00 (ISBN 0-316-05056-3). Little.

Areeda, Phillip E. & Turner, Donald F. Antitrust Law. lawyers ed. 1980. Vol, I-V. text ed. 250.00 set (ISBN 0-316-05052-0); 50.00 ea. Little.

Areen, Judith. Cases & Materials on Family Law: 1983 Supplement. (University Casebook Ser.). 393p. 1982. pap. text ed. write for info. (ISBN 0-88277-107-8). Foundation Pr.

--Standards Relating to Youth Service Agencies. LC 77-14496. (IJA-ABA Juvenile Justice Standards Project Ser.). 140p. 1980. prof ref 20.00x (ISBN 0-88410-756-6); pap. 10.00x (ISBN 0-88410-804-X). Ballinger Pub.

Arellanes, Audrey S., ed. Bookplates: A Selected, Annotated Bibliography of the Periodical Literature. LC 71-123720. 1971. 33.00x (ISBN 0-8103-0340-X). Gale.

Arellano, Annette B. Ramirez de see Arbona, Guillermo & Ramirez de Arellano, Annette B.

Arena, Jay. Dangers to Children and Youth. LC 74-99141. (Illus.). 1970. 25.00 (ISBN 0-87716-025-2, Pub. by Moore Pub Co). F Apple.

Arendson. Living & Leaving It. 385p. (Orig.). 1982. 12.50. P Arendson.

Arendson, Peter. The Vision. 348p. (Orig.). 1982. 12.50. P Arendson.

Arendt, Hannah. The Jew As Pariah: Hannah Arendt on the Modern Jewish Condition. Feldman, Ron, ed. 1978. pap. 6.95 o.p. (ISBN 0-394-17042-3, E711, Ever). Grove.

--Lectures on Kant's Political Philosophy. Beiner, Ronald & Beiner, Ronald, eds. LC 82-4817. 192p. 1982. 15.00x (ISBN 0-226-02594-2). U of Chicago Pr.

--The Life of the Mind. LC 80-25403. 1981. pap. 9.95 (ISBN 0-15-651992-5, Harv). HarBraceJ.

--Rahel Varnhagen: The Life of a Jewish Woman. Winston, Richard & Winston, Clara, trs. from Ger. LC 74-6478. (Illus.). 236p. 1974. pap. 3.95 (ISBN 0-15-676100-9, HB287, Harv). HarBraceJ.

--Totalitarianism. LC 66-22273. Orig. Title: Origins of Totalitarianism Pt. 3. (3). 1968. pap. 3.50 (ISBN 0-15-690650-3, Harv). HarBraceJ.

Arendt, Hannah, ed. see Jaspers, Karl.

Arens, Alvin A. & Loebbecke, James K. Applications of Statistical Sampling to Auditing. (Illus.). 400p. 1981. 27.95 (ISBN 0-13-039156-5). P-H.

Arens, Richard, ed. Genocide in Paraguay. LC 76-5726. 171p. 1976. 12.95 (ISBN 0-87722-088-3). Temple U Pr.

Arens, W. The Man-Eating Myth: Anthropology & Anthropophagy. (Illus.). 1980. pap. 5.95 (ISBN 0-19-502793-0, GB 615). Oxford U Pr.

Arensberg, Conrad M. Irish Countryman. LC 68-13630. 1968. pap. 3.95 (ISBN 0-385-09075-7, B18, AMS). Natural Hist.

Arensman, Jeanne M. On My Way to Almost There. 1978. 4.50 o.p. (ISBN 0-533-03112-5). Vantage.

Arentewicz, Gerd & Schmidt, Gunter, eds. The Treatment of Sexual Disorders: Concepts & Techniques of Couple Therapy. 1983. 25.00x (ISBN 0-465-08748-5). Basic.

Arents, J. S., jt. auth. see Labowitz, L. C.

Aresty, Esther B. Best Behavior. LC 71-116500. 1970. 7.95 o.p. (ISBN 0-671-20336-3). S&S.

--The Exquisite Table. LC 79-55441. (Illus.). 170p. 1980. 8.95 o.p. (ISBN 0-672-52307-8). Bobbs.

Aretz, Isabel, ed. Latin America in Its Music. (Latin America in Its Culture Ser.). 370p. 1983. 36.00 (ISBN 0-8419-0533-9). Holmes & Meier.

Arewa, E. O., jt. auth. see Shreve, G. M.

Arfken, George. Mathematical Methods for Physicists. 2nd ed. 1970. text ed. 24.00 (ISBN 0-12-059851-5); SBP 32.50. Acad Pr.

Arfwedson, Carl D. The United States & Canada, in Eighteen Thirty-Two, Eighteen Thirty-Three & Eighteen Thirty-Four, 2 Vols. Repr. of 1834 ed. Set. lib. bdg. 65.00 (ISBN 0-384-01900-5). Johnson Repr.

Argall, George O., Jr., ed. see +019.

Argan, Giulio. The Renaissance City. LC 70-90409. (Planning & Cities Ser). (Illus.). 1969. 7.95 (ISBN 0-8076-0517-4). Braziller.

Argentesi, F. & Avenhaus, R., eds. Mathematical & Statistical Methods in Nuclear Safeguards. (Ispra Courses on Nuclear Engineering & Technology Ser.). 440p. 1982. 87.50 (ISBN 3-7186-0124-9). Harwood Academic.

Argenti, John. Practical Corporate Planning. 221p. 1980. text ed. 24.95x (ISBN 0-04-658230-4); pap. text ed. 10.95x (ISBN 0-04-658231-2). Allen Unwin.

Argetsinger, Gerlad S. Ludvig Holberg's Comedies. 1983. 17.95x (ISBN 0-8093-1058-9). S Ill U Pr.

Argez, Samuel. Historia, Indice, y Prologo de la Revista: La Palabra y el Hombre (1957-1970) (Coleccion Polymita Ser.). (Orig., Span.). 1982. pap. write for info. (ISBN 0-89729-315-0). Ediciones.

Argo, Ellen. The Crystal Star. LC 78-13325. 1979. 12.50 o.p. (ISBN 0-399-12297-4). Putnam Pub Group.

--Jewel of the Seas. LC 77-3180. 1977. 8.95 o.p. (ISBN 0-399-11959-0). Putnam Pub Group.

--The Yankee Girl. 372p. 1981. 13.95 (ISBN 0-399-12528-0). Putnam Pub Group.

Argon, A. S., jt. auth. see McClintock, F. A.

Argon, Ali. Constitutive Equations in Plasticity. 1975. text ed. 25.00x (ISBN 0-262-01042-9). MIT Pr.

Argonne National Laboratory. Reactor Physics Constants. 2nd ed. (AEC Technical Information Center SEr.). 876p. 1963. pap. 58.00 (ISBN 0-87079-337-3, ANL-5800 (2ND ED.)); microfiche 4.50 (ISBN 0-87079-497-3, ANL-5800 (2ND ED.)). DOE.

--Thermal Energy Storage: Design & Installation Manual. rev., 2nd ed. 372p. 1983. 44.50x (ISBN 0-89934-009-1, H.929); pap. 32.50x (ISBN 0-89934-010-5, H.029). Solar Energy Info.

Argote, M. L., jt. auth. see Conesa, Salvador H.

Arguedas, Jose M. & Stephan, Ruth, eds. The Singing Mountaineers: Songs & Tales of the Quechua People. 212p. 1971. Repr. of 1957 ed. 12.50x (ISBN 0-292-70126-8). U of Tex Pr.

Argy, Victor. Exchange-Rate Management in Theory & Practice. LC 82-12015. (Princeton Studies in International Finance: No. 50). 1982. pap. text ed. 4.50x (ISBN 0-88165-221-0). Princeton U Int Finan Econ.

Argyle, M. & Cook, M. Gaze & Mutual Gaze. LC 75-12134. (Illus.). 160p. 1976. 32.50 (ISBN 0-521-20865-3). Cambridge U Pr.

Argyle, M., et al. Social Situations. (Illus.). 450p. 1981. 54.50 (ISBN 0-521-23260-0); pap. 18.95 (ISBN 0-521-29881-4). Cambridge U Pr.

Argyle, Michael. The Scientific Study of Social Behaviour. LC 73-13021. (Illus.). 239p. 1974. Repr. of 1957 ed. lib. bdg. 17.75x (ISBN 0-8371-7108-3, ARSS). Greenwood.

Argyris, C. The Applicability of Organizational Sociology. (Illus.). 138p. 1974. 27.95 (ISBN 0-521-08448-2); pap. 9.95x (ISBN 0-521-09894-7). Cambridge U Pr.

--Management & Organizational Development: The Paths from XA to YB. 1971. 26.95 o.p. (ISBN 0-07-002219-4, P&RB). McGraw.

Argyris, Chris. Increasing Leadership Effectiveness. LC 76-12784. (Wiley Ser. in Behavior). 286p. 1976. 29.95 (ISBN 0-471-01668-3, Pub. by Wiley-Interscience). Wiley.

--Integrating the Individual & the Organization. LC 64-13209. 330p. 1964. 31.95x (ISBN 0-471-03315-4). Wiley.

--Intervention Theory & Method: A Behavioral Science View. LC 79-114331. (Business Ser). 1970. text ed. 24.95 (ISBN 0-201-00342-2). A-W.

Argyris, Chris & Schon, Donald A. Organizational Learning: A Theory of Action Perspective. LC 77-81195. 1978. text ed. 15.95 (ISBN 0-201-00174-8). A-W.

Arian, Philip, jt. auth. see Eisenberg, Azriel.

Arian, Phillip & Eisenberg, Azriel. The Story of the Prayer Book. (gr. 7-9). 1971. pap. 5.95x (ISBN 0-87677-017-0). Prayer Bk.

Arias, I. M. & Frenkel, M., eds. The Liver Annual. (Liver Ser.: Vol. 1). 1982. 78.75 (ISBN 0-444-90241-4). Elsevier.

Arias, I. M., et al, eds. The Liver Annual. (Liver Ser.: Vol. 1). 1981. 78.75 (ISBN 0-444-90182-5). Elsevier.

Arias, Irwin, et al, eds. The Liver: Biology & Pathobiology. 888p. 1982. text ed. 95.00 (ISBN 0-89004-575-5). Raven.

Arias, M. M., jt. auth. see Lubian, Rafael.

Arias, Ricardo. Spanish Sacramental Plays. (World Authors Ser.). 15.95 (ISBN 0-8057-6414-3, Twayne). G K Hall.

Arias, Toby & Frassanito, Elaine. Fiesta Mexicana. (Illus.). 90p. 1982. pap. 6.95 (ISBN 0-9609942-0-3). T & E Ent.

Arias-Misson, Alain. Confessions of a Murderer, Rapist, Fascist, Bomber, Thief. LC 74-81095. (Illus.). 1974. 8.95 o.p. (ISBN 0-914090-05-4). Chicago Review.

Aricha, Amos & Landau, Eli. Phoenix. 1979. 9.95 o.p. (ISBN 0-453-00371-0, H371). NAL.

Arichea, D. C. & Nida, E. A. Translator's Handbook on the First Letter from Peter. (Helps for Translators Ser.). 1980. softcover 2.35x (ISBN 0-8267-0152-3, 08624). United Bible.

Arichea, D. C., Jr. & Nida, E. A. Translator's Handbook on Paul's Letter to the Galatians. (Helps for Translators Ser.). 1979. Repr. of 1976 ed. soft cover 2.55x (ISBN 0-8267-0142-6, 08527). United Bible.

Aridas, Chris. Discernment: Seeking God in Every Situation. (Orig.). 1981. pap. 3.50 (ISBN 0-914544-37-3). Living Flame Pr.

Ariel, Irving, ed. Progress in Clinical Cancer, Vols. 2, 4-7. Incl. Vol. 2. (Illus.). 392p. 1966. 69.50 o.p. (ISBN 0-8089-0014-5); Vol. 4. (Illus.). 424p. 1970. 96.50 o.p. (ISBN 0-8089-0016-1); Vol. 5. (Illus.). 296p. 1973. 76.50 o.p. (ISBN 0-8089-0777-8); Vol. 6. 240p. 1975. 73.50 o.p. (ISBN 0-8089-0906-1); Vol. 7. 288p. 1977. 56.50 o.p. (ISBN 0-8089-1087-6). LC 64-24793. Grune.

--Progress in Clinical Cancer, Vol. 8. Date not set. price not set. Grune.

Ariens-Kappers, J. Topics in Neuroendocrinology. (Progress in Brain Research: Vol. 38). 1973. 88.00 (ISBN 0-444-41049-X, North Holland). Elsevier.

Ariens-Kappers, J. & Pevet, P., eds. The Pineal Gland of Vertebrates Including Man. (Progress in Brain Research Ser.: Vol. 52). 534p. 1979. 116.25 (ISBN 0-444-80114-6). Elsevier.

Aries, R. S. & Newton, R. D. Chemical Engineering Cost Estimation. (Chemical Engineering Ser). 1955. 19.95 o.p. (ISBN 0-07-002200-3, C). McGraw.

Arieti, Silvano. Abraham & the Contemporary Mind. LC 80-68187. 187p. 1981. 13.50 (ISBN 0-465-00005-3). Basic.

--Interpretation of Schizophrenia. 2nd ed. LC 73-91078. 1974. 35.00x (ISBN 0-465-03429-2). Basic.

--Understanding & Helping the Schizophrenic: A Guide for Family & Friends. 1981. pap. 6.75 (ISBN 0-671-41252-3, Touchstone Bks). S&S.

Arietti, Silvano & Chrzanowski, Gerard, eds. New Dimensions in Psychiatry: A World View, 2 vols. LC 74-16150. 448p. 1975. Vol. 1. 35.00 o.p. (ISBN 0-471-03317-0, Pub. by Wiley-Interscience); Vol. 2. 53.95x (ISBN 0-471-03318-9). Wiley.

Arif, Abu A., jt. auth. see Ali, Syed A.

Ariga, Shinobu. Who Has the Yellow Hat? (Surprise Bks.). 22p. 1982. 4.95 (ISBN 0-8431-0638-7). Price Stern.

Arijon, Daniel. Grammar of the Film Language. (Illus.). 650p. 1976. 38.95 (ISBN 0-240-50779-7). Focal Pr.

Arin, M. K. Successful Wedding Photography. 1967. 10.95 o.p. (ISBN 0-8174-0461-9, Amphoto). Watson-Guptill.

ARINC Research Corporation. Thirty Twenty GHz Communications Satellite Trunking Network Study. 1981. 100.00 (ISBN 0-686-37982-9). Info Gatekeepers.

Ariosto. The Comedies of Ariosto. Beame, Edmond & Sbrocchi, Leonard G., eds. LC 74-5739. xlvi, 322p. 1975. text ed. 20.00x o.s.i. (ISBN 0-226-02649-3). U of Chicago Pr.

Ariosto, Ludovico. Orlando Furioso. Waldman, Guido, tr. (The World's Classics Ser.). 647p. 1983. pap. 12.95 (ISBN 0-19-281636-5, GB). Oxford U Pr.

--Orlando Furioso: Vol. Two. Reynolds, Barbara, tr. from It. (Classics Se.). 1977. pap. 9.95 (ISBN 0-14-044310-X). Penguin.

Ariotti, Piero, ed. see Bronowski, Jacob.

Aris, Rutherford. Mathematical Modeling Techniques. (Research Notes in Mathematics Ser.: No. 24). 191p. 1978. pap. text ed. 23.00 (ISBN 0-273-08413-5). Pitman Pub MA.

Aris, Rutherford & Davis, H. Ted, eds. Springs of Scientific Creativity: Essays on Founders of Modern Science. LC 82-23715. (Illus.). 352p. 1983. 32.50x (ISBN 0-8166-1087-8). U of Minn Pr.

Arisian, Khoren. The New Wedding: Creating Your Own Marriage Ceremony. 1973. 13.50 (ISBN 0-394-48334-0). Knopf.

--The New Wedding: Creating Your Own Marriage Ceremony. 160p. 1973. pap. 8.95 (ISBN 0-394-71919-0, Vin). Random.

Aristophanes. The Birds. Arnott, Peter D., ed. & tr. Bd. with The Brothers Menaechmus. Plautus. LC 58-12716. (Crofts Classics Ser.). 1958. pap. text ed. 3.25x (ISBN 0-88295-004-5). Harlan Davidson.

--The Clouds. Arnott, Peter D., ed. & tr. Bd. with The Pot of Gold. Plautus. LC 67-17194. (Crofts Classics Ser.). 1967. pap. text ed. 3.25x (ISBN 0-88295-005-3). Harlan Davidson.

--Clouds. Arrowsmith, William, ed. 1970. pap. 2.25 (ISBN 0-451-62231-6, ME2231, Ment). NAL.

--The Complete Plays of Aristophanes. Hadas, Moses, intro. by. & tr. (Bantam Classics Ser.). (gr. 9-12). 1981. pap. 2.95 (ISBN 0-553-21064-5). Bantam.

--Four Comedies: Lysistrata, the Congresswomen, the Acharnians, the Frogs. Arrowsmith, William, ed. (Illus.). 432p. 1969. pap. 7.95 (ISBN 0-472-06152-6, 152, AA). U of Mich Pr.

--Lysistrata. Parker, Douglass, tr. 1970. pap. 2.25 (ISBN 0-451-62219-7, ME2219, Ment). NAL.

Aristophanes see Hadas, Moses.

Aristotele, Pseudo. Poridat de las Poridades. Kasten, Lloyd, ed. 94p. 1957. pap. 1.50 (ISBN 0-942260-00-7). Hispanic Seminary.

Aristotle. An Analysis of the Soul of Man. (The Most Meaningful Classics in World Culture Ser.). (Illus.). 129p. 1983. 57.85 (ISBN 0-89920-052-4). Am Inst Psych.

--Aristotle on His Predecessors. 2nd ed. Taylor, A. E., tr. from Gr. 159p. 1969. 16.00 (ISBN 0-87548-001-2); pap. 5.00 (ISBN 0-87548-002-0). Open Court.

--Aristotle: Poetics. Telford, Kenneth, tr. LC 60-53611. 192p. 1978. pap. 5.95 (ISBN 0-89526-932-5). Regnery-Gateway.

--Aristotle's Physics. Hope, Richard, tr. LC 61-5498. xiv, 242p. 1961. pap. 6.25x (ISBN 0-8032-5093-2, BB122, Bison). U of Nebr Pr.

--Aristotle's Poetics. Butcher, S. H., tr. 118p. (Orig.). 1961. pap. 3.75 (ISBN 0-8090-0527-1, Drama). Hill & Wang.

--Aristotle's Poetics. Kirkwood, G. M., ed. Hutton, James. 120p. 1982. text ed. 15.95 (ISBN 0-393-01599-8); pap. text ed. 4.95x (ISBN 0-393-95216-9). Norton.

--Introduction to Aristotle. McKeon, Richard, ed. (YA) 1965. pap. 4.50x (ISBN 0-394-30973-1, T73, Mod LibC). Modern Lib.

--On Poetry & Style. Grube, G. M., tr. LC 58-13827. 1958. pap. 4.95 (ISBN 0-672-60244-X, LLA68). Bobbs.

--On the Art of Poetry. Bywater, Ingram, tr. 1920. pap. 5.50 (ISBN 0-19-814110-6). Oxford U Pr.

--Physics. rev. ed. Ross, W. David, ed. 1936. 65.00x (ISBN 0-19-814109-2). Oxford U Pr.

--The Pocket Aristotle. Kaplan, Justin, ed. 400p. 1983. pap. 5.95 (ISBN 0-671-46377-2). WSP.

--Poetics. 1978. Repr. of 1963 ed. 8.95x (ISBN 0-460-00901-X, Evman). Biblio Dist.

--Poetics. Else, Gerald F., tr. LC 67-11980. 1967. 4.95 (ISBN 0-472-06166-6). U of Mich Pr.

--Poetics. 1970. pap. 4.95 (ISBN 0-472-06166-6, 166, AA). U of Mich Pr.

--The Poetics of Aristotle. Epps, Preston H., tr. 84p. 1967. pap. 4.00x (ISBN 0-8078-4017-3). U of NC Pr.

--The Rhetoric & Poetics. LC 54-9971. 6.95 (ISBN 0-394-60425-3). Modern Lib.

Aristotle, Pseudo. Aragonese Version of the Secreto Secretorum. 1983. 12.00 (ISBN 0-942260-30-9). Hispanic Seminary.

Ariza, A. K. & Ariza, I. F., eds. Lauro Olmo: La Camisa. 1968. 8.00 o.s.i. (ISBN 0-08-012616-2); pap. 3.50 (ISBN 0-08-012615-4). Pergamon.

Ariza, I. F., jt. ed. see Ariza, A. K.

Arizona ASBO, ed. Warehousing & Distributing Guidelines. 0.69 (ISBN 0-685-05645-7). Assn Sch Busn.

Arizona State University Library. Solar Energy Index: Supplement I. 250p. 1982. 95.00 (ISBN 0-08-028832-4). Pergamon.

Arjmand, Mihdi. Gulshan-i Haqayiq. 320p. (Persian.). 1982. Repr. 12.95 (ISBN 0-933770-15-4). Kalimat.

Arkham, Candace. Dare to Love. (Orig.). 1980. pap. 1.50 o.s.i. (ISBN 0-440-11592-2). Dell.

--Forbidden Yearnings. 1978. pap. 1.25 o.s.i. (ISBN 0-440-12736-X). Dell.

--Splendors of the Heart. 1979. pap. 1.25 o.s.i. (ISBN 0-440-11890-5). Dell.

Arkhurst, Frederick S., ed. U. S. Policy Toward Africa. LC 74-33028. (Illus.). 272p. 1975. 33.95 o.p. (ISBN 0-275-05330-X); pap. 9.95 o.p. (ISBN 0-275-64250-X). Praeger.

Arkin, Alan. Tony's Hard Work Day. LC 76-183161. (Illus.). 32p. (ps-3). 1972. 9.57i o.p. (ISBN 0-06-020137-1, HarpJ); PLB 10.89 (ISBN 0-06-020138-X). Har-Row.

Arkin, Herbert. Handbook of Sampling for Auditing & Accounting. 2nd ed. (Accounting Ser.). (Illus.). 576p. 1974. 39.95 (ISBN 0-07-002212-7, P&RB). McGraw.

--Sampling Methods for the Auditor: An Advanced Treatment. (Illus.). 288p. 1982. 27.50 (ISBN 0-07-002194-5). McGraw.

Arkin, Herbert & Colton, Raymond R. Statistical Methods. 5th ed. 344p. (Orig.). 1970. pap. 5.95 (ISBN 0-06-460027-0, CO 27, COS). Har-Row.

Arkoff, Abe. Adjustment & Mental Health. 1968. 20.00 o.p. (ISBN 0-07-002221-6, C); questions 12.95 o.p. (ISBN 0-07-002223-2). McGraw.

Arksey, Laura & Pries, Nancy, eds. American Diaries: An Annotated Bibliography of Published American Diaries & Journals to 1980, 2 Vols. Incl. Vol. 1. Diaries Written from 1492 to 1844 (ISBN 0-8103-1800-8); Diaries Written from 1845 to 1980 (ISBN 0-8103-1801-6). 600p. 1983. 60.00x ea. Gale.

Arlen, Leslie. Fate & Dreams. (Borodins Ser.: No. 3). 384p. (Orig.). 1981. pap. 3.50 (ISBN 0-515-06898-5). Jove Pubns.

--Rage & Desire. (The Borodins Bk.: No. V). 336p. 1982. pap. 3.50 (ISBN 0-515-05852-1). Jove Pubns.

Arlen, Michael J. Living-Room War. 256p. 1982. pap. 5.95 (ISBN 0-14-006081-2). Penguin.

--Passage to Ararat & Exiles. 1982. pap. 8.95 (ISBN 0-14-006311-0). Penguin.

--Thirty Seconds. 224p. 1981. pap. 3.95 (ISBN 0-14-005810-9). Penguin.

Arlen, R., jt. auth. see Woltz, P.

Arlen, Richard T., jt. auth. see Woltz, Phebe M.

Arlens, Hans. Aristotle's Linguistic Theory & its Medieval Tradition. (Studies in the History of Linguistics: No. 29). 330p. 1982. 38.00 (ISBN 9-02724-511-8). Benjamins North Am.

Arlin, M., et al. Music Sources: A Collection of Excerpts & Complete Movements. 1979. pap. 22.95 (ISBN 0-13-607168-6). P-H.

Arlin, Marian T. The Science of Nutrition. 2nd ed. (Illus.). 352p. 1977. text ed. 21.95x (ISBN 0-02-303840-3, 30384). Macmillan.

Arlingaus, Bruce E. Military Development in Africa: Political & Economic Risks of Arms Transfers. (Special Studies on Africa). 175p. 1983. lib. bdg. 23.50 (ISBN 0-86531-434-9). Westview.

Arlinghaus, Bruce, ed. Africa Security Issues: Sovereignty, Stability, & Solidarity. 200p. Date not set. price not set. Westview.

Arlinghaus, Bruce E., ed. Arms for Africa: Military Assistance & Foreign Policy in the Developing World. LC 81-48668. 256p. 1982. 26.95x (ISBN 0-669-05527-1). Lexington Bks.

Arlington, R. Rene, jt. auth. see Murphy, Paul I.

Arlott & Fitter. The Complete Guide to British Wildlife. pap. 18.95 (ISBN 0-686-42744-0, Collins Pub England). Greene.

Arlott, jt. auth. see Williams.

Arlott, John. Island Camera: The Isles of Scilly in the Photography of the Gibson Family. (Illus.). 112p. 1983. 17.50 (ISBN 0-7153-8391-4). David & Charles.

Arlotti, John, et al. Island Camera. (Illus.). 110p. 1983. pap. 17.50 (ISBN 0-7153-8391-4). David & Charles.

Arlotto, Anthony. Introduction to Historical Linguistics. LC 80-6309. 284p. 1981. lib. bdg. 22.25 (ISBN 0-8191-1459-6); pap. text ed. 11.00 (ISBN 0-8191-1460-X). U Pr of Amer.

Arlt, W., jt. auth. see Sorensen, J. M.

Arlt, W., jt. auth. see Sorenson, J. M.

Arma, Paul, jt. auth. see Poston, Elizabeth.

Armajani, Yahya. Middle East-Past & Present. (Illus.). 1969. text ed. 22.95 (ISBN 0-13-581579-7). P-H.

Arman, Mike & Heinrichs, Kurt. What Fits What on Harley Davidson 1936-1981. 5th ed. (Illus.). 1982. pap. 5.00 (ISBN 0-933078-06-4). M Arman.

Arman, Mike, ed. see Shenton, Stan.

Armandi, Barry R. Organizational Structure & Efficiency. LC 80-69049. 276p. 1981. lib. bdg. 20.50 (ISBN 0-8191-1610-6); pap. text ed. 11.50 (ISBN 0-8191-1611-4). U Pr of Amer.

Armandi, Barry R. & Barbera, John J. Organizational Behavior: Classical & Contemporary Readings. 368p. 1982. pap. text ed. 17.95 (ISBN 0-8403-2807-9). Kendall-Hunt.

Armarego, W. L. F. Stereochemistry of Heterocyclic Compounds: Nitrogen Heterocycles, Pt.1. 433p. Repr. of 1977 ed. text ed. 63.50 (ISBN 0-471-02627-1). Krieger.

Armarego, W. L. F., ed. Stereochemistry of Heterocyclic Compounds. Incl. Pt. 1. Nitrogen Heterocycles. 1976. 71.50 o.p. (ISBN 0-471-01892-9); Pt. 2. Oxygen; Sulfur; Mixed N, D, & S; & Phosphorus Heterocycles. o.p. (ISBN 0-471-03322-7). LC 36-26023. (General Heterocyclic Chemistry Ser., Pub. by Wiley-Interscience). Wiley.

Armbruster, jt. auth. see Rembold.

Armbruster, Franz O., jt. auth. see Pedersen, Jean J.

Armeding, Carl E. The Old Testament & Criticism. 144p. 1983. pap. 6.95 (ISBN 0-8028-1951-6). Eerdmans.

Armelagos, George, jt. auth. see Farb, Peter.

Armendariz, Efraim P. & McAdam, Stephen J. Elementary Number Theory. (Illus.). 1980. text ed. 23.95 (ISBN 0-02-303850-0). Macmillan.

Armentani, Andy & Donatelli, Gary. The Monday Night Football Cookbook & Restaurant Guide. LC 82-71965. (Illus.). 176p. 1982. pap. 9.95 (ISBN 0-8019-7270-1). Chilton.

Armentano, Dominick T. Antitrust & Monopoly: Anatomy of a Policy Failure. LC 81-16440. 292p. 1982. 22.95x (ISBN 0-471-09931-7, Pub. by Wiley-Interscience); pap. 12.95x (ISBN 0-471-09930-9). Wiley.

--Antitrust & Monopoly: Anatomy of a Policy Failure. 304p. 1982. 22.95 (ISBN 0-686-98110-3). Telecom Lib.

Armento, Richard. Automotive Cooling System Training & Reference Manual. (Illus.). 1979. text ed. 22.95 (ISBN 0-8359-0265-X); pap. text ed. 14.95 (ISBN 0-8359-0264-1). Reston.

Armer, Alberta. Screwball. (Illus.). (gr. 4-7). 1981. 4.95 (ISBN 0-399-20837-2, Philomel). Putnam Pub Group.

Armer, Don. Hop Aboard - It's Later Than You Think. 1978. 5.95 o.p. (ISBN 0-533-03549-X). Vantage.

Armer, Laura A. Waterless Mountain. (Illus.). (gr. 5-8). 1931. 9.95 (ISBN 0-679-20233-1). McKay.

Armer, Michael. African Social Psychology: Review & Annotated Bibliography. LC 74-23711. (African Bibliography Ser.: No. 2). 400p. 1975. text ed. 45.00x (ISBN 0-8419-0164-3, Africana). Holmes & Meier.

Armer, Michael & Grimshaw, Allen D. Comparative Social Research: Methodological Problems & Strategies. LC 73-7604. 496p. 1973. 27.50 (ISBN 0-471-03321-9). Krieger.

Armerding, Hudson T. Leadership. 1978. 6.95 (ISBN 0-8423-2126-8); pap. 4.95 (ISBN 0-8423-2125-X). Tyndale.

Armes, Roy. The Ambiguous Image: Narrative Style in Modern European Cinema. LC 75-37266. (Illus.). 256p. 1976. 15.00x o.p. (ISBN 0-253-30560-8). Ind U Pr.

Armfelt, Roger. The Structure of English Education. 1955. 11.25x o.p. (ISBN 0-7100-1024-9, Cohen & West). Routledge & Kegan.

Armiger, William B., ed. Computer Applications in Fermentation Technology, No. 9. (Biotechnology & Bioengineering Symposium). 398p. 1980. pap. 30.95 o.p. (ISBN 0-471-05746-0, Pub. by Wiley-Interscience). Wiley.

Armijo, Moses A., jt. auth. see Harcharik, Kathleen.

Armington, Stan. Trekking in the Himalayas. 3rd ed. (Lonely Planet Travel Ser.). 224p. 1982. pap. 6.95 (ISBN 0-908086-06-7, Pub. by Lonely Planet Australia). Hippocrene Bks.

Armistead, J. M. Nathaniel Lee. (English Authors Ser.). 1979. 14.95 (ISBN 0-8057-6748-7, Twayne). G K Hall.

Armistead, John, jt. auth. see Birch, Clive.

Armitage, Andrew D. & Tudor, Dean. Annual Index to Popular Music Record Reviews 1972. LC 73-8909. 1973. 16.50 o.p. (ISBN 0-8108-0636-3). Scarecrow.

--Annual Index to Popular Music Record Reviews 1973. LC 73-8909. 1974. 24.00 o.p. (ISBN 0-8108-0774-2). Scarecrow.

--Annual Index to Popular Music Record Reviews 1974. LC 73-8909. 1976. 24.00 o.p. (ISBN 0-8108-0865-X). Scarecrow.

--Annual Index to Popular Music Record Reviews 1975. LC 73-8909. 1976. 24.00 o.p. (ISBN 0-8108-0934-6). Scarecrow.

Armitage, Andrew D. & Tudor, Nancy, eds. Canadian Essay & Literature Index 1973. LC 75-7703. 1975. 40.00 o.p. (ISBN 0-8020-4518-9). U of Toronto Pr.

Armitage, J. V., ed. Journees Arithmetiques Nineteen Eighty. LC 81-18032. (London Mathematical Society Lecture: No. 56). 350p. 1982. pap. 29.50 (ISBN 0-521-28513-5). Cambridge U Pr.

Armitage, Kenneth B. Investigations in General Biology. 1970. text ed. 9.50 o.s. (ISBN 0-12-062460-5); SBP 11.00 (ISBN 0-686-96638-4). Acad Pr.

Armitage, M. M. & Mason, R. A. Air Power in the Nuclear Age. LC 82-17551. (Illus.). 264p. 1983. 24.95 (ISBN 0-252-01030-2). U of Ill Pr.

Armitage, Merle, ed. Martha Graham: The Early Years. LC 78-17608. (Series in Dance). (Illus.). 1978. lib. bdg. 21.50 (ISBN 0-306-79504-3); pap. 5.95 (ISBN 0-306-80084-5). Da Capo.

Armitage, Paul. The Common Market. LC 78-61095. (Countries Ser.). (Illus.). 1978. PLB 12.68 (ISBN 0-382-06199-3). Silver.

Armitage, Philip. Laboratory Safety: A Science Teacher's Source Book. 1977. pap. text ed. 6.50x o.p. (ISBN 0-435-57050-1). Heinemann Ed.

Armitage, Richard, et al. Beginning Spanish: A Cultural Approach. 4th ed. (Illus.). 1979. pap. text ed. 19.95 (ISBN 0-395-27507-5); exercise bk. 8.50 (ISBN 0-395-27508-3); recordings-13 reels 280.00. HM.

Armor, David J. The American School Counselor: A Case Study in the Sociology of Professions. LC 68-58127. 228p. 1969. 10.00x (ISBN 0-87154-069-X). Russell Sage.

Armor, David J., jt. auth. see Polich, J. Michael.

Armor, David J., et al. Alcoholism & Treatment. LC 77-17421. (Personality Processes Ser.). 348p. 1978. 31.95x (ISBN 0-471-02558-5, Pub. by Wiley-Interscience). Wiley.

Armore, Sidney J. Introduction to Statistical Analysis & Inference for Psychology & Education. 546p. 1966. text ed. 24.95 o.p. (ISBN 0-471-03343-X). Wiley.

Armour, Graham. Super Profile: Lotus Elan. 56p. Date not set. 9.95 (ISBN 0-85429-330-2). Haynes Pubns.

Armour, L. A. & Samuel, G. H. Cases in Tort. 352p. 1977. 30.00x (ISBN 0-7121-0356-2, Pub. by Macdonald & Evans). State Mutual Bk.

Armour, Philip K. The Cycles of Social Reform: Mental Health Policy Making in the United States, England, & Sweden. LC 80-6187. 374p. (Orig.). 1982. lib. bdg. 25.50 (ISBN 0-8191-2033-2); pap. text ed. 14.00 (ISBN 0-8191-2034-0). U Pr of Amer.

Armour, R. American Lit Relit. 1970. pap. 2.95 (ISBN 0-07-002283-6). McGraw.

--It All Started With Columbus. rev. ed. 1971. pap. 2.95 (ISBN 0-07-002298-4). McGraw.

--It All Started with Hippocrates: A Mercifully Brief History of Medicine. 1972. pap. 2.95 (ISBN 0-07-002284-4). McGraw.

--It All Started with Nudes: An Artful History of Art. 1977. pap. 7.95 (ISBN 0-07-002271-2). McGraw.

--Twisted Tales from Shakespeare. pap. 4.95 (ISBN 0-07-002251-8). McGraw.

Armour, Richard. Anyone for Insomnia? A Playful Look at Sleeplessness. LC 82-9996. 128p. (Orig.). 1982. pap. 4.95 (ISBN 0-912800-69-0). Woodbridge Pr.

--Classics Reclassified. (Illus.). 1960. 6.95 o.p. (ISBN 0-07-002256-9, GB); pap. 3.95 o.p. (ISBN 0-07-002257-7). McGraw.

--Dozen Dinosaurs. (gr. k-3). 1967. 9.95 o.p. (ISBN 0-07-002226-7, GB). McGraw.

--Drug Store Days: My Youth Among the Pills & Potions. LC 59-10701. (Illus.). 192p. 1974. pap. 2.45 o.p. (ISBN 0-07-002287-9, SP). McGraw.

--Drug Store Days: My Youth Among the Pills & Potions. rev. ed. LC 82-23762. (Illus.). 192p. 1983. pap. 5.95 (ISBN 0-88007-125-7). Woodbridge Pr.

--Educated Guesses: Light-Serious Suggestions for Parents & Teachers. LC 82-17670. 192p. (Orig.). 1983. 9.95 (ISBN 0-88007-126-5); pap. 5.95 (ISBN 0-88007-127-3). Woodbridge Pr.

--Our Presidents. rev. ed. LC 82-23762. (Illus.). 96p. 1983. 9.95 (ISBN 0-88007-133-8); pap. 5.95 (ISBN 0-88007-134-6). Woodbridge Pr.

Armour, Richard & Galdone, P. Insects All Around Us. 1981. 8.95 (ISBN 0-07-002266-6). McGraw.

Armour, Robert. Fritz Lang. (Filmmakers Ser.). 1978. lib. bdg. 12.95 (ISBN 0-8057-9259-7, Twayne). G K Hall.

Armour, William J., jt. auth. see Colson, John H.

Arms, George, ed. Selected Letters of W. D. Howells, Vol. 2: 1873-1881. (Critical Editions Program). lib. bdg. 30.00 (ISBN 0-8057-8528-0, Twayne). G K Hall.

Arms, George, et al, eds. The Writer's World: Readings for College Composition. LC 77-86290. 1978. pap. text ed. 10.95x (ISBN 0-312-89433-3); Instr. manual avail (ISBN 0-312-89434-1). St Martin.

Arms, George, et al, eds. see Howells, W. D.

Arms, Richard W., Jr. Volume Cycles in the Stock Market. LC 82-73619. 200p. 1983. 30.00 (ISBN 0-87094-405-3). Dow Jones-Irwin.

Arms, Suzanne. Immaculate Deception: A New Look at Childbirth in America. LC 74-28129. (A San Francisco Ser.). 336p. 1975. 11.95 o.s.i. (ISBN 0-395-19893-3); pap. 6.95 (ISBN 0-395-19973-5). HM.

Arms, W. Y., et al. A Practical Approach to Computing. LC 75-15787. 353p. 1976. 46.50 o.p. (ISBN 0-471-03324-3); pap. 24.00 o.p. (ISBN 0-471-99736-6). Wiley.

Armstron, Michael. The Personnel & Trading Databook 1982. 422p. 1981. 38.00 (ISBN 0-85038-493-1). Nichols Pub.

Armstrong, et al. Education. 1981. 21.95x (ISBN 0-02-304050-5). Macmillan.

Armstrong, A. Stability & Change in an English County Town. LC 73-92785. (Illus.). 272p. 1974. 27.95 (ISBN 0-521-20423-2). Cambridge U Pr.

Armstrong, A. H. Cambridge History of Later Greek & Early Medieval Philosophy. 1967. 75.00 (ISBN 0-521-04054-X). Cambridge U Pr.

Armstrong, Allen. Belief, Truth & Knowledge. LC 72-83586. 240p. 1973. 37.50 (ISBN 0-521-08706-6); pap. 11.95 (ISBN 0-521-09737-1). Cambridge U Pr.

Armstrong, C. A., jt. ed. see Allmand, C. T.

Armstrong, C. N. & Marshall, A. J. Intersexuality in Vertebrates Including Man. 1964. 62.00 o.p. (ISBN 0-12-063150-4). Acad Pr.

Armstrong, Carolyn T. Leather & Lace, No. 6: Honeysuckle Love. 1983. pap. 2.50 (ISBN 0-686-82614-0). Zebra.

Armstrong, Christa, tr. see Von Lang, Jochen & Sibyll, Claus.

Armstrong, D. & Kappang, N. Ceroid Liposfucsinosis: Batten Disease. 1982. 99.75 (ISBN 0-444-80329-7). Elsevier.

Armstrong, D. M. Universals & Scientific Realism: Vol. 1, Nominalism & Realism. LC 77-80824. 1978. 29.95 (ISBN 0-521-21741-5). Cambridge U Pr.

--Universals & Scientific Realism: Vol. 2, a Theory of Universals. LC 77-80824. 1978. 29.95 (ISBN 0-521-21950-7). Cambridge U Pr.

Armstrong, David. Political Anatomy of the Body: Medical Knowledge in Britain in the Twentieth Century. LC 82-9546. 176p. Date not set. 29.95 (ISBN 0-521-24746-2). Cambridge U Pr.

--The Rise of International Organization. LC 82-16767. (Making of the 20th Century Ser.). 180p. 1982. 22.50x (ISBN 0-312-68427-4). St Martin.

Armstrong, David A. Bullets & Bureaucrats: The Machine Gun & the United States Army, 1861-1916. LC 81-7226. (Contributions in Military History Ser.: No. 29). (Illus.). 232p. 1982. lib. bdg. 27.50 (ISBN 0-313-23029-3, ABU). Greenwood.

Armstrong, David G. Social Studies in Secondary Education. (Illus.). 1980. text ed. 22.95 (ISBN 0-02-303980-9). Macmillan.

Armstrong, David G. & Savage, Tom V. Secondary Education: An Introduction. 1st ed. 576p. 1983. 22.95 (ISBN 0-02-304070-X). Macmillan.

Armstrong, Donald, tr. see Hoerni, B., et al.

Armstrong, E. F. & Armstrong, Sara. In a Copper Kettle. 15th ed. (Illus.). 1958. pap. 4.95x (ISBN 0-87315-019-8). Golden Bell.

Armstrong, Edward. Prayer & God's Infinate Power. 119p. pap. 0.45 o.p. (ISBN 0-87509-120-2). Chr Pubns.

Armstrong, Edward A. St. Francis, Nature Mystic: The Derivation & Significance of the Nature Stories in the Franciscan Legend. LC 74-149949. (Hermeneuties: Studies in the History of Religions). 1973. 33.00x (ISBN 0-520-01966-0); pap. 5.95 (ISBN 0-520-03040-0). U of Cal Pr.

--Shakespeare's Imagination: A Study of the Psychology of Association & Inspiration. landmark ed. LC 63-8165. vi, 230p. 1963. 22.95x (ISBN 0-8032-1005-1). U of Nebr Pr.

Armstrong, Edward C. French Metrical Versions of Barlaam & Josaphat. (Elliott Monographs: Vol. 10). 1922. pap. 12.00 (ISBN 0-527-02614-X). Kraus Repr.

Armstrong, Emma P. see Pryor, Harold.

Armstrong, Fiona & Baum, Myra. Getting Ready for the World of Work. (Illus.). 1980. pap. text ed. 6.40 (ISBN 0-07-002517-7). McGraw.

--A Realistic Job Search. (Lifeworks Ser.). (Illus.). 1980. pap. 6.40 (ISBN 0-07-002518-5). McGraw.

Armstrong, Fiona, et al. The Real Me & the World of Work. (Lifeworks Ser.). (Illus.). 1979. pap. text ed. 5.28 (ISBN 0-07-002515-0). McGraw.

--The Reality of Work & Promotion. (Illus.). 208p. 1980. pap. text ed. 6.40 (ISBN 0-07-002519-3). McGraw.

--Realizing What's Available in the World of Work. (Lifeworks Ser.). (Illus.). 1980. pap. text ed. 5.96 (ISBN 0-07-002516-9). McGraw.

Armstrong, Frank B. Biochemistry. 2nd ed. (Illus.). 1982. 22.95x (ISBN 0-19-503109-1). Oxford U Pr.

Armstrong, Frank B. & Bennett, Thomas P. Biochemistry. (Illus.). 1979. text ed. 24.95x o.p. (ISBN 0-19-502406-0). Oxford U Pr.

Armstrong, Frederick H., et al. Bibliography of Canadian Urban History: Part V: Western Canada. (Public Adminstration Ser.: Bibliography P-542). 72p. 1980. pap. 7.50 (ISBN 0-88066-078-3). Vance Biblios.

Armstrong, Herbert. Tomorrow...What It Will Be Like. LC 79-54748. 1980. 7.95 o.p. (ISBN 0-89696-077-3, An Everest House Book). Dodd.

Armstrong, Herbert W. The Incredible Human Potential. LC 78-70513. 1979. 8.95 o.p. (ISBN 0-89696-056-0, An Everest House Book). Dodd.

--The Missing Dimension in Sex. 288p. 1981. 10.00 o.p. (ISBN 0-89696-128-1, An Everest House Book). Dodd.

--U. S. & Britain in Prophecy. LC 80-80799. 240p. 1980. 10.00 o.p. (ISBN 0-89696-102-8, An Everest House Book). Dodd.

--A Voice Cries Out Amid Religious Confusion. 216p. 1981. 10.00 o.p. (ISBN 0-89696-129-X, An Everest House Book). Dodd.

Armstrong, Isobel. Language as Living Form in Nineteenth Century Poetry. LC 82-6694. 234p. 1982. text ed. 27.50x (ISBN 0-389-20293-2). B&N Imports.

Armstrong, Isobel, ed. Writers & Their Background: Robert Browning. LC 72-96846. (Writers & Their Background Ser). xxvi, 365p. 1975. 18.00x (ISBN 0-8214-0131-9, 82-81347); pap. 7.50x (ISBN 0-8214-0132-7, 82-81354). Ohio U Pr.

Armstrong, J. D. Revolutionary Diplomacy: Chinese Foreign Policy & the United Front Doctrine. LC 76-14315. 259p. 1977. 32.00x (ISBN 0-520-03251-9); pap. 7.95x (ISBN 0-520-04273-5). U of Cal Pr.

Armstrong, J. Scott. Long-Range Forecasting: From Crystal Ball to Computer. LC 77-25176. 612p. 1978. 39.95x (ISBN 0-471-03002-3, Pub. by Wiley-Interscience). Wiley.

Armstrong, James W., jt. auth. see Sarafino, Edward P.

Armstrong, Joe E. & Harman, Willis W. Strategies for Conducting Technology Assessments. (Westview Special Studies in Science, Technology, & Public Policy). 130p. 1980. lib. bdg. 17.50 (ISBN 0-89158-672-5). Westview.

Armstrong, John. The Idea of Holiness & the Humane Response: A Study of the Concept of Holiness & Its Social Consequences. 177p. 1982. 16.95 (ISBN 0-04-294122-9). Allen Unwin.

Armstrong, John A. Ukrainian Nationalism. 2nd ed. LC 79-25529. 361p. 1980. Repr. of 1963 ed. 30.00 (ISBN 0-87287-193-2). Libs Unl.

Armstrong, John H. Tailor-Made Model Railroad Track Plans. Hayden, Bob, ed. (Illus., Orig.). 1983. pap. price not set (ISBN 0-89024-040-X). Kalmbach.

Armstrong, John M. & Ryner, Peter. Coastal Waters: A Management Analysis. LC 77-95236. 1978. 24.00 o.p. (ISBN 0-250-40238-6). Ann Arbor Science.

Armstrong, John M. & Ryner, Peter C. Ocean Management: A New Perspective. LC 81-66620. 206p. 1981. text ed. 22.50 (ISBN 0-250-40470-2). Ann Arbor Science.

Armstrong, L. The Home Front: Notes from the Family War Zone. 240p. 1983. 14.95 (ISBN 0-07-002276-3). McGraw.

Armstrong, L. & Guy, P. K. Metalcraft Today. 1975. pap. text ed. 5.00x o.p. (ISBN 0-435-75700-8). Heinemann Ed.

Armstrong, Lee H., jt. auth. see Pettofrezzo, Anthony J.

Armstrong, Lilian. The Paintings & Drawings of Marco Zoppo. LC 75-23779. (Outstanding Dissertations in the Fine Arts - 15th Century). (Illus.). 1976. lib. bdg. 60.50 o.s.i. (ISBN 0-8240-1976-8). Garland Pub.

--Renaissance Miniature Painters & Classical Imagery: The Master of the Putti & His Venetian Workshop. (Harvey Miller Publications). (Illus.). 1981. 55.00x (ISBN 0-19-921023-3). Oxford U Pr.

Armstrong, Lilias E. Phonetic & Tonal Structure of Kikuyu. (African Language & Lingustics Ser). 1967. 25.00x o.p. (ISBN 0-7129-0204-X). Intl Pubns Serv.

Armstrong, Louise. Arthur Gets What He Spills. LC 78-32029. (Let Me Read Ser.). (Illus.). (gr. 6-10). 1979. 4.95 (ISBN 0-15-204106-0, HJ); pap. 1.95 (ISBN 0-15-607945-3, VoyB). HarBraceJ.

--How to Turn Lemons into Money. LC 75-43785. (Illus.). (gr. 3-6). 1976. pap. 2.95 (ISBN 0-15-237251-2, VoyB). HarBraceJ.

--How to Turn Up into Down into Up: A Child's Guide to Inflation, Depression, & Economic Recovery. LC 77-13278. (Illus.). (gr. 3-6). 1978. 4.95 (ISBN 0-15-236838-8, HJ); pap. 1.95 (ISBN 0-15-642204-2, VoyB). HarBraceJ.

--How to Turn War into Peace: A Child's Guide to Conflict Resolution. LC 79-11797. (Let Me Read Ser.). (Illus.). (gr. 3-6). 1979. 4.95 (ISBN 0-15-236840-X, HJ); pap. 1.95 (ISBN 0-15-642206-9, VoyB). HarBraceJ.

Armstrong, Louise V. We Too Are the People. LC 74-168679. (FDR & the Era of the New Deal Ser.). 1972. Repr. of 1938 ed. lib. bdg. 55.00 (ISBN 0-306-70367-X). Da Capo.

Armstrong, Lynne. Christmas. LC 81-52496. (Starters Ser.). PLB 8.00 (ISBN 0-382-06486-0). Silver.

Armstrong, M., et al. McGraw-Hill Nursing Dictionary. 1979. thumb-indexed 19.95 (ISBN 0-07-045019-6, HP). McGraw.

--McGraw-Hill's Handbook of Clinical Nursing. (Illus.). 1979. 38.50 (ISBN 0-07-045020-X, HP). McGraw.

Armstrong, Mark A. Basic Topology. (Illus.). 1980. pap. text ed. 29.95 (ISBN 0-07-084090-3, C). McGraw.

Armstrong, Marsha F., jt. auth. see Cohen, Stanley N.

Armstrong, Matthew W. Twenty-One Songs for Jesus That Anyone Can Sing & Play, 2 Vols. 30p. (Orig.). 1982. Vol. I: Great & Marvelous. 6.95 (ISBN 0-941148-01-7); Vol. II: Angels are Singing in the Sun. 6.95 (ISBN 0-941148-03-3); Set. 12.95 (ISBN 0-941148-04-1). Altar Bks.

Armstrong, Michael. Closely Observed Children. 224p. 1980. pap. 7.45x (ISBN 0-906495-21-0, Pub. by Writers & Readers). Boynton Cook Pub.

Armstrong, Nancy M., jt. auth. see Wood, Jean.

Armstrong, Patricia M. Good Causes & Warm Corners. LC 76-24189. 1976. 5.50 (ISBN 0-911838-47-3). Windy Row.

--The Rain Bids Me Listen. 64p. 1980. 5.50 (ISBN 0-911838-55-4). Windy Row.

Armstrong, Peter. Critical Problems in Diagnostic Radiology. (Illus.). 304p. 1983. text ed. 35.00 (ISBN 0-397-50496-9, Lippincott Medical). Lippincott.

Armstrong, R. Personal Income Tax Practice Set: 1983 Edition. 1983. 6.50 (ISBN 0-07-002525-8, G); free avail. McGraw.

Armstrong, R. B., ed. see Regional Plan Association.

Armstrong, R. W. & Lewis, H. T., eds. Human Ecology: North Kohala Studies. (Social Science & Linguistics Institute Special Publications). (Illus.). 144p. 1972. pap. 6.00x (ISBN 0-8248-0247-0). UH Pr.

Armstrong, Regis J. & Brady, Ignatius C., eds. Francis & Clare: The Complete Works. (Classics of Western Spirituality Ser.). 1983. 11.95 (ISBN 0-8091-0330-3); pap. 7.95 (ISBN 0-8091-2446-7). Paulist Pr.

Armstrong, Richard. Four Californians: Christopher Georgesco, Patsy Krebs, Andrew Spence, Robert Therrien. LC 77-82831. (Illus.). 44p. 1977. pap. 3.50x (ISBN 0-934418-03-9). La Jolla Mus Contemp Art.

--Kim MacConnel: Collection Applied Design. 1976. 3.00x (ISBN 0-686-99808-1). La Jolla Mus Contemp Art.

--The Modern Chair: Its Origins & Evolution. LC 77-84973. (Illus.). 62p. 1977. pap. 7.00x (ISBN 0-934418-05-5). La Jolla Mus Contemp Art.

--Richard Anuszkiewicz. (Illus.). 28p. 1976. 2.00x (ISBN 0-686-99811-1). La Jolla Mus Contemp Art.

Armstrong, Richard S. Service Evangelism. LC 78-26701. 1979. pap. 6.95 (ISBN 0-664-24252-9). Westminster.

Armstrong, Robert. Dave Cowens. (Sports Superstars Ser.). (Illus.). (gr. 3-9). 1978. PLB 5.95 o.p. (ISBN 0-87191-668-1); pap. 3.25 (ISBN 0-89812-182-5). Creative Ed.

--Rick Barry. (Sports Superstars Ser.). (Illus.). (gr. 3-9). 1977. PLB 6.95 o.p. (ISBN 0-87191-539-1); pap. 3.25 (ISBN 0-89812-185-X). Creative Ed.

Armstrong, Robert P. Wellspring: On the Myth & Source of Culture. LC 73-85781. (Illus.). 100p. 1975. 24.50x (ISBN 0-520-02571-7). U of Cal Pr.

Armstrong, Roger. Wax & Casting: A Notebook of Process & Technique. (Illus.). 160p. 1983. pap. write for info. (ISBN 0-89863-038-X). Star Pub CA.

Armstrong, Roger, et al. Laboratory Chemistry: A Life Science Approach. (Illus.). 1980. pap. text ed. 11.95x (ISBN 0-02-303920-5). Macmillan.

Armstrong, Russell M. Modular Programming in COBOL. LC 73-4030. (Business Data Processing Ser.). 224p. 1973. 39.50x (ISBN 0-471-03325-1, Pub. by Wiley-Interscience). Wiley.

Armstrong, Sara, jt. auth. see Armstrong, E. F.

Armstrong, Scott, jt. auth. see Woodward, Bob.

Armstrong, Seth. Consumer Rights in Washington. 149p. 1978. 4.50 (ISBN 0-88908-707-5). Self Counsel Pr.

Armstrong, Thomas H. Dental Hygiene Examination Review. LC 78-21854. 1979. pap. text ed. 10.00x o.p. (ISBN 0-668-04283-4). Arco.

Armstrong, Thomas H. & Barnes, Caren M. Dental Hygiene Examination Review. LC 82-8760. (Illus.). 320p. 1982. pap. text ed. 12.00x (ISBN 0-668-05483-2, 5483). Arco.

Armstrong, Tillie. Joy Runs High. (Orig.). 1980. pap. 1.25 o.s.i. (ISBN 0-440-14273-3). Dell.

Armstrong, Tom & Field Enterprises. Marvin: A Star is Born. LC 82-40388. (Field Enterprises Ser.). (Illus.). 96p. 1982. 3.95 (ISBN 0-89480-237-2). Workman Pub.

Armstrong, Tom & Whitney Museum of American Art. Two Hundred Years of American Sculpture. LC 75-41717. (Illus.). 544p. (Orig.). 1980. pap. 12.50 (ISBN 0-87923-186-6). Godine.

Armstrong, Tom, jt. auth. see Lipman, Jean.

Armstrong, Virginia I., ed. I Have Spoken: American History Through the Voices of the Indians. LC 82-72684. xxii, 206p. 1971. 10.00 o.p. (ISBN 0-8040-0529-X); pap. 6.95 (ISBN 0-8040-0530-3, SB). Swallow.

Armstrong, Virginia W. Gone Away with the Winmills. 1977. 18.00 (ISBN 2-902704-01-1, Pub. by V W Armstrong Switzerland). A Robinson.

--Our Science Book. Bodle, Marie, tr. from Fr. (Illus.). 27p. (gr. 2-5). 1982. pap. 6.00x (ISBN 2-88089-001-2). A Robinson.

Armstrong, Virginia W. L. Guest of China: English-Chinese Phrases. (Illus.). 120p. 1982. pap. 10.00x (ISBN 2-88089-000-4). A Robinson.

Armstrong, Warren. True Book About Lighthouses & Light Ships. 12.75x (ISBN 0-392-09138-0, SpS). Sportshelf.

--True Book About Whaling. 12.75x (ISBN 0-392-14467-0, SpS). Sportshelf.

Armstrong, William. The Tale of Tawny & Dingo. LC 78-19486. (Illus.). 48p. (gr. 1-4). 1979. 7.95 o.p. (ISBN 0-06-020113-4, HarpJ); PLB 7.89 (ISBN 0-06-020114-2). Har-Row.

Armstrong, William H. The Education of Abraham Lincoln. 128p. (gr. 5-10). 1974. PLB 4.64 o.p. (ISBN 0-698-30525-6, Coward). Putnam Pub Group.

--Eighty-Seven Ways to Help Your Child in School: The Parents' Commonsense Guide to Sound Elementary Education. new ed. 1984. pap. text ed. 5.95 (ISBN 0-8120-2270-X). Barron.

--Sounder. 1969. pap. 2.95i (ISBN 0-06-080379-7, P379, PL). Har-Row.

--Study Tactics. 272p. (gr. 10-12). 1983. pap. text ed. 4.95 (ISBN 0-8120-2590-3). Barron.

--Study Tips: How to Study Effectively & Get Better Grades. (gr. 9-12). 1983. pap. text ed. 3.95 (ISBN 0-8120-2366-8). Barron.

--Through Troubled Waters: A Young Father's Struggles with Grief. 96p. (Orig.). 1983. pap. 2.50 (ISBN 0-687-41895-X, Festival). Abingdon.

--Word Power in Five Easy Lessons: A Self Help Workbook for Elementary School Pupils. rev. ed. LC 68-25868. (gr. 3-6). 1969. pap. text ed. 4.95 (ISBN 0-8120-0317-9). Barron.

Armstrong, William M., ed. The Gilded Age Letters of E. L. Godkin. LC 74-6462. (Illus.). 1974. 49.50x (ISBN 0-87395-246-4). State U NY Pr.

Arnall, Franklin M. The Padlock Collector. 3rd ed. LC 77-74542. (Illus.). 1977. pap. 3.95 o.p. (ISBN 0-914638-02-5). Arnall.

--The Padlock Collector. 4th ed. (Illus.). 140p. 1982. pap. 8.95 (ISBN 0-914638-03-3). Collector.

Arnall, L. & Keymer, I. F. Bird Diseases: An Introduction to the Study of Birds in Health & Disease. (Illus.). 1975. 34.95 (ISBN 0-87666-950-X, H-964). TFH Pubns.

Arnandez, Richard, tr. see Leclerc, Eloi.

Arnason, H. Horvard. History of Modern Art. 2nd ed. (Illus.). 1976. 26.95 (ISBN 0-13-390351-6). P-H.

Arnason, K. Quantity in Historical Phonology. LC 79-41363. (Cambridge Studies in Linguistics: No. 30). (Illus.). 256p. 1980. 47.50 (ISBN 0-521-23040-3). Cambridge U Pr.

Arnaud, Camille. Du Livret d'Ouvrier. (Conditions of the 19th Century French Working Class Ser.). 103p. (Fr.). 1974. Repr. of 1856 ed. lib. bdg. 36.00x o.p. (ISBN 0-8287-0036-2, 1096). Clearwater Pub.

Arnaud, Jean-Claude. L' Economie Maraichere et Fruitiere dans la Region du Cap-Vert, Grande Banlieue de Dakar. (Black Africa Ser.). 298p. (Fr.). 1974. Repr. of 1970 ed. lib. bdg. 79.00x o.p. (ISBN 0-8287-0037-0, 71-2019). Clearwater Pub.

Arnaudet, Martin L. & Barrett, Mary E. Paragraph Development: A Guide for Students of English As a Second Language. (ESL Ser.). (Illus.). 160p. 1981. pap. text ed. 9.95 (ISBN 0-13-648618-5). P-H.

Arnauld, A., jt. auth. see Lancelot, G.

Arnberger, Leslie P. Flowers of the Southwest Mountains. rev. ed. Priehs, T. J., ed. LC 81-86380. 1983. pap. write for info. (ISBN 0-911408-61-4). SW Pks Mnmts.

Arndt, Elise. A Mother's Touch. 156p. 1983. pap. 4.95 (ISBN 0-88207-101-7). Victor Bks.

Arndt, Karl J. & Olson, May. German Language Press of the Americas, 3 vols. 1980. Set. text ed. 321.00x (ISBN 0-686-77582-1, Pub. by K G Saur). Gale.

Arndt, R. E., jt. ed. see Billet, M. L.

Arndt, Rolf D., et al. Clinical Arthrography. (Illus.). 223p. 1981. 33.00 (ISBN 0-686-77736-0, 0253-8). Williams & Wilkins.

Arndt, Sven W., ed. Political Economy of Austria. 1982. 16.95 (ISBN 0-8447-2241-3); pap. 8.95 (ISBN 0-8447-2240-5). Am Enterprise.

Arndt, Thomas. Encyclopedia of Conures: The Aratingas. (Illus.). 176p. 1982. 29.95 (ISBN 0-87666-873-2, H-1042). TFH Pubns.

Arndt, U. W. & Wonacott, A. J. The Rotation Method in Crystallography. 1977. 70.25 (ISBN 0-7204-0594-7, North-Holland). Elsevier.

Arndt, Walter, ed. see Busch, William.

Arndt, Walter, tr. see Goethe, Johann W. Von.

Arndt, Walter, tr. see Pushkin, Alexander.

Arndt, William. Fundamental Christian Beliefs. pap. text ed. 3.25 (ISBN 0-570-06324-8, 22-1144); pap. 3.75 guide (ISBN 0-570-06325-6, 22-1146); pap. tests 1.25 (ISBN 0-570-06362-0, 22-1145). Concordia.

Arndt, William F. Bible Difficulties. 1981. 4.25 (ISBN 0-570-03120-6, 12-2357). Concordia.

Arndt, William F., tr. see Bauer, Walter, et al.

Arnebeck, Bob. Proust's Last Beer: A History of Curious Demises. 160p. (Orig.). 1980. pap. 8.95 o.p. (ISBN 0-14-005022-1). Penguin.

Arnell & Groucutt. Music for TV & Films. (Illus.). 1983. 31.95x (ISBN 0-240-51196-4). Focal Pr.

Arnell, Peter & Bickford, Ted, eds. James Stirling. LC 82-50500. (Illus.). 320p. 1983. 45.00 (ISBN 0-8478-0448-8); pap. 29.95 (ISBN 0-8478-0449-6). Rizzoli Intl.

--Southwest Center: The Houston Competition. (Illus.). 120p. 1983. pap. 12.50 (ISBN 0-8478-0488-7). Rizzoli Intl.

Arnell, Peter, jt. ed. see Wheeler, Karen.

Arner, Douglas G. Perception, Reason, & Knowledge: An Introduction to Epistemology. 1972. pap. 8.95x (ISBN 0-673-05897-2). Scott F.

Arneson, Ben A. The Democratic Monarchies of Scandinavia. LC 74-4728. (Illus.). 294p. 1975. Repr. of 1949 ed. lib. bdg. 20.50x (ISBN 0-8371-7485-6, ARDM). Greenwood.

Arneson, D. J. Friend Indeed. LC 80-23062. (gr. 4 up). 1981. PLB 7.90 (ISBN 0-531-04257-X). Watts.

--The Official Computer Hater's Handbook. (Orig.). 1983. pap. price not set (ISBN 0-440-56619-3, Dell Trade Pbks). Dell.

--Sometimes in the Dead of Night. Schneider, Meg, ed. (Chiller Ser.). (gr. 3-7). 1983. pap. 3.95 (ISBN 0-671-45593-1). Wanderer Bks.

--Sometimes in the Dead of Night... (Chiller Ser.). 128p. (gr. 8-12). 1983. PLB 8.79 (ISBN 0-671-46782-4). Messner.

Arnett. Ancient Greek Theatre. write for info. (ISBN 0-685-84261-4). Phila Bk Co.

Arnett, Harold E. Proposed Funds Statements for Managers & Investors. 137p. pap. 12.95 (ISBN 0-86641-019-8, 79114). Natl Assn Accts.

Arnett, Mary E., jt. ed. see Arnett, Ross H., Jr.

Arnett, Ross H., Jr. Bibliography of Coleoptera of North America North of Mexico. 184p. 1978. pap. 17.50x (ISBN 0-916846-07-5). Flora & Fauna.

--Directory of Coleoptera, Collections of North America: Canada Throuth Panama. 122p. 1969. 6.95x (ISBN 0-916846-05-9). Flora & Fauna.

--Entomological Information Storage & Retrieral. 210p. 1970. 7.95x (ISBN 0-916846-00-8). Flora & Fauna.

Arnett, Ross H., Jr. & Arnett, Mary E., eds. The Naturalists' Directory of Insect Collectors & Identifiers, International, Pt. I. 44th ed. (The Naturalists' Directory (International) Ser.). 96p. (Orig.). 1983. pap. 9.95x (ISBN 0-916846-15-6). Flora & Fauna.

--The Naturalists' Directory of Plant Collectors & Identifiers, International, Pt. II. 4th ed. (Naturalists' Directory (International) Ser.). 96p. (Orig.). 1983. pap. 9.95x (ISBN 0-916846-16-4). Flora & Fauna.

Arnett, W. David, jt. ed. see Schramm, David N.

Arnett, Willard E. George Santayana. (World Leaders Ser). lib. bdg. 9.95 o.p. (ISBN 0-8057-3718-9, Twayne). G K Hall.

Arnett, William S. The Predynastic Origin of Egyptian Hieroglyphs: Evidence for the Development of Rudimentary Forms of Hieroglyphs in Upper Egypt in the Fourth Millennium B.C. LC 82-17562. (Illus.). 176p. (Orig.). 1983. lib. bdg. 19.00 (ISBN 0-8191-2775-2); pap. text ed. 8.25 (ISBN 0-8191-2776-0). U Pr of Amer.

Arney, William R. Power & the Profession of Obstetrics. LC 82-8410. (Illus.). 280p. 1983. lib. bdg. 25.00x (ISBN 0-226-02728-7). U of Chicago Pr.

Arnez, John A. Slovenian Lands & Their Economies, 1848-1873. (Studia Slovenica Ser.: No. 15). 321p. 1983. soft cover 16.00 (ISBN 0-686-38857-7). Studia Slovena.

Arnez, Nancy L. The Besieged School Superintendent: A Case Study of School Superintendent-School Board Relations in Washington, D. C. 1973-75. LC 80-69044. (Illus.). 815p. (Orig.). 1981. lib. bdg. 31.75 (ISBN 0-8191-1634-3); pap. text ed. 23.75 (ISBN 0-8191-1635-1). U Pr of Amer.

Arnez, Nancy Levi. Moll Flanders Notes. (Orig.). 1969. pap. text ed. 2.75 (ISBN 0-8220-0854-8). Cliffs.

Arnheim, Daniel D. & Klafs, Carl E. Athletic Training: A Study & Laboratory Guide. LC 78-145. 1978. pap. text ed. 11.50 o.p. (ISBN 0-8016-0329-3). Mosby.

Arnheim, Daniel D. & Sinclair, William A. The Clumsy Child: A Program of Motor Therapy. 2nd ed. LC 78-2. (Illus.). 1979. pap. 15.95 (ISBN 0-8016-0310-2). Mosby.

Arnheim, Daniel D., jt. auth. see Klafs, Carl E.

Arnheim, Rudolf. Entropy & Art: An Essay on Disorder & Order. LC 71-128585. (Illus.). 1971. 10.95x (ISBN 0-520-01803-6); pap. 4.95 (ISBN 0-520-02617-9). U of Cal Pr.

--The Genesis of a Painting: Picasso's Guernica. (Illus.). 1980. 34.50x (ISBN 0-520-00037-4); pap. 10.95 (ISBN 0-520-04266-2, CAL465). U of Cal Pr.

--Radio: The Psychology of an Art of Sound. LC 73-164504. (Cinema Ser). 1972. Repr. of 1936 ed. lib. bdg. 32.50 (ISBN 0-306-70291-6). Da Capo.

--Toward a Psychology of Art: Collected Essays. LC 66-10692. 1966. 27.50x (ISBN 0-520-00038-2); pap. 5.95 (ISBN 0-520-02161-4, CAL242). U of Cal Pr.

--Visual Thinking. LC 71-76335. (Illus.). 1980. 22.50x (ISBN 0-520-01378-6); pap. 7.95 (ISBN 0-520-01871-0, CAL227). U of Cal Pr.

Arnikar, Hari J. Essentials of Nuclear Chemistry. LC 81-6818. 335p. 1982. 17.95x (ISBN 0-470-27176-0). Halsted Pr.

Arno, Peter. Peter Arno. LC 79-19540. (Illus.). 1979. 10.95 o.p. (ISBN 0-396-07772-2). Dodd.

Arnold. Lectures & Essays in Criticism. Super, R. H., ed. 1980. 19.95 (ISBN 0-472-11653-3). U of Mich Pr.

Arnold & Burton. A Field Guide to Reptiles & Amphibians of Britain & Europe. 29.95 (ISBN 0-686-42777-7, Collins Pub England). Greene.

Arnold & Luke. Riders of the Range. 8.95 (ISBN 0-392-09348-0, SpS). Sportshelf.

Arnold, jt. auth. see Crowther, Patricia.

Arnold, A. Pearls of the Faith. pap. 2.75 (ISBN 0-686-18468-8). Kazi Pubns.

Arnold, Alvin, et al. Modern Real Estate. LC 79-67657. 570p. 1980. text ed. 19.75 (ISBN 0-88262-389-3). Wiley.

Arnold, Alvin L. & Smith, Owen T. Modern Ownership & Investment Forms. 2nd. ed. 1976. 56.00 (ISBN 0-88262-026-6). Warren.

Arnold, Alvin L. & Wurtzebach, Charles H. Modern Real Estate. LC 79-67657. 570p. 1982. text ed. 27.50 o.p. (ISBN 0-471-87751-4); write for info. tchrs.' manual o.p. (ISBN 0-471-89516-4). Warren.

Arnold, Annemarie, jt. auth. see Arnold, Heini.

Arnold, Anthony. Afghanistan's Two-Party Communism: Parcham & Khalq. (Publication Ser.: No. 279). 260p. 1983. pap. 10.95 (ISBN 0-8179-7792-9). Hoover Inst Pr.

Arnold, Armin. Casar Von Arx: Briefe An Den Vater. 182p. (Ger.). 1982. write for info. (ISBN 3-261-05000-4). P Lang Pubs.

--Friedrich Durrenmatt. LC 78-178169. (Literature and Life Ser.). 128p. 1972. 11.95 (ISBN 0-8044-2000-9). Ungar.

Arnold, Arnold. The Crowell Book of Arts & Crafts for Children. LC 75-2333. (Illus.). 356p. (YA) 1975. 12.45i (ISBN 0-690-00567-9). T Y Crowell.

Arnold, Bruce. Orpen: Mirror to an Age. (Illus.). 448p. 1982. 49.95 (ISBN 0-224-01581-8, Pub. by Chatto-Bodley-Jonathan). Merrimack Bk Serv.

--Running to Paradise. 320p. 1983. 16.95 (ISBN 0-241-10998-1, Pub. by Hamish Hamilton England). David & Charles.

Arnold, C. J. The Anglo-Saxon Cemeteries of the Isle of Wight. 208p. 1982. 99.00x (ISBN 0-7141-1359-X, Pub. by Brit Mus Pubns England). State Mutual Bk.

Arnold, C. P., jt. auth. see Arrillaga, J.

Arnold, Caroline. Animals that Migrate. LC 82-1253. (On My Own Bks.). (Illus.). 56p. (gr. 1-4). 1982. lib. bdg. 6.95g (ISBN 0-87614-194-7). Carolrhoda Bks.

--Electric Fish. LC 80-12479. (Illus.). 64p. (gr. 4-6). 1980. 8.75 (ISBN 0-688-22237-4); PLB 8.40 (ISBN 0-688-32237-9). Morrow.

--How Do We Communicate? (Easy-Read Community Bks.). (Illus.). 32p. (gr. k-3). 1983. PLB 7.90 (ISBN 0-531-04505-6). Watts.

--How Do We Have Fun? (Easy-Read Community Bks.). (Illus.). 32p. (gr. k-3). 1983. PLB 7.90 (ISBN 0-531-04506-4). Watts.

--How Do We Travel? (Easy-Read Community Bks.). (Illus.). 32p. (gr. k-3). 1983. PLB 7.90 (ISBN 0-531-04507-2). Watts.

--Sex Hormones: Why Males & Females Are Different. LC 81-38388. (Illus.). 128p. (gr. 7-9). 1981. 8.95 (ISBN 0-688-00696-5); PLB 8.59 (ISBN 0-688-00697-3). Morrow.

--What Will We Buy? (Easy-Read Community Bks.). (Illus.). 32p. (gr. k-3). 1983. PLB 7.90 (ISBN 0-531-04508-0). Watts.

--Why Do We Have Rules? (Easy-Read Community Bks.). (Illus.). 32p. (gr. k-3). 1983. PLB 7.90 (ISBN 0-531-04509-9). Watts.

Arnold, Carroll C., et al. Speaker's Resource Book. rev. ed. 1966. pap. 9.95x (ISBN 0-673-05718-6). Scott F.

Arnold, Danny R., et al. Strategic Retail Management. LC 82-8852. 752p. Date not set. text ed. 23.95 (ISBN 0-686-82088-6); instrs' manual avail. A-W.

Arnold, David O., ed. Subcultures. 171p. 1970. pap. cancelled (ISBN 0-87835-100-0). Boyd & Fraser.

Arnold, Dean, jt. auth. see Neuenswander, Helen.

Arnold, Denis. Monteverdi Church Music. LC 81-71298. (BBC Music Guides Ser.). 64p. (Orig.). 1983. pap. 4.95 (ISBN 0-295-95923-1). U of Wash Pr.

Arnold, Denis, ed. see Lassus, Orlandus.

Arnold, Denis V. The Management of the Information Department. 144p. 1976. 20.00 (ISBN 0-233-96652-8, 05767-3, Pub. by Gower Pub Co England). Lexington Bks.

Arnold, Dieter. The Temple of Mentuhotep at Dier El Bahari. (Publications of the Metropolitan Museum of Art Egyptian Expedition: Vol. XXI). (Illus.). 1979. 60.00 (ISBN 0-87099-163-9). Metro Mus Art.

Arnold, Don E. Legal Considerations in the Administration of Public School Physical Education & Athletic Programs. 392p. 1982. 28.50x (ISBN 0-398-04518-6). C C Thomas.

Arnold, Douglas M., ed. see Franklin, Benjamin.

Arnold, Dovie & Posey, Kayte Lee. Do It Yourself. 1971. pap. 2.25x (ISBN 0-88323-007-0, 187). Richards Pub.

Arnold, Duane W. & Fry, C. George. The Way, the Truth, & the Life: An Introduction to Lutheran Christianity. (Illus.). 204p. (Orig.). 1982. pap. 9.95 (ISBN 0-8010-0189-7). Baker Bk.

Arnold, Eberhard. Eberhard Arnold: A Testimony to the Church Community from His Life & Writings. 2nd ed. LC 73-11605. 107p. 1973. 3.95 (ISBN 0-87486-112-8). Plough.

--History of the Baptizer Movement in Reformation Times. 1970. pap. 1.25 o.p. (ISBN 0-87486-108-X). Plough.

--Salt & Light: Talks & Writings on the Sermon on the Mount. LC 67-18009. 1967. 7.95 (ISBN 0-87486-105-5). Plough.

--Why We Live in Community. 1976. pap. 1.50 (ISBN 0-87486-168-3). Plough.

Arnold, Eberhard, et al. The Heavens Are Opened. LC 73-20715. (Illus.). 190p. 1974. 7.95 (ISBN 0-87486-113-6). Plough.

Arnold, Eddie & Stocks, Broan. Men's Gymnastics. (EP Sport Ser.). (Illus.). 1979. 12.95 (ISBN 0-7158-0602-5, Pub. by EP Publishing England); pap. 6.95 (ISBN 0-7158-0668-8). Sterling.

Arnold, Edmund C. Editing the Organizational Publication. LC 82-60043. (Communications Library). 283p. (Orig.). 1982. pap. 25.00 (ISBN 0-931368-09-X); pap. text ed. 18.75 (ISBN 0-686-82102-5). Ragan Comm.

--Modern Newspaper Design. LC 69-15294. (Illus.). 1969. 13.95i (ISBN 0-06-030241-0, HarpT). Har-Row.

Arnold, Edwin. The Light of Asia or, the Great Renunciation (Mahabhinishkramana) Being the Life & Teaching of Gautama, Prince of India, Founder of Buddhism. x, 176p. 1972. pap. 5.00 (ISBN 0-7100-7006-3). Routledge & Kegan.

Arnold, Edwin, tr. The Song Celestial or Bhaggvad-Gita: From the Mahabharata, Being a Discourse Between Arjuna, Prince of India, & the Supreme Being Under the Form of Krishna. 1967. pap. 5.00 (ISBN 0-7100-6268-0). Routledge & Kegan.

Arnold, Elliot. The Commandos. 304p. 1982. pap. 2.75 o.p. (ISBN 0-505-51859-7). Tower Bks.

Arnold, Emmy. Torches Together: The Beginning & Early Years of the Bruderhof Communities. LC 63-23426. 1971. 8.95 o.p. (ISBN 0-87486-109-8). Plough.

Arnold, Emmy, ed. Inner Words for Every Day of the Year. LC 77-164915. 1963. 3.50 (ISBN 0-87486-101-2). Plough.

Arnold, Emmy. Ein Inneres Wort Fur Jeden Tag Des Jahres. LC 76-10987. 192p. 1976. 3.50 (ISBN 0-87486-166-7). Plough.

Arnold, Eric A. Fouche, Napoleon, & the General Police. LC 79-62894. 1979. pap. text ed. 10.50 (ISBN 0-8191-0716-6). U Pr of Amer.

Arnold, F. C. Gesammelte Lichenologische Schriften. Incl. Vol. 3. Lichenologische Ausfluege in Tirol, 30 pts. & register. 80.00 (ISBN 3-7682-0707-2). 1971. Lubrecht & Cramer.

Arnold, Francena. Road Winds On. (Giant Ser). 1970. pap. 3.95 (ISBN 0-8024-0066-3). Moody.

Arnold, Francena H. Brother Beloved. 1967. pap. 3.95 (ISBN 0-8024-0050-7). Moody.

--Straight Down a Crooked Lane. (gr. 9-12). 1959. pap. 3.95 (ISBN 0-8024-0041-8). Moody.

--Then Am I Strong. 1969. pap. 3.95 (ISBN 0-8024-0060-4). Moody.

--Three Shall Be One. (Orig.). (gr. 9-12). 1966. pap. 3.95 (ISBN 0-8024-0085-X). Moody.

Arnold, Fred, et al. The Value of Children: A Cross-National Study. Incl. Vol. 1. Introduction & Comparative Analysis. Arnold, Fred, et al. 120p. pap. 2.75x (ISBN 0-8248-0383-3); Vol. 2. Philippines. Bulatao, Rodolfo A. 230p. pap. 3.00x (ISBN 0-8248-0384-1); Vol. 3. Hawaii. Arnold, Fred & Fawcett, James T. 160p. pap. 3.00x (ISBN 0-8248-0382-5). 1975. pap. (Eastwest Ctr). UH Pr.

Arnold, G. W. & Dudzinski, M. L. Ethology of Free Ranging Domestic Animals. (Developments in Animal & Veterinary Sciences Ser.: Vol. 2). 1979. 53.25 (ISBN 0-444-41700-1). Elsevier.

Arnold, Grant. Creative Lithography & How to Do It. (Illus.). 1941. pap. 4.50 (ISBN 0-486-21208-4). Dover.

Arnold, Guy & Weiss, Ruth. Strategic Highways of Africa. LC 76-53953. (Illus.). 1977. 20.00 (ISBN 0-312-76431-6). St Martin.

Arnold, Harry L. Poisonous Plants of Hawaii. LC 68-15017. (Illus.). (gr. 9 up). 1968. 5.95 (ISBN 0-8048-0474-5). C E Tuttle.

Arnold, Harry L., Jr., jt. auth. see Domonkos, Anthony N.

Arnold, Heini. Freedom from Sinful Thoughts: Christ Alone Breaks the Curse. LC 73-20199. 130p. 1973. 3.50 (ISBN 0-87486-115-2). Plough.

Arnold, Heini & Arnold, Annemarie. Living in Community: A Way to True Brotherhood. 26p. 1974. pap. 1.50 (ISBN 0-87486-121-7). Plough.

Arnold, Henri & Lee, Bob. Jumble--That Scrambled Word Game, No. 20. 1981. pap. 1.95 (ISBN 0-451-12319-0, AJ2319, Sig). NAL.

--Jumble--That Scrambled Word Game, No. 11. (Orig.). 1977. pap. 1.50 (ISBN 0-451-11588-0, AW1588, Sig). NAL.

--Jumble--That Scrambled Word Game, No. 12. (Orig.). 1978. pap. 1.75 (ISBN 0-451-11226-1, AE1226, Sig). NAL.

--Jumble--That Scrambled Word Game, No.10. (Orig.). 1976. pap. 1.75 (ISBN 0-451-11683-6, AE1683, Sig). NAL.

--Jumble: That Scrambled Word Game, No.4. (Orig.). 1970. pap. 1.25 o.p. (ISBN 0-451-08377-6, Y8377, Sig). NAL.

--Jumble: That Scrambled Word Game, No. 15. (Orig.). 1980. pap. 1.50 (ISBN 0-451-09831-5, W9831, Sig). NAL.

--Jumble: That Scrambled Word Game, No. 16. 128p. (Orig.). 1980. pap. 1.75 (ISBN 0-451-11331-4, AE1331, Sig). NAL.

--Jumble: That Scrambled Word Game, No. 17. (Orig.). 1980. pap. 1.75 (ISBN 0-451-11333-0, AE1333, Sig). NAL.

--Jumble: That Scrambled Word Game, No. 21. (Orig.). 1982. pap. 1.75write for info. (ISBN 0-451-11284-9, AE1284, Sig). NAL.

--Jumble: That Scrambled Word Game, No. 19. (Orig.). 1981. pap. 1.95 (ISBN 0-451-12170-8, AJ2170, Sig). NAL.

--Jumble: That Scrambled Word Game, No. 7. (Orig.). 1973. pap. 1.25 o.p. (ISBN 0-451-08498-5, Y8498, Sig). NAL.

--Jumble: That Scrambled Word Game, No. 9. (Orig.). 1975. pap. 1.25 o.p. (ISBN 0-451-08484-5, Y8484, Sig). NAL.

Arnold, Henri & Lee, Bob, eds. Jumble: That Scrambled Word Game, No. 1. (Orig.). 1967. pap. 0.95 o.p. (ISBN 0-451-08186-2, Q8186, Sig). NAL.

--Jumble: That Scrambled Word Game, No. 3. (Orig.). pap. 1.25 o.p. (ISBN 0-451-08728-3, Y8728, Sig). NAL.

--Jumble: That Scrambled Word Game, No. 5. (Orig.). 1971. pap. 1.25 o.p. (ISBN 0-451-08376-8, Y8376, Sig). NAL.

--Jumble: That Scrambled Word Game, No. 8. (Orig.). 1974. pap. 1.25 o.p. (ISBN 0-451-08785-2, Y8785, Sig). NAL.

Arnold, Henry F. Trees in Urban Design. 256p. 1982. pap. 14.95 (ISBN 0-442-20340-3). Van Nos Reinhold.

Arnold, Hugh J., jt. auth. see Feldman, Daniel.

Arnold, Ign F. Gallerie der beruhmtesten Tonkunstler des Eighteen und Nineteen Jahrhunderts: Biographien, Anekdoten, und Darstellung ihrer Werke. (Facsimiles of Early Biographies Ser.: Vol. 7). 1981. Repr. of 1810 ed. 70.00 o.s.i. (ISBN 90-6027-140-8, Pub. by Frits Knuf Netherlands). Pendragon NY.

Arnold, Janet. A Handbook of Costume. (Illus.). 336p. (Orig.). 1980. pap. text ed. 14.95x (ISBN 0-87599-231-5). S G Phillips.

Arnold, John. Shooting the Executive Rapids: The First Year in a New Assignment. Newton, William R., ed. (Illus.). 288p. 1981. 19.95 (ISBN 0-07-002312-3, P&RB). McGraw.

Arnold, John & Harmer, Jeremy. Advanced Speaking Skills. (English As a Second Language Bk.). 1978. pap. text ed. 6.95x (ISBN 0-582-51510-6). Longman.

--Advanced Writing Skills. (English As a Second Language Bk.). 1978. pap. text ed. 6.95x (ISBN 0-582-55481-0). Longman.

Arnold, John, jt. auth. see Waterson, D. B.

Arnold, Joseph & Schank, Kenneth, eds. Exploratory Electricity. (gr. 9-12). 1960. text ed. 5.28 o.p. (ISBN 0-87345-276-3). McKnight.

Arnold, Judith M., jt. auth. see Jacob, Diane B.

Arnold, Katrin. Anna Joins in. 28p. Date not set. text ed. 9.95 (ISBN 0-687-01530-8). Abingdon.

Arnold, Kenneth J., jt. auth. see Beck, James V.

Arnold, L. E. & Cinningham, Lavern L., eds. Preventing Adolescent Alienation: An Interprofessional Approach. LC 82-48532. 160p. 1983. 19.95 (ISBN 0-669-06269-3). Lexington Bks.

Arnold, Lee E., Jr. Commercial-Investment Real Estate: Marketing & Management. Gerth, Dawn M., ed. LC 82-62949. (Illus.). 250p. text ed. 19.95 (ISBN 0-913652-53-9, BK 161). Realtors Natl.

Arnold, Lloyd. Hemingway: High on the Wild. (Illus.). 1977. 5.95 (ISBN 0-448-14290-2, G&D). Putnam Pub Group.

Arnold, Lloyd R. Hemingway: High on the Wild. (Illus.). 176p. 1982. 9.95 (ISBN 0-448-12334-7, G&D). Putnam Pub Group.

Arnold, Lorna, jt. auth. see Gowing, Margaret.

Arnold, Ludwig. Stochastic Differential Equations: Theory & Applications. LC 73-22256. 228p. 1974. 39.95x (ISBN 0-471-03359-6, Pub. by Wiley-Interscience). Wiley.

Arnold, M. H. Agricultural Research for Development. 368p. 1976. 60.00 (ISBN 0-521-21051-8). Cambridge U Pr.

Arnold, Margot. Affairs of State. 352p. 1983. pap. 3.50 (ISBN 0-449-12384-7, GM). Fawcett.

--Zadok's Treasure. LC 80-80980. 192p. (Orig.). 1980. pap. 2.50 (ISBN 0-86721-228-4). Playboy Pbks.

Arnold, Mark, jt. ed. see Windling, Terry.

Arnold, Mark A., jt. auth. see Windling, Terri.

Arnold, Matthew. Arnold: Selected Poems. Brown, E. K., ed. LC 51-6752. (Crofts Classics Ser.). 1951. pap. text ed. 3.75x (ISBN 0-88295-007-X). Harlan Davidson.

--Culture & Anarchy. 1932. 39.95 (ISBN 0-521-04061-2); pap. 8.95 (ISBN 0-521-09103-9). Cambridge U Pr.

--Poetical Works. Tinker, C. B. & Lowry, H. F., eds. (Standard Authors Ser). 1950. 29.95 (ISBN 0-19-254110-2). Oxford U Pr.

--Poetry & Criticism of Matthew Arnold. Culler, A. D., ed. LC 61-19991. (YA) (gr. 9 up). 1961. pap. 5.75 (ISBN 0-395-05152-5, B55, RivEd, 3-47689). HM.

--The Portable Matthew Arnold. Trilling, Lionel, ed. (Viking Portable Library). 1980. pap. 6.95 (ISBN 0-14-015045-5). Penguin.

Arnold, Mildred. Taking a Look at my Faith. 80p. 1982. pap. 5.95 (ISBN 0-8170-0966-3). Judson.

Arnold, Peter & Pendagast, Edward, Jr. Emergency Handbook: A First Aid Manual for Home & Travel. (Medical Library). 272p. 1982. pap. 5.95 (ISBN 0-452-25372-1). Mosby.

Arnold, Peter & Pendagast, Edward L. Emergency Handbook: A First Aid Manual for Home & Travel. 1981. pap. 6.95 (ISBN 0-452-25372-1, Z5372, Plume). NAL.

Arnold, Peter, jt. auth. see Germann, Richard.

Arnold, Richard. Better Roller Skating. LC 76-51164. (Illus.). 96p. 1980. pap. 4.95 o.p. (ISBN 0-8069-8902-5). Sterling.

--Better Roller Skating: The Key to Improved Performance. (Illus.). (gr. 7 up). 1977. 8.95 (ISBN 0-8069-4106-5); PLB 10.99 (ISBN 0-8069-4107-3). Sterling.

--Come Sea Fishing with Me. 10.50x (ISBN 0-392-06448-0, SpS). Sportshelf.

Arnold, Richard, jt. auth. see Lamb, Pose.

Arnold, Robert E. What to Do About Bites & Stings of Venomous Animals. 128p. 1973. 9.95 o.s.i. (ISBN 0-02-503250-X). Macmillan.

Arnold, Robert R., et al. Modern Data Processing. 3rd ed. LC 77-14941. 435p. 1978. 25.95x (ISBN 0-471-03361-8); wkbk. 11.95 (ISBN 0-471-03362-6); avail. tchrs. manual (ISBN 0-471-03405-3). Wiley.

Arnold, Ron. At the Eye of the Storm: James Watt. LC 82-60660. 312p. 1982. 14.95 (ISBN 0-89526-634-2). Regnery Gateway.

Arnold, Steven F. The Theory of Linear Models & Multivariate Analysis. LC 80-23017. (Probability & Math Statistics Ser.). 475p. 1981. 39.95x (ISBN 0-471-05065-2). Wiley.

Arnold, Steven H. Implementing Development Assistance European Approaches to Basic Needs. (Replica Edition Ser.). (Illus.). 190p. 1982. lib. bdg. 20.00 (ISBN 0-86531-904-9). Westview.

Arnold, Sue. Little Princes: From Cradle to Crown. (Illus.). 208p. 1983. 15.95 (ISBN 0-283-98598-4, Pub by Sidgwick & Jackson). Merrimack Bk Serv.

Arnold, Thurman W. The Bottlenecks of Business. LC 72-2363. (FDR & the Era of the New Deal Ser.). 352p. 1973. Repr. of 1940 ed. lib. bdg. 42.50 (ISBN 0-306-70470-6). Da Capo.

Arnold, Ulli. Strategische Beschaffungspolitik. 311p. (Ger.). 1982. write for info. (ISBN 3-8204-5842-5). P Lang Pubs.

Arnold, V. I. Geometrical Methods in the Theory of Ordinary Differential Equations. (Grundlehren der Mathematischen Wissenschaften: Vol. 250). (Illus.). 384p. 1983. 36.00 (ISBN 0-387-90681-9). Springer-Verlag.
--Singularity Theory. LC 81-6091. (London Mathematical Society Lecture Notes Ser.: No. 53). (Illus.). 280p. 1981. pap. 29.95 (ISBN 0-521-28511-9). Cambridge U Pr.
Arnold, Victor L., ed. Alternatives to Confrontation: National Policy Toward Regional Change. LC 79-2374. 400p. 1980. 34.95x (ISBN 0-669-03165-8). Lexington Bks.
Arnold, Walter M. see Brooking, Walter J.
Arnold, Wesley F. & Cardy, Wayne C. Fun with Next to Nothing: Handicraft Projects for Boys & Girls. LC 62-8039. (Illus.). (gr. 2-6). 1962. PLB 10.89 (ISBN 0-06-020146-0, HarpJ). Har-Row.
Arnold, William. Shadowland. 1979. pap. 2.25 o.s.i. (ISBN 0-515-05124-1). Jove Pubns.
Arnold, William & Brungardt, Terrence. Juvenile Misconduct & Delinquency. LC 82-82284. 512p. 1983. pap. text ed. 16.95 (ISBN 0-395-32562-5); instrs.' manual avail. (ISBN 0-395-32563-3). HM.
Arnold, William E. Crisis Communication. (Illus.). 90p. (Orig.). 1980. pap. text ed. 6.95 (ISBN 0-89787-302-5). Gorsuch Scarisbrick.
Arnold, William R. Juveniles on Parole: A Sociological Perspective. 1970. text ed. 6.95 (ISBN 0-394-30001-7). Phila Bk Co.
Arnold, William V., et al. Divorce: Prevention or Survival. LC 77-22066. 1977. pap. 5.95 (ISBN 0-664-24142-5). Westminster.
Arnold-Foster, Mark. World at War. (RL 8). 1974. pap. 3.50 (ISBN 0-451-11294-6, AE1294, Sig). NAL.
Arnoldi, Mary Jo, jt. auth. see Anderson, Martha G.
Arnolds, Eef. Ecology & Coenology of Macrofungi in Grasslands & Moist Heathlands in Drenthe, the Netherlands: Pt. 1: Introduction & Synecology. (Bibliotheca Mycologica: Vol. 83). (Illus.). 410p. 1981. text ed. 48.00x (ISBN 3-7682-1314-5). Lubrecht & Cramer.
--Ecology & Coenology of Macrofungi in Grasslands & Moist Heathlands in Drenthe, the Netherlands. (Illus.). 510p. (Orig.). 1982. Pt. 2. lib. bdg. 80.00x; Pt. 3 Taxonomy. lib. bdg. 90.00 (ISBN 3-7682-1346-3). Lubrecht & Cramer.
Arnon, I. Modernization of Agriculture in Developing Countries: Resources, Potentials & Problems. LC 80-41588. (Environmental Monographs & Symposia: A Series in Environmental Science). 592p. 1981. 78.95x (ISBN 0-471-27928-5, Pub. by Wiley-Interscience). Wiley.
Arnon, Isaac. Organisation & Administration of Agricultural Research. 1968. 39.00 (ISBN 0-444-20028-2, Pub. by Applied Sci England). Elsevier.
Arnon-Ohanna, Yuval, jt. auth. see Yodfat, Aryeh.
Arnopoulos, Sheila M. Voices from French Ontario. 216p. 1982. 17.50 (ISBN 0-7735-0405-2); pap. 6.95 (ISBN 0-7735-0406-0). McGill-Queens U Pr.
Arnopoulos, Sheila M. & Clift, Dominique. The English Fact in Quebec. 255p. 1980. 17.95 o.p. (ISBN 0-7735-0358-7); pap. 10.95 (ISBN 0-7735-0359-5). McGill-Queens U Pr.
Arnosky, Jim. Drawing from Nature. LC 82-15327. (Illus.). 64p. (gr. 5 up). 1982. 10.00 (ISBN 0-688-01295-7). Lothrop.
--Drawing from Nature. (Illus.). (gr. 5 up). 1982. 10.50 (ISBN 0-686-94033-4). Morrow.
--I Was Born in a Tree & Raised by Bees. LC 76-12632. (Illus.). (gr. k-4). 1977. PLB 4.99 o.p. (ISBN 0-399-61018-9). Putnam Pub Group.
--A Kettle of Hawks: And Other Wildlife Groups. LC 78-10212. (Illus.). (gr. k-3). 1979. 7.50 o.p. (ISBN 0-698-20469-7, Coward). Putnam Pub Group.
--Outdoors on Foot. (Illus.). (ps-1). 1978. PLB 4.99 o.p. (ISBN 0-698-30684-8, Coward). Putnam Pub Group.
Arnot, Madeleine, jt. ed. see Whitelegg, E.
Arnot, Michelle. Foot Notes: The Complete Guide for Everyone Who Runs, Dances, Walks or Stands on Their Own Two Feet. LC 79-7857. (Illus.). 192p. 1980. pap. 5.95 o.p. (ISBN 0-385-14944-1, Dolp). Doubleday.
Arnot, Phil & Monroe, Elvira. Exploring Point Reyes: A Trailguide to Point Reyes National Seashore. Rev. ed. LC 82-51259. (Illus.). 144p. 1983. pap. 4.95 (ISBN 0-933174-16-0). Wide World-Tetra.
Arnot, R. Page, tr. see Varga, Eugen.
Arnott, Anna L. People Speak. 64p. (Orig.). 1982. pap. 4.50 (ISBN 0-682-49857-2). Exposition.
Arnott, James, ed. Sale Catalogues of Libraries of Eminent Persons: Actors, Vol. 12. 601p. 1975. 29.00 o.p. (ISBN 0-7201-0451-3, Pub. by Mansell England). Wilson.
Arnott, Kathleen. Dragons, Ogres, & Scary Things: Two African Folktales. LC 74-9876. (Venture Ser). (Illus.). 64p. (gr. 2). 1974. PLB 6.89 (ISBN 0-8116-6978-5). Garrard.
--Spiders, Crabs, & Creepy Crawlers: Two African Folktales. LC 78-1057. (Imagination Ser.). (Illus.). (gr. k-6). 1978. PLB 6.69 (ISBN 0-8116-4412-X). Garrard.
Arnott, Marilyn S., et al, eds. Molecular Interrelations of Nutrition & Cancer. (M. D. Anderson Symposium on Fundamental Cancer Research Ser.: 34th Annual). 480p. 1982. text ed. 64.00 (ISBN 0-89004-701-4). Raven.
Arnott, Peter, jt. auth. see Reinert, Otto.
Arnott, Peter, jt. ed. see Reinert, Otto.
Arnott, Peter D. Greek Scenic Conventions in the Fifth Century B.C. LC 78-5950. 1978. Repr. of 1962 ed. lib. bdg. 20.25x (ISBN 0-313-20401-2, ARGS). Greenwood.
Arnott, Peter D., ed. & tr. see Aristophanes.
Arnould, Michel & Zubini, Fabio. English-French Petroleum Dictionary. 267p. 1983. pap. 37.00x (ISBN 0-8448-1432-6). Crane-Russak Co.
Arnout, Susan. The Frozen Lady. LC 81-71662. 581p. 1983. 15.95 (ISBN 0-87795-368-6). Arbor Hse.
Arnov, Boris. Water: Experiments to Understand It. (gr. 5 up). 1980. 8.75 (ISBN 0-688-41927-5); lib. bdg. 8.40 (ISBN 0-688-51927-X). Morrow.
Arnove, Robert F., ed. Philanthropy & Cultural Imperialism: The Foundations at Home & Abroad. LC 82-48055. (Midland Bks.: No. 303). 488p. 1982. pap. 10.95x (ISBN 0-253-20303-1). Ind U Pr.
--Philanthropy & Cultural Imperialism: The Foundations at Home & Abroad. 1980. lib. bdg. 24.95 (ISBN 0-8161-8259-0, Univ Bks). G K Hall.
Arnow, Harriette S. Seedtime on the Cumberland. LC 82-40464. (Illus.). 480p. 1983. 28.00x (ISBN 0-8131-1487-X); pap. 13.00x (ISBN 0-8131-0146-8). U Pr of Ky.
Arnow, Jan. Handbook of Alternative Photographic Processes. LC 81-1237. 256p. 1982. 35.00 (ISBN 0-442-24850-4). Van Nos Reinhold.
Arnow, L. Earle. Introduction to Laboratory Chemistry. 9th ed. (Illus.). 102p. 1976. pap. text ed. 8.50 o.p. (ISBN 0-8016-0325-0). Mosby.
Arnowitt, Richard & Nath, Pran, eds. Gauge Theories & Modern Field Theory. LC 76-5836. 423p. 1976. text ed. 23.00x o.p. (ISBN 0-262-01046-1). MIT Pr.
Arnstein, Walter, ed. The Past Speaks: Sources & Problems in British History Since 1688. 448p. 1981. pap. text ed. 9.95 (ISBN 0-669-02919-X). Heath.
Arnstein, Walter L. A History of England, Vol. IV: Britain Yesterday & Today 1830 to Present. Smith, Lacey B., ed. 304p. 1983. pap. text ed. 10.95 (ISBN 0-669-04380-X). Heath.
Arnstein, Walter L., jt. auth. see Willcox, William B.
Arnts, Robt R., jt. auth. see Bufalini, Joseph J.
Arntson, L. Joyce. Word-Information Processing: Vol. 1 Concepts Procedures. 1982. pap. text ed. 17.95x (ISBN 0-534-01346-5). Kent Pub Co.
--Word-Information Processing: Vol. 2 Applications Skill Procedures. 1983. pap. text ed. 14.95x (ISBN 0-534-01345-7). Kent Pub Co.
Arntzenius, A. C., jt. auth. see Baan, J.
Arny, Mary T. & Reaske, Christopher R. Ecology: A Writer's Handbook. 1972. pap. 2.50x (ISBN 0-685-26283-9). Phila Bk Co.
Arny, Thomas, jt. auth. see Pananides, Nicholas A.
Aron, Joan B. The Quest for Regional Cooperation: A Study of the New York Metropolitan Regional Council. LC 69-16738. (California Studies in Urbanization & Environmental Design). 1969. 31.50x (ISBN 0-520-01505-3). U of Cal Pr.
Aron, Joel D. The Program Development Process: Pt. II: The Programming Team. LC 74-2847. (Illus.). 704p. 1983. text ed. 28.95 (ISBN 0-201-14463-8). A-W.
--Program Development Process, Pt. 1: The Individual Programmer. (IBM Systems Programming Ser.). (Illus.). 280p. 1974. text ed. 22.95 (ISBN 0-201-14451-4). A-W.
Aron, Jon, jt. auth. see Linsley, Leslie.
Aron, Milton. Ideas & Ideals of the Hassidim. 1969. 7.95 o.p. (ISBN 0-8065-0319-X). Citadel Pr.
Aron, Raymond. The Imperial Republic: The United States & the World 1945-1973. Jellinek, Frank, tr. from Fr. LC 81-40938. Orig. Title: Republique Imperiale; les Etats-Unis Dans le Monde, 1945-1972. 378p. 1982. lib. bdg. 25.50 (ISBN 0-8191-2101-0); pap. text ed. 114.00 (ISBN 0-8191-2102-9). U Pr of Amer.
--Main Currents in Sociological Thought: Montesquieu, Comte, Marx, Tocqueville, the Sociologists, & the Revolution of 1848, Vol. 1. LC 68-14142. 1968. pap. 5.95 (ISBN 0-385-08804-3, A600A, Anch). Doubleday.
--Peace & War. LC 81-14296. 838p. 1981. Repr. of 1966 ed. 37.50 (ISBN 0-89874-391-5). Krieger.
Aronin, Eugene L., jt. auth. see Yawkey, Thomas D.
Aronoff, Craig. Business & the Media. LC 78-10394. 1979. text ed. 24.50x case ed. (ISBN 0-673-16071-8). Scott F.
Aronoff, Craig, et al. Getting Your Message Across: A Practical Guide to Business Communication. (Illus.). 500p. 1981. text ed. 19.50 (ISBN 0-8299-0362-3). West Pub.
Aronoff, Mark & Kean, Mary-Louise, eds. Juncture. (Studia Linguistica et Philologica: Vol. 7). 144p. 1980. pap. 25.00 (ISBN 0-915838-46-X). Anma Libri.
Aronoff, Myron J., ed. Culture & Political Change. (Political Anthropology Ser.: Vol. II). 224p. 1982. 29.95 (ISBN 0-87855-434-3). Transaction Bks.
--Freedom & Constraint: A Memorial Tribute to Max Gluckman. (Illus.). 1976. pap. text ed. 22.25x o.p. (ISBN 90-232-1392-0). Humanities.
Aronofsky, J. S., ed. Progress in Operations Research, Vol. 3. LC 61-10415. 570p. 1969. 32.50 (ISBN 0-471-03355-3, Pub. by Wiley). Krieger.
Aronofsky, J. S., et al. Managerial Planning with Linear Programming: In Process Industry Operations. 379p. 1978. 55.95x (ISBN 0-471-03360-X, Pub. by Wiley-Interscience). Wiley.
Aronofsky, Julius S., et al. Programmed Calculators: Business Applications. (Illus.). 1978. pap. text ed. 11.95 (ISBN 0-07-002317-4, T&D). McGraw.
Aronosky, Jim. Crinkleroot's Book of Animal Tracks & Wildlife Signs. LC 78-13081. (Illus.). (gr. 1-4). 1979. 7.95 o.p. (ISBN 0-399-20663-9); PLB 6.99 1980 guaranteed bind. o.p. (ISBN 0-399-61171-1). Putnam Pub Group.
Aronow, edward & Reznikoff, Marvin, eds. A Rorschach Introduction: Content & Perceptual Approaches. Date not set. price not set (ISBN 0-8089-1516-9). Grune.
Aronowicz, Annette, et al, trs. see Dumezil, Georges.
Aronowitz, Dennis S. Legal Aspects of Arms Control Verification in the United States. LC 65-26174. 1965. 15.00 (ISBN 0-379-00279-5). Oceana.
Aronowitz, Stanley. Class, Politics, & Culture. 372p. 1981. 25.95 (ISBN 0-03-059031-0). Praeger.
--False Promises: The Shaping of American Working-Class Consciousness. LC 73-5679. 480p. 1973. 12.50 (ISBN 0-07-002315-8, GB); pap. 5.95 (ISBN 0-07-002316-6). McGraw.
Arons, S. Compelling Belief: The Culture of American Schooling. 256p. 19.95 (ISBN 0-07-002326-3). McGraw.
Arons, Stephen, jt. auth. see Herr, Stanley S.
Aronsohn, Alan J. Partnership Income Taxes. 7th ed. LC 77-93944. 1978. text ed. 20.00 (ISBN 0-685-86797-8, J1-1420). PLI.
Aronson, E., jt. auth. see Lindzey, Gardner.
Aronson, Elliot & Helmreich, Robert. Social Psychology. (Transaction Ser.). 1973. pap. text ed. 10.95 (ISBN 0-442-20357-8). Van Nos Reinhold.
Aronson, Harvey. The Golden Shore. 256p. 1982. 14.95 (ISBN 0-399-12731-3). Putnam Pub Group.
Aronson, Harvey & McGrady, Mike. The Establishment of Innocence. LC 75-21938. 1976. 8.95 o.p. (ISBN 0-399-11540-4). Putnam Pub Group.
Aronson, Howard I. Georgian: A Reading Grammar. (Illus.). 526p. 1982. 22.95 (ISBN 0-89357-100-8). Slavica.
Aronson, J. Richard, jt. auth. see Maxwell, James A.
Aronson, J. Richard & Schwartz, Eli, eds. Management Policies in Local Government Finance. rev. 2nd ed. LC 81-2934. (Municipal Management Ser.). (Illus.). 493p. 1981. text ed. 34.00 (ISBN 0-87326-022-8). Intl City Mgt.
Aronson, Jonathan D., ed. Debt & the Less Developed Countries. (Special Studies in National Security & Defense Policy). 1979. lib. bdg. 33.00 o.p. (ISBN 0-89158-370-X); text ed. 13.50 o.p. Westview.
--Profit & the Pursuit of Energy: Economic Structures for Energy Transition. Cowhey, Peter F. (Special Studies in Economics). 200p. 1983. lib. bdg. 22.00 (ISBN 0-86531-216-8). Westview.
Aronson, Miriam K. & Bennett, Ruth, eds. The Acting-Out Elderly: Issues for Helping Professionals. Gurland, Barry. LC 82-23430. (Advanced Models & Practice in Aged Care: No. 1). 92p. 1983. text ed. 20.00 (ISBN 0-917724-76-3). Haworth Pr.
Aronson, Nicole. Mademoiselle De Scudery. (World Authors Ser.). 1978. 15.95 (ISBN 0-8057-6278-7, Twayne). G K Hall.
Aronson, Robert L., ed. The Localization of Federal Manpower Planning. LC 73-620149. 112p. 1973. pap. 4.50 (ISBN 0-87546-053-4); pap. 7.50 special hard bdg. (ISBN 0-87546-283-9). ILR Pr.
Aronson, Sara P. Communicable Disease Nursing. (Nursng Outline Ser.). 1978. pap. 12.75 (ISBN 0-87488-387-3). Med Exam.
Aronson, Steven M. Hype. 464p. 1983. 15.95 (ISBN 0-688-01228-0). Morrow.
Aronson, Virginia. A Practical Guide to Optimal Nutrition: Nutri-Plan. (Orig.). 1982. pap. text ed. 17.50 (ISBN 0-7236-7018-8). Wright-PSG.
Arora, Jasbir S., jt. auth. see Haug, Edward J.
Arora, S. K. Chemistry & Biochemistry of Legumes. 400p. 1982. text ed. 49.50 (ISBN 0-7131-2854-2). E Arnold.
Arora, S. P. Office Organization & Management. 1980. text ed. 22.50x (ISBN 0-7069-0795-7, Pub. by Vikas India). Advent NY.
Arotsky, J. & Glassbrook, D. W. An Introduction to Microcomputing with PET. 288p. 1983. pap. text ed. 14.95 (ISBN 0-7131-3475-5). E Arnold.
Arp, Claudia, jt. auth. see Arp, Dave.
Arp, Dave & Arp, Claudia. Ten Dates for Mates. 176p. 1983. pap. 6.95 (ISBN 0-8407-5845-6). Nelson.
Arpaci, Vedat S. Conduction Heat Transfer. 1966. 33.95 (ISBN 0-201-00359-7). A-W.
Arpan, Jeffrey & Radebaugh, Lee. International Accounting & Multinational Enterprises. 400p. 1980. text ed. 21.50 o.p. (ISBN 0-88262-539-X). Warren.
Arpan, Jeffrey S. & Radebaugh, Lee H. International Accounting & Multinational Enterprises. LC 80-26070. 400p. 1982. text ed. 27.95 (ISBN 0-471-87746-8); tchr's manual avail. (ISBN 0-471-89512-1). Wiley.
Arpel, Adrien. How to Look Ten Years Younger. (Illus.). 1981. pap. 9.95 (ISBN 0-446-37706-6). Warner Bks.
Arpin, Gary Q. John Berryman: A Reference Guide. 1976. lib. bdg. 19.50 (ISBN 0-8161-7804-6, Hall Reference). G K Hall.
--Master of the Baffled House: The Dream Songs of John Berryman. LC 76-9566. 80p. 1976. pap. 2.95 o.p. (ISBN 0-916684-03-2). Rook Pr.
Arps, Louisa W. Denver in Slices. LC 59-8214. (Illus.). 268p. 1983. write for info. Swallow.
--Denver in Slices. LC 59-8214. (Illus.). 268p. 1983. 15.95 (ISBN 0-686-84821-7, 82-76123); pap. 9.95 (ISBN 0-686-84822-5, 82-76131). Ohio U Pr.
Arrabal, Fernando. Architect & the Emperor of Assyria. D'Harnoncourt, Everard & Shank, Adele, trs. from Fr. 1969. pap. 3.95 o.s.i. (ISBN 0-394-17364-3, E486, Ever). Grove.
Arrants, Cheryl. Sew Wonderful Gourmet Garments. St. Amant, Kristi, ed. (Illus.). 96p. (Orig.). 1982. pap. text ed. write for info. (ISBN 0-943704-01-4). Sew Wonderful.
Arrants, Cheryl & Asbjornsen, Jan. Sew Wonderful Silk. rev. ed. Amant, Kristi, ed. (Illus.). 128p. 1981. pap. text ed. 5.95 (ISBN 0-943704-02-2). Sew Wonderful.
Arras, John & Hunt, Robert. Ethical Issues in Modern Medicine. 2nd ed. 574p. 1983. pap. 18.95 (ISBN 0-87484-574-2). Mayfield Pub.
Arras, John, jt. ed. see Hunt, Robert.
Arrastia, Cecilio. Itinerario De la Pasion: Meditaciones De la Semana Santa. 1981. Repr. of 1978 ed. pap. 2.95 (ISBN 0-311-43036-8). Casa Bautista.
Arredondo, Larry. How to Choose & Successfully Use a Microcomputer: A Personal Computer, a Small Business Computer, a Professional Computer, a Desktop Computer, a Home Computer, a Portable Computer, etc. (Orig.). 1982. pap. text ed. write for info. (ISBN 0-936648-16-3, Pub. by Comp Know Ctr). Telcom Lib.
Arrens, Christa, tr. see Bielfeld, Horst & Heidenreich, Manfred.
Arrick, Fran. Chernowitz! LC 81-7712. 176p. (gr. 7 up). 1981. 9.95 (ISBN 0-02-705720-8). Bradbury Pr.
--God's Radar. 192p. (gr. 5-10). 1983. 10.95 (ISBN 0-02-705710-0). Bradbury Pr.
--Steffie Can't Come Out to Play. LC 78-4423. 192p. (YA) (gr. 8 up). 1978. 9.95 (ISBN 0-87888-163-8). Bradbury Pr.
Arrighi, Frances E., et al, eds. see M. D. Anderson Symposia on Fundamental Cancer Research, 33rd.
Arrighi, Giovanni, et al, eds. see Amin, Samir.
Arrighi, Mel. Alter Ego: A Hank & Biff Mystery. 176p. 1983. 11.95 (ISBN 0-312-02144-5). St Martin.
--Delphine. LC 77-15828. 1978. 10.95 o.p. (ISBN 0-689-10862-1). Atheneum.
--Delphine. 1980. pap. 2.25 o.p. (ISBN 0-451-09066-7, E9066, Sig). NAL.
Arrigo, Joseph A. & Batt, Cara M. Plantations: Fourty-Four of Louisiana's Most Beautiful Antebellum Plantation Houses. (Illus.). 96p. (Orig.). Date not set. pap. 5.95 (ISBN 0-938530-19-4, 19-4). Lexikos.
Arrigoni, Enrico. The Totalitarian Nightmare. 280p. pap. 4.00 (ISBN 0-686-35963-1). West World Pr.
Arrillaga, J. & Arnold, C. P. Computer Modelling of Electrical Power Systems. 456p. 1983. 58.25 (ISBN 0-471-10406-X, Pub. by Wiley-Interscience). Wiley.
Arrington, French. Maintaining the Foundations. 1983. pap. 4.95 (ISBN 0-8010-0192-7). Baker Bk.
Arrington, French L. New Testament Exegesis: Examples. 1977. 8.25 (ISBN 0-8191-0108-7). U Pr of Amer.
--Paul's Aeon Theology in First Corinthians. 1977. pap. text ed. 9.75 (ISBN 0-8191-0119-2). U Pr of Amer.
Arriola, Gus. Gordo's Critters. (Illus.). 132p. (Orig.). Date not set. pap. 6.95 (ISBN 0-86679-001-2). Oak Tree Pubns. Postponed.
Arrow & Intriligator. Handbook of Mathematical Economics, Vol. 3. Date not set. 50.00 (ISBN 0-444-86128-9). Elsevier.
Arrow, K. J. & Hurwicz, L., eds. Studies in Resource Allocation Process. LC 76-9171. (Illus.). 1977. 54.50 (ISBN 0-521-21522-6). Cambridge U Pr.
Arrow, Kenneth J. Social Choice & Individual Values. 2nd ed. (Cowles Foundation Monograph: No. 12). 1970. 17.50x (ISBN 0-300-01363-9); pap. 4.95x (ISBN 0-300-01364-7, Y233). Yale U Pr.
Arrowsmith, D. K. & Place, C. M. Ordinary Differential Equations. 1982. 35.00x (ISBN 0-412-22600-6, Pub. by Chapman & Hall); pap. 17.95x (ISBN 0-412-22610-3). Methuen Inc.
Arrowsmith, Don. Princess's Birthday Party. (Illus.). (gr. 2-4). 1975. pap. 2.95 (ISBN 0-913270-46-6). Sunstone Pr.
Arrowsmith, William, ed. see Aristophanes.
Arrowsmith, William, tr. The Storm & Other Poems. 250p. 1983. 20.00 (ISBN 0-8180-1582-9); pap. 9.95 (ISBN 0-8180-1585-3). Horizon.
Arrowsmith, William, tr. see Euripides.
Arrowsmith, William see Euripides.
Arroyo, Stephen. Astrology, Psychology & the Four Elements. LC 75-27828. 208p. (Orig.). 1975. 11.95 (ISBN 0-916360-02-4); pap. 7.95 (ISBN 0-916360-01-6). CRCS Pubns NV.

Arroyo, Stephen & Greene, Liz. The Jupiter-Saturn Conference Lectures. LC 82-45632. (Lectures on Modern Astrology: Vol. I). 1982. pap. 8.95 (ISBN 0-916360-16-4). CRCS Pubns NV.
Arruda, A. L., et al, eds. Mathematical Logic in Latin America. (Studies in Logic & the Foundations of Mathematics: Vol. 99). 392p. 1979. 59.75 (ISBN 0-444-85402-9, North Holland). Elsevier.
ARS Electronics. Directory of Collectors & Suppliers: Including Phonograph & TV Collectors. 7th ed. (Orig.). 1982. pap. 4.00 (ISBN 0-938630-02-4). ARS Electronics.
ARS Electronics Editors. Most-Often-Needed 1926-38 Radio Diagrams & Servicing Information. 192p. 11.00 (ISBN 0-938630-17-2). ARS Electronics.
Arsan, Emmanuelle. Emmanuelle Two. Hollo, Anselm, tr. from Fr. LC 74-24995. 1974. 3.95 (ISBN 0-394-17891-2, B453, BC). Grove.
Arsdale, Mary Van see Van Arsdale, Mary G.
Arsdale, Robert S. Van see Van Arsdale, Robert S.
Arsdale, Tom Van see Van Arsdale, Tom, et al.
Arsdell, Paul M. Van see Van Arsdell, Paul M.
Arsene, Gr., ed. Invariant Subspaces & Other Topics. (Operator Theory: Advances & Applications Ser.: No. 6). 229p. Date not set. text ed. 26.95 (ISBN 3-7643-1360-9). Birkhauser.
Arsenin, E. Basic Equations & Special Functions of Mathematical Physics. 1968. 13.50 (ISBN 0-444-19778-8). Elsevier.
Arstila, A. U., jt. ed. see Trump, Benjamin F.
Art Address Verlag. International Directory of the Arts, 1983-1984. 2000p. 1983. 110.00 (ISBN 3-921529-03-4). Bowker.
Art & Antiques Magazines Editors, ed. Nineteenth Century Furniture: Innovation, Revival & Reform. (Illus.). 160p. 1982. 25.00 (ISBN 0-8230-8004-8). Watson-Guptill.
Art Directors Club of New York. The Fifty-Ninth Art Directors Annual. Solomon, Miriam L., ed. (Illus.). 672p. 1980. 34.95 o.p. (ISBN 0-937414-00-X). ADC Pubns.
Art Directors Club of Tokyo, ed. Annual of Advertising Art in Japan, 1979. LC 61-66515. (Illus.). 336p. 1979. 72.50x o.p. (ISBN 0-8002-2325-X). Intl Pubns Serv.
Art Institute of Chicago, Ryerson Library. Index to Art Periodicals, 11 Vols. 1962. Set. 990.00 (ISBN 0-8161-0627-4, Hall Library). G K Hall.
--Index to Art Periodicals, 1st Supplement. 1975. lib. bdg. 105.00 (ISBN 0-8161-0727-0, Hall Library). G K Hall.
Artaega, Robert F. Building of the Arch. 28p. 1967. pap. 2.00 (ISBN 0-686-95726-1). Jefferson Natl.
Artaud, Antonin. Cenci. Taylor, Simon W., tr. from Fr. LC 75-97158. (Orig.). 1970. pap. 3.95 o.s.i. (ISBN 0-394-17282-5, E532, Ever). Grove.
--Collected Works. Corti, V. & Hamilton, A., trs. Incl. Vol. 1. Correspondence with J. Riviere-Umbilical Limbo-Nerve Scales- Art & Death-Cup & Ball-Seven Letters-Unpublished Prose & Poetry. 247p. 1968. 17.50x (ISBN 0-7145-0169-7); pap. 7.50 (ISBN 0-7145-0170-0); Vol. 2. The Alfred Jarry Theatre-Two Stage Scenarios & Two Production Plans-Reviews-On Literature & the Plastic Arts. (Illus.). 240p. 1971. 13.50x (ISBN 0-7145-0171-9); pap. 7.50 (ISBN 0-7145-0172-7); Vol. 3. Scenarios-On the Cinema-Interviews-Letters. (Illus.). 255p. 1972. 15.00x (ISBN 0-7145-0778-4); pap. 7.50 (ISBN 0-7145-0779-2); Vol. 4. The Theatre & Its Double-The Cenci-Documents. 1974. 15.00x (ISBN 0-7145-0622-2); pap. 7.50 (ISBN 0-7145-0623-0). LC 76-369595. (French Surrealism Ser.). Intl Pubns Serv.
Artedi, P. Genera Piscium: Emendata & Aucta. 1967. Repr. of 1792 ed. 48.00 (ISBN 3-7682-0190-2). Lubrecht & Cramer.
--Ichthyolgia. Linnaeus, C., ed. 1961. Repr. of 1738 ed. 40.00 (ISBN 3-7682-0082-5). Lubrecht & Cramer.
Arterburn, S. Write English, Bk. 6. (Speak English Ser.). (Illus.). 64p. (Orig.). 1983. pap. text ed. 4.95 (ISBN 0-88499-689-1). Inst Mod Lang.
Arterburn, Yvonne. The Loom of Interdependence: Silkweaving Cooperatives in Kanchipuram. (Studies in Sociology & Social Anthropology). 220p. 1982. text ed. 13.75x (ISBN 0-391-02749-2, Pub. by Hindustan India). Humanities.
Artese, Robert N., jt. auth. see Nash, Constance.
Arth, Marvin & Ashmore, Helen. The Newsletter Editor's Desk Book. 3rd ed. 136p. 1982. softcover 10.00 (ISBN 0-938270-03-6). Parkway Pr.
Arthanari, Subramanyam & Dodge, Yadolah. Mathematical Programming in Statistics. LC 80-21637. (Probability & Math Statistics Ser.: Applied Probability & Statistics). 413p. 1981. 34.95x (ISBN 0-471-08073-X, Pub. by Wiley-Interscience). Wiley.
Arthos, John. Dante, Michelangelo, & Milton. LC 78-32053. 1979. Repr. of 1963 ed. lib. bdg. 16.00x (ISBN 0-313-20979-0, ARDA). Greenwood.
Arthur. Application of On-Line Analytical Instrumentation to Process Control. LC 82-70694. (Activated Sludge Process Control Ser.). 222p. 1982. 29.95 (ISBN 0-250-40539-3). Ann Arbor Science.
--New Concepts & Practices in Activated Sludge Process Control. LC 81-69767. (Activated Sludge Process Control Ser.). 125p. 1982. 29.95 (ISBN 0-250-40528-8). Ann Arbor Science.
Arthur Andersen & Co. Interest Rate Futures: The Corporate Decision. LC 82-82392. 1982. 4.50 (ISBN 0-910586-46-2). Finan Exec.
Arthur, Anthony. Critical Essays on Wallace Stegner. (Critical Essays on American Literature). 1982. lib. bdg. 28.50 (ISBN 0-8161-8487-9, Twayne). G K Hall.
Arthur, Anthony, jt. ed. see Brier, Peter A.
Arthur, Bonnie. Unicorns in Soft Sculpture, Bk. 1. (Illus., Orig.). 1982. pap. 3.50 (ISBN 0-941284-14-X). Deco Design Studio.
Arthur, Charles S., jt. auth. see Graham, John R.
Arthur D. Little, Inc. Health Care Cost Containment: Challenge to Industry. LC 80-6830. 1980. 5.20 (ISBN 0-910586-34-9). Finan Exec.
Arthur, Donald, tr. see Sevela, Efraim.
Arthur, Elizabeth. Island Sojourn. LC 79-2611. (Illus.). 1980. 11.49i (ISBN 0-06-010156-3, HarpT). Har-Row.
Arthur, Geoffrey H. Veterinary Reproduction & Obstetrics. 5th ed. (Illus.). 616p. 1982. text ed. write for info. o.p. (ISBN 0-8121-0778-0). Lea & Febiger.
Arthur, Henry B. Commodity Futures As a Business Management Tool. LC 71-162634. (Illus.). 1971. 20.00x (ISBN 0-87584-092-2). Harvard Busn.
Arthur, Humphrey, jt. auth. see Morris, Norman.
Arthur, J. Morality & Moral Controversies. 1981. pap. 15.95 (ISBN 0-13-601278-7). P-H.
Arthur, John & Shaw, William, eds. Justice & Economic Distribution. 1978. pap. text ed. 13.95 (ISBN 0-13-514166-4). P-H.
Arthur, Lowell J. Programmer Productivity: Myths, Methods & Morphology - A Guide for Managers, Analysts & Programmers. 300p. 1983. 22.95 (ISBN 0-471-86434-X, Pub. by Wiley-Interscience). Wiley.
Arthur, Phyllis. Goddess in the Home. (YA) 1971. 6.95 (ISBN 0-685-03334-1, Avalon). Bouregy.
Arthur, Robert. Alfred Hitchcock & the Three Investigators in the Mystery of the Whispering Mummy. Hitchcock, Alfred, ed. (Three Investigators Ser.: No. 3). (Illus.). (gr. 4-8). 1965. 2.95 o.p. (ISBN 0-394-81220-4, BYR); PLB 5.39 (ISBN 0-394-91220-9); pap. 1.95 o.p. (ISBN 0-394-83768-1). Random.
--Thrillers & More Thrillers. (Illus.). (gr. 7-11). 1968. 6.99 (ISBN 0-394-91561-5); pap. 2.95 (ISBN 0-394-81561-0). Random.
Arthur, Robert P., jt. auth. see Weinstock, E. B.
Arthur, William. Etymological Dictionary of Family & Christian Names. LC 68-17911. 1969. Repr. of 1857 ed. 40.00x (ISBN 0-8103-3107-1). Gale.
Arthur, William J. A Financial Planning Model for Private Colleges: A Research Report. LC 72-92879. 150p. 1973. 8.50x o.p. (ISBN 0-8139-0409-9). U Pr of Va.
Arthurs, A. M. & Bhagavan, M. R., eds. Functional Integration & Its Applications. 1975. 59.00x (ISBN 0-19-853346-2). Oxford U Pr.
Artigas, J. Llorens & Corredor-Matheos, J. Spanish Folk Ceramics. (Illus.). 235p. 1982. 35.00 (ISBN 84-7031-362-2, Pub. by Editorial Blume Spain). Intl Schol Bk Serv.
Artin, E. Algebraic Numbers & Algebraic Functions. 364p. 1969. pap. 36.00 (ISBN 0-677-00635-7). Gordon.
--Geometric Algebra: Pure & Applied Mathematics. (A Wiley-Interscience Ser. of Texts, Monographs & Tracts). 214p. 1957. 32.95x (ISBN 0-470-03432-7, Pub. by Wiley-Interscience). Wiley.
Artin, M. see Zariski, Oscar.
Artinian, Robert Willard. La Technique Descriptive Chez Guy de Maupassant. 1973. lib. bdg. 12.95 (ISBN 0-916948-01-3). Augustan Lib.
Artino, Ralph A. & Gaglione, Anthony M. Contest Problem Book IV: Annual High School Examinations 1973-1982. LC 82-51076. (New Mathematical Library Ser.: No. 29). 200p. 1982. write for info. (ISBN 0-88385-629-8). Math Assn.
Artis, M. J., et al. Demand Management Supply Constraints & Inflation. LC 81-16373. 256p. 1982. pap. 18.95x (ISBN 0-470-27287-2). Halsted Pr.
Artis, Vicki K. Brown Mouse & Vole. LC 74-14387. (See & Read Storybooks). (Illus.). (gr. k-4). 1975. PLB 5.29 o.p. (ISBN 0-399-60922-9). Putnam Pub Group.
Artis, Vicky K. Gray Duck Catches a Friend. LC 73-86475. (See & Read Storybooks). (Illus.). 48p. (gr. 1-4). 1974. PLB 5.29 o.p. (ISBN 0-399-60871-0). Putnam Pub Group.
Artiss, David. Theodor Storm: Studies in Ambivalence. (German Language & Literature Monographs). xix, 215p. 1978. 23.00 (ISBN 90-272-0965-0, 5). Benjamins North Am.
Artman, John. Cowboys: An Activity Book. (gr. 4-8). 1982. 5.95 (ISBN 0-86653-068-1, GA 417). Good Apple.
--Good Apple & Reading Fun. (gr. 3-7). 1981. 9.95 (ISBN 0-86653-046-0, GA 278). Good Apple.
--Indians: An Activity Book. (gr. 4-8). 1981. 5.95 (ISBN 0-86653-012-6, GA 240). Good Apple.
Artos. Jonah. (Illus.). 80p. (Orig.). 1982. pap. 4.00 o.p. (ISBN 0-934852-24-3). Lorien Hse.
Artos, John, ed. see Keats, John.
Arts & Antiques Magazines Editors, ed. Americana: Folk & Decorative Art. (Illus.). 160p. 1982. 25.00 (ISBN 0-8230-8005-6). Watson-Guptill.
Arts Council Of Great Britain - Conference. Obscenity Laws: Proceedings. 1970. 6.95 o.p. (ISBN 0-233-96204-2). Transatlantic.
Arts, Education & Americans Panel. Coming to Our Senses: The Significance of the Arts for American Education. 1977. 17.95 (ISBN 0-07-002360-3, P&RB); pap. 7.95 (ISBN 0-07-002361-1). McGraw.
Arts, Herwig. With Your Whole Soul: On the Christian Experience of God. LC 82-61419. 192p. 1983. pap. 7.95 (ISBN 0-8091-2517-X). Paulist Pr.
Artusio, Joseph F., jt. ed. see Yao, Fun-Sun F.
Artwick, B. Microcomputer Interfacing. 1980. 31.95 (ISBN 0-13-580902-9). P-H.
Artz, Frederick B. From the Renaissance to Romanticism: Trends in Style in Art, Literature, & Music 1300-1830. LC 62-20021. 1962. 16.00x (ISBN 0-226-02837-2). U of Chicago Pr.
--From the Renaissance to Romanticism: Trends in Style, in Art, Literature & Music, 1300-1830. LC 62-20021. 1962. pap. 8.00x (ISBN 0-226-02838-0, P186, Phoen). U of Chicago Pr.
--The Mind of the Middle Ages: An Historical Survey: A. D. 200-1500. 3rd rev. ed. LC 79-16259. 1980. lib. bdg. 25.00x (ISBN 0-226-02839-9); pap. 9.95 (ISBN 0-226-02840-2, P859, Phoen). U of Chicago Pr.
Artz, Robert J. Experimental Chemistry: An Introduction. 1980. 9.95 o.p. (ISBN 0-316-05278-7); instr. manual avail. o.p. Little.
--Experimental Chemistry: An Introduction. 1982. 9.95 (ISBN 0-316-05278-7); pap. avail. instrs' manual (ISBN 0-316-05279-5). Little.
Artzibashev, Michael. The Doctor. Goldberg, Isaac, ed. Pinkerton, Percy, tr. (International Pocket Library). pap. 3.00 (ISBN 0-686-77235-0). Branden.
Artzy, Rafael. Linear Geometry. 1965. 19.50 (ISBN 0-201-00362-7, Adv Bk Prog). A-W.
Arum, Nancy. Ice Cream & Ices. LC 82-48653. (Great American Cooking School Ser.). (Illus.). 80p. 1983. 8.61i (ISBN 0-06-015148-X, HarpT). Har-Row.
Arundel, Honor. The Longest Weekend. 160p. (gr. 7-9). 1973. pap. 0.95 o.p. (ISBN 0-448-05574-0, G&D). Putnam Pub Group.
--The Terrible Temptation. LC 74-160149. 174p. (gr. 7 up). 1971. 7.95 o.p. (ISBN 0-525-66160-3). Lodestar Bks.
Arundell, Dennis. The Critic at the Opera: Contemporary Comments on Opera in London Over Three Centuries. (Music Reprint Ser.: 1980). (Illus.). 1980. Repr. of 1957 ed. lib. bdg. 35.00 (ISBN 0-306-76026-6). Da Capo.
Arup, Jens see Ibsen, Henrik.
Arvin, Newton. Herman Melville. LC 72-7818. (Illus.). 316p. 1973. Repr. of 1950 ed. lib. bdg. 19.75x (ISBN 0-8371-6524-5, ARHM); pap. 5.95 (ISBN 0-8371-8952-7, ARH:). Greenwood.
Arvine, Kazlitt. Cyclopedia of Anecdotes of Literature. LC 67-14020. 1967. Repr. of 1851 ed. 40.00x (ISBN 0-8103-3296-5). Gale.
Arwas, Victor. Lalique. LC 79-92368. (All Color Paperbacks Ser.). (Illus.). 88p. 1980. pap. 8.95 (ISBN 0-8478-0282-5). Rizzoli Intl.
Arx, J. A. von. The Genera of Fungi Sporulating in Pure Culture. 3rd rev. ed. (Illus.). 410p. 1981. lib. bdg. 48.00x (ISBN 3-7682-0693-9). Lubrecht & Cramer.
--Pilzkunde: Ein Kurzer Abriss der Mykologie Unter Besonderer Beruecksichtigung der Pilze in Reinkultur. 3rd ed. (Illus.). 1976. 12.00 (ISBN 3-7682-1067-7). Lubrecht & Cramer.
Arx, J. A. Von see Von Arx, J. A.
Arx, William S. Von see Von Arx, William S.
Arya, Atam P. Introductory College Physics. (Illus.). 1979. text ed. 31.95 (ISBN 0-02-304000-9); instrs' manual avail.; student study guide avail. Macmillan.
Arya, J. C. & Lardner, R. W. Mathematics for the Biological Sciences. (Illus.). 1979. 28.95 (ISBN 0-13-562439-8). P-H.
Arya, Jagdish C. & Lardner, Robin W. Applied Calculus for Business & Economics. (Illus.). 528p. 1981. text ed. 23.95 (ISBN 0-13-039255-3). P-H.
Arya, Pandit U. Superconcious Meditation. 2nd ed. LC 78-102982. 1977. pap. 4.95 (ISBN 0-89389-035-9). Himalayan Intl Inst.
Arya, Suresh C., et al. Design of Structures & Foundations for Vibrating Machines. 190p. 1979. 34.95x (ISBN 0-87201-294-8). Gulf Pub.
Arya, V. K. & Aggarwal, J. K., eds. Deconvolution of Seismic Data. LC 81-6311. (Benchmark Papers in Electrical Engineering & Computer Science Ser.: Vol. 24). 336p. 1982. 45.00 (ISBN 0-87933-406-1). Hutchinson Ross.
Arzt, Max. Joy & Remembrance. LC 79-63435. 1979. 10.00 (ISBN 0-686-37150-X). Hartmore.
Arzt, Max, jt. auth. see Silverman, Morris.
Asada, Y., et al, eds. Plant Infection: The Physiological & Biochemical Basis. 362p. 1983. 56.00 (ISBN 0-387-11873-X). Springer-Verlag.
Asafiev. A Book about Stravinsky. Brown, Malcolm, ed. French, Richard F., tr. from Rus. LC 82-4810. (Studies in Russian Music: No. 5). 316p. 1982. 44.95 (ISBN 0-8357-1320-2, Pub. by UMI Res Pr). Univ Microfilms.
Asalache, Khadambi. Calabash of Life. (Orig.). 1967. pap. text ed. 4.95x (ISBN 0-582-64001-6). Humanities.
Asano, Osamu & Ishiwata, Mutsuko, eds. The Japanese Press, 1980. 32nd ed. Henshu-sha, Century E. & Higashi, Shinbu, trs. from Japanese. LC 49-25552. (Illus.). 172p. (Orig.). 1980. pap. 25.00x o.p. (ISBN 0-8002-2699-2). Intl Pubns Serv.
--The Japanese Press 1981. 33rd ed. Henshu-sha, Century & Higashi, Shinbu, trs. from Japanese. LC 49-25552. (Illus.). 172p. (Orig.). 1981. pap. 28.50x o.p. (ISBN 0-8002-3018-3). Intl Pubns Serv.
--The Japanese Press, 1982. 34th ed. Henshu-sha, Century Eibun & Higashi, Shinbu, trs. LC 49-25552. (Illus.). 192p. 1982. pap. 28.50x (ISBN 0-8002-3022-1). Intl Pubns Serv.
Asanuma, T. Flow Visualization. 1979. 69.50 (ISBN 0-07-002378-6). McGraw.
Asare, Bediako. Mwasi. (Swahili Literature). (Orig., Swahili.). 1978. pap. text ed. 3.50x o.p. (ISBN 0-686-74453-5, 00610). Heinemann Ed.
Asbell, Bernard, ed. Mother & Daughter: The Letters of Eleanor & Anna Roosevelt. LC 81-22051. 352p. 1982. 17.95 (ISBN 0-698-11161-3, Coward). Putnam Pub Group.
Asbjorn, Nesheim. Introducing the Lapps. 2nd ed. (Norwegian Guides Ser). (Illus., Orig.). 1966. pap. 8.50x (ISBN 0-8002-1585-0). Intl Pubns Serv.
Asbjornsen, Jan, jt. auth. see Arrants, Cheryl.
Asbjornsen, P. C. The Squire's Bride: A Norwegian Folk Tale. LC 74-19316. (Illus.). 32p. (gr. k-2). 1975. 6.95 o.p. (ISBN 0-689-30463-3). Atheneum.
ASBO-ASFSA, jt. auth. see Ponti.
ASBO-CESP. Educational Facilities Abstract Journal. 1969. pap. 0.50 o.p. (ISBN 0-685-57194-7). Assn Sch Busn.
ASBO Management Techniques Research Committee. Control Points in School Business Management. 1979. 3.00 (ISBN 0-910170-10-X). Assn Sch Busn.
ASBO's Maintenance & Operations Research Committee. Custodial Methods & Procedures Manual. 1981. 12.95 (ISBN 0-910170-19-3). Assn Sch Busn.
ASBO's Management Techniques Research Committee. Compendium of Management Techniques. 1982. 5.95 (ISBN 0-910170-23-1). Assn Sch Busn.
ASBO's Negotiations Research Committee. Negotiations & the Manager in Public Education. 1980. 27.50 (ISBN 0-910170-16-9). Assn Sch Busn.
ASBO's Purchasing & Supply Management Research Committee. Cooperative Purchasing Guidelines. 1979. 5.00 (ISBN 0-910170-09-6). Assn Sch Busn.
ASBO's School Facilities Council Division Staff. Schoolhouse Planning. 1980. 8.50 (ISBN 0-910170-12-6). Assn Sch Busn.
ASBO's Student Activity Research Committee. Internal Auditing for Student Activity Funds. 1981. 5.95 (ISBN 0-910170-18-5). Assn Sch Busn.
Asbury, Herbert. Great Illusion: An Informal History of Prohibition. LC 68-8051. (Illus.). 1968. Repr. of 1950 ed. lib. bdg. 21.00x (ISBN 0-8371-0008-9, ASGI). Greenwood.
--Suckers Progress: An Informal History of Gambling in America from the Colonies to Canfield. LC 69-14909. (Criminology, Law Enforcement, & Social Problems Ser.: No. 51). (Illus.). 1969. Repr. of 1938 ed. 17.50x (ISBN 0-87585-051-0). Patterson Smith.
Ascani, Sparky. Ransomed Heart. 208p. pap. 2.95 (ISBN 0-380-83287-9). Avon.
ASCAP Staff, ed. American Society of Composers, Authors, & Publishers Copyright Law Symposium, No. 29. 250p. 1983. 20.00 (ISBN 0-231-05554-4). Columbia U Pr.
--American Society of Composers, Authors, & Publishers Copyright Law Symposium, No. 30. (ASCAP Copyright Symposium Ser.). 200p. 1983. text ed. 20.00x (ISBN 0-231-05582-X). Columbia U Pr.
ASCE Geotechnical Engineering Division Conference, Ann Arbor, June 1977. Geotechnical Practice for Disposal of Solid Waste Materials: Proceedings. American Society of Civil Engineers, compiled By. 896p. 1977. pap. text ed. 29.00 o.p. (ISBN 0-87262-078-6). Am Soc Civil Eng.
ASCE Irrigation & Drainage Division, July 1976. Environmental Aspects of Irrigation & Drainage: Proceedings. American Society of Civil Engineers, compiled By. 752p. 1976. pap. text ed. 37.50 o.p. (ISBN 0-87262-171-5). Am Soc Civil Eng.
ASCE Technical Council on Computer Practices, June 1978. Computing in Civil Engineering: Proceedings. American Society of Civil Engineers, compiled By. 864p. 1978. pap. text ed. 42.50 o.p. (ISBN 0-87262-127-8). Am Soc Civil Eng.
Asch, Berta & Mangus, A. R. Farmers on Relief & Rehabilitation. LC 78-165678. (Research Monograph). 1971. Repr. of 1937 ed. lib. bdg. 27.50 (ISBN 0-306-70340-8). Da Capo.
Asch, Frank. City Sandwich. LC 77-18902. (Illus.). 48p. (gr. 1-4). 1978. 8.75 (ISBN 0-688-80156-0); PLB 8.40 (ISBN 0-688-84156-2). Greenwillow.
--George's Store. (Illus.). 48p. (ps-3). 1983. 5.50 (ISBN 0-8193-1101-4); PLB 5.95 (ISBN 0-8193-1102-2). Parents.
--Gia & the One Hundred Dollars Worth of Bubble Gum. LC 73-17437. (Illus.). 40p. (gr. k-2). 1974. PLB 7.95 o.p. (ISBN 0-07-002418-9, GB). McGraw.

--Goodnight Horsey. (Illus.). (ps-3). 1981. 8.95 (ISBN 0-13-360461-6). P-H.

--The Last Puppy. (Illus.). 32p. (ps-3). 1983. pap. 3.95 (ISBN 0-13-524041-7). P-H.

--Mooncake. (Illus.). 32p. (ps-3). 1983. 9.95 (ISBN 0-13-601013-X). P-H.

Asch, Peter. Economic Theory & the Antitrust Dilemma. LC 78-127658. (Illus.). 414p. 1970. 33.95 (ISBN 0-471-03443-6, Pub. by Wiley-Interscience). Wiley.

--Industrial Organization & Antitrust Policy. rev. ed. LC 82-20012. 399p. 1983. text ed. 26.95 (ISBN 0-471-09762-4). Wiley.

Aschaffenburg, Gustav. Crime & Its Repression. Albrecht, Adalbert, tr. LC 68-55767. (Criminology, Law Enforcement, & Social Problems Ser.: No. 11). 1968. Repr. of 1913 ed. 20.00x (ISBN 0-87585-011-1). Patterson Smith.

Ascham, Anthony. Of the Confusions & Revolutions of Governments. LC 75-33731. 226p. 1975. lib. bdg. 30.00x (ISBN 0-8201-1161-9). Schol Facsimiles.

Aschbacher, Michael. The Finite Simple Groups & Their Classifications. LC 79-20927. (Yale Mathematical Monograph: No. 7). (Orig.). 1980. pap. text ed. 8.95x (ISBN 0-300-02449-5). Yale U Pr.

Aschburner, Steve. Ted Kennedy: The Politician & the Man. LC 79-27299. (Illus.). 48p. (gr. 4-8). 1980. PLB 10.65 o.p. (ISBN 0-8172-0430-X). Raintree Pubs.

Aschenbach, Sarah, ed. see Muhaiyaddeen, Bawa M.

Aschenbrenner, Karl. Analysis of Appraisive Characterization. 1983. lib. bdg. 48.00 (ISBN 90-277-1452-5, Pub. by Reidel Holland). Kluwer Boston.

Ascher, Carol. Simone De Beauvoir: A Life of Freedom. LC 80-70361. 1982. 15.14 (ISBN 0-8070-3240-9); pap. 6.97 (ISBN 0-8070-3241-7). Beacon Pr.

Ascher, Scott & Shadburne, William. Scuba Handbook for Humans. 2nd ed. LC 75-3832. (Illus.). 1977. pap. text ed. 7.95 (ISBN 0-8403-1126-5). Kendall-Hunt.

Ascherson, Neil. Polish August. 1982. pap. 5.95 (ISBN 0-14-005931-8). Penguin.

Aschheim, Joseph & Ching-Yao Hsieh. Macroeconomics: Income & Monetary Theory. LC 80-5519. 279p. 1980. pap. text ed. 11.50 (ISBN 0-8191-1128-7). U Pr of Amer.

Aschheim, Steven E. Brothers & Strangers: The East European Jew in German & German Jewish Consciousness, 1800-1923. LC 81-69812. 331p. 1983. text ed. 25.00 (ISBN 0-299-09110-4). U of Wis Pr.

Aschmann, Bessie, jt. auth. see Aschmann, Herman.

Aschmann, Herman & Aschmann, Bessie. Diccionario Totonaco De Papantla. (Vocabularios Indigenas Ser.: No. 16). 268p. 1973. pap. 5.00x (ISBN 0-88312-750-4); microfiche 3.00x (ISBN 0-88312-585-4). Summer Inst Ling.

Aschmann, Herman P. Vocabulario Totonaco de la Sierra. (Vocabularios Indigenas Ser.: No. 7). 171p. 1962. pap. 3.00x (ISBN 0-88312-666-4); 2.25 (ISBN 0-88312-568-4). Summer Inst Ling.

Aschner, Kath. Word Processing Handbook: A Step-by-Step to Automating Your Office. Rev. ed. 1983. pap. write for info. (ISBN 0-88908-913-2). Self Counsel Pr.

Aschner, Katherine. The Word Processing Handbook: A Step-by-Step Guide to Automating Your Office. (Information & Comunications Management Guides Ser.). 193p. 1982. text ed. 32.95 (ISBN 0-86729-017-X); pap. text ed. 22.95 (ISBN 0-86729-018-8). Knowledge Indus.

Aschner, Katherine, ed. Taking Control of Your Office Records. 150p. 1983. 32.95 (ISBN 0-86729-057-9); pap. 22.95 (ISBN 0-86729-058-7). Knowledge Indus.

Ascoli, David. The Queen's Peace. (The Origins & Development of the Metropolitan Police, 1829-1979). (Illus.). 364p. 1980. 30.00 o.p. (ISBN 0-241-10296-0, Pub. by Hamish Hamilton England). David & Charles.

Ascoli, Max, ed. see Mussolini, Benito.

Aseltine, J. A. Transform Method in Linear System Analysis. (Electrical & Electronic Eng. Ser). 1958. 42.50 (ISBN 0-07-002389-1, C). McGraw.

Asencio, Diego & Asencio, Nancy. Our Man Is Inside. 288p. 1983. 17.00i (ISBN 0-316-05294-9, Pub. by Atlantic Monthly Pr). Little.

Asencio, Nancy, jt. auth. see Asencio, Diego.

Aseshananda, Swami, tr. see Saradananda, Swami.

Ash, Douglas. Dictionary of British Antique Glass. (Illus.). 210p. 1976. 14.00 o.p. (ISBN 0-7207-0837-0). Transatlantic.

Ash, I., jt. auth. see Ash, M.

Ash, James L., Jr. Protestantism & the American University: An Intellectual Biography of William Warren Sweet. (Illus.). 180p. 1982. 15.00 (ISBN 0-87074-183-7). SMU Press.

Ash, John. The Goodbyes. 63p. 1982. pap. text ed. 7.00x (ISBN 0-85635-423-6, 60777, Pub. by Carcanet New Pr England). Humanities.

--Grammatical Institutes. LC 79-15248. (American Linguistics Ser.). 1979. Repr. of 1785 ed. 30.00x (ISBN 0-8201-1339-5). Schol Facsimiles.

Ash, John, jt. auth. see Turner, Louis.

Ash, Kathleen. Beyond Pride, No. 77. 1982. pap. 1.75 o.p. (ISBN 0-515-06688-5). Jove Pubns.

Ash, M. & Ash, I. Encyclopedia of Chemical Additives Vol. 1, A-M. 1983. 75.00 (ISBN 0-8206-0299-X). Chem Pub.

--Encyclopedia of Plastics, Polymers & Resins Vol. 1, A-G. 1981. 75.00 (ISBN 0-8206-0290-6). Chem Pub.

--Encyclopedia of Plastics, Polymers & Resins Vol. 2, H-P. 1982. 75.00 (ISBN 0-8206-0296-5). Chem Pub.

--Encyclopedia of Plastics, Polymers & Resins Vol. 3, Q-Z. 1983. 75.00 (ISBN 0-8206-0303-1). Chem Pub.

--Formulary of Cosmetic Preparations. 1977. text ed. 35.00 (ISBN 0-8206-0218-3). Chem Pub.

--Formulary of Detergents & Other Cleaning Agents. 1980. 35.00 (ISBN 0-8206-0247-7). Chem Pub.

--Formulary of Paints & Other Coatings, Vol. 1. 1978. text ed. 35.00 (ISBN 0-8206-0248-5). Chem Pub.

--Formulary of Paints & Other Coatings Vol. 2. 1982. 35.00 (ISBN 0-8206-0292-2). Chem Pub.

Ash, Major M., Jr. & Ramfjord, Sigurd P. An Introduction to Functional Occlusion. LC 81-5275. (Illus.). 240p. 1982. 15.95 (ISBN 0-7216-1428-0). Saunders.

Ash, Major M., Jr., jt. auth. see Kerr, Donald A.

Ash, Maurice. Regions of Tommorrow: Towards the Open City. LC 70-85676. (Illus.). 1969. 5.95x o.p. (ISBN 0-8052-3221-4). Schocken.

Ash, Michael. The Handbook of Natural Healing. 1982. 25.00x (ISBN 0-906186-00-5, Pub. by Element Bks). State Mutual Bk.

Ash, Michael J., jt. ed. see Magill, Richard A.

Ash, R. Alma-Tadema. (Illus.). Date not set. pap. 3.50 o.s.i. (ISBN 0-912728-56-6). Newbury Bks.

Ash, R. B. Information Theory. LC 65-24284. (Pure & Applied Mathematics Ser.). 339p. 1965. 40.95x (ISBN 0-470-03445-9, Pub. by Wiley-Interscience). Wiley.

Ash, Robert B. Basic Probability Theory. LC 76-109394. 337p. 1970. 31.95x o.p. (ISBN 0-471-03450-9). Wiley.

--Complex Variables. 1971. text ed. 18.50 (ISBN 0-12-065250-1); SBP 25.00. Acad Pr.

--Real Analysis & Probability. (Probability & Mathematical Statistics Ser.). 476p. 1972. 21.00 (ISBN 0-12-065201-3); SBP 28.00; solutions to problems 3.00 (ISBN 0-12-065240-4). Acad Pr.

Ash, Sarah. Moment in Time. 80p. 1972. 4.00 o.p. (ISBN 0-8233-0173-7). Golden Quill.

Ashabraner, Joan, jt. auth. see DeWein, Sibyl.

Ashabranner, Brent. The New Americans: Changing Patterns in U. S. Immigration. LC 82-45999. (Illus.). 160p. (gr. 7 up). 1983. PLB 12.95 (ISBN 0-396-08140-1). Dodd.

Ashall, C. & Ellis, P. E. Studies on Numbers & Mortality in Field Populations of the Desert Locust (Schistocerca Gregaria Forskal) 1962. 35.00x (ISBN 0-85135-004-6, Pub. by Centre Overseas Research). State Mutual Bk.

Ashall, C., jt. auth. see Clark, D. P.

Ashani, Y., jt. auth. see Green, B. S.

Ashbee, C. R. Craftsmanship in Competitive Industry. Stansky, Peter & Shewan, Rodney, eds. LC 76-17772. (Aesthetic Movement & the Arts & Crafts Movement Ser.). 1978. Repr. of 1908 ed. lib. bdg. 44.00x o.s.i. (ISBN 0-8240-2477-X). Garland Pub.

--Manual of the Guild of Handicraft. Stansky, Peter & Shewan, Rodney, eds. LC 76-17776. (Aesthetic Movement & the Arts & Crafts Movement Ser.: Vol. 32). 1978. Repr. of 1892 ed. lib. bdg. 44.00 o.s.i. (ISBN 0-8240-2481-8). Garland Pub.

--Should We Stop Teaching Art? Stansky, Peter & Shewan, Rodney, eds. LC 76-17774. (Aesthetic Movement & the Arts & Crafts Movement Ser.). 1978. Repr. of 1911 ed. lib. bdg. 44.00x o.s.i. (ISBN 0-8240-2478-8). Garland Pub.

Ashbee, F., tr. see Shingarev, A. I.

Ashbee, F., tr. see Zhdanov, Andrei.

Ashberry, John, tr. see Dupin, Jacques.

Ashbery, Elmslie J., et al. ZZZZZ, Vol. 5. Elmslie, Kenward, ed. (Illus.). 1977. pap. 5.00 (ISBN 0-915990-08-3). Z Pr.

Ashbery, John. Self-Portrait in a Convex Mirror. (Poets Ser.). 1976. pap. 4.50 (ISBN 0-14-042201-3). Penguin.

--The Tennis Court Oath. 94p. 1981. pap. 6.95 (ISBN 0-8195-1013-0, Pub. by Wesleyan U Pr). Columbia U Pr.

--Three Plays. 1978. 15.00 (ISBN 0-915990-12-1); pap. 7.50 (ISBN 0-915990-13-X). Z Pr.

Ashbery, John & Moffett, Kenworth. Fairfield Porter. (Illus.). 108p. 1983. pap. 25.00 (ISBN 0-87846-231-7). Mus Fine Arts Boston.

Ashbery, John & Myers, John B. Fairfield Porter. (Illus.). 108p. 1983. 32.50 (ISBN 0-686-83106-3). NYGS.

Ashbery, John & Schuyler, James. A Nest of Ninnies. LC 75-28625. 191p. (Orig.). 1976. pap. 5.00 (ISBN 0-915990-02-4). Z Pr.

Ashbery, John, ed. see Snow, Richard.

Ashbery, John, et al, trs. see Jacob, Max.

Ashbrook, A. W., jt. auth. see Ritcey, G. M.

Ashbrook, A. W., jt. ed. see Ritcey, G. M.

Ashburner, Jenni, jt. auth. see Green, David.

Ashburner, M. & Carson, H. L., eds. The Genetics & Biology of Drosophilia. Date not set. price not set (ISBN 0-12-064947-0). Acad Pr.

Ashburner, M. & Novitski, E., eds. The Genetics & Biology of Drosophila. Incl. Vol. 1, 3 pts. 1976. Pt. A. 82.50 (ISBN 0-12-064901-2); Pt. B. 60.50 (ISBN 0-12-064902-0); Pt. C. 82.50 (ISBN 0-12-064903-9); Vol. 2, 5 pts. 1978-79. Pt. A. 107.00 (ISBN 0-12-064940-3); Pt. B. 86.50 (ISBN 0-12-064941-1); Pt. C. 93.50 (ISBN 0-12-064942-X); Pt. D. 124.50 (ISBN 0-12-064943-8); Pt. E. write for info. (ISBN 0-12-064944-6). Acad Pr.

Ashburner, M., et al, eds. The Genetics & Biology of Drosophila, Vol. 3B. 1982. 88.50 (ISBN 0-12-064946-2). Acad Pr.

Ashby, Bernice M. Shenandoah County, Virginia: Marriage Bonds 1772-1850. LC 66-14986. 418p. 1967. write for info 0.00 (ISBN 0-685-65056-1). Va Bk.

Ashby, Cliff. The Dogs of Dewsbury. (Poetry Ser.). 1979. 5.95 o.p. (ISBN 0-685-96487-6, Pub. by Carcanet New Pr England). Humanities.

--Lies & Dreams. 95p. 1980. pap. text ed. write for info (ISBN 0-85635-297-7, Pub. by Carcanet New Pr England). Humanities.

Ashby, E. Technology & the Academics: Essays on Universities & the Scientific Revolution. 1958. pap. 8.95 o.p. (ISBN 0-312-78820-7). St Martin.

Ashby, Eric. Adapting Universities to a Technological Society. LC 73-22555. (Higher Education Ser.). 200p. 1974. 15.95x (ISBN 0-87589-222-1). Jossey-Bass.

Ashby, Gene, ed. see Micronesian Community College Students.

Ashby, Gwynneth. Take a Trip to Japan. LC 80-52719. (Take a Trip Ser.). (gr. 1-3). 1981. PLB 8.40 (ISBN 0-531-00990-4). Watts.

Ashby, M. F., jt. auth. see Frost, H. J.

Ashby, M. K. Changing English Village. 1980. 18.00x o.p. (ISBN 0-900093-35-8, Pub. by Roundwood). State Mutual Bk.

Ashby, Maurice. Introduction to Plant Ecology. 2nd ed. (Illus.). 1969. text ed. 17.95 o.p. (ISBN 0-312-43120-1). St Martin.

Ashby, Neil. Introductory Modern Physics Experiments. 2nd ed. (Illus.). 1971. pap. text ed. 4.50x o.p. (ISBN 0-87108-102-4). Pruett.

Ashby, Susan. Granny's Muffin House. 1983. pap. 8.95 (ISBN 0-930440-18-8). Royal Pub Co.

Ashby, W. R. Design for a Brain: The Origin of Adaptive Behavior. 2nd ed. 286p. 1966. pap. 11.95x (ISBN 0-412-20090-2, Pub. by Chapman & Hall England). Methuen Inc.

Ashby, W. Ross. Introduction to Cybernetics. 1964. pap. 14.95x (ISBN 0-416-68300-2). Methuen Inc.

Ashcroft-Nowicki, Dolores. First Steps in Ritual: Safe, Effective Techniques for Experiencing the Inner Worlds. 96p. 1983. pap. 6.95 (ISBN 0-85030-314-1). Newcastle Pub.

Ashdown. Color Atlas of the Ruminants. 240p. 1982. text ed. 75.00 (ISBN 0-8391-1760-4). Univ Park.

Ashe, Amy E., jt. auth. see Bossone, Richard M.

Ashe, Arthur & Amdur, Neil. Off the Court. 1982. pap. 3.50 (ISBN 0-451-11766-2, AE1766, Sig). NAL.

Ashe, Geoffrey. A Guidebook to Arthurian Britain. (Longman Travellers Ser.). (Illus.). 1983. text ed. 15.95x (ISBN 0-582-50282-9). Longman.

--The Virgin. (Illus.). 1976. 15.00x o.p. (ISBN 0-7100-8342-4). Routledge & Kegan.

Ashe, Kaye. New Women, New Church. 1983. 10.95 (ISBN 0-88347-145-0). Thomas More.

Ashe, Penelope. Naked Came the Stranger. LC 69-20279. 1969. 5.95 o.p. (ISBN 0-8184-0114-1). Lyle Stuart.

Ashe, Rosalind. Literary Houses. 144p. 1982. 17.95x (ISBN 0-87196-676-X). Facts on File.

Asheim, Lester, ed. Persistent Issues in American Librarianship. LC 61-15050. vi, 114p. 1961. lib. bdg. 7.00 (ISBN 0-226-02960-3). U of Chicago Pr.

Asheim, Lester, et al. Reading & Successful Living: The Family-School Partnership. 150p. 1983. write for info. (ISBN 0-208-02003-9, Lib Prof Pubns); pap. 11.50x (ISBN 0-208-02004-7, Lib Prof Pubns). Shoe String.

Ashenhurst, Robert L., jt. auth. see AFIPS Taxonomy Committee.

Asher, C. Postural Variations in Childhood. (Postgraduate Pediatric Ser.). 1975. 14.95 o.p. (ISBN 0-407-00032-1). Butterworth.

Asher, Don. Blood Summer. LC 77-7993. 1977. 8.95 o.p. (ISBN 0-399-12028-9). Putnam Pub Group.

Asher, Gerald. On Wine. 1982. 15.95 (ISBN 0-394-52737-2). Random.

Asher, Harry. Photographic Principles & Practices. 224p. 1975. 11.95 (ISBN 0-13-665539-4, Spec); pap. text ed. write for info. (ISBN 0-13-665497-5, Spec). P-H.

Asher, Kenneth. Living Relics: Oregon's Old Hotels. (Illus.). 120p. (Orig.). 1982. pap. 5.95 cancelled (ISBN 0-89288-077-5). Maverick.

Asher, Oksana D. Letters from the Gulag. 1983. 15.00 (ISBN 0-8315-0187-1). Speller.

Asher, Robert E., jt. auth. see Mason, Edward S.

Asher, Sandy. Daughters of the Law. (YA) (gr. 7-12). 1983. pap. 1.95 (ISBN 0-440-92098-1, LFL). Dell.

--Summer Begins. 176p. 1982. 1.95 (ISBN 0-553-22512-X). Bantam.

--Things Are Seldom What They Seem. LC 82-72819. 144p. (YA) (gr. 7 up). 1983. 11.95 (ISBN 0-440-08932-8). Delacorte.

Asher, Shirley J., jt. ed. see Bloom, Bernard L.

Asher, Spring & Chambers, Wicke. The Moneymaking Book for Kids. (Illus.). (gr. 5-9). 1980. pap. 2.95 o.p. (ISBN 0-671-95473-3). Wanderer Bks.

Asher, Spring, jt. ed. see Chambers, Wicke.

Asher, Steven & Gottman, John, eds. The Development of Children's Friendships. LC 80-25920. (Cambridge Studies in Social & Emotional Development). (Illus.). 336p. 1981. 37.50 (ISBN 0-521-23103-5); pap. 13.95 (ISBN 0-521-29806-7). Cambridge U Pr.

Asher, W. Michael, jt. auth. see Leopold, George R.

Asheri, Michael. Living Jewish. enl. deluxe ed. 1980. 14.95 (ISBN 0-89696-072-2, An Everest House Book). Dodd.

--Living Jewish: The Lore & Law of the Practicing Jew. 1978. 14.95 o.p. (ISBN 0-89696-003-X, An Everest House Book). Dodd.

Ashfield, Helen. Beau Barron's Lady. 192p. 1981. 9.95 o.p. (ISBN 0-312-07057-8). St Martin.

--The Loving Highwaymany. 192p. 1983. 10.95 (ISBN 0-312-49973-6). St Martin.

Ashford, Ann. If I Found a Wistful Unicorn. LC 78-59094. (Illus.). 1978. 8.95 (ISBN 0-931948-00-2). Peachtree Pubs.

Ashford, Bob, jt. auth. see Gibbons, Robert.

Ashford, Douglas. Financing Urban Government in the Welfare State. LC 80-12166. 1980. 30.00 (ISBN 0-312-28985-5). St Martin.

Ashford, Douglas, ed. Comparative Policy Studies. 1977. pap. 6.00 (ISBN 0-918592-24-0). Policy Studies.

Ashford, Douglas E. National Resources & Urban Policy. LC 77-94185. (Illus.). 320p. 1980. 27.50 (ISBN 0-416-60181-2). Methuen Inc.

--Policy & Politics in Britain: The Limits of Consensus. (Policy & Politics in Industrial States Ser.). 330p. 1980. 29.95 (ISBN 0-87722-194-4); pap. text ed. 12.95 (ISBN 0-87722-195-2). Temple U Pr.

--Policy & Politics in France: Living With Uncertainty. LC 82-5771. (Policy & Politics in Industrial States Ser.). 365p. 1982. 29.95 (ISBN 0-87722-261-4); pap. text ed. 12.95x (ISBN 0-87722-262-2). Temple U Pr.

Ashford, Jane. The Marchington Scandal. 1982. pap. 2.25 (ISBN 0-451-11623-2, AE1623, Sig). NAL.

--The Three Graces. 1982. pap. 2.25 (ISBN 0-451-11418-3, AE1418, Sig). NAL.

Ashford, Janet I. The Whole Birth Catalog. (Illus.). 325p. (Orig.). 1983. 28.95 (ISBN 0-89594-108-2); pap. 14.95 (ISBN 0-89594-107-4). Crossing Pr.

Ashford, Jeffrey. Dick Knox at Le Mans. (Putnam Sports Shelf). 160p. (gr. 5 up). 1974. PLB 6.29 o.p. (ISBN 0-399-60893-1). Putnam Pub Group.

--Grand Prix Britain. new ed. (Putnam Sports Shelf). 160p. (gr. 6 up). 1973. PLB 4.97 o.p. (ISBN 0-399-60821-4). Putnam Pub Group.

--Slow Down the World. 186p. 1983. pap. 2.95 (ISBN 0-8027-3015-9). Walker & Co.

--Three Layers of Guilt. 185p. 1983. pap. 2.95 (ISBN 0-8027-3016-7). Walker & Co.

Ashford, Nicholas A. Crisis in the Workplace: Occupational Disease & Injury - (a Report to the Ford Foundation) LC 75-28424. 1976. 30.00x (ISBN 0-262-01045-3). MIT Pr.

Ashford, Norman & Wright, Paul H. Airport Engineering. LC 78-25930. 449p. 1979. 44.95x (ISBN 0-471-07255-9, Pub. by Wiley-Interscience). Wiley.

Ashford, Norman & Bell, W. G., eds. Mobility & Transport for Elderly & Handicapped Persons: International Conference Held in Cambridge, England, July, 1981. (Transportation Studies: Vol. 2). Date not set. price not set (ISBN 0-677-16380-0). Gordon.

Ashihara, Yoshinobu & Riggs, Lynne E. The Aesthetic Townscape. (Illus.). 196p. 1983. 20.00 (ISBN 0-262-01069-0). MIT Pr.

Ashkar, F., et al, eds. A Study Guide in Nuclear Medicine. (Illus.). 488p. 1975. 29.00x (ISBN 0-398-03029-4); pap. 22.25x (ISBN 0-398-03060-X). C C Thomas.

Ashkar, F. S., ed. Thyroid & Endocrine System Investigations with Radionuclides & Radioassays. LC 79-84782. (Illus.). 544p. 1979. 46.75x (ISBN 0-89352-070-5). Masson Pub.

Ashkenas, Thais L. Aids & Deterrents to the Performance of Associate Degree Graduates in Nursing. (League Exchange Ser.: No. 99). 168p. 1973. 6.95 (ISBN 0-686-38359-1, 23-1465). Natl League Nurse.

Ashkenasi, Abraham. Modern German Nationalism. LC 75-33702. 222p. 1976. 14.95x o.p. (ISBN 0-470-03492-0). Halsted Pr.

Ashleigh, E. A., jt. auth. see Utley, Joe R.

Ashley. Hospitals, Paternalism & the Role of the Nurse. pap. text ed. 8.50 (ISBN 0-686-97980-X, Lippincott Nursing). Lippincott.

Ashley, Benedict M. & O'Rourke, Kevin D. Health Care Ethics: A Theological Analysis. LC 77-88355. 1978. pap. 14.00 o.p. (ISBN 0-87125-044-6). Cath Health.

--Health Care Ethics: A Theological Analysis. 2nd ed. LC 81-17973. 1982. 25.00 (ISBN 0-87125-075-6); pap. 16.00 (ISBN 0-87125-070-5). Cath Health.

Ashley, Bernard. All My Men. LC 78-12683. (gr. 6 up). 1978. 10.95 (ISBN 0-87599-228-5). S G Phillips.

--A Break in the Sun. (Illus.). 186p. (gr. 6 up). 1980. 10.95 (ISBN 0-87599-230-7). S G Phillips.

--A Kind of Wild Justice. LC 78-10899. (Illus.). (gr. 7 up). 1979. 10.95 (ISBN 0-87599-229-3). S G Phillips.
--Linda's Lie. (Julia MacRae Blackbird Bks.). (Illus.). 48p. (gr. k-3). 1983. 5.95 (ISBN 0-531-04576-5, MacRae). Watts.
--Terry on the Fence. LC 76-39898. (Illus.). (gr. 5-9). 1977. 10.95 (ISBN 0-87599-222-6). S G Phillips.
Ashley, C. C. & Campbell, A. K. Measurement of Free Calcium in Cells. 1980. 81.00 (ISBN 0-444-80185-5). Elsevier.
Ashley, Clifford W. Ashley Book of Knots. 1944. 24.95 (ISBN 0-385-04025-3). Doubleday.
Ashley, Jo Ann. Hospitals, Paternalism, & the Role of the Nurse. LC 76-7908. 1976. pap. 8.50x o.p. (ISBN 0-686-82987-5); pap. 7.95x o.p. (ISBN 0-8077-2470-X). Tchrs Coll.
Ashley, John. Principles of Intermediate Algebra. 1977. text ed. 17.95 (ISBN 0-02-473170-6). Macmillan.
Ashley, John P. & Harvey, E. R. Modern Geometry: Complete Course. Maier, Eugene, ed. (Mathematics for Individualized Instruction Ser). (Orig., Prog. Bk.). 1970. pap. text ed. 13.95x (ISBN 0-02-473490-X, 47349); dupl. masters 12.95x (ISBN 0-02-473400-4, 47340). Macmillan.
Ashley, June e. Scout of Santa Fe. (Illus.). 1981. 8.95 (ISBN 0-8062-1677-8). Carlton.
Ashley, Leonard R. Colley Cibber. (English Authors Ser.: No. 17). lib. bdg. 14.95 (ISBN 0-8057-1092-2, Twayne). G K Hall.
Ashley, Maurice. Charles Two. (Illus.). 368p. 1981. pap. 4.95 (ISBN 0-586-03805-1, Pub. by Granada England). Academy Chi Ltd.
--The People of England: A Short Short Social & Economic History. (Illus.). 214p. 1983. text ed. 20.00x (ISBN 0-8071-1105-8). La State U Pr.
Ashley, Meg. The Secret of the Old House. (A Boarding House Adventure Ser.). 1982. pap. 3.95 (ISBN 0-8307-0845-6, 5900014). Regal.
Ashley, Nova. Call Me Grandma! 1982. 5.50 (ISBN 0-8378-1716-1). Gibson.
Ashley, P. P. Oh Promise Me But Put It in Writing: Living Together Agreements Without, Before, During & After Marriage. 1980. pap. 3.95 (ISBN 0-07-002414-6). McGraw.
Ashley, Paul P. Oh Promise Me, but Put It in Writing: Living Together Arrangements Without, During & After Marriage. (Illus.). 1978. 14.95 (ISBN 0-07-002409-X, P&RB). McGraw.
--You & Your Will: The Planning & Management. 1976. Repr. lib. bdg. 11.95 o.p. (ISBN 0-8161-6420-7, Large Print Bks). G K Hall.
--You & Your Will: The Planning & Management of Your Estate. (Illus.). 252p. (Orig.). 1975. 18.95 (ISBN 0-07-002407-3, P&RB). McGraw.
--You & Your Will: The Planning & Management of Your Estate. rev. ed. 1978. 19.95 o.p. (ISBN 0-07-002415-4, P&RB). McGraw.
Ashley, R. Background Math for a Computer World. 2nd ed. LC 80-11562. (Wiley Self-Teaching Guides). 308p. 1980. pap. text ed. 8.95 (ISBN 0-471-08086-1). Wiley.
Ashley, Ray. Electrical Estimating. 3rd ed. 1961. 51.50 (ISBN 0-07-002403-0, P&RB). McGraw.
Ashley, Richard. The Trouble with Cocaine. 200p. (Orig.). 1982. pap. 9.95 o.p. (ISBN 0-933328-44-3). Delilah Bks.
Ashley, Ruth. ANS Cobol. 2nd ed. LC 78-27717. (Self-Teaching Guide Ser.). 265p. 1979. pap. text ed. 9.50 (ISBN 0-471-05136-5). Wiley.
--Human Anatomy. LC 76-65. (Self-Teaching Guides). 274p. 1976. pap. text ed. 7.95 (ISBN 0-471-03508-4). Wiley.
--Structured Cobol. LC 79-27340. (Self-Teaching Guides Ser.). 295p. 1980. pap. text ed. 10.95 (ISBN 0-471-05362-7). Wiley.
Ashley, Ruth & Fernandez, Judi. COBOL for Microcomputers. (Self-Teaching Guide Ser.). 288p. 1983. pap. text ed. 10.95 (ISBN 0-471-87241-5). Wiley.
--PC Dos: Using the IBM PC Operating System A Self Teaching Guide. 188p. 1983. pap. text ed. 14.95 (ISBN 0-471-89718-3). Wiley.
Ashley, Ruth & Fernandez, Judi N. Job Control Language. LC 77-27316. (Self-Teaching Guide Ser.). 161p. 1978. pap. text ed. 7.95 (ISBN 0-471-03205-0). Wiley.
Ashley, Ruth & Kirby, Tess. Dental Anatomy & Terminology. LC 76-49088. (Self-Teaching Guides). 242p. 1977. text ed. 4.95x (ISBN 0-471-01348-X). Wiley.
Ashley, Ruth, jt. auth. see Fernandes, Judi N.
Ashley, Ruth, ed. see Fernandez, Judi N.
Ashley, Steven. The Last Brigade. 320p. 1982. pap. 2.95 (ISBN 0-515-05559-X). Jove Pubns.
Ashley Montagu. Life Before Birth. rev ed. pap. 2.25 (ISBN 0-451-09184-1, E9184, Sig). NAL.
--Man, His First Two Million Years. pap. 2.95 o.s.i. (ISBN 0-440-55144-7, Delta). Dell.
--On Being Human. (gr. 9-12). 1967. pap. 3.60 (ISBN 0-8015-5514-0, Hawthorn). Dutton.
Ashley Montagu, jt. auth. see Steen, Edwin B.
Ashlock, Patrick & Grant, Sister Marie. Educational Therapy Materials from the Ashlock Learning Center. (Illus.). 440p. 1976. spiral 34.50x (ISBN 0-398-02218-6). C C Thomas.
Ashlock, Robert. Error Patterns in Computation. 3rd ed. 208p. 1982. pap. text ed. 9.95 (ISBN 0-675-09880-7). Merrill.
Ashlock, Robert B. & Johnson, Martin L. Guide Each Child's Learning of Mathematics: A Diagnostic Approach to Instruction. 612p. 1983. text ed. 21.95 (ISBN 0-675-20023-7). Additional supplements may be obtained from publisher. Merrill.
Ashman, Howard. Flash Gordon Puzzlers. (Flash Gordon Puzzles Ser.). (gr. 3-6). 1979. pap. 0.95 o.s.i. (ISBN 0-448-15999-6, G&D). Putnam Pub Group.
--Godzilla Puzzlers. (Illus.). (gr. 3-6). 1979. pap. 0.95 o.s.i. (ISBN 0-448-15919-8, G&D). Putnam Pub Group.
Ashman, Iain. Make This Model Castle. (Illus.). (gr. 4-9). 1983. pap. 5.95 (ISBN 0-13-545947-8). P-H.
--Make This Model Village. (Illus.). (gr. 4-9). 1983. pap. 5.95 (ISBN 0-13-545954-0). P-H.
Ashmole, Bernard, jt. auth. see Groenewegen Frankfort, Mrs. H.
Ashmore, Harry. Hearts & Minds: The Anatomy of Racism From Roosevelt to Reagan. 1982. pap. 15.95 (ISBN 0-686-97692-4). Mcgraw.
Ashmore, Helen, jt. auth. see Arth, Marvin.
Ashmore, Owen. The Industrial Archaeology of North-West England. (Illus.). 272p. Date not set. 25.00 (ISBN 0-7190-0820-4). Manchester.
Ashmore, Richard & McConahay, John B. Psychology & America's Urban Problems. LC 74-9519. (Psychology Ser.). 204p. 1975. 7.95 o.p. (ISBN 0-07-002453-7, C). McGraw.
Ashmun, Margaret E. Singing Swan: An Account of Anna Seward & Her Acquaintance with Doctor Johnson, Boswell & Others of Their Time. LC 68-57589. (Illus.). 1969. Repr. of 1931 ed. lib. bdg. 17.50x (ISBN 0-8371-0287-1, ASSS). Greenwood.
Ashmun, Richard, jt. auth. see Ernest, John.
Ashmun, Richard D., jt. auth. see Ernest, John W.
Ashner, S. Shapiro, jt. auth. see Christensen, J. Ippolito.
Ashnorth, Georgina, ed. World Minorities, Vol. 2. pap. 8.95 o.p. (ISBN 0-905898-01-X). Transatlantic.
Ashour, Y., jt. auth. see Wardhaugh, K.
Ashton, Ann. Star Eyes. LC 82-45282. (Starlight Romance Ser.). 192p. 1983. 11.95 (ISBN 0-385-18130-2). Doubleday.
Ashton, Anne. Concession. LC 79-7484. (Romantic Suspense Ser.). 192p. 1981. 10.95 o.p. (ISBN 0-385-13210-7). Doubleday.
Ashton, D. L., jt. auth. see McPherson, E.
Ashton, Dave, jt. auth. see Delehanty, Suzanne.
Ashton, Dore. Picasso on Art. 1977. pap. 6.95 (ISBN 0-14-004528-7). Penguin.
Ashton, Dore & Marter, Jean M. Jose de Rivera Constructions. LC 79-56553. (Illus.). 254p. 1983. 85.00 (ISBN 0-8390-0311-0). Allanheld & Schram.
Ashton, Elizabeth. La Plus Douce Des Musiques. (Harlequin Romantique Ser.). 192p. 1983. pap. 1.95 (ISBN 0-373-41189-8). Harlequin Bks.
Ashton, Floyd M. & Crafts, Alden S. Mode of Action of Herbicides. 2nd ed. LC 80-23077. 525p. 1981. 47.95x (ISBN 0-471-04847-X, Pub. by Wiley-Interscience). Wiley.
Ashton, Floyd M., jt. auth. see Klingman, GLenn C.
Ashton, Floyd M., jt. auth. see Klingman, Glenn C.
Ashton, Heather & Stepney, Rod. Smoking: Psychology & Pharmacology. 1982. 22.00x (ISBN 0-422-77700-5, Pub. by Tavistock). Methuen Inc.
Ashton, Jean. Harriet Beecher Stowe: A Reference Guide. 1977. lib. bdg. 21.00 (ISBN 0-8161-7833-X, Hall Reference). G K Hall.
Ashton, John. Adventures & Discourses of Captain John Smith. LC 76-78108. (Illus.). 1969. Repr. of 1883 ed. 30.00x (ISBN 0-8103-3565-4). Gale.
--Century of Ballads. LC 67-23925. 1968. Repr. of 1887 ed. 34.00x (ISBN 0-8103-3406-2). Gale.
--Curious Creatures in Zoology. LC 68-57297. 1968. Repr. of 1890 ed. 37.00x (ISBN 0-8103-3525-5). Gale.
--Dawn of the Nineteenth Century in England. LC 67-23941. (Social History Reference Ser). 1968. Repr. of 1886 ed. 34.00x (ISBN 0-8103-3247-7). Gale.
--Devil in Britain & America. LC 73-18391. Repr. of 1896 ed. 45.00x (ISBN 0-8103-3626-X). Gale.
--Eighteenth Century Waifs. LC 68-58971. 1968. Repr. of 1887 ed. 34.00 (ISBN 0-8103-3517-4). Gale.
--English Caricature & Satire on Napoleon 1st. LC 67-24349. (Social History Reference Ser). 1968. Repr. of 1888 ed. 34.00x (ISBN 0-8103-3248-5). Gale.
--Fleet: Its River, Prison, & Marriages. LC 68-21753. 1969. Repr. of 1888 ed. 37.00x (ISBN 0-8103-3414-3). Gale.
--Gossip in the First Decade of Victoria's Reign. LC 67-23942. 1968. Repr. of 1903 ed. 30.00x (ISBN 0-8103-3249-3). Gale.
--History of English Lotteries. LC 67-23945. (Illus.). 1969. Repr. of 1893 ed. 34.00x (ISBN 0-8103-3250-7). Gale.
--History of Gambling in England. LC 68-21520. 1968. Repr. of 1899 ed. 30.00x (ISBN 0-8103-3501-8). Gale.
--History of Gambling in England. LC 69-14910. (Criminology, Law Enforcement, & Social Problems Ser.: No. 73). 1969. Repr. of 1898 ed. 10.00x (ISBN 0-87585-073-1). Patterson Smith.
--Humour, Wit & Satire of the Seventeenth Century. LC 67-24350. (Social History Reference). 1968. Repr. of 1883 ed. 30.00x (ISBN 0-8103-3251-5). Gale.
--Modern Street Ballads. LC 67-23926. (Illus.). 1968. Repr. of 1888 ed. 34.00x (ISBN 0-8103-3407-0). Gale.
--Old Times. LC 67-23944. (Illus.). 1969. Repr. of 1885 ed. 30.00x (ISBN 0-8103-3252-3). Gale.
--Social England Under the Regency. LC 67-23940. 1968. Repr. of 1899 ed. 30.00x (ISBN 0-8103-3253-1). Gale.
--Varia. LC 68-9573. (Illus.). 1968. Repr. of 1894 ed. 30.00x (ISBN 0-8103-3502-6). Gale.
--When William Fourth Was King. LC 67-23943. (Social History Reference Ser). 1968. Repr. of 1896 ed. 30.00x (ISBN 0-8103-3255-8). Gale.
Ashton, John, jt. auth. see Mew, James.
Ashton, Marvin J. Ye Are My Friends. 151p. 1982. 6.95 (ISBN 0-87747-934-8). Deseret Bk.
Ashton, Patricia M. & Henderson, Euan S. Teacher Education in the Classroom. 144p. 1983. text ed. 21.50x (ISBN 0-7099-1248-X, Pub. by Croom Helm Ltd England). Biblio Dist.
Ashton, R. The City & the Court: Sixteen Hundred & Three to Sixteen Forty-Three. LC 78-67296. 1979. 34.50 (ISBN 0-521-22419-5). Cambridge U Pr.
Ashton, Robert H. Human Information Processing in Accounting, Vol. 17. (Studies in Accounting Research). 215p. 1982. 6.00 (ISBN 0-86539-038-X). Am Accounting.
Ashton, Sharon, jt. auth. see Van Slyke, Helen.
Ashton, Sylvia, ed. see Bowler, Marion.
Ashton, Sylvia, ed. see Brink, Vonder Marylou.
Ashton, Sylvia, ed. see Cole, Bruce.
Ashton, Sylvia, ed. see Farrar, Kenneth G.
Ashton, Sylvia, ed. see Goodman, Marguerite.
Ashton, Sylvia, ed. see Jonathan, Stephen.
Ashton, Sylvia, ed. see Kimball, Gitele.
Ashton, Sylvia, ed. see Miller, Alan C., et al.
Ashton, Thomas L., ed. Heath Ten Short Novels. 704p. 1978. pap. text ed. 13.95 (ISBN 0-669-01029-4). Heath.
Ashton, Winifred. Legend. LC 78-17053. 1978. Repr. of 1919 ed. lib. bdg. 18.00x (ISBN 0-313-20572-8, ASLE). Greenwood.
Ashtor, E. A Social & Economic History of the Near East in the Middle Ages. LC 74-29800. (Near Eastern Center Series, UCLA). 1976. 37.50x (ISBN 0-520-02962-3). U of Cal Pr.
Ashurst, F. Gareth. Founders of Modern Mathematics. 128p. 1982. 39.00x (ISBN 0-584-10380-8, Pub. by Muller Ltd). State Mutual Bk.
Ashwell, D. G. & Gallagher, R. H., eds. Finite Elements for Thin Shells & Curved Members. LC 75-37654. (Studies in Social & Cognitive Development). 268p. 1976. 53.95x o.p. (ISBN 0-471-01648-9, Pub. by Wiley-Interscience). Wiley.
Ashwood, M. J. & Farrant, Smith J. Low Temperature Preservation in Medicine & Biology. 336p. 1980. text ed. 39.50 o.p. (ISBN 0-8391-1492-3). Univ Park.
Ashworth. Advanced Quantity: Surveying. 1983. text ed. write for info (ISBN 0-408-01192-0). Butterworth.
Ashworth, jt. auth. see Bourbousson.
Ashworth, Gregory, jt. auth. see Riley, R. C.
Ashworth, J. M. Cell Differentiation. 1973. pap. 6.50x (ISBN 0-412-11760-6, Pub. by Chapman & Hall). Methuen Inc.
Ashworth, M. R., tr. see Stahl, E.
Ashworth, P. D. Social Interaction & Consciousness. LC 78-27252. 227p. 1979. 44.95x (ISBN 0-471-27567-0, Pub. by Wiley-Interscience); pap. 21.00x (ISBN 0-471-27566-2). Wiley.
Ashworth, Robert. Highway Engineering. 1966. pap. text ed. 18.50x o.p. (ISBN 0-435-72302-2). Heinemann Ed.
Ashworth, Tony. Trench Warfare. LC 80-13696. 258p. 1980. text ed. 43.50x o.p. (ISBN 0-8419-0615-7). Holmes & Meier.
Ashworth, William. Nor Any Drop to Drink. 256p. 1982. 17.25 (ISBN 0-671-43551-5); pap. 6.75 (ISBN 0-671-45950-3). Summit Bks.
Asian Development Bank. Asian Energy Problems. 304p. 1982. 26.95 (ISBN 0-03-061566-6). Praeger.
Asian Regional Team for Employment Promotion, Bangkok. Employment Expansion Through Local Resource Mobilisation: Papers & Poceedings of a Workshop, Comilla, Bangladesh, 1-3 July 1981. iv, 45p. 1981. 5.00 (ISBN 92-2-102696-5). Intl Labour Office.
Asiedu, E. S., ed. Public Administration in English-Speaking West Africa: An Annotated Bibliography. 1977. lib. bdg. 55.00 (ISBN 0-8161-7811-9, Hall Reference). G K Hall.
Asiedu-Akrofi, K. A Living Classroom. (Illus.). 128p. (Orig.). 1981. pap. 10.00x (ISBN 0-04-370110-8). Allen Unwin.
Asija, S. P. How to Patent Computer Programs. 100p. 1982. 50.00 (ISBN 0-686-36935-1). Res Pr KS.
Asimakopulos, A. An Introduction to Economic Theory: Microeconomics. (Illus.). 1978. text ed. 18.95x (ISBN 0-19-540281-2). Oxford U Pr.
Asimov, Isaac. Adding a Dimension. 1975. pap. 1.50 o.p. (ISBN 0-380-00278-7, 36871, Discus). Avon.
--Animals of the Bible. LC 77-16893. (gr. 2-5). 1978. 9.95a (ISBN 0-385-07195-7); PLB (ISBN 0-385-07215-5). Doubleday.
--Asimov on Astronomy. LC 73-80946. (Illus.). 288p. 1975. pap. 5.50 (ISBN 0-385-06881-6, Anch). Doubleday.
--Asimov's Biographical Encyclopedia of Science & Technology. 2nd. rev. ed. LC 81-47861. (Illus.). 984p. 1982. 29.95 (ISBN 0-385-17771-2). Doubleday.
--Asimov's Guide to the Bible: The New Testament. 1971. pap. 7.95 (ISBN 0-380-01031-3, 59774-8). Avon.
--The Best Fantasy of the Nineteenth Century. Waugh, Charles G. & Greenberg, Martin H., eds. 357p. 1982. 15.95 (ISBN 0-686-82284-6). Beaufort Bks NY.
--Chemicals of Life. pap. 1.95 (ISBN 0-451-62037-2, MJ2037, Ment). NAL.
--A Choice of Catastrophes. 1979. 11.95 o.p. (ISBN 0-671-22701-7). S&S.
--Comets & Meteors. LC 72-2499. (Beginning Science Ser.). (Illus.). 32p. (gr. 2-5). 1972. 2.50 (ISBN 0-695-80047-7, Dist. by Caroline Hse); PLB 2.95 titan ed. (ISBN 0-695-40047-9). Follett.
--David Starr, Space Ranger. 9.95 (ISBN 0-8398-2486-6, Gregg). G K Hall.
--David Starr: Space Ranger. (David Starr Ser). (RL 5). 1971. pap. 0.95 o.p. (ISBN 0-451-06771-1, Q6771, Sig). NAL.
--Eight Stories from the Rest of the Robots. 1978. pap. 1.50 o.s.i. (ISBN 0-515-04551-9). Jove Pubns.
--Extraterrestrial Civilizations. Date not set. pap. 5.95 (ISBN 0-449-90020-7, Columbine). Fawcett.
--Foundation. 1968. pap. 2.95 (ISBN 0-380-00914-5, 61952-0). Avon.
--Foundation. 256p. 1983. pap. 2.75 (ISBN 0-345-30899-9, Del Rey). Ballantine.
--Foundation & Empire. 1968. pap. 2.50 o.p. (ISBN 0-380-00774-6, 61465). Avon.
--Foundation & Empire. 256p. 1983. pap. 2.75 (ISBN 0-345-30900-6, Del Rey). Ballantine.
--Foundation Trilogy. (Science Fiction Ser.). 684p. 1982. 17.95 (ISBN 0-385-18830-7). Doubleday.
--Foundation's Edge. LC 82-45450. 384p. 1982. 14.95 (ISBN 0-385-17725-9). Doubleday.
--Foundation's Edge. signed & numbered ed. 1982. leather spine 51.00x (ISBN 0-918372-10-0). Whispers.
--Genetic Code. pap. 2.50 (ISBN 0-451-62110-7, ME2110, Ment). NAL.
--How Did We Find Out About the Universe? (History of Science Ser.). (Illus.). 64p. (gr. 5-8). 1983. 7.95 (ISBN 0-8027-6476-2); lib. bdg. 8.85 (ISBN 0-8027-6477-0). Walker & Co.
--Human Body. (Illus.). 1964. pap. 2.95 (ISBN 0-451-62116-6, ME2116, Ment). NAL.
--Human Brain: Its Capacities & Functions. pap. 3.50 (ISBN 0-451-62187-5, ME2187, Ment). NAL.
--In the Beginning: Science Faces God in the Book of Genesis. 240p. 1981. 17.95 (ISBN 0-517-54336-2). Crown.
--Isaac Asimov's Book of Facts. 1979. 12.95 o.p. (ISBN 0-448-15776-4, G&D). Putnam Pub Group.
--Isaac Asimov's Treasury of Humor. 1979. pap. 8.95 (ISBN 0-395-28412-0). HM.
--The Key Word & Other Mysteries. (Illus.). (gr. 2-6). 1979. pap. 1.95 (ISBN 0-380-43224-2, 63776-6, Camelot). Avon.
--Lucky Starr & the Big Sun of Mercury. 9.95 (ISBN 0-8398-2489-0, Gregg). G K Hall.
--Lucky Starr & the Moons of Jupiter. 9.95 (ISBN 0-8398-2490-4, Gregg). G K Hall.
--Lucky Starr & the Oceans of Venus. 9.95 (ISBN 0-8398-2488-2, Gregg). G K Hall.
--Lucky Starr & the Pirates of the Asteroids. 9.95 (ISBN 0-8398-2487-4, Gregg). G K Hall.
--Lucky Starr & the Rings of Saturn. 9.95 (ISBN 0-8398-2491-2, Gregg). G K Hall.
--The Lucky Starr Series. 50.00 (ISBN 0-444-47070-0, Gregg). G K Hall.
--The Martian Way & Other Stories. LC 81-15009. 224p. 1982. Repr. of 1955 ed. 12.50x (ISBN 0-8376-0463-X). Bentley.
--The Measure of the Universe. LC 82-48654. (Illus.). 224p. 1983. 13.41i (ISBN 0-06-015129-3, HarpT). Har-Row.
--Moon. (Beginning Science Ser.). (Illus.). (gr. 2-4). 1966. 2.94 (ISBN 0-695-45875-2). Follett.
--More... Would You Believe? LC 80-84450. (Illus.). 64p. 1982. 5.95 (ISBN 0-448-04472-2, G&D). Putnam Pub Group.
--Near East: 10,000 Years of History. (Illus.). (gr. 7 up). 1968. 4.95 o.p. (ISBN 0-395-06562-3). HM.
--Of Time, Space, & Other Things. 1975. pap. 1.75 o.s.i. (ISBN 0-380-00325-2, 35584, Discus). Avon.
--Pebble in the Sky. LC 81-15516. 224p. 1982. Repr. of 1950 ed. 12.50x (ISBN 0-8376-0462-1). Bentley.
--Realm of Algebra. 144p. 1981. pap. 2.50 (ISBN 0-449-24398-2, Crest). Fawcett.
--The Roving Mind. 325p. 1983. 17.95 (ISBN 0-87975-201-7). Prometheus Bks.
--Second Foundation. 1976. pap. 2.50 o.p. (ISBN 0-380-00823-8, 59105). Avon.
--Second Foundation. 256p. 1983. pap. 2.75 (ISBN 0-345-30901-4, Del Rey). Ballantine.
--A Short History of Biology. LC 80-15464. (American Museum Science Bks.). (Illus.). ix, 189p. 1980. Repr. of 1964 ed. lib. bdg. 19.00x (ISBN 0-313-22583-4, ASSB). Greenwood.
--The Solar System. LC 73-93548. (Beginning Science Ser.). 32p. (gr. 2-4). 1974. PLB 2.94 (ISBN 0-695-40473-3). Follett.

--The Solar System & Back. 256p. 1972. pap. 1.50 o.p. (ISBN 0-380-01444-0, 36012). Avon.
--The Sun. LC 70-184458. (Beginning Science Ser.). (Illus.). 32p. (gr. 2-5). 1972. 2.49 (ISBN 0-695-80320-4). Follett.
--The Sun Shines Bright. 256p. 1983. pap. 2.95 (ISBN 0-380-61390-5, 61390-5, Discus). Avon.
--Understanding Physics: Light, Magnetism & Electricity. (Signet Science Ser). 1969. pap. 2.75 (ISBN 0-451-62121-2, ME2121, Ment). NAL.
--Understanding Physics: Motion, Sound & Heat. (Signet Science Ser.). 1969. pap. 3.95 (ISBN 0-451-62202-2, ME2202, Ment). NAL.
--Understanding Physics: The Electron, Proton & Neutron. (Signet Science Ser). 1969. pap. 3.95 (ISBN 0-451-62190-5, ME2190, Ment). NAL.
--The Universe: From Flat Earth to Quasar. 1976. pap. 3.95 (ISBN 0-380-01596-X, 62208-4, Discus). Avon.
--The Winds of Change & Other Stories. LC 81-43912. 288p. 1983. 15.95 (ISBN 0-385-18099-3). Doubleday.
--Words from the Myths. (Illus.). (RL 6). 1969. pap. 1.75 (ISBN 0-451-11326-8, AE1326, Sig). NAL.
--Words of Science & the History Behind Them. (Illus.). (RL 7). 1969. pap. 1.95 (ISBN 0-451-61799-1, MJ1799, Ment). NAL.
Asimov, Isaac & Greenberg. Asimov Presents the Great SF Stories (1942, No. 4. (Science Fiction Ser.). 1980. pap. 2.50 o.p. (ISBN 0-87997-570-9, UE1570). DAW Bks.
Asimov, Isaac & Greenberg, Martin H. Dragon Tales. 320p. 1982. pap. 2.95 (ISBN 0-686-98388-2, Crest). Fawcett.
Asimov, Isaac see Dr. A., pseud.
Asimov, Isaac, ed. The Annotated Gulliver's Travels. (Illus.). 416p. 1980. 19.95 (ISBN 0-517-53949-7, C N Potter Bks). Crown.
Asimov, Isaac, intro. by. Astronauts & Androids. LC 77-81938. 1977. pap. 1.50 o.s.i. (ISBN 0-89559-005-0). Davis Pubns.
--Black Holes & Bug-Eyed-Monsters. LC 77-82629. 1977. pap. 1.50 o.s.i. (ISBN 0-89559-007-7). Davis Pubns.
Asimov, Isaac, ed. Soviet Science Fiction. (Orig.). 1962. pap. 1.75 o.p. (ISBN 0-02-016550-1, Collier). Macmillan.
Asimov, Isaac & Greenberg, Martin H., eds. Isaac Asimov Presents the Great SF Stories, No. 1. (Science Fiction Ser.). 1979. pap. 2.95 (ISBN 0-87997-700-0, UE1700). DAW Bks.
--Isaac Asimov Presents the Great SF Stories, No. 3. 1980. pap. 2.25 o.p. (ISBN 0-87997-523-7, UE1523). Daw Bks.
--Isaac Asimov Presents the Great SF Stories, No. 5. 1981. pap. 2.75 (ISBN 0-87997-604-7, UE1604). Daw Bks.
--Isaac Asimov Presents the Great SF Stories, No. 6. (Science Fiction Ser.). 1981. pap. 2.95 (ISBN 0-87997-670-5, U E 1670). DAW Bks.
--Isaac Asimov Presents the Great SF Stories, No. 7. 368p. 1982. pap. 3.50 (ISBN 0-87997-746-9, UE1746). DAW Bks.
--Isaac Asimov Presents the Great SF Stories, No. 8. 1982. pap. 3.50 (ISBN 0-87997-780-9, UE1780). DAW Bks.
--Isaac Asimov Presents the Great SF Stories, No. 9. 368p. 1983. pap. 3.50 (ISBN 0-686-84671-0). DAW Bks.
--Miniature Mysteries: 100 Malicious Little Mystery Stories. LC 80-28667. 1983. pap. 9.95 (ISBN 0-8008-5252-4). Taplinger.
Asimov, Isaac & Laurance, Alice, eds. Speculations. 312p. 1982. 13.95 (ISBN 0-395-32065-8). HM.
Asimov, Isaac & Martin, George R., eds. The Science Fiction Weightloss Book. 1983. 12.95 (ISBN 0-517-54978-6). Crown.
Asimov, Isaac & Waugh, Charles G., eds. Isaac Asimov Presents the Best Fantasy of the 19th Century. LC 82-4480. (Isaac Asimov Presents Anthologies). 368p. 1982. 16.95 (ISBN 0-8253-0099-1). Beaufort Bks NY.
Asimov, Isaac, et al, eds. Caught in the Organ Draft: Biology in Science Fiction. 186p. 1983. 10.95 (ISBN 0-374-31228-1). FS&G.
--Hallucination Orbit: Psychology in Science Fiction. 186p. 1983. 10.95 (ISBN 0-374-32835-8). FS&G.
--Fantastic Creatures. LC 81-10412. 160p. (gr. 7 up). 1981. lib. bdg. 9.90 (ISBN 0-531-04342-8). Watts.
--One Hundred Great Science Fiction Short Short Stories. 1980. pap. 2.95 (ISBN 0-380-58735-1, 60483-3). Avon.
--Starships. 432p. (Orig.). 1983. pap. 3.50 (ISBN 0-449-20126-0, Crest). Fawcett.
ASIS Annual Meeting, 37th. Information Utilities: Proceedings. Zunde, Pranas, ed. LC 64-8303. (Proceedings of the ASIS Annual Meeting Ser: Vol. 11). 278p. 1974. 17.50 (ISBN 0-87715-411-2). Am Soc Info Sci.
ASIS Annual Meeting 38th. Information Revolution: Proceedings. Husbands, Charles & Tighe, Ruth, eds. LC 64-8303. (Annual Meeting Ser.: Vol. 12). 1975. 17.50 (ISBN 0-87715-412-0). Am Soc Info Sci.
ASIS Mid-Year Meeting, 4th. Information Roundup on Microforms & Data Processing in the Library & Information Center: Costs-Benefits-History-Trends-Proceedings. Spigai, Frances, et al, eds. LC 75-29520. 1975. 14.00 (ISBN 0-87715-112-1). Am Soc Info Sci.
ASIS Workshop on Computer Composition. Proceedings. Landau, Robert M., ed. LC 78-151299. 1971. 12.50 (ISBN 0-87715-002-8). Am Soc Info Sci.
Askey, Richard. Orthogonal Polynomials & Special Functions. (CBMS Regional Conference Ser.: Vol. 21). vii, 110p. (Orig.). 1975. pap. text ed. 14.50 (ISBN 0-89871-018-9). Soc Indus-Appl Math.
Askham, Janet. Fertility & Deprivation. LC 75-2718. (Papers in Sociology Ser.: No. 5). (Illus.). 192p. 1975. 27.95 (ISBN 0-521-20795-9). Cambridge U Pr.
Askim, P. Norwegian-English, English-Norwegian Maritime-Technical Dictionary, 2 vols. 1977. Set. 45.00 (ISBN 82-504-0031-3). Heinman.
Askin, A. Bradley, ed. How Energy Affects the Economy. LC 77-70084. 1978. 18.95x o.p. (ISBN 0-669-01365-X). Lexington Bks.
Asmussen, E. Biomechanics. 1978. VI-A. 44.50 (ISBN 0-8391-1242-4); VI-B. 44.50 (ISBN 0-8391-1243-2). Univ Park.
Asmussen, N. W., et al, eds. Aldosterone Antagonists in Clinical Medicine. (International Congress Ser.: No. 460). 1979. 90.25 (ISBN 0-444-90062-4, Excerpta Medica). Elsevier.
Asp, C. Elliott, jt. auth. see Garbarino, James.
Aspaklaria, Shelley & Geltner, Gerson. Everything You Want to Know About Your Husband's Money...& Need to Know Before the Divorce. LC 78-22456. (Illus.). 1980. 10.95i o.p. (ISBN 0-690-01807-X). T Y Crowell.
Aspden, George. One Piece of Card. 1973. 14.95 o.p. (ISBN 0-7134-2866-X, Pub. by Batsford England). David & Charles.
Aspe, Pedro & Sigmund, Paul, eds. Political Economy of Income Distribution in Mexico. 1983. write for info. (ISBN 0-8419-0634-3). Holmes & Meier.
Aspen Systems Corporation. Collective Index to the Journal of the American Society for Information Science Vol. 1-25, 1950-1974. LC 75-34696. 1975. 60.00 (ISBN 0-87715-113-X). Am Soc Info Sci.
--National Directory of Health-Medicine Organizations, 1982-83. 234p. 1982. 38.50 (ISBN 0-89443-691-0). Aspen Systems.
Asperheim, Mary K. Pharmacology: An Introduction Text. 5th ed. (Illus.). 272p. 1981. text ed. 13.50 (ISBN 0-7216-1446-9). Saunders.
Asperheim, Mary K. & Eisenhauer, Laurel A. The Pharmacologic Basis of Patient Care. 4th ed. (Illus.). 624p. 1981. text ed. 24.50 (ISBN 0-7216-1438-8). Saunders.
Aspey, Wayne P. & Lustick, Sheldon I., eds. Behavioral Energetics: The Cost of Survival in Vertebrates. (Ohio State Univ. Biosciences Colloquia: No. 7). (Illus.). 400p. 1983. 27.50x (ISBN 0-8142-0332-9). Ohio St U Pr.
Aspilden, C., jt. auth. see Rainey, R. C.
Aspin, B. Terry. Foundrywork for the Amatuer. 94p. 7.50x (ISBN 0-85344-105-7). Intl Pubns Serv.
Aspin, Robert. Myth Directions. Stine, Hank, ed. LC 82-12776. (Myth Trilogy Ser.: Vol. 3). (Illus.). 176p. (Orig.). 1982. pap. 5.95 (ISBN 0-89865-250-2, Starblaze). Donning Co.
Aspinall, D., ed. The Microprocessor & Its Application. LC 78-54572. (Illus.). 402p. 1980. pap. 17.95 (ISBN 0-521-29798-2). Cambridge U Pr.
--The Microprocessor & Its Application. LC 78-54572. (Illus.). 1978. 49.50 (ISBN 0-521-22241-9). Cambridge U Pr.
Aspinall, G. O., ed. The Polysaccharides, Vol. 1. (Molecular Biology Ser.). 330p. 1982. 47.00 (ISBN 0-12-065601-9). Acad Pr.
Aspinall, Mary J. Nursing the Open-Heart Surgery Patient. (Illus.). 288p. 1973. 17.95 o.p. (ISBN 0-07-002410-3, HP). McGraw.
Aspinall, Richard. Radio Programme Production: A Manual for Training. 151p. 1971. pap. 9.25 (ISBN 92-3-101030-1, U516, UNESCO). Unipub.
Aspinwall, Margaret, ed. The Painterly Print: Monotypes from the Seventeenth to the Twentieth Century. (Illus.). 262p. 1980. 29.95 o.p. (ISBN 0-87099-223-6); pap. 14.95 o.p. (ISBN 0-87099-224-4). Metro Mus Art.
Aspler, Tony, jt. auth. see Pape, Gordon.
Asplund, Gisele, jt. auth. see Asplund, Goran.
Asplund, Goran & Asplund, Gisele. An Integrated Development Strategy. LC 81-14822. 136p. 1982. 26.95x (ISBN 0-471-10075-7, Pub. by Wiley-Interscience). Wiley.
Asprey, Robert B. The First Battle of the Marne. LC 78-10667. 1979. Repr. of 1962 ed. lib. bdg. 18.75x (ISBN 0-313-21229-5, ASFB). Greenwood.
Asprin, Robert. Another Fine Myth. Freas, Polly & Freas, Kelly, eds. LC 78-2630. (Illus.). 1978. pap. 5.95 (ISBN 0-915442-54-X, Starblaze). Donning Co.
--Myth Conceptions. Freas, Polly & Freas, Kelly, eds. LC 79-9216. (Illus.). 1980. pap. 5.95 (ISBN 0-915442-94-9, Starblaze). Donning Co.
Asprin, Robert, ed. Storm Season. 1982. pap. 2.95 (ISBN 0-441-78710-X, Pub. by Ace Science Fiction). Ace Bks.
--Tales from the Vulgar Unicorn. 1982. pap. 2.75 (ISBN 0-441-79577-3, Pub. by Ace Science Fiction). Ace Bks.
Asprin, Robert L., ed. Shadows of Sanctuary. 320p. (Orig.). 1981. pap. 2.75 (ISBN 0-441-76028-7, Pub. by Ace Science Fiction). Ace Bks.
--Thieves World. 320p. 1981. pap. 2.75 (ISBN 0-441-80579-5, Pub. by Ace Science Fiction). Ace Bks.
Asquith, George. Log Analysis by Microcomputer. 104p. 1980. 33.95x (ISBN 0-87814-118-9). Pennwell Pub.
Asquith, George B. Subsurface Carbonate Depositional Models. 121p. 1979. 33.95x (ISBN 0-87814-104-9). Pennwell Book Division.
Asquith, P. D., ed. see Philosophy of Science Association, Biennial Meeting, 1976.
Asquith, Peter D., ed. see Philosophy of Science Biennial Meeting, 1976.
Asquith, Stewart. Children & Justice. 200p. 1982. 20.00x (ISBN 0-85224-429-0, Pub. by Edinburgh U Pr Scotland). Columbia U Pr.
Asquith, Stewart, jt. ed. see Adler, Michael.
Asratyan, E. A. Brain Reflexes. (Progress in Brain Research Ser.: Vol. 22). 1968. 145.75 (ISBN 0-444-40018-4). Elsevier.
Assael, Henry. Consumer Behavior & Marketing Action. (Business Ser.). 641p. 1981. text ed. 23.95x (ISBN 0-534-00958-1). Kent Pub Co.
Assai, T., jt. ed. see Agee, E. M.
Assaiante, Paul, ed. Championship Tennis by the Experts. LC 80-83978. (Illus.). 208p. (Orig.). 1981. pap. text ed. 6.95 (ISBN 0-918438-23-3). Leisure Pr.
Asscher, A. W., et al. Nephrology Illustrated: An Integrated Text & Colour Atlas. (Pergamon Medical Publications Ser.). (Illus.). 256p. 1982. 96.00 (ISBN 0-08-028851-0). Pergamon.
Assefi, Touraj. Stochastic Processes & Estimation Theory with Applications. LC 79-17872. 291p. 1979. 32.50x (ISBN 0-471-06454-8, Pub. by Wiley-Interscience). Wiley.
Asselineau, Roger. Evolution of Walt Whitman: The Creation of a Book. 1962. 15.00x o.p. (ISBN 0-674-27201-3, Belknap Pr). Harvard U Pr.
--Studies in the House of Seven Gables. LC 73-146037. 1971. pap. text ed. 3.50x (ISBN 0-675-09246-9). Merrill.
Asselmann, Teresa & Britto, Rudolf. Earth. LC 81-52655. (Starters Ser.). PLB 8.00 (ISBN 0-382-06492-5). Silver.
Assendelft, Van & England, J. M. Advances in Hematological Methods: The Blood Count. 272p. 1982. 72.00 (ISBN 0-8493-6596-1). CRC Pr.
Assiac. Opening Preparation. 1982. 15.90 (ISBN 0-08-024095-X); pap. 8.95 (ISBN 0-08-024096-8). Pergamon.
Assimakopoulos, Pat. Both Feet in the Water. LC 79-50943. 1980. 7.95 o.p. (ISBN 0-915684-31-4). Christian Herald.
Assis, Joaquim M. The Attendant's Confession, the Fortune Teller, & Life. Goldberg, Isaac, ed. & tr. (International Pocket Library). pap. 3.00 (ISBN 0-686-77236-9). Branden.
Assis, Joaquim M. Machado De see Machado de Assis, Joaquim M.
Associated Press, jt. auth. see Cappon, Rene J.
Associated Press, jt. auth. see Goldstein, Norm.
Associated Press, ed. The Associated Press Sunday Crossword Puzzle Book. (Illus.). 96p. (Orig.). 1983. 4.95 (ISBN 0-8092-5573-1). Contemp Bks.
Associated Writing Programs Staff, ed. Intro Thirteen. (Intro Ser.). 224p. (Orig.). 1982. pap. 7.95x (ISBN 0-936266-03-1). Assoc Writing Progs.
Association for Advancement of Medical Instrumentation. Cardiac Monitering in a Complex Patient Care Environment. 96p. (Orig.). 1982. pap. text ed. 30.00 (ISBN 0-910275-09-2); 20.00 (ISBN 0-686-36661-1). Assn Adv Med Instrs.
Association for Asian Studies. Cumulative Bibliography of Asian Studies, 1966-1970. Incl. Author Bibliography, 3 vols. 1973. lib. bdg. 395.00 (ISBN 0-8161-0959-1); Subject Bibliography, 3 vols. 1972. lib. bdg. 395.00 (ISBN 0-8161-0235-X). Hall Library). G K Hall.
--Cumulative Bibliography of Asian Studies, 1941-1965, Author Bibliography, 4 Vols. 1969. Set. 390.00 (ISBN 0-8161-0805-6, Hall Library). G K Hall.
--Cumulative Bibliography of Asian Studies, 1941-1965, Subject Bibliography, 4 Vols. 1970. Set. 395.00 (ISBN 0-8161-0127-2, Hall Library). G K Hall.
Association for Childhood Education International. Bibliography of Books for Children. rev. ed. Sunderlin, Sylvia, ed. LC 42-21946. 1980. 5.95 (ISBN 0-87173-095-2). ACEI.
Association for Counselor Education & Supervision. The Professional Counselor: Competencies, Performance Guidelines & Assessment. 1980. 6.50 (ISBN 0-686-36436-8, 72141); nonmembers 7.25 (ISBN 0-686-37319-7). Am Personnel.
Association for Counselor Education & Supervision Committee on Accreditation. Standards for Preparation in Counselor Education. 1979. 2.00 (ISBN 0-686-36441-4, 72128); nonmembers 2.50 (ISBN 0-686-37320-0). Am Personnel.
Association for Educational Communications & Technology. Task Force on Definition & Terminology. The Definition of Educational Technology. Silber, Kenneth, ed. LC 79-53125. 1979. pap. 10.95 (ISBN 0-89240-006-4). Assn Ed Comm Tech.
--Educational Technology: A Glossary of Terms. Silber, Kenneth, ed. LC 79-53125. 1979. pap. text ed. 21.00 (ISBN 0-89240-007-2). Assn Ed Comm Tech.
Association for Holistic Health Staff. The National Directory of Holistic Health Professionals. 269p. 1982. pap. 7.95 (ISBN 0-686-38102-5). Assn Holistic.
Association for Radiation Research, Winter Meeting Jan.3-5, 1979. Radiation Biology & Chemistry: Research Developments: Proceedings. Edwards, H. E., et al, eds. LC 79-15532. (Studies in Physical & Theoretical Chemistry Ser.: Vol. 6). 505p. 1979. 85.00 (ISBN 0-444-41821-0). Elsevier.
Association For Recorded Sound Collections. Preliminary Directory of Sound Recordings Collections in the United States & Canada. LC 67-31297. 1967. pap. 5.00 o.p. (ISBN 0-87104-144-8). NY Pub Lib.
Association for Research & Enlightenment, Inc. Virginia Beach, Va. Study Groups, et al, eds. Search for God, 2 Bks. 1942-1950. 4.95 ea. Bk. 1 (ISBN 0-87604-000-8). Bk. 2 (ISBN 0-87604-001-6). ARE Pr.
Association for Research in Nervous & Mental Disease. Biology of the Major Psychoses: A Comparative Analysis. Freedman, D. X., ed. LC 75-14571. (Research Publications: Vol. 54). 384p. 1975. 34.50 (ISBN 0-89004-034-6). Raven.
--Brain Dysfunction in Metabolic Disorders, Vol. 53. Plum, Fred, ed. LC 74-79190. 336p. 1974. 38.00 (ISBN 0-911216-81-2). Raven.
Association For Science Education. Teaching Science at the Secondary Stage. text ed. 8.50x o.p. (ISBN 0-7195-1707-9). Transatlantic.
Association for the Advancement of Medical Instrumentation. Inhospital Sterility Assurance: Current Perspectives. (Illus.). 80p. (Orig.). 1982. pap. 20.00 members (ISBN 0-910275-14-9); pap. 30.00 nonmembers (ISBN 0-686-38440-7). Assn Adv Med Instrs.
Association for the Library Service to Children. The Arbuthnot Lectures Nineteen-Seventy to Nineteen Seventy-Nine. LC 79-26095. 214p. 1980. 15.00 (ISBN 0-8389-3240-1). ALA.
Association of American Law Schools. Selected Essays in Anglo-American Legal History 1907-09, 3 Vols. 1968. Set. 120.00 (ISBN 0-379-00426-7). Oceana.
Association of College & Research Libraries & American Library Association. Books for College Libraries, 6 vols. 2nd ed. LC 74-13743. 2000p. 1975. pap. 80.00 set (ISBN 0-8389-0178-6). ALA.
Association of Commonwealth Universities. Schedule of Postgraduate Courses in United Kingdom Universities, 1980-81. 17th ed. LC 75-644246. 114p. (Orig.). 1980. pap. 10.00x o.p. (ISBN 0-85143-070-8). Intl Pubns Serv.
--Schedule of Postgraduate Courses in United Kingdom Universities, 1981-82. 18th ed. LC 75-644246. 114p. 1981. pap. 10.00x (ISBN 0-85143-075-9). Intl Pubns Serv.
--Scholarships Guide for Commonwealth Postgraduate Students, 1980-82. 4th ed. LC 77-643818. 326p. (Orig.). 1979. pap. 13.50x (ISBN 0-85143-062-7). Intl Pubns Serv.
Association of Desk & Derrick Clubs of America. D & D Standard Oil Abbreviator. 2nd ed. LC 72-96172. 256p. 9.50 (ISBN 0-87814-017-4). Pennwell Book Division.
Association of Energy Engineers. Advances in Energy Cost Savings for Industry & Buildings. Payne, F. William, ed. (Illus.). 500p. 1983. text ed. 45.00 (ISBN 0-915586-78-9); pap. text ed. 30.00 (ISBN 0-915586-79-7). Fairmont Pr.
Association of Independent Producers. Independent Production Handbook. (Illus.). 1982. 25.95 (ISBN 0-240-51204-9). Focal Pr.
Association of International Education, Japan. ABC's of Study in Japan, 1982-83. (Illus.). 154p. (Orig.). 1981. pap. 5.00x (ISBN 0-8002-3041-8). Intl Pubns Serv.
Association of Licensed Automobile Manufacturers. Handbook of Automobiles Nineteen Fifteen to Nineteen Sixteen. (Illus.). 6.50 o.p. (ISBN 0-8446-0126-8). Peter Smith.
Association of Manufacturers. Handbook of Automobiles Nineteen Twenty-Five to Nineteen Twenty-Six. (Illus.). 7.00 o.p. (ISBN 0-8446-0127-6). Peter Smith.
Association of Pediatric Oncology. Nursing Care of the Child With Cancer. 1982. text ed. write for info. (ISBN 0-316-04884-4). Little.
Association of Specialized & Cooperative Library Agencies. Standards of Service for the Library of Congress Network of Libraries for the Blind & Physically Handicapped. LC 79-22963. 76p. 1980. pap. 5.00 (ISBN 0-8389-0298-7). ALA.
Association of Student International Law Societies & American Society of International Law. Philip C. Jessup International Law Moot Court Competition, 1960-1980, 12 vols. LC 80-85091. 1980-81. Set. lib. bdg. 545.00 (ISBN 0-89941-094-4). W S Hein.
Association of the Bar of the City of New York, ed. Professional Responsibility of the Lawyer: The Murky Divide Between Right & Wrong. LC 76-5391. 1976. lib. bdg. 38.00 (ISBN 0-379-00775-4); pap. 8.50 (ISBN 0-379-00776-2). Oceana.
Association of the Bar of the City of New York. Report of the Special Committee on the Federal Loyalty Security Program. LC 74-6494. (Civil Liberties in American History Ser.). 301p. 1974. Repr. of 1956 ed. lib. bdg. 39.50 (ISBN 0-306-70596-6). Da Capo.

Association of the commonwealth Universities. Compendium of University Entrance Requirements for First Degree Courses in the United Kingdom, 1983-84. 20th ed. LC 74-648109. (Illus.). 355p. (Orig.). 1982. pap. text ed. 18.50x (ISBN 0-85143-077-5). Intl Pubns Serv.

Assorodobraj-Kula, N., et al, eds. Studies in Economic Theory & Practice: Essays in Honor of Honor of Edward Lipinski. 1981. 55.50 (ISBN 0-444-86010-X). Elsevier.

Astaire, Fred. Steps in Time. (Series in Dance). 1979. Repr. of 1959 ed. 22.50 (ISBN 0-306-79575-2). Da Capo.

Astaldi, G., et al, eds. Current Studies on Standardization Problems in Clinical Pathology, Haematology & Radiation Therapy for Hodgkins' Disease. (International Congress Ser.: No. 400). (Proceedings). 1975. pap. 72.00 (ISBN 0-444-15162-1). Elsevier.

Astarita, G. & Marrucci, G. Principles of Non-Newtonian Fluid Mechanics. 1974. 22.95 o.p. (ISBN 0-07-084022-9, C). McGraw.

Astarita, Gianni, et al. Gas Treating With Chemical Solvents. 512p. 1983. 49.95 (ISBN 0-471-05768-1, Pub. by Wiley-Interscience). Wiley.

Astbury, Raymond. The Writer in the Market Place. 1969. 15.00 (ISBN 0-208-00635-4, Archon). Shoe String.

Aste, H., jt. auth. see Cheli, R.

Aste, Mario. Two Novels of Pirandello: An Essay. 1979. pap. text ed. 8.25 (ISBN 0-8191-0735-2). U Pr of Amer.

Asten, H. Keller-von. Encounters with the Infinite: Geometrical Experiences Through Active Comtemplation. Juhr, Gerald, tr. from Germ. (Illus.). 364p. 1971. 19.95 (ISBN 0-88010-040-0, Pub. by Verlag Walter Keller Switzerland). Anthroposophic.

Asten, Kenneth J. Data Communications for Business Information Systems. (Illus.). 384p. 1973. text ed. 22.95x (ISBN 0-02-304440-3, 30444). Macmillan.

Asthana, Rama K. Henry James: A Study in the Aesthetics of the Novel. 130p. 1980. Repr. of 1936 ed. text ed. 11.75x (ISBN 0-391-02180-X). Humanities.

Asthana, Shashi P. History & Archeology of India's Contacts with Other Countries from the Earliest Times to 300 B.C. LC 76-903130. 1976. 27.00x o.p. (ISBN 0-88386-787-7). South Asia Bks.

Asthma & Allergy Foundation of America & Norback, Craig T., eds. The Allergy Encyclopedia. (Medical Library). 256p. 1982. pap. 7.95 (ISBN 0-452-25345-4, 3717-1). Mosby.

--The Allergy Encylopedia. (Illus.). 1981. pap. 7.95 (ISBN 0-452-25270-9, Z5270, Plume). NAL.

Astill, Kenneth N., jt. auth. see Arden, Bruce W.

Astin, Alexander W. Minorities in American Higher Education: Recent Trends, Currect Prospects, & Recommendations. LC 81-48663. (Higher Education Ser.). 1982. 16.95x (ISBN 0-87589-523-9). Jossey-Bass.

Astin, Helen S., ed. Some Action of Her Own. LC 75-43476. 208p. 1976. 20.95x (ISBN 0-669-00567-3). Lexington Bks.

Astiz, Carlos A., tr. see Ciria, Alberto.

Astiz, Carlos A., tr. see De Imaz, Jose L.

Astley, Juliet. Copsi Castle. y ed. LC 78-484. (Fic). 1978. 9.95 o.p. (ISBN 0-698-10913-9, Coward). Putnam Pub Group.

--Copsi Castle. (General Ser.). 1979. lib. bdg. 16.95 (ISBN 0-8161-6669-2, Large Print Bks). G K Hall.

--The Fall of Midas. 256p. 1975. 7.95 o.p. (ISBN 0-698-10680-6, Coward). Putnam Pub Group.

Astmann, Herbert K. Four Big Steps to Success: Reading, Writing, Speaking, Listening. 1978. pap. text ed. 8.95 (ISBN 0-8403-1916-9). Kendall-Hunt.

Aston, Clive C. A Contemporary Crisis: Political Hostage-Taking & the Experience of Western Europe. LC 82-6165. (Contributions in Political Science Ser.: No. 84). 1982. lib. bdg. 27.50 (ISBN 0-313-23289-X, ASP/). Greenwood.

Aston, Melba. Developing Sentence Skills. (English Ser.). 24p. (gr. 4-7). 1980. wkbk. 5.00 (ISBN 0-8209-0182-2, E-10). ESP.

--Learning to Outline & Organize: Grades 7-12. (Language Arts Ser.). 24p. 1977. wkbk. 5.00 (ISBN 0-8209-0321-3, LA-7). ESP.

--Understanding Punctuation: Grades 7-12. (English Ser.). 24p. (gr. 7-12). 1977. wkbk. 5.00 (ISBN 0-8209-0184-9, E12). ESP.

Aston, P., jt. auth. see Paynter, J.

Aston, Sherrell., et al. Third International Symposium of Plastic & Reconstructive Surgery of the Eye & Adnexa. (Illus.). 470p. 1982. lib. bdg. write for info. (ISBN 0-683-05951-3). Williams & Wilkins.

Aston, Sherrell J. & Hornblass, Albert. Third International Symposium of Plastic & Reconstructive Surgery of the Eye & Adnexa. 380p. 1982. 65.00. Williams & Wilkins.

Aston, Trevor, ed. Crisis in Europe 1560-1660: Essays from "Past & Present". 376p. 1980. pap. 7.95 (ISBN 0-7100-6889-1). Routledge & Kegan.

Aston, W. G. Shinto: The Ancient Religion of Japan. 83p. 1982. lib. bdg. 25.00 (ISBN 0-89760-018-5). Telegraph Bks.

Astor, Brooke. Footprints. LC 78-20053. (Illus.). 1980. 13.95 o.p. (ISBN 0-385-14377-X). Doubleday.

Astor, Saul D. Loss Prevention: Controls & Concepts. LC 77-28164. 1978. 18.95 (ISBN 0-913708-29-1). Butterworth.

Astrand, Per-Olof & Rodahl, Kaare. Textbook of Work Physiology: Physiological Basis of Exercisers. 2nd ed. (McGraw-Hill Series in Health, Physical Education & Recreation). 1977. text ed. 35.00 (ISBN 0-07-002406-5, C). McGraw.

Astro Analysts Insitute. Astroanalysis Nineteen Eighty Forecasts. (Illus.). 1979. pap. 6.95 o.p. (ISBN 0-448-16290-3, G&D). Putnam Pub Group.

Astro Publishers. Military Competency Test, with Explanations. 1979. pap. 8.95 (ISBN 0-686-70926-8, Pub. by Astro). Aviation.

Astrom, Paul, jt. auth. see Gullberg, Elsa.

Astroms, P. & Eriksson, A. Fingerprints & Archaeology. (Studies in Mediterranean Archaeology Ser.: Vol. XXVIII). 88p. 1981. pap. text ed. 45.00x (Pub. by Paul Astroms Sweden). Humanities.

Asturias, Miguel A. Leyendas De Guatemala. (Easy Readers, C). 1977. pap. text ed. 3.95 (ISBN 0-88436-290-6). EMC.

Astwood, E. B. see Laurentian Hormone Conferences.

Astwood, Edwin B., ed. see American Physiological Society.

Asua, L. Jimenez de see Jimenez de Asua, L.

Atack, Sally M. Art Activities for the Handicapped: A Guide for Parents & Teachers. LC 82-5282. (Illus.). 131p. 1982. 13.95 (ISBN 0-13-046995-5); pap. 6.95 (ISBN 0-13-046987-4). P-H.

Atal, Yogesh. Social Sciences: The Indian Scene. 1976. 12.00x o.p. (ISBN 0-88386-883-0). South Asia Bks.

Atangana, Englebert, jt. auth. see Bahoken, J. C.

Atassi, M. Z. & Benjamini, E., eds. Immunobiology of Proteins & Peptides-II, Vol.150. (Advances in Experimental Medicine & Biology). 238p. 1982. 35.00x (ISBN 0-306-41110-5, Plenum Pr). Plenum Pub.

Atcheson, Marguerite. The Mouse Who Didn't Believe. (Illus.). 60p. 1980. 2.50 (ISBN 0-9603118-6-6). MD Bks.

Atcheson, Richard, ed. see Urvater, Michele.

Atchinson, Joseph E. Nonwood Plant Fiber Pulping Progress Report. (No. 13). 148p. 1983. pap. 48.95 (ISBN 0-89852-404-0, 01 01 R104). TAPPI.

Atchison, Evelyn, jt. auth. see Glass, Marion.

Atchison, Joseph E., et al, eds. Nonwood Plant Fiber Pulping, 13 Vols. 1835p. 1983. soft cover 297.95 (ISBN 0-686-98535-4, 01-01-NPFS). TAPPI.

Atchison, Thomas J. & Hill, Winston W. Management Today: Managing Work in Organizations. 575p. 1978. text ed. 24.95 (ISBN 0-15-554780-1, HC); instructor's manual avail. (ISBN 0-15-554781-X). HarBraceJ.

Atchley, Robert C. Social Forces in Later Life. 3rd ed. 480p. 1980. text ed. 21.95x (ISBN 0-534-00828-3). Wadsworth Pub.

Atchley, W. R. & Woodruff, David S., eds. Evolution & Speciation: Essays in Honor of M.J.D. White. (Illus.). 496p. 1981. 59.50 (ISBN 0-521-23823-4). Cambridge U Pr.

Aten, Jerry. Americans, Too! (gr. 4-8). 1982. 6.95 (ISBN 0-86653-099-1, GA 444). Good Apple.

--Good Apple & Math Fun. 1981. 9.95 (ISBN 0-86653-023-1, GA 279). Good Apple.

--Maptime... U. S. A. (gr. 4-8). 1982. 5.95 (ISBN 0-86653-093-2, GA 422). Good Apple.

--A Part of Something Great. (gr. 4-8). 1981. 5.95 (ISBN 0-916456-97-8, GA 226). Good Apple.

Aten, Lawrence. Indians of the Upper Texas Coast. LC 82-13828. (New World Archaeological Record Ser.). 338p. 1982. 39.50 (ISBN 0-12-065740-6). Acad Pr.

Aten, Marilyn J. & McAnarney, Elizabeth R. A Behavioral Approach to the Care of Adolescents. LC 81-1959. 179p. 1981. pap. text ed. 13.50 (ISBN 0-8016-3201-3). Mosby.

Athanasopulos, Christos G. Contemporary Theater: Evolution & Design. 350p. 1983. 60.00 (ISBN 0-471-87319-5, Pub. by Wiley-Interscience). Wiley.

Athanasoulis, Christos A., et al. Interventional Radiology. LC 77-11329. (Illus.). 806p. 1982. text ed. 98.00 (ISBN 0-7216-1448-5). Saunders.

Athans, Michael & Falb, P. Optimal Controls. 1966. 48.95 (ISBN 0-07-002413-8, C). McGraw.

Athans, Michael, et al. Systems, Networks & Computations: Multivariable Methods. (Illus.). 592p. 1974. text ed. 38.00 (ISBN 0-07-002430-8, C). McGraw.

Athearn, James L. Risk & Insurance. (Illus.). 1977. text ed. 18.95 o.s.i. (ISBN 0-8299-0132-9). West Pub.

--Risk & Insurance. 4th ed. (Illus.). 512p. 1981. text ed. 24.95 (ISBN 0-8299-0298-8). West Pub.

Athens, Lonnie. Violent Criminal Acts & Actors: A Symbolic Interactionist Study. (International Library of Sociology). 1980. 16.95x (ISBN 0-7100-0342-0). Routledge & Kegan.

Atherly, Gordon. Occupational Health & Safety Concepts. 1978. text ed. 33.00 (ISBN 0-85334-848-0, Pub. by Applied Sci England). Elsevier.

Atherton. Stability of Nonlinear Systems. LC 80-40947. (Control Theory & Applications Studies Ser.). 208p. 1981. 45.95x (ISBN 0-471-27856-4, Pub. by Research Studies Pr). Wiley.

Atherton, Alexine L., ed. International Organizations: A Guide to Information Sources. LC 73-17502. (International Relations Guide Ser.: Vol. 1). 1976. 42.00x (ISBN 0-8103-1324-3). Gale.

Atherton, Charles P., jt. auth. see Prigmore, Charles S.

Atherton, Charles R. & Klemmack, David L. Methods of Social Work Research. 496p. 1982. text ed. 19.95 (ISBN 0-669-03473-8). Heath.

Atherton, Derek P. Stability of Nonlinear Systems. (Control Theory & Applications Studies Ser.). 231p. 1981. 45.95x (ISBN 0-471-27856-4). Res Stud Pr.

Atherton, Gertrude. California: An Intimate History. 330p. 1983. Repr. of 1914 ed. lib. bdg. 65.00 (ISBN 0-89987-041-4). Darby Bks.

Atherton, Gertrude, et al. The Spinners' Book of Fiction. 1979. lib. bdg. 9.95 (ISBN 0-8398-2582-X, Gregg). G K Hall.

Atherton, Lewis E. The Pioneer Merchant in Mid-America. LC 75-77700. (American Scene Ser). 1969. Repr. of 1939 ed. 24.50 (ISBN 0-306-71338-1). Da Capo.

Atherton, M. P. & Gribble, C. J., eds. Migmatitxes, Melting & Metamorphism. 200p. Date not set. text ed. 24.95 (ISBN 0-906812-26-7). Birkhauser.

Atherton, M. P. & Tarney, J., eds. Origin of Granite Batholiths, Geochemical Evidence. 152p. (Orig.). 1979. pap. text ed. 12.50 (ISBN 0-906812-00-3, Pub. by Shiva Pub England). Imprint Edns.

Atherton, Roy. Structured Programming with Comal. (Computers & Their Applications Ser.). 192p. 1982. 49.95x (ISBN 0-470-27318-6); pap. 24.95 (ISBN 0-470-27359-3). Halsted Pr.

Athey, Irene J. & Rubadeau, Duane O., eds. Educational Implications of Piaget's Theory. LC 82-101. 400p. 1983. Repr. of 1970 ed. lib. bdg. write for info (ISBN 0-89874-475-X). Krieger.

Athey, Jackie, ed. see Hasegawa, Hideo.

Athey, Robert D., Jr., et al. Water Resistance in Paper Coatings. (TAPPI PRESS Reports). 27p. 1979. pap. 19.95 (ISBN 0-89852-382-6, 01-01-R082). TAPPI.

Athey, Thomas H. Systematic Systems Approach: An Integrated Method for Solving Systems Problems. (Illus.). 416p. 1982. text ed. 26.95 (ISBN 0-13-880914-3). P-H.

Athos, Anthony G., jt. auth. see Pascale, Richard T.

Ati, H. A. Islam in Focus. pap. 6.50 o.p. (ISBN 0-686-18504-8). Kazi Pubns.

Atil, Esin. Art of the Arab World. LC 75-7730. (Illus.). 1975. pap. 20.00 (ISBN 0-934686-28-9). Freer.

Atil, Esin, ed. Turkish Art. (Illus.). 386p. 1980. 65.00 o.p. (ISBN 0-686-62717-2, 1659-2). Abrams.

Atiya, Aziz S. Crusade in the Later Middle Ages. LC 67-28472. (Illus.). 1965. 22.00 o.s.i. (ISBN 0-527-03700-1). Kraus Repr.

Atiya, Nayra. Khul-Khaal: Five Egyptian Women Tell Their Stories. LC 82-5773. (Contemporary Issues in the Middle East Ser.). (Illus.). 216p. 1982. text ed. 20.00x (ISBN 0-8156-0177-8); pap. 11.95 (ISBN 0-8156-0181-6). Syracuse U Pr.

Atiyah, M. F., et al. Representation Theory of Lie Groups. LC 78-73820. (London Mathematical Society Lecture Note: No. 34). 1980. pap. 32.50x (ISBN 0-521-22636-8). Cambridge U Pr.

Atiyah, P. S. Law & Modern Society. 240p. 1983. 22.00 (ISBN 0-19-219166-7). Oxford U Pr.

Atiyah, Patrick S. An Introduction to the Law of Contract. 3rd ed. (Claredon Law Ser.). 1981. pap. 39.95x (ISBN 0-19-876140-6); pap. text ed. 14.50x (ISBN 0-19-876141-4). Oxford U Pr.

Atiyeh, George N., compiled by. The Contemporary Middle East, Nineteen Forty-Eight to Nineteen Seventy-Three: An Selective & Annotated Bibliography. 775p. 1975. lib. bdg. 55.00 (ISBN 0-8161-1085-9, Hall Reference). G K Hall.

Atiyeh, Wadeeha. Fourth Wise Man. (gr. 4 up). 1959. pap. 2.00 (ISBN 0-8315-0038-7). Speller.

Atkeson, Ray, photos by. Oregon II. LC 74-75124. (Belding Imprint Ser.). (Illus.). 192p. (Text by Archie Satterfield). 1974. 32.50 (ISBN 0-912856-15-7). Graphic Arts Ctr.

Atkin, J. K. Computer Science. 272p. 1981. 19.00 (ISBN 0-7121-0396-1, Pub. by Macdonald & Evans). State Mutual Bk.

Atkin, John. Practical Boat Designs. LC 82-48618. (Illus.). 192p. 1983. 17.50 (ISBN 0-87742-160-9). Intl Marine.

Atkin, William W. Architectural Presentation Techniques. 196p. 1982. pap. 10.95 (ISBN 0-442-21074-4). Van Nos Reinhold.

Atkins, jt. auth. see Spence.

Atkins, A. G., jt. ed. see Alsmeyer, D.

Atkins, Andrew. Skipper Butterflies of the World. 544p. 395.00 (ISBN 0-686-98245-2, Pub. by E W Classey England). State Mutual Bk.

Atkins, Guy, jt. auth. see Anderson, Troels.

Atkins, Irene K. Source Music in Motion Pictures. LC 81-65338. (Illus.). 192p. 1983. 22.50 (ISBN 0-8386-3076-6). Fairleigh Dickinson.

Atkins, John F. The Paper Machine Wet Press Manual. LC 79-6366. (TAPPI PRESS Books). (Illus.). 120p. 1979. 14.95 (ISBN 0-89852-042-8, 01-02 B042). TAPPI.

Atkins, John W. Literary Criticism in Antiquity, 2 vols. Incl. Vol. 1. Greek. 9.00 (ISBN 0-8446-1033-X); Vol. 2. Graeco-Roman. 9.00. Peter Smith.

Atkins, Kenneth R. Physics. 3rd ed. LC 75-11677. 818p. 1976. text ed. 27.95x o.p. (ISBN 0-471-03629-3). Wiley.

Atkins, Kenneth R., et al. Essentials of Physical Science. LC 77-12507. 546p. 1978. text ed. 28.50 (ISBN 0-471-03617-X); study guide 8.95 (ISBN 0-471-03551-3); avail. tchrs. manual (ISBN 0-471-03552-1). Wiley.

Atkins, M. Atlas of Continuous Cooling Transformation Diagrams for Engineering Steels. 1980. 90.00 (ISBN 0-87170-093-X). ASM.

Atkins, Michael D. Insect Behavior. 1980. pap. 15.95 o.p. (ISBN 0-02-304510-8). Macmillan.

--Insects in Perspectives. (Illus.). 1978. text ed. 24.95 (ISBN 0-02-304500-0). Macmillan.

--Introduction to Insect Behavior. (Illus.). 1980. pap. text ed. 19.95x o.p. (ISBN 0-686-65947-3). Macmillan.

Atkins Research & Development Corp. The Control of Noise in Ventillation Systems: A Designer's Guide. Iqbal, M. A., ed. 1982. 29.00x (ISBN 0-419-11050-X, Pub. by E & FN Spon). Methuen Inc.

Atkins, Robert, et al. Dr. Atkins Super-Energy Cookbook. (Orig.). 1978. pap. 3.95 (ISBN 0-451-12176-7, AE2176, Sig). NAL.

Atkins, Stuart. The Name of your Game: Four Game Plans for Success at Home & at Work. LC 81-71849. (Illus.). 1982. 16.95 (ISBN 0-942532-00-7); pap. 4.95. Ellis & Stuart Pub.

Atkins, Thomas R. Frederick Wiseman. (Monarch Film Studies). 1976. pap. 2.95 o.p. (ISBN 0-671-08101-2). Monarch Pr.

--Science Fiction Films. (Monarch Film Studies). 1976. pap. 2.95 o.p. (ISBN 0-671-08100-4). Monarch Pr.

Atkins, Walter J., Jr., jt. auth. see Anderson, Ron.

Atkinson, A. B. The Economics of Inequality. (Illus.). 1975. pap. 11.95x (ISBN 0-19-877076-6). Oxford U Pr.

--Poverty in Britain & the Reform of Social Security. LC 76-85711. (Department of Applied Economic, Occasional Papers Ser). 1969. 17.95 (ISBN 0-521-07522-X); pap. 9.95 (ISBN 0-521-09607-3, 607). Cambridge U Pr.

--Social Justice & Public Policy. 480p. 1982. 37.50x (ISBN 0-262-01067-4). MIT Pr.

Atkinson, A. B. & Harrison, A. J. Distribution of Personal Wealth in Britain. LC 77-2715. 1978. 47.50 (ISBN 0-521-21735-0). Cambridge U Pr.

Atkinson, Anthony & Stiglitz, Joseph. Lectures on Public Economies. (McGraw-Hill Economics Handbook Ser.). 640p. 1980. text ed. 31.95 (ISBN 0-07-084105-5). McGraw.

Atkinson, Anthony B., ed. The Personal Distribution of Incomes. LC 75-34050. 1976. 36.50 o.p. (ISBN 0-89158-526-5). Westview.

Atkinson, B. F. Biochemical Reactors. (Advanced Biochemistry Ser.). 264p. 1974. 21.00x (ISBN 0-85086-042-3, Pub. by Pion England). Methuen Inc.

Atkinson, Betty J. The Medical Assistant: Clinical Practice. LC 76-5301. 1976. pap. 12.00 (ISBN 0-8273-0351-3); instructor's guide 2.50 (ISBN 0-8273-0352-1). Delmar.

Atkinson, Brooks. New Voices in the American Theatre. 1955. 3.95 o.s.i. (ISBN 0-394-60258-7, M258). Modern Lib.

--Sean O'Casey: From Times Past. Lowery, Robert G., ed. 1982. 26.50x (ISBN 0-389-20005-0). B&N Imports.

Atkinson, Brooks, ed. see Emerson, Ralph Waldo.

Atkinson, Brooks, ed. see Thoreau, Henry D.

Atkinson, Brooks, ed. & intro. by see Thoreau, Henry David.

Atkinson, Charles M. Jeremy Bentham: His Life & Work. LC 68-55464. Repr. of 1905 ed. 22.50x (ISBN 0-678-00544-3). Kelley.

Atkinson, D., et al, eds. Mineral Nutrition of Fruit Trees. LC 79-41647. (Studies in the Agricultural & Food Sciences). 1980. text ed. 89.95 (ISBN 0-408-10662-X). Butterworth.

Atkinson, David. The Wings of Refuge: The Message of Ruth. (Bible Speaks Today Ser.). 128p. 1983. pap. 4.95 (ISBN 0-87784-820-3). Inter-Varsity.

Atkinson, Dorothy. The End of the Russian Land Commune, 1905-1930. LC 81-84457. 472p. 1983. 29.50x (ISBN 0-8047-1148-8). Stanford U Pr.

Atkinson, Ernest E. A Selected Bibliography of Hispanic Baptist History. LC 81-81174. 103p. (Orig.). 1982. pap. 10.00 o.p. (ISBN 0-939804-11-5). Hist Comm S Baptist.

Atkinson, Frank. The Public Library. (Local Search Ser). (Illus.). 1970. 8.95 o.p. (ISBN 0-7100-6690-2). Routledge & Kegan.

Atkinson, Geoffroy. The Sentimental Revolution: French Writers of 1690-1740. Keller, Abraham C., ed. LC 64-18424. 200p. 1966. 13.50 (ISBN 0-295-74024-8). U of Wash Pr.

Atkinson, Gerald M. Arab Banks & the Financial Leadership of the World. (The Great Currents of History Library Bk.). (Illus.). 137p. 1983. 97.85 (ISBN 0-86722-029-5). Inst Econ Pol.

Atkinson, J. Brooks. Broadway Scrapbook. LC 71-104221. Repr. of 1947 ed. lib. bdg. 15.75x (ISBN 0-8371-3331-9, ATBS). Greenwood.

Atkinson, J. Edward, ed. Black Dimensions in Contemporary American Art. 3.95 o.p. (ISBN 0-452-25041-2, Z5041, Plume). NAL.

Atkinson, James, tr. see Firdawsi.

Atkinson, Jennifer, ed. see O'Neill, Eugene.

Atkinson, John W. Introduction to Motivation. 2d ed. (Illus.). 1978. text ed. 16.95x (ISBN 0-442-00368-4). Van Nos Reinhold.

Atkinson, K. B. Developments in Close Range Photogrammetry, Vol. 1. 1982. 45.00 (ISBN 0-85334-882-0, Pub. by Applied Sci England). Elsevier.

Atkinson, Kendall E. A Survey of Numerical Methods for the Solution of Fredholm Integral Equations of the Second Kind. LC 75-28900. (Illus.). vii, 230p. (Orig.). 1976. pap. text ed. 25.50 (ISBN 0-89871-034-0). Soc Indus-Appl Math.

Atkinson, L. Hit & Run. 1981. 8.90 (ISBN 0-531-04265-0). Watts.

Atkinson, L. J. & Kohn, M. J. Berry & Kohn's Introduction to Operating Room Technique. 1978. pap. text ed. 25.00 (ISBN 0-07-002540-1, HP). McGraw.

Atkinson, Laurence. PASCAL Programming. LC 80-40126. (Computing Ser.). 428p. 1980. 49.95x (ISBN 0-471-27773-8); pap. 16.95 (ISBN 0-471-27774-6). Wiley.

Atkinson, Leslie D. & Murray, Mary E. Understanding the Nursing Process. 2nd ed. (Illus.). 1983. write for info. (ISBN 0-02-304580-9); pap. text ed. write for info. (ISBN 0-02-304600-7). Macmillan.

Atkinson, Linda. Alternatives to College. LC 78-5957. (Career Concise Guides Ser.). (Illus.). 1978. lib. bdg. 7.90 s&l o.p. (ISBN 0-531-01495-9). Watts.

--Have We Lived Before? (High Interest, Low Vocabulary Ser.). (Illus.). 112p. (gr. 4 up). 1982. PLB 7.95 (ISBN 0-396-07999-7). Dodd.

--Incredible Crimes. (Triumph Bks.). (gr. 5 up). 1980. PLB 8.90 (ISBN 0-531-04170-0, F21). Watts.

--Mother Jones: The Most Dangerous Woman in America. LC 77-15863. (Illus.). (gr. 7 up). 1978. 10.95 (ISBN 0-517-53201-8). Crown.

--Psychic Stories Strange but True. (Triumph Ser.). (Illus.). (gr. 5 up). 1979. PLB 8.90 s&l (ISBN 0-531-02861-5). Watts.

--Your Legal Rights. LC 82-6963. (Triumph Ser.). (Illus.). 96p. (gr. 7). 1982. lib. bdg. 8.90 (ISBN 0-531-04495-5). Watts.

Atkinson, Lloyd C. Economics: The Science of Choice. (Student Guide by Dennis Sullivan). 1982. 23.95x (ISBN 0-256-02486-3); write for info. student guide (ISBN 0-256-02487-1). Irwin.

Atkinson, M. J., ed. A Commentary on Plotinus: Emnead, Vol. I. (Classical & Philosophical Monographs). 1982. 59.50 (ISBN 0-19-814719-8). Oxford U Pr.

Atkinson, Mary. Maria Teresa. LC 79-90393. (Illus.). 40p. (gr. k-3). 1979. pap. 3.25 (ISBN 0-914996-21-5). Lollipop Power.

Atkinson, Mary W. Johnny Smith Goes to His Speech Therapist. 32p. (gr. k-6). 1982. pap. 7.95 (ISBN 0-88450-734-3). Communication Skill.

Atkinson, Michael M. & Chandler, Marsha A., eds. The Politics of Canadian Public Policy. 320p. 1983. 30.00x (ISBN 0-8020-2485-8); pap. 12.50 (ISBN 0-8020-6517-1). U of Toronto Pr.

Atkinson, P. see Heath, C.

Atkinson, Paul. The Clinical Experience. 160p. 1981. text ed. 34.25x (ISBN 0-566-00413-5). Gower Pub Ltd.

Atkinson, Paul, jt. auth. see Rees, Teresa L.

Atkinson, R. F. Knowledge & Explanation in History: An Introduction to the Philosophy of History. LC 77-90896. 1978. 29.50x (ISBN 0-8014-1116-5); pap. 7.95x (ISBN 0-8014-9171-1). Cornell U Pr.

Atkinson, R. S. & Rushman, G. B. A Synopsis of Anaesthesia. 9th ed. (Illus.). 976p. 1982. pap. text ed. 33.50 (ISBN 0-7236-0621-8). Wright-PSG.

Atkinson, Ruth A., jt. ed. see Appenzeller, Otto.

Atkinson, Terry & Cerf, Martin. Billy Squier: An Illustrated History. (Illus.). 48p. (Orig.). 1983. pap. 6.95 (ISBN 0-89524-174-9, 8615). Cherry Lane.

Atkinson, Ti-Grace. Amazon Odyssey: The First Collection of Writings by the Political Pioneer of the Women's Movement. LC 73-80394. (Illus.). 1974. 15.00 (ISBN 0-8256-3023-1, Quick Fox); pap. 5.95 (ISBN 0-8256-3016-9, Links Bks). Putnam Pub Group.

Atkisson, Harold F. Basic Counterpoint. (Music Ser). 1956. 32.00 (ISBN 0-07-002412-X, C). McGraw.

Atlantic Council. The Common Security Interests of Japan, the United States, & NATO. 256p. 1981. prof ref 25.00x (ISBN 0-88410-698-5). Ballinger Pub.

--Strengthening Deterrence: NATO & the Credibility of Western Defense in the 1980's. Rush, Kenneth & Scowcroft, Brent, eds. 288p. 1982. prof ref 24.50x (ISBN 0-88410-868-6). Ballinger Pub.

--U. S. Energy Policy & U.S. Foreign Policy in the Nineteen Eighties. 336p. 1981. prof ref 25.00x (ISBN 0-88410-901-1). Ballinger Pub.

Atlantic Council, ed. The Soviet Merchant Marine: Economic Aid & Strategic Challenge to the West. 1979. pap. text ed. 6.50 (ISBN 0-686-59447-9). Westview.

Atlantic Council of the United States. GATT Plus-A Proposal for Trade Reform: With the Text of the General Agreement. LC 76-126. (Special Studies). 208p. 1976. text ed. 27.95 o.p. (ISBN 0-275-23010-4). Praeger.

Atlantic Council Working Group on Nuclear Fuels Policy. Nuclear Power & Nuclear Weapons Proliferation. 2 vols. Gray, John E. & Harned, Joseph W., eds. (Atlantic Council Policy Papers). (Illus.). 1978. pap. text ed. 8.25x ea. o.p. Vol. 1 (ISBN 0-917258-13-4). Vol. 2. Westview.

Atlantic Council Working Group on the U.S. & the Developing Countries & Martin, Edwin M. The United States & the Developing Countries. LC 77-9102. (Atlantic Council Policy Ser.). 1977. lib. bdg. 20.00 (ISBN 0-89158-400-5); pap. 9.25x o.p. (ISBN 0-89158-401-3). Westview.

Atlantic Council's Special Committee on Intergovernmental Organization & Reorganization. Beyond Diplomacy. 81p. pap. text ed. 4.50 (ISBN 0-87855-744-X). Transaction Bks.

Atlas, James, ed. Ten American Poets: An Anthology of Poems. (Poetry Ser.). 1979. 6.95 o.p. (ISBN 0-85635-048-6, Pub. by Carcanet New Pr England); pap. 3.95 o.p. (ISBN 0-85635-049-4, Pub. by Carcanet New Pr England). Humanities.

Atlas, James, jt. ed. see Gomori, George.

Atleson, James B. Values & Assumptions in American Labor Law. LC 82-21993. 240p. 1983. lib. bdg. 25.00x (ISBN 0-87023-389-0). U of Mass Pr.

Atleson, James B., et al see Labor Law Group.

Atluri, S. N. & Gallagher, R. H. Hybrid & Mixed Finite Element Methods. (Numerical Methods in Engineering). 450p. 1983. 69.95 (ISBN 0-471-10486-8, Pub. by Wiley-Interscience). Wiley.

Atmananda & Lenz, Frederick, eds. Samadhi Is Loose in America! LC 82-83869. 500p. (Orig.). 1982. pap. text ed. 9.00 (ISBN 0-941868-02-8). Lakshmi.

Atmore, A., jt. auth. see Oliver, Roland.

Atmore, Anthony & Stacey, Gillian. Black Kingdoms, Black Peoples. LC 78-71755. (Illus.). 1980. 14.95 o.p. (ISBN 0-399-12254-0). Putnam Pub Group.

Atnassova, T., et al. Bulgarian-English Dictionary. 1050p. (Bulgarian & Eng.). 1980. 65.00 (ISBN 0-686-97393-3, M-9829). French & Eur.

Atre, Shakuntala. Data Base Structured Techniques to Designing Performance & Management: With Case Studies. LC 80-14808. (Business Data Processing Ser.). 442p. 1980. 31.95x (ISBN 0-471-05267-1, Pub. by Wiley-Interscience). Wiley.

Atrens, D. M. & Curthoys, J. S., eds. Neuroscience & Behavior: An Introduction. 2nd ed. 214p. 1982. 8.00 (ISBN 0-686-81705-2); subscription 9.95. Acad Pr.

Atshul, B. J., ed. see Baldwin, Barbie.

Atsuta, T., jt. auth. see Chen Wai-Fah.

Atsuta, Toshio, jt. auth. see Chen Wai-Fah.

Atta, Dale Van see Bradlee, Ben, Jr. & Van Atta, Dale.

Atta, Frieda Van see Van Atta, Frieda.

Atta, Jacob K. A Macroeconometric Model of a Developing Economy: Ghana (Simulations & Policy Analysis) LC 80-67178. 346p. (Orig.). 1981. pap. text ed. 13.75 o.p. (ISBN 0-8191-1504-5). U Pr of Amer.

Atta, Jacob K., jt. auth. see El Mallakh, Ragai.

Atta, Robert E. Van see Van Atta, Robert E.

Atta, Winfred Van see Van Atta, Winfred.

Attal, Pierre & Muller, Claude, eds. Actes du Colloque de Linquistique de Rennes, Nov. 17-19, 1979. (Lingvisticae Investigationes Supplementa: 8). 250p. (French.). 1983. 28.00 (ISBN 9-02723-118-4). Benjamins North Am.

Attalides, Michael A. Cyprus: Nationalism & International Politics. LC 79-1388. 1979. 25.00 (ISBN 0-312-18057-8). St Martin.

Attanasio, Salvator, tr. see Danielou, Jean.

Attanasio, Salvatore, tr. see Pedraz, Juan L.

Attar, Farid Al-Din. Muslim Saints & Mystics. 300p. 1976. pap. 7.95 (ISBN 0-7100-7821-8). Routledge & Kegan.

Atta-Ur-Rahman & Basha, Anwar. Biosynthesis of Indole Alkaloids. (International Series of Monographs on Chemistry). (Illus.). 1982. 39.50x (ISBN 0-19-855610-1). Oxford U Pr.

Atteberry, William L., et al. Real Estate Law. 2nd ed. 380p. 1978. text ed. 28.95 (ISBN 0-471-87005-6); tchr's ed. avail. (ISBN 0-471-87006-4); wkbk. o.p. 9.95 (ISBN 0-471-87007-2). Wiley.

Atteia, M., et al. Nonlinear Problems of Analysis in Geometry & Mechanics. LC 80-21647. (Research Notes in Mathematics: No. 46). 288p. (Orig.). 1981. pap. text ed. 25.00 (ISBN 0-273-08493-3). Pitman Pub MA.

Attenberger, Walburga. Who Knows the Little Man? (Illus.). (ps-1). 1972. PLB 3.99 (ISBN 0-394-92427-4); pap. 1.95 (ISBN 0-394-82427-X). Random.

Attenborough, David. Journeys to the Past. 1983. 21.95 (ISBN 0-686-38869-0, Pub. by Salem Hse Ltd). Merrimack Bk Serv.

--The Zoo Quest Expeditions. 1983. pap. 4.95 (ISBN 0-14-005765-X). Penguin.

--Zoo Quest Expeditions. 1983. 21.95 (ISBN 0-686-38870-4, Pub. by Salem Hse Ltd). Merrimack Bk Serv.

Attenborough, Richard. In Search of Gandhi. (Illus.). 240p. 1983. 17.95 (ISBN 0-8329-0237-3). New Century.

Attenborough, Richard, intro. by. The Words of Gandhi. LC 82-14403. (Illus.). 111p. 1982. 8.95 (ISBN 0-937858-14-5). Newmarket.

Atterbury, Paul. The History of Porcelain. LC 82-2275. (Illus.). 256p. 1982. 35.00 (ISBN 0-688-01402-X). Morrow.

Atterbury, Paul, ed. English Pottery & Porcelain. (Antiques Magazine Library). (Illus.). 1979. 14.50x o.p. (ISBN 0-87663-314-9, Main St); pap. 8.95 (ISBN 0-87663-984-8). Universe.

Atthill, Catherine, tr. see Zanetti, Adriano.

Atthill, Robin. Old Mendip. (Old... Ser.). (Illus.). 6.50 o.p. (ISBN 0-7153-4050-6). David & Charles.

Attia, E. L., jt. auth. see Marshall, Kenneth G.

Attig, Thomas, jt. auth. see Scherer, Donald.

Attir, Mustafa O., et al, eds. Directions of Change: Modernization Theory, Research, & Realities. (Special Study Ser.). 300p. (Orig.). 1981. 23.50 (ISBN 0-86531-223-0); pap. 10.95 (ISBN 0-86531-274-5). Westview.

Attix, Frank H., ed. Luminescence Dosimetry: Proceedings. LC 67-60038. (AEC Symposium Ser.). 532p. 1967. pap. 21.25 (ISBN 0-87079-263-6, CONF-650637); microfiche 4.50 (ISBN 0-87079-264-4, CONF-650637). DOE.

Attiyeh, Richard E., et al. Macroeconomics: A Programmed Book. 3rd ed. (Illus.). 272p. (Prog. Bk.). 1974. pap. 9.95 ref. ed. o.p. (ISBN 0-13-542662-6). P-H.

Attman, Artu. The Struggle for Baltic Markets: Powers in Conflict 1558-1618. (Acta Regiae Societatis Scientiarum et Litterarum, Goteborg, Humaniora: No. 14). (Illus.). 1980. pap. text ed. 18.50x (ISBN 91-85252-15-8). Humanities.

Attner, Raymond F., jt. auth. see Plunkett, Warren R.

Attoe, Wayne. Architecture & Critical Imagination. 188p. 1978. 34.95x (ISBN 0-471-99574-6, Pub. by Wiley-Interscience). Wiley.

--Skylines: Understanding & Molding Urban Silhouettes. LC 80-41684. 128p. 1981. 41.95x (ISBN 0-471-27940-4, Pub. by Wiley-Interscience). Wiley.

Attridge, D. Well-Weighed Syllables. LC 74-80362. (Illus.). 280p. 1975. 42.50 (ISBN 0-521-20530-1); pap. 14.95 (ISBN 0-521-29722-2). Cambridge U Pr.

Attridge, G. G., jt. auth. see Walls, H. J.

Attwater, Donald. Names & Name-Days: A Dictionary of Catholic Christian Names in Alphabetical Order with Origins & Meanings. LC 68-30595. 1968. Repr. of 1939 ed. 34.00x (ISBN 0-8103-3108-X). Gale.

Attwater, Donald, ed. Catholic Dictionary. (Orig.). 1961. pap. 2.45 o.p. (ISBN 0-685-14837-8). Macmillan.

Attwater, Donald, tr. see Lawrence, Bro.

Attwater, Donald, tr. see Solovyev, Vladimir.

Attwell, Arthur A. & Jamison, Colleen B. The Mentally Retarded: Answers to Questions About Sex. LC 76-48563. 153p. 1977. pap. 9.90x o.p. (ISBN 0-87424-143-X). Western Psych.

Attwell, Peter & Farmer, Ian. Principles of Engineering Geology. 1976. 85.00x (ISBN 0-412-11280-9, Pub. by Chapman & Hall). Methuen Inc.

Attwood, D. & Florence, A. T. Surfactant Systems. 1982. 99.00x (ISBN 0-412-14840-4, Pub. by Chapman & Hall). Methuen Inc.

Attwood, D., jt. auth. see Florence, A. T.

Atwan, Robert, jt. ed. see McQuade, Donald.

Atwan, Robert, et al. Edsels, Luckies & Frigidaires. 1979. pap. 9.95 o.s.i. (ISBN 0-440-53487-9, Delta). Dell.

Atwater, Eastwood. I Hear You: Listening Skills to Make You a Better Manager. 127p. 1982. 11.95 (ISBN 0-13-450684-7); pap. 5.95 (ISBN 0-13-450676-6). P-H.

--Psychology of Adjustment: Personal Growth in a Changing World. 2nd ed. (Illus.). 448p. 1983. pap. 19.95 (ISBN 0-13-734855-X). P-H.

Atwater, Florence, jt. auth. see Atwater, Richard.

Atwater, James D., jt. auth. see Ford Foundation.

Atwater, M. Shuttle-Craft Book of American Hand Weaving. 16.95 o.p. (ISBN 0-87245-026-0). Textile Bk.

Atwater, Mary M. Design & the Handweaver. LC 61-4138. (Shuttle Craft Guild Monograph: No. 3). (Illus.). 26p. 1961. pap. 6.45 (ISBN 0-916658-03-1). HTH Pubs.

--Guatemala Visited. LC 47-24720. (Shuttle Craft Guild Monograph: No. 15). (Illus.). 46p. 1965. pap. 7.45 (ISBN 0-916658-15-5). HTH Pubs.

--Handwoven Rugs. LC 76-24018. (Shuttle Craft Guild Monograph: No. 29). (Illus.). 28p. 1948. pap. 7.45 (ISBN 0-916658-29-5). HTH Pubs.

Atwater, Maxine H. Rollin' On: A Wheelchair Guide to U. S. Cities. LC 78-15289. (Illus.). 1978. 9.95 o.p. (ISBN 0-396-07548-7). Dodd.

Atwater, Montgomery. Avalanche Hunters. LC 68-31147. (Illus.). 1968. 6.95 (ISBN 0-8255-1345-6). Macrae.

Atwater, Richard & Atwater, Florence. Mr. Popper's Penguins. 1978. pap. 2.25 (ISBN 0-440-45934-6, YB). Dell.

--Mr. Popper's Penguins. (Illus.). (gr. 3 up). 1938. 9.95 (ISBN 0-316-05842-4). Little.

Atwater, Richard, tr. see Procopius.

Atwater, Warren E. Psychology of Adjustment: Personal Growth in a Changing World. (Illus.). 1979. pap. 19.95 (ISBN 0-13-734830-4). P-H.

Atwell, Lee. G. W. Pabst. (Filmmakers Ser.). 1977. lib. bdg. 12.95 (ISBN 0-8057-9251-1, Twayne). G K Hall.

Atwell, Susan, ed. see Petit, Ronald E.

Atwood, A. C., jt. auth. see Blake, S. F.

Atwood, Calvin. Squadron of Roses. LC 78-65165. 1978. 8.95 (ISBN 0-87716-095-3, Pub. by Moore Pub Co). F Apple.

Atwood, Charles. A Doughnut on the Nose is Better than Mustard on the Toes. 96p. (Orig.). 1983. pap. 3.95 (ISBN 0-89815-088-4). Ten Speed Pr.

Atwood, Evangeline. Anchorage: Star of the North. Silvey, Kitty & Alexander, Lynn, eds. LC 81-86568. (American Portrait Ser.). (Illus.). 240p. 1982. 29.95 (ISBN 0-932986-25-0). Continent Herit.

Atwood, H. L., jt. ed. see Bliss, Dorothy.

Atwood, June, jt. auth. see Cronan, Marion.

Atwood, June, jt. auth. see Cronan, Marion L.

Atwood, Kathryn. Renegade Lady. 352p. 1982. pap. 3.25 (ISBN 0-515-06045-3). Jove Pubns.

--Satan's Angel. 384p. (Orig.). 1981. pap. 2.95 o.s.i. (ISBN 0-515-05510-7). Jove Pubns.

Atwood, Kenneth W., jt. auth. see Alley, Charles L.

Atwood, L. Erwin, et al, eds. International Perspectives on News. 192p. 1982. 13.95x (ISBN 0-8093-1069-4). S Ill U Pr.

Atwood, Margaret. The Circle Game. (House of Anansi Poetry Ser.: No. 3). 1967. 9.95 (ISBN 0-88784-070-1, Pub. by Hse Anansi Pr Canada); pap. 3.95 (ISBN 0-686-86816-1). U of Toronto Pr.

--The Edible Woman. 288p. 1983. pap. 3.50 (ISBN 0-446-31105-7). Warner Bks.

--Lady Oracle. 1977. pap. 3.50 (ISBN 0-380-01799-7, 35444, Bard). Avon.

--Life Before Man. 1980. 11.95 o.p. (ISBN 0-671-25115-5). S&S.

--Life Before Man. 304p. 1983. pap. 3.50 (ISBN 0-446-31106-5). Warner Bks.

--Second Words: Selected Critical Prose. 448p. 1982. 22.95 (ISBN 0-88784-095-7, Pub. by Hse Anansi Pr Canada). U of Toronto Pr.

--Selected Poems. 1978. 10.95 o.p. (ISBN 0-671-22885-4); pap. 5.95 o.p. (ISBN 0-671-24199-0). S&S.

--Surfacing. 224p. 1983. pap. 3.50 (ISBN 0-446-31107-3). Warner Bks.

--Two-Headed Poems. 1981. 10.95 o.p. (ISBN 0-671-25370-0, Touchstone Bks); pap. 5.95 (ISBN 0-671-25373-5). S&S.

Atwood, Rodney. The Hessians: Mercenaries from Hessen Kassel in the American Revolution. LC 79-20150. 1980. 32.50 (ISBN 0-521-22884-0). Cambridge U Pr.

Atwood, Stephen J. A Doctor's Guide to Feeding Your Child: Complete Nutrition for Healthy Growth. (Illus.). 288p. 1982. 12.95 (ISBN 0-02-504400-1). Macmillan.

Atwood, Valdine, ed. Maine D.A.R. Cook Book. LC 82-73245. 310p. (Orig.). 1982. pap. 7.00 (ISBN 0-941216-04-7). Cay-bel.

Atwood, W. B. & Bjorken, J. D. Lectures on Lepton Nucleon Scattering & Quantum Chromo-Dynamics. (Progress in Physics Ser.: Vol. 4). 1982. 34.95 (ISBN 3-7643-3079-1). Birkhauser.

Aubert, H. & Pinta, M. Trace Elements in Soils. (Developments in Soil Science: Vol. 7). 1977. 81.00 (ISBN 0-444-41511-4). Elsevier.

Aubert, Louis. Reconstruction of Europe. 1925. text ed. 37.50x (ISBN 0-686-83724-X). Elliots Bks.

Aubert, Marcel. The High Gothic Era. (Art of the World Ser.). 7.95 (ISBN 0-517-50843-5). Crown.

Aubert, Vilhelm. The Hidden Society. LC 80-18939. (Social Science Classics Ser.). 359p. 1982. pap. 12.95 (ISBN 0-87855-730-X). Transaction Bks.

--In Search of Law. 220p. 1983. text ed. 26.50x (ISBN 0-389-20385-8). B&N Imports.

Aubin, J. P. Mathematical Methods of Game & Economic Theory. (Studies in Mathematics & Its Applications: Vol. 7). 1980. 106.50 (ISBN 0-444-85184-4, North-Holland). Elsevier.

Aubin, J. P. & Vinter, R. B. Convex Analysis & Optimization. (Research Notes in Mathematics Ser.: No. 57). 240p. 1982. pap. text ed. 21.95 (ISBN 0-273-08547-6). Pitman Pub MA.

Aubin, Jean-Pierre. Applied Abstract Analysis. LC 77-2382. (Pure & Applied Mathematics, a W-I Ser. of Texts, Monographs & Tracts). 263p. 1977. 42.50x (ISBN 0-471-02146-6, Pub. by Wiley-Interscience). Wiley.

--Applied Functional Analysis. LC 78-20896. (Pure & Applied Mathematics: Texts, Monographs & Tracts). 1979. 42.50x (ISBN 0-471-02149-0, Pub. by Wiley-Interscience). Wiley.

Aubin, Penelope. The Life of Madam De Beaumont, a French Lady. Bd. with The Strange Adventures of the Count De Vinevil & His Family. LC 75-170548. (Foundations of the Novel 1700-1739). lib. bdg. 50.00 o.s.i. (ISBN 0-8240-0548-1). Garland Pub.

Aubin, T. Nonlinear Analysis on Manifolds: Monge-Ampere Equations. (Grundlehren der mathematischen Wiszenschaften Ser.: Vol. 252). 204p. 1983. 29.50 (ISBN 0-387-90704-1). Springer-Verlag.

Aublet, J. B. Histoire des Plantes de la Guiane Francaise, 4 vols. bd. in one. (Historia Naturalis Classica Ser.: No. 100). 1977. Repr. of 1775 ed. lib. bdg. 200.00x (ISBN 3-7682-1105-3). Lubrecht & Cramer.

Auboyer, Jeannine, intro. by. Rarities of the Musee Guimet. LC 74-81967. (Illus.). 124p. 1975. 19.50 o.p. (ISBN 0-87848-043-9). Asia Soc.

Aubrey, Henry G. Coexistence: Economic Challenge & Response. LC 75-28675. 323p. 1976. Repr. of 1961 ed. lib. bdg. 19.25x (ISBN 0-8371-8471-1, AUCO). Greenwood.

Aubrey, John. Aubrey's Brief Lives. Dick, Oliver L., ed. 1982. pap. 6.95 (ISBN 0-14-043079-2). Penguin.

--Brief Lives (Modern English Version) Barber, Richard, ed. LC 82-24416. 200p. 1983. text ed. 22.50x (ISBN 0-389-20366-1). B&N Imports.

Aubrey, Vickey. Chinese Brush Painting for Children. (Illus.). 32p. (gr. 2 up). 1982. 9.95 (ISBN 0-8149-0851-9). Vanguard.

Aubry, M. P. Handbook of Cenozoic Calcareous Nannoplankton, 7 vols. Date not set. 50.00 ea. Am Mus Natl Hist.

Auburn, Mark & Burkman, Katherine. Drama Through Performance. LC 76-19458. (Illus.). 1977. pap. text ed. 15.95 (ISBN 0-395-24548-6); instr's manual 1.35 (ISBN 0-395-24550-8). HM.

Auchincloss, Louis. The House of the Prophet. (General Ser.). 1980. lib. bdg. 14.95 (ISBN 0-8161-3133-3, Large Print Bks). G K Hall.

--The House of the Prophet. 1981. pap. 3.95 (ISBN 0-395-30520-9). HM.

--Life, Law & Letters: Essays & Sketches. 1979. 8.95 o.s.i. (ISBN 0-395-28151-2). HM.

--Narcissa & Other Fables. 1984. 13.95 (ISBN 0-395-33114-5). HM.

--Sister Carrie. LC 69-13798. (gr. 9-12). 1969. text ed. 7.95x o.s.i. (ISBN 0-686-86343-7); pap. text ed. 3.50 (ISBN 0-675-09528-X). Merrill.

--Sybil. LC 75-108840. 284p. 1972. Repr. of 1952 ed. lib. bdg. 20.50x (ISBN 0-8371-3728-4, AUSY). Greenwood.

Auchterlonie, Paul & Safadi, Yasin H., eds. Union Catalogue of Arabic Serials & Newspapers in British Libraries. 164p. 1977. 20.00 o.p. (ISBN 0-7201-0636-2, Pub. by Mansell England). Wilson.

Audah, A. Q. Islam Between Ignorant Followers & Incapable Scholars. pap. 3.75 o.p. (ISBN 0-686-18505-6). Kazi Pubns.

Audebert, A. J., jt. ed. see Hafez, E. S.

Audemars, Pierre. Slay Me a Sinner. (Scene of the Crime Ser.: No. 62). 1983. pap. 2.95 (ISBN 0-440-18191-7). Dell.

Auden, W. H. Collected Shorter Poems: 1927 to 1957. 352p. Date not set. pap. 22.50 (ISBN 0-394-40333-9, V-2015, Vin). Random.

--The Double Man. LC 79-4323. 1979. Repr. of 1941 ed. lib. bdg. 17.75x (ISBN 0-313-21073-X, AUDM). Greenwood.

Auden, W. H. & Kallman, Chester. An Elizabethan Song Book. Greenberg, Noah, ed. 240p. 1968. pap. 7.95 (ISBN 0-686-16377-X). Faber & Faber.

Auden, W. H., ed. Portable Greek Reader. (Viking Portable Library: No. 39). 1977. pap. 6.95 (ISBN 0-14-015039-0, P39). Penguin.

Auden, W. H. & Pearson, Norman H., eds. Poets of the English Language, Vol. 4: Romantic Poets. (Viking Portable Library: No. 52). 1977. pap. 5.95 o.p. (ISBN 0-14-015052-8, P52). Penguin.

--The Portable Elizabethan & Jacobean Poets. (Viking Portable Library: No. 50). 1977. pap. 6.95 (ISBN 0-14-015050-1). Penguin.

Auden, W. H., ed. see Byron, George G.

Auden, W. H., ed. see Campion, Thomas.

Auden, W. H., ed. see Dryden, John.

Auden, W. H., tr. see Brecht, Bertolt.

Auden, W. H., tr. see Von Goethe, Johann W.

Audet, Thelma, jt. auth. see Dreizen, LaVerne.

Audette, Larry. Bjorn Borg. (Illus.). 1979. pap. 3.95 (ISBN 0-8256-3931-X, Quick Fox). Putnam Pub Group.

Audette, Vicki. Dress Better for Less. Grooms, Kathe, ed. LC 81-11246. (Illus.). 192p. 1981. 9.95 (ISBN 0-915658-44-5); pap. 4.95 (ISBN 0-915658-33-X). Meadowbrook Pr.

Audfray, Annie, tr. see Getz, Gene A.

Audiganne, A. Memoires d'un Ouvrier de Paris, 1871-1872. (Conditions of the 19th Century French Working Class Ser.). 320p. (Fr.). 1974. Repr. of 1873 ed. lib. bdg. 84.00x o.p. (ISBN 0-8287-0176-8, 1092). Clearwater Pub.

--Les Ouvriers a Present et la Nouvelle Economie du Travail. (Conditions of the 19th Century French Working Class Ser.). 492p. (Fr.). 1974. Repr. of 1865 ed. lib. bdg. 118.00 o.p. (ISBN 0-8287-0041-9, 1103). Clearwater Pub.

--Les Ouvriers en Famille, Cinquieme Edition Augmentee d'un Manuel Elementaire des Societes de Secours Mutuel. (Conditions of the 19th Century French Working Class Ser.). 263p. (Fr.). 1974. Repr. of 1858 ed. lib. bdg. 71.25x o.p. (ISBN 0-8287-0042-7, 1039). Clearwater Pub.

--Les Populations Ouvrieres et les Industries de la France, 2 vols. (Conditions of the 19th Century French Working Class Ser.). 860p. (Fr.). 1974. Repr. of 1860 ed. Set. lib. bdg. 217.00x o.p. (ISBN 0-8287-0043-5). Vol. 1 (1168). Vol. 2 (1169). Clearwater Pub.

--Le Travail et les Ouvriers sous la Troisieme Republique. (Conditions of the 19th Century French Working Class Ser). 36p. (Fr.). 1974. Repr. of 1873 ed. 26.00x o.p. (ISBN 0-8287-1424-X, 1086). Clearwater Pub.

Audretsch, H. Supervision in European Community Law: Observance by the Member States of Their Treaty Obligations - a Treatise on International & Supranational Supervision. 1978. 61.75 (ISBN 0-444-85037-6, North-Holland). Elsevier.

Audsley, G., jt. auth. see Audsley, W.

Audsley, W. & Audsley, G. Designs & Patterns from Historic Ornament. Orig. Title: Outlines of Ornament in the Leading Styles. 1968. pap. 5.00 (ISBN 0-486-21931-3). Dover.

--Designs & Patterns from Historic Ornaments. Orig. Title: Outlines of Ornament in the Leading Styles. (Illus.). 9.50 (ISBN 0-8446-1565-X). Peter Smith.

Audubon, John J. Audubon's Birds of America Coloring Book. 48p. 1974. pap. 2.00 (ISBN 0-486-23049-X). Dover.

Audubon Society. Encyclopedia of Animal Life. Farrand, John, Jr., ed. (Illus.). 1982. 45.00 o.p. (ISBN 0-686-83058-X, C N Potter Bks). Crown.

--One Hundred Two Favorite Audubon Birds of America. 1979. 17.95 o.p. (ISBN 0-517-53545-9). Crown.

Audy dos Santos, Joyce. Giants of Smaller Worlds: Drawn in Their Natural Sizes. LC 82-45993. (Illus.). 48p. (gr. 2-5). 1983. PLB 10.95 (ISBN 0-396-08143-6). Dodd.

Aue, Hartmann Von see Hartman, Von Aue.

Aue, Hartmann Von see Hartmann Von Aue.

Aue, Maximilian A. E., tr. see Wittgenstein, Ludwig.

Auer, J. Jeffery, ed. Brigance's Speech Communication. 3rd ed. Orig. Title: Speech Communication. 1967. pap. 14.95 (ISBN 0-13-082933-1). P-H.

Auer, Jim. Sorting it Out with God. 64p. 1982. pap. 1.95 (ISBN 0-89243-163-6). Liguori Pubns.

Auer, Peter L., ed. Advances in Energy Systems & Technology, Vol. 3. 308p. 1982. 39.50 (ISBN 0-12-014903-6). Acad Pr.

Auerbach & Geehr. Management of Wilderness & Environmental Emergency. 1983. price not set (ISBN 0-02-304630-9). Macmillan.

Auerbach, ed. Best Computer Papers, 1979. (Annual Computer Papers Ser.). 1980. 49.00 (ISBN 0-444-00350-9). Elsevier.

--Best Computer Papers, 1980. (Annual Computer Papers Ser.). 1980. 58.00 (ISBN 0-444-00447-5). Elsevier.

Auerbach, Arnold. Basketball for the Player, the Fan, & the Coach. (Illus.). 1976. 9.95 o.p. (ISBN 0-671-22155-8). S&S.

Auerbach, Arnold Red & Fitzgerald, Joe. Red Auerbach: An Autobiography. LC 76-51377. (Illus.). 1977. 9.95 o.p. (ISBN 0-399-11893-4). Putnam Pub Group.

Auerbach, Charlotte. Mutation Research: Problems, Results & Perspectives. 1976. 46.00x (ISBN 0-412-11280-9, Pub. by Chapman & Hall). Methuen Inc.

Auerbach, Debbie, jt. ed. see Satterlee, Sarah.

Auerbach, Doris. Sam Shepard, Arthur Kopit, & the Off-Broadway Theater. (United States Authors Ser.). 1982. lib. bdg. 13.95 (ISBN 0-8057-7371-1, Twayne). G K Hall.

Auerbach, Erich. Dante, Poet of the Secular World. Silverstein, Theodore, ed. Manheim, Ralph, tr. 1961. 7.00x o.s.i. (ISBN 0-226-03207-8). U of Chicago Pr.

Auerbach, Jerold S. Justice Without Law? (Illus.). 224p. 1983. 16.95 (ISBN 0-19-503175-X). Oxford U Pr.

--Unequal Justice: Lawyers & Social Change in Modern America. LC 75-7364. 1977. pap. 8.95 (ISBN 0-19-502170-3, 490, GB). Oxford U Pr.

Auerbach, Jerold S., ed. American Labor: The Twentieth Century. LC 69-14822. (American Heritage Ser). 1969. pap. 9.95 (ISBN 0-672-60128-1, 78). Bobbs.

Auerbach, Nina. Woman & the Demon: The Life of a Victorian Myth. (Illus.). 256p. 1982. text ed. 17.50x (ISBN 0-674-95406-8). Harvard U Pr.

Auerbach, Paul & Budassi, Susan, eds. Cardiac Arrest & CPR: Assessment, Planning & Intervention. 2nd ed. 230p. 1982. 29.00 (ISBN 0-89443-841-7). Aspen Systems.

Auerbach, Stanley I., jt. ed. see Francis, Chester.

Auerbach, Stevanne. The Whole Child: A Source Book. 320p. 1982. pap. 8.95 (ISBN 0-399-50554-7, Perige). Putnam Pub Group.

--The Whole Child: A Sourcebook. (Illus.). 320p. 1981. 18.95 (ISBN 0-399-12364-4). Putnam Pub Group.

Auernheimer, Leonardo & Ekelund, Robert B. The Essential of Money & Banking. LC 81-11466. 445p. 1982. 23.95 (ISBN 0-471-02103-2); avail. instrs' manual (ISBN 0-471-87633-X). Wiley.

Aufermann, B. Zur Chemotaxonomie Mariner Rhodophyceen am Beispiel Einer Leucin-Decarboxylase. (Bibliotheca Phycologica Ser.: No. 43). (Illus.). 1978. pap. text ed. 16.00x (ISBN 3-7682-1206-8). Lubrecht & Cramer.

Aufhammer & Bergal. Barley Varieties. 3rd ed. 1968. 20.00 (ISBN 0-444-40023-0). Elsevier.

Aufmann, jt. auth. see Barker.

Aufmann, Richard N. & Barker, Vernon C. Arithmetic: An Applied Approach. LC 77-77005. (Illus.). 1978. pap. text ed. 20.95 (ISBN 0-395-25791-3); instr's. manual 0.55 (ISBN 0-395-25790-5). HM.

--Basic College Mathematics: An Applied Approach. 2nd ed. LC 81-84253. 1982. pap. 20.50; instr's annotated ed. 21.50 (ISBN 0-395-32322-3); instr's alt. test program 1.95 (ISBN 0-395-31680-4); solutions manual 6.50 (ISBN 0-395-32023-2). HM.

--Introductory Algebra: An Applied Approach. LC 82-82886. 512p. 1983. pap. text ed. 19.95 (ISBN 0-395-32593-5); write for info. supplementary materials. HM.

Aufmann, Richard N., jt. auth. see Baker, Vernoon C.

Aufrecht, Walter E. & Hurd, John. A Synoptic Concordance of Aramaic Inscriptions. (International Concordance Library: Vol. I). 1975. pap. 20.00 (ISBN 0-935106-24-3). Biblical Res Assocs.

Auge-Laribe, Michel & Pinot, Pierre. Agriculture & Food Supply in France During the War. (Economic & Social History of the World War Ser.). 1927. text ed. 75.00x (ISBN 0-686-83458-5). Elliots Bks.

Augelli, John P. Caribbean Lands. rev. ed. LC 77-84154. (American Neighbors Ser.). (Illus.). (gr. 5 up). 1978. text ed. 11.20 ea. 1-4 copies (ISBN 0-88296-112-8); text ed. 8.96 ea. 5 or more; tchrs'. guide 8.96 (ISBN 0-88296-353-8). Fideler.

Augelli, John P. & West, Robert C. Middle America: Its Lands & Peoples. 2nd ed. (Anthropology Ser.). (Illus.). 576p. 1976. text ed. 28.95 (ISBN 0-13-581546-0). P-H.

Augelli, John P., ed. American Neighbors. rev ed. LC 81-71296. (American Neighbors Ser.). (Illus.). (gr. 5 up). 1982. text ed. 16.18 1-4 copies (ISBN 0-88296-086-5); text ed. 12.94 5 or more copies (ISBN 0-686-98159-6); tchr's guide 8.96 (ISBN 0-88296-354-6). Fideler.

Augenstein, Moshe & Tenenbaum, Aaron. Data Structures & PL-1 Programming. (Illus.). 1979. text ed. 27.95 (ISBN 0-13-197731-8); exercise manual 8.95 (ISBN 0-13-197756-3). P-H.

Augenstein, Moshe & Tenenbaum, Aaron M. Data Structures Using PASCAL. (Illus.). 528p. 1981. text ed. 27.95 (ISBN 0-13-196501-8). P-H.

Auger, C. P. Use of Reports in Literature. 1975. 37.95 (ISBN 0-408-70666-X). Butterworth.

Auger, J. Behavioral Systems & Nursing. (Illus.). 224p. 1976. ref. ed. 19.95x (ISBN 0-13-074484-0). P-H.

Augerbauer, George J. Electronics for Modern Communication. (Illus.). 672p. 1974. ref. ed. 24.95 (ISBN 0-13-252338-8). P-H.

Aughey, Arthur, jt. auth. see Norton, Philip.

Augier, F. R. & Gordon, Shirley C., eds. Sources of West Indian History: A Compilation of Writings of Historical Events in the West Indies. (Orig.). (YA) 1962. pap. text ed. 4.25x (ISBN 0-582-76303-7). Humanities.

Augier, F. R., et al. The Making of the West Indies. (Illus.). 310p. (Orig.). (gr. 10-12). 1960. pap. text ed. 7.50 (ISBN 0-582-76304-5). Longman.

Augsburger, David. Caring Enough to Forgive Caring Enough Not to Forgive. 160p. (Orig.). 1981. pap. 4.95 (ISBN 0-8361-1965-7). Herald Pr.

--Cherishable: Love & Marriage. 1975. pap. write for info (ISBN 0-515-09265-7, PV065). Jove Pubns.

--From Here to Maturity. 1982. pap. 2.50 (ISBN 0-8423-0938-1). Tyndale.

--Perdonar Para Ser Libre: The Freedom of Forgiveness. Powell, David R., tr. from Eng. (Spanish Ser.). 1977. pap. 2.95 (ISBN 0-8024-6599-4). Moody.

Augsburger, Myron S. Quench Not the Spirit. LC 62-7330. 178p. 1975. pap. 1.75 o.p. (ISBN 0-87983-107-3). Keats.

Augur, Helen. The Book of Fairs. LC 75-159875. (Tower Bks). (Illus.). xviii, 308p. 1972. Repr. of 1939 ed. 37.00x (ISBN 0-8103-3927-7). Gale.

August, Gilbert P., jt. auth. see Hung, Wellington.

August, J. T., ed. Monoclonal Antibodies in Drug Development. (Illus.). 237p. (Orig.). 1982. lexitone 24.00 (ISBN 0-9609094-0-0). Am Phar & Ex.

Augustan Reprint Society. Publications, 18 vols. nos. 1-108. 1974. Set. 608.00 (ISBN 0-527-03250-6); pap. 36.00 per year. Kraus Repr.

Augusteyn, R. C. & Collin, H. B. The Eye, Vol. 2. Horrobin, David F., ed. LC 79-32253. (Annual Research Reviews). 344p. 1980. 36.00 (ISBN 0-88831-083-8). Eden Pr.

Augusteyn, R. C., et al. The Eye, Vol 1. Horrobin, D. F., ed. (Annual Research Reviews Ser.). 1979. 22.00 (ISBN 0-88831-057-9). Eden Pr.

Augustijn, Cornelis & Fraenkel, Pierre, eds. Martini Buceri (Opera Latina) Vol. 1 Opera Omia, Series II. (Studies in Medieval & Reformation Thought Ser.: Vol. 30). viii, 296p. 1982. write for info. (ISBN 90-04-06490-7). E J Brill.

Augustin, John S. The Indian Family in Transition. 256p. 1982. text ed. 25.00x (ISBN 0-7069-1970-X, Pub. by Vikas India). Advent NY.

Augustine. Basic Writings of Saint Augustine, 2 vols. Oates, Whitney J., ed. 1981. Repr. of 1948 ed. 45.00 o.p. (ISBN 0-8010-0164-1). Baker Bk.

--Of True Religion. pap. 3.95 o.s.i. (ISBN 0-89526-926-0). Regnery-Gateway.

Augustine, Aurelius. What Augustine Says. Geisler, Norman L., ed. 204p. (Orig.). 1982. pap. 8.95 (ISBN 0-8010-0185-4). Baker Bk.

Augustine, James R. Medical Neuroanatomy. (Illus.). 500p. 1982. write for info. o.p. (ISBN 0-8121-0801-9). Lea & Febiger.

Augustine, Saint Against the Academicians. Garvey, Sr. M. Patricia, tr. 1957. pap. 7.95 (ISBN 0-87462-202-6). Marquette.

--Confessions of Saint Augustine. Sheed, Frank, tr. 1969. Bks. 1-10. pap. text ed. 5.95 o.s.i. (ISBN 0-8362-0482-4). Andrews & McMeel.

--Confessions of Saint Augustine. Pusey, Edward B., tr. 1961. pap. 2.95 (ISBN 0-02-064230-X, Collier). Macmillan.

--Confessions of Saint Augustine. Warner, Rex, tr. pap. 3.95 (ISBN 0-451-62188-3, ME2188, Ment). NAL.

--Enchiridion on Faith, Hope & Love. Paolucci, Henry, ed. 177p. 1961. pap. 4.95 (ISBN 0-89526-938-4). Regnery-Gateway.

--The Essential Augustine. Bourke, Vernon J., commentary by. 1973. 12.50 (ISBN 0-915144-08-5); pap. text ed. 4.50 (ISBN 0-915144-07-7). Hackett Pub.

Augustine, St. From the Sermon on the Mount. Bd. with Related Sermons. (Fathers of the Church Ser.: Vol. 11). 1951. 19.00 (ISBN 0-8132-0011-3). Cath U Pr.

Augustine, Saint On the Two Cities: Selections from the City of God. Strothmann, F. W., ed. LC 57-13344. (Milestones of Thought Ser.). 1958. 4.50 o.p. (ISBN 0-8044-5827-8); pap. 3.95 o.p. (ISBN 0-8044-6791-9). Ungar.

Augustine, St. The Teacher. Bd. with Two Works on Free Will. (Fathers of the Church Ser.: Vol. 59). 1968. 17.00 (ISBN 0-8132-0059-8). Cath U Pr.

--Treatises on Marriage & Other Subjects. (Fathers of the Church Ser.: Vol. 27). 1955. 23.00 (ISBN 0-8132-0027-X). Cath U Pr.

Augustithis, S. S. Atlas of the Textural Patterns of Basalts & Their Genetic Significance. 1978. 93.75 (ISBN 0-444-41566-1). Elsevier.

--Atlas of the Textural Patterns of Granites, Gneisses & Associated Rock Types. 1973. 102.25 (ISBN 0-444-40977-7). Elsevier.

Augustus, Frederick. The Emperor Akbar: A Contribution Towards the History of India in the 16th Century, 2 vols. Beveridge, Annette S., tr. 1973. Repr. of 1890 ed. 18.75x ea. Vol. 1, 348p (ISBN 0-8002-0595-2). Vol. 2, 454p (ISBN 0-8002-0596-0). Intl Pubns Serv.

Augustus, John. John Augustus, First Probation Officer. LC 79-129308. (Ser. in Criminology, Law Enforcement & Social Problems: No. 130). (Illus.). 10.00x (ISBN 0-87585-130-4). Patterson Smith.

Augustyniak, J., ed. Biological Implications of Protein-Nucleic Acid Interactions. 1981. 81.00 (ISBN 0-444-80292-4). Elsevier.

Auker, Jim & Cey, Ron. How to Play Third Base. 1977. pap. 2.50 o.s.i. (ISBN 0-695-80867-2). Follett.

Aukerman, Louise R., jt. auth. see Aukerman, Robert C.

Aukerman, Robert C. Approaches to Beginning Reading. LC 70-144330. (Illus.). 509p. 1971. pap. text ed. 18.50x (ISBN 0-471-03691-9); avail. tchrs. manual (ISBN 0-471-04850-X). Wiley.

--The Basal Reader Approach to Reading. LC 80-28174. 339p. 1981. text ed. 15.95 (ISBN 0-471-03082-1); pap. text ed. 10.95 (ISBN 0-471-09066-2). Wiley.

--Reading in the Secondary School Classroom. (Illus.). 425p. 1972. text ed. 22.95 (ISBN 0-07-002483-9, C). McGraw.

Aukerman, Robert C. & Aukerman, Louise R. How Do I Teach Reading. LC 80-23380. 543p. 1981. text ed. 21.95 (ISBN 0-471-03687-0). Wiley.

Aulanger, G. & Plasse, J. C., eds. Progress in Clinical Pharmacy, Vol. 2. 1980. 50.75 (ISBN 0-444-80250-9). Elsevier.

Auld, A. Graeme. Joshua, Moses & the Land: Tretrateuch-Pentateuch-Hexateuch in a Generation Since 1938. 156p. 1980. Repr. text ed. 20.00x o.p. (ISBN 0-567-09306-9). Attic Pr.

Auld, B. Acoustic Fields & Waves in Solids, 2 vols. LC 72-8926. 1973. Set. 96.00x (ISBN 0-471-03702-8); 52.00x ea. Vol. 1 (ISBN 0-471-03700-1). Vol. 2 (ISBN 0-471-03701-X, Pub. by Wiley-Interscience). Wiley.

Auld, Douglas & Bannock, Graham. The American Dictionary of Economics. 352p. 1983. 15.95x (ISBN 0-87196-532-1). Facts on File.

Auld, John W. Canadian Housing References, Nineteen Seventy-Five to Nineteen Seventy-Seven. (Public Administration Ser.: P 11). 1978. pap. 12.50 o.p. (ISBN 0-88066-002-3). Vance Biblios.

Auld, William M. Christmas Traditions. LC 68-58167. 1968. Repr. of 1931 ed. 37.00x (ISBN 0-8103-3353-8). Gale.

Aulen, Gustaf E. Reformation & Catholicity. Wahlstrom, Eric H., tr. from Swedish. LC 78-25981. 1979. Repr. of 1961 ed. lib. bdg. 19.25x (ISBN 0-313-20809-3, AURC). Greenwood.

Auleta, Michael S. Foundations of Early Childhood Education: Readings. 1969. pap. text ed. 6.95x (ISBN 0-685-77205-5). Phila Bk Co.

Auletta, Ken. The Underclass. 1982. 17.50 (ISBN 0-394-52343-1). Random.

--The Underclass. LC 82-40433. 368p. 1983. pap. 6.95 (ISBN 0-394-71388-5, Vin). Random.

Aulicino, Armand. The Nouvelle Cuisine Cookbook. LC 76-1447. (Illus.). 295p. (Orig.). 1981. pap. 7.95 (ISBN 0-448-14418-2, G&D). Putnam Pub Group.

Aulnoy, Marie C. The Prince of Carency. LC 70-170541. (Novel in England, 1700-1775 Ser). lib. bdg. 50.00 o.s.i. (ISBN 0-8240-0542-2). Garland Pub.

Aulock, Wilhelm H. Von see Von Aulock, Wilhelm H.

Aulson, Pam. Crafty Ideas with Placemats. (Illus.). 24p. 1979. pap. 2.50 (ISBN 0-9601896-3-7). Patch As Patch.

--Placemat Pets 'n Playmates. (Illus.). 24p. 1980. pap. 2.75 (ISBN 0-9601896-2-9). Patch As Patch.

--Placement Plus & Plenty More. (Illus.). 64p. 1982. pap. 3.00 (ISBN 0-9601896-5-3). Patch As Patch.

--Pretty as a Picture: Fabric Frames. (Illus.). 24p. 1981. pap. 2.50 (ISBN 0-9601896-4-5). Patch As Patch.

Ault, Addison & Ault, Margaret R. A Handy & Systematic Catalog of NMR Spectra: Instruction Through Examples. LC 79-57227. 425p. 1980. 18.00x (ISBN 0-935702-00-8). Univ Sci Bks.

Ault, Addison & Dudek, Gerald. An Introduction to Proton NMR Spectroscopy. LC 75-26286. 141p. 1976. pap. text ed. 8.50x (ISBN 0-8162-0331-8). Holden-Day.

Ault, Frederick K. & Lawrence, Richard M. Chemistry: A Conceptual Introduction. 1976. 15.50x (ISBN 0-673-07903-1). Scott F.

Ault, Karuna, ed. see Hari Dass, Baba.

Ault, Leslie. The Official Mastermind Handbook. 1976. pap. 1.50 o.p. (ISBN 0-451-07921-3, W7921, Sig). NAL.

--The Official Mastermind Puzzle Book. (Orig.). 1978. pap. 1.75 o.p. (ISBN 0-451-08536-1, E8536, Sig). NAL.

Ault, Margaret R., jt. auth. see Ault, Addison.

Ault, Nelson A., jt. auth. see Magill, L. M.

Ault, Norman. New Light on Pope, with Some Additions to His Poetry Hitherto Unknown. viii, 379p. 1967. Repr. of 1949 ed. 19.50 o.p. (ISBN 0-208-00269-3, Archon). Shoe String.

Ault, Ruth L. Children's Cognitive Development. 2nd ed. (Illus.). 1982. 15.00x (ISBN 0-19-503183-0); pap. 6.00 (ISBN 0-19-503184-9). Oxford U Pr.

Ault, Ruth L., ed. Developmental Perspectives. text ed. 18.95x (ISBN 0-673-16187-0). Scott F.

Ault, Warren O. Private Jurisdiction in England. Helmholz, R. H. & Reams, Bernard D., Jr., eds. LC 80-84955. (Historical Writings in Law & Jurisprudence: No. 25, Bk. 39). 370p. 1981. Repr. of 1923 ed. lib. bdg. 35.00 (ISBN 0-89941-091-X). W S Hein.

Aultman, Dick, jt. auth. see Jacobs, John.

Aultman, Dick, jt. auth. see Toski, Bob.

Auluck, Sunita V. Intracity Residential Mobility in an Industrial City: A Case Study of Ludhiana. 180p. 1980. text ed. 10.75x (ISBN 0-391-02134-6). Humanities.

Aumann, Francis R. Changing American Legal System: Some Selected Phases. LC 79-92625. (Law, Politics, & History Ser). 1969. Repr. of 1940 ed. 39.50 (ISBN 0-306-71762-X). Da Capo.

Aumann, Jordan & Dongan, Margaret. Teresa of Avila. LC 82-10795. (Word & Spirit Ser.: Vol. 4). 1983. pap. 6.00 (ISBN 0-932506-19-4). St Bedes Pubns.

Aumiaux, M. The Use of Microprocessors. LC 79-42904. (Wiley Series in Computing). 198p. 1980. 29.95x (ISBN 0-471-27689-8, Pub. by Wiley Interscience). Wiley.

Aune, A. B. & Vlietstra, J. Automation for Safety in Shipping & Offshore Petroleum Operations. 1980. 89.50 (ISBN 0-444-85498-3). Elsevier.

--Automation for Safety in Shipping & Off-Shore Petroleum Operations. (Computer Applications in Shipping & Shipbuilding Ser.: Vol. 8). 1980. 89.75 (ISBN 0-444-85498-3). Elsevier.

Aune, B. A. Knowledge, Mind & Nature. 1979. lib. bdg. 24.00 (ISBN 0-917930-27-4); pap. text ed. 8.50x (ISBN 0-917930-07-X). Ridgeview.

Aune, Bruce A. Rationalism, Empiricism & Pragmaticism: An Introduction. 1970. pap. text ed. 6.00x (ISBN 0-394-30017-3, RanC). Random.

Aune, David E. Jesus & the Synoptic Gospels: A Bibliographic Study Guide. Branson, Mark L., ed. (TSF - IBR Bibliographic Study Guides Ser.). 99p. (Orig.). 1981. pap. 2.95 (ISBN 0-8308-5498-3). Inter-Varsity.

--Prophecy & Early Christianity. 400p. 1983. 24.95 (ISBN 0-8028-3584-8). Eerdmans.

AUPHA Task Force on Financial Management. Financial Management of Health Care Organizations: A Referenced Outline & Annotated Bibliography. 237p. 1978. 8.00 (ISBN 0-686-68588-1, 14921). Healthcare Fin Man Assn.

Auping, Michael. John Chamberlain: Wall Reliefs 1960-1983. LC 82-83513. (Illus.). 85p. (Orig.). 1983. pap. 15.00 (ISBN 0-916758-10-9). Ringling Mus Art.

Aurand, Harold W. From the Molly Maguires to the United Mine Workers: The Social Ecology of an Industrial Union, 1869-97. LC 73-157737. 1971. 29.95 (ISBN 0-87722-006-9). Temple U Pr.

Aurandt, Paul. Paul Harvey's the Rest of the Story. LC 77-75381. 1977. 11.95 (ISBN 0-385-12768-5). Doubleday.

Aurelio, John R. Story Sunday: Christian Fairy Tales for Children, Parents & Educators. LC 78-51587. 104p. 1978. pap. 3.95 (ISBN 0-8091-2115-8). Paulist Pr.

Aurelius, Marcus. Meditations. Long, George, tr. Bd. with Enchiridion. Epictetus. 224p. 1956. pap. 3.95 o.s.i. (ISBN 0-89526-922-8). Regnery-Gateway.

Auriche, M. & Burke, J., eds. Drug Safety: Proceeding of the Fourth International Congress of Pharmaceutical Physicians by the Association des Medecins de l'Industrie Pharmaceutique (AMPI) under the Auspices of the International Federation of the Association of the Pharmaceutical Physicians (IFAPP) in Paris, April 1981. 320p. 1982. 60.50 (ISBN 0-08-027073-5); pap. 36.00 (ISBN 0-08-027074-3). Pergamon.

Aurobindo, Sri. The Essential Aurobindo. McDermott, Robert, ed. LC 73-81341. 256p. 1973. 10.50x o.p. (ISBN 0-8052-3515-9); pap. 5.50 (ISBN 0-8052-0398-2). Schocken.

--Future Evolution of Man: The Divine Life upon Earth. 2nd ed. 1971. 7.50x (ISBN 0-391-00496-4). Humanities.

--The Mother. 62p. 1980. 1.00 (ISBN 0-89744-148-6, Pub. by Sri Aurobindo Ashram Trust India); pap. 0.75 miniature size (ISBN 0-686-96666-X). Auromere.

--Sri Aurobindo on the Tantra. Pandit, Sri M. P., compiled by. 47p. (Orig.). 1979. pap. 2.00 (ISBN 0-941524-17-5). Lotus Light.

Aurthur, Jonathan. Socialism in the Soviet Union. LC 77-5727. 1977. 5.95 (ISBN 0-917348-15-X); pap. 5.95 (ISBN 0-917348-14-1). Workers Pr.

Ausband, John R., ed. Ear, Nose and Throat Disorders: Essentials of Primary Care. 2nd ed. 1982. spiral bdg. 12.00 (ISBN 0-87488-705-4); pap. 23.50. Med Exam.

Ausberger, Carlyn & Green, Mary J. Here's How to Handle "S". 1979. 50.00 (ISBN 0-88450-708-4, 3057-B). Communications Skill.

Ausberger, Carolyn. Syntax One: Syntactic Skills Development. 112p. 1982. 3-ring binder 75.00 (ISBN 0-88450-675-4, 3018-B). Communication Skill.

--Syntax Two: Interaction with 'WH' Questions. 208p. 1980. 3-ring binder 75.00 (ISBN 0-88450-717-3, 4000-B). Communication Skill.

Ausberger, Carolyn & Green, Mary J. Here's How to Handle "R". 1975. 50.00 (ISBN 0-88450-707-6, 2023-B). Communication Skill.

Ausberger, Carolyn & Martin, Margaret J. Learning to Talk is Child's Play. 120p. 1982. pap. text ed. 11.95 (ISBN 0-88450-826-9, 3000-B). Communication Skill.

Ausberger, Carolyn & Martin, Margaret. Speaking from Experiences: A Language Interaction Kit. 1982. 49.95 (ISBN 0-88450-817-X, 2525-B). Communication Skill.

Ausberger, Carolyn & Mullica, Karyn. Group Games Galore: Wkbk. (Worksheets Unlimited Ser.). 120p. (gr. k-7). wkbk. 27.00 (ISBN 0-686-84661-3). Communication Skill.

--My Own Notebook: Wkbk. (Worksheets Unlimited Ser.). 120p. (gr. k-8). 1982. wkbk. 27.00 (ISBN 0-88450-840-4). Communication Skill.

Ausberger, Carolyn, jt. auth. see Martin, Margaret J.

Ausbund. Das ist: Etliche schone Christliche Lieder, wie sie in dem Gefangnis zu Passau in dem Schloss von den Schweitzer-Brudern und von anderen rechtglaubigen Christen hin und her gedichtet worden. facsimile ed. (Mennonite Songbks., American Ser.: Vol. 1). x, 818p. 1971. Repr. of 1742 ed. 62.50 o.s.i. (ISBN 90-6027-244-7, Pub. by Frits Knuf Netherlands). Pendragon NY.

--Etliche schone christliche Gesang, wie dieselbigen zu Passau von der Schweizer Brudern in der Gefenknus im Schloss durch gottliche Gnade gedicht und gesungen worden. facsimile ed. (Mennonite Songbks., German Ser.: Vol. 1). 1973. Repr. of 1564 ed. 25.00 o.s.i. (ISBN 90-6027-160-2, Pub. by Frits Knuf Netherlands). Pendragon NY.

Ausland, John C. Norway, Oil & Foreign Policy. (Westview Special Study). 1979. lib. bdg. 20.00 o.p. (ISBN 0-89158-357-2). Westview.

Auslander, et al. Introducing Systems & Control. (Illus.). 400p. 1974. text ed. 39.50 (ISBN 0-07-002491-X, C). McGraw.

Auslander, Louis & Mackenzie, Robert E. Introduction to Differentiable Manifolds. 1977. pap. 4.50 (ISBN 0-486-63455-8). Dover.

Auslander, M. & Lluis, E., eds. Representations of Algebras, Workshopnotes, Puebla, Mexico 1980. (Lecture Notes in Mathematics: Vol. 944). 258p. 1982. pap. 14.00 (ISBN 0-387-11577-3). Springer-Verlag.

Ausloos, P. Fundamental Processes in Radiation Chemistry. LC 68-21488. 753p. 1968. text ed. 36.50 (ISBN 0-470-03834-9, Pub. by Wiley). Krieger.

Ausmus, Harry J. The Polite Escape: On the Myth of Secularization. LC 81-16924. xii, 189p. 1982. lib. bdg. 20.95x (ISBN 0-8214-0650-7, 82-84192). Ohio U Pr.

Austen, D. E. & Rhymes, I. L. A Laboratory Manual of Blood Coagulation. (Illus.). 160p. 1976. 19.95 (ISBN 0-632-00781-8, B 0376-5, Blackwell). Mosby.

Austen, Jane. The Complete Novels of Jane Austen. 10.95 (ISBN 0-394-60436-9). Modern Lib.

--Emma. (Bantam Classics Ser.). 446p. (gr. 9-12). 1981. pap. 1.75 (ISBN 0-553-21019-X). Bantam.

--Emma. (Illus.). 1976. pap. 2.75x (ISBN 0-460-01024-7, Evman). Biblio Dist.

--Emma. lib. bdg. 16.95 (ISBN 0-89966-242-0). Buccaneer Bks.

--Emma. Trilling, Lionel, ed. 1957. pap. 5.25 (ISBN 0-395-05115-0, RivEd). HM.

--Emma. Parrish, Stephen, ed. (Norton Critical Editions). 430p. 1972. pap. 6.95x (ISBN 0-393-09667-X). Norton.

--Letters: Seventeen Ninety-Six to Eighteen-Seventeen. Chapman, R. W., ed. 9.95 (ISBN 0-19-250549-1). Oxford U Pr.

--Mansfield Park. lib. bdg. 17.95 (ISBN 0-89966-244-7). Buccaneer Bks.

--Mansfield Park. 1964. pap. 3.50 (ISBN 0-451-51752-0, CE1752, Sig Classics). NAL.

--Northanger Abbey. pap. 2.50 (ISBN 0-451-51748-2, CE1748, Sig Classics). NAL.

--Northanger Abbey & Persuasion. 1974. Repr. of 1906 ed. 9.95x (ISBN 0-460-00025-X, Evman). Biblio Dist.

--The Oxford Illustrated Jane Austen, 6 vols. 3rd ed. Chapman, R. W., ed. Incl. Sense & Sensibility. 1933. Vol. 1. 16.95x (ISBN 0-19-254701-1); Pride & Prejudice. 1932. Vol. 2. 16.95x (ISBN 0-19-254702-X); Mansfield Park. 1934. Vol. 3. 18.50x (ISBN 0-19-254703-8); Emma. 1933. Vol. 4. 17.95x (ISBN 0-19-254704-6); Northanger Abbey & Persuasion. 1933. Vol. 5. 17.95x (ISBN 0-19-254705-4); Minor Works. (1st ed.). 1954. Vol. 6. 16.95x (ISBN 0-19-254706-2). 16.95 (ISBN 0-686-86549-9). Oxford U Pr.

--Persuasion. pap. 2.95 (ISBN 0-451-51715-6, CE1715, Sig Classics). NAL.

--Pride & Prejudice. (Bantam Classics Ser.). 304p. (gr. 9-12). 1981. pap. 1.50 (ISBN 0-553-21018-1). Bantam.

--Pride & Prejudice. lib. bdg. 16.95x (ISBN 0-89966-243-9). Buccaneer Bks.

--Pride & Prejudice. 1959. pap. 2.25 o.p. (ISBN 0-440-37106-6, LFL). Dell.

--Pride & Prejudice. Schorer, Mark, ed. LC 56-13877. (YA) (gr. 9 up). 1956. pap. 4.75 (ISBN 0-395-05101-0, B1, RivEd, 3-47635). HM.

--Pride & Prejudice. 1962. pap. 1.50 (ISBN 0-451-51662-1, CW1662, Sig Classics). NAL.

--Sanditon. 1976. pap. 1.95 o.p. (ISBN 0-451-06945-5, J6945, Sig). NAL.

--Sense & Sensibility. Tanner, Tony, ed. (English Library Ser.). 1969. pap. 2.95 (ISBN 0-14-043047-4). Penguin.

--Sense & Sensibility. (Bantam Classics Ser.). 352p. (YA) (gr. 9-12). 1983. pap. 2.50 (ISBN 0-553-21110-2). Bantam.

--Sense & Sensibility with Lady Susan & the Watsons. (Macdonald Classics Ser.). 528p. 1974. 12.95x o.p. (ISBN 0-8464-0837-6). Beekman Pubs.

--The Works of Jane Austen. (Spring Books Ser. of Classics). 1979. 14.00 o.p. (ISBN 0-600-00603-4). Transatlantic.

Austen, Jane & Coates, John. The Watsons. 1977. pap. 1.95 o.p. (ISBN 0-451-07522-6, J7522, Sig). NAL.

Austen, Jane & Hemmant, Lynette. Pride & Prejudice. 1980. 14.95 (ISBN 0-437-24575-6, Pub. by World's Work). David & Charles.

Austen, Jane see Eyre, A. G.

Austen, Jane see Swan, D. K.

Auster, Paul. The Invention of Solitude. LC 82-16757. (Illus.). 174p. (Orig.). 1982. pap. 6.00 (ISBN 0-915342-37-5). SUN.

Auster, Paul, ed. & tr. see Joubert, Joseph.

Austin, Albert G. Australian Education: 1788-1900. LC 75-36359. (Illus.). 300p. 1976. Repr. of 1972 ed. lib. bdg. 19.75x (ISBN 0-8371-8629-3, AUAE). Greenwood.

Austin, Allan E. Roy Fuller. (English Authors Ser.). 1979. lib. bdg. 14.95 (ISBN 0-8057-6743-6, Twayne). G K Hall.

Austin, C. K. Site Carpentry. (Illus.). 1979. 25.00x (ISBN 0-7198-2730-2); wire bdg. o.p. 17.95x (ISBN 0-686-82927-1). Intl Ideas.

Austin, C. R. & Short, R. V., eds. Artificial Control of Reproduction. LC 70-185569. (Reproduction in Mammals Ser.: Bk. 5). (Illus.). 1973. 27.50 (ISBN 0-521-08505-5); pap. 7.95x (ISBN 0-521-09713-4). Cambridge U Pr.

--Embryonic & Fetal Development. (Reproduction in Mammals Ser.: Bk. 2). (Illus.). 1972. 27.95 (ISBN 0-521-08373-7); pap. 7.95x (ISBN 0-521-09682-0). Cambridge U Pr.

--Embryonic & Fetal Development. 2nd ed. LC 81-18060. (Reproduction in Mammals Ser.: Bk. 2). (Illus.). 200p. 1983. 29.95 (ISBN 0-521-24786-1); pap. 12.95 (ISBN 0-521-28962-9). Cambridge U Pr.

--The Evolution of Reproduction. LC 76-8170. (Reproduction in Mammals Ser.: Bk. 6). (Illus.). 1975. 27.95 (ISBN 0-521-21286-3); pap. 7.95x (ISBN 0-521-29085-6). Cambridge U Pr.

--Germ Cells & Fertilization. 2nd ed. LC 81-18060. (Reproduction in Mammals Ser.: No. 1). (Illus.). 180p. 1982. 24.50 (ISBN 0-521-24628-8); pap. 11.95 (ISBN 0-521-28861-4). Cambridge U Pr.

--Hormones in Reproduction. LC 73-178279. (Reproduction in Mammals Ser.: Bk. 3). (Illus.). 1972. 27.95 (ISBN 0-521-08438-5); pap. 7.95x (ISBN 0-521-09696-0). Cambridge U Pr.

--Human Sexuality. LC 78-18959. (Reproduction in Mammals Ser.: Bk. 8). (Illus.). 110p. 1980. 27.95 (ISBN 0-521-22361-X); pap. 8.95 (ISBN 0-521-29461-4). Cambridge U Pr.

--Mechanisms of Hormone Action. LC 79-16287. (Reproduction in Mammals Ser.: Bk. 7). (Illus.). 1980. 37.50 (ISBN 0-521-22945-6); pap. 9.95x (ISBN 0-521-29737-0). Cambridge U Pr.

--Reproductive Patterns. LC 78-189597. (Reproduction in Mammals Ser.: Bk. 4). (Illus.). 120p. 1973. 27.95 (ISBN 0-521-08578-0); pap. 7.95x (ISBN 0-521-09616-2). Cambridge U Pr.

Austin, Clifford. I Left My Hat in Andamooka: An Odyssey Through the Australian Outback. 1974. 6.50 o.p. (ISBN 0-85885-024-9). David & Charles.

Austin, Daniel J., jt. auth. see Smith, Brian R.

Austin, David R. Therapeutic Recreation Processes & Techniques. 241p. 1982. text ed. 16.95 (ISBN 0-471-08666-5). Wiley.

Austin, Dennis. Politics in Africa. LC 77-95397. 212p. 1978. text ed. 15.00x (ISBN 0-87451-150-X); pap. text ed. 8.50x (ISBN 0-87451-152-6). U Pr of New Eng.

Austin, Diana J. The Maker. 4.95 (ISBN 0-8062-1995-5). Carlton.

Austin, Ellis H. Drilling Engineering Handbook. (Short Course Handbooks). (Illus.). 288p. 1983. text ed. 29.00 (ISBN 0-934634-46-7); pap. text ed. 22.00 (ISBN 0-934634-54-8). Intl Human Res.

Austin, Evelyn. Secretarial Services. 208p. 1982. pap. text ed. 11.00 (ISBN 0-7121-1984-1). Intl Ideas.

Austin, Glenn, ed. The Parents' Guide to Child Raising. LC 77-28168. (Illus.). 1978. 15.95 (ISBN 0-13-650028-5, Spec); pap. 7.95 o.p. (ISBN 0-13-650010-2, Spec). P-H.

Austin, H. & Kutscher, Lillian G. Religion & Bereavement. 255p. 1972. 12.50 (ISBN 0-930194-78-0). Ctr Thanatology.

Austin, James, jt. ed. see Krisberg, Barry.

Austin, James C. Bill Arp. (United States Authors Ser.). 12.95 (ISBN 0-8057-0024-2, Twayne). G K Hall.

Austin, James E. & Hitt, Christopher. Nutrition Intervention in the United States: Cases & Concepts. LC 79-14494. 416p. 1979. prof ref 32.50x (ISBN 0-88410-370-6). Ballinger Pub.

Austin, James E., ed. Global Malnutrition & Cereal Fortification. LC 78-21224. 336p. 1979. prof ref 35.00x (ISBN 0-88410-366-8). Ballinger Pub.

Austin, James T. The Life of Elbridge Gerry, 2 Vols. LC 77-99470. (American Public Figures Ser). 1970. Repr. of 1828 ed. Set. lib. bdg. 89.50 (ISBN 0-306-71841-3). Da Capo.

Austin, John L. Sense & Sensibilia. Warnock, Geoffrey J., ed. 1962. pap. 5.95x (ISBN 0-19-500307-1). Oxford U Pr.

Austin, Karen O., tr. see Galdos, Benito P.

Austin, Karl L., tr. see Dexeus, Santiago, Jr., et al.

Austin, Lou. A Lou Austin Anthology. 1983. write for info. Partnership Foundation.

Austin, M. M. & Vidal-Naquet, P. Economic & Social History of Ancient Greece. 1978. 39.75x (ISBN 0-520-02658-6); pap. 8.95 (ISBN 0-520-04267-0). U of Cal Pr.

Austin, Margaret F. & Vines, Harriet M. Bridges to Success: Finding Jobs & Changing Careers. (Illus.). 300p. 1983. 15.95 (ISBN 0-471-87062-5); pap. text ed. 10.95 (ISBN 0-471-86577-X). Wiley.

Austin, Marilyn. A Dream for Tomorrow. (YA) 1980. 6.95 (ISBN 0-686-73927-2, Avalon). Bouregy.

--Karen Connors, Family Therapist. (YA) 1978. 6.95 (ISBN 0-685-19059-5, Avalon). Bouregy.

Austin, Mary. The Land of Journeys' Ending. 500p. 1983. 24.50x (ISBN 0-8165-0807-0); pap. 14.50 (ISBN 0-8165-0808-9). U of Ariz Pr.

Austin, Mary & Jenkins, Esther. Promoting World Understanding Through Literature, K-8. 300p. 1983. lib. bdg. 22.50 (ISBN 0-87287-356-0). Libs Unl.

Austin, Mary S. Philip Freneau, the Poet of the Revolution. Vreeland, Helen K., ed. LC 67-23885. 1968. Repr. of 1901 ed. 30.00x (ISBN 0-8103-3040-7). Gale.

Austin, Michael J. Management Simulations for Mental Health & Human Services Administration. LC 78-12172. 432p. (Orig.). 1978. pap. 16.95 wkbk. (ISBN 0-917724-07-0, B7). Haworth Pr.

--Supervisory Management for the Human Services. (P-H Ser. in Social Work Practices). 352p. 1981. text ed. 21.95 (ISBN 0-13-877068-9). P-H.

Austin, Michael J. & Cox, Gary. Evaluating Your Agency's Programs. (Sage Human Services Guides: Vol. 29). 176p. 1982. pap. 8.50 (ISBN 0-8039-0989-6). Sage.

Austin, Michael J., jt. auth. see Giddan, Norman S.

Austin, Michael J. & Hershey, William E., eds. Handbook on Mental Health Administration. (Social & Behavioral Science Ser.). 1982. text ed. 29.95x (ISBN 0-87589-544-1). Jossey Bass.

Austin, Michael J., et al. Delivering Human Services: An Introductory Programmed Text. new ed. (Ser. in Social Work). 1977. pap. text ed. 16.50 scp o.p. (ISBN 0-06-040396-9, HarpC). Har-Row.

Austin, Nancy, jt. auth. see Phelps, Stanlee.

Austin, Norman. Archery at the Dark of the Moon: Poetic Problems in Homer's Odyssey. LC 73-94442. 300p. 1975. 29.95x (ISBN 0-520-02713-2). U of Cal Pr.

--Archery at the Dark of the Moon: Poetic Problems in Homer's Odyssey. 311p. 1982. 29.75x (ISBN 0-520-02713-2); pap. 9.95x. U of Cal Pr.

Austin, O. L., ed. Antarctic Bird Studies. LC 68-61438. (Antarctic Research Ser.: Vol. 12). 1968. 21.00 (ISBN 0-87590-112-3). Am Geophysical.

Austin, Phylis A. & Thrash, Agatha M. Natural Remedies: A Manual. 283p. (Orig.). 1983. pap. price not set (ISBN 0-942658-05-1). Yuchi Pines.

Austin, R. G. Creatures of the Dark. (Which Way Bks.: No. 9). (Illus., Orig.). (gr. 3-6). 1982. pap. 1.95 (ISBN 0-686-91918-1). Archway.

--Creatures of the Deck. (Which Way Book Ser.: No. 9). (gr. 6). 1982. pap. 1.95 (ISBN 0-671-46021-8). Archway.

--Vampires, Spies & Alien Beings. (Which Way Bks.: No. 2). (Illus.). (gr. 3-6). 1982. pap. 1.75 (ISBN 0-686-85654-6). Archway.

Austin, R. W. Sufis of Andalusia: The Ruh Al-Quds & Al-Durrat Al-Fakhirah of Ibn 'arabi. Austin, R. W., tr. LC 77-165230. (California Library Reprint Ser.: Vol. 91). 1978. Repr. of 1971 ed. 24.50x (ISBN 0-520-03553-4). U of Cal Pr.

Austin, Reid, jt. auth. see Vargas, Alberto.

Austing, John F. & Austing, June. Semantics of Omie Discourse. (Language Data-Asia Pacific Ser.: No. 11). 72p. (Orig.). 1977. pap. text ed. 3.50x (ISBN 0-88312-211-1); microfiche 1.50x (ISBN 0-88312-311-8). Summer Inst Ling.

Austing, June, jt. auth. see Austing, John F.

Austin-Lett, Genelle & Sprague, Janet. Talk to Yourself: Experiencing Intrapersonal Communication. LC 75-31037. (Illus.). 160p. 1976. pap. text ed. 9.50 o.p. (ISBN 0-395-18576-9). HM.

Australia Bureau of Statistics. Yearbook Australia 1981. 65th ed. LC 9-6317. (Illus.). 843p. (Orig.). 1981. pap. 30.00x (ISBN 0-8002-3012-4). Intl Pubns Serv.

--Yearbook Australia, 1982. 66th ed. LC 9-6317. (Illus.). 843p. (Orig.). 1982. pap. 35.00x (ISBN 0-8002-3026-4). Intl Pubns Serv.

Australian Academy of Science, ed. see Commonwealth Scientific & Industrial Research Institute (CSIRO).

Australian Information Service. Australia Handbook, 1981-1982. 20th ed. LC 70-7283. (Illus.). 160p. (Orig.). 1981. pap. 10.00x o.p. (ISBN 0-642-06526-8). Intl Pubns Serv.

Australian Society. Animal Production: Proceedings of the Australian Society of Animal Production 13th Biennial Conference, Perth, August 1980. (Illus.). 544p. 1980. 72.00 (ISBN 0-08-024812-8). Pergamon.

Australian Society of Animal Production 14th Biennial Conference, Brisbane, Queensland, May 1982. Animal Production in Australia: Proceeding. (Illus.). 708p. 1982. 59.50 (ISBN 0-686-81910-1). Pergamon.

Austrin, Miriam G. Young's Learning Medical Terminology Step by Step: Textbook & Workbook. (Illus.). 416p. 1983. pap. 18.95 (ISBN 0-8016-5662-1). Mosby.

Ausubel, David P., et al. Theory & Problems of Adolescent Development. 2nd ed. 576p. 1977. 29.50 (ISBN 0-8089-1031-0). Grune.

Ausubel, Nathan, ed. Treasury of Jewish Humor. LC 51-10639. 1951. 17.95 (ISBN 0-385-04499-2). Doubleday.

Auth, Susan H. Ancient Glass at the Newark Museum. LC 76-47222. 1977. 15.95 (ISBN 0-932828-02-7); pap. 9.95 (ISBN 0-932828-08-6). Newark Mus.

Author Aid-Research Associates International. Freelancers of North America: Editors, Ghost-Writers-Collaborators, Copywriters, Speechwriters, Business-Technical-Medical Writers 1983-84. 350p. Date not set. pap. price not set (ISBN 0-911085-01-7). Author Aid.

Author Aid-Research Associates International, ed. Literary Agents of North America: Marketplace 1983-84. 128p. (Orig.). 1983. pap. 14.95 (ISBN 0-911085-00-9, 0082-1). Author Aid.

Author's Guild Inc. Creation & Annihilation Operators. 1977. text ed. 35.50x (ISBN 0-07-002504-5, C). McGraw.

Autocar Editors, ed. see Garnier.

Automation Technology Symposium. Automation Technology for Management & Productivity Advancements through CAD-CAM & Engineering Data Handling. Wang, Peter, ed. (Illus.). 336p. 1983. text ed. 24.95 (ISBN 0-13-054593-7). P-H.

Automobile Association. AA Guesthouses, Farmhouses & Inns in Europe. (Illus.). 256p. 1982. pap. 9.75 o.p. (ISBN 0-86145-046-9, Pub. by Auto Assn-British Tourist Authority England). Merrimack Bk Serv.

--AA Motoring in Europe. rev. ed. (Illus.). 416p. 1981. pap. 9.95 o.p. (ISBN 0-686-31830-7, Pub. by Auto Assn-British Tourist Authority England). Merrimack Bk Serv.

Automobile Association & British Tourist Authority. AA Camping & Caravanning in Britain. (Illus.). 256p. 1982. pap. 8.95 o.p. (ISBN 0-86145-083-3, Pub. by Auto Assn-British Tourist Authority England). Merrimack Bk Serv.

--AA Camping & Caravanning in Europe. (Illus.). 432p. 1982. pap. 9.95 o.p. (ISBN 0-86145-047-7, Pub. by Auto Assn-British Tourist Authority England). Merrimack Bk Serv.

--AA Eat Out for Around Five Pounds. (Illus.). 288p. 1982. pap. 6.95 o.p. (ISBN 0-86145-090-6, Pub. by Auto Assn-British Tourist Authority England). Merrimack Bk Serv.

--AA Guesthouses, Farmhouses & Inns in Britain. (Illus.). 296p. 1982. pap. 8.95 o.p. (ISBN 0-86145-085-X, Pub. by Auto Assn-British Tourist Authority England). Merrimack Bk Serv.

--AA Hotels & Restaurants in Britain. (Illus.). 624p. 1982. pap. 12.95 o.p. (ISBN 0-86145-082-5, Pub. by Auto Assn-British Tourist Authority England). Merrimack Bk Serv.

--AA Self Catering in Britain. 256p. 1982. pap. 6.95 o.p. (ISBN 0-86145-084-1, Pub. by Auto Assn-British Tourist Authority England). Merrimack Bk Serv.

--AA Stately Homes, Museums, Castles & Gardens in Great Britain. (Illus.). 272p. 1982. pap. 8.95 o.p. (ISBN 0-86145-086-8, Pub. by Auto Assn-British Tourist Authority England). Merrimack Bk Serv.

Automobile Association (Britain) Hotels & Restaurants in Britain 1981. LC 52-21171. 600p. 1981. 10.00 o.p. (ISBN 0-7095-0579-5). Intl Pubns Serv.

Automobile Association - British Tourist Authority. AA Wildlife in Great Britain. (Illus.). 1979. 9.95 o.p. (ISBN 0-09-126390-5, Pub. by B T a). Merrimack Bk Serv.

--Walks & Trails in Scotland. 1979. pap. 2.50 o.p. (ISBN 0-7095-0121-8, Pub. by B T a). Merrimack Bk Serv.

Automobile Association of England Staff. Discovering Britain. 1983. 24.95 (ISBN 0-393-01741-9). Norton.

Automobile Club of Italy. World Cars, 1972. Orig. Title: World Car Catalogue. (Illus.). 440p. 1972. 45.00 (ISBN 0-910714-04-5). Herald Bks.

Automobile Club of Italy, ed. World Car Catalogue, 1971. (Illus.). 1971. 32.00 (ISBN 0-910714-03-7). Herald Bks.

--World Cars 1973. LC 73-3055. (Illus.). 440p. 1973. 45.00 (ISBN 0-910714-05-3). Herald Bks.

--World Cars 1974. LC 74-3055. (Illus.). 440p. 1974. 45.00 (ISBN 0-910714-06-1). Herald Bks.

--World Cars, 1975. annual LC 74-643381. (Illus.). 440p. 1975. 48.50 (ISBN 0-910714-07-X). Herald Bks.

--World Cars 1978. LC 74-643381. (Illus.). 1978. 37.50 (ISBN 0-910714-10-X). Herald Bks.

--World Cars 1979. LC 7-643381. (Illus.). 1979. 37.50 (ISBN 0-910714-11-8). Herald Bks.

--World Cars 1980. LC 74-643381. (Illus.). 1980. 37.50 (ISBN 0-910714-12-6). Herald Bks.

Automotive Invoice Service Editors. Car Cost Guide, 1983. Rev. ed. 250p. 1982. looseleaf binder 60.00 (ISBN 0-88098-013-3, Pub. by Chek-Chart). Har-Row.

Auton, Graeme P., jt. auth. see Hanrieder, Wolfram.

Autor, Anne, ed. Pathology of Oxygen. 360p. 1982. 59.50 (ISBN 0-12-068620-1). Acad Pr.

Autore, Donald D., jt. auth. see Beakley, George C.

Autry, Gene & Herskowitz, Mickey. Back in the Saddle Again. LC 76-18332. (Illus.). 1978. 9.95 o.p. (ISBN 0-385-03234-X). Doubleday.

Autry, Gloria D. & Allen, T. D. The Color Coded Allergy Cookbook. new ed. 400p. 1983. 16.95 (ISBN 0-672-52746-4). Bobbs.

Autry, William O., Jr. An Archaeological, Architectural, & Historic Cultural Resources Reconnaissance of the Northeast Metropolitan Nashville Transportation Corridor. (Illus.). vii, 120p. (Orig.). 1982. pap. 12.00 (ISBN 0-940148-04-8). TARA.

Autry, William O., Jr., et al. Archaeological Investigations at the Tennessee Valley Authority Hartsville Nuclear Plants Off-Site Borrow Areas: The Taylor Tract. (T.A.R.A. Report Ser.: No. 2). (Illus.). 125p. (Orig.). 1983. pap. price not set (ISBN 0-940148-03-X). TARA.

Autumn, Violeta. A Russian Jew Cooks in Peru. LC 73-81086. (Illus.). 192p. 1973. 7.95 o.s.i. (ISBN 0-912238-42-9); pap. 4.95 o.s.i. (ISBN 0-912238-41-0). One Hund One Prods.

Auty, R. & Obolensky, D., eds. Companion to Russian Studies: An Introduction to Russian Art & Architecture, Vol. 3. LC 75-10691. (Illus.). 1980. 37.50 (ISBN 0-521-20895-5). Cambridge U Pr.

--Companion to Russian Studies: An Introduction to Russian History. LC 75-10688. 403p. 1981. pap. 17.95 (ISBN 0-521-28038-9). Cambridge U Pr.

--Companion to Russian Studies: An Introduction to Russian History, Vol. 1. LC 75-10688. 1976. 49.50 (ISBN 0-521-20893-9). Cambridge U Pr.

--Companion to Russian Studies: An Introduction to Russian Language & Literature. LC 75-10688. 300p. 1981. pap. 16.95x (ISBN 0-521-28039-7). Cambridge U Pr.

--Companion to Russian Studies: An Introduction to Russian Language & Literature, Vol. 2. LC 75-10691. (Illus.). 1977. 37.50 (ISBN 0-521-20894-7). Cambridge U Pr.

Auty, Robert. Handbook of Old Church Slavonic, Text & Glossary. (London East European Ser.). 1977. pap. text ed. 23.25x (ISBN 0-485-17518-5, Athlone Pr). Humanities.

Auvenshine, Charles D. & Noffsinger, Anne-Russell L. Counseling: Issues & Procedures in the Human Services. (Illus.). 1983. pap. text ed. price not set (ISBN 0-8391-1793-0, 14230). Univ Park.

Auvil, D. L. Calculus with Applications. LC 81-14914. 1982. text ed. 24.95 (ISBN 0-201-10063-0); write for info. student supplement (ISBN 0-201-10064-9). A-W.

Auvil, Daniel L. Intermediate Algebra. LC 78-18643. (Illus.). 1979. text ed. 19.95 (ISBN 0-201-00135-7); student supplement 3.95 (ISBN 0-201-00136-5). A-W.

Auvil, Daniel L. & Poluga, Charles. Elementary Algebra. LC 77-76194. (Illus.). 1978. text ed. 19.95 (ISBN 0-201-00137-3); student supplement 3.95 (ISBN 0-201-00138-1). A-W.

Auvil, Kenneth W. Serigraphy: Silk Screen Techniques for the Artist. (Illus., Orig.). 1965. 12.95 (ISBN 0-13-807164-0). P-H.

Auvinen, Jewell S. Ringer the Kitten Learns to Read. (Illus.). 22p. (ps-3). 1982. pap. 2.95 (ISBN 0-9610158-0-2). J S Auvinen.

Auvray, Louis, jt. auth. see De La Chavignerie, Emile B.

Auxier, John A. Ichiban: Radiation Dosimetry for the Survivors of the Bombings of Hiroshima & Nagasaki. LC 76-30780. (ERDA Critical Review Ser.). 128p. 1977. pap. 11.25 (TID-27080); microfiche 4.50 (ISBN 0-87079-244-X, TID-27080). DOE.

Avakian, Arra, ed. see Shoehmelian, O.

Avakian, Arra S. The Armenians in America. LC 77-73739. (In America Bks). (Illus.). (gr. 5 up). 1977. PLB 6.95g (ISBN 0-8225-0228-3). Lerner Pubns.

Avakian, Bob. For Decades to Come: On a World Scale. 130p. (Orig.). pap. 5.95 o.p. (ISBN 0-89851-054-6). RCP Pubns.

--Leadership. Incl. If There is to be Revolution, There Must be a Revolutionary Party. 74p. 1982. 2.00 (ISBN 0-686-82470-9); Anarchism. Avakian, Bob. 1982. 1.00 (ISBN 0-686-82471-7); Bob Avakian Speaks on the Mao Defendants' Railroad & the Historic Battles Ahead. 69p. 1981. 1.50 (ISBN 0-686-82472-5); Summing Up the Black Panther Party. 1980. 0.60 (ISBN 0-686-82473-3); Communists are Rebels. 1980. 0.50 (ISBN 0-686-82474-1); Important Struggles in Building the RCP. 55p. 1978. 1.00 (ISBN 0-686-82475-X); New Constitution of the RCP, U. S. A. 1981. 0.75 (ISBN 0-686-82476-8). 5.00 (ISBN 0-686-82469-5). RCP Pubns.

Avalos, B. & Haddad, W. Resena de la Investigacion sobre Efectividad de los Maestros en Africa, America Latina, Filipinas, India, Malasia, Medio Oriente y Tailandia: Sintesis de Resultados. 118p. 1981. pap. 10.00 o.p. (ISBN 0-88936-259-9, IDRC-TS23S, IDRC). Unipub.

Avanesov, R. I. Modern Russian Stress. (Pergamon Oxford Russian Ser.). 1965. pap. 4.40 o.p. (ISBN 0-08-010300-6). Pergamon.

Avant-Garde Creations. The Creativity Life Dynamic Book. (Illus.). 84p. 1980. pap. 9.95 (ISBN 0-930182-07-3); pkg. including book, 2 drawing cards & program disk 24.95 (ISBN 0-930182-08-1). Avant Garde CR.

Avant, Gayle. American Government. (College Outlines Ser). pap. 4.95 o.p. (ISBN 0-671-08051-2). Monarch Pr.

Avary, Myrta L. Dixie After the War: An Exposition of Social Conditions Existing in the South, During the 12 Years Succeeding the Fall of Richmond. LC 79-77701. (American Scene Ser). (Illus.). 1970. Repr. of 1937 ed. 49.50 (ISBN 0-306-71339-X). Da Capo.

Avary, Myrta L., ed. Recollections of Alexander H. Stephens: His Diary Kept When a Prisoner at Fort Warren, Boston Harbor, 1865. LC 76-124914. (American Public Figures Ser). 1971. Repr. of 1910 ed. lib. bdg. 69.50 (ISBN 0-306-71984-3). Da Capo.

Avedon, Burt. Ah, Men! LC 78-74675. 1980. 10.95 o.s.i. (ISBN 0-89479-048-X). A & W Pubs.

Avedon, Elliott M. Socio-Recreative Programming for the Retarded: A Handbook for Sponsoring Groups. LC 64-15576. (Orig.). 1964. pap. 7.50x (ISBN 0-8077-1041-5). Tchrs Coll.

--Therapeutic Recreation Service: An Applied Behavioral Science Approach. 256p. 1974. ref. ed. 20.95 (ISBN 0-13-914879-5). P-H.

Avedon, Elliott M. & Sutton-Smith, Brian. The Study of Games. LC 79-21194. 544p. 1979. Repr. of 1971 ed. lib. bdg. 27.50 (ISBN 0-89874-045-2). Krieger.

Avedon, Richard. Portraits. 142p. 1976. 25.00 (ISBN 0-374-23638-0); pap. 15.00 (ISBN 0-374-51412-7). FS&G.

Ave-Lallemant, E., jt. auth. see Spiegelberg, H.

Aveling, Eleanor M., tr. see Lissagaray, P. O.

Aveling, Harry. Contemporary Indonesian Poetry. (Asian & Pacific Writing Ser.). 1975. 14.95x o.p. (ISBN 0-7022-0931-7); pap. 8.50x o.s.i o.p. (ISBN 0-7022-0932-5). U of Queensland Pr.

Aveling, Harry, ed. The Development of Indonesian Society. LC 79-11452. 1979. 30.00 (ISBN 0-312-19661-X). St Martin.

Aveling, Harry, tr. see Toer, Pramoedya A.

Avellani, Pamela B., jt. auth. see Vandergoot, David.

Avellani, Pamela B., jt. auth. see Jacobsen, Richard J.

Aven, Del. God Has Special Places. (Illus.). (gr. k-3). 1979. 4.95 (ISBN 0-8054-4253-7). Broadman.

Avenhaus, R., jt. ed. see Argentesi, F.

Avenhaus, Rudolf. Material Accountability: Theory, Verification & Applications. LC 77-9356. (Wiley International Series on Applied Systems Analysis). 187p. 1977. 34.95x (ISBN 0-471-99528-2, Pub. by Wiley-Interscience). Wiley.

Aveni, A. F., ed. Archaeoastronomy in the New World: American Primitive Astronomy. LC 82-1344. 230p. 1982. 29.95 (ISBN 0-521-24731-4). Cambridge U Pr.

Aveni, Anthony F. Skywatchers of Ancient Mexico. (Texas Pan American Ser.). (Illus.). 369p. 1980. text ed. 30.00x (ISBN 0-292-77557-1); pap. 6.95 cancelled (ISBN 0-686-96908-1). U of Tex Pr.

Avenoso, jt. auth. see Cheifetz.

Avenoso, Frank, ed. see DeSanto, et al.

Avens, Roberts. Imaginal Body: Para-Jungian Reflections on Soul, Imagination & Death. LC 81-43814. 264p. (Orig.). 1982. lib. bdg. 23.00 (ISBN 0-8191-2411-7); pap. text ed. 11.50 (ISBN 0-8191-2412-5). U Pr of Amer.

--Imagination Is Reality. rev. ed. Severson, R. & Bedford, G., eds. 127p. 1980. pap. 7.50 (ISBN 0-88214-311-5). Spring Pubns.

Avento, Genarro P. The Church's Moral Teaching, Bk. III. pap. 3.95 (ISBN 0-941850-08-0). Sunday Pubn.

Averbakh, Y. & Checkover, V. Comprehensive Chess Endings: Bishop Endings & Knight Endings, Vol. 1. Neat, K. P., tr. from Rus. (Russian Chess Ser.). 232p. 1983. 24.95 (ISBN 0-08-026900-1). Pergamon.

Averchenko, Arkadii. Tri Knigi: Nechistaia Sila, Panteon Sovetov Molodym Liudiam, Deti. LC 79-65800. (Rus.). pap. 6.95 o.p. (ISBN 0-89830-009-6). Russica Pubs.

Averett, Tanner F. Basic Drama Projects. 4th ed. (Illus.). 286p. 1982. pap. text ed. 7.50 (ISBN 0-931054-06-0). Clark Pub.

--Creative Communication. rev. ed. (Illus.). 379p. 1979. pap. text ed. 8.95 (ISBN 0-931054-09-5). Clark Pub.

Averill, Deborah M. The Irish Short Story from George Moore to Frank O'Connor. LC 81-40188. 338p. (Orig.). 1982. lib. bdg. 24.25 (ISBN 0-8191-2133-9); pap. text ed. 12.75 (ISBN 0-8191-2134-7). U Pr of Amer.

Averill, Esther. Captains of the City Streets: A Story of the Cat Club. LC 72-76500. (Illus.). 128p. (gr. k-3). 1972. 5.95 o.p. (ISBN 0-06-020176-2, HarpJ); PLB 8.89 (ISBN 0-06-020177-0). Har-Row.

--Cartier Sails the St. Lawrence. LC 56-5159. (Illus.). (gr. 4 up). 1956. PLB 12.89 (ISBN 0-06-020161-4, HarpJ). Har-Row.

--Jenny & the Cat Club: A Collection of Favorite Stories About Jenny Linsky. LC 72-9862. (Illus.). 168p. (ps-3). 1973. PLB 8.89 o.p. (ISBN 0-06-020223-8, HarpJ). Har-Row.

--Jenny Goes to Sea. LC 57-9261. 128p. (gr. k-3). 1957. PLB 8.89 o.p. (ISBN 0-06-020220-3, HarpJ). Har-Row.

--Jenny's Birthday Book. LC 54-6589. (Illus.). (gr. k-3). 1954. PLB 10.89 (ISBN 0-06-020251-3, HarpJ). Har-Row.

--Jenny's Moonlight Adventure. LC 49-8288. (Illus.). (gr. k-3). 1949. PLB 8.89 o.p. (ISBN 0-06-020266-1, HarpJ). Har-Row.

Averill, James R. Anger & Aggression: An Essay on Emotion. (Springer Series in Social Psychology). (Illus.). 402p. 1983. 29.90 (ISBN 0-387-90719-X). Springer-Verlag.

Averill, Lawrence H. Estate Valuation Handbook. (Tax Library Ser.). 448p. 1983. 65.00 (ISBN 0-471-89859-7). Wiley.

Averintsev, Sergei. Religya i Literatura: Religion & Literatura. 140p. (Rus.). 1981. pap. 7.00 (ISBN 0-938920-02-2). Hermitage MI.

Averroes, Rushd Ibn. Averroes' Middle Commentary on Aristole's de Interpretation. Kassem, Mahmoud M., et al, eds. (Corpus Commentariorum Averroes in Aristotelem Ser.: Vol. 2). 150p. (Orig.). 1981. pap. 13.50x (ISBN 0-936770-05-8, Pub. by Am Res Ctr Egypt). Undena Pubns.

Avers, Charlotte. Cell Biology. 1976. 20.95 (ISBN 0-442-20382-9). Van Nos Reinhold.

--Genetics, Revised Edition. 657p. 1980. text ed. write for info (ISBN 0-87150-759-5). Grant Pr.

Avers, Charlotte G. Genetics. (Illus.). 659p. 1980. text ed. 21.95 (ISBN 0-442-26233-7). Van Nos Reinhold.

Avers, Charlotte J. Cell Biology. 2nd ed. 1981. text ed. write for info. (ISBN 0-442-25770-8). Van Nos Reinhold.

Avery, A. J., jt. auth. see Lovell, M. C.

Avery, C. The New Century Italian Renaissance Encyclopedia. 1972. 42.95 o.p. (ISBN 0-13-612051-2, Spec). P-H.

Avery, Charles. Florentine Renaissance Sculpture. LC 78-148429. (Icon Editions). (Illus.). 282p. 1971. pap. 5.95xi o.p. (ISBN 0-06-430038-2, IN-38, HarpT). Har-Row.

Avery, Clarence G., jt. auth. see Istvan, Donald F.

Avery, David D. & Cross, Henry, Jr. Experimental Methodology in Psychology. LC 77-21641. (Illus.). 1978. text ed. 20.95 (ISBN 0-8185-0245-2). Brooks-Cole.

Avery, David R., jt. auth. see McDonald, Ralph E.

Avery, Emmett L. & Scouten, Arthur H. London Stage, Sixteen Sixty to Seventeen-Hundred: A Critical Introduction, Pt. 1. LC 60-6539. (Arcturus Books Paperbacks Ser.). (Illus.). 203p. 1968. pap. 5.95 o.p. (ISBN 0-8093-0336-1). S Ill U Pr.

Avery, Gillian, ed. & intro. by. Victorian Doll Stories. Incl. Victoria-Bess. Brenda; Aunt Sally's Life. Gatty, Mrs.; Racketty-Packetty House. Burnett, Frances H. LC 69-14797. (Victorian Revival Ser). (Illus.). 140p. (gr. 4 up). 1969. 4.50x o.p. (ISBN 0-8052-3275-3); pap. 2.95 (ISBN 0-8052-0224-2). Schocken.

Avery, Ira. The Miracle of Dommatina. LC 77-28031. 1978. 7.95 o.p. (ISBN 0-399-12006-8). Putnam Pub Group.

Avery, J. H. & Ingram, A. W. Modern Laboratory Physics. 1971. text ed. 22.50x o.p. (ISBN 0-435-68044-7). Heinemann Ed.

Avery, Laurence G., ed. see Anderson, Maxwell.

Avery, Mary E. & Litwack, Georgia. Born Early: The Story of a Premature Baby. (Illus.). 160p. 1983. 15.00i (ISBN 0-686-84515-3). Little.

Avery, Michael. Police Misconduct: Law & Litigation. 2nd ed. LC 80-23165. 1980. looseleaf 60.00 (ISBN 0-87632-112-0). Boardman.

Avery, Michel, et al. Building United Judgement: A Handbook for Consensus Decision Making. 124p. (Orig.). 1981. pap. text ed. 5.00 (ISBN 0-941492-01-X). Ctr Conflict Resol.

Avery, Paul & McLellan, Vin. The Voices of Guns. (Illus.). 388p. 1977. 14.95 o.p. (ISBN 0-399-11738-5). Putnam Pub Group.

Avery, T. E. Natural Resources Measurements. 2nd ed. (The American Forestry Ser). 1975. 32.50 (ISBN 0-07-002502-9, C). McGraw.

Avery, Thomas E. & Burkhart, Harold E. Forest Measurements. 3rd ed. (McGraw-Hill Ser. in Forest Measurements). (Illus.). 384p. 1983. text ed. 29.95x (ISBN 0-07-002503-7, C). McGraw.

Averyt, William F., Jr. Agropolitics in the European Community: Interest Groups & the Common Agricultural Policy. LC 77-10619. 144p. 1977. 24.95 (ISBN 0-03-039666-2). Praeger.

Aves, Diane K. & Anderson, Debra. Planning Your Job Search: Making the Right Moves. 84p. 1982. 9.75 (ISBN 0-88440-036-0). Sis Kenny Inst.

Avesthi, Rajendra. Nature of Politics. 10.00x (ISBN 0-210-22288-3). Asia.

Avett, Elizabeth M. Today's Business Letter Writing. (Illus.). 1977. pap. 12.95 (ISBN 0-13-924027-6). P-H.

Aveyard, R. & Haydon, D. A. An Introduction to the Principles of Surface Chemistry. LC 72-89802. (Illus.). 200p. 1973. 45.00 (ISBN 0-521-20110-1); pap. 19.95x (ISBN 0-521-09794-0). Cambridge U Pr.

Avez, A. & Blaquiere, A. Dynamical Systems & Microphysics: Symposium. 465p. 1982. 34.50 (ISBN 0-12-068720-8). Acad Pr.

Avi. Shadrach's Crossing. LC 82-19008. 192p. (gr. 5 up). 1983. 10.95 (ISBN 0-394-85816-6); PLB 10.99 (ISBN 0-394-95816-0). Pantheon.

Aviad, Janet. Return to Judaism: Religious Renewal in Israel. LC 82-17663. 208p. 1983. lib. bdg. 20.00x (ISBN 0-226-03236-1). U of Chicago Pr.

Aviad, Janet O., jt. auth. see O'Dea, Thomas F.

Aviado, Domingo M. Pharmacologic Principles of Medical Practice. 8th ed. LC 72-84836. 1366p. 1977. Repr. of 1972 ed. 39.50 (ISBN 0-686-86261-9). Krieger.

Aviation Book Company Staff, ed. see Federal Aviation Administration.

Aviation Consumer Staff. The Aviation Consumer Used Aircraft Guide. 1981. 24.75 (ISBN 0-07-002543-6). McGraw.

Avicenne, Paul, ed. Bibliographical Services Throughout the World, Nineteen Sixty Five to Nineteen Sixty-Nine. LC 72-79748. (Documentation, Libraries & Archives Ser.: Bibliographies & Reference Works). 311p. 1973. 12.50 o.p. (ISBN 92-3-100974-5, U45, UNESCO). Unipub.

Aviel, Joanne F. Resource Shortages & World Politics. 162p. 1977. pap. text ed. 9.00 (ISBN 0-8191-0263-6). U Pr of Amer.

Aviel, S. David. The Politics of Nuclear Energy. LC 81-40875. (Illus.). 274p. (Orig.). 1982. lib. bdg. 23.25 (ISBN 0-8191-2201-7); pap. text ed. 11.50 (ISBN 0-8191-2202-5). U Pr of Amer.

Aviel, S. David, jt. auth. see Duncan, Doris G.

Avigad, Nahman. Beth She'Arim, Vol. 3: The Excavations, 1953-58. 312p. 1976. 35.00x o.p. (ISBN 0-8135-0763-4). Rutgers U Pr.

Avi-Itzhak, Benjamin. Developments in Operations Research, 2 vols. LC 78-141897. (Illus.). 642p. 1971. Set. 136.00 (ISBN 0-677-30510-9); Vol. 1,308p. 70.00x (ISBN 0-677-30830-2); Vol 2.,344p. 81.00x (ISBN 0-677-30840-X). Gordon.

Avi-Itzhak, Benjamin, jt. auth. see Vardi, Joseph.

Avila, Kay, et al. Harian Creative Awards - I: Featuring the Gospel According to Everyman by Baron Mikan. Barba, Harry, ed. 220p. 1981. lib. bdg. 8.95 (ISBN 0-911906-09-6); pap. 5.95 (ISBN 0-911906-16-9). Harian Creative.

Avineri, Shlomo. Hegel's Theory of the Modern State. LC 70-186254. (Cambridge Studies in the History & Theory of Politics Ser.). 266p. 1973. 37.50 (ISBN 0-521-08513-6); pap. 10.95 (ISBN 0-521-09832-7). Cambridge U Pr.

--The Making of Modern Zionism: Intellectual Origins of the Jewish State. LC 81-66102. 272p. 1981. 15.50 (ISBN 0-465-04328-3). Basic.

--Social & Political Thought of Karl Marx. LC 68-12055. (Studies in the History & Theory of Politics). 1971. 37.50 (ISBN 0-521-04071-X); pap. 10.95x (ISBN 0-521-09619-7). Cambridge U Pr.

Avins, Carol. Border Crossings: The West & Russian Identity in Soviet Literature, Nineteen Seventeen through Nineteen Thirty-Four. LC 81-19729. 200p. 1983. 22.50x (ISBN 0-520-04233-6). U of Cal Pr.

Avioli, Louis V. The Osteoporatic Syndrome: Detection & Prevention. write for info (ISBN 0-8089-1548-7). Grune.

Avioli, Louis V. & Krane, Stephen M., eds. Metabolic Bone Disease. LC 76-27431. 1977-78. Vol. 1. 52.50 (ISBN 0-12-068701-1); Vol. 2. 68.50 (ISBN 0-12-068702-X). Acad Pr.

Aviram, Uri, jt. auth. see Segal, Steven P.

Avirgan, Tony & Honey, Martha. War in Uganda: The Legacy of Idi Amin. 320p. 1982. 16.95 (ISBN 0-88208-136-5); pap. 9.95 (ISBN 0-88208-137-3). Lawrence Hill.

Avis, Kenneth E. & Akers, Michael J. Sterile Preparation for the Hospital Pharmacist: An Illustrated Manual of Procedures. LC 81-69246. 1982. pap. text ed. 9.95 (ISBN 0-250-40518-0). Ann Arbor Science.

Avis, Paul D. The Church in the Theology of the Reformers. Toon, Peter & Martin, Ralph, eds. LC 80-16186. (New Foundations Theological Library). 256p. 1981. 12.95 (ISBN 0-8042-3708-5); pap. 11.95 (ISBN 0-8042-3728-X). John Knox.

Avis, Peter, jt. auth. see Chester, Joyce.

Avishai, Bernard. The Tragedy of Zionism. 300p. 1982. 14.50 (ISBN 0-374-27863-6). FS&G.

Avital, Samuel. The Mime Workbook. 3rd ed. (Illus.). 158p. 1982. pap. 9.95 (ISBN 0-941524-19-1). Lotus Light.

Avitzur, Betzalel. Handbook of Metal Forming Processes. 1056p. 1983. 77.50 (ISBN 0-471-03474-6, Pub. by Wiley-Interscience). Wiley.

--Metal Forming: Processes & Analysis. LC 78-2767. 522p. 1968. Repr. of 1979 ed. lib. bdg. 29.50 (ISBN 0-88275-673-7). Krieger.

Avi-Yonah, Michael. Ancient Scrolls. LC 72-10792. (The Lerner Archaeology Ser.: Digging up the Past). (Illus.). 96p. (gr. 5 up). 1974. PLB 7.95g (ISBN 0-8225-0827-3). Lerner Pubns.

--The Art of Mosaics. LC 72-10793. (The Lerner Archaeology Ser.: Digging up the Past). (Illus.). 96p. 1975. PLB 7.95g (ISBN 0-8225-0828-1). Lerner Pubns.

Avi-Yonah, Michael & Braun, Werner. Jerusalem the Holy. LC 75-24510. (Illus.). 130p. 1976. 10.00 o.p. (ISBN 0-8052-3604-X). Schocken.

Avi-Yonah, Michael, jt. auth. see Aharoni, Yohanan.

Avi-Yonah, Michael, jt. auth. see Aharoni, Yohanon.

Avi-Yonah, Michael, jt. auth. see Mazar, Benjamin.

Avi-Yonah, Michael see Mazar, Benjamin & Avi-Yonah, Michael.

Avner, Sidney H. Introduction to Physical Metallurgy. 2nd ed. (Illus.). 672p. 1974. text ed. 26.95 (ISBN 0-07-002499-5, G). McGraw.

Avogaro, Pietro, et al, eds. Phospholipids & Atherosclerosis. 1982. text ed. write for info. (ISBN 0-89004-842-8). Raven.

Avon, Dennis & Hawkins, Andrew. Photography: A Complete Guide to Technique. (Illus., Orig.). 1979. 25.00 o.p. (ISBN 0-8174-2527-6, Amphoto); pap. 16.95 (ISBN 0-8174-2191-2). Watson-Guptill.

Avon Products. Looking Good, Feeling Beautiful. 1981. 14.95 o.p. (ISBN 0-671-25224-0). S&S.

Avondo-Bodino, G. Economic Applications of the Theory of Graphs. 126p. 1962. 32.00 (ISBN 0-677-00030-8). Gordon.

Avram, C., et al. Concrete Strength & Strains. (Developments in Civil Engineering Ser.: Vol. 3). 1982. 91.50 (ISBN 0-444-99733-4). Elsevier.

Avram, M. M., ed. Prevention of Kidney Disease & Long-Term Survival. 304p. 1982. 35.00x (ISBN 0-306-40965-8, Plenum Med Bk). Plenum Pub.

Avram, Margareta & Mateescu, Gh. Infrared Spectroscopy: Applications in Organic Chemistry. LC 78-16322. 532p. 1978. Repr. of 1972 ed. lib. bdg. 33.00 (ISBN 0-88275-711-3). Krieger.

Avrett, Roz. My Turn. 1983. 14.50 (ISBN 0-87795-476-3). Arbor Hse.

Avrich, Paul. Bakunin & Nechaev. 32p. 1974. pap. 1.00 (ISBN 0-900384-09-3). Left Bank.

--The Russian Anarchists. 1978. pap. 4.95 o.s.i. (ISBN 0-393-00897-5, N897, Norton Lib). Norton.

Avriel, Mordecai & Amit, Raphael, eds. Perspectives on Resource Policy Modeling: Theory & Applications. 456p. 1982. prof ref 42.00x (ISBN 0-88410-837-6). Ballinger Pub.

Avtgis, Alexander, jt. auth. see Villanucci, Robert.

Aw, S. E. Chemical Evolution. LC 81-70575. 1982. pap. 9.95 (ISBN 0-89051-082-2, Pub. by Master Bks). CLP Pubs.

Awad, Elias M. Business Data Processing. 5th ed. (Illus.). 1980. text ed. 23.95 (ISBN 0-13-093807-6); student wkbk. 8.95 (ISBN 0-13-093757-6). P-H.

--Introduction to Computers. 2nd ed. (Illus.). 496p. 1983. text ed. 19.95 (ISBN 0-13-479444-3). P-H.

Awad, Elias M. & Data Processing Management Association. Automatic Data Processing: Principles & Procedures. 3rd ed. (Illus.). 576p. 1973. text ed. 23.95 (ISBN 0-13-054718-2); wkbk. 5.95 (ISBN 0-13-055418-9). P-H.

Awad, Elias M., jt. auth. see Cascio, Wayne F.

Awani, Alfred O. Project Management Techniques. (Illus.). 192p. 19.95 (ISBN 0-89433-197-3). Petrocelli.

Awashti, D. D. Catalogue of the Lichens from India, Nepal, Pakistan & Ceylon. 1965. 16.00 (ISBN 3-7682-5417-8). Lubrecht & Cramer.

Awasthi, D. D. A Monograph of the Lichen Genus Dirinaria. 1975. 16.00 (ISBN 3-7682-0957-1). Lubrecht & Cramer.

Awbery, Gwen. The Syntax of Welsh. LC 76-11489. (Cambridge Studies in Linguistics: No. 18). 1977. 39.50 (ISBN 0-521-21341-X). Cambridge U Pr.

Awevera, Johan Van der see Van der Awevera, Johan.

Awh, Robert Y. Microeconomics: Theory & Applications. LC 75-38643. 492p. 1976. text ed. 30.95x (ISBN 0-471-03849-0); wkbk., micro 11.95x (ISBN 0-471-03853-9); tchrs. manual avail. (ISBN 0-471-03854-7). Wiley.

Awooner, Kofi, et al. There Is a Song, We Shall Sing It. (African Poetry Ser.). write for info. Greenfld Rev Pr.

AWS A2 Committee on Definitions & Symbols. Symbols for Welding & Nondestructive Testing: AWS A2.4-79. new ed. LC 78-74600. 1979. pap. text ed. 20.00 (ISBN 0-87171-170-2). Am Welding.

AWS A5 Committee on Filler Metal. Specification for Carbon Steel Electrodes for Flux Cored Arc Welding: AWS A5.20-79. rev. ed. LC 78-74839. 24p. 1979. pap. 8.00 (ISBN 0-87171-171-0). Am Welding.

AWS Committee on Automotive Welding. Standard for Automobile Weld Quality-Resistance Spot Welding. LC 78-51369. 24p. 1978. pap. 8.00 (ISBN 0-87171-149-4). Am Welding.

AWS Committee on Definitions, Symbols & Metric Practice. Welding Terms & Definitions: A3.0-76. 2nd ed. (Illus.). 96p. 1976. pap. 8.00 o.p. (ISBN 0-87171-131-1). Am Welding.

AWS Committee on Machinery & Equipment. Specification for Welding Earthmoving & Construction Equipment: D14.3-77. (Illus.). 1977. pap. 18.00 (ISBN 0-87171-119-2). Am Welding.

AWS Committee on Qualification. Welding Procedure & Performance Qualification: B3.0-77. LC 77-90987. 1978. pap. 12.00 o.p. (ISBN 0-87171-146-X). Am Welding.

AWS Conference on Welding for the Aerospace Industry, October 1980. Welding Technology for the Aerospace Industry: Proceedings. (Welding Technology Ser.). 176p. 1981. 25.00 (ISBN 0-686-95643-5). Am Welding.

AWS Conference, 1979. Maintenance Welding in Nuclear Power Plants: Proceedings. 176p. 1980. 25.00 (ISBN 0-686-95646-X). Am Welding.

AWS Conference, 1980. Underwater Welding of Offshore Platforms & Pipelines: Proceedings. 189p. 1981. 28.00 (ISBN 0-686-95652-4). Am Welding.

AWS C5 Committee on Arc Welding & Arc Cutting. Recommended Practices for Gas Metal Arc Welding: AWS C5.6-79. LC 78-73281. (Illus.). 1979. pap. text ed. 18.00 (ISBN 0-87171-166-4). Am Welding.

AWS Pipeline Conference, 1980. Pipeline Welding & Inspection: Proceedings. 108p. 1980. 25.00 (ISBN 0-686-95655-9). Am Welding.

AWS-SAE Joint Committee on Automotive Welding. Standard for Automotive Resistance Spot Welding Electrodes. (Illus.). 1977. pap. 18.00 (ISBN 0-87171-136-2). Am Welding.

AWS Structural Welding Committee. Structural Welding Code--Steel: AWS D1.1-79. 3rd ed. LC 78-64973. 1978. pap. text ed. 18.00 o.p. (ISBN 0-87171-164-8). Am Welding.

--Structural Welding Code-Reinforcing Steel: AWS D1-1. (Illus.). 1979. 15.00 (ISBN 0-87171-125-7). Am Welding.

AWS Subcommittee on Soldering. Soldering Manual. 2nd ed. 1978. 20.00 (ISBN 0-87171-151-6). Am Welding.

Awtrey, Amy & Markos, Carol. The Reading Program: Critical Reading, Bk. G. 72p. 1982. pap. 3.50x (ISBN 0-88069-006-2). L A Meyer.

--The Reading Program: Essay Structures, Bk. F. 72p. 1982. pap. 3.50x (ISBN 0-88069-005-4). L A Meyer.

--The Reading Program: Relationships, Bk. E. 58p. 1982. pap. 3.50x (ISBN 0-88069-004-6). L A Meyer.

--The Reading Program: Sentence Structure. 48p. 1982. pap. 3.50x (ISBN 0-88069-002-X). L A Meyer.

--The Reading Program: Signals, Bk. D. 62p. 1982. pap. 3.50x (ISBN 0-88069-003-8). L A Meyer.

--The Reading Program: Vocabulary, Bk. B. 48p. 1982. pap. 3.50x (ISBN 0-88069-001-1). L A Meyer.

--The Reading Program: Word Patterns, Bk. A. 48p. 1982. pap. 3.50 (ISBN 0-88069-000-3). L A Meyer.

Axe, John. Collectible Black Dolls. 48p. 1978. pap. 4.95 (ISBN 0-87588-138-6). Hobby Hse.

--The Encyclopedia of Celebrity Dolls. 420p. 1983. 27.50 (ISBN 0-87588-186-6). Hobby Hse.

Axe, John, ed. Collecting Modern Dolls. 64p. 1981. pap. 7.95 (ISBN 0-87588-175-5). Hobby Hse.

Axel, Helen, ed. Regional Perspectives on Energy Issues. (Report Ser.: No. 825). (Illus.). vii, 63p. (Orig.). 1982. pap. text ed. 30.00 (ISBN 0-8237-0264-2). Conference Bd.

Axelrad, D. R. Micromechanics of Solids. 1978. 53.25 (ISBN 0-444-99806-3). Elsevier.

Axelrad, Jacob. Patrick Henry: The Voice of Freedom. LC 75-23310. (Illus.). 318p. 1975. Repr. of 1947 ed. lib. bdg. 20.00x (ISBN 0-8371-8331-6, AXPH). Greenwood.

Axelrod & Vorderwinkler. Goldfish & Koi in Your Home. (Illus.). 1970. 12.95 (ISBN 0-87666-075-8, H909). TFH Pubns.

Axelrod, jt. auth. see Burghardt.

Axelrod, Alan. Charles Brockden Brown: An American Tale. 224p. 1983. text ed. 22.50x (ISBN 0-292-71076-3). U of Tex Pr.

Axelrod, Allan & Berger, Curtis J. Land Transfer & Finance. 1982. pap. 6.95 (ISBN 0-316-06034-8). Little.

Axelrod, Allan, et al. Land Transfer & Finance. 1978. 27.50 (ISBN 0-316-06032-1); 1982 supplement 6.95 (ISBN 0-316-06031-3). Little.

Axelrod, Daniel I. Contributions to the Neogene Paleobotany of Central California. (U. C. Publications in Geological Sciences: Vol. 121). 222p. 1981. pap. 21.50x (ISBN 0-520-09621-5). U of Cal Pr.

--History of the Maritime Closed-Cone Pines, Alta & Baja California. (U. C. Publications in Geological Sciences: Vol. 120). 1980. pap. 12.50x (ISBN 0-520-09620-7). U of Cal Pr.

Axelrod, Glen S. Rift Lake Cichlids. (Illus.). 1979. 3.95 o.p. (ISBN 0-87666-514-8, KW-035). TFH Pubns.

Axelrod, H., et al. Exotic Tropical Fishes. rev. ed. (Illus.). 1302p. 1980. 39.95 (ISBN 0-87666-543-1, H-1028); looseleaf 49.95 (ISBN 0-87666-537-7, H-1028L). TFH Pubns.

Axelrod, Herbert & Shaw, Susan. Breeding Aquarium Fishes, Bk. 1. 1968. 16.95 (ISBN 0-87666-006-5, H930). TFH Pubns.

Axelrod, Herbert & Vorderwinkler, W. Tropical Fish in Your Home. LC 56-7698. (gr. 10 up). 9.95 (ISBN 0-8069-3710-6); PLB 12.49 (ISBN 0-8069-3711-4). Sterling.

Axelrod, Herbert, jt. auth. see Emmens, C. W.

Axelrod, Herbert, ed. see Ginsberg, Lev.

Axelrod, Herbert P., jt. auth. see Gorden, Myron.

Axelrod, Herbert R. African Cichlids of Lakes Malawi & Tanganyika. (Illus.). 224p. 1973. 19.95 (ISBN 0-87666-515-6, PS-703). TFH Pubns.

--Breeding Aquarium Fishes, Bk. 2. 1971. 16.95 (ISBN 0-87666-007-3, H-941). TFH Pubns.

--Breeding Aquarium Fishes, Bk. 4. (Illus.). 320p. 1976. 16.95 (ISBN 0-87666-451-6, H-963). TFH Pubns.

--Breeding Aquarium Fishes, Bk. 5. (Illus.). 1978. 16.95 (ISBN 0-87666-469-9, H-986). TFH Pubns.

--Breeding Aquarium Fishes, Bk.6. (Illus.). 288p. 1980. 16.95 (ISBN 0-87666-536-9, H-995). TFH Pubns.

--Koi of the World. (Illus.). 239p. 1973. 39.95 (ISBN 0-87666-092-8, H-947). TFH Pubns.

--Sand Painting for Aquariums & Terrariums. (Illus.). 128p. 1975. pap. 1.00 o.p. (ISBN 0-87666-626-8, P-902). TFH Pubns.

--Tropical Fish. (Illus.). 1979. 4.95 (ISBN 0-87666-510-5, KW-020). TFH Pubns.

--Tropical Fish As a Hobby. rev. ed. 1969. 13.50 (ISBN 0-07-002606-8, GB). McGraw.

--Tropical Fish for Beginners. (Illus.). 1972. 7.95 (ISBN 0-87666-752-3, PS-304). TFH Pubns.

Axelrod, Herbert R. & Burgess, Lourdes. Breeding Aquarium Fishes, Bk. 3. 1973. 16.95 (ISBN 0-87666-025-1, H-946). TFH Pubns.

Axelrod, Herbert R. & Burgess, Warren. Pacific Marine Fishes, 7 bks. Incl. Book 1. (Illus.). 1972 (ISBN 0-87666-123-1, PS-697); Book 2. (Illus.). 1973 (ISBN 0-87666-124-X, PS-699). 29.95 ea. TFH Pubns.

--Pacific Marine Fishes, Bk. 6. (Illus.). 1976. text ed. 29.95 (ISBN 0-87666-128-2, PS-722). TFH Pubns.

--Pacific Marine Fishes, Bk. 7. (Illus.). 1976. text ed. 29.95 (ISBN 0-87666-129-0, PS723). TFH Pubns.

--Saltwater Aquarium Fishes. 12.95 (ISBN 0-87666-138-X, H914). TFH Pubns.

Axelrod, Herbert R. & Burgess, Dr. Warren. Marine Fishes. (Illus.). 1979. 4.95 (ISBN 0-87666-513-X, KW-031). TFH Pubns.

Axelrod, Herbert R. & Burgess, Warren E. Angelfish. (Illus.). 1979. 4.95 (ISBN 0-87666-516-4, KW-048). TFH Pubns.

Axelrod, Herbert R. & Vorderwinkler, W. Encyclopedia of Tropical Fish. new ed. 1975. 14.95 (ISBN 0-87666-158-4, H905). TFH Pubns.

Axelrod, Herbert R. & Welty, Edwin C., Jr. Pigeon Racing. LC 72-81050. 160p. (gr. 10 up). 1973. 11.95 (ISBN 0-8069-3720-3); PLB 14.49 (ISBN 0-8069-3721-1). Sterling.

Axelrod, Herbert R. & Whitern, Wilfred H. Guppies. (Orig.). pap. 2.95 (ISBN 0-87666-082-0, M505). TFH Pubns.

Axelrod, Herbert R., jt. auth. see Burgess, Warren E.

Axelrod, Herbert R., jt. auth. see Gordon, Myron.

Axelrod, Herbert R., jt. auth. see Vriends, Matthew M.

Axelrod, Herbert R., ed. Heifetz. 2nd ed. (Illus.). 640p. 1981. 25.00 (ISBN 0-87666-600-4, Z-24). Paganiniana Pubns.

Axelrod, Herbert R., ed. see Anderson, Douglas P.

Axelrod, Herbert R., ed. see Ginsburg, Lev.

Axelrod, Herbert R., ed. see Neish, Gordon A. & Hughes, Gilbert C.

Axelrod, Herbert R., et al. Exotic Tropical Fishes. 19.95 (ISBN 0-87666-051-0, H-907); looseleaf 29.95 (ISBN 0-87666-052-9, H-907L). TFH Pubns.

--Exotic Marine Fishes. (Illus.). 608p. 1973. 19.95 (ISBN 0-87666-102-9, H938); looseleaf bdg. 20.00 (ISBN 0-87666-103-7, H-938L). TFH Pubns.

Axelrod, Herbet R. Cardinal Tetras. (Illus.). 1980. 4.95 (ISBN 0-87666-517-2, KW-050). TFH Pubns.

Axelrod, Jennifer. Breeding Guinea Pigs. 1980. 4.95 (ISBN 0-87666-929-1, KW-073). TFH Pubns.

Axelrod, Jerold L. The Arco Book of Home Plans. LC 79-14620. (Illus.). 1979. lib. bdg. 8.95 o.p. (ISBN 0-668-04728-3); pap. 4.95 o.p. (ISBN 0-668-04732-1). Arco.

Axelrod, M. Creative Timed Writings. 1975. 7.88 (ISBN 0-07-002610-6, G). McGraw.

Axelrod, Nathan. Executive Leadership. 1969. pap. text ed. 10.95 (ISBN 0-672-96054-0); tchr's manual 6.67 (ISBN 0-672-96055-9). Bobbs.

Axelrod, Paul. Scholars & Dollars: Politics, Economics, & the Universities of Ontario 1945-1980. (State & Economic Life Ser.). 388p. 1982. 35.00x (ISBN 0-8020-5609-1); pap. 12.50 (ISBN 0-8020-6492-2). U of Toronto Pr.

Axelrod, R. Herbert, jt. auth. see Sheppard, Leslie.

Axelrod, Regina. Conflict Between Energy & Urban Environment: Consolidated Edison Versus the City of New York. LC 80-67179. 214p. (Orig.). 1982. lib. bdg. 23.00 (ISBN 0-8191-2376-5); pap. text ed. 10.75 (ISBN 0-8191-2377-3). U Pr of Amer.

Axelrod, Regina S., ed. Environment, Energy, & Public Policy: Conflict & Resolution. LC 79-3523. (Conflict & Resolution). (Illus.). 1981. 22.95x (ISBN 0-669-03460-6). Lexington Bks.

Axelrod, Robert M. Framework for a General Theory of Cognition & Choice. LC 72-619609. (Research Ser.: No. 18). (Illus.). 1972. pap. 1.50x o.p. (ISBN 0-87725-118-5). U of Cal Intl St.

Axelrod, Saul. Behavior Modification for the Classroom Teacher. (McGraw-Hill Series in Special Education). (Illus.). 1977. pap. text ed. 13.50 (ISBN 0-07-002570-3, C). McGraw.

--Behavior Modification for the Classroom Teacher. 2nd ed. (Illus.). 272p. 1983. pap. text ed. 13.50x (ISBN 0-07-002572-X, C). McGraw.

Axelrod, Saul, ed. The Effects of Punishment on Human Behavior. Apsche, Jack. LC 82-13892. 342p. 1982. 34.50 (ISBN 0-12-068740-2). Acad Pr.

Axelrod, Steven G. & Deese, Helen. Robert Lowell: A Reference Guide. 460p. 1982. lib. bdg. 35.00 (ISBN 0-8161-7814-3, Pub by Hall Reference). G K Hall.

Axelsson, O., et al, eds. Analytical & Numerical Approaches to Asymptotic Problems in Analysis. (North Holland Mathematical Studies: Vol. 47). 1981. 64.00 (ISBN 0-444-86131-9). Elsevier.

Axford, H. William. Gilpin County Gold: Peter McFarlane, 1848-1929 Mining Entrepreneur in Central City, Colorado. LC 82-72825. (Illus.). xii, 210p. 1976. 12.95 (ISBN 0-8040-0550-8, SB). Swallow.

Axford, Lavonne, ed. English Language Cookbooks, Sixteen Hundred to Nineteen Seventy-Three. LC 76-23533. 1976. 82.00x (ISBN 0-8103-0534-8). Gale.

Axford, Roger W. Adult Education: The Open Door to Lifelong Learning. rev. ed. 504p. 1980. pap. 12.50x (ISBN 0-935648-01-1). Halldin Pub.

--Native Americans: 23 Indian Biographies. (Illus.). 128p. Date not set. pap. 4.50 o.p. (ISBN 0-935648-02-X). Halldin Pub.

Axinn, Donald E. Sliding Down the Wind. LC 77-90082. 1977. 5.95 o.p. (ISBN 0-8040-0793-4); pap. 3.50 o.p. (ISBN 0-8040-0794-2). Swallow.

Axinn, June & Levin, Herman. Social Welfare: A History of the American Response to Need. 2nd ed. 351p. 1982. pap. text ed. 10.50 scp o.p. (ISBN 0-06-040403-5, HarpC). Har-Row.

Axler, Bruce H. Showmanship in the Dining Room. 1974. pap. 4.50 (ISBN 0-672-96117-2). Bobbs.

--Tableservice Techniques. 1974. pap. 3.95 o.p. (ISBN 0-672-96116-4). Bobbs.

Axline, Andrew W., jt. auth. see Stegenga, James A.

Axon, Gordon V. Let's Go to a Stock Exchange. (Let's Go Ser). (Illus.). 48p. (gr. 3-5). 1973. PLB 4.29 o.p. (ISBN 0-399-60813-3). Putnam Pub Group.

Axsom, Richard H. The Prints of Frank Stella: A Catalogue Raisonne 1967-1982. LC 82-15729. (Illus.). 192p. 1983. 50.00 (ISBN 0-933920-40-7); pap. 19.50 for museum distribution only (ISBN 0-933920-41-5). Hudson Hills.

Axtell, James. The European & the Indian: Essays in the Ethnohistory of Colonial North America. (Illus.). 1982. pap. 7.95 (ISBN 0-19-502904-6, GB643). Oxford U Pr.

Axton, Marie. Three Tudor Classical Interludes: Thersites, Jacke Jugeler & Horestes. (Tudor Interludes Ser.: No. III). 246p. 1982. text ed. 47.50x (ISBN 0-8476-7193-3). Rowman.

Axton, Marie & Williams, R., eds. English Drama. LC 76-57099. 1977. 32.50 (ISBN 0-521-21588-9). Cambridge U Pr.

Aya, R. & Miller, N. New American Revolution. LC 74-142353. 1971. pap. text ed. 4.50 (ISBN 0-02-901090-X). Free Pr.

Ayad, Foaud, tr. see Hazm, Imam Ibn.

Ayal, Eliezer B., ed. The Study of Thailand: Analyses of Knowledge. LC 79-4544. (Papers in International Studies: Southeast Asia: No. 54). 1979. pap. 13.50 (ISBN 0-89680-079-2, Ohio U Ctr Intl). Ohio U Pr.

Ayal, Ora & Nakao, Naomi. The Adventures of Chester the Chest. LC 81-48642. (Illus.). 32p. (gr. k-3). 1982. 8.61i (ISBN 0-06-020304-8, HarpJ); PLB 8.89g (ISBN 0-06-020306-4). Har-Row.

Ayala. Evolutionary & Population Genetics: A Primer. 1982. 13.95 (ISBN 0-8053-0315-4). Benjamin-Cummings.

Ayala, F. J. Genetic Variation & Evolution. Head, J. J., ed. LC 81-67985. (Carolina Biology Readers Ser.). 16p. (Orig.). (gr. 10 up). 1983. pap. 1.60 (ISBN 0-89278-326-5, 45-9726). Carolina Biological.

--Origin of Species. Head, J. J., ed. LC 81-67980. (Carolina Biology Readers Ser.). (Illus.). 16p. (gr. 10 up). 1983. pap. 1.60 (ISBN 0-89278-269-2, 45-9669). Carolina Biological.

Ayala, Francisco & Kiger, John. Modern Genetics. 1980. 27.95 (ISBN 0-8053-0312-X); solutions manual 4.95 (ISBN 0-8053-0313-8). Benjamin-Cummings.

Ayala, Francisco J. & Valentine, James W. Evolving: The Theory & Processes of Organic Evolution. 1979. text ed. 22.95 (ISBN 0-8053-0310-3). Benjamin-Cummings.

Ayala, Ramon P. De see De Ayala, Ramon P.

Ayalon, Ofra, jt. auth. see Segal, Zev.

Ayalti, Hanan J., ed. Yiddish Proverbs. LC 49-11135. (Illus., Bilingual). 1963. pap. 3.95 (ISBN 0-8052-0050-9). Schocken.

Ayanaba, A. & Dart, P. J., eds. Biological Nitrogen Fixation in Farming Systems of the Tropics. LC 77-1304. 377p. 1978. 74.95x (ISBN 0-471-99499-5, Pub. by Wiley-Interscience). Wiley.

Ayandele, E. A. Holy Johnson: Pioneer of African Nationalism, 1836-1917. (Africana Modern Library: No. 13). 1970. text ed. 17.50x (ISBN 0-391-00041-1). Humanities.

Ayars, Christine M. Contributions to the Art of Music in America by the Music Industries of Boston: 1640-1936. 27.00 (ISBN 0-384-02825-X). Johnson Repr.

Ayatey, Siegfried B. Essentials of Economic Analysis: Vol. 1, Microeconomics. LC 79-66234. 1979. pap. text ed. 11.00 o.p. (ISBN 0-8191-0803-0). U Pr of Amer.

--Essentials of Economic Analysis: Vol. 2, Macroeconomics. LC 79-66234. 1979. pap. text ed. 9.50 o.p. (ISBN 0-8191-0804-9). U Pr of Amer.

Aybar de Soto, Jose. Dependency & Intervention: The Case of Guatemala in 1954. 1978. softcover 24.00 (ISBN 0-89158-192-8). Westview.

Aycock, Don M. The E. Y. Mullins Lectures on Preaching with Reference to the Aristotelian Triad. LC 79-6080. 113p. 1980. text ed. 18.00 (ISBN 0-8191-0981-9); pap. text ed. 8.25 (ISBN 0-8191-0982-7). U Pr of Amer.

Aycock, Shirley. About Frogs. 28p. 1981. stapled chapbook 1.00 (ISBN 0-942432-03-7). M O P Pr.

--The Bus Stop. 20p. 1981. 1.25 (ISBN 0-942432-04-5). M O P Pr.

--Close-Ups. 24p. 1983. stapled chapbook 2.00 (ISBN 0-942432-08-8). M O P Pr.

--Comma. 50p. 1982. stapled chapbook 3.25 (ISBN 0-942432-05-3). M O P Pr.

--Diet-Notes. 30p. 1983. stapled chapbook 2.50 (ISBN 0-942432-07-X). M O P Pr.

--Of Chimes & Wind. 24p. 1980. stapled chapbook 1.00 (ISBN 0-942432-02-9). M O P Pr.

--Ripcord. 24p. 1978. stapled chapbook 2.25 (ISBN 0-942432-00-2). M O P Pr.

--Winging It. 24p. 1979. stapled chapbook 1.25 (ISBN 0-942432-01-0). M O P Pr.

Aycock, Wendell M. & Cravens, Sydney P., eds. Calderon de la Barca at the Tercentenary: Comparative Views, Vol. 14. LC 82-80309. (Proceedings of the Comparative Literature Symposium: Vol. 14). 195p. 1982. pap. 24.95 (ISBN 0-89672-101-9). Tex Tech Pr.

Ayd, Frank J., ed. Medical, Moral & Legal Issues in Mental Health Care. LC 74-11375. 220p. 1974. 14.50 (ISBN 0-683-00295-3, Pub. by W & W). Krieger.

Ayed, Sabine L., tr. see Cranefield, Paul F.

Ayeni, Bola. Concepts & Techniques in Urban Analysis. LC 78-19219. 1979. 30.00 (ISBN 0-312-16044-5). St Martin.

Ayensu, Edward S. Medicinal Plants of West Africa. Irvine, Keith, ed. LC 78-3110. (Medicinal Plants of the World Ser.: No. 1). (Illus.). 1978. 29.95 (ISBN 0-917256-07-7). Ref Pubns.

Ayensu, Edward S., ed. see Boulos, Loutfy.

Ayer, A. J. The Concept of a Person. 1973. 17.95 o.p. (ISBN 0-312-15995-1). St Martin.

Ayer, Alfred J. Language, Truth & Logic. 2nd ed. 1936. pap. 2.50 (ISBN 0-486-20010-8). Dover.

Ayer, Frederick, Jr. Before the Colors Fade; Portrait of a Soldier: George Patton. LC 64-18329. 1971. 14.95 (ISBN 0-910220-61-1). Berg.

Ayer, Jacqueline. Wish for Little Sister. LC 60-7032. (Illus.). (gr. k-3). 1960. 6.50 o.p. (ISBN 0-15-298213-2, HJ). HarBraceJ.

Ayer, Jacqueline, jt. ed. see Grimm Brothers.

Ayers, A. J. Philosophy in the Twentieth Century. LC 82-40131. 283p. 1982. 22.50 (ISBN 0-394-50454-2). Random.

Ayers, Chesley. Specifications: An Introduction for Architecture & Construction. (Illus.). 448p. 1975. 32.50 (ISBN 0-07-002638-6, P&RB). McGraw.

Ayers, Gwendoline M. England's First State Hospitals & the Metropolitan Asylums Board 1867-1930. LC 75-126766. (Wellcome Institute of the History of Medicine). (Illus.). 1971. 46.50x (ISBN 0-520-01792-7). U of Cal Pr.

Ayers, Rose. The Street Sparrows. LC 78-9354. 1978. 10.95 o.p. (ISBN 0-698-10935-X, Coward). Putnam Pub Group.

Ayers, Tim, ed. Art at Auction: The Year at Sotheby's 1981-82; Two Hundred Forty Eighth Season. 392p. 1982. text ed. 45.00 (ISBN 0-85667-165-7, Pub. by Sotheby Pubns England). Biblio Dist.

Aykac, A., ed. see CEDEP-INSEAD Conference, Jun. 1976.

Aykroyo, W. R. & Doughty, J. Legumes in Human Nutrition. (FAO Nutritional Studies, No. 19; FAO Food & Nutrition Ser.: No. 12). 138p. 1964. pap. 7.25 (ISBN 0-686-92935-7, F257, FAO). Unipub.

Aylen, Leo. Discontinued Design. 1983. pap. text ed. 7.95x (ISBN 0-8290-1303-2). Irvington.

--Greek Tragedy & the Modern World. 1983. Repr. of 1964 ed. text ed. 24.50x (ISBN 0-8290-1299-0). Irvington.

--I, Odysseus. 1983. pap. text ed. 7.95x (ISBN 0-8290-1301-6). Irvington.

--Red Alert: This is a God Warning. 1983. pap. text ed. 7.95x (ISBN 0-8290-1304-0). Irvington.

--Return to Zululand. 1983. pap. text ed. 7.95x (ISBN 0-8290-1302-4). Irvington.

--Sunflower. 1983. pap. text ed. 7.95x (ISBN 0-8290-1300-8). Irvington.

Aylesworth, Jim. Siren in the Night. Fay, Ann, ed. (Self-Starter Bks.). (Illus.). 32p. (ps-2). 1983. PLB 7.75 (ISBN 0-8075-7374-4). A Whitman.

Aylesworth, Owen R. Caleb Sheldon Butts Aylesworth, His Descendants. (Illus.). 287p. 1982. text ed. 25.00 (ISBN 0-9609312-0-1). O R Aylesworth.

Aylesworth, T. G. The Story of Werewolves. 1982. 8.95 (ISBN 0-07-002645-9). McGraw.

Aylesworth, Thomas. Spoon Bending & Other Impossible Feats. LC 80-20901. (Monsters & Mysteries Ser.). (gr. 4-10). 1980. pap. 2.25 (ISBN 0-88436-767-3). EMC.

Aylesworth, Thomas C. & Klein, Stanley, eds. Science Update: 1978 Issue. pap. 29.95 o.p. (ISBN 0-915794-11-X, 9365/78). Gaylord Prof Pubns.

Aylesworth, Thomas G. Geological Disasters: Earthquakes & Volcanoes. (Impact Bks.). (Illus.). 1979. PLB 8.90 s&l (ISBN 0-531-02288-9). Watts.

--The Story of Vampires. (Illus.). (gr. 4-6). 1977. 7.95 o.p. (ISBN 0-07-002647-5, GB). McGraw.

--The Story of Witches. LC 79-12321. (Illus.). (gr. 5-8). 1979. 7.95 o.p. (ISBN 0-07-002649-1). McGraw.

--Understanding Body Talk. LC 78-12446. (Impact Bks.). (Illus.). (gr. 7 up). 1979. PLB 8.90 s&l (ISBN 0-531-02200-5). Watts.

--Who's Out There? The Search for Extraterrestrial Life. (gr. 9-12). 1975. PLB 7.95 o.p. (ISBN 0-07-002637-8, GB). McGraw.

Aylesworth, Thomas G. & Aylesworth, Virginia L. The Mount St. Helens Disaster: What We've Learned. (Impact Ser.). 96p. (gr. 7 up). 1983. PLB 8.90 (ISBN 0-531-04488-2). Watts.

Aylesworth, Virginia L., jt. auth. see Aylesworth, Thomas G.

Aylett, B. J. Organometallic Compounds, Vol. 1, Pt. 2: Groups IV & V. 4th ed. 1979. 82.00x (ISBN 0-412-13020-3, Pub. by Chapman & Hall). Methuen Inc.

Aylett, B. J., ed. Fundamentals of Inorganichemistry: A Programmed Introduction. 29.95 (ISBN 0-471-25587-4, Pub. by Wiley Heyden). Wiley.

Ayliffe, G. A. & Taylor, L. J. Hospital-Acquired Infection: Principles & Prevention. (Illus.). 144p. 1982. pap. text ed. 15.00 (ISBN 0-7236-0608-0). Wright-PSG.

Ayliffe, Jerry. American Premium Guide to Coin-Operated Machines: Identification & Values. (Illus.). 400p. 1981. pap. 9.95 (ISBN 0-517-54407-5, Americana). Crown.

Ayling, Ronald, ed. see O'Casey, Sean.

Ayling, Stanley. John Wesley. 1983. 16.95 (ISBN 0-687-20376-7). Abingdon.

Ayling, Tony & Cox, Geoffrey J. The Collins Guide to the Sea Fishes of New Zealand. (Illus.). 384p. 1983. 19.95 (ISBN 0-00-216987-8, Pub. by W Collins Australia). Intl Schol Bk Serv.

Ayllon, Candido & Smith, Paul. Spanish Composition Through Literature. 1968. text ed. 18.95 (ISBN 0-13-824052-3). P-H.

Ayllon, Teodoro & Azrin, Nathan H. Token Economy: A Motivational System for Therapy & Rehabilitation. (Orig.). 1968. pap. 14.95 (ISBN 0-13-919357-X). P-H.

Ayllon, Teodoro & Milan, Michael A. Correctional Rehabilitation & Management: A Psychological Approach. LC 78-21703. (Wiley Ser. in Behavior). 280p. 1979. 29.95 (ISBN 0-471-03843-1, Pub. by Wiley-Interscience). Wiley.

Aylmer, G. E. The King's Servants: The Civil Service of Charles I, 1625-1645. 2nd rev ed. 1974. 46.95x (ISBN 0-7100-1037-0). Routledge & Kegan.

--The State's Servants: The Civil Service of the English Republic, 1649-1660. (Illus.). 498p. 1973. 36.95x (ISBN 0-7100-7637-1). Routledge & Kegan.

Aylward. Ships & How to Draw Them. (The Grosset Art Instruction Ser.: No. 24). (Illus.). 48p. 1981. pap. 2.50 (ISBN 0-448-00533-6, G&D). Putnam Pub Group.

Aylward, Gladys & Hunter, Christine. Gladys Aylward. 1970. pap. 2.95 (ISBN 0-8024-2986-6). Moody.

Aynesworth, Hugh, jt. auth. see Michaud, Stephen G.

Aynsley, R. M. Architectural Aerodynamics. 1977. 41.00 (ISBN 0-85334-698-4, Pub. by Applied Sci England). Elsevier.

Ayoade, J. O. Introduction to Climatology for the Tropics. 200p. 1983. 28.95 (ISBN 0-471-10349-7, Pub. by Wiley-Interscience); pap. 13.95 (ISBN 0-471-10407-8, Pub. by Wiley-Interscience). Wiley.

Ayoob, Mohadded. Conflict & Intervention in the Third World. 1980. 29.00 (ISBN 0-312-16228-6). St Martin.

Ayoob, Mohammed, ed. The Middle East in World Politics. LC 80-22312. 224p. 1981. 26.00 (ISBN 0-312-53184-2). St Martin.

Ayres, Frank, Jr. Calculus. 2nd ed. (Schaum Outline Ser.). 1968. pap. 7.95 (ISBN 0-07-002653-X, SP). McGraw.

--Differential Equations. (Schaum's Outline Ser). (Orig.). 1952. pap. 6.95 (ISBN 0-07-002654-8, SP). McGraw.

--First Year College Mathematics. (Schaum's Outline Ser). (Orig.). 1958. pap. 7.95 (ISBN 0-07-002650-5, SP). McGraw.

--Mathematics of Finance. (Schaum's Outline Ser). (Orig.). 1963. pap. 6.95 (ISBN 0-07-002652-1, SP). McGraw.

--Matrices. (Schaum's Outline Ser). (Orig.). 1968. pap. 5.95 (ISBN 0-07-002656-4, SP). McGraw.

--Modern Algebra. (Schaum's Outline Ser). (Orig.). 1965. pap. 6.95 (ISBN 0-07-002655-6, SP). McGraw.

--Projective Geometry. (Schaum's Outline Ser). (Orig.). 1967. pap. 6.95 (ISBN 0-07-002657-2, SP). McGraw.

--Trigonometry. (Schaum's Outline Ser). (Orig.). 1954. pap. 6.95 (ISBN 0-07-002651-3, SP). McGraw.

Ayres, Gilbert. Analisis Quimico Cuantativo. (Span.). 1970. 17.60 o.p. (ISBN 0-06-310050-9, IntlDept). Har-Row.

Ayres, J. A., ed. Decontamination of Nuclear Reactors & Equipment. (Illus.). 815p. 1970. 71.95x (ISBN 0-471-06687-7, Pub. by Wiley-Interscience). Wiley.

Ayres, James. The Shell Book of the Home in Britain: Decoration, Design & Construction of Vernacula Interiors, 1500-1850. LC 81-670125. (Shell Book Ser.). (Illus.). 240p. 1981. write for info (ISBN 0-571-11625-6). Faber & Faber.

Ayres, Jane. Une Merveilleuse Odyssee. (Harlequin Seduction Ser.). 332p. 1983. pap. 3.25 (ISBN 0-373-45019-2). Harlequin Bks.

Ayres, Joe & Miller, Janice. Effective Public Speaking. 300p. 1983. pap. text ed. write for info. (ISBN 0-697-04229-4); instrs.' manual avail. (ISBN 0-697-04230-8). Wm C Brown.

Ayres, Phillip J., ed. see Munday, Anthony.

Ayres, R. U. Resources, Environment, & Economics: Applications of the Materials-Energy Balance Principle. 207p. Repr. of 1978 ed. text ed. 40.00 (ISBN 0-471-02627-1). Krieger.

Ayres, Robert L. Banking on the Poor: The World Bank & World Poverty. 296p. 1983. 17.50x (ISBN 0-262-01070-4). MIT Pr.

Ayres, Robert U. Resources, Environment & Economics: Applications of the Materials-Energy Balance Principle. LC 77-20049. 207p. 1978. 44.95 o.p. (ISBN 0-471-02627-1, Pub. by Wiley-Interscience). Wiley.

--Uncertain Futures: Challenges for Decision-Makers. LC 78-10252. 429p. 1979. 36.95 (ISBN 0-471-04250-1, Pub. by Wiley-Interscience). Wiley.

Ayres, Robert U. & Miller, Steven M. Robotics: Applications & Social Implications. 368p. 1982. prof ref 32.50x (ISBN 0-88410-891-0). Ballinger Pub.

Ayres, Ronald F. VLSI Design: Silicon Compilation & the Art of Automatic Microchip Design. (Illus.). 496p. 1983. text ed. 39.95 (ISBN 0-13-942680-9). P-H.

Ayrton, Pete, ed. World View 1983: What the Press & Television Have Not Told You about the Year's Mega-Issues. (Illus.). 500p. 1983. 22.50 (ISBN 0-394-53072-1); pap. 9.95 (ISBN 0-394-71419-9). Pantheon.

Ayscough, Florence. Chinese Women: Yesterday & Today. LC 74-32095. (China in the 20th Century Ser). (Illus.). xiv, 324p. 1975. Repr. of 1937 ed. lib. bdg. 42.50 (ISBN 0-306-70700-4). Da Capo.

Ayscough, P. B. Electron Spin Resonance, Vol. 6. 372p. 1982. 195.00x (ISBN 0-85186-801-0, Pub. by Royal Soc Chem England). State Mutual Bk.

Ayubi, Shaheen & Bissell, Richard E. Economic Sanctions in U. S. Foreign Policy. (Philadelphia Policy Papers). 1982. pap. 3.95 (ISBN 0-910191-01-8). For Policy Res.

Ayyar, R. S. Manu's Land & Trade Laws. 1976. Repr. 12.50x o.p. (ISBN 0-88386-852-0). South Asia Bks.

Azaad, Meyer. The Tale of Ringy. Ghanoonparvar, Mohammad R. & Wilcox, Diane L., trs. Orig. Title: Persian. (Illus.). 24p. (Orig.). (gr. 3 up). 1983. pap. 5.95 (ISBN 0-686-43078-6). Mazda Pubs.

Azaad, Meyer, jt. auth. see Farjam, Farideh.

Azad, A. K. Tarjaman-ul-Quran, 3 vols. Vol. 1. 9.50 (ISBN 0-686-18512-9); Vol. 2. 15.95 (ISBN 0-686-67787-0). Vol. 3. Kazi Pubns.

Azad, Hardam S. Industrial Wastewater Management Handbook. 1976. 49.95 (ISBN 0-07-002661-0, P&RB). McGraw.

Azadi, S. Turkoman Carpets. 1982. 95.00x (ISBN 0-903580-30-6, Pub. by Element Bks). State Mutual Bk.

Azam, Salem. Concept of Islamic State. 42p. 1980. pap. 2.95 (ISBN 0-906041-13-9, Pub. by Islamic Council of Europe England). Intl Schol Bk Serv.
--Muslim Communities in Non-Muslim States. 169p. 1982. 8.95 (ISBN 0-907163-01-7, Pub. by Islamic Council of Europe England); pap. 14.95 (ISBN 0-686-98297-5). Intl Schol Bk Serv.
Azami, M. M. Early Hadith Literature. LC 77-90341. 1978. 8.25 (ISBN 0-89259-012-2). Am Trust Pubns.
Azana, Manuel M., jt. auth. see Sedwick, Frank.
Azar, J. J., jt. auth. see Peery, D. J.
Azariah, Isaiah. Lord Bentinck & Indian Education, Crime, & Status of Women. LC 78-64822. 1978. pap. text ed. 10.00 (ISBN 0-8191-0641-0). U Pr of Amer.
Azarian, Barbara. The American Teachers Nineteen Eighty-Two Tax Guide & Portfolio for Your Nineteen Eighty-Three Filing. 128p. (Orig.). 1982. pap. 8.95 (ISBN 0-89529-168-1). Avery Pub.
Azarian, Mary. The Tale of John Barleycorn: or From Barley to Beer. LC 82-3130. (Illus.). 32p. 1982. 12.95 (ISBN 0-87923-446-6); pap. 6.95 (ISBN 0-87923-447-4). Godine.
Azarnoff, Daniel L. Steroid Therapy. LC 74-24511. (Illus.). 340p. 1975. 15.50 o.p. (ISBN 0-7216-1469-8). Saunders.
Azarnoff, Pat. Best Books on Health For Children. 600p. 1983. 60.00 (ISBN 0-8352-1518-0). Bowker. Postponed.
Azarnoff, Pat & Hardgrove, Carol. The Family in Child Health Care. LC 80-26586. 272p. 1981. pap. 17.95x (ISBN 0-471-08663-0, Pub. by Wiley-Med). Wiley.
Azaroff, Leonid V. Elements of X-Ray Crystallography. LC 82-15204. 628p. 1983. Repr. of 1968 ed. price not set (ISBN 0-89874-338-9). Krieger.
--Introduction to Solids. LC 75-20462. 474p. 1975. Repr. of 1960 ed. 25.50 (ISBN 0-88275-345-2). Krieger.
Azaroff, Leonid V. & Brophy, J. J. Electronic Processes in Materials. 1963. text ed. 39.50 (ISBN 0-07-002669-6, C). McGraw.
Azaroff, Leonid V. & Buerger, M. L. Powder Method in X-Ray Crystallography. 1958. 25.95 o.p. (ISBN 0-07-002670-X, C). McGraw.
Azaroff, Leonid V. & Buerger, Martin J. Powder Method in X-Ray Crystallography. LC 82-6520. 352p. 1983. Repr. of 1958 ed. write for info. (ISBN 0-89874-422-9). Krieger.
Azaroff, Leonid V. & Donahue, R. J. X-Ray Diffraction. (International Series in Pure & Applied Physics). (Illus.). 544p. 1974. text ed. 40.50 o.p. (ISBN 0-07-002672-6, C). McGraw.
--X-Ray Spectroscopy. (International Series in Pure & Applied Physics). (Illus.). 576p. 1974. 45.00 o.p. (ISBN 0-07-002674-2, C). McGraw.
Azbel. Chemical & Process Equipment Design: Vessel Design & Selection. LC 81-70863. 791p. 1982. 69.95 (ISBN 0-250-40478-8). Ann Arbor Science.
Azbel, David S., jt. auth. see Cheremisinoff, Nicholas P.
Azbel, David S., jt. ed. see Cheremisinoff, Nicholas P.
Azen, Stanley P., jt. auth. see Afifi, A. A.
Azevedo, Carlos de. Baroque Organ-Cases of Portugal. (Bibliotheca Organologica Ser.: Vol. 50). (Illus.). 160p. 1972. 32.50 o.s.i. (ISBN 90-6027-238-2, Pub. by Frits Knuf Netherlands). Pendragon NY.
Azevedo, M. T., jt. auth. see Bicudo, C. E.
Azevedo, Milton M. & Kerr, Herminia J. Self-Paced Exercises in Spanish. 176p. (Span.). 1982. pap. text ed. 14.00 (ISBN 0-8403-2803-6). Kendall-Hunt.
Azevedo, Milton M. & McMahon, Kathryn K. Lecturas Periodisticas. 1978. pap. text ed. 9.95x o.p. (ISBN 0-669-85613-4). Heath.
Azevedo, Ross. Labor Economics: A Guide to Information Sources. LC 73-17568. (Economics Information Guide Ser.: Vol. 8). 1978. 42.00x (ISBN 0-8103-1297-2). Gale.
Azevedo, Warren L., ed. The Traditional Artist in African Societies. LC 79-160126. (Illus.). 480p. 1973. pap. 5.95x o.p. (ISBN 0-253-39902-5). Ind U Pr.
Aziz, K. & Settari, A. Petroleum Reservoir Simulation. (Illus.). 1979. 92.25x (ISBN 0-85334-787-5, Pub. by Applied Sci England). Elsevier.
Aziz, Khalid, jt. auth. see Govier, George W.
Aziz, Maqbool, ed. see James, Henry.
Azizullah. Glimpses of Hadith, 3. pap. 4.95 (ISBN 0-686-18380-0). Kazi Pubns.
Aznar, J., ed. see International Congress on Thrombosis, 7th, Valencia, Spain, October, 1982.
Azrin, Nathan & Besalel, Victoria B. Finding a Job. LC 82-50904. 160p. (Orig.). 1983. pap. 6.95 (ISBN 0-89815-049-3). Ten Speed Pr.
Azrin, Nathan H. A Parent's Guide to Bedwetting Control. 1980. 9.95 o.p. (ISBN 0-671-24804-9). S&S.
Azrin, Nathan H. & Besalel, Victoria A. Job Club Counselor's Manual. 224p. 1979. pap. text ed. 17.95 (ISBN 0-8391-1535-0). Univ Park.
Azrin, Nathan H. & Foxx, Richard M. Toilet Training in Less Than a Day. 1974. 7.95 o.p. (ISBN 0-671-21701-1). S&S.
Azrin, Nathan H. & Nunn, R. Gregory. Habit Control in a Day. 1977. 8.95 o.p. (ISBN 0-671-22752-1). S&S.
Azrin, Nathan H., jt. auth. see Ayllon, Teodoro.
Azuelo, Mariano. Underdogs. Munguia, E., Jr., tr. (Orig.). pap. 2.50 (ISBN 0-451-51741-5, CE1741, Sig Classics). NAL.
Azur, Betty S. Understanding & Using English Grammar. (Illus.). 416p. 1981. pap. text ed. 13.50 (ISBN 0-13-936492-7, Spec). P-H.
Azzam, Salem. Islam & Contemporary Society. 256p. 1982. 35.00 (ISBN 0-582-78323-2); pap. 15.00 (ISBN 0-582-78322-4). Longman.
Azzolina, L. S., ed. Comparative Immunology: Proceedings of the Verona Workshop, 16-17 July 1980, Verona, Italy. (Illus.). 180p. 1982. pap. 25.00 (ISBN 0-08-028019-6). Pergamon.
Azzone, G. F., ed. see Symposium on Biochemistry & Biophysics of Mitochondrial Membranes.
Azzone, G. F., et al, eds. The Proton & Calcium Pumps: Proceedings of the Int'l Symposium on Mechanisms of Proton & Calcium Pumps Held in Padova, Italy, Sept. 1977. (Developments in Bioenergetics & Biomembranes: Vol. 2). 1978. 67.00 (ISBN 0-444-80037-9, Biomedical Pr). Elsevier.

B

B & W Associates, ed. Double Play Reading Series, 5 kits. Incl. Kit 1. The Thief Who Liked Baseball, Showdown (ISBN 0-8372-2542-6); Kit 2. The Golden Puma, Grunk's Fantastic Basketball Team (ISBN 0-8372-2543-4); Kit 3. Fire on 7th Street, King Toop's Revenge (ISBN 0-8372-2544-2); Kit 4. Ten Speed Thieves, the Visitors (ISBN 0-8372-2545-0); Kit 5. Juan's Story, the Millville Lions (ISBN 0-8372-2546-9). (Illus.). 1977. one of ea. kit 159.90 (ISBN 0-8372-2559-0). kit 34.95 ea. Bowmar-Noble.
Baade, Walter. Evolution of Stars & Galaxies. Payne-Gaposchkin, Cecilia, ed. LC 75-24679. (Paperback Ser: No. 284). 352p. 1975. pap. 6.95 o.p. (ISBN 0-262-52033-8). MIT Pr.
Baader, Horst, ed. Onze Etudes sur L'Esprit de la Satire. (Etudes Litteraires Francaise Ser.: No. 3). 219p. (Orig., Fr.). 1978. pap. 19.00 (ISBN 3-87808-882-5). Benjamins North Am.
Baaklini, Abdo I. & Heaphy, James J., eds. Comparative Legislative Reforms & Innovations. LC 77-4249. 1977. 29.50x (ISBN 0-87395-805-5). State U NY Pr.
Ba'Albaki. English-Arabic Student Dictionary: Al-Muyassar/Munir. 12.00x (ISBN 0-86685-061-9). Intl Bk Ctr.
Ba'Albaki, Munir, jt. auth. see Al-Mawrid.
Baan, J. & Arntzenius, A. C. Basic & Clinical Aspects of Cardiac Dynamics. (International Congress Ser.: No. 453). (Abstracts). 1978. pap. 18.75 (ISBN 0-444-90037-3). Elsevier.
Baan, Jan, et al, eds. Cardiac Dynamics: A Selection of Papers Presented at the Third International Conference on Cardiovascular System Dynamics Held at the Univ. of Leiden, the Netherlands, August 1978. (Developments in Cardiovascular Medicine Ser.: No. 2). 545p. 1980. lib. bdg. 81.50 (ISBN 90-247-2212-8). Kluwer Boston.
--Cardiovascular System Dynamics. 1978. 90.00x (ISBN 0-262-18078-2). MIT Pr.
Baar, C. A. Applied Salt Rock Mechanics: Vol. 1, The in-Situ Behavior of Salt Rocks, Vol. 16A. (Developments in Geotechnical Engineering). 1977. 61.75 (ISBN 0-444-41500-9). Elsevier.
Baarli, jt. auth. see International School of Physics "Enrico Fermi" Course 66.
Baars, Conrad W. & Terruwe, Anna A. Healing the Unaffirmed: Recognizing the Deprivation Neurosis. LC 76-7897. 214p. 1979. pap. 4.95 (ISBN 0-8189-0393-7). Alba.
Baars, Donald L. The Colorado Plateau: A Geologic History. rev. ed. LC 81-52050. 272p. 1983. 18.95 (ISBN 0-8263-0598-9); pap. 9.95 (ISBN 0-8263-0599-7). U of NM Pr.
Baas, John H. History of Medicine, 2 vols. LC 70-154541. 1971. Repr. of 1889 ed. Set. leather bdg. 90.00 (ISBN 0-88275-983-3); lib. bdg. 62.50 set (ISBN 0-88275-001-1). Krieger.
Baas, P. New Perspectives in Wood Anatomy. 1982. 54.00 (ISBN 90-247-2526-7, Pub. by Martinus Nijhoff Netherlands). Kluwer Boston.
Baasel, William D. Preliminary Chemical Engineering Plant Design. LC 74-19453. xiv, 490p. 1976. 38.95 (ISBN 0-444-00152-2). Elsevier.
Baatz, Charles A., ed. Philosophy of Education: A Guide to Information Sources. (Education Information Guide Ser.: Vol. 6). 1980. 42.00x (ISBN 0-8103-1452-5). Gale.
Baatz, Charles A. & Baatz, Olga K., eds. The Psychological Foundations of Education: A Guide to Information Sources. (Education Information Guide Ser.: Vol. 10). 350p. 1981. 42.00x (ISBN 0-8103-1467-3). Gale.
Baatz, Olga K., jt. ed. see Baatz, Charles A.
Bab, Werner. The Uses of Psychology in Geriatric Ophthalmology. photocopy ed. 104p. 1964. spiral 11.75x (ISBN 0-398-00074-3). C C Thomas.
Baba, Bangali. The Yogasutra of Patanjali. 2nd rev. ed. 1979. pap. 8.50 (ISBN 0-8426-0916-4, Pub. by Motilal Banarsidass India). Orient Bk Dist.
Babad, Elisha Y. & Birnbaum, Max. The Social Self: Group Influences on Personal Identity. (Sage Library of Social Research). (Illus.). 320p. 25.00 (ISBN 0-8039-1938-7); pap. 12.50 (ISBN 0-8039-1939-5). Sage.
Babary, J. P., ed. see IFAC.
Babb, Janice B. & Dordick, B. F., eds. Real Estate Information Sources. LC 63-16246. (Management Information Guide Ser.: No. 1). 1963. 42.00x (ISBN 0-8103-0801-0). Gale.
Babbage, Charles. On the Economy of Machinery & Manufactures. 4th ed. LC 74-22019. Repr. of 1835 ed. 37.50x (ISBN 0-678-00001-8). Kelley.
--Passages from the Life of a Philosopher. LC 67-30854. Repr. of 1864 ed. 37.50x (ISBN 0-678-00479-X). Kelley.
--Reflections on the Decline of Science in England. LC 77-115928. Repr. of 1830 ed. 25.00x (ISBN 0-678-00645-8). Kelley.
Babbage, Henry P., ed. Babbage's Calculating Engines. (The Charles Babbage Institute Reprint Series for the History of Computing: Vol. 2). (Illus.). 1982. Repr. of 1889 ed. write for info. set limited edition (ISBN 0-938228-04-8). Tomash Pubs.
Babbage, Stuart B. Sex & Sanity: A Christian View of Sexual Morality. LC 67-11492. 1967. pap. 1.45 (ISBN 0-664-24744-X). Westminster.
Babbel, Ulrich & Giddens, Craig. Bibliographical Reference List of the Published Works of Rudolf Steiner in English Translation, 2 Vols, Vol. 1. 51p. 1977. pap. 1.95 (ISBN 0-88010-038-9, Pub. by Steinerbooks). Anthroposophic.
Babbidge, Homer D. & Rosenzweig, Robert M. The Federal Interest in Higher Education. LC 74-25991. 214p. 1975. Repr. of 1962 ed. lib. bdg. 15.50x (ISBN 0-8371-7882-7, BAFI). Greenwood.
Babbidge, Homer D., intro. by see Dodge, Marshall & Bryan, Robert.
Babbidge, Irene. Beginning in Bookselling: A Handbook of Bookshop Practice. 96p. 1972. 7.50 (ISBN 0-233-96019-8, 05768-1, Pub. by Gower Pub Co England); pap. 4.50 (ISBN 0-686-94102-0, 05770-3). Lexington Bks.
Babbie, Earl R. Practice of Social Research. 2nd ed. 1979. text ed. 24.95x (ISBN 0-534-00630-2); wkbk. 9.95x (ISBN 0-534-00702-3). Wadsworth Pub.
--The Practice of Social Research. 3rd ed. 576p. 1982. text ed. 24.95x (ISBN 0-534-01255-8). Wadsworth Pub.
--Understanding Sociology: A Context for Action. 464p. 1981. pap. text ed. 16.95x (ISBN 0-534-01024-5). Wadsworth Pub.
Babbin, Kenneth & Oleksy, Walter. Reach For The Stars: Helping Yourself With Personal Astrology. 1982. pap. 4.95 (ISBN 0-686-97517-0, Reward). P-H.
Babbit, Natalie. Goodyhall. 1976. pap. 1.25 o.p. (ISBN 0-380-30163-6, 30163, Camelot). Avon.
Babbitt, Diane H. & Haas, Werner. Gymnastic Apparatus Exercises for Girls. (Illus.). 130p. 1964. 13.50 o.p. (ISBN 0-471-07114-5). Wiley.
Babbitt, Harold E. Plumbing. 3rd ed. 1959. 46.50 (ISBN 0-07-002688-2, P&RB). McGraw.
Babbitt, Irving. Irving Babbitt: Representative Writings. Panichas, George A., ed. LC 81-2968. xl, 316p. 1981. 19.50x (ISBN 0-8032-3655-7). U of Nebr Pr.
Babbitt, Irving, tr. see Buddha, Gautama.
Babbitt, Natalie. Herbert Rowbarge. 192p. (gr. 9 up). 1982. 11.95 (ISBN 0-374-32959-1). FS&G.
--The Search for Delicious. (gr. 3-7). 1974. pap. 1.50 o.p. (ISBN 0-380-01541-2, 42085, Camelot). Avon.
Babbitt, Theodore. Cronica de Veinte Reyes. 1936. text ed. 12.50x (ISBN 0-686-83515-8). Elliots Bks.
Babcock, Arthur E. Portraits of Artists: Reflexivity in Gidean Fiction, 1902-1936. 16.00 (ISBN 0-917786-26-2). French Lit.
Babcock, Barbara A., jt. auth. see Carrington, Paul.
Babcock, Barbara A., et al. Sex Discrimination & the Law: Causes & Remedies. 1092p. 1975. 27.00 (ISBN 0-316-07420-9); Suppl., 1978. pap. 6.95 (ISBN 0-316-07421-7). Little.
Babcock, C. L. Silicate Glass Technology Methods. LC 76-30716. (Pure & Applied Optics Ser). 326p. 1977. 55.50x (ISBN 0-471-03965-9, Pub. by Wiley-Interscience). Wiley.
Babcock, Dennis & Boyd, Preston. Careers in the Theater. LC 74-11907. (Early Career Bks.). (Illus.). 36p. (gr. 2-5). 1975. PLB 5.95g (ISBN 0-8225-0324-7). Lerner Pubns.
Babcock, Diane S. Cranial Ultrasonography of Infants. (Illus.). 262p. 1981. lib. bdg. 36.00 (ISBN 0-683-00300-3). Williams & Wilkins.
Babcock, Dorothy E. & Keepers, Terry D. Raising Kids O. K. 1977. pap. 1.95 o.p. (ISBN 0-380-00937-4, 319896). Avon.
Babcock, James C., tr. & intro. by see Huysmans, J. K.
Babcock, James C., et al, eds. Gorostiza's Contigo Pan y Cebolla. LC 49-8551. (Graded Spanish Readers, Bk. 3). (Span). (gr. 10-11). 1953. pap. text ed. 5.50 (ISBN 0-395-04126-0). HM.
--Marmol's Amalia. LC 49-8551. (Graded Spanish Readers, Bk. 1). (Span). (gr. 10-11). 1949. pap. text ed. 5.50 (ISBN 0-395-04124-4). HM.
Babcock, Judy & Kennedy, Judy. The Spa Book: A Guided, Personal Tour of Health Resorts & Beauty Spas for Men & Women. LC 82-18249. (Illus.). 288p. 1983. 14.95 (ISBN 0-517-54950-6). Crown.
Babcock, Kendric C. Rise of American Nationality, 1811-1819. LC 69-13805. Repr. of 1906 ed. lib. bdg. 15.00 o.p. (ISBN 0-8371-1346-6, BAAN). Greenwood.
Babcock, R. F. Billboards, Glass Houses & the Law. 1977. pap. 9.00 (ISBN 0-07-002801-X). McGraw.
Babcock, Richard F., jt. auth. see Weaver, Clifford L.
Babcock, Robert J., jt. auth. see Gerbracht, Carl.
Babcock, U. C., ed. see Eoff, Sherman, et al.
Babcock, Winifred. Jung, Hesse, Harold: Contributions of C. G. Jung, Hermann Hesse, and Preston Harold to Spiritual Psychology. LC 83-12945. 1983. 14.95 (ISBN 0-396-08082-0); pap. 8.95 (ISBN 0-396-08113-4). Dodd.
Babeau, Albert A. La Province sous l'ancien regime, 2 vols. LC 77-161720. Date not set. 49.50 set (ISBN 0-404-07506-1). AMS Pr.
Babel, Isaac. Collected Stories. Morison, Walter, ed. & tr. pap. 7.95 (ISBN 0-452-00594-9, F594, Mer). NAL.
--A Letter. Goldberg, Isaac, ed. Deutsch, Babette, tr. (International Pocket Library). pap. 3.00 (ISBN 0-686-77237-7). Branden.
--You Must Know Everything. Babel, Nathalie, ed. Hayward, Max, tr. from Rus. 1969. 10.95 o.p. (ISBN 0-374-29408-9); pap. 6.95 (ISBN 0-374-51580-8). FS&G.
Babel, Isaac see Goldberg, Isaac.
Babel, Nathalie, ed. see Babel, Isaac.
Babenco, Maurice. Toward a Better World. 1978. 6.50 o.p. (ISBN 0-533-03653-4). Vantage.
Baber, Adin. Sarah & Abe in Indiana. LC 73-99295. (Illus.). (gr. 4-7). 1970. 9.95 (ISBN 0-87716-016-3, Pub. by Moore Pub Co). F Apple.
Baber, Frank, illus. Frank Baber's Mother Goose. (Illus.). (gr. k-2). 1976. 4.95 o.p. (ISBN 0-517-52819-3). Crown.
Baber, Lina G. Office Practices & Procedures. 544p. 1982. text ed. 18.50 (ISBN 0-675-09846-7); practice set 6.95 (ISBN 0-675-20007-5). Additional supplements may be obtained from publisher. Merrill.
Baber, R. L. Software Reflected: A Socially Responsible Programming of Computers. 1982. 34.00 (ISBN 0-444-86372-9). Elsevier.
Baber, Shirley G. Survival In Your Own Backyard. LC 82-99943. (First Edition). (Illus.). 60p. (Orig.). 1982. pap. 10.00 (ISBN 0-686-42957-5). Shirleys Pub.
Baber, Walter F. Organizing the Future: Matrix Models for the Postindustrial Polity. (Illus.). 176p. 1983. text ed. 14.50 (ISBN 0-8173-0123-2). U of Ala Pr.
Babeuf, Francois-Noel. Le Tribun du Peuple: ou le Defenseur de L'homme. Soboul, Albert, ed. (Babeuf & Babouvism Ser.). 96p. 1975. pap. 25.00x o.p. (ISBN 0-8287-1426-6). Clearwater Pub.
Babic, S. Serbo-Croatian for Foreigners, Vol. 1. Rev. & enl. ed. (Illus.). 1981. pap. 25.00 (ISBN 0-686-64047-0). Heinman.
Babic, Slavna. Serbo Croat for Foreigners. (Illus.). 231p. 1973. pap. text ed. 18.50x (ISBN 0-89918-702-1, Y702). Vanous.
Babiiha, Thaddeo K. The James-Hawthorne Relation: Biographical Essays. 1980. lib. bdg. 22.00 (ISBN 0-8161-8431-3, Hall Reference). G K Hall.
Babin, Claude. Elements of Palaeontology. LC 79-1323. 446p. 1980. 57.00 (ISBN 0-471-27577-8, Pub. by Wiley-Interscience); pap. 24.00x (ISBN 0-471-27576-X). Wiley.
Babin, Edith H. & Cordes, Carole V. TOEFL (Test of English as a Foreign Language) 3rd ed. 288p. 1983. pap. 7.95 (ISBN 0-668-05446-8); cassette 7.95 (ISBN 0-668-05743-2). Arco.
Babior, Bernard M., ed. Cobalamin: Biochemistry & Pathophysiology. LC 74-32499. 477p. 1975. 42.50 o.p. (ISBN 0-471-03970-5, Pub. by Wiley-Interscience). Wiley.
Bablet, Denis. Edward Gordon Craig. Woodward, D., tr. LC 66-23134. (Illus.). 1966. 9.95 o.s.i. (ISBN 0-87830-042-2). Theatre Arts.
Babson, J. H. Disease Costing. 1973. 11.00 (ISBN 0-7190-0524-8). Manchester.
Babson, Marian. Dangerous to Know. 168p. 1983. pap. 2.95 (ISBN 0-8027-3029-9). Walker & Co.
--Death Beside the Sea. 176p. 1983. 12.95 (ISBN 0-8027-5490-2). Walker & Co.
--The Lord Mayor of Death. 193p. 1983. pap. 2.95 (ISBN 0-8027-3026-4). Walker & Co.
Babson, S. Gorham, et al. Diagnosis & Management of the Fetus & Neonate at Risk: A Guide for Team Care. 4th ed. LC 79-16957. (Illus.). 1979. text ed. 36.50 (ISBN 0-8016-0415-X). Mosby.
Babu, Mohammed. African Socialism. 224p. (Orig.). 1981. 20.00 (ISBN 0-905762-19-3, Pub. by Zed Pr England); pap. 9.95 (ISBN 0-905762-39-8, Pub. by Zed Pr England). Lawrence Hill.
Babunakis, Michael. Budget Reform for Government: A Comprehensive Allocation & Management System Cams. LC 82-354. 248p. 1982. lib. bdg. 29.95 (ISBN 0-686-97994-X, BBG/, Quorum). Greenwood.
--Budgets: An Analytical & Procedural Handbook for Government & Non-Profit Organizations. LC 76-5323. (Illus.). 228p. 1976. lib. bdg. 27.50x (ISBN 0-8371-8900-4, BBP). Greenwood.

Babusis, Vytautas, ed. see Love, Richard H.

Babyonyshev, Alexander, ed. On Sakharov. LC 82-40034. 224p. 1982. pap. 6.95 (ISBN 0-394-71033-9, Vin). Random.

--On Sakharov. LC 81-48259. 1983. 15.95 (ISBN 0-394-52469-1); pap. 6.95 (ISBN 0-394-71033-9). Knopf.

Baca, Jimmy S. What's Happening. LC 82-5089. 36p. (Orig.). 1982. pap. 4.50 (ISBN 0-915306-27-1). Curbstone.

Baca, Murtha, tr. see Pignatti, Terisio.

Bacardi, Amalia E., tr. see Santa Cruz, Mercedes.

Baccheschi, Edi. El Greco. Piper, David, ed. Carroll, Jane, tr. from Ital. LC 79-64901. (Every Painting Ser.). (Illus.). 96p. 1980. pap. 5.95 o.p. (ISBN 0-8478-0265-5). Rizzoli Intl.

Bacchi, Carol L. Liberation Deferred? The Ideas of the English-Canadian Suffragists, 1877-1918. (Social History of Canada Ser.). 222p. 1983. 25.00x (ISBN 0-8020-2455-6); pap. 8.95 (ISBN 0-8020-6466-3). U of Toronto Pr.

Bacchus, Habeeb. Essentials of Gynecologic & Obstetric Endocrinology. (Illus.). 240p. 1975. pap. 16.50 o.p. (ISBN 0-8391-0814-1). Univ Park.

Bacchus, M. K. Education for Development or Underdevelopment? Guyana's Educational System & Its Implications for the Third World. Boyd, Rosalind E., ed. (Development Perspectives Ser.: No. 2). 302p. 1980. text ed. 17.25 (ISBN 0-88920-084-X, Pub. by Wilfrid Laurier U Pr Canada); pap. text ed. 10.75x (ISBN 0-88920-085-8). Humanities.

Bach, Alice. Millicent the Magnificent. LC 77-11840. (Illus.). 1978. PLB 8.61i (ISBN 0-06-020309-9, HarpJ); PLB 8.89 o.p. (ISBN 0-06-020312-9). Har-Row.

--Mollie Make-Believe. LC 73-14334. 160p. (gr. 7 up). 1974. PLB 9.89 o.p. (ISBN 0-06-020316-1, HarpJ). Har-Row.

--They'll Never Make a Movie Starring Me. LC 72-12240. 208p. (gr. 7 up). 1973. 10.89 (ISBN 0-06-020323-4, HarpJ). Har-Row.

--Waiting for Johnny Miracle. LC 79-2813. 256p. (YA) (gr. 7 up). 1980. 9.57i (ISBN 0-06-020348-X, HarpJ); PLB 10.89 (ISBN 0-06-020349-8). Har-Row.

Bach, Bert C. & Browning, Gordon. Drama for Composition. 1973. pap. 8.95x (ISBN 0-673-07640-7). Scott F.

Bach, Bob & Mercer, Ginger. Our Huckleberry Friend: The Life, Times & Lyrics of Johnny Mercer. 256p. 1982. 24.95 (ISBN 0-8184-0331-4). Lyle Stuart.

Bach, Emmon. Syntactic Theory. LC 81-40918. 310p. 1982. pap. text ed. 12.75 (ISBN 0-8191-2258-0). U Pr of Amer.

Bach, George & Goldberg, Herb. Creative Aggression: The Art of Assertive Living. 1975. pap. 2.95 o.p. (ISBN 0-380-00373-2, 57299-0). Avon.

--Creative Aggression: The Art of Creative Living. LC 82-45621. 432p. 1983. pap. 8.95 (ISBN 0-385-18442-5, Anch). Doubleday.

Bach, George R. & Deutsch, Ronald M. Pairing. 1971. pap. 3.50 (ISBN 0-380-00394-5, 62174-6). Avon.

--Stop! You're Driving Me Crazy. LC 79-12611. 1980. 9.95 o.p. (ISBN 0-399-11834-9). Putnam Pub Group.

Bach, George R. & Torbet, Laura. The Inner Enemy: How to Fight Fair with Yourself. LC 82-14397. 224p. 1983. 11.95 (ISBN 0-688-01557-3). Morrow.

Bach, Ira J. & Gray, Mary L. A Guide to Chicago's Public Sculpture. LC 82-20214. (Illus.). 384p. 1983. lib. bdg. 20.00x (ISBN 0-226-03398-8); pap. 8.95 (ISBN 0-226-03399-6). U of Chicago Pr.

Bach, Ira J. & Wolfson, Susan. A Guide to Chicago's Historic Suburbs on Wheels & on Foot. LC 81-75216. (Illus.). xvi, 726p. 1981. 29.95 (ISBN 0-8040-0374-2); pap. 16.95 (ISBN 0-8040-0384-X). Swallow.

Bach, J. S. Keyboard Music. 312p. 1970. pap. 7.95 (ISBN 0-486-22360-4). Dover.

Bach, Jean. Collecting German Dolls. 192p. Date not set. 22.50 (ISBN 0-8184-0333-0). Lyle Stuart. Postponed.

Bach, Jean-Francis. Immunology. 2nd ed. LC 81-11503. 1014p. 1982. 70.00 (ISBN 0-471-08044-6, Pub. by Wiley Med). Wiley.

Bach, Jean-Francois, ed. Immunology. LC 77-12139. 1978. 73.50x o.p. (ISBN 0-471-01760-4, Pub. by Wiley Medical). Wiley.

Bach, Johann S. Eleven Great Cantatas in Full Vocal & Instrumental Score. 352p. 1976. pap. 10.00 (ISBN 0-486-23268-9). Dover.

--Sonaten und Partiten fur Violine Allein. Stobla, K. Marie, tr. (Music Reprint Ser.). 80p. 1981. Repr. of 1962 ed. 17.50 (ISBN 0-306-76085-1). Da Capo.

Bach, Kent & Harnish, Robert M. Linguistic Communication & Speech Acts. (Illus.). 1979. text ed. 22.50x (ISBN 0-262-02136-6). MIT Pr.

Bach, Laurence & Goolrich, Robert. Paros Dream Book. LC 82-51223. (Artists' Bk.). 72p. (Orig.). 1983. pap. 7.95. Visual Studies.

Bach, Linda. Awake! Aware! Alive! (Illus.). 1973. 12.95 o.p. (ISBN 0-394-48685-4, BYR); pap. 7.95 (ISBN 0-394-70830-X). Random.

Bach, Marcus. Strange Sects & Curious Cults. LC 76-52474. Repr. of 1962 ed. lib. bdg. 18.75x o.s.i. (ISBN 0-8371-9457-1, BASS). Greenwood.

--The Unity Way. LC 82-50085. 387p. 1982. 4.95 (ISBN 0-87159-164-2). Unity Bks.

Bach, Peter, ed. Collector's Treasury of Antique Slot Machines from Contemporary Advertising 1925-1950. LC 80-82463. (Illus.). 1980. 22.00 (ISBN 0-911160-61-2). Post-Era.

Bach, Richard. Illusions: The Adventures of a Reluctant Messiah. 1977. 10.95 (ISBN 0-440-04318-2, E Friede). Delacorte.

--Illusions: The Adventures of a Reluctant Messiah. 1977. lib. bdg. 10.95 o.p. (ISBN 0-8161-6520-3, Large Print Bks). G K Hall.

--Jonathan Livingston Seagull. LC 75-119617. (Illus.). 1970. 9.95 (ISBN 0-02-504540-7). Macmillan.

Bach, Shirley J., jt. auth. see Binkin, Martin.

Bach, Stanley & Sulzner, George T. Perspectives on the Presidency. 1974. pap. text ed. 9.95x o.p. (ISBN 0-669-85613-4). Heath.

Bach, W., et al, eds. see Conference on Non-Fossil Fuel & Non-Nuclear Fuel Energy Strategies, Honolulu, USS, January 1979.

Bach, Wilfred & Daniels, Anders. Handbook of Air Quality in the United States. LC 75-8390. 1975. text ed. 14.95x (ISBN 0-8248-0574-7). UH Pr.

Bach, Wilfrid. Atmospheric Pollution. Taaffe, Edward J., ed. LC 78-170869. (Illus.). 160p. 1971. pap. text ed. 6.50 o.p. (ISBN 0-07-002819-2, C). McGraw.

Bacha, Edmar L. & Diaz Alejandro, Carlos F. International Financial Intermediation: A Long & Tropical View. LC 82-3096. (Essays in International Finance Ser.: No. 147). 1982. pap. text ed. 2.50x (ISBN 0-88165-054-4). Princeton U Int Finan Econ.

Bacham & Udris. Mental Load & Stress in Activity. Date not set. 34.00 (ISBN 0-444-86349-4). Elsevier.

Bachand, Shirley, jt. auth. see Catlin, Alberta P.

Bacharach, A. L. & Pearce, J. R., eds. The Musical Companion. (Illus.). 800p. 1982. Repr. of 1977 ed. 24.95 (ISBN 0-575-02263-9, Pub by Gollancz England). David & Charles.

Bacharach, A. L., jt. ed. see Laurence, D. R.

Bacharach, Bert. How to Do Almost Everything. 1979. 9.95 o.p. (ISBN 0-671-24384-5). S&S.

Bacharach, M. Biproportional Matrices & Input Output Change. LC 77-75823. (Department of Applied Economics Monographs: No. 16). (Illus.). 1970. 32.50 (ISBN 0-521-07594-7). Cambridge U Pr.

Bacharach, M. O., jt. ed. see Malinvaud, E.

Bacharach, Michael. Economics & the Theory of Games. LC 76-27665. 1977. lib. bdg. 23.50 o.p. (ISBN 0-89158-704-7). Westview.

Bacharach, Samuel B., ed. Research in the Sociology of Organizations, Vol. 1. 350p. 1981. 40.00 (ISBN 0-89232-170-9). Jai Pr.

Bacharach, Samuel B., jt. ed. see Hammer, Tove H.

Bacharach, Stephen L. & Alpert, Nathaniel M., eds. Nuclear Cardiology: Selected Computers Aspects, 1978 Symposium Proceedings. LC 78-58477. 214p. pap. 15.00 (ISBN 0-932004-00-8). Soc Nuclear Med.

Bache, Constance, tr. see Von Bulow, Marie.

Bachelard, Gaston. On Poetic Imagination & Reverie: Selections from the Works of Gaston Bachelard. Gaudin, C., ed. LC 73-148015. (Library of Liberal Arts Ser). 1971. pap. 4.95 o.p. (ISBN 0-672-61187-2). Bobbs.

Bachelard, H. S. Brain Biochemistry. 2nd ed. 1981. pap. 6.50x (ISBN 0-412-23470-X, Pub. by Chapman & Hall). Methuen Inc.

Bachelis, Faren, ed. see Davis, Hilarie.

Bachelis, Faren, ed. see Draze, Dianne.

Bachelis, Faren, ed. see Keene, Donna & Keene, Dathy.

Bacheller, Martin A., ed. Ambassador World Atlas. new census ed. LC 82-81114. (Illus.). 500p. 1982. 34.95 (ISBN 0-8437-1251-1). Hammond Inc.

--Citation World Atlas: New World Census Edition. rev. ed. LC 82-81115. (Hammond World Atlas Ser.). (Illus.). 376p. 1982. 19.95 (ISBN 0-8437-1254-6); pap. 14.95 lexotone cover (ISBN 0-8437-1255-4). Hammond Inc.

--The Hammond Almanac of a Million Facts & Records 1983. (Illus.). 1040p. 1982. 7.95 (ISBN 0-8437-4032-9). Hammond Inc.

--Hammond Almanac of a Million Facts, Records, Forecasts 1981. (Illus.). 1982. 7.95 o.p. (ISBN 0-8437-4028-0). Hammond Inc.

--The Whole Earth Atlas: New Census Edition. (Illus.). 256p. 1983. pap. 8.95 (ISBN 0-8437-2499-4). Hammond Inc.

Bachelor, A. & Haley, J. Practice of English Fundamentals: V. Form. 1945. pap. text ed. 11.95 (ISBN 0-13-689281-7). P-H.

Bachem, A., et al, eds. Bonn Workshop on Combinatorial Optimization. (North-Holland Mathematics Studies: Vol. 66). 312p. 1982. pap. 51.00 (ISBN 0-444-86366-4, North Holland). Elsevier.

Bachem, Michael. Heimito von Doderer. (World Authors Ser.). 1981. lib. bdg. 14.95 (ISBN 0-8057-6437-2, Twayne). G K Hall.

Bacher, June M. Great Gifts of Christmas Joy. 96p. 1983. pap. 4.95 (ISBN 0-8054-5707-0). Broadman.

--Kitchen Delights. LC 82-81649. 176p. 1982. 7.95 (ISBN 0-89081-358-2). Harvest Hse.

--Love is a Gentle Stranger. LC 82-83839. 160p. (YA) (gr. 10 up). 1983. pap. 3.95 (ISBN 0-89081-374-4). Harvest Hse.

Bacher, Wilhelm. Die Anfaenge der Hebraeischen Grammatik (1895) Together with Die Hebraeische Sprachwissenschaft Vom 10. Bis Zum 16. Jahrhundert (1892) (Studies in the History of Linguistics Ser.). xix, 235p. 1974. pap. 35.00 (ISBN 90-272-0895-6, 4). Benjamins North Am.

Bachert, Russel E., Jr. Hundreds of Ideas for Outdoor Education. 152p. 1979. pap. text ed. 8.50x (ISBN 0-8134-2095-4). Interstate.

Bachhofer, Ludwig. Early Indian Sculpture, 2 vols. in 1. LC 79-143338. (Illus.). 1972. Repr. of 1929 ed. 60.00 o.s.i. (ISBN 0-87817-058-8). Hacker.

Bachhuber, Andrew H. Introduction to Logic. (Illus.). 1957. text ed. 15.95 (ISBN 0-13-487280-0). P-H.

Bachhuber, Thomas D. & Harwood, Richard K. Directions: A Guide to Career Planning. LC 77-78015. (Illus.). 1978. pap. text ed. 12.50 (ISBN 0-395-25385-3). HM.

Bachman, Christian G. Radar Sensor Engineering. LC 81-48004. 304p. 1982. 34.95x o.p. (ISBN 0-669-05233-7). Lexington Bks.

Bachman, David C. & Noble, H. Bates. The Diet that Lets You Cheat. 1983. pap. 7.95 (ISBN 0-517-54987-5). Crown.

Bachman, Jerald G., jt. auth. see Herzog, A. Regula.

Bachman, Jerald G., et al. Youth in Transition. Incl. Vol. 3. Dropping Out-- Problem or Symptom? LC 67-66009. 263p. 1971. 14.00x (ISBN 0-87944-112-7); Vol. 5. Young Men & Military Service. LC 67-66009. 260p. 1972. 12.00x (ISBN 0-87944-119-4); pap. 8.00x (ISBN 0-87944-118-6); Vol. 6. Adolescence to Adulthood: Change & Stability in the Lives of Young Men. 350p. 1978. 18.00x (ISBN 0-87944-224-7). Inst Soc Res.

Bachman, Jerald G., jt. auth. see Johnston, Lloyd D.

Bachman, Manfred & Hansmann, Klaus. Dolls the Wide World Over. (Illus.). 204p. 1973. 19.95 o.p. (ISBN 0-517-50307-7). Crown.

Bachman, Mary. Choosing Is Fun. Sparks, Judith, ed. LC 81-86704. (Happy Day Bks.). (Illus.). 24p. (Orig.). (ps-3). 1982. pap. 1.29 (ISBN 0-87239-534-0, 3580). Standard Pub.

--God's World of Colors. Sparks, Judith, ed. (A Happy Day Book). (Illus.). 24p. (gr. k-2). 1980. 1.29 (ISBN 0-87239-408-5, 3640). Standard Pub.

Bachman, Richard. Roadwork: A Novel of the First Energy Crisis. (Orig.). 1981. pap. 2.50 o.p. (ISBN 0-451-09668-1, Sig). NAL.

--The Running Man. 1982. pap. 2.50 (ISBN 0-451-11508-2, AE1508, Sig). NAL.

Bachmann, Alberto. An Encyclopedia of the Violin. Weir, Albert E., ed. Martens, Frederick H., tr. from Ger. LC 65-23406. (Music Ser.). 1966. Repr. of 1925 ed. lib. bdg. 35.00 (ISBN 0-306-70912-0). Da Capo.

Bachmann, E. Theodore, tr. see Bornkamm, Heinrich.

Bachmann, Manfred, jt. auth. see Fritzsch, Karl E.

Bachmann, Paul. Zahlentheorie, 5 vols. (Nos. 15-20). (Ger). Repr. Set. 175.00 (ISBN 0-384-02990-6). Johnson Repr.

Bachmeyer, jt. auth. see Hauenstein.

Bachmeyer, T. J., jt. auth. see Everett, William W.

Bachner, Jane, jt. auth. see Stone, Janet.

Bachner, John P. & Hutslar, Donald. Call to Colors, a History of Military Recruiting, the Draft in the American Civil War as Told Through Posters & Broadsides. (Illus.). Date not set. cancelled (ISBN 0-685-09638-6). Flayderman.

Bachofen, R. & Mislin, H., eds. New Trends in Research & Utilization of Solar Energy Through Biological Systems. (Experientia Supplementum: Vol. 43). 156p. 1982. text ed. 24.95 (ISBN 3-7643-1335-8). Birkhauser.

Bachrach, Ann W. & Swindle, Fay L. Developmental Therapy for Young Children with Autistic Characteristics. LC 77-16370. 200p. 1978. pap. 19.95 (ISBN 0-8391-1186-X). Univ Park.

Bachrach, Judy & DeMonte, Claudia. The Height Report: A Tall Woman's Handbook. 72p. 1983. pap. 5.95 (ISBN 0-8362-6406-1). Andrews & McMeel.

Bachrach, Peter. The Theory of Democratic Elitism: A Critique. LC 80-5747. 125p. 1980. lib. bdg. 17.50 (ISBN 0-8191-1184-8); pap. text ed. 7.25 (ISBN 0-8191-1185-6). U Pr of Amer.

Back, Kurt W. Beyond Words: The Story of Sensitivity Training & the Encounter Movement. LC 73-182935. 266p. 1972. 9.95x (ISBN 0-87154-077-0). Russell Sage.

--Social Psychology. LC 76-30835. 498p. 1977. text ed. 27.95 (ISBN 0-471-03983-7); instructor's manual 6.00 (ISBN 0-471-02656-5). Wiley.

Back, Kurt W., ed. In Search for Community. LC 77-90415. (AAAS Selected Symposium Ser.: No. 4). 1978. lib. bdg. 25.00x o.p. (ISBN 0-89158-431-5). Westview.

Back, Nathan & Dietze, Gunther, eds. Kinins III. (Advances in Experimental Medicine & Biology: Vol. 156). 1190p. 1983. 145.00x (ISBN 0-306-41167-9, Plenum Pr). Plenum Pub.

Back, P. De see De Back, P.

Back, Philippa. Herbs for Cleaning, Canning & Sundry Household Chores. write for info. o.p. Keats.

Back, W. & Letolle, R., eds. Geochemistry of Groundwater. (Developments in Water Science Ser.: Vol. 16). 1982. 64.00 (ISBN 0-444-42036-3). Elsevier.

Back, W., jt. ed. see Freeze, R. A.

Back, William, ed. Chemical Hydrogeology. Freeze, Allan. LC 81-11853. (Benchmark Papers in Geology Ser.: Vol. 73). 432p. 1983. 49.00 (ISBN 0-87933-440-1). Hutchinson Ross.

Backer, Barbara, jt. auth. see Larkin, Patricia.

Backer, Barbara A., et al. Death & Dying: Individuals & Institutions. 332p. 1982. 16.95 (ISBN 0-471-08715-7, Pub. by Wiley Medical). Wiley.

Backer, Morton & Gosman, Martin L. Financial Reporting & Business Liquidity. 305p. pap. 24.95 (ISBN 0-86641-020-1, 78110). Natl Assn Accts.

Backer, Thomas E., jt. auth. see Farmer, Helen S.

Backer-Grondahl, Agathe. Piano Music. (Women Composers Ser.: No. 9). 1983. lib. bdg. 22.50 (ISBN 0-306-76133-5). Da Capo.

Backhouse, Andrew. Illustrated Card Games. LC 75-24120. (Illus.). 160p. (gr. 7 up). 1976. 7.95 o.p. (ISBN 0-525-66481-5). Lodestar Bks.

Backhouse, Constance & Cohen, Leah. Sexual Harassment on the Job: How to Avoid the Working Woman's Nightmare. 240p. 1981. 12.95 (ISBN 0-13-807545-X, Spec); pap. 5.95 (ISBN 0-13-807537-9). P-H.

Backhouse, R. Syntax of Programming Languages Theory & Practice. 1979. 27.95 (ISBN 0-13-879999-7). P-H.

Backhurst, J. R. & Harker, J. H. Process Plant Design. LC 72-12561. 411p. 1973. 46.95 (ISBN 0-444-19566-1). Elsevier.

Backman, Carl W., jt. auth. see Secord, Paul F.

Backman, Jules. Entrepreneurship & the Outlook for America. 1982. text ed. 12.95 (ISBN 0-02-922940-5). Free Pr.

--Regulation & Deregulation. (ITT Key Issues Lecture Ser.). 188p. (Orig.). 1981. pap. text ed. 6.95 (ISBN 0-672-97879-2). Bobbs.

Backman, Jules, ed. Economic Growth or Stagnation. LC 78-10874. (ITT Key Issue Lecture Ser.). 1979. text ed. 11.95 (ISBN 0-672-97323-5); pap. text ed. 6.50x (ISBN 0-672-97322-7). Bobbs.

Backmund, jt. auth. see Decker.

Backpacking Journal Editors, jt. auth. see Schreiber, Lee.

Backscheider, P. R., jt. ed. see Borkat, Roberta F.

Backscheider, P. R., jt. ed. see Cohan, Steven.

Backscheider, P. R., jt. ed. see Kenny, Shirley S.

Backscheider, P. R., jt. ed. see Liesenfeld, Vincent J.

Backscheider, P. R., jt. ed. see Rudolph, Valerie C.

Backscheider, P. R., jt. ed. see Steeves, Edna L.

Backscheider, Paula R. The Plays of Elizabeth Inchbald, 2 Vols. LC 78-66648. (Eighteenth Century English Drama Ser.). lib. bdg. 50.00 (ISBN 0-8240-3597-6). Garland Pub.

Backscheider, Paula R., jt. ed. see Malek, James S.

Backsheider, P. R., jt. ed. see Parke, Catherine N.

Backstrom, Charles H. & Hursch-Cesar, Gerald. Survey Research. 2nd ed. LC 81-1738. 436p. 1981. text ed. 15.95x (ISBN 0-471-02543-7). Wiley.

Backus, Charles. The Nan-Chao Kingdom & T'ang China's Southwestern Frontier. LC 81-6138. (Cambridge Studies in Chinese History, Literature & Institutions). (Illus.). 200p. 1982. 37.50 (ISBN 0-521-22733-X). Cambridge U Pr.

Backus, Charles E. Solar Cells. LC 75-46381. (IEEE Press Selected Reprint Ser.). 504p. 1976. 32.95x (ISBN 0-471-01981-X); pap. 19.50 o.p. (ISBN 0-471-01980-1, Pub. by Wiley-Interscience). Wiley.

Backus, Isaac. Isaac Backus on Church, State, & Calvinism: Pamphlets, 1754-1789. McLoughlin, William G., ed. LC 68-14268. (The John Harvard Library). 1968. 25.00x o.p. (ISBN 0-674-46750-7). Harvard U Pr.

Backus, Jean L. Letters From Amelia: An Intimate Portrait of Amelia Earhart. LC 81-68356. (Illus.). 262p. 1983. pap. 9.57 (ISBN 0-8070-6703-2, BP 655). Beacon Pr.

Backus, Jean L., ed. Letters from Amelia: An Intimate Portrait of Amelia Earhart. LC 81-68356. (Illus.). 224p. 1982. 14.37 (ISBN 0-8070-6702-4). Beacon Pr.

Backus, John. Acoustical Foundations of Music. 2nd ed. LC 68-54957. (Illus.). 1978. 17.95x (ISBN 0-393-09096-5, NortonC); wkbk., questions & problems avail. Norton.

Backus, Richard H., jt. auth. see Lineaweaver, Thomas H., 3rd.

Backus, William & Chaplan, Marie. Digase la Verdad. 1983. 3.25 (ISBN 0-88113-049-4). Edit Betania.

Baclawski, K., ed. see Kac, Mark.

Bacmeister, Rhoda. People Downstairs & Other City Stories. (Illus.). (gr. k-3). 1964. PLB 4.97 o.p. (ISBN 0-698-30415-2, Coward). Putnam Pub Group.

Bacon & Boyce. Towns & Cities. rev. ed. (People: Cultures, Times, Places). (gr. 2-4). 1976. text ed. 13.68 (ISBN 0-201-42474-6, Sch Div); tchr's. ed. 19.28 (ISBN 0-201-42475-4). A-W.

Bacon, jt. auth. see Johnston.

Bacon, jt. auth. see Valencia.

Bacon, Banjamin W. Non-Resistance: Christian or Pagan. 1918. pap. text ed. 19.50x (ISBN 0-686-83649-9). Elliots Bks.

Bacon, Benjamin W. Christianity, Old & New. 1914. text ed. 24.50x (ISBN 0-686-83503-4). Elliots Bks.

--The Teaching Ministry for Tomorrow. 1923. 19.50x (ISBN 0-686-51320-7). Elliots Bks.

Bacon, D. H. Engineering Thermodynamics. 1972. text ed. 39.95 (ISBN 0-408-70230-3); pap. text ed. 10.95 (ISBN 0-408-70231-1). Butterworth.

Bacon, David & Maslov, Norman. The Beatles' England: There Are Places I'll Remember. LC 81-82555. (Illus.). 144p. 1982. 20.00 (ISBN 0-9606736-0-1); pap. 12.95 (ISBN 0-9606736-1-X). Nine Hundred-Ten Pr.

Bacon, E. M. Principles of Wheel Alignment Service: A Text-Workbook. 2nd ed. (Illus.). 1977. pap. text ed. 15.75 (ISBN 0-07-002855-9, G); instructor's guide 4.50 (ISBN 0-07-002856-7); instructor's kit 160.00 (ISBN 0-07-079364-6). McGraw.

--Principles of Wheel Alignment Service. 1971. pap. text ed. 7.95 o.p. (ISBN 0-07-002851-6, G). McGraw.

Bacon, Ernst. Notes on the Piano. LC 63-13887. 1963. 12.95x (ISBN 0-8156-0030-5). Syracuse U Pr.

Bacon, Francis. Great Instauration & New Atlantis. Weinberger, J., ed. (Croft Classics Ser.). 1980. text ed. 10.95x (ISBN 0-88295-115-7); pap. text ed. 3.75x (ISBN 0-88295-113-0). Harlan Davidson.

--New Organon & Related Writings. Anderson, Fulton H., ed. LC 60-11682. 1960. pap. 7.95 (ISBN 0-672-60289-X, LLA97). Bobbs.

Bacon, Lenice I. American Patchwork Quilts. (Illus.) 7.98 o.p. (ISBN 0-517-30940-8). Crown.

--American Patchwork Quilts. 190p. 1980. 7.98 (ISBN 0-686-36470-8). Md Hist.

Bacon, Margaret. The Kingdom of the Rose. 530p. 1982. 27.00x o.p. (ISBN 0-86188-117-6, Pub. by Judy Piatkus). State Mutual Bk.

--Quakers & the Struggle for Liberation. 1976. pap. 0.25 (ISBN 0-686-95381-9). Am Fr Serv Comm.

Bacon, Margaret H. I Speak for My Slave Sister: The Life of Abby Kelley Foster. LC 74-4042. (gr. 5-12). 1974. 10.53i (ISBN 0-690-00515-6, TYC-J). Har-Row.

Bacon, Nancy. Bayou Lady. 320p. (Orig.). 1980. pap. 2.25 o.p. (ISBN 0-523-40614-2). Pinnacle Bks.

--Winter Morning. (Love & Life Romance Ser.). 176p. (Orig.). 1982. pap. 1.75 (ISBN 0-345-29760-1). Ballantine.

Bacon, P. Regions Around the World. rev. ed. (People, Cultures, Times, Places). (gr. 1-8). 1976. text ed. 13.68 (ISBN 0-201-42478-9, Sch Div); tchrs ed 19.28 (ISBN 0-201-42479-7). A-W.

Bacon, P. R., ed. see Cooper, St. G.

Bacon, Paul & Hadler, Norton M. Kidney & Rheumatic Disease. (BIMR Rheumatology Ser.: Vol. 1). 498p. 1982. text ed. 39.95 (ISBN 0-407-02352-6). Butterworth.

Bacon, R. L. & Niles, N. R. Medical Histology: A Text-Atlas with Introductory Pathology. (Illus.). 368p. 1983. 34.50 (ISBN 0-387-90734-3). Springer-Verlag.

Bacon, Richard M. The Art & Craft of Wall Stenciling. LC 76-41361. (Funk & W Bk.). 1977. 9.95i o.p. (ISBN 0-308-10274-6). T Y Crowell.

Bacon, Robert & Eltis, Walter. Britain's Economic Problem: Too Few Producers. 2nd ed. LC 78-52386. 1978. 27.50 (ISBN 0-312-09941-X). St Martin.

Bacon, Roy. The Motorcycle Manual. 1977. pap. 12.50 o.s.i. (ISBN 0-408-00260-3). Transatlantic.

Bacon, Stephens. Fluid Mechanics for Tech 3-4. 1983. text ed. 14.95 (ISBN 0-408-01115-7). Butterworth.

Bacon, Susan, jt. auth. see Valencia, Pablo.

Bacon, Theo. D. Leonard Bacon: A Statesman in the Church. 1931. 49.50x (ISBN 0-685-69788-6). Elliots Bks.

Bacou, Roseline & Viatte, Francoise. Italian Renaissance Drawings from the Musee du Louvre. LC 74-12141. (Illus.). 160p. 1974. pap. 2.95 o.s.i. (ISBN 0-87099-094-2). Metro Mus Art.

Bacow, Lawrence S. Bargaining for Job Safety & Health. 208p. 1980. text ed. 20.00x (ISBN 0-262-02152-8). MIT Pr.

Bacq, Z. M. Sulfur Containing Radio-Protective Agents. 344p. 1975. text ed. 100.00 (ISBN 0-08-016298-3). Pergamon.

Baczynsky, Mark. Camera Repair, Restoration & Adaptation. (Illus.). 52p. 1982. pap. 9.95 (ISBN 0-89816-009-X). Embee Pr.

--Creative Projects & Processes. (Illus.). 54p. 1982. pap. 9.95 (ISBN 0-89816-007-3). Embee Pr.

--How to Make a Comfortable Living with Your Computer. 1983. pap. 4.95 (ISBN 0-89816-010-3). Embee Pr.

--Making Custom Cameras & Equipment. (Illus.). 44p. 1982. pap. 9.95 (ISBN 0-89816-008-1). Embee Pr.

--Making Money with Photography. (Illus.). 86p. 1982. pap. 14.95 (ISBN 0-89816-006-5). Embee Pr.

Badalamenti, Rosalyn T., jt. auth. see Klein, Diane.

Badalato, Billy & Richards, Charlie R. Comedy Realm. 140p. (Orig.). (gr. 5-12). 1982. pap. 10.50 (ISBN 0-9609224-0-7). Comedy Writ.

Badauni, M. T. Seerat-un-Nabi: 2 Vols-Shibli Numani. 18.95 ea. (ISBN 0-686-18339-8). Kazi Pubns.

Badawi, G. A. Polygamy in Islamic Law. pap. 1.00 (ISBN 0-686-18440-8). Kazi Pubns.

Badawi, Gamal. The Status of Woman in Islam. Al-Jarrahi, Abdussamad, ed. Bekkari, Muhammad, tr. from English. 20p. (Orig.). 1982. pap. 2.00 (ISBN 0-89259-036-X). Am Trust Pubns.

Badawi, Gamal A. The Status of Woman in Islam: (French Edition) Quinlan, Hamid, ed. LC 82-74127. (Illus.). 28p. 1983. pap. 0.75 (ISBN 0-89259-039-4). Am Trust Pubns.

Badawy, Alexander. Coptic Art & Archaeology: The Art of the Christian Egyptians from the Late Antique to the Middle Ages. 1978. 55.00x (ISBN 0-262-02025-4). MIT Pr.

--The Tomb of Nyhetep-Ptah at Giza & the Tomb of 'Ankhm' Ahor at Saqqara. (Occasional Papers Archaeology Ser.: Vol. 11). 1978. pap. 23.00x (ISBN 0-520-09575-8). U of Cal Pr.

Badayum, T. B. A Short Handbook of Fiqh. pap. 2.95 (ISBN 0-686-63895-6). Kazi Pubns.

Badayuni, T. B. Sirat-un-Nabi, Vol. II. 1981. 18.00 (ISBN 0-686-97877-3). Kazi Pubns.

Badcock, W. & Reynolds, J. A New Touch-Stone for Gold & Silver Wares. 390p. 1970. Repr. of 1679 ed. 10.00x (ISBN 0-7165-0056-6, Pub. by Irish Academic Pr). Biblio Dist.

Baddeley, Allan. Your Memory: A Users Guide. 224p. 1982. 16.95 (ISBN 0-02-504660-8). Macmillan.

Baddeley, W. Hugh. Technique of Documentary Film Production. 4th ed. (Library of Communication Techniques Ser). 1975. 27.95 (ISBN 0-240-50918-8). Focal Pr.

Baddeley, Welbore S. A Cotteswold Manor Being the History of Painswick. 261p. 1980. Repr. of 1929 ed. text ed. 27.00x (ISBN 0-904387-54-2, Pub. by Alan Sutton England). Humanities.

Baddour, Raymond F. & Timmins, Robert S., eds. Application of Plasmas to Chemical Processing. 1967. 25.00x (ISBN 0-262-02027-0). MIT Pr.

Bade, jt. auth. see Blakely.

Bade, William F., ed. see Muir, John.

Baden, Clifford, jt. auth. see Aharoni, Yair.

Baden, John, jt. auth. see Stroup, Richard.

Baden, Marian. Being in God's Family. (Concordia Weekday Ser. - Gr. 3-4. Bk. 4, 2-V). 1967. pap. text ed. 2.55 (ISBN 0-570-06658-1, 22-2028); manual 5.65 (ISBN 0-686-82886-0, 22-2029). Concordia.

Baden, Michael M., jt. auth. see Haberman, Paul W.

Baden, Nancy T., ed. Social Responsibility & Latin America. (Proceedings of the Pacific Coast Council on Latin American Studies: Vol. 8). (Illus.). 190p. (Orig.). 1981. pap. 12.00 (ISBN 0-916304-53-1). Campanile.

Baden, R. Kramer, jt. auth. see Seltzer, M. Seligson.

Baden, Wayne F., et al. Primary Health Care for Obstetricians & Gynecologists. (Illus.). 208p. 1980. lib. bdg. 25.00 (ISBN 0-683-00301-1). Williams & Wilkins.

Baden-Fuller, A. J. Engineering Field Theory. 272p. 1973. text ed. 34.00 o.s.i. (ISBN 0-08-017033-1); pap. text ed. 16.25 (ISBN 0-08-017034-X). Pergamon.

--Microwaves. LC 74-94930. 1969. text ed. 14.30 o.p. (ISBN 0-08-006617-8); pap. text ed. 9.90 o.p. (ISBN 0-08-006616-X). Pergamon.

Bader. Practical Quality Management in the Chemical Process Industry. (Industrial Engineering Ser.). 168p. 1983. price not set (ISBN 0-8247-1903-4). Dekker.

Bader, Iva M., jt. auth. see Morris, Woodrow W.

Bader, Julia. Crystal Land: Patterns of Artifice in Vladimir Nabokov's English Novels. LC 72-182277. 1973. 23.50x o.p. (ISBN 0-520-02167-3). U of Cal Pr.

Bader, Lois A. Reading Diagnosis & Remediation in Classroom & Clinic. (Illus.). 1980. pap. text ed. 14.95 (ISBN 0-02-305100-0). Macmillan.

Bader, Robert S. The Great Kansas Bond Scandal. LC 82-9056. (Illus.). xiv, 398p. 1982. 25.00x (ISBN 0-7006-0223-2). Univ Pr KS.

Bader, William & Burt, Daniel S. Miller Analogies Test. LC 81-152. 160p. 1982. lib. bdg. 10.00 o.p. (ISBN 0-668-04989-8); pap. 5.00 (ISBN 0-668-04990-1). Arco.

Badescu, Mario. Mario Badescu's Skin Care Program for Men. 224p. 1981. 10.95 (ISBN 0-89696-032-3, An Everest House Book). Dodd.

Badger, Carl B. Badger's Illustrated Catalogue of Cast-Iron Architecture. 1982. pap. 8.95 (ISBN 0-486-24223-4). Dover.

Badger, Daniel & Belgrave, Robert. Oil Supply & Price: What Went Right in 1980? (Atlantic Papers Ser.: No. 47). 70p. 1982. pap. text ed. 6.50x (ISBN 0-86598-110-8). Allanheld.

Badger, Geoffrey M. Aromatic Character & Aromaticity. LC 68-29650. (Chemistry Texts Ser). (Illus., Orig.). 1969. 27.50 (ISBN 0-521-07339-1). Cambridge U Pr.

Badger, John. The Arthuriad. 1972. 10.00 (ISBN 0-916988-02-3). Pendragon Hse.

--British Destiny. 1983. pap. 8.00 (ISBN 0-906158-30-3). Pendragon Hse.

Badgley, F. I., et al. Profiles of Wind, Temperature, & Humidity Over the Arabian Sea. LC 70-129539. (International Indian Ocean Expedition Meteorological Monographs: No. 6). (Illus.). 1972. text ed. 15.00x (ISBN 0-8248-0101-6, Eastwest Ctr). UH Pr.

Badia, Leonard F. The Qumran Baptism & John the Baptist's Baptism. LC 80-5438. 97p. 1980. lib. bdg. 15.50 (ISBN 0-8191-1095-7); pap. text ed. 7.25 (ISBN 0-8191-1096-5). U Pr of Amer.

Badian, E. Publicans & Sinners: Private Enterprise in the Service of the Roman Republic, With a Critical Bibliography. (Orig.). 1983. pap. 5.95x (ISBN 0-8014-9241-6). Cornell U Pr.

--Roman Imperialism in the Late Republic. 2nd ed. 1969. 8.50x o.p. (ISBN 0-8014-0024-4); pap. 4.95x (ISBN 0-8014-9109-6, CP109). Cornell U Pr.

Badie, Bertrand. Strategie de la Greve: Pour une Approchefonctionnaliste du Parti Communiste Francais. (Travaux et Recherches Ser.: No. 40). (Fr.). lib. bdg. 27.50x o.p. (ISBN 2-7246-0348-6, Pub by Presses de la Fondation Nationale des Sciences Politiques); pap. text ed. 19.50x o.p. (ISBN 2-7246-0341-9). Clearwater Pub.

Badie, Bertrand & Birnbaum, Pierre. The Sociology of the State: Chicago Original Ser. Goldhammer, Arthur, tr. from Fr. LC 82-20249. 1983. lib. bdg. 24.00x (ISBN 0-226-03548-4); pap. text ed. 10.95x (ISBN 0-226-03549-2). U of Chicago Pr.

Badinter, Elisabeth. Mother Love: Myth & Reality. DeGaris, Roger, tr. (Illus.). 360p. 1981. 13.95 (ISBN 0-02-504610-1). Macmillan.

--Mother Love: Myth & Reality. Gray, Francine, frwd. by. 384p. 1982. pap. 8.95 (ISBN 0-02-048350-3). Macmillan.

Badley, J. H. The Bible for Modern Readers: New Testament. 746p. 1961. 9.00 (ISBN 0-227-67541-X). Attic Pr.

Badmajew, Peter, Jr. & Badmajew, Vladimir, Jr. Healing Herbs: The Heart of Tibetan Medicine. LC 82-81022. (Illus.). 96p. 1982. pap. 2.95 (ISBN 0-943014-00-X, 607). Red Lotus Pr.

Badmajew, Vladimir, Jr., jt. auth. see Badmajew, Peter, Jr.

Badough, Rose M., jt. ed. see Lilley, Dorothy B.

Badovici, Jean, ed. L' Architecture Vivante, 5 vols. LC 75-5874. (Architecture & Decorative Arts Ser.). (Illus.). 885p. 1975. 695.00 set (ISBN 0-306-70540-0). Da Capo.

Badra, Robert. Meditations for Spiritual Misfits. 93p. (Orig.). 1982. pap. 7.95 (ISBN 0-9610274-0-1). JCL Hse.

Badre, Albert & Shneiderman, Ben, eds. Directions in Human-Computer Interaction. 240p. 1982. text ed. 27.50 (ISBN 0-89391-144-5). Ablex Pub.

Badrig, Robert H. Florenz Ziegfeld, Twentieth Century Showman. 1st ed. Rahmas, D. Steve, ed. (Outstanding Personalities Ser.: No. 37). 32p. (Orig.). (gr. 7-12). 1972. lib. bdg. 2.95 incl. catalog cards (ISBN 0-87157-537-X); pap. 1.95 vinyl laminated covers (ISBN 0-87157-037-8). SamHar Pr.

Badskey, Lorin J. Unaccustomed As I Am. 2nd ed. 1974. pap. 7.95 (ISBN 0-686-81687-0). Loru Co.

Badura-Skoda, Eva, ed. Beethoven Remembered: The Biographical Notes of Franz Wegeler & Ferdinand Ries. Noonan, Frederick, tr. (Illus.). 1983. 14.95 (ISBN 0-915556-08-1). Great Ocean.

Badura-Skoda, Eva & Branscombe, Peter, eds. Schubert Studies: Problems of Style & Chronology. LC 81-38528. (Illus.). 350p. 1982. 34.50 (ISBN 0-521-22606-6). Cambridge U Pr.

Badura-Skoda, Paul, ed. see Czerny, Carl.

Badzinski, S. Carpentry in Commercial Construction. 2nd ed. 1980. 16.95 (ISBN 0-13-115220-3). P-H.

Badzinski, S., Jr. Carpentry in Residential Construction. 1981. 17.95 (ISBN 0-13-115238-6). P-H.

Bae, Yoong. Pinwheels. (Illus.). 48p. 1980. pap. 2.50 (ISBN 0-89844-015-7). Troubador Pr.

Baechler, Jean. The Origins of Capitalism. LC 75-21971. 200p. 1976. 18.95 o.p. (ISBN 0-312-58835-6). St Martin.

Baechtold, Marquerite, jt. auth. see McKinney, Eleanor.

Baeck. Studies of the Leo Baeck Institute. Kreutzberger, Max, ed. LC 67-25839. 12.50 (ISBN 0-8044-5047-1). Ungar.

Baedecker. The Baedecker Guide to Germany. (The Baedecker Travel Ser.). 320p. 1981. 19.95 (ISBN 0-13-055848-6); pap. 11.95 (ISBN 0-13-055830-3). P-H.

Baedeker. Baedeker's Caribbean. (Illus.). 250p. 1983. pap. 14.95 (ISBN 0-13-056143-6). P-H.

--Baedeker's Israel. (Baedeker Ser.). (Illus.). 250p. 1983. pap. 12.95 (ISBN 0-13-056176-2). P-H.

--Baedeker's Yugoslavia. (Baedeker). (Illus.). 250p. 1983. pap. 14.95 (ISBN-0-13-056184-3). P-H.

Baedeker, Karl, ed. Baedeker's United States. LC 76-77703. (American Scene Ser.). Orig. Title: The United States with an Excursion into Mexico. (Illus.). 520p. 1971. Repr. of 1893 ed. lib. bdg. 25.00 (ISBN 0-306-71341-1). Da Capo.

Baeder, John. Gas, Food & Lodging: A Postcard Odyssey Through the Great American Roadside. (Illus.). 1981. 19.95 (ISBN 0-89893-502-4); pap. 9.95 (ISBN 0-89893-300-5). CDP.

Baegert, Jacob. The Letters of Jacob Baegert 1749-1761. Schulz-Bischof, Elsbeth, et al, trs. 1982. 36.00 (ISBN 0-686-91821-5). Dawsons.

Baegert, Johann J. Observations in Lower California. Brandenburg, M. M. & Baumann, Carl L., trs. from Ger. (Library Reprint Ser.: No. 100). 1979. Repr. of 1952 ed. 28.50x (ISBN 0-520-03873-8). U of Cal Pr.

Baeher, Helen, ed. Women & Media. LC 80-41424. (Illus.). 150p. 1980. 19.00 (ISBN 0-08-026061-6). Pergamon.

Baehr, Consuelo. Best Friends. 1980. 11.95 o.s.i. (ISBN 0-440-00841-7). Delacorte.

--Nothing to Lose. 224p. 1982. 15.95 (ISBN 0-399-12749-6). Putnam Pub Group.

Baehr, Patricia G. The Dragon Prophecy. LC 80-11597. 128p. (gr. 4-7). 1980. 7.95 o.p. (ISBN 0-7232-6187-3). Warne.

Baehr, Tom. New Tunes-Old Friends. (Illus.). 40p. (Orig.). 1979. music book 4.95 (ISBN 0-9608842-0-3). Hogfiddle Pr.

--A Pleasant Addiction. (Illus.). 48p. (Orig.). 1982. 5.95 (ISBN 0-9608842-1-1). Hogfiddle Pr.

Baelz, Peter. Does God Answer Prayer? (Illus.). 128p. (Orig.). 1983. pap. 6.95 (ISBN 0-87243-117-7). Templegate.

--Ethics & Belief. LC 76-15425. 128p. 1977. pap. 4.95 (ISBN 0-8164-1229-4). Seabury.

Baender, Margaret W. Tail Waggings of Maggie. (Illus.). 64p. (gr. 8-10). 1982. pap. 6.00 (ISBN 0-88100-012-4). Philmar Pub.

Baer, Adela S. Heredity & Society: Readings in Social Genetics. 2nd ed. 352p. 1977. pap. text ed. 14.95x (ISBN 0-02-305160-4, 30516). Macmillan.

Baer, Barbara. Very New Christmas-Make It Book. LC 68-8523. (Illus.). 1968. 4.95 (ISBN 0-8208-0328-6). Hearthside.

Baer, Betty & Federico, Ronald C., eds. Educating the Baccalaureate Social Worker Vol. I: Report of the Undergraduate Social Work Curriculum Development Project. LC 77-16189. 256p. 1978. prof ref 22.50x (ISBN 0-88410-666-7). Ballinger Pub.

Baer, Betty L. & Federico, Ronald C., eds. Educating the Baccalaureate Social Worker: Vol. II: a Curriculum Development Resource Guide. LC 79-11681. 288p. 1979. prof ref 25.00x (ISBN 0-88410-674-8). Ballinger Pub.

Baer, Charles J. Electrical & Electronics Drawing. 3rd ed. 1972. 16.25 o.p. (ISBN 0-07-003008-1, G); solutions manual 2.00 o.p. (ISBN 0-07-003009-X). McGraw.

Baer, Charles J. & Ottaway, John R. Electrical & Electronics Drawing. 4th ed. LC 79-15837. (Illus.). 1980. text ed. 24.95 (ISBN 0-07-003010-3); instr's manual 2.00 (ISBN 0-07-003011-1). McGraw.

Baer, D. Richard. Movie Almanac 1983-84. (Illus.). 360p. 1983. 19.95 (ISBN 0-913616-05-2); lib. bdg. 29.95 (ISBN 0-913616-06-0). Hollywd Film Arch.

Baer, Earl E. Salesmanship. 1972. 18.50 o.p. (ISBN 0-07-003012-X, C); instructor's manual 6.95 o.p. (ISBN 0-07-003013-8). McGraw.

--The Sensitive I: People in Business. LC 74-28164. 512p. 1975. text ed. 7.00x o.p. (ISBN 0-471-04004-5); instructor's manual 3.50 o.p. (ISBN 0-471-04001-0). Wiley.

Baer, Elizabeth, jt. ed. see Fowler, Laurence H.

Baer, Eric, ed. Engineering Design for Plastics. LC 75-1222. 1216p. 1975. Repr. of 1964 ed. 59.50 (ISBN 0-88275-281-2). Krieger.

Baer, Eva. Metalwork in Medieval Islamic Art. LC 81-23243. (Illus.). 490p. 1983. 38.50x (ISBN 0-87395-602-8). State U NY Pr.

Baer, Frank. Max's Gang. 324p. (gr. 7 up). 1983. 15.45i (ISBN 0-316-07517-5). Little.

Baer, George W. Coming of the Italian-Ethiopian War. 1967. 22.50x o.p. (ISBN 0-674-14450-3). Harvard U Pr.

--International Organizations, Nineteen Eighteen to Nineteen Forty-Five: A Guide to Research & Research Materials. Kimmich, Christoph M., ed. LC 80-53893. 261p. 1981. lib. bdg. 17.50 (ISBN 0-8420-2179-5). Scholarly Res Inc.

Baer, Herbert R. Admiralty Law of the Supreme Court. 3rd ed. 1982. 50.00 (ISBN 0-87215-216-2); 1981 supplement 17.50 (ISBN 0-87215-429-7). Michie-Bobbs.

Baer, J., jt. auth. see Fensterheim, H.

Baer, Jean. How to Be an Assertive (Not Aggressive) Woman in Life, in Love, & on the Job. 2.95 o.p. (ISBN 0-686-92342-1, 6459). Hazelden.

Baer, Jean, jt. auth. see Fensterheim, Herbert.

Baer, Jean-Loup. Computer Systems Architecture. LC 72-27039. (Illus.). 1980. text ed. 28.95x (ISBN 0-914894-15-3). Computer Sci.

Baer, Judith A. The Chains of Protection: The Judicial Response to Women's Labor Legislation. LC 77-82695. (Contributions in Women's Studies: No. 1). 1978. lib. bdg. 25.00x (ISBN 0-8371-9785-6, BCP/). Greenwood.

Baer, Larry L. The Parker Gun. 29.95 (ISBN 0-686-43087-5). Gun Room.

Baer, Louis S. Better Health with Fewer Pills. LC 82-8394. 132p. 1982. pap. 5.95 (ISBN 0-664-24425-4). Westminster.

Baer, Max F. & Roeber, Edward C. Occupational Information: The Dynamics of Its Nature & Use. 1977. text ed. 15.93 o.s.i. (ISBN 0-574-50069-3, 5-0069). SRA.

Baer, Melvyn J., et al. The Postnatal Development of the Rat Skull. LC 81-19837. 1983. text ed. 125.00x (ISBN 0-472-10011-4). U of Mich Pr.

Baer, Mervin. The Christian Home. 1976. 1.75 (ISBN 0-686-11147-8). Rod & Staff.

Baer, Mervin J. The Doctrine of Salvation. 1980. 2.90 (ISBN 0-686-30768-2). Rod & Staff.

--El Hogar Cristiano. (Span.). pap. 1.75 (ISBN 0-686-32324-6). Rod & Staff.

Baer, Morley, et al. Painted Ladies: The Art of San Francisco's Victorian Houses. (Illus.). 1978. pap. 11.50 (ISBN 0-525-47523-0, 01117-330). Dutton.

Baer, Phil & Merrifield, William R. Two Studies on the Lacandones of Mexico. (Publications in Linguistics & Related Fields Ser.: No. 33). 272p. 1971. pap. 4.00x o. p. (ISBN 0-88312-035-6); microfiche 3.00 (ISBN 0-88312-435-1). Summer Inst Ling.

Baer, Ruth. Ancient History, Bk. 1. (gr. 7). 1979. 10.95 (ISBN 0-686-30770-4); tchr's ed. avail. 3.85 (ISBN 0-686-30771-2). Rod & Staff.

Baer, Walt. Winning in Labor Arbitration. LC 82-70973. 192p. 1982. 21.95 (ISBN 0-87251-071-9). Crain Bks.

Baer, Walter E. The Operating Manager's Labor Relations Guidebook. 1978. pap. text ed. 9.95 (ISBN 0-8403-1936-3). Kendall Hunt.

Baer, Werner. Industrialization & Economic Development in Brazil. (Economic Growth Center Pubns.). 309p. 1975. 25.50x o.p. (ISBN 0-300-01926-2). Yale U Pr.

Baerends, Gerard, et al, eds. Function & Evolution in Behaviour. (Illus.). 1975. 59.00x (ISBN 0-19-857382-0). Oxford U Pr.

Baerheim-Svendsen, A. Chromatography of Alkaloids, Pt. A. (Journal of Chromatography Library: Vol. 23A). Date not set. 104.25 (ISBN 0-686-43094-8). Elsevier.

Baernreither, Joseph M. English Associations of Working Men. Taylor, A., tr. LC 66-28040. 1966. Repr. of 1889 ed. 40.00x (ISBN 0-8103-3078-4). Gale.

Baert, A. L., jt. auth. see Bulcke, J. A.

Baert, Andre E., jt. ed. see Mednick, Sarnoff A.

Baertschi, A. J. & Dreifus, J. J., eds. Neuroendocrinology of Vasopressin Carticolberin & Optimelanocortins. 1982. 33.00 (ISBN 0-12-072440-5). Acad Pr.

Baerwald, H. H. Japan's Parliament: An Introduction. LC 73-90810. 200p. 1974. 27.95x (ISBN 0-521-20387-2). Cambridge U Pr.

Baes, Charles F., Jr. & Mesmer, Robert E. The Hydrolysis of Cations. LC 75-44393. 496p. 1976. 59.50x (ISBN 0-471-03985-3, Pub. by Wiley-Interscience). Wiley.

Baesemann, Robert, jt. auth. see Braeutigam, Ronald R.

Baez, Tony, et al. Desegregation & Hispanic Students: A Community Perspective. LC 80-80311. 96p. (Orig.). 1980. pap. 5.25 (ISBN 0-89763-023-8). Natl Clearinghse Bilingual Ed.

Bafaro, Johanna, ed. see Freedman, Melvin H. & Silver, Samuel M.

Bagai, Eric, ed. see Los Angeles Unified School District, et al.

Bagai, Eric, ed. see West Linn Unified School District.

Bagai, Judith, ed. see Los Angeles Unified School District, et al.

Bagai, Judith, ed. see West Linn Unified School District.

Bagarozzi, Dennis, et al, eds. Marital & Family Therapy: New Perspectives in Theory, Research & Practice. (Illus.). 128p. 1982. text ed. 16.95x (ISBN 0-89885-069-X). Human Sci Pr.

Bagby, George. The Golden Creep. LC 81-43913. 192p. 1982. 10.95 (ISBN 0-385-18142-6). Doubleday.

--A Question of Quarry. LC 80-1668. (Crime Club Ser.). 192p. 1981. 10.95 o.p. (ISBN 0-385-17294-X). Doubleday.

--The Sitting Duck. LC 81-43251. (Crime Club Ser.). 1981. 10.95 (ISBN 0-385-17802-6). Doubleday.

Bagby, Joseph R. Real Estate Financing Desk Book. 3rd ed. LC 81-170. 454p. 1981. 54.50 (ISBN 0-87624-493-2). Inst Busn Plan.

Bagby, Philip. Culture & History. LC 76-3680. (Illus.). 244p. 1976. Repr. of 1963 ed. lib. bdg. 17.50x (ISBN 0-8371-8797-4, BACH). Greenwood.

Bagby, Wesley M. Contemporary International Problem. 248p. 1983. 19.95 (ISBN 0-88229-774-0); pap. text ed. 9.95 (ISBN 0-88229-775-9). Nelson-Hall.

Bagdikian, Ben H. The Media Monopoly. LC 82-72503. 320p. 1983. 14.18 (ISBN 0-8070-6162-X). Beacon Pr.

Bage, Robert & Paulson, Ronald. Man As He Is, 4 vols. LC 78-60853. (Novel 1720-1805 Ser.: Vol. 12). 1979. Set. 124.00 o.s.i. (ISBN 0-8240-3661-1); lib. bdg. 31.00 ea. o.s.i. Garland Pub.

Bagehot, Walter. Economic Studies. 2nd ed. Hutton, Richard H., ed. LC 68-55465. Repr. of 1898 ed. 25.00x (ISBN 0-678-00852-3). Kelley.

--English Constitution. (World's Classics Ser.). 1968. 12.95 (ISBN 0-19-250330-8). Oxford U Pr.

Bagelon, Bruce S. Defending the Commonwealth: Catalogue of the Militia Exhibit at the Will Penn Memorial Museum in Harrisburg, PA. (Illus.). 28p. 1980. pap. 4.00 (ISBN 0-917218-14-0). Mowbray Co.

Bagenal, Philip H. The American Irish & Their Influence on Irish Politics. LC 74-145469. (The American Immigration Library). viii, 252p. 1971. Repr. of 1882 ed. lib. bdg. 14.95x (ISBN 0-89198-001-6). Ozer.

Bagenal, T. B. Ageing of Fish. 240p. 1982. 40.00 (ISBN 0-686-84445-9, Pub. by Gresham England). State Mutual Bk.

Bagg, Alan. Fifty Short Climbs in the Midwest. LC 77-91194. 1978. 9.95 o.p. (ISBN 0-8092-7668-2); pap. 6.95 o.p. (ISBN 0-8092-7667-4). Contemp Bks.

Bagg, Elma W. Cooking Without a Grain of Salt. LC 64-13870. 1964. 10.95 (ISBN 0-385-05432-7). Doubleday.

Bagg, Lyman H. Ten Thousand Miles on a Bicycle. rev. ed. 911p. 1982. 20.00x (ISBN 0-9610060-0-5). E Rosenblatt.

Bagg, Robert, tr. see Sophocles.

Baggaley, Andrew R. Mathematics for Introductory Statistics: A Programmed Review. 203p. 1969. pap. 15.95x (ISBN 0-471-04008-8). Wiley.

Bagge, U. & Born, G. V. White Blood Cells. 1982. 34.50 (ISBN 90-247-2681-6, Pub. by Martinus Nijhoff Netherlands). Kluwer Boston.

Bagger, Jonathan, jt. auth. see Wess, Julius.

Baggeroer, Arthur. State Variables & Communication Theory. 1970. 22.50x (ISBN 0-262-02060-2). MIT Pr.

Baggett, Glick. Dollhouse Kit & Dining Room Accessories. 30p. pap. 1.95 (ISBN 0-87588-150-5). Hobby Hse.

--Dollhouse Lamps & Chandeliers. 30p. pap. 1.95 (ISBN 0-87588-149-1). Hobby Hse.

Baggett, Richard C. Programmed Approach to Good Spelling! 160p. 1981. pap. text ed. 9.95 (ISBN 0-13-729764-5). P-H.

Baggish, Michael S. Atlas Hysteroscopy: Contact & Conventional. 1982. cancelled (ISBN 0-8067-0281-8). Urban & S.

Baghio'o, Jean-Louis. The Blue-Flowered Tree. Romer, Stephen, tr. from Fr. 192p. 1983. Repr. of 1973 ed. text ed. 14.75x (ISBN 0-85635-470-8, Pub. by Carcanet New Pr England). Humanities.

Baglee, Chris & Morley, Andrew. Enamelled Street Signs. LC 78-74585. (Illus.). 1979. pap. 7.95 (ISBN 0-89696-055-2, An Everest House Book). Dodd.

--Street Signs. 1979. pap. cancelled (ISBN 0-8256-3151-3, Quick Fox). Putnam Pub Group.

Bagley, Christopher. Child Welfare & Adoption: International Perspectives. LC 82-16873. 208p. 1982. 26.00x (ISBN 0-312-13232-8). St Martin.

Bagley, Christopher, jt. ed. see Verma, Gajendra K.

Bagley, Desmond. Flyaway. LC 78-22226. 1979. 12.95 o.p. (ISBN 0-385-14911-5). Doubleday.

--Windfall. 320p. 1982. 14.95 (ISBN 0-671-43454-3). Summit Bks.

Bagley, F. R., ed. see Chubak, Sadeq.

Bagley, F. R., tr. see Ghazali.

Bagley, Helen G. Sand in My Shoe: Homestead Days in Twentynine Palms. 2nd ed. Weight, Harold & Weight, Lucile, eds. LC 77-94990. (Illus.). 269p. 1980. Repr. of 1978 ed. 11.95 (ISBN 0-912714-08-5). Homestead Pub.

Bagley, J. J. Historical Interpretation. Incl. Vol. 1. Sources of English Medieval History, 1066-1540. 285p (ISBN 0-312-38045-3); Vol. 2. Sources of English History, 1540 to Present Day. 296p (ISBN 0-312-38080-1). LC 72-85263. (Illus.). 1973. 10.00x ea. o.p. St Martin.

Bagley, Peter. Making Silver Jewellery. (Illus.). 144p. 1983. 29.95 (ISBN 0-7134-2580-6, Pub. by Batsford England). David & Charles.

Bagley, Vicky & Cohen, Rona. Dining In: Washington, D. C. (Dining in Ser.). (Orig.). 1982. pap. 8.95 (ISBN 0-89716-038-X). Peanut Butter.

Bagnal, K. Actinide Elements. 1979. 39.00 (ISBN 0-444-41041-4). Elsevier.

Bagnall, Jim, jt. auth. see Koberg, Don.

Bagnall, Nicholas, ed. New Movements in the Study & Teaching of English. 1977. 12.00 o.s.i. (ISBN 0-85117-044-7). Transatlantic.

--Parent Power: A Dictionary Guide to Your Child's Education & Schooling. 146p. 1974. 8.95 o.p. (ISBN 0-7100-7944-3). Routledge & Kegan.

Bagnall, Oscar. Origin & Properties of the Human Aura. LC 74-84848. 1981. 3.50 (ISBN 0-87728-284-6). Weiser.

Bagnall, Roger, ed. Research Tools for the Classics. LC 80-25766. (APA Pamphlets). 1980. pap. 7.50 (ISBN 0-89130-452-5, 40-06-06). Scholars Pr CA.

Bagnold, Enid. Loved & Envied. LC 75-110820. Repr. of 1951 ed. lib. bdg. 15.75x (ISBN 0-8371-2700-9, BALE). Greenwood.

--National Velvet. (gr. 7-9). 1971. pap. 2.50 (ISBN 0-671-46528-7). Archway.

--National Velvet. (Illus.). (gr. 7 up). 1949. Repr. of 1935 ed. 11.25 (ISBN 0-688-21422-3); PLB 10.80 (ISBN 0-688-31422-8). Morrow.

Bagnold, R. A. Physics of Blown Sand & Sand Dunes. 1971. 38.00x (ISBN 0-412-10270-6, Pub. by Chapman & Hall). Methuen Inc.

Bagnole, John W. Cultures of the Islamic Middle East. (America-Mideast Educational & Training Servies, Inc. - Occasional Paper: No. 4). 86p. (Orig.). 1978. pap. text ed. 4.00 o.p. (ISBN 0-89192-296-2). Interbk Inc.

Bagozzi, Richard P. Casual Models in Marketing. LC 79-11622. (Theories in Marketing Ser.). 303p. 1980. text ed. 30.50 (ISBN 0-471-01516-4). Wiley.

Bagshaw, C. R. Muscle Contraction. 1982. pap. 6.50x (ISBN 0-412-13450-0, Pub. by Chapman & Hall). Methuen Inc.

Bagshaw, Norman E. Batteries on Ships. (Battery Applications Bk.). 215p. 1983. write for info. (ISBN 0-471-90021-4). Res Stud Pr.

Bagshaw, T. W. Worked Examples in Relative Radar Plotting. 1981. 25.00x (ISBN 0-85174-330-7, Pub. by Brown, Son & Ferguson). State Mutual Bk.

Bagshawe, L. E., tr. The Maniyadanabon of Shin Sandalinka. 152p. 1981. 7.00 (ISBN 0-87727-115-1). Cornell SE Asia.

Bagwell, Beth. Oakland: The Story of a City. (Illus.). 288p. 1982. 16.95 (ISBN 0-89141-146-1). Presidio Pr.

Bagwell, Elizabeth, jt. auth. see Meeks, Esther.

Bahadur, K. P., tr. Rasikapriya of Keshavadasa. 1972. 12.50 (ISBN 0-89684-303-3). Orient Bk Dist.

Bahadur, R. R. Some Limit Theorems in Statistics. (CBMS-NSF Regional Conference Ser.: No. 4). v, 42p. 1971. pap. 7.00 (ISBN 0-89871-175-4). Soc Indus-Appl Math.

Bahadur Singh, I., ed. Inidans in Southeast Asia. 232p. 1982. 34.95 (ISBN 0-940500-53-1, Pub. by Sterling India). Asia Bk Corp.

Bahar, Mehrdad. Bastoor. new & rev. ed. Jabbari, Ahmad, ed. Alyeshmreni, Mansoor, tr. from Persian. (Illus.). 24p. (Orig.). (gr. 1 up). 1983. pap. 6.95 (ISBN 0-939214-17-2). Mazda Pubs.

Bahathy, Bela H. Developing a System View of Education. (Systems Inquiry Ser.). 92p. (Orig.). 1980. pap. text ed. 7.95 (ISBN 0-686-36600-X). Intersystems Pubns.

Bahau'lah & Abdu'l-Baha. Ayyam-i Tis'ih (The Nine Days) 580p. (Persian & Arabic.). 1981. Repr. of 1946 ed. 12.95 (ISBN 0-933770-24-3). Kalimat.

Baha'u'llah. The Seven Valleys & the Four Valleys. 3rd rev. ed. Gail, Marzieh, tr. LC 77-23326. 1978. 5.95 (ISBN 0-87743-113-2, 103-015); pap. 2.95 o.s. (ISBN 0-87743-114-0, 103-016). Baha'i.

Baha'u'llah, The Bab & Abdu'l-Baha. Baha'i Prayers: A Selection of Prayers Revealed by Baha'u'llah, the Bab & Abdu'l-Baha. LC 82-11502. 1982. 8.95 (ISBN 0-87743-175-2, 115-070); pap. 5.00 (ISBN 0-87743-176-0, 315-072). Baha'i.

Baheri, Antti, et al, eds. Fibroblast Surface Protein. (Annals of the New York Academy of Sciences: Vol. 312). 456p. 1978. pap. 54.00x (ISBN 0-89072-068-1). NY Acad Sci.

Bahill, A. Terry. Bioengineering: Biomedical, Medical, & Clinical Engineering. (Illus.). 336p. 1981. text ed. 31.00 (ISBN 0-13-076380-2). P-H.

Bahl, Roy W. The Taxation of Urban Property in Less Developed Countries. LC 78-65018. (Illus.). 298p. 1979. 25.00 (ISBN 0-299-07860-4). U of Wis Pr.

Bahl, Roy W. & Vogt, Walter. Fiscal Centralization & Tax Burdens: State and Regional Finance of City Services. LC 75-31649. 192p. 1976. prof ref 25.00x (ISBN 0-88410-423-0). Ballinger Pub.

Bahl, Roy W. & Burkhead, Jesse, eds. Public Employment & State & Local Government Finance. 256p. 1980. prof ref 30.00x (ISBN 0-88410-683-7). Ballinger Pub.

Bahlman, Dudley W., ed. see Hamilton, Edward W.

Bahm, Archie J. Ethics as a Behavioral Science. 216p. 1974. 17.25x (ISBN 0-398-03043-X); pap. 12.50x (ISBN 0-398-03044-8). C C Thomas.

--The Philosopher's World Model. LC 78-67569. (Contributions in Philosophy: No. 12). (Illus.). 1979. lib. bdg. 29.95x (ISBN 0-313-21198-1, BPW/). Greenwood.

--The Philosophy of the Buddha. 175p. 1982. text ed. 18.95x (ISBN 0-7069-2017-1, Pub. by Vikas India). Advent NY.

Bahn, G. S. High Temperature Systems, Vol. II. 360p. 1969. 89.00x (ISBN 0-677-12960-2). Gordon.

Bahn, Gilbert S., ed. see Conference on High-Temperature Systems, 3rd.

Bahne, Siegfried. Archives de Jules Humbert-Droz: Nineteen Twenty-Three to Nineteen Twenty-Seven, Vol. II. 1983. 120.00 (ISBN 90-277-1241-7, Pub. by Reidel Holland). Kluwer Boston.

Bahoken, J. C. & Atangana, Englebert. Cultural Policy in the United Republic of Cameroon. (Studies & Documents on Cultural Policies). (Illus.). 91p. 1976. pap. 5.00 (ISBN 92-3-101316-5, U143, UNESCO). Unipub.

Bahr, A. J. & McGonnagle, Warren J. Microwave Nondestructive Testing Methods. (Nondestructive Monographs: Vol. 1). Date not set. price not set. Gordon.

Bahr, Alice H. Automated Library Circulation Systems, 1979-1980. LC 79-16189. (Professional Librarian Ser.). (Illus.). 1979. pap. text ed. 24.50x softcover (ISBN 0-914236-34-2). Knowledge Indus.

--Book Theft & Library Security Systems: 1981-82. 2nd ed. LC 77-25284. (Illus.). 156p. 1980. pap. text ed. 27.50 (ISBN 0-914236-71-7). Knowledge Indus.

Bahr, Amy, ed. see Nichols, Faith.

Bahr, Ehrhard & Kunzer, Ruth G. Georg Lukacs. LC 70-190350. (Literature and Life Ser.). 1972. 11.95 (ISBN 0-8044-2014-9). Ungar.

Bahr, Gisela, ed. see International Brecht Society.

Bahr, Gunter F., jt. auth. see Wied, George.

Bahr, Howard M. Skid Row: An Introduction to Disaffiliation. (Illus.). 1973. pap. text ed. 8.95x (ISBN 0-19-501712-9). Oxford U Pr.

Bahr, Howard M., jt. auth. see Harvey, Carol D.

Bahr, Howard M., et al. Life in Large Families: Views of Mormon Women. LC 82-45005. 264p. (Orig.). 1982. lib. bdg. 23.25 (ISBN 0-8191-2551-2); pap. text ed. 11.50 (ISBN 0-8191-2552-0). U Pr of Amer.

Bahr, Jerome. The Lonely Scoundrel: A Supplement to the Perishing Republic. LC 73-80240. 89p. 1974. 8.00 o.p. (ISBN 0-686-63592-2). Trempealeau.

Bahr, Robert. The Blizzard. LC 80-14956. 1980. 9.95 o.p. (ISBN 0-13-077842-7). P-H.

--Virility Factor: Masculinity Through Testosterone, the Male Sex Hormone. 1976. 8.95 o.p. (ISBN 0-399-11808-X). Putnam Pub Group.

Bahr, Stephen J., ed. Economics & the Family. LC 79-47985. 208p. 1980. 22.95x (ISBN 0-669-03623-4). Lexington Bks.

Bahre, Conrad J. Destruction of the Natural Vegetation of North-Central Chile. LC 78-50836. (Publications in Geography Ser.: Vol. 23). 1979. 14.50x (ISBN 0-520-09594-4). U of Cal Pr.

Bahri, Vijal S. Introductory Course in Spoken Punjabi. (Ser. in Indian Languages & Linguistics). 1977. 15.95 o.p. (ISBN 0-89684-254-1, Pub. by Bahri Pubns India); pap. 5.00 o.s.i. (ISBN 0-89684-255-X). Orient Bk Dist.

Bahri, Vijal S. & Jagannathan, V. R. Introductory Course in Spoken Hindi. (India Languages & Linguistics Ser.). 280p. 1978. 15.95 o.p. (ISBN 0-89684-252-5, Pub. by Bahri Pubns India); pap. text ed. 7.00 o.s.i. (ISBN 0-89684-253-3). Orient Bk Dist.

Bahro, Rudolf. Socialism & Survival. 160p. (Orig.). 1982. 13.00 (ISBN 0-946097-02-X); pap. 6.50 (ISBN 0-946097-00-3). Heretic Bks.

Bahti, Tom. Southwest Indian Arts & Crafts. 1977. pap. 2.00 (ISBN 0-686-95836-5). Jefferson Natl.

--Southwest Indian Ceremonials. 1970. pap. 3.00 (ISBN 0-686-95839-X). Jefferson Natl.

Baiardi, John C. & Ruggieri, George D., eds. Aquatic Sciences. (Annals of the New York Academy of Sciences: Vol. 245). 70p. 1974. 17.00x (ISBN 0-89072-759-7). NY Acad Sci.

Baides, J., jt. auth. see Porter, Q. N.

Baier, Lesley K. & Shestack, Alan. The Katherine Ordway Collection, Yale University Art Gallery. (Illus.). 128p. 1983. pap. write for info. (ISBN 0-89467-025-5). Yale Art Gallery.

Baierlein, Ralph. Newtonian Dynamics. (Illus.). 384p. 1983. text ed. 29.90 (ISBN 0-07-003016-2, C); instructor's manual 16.00 (ISBN 0-07-003017-0). McGraw.

Baigell, Matthew. Dictionary of American Art. 390p. 1979. 17.95i (ISBN 0-06-433254-3, Icon Edns); pap. 8.95i (ISBN 0-06-430078-1, IN 78, Icon Edns). Har-Row.

Baigent, Michael, et al. Holy Blood, Holy Grail. 1983. pap. 3.95 (ISBN 0-440-13648-2). Dell.

Baijal, Mahendra D., ed. Plastic Polymers Science & Technology. LC 31-13066. (Society of Plastic Engineers Monographs). 992p. 1982. 150.00x (ISBN 0-471-04044-4, Pub. by Wiley-Interscience). Wiley.

Baijal, S. K. Flow Behavior of Polymers in Porous Media. 116p. 1982. 29.95x (ISBN 0-87814-188-X). Pennwell Books Division.

Baikie, A. G., jt. ed. see Gunz, Frederick W.

Baikow, V. E. Manufacture & Refining of Raw Cane Sugar. 2nd ed. (Sugar Ser.: Vol. 2). 1982. 159.75 (ISBN 0-444-41896-2). Elsevier.

Bailar, John C., et al. Chemistry. 940p. 1978. 24.00 (ISBN 0-12-072850-8); instr's. manual 2.50 (ISBN 0-12-072852-4); study guide 8.00 (ISBN 0-12-072854-0); solution manual 5.00 (ISBN 0-12-072853-2). Acad Pr.

Bailard, Thomas E. & Biehl, David L. Personal Money Management. 4th ed. 640p. 1983. text ed. write for info. (ISBN 0-574-19525-4, 13-2525); write for info. instr's guide (ISBN 0-574-19526-2, 13-2526); write for info. study guide (ISBN 0-574-19527-0, 13-2527). SRA.

Bailard, Thomas E., et al. Personal Money Management. 3rd ed. 1979. text ed. 19.95 (ISBN 0-574-19395-2, 13-2395); instr's guide avail. (ISBN 0-574-19396-0, 13-2396); study guide 7.95 (ISBN 0-574-19397-9, 13-2397). SRA.

Bailey. Analysis with Ion-Selective Electrodes. 2nd ed. 29.95 (ISBN 0-471-25590-4, Pub. by Wiley Heyden). Wiley.

--Prisoners of War. LC 81-9403. (World War II Ser.). PLB 19.92 (ISBN 0-8094-3392-3). Silver.

Bailey, jt. auth. see Draper.

Bailey, Adrian. Cooking of the British Isles. LC 69-19833. (Foods of the World Ser.). (Illus.). (gr. 6 up). 1969. PLB 17.28 (ISBN 0-8094-0065-0, Pub. by Time-Life). Silver.

--Walt Disney's World of Fantasy. (Illus.). 256p. 1982. 35.00 o.p. (ISBN 0-686-30957-X, An Everest House Book). Dodd.

--Walt Disney's World of Fantasy. Ridgeway, Julie & Ridgeway, Steve, eds. LC 82-1547. (Illus.). 252p. 1982. 35.00 (ISBN 0-89696-117-6, An Everest House Book). Dodd.

Bailey, Adrian, ed. Mrs. Bridges' Upstairs Downstairs Cookery Book. LC 74-32163. (Illus.). 192p. 1975. 9.95 o.p. (ISBN 0-671-22029-2); pap. 3.95 o.s.i. (ISBN 0-671-22030-6). S&S.

Bailey, Alice A. A Compilation on Sex. 160p. (Orig.). pap. 5.50 (ISBN 0-85330-136-0). Lucis.

--Consciousness of the Atom. 1972. 11.00 (ISBN 0-85330-001-1); pap. 5.00 (ISBN 0-85330-101-8). Lucis.

--The Destiny of the Nations. 1968. 11.00 (ISBN 0-85330-002-X); pap. 5.00 (ISBN 0-85330-102-6). Lucis.

--Discipleship in the New Age, 2 Vols. Vol. 1, 1971. 13.50 (ISBN 0-85330-003-8); Vol. 2, 1968. 22.00 (ISBN 0-85330-004-6); Vol. 1. pap. 10.50 (ISBN 0-85330-103-4); Vol. 2. pap. 10.50 (ISBN 0-85330-104-2). Lucis.

--Education in the New Age. 1971. 11.00 (ISBN 0-85330-005-4); pap. 5.00 (ISBN 0-85330-105-0). Lucis.

--The Externalisation of the Hierarchy. 1968. 26.00 (ISBN 0-85330-006-2); pap. 10.50 (ISBN 0-85330-106-9). Lucis.

--From Intellect to Intuition. 1972. 7.50 (ISBN 0-85330-008-9); pap. 5.00 (ISBN 0-85330-108-5). Lucis.

--Glamour: A World Problem. 1973. 11.00 (ISBN 0-85330-009-7); pap. 5.00 (ISBN 0-85330-109-3). Lucis.

--Initiation, Human & Solar. 1977. 11.25 (ISBN 0-85330-010-0); pap. 5.00 (ISBN 0-85330-110-7). Lucis.

--Letters on Occult Meditation. 1973. 11.25 (ISBN 0-85330-011-9); pap. 5.50 (ISBN 0-85330-111-5). Lucis.

--The Light of the Soul. 1972. 12.50 (ISBN 0-85330-012-7); pap. 5.75 (ISBN 0-85330-112-3). Lucis.

--Ponder on This: A Compilation. 432p. 1980. pap. 7.00 (ISBN 0-85330-131-X). Lucis.

--Problems of Humanity. 1972. pap. 5.00 (ISBN 0-85330-113-1). Lucis.

--The Reappearance of the Christ. 1978. 12.00 (ISBN 0-85330-014-3); pap. 5.00 (ISBN 0-85330-114-X). Lucis.

--Serving Humanity: A Compilation. 1977. pap. 7.00 (ISBN 0-85330-133-6). Lucis.

--The Soul & Its Mechanism. 1971. 11.00 (ISBN 0-85330-015-1); pap. 5.00 (ISBN 0-85330-115-8). Lucis.

--The Soul, the Quality of Life. 1979. pap. 7.00 (ISBN 0-85330-132-8). Lucis.

--Telepathy & the Etheric Vehicle. 1971. 11.00 (ISBN 0-85330-016-X); pap. 5.00 (ISBN 0-85330-116-6). Lucis.

--Treatise on Cosmic Fire. 1973. 28.00 (ISBN 0-85330-017-8); pap. 15.00 (ISBN 0-85330-117-4). Lucis.

--A Treatise on the Seven Rays, 5 vols. Incl. Vol. 1. Esoteric Psychology. 1979. 17.00 (ISBN 0-85330-018-6); pap. 6.00 (ISBN 0-85330-118-2); Vol. 2. Esoteric Psychology. 1970. 26.00 (ISBN 0-85330-019-4); pap. 10.50 (ISBN 0-85330-119-0); Vol. 3. Esoteric Astrology. 1975. 26.00 (ISBN 0-85330-020-8); pap. 10.50 (ISBN 0-85330-120-4); Vol. 4. Esoteric Healing. 1978. 26.00 (ISBN 0-85330-021-6); pap. 10.50 (ISBN 0-85330-121-2); Vol. 5. The Rays & the Initiations. 1970. 26.00 (ISBN 0-85330-022-4); pap. 10.50 (ISBN 0-85330-122-0). Lucis.

--Treatise on White Magic. 1979. 26.00 (ISBN 0-85330-023-2); pap. 10.50 (ISBN 0-85330-123-9). Lucis.

--Unfinished Autobiography. 1970. 11.00 (ISBN 0-85330-024-0); pap. 7.50 (ISBN 0-85330-124-7). Lucis.

Bailey, Alison, tr. see Zhou Erfu.

Bailey, Andrew D., Jr. Statistical Auditing: Review, Concepts & Problems. 308p. 1981. pap. text ed. 13.95 o.p. (ISBN 0-15-583758-3, HC); solutions manual 5.95 o.p. (ISBN 0-15-583759-1). HarBraceJ.

Bailey, Anita, ed. see Tozer, Aiden W.

Bailey, Arthur W., jt. auth. see Wright, Henry A.

Bailey, Barbara R. Main Street, Northeastern Oregon: The Founding & Development of Small Towns. LC 80-84483. (Illus.). 240p. 1982. 12.95 (ISBN 0-87595-105-8, Western Imprints); pap. 7.95 (ISBN 0-87595-073-6, Western Imprints). Oreg Hist Soc.

Bailey, C. J. Nineteenth Century German Drawings from the Ashmolean. 55.00x (ISBN 0-900090-96-0, Pub. by Ashmolean Mus Oxford). State Mutual Bk.

Bailey, Carolyn S. Stories for Every Holiday. LC 73-20149. 277p. 1974. Repr. of 1918 ed. 44.00x (ISBN 0-8103-3957-9). Gale.

Bailey, Carolyn S. & Lewis, Clara M. For the Children's Hour. LC 73-20186. (Illus.). 336p. 1974. Repr. of 1920 ed. 44.00x (ISBN 0-8103-3958-7). Gale.

Bailey, Charles-James N. On the Yin & Yang Nature of Language. viii, 120p. 1982. pap. 10.95 (ISBN 0-89720-060-8). Karoma.

Bailey, Chris H., ed. Illustrated Catalogue of Seth Thomas Clocks, Regulators & Time Pieces, 1863. 1973. 5.00 (ISBN 0-913602-07-8). K Roberts.

Bailey, Conner. Broker, Mediator, Patron, & Kinsman: An Historical Analysis of Key Leadership Roles in a Rural Malaysian District. LC 75-620141. (Papers in International Studies: Southeast Asia: No. 38). (Illus.). 1976. pap. 7.00 (ISBN 0-89680-024-5, Ohio U Ctr Intl). Ohio U Pr.

Bailey, Covert. Fit or Fat. 1978. 6.95 o.s.i. (ISBN 0-395-27161-4); pap. 4.75 (ISBN 0-395-27162-2). HM.

Bailey, Cyril. Greek Atomists & Epicurus: A Study. LC 64-11844. 1964. Repr. of 1928 ed. 18.00x o.p. (ISBN 0-8462-0427-4). Russell.

Bailey, D. L. & Clayton, P. The Measurement of Suspended Particulate & Carbon Concentrations in the Atmosphere Using Standard Smoke Shade Methods, 1980. 1982. 45.00x (ISBN 0-686-97112-4, Pub. by W Spring England). State Mutual Bk.

Bailey, D. R., ed. see Cicero.

Bailey, Dan E. WW II Wrecks of the Kwajalein & Truk Lagoons. LC 82-63006. (Illus.). 152p. 1983. pap. text ed. 15.95 (ISBN 0-911615-00-8). North Valley.

Bailey, David. How to Take Better Pictures. (Illus.). 212p. 1983. 29.50 (ISBN 0-937950-03-3). Xavier-Moreau.

Bailey, David, ed. Productivity Measurement: An International Review of Concepts, Techniques, Programs & Current Issues. Hubert, Tony. 284p. 1981. text ed. 44.50x (ISBN 0-566-02230-3). Gower Pub Ltd.

Bailey, David H. & Gottlieb, Louise. Rotary Basic Library, 7 vols. White, Willmon L. & Perlberg, Mark, eds. (Illus.). 506p. 1982. 14.50 (ISBN 0-915062-08-9). Rotary Intl.

Bailey, Derek. Musical Improvisation. 154p. 1983. 14.95 (ISBN 0-686-82656-6); pap. 6.95 (ISBN 0-686-82657-4). P-H.

Bailey, F. G. Stratagems & Spoils: A Social Anthropology of Politics. LC 70-75221. (Pavilion Social Anthropology Ser.). 1973. 10.00x o.p. (ISBN 0-8052-3254-0). Schocken.

Bailey, F. G., ed. Gifts & Poison: The Politics of Reputation. LC 78-151824. (Pavilion Social Anthropology Ser.). 1971. 9.50x o.p. (ISBN 0-8052-3409-8). Schocken.

Bailey, F. Lee. The Defense Never Rests. pap. 2.50 (ISBN 0-451-09236-8, E9236, Sig). NAL.

--How to Protect Yourself Against Cops In California & Other Strange Places. LC 82-48516. 96p. 1983. 9.95 (ISBN 0-8128-2891-7). Stein & Day.

Bailey, F. Lee & Greenya, John. Cleared for the Approach: In Defense of Flying. 1978. pap. 2.50 o.p. (ISBN 0-451-08286-9, E8286, Sig). NAL.

Bailey, Faith C. Adoniram Judson. (Golden Oldies Ser.). 128p. 1980. pap. 2.95 (ISBN 0-8024-0287-9). Moody.

--D. L. Moody. (Golden Oldies Ser.). 1959. pap. 3.95 (ISBN 0-8024-0039-6). Moody.

Bailey, Foster. Reflections. 1979. pap. 5.00 (ISBN 0-85330-134-4). Lucis.

--Running God's Plan. 190p. (Orig.). 1972. pap. 5.00 (ISBN 0-85330-128-X). Lucis.

--The Spirit of Masonry. rev. ed. 143p. 1979. pap. 5.00 (ISBN 0-85330-135-2). Lucis.

--Things to Come. 264p. (Orig.). 1974. pap. 5.00 (ISBN 0-85330-129-8). Lucis.

Bailey, Frank. Small Boat Design for Beginners. (Illus.). 88p. (Orig.). 1980. pap. 6.75 o.p. (ISBN 0-589-50203-4, Pub. by Reed Bks Australia). C E Tuttle.

Bailey, Frank A. Basic Mathematics. 1977. pap. 13.50x (ISBN 0-673-15064-X). Scott F.

--Basic Mathematics for Automotive Technology. 1977. pap. 8.95x (ISBN 0-673-15065-8). Scott F.

--Basic Mathematics for Electricity & Electronics. 1977. pap. 8.95x (ISBN 0-673-15067-4). Scott F.

Bailey, G. M. Studies in the Mythology of Brahma. 1982. 24.95x (ISBN 0-19-561411-9). Oxford U Pr.

Bailey, Geoffrey, jt. auth. see Landau, Suzanne.

Bailey, George, ed. Kontinent Four: Contemporary Russian Writers. 528p. 1982. pap. 4.95 (ISBN 0-380-81182-0, 81182, Bard). Avon.

Bailey, George W., jt. ed. see Schaller, Frank W.

Bailey, Glen. An Analysis of the Ethiopian Revolution. LC 80-13961. (Papers in International Studies, Africa Ser.: No. 40). 150p. (Orig.). 1980. pap. 12.00 (ISBN 0-89680-104-7, Ohio U Ctr Intl). Ohio U Pr.

Bailey, Harold W. Culture of the Sakas in Ancient Iranian Khotan. LC 82-1236. (Columbia Lectures on Iranian Studies). 1983. 25.00x (ISBN 0-88206-053-8). Caravan Bks.

Bailey, Harry A., ed. Classics of the American Presidency. LC 80-61. (Classics Ser.). (Orig.). 1980. pap. 12.50x (ISBN 0-935610-10-3). Moore Pub IL.

Bailey, Helen M. & Nasatir, Abraham P. Latin America: The Development of Its Civilization. 3rd ed. (Illus.). 896p. 1973. ref. ed. 24.95 (ISBN 0-13-524264-9). P-H.

Bailey, Henry T. & Pool, Ethel. Symbolism for Artists. LC 68-18018. (Illus.). 239p. 1973. Repr. of 1925 ed. 27.00 o.p. (ISBN 0-8103-3870-X). Gale.

Bailey, Herbert. Vitamin E: Your Key to a Healthy Heart. LC 64-23349. (Orig.). 1968. pap. 1.65 o.p. (ISBN 0-668-01514-4). Arco.

--Vitamin Pioneers. 1970. pap. 0.95 o.s.i. (ISBN 0-515-02239-X). Jove Pubns.

Bailey, J. C. & Bedborough, D. R. Tests on the Efficiency of Odour Removal of a Pilot-Scale Boiler Incinerator at an Activated Carbon Plant, 1979. 1981. 40.00x (ISBN 0-686-97145-0, Pub. by W Spring England). State Mutual Bk.

Bailey, J. C. & Viney, N. J. Analysis of Odours by Gas Chromatography & Allied Techniques, 1979. 1981. 75.00x (ISBN 0-686-97023-3, Pub. by W Spring England). State Mutual Bk.

Bailey, J. O. Thomas Hardy & the Cosmic Mind: A New Reading of "the Dynasts". LC 77-24118. 1977. Repr. of 1956 ed. lib. bdg. 20.00x (ISBN 0-8371-9743-0, BATH). Greenwood.

Bailey, J. O., jt. ed. see Brown, Edward K.

Bailey, Jack. The British Co-Operative Movement. LC 73-19302. (Illus.). 178p. 1974. Repr. of 1955 ed. lib. bdg. 17.75x (ISBN 0-8371-7116-4, BABC). Greenwood.

Bailey, James. Sermons from the Parables. 128p. (Orig.). 1981. pap. 2.95 (ISBN 0-8341-0730-9). Beacon Hill.

Bailey, James & Ollis, David F. Biochemical Engineering Fundamentals. (McGraw-Hill Chemical Engineering Ser.). (Illus.). 1977. text ed. 39.95 (ISBN 0-07-003210-6, C); solutions manual 19.00 (ISBN 0-07-003211-4). McGraw.

Bailey, James E., jt. auth. see Bedworth, David D.

Bailey, Jim, jt. auth. see Henry, Orville.

Bailey, John, ed. Great Cartoons of the World: Fifth Series. (Illus.). 144p. (YA) 1971. 6.95 o.p. (ISBN 0-517-50719-6). Crown.

Bailey, John W. Pacifying the Plains: General Alfred Terry & the Decline of the Sioux, 1866-1890. LC 78-19300. (Contributions in Military History: No. 17). 1979. lib. bdg. 25.00x (ISBN 0-313-20625-2, BAT/). Greenwood.

Bailey, Joseph A., 2nd. Disproportionate Short Stature: Diagnosis & Management. LC 72-78953. (Illus.). 590p. 1973. 22.50 o.p. (ISBN 0-7216-1470-1). Saunders.

Bailey, Joyce W. Handbook of Latin American Art: Comprehensive, Annotated Bibliography, 1942-1980, 3 vols. 1983. write for info. Holmes & Meier.

Bailey, June T., jt. auth. see Claus, Karen E.

Bailey, K. M. Christ's Coming & His Kingdom. LC 80-70733. 175p. 1981. pap. 5.95 (ISBN 0-87509-296-9); Leader's Guide. 2.95 (ISBN 0-87509-309-4). Chr Pubns.

Bailey, K. M., ed. Church Planters' Manual. 86p. 1981. pap. 3.50 o.p. (ISBN 0-87509-302-7). Chr Pubns.

Bailey, Kathleen M. & Long, Michael H. Second Language Acquistion Studies. 256p. 1983. pap. text ed. 19.95 o.p. (ISBN 0-88377-259-0). Newbury Hse.

Bailey, Keith M. Aprender a Vivir: Learning to Live. Bucher, Dorothy, tr. 125p. (Spanish.). 1980. 1.50 (ISBN 0-87509-299-3). Chr Pubns.

--Learning to Live. 64p. (Orig.). 1978. pap. 1.25 (ISBN 0-87509-158-X). Chr Pubns.

--Servants in Charge. 123p. 1979. pap. 3.50 (ISBN 0-87509-160-1); Leader's Guide. 0.95 (ISBN 0-87509-261-6). Chr Pubns.

Bailey, Kenneth. Through Peasant Eyes: More Lucan Parables. LC 80-14297. 208p. 1980. 16.95 o.p. (ISBN 0-8028-3528-7). Eerdmans.

Bailey, L. R. Indian Slave Trade in the Southwest: A Study of Slave-Taking & the Traffic in Indian Captives from 1700-1935. LC 66-2888. (Illus.). 9.95 (ISBN 0-87026-028-6). Westernlore.

Bailey, Lee. Country Weekends. 1983. 18.95 (C N Potter Bks). Crown.

--Lee Bailey's Country Weekends. 1983. 18.95 (ISBN 0-517-54880-1, C N Potter Bks). Crown.

Bailey, Lee, jt. ed. see Biklen, Douglas.

Bailey, Liberty H. How Plants Get Their Names. (Illus.). 1933. pap. 3.50 (ISBN 0-486-20796-X). Dover.

--How Plants Get Their Names. LC 73-30611. 1975. Repr. of 1933 ed. 30.00x (ISBN 0-8103-3763-0). Gale.

--How Plants Get Their Names. (Illus.). 8.00 (ISBN 0-8446-1574-9). Peter Smith.

Bailey, Lloyd R., ed. see Fretheim, Terence E.

Bailey, Lloyd R., ed. see Murphy, Roland E.

Bailey, Lorraine H. Time to Spare. (Gregg-McGraw-Hill Series for Independent Living). 1978. pap. text ed. 7.96 (ISBN 0-07-003223-8, G); tchr's. manual 4.00 (ISBN 0-07-003225-4); wkbk 3.96 (ISBN 0-07-003224-6). McGraw.

Bailey, Lynn R. The Long Walk: A History of the Navajo Wars, 1846-1868. (Illus.). 300p. 1979. 9.95 (ISBN 0-87026-047-2). Westernlore.

Bailey, M. J. National Income & the Price Level: A Study in Macroeconomic Theory. 2nd ed. 1970. text ed. 31.95 (ISBN 0-07-003221-1, C). McGraw.

Bailey, M. R. British Railway Headcodes. pap. 4.00x (ISBN 0-392-15733-0, SpS). Sportshelf.

Bailey, Mark W. Electricity. LC 77-27324. (Read About Science Ser.). (Illus.). (gr. k-3). 1978. PLB 13.30 (ISBN 0-8393-0085-9). Raintree Pubs.

Bailey, Nathan. Divers Proverbs with Their Explication & Meaning. 1917. 29.50x (ISBN 0-686-51373-8). Elliots Bks.

Bailey, Norman T. Elements of Stochastic Processes with Applications to the Natural Sciences. LC 63-23220. (Probability & Mathematical Statistics Ser.: Applied Probability & Statistics Section). 249p. 1964. 39.95x (ISBN 0-471-04165-3, Pub. by Wiley-Interscience). Wiley.

--Mathematics, Statistics & Systems for Health. LC 77-1307. (Wiley Series Probability & Mathematical Statistics: Applied Probability & Statistics). 222p. 1977. 36.95x (ISBN 0-471-99500-2, Pub. by Wiley-Interscience). Wiley.

Bailey, Patricia. The Summer of the Flea. LC 81-80163. 160p. 1983. 10.95 (ISBN 0-86666-013-5). GWP.

Bailey, Patricia A., jt. auth. see Kramer, Victor A.

Bailey, Paul. City in the Sun: The Japanese Concentration Camp at Poston, Arizona. (Illus.). 1979. 9.00 (ISBN 0-87026-026-X). Westernlore.

--Polygamy Was Better Than Monotony: To My Grandfathers & Their Plural Wives. LC 72-83538. (Illus.). 8.95 (ISBN 0-87026-027-8). Westernlore.

Bailey, Percival & Cushing, Harvey. Classification of the Tumors of the Glioma Group on a Histogenetic Basis with a Correlated Study of Prognosis. (Illus.). 1970. Repr. of 1926 ed. 15.00 (ISBN 0-87266-049-4). Argosy.

Bailey, Peter. Forts & Castles. LC 80-52515. (Starters Ser.). PLB 8.00 (ISBN 0-382-06490-9). Silver.

Bailey, Peter & Farmer, David. Materials Management Handbook. 300p. 1982. text ed. 47.50x (ISBN 0-566-02272-9). Gower Pub Ltd.

Bailey, R. The European Connection: Britain's Relationship with the European Community. (Illus.). 250p. 1983. 21.00 (ISBN 0-08-026775-0); pap. 14.00 (ISBN 0-08-026774-2). Pergamon.

Bailey, R. W. Computers in the Humanities. 1982. not set 42.75 (ISBN 0-444-86423-7). Elsevier.

Bailey, Raymond C. Popular Influence Upon Public Policy: Petitioning in Eighteenth-Century Virginia. LC 78-73792. (Contributions in Legal Studies: No. 10). (Illus.). 1979. lib. bdg. 27.50x (ISBN 0-313-20892-1, BPP/). Greenwood.

Bailey, Richard. Africa's Industrial Future. LC 76-30919. 1977. lib. bdg. 26.25x o.p. (ISBN 0-89158-726-8). Westview.

Bailey, Richard M. Clinical Laboratories & the Practice of Medicine: An Economic Perspective. LC 78-70545. (Health Care Ser.). 1979. 23.00 (ISBN 0-8211-0132-3); text ed. 20.75 in ten or more copies (ISBN 0-685-63680-1). McCutchan.

Bailey, Richard W. & Burton, Dolores M. English Stylistics: A Bibliography. 1968. 18.50x o.p. (ISBN 0-262-02033-5). MIT Pr.

Bailey, Richard W. & Robinson, Jay L. Varieties of Present-Day English. (Illus.). 416p. 1973. pap. text ed. 16.95x (ISBN 0-02-305200-7, 30520). Macmillan.

Bailey, Robert & Childers, Milton. Applied Mineral Exploration with Special Reference to Uranium. LC 76-30874. (Illus.). 1977. lib. bdg. 80.00 o.p. (ISBN 0-89158-210-X); text ed. 35.00 o.p. (ISBN 0-686-67660-2). Westview.

Bailey, Robert L. The Career Education & Financial Aid Guide. LC 82-1696. 192p. 1982. 12.95 (ISBN 0-668-05289-9); pap. 7.95 (ISBN 0-668-05292-9). Arco.

--Disciplined Creativity for Engineers. LC 78-50310. 1978. 29.95 (ISBN 0-250-40246-7); pap. 19.95 (ISBN 0-250-40615-2). Ann Arbor Science.

--Disciplined Creativity for Engineers. LC 78-50310. (Illus.). 614p. 1982. pap. 19.95 (ISBN 0-250-40615-2). Ann Arbor Science.

--Solar-Electrics Research & Development. LC 79-54871. (Illus.). 1980. 39.95 (ISBN 0-250-40346-3). Ann Arbor Science.

Bailey, Robert L. & Hafner, Anne L. Minority Admissions. LC 77-18360. (Illus.). 1978. 22.95x (ISBN 0-669-02095-8). Lexington Bks.

Bailey, Robert W. God's Questions & Answers: Contemporary Studies in Malachi. LC 76-56513. 1977. pap. 3.95 (ISBN 0-8164-1228-6); pap. 2.00 (ISBN 0-8164-1231-6). Seabury.

--Human Error in Computer Systems. (Illus.). 160p. 1983. pap. 15.95 (ISBN 0-13-445056-6). P-H.

Bailey, Roger B. Guide to Chinese Poetry & Drama. 1973. lib. bdg. 15.00 (ISBN 0-8161-1102-2, Hall Reference). G K Hall.

Bailey, Ronald. The Air War in Europe. LC 78-2937. (World War II Ser.). (Illus.). 1979. lib. bdg. 19.92 (ISBN 0-686-51053-4). Silver.

--Glacier. (Planet Earth Ser.). 1982. lib. bdg. 19.92 (ISBN 0-8094-4317-1, Pub. by Time-Life). Silver.

--The Home Front: U. S. A. LC 77-87556. (World War II Ser.). (Illus.). 1977. lib. bdg. 19.92 (ISBN 0-8094-2479-7). Silver.

--Partisans & Guerrillas. LC 78-2949. (World War II Ser.). (Illus.). 1978. lib. bdg. 19.92 (ISBN 0-8094-2491-6). Silver.

--The Role of the Brain. LC 75-939. (Human Behavior). (Illus.). (gr. 6 up). 1975. PLB 13.28 (ISBN 0-8094-1921-1, Pub. by Time-Life). Silver.

Bailey, Rosalie F. Pre-Revolutionary Dutch Houses & Families in Northern New Jersey & Southern New York. (Illus.). 1968. pap. 6.00 o.p. (ISBN 0-486-21985-2). Dover.

Bailey, Ross R., ed. Single Dose Treatment of Urinary Tract Infection. 1982. text ed. write for info. (ISBN 0-86792-007-6, Pub by Adis Pr Australia). Wright-PSG.

Bailey, S. K. Speaking of School Governance. (Distinguished Scholar Ser). 1975. 32.50 o.p. (ISBN 0-07-079434-0, P&RB). McGraw.

Bailey, Sandra B. Big Book of Baby Names. 160p. 1982. pap. 5.95 (ISBN 0-89586-191-7). H P Bks.

Bailey, Shackleton, ed. Harvard Studies in Classical Philology, Vol. 84. LC 44-32100. 1981. text ed. 30.00x (ISBN 0-674-37931-4). Harvard U Pr.

Bailey, Sherwin. Canonical Houses of Wells. 192p. 1982. text ed. 18.75x (ISBN 0-904387-91-7, Pub. by Sutton England). Humanities.

Bailey, Stephen K. Congress in the Seventies. (American Politics Ser.). 1970. pap. text ed. 7.95 o.p. (ISBN 0-312-16240-5). St Martin.

--Education Interest Groups in the Nation's Capital. 87p. 1975. 7.50 o.p. (ISBN 0-8268-1265-1). ACE.

Bailey, Stephen K., ed. Higher Education in the World Community. 1976. 15.00 o.p. (ISBN 0-8268-1321-6). ACE.

Bailey, Sturges M. History of Columbia County, Wisconsin, Illnois, 1914: Index. 27p. (Orig.). 1982. pap. 5.00 (ISBN 0-910255-35-0). Wisconsin Gen.

Bailey, Sturges W. Index to Portrait & Biographical Album of Green Lake, Marquette, & Waushara Cos., Wis., 1890. (Illus.). 44p. (Orig.). 1983. pap. text ed. write for info. (ISBN 0-910255-38-5). Wisconsin Gen.

Bailey, Sydney D. How Wars End: The United Nations & the Termination of Armed Conflict, 1946-1964, 2 vols. 400p. 1982. Vol. I, 82.00x (ISBN 0-19-827424-6); Vol. II, 105.00x (ISBN 0-19-827462-9). Oxford U Pr.

Bailey, T. E. & Lundgaard, Kris. Program Design with Pseudocode. LC 82-17802. (Computer Science Ser.). 160p. 1983. pap. text ed. 13.95 (ISBN 0-534-01361-9). Brooks-Cole.

Bailey, Thomas A. America Faces Russia. 1964. 9.00 (ISBN 0-8446-1037-2). Peter Smith.

--The American Spirit: American History As Seen by Contemporaries, 2 vols. 4th ed. 1978. Vol. 1. pap. text ed. 11.95 (ISBN 0-669-01001-4); Vol. 2. pap. 9.95x (ISBN 0-669-01002-2). Heath.

--A Diplomatic History of the American People. 10th ed. (Illus.). 1980. text ed. 26.95 (ISBN 0-13-214726-2). P-H.

Bailey, Thomas A. & Kennedy, David M. The American Pageant. 7th ed. 1982. lib. bdg. 24.95 case bd. 1020 p. (ISBN 0-669-05270-1); Vol. I, 592 p. lib. bdg. 16.95 (ISBN 0-669-05266-3); Vol. II, 512 p. lib. bdg. 16.95 (ISBN 0-669-05267-1). Heath.

Bailey, Thoms A. Probing America's Past: A Critical Examination of Major Myths & Misconceptions, 2 vols. 1973. pap. text ed. 11.95x ea.; Vol. 1. (ISBN 0-669-84350-4); Vol. 2. (ISBN 0-669-84368-7). Heath.

Bailey, Vicki, jt. ed. see Huisingh, Donald.

Bailey, Wayne, jt. auth. see Brown, F. Martin.

Bailey, William A. The Powers. 288p. 1982. 14.95 (ISBN 0-399-12753-4). Putnam Pub Group.

Bailey, William J. & Guynn, J. Bibliographic Index of Health Education Periodicals (BIHEP) 1980 Cumulative Edition. 428p. 1982. lib. bdg. 75.00x (ISBN 0-941636-00-3). IN U Dept Health.

Bailey, William J. & Guynn, Stephen J. Bibliographic Index of Health Education Periodicals (BIHEP) Vol. 2, 1981 Cumulative Edition. 650p. 1982. lib. bdg. 75.00x (ISBN 0-941636-01-1). IN U Dept Health.

Bailey, William J., ed. Health Education-Risk Reduction: Proceedings of a Colloquium on Health Education-Risk Reduction held June 17, 1982, Indiana University. 125p. 1982. pap. 10.00x (ISBN 0-941636-51-8). IN U Dept Health.

Bailie, Anne. In the Soul's Riptide. LC 82-4442. (Orig.). 1982. pap. 5.00 (ISBN 0-941608-02-6). Chantry Pr.

Bailie, Richard C. Energy Conversion Engineering. LC 78-11969. (Ser. of Graduate Textbooks, Monographs & Research Papers). (Illus.). 1978. text ed. 29.50 (ISBN 0-201-00840-8). A-W.

Bailkey, Nels, ed. Readings in Ancient History: From Gilgamesh to Diocletian. 2nd ed. 1977. pap. text ed. 11.95x (ISBN 0-669-00249-6). Heath.

Bailleul, C. Dictionnaire Bambara-Francais - Francais-Bambara. 75.00x o.p. (ISBN 0-686-79109-6, Pub. by Avebury Pub England). State Mutual Bk.

Bailleul, Pere C. Petit Dictionnaire Bambara-Francais Francais-Bambara. 1981. 100.00x o.p. (ISBN 0-686-75433-6, 0-86127-220-X, Pub. by Avebury Pub England). State Mutual Bk.

Baillie, Joanna. The Family Legend, Repr. Of 1810 Ed. Bd. with Metrical Legends of Exalted Characters. Repr. of 1821 ed. LC 75-31147. (Romantic Context: Poetry 1789-1830 Ser.: Vol. 4). 1977. lib. bdg. 47.00 o.s.i. (ISBN 0-8240-2103-7). Garland Pub.

--A Series of Plays: In Which It Is Attempted to Delineate the Strongest Passions of the Mind, 3 vols. LC 75-31145. (Romantic Context: Poetry 1789-1830 Ser.: Vol. 2). 1977. Repr. of 1812 ed. Set. lib. bdg. 47.00 ea. o.s.i. (ISBN 0-8240-2101-0). Garland Pub.

Baillie, N. A Digest of Muhammadan Law, 2 vols. 39.50 set (ISBN 0-686-18561-7). Kazi Pubns.

Baillie, William M., ed. A Choice Ternary of English Plays: Gratiae Theatrales, 1662. 1983. write for info. (ISBN 0-86698-054-7). Medieval & Renaissance NY.

Baillif, Jean-Claude. Superpuzzles. LC 81-21112. (Illus.). 125p. 1982. 10.95 (ISBN 0-13-876201-5); pap. 4.95 (ISBN 0-13-876193-0). P-H.

Baillio, Joseph. Elisabeth Louise Vigee Le Brun 1755-1842. LC 82-81554. 148p. 1982. 29.95 (ISBN 0-912804-06-8, Dist. by U of Wash Pr). Kimbell Art.

Baillon, D. Direction des Etudes de Developpement Population Rurale et Urbaine par Departement et par Sous-Prefecture. (Black Africa Ser.). 23p. (Fr.). 1974. Repr. of 1970 ed. 10.00x o.p. (ISBN 0-8287-1361-8, 71-2069). Clearwater Pub.

--Erreurs Systematiques de Recensement en Milieu Rural Traditionnel. (Black Africa Ser.). (Illus.). 55p. (Fr.). 1974. Repr. of 1970 ed. lib. bdg. 30.00x o.p. (ISBN 0-8287-0050-8, 71-2068). Clearwater Pub.

Baillon, D., jt. auth. see Castella, P.

Bailly-Herzberg, Janine, jt. auth. see Fidell-Beaufort, Madeleine.

Bails, Dale G. & Peppers, Larry C. Business Fluctuations: Forecasting Techniques & Applications. (Illus.). 480p. 1982. 27.95 (ISBN 0-13-098400-0). P-H.

Baily, Charles M. Faint Praise: The Development of American Tanks & Tank Destroyers During World War II. (Illus.). 224p. 1983. 24.00 (ISBN 0-208-02006-3, Archon). Shoe String.

Baily, Keith M. Care of Converts. 95p. (Orig.). 1979. pap. 1.75 (ISBN 0-87509-156-3); leader's guide 0.95 (ISBN 0-87509-157-1). Chr Pubns.

Baily, Martin & Okun, Arthur M. Battle Against Unemployment & Inflation. 3rd ed. 1982. 19.00 (ISBN 0-393-01381-2); pap. 6.95x (ISBN 0-393-95055-7). Norton.

Baily, Martin N., ed. Workers, Jobs, & Inflation. 365p. 1982. 31.95 (ISBN 0-8157-0764-9); pap. 12.95 (ISBN 0-8157-0763-0). Brookings.

Baily, P. J. Purchasing Supply Management. 1978. pap. 18.50x (ISBN 0-412-15690-3, Pub. by Chapman & Hall England). Methuen Inc.

Baily, Peter & Farmer, David. Managing Materials in Industry. (Illus.). 341p. 1972. text ed. 33.75x (ISBN 0-7161-0113-0). Gower Pub Ltd.

Baily, Thelma F. & Baily, Walter H. Child Welfare Practice: A Guide to Providing Effective Services for Children & Families. LC 82-49034. (Social & Behavioral Science Ser.). 1983. text ed. 15.95x (ISBN 0-87589-558-1). Jossey-Bass.

Baily, Walter H, jt. auth. see Baily, Thelma F.

Bailyn, Bernard. Origins of American Politics. LC 68-12665. 1970. pap. 3.95 (ISBN 0-394-70865-2, V604, Vin). Random.

Bailyn, Bernard, et al. The Great Republic: A History of the American People. 2nd ed. 1008p. 1981. text ed. 23.95 (ISBN 0-669-02753-7); pap. text ed. 15.95 vol. 1 (ISBN 0-669-02754-5); pap. text ed. 15.95 vol. 2 (ISBN 0-669-02755-3); instr's guide 1.95 (ISBN 0-669-02757-X); student guide 6.95 (ISBN 0-669-02756-1). Heath.

Bailyn, Lotte & Schein, Edgar H. Living with Technology: Issues at Mid-Career. 160p. 1980. text ed. 17.50x (ISBN 0-262-02153-6). MIT Pr.

Bain, jt. auth. see Froebe, Doris J.

Bain, A. G. & Bonnington, S. T. Hydraulic Transport of Solids by Pipelines. 1971. text ed. inquire for price o.p. (ISBN 0-08-015778-5). Pergamon.

Bain, Alexander. James Mill: A Biography. LC 66-19689. Repr. of 1882 ed. 35.00x (ISBN 0-678-00214-2). Kelley.

--John Stuart Mill: A Criticism with Personal Recollections. LC 69-16521. Repr. of 1882 ed. 19.50x (ISBN 0-678-00468-4). Kelley.

Bain, Carl E., et al, eds. The Norton Introduction to Literature. 3rd ed. 1536p. 1981. pap. text ed. 13.95x (ISBN 0-393-95146-4); classroom guide 2.95x (ISBN 0-393-95158-8). Norton.

Bain, David. Masters, Servants, & Orders in Greek Tragedy: Some Aspects of Dramatic Technique & Convention. 84p. 1982. 15.00 (ISBN 0-7190-1296-1). Manchester.

Bain, E C. Pioneering in Steel Research. 1975. 16.00 (ISBN 0-686-95117-4). ASM.

Bain, E. C. & Paxton, H. W. Alloying Elements in Steel. 1966. 35.00 (ISBN 0-686-95098-4). ASM.

Bain, George. Celtic Art: The Methods of Construction. LC 73-75875. 1973. lib. bdg. 15.00x (ISBN 0-88307-590-3). Gannon.

Bain, George S. & Price, Robert. Profiles of Union Growth: A Comparative Statistical Portrait of Eight Countries. (Warwick Studies in Industrial Relations). (Illus.). 304p. 1981. 62.50x (ISBN 0-631-12633-3, Pub. by Basil Blackwell England). Biblio Dist.

Bain, Ian. Mountains & People. LC 82-50392. (Nature's Landscape Ser.). PLB 15.96 (ISBN 0-382-06673-1). Silver.

Bain, J. A. Soren Kierkegaard: His Life & Religious Teaching. Repr. of 1935 ed. 13.00 o.s.i. (ISBN 0-527-04400-8). Kraus Repr.

Bain, J. Paul, ed. Rehabilitation & Handicapped Literature 1981 Update: A Bibliographic Guide to the Microfiche Collection. 38p. 1982. reference bk. 25.00 (ISBN 0-667-00678-8). Microfilming Corp.

Bain, J. S. & Jain, R. B., eds. Contemporary Political Theory. 300p. 1980. text ed. 14.00x (ISBN 0-391-01901-5). Humanities.

--Perspectives in Political Theory. 275p. 1980. text ed. 14.00x (ISBN 0-391-01900-7). Humanities.

Bain, John A. The Foundations of Christian Faith. 112p. Repr. of 1936 ed. 3.95 o.p. (ISBN 0-567-02015-0). Attic Pr.

Bain, John, Jr. Tobacco in Song & Story. (Arents Tobacco Pub., No. 4). 1953. 10.00 o.p. (ISBN 0-87104-209-6). NY Pub Lib.

Bain, Mildred & Lewis, Ervin, eds. From Freedom to Freedom: African Roots in American Soil. new ed. LC 77-73176. (Illus.). lib. bdg. 52.60 (ISBN 0-8393-6001-0); study guide 19.93 (ISBN 0-8393-6002-9). Purnell Ref Bks.

Bain, Richard C. & Parris, Judith H. Convention Decisions & Voting Records. rev. 2nd ed. (Studies in Presidential Selection). 500p. 1973. 18.95 (ISBN 0-8157-0768-1). Brookings.

Bain, Willard S. Informed Sources: Day East Received. Date not set. price not set (ISBN 0-914994-04-2); pap. price not set (ISBN 0-914994-05-0). Cider Pr.

Bainbridge, Beryl. Harriet Said. pap. 2.95 (ISBN 0-451-11957-6, AE1957, Sig). NAL.

--A Quiet Life. 1978. pap. 1.75 o.p. (ISBN 0-451-07969-8, E7969, Sig). NAL.

Bainbridge, William S. Satan's Power: A Deviant Psychotherapy Cult. LC 77-80466. 1978. 26.50x (ISBN 0-520-03546-1). U of Cal Pr.

--The Space Revolution: A Sociological Study. LC 82-21725. 304p. (Orig.). 1983. Repr. of 1976 ed. 24.50 (ISBN 0-89874-501-2). Krieger.

--The Spacefight Revolution: A Sociological Study. LC 76-21349. (Science, Culture, & Society Ser.). 294p. 1976. 34.95 o.p. (ISBN 0-471-04306-0, Pub. by Wiley-Interscience). Wiley.

Bainbrigge, Marion S. A Walk in Other Worlds in Dante. 253p. 1982. Repr. of 1914 ed. lib. bdg. 30.00 (ISBN 0-686-98149-9). Darby Bks.

--A Walk in Other Worlds with Dante. 253p. 1982. Repr. of 1914 ed. lib. bdg. 40.00 (ISBN 0-89760-092-4). Telegraph Bks.

Baines, J. Fecundity Figures: Egyptian Personification & the Iconology of a Genre. 200p. 1982. text ed. 75.00x (ISBN 0-85668-087-7, 40651, Pub. by Aris & Phillips England). Humanities.

Baines, Jennifer. Mandelstam: The Later Poetry. LC 76-8515. 1977. 39.50 (ISBN 0-521-21273-1). Cambridge U Pr.

Baines, Jocelyn. Joseph Conrad: A Critical Biography. LC 75-17476. 507p. 1975. Repr. of 1961 ed. lib. bdg. 45.00x (ISBN 0-8371-8304-9, BAJOC). Greenwood.

Baines, John & Malek, Jaromir. Atlas of Ancient Egypt. (Illus.). 240p. 1980. 35.00 (ISBN 0-87196-334-5). Facts on File.

Baines, John, jt. tr. see Hornung, Erik.

Baines, Keith, tr. see Malory, Thomas.

Baines, M. J., jt. ed. see Morton, K. M.

Baines, Patricia. Spinning Wheels, Spinners & Spinning. 1980. pap. 10.95 (ISBN 0-686-27277-3). Robin & Russ.

--Spinning Wheels, Spinners & Spinning. new ed. pap. 10.95 (ISBN 0-686-37658-7). Robin & Russ.

Bainton, Roland. The Martin Luther Easter Book. LC 82-15996. 88p. 1983. pap. 3.50 (ISBN 0-8006-1685-5). Fortress.

Bainton, Roland, jt. auth. see Brokering, Herb.

Bainton, Roland H. Christendom: A Short History of Christianity & Its Impact on Western Civilization, Vol. 2. rev. ed. (Illus.). pap. 5.95xi (ISBN 0-06-130132-9, TB132, Torch). Har-Row.

--Here I Stand: A Life of Martin Luther. pap. 2.95 (ISBN 0-451-62103-4, ME2103, Ment). NAL.

Bainton, Roland H., tr. see Holborn, Hajo.

Bainum, Peter M. & Koelle, Dietrich E., eds. Spacelab, Space Platforms & the Future. LC 57-43769. (Advances in the Astronautical Sciences Ser.: Vol. 49). (Illus.). 502p. (Orig.). 1982. lib. bdg. 55.00x (ISBN 0-87703-174-6); pap. text ed. 45.00x (ISBN 0-87703-175-4); microfiche supplement 5.00. Am Astronaut.

Bair, Bill. Love Is an Open Door. 258p. 1974. PLB 6.95 o.p. (ISBN 0-912376-07-4). Chosen Bks Pub.

Bair, Dierdre. Samuel Beckett. LC 79-24485. (Illus.). 1980. 7.95 (ISBN 0-15-679241-9, Harv). HarBraceJ.

Bair, Frank, jt. ed. see Ruffner, James.

Bair, Frank E., ed. International Marketing Handbook: Supplement. 1232p. 1982. 75.00x (ISBN 0-8103-0546-1). Gale.

--International Marketing Handbook, 1981, 2 vols. LC 80-28549. (Illus.). 2380p. 1981. Set. 150.00x (ISBN 0-8103-0544-5). Gale.

Bair, Frank E., jt. ed. see Ruffner, James A.

Bair, Lowell, ed. see Flaubert, Gustave.

Bair, Lowell, tr. see Hugo, Victor.

Bair, Lowell, tr. see Voltaire.

Bair, Marjorie, jt. auth. see Bry, Adelaide.

Bair, Robert, tr. see Munoz, Hector.

Bairacli-Levy, Julie de see De Bairacli-Levy, Juliette.

Bairacli-Levy, Juliette De see De Bairacli-Levy, Juliette.

Baird. Orientations to Organizational Communication. Applbaum, Ronald & Hart, Roderick, eds. LC 77-21002. (MODCOM - Modules in Speech Communication). 1978. pap. text ed. 2.75 (ISBN 0-574-22533-1, 13-5533). SRA.

Baird, A. Craig, et al. Essentials of General Speech Communication. 4th ed. (Speech Ser.). (Illus.). 288p. 1973. text ed. 27.00 (ISBN 0-07-003252-1, C); tchr's manual 15.00 (ISBN 0-07-003253-X). McGraw.

Baird, Arthur, ed. see Morton, A. Q. & Michaelson, S.

Baird, Bruce F. The Engineering Manager: How to Manage People & Make Decisions. (Illus.). 224p. 1983. 22.50 (ISBN 0-534-97925-4). Lifetime Learn.

Baird, Charles W. Elements of Macroeconomics. 1977. pap. text ed. 12.95 o.s.i. (ISBN 0-8299-0069-1). West Pub.

--Prices & Markets: Intermediate Microeconomics. 2nd ed. (Illus.). 396p. 1982. text ed. 22.95 (ISBN 0-314-63156-9). West Pub.

Baird, Charles W. & Cassuto, Alexander E. Macroeconomics. 2nd ed. 336p. 1980. text ed. 19.95 (ISBN 0-574-19400-2, 13-2400); instr's. guide avail. (ISBN 0-574-19401-0, 13-2401). SRA.

Baird, Charles W., jt. auth. see Main, Robert S.

Baird, D. H., jt. ed. see Dodge, D.

Baird, David, jt. auth. see Baird, Ronald J.

Baird, David C. Experimentation: An Introduction to Measurement Theory & Experiment Design. 1962. text ed. 12.95 (ISBN 0-13-295345-5). P-H.

Baird, Duncan H., jt. ed. see Dodge, Dorothy.

Baird, Eva-Lee & Wyler, Rose. Going Metric the Fun Way. LC 77-16895. (Illus.). (gr. 8-9). 1980. 7.95 (ISBN 0-385-13642-0). Doubleday.

Baird, J. Arthur, ed. see Andersen, Francis & Forbes, A. Dean.

Baird, J. Arthur, ed. see Morton, A. Q., et al.

Baird, J. W. From Nuremberg to My Lai. (Problems in European Civilization Ser.). 1972. pap. text ed. 5.95x (ISBN 0-669-82081-4). Heath.

Baird, Jack, jt. auth. see Sopher, Charles.

Baird, James, et al see Kurtz, David L. & Boone, Louis E.

Baird, James W. Thunder over Scotland: George Wishart, Mentor of John Knox. LC 82-81516. (Illus.). 1982. text ed. 7.95 (ISBN 0-938462-04-0). Green Leaf CA.

Baird, John A., Jr. Horn of Plenty. 1982. pap. 6.95 (ISBN 0-8423-1451-2). Tyndale.

Baird, John C. & Noma, Elliot. Fundamentals of Scaling & Psychophysics. LC 78-6011. (Wiley Ser. in Behavior). 287p. 1978. 33.95x (ISBN 0-471-04169-6, Pub. by Wiley-Interscience). Wiley.

Baird, John C. & Lutkus, Anthony, eds. Mind Child Architecture. LC 81-69937. (Illus.). 224p. 1982. text ed. 18.00x (ISBN 0-87451-233-6, Pub. by Dartmouth College). U Pr of New Eng.

Baird, John E. Corinthians Study Guide. (Search & Discover Bible Study). 104p. 1975. wkbk. 2.50 (ISBN 0-87239-024-1, 40016). Standard Pub.

--Hebrews, James, Peter, John, & Jude Study Guide. (Search-&-Discover Bible Study Guide). 1976. pap. 2.50 (ISBN 0-87239-026-8, 40018). Standard Pub.

--Matthew Study Guide. (Search & Discover Bible Study). 104p. 1975. wkbk. 2.50 (ISBN 0-87239-020-9, 40010). Standard Pub.

--Romans, Thessalonians Study Guide. (Search & Discover Bible Study). 96p. 1975. wkbk. 2.50 (ISBN 0-87239-002-0, 40015). Standard Pub.

Baird, John E., Jr. Quality Circles: Leaders Manual. 256p. 1982. pap. 11.95. Waveland Pr.

Baird, John E., Jr. & Rittof, David J. Quality Circles: Facilitator's Manual. (Illus.). 247p. (Orig.). 1983. pap. 34.95X (ISBN 0-88133-010-8). Waveland Pr.

Baird, John E., Jr., jt. auth. see Bradley, Patricia H.

Baird, John W. & Stull, James B. Business Communication: A Problem-Solving Approach. (Illus.). 416p. 1983. text ed. 21.95x (ISBN 0-07-003281-5, C); write for info. instr's manual (ISBN 0-07-003282-3); write for info. wkbk. (ISBN 0-07-003283-1). McGraw.

Baird, Joseph A., Jr. The Churches of Mexico, 1530-1810. (Illus.). 1962. 60.00x (ISBN 0-520-00066-8). U of Cal Pr.

Baird, Joseph L. & Kane, John R. Rossignol. LC 78-38. 1978. 13.00x (ISBN 0-87338-211-0). Kent St U Pr.

Baird, Julia L., jt. auth. see Weaver, Donald B.

Baird, Leonard. The Elite Schools: A Profile of Prestigious Independent College Preparatory Schools. LC 76-48376. 1977. 18.95x o.p. (ISBN 0-669-01146-0). Lexington Bks.

Baird, Lorrayne Y. Bibliography of Chaucer, Nineteen Sixty-Four to Nineteen Seventy-Three. 1977. lib. bdg. 22.00 o.p. (ISBN 0-8161-8005-9). G K Hall.

Baird, Macaran A., jt. auth. see Doherty, William J.

Baird, Martha, ed. see Siegel, Eli, et al.

Baird, Ronald J. Contemporary Industrial Teaching. LC 78-185957. (Illus.). 200p. 1972. text ed. 10.64 (ISBN 0-87006-130-5). Goodheart.

--Oxyacetylene Welding. LC 79-6555. (Illus.). 1980. pap. text ed. 6.00 (ISBN 0-87006-290-5). Goodheart.

Baird, Ronald J. & Baird, David. Industrial Plastics. LC 81-13514. (Illus.). 320p. 1982. 14.00 (ISBN 0-87006-402-9). Goodheart.

Baird, Ronald J., jt. auth. see Roth, Alfred C.

Baird, Ronald J., ed. see Kicklighter, Clois E.

Baird, Russel N., jt. auth. see Click, J. W.

Baird, Scott, tr. see Fujiwara, Yoichi.

Baird, Thomas. Finding Out. 1979. pap. 1.95 o.p. (ISBN 0-380-44248-5, 44248). Avon.

Baird, W. David. Medical Education in Arkansas, Eighteen Seventy Nine-Nineteen Seventy Eight. LC 79-126280. (Illus.). 1979. 21.95x o.p. (ISBN 0-87870-052-8). Memphis St Univ.

Baird, W. David, intro. by see James, Frank L.

Baird, William see Hayes, John.

Baird, William, ed. see Bassler, Jouette M.

Bairstow, Jeffrey. Camping Year Round: A Guide to Equipment & Technique. LC 82-40019. (Illus.). 288p. (Orig.). 1983. pap. 5.95 (ISBN 0-686-43023-9, Vin). Random.

Bairstow, Jeffrey, jt. auth. see Lott, George.

Baitsell, George A., ed. The Centennial of the Sheffield Scientific School (Yale University) 1950. 18.50x (ISBN 0-686-51350-9). Elliots Bks.

Baiulescu, G. E., et al. ed. Education & Teaching in Analytical Chemistry. (Series in Analytical Chemistry). 160p. 1982. 44.95x (ISBN 0-470-27283-X). Halsted Pr.

Baizer, M. M., ed. Organic Electrochemistry: An Introduction & a Guide. 1096p. 1973. 110.25 o.p. (ISBN 0-8247-1029-0). Dekker.

Bajaj, J. S., ed. Insulin & Metabolism. 1977. 72.00 (ISBN 90-219-2105-7, North Holland). Elsevier.

Bajaj, Satish K. Secondary Social Science Workbook. (Illus.). 236p. 1981. pap. text ed. 7.95x (ISBN 0-86131-271-6, Pub. by Orient Longman Ltd India). Apt Bks.

Bajaria, Hans J., ed. Quality Assurance: Methods, Management & Motivation. LC 81-50392. (Manufacturing Update Ser.). (Illus.). 265p. 1981. 32.00 (ISBN 0-87263-067-6). SME.

Bajec, A. & Kalan, P. Dizionario Italian-Slovar. 843p. (Ital. & Slovene.). 1980. 49.95 (ISBN 0-686-97337-2, M-9692). French & Eur.

Bajema, Carl J., ed. Artificial Selection & Development of Evolutionary Theory. LC 80-10784. (Benchmark Papers in Systematic & Evolutionary Biology: Vol. 4). 384p. 1982. 47.00 (ISBN 0-87933-369-3). Hutchinson Ross.

--Natural Selection Theory: From the Speculations of the Greeks to the Quantitative Measurements of the Biometricians. LC 82-15633. (Benchmark Papers in Systematic and Evolutionary Biology: Vol. 5). 400p. 1983. 42.00 (ISBN 0-87933-412-6). Hutchinson Ross.

Bajkai, Louis A. Teachers' Guide to Overseas Teaching: A Complete & Comprehensive Guide of English-Language Schools & Colleges Overseas. LC 77-81788. (Illus., Orig.). 1982. pap. 19.95x o.p. (ISBN 0-9601550-1-5). Friends World Teach.

--Teachers Guide to Overseas Teaching: A Complete & Comprehensive Guide of English-Language Schools & Colleges Overseas. 3rd, Rev. ed. LC 77-81788. (Illus.). 192p. 1983. pap. 19.95 (ISBN 0-9601550-2-3). Friends World Teach.

Bajpai, A. C., et al. Numerical Methods for Engineers & Scientists. (Ser. on Programmes on Mathematics for Scientist & Technologist). 380p. 1977. 22.95x (ISBN 0-471-99542-8, Pub. by Wiley-Interscience). Wiley.

--Statistical Methods for Engineers & Scientists: A Students' Course Book. LC 78-2481. (Programmes on Mathematics for Scientists & Technologists Ser.). 444p. 1978. 25.00x (ISBN 0-471-99644-0). Wiley.

--Engineering Mathematics. LC 73-21230. 793p. 1974. text ed. 52.50 o.p. (ISBN 0-471-04375-3); pap. text ed. 22.95x (ISBN 0-471-04376-1, Pub. by Wiley-Interscience). Wiley.

--Specialist Techniques in Engineering Mathematics. LC 80-41274. 401p. 1980. 59.00x (ISBN 0-471-27907-2, Pub. by Wiley-Interscience); pap. 29.95x (ISBN 0-471-27908-0). Wiley.

Bajpai, Avi C., et al. Advanced Engineering Mathematics. LC 77-2198. 578p. 1977. 55.00 (ISBN 0-471-99521-5); pap. 22.95x (ISBN 0-471-99520-7). Wiley.

Bajpai, S. C. The Northern Frontier of India. (Illus.). 223p. 1970. 7.00x o.p. (ISBN 0-8188-1157-9). Paragon.

Bajusz, E., ed. Physiology & Pathology of Adaptation Mechanisms: Neural-Neuroendocrine-Hormonal. 598p. 1969. text ed. 97.00 (ISBN 0-08-012023-7). Pergamon.

Bajza, Charles C. & Schroeder, Mayme. At Home & Far Away. (Illus.). (gr. 3). 1966. text ed. 6.24 (ISBN 0-87443-049-6); tchr's ed. 4.68 (ISBN 0-87443-050-X); preprinted masters 4.95 (ISBN 0-87443-051-8). Benson.

Bakal, Donald A. Psychology & Medicine: Psychobiological Dimensions of Health & Illness. LC 78-23439. 1979. text ed. 23.95 (ISBN 0-8261-2580-8); pap. text ed. 14.95 (ISBN 0-8261-2581-6). Springer Pub.

Bakal, Yitzhak & Polsky, Howard W. Reforming Corrections for Juvenile Offenders. LC 73-11680. 1979. 19.95x (ISBN 0-669-90209-8). Lexington Bks.

Bakal, Yitzhak, jt. auth. see Vachss, Andrew H.

Bakal, Yitzhak, ed. Closing Correctional Institutions. LC 73-998. 275p. 1973. 17.95x o.p. (ISBN 0-669-86140-5). Lexington Bks.

Bakalar, James B., jt. auth. see Grinspoon, Lester.

Bakalar, James B., jt. ed. see Grinspoon, Lester.

Bakalinsky, Adah. Stairway Walks in San Francisco. LC 82-81462. (Illus.). 128p. (Orig.). 1983. pap. 5.95 (ISBN 0-938530-10-0, 10-0). Lexikos.

Bakalla, Muhammad H. Arabic Linguistics: An Introduction & Bibliography. 600p. 1982. 44.00 (ISBN 0-7201-1583-3, Pub. by Mansell England). Wilson.

Bakamis, William A. Improving Instruction in Industrial Arts. 1966. 8.95 o.p. (ISBN 0-02-810270-3). Glencoe.

Bakan, David. And They Took Themselves Wives: The Emergence of Patriarchy in Western Society. LC 79-1763. 1979. 10.00i o.p. (ISBN 0-06-060360-7, HarpR). Har-Row.

Bakara, Amiri & Baraka, Amina, eds. Confirmation: An Anthology of African-American Women. 416p. 1983. pap. 9.95 (ISBN 0-688-01582-4). Quill NY.

Bake, William A., photos by. The American South: Towns & Cities. Kilpatrick, James J. LC 82-80593. (Illus.). 224p. 1982. 28.80i (ISBN 0-8487-0533-5). Oxmoor Hse.

Bakeless, John, jt. auth. see Bakeless, Katherine.

Bakeless, John, jt. auth. see Bakeless, Katherine L.

Bakeless, John, ed. Report of the Round Tables & General Conferences at the Twelfth Session (Institute of Politics, Williams College) 1932. 49.50x (ISBN 0-686-51301-0). Elliots Bks.

Bakeless, John, ed. see Lewis, Meriwether & Clark, William.

Bakeless, Katherine & Bakeless, John. Confederate Spy Stories. LC 73-15915. 160p. (gr. 7 up). 1973. 9.95i o.p. (ISBN 0-397-31230-X, JBL-J). Har-Row.

Bakeless, Katherine L. & Bakeless, John. They Saw America First. (Illus.). (gr. 7-9). 1957. PLB 10.89 o.p. (ISBN 0-397-31377-2, JBL-J). Har-Row.

Baker. Evaluation of Analytical Systems, Pt. A. (Techniques & Instrumentation in Analytical Chemistry Ser.: Vol. 4). 1982. 70.25 (ISBN 0-444-42110-6). Elsevier.

Baker, jt. auth. see Bellak.

Baker, A. Baptist Source Book. LC 66-22076. 1974. pap. 6.95 (ISBN 0-8054-6519-7). Broadman.

Baker, A. A. Border War. 192p. (YA) 1976. 6.95 (ISBN 0-685-61051-9, Avalon). Bouregy.

--Rebel Guns. 192p. (YA) 1975. 6.95 (ISBN 0-685-52653-4, Avalon). Bouregy.

Baker, A. B. & Baker, Lowell H., eds. Clinical Neurology, 3 vols. (Annual Revision Service). loose leaf 300.00 (ISBN 0-686-97871-4, Harper Medical); revision pages 40.00 (ISBN 0-686-97872-2). Lippincott.

Baker, A. E., ed. see Temple, William.

Baker, A. J., et al. More Spectroscopic Problems in Organic Chemistry. 2nd ed. 1975. 29.95 (ISBN 0-471-25591-2, Wiley Heyden). Wiley.

Baker, Abe B., et al, eds. see Loose Leaf Reference Services.

Baker, Al. TRS-80 Programs & Applications. (Illus.). 1982. text ed. 18.95 (ISBN 0-8359-7871-0); pap. 14.95 (ISBN 0-686-82960-3). Reston.

Baker, Alan. Benjamin's Book. LC 82-4605. (Illus.). 32p. (ps-1). 1983. 9.00 (ISBN 0-688-01697-9). Lothrop.

Baker, Alan J. Business Decision Making. 228p. 1981. 30.00 (ISBN 0-312-10902-4). St Martin.

--Investment, Valuation & the Managerial Theory of the Firm. 336p. 1978. text ed. 30.25x (ISBN 0-566-00192-6). Gower Pub Ltd.

Baker, Alan R. Transcendental Number Theory. LC 74-82591. 148p. 1975. 29.95x (ISBN 0-521-20461-5). Cambridge U Pr.

Baker, Alan R. & Butlin, R. A., eds. Studies of Field Systems in the British Isles. (Illus.). 728p. 1980. pap. 32.50 (ISBN 0-521-29790-7). Cambridge U Pr.

--Studies of Field Systems in the British Isles. LC 72-91359. (Illus.). 744p. 1973. 87.50 (ISBN 0-521-20121-7). Cambridge U Pr.

Baker, Alton, jt. auth. see Sartain, Aaron.

Baker, Ann. Introducing English Pronunciation: A Teacher's Guide to Tree or Three? & Ship or Sheep. 1982. 7.95 (ISBN 0-686-81782-6). Cambridge U Pr.

Baker, Archibald G., ed. Short History of Christianity. LC 40-34185. (Midway Reprints Ser.). 1983. 10.00 o.s.i. (ISBN 0-226-03529-8); pap. 8.00x (ISBN 0-226-03530-1); price not set (ISBN 0-226-03527-1). U of Chicago Pr.

Baker, Arthur. Arthur Baker's Foundational Calligraphy Manual. (Illus.). 96p. 1982. pap. 5.95 (ISBN 0-686-83696-0, ScribT). Scribner.

--The Calligraphic Art of Arthur Baker. (Illus.). 64p. 1983. 9.95 (ISBN 0-686-83809-2, ScribT). Scribner.

--Calligraphic Cut-Paper Designs for Artists & Craftsmen. (Pictorial Archive Ser.). (Illus.). 80p. (Orig.). 1983. pap. 2.50 (ISBN 0-486-20306-9). Dover.

--Calligraphic Swash Initials. (Illus.). 96p. (Orig.). (gr. 7 up). 1983. pap. 3.50 (ISBN 0-486-24427-X). Dover.

--Celtic Hand Stroke by Stroke (Irish Half-Uncial from "The Book of Kells") (An Arthur Baker Calligraphy Manual: Lettering, Calligraphy, Typography Ser.). (Illus.). 48p. (Orig.). Date not set. pap. 2.25 (ISBN 0-486-24336-2). Dover. Postponed.

--Classic Roman Capitals Stroke By Stroke: An Arthur Baker Calligraphy Manual. (Illus.). 64p. (Orig.). (gr. 6 up). 1983. pap. 2.95 (ISBN 0-486-24450-4). Dover.

--The House Is Sitting. LC 74-68. (Illus.). 264p. 1974. Repr. of 1958 ed. lib. bdg. 15.75x (ISBN 0-8371-7364-7, BAHS). Greenwood.

Baker, Augusta & Greene, Ellin. Storytelling: Art & Technique. LC 77-16481. 1977. pap. 9.25 (ISBN 0-8352-0840-0). Bowker.

Baker, Betty. All-by-Herself. (Illus.). (gr. 1-3). 1980. 5.95 (ISBN 0-688-80242-7); lib. bdg. 5.71 (ISBN 0-688-84242-9). Greenwillow.

--And Me, Coyote! LC 82-7134. (Illus.). 32p. (gr. k-4). 1982. 8.95 (ISBN 0-02-708280-6). Macmillan.

--The Big Push. (Break of Day Bk). (Illus.). (gr. 1-4). 1972. PLB 4.89 o.p. (ISBN 0-698-30416-0, Coward). Putnam Pub Group.

--Dunderhead War. LC 67-18551. (gr. 5 up). 1967. PLB 10.89 (ISBN 0-06-020328-5, HarpJ). Har-Row.

--Killer-Of-Death. LC 63-13676. (gr. 7 up). 1963. PLB 10.89 (ISBN 0-06-020331-5, HarpJ). Har-Row.

--Shaman's Last Raid. LC 63-8004. (Illus.). (gr. 3-6). 1963. PLB 10.89 (ISBN 0-06-020351-X, HarpJ). Har-Row.

--The Turkey Girl. LC 82-17285. (Ready-to-Read Ser.). (Illus.). 64p. (gr. 1-4). 1983. 8.95 (ISBN 0-02-708260-1). Macmillan.

--Walk the World's Rim. LC 65-11458. (gr. 5 up). 1965. PLB 10.89 (ISBN 0-06-020381-1, HarpJ). Har-Row.

Baker, Bill. How to Beat the Energy Crisis & Still Live in Style. LC 77-22717. 1979. 12.95 o.p. (ISBN 0-399-12020-3); pap. 6.95 o.p. (ISBN 0-399-12337-7). Putnam Pub Group.

Baker, Bonnie Jeanne. A Pear by Itself. LC 82-4430. (Rookie Readers Ser.). (ps-2). 1982. 8.65 (ISBN 0-516-02032-3); pap. 1.95 (ISBN 0-516-42032-1). Childrens.

Baker, Brian H. Fundamental Skills in Hematology. 508p. 1980. spiral 28.50x (ISBN 0-398-04101-6). C C Thomas.

Baker, C. L. Introduction to Generative-Transformational Syntax. 1977. text ed. 22.95 (ISBN 0-13-484410-6). P-H.

Baker, C. L. & McCarthy, John J., eds. The Logical Problem of Language Acquisition. (Cognitive Theory & Mental Representation Ser.). 358p. 1981. 30.00x (ISBN 0-262-02159-5). MIT Pr.

Baker, C. R. & Hayes, R. S. Lease Financing: Alternative to Buying. LC 8-1576. 200p. 1981. 24.95x (ISBN 0-471-06040-2, Pub. by Wiley-Interscience). Wiley.

Baker, C. R., jt. auth. see Hayes, R. S.

Baker, Caleb. Two Roads & Two Breaths. 59p. pap. 0.50 (ISBN 0-937396-51-6); chart 1.00 (ISBN 0-937396-52-4). Walterick Pubs.

Baker, Carlos. Ernest Hemingway: A Life Story. 1980. pap. 5.95 (ISBN 0-380-50039-6, 57877-8, Discus). Avon.

Baker, Carol, jt. ed. see Fingerhut, Astri.

Baker, Catherine J., ed. see Schweiker, Roioli.

Baker, Charlotte. Cockleburr Quarters. (Illus.). (gr. 3-7). 1973. pap. 1.50 o.p. (ISBN 0-380-01108-5, 35857, Camelot). Avon.

Baker, Christopher T. & Miller, Geoffrey F. Treatment of Integral Equations by Numerical Methods. Date not set. 37.00 (ISBN 0-12-074120-2). Acad Pr.

Baker, D., ed. Heresy, Schism & Religious Protest. LC 75-184899. (Studies in Church History: Vol. 9). 1972. 54.50 (ISBN 0-521-08486-5). Cambridge U Pr.

Baker, D. A. Transport Phenomena in Plants. (Outline Studies in Biology Ser.). 1978. pap. 6.50x (ISBN 0-412-15360-2, Pub. by Chapman & Hall). Methuen Inc.

Baker, D. A., jt. auth. see Sutcliffe, J. F.

Baker, D. K., jt. auth. see Goble, Alfred T.

Baker, D. L. Two Testaments: One Bible. 1977. pap. 7.95 o.p. (ISBN 0-87784-872-6). Inter-Varsity.

Baker, D. Phillip. School & Public Library Media Programs for Children & Young Adults. 300p. 1976. pap. 14.50 o.s.i. (ISBN 0-915794-09-8). Gaylord Prof Pubns.

Baker, Darrel. Bugs Bunny & Friends. (How to Draw Ser.: No. 2150). (Illus.). 48p. (gr. 2-5). 1983. pap. 0.99 (ISBN 0-307-20150-3). Western Pub.

Baker, David. The Rocket. (Illus.). 1978. 17.95 o.p. (ISBN 0-517-53404-5). Crown.

Baker, Dennis, jt. auth. see Boone, Debby.

Baker, Dennis, jt. auth. see Sutcliffe, James.

Baker, Denys V., ed. A View From Land's End: Writers Against a Cornish Background. 1982. 39.00x (ISBN 0-686-82341-9, Pub. by W Kimber). State Mutual Bk.

Baker, Derek & Wilks, Michael, eds. The World of John of Salisbury. (Studies in Church History: Subsidia 3). 400p. 1983. text ed. 36.00x (ISBN 0-631-13122-1, Pub. by Basil Blackwell England). Biblio Dist.

Baker, Derek, jt. ed. see Cuming, G. J.

Baker, Derek, jt. ed. see Sheils, W. J.

Baker, Don & Nester, Emery. Depression: Finding Hope & Meaning in Life's Darkest Shadow. (Critical Concern Ser.). 1983. write for info. (ISBN 0-88070-011-4). Multnomah.

Baker, Donald G. & Sheldon, Charles H. Postwar America: The Search for Identity. (Insight Series: Studies in Contemporary Issues). 1969. pap. 7.95x (ISBN 0-02-473840-9, 47384). Macmillan.

Baker, Donald I., jt. auth. see Penney, Norman.

Baker, Donald R. Cooling Tower Performance. (Illus.). 1983. 40.00 (ISBN 0-8206-0300-7). Chem Pub.

Baker, Donald W. Formal Application. LC 81-71435. 64p. (Orig.). 1982. pap. 6.95 (ISBN 0-935306-14-5). Barnwood Pr.

Baker, Dorothy D. Trio. LC 77-5686. 1977. lib. bdg. 19.25x (ISBN 0-8371-9647-7, BATR). Greenwood.

Baker, Doug. River Place. LC 79-27119. 176p. 1980. pap. 8.50 (ISBN 0-917304-57-8). Timber.

Baker, Douglas, ed. Karmic Laws: The Esoteric Philosophy of Disease & Rebirth. 96p. 1983. pap. 6.95 (ISBN 0-85030-299-4). Newcastle Pub.

Baker, Elijah. Introduction to Steel Shipbuilding. 2nd ed. (Illus.). 1953. 26.95 (ISBN 0-07-003359-5). McGraw.

Baker, Elizabeth. Love Around the House. 1979. pap. 3.95 (ISBN 0-88207-603-5). Victor Bks.

Baker, Elizabeth F. Henry Wheaton: 1785-1848. LC 70-154698. (American Constitutional & Legal History Ser.). 1971. Repr. of 1937 ed. lib. bdg. 49.50 (ISBN 0-306-70152-9). Da Capo.

Baker, Ernest A. A History of the English Novel, 11 vols. Incl. Vol. 1. The Age of Romance: From the Beginnings to the Renaissance. 336p. 1977. Repr. of 1924 ed. 19.50x (ISBN 0-06-480046-6); Vol. 2. The Elizabethan Age & After. 303p. 1966. Repr. of 1936 ed. 19.50x (ISBN 0-06-480047-4); Vol. 3. The Later Romances & the Establishment of Realism. 278p. 1969. Repr. of 1929 ed. 19.50x (ISBN 0-06-480048-2); Vol. 4. Intellectual Realism: From Richardson to Sterne. 297p. 1976. Repr. of 1936 ed. 19.50x (ISBN 0-06-480049-0); Vol. 5. The Novel of Sentiment & the Gothic Romance. 300p. 1975. Repr. of 1929 ed. 19.50x (ISBN 0-06-480050-4); Vol. 6. Edgeworth, Austen, Scott. 277p. 1979. Repr. of 1929 ed. 19.50x (ISBN 0-06-480051-2); Vol. 7. The Age of Dickens & Thackeray. 404p. 1968. Repr. of 1936 ed. 19.50x (ISBN 0-06-480052-0); Vol. 8. From the Brontes to Meredith: Romanticism in the English Novel. 411p. 1972. Repr. of 1936 ed. 19.50x (ISBN 0-06-480053-9); Vol. 9. The Day Before Yesterday. 364p. 1975. **Repr. of 1936 ed. 19.50x (ISBN 0-06-480054-7); Vol. 10. Yesterday. 420p. 1976. Repr. of 1936 ed. 19.50x (ISBN 0-06-480055-5); Vol. 11. Yesterday & After. Stevenson, Lionel. 431p. 1975. Repr. of 1967 ed. 19.50x (ISBN 0-686-76930-9). Set. 214.50x (ISBN 0-686-66645-3). B&N Imports.**

Baker, Eugene. At the Scene of the Crime. (Junior Detective Bks.). (Illus.). 32p. (gr. 2-6). 1980. PLB 8.60g (ISBN 0-516-06470-3). Childrens.

--I Want to Be a Football Player. LC 79-178492. (I Want to Be Books). (Illus.). 32p. (gr. k-4). 1972. PLB 7.95 (ISBN 0-516-01796-9). Childrens.

--In the Detective's Lab. LC 80-17787. (Junior Detective Bks.). (Illus.). 32p. (gr. 2-6). 1980. 8.60g (ISBN 0-516-06471-1). Childrens.

--Master of Disguise. LC 80-11297. (Junior Detective Bks.). (Illus.). 32p. (gr. 2-6). 1980. 8.60g (ISBN 0-516-06472-X). Childrens.

--Secret Writing-Codes & Messages. LC 80-11416. (Junior Detective Bks.). (Illus.). 32p. (gr. 2-6). 1980. 8.60g (ISBN 0-516-06473-8). Childrens.

--Shadowing the Suspect. LC 80-13982. (Junior Detective Bks.). (Illus.). 32p. (gr. 2-6). 1980. 8.60g (ISBN 0-516-06474-6). Childrens.

--Spotting the Fakes-Forgeries & Counterfeits. LC 80-15998. (Junior Detective Bks.). (Illus.). 32p. (gr. 2-6). 1980. 8.60g (ISBN 0-516-06475-4). Childrens.

--What's Right? Buerger, Jane, ed. LC 80-17552. (Illus.). 112p. 1980. 5.95 (ISBN 0-89565-175-0, 4932). Standard Pub.

Baker, Eva, jt. auth. see Popham, James.

Baker, Eva, jt. auth. see Popham, W.

Baker, F. C. The Fresh Water Mollusca of Wisconsin. 1973. Repr. of 1928 ed. lib. bdg. 80.00 (ISBN 3-7682-0764-1). Lubrecht & Cramer.

Baker, F. J. & Silverton, R. E. Introduction to Medical Laboratory Technology. 5th ed. 1976. 34.95 (ISBN 0-407-73251-9). Butterworth.

Baker, Frank & Northman, John E. Helping: Human Services for the 80's. LC 80-27524. 241p. 1981. pap. text ed. 13.95 (ISBN 0-8016-0424-9). Mosby.

Baker, Frank H., ed. Beef Cattle Science Handbook: International Stockmen's School Handbooks, Vol. 19. 800p. 1982. 45.00 (ISBN 0-86531-509-4, Pub. in Cooperation with Winrock International). Westview.

--Dairy Science Handbook: International Stockmen's School Handbooks, Vol. 15. 500p. 1982. lib. bdg. 35.00X (ISBN 0-86531-508-6, Pub. in Cooperation with Winrock International). Westview.

--Sheep & Goat Handbook: International Stockmen's School Handbooks, Vol. 3. 600p. 1982. lib. bdg. 35.00 (ISBN 0-86531-510-8, Pub. with Winrock International). Westview.

--Stud Manager's Handbook: International Stockmen's School Handbooks, Vol. 18. 500p. 1982. lib. bdg. 30.00 (ISBN 0-86531-507-8, Pub. with Winrock International). Westview.

Baker, Frank J. How to Make Your Camera Pay for Your Vacation. LC 81-10843. 1983. 12.95 (ISBN 0-87949-208-2). Ashley Bks.

--One Hundred One Ways to Make Money in Photography. 1980. 14.95 o.p. (ISBN 0-8092-7043-9); pap. 7.95 (ISBN 0-8092-7042-0). Contemp Bks.

Baker, Frank J., jt. auth. see Rosen, Peter.

Baker, Fred. Ptolia, Bk. 1. LC 82-81453. 175p. (Orig.). 1982. pap. 4.95 (ISBN 0-914766-83-X, 0197). IWP Pub.

Baker, G. A., Jr. & Graves-Morris, P. R. Encyclopedia of Mathematics & Its Applications, Vol. 13, Pt. 1: Basic Theory. 1981. 34.50 (ISBN 0-201-13512-4). A-W.

--Encyclopedia of Mathematics & Its Applications, Vol. 14, Pt. 2: Extension & Applications. 1981. 32.50 (ISBN 0-201-13513-2). A-W.

Baker, George, jt. ed. see Needleman, Jacob.

Baker, George P. Dramatic Technique. LC 77-77706. (Theatre, Film & the Performing Arts Ser). 532p. 1971. Repr. of 1919 ed. lib. bdg. 39.50 (ISBN 0-306-71344-6). Da Capo.

--Dramatic Technique. LC 75-31999. (Theatre, Film & the Performing Arts Ser.). 1976. pap. 8.95 (ISBN 0-306-80030-6). Da Capo.

--Dramatic Technique. LC 74-100220. Repr. of 1919 ed. lib. bdg. 18.50x (ISBN 0-8371-3005-0, BADT). Greenwood.

--Formation of the New England Railroad Systems: A Study of Railroad Combination in the Nineteenth Century. LC 68-8936. (Illus.). 1968. Repr. of 1937 ed. lib. bdg. 16.25x (ISBN 0-8371-0009-7, BANE). Greenwood.

Baker, George T., jt. ed. see Rockstein, Morris.

Baker, Glenn E. & Miller, Rex. Carpentry Fundamentals. (Contemporary Construction Ser.). (Illus.). 512p. (gr. 10-12). 1981. 22.96 (ISBN 0-07-003361-7, G); tchrs. manual & key 2.00 (ISBN 0-07-003363-3); wkbk. 7.96 (ISBN 0-07-003362-5). McGraw.

Baker, Gordon E. Reapportionment Revolution: Representation, Political Power & the Supreme Court. 1966. pap. text ed. 2.95 (ISBN 0-685-19761-1). Phila Bk Co.

Baker, Gwendolyn C. Planning & Organizing for Multicultural Instruction. LC 82-8910. (Illus.). 288p. 1983. pap. text ed. 10.95 (ISBN 0-201-10188-2). A-W.

Baker, H. A. Black Literature in America. 1971. 18.95 (ISBN 0-07-003365-X). McGraw.

Baker, H. A., jt. auth. see Lerner, Joel V.

Baker, H. F. Introduction to Plane Geometry. LC 70-141879. 1971. text ed. 18.50 (ISBN 0-8284-0247-7). Chelsea Pub.

Baker, Herschel, ed. Later Renaissance in England: Nondramatic Verse & Prose, 1600-1660. 1975. text ed. 26.50 (ISBN 0-395-16038-3). HM.

Baker, Herschel C. John Philip Kemble: The Actor in His Theatre. LC 76-90701. Repr. of 1942 ed. lib. bdg. 17.00x (ISBN 0-8371-2279-1, BAJK). Greenwood.

Baker, Houston A. Singers of Daybreak: Studies in Black American Literature. LC 74-1106. 128p. 1975. 8.95 (ISBN 0-88258-017-5); pap. 6.95 (ISBN 0-88258-025-6). Howard U Pr.

Baker, Houston A., Jr., ed. Three American Literatures: Essays in Chicano, Native American, & Asian-American Literature for Teachers of American Literature. LC 82-63420. iii, 265p. 1982. 19.50x (ISBN 0-87352-353-9); pap. 9.50x (ISBN 0-87352-352-0). Modern Lang.

Baker, Howard. Howard Baker's Washington. (Illus.). 1982. 19.95 (ISBN 0-393-01562-9). Norton.

--Ode to the Sea & Other Poems. LC 82-71561. 77p. 1966. 5.95 (ISBN 0-8040-0228-2). Swallow.

Baker, Ian F., ed. see Micklem, et al.

Baker, J., tr. see Eichrodt, Walther.

Baker, J. G. Flora of Mauritius & the Seychelles. 1971. Repr. of 1877 ed. 80.00 (ISBN 3-7682-0677-7). Lubrecht & Cramer.

--Handbook of the Amaryllideae: Including the Alstromeriae & Agaveae. (Plant Monograph: No.7). 1972. Repr. of 1888 ed. 16.00 (ISBN 3-7682-0677-7). Lubrecht & Cramer.

--Handbook of the Bromeliaceae. (Plant Monograph: No.8). 1972. Repr. of 1889 ed. 16.00 (ISBN 3-7682-0752-8). Lubrecht & Cramer.

--Handbook of the Irideae. (Plant Monograph Ser.: No.9). 1972. Repr. of 1892 ed. 16.00 (ISBN 3-7682-0753-6). Lubrecht & Cramer.

Baker, J. H. Manual of Law French. 1979. 45.00x o.p. (ISBN 0-86127-401-6, Pub. by Avebury Pub England). State Mutual Bk.

Baker, J. K. & Juergenson, E. M. Approved Practices in Swine Production. 6th ed. LC 79-142330. 1979. 16.50 (ISBN 0-8134-2038-5, 2038); text ed. 12.50x. Interstate.

Baker, J. R. Cytological Technique. 1981. pap. 7.95x (ISBN 0-412-20300-6, Pub. by Chapman & Hall). Methuen Inc.

--Parasitic Protozoa. (Biological Sciences Ser). 1969. pap. text ed. 6.50x o.p. (ISBN 0-09-099161-3, Hutchinson U Lib). Humanities.

Baker, J. R. & Muller, R. Advances in Parasitology, Vol. 21. (Serial Publication). 336p. 1982. 52.00 (ISBN 0-12-031721-4). Acad Pr.

Baker, J. Stannard. Traffic Accident Investigation Manual. 1975. 30.00 (ISBN 0-912642-01-7). Traffic Inst.

Baker, J. Wayne. Heinrich Bullinger & the Covenant: The Other Reformed Tradition. LC 80-14667. xxvi, 300p. 1980. 21.00x (ISBN 0-8214-0554-3, 82-834075). Ohio U Pr.

Baker, James. Eric Hoffer. (United States Authors Ser.). 1982. lib. bdg. 13.95 (ISBN 0-8057-7359-2, Twayne). G K Hall.

--International Bank Regulation. LC 76-19545. (Praeger Special Studies). 240p. 1978. 26.95 o.p. (ISBN 0-03-028936-X). Praeger.

Baker, James, jt. auth. see Kearny, Mary Ann.

Baker, James H., ed. Poems of Bishop Henry King. LC 60-8067. 138p. 1960. 5.95 (ISBN 0-8040-0249-5); pap. 3.95 o.p. (ISBN 0-686-82979-4). Swallow.

Baker, James L. & Goodkind, Richard J. Theory & Practice of Precision Attachments Removable Partial Dentures. LC 81-2393. (Illus.). 282p. 1981. text ed. 54.50 (ISBN 0-8016-0427-3). Mosby.

Baker, James R. & Siegler, Arthur B., Jr., eds. Lord of the Flies: Text, Notes & Criticism. casebook ed. 1964. pap. text ed. 4.95 (ISBN 0-399-30002-3). Putnam Pub Group.

Baker, Janice, jt. auth. see Carpenter, Allan.

Baker, Jarry. The Impatient Gardener. 288p. (Orig.). 1983. pap. 6.95 (ISBN 0-345-30949-9). Ballantine.

Baker, Jean H. Affairs of Party: The Political Culture of Northern Democrats in the Mid-19th Century. (Illus.). 368p. 1983. 39.50x (ISBN 0-8014-1513-6); pap. 14.95x (ISBN 0-8014-9883-X). Cornell U Pr.

--Ambivalent Americans: The Know-Nothing Party in Maryland. 206p. 1977. 14.00 (ISBN 0-686-36821-5). Md Hist.

Baker, Jeannie. One Hungry Spider. (Illus.). 32p. (ps-1). 1982. 9.95 (ISBN 0-233-97429-6). Andre Deutsch.

Baker, Jeffrey J. & Allen, Garland A. The Study of Biology. 4th ed. LC 81-17550. (Illus.). 900p. 1982. text ed. 27.95 (ISBN 0-201-10180-7); instr's. manual 3.50 (ISBN 0-201-10181-5); write for info. study guide (ISBN 0-201-10182-3). A-W.

Baker, Jeffrey J. W. & Allen, Garland E. Matter, Energy, & Life: An Introduction to Chemical Concepts, 4-E. LC 80-17946. (Life Sciences Ser.). 256p. 1981. 12.95 (ISBN 0-201-00169-1). A-W.

Baker, Jennifer. Saddlery & Horse Equipment. LC 82-11468. (Illus.). 96p. 1982. 7.95 (ISBN 0-668-05633-9, 5633). Arco.

Baker, Jim. O. J. Simpson's Most Memorable Games. LC 78-1304. (Illus.). 1978. 8.95 o.p. (ISBN 0-399-12108-0). Putnam Pub Group.

Baker, Joe. Coping with Drug Abuse: A Lifeline for Parents. LC 82-12723. (Illus.). 60p. 1982. pap. 9.95 (ISBN 0-943690-00-5). DARE.

Baker, John. The Neighbourhood Advice Centre: A Community Project in Camden. (Reports of the Institute of Community Studies). 1978. 25.50x (ISBN 0-7100-8731-4). Routledge & Kegan.

Baker, John & Heyman, J. Plastic Design of Frames, 2 vols. Incl. Vol. 1. Fundamentals. 32.95 (ISBN 0-521-07517-3); pap. 17.95 (ISBN 0-521-29778-8); Vol. 2. Applications. 40.75 (ISBN 0-521-07984-5). LC 69-19370. (Illus.). 1969-1971. Cambridge U Pr.

Baker, John A., tr. see Danielou, Jean.

Baker, John B. & Soroka, Marguerite C., eds. Library Conservation: Preservation in Perspective. LC 78-16133. (Publications in the Informtion Sciences Ser.). 459p. 1978. 50.00 (ISBN 0-87933-332-4). Hutchinson Ross.

Baker, John C., jt. auth. see Berman, Robert P.

Baker, John R. The Biology of Protozoa. (Studies in Biology: No. 138). 64p. 1982. pap. text ed. 8.95 (ISBN 0-7131-2837-2). E Arnold.

Baker, John R. & Trypanosomiasis Seminar. Perspectives in Trypanosomiasis Research: Proceedings of the Twenty-First Trypanosomiasis Seminar: London 24 September 1981. (Tropical Medicine Research Studies). 105p. 1982. 29.95 (ISBN 0-471-10478-7, Pub. by Res Stud Pr). Wiley.

Baker, John T., jt. auth. see Barnett, Nancy B.

Baker, Justine. Microcomputers in the Classroom. LC 82-60799. (Fastback Ser.: No. 179). 50p. 1982. pap. 0.75 (ISBN 0-87367-179-1). Phi Delta Kappa.

Baker, K. F. & Cook, R. J. Biological Control of Plant Pathogens. LC 82-70786. 451p. Repr. of 1974 ed. text ed. 32.00 (ISBN 0-89054-045-4). Am Phytopathol Soc.

Baker, Karle W. Old Coins (Poetry) 1923. text ed. 24.50x (ISBN 0-686-83652-9). Elliots Bks.

Baker, Keith & Rubel, Tobert J. Violence & Crime in the Schools. LC 79-5325. 320p. 1980. 18.95x (ISBN 0-669-03389-8). Lexington Bks.

Baker, Keith, et al. Comprehensive Services to Rural Poor Families: An Evaluation of the Arizona Job College Program. LC 75-36414. (Illus.). 1976. text ed. 25.95 o.p. (ISBN 0-275-56310-3). Praeger.

Baker, Keith A., ed. Bilingual Education: A Reappraisal of Federal Policy. Kenter, Adriana A. LC 82-48040. 272p. 1982. 21.95x (ISBN 0-669-05885-8). Lexington Bks.

Baker, Keith M. Condorcet: From Natural Philosophy to Social Mathematics. LC 74-5725. 538p. 1982. 15.00x (ISBN 0-226-03533-6). U of Chicago Pr.

Baker, Kenneth. Fundamentals of Catholicism, Vol. 1. LC 82-80297. 282p. (Orig.). 1982. pap. 8.95 (ISBN 0-89870-017-5). Ignatius Pr.

--I Have No Gun But I Can Spit. 1982. pap. write for info. o.p. Methuen Inc.

Baker, Kenneth G., jt. auth. see Udell, Gerald G.

Baker, Kenneth R. Introduction to Sequencing & Scheduling. LC 74-8010. 305p. 1974. text ed. 32.95x (ISBN 0-471-04555-1). Wiley.

Baker, Kenneth S. Fundamentals of Catholicism, Vol. 2. LC 82-80297. 387p. (Orig.). 1983. pap. 10.95 (ISBN 0-89870-019-1). Ignatius Pr.

Baker, L. E., jt. auth. see Geddes, L. A.

Baker, Leonard. Days of Sorrow & Pain: Leo Baeck & the Berlin Jews. 1978. 19.95 o.s.i. (ISBN 0-02-506340-5). Macmillan.

--Days of Sorrow & Pain: Leo Baeck & the Berlin Jews. (Illus.). 412p. 1980. pap. 9.95 (ISBN 0-19-502800-7, GB 611). Oxford U Pr.

Baker, Leslie A. The Art Teacher's Resource Book. (Illus.). 1978. ref. 19.95 (ISBN 0-87909-022-7). Reston.

Baker, Liva. Miranda. LC 81-69127. 320p. 1983. 16.95 (ISBN 0-689-11240-8). Atheneum.

Baker, Lowell H., jt. ed. see Baker, A. B.

Baker, Lucinda. Memoirs of the First Baroness. LC 78-1320. 1978. 10.00 o.p. (ISBN 0-399-12162-5). Putnam Pub Group.

--The Place of Devils. LC 76-3640. 1976. 8.95 o.p. (ISBN 0-399-11701-6). Putnam Pub Group.

--Walk the Night Unseen. LC 76-57220. 1977. 8.95 o.p. (ISBN 0-399-11896-9). Putnam Pub Group.

Baker, Lynn S. The Fertility Fallacy: Sexuality in the Post-Pill Age. LC 80-50715. 224p. 1981. 11.95 o.p. (ISBN 0-7216-1492-2). Saunders.

Baker, M. A., et al. Women Today: A Multidisciplinary Approach to Women's Studies. LC 79-11834. 1979. pap. text ed. 14.95 (ISBN 0-8185-0341-6). Brooks-Cole.

Baker, M. C., jt. auth. see Winn, Charles S.

Baker, M. J. Perceiving, Explaining & Acting. 1979. 9.95 o.p. (ISBN 0-533-03995-9). Vantage.

Baker, M. Joyce. Images of Women in Film: The War Years, 1941-1945. Berkhofer, Robert, ed. LC 80-39795. (Studies in American History & Culture: No. 21). 196p. 1981. 39.95 (ISBN 0-8357-1153-6, Pub. by UMI Res Pr). Univ Microfilms.

Baker, M. Pauline, jt. auth. see Hearn, D. Donald.

Baker, Mariam. Woman as Divine: Tales of the Goddess. (Illus., Orig.). 1982. pap. 8.95 (ISBN 0-9609916-0-3). Crescent Heart.

Baker, Mark. Nam. 320p. 1983. pap. 3.50 (ISBN 0-425-06000-4). Berkley Pub.

Baker, Maryn. The Short Change Game: How to Stop the School from Depriving Your Retarded or Handicapped Child. LC 81-3653. 1983. 13.95 (ISBN 0-87949-211-2). Ashley Bks.

Baker, Michael. The Book of Braintree. 1981. 39.50x o.p. (ISBN 0-86023-135-6, Pub. by Barracuda England). State Mutual Bk.

Baker, Michael A. Visa Qualifying Examination Review, Vol. 2: Clinical Sciences. LC 78-61618. 1978. pap. 15.50 (ISBN 0-87488-125-0). Med Exam.

Baker, Michael A., ed. Medicine. 7th ed. (Medical Examination Review Ser.: Vol. 2). 1980. pap. 11.95 (ISBN 0-87488-102-1). Med Exam.

Baker, Miriam. Our Angels & Our Mysteries. (Illus.). 131p. 1978. pap. 4.95 (ISBN 0-686-32024-7, TX-134-317). Automatic Print.

Baker, Muriel L. Handbook of American Crewel Embroidery. LC 66-16722. (Illus.). 1966. 10.95 (ISBN 0-8048-0230-0). C E Tuttle.

Baker, Norman, jt. auth. see Murphy, Barbara.

Baker, Oleda. How to Renovate Yourself from Head to Toe. LC 77-27671. (Illus.). 224p. 1980. 10.95 o.p. (ISBN 0-385-12894-0). Doubleday.

Baker, P. F. & Reute, H. Calcium Movement in Excitable Cells. 1975. pap. text ed. 11.25 (ISBN 0-08-018298-4). Pergamon.

Baker, Pat. I Now Pronounce You Parent: What Other Books Don't Tell You About Babies. 96p. (Orig.). 1983. pap. 4.95 (ISBN 0-8010-0850-6). Baker Bk.

Baker, Paul R. Richard Morris Hunt. (Illus.). 1980. 45.00x (ISBN 0-262-02139-0). MIT Pr.

Baker, Pauline H. Urbanization & Political Change: The Politics of Lagos, 1917-1967. LC 70-162001. 1975. 41.00x (ISBN 0-520-02066-9). U of Cal Pr.

Baker, Philip & Corne, Chris. Isle de France Creole: Affinities & Origins. viii, 299p. 23.50 (ISBN 0-89720-049-7); pap. 15.50 (ISBN 0-89720-048-9). Karoma.

Baker, R. A. Compendio De la Historia Cristiana. Almanza, Francisco G., tr. Orig. Title: A Summary of Christian History. 372p. (Span.). 1981. pap. 9.50 (ISBN 0-311-15032-2). Casa Bautista.

Baker, R. J. Administrative Theory & Public Administration. 208p. 1972. pap. text ed. 8.25x o.p. (ISBN 0-09-110680-X, Hutchinson U Lib); pap. text ed. 3.75x o.p. (ISBN 0-09-110681-8, Hutchinson U Lib). Humanities.

Baker, R. Robin. Human Navigation & the Sixth Sense. 1982. pap. 4.80 (ISBN 0-671-44129-9, Touchstone Bks). S&S.

--Migration Paths Through Time & Space. (Illus.). 1983. text ed. 15.95x (ISBN 0-8419-0822-2). Holmes & Meier.

Baker, Ralph & Meyer, Fred, eds. Evaluating Alternative Law-Enforcement Policies. LC 79-1541. (Policy Studies Organization Bk.). (Illus.). 240p. 1979. 22.95x (ISBN 0-669-02898-3). Lexington Bks.

Baker, Ralph, jt. ed. see Meyer, Fred.

Baker, Rance G. & Phillips, Billie R. The Sampler: Patterns for Composition. 1979. pap. text ed. 6.95x (ISBN 0-669-02267-5). Heath.

Baker, Ray J. Hawaiian Yesterdays. Van Dyke, Robert E. & Ronck, Ronn, eds. 256p. 1982. 28.95 (ISBN 0-935180-03-6). Mutual Pub HI.

Baker, Richard & Hayes, Rick S. Accounting for Small Manufacturers. LC 80-12001. (Small Business Management Ser.). 197p. 1980. 31.95x (ISBN 0-471-05704-5). Wiley.

Baker, Richard & Miall, Antony, eds. Everyman's Book of Sea Songs. 278p. 1983. 24.95 (ISBN 0-460-04470-2, Pub. by Evman England). Biblio Dist.

Baker, Robert, jt. auth. see Fredrick, Laurence.

Baker, Robert & Elliston, Frederick, eds. Philosophy & Sex. LC 75-21670. 397p. 1975. 11.95 (ISBN 0-87975-050-2); pap. 8.95 (ISBN 0-87975-055-3). Prometheus Bks.

Baker, Robert A. Contaminants & Sediments: Analysis, Chemistry, Biology, Vol. 2. LC 79-53424. 1980. 49.95 (ISBN 0-250-40307-2). Ann Arbor Science.

Baker, Robert A. & Craven, Paul J., Jr. Adventure in Faith: The First Three Hundred Years of First Baptist Church, Charleston, South Carolina. LC 82-71559. 1982. 9.95 (ISBN 0-8054-6563-4). Broadman.

Baker, Robert A., ed. Contaminants & Sediments: Fate & Transport, Case Studies, Modeling, Toxicity, Vol. 1. LC 79-53422. 1980. 49.95 (ISBN 0-250-40270-X); Set. 99.90 (ISBN 0-250-40308-0). Ann Arbor Science.

Baker, Robert D., jt. auth. see Maxwell, Robert S.

Baker, Robert F. Handbook of Highway Engineering. Bryd, L. G. & Grant, D., eds. LC 82-8922. 904p. 1982. Repr. lib. bdg. 62.50 (ISBN 0-89874-482-2). Krieger.

Baker, Robert F., et al. Public Policy Development: Linking the Technical & Political Processes. LC 74-32157. (Cambridges Studies on Applied Econometrics). 315p. 1975. 31.95 o.p. (ISBN 0-471-04435-0, Pub. by Wiley-Interscience). Wiley.

Baker, Robert H., jt. auth. see Fredrick, Laurence W.

Baker, Robert J. God Healed Me. LC 74-17801. (Pivot Family Reader Ser). 176p. (Orig.). 1974. pap. 1.75 o.p. (ISBN 0-87983-101-4). Keats.

--I'm Listening Lord, Keep Talking. LC 81-4278. 200p. 1981. pap. 6.95 (ISBN 0-8361-1953-3). Herald Pr.

Baker, Robert K. Doing Library Research: An Introduction for Community College Students. LC 80-22943. (Westview Guides to Library Research Ser.). 260p. 1981. 28.50 (ISBN 0-89158-778-0). Westview.

Baker, Robin, ed. The Mystery of Migration. LC 80-16839. (Illus.). 256p. 1981. 35.00 o.p. (ISBN 0-670-50286-3, Studio). Viking Pr.

Baker, Roger D., et al. Human Infection with Fungi, Actinomycetes & Algae. LC 72-160588. (Illus.). 1971. 230.60 o.p. (ISBN 0-387-05378-6). Springer-Verlag.

Baker, Rollin H. Michigan Mammals. (Illus.). 700p. 1982. 60.00 (ISBN 0-87013-234-2). Wayne St U Pr.

--Michigan Mammals. (Illus.). 700p. 1982. 60.00 (ISBN 0-686-43260-6). Mich St U Pr.

Baker, Roscoe. The American Legion & American Foreign Policy. LC 74-39. (Illus.). 329p. 1974. Repr. of 1954 ed. lib. bdg. 18.25x (ISBN 0-8371-7360-4, BAAL). Greenwood.

Baker, Ross & Pomper, Gerald. American Government. 704p. 1983. text ed. 19.95 (ISBN 0-686-84129-8). Macmillan.

Baker, Russell. Growing Up. 256p. 1982. 15.00 (ISBN 0-312-92267-1). Congdon & Weed.

--Poor Russell's Almanac. 256p. 1981. 12.00 o.p. (ISBN 0-312-92651-0). St Martin.

Baker, S. Games Dogs Play. Date not set. pap. 5.95 (ISBN 0-07-003452-4). McGraw.

--Systematic Approach to Advertising Creativity. 288p. 1983. pap. 10.95 (ISBN 0-07-003353-6, GB). McGraw.

Baker, S. Josephine. Fighting for Life. LC 78-156075. 296p. 1980. Repr. of 1939 ed. lib. bdg. 17.50 (ISBN 0-88275-611-7). Krieger.

Baker, Samm S., jt. auth. see Stillman, Irwin M.

Baker, Scott. Dhampire. 1982. pap. 2.95 (ISBN 0-671-44666-5, Timescape). PB.

--Nightchild. LC 79-4358. 1979. 10.95 o.p. (ISBN 0-399-12377-6). Putnam Pub Group.

Baker, Sheridan. The Practical Stylist. 5th ed. 206p. 1981. pap. text ed. 9.95 scp (ISBN 0-06-040454-X, HarpC); instructor's manual avail. (ISBN 0-06-360289-X). Har-Row.

Baker, Sinclair, jt. auth. see Stillman, Irwin.

Baker, Stephen. Games Dogs Play. LC 79-12535. (Illus.). 1979. 9.95 o.p. (ISBN 0-07-003451-6); pap. 5.95 o.p. (ISBN 0-07-003452-4). McGraw.

--The Systematic Approach to Advertising Creativity. 1979. 34.95 (ISBN 0-07-003352-8). McGraw.

Baker, Susan. The Christmas Book. LC 79-51212. (gr. 1-5). 1979. 4.95 (ISBN 0-448-16563-5, G&D); PLB write for info. (ISBN 0-448-13612-0). Putnam Pub Group.

Baker, Theodore. Dictionary of Musical Terms. LC 75-124595. (BCL Ser.: No. 1). 1970. Repr. of 1923 ed. 8.00 (ISBN 0-404-00468-7). AMS Pr.

--On the Music of the North American Indians. Buckley, Ann, tr. from Ger. (Music Reprint Ser., 1977). 1978. lib. bdg. 19.50 (ISBN 0-306-70888-4). Da Capo.

--Uber die Musik der nordamerikanischen Wilden. (Source Materials & Studies in Ethnomusicology Ser.: Vol. 9). (Dutch & Eng.). 1976. Repr. of 1882 ed. 40.00 o.s.i. (ISBN 90-6027-163-7, Pub. by Frits Knuf Netherlands); wrappers 27.50 o.s.i. (ISBN 90-6027-162-9, Pub. by Frits Knuf Netherlands). Pendragon NY.

Baker, Thomas E. Another Such Victory. write for info. (ISBN 0-915992-06-X). Eastern Acorn.

Baker, Thomas H. Memphis Commercial Appeal: The History of a Southern Newspaper. LC 74-165066. viii, 336p. 1971. 25.00x (ISBN 0-8071-0944-4). La State U Pr.

Baker, Toni. Mastering Machine Code on Your ZX-81. 1982. 18.95 (ISBN 0-8359-4262-7); pap. text ed. 12.95 (ISBN 0-8359-4261-9). Reston.

Baker, V. R., ed. Catastrophic Flooding: The Origin of the Channeled Scabland. LC 79-22901. (Benchmark Papers in Geology: Vol. 55). 384p. 46.00 (ISBN 0-87933-360-X). Hutchinson Ross.

Baker, Vernoon C. & Aufmann, Richard N. Essential Mathematics with Applications. LC 82-82928. 288p. 1982. pap. text ed. 20.95 (ISBN 0-395-33195-1); write for info. answer booklet (ISBN 0-395-33196-X). HM.

Baker, Victor R., jt. auth. see Costa, John E.

Baker, W., et al. Avoidance of Failure. 1970. 12.00 (ISBN 0-444-19653-6). Elsevier.
Baker, W. M. Bell's Acrostic Dictionary. LC 77-141772. 1971. Repr. of 1927 ed. 30.00x (ISBN 0-8103-3379-1). Gale.
Baker, W. P., ed. Compendium of Homoeotherapeutics. 1974. 6.00x (ISBN 0-685-85698-4, Pub. by American Foundation for Homoepathy). Formur Intl.
Baker, Wallace H., ed. Grouting in Geotechnical Engineering. LC 81-71798. 1032p. 1982. pap. text ed. 69.00 (ISBN 0-87262-295-9). Am Soc Civil Eng.
Baker, Wilfred E. Explosions in Air. (Illus.). 282p. 1973. 22.50x o.p. (ISBN 0-292-72003-3). U of Tex Pr.
Baker, William, jt. auth. see Smith, Harold.
Baker, William C., jt. auth. see Kelly, James C.
Baker, William D. Reading Skills. 2nd ed. LC 73-17161. (Illus.). 176p. 1974. pap. text ed. 9.95 (ISBN 0-13-762062-4). P-H.
Baker, William E. Jacques Prevert. (World Authors Ser.). 1967. 15.95 (ISBN 0-8057-2714-0, Twayne). G K Hall.
Baker, William H., jt. auth. see Lewis, Philip V.
Baker, William J. Sports in the Western World. LC 82-3669. 368p. 1983. text ed. 19.95 (ISBN 0-8476-7075-9); pap. 9.50x (ISBN 0-8476-7194-1). Rowman.
Baker, William M. Timothy Warren Anglin, 1822-96: Irish Catholic Canadian. LC 76-49480. 35.00x (ISBN 0-8020-5368-8). U of Toronto Pr.
Baker, William S. Bibliotheca Washingtoniana. LC 67-14022. 1967. Repr. of 1889 ed. 30.00x (ISBN 0-8103-3318-X). Gale.
Bakescu, R., tr. see Klimontovich, Yu L.
Bakewell, Dennis, ed. The Charter of the Heart Mountain Relocation Center, Wyoming. (Santa Susana Pr California Masters Ser.: No. 4). (Illus.). 56p. 1983. 30.00 (ISBN 0-937048-32-1). CSUN.
Bakewell, K. G., jt. auth. see Hunter, Eric.
Bakewell, K. G., ed. Management Principles & Practice: A Guide to Information Sources. LC 76-16127. (Management Information Guide Series: No. 32). 1977. 42.00x (ISBN 0-8103-0832-0). Gale.
Bakewell, P. J. Silver Mining & Society in Colonial Mexico, Zacatecas, 1546-1700. LC 78-158553. (American Latin Studies: No. 15). (Illus.). 1972. 42.50 (ISBN 0-521-08227-7). Cambridge U Pr.
Bakhash, Shaul. The Politics of Oil & Revolution in Iran. LC 82-72116. 61p. 1982. pap. 5.95 (ISBN 0-8157-0781-9). Brookings.
Bakhtin, M. Rabelais & His World. Iswolsky, Helene, tr. from Rus. 1968. pap. 6.95 o.p. (ISBN 0-262-52024-9). MIT Pr.
Bakhtin, M. M. The Dialogic Imagination: Four Essays. Holquist, Michael, ed. Emerson, Caryl, tr. from Rus. LC 80-15450. (University of Texas Press Slavic Ser.: No. 1). 478p. 1981. 27.50x o.p. (ISBN 0-292-71527-7). U of Tex Pr.
Bakir, A. M. Notes on Late Egyptian Grammar: A Semitic Approach. 144p. 1982. pap. text ed. 16.00x (ISBN 0-85668-214-4, Pub. by Aris & Phillips England). Humanities.
Bakish, David. Richard Wright. LC 71-190353. (Literature and Life Ser.). 121p. 1973. 11.95 (ISBN 0-8044-2015-7). Ungar.
Bakish, David, jt. ed. see Margolies, Edward.
Bakish, R. see Winkler, O.
Bakke, Karen. Sewing Machine As a Creative Tool. (Illus.). 128p. 1976 (ISBN 0-13-807255-8, Spec). pap. 4.95 o.p. (ISBN 0-13-807248-5). P-H.
Bakken, Gordon M. The Development of Law on the Rocky Mountain Frontier: Civil Law & Society, 1850-1912. LC 82-10984. (Contributions in Legal Studies: No. 27). 208p. 1983. lib. bdg. 29.95 (ISBN 0-313-23285-7, BDL/). Greenwood.
Bakken, Lavolla J. Land of the North Umpquas: Peaceful Indians of the West. LC 73-84954. (Illus.). 32p. 1973. pap. 1.95 (ISBN 0-913508-03-9). Te Cum Tom.
Bakker, Dirk J., jt. ed. see Knights, Robert M.
Bakker, H. De see De Bakker, H.
Bakker, J., jt. auth. see Riewald, J. G.
Bakker, J. J., jt. ed. see Politiek, R. D.
Bakker, Jim & Bakker, Tammy. You Can Make It. 128p. (Orig.). Date not set. pap. 2.95 (ISBN 0-89221-098-2). New Leaf.
Bakker, Marilyn. Rim: Breakthrough Ahead, P-054. 1983. Set. 1750.00 (ISBN 0-89336-202-6). BCC.
Bakker, Tammy & Dudley, Cliff. Run to the Roar. LC 80-80656. 160p. 1980. 2.95 (ISBN 0-89221-073-7). New Leaf.
Bakker, Tammy, jt. auth. see Bakker, Jim.
Bakko, Darlene. Unusual Animals A to Z. LC 82-71047. (Illus.). 60p. (Orig.). (gr. k-5). 1982. pap. 2.50x (ISBN 0-943864-30-5). Davenport.
Bakounine, M. A. A Mes Amis Russes et Polonais. (Nineteenth Century Russia). 24p. (Fr.). 1974. Repr. of 1862 ed. 21.50x o.p. (ISBN 0-8287-0000-1, R4). Clearwater Pub.
Bakshian, Aram, Jr. The Candidates Nineteen Eighty. 1980. 12.95 o.p. (ISBN 0-87000-472-7, Arlington Hse). Crown.
Bakunin, Mikhail. From Out of the Dustbin: Articles & Speeches 1869-1871. Cutler, R., tr. from Rus. & intro. by. 212p. 1983. 22.50 (ISBN 0-88233-645-2). Ardis Pubs.
Bakutis, Alice R. Nurse Anesthetists Continuing Education Review. 2nd ed. 1981. pap. 20.00 (ISBN 0-87488-356-3). Med Exam.
Bakwin, Harry & Bakwin, Ruth M. Behavior Disorders in Children. 4th ed. LC 75-173330. (Illus.). 690p. 1972. 29.00 o.p. (ISBN 0-7216-1502-3). Saunders.
Bakwin, Ruth M., jt. auth. see Bakwin, Harry.
Balaam, L. N. Fundamentals of Biometry. 1972. 21.95x o.p. (ISBN 0-470-04571-X). Halsted Pr.
Balaban, M., ed. Molecular Structure & Dynamics. (Illus.). 368p. 1981. text ed. write for info. (ISBN 0-86689-001-7). Balaban Intl Sci Serv.
Balaban, M., et al, eds. Structural Aspects of Recognition & Assembly in Biological Macromolecules, 2 vols. 976p. Set. text ed. write for info. (ISBN 0-86689-004-1). Vol. 1 (ISBN 0-86689-002-5). Vol. 2 (ISBN 0-86689-003-3). Balaban Intl Sci Serv.
Balaban, Nancy, jt. auth. see Morey, G. B.
Balabanian, Norman & Bickart, T. Electrical Network Theory. LC 69-16122. 931p. 1969. 59.50x (ISBN 0-471-04576-4). Wiley.
Balabanian, Norman & Bickart, Theodore. Electrical Network Theory. LC 82-21224. 954p. 1983. Repr. of 1969 ed. lib. bdg. 59.50 (ISBN 0-89874-581-0). Krieger.
Balabanian, Norman & LePage, Wilbur. Electrical Science: No. 2-Dynamic Networks. (Illus.). 640p. 1973. 22.50 (ISBN 0-07-003544-X, C). McGraw.
Balabanoff, Angelica. My Life As a Rebel. LC 68-23270. 1968. Repr. of 1938 ed. lib. bdg. 17.75x (ISBN 0-8371-0011-9, BARB). Greenwood.
Balabkins, Nicholas. Germany under Direct Controls: Economic Aspects of Industrial Disarmament, 1945-1948. 1964. 22.50 (ISBN 0-8135-0449-X). Rutgers U Pr.
Balachandran, M., ed. Regional Statistics: A Guide to Information Sources. LC 80-14260. (Economics Information Guide Ser.: Vol. 13). 230p. 1980. 42.00x (ISBN 0-8103-1463-0). Gale.
Balachandran, Sarojini. Directory of Publishing Sources: The Researcher's Guide to Journals in Engineering & Technology. 386p. 1982. 27.50x (ISBN 0-471-09200-2, Pub. by Wiley-Interscience). Wiley.
Balachandran, Sarojini, ed. Energy Statistics: A Guide to Information Sources. LC 80-13338. (Natural World Information Guide Ser.: Vol. 1). 272p. 1980. 42.00x (ISBN 0-8103-1419-3). Gale.
--New Product Planning. LC 79-24046. (Management Information Guide Ser.: No. 38). 1980. 42.00x (ISBN 0-8103-0838-X). Gale.
Balagum, Olga. Nigeria, Magic of a Land. (Illus.). 1980. 60.00 o.p. (ISBN 2-85258-106-X). Hippocrene Bks.
Balakian, A. A., ed. The Symbolist Movement in the Literature of European Languages. (Comparative History of Literatures in European Language Ser.: Vol. 2). 732p. 1982. text ed. 53.00x (ISBN 963-05-2694-8, Pub. by Kultura Pr Hungary). Humanities.
Balakian, Anna. Literary Origins of Surrealism: A New Mysticism in French Poetry. 1966. 15.00x o.p. (ISBN 0-8147-0024-1); pap. 7.50x o.p. (ISBN 0-8147-0025-X). NYU Pr.
Balakian, Peter. Sad Days of Light. 72p. 1983. 13.95 (ISBN 0-935296-33-6); pap. 7.95 (ISBN 0-935296-34-4). Sheep Meadow.
Balakrishnan, A. V. Stochastic Differential Systems One Filtering & Control: A Function Space Approach. LC 73-79363. (Lecture Notes in Economics & Mathematical Systems: Vol. 84). 252p. 1973. pap. 14.00 o.p. (ISBN 0-387-06303-X). Springer-Verlag.
Balam, Pablo, ed. see Luxton, Richard.
Balas, Robert S. Qu'est-ce qui se Passe? Conversation-Revision de Grammaire. 448p. 1979. pap. 15.95 (ISBN 0-395-30955-7); tchr's manual 2.00 (ISBN 0-395-30956-5); cahier d'exercises et de laboratoire 8.50 (ISBN 0-395-30957-3); recordings 170.00 (ISBN 0-395-30958-1). HM.
Balaskas, Arthur. Bodylife. LC 77-79106. (Health, Nutrition, & Well Being Bks). 1979. 10.00 o.p. (ISBN 0-448-14500-6, G&D); pap. 6.95 o.p. (ISBN 0-448-16803-0, Today Pr). Putnam Pub Group.
Balassa, B. & Nelson, R., eds. Economic Progress, Private Values, & Public Policy: Essays in Honor of William Fellner. 1977. 64.00 (ISBN 0-7204-0515-7, North-Holland). Elsevier.
Balassa, Bela. The Newly Industrialized Countries in the World Economy. LC 80-20787. 450p. 1981. 27.50 (ISBN 0-08-026336-4); pap. 18.50 (ISBN 0-08-026335-6). Pergamon.
--The Newly-Industrializing Developing Countries after the Oil Crisis. (Working Paper: No.437). 57p. 1980. 5.00 (ISBN 0-686-36173-3, WP-0437). World Bank.
--The Process of Industrial Development & Alternative Development Strategies. LC 81-1033. (Essays in International Finance Ser.: No. 141). 1980. pap. text ed. 2.50x (ISBN 0-88165-048-X). Princeton U Int Finan Econ.
Balasubramanyam, V. N., jt. auth. see MacBean, Alasdair.
Balasz, R., jt. auth. see Di Benedetta, C.
Balaz, S. & Blaysek, J. Control of Cell Proliferation by Endogenous Inhibitors. 1979. 62.25 (ISBN 0-444-80127-8, North Holland). Elsevier.
Balazs, Endre A., jt. ed. see Jeanloz, Roger W.
Balbaki, M. Al-Mawrid: Dictionary. 49.00 (ISBN 0-686-18367-3). Kazi Pubns.
Balbkins, Nicholas. Indigenization & Economic Development: The Nigerian Experience, Vol. 33. Altman, Edward I. & Walter, Ingo, eds. LC 81-81654. (Contemporary Studies in Economic & Financial Analysis). 300p. 1981. 40.00 (ISBN 0-89232-227-6). Jai Pr.
Balbus, Isaac D. The Dialectics of Legal Repression: Black Rebels Before the American Criminal Courts. LC 73-76762. 270p. 1973. 12.50x (ISBN 0-87154-081-9). Russell Sage.
Balbus, Issac D. The Dialectics of Legal Repression: Black Rebels Before the American Criminal Courts. new ed. LC 75-44825. (Law & Society Ser.). 269p. 1977. pap. text ed. 6.95 (ISBN 0-87855-609-5). Transaction Bks.
Balch, Dianne. All Joy. 175p. 1982. pap. 4.95 (ISBN 0-86605-098-1). Here's Life.
Balch, Emily. Innocence Abroad. LC 74-2796. (Illus.). 270p. 1975. Repr. of 1931 ed. lib. bdg. 19.00x (ISBN 0-8371-7433-3, BAIB). Greenwood.
Balchin, Paul N. Housing Improvement & Social Inequality. 1979. text ed. 36.25x (ISBN 0-566-00274-4). Gower Pub Ltd.
Balcolm, Kenneth C., III, jt. auth. see Angell, Tony.
Balcom, Mary. Ketchikan: Alaska's Totemland. (Illus.). 1973. 4.00 o.p. (ISBN 0-685-30785-9). Balcom.
Balcom, Mary G. Ghost Towns of Alaska. 6th ed. (Illus.). 1982. pap. 3.75 o.p. (ISBN 0-686-59779-6). Balcom.
Balcomb, J. D., et al. Passive Solar Heating & Cooling: Proceedings of the Conference & Workshop, May 1976, Albuquerque, New Mexico. Keller, M. H., ed. 355p. 1983. pap. text ed. 27.00x (ISBN 0-89553-108-9). Am Solar Energy.
Balcomb, J. Douglas, et al. Passive Solar Design Handbook. Jones, R., ed. (Passive Solar Design Handbook Ser.: Vol. 3, 1980). 668p. 1983. text ed. 59.00 (ISBN 0-89553-124-0); pap. text ed. 25.00x (ISBN 0-89553-106-2); pap. text ed. 15.00 pap. suppl. (ISBN 0-89553-123-2). Am Solar Energy.
Bald, R. C., ed. see Coleridge, Samuel T.
Bald, Robert C. Donne's Influence in English Literature. 1932. 7.50 o.p. (ISBN 0-8446-1040-2). Peter Smith.
Bald, Suresht R. Novelists & Political Consciousness: Literary Expression of Indian Nationalism, 1919-1947. 1982. 17.50x (ISBN 0-8364-0921-3, Pub. by Chanakya). South Asia Bks.
Baldamus, C. A. & Koch, K. M., eds. Biocompatibility in Hemodialysis. (Contributions to Nephrology: Vol. 36). (Illus.). viii, 140p. 1983. pap. 57.50 (ISBN 3-8055-3601-1). S Karger.
Baldanza, Frank. Iris Murdoch. (English Authors Ser.: No. 169). 169p. 1974. lib. bdg. 10.95 o.p. (ISBN 0-8057-1410-3, Twayne). G K Hall.
--Ivy Compton-Burnett. (English Authors Ser.). 13.95 (ISBN 0-8057-1112-0, Twayne). G K Hall.
Baldassare, Mark. The Growth Dilemma: Residents' Views & Local Population Change in the United States. LC 81-1499. 224p. 1981. 22.00x (ISBN 0-520-04302-2). U of Cal Pr.
--Residential Crowding in Urban America. LC 77-83102. 1979. 19.95x (ISBN 0-520-03563-1). U of Cal Pr.
Baldauski, Karen. The Cat Coloring Book. (Illus.). pap. 2.25 (ISBN 0-486-24011-8). Dover.
Balderson, Margaret. When Jays Fly to Barbmo. 1980. PLB 9.95 (ISBN 0-8398-2601-X, Gregg). G K Hall.
Balderston, Daniel, tr. see Bianco, Jose.
Balderston, Katherine C. The History & Sources of Percy's Memoir of Goldsmith, 1926. Bd. with Collected Letters. Goldsmith. 1928. 18.00 (ISBN 0-527-04700-7). Kraus Repr.
Balderston, Katherine G., ed. see Goldsmith, Oliver.
Baldessarini, Ross J. Biomedical Aspects of Depression & Its Treatment. LC 82-22659. (Illus.). 140p. 1983. casebound 18.00x (ISBN 0-88048-004-1). Am Psychiatric.
Baldi, Philip. An Introduction to the Indo-European Languages. 208p. 1983. price not set (ISBN 0-8093-1090-2); pap. price not set (ISBN 0-8093-1091-0). S Ill U Pr.
Baldi, Philip & Werth, Ronald N., eds. Readings in Historical Phonology: Chapters in the Theory of Sound Change. LC 77-13895. 1978. lib. bdg. 18.50x (ISBN 0-271-00525-4); pap. text ed. 10.00x (ISBN 0-271-00539-4). Pa St U Pr.
Baldick, Robert. The Duel: The History of Dueling. (Illus.). 252p. 1966. 8.50 o.p. (ISBN 0-517-01978-7). Crown.
Baldinger, Kurt. Semantic Theory. 1980. 30.00 (ISBN 0-312-71258-8). St Martin.
Baldini, Gabriele. The Story of Giuseppe Verdi. Parker, Roger, tr. from Ital. LC 79-41376. 330p. 1980. 42.50 (ISBN 0-521-22911-1); pap. 11.95 (ISBN 0-521-29712-5). Cambridge U Pr.
Baldini, Pier R., jt. auth. see Lebano, Edoardo A.
Baldini, Umberto. The Sculpture of Michelangelo. LC 82-60032. (Illus.). 294p. 1982. cancelled 45.00 (ISBN 0-8478-0447-X). Rizzoli Intl.
Baldinucci, Filippo. Vocabolario toscano dell'arte del disegno. (Documents of Art & Architectural History, Ser. 1: Vol. 5). (Ital.). 1980. Repr. of 1681 ed. 35.00x (ISBN 0-89371-105-5). Broude Intl Edns.
Baldo-Ceolin, M. Weak Interactions. (Enrico Fermi Summer School Ser.: Vol. 71). 1980. 102.25 (ISBN 0-444-85286-7). Elsevier.
Baldock, Cora V. & Lally, James. Sociology in Australia & New Zealand: Theory & Methods. LC 72-778. (Contributions in Sociology: No. 16). (Illus.). 328p. 1975. lib. bdg. 29.95x (ISBN 0-8371-6126-6, BSA/). Greenwood.
Baldock, Peter. Community Work & Social Work. (Library of Social Work). 1974. 16.95x (ISBN 0-7100-8026-3); pap. 7.95 (ISBN 0-7100-8027-1). Routledge & Kegan.
Baldonado, Ardelina A. & Stahl, Dulcelina A. Cancer Nursing. 2nd ed. (Nursing Outline Ser.). 1982. pap. 21.50 o.p. (ISBN 0-87488-374-1). Med Exam.
Baldridge, H. David. Shark Attack. LC 74-79073. 1974. 8.95 o.p. (ISBN 0-8375-6780-7). H D Baldridge.
Baldridge, J. Victor. Sociology: A Critical Approach to Power, Conflict, & Change. 2nd ed. 547p. 1980. text ed. 21.95 (ISBN 0-471-04708-2); study guide 10.95 (ISBN 0-471-07689-9); test avail. (ISBN 0-471-04568-3). Wiley.
Baldridge, J. Victor, et al, eds. Managing Change in Educational Organizations: Sociological Perspectives Stragegies & Case Studies. LC 74-24479. 500p. 1975. 25.50 (ISBN 0-8211-0128-5); text ed. 23.00 (ISBN 0-685-51463-3). McCutchan.
Baldridge, Letitia. Amy Vanderbilt Complete Book of Etiquette. rev. ed. LC 77-16896. 1978. 15.95 (ISBN 0-385-13375-8); thumb-indexed 16.95 (ISBN 0-385-14238-2). Doubleday.
Baldridge, Victor J., jt. ed. see Riley, Gary L.
Baldry, P. E. The Battle Against Bacteria: A Fresh Look. LC 76-639. (Illus.). 140p. 1976. 24.95 (ISBN 0-521-21268-5). Cambridge U Pr.
--Battle Against Heart Disease. LC 75-108098. (Illus.). 1971. 37.50 (ISBN 0-521-07490-8). Cambridge U Pr.
Balducci, Carolyn. A Self-Made Woman: Biography of Nobel-Prize-Winner Grazia Deledda. 256p. (gr. 7 up). 1975. 6.95 o.p. (ISBN 0-395-21914-0). HM.
Baldwin. Makin' Things for Kids. LC 78-73845. 1981. 12.95 (ISBN 0-916752-46-1). Dorison Hse.
Baldwin, A., et al. Introduction to Sixteen-Bit Microprocessors. LC 81-50564. 1981. pap. 15.95 (ISBN 0-672-21805-4). Sams.
Baldwin, Agnew. Facing Heads on Ancient Greek Coins. (Illus.). 1981. pap. 10.00 o.p. (ISBN 0-915262-47-9). S J Durst.
Baldwin, Alfred L. Theories of Child Development. 2nd ed. LC 80-24517. 582p. 1980. text ed. 24.95 (ISBN 0-471-04583-7). Wiley.
Baldwin, Barbie. Famous Florida! Underground Gourmet Restaurants & Recipes. Atshul, B. J. & LaFray, J., eds. (Famous Florida! Ser.). (Illus.). 280p. 1982. pap. write for info. (ISBN 0-942084-01-2). LaFrey Pub.
Baldwin, Charles C. Stanford White. LC 78-150512. (Architecture & Decorative Art Ser.: Vol. 39). 1971. Repr. of 1931 ed. lib. bdg. 42.50 (ISBN 0-306-70138-3). Da Capo.
Baldwin, Charles S. Composition: Oral & Written. LC 69-13806. Repr. of 1909 ed. lib. bdg. 18.00x (ISBN 0-8371-0294-4, BAC). Greenwood.
Baldwin, Christina. One to One: Self-Understanding Through Journal Writing. LC 76-58537. 204p. 1977. 8.95 (ISBN 0-87131-232-8); pap. 4.95 (ISBN 0-87131-294-8). M Evans.
Baldwin, Claudia. Nigerian Literature: A Bibliography of Criticism, 1952-1976. 1980. lib. bdg. 21.00 (ISBN 0-8161-8418-6, Hall Reference). G K Hall.
Baldwin, Deirdra. The Emerging Detail. LC 77-74622. 1977. perfect binding 9.95 o.p. (ISBN 0-915380-03-X); ltd. ed. 100.00 o.p. (ISBN 0-686-77069-2). Word Works.
Baldwin, Deirdra & Davis, Gene. Inside Outside. spec. signed ed. 35.00 (ISBN 0-915380-17-X); saddle stitch 8.00. Word Works.
Baldwin, Dierdra. Totemic. (Burning Deck Poetry Ser.). 32p. 1983. pap. 3.00 (ISBN 0-930901-13-4). Burning Deck.
Baldwin, Ed & Baldwin, Stevie. Scrap Fabric Crafts. (Illus.). 160p. 1982. pap. 7.95 (ISBN 0-89586-168-2). H P Bks.
Baldwin, Ed, jt. ed. see Baldwin, Stevie.
Baldwin, Ernest. Nature of Biochemistry. 2nd ed. (Orig.). 1962. 19.95 (ISBN 0-521-04097-3); pap. 8.95x (ISBN 0-521-09177-2, 177). Cambridge U Pr.
Baldwin, Faith. Adam's Eden. 1977. lib. bdg. 11.50 o.p. (ISBN 0-8161-6533-5, Large Print Bks). G K Hall.
Baldwin, Gordon C. Indians of the Southwest. (American Indians Then & Now Ser.). (Illus.). (gr. 6-8). 1970. 6.75 o.p. (ISBN 0-399-20105-X). Putnam Pub Group.
--Pyramids of the New World. (Illus.). (gr. 7 up). 1971. PLB 5.49 o.p. (ISBN 0-399-60526-6). Putnam Pub Group.
Baldwin, Hanson W. World War One: An Outline History. (Illus.). 1962. 12.45i (ISBN 0-06-010190-3, HarpT). Har-Row.
Baldwin, Hare, et al. The Preparation of a Products Liability Case. 1054p. 1981. 60.00 (ISBN 0-316-07923-5). Little.
Baldwin, Helene L. Samuel Beckett's Real Silence. LC 80-21465. 184p. 1981. 16.50x (ISBN 0-271-00301-4). Pa St U Pr.

Baldwin, Henry. A General View of the Origin & Nature of the Constitution & Government of the United States. LC 72-118027. (American Constitutional & Legal History Ser). 1970. Repr. of 1837 ed. lib. bdg. 27.50 (ISBN 0-306-71944-4). Da Capo.

Baldwin, Horace S. Our Host the World. LC 78-66223. 1980. 6.95 o.p. (ISBN 0-533-04152-X). Vantage.

Baldwin, Huntley. Creating Effective TV Commercials. LC 81-66509. (Illus.). 200p. 1982. 24.95 (ISBN 0-87251-063-8). Crain Bks.

Baldwin, Ian & Stanley, John. The Garden Centre Manuel. (Illus.). 250p. 1982. pap. text ed. 29.95 (ISBN 0-686-84094-1). Timber.

Baldwin, J. N. Microprocessors for Industry. 144p. 1982. text ed. 19.95 (ISBN 0-408-00517-3). Butterworth.

Baldwin, James. Horse Fair. LC 76-9890. (Children's Literature Reprint Ser). (Illus.). (gr. 5-6). 1976. 19.75x o.p. (ISBN 0-8486-0201-3). Core Collection.

--If Beale Street Could Talk. (RL 10). 1975. pap. 2.95 (ISBN 0-451-12044-2, AE2044, Sig). NAL.

Baldwin, James M. Dictionary of Philosophy & Psychology, 3 vols. bound in 4. Incl. Vols. 1 & 2. 22.50 ea.; Vol. 1. (ISBN 0-8446-1047-X); Vol. 2. (ISBN 0-8446-1048-8); Vol. 3., 2 Pts. Bibliography of Philosophy, Psychology and Cognate Subjects. 20.00 ea.; Pt. 1. (ISBN 0-8446-1049-6); Pt. 2. (ISBN 0-8446-1050-X). Set. 85.00 (ISBN 0-8446-1046-1). Peter Smith.

Baldwin, James Mark. Mental Development in the Child & the Race. 3rd ed. LC 66-19690. Repr. of 1906 ed. 35.00x (ISBN 0-678-00396-3). Kelley.

Baldwin, Janice I., jt. auth. see Baldwin, John D.

Baldwin, John. Ice Pick. LC 82-14369. 228p. 1983. 12.50 (ISBN 0-688-00679-5). Morrow.

Baldwin, John & McConville, Michael. Jury Trials. 1979. 19.95x (ISBN 0-19-825350-8). Oxford U Pr.

Baldwin, John & McConville, Michael J. Negotiated Justice: Pressure to Plead Guilty. (Law in Society Ser.). 128p. 1977. 19.00x o.p. (ISBN 0-85520-171-1, Pub. by Martin Robertson England). Biblio Dist.

Baldwin, John D. & Baldwin, Janice I. Behavior Principles in Everyday Life. (Illus.). 336p. 1981. text ed. 19.95 (ISBN 0-13-072751-2). P-H.

Baldwin, John R. The Regulatory Agency & the Public Corporation: The Canadian Air Transport Industry. LC 75-8916. 256p. 1975. prof ref 25.00x (ISBN 0-88410-262-9). Ballinger Pub.

Baldwin, Leland D. The Keelboat Age on Western Waters. LC 41-10342. 1941. 7.95 o.p. (ISBN 0-8229-1027-6). U of Pittsburgh Pr.

Baldwin Library of Childrens Literature, Universityof Florida, Gainesville. Index to Children's Literature in English Before 1900: Catalog of the Baldwin Library of the University of Florida at Gainesville. (Library Catalogs Supplements). 1981. lib. bdg. 325.00 (ISBN 0-8161-0370-4, Hall Library). G K Hall.

Baldwin, Lindley. Samuel Morris. 74p. Date not set. 1.75 (ISBN 0-88113-319-1). Edit Betania.

Baldwin, Margaret. Kisses of Death: A Great Escape Story of World War II. (Jem - High Interest-Low Reading Level Ser.). (Illus.). 64p. (gr. 7-9). 1983. PLB 9.29 (ISBN 0-671-43850-6). Messner.

--Thanksgiving. (First Bks.). (Illus.). 72p. (gr. 4 up). 1983. PLB 8.90 (ISBN 0-531-04532-3). Watts.

Baldwin, Michael, ed. Poems by Children. (Illus.). 1962. 11.95 o.p. (ISBN 0-7100-1041-9). Routledge & Kegan.

Baldwin, Neil & Meyers, Steven L., eds. The Manuscripts & Letters of William Carlos Williams in the Poetry Collection of the Lockwood Memorial Library, State University of New York at Buffalo. lib. bdg. 35.00 (ISBN 0-8161-8047-4, Hall Reference). G K Hall.

Baldwin, Orrel. Makers of American History. rev. ed. (Illus.). 480p. (gr. 4-6). 1979. text ed. 9.57 (ISBN 0-8372-3692-4); tchrs' guide 2.58 (ISBN 0-8372-3672-X). Bowmar-Noble.

Baldwin, Pat. Bob Barnes Revenge. 1970. pap. 1.25 (ISBN 0-87508-646-2). Chr Lit.

--Drumbeats in the Forest. 1970. pap. 0.69 o.p. (ISBN 0-87508-661-6). Chr Lit.

--Hideaway. 1970. pap. 0.69 o.p. (ISBN 0-87508-678-0). Chr Lit.

--Race Against Time. 1970. pap. 0.69 o.p. (ISBN 0-87508-749-3). Chr Lit.

Baldwin, R. L., ed. Animals, Feed, Food & People: An Analysis of the Role of Animals in Food Production. (AAAS Selected Symposium: No. 42). 150p. 1980. lib. bdg. 17.00 (ISBN 0-89158-779-9). Westview.

Baldwin, Rebecca. A Matter of Honor. 176p. (Orig.). 1983. pap. 2.25 (ISBN 0-449-20102-3, Crest). Fawcett.

Baldwin, Robert, jt. auth. see Paris, Ruth.

Baldwin, Robert E. The Inefficacy of Trade Policy. LC 82-23425. (Essays in International Finance Ser.: No. 150). 1982. pap. text ed. 2.50x (ISBN 0-88165-057-9). Princeton U Int Finan Econ.

Baldwin, Robert E., jt. auth. see Meier, Gerald M.

Baldwin, Roger & Brakeman, Louis. Expanding Faculty Options: Career Development Projects at Colleges & Universities. 116p. 1981. 7.95. Impact VA.

Baldwin, Roger, ed. see Kropotkin, Peter.

Baldwin, Sally, jt. ed. see Jones, Kathleen.

Baldwin, Shirley. First Aid for the Office & Workplace. (Illus.). 192p. 1983. 15.75 (ISBN 0-87527-258-4). Green.

Baldwin, Simeon E. Life & Letters of Simeon Baldwin. 1919. 65.00x (ISBN 0-685-89762-1). Elliots Bks.

Baldwin, Stanley C. A True View of You. LC 81-84569. (Orig.). 1982. pap. 4.95 (ISBN 0-8307-0779-4, 5414602). Regal.

--What Did Jesus Say About That? 156p. 1975. pap. 4.95 (ISBN 0-88207-718-X). Victor Bks.

Baldwin, Stevie, jt. auth. see Baldwin, Ed.

Baldwin, Stevie & Baldwin, Ed, eds. The Great Panty Hose Craft Book. (Illus.). 160p. 1982. 14.95 (ISBN 0-307-46615-9, Golden Pr); pap. 9.95 (ISBN 0-307-46616-7). Western Pub.

Baldwin, Summerfield. Business in the Middle Ages. LC 68-25172. (Berkshire Studies in European History Ser.). 1968. Repr. of 1937 ed. 12.50x (ISBN 0-8154-0015-2). Cooper Sq.

Baldwin, Thomas F. & McVoy, D. Stevens. Cable Communication. (Illus.). 432p. 1983. 24.95 (ISBN 0-13-110171-4). P-H.

Baldwin, Thomas W. Organization & Personnel of the Shakespearean Company. LC 60-6036. 1961. Repr. of 1927 ed. 15.00x (ISBN 0-8462-0115-1). Russell.

Baldwin, W. W. The Price of Power. LC 76-990. 361p. 1976. Repr. of 1948 ed. lib. bdg. 39.50 (ISBN 0-306-70803-5). Da Capo.

Baldwin, William. Treatise of Morall Philosophie. rev. ed. LC 67-10126. 1967. Repr. of 1620 ed. 46.00x (ISBN 0-8201-1003-5). Schol Facsimiles.

Baldwin, William L. The World Tin Market: Political Pricing & Economic Competition. (Duke Press Policy Studies). 440p. 1983. 55.00 (ISBN 0-8223-0505-4). Duke.

Bale, Don, Jr. The Fabulous Investment Potential of Singles. rev. 3rd ed. 1975. pap. 5.00 o.p. (ISBN 0-912070-13-7). Bale Bks.

--The Fabulous Investment Potential of Uncirculated Singles. rev. 3rd ed. 1975. pap. 5.00 o.p. (ISBN 0-912070-11-0). Bale Bks.

--How to Invest in Singles. rev. 3rd ed. 1975. pap. 5.00 o.p. (ISBN 0-912070-09-9). Bale Bks.

--How to Invest in Uncirculated Singles. rev. 3rd ed. 1975. pap. 5.00 o.p. (ISBN 0-912070-10-2). Bale Bks.

--Out of Little Coins, Big Fortunes Grow. rev. 3rd ed. 1975. pap. 5.00 o.p. (ISBN 0-912070-08-0). Bale Bks.

Bale, Shelby G., jt. ed. see Friis, Herman R., Jr.

Balek, Jaroslav. Hydrology & Water Resources in Tropical Africa. (Developments in Water Science: Vol. 8). 1977. 64.00 (ISBN 0-444-99814-4). Elsevier.

Balekjian, Wahe H. Legal Aspects of Foreign Investment in the European Economic Community. LC 67-15827. 356p. 1967. 10.80 (ISBN 0-379-00312-0). Oceana.

Balentine, J. Douglas. Pathology of Oxygen Toxicity. 346p. 1982. 45.00 (ISBN 0-12-077080-6). Acad Pr.

Balentine, Samuel E. The Hidden God: The Hiding of the Face of God in the Old Testament. (Oxford Theological Monographs). 192p. 1983. 29.95 (ISBN 0-19-826719-3). Oxford U Pr.

Balescu, R. Statistical Mechanics of Charged Particles. LC 63-17454. (Monographs in Statistical Physics & Thermodynamics: Vol. 4). 477p. 1963. 26.00 (ISBN 0-470-04602-3, Pub. by Wiley). Krieger.

Balescu, Radu C. Equilibrium & Non-Equilibrium Statistical Mechanics. LC 74-20907. 768p. 1975. 59.00x (ISBN 0-471-04600-0, Pub. by Wiley-Interscience). Wiley.

Balestrino, Philip. Skeleton Inside You. LC 72-132290. (A Let's-Read-and-Find-Out Science Bk). (Illus.). (gr. k-3). 1971. PLB 10.89 (ISBN 0-690-74123-5, TYC-J). Har-Row.

Balet, Jan. The King & the Broom Maker. LC 68-28672. (Illus.). (gr. k-3). 1969. 4.95 o.s.i. (ISBN 0-440-04523-1, Sey Lawr); PLB 4.58 o.s.i. (ISBN 0-440-04520-7, Sey Lawr). Delacorte.

Baley, B. A., jt. ed. see Jaeger, T. A.

Baley, James A. Illustrated Guide to Developing Athletic Strength, Power, & Agility. (Illus.). 1977. 14.95 o.p. (ISBN 0-13-450999-4, Parker). P-H.

Baley, John D. Semi-Programmed Arithmetic for College Students. 144p. 1975. pap. text ed. 8.95x o.p. (ISBN 0-669-90886-X). Heath.

Balfour, A. J. Speeches on Zionism. Cohen, I., ed. Repr. of 1928 ed. 19.00 o.s.i. (ISBN 0-527-04800-3). Kraus Repr.

Balfour, Alan H. Rockefeller Center: Architecture As Theatre. (Illus.). 1978. 32.50 (ISBN 0-07-003480-X). McGraw.

Balfour, Campbell. Industrial Relations in the Common Market: France, Germany, Italy, Netherlands, Belgium, Luxembourg, Denmark, Norway, Ireland & Britain. (Illus.). 142p. 1972. 10.95x o.p. (ISBN 0-7100-7436-0); pap. 4.75 (ISBN 0-7100-7437-9). Routledge & Kegan.

Balfour, D., jt. ed. see Grant, W. A.

Balfour, Isaac B., ed. see Sachs, Julius Von.

Balfour, Issac B., tr. see Goebel, K.

Balfour, Michael. The Adversaries. 276p. 1983. pap. 11.95 (ISBN 0-7100-0753-1). Routledge & Kegan.

Balgopal, Pallassana R. & Vassil, Thomas V. Groups in Social Work: An Ecological Approach. 300p. 1983. text ed. 20.95 (ISBN 0-02-305530-8). Macmillan.

Balian. Sometimes it's Turkey, Sometimes it's Feathers. 1982. pap. 4.95 (ISBN 0-687-39073-7). Abingdon.

Balian, Edward S. How to Design, Analyze, & Write Doctoral Research: The Practical Guidebook. LC 82-20164. (Illus.). 268p. (Orig.). 1983. lib. bdg. 22.75 (ISBN 0-8191-2879-1); pap. text ed. 11.75 (ISBN 0-8191-2880-5). U Pr of Amer.

Balian, Lorna. Bah! Humbug? LC 76-50625. (Illus.). (gr. k-3). 1982. pap. 3.95. Abingdon.

--Humbug Rabbit. LC 73-9555. (Illus.). 32p. (gr. k-2). 1974. 9.95 o.p. (ISBN 0-687-18046-5). Abingdon.

--Sometimes It's Turkey, Sometimes It's Feathers. LC 72-3867. (Illus.). 32p. (gr. k-11). 1973. 8.95 o.p. (ISBN 0-687-39074-5). Abingdon.

--A Sweetheart for Valentine. LC 79-3957. (Illus.). 32p. (gr. k-3). 1979. 8.95 o.p. (ISBN 0-687-40771-0). Abingdon.

Balian, R. & Adam, J. G. Laser-Plasma Interactions. (Les Houches Summer School Ser.: Vol. 34). 1982. 159.75 (ISBN 0-444-86215-3). Elsevier.

Balian, R. & Adouse, J. Physical Cosmology. (Les Houches Summer School Ser.: Vol. 32). 1980. 106.50 (ISBN 0-444-85433-9). Elsevier.

Balian, R., ed. Fluid Dynamics. (Les Houches Lectures: 1973). 1977. 113.00 o.p. (ISBN 0-677-10170-8). Gordon.

Balian, R. & Iagolnitzer, D., eds. Structural Analysis of Collision Amplitudes: Proceedings, les Houches June Institute of Physics, June 2-27, 1975. LC 76-17583. 1976. 95.75 (ISBN 0-7204-0506-8, North-Holland). Elsevier.

Balian, R., ed. see Summer School on Weak & Electromagnetic Interactions at High Energy, Session XXIX, les Houches, July 5-August 14, 1976.

Balian, R., et al, eds. Atomic & Molecular Physics & the Interstellar Matter, 2 vols. LC 75-23253. (Les Houches Summer School Ser.: Vol. 26). 1975. Set. 106.50 (ISBN 0-444-10856-4, North-Holland). Elsevier.

--Claude Bloch Scientific Works, 2 vols. LC 74-84212. 1975. Set. 234.00 (ISBN 0-444-10853-X, North-Holland). Elsevier.

--Physics of Defects: Proceedings of the Les Houches Summer School Session, XXXV. (Les Houches Summer School Proceedings 1982 Ser.: Vol. 35). 884p. 1982. 159.75 (ISBN 0-444-86225-0). Elsevier.

Balibar, Etienne, jt. auth. see Althusser, Louis.

Balika, Susan S. Jesus Is My Special Friend. Sparks, Judith, ed. LC 81-86702. (Happy Day Bks.). (Illus.). 24p. (Orig.). (ps-3). 1982. pap. 1.29 (ISBN 0-87239-541-3, 3587). Standard Pub.

Balikci, Asen. Netsilik Eskimo. LC 71-114660. 1971. pap. 6.95 (ISBN 0-385-05766-0). Natural Hist.

Balin, Peter. Flight of the Feathered Serpent. (Illus.). 184p. 1983. pap. 10.95 (ISBN 0-910261-01-6). Arcana Pub.

Balinski, M. L. & Cottle, R. W., eds. Complementary & Fixed Point Problems. (Mathematical Programming Studies: Vol. 7). 1978. pap. 30.00 (ISBN 0-444-85123-2, North-Holland). Elsevier.

Balint, John A, et al. Gastrointestinal Bleeding: Diagnosis & Management. LC 77-4423. (Clinical Gastroenterology Monographs). 101p. 1977. 30.00 o.p. (ISBN 0-471-04607-8, Pub. by Wiley Medical). Wiley.

Balio, Tino. United Artists: The Company Built by the Stars. LC 75-12208. (Illus.). 344p. 1976. 22.50x (ISBN 0-299-06940-0); pap. 9.95 (ISBN 0-299-06944-3). U of Wis Pr.

Balio, Tino, ed. The American Film Industry. LC 75-32070. (Illus.). 512p. 1976. 25.00 (ISBN 0-299-07000-X); pap. 12.50 (ISBN 0-299-07004-2). U of Wis Pr.

Balio, Tino, jt. ed. see Behlmer, Rudy.

Balitas, Maggie, ed. see Wade, Herb.

Balitzer, Alfred, ed. A Time for Choosing. 512p. 1983. 15.00 (ISBN 0-89526-622-9). Regnery-Gateway.

Balje, O. E. Turbomechanics: A Guide to Design, Selection & Theory. LC 80-21524. 513p. 1981. 57.95x (ISBN 0-471-06036-4, Pub. by Wiley-Interscience). Wiley.

Balka, Don. Polyhedra Dice Games for Grades K to 6. Savage, Lyn, ed. (Illus.). (gr. k-6). 1978. 7.25 (ISBN 0-88488-102-4). Creative Pubns.

Balkam, Jean & Moran, Cathleen. Pediatric Ambulatory Care Guidelines. 384p. 1983. pap. text ed. 17.95 (ISBN 0-89303-263-8). R J Brady.

Balkan, Sheila & Berger, Ronald. Crime & Deviance in America. 416p. 1980. pap. text ed. 17.95x (ISBN 0-534-00803-8). Wadsworth Pub.

Balkanski, M. & Moss, T. S. Handbook on Semiconductors, Vol. 2: Optical Properties of Semiconductors. 1980. 117.00 (ISBN 0-444-85273-5). Elsevier.

Balkema, John, ed. Services for the Aging: Source & Resource. 1983. pap. 34.95 (ISBN 0-915794-19-5). Gaylord Prof Pubns.

Balkey, Rita. Prince of Passion. 352p. (Orig.). 1980. pap. 2.50 o.p. (ISBN 0-523-40662-2). Pinnacle Bks.

--Tears of Glory. 384p. (Orig.). 1981. pap. 2.75 o.p. (ISBN 0-523-41014-X). Pinnacle Bks.

Ball. Architectural Drafting. (Illus.). 320p. 1980. text ed. 20.95 (ISBN 0-8359-0255-2). Reston.

--Light Construction Techniques: From Foundation to Finish. (Illus.). 416p. 1980. ref. ed. 25.95 (ISBN 0-8359-4035-7); text ed. 19.95. Reston.

Ball, jt. auth. see Galloway.

Ball, A. H., ed. see Ruskin, John.

Ball, A. P. Antibacterial Drugs Today. 2nd ed. 180p. 1978. pap. text ed. 16.95 (ISBN 0-8391-1333-1). Univ Park.

Ball, Avis J. What Shall I Do with a Hundred Years? 130p. (Orig.). 1982. pap. 6.95 (ISBN 0-932910-44-0). Potentials Development.

Ball, Baron V. Alpha Backgammon. LC 80-19226. (Illus.). 1980. pap. 5.95 (ISBN 0-688-08714-0). Quill NY.

Ball, Bryan W. The English Connection: The Puritan Roots of Seventh-day Adventist Belief. 252p. text ed. 15.95 (ISBN 0-227-67844-3). Attic Pr.

Ball, C. J. Introduction to the Theory of Diffraction. 1971. text ed. 27.00 o.s.i. (ISBN 0-08-015787-4); pap. text ed. 12.75 (ISBN 0-08-015786-6). Pergamon.

Ball, Charles E. Saddle Up: The Farm Journal Book of Western Horsemanship. LC 71-11065. (Illus.). 1970. 12.45i (ISBN 0-397-00668-3); pap. 7.95i (ISBN 0-397-00990-9, LP-083). Har-Row.

Ball, Charles F. Heaven. 120p. 1980. pap. 3.95 (ISBN 0-89693-004-1). Victor Bks.

Ball, David. Backwards & Forwards: A Technical Manual for Reading Plays. 128p. (Orig.). 1983. pap. price not set (ISBN 0-8093-1110-0). S Ill U Pr.

Ball, David, jt. ed. see Lion, Eugene.

Ball, Derek S. An Introduction to Real Analysis. LC 72-84200. (Mathematical Topics). (Illus.). 324p. 1973. text ed. 23.00 o.p. (ISBN 0-08-016936-8); pap. text ed. 9.90 o.p. (ISBN 0-08-016937-6). Pergamon.

Ball, Desmond. Strategy & Defence: Australian Essays. 400p. 1983. text ed. 37.50x (ISBN 0-86861-316-9). Allen Unwin.

Ball, Desmond J. Politics & Force Levels: The Strategic Missile Program of the Kennedy Administration. LC 78-57302. 400p. 1981. 32.50x (ISBN 0-520-03698-0). U of Cal Pr.

Ball, Don, Jr. America's Colorful Railroads. LC 78-51055. (Illus.). 1978. 30.00 (ISBN 0-89169-517-6). Reed Bks.

--America's Railroads: The Second Generation-the60's & 70's. LC 79-51794. (Illus.). cancelled (ISBN 0-89169-527-3). Reed Bks.

Ball, Edith L. & Cipriano, Robert E. Leisure Services Preparation: A Competency Based Approach. (Illus.). 1978. ref. ed. 22.95 (ISBN 0-13-528273-X). P-H.

Ball, Frances. The Development of Reading Skills: A Book of Resources for Teachers. 120p. 1977. 18.00x o.p. (ISBN 0-631-17660-8, Pub. by Basil Blackwell); pap. 9.50x o.p. (ISBN 0-631-18290-X, Pub. by Basil Blackwell). Biblio Dist.

Ball, George. Diplomacy for a Crowded World. 1976. pap. 4.95 (ISBN 0-316-07956-1, Pub. by Atlantic Monthly). Little.

Ball, Geraldine. Having Good Feelings in the Magic Circle at School: Story & Activity Booklet. (Illus.). 1972. pap. 0.40 o.p. (ISBN 0-86584-016-4); pap. 3.95 set of 10 o.p. (ISBN 0-86584-015-6). Human Dev Train.

--Magic Circle: An Overview of the Human Development Program. 1974. 4.95 o.p. (ISBN 0-86584-007-5). Human Dev Train.

Ball, H. W., pref. By. British Palaeozoic Fossils. 4th ed. (Illus.). vi, 203p. 1975. pap. 5.50x (ISBN 0-686-27503-9, Pub. by Brit Mus Nat Hist). Sabbot-Natural Hist Bks.

Ball, Howard. Courts & Politics: The Federal Judicial System. 1980. pap. text ed. 13.95 (ISBN 0-13-184655-8). P-H.

--Judicial Craftsmanship or Fiat? Direct Overturn by the United States Supreme Court. LC 77-91102. (Contributions in Political Science: No. 7). 1978. lib. bdg. 25.00x (ISBN 0-313-20035-1, BJC/). Greenwood.

Ball, J. Dyer. Things Chinese: Or Notes Connected with China. rev. 5th ed. Werner, Chalmers, ed. LC 74-164085. (Tower Bks). 1971. Repr. of 1926 ed. 56.00x (ISBN 0-8103-3917-X). Gale.

Ball, J. N. Merchants & Merchandise: The Expansion of Trade in Europe, 1500-1630. LC 77-74803. 1977. 23.00 (ISBN 0-312-53008-0). St Martin.

Ball, Jeff. The Self-Sufficient Suburban Gardener: A Step-by-Step Planning & Management Guide to Backyard Food Production. Halpin, Anne, ed. (Illus.). 256p. 1983. 14.95 (ISBN 0-87857-457-3, 01-083-0). Rodale Pr Inc.

Ball, John, jt. auth. see McDonnell, Leo.

Ball, John A. Algorithms for RPN Calculators. LC 77-14977. 330p. 1978. 29.95x (ISBN 0-471-03070-8, Pub. by Wiley-Interscience). Wiley.

Ball, John E. Architectural Drafting Fundamentals. (Illus.). 336p. 1980. text ed. 17.95 (ISBN 0-8359-0254-4). Reston.

--Carpenters & Builders Library, Vol. 1. 5th ed. LC 82-1340. 1982. 10.95 (ISBN 0-672-23365-7). Bobbs.

--Carpenters & Builders Library, Vol. 2. 5th ed. LC 82-1341. 1982. 10.95 (ISBN 0-672-23366-5). Bobbs.

--Carpenters & Builders Library, Vol. 3. 5th ed. LC 82-1339. 1982. 10.95 (ISBN 0-672-23367-3). Bobbs.

--Carpenters & Builders Library, Vol. 4. 5th ed. LC 82-1332. 1982. 10.95 (ISBN 0-672-23368-1). Bobbs.
--Exterior & Interior Trim. LC 75-6060. 192p. 1975. pap. 11.80 (ISBN 0-8273-1120-6); instr.'s guide 2.00 (ISBN 0-8273-1121-4). Delmar.
--Practical Problems in Mathematics for Masons. LC 78-74431. (Mathematics - Construction Ser.). 200p. 1980. 7.80 (ISBN 0-8273-1283-0); instructor's guide 3.25 (ISBN 0-8273-1284-9). Delmar.
Ball, John M., et al. The Social Sciences & Geographic Education: A Reader. LC 73-140549. 329p. 1971. pap. 14.00 (ISBN 0-471-04631-0, Pub. by Wiley). Krieger.
Ball, Marion J. & Charp, Sylvia. Be a Computer Literate. LC 78-52055. pap. 4.95 (ISBN 0-916688-08-9). Creative Comp.
Ball, Nancy, ed. Architect's Guide to International Practice. LC 78-74736. 1978. pap. 17.50x (ISBN 0-913962-19-8). Am Inst Arch.
Ball, Nicole, jt. ed. see Leitenberg, Milton.
Ball, Patricia M. The Heart's Events: The Victorian Poetry of Relationships. 240p. 1976. text ed. 30.50x (ISBN 0-485-11163-2, Athlone Pr). Humanities.
Ball, R. J. Money & Employment. 450p. 1982. 27.95 (ISBN 0-470-27290-2). Halsted Pr.
Ball, Robert. The Crown, the Sages & Supreme Morality. 176p. 1983. 22.50 (ISBN 0-7100-9317-9). Routledge & Kegan.
Ball, S. Beachside Comprehensive: A Case Study in Secondary Schooling. (Illus.). 280p. 1981. 54.50 (ISBN 0-521-23238-4); pap. 18.95 (ISBN 0-521-29878-4). Cambridge U Pr.
Ball, Samuel. An Account of the Cultivation & Manufacture of Tea in China. LC 78-74309. (The Modern Chinese Economy Ser.). 382p. 1980. lib. bdg. 42.00 (ISBN 0-8240-4250-6). Garland Pub.
Ball, T. H., jt. auth. see Halbert, H. S.
Ball, V. A. & Halvorson, E. W. Managing the Dental Practice. LC 74-602. 200p. 1974. 11.50 (ISBN 0-03-010416-5, Pub. by HR&W). Krieger.
Ball, V. K. Architecture & Interior Design: Europe & America from the Colonial Era to Today, 2 vol. set. LC 79-24851. 890p. 1980. Set. 100.00 (ISBN 0-471-08721-1, Pub. by Wiley-Interscience); Set. pap. 56.95 (ISBN 0-471-08720-3). Wiley.
Ball, Victoria K. Architecture & Interior Design: A Basic History Through the Seventeenth Century. LC 79-21371. 448p. 1980. 57.50 (ISBN 0-471-05162-4, Pub. by Wiley-Interscience); pap. 30.95 (ISBN 0-471-08719-X). Wiley.
--Architecture & Interior Design: Europe & America from the Colonial Era to Today. LC 79-24851. 442p. 1980. 57.50 (ISBN 0-471-05161-6, Pub. by Wiley-Interscience); pap. 30.95 (ISBN 0-471-08722-X). Wiley.
--The Art of Interior Design. 2nd ed. 288p. 1982. 24.95x (ISBN 0-471-09679-2, Pub. by Wiley-Interscience). Wiley.
Ball, W. R; see Ball, W. Rouse, et al.
Ball, W. Rouse, et al, eds. String Figures & Other Monographs, 4 vols. in 1. Incl. String Figures. Ball, W. R; History of the Slide Rule. Cajori, F; Non Euclidean Geometry. Carslaw, Horatio S; Methods Geometrical Construction. Petersen, Julius. LC 59-11780. 15.95 (ISBN 0-8284-0130-6). Chelsea Pub.
Ball, W. W. Short Account of the History of Mathematics. 4th ed. 1908. pap. 7.50 (ISBN 0-486-20630-0). Dover.
Ball, Wendy A., ed. Rare Afro-Americana: A Reconstruction of the Adger Library. 1981. 27.50 (ISBN 0-8161-8175-6, Hall Reference). G K Hall.
Balla, D., jt. auth. see Zigler, E.
Ballabon, M. B., ed. Economic Perspectives: An Annual Survey of Economics, Vol. 2. 276p. 1981. lib. bdg. 59.00 (ISBN 3-7186-0036-6). Harwood Academic.
Ballagh, James C., ed. The Letters of Richard Henry Lee, 2 Vols. LC 79-107678. (Era of the American Revolution Ser). 1970. Repr. of 1914 ed. Set. 115.00 (ISBN 0-306-71894-4). Da Capo.
Ballance, P. F. & Reading, H. G., eds. Sedimentation of Oblique-Slip Mobile Zones. (International Association of Sedimentologists & the Societ As Internationalis Limnological Symposium). 265p. 1980. pap. 64.95 (ISBN 0-470-26927-8). Halsted Pr.
Ballant, Art. The College Mascot Handbook. (Illus.). 192p. (Orig.). Date not set. pap. cancelled (ISBN 0-88011-056-2). Leisure Pr.
Ballantine, Alistair, jt. ed. see Blashford-Snell, John.
Ballantine, Christopher. Music, Society & Ideology. (Monographs on Musicology: Vol. 2). 1982. write for info. (ISBN 0-677-06050-5). Gordon.
Ballantine, Jeanne H. The Sociology of Education: A Systematic Analysis. (Illus.). 400p. 1983. 21.95 (ISBN 0-13-820860-3). P-H.
Ballantyne, J. Ear. Rob & Smith, eds. (Operative Surgery Ser). 1976. text ed. 69.95 (ISBN 0-407-00097-6). Butterworth.
Ballantyne, J. & Smith, Rodney, eds. Nose & Throat. 3rd ed. (Operative Surgery Ser). 1976. 99.95 (ISBN 0-407-00627-3). Butterworth.
Ballantyne, J. R., ed. see Patanjali.
Ballantyne, Janet. Desserts from the Garden. Chesman, Andrea, ed. (Illus.). 144p. (Orig.). 1983. pap. 5.95 (ISBN 0-88266-322-4). Garden Way Pub.
Ballantyne, R. M. see Eyre, A. G.
Ballantyne, Robert. The Coral Island. Lurie, Alison & Schiller, Justin G., eds. LC 75-32167. (Classics of Children's Literature Ser.: 1621-1932). PLB 38.00 o.s.i. (ISBN 0-8240-2280-7). Garland Pub.
Ballantyne, Sheila. Imaginary Crimes. 1983. pap. 4.95 (ISBN 0-14-006540-7). Penguin.
--Norma Jean the Termite Queen. 1983. pap. 5.95 (ISBN 0-14-006551-2). Penguin.
Ballantyne, Verne. How & Where to Find Gold: Secrets of the Forty Niners. LC 75-18878. (Illus.). 128p. 1976. 8.95 o.p. (ISBN 0-668-03859-4); pap. 4.95 o.p. (ISBN 0-668-04082-3). Arco.
Ballantyne, Verne H. How & Where to Find Gold. 2nd ed. LC 82-13734. (Illus.). 176p. 1983. 12.95 (ISBN 0-668-05377-1); pap. 6.95 (ISBN 0-668-05385-2). Arco.
Ballard, D. Lee, et al. More on the Deep & Surface Grammar of Interclausal Relations. (Language Data, Asian-Pacific Ser: No. 1). 61p. 1971. pap. 2.50x (ISBN 0-88312-201-4); microfiche 1.50x (ISBN 0-88312-301-0). Summer Inst Ling.
Ballard, E. John, pref. by. Diverse Images: Photographs from the New Orleans Museum of Art. (Illus.). 1979. 19.95 o.p. (ISBN 0-8174-2484-9, Amphoto); pap. 9.95 o.p. (ISBN 0-8174-2156-4). Watson-Guptill.
Ballard, George. Memoirs of Several Ladies of Great Britain. 47.50 (ISBN 0-404-18053-1). AMS Pr.
Ballard, George A. The Influence of the Sea on the Political History of Japan. LC 74-136516. (Illus.). 311p. 1973. Repr. of 1921 ed. lib. bdg. 19.75x (ISBN 0-8371-5435-9, BAIS). Greenwood.
Ballard, J. G. Re-Search: J. G. Ballard. Vale, V., ed. (Re-Search Ser.). (Illus.). 96p. 1983. pap. 6.95 (ISBN 0-940642-08-5). Re-Search Prods.
Ballard, Jack S. The Shock of Peace: Military & Economic Demobilization After World War II. LC 82-24860. (Illus.). 270p. (Orig.). 1983. lib. bdg. 23.50 (ISBN 0-8191-3029-X); pap. text ed. 11.75 (ISBN 0-8191-3030-3). U Pr of Amer.
Ballard, Juliet B. The Art of Living. 251p. 1982. pap. 7.95 (ISBN 0-87604-144-6). ARE Pr.
Ballard, M., ed. see Gissing, George.
Ballard, R. E. Photoelectron Spectroscopy & Molecular Orbital Theory. LC 78-40817. 1979. 69.95 (ISBN 0-470-26542-6). Halsted Pr.
Ballardo, Victoria M. Count Me Among the Living: The Story of My Wheelchair Liberation. 160p. 1983. 8.50 (ISBN 0-682-49945-5). Exposition.
Ballenger, A. F. A Believer's Guide to Christian Maturity. 256p. 1982. pap. 4.95 (ISBN 0-87123-278-2, 210278). Bethany Hse.
Ballenger, Dean W. The Sea Guerrillas. 1982. pap. 1.95 (ISBN 0-451-11413-2, AJ1413, Sig). NAL.
Ballenger, Sally, jt. auth. see Taylor, Joyce.
Ballentine, George K. Your Voice in Speech or Song. 1978. 5.95 o.p. (ISBN 0-533-03378-0). Vantage.
Ballentine, Rudolph. Essential Anatomy for Yoga Students. LC 78-78250. (Illus., Orig.). Date not set. pap. cancelled o.s.i. (ISBN 0-89389-058-8). Himalayan Intl Inst.
Ballentine, Rudolph M., ed. see Himalayan International Institute.
Ballentyne, D. W. & Lovett, D. R. Dictionary of Named Effects. 4th ed. 1982. 19.95x (ISBN 0-412-22390-2, Pub. by Chapman & Hall England). Methuen Inc.
--Dictionary of Named Effects & Laws in Chemistry, Physics & Mathematics. 4th ed. 1980. 25.00x o.p. (ISBN 0-412-22380-5, Pub. by Chapman & Hall England). Methuen Inc.
Baller, Warren B. Bed-Wetting: Origins & Treatment. rev. ed. 300p. 1975. 23.00 (ISBN 0-08-017859-6). Pergamon.
Ballerini, Luigi. Che Figurato Muore. Harrison, Thomas, tr. from It. LC 78-58982. 1982. 7.95 o.p. (ISBN 0-915570-11-4). Oolp Pr.
Ballester, Gonzalo T. Don Juan. 1983. 17.95 (ISBN 0-914366-10-6). Vanguard.
Ballew, Hunter. Teaching Children Mathematics. LC 73-75000. 1973. text ed. 19.95 (ISBN 0-675-08982-4). Merrill.
Ballhatchet, Kenneth. Race, Sex & Class under the Raj: Imperial Attitudes & Policies & Their Critics, 1793-1905. LC 79-9604. 1980. 22.50x (ISBN 0-312-66144-4). St Martin.
Ballhausen, C. J. Molecular Electronic Structures of Transition Metal Complexes. 1979. 38.95 (ISBN 0-07-003495-8). McGraw.
Balliet, L. D. Number Vibration in Question & Answer. 104p. 4.50 (ISBN 0-686-38231-5). Sun Bks.
--Vibration: A System of Numbers As Taught by Pythagoras. 80p. 3.50 (ISBN 0-686-38237-4). Sun Bks.
Balliet, Lee. Survey of Labor Relations. 208p. 1981. text ed. 14.00 (ISBN 0-87179-347-4); pap. text ed. 10.00 (ISBN 0-87179-351-2). BNA.
Balliett, Whitney. Alec Wilder & His Friends. (The Roots of Jazz Ser.). (Illus.). 205p. 1983. Repr. of 1974 ed. lib. bdg. 25.00 (ISBN 0-306-76153-X). Da Capo.
--American Singers. 1979. 15.00 (ISBN 0-19-502524-5). Oxford U Pr.
--Ecstasy at the Onion: Thirty-pieces on Jazz. LC 82-6249. 284p. 1982. Repr. of 1971 ed. lib. bdg. 29.75 (ISBN 0-313-22577-X, BAEO). Greenwood.
--Improvising: Sixteen Jazz Musicians & Their Art. LC 76-42635. 1977. 17.95 (ISBN 0-19-502149-5). Oxford U Pr.
--Jelly Roll, Jabbo & Fats: Nineteen Portraits in Jazz. 224p. 1983. 19.95 (ISBN 0-19-503275-6). Oxford U Pr.
--New York Notes: A Journal of Jazz in the Seventies. LC 76-51396. (Quality Paperback Ser.). 1977. pap. 6.95 (ISBN 0-306-80037-3). Da Capo.
--Night Creature: A Journal of Jazz, 1975-1980. (Illus.). 1981. 17.95 (ISBN 0-19-502908-9). Oxford U Pr.
--The Sound of Surprise. LC 77-17852. (Roots of Jazz Ser.). 1978. Repr. of 1961 ed. lib. bdg. 22.50 (ISBN 0-306-77543-3). Da Capo.
Ballieux, R., jt. ed. see Fauci, A. S.
Balling, L. Christian. The Fourth Shot. 228p. 1982. 14.00i (ISBN 0-316-07968-5, Pub. by Atlantic Monthly Pr). Little.
Balling, Michael, ed. see Wagner, Richard.
Ballinger, Philip W. Merrill's Atlas of Radiographic Positions & Radiologic Procedures, 3 Vols. 5th ed. (Illus.). 950p. 1982. text ed. 99.95 (ISBN 0-8016-3408-3). Mosby.
Ballinger, R., ed. see Visigli, R.
Ballinger, Raymond A. Design with Paper in Art & Graphic Design. 144p. 1982. 29.95 (ISBN 0-442-24491-6). Van Nos Reinhold.
Ballinger, Rex E., ed. see Usigli, Rodolfo.
Ballinger, Royce E & Lynch, John D. How to Know the Amphibians & Reptiles. (Pictured Key Nature Ser.). 300p. 1983. write for info. wire coil (ISBN 0-697-04786-5). Wm C Brown.
Ballinger, Walter F., 2nd, et al, eds. The Management of Trauma. 2nd ed. LC 73-77933. (Illus.). 785p. 1973. text ed. 29.50 o.p. (ISBN 0-7216-1521-X). Saunders.
Ballmer, T. Logical Grammar. (North Holland Linguistic Ser.: Vol. 39). 1978. 59.75 (ISBN 0-444-85205-0, North Holland). Elsevier.
Ballmer, Thomas. Biological Foundations of Linguistic Communication: Towards a Biocybernetics of Language. (Pragmatics & Beyond: III-7). 120p. (Orig.). 1982. pap. 16.00 (ISBN 90-272-2520-6). Benjamins North Am.
Ballon, Samuel C. Gynecologic Oncology: Controversies in Cancer Treatment. 1981. lib. bdg. 49.95 (ISBN 0-8161-2156-7, Pub. by Hall Medical Bks). G K Hall.
Ballonoff, P. A., jt. ed. see Weiss, K. M.
Ballou, Adin. Christian Non-Resistance. LC 70-121104. (Civil Liberties in American History Ser). 1970. Repr. of 1910 ed. lib. bdg. 35.00 (ISBN 0-306-71980-0). Da Capo.
--Christian Non-Resistance in All Its Important Bearings, Illustrated & Defended. LC 76-137527. (Peace Movement in America Ser). 240p. 1972. Repr. of 1846 ed. lib. bdg. 16.95x (ISBN 0-89198-054-7). Ozer.
--History of The Hopedale Community. Heywood, W. S., ed. LC 76-187467. (The American Utopian Adventure Ser.). 415p. Repr. of 1897 ed. lib. bdg. 25.00x (ISBN 0-87991-007-0). Porcupine Pr.
Ballou, D. H., jt. auth. see Steen, Frederick H.
Ballou, John E., ed. Radiation & the Lymphatic System: Proceedings. LC 75-38685. (ERDA Symposium Ser.). 264p. 1976. pap. 14.50 (ISBN 0-87079-030-7, CONF-740930); microfiche 4.50 (ISBN 0-87079-317-9, CONF-740930). DOE.
Ballou, Judith. The Psychology of Pregnancy. LC 78-57242. 1978. 18.95x (ISBN 0-669-02377-9). Lexington Bks.
Ballou, Maturin M. Notable Thoughts about Women: A Literary Mosaic. LC 78-141602. 1971. Repr. of 1882 ed. 37.00x (ISBN 0-8103-3771-1). Gale.
Ballou, Patricia K. Women: A Bibliography of Bibliographies. 1980. lib. bdg. 17.00 (ISBN 0-8161-8292-2, Hall Reference). G K Hall.
Ballou, Ralph. Teaching Badminton. LC 81-68519. (Sport Teaching Ser.). 160p. (Orig.). 1982. pap. text ed. 7.95x (ISBN 0-8087-4068-7). Burgess.
Ballou, Richard. A Guide for Brass Bands in the Pacific. 1983. 9.95 (ISBN 0-939154-29-3). Inst Polynesian.
Ballou, Robert O. The Portable World Bible. (Viking Portable Library). 1977. pap. 6.95 (ISBN 0-14-015005-6). Penguin.
Ballou, Ronald H. Business Logistics Management. LC 72-1338. (International Management Ser). (Illus.). 496p. 1973. ref. ed. 25.95 (ISBN 0-13-104802-3). P-H.
Ballou, Stephen V. Model for Theses & Research Papers. LC 72-125125. (Illus., Orig.). 1970. pap. text ed. 8.50 o.p. (ISBN 0-395-10806-3, 3-02700). HM.
Balls, M. & Billett, F. S., eds. The Cell Cycle in Development & Differentiation. (British Society for Developmental Biological Symposia Ser.). (Illus.). 450p. 1973. 80.00 (ISBN 0-521-20136-5). Cambridge U Pr.
Balls, M. & Wild, A. E., eds. The Early Development of Mammals. (British Society for Developmental Biology Symposium Ser). (Illus.). 500p. 1975. 95.00 (ISBN 0-521-20771-1). Cambridge U Pr.
Balls, M., jt. ed. see Newth, D. R.
Ballweber, Duane. Practical Applications in Basic Autobody Repair. (Illus.). 288p. 1983. text ed. 15.95 (ISBN 0-13-689216-7). P-H.
Ballweg, Marie E. Reluctant Ronnie. LC 78-56174. (gr. 1-6). 1978. 15.00 (ISBN 0-89002-104-X); pap. 5.00 (ISBN 0-89002-103-1). Northwoods Pr.
Balma, M. J., jt. auth. see Lawshe, Charles H.
Balmain, K. G., jt. auth. see Jordan, Edward C.
Balmer, Edwin, jt. auth. see Wylie, Philip.
Balmer, Philip & Wylie, Edwin. When Worlds Collide. 192p. 1962. pap. 2.75 (ISBN 0-446-30539-1). Warner Bks.
Balmford, Rosemary. Learning about Australian Birds. (Illus.). 240p. 1982. 17.95 (ISBN 0-00-216440-X, Pub. by W Collins Australia). Intl Schol Bk Serv.
Balmforth, C. K. & Cox, N. S., eds. Interface: Library Automation with Special Reference to Computing Activity. 1971. 22.50x (ISBN 0-262-02084-X). MIT Pr.
Balmuth, Bernard. The Language of the Cutting Room. LC 81-84920. 90p. 1981. pap. text ed. 10.95 (ISBN 0-9607486-0-1). Rosallen Pubns.
Balmuth, Daniel. Censorship in Russia, Eighteen Sixty-Five to Nineteen Five. LC 79-52510. 1979. pap. text ed. 11.50 (ISBN 0-8191-0773-5). U Pr of Amer.
Balnaves, John & Biskup, Peter. Australian Libraries. 2nd ed. (Comparative Library Studies). 192p. 1975. 15.00 o.p. (ISBN 0-208-01361-X, Linnet). Shoe String.
Baloff, Marsha. Crosswords for Nurses. Paquet, Judith B., ed. 120p. 1982. 9.95 (ISBN 0-913590-94-0). Slack Inc.
Balon, Eugene K. African Fishes of Lake Kariba. (Illus.). 144p. 1974. 19.95 (ISBN 0-87666-073-1, PS-706). TFH Pubns.
Balough, Teresa. A Musical Genius from Australia. (Illus.). 161p. 1982. pap. 13.50 (ISBN 0-686-84841-1, Pub. by CSIRO Australia). Intl Schol Bk Serv.
Balow, James E., jt. ed. see Diamond, Louis H.
Baloyra, Enrique. El Salvador in Transition. LC 82-4815. xviii, 236p. 1982. 19.95x (ISBN 0-8078-1532-2); pap. 8.95 (ISBN 0-8078-4093-9). U of NC Pr.
BALPA Medical Study Group. Fit to Fly: A Medical Handbook for Pilots. 80p. 1980. pap. text ed. 5.25x (ISBN 0-246-11401-0, Pub. by Granada England). Renouf.
Bals, H., jt. auth. see Logan, G.
Balsam, M. S. & Sagarin, Edward, eds. Cosmetics: Science & Technology, 3 vols. 2nd ed. LC 75-177888. Set. 188.50x (ISBN 0-471-04650-7); Vol. 1, 1972, 605 Pgs. 67.50x (ISBN 0-471-04646-9); Vol. 2, 1972, 691 Pgs. 75.50x (ISBN 0-471-04647-7); Vol. 3, 1974, 787 Pgs. 67.50x (ISBN 0-471-04649-3, Pub. by Wiley-Interscience). Wiley.
Balsama, George D. The Politics of National Despair: French Royalism in the Post-Reformation Era. 1977. pap. text ed. 8.25 (ISBN 0-8191-0142-7). U Pr of Amer.
Balsdon, J. P. Roman Women. LC 82-48825. (Illus.). 354p. (gr. 11-12). 1983. pap. 6.95 (ISBN 0-06-464062-0, BN 4062). B&N NY.
Balseiro, Jose, ed. see Casona, Alejandro.
Balsekar, Ramesh s. Pointers from Nisargadatta Maharaj. LC 82-71505. xiv, 223p. 1983. 13.95 (ISBN 0-89386-004-2). Acorn NC.
Balshofer, Fred J. & Miller, Arthur C. One Reel a Week. LC 67-24119. (Illus.). 1968. 21.95 o.p. (ISBN 0-520-00073-0). U of Cal Pr.
Balsley, Gene. Pentax MX & ME. (Amphoto Pocket Companion Ser.). (Illus.). 1980. pap. 4.95 (ISBN 0-8174-2183-1, Amphoto). Watson-Guptill.
Balsom, Denis & Burch, Martin. Political & Electoral Handbook of Wales. 1980. text ed. 35.50x (ISBN 0-566-00236-1). Gower Pub Ltd.
Balstrino, Philip. Fat & Skinny. LC 74-12306. (A Let's-Read-&-Find-Out Science Bk). (Illus.). (gr. k-3). 1975. o. p. 8.95i (ISBN 0-690-00454-0, TYC-J); PLB 9.89 (ISBN 0-690-00665-9). Har-Row.
Baltaxe, Christiane A., tr. see Trubetzkoy, N. S.
Baltazar, Clare R. & Salazar, Nelia P. Philippine Insects: An Introduction. (Illus.). 1980. text ed. 17.00x (ISBN 0-8248-0675-1, Pub. by U of Philippines Pr); pap. text ed. 12.00x (ISBN 0-8248-0676-X). UH Pr.
Baltazzi, Evan S. Stickfighting: A Practical Guide for Self-Protection. (Illus.). 224p. 1983. 19.50 (ISBN 0-8048-1450-3). C E Tuttle.
Balter, Harry G. Tax Fraud & Evasion. 5th ed. 1982. 68.00 (ISBN 0-88262-796-1, 76-10629). Warren.
Baltes, H. P. & Hilf, E. R. Spectra of Finite Systems: A Review of Weyl's Problem--The Eigenvalue Distribution of the Wave Equation for Finite Domains & It Applications on the Physics of Small Systems. 116p. 1976. pap. 11.95x (ISBN 3-411-01491-1). Birkhauser.
Balthasar, Hans Urs von. The Glory of the Lord: A Theological Aesthetics-Seeing the Form, Vol. 1. 656p. (Orig.) 1983. 30.00 (ISBN 0-8245-0579-4). Crossroad NY.
Balthasur, Hans Von see Von Balthasar, Hans.
Balthazar, Vera & Batista, Joao, eds. Dictionario Biblico Buckland. Orig. Title: Buckland Bible Dictionary. (Illus.). 453p. text ed. 6.50 (ISBN 0-8297-0836-7); pap. 4.50 (ISBN 0-686-97837-4). Life Pubs Intl.
Balthazar, Vera, ed. see Williams, Moris.
Baltus, R. K. Personal Psychology for Life & Work. 1976. 12.05 (ISBN 0-07-003592-X, G); instructor's manual & key 5.30 (ISBN 0-07-003593-8). McGraw.

Baltzell, Edward D. Protestant Establishment: Aristocracy & Caste in America. 1966. pap. 4.95 (ISBN 0-394-70334-0, V334, Vin). Random.

Baltzer, Fritz. Theodor Boveri: The Life & Work of a Great Biologist, 1862-1915. Rudnick, Dorothea, tr. LC 67-21996. (Illus.). 1967. 28.50x (ISBN 0-520-00074-9). U of Cal Pr.

Baly. Professional Responsibility in the Community Health Services. 1981. 9.95 (ISBN 0-471-25592-0, Wiley Heyden). Wiley.

Baly, Dennis. God & History in the Old Testament. LC 76-9984. 256p. 1976. pap. 10.53i (ISBN 0-06-060369-0, RD 186, HarpR). Har-Row.

Balyoz, Harold. Signs of Christ. LC 79-64608. 1979. 18.00 (ISBN 0-9609710-0-9). Altai Pub.

Balzac. Le Pere Goriot. (Easy Reader, D). pap. 3.95 (ISBN 0-88436-043-1, 40280). EMC.

Balzac, Honore De. Eugenie Grandet. Marriage, Ellen, tr. 1973. Repr. of 1907 ed. 9.95x o.p. (ISBN 0-460-00169-8, Evman). Biblio Dist.

--Old Goriot. Crawford, Marion A., tr. (Classics Ser.). (Orig.). 1951. pap. 3.95 (ISBN 0-14-044017-8). Penguin.

--Pere Goriot. Bd. with Eugenie Grandet. 1950. pap. 4.50x (ISBN 0-394-30902-2, T2, Mod LibC). Modern Lib.

--Seraphita. 2nd ed. LC 76-12203. 192p. 1982. Repr. of 1976 ed. 10.00 (ISBN 0-89345-400-1, Spirit Fiction). Garber Comm.

--The Wild Ass's Skin. Hunt, Herbert J., tr. (Classic Ser.). 1977. pap. 3.95 (ISBN 0-14-044330-4). Penguin.

Balzac, Honore De see De Balzac, Honore.

Balzac De, Honore see Balzac, Honore De.

Balzhiser, R. E. & Samuels, M. R. Engineering Thermodynamics. (Illus.). 1977. text ed. 31.95 (ISBN 0-13-279570-1). P-H.

Balzhiser, R. E., et al. Chemical Engineering Thermodynamics. (International Physical & Chemical Engineering Sciences Ser). (Illus.). 1972. ref. ed. 32.95 (ISBN 0-13-128603-X). P-H.

Bambas, L. L. Five-Membered Heterocyclic Compounds with Nitrogen & Sulfur or Nitrogen, Sulfur & Oxygen--Except Thrazole, Vol. 4. 416p. 1952. 58.50 o.p. (ISBN 0-686-74353-9, Pub. by Wiley-Interscience). Wiley.

Bamberg, Robert D., ed. see James, Henry.

Bamberger, Bernard J. The Search for Jewish Theology. new ed. LC 77-28457. 1978. 7.95x o.p. (ISBN 0-87441-295-1); pap. 3.95x (ISBN 0-87441-300-1). Behrman.

--Story of Judaism. rev. 3rd ed. LC 64-16463. 1964. pap. 8.95 (ISBN 0-8052-0077-0). Schocken.

Bambert, Arnold. Africa: Tribal Art of Forest & Savanna. (Illus.). 332p. 1980. 29.98 (ISBN 0-500-23318-7). Thames Hudson.

Bamborough, J. B; see Henderson, Philip.

Bambrough, Renford, ed. Philosophy of Aristotle: A New Selection. (Orig.). pap. 3.95 (ISBN 0-451-62180-8, ME2180, Ment). NAL.

Bament, R. C., jt. auth. see Casimir, M.

Bamford, C. & Tipper, C., eds. Comprehensive Chemical Kinetics, Vol. 20: Complex Catalytic Processes. 1978. 119.25 (ISBN 0-444-41651-X). Elsevier.

--Comprehensive Chemical Kinetics, Vol. 22: Reactions in the Solid State. 1980. 110.75 (ISBN 0-444-41807-5). Elsevier.

Bamford, C. G., jt. auth. see Robinson, H.

Bamford, C. H. & Tipper, C. F., eds. Comprehensive Chemical Kinetics, Vol. 11: Reactions of Carbonyl Compounds. Date not set. price not set (ISBN 0-685-84869-8). Elsevier.

--Comprehensive Chemical Kinetics, Vol. 24: Modern Methods in Kinetics. 528p. 1982. 197.75 (ISBN 0-444-42028-2). Elsevier.

Bamford, C. R. Color Generation & Control in Glass. (Glass Science & Technology Ser.: Vol. 2). 1977. 53.25 (ISBN 0-444-41614-5). Elsevier.

Bamford, James. The Puzzle Palace: A Report on America's Most Secret Agency. (Illus.). 436p. 1982. 16.95 (ISBN 0-395-31286-8). HM.

Bamford, T. W. Thomas Arnold on Education. LC 79-108099. (Texts & Studies in the History of Education: No. 8). 1970. 24.95 (ISBN 0-521-07785-0). Cambridge U Pr.

Bamman, et al. Target Spelling Skills Program, 2 pts. (gr. 3-12). 1977. 325.00 ea. (Sch Div); Pt. 1. (ISBN 0-201-21050-9); Pt. 2. (ISBN 0-201-21100-9); tchr's man. incl. A-W.

Bamman, H. A., et al. Free to Read: A Guide to Effective Reading. rev. ed. LC 74-84819. 1975. 12.95 (ISBN 0-8465-5835-1, 55835); instr's. guide 6.95 (ISBN 0-8465-5836-X, 55836). Benjamin-Cummings.

Bamman, Henry A. & Whitehead, R. J. Top Flight Readers Series, 7 bks. Incl. Chopper (ISBN 0-201-21501-2); Test Pilot (ISBN 0-201-21502-0); Hang Glider (ISBN 0-201-21503-9); Bush Pilot.; Barnstormers. (ISBN 0-201-21505-5); Balloon. (ISBN 0-201-21506-3). (gr. 5-12). 1977. pap. text ed. 8.16 ea. (Sch Div); tchr's. ed. 4.92 (ISBN 0-201-21500-4). A-W.

Bamman, Henry A., ed. see Dawson, Mildred A., et al.

Bamman, Henry A., et al. Beyond Barriers. (Passport to Reading Ser.). (Illus., Orig.). (gr. 7-12). 1982. pap. 3.25 (ISBN 0-88436-723-1, 35675). EMC.

--Challenges. (Passport to Reading Ser.). (Illus.). 64p. (Orig.). (gr. 7-12). 1982. pap. 3.25 (ISBN 0-88436-725-8, 35676). EMC.

--Daredevils & Dreamers. (Passport to Reading Ser.). (Illus.). 64p. (Orig.). (gr. 7-12). 1982. pap. 3.25 (ISBN 0-88436-727-4, 35677). EMC.

--Extraordinary Episodes. (Passport to Reading Ser.). (Illus.). 64p. (Orig.). (gr. 7-12). 1982. pap. 3.25 (ISBN 0-88436-729-0, 35678). EMC.

--Fantastic Flights. (Passport to Reading Ser.). (Illus.). 64p. (gr. 7-12). 1982. pap. 3.25 (ISBN 0-88436-731-2, 35679). EMC.

Bamman, Henry S., et al. Amazing. (Passport to Reading Ser.). (Illus.). 64p. (Orig.). (gr. 7-12). 1982. pap. 3.25 (ISBN 0-88436-721-5, 35674). EMC.

Bammate, Haidar. Muslim Contribution to Civilization. LC 82-72577. 62p. (Orig.). 1982. pap. 2.00 o.p. (ISBN 0-686-92018-X). Contemp Bks.

--Muslim Contribution to Civilization. Date not set. price not set (ISBN 0-89259-029-7). Am Trust Pubns.

Ban, Ioan A. Zang-Bloemzel...(Theoretical Parts) & Kort Sangh-Bericht... (Early Music Theory in the Low Countries Ser.: Vol. 1). wrappers 20.00 o.s.i. (ISBN 90-6027-077-0, Pub. by Frits Knuf Netherlands). Pendragon NY.

Ban, Jeno. The Tactics of End-Games. 2nd & rev. ed. Bochkor, Jeno, tr. from Hung. 215p. 1972. 8.00 (ISBN 0-8283-1506-X). Branden.

Ban, Joseph D., jt. ed. see Dekar, Paul R.

Ban, Thomas A. Psychopharmacology. LC 69-16711. 502p. 1969. 24.00 (ISBN 0-683-00419-0, Pub. by Williams & Wilkins). Krieger.

--Psychopharmacology of Thiothixene. LC 75-43191. 1978. 22.50 (ISBN 0-89004-108-3). Raven.

Banach, Stefan. Theorie Des Operations Lineaires. 2nd ed. LC 63-21849. (Fr). 10.95 (ISBN 0-8284-0110-1). Chelsea Pub.

Banahan, Mark & Rutter, Andy. The Unix-tm Book. 224p. 1983. pap. 16.95 (ISBN 0-471-89676-4). Wiley.

Banas, Norma & Wills, I. H. H.E.L.P. LC 78-62104. 1979. pap. 7.95 (ISBN 0-89334-018-9). Humanics Ltd.

Banat, Gabriel, ed. see Cassanea de Mondonville, Jos.

Banbery, Alan, jt. auth. see Huber, Martin.

Bance, Alan. Theodor Fontane: The Major Novels. LC 81-21688. (Anglica Germanica Ser.: No. 2). 250p. 1982. 44.50 (ISBN 0-521-24532-X). Cambridge U Pr.

Bance, S. Handbook of Practical Organic Micro-Analysis: Recommended Methods for Determining Elements & Groups. LC 80-40145. (Ellis Horwood Ser. in Analytical Chemistry). 206p. 1980. 69.95 (ISBN 0-470-26972-3). Halsted Pr.

Bancheri, Louis, et al. Biology. (Arco's Regents Review Ser.). 288p. (Orig.). 1983. pap. 3.95 (ISBN 0-668-05697-5, 5697). Arco.

Banchieri, Adriano. L' Organo Suonarino: Venezia 1605, 1611, & 1638. (Bibliotheca Organologica Ser.: Vol. 27). 1969. 32.50 o.s.i. (ISBN 90-6027-076-2, Pub. by Frits Knuf Netherlands). Pendragon NY.

Banchoff, T., et al. Cusps of Gauss Mappings. (Research Notes in Mathematics Ser.: No. 55). 120p. (Orig.). 1981. pap. text ed. 14.50 (ISBN 0-273-08536-0). Pitman Pub MA.

Bancroft, Caroline. Grand Lake: From Utes to Yachts. (Bancroft Booklet Ser.). (Illus.). 40p. (Orig.). 1982. pap. 2.50 (ISBN 0-933472-68-4). Johnson Bks.

--Tabor's Matchless Mine & Lusty Leadville. 1960. pap. 2.00 (ISBN 0-933472-23-4). Johnson Bks.

Bancroft, G. M. Mossbauer Spectroscopy: An Introduction for Chemists & Geochemists. LC 73-3326. 252p. 1974. text ed. 34.95 (ISBN 0-470-04665-1). Halsted Pr.

Bancroft, G. Thomas & Woolfenden, Glen E. Molt of Scrub Jays & Blue Jays in Florida. 51p. 1982. write for info. (ISBN 0-943610-29-X). Am Ornithologists.

Bancroft, George. The Life & Letters of George Bancroft, 2 Vols. in 1. Howe, Mark D., ed. LC 78-106990. (American Public Figures Ser). 1970. Repr. of 1908 ed. lib. bdg. 79.50 (ISBN 0-306-71877-4). Da Capo.

Bancroft, H. H. History of Utah: 1888. (Illus.). 1982. 25.00 (ISBN 0-913814-49-0). Nevada Pubns.

--Reproduction of Bancroft History of Nevada, 1888. (Illus.). 1982. 25.00 (ISBN 0-913814-44-X). Nevada Pubns.

Bancroft, Henrietta. Down Come the Leaves. LC 61-10496. (A Let's-Read-&-Find-Out Science Bk). (Illus.). (gr. k-3). 1961. PLB 10.89 (ISBN 0-690-24313-8, TYC-J). Har-Row.

Bancroft, Hubert H. History of California, 7 vols. LC 67-29422. Repr. of 1888 ed. Set. 100.00 (ISBN 0-914888-20-X). Bancroft Pr.

Bancroft, Iris. Rapture's Rebel. 384p. (Orig.). 1980. pap. 2.50 o.p. (ISBN 0-523-40521-9). Pinnacle Bks.

--Whispering Hope. 1983. pap. 3.50 (ISBN 0-553-22862-5). Bantam.

Bancroft, John. Deviant Sexual Behaviour: Modification & Assessment. (Illus.). 1974. text ed. 27.50x (ISBN 0-19-857367-7). Oxford U Pr.

Bancroft, Keith. Amphoto Guide to Lenses. (Illus.). 169p. 1981. pap. 12.95 (ISBN 0-8174-3528-X, Amphoto); pap. 7.95. Watson-Guptill.

Bancroft Library, University of California, Berkeley. University of California, Berkeley, Bancroft Library: Index to Printed Maps, 1st Suppl. 1975. lib. bdg. 105.00 (ISBN 0-8161-1172-3, Hall Library). G K Hall.

Bancroft, Mary. Autobiography of a Spy. (Illus.). 320p. 1983. 15.95 (ISBN 0-688-02019-4). Morrow.

Bancroft-Hunt, Norman & Forman, Werner. People of the Totem. LC 78-57977. (Illus.). 1979. 14.95 (ISBN 0-399-11991-4). Putnam Pub Group.

Bancroft-Hunt, Norman & Werner, Forman. The Indians of the Great Plains. LC 81-85585. (Illus.). 128p. 1982. 25.00 (ISBN 0-688-01215-9). Morrow.

Band, Arnold J. Nostalgia & Nightmare: A Study in the Fiction of S. Y. Agnon. LC 67-22714. (Near Eastern Center, UCLA). 1968. 40.00x (ISBN 0-520-00076-5). U of Cal Pr.

Band, Ora, et al. Hebrew: A Language Course. 256p. 1982. pap. text ed. 6.95x (ISBN 0-87441-331-1). Behrman.

Bandelier, Adolph F. & Hewett, Edgar L. Indians of the Rio Grande Valley. LC 72-95268. (Illus.). 274p. 1973. Repr. of 1939 ed. lib. bdg. 16.50x o.p. (ISBN 0-8154-0462-X). Cooper Sq.

Bander, David F., jt. auth. see Bander, Edward.

Bander, Edward & Bander, David F. Legal Research & Education Abridgment: A Manual for Law Students, Paralegals & Researchers. LC 78-2408. 240p. 1978. prof ref 25.00x (ISBN 0-88410-794-9). Ballinger Pub.

Bander, Edward J. Dictionary of Selected Legal Terms & Maxims, Vol. 58. 2nd ed. LC 79-19266. (Legal Almanac Ser.: No. 58). 140p. 1979. 5.95 (ISBN 0-379-11119-5). Oceana.

Bander, Edward J., jt. auth. see Marke, Julius J.

Banderly, Mark B. Name It! (Illus.). 128p. (Orig.). 1980. pap. 7.95 o.s.i. (ISBN 0-89104-145-1, A & W Visual Library). A & W Pubs.

--Super Cryptograms. 96p. (Orig.). 1979. pap. 2.95 o.s.i. (ISBN 0-89104-250-4, A & W Visual Library). A & W Pubs.

--Wordplay. 224p. (Orig.). 1979. pap. 5.95 o.s.i. (ISBN 0-89104-149-4, A & W Visual Library). A & W Pubs.

Bandi, Hans-George. Art of the Stone Age. (Art of the World Library). (Illus.). 6.95 o.p. (ISBN 0-517-50854-0). Crown.

Band-Kuzmany, K. R. Glossary of the Theatre. (Eng. Fr. Ital. & Ger.). 1970. 30.00 (ISBN 0-444-40716-2). Elsevier.

Bandler, Leslie C. They Lived Happily Ever After. LC 78-71281. 1978. 10.95x (ISBN 0-916990-05-2). Meta Pubns.

Bandlow, Richard F., jt. auth. see Yehl, Joan K.

Bandopadhyaya, J. North Over South: A NonWestern Perspective of International Relations. 1982. 26.00x (ISBN 0-8364-0894-2). South Asia Bks.

Bandt, Jacques de see De Bandt, Jacques, et al.

Bandura, A. Social Learning Theory. 1977. text ed. 19.95 (ISBN 0-13-816751-6); pap. text ed. 13.95 (ISBN 0-13-816744-3). P-H.

Bandura, Albert. Aggression: A Social Learning Analysis. (P-H Social Learning Ser). (Illus.). 368p. 1973. ref. ed. 24.95 (ISBN 0-13-020743-8). P-H.

Bandy, Anastasius. Ioannes Lydus on Powers or the Magistracies of the Roman State. LC 80-68491. (Memoirs Ser.: Vol. 149). 1982. 35.00 (ISBN 0-686-82856-9). Am Philos.

Bandy, Dale & Swad, Randy. Federal Income Tax Procedures, 1982. 2nd ed. 800p. 1982. pap. text ed. 17.95 (ISBN 0-13-308494-9). P-H.

--Federal Income Tax Procedures, 1983. 320p. 1983. pap. text ed. 19.00 (ISBN 0-13-309104-X). P-H.

Bandy, Mary Lea, ed. Rediscovering French Film. (Illus.). 240p. 1982. pap. 14.95 (ISBN 0-87070-335-8, Pub. by Museum Mod Art). NYGS.

Bandyopadhyay. Metal Sculptures of Eastern India. 1981. 44.00x o.p. (ISBN 0-8364-0732-6, Pub. by Sundeep). South Asia Bks.

Bandyopadhyaya, S. The Origin of Raga. 1978. 7.50x o.p. (ISBN 0-8364-0255-3). South Asia Bks.

Bane, Allyne. Creative Clothing Construction. 3rd ed. (Illus.). 448p. 1972. text ed. 32.50 (ISBN 0-07-003615-2, C). McGraw.

--Flat Pattern Design. (Illus.). 288p. (gr. 9-12). 1972. text ed. 28.50 (ISBN 0-07-003609-5, C). McGraw.

--Tailoring. 3rd ed. LC 74-5755. (Illus.). 560p. 1974. text ed. 32.50 (ISBN 0-07-003608-X, C). McGraw.

Bane, Mary J. Here to Stay: American Families in the 20th Century. LC 76-44877. 1978. pap. 5.95x (ISBN 0-465-09726-X, CN-5026). Basic.

Bane, Mary Jo, jt. auth. see Masnick, George.

Bane, Michael. Who's Who in Rock. (Illus.). 260p. 1982. pap. 10.95 (ISBN 0-89696-184-2, An Everest House Book). Dodd.

Bane, Michael & Moore, Ellen. Tampa: Yesterday, Today & Tomorrow. (Illus.). 180p. (Orig.). 1982. 19.95 (ISBN 0-9609530-0-0); pap. 12.95 (ISBN 0-9609530-2-7). Mishler & King.

Bane, Michael, jt. auth. see Williams, Hank, Jr.

Banek, Reinhold & Scoville, Jon. Sound Designs: A Handbook of Musical Instrument Building. LC 80-65364. (Illus.). 224p. (Orig.). 1980. pap. 6.95 (ISBN 0-89815-011-6). Ten Speed Pr.

Banel, Joseph. Lee Wong, Boy Detective. LC 72-1923. (Venture Ser). (Illus.). 64p. (gr. 2). 1972. PLB 6.89 (ISBN 0-8116-6967-X). Garrard.

Banerjee, A. C. Two Nations: The Philosophy of Muslim Nationalism. 268p. 1981. text ed. 16.25x (ISBN 0-391-02210-5, Pub. by Concept India). Humanities.

Banerjee, Gauranga N. Hellenism in Ancient India. rev. ed. 276p. 1981. text ed. 20.00x (ISBN 0-391-02417-5, Pub. by Munshiram Manoharlal India). Humanities.

Banerjee, H. N. Americans Who Have Been Reincarnated. 1980. 11.95 o.s.i. (ISBN 0-02-506740-0). Macmillan.

Banerjee, J. India in Soviet Global Strategy. 1977. 12.50x o.p. (ISBN 0-88386-908-X). South Asia Bks.

Banerjee, K. K., ed. Logic, Ontology & Action. (Jadavpur Studies in Philosophy: Vol. 1). 269p. 1982. text ed. 12.50x (ISBN 0-391-02490-6). Humanities.

--Mind, Language & Necessity. (Jadavpur Studies in Philosophy: Vol. 3). 275p. 1982. text ed. 12.50x (ISBN 0-391-02504-X). Humanities.

Banerjee, P. K. Development in Boundary Element Methods. (Vol. 2). 1982. 69.75 (ISBN 0-85334-112-5, Pub. by Applied Sci England). Elsevier.

--Developments in Boundary Element Methods, Vol. 1. 1979. 74.00 (ISBN 0-85334-845-6, Pub. by Applied Sci England). Elsevier.

Banerjee, P. K. & Butterfield, R. Boundary Element Methods in Engineering Science. 512p. 1982. text ed. 32.50 (ISBN 0-07-084120-9). McGraw.

Banerjee, S. Deferred Hopes: Blacks in Contemporary America. 425p. 1983. text ed. 30.00x (ISBN 0-391-02800-6, Pub. by Radiant Pub India). Humanities.

Banerjee, S. K., jt. auth. see Stacey, F. D.

Banerjee, Sikhar N. Rehabilitation Management of Amputees. (Rehabilitative Medicine Library). (Illus.). 464p. 1982. lib. bdg. 48.00 (ISBN 0-683-00470-0). Williams & Wilkins.

Banerjee, Sumanta. Family Planning Communication: A Critique of the Indian Programme. (Illus.). 218p. 1980. text ed. 11.00x (ISBN 0-391-02169-9). Humanities.

--India's Simmering Revolution: The Naxalite Uprising. 464p. (Orig.). 1983. pap. 14.50 (ISBN 0-86232-038-0, Pub. by Zed Pr England). Lawrence Hill.

Banerjee, Utpal K. Operational Analysis & Indian Defence. 1980. text ed. 42.50x (ISBN 0-391-01839-6). Humanities.

Banerji, Arun. Aspects of Indo-British Economic Relations, 1858-98. (Illus.). 272p. 1981. text ed. 24.95 (ISBN 0-19-561341-4). Oxford U Pr.

Banerji, Dilip & Raymond, Jacque. Elements of Microprogramming. (Illus.). 416p. 1982. text ed. 26.95 (ISBN 0-13-267146-8). P-H.

Banerji, M. L. Orchids of Nepal. (Illus.). 135p. (Orig.). 1982. text ed. 12.50 (ISBN 0-934454-95-7). Lubrecht & Cramer.

Banes, Daniel. Shakespeare, Shylock & Kabbalah. LC 78-58912. 1978. 9.99 (ISBN 0-686-10284-3); pap. 3.60 (ISBN 0-686-10285-1). Malcolm Hse.

Banet, Anthony G., Jr., ed. Creative Psychotherapy: A Source Book. LC 75-32382. 358p. 1976. pap. 7.50 (ISBN 0-88390-109-9). Univ Assocs.

Banet, Doris. Flicker, the Discontented Firefly. (Nature & Science Bk.). (Illus.). (gr. k-6). PLB 5.95 o.p. (ISBN 0-513-00329-0). Denison.

Banfield, Beryl. Africa in the Curriculum. LC 37-475. 1968. pap. text ed. 5.50 tchr's. guide o.p. (ISBN 0-914110-00-4). Blyden Pr.

Banfield, Beryle, jt. ed. see Meyers, Ruth S.

Banfield, Edward C. Big City Politics: A Comparative Guide to the Political Systems of Nine American Cities. 1965. pap. text ed. 3.40x (ISBN 0-394-30848-4). Phila Bk Co.

Banfield, Thomas C. Organization of Industry. 2nd ed. LC 68-55469. Repr. of 1848 ed. 22.50x (ISBN 0-678-00964-3). Kelley.

Bang & Dahlstrom. Collins Guide to Animal Tracks & Signs. 29.95 (ISBN 0-686-42775-0, Collins Pub England). Greene.

Bang, B., jt. ed. see Sladen, F.

Bang, Im & Ryuk, Yi. Korean Folk Tales: Imps, Ghosts & Fairies. Gale, James S., tr. LC 62-21538. 1962. pap. 4.95 (ISBN 0-8048-0935-6). C E Tuttle.

Bang, Kirsten. Yougga Finds Mother Teresa: The Adventures of a Beggar Boy in India. Spink, Kathryn, tr. from Fr. 176p. (Orig.). 1983. pap. price not set (ISBN 0-8164-2469-1). Seabury.

Bangert, Ethel. Child of the Wind. (Silver Bell Ser.). 192p. (Orig.). 1982. pap. 1.95 o.s.i. (ISBN 0-8439-1128-X, Leisure Bks). Nordon Pubns.

--The Hauntin Fear. 1981. pap. 6.95 (ISBN 0-686-84676-1, Avalon). Bouregy.

Bangert, William V. A History of the Society of Jesus. LC 78-188687. (Original Studies Composed in English Ser.: No. 3). (Illus.). 570p. 1972. 14.75 o.s.i. (ISBN 0-912422-05-X); pap. 9.00 (ISBN 0-686-76928-7) (ISBN 0-912422-23-8). Inst Jesuit.

Bangerter, Lowell A. Hugo Von Hofmannsthal. LC 76-20408. (Literature and Life Ser.). 1977. 11.95 (ISBN 0-8044-2028-9). Ungar.

Bangley, Bernard. Growing in His Image. 160p. 1983. pap. 2.95 (ISBN 0-87788-328-9). Shaw Pubs.

Bangor Public Library. Bibliography of the State of Maine. 1962. 95.00 (ISBN 0-8161-0636-3, Hall Library). G K Hall.

Bangs, Lester & Ochs, Michael. Rock Secrets. (Illus.). 192p. (Orig.). 1982. pap. 9.95 (ISBN 0-933328-45-1). Delilah Bks.

Bangs, Lester, jt. auth. see Nelson, Paul.

Bangs, Robert B. Men, Money, & Markets. (Illus.). 312p. (Orig.). 1972. text ed. 3.75x o.p. (ISBN 0-910286-18-3); pap. text ed. 2.95x o.p. (ISBN 0-910286-17-5). Boxwood.

Bangs, Tina E. Language & Learning Disorders of the Pre-Academic Child. (Illus.). 1968. 23.95 (ISBN 0-13-522797-6). P-H.

--Language & Learning Disorders of the Pre-Academic Child: With Curriculum Guide. 2nd ed. (Illus.). 304p. 1982. 22.95 (ISBN 0-13-523001-2). P-H.

Banica, Constantin & Stanasila, Octavian. Algebraic Methods in the Gobal Theory of Complex Spaces. LC 76-5823. 296p. 1976. 53.95x (ISBN 0-471-01809-0, Pub. by Wiley-Interscience). Wiley.

Banik, Allan E. & Wade, Carlson. Your Water & Your Health. LC 81-81289. (Pivot Original Health Bk). 128p. 1974. pap. 2.95 o.p. (ISBN 0-87983-073-5). Keats.

Banis, Carolyn S., jt. auth. see Shipley, Kenneth G.

Banis, William J. & Krannich, Ronald L. Network Your Way to a New Job. 1981. write for info. (ISBN 0-940010-03-8). Impact VA.

Banis, William J., jt. auth. see Krannich, Ronald L.

Banister, David. Transport Mobility & Deprivation in Inter-Urban Areas. 1980. text ed. 29.50x (ISBN 0-566-00307-4). Gower Pub Ltd.

Banister, Judith. Late Georgian & Regency Silver. (Country Life Collectors Guides Ser). 1972. 4.95 o.p. (ISBN 0-600-43203-3). Transatlantic.

--Mid-Georgian Silver. (Country Life Collector's Guides Ser). 1972. 4.95 o.p. (ISBN 0-600-43129-0). Transatlantic.

Banister, Manly. Making Picture Frames in Wood. LC 81-50985. (Illus.). 128p. 1981. 13.95 o.p. (ISBN 0-8069-5450-7); lib. bdg. 16.79 o.p. (ISBN 0-8069-5451-5); pap. text ed. 6.95 o.p. (ISBN 0-8069-7542-3). Sterling.

Banister, Margaret. Burn Then, Little Lamp. 320p. 1982. pap. 2.95 (ISBN 0-686-96930-8). Popular Lib.

Bank for International Settlements, ed. Payment Systems in Eleven Developed Countries. 312p. 1980. 70.00x (ISBN 0-7121-5483-3, Pub. by Macdonald & Evans). State Mutual Bk.

Bank, Ira M. Community Careering Gamebook. new ed. 59p. (gr. 3-6). 1974. wkbk. 2.00 (ISBN 0-912578-15-7). Chron Guide.

--Curriculum Careering Gamebook. (Illus.). 60p. (gr. 4-6). 1978. Repr. 2.00 (ISBN 0-912578-16-5). Chron Guide.

Bank Street College of Education, jt. auth. see Brenner, Barbara.

Banker, Gilbert S. & Chalmers, Robert K., eds. Pharmaceutics & Pharmacy Practice. (Illus.). 421p. 1981. text ed. 27.50 (ISBN 0-397-50483-7, Lippincott Medical). Lippincott.

Banker, John, et al. Bahnar Dictionary. 202p. (Orig.). 1979. pap. 9.00x (ISBN 0-88312-997-3); microfiche (3) 3.00 (ISBN 0-686-96898-0). Summer Inst Ling.

Banker, John, et al see Linguistic Circle of Saigon & Summer Institute of Linguistics.

Bankes, J. & Kerridge, E. The Early Records of the Bankes Family at Winstanley. 1973. 19.00 (ISBN 0-7190-1158-2). Manchester.

Bankier, Joanna, et al, eds. The Other Voice. 1976. pap. 5.95 (ISBN 0-393-04421-1). Norton.

Banking Law Journal Editors, ed. Banking Law Journal Digest, 2 vols. 6th ed. 1982. Set. 96.00 (ISBN 0-88262-752-X). Warren.

Bankoff, S. G., jt. ed. see Jones, O. C., Jr.

Banks. Feminism & Family Planning in Victorian England. 154p. 1982. 39.00x (ISBN 0-85323-281-4, Pub. by Liverpool Univ England). State Mutual Bk.

--Killey's Fractures of the Middle Third of the Facial Skeleton. 4th ed. (Dental Practioner Handbook: No. 3). (Illus.). 614p. 1983. text ed. 13.95 (ISBN 0-7236-0625-0). Wright-PSG.

--Political Handbook of the World: 1982. 1983. write for info. (ISBN 0-07-003631-4). McGraw.

Banks, jt. auth. see Pfeiffer.

Banks, Arthur S. Cross-Polity Time-Series Data. 328p. 1971. 55.00x (ISBN 0-262-02071-8). MIT Pr.

Banks, Arthur S., ed. Political Handbook of the World, 1976. LC 75-4083. 1976. 30.95 o.p. (ISBN 0-07-003640-3, P&RB). McGraw.

Banks, Arthur S., et al. Economic Handbook of the World: 1981. 608p. 1981. 39.95 (ISBN 0-07-003691-8, P&RB). McGraw.

--Economic Handbook of the World: 1982. 640p. 1982. 44.95 (ISBN 0-07-003692-6, P&RB). McGraw.

Banks, Barbara. Dragonseeds. LC 76-29854. 1977. 7.95 o.p. (ISBN 0-312-21927-X). St Martin.

Banks, Bill & Banks, Sue. Ministering to Abortion's Aftermath. 144p. (Orig.). 1982. pap. 3.95 (ISBN 0-89228-057-3). Impact Bks MO.

Banks, Carl. Teach Your Child to Read. LC 81-86350. 64p. 1983. pap. 3.95 (ISBN 0-86666-049-6). GWP.

Banks, Caroline, jt. auth. see Logan, Gerald E.

Banks, Carolyn. Mr. Right. 1980. pap. 2.50 o.p. (ISBN 0-446-91191-7). Warner Bks.

Banks, David J. Malay Kinship. LC 82-2899. (Illus.). 210p. 1983. text ed. 25.00 (ISBN 0-89727-037-1). Inst Study Human.

Banks, Ferdinand E. Bauxite & Aluminum: An Introduction to the Economics of Non-Fuel Minerals. LC 78-24632. 208p. 1979. 22.95x (ISBN 0-669-02771-5). Lexington Bks.

--The International Economy: A Modern Approach. LC 77-26560. (Illus.). 1979. 19.95x (ISBN 0-669-01504-0). Lexington Bks.

--The Political Economy of Oil. LC 79-3340. 1980. 27.95x (ISBN 0-669-03402-9). Lexington Bks.

--Resources & Energy: An Economic Analysis. LC 81-47967. 368p. 1983. 34.95x (ISBN 0-669-05203-5). Lexington Bks.

--Scarcity, Energy and Economic Progress. LC 77-4630. 1977. 21.95x o.p. (ISBN 0-669-01781-7). Lexington Bks.

Banks, Howard. The Rise & Fall of Freddie Laker. 256p. 1982. 14.95 (ISBN 0-571-11986-7); pap. 6.95 (ISBN 0-571-13077-1). Faber & Faber.

Banks, J. A. The Sociology of Social Movements. (Studies in Sociology). 1972. pap. text ed. 6.00x (ISBN 0-333-13433-8). Humanities.

Banks, J. A. & Banks, Olive. Feminism & Family Planning in Victorian England. LC 63-18387. (Studies in the Life of Women). 154p. 1972. pap. 5.95 (ISBN 0-8052-0350-8). Schocken.

Banks, J. Houston, jt. auth. see Sobel, Max A.

Banks, J. Houston, et al. Geometry: Its Elements & Structure. (Illus.). (gr. 10). 1972. text ed. 12.56 o.p. (ISBN 0-07-003681-0, W); tchr's ed. 14.00 o.p. (ISBN 0-07-003682-9); tests 2.64 o.p. (ISBN 0-686-60800-3). McGraw.

Banks, James A., ed. Teaching Ethnic Studies: Concepts & Strategies, 43rd Yearbook. LC 73-75298. (Illus.). 320p. 1973. 9.00 (ISBN 0-87986-000-6, 490-15278); pap. 8.25 (ISBN 0-87986-036-7, 490-15276). Coun Soc Studies.

Banks, Jane, jt. auth. see Dong, Collin H.

Banks, Lynne R. Backward Shadow. LC 73-129876. 1970. 6.95 o.p. (ISBN 0-671-20671-0). S&S.

--The Indian in the Cupboard. (Illus.). 1982. pap. 2.25 (ISBN 0-380-60012-9, 60012, Camelot). Avon.

--My Darling Villain. LC 76-58718. (gr. 12 up). 1977. 10.95 (ISBN 0-06-020392-7, HarpJ); PLB 10.89 (ISBN 0-06-020393-5). Har-Row.

--Two Is Lonely. 1974. 7.95 o.p. (ISBN 0-671-21732-1). S&S.

Banks, Michael. Second Stage Advanced Model Rocketry. Angle, Burr, ed. (Illus., Orig.). 1984. pap. price not set (ISBN 0-89024-057-4). Kalmbach.

Banks, Michael A. Understanding Science Fiction. 180p. 1982. 10.20 (ISBN 0-382-29074-7). Silver.

Banks, Natalie N. The Golden Thread. 1979. pap. 3.50 (ISBN 0-85330-127-1). Lucis.

Banks, Noel. Six Inner Hebrides. 1977. 16.95 o.p. (ISBN 0-7153-7368-4). David & Charles.

Banks, Olive, jt. auth. see Banks, J. A.

Banks, Oliver. The Rembrandt Panel. 1980. 11.95 (ISBN 0-316-08021-7). Little.

Banks, P., et al. The Biochemistry of the Tissues. 2nd ed. LC 75-26739. 493p. 1976. 74.95x (ISBN 0-471-05471-2, Pub. by Wiley-Interscience); pap. 27.95 (ISBN 0-471-01923-2, Pub. by Wiley-Interscience). Wiley.

Banks, Paul N. A Selective Bibliography on the Conservation of Research Library Materials. 150p. 1981. member 8.00 (ISBN 0-686-95761-X, 5003); non-member 10.00 (ISBN 0-686-99604-6). Soc Am Archivists.

Banks, Peter M. & Doupnik, Joseph. Introduction to Computer Science. LC 75-20407. 384p. 1976. text ed. 24.95 o.p. (ISBN 0-471-04710-4). Wiley.

Banks, R. E. Organofluorine Chemicals & Their Industrial Applications. LC 79-40251. (Industrial Chemistry Ser.). 255p. 1979. 69.95 (ISBN 0-470-26720-8). Halsted Pr.

--Preparation Properties & Industrial Applications of Organofluorine Compounds. (Ser. in Chemical Science). 352p. 1982. 84.95 (ISBN 0-470-27526-X). Halsted Pr.

Banks, R. W. The Battle of Franklin. 88p. 1982. 15.00 (ISBN 0-686-97674-6). Pr of Morningside.

Banks, Richard C., et al. Introductory Problems in Spectroscopy. 1979. 16.95 (ISBN 0-8053-0572-6). Benjamin-Cummings.

Banks, Robert F. & Stieber, Jack, eds. Multinationals, Unions, & Labor Relations in Industrialized Countries. LC 77-4463. (International Report Ser.: No. 9). 208p. 1977. 10.00 (ISBN 0-87546-064-X). ILR Pr.

Banks, Ronald F. Maine Becomes a State: The Movement to Separate Maine from Massachusetts, 1785-1820. LC 73-82845. 1973. pap. 6.95 o.p. (ISBN 0-915592-08-8). Maine Hist.

Banks, Russell. Family Life. (Orig.). 1975. pap. 2.95 o.p. (ISBN 0-380-00258-2, 22855). Avon.

Banks, Sue, jt. auth. see Banks, Bill.

Banks, Sydney. Second Chance. 146p. 1983. pap. 4.95 (ISBN 0-686-43270-3). Pine Mntn.

Banks, William. Daily Manna. 380p. 1981. 8.95 o.p. (ISBN 0-8024-5607-3). Moody.

Banks, William J. Applied Veterinary Histology. 2nd ed. (Illus.). 540p. 1981. 39.00 (ISBN 0-686-77705-0, 0410-7). Williams & Wilkins.

Banks, William L. Jonah, the Reluctant Prophet. (Everyman's Bible Commentary Ser). 1968. pap. 4.50 (ISBN 0-8024-2032-X). Moody.

--Now I See. 1971. pap. 1.50 o.p. (ISBN 0-87508-009-X). Chr Lit.

Bankson, Nicholas W., jt. auth. see Bernthal, John E.

Bann, Stephen, jt. auth. see Finlay, Ian H.

Banna, M. Clinical Neuroradiology. (Illus.). 1983. text ed. price not set (ISBN 0-8391-1809-0, 17523). Univ Park.

Bannatyne, Alexander. Language, Reading & Learning Disabilities: Psychology, Neuropsychology, Diagnosis & Remediation. (Illus.). 800p. 1976. 21.50x o.p. (ISBN 0-398-02182-1). C C Thomas.

Banner, David K., et al. The Politics of Social Program Evaluation. LC 74-28452. 192p. 1975. prof ref 17.50x (ISBN 0-88410-009-X). Ballinger Pub.

Banner, F. T. & Collins, M. B. Northwest European Shelf Seas: The Sea-Bed & the Sea in Motion, Vol. 2, Physical & Chemical Oceanography & Physical Resources. (Oceanography Ser.: Vol. 24B). 1980. 85.00 (ISBN 0-444-41739-7); Vols. 1 & 2. 151.00 (ISBN 0-444-41740-0). Elsevier.

Banner, F. T. & Lord, A. R., eds. Aspects of Micropalaeontology. (Illus.). 362p. 1982. text ed. 50.00x (ISBN 0-04-562003-2). Allen Unwin.

Banner, F. T., et al, eds. The North-West European Shelf Seas: The Sea-Bed & the Sea in Motion, Vol. 1, Geology & Sedimentology. LC 78-14524. (Elsevier Oceanography Ser.: Vol. 24A). 300p. 1979. 66.00 (ISBN 0-444-41693-5). Elsevier.

Banner, Hubert S. Calamities of the World. LC 74-159880. (Tower Bks). (Illus.). 1971. Repr. of 1932 ed. 34.00x (ISBN 0-8103-3918-8). Gale.

Banner, Lois W. American Beauty. LC 82-4738. 352p. 1983. 17.95 (ISBN 0-394-51923-X). Knopf.

--Elizabeth Cady Stanton: A Radical for Women's Rights. (Library of American Biography). 189p. 1980. pap. text ed. 5.95 (ISBN 0-316-08030-6). Little.

Banner, Melvin. The Black Pioneer in Michigan. LC 73-91313. 1973. pap. 7.00 o.s.i. (ISBN 0-87812-053-X). Pendell Pub.

Bannerman, David & Bannerman, W. Mary. Birds of the Balearics. (Illus.). 450p. 1983. 45.00 (ISBN 0-686-38404-0). Tanager Bks.

Bannerman, Glenn & Fakkema, Robert. Guide for Recreation Leaders. LC 74-28523. 120p. (Orig.). 1975. pap. 4.95 (ISBN 0-8042-2154-5). John Knox.

Bannerman, W. Mary, jt. auth. see Bannerman, David.

Bannister & Hill. Superoxide & Superoxide Dismutase, 2 Vols. (Developments in Biochemistry: Vol. 11). 1980. Set. 98.95 (ISBN 0-686-95307-X). Elsevier.

Bannister, Anthony & Johnson, Peter. Namibia: Africa's Harsh Paradise. Gordon, Rene, ed. LC 79-10312. (Illus.). 240p. 1979. 37.50 o.p. (ISBN 0-89196-060-0, Domus Bks). Quality Bks IL.

Bannister, D. & Fransella, F. Inquiring Man. LC 82-13016. 218p. 1982. lib. bdg. 11.50 (ISBN 0-89874-541-1). Krieger.

Bannister, D., jt. auth. see Fransella, F.

Bannister, Henry S. Donn Byrne: A Descriptive Bibliography, 1912-1935. LC 80-8485. 350p. 1982. lib. bdg. 50.00 (ISBN 0-8240-9502-2). Garland Pub.

Bannister, John, jt. auth. see Lemmons, Reuel.

Bannister, Kathleen & Pincus, Lily. Shared Phantasy in Marital Problems: Therapy in a Four Person Relationship. 80p. 1971. 3.50x o.p. (ISBN 0-686-77025-0, CBO-903-C). Natl Assn Soc Wkrs.

Bannister, Peter. Introduction to Physiological Plant Ecology. LC 76-16743. 1978. pap. text ed. 22.95 (ISBN 0-470-99389-8). Halsted Pr.

Bannister, Robert C. Social Darwinism: Science & Myth in Anglo-American Social Thought. Davis, Allen F., ed. LC 79-615. (American Civilization Ser.). 292p. 1979. lib. bdg. 29.95 (ISBN 0-87722-155-3). Temple U Pr.

Bannister, Roger, ed. Brain's Clinical Neurology. 5th ed. (Illus.). 1978. 29.50x (ISBN 0-19-519957-X); pap. 19.95x (ISBN 0-19-261308-1). Oxford U Pr.

Bannius, Ioan A. see Ban, Ioan A.

Bannock, Graham, jt. auth. see Auld, Douglas.

Bannon, Edward. Operational Amplifiers: Theory & Servicing. (Illus.). 208p. 1975. 19.95 (ISBN 0-87909-585-7). Reston.

Bannon, John F. Spanish Borderlands Frontier, 1513-1821. LC 74-110887. (Histories of the American Frontier Series). (Illus.). 308p. 1974. pap. 9.95x (ISBN 0-8263-0309-9). U of NM Pr.

Bannon, Joseph J. Leisure Resources: Its Comprehensive Planning. (Illus.). 512p. 1976. 22.95 (ISBN 0-13-528208-X). P-H.

--Problem Solving in Recreation & Parks. 2nd ed. 400p. 1981. text ed. 20.95 (ISBN 0-13-711770-1). P-H.

Bannon, Laura. When the Moon Is New. LC 53-7925. (Illus.). (gr. 3-5). 1953. 5.95g o.p. (ISBN 0-8075-8896-2). A Whitman.

Bannon, Lois & Carr, Martha. History of Magnolia Mound Plantation. 1983. pap. 5.95 (ISBN 0-88289-381-5). Pelican.

Banov, A. Paints & Coating Handbook. 1981. 36.50 (ISBN 0-07-003664-0). McGraw.

Banovetz, James M., ed. Managing the Modern City. LC 58-9090. (Muncipal Management Ser.). 1971. text ed. 26.00 (ISBN 0-87326-004-X). Intl City Mgt.

Banowsky, William S., jt. auth. see Decazes, Daisy.

Banskota, N. P. Indo-Nepal Trade & Economic Relations. 299p. 1981. text ed. 19.00x (ISBN 0-391-02337-3, Pub. by Concept India). Humanities.

Bantel, Linda, ed. William Rush: American Sculptor. LC 82-80636. (Illus.). 211p. (Orig.). 1982. 21.95x (ISBN 0-943836-00-X, Pub. by Penn Acad Fine Arts). U Pr of Va.

Bantens, Robert J. Eugene Carriere: His Work & His Influence. Foster, Stephen, ed. LC 82-4919. (Studies in Fine Arts: The Avant-Garde: No. 29). 290p. 1983. 39.95 (ISBN 0-8357-1329-6, Pub. by UMI Res Pr). Univ Microfilms.

Banti, Alberto & Simonetti, L. Corpus Nummorum Romanorum (Roman Imperial, 18 Vol. 1978. Set. 750.00 (ISBN 0-686-37929-2). Numismatic Fine Arts.

Banti, Marco, ed. Italy in Colour. LC 73-155752. (Illus.). 254p. 1972. pap. 30.00x (ISBN 0-8002-0834-X). Intl Pubns Serv.

Banting, Keith G. The Welfare State & Canadian Federalism. 216p. 1982. 22.50x (ISBN 0-7735-0380-3); pap. 12.95 (ISBN 0-7735-0384-6). McGill-Queens U Pr.

Bantock, G. H. Dilemmas of the Curriculum. LC 80-11764. 146p. 1980. 19.95 (ISBN 0-470-26920-0). Halsted Pr.

--T. S. Eliot & Education. 1969. pap. text ed. 2.95 (ISBN 0-685-19775-1). Phila Bk Co.

Banton, Michael, ed. Anthropological Approaches to the Study of Religion. 1968. pap. 11.50x (ISBN 0-422-72510-2, Pub. by Tavistock England). Methuen Inc.

Banton, Michael P. White & Coloured: The Behavior of the British People Towards Coloured Immigrants. LC 76-43335. 1976. Repr. of 1960 ed. lib. bdg. 18.00x (ISBN 0-8371-9290-0, BAWAC). Greenwood.

Bants, William J., jt. auth. see Krannich, Ronald L.

Banville, John. Kepler. 192p. 1983. 12.95 (ISBN 0-87923-438-5). Godine.

Banwart, George J. Basic Food Microbiology. abr. ed. (Illus.). 1981. text ed. 21.50 (ISBN 0-87055-384-4). AVI.

Bany, Mary A. & Johnson, Lois V. Educational Social Psychology. (Illus.). 480p. 1975. pap. text ed. 14.95 (ISBN 0-02-305780-7, 30578). Macmillan.

Banz, G. Elements of Urban Form. 1970. 31.50 (ISBN 0-07-003637-3, P&RB). McGraw.

Banz, Hans. Building Construction Details: Practical Drawings. 272p. pap. 14.95 (ISBN 0-442-21325-5). Van Nos Reinhold.

Banzhaf, Jane C., jt. auth. see Greendyke, Robert M.

Banzhaf, Jane C. & Wallas, Charles H., eds. Strategies for Instruction in the Blood Bank. 120p. 1982. 17.00 (ISBN 0-914404-79-2); non-members 19.00 (ISBN 0-686-83052-0). Am Assn Blood.

Banzhaf, Robert A. Screen Process Printing. 1983. text ed. 10.00 (ISBN 0-87345-206-2). McKnight.

Baptista, Bob & Baptista, Martha. Ric. 150p. 1981. 8.95 o.p. (ISBN 0-8024-7351-2). Moody.

Baptista, Martha, jt. auth. see Baptista, Bob.

Baptista, W. S., tr. see Glaucia, Daria.

Baptista Mantuanus. The Eclogues of Mantuan. Bush, Douglas, ed. Turbervile, George, tr. LC 38-12665. 208p. 1977. Repr. of 1567 ed. 30.00x (ISBN 0-8201-1181-3). Schol Facsimiles.

Baptiste, H. Prentice, Jr. Multicultural Education: A Synopsis. LC 79-89924. 1979. pap. text ed. 7.00 (ISBN 0-8191-0851-0). U Pr of Amer.

Baptiste, H. Prentice, Jr. & Baptiste, Mira L. Developing the Multicultural Process in Classroom Instruction: Competencies for Teachers. LC 79-89993. 1979. pap. text ed. 12.75 (ISBN 0-8191-0855-3). U Pr of Amer.

Baptiste, Mira L., jt. auth. see Baptiste, H. Prentice, Jr.

Baptist-Metz, Johannes, jt. auth. see Schillebeeckx, Edward.

Bar, Hans, ed. see Schad, N., et al.

Bara, Nina see Linke, Frances, pseud.

Barach, Jeffrey. The Individual, Business & Society. (Illus.). 1977. 16.95 (ISBN 0-13-458075-3); pap. text ed. 14.95 (ISBN 0-13-458067-2). P-H.

Barad, Diane S. More Games Kids Like. 1975. loose-leaf text 15.95 (ISBN 0-88450-751-3, 2125-B). Communication Skill.

Barad, Dianne S. K-Speech News. (gr. 7-12). 1981. manual 15.95 (ISBN 0-686-69810-X, 3135-B). Communication Skill.

--Unfamiliar Fables. 1979. pap. text ed. 15.95 (ISBN 0-88450-702-5, 3102-B). Communication Skill.

Baradat, Leon P. Political Ideologies: Their Origins & Impact. (Illus.). 1979. pap. 14.95 ref. (ISBN 0-13-684985-7). P-H.

Baragwanath, Albert K. Currier & Ives. LC 79-57412. (Abbeville Library of Art: No. 6). (Illus.). 112p. (Orig.). 1980. pap. 4.95 o.p. (ISBN 0-89659-092-5). Abbeville Pr.

--One Hundred Currier & Ives Favorites. (Illus.). 1979. 17.95 o.p. (ISBN 0-517-53547-5). Crown.

Barak, Michael. Double Cross. 1982. pap. 2.95 (ISBN 0-451-11547-3, AE1547, Sig). NAL.

--The Enigma. 1980. pap. 1.95 o.p. (ISBN 0-451-08920-0, J8920, Sig). NAL.

--The Phantom Conspiracy. 1981. pap. 2.95 o.p. (ISBN 0-451-11014-5, AE1014, Sig). NAL.

Baraka, Amina, jt. ed. see Bakara, Amiri.

Baraka, Amina, jt. ed. see Baraka, Amiri.

Baraka, Amiri & Baraka, Amina, eds. Confirmation: An Anthology of African-American Women. 416p. 1983. 17.95 (ISBN 0-688-01580-8). Morrow.

Barakat, Gamal. English-Arabic Dictionary of Diplomacy & Related Terminology. 1982. 25.00x (ISBN 0-86685-290-5). Intl Bk Ctr.

Baral, Jaya K. The Pentagon & the Making of US Foreign Policy: A Case Study of Vietnam 1960-1968. LC 77-13333. 1978. text ed. 16.25x (ISBN 0-391-00549-9). Humanities.

Baralt, Guillermo A. Esclavos Rebeldes. LC 81-70982. (Coleccion Semilla Ser.). 190p. 1982. pap. 4.95 (ISBN 0-940238-07-1). Ediciones Huracan.

Baram, Michael, et al. Marine Mining of the Continental Shelf: An Assessment of Legal, Technical & Environmental Feasibilities. LC 77-23831. 328p. 1978. prof ref 35.00x (ISBN 0-88410-616-0). Ballinger Pub.

Baram, Michael S. Alternatives to Regulation: Managing Risks to Health, Safety, & the Environment. LC 81-47560. 256p. 1981. 24.95x (ISBN 0-669-04666-3). Lexington Bks.

--Environmental Law & the Siting of Facilities: Issues in Land Use & Coastal Zone Management. LC 76-2664. 272p. 1976. prof ref 17.50 (ISBN 0-88410-417-6). Ballinger Pub.

Baramki, D. C., jt. auth. see Sellers, O. R.

Baramki, Dimitri, jt. auth. see Kelso, James L.

Baran, Elaine A. Modern Spoken Italian: Active Italian Conversation, Part A. 144p. (Orig.). 1981. pap. text ed. 125.00 (ISBN 0-686-73214-6, Z501); 8 audio cassettes incl. J Norton Pubs.

--Modern Spoken Italian: Active Italian Communication, Part B. 144p. (Orig.). 1981. pap. 125.00 (ISBN 0-88432-074-X, Z551); 8 audio cassettes incl. J Norton Pubs.

Baran, Kathryn Kavanaugh see Adams, Bruce & Kavanaugh-Baran, Kathryn.

Baran, Paul A. Political Economy of Growth. LC 57-7953. 1957. pap. 7.50 (ISBN 0-85345-076-5, PB-0765). Monthly Rev.

Barancourt, Petit De see De Barancourt, Petit.

Baranov, A. Basic Latin for Plant Taxonomists. 1971. pap. text ed. 16.00 (ISBN 3-7682-0727-7). Lubrecht & Cramer.

Baranov, Alvin B. Divorces California Style. 4th ed. 90p. pap. 7.95 (ISBN 0-686-36139-3). Legal Pubns CA.

--How to Evict a Tenant. 11th ed. (Illus.). 147p. 1982. Repr. of 1978 ed. 9.95 (ISBN 0-910531-04-8). Wolcotts.

Baranov, Alvin B. & Sirkin, Esther. What Every Husband & Wife Should Know Before It's Too Late. 165p. pap. 3.00 (ISBN 0-686-36142-3). Legal Pubns CA.

Baranski, Johnny. Pencil Flowers. LC 82-12057. (Kestrel Ser.). 24p. 1983. 3.00 (ISBN 0-914974-36-X). Holmgangers.

Baranson, Jack. The Japanese Challenge to U. S. Industry. (Illus.). 208p. 1981. 20.95x (ISBN 0-669-04402-4). Lexington Bks.

--Technology & the Multinationals. LC 77-14699. 1978. 21.95x (ISBN 0-669-02021-4). Lexington Bks.

Barante, Guillaume-Prosper De. Notes sur la Russie, 1835-1840. (Nineteenth Century Russia Ser.). 464p. (Fr.). 1974. Repr. of 1875 ed. lib. bdg. 116.00 o.p. (ISBN 0-8287-0054-0, R5). Clearwater Pub.

Baranwal, S. P., ed. Military Year Book, 1978-1979. 13th ed. (Illus.). 1979. 25.00x o.p. (ISBN 0-8002-0984-2). Intl Pubns Serv.

Baranzini, Mauro. Advances In Economic Theory. LC 82-42613. 330p. 1982. 35.00 (ISBN 0-312-00636-5). St Martin.

Baras, Victor, jt. ed. see Himmelfarb, Milton.

Barasch, Clarence S., jt. ed. see Biskind, Elliott L.

Barasch, Marc, ed. Breaking One Hundred: Americans Who Have Lived Over a Century. (Illus.). 64p. 1983. pap. 4.95 (ISBN 0-688-01926-9). Quill NY.

Barasch, Marc & Aguilera-Hellweg, Max, eds. Breaking One Hundred: Americans Who Have Lives Over a Century. (Illus.). 64p. (Orig.). 1983. 9.95 (ISBN 0-688-01925-0). Morrow.

Barasch, Moshe. Gestures of Despair in Medieval & Early Renaissance Art. LC 76-4601. 1976. 28.50x o.p. (ISBN 0-8147-1006-9). NYU Pr.

Barasch, Seymour. High School Equivalency Diploma Test. LC 81-1618. (Arco's Preparation for the GED Examination Ser.). 480p. 1983. lib. bdg. 12.95 (ISBN 0-668-05375-5); pap. 6.95 (ISBN 0-668-05382-8). Arco.

Barash, David. The Whisperings Within: Evolution & the Origin of Human Nature. LC 78-20155. 1979. 13.41i (ISBN 0-06-010341-8, HarpT). Har-Row.

Barash, David P. Aging: An Exploration. 232p. 1983. 14.95 (ISBN 0-295-95993-2). U of Wash Pr.

Barash, Meyer, tr. see Caillois, Roger.

Barass, R. Scientists Must Write: A Guide to Better Writing for Scientists, Engineers & Students. 1978. pap. 9.75x (ISBN 0-412-15440-4, Pub. by Chapman & Hall England). Methuen Inc.

Barat, Morton S. The Union & the Coal Industry. LC 82-25141. (Yale Studies in Economics: Vol. 4). xvii, 170p. 1983. Repr. of 1955 ed. lib. bdg. 29.75x (ISBN 0-313-23698-4, BAUC). Greenwood.

Baratt, Andrew, tr. see Levitin, Yevgeny.

Baratta, Ron & Stone, Linda. How to Win With Women. Orig. Title: How to Take Advantage of A Woman. 200p. (Orig.). 1982. pap. 11.95 (ISBN 0-9605628-1-8). Mutual Pr IL.

--Sex Power. 200p. (Orig.). 1983. pap. 11.95 (ISBN 0-9605628-2-6). Mutual Pr IL.

Baratta-Lorton, Mary. Workjobs for Parents. (preprimer-2). 1975. 7.50 (ISBN 0-201-04303-3, Sch Div). A-W.

--Workjobs II. 1978. 11.25 (ISBN 0-201-04302-5, Sch Div). A-W.

Baratta-Lorton, Mary B. Workjobs: Activity-Centered Learning for Early Childhood Education. 1972. text ed. 13.25 (ISBN 0-201-04311-4, Sch Div). A-W.

Baratta-Lorton, Robert. Mathematics: A Way of Thinking. new ed. (gr. 1-8). 1977. tchr's. ed. 22.50 (ISBN 0-201-04322-X, Sch Div). A-W.

Baravalle, Hermann Von see Von Baravalle, Hermann.

Baravykas, V., jt. auth. see Piesarskas, B.

Barba, Harry. The Day the World Went Sane: A Fictive Ballet & a Dramatic Opera by Harry Barba. LC 78-70762. 1979. 9.95 (ISBN 0-911906-14-2); pap. 4.95 (ISBN 0-911906-13-4). Harian Creative.

Barba, Harry & Barba, Marian, eds. What's Cooking in Congress, Vol. II. LC 79-83777. (What's Cooking Ser.). (Illus.). 250p. (Orig.). 1982. 12.95 (ISBN 0-911906-20-7, 0278-4947); pap. 7.95 (ISBN 0-911906-21-5). Harian Creative.

Barba, Harry, ed. see Avila, Kay, et al.

Barba, Marian, jt. ed. see Barba, Harry.

Barba, Preston A., jt. auth. see Treher, Charles H.

Barbacci, Mario, jt. auth. see Siewiorek, Daniel P.

Barbach, Lonnie. For Each Other: Sharing Sexual Intimacy. LC 81-43538. 320p. 1982. 13.95 (ISBN 0-385-17296-6, Anchor Pr). Doubleday.

Barbach, Lonnie G. For Yourself: Fulfillment of Female Sexuality - a Guide to Orgasmic Response. 1976. pap. 2.95 (ISBN 0-451-11947-9, AE1947, Sig). NAL.

Barbara, Dominick A. The Psychodynamics of Stuttering. 96p. 1982. 13.75x (ISBN 0-398-04714-6). C C Thomas.

Barbarena, Celia, jt. auth. see Whimbey, Arthur.

Barbaresi, Sara M. How to Raise & Train a Boxer. pap. 2.95 (ISBN 0-87666-253-X, DS1006). TFH Pubns.

--How to Raise & Train a Collie. pap. 2.95 (ISBN 0-87666-272-6, DS1010). TFH Pubns.

--How to Raise & Train a German Shepherd. pap. 2.95 (ISBN 0-87666-296-3, DS1017). TFH Pubns.

Barbaresi, Sara M., jt. auth. see Ferguson, Estelle.

Barbaresi, Sara M., jt. auth. see Martin, Leda B.

Barbaresi, Sara M., jt. auth. see Meistrell, Lois.

Barbaresi, Sara M., jt. auth. see Shay, Sunny.

Barbaresi, Sara M., jt. auth. see Stebbins, Natalie.

Barbaresi, Sara M., jt. auth. see Ward, Mary A.

Barbash, Heather, jt. auth. see Marshall, John L.

Barbash, Joseph & Feerick, John D. Employment Law: New Problems in the Workplace. 256p. 1981. softcover 30.00 (ISBN 0-686-79680-2, H4-4861). PLI.

--Unjust Dismissal & At Will Employment. (Litigation & Administrative Practice Course Handbook Ser.). 343p. 1982. pap. 30.00 (H4-4885). PLI.

Barbata, Jean, jt. auth. see Koch, Marianna.

Barbe, jt. auth. see St. Barbe, Richard.

Barbe, D. F., ed. Very Large Scale Integration (VLSI) Fundamentals & Applications: Fundamentals & Applications. (Springer Series in Electrophysics: Vol. 5). (Illus.). 279p. 1980. 31.00 o.p. (ISBN 0-387-10154-3). Springer-Verlag.

Barbe, Walter B. & Lucas, Virginia H. Zaner-Bloser Handwriting: Basic Skills & Applications. 1984. write for info pupil texts grade 1-8; write for info tchr's. eds. grade 1-8. Zaner-Bloser.

Barbe, Walter B., ed. Fables & Folktales from Many Lands. (Highlights Handbooks Ser.). (Illus.). 33p. (gr. 2-6). 1972. pap. 1.95 o.p. (ISBN 0-87534-147-0). Highlights.

Barbe, Walter B., jt. ed. see Myers, Caroline C.

Barbe, Walter B., et al. Zaner-Bloser Spelling: Skills & Applications. 1983. write for info pupil texts grade 1-8; write for info tchr's eds. grade 1-8. Zaner-Bloser.

--Creative Growth with Handwriting. Incl. Readiness. tchrs.' manual 11.95 (ISBN 0-88309-244-1); consumable; non-consumable (ISBN 0-88309-255-7); Grade One. t chrs.' manual 11.95 (ISBN 0-88309-245-X); consumable (ISBN 0-88309-234-4); non-consumable (ISBN 0-88309-256-5); Grade Two. tchrs.' manual 11.95 (ISBN 0-88309-246-8); consumable (ISBN 0-88309-235-2); non-consumable (ISBN 0-88309-257-3); Book 2T. tchrs.' manual 11.95 (ISBN 0-88309-247-6); consumable (ISBN 0-88309-236-0); non-consumable (ISBN 0-88309-258-1); Grade 3T. tchrs.' manual 11.95 (ISBN 0-88309-248-4); consumable (ISBN 0-88309-237-9); non-consumable (ISBN 0-88309-259-X); Grade 4. tchrs.' manual 11.95 (ISBN 0-88309-250-6); consumable (ISBN 0-88309-239-5); non-consumable (ISBN 0-88309-261-1); Grade 5. tchrs.' manual 11.95 (ISBN 0-88309-251-4); consumable (ISBN 0-88309-240-9); non-consumable (ISBN 0-88309-262-X); Grade 6. tchrs.' manual 11.95 (ISBN 0-88309-252-2); consumable (ISBN 0-88309-241-7); non-consumable (ISBN 0-88309-263-8); Grade 7. tchrs.' manual 7.95 (ISBN 0-88309-253-0); consumable (ISBN 0-88309-242-5); non-consumable (ISBN 0-88309-264-6); Grade 8. tchrs.' manual 7.95 (ISBN 0-88309-254-9); consumable (ISBN 0-88309-243-3); non-consumable (ISBN 0-88309-265-4). (Illus.). 1979. pupil bk., consumable 2.57 ea.; non-consumable 2.87 ea. Zaner-Bloser.

Barbe, Walter B., et al, eds. Spelling: Basic Skills for Effective Communication. 1982. 10.00 (ISBN 0-88309-118-6). Zaner-Bloser.

Barbeau, A., ed. see Canadian-American Conference on Parkinson's Disease, 2nd.

Barbeau, A., et al, eds. Huntington's Chorea: Advances in Neurology, Vol. 1. LC 72-93317. 848p. 1973. 81.00 (ISBN 0-911216-40-5). Raven.

Barbeau, Andre & Huxtable, Ryan, eds. Taurine & Neurological Disorders. LC 77-85076. 482p. 1978. 49.50 (ISBN 0-89004-202-0). Raven.

Barbeau, Andre, jt. ed. see Huxtable, Ryan.

Barbeau, Andre, et al, eds. Choline & Lecithin in Brain Disorders. LC 78-68608. (Nutrition & the Brain Ser.: Vol. 5). 474p. 1979. text ed. 52.50 (ISBN 0-89004-366-3). Raven.

Barbeau, Arthur E. & Henri, Florette. Unknown Soldiers: Black American Troops in World War I. LC 72-95880. (Illus.). 303p. 1974. 24.95 (ISBN 0-87722-063-8). Temple U Pr.

Barbeau, C., ed. Future of the Family. 1971. pap. 2.95 o.p. (ISBN 0-685-07635-0, 80009). Glencoe.

--Generation of Love. 1969. pap. 2.95 o.p. (ISBN 0-685-07637-7, 80008). Glencoe.

Barber. Electron Transport. (Topics in Photosynthesis Ser.: Vol. 4). 1982. 82.25 (ISBN 0-444-80375-0). Elsevier.

Barber, jt. tr. see Elstob.

Barber, A. J., ed. see CCOP-IOC SEATAR Working Group Meeting, July 1979, Bandung, Indonesia.

Barber, Albert A., jt. auth. see Grinnell, Alan.

Barber, Aldyth & Barber, Cyril. Your Marriage Has Real Possibilities. 200p. (Orig.). 1981. pap. 4.95 o.p. (ISBN 0-89840-015-5). Heres Life.

Barber, Antonia. The Ghosts. (gr. 5-7). 1975. pap. 2.25 (ISBN 0-671-42454-8). Archway.

Barber, Bernard. The Logic & Limits of Trust. 203p. 1983. 19.00x (ISBN 0-8135-0958-0). Rutgers U Pr.

Barber, Bernard & Barber, Elinor G. European Social Class: Stability & Change. LC 77-13508. (Main Themes in European History). 1977. Repr. of 1965 ed. lib. bdg. 16.00x (ISBN 0-8371-9860-7, BAEU). Greenwood.

Barber, Bernard & Lambert, Richard D., eds. Medical Ethics & Social Change. new ed. LC 77-26530. (Annals: No. 437). 1978. pap. 6.00 o.p. (ISBN 0-87761-227-7). Am Acad Pol Soc Sci.

Barber, Bernard, et al. Research on Human Subjects: Problems of Social Control in Medical Experimentation. LC 70-83831. 264p. 1973. 10.50x (ISBN 0-87154-090-8). Russell Sage.

Barber, Bruce, jt. auth. see Nennsberg, Tatiana O.

Barber, Charles. Early Modern English. (Andre Deutsch Language Library). (Illus.). 360p. 1977. 20.00 o.p. (ISBN 0-233-96262-X). Westview.

Barber, Colin. Evoked Potentials. 636p. 1980. text ed. 49.50 (ISBN 0-8391-1491-5). Univ Park.

Barber, Cyril. The Effective Parent. Strauss, Gary, ed. 200p. 1980. pap. 4.95 o.p. (ISBN 0-89840-012-0). Campus Crusade.

Barber, Cyril & Strauss, Gary. The Effective Parent: Biblical Principles of Parenting. 200p. (Orig.). 1980. pap. 4.95 o.p. (ISBN 0-89840-012-0). Heres Life.

Barber, Cyril, jt. auth. see Barber, Aldyth.

Barber, Cyril J. Dynamic Personal Bible Study: Principles of Inductive Bible Study Based on the Life of Abraham. LC 81-8443. 1981. pap. 4.95 (ISBN 0-87213-023-1). Loizeaux.

--Nehemias, Dinamica de un Lider. Carrodeguas, Andy & Marosi, Esteban, eds. Taracido, Frank, tr. from Eng. Orig. Title: Nehemiah & the Dynamics of Effective Leadership. 174p. (Span.). 1982. pap. 3.00 (ISBN 0-8297-1206-2). Life Pubs Intl.

--Ruth: An Expositional Commentary. 1983. pap. 6.95 (ISBN 0-8024-0184-8). Moody.

--Vital Encounter. LC 79-89026. 1980. pap. 3.95 o.p. (ISBN 0-89840-004-X). Heres Life.

Barber, Cyril J. & Strauss, Gary H. Leadership: The Dynamics of Success. 126p. pap. 4.95 (ISBN 0-87921-068-0). Attic Pr.

Barber, Cyril L., jt. auth. see Towns, Elmer L.

Barber, D. L., jt. auth. see Davies, D. W.

Barber, E. A., jt. ed. see Powell, J. U.

Barber, Edward A. & Lockwood, Luke V. The Ceramic Furniture & Silver Collectors' Glossary. (Architecture & Decorative Art Ser.). 1976. pap. 6.95 (ISBN 0-306-80049-7). Da Capo.

Barber, Edwin A. The Ceramic Collectors' Glossary. LC 76-8172. (Architecture & Decorative Art Ser). 1967. Repr. of 1914 ed. 16.50 (ISBN 0-306-70521-4). Da Capo.

Barber, Elinor G., jt. auth. see Barber, Bernard.

Barber, Ezekiel. The Bene-Israel of India: Images & Reality. LC 81-40006. (Illus.). 176p. 1981. lib. bdg. 19.00 (ISBN 0-8191-1594-0); pap. text ed. 9.50 (ISBN 0-8191-1645-9). U Pr of Amer.

Barber, H. R. Immunobiology for the Clinician. LC 76-23386. 310p. 1977. 44.95 o.p. (ISBN 0-471-04785-6). Wiley.

Barber, Harry L. How to Steal a Million Dollars in Free Publicity. LC 81-90285. 66p. (Orig.). 1982. pap. 8.97 (ISBN 0-940008-01-7). Newport Pub.

Barber, Hugh O. & Stockwell. Manual of Electronystagmography. 2nd ed. LC 80-17349. (Illus.). 232p. 1980. text ed. 42.50 (ISBN 0-8016-0449-4). Mosby.

Barber, Hugh O. & Stockwell, Charles W. Manual of Electronystagmography. LC 76-17897. (Illus.). 1976. 29.50 o.p. (ISBN 0-8016-0446-X). Mosby.

Barber, Hugh R. Ovarian Carcinoma: Etiology, Diagnosis, & Treatment. 2nd ed. LC 82-7176. (Illus.). 420p. 1982. 59.50x (ISBN 0-89352-168-X). Masson Pub.

Barber, Hugh R. & Graber, Edward A. Surgical Disease in Pregnancy. LC 73-89171. (Illus.). 720p. 1974. text ed. 39.00 o.p. (ISBN 0-7216-1539-2). Saunders.

Barber, Hugh R. K. & Sommers, Sheldon C., eds. Carcinoma of the Endometrium: Etiology, Diagnosis & Treatment. LC 81-14264. (Illus.). 248p. 1981. 41.50x (ISBN 0-89352-072-1). Masson Pub.

Barber, J., ed. The Intact Chloroplast. (Topics in Photosynthesis: Vol. 1). 1976. 95.75 (ISBN 0-444-41451-7, North Holland). Elsevier.

--Photosynthesis in Relation to Model Systems. (Topics in Photosynthesis: Vol. 3). 1979. 119.75 (ISBN 0-444-80066-2, North Holland). Elsevier.

--Primary Processes of Photosynthesis. (Topics in Photosynthesis: Vol. 2). 1977. 119.75 (ISBN 0-444-41585-8, North Holland). Elsevier.

Barber, James. Fear of Frying. (Illus.). 96p. (Orig.). 1978. pap. 6.95 (ISBN 0-88894-281-8, Pub. by Douglas & McIntyre Canada). Madrona Pubs.

--Flash in the Pan. (Illus.). 96p. (Orig.). 1982. pap. 6.95 (ISBN 0-88894-331-8, Pub. by Douglas & McIntyre Canada). Madrona Pubs.

Barber, James, jt. auth. see Hill, Christopher.

Barber, James D. Erasmus: A Play on Words. LC 81-40002. 80p. (Orig.). 1982. lib. bdg. 18.50 (ISBN 0-8191-1868-0); pap. text ed. 5.00 (ISBN 0-8191-1869-9). U Pr of Amer.

--The Presidential Character: Predicting Performance in the White House. 2nd ed. LC 77-4094. 1977. pap. 14.95 (ISBN 0-13-697847-9). P-H.

Barber, James D., ed. Race for the Presidency: The Media & the Nominating Process. (American Assembly Ser.). (Illus.). 1978. 10.95 o.p. (ISBN 0-13-750141-2, Spec); pap. 4.95 o.p. (ISBN 0-13-750133-1). P-H.

Barber, John W. & Howe, Henry. Historical Collections of the State of New York. LC 78-118780. (Empire State Historical Publications Ser.). (Illus.). 1970. Repr. of 1841 ed. 35.00x o.p. (ISBN 0-87198-083-5). Friedman.

Barber, Joseph & Adrian, Cheri, eds. Psychological Approaches to the Management of Pain. LC 82-45471. 224p. 1982. 20.00 (ISBN 0-87630-303-3). Brunner-Mazel.

Barber, Lynn. The Heyday of Natural History. LC 79-6533. (Illus.). 324p. 1980. 19.95 (ISBN 0-385-12574-7). Doubleday.

Barber, M. C. The Trial of the Templars. LC 77-85716. 320p. 1978. 47.50 (ISBN 0-521-21896-9); pap. 12.95x (ISBN 0-521-28018-4). Cambridge U Pr.

Barber, Melanie, ed. Index to the Letters & Papers of Frederick Temple, Archbishop of Canterbury, 1896-1902, in Lambeth Palace Library, Vol. 1. LC 75-321735. 174p. 1975. 24.00 o.p. (ISBN 0-7201-0520-X, Pub. by Mansell England). Wilson.

Barber, Noel. The Black Hole of Calcutta: A Reconstruction. (Illus.). 256p. 1982. 6.95 (ISBN 0-02-030390-4). Macmillan.

--The Fall of Shanghai. LC 79-17523. 1979. 10.95 (ISBN 0-698-10996-1, Coward). Putnam Pub Group.

--A Farewell to France. 704p. 1983. 17.95 (ISBN 0-02-506830-X). Macmillan.

--Tanamera. 688p. 1982. 3.95 (ISBN 0-553-20921-3). Bantam.

Barber, Peggy, ed. Sixty-Eight Great Ideas. LC 82-11518. 72p. Date not set. pap. 5.00 (ISBN 0-8389-0376-2). ALA.

Barber, Richard. A Companion to World Mythology. LC 79-16843. (Illus.). (gr. 4 up). 1980. 14.95 o.s.i. (ISBN 0-440-00750-X). Delacorte.

--The Knight & Chivalry. 2nd ed. (Illus.). 400p. 1975. 22.50x (ISBN 0-87471-653-5). Rowman.

--The Pastons: A Family. 1983. pap. price not set (ISBN 0-14-006599-7). Penguin.

Barber, Richard, ed. Arthurian Literature II. (Illus.). 224p. 1983. text ed. 42.50x (ISBN 0-8476-7196-8). Rowman.

Barber, Richard, ed. see Aubrey, John.

Barber, Russell J. The Wheeler's Site: A Specialized Shellfish Processing Station on the Merrimack River. (Peabody Museum Monographs: No. 7). (Illus.). 96p. 1983. pap. text ed. 10.00x (ISBN 0-87365-907-4). Peabody Harvard.

Barber, Sotirios, et al. Introduction to Problem Solving in Political Science. LC 74-150128. 1971. pap. text ed. 3.95x (ISBN 0-675-09207-8). Merrill.

Barber, Theodore X. Pitfalls in Human Research: Ten Pivotal Points. LC 76-13488. 128p. 1977. 10.25 (ISBN 0-08-020935-1). Pergamon.

Barber, Theodore X., et al, eds. Advances in Altered States of Consciousness & Human Potentialities, Vol. 1. 700p. 1980. 69.95 (ISBN 0-88437-002-X). Psych Dimensions.

Barber, Thomas K. & Luke, Larry S., eds. Pediatric Dentistry. (Illus.). 512p. 1982. 49.50 (ISBN 0-88416-167-6). Wright-PSG.

Barber, Triphy & Langfitt, Dot E. Teaching the Medical-Surgical Patient: Diagnostics & Procedures. (Illus.). 384p. 1983. pap. text ed. 19.95 (ISBN 0-89303-250-6). R J Brady.

Barber, Virginia & Skaggs, Merrill M. The Mother Person. LC 76-48850. 1977. pap. 5.95 (ISBN 0-8052-0565-9). Schocken.

Barbera, John J., jt. auth. see Armandi, Barry R.

Barberet, J. Les Greves et la Loi sur les Coalitions. (Conditions of the 19th Century French Working Class Ser.). 189p. (Fr.). 1974. Repr. of 1873 ed. lib. bdg. 55.00x o.p. (ISBN 0-8287-0055-9, 1104). Clearwater Pub.

--Le Travail en France, Monographies Professionnelles, 7 vols. (Conditions of the 19th Century French Working Class Ser.). (Fr.). 1974. Repr. of 1866 ed. Set. lib. bdg. 860.00x, order nos. 1176-1182 o.p. (ISBN 0-8287-1423-1). Clearwater Pub.

Barberis, France. Would You Like a Parrot? LC 67-28671. (Illus.). 32p. (ps-k). 5.95 (ISBN 0-87592-060-8). Scroll Pr.

Barbet, Pierre. Cosmic Crusaders. (Science Fiction Ser.). 1980. pap. 2.25 o.p. (ISBN 0-87997-583-0, UE1583). DAW Bks.

--Doctor at Calvary. pap. 3.95 (ISBN 0-385-06687-2, Im). Doubleday.

Barbeu-Dubourg, Jacques. Petit Code de la Raison Humaine. (Holbach & His Friends Ser). 54p. (Fr.). 1974. Repr. of 1774 ed. lib. bdg. 24.00x o.p. (ISBN 0-8287-0056-7, 1588). Clearwater Pub.

Barbier, E., ed. Cerro Prieto Geothermal Field: Proceedings of the Second Symposium, 17-19 October 1979, Mexicali, Mexico-Selected Papers. 144p. 1982. pap. 38.50 (ISBN 0-08-028746-8). Pergamon.

Barbier, J. L., ed. see De Lamartine.

Barbier, Ken. CP-M Assembly Language Programming: A Guide to Intergrated Learning of the CP-M Operating & Assembly Language Programming. (Illus.). 226p. 1982. 19.95 (ISBN 0-13-188268-6); pap. 12.95 (ISBN 0-13-188250-3). P-H.

Barbier, Maurice. The Mini Sosie Method. LC 82-80775. (Illus.). 96p. 1983. text ed. 24.00 (ISBN 0-934634-41-6). Intl Human Res.

Barbier, Maurice G. Pulse Coding. LC 82-80776. (Short Course Handbooks). (Illus.). 96p. (Orig.). 1982. text ed. 26.00 (ISBN 0-934634-52-1); pap. 16.00 (ISBN 0-934634-40-8). Intl Human Res.

Barbieri, Elaine. Love's Fiery Jewel. 1983. pap. 3.75 (ISBN 0-8217-1128-8). Zebra.

Barbieri, Franco. Basilica of Andrea Palladio. LC 75-79835. (Corpus Palladianum, Vol. 2). (Illus.). 1970. 42.50x (ISBN 0-271-00087-2). Pa St U Pr.

Barbieri, Louis. First & Second Peter. (Everyman's Bible Commentary Ser.). 1977. pap. 4.50 (ISBN 0-8024-2061-3). Moody.

Barbieri, Santa U. Anthology of Poetry & Prose. LC 82-70400. 1983. 4.95 (ISBN 0-8358-0441-0). Upper Room.

Barbira-Freedman, Francois, jt. auth. see Kroeger, Axel.

Barborka, Geoffrey A. Glossary of Sanskrit Terms & Key to Their Correct Pronunciation. 76p. (Orig.). 1972. pap. 1.75 (ISBN 0-913004-04-9). Point Loma Pub.

Barbour. Energy & American Values. 256p. 1982. 27.95 (ISBN 0-03-062468-1); pap. 12.95 (ISBN 0-03-062469-X). Praeger.

Barbour, Alan G. Cliffhanger. 256p. 1977. 14.95 o.s.i. (ISBN 0-89104-070-6); pap. 8.95 o.s.i. (ISBN 0-686-85467-5). A & W Pubs.

Barbour, Beverly. Cooking with Spirits. LC 76-6838. (Illus.). 192p. (Orig.). 1976. 7.95 o.s.i. (ISBN 0-912238-83-6); pap. 4.95 o.s.i. (ISBN 0-912238-82-8). One Hund One Prods.

Barbour, Brian M., ed. Benjamin Franklin: A Collection of Critical Essays. (Twentieth Century Views Ser.). 1979. text ed. 12.95 (ISBN 0-13-074856-0, Spec); pap. 3.95 o.p. (ISBN 0-13-074849-8). P-H.

Barbour, Harriet & Freeman, Warren S. The Children's Record Book. LC 78-6156. 1978. Repr. of 1947 ed. lib. bdg. 18.75x (ISBN 0-313-20424-1, BACB). Greenwood.

Barbour, Harriot B. & Freeman, Warren S. Story of Music. rev. ed. (Illus.). (gr. 7-9). text ed. 13.95 (ISBN 0-87487-033-X). Summy.

Barbour, Ian G. Myths, Models, & Paradigms. LC 73-18690. 1976. pap. text ed. 6.95i (ISBN 0-06-060388-7, RD 183, HarpR). Har-Row.

--Technology, Environment & Human Values. 344p. 1980. 29.95 (ISBN 0-03-055886-7); pap. 12.95 (ISBN 0-686-92513-0). Praeger.

Barbour, James M. The Church Music of William Billings. LC 72-39000. 167p. 1972. Repr. of 1960 ed. lib. bdg. 19.50 (ISBN 0-306-70434-X). Da Capo.

Barbour, James Murray. Tuning & Temperament: A Historical Survey. LC 74-37288. (Illus.). 228p. 1972. Repr. of 1951 ed. lib. bdg. 23.50 (ISBN 0-306-70422-6). Da Capo.

Barbour, K. M., et al, eds. Nigeria in Maps. Oguntoyinbo, J. S. & Onyenelukwe, J. C. 160p. 1982. 35.00x (ISBN 0-8419-0763-3). Holmes & Meier.

Barbour, Michael, et al. Botany: A Laboratory Manual for Weier. 5th ed. 263p. 1975. 13.50x (ISBN 0-471-04800-3). Wiley.

Barbour, Michael G. & Major, Jack, eds. Terrestrial Vegetation of California. LC 76-53769. 1002p. 1977. 81.50x (ISBN 0-471-56536-9, Pub. by Wiley-Interscience). Wiley.

Barbour, Michael G., et al. Terrestrial Plant Ecology. 1980. 24.95 (ISBN 0-8053-0540-8). Benjamin-Cummings.

--Coastal Ecology: Bodega Head. LC 70-173902. (Illus.). 1974. 24.50x (ISBN 0-520-02147-9); pap. 9.95x (ISBN 0-520-03276-4). U of Cal Pr.

Barbour, Pamela G. & Spivey, Morma G. The Exchange Cookbook for Diabetic & Weight Control Programs. Davidson, Paul C., ed. LC 82-83512. (Illus.). 198p. (Orig.). 1982. pap. 9.95 (ISBN 0-9610028-0-8). G&G Pub.

Barbour, Philip L., tr. see Pushkin, Alexander.

Barbour, R. Glassblowing for Laboratory Technicians. 2nd ed. 1979. text ed. 48.00 (ISBN 0-08-022155-6); pap. text ed. 14.00 (ISBN 0-08-022156-4). Pergamon.

Barbour, Richmond. Dear Dr. Barbour. LC 77-87418. 1977. 8.95 (ISBN 0-89325-007-4). Joyce Pr.

Barbrook, Alec. Patterns of Political Behaviour. 1976. pap. text ed. 8.50 (ISBN 0-87581-191-4, 191). Peacock Pubs.

Barbrook, Alec & Bolt, Christine. Power & Protest in American Life. 1980. 29.00 (ISBN 0-312-63369-6). St Martin.

Barca, Pedro C. de la see De la Barca, Pedro C.

Barchas, Jack D., et al, eds. Psychopharmacology: From Theory to Practice. (Illus.). 1977. text ed. 21.95x o.p. (ISBN 0-19-502214-9); pap. text ed. 17.95x (ISBN 0-19-502215-7). Oxford U Pr.

Barchilon, Jacques & Flinder, Peter. Charles Perrault. (World Authors Ser.). 15.95 (ISBN 0-8057-6483-6, Twayne). G K Hall.

Barcia, Jose R. Americo Castro & the Meaning of Spanish Civilization. LC 74-27282. 1977. 33.00x (ISBN 0-520-02920-8). U of Cal Pr.

Barcia, Jose R., tr. see Vallejo, Cesar.

Barck, Oscar T. & Blake, Nelson M. Since Nineteen Hundred: A History of the United States in Our Times. 5th ed. 1974. 24.95x (ISBN 0-02-305930-3, 30593). Macmillan.

Barclay, Cyril N. The New Warfare. LC 82-18375. x, 66p. 1983. Repr. of 1953 ed. lib. bdg. 24.50x (ISBN 0-313-23793-X, BANW). Greenwood.

Barclay, G. The Rise & Fall of the New Roman Empire. 1973. 8.95 o.p. (ISBN 0-312-68320-0). St Martin.

Barclay, Glen St. John see St. John Barclay, Glen.

Barclay, Ian. Living & Enjoying the Fruit of the Spirit. 1978. pap. 2.95 (ISBN 0-8024-4911-5). Moody.

Barclay, James R. Foundations of Counseling Strategies. LC 78-15407. 480p. 1978. Repr. of 1971 ed. lib. bdg. 25.50 (ISBN 0-88275-709-1). Krieger.

Barclay, Janet M., ed. Emily Bronte Criticism Nineteen Hundred to Nineteen Eighty: An Annotated Check List. 1983. 40.00X (ISBN 0-930466-63-2). Meckler Pub.

Barclay, Marion S., et al. Teen Guide to Homemaking. 3rd ed. (gr. 7-9). text ed. 16.72 (ISBN 0-07-003644-6, W); tchr's manual 3.40 (ISBN 0-07-003646-2). McGraw.

Barclay, Virginia. Emergency. (Mid-City Hospital Ser.: No. 1). (Orig.). 1981. pap. 2.25 o.p. (ISBN 0-686-72815-7, AE1070, Sig). NAL.

--Mid-City Hospital, No. 4: Crisis. 1982. pap. 2.25 (ISBN 0-451-11415-9, AE1415, Sig). NAL.

--Mid-City Hospital, No. 5: Double Face. 1982. pap. 2.25 (ISBN 0-451-11554-6, AE1554, Sig). NAL.

--Mid-City Hospital, No. 6: Life Support. 1982. pap. 2.50 (ISBN 0-451-11769-7, AE1769, Sig). NAL.

Barclay, William. And Jesus Said: A Handbook on the Parables of Jesus. LC 77-120410. 1970. pap. 5.95 (ISBN 0-664-24898-5). Westminster.

--The Beatitudes & the Lord's Prayer for Everyman. LC 75-9309. 256p. 1975. pap. 6.95i (ISBN 0-06-060393-3, RD112, HarpR). Har-Row.

--The Daily Study Bible, 18 vols. rev. ed. Incl. The Gospel of Matthew, Vol. 1. (ISBN 0-664-21300-6); softcover (ISBN 0-664-24100-X); The Gospel of Matthew, Vol. 2. (ISBN 0-664-21301-4); softcover (ISBN 0-664-24101-8); The Gospel of Mark. (ISBN 0-664-21302-2); softcover (ISBN 0-664-24102-6); The Gospel of Luke. (ISBN 0-664-21303-0); softcover (ISBN 0-664-24103-4); The Gospel of John, Vol. 1. (ISBN 0-664-21304-9); softcover (ISBN 0-664-24104-2); The Gospel of John, Vol. 2. (ISBN 0-664-21305-7); softcover (ISBN 0-664-24105-0); The Acts of the Apostles. (ISBN 0-664-21306-5); softcover (ISBN 0-664-24106-9); The Letter to the Romans. (ISBN 0-664-21307-3); softcover (ISBN 0-664-24107-7); The Letters to the Corinthians. (ISBN 0-664-21308-1); softcover (ISBN 0-664-24108-5); The Letters to the Galatians & Ephesians. (ISBN 0-664-21309-X); softcover (ISBN 0-664-24109-3); The Letters to the Philippians, Colossians & Thessalonians. (ISBN 0-664-21310-3); softcover (ISBN 0-664-24110-7); The Letters to Timothy, Titus & Philemon. (ISBN 0-664-21311-1); softcover (ISBN 0-664-24111-5); The Letter to the Hebrews. (ISBN 0-664-21312-X); softcover (ISBN 0-664-24112-3); The Letters of James & Peter. (ISBN 0-664-21313-8); softcover (ISBN 0-664-24113-1); The Letters of John & Jude. (ISBN 0-664-21314-6); softcover (ISBN 0-664-24114-X); The Revelation of John, Vol. 1. (ISBN 0-664-21315-4); softcover (ISBN 0-664-24115-8); The Revelation of John, Vol. 2. (ISBN 0-664-21316-2); softcover (ISBN 0-664-24116-6). 1977. Set. deluxe ed. 203.00 (ISBN 0-664-21318-9); Set. 99.95 (ISBN 0-664-24098-4); deluxe ed. 11.95 ea.; 5.95 ea.; Index Vol. (ISBN 0-664-21370-7); softcover (ISBN 0-664-24215-4). Westminster.

--Fishers of Men. LC 66-22246. 1979. pap. 4.95 (ISBN 0-664-24224-3). Westminster.

--Introducing the Bible. (Festival Bks). 1979. pap. 2.25 (ISBN 0-687-19488-1, Festival). Abingdon.

--Letters to the Seven Churches. LC 82-2760. 1982. pap. 5.95 (ISBN 0-664-24433-5). Westminster.

--The Life of Jesus for Everyman. LC 75-12282. 96p. 1975. pap. 5.72i (ISBN 0-06-060404-2, RD 319, HarpR). Har-Row.

--The Lord Is My Shepherd: Expositions of Selected Psalms. LC 79-27096. 1980. pap. 5.95 (ISBN 0-664-24317-7). Westminster.

--The Lord's Supper. LC 82-2774. 1982. pap. 5.95 (ISBN 0-664-24432-7). Westminster.

--The Master's Men. (Orig.). pap. write for info o.s.i. (ISBN 0-515-09610-5). Jove Pubns.

--Meditations on Communicating the Gospel. 1971. pap. 2.25x (ISBN 0-8358-0253-1). Upper Room.

--The Mind of Jesus. LC 61-7332. 352p. 1976. pap. 7.95i (ISBN 0-06-060451-4, RD143, HarpR). Har-Row.

--The Mind of St. Paul. LC 75-9310. 256p. 1975. pap. 7.64i (ISBN 0-06-060471-9, RD110, HarpR). Har-Row.

--The New Testament: A New Translation. 1980. pap. 5.95 (ISBN 0-664-24358-4). Westminster.

--Palabras Griegas Del Nuevo Testamento. Marin, Javier J., tr. 1979. pap. 4.50 (ISBN 0-311-42052-4). Casa Bautista.

--Prayers for the Christian Year. (Student Christian Movement Press). (Orig.). 1964. pap. 6.95x (ISBN 0-19-520290-2). Oxford U Pr.

--The Ten Commandments for Today. 1977. pap. 2.25 o.p. (ISBN 0-8028-1666-5). Eerdmans.

--Ten Commandments for Today. 1977. pap. 1.25 o.s.i. (ISBN 0-89129-228-4). Jove Pubns.

Barcomb, David. Office Automation: A Survey of Tools & Technology. 288p. 1981. pap. 15.00 (ISBN 0-932376-16-9); 24.00 (ISBN 0-932376-15-0). Digital Pr.

--Office Automation: A Survey of Tools & Technology. 256p. 1981. 15.00 (ISBN 0-686-98086-7). Telecom Lib.

Barcus, F. Earle & Wolkin, Rachel. Children's Television: An Analysis of Programming & Advertising. LC 76-12843. 1977. text ed. 28.95 o.p. (ISBN 0-275-23210-7). Praeger.

Bard, Allen J. Chemical Equilibrium. (Illus.). 1968. pap. text ed. 12.95 scp (ISBN 0-06-040451-5, HarpC). Har-Row.

Bard, Allen J. & Faulkner, Larry R. Electrochemical Methods: Fundamentals & Applications. LC 79-24712. 718p. 1980. text ed. 37.95x (ISBN 0-471-05542-5). Wiley.

Bard, Allen J., ed. Electroanalytical Chemistry: A Series of Advances, Vol. 1. 1966. 55.00 o.p. (ISBN 0-8247-1035-5). Dekker.

--Electroanalytical Chemistry: A Series of Advances, Vol. 3. 1969. 49.25 o.p. (ISBN 0-8247-1037-1). Dekker.

Bard, James A. Rational-Emotive Therapy in Practice. pap. 8.95 (ISBN 0-686-36793-6). Inst Rat Liv.

Bard, Lund. Encyclopedia of Electrochemistry of the Elements, Vol. 9B. 1983. price not set (ISBN 0-8247-2519-0). Dekker.

Bard, Martin. The Peril of Faith. 166p. (Orig.). 1982. pap. 5.00 (ISBN 0-910309-05-1). Am Atheist.

Bard, Morton & Sangrey, Dawn. The Crime Victim's Book. LC 78-19941. 1979. 11.95 o.s.i. (ISBN 0-465-01470-4). Basic.

Bardach, Eugene. The Implementation Game: What Happens After a Bill Becomes Law. 1977. 22.00x (ISBN 0-262-02125-0); pap. 5.95x (ISBN 0-262-52049-4). MIT Pr.

--The Skill Factor in Politics: Repealing the Mental Commitment Laws in California. LC 79-157820. 300p. 1972. 26.50x (ISBN 0-520-02042-1). U of Cal Pr.

Bardach, Eugene & Angelides, Sotirios. Water Banking: How to Stop Wasting Agricultural Water. LC 78-50766. 56p. 1978. pap. 2.00 (ISBN 0-917616-26-X). ICS Pr.

Bardach, Eugene & Kagan, Robert A. Going by the Book: The Problem of Regulatory Unreasonableness. 375p. 1982. 22.95x (ISBN 0-87722-251-7); pap. 10.95 (ISBN 0-87722-252-5). Temple U Pr.

Bardach, Eugene & Kagan, Robert A., eds. Social Regulation: Strategies for Reform. LC 81-85279. 420p. 1982. text ed. 19.95 (ISBN 0-917616-47-2); pap. text ed. 8.95 (ISBN 0-917616-46-4). ICS Pr.

Bardach, Eugene, et al. The California Coastal Plan: A Critique. LC 76-7715. (Illus.). 1976. pap. 5.95 o.p. (ISBN 0-917616-04-9). ICS Pr.

Bardach, John E., et al. Aquaculture: The Farming & Husbandry of Freshwater & Marine Organisms. LC 72-2516. 976p. 1972. pap. 29.50x (ISBN 0-471-04826-7, Pub. by Wiley-Interscience). Wiley.

Bar-David, Molly L. Israeli Cook Book. (International Cook Book Ser). 1964. 5.95 o.p. (ISBN 0-517-50667-X). Crown.

Barden, John A., jt. auth. see Halfacre, Gordon.

Barden, William, Jr. Guidebook to Small Computers. 1980. pap. 6.95 (ISBN 0-672-21698-1). Sams.

--TRS-80 Assembly Language Subroutines. (Illus.). 282p. Date not set. pap. 18.95 (ISBN 0-13-931188-2). P-H. Postponed.

--Z-80 Microcomputer Design Projects. 1980. pap. 13.95 (ISBN 0-672-21682-5). Sams.

Barder, Richard C. Grandfather Clocks: The English Country Longcase, 1660-1830. (Illus.). 192p. 1983. 31.50 (ISBN 0-7153-8314-0). David & Charles.

Bardham Roy, B K., jt. auth. see Abeles, P W.

Bardi, Edward, jt. auth. see Coyle, John J.

Bardi, Edward J., jt. auth. see Coyle, John J.

Bardin, C. Wayne, jt. ed. see Krieger, Dorothy T.

Bardis, Panos D. History of Thanatology: Philosophical, Religious, Psychological, & Sociological Ideas Concerning Death from Primitive Times to the Present. LC 81-43026. 102p. (Orig.). 1981. lib. bdg. 16.75 (ISBN 0-8191-1648-3); pap. text ed. 7.00 (ISBN 0-8191-1649-1). U Pr of Amer.

Bardon, Jack I. & Bennett, Virginia C. School Psychology. LC 73-11419. (Foundations of Modern Psychology Ser). (Illus.). 224p. 1973. pap. text ed. 10.95 (ISBN 0-13-794412-8). P-H.

Bardos, T. J. & Kalman, T. I., eds. New Approaches to the Design of Antineoplastic Agents. 344p. Date not set. p.n.s. (ISBN 0-444-00724-5, Biomedical Pr). Elsevier.

Bardossy, G. Karst Bauxites: Bauxite Deposits on Carbonate Rocks. (Developments in Economic Geology Ser.: Vol. 14). 1982. 83.00 (ISBN 0-444-99727-X). Elsevier.

Bardsley, Charles W. Curiosities of Puritan Nomenclature. LC 76-140409. 1971. Repr. of 1897 ed. 27.00 o.p. (ISBN 0-8103-3715-0). Gale.

--Romance of the London Directory. LC 72-78115. 1971. Repr. of 1879 ed. 34.00x (ISBN 0-8103-3782-7). Gale.

Bardsley, Kathryn, ed. see Esposito, Barbara, et al.

Bardsley, W., et al, eds. Crystal Growth: A Tutorial Approach. (North Holland Series in Crystal Growth: Vol. 2). 408p. 1979. 64.00 (ISBN 0-444-85371-5, North Holland). Elsevier.

Bardwell, Denver. Calamity at Devil's Crossing. (YA) 1973. 6.95 (ISBN 0-685-28397-6, Avalon). Bouregy.

Bardwell, George, jt. auth. see Seligson, Harry.

Bardwick, Judith M. Psychology of Women: A Study of Biocultural Conflicts. 1971. pap. text ed. 13.50 scp o.p. (ISBN 0-06-040497-3, HarpC). Har-Row.

Bardwick, Judith M., et al. Feminine Personality & Conflict. LC 75-131872. (Contemporary Psychology Ser.). (Orig.). 1970. pap. text ed. 6.95 o.p. (ISBN 0-8185-0303-3). Brooks-Cole.

Bare, Colleen S. Rabbits & Hares. LC 82-45992. (Illus.). 80p. (gr. 4 up). 1983. PLB 9.95 (ISBN 0-396-08127-4). Dodd.

Bare, William K. Fundamentals of Fire Prevention. LC 76-23221. (Fire Science Ser.). 213p. 1977. text ed. 18.95 (ISBN 0-471-04835-6). Wiley.

--Introduction to Fire Science & Fire Prevention. LC 77-14002. (Fire Science Ser.). 290p. 1978. text ed. 19.95x (ISBN 0-471-01708-6); tchrs. manual (ISBN 0-471-03779-6). Wiley.

Barefoot, A. C. & Hankins, Frank W. Identification of Modern Tertiary Woods. (Illus.). 1982. 98.00x (ISBN 0-19-854378-6). Oxford U Pr.

Barefoot, J. Kirk. Employee Theft Investigation. LC 79-9764. 1979. 18.95 (ISBN 0-913708-33-X). Butterworth.

Barefoot, Patience. Community Services. 280p. 1977. pap. 7.95 o.p. (ISBN 0-571-11052-5). Faber & Faber.

Bareiss, Karl-Heinz. Comoedia. 525p. (Ger.). 1982. write for info. (ISBN 3-8204-5986-3). P Lang Pubs.

Barell, John. Playgrounds of Our Minds. LC 79-27084. 1980. pap. text ed. 10.50x (ISBN 0-8077-2580-3). Tchrs Coll.

Baren, Martin, et al. Overcoming Learning Disabilities: A Team Approach (Parent-Teacher-Physician-Child) 1978. text ed. 19.95 (ISBN 0-8359-5365-3). Reston.

Barentsen, A., ed. South Slavic & Balkan Linguistics. (Studies in Slavic & General Linguistics: Vol. 2). 340p. 1982. pap. text ed. 32.25x (ISBN 90-6203-634-1, Pub. by Rodopi Holland). Humanities.

--Studies in Slavic & General Linguistics, Vol. 1. 472p. 1980. pap. text ed. 46.00x (ISBN 90-6203-523-X, Pub. by Rodopi Holland). Humanities.

Barer, R., jt. ed. see Cosslett, V. E.

Bares, Jiri, et al. Collection of Problems in Physical Chemistry. 1962. text ed. 29.00 o.p. (ISBN 0-08-009577-1). Pergamon.

Bares, R. A., ed. Plastics in Material & Structural Engineering: Proceedings ICP-RILEM-IBK International Symposium, Prague, June 23-25, 1981. (Developments in Civil Engineering Ser.: Vol. 5). 962p. 1982. 164.00 (ISBN 0-444-99710-5). Elsevier.

Barett, B., jt. ed. see Learning Technology Inc.

Barfield, O. Speaker's Meaning. 118p. 1967. pap. 5.00 (ISBN 0-85440-249-7). Anthroposophic.

Barfield, Owen. Orpheus: A Poetic Drama. LC 82-83247. 160p. (Orig.). 1983. pap. 6.95 (ISBN 0-940262-01-0). Lindisfarne Pr.

Barfield, Owen, tr. see Steiner, Rudolf.

Barfield, Richard E. & Morgan, James N. Early Retirement: The Decision & the Experience & A Second Look. LC 70-626137. 345p. 1970. pap. 12.00x (ISBN 0-87944-067-8). Inst Soc Res.

Barfoot, K. M., jt. auth. see Mitchell, I. V.

Bargar, Bradley D. Lord Dartmouth & the American Revolution. LC 65-28498. (Illus.). xiii, 222p. 1965. 17.95x o.s.i. (ISBN 0-87249-100-5). U of SC Pr.

Bargellini, Clara, tr. see Tintoretto.

Barger, Gerald L., jt. ed. see Jen-Yu Wang.

Barger, James. Ernest Hemingway: American Literary Giant. new ed. Rahmas, D. Steve, ed. (Outstanding Personalities Ser.). 32p. 1975. lib. bdg. 2.95 incl. catalog cards (ISBN 0-87157-580-9); pap. 1.95 vinyl laminated covers (ISBN 0-87157-080-7). SamHar Pr.

--James Joyce, Modern Irish Writer. Rahmas, D. Steve, ed. LC 74-14701. (Outstanding Personalities Ser.). 32p. 1974. lib. bdg. 2.95 incl. catalog cards (ISBN 0-87157-577-9); pap. 1.95 vinyl laminated covers (ISBN 0-87157-077-7). SamHar Pr.

--William Faulkner, Modern American Novelist & Nobel Prize Winner. Rahmas, D. Steve, ed. (Outstanding Personalities Ser.: No. 63). 32p. (Orig.). (gr. 7-12). 1973. lib. bdg. 2.95 incl. catalog cards (ISBN 0-87157-563-9); pap. 1.95 vinyl laminated covers (ISBN 0-87157-063-7). SamHar Pr.

Barger, V., et al, eds. see AIP Conference, 85th, Madison, Wisconsin, 1982.

Barger, Vernon D. & Olsson, Martin G. Classical Mechanics: A Modern Perspective. LC 72-5697. (Illus.). 352p. 1973. text ed. 29.95 (ISBN 0-07-003723-X, C); instructor's manual 9.95 (ISBN 0-07-003724-8). McGraw.

Barghahn, Barbara Von see Von Barghahn, Barbara.

Barghoorn, Frederick C. Politics in the U.S.S.R. 2nd ed. (Ser. in Comparative Politics). 1972. pap. 10.95 (ISBN 0-316-08089-6). Little.

Bargmann, Eve & Wolfe, Sidney M. Stopping Valium: And Ativan, Centrax, Dalmane, Librium, Paxipam, Restoril, Serax, Tranxene, Xanax. 1983. pap. 5.95 (ISBN 0-446-37582-9). Warner Bks.

Bargmann, W. & Schade, J. P., eds. Lectures on the Diencephalon. (Progress in Brain Research: Vol. 5). 1964. 63.00 (ISBN 0-444-40029-X). Elsevier.

--Rhinencephalon & Related Structures. (Progress in Brain Research: Vol. 3). 1963. 65.75 (ISBN 0-444-40030-3). Elsevier.

Bargmann, Wolfgang & Schade, J. P., eds. Topics in Basic Neurology. (Progress in Brain Research: Vol. 6). 1964. 65.75 o.p. (ISBN 0-444-40028-1). Elsevier.

Bargo, Michael, Jr. Choices & Decisions: A Guidebook for Constructing Values. LC 76-67019. 164p. 1980. pap. 12.00 (ISBN 0-88390-153-6); facilitator's manual with guidebook 25.00 (ISBN 0-88390-152-8). Univ Assocs.

Bargyla, ed. see Hainsworth, P. H.

Barham, Jerry N. & Thomas, William L. Anatomical Kinesiology: A Programmed Text. (Illus., Prog. Bk.). 1969. pap. text ed. 12.95x (ISBN 0-02-306010-7, 30601). Macmillan.

Barham, Jerry N. & Wooten, Edna L. Structural Kinesiology. (Illus.). 448p. 1973. text ed. 24.95x (ISBN 0-02-306000-X, 30600). Macmillan.

Barham, Martha. Bridging Two Worlds. Greene, Tom, ed. 246p. (Orig.). 1981. pap. 6.95x (ISBN 0-9609680-0-8). MJB Bks.

Barhes, Harold, ed. Proceedings of the Ninth European Marine Biology Symposium, Oban, 1974. 1976. 65.00x (ISBN 0-900015-34-9). Taylor-Carlisle.

Bar-Hillel, Yehoshua. Aspects of Language: Essays & Lectures on Philosophy of Language, Linguistic Philosophy & Methodology of Linguistics. 1970. text ed. 30.00x o.p. (ISBN 0-7204-6033-6, Pub. by North Holland). Humanities.

Barich, Madeline C. Confetti. 64p. 1983. 5.50 (ISBN 0-682-49981-1). Exposition.

Barickman, Richard, et al. Corrupt Relations: Dickens, Thackeray, Trollope, Collins & the Victorian Sexual System. 1982. 25.00 (ISBN 0-686-82110-6). Columbia U Pr.

Barigozzi, Claudio, ed. Mechanisms of Speciation. LC 82-13014. (Progress in Clinical & Biological Research Ser.: Vol. 96). 560p. 1982. 88.00 (ISBN 0-8451-0096-3). A R Liss.

Barincou, Edmond. Machiavelli. Lane, Helen, tr. LC 75-11427. 192p. 1975. Repr. of 1962 ed. lib. bdg. 17.00x (ISBN 0-8371-8185-2, BAMA). Greenwood.

Baring-Gould, Cecil, jt. ed. see Baring-Gould, William S.

Baring-Gould, Ceil, jt. auth. see Baring-Gould, William S.

Baring-Gould, S. A Book of Cornwall. 304p. 1982. 30.00x (ISBN 0-7045-0419-7, Pub. by Wildwood House). State Mutual BK.

Baring-Gould, Sabine. Book of Folklore. LC 69-16807. Repr. of 1913 ed. 31.00 o.p. (ISBN 0-8103-3603-0). Gale.

--Book of Nursery Songs & Rhymes. LC 68-23135. 1969. Repr. of 1895 ed. 30.00x (ISBN 0-8103-3471-2). Gale.

--Book of Werewolves: Being an Account of Terrible Superstition. Repr. of 1865 ed. 30.00x (ISBN 0-685-32595-4). Gale.

--Cliff Castles & Cave Dwellings of Europe. LC 68-17983. (Illus.). 1968. Repr. of 1911 ed. 30.00x (ISBN 0-8103-3423-2). Gale.

--Family Names & Their Story. LC 68-23136. 1969. Repr. of 1910 ed. 30.00x (ISBN 0-8103-0151-2). Gale.

--Freaks of Fanaticism & Other Strange Events. LC 68-21754. 1968. Repr. of 1891 ed. 34.00x (ISBN 0-8103-3503-4). Gale.

--Further Reminiscences, Eighteen Sixty-four to Eighteen Ninety-four. LC 67-23869. 1967. Repr. of 1925 ed. 30.00x (ISBN 0-8103-3050-4). Gale.

--Old Country Life. LC 78-77086. 1969. Repr. of 1890 ed. 34.00x (ISBN 0-8103-3848-3). Gale.

--Old English Home & Its Dependencies. LC 74-77085. 1969. Repr. of 1898 ed. 34.00x (ISBN 0-8103-3847-5). Gale.

--Strange Survivals, Some Chapters in the History of Man. LC 67-23909. (Illus.). 1968. Repr. of 1892 ed. 30.00x (ISBN 0-8103-3422-4). Gale.

Baring-Gould, William S. Lure of the Limerick. (Illus.). 1967. 8.95 (ISBN 0-517-08323-X, C N Potter Bks); pap. 4.95 (ISBN 0-517-53856-3). Crown.

Baring-Gould, William S. & Baring-Gould, Ceil. Annotated Mother Goose. (Illus.). 352p. 1982. 25.00 (ISBN 0-517-54629-9, C N Potter Bks). Crown.

Baring-Gould, William S. & Baring-Gould, Cecil, eds. Annotated Mother Goose. (Illus.). 1967. pap. 4.95 (ISBN 0-452-00520-5, F520, Mer). NAL.

Baring-Gould, William S., ed. see Doyle, Arthur C.

Barish & Schla. Seeing the Real London. 1983. pap. cancelled (ISBN 0-8120-2241-6). Barron.

Barish, Norman N. Economic Analysis for Engineering & Managerial Decision Making. (Industrial Engineering & Management Science). (Illus.). 1978. text ed. 32.95 (ISBN 0-07-003649-7, C). McGraw.

Barish, Wendy, jt. auth. see Rotsler, William.

Barish, Wendy, ed. see Alcott, Louisa M.

Barish, Wendy, ed. see Appleton, Victor.

Barish, Wendy, ed. see Berger, Melvin & Berger, Gilda.

Barish, Wendy, ed. see Brothers Grimm.

Barish, Wendy, ed. see Carroll, Lewis.

Barish, Wendy, ed. see Daly, Kathleen N.

Barish, Wendy, ed. see Dixon, Franklin W.

Barish, Wendy, ed. see Heck, Joseph.

Barish, Wendy, ed. see Hope, Laura Lee.

Barish, Wendy, ed. see Rotsler, William.

Barish, Wendy, ed. see Saunders, Rubie.

Barish, Wendy, ed. see Sewell, Anna.

Barish, Wendy, ed. see Sheldon, Ann.

Barish, Wendy, ed. see Smith, Frank.

Barish, Wendy, ed. see Spyri, Johanna.

Barish, Wendy, ed. see Taylor, L. B., Jr.

Barish, Wendy, ed. see Twain, Mark.

Barisi, B., jt. auth. see Sala, F.

Barjon, J. Radio-Diagnosis of Pleuro-Pulmonary Affections. 1918. 57.50x (ISBN 0-685-89775-3). Elliots Bks.

Bark & Allen. Analysis of Polymer Systems. (Applied Science Ser.). 1982. 57.50 (ISBN 0-85334-122-2). Elsevier.

Bark, Voss. West Country Fly Fishing. (Illus.). 192p. 1983. 22.50 (ISBN 0-7134-1882-6, Pub. by Batsford England). David & Charles.

Barkai, Haim. Growth Patterns of the Kibbutz Economy. LC 76-44024. (Contributions to Economic Analysis: Vol. 108). 1977. 64.00 (ISBN 0-7204-0556-4, North-Holland). Elsevier.

Barkan, Joel D., jt. auth. see Kim, Chong Lim.

Barke, James. The Wind That Shakes the Barley: A Novel of the Life & Loves of Robert Burns. 384p. 1982. Repr. of 1945 ed. lib. bdg. 30.00 (ISBN 0-89987-087-2). Darby Bks.

Barke, James, ed. Poems & Songs of Robert Burns. 736p. 1983. 16.95 (ISBN 0-00-420224-4, Collins Pub England). Greene.

Barkely, William D., jt. auth. see Martin, Alexander C.

Barker & Aufmann. Essential Mathematics with Applications. 1982. 9.95 (ISBN 0-686-84648-6); supplementary materials avail. HM.

Barker, et al. Modus Operandi Poetry Anthology. new ed. Jensen, Sheila R., ed. LC 77-83531. 1977. pap. 2.00 (ISBN 0-932044-02-6). M O Pub Co.

Barker, A. J. British & American Infantry Weapons of World War Two. LC 69-13594. (Illus.). 1978. pap. 2.95 o.p. (ISBN 0-668-04526-4, 4526). Arco.

Barker, Allen, ed. see Barker, Diana L.

Barker, Anthony, ed. Quangos in Britain: Government & the Networks of Public Policy-Making. 200p. 1982. 49.00x (ISBN 0-333-29468-8, Pub. by Macmillan England). State Mutual Bk.

Barker, Arthur E., compiled by. The Seventeenth Century: Bacon Through Marvell. LC 76-4657. (Goldentree Bibliographies in Language & Literature). 1980. text ed. 22.50x (ISBN 0-88295-570-5); pap. text ed. 13.95 (ISBN 0-88295-548-9). Harlan Davidson.

Barker, Ben D., jt. ed. see DeFriese, Gordon H.

Barker, Berta L. Dr. Laurie's Conquest. (YA) 1980. 6.95 (ISBN 0-686-73930-2, Avalon). Bouregy.

--A Dream House for Nurse Rhonda. (YA) 1979. 6.95 (ISBN 0-685-65269-6, Avalon). Bouregy.

--Lianne's Island Love. (YA) 1979. 6.95 (ISBN 0-686-52552-3, Avalon). Bouregy.

--Lost in a Mist. (YA) 1981. 6.95 (ISBN 0-686-73954-X, Avalon). Bouregy.

--The Magic of Paris. (YA) 1981. 6.95 (ISBN 0-686-73958-2, Avalon). Bouregy.

Barker, Berta LaVan. Dangerous Waters. (YA) 1978. 6.95 (ISBN 0-685-19056-0, Avalon). Bouregy.

--A Nurse for Dr. Turner. (YA) 1979. 6.95 (ISBN 0-685-93877-8, Avalon). Bouregy.

--A Thousand Happiness. (YA) 1978. 6.95 (ISBN 0-685-87351-X, Avalon). Bouregy.

Barker, C. Edward. Psychology's Impact on the Christian Faith. 1963. 7.50 o.p. (ISBN 0-04-210001-1). Transatlantic.

Barker, Carol. An Oba of Benin. 1977. PLB 6.95 (ISBN 0-201-00423-2, 0423). A-W.

Barker, Carol, ed. see Savannah Junior Auxiliary.

Barker, Carol M. & Fox, Matthew H. Classified Files: The Yellowing Pages. LC 72-80587. 1974. pap. 6.00 o.s.i. (ISBN 0-527-02850-9). Kraus Repr.

Barker, Chris A. Tomorrow May Never Come. (Illus.). 415p. Date not set. 15.00x (ISBN 0-9609382-0-6). Susquehanna.

Barker, Cicely M. The Flower Fairies Miniature Library, 4 vols. (Illus.). 1981. boxed set 6.95 (ISBN 0-399-20823-2, Philomel). Putnam Pub Group.

Barker, Clive. Theatre Games. LC 78-665. (Illus.). 240p. 1978. pap. 9.95 (ISBN 0-910482-93-4). Drama Bk.

Barker, Craig. Starting a Marine Aquarium. 1972. 5.95 (ISBN 0-87666-751-5, PS-305). TFH Pubns.

Barker, Danny, jt. auth. see Buerkle, Jack V.

Barker, Dave. TA & Training: The Theory & Use of Transactional Analysis. 225p. 1980. text ed. 34.25x (ISBN 0-566-02118-8). Gower Pub Ltd.

Barker, Diana L. Sexual Divisions & Society. Barker, Allen, ed. 1976. 12.95x (ISBN 0-422-74820-X, Pub. by Tavistock England); pap. 10.95 (ISBN 0-422-74830-7, Pub. by Tavistock England). Methuen Inc.

Barker, E. G. Diagnostic Radiology Continuing Education Review. 1976. spiral bdg. 12.00 o.p. (ISBN 0-87488-372-5). Med Exam.

Barker, Edmund S. Webb Society Deep-Sky Observer's Handbook: Vol. 4, Galaxies. Glyn-Jones, Kenneth, ed. 250p. 1982. 40.00x (ISBN 0-7188-2527-6, Pub. by Lutterworth Pr England). State Mutual Bk.

Barker, Eileen, ed. New Religious Movements: A Perspective for Understanding Society. (Studies in Religion & Society: Vol. 3). 440p. 1982. 44.95 (ISBN 0-686-84111-5). E Mellen.

Barker, Elisabeth. Macedonia: Its Place in Balkan Power Politics. LC 80-16769. (Illus.). 129p. 1980. Repr. of 1950 ed. lib. bdg. 19.25x (ISBN 0-313-22587-7, BAMI). Greenwood.

Barker, Elliott S. Smokey Bear & the Great Wilderness. Hausman, Gerald, ed. LC 82-19373. (Illus.). 176p. (Orig.). 1982. pap. 12.95 (ISBN 0-86534-017-X). Sunstone Pr.

Barker, Eric J. & Millard, W. F. Materials & Elements. LC 66-22904. (Science Projects & Experiments Ser.). (Illus.). 80p. (gr. 7 up). 1972. PLB 4.50 o.p. (ISBN 0-668-01498-9). Arco.

Barker, Eric J., jt. auth. see Williams, Lawrence.

Barker, Ernest. Britain & the British People. LC 75-28660. (Illus.). 1978. Repr. of 1955 ed. lib. bdg. 19.75x (ISBN 0-8371-8483-5, BABB). Greenwood.

Barker, Eugene C. Life of Stephen F. Austin, Founder of Texas, 1793-1836. LC 68-27723. (American Scene Ser). (Illus.). 1968. Repr. of 1925 ed. 65.00 (ISBN 0-306-71153-2). Da Capo.

Barker, Evelyn M. Everyday Reasoning. (Illus.). 304p. 1981. pap. text ed. 12.95 (ISBN 0-13-293407-8). P-H.

Barker, F., ed. Trondhjemites, Dacites, & Related Rocks. LC 78-24338. (Developments in Petrology Ser.: Vol. 6). 1979. 70.25 (ISBN 0-444-41765-6). Elsevier.

Barker, Forrest L. & Wheeler, Gershon J. Mathematics for Electronics. 2nd ed. LC 77-80492. 1978. 24.95 (ISBN 0-8053-0340-5); instr's guide 6.95 (ISBN 0-8053-0341-3). Benjamin-Cummings.

Barker, Frank G. The Flying Dutchman. LC 80-52507. (Masterworks of Opera Ser.). PLB 15.96 (ISBN 0-382-06430-5). Silver.

Barker, G. R. Chemistry of the Cell. (Studies in Biology: No. 13). 72p. 1982. pap. text ed. 8.95 (ISBN 0-7131-2841-0). E Arnold.

Barker, George E. Death & After Death. LC 78-65349. 1978. pap. text ed. 8.00 (ISBN 0-8191-0653-4). U Pr of Amer.

Barker, Gerard A. Henry Mackenzie. (English Authors Ser.). 1975. lib. bdg. 14.95 (ISBN 0-8057-6651-0, Twayne). G K Hall.

--Twice-Told Tales: An Anthology of Short Fiction. LC 78-69561. 1979. pap. text ed. 12.50 (ISBN 0-395-26635-1); instr's. manual 1.00 (ISBN 0-395-26636-X). HM.

Barker, Graham H. Your Search for Fertility: A Sympathetic Guide to Achieving Pregnancy for Childless Couples. Bronson, Richard A., frwd. by. LC 82-61676. 208p. 1983. pap. 5.95 (ISBN 0-688-01593-X). Quill NY.

Barker, Gray. The Secret Terror Among Us. (Illus., Orig.). 1982. pap. 9.95 (ISBN 0-911306-29-3). G Barker Bks.

Barker, Harley G. Prefaces to Shakespeare: Othello. 160p. 1982. pap. 9.95 (ISBN 0-686-97290-2, Pub. by Batsford England). David & Charles.

Barker, Harold R. History of the Forty-Third Division Artillery: World War II, 1941-1945. (Illus.). 251p. 1961. 12.95 (ISBN 0-917012-45-3). RI Pubns Soc.

--History of the Rhode Island Combat Units in the Civil War, 1861-1865. (Illus.). 338p. 1964. 12.95 (ISBN 0-917012-44-5). RI Pubns Soc.

Barker, Harriett. Supermarket Backpacker. (Illus.). 1977. 7.70 (ISBN 0-8092-7307-1). Contemp Bks.

Barker, Howard. The Love of a Good Man. 1982. pap. 9.95 (ISBN 0-7145-3767-5). Riverrun NY.

Barker, J. S., ed. Future Developments in the Genetic Improvement of Animals. 256p. 1982. 24.50 (ISBN 0-12-078830-6). Acad Pr.

Barker, J. S. & Starmer, T., eds. Ecological Genetics & Evolutions: The Cactus-Yeast-Drosophilia Model. 376p. 1982. 47.00 (ISBN 0-12-078820-9). Acad Pr.

Barker, Jane. Love's Intrigues. Bd. with The Lovers Week. Hearne, Mary; The Female Deserters. Hearne, Mary. LC 70-170528. (Foundations of the Novel 1700-1739). lib. bdg. 50.00 o.s.i. (ISBN 0-8240-0531-7). Garland Pub.

--A Patchwork Screen for the Ladies. Bd. with The Prude: A Novel by a Young Lady. LC 74-170553. (Novel in England, 1700-1775 Ser). lib. bdg. 50.00 o.s.i. (ISBN 0-8240-0551-1). Garland Pub.

Barker, Jane V. & Downing, Sybil. Wagons & Rails. (Colorado Heritage Ser.: Bk. 9). (Illus.). 44p. (gr. 3-4). 1980. pap. 3.50x o.p. (ISBN 0-87108-225-X). Pruett.

Barker, John A. A Formal Analysis of Conditions. (Monographs-Humanities: No. 3). 101p. 1969. pap. 4.95x o.p. (ISBN 0-8093-9801-X). S Ill U Pr.

Barker, John N. & Bray, John. The Indian Princess, 2 vols in 1. LC 77-169587. (Earlier American Music Ser.: No. 11). 1973. Repr. of 1808 ed. 21.50 (ISBN 0-306-77311-2). Da Capo.

Barker, John W. Manuel II Palaeologus, 1391-1425: A Study in Late Byzantine Statesmanship. 1969. 47.50x o.p. (ISBN 0-8135-0582-8). Rutgers U Pr.

Barker, Joseph. Hellish Dictionary. LC 81-84054. 84p. 1981. pap. 2.95 (ISBN 0-686-35984-4). J Barker.

Barker, Kenneth. Seven Dramatic Moments in the Life of Christ: Plays for Church Events. LC 78-52443. 1978. pap. 3.49 (ISBN 0-8042-1432-8). John Knox.

Barker, Kenneth & Breland, O. P. Laboratory Manual of Comparative Anatomy. (Organismal Ser.). (Illus.). 208p. 1980. 16.50 (ISBN 0-07-003656-X). McGraw.

Barker, Larry. Communication in the Classroom. 208p. 1982. 15.95 (ISBN 0-13-153551-X). P-H.

Barker, Larry & Edwards, Renee. Intrapersonal Communication. (Comm Comp Ser.). (Illus.). 52p. 1979. pap. text ed. 2.95 (ISBN 0-89787-301-7). Gorsuch Scarisbrick.

Barker, Larry L. Communication Vibrations. (Speech Communication Ser.). (Illus.). 160p. 1974. pap. text ed. 14.95 (ISBN 0-13-153007-0). P-H.

Barker, Larry L., jt. auth. see Malandro, Loretta A.

Barker, Larry L. & Kibler, Robert J., eds. Speech Communication Behavior: Perspectives & Principles. LC 74-143585. 1971. pap. text ed. 18.95 (ISBN 0-13-827337-5). P-H.

Barker, Larry L., et al. Groups in Process: An Introduction to Small Group Communication. LC 78-17202. 1979. 21.95 (ISBN 0-13-365361-7). P-H.

Barker, Larry L., jt. auth. see Steil, Lyman K.

Barker, Lee R. Principles of Ambulatory Medicine. (Illus.). 1142p. 1982. lib. bdg. 65.00 (ISBN 0-683-00435-2). Williams & Williams.

Barker, Louisa & Poe, Tina. The Diet Cookbook. 45p. (Orig.). 1983. pap. 6.50 (ISBN 0-943938-00-7). Res Assocs.

Barker, Lucius J. & McCorry, Jesse J., Jr. Black Americans & the Political System. 2nd ed. (Orig.). 1980. pap. text ed. 13.95 (ISBN 0-316-08095-0). Little.

Barker, Lucius J., Jr. & Barker, Twiley W. Civil Liberties & the Constitution. 736p. 1982. 22.95 (ISBN 0-13-134882-5). P-H.

Barker, Michael. State Taxation Policy & Economic Growth, No. 1. (Duke Press Policy Studies). 290p. Date not set. 22.75 (ISBN 0-8223-0535-6). Duke.

Barker, Michael, ed. Financing State Economic Development. (Duke Press Policy Studies). 490p. Date not set. 35.00 (ISBN 0-8223-0536-4). Duke.

--The Politics of State-Level Economic Development. (Duke Press Policy Studies). 390p. 1983. cancelled (ISBN 0-8223-0537-2). Duke.

--Rebuilding America's Infrastructure: An Agenda for the 1980's. (Press Policy Studies). 390p. 1983. 30.00 (ISBN 0-8223-0568-2). Duke.

--State Employment Policy in Hard Times. (Duke Press Policy Studies). 260p. Date not set. 20.00 (ISBN 0-8223-0538-0). Duke.

Barker, Michael B. Building Underground for People. (Illus.). 1978. pap. 7.75X (ISBN 0-913962-27-9). Am Inst Arch.

Barker, Muhammad & Hamdani. Spoken Urdu, Vol. 1. 497p. 1975. with 9 cassettes 135.00x (ISBN 0-88432-106-1, U200). J Norton Pubs.

--Spoken Urdu, Vol. 2. 568p. Date not set. with 5 cassettes 115.00x (ISBN 0-88432-107-X, U250). J Norton Pubs.

Barker, Nancy N. Distaff Diplomacy: The Empress Eugenie & the Foreign Policy of the Second Empire. 268p. 1967. 16.95x o.p. (ISBN 0-292-73694-0). U of Tex Pr.

Barker, Nicholas P. Purpose & Function in Prose. 1970. pap. text ed. 4.75x (ISBN 0-685-77214-4, 0-394-30030). Phila Bk Co.

Barker, Nicolas. The Oxford University Press & the Spread of Learning: An Illustrated History, 1478-1978. (Illus.). 1978. 35.00 (ISBN 0-19-951086-5). Oxford U Pr.

Barker, Paul, ed. The Other Britain. 280p. 1982. 22.50 (ISBN 0-7100-9308-X); pap. 10.95 (ISBN 0-7100-9340-3). Routledge & Kegan.

Barker, Peter. Eastern Europe. LC 79-65841. (Countries Ser.). PLB 12.68 (ISBN 0-382-06326-0). Silver.

Barker, Peter & Button, Kenneth. Case Studies in Cost Benefit Analysis. 1975. pap. text ed. 5.50x o.p. (ISBN 0-435-84049-5); tchr's guide 9.00x o.p. (ISBN 0-435-84050-9). Heinemann Ed.

Barker, Phil. Alexander the Great's Campaigns: A Wargamers Guide to Ancient Greek Political & Military Wargaming. (Illus.). 1979. pap. 9.95 (ISBN 0-85059-553-3). Aztex.

Barker, Philip. Basic Child Psychiatry. 3rd ed. 288p. 1979. pap. text ed. 16.95 (ISBN 0-8391-1437-0). Univ Park.

--Basic Family Therapy. 224p. (Orig.). 1981. pap. 19.95 (ISBN 0-8391-1673-X). Univ Park.

--Techniques of Archaeological Excavation. 2nd, rev., & extended ed. LC 82-23792. (Illus.). 288p. 1983. text ed. 25.00x (ISBN 0-87663-399-8); pap. text ed. 12.50x (ISBN 0-87663-587-7). Universe.

Barker, Philip, ed. The Residential Psychiatric Treatment of Children. LC 74-7208. 354p. 1974. 42.95 (ISBN 0-470-04910-3). Halsted Pr.

Barker, Philip J. Behaviour Therapy Nursing. 286p. 1982. pap. text ed. 17.00x (ISBN 0-7099-0637-4, Pub. by Croom Helm Ltd England). Biblio Dist.

Barker, Rachel. Conscience, Government, & War: Conscientious Objection in Great Britain, 1939-1945. 180p. (Orig.). 1982. pap. 14.95 (ISBN 0-7100-9000-5). Routledge & Kegan.

Barker, Ralph. The RAF at War. LC 81-5207. (Epic of Flight Ser.). PLB 19.96 (ISBN 0-8094-3292-7). Silver.

Barker, Raymond J. & McDole, Robert E. Idaho Soils Atlas. LC 82-60201. (Illus.). 1983. 18.95 (ISBN 0-89301-088-X). U Pr of Idaho.

Barker, Richard H. Thomas Middleton. LC 74-12880. 216p. 1975. Repr. of 1958 ed. lib. bdg. 16.25x (ISBN 0-8371-7767-7, BATM). Greenwood.

Barker, Robert. Organic Chemistry of Biological Compounds. (Modern Biochemistry Ser). (Illus.). 1971. pap. 13.95x ref. ed. o.p. (ISBN 0-13-640623-8). P-H.

Barker, Rodney. Political Ideas in Modern Britain. 1978. 24.00x (ISBN 0-416-76250-6); pap. 15.95x (ISBN 0-416-76260-3). Methuen Inc.

Barker, Rodney, ed. Studies in Opposition. LC 70-167757. 300p. 1972. 25.00 (ISBN 0-312-77105-3). St Martin.

Barker, Roger G., et al. Habitats, Enviroments, & Human Behavior: Studies in Ecological Psychology & Eco-Behavioral Science. LC 77-82912. (Social & Behavioral Science Ser). 1978. text ed. 23.95x (ISBN 0-87589-356-2). Jossey-Bass.

Barker, Stephen F. Elements of Logic. 3rd ed. (Illus.). 1980. text ed. 19.95 (ISBN 0-07-003720-5); instr's manual 9.95 (ISBN 0-07-003721-3); study guide 13.50 (ISBN 0-07-003722-1). McGraw.

Barker, Stephen F. & Beauchamp, Tom L. Thomas Reid: Critical Interpretations. 148p. 1976. pap. 19.95 (ISBN 0-87722-124-3). Temple U Pr.

Barker, T. E., et al, eds. Perspectives on Economic Development: Essays in the Honour of W. Arthur Lewis. LC 81-43790. (Illus.). 324p. (Orig.). 1982. PLB 24.25 (ISBN 0-8191-2381-1); pap. text ed. 12.75 (ISBN 0-8191-2382-X). U Pr of Amer.

Barker, T. S., ed. Economic Structure & Policy. 1976. 40.00x (ISBN 0-412-14390-9, Pub. by Chapman & Hall). Methuen Inc.

Barker, Theo & Drake, Michael, eds. Population & Society in Britain, 1850-1980. 240p. 1982. 30.00 (ISBN 0-8147-1043-3). Columbia U Pr.

Barker, Thomas M. The Military Intellectual & Battle: Raimondo Montecuccoli & the Thirty Years War. LC 74-837. (Illus.). 1975. 39.50x (ISBN 0-87395-250-2). State U NY Pr.

Barker, Twiley W., jt. auth. see Barker, Lucius J., Jr.

Barker, Vernon C., jt. auth. see Aufmann, Richard N.

Barker, Wade. Death's Door. pap. cancelled (ISBN 0-446-00000-0). Warner BKs.

--Ninja Master No. 2: Mountain of Fear. (Men of Action Ser.). 160p. (Orig.). 1981. pap. 1.95 o.p. (ISBN 0-446-30064-0). Warner Bks.

--Ninja Master No. 5: Black Magician. (Men of Action Ser.). 160p. (Orig.). 1982. pap. 1.95 (ISBN 0-446-30178-7). Warner Bks.

--Ninja Master No. 6: Death's Door. (Men of Action Ser.). 175p. (Orig.). 1982. pap. 1.95 o.s.i. (ISBN 0-446-30229-5). Warner Bks.

--Ninja Master, No. 7: The Skin Swindle. (Men of Action Ser.). 176p. (Orig.). 1983. pap. 1.95 (ISBN 0-446-30227-9). Warner Bks.

--Ninja Master, No. 8: Only the Good Die. 176p. (Orig.). 1983. pap. 2.25 (ISBN 0-446-30239-2). Warner Bks.

Barker, Wiley F. Peripheral Arterial Disease. 2nd ed. LC 72-78954. (Major Problems in Clinical Surgery Ser.: Vol. 4). (Illus.). 1975. text ed. 18.75 o.p. (ISBN 0-7216-1546-5). Saunders.

Barker, Wiley F., jt. auth. see Gaspar, Max R.

Barker, William F. & Doeff, Annick M. Preschool Behavior Rating Scale. LC 80-11444. (Orig.). 1980. pap. text ed. 4.35 instructions & scoring sample (ISBN 0-87868-148-5, J-60A); blank scale 0.60 (ISBN 0-87868-185-X, J-60B); Methodology 2.25 (ISBN 0-87868-187-6, J-60C). Child Welfare.

Barker, William H., ed. Teaching Preventive Medicine in Primary Care, Vol. 5. (Springer Series in Medical Education: Vol. 5). 336p. 1983. text ed. 41.50 (ISBN 0-8261-4080-7). Springer Pub.

Barker, William P. Everyone in the Bible. 384p. 1966. 14.95 (ISBN 0-8007-0084-8). Revell.

Barker, William P., jt. ed. see Mead, Frank S.

Barkhouse, Bob. Engine Repair: Head Assembly & Valve Gear. LC 74-21562. 500p. (gr. 10-12). 1974. text ed. 19.96 (ISBN 0-87345-101-5). McKnight.

Barkin, David & King, Timothy. Regional Economic Development: The River Basin Approach in Mexico. LC 76-111122. (Cambridge Latin American Studies, No. 7). (Illus.). 1970. 37.50 (ISBN 0-521-07837-7). Cambridge U Pr.

Barkin, Solomon, ed. Worker Militancy & Its Consequences, 1965-75: New Directions in Western Industrial Relations. LC 75-3745. (Illus.). 448p. 1975. 31.95 o.p. (ISBN 0-275-07410-2); pap. 13.95 o.p. (ISBN 0-275-89440-1). Praeger.

Barkins, Evelyn. Hospital Happy. 112p. 1976. pap. 4.95 (ISBN 0-8119-0404-0). Fell.

Barklem, Jill. Autumn Story. LC 80-15433. (The Brambly Hedge Bks.). (Illus.). 32p. (gr. 1 up). 1980. 6.95 (ISBN 0-399-20745-7, Philomel); PLB 6.99 (ISBN 0-399-61155-X). Putnam Pub Group.

--The Big Book of Brambly Hedge. (Illus.). 24p. 1981. pap. 10.95 (ISBN 0-399-20833-X, Philomel). Putnam Pub Group.

--Spring Story. LC 80-15300. (The Brambly Hedge Bks.). (Illus.). 32p. (gr. 1 up). 1980. 6.95 (ISBN 0-399-20746-5, Philomel); PLB 6.99 (ISBN 0-399-61156-8). Putnam Pub Group.

--Summer Story. LC 80-15423. (The Brambly Hedge Bks.). (Illus.). 32p. (gr. 1 up). 1980. 6.95 (ISBN 0-399-20747-3, Philomel); PLB 6.99 (ISBN 0-399-61157-6). Putnam Pub Group.

--Winter Story. LC 80-15422. (The Brambly Hedge Bks.). (Illus.). 32p. (gr. 1 up). 1980. 6.95 (ISBN 0-399-20748-1, Philomel); PLB 6.99 (ISBN 0-399-61158-4). Putnam Pub Group.

Barkley, Richard A. Oceanographic Atlas of the Pacific Ocean. (Illus.). 1969. text ed. 50.00x (ISBN 0-87022-050-0). UH Pr.

Barkley, T. M. Field Guide to the Common Weeds of Kansas. LC 82-21914. (Illus.). 160p. 1983. text ed. 17.95x (ISBN 0-7006-0233-X); pap. 7.95 (ISBN 0-7006-0224-0). Univ Pr KS.

Barkman, Alma. Days Remembered. (Illus.). 96p. 1983. pap. price not set (ISBN 0-8024-0188-0). Moody.

--Sunny-Side up. (Quiet Time Ser.). 1977. pap. 2.50 o.p. (ISBN 0-8024-8431-X). Moody.

--Times to Treasure. LC 80-22835. 96p. 1980. text ed. 14.95 (ISBN 0-8024-2072-9). Moody.

Bar-Kochva, B. The Seleucid Army. (Cambridge Classical Studies Ser.). 1976. 29.95 (ISBN 0-521-20667-7). Cambridge U Pr.

Barkow, Al, jt. auth. see Low, George.

Barkow, Al, jt. auth. see Venturi, Ken.

Barks, Carl, illus. Donald Duck & the Magic Hourglass. LC 80-68946. (Illus.). 36p. 1981. 3.95 o.p. (ISBN 0-89659-177-8). Abbeville Pr.

--Uncle Scrooge & the Secret of Old Castle. (Illus.). 36p. 1981. 3.95 o.p. (ISBN 0-89659-180-8). Abbeville Pr.

Barks, Coleman, tr. see Rumi.

Barksdale, A. Beverly. The Printed Note: Five Hundred Years of Music Printing & Engraving. (Music Ser.). (Illus.). 145p. 1981. Repr. of 1957 ed. lib. bdg. 22.50 (ISBN 0-306-76087-8). Da Capo.

Barksdale, Jelks. Titanium: Its Occurrence, Chemistry & Technology. 2nd ed. LC 66-20080. 702p. 1966. 43.50 (ISBN 0-686-74184-6). Krieger.

Barksdale, Richard & Kinnamon, Keneth. Black Writers of America: A Comprehensive Anthology. 980p. 1972. text ed. 22.95x (ISBN 0-02-306080-8, 30608). Macmillan.

Barkus, Philip. How to Prepare for the Postal Clerk Carrier Examination. 256p. 1982. pap. 6.95 (ISBN 0-8120-2524-5). Barron.

Barlaus, A. Rivers of Norway. (Illus.). 1966. 15.00x o.p. (ISBN 82-09-00841-2, N447). Vanous.

Barlay, Stephen. Blockbuster. 1978. pap. 2.25 o.p. (ISBN 0-451-08111-0, E8111, Sig). NAL.

Bar-Lev, A. Semiconductors & Electronic Devices. 1979. 31.95 (ISBN 0-13-806299-4). P-H.

Barley, Elizabeth G. & Bloom, Mark. Young Runner's Handbook. (Illus.). 128p. 1981. pap. 3.00 (ISBN 0-686-75679-7, Quick Fox). Putnam Pub Group.

Barlin, G. B. Chemistry of Heterocyclic Compounds, Vol. 41: Pyrazines - A Series of Monographs. 712p. 1982. 168.95x (ISBN 0-471-38119-5, Pub. by Wiley-Interscience). Wiley.

Barling, Tom, ed. Dracula. pap. 1.99 o.p. (ISBN 0-448-12637-0, G&D). Putnam Pub Group.

Barlotti, A. Combinatorial & Geometric Structures & Their Applications. (Mathematical Studies Ser.: Vol. 63). Date not set. 40.50 (ISBN 0-444-86384-2, North Holland). Elsevier.

Barlotti, A. & Ceccerini, P. V. Combinatorics, 1981. (Mathematical Studies: Vol. 78). Date not set. 89.50 (ISBN 0-444-86546-2, North Holland). Elsevier.

Barlough, J. Ernest. The Archaicon: A Collection of Unusual Archaic English. LC 73-14926. 1974. 12.00 o.p. (ISBN 0-8108-0683-5). Scarecrow.

--Minor British Poetry 1680-1800: An Anthology. LC 73-4878. 1973. 13.00 o.p. (ISBN 0-8108-0619-3). Scarecrow.

Barlow, A. Analysis of the Absorption Process & of Desiccant Cooling Systems: A Pseudo-Steady State Model for Coupled Heat & Mass Transfer. (Progress in Solar Energy Supplements Ser.). 160p. 1983. pap. text ed. 15.00x (ISBN 0-89553-069-4). Am Solar Energy.

Barlow, C. W. & Eisen, Glen P. Purchasing Negotiations. 200p. 1983. 18.95 (ISBN 0-8436-0881-1). CBI Pub.

Barlow, David. Sexually Transmitted Diseases: The Facts. (Illus.). 1979. text ed. 14.95x (ISBN 0-19-261157-7). Oxford U Pr.

Barlow, David H. & Hayes, Steven C. The Scientist Practitioner: Research & Accountability in Mental Health & Education. 400p. 1983. 35.00 (ISBN 0-08-027217-7); pap. 14.95 (ISBN 0-08-027216-9). Pergamon.

Barlow, Frank. Edward the Confessor. LC 70-104107. (English Monarchs Series). (Illus.). 1970. 30.00x (ISBN 0-520-01671-8). U of Cal Pr.

Barlow, Fred. Mental Prodigies. LC 70-88982. Repr. of 1951 ed. lib. bdg. 17.50x (ISBN 0-8371-2092-6, BAMP). Greenwood.

Barlow, G. The Genius of Dickens. LC 75-22401. (Studies in Dickens, No. 52). 1975. lib. bdg. 40.95x (ISBN 0-8383-2091-0). Haskell.

Barlow, George W. & Silverberg, James, eds. Sociobiology: Beyond Nature-Nurture. (AAAS Selected Symposium: No. 35). 625p. 1980. lib. bdg. 37.00 (ISBN 0-89158-372-6); pap. text ed. 16.00 (ISBN 0-89158-960-0). Westview.

Barlow, H. B. & Mollon, J. D., eds. The Senses. LC 81-17007. (Cambridge Texts in the Physiological Sciences Ser.: No. 3). (Illus.). 400p. 1982. 59.50 (ISBN 0-521-24474-9); pap. 19.95 (ISBN 0-521-28714-6). Cambridge U Pr.

Barlow, Harold & Morgenstern, Sam, eds. Dictionary of Musical Themes. rev. ed. (Illus.). 1976. 14.95 (ISBN 0-517-52446-5). Crown.

--Dictionary of Opera & Song Themes. rev. ed. 1976. 15.95 (ISBN 0-517-52503-8). Crown.

Barlow, I. M. Spatial Dimensions of Urban Government. LC 80-41972. (Geographical Research Studies). 199p. 1981. 52.95x (ISBN 0-471-27978-1, Pub. by Res Stud Pr). Wiley.

Barlow, Jeffrey G. Sun Yat-Sen & the French, 1900-1908. LC 79-620017. (China Research Monographs: No. 14). 1979. pap. 4.00x (ISBN 0-912966-19-X). IEAS.

Barlow, Joel. Works 2 Vols: Vol. 1. Prose, Vol. 2. Poetry. LC 68-17012. 1970. Set. 130.00x (ISBN 0-8201-1062-0). Schol Facsimiles.

Barlow, John D. German Expressionist Film. (Twayne's Filmmakers Ser.). 1982. lib. bdg. 16.95 (ISBN 0-8057-9284-8, Twayne). G K Hall.

Barlow, Lawrence E. The Job-Seekers' Bible. LC 81-11494. 320p. (Orig.). 1981. pap. 8.95 (ISBN 0-940150-00-X). Voc Career Assess.

Barlow, Nora, ed. Darwin & Henslow: The Growth of an Idea, Letters 1831-1860. LC 67-18368. 1967. 28.50x (ISBN 0-520-00080-3). U of Cal Pr.

Barlow, Nora, ed. see Darwin, Charles R.

Barlow, R. An Assessment of Dehumidifier Geometries for Dessicant Cooling Systems. (Progress in Solar Energy Supplements SERI Ser.). 75p. 1983. pap. text ed. 9.00x (ISBN 0-89553-082-1). Am Solar Energy.

Barlow, R., jt. auth. see Kutscher, C.

Barlow, R. B. Quantitative Aspects of Chemical Pharmacology. 256p. 1980. text ed. 19.95 o.p. (ISBN 0-8391-1388-9). Univ Park.

Barlow, R. E., et al. Statistical Inference Under Order Restrictions: The Theory & Application of Isotonic Regression. LC 74-39231. (Probability & Statistics Ser.). (Illus.). 400p. 1972. 64.95x (ISBN 0-471-04970-0, Pub. by Wiley-Interscience). Wiley.

Barlow, Richard M. & Patterson, Deryck S. Border Disease of Sheep: A Virus-Induced Teratogenic Disorder. (Advances in Veterinary Medicine Ser.: Vol. 36). (Illus.). 36p. 1982. pap. text ed. 24.00 (ISBN 0-686-35822-8). Parey Sci Pubs.

Barlow, Robert H. A Dim-Remembered Story. 1.50 o.p. (ISBN 0-686-31247-3). Necronomicon.

Barlow, Ron & Stewart, Bhob, eds. EC Horror Comics of the 1950s. (Illus.). 1976. 24.95 o.p. (ISBN 0-517-52578-X). Crown.

Barlow, Ronald S. How to be Successful in the Antique Business. (Illus.). 256p. 1982. pap. 6.95 (ISBN 0-686-83705-3, ScribT). Scribner.

Barlow, S. M. & Stansby, M. E., eds. Nutritional Evaluation of Long-Chain Fatty Acids in Fish Oil. 1982. 30.00 (ISBN 0-12-078920-5). Acad Pr.

Barlow, S. M. & Sullivan, F. M., eds. Reproductive Hazards of Industrial Chemicals. 610p. 1982. 75.00 (ISBN 0-12-078960-4). Acad Pr.

Barlow, W. A. Langmuir-Blodgett Films. (Thin Films Science & Technology Ser.: Vol. 1). 1980. 70.25 (ISBN 0-444-41901-2). Elsevier.

Barlow, Wilfred. Alexander Technique. 240p. 1980. pap. 6.95 (ISBN 0-446-37312-5). Warner Bks.

Barlow, William. Summe & Substance of the Conference. LC 65-10395. 1965. Repr. of 1604 ed. 25.00x (ISBN 0-8201-1004-3). Schol Facsimiles.

Barlowe, Raleigh. Land Resource Economics: The Economics of Real Estate. 3rd ed. (Illus.). 1978. ref. ed. 26.95 (ISBN 0-13-522532-9). P-H.

Barlowe, Wayne D. & Summers, Ian. Barlowe's Guide to Extraterrestrials. LC 79-64782. (Illus.). 148p. 1979. 14.95 o.p. (ISBN 0-89480-113-9); pap. 7.95 (ISBN 0-89480-112-0). Workman Pub.

Barltrop, J. A. & Coyle, J. D. Excited States in Organic Chemistry. LC 74-22400. 376p. 1975. 79.95 (ISBN 0-471-04995-6, Pub. by Wiley-Interscience). Wiley.

--Principles of Photochemistry. LC 78-16622. 213p. 1979. pap. 22.95x (ISBN 0-471-99687-4, Pub. by Wiley-Interscience). Wiley.

Barmada, Riad, jt. auth. see Ray, Robert D.

Barmann, Lawrence F. Baron Friedrich Von Hugel & the Modernist Crisis in England. LC 77-153014. 1972. 44.50 (ISBN 0-521-08178-5). Cambridge U Pr.

Barmark, Jan, ed. Perspectives in Metascience. (Regiae Societatis-Interdisciplinaria: No. 2). 199p. 1980. text ed. 21.00x (ISBN 91-85252-21-2). Humanities.

Barmash, Isadore. More Than They Bargained for: The Rise & Fall of Korvettes. 272p. 1982. 14.95 (ISBN 0-448-21012-6, G&D). Putnam Pub Group.

Barna, A. A. VHSIC (Very High Speed Integrated Circuits) Technologies & Tradeoffs. LC 81-4356. 114p. 1981. 19.95x (ISBN 0-471-09463-3, Pub. by Wiley-Interscience). Wiley.

Barna, Arpad. High Speed Pulse & Digital Techniques. LC 79-26264. 185p. 1980. 24.95x (ISBN 0-471-06062-3, Pub. by Wiley-Interscience). Wiley.

--Operational Amplifiers. LC 70-150608. 148p. 1971. 25.95x (ISBN 0-471-05030-X, Pub. by Wiley-Interscience). Wiley.

Barna, Arpad & Porat, Dan I. Integrated Circuits in Digital Electronics. LC 73-6709. 483p. 1973. 42.50x (ISBN 0-471-05050-4, Pub. by Wiley-Interscience). Wiley.

--Introduction to Microcomputers & Microprocessors. LC 75-31675. 108p. 1976. 19.95x (ISBN 0-471-05051-2, Pub. by Wiley-Interscience). Wiley.

Barna, Arpad, jt. auth. see Porat, Dan I.

Barna, Victor. Your Book of Table Tennis. (gr. 7 up). 1971. 6.50 o.p. (ISBN 0-571-09345-0). Transatlantic.

Barnabas. Gospel of Barnabas. 1981. pap. 5.50 (ISBN 0-686-77427-2). Kazi Pubns.

Barnaby, C. F. & Boserup, A., eds. Implications of Anti-Ballistic Missile Systems. (Pugwash Monographs Ser: No. 2). 1969. text ed. 15.00x (ISBN 0-285-50260-3). Humanities.

Barnaby, Frank & Thomas, Geoffrey, eds. The Nuclear Arms Race: Control or Catastrophe. LC 81-21282. 265p. 1982. 25.00x (ISBN 0-312-57974-8). St Martin.

Barnard, A. J., Jr., jt. ed. see Flaschka, H. A.

Barnard, A. J., Jr., jt. ed. see Flashka, H. A.

Barnard, C. S. & Nix, J. S. Farm Planning & Control. 2nd ed. LC 79-10572. 1980. 75.00 (ISBN 0-521-22658-9); pap. 27.95x (ISBN 0-521-29604-8). Cambridge U Pr.

Barnard, Caroline K. Sylvia Plath. (United States Authors Ser.). 1978. lib. bdg. 11.95 (ISBN 0-8057-7219-7, Twayne). G K Hall.

Barnard, Chester I. Functions of the Executive. 30th anniversary ed. LC 68-28690. 1968. 18.50x o.p. (ISBN 0-674-32800-0); pap. 5.95x (ISBN 0-674-32803-5). Harvard U Pr.

Barnard College Women's Center. Women's Work & Women's Studies. 370p. 1976. 12.50x o.p. (ISBN 0-685-77282-9). Feminist Pr.

Barnard, David & Crawford, Robert. PASCAL Programming Problems & Applications. 1982. pap. text ed. 12.95 (ISBN 0-8359-5467-6). Reston.

--PL-One Programming Problems & Applications. 1982. pap. text ed. 10.95 (ISBN 0-8359-5554-0). Reston.

Barnard, F. M., ed. J. G. Herder on Social & Political Culture. LC 69-11022. (Cambridge Studies in the History & Theory of Politics). (Illus.). 1969. 44.50 (ISBN 0-521-07336-7). Cambridge U Pr.

Barnard, Francis P. Edward IV's French Expedition of Fourteen Seventy Five. (Illus.). 162p. 1982. Repr. of 1925 ed. text ed. 21.00x (ISBN 0-904586-01-4, Pub. by Alan Sutton England). Humanities.

Barnard, Gwen. The Shapes of the River. 44p. 1955. 15.00x o.p. (ISBN 0-85247-026-6, Pub. by Baberbocchus). State Mutual Bk.

Barnard, H. C. Education & the French Revolution. (Cambridge Texts & Studies in the History of Education: No. 5). 1969. 36.00 (ISBN 0-521-07256-5). Cambridge U Pr.

--Fenelon on Education. (Cambridge Texts & Studies in the History of Education: No. 1). 1966. 26.50 (ISBN 0-521-04107-4). Cambridge U Pr.

--Were Those the Days? 1970. 17.25 (ISBN 0-08-007107-4). Pergamon.

Barnard, Helen. Advanced English Vocabulary. 1971. tchrs' bk 2.95 (ISBN 0-912066-19-9); wkbk 1 6.95 (ISBN 0-686-96805-0). Newbury Hse.

Barnard, John. Walter Reuther & the Rise of the Auto Workers. 1983. 13.00i (ISBN 0-316-08141-8). Little.

Barnard, Kathryn E. & Erickson, Marcene L. Teaching Children with Developmental Problems: A Family Care Approach. 2nd ed. LC 75-31520. (Illus.). 182p. 1976. pap. 10.50 o.p. (ISBN 0-8016-0486-9). Mosby.

Barnard, Marjorie. Miles Franklin. (World Authors Ser.). lib. bdg. 13.95 (ISBN 0-8057-2328-5, Twayne). G K Hall.

Barnard, Martha, jt. auth. see Hymovich, Debra.

Barnard, Martha U., et al. Handbook of Comprehensive Pediatric Nursing. (Illus.). 592p. 1981. pap. text ed. 14.50 (ISBN 0-07-003740-X). McGraw.

Barnard, Mary. Mythmakers. LC 66-20061. 213p. 1979. 16.95 (ISBN 0-8214-0024-X, 82-80265); pap. 6.50 (ISBN 0-8214-0562-4, 82-80273). Ohio U Pr.

Barnard, Mary, tr. see Sappho.

Barnard, Max, jt. auth. see Herbert, Frank.

Barnard, Robert. Blood Brotherhood. 1983. pap. 2.95 (ISBN 0-14-006552-0). Penguin.

--The Case of the Missing Bronte: A Perry Trethowan Mystery. 192p. 1983. 11.95 (ISBN 0-686-83668-5, ScribT). Scribner.

--Death by Sheer Torture. (Nightingale Ser.). 1982. pap. 9.95 (ISBN 0-8161-3456-1, Large Print Bks). G K Hall.

--Death by Sheer Torture. 1983. pap. 2.95 (ISBN 0-440-11976-6). Dell.

--A Little Local Murder. 192p. 1983. 11.95 (ISBN 0-684-17882-6, ScribT). Scribner.

Barnard, S. A., jt. auth. see Beagley, H. A.

Barnard, Simon. The Dragon of St. Pancras. (Illus.). 1976. PLB 2.00 o.p. (ISBN 0-685-86594-0, 901720127). State Mutual Bk.

Barnave, A. P. Rapport sur les Affaires de Saint-Domingue Fait les 11 et 12 Octobre, 1790. (Slave Trade in France Ser., 1744-1848). 103p. (Fr.). 1974. Repr. lib. bdg. 36.00x o.p. (ISBN 0-8287-0057-5, TN115). Clearwater Pub.

--Rapport sur les Colonies, et Decret Rendu sur Cette Affaire... le 28 Septembre 1791. (Slave Trade in France Ser., 1744-1848). 63p. (Fr.). 1974. Repr. lib. bdg. 27.00x o.p. (ISBN 0-8287-0058-3, TN116). Clearwater Pub.

Barndorff-Nielsen, O. Information & Exponential Families in Statistical Theory. LC 77-9943. (Probability & Mathematical Statistics, Tracts). 238p. 1978. 54.95x (ISBN 0-471-99545-2, Pub. by Wiley-Interscience). Wiley.

Barndt, Deborah. Education & Social Change: A Photographic Study of Peru. LC 80-82833. 1980. pap. text ed. 20.95 (ISBN 0-8403-2283-6). Kendall-Hunt.

Barndt, Stephen E. & Carvey, Davis W. Essentials of Operations Management. (Illus.). 192p. 1982. 18.95 (ISBN 0-13-286534-3); pap. text ed. 12.95 (ISBN 0-13-286526-2). P-H.

Barne, Weston La see La Barre, Weston.

Barner, Herbert E. & Scheuerman, Richard V. Handbook of Thermochemical Data for Compounds & Aqueous Species. LC 77-20244. 192p. 1978. 39.95x (ISBN 0-471-03238-7, Pub. by Wiley-Interscience). Wiley.

Barnes. Applications of Plasma Emission Spectrochemistry. 1980. 39.95 (ISBN 0-471-25595-5, Pub. by Wiley Heyden). Wiley.

Barnes, A. J. & Orville-Thomas, W. J., eds. Vibrational Spectroscopy: Modern Trends. 1977. 66.00 (ISBN 0-444-42001-0). Elsevier.

Barnes, Albert. Barnes' Notes on the Old & New Testaments, 14 vols. 249.50 (ISBN 0-8010-0834-4). Baker Bk.

Barnes, Ann, jt. ed. see Berkeley, A. Eliot.

Barnes, Asa, ed. Hemotherapy in Trauma & Surgery. 87p. 1979. 12.00 (ISBN 0-914404-48-2). Am Assn Blood.

Barnes, Asa & Nelson, Ilene F., eds. Safe Transfusion. (Illus.). 104p. 1981. 19.00 (ISBN 0-914404-68-7). Am Assn Blood.

Barnes, Asa, Jr., jt. ed. see Judd, W. John.

Barnes, B. A. & Murphy, G. J. Riesz & Fredholm Theory in Banach Algebras. (Research Notes in Mathematics Ser.: No. 67). 300p. 1982. pap. text ed. 18.95 (ISBN 0-273-08563-8). Pitman Pub MA.

Barnes, B. J., jt. ed. see Hill, Shirley.

Barnes, Barry. Scientific Knowledge & Sociological Theory. (Monographs in Social Theory). 204p. 1974. 16.50 (ISBN 0-7100-7961-3); pap. 8.95 (ISBN 0-7100-7962-1). Routledge & Kegan.

Barnes, Ben, jt. auth. see Gay, Kathlyn.

Barnes, Ben E. & Gay, Kathlyn. Beginner's Guide to Better Boxing. (gr. 6 up). 1980. 7.95 o.p. (ISBN 0-679-20533-0). McKay.

Barnes, Bernard. Man & the Changing Landscape. (Work Notes 3). (Illus.). 144p. pap. text ed. 14.00x (ISBN 0-906367-12-3, Merseyside County Mus of Liverpool England). Smithsonian.

Barnes, Bill. New A to Z on Fuchsias. (Illus.). Date not set. pap. 9.95. Natl Fuchsia.

Barnes, Broda. Hope for Hypoglycemia. 4.00x (ISBN 0-686-29861-6). Cancer Control Soc.

Barnes, Broda & Galton, Lawrence. Hypothyroidism: The Unsuspected Illness. LC 75-29251. 224p. 1976. 12.45i (ISBN 0-690-01029-X). T Y Crowell.

Barnes, Burton V., jt. auth. see Spurr, Stephen H.

Barnes, C. D. & Eltherington, L. G. Drug Dosage in Laboratory Animals: A Handbook. 2nd rev. & enl. ed. 1973. 39.00x (ISBN 0-520-02273-4). U of Cal Pr.

Barnes, C. D & Kircher, Christopher, eds. Readings in Neurophysiology. LC 68-15458. 482p. 1968. text ed. 18.50 (ISBN 0-471-05060-1, Pub. by Wiley). Krieger.

Barnes, C. D., jt. ed. see Orem, J.

Barnes, Caren M., jt. auth. see Armstrong, Thomas H.

Barnes, Carl F., Jr. Villard de Honnecourt-The Artist & His Drawings: A Critical Bibliography. 1982. lib. bdg. 28.95 (ISBN 0-8161-8481-X, Hall Reference). G K Hall.

Barnes, Carol P., jt. auth. see Ellner, Carolyn L.

Barnes, Caroline. The Star Wars Book about Flight. LC 82-20423. (Illus.). 32p. (gr. 3-8). 1983. pap. 1.25 (ISBN 0-394-85689-9). Random.

Barnes, Charles & Blake, David. Bargello & Related Stichery. LC 71-151458. (Illus.). 1971. 8.95 (ISBN 0-8208-0337-5). Hearthside.

Barnes, Charles A., et al, eds. Essays in Nuclear Astrophysics. LC 81-9992. 555p. 1982. 75.00 (ISBN 0-521-24410-2); pap. 29.95 (ISBN 0-521-28876-2). Cambridge U Pr.

Barnes, Charles D., jt. ed. see Hughes, Maysie J.

Barnes, Charles D., jt. ed. see McGrath, James J.

Barnes, Chester. Advanced Table Tennis Techniques. LC 76-52386. (Illus.). 1977. 8.95 o.p. (ISBN 0-668-04233-8); pap. 5.95 o.p. (ISBN 0-668-04236-2). Arco.

Barnes, Clive. Inside American Ballet Theatre. (Quality Paperbacks Ser.). (Illus.). 192p. 1983. pap. 11.95 (ISBN 0-306-80192-2). Da Capo.

--Nureyev. (Illus.). 272p. 1982. 35.00 (ISBN 0-9609736-2-1). Helene Obolensky Ent.

Barnes, Clive, ed Best American Plays. (The John Gossner Best Plays Ser.: Eighth Ser. 1974-1982). 512p. 1983. 24.95 (ISBN 0-517-54480-6). Crown.

Barnes, D. & Wilson, F. Chemistry & Unit Operations in Sewage Treatment. (Illus.). 1978. text ed. 51.30x (ISBN 0-85334-783-2, Pub. by Applied Sci England). Elsevier.

--The Design & Operation of Small Sewage Works. 180p. 1976. 26.00x (ISBN 0-419-10980-3, Pub. by E & FN Spon England). Methuen Inc.

Barnes, Djuna. Smoke & Other Early Stories. Messerli, Douglas, ed. (Illus.). 184p. 1982. 12.95 (ISBN 0-940650-17-7); pap. 8.00 (ISBN 0-940650-12-6). Sun & Moon MD.

Barnes, Djuna, et al see Andre, Michael.

Barnes, Dorothy L., jt. auth. see Stephens, Irving E.

Barnes, Douglas. Practical Curriculum Study. (Rutledge Education Bks.). 160p. 1983. pap. 19.95 (ISBN 0-7100-0979-8). Routledge & Kegan.

Barnes, Douglas & Britton, James. Language, the Learner & the School. 176p. (Orig.). 1971. pap. 6.75x (ISBN 0-14-080094-8). Boynton Cook Pubs.

Barnes, Emilie. More Hours in My Day. (Orig.). 1982. pap. 4.95 (ISBN 0-89081-355-8). Harvest Hse.

Barnes, F. A. Canyon Country Geology for the Layman & Rockhound. new ed. LC 77-95050. (Illus.). 1978. pap. 4.50 (ISBN 0-915272-17-2). Wasatch Pubs.

--Canyon Country Prehistoric Rock Art. LC 82-60129. (Canyon Country Ser.). (Illus.). 304p. 1982. pap. 7.50 (ISBN 0-915272-25-3). Wasatch Pubs.

Barnes, Frank C. Cartridges of the World. 4th ed. 352p. 1980. pap. 9.95 o.s.i. (ISBN 0-695-81417-6). Follett.

Barnes, Gilbert H. Anti-Slavery Impulse, Eighteen Thirty to Forty-Four. 9.00 (ISBN 0-8446-4020-4). Peter Smith.

Barnes, Gilbert H. & Dumond, Dwight L., eds. Letters of Theodore Dwight Weld, Angelina Grimke Weld, & Sarah Grimke. LC 77-121103. (American Public Figures Ser). 1970. Repr. of 1934 ed. lib. bdg. 95.00 (ISBN 0-306-71981-9). Da Capo.

Barnes, Grace M., compiled by. Alcohol & Youth: A Comprehensive Bibliography. LC 82-15397. 464p. 1982. lib. bdg. 45.00 (ISBN 0-313-23136-2, BAY/). Greenwood.

Barnes, Gregory. Crisscross: Structured Writing in Context. (Illus.). 208p. 1981. pap. text ed. 11.95 (ISBN 0-13-193920-3). P-H.

Barnes, H. L., ed. Geochemistry of Hydrothermal Ore Deposits. 2nd ed. LC 79-354. 798p. 1979. 38.95x (ISBN 0-471-05056-3, Pub. by Wiley-Interscience). Wiley.

Barnes, Harold, ed. Oceanography & Marine Biology: An Annual Review, Vol. 15. 1977. 75.00 (ISBN 0-900015-39-X). Taylor-Carlisle.

--Oceanography & Marine Biology: An Annual Review, Vol. 16. 1978. 80.00 (ISBN 0-900015-44-6). Taylor-Carlisle.

--Oceanography & Marine Biology: Annual Review, Vol. 14. 1976. 75.00 (ISBN 0-900015-37-3). Taylor-Carlisle.

Barnes, Harry E. Evolution of Penology in Pennsylvania, a Study in American Social History. LC 68-55768. (Criminology, Law Enforcement, & Social Problems Ser.: No. 21). (Illus.). 1968. Repr. of 1927 ed. 20.00x (ISBN 0-87585-021-9). Patterson Smith.

--In Quest of Truth & Justice: Debunking the War Guilt Myth. LC 72-78407. 1972. 17.50 (ISBN 0-87926-011-4); pap. 2.95 (ISBN 0-87926-012-2). R Myles.

--Perpetual War for Perpetual Peace. rev. & enl. ed. 1982. lib. bdg. 79.95 (ISBN 0-87700-454-4). Revisionist Pr.

--Repression of Crime, Studies in Historical Penology. LC 69-14911. (Criminology, Law Enforcement, & Social Problems Ser.: No. 56). 1969. Repr. of 1926 ed. 16.00x (ISBN 0-87585-056-1). Patterson Smith.

--Story of Punishment: A Record of Man's Inhumanity to Man. 2nd rev. ed. LC 74-108229. (Criminology, Law Enforcement, & Social Problems Ser.: No. 112). (Illus.). 1972. 20.00x (ISBN 0-87585-112-6); pap. 7.50x (ISBN 0-87585-913-5). Patterson Smith.

Barnes, Harry E., ed. Perpetual War for Perpetual Peace. 680p. 1982. pap. 11.00 (ISBN 0-939484-01-3). Inst Hist Rev.

Barnes, Hazel E., tr. see Sartre, Jean-Paul.

Barnes, Irston R. Public Utility Control in Massachusetts. 1930. 52.50x (ISBN 0-685-89774-5). Elliots Bks.

Barnes, J. A. Three Styles in the Study of Kinship. LC 74-142057. 1972. 26.00x (ISBN 0-520-01879-6); pap. 6.95x (ISBN 0-520-02481-8). U of Cal Pr.

--Who Should Know What? LC 79-9656. 232p. 1980. 19.95 (ISBN 0-521-23359-3); pap. 5.95 (ISBN 0-521-29934-9). Cambridge U Pr.

Barnes, J. G. Rtl-2 Design and Philosophy. 1976. 42.95 (ISBN 0-471-25596-3, Wiley Heyden). Wiley.

Barnes, J. Wesley, jt. auth. see Jensen, Paul A.

Barnes, James. David G. Farragut. 132p. 1982. Repr. of 1899 ed. lib. bdg. 25.00 (ISBN 0-686-81844-X). Darby Bks.

Barnes, James J. & Barnes, Patience P. Hitler's Mein Kampf in Britain & America: A Publishing History, 1930-39. LC 79-54014. 1980. pap. 22.95 (ISBN 0-521-22691-0). Cambridge U Pr.

Barnes, James N. Let's Save Antarctica! (Illus.). 112p. 1983. pap. 6.95 (ISBN 0-87663-581-8). Universe.

Barnes, Jane. Double Lives. LC 79-7795. 264p. 1981. 11.95 o.p. (ISBN 0-385-15647-2). Doubleday.

Barnes, Jennifer, tr. see Hinz, Walther.

Barnes, John. More Money for Your Retirement. 320p. 1980. pap. 4.95 o.p. (ISBN 0-686-61976-5, EH 514, EH). B&N NY.

Barnes, John E. & Waring, Alan J. Pocket Programmable Calculators in Biochemistry. LC 79-2547. 363p. 1980. 40.95x (ISBN 0-471-06434-3, Pub. by Wiley-Interscience); pap. 29.95 (ISBN 0-471-04713-9). Wiley.

Barnes, Johnathan. Aristotle. Thomas, Keith, ed. (Past Masters Ser.). 96p. 1983. pap. 3.95 (ISBN 0-19-287581-7, GB). Oxford U Pr.

Barnes, Jonathan. Aristotle. (Past Masters Ser.). 96p. 1982. 13.95 (ISBN 0-19-287582-5). Oxford U Pr.

--The Presocratic Philosophers. Rev. ed. (Arguments of the Philosophers Ser.). 680p. 1982. pap. text ed. 19.95 (ISBN 0-7100-9200-8). Routledge & Kegan.

Barnes, Jonathan, et al. Science & Speculation. LC 82-4221. (Studies in Hellinistic Theory & Practice). 352p. Date not set. 44.50 (ISBN 0-521-24689-X). Cambridge U Pr.

Barnes, Jonathan, et al, eds. Articles on Aristotle: Ethics & Politics, Vol. 2. LC 77-2064. 1979. 27.50 (ISBN 0-312-05478-5). St Martin.

--Articles on Aristotle: Vol. I: Metaphysics. LC 77-20604. 1979. 27.50 (ISBN 0-312-05479-3). St Martin.

--Articles on Aristotle: Vol. IV: Psychology & Aesthetics. LC 77-20604. 27.50 (ISBN 0-312-05480-7). St Martin.

Barnes, K. R. Optical Transfer Function. (Applied Optics Monographs: No. 3). 1971. 20.95 (ISBN 0-444-19592-0). Elsevier.

Barnes, Ken. The Crosby Years. (Illus.). 216p. 1980. 12.95 o.p. (ISBN 0-312-17663-5). St Martin.

Barnes, Leo & Feldman, Stephen. Handbook of Wealth Management. (Illus.). 1977. 59.95 (ISBN 0-07-003765-5, P&RB). McGraw.

Barnes, Linda J. Bitter Finish. 192p. 1983. 11.95 (ISBN 0-312-08236-3). St Martin.

Barnes, M. Oceanography & Marine Biology: An Annual Review, Vol. 20. (Illus.). 778p. 1982. 82.80 (ISBN 0-08-028460-4). Pergamon.

Barnes, Malcolm, tr. see Descola, Jean.

Barnes, Margaret A. Murder in Coweta County. 287p. 1983. Repr. of 1976 ed. 12.95 (ISBN 0-88289-419-6). Pelican.

Barnes, Margaret C. Brief Gaudy Hour. 336p. 1972. 6.95 (ISBN 0-8255-1520-3). Macrae.

--Isabel the Fair. 352p. 1972. 6.95 (ISBN 0-8255-1530-0). Macrae.

--My Lady of Cleves. 352p. 1972. 6.95 (ISBN 0-8255-1540-8). Macrae.

--The Passionate Brood. 300p. 1972. 6.95 (ISBN 0-8255-1542-4). Macrae.

--Tudor Rose. LC 53-7889. 1971. 6.95 (ISBN 0-8255-1533-5). Macrae.

--With All My Heart. 288p. 1973. 6.95 (ISBN 0-8255-1545-9). Macrae.

--Within the Hollow Crown. 360p. 1971. 6.95 (ISBN 0-8255-1547-5). Macrae.

Barnes, Marvin P. Computer-Assisted Mineral Appraisal & Feasibility. LC 79-52270. (Illus.). 167p. 1980. text ed. 33.00x (ISBN 0-89520-262-X). Soc Mining Eng.

Barnes, Mary. Is There a Chef in the Kitchen. (Illus., Orig.). 1969. pap. 8.50x (ISBN 0-392-06983-0, AUS68-2523, ABC). Sportshelf.

Barnes, Michael, jt. auth. see Ely, Vivian.

Barnes, Mildred. Girl's Basketball. rev. ed. LC 65-24381. (Athletic Institute Ser.). (Illus.). 144p. (gr. 5 up). 1975. 8.95 (ISBN 0-8069-4308-4); PLB 10.99 (ISBN 0-8069-4309-2). Sterling.

Barnes, Mildred, jt. ed. see Barnes, Virgil.

Barnes, N. Sue, jt. auth. see Curtis, Helena.

Barnes, Patience P., jt. auth. see Barnes, James J.

Barnes, Peter. The Bewitched. 1974. pap. 5.00x (ISBN 0-435-23062-X). Heinemann Ed.

Barnes, R. A. Fundamentals of Music: A Program for Self-Instruction. 1964. pap. text ed. 18.50 (ISBN 0-07-003771-X, C). McGraw.

Barnes, R. J. Economic Analysis: An Introduction. 412p. 1971. 12.95 o.p. (ISBN 0-408-70220-6); pap. 7.95 o.p. (ISBN 0-408-70233-8). Butterworth.

Barnes, R. J., jt. ed. see Johnson, T. B.

Barnes, R. P., jt. auth. see White, J. M.

Barnes, R. S. Coastal Lagoons. LC 80-40041. (Cambridge Studies in Modern Biology: No. 1). (Illus.). 130p. 1980. 32.50 (ISBN 0-521-23422-0); pap. 12.95 (ISBN 0-521-29945-4). Cambridge U Pr.

--Estuarine Biology. (Studies in Biology: No. 49). 80p. 1974. pap. text ed. 8.95 (ISBN 0-7131-2466-0). E Arnold.

Barnes, R. S. & Hughes, R. N. An Introduction to Marine Ecology. (Illus.). 234p. 1982. pap. text ed. 21.95 (ISBN 0-632-00892-X, B0536-9). Mosby.

Barnes, R. S., ed. The Coastline: A Contribution to Our Understanding of Its Ecology & Physiography in Relation to Land-Use & Management & the Pressures to Which It Is Subject. LC 76-51343. 356p. 1977. 55.95x (ISBN 0-471-99470-7, Pub. by Wiley-Interscience). Wiley.

--Estuarine Environment. Green, J. (Illus.). 1972. 26.75x (ISBN 0-85334-539-2, Pub. by Applied Sci England). Elsevier.

Barnes, Ralph M. Motion & Time Study: Design & Measurement of Work. 6th ed. LC 68-20097. 1968. 12.95 o.p. (ISBN 0-471-05350-3). Wiley.

--Motion & Time Study: Design & Measurement of Work. 7th ed. LC 80-173. 689p. 1980. text ed. 36.95x (ISBN 0-471-05905-6). Wiley.

Barnes, Richard. The Who: Maximum R&B. (Illus.). 168p. 1982. pap. 12.95 (ISBN 0-312-86989-4); 20 copy floor display 259.00 (ISBN 0-312-86990-8). St Martin.

Barnes, Richard, jt. auth. see Giffin, Kim.

Barnes, Richard, jt. auth. see Mabry, Edward.

Barnes, Richard, jt. auth. see Williams, George A.

Barnes, Richard E., jt. auth. see Mabry, Edward A.

Barnes, Robert M. Taming the Pits: A Technical Approach to Commodity Trading. LC 79-12107. 272p. 1979. 44.95x (ISBN 0-471-05795-9, Pub. by Wiley-Interscience). Wiley.

Barnes, Sam M., ed. Poems & Things. (Illus.). 1983. pap. price not set (ISBN 0-910257-00-0). Woodgreene Pr.

Barnes, Simon. China in Focus. (The "In Focus" Ser.). (Illus.). 64p. (Orig.). 1981. pap. 5.95 (ISBN 962-7031-12-7). C E Tuttle.

--Philippines in Focus. (The "In Focus" Ser.). (Illus.). 64p. (Orig.). 1981. pap. 5.95 (ISBN 0-686-42860-9). C E Tuttle.

--Singapore in Focus. (The "In Focus" Ser.). (Illus.). 64p. (Orig.). 1981. pap. 5.95 (ISBN 962-7031-11-9). C E Tuttle.

--Thailand in Focus. (The "In Focus" Ser.). (Illus.). 64p. (Orig.). 1983. pap. 5.95 (ISBN 962-7031-23-2). C E Tuttle.
Barnes, Thomas. Origin & Destiny of the Earth's Magnetic Field. LC 73-79065. (ICR Technical Monograph: No. 4). (Illus.). 64p. 1973. pap. 5.95 (ISBN 0-89051-013-X). CLP Pubs.
Barnes, Thomas G. Somerset, 1625-1640: A County's Government During the "Personal Rule". LC 82-11012. (Midway Reprint Ser.). xviii, 370p. 1982. pap. 21.00x (ISBN 0-226-03719-3). U of Chicago Pr.
Barnes, Thomas G. & Feldman, Gerald D., eds. Nationalism, Industrialization, & Democracy, 1815-1914: A Documentary History of Modern Europe, Vol. III. LC 80-5383. 331p. 1980. pap. text ed. 11.75 (ISBN 0-8191-1079-5). U Pr of Amer.
--Rationalism & Revolution Sixteen Sixty to Eighteen Fifteen, Vol. II. LC 79-66686. 1979. pap. text ed. 10.50 (ISBN 0-8191-0850-2). U Pr of Amer.
--Renaissance, Reformation, & Absolutism Fourteen Hundred to Sixteen Sixty, Vol. I. LC 79-66685. 1979. pap. text ed. 10.00 (ISBN 0-8191-0847-2). U Pr of Amer.
Barnes, V. E. Geologic Atlas of Texas: Amarillo Sheet, Leroy Thompson Patten Memorial Edition. 1969. 4.00 (ISBN 0-686-36619-0). Bur Econ Geology.
--Geologic Atlas of Texas: Austin Sheet, Francis Luther Whitney Memorial Edition. 1974. 4.00 (ISBN 0-686-36621-2). Bur Econ Geology.
Barnes, Virgil & Barnes, Mildred, eds. Tektites. LC 72-95942. (Benchmark Papers in Geology Ser). 400p. 1973. 55.50 (ISBN 0-12-786138-6). Acad Pr.
Barnes, W. Anderson. Downtown Development: Plan & Implementation. LC 82-60313. (Development Component Ser.). (Illus.). 32p. 1982. pap. 10.00 (ISBN 0-87420-608-1, D21). Urban Land.
Barnes, W. Emery. Gospel Criticism & Form Criticism. 83p. 1936. pap. text ed. 4.95 o.p. (ISBN 0-567-02020-7). Attic Pr.
Barnes, William. A Prose Anthology. Hearl, Trevor, ed. 384p. 1983. text ed. 21.00x (ISBN 0-85635-407-4, Pub. by Carcanet Pr England). Humanities.
--William Barnes: A Selection of Poems. Nye, Robert, ed. (Fyfield). 1979. 7.95 o.p. (ISBN 0-85635-031-1, Pub. by Carcanet New Pr England). Humanities.
Barnes-Ostrander, Marilyn. Music: Reflections in Sound. 1976. text ed. 18.50 scp o.p. (ISBN 0-06-383890-7, HarpC); instr. manual avail. o.p. (ISBN 0-06-371056-0). Har-Row.
Barness, Lewis. Advances in Pediatrics, Vol. 28. 1981. 49.50 (ISBN 0-8151-0500-2). Year Bk Med.
Barness, Lewis A., ed. Advances in Pediatrics, Vol. 29. 1982. 49.50 (ISBN 0-8151-0501-0). Year Bk Med.
Barness, Richard. Graystone College. LC 72-7654. (Adult & Young Adult Bks.). (Illus.). (gr. 9 up). 1973. PLB 5.95g (ISBN 0-8225-0753-6). Lerner Pubns.
--Listen to Me! LC 74-11901. (Books for Adults & Young Adults Ser.). 96p. (gr. 6 up). 1976. PLB 5.95g (ISBN 0-8225-0758-7). Lerner Pubns.
Barnet & Muller. Global Reach. 1976. 9.40 (ISBN 0-671-22104-3, Touchstone Bks). S&S.
Barnet, Richard. Real Security: Restoring American Power in a Dangerous Decade. 1981. 10.95 (ISBN 0-671-43172-2, Touchstone Bks); pap. 4.95 (ISBN 0-671-43166-8, Touchstone Bks). S&S.
--Roots of War. 1973. pap. 6.95 (ISBN 0-14-021698-7, Pelican). Penguin.
Barnet, Richard J. The Giants: Russia & America. 1977. 10.95 o.p. (ISBN 0-671-22741-6, Touchstone Bks); pap. 4.95 (ISBN 0-671-24403-5). S&S.
--Intervention & Revolution: The United States in the Third World. 1969. pap. 6.95 (ISBN 0-452-00610-4, F610, Mer). NAL.
--The Lean Years: Politics in the Age of Scarcity. 1982. pap. 6.95 (ISBN 0-671-43829-8, Touchstone Bks). S&S.
Barnet, Richard J. & Muller, Ronald E. Global Reach: The Power of the Multinational Corporations. LC 74-2794. 1975. 15.95 o.p. (ISBN 0-671-21835-2); pap. 7.95 o.p. (ISBN 0-671-22104-3). S&S.
Barnet, Sylvan. A Short Guide to Shakespeare. new ed. LC 73-13359. (Orig.). 1974. pap. 3.50 o.p. (ISBN 0-15-681800-0, HB268, Harv). HarBraceJ.
--A Short Guide to Writing About Art. (Orig.). 1981. pap. 5.95 (ISBN 0-316-08214-7). Little.
--A Short Guide to Writing About Literature. 4th ed. 282p. 1979. pap. text ed. 6.95 (ISBN 0-316-08159-0). Little.
Barnet, Sylvan & Stubbs, Marcia. Barnet & Stubbs's Practical Guide to Writing with Additional Readings. 3rd ed. 642p. 1980. pap. text ed. 11.95 o.p. (ISBN 0-316-08158-2); instructor's manual free o.p. (ISBN 0-316-08156-6). Little.
Barnet, Sylvan, ed. see Marlowe, Christopher.
Barnet, Sylvan, ed. see Shakespeare, William.
Barnet, Sylvan, et al. A Dictionary of Literary, Dramatic, & Cinematic Terms. 2nd ed. 124p. 1971. pap. 5.95 (ISBN 0-316-08194-9). Little.
Barnet, Sylvan, et al, eds. Eight Great Comedies: Clouds, Mandragola, Twelfth Night, Miser, Beggar's Opera, Importance of Being Earnest, Uncle Vanya, Arms & the Man. pap. 3.95 (ISBN 0-451-62191-3, ME2191, Ment). NAL.
--Eight Great Tragedies: Prometheus Bound, Oedipus the King, Hippolytus, King Lear, Ghosts, Miss Julie, On Bailles Strand, Desire Under the Elms. pap. 2.95 (ISBN 0-451-62074-7, ME2074, Ment). NAL.
--Genius of the Early English Theater: Abraham & Isaac, Second Shepherd's Play, Everyman, Doctor Faustus, Macbeth, Volpone, Samson Agonistes. 1962. pap. 3.95 (ISBN 0-451-62221-9, ME2221, Ment). NAL.
Barnett, jt. ed. see Barnett, Vic.
Barnett, A. & Bell, R. M. Rural Energy & the Third World: A Review of Social Science Research & Technology Policy Problems. (Illus.). 302p. 1982. 36.00 (ISBN 0-08-028953-3); 18.00 (ISBN 0-08-028954-1). Pergamon.
Barnett, A. & Pyle, L. Biogas Technology in the Third World: A Multidisciplinary Review. 132p. 1978. pap. 10.00 (ISBN 0-88936-162-2, IDRC103, IDRC). Unipub.
Barnett, A. Doak. Cadres, Bureaucracy, & Political Power in Communist China. LC 67-15895. (Studies of the East Asian Institute Ser.). 565p. 1967. 26.50x (ISBN 0-231-03035-5). Columbia U Pr.
--China & the Major Powers in East Asia. 1977. 24.95 (ISBN 0-8157-0824-6); pap. 9.95 (ISBN 0-8157-0823-8). Brookings.
--China Policy: Old Problems & New Challenges. LC 76-51538. 1977. 12.95 (ISBN 0-8157-0822-X); pap. 5.95 (ISBN 0-8157-0821-1). Brookings.
--Communist Economic Strategy: The Rise of Mainland China. LC 75-28661. (Economics of Competive Coexistence Ser). 106p. 1976. Repr. of 1959 ed. lib. bdg. 19.25x (ISBN 0-8371-8478-9, BACE). Greenwood.
--The FX Decision: Another Crucial Moment in U. S.-China-Taiwan Relations. LC 81-70778. (Studies in Defense Policy). 60p. 1981. pap. 5.9501151952x (ISBN 0-8157-0827-0). Brookings.
--U. S. Arms Sales: The China-Taiwan Tangle. LC 82-72117. (Studies in Defense Policy). 70p. 1982. pap. 5.95 (ISBN 0-8157-0829-7). Brookings.
Barnett, Alan W. Community Murals. LC 79-21552. (Illus.). 520p. 1983. 60.00. Art Alliance.
--Community Murals. LC 79-21552. (Illus.). 520p. 1983. 60.00 (ISBN 0-8453-4731-4). Cornwall Bks.
Barnett, Anthony. The Cambodian Revolutions. Date not set. cancelled o.p. (ISBN 0-8052-7065-5, Pub. by NLB). Schocken. Postponed.
Barnett, Correlli. The Desert Generals. LC 82-47957. (Illus.). 352p. 1983. 17.95x (ISBN 0-253-11600-7). Ind U Pr.
--The Great War. (Illus.). 1980. 19.95 o.p. (ISBN 0-399-12386-5). Putnam Pub Group.
Barnett, Dick. Inside Basketball. (Inside Sports Ser.). (Illus.). 96p. 1971. 7.95 (ISBN 0-8092-8861-3); PLB avail (ISBN 0-685-28676-2); pap. 6.95 (ISBN 0-8092-8860-5). Contemp Bks.
Barnett, Donald F. & Schorsch, Louis. Steel: Upheaval in a Basic Industry. 300p. 1983. prof ref 28.00x (ISBN 0-88410-397-8). Ballinger Pub.
Barnett, Eugene H. Programming Time-Shared Computers in BASIC. LC 72-175798. 366p. 1972. 27.95x (ISBN 0-471-05400-3, Pub. by Wiley-Interscience). Wiley.
Barnett, G. J., tr. see Moreau, J. J., et al.
Barnett, Gary L. A Manual for the Identification of Fish Bones. (Department of Prehistory Research School of Pacific Studies Technical Bulletin: No. 1). 60p. 1978. pap. text ed. 17.00 (ISBN 0-686-35910-0, Pub by ANUP Australia). Bks Australia.
Barnett, Gene A. Denis Johnston. (English Author Ser.). 1978. 14.95 (ISBN 0-8057-6701-0, Twayne). G K Hall.
Barnett, George L. Charles Lamb. (English Author Ser.). 1976. lib. bdg. 12.95 (ISBN 0-8057-6668-5, Twayne). G K Hall.
Barnett, H. J., et al, eds. Acetylsalicylic Acid: New Uses for an Old Drug. 295p. 1982. text ed. 43.00 (ISBN 0-89004-647-6). Raven.
Barnett, H. P., et al, eds. Cerebrovascular Diseases: New Trends in Surgical & Medical Aspects. (Symposium of the Giovanni Lorenzini Foundation: Vol. 12). 408p. 1981. 78.50 (ISBN 0-444-80381-5). Elsevier.
Barnett, H. Villiers, tr. see Massenet, Jules E.
Barnett, Henry L. see Walcher, Dwain N., et al.
Barnett, Herbert E. & Fraser, Hugh, eds. Who's Who in Canada 1980-81. 70th ed. (Illus.). 1496p. 1980. 75.00x o.p. (ISBN 0-8002-2744-1). Intl Pubns Serv.
Barnett, Hert E. & Fraser, Hugh, eds. Who's Who in Canada, 1982-83. LC 17-16282. (Illus.). 1608p. 1982. 75.00x (ISBN 0-919339-02-6). Intl Pubns Serv.
Barnett, J. A., et al. A Guide to Identifying & Classifying Yeasts. LC 79-11136. (Illus.). 1979. 90.00 (ISBN 0-521-22762-3). Cambridge U Pr.
Barnett, James. Backfire Is Hostile. LC 79-5164. 1979. 8.95 o.p. (ISBN 0-312-06481-0). St Martin.
Barnett, Jonathan, jt. auth. see Portman, John.
Barnett, Linda D. Bret Harte: A Reference Guide. 1980. lib. bdg. 38.00 (ISBN 0-8161-8197-7, Hall Reference). G K Hall.
Barnett, Louise K. Ignoble Savage: American Literary Racism, 1790-1890. LC 75-16964. (Contributions in American Studies: No. 18). 220p. 1975. lib. bdg. 25.00x (ISBN 0-8371-8281-6, BIG/). Greenwood.
Barnett, Louise K., jt. ed. see Jeannet, Angela M.
Barnett, M. E., jt. auth. see Klemperer, O. E.
Barnett, Marva T. Writing for Technicians. Rev. ed. LC 80-69550. (Technical Communications Ser.). 358p. 1982. pap. text ed. 11.00 (ISBN 0-8273-1867-7); instr's. guide 3.75 (ISBN 0-8273-1868-5). Delmar.
Barnett, Mary, ed. see Bernier, Olivier.
Barnett, Nancy B. & Baker, John T. Texas Instruments Compact Computer Forty User's Guide. 336p. (Orig.). 1983. pap. 14.95 (ISBN 0-89512-057-7). Tex Instr Inc.
Barnett, Naomi. I Know a Dentist. LC 77-24968. (Community Helper Bks.). (Illus.). (gr. k-4). 1978. PLB 4.29 o.p. (ISBN 0-399-61097-9). Putnam Pub Group.
Barnett, Pankhurst. A New Key to the Yeasts. LC 73-86076. 120p. 1974. 98.75 (ISBN 0-444-10580-8, North-Holland); pap. 11.00 o.p. (ISBN 0-444-10624-3). Elsevier.
Barnett, Peggy, jt. auth. see Spicer, Jerry.
Barnett, Peter, et al. Parenting Children of Divorce. LC 80-11044. (Workshop Models for Family Life Education Ser.). 111p. 1980. plastic comb 10.95 (ISBN 0-87304-178-X). Family Serv.
Barnett, R., jt. auth. see Baruch, G.
Barnett, Randy & Hagel, John, eds. Assessing the Criminal: Restitution, Retribution & the Legal Process. LC 77-21388. 432p. 1977. prof ref 25.00x (ISBN 0-88410-785-X). Ballinger Pub.
Barnett, Raymond. Analytic Trigonometry with Applications. 2nd ed. 1980. pap. text ed. 21.95x (ISBN 0-534-00728-7). Wadsworth Pub.
Barnett, Raymond A. College Algebra. 2nd ed. (Illus.). 1979. text ed. 21.00 (ISBN 0-07-003778-7, C); ans. manual 9.95 (ISBN 0-07-003779-5); tests 15.00 (ISBN 0-07-003784-1). McGraw.
--College Algebra. 1975. text ed. 13.95 o.p. (ISBN 0-07-003764-7, C). McGraw.
--College Algebra with Trigonometry. 2nd ed. (Illus.). 1979. text ed. 22.95 (ISBN 0-07-003809-0, C); answer manual 9.95 (ISBN 0-07-003810-4); tests 13.95 (ISBN 0-07-003813-9). McGraw.
--Elementary Algebra: Structure & Use. 2nd ed. (Illus.). 352p. 1975. text ed. 19.95 (ISBN 0-07-003781-7, C). McGraw.
--Essentials of Algebra for College Students. 1976. text ed. 21.00 (ISBN 0-07-003756-6, C); instructor's manual 7.95 (ISBN 0-07-003757-4). McGraw.
--Intermediate Algebra. 2nd ed. (Illus.). 1980. text ed. 22.00 (ISBN 0-07-003750-7). McGraw.
--Intermediate Algebra: Structure & Use. 1971. text ed. 15.50 o.p. (ISBN 0-07-003786-8, C); instructors' manual 3.95 o.p. (ISBN 0-07-003795-7). McGraw.
Barnett, Raymond A. & Burke, Charles J. Applied Mathematics for Business & Economics, Life Sciences & Social Sciences. (Illus.). 1983. text ed. 27.95 (ISBN 0-89517-049-3). Dellen Pub.
Barnett, Regina R. Create, One. 31p. (Orig.). (ps). 1978. pap. text ed. 4.95 student work pad (ISBN 0-697-01678-1); tchrs.' manual 10.75 (ISBN 0-697-01677-3). Wm C Brown.
--Create, Two. 31p. (Orig.). (ps). 1979. pap. text ed. 4.95 student work pad (ISBN 0-697-01705-2); tchrs.' manual 10.75 (ISBN 0-697-01706-0). Wm C Brown.
--Let Out the Sunshine. 144p. (Orig.). 1981. pap. text ed. 12.00 (ISBN 0-697-01762-1). Wm C Brown.
Barnett, Richard B. North India Between Empires: Awadh, the Mughals, & the British, 1720-1801. LC 78-64459. (Center for South & Southeast Asian Studies). 294p. 1980. 30.00x (ISBN 0-520-03787-1). U of Cal Pr.
Barnett, Robert M. Analysis, Computation, Presentation of Engineering Information. 8.50 (ISBN 0-89741-000-9); pap. 5.00 (ISBN 0-686-96874-3). Roadrunner Tech.
Barnett, Rosalind & Baruch, Grace K. The Competent Woman: Perspectives on Development. (Social Relations Ser.). 1978. 12.95X (ISBN 0-470-26424-1). Halsted Pr.
Barnett, S. A., ed. Lessons from the Animal Behavior for the Clinician. (Clinics in Developmental Medicine Ser.: Vol. 7). 53p. 1962. text ed. 4.00 (ISBN 0-686-97932-X, Pub. by Spastics Intl England). Lippincott.
Barnett, Snowdon. Last Entry. 1982. pap. 8.95 (ISBN 0-85362-194-2). Routledge & Kegan.
Barnett, Stephen. Introduction to Mathematical Control Theory. (Oxford Applied Mathematics & Engineering Sciences Ser). (Illus.). 280p. 1975. 27.50x o.p. (ISBN 0-19-859618-9); pap. 18.95x. Oxford U Pr.
--Matrices in Control Theory. rev. ed. 236p. 1984. lib. bdg. price not set (ISBN 0-89874-590-X). Krieger.
--Matrix Methods for Engineers & Scientists. 185p. 1979. pap. text ed. 11.95 (ISBN 0-07-084084-9, C). McGraw.
Barnett, Ursula A. Ezekiel Mphahlele. (World Authors Ser). 1976. lib. bdg. 15.95 (ISBN 0-8057-6257-4, Twayne). G K Hall.
Barnett, V. Comparative Statistical Inference. LC 73-1833. (Probability & Mathematical Statistics Ser.: Probability Section). 287p. 1973. 46.95x (ISBN 0-471-05401-1, Pub. by Wiley-Interscience). Wiley.
Barnett, Vic. Comparative Statistical Inference. 2nd ed. (Probability & Mathematical Statistics Ser.: Applied Probability & Statistics Section). 344p. 1982. 38.00x (ISBN 0-471-10076-5, Pub. by Wiley Interscience). Wiley.
Barnett, Vic & Lewis, Toby. Outliers in Statistical Data. LC 77-21024. (Probability & Mathematical Statistics Ser.: Applied Section). 365p. 1978. 69.95x (ISBN 0-471-99599-1, Pub. by Wiley-Interscience). Wiley.
Barnett, Vic & Barnett, eds. Interpreting Multivariate Data: Proceedings. (Wiley Ser. in Probability & Mathematical Statistics - Applied Probability & Statistics Section). 374p. 1982. 54.95x (ISBN 0-471-28039-9, Pub. by Wiley-Interscience). Wiley.
Barnett, Vivian E. The Guggenheim Museum: Justin K. Thannhauser Collection. new ed. LC 78-66357. (Illus.). 1978. 24.50 (ISBN 0-89207-016-1); pap. 15.50 o.p. (ISBN 0-685-91431-3). S R Guggenheim.
Barnett, W. A. Consumer Demand & Labor Supply: Goods, Monetary Assets & Time. (Studies in Mathematical & Managerial Economics: Vol. 29). 1981. 66.00 (ISBN 0-444-86097-5). Elsevier.
Barnett, Walter. Homosexuality & the Bible: An Interpretation. LC 79-84920. 1979. pap. 1.50 o.p. (ISBN 0-87574-226-2). Pendle Hill.
Barnett, Walter E. Sexual Freedom & the Constitution. LC 72-94661. 333p. 1973. 12.95x o.p. (ISBN 0-8263-0255-6). U of NM Pr.
Barnett, Winston & Winskell, Cyril. A Study in Conservation. 1978. 14.00 (ISBN 0-85362-168-3, Oriel); pap. 8.95 (ISBN 0-85362-172-1). Routledge & Kegan.
Barnette, David W. Map Coloring, Polyhedra & the Four-Color Problem. (Dolciani Mathematical Expositions Ser.: Vol. 8). Date not set. pap. price not set (ISBN 0-88385-309-4). Math Assn.
Barnett-Mizrahi, Carol, jt. ed. see Trueba, Henry T.
Barnewall, Gordon G. Succeed as a Job Applicant. LC 75-18877. (Career Guidance Ser.). 160p. (YA) 1976. pap. 4.50 (ISBN 0-668-03861-6). Arco.
Barney, C. W., jt. auth. see Goor, A. Y.
Barney, Frances. Summer of Awakening. (YA) 1979. 6.95 (ISBN 0-685-93879-4, Avalon). Bouregy.
Barney, G. C. & Dos Santos, S. M. Lift (Elevator) Traffic Analysis, Design & Control. (IEE Control Engineering Ser.: No. 2). (Illus.). 331p. 1977. casebound 53.25 (ISBN 0-901223-86-7). Inst Elect Eng.
Barney, Gerald O. Entering the 21st Century, 2 vols. Incl. Vol. 1. Summary Report. 20.00 (ISBN 0-08-024617-6); pap. 7.50 (ISBN 0-08-024616-8); Vol. 2. Technical Supplement. 40.00 (ISBN 0-08-024618-4). (Pergamon Policy Studies). 1981. Set. 50.00 (ISBN 0-08-024626-5). Pergamon.
Barney, Gerald O., ed. The Global Two Thousand Report to the President of the U. S.-Entering the 21st Century: The Summary Report--Special Edition with Environment Projections & the Government's Global Model, Vol. 1. (Pergamon Policy Studies Ser.). 200p. 1981. 30.00 (ISBN 0-08-024617-6); pap. 10.95 (ISBN 0-08-024616-8). Pergamon.
--The Unfinished Agenda. LC 76-30486. 1977. 8.95 o.p. (ISBN 0-690-01481-3, TYC-T); pap. 3.95i (ISBN 0-690-01482-1). T Y Crowell.
Barney, Kenneth D. Directions, Please. LC 82-82080. 108p. (Orig.). 1983. pap. 2.50 (ISBN 0-88243-856-5, 02-0856); tchr's. ed. 3.95 (ISBN 0-88243-197-8, 32-0197). Gospel Pub.
--Mais Croyez Donc! 1981. 2.00 (ISBN 0-8297-1052-3). Life Pubs Intl.
Barney, Philip L. Pathology of the Nose & Paranasal Sinuses. LC 82-720085. (Atlases of the Pathology of the Head & Neck Ser.). 1982. includes slides 100.00 (ISBN 0-89189-082-3, 15102900). Am Soc Clinical.
Barney, William L. Flawed Victory: A New Perspective on the Civil War. LC 80-68972. 225p. 1980. lib. bdg. 21.50 (ISBN 0-8191-1273-9); pap. text ed. 9.50 (ISBN 0-8191-1274-7). U Pr of Amer.
Barnhardt, Marion I., jt. auth. see Lusher, Jeanne M.
Barnhart, Clarence L., ed. The World Book Dictionary, 2 vols. rev. ed. Barnhart, Robert K. LC 79-53618. (Illus.). (gr. 4-12). 1980. Set. PLB write for info. o.p. (ISBN 0-7166-0280-6). World Bk.
Barnhart, Clarence L. & Barnhart, Robert K., eds. The World Book Dictionary, 2 vols. LC 80-2556. 2554p. (gr. 4-12). 1981. write for info. o.p. (ISBN 0-7166-0281-4). World-Bk.
--The World Book Dictionary, 2 vols. LC 81-43325. (Illus.). 2554p. (gr. 4-12). 1982. Set. PLB write for info. o.p. (ISBN 0-7166-0282-2). World Bk.
--The World Book Dictionary, 2 vols. LC 78-66881. (Illus.). 1979. write for info. o.p. (ISBN 0-7166-0279-2). World Bk.
--The World Book Dictionary, 2 Vols. LC 82-45610. (Illus.). 2554p. (gr. 4-12). 1983. lib. bdg. write for info. (ISBN 0-7166-0283-0). World Bk.
Barnhart, Helene S. Writing Romance Fiction-For Love & Money. 256p. 1983. 14.95 (ISBN 0-89879-105-7). Writers Digest.
Barnhart, Marion I., jt. ed. see Lusher, Jeanne M.
Barnhart, Robert K. see Barnhart, Clarence L.
Barnhart, Robert K., jt. ed. see Barnhart, Clarence L.
Barnhart, Russell, tr. see Villiod, Eugene.

Barnhart, Russell T. Gamblers of Yesteryear. LC 82-83031. (Illus.). 280p. (Orig.). 1983. pap. 14.95 (ISBN 0-89650-708-4). Gamblers.

Barnhart, Sarah A. Introduction to Interpersonal Communication. 1976. pap. text ed. 8.50 scp o.p. (ISBN 0-690-00855-4, HarpC). Har-Row.

Barnhill, Laurence, jt. ed. see Hansen, James C.

Barnhouse, Margaret N. That Man Barnhouse. 1983. pap. 7.95 (ISBN 0-8423-7033-1). Tyndale.

Barnouw. Plaid for Cultural Anthropology. rev. ed. 1978. 4.95 (ISBN 0-256-02100-7). Dow Jones-Irwin.

Barnouw, Adriaan J. & Wohlrabe, Raymond A. Land & People of Holland. rev. ed. LC 79-37249. (Ports. of the Nations Ser.). (Illus.). (gr. 6 up). 1972. PLB 9.89 (ISBN 0-397-31254-7, JBL-J). Har-Row.

Barnouw, Erik. Documentary: A History of the Non-Fiction Film. (Illus.). 1974. 19.95 (ISBN 0-19-501835-4). Oxford U Pr.

--Documentary: A History of the Non-Fiction Film. rev. ed. (Illus.). 368p. 1983. pap. 8.95 (ISBN 0-19-503301-9, GB 451, GB). Oxford U Pr.

--The Magician & the Cinema. (Illus.). 138p. 1981. 14.95 (ISBN 0-19-502918-6). Oxford U Pr.

--The Sponsor: Notes on a Modern Potentate. (Illus.). 1979. pap. 5.95 (ISBN 0-19-502614-4, GB 580, GB). Oxford U Pr.

--Tube of Plenty: The Evolution of American Television. LC 75-7362. (Illus.). 1977. pap. 7.95 o.p. (ISBN 0-19-502180-0, 481, GB). Oxford U Pr.

Barnouw, Erik & Krishnaswamy, S. Indian Film. 2nd ed. (Illus.). 1980. 16.95 (ISBN 0-19-502682-9, GB 592, GB); pap. 8.95 (ISBN 0-19-502683-7). Oxford U Pr.

Barnouw, Victor. Anthropology: A General Introduction. 1979. 21.95x (ISBN 0-256-02113-9); text ed. 3.50x study guide (ISBN 0-686-96704-6). Dorsey.

--An Introduction to Anthropology, 2 vols. 4th ed. 1982. pap. 15.50x Vol. 1 (ISBN 0-256-02658-0); pap. 15.50x Vol. 2 (ISBN 0-256-02659-9). Dorsey.

--Wisconsin Chippewa Myths & Tales & Their Relation to Chippewa Life. LC 76-53647. 304p. 1977. 25.00 (ISBN 0-299-07310-6); pap. 9.95 (ISBN 0-299-07314-9). U of Wis Pr.

Barns, Florence E. Texas Writers of Today. LC 70-157491. Repr. of 1935 ed. 47.00x (ISBN 0-685-44091-5). Gale.

Barns, R. E. The Answer Is One, the First One. (Illus.). (gr. 2-12). 1977. wkbk. 6.95 (ISBN 0-88488-068-0). Creative Pubns.

--The Answer Is One, the Third One. (gr. 2-12). 1977. wkbk. 6.95 (ISBN 0-88488-070-2). Creative Pubns.

Barns, R. E. & Eral, Bill. The Answer Is One, the Second One. (gr. 2-12). 1977. wkbk. 6.95 (ISBN 0-88488-069-9). Creative Pubns.

Barns, Robert E. Tangle Table. 1973. pap. 7.95 wkbk. cancelled (ISBN 0-88488-022-2). Creative Pubns.

Barnsley, Pam, et al. Hiking Trails of the Sunshine Coast. (Illus.). 1979. pap. 5.95 (ISBN 0-913140-41-4). Signpost Bk Pub.

Barnstead, John, tr. see Kuzmin, Mikhail.

Barnstone, Aliki & Barnstone, Willis. A Book of Women Poets, Book of Puzzlements: From Antiquity to Now. 640p. (Orig.). 1981. 29.95 (ISBN 0-8052-3693-7); pap. 11.95 (ISBN 0-8052-0680-9). Schocken.

Barnstone, Willis. The Poetics of Ecstasy. 320p. 1983. text ed. cancelled (ISBN 0-8419-0814-1); pap. text ed. 19.50x (ISBN 0-8419-0849-4). Holmes & Meier.

Barnstone, Willis, jt. auth. see Barnstone, Aliki.

Barnstone, Willis, tr. from Span. The Dream Below the Sun: Selected Poems of Antonio Machado. rev., enl ed. LC 80-28613. (Illus.). 176p. (Span., Eng.). 1981. 16.95 (ISBN 0-89594-048-5); pap. 7.95 (ISBN 0-89594-047-7). Crossing Pr.

Barnstone, Willis, tr. see Aleixandre, Vicente.

Barnstone, Willis, tr. see De Leon, Fray L.

Barnum, H. L. The Spy Unmasked: Or, the Memoirs of Enoch Crosby, Alias Harvey Birch, the Hero of James Fenimore Cooper's "the Spy". facsimile ed. LC 75-29452. (Illus.). 264p. 1975. Repr. of 1828 ed. 11.50 (ISBN 0-916346-15-3). Harbor Hill Bks.

Barnum, Marrin R. Human Form & Function: A Health Science. LC 78-23374. 1979. 23.50x (ISBN 0-673-16247-8); study guide avail. (ISBN 0-673-16248-6). Scott F.

Barnum, Marvin R., et al. Audio-Tutorial Introductory Biology: Principles. rev. ed. (Illus., Orig.). 1969. text ed. 6.95x o.p. (ISBN 0-02-473600-7, 47360); tapes 433.95 o.p. (ISBN 0-02-473580-9, 47358); tape script 7.95 o.p. (ISBN 0-02-473610-4, 47361). Macmillan.

Barnum, Phineas T. Humbugs of the World. LC 68-21755. 1970. Repr. of 1865 ed. 30.00x (ISBN 0-8103-3580-8). Gale.

Barnum, Priscilla H., ed. Dives & Pauper, Vol. I, Pt. 2. (Early English Text Society Original Ser.). (Illus.). 1980. 29.50x (ISBN 0-19-722282-X). Oxford U Pr.

Barnwell. Writing for a Reason. 1983. pap. text ed. 12.95 (ISBN 0-686-84569-2, RM86); instr's manual avail. (RM87). HM.

Barnwell, H. T. The Tragic Drama of Corneille & Racine: An Old Parallel Revisited. 1982. 42.00x (ISBN 0-19-815779-7). Oxford U Pr.

Barnwell, William. Writing for a Reason. LC 82-83174. 432p. 1983. pap. text ed. 12.95 (ISBN 0-395-32597-8); write for info. instr's. manual (ISBN 0-395-32598-6). HM.

Baro, Gene. Twenty-Second National Print Exhibition. (Illus.). 100p. 1981. pap. 6.95 (ISBN 0-87273-084-0). Bklyn Mus.

Baro, Gene, ed. Famous American Poets. (Pocket Poet Ser.). 1962. pap. 1.25 (ISBN 0-8023-9038-2). Dufour.

Barocas, Claudie. Egypt. LC 70-179259. (Monuments of Civilization Ser). (Illus.). 192p. 1972. 25.00 (ISBN 0-448-02018-1, G&D). Putnam Pub Group.

Barocci, Thomas A. Non-Profit Hospitals: Their Structure, Human Resources, & Economic Importance. LC 80-22075. 256p. 1981. 21.00 (ISBN 0-86569-054-5). Auburn Hse.

Barocio, Ernesto. Bosquejos de Sermones Selectos. 144p. pap. 5.25 (ISBN 0-311-43039-2). Casa Bautista.

Barocio, Ernesto, tr. see Broadus, J. A.

Barocio, Teofilo, tr. see Vedder, Enrique C.

Barofsky, I. & Budson, R. D., eds. The Chronic Psychiatric Patient in the Community: Principles of Treatment. 400p. 1983. text ed. 49.95 (ISBN 0-89335-164-4). SP Med & Sci Bks.

Baroja. Las Inquietudes de Shanti Andia. (Easy Reader, B). 1973. pap. 3.95 (ISBN 0-88436-062-8, 70265). EMC.

Baroja, Julio C. The World of Witches. Glendinning, O. N., tr. LC 64-15829. (Nature of Human Society Ser.). xiv, 314p. 1973. pap. 10.00x (ISBN 0-226-03763-0, P497, Phoen). U of Chicago Pr.

Barokas, Bernard. Alexander's Battle. LC 79-65862. (Children's Art Ser.). PLB 11.96 (ISBN 0-382-06328-7). Silver.

Baron. Essentials of Clinical Biochemistry. 1982. 26.95 (ISBN 0-444-00684-2). Elsevier.

Baron, Alvin. Bud's Easy Term Paper Typing Kit. 4th ed. 6p. (gr. 9-12). 1980. pap. text ed. 1.98 (ISBN 0-9609436-0-9). Lawrence Hse.

Baron, Bonnie D., ed. Bibliography of Books for Children. rev. ed. LC 42-21946. Repr. 3.75x o.p. (ISBN 0-87173-079-0). ACEI.

Baron, Carl E., ed. A Memoir of D. H. Lawrence: The Betrayal by G. H. Neville. LC 81-7656. (Illus.). 200p. 1982. 37.50 (ISBN 0-521-24097-2). Cambridge U Pr.

Baron, David. Israel in the Plan of God. 320p. 1983. 12.95 (ISBN 0-8254-2241-8). Kregel.

--Types, Psalms & Prophecies. 1981. lib. bdg. 14.00 (ISBN 0-86524-077-9, 9511). Klock & Klock.

Baron, David P., ed. The Export-Import Bank: An Economic Analysis. (Mathematical Economics, Econometrics & Economic Theory Monograph). Date not set. price not set (ISBN 0-12-079080-7). Acad Pr.

Baron, Dennis E. Going Native: The Regeneration of Saxon English. (Publications of the American Dialect Society (PADS): No. 69). 63p. (Orig.). 1982. pap. text ed. 4.80 (ISBN 0-8173-0011-2). U of Ala Pr.

Baron, Hans. From Petrarch to Leonardo Bruni: Studies in Humanistic & Political Literature. LC 68-16686. 1968. 12.00x o.s.i. (ISBN 0-226-03801-7); pap. 3.25 (ISBN 0-226-03802-5). U of Chicago Pr.

Baron, Henrietta. Everybody Can Cook: Techniques for the Handicapped, Vol. 1: Breakfast. LC 74-84845. (Illus.). 1977. pap. 10.50x tchr's manual o.p. (ISBN 0-87562-041-8); pap. 5.00x student manual o.p. (ISBN 0-87562-042-6). Spec Child.

Baron, Howard C. & Gorin, Edward. Varicose Veins: A Commonsense Approach to Their Management. LC 78-31727. 160p. 1980. pap. 4.95 (ISBN 0-688-08459-1). Quill NY.

Baron, J. H. & Moody, F., eds. BIMR Gastroenterology: Foregut, Vol. 1. (Butterworth International Medical Reviews). 1981. text ed. 49.95 (ISBN 0-407-02287-2). Butterworth.

Baron, J. W. Blaze. 192p. (Orig.). 1983. pap. 2.25 (ISBN 0-523-41745-4). Pinnacle Bks.

Baron, Joan. Cat Couples. LC 82-48798. 160p. (Orig.). 1983. pap. 9.57i (ISBN 0-06-090986-2, CN 986, CN). Har-Row.

Baron, John, compiled by. Piano Music from New Orleans Eighteen Fifty-One to Eighteen Ninety-Eight. (Music Reprint Ser.). (Illus.). 194p. 1980. Repr. lib. bdg. 25.00 (ISBN 0-306-76034-7). Da Capo.

Baron, Judith P. Radiologic Technologists: A Study Guide. (Illus.). 560p. 1978. 8.95x (ISBN 0-398-03726-4). C C Thomas.

Baron, Mary. Letters for the New England Dead. Schreiber, Jan, ed. LC 73-84885. (Chapbook Series One). 32p. 1974. 5.00 (ISBN 0-87923-083-5). Godine.

Baron, Mary, jt. auth. see Richardson, H. D.

Baron, Michael. Water & Plant Life. 1967. pap. text ed. 5.95x o.p. (ISBN 0-435-61054-6). Heinemann Ed.

Baron, N. S. Language Acquisition & Historical Change. (North-Holland Linguistic Ser: Vol. 36). 1978. 53.25 (ISBN 0-444-85077-5, North-Holland). Elsevier.

Baron, Nancy. Getting Started in Calligraphy. LC 78-66311. (Illus.). (gr. 7 up). 1979. 14.95 (ISBN 0-8069-5392-6); spiral bdg. 8.95 (ISBN 0-8069-8840-1); PLB 17.79 (ISBN 0-8069-5393-4). Sterling.

Baron, Paul B. When the Company Is for Sale. LC 80-66938. 396p. 1980. three ring binder 85.00 o.p. (ISBN 0-936936-50-9). Ctr Busn Info.

Baron, Richard, et al. Raid: The Untold Story of Patton's Secret Mission. 288p. 1981. 12.95 (ISBN 0-399-12597-3). Putnam Pub Group.

Baron, Robert E., et al. Chemical Equilibria in Carbon-Hydrogen-Oxygen Systems. LC 75-44374. (Energy Laboratory Ser.). 120p. 1976. 20.00x (ISBN 0-262-02121-8). MIT Pr.

Baron, W. M. Organization in Plants. 3rd ed. LC 78-12085. 1979. pap. 27.95x (ISBN 0-470-26558-2). Halsted Pr.

Baron, William, jt. auth. see Perloff, William H.

Barondess, J. A. Diagnostic Approaches to Presenting Syndromes. LC 77-141764. 557p. 1971. 32.50 (ISBN 0-683-00418-2, Pub. by Williams & Wilkins). Krieger.

Barone, Antonio & Paterno, Gianfranco. The Physics & Applications of the Josephson Effect. 529p. 1982. 49.50x (ISBN 0-471-01469-9, Pub. by Wiley-Interscience). Wiley.

Barone, Michael, et al. Almanac of American Politics - 1972. LC 70-160417. (Illus.). 1972. 12.95 (ISBN 0-87645-053-2); pap. 4.95 (ISBN 0-87645-056-7). Gambit.

Barone, Steve. Aztec Uprising. (Illus.). 1975. 7.95 (ISBN 0-89325-000-7). Joyce Pr.

Barone, Steve, ed. see Sinor, John.

Barongo, Yolamu. Political Science in Africa. 272p. 1983. cancelled 26.95 (ISBN 0-86232-033-X, Pub. by Zed Pr England); pap. 11.50 (ISBN 0-86232-034-8, Pub. by Zed Pr England). Lawrence Hill.

Baroni, T. J. A Revision of the Genus Rhodocybe Maire (Agaricales) rev. ed. (Nova Hedwigia Beiheft). (Illus.). 300p. 1981. text ed. 48.00x (ISBN 3-7682-5467-4). Lubrecht & Cramer.

--A Revision of the Genus Rhodocybe Maire: Agaricales. (Nova Hedwigia Beiheft: No. 67). (Illus.). 300p. 1981. lib. bdg. 48.00x (ISBN 3-7682-5467-4). Lubrecht & Cramer.

Baronian, Hagop. The Perils of Politeness. Antreassian, Jack, tr. from Armenian. (Illus.). 160p. (Orig.). 1983. pap. 7.50 (ISBN 0-935102-10-8). Ashod Pr.

Baron Von Mullenheim-Rechberg, Burkhard. Battleship Bismarck: A Survivor's Story. LC 80-81093. 284p. 1980. 17.95 (ISBN 0-87021-096-3). Naval Inst Pr.

Barquero, J. A. Estampas Espanolas. (Span.). 10.50 (ISBN 84-241-5632-3). E Torres & Sons.

Barr, Alfred H., Jr. Matisse: His Art & His Public. rev. & enl. ed. LC 74-81656. (Illus.). 592p. 1974. pap. 14.95 (ISBN 0-87070-469-9). Museum Mod Art.

Barr, Allan. A Diagram of Synoptic Relationships. Repr. of 1938 ed. text ed. 12.95x o.p. (ISBN 0-567-02021-5). Attic Pr.

Barr, Alwyn & Calvert, Robert A. Black Leaders: Texans for their Times. 11.95 (ISBN 0-87611-055-3); pap. 8.95 (ISBN 0-87611-056-1). Tex St Hist Assn.

Barr, Amelia. Remember the Alamo. 1979. lib. bdg. 9.95 (ISBN 0-8398-2579-X, Gregg). G K Hall.

Barr, Andrew M. Master Guide to High-Income Real Estate Selling. 1974. pap. text ed. 11.95 (ISBN 0-13-560011-1). Exec Reports.

Barr, Bonnie & Leyden, Michael. Life Science. (gr. 7-8). 1980. text ed. 17.56 (ISBN 0-201-00312-0, Sch Div); tchrs'. materials 21.28 (ISBN 0-201-00313-9, Sch Div). A-W.

Barr, Charles. Ealing Studios. LC 79-15033. (Illus.). 200p. 1980. 19.95 (ISBN 0-87951-101-X). Overlook Pr.

Barr, Claude A. Jewels of the Plains: Wild Flowers of the Great Plains Grasslands & Hills. LC 82-13691. 256p. 1983. 19.95 (ISBN 0-8166-1127-0). U of Minn Pr.

Barr, Donald. Atomic Energy. (How & Why Wonder Bks.). (gr. 4-6). deluxe ed. 1.95 o.p. (ISBN 0-448-04012-3, G&D). Putnam Pub Group.

Barr, Donald R. & Zehna, Peter W. Probability: Modeling Uncertainty. (Illus.). 480p. Date not set. text ed. price not set (ISBN 0-201-10798-8). A-W.

Barr, George. Entertaining with Number Tricks. (Illus.). (gr. 4-6). 1971. PLB 7.95 o.p. (ISBN 0-07-003842-2, GB). McGraw.

--Research Ideas for Young Scientists. (gr. 5 up). 1958. PLB 6.50 o.p. (ISBN 0-07-003803-1, GB). McGraw.

Barr, James. The Bible in the Modern World. (Student Christian Movement Press). (Orig.). 1981. pap. 7.95x (ISBN 0-19-520305-4). Oxford U Pr.

--Holy Scripture: Canon Authority, Criticism. LC 82-20123. 192p. 1983. 18.95 (ISBN 0-664-21395-2); pap. 9.95 (ISBN 0-664-24477-7). Westminster.

Barr, Jean, et al. Standards for Clinical Education in Physical Therapy. 1981. pap. 5.00 (ISBN 0-912452-33-1). Am Phys Therapy Assn.

Barr, Jene. Good Morning, Teacher. rev. ed. LC 57-7754. (Career Awareness-Community Helpers Ser.). (Illus.). (gr. k-2). 1966. 5.25g o.p. (ISBN 0-8075-2991-5). A Whitman.

Barr, Jene, jt. auth. see Antonacci, Robert J.

Barr, Jennifer. Within a Dark Wood. LC 79-6976. 1979. 10.95 o.p. (ISBN 0-385-15228-0). Doubleday.

Barr, Justin, et al. Hellinger's Law. (Orig.). pap. 2.25 o.s.i. (ISBN 0-515-05809-2). Jove Pubns.

Barr, Larry, jt. auth. see McMullen, Haynes.

Barr, M. E. Diaporthales in North America with Emphasis on Gnomonia & Its Segregates. (Mycologia Memoirs: No. 7). (Illus.). 1977. lib. bdg. 32.00 (ISBN 3-7682-1189-4). Lubrecht & Cramer.

Barr, Mary & D'Aroy, Pat, eds. What's Going On? Language Learning Episode in British & American Classroom, Grades 4-13. LC 81-18119. (Illus.). 240p. 1981. pap. text ed. 9.00 (ISBN 0-86709-013-8). Boynton Cook Pubs.

Barr, Murray L. & Kiernan, John A. The Human Nervous System: An Anatomical Viewpoint. 4th ed. 1983. pap. text ed. price not set (ISBN 0-06-140311-3, Harper Medical). Lippincott.

Barr, N. R. The Hand: Principles & Techniques of Simple Splint Making in Rehabilitation. 1975. pap. 15.95 (ISBN 0-407-00010-0). Butterworth.

Barr, Pat. Jade: A Novel of China. 640p. 1982. 14.95 (ISBN 0-312-43943-1). St Martin.

--Japan. (Illus.). 160p. 1980. 22.50 (ISBN 0-7134-0578-3, Pub. by Batsford England). David & Charles.

--Taming the Jungle in British Malaya. 1977. 12.50 (ISBN 0-436-03365-8, Pub. by Secker & Warburg). David & Charles.

Barr, Pauline, et al. Advanced Reading Skills. (English As a Second Language Bk.). 1981. pap. text ed. 6.95x (ISBN 0-582-55904-9). Longman.

Barr, Robert see Lodge, James P., Jr.

Barr, Robert D., et al. Defining the Social Studies. LC 77-85192. (Bulletin Ser.: No. 51). (Illus.). 1977. pap. 7.25 (ISBN 0-87986-012-X, 498-15260). Coun Soc Studies.

Barr, Robert R., tr. see Buhlmann, Walbert.

Barr, Robert R., tr. see Carretto, Carlo.

Barr, Robert R., tr. see Esquivel, Adolfo P.

Barr, Robert R., tr. see Gutierrez, Gustavo.

Barr, Robert S., jt. auth. see Blecher, Melvin.

Barr, Stephen. Experiments in Topology. LC 64-10866. (Illus.). (gr. 7 up). 1964. 10.95 (ISBN 0-690-27862-4, TYC-J). Har-Row.

--Miscellany of Puzzles: Mathematical & Otherwise. LC 65-14905. (Illus.). (gr. 6 up). 1965. 10.95 (ISBN 0-690-54419-7, TYC-J). Har-Row.

Barr, Stringfellow. Three Worlds of Man. LC 63-9943. 104p. 1963. 5.00x (ISBN 0-8262-0019-2). U of Mo Pr.

Barr, Ted. Barr on Backgammon. (Illus.). 208p. 1981. text ed. 9.95 o.p. (ISBN 0-916076-52-0). Writing.

--Gambling Times Guide to Backgammon. (Illus., Orig.). 1983. pap. text ed. 5.95 (ISBN 0-89746-006-5). Gambling Times.

--Gambling Times Guide to Gambling Junkets. (Illus., Orig.). 1983. pap. text ed. cancelled (ISBN 0-89746-006-5). Gambling Times.

Barra, Donald. The Dynamic Performance: A Performer's Guide to Musical Expression & Interpretation. (Illus.). 192p. 1983. 16.95 (ISBN 0-13-221556-X). P-H.

Barracato, John S. Arson: How Can it be Curbed? (Vital Issues Ser.: Vol. XXXI, No. 1). 0.80 (ISBN 0-686-84133-6). Ctr Info Am.

Barraclough, Geoffrey. Factors in German History. LC 78-21483. (Illus.). 1979. Repr. of 1946 ed. lib. bdg. 20.75x (ISBN 0-313-21066-7, BAFG). Greenwood.

--From Agadir to Armageddon. 208p. 1982. text ed. 22.50x (ISBN 0-8419-0824-9). Holmes & Meier.

--Main Trends in History. 259p. 1979. 10.95 (ISBN 0-8419-0505-3). Holmes & Meier.

--The Times Concise Atlas of World History. LC 82-50111. (Illus.). 192p. 1982. 40.00 (ISBN 0-7230-0247-9). Hammond Inc.

Barraclough, Geoffrey, ed. The Times Atlas of World History. 1979. 70.00 (ISBN 0-7230-0161-8). Hammond Inc.

Barraclough, Geoffrey, ed. see Pollard, Sidney.

Barradas, Efrain, ed. Apalabramiento: Cuentos puertorriquenos de hoy. (Span.). Date not set. pap. 9.00 (ISBN 0-910061-09-2). Ediciones Norte.

Barral, R. M. Progressive Neutralism: A Philosophical Aspect of American Education. Matczak, Sebastian A., ed. LC 72-80678. (Philosophical Questions Ser.: No. 6). 1970. 18.00x (ISBN 0-912116-03-X). Learned Pubns.

Barranger, Milly S. Theatre: A Way of Seeing. 320p. 1980. pap. text ed. 16.95x (ISBN 0-534-00763-5). Wadsworth Pub.

Barrante, James R. Applied Mathematics for Physical Chemistry. (Illus.). 160p. 1974. pap. text ed. 16.95 (ISBN 0-13-041384-4). P-H.

Barrante, Paul. Physical Chemistry for the Life Sciences. (Illus.). 1977. text ed. 28.95 (ISBN 0-13-665984-5). P-H.

Barrass, Robert. Biology: Food & People. LC 74-21791. 224p. 1975. 18.95 o.p. (ISBN 0-312-08050-6). St Martin.

--The Locust. (Illus.). 73p. (gr. 10 up). 1975. 8.95x o.p. (ISBN 0-903330-11-3). Transatlantic.

Barrat, John & Louw, Michael, eds. International Aspects of Overpopulation. LC 71-179498. 1972. 26.00 (ISBN 0-312-41965-1). St Martin.

Barratt, Glen. The Russians at Port Jackson. 1980. text ed. 15.50x (ISBN 0-391-02165-6); pap. text ed. 0.50x Write For Info. (ISBN 0-391-02166-4). Humanities.

Barratt, John, jt. ed. see Hero, Alfred O.

Barratt, John, jt. ed. see Rotberg, Robert I.

Barratt, John, et al, eds. Accelerated Development in Southern Africa. LC 73-82636. 300p. 1974. 27.50 (ISBN 0-312-00210-6). St Martin.

--Strategy for Development. LC 76-1339. 320p. 1976. 25.00 (ISBN 0-312-76475-8). St Martin.

Barratt, Mike. Questions & Answers: Cameras. 128p. 1981. pap. 4.95 (ISBN 0-408-01138-6). Focal Pr.

Barraud, Cecile. Tanebar-Evav. LC 78-56176. (Atelier D'anthropologie Sociale). (Illus.). 1980. 42.50 (ISBN 0-521-22386-5). Cambridge U Pr.

Barrault, Jean-Louis, jt. auth. see Gide, Andre.

Barre, jt. auth. see Radet.

Barre, George La see La Barre, George.

Barre, Michael. The Case Against the Andersons. 1983. 15.95 (ISBN 0-440-01125-6). Delacorte.

Barre, W. La see La Barre, W.

Barre, Weston La see La Barre, Weston.

Barreau, Jean C. Religious Impulse. LC 78-71436. 80p. 1979. pap. 1.95 o.p. (ISBN 0-8091-2186-7). Paulist Pr.

Barreiro, Jose & Wright, Robin M., eds. Native Peoples in Struggle: Russell Tribunal & Other International Forums. LC 82-72533. (Illus.). 166p. 1982. pap. 12.00 (ISBN 0-932978-07-X). Anthropology Res.

Barrell, J. The Dark Side of the Landscape. LC 78-72334. (Illus.). 1980. 42.50 (ISBN 0-521-22509-4). Cambridge U Pr.

Barrendregt, H. P. The Lambda Calculus: Its Syntax & Semantics. (Studies in Logic & the Foundation of Mathematics Ser.: Vol. 103). 1981. 95.75 (ISBN 0-444-85490-8). Elsevier.

Barrer, R. M. Hydrothermal Chemistry of Zeolites: Synthesis, Isomorphous Replacelments & Transformations. 1982. 57.50 (ISBN 0-12-079360-1). Acad Pr.

Barrera, Mario, ed. Work Family Sex Roles Language. LC 80-53691. 1980. pap. 6.00 (ISBN 0-89229-007-2). Tonatiuh-Quinto Sol Intl.

Barrera-Benitez, Heriberto, jt. ed. see Teranishi, Roy.

Barrere, Albert. Dictionary of Slang, Jargon & Cant, 2 Vols. Leland, Charles G., ed. LC 66-27828. 1967. Repr. of 1889 ed. Set. 78.00x (ISBN 0-8103-3242-6). Gale.

Barrere, Dorothy B., ed. see Kamakau, S. M.

Barrere, Dorothy B., ed. see Papa, John.

Barres, Maurice. Colline Inspiree. (Classiques Larousse). (Illus., Fr.). pap. 1.95 o.p. (ISBN 0-685-13833-X, 19). Larousse.

--Les Traits Eternels de la France. 1918. 19.50x (ISBN 0-685-89791-5). Elliots Bks.

--The Undying Spirit of France. 1917. 19.50x (ISBN 0-686-51322-3). Elliots Bks.

Barret, P., ed. see International Meeting of the Societe de Chimie Physique, 25th, July, 1974.

Barrett & Hanson, Marvin L. Oral Myofunctional Disorders. 2nd ed. LC 78-7029. 1978. text ed. 44.50 o.p. (ISBN 0-8016-0497-4). Mosby.

Barrett & Ovenden. The Seacoast. pap. 8.95 (ISBN 0-686-42741-6, Collins Pub England). Greene.

Barrett & Yonge. Collins Pocket Guide to the Seashore. 29.95 (ISBN 0-686-42767-X, Collins Pub England). Greene.

Barrett, A. J., ed. Proteinases in Mammalian Cells & Tissues. (Research Monographs in Cell & Tissue Physiology: Vol. 2). 1977. 110.25 (ISBN 0-7204-0619-6, North-Holland). Elsevier.

Barrett, Alan H., ed. see Bekefi, George.

Barrett, Benjamin, ed. see Brewer, J. E.

Barrett, Benjamin, ed. see Salinger, John. P.

Barrett, Benjamin, ed. see Salinger, John P.

Barrett, Bernard M., ed. Manual of Patient Care in Plastic Surgery. (Spiral Manual Ser.). 1982. spiralbound 18.95 (ISBN 0-316-08217-1). Little.

Barrett, C. K. Essays on John. LC 82-2759. 180p. 1982. 18.95 (ISBN 0-664-21389-8). Westminster.

--Essays on Paul. LC 82-2764. 180p. 1982. 18.95 (ISBN 0-664-21390-1). Westminster.

Barrett, Charles D. Understanding the Christian Faith. (Illus.). 1980. text ed. 18.95 (ISBN 0-13-935882-X). P-H.

Barrett, Clotilde. Summer & Winter & Beyond. Rev. ed. 50p. 1982. pap. 5.00 (ISBN 0-937452-05-X). Colo Fiber.

Barrett, David, et al. Financing the Solar Home. LC 77-3858. 1977. 24.95x (ISBN 0-669-01684-5). Lexington Bks.

Barrett, David D. Dixie Mission: The United States Army Observer Group in Yenan, 1944. (China Research Monographs: No. 6). 92p. 1970. pap. 4.00x (ISBN 0-912966-07-6). IEAS.

Barrett, E. C. Climatology from Satellites. (Illus.). 418p. 1974. 53.00x (ISBN 0-416-65940-3); pap. 17.95x (ISBN 0-416-72150-8). Methuen Inc.

Barrett, Eaton S. All the Talents; a Satirical Poem, in Four Dialogues. to Which Is Added, a Pastoral Epilogue, Repr. Of 1807. Reiman, Donald H., ed. Bd. with The Second Titan War Against Heaven; or, the Talents Buried Under Portland-Isle. Repr. of 1807 ed; The Talents Run Mad; or, Eighteen Hundred & Sixteen. a Satirical Poem. Repr. of 1816 ed. LC 75-31150. (Romantic Context Ser.: Poetry 1789-1830). 1979. lib. bdg. 47.00 o.s.i. (ISBN 0-8240-2104-5). Garland Pub.

--Women, a Poem, Repr. Of 1810 Ed. Reiman, Donald H., ed. Bd. with Henry Schultze. a Tale, the Savoyard, a French Republican's Story. with Other Poems. Repr. of 1821 ed. LC 75-31150. 1979. lib. bdg. 43.00 o.s.i. (ISBN 0-8240-2105-3). Garland Pub.

Barrett, Elizabeth. Elizabeth Barrett to Miss Mitford. Miller, ed. 1954. 42.50x (ISBN 0-685-69789-4). Elliots Bks.

Barrett, Ethel. Abraham: God's Faithful Pilgrim. 128p. (Orig.). (gr. 3 up). 1982. pap. 2.50 (ISBN 0-8307-0769-7, 5810906). Regal.

--Historias Biblicas. (No. 1). (Span.). 2.25 o.p. (ISBN 0-686-76293-2). Life Pubs Intl.

--Historias Biblicas: Juego. (Span.). 6.25 o.p. (ISBN 0-686-76295-9). Life Pubs Intl.

--Historias De la Biblia Lujo. (Span.). Date not set. 19.95 (ISBN 0-8297-1115-5). Life Pubs Intl.

--If I Had a Wish. LC 74-83139. 144p. (Orig.). (gr. 4-8). 1975. pap. 1.95 o.p. (ISBN 0-8307-0314-4, 57-001-08). Regal.

--Moses: Mission Impossible! (Bible Biographies Ser.). 1982. pap. text ed. 2.50 (ISBN 0-8307-0772-7, 5811201). Regal.

Barrett, Francis D., Jr. Accountant's Guide to Insurance & Risk Management. LC 77-90645. 39.50 (ISBN 0-931372-02-X). Compton & Rowe.

--Professional's Guide to Insurance & Risk Management. LC 77-90648. 1978. 39.50 (ISBN 0-931372-00-3). Compton & Rowe.

Barrett, G. Vincent & Blair, John P. Foundations of Real Estate Analysis. 1981. 24.95 (ISBN 0-02-306140-5). Macmillan.

Barrett, G. W. Ancient China. Reeves, Marjorie, ed. (Then & There Ser.). (Illus.). 96p. (gr. 7-12). 1969. pap. text ed. 3.10 (ISBN 0-582-20453-4). Longman.

Barrett, Gary W. Stress Effects on Natural Ecosystems. Rosenberg, Rutger, ed. LC 80-40851. (Environmental Monographs & Symposia, Environmental Science). 305p. 1982. 47.95x (ISBN 0-471-27834-3, Pub. by Wiley-Interscience). Wiley.

Barrett, Gwynn W., jt. auth. see Adler, Jacob.

Barrett, H. J., jt. auth. see Rohl, J. S.

Barrett, Harold. Daring to Be: Love & the Art of Rhetorical Intercourse. LC 82-2237. 152p. 1982. text ed. 15.95x (ISBN 0-88229-609-4). Nelson-Hall.

Barrett, Helena M. One Way to Write Anything. 144p. (Orig.). 1982. pap. 4.09 (ISBN 0-06-463551-1, EH 551, EH). B&N NY.

Barrett, Ian. Tundra & People. LC 82-50395. (Nature's Landscape Ser.). PLB 15.96 (ISBN 0-382-06670-7). Silver.

Barrett, J. W. Immediate Prehospital Care. 551p. 1980. 39.50 (ISBN 0-471-05645-6, AG30, Pub. by Wiley-Interscience). Wiley.

Barrett, James E., ed. Stress & Mental Disorder. LC 79-2202. (American Psychopathological Association Ser.). 310p. 1979. text ed. 31.00 (ISBN 0-89004-384-1). Raven.

Barrett, James E., jt. ed. see Clayton, Paula J.

Barrett, James E., jt. ed. see Cole, Jonathan O.

Barrett, Janice R. & Schuller, Linda J. Illinois Artisans & Craftsmen: A Guide, Resource, & Reference. (Illinois Artisans & Craftsmen Ser.: No. 1). (Illus.). 200p. 1982. 35.00 (ISBN 0-943902-00-2); pap. 14.95 (ISBN 0-943902-01-0). Insearch Pr.

Barrett, Jean. Archery. 3rd ed. 1980. 7.95x (ISBN 0-673-16181-1). Scott F.

Barrett, John G. The Civil War in North Carolina. LC 63-22810. xi, 484p. 1963. 14.95 (ISBN 0-8078-0874-1). U of NC Pr.

Barrett, Jon H. Individual Goals & Organizational Objectives. LC 77-632403. 119p. 1970. 12.00x (ISBN 0-87944-080-5). Inst Soc Res.

Barrett, Judi. What's Left? LC 82-12824. (Illus.). 32p. (ps). 1983. 10.95 (ISBN 0-689-30874-4). Atheneum.

Barrett, Keith E. Dispersion Polymerization in Organic Media. LC 74-5491. 388p. 1975. 69.95x (ISBN 0-471-05418-6, Pub. by Wiley-Interscience). Wiley.

Barrett, Laurence. Gambling with History: The Reagan White House. LC 82-46057. (Illus.). 288p. 1983. 17.95 (ISBN 0-385-17939-1). Doubleday.

Barrett, Lindsay. Song for Mumu. LC 73-99065. 1974. 6.95 (ISBN 0-88258-006-X). Howard U Pr.

Barrett, Louis C., jt. auth. see Wylie, C. Ray.

Barrett, M. Edgar & Cormack, Mary P. Management Strategy in the Oil & Gas Industries: Cases & Readings. 1982. text ed. 34.95 (ISBN 0-87201-506-8). Gulf Pub.

Barrett, Margaret W., jt. auth. see Marram, Gwen.

Barrett, Martha B. Maggie's Way. (Orig.). 1981. pap. 2.75 o.p. (ISBN 0-451-09601-0, E9601, Sig). NAL.

Barrett, Marvin. Meet Thomas Jefferson. (Step-up Books Ser.). (gr. 2-6). 1967. 4.95 (ISBN 0-394-80067-2, BYR); PLB 5.99 (ISBN 0-394-90067-7). Random.

--Rich News, Poor News: The Sixth Alfred I. duPont - Columbia University Survey of Broadcast Journalism. LC 77-95161. 1978. 14.37i (ISBN 0-690-01740-5); pap. 5.95i (ISBN 0-690-01741-3, TYC-T). T Y Crowell.

Barrett, Marvin, ed. Broadcast Journalism. LC 82-5067. 256p. 1982. 15.95 (ISBN 0-89696-160-5, An Everest House Book). Dodd.

Barrett, Mary E., jt. auth. see Arnaudet, Martin L.

Barrett, Michele & McIntosh, Mary. The Anti-Social Family. 164p. 1983. 18.50 (ISBN 0-686-37927-6); pap. 7.50 (ISBN 0-686-37928-4). Schocken.

--The Anti-Social Family. 160p. 1982. 18.50 (ISBN 0-8052-7134-1, Pub. by NLB England); pap. 7.50 (ISBN 0-686-38371-0). Nichols Pub.

Barrett, Michele, intro. by see Woolf, Virginia.

Barrett, Michele, et al, eds. Ideology & Cultural Production. LC 78-26901. 1979. 26.00x (ISBN 0-312-40451-4). St Martin.

Barrett, Nancy S. The Theory of Microeconomic Policy. 1974. text ed. 13.95x o.p. (ISBN 0-669-83170-0). Heath.

Barrett, Neal, Jr. Aldair in Albion. (Science Fiction Ser.). 1976. pap. 1.25 o.p. (ISBN 0-87997-235-1, UY1235). DAW Bks.

Barrett, Paul. The Automobile & Urban Transit: The Formation of Public Policy in Chicago. 1983. write for info. (ISBN 0-87722-294-0). Temple U Pr.

Barrett, Paul, tr. see Dumery, Henry.

Barrett, Paul H., ed. The Collected Papers of Charles Darwin, 2 vols. in 1. LC 76-606. (Illus.). 1980. pap. 12.50 (ISBN 0-226-13658-2, P886, Phoen); 40.00x. U of Chicago Pr.

Barrett, R. Developments in Optical Disc Technology & the Implications for Information Storage & Retrieval. 80p. 1981. pap. 170.00x (ISBN 0-905984-71-4, Pub. by Brit Lib England). State Mutual Bk.

Barrett, Richard. The Commission. LC 82-72373. (Illus.). 438p. 1982. 25.00 (ISBN 0-9609396-0-1). Barrett.

Barrett, Roger C. & Jackson, Daphne F. Nuclear Sizes & Structure. (International Series of Monographs on Physics). 1977. 84.00x (ISBN 0-19-851272-4). Oxford U Pr.

Barrett, Rowland P., jt. ed. see Matson, Johnny L.

Barrett, S. A. Pomo Indian Basketry. LC 76-147075. (Beautiful Rio Grande Classics Ser.). lib. bdg. 12.50 o.s.i. (ISBN 0-87380-099-0). Rio Grande.

Barrett, Stanley R. The Rise & Fall of an African Utopia: A Wealthy Theocracy in Comparative Perspective. Boyd, Rosalind E., ed. (Development Perspectives Ser.: No. 1). 251p. 1977. text ed. 12.75 (ISBN 0-88920-054-8, Pub. by Wilfred Laurier U Pr Canada); pap. text ed. 8.75x (ISBN 0-88920-053-X). Humanities.

Barrett, Stephen, jt. auth. see Cornacchia, Harold J.

Barrett, Susan & Fudge, Colin, eds. Policy & Action: Essays on the Implementation of Public Policy. 1981. 33.00x (ISBN 0-416-30670-5); pap. 16.95x (ISBN 0-416-30680-2). Methuen Inc.

Barrett, Theodosia. Russel County. LC 81-69331. 148p. 1981. 10.95 (ISBN 0-89227-047-0). Commonwealth Pr.

Barrett, Thomas J. Harnessing the Earthworm. (Illus.). 192p. 1976. 7.95 (ISBN 0-916302-14-8); pap. 5.95 (ISBN 0-916302-09-1). Bookworm NY.

Barrett, Thomas S. & Livermore, Putnam. The Conservation Easement in California. 256p. 1983. 44.95 (ISBN 0-933280-20-3); pap. 24.95 (ISBN 0-933280-19-X). Island CA.

Barrett, W. H. & Garrod, R. P. East Anglian Folklore & Other Tales. (Illus.). 1976. 16.95 (ISBN 0-7100-8300-9). Routledge & Kegan.

Barrett, William. The History & Antiquities of the City of Bristol. 704p. 1982. text ed. 75.00x (ISBN 0-904387-48-8, Pub. by Sutton England). Humanities.

--The Illusion of Technique: A Search for Meaning in a Technological Civilization. 1978. pap. 6.95 (ISBN 0-385-11202-5, Anch). Doubleday.

--The Left Hand of God. 1976. Repr. of 1951 ed. lib. bdg. 16.95x (ISBN 0-89244-017-1). Queens Hse.

--The Lilies of the Field. 128p. 1982. pap. 2.50 (ISBN 0-446-31042-5). Warner Bks.

--Time of Need: Forms of Imagination in the Twentieth Century. (Illus.). 416p. 1973. pap. 4.95xi o.p. (ISBN 0-06-131754-3, TB 1754, Torch). Har-Row.

--The Truants: Adventures Among the Intellectuals. 296p. 1983. pap. 8.95 (ISBN 0-385-17328-8, Anch). Doubleday.

Barrett, William A. & Couch, John D. Compiler Construction: Theory & Practice. LC 78-26183. 512p. 1979. text ed. 26.95 (ISBN 0-574-21335-X, 13-4335); inst. guide o.p. 2.00 (ISBN 0-574-18508-9, 13-4161). SRA.

Barrett, William E. The Left Hand of God. 1968. 3.95 (ISBN 0-385-04253-1). Doubleday.

--Lilies of the Field. LC 62-8085. (Illus.). (YA) (gr. 7 up). 1962. 8.95 (ISBN 0-385-01785-5); pap. 2.50 (ISBN 0-385-07246-5). Doubleday.

Barrett-Connor, Elizabeth, et al, eds. Epidemiology for the Infection Control Nurse. LC 77-13128. (Illus.). 1978. text ed. 19.95 o.p. (ISBN 0-8016-0744-2). Mosby.

Barrette, Paul & Braun, Theodore. First French: Le Francais Non sans Peine. rev. ed. 1970. 14.95x o.p. (ISBN 0-673-05113-7). Scott F.

--Second French: Le Francais Non sans Peine. 1968. 14.95x o.p. (ISBN 0-673-05110-2). Scott F.

Barrette, Paul & Fol, Monique. Certain Style Ou un Style Certain. 1969. pap. 11.95x (ISBN 0-19-500824-3). Oxford U Pr.

Barrette, Pierre, ed. Microcomputers in K-Twelve Education, Second Annual Congerence Proceedings. 1983. pap. write for info. (ISBN 0-914894-87-0). Computer Sci.

Barrette, Roy. A Countryman's Journal: Views of Life & Nature from a Maine Coastal Farm. (Illus.). 7.50 (ISBN 0-686-84139-5). Down East.

Barricelli, Gian P. Alessandro Manzoni. (World Authors Ser.). 1976. lib. bdg. 15.95 (ISBN 0-8057-6251-5, Twayne). G K Hall.

Barricelli, Jean-Pierre, et al. Interrelations of Literature. Gibaldi, Joseph, ed. LC 82-7956. vi, 329p. 1982. 18.50x (ISBN 0-87352-090-4); pap. 9.50x (ISBN 0-87352-091-2). Modern Lang.

Barrie, Donald S. Directions in Managing Construction: A Critical Look at Present & Future Industry Practices, Problems & Policies. (Construction Management & Engineering Ser.). 500p. 1981. 49.95x (ISBN 0-471-04642-6, Pub. by Wiley-Interscience). Wiley.

Barrie, Donald S., jt. auth. see Paulson, Boyd C.

Barrie, Donald S., jt. auth. see Parker, Albert D.

Barrie, J. M. The Little Minister. 232p. 1981. Repr. PLB 16.95 (ISBN 0-89966-329-X). Buccaneer Bks.

--Peter Pan. Frank, Josette, adapted by. LC 82-13288. (The Looking Glass Library). (Illus.). 72p. (ps-4). 1983. PLB 7.99 (ISBN 0-394-95717-2); pap. 6.95 (ISBN 0-394-85717-8). Random.

Barrie, James M. Peter Pan. (Silver Dollar Library Ser.). (Illus.). (gr. 2-6). 1970. 1.95 o.p. (ISBN 0-448-02137-4, G&D). Putnam Pub Group.

Barrie, Monica. Run on the Wind. (Orig.). 1983. pap. 3.50 (ISBN 0-440-01977-X, Emerald). Dell.

Barrientos, Parra O. Revision der Gattung Pediastrum Meyen (Chlorophyta) (Bibliotheca Phycologica: No. 48). (Illus.). 1979. pap. text ed. 24.00x (ISBN 3-7682-1254-8). Lubrecht & Cramer.

Barrier, Michael. Carl Barks & the Art of the Comic Book. (Illus.). 228p. 1982. 49.95 (ISBN 0-9607652-0-4). M Lilien.

Barriga, Omar O. Immunology of Parasitic Infections. 368p. (Orig.). 1981. pap. text ed. 29.50 (ISBN 0-8391-1621-7). Univ Park.

Barrile, Jackie. Confessions of a Closet Eater. 1983. 12.95 (ISBN 0-941018-09-1). P Hanson.

Barrili, Anton G. Capitan Dodero. Cotterill, H. R., tr. from Span. (Harrap's Bilingual Ser.). 128p. Date not set. pap. 5.00 (ISBN 0-911268-50-2); price not set pocket size. Rogers Bk.

Barrilleaux, Doris & Murray, Jim. Inside Weight Training for Women. 1978. pap. 5.95 (ISBN 0-8092-7500-7). Contemp Bks.

Barrington, E. J. Chemical Basis of Physiological Regulation. 1968. pap. 8.95x (ISBN 0-673-05167-6). Scott F.

--Environmental Biology. LC 80-12090. (Resource & Environmental Science Ser.). 244p. 1980. pap. 19.95X (ISBN 0-470-26967-7). Halsted Pr.

--Intervertebrate Structure & Function. 2nd ed. 1979. 32.95 o.p. (ISBN 0-470-26502-7); pap. 20.95 (ISBN 0-470-26503-5). Halsted Pr.

Barrington, Mollie. Extending Skills in Handwriting. (Handwriting for Daily Use Ser.). (Illus., Non-consumable). (gr. 5). Date not set. pap. text ed. write for info. o.s.i. (ISBN 0-685-47735-5); tchr's ed. 0.60 o.s.i. (ISBN 0-686-67002-7). Benson.

--Learning More About Writing. (Handwriting for Daily Use Ser.). (Illus., Non-consumable). (gr. 7). Date not set. pap. text ed. cancelled o.s.i. (ISBN 0-685-47731-2); tchr's ed. pap. cancelled o.s.i. (ISBN 0-685-47732-0). Benson.

Barris, Alex. Hollywood's Solid Gold Year, 1939. (Illus.). 272p. 1982. cancelled (ISBN 0-498-02588-8). A S Barnes.

Barrister, Amanda M. A Practical Guide to Trade Marks. 216p. 1982. 39.00x (ISBN 0-686-97894-3, Pub. by ESC Pub England). State Mutual Bk.

Barristers Committee for the Arts, jt. auth. see Beverly Hills Bar Association.

Barro, R. J. & Grossman, H. I. Money, Employment & Inflation. LC 75-13449. (Illus.). 304p. 1976. 29.95x (ISBN 0-521-20906-4). Cambridge U Pr.

Barrodale, Ian, et al. Elementary Computer Applications: In Science, Engineering & Business. LC 74-150609. 254p. 1971. pap. 21.95x (ISBN 0-471-05423-2). Wiley.

Barroitt, Denis P. & Carter, Charles F. The Northern Ireland Problem: A Study in Group Relations. LC 82-15568. 163p. 1982. Repr. of 1962 ed. lib. bdg. 22.50x (ISBN 0-313-23262-8, BANI). Greenwood.

Barroll, J. Leeds, et al. Revels History of Drama in English, Vol. 3: 1576-1613. LC 74-15177. (Revels History of the Drama in English Ser.). 400p. 1975. 53.00x (ISBN 0-416-13040-2); pap. 18.95x (ISBN 0-416-81350-X). Methuen Inc.

Barron, C. H. Numerical Control for Machine Tools. 1971. 24.95 (ISBN 0-07-003824-4, G); answer key 4.00 (ISBN 0-07-003831-7). McGraw.

Barron, Colin see Bates, Martin & Dudley-Evans, Tony.

Barron, D. Assemblers & Loaders. 3rd ed. 1978. 22.00 (ISBN 0-444-19462-2). Elsevier.

Barron, D. W. Computer Operating Systems. 2nd ed. 1983. pap. 17.00x (ISBN 0-412-15630-X, Pub. by Chapman & Hall). Methuen Inc.

--An Introduction to the Study of Programming Languages. LC 76-11070. (Cambridge Computer Science Texts Ser.: No. 7). (Illus.). 1977. 24.95 (ISBN 0-521-21317-7); pap. 9.95x (ISBN 0-521-29101-1). Cambridge U Pr.

Barron, David W. Anaesthesia & Related Subjects in Orthopaedic Surgery. (Illus.). 216p. 1982. text ed. 24.95 (ISBN 0-632-00675-7, B0512-1). Mosby.

Barron, Don. Creativity, Six. LC 59-14827. (Creativity Ser.: Vol. 6). (Illus.). 1977. 27.50 o.p. (ISBN 0-910158-25-8). Art Dir.

Barron, Frank. LSD, Man & Society. DeBold, Richard C. & Leaf, Russell C., eds. LC 73-15314. (Illus.). 219p. 1975. Repr. of 1967 ed. lib. bdg. 15.00 o.p. (ISBN 0-8371-7195-4, BALS). Greenwood.

Barron, George L. Genera of Hyphomycetes from Soil. LC 68-14275. 378p. 1977. Repr. of 1968 ed. 25.50 (ISBN 0-88275-004-6). Krieger.

Barron, Greg. Groundrush. 1982. 13.50 (ISBN 0-394-52214-1). Random.

Barron, J. & Paul, A. Murder of a Gentle Land. 1977. 9.95 (ISBN 0-07-003849-X). McGraw.

Barron, Jerome A. & Dienes, C. Thomas. Constitutional Law: Principles & Policy, Cases & Materials. LC 74-2945. (Contemporary Legal Education Ser.). 1982. text ed. 28.50 (ISBN 0-87215-411-4, Bobbs-Merrill Law); 1980 cum. suppl. o.p. 8.00 (ISBN 0-672-83549-5). Michie-Bobbs.

--Handbook of Free Speech & Free Press. 1979. text ed. 50.00 (ISBN 0-316-08230-9). Little.

Barron, John. An Introduction to Greek Sculpture. 176p. 1981. text ed. 31.50x o.p. (ISBN 0-485-11196-9, Athlone Pr); pap. text ed. 12.50x o.p. (ISBN 0-485-12033-X, Athlone Pr). Humanities.

Barron, John & Paul, Anthony. Murder of a Gentle Land. 1977. 9.95 o.p. (ISBN 0-88349-129-X). Readers Digest Pr.

Barron, L. D. Molecular Light Scattering & Optical Activity. 425p. Date not set. price not set (ISBN 0-521-24602-4). Cambridge U Pr.

Barron, Linda. Mathematics Experiences for the Early Childhood Years. 1979. pap. text ed. 14.95 (ISBN 0-675-08284-6). Merrill.

Barron, Sr. Mary C. Unveiled Faces: Men & Women of the Bible. LC 80-27728. 95p. 1981. softcover 4.50 (ISBN 0-8146-1212-1). Liturgical Pr.

Barron, Neil & Doiron, Peter, eds. Anatomy of Wonder: Science Fiction. LC 76-10260. (Bibliographic Guides for Comtemporary Collections Ser.). 464p. 1976. 17.50 o.p. (ISBN 0-8352-0884-2); pap. 9.50 o.p. (ISBN 0-8352-0949-0). Bowker.

Barron, Robert, jt. auth. see Fisk, Jim.

Barron, Stephanie & Tuchman, Maurice, eds. Avant-Garde in Russia, 1910-1930: New Perspectives. (Illus.). 288p. 1980. 27.50 (ISBN 0-262-20040-6); pap. 12.50 (ISBN 0-262-52077-X). MIT Pr.

Barron, Stephanie, et al. The Avant-Garde in Russia, 1910-1930: New Perspectives. D'Andrea, Jeanne & West, Stephen, eds. Hirshman, Jack & Wojciechowski, Andrzej, trs. (Illus.). 288p. (Orig., Rus. Ger. Fr. Pol.). 1980. pap. 11.95 (ISBN 0-87587-095-3). LA Co Art Mus.

Barron, Terry. The Aluminum Industry of Texas. (Mineral Resource Circular Ser.: No. 67). (Illus.). 16p. 1982. 1.50 (ISBN 0-686-36996-3). U of Tex Econ Geology.

Barron, W. R., jt. auth. see Rothwell, W.

Barron, W. R., ed. Sir Gawain & the Green Knight. LC 74-21. (Manchester Medieval Classics Ser). 179p. 1976. pap. text ed. 9.50x (ISBN 0-06-490311-7). B&N Imports.

Barron, W. R., ed. see Henryson, Robert.

Barron's Educational Series, Inc., College Division. Barron's Compact Guide to Colleges. 352p. (gr. 10-12). 1982. pap. 2.95 (ISBN 0-8120-2475-3). Barron.

Barron's Educational Series, Inc College Division. Barron's Guide to the Best, Most Popular, & Most Exciting Colleges. Rev. ed. LC 81-17573. 416p. (gr. 10-12). 1982. pap. 6.95 (ISBN 0-8120-2607-1). Barron.

--Barron's Guide to the Most Prestigious Colleges. rev. ed. LC 81-17573. 272p. (gr. 10-12). 1982. pap. 6.95 (ISBN 0-8120-2606-3). Barron.

--Barron's Profiles of American Colleges: Descriptions of the Colleges, Vol. 1. rev. ed. LC 81-21243. 1088p. 1982. 25.95 (ISBN 0-8120-5449-0); pap. 11.95 (ISBN 0-8120-2459-1). Barron.

--Barron's Profiles of American Colleges: Index to College Majors, Vol. 2. 13th ed. 256p. (gr. 10-12). 1982. 17.95 (ISBN 0-8120-5450-4); pap. 9.95 (ISBN 0-8120-2460-5). Barron.

--Barrons Profiles of American Colleges: The Northeast. Rev. ed. 336p. (gr. 10-12). 1982. pap. 6.95 (ISBN 0-8120-2467-2). Barron.

Barros, James. Britain, Greece & the Politics of Sanctions. (Royal Historical Society, Studies in History: No. 33). 248p. 1982. text ed. 30.00x (ISBN 0-391-02690-9, Pub. by Swiftbks England). Humanities.

Barros, Leda Watson de see Sutton, Joan L. & Watson de Barros, Leda.

Barroso, J. A., ed. Advances in Holomorphy. (North Holland Mathematics Studies: Vol. 34). 1979. 76.75 (ISBN 0-444-85265-4, North Holland). Elsevier.

--Functional Analysis, Holomorphy & Approximation Theory: Proceedings of the Seminario de Analise Funcional, Holomorfia e Teoria da Approximacao, Universidade Federal do Rio de Janeiro, Aug. 4-8, 1980. (North Holland Mathematics Studies: Vol. 71). 486p. 1982. 63.75 (ISBN 0-444-86527-6, North Holland). Elsevier.

Barroso, Memo. Yucatan: The Hidden Beaches. 1983. pap. 8.95 (ISBN 0-517-54789-9, Harmony). Crown.

Barrot, J. & Martin, F. Eclipse & Re-Emergence of the Communist Movement. 1974. 1.90 o.p. (ISBN 0-934868-04-2). Black & Red.

Barrow, Andrew. Gossip: A History of High Society, 1920-1970. LC 78-24509. 1979. 16.95 o.p. (ISBN 0-698-10977-5, Coward). Putnam Pub Group.

Barrow, Christopher J., jt. auth. see Saha, Suranjit K.

Barrow, G. W. S. Robert Bruce & the Community of the Realm of Scotland. 1965. 32.50x o.p. (ISBN 0-520-00083-8). U of Cal Pr.

Barrow, Georgia & Smith, Patricia. Aging, Ageism, & Society. (Illus.). 1979. pap. text ed. 16.95 (ISBN 0-8299-0237-6); instrs.' manual avail. (ISBN 0-8299-0458-1). West Pub.

Barrow, Georgia M. & Smith, Patricia A. Aging: The Individual & Society. 2nd ed. (Illus.). 400p. 1983. pap. text ed. 15.95 (ISBN 0-314-69635-0). West Pub.

Barrow, Gordon. Physical Chemistry. 4th ed. (Illus.). 1979. text ed. 31.00 (ISBN 0-07-003825-2, C). McGraw.

--Physical Chemistry for the Life Sciences. 2nd ed. (Illus.). 448p. 1981. text ed. 26.95 (ISBN 0-07-003858-9, C); solutions manual 7.95 (ISBN 0-07-003859-7). McGraw.

Barrow, Gordon M. Introduction to Molecular Spectroscopy. 1962. 21.00 o.p. (ISBN 0-07-003870-8, C). McGraw.

--Physical Chemistry for the Life Sciences. (Illus.). 416p. 1974. text ed. 18.00 o.p. (ISBN 0-07-003855-4, C); 5.95 o.p. (ISBN 0-07-003859-7). McGraw.

Barrow, Harold M. Man & Movement: Principles of Physical Education. 3rd ed. LC 82-20398. 410p. 1983. text ed. write for info. (ISBN 0-8121-0861-2). Lea & Febiger.

Barrow, Sir John. Mutiny of the Bounty. Kennedy, Gavin, ed. LC 80-66459. (Illus.). 208p. 1980. 17.95 (ISBN 0-87923-343-5). Godine.

Barrow, M. H., jt. auth. see Rase, H. F.

Barrow, R. St., jt. auth. see Woods, R. G.

Barrow, Robin. Happiness & Schooling. 175p. 1980. 25.00x (ISBN 0-312-36177-7). St Martin.

--Moral Philosophy for Education. 214p. 1975. 17.50 o.p. (ISBN 0-208-01502-7, Linnet). Shoe String.

--Philosphy of Schooling. LC 81-7445. 250p. 1981. 16.95 (ISBN 0-470-27180-9). Halsted Pr.

--Plato & Education. (Students Library of Education Ser.). 1976. 12.95x (ISBN 0-7100-8343-2). Routledge & Kegan.

--Radical Education: A Critique of Freeschooling & Deschooling. LC 78-1972. 1978. 27.95 o.p. (ISBN 0-470-26329-6); pap. 20.95x o.p. Halsted Pr.

Barrow, S. M. Major Companies of the Far East, 1983, Vol. 1. (Major Companies Ser.). 350p. 1983. 90.00 (ISBN 0-86010-324-2). Nichols Pub.

--Major Companies of the Far East 1983, Vol. 2. (Major Companies Ser.). 350p. 1983. 90.00 (ISBN 0-86010-326-9). Nichols Pub.

Barrow, Thomas C; see Weaver, Glenn.

Barrow, Thomas F., et al, eds. Reading into Photography: Selected Essays, 1959-81. 320p. 1982. 24.95x (ISBN 0-8263-0597-0); pap. 12.50x (ISBN 0-8263-0647-0). U of NM Pr.

Barrows & Hall. An American Phonetic Reader. 1973. text ed. 1.75 o.p. (ISBN 0-686-09410-7). Expression.

Barrows, Anita, tr. see Milani, Felix.

Barrows, Howard S. Simulated Patients (Programmed Patients) The Development & Use of a New Technique in Medical Education. (Illus.). 80p. 1971. spiral 9.75x (ISBN 0-398-02227-5). C C Thomas.

Barrows, Marjorie. One Thousand Beautiful Things. (Library of Beautiful Things: Vol. 1). (gr. 7 up). 1955. 9.95 o.p. (ISBN 0-8015-5562-0, Hawthorn). Dutton.

Barrows, Sarah T. An Introduction to the Phonetic Alphabet. 1973. text ed. 1.75 o.p. (ISBN 0-686-09409-3). Expression.

Barrows, Suzanne S., jt. ed. see Goode, John W., Jr.

Barrows, Walter. Grassroots Politics in an African State: Integration & Development in Sierra Leone. LC 74-84655. 250p. 1976. text ed. 35.00x (ISBN 0-8419-0183-X, Africana). Holmes & Meier.

Barrs, Jerram. Shepherds & Sheep. 96p. (Orig.). 1983. pap. 2.95 (ISBN 0-87784-395-3). Inter-Varsity.

Barrs, Jerram, jt. auth. see Macaulay, Ranald.

Barruel-Beauvert, Antoine-Joseph. Vie De J. J. Rousseau, Precedee De Quelques Lettres Relatives Au Meme Sujet. (Rousseauism, 1788-1797). 1978. Repr. lib. bdg. 118.00x o.p. (ISBN 0-8287-0060-5). Clearwater Pub.

Barrutia, Richard & Terrell, Tracy David. Fonetica y Fonologia Espanolas. LC 81-13155. 189p. 1982. text ed. 20.95x (ISBN 0-471-08461-1); avail. tapes. Wiley.

Barry. Dermatological Formation. (Drugs & the Pharmaceutical Science Ser.). 472p. 1983. price not set (ISBN 0-8247-1729-5). Dekker.

Barry, B. Austin. Construction Measurements. LC 72-13073. (Practical Construction Guides Ser.). 352p. 1973. 35.95x (ISBN 0-471-05428-3, Pub. by Wiley-Interscience). Wiley.

--Errors in Practical Measurement in Science, Engineering & Technology. LC 78-9751. 183p. 1978. 27.95x (ISBN 0-471-03156-9, Pub. by Wiley-Interscience). Wiley.

Barry, Brian. The Liberal Theory of Justice: A Critical Examination of the Principal Doctrines in - A Theory of Justice by John Rawls. (Illus.). 1973. pap. text ed. 6.95x o.p. (ISBN 0-19-875032-3). Oxford U Pr.

--Power & Political Theory: Some European Perspectives. LC 74-20693. 322p. 1976. 41.95x (ISBN 0-471-05424-0, Pub. by Wiley-Interscience). Wiley.

Barry, Brian, jt. ed. see Sikora, R. I.

Barry, Elaine. Robert Frost. LC 72-79942. (Literature and Life Ser.). 1973. 11.95 (ISBN 0-8044-2016-5). Ungar.

--Robert Frost on Writing. 1974. 18.00x o.p. (ISBN 0-8135-0692-1); pap. 4.95x o.p. (ISBN 0-8135-0789-8). Rutgers U Pr.

Barry, Florence V. A Century of Children's Books. LC 68-23467. 31.00 o.p. (ISBN 0-8103-3472-0). Gale.

Barry, Jackson G. Dramatic Structure: The Shaping of Experience. LC 78-100607. 1970. 32.00x (ISBN 0-520-01624-6). U of Cal Pr.

Barry, Jean. Emergency Nursing. LC 77-1436. (Illus.). 1977. pap. text ed. 26.00 (ISBN 0-07-003839-2, HP). McGraw.

Barry, John R. & Wingrove, C. Ray, eds. Let's Learn About Aging: A Book of Readings. LC 76-45168. 1977. text ed. 18.50 (ISBN 0-470-98965-3); pap. text ed. 12.95 (ISBN 0-470-98967-X). Halsted Pr.

Barry, John W. & Henry, Porter J. Effective Sales Incentive Compensation. (Illus.). 192p. 1980. 18.95 (ISBN 0-07-003860-0, P&RB). McGraw.

Barry, Katharina, jt. auth. see Joslin, Sesyle.

Barry, Kathleen. Female Sexual Slavery. LC 79-16035. 1979. 10.95 o.p. (ISBN 0-13-314302-3). P-H.

Barry, Les. Getting Started in Photography. (Illus.). 96p. 1975. pap. 4.95 o.p. (ISBN 0-8174-0187-3, Amphoto). Watson-Guptill.

Barry, Louise. The Beginning of the West: Annals of the Kansas Gateway to the American West 1540-1854. LC 78-172252. (Illus.). 1972. 10.95 (ISBN 0-87726-001-X). Kansas St Hist.

Barry, Nora. Sherbourne's Folly. LC 77-76220. 1978. 10.95 o.p. (ISBN 0-385-12882-7). Doubleday.

Barry, Norman P. An Introduction to Modern Political Theory. 1980. 25.00 (ISBN 0-312-43098-1). St Martin.

Barry, R. G. & Perry, A. H. Synoptic Climatology: Methods & Applications. 500p. 1973. 55.00x (ISBN 0-416-08500-8). Methuen Inc.

Barry, Richard, tr. see Hoffmann, Peter.

Barry, Roger D. Basic Chemistry. LC 74-79831. (Health Occupations Ser.). 1975. pap. text ed. 11.50 (ISBN 0-672-61376-X); lab manual 7.50 (ISBN 0-672-61377-8); answer key 3.33 (ISBN 0-672-61432-4). Bobbs.

Barry, Roger G. Mountain, Weather & Climate. LC 80-42348. 1981. 38.00x (ISBN 0-416-73730-7). Methuen Inc.

Barry, Roger G. & Chorley, R. J. Atmosphere, Weather & Climate. 4th ed. 1983. 31.00x (ISBN 0-416-33690-6); pap. 13.95x (ISBN 0-416-33700-7). Methuen Inc.

Barry, Ruth & Wolf, Beverly. Motives, Values, & Realities: A Framework for Counseling. LC 76-40268. 1976. Repr. of 1965 ed. lib. bdg. 20.50x (ISBN 0-8371-9066-5, WOMV). Greenwood.

Barry, Scott. The Kingdom of Wolves. LC 78-9895. (Illus.). (gr. 6-8). 1979. 9.95 (ISBN 0-399-20657-4). Putnam Pub Group.

Barry, Sheila A. Super-Colossal Book of Puzzles, Tricks & Games. LC 77-93325. (Illus.). 640p. (gr. 4 up). 1981. 19.95 (ISBN 0-8069-4580-X); PLB 23.59 (ISBN 0-8069-4581-8); pap. 12.95 (ISBN 0-8069-7524-5). Sterling.

Barry, Sheila A., ed. Our New Home. LC 81-8801. 128p. (Orig.). 1981. pap. 5.95 (ISBN 0-8069-7550-4). Sterling.

Barry, Sheila M., jt. ed. see Oxley, T. A.

Barry, Stephen. Royal Service: My Twelve Years as Valet to Prince Charles. (Illus.). 320p. 1983. 14.95 (ISBN 0-02-507490-3). Macmillan.

Barry, Tim, ed. see McCabe, C. Kevin.

Barry, Tim, ed. see Townsend, Carl.

Barry, Tom & Wood, Beth. Dollars & Dictators: A Guide to Central America. 272p. (Orig.). 1982. pap. 5.95 (ISBN 0-686-37896-2). Resource Ctr.

Barry, Vincent. Good Reason for Writing: A Text with Readings. 400p. 1982. pap. text ed. 12.95x (ISBN 0-534-01232-9). Wadsworth Pub.

--Philosophy: A Text with Readings. 544p. 1980. text ed. 21.95x (ISBN 0-534-00767-8). Wadsworth Pub.

--Philosophy: A Text with Readings. 2nd ed. 544p. 1982. text ed. 21.95x (ISBN 0-534-01216-7). Wadsworth Pub.

Barry, W. R., ed. Architectural, Construction, Manufacturing & Engineering Glossary of Terms. 519p. 1979. pap. 40.00 (ISBN 0-930284-05-4). Am Assn Cost Engineers.

Barry, Wallace. Structural Functions in Music. (Illus.). 512p. 1976. 24.95 (ISBN 0-13-853903-0). P-H.

Barry, William, jt. auth. see Dominic, Randolph.

Barrymore, Lionel. We Barrymores. LC 74-7602. (Illus.). 311p. 1974. Repr. of 1951 ed. lib. bdg. 20.00x (ISBN 0-8371-7550-X, BAB). Greenwood.

Barsch, Ray H. Enriching Perception & Cognition. LC 68-282. (Perceptual-Motor Curriculum: Vol. 2). 1969. 18.00x o.p. (ISBN 0-87562-010-8). Spec Child.

Barsh, Elizabeth T., jt. auth. see Blackard, M. Kay.

Barsh, Russel L. & Henderson, J. Youngblood. The Road: Indian Tribes & Political Liberty. 1980. 17.95x (ISBN 0-520-03629-8). U of Cal Pr.

Barshay, Robert H. Philip Wylie: The Man & His Work. LC 79-63682. 1979. pap. text ed. 8.25 (ISBN 0-8191-0733-6). U Pr of Amer.

Bar-Siman-Tov, Yaacov. Linkage Politics in the Middle East: Syria Between Domestic & External Conflict, 1961-1970. (Replica Edition Ser.). 225p. 1983. softcover 18.50x (ISBN 0-86531-945-6). Westview.

Barskaya, Anna, compiled By. Monet. (Illus.). 50p. 1982. pap. 14.95 o.p. (ISBN 0-8109-2265-7, 2219-3). Abrams.

Barsocchini, Peter, jt. auth. see Griffin, Merv.

Barson. Laboratory Investigation of Fetal Disease. 520p. 1981. 54.00 (ISBN 0-7236-0563-7). Wright-PSG.

Barsoum, R. S., ed. Simplified Methods in Pressure Vessel Analysis, PVP-PB-029. (Pressure Vessel & Piping Division Ser.: Bk. No. G00137). 1978. 18.00 (ISBN 0-685-37581-1). ASME.

Barston, R. P. & Birnie, Patricia, eds. The Maritime Dimension. (Illus.). 272p. 1981. text ed. 27.50x (ISBN 0-04-341015-4); pap. text ed. 12.50x (ISBN 0-04-341016-2). Allen Unwin.

Barstow, Anne L. Married Priests & the Reforming Papacy: The 11th Century Debates. LC 82-7914. (Texts & Studies in Religion: Vol. 12). 344p. 1982. 39.95x (ISBN 0-88946-987-3). E Mellen.

Barstow, D. R. Knowledge-Based Program Construction. (Programming Language Ser.: Vol. 6). 1979. 25.00 (ISBN 0-444-00340-1, North Holland); pap. 15.50 (ISBN 0-444-00341-X). Elsevier.

Barsuhn, Rochelle N. Afraid. LC 82-4559. (What Does it Mean? Ser.). (Illus.). 32p. (gr. 1-2). 1982. PLB 4.95 (ISBN 0-89565-235-8, 4894, Pub. by Childs World). Standard Pub.

--Angry. LC 82-4570. (What Does it Mean? Ser.). (Illus.). 32p. (gr. 1-2). 1982. PLB 4.95 (ISBN 0-89565-234-X, 4895, Pub. by Childs World). Standard Pub.

Barswell, C. N. Fundamentals of Molecular Spectroscopy. 2nd ed. 1973. text ed. 15.95 o.p. (ISBN 0-07-084007-5, P&RB). McGraw.

Barsy, Kalman. Cuento del coqui valiente. LC 81-68705. (Illus.). 75p. 1982. pap. text ed. cancelled (ISBN 0-940238-53-5). Ediciones Huracan.

Bart, Benjamin F. Flaubert. LC 67-27410. (Illus.). 1967. 16.00 o.p. (ISBN 0-8156-0057-7); pap. 11.95 (ISBN 0-8156-0087-9). Syracuse U Pr.

Bart, Pauline B. & Frankel, Linda. The Student Sociologist's Handbook. 3rd ed. 1981. pap. text ed. 6.95x o.p. (ISBN 0-673-15367-3). Scott F.

Bart, Philip, et al, eds. Highlights of a Fighting History: Sixty Years of the Communist Party, U.S.A. LC 79-14000. (Illus.). 1979. 15.00 (ISBN 0-7178-0559-X); pap. 5.25 (ISBN 0-7178-0502-6). Intl Pub Co.

Bar-Tal, Daniel & Saxe, Leonard. Social Psychology of Education: Theory & Research. LC 77-28746. 1978. text ed. 16.95 (ISBN 0-470-26306-7). Halsted Pr.

Bartas, Guillaume D. Du see Du Bartas, Guillaume D.

Bartee, T. C., jt. auth. see Birkhoff, G.

Bartee, Thomas. Digital Computer Fundamentals. 5th ed. (Illus.). 576p. 1980. text ed. 28.95 (ISBN 0-07-003894-5, C); instr's manual 8.50 (ISBN 0-07-003895-3). McGraw.

Bartee, Thomas C. Digital Computer Fundamentals. 4th ed. (Illus.). 1977. text ed. 18.95 o.p. (ISBN 0-07-003892-9, C); instructor's manual 4.95 o.p. (ISBN 0-07-003893-7). McGraw.

--Introduction to Computer Science. 1974. 29.95 (ISBN 0-07-003880-5, C); instructor's manual 7.95 (ISBN 0-07-069265-3). McGraw.

Bartek, Edward J. Mind of Future Man. 111p. 1965. pap. 3.00 (ISBN 0-934310-00-9). Trinity Bks.

--Philosophy of Trinityism, 2 vols. rev. ed. 540p. 1978. Vol. I. 8.00 (ISBN 0-934310-02-5); Vol. II. 10.00 (ISBN 0-934310-03-3); 20.00 set (ISBN 0-934310-01-7). Trinity Bks.

--Trinitarian Philosophical Psychology, 2 vols. 1978. Vol. I. 8.00 (ISBN 0-934310-06-8); Vol. II. 8.00 (ISBN 0-934310-07-6); 20.00 set (ISBN 0-934310-05-X). Trinity Bks.

--Trinitarian Philosophy - Psychology Poems. rev. ed. 1978. 10.00 (ISBN 0-934310-08-4). Trinity Bks.

--Truth & Wisdom, 4 vols, Nos. 1-4. 156p. 1968. Ea. pap. 5.00 (ISBN 0-934310-09-2). Vol. 1 (ISBN 0-934310-10-6). Vol. 2 (ISBN 0-934310-11-4). Vol. 3 (ISBN 0-934310-12-2). Vol. 4 (ISBN 0-934310-13-0). Set. Trinity Bks.

--Ultimate Philosophy: Trinityism. 103p. 1968. pap. 3.00 (ISBN 0-934310-14-9). Trinity Bks.

--Unifying Principles of the Mind. 190p. 1969. pap. 4.00 (ISBN 0-934310-15-7). Trinity Bks.

Bartell, Steven M., jt. ed. see Fontaine, Thomas D., III.

Bartels, J. see Fluegge, E.

Bartels, Michael M., jt. auth. see Reisdorff, James J.

Bartels, Michael M., et al. A Railfan's Guide to Nebraska. 48p. 1975. pap. 1.75 o.p. (ISBN 0-685-57652-3). J-B Pubs.

Bartels, Susan L. Step Carefully in Night Grass. LC 74-75750. 64p. 1974. 5.95 (ISBN 0-910244-76-6). Blair.

Bartelt, Victor A. Living Our Lives for God. 1957. pap. 0.75 o.p. (ISBN 0-8100-0039-3, 15-0316). Northwest Pub.

Barten, Harvey H. Brief Therapies. LC 78-140053. 250p. 1971. text ed. 22.95 o.p. (ISBN 0-87705-017-1). Human Sci Pr.

Barten, Harvey H., jt. ed. see Bellak, Leopold.

Bartene, I., jt. auth. see Fyodorov, B.

Bartenev, G. M. Friction & Wear of Polymers. (Tribilogy Ser.: Vol. 6). 1981. 70.25 (ISBN 0-444-42000-2). Elsevier.

Bartenieff, I. & Lewis, D. Body Movement: Coping with the Environment. 304p. 1980. 43.00 (ISBN 0-677-05500-5). Gordon.

Barter Publishing Staff. Barter Alert. 60p. 1983. pap. text ed. 9.95 (ISBN 0-686-37637-4). Barter Pub.

--Barter Referral Directory. 300p. Date not set. pap. text ed. 29.95 (ISBN 0-686-37635-8). Barter Pub.

--Business Bartering: A Bibliography. 15p. 1983. pap. text ed. 4.95 (ISBN 0-686-37639-0). Barter Pub.

--The Piggy Back Concept: Reference Pages. 25p. 1983. pap. text ed. 3.00 (ISBN 0-686-37638-2). Barter Pub.

Barter Publishing Staff, ed. Directory of Barter Associations & Organizations Based in Arizona. 50p. 1983. pap. 9.95 (ISBN 0-911617-05-1). Barter Pub.

--Directory of Barter Associations & Organizations Based in California. 25p. 1983. pap. 9.95 (ISBN 0-911617-07-8). Barter Pub.

--Directory of Barter Associations & Organizations Based in Colorado. 50p. 1983. pap. 9.95 (ISBN 0-911617-08-6). Barter Pub.

--Directory of Barter Associations & Organizations Based in Florida. 50p. 1983. pap. 9.95 (ISBN 0-911617-12-4). Barter Pub.

--Directory of Barter Associations & Organizations Based in Maryland. 30p. 1983. pap. 9.95 (ISBN 0-911617-21-3). Barter Pub.

--Directory of Barter Associations & Organizations Based in Massachusetts. 35p. 1983. pap. 9.95 (ISBN 0-911617-22-1). Barter Pub.

--Directory of Barter Associations & Organizations Based in North Carolina. 40p. 1983. pap. 9.95 (ISBN 0-911617-36-1). Barter Pub.

--Directory of Barter Associations & Organizations Based in Ohio. 35p. Date not set. pap. 9.95 (ISBN 0-911617-38-8). Barter Pub.

--Directory of Barter Associations & Organizations Based in Pennsylvania. 50p. 1983. pap. 9.95 (ISBN 0-911617-40-X). Barter Pub.

--Directory of Barter Associations & Organizations Based in Washington. 50p. Date not set. pap. 9.95 (ISBN 0-911617-49-3). Barter Pub.

--Directory of Barter Associations Organizations Based in New York. 60p. 1983. pap. 9.95 (ISBN 0-911617-35-3). Barter Pub.

Bartfai, P. & Tomko, J. Point Process Queuing Problems. (Colloquia Mathematics Ser.: Vol. 24). 1981. 76.75 (ISBN 0-444-85432-0). Elsevier.

Barth & Deal. The Effective Principal: A Research Summary. Lucas, Pat, ed. 48p. 1982. pap. text ed. 4.00 (ISBN 0-88210-141-2). Natl Assn Principals.

Barth, A. Religions of India. 6th ed. Wood, J., tr. from Fr. 309p. 1980. Repr. of 1880 ed. 23.95x (ISBN 0-940500-64-7). Asia Bk Corp.

Barth, Alan. The Price of Liberty. LC 74-176486. (Civil Liberties in American History Ser.). 1972. Repr. of 1961 ed. lib. bdg. 29.50 (ISBN 0-306-70416-1). Da Capo.

Barth, E. M. & Krabbe, E. C., eds. From Axiom to Dialogue: Foundations of Communication Ser. xi, 337p. 1982. 69.00x (ISBN 3-11-008489-9). De Gruyter.

Barth, E. M., ed. see Symposium on Theory of Argumentation, Groningen, October 11-13, 1978.

Barth, Edna. Cupid & Psyche: A Love Story. LC 76-8821. (Illus.). 64p. (gr. 3-6). 1976. 10.95 (ISBN 0-395-28840-1, Clarion). HM.

--Shamrocks, Harps, & Shillelaghs: The Story of the St. Patrick's Day Symbols. LC 77-369. (Illus.). 96p. (gr. 3-6). 1977. 9.95 (ISBN 0-395-28845-2, Clarion). HM.

--Turkeys, Pilgrims, & Indian Corn: The Story of the Thanksgiving Symbols. LC 75-4703. (Illus.). 96p. (gr. 3-6). 1975. 9.95 (ISBN 0-395-28846-0, Clarion). HM.

Barth, Gunther. Instant Cities: Urbanization & the Rise of San Francisco & Denver. (Urban Life in America Ser). (Illus.). 384p. 1975. 19.95 (ISBN 0-19-501899-0). Oxford U Pr.

Barth, Gunther P. Bitter Strength: A History of the Chinese in the United States, 1850-1870. LC 64-21785. (Center for the Study of the History of Liberty in America Ser). 1964. 16.50x o.p. (ISBN 0-674-07600-1). Harvard U Pr.

Barth, Hans. Truth & Ideology. LC 74-81430. Orig. Title: Wahrheit und Ideologie. 1977. 28.50x (ISBN 0-520-02820-1). U of Cal Pr.

Barth, J. Robert, ed. Religious Perspectives in Faulkner's Fiction: Yoknapatawpha & Beyond. LC 75-185896. 244p. 1972. 8.95x o.p. (ISBN 0-268-00464-1); pap. 3.25x o.p. (ISBN 0-268-00512-5). U of Notre Dame Pr.

Barth, James L. Elementary & Middle School Social Studies Curriculum Program, Activities, Materials. LC 78-71367. 1979. pap. text ed. 12.00 (ISBN 0-8191-0667-4). U Pr of Amer.

--Methods of Instruction in Social Studies Education. LC 79-66224. 1979. pap. text ed. 12.25 (ISBN 0-8191-0817-0). U Pr of Amer.

Barth, James L., ed. Principles of Social Studies: The Why, What, & How of Social Studies Instruction. LC 79-5513. 1980. pap. text ed. 9.25 (ISBN 0-8191-0902-9). U Pr of Amer.

Barth, John. The End of the Road. LC 58-9381. 1967. 4.95 (ISBN 0-385-09026-9). Doubleday.

--Letters. 1982. pap. write for info. (ISBN 0-449-90090-8, Columbine). Fawcett.

--Letters: A Novel. LC 79-13503. 1979. 16.95 (ISBN 0-399-12425-X). Putnam Pub Group.

--The Literature of Exhaustion. Bd. with The Literature of Replenishment. 100p. 1982. deluxe ed. 75.00 signed (ISBN 0-935716-16-5). Lord John.

--Sabbatical: A Romance. 352p. 1982. 14.95 (ISBN 0-399-12717-8). Putnam Pub Group.

--Sabbatical: A Romance. 1983. pap. 5.95 (ISBN 0-14-006619-5). Penguin.

Barth, Karl. Church Dogmatics. Incl. Vol. 4, Pt. 3. Doctrine of Reconciliation, 2 sections. Section II Repr. Of 1962 Ed., 492p. text ed. 26.00x o.p. (ISBN 0-567-09044-2); Pt. 4, Repr. Of 1969 Ed., 240p. 13.95x o.p. (ISBN 0-567-09045-0); Vol. 5. Index: with Aids to the Preacher. Bromiley, G. W. & Torrance, G. F. 584p. Repr. of 1977 ed. 32.00x o.p. (ISBN 0-567-09046-9). Attic Pr.

--Church Dogmatics: A Selection. abr ed. pap. 5.95xi (ISBN 0-06-130095-0, TB95, Torch). Har-Row.

--Church Dogmatics: A Selection. 12.00 (ISBN 0-8446-5842-1). Peter Smith.

--Deliverance to the Captives. LC 78-12767. 1979. Repr. of 1978 ed. lib. bdg. 16.25x (ISBN 0-313-21179-5, BADC). Greenwood.

--Dogmatics in Outline. pap. 4.95xi o.p. (ISBN 0-06-130056-X, TB56, Torch). Har-Row.

--The Theology of Schleiermacher. Bromiley, Geoffrey W., tr. 1982. 10.95 (ISBN 0-8028-3565-1). Eerdmans.

Barth, Karl & Zuckmayer, Carl. A Late Friendship: The Letters of Carl Zuckmayer & Karl Barth. Bromiley, Geoffrey W., tr. 80p. 1983. 7.95 (ISBN 0-8028-3574-0). Eerdmans.

Barth, Peter S. & Hunt, H. Allen. Workers' Compensation & Work-Related Illnesses & Diseases. 1980. text ed. 35.00x (ISBN 0-262-02141-2). MIT Pr.

Barth, R. L. Forced-Marching to the Styx. (Poetry Chapbks.). 20p. 1983. pap. 2.50 (ISBN 0-912288-21-3, PER-17). Perivale Pr.

--Looking for Peace. 56p. (Orig.). 1982. pap. 3.25 o.p. (ISBN 0-941150-00-3). Barth.

Barth, T. Potential Theory: An Introduction. (Research Notes in Mathematics). 150p. 1984. pap. text ed. price not set (ISBN 0-273-08524-7). Pitman Pub MA.

Barthel, J. Thermometric Titrations. (Chemical Analysis Ser: Vol. 45). 209p. 1975. 34.50 o.p. (ISBN 0-471-05448-8, Pub. by Wiley-Interscience). Wiley.

Barthel, Manfred. What the Bible Really Says: Casting New Light on the Book of Books. Howson, Mark, tr. from Ger. (Illus.). 416p. 1983. pap. 7.50 (ISBN 0-688-01979-X). Quill NY.

Barthel, Thomas. The Eighth Land: The Polynesian Discovery & Settlement of Easter Island. Martin, Anneliese, tr. from Ger. LC 78-21945. 1978. text ed. 20.00x (ISBN 0-8248-0553-4). UH Pr.

Barthelme, Donald. Sixty Stories. 480p. 1981. 15.95 (ISBN 0-399-12659-7); limited deluxe boxed 50.00 (ISBN 0-399-12675-9). Putnam Pub Group.

--Sixty Stories. Whitehead, Bill, ed. 464p. 1982. pap. 8.95 (ISBN 0-525-48018-8, 0869-260, Obelisk). Dutton.

--Slightly Irregular Fire Engine, or the Hithering Thithering Djinn. LC 70-162793. (Illus.). 32p. (ps-3). 1971. 4.95 o.p. (ISBN 0-374-37038-9). FS&G.

--Unspeakable Practices, Unnatural Acts. LC 68-14918. 170p. 1968. 6.95 o.p. (ISBN 0-374-28176-9). FS&G.

Barthelmeh, Volker. Street Murals. LC 82-80836. 1982. 20.00 (ISBN 0-394-52783-6); pap. 11.95 (ISBN 0-394-71196-3). Knopf.

Barthes, Roland. Barthes Reader. Sontag, Susan, intro. by. LC 80-26762. (Illus.). 495p. 1982. 20.00 (ISBN 0-8090-2815-8); pap. 9.95 o.p. (ISBN 0-8090-1394-0). Hill & Wang.

--Empire of Signs. Howard, Richard, tr. from Fr. (Illus.). 1982. 12.95 (ISBN 0-8090-4222-3). Hill & Wang.

--S-Z. Miller, Richard, tr. 271p. 1974. 10.95 (ISBN 0-8090-8375-2); pap. 7.95 (ISBN 0-8090-1377-0). Hill & Wang.

Barthes, Roland, jt. auth. see Lambert, Yvon.

Barthes, Ronald. The Fashion System. Ward, Matthew & Howard, Richard, trs. from Fr. 1983. 20.50 (ISBN 0-8090-4437-4). Hill & Wang.

Barthlolmew, Mel. Square Foot Gardening. (Illus.). 360p. 14.95 (ISBN 0-87857-340-2); pap. 11.95 (ISBN 0-87857-341-0). Rodale Pr Inc.

Bartholic, Edward L. Cricket & Sparrow. LC 78-13141. (Illus.). 48p. (ps-3). 1979. 6.95 o.s.i. (ISBN 0-529-05512-0, Philomel); PLB 6.99 o.s.i. (ISBN 0-529-05513-9). Putnam Pub Group.

Bartholmer, Barbara. Anne & Jay. 1982. pap. 1.75 (ISBN 0-451-11655-0, AE1655, Sig Vista). NAL.

Bartholomaeo, S., jt. auth. see Paulinus.

Bartholomeusz, Dennis. Macbeth & the Players. LC 69-10270. (Illus.). 1969. 49.50 (ISBN 0-521-06925-4, 4); pap. 12.95 (ISBN 0-521-29322-7). Cambridge U Pr.

--The Winter's Tale in Performance in England & America, 1611-1976. LC 81-24198. (Illus.). 324p. 1982. 44.50 (ISBN 0-521-24529-X). Cambridge U Pr.

Bartholomew. Jimmy & the White Lie. (Illus.). 32p. (gr. k-9). 1976. 3.50 (ISBN 0-570-03460-4, 56-1294). Concordia.

Bartholomew & Orr. Learning to Read & Make Mechanical Drawings. (gr. 7-9). 1982. pap. text ed. 5.20 (ISBN 0-87002-371-3). Bennett IL.

Bartholomew, Cecilia. Outrun the Dark. LC 77-8975. 1977. 8.95 o.p. (ISBN 0-399-12047-5). Putnam Pub Group.

--Second Sight. 1981. pap. 2.75 o.p. (ISBN 0-425-04798-9). Berkley Pub.

--Second Sight. 1980. 10.95 o.p. (ISBN 0-399-12441-1). Putnam Pub Group.

Bartholomew, D. J. Stochastic Models for Social Processes. 3rd ed. (Wiley Ser. in Probability & Mathematical Statistics: Applied Probability & Statistics Section). 365p. 1982. 44.95x (ISBN 0-471-28040-2, Pub. by Wiley-Interscience). Wiley.

--Stochastic Models for Social Processes. 2nd ed. LC 73-2776. (Probability & Mathematical Statistics Ser.: Applied Probability & Statistic Section). 408p. 1974. 57.50 (ISBN 0-471-05451-8, Pub. by Wiley-Interscience). Wiley.

Bartholomew, D. J. & Morris, B. R. Aspects of Manpower Planning. (NATO Ser). 1971. 21.95 o.p. (ISBN 0-444-19603-X). Elsevier.

Bartholomew, David. Mathematical Methods in Social Scientists. LC 80-41593. (Handbook of Applicable Mathematics Ser.). 148p. 1981. 29.95 (ISBN 0-471-27932-3, Pub. by Wiley-Interscience); pap. 16.95 (ISBN 0-471-27933-1, Pub. by Wiley-Interscience). Wiley.

Bartholomew, David J. & Forbes, Andrew F. Statistical Techniques for Manpower Planning. LC 78-8604. (Probability & Mathematical Statistics: Applied Section Ser.). 288p. 1979. 59.95x (ISBN 0-471-99670-X, Pub. by Wiley-Interscience). Wiley.

Bartholomew, Doris. A Manual for Practical Grammars. 44p. 1976. pap. 4.00x o. p. (ISBN 0-685-51606-7); microfiche 1.50 (ISBN 0-88312-330-4). Summer Inst Ling.

Bartholomew, J. G. A Literary Historical Atlas of Europe. 253p. 1983. Repr. of 1982 ed. lib. bdg. 30.00 (ISBN 0-89984-092-2). Century Bookbindery.

Bartholomew, Mel. How to Plant a Vegetable Garden. 144p. 1982. write for info.; pap. cancelled (ISBN 0-88453-036-1). Berkshire Traveller.

Bartholomew, Paul C. Summaries of Leading Cases on the Constitution. 10th ed. Menez, Joseph F., rev. by. LC 68-7178. (Quality Paperback: No. 50). 1979. pap. 5.95 o.p. (ISBN 0-8226-0050-1). Littlefield.

Bartholomew, Robert, et al. Child Care Centers: Indoor Lighting - Outdoor Playspace. LC 72-90516. (Illus.). 1973. pap. 2.90 (ISBN 0-87868-099-3, J-57). Child Welfare.

Bartholomew, Rolland & Crawley, Frank. Science Laboratory Techniques. (gr. 9-12). 1980. pap. text ed. 14.50 (ISBN 0-201-00354-6, Sch Div). A-W.

Bartholomew, Roy A. & Orr, Francis S. Learning to Read & Make Mechanical Drawings. rev. ed. (gr. 9-12). 1970. pap. text ed. 5.20 o.p. (ISBN 0-87002-040-4); tchr. guide free o.p. Bennett IL.

Bartholomew's Cartographic Staff, illus. Bartholomew World Atlas. rev. ed. (Illus.). 168p. 1982. 35.00 (ISBN 0-7028-0404-5). Hammond Inc.

Bartholomy, David. Sometimes You Just Have to Stand Naked: A Guide to Interesting Writing. (Illus.). 224p. 1983. pap. text ed. 8.95 (ISBN 0-13-822593-1). P-H.

Bartik, M. & Piskac, A., eds. Veterinary Toxicology: Developments in Animal & Veterinary Science Ser. (Vol. 7). 1981. 61.75 (ISBN 0-444-99757-1). Elsevier.

Bartke, Wolfgang. China's Economic Aid. LC 74-78315. 206p. 1975. 30.00x (ISBN 0-8419-0179-1). Holmes & Meier.

--Who's Who in the People's Republic of China. LC 80-27599. (Illus.). 750p. 1981. 125.00 (ISBN 0-87332-183-9). M E Sharpe.

Bartkowiak, Robert A. Electric Circuits. LC 72-14366. 478p. 1973. text ed. 26.50 scp (ISBN 0-7002-2421-1, HarpC); solution manual avail. (ISBN 0-7002-2530-7). Har-Row.

Bartl, R. & Frisch, B. Bone Marrow Biopsies Revisited. (Illus.). x, 94p. 1982. 34.75 (ISBN 3-8055-3572-4). S Karger.

Bartle, Dorothy B., ed. see Wait, George W.

Bartle, Robert G. Elements of Integration. LC 75-15979. 129p. 1966. 22.95x (ISBN 0-471-05457-7). Wiley.

--The Elements of Real Analysis. 2nd ed. LC 75-15979. 480p. 1976. text ed. 30.50x (ISBN 0-471-05464-X); arabic translation avail. (ISBN 0-471-06391-6). Wiley.

Bartle, Wilmot T., ed. see Spencer, Anne M.

Bartleson, James, jt. ed. see Grum, Fran.

Bartlett, A., jt. ed. see Voller, A.

Bartlett, A. J., jt. auth. see Garbutt, J. W.

Bartlett, Bruce R. Reaganomics: Supply-Side Economics in Action. LC 82-472. 264p. 1982. pap. 7.50 (ISBN 0-688-01182-9). Quill NY.

--Reagonomics: Supply-Side Economics in Action. 1982. pap. 7.00 (ISBN 0-686-94035-0). Morrow.

--A Walk on the Supply Side: Economic Policies for the Eighties & Beyond. 256p. 1981. 14.95 o.p. (ISBN 0-87000-505-7, Arlington Hse). Crown.

Bartlett, C. J. The Rise & Fall of the Pax Americana: U. S. Foreign Policy in the Twentieth Century. LC 74-24742. 300p. 1975. 23.00 (ISBN 0-312-68355-3). St Martin.

Bartlett, C. J., ed. Britain Pre-Eminent: Studies in British World Influence in the Nineteenth Century. LC 75-93447. (Problems in Focus Ser). 1969. 22.50 (ISBN 0-312-09835-9). St Martin.

--The Long Retreat. LC 79-177925. 1972. 25.00 (ISBN 0-312-49665-6). St Martin.

Bartlett, Catherine T. My Dear Brother. 224p. 1952. 7.00 (ISBN 0-686-36718-9). Md Hist.

--Three Under Three: A Baltimore Tale. 70p. 1970. 5.00 (ISBN 0-686-36719-7). Md Hist.

--Two Links in a Chain: A Nostalgic Narrative. 119p. 1977. 12.00 (ISBN 0-686-36720-0). Md Hist.

Bartlett, David F., ed. The Metric Debate. LC 79-53270. 15.00x (ISBN 0-87081-083-9). Colo Assoc.

Bartlett, Elizabeth. Memory Is No Stranger. LC 81-1484. xii, 68p. 1981. text ed. 13.95x (ISBN 0-8214-0602-7, 82-83863); pap. 7.95 (ISBN 0-8214-0645-0, 82-83871). Ohio U Pr.

Bartlett, Frederic C. Remembering: A Study in Experimental & Social Psychology. 1932. 39.50 (ISBN 0-521-04114-7); pap. 10.95x (ISBN 0-521-09441-0). Cambridge U Pr.

Bartlett, Hazel & Gregory, Julia. Catalogue of Early Books on Music (Before 1800) LC 69-12684. (Music Ser). 1969. Repr. of 1913 ed. lib. bdg. 37.50 (ISBN 0-306-71223-7). Da Capo.

Bartlett, Henrietta C. Mr. William Shakespeare Original & Early Editions of His Quartos & Folios, His Source Books & Those Containing Contemporary Notices. 1922. 7.50x (ISBN 0-685-89767-2). Elliots Bks.

Bartlett, Irving H. American Mind in the Mid-nineteenth Century. LC 67-14299. (AHM American History Ser.). (Orig.). 1967. pap. 5.95 o.p. (ISBN 0-88295-701-5). Harlan Davidson.

--Wendell & Ann Phillips: The Community of Reform, 1840-1880. (Illus.). 256p. 1982. pap. 5.95x (ISBN 0-393-00061-3). Norton.

--Wendell Phillips, Brahmin Radical. LC 73-11849. 438p. 1973. Repr. of 1961 ed. lib. bdg. 20.75x (ISBN 0-8371-7071-0, BAWP). Greenwood.

Bartlett, J. L., jt. auth. see Helmrath, M. O.

Bartlett, J. V. Handy Farm & Home Devices & How to Make Them. (Illus.). 320p. (Orig.). 1981. pap. 9.95 (ISBN 0-262-52064-8). MIT Pr.

Bartlett, Jerry F. Getting Started in Alabama Real Estate. (Real Estate Ser.). 1978. pap. text ed. 14.50 (ISBN 0-8403-1879-0). Kendall-Hunt.

Bartlett, John. Jericho. 128p. 1982. 35.00x (ISBN 0-7188-2456-3, Pub. by Lutterworth Pr England). State Mutual Bk.

Bartlett, John, ed. Complete Concordance to Shakespeare. 1910p. 1973. 50.00 (ISBN 0-312-15645-6). St Martin.

Bartlett, Joseph W. The Law Business: A Tired Monopoly. LC 82-11309. vii, 198p. 1982. text ed. 17.50x (ISBN 0-8377-0324-7). Rothman.

Bartlett, Laurence. William Congreve: A Reference Guide. 1979. lib. bdg. 24.00 (ISBN 0-8161-8142-X, Hall Reference). G K Hall.

Bartlett, M. S. Introduction to Stochastic Processes. 3rd ed. LC 76-57094. (Illus.). 404p. 1981. pap. 19.95 (ISBN 0-521-28085-0). Cambridge U Pr.

--Probability, Statistics & Time: A Collection of Essays. (Monographs on Applied Probability & Statistics). 1975. 17.95x (ISBN 0-412-14150-7, Pub. by Chapman & Hall England); pap. 12.95x (ISBN 0-412-22260-4). Methuen Inc.

--Statistical Analysis of Spatial Pattern. (Monographs in Applied Probability & Statistics). 1976. 17.50x (ISBN 0-412-14290-2, Pub. by Chapman & Hall). Methuen Inc.

Bartlett, Margaret F. Clean Brook. LC 60-8257. (A Let's-Read-&-Find-Out Science Bk). (Illus.). (gr. k-3). 1960. PLB 10.89 (ISBN 0-690-19556-7, TYC-J). Har-Row.

--Rock All Around. (Science Is What & Why Ser). (Illus.). (gr. k-3). 1970. PLB 4.49 o.p. (ISBN 0-698-30297-4, Coward). Putnam Pub Group.

--Where Does All the Rain Go? (Science Is What & Why Ser.). (Illus.). 48p. (gr. k-3). 1974. PLB 5.99 o.p. (ISBN 0-698-30509-4, Coward). Putnam Pub Group.

--Who Will Answer the Owl? LC 74-79704. (Illus.). 64p. (gr. 3-5). 1976. PLB 5.96 o.p. (ISBN 0-698-30555-8, Coward). Putnam Pub Group.

Bartlett, R. B. Wastewater Treatment: Public Engineering Design in Metric. 1971. 39.00 (ISBN 0-85334-504-X, Pub. by Applied Sci England). Elsevier.

Bartlett, R. E. & Madill, W. Hydraulics for Public Health Engineers. (Illus.). 198p. 1982. 33.00 (ISBN 0-85334-148-6, Pub. by Applied Sci England). Elsevier.

Bartlett, R. E., ed. Developments in Sewerage, Vol. 1. 1979. 33.00 (ISBN 0-85334-831-6, Pub. by Applied Sci England). Elsevier.

Bartlett, R. P. Human Capital: The Settlement of Foreigners in Russia, 1762-1804. LC 78-68337. 1980. 59.50 (ISBN 0-521-22205-2). Cambridge U Pr.

Bartlett, Raymond C. Medical Microbiology: Quality Cost & Clinical Relevance. LC 73-18482. (Quality Control Methods in the Clinical Laboratory Ser.). 272p. 1974. 47.95x o.p. (ISBN 0-471-05475-5, Pub. by Wiley Medical). Wiley.

Bartlett, Richard & Keller, Clair. Freedom's Trail. LC 78-53884. (Illus., Gr. 8). 1979. text ed. 19.24 (ISBN 0-395-26197-X); tchr's ed. 19.80 (ISBN 0-395-26198-8). HM.

Bartlett, Richard A. The New Country: A Social History of the American Frontier 1776-1890. LC 74-79619. (Illus.). 495p. 1976. pap. 10.95 (ISBN 0-19-502021-9, 452, GB). Oxford U Pr.

Bartlett, Robert M. Pilgrim House by the Sea. (Illus.). 327p. 1973. 6.95 o.p. (ISBN 0-8158-0298-6). Chris Mass.

Bartlett, Roger W. Power Base Attribution & the Perceived Legitimacy of Managerial Accounting. Farmer, Richard N., ed. LC 82-23697. (Research for Business Decisions Ser.: No. 57). 1983. write for info. (ISBN 0-8357-1393-8). Univ Microfilms.

Bartlett, Roland W. The Fans Vote! One Hundred Baseball Superstars. LC 82-5118. (Illus.). 256p. 1983. 17.95 (ISBN 0-88280-088-4); pap. 9.95 (ISBN 0-88280-089-2). ETC Pubns.

Bartlett, Ronald & Wolfson, Marty. Galbraiths Garbled Economics. (Illus.). 1974. pap. 1.95 (ISBN 0-916114-03-1). Wolfson.

Bartlett, Ronald E. Public Health Engineering: Sewerage. 2nd ed. (Illus.). 1979. 33.00 (ISBN 0-85334-796-4, Pub. by Applied Sci England). Elsevier.

--Pumping Stations for Water & Sewage. LC 73-22472. 150p. 1974. 34.95 (ISBN 0-470-05477-8). Halsted Pr.

--Surface Water Sewerage. 2nd ed. LC 80-42202. 147p. 1981. 34.95 (ISBN 0-470-27144-2). Halsted Pr.

Bartlett, Ruhl J. John C. Fremont & the Republican Party. LC 73-87663. (American Scene Ser). 1970. Repr. of 1930 ed. lib. bdg. 24.50 (ISBN 0-306-71763-8). Da Capo.

Bartlett, Truman H. The Art Life of William Rimmer: Sculptor, Painter, & Physician. LC 68-27718. (Library of American Art Ser.). (Illus.). 1970. Repr. of 1890 ed. lib. bdg. 29.50 (ISBN 0-306-71166-4). Da Capo.

Bartlett, Virginia. Pickles & Pretzels: Pennsylvania's World of Food. LC 79-3996. 1980. 9.95 (ISBN 0-8229-3400-0); pap. 5.95 (ISBN 0-8229-5308-0). U of Pittsburgh Pr.

Bartlett, William I. Jones Very, Emerson's Brave Saint. LC 68-29741. (Illus.). 1968. Repr. of 1942 ed. lib. bdg. 18.55x (ISBN 0-8371-0296-0, BAJV). Greenwood.

Bartley, Douglas. Job Evaluation-Wage & Salary Administration. LC 80-21099. 272p. 1981. text ed. 18.95 (ISBN 0-201-00095-4); manual 2.50instr's. (ISBN 0-201-11200-0). A-W.

Bartley, W. W. Lewis Carroll's Symbolic Logic. (Illus.). 1978. pap. 6.95 o.p. (ISBN 0-517-53363-4, C N Potter Bks). Crown.

Bartley, W. W., ed. see Carroll, Lewis.

Bartley, W. W., III, ed. see Popper, Karl.

Bartmann, W., jt. auth. see Workshop Conference Hoechst Schloss Reisenburg, 11th, October 11-15, 1981.

Bartok, B. & Suchoff, B. Rumanian Music: 1967-1975. 5 vols. 450.00 set o.p. (ISBN 0-686-91774-X). Heinman.

Bartok, Bela. The Hungarian Folk Song. Suchoff, Benjamin, ed. Calvocoressi, M. D., tr. (Bartok Studies in Musicology). 1980. 59.50x (ISBN 0-87395-410-6); pap. text ed. 18.50x (ISBN 0-87395-439-4). State U NY Pr.

--Piano Music of Bela Bartok. Suchoff, Benjamin, ed. (Series I-Archive Edition). 13.50 (ISBN 0-8446-5875-8). Peter Smith.

--Piano Music of Bela Bartok. Suchoff, Benjamin, ed. (Series II-Archive Edition). 13.50 (ISBN 0-8446-5876-6). Peter Smith.

Bartok, Suchoff B. Rumanian Music 1965-1975, 5 vols. 450.00 (ISBN 0-686-97884-6). Heinman.

Bartol, Curt R. Criminal Behavior: A Psychosocial Approach. (Criminal Justice Ser.). (Illus.). 1980. text ed. 23.95 (ISBN 0-13-193169-5). P-H.

--Psychology & American Law. 384p. 1982. text ed. 22.95x (ISBN 0-534-01217-5). Wadsworth Pub.

Bartollas, C., et al. Juvenile Victimization: The Institutional Paradox. LC 76-3476. 324p. 1976. 18.95 (ISBN 0-470-05490-5). Halsted Pr.

Bartollas, Clemens & Miller, Stuart J. Correctional Administration: Theory & Practice. (Illus.). 1978. text ed. 21.50 (ISBN 0-07-003950-X, G); tchr's manual & key 4.50 (ISBN 0-07-003951-8). McGraw.

Bartolo, Dick De see De Bartolo, Dick & Clarke, Bob.

Barton & Ellis. Maintenance & Repair of Buildings. 1975. 27.50x (ISBN 0-408-00372-3). Butterworth.

Barton, jt. auth. see Hutchinson.

Barton, A. F. Resource Recovery & Recycling. LC 78-13601. (Environmental Science & Technology Ser.). 418p. 1979. 56.95x (ISBN 0-471-02773-1, Pub. by Wiley-Interscience). Wiley.

Barton, Allen, et al. Decentralizing City Government. (Illus.). 1977. 23.95x o.p. (ISBN 0-669-01098-7). Lexington Bks.

Barton, Allen H. Organizational Measurement & Its Bearing on the Study of College Environments. (Research Monograph: No. 2). 1961. pap. 5.00 (ISBN 0-87447-067-6, 254730). College Bd.

Barton, Andrew. The Disappointment, or, the Force of Cruelty. Mays, David, ed. LC 76-26470. 1976. 6.50 (ISBN 0-8130-0562-0). U Presses Fla.

Barton, Anne. Shakespeare & the Idea of the Play. LC 76-58419. 1977. Repr. of 1962 ed. lib. bdg. 18.75x (ISBN 0-8371-9446-6, BASI). Greenwood.

Barton, Beranrd. Metrical Effusions: Or, Verses on Various Occasions, Repr. Of 1812 Ed. Bd. with The Triumph of the Orwell. Repr. of 1817 ed; The Convict's Appeal. Repr. of 1818 ed. LC 75-31151. (Romantic Context: Poetry 1789-1830 Ser.: Vol. 7). 1977. lib. bdg. 43.00 o.s.i. (ISBN 0-8240-2106-1). Garland Pub.

Barton, Bernard. A Day in Autumn: A Poem, Repr. Of 1820 Ed. Bd. with Napoleon, & Other Poems. Repr. of 1822 ed; Verses on the Death of Percy Bysshe Shelley. Repr. of 1822 ed. LC 75-31153. (Romantic Context: Poetry 1789-1830 Ser.: Vol. 9). 1977. lib. bdg. 47.00 o.s.i. (ISBN 0-8240-2108-8). Garland Pub.

Barton, Byron. Hester. (Picture Puffins Ser.). (Illus.). (gr. 1-3). 1978. pap. 3.50 (ISBN 0-14-050281-5, Puffin). Penguin.

--Wheels. LC 78-20541. (Illus.). (ps-3). 1979. o. p. 9.57i (ISBN 0-690-03951-4, TYC-J); PLB 10.89 (ISBN 0-690-03952-2). Har-Row.

Barton, Crawford. Beautiful Men. (Illus.). 1976. pap. 15.00 o.p. (ISBN 0-917076-01-X). Liberation Pubns.

Barton, D. H., ed. see Jung, M.

Barton, David. Dying & Death. 1977. pap. text ed. 17.95 o.p. (ISBN 0-683-00440-9). Williams & Wilkins.

--Notes from the Exile. LC 82-84118. 70p. (Orig.). Date not set. pap. 3.95 (ISBN 0-941692-05-1). Elysian Pr.

Barton, David K. Radar Systems Analysis. LC 76-45811. (Artech Radar Library). 1976. Repr. of 1964 ed. 33.00x (ISBN 0-89006-043-6). Artech Hse.

Barton, Derek, et al. Tetrahedron Reports on Organic Chemistry, Vols. 1 & 4. LC 76-16352. 1977-78. Vol. 1. text ed. 81.00 (ISBN 0-08-021154-2); Vol. 4. text ed. 81.00 (ISBN 0-08-022093-2). Pergamon.

Barton, Donald K., et al. Beginning Spanish Course. 3rd ed. 1976. text ed. 21.95x (ISBN 0-669-96776-9); wkbk. 8.95x (ISBN 0-669-96784-X); tape set 8 reels 50.00 (ISBN 0-669-96792-0); 8 cassettes 30.00 (ISBN 0-669-00082-5). Heath.

Barton, Dorothea M., ed. see Kummel, W. G.

Barton, Felix. The Most Beautiful Women in British History. (Illus.). 1978. deluxe ed. 47.75 o.p. (ISBN 0-930582-07-1). Gloucester Art.

Barton, G. Introduction to Advanced Field Theory, Vol. 22. LC 63-22253. 163p. 1963. text ed. 9.50 (ISBN 0-470-05497-2, Pub. by Wiley). Krieger.

Barton, G., tr. see Pfeuty, Pierre & Toulouse, Gerard.

Barton, G. A. Sumerian Business & Administrative Documents from the Earliest Times to the Dynasty of Agade. (Publications of the Babylonian Section Ser.: Vol. 9). (Illus.). 1915. 7.00x (ISBN 0-686-24095-2). Univ Mus of U.

Barton, Gail M., jt. auth. see Barton, Walter E.

Barton, George A. Religions of the World. LC 74-90469. Repr. of 1929 ed. lib. bdg. 17.74x (ISBN 0-8371-2216-3, BARW). Greenwood.

Barton, H. Arnold. Count Hans Axel Von Fersen. (International Studies & Translations Ser.). 1975. lib. bdg. 12.50 (ISBN 0-8057-5363-X, Twayne). G K Hall.

--The Search for Ancestors: A Swedish-American Family Saga. LC 78-15537. (Illus.). 189p. 1979. 13.95 (ISBN 0-8093-0893-2). S Ill U Pr.

Barton, J. Amos' Oracles Against the Nations. LC 78-67630. (Society for Old Testament Study Ser.). 1980. 19.95 (ISBN 0-521-22501-9). Cambridge U Pr.

Barton, Jack S., et al. Future Technical Needs & Trends in the Paper Industry-II. (TAPPI PRESS Reports). (Illus.). 82p. 1976. pap. 19.95 (ISBN 0-89852-364-8, 01-01-R064). TAPPI.

Barton, Joel R., III & Grice, William A. Tennis. (Illus.). 88p. 1981. pap. text ed. 3.95x (ISBN 0-89641-065-X). American Pr.

Barton, John, adapted by see Schnitzler, Arthur.

Barton, John H., ed. see Stanford Arms Control Group.

Barton, John H., et al. Law in Radically Different Cultures. LC 82-24802. (American Casebook Ser.). 960p. 1983. text ed. write for info. (ISBN 0-314-70396-9). West Pub.

Barton, Karel. Protection Against Atmospheric Corrosion: Theories & Methods. LC 75-26570. 224p. 1976. 46.95x (ISBN 0-471-01349-8, Pub. by Wiley-Interscience). Wiley.

Barton, L., et al, eds. Schooling, Ideology & the Curriculum. 208p. 1981. write for info. (ISBN 0-905273-13-3, Pub. by Taylor & Francis); pap. write for info. (ISBN 0-905273-12-5). Intl Pubns Serv.

Barton, Len & Walker, Stephen. Race, Class & Education. 256p. 1983. text ed. 27.25 (ISBN 0-7099-0683-8, Pub. by Croom Helm Ltd England). Biblio Dist.

Barton, Lois. Spencer Butte Pioneers: One Hundred Years on the Sunny Side of the Butte 1850-1950. Mills, Charlotte & Northwest Matrix, eds. LC 82-61837. (Illus.). 144p. 1982. pap. write for info. (ISBN 0-9609420-0-9). S Butte Pr.

Barton, Lucy, frwd. by see O'Donnol, Shirley M.

Barton, Marianne, ed. British Music Yearbook 1982. 8th ed. 512p. 1982. pap. text ed. 24.50x (ISBN 0-8476-4523-1). Rowman.

Barton, Michael. Goodmen: The Character of Civil War Soldiers. LC 81-139. 144p. 1981. 14.95x (ISBN 0-271-00284-0). Pa St U Pr.

Barton, Michael, jt. ed. see Blain, Daniel.

Barton, Paul E. Worklife Transitions. 1982. 16.95 (ISBN 0-07-003974-7). McGraw.

Barton, R. F. Religion of the Ifugaos. LC 48-3664. (American Anthropological Association Memoirs Ser). Repr. of 1946 ed. pap. 23.00 (ISBN 0-527-00564-9). Kraus Repr.

Barton, R. M. Life in Cornwall: Early Nineteenth Century. 248p. 1981. 29.00x (ISBN 0-686-97157-4, Pub. by D B Barton England). State Mutual Bk.

--Life in Cornwall: Late 19th Century. 280p. 1981. 29.00x (ISBN 0-686-97163-9, Pub. by D B Barton England). State Mutual Bk.

--Life in Cornwall: Mid Nineteenth Century. 244p. 1981. 29.00x (ISBN 0-686-97164-7, Pub. by D B Barton England). State Mutual Bk.

--Waterfalls of the World. 1981. 30.00x (ISBN 0-686-97153-1, Pub. by D B Barton England). State Mutual Bk.

Barton, Roger. Handbook of Advertising Management. 1970. 59.95 (ISBN 0-07-003966-6, P&RB). McGraw.

Barton, Roger E., jt. auth. see Richardson, Richard E.

Barton, Roy F. Ifugao Law. LC 78-76334. (Illus.). 1969. Repr. of 1919 ed. 21.95x (ISBN 0-520-01427-8). U of Cal Pr.

Barton, S. R., jt. auth. see O'Rourke, Karen.

Barton, S. W., jt. auth. see Kurland, Michael.

Barton, Walter E. & Barton, Gail M. Mental Health Administration: Principles & Practice, 2 vols. LC 81-7064. 1008p. 1982. 45.00 ea. Vol. I (ISBN 0-89885-061-4). Vol. II (ISBN 0-89885-062-2). Set. 90.00 (ISBN 0-89885-110-6). Human Sci Pr.

Barton, William B., Jr. A Calendar to the Complete Edition of the Sermons of Ralph Waldo Emerson. LC 77-23714. 1977. 6.95 (ISBN 0-930898-01-X). Bee Bks.

Barton, William E. Safed & Keturah. LC 69-19473. 1969. pap. 2.95 (ISBN 0-8042-3425-6). John Knox.

--Safed the Sage: Selections from Wit & Wisdom of Safed the Sage. LC 65-13377. 1965. pap. 2.95 (ISBN 0-8042-3424-8). John Knox.

Barton, Winifred W. John P. Williamson: A Brother to the Sioux. LC 80-53176. (Illus.). 308p. 1980. Repr. of 1919 ed. 16.00 (ISBN 0-9610012-0-8). Sunnycrest Pub.

Bartone, J. C., ed. see American Health Research Institute.

Bartone, J. C., ed. see American Health Research Institute Ltd.

Bartone, J. C., ed. see Reynolds, Brenda, et al.

Bartone, J. C., et al, eds. see American Health Research Institute.

Bartone, J. C., et al, eds. see American Health Research Institute, Ltd.

Bartone, J. C., et al, eds. see American Health Research Institute Ltd.

Bartone, John C., ed. see American Health Research Institute, Ltd.

Bartoo, Grover C., et al. Foundation Mathematics. 3rd ed. (gr. 9). 1968. text ed. 10.60 (ISBN 0-07-003989-5, W). McGraw.

Bartos, ed. Bond in Concrete. (Applied Science Ser.). 1982. 80.00 (ISBN 0-85334-156-7). Elsevier.

Bartos, Beth, ed. see Junior Service League of Brooksville Florida.

Bartos, Rena. The Moving Target: What Every Marketer Should Know About Women. LC 81-70148. (Illus.). 320p. 1982. text ed. 17.95 (ISBN 0-02-901700-9). Free Pr.

Bartos, V., jt. ed. see Malek, P.

Bartosek, I., et al, eds. Isolated Liver Perfusion & Its Applications. LC 72-95635. (Mario Negri Institute for Pharmacological Research Monographs). (Illus.). 303p. 1973. 28.00 (ISBN 0-911216-43-X). Raven.

Bartosek, Ivan, et al, eds. Animals in Toxicological Research. (Monographs of the Mario Negri Institute for Pharmacological Research). 224p. 1982. text ed. 29.00 (ISBN 0-89004-811-8). Raven.

Bartow, Arthur, jt. ed. see Zesch, Lindy.

Bartow, Maxine, jt. ed. see Allen, Celine.

Bartram, E. B. Mosses of the Phillipines. (Illus.). 437p. 1972. Repr. of 1939 ed. lib. bdg. 54.00x (ISBN 3-87429-033-6). Lubrecht & Cramer.

Bartram, G. & Waine, A. Brecht in Perspective. LC 81-13755. (Illus.). 288p. (Orig.). 1982. pap. text ed. 12.95x (ISBN 0-582-49205-X). Longman.

Bartram, George. The Sunset Gun. 1983. pap. 3.50 (ISBN 0-523-41867-1). Pinnacle Bks.

Bartram, Graham & Waine, Anthony, eds. Brecht in Perspective. (German Literature & Society: Vol. 2). text ed. cancelled o.s.i. (ISBN 0-85496-076-7). Humanities.

Bartram, John. Diary of a Journey Through the Carolinas, Georgia, & Florida from July 1, 1765, to April 10, 1766. Harper, Francis, ed. LC 82-62493. (Historic Byways of Florida Ser.: Vol. VIII). (Illus.). 152p. 1982. pap. 12.95 (ISBN 0-941948-08-0). St Johns-Oklawaha.

Bartram, William. Travels. Van Doren, Mark, ed. (Illus.). 9.50 (ISBN 0-8446-1600-1). Peter Smith.

Bartrum, Douglas. Foliage Plants for Your Garden. 5.50x (ISBN 0-392-06787-0, LTB). Sportshelf.

Bartsch, Karl & Sandmeyer, Louise. Skills in Life-Career Planning. LC 78-24615. (Psychology Ser.). (Illus.). 1979. pap. text ed. 13.95 o.p. (ISBN 0-8185-0322-X). Brooks-Cole.

Bartsch, R. Grammar of Adverbials. (Linguistics Ser.: Vol. 16). 1976. 59.75 (ISBN 0-444-10964-1, North-Holland). Elsevier.

Bartsch, R. & Vennemann, T. Linguistics & Neighboring Disciplines, Vol. 4. LC 74-24347. (North-Holland Linguistics Ser.). 250p. 1975. 35.00 (ISBN 0-444-10891-2, North-Holland); pap. 17.00 (ISBN 0-444-10786-X). Elsevier.

Bartsocas, Christos S., jt. ed. see Papadatos, Costas J.

Barty-King, Hugh. Girdle Round the Earth-Story of Cable & Wireless. 1979. 21.50 (ISBN 0-434-04902-6, Pub. by Heinemann). David & Charles.

Bartz, Wayne R., jt. auth. see Vogler, Roger E.

Baruah, H. K. Textbook of Plant Pathology. 486p. 1979. 50.00 (ISBN 0-686-84470-X, Pub. by Oxford & I B H India). State Mutual Bk.

Baruch, Dorothy W. New Ways in Discipline. 1949. 12.95 (ISBN 0-07-004040-0, GB). McGraw.

Baruch, G. & Barnett, R. Lifeprints: New Patterns of Love & Work for Today's Women. 368p. 1983. 16.95 (ISBN 0-07-052981-7). McGraw.

Baruch, Grace, jt. auth. see Rivers, Caryl.

Baruch, Grace K., jt. auth. see Barnett, Rosalind.

Baruch, Knei-Paz see Knei-Paz, Baruch.

Barukinamwo, Matthieu. Edith Stein: Pour une Ontologie Dynamique, Ouverte a la Transcendance Totale. 184p. (Fr.). 1982. write for info. (ISBN 3-8204-5974-X). P Lang Pubs.

Barut, A. O. & Brittin, Wesley E., eds. Lectures in Theoretical Physics, Vol. 14A: Topics in Strong Interactions. (Lectures in Theoretical Physics Ser.). (Illus.). 455p. 1972. text ed. 19.50x (ISBN 0-87081-043-X). Colo Assoc.

Barut, Asim O. & Brittin, Wesley E., eds. Lectures in Theoretical Physics Vol. 13: Desitter & Conformal Groups & Their Applications. 1971. 19.50x (ISBN 0-87081-014-6); pap. text ed. 7.50 (ISBN 0-87081-039-1). Colo Assoc.

Baruth & Duff, eds. Early Childhood Education. (Special Education Ser.). (Illus., Orig.). 1979. pap. text ed. 15.00 (ISBN 0-89568-100-5). Spec Learn Corp.

Baruth & Lane, eds. Child Psychology. (Special Education Ser.). (Illus., Orig.). 1979. pap. text ed. 15.00 (ISBN 0-89568-101-3). Spec Learn Corp.

Baruth, Leroy G. A Single Parent's Survival Guide: How to Raise the Children. 1979. pap. text ed. 6.95 (ISBN 0-8403-2053-1). Kendall-Hunt.

Baruth, Leroy G. & Eckstein, Daniel G. Life Style: Theory, Practice, & Research. 2nd ed. 224p. 1981. pap. text ed. 11.95 (ISBN 0-8403-2375-1, 40237501). Kendall-Hunt.

Barutio, William H., jt. auth. see Eizenstat, Stuart E.

Barvenel, J. C. & Forbes, C. D., eds. Pressure Sores. 270p. 1981. 85.00x (ISBN 0-333-31889-7, Pub. by Macmillan England). State Mutual Bk.

Barwick, Diane & Urry, James, eds. Aboriginal History, Vol. 5. 178p. (Orig.). 1982. pap. text ed. 14.95 (ISBN 0-686-37604-8, 1188, Pub. by ANUP Australia). Bks Australia.

Barwick, James. The Hangman's Crusade. 320p. 1981. 12.95 (ISBN 0-698-11037-4, Coward). Putnam Pub Group.

--Shadow of the Wolf. LC 78-31203. 1979. 9.95 o.p. (ISBN 0-698-10966-X, Coward). Putnam Pub Group.

Barwin, Norman B. & Belisle, Serge, eds. Adolescent Gynecology & Sexuality. LC 82-6583. (Illus.). 128p. 1982. flexicover 15.75x (ISBN 0-89352-167-1). Masson Pub.

Barwise, J., ed. Handbook of Mathematical Logic. (Studies in Logic: Vol. 90). 1977. 106.50 (ISBN 0-7204-2285-X, North-Holland). Elsevier.

Barwise, J. & Keisler, H. J., eds. Kleene Symposium. (Studies in Logic: Vol. 101). 1980. 70.25 (ISBN 0-444-85345-6). Elsevier.

Barwise, Jon & Perry, John. Situations & Attitudes. 256p. 1983. 17.50x (ISBN 0-262-02189-7). MIT Pr.

Bary, William T. De see De Bary, William T.

Bar-Yosef, Rivkah, jt. auth. see Eisenstadt, Samuel N.

Barz, P. Le & Hervier, Y., eds. Enumerative Geometry & Classical Algebra. (Progress in Mathematics Ser.: Vol. 24). 246p. 1982. text ed. 20.00 (ISBN 3-7643-3106-2). Birkhauser.

Barzel, Uriel S., ed. Osteoporosis. LC 71-109575. (Illus.). 304p. 1970. 69.50 o.p. (ISBN 0-8089-0032-3). Grune.

Barzini, Luigi, Jr., ed. see Barzini, Luigi S.

Barzini, Luigi S. Peking to Paris. Barzini, Luigi, Jr., ed. Castelvecchio, tr. LC 72-6279. (Illus.). 1973. 21.00x (ISBN 0-912050-26-8, Library Pr). Open Court.

Bar-Zohar, Michael & Haber, Eitan. The Quest for the Red Prince. (Illus.). 320p. 1983. 15.95 (ISBN 0-688-02043-7). Morrow.

Barzun, J., ed. see Kuttner, Henry.

Barzun, J., ed. see Priestley, J. B.

Barzun, J., ed. see Tyrer, Walter.

Barzun, Jacques. God's Country & Mine. LC 73-3919. 344p. 1973. Repr. of 1954 ed. lib. bdg. 17.50x (ISBN 0-8371-6860-0, BAGC). Greenwood.

--Of Human Freedom. rev., 2nd ed. LC 76-47651. 1977. Repr. of 1964 ed. lib. bdg. 17.75x (ISBN 0-8371-9321-4, BAOH). Greenwood.

--A Stroll with William James. LC 82-48108. 288p. 1983. 16.50 (ISBN 0-06-015090-4, HarpT). Har-Row.

Barzun, Jacques, ed. see Follett, Wilson.

Barzun, Jacques, tr. & intro. by see Berlioz, Hector.

Bas, M. J. Le see Le Bas, M. J.

Basa, Eniko M. Sandor Petofi. (World Authors Ser.). 1980. lib. bdg. 15.95 (ISBN 0-8057-6429-1, Twayne). G K Hall.

Basagni, Fabio. International Monetary Relations After Jamaica. (The Atlantic Papers: No. 76/4). (Orig.). 1977. pap. text ed. 4.75x (ISBN 0-686-83641-3). Allanheld.

Basagni, Fabio & Sauzey, Francois. Employee Participation & Company Reform. (The Atlantic Papers: No. 75/4). (Orig.). 1976. pap. text ed. 4.75x (ISBN 0-686-83643-X). Allanheld.

Basar. EEG Brain Dynamics. 1980. 86.75 (ISBN 0-444-80249-5). Elsevier.

Basar, E. Vasculature & Circulation: The Roll of Myogenic Reactivity in the Regulation of Blood Flow. Weiss, C., ed. 1981. 90.00 (ISBN 0-444-80271-1). Elsevier.

Basar, Erol. Biophysical & Physiological Systems Analysis: Based on Lectures for Graduate Students. 448p. 1976. text ed. 29.50 (ISBN 0-201-00846-7, Adv Bk Prog); pap. text ed. 19.50 (ISBN 0-201-00847-5). A-W.

Basart, Ann. Serial Music: A Classified Bibliography of Writings on 12 Tone & Electronic Music. LC 75-45460. 151p. 1976. Repr. of 1961 ed. lib. bdg. 18.25x (ISBN 0-8371-8753-2, BASM). Greenwood.

Basawa, I. V. & Scott, D. J. Asymptotic Optimal Inference for Non-Ergodic Models. (Lecture Notes in Mathematics Ser.: Vol. 17). 170p. 1983. pap. 15.00 (ISBN 0-387-90810-2). Springer-Verlag.

Basawa, Ishwar & Rao, Prakasa, eds. Statistical Interference for Stochastic Processes. LC 79-50533. (Probability & Mathematical Statistics Ser.). 1980. 71.50 (ISBN 0-12-080250-3). Acad Pr.

Basch, Lester D. & Finkelstein, Milton. Spelling Made Easy. 1974. pap. 3.00 (ISBN 0-87980-288-X). Wilshire.

Basch, Norma. In the Eyes of the Law: Women, Marriage, & Property in Nineteenth Century New York. LC 82-2454. 1982. 19.50x (ISBN 0-8014-1466-0). Cornell U Pr.

Basch, Paul F. International Health. 1978. text ed. 24.95x (ISBN 0-19-502328-5); pap. text ed. 12.95x (ISBN 0-19-502329-3). Oxford U Pr.

Basch, Peter & Rey, Jack. Peter Basch's Guide to Nude Figure Photography. 1961. 8.95 o.p. (ISBN 0-8174-0481-3, Amphoto). Watson-Guptill.

Bascom, W. R. The Sociological Role of the Yoruba Cult-Group. LC 44-47266. 1976. Repr. of 1944 ed. 8.00 (ISBN 0-527-00562-2). Kraus Repr.

Bascom, William. IFA Divination: Communication Between Gods & Men in West Africa. LC 69-10349. (Illus.). 604p. 1969. 35.00x (ISBN 0-253-32890-X). Ind U Pr.

Bascom, William R., ed. Frontiers of Folklore. LC 77-12784. (AAAS Selected Symposium Ser.: No. 5). (Illus.). 1978. lib. bdg. 17.00 o.p. (ISBN 0-89158-432-3). Westview.

Basdevant, J. L. & Gastmans, R., eds. Fundamental Interactions: Cargese 1981. (NATO Advanced Study Ser. B, Physics: Vol. 85). 712p. 1982. 89.50 (ISBN 0-306-41116-4, Plenum Pr). Plenum Pub.

Basel, G. I. Pak Six, A Story of the Air-War Over North Vietnam. LC 82-72150. 176p. (Orig.). 1982. pap. 7.95 (ISBN 0-933362-07-2). Assoc Creative Writers.

Baserga, Renato, ed. see Conference in Honor of Anna Goldfeder, Feb 17-19, 1982.

Basevi, Giorgio, jt. auth. see Kohl, Wilfied L.

Basgoz, Ilhan. Turkish Folklore Reader. (Uralic & Altaic Ser: Vol. 120). 1971. pap. text ed. 8.00x o.p. (ISBN 0-87750-164-5). Res Ctr Lang Semiotic.

Bash, Deborah M. & Gold, Winifred A. The Nurse & the Childbearing Family. LC 80-22945. 718p. 1981. 23.50 (ISBN 0-471-05520-4). Wiley.

Bash, Frank N. Astronomy. (Illus.). 1977. pap. text ed. 20.95 scp (ISBN 0-06-043853-3, HarpC). Har-Row.

Bash, Michael R., et al. Ingles Para Sobrevivir, 2 vols. (Vol. 1, 135 p.; vol. 2, 120 p.). 1979. Repr. of 1973 ed. 6.95 ea. o.p. Vol. 1 (ISBN 0-89196-070-8). Vol. 2 (ISBN 0-89196-071-6). tchr's ed. 4.95 o.p. (ISBN 0-89196-072-4). Quality Bks IL.

Basha, Anwar, jt. auth. see Atta-Ur-Rahman.

Basham, A. L. The Wonder That Was India. (Illus.). 568p. 1983. 34.95 (ISBN 0-283-35457-7, Pub by Sidgwick & Jackson). Merrimack Bk Serv.

Basham, A. L., ed. A Cultural History of India. (Illus.). 1975. 39.50x (ISBN 0-19-821914-8). Oxford U Pr.

Basham, Don. Libranos del Mal. 240p. Date not set. 2.95. Edit Betania.

Basham, Richard. Urban Anthropology: The Cross-Cultural Study of Complex Societies. LC 78-51942. 353p. 1978. text ed. 17.95 (ISBN 0-87484-393-6). Mayfield Pub.

Bashaw, W. L. Mathematics for Statistics. LC 69-16123. 326p. 1969. pap. 18.50x (ISBN 0-471-05531-X). Wiley.

Bashkin, S. & Stonar, J. O., Jr. Atomic Energy-Level & Grotrian Diagrams: Vol. 3: Vanadium I - Chromium XXIV. 1981. 106.50 (ISBN 0-686-80530-5). Elsevier.

Bashkin, S. & Stoner, J. O., Jr. Atomic Energy-Level & Grotrian Diagrams, Vol. 4: Manganese I-XXV. 354p. 1983. 72.50 (ISBN 0-444-86463-6, North Holland). Elsevier.

--Atomic Energy Levels & Grotrian Diagrams, Vol. 2: Sulphur I - Calcium XX. 1978. 106.50 (ISBN 0-444-85149-6, North-Holland). Elsevier.

Bashkin, S., ed. Beam-Foil Spectroscopy. (Proceedings - 3rd Conference). 1972. 109.75 (ISBN 0-7204-0277-8, North Holland). Elsevier.

Bashlor, Carolyn. Getting It All Together. 1980. pap. 3.95 o.p. (ISBN 0-88270-423-0, Pub. by Logos). Bridge Pub.

Basho. The Narrow Road to the Deep North & Other Travel Sketches. Yuasa, Nobuyuki, tr. lib. bdg. 10.50x (ISBN 0-88307-304-8). Gannon.

Basho see Shan, Han.

Bashour, Dora, jt. auth. see Ernst, Frederic.

Basi, Santokh. Semiconductor Pulse & Switching Circuits. LC 79-15379. (Electronic Technology Ser.). 538p. 1980. text ed. 23.95x (ISBN 0-471-05539-5); avail. solutions manual (ISBN 0-471-05831-9). Wiley.

Basic Environmental Problems of Man in Space II, 6th International Symposium, Bonn, Germany, 3-6 November 1980. Proceedings. Klein, K. E. & Hordinsky, J. R., eds. 250p. 1982. pap. 64.00 (ISBN 0-08-028697-6, A140). Pergamon.

Basichis, Gordon A. The Constant Travellers. LC 77-17432. 1978. 9.95 o.p. (ISBN 0-399-12109-9). Putnam Pub Group.

Basil, Cynthia. Breakfast in the Afternoon. LC 78-10366. (Illus.). (gr. k-3). 1979. PLB 8.88 (ISBN 0-688-32175-5). Morrow.

--How Ships Play Cards, a Beginning Book of Homonyms. LC 79-18420. (Illus.). 32p. (gr. k-3). 1980. 9.75 (ISBN 0-688-22217-X); PLB 9.36 (ISBN 0-688-32217-4). Morrow.

--Nailheads & Potato Eyes. LC 75-23180. (Illus.). 32p. (gr. k-3). 1976. PLB 9.36 (ISBN 0-688-32056-2). Morrow.

Basil, Douglas & Cook, Curtis W. The Management of Change. 1974. 29.50 (ISBN 0-07-084440-2, P&RB). McGraw.

Basil, Douglas C., et al, eds. Purchasing Information Sources. LC 76-7037. (Management Information Guide Ser.: No. 30). 380p. 1977. 42.00x (ISBN 0-8103-0830-4). Gale.

Basile, Frank M. Back to Basics with Basile. Glick, Marianne, ed. 305p. (Orig.). 1979. pap. 14.00 (ISBN 0-937008-01-X). Charisma Pubns.

--Beyond the Basics. Basile, Marianne G., ed. (Illus.). 76p. (Orig.). 1980. pap. 12.00 (ISBN 0-937008-02-8). Charisma Pubns.

--Flying to Your Success. (Illus.). 210p. (Orig.). 1982. pap. 15.00 (ISBN 0-937008-03-6). Charisma Pubns.

Basile, Giambattista. Petrosinella. LC 80-25840. (Illus.). 32p. 1981. 11.95 (ISBN 0-7232-6196-2). Warne.

Basile, Gloria. The Manipulators, Part 1. 1979. pap. 2.50 o.p. (ISBN 0-523-40389-5). Pinnacle Bks.

Basile, Gloria V. Appassionato. 1980. pap. 2.50 o.p. (ISBN 0-523-40072-1). Pinnacle Bks.

--Born to Power: Manipulators II. (Orig.). 1979. pap. 3.50 (ISBN 0-523-41822-1). Pinnacle Bks.

--Giants in the Shadows. (Orig.). 1979. pap. 2.75 o.p. (ISBN 0-523-40708-4). Pinnacle Bks.

Basile, Marianne G., ed. see Basile, Frank M.

Basilevsky. Applied Matrix Algebra in the Statistical Sciences. Date not set. price not set (ISBN 0-444-00756-3). Elsevier.

Basinger, Jeanine. Anthony Mann. (Filmmakers Ser.). 1979. lib. bdg. 12.95 (ISBN 0-8057-9263-5, Twayne). G K Hall.

Baskett, P. J. Immediate Prehospital Care. 290p. 1981. 45.00 (ISBN 0-471-28035-6, MD36, Pub. by Wiley-Interscience). Wiley.

Baskin, Barbara & Harris, Karen. Mainstreamed Library. 324p. 1983. text ed. 35.00. ALA.

Baskin, Leonard. Leonard Baskin's Miniature Natural History, 4 vols. LC 82-12612. (Illus., Each vol. 32 pages). 1983. Set. slipcased 9.95 (ISBN 0-394-85567-1). Pantheon.

Baskin, Wade, ed. Classics in Chinese Philosophy from Mo Tzu to Mao Tse-Tung. (Quality Paperback: No. 274). 737p. 1974. pap. 7.95 (ISBN 0-8226-0274-1). Littlefield.

Baskin, Wade see Brehier, Emile.

Basler, Beatrice K. & Basler, Thomas G., eds. Health Sciences Librarianship: A Guide to Information Sources. LC 74-11552. (Books, Publishing, & Libraries Information Guide Ser.: Vol. 1). 180p. 1977. 42.00x (ISBN 0-8103-1284-0). Gale.

Basler, Roy P. The Muse & the Librarian. LC 72-780. (Contributions in American Studies: No. 10). 1974. lib. bdg. 25.00x (ISBN 0-8371-6134-7, BML/). Greenwood.

--A Touchstone for Greatness: Essays, Addresses & Occasional Pieces About Abraham Lincoln. LC 72-781. (Contributions in American Studies: No. 4). 1973. lib. bdg. 25.00x (ISBN 0-8371-6135-5, BTG/). Greenwood.

Basler, Thomas G., jt. ed. see Basler, Beatrice K.

Basmajian. Biofeedback: Principles & Practice for Clinicians. (Illus.). 1979. 35.00 o.p. (ISBN 0-683-00357-7). Williams & Wilkins.

Basmajian, et al. Computers in Electromyography. (Computers in Medicine Ser.). 1975. 15.95 o.p. (ISBN 0-407-50005-7). Butterworth.

Basmajian, J. V. & MacConaill, M. A. Muscles & Movements: A Basis for Human Kinesiology. rev. ed. LC 76-6883. 412p. 1977. 25.50 (ISBN 0-88275-398-3). Krieger.

Basmajian, John V. Biofeedback: Principles & Practice for Clinicians. 330p. Date not set. lib. bdg. price not set (ISBN 0-683-00356-9). Williams & Wilkins.

--Primary Anatomy. 8th ed. (Illus.). 436p. 1982. text ed. 22.50 (ISBN 0-683-00550-2). Williams & Wilkins.

--Surface Anatomy: An Instruction Manual. 2nd ed. LC 77-3831. (Illus.). 78p. 1983. pap. 5.95 (ISBN 0-683-00359-3). Williams & Wilkins.

Basmajian, John V., jt. auth. see Lehmann, Justus F.

Basmajian, John V., jt. auth. see Smorto, Mairo P.

Basmajian, John V., ed. see Roy, Ranjan & Tucks, E.

Basmann, R. L. & Rhodes, George F., eds. Advances in Econometrics, Vol. 1. (Orig.). 1982. lib. bdg. 49.50 (ISBN 0-89232-138-5). Jai Pr.

Basolo, F., jt. auth. see Eliel, E. L.

Basolo, Fred. Inorganic Syntheses, Vol. 16. LC 79-642684. 270p. 1982. Repr. of 1976 ed. lib. bdg. write for info. (ISBN 0-89874-540-3). Krieger.

Basolo, Fred & Pearson, R. G. Mechanisms of Inorganic Reactions. 2nd ed. LC 66-28755. 701p. 1967. 55.00x (ISBN 0-471-05545-X, Pub. by Wiley-Interscience). Wiley.

Bason, Lillian. Those Foolish Molboes! LC 76-42459. (A Break-of-Day Bk.). (Illus.). 47p. (gr. 2-3). Date not set. 4.98 o.p. (ISBN 0-698-20397-6, Coward). Putnam Pub Group.

--Those Foolish Molboes! (Break of Day Ser.). (Illus.). (gr. k-4). 1977. PLB 6.99 o.p. (ISBN 0-698-30642-2, Coward). Putnam Pub Group.

Basov, N. G., ed. Stimulated Raman Scattering. Adashko, J. George, tr. (Proceedings (Trudy) of the Lebedev Physics Institute: Vol. 99). 175p. 1982. 45.00x (ISBN 0-306-10968-9, Plenum Pr). Plenum Pub.

Basow, Susan. Sex Role Stereotypes: Traditions & Alternatives. LC 80-19086. 320p. (Orig.). 1980. pap. text ed. 13.95 (ISBN 0-8185-0394-7). Brooks-Cole.

Basquette, Lina. How to Raise & Train a Great Dane. (Illus.). pap. 2.95 (ISBN 0-87666-308-0, DS1019). TFH Pubns.

Bass, jt. auth. see Smith.

Bass, Alan, tr. see Derrida, Jacques.

Bass, Bernard, jt. ed. see Klauss, Rudi.

Bass, Bernard M. Stogdill's Handbook of Leadership. 2nd ed. (Illus.). 1057p. 1981. text ed. 39.95. Free Pr.

Bass, Bernard M. & Vaughan, James A. Training in Industry: The Management of Learning. LC 66-24534. (Behavioral Science in Industry Ser). (Orig.). 1968. pap. text ed. 7.95 o.p. (ISBN 0-8185-0319-X). Brooks-Cole.

Bass, Billy O., jt. auth. see Glades County Commissioners.

Bass, Clarence. Ripped: The Sensible Way to Achieve Ultimate Muscularity. (Illus.). 104p. 1980. pap. 9.95 (ISBN 0-9609714-0-8). Bear & Co.

--Ripped Two. (Illus.). 179p. 1982. pap. 12.95 (ISBN 0-9609714-1-6). Clarence Bass.

Bass, David A., jt. auth. see Beeson, Paul B.

Bass, Eben E. Aldous Huxley: An Annotated Bibliography. LC 79-7907. (Garland Reference Library of Humanities). 275p. 1981. 30.00 o.s.i. (ISBN 0-8240-9525-1). Garland Pub.

Bass, George F., et al. Yassi Ada, Volume I: A Seventh-Century Byzantine Shipwreck. LC 81-40401. (Nautical Archaeology Ser.: No. 1). (Illus.). 368p. 1982. 79.50x (ISBN 0-89096-063-1). Tex A&M Univ Pr.

Bass, Helen, jt. auth. see Gulati, Bodh R.

Bass, J. & Fischer, K. H. Metals: Electronic Transport Phenomena. (Landolt Boernstein Ser.: Group III, Vol. 15, Subvol. A). (Illus.). 400p. 1983. 271.10 (ISBN 0-387-11082-8). Springer-Verlag.

Bass, Jack. Unlikely Heroes. 1982. pap. 5.95 (ISBN 0-671-44755-6, Touchstone Bks). S&S.

--Unlikely Heroes: The Southern Judges Who Made the Civil Rights Revolution. 1981. 14.95 o.p. (ISBN 0-671-25064-7). S&S.

Bass, Lawrence W. Management by Task Forces: A Manual on the Operation of Interdisciplinary Teams. LC 74-82702. 1975. 20.00 (ISBN 0-912338-09-1); microfiche 9.50 (ISBN 0-912338-10-5). Lomond.

Bass, Mary Ann & Wakefield, Lucille. Community Nutrition & Individual Food Behavior. LC 78-67116. 1979. text ed. 14.95x (ISBN 0-8087-0299-8). Burgess.

Bass, Milton R. Mister Jory. LC 75-34335. 1976. 7.95 o.p. (ISBN 0-399-11702-4). Putnam Pub Group.

--Not Quite a Hero. LC 77-4749. 1977. 8.95 o.p. (ISBN 0-399-12007-6). Putnam Pub Group.

Bass, Robert D. Ninety-Six: The Struggle for the South Carolina Back Country. LC 77-20551. (Illus.). 1978. 12.50 (ISBN 0-87844-039-9); ltd. signed 15.00 (ISBN 0-87844-017-8). Sandlapper Store.

Bass, Ronald. Lime's Crisis. LC 81-22470. 352p. 1982. 15.50 (ISBN 0-688-01025-3). Morrow.

Bass, William G., jt. auth. see Maurer, Stephen G.

Bassanese, Fiore A. Gaspara Stampa. (World Authors Ser.). 1982. lib. bdg. 18.95 (ISBN 0-8057-6501-8, Twayne). G K Hall.

Bassani, F. & Parravicini, Pastori. Electron States & Optical Transitions in Solids. 312p. 1975. text ed. 47.00 (ISBN 0-08-016846-9). Pergamon.

Bassani, Giorgio. Behind the Door. Weaver, William, tr. from It. LC 75-29308. 150p. (A/Helen & Kurt Wolff Bk.). 1976. pap. 2.25 (ISBN 0-15-611685-5, Harv). HarBraceJ.

Bass de Martinez, Bernice B., jt. auth. see Sims, William E.

Bassell, G. M., jt. auth. see Marx, G. F.

Bassett. Developments in Crystalline Polymers, Vol. 1. 1982. 65.75 (ISBN 0-85334-116-8, Pub. by Applied Sci England). Elsevier.

Bassett, Bernard. And Would You Believe It! Thoughts about the Creed. 1978. pap. 3.50 o.p. (ISBN 0-385-13367-7, Im). Doubleday.

Bassett, D. C. Principles of Polymer Morphology. (Cambrige Solid State Science Ser.). (Illus.). 220p. 1981. 57.50 (ISBN 0-521-23270-8); pap. 21.95 (ISBN 0-521-29886-5). Cambridge U Pr.

Bassett, Edward, ed. see Miles International Symposium, 12th.

Bassett, Edward G., jt. ed. see Beers, Roland F.

Bassett, Edward G., jt. ed. see Beers, Roland F., Jr.

Bassett, Fletcher S. Legends & Superstitions of the Sea & of Sailors, in All Lands & at All Times. LC 70-119444. (Illus.). 1974. Repr. of 1885 ed. 44.00 o.p. (ISBN 0-8103-3375-9). Gale.

Bassett, G. W. & Jack, Brian. The Modern Primary School in Australia. 280p. 1982. text ed. 28.50x (ISBN 0-86861-140-9). Allen Unwin.

Bassett, J. Inorganic Chemistry. 1965. text ed. 25.00 o.p. (ISBN 0-08-011207-2); pap. text ed. 9.75 o.p. (ISBN 0-08-011206-4). Pergamon.

Bassett, John S. Federalist System, 1789-1801. LC 68-55870. 1968. Repr. of 1906 ed. lib. bdg. 17.00x (ISBN 0-8371-2065-9, BAFS). Greenwood.

--Makers of a New Nation. 1928. text ed. 22.50x (ISBN 0-686-83612-X). Elliots Bks.

Bassett, Lawrence W. & Gold, Richard H., eds. Mammography, Thermography & Ultrasound in Breast Cancer Detention. Date not set. price not set (ISBN 0-8089-1509-6). Grune.

Bassett, Lee. The Mapmaker's Lost Daughter. 32p. 1980. pap. 3.50 (ISBN 0-937160-00-8). Dooryard.

Bassett, Margaret. Abraham & Mary Todd Lincoln. (Illus.). 64p. 1974. 3.75 (ISBN 0-87027-153-9); pap. 2.50 (ISBN 0-87027-148-2). Cumberland Pr.

Bassett, Michael. The American Deal. (Studies in 20th Century History). 48p. 1977. pap. text ed. 4.50x o.p. (ISBN 0-435-31763-6). Heinemann Ed.

Bassett, Paul M. Keep the Wonder. 61p. 1979. pap. 1.95 (ISBN 0-8341-0608-6). Beacon Hill.

Bassett, R. L., jt. auth. see Gustavson, T. C.

Bassett, S. R. Saffron Walden: Excavations & Research 1972-1980. (CBA Research Report: No. 45). 134p. 1982. pap. text ed. 38.00x (ISBN 0-906780-15-2, 41417, Pub. by Coun Brit Archaelolgy England). Humanities.

Bassett, T., ed. Vermont: A Bibliography of Its History. Seymour, D. 1981. lib. bdg. 35.00 (ISBN 0-8161-8567-0, Hall Reference). G K Hall.

Bassett, William B. Historic American Buildings Survey of New Jersey. (Illus.). 210p. 1977. 13.95 (ISBN 0-686-81818-0); pap. 9.95 (ISBN 0-686-81819-9). NJ Hist Soc.

Bassi, Elena. The Convento della Carita. LC 72-1140. (Corpus Palladianum: Vol. 6). (Illus.). 252p. 1974. 42.50x (ISBN 0-271-01155-6). Pa St U Pr.

Bassichis, William H. Don't Panic: A Guide to Introductory Physics for Students of Science & Engineering. pilot ed. 712p. (Orig.). 1979. pap. text ed. 14.95x (ISBN 0-8162-0389-X). Holden-Day.

Bassin, Alexander & Bratter, Thomas E. The Reality Therapy Reader: A Survey of the Work of William Glasser, M. D. 15.00 o.p. (ISBN 0-686-92212-3, 6261). Hazelden.

Bassin, Alexander, et al, eds. The Reality Therapy Reader: A Survey of the Work of William Glasser. LC 74-1789. 704p. 1976. 16.30i (ISBN 0-06-010238-1, HarpT). Har-Row.

Bassin, Ethel. The Old Songs of Skye: Frances Tolmie & Her Circle. Bowman, Derek, ed. 1977. 17.95 (ISBN 0-7100-8546-X). Routledge & Kegan.

Bassin, Milton G., et al. Statics & Strength of Materials. 2nd ed. LC 68-29909. (Illus.). 1969. text ed. 24.05 o.p. (ISBN 0-07-004035-4, G); solutions manual for selected problems 1.50 o.p. (ISBN 0-07-004034-6). McGraw.

Bassiouni, M. C., ed. International Extradition: U. S. Law & Practice, Release 1, Binder 1. 1983. loose-leaf 85.00 (ISBN 0-379-20746-X). Oceana.

--The Islamic Criminal Justice System. LC 81-22370. 255p. 1982. lib. bdg. 30.00 (ISBN 0-379-20745-1); pap. 8.00 (ISBN 0-379-20749-4). Oceana.

Bassiouni, M. Cherif & Savitski, V. M. The Criminal Justice System of the USSR. 296p. 1979. 27.50x (ISBN 0-398-03868-6). C C Thomas.

Bassis, Michael S. & Gelles, Richard J. Social Problems. Merton, Robert K., ed. 586p. 1982. text ed. 21.95 (ISBN 0-15-581430-3, HC); tests 4.95 (ISBN 0-15-581431-1); study guide 7.95 (ISBN 0-15-581432-X). HarBraceJ.

Bassis, Michael S., et al. Sociology: An Introduction. 512p. 1980. text ed. 21.00 (ISBN 0-394-32259-2); wkbk. 8.95 (ISBN 0-394-32510-9). Random.

Bassity, Matthew A. Magic World of Roses. (Illus.). 1966. 6.95 (ISBN 0-8208-0046-5). Hearthside.

Bassler, G. Clayton, jt. auth. see Silverstein, Robert M.

Bassler, Jouette M. Divine Impartiality: Paul & a Theological Axiom. Baird, William, ed. LC 81-1367. (Society of Biblical Literature Dissertation Ser.). 1981. pap. text ed. 13.50 (ISBN 0-89130-475-4, 0-06-01-59). Scholars Pr CA.

Bassler, U. Neural Basis of Elementary Behavior in Stick Insects. Strausfeld, C., tr. (Studies in Brain Function: Vol.10). (Illus.). 180p. 1983. 32.60 (ISBN 0-387-11918-3). Springer-Verlag.

Basso, Daivd T. & Schwartz, Ronald D. Programming with FORTRAN-WATFOR-WATFIV. (Orig.). 1981. pap. text ed. 14.95 (ISBN 0-316-08315-1); tchr's ed. avail. (ISBN 0-316-08317-8). Little.

Basso, Dave, ed. Nevada's Public Museums: A Guide. (Nevada Classics Ser.). (Illus.). 88p. (Orig.). 1982. pap. 5.95 (ISBN 0-936332-08-5). Falcon Hill Pr.

Basso, Dave, ed. see DeGroot, Henry.

Basso, Dave, ed. see DeQuille, Dan.

Basso, Dave, ed. see Taylor, Alexander S.

Basso, David T. & Schwartz, Ronald D. Programming in FORTRAN, WATFOR, WATFIV. (Corporate Science Ser.). 352p. 1980. 14.95 o.p. (ISBN 0-316-08315-1). Little.

Basso, Hamilton. The View from Pompey's Head. LC 79-110821. 409p. Repr. of 1954 ed. lib. bdg. 19.50 o.p. (ISBN 0-8371-3207-X, BAPH). Greenwood.

Basso, Keith H. Portraits of the Whiteman. LC 78-31535. 1979. 19.95 (ISBN 0-521-22640-6); pap. 6.50 (ISBN 0-521-29593-9). Cambridge U Pr.

Basso, Keith H., ed. see Goodwin, Grenville.

Bassoli, F., jt. auth. see Gareff, G.

Bassols, C. & Blanco, L. Ingles, Primer Curso. 1974. text ed. 2.20 o.p. (ISBN 0-07-090582-7, W). McGraw.

Bassuk, Ellen L. & Fox, Sandra S. Behavioral Emergencies: A Field Guide for EMT's & Paramedics. 1983. pap. text ed. write for info. (ISBN 0-316-08330-5); instrs.' manual avail. (ISBN 0-316-08331-3). Little.

Bassuk, Ellen L. & Gelenberg, Alan J., eds. The Practitioner's Guide to Psychoactive Drugs. (Topics in General Psychiatry Ser.). 410p. 1983. 27.50x (ISBN 0-306-41093-1, Plenum Pr). Plenum Pub.

Bast, Herbert. New Essentials of Modern Upholstery. (gr. 9-12). 1970. 10.95 o.p. (ISBN 0-02-810420-X). Glencoe.

Bast, Rochelle, ed. Handbook for Senior Adult Camping. 68p. 1977. pap. 4.00 (ISBN 0-686-84032-1). U OR Ctr Leisure.

Basta, Daniel J. & Bower, Blair T., eds. Analyzing Natural Systems: Analysis for Regional Residuals--Environmental Quality Management. LC 81-48248. (Research Paper). 564p. 1982. pap. 30.00 (ISBN 0-8018-2820-1). Johns Hopkins.

Basta, Lofty L. Cardiovascular Diseases: Essentials of Primary Care. 1983. pap. text ed. price not set (ISBN 0-87488-738-0). Med Exam.

Bastable, Patrick K. Logic: Depth Grammar of Rationality, a Textbook on the Science & History of Logic. 429p. 1975. text ed. 32.50x o.p. (ISBN 0-7171-0710-8). Humanities.

Bastenie, P. A. & Bonnyns, M., eds. Recent Progress in the Diagnosis & Treatment of Hypothyroid Conditions. (International Congress Ser.: Vol. 529). 1980. 42.25 (ISBN 0-444-90161-2). Elsevier.

Bastian, Marlene Y. How to Shop Wisely. 108p. (Orig.). 1982. pap. 5.95x (ISBN 0-9609058-0-4). M Y Bastian.

Bastias, John C., jt. ed. see Christopoulos, George A.

Bastias, John C., ed. see Christopoulos, George A.

Bastiat, Frederic. Economic Harmonies. 596p. 1968. pap. 7.00 (ISBN 0-910614-13-X). Foun Econ Ed.

--Economic Sophisms. 291p. 1968. pap. 5.00 (ISBN 0-910614-14-8). Foun Econ Ed.

--Selected Essays on Political Economy. 352p. 1968. pap. 6.00 (ISBN 0-910614-15-6). Foun Econ Ed.

Bastick, Tony. Intuition: How We Think & Act. LC 80-42060. 520p. 1982. 47.95x (ISBN 0-471-27992-7, Pub. by Wiley-Interscience). Wiley.

Bastide, Roger. The African Religions of Brazil: Toward a Sociology of the Interpenetration of Civilizations. Sebba, Helen, tr. (Johns Hopkins Studies in Atlantic History & Culture Ser.). 1978. text ed. 35.00x (ISBN 0-8018-2130-4); pap. text ed. 9.95x (ISBN 0-686-82930-1). Johns Hopkins.

Bastien, James W. How to Teach Piano Successfully. 2nd ed. LC 77-75481. (Illus.). 1977. pap. text ed. 17.95 (ISBN 0-8497-6109-3, GP40, Pub. by GWM). Kjos.

Bastien, James W. & Bastien, Jane S. Beginning Piano for Adults. LC 68-25633. (Illus.). 1968. 12.95 (ISBN 0-910842-02-7, GP23, Pub. by GWM). Kjos.

Bastien, Jane S., jt. auth. see Bastien, James W.

Bastien, Joseph W. Mountain of the Condor: Metaphor & Ritual in an Andean Ayllu. (The American Ethnological Society Ser.). (Illus.). 1978. text ed. 23.95 (ISBN 0-8299-0175-2). West Pub.

Bastien, Joseph W. & Donahue, John N., eds. Health in the Andes. 1981. pap. 15.00 (ISBN 0-686-36592-5). Am Anthro Assn.

Bastin, E. W., ed. Quantum Theory & Beyond: Essays & Discussions Arising from a Colloquium. LC 77-127237. (Illus.). 1971. 47.50 (ISBN 0-521-07956-X). Cambridge U Pr.

Baston, Abbe. Voltairimeros, Ou Premiere Jounee De M. De V. Dans L'autre Monde. Repr. of 1779 ed. 132.00 o.p. (ISBN 0-8287-0062-1). Clearwater Pub.

Basu, Romen. Candles & Roses. 204p. 1978. write for info. Sterling.

--Canvas & the Brush. 116p. 1970. write for info. (Pub. by Filma K L Mukhopadhyay India). R Basu.

--A Gift of Love. 176p. 1974. write for info. (Pub. by Writers Wksp India). R Basu.

--A House Full of People. 186p. 1968. write for info. Navana Pub.

--Portrait on the Roof. 151p. 1980. write for info. Sterling.

--Rustling of Many Winds. 204p. 1982. write for info. Sterling.

--The Tamarind Tree. 227p. 1976. write for info. (Pub. by Writers Wksp India). R Basu.

--Your Life to Live. 180p. 1972. write for info. (Pub. by Filma K L Mukhopadhyay India). R Basu.

Basu, S. K. Economics of Hire Purchase Credit. 1971. 12.50x o.p. (ISBN 0-210-98135-0). Asia.

Bataille, F. Les Reactions Macrochimiques Chez les Champignons Suives D'Indications Sur la Morphologie Des Spores. 1969. Repr. of 1948 ed. 16.00 (ISBN 3-7682-0654-8). Lubrecht & Cramer.

Bataille, Leon, ed. A Turning Point for Literacy-Adult Education for Development-Spirit & Declaration of Persepolis: Proceedings of the International Symposium for Literacy, Iran, 1975. LC 76-46206. 1977. text ed. 31.00 (ISBN 0-08-021385-5); pap. text ed. 17.25 (ISBN 0-08-021386-3). Pergamon.

Batalden, Stephen K. Catherine II's Greek Prelate: Eugenios Voulgaris in Russia, 1771-1806. (East European Monographs: No. 115). 288p. 1982. 25.00x (ISBN 0-88033-006-6). East Eur Quarterly.

Batchelder, Alan & Haitani, Kanji. International Economics: Theory & Practice. LC 70-21770. (Economics Ser.). 471p. 1981. text ed. 26.95 o.p. (ISBN 0-88244-231-7). Grid Pub.

Batchelder, Marjorie H. Puppet Theatre Handbook. LC 47-30105. (Illus.). 1947. 11.49xi (ISBN 0-06-000270-0, HarpT). Har-Row.

Batchelder, Martha. The Art of Hooked-Rug Making. (Illus.). 160p. 1983. pap. 7.95t (ISBN 0-89272-138-3). Down East.

Batcheller, John M. & Monsour, Sally. Music in Recreation & Leisure. 2nd ed. 168p. 1982. write for info. wire coil (ISBN 0-697-03561-1). Wm C Brown.

Batchelor, Edward, Jr., ed. Homosexuality & Ethics. rev. ed. LC 80-10533. 1982. 12.95 (ISBN 0-8298-0392-0); pap. 8.95 (ISBN 0-8298-0615-6). Pilgrim NY.

Batchelor, George K. Introduction to Fluid Dynamics. (Illus.). 634p. 1967. 82.50 (ISBN 0-521-04118-X); pap. 27.95x (ISBN 0-521-09817-3). Cambridge U Pr.

Batchelor, Ivor R., ed. see Henderson, David & Gillespie, R. D.

Batchelor, John & Batchelor, Julie. The Congo. LC 80-50938. (Rivers of the World Ser.). PLB 12.68 (ISBN 0-382-06370-8). Silver.

--The Euphrates. LC 80-53605. (Rivers of the World Ser.). PLB 12.68 (ISBN 0-382-06518-2). Silver.

Batchelor, John, jt. auth. see Forty, George.

Batchelor, John C. The Further Adventures of Halley's Comet. 384p. 1980. 17.95 o.p. (ISBN 0-312-92231-0); pap. 8.95 (ISBN 0-312-92232-9). St Martin.

Batchelor, Julie, jt. auth. see Batchelor, John.

Batchelor, Julie F. Communication: From Cave Writing to Television. LC 53-7860. (gr. 4-6). 1953. 7.95 (ISBN 0-15-219832-6, HJ). HarBraceJ.

Batchelor, Julie F. & De Lys, Claudia. Superstitious? Here's Why! LC 54-566. (Illus.). (gr. 5 up). 1954. 5.95 o.p. (ISBN 0-15-283179-7, HJ). HarBraceJ.

--Superstitious? Here's Why! LC 54-8566. (Illus.). (gr. 5 up). 1966. pap. 1.25 (ISBN 0-15-686793-1, VoyB). HarBraceJ.

Batchelor, Peter. People in Rural Development. 160p. pap. text ed. 7.95 (ISBN 0-85364-310-5). Attic Pr.

Batchelor, R. A., et al. Industrialisation & the Basis for Trade. LC 79-41582. (Economic & Social Studies: No. 32). 350p. 1980. 44.50 (ISBN 0-521-23302-X). Cambridge U Pr.

Batchelor, Roy. Edwardian Novelists. 1982. 25.00 (ISBN 0-312-23907-6). St Martin.

Batchelor, Roy A. & Wood, Geoffrey E., eds. Exchange Rate Policy. LC 81-23262. 265p. 1982. 27.50x (ISBN 0-312-27389-4). St Martin.

Batchelor, Stephen. Alone with Others. Rosset, Hannelore, ed. (Grove Press Eastern Philosophy & Religion Ser.). 144p. 1983. pap. 5.95 (ISBN 0-394-62457-2, Ever). Grove.

Bate, Marjorie & Casey, Mary. Legal Office Procedures. (Illus.). 448p. 1975. pap. text ed. 17.05 o.p. (ISBN 0-07-004056-7, G); instructor's manual & key 8.85 o.p. (ISBN 0-07-004057-5). McGraw.

Bate, Marjorie D. & Casey, Mary C. Legal Office Procedures. 2nd ed. (Illus.). 544p. 1980. pap. text ed. 18.80 (ISBN 0-07-004058-3, G); instructor's manual & key 8.00 (ISBN 0-07-004059-1). McGraw.

Bate, Paul & Mangham, Ian. Exploring Participation. LC 80-41415. 320p. 1981. 35.95x (ISBN 0-471-27921-8, Pub. by Wiley-Interscience). Wiley.

Bate, Philip. The Flute. rev. ed. (Instruments of the Orchestra Ser.). 1979. 17.95x o.p. (ISBN 0-393-01292-1). Norton.

Bate, R. H. & Robinson, E. A Stratigraphical Index of British Ostracada: Geological Journal Special Issue, No. 8. (Liverpool Geological Society & the Manchester Geological Association). 538p. 1980. 139.95x (ISBN 0-471-27755-X, Pub. by Wiley-Interscience). Wiley.

Bate, R. H., et al. Fossil & Recent Ostracods. 350p. 1982. 105.00 (ISBN 0-470-27314-3). Halsted Pr.

Bate, W. J., ed. see Johnson, Samuel.

Bate, W. J., et al, eds. see Johnson, Samuel.

Bateman, A. M., jt. auth. see Jensen, M. L.

Bateman, Barbara. So You're Going to Hearing: Preparing for a Public Law 94-142 Due Process Hearing. 36p. 1980. pap. 2.95 (ISBN 0-686-82958-1, 4001). Res Press.

Bateman, Barbara, jt. auth. see Haring, Norris.

Bateman, Barbara D. Interpretation of the Nineteen Sixty-One Illinois Test of Psycholinguistic Abilities. LC 68-57926. (Orig.). 1968. pap. 5.00x o.p. (ISBN 0-87562-012-4). Spec Child.

Bateman, Barbara D., ed. Learning Disorders, Vol. 4. LC 68-85. (Illus.). 1971. text ed. 10.50 o.p. (ISBN 0-87562-023-X); pap. 9.00 o.p. (ISBN 0-87562-024-8). Spec Child.

--Reading Performance & How to Achieve It. LC 72-79162. 385p. (Orig.). 1973. pap. 9.00x o.p. (ISBN 0-87562-039-6). Spec Child.

Bateman, Barry L. & Pitts, Gerald N. Essentials of COBOL Programming: A Structured Approach. 1982. text ed. 14.95 (ISBN 0-914894-34-X). Computer Sci.

Bateman, David N., jt. auth. see Sigband, Norman B.

Bateman, Donald & Zidonis, Frank. Effect of a Study of Transformational Grammar on the Writing of Ninth & Tenth Graders. 1966. pap. 2.45 (ISBN 0-8141-1295-1); pap. 1.75 members (ISBN 0-686-86406-9). NCTE.

Bateman, Glenn. MHD Instabilities. 1978. text ed. 29.95x (ISBN 0-262-02131-5). MIT Pr.

Bateman, Harry. Differential Equations. LC 66-23754. 1967. 14.95 (ISBN 0-8284-0190-X). Chelsea Pub.

Bateman, Hugh E. A Clinical Approach to Speech Anatomy & Physiology. (Illus.). 440p. 1977. 33.75x (ISBN 0-398-03633-0); pap. 26.75x (ISBN 0-398-03634-9). C C Thomas.

Bateman, James E., ed. Foot Science: A Selection of Papers from the Proceedings of the American Orthopaedic Foot Society, Inc., 1974 & 1975. LC 75-14780. (Illus.). 290p. 1976. text ed. 31.75 o.p. (ISBN 0-7216-1580-5). Saunders.

Bateman, Paul, et al. Deepest Valley: A Guide to Owens Valley, Its Roadsides & Mountain Trails. rev. ed. Smith, Genny, ed. LC 78-50975. (Illus.). 1978. pap. 7.95 o.p. (ISBN 0-931378-01-X, Dist. by W. Kaufmann Inc.). Genny Smith Bks.

Bateman, Robert. The Art of Robert Bateman. LC 81-43019. (Illus.). 180p. 1981. 45.00 (ISBN 0-670-13497-X, Studio). Viking Pr.

Bateman, Wayne. Introduction to Computer Music. LC 79-26361. 314p. 1980. 29.95x (ISBN 0-471-05266-3, Pub. by Wiley-Interscience). Wiley.

--Introduction to Computer Music. 314p. 1982. pap. 14.95 (Pub. by Wiley-Interscience). Wiley.

Bates, Alan P. & Julian, Joseph. Sociology: Understanding Social Behavior. 1975. text ed. 24.95 (ISBN 0-395-18652-8); instr's. guide & resource manual by Patricia Harvey 1.90 (ISBN 0-395-18794-X). HM.

Bates, Albert D. Retailing & Its Environment. (Illus.). 1978. text ed. 11.95 (ISBN 0-442-80429-6). Van Nos Reinhold.

Bates, Barbara. A Guide to Physical Examination. 2nd ed. LC 78-21634. 1979. text ed. 29.00x o.p. (ISBN 0-397-54224-0, Lippincott Medical). Lippincott.

--A Guide to Physical Examination. 3rd ed. (Illus.). 580p. 1983. text ed. 32.50 (ISBN 0-397-54399-9, Lippincott Medical). Lippincott.

Bates, Betty. Bugs in Your Ears. LC 77-3821. (gr. 5 up). 1977. 9.95 (ISBN 0-8234-0304-1). Holiday.

--Love Is Like Peanuts. (gr. 7-9). 1981. pap. 1.75 (ISBN 0-671-56109-X). Archway.

--My Mom, the Money Nut. LC 78-24213. (gr. 4-6). 1979. 9.95 (ISBN 0-8234-0347-5). Holiday.

Bates, Billy P. I. S. Q. D. (Identification System for Questioned Documents) (Illus.). 112p. 1970. photocopy ed. spiral 11.25x (ISBN 0-398-00108-1). C C Thomas.

Bates, C. C. & Gaskell, T. F. Geophysics in the Affairs of Man: A Personalized History of Exploration Geophysics & Its Allied Sciences of Seismology & Oceanography. (Illus.). 536p. 1982. 60.00 (ISBN 0-08-024026-7); pap. 25.00 (ISBN 0-08-024025-9). Pergamon.

Bates, D. R. Carpentry & Joinery. (Illus.). 208p. 1982. pap. text ed. 13.95x (ISBN 0-7121-0394-5). Intl Ideas.

Bates, Daniel & Rassam, Amal. Peoples & Cultures of the Middle East. (Illus.). 288p. 1983. pap. 12.95 (ISBN 0-13-656793-2). P-H.

Bates, David. A Citizen's Guide to Air Pollution. (Environmental Damage & Control in Canada Ser.: Vol. 2). 250p. 1972. 6.75x (ISBN 0-7735-0144-4); pap. 4.00 (ISBN 0-7735-0145-2). McGill-Queens U Pr.

Bates, David & Bederson, Benjamin. Advances in Atomic & Molecular Physics, Vol. 18. (Serial Publication). 1982. 83.50 (ISBN 0-12-003818-8); Lib. ed. 64.00 (ISBN 0-12-003888-9); Microfiche 44.80 (ISBN 0-12-003889-7). Acad Pr.

Bates, David R. & Bederson, Benjamin, eds. Advances in Atomic & Molecular Physics, Vol. 15. LC 65-18423. (Serial Publication). 1979. 63.00 (ISBN 0-12-003815-3); lib. ed. 77.00 (ISBN 0-12-003882-X); microfiche 42.00 (ISBN 0-12-003883-8). Acad Pr.

Bates, Sir David R. & Bederson, Benjamin, eds. Advances in Atomic & Molecular Physics, Vol. 16. LC 65-18423. 1980. 50.00 (ISBN 0-12-003816-1); lib. ed. 64.00 (ISBN 0-12-003884-6); microfiche 36.00 (ISBN 0-12-003885-4). Acad Pr.

Bates, David V., et al. Respiratory Function in Disease. 2nd ed. LC 78-135319. (Illus.). 1971. 30.00 o.p. (ISBN 0-7216-1591-0). Saunders.

Bates, E. S. The Bible Designed to Be Read As Living Literature. 1972. pap. 9.95 o.p. (ISBN 0-671-21407-1, Touchstone Bks). S&S.

Bates, Elizabeth B., jt. auth. see Fairbanks, Jonathan.

Bates, Enid & Lowes, Ruth. Potpourri of Puppetry. LC 76-24151. 1976. pap. 4.50 o.p. (ISBN 0-8224-5500-5). Pitman Learning.

Bates, Ernest. This Land of Liberty. LC 73-19817. (Civil Liberties in American History Ser.). 383p. 1974. Repr. of 1930 ed. lib. bdg. 42.50 (ISBN 0-306-70597-4). Da Capo.

Bates, Frank & Douglas, Mary L. Programming Language One: With Structured Programming. 3rd ed. 1975. pap. 17.95 (ISBN 0-13-730473-0). P-H.

Bates, G. L., jt. auth. see Gill, F. W.

Bates, Grace K. Alaska & Back in Three Weeks (We Drove the Alcan) 1978. 4.95 o.p. (ISBN 0-533-03465-5). Vantage.

Bates, Henry & Busenbark, R. Finch & Softbilled Birds. 19.95 (ISBN 0-87666-421-4, H908). TFH Pubns.

Bates, Henry & Busenbark, Robert. Guide to Mynahs. (Orig.). 5.95 (ISBN 0-87666-769-8, PS633). TFH Pubns.

--Introduction to Finches & Softbilled Birds. (Orig.). 7.95 (ISBN 0-87666-762-0, PS648). TFH Pubns.

--Parrots. (Orig.). pap. 2.95 (ISBN 0-87666-427-3, M506). TFH Pubns.

Bates, Henry J. & Busenbark, Robert I. Parrots & Related Birds. (Illus.). 543p. 16.95 (ISBN 0-87666-967-4, TFH H-912). TFH Pubns.

Bates, James & Parkinson, J. R., eds. Business Economics. (Illus.). 36p. 1982. text ed. 22.50x (ISBN 0-631-13146-9, Pub. by Basil Blackwell England); pap. text ed. 9.50x (ISBN 0-631-13147-7, Pub. by Basil Blackwell England). Biblio Dist.

Bates, Joseph D., Jr. Fishing: An Encyclopedic Guide to Tackle & Tactics for Fresh & Salt Water. 1974. 19.95 (ISBN 0-87690-110-0). Dutton.

--How to Find Fish & Make Them Strike. LC 73-93268. (An Outdoor Life Bk). (Illus.). 224p. 1975. 11.49i (ISBN 0-06-010241-1, HarpT). Har-Row.

--Outdoor Cook's Bible. LC 63-19269. 1964. 4.50 (ISBN 0-385-02107-0). Doubleday.

Bates, Leonard J. United States Eighteen Ninety-Eight to Nineteen Twenty-Eight. (Modern America Ser.). (Illus.). 350p. 1975. pap. text ed. 17.95 (ISBN 0-07-004050-8, C). McGraw.

Bates, M. Searle. Religious Liberty: An Inquiry. LC 77-166096. (Civil Liberties in American History Ser.). 1972. Repr. of 1945 ed. lib. bdg. 59.50 (ISBN 0-306-70235-5). Da Capo.

Bates, Marston. The Land & Wildlife of South America. rev. ed. LC 80-52259. (Life Nature Library). PLB 13.40 (ISBN 0-8094-3863-1). Silver.

Bates, Martin see Bates, Martin & Dudley-Evans, Tony.

Bates, Martin & Dudley-Evans, Tony, eds. Nucleus: English for Science & Technology. Incl. Biology. Adamson, Donald & Bates, Martin. pap. text ed. 6.25x student's bk. (ISBN 0-582-51302-2); tchr's notes 3.75x (ISBN 0-582-55354-7); cassette 13.50x (ISBN 0-582-74825-9); Engineering. Dudley-Evans, Tony, et al. pap. text ed. 6.25x student's bk. (ISBN 0-582-51304-9); tchr's notes 3.75x (ISBN 0-582-55281-8); cassette 13.50x (ISBN 0-582-74824-0); General Science. Bates, Martin & Dudley-Evans, Tony. pap. text ed. 6.50x student's bk. (ISBN 0-582-51300-6); tchr's notes 3.75x (ISBN 0-582-55262-1); tapescript 3.75x (ISBN 0-582-74801-1); 3 cassettes 48.00x (ISBN 0-582-74802-X); Geology. Barron, Colin & Stewart, Ian. pap. text ed. 6.25x student's bk. (ISBN 0-582-51305-7); tchr's notes 3.75x (ISBN 0-582-55286-9); cassette 13.50x (ISBN 0-582-74823-2); Mathematics. Hall, David. pap. text ed. 6.25x student's bk. (ISBN 0-582-51306-5); tchr's notes 3.75x (ISBN 0-582-55282-6); cassette 13.50x (ISBN 0-582-74829-1); Medicine. Kirwan, David **& O'Brien, Tony. pap. text ed. 6.25x student's bk. (ISBN 0-582-51307-3); tchr's notes 3.75x (ISBN 0-582-55285-0); cassette 13.50x (ISBN 0-582-74828-3); Nursing Science. Kerr, Rosalie & Smith, Jennifer. pap. text ed. 6.25x student's bk. (ISBN 0-582-51309-X); tchr's notes 3.75x (ISBN 0-582-55280-X); cassette 13.50x (ISBN 0-582-74822-4). (English As a Second Language Bk.). 1976-80. Longman.**

Bates, Myrtle & Stern, Renee. The Grammar Game. (Illus.). 368p. (Orig.). 1983. pap. text ed. 8.95 (ISBN 0-686-82307-9); instr's. guide 3.33 (ISBN 0-686-82308-7). Bobbs.

Bates, Paul A., ed. Faust: Sources, Works, Criticism. (Harbrace Sourcebook Ser.). 218p. (Orig.). 1968. pap. text ed. 8.95 o.p. (ISBN 0-15-527102-4, HC). HarBraceJ.

Bates, R. W. & Fraser, N. M. Investment Decisions in the Nationalized Fuel Industries. LC 74-76575. (Illus.). 208p. 1974. 32.50 (ISBN 0-521-20455-0). Cambridge U Pr.

Bates, Richard O. The Gentleman from Ohio: A Biography of James A. Garfield. LC 72-90712. 1973. 12.95 (ISBN 0-87716-039-2, Pub. by Moore Pub Co). F Apple.

Bates, Robert C., ed. see De Blois, Pierre.

Bates, Robert L. & Sweet, Walter C. Geology: An Introduction. 2nd ed. 1973. text ed. 24.95 o.p. (ISBN 0-669-74328-3). Heath.

Bates, Roger G. Determination of pH: Theory & Practice. 2nd ed. LC 72-8779. 510p. 1973. 43.50x (ISBN 0-471-05647-2, Pub. by Wiley-Interscience). Wiley.

Bates, Sandra, jt. ed. see Sjoden, Per-Olow.

Bates, Scott. Guillaume Apollinaire. (World Authors Ser.: France: No. 14). lib. bdg. 10.95 o.p. (ISBN 0-8057-2052-9, Twayne). G K Hall.

Bates, Shirley. Popular Pottery. (Illus.). 128p. 1982. 14.95 (ISBN 0-7134-4168-2, Pub. by Batsford England). David & Charles.

Bates, Steven L. & Orr, Sidney D. Concordance to the Poems of Ben Jonson. LC 76-25613. xiv, 878p. 1978. 40.00x (ISBN 0-8214-0359-1, 82-82493). Ohio U Pr.

Bates, Sylvia. Religions of the World. LC 80-50957. (New Reference Library Ser.). PLB 11.96 (ISBN 0-382-06398-8). Silver.

Bates, William. The Computer Cookbook. (Illus.). 1983. 21.95 (ISBN 0-13-164558-7); pap. 12.95 (ISBN 0-13-165167-6). P-H.

Bateson. Introduction to Control Systems Technology. 2nd ed. (Technology Ser.). 560p. 1980. text ed. 26.95 (ISBN 0-675-08255-2). Additional supplements may be obtained from publisher. Merrill.

Bateson, P. P. & Klopfer, Peter H., eds. Perspectives in Ethology, Vol. 5: Ontogeny. 500p. 1982. 39.50x (ISBN 0-306-41063-X, Plenum Pr). Plenum Pub.

Bates-Yakobson, Helen, jt. auth. see Von Gronicka, Andre.

Batey, Mavis. Oxford Gardens. 1981. 50.00x o.p. (ISBN 0-86127-002-9, Pub. by Avebury Pub England). State Mutual Bk.

Batey, P. W. Theory & Method in Urban & Regional Analysis. (London Papers in Regional Science). 184p. 1978. pap. 16.00x (ISBN 0-85086-066-0, Pub. by Pion England). Methuen Inc.

Batey, P. W., jt. ed. see Massey, Doreen B.

Bath, M. Spectral Analysis in Geophysics. (Development in Solid Earth Geophysics: Vol. 7). 208p. 1974. 81.00 (ISBN 0-444-41222-0). Elsevier.

Bathe, K. J., ed. Nonlinear Finite Element Analysis & Adina: Proceedings of the 3rd Adina Conference, Massachussetts, USA, 10-12 June 1981. 206p. 1981. 112.00 o.p. (ISBN 0-08-027594-X). Pergamon.

Bathe, Klaus, et al, eds. Formulations & Computational Algorithms in Finite-Element Analysis: U. S. German Symposium. 1977. 57.50x (ISBN 0-262-02127-7). MIT Pr.

Bathgate, M. A., et al. Change in the Solomons. (Illus.). 400p. 1982. 27.50x (ISBN 0-19-558031-1). Oxford U Pr.

Batho, Margot. Sandcasting. LC 72-13345. (Early Crafts Bks.). (Illus.). 36p. (gr. 1-4). 1973. PLB 3.95g (ISBN 0-8225-0860-5). Lerner Pubns.

Bathurst, R. G. Carbonate Sediments & Their Diagenesis. 2nd ed. (Developments in Sedimentology: Vol. 12). 658p. 1975. pap. text ed. 30.00 (ISBN 0-444-41353-7). Elsevier.

Batist, Bessie, ed. A Treasure for My Daughter. pap. 5.95 (ISBN 0-8015-7939-2, 0577-180, Hawthorn). Dutton.

Batista, Joao, ed. see Eskelin, Neil.

Batista, Joao, ed. see Nee, Watchman.

Batista, Joao, tr. see Bennett, Rita & Bennett, Dennis.

Batista, Joao, tr. see Hutchison, Becky & Farish, Kay.

Batista, Joao, jt. ed. see Balthazar, Vera.

Batki, John, tr. see Gomori, George & Atlas, James.

Batley, Richard. Power Through Bureaucracy: Urban Political Analysis in Brazil. LC 82-16872. 240p. 1982. 27.50x (ISBN 0-312-63437-4). St Martin.

Batley, Richard, jt. auth. see Edwards, John.

Bator, Paul M. The International Trade in Art. LC 82-17405. vii, 128p. 1982. pap. 6.95 (ISBN 0-226-03910-2). U of Chicago Pr.

Batra, Gretchen, jt. ed. see Markson, Elizabeth.

Batra, Lekh R., ed. Insect-Fungus Symbiosis: Nutrition, Mutualism & Commensalism. LC 78-20640. (Illus.). 276p. 1979. text ed. 39.95 (ISBN 0-470-26671-6). Halsted Pr.

Batra, Neelam. Clinical Pathology for Medical Students. 240p. 1982. text ed. 37.50x (ISBN 0-7069-1117-2, Pub. by Vikas India). Advent NY.

Batra, R. N. The Pure Theory of International Trade Under Uncertainty. LC 74-4820. 1975. text ed. 29.95x o.p. (ISBN 0-470-05687-8). Halsted Pr.

Batra, Ravi. Muslim Civilization & the Crisis in Iran. LC 80-53736. 218p. (Orig.). 1981. 15.00 (ISBN 0-939352-00-1); pap. 8.00 (ISBN 0-686-36905-X). Venus Bks.

--Muslim Civilization & the Crisis in Iran. 218p. 1980. pap. 2.00 (ISBN 0-686-95468-8). Ananda Marga.

--Prout: The Alternative to Capitalism & Marxism. LC 80-67184. 221p. 1980. lib. bdg. 19.50 (ISBN 0-8191-1187-2); pap. text ed. 9.50 (ISBN 0-8191-1188-0). U Pr of Amer.

Batschelet, E. Introduction to Mathematics for Life Scientists. 2nd ed. LC 75-11755. (Biomathematics Ser.: Vol. 2). (Illus.). 643p. 1975. 43.00 (ISBN 0-387-09662-0); pap. text ed. o.p. (ISBN 0-387-07350-7). Springer-Verlag.

Batschelet, Edward. Circular Statistics in Biology. LC 81-66364. (Mathematics in Biology Ser.). 1981. 69.50 o.s.i. (ISBN 0-12-081050-6). Acad Pr.

Batson, Benjamin A., ed. Siam's Political Future: Documents from the End of the Absolute Monarchy. 102p. 1974. 4.00 o.p. (ISBN 0-87727-096-1, DP 96). Cornell SE Asia.

Batson, Larry. Walt Frazier. LC 74-2013. (Creative Superstars Ser.). 32p. 1974. PLB 6.95 o.p. (ISBN 0-87191-348-8); pap. 2.95 o.p. (ISBN 0-89812-179-5). Creative Ed.

Batson, Robert G., tr. see Masaryk, Thomas G.

Batson, Wade T. Genera of the Eastern Plants. 3rd ed. LC 77-24339. 203p. 1977. pap. text ed. 11.95x (ISBN 0-471-03497-5). Wiley.

Batt, Cara M., jt. auth. see Arrigo, Joseph A.

Batt, Elisabeth. The Moncks & Charleville House: A Wicklow Family in the Nineteenth Century. 1981. 40.00x (ISBN 0-686-97834-X, Pub. by Blackwater Pr Ireland). State Mutual Bk.

Batt, Elizabeth. Birthday Plan. 1971. pap. 1.50 (ISBN 0-87508-647-0). Chr Lit.

Battaglia, Aurelius, ed. Mother Goose. (ps-1). 1973. pap. 1.50 (ISBN 0-394-82661-2, BYR). Random.

Battaglia, Carmelo L. Dog Genetics. (Illus.). 1978. 12.95 (ISBN 0-87666-662-4, H-976). TFH Pubns.

Battaglia, J. & Fisher, M., eds. Yoshi Goes To New York: Authentic Discourse for Listening Comprehension. (Materials for Language Practice Ser.). (Illus.). 64p. 1982. 3.95 (ISBN 0-08-028648-8). Pergamon.

Battaglia, R. A. & Mayrose, V. Handbook of Livestock Management Techniques. 1981. text ed. 24.95x (ISBN 0-8087-2957-8). Burgess.

Battan, Louis J. Cloud Physics & Cloud Seeding. LC 78-25711. (Illus.). 1979. Repr. of 1962 ed. lib. bdg. 18.25x (ISBN 0-313-20770-4, BACL). Greenwood.

--Fundamentals of Meteorology. 1979. 26.95 (ISBN 0-13-341131-1). P-H.

--Radar Observation of the Atmosphere. rev. ed. (Illus.). 1981. text ed. 16.50x o.s.i. (ISBN 0-226-03919-6); pap. 15.00x (ISBN 0-226-03921-8). U of Chicago Pr.

Battcock, Gregory, ed. Breaking the Sound Barrier: A Critical Anthology of the New Music. (Illus.). 288p. 1981. pap. 12.50 (ISBN 0-525-47640-7, 01214-360). Dutton.

--Idea Art: A Critique. 1973. pap. 5.50 (ISBN 0-525-47344-0, 0533-120). Dutton.

--Minimal Art: A Critical Anthology. 1968. pap. 9.95 (ISBN 0-525-47211-8, 0966-290). Dutton.

--The New Art: A Critical Anthology. rev. ed. 1973. pap. 5.75 (ISBN 0-525-47361-0, 0558-170). Dutton.

--Super Realism: A Critical Anthology. 352p. 1975. pap. 10.95 o.p. (ISBN 0-525-47377-7). Dutton.

Battcock, Gregory & Nickas, Robert, eds. The Art of Performance: A Critical Anthology. LC 79-53323. (Illus.). 256p. 1983. pap. 11.95 (ISBN 0-525-48039-0, 01064-310). Dutton.

Batteau, Allen, ed. Applachia & America: Autonomy & Regional Dependence. LC 82-40462. (Illus.). 296p. 1983. 26.00x (ISBN 0-8131-1480-2). U Pr of Ky.

Battelle Columbus Laboratories. Solar Energy Employment & Requirements: 1978-1983. 200p. 1981. pap. 29.50x (ISBN 0-89934-102-0, V.065). Solar Energy Info.

Batten, A. H. Binary & Multiple Systems of Stars. LC 72-88026. 288p. 1973. write for info. (ISBN 0-08-016986-4). Pergamon.

Batten, Charles L., Jr. Pleasurable Instruction: Form & Convention in Eighteenth-Century Travel Literature. LC 76-14316. 1978. 23.50x (ISBN 0-520-03260-8). U of Cal Pr.

Batten, David F. Spatial Analysis of Interacting Economies. 1982. lib. bdg. 26.00 (ISBN 0-89838-109-6). Kluwer-Nijhoff.

Batten, H. Mortimer. Romances of the Wild. (Illus.). (gr. 4-6). 1977. pap. 2.95 o.p. (ISBN 0-216-90279-7). Transatlantic.

--Tales of Wild Bird Life. (gr. 4-6). 1977. pap. 2.95 o.p. (ISBN 0-216-90277-0). Transatlantic.

Batten, Jack. The Complete Jogger. LC 76-55527. (Illus.). 1977. pap. 4.95 (ISBN 0-15-120699-6, Harv). HarBraceJ.

Batten, Leo, et al. Birdwatchers' Year. (Illus.). 1973. 16.00 o.p. (ISBN 0-85661-003-8, Pub by T & A D Poyser). Buteo.

Batten, R. L., tr. see Heim, U., et al.

Batten, Robert W. Mortality Table Construction. LC 77-12349. (Risk, Insurance & Security Ser.). (Illus.). 1978. 23.95 (ISBN 0-13-601302-3). P-H.

Batten, Roger L., jt. auth. see Dott, Robert H.

Batterberry, M. Twentieth Century Art. 1969. 9.95 (ISBN 0-07-004080-X). McGraw.

Batterberry, Michael. Art of the Early Renaissance. (Discovering Art Ser.). (Illus.). (gr. 7-8). 1970. 11.95 (ISBN 0-07-004081-8, GB). McGraw.

--Chinese & Oriental Art. (Discovering Art Ser). (Illus.). (gr. 7 up). 1969. 11.95 (ISBN 0-07-004078-8, GB). McGraw.

Batterberry, Michael & Ruskin, Ariane. Primitive Art. (Illus.). 192p. (gr. 3 up). 1972. 11.95 (ISBN 0-07-004073-7, GB). McGraw.

Batterberry, Michael. Art of the Middle Ages. (Discovering Art Ser.). (Illus.). 192p. (gr. 9-12). 1972. 9.95 o.p. (ISBN 0-07-004082-6, GB). McGraw.

Batterham, T. J. NMR Spectra of Simple Heterocycles. LC 80-11724. 560p. 1982. Repr. of 1973 ed. lib. bdg. 64.50 (ISBN 0-89874-140-8). Krieger.

Batterman, Charles A. Techniques of Springboard Diving. LC 68-14457. (Illus.). 1968. 20.00x (ISBN 0-262-02038-6); pap. 4.95 (ISBN 0-262-52043-5). MIT Pr.

Battersby, A. R., jt. ed. see Taylor, W. I.

Battersby, James J. Elder Olson: An Annotated Bibliography. LC 82-48273. 250p. 1982. lib. bdg. 30.00 (ISBN 0-8240-9254-6). Garland Pub.

Battersby, Martin. Decorative Twenties. LC 71-84213. 1969. 20.00 o.s.i. (ISBN 0-8027-0078-0, 11045). Walker & Co.

--Trompe l'Oeil: The Eye Deceived. LC 73-89208. (Illus.). 176p. 1974. 25.00 o.p. (ISBN 0-312-81900-5). St Martin.

Battie & Turner. Price Guide to Nineteenth & Twentieth Century British Porcelain. (Illus.). 1980. 29.50 (ISBN 0-902028-38-3). Apollo.

Battig, William F., jt. auth. see Toglia, Michael P.

Battin, B. W. Angel of the Night. 256p. (Orig.). 1983. pap. 2.95 (ISBN 0-449-12380-4, GM). Fawcett.

Battin, Margaret P. Ethical Issues in Suicide. 250p. 1982. 11.95 (ISBN 0-13-290155-2). P-H.

Battison, Edward A. & Kane, Patricia E. The American Clock, 1725-1865: From the Mabel Brady Garvan & Other Collections at Yale University. LC 72-93856. (Illus.). 208p. 1973. 19.95 o.p. (ISBN 0-8212-0493-9, 036706). NYGS.

Battista, O. A. Quotoons: A Speakers Dictionary. 472p. 1981. 12.95 (ISBN 0-399-12573-6, Perige); 5.95 (ISBN 0-399-50514-8). Putnam Pub Group.

Battista, O. A., ed. Business-One Thousand Directory, 1983. LC 80-642221. 504p. 1983. 30.00 (ISBN 0-915074-10-9). Research Servs Corp.

Battista, Orlando A., ed. Synthetic Fibers in Papermaking. LC 64-13211. 340p. 1964. text ed. 21.00 (ISBN 0-470-05894-3, Pub. by Wiley). Krieger.

Battistella, Roger M. & Rundall, Thomas G., eds. Health Care Policy in a Changing Environment. LC 78-57148. 1979. 25.00 (ISBN 0-8211-0131-5); text ed. 22.95 in ten or more copies (ISBN 0-686-67039-6). McCutchan.

Battisto, Jack R., ed. see New York Academy of Sciences Annals of, October 19-21, 1981.

Battistone, Joseph. The Great Controversy Theme in E. G. White Writings. xiv, 134p. 1978. pap. 3.95 (ISBN 0-943872-76-6). Andrews Univ Pr.

Battle, Dennis M. America's Future in Symbolic Prophecy. (Illus.). 52p. 1981. pap. 3.00 o.s.i. (ISBN 0-933464-10-X). D M Battle Pubns.

--Armageddon: Heaven's Holy War on Earth. LC 80-65197. 56p. 1980. pap. 2.50 (ISBN 0-933464-07-X). D M Battle Pubns.

--God's True Sabbath: Is It Sunday or Saturday? LC 79-50721. (Illus.). 1979. 5.00 o.s.i. (ISBN 0-933464-04-5); pap. 2.50 (ISBN 0-933464-03-7). D M Battle Pubns.

--The Gospel Religion of Jesus Christ. LC 80-65198. 52p. 1980. pap. 2.25 (ISBN 0-933464-08-8). D M Battle Pubns.

--Life After Death? LC 81-65426. (Illus.). 52p. 1981. pap. 3.00x (ISBN 0-933464-13-4). D M Battle Pubns.

--Sunday: Is It the Lord's Day? 52p. 1982. pap. text ed. 2.50 (ISBN 0-933464-20-7). D M Battle Pubns.

--Wings of Hope & Praise. LC 79-83640. 1979. pap. 2.50 (ISBN 0-933464-00-2). D M Battle Pubns.

Battle, Lois. Season of Change. 288p. 1983. pap. 2.95 (ISBN 0-449-20054-X, Crest). Fawcett.

--War Brides. large type ed. LC 82-7347. 693p. 1982. Repr. of 1982 ed. 13.95 (ISBN 0-89621-374-9). Thorndike Pr.

Battle, Vincent M. & Lyons, Vincent, eds. Essays in the History of African Education. LC 73-126535. 1970. pap. 4.50x o.p. (ISBN 0-8077-1054-7). Tchrs Coll.

Battles, Edith. The Secret of Castle Drai. 192p. (Orig.). 1980. pap. 1.95 o.p. (ISBN 0-523-40848-X). Pinnacle Bks.

Battles, Ford L. & Miller, Charles. A Concordance to Calvin's Institutio. LC 73-206014. 246p. 1974. 80.00 (ISBN 0-931222-07-9); prepub. 7 microfilm reels incl. Pitts Theolog.

Battley, Harry. Single Finger Prints: A New & Practical Method of Classifying & Filing Single Finger Prints & Fragmentary Impressions. (Illus.). 1931. 42.50x o.p. (ISBN 0-686-51311-8). Elliots Bks.

Battocletti, Joseph H. Electromagnetism, Man, & the Environment. LC 76-7905. (Westview Environmental Studies Ser.). 1976. 17.50 (ISBN 0-89158-612-1). Westview.

Batts, Michael S. Gottfried von Strassburg. (World Authors Ser.: Germany: No. 167). lib. bdg. 15.95 (ISBN 0-8057-2866-X, Twayne). G K Hall.

Battson, R. K. Period Ship Modelling. (Illus.). 80p. 1979. 5.00x (ISBN 0-85242-691-7). Intl Pubns Serv.

Battuta, Ibn. Ibn Battuta in Black Africa. Hamdun, Said & King, Noel, trs. from Arabic. 99p. (Orig.). 1978. pap. 5.00x o.s.i. (ISBN 0-901720-57-7, Dist. for Rex Collings, London). Three Continents.

Batty, C. D. The Electronic Library. 160p. 1983. price not set (Pub. by Bingley England). Shoe String.

Batty, Eric G., ed. International Football (Soccer) Book, No. 24. 144p. 1983. text ed. 23.50x (ISBN 0-285-62533-0, SpS). Sportshelf.

Batty, I., jt. auth. see Sterne, M.

Batty, J. Management Accountancy. 5th ed. 896p. 1982. pap. text ed. 29.95x (ISBN 0-7121-1272-3). Intl Ideas.

Batty, J., ed. Developments in Office Management. (Illus.). 314p. 1972. 15.00x o.p. (ISBN 0-434-90109-1). Intl Pubns Serv.

Batty, M. Urban Modelling. (Urban & Architectural Studies). (Illus.). 384p. 1976. 69.50 (ISBN 0-521-20811-4). Cambridge U Pr.

Baturin, G. N. Phosphorites on the Sea Floor: Origin, Composition & Distribution. (Developments in Sedimentology: Vol. 33). 344p. 1982. 93.50 (ISBN 0-444-41990-X). Elsevier.

Baty, Gordon. Entrepreneurship in the Eighties. 1981. text ed. 17.95 (ISBN 0-8359-1745-2); pap. text ed. 14.95 (ISBN 0-8359-1744-4). Reston.

Baty, Wayne M., jt. auth. see Himstreet, William C.

Batzer, Hans & Lohse, Friedrich. Introduction to Macromolecular Chemistry. 2nd ed. LC 78-6175. 297p. 1979. 51.00x (ISBN 0-471-99645-9, Pub. by Wiley-Interscience). Wiley.

Batzler, L. Richard. Journeys on Your Spiritual Path. 1982. 7.95 (ISBN 0-935710-04-3). Hidden Valley.

Batzler, L. Richard, jt. auth. see Tauraso, Nicola M.

Bau, Gerald. Dee-Dee's Mushrooms. 1978. 4.50 o.p. (ISBN 0-533-03719-0). Vantage.

Baucom, Marta E. & Causby, Ralph E. Total Communication Used in Experience Based Speech Reading & Auditory Training Lesson Plans: For Hard of Hearing & Deaf Individuals. (Illus.). 160p. 1981. 12.50x (ISBN 0-398-04124-5); pap. 7.75x (ISBN 0-398-04125-3). C C Thomas.

Baudelaire, tr. see Poe, Edgar Allan.

Baudelaire, Charles. Les Fleurs du Mal. Howard, Richard, tr. from Fr. LC 81-13283. (Illus.). 384p. 1982. 22.50 (ISBN 0-87923-425-3); date not set, limited edition 60.00 (ISBN 0-87923-435-0). Godine.

Baudelaire, Charles P. Baudelaire on Poe: Critical Papers. Hyslop, Lois & Hyslop, Francis, trs. (Bald Eagle Ser.). 1952. 15.00x (ISBN 0-271-00317-0, Pub. by Bald Eagle). Pa St U Pr.

Baudelaive, Charles. Intimate Journals. 124p. 1983. 10.95 (ISBN 0-87286-147-3); pap. 4.95 (ISBN 0-87286-146-5). City Lights.

Bauder, Thomas. Write English, Bk. 4. (Speak English Ser.). (Illus.). 64p. (Orig.). 1983. pap. text ed. 4.95 (ISBN 0-88499-687-5). Inst Mod Lang.

Baudhuin, John & Hawks, Linda. Living Longer, Living Better. 144p. 1983. pap. 6.95 (ISBN 0-86683-671-3). Winston Pr.

Baudouin, Jean. Mythologie, 2 vols. LC 75-27871. (Renaissance & the Gods Ser.: Vol. 26). (Illus.). 1976. Repr. of 1627 ed. Set. lib. bdg. 146.00 o.s.i. (ISBN 0-8240-2075-8); lib. bdg. 73.00 ea. o.s.i. Garland Pub.

Baudouin, Jean, tr. see Ripa, Cesare.

Baudouy, Michel-Aime. More Than Courage. Ponsot, Marie, tr. LC 61-13241. (gr. 7 up). 1966. pap. 1.65 (ISBN 0-15-662145-2, VoyB). HarBraceJ.
Bauemler, Ernest. Paul Ehrlich: Life Scientists. 350p. 1983. text ed. 39.50x (ISBN 0-8419-0837-0). Holmes & Meier.
Bauer, A. J. Chilean Rural Society from the Spanish Conquest to 1930. LC 75-2724. (Cambridge Latin American Studies: No. 21). (Illus.). 311p. 1975. 37.50 (ISBN 0-521-20727-4). Cambridge U Pr.
Bauer, Armand, tr. see Sallet, Richard.
Bauer, Arnold. Carl Zuckmayer. LC 75-29600. (Literature and Life Ser.). 1976. 11.95 (ISBN 0-8044-2026-2). Ungar.
--Rainer Maria Rilke. Lamm, Ursula, tr. LC 75-163151. (Literature and Life Ser.). 128p. 1972. 11.95 (ISBN 0-8044-2025-4). Ungar.
--Thomas Mann. Henderson, Alexander & Henderson, Elizabeth, trs. from Ger. LC 71-139221. (Literature and Life Ser.). 1971. 11.95 (ISBN 0-8044-2023-8); pap. 4.95 (ISBN 0-8044-6018-3). Ungar.
Bauer, Bruce S., ed. see Kernahan, Desmond A. & Thomson, Hugh G.
Bauer, C. E. & Thompson, R. L. Comprehensive General Shop One. 1959. 7.00 o.p. (ISBN 0-02-810480-3). Glencoe.
Bauer, Camille & Bond, Otto F. Graded French Reader, Deuxieme Etape. 2nd ed. 240p. 1982. pap. text ed. 7.95 (ISBN 0-669-04337-0). Heath.
Bauer, Caroline F. Handbook for Storytellers. LC 76-56385. (Illus.). 1977. text ed. 20.00 (ISBN 0-8389-0225-1); pap. 15.00 (ISBN 0-8389-0293-6). ALA.
--This Way to Books. 376p. 1983. 30.00 (ISBN 0-8242-0678-9). Wilson.
Bauer, D. J. Chemotherapy of Virus Diseases. 1972. text ed. 69.00 (ISBN 0-08-016961-9). Pergamon.
Bauer, Dennis E. & Strahl, John W. Office Reproduction Processes. LC 75-2381. 1975. pap. text ed. 14.95 scp (ISBN 0-06-453000-0, HarpC). Har-Row.
Bauer, Douglas. Prairie City, Iowa. LC 79-10314. 1979. 10.95 o.p. (ISBN 0-399-12359-8). Putnam Pub Group.
--Prairie City, Iowa: Three Seasons at Home. 330p. 1982. pap. 8.95 (ISBN 0-8138-1329-8). Iowa St U Pr.
Bauer, E. Charles. Little Lessons to Live by. LC 79-175143. 150p. (Orig.). (gr. 1-4). 1972. pap. 3.95 (ISBN 0-570-03131-1, 12-2379). Concordia.
Bauer, Eddie, jt. auth. see Satterfield, Archie.
Bauer, Eddie, Sr., jt. auth. see Satterfield, Archie, Sr.
Bauer, Erwin. The Digest Book of Camping. (Sports & Leisure Library). (Illus.). 1979. pap. 2.95 o.s.i. (ISBN 0-695-81281-5). Follett.
--Hunter's Digest. (DBI Bks). 1973. pap. 7.95 o.s.i. (ISBN 0-695-80431-6). Follett.
--Saltwater Fisherman's Bible. rev. ed. (Illus.). 208p. 1983. pap. text ed. 5.95 (ISBN 0-385-17220-6). Doubleday.
Bauer, Erwin & Bauer, Peggy. Camper's Digest. 3rd ed. (DBI Bks). 1974. pap. 5.95 o.s.i. (ISBN 0-695-80452-9). Follett.
Bauer, Erwin, jt. auth. see Bauer, Peggy.
Bauer, Erwin A. The Bass Fisherman's Bible. rev. ed. LC 79-7680. (Outdoor Bible Ser.). (Illus.). 1980. pap. 4.95 (ISBN 0-385-14993-X). Doubleday.
--The Cross-Country Skier's Bible. LC 76-52001. (Illus.). 1977. pap. 4.50 (ISBN 0-385-01321-3). Doubleday.
--Cross-Country Skiing & Snowshoeing. (Stoeger Bks). (Illus.). 208p. 1976. pap. 5.95 o.s.i. (ISBN 0-685-67176-3). Follett.
--The Digest Book of Cross-Country Skiing. (Illus.). 96p. 1979. pap. 2.95 o.s.i. (ISBN 0-695-81321-8). Follett.
--The Digest Book of Deer Hunting. (The Sports & Leisure Library). (Illus.). 96p. 1979. pap. 2.95 o.s.i. (ISBN 0-686-60304-4). Follett.
--Duck Hunter's Bible. LC 65-15543. pap. 4.50 (ISBN 0-385-04373-2). Doubleday.
--Salt-Water Fisherman's Bible. LC 62-14182. (Illus.). 1962. pap. 3.95 (ISBN 0-385-02337-5). Doubleday.
Bauer, Erwin A., ed. Fishermen's Digest. 10th rev. ed. (DBI Bks). (Illus.). 1977. pap. 7.95 o.s.i. (ISBN 0-695-80717-X). Follett.
--Hunter's Digest. 2nd ed. (Illus.). 288p. 1979. pap. 7.95 o.s.i. (ISBN 0-695-81314-5). Follett.
Bauer, F., ed. Software Engineering. (Lecture Notes in Computer Science Ser.: Vol. 30). xii, 545p. 1975. pap. 20.90 o.p. (ISBN 0-387-07168-7). Springer-Verlag.
Bauer, F., et al. Supercritical Wing Sections: A Handbook. LC 74-34333. (Lecture Notes in Economics & Mathematical Systems: Vol. 108). (Illus.). v, 296p. 1975. pap. 17.00 o.p. (ISBN 0-387-07029-X). Springer-Verlag.
--Supercritical Wing Sections III. (Lecture Notes in Economics & Mathematical Systems Ser: Vol. 150). 1977. pap. 12.00- (ISBN 0-387-08533-5). Springer-Verlag.
--A Theory of Supercritical Wing Sections, with Computer Programs & Examples. LC 72-79583. (Lecture Notes in Economics & Mathematical Systems: Vol. 66). (Illus.). 216p. 1972. pap. 9.00 o.p. (ISBN 0-387-05807-9). Springer-Verlag.
Bauer, F. L. & Woessner, H. Algorithmic Language & Program Development. (Texts & Monographs in Computer Science). (Illus.). 520p. 1982. pap. 29.00 (ISBN 0-387-11148-4). Springer-Verlag.
Bauer, F. L., ed. Software Engineering. 1977. 17.50 o.p. (ISBN 0-387-08364-2). Springer-Verlag.
Bauer, Fred, jt. auth. see Van Buskirk, Robert.
Bauer, Frederick, jt. auth. see Bollinger, Edward T.
Bauer, Gerhard. How to Succeed at Soccer. (Illus.). 128p. 1982. 12.95 (ISBN 0-8069-4160-X); lib. bdg. 15.69 (ISBN 0-8069-4161-8); pap. 6.95 (ISBN 0-8069-4148-0). Sterling.
Bauer, Gerhard, jt. auth. see Breitmaier, Eberhard.
Bauer, H. Wirtschaftsgeschichte. 304p. 1982. 42.90 (ISBN 3-7643-1225-4). Birkhauser.
Bauer, Hanna. Learning to Be: The Psychoeducational Management of Severely Dysfunctional Children. LC 73-81604. 150p. 1974. pap. 5.50 o.p. (ISBN 0-87562-044-2). Spec Child.
Bauer, Helen. Hawaii: The Aloha State. rev. ed. (Illus.). 192p. (gr. 4-7). 1982. 12.95 (ISBN 0-935848-13-4); pap. 9.95 (ISBN 0-935848-15-0). Bess Pr.
Bauer, Jeffrey C., jt. auth. see Domer, Larry R.
Bauer, Jeffrey C., jt. auth. see Luke, Roice D.
Bauer, K. Jack, ed. Soldiering: The Civil War Diary of Rice C. Bull. LC 76-58758. (Illus.). 1978. 12.95 o.p. (ISBN 0-89141-014-7). Presidio Pr.
Bauer, Marion. Twentieth Century Music: How It Developed, How to Listen to It. (Music Ser.). 354p. 1978. Repr. of 1933 ed. lib. bdg. 29.50 (ISBN 0-306-79503-5). Da Capo.
Bauer, Marion D. Foster Child. pap. 1.50 o.p. (ISBN 0-440-92861-3, LFL). Dell.
--Tangled Butterfly. LC 79-23405. 162p. (gr. 6 up). 1980. 8.95 (ISBN 0-395-29110-0, Clarion). HM.
Bauer, Max. Precious Stones, 2 vols. (Illus.). Vol. 1. 15.00 (ISBN 0-8446-1608-7); Vol. 2. 10.00 (ISBN 0-686-96852-2). Peter Smith.
--Precious Stones: A Popular Account of Their Characters, Occurence & Applications. Spencer, L. J., tr. LC 69-12082. (Illus.). 1969. 52.50 (ISBN 0-8048-0489-3). C E Tuttle.
Bauer, N. S., ed. William Wordsworth: A Reference Guide to British Criticism, 1793-1899. 1978. lib. bdg. 40.00 (ISBN 0-8161-7828-3, Hall Reference). G K Hall.
Bauer, Oswald G. Richard Wagner. (Illus.). 288p. 1983. 60.00 (ISBN 0-8478-0478-X). Rizzoli Intl.
Bauer, P. T. Equality, the Third World & Economic Delusion. 304p. 1983. pap. text ed. 7.95x (ISBN 0-674-25986-6). Harvard U Pr.
Bauer, Peggy & Bauer, Erwin. Campers' Digest. 3rd ed. 288p. 1980. pap. 7.95 o.s.i. (ISBN 0-695-81416-8). Follett.
Bauer, Peggy, jt. auth. see Bauer, Erwin.
Bauer, Peter T. Economic Analysis & Policy in Underdeveloped Countries. LC 81-13361. (Duke University Commonwealth-Studies Center Publication: No. 4). xiii, 145p. 1982. Repr. of 1957 ed. lib. bdg. 20.75x (ISBN 0-313-23272-5, BACA). Greenwood.
Bauer, R. & Loeschen, R. Chemistry for the Allied Health Sciences. 1980. 25.95 (ISBN 0-13-129205-6); lab manual 14.95 (ISBN 0-13-129213-7); student guide 9.95 (ISBN 0-13-129197-1). P-H.
Bauer, Raymond A. New Man in Soviet Psychology. LC 52-5385. (Russian Research Center Studies: No. 7). 1952. 12.50x o.p. (ISBN 0-674-61700-2). Harvard U Pr.
Bauer, Raymond A. & Fenn, Dan H., Jr. The Corporate Social Audit. LC 72-83832. (Social Science Frontiers Ser.). 109p. 1972. pap. 4.95x (ISBN 0-87154-103-3). Russell Sage.
Bauer, Raymond A. & Wasiolek, Edward. Nine Soviet Portraits. LC 79-4609. (Illus.). 1979. Repr. of 1965 ed. lib. bdg. 20.75x (ISBN 0-313-20929-4, BANS). Greenwood.
Bauer, Raymond A., ed. Some Views on Soviet Psychology. LC 75-26671. (Illus.). 285p. 1975. Repr. of 1962 ed. lib. bdg. 19.75x (ISBN 0-8371-8363-4, BASV). Greenwood.
Bauer, Robert F. & Kafka, Doris M. U. S. Federal Election Law: Federal Regulation of Political Campaign Finance & Participation. LC 82-12455. 1982. loose-leaf 85.00 (ISBN 0-379-20743-5). Oceana.
Bauer, Steven. Satyrday. (Illus.). 228p. 1980. 11.95 (ISBN 0-399-12533-7). Putnam Pub Group.
Bauer, Walter, et al, eds. A Greek-English Lexicon of the New Testament & Other Early Christian Literature. Arndt, William F., tr. from Ger. LC 78-14293. (2nd rev. & augmented edition). 1979. lib. bdg. 37.50x (ISBN 0-226-03932-3). U of Chicago Pr.
Bauer, Yehuda. American Jewry & the Holocaust: The American Jewish Joint Distribution Committee, 1939-1945. LC 80-26035. 550p. 1981. 25.00 (ISBN 0-8143-1672-7). Wayne St U Pr.
Bauer, Yehuda & Rotenstreich, Nathan, eds. Holocaust as Historical Experience. 300p. 1981. text ed. 24.50x (ISBN 0-8419-0635-1); pap. text ed. 12.50x (ISBN 0-8419-0636-X). Holmes & Meier.
Bauerle, Richard E. I, the Prophet. 1981. pap. 6.25 (ISBN 0-570-03835-9, 12YY2800). Concordia.
Bauer-Lechner, Natalie. Recollections of Gustav Mahler. Franklin, P., ed. Newlin, D., tr. from Ger. LC 80-834. (Illus.). 241p. 1980. 24.95 (ISBN 0-521-23572-3). Cambridge U Pr.
Baues, H. J. Commutator Calculus & Groups of Homotopy Classes. (London Mathematical Society Lecture Note Ser.: No. 50). (Illus.). 220p. 1981. pap. 24.95 (ISBN 0-521-28424-4). Cambridge U Pr.
Baugh, A., et al, eds. Literary History of England. 2nd student ed. 1967. 49.00 (ISBN 0-13-537605-X). P-H.
Baugh, Albert C. & Cable, Thomas. History of the English Language. 3rd ed. LC 77-26324. (Illus.). 1978. ref. ed. 20.95 (ISBN 0-13-389239-5). P-H.
Baugh, Edward, ed. Critics on Caribbean Literature: Readings in Literary Criticism. LC 76-21943. 1978. text ed. 15.95 o.p. (ISBN 0-312-17605-8). St Martin.
Baughan, Michalina, et al. Social Change in France. 1980. 26.00x (ISBN 0-312-73161-2). St Martin.
Baughen, Michael. The Moses Principle: Leadership & the Venture of Faith. LC 78-27498. 1978. pap. 2.95 (ISBN 0-87788-558-3). Shaw Pubs.
Baughman, Dorothy. Piney's Summer. LC 76-13019. (Illus.). (gr. 3-5). 1976. 5.95 o.p. (ISBN 0-698-20380-1, Coward). Putnam Pub Group.
--Secret of Montoya Mission. (YA) 1981. 6.95 (ISBN 0-686-73950-7, Avalon). Bouregy.
Baughman, Gary L., jt. ed. see Raese, Jon W.
Baughman, Kenneth L. & Green, Bruce M. Clinical Diagnostic Manual for the House Officer. (House Officer Ser.). (Illus.). 176p. 1981. softcover 9.95 (ISBN 0-683-00479-4). Williams & Wilkins.
Baughman, Martin L., et al. Electric Power in the United States: Models & Policy Analysis. 1979. text ed. 37.50x (ISBN 0-262-02130-7). MIT Pr.
Baughn, William H. & Walker, Charls E., eds. The Banker's Handbook. rev. ed. LC 77-89797. 1978. 45.00 (ISBN 0-87094-154-2). Dow Jones-Irwin.
Baugmartner, Ted A. & Jackson, Andrew S. Measurement for Evaluation in Physical Education. 2nd ed. 540p. 1982. write for info. o.p. (ISBN 0-697-07194-4); write for info. o.p. (ISBN 0-697-07195-2). Wm C Brown.
Baulch, D. L., et al. Evaluated Kinetic Data for High Temperature Reactions, Vol. 3. 1977. 99.95 o.p. (ISBN 0-408-70787-9). Butterworth.
Bauly, C. B., jt. ed. see Bauly, J. A.
Bauly, J. A. & Bauly, C. B., eds. World Energy Directory: A Guide to Organizations & Research Activities in Non-Atomic Energy. 600p. 1981. 195.00x (ISBN 0-686-76211-8, Pub. by Longman). Gale.
Baum, jt. ed. see Kuttin.
Baum, A. & Singer, J. E., eds. Issues in Child Health & Adolescent Health: Handbook of Psychology & Health. (Vol. 2). (Illus.). 304p. 1982. text ed. 29.95 (ISBN 0-89859-184-8). L Erlbaum Assocs.
Baum, Andrew & Mackmin, David. The Income Approach to Property Valuation. 1979. pap. 12.00 o.p. (ISBN 0-7100-0018-9). Routledge & Kegan.
Baum, Andrew & Valins, Stuart. Architecture & Social Behavior: Psychological Studies of Social Density. (Complex Human Behavior Ser.). 1977. 11.95 (ISBN 0-470-99300-6). Halsted Pr.
Baum, Andrew, jt. auth. see Krantz, David S.
Baum, Andrew & Epstein, Yakov M., eds. Human Response to Crowding. LC 78-6875. (Environmental Psychology Ser.). 1978. 24.95 (ISBN 0-470-26374-1). Halsted Pr.
Baum, Andrew & Singer, Jerome E., eds. Environment & Health. (Advances in Environmental Psychology Ser.: Vol. 4). (Illus.). 352p. 1982. text ed. 39.95x (ISBN 0-89859-174-0). L Erlbaum Assocs.
Baum, Andrew, et al, eds. Advances in Environmental Psychology: The Urban Environment, Vol. 1. LC 78-13289. 1978. 14.95 (ISBN 0-470-26545-0). Halsted Pr.
Baum, Mrs. C. L. Studies in Divine Science. 1964. 6.50 (ISBN 0-686-24362-5). Divine Sci Fed.
Baum, Claude. The System Builders: The Story of SDC. (Illus.). ix, 302p. 1981. 20.00x (ISBN 0-916368-02-5). System Dev CA.
Baum, David, jt. ed. see Buckley, Mary.
Baum, Edward & Gagliano, Felix. Chief Executives in Black Africa & Southeast Asia: A Descriptive Analysis of Social Background Characteristics. LC 76-620039. (Illus.). 1976. pap. 4.00x (ISBN 0-89680-025-3, Ohio U Ctr Intl). Ohio U Pr.
Baum, Edward, compiled by. A Comprehensive Periodical Bibliography of Nigeria: 1960-1970. LC 75-620025. (Papers in International Studies: Africa: No. 24). 1975. pap. 13.00x (ISBN 0-89680-057-1, Ohio U Ctr Intl). Ohio U Pr.
Baum, Gilbert. Fundamentals of Medical Ultrasonography. 1975. 50.00 o.p. (ISBN 0-399-40045-1). Putnam Pub Group.
Baum, Gregory. New Horizon. LC 74-188284. 160p. 1972. pap. 2.95 o.p. (ISBN 0-8091-1724-X). Paulist Pr.
--Truth Beyond Relativism: Karl Mannheim's Sociology of Knowledge. LC 77-76605. (Pere Marquette Ser.). 1977. 7.95 (ISBN 0-87462-509-2). Marquette.
Baum, Gregory, ed. Sociology & Human Destiny: Studies in Sociology, Religion & Society. 224p. 1980. 14.50 (ISBN 0-8164-0110-1). Seabury.
--Work & Religion. (Concilium Ser.: Vol. 131). 128p. (Orig.). 1980. pap. 5.95 (ISBN 0-8164-2273-7). Seabury.
Baum, Gregory & Coleman, John, eds. New Religious Movements. (Concilium 1983: Vol. 161). 128p. (Orig.). 1983. pap. 6.95 (ISBN 0-8164-2441-1); pap. 62.55 10 Volume Subscription (ISBN 0-8164-2453-5). Seabury.
Baum, Gregory, ed. see Vatican Council Two.
Baum, H. The Biochemist's Songbook. (Illus.). 64p. 1982. pap. 4.95 (ISBN 0-08-027370-X). Pergamon.
Baum, H. & Gergely, J., eds. Molecular Aspects of Medicine, Vol. 4. (Illus.). 452p. 1982. 150.00 (ISBN 0-08-030007-3). Pergamon.
Baum, Herman. House Doctor's Book of Simple Home Repairs. 192p. 1982. pap. 2.50 o.p. (ISBN 0-523-41270-3). Pinnacle Bks.
--The House Doctor's Guide to Simple Home Repair. 240p. 1983. pap. 2.95 (ISBN 0-523-41270-3). Pinnacle Bks.
Baum, Joseph L. Beginner's Handbook of Dowsing. LC 73-89055. (Illus.). 32p. 1974. 3.95 o.p. (ISBN 0-517-51468-0). Crown.
Baum, Kenneth H & Schertz, Lyle P. Modeling Farm Decisions for Policy Analysis. 500p. 1983. lib. bdg. 20.00x (ISBN 0-86531-589-2). Westview.
Baum, L. Frank. The Life & Adventures of Santa Claus. 8.50 (ISBN 0-8446-5450-7). Peter Smith.
--Magic of Oz. LC 77-75851. (Wonderful World of the Wizard of Oz Ser.). 1977. pap. 3.95 o.p. (ISBN 0-8092-7768-9). Contemp Bks.
--The Wizard of Oz. (Elephant Bks.). pap. 2.95 (ISBN 0-448-12432-7, G&D). Putnam Pub Group.
--Wizard of Oz. (Illus.). (gr. 4-6). 1956. il. jr. lib. 5.95 (ISBN 0-448-05826-X, G&D); deluxe ed. 8.95 (ISBN 0-448-06026-4); Companion Lib. Ed. 2.95 (ISBN 0-448-05470-1). Putnam Pub Group.
--Wizard of Oz. Chaffee, Allen, ed. (Illus.). (gr. k-3). 1950. 4.95 (ISBN 0-394-80689-1, BYR); PLB 4.99 (ISBN 0-394-90689-6). Random.
--The Wizard of Oz. 1983. pap. 1.95 (ISBN 0-14-035001-2, Puffin). Penguin.
--Wonderful Wizard of Oz. (Illus.). (gr. k-6). 1960. pap. 4.50 (ISBN 0-486-20691-2). Dover.
Baum, Lawrence. The Supreme Court. O'Connor, Ann & Woy, Jean, eds. LC 80-607841. (Politics & Public Policy Ser.). 264p. (Orig.). 1981. pap. 8.95 (ISBN 0-87187-160-2). Congr Quarterly.
Baum, Lloyd, ed. Restorative Techniques for Individual Teeth. LC 80-81989. (Masson Monographs in Dentistry: Vol. 2). (Illus.). 224p. 1980. 34.25x (ISBN 0-89352-113-2). Masson Pub.
Baum, Lloyd, et al. Textbook of Operative Dentistry. (Illus.). 450p. 1981. text ed. 35.00 (ISBN 0-7216-1601-1). Saunders.
Baum, M. & Kay, R., eds. Clinical Trails in Early Breast Cancer. (Experientia Supplementum: Vol. 41). 676p. Date not set. text ed. 49.95 (ISBN 3-7643-1358-7). Birkhauser.
Baum, Martha, jt. auth. see Baum, Rainer.
Baum, Maud G. In Lands Other Than Ours. LC 82-10254. 1983. 25.00 (ISBN 0-8201-1385-9). Schol Facsimiles.
Baum, Michael. Breast Cancer: The Facts. (The Facts Ser.). (Illus.). 124p. 1981. text ed. 12.95x (ISBN 0-19-261265-4). Oxford U Pr.
Baum, Myra, jt. auth. see Armstrong, Fiona.
Baum, Patricia. Dictators of Latin America. (Illus.). (gr. 6 up). 1972. PLB 5.29 o.p. (ISBN 0-399-60720-X). Putnam Pub Group.
Baum, Rainer & Baum, Martha. Growing Old: A Social Perspective. (Ser. in Sociology). (Illus.). 1980. pap. text ed. 15.95 (ISBN 0-13-367797-4). P-H.
Baum, Robert J., ed. Philosophy & Mathematics: From Plato to the Present. LC 73-84704. 320p. 1973. pap. 11.00x (ISBN 0-87735-514-2). Freeman C.
Baum, S. J., et al, eds. Experimental Hematology Today, 1982. (Illus.). xx, 270p. 1982. 118.75 (ISBN 3-8055-3486-8). S Karger.
Baum, Stuart, et al. Exercises in Organic & Biological Chemistry. 2nd ed. 1981. 14.95x (ISBN 0-02-306540-0). Macmillan.
Baum, Stuart J. Introduction to Organic & Biological Chemistry. 3rd ed. 1981. 26.95 (ISBN 0-02-306640-7); pap. 2.95 answer bk. (ISBN 0-02-306580-X). Macmillan.
Baum, Stuart J. & Scaife, Charles W. Chemistry: A Life Science Approach. 2nd ed. (Illus.). 1980. text ed. 26.95 (ISBN 0-02-306610-5). Macmillan.
Baum, Thomas. Carny. 224p. (Orig.). 1980. pap. 2.50 o.s.i. (ISBN 0-515-05431-3). Jove Pubns.
Baum, Warren C. The French Economy & the State. LC 82-15539. xvi, 391p. 1982. lib. bdg. 39.95 (ISBN 0-313-23650-X, BAFE). Greenwood.
Baum, Willa K. Oral History for the Local Historical Society. rev. ed. (Illus.). 1971. pap. 4.00 (ISBN 0-910050-06-6). AASLH.
--Transcribing & Editing Oral History. LC 77-3340. (Illus.). 1977. pap. 8.00 o.p. (ISBN 0-910050-26-0). AASLH.
Bauman, Chester W. Faith & Works. 1976. pap. 1.75 (ISBN 0-686-15483-5). Rod & Staff.
Bauman, Edward J., jt. ed. see Culp, Robert D.
Bauman, Edward W. Life & Teaching of Jesus. LC 60-7038. 1978. softcover 6.95 (ISBN 0-664-24221-9). Westminster.
Bauman, Elizabeth. Ascuas de Fuego. Patzan, Flora, tr. 128p. (Span.). 1982. pap. 3.50 (ISBN 0-8361-3315-3). Herald Pr.

Bauman, John W. & Chinard, Francis P. Renal Function: Physiological & Medical Aspects. LC 74-28278. 1975. pap. 10.45 o.p. (ISBN 0-8016-0509-1). Mosby.

Bauman, Karl E. Research Methods for Community Health & Welfare: An Introduction. 1980. 19.95x (ISBN 0-19-502698-5); pap. 9.95x (ISBN 0-19-502699-3). Oxford U Pr.

Bauman, Kurt, jt. auth. see Wilkon, Jozef.

Bauman, Mary K., ed. Blindness, Visual Impairment, Deaf-Blindness: Annotated Listing of the Literature, 1953-75. LC 76-14724. 553p. 1976. 39.95 (ISBN 0-87722-067-0). Temple U Pr.

Bauman, Richard, jt. ed. see Paredes, Americo.

Bauman, W. Scott, jt. auth. see Hayes, Douglas A.

Bauman, William A. The Ministry of Music: A Guide for the Practicing Church Musician. rev. ed. Rendler, Elaine, ed. 1979. pap. 7.95 (ISBN 0-918208-93-9). Liturgical Conf.

Bauman, Zygmunt. Between Class & Elite: The Evolution of the British Labour Movement - a Sociological Study. Patterson, Sheila, tr. (Illus.). 334p. 1972. text ed. 16.00x o.p. (ISBN 0-7190-0502-7). Humanities.

--Memories of Class. (International Library of Sociology Ser.). 224p. 1983. 21.95 (ISBN 0-7100-9196-6). Routledge & Kegan.

Baumann, Carl L., tr. see Baegert, Johann J.

Baumann, Duane D. & Dworkin, Daniel M., eds. Planning for Water Reuse. LC 77-83289. (Illus.). 1978. text ed. 22.95x (ISBN 0-88425-008-3). Maaroufa Pr.

Baumann, Duane D., jt. ed. see Sims, John H.

Baumann, Edward W., jt. auth. see O'Brien, John.

Baumann, Elwood. The Loch Ness Monster. LC 72-182896. (Illus.). 160p. (gr. 6 up). 1972. PLB 7.90 (ISBN 0-531-02031-2). Watts.

Baumann, Elwood D. An Album of Motorcycles & Motorcycle Racing. (Picture Albums Ser.). (Illus.). 96p. (gr. 5 up). 1982. PLB 9.60 (ISBN 0-531-04469-6). Watts.

--The Devil's Triangle. LC 75-22020. (Illus.). 160p. (gr. 7 up). 1976. PLB 7.90 (ISBN 0-531-01094-5). Watts.

Baumann, Kurt. The Pied Piper of Hamelin. LC 78-62168. (Illus.). (gr. k-4). 1979. 8.95 o.p. (ISBN 0-416-30521-0). Methuen Inc.

--Puss in Boots. (Illus.). 24p. (gr. 1-3). 1982. lib. bdg. 8.95 (ISBN 0-571-12511-5). Faber & Faber.

Baumann, N. Neurological Mutants Affecting Myclination. (Inserm Symposia Ser.: Vol. 14). 1980. 92.00 (ISBN 0-444-80270-3). Elsevier.

Baumann, P., et al, eds. Les Alpha-Bloquants: Pharmacologie Experimentale & Clinique. (Illus.). 418p. 1981. write for info. (ISBN 2-225-68618-1). Masson Pub.

Baumann, Winfried. Erinnerung und Erinnertes In Gor'kijs "Kindheit". 196p. (Ger.). 1982. write for info. (ISBN 3-8204-5760-7). P Lang Pubs.

Baumbach, Jonathan. My Father More or Less. 256p. 1982. 11.95 (ISBN 0-914590-66-9); pap. 5.95 (ISBN 0-914590-67-7). Fiction Coll.

Baumback, Clifford M. & Mancuso, Joseph R. Entrepreneurship & Venture Management: Text & Readings. (Illus.). 368p. 1975. pap. text ed. 15.95 (ISBN 0-13-283119-8). P-H.

Baumeister, E. T., ed. Standard Handbook for Mechanical Engineers. 8th ed. (Bk. No. E00028). 1978. pap. 58.00 (ISBN 0-685-99211-X). ASME.

Baumeister, Theodore. Marks' Standard Handbook for Mechanical Engineers. 8th ed. (Illus.). 1978. 58.00 (ISBN 0-07-004123-7, P&RB). McGraw.

Baumer, Franklin L. Modern European Thought: Continuity & Change in Ideas, 1600-1950. (Illus.). 1978. 15.95 (ISBN 0-02-306450-1). Macmillan.

Baumer, Franz. Hermann Hesse. Conway, John, tr. LC 68-31446. (Literature and Life Ser.). 1969. 11.95 (ISBN 0-8044-2027-0). Ungar.

Baumer, Mary P. Seasonal Kindergarten Units. 1972. pap. 6.95 (ISBN 0-8224-6330-X). Pitman Learning.

Baumer, Rachel & Brandon, James R. Sanskrit Drama in Performance. LC 80-26900. (Illus.). 334p. 1981. text ed. 27.50x (ISBN 0-8248-0688-3). UH Pr.

Baumer, Rachel, ed. Aspects of Bengali History & Society. LC 73-90491. (Asian Studies at Hawaii Ser.: No. 12). 1975. pap. text ed. 9.50x (ISBN 0-8248-0318-3). UH Pr.

Baumgaertner, John H. Meet the Twelve. rev. ed. LC 60-6440. (Illus., Orig.). 1960. pap. 4.50 (ISBN 0-8066-0604-5, 10-4311). Augsburg.

Baumgardner, jt. auth. see Perls, Fritz.

Baumgardner, Patricia see Perls, Fritz & Baumgardner.

Baumgardner, Robert W., et al. Report of Investigations No. 114: The Wink Sink, a Salt Dissolution & Collapse Feature, Winker County, Texas. (Illus.). 38p. 1982. 1.50 (ISBN 0-686-37544-0). U of Tex Econ Geology.

Baumgardt, John P. How to Identify Flowering Plant Families. (Illus.). 269p. 1982. pap. 22.95 (ISBN 0-917304-21-7). Timber.

--The Practical Vegetable Gardener. LC 77-88751. 1978. (ISBN 0-685-88354-X, Quick Fox); pap. 5.95 o.p. (ISBN 0-8256-3094-0). Putnam Pub Group.

Baumgarner, James, ed. see Levin, Paul.

Baumgart, Winfried. Imperialism: The Idea & Reality of British & French Colonial Expansion, 1880-1914. Mast, Ben V., tr. (Illus.). 1982. 34.95x (ISBN 0-19-873040-3); pap. 9.95x (ISBN 0-19-873041-1). Oxford U Pr.

Baumgart, Winfried, ed. see Saab, Ann P.

Baumgartel, Elise. Petrie's Naqada Excavation a Supplement. 75p. 1970. text ed. 40.00x (ISBN 0-85388-005-0, Pub. by Aris & Phillips England). Humanities.

Baumgarten, Henry E., jt. auth. see Linstromberg, Walter W.

Baumgarten, Henry F., jt. auth. see Linstromberg, Walter W.

Baumgarten, Murray, tr. see De Ayala, Ramon P.

Baumgarten, Paul, jt. auth. see Farber, Donald C.

Baumgarten, Paul A. & Leavy, Morton L. Legal & Business Problems of Financing Motion Pictures, 1979. LC 78-88389. (Patents, Copyrights, Trademarks, & Literary Property Course Handbook Ser.: 1978-1979). 1979. pap. text ed. 20.00 o.p. (ISBN 0-686-59550-5, G4-3658). PLI.

Baumgarten, Reuben L. Organic Chemistry: A Brief Survey. LC 74-22533. 475p. 1978. 25.95x (ISBN 0-471-06716-4); instructors manual o.p. (ISBN 0-471-07576-0). Wiley.

Baumgartner, A. & Reichel, E. World Water Balance. (Eng. & Ger.). 1975. 83.00 (ISBN 0-444-99858-6). Elsevier.

Baumgartner, J. S. Systems Management. 522p. 1979. 22.00 (ISBN 0-87179-297-4). BNA.

Baumgartner, Leona, et al. The Parent's Book of Baby Care. (Good Health Books). (Illus.). 1978. pap. 2.50 (ISBN 0-448-14823-4, G&D). Putnam Pub Group.

Baumgartner, Richard A., ed. & intro. by see Rizzi, Joseph N.

Baumgartner, Thomas, ed. Transitions to Alternative Energy Systems. (Replica Edition Ser.). 270p. 1982. lib. bdg. 22.50 (ISBN 0-86531-907-3). Westview.

Baumgartner, Victor. Graphic Games: From Pattern to Composition. (Illus.). 160p. 1983. text ed. 12.95 (ISBN 0-13-363333-0). P-H.

Baumhoff, Martin A., jt. auth. see Heizer, Robert F.

Baumhover, Lorin S. & Jones, Joan D., eds. Handbook of American Aging Programs. LC 76-28641. 1977. lib. bdg. 25.00x (ISBN 0-8371-9287-0, BAA/). Greenwood.

Baumol, W. Economic Theory & Operations Analysis. 4th ed. 1977. 27.95 (ISBN 0-13-227132-X). P-H.

Baumol, William J. Economic Dynamics. 3rd ed. (Illus.). 1970. text ed. 25.95x (ISBN 0-02-306660-1, 30666). Macmillan.

Baumol, William J. & Marcus, Matityahu. Economics of Academic Libraries. 112p. 1973. 6.50 o.p. (ISBN 0-8268-1257-0). ACE.

Baumol, William J. & Oates, Wallace E. The Theory of Environmental Policy: The Externalities, Public Outlays, & the Quality of Life. LC 74-11205. (Illus.). 304p. 1975. ref. ed. 24.95 (ISBN 0-13-913673-8). P-H.

Baumol, William J. & Panzar, John C. Contestable Markets & the Theory of Industry Structure. 512p. 1982. text ed. 31.95 (ISBN 0-15-513910-X, HC). HarBraceJ.

Baumol, William J see Knorr, Klaus E.

Baumol, William J., ed. Public & Private Enterprise in a Mixed Economy. LC 79-24732. 300p. 1980. 40.00x (ISBN 0-312-65397-2). St Martin.

Baumol, William J., et al. Economics, Environmental Policy & the Quality of Life. 1979. 18.95 (ISBN 0-13-231365-0); pap. 14.95 (ISBN 0-13-231357-X). P-H.

Baumsiag, C. B. & Chandler, B. Group Theory. LC 68-6033. (Schaum's Outline Ser). (Illus.). 1968. pap. 7.95 (ISBN 0-07-004124-5, SP). McGraw.

Baumslag, Naomi, ed. Family Care. LC 73-4556. 392p. 1973. 15.00 (ISBN 0-683-00412-3, Pub. by W & W). Krieger.

Baur, Arthur, tr. see Wodehouse, P. G.

Baur, F. J., ed. Bird Control in Plants: It's a Flying Shame. LC 81-71370. 90p. 1982. pap. text ed. 12.00 (ISBN 0-913250-27-9). Am Assn Cereal Chem.

Baur, Francis. Life in Abundance: A Contemporary Spirituality. 240p. 1983. pap. 7.95 (ISBN 0-8091-2507-2). Paulist Pr.

Baur, Karla, jt. auth. see Crooks, Robert.

Baur, P. V. Preliminary Catalogue of the Rebecca Darlington Stoddard Collection of Greek & Italian Vases. 1914. pap. 22.50x (ISBN 0-686-51289-8). Elliots Bks.

Baur, P. V., jt. auth. see Hopkins, C.

Baur, Robert C. Gardens in Glass Containers. LC 76-92493. (Illus.). 1970. 7.95 (ISBN 0-8208-0064-3). Hearthside.

Baurley, George L., tr. see Stempell, Dieter.

Baurmeister, Carl L. Revolution in America: Confidential Letters & Journals, 1776-1784. Uhlendorf, Bernhard A., tr. LC 72-11301. (Illus.). 640p. 1973. Repr. of 1957 ed. lib. bdg. 29.50x o.p. (ISBN 0-8371-6651-9, BARE). Greenwood.

Baus, Herb. Best Restaurants, Orange County. LC 82-81766. (Best Restaurants Ser.). (Illus.). 224p. (Orig.). 1982. pap. 4.95 (ISBN 0-89286-199-1). One Hund One Prods.

Baus, Herbert M. The Experts Crossword Puzzle Dictionary. LC 72-84960. pap. 6.95 (ISBN 0-385-04788-6, Dolp). Doubleday.

Bausch, Richard. Real Presence. 288p. 1981. pap. 2.75 o.p. (ISBN 0-523-41540-0). Pinnacle Bks.

Bausch, William. A New Look at the Sacraments. 2nd ed. 288p. 1983. pap. 5.95 (ISBN 0-89622-174-1). Twenty-Third.

Bausch, William J., jt. auth. see Pantoga, Fritzie.

Bausell, R. Barker, et al. The Bausell Home Learning Guide: Teach Your Child to Write. 1981. 12.95 (ISBN 0-7216-1596-1). Saunders.

--Teach Your Child to Write. (Illus.). 224p. text ed. 12.95 o.p. (ISBN 0-7216-1596-1). Saunders.

Bausert, John. Complete Book of Wicker & Cane Furniture Making. LC 75-36148. (Illus.). 1976. pap. 8.95 (ISBN 0-8069-8240-3). Sterling.

Bautista, Romeo M. Exhange Rate Adjustment under Generalized Currency Floating: Comparative Analysis among Developing Countries. (Working Paper: No. 436). 99p. 1980. 5.00 (ISBN 0-686-36172-5, WP-0436). World Bank.

Bautista, Romeo M., et al, eds. Capital Utilization in Manufacturing: Colombia, Israel, Malaysia & the Philippines. (World Bank Research Publications Ser.). (Illus.). 1981. 27.50x (ISBN 0-19-520268-6). Oxford U Pr.

Bautista, Sara, tr. see Collingwood, Guillermo.

Bautista, Sara, tr. see Cutting, Jorge.

Bautista, Sara, tr. see Mackintosh, Carlos H.

Bautista, Sara, tr. see Marshall, Alejandro & Bennett, Gordon H.

Bautista, SAra, tr. see Pollock, Algernon J.

Bautista, Sara, tr. see Pollock, Algernon J. & Bennett, Gordon H.

Bautista, Sara, tr. see Rossier, H.

Bautista, Sara, tr. see Voorehoeve, H. C. & Bennett, Gordon H.

Bauwens, Eleanor E., jt. auth. see Anderson, Sandra V.

Bauwens, Eleanor E., ed. The Anthropology of Health. LC 78-6776. 1978. pap. text ed. 11.95 o.p. (ISBN 0-8016-0516-4). Mosby.

Bavarel, Michel. New Communities, New Ministries: The Church Resurgent in Africa, Asia, & Latin America. Martin, Francis, tr. from Fr. LC 82-22318. Orig. Title: Chretienes Du Bout Du Monde. 128p. (Orig.). 1983. pap. 5.95 (ISBN 0-88344-337-6). Orbis Bks.

Bavel, Zamir. Introduction to the Theory of Automata & Sequential Machines. 1982. text ed. 27.95 (ISBN 0-8359-3271-0); cancelled instr's. manual (ISBN 0-8359-3272-9). Reston.

--A Math Companion for Computer Science. 1981. 21.95 (ISBN 0-8359-4300-3); pap. 16.95 (ISBN 0-8359-4299-6); solutions manual avail. (ISBN 0-8359-4301-1). Reston.

Bavelas, Janet. Personality: Current Theory & Research. LC 77-13213. 1978. text ed. 18.95 o.p. (ISBN 0-8185-0253-3). Brooks-Cole.

Bavendam, Fred. Beneath Cold Waters: The Marine Life of New England. LC 79-67413. (Illus.). 128p. 1980. 18.95 (ISBN 0-89272-068-9, PIC449). Down East.

Baver, Leonard D., et al. Soil Physics. 4th ed. LC 72-5318. 498p. 1972. 34.95x (ISBN 0-471-05974-9). Wiley.

Bavetta, Lucien A., jt. ed. see Slavkin, Harold C.

Bavier, Robert N., Jr. Keys to Racing Success. LC 82-2358. (Illus.). 1982. 19.95 (ISBN 0-396-08064-2). Dodd.

--New Yacht, Rules - Racing. 1969. 5.95 (ISBN 0-393-03135-7). Norton.

--Sailing to Win. LC 82-22040. (Illus.). 1983. 17.95 (ISBN 0-396-08050-2). Dodd.

Bavouse, Glenn B. More World War II Aircraft in Combat. LC 80-12082. (Illus.). 256p. 1981. 15.00 o.p. (ISBN 0-668-04550-7); pap. 8.95 o.p. (ISBN 0-668-04563-9). Arco.

Bavousett, Glenn. World War II Aircraft in Combat. LC 75-7167. (Illus.). 1976. 11.95 o.p. (ISBN 0-668-03823-3); pap. 6.95 (ISBN 0-668-03824-1). Arco.

Bawa, Vasant K. Latin American Integration. 225p. 1980. text ed. 13.00x (ISBN 0-391-01899-X). Humanities.

Bawa Muhaivaddeen, M. R. The Truth & Unity of Man: Letters in Response to a Crisis. LC 80-18050. 144p. 1980. 10.00 (ISBN 0-914390-15-5); pap. 4.00 (ISBN 0-914390-14-7). Fellowship Pr PA.

Bawa Muhaiyaddeen, M. R. The Asma'ul-Husna: The 99 Beautiful Names of Allah. LC 79-19619. (Illus.). 211p. 1979. pap. 5.00 (ISBN 0-914390-13-9). Fellowship Pr PA.

--A Book of God's Love. LC 81-4503. (Illus.). 126p. 1981. 8.00 (ISBN 0-914390-19-8). Fellowship Pr.

--The Divine Luminous Wisdom That Dispels the Darkness God-Man Man-God. rev. ed. (Illus.). 288p. 1977. pap. 7.00 (ISBN 0-914390-11-2). Fellowship Pr PA.

--Four Steps to Pure Iman. 65p. 1979. pap. 4.00 (ISBN 0-914390-17-1). Fellowship Pr PA.

--God, His Prophets & His Children. LC 78-12891. (Illus.). 1978. pap. 6.00 (ISBN 0-914390-09-0). Fellowship Pr PA.

--The Guidebook to the True Secret of the Heart, 2 vols. LC 75-44557. (Illus.). 1976. pap. 6.00 ea. Vol. 1, 224p (ISBN 0-914390-07-4). Vol. 2, 232p (ISBN 0-914390-08-2). Fellowship Pr PA.

Bawa Muhaiy addeen, M. R. Songs of God's Grace. LC 73-91016. (Illus.). 154p. 1974. pap. 4.00 (ISBN 0-914390-02-3). Fellowship Pr PA.

Bawa Muhaiyaddeen, M. R. Truth & Light: Brief Explanations. LC 74-76219. (Illus.). 144p. 1974. pap. 3.50 (ISBN 0-914390-04-X). Fellowship Pr PA.

--Wisdom of Man: Selected Discourses. LC 80-20541. (Illus.). 168p. 1980. 8.00 (ISBN 0-914390-16-3). Fellowship Pr PA.

Bawden, F. C. Plant Viruses & Virus Diseases. 4th ed. (Illus.). 361p. 1964. 21.50x (ISBN 0-471-06804-7, Pub. by Wiley-Interscience). Wiley.

Bawden, Nina. Carrie's War. LC 72-13253. (gr. 7 up). 1973. lib. bdg. 10.89 (ISBN 0-397-31450-7, JBL-J). Har-Row.

--Devil by the Sea. 1978. pap. 1.95 o.p. (ISBN 0-380-01922-1, 57695). Avon.

--Devil by the Sea. LC 76-13177. (gr. 7-12). 1976. 10.53i (ISBN 0-397-31683-6, JBL-J). Har-Row.

--Kept in the Dark. (gr. 4-7). 1982. 9.50 (ISBN 0-686-94036-9). Morrow.

--The Peppermint Pig. LC 74-26922. (gr. 3-6). 1975. lib. bdg. 10.53i (ISBN 0-397-31618-6, JBL-J). Har-Row.

--Squib. (gr. 4-6). 1982. 9.50 (ISBN 0-688-01299-X). Morrow.

--Witch's Daughter. LC 66-10349. (Illus.). (gr. 4-6). 1966. 10.53i (ISBN 0-397-30922-8, JBL-J). Har-Row.

Bax, E. Belfort. The Social Side of the Reformation in Germany, 3 vols. Incl. Vol. 1. German Society at the Close of the Middle Ages. LC 67-25997. 276p. Repr. of 1894 ed. lib. bdg. 22.50x (ISBN 0-678-00312-2); Vol. 2. The Peasants' War in Germany 1525-1526. LC 68-57371. 367p. Repr. of 1899 ed. lib. bdg. 25.00x (ISBN 0-678-00445-5); Vol. 3. The Rise & Fall of the Anapabtists. LC 75-101125. 407p. Repr. of 1903 ed. lib. bdg. 27.50x (ISBN 0-678-00593-1). lib. bdg. 65.00x set (ISBN 0-678-00772-1). Kelley.

Baxandall, Michael. The Limewood Sculptors of Renaissance Germany Fourteen Seventy-Five to Fifteen Twenty-Five. LC 79-23258. (Illus.). 1980. 65.00x (ISBN 0-300-02423-1); pap. 16.95x (ISBN 0-300-02829-6, Y-414). Yale U Pr.

Baxendale, J. & Busi, F. The Study of Fast Processes & Transient Species by Electron Pulse Radiolysis. 1982. 74.50 (ISBN 90-277-1431-2, Pub. by Reidel Holland). Kluwer Boston.

Baxi, Upendra. Alternatives in Developmental Law: The Crisis of the Indian Legal System. 200p. 1981. text ed. 35.00x (ISBN 0-7069-1369-8, Pub. by Vikas India). Advent NY.

Baxter, Angus. In Search of Your British & Irish Roots: A Complete Guide to Tracing Your English, Welsh, & Scottish & Irish Ancestors. LC 82-7895. 320p. 1982. 15.00 (ISBN 0-688-01350-3). Morrow.

Baxter, Anne. Intermission: A True Story. LC 75-45285. 1976. 10.00 (ISBN 0-399-11577-3). Putnam Pub Group.

Baxter, Batsell B. When Life Tumbles in. (Direction Bks.). 136p. 1976. pap. 3.95 (ISBN 0-8010-0630-9). Baker Bk.

Baxter, Batsell B. & Hazelip, Harold. Anchors in Troubled Waters. Abr. ed. LC 82-50267. (Journey Adult Ser.). 124p. pap. text ed. 2.95 (ISBN 0-8344-0120-7). Sweet.

Baxter, Bob. Confidence: How to Get It, How to Keep It, How to Use It. (Illus.). 176p. 1981. pap. cancelled (ISBN 0-8256-3223-4, Quick Fox). Putnam Pub Group.

Baxter, Carol. Business Report Writing. 392p. 1983. text ed. 20.95x (ISBN 0-534-01392-9). Kent Pub Co.

Baxter, Claude & Melnechuk, Theodore, eds. Perspectives in Schizophrenia Research. 463p. 1980. text ed. 56.00 (ISBN 0-89004-517-8). Raven.

Baxter, Ellen & Hopper, Kim. Private Lives-Public Spaces: Homeless Adults on the Streets of New York City. 129p. (Orig.). 1981. pap. 6.50 (ISBN 0-88156-002-2). Comm Serv Soc NY.

Baxter, Glen. Atlas. 1983. 7.95 (ISBN 0-394-52994-4). Knopf.

Baxter, J. Sidlow. A New Call to Holiness. 256p. 1973. pap. 6.95 (ISBN 0-310-20581-6). Zondervan.

Baxter, James K. The Bone Chanter. Weir, J. E., ed. 1977. pap. 9.95x o.p. (ISBN 0-19-558019-2). Oxford U Pr.

Baxter, James P., ed. The British Invasion from the North: The Campaigns of Generals Carleton & Burgoyne from Canada, 1776-1777. LC 74-114756. (Era of the American Revolution Ser). 1970. Repr. of 1887 ed. 49.50 (ISBN 0-306-71926-6). Da Capo.

Baxter, John. Black Yacht. 336p. 1982. pap. 2.95 (ISBN 0-515-06159-X). Jove Pubns.

--King Vidor. (Monarch Film Studies). 1975. pap. 2.95 o.p. (ISBN 0-671-08103-9). Monarch Pr.

Baxter, Maurice G. Steamboat Monopoly: Gibbons Vs Ogden, 1824. 1972. pap. text ed. 3.10x (ISBN 0-394-31491-3). Phila Bk Co.

Baxter, P. T. & Almagor, Uri, eds. Age, Generation & Time: Some Features of East African Age Organizations. LC 78-18952. (Illus.). 1978. 30.00 (ISBN 0-312-01172-5). St Martin.

Baxter, Pam, jt. auth. see Need, Jeffrey.

Baxter, R., jt. ed. see Perraton, J.

Baxter, R. R. & Carroll, D. The Panama Canal: Background Papers & Proceedings. LC 65-22162. (Hammarskjold Forum Ser.: No. 6). 118p. 1965. 10.00 (ISBN 0-379-11806-8). Oceana.

Baxter, Richard. The Reformed Pastor: A Pattern for Personal Growth & Ministry. rev. ed. Houston, James M., ed. LC 82-18825. (Classics of Faith & Devotion Ser.). 150p. 1983. 9.95 (ISBN 0-88070-003-3). Multnomah.

Baxter, Richard S. Computer & Statistical Techniques for Planners. 1976. 39.00x (ISBN 0-416-84620-3); pap. 22.00x (ISBN 0-416-84630-0). Methuen Inc.

Baxter, Robert. Baxter's Alaska. 1983. 9.95 (ISBN 0-913384-47-X). Rail Europe-Baxter.

--Baxter's California: Vol. 1, Southern California. 1983. 9.95 (ISBN 0-913384-51-8). Rail-Europe-Baxter.

--Baxter's California: Vol. 2, Northern California. 1983. 9.95 (ISBN 0-913384-52-6). Rail-Europe-Baxter.

--Baxter's Eurailpass Travel Guide. LC 74-169913. 1983. 9.95 (ISBN 0-913384-65-8). Rail-Europe-Baxter.

--Baxter's Florida. 1983. 9.95 (ISBN 0-913384-34-8). Rail-Europe-Baxter.

--Baxter's Mexico. 1983. 9.95 (ISBN 0-913384-42-9). Rail-Europe-Baxter.

--Baxter's Western Canada. 1983. 9.95 (ISBN 0-913384-41-0). Rail-Europe-Baxter.

Baxter, Robert E. Aim High! 3rd ed. LC 78-70660. 1978. pap. 2.95 o.p. (ISBN 0-89221-045-1). New Leaf.

Baxter, Stephen, ed. England's Rise to Greatness, 1660-1763. LC 82-40095. (Clark Library Professorship Ser.). (Illus.). 400p. 1983. text ed. 30.00x (ISBN 0-520-04572-6). U of Cal Pr.

Baxter, William D., jt. auth. see Bowen, William R.

Baxter, William T. Jewelry, Gem Cutting & Metalcraft. 3rd ed. 1950. 13.95 (ISBN 0-07-004149-0, GB). McGraw.

Bay, Bill. Mel Bay's Deluxe Guitar Praise Book. 64p. (Orig.). 1973. pap. 2.95 (ISBN 0-89228-007-7). Impact Bks MO.

--Mel Bay's Guitar Hymnal. 80p. (Orig.). 1972. pap. 2.95 (ISBN 0-89228-009-3). Impact Bks MO.

Bay, Timothy. Fake Giants & Other Great Hoaxes. LC 80-21132. (Monsters & Mysteries Ser.). (gr. 4-10). 1980. pap. 2.25 (ISBN 0-88436-766-5). EMC.

Bayard, James A. Papers of James A. Bayard. Donnan, Elizabeth, ed. LC 75-75312. (The American Scene: Comments & Commentators Ser.). 1971. Repr. of 1915 ed. lib. bdg. 59.50 (ISBN 0-306-71273-3). Da Capo.

Bayard, Jean, jt. auth. see Bayard, Robert T.

Bayard, Robert T. & Bayard, Jean. How to Deal with Your Acting-Up Teenager: Pratical Help for Desperate Parents. 228p. 1983. 11.95 (ISBN 0-87131-407-X). M Evans.

Bayard, Samuel P. Dance to the Fiddle-March to the Fife: Instrumental Folk Tunes in Pennsylvania. LC 81-83146. 628p. 1982. 28.50x (ISBN 0-271-00299-9). Pa St U Pr.

Bayat, Mangol. Mysticism & Dissent: Socioreligious Thought in Qajar Iran. LC 82-5498. 320p. 1982. 25.00x (ISBN 0-8156-2260-0). Syracuse U Pr.

Baybars, Taner, tr. see Hikmet, Nazim.

Baybutt, Ron. Camera in Colditz. (Illus.). 128p. 1983. 14.45i (ISBN 0-316-08394-1). Little.

Baydo, G. R. U. S. A.-A Synoptic History of America's Past, 2 vols. 1981. pap. 19.95 combined (ISBN 0-471-06432-7); Vol. 1, 325 pgs. pap. 14.95 (ISBN 0-471-06433-5); Vol. 2, 336 pgs. pap. 14.95 (ISBN 0-471-06431-9). Wiley.

Baydo, Gerald, ed. The Evolution of Mass Culture in America, 1877 to the Present. 1982. pap. text ed. 10.95x (ISBN 0-88273-260-9). Forum Pr IL.

Baydo, Gerald R. A Topical History of the United States. (Illus.). 1978. pap. text ed. 14.95x (ISBN 0-88273-008-8). Forum Pr IL.

Baydun, M., ed. Quran. (Arabic.). 30.00x (ISBN 0-86685-133-X). Intl Bk Ctr.

--Quran. (Arabic.). medium sized. 25.00x (ISBN 0-86685-134-8). Intl Bk Ctr.

Bayer, Marc J. Toxicologic Emergencies. (Illus.). 384p. 1983. pap. text ed. 19.95 (ISBN 0-89303-188-7). R J Brady.

Bayer, Marc J. & Rumack, Barry H., eds. Poisoning & Overdose. LC 82-13770. 145p. 1982. 22.95 (ISBN 0-89443-809-3). Aspen Systems.

Bayer, William. The Great Movies. LC 73-75614. (Illus.). 256p. 1973. 7.95 o.p. (ISBN 0-448-02217-6, G&D). Putnam Pub Group.

--Peregrine. 256p. 1983. pap. 2.95 (ISBN 0-345-30618-X). Ballantine.

Bayer, William S. Breaking Through Selling Out Dropping Dead. 1973. pap. 2.45 o.s.i. (ISBN 0-440-51334-0, Delta). Dell.

Bayerschmidt, Carl F., tr. see Reuter, Fritz.

Bayes, Jane H. Ideologies & Interest-Group Politics: The United States as a Special-Interest State in a Global Economy. Jones, Victor, ed. (Chandler & Sharp Publications in Political Science Ser.). 288p. (Orig.). 1982. pap. text ed. 8.95x (ISBN 0-88316-547-3). Chandler & Sharp.

--Minority Politics & Ideologies in the United States. Jones, Victor, ed. (Chandler & Sharp Publications in Political Science Ser.). 144p. (Orig.). 1982. pap. text ed. 5.95 (ISBN 0-88316-551-1). Chandler & Sharp.

Bayes, Marjorie, jt. ed. see Howell, Elizabeth.

Bayes, Pat, jt. auth. see Magee, Michael.

Bayes, Ronald H., jt. auth. see Gibson, Grace L.

Bayes, Ronald H., ed. see Blackburn, Kate & McDonald, Agnes.

Bayes, Ronald H., ed. see Fortner, Ethel.

Bayes, Ronald H., ed. see Gibson, Grace E.

Bayes, Ronald H., ed. see Oppenheimer, Joel.

Bayes, Ronald H., ed. see Ragan, Sam.

Bayh, Marvella & Kotz, Mary L. Marvella: A Personal Journey. LC 80-25195. 1981. pap. 4.95 (ISBN 0-15-657402-0, Harv). HarbraceJ.

Baylac, G., ed. Inelastic Analysis & Life Prediction In Elevated Temperature Design. (PVP Ser.: Vol. 59). 250p. 1982. 44.00 (H00216). ASME.

Bayle, Pierre. Selections from Bayle's Dictionary. Beller, Elmer A. & Lee, M. D., eds. LC 69-13810. Repr. of 1952 ed. lib. bdg. 17.00x (ISBN 0-8371-1068-8, BABD). Greenwood.

Baylen, J. O. & Grossman, N. J. The Biographical Dictionary of Modern British Radicals Since 1770: 1833-1914, Vol.2. 1980. text ed. price not set (ISBN 0-391-01058-1). Humanities.

Baylen, J. O. & Gossman, N. J., eds. The Biographical Dictionary of Modern British Radicals Since 1770: 1915-1970, Vol. 3. 1980. text ed. price not set (ISBN 0-391-01059-X). Humanities.

Bayles, Michael D. Professional Ethics. 176p. 1981. pap. text ed. 11.95x (ISBN 0-534-00998-0). Wadsworth Pub.

Bayles, Michael D., ed. Ethics & Population. LC 76-7840. 250p. 1976. text ed. 15.25x o.p. (ISBN 0-87073-405-9). Schenkman.

--Medical Treatment of the Dying: Moral Issues. 180p. 1982. pap. 8.95 (ISBN 0-87073-366-4). Schenkman.

Bayles, Michael D. & High, Dallas M., eds. Medical Treatment of the Dying: Moral Issues. 1978. 17.50 (ISBN 0-8161-2128-1, Hall Medical). G K Hall.

Bayless, Kathleen M. & Ramsey, Marjorie E. Music: A Way of Life for the Young Child. 2nd ed. LC 81-14055. (Illus.). 251p. 1982. pap. text ed. 14.95 (ISBN 0-8016-0521-0). Mosby.

--Music: A Way of Life for the Young Child. LC 77-14310. (Illus.). 1978. pap. text ed. 12.95 o.p. (ISBN 0-8016-0515-6). Mosby.

Bayless, Kathleen M., jt. auth. see Ramsey, Marjorie E.

Bayley, Barrington J. Annihilation Factor. 144p. 1980. 11.95 (ISBN 0-8052-8018-9, Pub. by Allison & Busby England); pap. 4.95 (ISBN 0-8052-8017-0, Pub. by Allison & Busby England). Schocken.

--Empire of Two Worlds. 160p. 1980. 11.95 (ISBN 0-8052-8016-2, Pub. by Allison & Busby England); pap. 4.95 (ISBN 0-8052-8015-4, Pub. by Allison & Busby England). Schocken.

--The Seed of Evil. 176p. 1980. 11.95 (ISBN 0-8052-8013-8, Pub. by Allison & Busby England); pap. 4.95 (ISBN 0-8052-8014-6, Pub. by Allison & Busby England). Schocken.

Bayley, D. H. & Mendelsohn, H. Minorities & the Police. LC 69-12119. 1969. pap. 3.50 (ISBN 0-02-901970-2). Free Pr.

Bayley, David H. Forces of Order: Police Behavior in Japan & the United States. LC 75-17304. 1976. 24.50x (ISBN 0-520-03069-9); pap. 6.95 (ISBN 0-520-03641-7). U of Cal Pr.

Bayley, Edwin. Joe McCarthy & the Press. LC 81-50824. 288p. 1981. 17.50 (ISBN 0-299-08620-8). U of Wis Pr.

Bayley, James R. A Brief Sketch of the Early History of the Catholic Church on the Island of New York. LC 77-359171. (Monograph Ser.: No. 29). 1973. Repr. of 1870 ed. 8.50x (ISBN 0-930060-09-1). US Cath Hist.

Bayley, John. An Essay on Hardy. LC 77-80826. 1978. 27.95 (ISBN 0-521-21814-4). Cambridge U Pr.

Bayley, Linda, et al. Jail Library Service: A Guide for Librarians & Jail Administrators. LC 81-2023. 126p. 1981. pap. 17.50 (ISBN 0-8389-3258-4). ALA.

Bayley, Monica & Perl, Susan. Susan Perl's Park Peepl. LC 81-67306. (Illus.). 5.95 (ISBN 0-915696-25-8). Determined Prods.

Bayley, Monica & Schulz, Charles M. Snoopy Omnibus. LC 82-71285. (Illus.). 1982. 6.95 (ISBN 0-915696-54-1). Determined Prods.

Bayley, Peter & Coleman, Dorothy G., eds. The Equilibrium of Wit: Essays for Odette de Mourgues. LC 81-71433. (French Forum Monographs: No. 36). 286p. (Orig.). 1982. pap. 25.00x (ISBN 0-917058-35-6). French Forum.

Bayley, S. C., jt. auth. see Sheeler, W. D.

Baylis, Maggie. House Plants for the Purple Thumb. Rev. ed. LC 81-11174. (Illus.). 192p. (Orig.). 1981. pap. 6.95 (ISBN 0-89286-194-0). One Hund One Prods.

--House Plants for the Purple Thumb. LC 72-94894. (Illus.). 192p. (Orig.). 1973. pap. write for info. o.p.; pap. write for info. o.p. One Hund One Prods.

Baylis, Maggie & Castle, Coralie. Real Bread. LC 80-21929. (Illus.). 240p. (Orig.). 1980. pap. 7.95 (ISBN 0-89286-179-7). One Hund One Prods.

Baylis, Robert. Ephesians: Living in God's Household. LC 76-43523. (Fisherman Bible Studyguide). 1976. saddle stitched 2.50 (ISBN 0-87788-223-1). Shaw Pubs.

Baylis, Thomas A. The Technical Intelligentsia & the East German Elite: Legitimacy & Social Change in Mature Communism. LC 72-95306. (Illus.). 1974. 33.00x (ISBN 0-520-02395-1). U of Cal Pr.

Bayliss, B. T. & Philip, A. Butt. Capital Markets & Industrial Investment in Germany & France: Lessons for the U. K. 1979. text ed. 29.50x (ISBN 0-566-00335-X). Gower Pub Ltd.

Bayliss, Brian. Planning & Control in the Transport Sector. 202p. 1981. text ed. 47.00x (ISBN 0-566-00407-0). Gower Pub Ltd.

Bayliss, R. I. Thyroid Disease: The Facts. (Illus.). 124p. (Orig.). 1982. 12.95x (ISBN 0-19-261350-2). Oxford U Pr.

Bayliss-Smith, T. P. The Ecology of Agricultural Systems. 2nd ed. LC 82-1132. (Cambridge Topics in Geography Ser.: No. 2). (Illus.). 96p. 1982. 12.95 (ISBN 0-521-23125-6); pap. 6.95 (ISBN 0-521-29829-6). Cambridge U Pr.

Baylor, Robert & Moore, James. People & Ideas: A Rhetoric Reader. (Illus.). 1980. text ed. 12.95 (ISBN 0-07-004162-8). McGraw.

Baylor, Robert A. Detail & Pattern: Essays for Composition. 3rd rev. ed. (Illus.). 224p. 1975. text ed. 13.95 (ISBN 0-07-004145-8, C); instructors' manual 9.95 (ISBN 0-07-004146-6). McGraw.

Bayly, Brian. Introduction to Petrology. 1968. text ed. 28.95 (ISBN 0-13-491621-2). P-H.

Bayly, C. A. Rulers, Merchants & Bazaars: North Indian Society in the Age of British Expansion, 1780-1880. LC 82-4420. (South Asian Studies: No. 28). (Illus.). 488p. Date not set. price not set (ISBN 0-521-22932-4). Cambridge U Pr.

Bayly, Thomas H. Epistles from Bath, or, Q's Letters to His Yorkshire Relations, Repr. Of 1817. Bd. with Rough Sketches of Bath, Imitations of Horace & Other Poems. Repr. of 1817 ed; Parliamentary Letters, & Other Poems. Repr. of 1818 ed; The Dandies of the Present & the Macaronies of the Past: A Rough Sketch. Repr. of 1819 ed; The Tribute of a Friend. Repr. of 1819 ed; Mournful Recollections. Repr. of 1820 ed; Small Talk. Repr. of 1820 ed; Erin, & Other Poems. Repr. of 1822 ed; Outlines of Edinburgh, & Other Poems. Repr. of 1822 ed. LC 75-31154. (Romantic Context Ser.: Poetry 1789-1830: Vol. 10). 1979. lib. bdg. 47.00 o.s.i. (ISBN 0-8240-2109-6). Garland Pub.

Baym, Nina, ed. see Chopin, Kate.

Bayne, Neil & Sarginson, Wes. Fast Eddie. 320p. (Orig.). 1983. pap. 3.50 (ISBN 0-8439-1070-4, Leisure Bks). Dorchester Pub Co.

Bayne, Pauline S., ed. Basic Music Library. LC 78-11997. 1978. pap. text ed. 7.00 (ISBN 0-8389-0281-2). ALA.

Bayne, Stephen. Now Is the Accepted Time. Woodhams, Wilbur, ed. 80p. (Orig.). 1983. pap. 1.85 (ISBN 0-88028-022-0). Forward Movement.

Bayne, Stephen F., Jr. Christian Living. (Orig.). 1956. pap. 1.00 (ISBN 0-8164-2007-6, SP5). Seabury.

Baynes, Cary F., tr. see Jung, Emma.

Baynes, Kate, jt. ed. see Baynes, Ken.

Baynes, Ken, ed. Attitudes in Design Education. LC 75-463351. (Illus.). 1969. 15.75x o.p. (ISBN 0-85331-246-X). Intl Pubns Serv.

Baynes, Ken & Baynes, Kate, eds. The Shoe Show: British Shoes Since Seventeen Ninety. 96p. 1979. 24.00x (ISBN 0-903798-37-9, Pub. by Jolly & Barber England). State Mutual Bk.

Baynes, Richard. The Happy Shepherd. (Illus.). 24p. (Orig.). (gr. k-3). 1979. pap. 1.49 (ISBN 0-87239-305-4, 2924). Standard Pub.

--Jesus Loves Me. (Illus.). 24p. (Orig.). (gr. k-3). 1979. pap. 1.69 (ISBN 0-87239-306-2, 2925). Standard Pub.

Baynes, Richard W. God's OK-You're OK? Perspective on Christian Worship. LC 79-67440. 96p. (Orig.). 1981. pap. 1.95 (ISBN 0-87239-382-8, 40088). Standard Pub.

Baynton-Power, Henry. How to Compose Music: A Simple Guide for the Amateur to the Composition of Melodies & to Their Effective Harmonization. 2nd ed. LC 79-23654. (Illus.). 1980. Repr. of 1948 ed. lib. bdg. 16.25x (ISBN 0-313-22214-2, BPHC). Greenwood.

Baynton-Williams, Roger. Investing in Maps. 1969. 5.98 o.p. (ISBN 0-517-02659-7, C N Potter). Crown.

Bayo, J. W., tr. see Gottinger, W.

Bayon, Damian & Gasparini, Paolo. The Changing Shape of Latin American Architecture: Conversations with Ten Leading Architects. LC 78-31583. 254p. 1979. 56.95x (ISBN 0-471-27568-9, Pub. by Wiley-Interscience). Wiley.

Bayon, Damian, ed. Latin America in Its Art. (Latin America in Its Culture Ser.). 250p. 1983. 28.00 (ISBN 0-8419-0531-2). Holmes & Meier.

Bayrak, Tosun, tr. see Al-Husayn al-Sulami, Ibn.

Bayrd, Edwin, ed. see Greenberg, Mark.

Bayrd, Edwin, ed. see Hibbert, Christopher.

Bayrd, Ned, ed. see Kemper, Rachel H.

Baysinger, Barry D., et al. Barriers to Corporate Growth. LC 80-8603. 144p. 1981. 18.95x (ISBN 0-669-04323-0). Lexington Bks.

Baysinger, Patricia R. see Dewey, John.

Bayt, Phyllis T. Administering Medications. (Health Occupations Ser.). 1982. pap. 14.50 (ISBN 0-672-61522-3); answer key 3.33 (ISBN 0-672-61538-X). Bobbs.

Bayvel, L. Electronic Scattering & Its Applications. 1981. 63.75 (ISBN 0-85334-955-X, Pub. by Applied Sci England). Elsevier.

Bayvel, L. P. & Jones, A. R. Electromagnetic Scattering & Its Applications. (Illus.). xvi, 289p. 1981. 63.75 (ISBN 0-85334-955-X, Pub. by Applied Sci England). Elsevier.

Bazan, N. G. & Lolley, R. N., eds. Neurochemistry of the Retina: Proceedings of the International Symposium on the Neurochemistry of the Retina, 28 August - 1 September 1979, Athens, Greece. (Illus.). 584p. 1980. 96.00 (ISBN 0-08-025485-3). Pergamon.

Bazan, Nicolas, jt. ed. see Sun, Grace Y.

Bazant, J. A Concise History of Mexico from Hidalgo to Cardenas 1805-1940. (Illus.). 1977. 34.50 (ISBN 0-521-21495-5); pap. 9.95x (ISBN 0-521-29173-9). Cambridge U Pr.

Bazant, Jan. Alienation of Church Wealth in Mexico. (Cambridge Latin American Studies: No. 11). 37.50 (ISBN 0-521-07872-5). Cambridge U Pr.

Bazant, Z. Methods of Foundation Engineering. LC 78-15933. (Developments in Geotechnical Engineering Ser.: Vol. 24). 616p. 1979. 93.75 (ISBN 0-444-99789-X). Elsevier.

Bazant, Z. P. & Wittmann, F. H. Creep & Shrinkage in Concrete Structures. LC 82-4766. (Numerical Methods in Engineering Ser.). 350p. 1983. 54.95 (ISBN 0-471-10409-4, Pub. by Wiley Interscience). Wiley.

Bazaraa, Mokhtar S. & Jarvis, John J. Linear Programming & Network Flows. LC 76-42241. 565p. 1977. text ed. 40.95x (ISBN 0-471-06015-1). Wiley.

Bazaraa, Mokhtar S. & Shetty, C. M. Nonlinear Programming: Theory & Algorithms. LC 78-986. 560p. 1979. text ed. 40.95 (ISBN 0-471-78610-1). Wiley.

Bazaz, Prem N. Secular Morality: A Solvent of Contemporary Spiritual Crisis. 1978. 6.95 o.p. (ISBN 0-533-03602-X). Vantage.

Bazen, Frances, jt. auth. see Ziegler, Ann.

Bazerman, jt. auth. see Wiener.

Bazerman, Charles. The Informed Writer. LC 80-68140. 320p. 1981. pap. text ed. 12.95 (ISBN 0-395-29715-X); instr's manual 1.00 (ISBN 0-395-29716-8). HM.

Bazerman, Charles, jt. auth. see Wiener, Harvey.

Bazerman, Charles, jt. auth. see Wiener, Harvey S.

Bazin, Andre. The Cinema of Cruelty. LC 75-18604. Date not set. 8.95 o.p. (ISBN 0-89388-208-9). Okpaku Communications.

--The Cinema of Cruelty. Fliss, Tiffany, tr. from Fr. LC 81-13545. Orig. Title: La Cinema De la Cruaute. 224p. 1982. 17.95 (ISBN 0-394-51808-X); pap. 9.95 (ISBN 0-394-17826-2). Seaver Bks.

--Jean Renoir. Truffaut, Francois, ed. LC 72-84984. (Illus.). 1973. 10.00 o.p. (ISBN 0-671-21464-0). S&S.

--What Is Cinema, Vol. 1. Gray, Hugh, tr. LC 67-18899. 1967. 16.95x (ISBN 0-520-00091-9); pap. 5.95 (ISBN 0-520-00092-7, CAL151). U of Cal Pr.

Bazin, Herve. Madame Ex. Crant, Phillip & Platt, Helen, trs. from Fr. 11.00 (ISBN 0-917786-06-8). French Lit.

Bazire, Joyce & Cross, James E. Eleven Old English Rogationtide Homilies. (Toronto Old English Ser.). 176p. 1982. 32.50x (ISBN 0-8020-5575-3). U of Toronto Pr.

Bazley, John D., jt. auth. see Nikolai, Loren A.

BBC Publications, ed. BBC Music Library, 4 vols. (Orchestral Catalogue Ser.). 1982. 300.00x ea. (BBC Pubns); Set. 1200.00x. State Mutual Bk.

--The Computer Book. 208p. 1982. pap. 30.00x (ISBN 0-563-16484-0, BBC Pubns). State Mutual Bk.

--Gardeners' World Cottage Garden. 1982. 29.00x (ISBN 0-563-20059-6, BBC Pubns). State Mutual Bk.

--Grand Slam. 144p. 1982. 25.00x (ISBN 0-563-20047-2, BBC Pubns). State Mutual Bk.

--Priestland's progress. 180p. 1981. 30.00x (ISBN 0-563-17968-6, BBC Pubns). State Mutual Bk.

--Taking the Strain. 1982. pap. 25.00x (ISBN 0-563-16499-9, BBC Pubns). State Mutual Bk.

BCC Staff. The Dynamic Telephone Hardware Business. 1982. cancelled (ISBN 0-89336-338-3). BCC.

--Electronic Display Materials & Design: G-072. 1983. 1250.00 (ISBN 0-89336-339-1). BCC.

--EMI Shielding: Materials, Markets. 1982. 1500.00 (ISBN 0-89336-341-3, GB-066). BCC.

--Engineering Thermoplastics. 1983. 1500.00 (ISBN 0-89336-342-1, P-015). BCC.

--Engineering Thermoplastics, P-015r. 1979. 750.00 (ISBN 0-89336-152-6). BCC.

--Fuel & Lubricant Additives. 1983. 975.00 (ISBN 0-89336-239-5, C-027). BCC.

--Growth Opportunities in Telecommunications. 1983. 1250.00 (ISBN 0-89336-241-7, G-009N). BCC.

--Industrial Energy Conservation E-033. 1982. text ed. 950.00 (ISBN 0-89336-167-4). BCC.

--Magnetic Recording Equipment-Tapes 1977-85. 1983. 1250.00 (ISBN 0-89336-336-7, G-073). BCC.

--Markets & Materials for High Temp. Wire & Cable: G-070. 1983. 1250.00 (ISBN 0-89336-337-5). BCC.

--Markets for Bugs & Enzymes, C-008: C-008. 1982. 1250.00 (ISBN 0-89336-101-1). BCC.

--Modern Adhesives & Sealants: C-009. 1983. 975.00 (ISBN 0-89336-108-9). BCC.

--Nutritional Food Additives, GA-040. 1983. 1250.00 (ISBN 0-89336-119-4). BCC.

--The Pet Industry: Outlook. 1982. 750.00 (ISBN 0-89336-164-X, GA-034). BCC.

--Plastics vs. Paper P-027. 1980. text ed. 950.00 (ISBN 0-89336-161-5). BCC.

--Polyester Growth Markets, P-047. (Illus.). 1983. 1250.00 (ISBN 0-89336-100-3). BCC.

BCC Staff, ed. Thermoplastics Elastomers: Rubber Substitutes, P-026. 1983. 1500.00 (ISBN 0-89336-043-0). BCC.

Beable, William H. Epitaphs: Graveyard Humour & Eulogy. LC 79-154494. 246p. Repr. of 1925 ed. 30.00x (ISBN 0-8103-3374-0). Gale.

Beach, Amy. Piano Music. (Women Composers Ser.: No. 10). 1982. Repr. lib. bdg. 22.50 (ISBN 0-306-76088-6). Da Capo.

--Quintet for Piano & Strings in F-Sharp Minor. (Women Composers Ser.: No. 1). 1979. Repr. of 1909 ed. lib. bdg. 19.95 (ISBN 0-306-79550-7). Da Capo.

Beach, Beatrice, jt. auth. see Hu, C. T.

Beach, Belle. Riding & Driving for Women. LC 77-3505. (Illus.). 1978. Repr. of 1912 ed. 30.00 (ISBN 0-88427-028-9). North River.

Beach, Charles & Fordyce, Edward, eds. A Solar World: Proceedings of the Annual Meeting of the International Solar Energy Society, 3 vols. 1977. pap. text ed. 115.00x (ISBN 0-89553-004-X). Am Solar Energy.

Beach, Dale S. Managing People at Work: Readings in Personnel. 3rd ed. (Illus.). 1980. pap. text ed. 13.95x (ISBN 0-02-307030-7). Macmillan.

--Personnel: The Mangement of People at Work. 4th ed. (Illus.). 1980. text ed. 24.95x (ISBN 0-02-307040-4). Macmillan.

Beach, David. Aspects of Schenkerian Theory. LC 82-13498. 240p. 1983. text ed. 25.00x (ISBN 0-300-02800-8); pap. text ed. 7.95x (ISBN 0-300-02803-2). Yale U Pr.

Beach, Don M., et al. Applications of the Learning Process: A Laboratory Approach. 1979. pap. 10.95 (ISBN 0-8403-2085-X). Kendall-Hunt.

Beach, E. F. Economic Models: An Exposition. LC 57-10800. 227p. 1957. text ed. 12.50 (ISBN 0-471-06072-0, Pub. by Wiley). Krieger.

Beach, Edward. Dance of the Dialectic: A Dramatic Dialogue Presenting Hegel's Philosophy of Religion. LC 78-63255. pap. text ed. 6.25 (ISBN 0-8191-0615-1). U Pr of Amer.

Beach, Edward L. Keepers of the Sea: A Profile. (Illus.). 256p. 1983. write for info. (ISBN 0-87021-727-5). Naval Inst Pr.

Beach, Frank A., ed. Sex & Behavior. LC 73-92863. 608p. 1974. Repr. of 1965 ed. 25.00 (ISBN 0-88275-147-6). Krieger.

Beach, Janet. How to Get a Job in the San Francisco Bay Area. 256p. (Orig.). 1983. pap. 8.95 (ISBN 0-8092-5692-4). Contemp Bks.

Beach, Joseph W. Outlook for American Prose. LC 26-19094. (Illus.). 1969. Repr. of 1926 ed. lib. bdg. 15.50x (ISBN 0-8371-0299-5, BEAP). Greenwood.

Beach, Kenneth M; see Mager, Robert F.

Beach, Kenneth M., Jr., jt. auth. see Mager, Robert F.

Beach, Marie H., ed. Guide to Richmond. rev. ed. Date not set. pap. price not set (ISBN 0-9607442-0-7). Guide to Rich.

Beach, Mark. A Bibliographic Guide to American Colleges & Universities: From Colonial Times to the Present. LC 74-11704. 315p. 1975. lib. bdg. 29.95x (ISBN 0-8371-7690-5, BCU/). Greenwood.

Beach, Milo C. The Adventures of Rama. (Illus.). 64p. (Orig.). 1983. 13.00 (ISBN 0-934686-51-3). Freer.

--The Imperial Image: Paintings for the Mughal Court. LC 81-8762. (Illus.). 240p. 1982. 45.00x (ISBN 0-934686-37-8); pap. 22.50x (ISBN 0-934686-38-6). Freer.

Beach, Phil R. The Satellite Services Sourcebook. 336p. (Orig.). 1982. pap. 75.00 (ISBN 0-910339-00-7). Beach Assocs.

Beach, Sean C., jt. auth. see Hicks, Tyler G.

Beach, Stewart. Good Morning-Sun's Up. LC 79-108178. (Illus.). 32p. (ps-3). 6.50 (ISBN 0-87592-021-7). Scroll Pr.

Beach, Sunny. Stan Goes on Safari. 1981. 4.95 o.p. (ISBN 0-533-04641-6). Vantage.

Beach, Waldo & Niebuhr, H. Richard, eds. Christian Ethics-Sources of the Living Tradition. 2nd ed. 550p. 1973. text ed. 23.95x (ISBN 0-471-07007-6). Wiley.

Beach, Walter E. British International Gold Movements & Banking Policy, 1881-1913. LC 76-138201. (Illus.). xiv, 218p. Repr. of 1935 ed. lib. bdg. 17.25x (ISBN 0-8371-5554-1, BEBG). Greenwood.

Beacham, Hans. Architecture of Mexico: Yesterday & Today. 1969. 15.00 o.s.i. (ISBN 0-8038-0013-4). Architectural.

Beacham, Walton, ed. see Janowitz, Phyllis.

Beachem, C. D. Source Book, Hydrogen Damage. 1977. 46.00 (ISBN 0-87170-042-5). ASM.

Beachey, Duane. Faith in a Nuclear Age. LC 82-11785. (Christian Peace Shelf Ser.). 136p. (Orig.). 1983. pap. 6.95 (ISBN 0-8361-3308-0). Herald Pr.

Beachey, E. H., ed. Bacterial Adherence. (Receptors & Recognition Series B: Vol. 6). 1980. 69.95x (ISBN 0-412-21730-9). Methuen Inc.

Beachey, R. W. The British & West Indies Sugar Industry in the Late 19th Century. LC 77-26800. (Illus.). 1978. Repr. of 1957 ed. lib. bdg. 21.00x (ISBN 0-313-20165-X, BEBW). Greenwood.

--The Slave Trade of Eastern Africa. LC 76-15786. (Illus.). 324p. 1976. text ed. 19.50x o.p. (ISBN 0-06-490326-5). B&N Imports.

Beacon Hill Staff. One Corinthians, Living as a Responsible Christian. (Beacon Small Group Bible Studies). 60p. 1982. pap. 2.25 (ISBN 0-8341-0755-4). Beacon Hill.

Beacon Presse Staff, ed. Who's Who in Puerto Rico, Virgin Islands & American Samoa, 1982. LC 81-70647. (Who's Who Reference Ser.: No. 48). 211p. 1982. lib. bdg. 59.95 (ISBN 0-935954-59-7). Beacon Presse IA.

Beacon Publishing, ed. The Arabian Transport Directory, 1981. 1982. 110.00x (ISBN 0-686-98473-0, Pub. by Parrish-Rogers England). State Mutual Bk.

--The Jeddah Commercial Directory, 1981. 1982. 125.00 (ISBN 0-686-98474-9, Pub. by Parrish-Rogers England). State Mutual Bk.

--The Oman Business Directory. 1982. 90.00x (ISBN 0-686-92070-8, Pub. by Parrish-Rogers England). State Mutual Bk.

Beacroft, B. W. The Last Fighting Indians of the American West. Reeves, Marjorie, ed. (Then & There Ser.). (Illus.). 96p. (Orig.). (gr. 7-12). 1976. pap. text ed. 3.10 (ISBN 0-582-20538-7). Longman.

Beacroft, Bernard. The Voyages of Christopher Columbus. Reeves, Marjorie, ed. (Then & There Ser.). (Illus.). 96p. (Orig.). (gr. 7-12). 1978. pap. text ed. 3.10 (ISBN 0-582-21727-X). Longman.

Beadle, George W., jt. auth. see Sturtevant, Alfred H.

Beadle, Jeremy. Today's the Day. (Orig.). 1981. pap. 3.50 o.p. (ISBN 0-686-72826-2, AE1078, Sig). NAL.

Beadle, Jeremy, jt. auth. see Winn, Chris.

Beadle, Muriel. The Cat: History, Biology & Behavior. LC 76-53770. 1977. 9.95 o.p. (ISBN 0-671-22451-4). S&S.

Beadle, Richard, ed. The York Cycle of Plays. 600p. 1982. text ed. 98.50 (ISBN 0-7131-6326-7). E Arnold.

Beadle, Robert W., jt. ed. see Semonin, Richard W.

Beadnell, Charles M. Encyclopaedic Dictionary of Science & War. LC 74-164093. 1971. Repr. of 1943 ed. 37.00x (ISBN 0-8103-3753-3). Gale.

Beaglehole, Ernest & Beaglehole, Pearl. Hopi of the Second Mesa. LC 36-5468. 1935. pap. 8.00 (ISBN 0-527-00543-6). Kraus Repr.

Beaglehole, Pearl, jt. auth. see Beaglehole, Ernest.

Beagley, H. A. & Barnard, S. A. Manual of Audiometric Techniques. (Illus.). 96p. 1983. pap. 12.95 (ISBN 0-19-261372-3). Oxford U Pr.

Beahrs, John O. Unity & Multiplicity: Multilevel Consciousness of Self in Hypnosis, Psychiatric Disorder & Mental Health. LC 81-38538. 256p. 1981. 22.50 (ISBN 0-87630-273-8). Brunner-Mazel.

Beahrs, Oliver H., jt. auth. see Jackman, Raymond J.

Beahrs, Oliver H., ed. see American Joint Committee on Cancer.

Beak, Linda. Wire Fox Terriers. Foyle, Christina, ed. (Foyle's Handbks.). 1973. 3.95 (ISBN 0-685-55789-8). Palmetto Pub.

Beakley, George C. Electronic Drafting. 1982. pap. text ed. 13.50 (ISBN 0-672-97971-3). Bobbs.

--Electronic Hand Calculators. 4th ed. 1983. pap. 10.95 cancelled (ISBN 0-686-82939-5). Macmillan.

--Freehand Drawing & Visualization. LC 81-3803. (gr. 12). 1982. pap. text ed. 9.95 (ISBN 0-672-97972-1). Bobbs.

--Introduction to Engineering Graphics. (Illus.). 341p. 1975. pap. text ed. 19.95 (ISBN 0-02-307210-5, 30721). Macmillan.

Beakley, George C. & Autore, Donald D. Graphics for Design & Visualization: Problem Series B. 1975. pap. 15.95 (ISBN 0-02-307270-9, 30727). Macmillan.

--Technical Illustration. (Illus.). 256p. (Orig.). 1983. pap. text ed. 18.95 (ISBN 0-672-97993-4). Bobbs.

Beakley, George C. & Leach, H. W. Careers in Engineering & Technology. 2nd ed. (Illus.). 1978. pap. text ed. 15.95 (ISBN 0-02-307170-2); instrs'. manual avail. Macmillan.

--Engineering: An Introduction to a Creative Profession. 4th ed. 1982. text ed. 26.95 (ISBN 0-02-307130-3). Macmillan.

Beakley, George C. & Lovell, Robert E. Computation, Calculators & Computers: Tools of Engineering Problem Solving -- Including FORTRAN. 368p. 1983. pap. text ed. 17.95 (ISBN 0-686-83141-1). Macmillan.

Beakley, George C., Jr. Graphics for Design & Visualization: Problem Series A. (Illus.). 120p. 1973. pap. text ed. 15.95x (ISBN 0-02-307260-1, 30726). Macmillan.

Beal, Fred E. Proletarian Journey. LC 70-146158. (Civil Liberties in American History Ser). 1971. Repr. of 1937 ed. lib. bdg. 45.00 (ISBN 0-306-70096-4). Da Capo.

Beal, George. See Inside a TV Studio. (See Inside Bks.). (Illus.). (gr. 5 up). 1978. PLB 9.40 s&l (ISBN 0-531-09064-7, Warwick Press). Watts.

Beal, George M., et al, eds. Sociological Perspectives of Domestic Development. (Illus.). 1971. 8.95x o.p. (ISBN 0-8138-1405-7). Iowa St U Pr.

Beal, J. D. Adventurous Film Making. (Illus.). 224p. 1980. 27.95 (ISBN 0-240-51047-X). Focal Pr.

Beal, John M. Critical Care for Surgical Patients. (Illus.). 704p. 1982. text ed. 48.00 (ISBN 0-02-307410-8). Macmillan.

Beal, Mary R. & Gilbert, Janet P. Music Curriculum Guidelines For Moderately Retarded Adolescents. 122p. 1982. spiral 14.75x (ISBN 0-398-04757-X). C C Thomas.

Beal, Richard S. Systems Analysis of International Crises. LC 79-66860. 1979. text ed. 21.25x (ISBN 0-8191-0858-8); pap. text ed. 15.00 (ISBN 0-8191-0859-6). U Pr of Amer.

Beal, Virginia A. Nutrition in the Life Span. LC 79-24610. 467p. 1980. text ed. 26.95 (ISBN 0-471-03664-1). Wiley.

Beale, jt. auth. see Griffin.

Beale, E. Applications of Mathematical Programming Techniques. (Nato Ser.). 1970. 21.50 (ISBN 0-444-19716-8). Elsevier.

Beale, Erica, ed. see Kyasht, Lydia.

Beale, Geoffrey. Extranuclear Genetics. 152p. 1979. pap. text ed. 19.95 o.p. (ISBN 0-8391-1368-4). Univ Park.

Beale, Griffin. TV & Video. (Electronic World Ser.). 32p. (gr. 5-9). 1983. 6.95 (ISBN 0-86020-640-8); PLB 9.95 (ISBN 0-88110-000-5); pap. 3.95 (ISBN 0-86020-639-4). EDC.

Beale, Howard K., ed. The Diary of Edward Bates: 1859-1866. LC 75-75304. (American History, Politics & Law Ser). 1971. Repr. of 1933 ed. lib. bdg. 85.00 (ISBN 0-306-71260-1). Da Capo.

Beale, T. The Natural History of the Sperm Whale. 1981. 75.00x (ISBN 0-686-97096-9, Pub. by Corner Place England). State Mutual Bk.

Beale, Walter H. Old & Middle English Poetry: A Guide to Information Sources. LC 74-11538. (American Literature, English Literature & World Literatures in English Information Guide Ser.: Vol. 7). 1976. 42.00x (ISBN 0-8103-1247-6). Gale.

Beale, Walter H., et al. Stylistic Options: The Sentence & the Paragraph. 1981. pap. text ed. 10.95x (ISBN 0-673-15444-0). Scott F.

--Real Writing: Argumentation, Reflection, Information, with Stylistic Options: The Sentence & the Paragraph. 1981. text ed. 16.95x (ISBN 0-673-15585-4); pap. text ed. 12.95x (ISBN 0-673-15446-7). Scott F.

Bealer, Alex. The Tools That Built America. (Illus.). 1976. 12.50 (ISBN 0-517-52405-8, C N Potter Bks). Crown.

Bealer, Alex W. Old Ways of Working Wood. rev. ed. (Illus.). 1980. 12.50 (ISBN 0-517-54047-9, C N Potter Bks). Crown.

Bealer, Alex W., 3rd. The Art of Blacksmithing. LC 76-4546. (Funk & W Bk.). (Illus.). 448p. 1976. 19.18i (ISBN 0-308-10254-1). T Y Crowell.

Beales, Derek. From Castlereagh to Gladstone, Eighteen Fifteen to Eighteen Eighty-Five. (History of England Ser.). (Illus.). 1969. pap. 7.95x (ISBN 0-393-00367-1, Norton Lib). Norton.

Beales, Philip. Otosclerosis. (Illus.). 216p. 1981. text ed. 29.95 (ISBN 0-7236-0598-X). Wright-PSG.

Bealey, Frank & Pelling, Henry. Labour & Politics, 1900-1906: A History of the Labour Representation Committee. LC 82-15828. xi, 317p. 1982. lib. bdg. 45.00x (ISBN 0-313-23693-3, BELAP). Greenwood.

Beall, C. M., ed. Cross-Cultural Studies of Biological Aging. 100p. 1982. 19.50 (ISBN 0-08-028946-0). Pergamon.

Beall, Gildon N. Allergy & Clinical Immunology. (UCLA Internal Medicine Today Ser.). 352p. 1983. 29.50 (ISBN 0-471-09568-0, Pub. by Wiley Med). Wiley.

Beall, H. W., jt. auth. see Bene, J. G.

Beall, James. Laying the Foundation. 389p. 1977. pap. 5.95 (ISBN 0-88270-198-3, Pub. by Logos). Bridge Pub.

Beall, James L. Your Pastor, Your Shepherd. 1977. pap. 4.95 (ISBN 0-88270-216-5, Pub. by Logos). Bridge Pub.

Beall, Karen F., ed. Cries & Itinerant Trades: A Bibliography. 1975. 235.00x (ISBN 0-685-67341-3, Pub. by Dr. E. Hauswedell). Gale.

Beall, Pamela & Nipp, Susan. Wee Sing. 1982. pap. 2.25 (ISBN 0-686-82010-X). Price Stern.

Beals, Carleton. Mexican Maze. LC 71-156174. (Illus.). 1971. Repr. of 1931 ed. lib. bdg. 19.25x (ISBN 0-8371-6117-7, BEMM). Greenwood.

Beals, Judy. Miniature Furniture & Room Settings. Stern, Marcia, ed. (Illus.). 88p. (Orig.). 1983. pap. 8.95 (ISBN 0-89024-044-2). Kalmbach.

Beals, Ralph E. see Gillis, S. Malcolm.

Beals, Ralph L. Cheran: A Sierra Tarascan Village. LC 72-95137. (Illus.). 225p. 1973. Repr. of 1946 ed. lib. bdg. 17.50x (ISBN 0-8154-0466-2). Cooper Sq.

Beals, Ralph L., ed. see Driver, Harold, et al.

Beals, Richard. National Real Estate Examination Study Guide. 1982. pap. text ed. 10.95 (ISBN 0-89764-002-0). Lincoln's Leadership.

Beam, Burton T., Jr. Group Insurance: Basic Concepts & Alternatives. Date not set: price not set (ISBN 0-943590-00-0). Amer College.

Beam, George, jt. auth. see Simpson, Dick.

Beam, Robert D., jt. auth. see Kuhn, Alfred.

Beam, Thomas R., jt. auth. see Allen, James C.

Beam, Victoria R., jt. auth. see Ellis, John T.

Beaman, Bruce R., ed. The Sherlock Holmes Book of Quotations. LC 79-55659. (Sherlock Holmes Reference Ser.). 88p. 1980. 8.95x o.p. (ISBN 0-934468-02-8). Gaslight.

Beaman, John. BF One-Zero-Nine in Action, Part 2. (Illus.). 58p. 1983. 4.95 (ISBN 0-89747-138-5). Squad Sig Pubns.

Beaman, Joyce. Bloom Where You Are Planted. LC 75-34645. 1976. 7.95 (ISBN 0-87716-060-0, Pub. by Moore Pub Co). F Apple.

Beaman, Joyce P. All for the Love of Cassie. LC 73-86471. 1973. 6.95 (ISBN 0-87716-046-5, Pub. by Moore Pub Co). F Apple.

Beame, Edmond, ed. see Ariosto.

Beament, J. W., et al, eds. Advances in Insect Physiology. Incl. Vol. 2. 1964. 57.50 (ISBN 0-12-024202-8); Vol. 3. 1966. 60.00 (ISBN 0-12-024203-6); Vol. 4. 1967. 66.00 (ISBN 0-12-024204-4); Vol. 5. 1968. 57.00 (ISBN 0-12-024205-2); Vol. 6, 1969. 46.00 (ISBN 0-12-024206-0); Vol. 7. 1970. 73.50 (ISBN 0-12-024207-9); Vol. 8. 1972. 60.50 (ISBN 0-12-024208-7); Vol. 9. Treherne, J. E. & Berridge, M. J., eds. 1972. 70.00 (ISBN 0-12-024209-5); Vol.10. 1974. 63.50 (ISBN 0-12-024210-9); Vol. 11. 1975. 68.50 (ISBN 0-12-024211-7); Vol. 12. 1977. 55.50 (ISBN 0-12-024212-5); Vol. 13. 1978. 60.00 (ISBN 0-12-024213-3). Acad Pr.

Beamer, Charles. Joshua Wiggins & the Tough Challenge. (Joshua Wiggins Ser.: No. 2). 144p. (Orig.). 1983. pap. 3.95 (ISBN 0-87123-266-9). Bethany Hse.

--Love's Majesty. LC 82-84071. 192p. 1983. pap. 4.95 (ISBN 0-89081-325-6). Harvest Hse.

Beamesderfer, Alice O., jt. auth. see Gray, Lois S.

Beamon, Bob, jt. auth. see Schaap, Dick.

Beams, Floyd A. Advanced Accounting. 2nd ed. (Illus.). 880p. 1982. text ed. 28.95 (ISBN 0-13-010157-5). P-H.

Beams, J. W., et al. Developments in the Centrifuge Separation Project. (National Nuclear Energy Ser.: Div. X, Vol. 1). 269p. 1951. pap. 21.00 (ISBN 0-87079-179-6, TID-5230); microfilm 4.50 (ISBN 0-87079-180-X, TID-5230). DOE.

Bean, A. R. & Simons, R. H. Lighting Fittings, Performance & Design. (International Series in Electrical Engineering: Vol. 1). 1968. inquire for price o.p. (ISBN 0-08-012594-8). Pergamon.

Bean, Barbara, jt. auth. see Erdstein, Erich.

Bean, Constance A. Methods of Childbirth: A Complete Guide to Childbirth Classes & the New Maternity Care. LC 78-187123. 240p. 1974. pap. 4.95 o.p. (ISBN 0-385-06228-1, Dolp). Doubleday.

Bean, Elwood L., jt. auth. see Hopkins, Edward S.

Bean, H. S., et al. Advances in Pharmaceutical Sciences. Vol. 1. 1964. 53.00 (ISBN 0-12-032301-X); Vol. 2. 1967. 52.00 (ISBN 0-12-032302-8); Vol. 3. 1971. 38.50 (ISBN 0-12-032303-6); Vol. 4 1975. 73.50 (ISBN 0-12-032304-4). Acad Pr.

Bean, Jacob & Stampfle, Felice. Drawings from New York Collections: Vol. 3, The Eighteenth Century in Italy. LC 77-134891. (Illus.). 1971. 4.95 (ISBN 0-87099-021-7). Metro Mus Art.

Bean, Jacob & Turcic, Lawrence. Fifteenth & Sixteenth Century Drawings in the Metropolitan Museum of Art. Preuss, Anne M., ed. (Illus.). 332p. 1982. 35.00 (ISBN 0-87099-314-3); pap. 19.95 (ISBN 0-87099-315-1). Metro Mus Art.

Bean, John E. & Bean, Ruth E. To Seattle with Love: A Very Unofficial Guidebook. LC 82-50381. (Illus.). 128p. (Orig.). 1982. pap. 4.95 (ISBN 0-9608430-0-0). Sheba Pub.

Bean, John L., Jr., jt. auth. see Jordan, Terry G.

Bean, L. Lee. Domestic Relations: A Virginia Law Practice System. 400p. 1982. 75.00 (ISBN 0-87215-508-0). Michie-Bobbs.

Bean, Lowell J. Mukat's People: The Cahuilla Indians of Southern California. LC 78-145782. (Illus.). 300p. 1972. 18.95x (ISBN 0-520-01912-1); pap. 6.25x (ISBN 0-520-02627-6). U of Cal Pr.

Bean, Marian C. The Development of Word Order Patterns in Old English. (Illus.). 150p. 1983. text ed. 25.75x (ISBN 0-389-20356-4). B&N Imports.

Bean, Philip. Compulsory Admissions to Mental Hospitals. LC 79-41786. 278p. 1980. 53.95x (ISBN 0-471-27758-4, Pub. by Wiley-Interscience). Wiley.

--Mental Illness: Changes & Trends. 500p. 1983. 64.95 (ISBN 0-471-10240-7, Pub. by Wiley-Interscience). Wiley.

--Rehabilitation & Deviance. (Radical Social Policy Ser.). 180p. 1976. 18.95x (ISBN 0-7100-8270-3); pap. 7.95 (ISBN 0-7100-8271-1). Routledge & Kegan.

Bean, Philip & MacPherson, Stewart, eds. Approaches to Welfare. 300p. 1983. 27.95 (ISBN 0-7100-9423-X); pap. 14.95 (ISBN 0-7100-9424-8). Routledge & Kegan.

Bean, Reynold, jt. auth. see Clemes, Harris.

Bean, Robert B. & Bean, William B. Sir William Osler: Aphorisms from His Bedside Teachings & Writings. 160p. 1968. photocopy ed. spiral 14.50x (ISBN 0-398-04202-0). C C Thomas.

Bean, Ruth E., jt. auth. see Bean, John E.

Bean, Thomas W. & Bishop, Ashley. Rapid Reading for Professional Success. 176p. 1983. pap. text ed. 10.95 (ISBN 0-8403-2882-6). Kendall-Hunt.

Bean, Walton. California: An Interpretive History. 3rd ed. (Illus.). 1978. text ed. 26.50 (ISBN 0-07-004241-1, C); instructor's manual 15.00 (ISBN 0-07-004242-X). McGraw.

Bean, Walton & Rawls, James J. California: An Interpretive History. 4th ed. (Illus.). 544p. 1982. text ed. 24.95 (ISBN 0-07-004206-3, C); instr's. manual 16.00 (ISBN 0-07-004207-1). McGraw.
Bean, William B. Vascular Spiders & Related Lesions of the Skin. (Illus.). 338p. 1959. photocopy ed. spiral 37.50x (ISBN 0-398-04204-7). C C Thomas.
--Walter Reed: A Biography. LC 81-16123. (Illus.). 1982. 12.95x (ISBN 0-8139-0913-9). U Pr of Va.
Bean, William B., jt. auth. see Bean, Robert B.
Beanblossom, Ronald E., ed. see Reid, Thomas.
Beane, Leona, jt. auth. see Lakin, Leonard.
Beane, Wendell C., ed. see Eliade, Mircea.
Beaney, Wiliam M., jt. auth. see Mason, A. T.
Beaney, William M., jt. auth. see Mason, Alpheus T.
Beangcheon, Yul. Natsume Soseki. (World Authors Ser.). 15.95 (ISBN 0-8057-2850-3, Twayne). G K Hall.
Bear, David. Keeping Time. LC 79-16368. 1979. 9.95 o.p. (ISBN 0-312-45110-5). St Martin.
Bear, F. E., ed. Chemistry of the Soil. 3rd ed. 544p. 1981. 40.00x o.p. (ISBN 0-686-76628-8, Pub. by Oxford & IBH India). State Mutual Bk.
Bear, Firman E. Soils in Relation to Crop Growth. LC 65-23863. 304p. 1977. Repr. of 1965 ed. 19.50 (ISBN 0-88275-927-2). Krieger.
Bear, Fred. The Archer's Bible. rev. ed. LC 79-7585. (Outdoor Bible Ser.). (Illus.). 1980. pap. 4.50 (ISBN 0-385-15155-1). Doubleday.
Bear, Greg. Lost Souls. 320p. 1982. pap. 2.95 (ISBN 0-441-49492-7, Pub. by Charter Bks). Ace Bks.
--The Wind from a Burning Woman. (Illus.). 270p. 1983. 13.95 (ISBN 0-87054-094-7). Arkham.
Bear, H. S. Introduction to Differential Equations. (Illus.). 490p. 1981. pap. text ed. 19.50 o.s.i. (ISBN 0-9605502-0-8). Manoa Pr.
Bear, Jacob. Hydraulics of Ground Water. (Water Resources & Environmental Engineering Ser.). (Illus.). 1979. text ed. 65.00 (ISBN 0-07-004170-9). McGraw.
Bear, John. How to Get the Degree You Want. LC 82-905. 256p. (Orig.). 1982. pap. 9.95 (ISBN 0-89815-080-9). Ten Speed Pr.
--United States of America. LC 75-44862. (Macdonald Countries). (Illus.). (gr. 6 up). 1976. PLB 12.68 (ISBN 0-382-06109-8, Pub. by Macdonald Ed). Silver.
Bear, Yogi. Survival Kit: Meditations & Exercises for Stress & Pressure of the Times. (Illus.). 74p. (Orig.). 1980. pap. text ed. cancelled (ISBN 0-940992-00-0). Khalsa.
Beard, Belle B. Juvenile Probation: An Analysis of the Case Records of Five Hundred Children Studies at the Judge Baker Guidance Clinic & Placed on Probation in the Juvenile Court of Boston. LC 69-16224. (Criminology, Law Enforcement, & Social Problems Ser.: No. 95). 1969. Repr. of 1934 ed. 12.00x (ISBN 0-87585-095-2). Patterson Smith.
Beard, Charles A. Economic Interpretation of the Constitution of the United States. 1965. pap. 8.95 (ISBN 0-02-902030-1). Free Pr.
Beard, Charles A. & Schultz, Birl E. Documents on the State-Wide Initiative, Referendum & Recall. LC 70-120853. (Law, Politics & History Ser). 1970. Repr. of 1912 ed. lib. bdg. 49.50 (ISBN 0-306-71958-4). Da Capo.
Beard, Charles A., ed. Whither Mankind. LC 78-109708. 408p. 1973. Repr. of 1934 ed. lib. bdg. 18.50x (ISBN 0-8371-4199-0, BEWM). Greenwood.
Beard, Charles R. Lucks & Talismans: A Chapter of Popular Superstition. LC 74-174903. xxii, 258p. Repr. of 1934 ed. 40.00x (ISBN 0-8103-3871-8). Gale.
Beard, Daniel C. The American Boy's Handy Book. (Illus.). 448p. 1983. pap. 9.95 (ISBN 0-87923-449-0). Godine.
--American Boys Handy Book-What to Do & How to Do It. facs. ed. LC 66-15858. (Illus.). (gr. 4 up). 1966. 11.95 (ISBN 0-8048-0006-5). C E Tuttle.
Beard, E., et al. Risk Theory: The Stochastic Basis of Insurance. 2nd ed. (Monographs on Applied Probability & Statistics). 1977. 17.50x (ISBN 0-412-15100-6, Pub. by Chapman & Hall). Methuen Inc.
Beard, Estle, jt. auth. see Carranco, Lynwood.
Beard, Frank A., et al. Maine's Historic Places. (Illus.). 1982. 9.95 (ISBN 0-89272-140-5). Down East.
Beard, Geoffrey. Stucco & Decorative Plasterwork in Europe. LC 82-49006. (Icon Editions). (Illus.). 165p. 1983. 50.00 (ISBN 0-06-430383-7, HarpT). Har-Row.
--The Work of Christopher Wren. (Illus.). 240p. 1982. 75.00x (ISBN 0-7028-8071-X, Pub. by Bartholomew & Son England). State Mutual Bk.
Beard, H. & McKie, R. Sailing: A Sailor's Dictionary. 96p. 1982. 17.50x (ISBN 0-333-32845-0, Pub. by Macmillan England). State Mutual Bk.
Beard, Helen. Women in Ministry Today. (Orig.). 1980. pap. 5.95 (ISBN 0-88270-447-8, Pub. by Logos). Bridge Pub.
Beard, Henry & McKie, Roy. Fishing. 96p. 1983. 8.95 (ISBN 0-89480-357-3); pap. 4.95 (ISBN 0-89480-355-7). Workman Pub.
Beard, Howard. New Approach to Etiology Diagnosis, Treatment & Prevention of the Degenerative Diseases. 1965. 10.00x (ISBN 0-943080-14-2). Cancer Control Soc.
Beard, Isobel R. Draw with Dots. (Activity Fun Books). (Illus., Orig.). (ps-3). 0.99 (ISBN 0-695-90180-X, Dist. by Caroline Hse). Follett.
--Join the Dots. (Activity Fun Bks.). (Illus.). (ps-3). 1969. 0.99 (ISBN 0-695-90390-X, Dist. by Caroline Hse). Follett.
--Link the Dots. 2nd ed. (Activity Fun Bks.). (Illus.). (ps-3). 1969. 0.99 (ISBN 0-695-90456-6, Dist. by Caroline Hse). Follett.
--Play with Dots. 2nd ed. (Activity Fun Books). (Illus.). (ps-3). 1969. 0.99 (ISBN 0-695-90625-9, Dist. by Caroline Hse). Follett.
--Purple Pussycat. (gr. 3up). pap. 0.99 (ISBN 0-695-90644-5, Dist. by Caroline Hse). Follett.
--Puzzles & Riddles. (Activity Fun Bks). (ps-3). 0.99 (ISBN 0-695-90643-7, Dist. by Caroline Hse). Follett.
Beard, J. Turfgrass: Science & Culture. (Illus.). 1972. ref. ed. 27.95 (ISBN 0-13-933002-X). P-H.
Beard, James. Beard on Food. 1974. 17.50 (ISBN 0-394-48505-X). Knopf.
--Beard on Pasta. LC 82-48727. 1983. 13.95 (ISBN 0-394-52291-5). Knopf.
--Delights & Prejudices. LC 80-24560. (Illus.). 1964. 6.95 (ISBN 0-689-00007-3); pap. 7.95 (ISBN 0-689-70605-7, 266). Atheneum.
--James Beard's Theory & Practice of Good Cooking. 1977. 16.95 (ISBN 0-394-48493-2). Knopf.
Beard, James, et al, eds. The Cooks' Catalogue. LC 75-6329. (Illus.). 576p. 1975. 21.10i (ISBN 0-06-011563-7, HarpT). Har-Row.
Beard, James A. James Beard's American Cookery. 1972. 19.95 (ISBN 0-316-08564-2); pap. 10.95. Little.
Beard, James B. Turf Management for Golf Courses. (Orig.). 1982. 45.00x (ISBN 0-8087-2872-5). Burgess.
Beard, James F., ed. see Cooper, James F.
Beard, Marna L. & McGahey, Michael J. Alternative Careers for Teachers. 192p. (Orig.). 1983. pap. 9.95 (ISBN 0-668-05571-5). Arco.
Beard, Mary R. Mary Ritter Beard: A Sourcebook. Lane, Anne J., ed. LC 77-3135. (Studies in the Life of Women). 1977. lib. bdg. 15.00x o.p. (ISBN 0-8052-3668-6); pap. 6.95 (ISBN 0-8052-0576-4). Schocken.
Beard, R. The Indo-European Lexicon: Synchronic Theory. (North Holland Linguistic Ser.: Vol. 44). 1981. 47.00 (ISBN 0-444-86214-5). Elsevier.
Beard, R. W. & Nathanielsz, P. W. Fetal Physiology & Medicine. LC 76-20126. (Illus.). 1976. text ed. 32.00 o.p. (ISBN 0-7216-1600-3). Saunders.
Beard, Ray, jt. auth. see Matthews, Velda.
Beard, Richard R. Walt Disney's EPCOT: Creating the New World of Tomorrow. (Illus.). 240p. 1982. 35.00 (ISBN 0-8109-0819-0). Abrams.
Beard, Robert S. Patterns in Space. 1973. pap. text ed. 14.95 (ISBN 0-88488-015-X). Creative Pubns.
Beard, Ross E., Jr. Carbine: The Story of David Marshall Williams. LC 76-20847. 1977. 0.00 o.p. (ISBN 0-87844-036-4); ltd ed, signed 15.00 (ISBN 0-87844-047-X). Sandlapper Pub Co.
Beard, Ruth M. An Outline of Piaget's Developmental Psychology. (Student's Library of Education). 144p. 1976. pap. 6.95 (ISBN 0-7100-6344-X). Routledge & Kegan.
Beard, Ruth M., jt. auth. see Verma, Gajendra K.
Beard, Thomas R., ed. Louisiana Economy. LC 69-7622. (University Studies, Social Science Ser.: Vol. 15). (Illus.). viii, 232p. 1969. 20.00x (ISBN 0-8071-0307-1). La State U Pr.
Beard, Timothy F. & Demong, Denise. How to Find Your Family Roots. 1978. 24.95 o.p. (ISBN 0-07-004210-1, GB). McGraw.
Beardall, Douglas & Beardall, Jewel, eds. Qualities of Love. (Orig.). 1978. pap. 3.95 o.p. (ISBN 0-89036-110-X). Hawkes Pub Inc.
Beardall, Jewel, jt. ed. see Beardall, Douglas.
Bearden, G., jt. auth. see Stolle, C.
Bearden, H. Joe, jt. auth. see Fuquay, John W.
Beardon, A. F. Complex Analysis: The Argument Principle in Analysis & Topology. LC 78-8540. 239p. 1979. 53.95x (ISBN 0-471-99671-8, Pub. by Wiley-Interscience). Wiley.
Beardon, Alan. A Primer on Riemann Surfaces. LC 82-4439. (London Mathematical Society Lecture Note Ser.: No. 78). 150p. Date not set. pap. price not set (ISBN 0-521-27104-5). Cambridge U Pr.
Beards, C. F. Vibration Analysis & Control System Dynamic. LC 81-6646. (Ser. in Engineering Science: Civil Engineering). 169p. 1981. 51.95 (ISBN 0-470-27255-4). Halsted Pr.
Beards, P. H., ed. see Robinson, Joseph F.
Beardsell, P. R., ed. Ricardo Guiraldes: Don Segundo Sombra. 252p. 1973. text ed. 8.65 o.s.i. (ISBN 0-08-017009-9); pap. text ed. 8.30 (ISBN 0-08-017010-2). Pergamon.
Beardshaw, John & Palfreman, David. The Organization in It's Environment. 2nd ed. 625p. 1982. pap. text ed. 21.95 (ISBN 0-7121-1541-2). Intl Ideas.
Beardslee, Edward C., jt. auth. see Jerman, Max E.
Beardslee, William A., ed. see Calloud, Jean.
Beardslee, William A., ed. see Detweiler, Robert.
Beardslee, William A., ed. see Polzin, Robert M.
Beardslee, William R. The Way Out Must Lead In: Life Histories in the Civil Rights Movement. rev. ed. 192p. 1983. 14.95 (ISBN 0-88208-153-5); pap. 6.95 (ISBN 0-88208-120-9). Lawrence Hill.
Beardsley, Aubrey. Early Work of Aubrey Beardsley. (Illus.). 10.50 (ISBN 0-8446-1616-8). Peter Smith.
--Later Work of Aubrey Beardsley. (Illus.). 11.50 (ISBN 0-8446-1617-6). Peter Smith.
Beardsley, Elizabeth L., jt. auth. see Beardsley, Monroe C.
Beardsley, John, jt. auth. see Livingston, Jane.
Beardsley, M. C. Writing with Reason: Logic for Composition. (Illus.). 176p. 1976. pap. text ed. 8.95 (ISBN 0-13-970301-2). P-H.
Beardsley, Monroe. Practical Logic. 1950. text ed. 16.95 (ISBN 0-13-692111-6). P-H.
Beardsley, Monroe C. The Aesthetic Point of View: Selected Essays. Callen, Donald M., ed. Wreen, Michael. LC 82-71601. 424p. 1983. 34.50x (ISBN 0-8014-1250-1); pap. 19.95x (ISBN 0-8014-9880-5). Cornell U Pr.
--Modes of Argument. LC 67-18663. 1967. pap. 2.95 o.p. (ISBN 0-672-60893-6). Bobbs.
--Thinking Straight: Principles of Reasoning for Readers & Writers. 4th ed. LC 74-16349. (Illus.). 1975. 8.50 o.p. (ISBN 0-13-918235-7); pap. text ed. 11.95 (ISBN 0-13-918227-6). P-H.
Beardsley, Monroe C. & Beardsley, Elizabeth L. Invitation to Philosophical Thinking. 178p. 1972. pap. text ed. 10.95 o.p. (ISBN 0-15-546902-9, HC). HarBraceJ.
Beardsley, Monroe C., ed. The European Philosophers from Descartes to Nietzsche. LC 60-10004. 8.95 (ISBN 0-394-60412-1). Modern Lib.
Beardsley, Monroe C., et al, eds. Theme & Form: An Introduction to Literature. 4th ed. 704p. 1975. text ed. 19.95 (ISBN 0-13-912972-3). P-H.
Beardsley, Philip L. Conflicting Ideologies in Political Economy: A Synthesis. LC 80-39916. (Sage Library of Social Research: Vol. 18). 200p. 1981. 22.00 (ISBN 0-8039-1528-4); pap. 10.95 (ISBN 0-686-96879-4). Sage.
Beardsley, R. K., jt. auth. see Hall, John.
Beardwell, C. Clinical Endocrinology: Pituitary, Vol. 1. (Butterworths International Medical Reviews Ser.). 1981. text ed. 59.95 (ISBN 0-407-02272-4). Butterworth.
Beare, Geraldine, compiled by. Index to the Strand Magazine, 1891-1950. LC 82-11769. 896p. 1982. lib. bdg. 75.00 (ISBN 0-313-23122-2, BIM/). Greenwood.
Beare, John B. Macroeconomics: Cycles, Growth, & Policy in a Monetary Economy. 299p. 1978. text ed. 25.95 (ISBN 0-02-307710-7). Macmillan.
Beare, Patricia G. & Rahr, Virginia A. Quick Reference to Nursing Implications of Diagnostic Tests. (Quick References for Nurses Ser.). (Illus.). 438p. 1982. pap. text ed. 12.50 (ISBN 0-397-54366-2, Lippincott Nursing). Lippincott.
Bearman, Toni C. & Kunberger, William. A Study of Coverage Overlap Among Major Science & Technology Abstracting & Indexing Services. 1977. 20.00 (ISBN 0-942308-12-3). NFAIS.
Bearns, Robert J. The Awakening Electromagnetic Spectrum. new ed. LC 74-76050. (Illus.). 128p. (Orig.). 1974. pap. 8.95 (ISBN 0-914706-00-4). Awakening Prods.
Bearth, Thomas. L' Enonce Toura (Cote d'Ivoire) (Publications in Linguistics & Related Fields Ser.: No. 30). 481p. (Fr.). 1971. pap. 7.00 o.p. (ISBN 0-88312-032-1); microfiche 4.50 (ISBN 0-88312-432-7). Summer Inst Ling.
Beasley, Conger, Jr., jt. ed. see Findlay, Ted.
Beasley, Jerry, ed. English Fiction, Sixteen Sixty to Eighteen Hundred: A Guide to Information Sources. LC 74-11526. (American Literature, English Literature & World Literatures in English Information Guide Ser.: Vol. 14). 1978. 42.00x (ISBN 0-8103-1226-3). Gale.
Beasley, Kenneth L., et al. The Administration of Sponsered Programs: Handbook for Developing & Managing Research Activities & Other Projects. LC 82-48074. (Higher Education & Social & Behavioral Science Ser.). 1982. text ed. 24.95x (ISBN 0-87589-542-5). Jossey Bass.
Beasley, Manley & Robinson, Ras. Laws for Liberated Living. 212p. 1980. pap. 5.00 (ISBN 0-937778-01-X); 3.00 (ISBN 0-937778-02-8). Fulness Hse.
Beasley, Maurine H. & Harlow, Richard R. Voices of Change: Southern Pulitzer Winners. LC 79-52511. 1979. pap. text ed. 9.00 (ISBN 0-8191-0771-9). U Pr of Amer.
Beasley, W. G., tr. Select Documents on Japanese Foreign Policy, 1853-1868. 1955. 27.50x o.p. (ISBN 0-19-713508-0). Oxford U Pr.
Beasley-Murray, Stephen. Toward a Metaphysics of the Sacred: Development of the Concept of the Holy. 7.95 (ISBN 0-86554-038-1). Mercer Univ Pr.
--Towards a Metaphysics of the Sacred. LC 82-8288. (Special Studies: No. 8). 1982. pap. 7.95 (ISBN 0-86554-038-1). Assn Baptist P.
Beath, O. A., jt. auth. see Rosenfeld, Irene.
Beatley, Janice C. Vascular Plants of the Nevada Test Site & Central-Southern Nevada: Ecologic & Geographic Distributions. LC 76-21839. (ERDA Technical Information Center Ser.). 316p. 1976. pap. 16.00 (ISBN 0-87079-033-1, TID-26881); microfiche 4.50 (ISBN 0-87079-216-4, TID-26881). DOE.
Beato, M., ed. Steroid Induced Utherine Proteins. (Developments in Endocrinology Ser.: Vol. 8). 1980. 68.00 (ISBN 0-444-80203-7). Elsevier.
Beaton, Leonard & Maddox, John. The Spread of Nuclear Weapons. LC 76-16061. (Studies in International Security: No. 5). 1976. Repr. of 1962 ed. lib. bdg. 17.25x (ISBN 0-8371-8949-7, BENW). Greenwood.
Beaton, Roderick. Folk Poetry of Modern Greece. LC 79-7644. (Illus.). 272p. 1980. 29.95 (ISBN 0-521-22853-0). Cambridge U Pr.
Beaton, William R., et al. Real Estate. 2nd ed. Ferguson, Jerry T., ed. 1982. text ed. 25.50x (ISBN 0-673-16003-3). Scott F.
Beatson, Ronald. Red Rage & China Shops. 1977. 6.95 o.p. (ISBN 0-533-02670-9). Vantage.
Beattie, Ann. Chilly Scenes of Winter. 320p. 1983. pap. 3.50 (ISBN 0-446-31108-1). Warner Bks.
--Distortions. 288p. 1983. pap. 3.50 (ISBN 0-446-31110-3). Warner Bks.
--Falling in Place. 320p. 1983. pap. 3.50 (ISBN 0-446-31112-X). Warner Bks.
--Jacklighting. (Metacom Limited Edition Ser.: No. 3). 24p. 1981. ltd. 25.00x (ISBN 0-911381-02-3). Metacom Pr.
--Secrets & Suprises. 320p. 1983. pap. 3.50 (ISBN 0-446-31114-6). Warner Bks.
--Secrets & Surprises. 1980. pap. 2.95. Popular Lib.
Beattie, Arthur H., ed. & tr. see Pascal, Blaise.
Beattie, J. A. & Oppenheim, J. Principles of Thermodynamics. (Studies in Modern Thermodynamics: Vol. 2). 1980. 41.75 (ISBN 0-444-41806-7). Elsevier.
Beattie, John. Other Cultures. LC 64-16952. 1968. 9.95 o.s.i. (ISBN 0-02-902040-9); pap. text ed. 10.95 (ISBN 0-02-902050-6). Free Pr.
Beattie, John M. English Court in the Reign of George First. 1967. 44.50 (ISBN 0-521-04126-0). Cambridge U Pr.
Beattie, Russell. Saddles. (Illus.). 800p. 55.00 (ISBN 0-87556-611-1). Saifer.
Beatts, Anne & Head, John, eds. Saturday Night Live. (Illus.). 1977. pap. 7.95 o.p. (ISBN 0-380-01801-2, 51342). Avon.
Beatty, jt. auth. see Davies.
Beatty, David. He That Wins Souls is Wise. 1982. pap. 0.75 (ISBN 0-88144-005-1, CPS-005). Christian Pub.
Beatty, Eleanor & Schnitger, Carol. Center in on Music: Individualized Learning Centers in the Elementary Classroom. LC 77-76865. (Illus.). 1977. pap. 10.95 (ISBN 0-916656-06-3); material packet 12.95 (ISBN 0-916656-07-1). Mark Foster Mus.
Beatty, Grace J., jt. auth. see Gardner, David C.
Beatty, J. Kelly & O'Leary, Brian, eds. The New Solar System. 2nd ed. LC 82-4396. (Illus.). 240p. 1982. 24.95 (ISBN 0-521-24988-0); pap. 13.95 (ISBN 0-521-27114-2). Cambridge U Pr.
Beatty, J. Kelly, et al, eds. The New Solar System. LC 81-2661. (Illus.). 208p. 1981. 22.95 o.p. (ISBN 0-521-23881-1). Cambridge U Pr.
Beatty, J. Kelly, jt. ed. see O'Leary, Brian.
Beatty, J. L. & Johnson, Oliver A. Heritage of Western Civilization, 2 vols. 4th ed. LC 76-14894. (Illus.). 1977. Vol. 1. pap. text ed. 10.95 o.p. (ISBN 0-13-387209-2); Vol. 2. pap. 10.95 o.p. (ISBN 0-13-387217-3). P-H.
Beatty, Jerome, Jr. Bob Fulton's Amazing Soda-Pop Stretcher. (Illus.). 208p. 1982. pap. 1.95 (ISBN 0-553-15083-9, Skylark). Bantam.
--Maria Looney on the Red Planet. (Illus.). (gr. 3-7). 1977. pap. 1.50 o.p. (ISBN 0-380-01729-6, 75523, Camelot). Avon.
--The Tunnel to Yesterday. 160p. (gr. 3-5). 1983. pap. 2.25 (ISBN 0-380-82537-6, 380-82537-6, Camelot). Avon.
Beatty, John. The Citizen-Solider. (Collector's Library of the Civil War). 1983. 26.60 (ISBN 0-8094-4258-2). Silver.
Beatty, John & Beatty, Patricia. Master Rosalind. LC 74-5050. 224p. (gr. 7 up). 1974. 9.95 (ISBN 0-688-21819-9); PLB 9.55 (ISBN 0-688-31819-3). Morrow.
Beatty, Patricia. The Bad Bell of San Salvador. (Illus.). 256p. (gr. 5-9). 1973. PLB 9.55 (ISBN 0-688-30081-2). Morrow.
--Billy Bedamned, Long Gone by. (gr. 5-9). 1977. 9.95 (ISBN 0-688-22101-7); PLB 9.55 (ISBN 0-688-32101-1). Morrow.
--I Want My Sunday, Stranger. (gr. 7 up). 1977. 10.95 (ISBN 0-688-22118-1); PLB 10.51 (ISBN 0-688-32118-6). Morrow.
--Jonathan Down Under. (gr. 5-9). 1982. 9.50 (ISBN 0-688-01467-4). Morrow.
--Just Some Weeds from the Wilderness. (gr. 7-9). 1978. 10.75 (ISBN 0-688-22137-8); PLB 10.32 (ISBN 0-688-32137-2). Morrow.
--Lacy Makes a Match. LC 79-9813. (gr. 7-9). 1979. 10.25 (ISBN 0-688-22200-5); PLB 9.84 (ISBN 0-688-32200-X). Morrow.
--Lupita Manana. (gr. 7-9). 1981. 9.95 (ISBN 0-688-00358-3); PLB 9.55 (ISBN 0-688-00359-1). Morrow.
--Red Rock Over the River. LC 72-5883. 256p. (gr. 7-9). 1973. PLB 10.08 (ISBN 0-688-30065-0). Morrow.
--Rufus, Red Rufus. LC 74-26981. (Illus.). 192p. (gr. 7 up). 1975. 9.95 (ISBN 0-688-22021-5); PLB 9.55 (ISBN 0-688-32021-X). Morrow.
--Something to Shout About. LC 76-22185. (gr. 5-9). 1976. PLB 9.55 (ISBN 0-688-32078-3). Morrow.

--The Staffordshire Terror. LC 79-21787. (gr. 7-9). 1979. 9.75 (ISBN 0-688-22201-3); PLB 9.36 (ISBN 0-688-32201-8). Morrow.
--That's One Ornery Orphan. LC 80-10200. 224p. (gr. 7-9). 1980. 9.75 (ISBN 0-688-22227-7); PLB 9.36 (ISBN 0-688-32227-1). Morrow.
--Wait for Me, Watch for Me, Eula Bee. (gr. 7-9). 1978. 10.75 (ISBN 0-688-22151-3); PLB 10.32 (ISBN 0-688-32151-8). Morrow.
Beatty, Patricia, jt. auth. see Beatty, John.
Beatty, Richard W. & Schneier, Craig E. Personnel Administration: An Experiential Skill-Building Approach. 576p. 1981. pap. text ed. 18.95 (ISBN 0-201-00172-1); implementor's manual 25.95 (ISBN 0-201-00176-4). A-W.
Beatty, Richard W., jt. auth. see Schneier, Craig E.
Beatty, Virginia & Consumer Guide Editors. Rating & Raising Indoor Plants. 1975. 8.95 o.p. (ISBN 0-671-22050-0); pap. 4.95 o.p. (ISBN 0-671-22051-9). S&S.
Beatty, Virginia L. & Consumer Guide Editors. Consumer Guide Rating & Raising Vegetables: A Practical Guide for Growing Vegetables, Herbs, Fruits & Sprouts. 8.95 o.p. (ISBN 0-671-22361-5); pap. 4.95 o.p. (ISBN 0-671-22362-3). S&S.
Beaty, Betty, jt. auth. see Beaty, David.
Beaty, David & Beaty, Betty. Wings of the Morning. 512p. 1982. 17.95 (ISBN 0-698-11141-9, Coward). Putnam Pub Group.
Beaty, H. Wayne, jt. auth. see Fink, Donald G.
Beaty, Janice J. Classroom Skills for Preschool Teachers: A Self-Taught Modular Training Program. (Early Childhood Education Ser.). 1979. pap. 10.95 (ISBN 0-675-08283-8). Merrill.
Beaty, Jerome, ed. The Norton Introduction to the Short Novel. (gr. 12). 1981. pap. text ed. 13.95x (ISBN 0-393-95187-1); classroom guide avail. (ISBN 0-393-95190-1). Norton.
Beaubier, Jeff. High Life Expectancy on the Island of Paros, Greece. LC 75-22948. (Illus.). 160p. 1976. 10.00 o.p. (ISBN 0-8022-2172-6). Philos Lib.
Beauchamp, Dan E. Beyond Alcoholism: Alcohol & Public Health Policy. 240p. 1980. 27.95 (ISBN 0-87722-189-8). Temple U Pr.
--Beyond Alcoholism: Alcohol & Public Health Policy. 222p. 1982. pap. 9.95 (ISBN 0-87722-286-X). Temple U Pr.
Beauchamp, Deanna, jt. auth. see Beauchamp, Gary.
Beauchamp, Edward. An American Teacher in Early Meiji Japan. (Asian Studies at Hawaii Ser: No. 17). 176p. 1976. pap. text ed. 7.00x (ISBN 0-8248-0404-X). UH Pr.
Beauchamp, Gary & Beauchamp, Deanna. Religiously Mixed Marriage. 4.75 (ISBN 0-89137-528-7). Quality Pubns.
Beauchamp, George A. Curriculum Theory. 4th ed. LC 80-84104. 219p. 1981. pap. text ed. 10.95 (ISBN 0-87581-270-8). Peacock Pubs.
Beauchamp, Gorman. Jack London. (Starmont Reader's Guide Ser.: No. 15). 96p. 1983. Repr. lib. bdg. 10.95x. Borgo Pr.
--Reader's Guide to Jack London. Schlobin, Roger C., ed. (Reader's Guides to Contemporary Science Fiction & Fantasy Authors Ser.: Vol. 15). (Illus., Orig.). 1983. 10.95x (ISBN 0-916732-40-1); pap. text ed. 4.95x (ISBN 0-916732-39-8). Starmont Hse.
Beauchamp, K. G. & Yuen, C. K. Digital Methods for Signal Analysis. (Illus.). 1979. text ed. 50.00x (ISBN 0-04-621027-X). Allen Unwin.
Beauchamp, Kenneth P., jt. auth. see McDorman, Ted L.
Beauchamp, Murray A. Elements of Mathematical Sociology. 1970. text ed. 6.35x (ISBN 0-685-19724-7). Phila Bk Co.
Beauchamp, Thom & Perlin, Seymour. Ethical Issues in Death & Dying. 1978. pap. 14.95 (ISBN 0-13-290114-5). P-H.
Beauchamp, Tom L. Case Studies in Business, Society & Ethics. 256p. 1983. pap. 12.95 (ISBN 0-13-119263-9). P-H.
--Ethics & Public Policy. 464p. 1975. ref. ed. 17.95 (ISBN 0-13-290601-5); pap. 15.95 (ISBN 0-13-290593-0). P-H.
--Philosophical Ethics: An Introduction to Moral Philosophy. Pace, Kaye, ed. 416p. 1982. 21.00x (ISBN 0-07-004203-9). McGraw.
Beauchamp, Tom L. & Bowie, Norman E. Ethical Theory & Business. 2nd ed. 640p. 1983. text ed. 22.95 (ISBN 0-13-290452-7). P-H.
Beauchamp, Tom L. & Rosenberg, Alexander. Hume & the Problem of Causation. 1981. 23.50x (ISBN 0-19-520236-8). Oxford U Pr.
Beauchamp, Tom L. & Walters, LeRoy. Contemporary Issues in Bioethics. 1978. 22.95x o.p. (ISBN 0-8221-0200-5). Dickenson.
--Contemporary Issues in Bioethics. 2nd ed. 624p. 1982. text ed. 23.95x (ISBN 0-534-01102-0). Wadsworth Pub.
Beauchamp, Tom L., jt. auth. see Barker, Stephen F.
Beauchamp, Tom L. & Bowie, Norman E., eds. Ethical Theory & Business. (Illus.). 1979. text ed. 20.95 o.p. (ISBN 0-13-290460-8). P-H.
Beauchamp, Tom L. & Pinkard, Terry P., eds. Ethics & Public Policy: Introduction to Ethics. (Illus.). 416p. 1983. pap. 14.95 (ISBN 0-13-290957-X). P-H.
Beauchamp, Tom L., et al. Philosophy & the Human Condition. (Illus.). 640p. 1980. text ed. 20.95 (ISBN 0-13-662528-2). P-H.
Beauchamp, Val, jt. auth. see Dale, Stan.
Beauchamp, William M. Aboriginal Place Names of New York. LC 68-17915. 333p. 1972. Repr. of 1907 ed. 38.00x (ISBN 0-8103-3231-0). Gale.
Beaudry, Antoinette. Desert of Desire. 320p. (Orig.). 1980. pap. 2.50 o.p. (ISBN 0-523-40672-X). Pinnacle Bks.
--River of Desire. (Orig.). 1979. pap. 2.50 o.p. (ISBN 0-523-40498-0). Pinnacle Bks.
--Strands of Desire. 288p. (Orig.). 1981. pap. 2.50 o.p. (ISBN 0-523-40925-7). Pinnacle Bks.
Beaudry, Jo & Ketchum, Lynne. Carla Goes to Court. LC 82-2854. (Illus.). 32p. 1982. 9.95 (ISBN 0-89885-088-6). Human Sci Pr.
Beaugrand, Honore. Jeanne la Fileuse. (Novels by Franco-Americans in New England 1850-1940 Ser.). 188p. (Fr.). (gr. 10 up). 1980. pap. 4.50 (ISBN 0-911409-17-3). Natl Mat Dev.
Beaugrande, Robert de. Text Production. Freedle, Roy O., ed. (Advances in Discourse Processes Ser.: Vol. 11). 400p. 1983. text ed. 37.50 (ISBN 0-89391-158-5); pap. text ed. 18.50 (ISBN 0-89391-159-3). Ablex Pub.
Beaugrande, Robert De see De Beaugrande, Robert.
Beaujean, Von Marion Herausgegeben see Von Marion Beaujean, Herausgegeben.
Beaulieu, Victor A. The Reconstruction of Pythagoras System on the Vibrational Theory of Number: The Essential Library of the Great Philosophers. (Illus.). 91p. 1983. Repr. of 1905 ed. 97.45 (ISBN 0-89920-050-8). Am Inst Psych.
Beauman, Sally. The Royal Shakespeare Company: A History of Ten Decades. 1982. 29.95 (ISBN 0-19-212209-6). Oxford U Pr.
Beaumont, A. P. Intermediate Mathematical Statistics. 225p. 1980. pap. 14.95x (ISBN 0-412-15480-3, Pub. by Chapmman & Hall England). Methuen Inc.
Beaumont, Charles. Best of Beaumont. 288p. 1982. pap. 2.95 (ISBN 0-686-82103-3). Bantam.
--A Modest Proposal. LC 70-79858. (Literary Casebook Ser.). 1969. pap. text ed. 3.50 (ISBN 0-675-09441-0). Merrill.
Beaumont, Cyril W., tr. see Levinson, Andre.
Beaumont, Francis & Fletcher, John. The Dramatic Works in the Beaumont & Fletcher Canon: Vol. V, The Mad Lover, The Loyal Subject, The Humorous Lieutenant, Women Pleased, The Island Princess. Bowers, Fredson, ed. LC 66-74421. 600p. Date not set. 89.50 (ISBN 0-521-20061-X). Cambridge U Pr.
Beaumont, John A., et al. Your Career in Marketing. 2nd ed. 1976. text ed. 15.04 (ISBN 0-07-004245-4, G); tchr's manual & key 4.56 (ISBN 0-07-004248-9); job activity guide 7.08 (ISBN 0-07-004246-2). McGraw.
Beaumont, John R. & Keys, Paul. Future Cities: Spatial Analysis of Energy Issues. (Geography & Public Policy Research Studies Ser.). 198p. 1982. 39.95 (ISBN 0-471-10451-5, Pub. by Res Stud Pr). Wiley.
Beaumont, P. B. Safety at Work & the Unions. 208p. 1983. text ed. 25.25x (ISBN 0-7099-0097-X, Pub. by Croom Helm Ltd England). Biblio Dist.
Beaumont, Peter, et al. The Middle East: A Georgraphical Study. LC 74-28284. 614p. 1976. 55.95x (ISBN 0-471-06117-4, Pub. by Wiley-Interscience); pap. 25.95 (ISBN 0-471-06119-0). Wiley.
Beaumont, Timothy, ed. Modern Religious Verse. (Pocket Poet Ser.). 1966. pap. 1.25 (ISBN 0-8023-9039-0). Dufour.
Beaupre, Normand R. L' Enclume et le Couteau: The Life & Work of Adelard Cote Folk Artist. (Illus.). 98p. (Eng. & Fr.). 1982. pap. 9.00 (ISBN 0-911409-13-0). Natl Mat Dev.
Beauregard, Raymond A. & Fraleigh, John B. A First Course in Linear Algebra. LC 72-5648. 1973. text ed. 26.50 (ISBN 0-395-14017-X); solutions manual 5.50 (ISBN 0-395-14018-8). HM.
Beaurline, L. A., ed. see Dryden, John.
Beauville, A. Complex Algebraic Surfaces. LC 82-9490. (London Mathematical Society Lecture Note Ser.: No. 68). 150p. Date not set. pap. price not set (ISBN 0-521-28815-0). Cambridge U Pr.
Beauvoir, Simone De see De Beauvoir, Simone.
Beaver, Edmund. Travel Games. (gr. 4 up). 1974. pap. 0.59 (ISBN 0-910208-01-8). Beavers.
--Word of Life: Scripture Selections. (Illus.). 1953. pap. 1.75 (ISBN 0-910208-02-6). Beavers.
Beaver, Frank. Dictionary of Film Terms. (Illus.). 320p. 1983. text ed. 15.95 (ISBN 0-07-004216-0, C); pap. text ed. 9.95 (ISBN 0-07-004212-8). McGraw.
--On Film: A History of the Motion Picture. 544p. 1982. 21.50 (ISBN 0-07-004219-5, C). McGraw.
Beaver, Harald, ed. see Poe, Edgar Allan.
Beaver, Marion L. Human Service Practice with the Elderly. (Illus.). 256p. 1983. 19.95 (ISBN 0-686-38827-5). P H.
Beaver, Patrick. The Spice of Life: Pleasures of the Victorian Age. (Illus.). 1979. 24.00 o.p. (ISBN 0-241-89366-6, Pub. by Hamish Hamilton England). David & Charles.
--Victorian Parlor Games. LC 78-12396. (Illus.). 1979. 7.95 o.p. (ISBN 0-525-66608-7). Lodestar Bks.
Beaver, Paul. U-Boats in the Atlantic. LC 81-65156. (World War Two Photo Album). (Illus.). 96p. 1982. pap. 5.95 (ISBN 0-89404-057-X). Aztex.
Beaver, R. Pierce, ed. The Native American Christian Community: A Directory of Indian, Aleut, & Eskimo Churches. 1979. text ed. 6.00 (ISBN 0-912552-25-5). MARC.
Beaver, S. H., jt. auth. see Stamp, L. Dudley.
Beaver, William H. Financial Reporting: An Accounting Revolution. (Contemporary Topics in Accounting Ser.). (Illus.). 240p. 1981. text ed. 15.95 (ISBN 0-13-316141-2); pap. text ed. 12.95 (ISBN 0-13-316133-1). P-H.
Beavers, Dorothy J. Autism: Nightmare Without End. Hammond, Debbie, ed. LC 79-27669. 1982. 15.95 (ISBN 0-87949-167-1). Ashley Bks.
Beavers, James E., ed. Earthquakes & Earthquake Engineering: The Eastern United States, 2 vols. LC 81-68244. 1191p. 1981. Set. text ed. 39.95 (ISBN 0-250-40496-6). Vol. 1 (ISBN 0-250-40512-1). Vol. 2 (ISBN 0-250-40511-3). Ann Arbor Science.
Beavers, Mary K. Essential Mathematics. 560p. 1983. pap. text ed. 21.50 scp (ISBN 0-06-040591-0, HarpC); instr's. manual & test bank avail. (ISBN 0-06-360553-8). Har-Row.
Beazley, E. & Haverson, M. Living with the Desert: Working Buildings of the Iranian Plateau. (Illus.). 140p. 1983. text ed. 44.00x (ISBN 0-85668-192-X, 60245, Pub. by Aris & Phillips England). Humanities.
Beazley, J. D. Attic Red-Figure Vase-Painters, 3 Vols. 2036p. 1982. Repr. of 1963 ed. Set. 125.00 (ISBN 0-87817-289-0). Hacker.
Beazley, Mary, jt. auth. see Scott, Margaret K.
Bebarta, Prafulla C. Family Type & Fertility in India. LC 76-4268. (Illus.). 224p. 1977. 8.95 o.p. (ISBN 0-8158-0339-7). Chris Mass.
Bebb, Russ. The Big Orange: A Story of Tennessee Football. LC 73-86998. (College Sports Ser.). 1980. 10.95 o.p. (ISBN 0-87397-032-2). Strode.
--The Big Orange: A Story of Tennessee Football. (College Sports Ser.). 1982. 10.95 (ISBN 0-87397-214-7). Strode.
Bebbington, Jum. Soccer. LC 80-50933. (Intersport Ser.). 13.00 (ISBN 0-382-06436-4). Silver.
Bebek, Borna. The Third City: Philosophy at War with Positivism. 352p. 1983. 29.95 (ISBN 0-7100-9042-0). Routledge & Kegan.
Bebel, August. My Life. 1973. 27.50x (ISBN 0-685-09582-7). Fertig.
--Woman under Socialism. De Leon, Daniel, tr. from Ger. LC 72-162286. (Studies in the Life of Women). 1971. pap. 3.95 o.p. (ISBN 0-8052-0323-0). Schocken.
Bebensee, Elisabeth L., jt. auth. see Adams, Anne.
Bebie, Phillip. Proclaim Her Name. 62p. 1982. pap. write for info (ISBN 0-911988-46-7). Ami Pr.
Bebout, D. G., et al. Depositional & Diagenetic History of the Sligo & Hosston Formations (Lower Cretaceous) in South Texas. (Report of Investigations Ser.: No. 109). (Illus.). 55p. 1982. 4.00 (ISBN 0-686-36993-9). U of Tex Econ Geology.
Beccaria, Cesare. On Crimes & Punishments. 1983. pap. 3.00 (ISBN 0-8283-1800-X). Branden.
Becerra, Rosina, jt. auth. see Giovannoni, Jeanne M.
Becerra, Rosina M. & Escobar, Javier I., eds. The Hispanic Patient: Mental Health Issues & Strategies. LC 81-22931. (Seminars in Psychiatry Ser.). 232p. 1982. 24.50 (ISBN 0-8089-1452-9). Grune.
Becher, Peter. Der Untergang Kakaniens. 410p. (Ger.). 1982. write for info. (ISBN 3-8204-6260-0). P Lang Pubs.
Becher, Tony & Kogan, Maurice. Process & Structure in Higher Education. (Studies in Social Policy & Welfare Ser.). 1980. text ed. 27.00x (ISBN 0-435-82507-0). Heinemann Ed.
Becherer, Richard, jt. ed. see Grum, Franc.
Bechet, Sidney. Treat It Gentle: An Autobiography. LC 74-23412. (Roots of Jazz Ser). (Illus.). vi, 245p. 1978. lib. bdg. 25.00 (ISBN 0-306-70657-1); pap. 6.95 (ISBN 0-686-77055-2). Da Capo.
Bechler, Leo & Rahm, B. Die Oboe und die Ihr Verwandten Istrumente, Nebst Biographischen Skizzen der Bedeutendsten Ihrer Meister: Ph. Losch, Musikliteratur fur Oboe. 1978. Repr. of 1914 ed. 35.00 o.s.i. (ISBN 90-6027-165-3, Pub. by Frits Knuf Netherlands); wrappers 22.50 o.s.i. (ISBN 90-6027-164-5, Pub. by Frits Knuf Netherlands). Pendragon NY.
Becht, J. Edwin & Belzung, L. D. World Resource Management: Key to Civilizations & Social Achievement. (Illus.). 336p. 1975. text ed. 26.95 (ISBN 0-13-968107-8). P-H.
Becht, R. Revision der Sektion Alopecuroideae DC. der Gattung Astragalus L. (Phanerogamarum Monographiae Ser: No. 10). (Illus.). 1979. lib. bdg. 24.00 (ISBN 3-7682-1188-6). Lubrecht & Cramer.
Bechtel, Helmut. Cage Bird Indentifier. LC 72-81049. (Identifier Ser.). (Illus.). 256p. (gr. 6 up). 1973. 9.95 (ISBN 0-8069-3718-1); PLB 12.49 (ISBN 0-8069-3719-X). Sterling.
--House Plant Identifier. LC 72-95203. (Identifier Bks.). (Illus.). 256p. (gr. 6 up). 1973. 9.95 o.p. (ISBN 0-8069-3056-X); PLB 9.29 o.p. (ISBN 0-8069-3057-8). Sterling.
Bechtel, John H. Slips of Speech. LC 77-159889. Repr. of 1901 ed. 34.00x (ISBN 0-8103-4041-0). Gale.
Bechtel National, Inc. Handbook for Battery Energy Storage in Photovoltaic Power Systems. 127p. 1982. pap. 19.50x o.p. (ISBN 0-89934-164-0, P046). Solar Energy Info.
Bechtel, Paul, ed. The Confessions of St. Augustine. LC 81-11163. 1981. 8.95 (ISBN 0-8024-1618-7). Moody.
Bechtereva, N. P. The Neurophysiological Aspects of Human Mental Activity. 2nd ed. (Illus.). 1978. text ed. 19.95x (ISBN 0-19-502131-2). Oxford U Pr.
Bechtold, Peter K. Politics in the Sudan: Parliamentary & Military Rule in an Emerging African Nation. LC 76-6466. (Illus.). 384p. 1976. text ed. 38.95 o.p. (ISBN 0-275-22730-8). Praeger.
Beck, A. E. Physical Principles of Exploration Methods: An Introductory Text for Geology & Geophysics Students. LC 81-80411. 234p. 1981. 34.95 (ISBN 0-470-27124-8); pap. 17.95 (ISBN 0-470-27128-0). Halsted Pr.
Beck, A. H. Handbook of Vacuum Physics. Vol. 2, Pt. 1 1965. pap. 21.00 o.p. (ISBN 0-08-010888-1); Vol. 3, Pts. 1-3. 1965. pap. 22.00 o.p. (ISBN 0-08-011051-7). Pergamon.
Beck, Aaron T. Cognitive Therapy & the Emotional Disorders. pap. 5.95 (ISBN 0-686-36687-5). Inst Rat Liv.
Beck, Alan & Katcher, Aaron, eds. New Perspectives on Our Lives with Companion Animals. LC 82-40484. 640p. 1983. 25.00x (ISBN 0-8122-7877-1). U of Pa Pr.
Beck, Art. Rilke. LC 82-84119. Orig. Title: Ger. 70p. (Orig.). Date not set. pap. 3.95 (ISBN 0-941692-06-X). Elysian Pr.
Beck, Barbara L. The Ancient Maya. rev. ed. (First Bks.). (Illus.). 72p. (gr. 4 up). 1983. PLB 8.90 (ISBN 0-531-04529-3). Watts.
--The Aztecs. rev. ed. (First Bks.). (Illus.). 72p. (gr. 4 up). 1983. PLB 8.90 (ISBN 0-531-04522-6). Watts.
--The Incas. rev. ed. (First Bks.). (Illus.). 72p. (gr. 4 up). 1983. PLB 8.90 (ISBN 0-531-04528-5). Watts.
Beck, Carl. Contempt of Congress: A Study of the Prosecutions Initiated by the Committee on Un-American Activities, 1945-1957. LC 75-166090. (Studies in American History & Government Ser.). 264p. 1974. Repr. of 1959 ed. lib. bdg. 32.50 (ISBN 0-306-70229-0). Da Capo.
Beck, Carl, jt. ed. see Mesa-Lago, Carmelo.
Beck, Clark L. & Burks, Ardath W. Aspects of Meiji Modernization: The Japan Helpers & the Helped. 45p. 1983. pap. text ed. 4.95x (ISBN 0-87855-936-1). Transaction Bks.
Beck, Dawn. Where To Go Dancing in Silicon Valley. LC 82-61728. 96p. 1982. pap. 4.95 (ISBN 0-9609740-0-8). Sharain Bks.
Beck, Earl R. A Time of Triumph & of Sorrow: Spanish Politics During the Reign of Alfonso XII, 1874-1885. LC 78-23282. 320p. 1979. 22.50x (ISBN 0-8093-0902-5). S Ill U Pr.
Beck, Elmer A. & Westburg, John, eds. The Sewer Socialists: A History of the Socialist Party of Wisconsin, 1897-1940, 2 Vols. Incl. Vol. 1. The Socialist Trinity of the Party, the Unions & the Press. 204p; The Nineteen Twenties & Nineteen Thirties. (Illus.). 168p. (Illus.). 1982. Set. pap. 20.00 (ISBN 0-87423-031-4). Westburg.
Beck, Eric R., et al. Differential Diagnosis: Internal Medicine. LC 82-71362. (Illus.). 229p. (Orig.). 1983. pap. text ed. 14.50x (ISBN 0-668-05622-3, 5622). Arco.
Beck, Eugen A., tr. see Bizzozero, Julius.
Beck, Evelyn T., jt. ed. see Sherman, Julia A.
Beck, Helen. How Books Get That Way: Athena Tells. (Illus.). 64p. (gr. 3-6). 1983. 9.95 (ISBN 0-940730-01-4). Athena Pr ND.
Beck, Henry J. & Parrish, Roy J., Jr. Computerized Accounting. (Business Ser.). 1977. pap. text ed. 9.95 (ISBN 0-675-08449-0). Additional supplements may be obtained from publisher. Merrill.
Beck, Horace. Folklore & the Sea. (Illus.). 480p. 1983. pap. 10.95 (ISBN 0-8289-0499-5). Greene.
Beck, Horace P. Gluskap the Liar & Other Indian Tales. (Illus.). 192p. 1966. 5.95 (ISBN 0-87027-083-4). Cumberland Pr.
Beck, Horace P., ed. Folklore in Action: Essays for Discussion in Honor of MacEdward Leach. LC 62-12687. (American Folklore Society Memoirs Ser). Repr. of 1962 ed. 23.00 (ISBN 0-527-01130-4). Kraus Repr.
Beck, J. M. Joseph Howe: Conservative Reformer 1804-1848, Vol. 1. 400p. 1983. 35.00x (ISBN 0-7735-0387-0). McGill-Queens U Pr.
--Joseph Howe: The Briton Becomes Canadian 1848-1873, Vol. 2. 448p. 1983. 37.50x (ISBN 0-7735-0388-9). McGill-Queens U Pr.
Beck, J. S. Biomembranes: Fundamentals in Relation to Human Biology. 1979. 24.95 (ISBN 0-07-004263-2). McGraw.
Beck, J. V. & Yao, L. S., eds. Heat Transfer in Porous Media. (HTD Ser.: Vol. 22). 1982. 24.00 (H00250). ASME.
Beck, Jacob. Organizational & Representation in Perception. 400p. 1982. text ed. 39.95 (ISBN 0-89859-175-9). L Erlbaum Assocs.
Beck, James. Massicio the Documents With the Collaboration of Gino Corth. LC 78-67679. 1978. 12.00 (ISBN 0-686-92649-8). J J Augustin.

Beck, James V. & Arnold, Kenneth J. Parameter Estimation in Engineering & Science. LC 77-40293. (Probability & Statistics: Applied Probability & Statistics Section). 501p. 1977. 45.95x (ISBN 0-471-06118-2, Pub. by Wiley-Interscience). Wiley.

Beck, Jane C., ed. Always in Season: Folk Art & Traditional Culture in Vermont. (Illus.). 144p. (Orig.). 1982. 8.75 (ISBN 0-916718-09-3). VT Council Arts.

Beck, Joan. Best Beginnings. 300p. 1983. 14.95 (ISBN 0-399-12683-X). Putnam Pub Group.

Beck, John & Cox, Charles. Advances in Management Education. LC 80-40117. 360p. 1980. 48.00x (ISBN 0-471-27775-4, Pub. by Wiley-Interscience). Wiley.

Beck, Julian. The Life of the Theatre: The Relation of the Artist to the Struggle of the People. LC 72-84229. 250p. 1972. pap. 4.00 o.p. (ISBN 0-87286-060-4). City Lights.

Beck, K. C., jt. auth. see Weaver, C. E.

Beck, Kirsten. Cultivating the Wasteland: Can Cable Put the Vision Back in TV? (Orig.). 1983. pap. 14.95 (ISBN 0-915400-34-0). Am Council Arts.

Beck, L. & Holms, R. Philosophic Inquiry: An Introduction to Philosophy. 2nd ed. 1968. 18.95 o.p. (ISBN 0-13-662494-4). P-H.

Beck, L. W., et al, trs. see Kant, Immanuel.

Beck, Leif C. The Physician's Office. LC 77-87555. (Illus.). 1977. 14.95 (ISBN 90-219-0346-6). Excerpta-Princeton.

Beck, Lewis W., ed. Kant Studies Today. LC 68-57207. ix, 516p. (Orig.). 1969. 27.50 (ISBN 0-87548-028-4). Open Court.

Beck, Lewis W., ed. see Kant, Immanuel.

Beck, Lewis W., ed. see Macmillan, R. A.

Beck, Lewis W., ed. see Watson, John.

Beck, Lewis W., tr. see Kant, Immanuel.

Beck, M. Susan. Kidspeak: How Your Child Develops Language Skills. 144p. 1982. pap. 4.95 (ISBN 0-452-25376-4, Plume). NAL.

Beck, Madeline H. & Williamson, Lamar, Jr. Mastering Old Testament Facts, Bk. 4: Isaiah-Malachi. (Mastering Old Testament Facts Ser.). (Illus.). 112p. (Orig.). (gr. 9-12). 1981. pap. 5.25 (ISBN 0-8042-0137-4). John Knox.

Beck, Malcolm & Judd, John, eds. Polyagglutination. 90p. 1980. 18.00 (ISBN 0-914404-58-X). Am Assn Blood.

Beck, Mary Ann, et al, eds. The Analysis of Hispanic Texts: Current Trends in Methodology. LC 76-5741. (First York College Colloquium). 1976. pap. 10.95x (ISBN 0-916950-00-X). Bilingual Pr.

Beck, Michael, ed. The Narcissistic Family Member. 1982. 8.95 (ISBN 0-932930-49-2). Pilgrimage Inc.

Beck, P. G. & Forster, M. C. Six Rural Problem Areas: Relief-Resources-Rehabilitation. LC 71-165679. (Research Monograph: Vol. 1). 1971. Repr. of 1935 ed. lib. bdg. 22.50 (ISBN 0-306-70333-5). Da Capo.

Beck, R. & Guers, K. Table of Laser Lines in Gases & Vapors. 2nd rev ed. LC 77-26659. (Springer Series in Optical Sciences: Vol. 2). 1978. 28.40 o.p. (ISBN 0-387-08603-X). Springer-Verlag.

Beck, R. H., et al. Introductory Soil Science: A Laboratory Manual. (Illus.). 276p. 1982. 9.40 (ISBN 0-87563-222-X). Stipes.

Beck, Robert, ed. see Brightman, Edgar S.

Beck, Robert C. Applying Psychology: Understanding People. (Illus.). 480p. 1982. 23.95 (ISBN 0-13-043463-9). P-H.

--Motivation: Theories & Principles. 1978. ref. ed. 23.95 (ISBN 0-13-603902-2). P-H.

--Motivation: Theories & Principles. (Illus.). 480p. 1983. text ed. 23.95 (ISBN 0-13-603910-3). P-H.

Beck, Robert N. Handbook in Social Philosophy. 1979. pap. text ed. 11.95 (ISBN 0-02-307820-0). Macmillan.

Beck, Robert N. & Steinkraus, Warren E., eds. Studies in Personalism: Selected Writings of Edgar Sheffield Brightman. LC 75-4133. (Philosophy Ser.: No. 603). 15.00 (ISBN 0-89007-603-0). C Stark.

Beck, Roger. Microeconomic Analysis of Issues in Business, Government & Society. (Illus.). 1978. pap. text ed. 15.95 (ISBN 0-07-004253-5, C); instr's manual 7.95 (ISBN 0-07-004254-3). McGraw.

Beck, Roger B. A Bibliography of Africana in the Institute for Sex Research, Indiana University. (Afican Humanities Ser.). 134p. (Orig.). 1979. pap. text ed. 5.00 (ISBN 0-941934-29-2). Ind U Afro-Amer Arts.

Beck, S. William. Gloves: Their Annals & Associations. LC 75-75801. 1969. Repr. of 1883 ed. 27.00 o.p. (ISBN 0-8103-3825-4). Gale.

Beck, Sandy. Alcoholic's Guide to Sobriety & Recovery. 109p. pap. 2.95 o.p. (ISBN 0-686-64749-1, Pub. by Ermine). Hippocrene Bks.

Beck, Simone. Simca's Cuisine. (Illus.). 1972. 17.95 (ISBN 0-394-47449-X). Knopf.

Beck, Thomas. French Legislators Eighteen Hundred to Eighteen Thirty-Four: A Study in Quantitative History. LC 73-83059. 1975. 33.00x (ISBN 0-520-02535-0). U of Cal Pr.

Beck, Warren. Man in Motion: Faulkner's Trilogy. 216p. (Orig.). 1961. pap. 7.50 (ISBN 0-299-02414-8). U of Wis Pr.

--Rest Is Silence & Other Stories. LC 82-71835. 132p. (Orig.). 1963. pap. 5.95 (ISBN 0-8040-0261-4). Swallow.

Beck, Warren A. & Clowers, Myles L. Understanding American History Through Fiction, 2 vols. 480p. 1975. Vol. 1. pap. text ed. 14.95 (ISBN 0-07-004217-9, C); Vol. 2. pap. text ed. 14.95 (ISBN 0-07-004218-7). McGraw.

Beck, William C. & Trier, James R. Programmed Course in Basic Algebra. (Mathematics Ser). 1971. 16.95 (ISBN 0-201-00445-3); pap. 3.95 (ISBN 0-201-00446-1). A-W.

Beck, William F., tr. New Testament in the Language of Today. LC 63-8909. (YA) (gr. 9 up). 1964. 7.95 o.p. (ISBN 0-570-00501-9, 2-1052); pap. 4.95 o.p. (ISBN 0-570-00502-7, 2-1066). Concordia.

Beck, William S., ed. Hematology. 3rd ed. (Illus.). 448p. 1981. text ed. 30.00x (ISBN 0-262-02163-3); pap. text ed. 15.00x (ISBN 0-262-52067-2). MIT Pr.

Becke, Louis. South Sea Supercargo. Day, A. Grove, ed. LC 68-18937. (YA) 1967. Repr. 8.50 (ISBN 0-87022-060-8). UH Pr.

Beckelhymer, Hunter, ed. The Word We Preach: Sermons in Honor of Dean Elmer D. Henson. 1970. 7.50 (ISBN 0-912646-29-2). Tex Christian.

Beckenbach, E. F. & Bellman, R. An Introduction to Inequalities. LC 61-6228. (New Mathematical Library: No. 3). 1975. pap. 7.50 (ISBN 0-88385-603-4). Math Assn.

Beckenbach, Edwin, et al. College Algebra. 4th ed. 1978. text ed. 20.95x o.p. (ISBN 0-534-00536-5); study guide 6.95x o.p. (ISBN 0-534-00537-3). Wadsworth Pub.

Beckenbauer, Franz. Franz Beckenbauer's Soccer Power. Saunders, Harry, tr. (Illus.). 1978. 7.95 o.p. (ISBN 0-87866-097-6, 0976). Petersons Guides.

Beckenstein, Alan, et al. Performance Measurement of the Petroleum Industry: Functional Profitability & Alternatives. LC 79-1951. (Illus.). 1979. 23.95x (ISBN 0-669-03017-1). Lexington Bks.

Beckenstein, E., et al. Topological Algebras. (North-Holland Mathematical Studies: Vol. 24). 1977. pap. 53.25 (ISBN 0-7204-0724-9, North-Holland). Elsevier.

Becker. Phosphates & Phosphoric Acid. (Fertilizer Science & Technology Ser.). 592p. 1983. price not set (ISBN 0-8247-1712-0). Dekker.

Becker, A. L. & Yengoyan, Aram, eds. The Imagination of Reality: Essays in Southeast Asian Coherence Systems. LC 79-15675. (Language & Being Ser.). (Illus.). 1979. 29.50x (ISBN 0-89391-021-X). Ablex Pub.

Becker, Abraham S. Military Expenditure Limitation for Arms Control: Problems & Prospects - With a Documentary History of Recent Proposals. LC 77-8224. 368p. 1977. prof ref 25.00x (ISBN 0-88410-470-2). Ballinger Pub.

--Soviet National Income, 1958-1964: National Accounts of the USSR in the Seven Year Plan Period. LC 70-77483. (Illus.). 1969. 49.50x (ISBN 0-520-01437-5). U of Cal Pr.

Becker, Betty G. & Fendler, Dolores T. Vocational & Personal Adjustments in Practical Nursing. 4th ed. LC 81-14041. (Illus.). 180p. 1982. pap. text ed. 11.50 (ISBN 0-8016-0566-0). Mosby.

Becker, Bruce. Backgammon for Blood. 1975. pap. 2.95 (ISBN 0-380-00384-8, 59444-7). Avon.

Becker, Calvin W. First & Second Timothy & Titus: Letters to Two Young Men. (Teach Yourself the Bible Ser). 1961. pap. 2.25 (ISBN 0-8024-2646-8). Moody.

Becker, Carl. Eve of the Revolution. 1918. text ed. 8.50x (ISBN 0-686-83540-9). Elliots Bks.

Becker, Carl L. Declaration of Independence: A Study in the History of Political Ideas. 1958. pap. 3.95 (ISBN 0-394-70060-0, V-60, Vin). Random.

--Freedom & Responsibility in the American Way of Life. LC 80-11156. (University of Michigan, William W. Cook Foundation Lectures: Vol. 1). 1980. Repr. of 1945 ed. lib. bdg. 18.25x (ISBN 0-313-22361-0, BEFA). Greenwood.

Becker, Carl M. The Village: A History of Germantown, Ohio, 1804-1976. LC 80-16683. (Historical Society of Germantown, Ohio Ser.). (Illus.). xvi, 209p. 1980. 15.00 o.p. (ISBN 0-8214-0550-0). Ohio U Pr.

Becker, Carol, jt. ed. see Spiegel, Stephen L.

Becker, David G. The New Bourgeoisie & the Limits of Dependency: Mining, Class, & Power in "Revolutionary" Peru. LC 82-61352. 368p. 1983. 35.00x (ISBN 0-691-07645-6); pap. 9.95 (ISBN 0-691-02213-5). Princeton U Pr.

Becker, Dennis & Becker, Nancy. How to Succeed with Your Money: Leader's Guide. (Leader's Guide Ser.). (Illus.). 1978. text ed. 4.95 (ISBN 0-8024-3661-7). Moody.

Becker, Dennis, ed. see Becker, Nancy & Braun, Jack.

Becker, E. Lovell, et al, eds. Nephrology - Cornell Seminars. 138p. 1971. pap. 7.50 o.p. (ISBN 0-683-00493-X, Pub. by Williams & Wilkins). Krieger.

Becker, Eric B., et al. Finite Elements: An Introduction, Vol. 1. (Illus.). 256p. 1981. 27.95 (ISBN 0-13-317057-8). P-H.

Becker, Ernest. The Structure of Evil. LC 68-12890. 1976. pap. 5.95 (ISBN 0-02-902290-8). Free Pr.

Becker, Ernest I. & Tsutsui, Minoru, eds. Organometallic Reactions, 2 vols. LC 74-92108. 1971. Vol. 1, 389pp. 29.50 (ISBN 0-471-06135-2); Vol. 2, 450pp. 32.50 (ISBN 0-471-06130-1). Krieger.

Becker, Ernest I., tr. see Lefevre, M. J.

Becker, Esther R. & Anders, Evelyn. The Successful Secretary's Handbook. LC 70-83584. (Illus.). 1971. 11.49i (ISBN 0-06-010267-5, HarpT). Har-Row.

Becker, Franklin D. Housing Messages. LC 76-21267. (Community Development Ser.: Vol. 30). (Illus.). 1977. 21.50 (ISBN 0-87933-259-X). Hutchinson Ross.

Becker, George C. Fishes of Wisconsin. LC 81-69813. (Illus.). 1000p. 1983. cloth 75.00 (ISBN 0-299-08790-5). U of Wis Pr.

Becker, George J. D. H. Lawrence. LC 79-48075. (Literature and Life Ser.). 160p. 1980. 11.95 (ISBN 0-8044-2029-7); pap. 4.95 (ISBN 0-8044-6033-7). Ungar.

--James Michener. LC 82-40279. (Literature & Life Ser.). 170p. 1983. 11.95 (ISBN 0-8044-2044-0). Ungar.

--John Dos Passos. LC 74-78437. (Literature and Life Ser.). 142p. 1974. 11.95 (ISBN 0-8044-2034-3). Ungar.

--Master European Realists of the Nineteenth Century. LC 81-70124. 225p. 1982. 15.95 (ISBN 0-8044-2046-7). Ungar.

--Shakespeare's Histories. LC 76-15644. (Literature & Life Ser.). (Illus.). 1977. 11.95 (ISBN 0-8044-2032-7). Ungar.

--Shakespeare's Histories. LC 76-15644. (Literature & Life Ser.). (Illus.). 192p. 1983. pap. 5.95 (ISBN 0-8044-6032-9). Ungar.

Becker, H. A. Dimensionless Parameters: Theory & Methodology. LC 76-1570. 128p. 1976. 31.95x (ISBN 0-470-15048-3). Halsted Pr.

Becker, Hal B. Functional Analysis of Information Networks: Astructured Approach to the Data Communications Environment. LC 80-15347. 296p. 1981. Repr. of 1973 ed. lib. bdg. 29.50 o.p. (ISBN 0-89874-028-2). Krieger.

--Functional Analysis of Information Networks: A Structured Approach to the Data Communications Environment. LC 73-14991. (Business Data Processing Ser.). 304p. 1973. 28.50 o.p. (ISBN 0-471-06124-7, Pub. by Wiley-Interscience). Wiley.

--Information Integrity: A Structure for Its Definition & Management. (Illus.). 256p. 1983. 26.95 (ISBN 0-07-004191-1, P&RB). McGraw.

Becker, Howard P. Through Values to Social Interpretation: Essays on Social Contexts, Actions, Types & Prospects. LC 69-10068. 1968. Repr. of 1950 ed. lib. bdg. 20.00x (ISBN 0-8371-0014-3, BESI). Greenwood.

Becker, Howard S., ed. Campus Power Struggle. 2nd, rev ed. LC 72-91466. 191p. 1970. 9.95 (ISBN 0-87855-059-3); pap. text ed. 3.95 (ISBN 0-87855-556-0). Transaction Bks.

--Culture & Civility in San Francisco. (Illus.). 164p. 1971. pap. text ed. 3.95 (ISBN 0-87855-568-4). Transaction Bks.

--Exploring Society Photographically. 1981. 10.00 (ISBN 0-941680-00-2, 04097-6, Distrib. for Block Gallery, Northwestern University). U. of Chicago Pr.

Becker, Howard S., et al, eds. Boys in White: Student Culture in Medical School. rev. ed. LC 76-26951. 456p. 1976. pap. text ed. 14.95 (ISBN 0-87855-622-2). Transaction Bks.

Becker, Irving, jt. auth. see Ellis, Albert.

Becker, J. Marxian Political Economy. LC 76-9172. (Illus.). 1977. 32.50x (ISBN 0-521-21349-5). Cambridge U Pr.

Becker, Jack D. Introduction to Business Data Processing: Supplement. 216p. 1982. pap. text ed. 11.95 (ISBN 0-8403-2829-X). Kendall-Hunt.

Becker, James M., ed. Schooling for a Global Age. (Illus.). 1979. text ed. 15.95 (ISBN 0-07-004190-3, P&RB). McGraw.

Becker, John. Jaimie. LC 80-65424. 176p. 1981. 10.00 (ISBN 0-87923-340-0). Godine.

Becker, Joseph & Hayes, Robert M. Information Storage & Retrieval: Tools, Elements & Theories. LC 62-12279. (Information Science Ser.). 448p. 1963. 32.95x o.p. (ISBN 0-471-06129-8, Pub. by Wiley-Interscience). Wiley.

Becker, Joseph, jt. auth. see Hayes, Robert M.

Becker, Joseph, ed. Interlibrary Communications & Information Networks. LC 70-185963. 1972. 15.00 o.p. (ISBN 0-8389-3123-5). ALA.

Becker, Judith. Traditional Music in Modern Java. LC 80-19180. (Illus.). 1980. text ed. 30.00x (ISBN 0-8248-0563-1). UH Pr.

Becker, Judith O., jt. ed. see Bruner, Edward M.

Becker, Julie. Animals of the Fields & Meadows. LC 77-8496. (Animals Around Us Ser.). (Illus.). (gr. 2-6). 1977. PLB 7.95 (ISBN 0-88436-394-5). EMC.

--Animals of the Ponds & Streams. LC 77-8497. (Animals Around Us Ser.). (Illus.). (gr. 2-6). 1977. PLB 7.95 (ISBN 0-88436-398-8). EMC.

--Animals of the Seashore. LC 77-8106. (Animals Around Us Ser.). (Illus.). (gr. 2-6). 1977. PLB 7.95 (ISBN 0-88436-392-9). EMC.

--Animals of the Woods & Forests. LC 77-8253. (Animals Around Us Ser.). (Illus.). (gr. 2-6). 1977. PLB 7.95 (ISBN 0-88436-396-1). EMC.

Becker, Lawrence C. Property Rights: Philosophic Foundations. 148p. 1980. pap. 5.95x (ISBN 0-7100-0606-3). Routledge & Kegan.

Becker, Lee, jt. auth. see McCombs, Maxwell E.

Becker, Leonard, Jr. & Gustafson, Clair. Encounter with Sociology: The Term Paper. 2nd ed. LC 76-8791. 1976. pap. cancelled (ISBN 0-87835-056-X). Boyd & Fraser.

Becker, Loftus E. & Goldstein, Joseph. Supplement to Criminal Law: Theory & Process. 1983. pap. 9.95x (ISBN 0-02-912320-8). Free Pr.

Becker, Lucille F. Georges Simenon. (World Authors Ser.). 1977. lib. bdg. 13.95 (ISBN 0-8057-6293-0, Twayne). G K Hall.

Becker, Manning H., jt. auth. see Castle, Emory N.

Becker, Marion R. & Rombauer, Irma. The Joy of Cooking, 2 vols, Vol. 1. Vol. 1. pap. 3.95 (ISBN 0-451-11710-7, AE1710, Sig); Vol. 2. pap. 3.95 (ISBN 0-451-11711-5, AE1711). NAL.

Becker, Marion R., jt. auth. see Rombauer, Irma.

Becker, Marion R., jt. auth. see Rombauer, Irma S.

Becker, Martin J. A History of Catholic Life in the Diocese of Albany, 1609-1864. LC 77-359170. (Monograph: No. 31). (Illus.). 1975. 15.00x (ISBN 0-930060-11-3). US Cath Hist.

Becker, Muriel R. Clifford D. Simak: A Primary & Secondary Bibliography. 1979. lib. bdg. 19.00 (ISBN 0-8161-8063-6, Hall Reference). G K Hall.

Becker, Nancy & Braun, Jack. Family Night at Home: A Manual for Growing Families. Martens, Phyllis & Becker, Dennis, eds. LC 81-67635. (Illus.). 100p. pap. 7.95 (ISBN 0-9606436-0-5); wkbk. 7.95 (ISBN 0-686-36034-6). Kindred Pr.

Becker, Nancy, jt. auth. see Becker, Dennis.

Becker, P. W. Recognitions of Patterns Using the Frequencies of Occurrence of Binary Words. 2nd, rev. ed. (Illus.). 230p. 1974. pap. 24.00 (ISBN 0-387-81506-6). Springer-Verlag.

Becker, Paul & Wood, Elizabeth C. Beard's Massage. 1981. pap. 15.95 (ISBN 0-7216-9592-2). Saunders.

Becker, R., et al, eds. Psychopathological & Neurological Dysfunctions Following Open-Heart Surgery, Milwaukee 1980: Proceedings. (Illus.). 384p. 1983. 57.00 (ISBN 0-387-11621-4). Springer-Verlag.

Becker, R. Frederick & Fix, James A. Outline of Functional Neuroanatomy. (Illus.). 1983. pap. text ed. price not set (ISBN 0-8391-1707-8, 16896). Univ Park.

Becker, Ralph S. & Wentworth, Wayne E. General Chemistry. 2nd ed. LC 79-87864. 1980. text ed. 28.50 (ISBN 0-395-25316-0); instr's. manual 1.20 (ISBN 0-395-25317-9); study guide 10.50 (ISBN 0-395-25318-7); practice problems 1.00 (ISBN 0-395-29341-3). HM.

Becker, Raymond De see De Becker, Raymond.

Becker, Robert. Out of the Tempest: Readings in U. S. History Before 1865. 205p. 1977. pap. text ed. 9.50 o.p. (ISBN 0-8191-0154-0). U Pr of Amer.

Becker, Robert A. Introduction to Theoretical Mechanics. LC 81-20948. 434p. 1983. write for info. (ISBN 0-89874-364-8). Krieger.

--Revolution, Reform, & the Politics of American Taxation, 1763-1783. LC 79-19729. viii, 312p. 1980. 25.00x (ISBN 0-8071-0654-2). La State U Pr.

Becker, Robert D. Pathways to the Present: The United States Since the Civil War. LC 78-68694. 1979. pap. text ed. 11.25 (ISBN 0-8191-0696-8). U Pr of Amer.

Becker, Robert H., ed. Wagner-Camp: The Plains & the Rockies, 1800-1865. rev. ed. LC 81-86051. 1982. 150.00 (ISBN 0-686-97817-X). J Howell.

Becker, Samuel L. Discovering Mass Communication. 1982. pap. text ed. 15.95x (ISBN 0-673-15159-X). Scott F.

Becker, Sarah & Glenn, Donna. How to Make the Most of Your Non-Profit Status. 1983. 14.95 (ISBN 0-910580-16-2). Farnswth Pub.

Becker, Seymour. Russia's Protectorates in Central Asia: Bukhara & Khiva, 1865-1924. LC 67-30825. (Russian Research Center Studies: No. 54). (Illus.). 1968. 22.50x o.p. (ISBN 0-674-78360-3). Harvard U Pr.

Becker, Sidney. Law Enforcement Inc. new ed. 191p. 1973. 8.95 (ISBN 0-89388-100-7). Okpaku Communications.

Becker, Theodore L. & Feeley, Malcolm M., eds. The Impact of Supreme Court Decisions: Empirical Studies. 2nd ed. 1973. pap. text ed. 7.95x (ISBN 0-19-501651-3). Oxford U Pr.

Becker, U. Dictionary of Commercial Law. 992p. 1980. 175.00x (ISBN 0-7121-5489-2, Pub. by Macdonald & Evans). State Mutual Bk.

Becker, Vivienne. Antique & Twentieth Century Jewellery. 336p. 1981. 65.00x o.p. (ISBN 0-7198-0081-1, Pub. by Northwood England). State Mutual Bk.

Becker, Wesley, et al. Teaching: A Course in Applied Psychology. LC 71-154208. 1971. pap. text ed. 16.95 (ISBN 0-574-18425-2, 13-1425); instr's manual 2.95 (ISBN 0-574-18427-9, 13-1427). SRA.

Becker, Wesley C., et al. Teaching 2: Cognitive Learning & Instruction. LC 75-5563. (Illus.). 306p. 1975. pap. text ed. 12.95 (ISBN 0-574-18030-3, 13-6030); instr's guide avail. (ISBN 0-574-18026-5, 13-6026). SRA.

--Teaching 1: Classroom Management. LC 74-31012. (Illus.). 1975. pap. text ed. 12.95 (ISBN 0-574-18025-7, 13-6025); instr's guide avail. (ISBN 0-574-18026-5, 13-6026). SRA.

Becker, William E., jt. ed. see Lewis, Darrell R.

Becker, William H. The Dynamics of Business-Government Relations: Industry, & Exports, 1893 to 1921. LC 81-10318. (Chicago Original Ser.). 1982. lib. bdg. 20.00x (ISBN 0-226-04121-2). U of Chicago Pr.

Becker-Cantarino, Baerbel. Daniel Heinsius. (World Author Ser.). 1978. lib. bdg. 15.95 (ISBN 0-8057-6318-X, Twayne). G K Hall.

Beckerley, James G., jt. ed. see Harrer, Joseph M.

Beckerman, Bernard, ed. see Clarke, Brenna K.

Beckerman, Jay, jt. auth. see Rosner, Bernard.

Beckerman, Wilfred. Two Cheers for the Affluent Society. LC 74-80214. 224p. 1976. pap. 4.95 o.p. (ISBN 0-312-82635-4). St Martin.

Beckers, C., ed. Thyroid Diseases. 236p. 1983. 25.00 (ISBN 0-08-027094-8). Pergamon.

Beckes, Shirley. Things That Go. (Scribbler Play Bks.). (Illus.). 20p. (ps). 1983. pap. write for info. (ISBN 0-307-20328-X). Western Pub.

Beckett. Worstward Ho. 48p. 1983. 8.95 (ISBN 0-394-53230-9). Grove.

Beckett, Arthur W. A see A Beckett, Arthur W.

Beckett, Derrick. Limit State Design of Reinforced Concrete Structures. LC 74-20975. 134p. 1975. 24.95 (ISBN 0-470-06128-6). Halsted Pr.

Beckett, Ian & Gooch, John, eds. Politicians & Defence: Studies in the Formulation of British Defence Policy. 224p. 1982. 20.00 (ISBN 0-7190-0818-2). Manchester.

Beckett, J. Management Dynamics: The New Synthesis. (Management Ser). 1971. text ed. 29.95 (ISBN 0-07-004255-1, C). McGraw.

Beckett, J. V. Coal & Tobacco. (Illus.). 280p. 1981. 49.50 (ISBN 0-521-23486-7). Cambridge U Pr.

Beckett, James C. Short History of Ireland. 6th ed. 1975. 17.50x o.p. (ISBN 0-391-02079-X, Hutchinson U Lib); pap. text ed. 10.25x o.p. (ISBN 0-391-02080-3). Humanities.

Beckett, Kenneth A. Growing Hardy Perennials. (Illus.). 182p. 1982. 14.95 (ISBN 0-7099-0621-8). Timber.

Beckett, Kenneth A. & Carr, David. The Contained Garden: A Complete Illustrated Guide to Growing Plants, Flowers, Fruits, & Vegetables Outdoors in Pots. (Illus.). 168p. 1983. 26.00 (ISBN 0-670-23960-7, Studio); pap. 12.95 (ISBN 0-670-23961-5). Viking Pr.

Beckett, Lucy. Wallace Stevens. 208p. 1974. 37.50 (ISBN 0-521-20278-7); pap. 11.50x (ISBN 0-521-29194-1). Cambridge U Pr.

Beckett, P. J., ed. see Buttle, J. W.

Beckett, Patrick, ed. see Mogollon Conference, March 27-28,1980, Las Cruces, New Mexico.

Beckett, Royce & Hurt, James. Numerical Calculations & Algorithms. LC 81-20894. 1983. write for info. (ISBN 0-89874-415-6). Krieger.

Beckett, Samuel. En Attendant Godot. Bree, Germaine & Schoenfeld, Eric, eds. (Orig.). 1963. pap. text ed. 7.95 (ISBN 0-02-307830-8). Macmillan.

--Ill Seen Ill Said. 50p. 1982. deluxe ed. 100.00 signed (ISBN 0-935716-19-X). Lord John.

--Rockaby & Other Works. 128p. 1981. pap. 3.95 (ISBN 0-686-98283-5, Ever). Grove.

Beckett, Samuel, et al, trs. see Bosquet, Alain.

Beckett, Wendy M., tr. from Latin. John of Ford: Sermons on the Final Verses of the Song of Songs, IV. (Cistercian Fathers Ser.: No. 44). 1983. write for info. (ISBN 0-87907-644-5). Cistercian Pubns.

--John of Ford: Sermons on the Final Verses of the Song of Songs, V (Sermons 62-82) (Cistercian Fathers Ser.: No. 45). 1983. write for info (ISBN 0-87907-645-3). Cistercian Pubns.

Beckey, H. D. Field Ionization & Field Desorption Mass Spectroscopy. 1978. text ed. write for info. (ISBN 0-08-020612-3). Pergamon.

--Principles of Field Ionization & Field Desorption Mass Spectrometry. LC 77-33014. 1971. 56.00 (ISBN 0-08-017557-0). Pergamon.

Beckford, George & Witter, Michael. Small Garden, Bitter Weed: Struggle & Change in Jamaica. 192p. 1982. 20.00 (ISBN 0-86232-003-8, Pub. by Zed Pr England); pap. 9.50 (ISBN 0-86232-008-9, Pub. by Zed Pr England). Lawrence Hill.

Beckford, Grania. Virtues & Vices. 304p. 1981. 13.95 o.p. (ISBN 0-312-84954-0); pap. 5.95 o.p. (ISBN 0-312-84955-9). St Martin.

Beckford, James A. The Trumpet of Prophecy: A Sociological Study of Jehovah's Witnesses. LC 75-14432. 246p. 1975. 29.95 (ISBN 0-470-06138-3). Halsted Pr.

Beckford, William. Modern Novel Writing, 4 vols. in 1. Incl. Azemia. Repr. of 1797 ed. LC 74-81366. 264p. 1970. Repr. of 1796 ed. 40.00x (ISBN 0-8201-1063-9). Schol Facsimiles.

--Vathek: The English Translation by Samuel Henley (1786) & the French Editions of Lausanne & Paris -1787, 3 vols. in 1. facs. ed. LC 72-4324. 768p. (Fr.). 1972. Repr. of 1786 ed. 75.00x (ISBN 0-8201-1102-3). Schol Facsimiles.

Beckham, Barry. Runner Mack. (Howard University Press Library of Contemporary Literature). 213p. 1983. pap. 6.95 (ISBN 0-88258-116-3). Howard U Pr.

Beckham, Barry & Soule, Sandra, eds. The Black Student's Guide to College. 384p. 1982. 15.95 (ISBN 0-525-93256-9, 01549-460); pap. 8.95 (ISBN 0-525-93257-7, 0869-260). Dutton.

Beckham, Stephen D., ed. Tall Tales from Rogue River: The Yarns of Hathaway Jones. LC 73-16524. (Illus.). 192p. 1974. 10.00x o.p. (ISBN 0-253-18654-4). Ind U Pr.

Beckhard, Richard, jt. ed. see Burke, W. Warner.

Beckinsale, Monica & Beckinsale, Robert. Southern Europe: A Systematic Geographical Study. LC 74-14940. (Illus.). 352p. 1975. text ed. 55.00x (ISBN 0-8419-0178-3). Holmes & Meier.

Beckinsale, R. P. Land, Air & Ocean. (Illus.). 1966. 14.95 o.p. (ISBN 0-7156-0203-9). Dufour.

Beckinsale, Robert, jt. auth. see Beckinsale, Monica.

Becklake, John. Man & the Moon. LC 81-51496. (Exploration & Discovery Ser.). PLB 13.80 (ISBN 0-382-06615-4). Silver.

Becklake, Susan. The Solar System. LC 81-51498. (Exploration & Discovery Ser.). PLB 13.80 (ISBN 0-382-06614-6). Silver.

Beckley, John L. Why Didn't Somebody Tell Us! Some Curious but Little-known Facts about the way We Make Our Living. Flint, Helen, ed. (Illus.). 128p. 1982. 12.95 (ISBN 0-910187-00-2). Economic Pr.

Beckley, Tim, jt. auth. see Machlin, Milt.

Becklund, Orville A., jt. auth. see Williams, Charles S.

Beckman, A. L., ed. The Neural Basis of Behavior. (Illus.). 350p. 1982. text ed. 45.00 (ISBN 0-89335-132-6). SP Med & Sci Bks.

Beckman, Bob. Giant Scale Radio Control Aircraft Modeling. Angle, Burr, ed. (Illus., Orig.). 1983. pap. price not set (ISBN 0-89024-049-3). Kalmbach.

Beckman, Delores. Who Loves Sam Grant? LC 82-18211. 160p. (gr. 5-9). 1983. 9.95 (ISBN 0-525-44055-0, 0966-290). Dutton.

Beckman, Ed. Love, Praise & Reward: The New Way to Train Your Dog. LC 78-23938. (Illus.). 1979. 9.95 (ISBN 0-698-10886-8, Coward). Putnam Pub Group.

Beckman, Ericka & Casebere, Jim. Cave Canem. (Illus.). 1982. 25.00x (ISBN 0-9607244-1-9); pap. 6.50x (ISBN 0-9607244-2-7). Cave Canem Bks.

Beckman, Frank S. Mathematical Foundations of Programming. LC 79-1453. 1980. text ed. 26.95 (ISBN 0-201-14462-X). A-W.

Beckman, Gail M., et al. Law for Business & Management. (Illus.). 480p. 1974. text ed. 21.00 (ISBN 0-07-004136-9, G); instructor's manual & key 8.65 (ISBN 0-07-004138-5). McGraw.

Beckman, J. E. & Phillips, J. P. Submillimetre Wave Astronomy. LC 82-4487. (Illus.). 370p. 1982. 47.50 (ISBN 0-521-24733-0). Cambridge U Pr.

Beckman, James. The Religious Dimension of Socrates' Thought. 266p. 1979. pap. text ed. 7.00x (ISBN 0-919812-09-0, Pub. by Wilfred Laurier U Pr Canada). Humanities.

Beckman, Linda, jt. ed. see Eiduson, Bernice T.

Beckman, Patti. The Beachcomber. 192p. (Orig.). 1980. pap. 1.50 (ISBN 0-671-57037-4, Pub. by Silhouette Bks). S&S.

--Captive Heart. 192p. (Orig.). 1980. pap. 1.50 (ISBN 0-671-57008-0, Pub. by Silhouette Bks). S&S.

--Shrimpers Woman. 192p. 1981. pap. 1.50 (ISBN 0-671-57054-4, Pub. by Silhouette Bks). S&S.

Beckman, Petr. The Health Hazards of Not Going Nuclear. 1980. pap. 2.50 (ISBN 0-686-97299-6). Ace Bks.

Beckman, Theodore N. & Foster, Ronald S. Credits & Collections. 8th ed. LC 68-55262. (Illus.). 1969. text ed. 29.95 (ISBN 0-07-004142-3, C); tchr's manual 19.95 (ISBN 0-07-004258-6). McGraw.

Beckman, Theodore N., et al. Wholesaling. 3rd ed. (Illus.). (gr. 9-12). 1959. 29.95 o.p. (ISBN 0-471-06585-4, Pub. by Ronald Pr). Ronald Pr.

Beckman, W. A., jt. auth. see Duffie, J. A.

Beckman, William A., et al. Solar Heating Design: By the F-Chart Method. LC 77-22168. 200p. 1977. 26.95x (ISBN 0-471-03406-1, Pub. by Wiley-Interscience). Wiley.

Beckmann, H., ed. Monoamine Oxidase & Its Selective Inhibitors. (Modern Problems of Pharmacopsychiatry: Vol. 19). (Illus.). 240p. 1983. 84.00 (ISBN 3-8055-3595-3). S Karger.

Beckmann, Martin, et al. Studies in the Economics of Transportation. 1956. 49.50x (ISBN 0-685-89787-7). Elliots Bks.

Beckmann, Peter. A History of Pi. 1976. pap. 4.95 o.p. (ISBN 0-312-38185-9). St Martin.

Beckmann, Petr. Elementary Queuing Theory & Telephone Traffic. 1976. 7.75 (ISBN 0-686-98072-7). Telecom Lib.

--Orthogonal Polynomials for Engineers & Physicists. LC 72-87318. 1973. 25.00x (ISBN 0-911762-14-0). Golem.

--The Structure of Language: A New Approach. LC 72-77116. (Illus.). 320p. 1972. 25.00x (ISBN 0-911762-13-2). Golem.

Beckmann, Petr, tr. see Shevchenko, Viktor V.

Beckmann, Petr, tr. see Weinstein, L. Albertovich.

Beckmann, Petr, tr. see Zakharyev, L. N., et al.

Beckmann, Till. Studien Zur Bestimmung Des Lebens In Meister Eckharts Deutschen Predigten. 244p. (Ger.). 1982. write for info. (ISBN 3-8204-5708-9). P Lang Pubs.

Beckmann, Uwe. Sky Diving. LC 78-66323. (Illus.). 1979. 12.95 o.p. (ISBN 0-8069-4140-5); lib. bdg. 11.69 o.p. (ISBN 0-8069-4141-3); pap. 7.95 (ISBN 0-8069-8852-5). Sterling.

Beckner, Morton. Money Plays. 1981. 10.95 o.p. (ISBN 0-671-25122-8). S&S.

Beckner, Weldon, jt. auth. see Cornett, Joe D.

Beckner, William, et al, eds. Conference on Harmonic Analysis in Honor of Antoni Zygmund. LC 82-11172. (Mathematics Ser.: Vols. I & II). 837p. 1983. 79.95 (ISBN 0-534-98043-0). Wadsworth Pub.

Beckoff, Samuel. English Literature One, 450-1798. (College Outlines Ser.). pap. 4.95 o.p. (ISBN 0-671-08019-9, 08019). Monarch Pr.

--English Literature Two, 1798 to the Present. (College Outines Ser.). pap. 4.95 o.p. (ISBN 0-671-08047-4). Monarch Pr.

Beckoff, Samuel, jt. ed. see Washington, William D.

Beckson, Karl & Ganz, Arthur. Literary Terms: A Dictionary. rev. ed. 228p. 1975. 10.00 o.p. (ISBN 0-374-18800-9); pap. 5.95 (ISBN 0-374-51225-6). FS&G.

Beckwith, B. P. Liberal Socialism Applied: The Applied Welfare Economics of a Liberal Socialist Economy. 1978. 12.00 o.p. (ISBN 0-9603262-0-0). Beckwith.

--Socialist Essays. 1980. 10.00 o.p. (ISBN 0-9603262-1-9). Beckwith.

Beckwith, George C. The Peace Manual; or, War & Its Remedies. LC 73-137529. (Peace Movement in America Ser). 1972. Repr. of 1847 ed. lib. bdg. 16.95x (ISBN 0-89198-056-3). Ozer.

Beckwith, George C., ed. The Book of Peace: A Collection of Essays on War & Peace. LC 70-137528. (Peace Movement in America Ser.). iv, 500p. 1972. Repr. of 1845 ed. lib. bdg. 25.95x (ISBN 0-89198-055-5). Ozer.

Beckwith, Howard B. Calculus for Business & Life. 1978. text ed. 24.95x (ISBN 0-534-00551-9). Wadsworth Pub.

Beckwith, J. Grant's Clinical Electrocardiography. 2nd ed. 1970. 19.95 o.p. (ISBN 0-07-004265-9, HP). McGraw.

Beckwith, John. Ivory Carvings in Early Medieval England. (Illus.). 168p. 1972. 49.00x (ISBN 0-19-921007-1). Oxford U Pr.

Beckwith, John & Kasemets, Udo, eds. The Modern Composer & His World. (Scholarly Reprint Ser.). 1980. Repr. of 1961 ed. 25.00x o.p. (ISBN 0-8020-7090-6). U of Toronto Pr.

Beckwith, Martha W. Hawaiian Mythology. LC 70-97998. 1977. pap. 8.95 (ISBN 0-8248-0514-3). UH Pr.

--The Kumulipo: A Hawaiian Creation Chant. 2nd ed. 260p. 1972. Repr. of 1951 ed. 9.50x o.p. (ISBN 0-8248-0201-2). UH Pr.

Beckwith, Martha W., ed. The Kumulipo: A Hawaiian Creation Chant. LC 79-188978. 276p. 1981. pap. 5.95 (ISBN 0-8248-0771-5). UH Pr.

Beckwith, Neil, et al, eds. AMA Educators Conference, 1979. LC 79-14547. (Proceedings Ser.: No. 44). (Illus.). pap. 24.00 (ISBN 0-87757-121-X). Am Mktg.

Beckwith, T. G., et al. Mechanical Measurements. 3rd ed. 1982. 32.95 (ISBN 0-201-00036-9); solutions manual avail. (ISBN 0-201-00037-7). A-W.

Becquart-Leclerq, Jeanne, ed. Paradoxes du Pouvoir Local. (Travaux et Recherches Ser: No. 38). 1977. lib. bdg. 28.75x o.p. (ISBN 2-7246-0346-X, Pub. by Presses De la Foundation Nationale Sciences Politiques); pap. text ed. 20.00x o.p. (ISBN 2-7246-0339-7). Clearwater Pub.

Becquer, G. A. The Inn of the Cats. Carey, J. R., tr. from Span. (Harrap's Bilingual Ser.). 110p. 1945. 5.00 (ISBN 0-911268-49-9). Rogers Bk.

Becraft, Melvin. Picasso's Guernica: Images within Images. 1983. 6.95 (ISBN 0-533-05440-0). Vantage.

Becton, F. Julian & Morschauser, Joseph, III. The Ship That Would Not Die. LC 80-16263. 1980. 11.95 o.p. (ISBN 0-13-808998-1). P-H.

Becvar, Dorothy S., jt. auth. see Becvar, Raphael J.

Becvar, Raphael J. & Becvar, Dorothy S. Systems Theory & Family Therapy: A Primer. LC 81-43721. 104p. (Orig.). 1982. PLB 19.50 (ISBN 0-8191-2443-5); pap. text ed. 8.25 (ISBN 0-8191-2444-3). U Pr of Amer.

Bedard, Hank. Lucky Thirteen. 1980. pap. 1.50 (ISBN 0-686-38385-0). Eldridge Pub.

--Lucky Thirteen. 1980. pap. 1.50 (ISBN 0-686-38752-X). Eldridge Pub.

Bedard, Roger L. Dramatic Literature for Children: A Century in Review. 1983. pap. text ed. 21.00 (ISBN 0-87602-020-1). Anchorage.

Bedarida, Francois. A Social History of England, Eighteen Fifty-One to Nineteen Seventy-Five. 448p. 1979. 14.95x (ISBN 0-416-85910-0); pap. 13.95x (ISBN 0-416-85920-8). Methuen Inc.

Bedau, Hugo. Justice & Equality. (Central Issues of Philosophy Ser). (Illus.). 1971. pap. 11.95 ref. ed. (ISBN 0-13-514125-7). P-H.

Bedborough, D. R. & Trott, P. E. The Sensory Measurement of Odours by Dynamic Dilution, 1979. 1981. 69.00x (ISBN 0-686-97168-X, Pub. by W Spring England). State Mutual Bk.

Bedborough, D. R., jt. auth. see Bailey, J. C.

Bedbrook, Gerald S. Keyboard Music from the Middle Ages to the Beginnings of the Baroque. 2nd ed. LC 69-15605. (Music Ser). (Illus.). 1973. Repr. of 1949 ed. 21.50 (ISBN 0-306-71056-0). Da Capo.

Beddington. Design for Shopping Centers. 1982. text ed. 59.95. Butterworth.

Beddoe, John. The Anthropological History Europe. 1982. 20.00 (ISBN 0-941694-07-0). Inst Study Man.

Beddoes, Thomas L. Thomas Lovell Beddoes: Selected Poems. Higgens, Judith, ed. 1979. 7.95 o.p. (ISBN 0-85635-192-X, Pub. by Carcanet New Pr England); pap. 4.95 o.p. (ISBN 0-85635-193-8). Humanities.

Beddome, R. H. The Ferns of British India, Vols. I & II. 702p. 1978. 99.00x (ISBN 0-686-84451-3, Pub. by Oxford & I B H India). State Mutual Bk.

Beddow. Testing & Characterization of Powders & Fine Particles. 1980. 49.95 (ISBN 0-471-25602-1, Wiley Heyden). Wiley.

Beddow, J. K. The Production of Metal Powders by Atomizaton. 1977. 52.95 (ISBN 0-471-25601-3, Wiley Heyden). Wiley.

Beddow, John K., ed. Particulate Systems: Technology & Fundamentals. LC 82-1099. (Illus.). 384p. 1983. text ed. 65.00 (ISBN 0-89116-241-0). Hemisphere Pub.

Beddow, Michael. The Fiction of Humanity: Studies in the 'Bildungsroman' from Wieland to Thomas Mann. LC 81-18057. (Anglica Germanica Ser.: No. 2). 250p. 1982. 49.50 (ISBN 0-521-24533-8). Cambridge U Pr.

Beddow, Virginia, ed. The Year of the Bible Manual. (Orig.). 1983. pap. 1.95 (ISBN 0-87239-646-0, 3036). Standard Pub.

Bede, Cuthbert. The Adventures of Mr. Verdant Green. (Illus.). 1982. pap. 9.95x (ISBN 0-19-281331-5). Oxford U Pr.

Bede, Elbert. Five Fifteen-Minute Talks. 1981. Repr. of 1972 ed. 4.50 (ISBN 0-686-43321-1). Macoy Pub.

--Three-Five-Seven Minute Talks on Freemasonry. 1981. Repr. of 1978 ed. 4.00 (ISBN 0-686-43320-3). Macoy Pub.

Bede The Venerable. Ecclesiastical History of the English People. Colgrave, Bertram & Minors, R. A., eds. (Oxford Medieval Texts Ser). 1969. 79.00x (ISBN 0-19-822202-5). Oxford U Pr.

Bedeian, Arthur G. & Glueck, William F. Management. 1977. text ed. 25.95 (ISBN 0-03-061239-X); 10.95 (ISBN 0-03-061242-X); rdgs. & cases 5.95x (ISBN 0-685-69559-X). Dryden Pr.

Bedekar, V. M., tr. see Frauwallner, Erich.

Bedell, Beverly. The Magic Little Ones. LC 75-2964. (Beginning-to-Read Bks). (Illus.). 32p. (gr. 1-3). 1975. PLB 4.39 (ISBN 0-695-80588-6, Dist. by Caroline Hse); pap. 1.95 (ISBN 0-695-30588-3). Follett.

Bedell, Clyde. How to Write Advertising That Sells. 2nd ed. 1952. 6.95 (ISBN 0-07-004299-3, P&RB). McGraw.

Bedell, Gary. Philosophizing with Socrates: An Introduction to the Study of Philosophy. LC 80-5626. 262p. 1980. pap. text ed. 8.75 (ISBN 0-8191-1203-8). U Pr of Amer.

Bedell, George C., et al. Religion in America. 2nd ed. 1982. text ed. 21.95x (ISBN 0-02-307810-3). Macmillan.

Bedell, Madelon. The Alcotts: Biography of a Family. (Illus.). 416p. 1980. 15.95 (ISBN 0-517-54031-2, C N Potter Bks). Crown.

Bedell, Meredith. Stella Benson. (English Authors Ser.). 172p. 1983. lib. bdg. 18.95 (ISBN 0-8057-6845-9, Twayne). G K Hall.

Bederson, Benjamin, jt. auth. see Bates, David.

Bederson, Benjamin, ed. Advances in Atomic & Molecular Physics, Vol. 17. LC 65-18423. (Serial Publication). 1982. 58.00 (ISBN 0-12-003817-X); lib. ed. 75.50 (ISBN 0-12-003886-2); microfiche 41.00 (ISBN 0-12-003887-0). Acad Pr.

Bederson, Benjamin, jt. ed. see Bates, David R.

Bederson, Benjamin, jt. ed. see Bates, Sir David R.

Bedeski, Robert E. The Fragile Entente: The Nineteen Seventy-Eight Japan-China Peace Treaty in a Global Context. (Replica Edition Ser.). 235p. 1983. softcover 18.50x (ISBN 0-86531-944-8). Westview.

--State Building in Modern China: The Kuomintang in the Prewar Period. (China Research Monographs: No. 18). 181p. 1981. pap. 8.00x (ISBN 0-912966-28-9). IEAS.

Bede The Venerable. Ecclesiastical History of the English Nation & Other Writings. Stevens, John, tr. 1978. Repr. of 1910 ed. 9.95x (ISBN 0-460-00479-4, Evman). Biblio Dist.

Bedford, A. D. Defence of Truth. 1979. 27.00 (ISBN 0-7190-0740-2). Manchester.

Bedford, Burnice D. & Hoft, R. G. Principles of Inverter Circuits. LC 64-20078. 413p. 1964. 39.95x (ISBN 0-471-06134-4, Pub. by Wiley-Interscience). Wiley.

Bedford, Emmett G. & Dilligan, Robert J., eds. Concordance to the Poems of Alexander Pope, 2 vols. LC 74-852. 1656p. 1974. Set. 160.00x (ISBN 0-8103-1008-2). Gale.

Bedford, F. W. & Dwivedi, T. D. Vector Calculus. 1970. 26.00 (ISBN 0-07-004720-0, C). McGraw.

Bedford, Frances & Conant, Robert. Twentieth-Century Harpsichord Music: A Classified Catalog. 1974. pap. 9.50 (ISBN 0-913574-08-2). Eur-Am Music.

Bedford, G., ed. see Avens, Roberts.

Bedford, Henry F. & Colbourn, Trevor. The Americans: A Brief History, 1 vol. ed. 3rd ed. 559p. 1980. pap. text ed. 18.95 (ISBN 0-15-502613-5, HC); test bklt. avail. HarBraceJ.

Bedford, John. Kibbutz Volunteer. 157p. (Orig.). pap. 7.95 (ISBN 0-901205-97-4, Pub. by Vaction-Work England). Writers Digest.

Bedford, Mary A., jt. auth. see Harlow, Clarissa.
Bedford, Norton M., et al. Advanced Accounting: An Organizational Approach. 4th ed. LC 78-6961. (Accounting & Information Systems Ser.). 892p. 1979. text ed. 32.95 (ISBN 0-471-02927-0). Wiley.
Bedford, Stewart. How to Teach Children Stress Management & Emotional Control: A Survival Kit for Teachers, Parents, & Kids. 1981. 29.50 (ISBN 0-935930-03-5). Scott Pubns CA.
--Instant Replay. (Illus.). pap. 2.95 (ISBN 0-686-36816-9). Inst Rat Liv.
--Little Sprouts for Health & Fun. Date not set. pap. 2.95 (ISBN 0-935930-04-3). Scott Pubns CA.
--Prayer Power & Stress Management. Date not set. pap. 8.95 (ISBN 0-935930-05-1). Scott Pubns CA.
Bedichek, Wendell M. & Tannahill, Neal. Public Policy in Texas. 1982. pap. text ed. 14.50x (ISBN 0-673-15475-0). Scott F.
Bedient, P. E., jt. auth. see Rainville, E. D.
Bedingfield, James. Accounting & Federal Regulation. (Illus.). 336p. 1982. text ed. 22.95 (ISBN 0-8359-0052-5); pap. text ed. 18.95 (ISBN 0-8359-0051-7). Reston.
Bedini, Silvio A. The Life of Benjamin Banneker. 434p. 1972. 14.95 (ISBN 0-686-36704-9). Md Hist.
Bedlar, Jean W. India in the Mind of Germany: Schelling, Schopenhauer & Their Times. LC 81-40842. 270p. (Orig.). Date not set. lib. bdg. 23.00 (ISBN 0-8191-2191-6); pap. text ed. 11.50 (ISBN 0-8191-2192-4). U Pr of Amer. Postponed.
Bednar, Michael J, ed. Barrier-Free Environments. LC 76-54798. (Community Development Ser.: Vol. 33). 1977. 35.00 (ISBN 0-87933-277-8). Hutchinson Ross.
Bednar, Michael J., ed. Proceedings of the Sixty-Seventh A.C.S.A. Annual Meeting. 288p. 1980. 25.00 o.p. (ISBN 0-686-77618-6); pap. 17.50 o.p. (ISBN 0-686-77619-4). Carrollton Pr.
Bednar, Zdenek F. Keep Your Chin Up. LC 82-73984. 144p. (Orig.). 1983. pap. write for info. (ISBN 0-89272-165-0). Down East.
Bednarek, A. R. & Cesari, L., eds. Dynamical Systems: Symposium, II. 1982. 49.00 (ISBN 0-12-084720-5). Acad Pr.
Bednarski, Gloriana, jt. auth. see Hitchcock, James.
Bednarski, Mary W. & Florczyk, Sandra E. Nursing Home Care As a Public Policy Issue. (Learning Packages in Policy Issues Ser.: No. 4). 62p. (Orig.). 1978. pap. text ed. 1.75x (ISBN 0-936826-13-4). Pol Stud Assocs.
Bednarski, Mary W., jt. auth. see Lubliner, Jerry.
Bedwell, C., ed. Developments in Electronics for Offshore Fields, Vol. 1. (Illus.). 1978. text ed. 42.60x (ISBN 0-85334-753-0, Pub. by Applied Sci England). Elsevier.
Bedwinek, Anne P. Supplemental Audio Cassettes: For Adults with Neurogenic Communicative Disorders. 1981. 75.00 (ISBN 0-88450-732-7, 3136-B). Communication Skill.
Bedworth. Computer Animation. 1983. write for info. (ISBN 0-07-004269-1). McGraw.
Bedworth, Albert E. & Bedworth, David A. Health for Human Effectiveness: A Holistic Approach. (Illus.). 432p. 1982. 23.95 (ISBN 0-13-385500-7). P-H.
Bedworth, David A., jt. auth. see Bedworth, Albert E.
Bedworth, David D. Industrial Systems: Planning, Analysis, Control. 504p. 1973. 32.95x (ISBN 0-471-06654-0); avail. tchrs. manual (ISBN 0-471-07495-0). Wiley.
Bedworth, David D. & Bailey, James E. Integrated Production Control Systems: Management, Analysis, Design. LC 81-10506. 433p. 1982. text ed. 28.95x (ISBN 0-471-06223-5); avail solutions. Wiley.
Bee, Helen S. The Developing Child. 3rd ed. 531p. 1981. text ed. 24.50 scp (ISBN 0-06-040579-1, HarpC); scp study guide 8.50 (ISBN 0-06-043847-9); instr. manual avail. (ISBN 0-06-363832-0). Har-Row.
Bee, Noah. In Spite of Everything: History of the State of Israel. LC 73-77304. (Illus.). 200p. 1973. 7.95 o.p. (ISBN 0-8197-0297-8). Bloch.
Bee, Ooi J. see Ooi Jin Bee.
Beebe, Ann. Easy Cooking, Simple Recipes for Beginning Cooks. (Illus.). 48p. (gr. 4-6). 1972. PLB 8.59 (ISBN 0-688-30039-1). Morrow.
Beebe, Brooke. Best Bets for Babies. (Orig.). 1981. pap. 5.95 (ISBN 0-440-50453-8, Dell Trade Pbks). Dell.
--Tips for Toddlers. (Orig.). 1983. pap. price not set (ISBN 0-440-58658-5, Dell Trade Pbks). Dell.
Beebe, John E., III, jt. ed. see Rosenbaum, C. Peter.
Beebe, Robert P. Voyaging Under Power. (Illus.). 256p. 1975. 12.50 (ISBN 0-915160-18-8). Seven Seas.
Beebe, Ruth. Sallets, Humbles & Shrewsbery Cakes: An Elizabethan Cookbook with Recipes Adapted for the Modern Kitchen. LC 76-14226. (Illus.). 1977. pap. 7.95 (ISBN 0-87923-238-2). Godine.
Beebe, Steven A. & Masterson, John T. Communicating in Small Groups. 1981. text ed. 16.50x (ISBN 0-673-15389-4). Scott F.
Beebee, Trevor J. The Natterjack Toad. (Illus.). 200p. 1983. 16.95 (ISBN 0-19-217709-5). Oxford U Pr.
Beech, D. Command Language Directions. 1980. 53.25 (ISBN 0-444-85450-9). Elsevier.
Beech, G., ed. Computer Assisted Learning in Science Education. 1979. pap. text ed. 45.00 (ISBN 0-08-023010-5). Pergamon.
Beech, Graham. Fortran IV in Chemistry: An Introduction to Computer-Assisted Methods. LC 75-2488. 303p. 1975. 62.95x (ISBN 0-471-06165-4, Pub. by Wiley-Interscience). Wiley.
--Successful Software for Small Computers. LC 82-10881. 182p. 1982. pap. text ed. 14.95 (ISBN 0-471-87458-2). Wiley.
Beech, H. R. & Vaughan, M. Behavioural Treatment of Obsessional States. LC 78-4552. 200p. 1978. 26.95x (ISBN 0-471-99646-7, Pub. by Wiley-Interscience). Wiley.
Beech, H. R., et al. A Behavioural Approach to the Management of Stress: A Practical Guide to Techniques. LC 81-11554. (Studies in Occupational Stress). 132p. 1982. 24.95x (ISBN 0-471-10054-4, Pub. by Wiley Med). Wiley.
Beecham, K. J. History of Cirencester. 344p. 1978. Repr. of 1887 ed. text ed. 24.75x (ISBN 0-904387-18-6, Pub. by Alan Sutton England). Humanities.
Beecham, Thomas. A Mingled Chime: An Autobiography. LC 76-40182. (The Lyric Stage Ser.). 1976. Repr. of 1943 ed. 29.50 (ISBN 0-306-70791-8). Da Capo.
Beechcroft, William. Position of Ultimate Trust. 1982. pap. 2.50 (ISBN 0-451-11551-1, AE1551, Sig). NAL.
Beecher, Addison & Whipple, Colvin. The Racing Yachts. LC 80-20463. (Seafarers Ser.). PLB 19.92 (ISBN 0-8094-2694-3). Silver.
Beecher, Donald, tr. see Caro, Annibal.
Beecher, Donald, tr. see De Turnebe, Odet.
Beecher, Marguerite, jt. auth. see Beecher, Willard.
Beecher, Willard & Beecher, Marguerite. The Sin of Obedience. 88p. (Orig.). 1982. pap. 4.75 (ISBN 0-942350-00-6). Beecher Found.
Beeching, Cyril L. A Dictionary of Eponyms. 2nd ed. 160p. 1983. price not set (ISBN 0-85157-329-0, Pub. by Bingley England). Shoe String.
Beeching, Jack. The Galleys at Lepanto. (Illus.). 272p. 1983. 15.95 (ISBN 0-686-83833-5, ScribT). Scribner.
--Open Path: Christian Missionaries 1515-1914. LC 80-21270. (Illus.). 350p. 1982. 19.95 (ISBN 0-915520-37-0); pap. 10.95 (ISBN 0-915520-53-2). Ross-Erikson.
Beeching, Jack, ed. see Hakluyt, Richard.
Beeching, L. J. Engineering Science: Questions & Answers. (Marine Engineering Ser.). 116p. 1975. pap. 9.95x (ISBN 0-540-07341-5). Sheridan.
Beechy, Winifred. The New China. LC 82-11800. 280p. (Orig.). 1982. pap. 6.95 (ISBN 0-8361-3310-2). Herald Pr.
Beeck, Frans J. van see Van Beeck, Frans J.
Beecroft, Glynis. Carving Techniques. LC 82-82918. (Illus.). 144p. 1983. pap. 7.95 (ISBN 0-668-05715-7, 5715). Arco.
Beede, Gretchen. Simple Sewing. LC 74-33536. (Early Craft Bks). (Illus.). 32p. (gr. 1-4). 1975. PLB 3.95g (ISBN 0-8225-0875-3). Lerner Pubns.
Beedell, Suzanne. Windmills. (Illus.). 222p. 1982. Repr. of 1975 ed. 21.50 (ISBN 0-7153-6811-7). David & Charles.
Beedle, Lynn S. Plastic Design of Steel Frames. LC 58-13454. 406p. 1958. 49.50x (ISBN 0-471-06171-9, Pub. by Wiley-Interscience). Wiley.
Beeforth, T. H. & Goldsmid, H. J. Physics of Solid State Devices. 1970. 15.50x o.p. (ISBN 0-85086-013-X, Pub. by Pion England); pap. text ed. 9.50x o.p. (ISBN 0-85086-014-8). Methuen Inc.
Beeghley, Leonard. Social Stratification in America. LC 78-1551. 1978. 17.95x o.p. (ISBN 0-673-16323-7). Scott F.
Beegle, Shirley. Bible Game Ideas. (Ideas Ser.). (Illus.). 1977. pap. text ed. 1.75 o.p. (ISBN 0-87239-118-3, 7958). Standard Pub.
--Good News Is Jesus. (Bible Puzzle Time Ser.). (Illus.). 16p. (Orig.). (gr. 3-6). 1982. pap. 0.50 (ISBN 0-87239-524-3, 2179). Standard Pub.
Beegle, Shirley, ed. see Sherlock, Connie.
Beehler, Paul J. Contemporary Cash Management: Principles, Practices, Perspectives. LC 77-18998. (Systems & Controls for Financial Management Ser.). 1978. 38.95x (ISBN 0-471-06172-7). Ronald Pr.
--Contemporary Cash Management: Principles, Practices, Perspectives. 2nd ed. (Systems & Control for Financial Management Ser.). 288p. 1983. 34.95x (ISBN 0-471-86861-2). Ronald Pr.
Beehler, Roger & Drengson, Alan R., eds. The Philosophy of Society. 1978. 39.95x (ISBN 0-416-83480-9); pap. 14.50x (ISBN 0-416-83490-6). Methuen Inc.
Beek, W. J. & Muttzall, K. M. Transport Phenomena. LC 74-4651. 332p. 1975. text ed. 43.25 o.p. (ISBN 0-471-06173-5, Pub. by Wiley-Interscience); pap. text ed. 23.00x (ISBN 0-471-06174-3, Pub. by Wiley-Interscience). Wiley.
Beek, Wil van. Hazrat Inayat Khan: Master of Life-Modern Sufi Mystic. 1983. 12.95 (ISBN 0-533-05453-2). Vantage.
Beekman, Allan. The Niihau Incident. (Illus.). 128p. 1982. 9.95 (ISBN 0-9609132-0-3). Heritage Pac.
Beekman, E. M., ed. see Alberts, A.
Beekman, E. M., ed. see Breton de Nijs, E.
Beekman, E. M., ed. see Dermout, Maria.
Beekman, E. M., ed. see Nieuwenhuys, Rob.
Beekman, E. M., ed. see Van Schendel, Arthur.
Beekman, John, ed. Notes on Translation with Drills. 346p. 1965. pap. 3.75 o. p. (ISBN 0-88312-792-X); microfiche 3.75 (ISBN 0-88312-336-3). Summer Inst Ling.
Beekun, Rifeek, jt. auth. see Unus, Iabal.
Beelen, Geertruida C., jt. auth. see Sadee, Wolfgang.
Beeler, J. R. Radiation Effects Computer Experiments. (Defects in Solids Ser.: Vol. 13). 960p. 1982. 168.00 (ISBN 0-444-86315-X, North Holland). Elsevier.
Beeler, Janet. Dowry: Poems. LC 77-18232. (Breakthrough Bks). 72p. 1978. text ed. 6.95 (ISBN 0-8262-0246-2). U of Mo Pr.
Beeler, Myrton F. & Catrou, Paul G. Interpretive Chemical Pathology. (Illus.). 272p. 1983. text ed. 35.00 (ISBN 0-89189-165-X, 45-2-040-00). Am Soc Clinical.
Beeler, Myrton F., jt. ed. see Freeman, James A.
Beeler, Samuel. Understanding Your Car. rev. ed. (gr. 10-12). 1967. 13.28 o.p. (ISBN 0-87345-471-5). McKnight.
Beeley, J. A., jt. ed. see Arbuthnott, J. P.
Beeley, P. R. Foundry Technology. 1972. text ed. 59.95 (ISBN 0-408-70348-2). Butterworth.
Beeman, D. L., ed. Industrial Power Systems Handbook. 1955. 62.00 (ISBN 0-07-004301-9, P&RB). McGraw.
Beemer, Halsey, jt. ed. see Plucknett, Donald L.
Beemster, A. & Dijkstra, J., eds. Viruses of Plants. 1966. 20.75 (ISBN 0-444-10138-1). Elsevier.
Beene, Wayne, jt. ed. see Woodhead, Daniel.
Beenhakker, Arie. A System for Development Planning & Budgeting. 208p. 1980. text ed. 31.25x (ISBN 0-566-00326-0). Gower Pub Ltd.
Beenhakker, Henri L. Handbook for the Analysis of Capital Investments. LC 76-5324. (Illus.). 416p. (Orig.). 1976. lib. bdg. 35.00x (ISBN 0-8371-8901-2, BCI). Greenwood.
Beenhakker, Henri L. & Chammari, Abderraouf. Identification & Appraisal of Rural Roads Projects. (Working Paper: No. 362). 74p. 1979. 5.00 (ISBN 0-686-36219-5, WP-0362). World Bank.
Beenstock, M. A Neoclassical Analysis of Macroeconomic Policy. LC 79-8961. 1981. 37.50 (ISBN 0-521-23077-2). Cambridge U Pr.
Beenstock, Michael. The Foreign Exchanges: Theory, Modelling & Policy. LC 78-1372. 1979. 26.00x (ISBN 0-312-29862-5). St Martin.
--Health, Migration & Development. 192p. 1980. text ed. 27.75x (ISBN 0-566-00369-4). Gower Pub Ltd.
--The World Economy in Transition. 240p. 1983. text ed. 25.00x (ISBN 0-04-339033-1). Allen Unwin.
Beer. Househusbands. LC 82-12079. 176p. 1983. 23.95 (ISBN 0-03-059978-4). Praeger.
Beer, A., jt. ed. see Willardson, Robert.
Beer, A. C., jt. ed. see Willardson, R. K.
Beer, A. C., jt. ed. see Willardson, Robert.
Beer, Alice S. & Graham, Richard. Teaching Music to the Exceptional Child: A Handbook for Mainstreaming. (Illus.). 1980. text ed. 20.95 (ISBN 0-13-893982-9); pap. text ed. 13.95 (ISBN 0-13-893974-8). P-H.
Beer, Barrett L. Northumberland: The Political Career of John Dudley, Earl of Warwick & Duke of Northumberland. LC 73-77386. 180p. 1974. 13.50x (ISBN 0-87338-140-8). Kent St U Pr.
Beer, E. S. de see Locke, John.
Beer, E. S. De see Locke, John.
Beer, F. P. & Johnston, E. R. Mechanics for Engineers, 2 vols. 3rd ed. 1976. Vol. 1: Statistics. 26.95 (ISBN 0-07-004271-3); solns. manual 18.50 (ISBN 0-07-004272-1); Vol. 2: Dynamics. 26.95 (ISBN 0-07-004273-X); solns. manual 25.00 (ISBN 0-07-004270-5); Combined ed. 35.50 (ISBN 0-686-84863-2). McGraw.
Beer, Ferdinand P. & Johnston, E. R. Vector Mechanics for Engineers: Statics. 3rd ed. 1977. text ed. 28.95 (ISBN 0-07-004278-0, C); manual 24.00instructor's (ISBN 0-07-004279-9). McGraw.
Beer, Ferdinand P. & Johnston, E. R., Jr. Vector Mechanics for Engineers Combined. 3rd ed. 1977. text ed. 38.95 (ISBN 0-07-004277-2, C). McGraw.
--Vector Mechanics for Engineers: Dynamics. 3rd ed. 1977. text ed. 28.95 (ISBN 0-07-004281-0, C); solutions manual 25.00 (ISBN 0-07-004282-9). McGraw.
Beer, Ferdinand P. & Johnston, E. Russell, Jr. Mechanics of Materials. (Illus.). 672p. 1981. text ed. 31.50x (ISBN 0-07-004284-5, C); solutions manual 20.00 (ISBN 0-07-004291-8). McGraw.
Beer, Gavin de see De Beer, Gavin.
Beer, Gavin R. De see Locke, John.
Beer, George L. British Colonial Policy, 1754-1765. 10.00 (ISBN 0-8446-1065-8). Peter Smith.
Beer, Gerald A. Applied Calculus for Business & Economics with an Introduction to Matrices. 1978. text ed. 19.95 (ISBN 0-316-08727-0); tchr's ed. avail. (ISBN 0-316-08728-9). Little.
Beer, Gretel. Austrian Cooking & Baking. 224p. 1975. pap. 3.50 (ISBN 0-486-23220-4). Dover.
Beer, J. B. The Achievement of E. M. Forster. 225p. 1982. Repr. of 1962 ed. lib. bdg. 35.00 (ISBN 0-686-98150-2). Darby Bks.
Beer, J. M. & Chigier, N. A. Combustion Aerodynamics. LC 82-13084. 274p. 1982. Repr. of 1972 ed. lib. bdg. 19.50 (ISBN 0-89874-545-4). Krieger.
Beer, John, ed. Coleridge's Variety: Bicentenary Studies. LC 74-2051. 1974. 14.95 (ISBN 0-8229-1114-0). U of Pittsburgh Pr.
Beer, Lawrence W., ed. Constitutionalism in Asia: Asian Views of the American Influence. LC 78-57303. 1979. 28.75x (ISBN 0-520-03701-4). U of Cal Pr.
Beer, Michael. Organizational Change & Development: A Systems View. 1980. pap. text ed. 24.50x (ISBN 0-673-16126-9). Scott F.
Beer, Patricia. Reader, I Married Him: A Study of the Women Characters of Jane Austen, Charlotte Bronte, Elizabeth Gaskell & George Eliot. 1979. pap. 3.95 o.p. (ISBN 0-06-464034-5, BN4034BN). B&N NY.
Beer, Peter H. see Leonard, Robert J. & De Beer, Peter H.
Beer, Peter H. de see Leonard, Robert J. & De Beer, Peter H.
Beer, Samuel H. City of Reason. LC 68-23274. (Harvard Political Studies Ser). 1968. Repr. of 1949 ed. lib. bdg. 16.25x (ISBN 0-8371-0016-X, BECR). Greenwood.
--Treasury Control: The Co-ordination of Financial & Economic Policy in Great Britain. LC 82-11843. viii, 138p. 1982. Repr. of 1957 ed. lib. bdg. 25.00x (ISBN 0-313-23626-7, BETRC). Greenwood.
Beer, Stafford. Decision & Control: The Meaning of Operational Research & Management Cybernetics. LC 66-25668. 556p. 1966. 41.95x (ISBN 0-471-06210-3, Pub. by Wiley-Interscience). Wiley.
--The Heart of Enterprise. LC 79-40532. 582p. 1980. 32.95 (ISBN 0-471-27599-9, Pub. by Wiley-Interscience). Wiley.
--Platform for Change. LC 73-10741. 460p. 1975. 41.95x (ISBN 0-471-06189-1, Pub. by Wiley-Interscience). Wiley.
Beer, T. Environmental Oceanography: An Introduction to the Behaviour of Coastal Waters. (PIL Ser.). (Illus.). 109p. 1983. 40.00 (ISBN 0-08-026291-0); pap. 14.00 (ISBN 0-08-026290-2). Pergamon.
Beer, William R. Househusbands: Men & Housework in American Families. (Illus.). 192p. 1982. text ed. 23.95x (ISBN 0-686-78910-5). J F Bergin.
--Language Policy & National Unity. LC 81-67475. 256p. 1983. text ed. 30.00x (ISBN 0-86598-058-6). Allanheld.
Beer, William R., tr. see Bloch, Mark.
Beerbohm, M. Lytton Strachey. LC 74-7186. (English Literature Ser., No. 33). 1974. lib. bdg. 40.95x (ISBN 0-8383-1936-X). Haskell.
Beerits, Henry. The United Nations & Human Survival. 1976. pap. 1.50 (ISBN 0-686-95386-X). Am Fr Serv Comm.
Beerman. Cell Differentiation & Morphogenesis. 1966. 14.75 (ISBN 0-444-10139-X). Elsevier.
Beer-Poitevin, F. Enciclopedia Medica para la Familia. Moderma. 1770p. (Span.). 1979. 250.00 (ISBN 0-686-97358-5, S-34968). French & Eur.
Beers, A. H., jt. auth. see Coker, W. C.
Beers, Burton F., jt. auth. see Clyde, Paul H.
Beers, Gil. Cats & Bats & Things Like That. 32p. (gr. 1-3). 1972. 5.95 o.p. (ISBN 0-8024-1211-4). Moody.
Beers, Gilbert. Victor Handbook of Bible Knowledge. 640p. 1981. 29.95 (ISBN 0-88207-811-9). Victor Bks.
--With Sails to the Wind. LC 77-24955. (Muffin Family Ser.). (Illus.). (gr. k-5). 1977. 9.95 (ISBN 0-8024-9570-2). Moody.
Beers, Gilbert V. Around the World with My Red Balloon. (ps-3). 1973. 5.95 o.p. (ISBN 0-8024-0303-4). Moody.
--The Book of Life. 6000p. 1980. 299.00x o.p. (ISBN 0-310-79908-2). Zondervan.
Beers, Henry A. The Connecticut Wits & Other Essays. 1920. 14.50x (ISBN 0-686-51360-6). Elliots Bks.
Beers, Henry S., Jr. Computer Leasing. (Data Processing Ser.). (Illus.). 320p. 1982. 30.00 (ISBN 0-534-97929-7). Lifetime Learn.
Beers, John C., jt. auth. see Gafney, Leo.
Beers, Roland F. & Bassett, Edward G., eds. Nutritional Factors: Modulating Effects on Metabolic Processes. (Miles International Symposium Ser.: Vol. 13). 582p. 1981. text ed. 60.50 (ISBN 0-89004-592-5). Raven.
Beers, Roland F., ed. see Miles International Symposium, 12th.
Beers, Roland F., Jr. & Bassett, Edward G., eds. Cell Membrane Receptors for Viruses, Antigens & Antibodies, Polypeptide Hormones, & Small Molecules. LC 75-25108. (Miles International Symposium Ser.: No.9). 554p. 1976. 54.50 (ISBN 0-89004-091-5). Raven.
--Recombinant Molecules: Impact on Science & Society. LC 77-5276. (Miles International Symposium Ser: 10th). 1977. 54.00 (ISBN 0-89004-131-8). Raven.
--The Role of Immunological Factors in Infectious, Allergic, & Autoimmune Processes. LC 75-25109. (Miles International Symposium Ser: No. 8). 556p. 1976. 49.50 (ISBN 0-89004-073-7). Raven.
Beers, V. Gilbert. Along Thimblelane Trails. LC 81-14197. (Muffin Family Ser.). 96p. 1981. 9.95 (ISBN 0-8024-0298-4). Moody.
--Captain Maxi's Secret Island. (Muffin Family Ser.: No. 11). 96p. 1983. 9.95 (ISBN 0-8024-9573-7). Moody.
--Coco's Candy Shop. 32p. (gr. 3-6). 1973. 5.95 o.p. (ISBN 0-8024-1586-5). Moody.

--A Gaggle of Green Geese. (Christian Home Library). (Illus.). 32p. (ps-3). 1974. 5.95 o.p. (ISBN 0-8024-2911-4). Moody.
--Honeyphants & Elebees. (Christian Home Library). 32p. (ps-3). 1974. 5.95 o.p. (ISBN 0-8024-3612-9). Moody.
--The House in the Hole in the Side of the Tree. 32p. (ps-6). 1973. 5.95 o.p. (ISBN 0-8024-3599-8). Moody.
--The Magic Merry-Go-Round. LC 72-94874. 32p. (gr. 2-4). 1973. 5.95 (ISBN 0-8024-5138-1). Moody.
--Muffkins on Parade. LC 82-6338. (Muffin Family Ser.). 96p. 1982. text ed. 9.95 (ISBN 0-8024-9572-9). Moody.
--My Picture Bible to See & to Share. (ps-4). 1982. text ed. 11.95 (ISBN 0-88207-818-6, Sonflower Bks). SP Pubns.
--My Picture Bible to See & to Share. (ps-3). text ed. 11.95 (ISBN 0-88207-818-6). Victor Bks.
--Out of the Treasure Chest. LC 81-1601. (Muffin Family Ser.). (Illus.). 96p. (ps-6). 1981. 9.95 (ISBN 0-8024-6099-2). Moody.
--Over Buttonwood Bridge. LC 78-13103. (Muffin Family Ser.). (ps-4). 1978. 9.95 (ISBN 0-8024-6266-9). Moody.
--Through Golden Windows. LC 75-25535. (Muffin Family Ser.). (Illus.). 144p. 1975. 9.95 (ISBN 0-8024-8753-X). Moody.
--Treehouse Tales. LC 81-19011. (Muffin Family Ser.). (Illus.). 96p. 1982. 9.95 (ISBN 0-8024-9571-0). Moody.
--Under the Tagalong Tree. LC 76-22173. (Muffin Family Ser.). (Illus.). (gr. k-5). 1976. 9.95 (ISBN 0-8024-9021-2). Moody.
--With Mini & Maxi in Muffkinland. LC 80-39767. (Muffin Family Ser.). 79p. (gr. k-4). 1981. 9.95 (ISBN 0-8024-4063-0). Moody.

Beery, Mary. Young Teens & Money. (Young Teens Ser). (gr. 5 up). 1970. PLB 6.95 (ISBN 0-07-005034-1, GB). McGraw.

Beeson, Harold, jt. auth. see Maddox, Bill.

Beeson, Marianne S., jt. auth. see Gurel, Lois M.

Beeson, Paul B. & Bass, David A. The Eosinophil. LC 77-84661. (Major Problems in Internal Medicine Ser.: Vol. 14). (Illus.). 1977. text ed. 16.00 o.p. (ISBN 0-7216-1650-X). Saunders.

Beeson, Paul B., et al. Cecil Textbook of Medicine, 2 vols. 15th ed. LC 77-16994. 1979. text ed. 55.00 single vol. ed. o.p. (ISBN 0-7216-1663-1); Vol. 1. text ed. 32.50 o.p. (ISBN 0-7216-1664-X); Vol. 2. text ed. 32.50 o.p. (ISBN 0-7216-1666-6); Set. text ed. 65.00 o.p. (ISBN 0-7216-1667-4). Saunders.

Beeston, A. F., ed. Selections from the Poetry of Bassar. LC 77-928. 1977. 29.95 (ISBN 0-521-21664-8); pap. 8.95x (ISBN 0-521-29223-9). Cambridge U Pr.

Beeston, Alfred F. Written Arabic: An Approach to the Basic Structures. (Orig.). 1968. 12.95 (ISBN 0-521-09559-X). Cambridge U Pr.

Beetham, William P., Jr., jt. auth. see Pieroni, Robert E.

Beethoven, Ludwig Van. Beethoven's Letters. Eaglefield-Hull, A., ed. Shedlock, J. S., tr. from Ger. LC 73-159687. 1972. pap. 5.95 (ISBN 0-486-22769-3). Dover.
--Complete String Quartets Transcribed for Four-Hand Piano, 2 series. unabr. ed. Ser. 1, 320p. pap. 8.95 (ISBN 0-486-23974-8); Ser. 2, 256p. pap. 7.95 (ISBN 0-486-23975-6). Dover.
--Eighth & Ninth Symphonies in Full Orchestral Score. 392p. 1976. pap. 7.95 (ISBN 0-486-23380-4). Dover.
--First, Second & Third Symphonies; in Full Orchestral Score. 368p. 1976. pap. 8.95 (ISBN 0-486-23377-4). Dover.

Beeton, Douglas R. & Dorner, Helene T. A Dictionary of English Usage in Southern Africa. 1976. 19.95x (ISBN 0-19-570069-4). Oxford U Pr.

Beeton, I. M. Hot & Cold Sweets. 13.50x (ISBN 0-392-03307-0, LTB). Sportshelf.

Beeton, Isabella. Beeton's Book of Household Management: Illustrated with 500 Engravings. 1112p. 1969. 15.00 o.p. (ISBN 0-374-21513-8); pap. 6.95 (ISBN 0-374-51404-6). FS&G.

Beeton, Isabella M. Mrs. Beeton's Cookery & Household Management. Rev. ed. LC 64-3849. (Illus.). 1606p. 1982. Repr. of 1980 ed. 37.50x (ISBN 0-7063-5743-4). Intl Pubns Serv.

Beeton, Mrs. Mrs. Beeton's All About Cookery. (Illus.). 10.95x o.s.i. (ISBN 0-8464-0649-7). Beekman Pubs.

Beets, M. G., ed. Structure-Activity Relationships in Human Chemoreception. (Illus.). 1978. text ed. 49.25x (ISBN 0-85334-746-8, Pub. by Applied Sci England). Elsevier.

Beets, Willem C. Multiple Cropping & Tropical Farming Systems. 250p. 1982. lib. bdg. 30.00 (ISBN 0-86531-518-3). Westview.

Beetz, Carl P. & Satterthwaite, Linton. The Monuments & Inscriptions of Caracol, Belize. (University Museum Monographs: Vol. 45). (Illus.). xiv, 188p. 1982. 25.00x (ISBN 0-934718-41-5). Univ Mus of U PA.

Befu, Ben. Ihara Saikaku: Worldly Mental Calculations. (Publications in Occasional Papers: No. 5). 1976. pap. 18.00x (ISBN 0-520-09406-9). U of Cal Pr.

Beg, M. A. S. Fine Arts in Islamic Civilisation. 5.95 (ISBN 0-686-83581-6). Kazi Pubns.

Beg, Mahmood A. Universal Humanism & One World Order: Philosociopolinomica. (Illus.). 1983. 8.95 (ISBN 0-533-05236-X). Vantage.

Begab, Michael J. & Haywood, H. Carl, eds. Psychosocial Influences in Retarded Performance, Vol. 1. (Issues & Theory in Development Ser.). 352p. 1981. text ed. 19.95 (ISBN 0-8391-1634-9). Univ Park.
--Psychosocial Influences in Retarded Performance, Vol. 2. (Strategies for Improving Competence Ser.). 352p. 1981. text ed. 19.95 (ISBN 0-8391-1635-7). Univ Park.

Begemann, H. & Rastetter, J. Atlas of Clinical Haematology. 2nd ed. Heilmeyer, L., ed. Hirsch, H. J., tr. from Ger. LC 72-86892. (Illus.). xv, 324p. 1972. 118.50 (ISBN 0-387-09404-0). Springer-Verlag.

Begeron, Leandre. The Quebecois Dictionary. 206p. 1983. 28.00 (ISBN 0-89490-092-7); pap. 17.95 (ISBN 0-89490-093-5). Enslow Pubs.

Begg, Ian, jt. auth. see Paivio, Allan.

Beggs, Denise M., jt. auth. see Ross, Cathy R.

Beggs, Donald L. & Lewis, Ernest L. Measurement & Evaluation in the Schools. 1975. 20.50 (ISBN 0-395-18609-9); instr's. manual 2.00 (ISBN 0-395-18795-8). HM.

Beggs, Joseph S. Kinematics. LC 82-15835. (Illus.). 1983. text ed. 24.50 (ISBN 0-89116-355-7). Hemisphere Pub.

Beghi, G., ed. Thermal Energy Storage. 1982. 59.50 (ISBN 90-277-1428-2, Pub. by Reidel Holland). Kluwer Boston.

Begle, Edward G. The Mathematics of the Elementary School. (Illus.). 576p. 1975. text ed. 28.00 (ISBN 0-07-004325-6, C); instructor's manual 5.50 (ISBN 0-07-004327-2). McGraw.

Begleiter, Henry & Kissin, Benjamin, eds. The Pathogenesis of Alcoholism: Biological Factors. (The Biology of Alcoholism Ser.: Vol. 7). 666p. 1983. 62.50x (ISBN 0-686-84491-2, Plenum Pr). Plenum Pub.

Begleiterr, Henry & Kissin, Benjamin, eds. The Pathogenesis of Alcoholism: Psychosocial Factors. (The Biology of Alcoholism Ser.: Vol. 6). 724p. 1983. 69.50x (ISBN 0-306-41053-2, Plenum Pr). Plenum Pub.

Begley, Eve. Of Scottish Ways. (Illus.). 1978. pap. 4.50 (ISBN 0-06-464020-5, BN4020, BN). B&N NY.

Begley, Kathleen A. Deadline. LC 77-2550. (gr. 5-8). 1977. 8.95. o.p. (ISBN 0-399-20611-6). Putnam Pub Group.

Begley, Monie. Rambles in Ireland. rev. ed. LC 79-27302. (Illus.). 1979. 9.95 o.p. (ISBN 0-416-00651-5). Methuen Inc.

Begner, Edith. Just off Fifth. 352p. 1981. pap. 2.95 (ISBN 0-380-77321-X, 77321). Avon.

Begon, Michael. Investigating Animal Abundance. 104p. 1979. pap. text ed. 13.95 (ISBN 0-8391-1387-0). Univ Park.

Beguin, Albert. Leon Bloy: A Study in Impatience. Riley, Edith M., tr. from Fr. 247p. 1982. Repr. of 1947 ed. lib. bdg. 45.00 (ISBN 0-686-94633-2). Century Bookbindery.

Begun, James W. Professionalism & the Public Interest: Price & Quality in Optometry. (Health & Public Policy Ser.). 152p. 1981. 20.00x (ISBN 0-262-02156-0). MIT Pr.

Begus, Sarah & Goodman, Allen C. An Annotated Bibliography of Recent Research on the Elderly. (Public Administration Ser.: Bibliography P 1083). 63p. 1982. pap. 9.75 (ISBN 0-88066-273-5). Vance Biblios.

Behague, Gerard. Music in Latin America: An Introduction. (History of Music Ser.). (Illus.). 1979. text ed. 19.95 (ISBN 0-13-608919-4); pap. text ed. 14.95 (ISBN 0-13-608901-1). P-H.

Behan, P. O. & Currie, S. Clinical Neuroimmunology. (Major Problems in Neurology: Vol. 8). 1978. text ed. 11.00 (ISBN 0-7216-1672-0). Saunders.

Behforooz, Ali, jt. auth. see Holoien, Martin O.

Behler, Donna M., jt. auth. see Tippert-Neilson, Terry E.

Behler, Donna M., jt. auth. see Tippett-Neilson, Terry E.

Behler, Ernst, tr. see Schlegel, Friedrich.

Behler, John, jt. auth. see King, F. Wayne.

Behling, John H. Guidelines for Preparing the Research Proposal. LC 78-54071. 1978. pap. text ed. 7.00 (ISBN 0-8191-0499-X). U Pr of Amer.
--Research Methods: Statistical Concepts & Research Practicum. 1977. pap. text ed. 6.75 (ISBN 0-8191-0084-6). U Pr of Amer.

Behling, Mary, jt. auth. see Gensemer, Robert.

Behlmer, Rudy & Balio, Tino, eds. The Adventures of Robin Hood. LC 79-3971. (Wisconsin-Warner Bros. Screenplay Ser.). (Illus.). 1979. 17.50 (ISBN 0-299-07940-6); pap. 6.95 (ISBN 0-299-07944-9). U of Wis Pr.

Behm, Carl, jt. auth. see Hahn, H. George.

Behm, Herbert C., jt. tr. see Place, Edwin B.

Behm, Richard. Simple Explanations. pap. 3.00 (ISBN 0-686-84328-2, JB40). Juniper Pr WI.

Behn, Aphra. Novels of Mrs. Aphra Behn. LC 72-98812. Repr. of 1913 ed. lib. bdg. 17.00x (ISBN 0-8371-2824-2, BENB). Greenwood.

Behn, Harry. The Faraway Lurs. 1981. PLB 8.95 (ISBN 0-8398-2722-9, Gregg). G K Hall.
--The Faraway Lurs. (Illus.). 192p. 1982. pap. 4.95 (ISBN 0-399-20860-7, Philomel). Putnam Pub Group.

Behn, Judith, ed. see Public Interest Economics Foundation, et al.

Behn, Noel. Big Stick-Up at Brink's! (Illus.). 1977. 10.00 o.p. (ISBN 0-399-11897-7). Putnam Pub Group.
--Seven Silent Men. 1983. 15.50 (ISBN 0-87795-499-2). Arbor Hse.

Behn, Wolfgang. Kurds in Iran: A Selected & Annotated Bibliography. 78p. 1977. pap. 16.00 o.p. (ISBN 0-7201-0700-8, Pub. by Mansell England). Wilson.

Behn, Wolfgang, ed. The Iranian Opposition in Exile: An Annotated Bibliography of Publications from 1962-1979. 249p. (Orig.). 1979. pap. text ed. 32.50x (ISBN 3-447-02064-4). Intl Pubns Serv.

Behnke, Albert R., Jr. & Wilmore, Jack H. Evaluation & Regulation of Body Build & Composition. (International Research Monograph Series in Physical Education). (Illus.). 224p. 1974. ref. ed. 16.95 (ISBN 0-13-292284-3). P-H.

Behnke, Donna A. Religious Issues in Nineteenth Century Feminism. LC 80-52544. 300p. 1982. 22.50x (ISBN 0-87875-203-X). Whitston Pub.

Behnke, H. & Courant, R., eds. Contributions to Functional Analysis. (Eng, Ger. & Fr.). 1966. 28.40 (ISBN 0-387-07768-5). Springer-Verlag.

Behnke, H., et al, eds. Fundamentals of Mathematics, 3 vols. Gould, S. H., tr. Incl. Vol. 1. Foundations of Mathematics: The Real Number System & Algebra. (ISBN 0-262-02048-3); Vol. 2. Geometry. (ISBN 0-262-02069-6); Vol. 3. Analysis. (ISBN 0-262-02049-1). 1974. Set. 60.00x (ISBN 0-262-02143-9); 25.00x ea. MIT Pr.

Behnke, John A., ed. Challenging Biological Problems: Directions Toward Their Solution. 1972. 25.00 (ISBN 0-19-501619-X). Oxford U Pr.

Behr, jt. auth. see Bowen.

Behr, Caroline. T. S. Eliot: A Chronology of His Life & Works. LC 82-16716. 250p. 1982. 25.00x (ISBN 0-686-84435-1). St Martin.

Behr, Edward. The Algerian Problem. LC 75-43947. (Illus.). 256p. 1976. Repr. of 1961 ed. lib. bdg. 20.25x (ISBN 0-8371-8722-2, BEAPR). Greenwood.

Behr, Marcia W., et al. Drama Integrates Basic Skills: Lesson Plans for the Learning Disabled. (Illus.). 144p. 1979. vinyl spiral 12.75x (ISBN 0-398-03881-3). C C Thomas.

Behrangi, Samad. The Little Black Fish & Other Modern Persian Stories. Hooglund, Mary & Hooglund, Eric, trs. from Persian. LC 75-42512. 1982. 14.00 (ISBN 0-914478-21-4); pap. 7.00 (ISBN 0-914478-22-2). Three Continents.

Behrend, Genevieve. Your Invisible Power. 1921. pap. 2.50 (ISBN 0-87516-004-2). De Vorss.

Behrend, George. Luxury Trains: From the Orient Express to the TGV. LC 81-10366. (Illus.). 1982. 35.00 (ISBN 0-86565-016-0). Vendome.

Behrendt, Alex. The Management of Angling Waters. (Illus.). 1978. 15.00 o.s.i. (ISBN 0-233-96857-1). Transatlantic.

Behrendt, Bill. Pocket Magic. 96p. 1982. 17.95 (ISBN 0-13-683847-2); pap. 9.95 (ISBN 0-13-683839-1). P-H.

Behrendt, Walter C. Modern Building: Its Nature, Problems & Forms. LC 78-59005. (Illus.). 1981. Repr. of 1937 ed. cancelled o.p. (ISBN 0-88355-681-2). Hyperion Conn.

Behrenfeld, William H. Accounting Desk Book. 6th ed. 1979. 49.50 o.p. (ISBN 0-87624-009-0). Inst Busn Plan.

Behrens, D., ed. see Gmehling, J., et al.

Behrens, D., ed. see Gmehling, J. & Onken, U.

Behrens, D., ed. see Sorensen, J. M. & Arlt, W.

Behrens, Dieter, ed. see Gmehling, J., et al.

Behrens, Dieter, ed. see Sorenson, J. M. & Arlt, W.

Behrens, Heinrich. Electron Radial Wave Functions & Nuclear Beta-Decay. (International Series of Monographs in Physics). (Illus.). 1982. 98.00x (ISBN 0-19-851297-X). Oxford U Pr.

Behrens, Herman D. & Maynard, Glenn. The Changing Child: Readings in Child Development. 1972. pap. 9.95x (ISBN 0-673-07645-8). Scott F.

Behrens, June. Gung Hay Fat Choy. LC 81-17077. (gr. 1-4). 1982. 9.25 (ISBN 0-516-08842-4). Childrens.
--Ronald Reagan: An All American, Easy Reading Biography. LC 81-9993. (Illus.). 32p. (gr. 2 up). 1981. PLB 8.65 (ISBN 0-516-03565-7). Childrens.

Behrens, Laurence & Rosen, Leonard. Writing & Reading Across the Curriculum. (Orig.). 1982. pap. text ed. 10.95 (ISBN 0-316-09132-4); tchrs'. guide avail. (ISBN 0-316-09133-2). Little.

Behrens, Robert H. Commercial Problem Loans: How to Identify, Supervise & Collect the Problem Loan. LC 74-13733. (Bank Study Ser). 1974. pap. 20.00 o.p. (ISBN 0-87267-021-X). Bankers.
--Commercial Problem Loans: How to Identify, Supervise, & Collect the Problem Loan. 2nd ed. LC 82-16416. 226p. 1983. 35.00 (ISBN 0-87267-039-2). Bankers.

Behrens, Robert H., jt. auth. see Frey, Thomas L.

Behringer, Marjorie P. Techniques & Materials in Biology. LC 80-12458. 608p. 1981. Repr. of 1973 ed. lib. bdg. 28.50 (ISBN 0-89874-175-0). Krieger.

Behrisch, R., et al, eds. Ion Surface Interaction, Sputtering & Related Phenomena. new ed. LC 73-85272. 334p. 1973. 70.00x (ISBN 0-677-15850-5). Gordon.

Behrman, Cynthia F. Victorian Myths of the Sea. LC 76-51694. 188p. 1977. 12.95 (ISBN 0-8214-0351-6, 82-82428). Ohio U Pr.

Behrman, Debra L. Family and-or Career: Plans of First-Time Mothers. Nathan, Peter, ed. LC 82-17572. (Studies in Clinical Psychology: No. 2). 176p. 1982. 34.95 (ISBN 0-8357-1381-4). Univ Microfilms.

Behrman, Howard T., et al. Common Skin Diseases: Diagnosis & Treatment. 3rd ed. LC 75-152649. (Illus.). 186p. 1978. 44.50 o.s.i. (ISBN 0-8089-1102-3). Grune.

Behrman, J. U. S. International Business & Governments. 12.95 o.p. (ISBN 0-07-004361-2, C). McGraw.

Behrman, J. R. Macroeconomic Policy in a Developing Country: Chilean Experience. (Contributions to Economic Analysis: Vol. 109). 1977. 68.00 (ISBN 0-7204-0548-3, North-Holland). Elsevier.

Behrman, J. R. & Hrubec, C. Socioeconomic Success: A Study of the Effects of Genetic Endowments, Family Environment & Schooling. (Contributions to Economic Analysis: Vol. 128). 1980. 59.75 (ISBN 0-444-85410-X). Elsevier.

Behrman, Jack N. Decision Criteria for Foreign Direct Investment in Latin America. LC 74-75185. 89p. 1974. pap. 5.00 (ISBN 0-685-56603-X, COA6, CoA). Unipub.

Behrman, Jere R., jt. auth. see Adams, F. Gerald.

Behrman, Jere R., jt. auth. see Adams, F. Gerard.

Behrman, Jere R. & Hanson, James A., eds. Short-Term Macroeconomic Policy in Latin America: Conference on Planning & Short-Term Marco-Economic Policy in Latin America. LC 78-24053. 400p. 1979. prof ref 30.00x (ISBN 0-88410-489-3, Pub for the National Bureau of Economic Research). Ballinger Pub.

Behrstock, Barry & Trubo, Richard. The Parent's When-Not-to Worry Book: Straight Talk About All Those Myths You've Learned from Your Parents, Friends-- & Even Doctors. LC 80-7894. 256p. 1981. 13.41i (ISBN 0-690-01972-6, HarpT). Har-Row.

Behrstock, Barry & Turbo, Richard. The Parent's When-Not-To-Worry Book. LC 80-7894. 272p. 1983. pap. 4.76i (ISBN 0-686-82652-3, CN 1043, CN). Har-Row.

Beichman, Arnold. Nine Lies About America. LC 76-37468. 345p. 1972. 21.50x (ISBN 0-912050-18-7, Library Pr). Open Court.

Beichman, Arnold & Bernstam, Mikhail. Andropov: New Challenge to the West. 1983. 14.95 (ISBN 0-8128-2921-2). Stein & Day.

Beichman, Janine. Masaoka Shiki. (World Authors Ser.). 1982. lib. bdg. 18.95 (ISBN 0-8057-6504-2, Twayne). G K Hall.

Beidelman, William. Story of the Pennsylvania Germans: Embracing an Account of Their Origin, Their History, Their Dialect. LC 70-81759. 1969. Repr. of 1898 ed. 37.00x (ISBN 0-8103-3571-9). Gale.

Beiderman, Charles & Johnston, William. The Beginner's Handbook of Woodcarving. (Illus.). 192p. 1983. 19.95 (ISBN 0-13-072116-6); pap. 10.95 (ISBN 0-13-072108-5). P-H.

Beidler, Peter G. Fig Tree John: An Indian in Fact & Fiction. LC 76-26345. 1977. 10.50x o.s.i. (ISBN 0-8165-0600-0); pap. 4.95x o.s.i. (ISBN 0-8165-0522-5). U of Ariz Pr.
--John Gower's Literary Transformations in the Confessio Amantis: Original Articles & Translations. 150p. (Orig.). 1982. lib. bdg. 19.75 (ISBN 0-8191-2596-2); pap. text ed. 8.25 (ISBN 0-8191-2597-0). U Pr of Amer.

Beier, Friedrich, ed. see Bochnovic, John.

Beier, Ulli. African Poetry. (Illus., Orig.). 1966. o. p. 10.95 (ISBN 0-521-04140-6); pap. 5.95x (ISBN 0-521-04141-4). Cambridge U Pr.
--The Stolen Images. 64p. 1976. pap. 2.95x (ISBN 0-521-20901-3). Cambridge U Pr.
--Voices of Independence. 1980. 20.00 (ISBN 0-686-42889-7). St Martin.
--Yoruba Myths. LC 79-7645. (Illus.). 88p. 1980. 14.95 (ISBN 0-521-22995-2); pap. 4.95 (ISBN 0-521-22865-4). Cambridge U Pr.

Beier, V. The Return of the Gods. LC 74-12969. (Illus.). 96p. 1975. 29.95 (ISBN 0-521-20717-7). Cambridge U Pr.

Beierle, Herbert L. Autobiography of God. 1979. 10.00 (ISBN 0-940480-05-0). U of Healing.
--How Much of God I Express Is How Much I Profess. 1982. 81.00 (ISBN 0-686-35834-1). U of Healing.
--How to Give a Healing Treatment. 1979. 1.00 (ISBN 0-940480-07-7). U of Healing.

Beigel, Hugo G. Dictionary of Psychology & Related Fields. LC 74-115063. (Ger. & Eng.). 15.00 (ISBN 0-8044-0042-3). Ungar.

Beighey, Clyde & Borchardt, Gordon C. Mathematics for Business, College Course. 5th ed. (Illus.). 256p. 1974. pap. text ed. 13.95 (ISBN 0-07-004370-1, G); instructor's ed. 13.50 (ISBN 0-07-004372-8); tests free (ISBN 0-07-004371-X). McGraw.

Beightler, Charles & Phillips, Donald. Applied Geometric Programming. LC 75-44391. 590p. 1976. 39.95x (ISBN 0-471-06390-8). Wiley.

Beightler, Charles S., et al. Foundations of Optimization. 2nd ed. (International Ser. in Industrial & Systems Engineering). (Illus.). 1979. text ed. 32.95 (ISBN 0-13-330332-2). P-H.

Beighton, John. Short Guide to Rome. 9.50 (ISBN 0-686-86757-2, SpS). Sportshelf.

Beighton, P., et al. Hypermobility of Joints. (Illus.). 105p. 1983. 44.00 (ISBN 0-387-12113-7). Springer-Verlag.

Beigie, Carl E. & Hero, Alfred O., Jr., eds. Natural Resources in U. S. - Canadian Relations: Patterns & Trends in Resource Supplies & Policies, Vol. 2. 1980. lib. bdg. 32.00 (ISBN 0-89158-555-9); pap. text ed. 12.00 (ISBN 0-89158-878-7). Westview.

--Natural Resources in U. S. - Canadian Relations: Perspectives, Prospects, & Policy Options, Vol. 3. 240p. 1983. lib. bdg. 18.50 cancelled (ISBN 0-89158-556-7); pap. text ed. 8.50 cancelled (ISBN 0-89158-879-5). Westview.

--Natural Resources in U. S. - Canadian Relations: The Evolution of Policies & Issues, Vol. 1. (Illus.). 362p. 1980. 30.00 (ISBN 0-89158-554-0); pap. text ed. 10.00x (ISBN 0-89158-877-9). Westview.

Beijing Bureau of Parks & Gardens, Staff. Chinese Chrysanthemums. (Illus.). 74p. (Orig.). 1981. pap. 13.95 (ISBN 0-8351-0965-8). China Bks.

Beijing Foreign Institute. The Pinyin Chinese English Dictionary. Wu Jingrong, ed. LC 79-2477. 976p. 1979. 68.95x (ISBN 0-471-27557-3, Pub. by Wiley-Interscience); pap. 15.00 (ISBN 0-471-86796-9). Wiley.

Beijing Institute of Foreign Trade Staff, jt. ed. see Beijing Language Institute.

Beijing Language Institute. Elementary Chinese-Supplement. (Elementary Chinese Readers). 277p. 1982. pap. 4.95 (ISBN 0-8351-1038-9). China Bks.

Beijing Language Institute & Beijing Institute of Foreign Trade Staff, eds. Business Chiness 500. 309p. (Orig.). 1982. pap. 4.95 (ISBN 0-8351-1039-7). China Bks.

Beijing Language Institute Staff, ed. Annotated Chinese Proverbs. (Elementary Chinese Readers). (Illus.). 178p. (Orig.). 1982. pap. 4.95 (ISBN 0-8351-1100-8). China Bks.

Beijing Symposium on Cardiothoracic Surgery & Brewer, Lyman A. Proceedings. 400p. 1982. 50.00x (ISBN 0-471-87327-6, Pub. by Wiley Med). Wiley.

Beil, Don. The Visicalc Book: Apple Edition. 1982. text ed. 22.95 (ISBN 0-8359-8398-6); pap. text ed. 14.95 (ISBN 0-8359-8397-8). Reston.

--The Visicalc Book: IBM PC Edition. 1982. text ed. 21.95 (ISBN 0-8359-8395-1); pap. text ed. 15.95 (ISBN 0-8359-8396-X). Reston.

Beil, Donald. The Visicalc Book: Atari Edition. 1982. text ed. 21.95 (ISBN 0-8359-8394-3); pap. text ed. 14.95 (ISBN 0-8359-8393-5). Reston.

Beil, Norman, et al, eds. see Beverly Hills Bar Association. Barristers Committee for the Arts.

Beilenson, Edna, ed. A Lover's Almanac. (Illus.). 64p. 1983. 3.95 (ISBN 0-88088-032-5). Peter Pauper.

Beilke, Marlan. Shining Clarity: God & Man in the Works of Robinson Jeffers. rev. ed. (Illus., Orig.). 1980. pap. write for info o.p. (ISBN 0-918466-05-9). Quintessence.

Beilner, H. & Gelenbe, E., eds. Measuring, Modelling & Evaluating Computer Systems: Proceedings of the Third International Workshop on Modelling & Performance Evaluation of Computer Systems, Bonn. 1978. 68.00 (ISBN 0-444-85058-9, North-Holland). Elsevier.

Beilstein Institute for Literature of Organic Chemistry. Beilstein-Leitfaden: Eine Anleitung Zur Benutzung Von Beilsteins Handbuch der Organischen Chemie. 56p. 1975. pap. 361.10 (ISBN 0-387-07431-7). Springer-Verlag.

Beim, George. Principles of Modern Soccer. LC 76-11986. (Illus.). 1977. pap. text ed. 21.95 (ISBN 0-395-24415-3). HM.

Beim, Jerrold. Andy & the School Bus. (Illus.). (gr. k-3). 1947. PLB 9.12 (ISBN 0-688-31022-2). Morrow.

--The Smallest Boy in the Class. (Illus.). (gr. k-3). 1949. PLB 9.12 (ISBN 0-688-31442-2). Morrow.

Beim, Jerrold, jt. auth. see Beim, Lorraine.

Beim, Lorraine. Triumph Clear. LC 46-3638. (gr. 7 up). 1966. pap. 0.65 (ISBN 0-15-691161-2, VoyB). HarBraceJ.

Beim, Lorraine & Beim, Jerrold. Two Is a Team. LC 73-12939. (Illus.). 58p. (gr. k-3). 1974. pap. 1.25 (ISBN 0-15-692050-6, VoyB). HarBraceJ.

Bein, Vic. Mountain Skiing. (Illus.). 192p. (Orig.). 1982. pap. 8.95 (ISBN 0-89886-034-2). Mountaineers.

Beinart, William. The Political Economy of Pondoland, 1860-1930: Production, Labour, Migrancy & Chiefs in Rural South Africa. LC 81-21619. (Afican Studies: No. 33). (Illus.). 232p. 1982. 39.50 (ISBN 0-521-24393-9). Cambridge U Pr.

Beineke, John A. Death & the Secondary School Student. LC 79-62895. 1979. pap. text ed. 6.50 o.p. (ISBN 0-8191-0715-8). U Pr of Amer.

Beiner, Ronald, ed. see Arendt, Hannah.

Beining, Guy R. The Raw-Robed Few & Other Poems. 1979. pap. 4.95 (ISBN 0-930090-11-X). Applezaba.

Beirne, Francis F. The Amiable Baltimoreans. LC 68-9401. xiv, 400p. 1968. Repr. 40.00x (ISBN 0-8103-5031-9). Gale.

Beirne, Gerald. The New England Sports Trivia Book. LC 82-50959. (Illus.). 176p. (Orig.). 1983. pap. 10.95 (ISBN 0-911658-47-5). Yankee Bks.

Beirne, Piers & Quinney, Richard. Marxism & Law. LC 81-15927. 381p. 1982. text ed. 16.95x (ISBN 0-471-08758-0). Wiley.

Beiser. Physics. 3rd ed. 1982. 25.95 (ISBN 0-8053-0381-2); study guide 8.95 (ISBN 0-8053-0383-9); instr's. manual with tests 4.95 (ISBN 0-8053-0382-0). Benjamin-Cummings.

Beiser, A. Schaum's Outline of Applied Physics. (Schaum's Outline Ser.). 1976. pap. 6.95 (ISBN 0-07-004377-9). McGraw.

Beiser, Arthur. Concepts of Modern Physics. 3rd ed. (Illus.). 544p. 1981. text ed. 25.50 (ISBN 0-07-004382-5). McGraw.

--The Earth. rev. ed. LC 80-52607. (Life Nature Library). PLB 13.40 (ISBN 0-8094-3935-2). Silver.

--The Earth. (Young Readers Library). (Illus.). 1977. PLB 6.80 (ISBN 0-8094-1368-X). Silver.

--Perspectives of Modern Physics. 1969. text ed. 33.50 (ISBN 0-07-004350-7, C). McGraw.

--Physical Science. (Schaum's Outline Ser.). 320p. 1974. pap. text ed. 5.95 (ISBN 0-07-004376-0, SP). McGraw.

--Physics. 2nd ed. LC 77-87340. 1978. 25.95 o.p. (ISBN 0-8053-0379-0); instr's guide 7.95 o.p. (ISBN 0-8053-0380-4). Benjamin-Cummings.

--Schaum's Outline of Mathematics for Electricity & Electronics. (Schaum's Outline Ser.). (Illus.). 208p. 1980. pap. 5.95 (ISBN 0-07-004378-7, SP). McGraw.

Beiser, Arthur & Krauskopf, Konrad B. Introduction to Earth Science. (Illus.). 320p. 1975. text ed. 27.50 (ISBN 0-07-004368-X, C); instructor's manual 15.00 (ISBN 0-07-004369-8). McGraw.

Beiser, Arthur, jt. auth. see Krauskopf, Konrad B.

Beiser, Karl. Twenty-Five Ski Tours in Maine: From Kittery to Caribou, A Cross-Country Skiers Guide. LC 79-64992. (Twenty-Five Ski Tours Ser.). (Illus.). 128p. 1979. pap. 5.95 (ISBN 0-89725-006-0). Backcountry Pubns.

Beisert, Heide H. Poor Fish. Koenig, Marion, tr. from Ger. (Illus.). 32p. (gr. 1-5). 1982. lib. bdg. 10.95 (ISBN 0-571-12514-X). Faber & Faber.

Beishir, Lois. Microbiology in Practice: Individualized Instruction for the Allied Health Sciences. 3rd ed. 320p. 1982. pap. text ed. 15.50 scp (ISBN 0-06-040587-2, HarpC); instrs'. manual avail. (ISBN 0-06-360636-4). Har-Row.

Beisner, Monika. Fantastic Toys. LC 74-79249. (Picture Bk). (Illus.). 24p. (gr. k-2). 1974. 5.95 o.s.i. (ISBN 0-695-80504-5); PLB 6.99 o.s.i. (ISBN 0-695-40504-7). Follett.

Beist, Van der see Van der Beist.

Beitler, Ethel J. & Lockhart, Bill C. Design for You. 2nd ed. LC 73-76050. 247p. 1969. 26.95x (ISBN 0-471-06337-1). Wiley.

Beitz, Donald & Hansen, R. G. Animal Products in Human Nutrition. (Nutrition Foundation Monograph). 1982. 62.00 (ISBN 0-12-086380-4). Acad Pr.

Beitzel, Wallace, jt. auth. see Harter, James.

Beja, Morris & Gontarski, S. E., eds. Samuel Beckett: Humanistic Perspectives. (Illus.). 237p. 1983. 20.00 (ISBN 0-8142-0334-5). Ohio St U Pr.

Bejan, Adrian. Entropy Generation Through Heat & Fluid Flow. LC 82-8414. 248p. 1982. 39.95 (ISBN 0-471-09438-2, Pub. by Wiley-Interscience). Wiley.

Bejarano & Sanchez. Obligaciones Civiles. 2nd ed. 608p. (Span.). 1983. pap. text ed. write for info (ISBN 0-06-310066-5, Pub. by HarLA Mexico). Har-Row.

Bejerot, Nils. Addiction & Society. (Illus.). 272p. 1970. photocopy ed. spiral 27.50x (ISBN 0-398-00126-X). C C Thomas.

Bekefi, George. Electromagnetic Vibrations, Waves, & Radiation. Barrett, Alan H., ed. LC 77-10421. 1978. pap. text ed. 21.95x (ISBN 0-262-52047-8). MIT Pr.

--Principles of Laser Plasmas. LC 76-28311. 736p. 1976. 71.95x (ISBN 0-471-06345-2, Pub. by Wiley-Interscience). Wiley.

Bekemeier, H., ed. Trends in Inflammation Research Two. Hirschelmann, R. (Agents & Actions Supplements: Vol. 10). 315p. 1982. text ed. 37.95 (ISBN 3-7643-1344-7). Birkhauser.

Beker, Henry & Piper, Fred. Cipher Systems: The Protection of Communications. 350p. 1983. 34.95 (ISBN 0-471-89192-4, Pub. by Wiley-Interscience). Wiley.

Beker, Simon, ed. Diagnostic Procedures in the Evaluation of Hepatic Diseases. LC 82-20324. (Laboratory & Research Methods in Biology & Medicine Ser.: Vol. 7). 620p. 1983. write for info. (ISBN 0-8451-1656-8). A R Liss.

Bekiroglu, Haluk, ed. Simulation in Inventory & Production Control. 1983. softbound 20.00 (ISBN 0-686-42972-9). Soc Computer Sim.

Bekkari, Muhammad, tr. see Badawi, Gamal.

Bekker, Leander J. De see Vizetelly, Frank H. & De Bekker, Leander J.

Bekkum, D. W. Van see VanBekkum, D. W.

Bekkum, O. Van see Van Bekkum, O. & De Vries, H.

Belady, L. A., jt. ed. see Maekawa, M.

Belair, Richard L. Double Take. LC 79-17056. 192p. (gr. 7-9). 1979. 9.75 (ISBN 0-688-22202-1); PLB 9.36 (ISBN 0-688-32202-6). Morrow.

Belais, Paul T. Belais' Master Index to Computer Programs in BASIC. LC 78-67465. (Orig.). 1979. pap. 9.95 (ISBN 0-932542-00-X). Falcon Pub.

Beland, Irene & Passos, Joyce. Clinical Nursing: Pathophysiological & Psychosocial Approaches. 4th ed. 1981. text ed. 39.95x (ISBN 0-02-307890-1). Macmillan.

Belanger, Maurice, jt. auth. see Purpel, David.

Belasco, Bernard. The Entrepreneur as Culture Hero: Pre-Adaptations in Nigerian Economic Development. 239p. 1980. 27.95x (ISBN 0-686-92307-3). J F Bergin.

Belasco, David. The Girl of the Golden West. 1978. lib. bdg. 11.95 (ISBN 0-8398-2457-2, Gregg). G K Hall.

Belasco, James A. & Hampton, David R. Management Today. 2nd ed. LC 80-28981. 460p. 1981. text ed. 22.95 (ISBN 0-471-08579-0); avail. tchrs. manual. Wiley.

Belasco, Leonard, ed. Northwords. 66p. (Orig.). 1981. pap. 12.95 (ISBN 0-915032-23-6). Natl Poet Foun.

Belasco, Warren J. Americans on the Road: From Autocamp to Motel. (Illus.). 1979. 20.00 (ISBN 0-262-52071-0); pap. 6.95 (ISBN 0-686-96795-X). MIT Pr.

Belash, Rachel P., tr. see Almendros, Nestor.

Belbin, R. M. Management Teams Why They Succeed or Fail. 179p. 1981. 24.95 (ISBN 0-470-27172-8). Halsted Pr.

Belch, Jean, ed. Contemporary Games: A Directory & Bibliography Describing Play Situations or Simulations, Vol. 1: Directory. LC 72-6353. 1973. 92.00x (ISBN 0-8103-0968-8). Gale.

--Contemporary Games: A Directory & Bibliography Describing Play Situations or Simulations, Vol. 2. LC 72-6353. 1974. 82.00x (ISBN 0-8103-0969-6). Gale.

Belchamber, David, tr. see Wein, Horst.

Belcher, David W. Compensation Administration. (Industrial Relations & Personnel Ser). (Illus.). 576p. 1974. ref. ed. 24.95 (ISBN 0-13-154161-7). P-H.

Belcher, E. H. & Vetter, H., eds. Radioisotopes in Medical Diagnosis. 2nd ed. (Illus.). 1971. 69.50 o.p. (ISBN 0-407-38400-6). Butterworth.

Belcher, James E., et al. Experiments & Problems for College Chemistry. 6th ed. (Illus., Orig.). 1961. pap. text ed. 18.95 (ISBN 0-13-295352-8). P-H.

Belcher, Richard. Layman's Guide to the Inerrancy Debate. LC 79-27015. 1980. pap. 2.95 (ISBN 0-8024-2379-5). Moody.

Belcher, Supply. The Harmony of Maine. Hitchcock, H. Wiley, ed. LC 77-169607. (Earlier American Music Ser: Vol. 6). 104p. 1972. Repr. of 1794 ed. lib. bdg. 21.50 (ISBN 0-306-77306-6). Da Capo.

Belden, Bernard R. The Eighth Day of the Week. 3rd ed. Henry, Bamman A., ed. (Kaleidoscope Ser.). 1978. pap. text ed. 7.48 (ISBN 0-201-40881-3, Sch Div); tchr's. ed. 8.04 (ISBN 0-201-40882-1). A-W.

Belden, Donald L. The Role of the Buyer in Mass Merchandising. LC 70-181779. (Chain Store Age Bks). (Illus.). 256p. 1971. 15.95 (ISBN 0-86730-510-X). Lebhar Friedman.

Belden, Jack. Retreat with Stillwell. (China in the 20th Century Ser). (Illus.). 368p. 1975. Repr. of 1943 ed. lib. bdg. 32.50 (ISBN 0-306-70734-9). Da Capo.

--Still Time to Die. (China in the 20th Century Ser). xi, 322p. 1975. Repr. of 1944 ed. lib. bdg. 32.50 (ISBN 0-306-70735-7). Da Capo.

Belden, Louise. Two Hundred Years of American Party Tables. (Illus.). 1983. 49.95 o.p. (ISBN 0-393-01618-8). Norton.

Belden, Louise C. The Festive Tradition: Table Decoration & Desserts in America, 1650-1900. (Winterthur Museum Book). (Illus.). 1983. 40.00 (ISBN 0-393-01618-8). Norton.

Belden, Wilanne S. The Rescue of Ranor. LC 82-13806. 192p. (gr. 5-8). 1983. 10.95 (ISBN 0-689-30951-1, Argo). Atheneum.

Belen, Hermogenes F. Philippine Creative Handicrafts. (Illus.). (gr. k-4). 1977. 6.75x o.p. (ISBN 0-686-09536-7). Cellar.

Belfast Free Library, ed. see Williamson, Joseph.

Belfield, W. O. & Zucker, M. The Very Healthy Cat Book. 264p. 1983. 14.95 (ISBN 0-07-004367-1, GB); pap. 6.95 (ISBN 0-07-004354-X). McGraw.

Belfield, Wendel & Zucker, Martin. How to Have a Healthier Dog. 1982. pap. 2.95 (ISBN 0-451-11833-2, AE1833, Sig). NAL.

Belfield, Wendel Q. & Zucker, Martin. How to Have a Healthier Dog: The Benefits of Vitamins & Minerals for Your Dog's Life Cycles. LC 80-1081. 288p. 1981. 13.50 (ISBN 0-385-15992-7) Doubleday.

Belfiglio, Valentine J. American Foreign Policy. LC 78-66047. (Illus.). 1979. pap. text ed. 8.50 o.p. (ISBN 0-8191-0681-X). U Pr of Amer.

--American Foreign Policy. 2nd ed. (Illus.). 152p. 1983. pap. text ed. 10.00 (ISBN 0-8191-2677-2) U Pr of Amer.

Belfiore, F. New Events & Facts in Diabetes. (Frontiers in Diabetes: Vol. 2). (Illus.). x, 190p. 1983. 68.50 (ISBN 3-8055-3541-4). S Karger.

Belford, G. & Liu, C. L. Structured Pascal. 384p. 1983. 13.95 (ISBN 0-07-038138-0); write for info. instr's manual (ISBN 0-07-038139-9). McGraw.

Belford, Lee A., ed. Religious Dimensions in Literature. 160p. (Orig.). 1982. pap. 6.95 (ISBN 0-8164-2360-1). Seabury.

Belford, Roz, ed. Collector Circle Gazette. 16p. 4.00 (ISBN 0-686-37039-2). Collector Circle.

Belfrage, Cedric, tr. see Selser, Gregorio.

Belgatom. Nuclear Fuel Supply Industry in the European Community. 141p. 85.00x (ISBN 0-686-97540-5, Pub. by Graham & Trotman England). State Mutual Bk.

Belgatom, ed. Nuclear Fuel Supply Industry in the European Community. 194p. 1983. pap. 35.00x (ISBN 0-8448-1424-5). Crane-Russak Co.

Belgrado, Fernando D., ed. Songs of the Synagogue of Florence, 2 Vols. Incl. Vol. 1. The Three Festivals (ISBN 0-87203-108-X); Vol. 2. The High Holy Days. 0p (ISBN 0-87203-109-8). (Illus.). 60p. 1982. 32.95 ea. Hermon.

Belgrano, Giovanni. Let's Make a Movie. LC 72-90235. (Illus.). 48p. (gr. 4-9). 1973. 6.95 (ISBN 0-87592-028-4). Scroll Pr.

Belgrave, Robert. Oil Supply & Price: Future Crisis Management. (Atlantic Papers: No. 48). 32p. (Orig.). 1982. pap. text ed. 6.50x (ISBN 0-86598-115-9). Allanheld.

Belgrave, Robert, jt. auth. see Badger, Daniel.

Belgum, David. Religion & Personality in the Spiral of Life. LC 79-66478. 1979. pap. text ed. 12.50 (ISBN 0-8191-0832-4). U Pr of Amer.

Beliaev, Alexander. Professor Dowell's Head. Bouis, Antonina W., tr. (Best of Soviet Science Fiction). 1981. 10.95 o.p. (ISBN 0-02-016580-3). Macmillan.

Belinfante, J. G. & Kolman, B. A Survey of Lie Groups & Lie Algebra. LC 72-77081. ix, 164p. 1972. 17.50 (ISBN 0-89871-044-8). Soc Indus-Appl Math.

Beling, Carl, ed. The LH - Releasing Hormone. LC 80-80300. (Illus.). 368p. 1980. text ed. 45.75x (ISBN 0-89352-045-4). Masson Pub.

Beling, Willard A., ed. King Faisal & the Modernisation of Saudi Arabia. LC 79-5134. 1979. lib. bdg. 32.50 (ISBN 0-89158-693-8); text ed. 16.00. Westview.

--The Middle East: Quest for an American Policy. LC 73-4281. (Illus.). 364p. 1973. 39.50 o.p. (ISBN 0-87395-228-6); microfiche 23.50 o.p. (ISBN 0-87395-229-4). State U NY Pr.

Belisle, Bertrand. The Myths of Satan. 64p. 1982. 6.95 (ISBN 0-89962-284-4). Todd & Honeywell.

Belisle, Serge, jt. ed. see Barwin, Norman B.

Belitt, Ben, ed. see Lorca, Federico G.

Belitt, Ben, ed. & tr. see Neruda, Pablo.

Belitt, Ben, tr. see Machado, Antonio.

Beljanski, M. The Regulation of DNA Replication & Transcription. (Experimental Biology & Medicine Ser.: Vol. 8). x, 180p. 1983. pap. 70.25 (ISBN 3-8055-3631-3). S Karger.

Belk, J. A., ed. Electron Microscopy & Microanalysis of Crystalline Materials. (Illus.). 1979. 41.00x (ISBN 0-85334-816-2, Pub. by Applied Sci England). Elsevier.

Belka, Bro. Marion S. Being & Becoming, An Action Approach to Group Guidance: Commitment. 1970. pap. text ed. 2.96 o.p. (ISBN 0-685-07622-9, 81061); leader's manual 3.76 o.p. (ISBN 0-02-810620-2). Glencoe.

Belka, Bro. Marion S., ed. Being & Becoming, An Action Approach to Group Guidance: Encounter. 1966. pap. text ed. 2.96 o.p. (ISBN 0-02-810570-2); leader's manual 3.76 o.p. (ISBN 0-02-810580-X). Glencoe.

--Being & Becoming, An Action Approach to Group Guidance: Identity. 1967. pap. text ed. 2.96 o.p. (ISBN 0-02-810600-8); leader's manual 3.76 o.p. (ISBN 0-685-07644-X). Glencoe.

--Being & Becoming, An Action Approach to Group Guidance: Involvement. 1968. pap. text ed. 2.96 o.p. (ISBN 0-02-810550-8); leader's manual 3.76 o.p. (ISBN 0-02-810560-5). Glencoe.

Belkaoui, Ahmed. Accounting Theory. 318p. 1981. pap. text ed. 14.95 (ISBN 0-15-500470-0, HC); solutions manual 2.95 (ISBN 0-15-500471-9). HarBraceJ.

--Cost Accounting: A Multidimensional Emphasis. 656p. 1983. text ed. 29.95 (ISBN 0-03-061121-0). Dryden Pr.

Belkin, Gary S. Comntemporary Psychotherapies. 1981. pap. 16.50 (ISBN 0-395-30781-3). HM.

Belkin, Gary S. & Goodman, N. Marriage, Family & Intimate Relationships. 1980. pap. text ed. 21.95 (ISBN 0-395-30560-8); Instr's. manual 1.00 (ISBN 0-395-30561-6). HM.

Belkin, Gary S. & Skydell, Ruth H. Foundations of Psychology. LC 78-69566. (Illus.). 1979. text ed. 21.95 o.p. (ISBN 0-395-25363-2); instr's. annotated ed. 22.95 o.p. (ISBN 0-395-25364-0); study guide 9.50 o.p. (ISBN 0-395-25365-9); test items 0.70 o.p. (ISBN 0-395-25366-7); test items manual II 1.30 o.p. (ISBN 0-395-28483-X); 9.50 o.p. (ISBN 0-395-25365-9). HM.

Belkin, Gary S., jt. auth. see Miller, Douglas R.

Belkin, John N. Fundamentals of Entomology. 220p. 1976. pap. 12.95x (ISBN 0-916846-10-5). Flora & Fauna.

Belkind, Allen, ed. Dos Passos, the Critics & the Writer's Intention. LC 70-156782. (Crosscurrents-Modern Critiques Ser.). 351p. 1971. 9.95 o.p. (ISBN 0-8093-0522-4). S Ill U Pr.

Belknap, George N. The Blue Ribbon University. 1976. pap. 1.25 (ISBN 0-87114-082-9). U of Oreg Bks.

--Henry Villard & the University of Oregon. 1976. pap. 2.00 (ISBN 0-87114-083-7). U of Oreg Bks.

--The University of Oregon Charter. 1976. pap. 1.25 (ISBN 0-87114-081-0). U of Oreg Bks.

Belknap, Jeremy. Foresters, an American Tale, 1792. LC 71-100127. 1969. Repr. of 1792 ed. 30.00x (ISBN 0-8201-1071-X). Schol Facsimiles.

Belknap, Jodi P. Majesty: The Exceptional Trees of Hawaii. Cazimero, Momi, ed. LC 82-60598. 72p. 1982. 12.95 (ISBN 0-686-38728-7). Outdoor Circle.

Belknap, Michael R. Cold War Political Justice: The Smith Act, the Communist Party, & American Civil Liberties. LC 77-4566. (Contributions in American History: No. 66). 1977. lib. bdg. 29.95x (ISBN 0-8371-9692-2, BCW/). Greenwood.

Bell. Fundamentals of Engineering Geology. 1983. text ed. write for info. (ISBN 0-408-01169-6). Butterworth.

--Industrial Noise Control. (Mechanical Engineering Ser.). 536p. 1982. 75.00 (ISBN 0-8247-1787-2). Dekker.

--One Thousand One Questions about Radiologic Technology, Vol. 2. 192p. 1982. pap. text ed. 9.95 (ISBN 0-8391-1774-4). Univ Park.

--Purdue Thirty-Sixth Industrial Waste Conference Proceedings. LC 77-84415. 997p. 1982. 69.95 (ISBN 0-250-40493-1). Ann Arbor Science.

Bell & Klammer. The Practicing Writer. 1983. pap. text ed. 11.95 (ISBN 0-686-84570-6, RM89); instr's. manual avail. (RM90). HM.

Bell & Weinber. Homosexualities. 1979. 5.95 o.p. (ISBN 0-671-25150-3, Touchstone Bks). S&S.

Bell & Hyman, eds. Mumby's Publishing & Bookselling in the 20th Century. 6th ed. 1982. 35.00 (ISBN 0-7135-1341-1). Bowker.

Bell, A., et al. Land & Water Resources. (Place & People Ser.: No. 6). 1977. pap. text ed. 4.95x o.p. (ISBN 0-435-34698-9). Heinemann Ed.

Bell, A. Craig, ed. & tr. see Dumas, Alexandre.

Bell, A. Fleming, jt. ed. see Burby, Raymond.

Bell, A. G. The Machine Plays Chess. 1978. text ed. 17.00 o.s.i. (ISBN 0-08-021221-2); pap. text ed. 8.95 (ISBN 0-08-021222-0). Pergamon.

Bell, Adam C. & Nerem, Robert M., eds. Advances in Bioengineering, 1975. 108p. 1975. pap. text ed. 12.00 o.p. (ISBN 0-685-62570-2, G00097). ASME.

Bell, Alan P. & Weinberg, Martin S. Homosexualities: A Study of Diversity Among Men & Women. 1978. 12.95 o.p. (ISBN 0-671-24212-1). S&S.

Bell, Alexander G. Memoir Upon the Formation of a Deaf Variety of the Human Race. 1969. 7.50 o.p. (ISBN 0-88200-083-7, L9109). Alexander Graham.

Bell, Alexis T. & Hegedus, L. Louis, eds. Catalysis Under Transient Conditions. (ACS Symposium Ser.: No. 178). 1982. write for info. (ISBN 0-8412-0688-0). Am Chemical.

Bell, Alexis T., jt. ed. see Hollahan, John R.

Bell & Howell Audio-Visual Products Division. Master It! with the Language Master. LC 78-52959. 1978. pap. 6.50 o.p. (ISBN 0-8224-4409-7). Pitman Learning.

Bell, Andrew. A History of Feudalism: British & Continental. 360p. 1982. Repr. of 1863 ed. lib. bdg. 75.00 (ISBN 0-686-81829-6). Darby Bks.

Bell, Ann O., ed. see Woolf, Virginia.

Bell, Ann Oliver, ed. The Diary of Virginia Woolf: Vol. 2, 1920-1924. LC 78-23882. 1980. pap. 5.95 (ISBN 0-15-626037-9, Harv). HarBraceJ.

Bell, Anne Oliver, ed. Diary of Virginia Woolf: Vol. 1, 1915-1919. LC 78-23882. 1979. pap. 3.95 (ISBN 0-15-626036-0, Harv). HarBraceJ.

--Diary of Virginia Woolf, Vol. 3: 1925-1930. LC 77-73111. 400p. 1981. pap. 8.95 (ISBN 0-15-626038-7, Harv). HarBraceJ.

Bell, Anthea, tr. see Andersen, H. C.

Bell, Anthea, tr. see Damjan, Mischa.

Bell, Anthea, tr. see Donnelley, Elfie.

Bell, Anthea, tr. see Pesek, Ludek.

Bell, Anthea, tr. see Sonnleitner, A. T.

Bell, Anthea, tr. see Wilkon, Jozef & Bauman, Kurt.

Bell, Arthur & Klammer, Thomas. The Practicing Writer. LC 82-83411. 224p. 1983. pap. text ed. 12.95 (ISBN 0-395-32564-1); write for info. instr's. manual (ISBN 0-395-32565-X). HM.

Bell, Arthur S., Jr. Peter Charlie: The Cruise of the PC 477. LC 82-71794. (Illus.). 384p. 1982. 14.95 (ISBN 0-910355-00-2). Courtroom Comp.

Bell, Aubrey F. Benito Arias Montano. 1922. pap. 2.50 (ISBN 0-87535-009-7). Hispanic Soc.

Bell, Betsy. Nurse Carrie's Island. 1982. 6.95 (ISBN 0-686-84162-X, Avalon). Bouregy.

Bell, Bob. The Digest Book of Upland Game Shooting. (The Sports & Leisure Library). (Illus.). 96p. 1979. pap. 2.95 o.s.i. (ISBN 0-686-66063-3). Follett.

Bell, Bruce A., jt. auth. see Mandt, Mikkel G.

Bell, Bruce W. A Little Dab of Color. (gr. 5 up). 1980. 9.75 (ISBN 0-688-51956-3); lib. bdg. 9.36 (ISBN 0-686-82942-5). Lothrop.

Bell, Bryan, ed. World Directory of Pharmaceutical Manufacturers. 4th ed. 316p. (Orig.). 1982. pap. 250.00x (ISBN 0-906184-03-7). Intl Pubns Serv.

Bell, C. F. & Lott, K. A. Modern Approach to Inorganic Chemistry. 3rd ed. 398p. 1972. pap. 18.95 o.p. (ISBN 0-408-70371-7). Butterworth.

Bell, C. G. & Newall, A. Computer Structures Readings & Examples. 1971. 42.95 (ISBN 0-07-004357-4, C). McGraw.

Bell, Carol, ed. Seminar on Antigen: Antigen-Antibody Reactions Revisited. 247p. 1982. 25.00 (ISBN 0-914404-80-6); non-members 27.00 (ISBN 0-686-83050-4). Am Assn Blood.

--A Seminar on Antigens on Blood Cells & Body Fluids. 205p. 1980. 21.00 (ISBN 0-914404-61-X). Am Assn Blood.

--A Seminar on Immune: Mediated Cell Destruction. (Illus.). 208p. 1981. 25.00 (ISBN 0-914404-70-9). Am Assn Blood.

--A Seminar on Laboratory Management of Hemolysis. 160p. 1979. 21.00 (ISBN 0-914404-44-X). Am Assn Blood.

Bell, Carol W. Columbiana County Ohio: 1860 Census Index. 57p. 1972. 5.00 o.s.i. (ISBN 0-941610-05-5). C W Bell.

--Muskingum County Ohio Genealogical Guide. 46p. 1979. 8.00 (ISBN 0-941610-01-2). C W Bell.

--Ohio Genealogical Guide. 2nd ed. 169p. 1979. 10.00 (ISBN 0-941610-02-0). C W Bell.

--Ohio Genealogical Periodical Index: A County Guide. 3rd ed. 80p. 1981. 8.00 (ISBN 0-941610-03-9). C W Bell.

--Wood County Ohio Genealogical Guide. 75p. 1979. 8.00 (ISBN 0-941610-04-7). C W Bell.

Bell, Charles. The Anatomy & Philosophy of Expression as Connected with the Fine Arts. 265p. 1982. Repr. of 1846 ed. lib. bdg. 100.00 (ISBN 0-89760-096-7). Telegraph Bks.

--Delta Return. rev. ed. LC 70-3119. 1969. 5.00 o.p. (ISBN 0-910220-04-2). Berg.

Bell, Charles H. Texas Real Estate. 3rd ed. LC 70-75612. (Illus.). 228p. 1977. 14.95 (ISBN 0-87201-845-8). Gulf Pub.

Bell, Sir Charles. Illustrations of the Great Operations of Surgery. 134p. 1975. 95.50 (ISBN 0-471-09474-9, Pub. by Wiley Med). Wiley.

Bell, Chip R. Influencing: Marketing the Ideas That Matter. LC 82-7772. 185p. 1982. text ed. 17.95 (ISBN 0-89384-051-3). Learning Concepts.

Bell, Chip R. & Nadler, Leonard. The Client-Consultant Handbook. (Building Blocks of Human Potential Ser.). 278p. 1979. 17.95 (ISBN 0-87201-113-5). Gulf Pub.

Bell, Clare. Ratha's Creature. LC 82-13875. 264p. (gr. 7 up). 1983. 11.95 (ISBN 0-689-50262-1, Argo). Atheneum.

Bell, Colin & Encel, Sol, eds. Inside the Whale: Ten Personal Accounts of Social Research. 1978. text ed. 20.00 (ISBN 0-08-022244-7); pap. text ed. 15.25 (ISBN 0-08-022243-9). Pergamon.

Bell, Coral. The Diplomacy of Detente: The Kissinger Era. LC 77-82634. 1977. 18.95x (ISBN 0-312-21122-8). St Martin.

--Negotiation from Strength: A Study in the Politics of Power. LC 77-1054. 1977. Repr. of 1963 ed. lib. bdg. 20.00x (ISBN 0-8371-9508-X, BENS). Greenwood.

Bell, Corydon, jt. auth. see Bell, Thelma.

Bell, D. J., ed. Recent Mathematical Developments in Control: Proceedings of University of Bath Conference, Sept. 1973. 1973. 66.00 o.s.i. (ISBN 0-12-085050-8). Acad Pr.

Bell, D. J. & Cook, P. A., eds. Design of Modern Control Systems. (IEE Control Engineering Ser.: No. 20). 400p. 1982. pap. 49.50 (ISBN 0-906048-74-5). Inst Elect Eng.

Bell, D. Rayford. The Philosophy of Christ. LC 81-90174. 165p. 1982. 6.95 (ISBN 0-9604820-5-9); pap. 4.95 (ISBN 0-686-37782-6). Adams Pr.

Bell, Daniel. Coming of Post-Industrial Society: A Venture in Social Forecasting. LC 72-89178. 1976. 18.95x o.p. (ISBN 0-465-01281-7); pap. 7.95x (ISBN 0-465-09713-8, CN-5013). Basic.

--The Cultural Contradictions of Capitalism. LC 75-7271. 384p. 1976. o.s. 17.95x (ISBN 0-465-01526-3); pap. 7.95 (ISBN 0-465-09727-8, CN-5027). Basic.

--The Social Sciences Since the Second World War. LC 80-27957. 104p. 1981. 16.95 (ISBN 0-686-82989-1); pap. text ed. 5.95 (ISBN 0-87855-872-1). Transaction Bks.

Bell, Daniel & Kristol, Irving, eds. The Crisis in Economic Theory. LC 80-70392. 242p. 1981. 15.50 (ISBN 0-465-01476-3); pap. 6.00 (ISBN 0-465-01477-1). Basic.

Bell, David. Frege's Theory of Judgement. 1979. text ed. 32.50x (ISBN 0-19-827423-8). Oxford U Pr.

--Fundamentals of Electric Circuits. 2nd ed. 688p. 1981. text ed. 24.95 (ISBN 0-8359-2128-X); instrs. manual avail. (ISBN 0-8359-2129-8); lab manual & study guide 8.95 (ISBN 0-8359-2131-X). Reston.

Bell, David A. Fundamentals of Electronic Devices. (Illus.). 480p. 1974. 22.95 (ISBN 0-87909-276-9); students manual avail. Reston.

Bell, David E. Conflicting Objectives in Decisions. LC 77-5064. (Wiley International Ser. on Applied Systems Analysis). 442p. 1977. pap. 41.00x (ISBN 0-471-99506-1, Pub. by Wiley-Interscience). Wiley.

Bell, David V. Power, Influence & Authority: An Essay in Political Linguistics. 1975. 12.95 (ISBN 0-19-501904-0); pap. 7.95x (ISBN 0-19-501903-2). Oxford U Pr.

Bell, Derrick, ed. Shades of Brown: New Perspectives on School Desegregation. LC 80-21877. 1980. text ed. 12.95x (ISBN 0-8077-2595-1). Tchrs Coll.

Bell, Derrick A., Jr. Race, Racism & American Law. 1973. 24.00 (ISBN 0-316-08821-8). Little.

Bell, Derrick, Jr. Race, Racism, & American Law. 2nd ed. 1980. text ed. 22.00 o.p. (ISBN 0-316-08821-8). Little.

Bell, Donald. Being a Man: The Paradox of Masculinity. 1982. 12.95 (ISBN 0-86616-013-2). Lewis Pub Co.

Bell, Eric T. Men of Mathematics. (Illus.). 1937. pap. 10.75 (ISBN 0-671-46401-9, Fireside). S&S.

Bell, Evelyn & Dunlop, Stewart. Industry & Resources. (Place & People Ser.: No. 5). (Illus.). 1977. pap. text ed. 4.95x o.p. (ISBN 0-435-34696-2). Heinemann Ed.

Bell, F. G. Engineering Properties of Soils & Rocks. (Illus.). 144p. 1981. pap. text ed. 13.95 (ISBN 0-408-00537-8). Butterworth.

--Foundation Engineering in Difficult Ground. 1978. 94.95 (ISBN 0-408-00311-1). Butterworth.

Bell, F. T. & Smith, F. Seymour. Library Bookselling: A History & Handbook of Current Practice. 128p. 1966. 10.50 (ISBN 0-686-94104-7, 05771-1, Pub. by Gower Pub Co England). Lexington Bks.

Bell, F. W., jt. auth. see Hazleton, J. E.

Bell, Frederick. Engineering Geology & Geotechnics. (Illus.). 1980. text ed. 67.95 (ISBN 0-408-00355-3). Butterworth.

Bell, Frederick & Canterbery, Ray. Aquaculture for Developing Countries: A Feasibility Study. 288p. 1976. 30.00x (ISBN 0-88410-296-3). Ballinger Pub.

Bell, Frederick W. Food from the Sea: The Economics & Politics of Ocean Fisheries. LC 77-28756. (Special Studies in Natural Resources & Energy Management Ser.). (Illus.). 1978. lib. bdg. 33.00 o.p. (ISBN 0-89158-403-X); pap. 13.50 o.p. (ISBN 0-89158-350-X). Westview.

Bell, Garrett De see DeBell, Garrett.

Bell, Gary & Seay, Davin R. Lost but Not Forever. LC 80-81472. 1981. pap. 4.95 o.p. (ISBN 0-89081-253-5). Harvest Hse.

Bell, Geoffrey. Eight Millimeter Film for Adult Audiences. 1968. pap. 2.25 o.p. (ISBN 92-3-100715-7, U215, UNESCO). Unipub.

Bell, Gertrude. First Crop. LC 72-89608. (Illus.). (gr. 5-8). 1973. 6.50 o.p. (ISBN 0-8309-0082-9). Ind Pr MO.

--A Ladder for Silvanus. (Illus.). 48p. (gr. 1-4). 1974. 5.00 o.p. (ISBN 0-8309-0126-4). Ind Pr MO.

--Roundabout Road. LC 72-4574. (Illus.). (gr. 4-8). 1972. 6.00 o.p. (ISBN 0-8309-0074-8). Ind Pr MO.

Bell, Gertrude L., jt. auth. see Ramsay, W. M.

Bell, Gwen, ed. Strategies for Human Settlements: Habitat & Environment. LC 76-5416. (Illus.). 200p. (Orig.). 1976. 9.95 o.p. (ISBN 0-8248-0414-7, Eastwest Ctr); pap. 3.95 (ISBN 0-8248-0469-4). UH Pr.

Bell, H. C., et al. Guide to British West Indian Archive Materials, in London & in the Islands, for the History of the United States. 1926. pap. 36.00 (ISBN 0-527-00688-2). Kraus Repr.

Bell, Harold I. Egypt, from Alexander the Great to the Arab Conquest. LC 77-8057. (Gregynog Lectures for 1946). 1977. Repr. of 1948 ed. lib. bdg. 19.75x (ISBN 0-8371-9093-2, BEEA). Greenwood.

Bell, Harold I., ed. Jews & Christians in Egypt. LC 79-97270. (Judaica Ser). (Illus.). 140p. 1972. Repr. of 1924 ed. lib. bdg. 15.50x (ISBN 0-8371-2587-1, BEJA). Greenwood.

Bell, Howard, ed. see Delany, M. R. & Campbell, Robert.

Bell, Ian F. Critic As Scientist: The Modernist Poetics of Ezra Pound. LC 80-41826. 320p. 1981. 29.95x (ISBN 0-416-31350-7). Methuen Inc.

Bell, Ian F. A., ed. Ezra Pound: Tactics for Reading. LC 82-11542. (Critical Studies Ser.). 248p. 1982. text ed. 28.50x (ISBN 0-389-20283-5). B&N Imports.

Bell, Inge P. CORE & the Strategy of Nonviolence. 1968. pap. text ed. 3.95x (ISBN 0-394-30776-3). Phila Bk Co.

Bell, Irene W. Literature Cross-A-Word Book II: Crossword Learning Experiences with Historical Fiction Mystery & Detective Stories, & Newbery Award Winners. (Illus.). 96p. 1982. pap. 12.50 (ISBN 0-89774-070-X). Oryx Pr.

Bell, Irene W. & Brown, Robert B. Gaming in the Media Center Made Easy. (Illus.). 200p. 1982. lib. bdg. 22.50 (ISBN 0-87287-336-6). Libs Unl.

Bell, Irene W. & Kirby, Keith E. Literature Cross-A-Word Book I: Crossword Learning Experiences with Animal Stories, Modern Fantasy, & Space & Time. (Illus.). 96p. (gr. 4-8). 1982. pap. 12.50 (ISBN 0-89774-062-9). Oryx Pr.

Bell, Irene W., jt. auth. see Wieckert, Jeanne E.

Bell, J. & Machover, M. A Course in Mathematical Logic. 1977. text ed. 42.75 (ISBN 0-7204-2844-0, North-Holland). Elsevier.

Bell, J., tr. see Nicod, Jean.

Bell, J. Bowyer. The Secret Army: The IRA, 1916-1979. rev. ed. (Illus.). 508p. 1980. text ed. 35.00x (ISBN 0-262-02145-5). MIT Pr.

Bell, J. G., jt. auth. see Stone, Wilfred.

Bell, J. L. & Slomson, A. B. Models & Ultra Products: An Introduction. 1972. pap. 28.00 (ISBN 0-444-10119-5, North-Holland). Elsevier.

Bell, James K. & Cohn, Adrian. Rhetoric in a Modern Mode, with Selected Readings. 3rd ed. 1976. pap. text ed. 13.95x (ISBN 0-02-470600-0). Macmillan.

--Rhetoric Three: The Rhetoric Section from Rhetoric in a Modern Mode. 3rd ed. 1976. pap. text ed. 7.95x (ISBN 0-02-470620-5). Macmillan.

Bell, James K. & Cohn, Adrian A. Handbook of Grammar, Style & Usage. 3rd ed. 1981. pap. text ed. 9.95x (ISBN 0-02-470640-X). Macmillan.

Bell, Jimmy, jt. ed. see Owens, Charles E.

Bell, John. An Employee Management Handbook. 384p. 1981. 40.00x (ISBN 0-85950-326-7, Pub. by Thornes England). State Mutual Bk.

Bell, John F. A History of Economic Thought: A Structured Approach to the Data Communications Environment. 2nd ed. LC 79-22893. 754p. 1980. Repr. of 1967 ed. lib. bdg. 32.50 (ISBN 0-89874-065-7). Krieger.

Bell, John L., Jr. Hard Times: Beginnings of the Great Depression in North Carolina, 1929-1933. (Illus.). xi, 87p. 1982. pap. 3.00 (ISBN 0-86526-196-2). NC Archives.

Bell, John M., ed. Thirty-Seven Purdue University Industrial Waste Conference, 1982. LC 77-84415. (Illus.). 1000p. 1983. 69.95 (ISBN 0-250-40592-X). Ann Arbor Science.

Bell, John M., ed. see Purdue University Industrial Waste Conference, 35th.

Bell, Joseph N. Love Theory in Later Hanbalite Islam. LC 78-5904. 1979. PLB 49.50x (ISBN 0-87395-244-8). State U NY Pr.

Bell, Josephine. A Deadly Place to Stay. 192p. 1983. 12.95 (ISBN 0-8027-5496-1). Walker & Co.

--Victim. 192p. 1983. pap. 2.95 (ISBN 0-8027-3021-3). Walker & Co.

Bell, Julius, jt. auth. see Fomon, Samuel.

Bell, K. W. & Parrish, R. G. Computational Skills with Applications. 448p. 1975. pap. text ed. 18.95 (ISBN 0-669-91082-1); instructor's manual 1.95 (ISBN 0-669-93237-X). Heath.

Bell, L. F., jt. auth. see Grant, Eugene L.

Bell Laboratories. Human Factors in Telecommunications International Symposium, 9th. 1980. 75.00 (ISBN 0-686-37981-0). Info Gatekeepers.

Bell, Laurel & Garthwiate, Elloyse M. Accelerated Grammar. 1982. pap. text ed. 17.95 (ISBN 0-8403-2778-1). Kendall-Hunt.

Bell, Linda. The Red Butterfly: Coping with Lupus Disease. 1983. pap. 4.95 (ISBN 0-8283-1880-8). Branden.

Bell, Lorna & Seyfer, Eudora. Gentle Yoga for People with Arthritis, Stroke Damage, Multiple Sclerosis & in Wheelchairs. (Illus.). 140p. 1982. pap. 6.50 (ISBN 0-911119-01-9). Igram Pr.

Bell, Madison S. The Washington Square Ensemble. 336p. 1983. 15.75 (ISBN 0-670-75005-0). Viking Pr.

Bell, Martin. Return of the Wolf. 1983. 8.95 (ISBN 0-8164-0545-X). Seabury.

--Songs from the Way of the Wolf. Seabury.

--Stories from the Way of the Wolf. Seabury.

--Way of the Wolf. (Epiphany Ser.). 144p. 1983. pap. 2.95 (ISBN 0-345-30522-1). Ballantine.

--Way of the Wolf: The Gospel in New Images. LC 77-120366. (Illus.). 1970. 7.95 (ISBN 0-8164-0202-7); 2 records 7.95 ea. Seabury.

Bell, Martin L. Marketing: Concepts & Strategy. 3rd ed. LC 78-69572. (Illus.). 1979. text ed. 26.50 (ISBN 0-395-26503-7); instr's. manual 1.65 (ISBN 0-395-26504-5). HM.

Bell, Marty. Breaking Balls. 1979. pap. 2.25 o.p. (ISBN 0-451-08549-3, E8549, Sig). NAL.

--The Legend of Dr. J: The Story of Julius Erving. LC 74-16636. (Illus.). 224p. 1975. 7.95 o.p. (ISBN 0-698-10639-3, Coward). Putnam Pub Group.

--The Legend of Dr. J. The Story of Julius Erving. (RL 8). 1976. pap. 2.95 (ISBN 0-451-12179-1, AE2179, Sig). NAL.

--No Hard Feelings. 264p. 1980. 11.95 o.p. (ISBN 0-670-36136-4). Viking Pr.

Bell, Marvin. Old Snow Just Melting: Essays & Interviews. (Poets on Poetry Ser.). 200p. 1983. pap. 7.95 (ISBN 0-472-06342-1). U of Mich Pr.

--Stars Which See: Stars Which Do Not See. LC 76-39922. 1977. pap. 4.95 (ISBN 0-689-10779-X). Atheneum.

Bell, Marvin, jt. auth. see Stafford, William.

Bell, Mervyn, ed. Britain's National Parks. LC 74-20450. (Illus.). 160p. 1975. 17.95 o.p. (ISBN 0-7153-6792-7). David & Charles.

Bell, Michael. The Sentiment of Reality. 224p. 1983. text ed. 22.50x (ISBN 0-04-801023-5). Allen Unwin.

Bell, Michael E. & Lande, Paul S., eds. Regional Dimensions of Industrial Policy. LC 80-8994. 224p. 1981. 23.95x (ISBN 0-669-04491-1). Lexington Bks.

Bell, Michael J. The World from Brown's Lounge: An Ethnography of Black Middle-Class Play. LC 82-4732. 208p. 1983. 14.95 (ISBN 0-252-00956-8). U of Ill Pr.

Bell, Millicent. Hawthorne's View of the Artist. LC 62-13566. 1962. 29.50x o.s.i. (ISBN 0-87395-008-9); microfiche 16.50 o.s.i. (ISBN 0-87395-108-5). State U NY Pr.

Bell, Millicent, ed. see Hawthorne, Nathaniel.

Bell, Mimi. Offbeat Oregon. (Orig.). 1983. pap. 6.95 (ISBN 0-87701-274-1). Chronicle Bks.

Bell, Muriel, tr. see Bianco, Lucien.

Bell, P. & Evans, J. Counseling the Black Client: Alcohol Use & Abuse in Black America. 1981. 3.95 (ISBN 0-89486-124-7). Hazelden.

Bell, P. R. & Woodcock, C. L. The Diversity of Green Plants. 1983. price not set. E Arnold.

Bell, Paul A., et al. Environmental Psychology. LC 77-84684. (Illus.). 1978. text ed. 16.95 o.p. (ISBN 0-7216-1706-9). Saunders.

Bell, Peter. Basic Teaching for Slow Learners. 1971. 10.50 o.p. (ISBN 0-584-10851-6). Transatlantic.

Bell, Philip W., jt. auth. see Edwards, Edgar O.

Bell, Quentin. On Human Finery. 2nd rev. & en. ed. LC 76-9129. (Illus.). 1978. 14.95x o.p. (ISBN 0-8052-3629-5); pap. 6.95 (ISBN 0-8052-0606-X). Schocken.

Bell, R. M., jt. auth. see Barnett, A.

Bell, R. P. The Proton in Chemistry. 2nd ed. LC 73-7174. (Baker Non-Resident Lectureship in Chemistry Ser.). 326p. 1973. 39.50x (ISBN 0-8014-0803-2). Cornell U Pr.

--The Tunnel Effect in Chemistry. 200p. 1980. 43.00x (ISBN 0-412-21340-0, Pub. by Chapman & Hall England). Methuen Inc.

Bell, Ralph B., jt. auth. see Winters, Robert W.

Bell, Rebecca S. & Severin, C. S., eds. The Whisper of Dreams: A Collection of Poetry. (CSS Collection of National Poetry Ser.). (Illus.). 232p. 1982. pap. 9.95 (ISBN 0-942170-04-0). CSS Pubns.

Bell, Richard Q. & Harper, Lawrence V. Child Effects on Adults. LC 77-24115. 1977. 16.50 (ISBN 0-470-99267-0). Halsted Pr.

Bell, Rivian & Koenig, Teresa. Careers at a Movie Studio. LC 82-20865. (Early Career Bks.). (Illus.). 36p. (gr. 2-5). 1983. PLB 5.95g (ISBN 0-8225-0347-6). Lerner Pubns.

--Careers in an Airplane Factory. LC 82-17136. (Early Career Bks.). (Illus.). 36p. (gr. 2-5). 1983. PLB 5.95g (ISBN 0-8225-0349-2). Lerner Pubns.

--Careers with a Record Company. LC 82-20840. (Early Career Bks.). (Illus.). 36p. (gr. 2-5). 1983. PLB 5.95g (ISBN 0-8225-0348-4). Lerner Pubns.

Bell, Robert & Grant, Nigel. Patterns of Education in the British Isles. (Unwin Education Books). 1977. text ed. 25.00x o.p. (ISBN 0-04-370082-9); pap. text ed. 9.95x o.p. (ISBN 0-04-370083-7). Allen Unwin.

Bell, Robert, ed. Early Ballads, Illustrative of History, Traditions, & Customs. LC 67-23928. 1968. Repr. of 1877 ed. 37.00x (ISBN 0-8103-3408-9). Gale.

Bell, Robert E. Dictionary of Classical Mythology: Symbols, Attributes, & Associations. LC 81-19141. 390p. 1982. text ed. 26.50 (ISBN 0-87436-305-5); pap. 15.95 (ISBN 0-87436-023-4). ABC Clio.

Bell, Robert V. Stranger in Dodge. 192p. (Orig.). 1983. pap. 2.25 (ISBN 0-345-30875-1). Ballantine.

Bell, Roger, et al, eds. Assessing Health & Human Service Needs: Concepts, Methods & Applications. LC 81-20249. (Community Psychology Ser.: Vol. VIII). (Illus.). 352p. 1983. 29.95 (ISBN 0-89885-057-6). Human Sci Pr.

Bell, Roger T. Sociolinguistics: Goals, Methods & Problems. LC 76-9423. 1976. 22.50x (ISBN 0-312-73955-9). St Martin.

Bell, Roseann P., et al. Sturdy Black Bridges: Visions of Black Women in Literature. LC 77-16898. 1979. pap. 7.95 o.p. (ISBN 0-385-13347-2, Anch). Doubleday.

Bell, Roy. One Thousand One Questions about Diagnostic Medical Sonography. 168p. 1982. pap. text ed. 9.95 (ISBN 0-8391-1749-3). Univ Park.

--One Thousand One Questions about Nuclear Medicine Technology. 168p. 1982. pap. text ed. 9.95 (ISBN 0-8391-1756-6). Univ Park.

Bell, Rudolf. Party & Faction in American Politics: The House of Representatives, 1789-1801. new ed. LC 72-782. (Contributions in American History: No. 32). 1974. lib. bdg. 27.50x (ISBN 0-8371-6356-0, BPF/). Greenwood.

Bell, Rudolph M., jt. auth. see Weinstein, Donald.

Bell, Ruth, et al. Changing Bodies, Changing Lives: A Book for Teens on Sex & Relationships. (Illus.). 1981. 15.95 (ISBN 0-394-50304-X); pap. 8.95 (ISBN 0-394-73632-X). Random.

Bell, Sally C. & Langdon, Dolly. Romper Room's Miss Sally Presents Two Hundred Fun Things to Do with Little Kids. LC 80-1807. (Illus.). 1983. pap. 7.95 (ISBN 0-385-15735-5, Dolp). Doubleday.

Bell, Sam, jt. auth. see Steben, Ralph E.

Bell, Sam H. The Theatre in Ulster. 147p. 1972. 10.00x o.p. (ISBN 0-87471-086-3). Rowman.

Bell, Samuel E. & Smallwood, James M. Zona Libre. (Southwestern Studies: No. 69). 100p. 1982. pap. 4.00 (ISBN 0-87404-129-5). Tex Western.

Bell, Steven & Kettell, Brian. Foreign Exchange Market Handbook. 250p. 1982. 92.00x (ISBN 0-86010-385-4, Pub. by Graham & Trotman England). State Mutual Bk.

Bell, Steven, jt. auth. see Kettell, Brian.

Bell, Terrel H. Active Parent Concern. Vezeris, Olga, ed. 1978. pap. 4.95 o.p. (ISBN 0-448-16804-9, 0-448-15504, G&D). Putnam Pub Group.

Bell, Thelma & Bell, Corydon. North Carolina. (States of the Nation Ser). (Illus.). (gr. 6-8). 1971. PLB 5.99 o.p. (ISBN 0-698-30262-1, Coward). Putnam Pub Group.

Bell, Vereen M. Robert Lowell: Nihilist as Hero. 272p. 1983. text ed. 17.50x (ISBN 0-674-77585-6). Harvard U Pr.

Bell, W. G., jt. ed. see Ashford, Norman.

Bell, W. J. The Laboratory Cockroach. (Illus.). 1982. pap. 15.95x (ISBN 0-412-23990-6, Pub. by Chapman & Hall). Methuen Inc.

Bell, Wendell. Jamaican Leaders: Political Attitudes in a New Nation. LC 64-19447. 1964. 29.50x (ISBN 0-520-00103-6). U of Cal Pr.

Bell, Wendell & Mau, James, eds. Sociology of the Future. LC 72-158565. 464p. 1971. 13.95x (ISBN 0-87154-106-8). Russell Sage.

Bell, William E. & McCormick, William. Neurologic Infections in Children. 2nd ed. (Major Problems in Clinical Pediatrics Ser.: Vol. 12). (Illus.). 600p. 1981. text ed. 60.00 (ISBN 0-7216-1676-3). Saunders.

Bell, William H., et al. Surgical Correction of Dentofacial Deformities. LC 76-27050. 1980. text ed. 195.00 (ISBN 0-7216-1671-2); Vol. 1. 100.00 (ISBN 0-7216-1675-5); Vol. 2. 100.00 (ISBN 0-7216-1707-7). Saunders.

Bell, William W. Secrets of a Professional Home Buyer. LC 82-21980. 160p. 1983. softcover 12.95 (ISBN 0-930294-00-9). World Wide OR.

Bellace, Janice, jt. auth. see Dunfee, Thomas W.

Bellack, Alan S. & Hersen, Michel. Behavior Modification: An Introductory Textbook. 1977. 19.95x (ISBN 0-19-502302-1). Oxford U Pr.

Bellack, Arno A., ed. Theory & Research in Teaching. LC 63-18839. (Orig.). 1963. pap. text ed. 5.25x (ISBN 0-8077-1065-2). Tchrs Coll.

Bellack, Arno A. & Kliebard, Herbert E., eds. Curriculum & Evaluation. LC 76-18040. (Readings in Educational Research Ser.). 1977. 30.75 (ISBN 0-8211-0129-3); text ed. 28.00 10 or more copies (ISBN 0-686-67488-X). McCutchan.

Bellack, Arno A., et al. Language of the Classroom. LC 66-22926. 1966. pap. 7.50x (ISBN 0-8077-1063-6). Tchrs Coll.

Bellafiore, Joseph. English Language Arts. rev. ed. (gr. 10-12). 1982. text ed. 18.33 (ISBN 0-87720-439-X); pap. text ed. 9.66 (ISBN 0-87720-438-1). AMSCO Sch.

--English Language Arts, Intermediate Level. (Illus.). (gr. 7-9). 1969. text ed. 11.25 o.p. (ISBN 0-87720-308-3); pap. text ed. 6.67 o.p. (ISBN 0-87720-307-5); wkbk. ed. 7.83 o.p. (ISBN 0-87720-347-4). AMSCO Sch.

--English Language Arts Workbook. 2nd ed. (Orig.). (gr. 9-12). pap. 9.25 (ISBN 0-87720-392-X). AMSCO Sch.

--Essentials of English. (gr. 7-9). 1970. pap. text ed. 5.33 o.p. (ISBN 0-87720-341-5); wkbk. 6.67 o.p. (ISBN 0-87720-349-0). AMSCO Sch.

--Essentials of English. 3rd ed. (Orig.). (gr. 9-12). 1983. pap. text ed. write for info. (ISBN 0-87720-448-9). AMSCO Sch.

--Essentials of English Workbook. 3rd ed. (gr. 10-12). 1982. 7.08 (ISBN 0-87720-441-1). AMSCO Sch.

Bellah, Robert N. Beyond Belief. LC 77-109058. 1976. pap. text ed. 5.95i (ISBN 0-06-060775-0, RD129, HarpR). Har-Row.

--The Broken Covenenant: American Civil Religion in Time of Trail. 1976. pap. 5.95 (ISBN 0-8164-2123-4). Seabury.

Bellah, Robert N., jt. ed. see Glock, Charles.

Bellaire, Arthur. Controlling Your TV Commercial Costs. LC 76-9377. 1977. 21.95 o.p. (ISBN 0-87251-026-3). Crain Bks.

--Controlling Your TV Commercial Costs. 2nd ed. 160p. 1982. 24.95 (ISBN 0-87251-075-1). Crain Bks.

Bellairs, jt. auth. see Carrington, R.

Bellairs, Donald W., jt. auth. see Steinbach, Robert C.

Bellairs, Herbert J., ed. see Helsel, James L.

Bellairs, John. The Curse of the Blue Figurine. LC 82-73217. (Illus.). 224p. (gr. 5 up). 1983. 10.95 (ISBN 0-8037-1119-0, 01063-320); lib. bdg. 10.89 (ISBN 0-8037-1265-0). Dial Bks Young.

--The Letter, the Witch & the Ring. (gr. 3-6). 1977. pap. 2.25 (ISBN 0-440-44722-4, YB). Dell.

Bellairs, R. & Gray, E. G., eds. Essays on the Nervous System: A Festschrift for Professor J. Z. Young. (Illus.). 1974. text ed. 50.00x (ISBN 0-19-857364-2). Oxford U Pr.

Bellairs, Ruth, et al, eds. Cell Behaviour: A Tribute to Michael Abercrombie. Ruth & Curtis, Dunn. LC 81-6119. (Illus.). 500p. 1982. 95.00 (ISBN 0-521-24107-3). Cambridge U Pr.

Bellak & Baker. Reading Faces. 1983. pap. 3.50 (ISBN 0-553-22851-X). Bantam.

Bellak, George. Come Jericho. 384p. 1983. pap. 2.95 (ISBN 0-425-05508-6). Berkley Pub.

Bellak, Leopold & Barten, Harvey H., eds. Progress in Community Mental Health, Vol. 3. LC 73-6067. 360p. 1975. 20.00 o.p. (ISBN 0-87630-100-6). Brunner-Mazel.

Bellak, Leopold, et al. Ego Functions in Schizophrenics, Neurotics, & Normals: A Systematic Study of Conceptual, Diagnostic, & Therapeutic Aspects. LC 73-3199. (Personality Processes Ser.). 688p. 1973. 52.95x (ISBN 0-471-06413-0, Pub. by Wiley-Interscience). Wiley.

Bellak, Rhoda & Voehl, Dick. Five Pennies Make a Nickel: A Child's First Savings Book. (Piggybank Bks.). 12p. (gr. k-2). 1981. text ed. 5.95 o.p. (ISBN 0-671-42562-5). Wanderer Bks.

Bellamy, Charles. Experiment in Marriage. LC 77-16040. 320p. 1977. Repr. of 1889 ed. 37.00x (ISBN 0-8201-1304-2). Schol Facsimiles.

Bellamy, D. J., jt. auth. see Moore, P. D.

Bellamy, David. Forces of Life. (Illus.). 1979. 15.95 o.p. (ISBN 0-517-53529-7). Crown.

Bellamy, Edward. Equality. LC 69-13816. Repr. of 1897 ed. lib. bdg. 17.00x (ISBN 0-8371-0994-9, BEEQ). Greenwood.

--Looking Backward. pap. 2.25 (ISBN 0-451-51666-4, CE1666, Sig Classics). NAL.

--Looking Backward: Two Thousand to Eighteen Eighty-Seven. Elliott, Robert C., ed. LC 67-2787. (YA) (gr. 9 up). 1966. pap. 4.75 (ISBN 0-395-05194-0, A99, RivEd, 3-47733). HM.

Bellamy, G. Thomas, jt. auth. see Wilcox, Barbara.

Bellamy, J. G. Law of Treason in England in the Later Middle Ages. LC 70-111123. (Cambridge Studies in English Legal History). 1970. 39.50 (ISBN 0-521-07830-X). Cambridge U Pr.

Bellamy, Joe D. The New Fiction: Interviews with Innovative American Writers. LC 74-14841. 225p. 1974. 12.95 (ISBN 0-252-00430-2); pap. 4.50 (ISBN 0-252-00555-4). U of Ill Pr.

Bellamy, Joe D. & Weingarten, Roger, eds. Love Stories-Love Poems. 300p. (Orig.). 1982. pap. 12.95 (ISBN 0-931362-07-5). Fiction Intl.

Bellamy, John. Digital Telephony. LC 81-11633. 526p. 1982. 48.50x (ISBN 0-471-08089-6, Pub. by Wiley-Interscience). Wiley.

Bellamy, John C. Digital Telephony. 526p. 1982. 37.50 (ISBN 0-686-98112-X). Telecom Lib.

Bellamy, Joyce M. & Saville, John, eds. Dictionary of Labour Biography, 5 vols. LC 78-185417. 1972. Vol. 1. lib. bdg. 25.00x (ISBN 0-678-07008-3); Vol. 2. lib. bdg. 47.50x (ISBN 0-678-07018-0); Vols. 3. lib. bdg. 37.50x (ISBN 0-333-14415-5); Vol. 4. lib. bdg. 37.50x (ISBN 0-333-19704-6); Vol. 5. lib. bdg. 37.50x (ISBN 0-333-22015-3). Kelley.

--Dictionary of Labour Biography, Vol. 6. LC 78-185417. 250p. 1982. PLB 37.50 (ISBN 0-333-24095-2). Kelley.

Bellamy, L. J. The Infrared Spectra of Complex Molecules, Vol. 1. 3rd ed. 1975. 38.00x (ISBN 0-412-13850-6, Pub. by Chapman & Hall). Methuen Inc.

--Infrared Spectra of Complex Molecules, Vol. 2. 2nd ed. 299p. 1980. 38.00x (ISBN 0-412-22350-3, Pub. by Chapman & Hall England). Methuen Inc.

Bellamy, Margot A. & Greenshields, Bruce L., eds. The Rural Challenge. 329p. 1981. text ed. 23.50x (ISBN 0-566-00472-0). Gower Pub Ltd.

Bellamy, Virginia W. And the Evening & the Morning. LC 76-41608. 1976. French style bdg. 4.50 (ISBN 0-87027-172-5). Cumberland Pr.

Bellamy, William. The Novels of Wells, Bennett & Galsworthy 1890-1910. 1971. 19.95x o.p. (ISBN 0-7100-7002-0). Routledge & Kegan.

Bellan, R. C. Excerpts from Principles of Economics & the Canadian Economy. 6th ed. (FLMI Insurance Education Program Ser.). (Illus.). 1981. pap. text ed. 4.00 (ISBN 0-915322-46-3). LOMA.

Bellan, R. M., et al, eds. Membranes & Intercellular Communication. (Les Houches Summer School Ser.: Vol. 33). 1981. 106.50 (ISBN 0-444-85469-X). Elsevier.

Bellante, Donald & Jackson, Mark. Labor Economics: Choice in Labor Markets. (Illus.). 1979. text ed. 21.95 (ISBN 0-07-004397-3, C); instructor's manual 19.95 (ISBN 0-07-004398-1). McGraw.

Bellante, Donald M. & Jackson, J. Mark, Jr. Labor Economics: Choice in Labor Markets. 2nd ed. (Illus.). 368p. 1983. text ed. 24.95x (ISBN 0-07-004399-X, C). McGraw.

Bellanti, J. A. & Dayton, D. H., eds. The Phagocytic Cell in Host Resistance. LC 74-14147. 365p. 1975. 34.50 (ISBN 0-911216-90-1). Raven.

Bellany, Ian & Blacker, Coit D., eds. Antiballistic Missile Defence in the 1980s. 200p. 1983. text ed. 30.00 (ISBN 0-7146-3207-4, F Cass Co). Biblio Dist.

Bellas, Patricia H. Your Career in the Business World: A Guide for Young Women. LC 80-27367. (Arco's Career Guidance Ser.). (Illus.). 128p. 1981. lib. bdg. 7.95 (ISBN 0-668-04745-3); pap. 4.50 (ISBN 0-668-04755-0). Arco.

Bellas, Ralph A. Christina Rossetti. (English Authors Ser.). 1977. lib. bdg. 12.95 (ISBN 0-8057-6671-5, Twayne). G K Hall.

Bellasis, Edward. Cherubini: Memorials Illustrative of His Life & Work. LC 70-138497. (Music Ser). 1971. Repr. of 1912 ed. lib. bdg. 35.00 (ISBN 0-306-70071-9). Da Capo.

Bellavance, Diane. Typing Made Easy. (Illus.). 20p. 1982. pap. 2.00 (ISBN 0-9605276-1-3). DBA Bks.

Bellay, Joachim du see Du'Bellay, Joachim.

Belle, O. C. Van see Bottcher, C. J., et al.

Bellecombe, L. Greyfie De see Roberts, Benjamin C. & De Bellecombe, L. Greyfie.

Bellenger, Danny N., jt. auth. see Robertson, Dan H.

Beller, Anne S. Fat & Thin: A Natural History of Obesity. 1978. pap. 4.95 o.p. (ISBN 0-07-004413-9, SP). McGraw.

Beller, Elmer A., ed. see Bayle, Pierre.

Belles, Donald W. Fire Hazard Analysis from Plastic Insulation in Exterior Walls of Buildings. Date not set. 5.35 (ISBN 0-686-37665-X, TR 82-1). Society Fire Protect.

Bellet, Samuel. Essentials of Cardiac Arrhythmias: Diagnosis & Management. LC 77-183444. (Illus.). 458p. 1972. 16.50 o.p. (ISBN 0-7216-1692-5). Saunders.

Bellett, J. G. Short Meditations, 3 vols. pap. 10.00 set (ISBN 0-88172-003-8); pap. 3.95 ea. Believers Bkshelf.

Belli, Melvin. The Belli Files. 275p. 1982. 14.95 (ISBN 0-13-077974-1, Busn). P-H.

Bellin, Robert. Queen's Pawn: Veresov System. (Illus.). 96p. 1983. pap. 13.50 (ISBN 0-7134-1877-X, Pub. by Batsford England). David & Charles.

Bellinger, Alfred R. Troy the Coins. (Illus.). 1980. Repr. of 1961 ed. lib. bdg. 35.00 (ISBN 0-915262-32-0). S J Durst.

Bellini, Enzo. The Middle Ages, 900-1300. Drury, John, ed. & tr. from Ital. (An Illustrated History of the Church). 126p. 16.95 (ISBN 0-03-056828-5). Winston Pr.

Bellini, Enzo, et al. The Catholic Church Today, 1920-1982. Drury, John, ed. & tr. from Ital. (Illustrated History of the Church). (Illus.). 126p. (gr. 6-12). 1982. 16.95 (ISBN 0-86683-160-6). Winston Pr.

--The Church & the Modern Nations, 1850-1920. Drury, John, ed. & tr. from Ital. (An Illustrated History of the Church). (Illus.). 216p. (gr. 6-12). 1982. 16.95 (ISBN 0-86683-159-2). Winston Pr.

--The Church Established, 180-381. Drury, John, ed. & tr. from Ital. (An Illustrated History of the Church). (Illus.). 126p. 16.95 (ISBN 0-03-056824-2). Winston Pr.

--The Church in Revolutionary Times. Drury, John, ed. & tr. from Ital. (An Illustrated History of the Church). (Illus.). 124p. (gr. 6-12). 1981. 16.95 (ISBN 0-86683-158-4). Winston Pr.

--The Church in the Age of Humanism, 1300-1500. Drury, John, ed. & tr. (An Illustrated History of the Church). 126p. 16.95 (ISBN 0-03-056829-3). Winston Pr.

--The End of the Ancient World, Three Hundred Eighty-One to Six Hundred. Drury, John, ed. & tr. from Ital. (Illustrated History of the Church). (Illus.). 126p. (gr. 6-12). 1982. 16.95 (ISBN 0-03-056826-9). Winston Pr.

--The First Christians: An Illustrated History of the Church. Drury, John, ed. & tr. from Ital. (Illus.). 124p. (gr. 4-9). 1980. 16.95 (ISBN 0-03-056823-4). Winston Pr.

--The Formation of Christian Europe: An Illustrated History of the Church. Drury, John, ed. & tr. (Illus.). (gr. 5-9). 1980. text ed. 16.95 (ISBN 0-03-056827-7). Winston Pr.

--Protestant & Catholic Reform. Drury, John, ed. & tr. from Ital. (An Illustrated History of the Church). (Illus.). 124p. (Orig.). (gr. 6-12). 1981. 16.95 (ISBN 0-03-056831-5). Winston Pr.

Bellini, Paolo, ed. Italian Masters of the Seventeenth Century, Vols. 46,47. (Illus.). 1982. 120.00 (ISBN 0-89835-046-8). Abaris Bks.

Bellink, Alan, jt. auth. see Kaplan, Donald.

Bellis, Herbert F. & Schmidt, Walter A. Architectural Drafting. 2nd ed. 1971. 19.95 (ISBN 0-07-004418-X, G). McGraw.

--Blueprint Reading for the Construction Trades. 2nd ed. (Illus.). 1978. pap. text ed. 17.95 (ISBN 0-07-004410-4, G); ans. key 1.50 (ISBN 0-07-004411-2). McGraw.

Bellisimo, Lou. The Bowler's Manual. 3rd ed. (Illus.). 128p. 1975. pap. text ed. 6.95 o.p. (ISBN 0-13-080432-0). P-H.

Bellisimo, Louis A. & Bennett, Jeanine. The Bowler's Manual. 4th ed. (Illus.). 176p. 1982. pap. 8.95 (ISBN 0-13-080507-6). P-H.

Belliston, Larry & Hanks, Kurt. Extra Cash for Kids. 192p. (Orig.). (gr. 4 up). 1982. pap. 6.95 (ISBN 0-89879-082-4). Writers Digest.

Belliveou, Jim & Belliveou, Mary. Riches Under Your Roof. LC 82-15420. 288p. 1983. 17.95 (ISBN 0-03-053016-4); pap. 9.95 (ISBN 0-03-053301-5). HR&W.

Belliveou, Mary, jt. auth. see Belliveou, Jim.

Bellman, James F. & Bellman, Kathryn. Antony & Cleopatra Notes. (Orig.). 1981. pap. 2.75 (ISBN 0-8220-0002-4). Cliffs.

Bellman, Kathryn, jt. auth. see Bellman, James F.

Bellman, R., jt. auth. see Beckenbach, E. F.

Bellman, R., et al. Mathematical Aspects of Scheduling & Applications. (I S Modern Applied Mathematics & Computer Sciences Ser.: Vol. 4). (Illus.). 300p. 1982. 35.00 (ISBN 0-08-026477-8); pap. 19.50 (ISBN 0-08-026476-X). Pergamon.

Bellman, Samuel I. Constance M. Rourke. (United States Authors Ser.). 1981. lib. bdg. 13.95 (ISBN 0-8057-7341-X, Twayne). G K Hall.

--Marjorie Kinnan Rawlings. (United States Authors Ser.). 1974. lib. bdg. 11.95 (ISBN 0-8057-0610-0, Twayne). G K Hall.

Bellman, Willard F. Scene Design, Stage Lighting, Sound, Costume, & Makeup: A Scenographic Approach. 672p. 1983. text ed. 33.50 scp (ISBN 0-06-040612-7, HarpC). Har-Row.

Bello, Ignacio. Contemporary Basic Mathematical Skills. (Illus.). 1978. pap. text ed. 20.95 scp o.p. (ISBN 0-06-040613-5, HarpC); solution & test manual avail. o.p. (ISBN 0-06-360610-0). Har-Row.

--Contemporary Basic Mathematical Skills. 2nd ed. 432p. 1982. pap. text ed. 22.50 scp (ISBN 0-06-040614-3, HarpC); answer manual avail. (ISBN 0-06-360611-9); Bank Test avail. (ISBN 0-06-360612-7). Har-Row.

Bello, Ignacio, jt. auth. see Britton, Jack R.

Bello, Walden & Kinley, David. Development Debacle: The World Bank in the Philippines. 272p. (Orig.). 1982. pap. 6.95 (ISBN 0-935028-12-9). Inst Food & Develop.

Belloc, Hilaire. Cautionary Tales. 1980. PLB 5.95 (ISBN 0-8398-2602-8, Gregg). G K Hall.
--Richelieu. LC 77-114466. (Illus.). 392p. Repr. of 1935 ed. lib. bdg. 20.75x (ISBN 0-8371-4762-X, BERI). Greenwood.
Belloc, Hillaire. The Path to Rome. LC 81-52214. pap. text ed. 5.95 cancelled (ISBN 0-89526-884-1). Regnery-Gateway.
Belloli, G. P., ed. Pediatric Cardiology & Cardiosurgery. (Modern Problems in Paediatrics: Vol. 22). (Illus.). viii, 216p. 1983. pap. 99.00 (ISBN 3-8055-3593-7). S Karger.
Belloli, Jay. Innovations: Contemporary Home Environments. (Illus.). 38p. 1973. 6.00x (ISBN 0-686-99821-9). La Jolla Mus Contemp Art.
--Jim Dine: The Summers Collection. (Illus.). 28p. 1974. 4.50x (ISBN 0-686-99817-0). La Jolla Mus Contemp Art.
--Ron Cooper. (Illus.). 38p. 1973. 6.00x (ISBN 0-686-99822-7). La Jolla Mus Contemp Art.
Belloli, Robert C. Contemporary Physical Science: Our Impact on Our World. (Illus.). 1978. 22.95 (ISBN 0-02-308070-1). Macmillan.
Bellomy, Mildred. Encyclopedia of Sea Horses. 1969. text ed. 14.95 (ISBN 0-87666-142-8, H936). TFH Pubns.
Bellon, Errol M. Radiologic Interpretation of ERCP: A Clinical Atlas. 1983. pap. text ed. price not set (ISBN 0-87488-707-0). Med Exam.
Bellon, Jerry & Handler, Janet R. Curriculum Development & Evaluation: A Design for Improvement. 96p. 1982. pap. text ed. 7.95 (ISBN 0-8403-2720-X). Kendall-Hunt.
Bellon, Jerry J., et al. Instructional Improvement: Principles & Processes. 1978. pap. text ed. 7.95 (ISBN 0-8403-1838-3). Kendall-Hunt.
Bellon De Saint-Quentin. Dissertation sur la Traite et le Commerce des Negres. (Slave Trade in France Ser., 1744-1848). 174p. (Fr.). 1974. Repr. of 1764 ed. lib. bdg. 51.50x o.p. (ISBN 0-8287-0073-7, TN104). Clearwater Pub.
Bellone, Enrico. The World on Paper: Studies on the Second Scientific Revolution. Giaconni, Mirella & Giaconni, Ricardo, trs. from Italian. Orig. Title: Il Mondo di Carta. 1980. text ed. 17.50x (ISBN 0-262-02147-1). MIT Pr.
Bellony-Rewald, Alice, jt. auth. see Peppiatt, Michael.
Bellosi. Giotto. pap. 12.50 (ISBN 0-935748-03-2). ScalaBooks.
Bellow, Gary, et al. Criminal Practice Institute Exclusionary Hearing Demonstration. 1966. 5.50 o.p. (ISBN 0-685-14177-2). Lerner Law.
Bellow, Saul. The Dean's December. 1983. pap. 3.95 (ISBN 0-671-45806-X). PB.
--Henderson the Rain King. 1976. pap. 4.95 (ISBN 0-14-004229-6). Penguin.
--The Portable Saul Bellow. (Viking Portable Library: No. 79). 672p. 1977. pap. 6.95 (ISBN 0-14-015079-X, P79). Penguin.
--Seize the Day. 1977. pap. 2.95 (ISBN 0-380-01649-4, 60202-4). Avon.
--Seize the Day. 1976. pap. 3.95 (ISBN 0-14-004311-X). Penguin.
Bellows, Emma L. Memoirs of a Town & Country Doctor. LC 81-51489. 198p. 1982. 10.00 (ISBN 0-533-05079-0). Vantage.
Bellows, Guy. Nontraditional Machining Guide. (Machining Process Ser.: MDC 76-101). (Illus.). 76p. (Orig.). 1976. pap. 8.00 o.p. (ISBN 0-936974-03-6). Metcut Res Assocs.
Bellows, John B., ed. Contemporary Ophthalomology. LC 72-166198. 554p. 1972. 34.75 o.p. (ISBN 0-683-00517-0, Pub. by W & W). Krieger.
Bellows, John G., ed. Glaucoma: Contemporary International Concepts. LC 79-88728. (Illus.). 448p. 1980. 63.00x (ISBN 0-89352-058-6). Masson Pub.
Bellows, Thomas J. The People's Action Party of Singapore: Emergence of a Dominant Party System. LC 73-114788. (Monograph Ser.: No. 14). xii, 195p. 1970. 8.25x (ISBN 0-686-30904-9). Yale U SE Asia.
Bellows, Thomas J., jt. auth. see Winter, Herbert R.
Bellusci, Joan L. The American Grown Italian Cookbook. LC 82-72309. (Illus.). 68p. (Orig.). 1982. pap. 6.95 (ISBN 0-9608570-0-1). Bellusci Pub.
Bellville, Cheryl W., jt. auth. see Bellville, Rod.
Bellville, Rod & Bellville, Cheryl W. Large Animal Veterinarians. LC 82-19750. (Illus.). 32p. (gr. 1-4). 1983. PLB 7.95g (ISBN 0-87614-211-0). Carolrhoda Bks.
Bellwood, Peter. Man's Conquest of the Pacific: The Prehistory of Southeast Asia & Oceania. 1979. 35.00x o.p. (ISBN 0-19-520103-5). Oxford U Pr.
Belmaker, Robert, jt. auth. see Gershon, Samuel.
Belman, A. Barry & Kaplan, George W. Urologic Problems in Pediatrics. (Major Problems in Clinical Pediatrics Ser.: Vol. 23). (Illus.). 200p. 1981. text ed. 39.50 (ISBN 0-7216-1678-X). Saunders.
Belman, H. S. & Shertzer, B. My Career Guidebook. 2nd ed. 1974. 3.00 o.p. (ISBN 0-02-800290-3); tchr's manual 0.80 o.p. (ISBN 0-02-800270-9). Glencoe.
Beloff, Max. The Great Powers: Essays in Twentieth Century Politics. LC 78-14402. 1979. Repr. of 1959 ed. lib. bdg. 20.00x (ISBN 0-8371-9297-8, BEGP). Greenwood.
--The Intellectual in Politics & Other Essays. LC 78-141854. 361p. 1971. 21.00x (ISBN 0-912050-02-0, Library Pr). Open Court.
Belohlavek, John M. George Mifflin Dallas: Jacksonian Patrician. LC 77-1415. 1977. 19.75x (ISBN 0-271-00510-6). Pa St U Pr.
Belotti, Elena G. What Are Little Girls Made of? The Roots of Feminine Stereotypes. LC 76-9136. 1978. 7.95 (ISBN 0-8052-3630-9); pap. 4.95 (ISBN 0-8052-0607-8). Schocken.
Belous, Russell E. & Weinstein, Robert A. Will Soule: Indian Photographers at Fort Hill. (Illus.). pap. 15.00 o.p. (ISBN 0-517-53770-2, Pub. by Ward Ritchie). Crown.
Beloussov, V. V. Continental Endogenous Regimes. 295p. 1981. 10.00 (ISBN 0-8285-2281-2, Pub. by Mir Pubs USSR). Imported Pubns.
Belov, N. V., jt. auth. see Shubnikov, A. V.
Belove, Charles & Drossman, Melvyn. Systems & Circuits for Electrical Engineering Technology. new ed. (Illus.). 1976. text ed. 36.00 (ISBN 0-07-004430-9). McGraw.
Belove, Charles, jt. auth. see Schilling, Donald.
Belove, Charles, et al. Digital Analog System Circulation Development. Wade, Charles R., ed. (Illus.). 448p. 1973. text ed. 38.50 (ISBN 0-07-004420-1, C); ans. bk. 7.95 (ISBN 0-07-004423-6). McGraw.
Belozerskaya-Bulgakova, L. E. My Life with Mikhail Bulgakov. Thompson, M., tr. from Rus. 120p. 1983. 16.50 (ISBN 0-88233-433-6). Ardis Pubs.
Bels, Albert. The Inspector. Cedrins, Inara, tr. from Latvian. 125p. 1983. 13.50 (ISBN 0-931556-08-2). Translation Pr.
Belshaw, Cyril S. Changing Melanesia: Social Economics of Culture Contact. LC 76-44881. (Illus.). 1976. lib. bdg. 17.00x (ISBN 0-8371-9039-8, BELM). Greenwood.
--Under the Ivi Tree: Society & Economic Growth in Rural Fiji. 1964. 26.50x (ISBN 0-520-00106-0). U of Cal Pr.
Belshaw, Michael. Economics of Underdeveloped Countries. LC 74-84420. (Real World of Economics Ser). Orig. Title: Economic Development. (Illus.). (gr. 5-11). 1970. PLB 4.95g (ISBN 0-8225-0617-3). Lerner Pubns.
Belsley, David A., et al. Regression Diagnostics: Identifying Influential Data & Sources of Collinearity. LC 79-19876. (Ser. in Probability & Mathematical Statistics: Applied Probability & Statistics). 292p. 1980. 29.95x (ISBN 0-471-05856-4, Pub. by Wiley-Interscience). Wiley.
Belson, Al. Fashion Photography Techniques. (Illus.). 1970. 11.95 o.p. (ISBN 0-8174-0529-1, Amphoto). Watson-Guptill.
Belson, David. What to Say & How to Say It: For All Occasions. 1961. pap. 2.95 (ISBN 0-8065-0027-1, 98). Citadel Pr.
Belson, W. A. & Thompson, B. A. Bibliography on Methods of Social & Business Research. LC 72-11488. 300p. 1973. 34.95 o.p. (ISBN 0-470-06420-X). Halsted Pr.
Belstock, Alan & Smith, Gerald. Consumer Mathematics with Calculator Applications. Gafney, Leo, ed. (gr. 10-12). 1980. text ed. 14.76x (ISBN 0-07-004436-8). McGraw.
Belt, E. R. Complete Electrical Estimating Course, 4 vols. 1976. Complete Course. 59.50 (ISBN 0-07-095030-X); Vol. 1: Electrical Estimating. 24.95 (ISBN 0-07-004454-6); Vol. 2: Electrical Pricing Units & Procedures. 24.95 (ISBN 0-07-004455-4); Vol. 3: Pricing Forms. 21.50 (ISBN 0-07-004456-2); Vol. 4: Take-Off Forms. 21.50 (ISBN 0-07-004457-0); study guide & final exam 12.00 (ISBN 0-07-004458-9). McGraw.
Belt, Forest & Taylor, Calton. Motorcycle Maintenance & Repair. (Mini Guide Ser.). 96p. 1974. pap. 0.99 o.p. (ISBN 0-672-23805-5). Audel.
--Small Engines Maintenance & Repair. 96p. 1974. pap. 0.99 o.p. (ISBN 0-672-23800-4). Audel.
Belth, Nathan C. A Promise to Keep: The American Encounter with Anti-Semitism. 305p. Repr. 6.95 (ISBN 0-686-95111-5). ADL.
Belting, Hans. Studies in the History of Art 1982, Vol. 12. (Illus.). pap. write for info. (ISBN 0-89468-063-3). Natl Gallery Art.
Belting, Paul E. & Clevenger, A. W. The High School at Work. 441p. 1982. Repr. of 1939 ed. lib. bdg. 30.00 (ISBN 0-89760-093-2). Telegraph Bks.
Beltman, H. A. Vegetative Strukturen der Parmeliaceae und Ihre Entwickelung. (Bibliotheca Lichenologica Ser.: No. 11). (Illus.). 1978. lib. bdg. 24.00x (ISBN 3-7682-1199-1). Lubrecht & Cramer.
Belton, John. Cinema Stylists. LC 82-10793. (Filmmakers Ser.: No. 2). (Illus.). 384p. 1983. 19.50 (ISBN 0-8108-1585-0). Scarecrow.
Beltrametti, E. G. & Cassinelli, G. Encyclopedia of Mathematics & Its Applications, Vol. 15: The Logic of Quantum Mechanics. 1981. 33.50 (ISBN 0-201-13514-0). A-W.
Beltrametti, Franco. Airmail Postcards. (Illus.). 28p. 1979. signed ed. 20.00 o.p. (ISBN 0-931428-07-6); pap. 6.00 o.p. (ISBN 0-931428-06-8). Vehicle Edns.
Beltrami, Edward. The High Cost of Clean Water: Models for Water Quality Management Ser. (The UMAP Expository Monograph). 53p. 1982. pap. text ed. 8.95 (ISBN 3-7643-3098-8). Birkhauser.
Beltramo, Mario & Longo, Giovanni E. The Italian Civil Code, Supplement, 1969-1978. LC 69-15387. 1978. lib. bdg. 25.00 (ISBN 0-379-20292-1). Oceana.
Beltran, Antonio. Rock Art of the Spanish Levant. LC 81-21694. (The Imprint of Man Ser.). 144p. 1982. 19.95 (ISBN 0-521-24568-0). Cambridge U Pr.
Beltran, Gonzalo A. Regions of Refuge, No. 12. 1979. pap. 6.00 (ISBN 0-686-36586-0). Am Anthro Assn.
Beltroy, Manuel, tr. see Hume, Roberto E.
Beltsville Symposia in Agricultural Research, ed. Animal Reproduction, No. 3. LC 78-65535. (Beltsville Symposia in Agricultural Research). (Illus.). 434p. 1979. text ed. 39.95 (ISBN 0-470-26672-4). Halsted Pr.
Beltsville Symposia in Agricultural Research. Biosystematics in Agriculture. Romberger, John A., ed. LC 77-84408. 1978. 39.95 (ISBN 0-470-26416-0). Halsted Pr.
Beltz, Walter. God & the Gods: Myths. 1983. pap. 5.95 (ISBN 0-14-022192-1, Pelican). Penguin.
Belu, C. Des Colonies et De la Traite Des Negres. (Slave Trade in France Ser., 1744-1848). 76p. (Fr.). 1974. Repr. of 1800 ed. lib. bdg. 22.50 o.p. (ISBN 0-8287-0076-1). Clearwater Pub.
Belytschko. Computational Methods for Transient Analysis. Date not set. price not set (ISBN 0-444-86479-2). Elsevier.
Belz, C. Cezanne. (Color Slide Program of the Great Masters Ser.). 1975. 14.95 (ISBN 0-07-004417-1, P&RB). McGraw.
Belz, Carl. The Story of Rock. 2nd ed. (Illus.). 1972. 17.50x (ISBN 0-19-501554-1). Oxford U Pr.
Belz, Herman. A New Birth of Freedom: The Republican Party & Freedmen's Rights, 1861 1866. LC 76-5257. (Contributions in American History: No. 52). 1976. lib. bdg. 25.00x (ISBN 0-8371-8902-0, BEO/). Greenwood.
Belz, R., jt. auth. see Maarse, H.
Belzer, Thomas J. Roadside Plants of Southern California. (Illus.). 172p. 1983. pap. 7.95 (ISBN 0-87842-158-0). Mountain Pr.
Belzung, L. D., jt. auth. see Becht, J. Edwin.
Bem, Daryl J. Beliefs, Attitudes, & Human Affairs. LC 71-95057. (Basic Concepts in Psychology Ser). (Orig.). 1970. pap. text ed. 7.95 o.p. (ISBN 0-8185-0295-9). Brooks-Cole.
Bem, Robyn. Everyone's Guide to Home Composting. 1978. 7.95 o.p. (ISBN 0-442-20682-8); pap. 3.95 (ISBN 0-442-20680-1). Van Nos Reinhold.
Beman, Lamar T., compiled by. Selected Articles on Censorship of Speech & the Press. LC 76-98813. 1971. Repr. of 1930 ed. lib. bdg. 19.75x (ISBN 0-8371-3073-5, BECE). Greenwood.
Beman, Lamar T., ed. Selected Articles on Censorship of the Theater & Moving Pictures. LC 78-160229. (Moving Pictures Ser). 385p. 1971. Repr. of 1931 ed. lib. bdg. 20.95x (ISBN 0-89198-030-X). Ozer.
Bembe, John P., jt. auth. see Darey-Bembe, Francoise.
Bemelmans, Ludwig. Madeline in London. (Illus.). 56p. (ps-3). 1977. pap. 3.50 (ISBN 0-14-050199-1, Puffin). Penguin.
BeMiller, J. N., jt. ed. see Whistler, R. L.
Bemis, Samuel F. John Quincy Adams & the Foundations of American Foreign Policy. (Illus.). 640p. 1973. pap. 4.95 o.p. (ISBN 0-393-00684-0, N684, Norton Lib). Norton.
--Pinckney's Treaty: America's Advantage from Europe's Distress, 1783-1800. LC 73-8148. (Illus.). xvi, 372p. 1973. Repr. of 1960 ed. lib. bdg. 20.50x (ISBN 0-8371-6954-2, BEPT). Greenwood.
Ben Lee Memorial International Conference on Parity Nonconservation, Weak Neutral Currents & Gauge Theories, Fermi National Accelerator Laboratory, October 20-22, 1977. The Unification of Elementary Forces & Gauge Theories: Proceedings. Cline, D. B. & Mills, F. E., eds. 792p. 1980. lib. bdg. 50.00 (ISBN 0-906346-00-2). Harwood Academic.
Benacerraf, Baruj & Unanue, Emil. Textbook of Immunology. (Illus.). 310p. 1979. pap. 13.95 (ISBN 0-683-00527-8). Williams & Wilkins.
Benagh, Jim. Picture Story of Wayne Gretzky. Anderson, Madelyn K., ed. (Sports Series--"Picture Story of..."). (Illus.). 64p. (gr. 4 up). 1982. PLB 7.97g (ISBN 0-671-45949-X). Messner.
--Terry Bradshaw: Superarm of Pro Football. new ed. LC 75-43585. (Putnam Sports Shelf). 128p. (gr. 3-5). 1976. PLB 5.49 o.p. (ISBN 0-399-60965-2). Putnam Pub Group.
Benamou, Michael & Ionesco, Eugene. Mise En Train: Premiere Annee De Francais. (gr. 11-12). 1969. text ed. 22.95x (ISBN 0-02-307970-3); wkbk. 7.95 (ISBN 0-02-307980-0). Macmillan.
Benamou, Michel & Carduner, Jean. Le Moulin a paroles. 2nd ed. LC 71-126958. (Illus.). 336p. (Fr.). 1975. pap. text ed. 11.95x (ISBN 0-471-06450-5); tapes o.p. (ISBN 0-471-00024-8). Wiley.
Benamou, Michel & Caramello, Charles, eds. Performance in Postmodern Culture. pap. 7.95 (ISBN 0-930956-00-1). Performing Arts.
Benarde, Melvin A., ed. Disinfection. 1970. 63.25 o.p. (ISBN 0-8247-1040-1). Dekker.
Ben-Ari. Amygdaloid Complex. (INSERM Symposia Ser.: Vol. 20). 1982. 90.00 (ISBN 0-444-80397-1). Elsevier.
Benarie, M. M. Atmospheric Pollution, 1982. (Studies in Environmental Science: Vol. 20). 1982. 81.00 (ISBN 0-444-42083-5). Elsevier.
Benarie, M. M., ed. Atmospheric Pollution, 1978: Proceedings of the 13th International Colloquium, UNESCO Building, Paris, France, April 1978. (Studies in Evironmental Science: No. 1). 1978. 56.00 (ISBN 0-444-41691-9). Elsevier.
--Atmospheric Pollution, 1980: Proceedings of the 14th International Colloquium, Paris, May 1980. (Studies in Environmental Science: Vol. 8). 1980. 78.75 (ISBN 0-444-41889-X). Elsevier.
Benarie, Michael M. Urban Air Pollution Modeling. (Illus.). 1980. text ed. 50.00x (ISBN 0-262-02140-4). MIT Pr.
Benarie, Michel, ed. see International Symposium, 12th, Paris, 1976.
Benario, Herbert W. A Commentary on the Vita Hadriana in the Historia Augusta. LC 80-11953. (American Classical Studies: No. 7). 1980. 13.50x o.p. (ISBN 0-89130-391-X, 40-04-07); pap. 10.50x (ISBN 0-89130-392-8). Scholars Pr CA.
Benaroya, Alfred. Fundamentals & Application of Centrifugal Pumps for the Practicing Engineer. 256p. 1978. 44.95x (ISBN 0-87814-040-9). Pennwell Pub.
Ben'Ary, Ruth. Touch Typing in Ten Lessons. rev. ed. (Illus., Orig.). 1982. pap. 3.95 (ISBN 0-448-01509-9, G&D). Putnam Pub Group.
Benary-Isbert, Margot. The Ark. Winston, Clara & Winston, Richard, trs. from Ger. LC 52-13677. (gr. 7 up). 1966. pap. 1.95 (ISBN 0-15-607921-6, VoyB). HarBraceJ.
--Blue Mystery. LC 57-6558. (gr. 4-7). 1957. 5.95 o.p. (ISBN 0-15-209092-4, HJ). HarBraceJ.
--Blue Mystery. LC 57-6558. (Illus.). (gr. 4-7). 1965. pap. 3.95 (ISBN 0-15-613225-7, VoyB). HarBraceJ.
Ben-Asher, David. Fighting Fit: The Official Israel Defense Force Guide to Physical Fitness & Self-Defense. (Illus.). 320p. 1983. pap. 6.95 (ISBN 0-399-50624-1, Perige). Putnam Pub Group.
Ben-Asher, Naomi & Leaf, Hayim, eds. Junior Jewish Encyclopedia. 9rev. ed. LC 79-66184. (Illus.). (gr. 9-12). 1979. 16.95 (ISBN 0-88400-066-4). Shengold.
Benassy, Jean-Pascal. Economics of Market Disequilibrium. (Mathematical Economics, Economic Theory & Econometric Ser.). 222p. 1982. 24.50 (ISBN 0-12-086420-7). Acad Pr.
Benatar, Stephen. Wish Her Safe at Home. LC 82-5815. 192p. 1982. 11.95 (ISBN 0-312-88419-2). St Martin.
Benavidez, Max, ed. see Schneider, Jerome.
Bencar, Gary R. Computers for Small Business: A Step by Step Guide on How to Buy. (Illus.). 148p. 1983. pap. 11.95 (ISBN 0-935222-05-7). La Cumbre.
Bence, Evelyn. Leaving Home: The Making of an Independent Woman. LC 82-15910. 192p. 1982. Pub. by Bridgebooks Pub. 9.95 (ISBN 0-664-27005-0). Westminster.
Bence, Richard. Handbook of Clinical Endodontics. 2nd ed. LC 80-15722. (Illus.). 262p. 1980. pap. text ed. 19.95 (ISBN 0-8016-0587-3). Mosby.
Bench, Carson E. The Collected Publications of Carson E. Bench, Vol. I & II. Write for info. o.p. Vol. I (ISBN 0-9608146-1-2). Vol. II (ISBN 0-9608146-2-0). Western Sun Pubns.
Benchimol, Alberto. Non-Invasive Diagnostic Techniques in Cardiology. LC 76-4843. 462p. 1977. 28.00 (ISBN 0-683-00525-1). Krieger.
--Non-Invasive Diagnostic Techniques in Cardiology. 2nd. ed. (Illus.). 576p. 1981. lib. bdg. 49.95 (ISBN 0-683-00523-5). Williams & Wilkins.
--Non-Invasive Diagnostic Techniques in Cardiology. 1977. 38.00 o.p. (ISBN 0-683-00525-1). Williams & Wilkins.
Benchley, Nathaniel. All Over Again. LC 80-1800. (Illus.). 240p. 1981. 12.95 o.s.i. (ISBN 0-385-15859-9). Doubleday.
--Beyond the Mists. LC 75-9389. 160p. (gr. 7 up). 1975. 10.95 (ISBN 0-06-020459-1, HarpJ); PLB 10.89 o.p. (ISBN 0-06-020460-5). Har-Row.
--Bright Candles. LC 73-5477. (gr. 7 up). 1974. 12.95 (ISBN 0-06-020461-3, HarpJ); PLB 8.79 o.p (ISBN 0-06-020462-1). Har-Row.
--Kilroy & the Gull. LC 76-24309. (Illus.). (gr. 5 up). 1977. 9.57i (ISBN 0-06-020502-4, HarpJ); PLB 6.89 o.p. (ISBN 0-06-020503-2). Har-Row.
--Only Earth & Sky Last Forever. LC 72-82891. 196p. (gr. 7 up). 1972. 10.95 o.p. (ISBN 0-06-020493-1, HarpJ); PLB 8.79 o.p. (ISBN 0-06-020494-X). Har-Row.
--Oscar Otter. LC 66-11499. (Illus.). 64p. (gr. k-2). 1966. 7.89i o.p. (ISBN 0-06-020471-0); PLB 4.79 o.p. (ISBN 0-06-020472-9). Har-Row.
--Portrait of a Scoundrel. (General Ser.). 1979. lib. bdg. 14.95 (ISBN 0-8161-3009-4, Large Print Bks). G K Hall.
--Portrait of a Scoundrel. (General Ser.). 1980. pap. 9.95 (ISBN 0-8161-3104-X, Large Print Bks). G K Hall.
--Snorri & the Strangers. LC 76-3290. (History I Can Read Book). (Illus.). 64p. (gr. k-3). 1976. 7.64i (ISBN 0-06-020457-5, HarpJ); PLB 8.89 o.p. (ISBN 0-06-020458-3). Har-Row.
--Sweet Anarchy. (General Ser.). 1980. lib. bdg. 15.50 (ISBN 0-8161-3134-1, Large Print Bks). G K Hall.

Benchley, Peter. The Girl of the Sea of Cortez. (General Ser.). 1983. lib. bdg. 14.95 (ISBN 0-8161-3487-1, Large Print Bks). G K Hall.
--The Girl of the Sea of Cortez. 1983. pap. 3.50 (ISBN 0-425-06005-5). Berkley Pub.

Bend, J. R., jt. ed. see Hodgson, E.

Benda, Julien. Belphegor. Lawson, S. J., tr. from Fr. LC 82-73432. 165p. Repr. of 1929 ed. lib. bdg. 15.00 (ISBN 0-88116-000-8). Brenner Bks.

Bendall, George P. & Nuetzel, Charles. Now the Time. (Religion Ser.). 179p. (Orig.). 1981. pap. 6.95 (ISBN 0-941018-00-8). Martin Pr.

Bendann, Effie. Death Customs: An Analytical Study of Burial Rites. 1971. 37.00x (ISBN 0-8103-3733-9). Gale.

Bendat, Julius S. Principles & Applications of Random Noise Theory. rev. ed. LC 77-7225. 456p. 1977. Repr. of 1958 ed. lib. bdg. 26.00 (ISBN 0-88275-556-0). Krieger.

Bendat, Julius S. & Piersol, Allan G. Engineering Applications of Correction & Spectral Analysis. LC 79-25926. 302p. 1980. 37.95x (ISBN 0-471-05887-4, Pub. by Wiley-Interscience). Wiley.
--Random Data: Analysis & Measurement Procedures. LC 71-160211. (Illus.). 407p. 1971. 40.95x (ISBN 0-471-06470-X, Pub. by Wiley-Interscience). Wiley.

Bendau, Clifford P. Colin Wilson: The Outsider & Beyond. LC 79-288. (The Milford Ser: Popular Writers of Today: Vol. 21). 1979. lib. bdg. 9.95x (ISBN 0-89370-129-7); pap. 3.95x (ISBN 0-89370-229-3). Borgo Pr.
--Still Worlds Collide: Philip Wylie & the End of the American Dream. LC 80-10756. (The Milford Ser.: Popular Writers of Today: Vol. 30). 1980. lib. bdg. 9.95x (ISBN 0-89370-144-0); pap. 3.95x (ISBN 0-89370-244-7). Borgo Pr.

Bendavid, Avrom. Regional Economic Analysis for Practitioners: An Introduction to Common Descriptive Methods. rev. ed. LC 73-22260. (Illus.). 1974. text ed. 17.95 o.p. (ISBN 0-275-08450-7); pap. text ed. 13.95 o.p. (ISBN 0-275-88820-7). Praeger.

Bendavid-Val, Avron. Regional & Local Economic Analysis for Practicioners. new ed. (Illus.). 208p. 1983. 29.95 (ISBN 0-03-062912-8); pap. 13.95 (ISBN 0-03-062913-6). Praeger.

Bendel, Stephanie B. Making Crime Pay: A Practical Guide to Mystery Writing. (Illus.). 204p. 1983. 13.95 (ISBN 0-13-545939-7); pap. 5.95 (ISBN 0-13-545921-4). P-H.

Bendeler, Johann P. Organopoeia, oder Unterweisung wie eine Orgel nach irhen Hauptstucken als Mensuriren, Abtheilung derer Laden, Zufall des Windes, Stimmung oder Temperatur etc., aus wahren Mathematischen Grunden zu erbauen. (Bibliotheca Organologica Ser.: Vol. 28). 1972. Repr. of 1690 ed. wrappers 22.50 o.s.i. (ISBN 90-6027-152-1, Pub. by Frits Knuf Netherlands). Pendragon NY.

Bender. Dictionary of Nutrition. 5th ed. 1983. text ed. write for info. Butterworth.

Bender, jt. auth. see Sabol.

Bender, A. E. Dictionary of Nutrition & Food Technology. 1977. 28.50 o.p. (ISBN 0-8206-0214-0). Chem Pub.
--Nutrition & Dietetic Foods. (Illus.). 1973. 30.00 o.p. (ISBN 0-8206-0231-0). Chem Pub.

Bender, A. E. & Bender, D. A. Nutrition for Medical Students. 380p. 1982. 38.00x (ISBN 0-471-28041-0, Pub. by Wiley-Interscience). Wiley.

Bender, A. E., et al, eds. Evaluation of Novel Protein Products. LC 70-99794. 1970. write for info. o.p. (ISBN 0-08-006635-6). Pergamon.

Bender, Arnold E. Dictionary of Nutrition & Food Technology. 4th ed. 1975. text ed. 29.95 (ISBN 0-408-00143-7). Butterworth.

Bender, Barbara. Farming in Prehistory from Hunter-Gatherer to Food-Producer. LC 75-13899. (Illus.). 288p. 1975. 21.50 o.p. (ISBN 0-312-28315-6). St Martin.

Bender, Byron W. Spoken Marshallese. (PALI Language Texts: Micronesian). (Orig., Marshallese & Eng.). 1969. pap. text ed. 10.00x (ISBN 0-87022-070-5). UH Pr.

Bender, Carl M. & Orszag, Steven A. Advanced Mathematical Methods for Scientists & Engineers. (International Series in Pure & Applied Mathematics). (Illus.). 1978. text ed. 38.00 (ISBN 0-07-004452-X, C). McGraw.

Bender, Coleman C., jt. auth. see Zacharis, John C.

Bender, D. A., jt. auth. see Bender, A. E.

Bender, David, jt. auth. see Glock, Marvin D.

Bender, David A. Amino Acid Metabolism. LC 74-20863. 234p. 1975. 56.95x (ISBN 0-471-06498-X, Pub. by Wiley-Interscience). Wiley.

Bender, David L. America's Prisons: Opposing Viewpoints. (Opposing Viewpoints Ser.). 140p. (gr. 12). 1980. lib. bdg. 10.95 (ISBN 0-89908-330-7); pap. text ed. 5.95 (ISBN 0-89908-305-6). Greenhaven.
--Constructing a Life Philosophy: Opposing Viewpoints. (Opposing Viewpoints Ser.). 144p. (gr. 12). 1980. lib. bdg. 10.95 (ISBN 0-89908-329-3); pap. text ed. 5.95 (ISBN 0-89908-304-8). Greenhaven.
--The Political Spectrum: Opposing Viewpoints. (Opposing Viewpoints Ser.). (gr. 12). 1981. lib. bdg. 10.95 (ISBN 0-89908-325-0); pap. text ed. 5.95 (ISBN 0-89908-300-5). Greenhaven.

Bender, David L., ed. American Values. (Opposing Viewpoints Ser.: Vol. 10). (Illus.). 1975. lib. bdg. 10.95 (ISBN 0-912616-35-0); pap. text ed. 5.95 (ISBN 0-912616-16-4). Greenhaven.
--The Arms Race: Opposing Viewpoints. (Opposing Viewpoints Ser.). 1982. lib. bdg. 10.95 (ISBN 0-89908-339-0); pap. 5.95 (ISBN 0-89908-314-5). Greenhaven.
--Death & Dying: Opposing Viewpoints. (Opposing Viewpoints Ser.). (gr. 12). 1980. lib. bdg. 10.95 (ISBN 0-89908-331-5); pap. text ed. 5.95 (ISBN 0-89908-306-4). Greenhaven.
--Liberals & Conservatives: A Debate on the Welfare State. rev. ed. (Opposing Viewpoints Ser.: Vol. 2). (Illus.). (gr. 9 up). 1973. lib. bdg. 10.95 (ISBN 0-912616-26-1); pap. 5.95 (ISBN 0-912616-08-3). Greenhaven.
--The Middle East: Opposing Views. (Opposing Views Ser.). 1982. lib. bdg. 10.95 (ISBN 0-89908-340-4); pap. 5.95 (ISBN 0-89908-315-3). Greenhaven.

Bender, David L. & McCuen, Gary E., eds. Economics in America: Opposing Viewpoints. (Opposing Viewpoints Ser.: Vol. 13). (Illus.). (gr. 9-12). 1976. lib. bdg. 10.95 (ISBN 0-912616-38-5); pap. text ed. 5.95 (ISBN 0-912616-19-9). Greenhaven.
--The Indochina War: Why Our Policy Failed. (Opposing Viewpoints Ser.: Vol. 11). (Illus.). 1975. lib. bdg. 10.95 (ISBN 0-912616-36-9); pap. text ed. 5.95 (ISBN 0-912616-17-2). Greenhaven.
--The Sexual Revolution: Traditional Mores Versus New Values. (Opposing Viewpoints Ser.: Vol. 7). (Illus.). (gr. 9 up). 1972. lib. bdg. 10.95 (ISBN 0-912616-31-8); pap. 5.95 (ISBN 0-912616-12-1). Greenhaven.

Bender, David L., ed. see Church, Carol B.

Bender, David L., ed. see Leone, Bruno.

Bender, David S., jt. auth. see Glock, Marvin D.

Bender, Edward A. An Introduction to Mathematical Modeling. LC 77-23840. 256p. 1978. 28.95x (ISBN 0-471-02951-3, Pub. by Wiley-Interscience); solutions manual 6.50 (ISBN 0-471-03407-X). Wiley.

Bender, F. Underground Siting of Nuclear Power Plants: Internationales Symposium, 1981. (Illus.). 409p. (Ger. & Eng.). 1982. pap. text ed. 63.25 (ISBN 3-510-65108-1). Lubrecht & Cramer.

Bender, Gerald J. Angola under the Portuguese: The Myth & the Reality. LC 76-7751. (Perspectives on Southern Africa Ser.: No. 23). 1978. 26.50x (ISBN 0-520-03221-7); pap. 8.50x (ISBN 0-520-04274-3). U of Cal Pr.

Bender, Harold S. Anabaptists & Religious Liberty in the Sixteenth Century. Anderson, Charles S., ed. LC 73-99611. (Facet Bks). 1970. pap. 0.50 o.p. (ISBN 0-8006-3058-0, 1-3058). Fortress.

Bender, Harold S. & Smith, C. Henry, eds. Mennonite Encyclopedia, 4vols. 1956-1969. Set. 108.00x (ISBN 0-8361-1018-8); 30.00x ea. Vol. 1 (ISBN 0-8361-1118-4). Vol. 2 (ISBN 0-8361-1119-2). Vol. 3 (ISBN 0-8361-1120-6). Vol. 4 (ISBN 0-8361-1121-4). Herald Pr.

Bender, James F. How to Sell Well: The Art & Science of Professional Salesmanship. 1971. pap. 4.95 (ISBN 0-07-004441-4, SP). McGraw.
--How to Talk Well. 1963. pap. 4.95 (ISBN 0-07-004446-5, SP). McGraw.
--N. B. C. Handbook of Pronunciation. 3rd, rev. ed. Crowell, Thomas, Jr., ed. 1964. 14.37i (ISBN 0-690-57472-X). T Y Crowell.

Bender, Jay & Shea, Edward. Physical Fitness: Tests & Excercises. 1983. Repr. of 1964 ed. write for info. (ISBN 0-89874-502-0). Krieger.

Bender, Lauretta. Aggression, Hostility & Anxiety in Children. (Illus.). 200p. 1953. photocopy ed. spiral 19.75x (ISBN 0-398-04631-X). C C Thomas.
--Child Psychiatric Techniques. (Illus.). 360p. 1952. photocopy ed. spiral 34.50x (ISBN 0-398-04632-8). C C Thomas.
--A Dynamic Psychopathology of Childhood. (Illus.). 296p. 1954. photocopy ed. spiral 29.75x (ISBN 0-398-04633-6). C C Thomas.
--Psychopathology of Children with Organic Brain Disorders. (Illus.). 168p. 1956. photocopy ed. spiral 16.75x (ISBN 0-398-04634-4). C C Thomas.

Bender, Leonard F. Prostheses & Rehabilitation After Arm Amputation. (Illus.). 196p. 1974. 19.75x (ISBN 0-398-03094-4). C C Thomas.

Bender, Mark, tr. Seventh Sister & Teh Serpent. (Illus.). 65p. 1982. pap. 2.95 (ISBN 0-8351-1044-3). China Bks.

Bender, Michael & Valletuhi, Peter J. Teaching the Moderately & Severely Handicapped: Curriculum, Objectives, Strategies & Activites, 3 vols. (Illus.). 1000p. 1976. Set. ed. 3 vol. set 50.00 (ISBN 0-686-77132-X). Vol. 1. 19.95 (ISBN 0-8391-0869-9); Vol. 2. 19.95 (ISBN 0-8391-0868-0); Vol. 3. 19.95 (ISBN 0-8391-0963-6). Univ Park.

Bender, Michael & Valletutti, Peter J. Teaching Functional Academics: A Curriculum Guide for Adolescents & Adults with Learning problems. 296p. 1981. pap. text ed. 19.95 (ISBN 0-8391-1662-4). Univ Park.

Bender, Michael, jt. auth. see Valletutti, J.

Bender, Myron L. & Brubacher, Lewis J. Catalysis. (Illus.). 256p. 1973. text ed. 18.95 (ISBN 0-07-004450-3, C); pap. text ed. 14.95 (ISBN 0-07-004451-1). McGraw.

Bender, Paul, jt. auth. see Dorsen, Norman.

Bender, Paul S. Resource Management: An Alternative View of the Management Process. (Systems Engineering & Analysis Ser.). 256p. 1982. 35.95x (ISBN 0-471-08179-5, Pub. by Wiley-Interscience). Wiley.

Bender, Roger J. Uniforms, Organization & History of the Waffen-SS, Vol. 1. (Illus.). 160p. 1969. 16.95 (ISBN 0-912138-02-5). Bender Pub CA.

Bender, Roger J., jt. auth. see Chalif, Don.

Bender, Sheldon R., jt. ed. see Kroman, Henry S.

Bender, Stephen J., jt. auth. see Sorochan, Walter D.

Bender, Thomas. Community & Social Change in America. LC 82-47981. 176p. (Orig.). 1982. pap. text ed. 5.95x (ISBN 0-8018-2924-0). Johns Hopkins.
--Toward an Urban Vision: Ideas & Institutions in Nineteenth-Century America. LC 82-47980. 296p. (Orig.). 1982. pap. text ed. 7.50x (ISBN 0-8018-2925-9). Johns Hopkins.

Bender, Todd K., jt. auth. see Briggum, Sue M.

Bendersky, David, et al. Resource Recovery Processing Equipment. LC 82-7882. (Pollution Technology Rev. 93). (Illus.). 417p. 1983. 42.00 (ISBN 0-8155-0911-1). Noyes.

Bendersky, Joseph W. Carl Schmitt, Theorist for the Reich. LC 82-61353. 336p. 1983. 27.50x (ISBN 0-691-05380-4). Princeton U Pr.

Bendick. The Big Strawberry Book of the Earth: Our Ever-Changing Planet. 110p. 1980. 6.95 (ISBN 0-07-004514-3). McGraw.

Bendick, James. Automobiles. rev. ed. LC 78-6252. (First Bks.). (Illus.). (gr. 4-6). 1978. PLB 8.90 signed & Hd (ISBN 0-531-02227-7). Watts.

Bendick, Jeanne. Airplanes. rev. ed. (First Bk.). (Illus.). 72p. (gr. 4-6). 1982. PLB 8.90 (ISBN 0-531-00455-4). Watts.
--Artificial Satellites. (First Bks.). (Illus.). 72p. (gr. 4 up). 1982. PLB 8.90 (ISBN 0-531-04381-9). Watts.
--Exploring an Ocean Tide Pool. LC 75-34469. (Good Earth Ser.). (Illus.). 64p. (gr. 2-6). 1976. PLB 7.22 (ISBN 0-8116-6105-9). Garrard.
--The First Book of Airplanes. rev. ed. LC 75-31880. (First Bks. Ser). (Illus.). 72p. (gr. 4). 1976. PLB 7.90 o.p. (ISBN 0-531-00455-4). Watts.
--Putting the Sun to Work. LC 78-6178. (Good Earth Ser.). (Illus.). (gr. 3). PLB 7.22 (ISBN 0-8116-6111-3). Garrard.
--Scare a Ghost, Tame a Monster. LC 82-23696. (Illus.). 120p. (gr. 3-6). 1983. price not set (ISBN 0-664-32701-X). Westminster.

Bendick, Jeanne & Lefkowitz, R. J. Electronics for Young People. 5th ed. (Illus.). 192p. (gr. 7 up). 1972. PLB 6.95 o.p. (ISBN 0-07-004495-3, GB). McGraw.

Bendick, Marc, Jr., et al. Toward Efficiency & Effectiveness in the WIC Delivery System. (An Institute Paper). 216p. 1976. pap. 4.50 o.p. (ISBN 0-685-99496-1, 14600). Urban Inst.

Bendiksen, Robert, jt. auth. see Fulton, Robert J.

Bendiner, Elmer. The Fall of Fortresses: A Personal Account of the Most Daring & Deadly American Air Battles of World War II. (Illus.). 1980. 11.95 o.p. (ISBN 0-399-12372-5). Putnam Pub Group.

Bendit, Laurence J., jt. auth. see Bendit, Phoebe D.

Bendit, Phoebe D. & Bendit, Laurence J. The Etheric Body of Man. LC 76-46930. 1977. pap. 3.50 (ISBN 0-8356-0489-6, Quest). Theos Pub Hse.

Bendix, Reinhard. Kings or People: Power & the Mandate to Rule. 1978. 35.00x o.p. (ISBN 0-520-02302-1); pap. 9.95 (ISBN 0-520-04090-2). U of Cal Pr.
--Max Weber: An Intellectual Portrait. 1978. 36.50x (ISBN 0-520-03503-8); pap. 8.50x (ISBN 0-520-03194-6). U of Cal Pr.
--Nation-Building & Citizenship: Studies of Our Changing Social Order. 2nd rev. ed. LC 73-91670. 400p. 1977. 38.50x (ISBN 0-520-02676-4); pap. 8.50x (ISBN 0-520-02761-2, CAMPUS 138). U of Cal Pr.

Bendle, S. C. Cricket. 1979. 4.95 o.p. (ISBN 0-533-03947-9). Vantage.

Ben-Dor, Gabriel. The Druzes in Israel: A Political Study. 287p. 1979. text ed. 23.00x (ISBN 965-223-333-1, Pub. by Magnes Israel). Humanities.
--State & Conflict in the Middle East. 200p. 1983. text ed. 30.00x (ISBN 0-7146-3224-4, F Cass Co). Biblio Dist.

Bendor-Samuel, David. Hierarchical Structures in Guajajara. (Publications in Linguistics & Related Fields, No. 37). 214p. 1972. pap. 4.50x (ISBN 0-88312-039-9); microfiche 3.00x (ISBN 0-88312-439-4). Summer Inst Ling.
--Tupi Studies I. (Publications in Linguistics & Related Fields Ser.: No. 29). 129p. 1971. pap. 3.00x (ISBN 0-88312-031-3); microfiche 2.25x (ISBN 0-88312-431-9). Summer Inst Ling.

Bendor-Samuel, John. Ten Nigerian Tone Languages. (Language Data, African Ser.: No. 4). 129p. 1974. pap. 7.00x (ISBN 0-88312-604-4); microfiche 2.25x (ISBN 0-88312-704-0). Summer Inst Ling.

Bendor-Samuel, John, et al. Duka Sentence, Clause & Phrase. (Language Data, African Ser.: No. 3). 1973. pap. 5.00x (ISBN 0-88312-603-6); microfiche 3.00x (ISBN 0-88312-703-2). Summer Inst Ling.

Bendt, Ingela & Downing, Jim. We Shall Return: Women of Palestine. (Illus.). 144p. (Orig.). 1982. 16.95 (ISBN 0-88208-154-3); pap. 8.50 (ISBN 0-88208-155-1). Lawrence Hill.

Bene, J. G. & Beall, H. W. Les Arbes dans l'Amenagement des Terres sous les Tropiques: Une solution a la Faim. 53p. 1978. pap. 4.00 o.p. (ISBN 0-88936-169-X, IDRC-084F, IDRC). Unipub.

Beneck, John. And Why Did You Come to the Emergency Room? LC 80-20360. 1983. pap. 10.95 (ISBN 0-87949-192-2). Ashley Bks.

Benecke, Gerhard. Germany in the Thirty Years War. LC 78-21443. (Illus.). 1979. 22.50x (ISBN 0-312-32626-2). St Martin.

Benedeit. The Anglo-Norman Voyage of St. Brendan. Short, I. & Merrilees, B., eds. (Medieval French Text Ser.). 1979. pap. 6.00 (ISBN 0-7190-0735-6). Manchester.

Benedek, P., ed. Steady-State Flow-Sheeting of Chemical Plants. (Chemical Engineering Monographs: Vol. 12). 1981. 68.00 (ISBN 0-444-99765-2). Elsevier.

Benedetta, C. di see Di Benedetta, C. & Balasz, R.

Benedetti, Edoardo De see De Benedetti, Edoardo.

Benedetti, Jean. Stanislavski: An Intoduction. 1982. pap. 5.95 (ISBN 0-87830-578-5). Theatre Arts.

Benedetti, Robert. The Actor at Work. 3rd ed. (Illus.). 1981. text ed. 18.95 (ISBN 0-13-003673-0). P-H.

Benedetti, Sergio De see DeBenedetti, Sergio.

Benedetto, Ubaldo di see Di Benedetto, Ubaldo.

Benedict, Brad. Cool Cats. 1982. 5.95 (ISBN 0-517-54760-0, Harmony Bks). Crown.

Benedict, Brad, ed. The Blue Book. (Illus.). 96p. 1983. 13.95 (ISBN 0-394-62439-4, E857, Ever). Grove.

Benedict, Dianne. Shiny Objects. LC 82-10853. (Iowa School of Letters Award for Short Fiction Ser.: No. 13). 176p. 1982. 12.95 (ISBN 0-87745-116-8); pap. 8.95 (ISBN 0-87745-117-6). U of Iowa Pr.

Benedict, Glen E., jt. auth. see Schulz, Wallace W.

Benedict, Madeline. Sudden Door. 1960. 2.75 o.p. (ISBN 0-8233-0005-6). Golden Quill.

Benedict, Manson, et al. Nuclear Chemical Engineering. 2nd ed. (Illus.). 1008p. 1981. text ed. 39.95 (ISBN 0-07-004531-3, C). McGraw.

Benedict, Paul K. Sino-Tibetan: A Conspectus. LC 78-154511. (Princeton-Cambridge Studies in Chinese Linguistics: No. 2). 1972. 82.50 (ISBN 0-521-08175-0). Cambridge U Pr.

Benedict, Philip. Rouen During the Wars of Religion. LC 79-50883. (Cambridge Studies in Early Modern History). (Illus.). 324p. 1981. 44.50 (ISBN 0-521-22818-2). Cambridge U Pr.

Benedict, R. Ralph. Electronics for Scientists & Engineers. 2nd ed. (Illus.). 1975. 31.95 (ISBN 0-13-252353-1). P-H.

Benedict, Robert P. Fundamentals of Temperature, Pressure, & Flow Measurements. 2nd ed. LC 76-54341. 517p. 1977. 47.95x (ISBN 0-471-06561-7, Pub. by Wiley-Interscience). Wiley.

Benedict, Ruth. Chrysanthemum & the Sword: Patterns of Japanese Culture. 1967. pap. 6.95 (ISBN 0-452-00611-2, F611, Mer). NAL.
--Patterns of Culture. 1961. 10.95 (ISBN 0-395-07405-3); pap. 4.95 (ISBN 0-395-08357-5). HM.
--Race: Science & Politics. 206p. 1982. Repr. of 1950 ed. lib. bdg. 27.50 (ISBN 0-313-23597-X, BENR). Greenwood.

Benedict, Ruth, ed. Cattails & Meadowlarks. LC 81-84103. (Illus.). 88p. 1981. pap. 3.95 (ISBN 0-89821-037-2). Reiman Assocs.
--Country People. LC 79-63698. (Illus.). 1979. pap. 7.95 (ISBN 0-89821-029-1). Reiman Assocs.
--Showers. LC 79-65360. (Orig.). 1980. pap. 7.95 (ISBN 0-89821-030-5). Reiman Assocs.

Benedict, Ruth F. Concept of the Guardian Spirit in North America. LC 24-872. 1923. pap. 12.00 (ISBN 0-527-00528-2). Kraus Repr.

Benedict, Stephen. Cultural Institutions Across America: Functions & Funding. 28p. 1982. pap. 3.00 (ISBN 0-943006-15-5). Seven Springs.

Benedict, Stephen, compiled by. Arts Management: An Annotated Bibliography. rev. ed. LC 80-25918. 48p. 1980. pap. 5.75 (ISBN 0-89062-049-0, Pub. by Ctr for Arts Info). Pub Ctr Cult Res.

Benedict, Stewart H., ed. Crime Solvers: Thirteen Classic Detective Stories. (Orig.). 1966. pap. 1.50 o.p. (ISBN 0-440-93078-2, LFL). Dell.

Benedictis, Daniel J. De see De Benedictis, Daniel J.

Benedikt, Michael. The Badminton at Great Barrington; Or, Gustave Mahler & the Chattanooga Choo-Choo. LC 80-5258. (Pitt Poetry Ser.). xii, 81p. 1980. 9.95 (ISBN 0-8229-3423-X); pap. 4.50 (ISBN 0-8229-5322-6). U of Pittsburgh Pr.

Benedikt, Michael & Wellwarth, George E., eds. Modern French Theatre: The Avant-Garde, Dada & Surrealism. Benedikt, Michael & Wellwarth, George E., trs. 1966. pap. 7.95 (ISBN 0-525-47176-6, 0772-230). Dutton.

Benedikt, Michael, tr. see Benedikt, Michael & Wellwarth, George E.

Benedikt, Moriz. Anatomical Studies upon Brains of Criminals. Fowler, E. P., tr. from Ger. (Historical Foundations of Forensic Psychiatry & Psychology Ser.). (Illus.). 185p. 1980. Repr. of 1881 ed. lib. bdg. 25.00 (ISBN 0-306-76071-1). Da Capo.

Benedikter, Helen. From Nursing Audit to Multidisciplinary Audit. 45p. 1977. 4.95 (ISBN 0-686-38333-8, 20-1673). Natl League Nurse.

Benediktsson, Thomas E. George Sterling. (United States Author Ser.). 1980. lib. bdg. 13.95 (ISBN 0-8057-7313-4, Twayne). G K Hall.

--George Sterling. (United States Author Ser.: No. 377). (gr. 10-12). 1980. lib. bdg. 11.95 o.p. (ISBN 0-8057-7313-4, Twayne). G K Hall.

Benedikz, S., tr. see Blondal, S.

Benefield, Larry D., jt. auth. see Judkins, Joseph F.

Benefield, Larry D., jt. auth. see Randall, Clifford W.

Benemann, John R. Biofuels: A Survey. 106p. 1980. pap. 16.95x (ISBN 0-89934-006-7, B045). Solar Energy Info.

Benenson, Abram S., ed. Control of Communicable Diseases in Man. 13th ed. LC 75-28217. 443p. 1981. pap. 7.50x (ISBN 0-87553-076-1, 079). Am Pub Health.

Benenson, Sharen. The New York Botanical Garden Cookbook. (Illus.). 256p. 1982. 16.95 (ISBN 0-686-83750-9). Hastings.

Benenzon, Rolando O. Music Therapy in Child Psychosis. (Illus.). 112p. 1982. 15.50x (ISBN 0-398-04646-8). C C Thomas.

Beneri, Marie L. Journey Through Utopia. 338p. 1982. pap. 4.00 (ISBN 0-900384-21-2). Left Bank.

Beneria, Lourdes. Women & Development: The Sexual Division of Labour in Rural Societies. 288p. 1982. 25.95 (ISBN 0-03-061802-9). Praeger.

Benes, J. Statistical Dynamics of Automatic Control Systems. text ed. 17.50x o.p. (ISBN 0-685-20634-3). Transatlantic.

Benes, P. & Majer, V. Trace Chemistry of Aqueous Solutions: General Chemistry & Radiochemistry. (Topics In Inorganic & General Chemistry: Vol. 18). 1980. 53.25 (ISBN 0-444-99798-9). Elsevier.

Benes, Vaclav. General Stochastic Processes in the Theory of Queues. (Illus.). 1963. 8.50 o.p. (ISBN 0-201-00510-7, Adv Bk Prog). A-W.

Benes, Vaclav & Porends, Norman J. Poland. (Nations of the Modern World Ser.). 1976. 27.00x o.p. (ISBN 0-510-38911-2). Westview.

Benes, Vaclav E. see Wets, Roger J.

Benesch, Friedrich. Easter. 1981. pap. 5.95 (ISBN 0-903540-44-4, Pub. by Floris Books). St George Bk Serv.

Benestad, J. Brian. The Pursuit of a Just Social Order: Policy Statements of the U. S. Catholic Bishops, 1966-80. LC 82-18326. 220p. (Orig.). 1982. 12.00 (ISBN 0-89633-060-5); pap. 7.00 (ISBN 0-89633-061-3). Ethics & Public Policy.

Benet, Juan. A Meditation. Rabassa, Gregory, tr. from Span. 372p. 1983. pap. 8.95 (ISBN 0-89255-065-1). Persea Bks.

Benet, William R. Perpetual Light. 1919. 34.50x (ISBN 0-686-51286-3). Elliots Bks.

Benet, William R., ed. Reader's Encyclopedia. 2nd ed. LC 65-12510. (Illus.). 1965. 16.95i (ISBN 0-690-67128-8); thumb indexed 21.10i (ISBN 0-690-67129-6). T Y Crowell.

Benet, William R., jt. ed. see Briggs, Wallace A.

Benevento, Nicole, jt. auth. see Appleton, Nicholas.

Benevolo, Leonardo. History of Modern Architecture, 2 vols. Incl. Vol. 1. The Tradition of Modern Architecture. pap. 12.50 (ISBN 0-262-52044-3); Vol. 2. The Modern Movement. pap. 15.00 (ISBN 0-262-52045-1). 1977. Set. pap. text ed. 25.00 (ISBN 0-262-52046-X). MIT Pr.

--The History of the City. (Illus.). 1980. 100.00x (ISBN 0-262-02146-3). MIT Pr.

--Origins of Modern Town Planning. Landry, Judith, tr. from It. 1971. pap. 5.95x (ISBN 0-262-52018-4). MIT Pr.

Benewick, Robert, et al, eds. Knowledge & Belief in Politics: The Problems of Ideology. LC 73-85266. 320p. 1973. 22.50 (ISBN 0-312-45885-1). St Martin.

Benfer, David W., jt. auth. see Spirn, Steven.

Benfey, O. Theodor. Classics in the Theory of Chemical Combination. LC 81-8300. 206p. 1981. Repr. of 1963 ed. 11.50 (ISBN 0-89874-368-0). Krieger.

Benfey, Otto T. Introduction to Organic Reaction Mechanisms. LC 80-12301. 224p. (Orig.). 1970. pap. text ed. 13.50 (ISBN 0-89874-173-4). Krieger.

--The Names & Structures of Organic Compounds. LC 82-10012. 228p. 1982. pap. text ed. 9.50 (ISBN 0-89874-520-9). Krieger.

Benforado, J., jt. ed. see Clarke, J. H.

Benford, Gregory. The Stars in Shroud. LC 78-242. 1978. 8.95 o.p. (ISBN 0-399-12229-X, Pub. by Berkley). Putnam Pub Group.

--Timescape. 1980. 12.95 o.p. (ISBN 0-671-25327-1). S&S.

Benford, Robert J., jt. auth. see Merriam, Alan P.

Benford, Timothy. The World War II Quiz & Fact Book. LC 82-47516. (Illus.). 224p. 1983. 12.45i (ISBN 0-06-015025-4, HarpT); pap. 7.64i (ISBN 0-06-090968-4, CN968, HarpT). Har-Row.

Bengesser, Gerhard. Wechselbeziehungen Zwischen Psychiatrie, Psychologie und Philosophie. 178p. (Ger.). 1982. write for info. (ISBN 3-261-05019-5). P Lang Pubs.

Bengtson, Athene, ed. see Newhouse, Flower A.

Bengtson, Hermann. The History of Greece. new ed. Bloedow, Edmund, tr. from Ger. Date not set. cancelled (ISBN 0-88866-576-8). Samuel Stevens. Postponed.

--Introduction to Ancient History. Frank, R. I. & Gilliard, Frank D., trs. LC 78-118685. (California Library Reprint Ser). 1976. 26.50x (ISBN 0-520-03150-4). U of Cal Pr.

Bengtson, Vern L. The Social Psychology of Aging. LC 73-4918. 1973. pap. 3.50 o.p. (ISBN 0-672-61339-5). Bobbs.

Bengtsson, Ingmar & Van Boer, Bertil H., Jr., eds. The Symphony in Sweeden, Pt. 1. (The Symphony 1720-1840 Series F: Vol. II). 1982. lib. bdg. 90.00 (ISBN 0-8240-3811-8). Garland Pub.

Ben Gurion, David & Pearlman, Moshe. Ben Gurion Looks Back: In Talks with Moshe Pearlman. LC 65-25283. 1970. pap. 2.25 o.p. (ISBN 0-8052-0274-9). Schocken.

Benham, Djamchid. Cultural Policy in Iran. LC 72-96471. (Studies & Documents on Cultural Policies). (Illus.). 46p. (Orig.). 1973. pap. 5.00 o.p. (ISBN 92-3-101002-6, U125, UNESCO). Unipub.

Benham, Harvey. Man's Struggle for Food. LC 80-67188. (Illus.). 506p. 1981. lib. bdg. 29.25 (ISBN 0-8191-1518-5); pap. text ed. 17.75 (ISBN 0-8191-1519-3). U Pr of Amer.

Benham, Hugh. Latin Church Music in England, Fourteen Sixty to Fifteen Seventy-Five. (Music Reprint Ser.: 1980). (Illus.). 1980. Repr. of 1977 ed. lib. bdg. 27.50 (ISBN 0-306-76025-8). Da Capo.

Benham, Jack L., ed. see Rickard, T. A.

Benham, P. P. Elementary Mechanics of Solids. (Illus.). 1966. 21.00 (ISBN 0-08-011216-1). Pergamon.

Benham, Phyllis S. Woodstove Cookery Cookbook: Soups, Stews, Chowders & Home-Made Breads, Vol. 2. 54p. 1981. pap. 3.95 (ISBN 0-686-81745-1). Country Cooking.

Ben-Horim, Moshe & Levy, Haim. Statistics: Decisions & Applications in Business & Economics. Incl. Mastering Business Statistics: A Student Guide to Problem Solving. Coccari, Ronald L. 320p. wkbk. 14.95 (ISBN 0-394-32484-6). 592p. 1981. text ed. 27.95 (ISBN 0-394-32297-5). Random.

Benice, Daniel D. Introduction to Computers & Data Processing. (Applied Mathematics Ser). 1970. ref. ed. 19.95 (ISBN 0-13-479543-1). P-H.

Benis, Leslie. This Is the Puli. (Illus.). 320p. 1976. 19.95 (ISBN 0-87666-368-4, PS709). TFH Pubns.

Benison, Saul, ed. Tom Rivers: Reflections on a Life in Medicine & Science. 1967. 25.00x o.p. (ISBN 0-262-02026-2). MIT Pr.

Ben-Israel, Adi & Greville, Thomas N. Generalized Inverses: Theory & Applications. LC 79-13385. 410p. 1980. Repr. of 1974 ed. lib. bdg. 26.00 (ISBN 0-88275-991-4). Krieger.

Ben-Israel, Adi, et al. Optimality in Nonlinear Programming: A Feasible Directions Approach. LC 80-36746. (Pure & Applied Mathematics Ser.). 144p. 1981. 24.95 (ISBN 0-471-08057-8, Pub. by Wiley-Interscience). Wiley.

Benitez, Fernando. In the Magic Land of Peyote. Upton, John, tr. from Span. LC 74-23171. (Texas Pan American Ser). (Illus.). 226p. 1975. 12.95 o.p. (ISBN 0-292-73806-4). U of Tex Pr.

Benitez, Zuleyka. Trouble in Paradise. LC 78-17909. (Lost Roads Ser.: No. 19). (Illus.). 56p. (Orig.). 1980. pap. 9.00 (ISBN 0-918786-20-7). Lost Roads.

Benjamin, A. Cooking with Conscience. 1977. pap. 4.95 (ISBN 0-8164-0902-1, Vineyard). Seabury.

Benjamin, A. Corne. Science, Technology & Human Values. LC 65-10698. 306p. 1965. 18.00x (ISBN 0-8262-0035-4). U of Mo Pr.

Benjamin, Alexander & Helal, Basil. Surgical Repair & Reconstruction in Rheumatoid Disease. 247p. 1980. 74.95x (ISBN 0-471-08291-0, Pub. by Wiley Med). Wiley.

Benjamin, Alfred D. The Helping Interview. 3rd ed. LC 80-81650. 208p. 1981. pap. text ed. 9.95 (ISBN 0-395-29648-X). HM.

Benjamin, Anna, tr. see Xenophon.

Benjamin, Asher. The Works of Asher Benjamin: Boston, 1806-1843, 7 vols. Incl. The Country Builder's Assistant: 1797. 84p. (ISBN 0-306-71027-7); The American Builder's Companion: 1806. 158p. (ISBN 0-306-71026-9); The Rudiments of Architecture: 1814. 162p. (ISBN 0-306-71031-5); The Practical House Carpenter: 1830. 248p. (ISBN 0-306-71029-3); The Practice of Architecture: 1833. 236p. (ISBN 0-306-71030-7); The Builder's Guide: 1839. 174p. 40.00 (ISBN 0-306-70971-6); Elements of Architecture: 1843. 290p. 40.00 (ISBN 0-306-71028-5). (Architecture & Decorative Art Ser.). 1974. 42.50 ea.; Set. 265.00 (ISBN 0-306-71032-3). Da Capo.

Benjamin, B. & Pollard, J. H. Analysis of Mortality & Other Actuarial Statistics. 212p. 1980. 31.50 (ISBN 0-434-90137-7, Pub. by Heinemann). David & Charles.

Benjamin, B., et al, eds. see Eugenics Society, 9th Symposium.

Benjamin, Ben. Listen to Your Pain. 1983. write for info. (ISBN 0-670-43017-X). Viking Pr.

--Listen to Your Pain. 1983. pap. 7.95 (ISBN 0-14-006687-X). Penguin.

Benjamin, Bernard. General Insurance. 1977. 18.95 (ISBN 0-434-90136-9, Pub. by Heinemann). David & Charles.

Benjamin, C. Running Basics. 1979. 7.95 o.p. (ISBN 0-13-783928-6); pap. 2.50 o.p. (ISBN 0-13-783910-3). P-H.

Benjamin, Carol. Cartooning for Kids. LC 81-43876. (Illus.). 80p. (gr. 3-7). 1982. pap. 3.80i (ISBN 0-690-04207-8, TYC-J); PLB 9.89g (ISBN 0-690-04208-6). Har-Row.

Benjamin, Carol L., jt. auth. see Haggerty, Arthur J.

Benjamin, David. Competitive Tennis. (Illus.). 168p. 1979. 5.00 o.p. (ISBN 0-686-37482-7). USTA.

--The Idol. LC 78-12844. 1979. 10.95 o.p. (ISBN 0-399-12287-7). Putnam Pub Group.

Benjamin, David A. Competitive Tennis: A Parent's & Young Players Guide. 1979. 12.45i (ISBN 0-397-01326-4). Har-Row.

Benjamin, Deborah V. A Road Map to Effective Planning & Time Management. rev. ed. 215p. 1982. pap. write for info. (ISBN 0-911347-00-3). Debron.

Benjamin, Don-Paul. Downhill. (Illus.). 1979. pap. 5.00 (ISBN 0-932624-01-4). Elevation Pr.

--Wait 'Til Next Year: The Football Fan's Handbook. (Illus.). 20p. (Orig.). 1982. pap. 2.00 (ISBN 0-932624-05-7). Elevation Pr.

--When You Live Alone: Things Dedicated Singles Do. (Illus.). 1979. pap. 3.00 (ISBN 0-932624-00-6). Elevation Pr.

Benjamin, Don-Paul, illus. Rado. (Illus.). 40p. (Orig.). 1982. pap. 2.00 (ISBN 0-932624-04-9). Elevation Pr.

Benjamin, Elsie. Man at Home in the Universe: A Study of the Great Evolutionary Cycle: the 'Globes', the 'Rounds', 'Races', 'Root-Races' & 'Sub-Races' (Study Ser.: No. 8). 36p. 1981. pap. 3.00 (ISBN 0-913004-43-X). Point Loma Pub.

--Search & Find: Theosophical Reference Index. Small, W. Emmett & Todd, Helen, eds. (Study Ser.: No. 1). 1978. pap. 5.95 (ISBN 0-913004-32-4). Point Loma Pub.

--The Stanzas of Dzyan: Notes for Study on Cosmogenesis & Anthropogenesis. (Study Ser.: No. 5). 45p. 1981. pap. 3.00 (ISBN 0-913004-40-5). Point Loma Pub.

--A Study of the Whole of Man: The Significance of the Seven Principles of Man & The Significance of the Monad. (Study Ser.: No. 6). 41p. 1981. pap. 3.00 (ISBN 0-913004-41-3). Point Loma Pub.

Benjamin, George J. Edward W. Blyden: Messiah of Black Revolution. 1978. 6.95 o.p. (ISBN 0-533-03651-8). Vantage.

Benjamin, J. & Cornell, C. A. Probability, Statistics, & Decisions for Civil Engineers. 1970. 39.50 (ISBN 0-07-004549-6, C). McGraw.

Benjamin, James J. & Kratchman, Stanley H. Practice Problem Two, for Use with Intermediate Accounting. (Illus.). 60p. (Orig.). 1981. pap. text ed. 5.95 (ISBN 0-931920-17-5). Dame Pubns.

Benjamin, James J., et al. Financial Accounting. 3rd ed. LC 80-67311. (Illus.). 737p. 1980. pap. text ed. 24.95 (ISBN 0-931920-21-3); practice problems 4.95x (ISBN 0-931920-51-5); study guide 5.95x (ISBN 0-686-70442-8); work papers 7.95x (ISBN 0-931920-52-3). Dame Pubns.

--Principles of Accounting. LC 80-67313. 1100p. 1981. text ed. 25.95x (ISBN 0-931920-24-8); study guide 5.95 (ISBN 0-931920-56-6); working papers o.p. 6.95 (ISBN 0-686-68563-6); practice problem o.p. 4.95 (ISBN 0-686-68564-4). Dame Pubns.

Benjamin, Jean K., jt. auth. see Roethel, Hans K.

Benjamin, Laura. Le Chemin de L'Inca. (Collection Colombine). 192p. 1983. pap. 1.95 (ISBN 0-373-48060-1). Harlequin Bks.

Benjamin, Linda. Ecstasy's Fury. 1983. pap. 3.50 (ISBN 0-8217-1126-1). Zebra.

Benjamin, Ludy T., ed. G. Stanley Hall Lecture Series, Vol.1. LC 81-66984. 1981. text ed. 12.00 (ISBN 0-912704-49-7). Am Psychol.

Benjamin, Ludy T. & Lowman, Kathleen D., eds. Activities Handbook for the Teaching of Psychology. LC 81-1648. (Orig.). 1981. pap. 13.00. Am Psychol.

Benjamin, Martin & Curtis, Joy. Ethics in Nursing. 1981. text ed. 19.95x (ISBN 0-19-502836-8); pap. text ed. 9.95x (ISBN 0-19-502837-6). Oxford U Pr.

Benjamin, Paul. Squeeze Play. 1982. 10.95 o.p. (ISBN 0-686-34662-9); pap. 5.95 o.p. (ISBN 0-686-35712-4). Caroline Hse.

--Squeeze Play. 200p. (Orig.). 1982. 10.95 (ISBN 0-938764-03-9); pap. 5.95 (ISBN 0-938764-04-7). Alpha-Omega Bks.

Benjamin, Philip S. The Philadelphia Quakers in the Industrial Age, 1865-1920. LC 75-22967. 309p. 1976. 19.95 (ISBN 0-87722-086-7). Temple U Pr.

Benjamin, Richard K. Introduction & Supplement to Thaxter's Contribution Towards a Monograph of the Laboulbeniacea. 1971. 12.80 (ISBN 3-7682-0708-0). Lubrecht & Cramer.

--The Merosporangiferous Mucorales. (Bibl. Myco.). (Illus.). 1967. Repr. of 1965 ed. 24.00 (ISBN 3-7682-0514-2). Lubrecht & Cramer.

Benjamin, Robert C. & Kemppainen, Rudolph C. Hospital Administrator's Desk Book. 270p. 1983. 41.50 (ISBN 0-13-394890-0, Busn). P-H.

Benjamin, Roger. The Limits of Politics: Collective Goods & Political Change in Post-Industrial Societies. LC 79-19473. 148p. 1982. pap. text ed. 5.00x (ISBN 0-226-04234-0). U of Chicago Pr.

Benjamin, Thomas. The Craft of Modal Counterpoint: A Practice Approach. LC 77-90012. 1979. pap. text ed. 12.95 (ISBN 0-02-870480-0). Schirmer Bks.

Benjamin, Thomas, et al. Music for Analysis: Examples from the Common Practice Period & the Twentieth Century. LC 77-78237. 1978. pap. text ed. 16.50 (ISBN 0-395-25507-4). HM.

Benjamin, Thomas E., et al. Techniques & Materials of Tonal Music: With an Introduction to Twentieth Century Techniques. 2nd ed. LC 78-69578. (Illus.). 1979. text ed. 20.50 (ISBN 0-395-27066-9). HM.

Benjamin, Walter. Illuminations. LC 68-24382. 1969. pap. 6.50 (ISBN 0-8052-0241-2). Schocken.

Benjamin, William A., ed. Harfax Directory of Industry Data Sources, 2 vol. set. 1440p. 1981. professional reference 175.00 o.p. (ISBN 0-88410-852-X). Ballinger Pub.

Benjamin, William A. & Kingston, Irene, eds. Directory of European Business Information. 608p. 1980. prof ref 110.00x (ISBN 2-85993-001-9). Ballinger Pub.

Benjamin, William P. Plastic Tooling: Techniques & Applications. LC 75-39845. (Illus.). 256p. 1972. 49.50 (ISBN 0-07-004554-2, P&RB). McGraw.

Benjamine, Elbert. How to Use Modern Ephemerides: Computed for Midnight & Noon & Eclipse Dates 1880-1990. 1981. pap. 1.50 (ISBN 0-933646-15-1). Aries Pr.

--The Influence of the Planet Pluto, Including an Ephemeris of Pluto, 1840-1990. 1981. pap. 1.50 (ISBN 0-933646-16-X). Aries Pr.

Benjamini, E., jt. ed. see Atassi, M. Z.

Benke, Ralph L., Jr. & Edwards, James Don. Transfer Pricing: Techniques & Uses. 154p. pap. 14.95 (ISBN 0-86641-012-0, 80118). Natl Assn Accts.

Benke, William. All About Land Investment. new ed. (Illus.). 1976. 27.50 (ISBN 0-07-004662-X, P&RB). McGraw.

Benkert, Joseph W. Introduction to Aviation Science. 1971. ref. ed. 25.95 (ISBN 0-13-478222-4). P-H.

Benkin, Richard. Sociology: A Way of Seeing. 432p. 1981. pap. text ed. 16.95x (ISBN 0-534-00929-8). Wadsworth Pub.

Benko, Stephen. Los Evangelicos, los Catolicos y la Virgen Maria. Olmedo, Alfonso, tr. from Eng. Orig. Title: Protestants, Catholics & Mary. 1981. pap. 6.75 (ISBN 0-311-05041-7). Casa Bautista.

Benkovitz, Miriam. Frederick Rolfe: Baron Corvo. LC 77-3671. (Illus.). 1977. 10.95 o.p. (ISBN 0-399-12009-2). Putnam Pub Group.

Benkovitz, Miriam J. Aubrey Beardsley: An Account of His Life. 1981. 11.95 (ISBN 0-686-72299-X). Putnam Pub Group.

Benkovitz, Miriam J., ed. A Bibliography of Ronald Firbank. 2nd ed. 122p. 1982. text ed. 42.00x (ISBN 0-19-818188-4). Oxford U Pr.

Benkovitz, Miriam J., ed. see Aldington, Richard.

Benlliure, F., tr. see Vardaman, Jerry.

Benlliure, Felix, tr. see Hester, H. I.

Benlliure, Felix, tr. see Mehl, Roger.

Benmaman, Virginia & Moore, Suzanne. Individualized Learning Program for En Camino! 1981. pap. text ed. 6.95x o.p. (ISBN 0-673-15392-4). Scott F.

Ben-Menachem, Yoram. Angiography in Trauma: A Work Atlas. (Illus.). 350p. 1981. text ed. 85.00 (ISBN 0-7216-1733-6). Saunders.

Benn, F. R. Production & Utilisation of Synthetic Fuels: An Energy Economics Study. Edewar, J. O., ed. LC 81-4528. 272p. 1981. 49.95 (ISBN 0-470-27171-X). Halsted Pr.

Benn Publications Ltd. Benn's Press Directory: The World Media Guide 1982, Vol. 1-2. (Benn Directories). 1982. 150.00 (ISBN 0-686-97956-7); lib. bdg. 97.00 (ISBN 0-686-97957-5). Nichols Pub.

--Chemical Industry Directory & Who's Who 1982. (Benn Directories). 1982. 84.00 (ISBN 0-686-97959-1). Nichols Pub.

--Chemist & Druggist Directory 1982. (Benn Directories). 1982. 65.00 (ISBN 0-686-97958-3). Nichols Pub.

--Phillips Paper Trade Directory 1982. (Benn Directories Ser.). 1982. 98.00 (ISBN 0-686-97961-3). Nichols Pub.

--Printing Trades Directory, 1982. 1982. 84.00 (ISBN 0-686-97962-1). Nichols Pub.

Bennassar, Bartolome. The Spanish Character: Attitudes & Mentalities from the Sixteenth to the Nineteenth Century. Keen, Benjamin, tr. LC 76-55563. 1979. 27.50x (ISBN 0-520-03401-5). U of Cal Pr.

Benne, Kenneth D., et al, eds. Laboratory Method of Changing & Learning: Theory & Application. LC 74-32598. 1975. 15.95 (ISBN 0-685-59371-1). Sci & Behavior.

Benne, Robert & Hefner, Philip. Defining America: A Christian Critique of the American Dream. LC 73-89062. 160p. 1974. pap. 1.00 o.p. (ISBN 0-8006-1075-X, 1-1075). Fortress.

Benneman, K. H. & Ketterson, J. B., eds. The Physics of Solid and Liquid Helium, Pt.1. 600p. Repr. of 1976 ed. text ed. 46.50 (ISBN 0-471-06600-1). Krieger.

--The Physics of Solid and Liquid Helium, Pt. 2. LC 75-20235. 760p. Repr. of 1978 ed. text ed. 80.95 (ISBN 0-471-06601-X). Krieger.

Bennemann, Karl H. & Ketterson, J. B., eds. Physics of Liquid & Solid Helium, 2 pts. LC 75-20235. (Interscience Monographs & Texts in Physics & Astronomy). 589p. Pt. 1, 1976, 608p. 46.50x (ISBN 0-471-06600-1, Pub. by Wiley-Interscience); Pt. 2, 1978, 750 Pgs. 92.50 (ISBN 0-471-06601-X). Wiley.

Benner, Judith A. Sul Ross: Soldier, Statesman, Educator. LC 82-45891. (Centennial Series of the Association of Former Students: No. 13). (Illus.). 344p. 1983. 19.50x (ISBN 0-89096-142-5). Tex A&M Univ Pr.

Benner, Margareta. The Emperor Says: Studies in the Rhetorical Style in Edicts of the Early Empire. (Studia Graeca et Latina Gothoburgensia: No. 33). 1975. pap. text ed. 14.50x o.p. (ISBN 91-7346-010-9). Humanities.

Benner, Margareta & Tengstrom, Emin. On the Interpretation of Learned Neo-Latin: An Explorative Study Based on Some Texts from Sweden 1611-1716. (Studia Graeca et Latina Goteborg: No. 39). 1977. 16.25x o.p. (ISBN 91-7346-044-3). Humanities.

Bennet, D. & Thomas, J. F. On Rational Grounds: Systems Analysis in Catchment & Land Use Planning. (Development in Landscape Planning & Urban Planning Ser.: Vol. 4). 1982. 81.00 (ISBN 0-444-42056-8). Elsevier.

Bennet, E. A. What Jung Really Said. LC 67-13153. (What They Really Said Ser). 1971. pap. 4.95 (ISBN 0-8052-0265-X). Schocken.

Bennet, Harold L. Glimpse at Wall Street & Its Markets: Descriptions of Important Railroad & Industrial Properties. LC 68-28616. 1968. Repr. of 1904 ed. lib. bdg. 16.00x (ISBN 0-8371-0307-X, BEGW). Greenwood.

Bennet, J. G. Enneagram. 160p. 1983. 6.95 (ISBN 0-87728-544-6). Weiser.

Bennet, John & Masia, Seth. Walks in the Catskills. LC 74-81304. (Illus.). 204p. 1974. pap. 7.95 (ISBN 0-914788-00-0). East Woods.

Bennet, John M., jt. auth. see Rosenthal, Susan N.

Bennet, Peter. The Illustrated Child. LC 79-5174. (Jonathan James Bk). (Illus.). 1980. 16.95 o.p. (ISBN 0-399-12481-0). Putnam Pub Group.

Bennet, S. & Bowers, D. An Introduction to Multivariate Techniques for Social & Behavioral Sciences. 156p. 1976. pap. 22.95 (ISBN 0-470-26428-4). Halsted Pr.

Bennett. Successful Communication & Effective Speaking. pap. 2.95 o.p. (ISBN 0-13-860437-1, Parker). P-H.

Bennett, A. International Organization: Principles & Issues. 2nd ed. (Illus.). 1980. text ed. 22.95 (ISBN 0-13-473447-5). P-H.

Bennett, A. E. & Siy, L. Blueprint Reading for Welders. 4th ed. 218p. 1983. text ed. 8.40 (ISBN 0-8273-2144-9); write for info. instr's. guide (ISBN 0-8273-2145-7). Delmar.

Bennett, A. Wayne. Introduction to Computer Simulation. LC 74-4509. 480p. 1974. text ed. 26.95 (ISBN 0-8299-0017-9); solutions manual avail. (ISBN 0-8299-0459-X). West Pub.

Bennett, A. Y. Picture Dictionary, ABCs, Telling Time, Counting Rhymes, Riddles & Finger Plays. (Illus.). (gr. k-3). 1970. 5.95 (ISBN 0-448-02813-1, G&D). Putnam Pub Group.

Bennett, Addison C. Improving Management Performance in Health Care Institutions: A Total Systems Approach. LC 78-8010. (Illus.). 256p. (Orig.). 1978. casebound 26.00 (ISBN 0-87258-246-9, AHA-001106); pap. 25.00 (ISBN 0-87258-229-9, AHA-001104). Am Hospital.

--Managing Hospital Costs Effectively As a System: A Primer for Hospital Administration. (Illus.). 72p. (Orig.). 1980. pap. 18.75 (ISBN 0-87258-327-9, AHA-001108). Am Hospital.

--Productivity & the Quality of Work Life in Hospitals. Dwight, Beryl M., ed. (Illus.). 96p. 1983. 30.00 (ISBN 0-87258-405-4). Am Hospital.

Bennett, Adrian A. Missionary Journalist in China: Young J. Allen & His Magazines, 1860-1883. LC 81-19761. (Illus.). 336p. text ed. 28.00x (ISBN 0-8203-0615-0). U of Ga Pr.

Bennett, Alan. Prostaglandins & the Gut, Vol. 1. 1977. 14.40 (ISBN 0-904406-49-0). Eden Pr.

Bennett, Alan H. Management of Male Impotence. (Illus.). 264p. 1982. lib. bdg. 36.00 (ISBN 0-683-00546-4). Williams & Wilkins.

Bennett, Alice S., jt. auth. see Mertens, Thomas.

Bennett, Angeline. Thinking is Good for the Mind. 22p. (Orig.). 1981. pap. 3.00 (ISBN 0-686-97501-4). Am Atheist.

Bennett, Archie, ed. New Illustrated Grosset Dictionary. LC 76-42144. (Illus.). (gr. k-5). 1977. pap. 6.95 (ISBN 0-448-14384-4, G&D). Putnam Pub Group.

Bennett, Arnold. Books & Persons: Being Comments on a Past Epoch, 1908-1911. LC 69-10069. 1969. Repr. of 1917 ed. lib. bdg. 18.75x (ISBN 0-8371-0018-6, BEBP). Greenwood.

--The Old Wives' Tale. 250p. 1983. pap. text ed. 3.95x (ISBN 0-460-01919-8, Pub. by Evman England). Biblio Dist.

--The Old Wives Tales. 1983. pap. 5.95 (ISBN 0-14-043163-2). Penguin.

Bennett, Barbara. A Rough Music. 294p. 1980. 11.95 o.p. (ISBN 0-312-69355-9). St Martin.

--Words Take Wing: A Teaching Guide to Creative Writing for Children. 260p. 1983. text ed. 15.00 (ISBN 0-8138-1932-6). Iowa St U Pr.

Bennett, Barbara R., jt. auth. see Jacobs, Lenworth M.

Bennett, Betty T., ed. British War Poetry in the Age of Romanticism: 1793-1815. LC 75-31144. (Romantic Context: Poetry 1789-1830 Ser.: Vol. 1). 1977. lib. bdg. 47.00 o.s.i. (ISBN 0-8240-2100-2). Garland Pub.

Bennett, Boyce M., Jr., ed. see Miller, Madeleine S. & Miller, J. Lane.

Bennett, Bruce, jt. auth. see Van Dalen, Deobold B.

Bennett, Bruce L. & Howell, Maxwell L. Comparative Physical Education & Sport. 2nd ed. LC 82-14957. 283p. 1983. pap. write for info (ISBN 0-8121-0864-7). Lea & Febiger.

Bennett, Bruce L., et al. Comparative Physical Education & Sport. LC 74-34006. 289p. 1975. pap. 9.75 o.p. (ISBN 0-8121-0518-4). Lea & Febiger.

Bennett, C. O. Momentum, Heat & Mass Transfer. 2nd ed. Myers, J. E., ed. (Chemical Engineering Ser.). (Illus.). 608p. 1974. 34.50 (ISBN 0-07-004667-0, C). McGraw.

Bennett, C. O. & Myers, J. E. Momentum, Heat & Mass Transfer. 3rd ed. (Chemical Engineering Ser.). 1981. 37.50 (ISBN 0-07-004671-9); solutions manual 28.00 (ISBN 0-07-004672-7). McGraw.

Bennett, C. Richard. Conscious Sedation in Dental Practice. 2nd ed. LC 78-4565. 1978. text ed. 29.50 o.p. (ISBN 0-8016-0612-8). Mosby.

--Monheim's Local Anesthesia & Pain Control in Dental Practice. 6th ed. LC 77-10994. (Illus.). 354p. 1978. text ed. 29.95 (ISBN 0-8016-0609-8). Mosby.

Bennett, Carl A. & Franklin, N. L. Statistical Analysis in Chemistry & the Chemical Industry. (Probability & Mathematical Statistics: Applied Probability & Statistics Section). 1954. 50.50 (ISBN 0-471-06633-8, Pub by Wiley-Interscience). Wiley.

Bennett, Cathereen. Will Rogers: The Cowboy Who Walked with Kings. LC 71-128806. (Real Life Bks). (Illus.). (gr. 5-11). 1971. PLB 3.95g (ISBN 0-8225-0704-8). Lerner Pubns.

Bennett, Charles A. History of Manual & Industrial Education, 2 Vols, Vol. 1. to 1870, Vol. 2. 1870-1917. Vol. 1. text ed. 22.60 (ISBN 0-87002-005-6); Vol. 2. text ed. 22.60 (ISBN 0-87002-006-4). Bennett IL.

Bennett, Charles E. Florida's French Revolution, Seventeen Ninety-Three to Seventeen Ninety-Five. LC 81-7431. x, 218p. 1981. 16.00 (ISBN 0-8130-0641-4). U Presses Fla.

Bennett, Charles E., ed. Dialogus de Oratoribus. 1983. pap. 10.00 (ISBN 0-89241-226-7). Caratzas Bros.

--On Old Age-De Senectutre: Cicero. (Bolchazy-Carducci Textbook). (Illus.). 446p. 1980. pap. text ed. 7.50x (ISBN 0-86516-001-5). Bolchazy-Carducci.

Bennett, Charles F. Conservation & Management of Natural Sources in the United States. 375p. 1983. text ed. 19.95 (ISBN 0-471-04652-3). Wiley.

Bennett, Charles F., Jr. Man & Earth's Ecosystems: An Introduction to the Geography of Human Modification of the Earth. LC 75-22330. 331p. 1976. text ed. 27.50x (ISBN 0-471-06638-9). Wiley.

Bennett, Clarence E. Physics Problems & How to Solve Them. 2nd ed. (Orig.). 1973. pap. 4.95 (ISBN 0-06-460149-8, CO 149, COS). B&N NY.

Bennett, Curtis. God As Form: Essays in Greek Mythology. LC 75-43851. 1976. 33.50x (ISBN 0-87395-325-8). State U NY Pr.

Bennett, D. M. An Open Letter to Jesus Christ. 1982. pap. 3.00 (ISBN 0-686-83177-2). Am Atheist.

Bennett, D. R., et al, eds. Atlas of Electroencephalography in Coma & Cerebral Death: EEG at the Bedside or in the Intensive Care Unit. LC 74-14470. 254p. 1976. 98.00 (ISBN 0-911216-91-X). Raven.

Bennett, David H. Cardiac Arrhythmias: Practical Notes on Interpretation & Treatment. (Illus.). 176p. 1981. pap. text ed. 19.50 (ISBN 0-7236-0590-4). Wright-PSG.

--Demagogues in the Depression: American Radicals & the Union Party, Nineteen Thirty-Two to Nineteen Thirty-Six. 10.00 o.p. (ISBN 0-8135-0590-9). Brown Bk.

Bennett, De Robigne M. Anthony Comstock: His Career of Cruelty & Crime. LC 73-121102. (Civil Liberties in American History Ser). 1971. Repr. of 1878 ed. lib. bdg. 22.50 (ISBN 0-306-71968-1). Da Capo.

Bennett, Dean B., ed. see Maine Studies Curriculum Project.

Bennett, Deborah. Jean's Black Diamond. (Teen Fiction Ser.). (gr. 7-10). pap. 1.25 o.p. (ISBN 0-87508-684-5). Chr Lit.

--Son of Diamond. (Teen Fiction Ser). (gr. 7-10). 1970. pap. 1.25 o.p. (ISBN 0-87508-759-0). Chr Lit.

Bennett, Dennis & Bennett, Rita. Trinity of Man. (Illus.). 1979. pap. text ed. 6.95 (ISBN 0-88270-287-4, Pub. by Logos). Bridge Pub.

Bennett, Dennis, jt. auth. see Bennett, Rita.

Bennett, Dorothea. The Jigsaw Man. 256p. 1976. 8.95 o.p. (ISBN 0-698-10729-2, Coward). Putnam Pub Group.

--The Maynard Hayes Affair. LC 78-26801. 1979. 8.95 (ISBN 0-698-10971-6, Coward). Putnam Pub Group.

Bennett, Dwight. Disaster Creek. LC 80-1061. (Double D Western Ser.). 192p. 1981. 10.95 o.p. (ISBN 0-385-15629-4). Doubleday.

--The Texans. LC 78-22788. (Double D Western Ser.). 1979. 10.95 o.p. (ISBN 0-385-14422-9). Doubleday.

Bennett, E. K. History of the German Novelle. rev. ed. Waidson, H. M., rev. by. (Orig.). 1961. 49.50 (ISBN 0-521-04152-X); pap. 12.95 (ISBN 0-521-09152-7). Cambridge U Pr.

Bennett, Earl, et al. Business Policy: Case Problems of the General Manager. 3rd ed. (Marketing & Management Ser.). 1978. text ed. 19.95x (ISBN 0-675-08401-6). Additional supplements may be obtained from publisher. Merrill.

Bennett, Edna. Nature Photography Simplified. (Illus.). 96p. 1975. pap. 4.95 o.p. (ISBN 0-8174-0184-9, Amphoto); Spanish Ed. pap. 6.95 o.p. (ISBN 0-8174-0312-4). Watson-Guptill.

Bennett, Edward H., jt. auth. see Burnham, Daniel H.

Bennett, Edward L., jt. ed. see Rosenzweig, Mark R.

Bennett, Edward M., jt. ed. see Burns, Richard D.

Bennett, Edward M., et al. As the Storm Clouds Gathered: European Perceptions of American Foreign Policy in the 1930's. LC 78-78074. 173p. 1979. pap. 6.95 (ISBN 0-87716-101-1, Pub. by Moore Pub Co). F Apple.

Bennett, Edward W. Germany & the Diplomacy of the Financial Crisis, 1931. LC 62-13261. (Historical Monographs Ser: No. 50). 1962. 18.00x (ISBN 0-674-35250-5). Harvard U Pr.

Bennett, Emerson. Forest Rose: A Tale of the Frontier. Facs. of 1885 Ed. LC 72-96394. li, 118p. 1973. 7.50 (ISBN 0-8214-0128-9, 82-81313). Ohio U Pr.

Bennett, Emma. By Passion Bound. (Candlelight Ecstasy Ser.: No. 135). (Orig.). 1983. pap. 1.95 (ISBN 0-440-10918-3). Dell.

--River Enchantment. (Candlelight Ecstasy Ser.: No. 139). (Orig.). 1983. pap. 1.95 (ISBN 0-440-17470-8). Dell.

--That Certain Summer. (Candlelight Ecstasy Ser.: No. 120). (Orig.). 1983. pap. 1.95 (ISBN 0-440-18579-3). Dell.

Bennett, Ernest N. Apparitions & Haunted Houses: A Survey of Evidence. LC 76-164100. Repr. of 1939 ed. 37.00 o.p. (ISBN 0-8103-3752-5). Gale.

Bennett, F. M. Religious Cults Associated with the Amazons. v, 79p. 1983. Repr. of 1912 ed. lib. bdg. 17.50x (ISBN 0-89241-204-6). Caratzas Bros.

Bennett, F. V. & Symmons, P. M. A Review of Estimates of the Effectiveness of Certain Control Techniques & Insecticides Against the Desert Locust. 1972. 35.00x (ISBN 0-85135-060-7, Pub. by Centre Overseas Research). State Mutual Bk.

Bennett, Gerald & Vourakis, Christine. Substance Abuse: Pharmacologic, Developmental & Clinical Perspectives. LC 82-13583. 453p. 1983. 24.95 (ISBN 0-471-08537-5, Pub. by Wiley Med). Wiley.

Bennett, Gordon. Aboriginal Rights in International Law. 1978. 29.00 (ISBN 0-686-98249-5, Pub. by Royal Anthro Ireland). State Mutual Bk.

--Huadong: The Story of a Chinese People's Commune. (Westview Special Studies on China & East Asia Ser.). 1978. lib. bdg. 24.00 (ISBN 0-89158-094-8); pap. text ed. 9.50 (ISBN 0-89158-095-6). Westview.

--Yundong: Mass Campaigns in Chinese Communist Leadership. LC 75-620060. (China Research Monographs: No. 12). 1976. pap. text ed. 4.50x (ISBN 0-912966-15-7). IEAS.

Bennett, Gordon, ed. China's Finance & Trade: A Policy Reader. LC 77-99080. 1978. pap. 10.95 (ISBN 0-87332-115-4). M E Sharpe.

Bennett, Gordon H. & Vedder, Eugene P., Jr. Missions Guidebook. (Illus.). 284p. 1983. write for info. (ISBN 0-942504-12-7); pap. write for info. (ISBN 0-942504-13-5). Overcomer Pr.

Bennett, Gordon H., jt. auth. see Marshall, Alejandro.

Bennett, Gordon H., jt. auth. see Pollock, Algernon J.

Bennett, Gordon H., jt. auth. see Voorehoeve, H. C.

Bennett, Gordon H., ed. El Futuro: En Los Anos de 1980 y adelante One Hundred Forty Preguntas y Respuestas. Flores, Rhode, tr. from Eng. 128p. (Orig., Span.). 1982. pap. write for info. (ISBN 0-942504-14-3). Overcomer Pr.

Bennett, Gordon H., ed. see Collingwood, Guillermo.

Bennett, Gordon H., ed. see Cutting, Jorge.

Bennett, Gordon H., ed. see Mackintosh, Carlos H.

Bennett, Gordon H., ed. see Rossier, H.

Bennett, Gregory R. Successful Convention Management. (Illus., Orig.). 1983. write for info. (ISBN 0-916732-59-2); pap. text ed. write for info. (ISBN 0-916732-58-4). Starmont Hse.

Bennett, H. Encyclopedia of Chemical Trademarks & Synonyms Vol. 2, F-O. 1982. 65.00 (ISBN 0-8206-0293-0). Chem Pub.

--Encyclopedia of Chemical Trademarks & Synonyms Vol. 3, P-Z. 1983. 65.00 (ISBN 0-8206-0302-3). Chem Pub.

Bennett, H., ed. Chemical Formulary, 24 vols. Incl. Vol. 1, 1933 (ISBN 0-8206-0259-0). Vol. 2, 1935 (ISBN 0-8206-0260-4). Vol. 3, 1936 (ISBN 0-8206-0261-2). Vol. 4, 1939 (ISBN 0-8206-0262-0). Vol. 5, 1941 (ISBN 0-8206-0263-9). Vol. 6, 1943 (ISBN 0-8206-0264-7). Vol. 7, 1945 (ISBN 0-8206-0265-5); Vol. 8, 1948 (ISBN 0-8206-0266-3). Vol. 9, 1950 (ISBN 0-8206-0267-1). Vol. 10, 1957 (ISBN 0-8206-0268-X). Vol. 11, 1961 (ISBN 0-8206-0269-8). Vol. 12, 1965 (ISBN 0-8206-0270-1). Vol. 13, 1967 (ISBN 0-8206-0271-X). Vol. 14, 1968 (ISBN 0-8206-0272-8); Vol. 15, 1970 (ISBN 0-8206-0273-6). Vol. 16, 1971 (ISBN 0-8206-0274-4). Vol. 17, 1973 (ISBN 0-8206-0275-2). Vol. 18, 1975 (ISBN 0-8206-0276-0). Vol. 19, 1976 (ISBN 0-8206-0277-9). Vol. 20, 1977 (ISBN 0-8206-0278-7). Vol. 21, 1979 (ISBN 0-8206-0279-5). Vol. 22, 1979 (ISBN 0-8206-0280-9). 35.00 ea. Chem Pub.

--Chemical Formulary, Vol. 23. 1981. 35.00 (ISBN 0-8206-0282-5). Chem Pub.

--Chemical Formulary, Vol. 24. 1982. 35.00 (ISBN 0-8206-0291-4). Chem Pub.

--Chemical Formulary, Vol. 25. 1983. 35.00 (ISBN 0-8206-0304-X). Chem Pub.

Bennett, H. O. The Last Drop. LC 70-88524. 1969. 9.95 (ISBN 0-87716-008-2, Pub. by Moore Pub Co). F Apple.

Bennett, Hal Z. Cold Comfort. 1979. pap. 4.95 o.p. (ISBN 0-517-53594-7, C N Potter Bks). Crown.

--The Complete Bicycle Commuter: The Sierra Club Guide to Wheeling to Work. LC 82-719. (Sierra Club Outdoors Activities Guides Ser.). (Illus.). 256p. (Orig.). 1982. pap. 8.95 (ISBN 0-87156-308-8). Sierra.

--The Doctor Within. 160p. 1981. 11.95 (ISBN 0-517-54178-5, C N Potter Bks); pap. 5.95 (ISBN 0-517-54299-4, C N Potter Bks). Crown.

--The Doctor Within. 1982. pap. 2.50 (ISBN 0-451-11626-7, AE1626, Sig). NAL.

--Sewing for the Outdoors. (Illus.). 160p. 1980. 14.95 o.p. (ISBN 0-517-54032-0, C N Potter Bks); pap. 8.95 o.p. (ISBN 0-517-54033-9). Crown.

Bennett, Harold. Saga of the Steam Plough. 18.50 (ISBN 0-392-15490-0, SpS). Sportshelf.

Bennett, Harold C. God's Awesome Challenge. LC 79-56692. 1980. 6.95 (ISBN 0-8054-6322-4). Broadman.

Bennett, Harold G. What It Means to Be a Southern Baptist. LC 81-67326. pap. cancelled o.s.i. (ISBN 0-8054-6565-0). Broadman.

Bennett, Henry S. English Books & Readers, 3 vols. 1970. Vol 1. 65.00 (ISBN 0-521-07609-9); Vol 2. 57.50 (ISBN 0-521-04153-8); Vol 3. 49.50 (ISBN 0-521-07701-X); 150.00 set (ISBN 0-521-08857-7). Cambridge U Pr.

--Life on the English Manor. (Cambridge Studies in Medieval Life & Thought). 1960. 37.50 (ISBN 0-521-04154-6); pap. 11.95x (ISBN 0-521-09105-5). Cambridge U Pr.

--Pastons & Their England. 2nd ed. LC 68-23175. (Cambridge Studies in Medieval Life & Thought). 1968. 39.50 (ISBN 0-521-07173-9); pap. 10.95x (ISBN 0-521-09513-1). Cambridge U Pr.

Bennett, J. A Packet of Poems. (Illus.). 112p. 1983. bds. 10.95 (ISBN 0-19-276049-1, Pub by Oxford U Pr Childrens). Merrimack Bk Serv.

Bennett, J. A. & Smithers, G. V., eds. Early Middle English Verse & Prose. 2nd ed. 1968. text ed. 27.95x (ISBN 0-19-811493-1). Oxford U Pr.

Bennett, J. M. & Kalman, R. E., eds. Computers in Developing Nations. 1981. 42.75 (ISBN 0-444-86270-6). Elsevier.

Bennett, J. V. Heat Engines: Questions & Answers. (Marine Engineering Ser.). 116p. 1975. pap. 9.95x (ISBN 0-540-07340-7). Sheridan.

Bennett, Jack A. Chaucer's Book of Fame: An Exposition of the House of Fame. 1968. 22.00x o.p. (ISBN 0-19-811655-1). Oxford U Pr.

Bennett, James & Pravitz, James. The Miracle of Sports Psychology: How to Win with Mental Dynamics. (Illus.). 169p. 1982. 16.95 (ISBN 0-13-585257-9); pap. 7.95 (ISBN 0-13-585240-4). P-H.

Bennett, James D. Frederick Jackson Turner. (United States Authors Ser.). 1975. lib. bdg. 12.95 (ISBN 0-8057-7150-6, Twayne). G K Hall.

Bennett, James D. & Harrison, Lowell H. Writing History Papers. (Orig.). 1979. pap. text ed. 3.50x (ISBN 0-88273-105-X). Forum Pr IL.

Bennett, James T. & DiLorenzo, Thomas J. Underground Government: The Off-Budget Public Sector. 184p. 1983. pap. 8.95 (ISBN 0-932790-37-2). Cato Inst.

Bennett, Jay. Say Hello to the Hit Man. LC 75-32919. 160p. (YA) 1976. 8.95 o.s.i. (ISBN 0-440-07675-7). Delacorte.

--Say Hello to the Hit Man. (gr. 7 up). 1977. pap. 1.95 (ISBN 0-440-97618-9, LFL). Dell.

Bennett, Jeanine, jt. auth. see Bellisimo, Louis A.

Bennett, Jill. Days Are Where We Live & Other Poems. (gr. k-2). 1982. 8.50 (ISBN 0-688-00852-6). Morrow.

Bennett, Joan. Five Metaphysical Poets: Donne, Herbert, Vaughan, Crashaw, Marvell. 1964. 29.95 (ISBN 0-521-04156-2); pap. 8.95x (ISBN 0-521-09238-8). Cambridge U Pr.

--George Eliot: Her Mind & Her Art. (Orig.). 1948. 29.95 (ISBN 0-521-04158-9); pap. 10.95x (ISBN 0-521-09174-8, 174). Cambridge U Pr.

--Virginia Woolf. 2nd ed. 1945. 19.95 o.p. (ISBN 0-521-04160-0); pap. 9.95x (ISBN 0-521-09951-X). Cambridge U Pr.

Bennett, John. Master Skylark. (Classics Ser). (gr. 5 up). 1.95 (ISBN 0-8049-0092-2, CL-92). Airmont.

--The Night of the Great Butcher. LC 75-19571. 1976. pap. 4.00 o.p. (ISBN 0-913204-05-6). December Pr.

Bennett, John & Cooley, Peter. The Struck Leviathan & The Company of Strangers: Poetry Readings by John Bennett & Peter Cooley. LC 76-741319. 1977. 7.95 (ISBN 0-8262-0220-9). U of Mo Pr.

Bennett, John C. & Seifert, Harvey. U. S. Foreign Policy & Christian Ethics. LC 77-5062. 1977. soft cover 7.95 (ISBN 0-664-24756-3). Westminster.

Bennett, John G. Witness. Date not set. price not set (ISBN 0-934254-05-2). Claymont Comm.

Bennett, John R., ed. Molodiya: A Soviet Russian L.P. Discography. LC 81-4247. 832p. 1981. write for info. o.p. (ISBN 0-313-22596-6). Greenwood.

Bennett, John W. Northern Plainsmen: Adaptive Strategy & Agrarian Life. LC 76-75043. (Worlds of Man Ser.). (Illus.). 1970. text ed. 17.95x (ISBN 0-88295-602-7); pap. text ed. 11.95x (ISBN 0-88295-603-5). Harlan Davidson.

Bennett, John W. & Ishino, Iwao. Paternalism in the Japanese Economy. LC 72-3538. 307p. 1972. Repr. of 1963 ed. lib. bdg. 17.75x (ISBN 0-8371-6424-9, BEJE). Greenwood.

Bennett, John W., jt. auth. see American Ethnological Society.

Bennett, Jonathan. Kant's Analytic. (Orig.). 1966. 39.50 (ISBN 0-521-04157-0); pap. 11.95x (ISBN 0-521-09389-9, 389). Cambridge U Pr.

--Kant's Dialectic. LC 73-89762. 290p. 1974. o. p. 38.50 (ISBN 0-521-20420-8); pap. 11.95x (ISBN 0-521-09849-1). Cambridge U Pr.

--Linguistic Behavior. LC 75-44575. 260p. 1976. 37.50 (ISBN 0-521-21168-9). Cambridge U Pr.

--Linguistic Behaviour. LC 75-44575. 1979. pap. 12.50x (ISBN 0-521-29751-6). Cambridge U Pr.

Bennett, Jonathan, ed. see Leibniz, G. W.

Bennett, Jonathan, tr. see Leibniz, G. W.

Bennett, Judith. Sex Signs. 1980. 12.95 o.p. (ISBN 0-312-71337-1). St Martin.

Bennett, Judith K. The Ahae Gang Meets Melvin. 1983. 7.95 (ISBN 0-533-05677-2). Vantage.

Bennett, Kenneth A., jt. auth. see Osborne, Richard H.

Bennett, L. Claire & Varga, Sarah S. Communicable Disease Handbook. LC 82-11062. 270p. 1982. 15.95 (ISBN 0-471-09271-1, Pub. by Wiley Med). Wiley.

Bennett, Linda L. Volunteers in the School Media Center. 350p. 1983. pap. text ed. 23.50 (ISBN 0-87287-351-X). Libs Unl.

Bennett, M. R. Automatic Neuromuscular Transmission. LC 76-182026. (Physiological Society Monographs: No. 30). (Illus.). 400p. 1973. 59.00 (ISBN 0-521-08463-6). Cambridge U Pr.

Bennett, M. V., ed. Synaptic Transmission & Neuronal Interaction. LC 73-83886. (Society of General Physiologists Ser: Vol. 28). 401p. 1974. 38.00 (ISBN 0-911216-56-1). Raven.

Bennett, Margaret. Biking for Grown Ups. 249p. Repr. of 1976 ed. 6.95 (ISBN 0-686-35966-6). Sugarfree.

--Cross-Country Skiing for the Fun of It. 206p. Repr. of 1973 ed. 5.95 (ISBN 0-686-35965-8). Sugarfree.

Bennett, Marian. Baby Jesus ABC's. (Little Happy Day Bks.). (Illus.). 24p. (Orig.). (gr. k-3). 1983. pap. 0.45 (ISBN 0-87239-651-7, 2121). Standard Pub.

--Bible Numbers. (Little Happy Day Bks.). (Illus.). 24p. (Orig.). (gr. k-3). 1983. pap. 0.45 (ISBN 0-87239-653-3, 2123). Standard Pub.

--God Made Kittens. Sparks, Judith, ed. (A Happy Day Book). (Illus.). 24p. (ps). 1980. 1.29 (ISBN 0-87239-404-2, 3636). Standard Pub.

--God Made Puppies. Sparks, Judith, ed. (A Happy Day Book). (Illus.). 24p. (ps). 1980. 1.29 (ISBN 0-87239-403-4, 3635). Standard Pub.

--My Book of Special Days. (Illus.). (gr. 4-8). 1977. 4.95 (ISBN 0-87239-156-6, 3049). Standard Pub.

--The Story of Baby Jesus. (Illus.). 24p. (Orig.). (ps-k). 1983. pap. 0.45 (ISBN 0-87239-654-1, 2124). Standard Pub.

Bennett, Marian, ed. Bible Heroes: Grade 4. rev. ed. (Basic Bible Readers Ser.). (Illus.). 128p. (gr. 4). 1983. text ed. 7.95 (ISBN 0-87239-664-9, 2954). Standard Pub.

Bennett, Marian, compiled by. Bible Memory Verses. (Little Happy Day Bks.). (Illus.). 24p. (Orig.). (gr. k-3). 1983. pap. 0.45 (ISBN 0-87239-652-5, 2122). Standard Pub.

Bennett, Marian, ed. see Falk, Cathy.

Bennett, Marilyn & Sanders, Sylvia. How We Talk: The Story of Speech. LC 65-25078. (Medical Bks for Children). (gr. 3-9). 1966. PLB 3.95g (ISBN 0-8225-0016-7). Lerner Pubns.

Bennett, Michael J. Community, Class & Careerism: Cheshire & Lancashire in the Age of Sir Gawain & the Green Knight. LC 82-4354. (Cambridge Studies in Medieval Life & Thought: No. 18). (Illus.). 312p. Date not set. price not set (ISBN 0-521-24744-6). Cambridge U Pr.

Bennett, Mildred. Death Comes for the Archbishop Notes. (Orig.). 1965. pap. 2.50 (ISBN 0-8220-0373-2). Cliffs.

Bennett, Mildred R. World of Willa Cather. LC 61-7235. (Illus.). xviii, 302p. 1961. 19.95x (ISBN 0-8032-1151-1); pap. 8.25 (ISBN 0-8032-5013-4, BB 112, Bison). U of Nebr Pr.

Bennett, Millard & Corrigan, John D. Successful Communications & Effective Speaking. 1972. 17.95 o.p. (ISBN 0-13-860445-2, Parker). P-H.

Bennett, Nicholas. Zig Zag to Timbuktu. 1963. 8.50 o.p. (ISBN 0-685-20654-8). Transatlantic.

Bennett, Noel. The Weaver's Pathway: A Clarification of the Spirit Trail in Navajo Weaving. LC 73-78002. (Illus.). 104p. 1974. 8.95 o.p. (ISBN 0-87358-108-3). Northland.

Bennett, Norman R. Arab Versus European: Diplomacy & War in Nineteenth-Century East Central Africa. 550p. 1983. 45.00 (ISBN 0-8419-0861-3). Holmes & Meier.

--A History of the Arab State of Zanzibar. (Studies in African History). 1978. 19.95x (ISBN 0-416-55080-0). Methuen Inc.

--Mirambo of Tanzania, 1840-1884. 1971. 12.50x (ISBN 0-19-501314-X). Oxford U Pr.

Bennett, P. What Happened on Lexington Green: An Inquiry into the Nature & Methods of History. Brown, Richard H. & Halsey, Van R., eds. (Amherst Ser.). (gr. 9-12). 1970. pap. text ed. 5.16 (ISBN 0-201-00461-5, Sch Div); tchr's. manual cancelled 1.92 (ISBN 0-201-00463-1). A-W.

Bennett, P. B. & Elliot, D. H., eds. The Physiology & Medicine of Diving & Compressed Air Work. 2nd ed. (Illus.). 1975. text ed. 59.00 o.p. (ISBN 0-02-857290-4, Pub. by Bailliere-Tindall). Saunders.

Bennett, Paul J. Conference under the Tamarind Tree: Three Essays in Burmese History. LC 77-137999. (Monograph Ser.: No. 15). (Illus.). viii, 153p. 1971. 8.25x (ISBN 0-686-30903-0). Yale U SE Asia.

--Conference Under the Tamarind Tree: Three Essays in Burmese History. (Illus.). 153p. 1971. 8.25 (ISBN 0-686-38050-9). Yale U SE Asia.

Bennett, Philip M., jt. auth. see Rosen, Harold J.

Bennett, R., jt. auth. see Ogston, D.

Bennett, R. J. Central Grants to Local Governments: The Politics & Economic Impact of the Rate Support Grant in England & Wales. LC 82-4378. (Cambridge Geographical Studies: No. 17). (Illus.). 300p. 1982. 49.50 (ISBN 0-521-24908-2). Cambridge U Pr.

--Spatial Time Series Analysis-Forecasting-Control. 674p. 1979. 87.50x (ISBN 0-85086-069-5, Pub. by Pion England). Methuen Inc.

Bennett, R. J., ed. European Progress in Spatial Analysis. 1982. 26.00x (ISBN 0-85086-091-1, Pub. by Pion Ltd England). Methuen Inc.

Bennett, Rainey. Secret Hiding Place. LC 60-7206. (Illus.). (ps-3). 1960. PLB 5.21 o.p. (ISBN 0-529-03540-5, 1837W, Philomel). Putnam Pub Group.

Bennett, Rebecca. A Merry Chase. (Candlelight Regency Special Ser.: No. 691). 256p. (Orig.). 1981. pap. 1.75 o.s.i. (ISBN 0-440-15596-7). Dell.

Bennett, Richard G., jt. ed. see Robins, Perry.

Bennett, Rita. I'm Glad You Asked That. 207p. 4.95 o.p. (ISBN 0-930756-56-8, 4290-BE6, Pub. by Logos). Women's Aglow.

Bennett, Rita & Bennett, Dennis. O Espiritu Santo E Voce. Caruso, Luis, ed. Batista, Joao, tr. 276p. (Port.). 1980. pap. 2.00 (ISBN 0-8297-0660-7). Life Pubs Intl.

Bennett, Rita, jt. auth. see Bennett, Dennis.

Bennett, Robert A. & Edwards, O. C. The Bible for Today's Church. (The Church's Teaching Ser.: Vol. 2). 320p. 1979. 5.95 (ISBN 0-8164-0419-4); pap. 3.95 (ISBN 0-8164-2215-X); users guide .95 (ISBN 0-8164-2222-2). Seabury.

Bennett, Roger. Managing Personnel & Performance: An Alternative Approach. LC 81-1819. 250p. 1981. pap. 18.95 (ISBN 0-470-27162-0). Halsted Pr.

Bennett, Ross S., ed. America's Wonderlands: Our National Parks. rev. ed. LC 80-12579. 464p. 1980. 12.95 (ISBN 0-87044-332-1). Natl Geog.

Bennett, Roy C. The Songwriter's Guide to Writing & Selling Hit Songs. 160p. 1983. 12.95 (ISBN 0-13-822783-7); pap. 6.95 (ISBN 0-13-822775-6). P-H.

Bennett, Russell, ed. see McLenighan, Valjean.

Bennett, Russell, ed. see McReynolds, Ginny.

Bennett, Russell, jt. ed. see Storr, Catherine.

Bennett, Russell, ed. see Swinburne, Laurence.

Bennett, Russell, ed. see Tripp, Jenny.

Bennett, Russell, ed. see Wilson, Lionel.

Bennett, Ruth, jt. ed. see Aronson, Miriam K.

Bennett, S. & Linkens, D. A., eds. Computer Control of Industrial Processes. (IEE Control Engineering Ser.: No. 21). 220p. 1982. pap. 40.00 (ISBN 0-906048-80-X). Inst Elect Eng.

Bennett, Susan see Allen, W. S.

Bennett, Thomas L. Brain & Behavior. LC 76-26091. (Illus.). 1977. text ed. 22.95 o.p. (ISBN 0-8185-0201-0). Brooks-Cole.

--The Sensory World: An Introduction to Sensation & Perception. LC 78-3613. (Psychology Ser.). (Illus.). 1978. pap. text ed. 18.95 o.p. (ISBN 0-8185-0262-2). Brooks-Cole.

Bennett, Thomas P. & Frieden, Earl. Modern Topics in Biochemistry. (Orig.). 1966. pap. text ed. 9.95x (ISBN 0-02-308200-3, 30820). Macmillan.

Bennett, Thomas P., jt. auth. see Armstrong, Frank B.

Bennett, Trevor, jt. auth. see Maguire, Mike.

Bennett, Virginia C., jt. auth. see Bardon, Jack I.

Bennett, W. A. Aspects of Language & Language Teaching. (Illus., Orig.). 1968. 24.95 o.p. (ISBN 0-521-04164-3); pap. 7.95x (ISBN 0-521-09512-3). Cambridge U Pr.

--Character & Tonnage of the Turk Magnesite Deposit. (Reports of Investigations Ser.: No. 7). (Illus.). 1943. 0.25 (ISBN 0-686-38465-2). Geologic Pubns.

Bennett, Wayne W. & Hess, Karen M. Criminal Investigation. (Criminal Justice Ser.). 511p. 1980. text ed. 23.50 (ISBN 0-8299-0342-9). West Pub.

Bennett, William H. Catholic Footsteps in Old New York: A Chronicle of Catholicity in the City of New York from 1524 to 1808. LC 77-359169. (Monograph Ser.: No. 28). 1973. Repr. of 1909 ed. 10.00x (ISBN 0-930060-08-3). US Cath Hist.

Bennett, William R. Introduction to Signal Transmission. (Electrical & Electronic Eng. Ser). 1970. 42.50 (ISBN 0-07-004678-6, C). McGraw.

--Scientific & Engineering Problem-Solving with the Computer. (Illus.). 512p. 1976. ref. ed 27.95x o.p. (ISBN 0-13-795807-2). P-H.

Bennett, William R. & Davey, J. R. Data Transmission. (Inter-University Electronics Ser). (Illus.). 1964. 36.50 o.p. (ISBN 0-07-004677-8, P&RB). McGraw.

Bennetts, Pamela. Don Pedro's Captain. LC 77-11740. 1978. 7.95 o.p. (ISBN 0-312-21677-7). St Martin.

Bennett-Sandler, Georgette, et al. Law Enforcement & Criminal Justice: An Introduction. LC 78-69537. (Illus.). 1979. text ed. 20.95 (ISBN 0-395-27467-2); instr's. manual 0.50 (ISBN 0-395-27466-4). HM.

Benney, David, jt. auth. see Greenspan, Harvey P.

Benni, C. A. & Bolza, Eleanor. South American Timbers. 1982. 60.00x (ISBN 0-686-97897-8, Pub. by CSIRO Australia). State Mutual Bk.

Bennigsen, Alexandre & Broxup, Marie. The Islamic Threat to the Soviet State. LC 82-16826. 224p. 1983. 27.50x (ISBN 0-312-43739-0). St Martin.

Benning, Calvin J. Plastic Foams, 2 Vols. LC 73-82971. (Physics & Chemistry of Product Performance & Process Technology Ser.). 1969. Set. 180.00 o.p. (ISBN 0-471-06640-0, Pub. by Wiley-Interscience). Wiley.

Benningfield, L. M., jt. auth. see Lago, G.

Bennington, Michael. Rossya: A Journey Through Siberia. (Travel Bks.: Vol. 12). (Illus.). 96p. (Orig.). 1982. 12.50 (ISBN 0-906672-10-4). Oleander Pr.

Bennion, Marion. Introductory Foods. 7th ed. (Illus.). 1980. text ed. 22.95x (ISBN 0-02-308170-8). Macmillan.

Bennis, Warren G., et al, eds. Leadership & Motivation: Essays of Douglas McGregor. 1966. pap. 6.95x (ISBN 0-262-63015-X). MIT Pr.

Benois, Alexandre. Reminiscences of the Russian Ballet. Britnieva, Mary, tr. LC 77-7791. (Da Capo Series in Dance). (Illus.). 1977. Repr. of 1941 ed. lib. bdg. 32.50 (ISBN 0-306-77426-7). Da Capo.

Benoist, Jean-Marie. The Structural Revolution. LC 78-5298. 1978. 22.50x (ISBN 0-312-76698-X). St Martin.

Benoist-Mechin, Jacques. History of the German Army Since the Armistice. 345p. 1983. Repr. of 1939 ed. 25.00X (ISBN 0-86527-094-5). Fertig.

Benoiston De Chateauneuf. Recherches sur les Consommations de Tout Genre de la Ville de Paris-Comparees a Ce Qu'Elles Etaient en 1789. (Conditions of the 19th Century French Working Class Ser.). 157p. (Fr.). 1974. Repr. of 1821 ed. lib. bdg. 48.00x o.p. (ISBN 0-8287-0079-6, 1120). Clearwater Pub.

Benoit. Le Dejeuner De Sousceyrac. (Easy Readers Ser. B). 1978. pap. text ed. 3.95 (ISBN 0-88436-293-0). EMC.

Benokraitis, Nijole V. & Feagin, Joe R. Affirmative Action & Equal Opportunity: Action, Inaction, Reaction. (Special Studies in Contemporary Social Issues). 1978. lib. bdg. 27.50 o.p. (ISBN 0-89158-168-5). Westview.

Benoliel, J. O. Death Education for the Health Professional. 1982. 39.95 (ISBN 0-07-004761-8). McGraw.

Benor, Daniel & Harrison, James Q. Agricultural Extension: The Training & Visit System. 55p. 1977. pap. 5.00 (ISBN 0-686-36060-5, PM-7701). World Bank.

Benouis, Mustapha K. Le Francais Economique et Commercial. 246p. (Fr.). 1982. pap. 9.95 o.p. (ISBN 0-15-528300-6). HarBraceJ.

Benowicz, Robert J. Non-Prescription Drugs & Their Side Effects. Zappler, Georg, ed. 1977. 10.00 (ISBN 0-448-14323-2, G&D); pap. 4.95 (ISBN 0-448-14324-0, Today Press). Putnam Pub Group.

--Vitamins & You. LC 77-87788. (Illus.). 1978. 10.00 o.p. (ISBN 0-448-14643-6, G&D); pap. 6.95 (ISBN 0-448-14644-4, Today Press). Putnam Pub Group.

Benoyendranath, Banerjea. The Practice of Freedom. 1983. 9.00x (ISBN 0-8364-0918-3, Pub. by Minerva India). South Asia Bks.

Ben-Porath, Yoram. Income Distribution & the Family. LC 82-61326. 248p. (Orig.). 1982. pap. 6.95 (ISBN 0-686-43273-8). Population Coun.

Bens, A. Active English: Pronunciation & Speech. 1977. pap. text ed. 12.95 (ISBN 0-13-003392-8). P-H.

Bensen, D. Mechanisms of Oxidation by Metal Ions. (Reaction Mechanisms in Organic Chemistry Monograph: Vol. 10). 1976. 53.25 (ISBN 0-444-41325-1). Elsevier.

Bensen, David W. & Sparrow, Arnold H., eds. Survival of Food Crops & Livestock in the Event of Nuclear War: Proceedings. LC 77-170334. (AEC Symposium Ser.). 745p. 1971. pap. 26.75 (ISBN 0-87079-219-9, CONF-700909); microfiche 4.50 (ISBN 0-87079-220-2, CONF-700909). DOE.

Bensen, Donald R., jt. ed. see Heineman, James H.

Bensen, Robert. In a Dream Museum. (Chapbook: No. 7). 18p. 1980. pap. 2.50 (ISBN 0-932884-06-7). Red Herring.

Ben-Shahar, Haim, jt. auth. see Lerner, Abba P.

Bensinger, Charles. The Video Guide. 3rd ed. (Illus.). 264p. 1982. pap. 17.95 (ISBN 0-931294-05-3, ScribT). Scribner.

Bensinger, Gad J. A Graphic Overview of the Organization & Process of the Criminal Justice System in Chicago & Cook County. (Illus.). 112p. 7.00 (ISBN 0-942854-02-0). Criminal Jus Dept.

Bension, Shmuel. The Producer's Master-Guide, 1983: The International Production Manual for Motion Picture, Television, Commercials, Cable & Videotape Industries in the United States & Canada. 624p. (Orig.). 1982. pap. 58.00 (ISBN 0-935744-02-9). NY Prod Manual.

Bension, Simuel, ed. New York Production Manual 1981. 2nd ed. 1981p. 1981. pap. 68.00x (ISBN 0-935744-01-0, Pub. by NY Prod Manual). Gale.

Ben-Sira, Zeev. Social Stratification: Components & Structure. 150p. 1983. write for info. (ISBN 0-88105-004-0). Cap & Gown.

Bensky, Dan, ed. see Shanghai College of Traditional Medicine.

Bensky, Dan, tr. see Shanghai College of Traditional Medicine.

Benson, jt. auth. see Frandsen.

Benson, Arthur C. Edward Fitzgerald. LC 69-13821. Repr. of 1905 ed. lib. bdg. cancelled o.p. (ISBN 0-8371-1069-6, BEEF). Greenwood.

--Walter Pater. LC 67-23876. (Library of Lives & Letters: British Writers Ser.). 1968. Repr. of 1906 ed. 30.00x (ISBN 0-8103-3054-7). Gale.

Benson, Ben. Critical Path Methods in Building Construction. 1970. pap. text ed. 16.95 (ISBN 0-13-194001-5). P-H.

Benson, Bernard. The Peace Book. 1982. pap. 9.95 (ISBN 0-686-82121-1). Bantam.

Benson, Brian J. & Dillard, Mabel M. Jean Toomer. (United States Authors Ser.). 1980. lib. bdg. 11.95 (ISBN 0-8057-7322-3, Twayne). G K Hall.

Benson, Carl & Andrews, Craig. The Newport Beach Answer Book. (Illus.). 65p. (Orig.). pap. 6.95x (ISBN 0-686-38111-4). L J Pubns.

Benson, Carl & Littleton, Taylor. The Idea of Tragedy. 1966. pap. 8.95x (ISBN 0-673-05644-9). Scott F.

Benson, Charles S. The Economics of Public Education. 3rd ed. LC 77-77670. (Illus.). 1978. text ed. 26.50 (ISBN 0-395-18619-6). HM.

Benson, Christopher. Careers in Agriculture. LC 80-22515. (Early Career Bks.). (Illus.). 36p. (gr. 2-5). 1974. PLB 5.95x (ISBN 0-8225-0316-6). Lerner Pubns.

--Careers in Animal Care. LC 73-22516. (Early Career Bks.). (Illus.). 36p. (gr. 2-5). 1974. PLB 5.95g (ISBN 0-8225-0317-4). Lerner Pubns.

--Careers in Auto Sales & Service. LC 73-22517. (Early Career Bks.). (Illus.). 36p. (gr. 2-5). 1974. PLB 5.95g (ISBN 0-8225-0318-2). Lerner Pubns.

--Careers in Conservation. LC 73-22519. (Early Career Bks.). (Illus.). 36p. (gr. 2-5). 1974. PLB 5.95g (ISBN 0-8225-0320-4). Lerner Pubns.

--Careers in Education. LC 73-22520. (Early Career Bks.). (Illus.). 36p. (gr. 2-5). 1974. PLB 5.95g (ISBN 0-8225-0321-2). Lerner Pubns.

--Careers with the City. LC 73-22158. (Early Career Bks.). (Illus.). 36p. (gr. 2-5). 1974. PLB 5.95g (ISBN 0-8225-0319-0). Lerner Pubns.

Benson, Dan. The Total Man. 1977. pap. 4.95 (ISBN 0-8423-7290-3). Tyndale.

Benson, Elizabeth P. The Maya World. rev. ed. LC 77-4955. (Illus.). 1977. 13.41i (ISBN 0-690-01673-5). T Y Crowell.

Benson, Elizabeth P., ed. Maya World. rev ed. LC 77-4955. (Apollo Eds.). 1977. pap. 4.95i (ISBN 0-8152-0423-X, A-423). T Y Crowell.

Benson, Eugene. J. M. Synge. 1982. 50.00x (ISBN 0-7171-1243-8, Pub. by Gill & Macmillan Ireland). State Mutual Bk.

--J. M. Synge. (Grove Press Modern Dramatists Ser.). (Illus.). 224p. (Orig.). 1983. pap. 9.95 (ISBN 0-394-62432-7, Ever). Grove.

Benson, Evelyn P. & DeVitt, Joan Q. Community Health & Nursing Practices. 2nd ed. (Illus.). 1980. text ed. 20.95 (ISBN 0-13-153171-9). P-H.

Benson, Ezra T. Farmers at the Crossroads. 1956. 8.95 (ISBN 0-8159-5501-4). Devin.

Benson, F. A. Problems in Electronics with Solutions. 5th ed. 1976. pap. 14.95x (ISBN 0-412-14770-X, Pub. by Chapman & Hall). Methuen Inc.

Benson, F. A. & Harrison, D. Electric-Circuit Theory. 470p. 1975. pap. text ed. 22.95 (ISBN 0-7131-3335-X). E Arnold.

Benson, F. A., ed. see Kraszewski, Andreej.

Benson, Forrest. The Saga of Seven Bays. 1979. 7.95 o.p. (ISBN 0-533-04032-9). Vantage.

Benson, Frank & Blumer, Diedrich, eds. Psychiatric Aspects of Neurologic Disease, Vol. 2. (Seminars in Psychiatry Ser.). 1982. 24.50 (ISBN 0-8089-1430-8). Grune.

Benson, George, jt. auth. see Sachs, William.

Benson, George C., et al. Political Corruption in America. LC 77-88815. 1978. 26.95x (ISBN 0-669-02008-7). Lexington Bks.

Benson, Harold J. Microbiological Applications: A Laboratory Manual in General Microbiology, Short Version. 3rd. ed. 288p. 1979. wire coil write for info. (ISBN 0-697-04658-3); instr. manual avail. (ISBN 0-697-04913-2). Wm C Brown.

--Microbiological Applications: A Laboratory Manual in General Microbiology, Complete Version. 3rd ed. 380p. 1979. wire coil write for info. (ISBN 0-697-04659-1); inst. manual avail. (ISBN 0-697-04913-2). Wm C Brown.

Benson, Harold J. & Gunstream, Stanley E. Revised Laboratory Report Edition for Anatomy & Physiology Laboratory Textbook. 2nd ed. 1981. write for info. wire coil (ISBN 0-697-04707-5); instr.'s manual avail. (ISBN 0-697-04710-5). Wm C Brown.

Benson, Harold J. & Kipp, Kenneth E. Dental Science Laboratory Guide. 4th ed. 224p. 1968. wire coil write for info (ISBN 0-697-05703-8); instr's manual avail. (ISBN 0-697-05711-9). Wm C Brown.

Benson, Harold J. & Talaro, Arthur. Physiological Applications. 318p. 1982. write for info. wire coil (ISBN 0-697-04717-2); instr's manual avail. 0.00 (ISBN 0-697-04723-7). Wm C Brown.

Benson, Harold J., et al. Anatomy & Physiology Laboratory Textbook: Short & Complete Version, 2 vols. 3rd ed. 350p. 1983. pap. text ed. write for info. wire coil short version (ISBN 0-697-04739-3); instrs' manual avail. (ISBN 0-697-04740-7); pap. text ed. write for info. complete version, 570p. (ISBN 0-697-04737-7); instrs' manual avail. (ISBN 0-697-04738-5). Wm C Brown.

Benson, Harrison J. Rate Your Own Personality. 192p. (Orig.). 1979. pap. 5.95 o.s.i. (ISBN 0-89104-150-8, A & W Visual Library). A & W Pubs.

Benson, Hazel B. Behavior Modification & the Child: An Annotated Bibliography. LC 79-7358. (Contemporary Problems of Childhood Ser.: No. 3). 1979. lib. bdg. 35.00 (ISBN 0-313-21489-1, BBM/). Greenwood.

Benson, Ian & Lloyd, John. New Technology & Industrial Change. 220p. 1982. 21.00 o.p. (ISBN 0-686-92621-8). Nichols Pub.

Benson, J. L. Horse, Bird, & Man: The Origins of Greek Painting. LC 70-95787. (Illus.). 256p. 1970. lib. bdg. 20.00x (ISBN 0-87023-053-0). U of Mass Pr.

Benson, Jackson. The True Adventures of John Steinbeck. 1983. write for info. (ISBN 0-670-16685-5). Viking Pr.

Benson, John. British Coalminers in the Nineteenth Century: A Social History. (Illus.). 1980. text ed. write for info. o.p. (ISBN 0-391-01041-7). Humanities.

Benson, John H. & Carey, A. G. Elements of Lettering. 2nd ed. 1962. text ed. 16.95 (ISBN 0-07-004775-8, G). McGraw.

Benson, John H., tr. First Writing Book: An English Translation & Facsimile Text of Arrighi's Operina. (Illus.). 1966. pap. 4.45 (ISBN 0-300-00020-0, Y178). Yale U Pr.

Benson, Kenneth R., jt. auth. see Frankson, Carl.

Benson, L. Images, Heroes & Self Perceptions: The Struggle for Identity from Maskwearing to Authenticity. 1974. 23.95 (ISBN 0-13-451187-5). P-H.

--Plant Taxonomy: Methods & Principles. (Illus.). 1962. 21.95 o.s.i. (ISBN 0-471-06805-5). Wiley.

Benson, Leonard. The Family Bond: Marriage, Love & Sex in America. 1971. pap. text ed. 9.95x (ISBN 0-685-77204-7). Phila Bk Co.

Benson, Leslie. Proletarians & Parties: Five Essays in Social Class. 1978. pap. 9.95x (ISBN 0-422-76580-5, Pub. by Tavistock England). Methuen Inc.

Benson, Lyman. Plant Classification. 2nd ed. 1979. text ed. 27.95x (ISBN 0-669-01489-3). Heath.

Benson, M. English-Serbocroatian Dictionary. 669p. (Eng. & Serbocroatian.). 1981. 75.00 (ISBN 0-686-97376-3, M-9635). French & Eur.

--Serbocroatian-English Dictionary. 770p. (Serbocroatian & Eng.). 1980. 75.00 (ISBN 0-686-97438-7, M-9630). French & Eur.

Benson, M. A. Measurement of Peak Discharge by Indirect Methods. (Technical Note Ser.). 1968. pap. 10.00 (ISBN 0-685-22318-3, W60, WMO). Unipub.

Benson, Murray & Ladd, Fred. Famous Fairy Tales. Duenewald, Doris, ed. LC 78-53666. (Illus.). (gr. k-5). 1978. 5.95 o.p. (ISBN 0-448-14728-9, G&D). Putnam Pub Group.

Benson, Nella. The Lady's Maid. 1982. pap. 2.95 (ISBN 0-553-20479-3). Bantam.

Benson, Nettie L., ed. Mexico & the Spanish Cortes, 1810-1822: Eight Essays. (Latin American Monograph Ser.: No. 5). 251p. 1966. 14.50x (ISBN 0-292-73606-1). U of Tex Pr.

Benson, Oscar H., jt. auth. see Tod, Osma G.

Benson, P. George, jt. auth. see McClave, James T.

Benson, Peter L., et al. Religion on Capitol Hill: Myths & Realities. 192p. 1982. 11.49i (ISBN 0-06-060780-7, HarpR). Har-Row.

Benson, Ragnar. Mantrappping. (Illus.). 88p. 1981. pap. 10.00 (ISBN 0-87364-215-5). Paladin Ent.

--Survivalist's Medicine Chest. (Illus.). 80p. 1982. pap. 5.95 (ISBN 0-87364-256-2). Paladin Ent.

Benson, Ralph C., ed. Current Obstetric & Gynecologic Diagnosis & Treatment. 4th ed. 1050p. 1982. 25.00 (ISBN 0-87041-213-2). Lange.

Benson, Robert, ed. see Johnston, William L.

Benson, Robert L. & Constable, Giles, eds. Renaissance & Renewal in the Twelfth Century. (Illus.). 832p. 1983. text ed. 50.00x (ISBN 0-674-76085-9). Harvard U Pr.

Benson, Rowland S. Thermodynamics & Gas Dynamics of Internal Combustion Engines, Vol. 1. Horlock, J. H. & Winterbone, D., eds. (Illus.). 600p. 1982. text ed. 125.00x (ISBN 0-19-856210-1). Oxford U Pr.

Benson, Sidney W. Chemical Calculations: An Introduction to the Use of Mathematics in Chemistry. 3rd ed. LC 76-146670. 2791p. 1971. text ed. 9.95 (ISBN 0-471-06769-5). Wiley.

--Foundations of Chemical Kinetics. LC 80-16099. 742p. 1982. Repr. of 1960 ed. lib. bdg. 39.50 (ISBN 0-89874-194-7). Krieger.

--Foundations of Chemical Kinetics. (Advanced Chemistry Ser.). 1959. text ed. 23.50 o.p. (ISBN 0-07-004778-2, C). McGraw.

--Thermochemical Kinetics: Methods for the Estimation of Thermochemical Data & Rate Parameters. 2nd ed. LC 76-6840. 320p. 1976. 42.50x (ISBN 0-471-06781-4, Pub. by Wiley-Interscience). Wiley.

Benson, Stella. The Far-Away Bride. LC 77-138606. 354p. 1972. Repr. of 1941 ed. lib. bdg. 18.50x (ISBN 0-8371-5714-5, BEFB). Greenwood.

Benson, Ted. Mother Lode Shortline. (Illus.). pap. 6.95 soft bound (ISBN 0-89685-025-0). Chatham Pub CA.

Benson, Vladimir. The Failure of the American Dream & the Moral Responsibility of the United States for the Crisis in the Middle East & for the Collapse of the World Order. (The Great Currents of History Library Bk.). (Illus.). 141p. 1983. 57.85 (ISBN 0-86722-025-2). Inst Econ Pol.

Benson, Warren, jt. ed. see Zuck, Roy B.

Benson, Warren S., jt. auth. see Gangel, Kenneth O.

Benson, William H. & Jacoby, Oswald. New Recreations with Magic Squares. (Illus.). 9.00 (ISBN 0-8446-5159-1). Peter Smith.

Bensousan, A. & Kleindorfer, P. R. Applied Stochastic Control in Econometrics & Management. (Contributions to Economic Analysis Ser.: Vol. 130). 1981. 55.50 (ISBN 0-444-85408-8). Elsevier.

Bensoussan, A. Stochastic Control by Functional Analysis Methods. (Studies in Mathematics & Its Applications: Vol. 11). 410p. 1982. 53.25 (ISBN 0-444-86329-X). Elsevier.

Bensoussan, A. & Lions, J. L. Applications of Variational Inequalities to Stochastic Control. (Studies in Mathematics & its Applications: Vol. 12). Orig. Title: Applications des Inequations Variationnelles en Controle Stochastique. 564p. 1982. Repr. of 1978 ed. 74.50 (ISBN 0-444-86358-3). Elsevier.

Bensoussan, A. & Lions, J. L., eds. Analysis & Optimization of Systems, Versailles, France, 1982: Proceedings. (Lecture Notes in Control & Information Sciences Ser.: Vol. 44). (Illus.). 987p. 1983. pap. 47.00 (ISBN 0-387-12089-0). Springer-Verlag.

Bensoussan, A., et al. Asymptotic Analysis for Periodic Structures. (Studies in Mathematics & Its Applications Ser.: Vol. 5). 1978. pap. text ed. 64.00 (ISBN 0-444-85172-0, North-Holland). Elsevier.

Benstead, C. R. Portrait of Cambridge. LC 68-99210. (Portrait Bks.). (Illus.). 1968. 11.50x (ISBN 0-7091-0112-0). Intl Pubns Serv.

Benstock, B., ed. Poems for James Joyce. 47p. 1981. pap. text ed. 4.25x (ISBN 0-905261-04-6, 51407, Pub. by Malton Pr Ireland). Humanities.

Benstock, Bernard, ed. The Seventh of Joyce. LC 81-47775. (Midland Bks Ser.: No. 282). 288p. (Orig.). 1982. 25.00X (ISBN 0-253-35184-7); pap. 12.50X (ISBN 0-253-20282-5). Ind U Pr.

Benstock, Bernard, jt. ed. see Staley, Thomas F.

Benston, George. Government Credit Allocation: Where Do We Go from Here? LC 75-32951. 208p. 1975. pap. text ed. 4.95 (ISBN 0-917616-02-2). ICS Pr.

Bent, Alan E. The Politics of Law Enforcement. 1977. pap. text ed. 8.95x o.p. (ISBN 0-669-01058-8). Heath.

Bent, Allen H. Bibliography of the White Mountains. rev. ed. Hanrahan, Jack, ed. LC 79-179457. (Bibliographies of New Hampshire History). (Illus.). 1972. Repr. of 1911 ed. pap. 10.00 (ISBN 0-912274-11-5). NH Pub Co.

Bent, Arthur C. Life Histories of North American Cardinals, Grosbeaks, Buntings, Towhees, Finches, Sparrows, & Their Allies, 3 Vols. (Illus.). 1968. pap. 7.95 ea.; Vol. 1 o.p. pap. (ISBN 0-486-21977-1); Vol. 2. pap. (ISBN 0-486-21978-X); Vol. 3. pap. (ISBN 0-486-21979-8). Dover.

--Life Histories of North American Gulls & Terns. (Illus.). 10.00 (ISBN 0-8446-1637-0). Peter Smith.

--Life Histories of North American Jays, Crows & Titmice, 2 vols. (Illus.). Set. 20.00 (ISBN 0-8446-1638-9). Peter Smith.

--Life Histories of North American Marsh Birds. (Illus.). 11.00 (ISBN 0-8446-1639-7). Peter Smith.

--Life Histories of North American Thrushes, Kinglets & Their Allies. (Illus.). 12.00 (ISBN 0-8446-1643-5). Peter Smith.

--Life Histories of North American Wagtails, Shrikes, Vireos & Their Allies. (Illus.). 10.50 (ISBN 0-8446-1644-3). Peter Smith.

--Life Histories of North American Wild Fowl, 2 Vols. (Illus.). Vol. 1. pap. 5.00 (ISBN 0-486-20285-2); Vol. 2. pap. 5.00 o.p. (ISBN 0-486-20286-0). Dover.

--Life Histories of North American Wood Warblers, 2 Vols. (Illus.). 11.00 ea. (ISBN 0-8446-1646-X). Peter Smith.

--Life Histories of North American Woodpeckers. (Illus.). 10.00 (ISBN 0-8446-1647-8). Peter Smith.

Bent, Bob & Bozzi. How to Cut Your Own or Anybody Else's Hair. LC 75-2295. 1975. 6.95 (ISBN 0-671-22012-8, Fireside). S&S.

Bent, Henry A. Second Law: An Introduction to Classical & Statistical Thermodynamics. 1965. 14.95x (ISBN 0-19-500829-4); pap. 11.95x (ISBN 0-19-500828-6). Oxford U Pr.

Bent, Ian, ed. Source Materials & the Interpretation of Music: A Memorial Volume to Thurston Dart. (Illus.). 474p. 1981. text ed. 70.00x (ISBN 0-8476-4785-4). Rowman.

Bent, R. D. & McKinley, J. L. Aircraft Basic Science. 5th ed. 1980. 20.05 (ISBN 0-07-004791-X); instr's. manual 4.00 (ISBN 0-07-002447-2); study guide & test bk. avail. McGraw.

Bent, R. D., jt. auth. see Casamassa, J. V.

Bent, R. K. & Dronenberg, D. H. Principles of Secondary Education. 6th ed. 1970. pap. text ed. 15.95 o.p. (ISBN 0-07-004810-X, C). McGraw.

Bent, Ralph D. & McKinley, James L. Aircraft Electricity & Electronics. rev. ed. (Aviation Technology Ser.). (Illus.). 432p. 1981. pap. text ed. 22.50 (ISBN 0-07-004793-6, G). McGraw.

--Aircraft Maintenance & Repair. 4th ed. (Aviation Technology). 1979. pap. text ed. 22.50 (ISBN 0-07-004794-4, G). McGraw.

--Aircraft Powerplants. 4th ed. Orig. Title: Powerplants for Aerospace Vehicles. (Illus.). 1978. pap. text ed. 22.50 (ISBN 0-07-004792-8, G). McGraw.

Bent, Robert J. & Sethares, George C. Basic: An Introduction to Computer Programming. 2nd ed. LC 81-17033. (Computer Science). 408p. 1982. pap. text ed. 18.95 (ISBN 0-534-01101-2). Brooks-Cole.

--Business Basic. LC 79-18502. 1980. pap. text ed. 18.95 (ISBN 0-8185-0359-9). Brooks-Cole.

--Fortran With Problem Solving. LC 80-28581. 448p. (Orig.). 1981. pap. text ed. 18.95 (ISBN 0-8185-0436-6). Brooks-Cole.

Bent, Samuel A., ed. Familiar Short Sayings of Great Men. LC 68-30643. 1968. Repr. of 1887 ed. 40.00x (ISBN 0-8103-3182-9). Gale.

Bente, F. Historical Introduction to the Book of Concord. 1965. 11.95 (ISBN 0-570-03287-3, 15-1926). Concordia.

Bente, Paul F., Jr., ed. Bio-Energy Directory, June 1978. 219p. (Orig.). 1978. pap. 10.00 o.p. (ISBN 0-940222-00-0). Bio Energy.

Bente, Thomas O. Spanish Conversation & Composition. 1976. text ed. 16.95 (ISBN 0-07-004808-8, C). McGraw.

Benteen, John. Run for Cover. (Sundance Ser.: No. 16). 176p. 1983. pap. 2.25 o.s.i. (ISBN 0-8439-1172-7, Leisure Bks). Dorchester Pub Co.

Bentham see Bentham, Jeremy & Mill, John S.

Bentham, C. G., jt. auth. see Haynes, R. M.

Bentham, G. The Botany of the Voyage of H. M. S. Sulphur: Under the Command of Captain Sir Edward Belcher 1836-42. (Illus.). 1968. 80.00 (ISBN 3-7682-0542-8). Lubrecht & Cramer.

--Plantae Hartwegianae: Plantas Hartwegianas Imprimis Mexicanas Adjectis Nonullis Grahamianis Enumerat Novasque Describit. 1971. Repr. of 1857 ed. 40.00 (ISBN 3-7682-0673-4). Lubrecht & Cramer.

Bentham, G. & Hooker, J. D. Genera Plantarum, 3 vols. 1966. 264.00 (ISBN 3-7682-0277-1). Lubrecht & Cramer.

--Supplemental Papers to Bentham & Hooker's Genera Plantarum. 1971. Repr. of 1881 ed. 88.00 (ISBN 3-7682-0706-4). Lubrecht & Cramer.

Bentham, Jeremy. Constitutional Code, Vol. 1. Rosen, F. & Burns, J. H., eds. (The Collected Works of Jeremy Bentham Ser.). 693p. 1983. 98.00 (ISBN 0-19-822608-X). Oxford U Pr.

--The Correspondence of Jeremy Bentham, 3 vols. Sprigge, T. L., ed. Incl. Vols. 1-2. 1752-1780. 1968 (ISBN 0-485-13201-X); Vol. 3. January 1781-October 1788. 1971 (ISBN 0-485-13203-6). text ed. 88.25x ea. (Athlone Pr). Humanities.

--Introduction to the Principles of Morals & Legislation. 1982. 15.95x (ISBN 0-416-41850-3). Methuen Inc.

--Limits of Jurisprudence Defined. LC 71-100143. Repr. of 1945 ed. lib. bdg. 20.75x (ISBN 0-8371-3249-5, BEJU). Greenwood.

--The Theory of Legislation. LC 75-39951. 294p. 1975. lib. bdg. 18.00 (ISBN 0-379-00587-5). Oceana.

Bentham, Jeremy & Mill, John S. The Utilitarians. Incl. Principles of Morals & Legislation. Bentham; Utilitarianism & on Liberty. Mill, John S. LC 62-2169. pap. 3.50 (ISBN 0-385-08256-8, C265, Anch). Doubleday.

Bentham, Jeremy see McReynolds, Paul.

Benthem, J. V. The Logic of Time. 1982. 49.50 (ISBN 90-277-1421-5, Pub. by Reidell Holland). Kluwer Boston.

Bentinck-Smith, William, ed. Harvard Book: Selections from Three Centuries. LC 53-11123. 1953. 16.50x o.p. (ISBN 0-674-37300-6). Harvard U Pr.

Bentivegna, F. C. Abbigliamento E Costume Nella Pittura Italiana, 2 Vols. (Illus.). boxed. 60.00 o.p. (ISBN 0-87817-138-X). Hacker.

Bentkover, Judith D., jt. auth. see Sloan, Frank A.

Bentley. National Health Care Controversy. (Impact Bks.). (gr. 7 up). 1979. PLB 8.90 (ISBN 0-531-04262-6). Watts.

Bentley, Arthur F. Process of Government. (Social Science Classics). 551p. 1983. pap. 19.95 (ISBN 0-87855-934-5). Transaction Bks.

Bentley, Beth. Phone Calls from the Dead. LC 76-122096. 78p. 1970. 8.95 (ISBN 0-8214-0076-2, 82-80802). Ohio U Pr.

Bentley, Christopher, ed. The Tragedy of Othello: The Moor of Venice. 166p. 1983. pap. 8.00 (ISBN 0-424-00093-8, Pub. by Sydney U Pr). Intl Schol Bk Serv.

Bentley, Clerihew. The First Clerihews. (Illus.). 59p. 1983. 14.95 (ISBN 0-19-212980-5). Oxford U Pr.

Bentley, Colin. Computer Project Management. 112p. 1983. 29.95 (ISBN 0-471-26208-0, Pub. by Wiley-Interscience). Wiley.

Bentley, E. C. Trent's Last Case. 1978. pap. 2.84i (ISBN 0-06-080440-8, P 440, PL). Har-Row.

--Trent's Own Case. LC 80-7836. 1980. pap. 2.84i (ISBN 0-06-080516-1, P 516, PL). Har-Row.

Bentley, Eric. Kleist Variations. 100p. (Orig.). 1982. pap. write for info. (ISBN 0-88127-010-5). Oracle Pr LA.

--Lord Alfred's Lover. (Drama Ser.). 128p. 1981. pap. 6.95 (ISBN 0-920510-41-8, Pub. by Personal Lib). Dodd.

--Modern Theatre, 6 Vols. Set. 54.00 (ISBN 0-8446-1653-2); 9.00 ea.; Vol. 1. (ISBN 0-8446-1654-0); Vol. 2. (ISBN 0-8446-1655-9); Vol. 3. (ISBN 0-8446-1656-7); Vol. 4. (ISBN 0-8446-1657-5); Vol. 5. (ISBN 0-8446-1658-3); Vol. 6. (ISBN 0-8446-1659-1). Peter Smith.

--Rallying Cries: Three Plays. LC 77-1973. 1977. o.s.i 10.00 (ISBN 0-915220-23-7); pap. 4.50 (ISBN 0-915220-24-5, 23034). New Republic.

--What Is Theatre. LC 68-56839. (Orig.). 1968. pap. 4.95 o.p. (ISBN 0-689-70012-1, 131). Atheneum.

Bentley, Eric, ed. The Theory of the Modern Stage. 496p. 1976. pap. 6.95 (ISBN 0-14-020947-6, Pelican). Penguin.

Bentley, Eric, ed. see Pirandello, Luigi.

Bentley, Eric, tr. see Brecht, Bertolt.

Bentley, G. Orthopedics, Vol. 1. (Operative Surgery Ser.). 1979. 140.00 (ISBN 0-407-00630-3). Butterworth.

Bentley, G., ed. Orthopedics, Vol. 2. (Operative Surgery Ser.). 1979. 140.00 (ISBN 0-407-00631-1). Butterworth.

Bentley, G. E. William Blake: Europe, a Prophecy. LC 73-93218. 1976. ltd. ed. 60.00 (ISBN 0-913130-30-3, American Blake Foundation). St Luke TN.

Bentley, G. E., Jr. Blake Books: Annotated Catalogues of His Writings in Illuminated Printing, in Conventional Typography & in Manuscript & Reprints Thereof; Reproductions of His Designs: Books with His Engravings: Catalogues: Books He Owned; & Scholarly & Critical Works About Him. 1977. 155.00x (ISBN 0-19-818151-5). Oxford U Pr.

Bentley, G. E., Jr., intro. by. William Blake: America; a Prophecy. LC 73-93217. 1974. 35.00 (ISBN 0-913130-03-6, American Blake Foundation). St Luke TN.

Bentley, George, ed. Orthopedics, 2 vols. 3rd ed. (Operative Surgery Ser.). (Illus.). 1979. Set. text ed. 270.00 (ISBN 0-407-00632-X). Butterworth.

Bentley, George, jt. ed. see Duthie, R. B.

Bentley, Gerald E., ed. see Jonson, Ben.

Bentley, Gerald E., Jr. Early Engravings of Flaxman's Classical Designs. LC 64-25357. (Illus., Orig.). 1964. pap. 5.00 o.p. (ISBN 0-87104-066-2). NY Pub Lib.

Bentley, Howard B., ed. Building Construction Information Sources. LC 64-16502. (Management Information Guide Ser.: No. 2). 1964. 42.00x (ISBN 0-8103-0802-9). Gale.

Bentley, James. Between Marx & Christ: The Dialogue in German-Speaking Europe, 1870-1970. 208p. 1982. 19.95 (ISBN 0-8052-7128-7, Pub. by NLB England); pap. 7.50 (ISBN 0-8052-7129-5, Pub. by NLB England). Schocken.

Bentley, John & Charlton, Bill. Finding out about Conservation. (Finding out about Ser.). (Illus.). 48p. (gr. 5-8). 1983. 12.50 (ISBN 0-7134-4287-5, Pub. by Batsford England). David & Charles.

--Finding Out about Villages. (Finding Out about Ser.). (Illus.). 48p. (gr. 5-8). 1983. 12.50 (ISBN 0-7134-4291-3, Pub. by Batsford England). David & Charles.

Bentley, John E. Problem Children: An Introduction to the Study of Handicapped Children in the Light of Their Psychological & Social Status. 437p. 1982. Repr. of 1936 ed. lib. bdg. 40.00 (ISBN 0-89760-094-0). Telegraph Bks.

Bentley, Judith. Busing: The Continuing Controversy. (Impact Ser.). (Illus.). 96p. (gr. 7 up). 1982. PLB 8.90 (ISBN 0-531-04482-3). Watts.

--State Government. (American Government Ser.). (Illus.). (gr. 7 up). 1978. PLB 8.90 s&l (ISBN 0-531-01343-X). Watts.

Bentley, K. W. & Kirby, G. W. Techniques of Chemistry: Vol. 4, 2 Pts. Elucidation of Organic Structures by Physical & Chemical Methods. 2nd ed. 689p. 1972. Pt. 1. 73.50x (ISBN 0-471-92896-8); Pt. 2, 1973, 561pgs. 75.50x (ISBN 0-471-92897-6). Wiley.

Bentley, K. W. see Weissberger, A.

Bentley, M. The Liberal Mind, 1914-1929. LC 76-11072. (Cambridge Studies in the History & Theory of Politics). 1977. 39.50 (ISBN 0-521-21243-X). Cambridge U Pr.

Bentley, Maxwell. Hydroponics Plus. (Illus.). 232p. 1982. 9.95. Timber.

Bentley, Nicholas. Nicholas Bentley's Book of Birds. (Illus.). (YA) (gr. 9 up). 1965. 7.50 o.p. (ISBN 0-685-20608-4). Transatlantic.

--Paybed. 1977. 5.00 o.s.i. (ISBN 0-233-96845-8). Transatlantic.

Bentley, P. J. Comparative Vertebrate Endocrinology. 2nd ed. LC 82-1205. (Illus.). 500p. 1982. 49.50 (ISBN 0-521-24653-9); pap. 19.95 (ISBN 0-521-28878-9). Cambridge U Pr.

Bentley, Peter J. Medical Pharmacology. (Medical Outline Ser.). 1982. pap. text ed. 15.95 (ISBN 0-87488-184-6). Med Exam.

Bentley, Sean. Into the Bright Oasis: The Great Knight Reason. 1976. 2.50 o.p. (ISBN 0-918116-01-5). Jawbone Pr.

Bentley, Toni. Winter Season: A Dancer's Journal. LC 81-23490. 160p. 1982. 11.95 (ISBN 0-394-52547-7). Random.

Bentley, Ursula. The Natural Order. 224p. 1983. 10.95 (ISBN 0-312-56147-4). St Martin.

Bentley, Virginia W. Bentley Farm Cook Book. LC 74-13108. 368p. 1975. pap. 11.95 (ISBN 0-395-19394-X). HM.

Bently, James. Simon & Schuster Children's Bible. (Children's Illustrated Bible Ser.). (Illus.). 240p. (gr. 2-5). 1983. 7.95 (ISBN 0-671-47089-2, Little). S&S.

Benton. An Atlas of the Fleas of Eastern U. S. 1980. 7.50 (ISBN 0-942788-08-7). Marginal Med.

--Keys to Mammals of Western N. Y. 1977. 0.50 (ISBN 0-942788-01-X). Marginal Med.

Benton & Pearl, eds. Dyslexia: An Appraisal of Current Knowledge. 1978. pap. 17.95x (ISBN 0-19-502710-8). Oxford U Pr.

Benton, Allen H. Keys to the Mammals of Western New York. (Marginal Media Bioguides Ser.: No. 2). (Illus.). 14p. 1977. pap. text ed. 1.00 (ISBN 0-942788-01-X). Marginal Med.

Benton, Allen H. & Bunting, Richard L. Young People's Nature Guide. (Illus.). 177p. (gr. 2-4). 1978. pap. text ed. 3.00 (ISBN 0-942788-05-2); 6.00 (ISBN 0-942788-06-0). Marginal Med.

Benton, Allen H. & Werner, William E. Field Biology & Ecology. 3rd ed. (Illus.). 480p. 1974. text ed. 37.50 (ISBN 0-07-004829-0, C). McGraw.

Benton, Allen H. & Werner, William, Jr. Manual of Field Biology & Ecology. 6th ed. 208p. 1982. 14.95x (ISBN 0-8087-4086-5). Burgess.

Benton, Angelo Ames. The Church Cyclopaedia: A Dictionary of Church Doctrine, History, Organization & Ritual, & Containing Original Articles on Special Topics, Written Expressly for This Work by Bishops, Presbyters, & Laymen. LC 74-31499. 810p. 1975. Repr. of 1883 ed. 56.00x (ISBN 0-8103-4204-9). Gale.

Benton, Arthur L., et al. Contributions to Neuropsychological Assessment: A Clinical Manual. (Illus.). 145p. 1983. text ed. 28.95x (ISBN 0-19-503192-X); pap. text ed. 18.95x (ISBN 0-19-503193-8). Oxford U Pr.

Benton, C. E., jt. auth. see Thomas, Elaine.

Benton, Chris. Chicagoland Nature Trails. LC 77-91183. 1978. pap. 7.95 o.p. (ISBN 0-8092-7662-3). Contemp Bks.

Benton, Dorothy G. Mountain Harvest. LC 72-92732. 64p. 1973. 4.00 (ISBN 0-911838-28-7). Windy Row.

Benton, Elbert J. The Movement for Peace Without a Victory During the Civil War. LC 70-176339. (The American Scene Ser.). 1972. Repr. of 1918 ed. lib. bdg. 17.50 (ISBN 0-306-70420-X). Da Capo.

Benton, Floria. Hollow Earth Mysteries & the Polar Shift. 100p. (Orig.). pap. 9.95 (ISBN 0-911306-25-0). G Barker Bks.

Benton, Joanna. Keeping Close. (Orig.). 1983. pap. 10.00 (ISBN 0-8065-0839-6). Citadel Pr.

Benton, John. Carmen. 192p. (Orig.). (gr. 7-12). 1974. pap. 1.95 o.p. (ISBN 0-8007-8159-7, New Hope Bks). Revell.

--Connie. 192p. (Orig.). (gr. 7-12). 1982. pap. 2.95 (ISBN 0-8007-8429-4, New Hope Bks). Revell.

--Debbie. (Orig.). (gr. 7-12). 1980. pap. 2.95 (ISBN 0-8007-8398-0, New Hope Bks). Revell.

--Denise. (gr. 7-12). 1982. pap. 2.50 (ISBN 0-8007-8451-0, New Hope Bks.). Revell.

--Lefty. (Orig.). (gr. 7-12). 1981. pap. 2.95 (ISBN 0-8007-8401-4, New Hope Bks). Revell.

--Lori. 160p. (Orig.). (gr. 7-12). 1980. pap. 2.50 o.p. (ISBN 0-8007-8385-9, New Hope Bks). Revell.

--Marji. (Orig.). (gr. 7-12). 1980. pap. 2.50 o.p. (ISBN 0-8007-8378-6, New Hope Bks). Revell.

--Marji & the Gangland Wars. 192p. (Orig.). (gr. 7-12). 1981. pap. 2.95 (ISBN 0-8007-8407-3, New Hope Bks). Revell.

--Patti. (Orig.). (gr. 7-12). 1979. pap. 2.50 o.p. (ISBN 0-8007-8346-8, New Hope Bks). Revell.

--Sheila. 192p. (gr. 7-12). 1982. pap. 2.95 (ISBN 0-8007-8419-7, New Hope Bks.). Revell.

--Teenage Runaway. 128p. 1977. pap. 1.95 (ISBN 0-8007-8309-3, Spire Bks). Revell.

--Terri. 192p. (gr. 7-12). 1981. pap. 2.95 (ISBN 0-8007-8408-1, New Hope Bks). Revell.

--Valarie. 192p. (Orig.). (gr. 7-12). 1982. pap. 2.95 (ISBN 0-8007-8430-8, New Hope Bks.). Revell.

Benton, Lewis. Supervision & Management. (Management Ser). 512p. 1972. text ed. 27.95 (ISBN 0-07-004813-4, C); instructor's manual by J. A. Kirklin 4.95 (ISBN 0-07-034830-8). McGraw.

Benton, Lewis, ed. Management for the Future. LC 77-22862. 1978. 27.50 (ISBN 0-07-004818-5). McGraw.

--Private Management & Public Policy: Reciprocal Impacts. LC 79-2040. 256p. 1980. 19.95x (ISBN 0-669-03063-5). Lexington Bks.

Benton, Mildred & Marks, Linda G., eds. Library & Reference Facilities in the Area of the District of Columbia. 9th ed. LC 75-7976. 248p. 1975. lexhide 14.50 (ISBN 0-87715-110-5). Am Soc Info Sci.

Benton, Peggie, tr. see Lyon, Ninette.

Benton, Richard A. Pangasinan Reference Grammar. McKaughan, Howard P., ed. LC 72-152458. (PALI Language Texts: Philippines). (Orig.). 1971. pap. text ed. 7.00x o.p. (ISBN 0-87022-072-1). UH Pr.

--Spoken Pangasinan. McKaughan, Howard P., ed. LC 79-152457. (PALI Language Texts: Philippines). (Orig.). 1971. pap. text ed. 12.00x o.p. (ISBN 0-87022-073-X). UH Pr.

Benton, Thomas H. An Artist in America. 4th rev. ed. LC 82-20279. (Illus.). 480p. 1983. text ed. 25.00 (ISBN 0-8262-0394-9); pap. 12.95 (ISBN 0-8262-0399-X). U of Mo Pr.

Benton, Wilbourn E. Texas: Its Government & Politics. 4th ed. 1977. pap. text ed. 13.95 (ISBN 0-13-912204-4). P-H.

Ben-Tor, Amnon. Cylinder Seals of Third Millennium Palestine. LC 77-13226. (American Schools of Oriental Research, Supplement Ser: Vol. 22). (Illus.). 121p. 1978. text ed. 12.50x (ISBN 0-89757-322-6, Am Sch Orient Res). Eisenbrauns.

Bentovim, A. Family Therapy: Complementary Frameworks of Theory & Practice, Vol. 2. 1982. 22.50 (ISBN 0-8089-1480-4). Grune.

Bentovim, A., ed. Family Therapy: Complementary Frameworks of Theory & Practice, Vol. 1. 1982. 22.50 (ISBN 0-8089-1479-0). Grune.

Bents, jt. ed. see Howey.

Bentz & Martin, eds. Salary Survey Eighty-One. 30p. (Orig.). pap. 5.00 (ISBN 0-686-92287-5). Tex Assn Mus.

Bentz, Edward J., Jr. & Salmon, Eliah J. Synthetic Fuels Technology Overview with Health & Environmental Impacts. LC 80-70756. 136p. 1981. text ed. 29.95 (ISBN 0-250-40423-0). Ann Arbor Science.

Benveniste, Guy. Bureaucracy. 2nd ed. 240p. 1983. pap. text ed. 8.95x (ISBN 0-87835-134-5). Boyd & Fraser.

Ben-Veniste, Richard & Frampton, George, Jr. Stonewall. 1978. pap. 5.95 o.p. (ISBN 0-671-24404-3, Touchstone Bks). S&S.

Benvenuti, Judi, jt. ed. see Cataldo, Mary A.

Benvenuto, Richard. Emily Bronte. (English Authors Ser.). 1982. lib. bdg. 11.95 (ISBN 0-8057-6813-0, Twayne). G K Hall.

Benward, Bruce. Ear Training: A Technique for Listening. 275p. 1978. wire coil write for info. o.p. (ISBN 0-697-03550-6); 14 tapes avail. o.p. (ISBN 0-697-03552-2); instrs.' man. avail. o.p. (ISBN 0-697-03551-4). Wm C Brown.

--Ear Training: A Technique for Listening. 2nd ed. 220p. 1983. write for info. (ISBN 0-697-03547-6); instr's dictation manual avail. (ISBN 0-697-03548-4); 14 tapes avail. Wm C Brown.

--Workbook in Advanced Ear Training. 190p. 1974. write for info. wire coil (ISBN 0-697-03589-1); tchrs.' dictation manual avail. (ISBN 0-697-03590-5); 10 tapes avail. (ISBN 0-697-03696-0). Wm C Brown.

Benward, Bruce & Jackson, Barbara G. Practical Beginning Theory. 4th ed. 475p. 1980. write for info. plastic comb o.p. (ISBN 0-697-03600-6); tchr's man. o.p. (ISBN 0-697-03604-9); 3 cassettes o.p. (ISBN 0-697-03553-0). Wm C Brown.

--Practical Beginning Theory. 5th ed. 464p. 1982. pap. text ed. write for info. plastic comb (ISBN 0-697-03545-X); write for info. instr's. manual (ISBN 0-697-03546-8). Wm C Brown.

Beny, Roloff. Iran: Elements of Destiny. LC 78-53014. (Illus.). 1978. 50.00 o.p. (ISBN 0-89696-000-5, An Everest House Book). Dodd.

Beny, Roloff & Gunn, Peter. The Churches of Rome. (Illus.). 1981. 35.00 (ISBN 0-671-43447-0); 29.95 (ISBN 0-686-82967-0). S&S.

Benyo, Richard. The Masters of the Marathon. LC 82-73028. 256p. 1983. 12.95 (ISBN 0-689-11340-4). Atheneum.

Benyo, Richard, jt. auth. see Herrin, Kym.

Benz, A. Finland: Facts About. 1976. pap. 4.50x o.p. (ISBN 9-5110-4105-3, F525). Vanous.

Benzaquin, Paul. Fire in Boston's Cocoanut Grove. 1967. 10.00 (ISBN 0-8283-1160-9). Branden.

Benzel, Kathryn N. & Goldbeck, Janne. The Little English Workbook. 190p. 1981. text ed. 8.95x (ISBN 0-673-15653-2). Scott F.

Benzie, William. Furnivall: Victorian Scholar Adventurer. 320p. 1983. 31.95 (ISBN 0-937664-57-X). Pilgrim Bks OK.

Benziger, Barbara F. Speaking Out: Therapists & Patients; How They Cure & Cope with Mental Illness Today. LC 74-31912. 320p. 1976. 15.00 o.s.i. (ISBN 0-8027-0484-0); pap. 5.95 (ISBN 0-8027-7146-7). Walker & Co.

Benziger, Theodore H., ed. Temperature, 2 pts. Incl. Pt. 1. Arts & Concept. 55.00 (ISBN 0-12-786141-6); Pt. 2. Thermal Homeostasis. 60.50 (ISBN 0-12-786142-4). (Benchmark Papers in Human Physiology: Vols. 9 & 10). 1977. Acad Pr.

Benzoni, Juliette. The Devil's Necklace. 416p. 1980. 12.95 o.p. (ISBN 0-399-12515-9). Putnam Pub Group.

--The Lure of the Falcon. LC 78-13154. 1978. 9.95 o.p. (ISBN 0-399-12048-3). Putnam Pub Group.

--Marianne & the Crown of Fire. 1976. 7.95 o.p. (ISBN 0-399-11798-9). Putnam Pub Group.

--Marianne & the Lords of the East. 256p. 1976. 7.95 o.p. (ISBN 0-399-11578-1). Putnam Pub Group.

Bequai, August. The Cashless Society: EFTS at the Crossroads. LC 80-21517. 298p. 1981. 27.95x (ISBN 0-471-05654-5, Pub. by Wiley-Interscience). Wiley.

--Organized Crime. LC 77-18574. 1979. 19.95x (ISBN 0-669-02104-0). Lexington Bks.

--White-Collar Crime. LC 77-11242. (Illus.). 1978. 18.95x (ISBN 0-669-01900-3); pap. 11.95 (ISBN 0-669-05907-2). Lexington Bks.

Beraha, E. & Shpigler, B. Color Metallography. (TN 690.b47). 1977. 81.00 (ISBN 0-87170-045-X). ASM.

Beram, Sandy. Back Before Bedtime. LC 77-88727. 1978. pap. 7.95 (ISBN 0-8256-3093-2, Quick Fox). Putnam Pub Group.

Beran, J. A. & Brady, J. E. Laboratory Manual for General Chemistry. 1978. pap. text ed. 21.95 (ISBN 0-471-03290-5); lab manual 15.50 (ISBN 0-471-07807-7). Wiley.

Beranek, Bernard. Annuale Mediaevele, Vol. 21. 138p. 1982. 13.50x (ISBN 0-686-82238-2). Humanities.

Beranek, Leo L. Noise & Vibration Control. 1971. 54.50 (ISBN 0-07-004841-X, P&RB). McGraw.

Beranek, Susan K. & Rapp, William F. An Industrial Archaeology of Nebraska. (Illus.). 50p. 1983. pap. write for info (ISBN 0-916170-00-4). J-B Pubs.

Berardo, Felix M., jt. auth. see Nye, F. Ivan.

Berberi, Dilaver & Berberi, Edel A., eds. Cortina-Grosset Basic Dictionary: Italian. 1977. pap. 2.95 (ISBN 0-448-14030-6, G&D). Putnam Pub Group.

--Cortina-Grosset Basic Italian Dictionary. LC 73-18524. 384p. 1975. limp bdg 2.95 o.p. (ISBN 0-448-11558-1, G&D). Putnam Pub Group.

Berberi, Dilaver, ed. see Laita, Luis M.

Berberi, Dilaver, ed. see Marcy, Teresa & Marcy, Michel.

Berberi, Edel A., jt. ed. see Berberi, Dilaver.

Berberi, Edel A., ed. see Laita, Luis M.

Berberi, Edel A., ed. see Marcy, Teresa & Marcy, Michel.

Berberian, Miriam, jt. ed. see Kasperson, Roger E.

Berberian, S. K. Lectures in Functional Analysis & Operator Theory. (Graduate Texts in Mathematics: Vol. 15). 370p. 1974. 32.00 (ISBN 0-387-90080-2). Springer-Verlag.

Berberian, Sterling K. Measure & Integration. LC 74-128871. 1970. Repr. of 1965 ed. text ed. 14.95 (ISBN 0-8284-0241-8). Chelsea Pub.

Berberoglu, B. Turkey in Crisis: From State Capitalism to Neocolonialism. 150p. 1982. 21.95 (ISBN 0-905762-56-8, Pub. by Zed Pr England); pap. 9.95 (ISBN 0-905762-61-4). Lawrence Hill.

Berberova, ed. see Tolstoy, Leo.

Berberova, Nina. Kursiv Moi, 2 vols. (Illus.). 720p. (Orig., Rus.). 1982. Set. pap. 34.00 (ISBN 0-89830-065-7). Vol. 1 (ISBN 0-89830-066-5). Vol.2 (ISBN 0-89830-067-3). Russica Pubs.

Berbrich, Joan D. Reading Today. (Orig.). (gr. 10-12). 1983. pap. write for info. (ISBN 0-87720-449-7). AMSCO Sch.

Berbrich, Joan D., ed. Stories of Crime & Detection. LC 73-8832. (Patterns in Literary Art Ser). (Illus.). 312p. (gr. 9-12). 1972. pap. text ed. 9.16 (ISBN 0-07-004826-6, W). McGraw.

Bercensi, Susan. Innocent Surrender. LC 82-45346. (Starlight Romance Ser.). (Illus.). 192p. 1983. 11.95 (ISBN 0-385-18258-9). Doubleday.

Berch, Bettina. The Endless Day: The Political Economy of Women & Work. 192p. 1982. pap. text ed. 8.95 (ISBN 0-15-517950-0, HC). HarBraceJ.

Berchem-Simon, Odette, ed. Ergonomics Glossary: Terms Commonly Used in Ergonomics. 264p. (Eng., Fr. & Ger.). 1982. 47.50x (ISBN 90-313-0500-6). Intl Pubns Serv.

Berchen, Ursula, jt. auth. see Berchen, William.

Berchen, William & Berchen, Ursula. Aspects of Boston. 1976. pap. 9.95 o.p. (ISBN 0-395-20549-2). HM.

Berchman, Evelyn. Victims of Piracy: The Admirality Court 1575-1678. 1978. 11.50 o.p. (ISBN 0-241-10105-0, Pub by Hamish Hamilton). David & Charles.

Berchoux, J. De. Voltaire Ou le Triomphe De la Philosophie Moderne. Repr. of 1814 ed. 96.00 o.p. (ISBN 0-8287-0080-X). Clearwater Pub.

Berchtold, R., ed. see Paquet, K. J., et al.

Berchtold, W., tr. see Hopper, A. G.

Berckman, Evelyn. The Beckoning Dream. 1974. pap. 0.95 o.p. (ISBN 0-451-05997-2, Q5997, Sig). NAL.

--The Crown Estate. 1978. pap. 1.75 o.p. (ISBN 0-380-01960-4, 38422). Avon.

--Do You Know This Voice? LC 60-11930. 1983. pap. 2.95 (ISBN 0-396-08161-4). Dodd.

--The Nightmare Chase. 1978. pap. 1.75 o.p. (ISBN 0-380-40501-6, 40501). Avon.

Bercoon, Norman, jt. auth. see Ullman, James M.

Bercovici. Barriers to Normalization: The Restrictive Management of Retarded Persons. 224p. 1982. pap. text ed. 19.95 (ISBN 0-8391-1766-3). Univ Park.

Bercovici, Eric. Wolftrap. LC 78-21598. 1979. 7.95 o.p. (ISBN 0-689-10949-0). Atheneum.

Bercovici, Konrad. Alexander, a Romantic Biography. 335p. 1982. Repr. of 1928 ed. lib. bdg. 30.00 (ISBN 0-686-81681-1). Century Bookbindery.

--Best Short Stories of the World. 25.00 (ISBN 0-89987-135-6). Darby Bks.

--The Story of the Gypsies. LC 78-164051. (Illus.). xii, 294p. 1975. Repr. of 1928 ed. 37.00x (ISBN 0-8103-4042-9). Gale.

Bercovitch, S. The American Puritan Imagination. LC 73-94136. 256p. 1974. 39.50 (ISBN 0-521-20392-9); pap. 11.95 (ISBN 0-521-09841-6). Cambridge U Pr.

Bercovitch, Sacvan. The American Jeremiad. LC 78-53283. 254p. 1979. 25.00 (ISBN 0-299-07350-5); pap. 9.95 (ISBN 0-299-07354-8). U of Wis Pr.

--The Puritan Origins of the American Self. LC 74-29713. 272p. 1975. 25.50x (ISBN 0-300-01754-5); pap. 8.95x (ISBN 0-300-02117-8). Yale U Pr.

Bercuson. Opening the Canadian West. (gr. 6-10). 1980. PLB 8.40 (ISBN 0-531-00448-1). Watts.

Berczeller, Richard. A Trip into the Blue & Other Stories from the New Yorker. LC 79-26955. 160p. 1980. 10.00 o.s.i. (ISBN 0-89479-066-8). A & W Pubs.

Berdahl, Robert O. Statewide Coordination of Higher Education. 1971. 8.50 o.p. (ISBN 0-8268-1383-6). ACE.

Berdes, Celia. Social Services for the Aged Dying & Bereaved in International Perspective. 82p. (Orig.). 1978. pap. text ed. 5.00 (ISBN 0-910473-04-8). Intl Fed Ageing.

Berdes, George R. Friendly Adversaries: The Press & Government. pap. 4.95 o.p. (ISBN 0-87462-427-4). Marquette.

--Up from Ashes: An American Journalist Reports from Germany. 1964. pap. 4.95 o.p. (ISBN 0-87462-426-6). Marquette.

Berdiaev, Nicolas. Leontiev. (Russian Ser.: Vol. 15). 1968. pap. 12.00x (ISBN 0-87569-004-1). Academic Intl.

Berdiaev, Nikolai. Solitude & Society. Reavey, George, tr. from Rus. LC 70-98211. 207p. 1976. Repr. of 1938 ed. lib. bdg. 17.00x (ISBN 0-8371-3250-9, BESS). Greenwood.

Berdiaev, Nikolai A. The Beginning & the End. French, R. M., tr. from Russian. LC 76-6083. 1976. Repr. of 1952 ed. lib. bdg. 18.25x (ISBN 0-8371-8837-7, BEBE). Greenwood.

Berdine, William H. & Cegelka, Patricia T. Teaching the Trainable Retarded. (Special Education Ser.). 312p. 1980. text ed. 19.50 (ISBN 0-675-08200-5). Merrill.

Berdine, William H., jt. auth. see Blackhurst, Edward A.

Berding, Andrew. The Making of Foreign Policy. LC 66-14226. (The U.S.A Survey Ser.). 102p. 1966. 4.95 (ISBN 0-87107-002-2). Potomac.

Berdjis, Charles C. What Should We Know About Health Hazards? LC 78-52763. 1979. 5.50 o.p. (ISBN 0-533-03695-X). Vantage.

Berdy, Janos. Antibiotics from Higher Forms of Life: Higher Plants, Vol. VIII. (CRC Handbook of Antibiotic Compounds Ser.). 248p. 1982. 64.00 (ISBN 0-8493-3460-8). CRC Pr.

Berdy, Janos, ed. Antibiotics from Higher Forms of Life: Lichens, Algae, & Animal Organisms, Vol. IX. (CRC Handbook of Antibiotic Compounds Ser.). 248p. 1982. 44.00 (ISBN 0-8493-3461-6). CRC Pr.

Bereano, Philip L. Technology As a Social & Political Phenomenon. LC 76-18723. 544p. 1976. text ed. 32.95x (ISBN 0-471-06875-6). Wiley.

Bereday, George Z. & Masui, Shigeo, eds. American Education Through Japanese Eyes. LC 72-91619. 1973. 15.00x (ISBN 0-8248-0249-7, Eastwest Ctr). UH Pr.

Bereday, George Z. & Pennar, Jaan, eds. The Politics of Soviet Education. LC 75-28662. 217p. 1976. Repr. of 1960 ed. lib. bdg. 16.25x (ISBN 0-8371-8477-0, BEPS). Greenwood.

Bereday, George Z. & Volpicelli, Luigi, eds. Public Education in America: A New Interpretation of Purpose & Practice. LC 77-23510. 1977. Repr. of 1958 ed. lib. bdg. 18.50x (ISBN 0-8371-9702-3, BEPU). Greenwood.

Berenberg, Ben R. Clock Book. (Play & Learn Bk). (Illus.). (gr. 1-3). 1967. 2.95 (ISBN 0-307-10730-2, Golden Pr). Western Pub.

Berenberg, Samuel R., ed. Liver Diseases in Infancy & Childhood. (Illus.). 1976. 25.00 o.p. (ISBN 0-683-00600-2). Williams & Wilkins.

Berenblum, I. Carcinogenesis as a Biological Problem. 1975. 100.50 (ISBN 0-444-10628-6). Elsevier.

Berend, Ivan & Ranki, Gyorgy. The European Periphery & Industrialisation 1780-1914. LC 81-3893. (Studies in Modern Capitalism). (Illus.). 200p. 1982. 27.50 (ISBN 0-521-24210-X). Cambridge U Pr.

Berendes, H. W., jt. ed. see Garattini, S.

Berends, Jan, tr. see Schouten, Alet.

Berends, Polly. Whole Child-Whole Parent. LC 81-480294. (Illus.). 384p. (Orig.). 1983. pap. 8.61i (ISBN 0-06-090949-8, CN 949, CN). Har-Row.

Berends, Polly B. Whole Child-Whole Parent: A Spiritual & Practical Guide to Parenthood. rev. ed. LC 81-48029. (Illus.). 1983. write for info. (ISBN 0-06-014971-X, HarpT). Har-Row.

--Who's That in the Mirror? (Early Bird Bks.). (Illus.). (ps-1). 1968. PLB 2.50 (ISBN 0-394-81782-6). Random.

Berendt, Joachim. The Jazz Book: From New Orleans to Rock & Free Jazz. rev. ed. Morgenstern, Dan, ed. & tr. from Ger. LC 73-81750. 480p. 1975. 12.95 o.p. (ISBN 0-88208-027-X); pap. 8.95 o.p. (ISBN 0-88208-028-8). Lawrence Hill.

Berendzen. Man Discovers the Galaxies. 1976. 15.95 (ISBN 0-07-004845-2). McGraw.

Berenson, F. M. Understanding Persons: Personal & Impersonal Relations. 22.50 (ISBN 0-312-83154-4). St Martin.

Berenson, Gerald & White, Harvey M., eds. Annual Review of Family Therapy, Vol. I. LC 81-4131. 494p. 1980. 34.95 (ISBN 0-87705-508-4). Human Sci Pr.

Berenson, Gerald S. Cardiovascular Risk Factors in Children. 1980. text ed. 39.50x (ISBN 0-19-502589-X). Oxford U Pr.

Berenson, Howard. Mostly BASIC Applications for Apple II, Bk. 2. Date not set. pap. 12.95 (ISBN 0-672-21864-X). Sams.

--Mostly BASIC Applications for your TRS-80, Bk.2. Date not set. pap. 12.95 (ISBN 0-672-21865-8). Sams.

Berenson, M. & Levine, D. Basic Business Statistics: Concepts & Applications. 1979. 25.95 (ISBN 0-13-057596-8); studyguide & wkbk. 8.50 (ISBN 0-13-057588-7). P-H.

Berenson, Mark L. & Levine, David M. Basic Business Statistics: Concepts & Applications. 2nd ed. (Illus.). 752p. 1983. text ed. 25.95 (ISBN 0-13-057620-4); study gd. & wkbk. 8.95. P-H.

Berenstain, Jan & Berenstain, Stan. The Berenstain Bears Get in a Fight. LC 81-15866. (Berenstain Bears First Time Bks.). (Illus.). 32p. (ps-1). 1982. PLB 4.99 (ISBN 0-394-95132-8); pap. 1.50 (ISBN 0-394-85132-3). Random.

Berenstain, Jan, jt. auth. see Berenstain, Stan.

Berenstain, Janice, jt. auth. see Berenstain, Stan.

Berenstain, Janice, jt. auth. see Berenstain, Stanley.

Berenstain, Stan & Berenstain, Jan. The Berenstain Bears & the Messy Room. (Berenstain Bears First Time Bks.). (Illus.). 32p. (gr. k-2). 1983. PLB 1.50 (ISBN 0-394-95639-7); pap. 1.50 (ISBN 0-394-85639-2). Random.

--The Berenstain Bears Go to the Doctor. LC 81-50043. (Berenstain Bears First Time Bks.). (Illus.). 32p. (ps-1). 1981. PLB 4.99 (ISBN 0-394-94835-1); pap. 1.50 (ISBN 0-394-84835-7). Random.

--The Berenstain Bears' Moving Day. LC 81-50044. (Berenstain Bears First Time Bks.). (Illus.). 32p. (ps-1). 1981. PLB o.p. (ISBN 0-394-94838-6); pap. 1.50 (ISBN 0-394-84838-1). Random.

--The Berenstains' Baby Book. (Illus.). 1983. 14.95 (ISBN 0-87795-509-3). Arbor Hse.

Berenstain, Stan & Berenstain, Janice. The Bears' Activity Book. (Illus.). (ps-4). 1979. pap. 4.95 (ISBN 0-394-84213-8, BYR). Random.

--The Bears' Nature Guide. LC 75-8070. (Now I Know! Ser). (Illus.). 72p. (ps-3). 1975. 6.95 (ISBN 0-394-83125-X, BYR); PLB 6.99 (ISBN 0-394-93125-4). Random.

--The Berenstain Bears & the Spooky Old Tree. LC 77-93771. (Bright & Early Bk). (Illus.). (ps-2). 1978. 4.95 (ISBN 0-394-83910-2, BYR); PLB 5.99 (ISBN 0-394-93910-7). Random.

--The Berenstain Bears' Counting Book. LC 75-36461. (Illus.). 14p. (ps-1). 1976. 3.50 (ISBN 0-394-83246-9, BYR). Random.

--The Berenstain Bears Go to School. LC 77-79853. (Picturebacks Ser.). (Illus.). (ps-2). 1978. PLB 4.99 (ISBN 0-394-93736-8, BYR); pap. 1.50 (ISBN 0-394-83736-3). Random.

--The Berenstain Bears' Science Fair. LC 76-8121. (Bear Facts Library: No. 2). (Illus.). (gr. 1-4). 1977. 5.95 (ISBN 0-394-83294-9, BYR); PLB 5.99 (ISBN 0-394-93294-3). Random.

Berenstain, Stan, jt. auth. see Berenstain, Jan.

Berenstain, Stanley & Berenstain, Janice. Bears' Christmas. LC 79-117542. (Illus.). (gr. k-3). 1970. 4.95 (ISBN 0-394-80090-7); PLB 4.99 (ISBN 0-394-90090-1). Beginner.

Berent, Irving. The Algebra of Suicide. LC 81-4131. 205p. 1981. 19.95 (ISBN 0-89885-006-1). Human Sci Pr.

Bereny, J. A., ed. see Central Intelligence Agency.

Bereny, Justin A. The Emerging Solar Technologies: An Investment Overview. 130p. 1983. 195.00x (ISBN 0-89934-146-2, V-972). Solar Energy Info.

--Survey of the Emerging Solar Energy Industry. De Winter, Francis, ed. LC 77-71664. (Illus.). 405p. 1977. 49.50x (ISBN 0-930978-00-5, V-901); pap. 34.50 (ISBN 0-930978-01-3). Solar Energy Info.

Bereny, Justin A., ed. Alcohol Fuels Information Series Vol. 1: U. S. Government Overviews. LC 80-51918. 1980. 54.95x (ISBN 0-89934-031-8, B941-SS); pap. 39.95x (ISBN 0-89934-032-6, B041-SS). Solar Energy Info.

Berenyi, D. & Hock, G., eds. High-Energy Ion-Atom Collisions: Proceedings of the International Seminar on High-Energy Ion-Atom Collision Processes, Debrecen, Hungary, Mar. 17-19, 1981, No. 2. (Nuclear Methods Monographs). 276p. 1982. 69.75 (ISBN 0-444-99703-2). Elsevier.

Beres, Louis R. People, States, & World Order. LC 80-83099. 237p. 1981. pap. text ed. 9.95 (ISBN 0-87581-267-8). Peacock Pubs.

--Terrorism & Global Security: The Nuclear Threat. (Westview Special Studies in National & International Terrorism). 1979. lib. bdg. 20.00 (ISBN 0-89158-557-5). Westview.

Beres, Zsuzsa, tr. see Andras, Szekely.

Beresford, Anne. Lair. 1971. pap. 2.95 o.p. (ISBN 0-85391-038-3). Transatlantic.

Beresford, J. D. The Hampdenshire Wonder. Del Rey, Lester, ed. LC 75-395. (Library of Science Fiction). 1975. lib. bdg. 17.50 o.s.i. (ISBN 0-8240-1401-4). Garland Pub.

Beresford, M. & Hurst, J. G. Deserted Medieval Villages. 1972. text ed. 35.00 o.p. (ISBN 0-312-19425-0). St Martin.

Beresford, M. W. & St. Joseph, J. K. Medieval England: An Aerial Survey. 2nd ed. LC 77-90200. (Cambridge Air Surveys). 1979. 32.50 (ISBN 0-521-21961-2). Cambridge U Pr.

Beresford, Maurice W. & Finberg, H. P. English Medieval Boroughs: A Handlist. 200p. 1973. 12.50x o.p. (ISBN 0-87471-201-7). Rowman.

Beresford, W. A. Chondroid Bone, Secondary Cartilage & Metaplasia. LC 80-13411. (Illus.). 470p. (Orig.). 1981. text ed. 45.00 (ISBN 0-8067-0261-3). Urban & S.

Beresford-Howe, Constance. A Population of One. LC 77-92976. 1978. 8.95 o.p. (ISBN 0-312-63150-2). St Martin.

Beresford-Jones, R. D. A Manual of Anglo-Gallic Gold Coins. 1964. 12.00 (ISBN 0-685-51544-3, Pub by Spink & Son England). S J Durst.

Beres Rene, Louis. Mimicking Sisyphus: America's Countervailing Nuclear Strategy. LC 82-48437. 160p. 1982. 19.95x (ISBN 0-669-06419-X); pap. 11.95 (ISBN 0-669-06137-9). Lexington Bks.

Berestyci, H. & Brezis, H. Recent Contributions to Nonlinear Partial Differential Equations. (Research Notes in Mathematics Ser.: No. 50). 288p. 1981. pap. text ed. 27.50 (ISBN 0-273-08492-5). Pitman Pub MA.

Bereswell, Joe, jt. auth. see Moriarty, Tim.

Berey, David, ed. Barron's Regents Exams & Answers Earth Science. rev. ed. LC 57-58736. 300p. (gr. 10-12). 1982. pap. text ed. 4.50 (ISBN 0-8120-3165-2). Barron.

Berezin, B. D. Coordination Compounds of Porphyrins & Phthalocyanine. LC 80-40958. 286p. 1981. 59.95x (ISBN 0-471-27857-2, Pub. by Wiley-Interscience). Wiley.

Berezin, Nancy, et al. The Gentle Birth Book. 1980. 12.95 o.p. (ISBN 0-671-24299-7). S&S.

Berfenstam, Ragnar & William-Olsson, Inger. Early Child Care in Sweden. (Intl. Monographs on Early Child Care). 166p. 1973. 30.00x (ISBN 0-677-04890-4). Gordon.

Berg, Alan. Malnourished People: A Policy View. 108p. 1981. 5.00 (ISBN 0-686-36129-6, BN-8104). World Bank.

--The Nutrition Factor: Its Role in National Development. 1973. 18.95 (ISBN 0-8157-0914-5); pap. 7.95 (ISBN 0-8157-0913-7). Brookings.

Berg, Barbara. The Remembered Gate: Origins of American Feminism - the Woman & the City 1800-1860. (Urban Life in America Ser.). 1978. 19.95x (ISBN 0-19-502280-7). Oxford U Pr.

Berg, Barbara J. The Remembered Gate: Origins of American Feminism - the Woman & the City, 1800-1860. (Illus.). 1980. pap. 6.95 (ISBN 0-19-502704-3, GB 595, GB). Oxford U Pr.

Berg, Cherney. Fixation: A Beginners Guide to Home Repairs. (Illus.). 192p. (Orig.). 1982. pap. 5.95 (ISBN 0-89893-308-0). CDP.

Berg, Dave. Dave Berg Looks Around. (Illus.). 192p. 1982. pap. 1.95 (ISBN 0-446-30432-8). Warner Bks.

--Mad's Dave Berg Looks at Modern Thinking. (Illus.). 192p. (Orig.). 1976. pap. 1.95 (ISBN 0-446-30434-4). Warner Bks.

Berg, David N., jt. auth. see Mirvis, Philip H.

Berg, Francie M. How to Be Slimmer, Trimmer & Happier. LC 82-90690. (Illus.). 180p. (Orig.). (YA) (gr. 9 up). 1983. 11.95 o.s.i. (ISBN 0-918532-10-8); pap. 6.95 o.s.i. (ISBN 0-918532-11-6); Leader's Guide 56p. 4.95 o.s.i. (ISBN 0-918532-12-4). Flying Diamond Bks.

--How to Lose Weight the Action Way: Young Adult-Teen Edition. LC 80-81578. (Illus.). 176p. 1980. 12.95 o.p. (ISBN 0-918532-03-5); pap. 8.95 o.p. (ISBN 0-918532-04-3); leaders guide for action groups, 48p. 4.95 o.p. (ISBN 0-918532-05-1). Flying Diamond Bks.

Berg, Gary. Using Calculators for Business Problems. LC 78-10173. 1979. pap. text ed. 12.95 (ISBN 0-574-20565-9, 13-3565); instr's guide avail. (ISBN 0-574-20566-7, 13-3566). SRA.

Berg, Gerald, et al, eds. Viruses in Water. LC 76-26638. 272p. 1976. 15.00x (ISBN 0-87553-076-1, 030). Am Pub Health.

Berg, Geri, ed. The Visual Arts & Medical Education. (Medical Humanities Ser.). 160p. 1983. price not set (ISBN 0-8093-1038-4). S Ill U Pr.

Berg, I. Industrial Sociology. 1979. op 12.95 (ISBN 0-13-463240-0); pap. 9.95 (ISBN 0-13-463232-X). P-H.

Berg, Ian, jt. ed. see Hersov, Lionel.

Berg, Jean. Wee Little Man. (Beginning-to-Read Ser.). (ps-3). 1963. 3.95 o.s.i. (ISBN 0-695-89220-7); lib. ed. 2.97 o.s.i. (ISBN 0-695-49220-9); pap. 1.50 o.s.i. (ISBN 0-695-39220-4). Follett.

Berg, Jean H. Joseph & His Brothers. (Illus.). 32p. (Ger.). (gr. k-2). 1976. pap. 2.75 (ISBN 0-87510-106-2). Chr Science.

--Little Red Hen. (Beginning-to-Read Ser.). (Illus.). (gr. 1-3). 1963. PLB 4.39 (ISBN 0-695-45257-6, Dist. by Caroline Hse); pap. 1.95 (ISBN 0-695-85256-6). Follett.

--Moses: Leader & Lawgiver. (Illus.). 40p. (gr. k-4). 1982. 4.95 (ISBN 0-87510-161-5). Chr Science.

--Moses: Leader & Lawgiver. (Illus.). 40p. (Fr.). (gr. k-4). 1982. 4.95 (ISBN 0-87510-163-1). Chr Science.

--Moses: Leader & Lawgiver. (Illus.). 40p. (Ger.). (gr. k-4). 1982. 4.95 (ISBN 0-87510-164-X). Chr Science.

--Moses: Leader & Lawgiver. (Illus.). 40p. (Span.). (gr. k-4). 4.95 (ISBN 0-87510-166-6). Chr Science.

--Story of Peter (Fr.) (Illus., Span.). (ps-3). 1979. pap. 2.75 o.p. (ISBN 0-87510-150-X). Chr Science.

Berg, Lee. Acusto-Optic Signal Processing. (Optical Engineering Ser.). 472p. 1983. 65.00 (ISBN 0-8247-1667-1). Dekker.

Berg, Leo S. Nomogenesis or Evolution Determined by Law. Rostovtsow, J. N., tr. 1969. 19.95x o.p. (ISBN 0-262-02043-2). MIT Pr.

Berg, Mark R., et al. Jobs & Energy in Michigan: The Next Twenty Years. LC 80-24884. (Illus.). 210p. 1981. 20.00x (ISBN 0-87944-264-6); pap. 14.00x (ISBN 0-87944-263-8). Inst Soc Res.

Berg, Maxine. The Machinery Question & the Making of Political Economy: 1815-1848. LC 79-51223. (Illus.). 1980. 44.50 (ISBN 0-521-22782-8). Cambridge U Pr.

Berg, Miguel, jt. auth. see Lebar, Lois.

Berg, Milton E., jt. auth. see Goff, Gerald K.

Berg, Norman. A History of Kern County Land Company. (Illus.). 50p. 1971. 5.00 (ISBN 0-943500-04-4). Kern Historical.

Berg, Paul C., jt. auth. see Spache, George D.

Berg, Paul W. & McGregor, James L. Elementary Partial Differential Equations. LC 66-28845. (Illus.). 1966. 26.95x (ISBN 0-8162-0584-1). Holden-Day.

Berg, Richard E. & Stork, David G. The Physics of Sound. (Illus.). 416p. 1982. 25.95 (ISBN 0-13-674283-1). P-H.

Berg, Robert L., jt. auth. see DeVries, Martin.

Berg, Roy T. & Butterfield, Rex M. New Concepts of Cattle Growth. 240p. 1978. text ed. 16.95 (ISBN 0-424-00002-4, Pub. by Sydney U Pr). Intl Schol Bk Serv.

Berg, Sanford V. Innovative Electric Rates: Issues in Cost-Benefit Analysis. LC 82-47751. 352p. 1983. 32.95x (ISBN 0-669-04835-6). Lexington Bks.

Berg, Scott A. Max Perkins. 1983. pap. 5.95 (ISBN 0-686-37704-4). WSP.

Berg, Stephen, ed. In Praise of What Persists. LC 81-47651. (Illus.). 320p. 1983. 14.95 (ISBN 0-06-014921-3, HarpT). Har-Row.

Berg, William M., jt. auth. see Ross, J. Michael.

Bergad, Laird W. Coffee & the Growth of Agrarian Capitalism in Nineteenth-Century Puerto Rico. LC 82-61354. (Illus.). 264p. 1983. 25.00x (ISBN 0-691-07646-4); pap. 12.50 (ISBN 0-691-10139-6). Princeton U Pr.

Bergal, jt. auth. see Aufhammer.

Bergamini, David. The Land & Wildlife of Australasia. rev. ed. LC 80-52258. (Life Nature Library). PLB 13.40 (ISBN 0-8094-3859-3). Silver.

--Mathematics. rev. ed. LC 80-52155. (Life Science Library). PLB 13.40 (ISBN 0-8094-4083-0). Silver.

Bergamini, John D. The Hundredth Year: The United States in 1876. LC 75-44328. (Illus.). 1976. 12.95 o.p. (ISBN 0-399-11703-2). Putnam Pub Group.

--The Spanish Bourbons: The History of a Tenacious Dynasty. LC 74-78006. (Illus.). 480p. 1974. 12.95 o.p. (ISBN 0-399-11365-7). Putnam Pub Group.

Bergan, John J. & Yao, James S., eds. Cerebrovascular Insufficiency. Date not set. price not set (ISBN 0-8089-1540-1). Grune.

Bergan, John R. & Dunn, James A. Psychology & Education: A Science for Instruction. LC 75-14321. 542p. 1976. text ed. 32.95 (ISBN 0-471-06910-8); tchrs. manual avail. (ISBN 0-471-06911-6). Wiley.

Bergan, John R., jt. auth. see Henderson, Ronald W.

Bergant, Dianne. Job, Ecclesiastes, Vol. 18. 1982. 12.95 (ISBN 0-89453-252-9); pap. 9.95 (ISBN 0-686-32771-3). M Glazier.

Bergau, Nancy, jt. auth. see Soedharno, R.

Bergaust, Erik. Colonizing Space. LC 77-11147. (Illus.). (gr. 6 up). 1978. PLB 4.96 o.p. (ISBN 0-399-61113-4). Putnam Pub Group.

--Colonizing the Planets: The Factual Story of Manned Interplanetary Flight into the 21st Century. (Illus.). 96p. (gr. 6-8). 1975. PLB 5.49 o.p. (ISBN 0-399-60961-X). Putnam Pub Group.

--Colonizing the Sea. LC 76-21355. (Illus.). (gr. 6 up). 1976. PLB 4.96 o.p. (ISBN 0-399-61035-9). Putnam Pub Group.

--Illustrated Nuclear Encyclopedia. (Illus.). (gr. 7 up). 1971. PLB 4.89 o.p. (ISBN 0-399-60296-8). Putnam Pub Group.

--The New Illustrated Space Encyclopedia. rev. ed. LC 68-26072. (Illus.). (gr. 5 up). 1970. PLB 5.79 o.p. (ISBN 0-399-60487-1). Putnam Pub Group.

--The Next Fifty Years on the Moon. new ed. LC 73-77419. (Illus.). 128p. (gr. 5 up). 1974. PLB 5.49 o.p. (ISBN 0-399-60851-6). Putnam Pub Group.

--Rescue in Space: Lifeboats for Astronauts & Cosmonauts. (Illus.). 1974. PLB 5.29 o.p. (ISBN 0-399-60894-X). Putnam Pub Group.

--The Russians in Space. LC 68-26552. (Illus.). (gr. 5-8). 1969. PLB 3.89 o.p. (ISBN 0-399-60551-7). Putnam Pub Group.

Bergaust, Erik & Foss, William. Oceanographers in Action. (Illus.). (gr. 7 up). 1968. PLB 4.89 o.p. (ISBN 0-399-60496-0). Putnam Pub Group.

Berge, C. Graphs & Hypergraphs. 2nd rev. ed. LC 72-88288. (Mathematical Library: Vol. 6). (Illus.). 555p. 1976. 68.00 (ISBN 0-7204-0479-7, North-Holland). Elsevier.

Berge, C. & Bresson, D., eds. Combinatorial Mathematics: Proceedings of the International Colloquium on Graph Theory & Combinatorics, Marseille-Luminy, June, 1981. (North-Holland Mathematics Studies: Vol. 75). 660p. 1983. 106.50 (ISBN 0-444-86512-8, North Holland). Elsevier.

Berge, Carol, ed. see Crews, Judson.

Bergelson, David. When All Is Said & Done. Martin, Bernard, tr. from Yiddish. LC 76-25614. xxi, 310p. 1978. 16.95 (ISBN 0-8214-0360-5, 82-82501); pap. 7.95 (ISBN 0-8214-0392-3, 82-82519). Ohio U Pr.

Bergelson, L. D. Lipid Biochemical Preparations. 1980. 82.75 (ISBN 0-444-80146-4); pap. 39.25 (ISBN 0-444-80261-4). Elsevier.

Bergen, Adrienne F. & Colangelo, Cheryl. Positioning the Client with Central Nervous System Deficits: The Wheelchair & Other Adapted Equipment. (Illus.). 191p. (Orig.). 1982. pap. text ed. 19.95 (ISBN 0-686-37672-2). Valhalla Rehab.

--Positioning the Client with Central Nervous System Deficits: The Wheelchair & Other Adapted Equiptment. (Illus.). 191p. (Orig.). 1982. pap. text ed. 19.95 (ISBN 0-686-38095-9). Valhalla Rehab.

Bergen, Frank & Papanikolas, Zeese. Looking Far West: The Search of the American West in History, Myth & Literature. (Illus., Orig.). (RL 9). 1978. pap. 3.95 (ISBN 0-451-62085-2, ME2085, Ment). NAL.

Bergen, Stephen F., jt. auth. see Preston, Jack D.

Bergen, W. Von see Von Bergen, W.

Bergen, Werner Von see Von Bergen, Werner.

Bergendorff, Fred & Smith, Charles H. Broadcast Advertising & Promotion: A Handbook for TV, Radio & Cable. (Communication Arts Bks.). (Illus.). 480p. (Orig.). 1983. pap. 21.00 (ISBN 0-8038-0801-1). Hastings.

Bergener, Manfred. Aging in the Eighties & Beyond. 1983. text ed. price not set (ISBN 0-8261-3690-7). Springer Pub.

Bergens, A. & Noakes, D., eds. Prevert Vous Parle. (Fr.). 1968. pap. 12.95 (ISBN 0-13-699231-5). P-H.

Berger. The Gifted & Talented. (gr. 7 up). 1980. PLB 8.90 (ISBN 0-531-04111-5). Watts.

--Programming of Control Systems: Step Five. 19.95 (ISBN 0-471-25603-X, Wiley Heyden). Wiley.

Berger & Hollerweger, eds. Celebrating the Easter Vigil. O'Connell, Matthew J., tr. 160p. (Ger.). 1983. pap. 9.95 (ISBN 0-916134-56-3). Pueblo Pub Co.

Berger, et al. Management for Nurses: A Multidisciplinary Approach. 2nd ed. LC 79-19965. 1980. pap. 15.50 (ISBN 0-8016-4815-7). Mosby.

--A Visit to the Doctor. (Illus.). pap. 2.95 o.p. (ISBN 0-448-14001-2, G&D). Putnam Pub Group.

Berger, Alan S. The City: Urban Communities & Their Problems. 540p. 1978. pap. text ed. write for info. (ISBN 0-697-07555-9); write for info. suppl resource man. & test item file (ISBN 0-697-07570-2). Wm C Brown.

Berger, Allen & Robinson, H. Alan, eds. Secondary School Reading: What Research Reveals for Classroom Practice. (Orig.). 1982. pap. 10.75 (ISBN 0-8141-4295-8). NCTE.

Berger & Associates Cost Consultants, Inc. The Berger Building & Design Cost File, 1983: General Construction Trades, Vol. 1. LC 83-70008. 477p. 1983. pap. 36.75 (ISBN 0-942564-02-2). Building Cost File.
--The Berger Building & Design Cost File, 1983: Mechanical, Electrical Trades, Vol. 2. LC 83-70008. 207p. 1983. pap. 26.45 (ISBN 0-942564-04-9). Building Cost File.
Berger, Andrew J. Hawaiian Birdlife. 2nd & rev. ed. LC 80-26332. (Illus.). 300p. 1981. 29.95 (ISBN 0-8248-0742-1). UH Pr.
Berger, Andrew J., jt. auth. see Van Tyne, Josselyn.
Berger, Arthur. Aaron Copland. LC 79-136055. (Illus.). 1971. Repr. of 1953 ed. lib. bdg. 18.25x (ISBN 0-8371-5205-4, BEAC). Greenwood.
Berger, Arthur A. Television As an Instrument of Terror. LC 78-55942. 214p. 1979. 6.95 (ISBN 0-87855-708-3). Transaction Bks.
Berger, B. A. & Gagnon, J. P. Management Handbook for Pharmacy Practitioners: A Practical Guide for Community Pharmacists. LC 82-48578. (Illus.). x, 204p. (Orig.). 1982. pap. text ed. 14.00x (ISBN 0-938938-08-8, 820-PB-066). Health Sci Consort.
Berger, Barbara. Animalia. 1982. 19.95 (ISBN 0-89087-342-9); pap. 12.95 o.p. (ISBN 0-686-99734-4). Celestial Arts.
Berger, Bennett M. The Survival of a Counterculture: Ideological Work & Everyday Life Among Rural Communards. 278p. 1983. pap. 8.95 (ISBN 0-520-04950-0, CAL 579). U of Cal Pr.
Berger, Bill & Anderson, Ken. Modern Petroleum. 2nd ed. 255p. 1981. 33.95x (ISBN 0-87814-172-3). Pennwell Books Division.
--Modern Petroleum: A Basic Primer of the Industry. 293p. 1978. 33.95x (ISBN 0-87814-081-6). Pennwell Pub.
--Petroleo Moderno. Pena, Gus, tr. from Eng. 284p. (Span.). 1980. 39.95 (ISBN 0-87814-136-7). Pennwell Pub.
Berger, Bill D. & Anderson, Ken E. Plant Operations Training, Vol. 1. 157p. 1980. 29.95x (ISBN 0-87814-109-X). Pennwell Pub.
--Plant Operations Training, Vol. 2. 165p. 1980. 29.95x (ISBN 0-87814-110-3). Pennwell Pub.
--Plant Operations Training, Vol. 3. 162p. 1981. 29.95x (ISBN 0-87814-111-1). Pennwell Pub.
Berger, Brigitte & Berger, Peter L. War Over the Family: Capturing the Middle Ground. LC 82-45237. 240p. 1984. pap. price not set (ISBN 0-385-18006-3, Anch). Doubleday. Postponed.
--War Over the Family: Capturing the Middle Ground. 240p. 1983. 14.95 (ISBN 0-385-18001-2, Anchor Pr). Doubleday.
Berger, Carl. Broadsides & Bayonets: The Propaganda War of the American Revolution. LC 76-27182. 1976. 12.95 o.p. (ISBN 0-89141-006-6). Presidio Pr.
--The Writing of Canadian History: Aspects of English-Canadian Historical Writing 1900-1970. 1976. pap. 6.95x o.p. (ISBN 0-19-540280-4). Oxford U Pr.
Berger, Carl, ed. Approaches to Canadian History. LC 23-16213. (Canadian Historical Readings Ser.: No. 1). 1967. pap. 4.00x (ISBN 0-8020-1459-3). U of Toronto Pr.
Berger, Charles J. How to Raise & Train an Alaskan Malamute. (Orig.). pap. 2.95 (ISBN 0-87666-235-1, DS1042). TFH Pubns.
Berger, Charles R. & Bradac, James J. Language & Social Knowledge Uncertainty in Interpersonal Relations. 208p. 1982. pap. text ed. 14.95 (ISBN 0-7131-6196-5). E Arnold.
Berger, Charles R., jt. auth. see Roloff, Michael E.
Berger, Curtis. Land Ownership & Use: Cases, Statutes, & Other Materials. 2nd ed. text ed. 28.00 (ISBN 0-316-09154-5). Little.
Berger, Curtis J., jt. auth. see Axelrod, Allan.
Berger, David L. Industrial Security. LC 79-628. 1979. 18.95 (ISBN 0-913708-32-1). Butterworth.
Berger, Dorothea. Jean Paul Friedrich Richter. (World Authors Ser.). lib. bdg. 15.95 (ISBN 0-8057-2762-0, Twayne). G K Hall.
Berger, Dorothea, jt. auth. see Berger, Erich W.
Berger, Erich W. & Berger, Dorothea. New German Self-Taught. 396p. (Ger.). 1982. pap. text ed. 4.76i (ISBN 0-06-463615-1, EH 615, EH). B&N NY.
Berger, Eugenia H. Parents As Partners in Education: The School & Home Working Together. LC 80-39691. (Illus.). 424p. 1981. pap. text ed. 14.95 (ISBN 0-8016-0637-3). Mosby.
Berger, F. Studying Deductive Logic. 1977. pap. 11.95 (ISBN 0-13-858811-2). P-H.
Berger, G., jt. auth. see Jackson, M.
Berger, Gary S., et al, eds. Second Trimester Abortion: Perspectives After a Decade of Experience. 364p. 1981. text ed. 35.00 (ISBN 0-88416-256-7). Wright-PSG.
Berger, Gilda. All in the Family: Animal Species Around the World. (Science Is What & Why Bk.). (Illus.). 48p. (gr. 7-10). 1981. PLB 6.99 (ISBN 0-698-30730-5, Coward). Putnam Pub Group.
--Apes in Fact & Fiction. LC 80-14061. (gr. 5 up). 1980. PLB 8.90 (ISBN 0-531-04152-2). Watts.
--The Coral Reef: What Lives There. (Illus.). 32p. (gr. 3-6). 1977. PLB 5.99 (ISBN 0-698-30660-0, Coward). Putnam Pub Group.
--Easter & Other Spring Holidays. (First Bks.). (Illus.). 72p. (gr. 4 up). 1983. PLB 8.90 (ISBN 0-531-04547-1). Watts.
--Kuwait & the Rim of Arabia: Kuwait, Bahrain, Quatar, United Arab Emirates, Yemen, Oman, People's Democratic Republic of Yemen. (First Bks). (Illus.). (gr. 4-6). 1978. PLB 8.90 s&l (ISBN 0-531-02235-8). Watts.
--Learning Disabilities & Handicaps. (Impact Bks.). (Illus.). (gr. 7 up). 1978. PLB 8.90 s&l o.p. (ISBN 0-531-01457-6). Watts.
--Mental Illness. (Illus.). 144p. (gr. 9 up). 1981. lib. bdg. 9.90 (ISBN 0-531-04343-6). Watts.
--Mountain Worlds: What Lives There. (What Lives There Ser.). (Illus.). (gr. 2-5). 1978. 5.99 (ISBN 0-698-30702-X, Coward). Putnam Pub Group.
--Physical Disabilities. LC 78-10106. (Illus.). 1979. s&l 8.90 (ISBN 0-531-02927-1). Watts.
--Religion. (A Reference First Bk.). 96p. (gr. 4 up). 1983. PLB 8.90 (ISBN 0-531-04538-2). Watts.
--Speech & Language Disorders. LC 80-85052. (Impact Bks.). (YA) (gr. 7 up). 1981. PLB 8.90 (ISBN 0-531-04263-4). Watts.
Berger, Gilda & Berger, Melvin. Bizarre Murders. (Illus.). 128p. (gr. 9-12). 1983. PLB 9.79 (ISBN 0-671-45583-4). Messner.
--Fitting in: Animals in Their Habitat. LC 75-22284. (Science Is What & Why Ser.). (Illus.). 48p. (gr. k-3). 1976. PLB 5.99 o.p. (ISBN 0-698-30606-6, Coward). Putnam Pub Group.
--The Whole World of Hands. (Illus.). (gr. 2-5). 1982. PLB 8.95 (ISBN 0-395-32862-4); 8.70. HM.
Berger, Gilda, jt. auth. see Berger, Melvin.
Berger, James L. & Wittich, Walter A., eds. Educators Guide to Free Audio & Video Materials. 29th rev. ed. LC 55-2784. 1982. 16.25 (ISBN 0-87708-123-9). Ed Prog.
Berger, James O., jt. ed. see Gupta, Shanti S.
Berger, Jason & Berger, Susanna. Italy in Your Pocket. Price, Diana, ed. (Grosset Travel Guide Ser.). 1979. pap. 1.95 (ISBN 0-448-16634-8, G&D). Putnam Pub Group.
--London in Your Pocket. Price, Diana, ed. (Grosset Travel Guide Ser.). 1979. pap. 1.95 (ISBN 0-448-16636-4, G&D). Putnam Pub Group.
--Paris in Your Pocket. (Grosset Travel Guide Ser.). 1979. pap. 1.95 (ISBN 0-448-16635-6, G&D). Putnam Pub Group.
--Spain in Your Pocket. Price, Diana, ed. (Grosset Travel Guide Ser.). 1979. pap. 1.95 (ISBN 0-448-16637-2, G&D). Putnam Pub Group.
Berger, Jason, ed. Serving Social Security. (Reference Shelf Ser.: Vol. 54, No. 4). 158p. pap. text ed. 6.25 (ISBN 0-8242-0668-1). Wilson.
Berger, Jean. Choral Etudes. 20p. 1982. pap. text ed. write for info. (ISBN 0-87487-738-5). Summy.
Berger, John. Nuclear Power: The Unviable Option. 384p. 1976. 4.50 (ISBN 0-686-43096-4). Ramparts.
Berger, John & Tanner, Alain. Jonah Who Will Be Twenty-Five in the Year Two-Thousand. Palmer, Michael, tr. from Fr. (Illus.). 150p. (Orig.). 1983. 19.95 (ISBN 0-913028-97-5); pap. 9.95 (ISBN 0-913028-98-3). North Atlantic.
Berger, John, tr. see Bielski, Nella.
Berger, Jordan C. & Brody, Marvin D. Professional's Guide to the Estate Tax Audit. LC 81-7147. 394p. 1982. 79.50 (ISBN 0-87624-440-1). Inst Busn Plan.
Berger, Joseph, et al. Types of Formalization in Small-Group Research. LC 79-27703. (Illus.). x, 159p. 1980. Repr. of 1962 ed. lib. bdg. 18.25x (ISBN 0-313-22328-9, BETF). Greenwood.
Berger, Joseph R., jt. auth. see Caprio, Frank S.
Berger, Karol. Theories of Chromatic & Enharmonic Music in Late Sixteenth Century Italy. Buelow, George, ed. LC 79-24734. (Studies in Musicology: No. 10). 1980. 34.95 (ISBN 0-8357-1065-3, Pub. by UMI Res Pub). Univ Microfilms.
Berger, Kathleen, ed. see Kemper, Rachel H.
Berger, Kathleen, ed. see Lebow, Jared.
Berger, Kathleen S. The Developing Person. (Illus.). 1980. 22.95x (ISBN 0-87901-117-3); study guide 7.95x (ISBN 0-87901-118-1). Worth.
Berger, M. L. & Berger, P. J., eds. Group Training Techniques: Cases, Applications & Research. LC 72-9008. 191p. 1973. 29.95 (ISBN 0-470-06960-0). Halsted Pr.
Berger, Marc A. & Sloan, Alan D. A Method of Generalized Characteristics. LC 82-8741. (Memoirs of the American Mathematical Society Ser.: No. 266). 4.00 (ISBN 0-8218-2266-7, MEMO/266). Am Math.
Berger, Margaret L. Aline Meyer Liebman: Pioneer Collector & Artist. (Illus.). 148p. 1982. 30.00 (ISBN 0-9605914-0-0). M L Berger.
Berger, Mark. Taking the Fifth: The Supreme Court & the Privilege Against Self-Incrimination. LC 78-55953. 304p. 1980. 25.95x (ISBN 0-669-02339-6). Lexington Bks.
Berger, Maxine, jt. auth. see Mays, Willie.
Berger, Melvin. Animal Hospital. LC 72-2418. (Scientists at Work Ser). (Illus.). 128p. (gr. 2-4). 1973. lib. bdg. 10.89 (ISBN 0-381-99941-6, A04400, JD-J). Har-Row.
--Atoms. (Science Is What & Why Ser). (Illus.). (gr. k-3). 1968. PLB 4.49 o.p. (ISBN 0-698-30021-1, Coward). Putnam Pub Group.
--Bionics. (Impact Books Ser.). (Illus.). (gr. 7 up). 1978. PLB 8.90 s&l (ISBN 0-531-01354-5). Watts.
--Censorship. LC 82-4754. (Impact Ser.). (Illus.). 96p. (gr. 7 up). 1982. PLB 8.90 (ISBN 0-531-04483-1). Watts.
--Comets, Meteors & Asteroids. (Illus.). 64p. (gr. 10 up). 1981. PLB 6.99 (ISBN 0-399-61148-7). Putnam Pub Group.
--Computers. (Science Is What & Why Ser.). (Illus.). (gr. k-3). 1972. PLB 4.49 o.p. (ISBN 0-698-30053-X, Coward). Putnam Pub Group.
--Consumer Protection Labs. LC 75-6686. (Scientists at Work Ser.). (Illus.). (gr. 2-4). 1975. PLB 10.89 (ISBN 0-381-99622-0, JD-J). Har-Row.
--Disastrous Floods & Tidal Waves. LC 81-2959. (First Bks.). (Illus.). 72p. (gr. 4 up). 1981. lib. bdg. 8.90 (ISBN 0-531-04326-6). Watts.
--Disastrous Volcanoes. LC 81-2995. (First Bks.). (Illus.). 72p. (gr. 4 up). 1981. lib. bdg. 8.90 (ISBN 0-531-04329-0). Watts.
--Disease Detectives. LC 77-26589. (Scientists at Work Ser.). (Illus.). (gr. 4 up). 1978. o. p. 9.57i (ISBN 0-690-03907-7, TYC-J); PLB 9.89 (ISBN 0-690-03908-5). Har-Row.
--Energy. (A Reference First Bk.). (Illus.). 96p. (gr. 4 up). 1983. PLB 8.90 (ISBN 0-531-04536-6). Watts.
--Exploring the Mind & Brain. LC 82-45582. (Scientists at Work Ser.). (Illus.). 128p. (gr. 5 up). 1983. 10.53i (ISBN 0-690-04251-5, TYC-J); PLB 10.89g (ISBN 0-690-04252-3). Har-Row.
--Jigsaw Continents. LC 77-6730. (Science Is What & Why Ser.). (Illus.). (gr. k-3). 1978. PLB 5.99 o.p. (ISBN 0-698-30670-8, Coward). Putnam Pub Group.
--Mad Scientists in Fact & Fiction. (gr. 5 up). 1980. PLB 8.90 (ISBN 0-531-04153-0). Watts.
--The New Water Book. LC 73-3395. (Illus.). 128p. (gr. 3-6). 1973. 9.57i o.p. (ISBN 0-690-58146-7, TYC-J). Har-Row.
--Planets, Stars & Galaxies. LC 78-16688. (Illus.). (gr. 6-8). 1978. PLB 6.99 (ISBN 0-399-61104-5). Putnam Pub Group.
--Quasars, Pulsars & Black Holes in Space. new ed. LC 76-50057. (Illus.). (gr. 3-6). 1977. PLB 6.99 (ISBN 0-399-61051-0). Putnam Pub Group.
--Sports. (A Reference First Bk.). (Illus.). 96p. (gr. 4 up). 1983. PLB 8.90 (ISBN 0-531-04540-4). Watts.
--Stars. (Science Is What & Why Ser). (Illus.). (gr. k-3). 1971. PLB 4.49 o.p. (ISBN 0-698-30328-8, Coward). Putnam Pub Group.
--Storms. LC 74-106930. (Science Is What & Why Ser). (Illus.). (gr. k-3). 1970. PLB 4.49 o.p. (ISBN 0-698-30331-8, Coward). Putnam Pub Group.
--The Story of Folk Music. LC 76-18159. (Illus.). (gr. 6 up). 1976. PLB 11.95 (ISBN 0-87599-215-3). S G Phillips.
--Time After Time. (Science Is What & Why Ser.). (Illus.). 48p. (gr. k-3). 1975. PLB 5.99 o.p. (ISBN 0-698-30558-2, Coward). Putnam Pub Group.
--Why I Cough, Sneeze, Shiver, Hiccup, & Yawn. LC 82-45587. (A Let's-Read-&-Find-Out Science Bk.). (Illus.). 40p. (gr. k-3). 1983. 9.57i (ISBN 0-690-04253-1, TYC-J); PLB 9.89g (ISBN 0-690-04254-X). Har-Row.
--The World of Dance. LC 78-14498. (Illus.). (gr. 5 up). 1978. 11.95 (ISBN 0-87599-221-8). S G Phillips.
Berger, Melvin & Berger, Gilda. Test & Improve. Barish, Wendy, ed. 64p. (gr. 8-12). 1983. pap. 2.95 (ISBN 0-671-43158-7). Wanderer Bks. Postponed.
Berger, Melvin, jt. auth. see Berger, Gilda.
Berger, Michael. Firearms in American History. LC 78-11652. (First Bks.). (Illus.). (gr. 5 up). 1979. PLB 8.90 (ISBN 0-531-02255-2). Watts.
Berger, Michail L. An Album of Modern Aircraft Testing. LC 81-7412. (Picture Album Ser.). (Illus.). 96p. (gr. 5 up). 1981. PLB 9.60 (ISBN 0-531-04341-X). Watts.
Berger, Morroe. Islam in Egypt Today: Social & Political Aspects of Popular Religion. LC 70-113597. 1970. 27.95 (ISBN 0-521-07834-2). Cambridge U Pr.
Berger, Morroe, et al. Benny Carter: A Life in American Music, 2 vols. LC 82-10634. (Studies in Jazz: No. 1). 877p. 1982. Set. 45.00 (ISBN 0-8108-1580-X). Vol. I, Biography, 456p. Vol. II, Discography, Filmography, & Bibliography, iv, 417p. Scarecrow.
Berger, Nomi. Devotions. 428p. Date not set. pap. 3.25 (ISBN 0-441-14619-8). Ace Bks.
Berger, P. J., jt. ed. see Berger, M. L.
Berger, Pam, jt. ed. see Dyer, Esther.
Berger, Paul & Searle, Leroy. Rational Space-Radical Time: Idea Networks in Contemporary Photography. (Illus.). 72p. (Orig.). 1983. pap. 14.95 (ISBN 0-686-42833-1). Henry Art.
Berger, Paul & Wadden, Douglas, eds. Photographic Constellations. (Illus., Orig.). 1983. pap. write for info. (ISBN 0-935558-10-1). Henry Art.
Berger, Peter. Protocol of a Damnation: A Novel. 250p. 1975. 3.00 (ISBN 0-8164-0280-9). Seabury.
Berger, Peter & Neuhaus, Richard J. Against the World for the World: The Hartford Appeal & the Future of American Religion. 180p. 1976. pap. 1.00 (ISBN 0-8164-2121-8). Seabury.
Berger, Peter L. The Precarious Vision. LC 76-1981. 238p. 1976. Repr. of 1961 ed. lib. bdg. 19.75x (ISBN 0-8371-8657-9, BEPV). Greenwood.
Berger, Peter L., jt. auth. see Berger, Brigitte.
Berger, Phil. Big Time. 288p. 1981. cancelled (ISBN 0-671-24708-5). Summit Bks.
Berger, Rainer, ed. Scientific Methods in Medieval Archaeology. LC 75-99771. (UCLA Center for Medieval & Renaissance Studies). (Illus.). 1971. 50.00x (ISBN 0-520-01626-2). U of Cal Pr.
Berger, Raoul. Government by Judiciary: The Transformation of the Fourteenth Amendment. 1977. 18.50x (ISBN 0-674-35795-7); pap. 7.95 (ISBN 0-674-35796-5). Harvard U Pr.
Berger, Raymond M. Computer Programmer Job Analysis Reference Text. (Illus.). 195p. 1974. pap. 10.00 o.p. (ISBN 0-88283-021-X). AFIPS Pr.
Berger, Renee A., jt. auth. see Fosler, Scott.
Berger, Robert O. Practical Accounting for Lawyers. LC 81-3319. (Modern Accounting Perspectives & Practice Ser.). 357p. 1981. 44.95 (ISBN 0-471-08486-7, Pub. by Wiley-Interscience). Ronald Pr.
Berger, Ronald, jt. auth. see Balkan, Sheila.
Berger, Stuart. Divorce Without Victims. 200p. 1983. 12.95 (ISBN 0-395-33115-3). HM.
Berger, Susanna, jt. auth. see Berger, Jason.
Berger, Suzanne & Piore, Michael. Dualism & Discontinuity in Industrial Societies. LC 79-25172. (Illus.). 176p. 1980. 21.95 (ISBN 0-521-23134-5). Cambridge U Pr.
Berger, Suzanne, ed. Organizing Interests in Western Europe: Pluralism, Corporatism & the Transformation of Politics. LC 80-16378. (Cambridge Studies in Modern Political Economies). (Illus.). 464p. 1981. 39.50 (ISBN 0-521-23174-4). Cambridge U Pr.
--Religion in West European Politics. 200p. 1982. text ed. 29.50x (ISBN 0-7146-3218-X, F Cass Co). Biblio Dist.
Berger, Terry. Ben's ABC Day. (gr. 1-3). 1982. 9.00 (ISBN 0-688-00881-X); PLB 9.50 (ISBN 0-688-00882-8). Morrow.
--Country Inns: The Rocky Mountains. 96p. 1983. pap. 10.95 (ISBN 0-03-062211-5). HR&W.
--I Have Feelings. (Illus.). (ps-4). 9.95 (ISBN 0-686-36814-2). Inst Rat Liv.
--Lucky. LC 73-16817. (Lead-off Bks.). 48p. (ps-3). 1976. 3.99 (ISBN 0-87955-110-0); PLB 2.99 (ISBN 0-87955-710-9). O'Hara.
Berger, Thomas. The Feud. 263p. 1983. 14.95 (ISBN 0-440-02833-7, Sey Lawr). Delacorte.
--Little Big Man. 1979. 10.95 o.s.i. (ISBN 0-440-05165-7, Sey Lawr). Delacorte.
--Neighbors. 1980. 9.95 o.s.i. (ISBN 0-440-06556-9, Sey Lawr). Delacorte.
--Reinhart in Love. 304p. 1982. pap. 8.95 (ISBN 0-440-57258-4, Delta). Dell.
--Reinhart in Love. 304p. 1982. 16.95 (ISBN 0-440-07343-X, Sey Lawr). Delacorte.
--Reinhart's Women. 1982. pap. 7.95 (ISBN 0-440-57408-0, Delta). Dell.
--Sneaky People. LC 74-22320. 320p. 1975. 8.95 o.p. (ISBN 0-671-21897-2). S&S.
--Sneaky People. 1983. pap. 7.95 (ISBN 0-440-57700-4, Delta). Dell.
Berger, Yves. Obsession: An American Love Story. O'Brien, Patrick, tr. LC 77-21666. 1978. 8.95 o.p. (ISBN 0-399-12049-1). Putnam Pub Group.
Bergeret, Annie & Tennaille, Mabel. Tales from China. LC 80-52512. (The World Folktale Library). PLB 12.68 (ISBN 0-382-06449-6). Silver.
Bergeron, Bill. Prairie State Blues: Comic Strips & Graphic Tales. LC 73-85174. (Illus.). 64p. 1975. pap. 2.95 o.p. (ISBN 0-914090-02-X). Chicago Review.
Bergeron, Dave. First Responder: Self-Instructional Workbook. (Illus.). 166p. 1982. 5.95 (ISBN 0-89303-227-1). R J Brady.
Bergeron, David M. English Civic Pageantry, 1558-1642. LC 70-163908. 338p. 1971. lib. bdg. 17.95x o.s.i. (ISBN 0-87249-238-9). U of SC Pr.
Bergeron, J. Self Instructional Workbook for Emergency Care. 2nd ed. (Illus.). 1978. pap. 7.95 o.p. (ISBN 0-87618-996-6). R J Brady.
Bergeron, J. D. Self-Instructional Workbook for Emergency Care. 3rd ed. (Illus.). 224p. 1982. pap. text ed. 7.95 (ISBN 0-89303-186-0). R J Brady.
Bergeron, J. David. First Responder. 336p. 1981. pap. text ed. 12.95 (ISBN 0-87619-998-8). R J Brady.
Bergeron, Paul H. Antebellum Politics in Tennessee. LC 82-40170. 224p. 1982. 18.50x (ISBN 0-8131-1469-1). U Pr of Ky.
Bergeron, Pierre. Les Voyages Fameux du Sieur Vincent le Blanc marseillais. (Bibliotheque Africaine Ser.). 625p. (Fr.). 1974. Repr. of 1649 ed. lib. bdg. 151.00x o.p. (ISBN 0-8287-0081-8, 72-2134). Clearwater Pub.
Bergeron, Victor J. Trader Vic's Bartender's Guide. rev. ed. LC 72-76212. (Illus.). 360p. 1972. 14.95 (ISBN 0-385-06805-0). Doubleday.
--Trader Vic's Book of Mexican Cooking. LC 72-96228. 272p. 1973. 11.95 (ISBN 0-385-01748-0). Doubleday.
--Trader Vic's Helluva Man's Cookbook. LC 75-21210. (Illus.). 176p. 1976. 6.95 o.p. (ISBN 0-385-09829-4). Doubleday.
--Trader Vic's Pacific Island Cookbook: With Side Trips to Hong Kong, Southeast Asia, Mexico & Texas. LC 68-10564. (Illus.). 1968. 14.95 (ISBN 0-385-02052-5). Doubleday.
Bergersen, F. J. Root Nodules of Legumes: Structure & Functions. 164p. 1982. 31.95x (ISBN 0-471-10456-6, Pub. by Res Stud Pr). Wiley.

Bergerud, Marly & Gonzalez, Jean. Word Information Processing Concepts: Careers Technology, & Applications. LC 80-22328. 387p. 1981. text ed. 18.95x (ISBN 0-471-08499-9); tchrs. manual avail. (ISBN 0-471-09430-7). Wiley.

--Word Processing: Concepts & Careers. 2nd ed. LC 80-29386. (Wiley Word Processing Ser.). 237p. 1981. pap. text ed. 16.95x (ISBN 0-471-06010-0). Wiley.

--Word Processing: Concepts & Careers. LC 77-15794. (Word Processing Ser.). 1978. pap. text ed. 13.95 o.p. (ISBN 0-471-02748-0); tchrs'. manual 2.95 o.p. (ISBN 0-471-03778-8). Wiley.

Bergerud, Mary & Gonzalez, Jean. Word Information Processing Concepts. 387p. 1981. 16.95 (ISBN 0-686-98088-3). Telecom Lib.

Bergesen, Albert, ed. Crises in the World-System. (Political Economy of the World-System Annuals: Vol. 6). (Illus.). 288p. 1983. 25.00 (ISBN 0-8039-1936-0); pap. 12.50 (ISBN 0-8039-1937-9). Sage.

--Studies of the Modern World System. LC 80-10871. (Studies in Social Discontinuity). 1980. 27.50 (ISBN 0-12-090550-7). Acad Pr.

Bergeson, J. B. & Miller, G. S. Learning Activities for Disadvantaged Children: Selected Readings. 1971. text ed. 19.95 (ISBN 0-02-308350-6, 30835). Macmillan.

Bergethon, Bjorner, jt. auth. see Nye, Robert E.

Bergethon, K. Roald & Finger, Ellis. Grammar for Reading German, Form C. rev. ed. 1979. pap. text ed. 9.40 (ISBN 0-395-26085-X); instr's. ans. key 7.00 (ISBN 0-395-26084-1). HM.

Bergevin, Patrick R., et al. A Guide to Therapeutic Oncology. 668p. 1979. lib. bdg. 60.00 (ISBN 0-683-00599-5). Williams & Wilkins.

Bergevin, Paul, et al. Adult Education Procedures: A Handbook of Tested Patterns for Effective Participation. 1963. pap. 5.95 (ISBN 0-8164-2000-9, SP29). Seabury.

Bergey, Alice & Obata. World God Made. LC 65-15145. (Arch Bks: Set 2). 1965. pap. 0.89 (ISBN 0-570-06011-7, 59-1114). Concordia.

Bergey, Alyce. Beggar's Greatest Wish. (Arch Bks: No. 6). (gr. 4-6). 1969. pap. 0.89 (ISBN 0-570-06040-0, 59-1155). Concordia.

--The Boy Who was Lost. (Arch Bks: Set 9). (Illus.). 32p. (ps-4). 1972. pap. 0.89 (ISBN 0-570-06065-6, 59-1183). Concordia.

--Fishermen's Surprise. (Arch Bks: Set 4). 1967. laminated cover 0.89 (ISBN 0-570-06028-1, 59-1139). Concordia.

--Great Promise. (Arch Bks: Set 5). (Illus.). (gr. 5). 1968. laminated cover 0.89 (ISBN 0-570-06034-6, 59-1147). Concordia.

--El Sueno de un Pordiosero. Villalobos, Fernando, tr. from Eng. (Libros Arco Ser.). (Illus.). 32p. (Span.). (gr. 1-3). 1978. pap. write for info. o.p. Edit Caribe.

Bergfeld, J., ed. see Wagner, Richard.

Bergfield, Philip B. Principles of California Real Estate Law. (Illus.). 480p. 1983. 24.95x (ISBN 0-07-004896-7). McGraw.

--Principles of Real Estate Law. (Illus.). 1979. text ed. 24.95 (ISBN 0-07-004890-8, C). McGraw.

Bergh, T. Van Den see Van Den Bergh, T.

Berghahn, V. R. Modern Germany: Society, Economy & Politics in the Twentieth Century. LC 82-4214. (Illus.). 352p. 1983. 34.50 (ISBN 0-521-23185-X); pap. 9.95 (ISBN 0-521-29859-8). Cambridge U Pr.

Berghahn, Volker R., tr. see Born, Karl B.

Berghe, Guido V. Political Rights for European Citizens. 245p. (Orig.). 1982. text ed. 38.00 (ISBN 0-566-00524-7). Gower Pub Ltd.

Berghe, Guido van den see Berghe, Guido V.

Berghe, Pierre L. Van Den see Van Den Berghe, Pierre L.

Berghorn, Forrest J., et al. Dynamics of Aging: Original Essays on the Process & Experience of Growing Old. 542p. 1980. lib. bdg. 35.00 (ISBN 0-89158-781-0); pap. 13.50 (ISBN 0-89158-782-9). Westview.

Bergiel, Blaise J., jt. auth. see Walters, C. Glenn.

Bergier, Jacques. Extraterrestrial Visitations from Prehistoric Times to the Present. 1974. pap. 1.50 o.p. (ISBN 0-451-05942-5, W5942, Sig). NAL.

Bergin, jt. auth. see Buchanek.

Bergin, Allen E., jt. auth. see Garfield, Sol L.

Bergin, Thomas G. Dante. LC 76-10974. (Illus.). 326p. 1976. Repr. of 1965 ed. lib. bdg. 21.00x (ISBN 0-8371-7973-4, BEDA). Greenwood.

--Giovanni Verga. 1931. text ed. 13.50x (ISBN 0-686-83557-3). Elliots Bks.

--Petrarch. (World Authors Ser.: Italy: No. 81). lib. bdg. 10.95 o.p. (ISBN 0-8057-2694-2, Twayne). G K Hall.

Bergin, Thomas G., ed. see Petrarch.

Bergin, Victoria. Special Education Needs in Bilingual Programs. 64p. (Orig.). 1980. pap. 4.50 (ISBN 0-89763-026-2). Natl Clearinghse Bilingual Ed.

Bergle, Rainer, jt. ed. see Libby, Leona M.

Bergler, Edmund. Divorce Won't Help. 1979. 12.95 (ISBN 0-87140-635-7); pap. 5.95 (ISBN 0-87140-124-X). Liveright.

--Selected Papers of Edmund Bergler. 992p. 1969. 12.00 o.p. (ISBN 0-8089-0057-9). Grune.

--The Superego - Unconscious Conscience. LC 52-12974. 378p. 1952. 42.50 o.p. (ISBN 0-8089-0056-0). Grune.

--Tensions Can Be Reduced to Nuisances. 1979. 12.95 (ISBN 0-87140-976-3); pap. 3.95 (ISBN 0-87140-123-1). Liveright.

Bergles, A. F. & Ishigai, S. Two Phase Flow Dynamics & Reactor Safety. 1981. 110.00 (ISBN 0-07-004904-1). McGraw.

Bergman, Abby, jt. auth. see Jacobson, Willard.

Bergman, Andrew. We're in the Money. 1975. pap. 4.95xi (ISBN 0-06-131948-1, TB1948, Torch). Har-Row.

Bergman, Bella. Hebrew Level Two. (Illus.). 243p. 1983. pap. text ed. 5.95 (ISBN 0-87441-360-5). Behrman.

Bergman, David, jt. auth. see Pantell, Robert.

Bergman, E. M. Eliminating Exclusionary Zoning. LC 73-18252. 1974. prof ref 25.00 (ISBN 0-88410-450-8). Ballinger Pub.

Bergman, Edward F. & Pohl, Thomas W. A Geography of the New York Metropolitan Region. LC 75-20816. (Illus.). 1975. perfect bdg. 6.95 (ISBN 0-8403-1263-6). Kendall Hunt.

Bergman, Elihu, et al, eds. American Energy Choices Before the Year Two Thousand. LC 78-7122. (Illus.). 1978. 18.95x (ISBN 0-669-02398-1). Lexington Bks.

Bergman, Elsie O., jt. auth. see Thorndike, Eard L.

Bergman, Hannah E. Luis Quinones de Benavente. (World Authors Ser.). lib. bdg. 15.95 (ISBN 0-8057-2140-1, Twayne). G K Hall.

Bergman, Ingmar. Fanny & Alexander. 220p. 1983. 13.95 (ISBN 0-686-38842-9); pap. 5.95 (ISBN 0-686-38843-7). Pantheon.

--A Project for the Theatre. Marker, Frederick J. & Marker, Lise-Lone, eds. LC 82-40258. (Ungar Film Library). (Illus.). 250p. 1983. 15.95 (ISBN 0-8044-2050-5). Ungar.

--Seventh Seal. (Film Scripts-Modern Ser.). 1969. pap. 2.95 o.p. (ISBN 0-671-20092-5). S&S.

Bergman, Ingrid & Burgess, Alan. Ingrid Bergman: My Story. 1980. 14.95 o.s.i. (ISBN 0-440-03299-7). Delacorte.

Bergman, Jay. Vera Zasulich: A Biography. LC 82-80927. 288p. 1983. 28.50x (ISBN 0-8047-1156-9). Stanford U Pr.

Bergman, Jerry. Understanding Educational Measurement & Evaluation. 1981. 20.95 (ISBN 0-395-30782-1). HM.

Bergman, Jules. Anyone Can Fly. rev. ed. LC 73-9141. 1977. 19.95 (ISBN 0-385-02830-X). Doubleday.

Bergman, Lee, jt. auth. see Daly, James.

Bergman, P. H. Concise Dictionary of Twenty-Six Languages in Simultaneous Translation. pap. 2.95 (ISBN 0-451-11478-7, AE1478, Sig). NAL.

Bergman, Peter M., compiled by. The Basic English-Chinese, Chinese-English Dictionary. (YA) 1980. pap. 2.25 (ISBN 0-451-11688-7, AE1688, Sig). NAL.

Bergman, R. N., jt. auth. see Cobelli, E.

Bergman, Samuel & Bruckner, Steven. Introduction to Computers & Computer Programming. LC 72-140834. 1972. text ed. 23.95 (ISBN 0-201-00552-2); instructor's guide & soultions manuals 2.50 (ISBN 0-201-00553-0). A-W.

Bergman, Samuel H. Faith & Reason: An Introduction to Modern Jewish Thought. LC 61-10414. 1963. pap. 3.95 (ISBN 0-8052-0056-8). Schocken.

Bergmann, Frank. Robert Grant. (United States Authors Ser.). 1982. lib. bdg. 15.50 (ISBN 0-8057-7360-6, Twayne). G K Hall.

Bergmann, Fred L. Essays. 2nd ed. 360p. 1975. pap. text ed. write for info. (ISBN 0-697-03818-1); instrs.' man. avail. (ISBN 0-697-03819-X). Wm C Brown.

Bergmann, Frederick L., jt. ed. see Pedicord, Harry W.

Bergmann, Fredrick L., jt. ed. see Pedicord, Harry W.

Bergmann, Leola N. Music Master of the Middle West: The Story of F. Melius Christiansen & the St. Olaf Choir. 2nd ed. LC 68-16222. (Music Ser). 1968. Repr. of 1944 ed. 25.00 (ISBN 0-306-71057-9). Da Capo.

Bergmann, Mark, jt. auth. see Otte, Elmer.

Bergmann, Wolfgang, ed. see Borchard, Franz.

Bergner, Erik E., et al, eds. Compartments, Pools & Spaces in Medical Physiology: Proceedings. LC 67-61865. (AEC Symposium Ser.). 521p. 1967. pap. 21.00 (ISBN 0-87079-167-2, CONF-661010); microfiche 4.50 (ISBN 0-87079-168-0, CONF-661010). DOE.

Bergner, Lawrence, jt. ed. see Eisenberg, Mickey.

Bergon, Frank, ed. see Burroughs, John.

Bergone, Frank, ed. see Burroughs, John.

Bergonzi, Bernard. Heroes Twilight. 241p. 1980. text ed. 25.00x (ISBN 0-333-28126-8, Pub. by Macmillan England). Humanities.

--Reading the Thirties: Texts & Contexts. LC 78-4262. (Critical Essays in Modern Literature Ser.). 1978. 10.95 (ISBN 0-8229-1135-3). U of Pittsburgh Pr.

Berg-Pan, Renata. Leni Riefenstahl. (Filmmakers Ser.). 1980. lib. bdg. 13.95 (ISBN 0-8057-9275-9, Twayne). G K Hall.

Bergquist, Lois M. Microbiology for the Hospital Environment. (Illus.). 719p. 1981. text ed. 26.95 scp (ISBN 0-06-040646-1, HarpC); scp lab manual 14.95 (ISBN 0-06-040644-5); inst's manual avail. (ISBN 0-06-360635-6). Har-Row.

Bergquist, M. Francille. Ibero-Romance: Comparative Phonology & Morphology. LC 81-40657. (Illus.). 186p. (Orig.). 1982. lib. bdg. 21.25 (ISBN 0-8191-2029-4); pap. text ed. 10.00 (ISBN 0-8191-2030-8). U Pr of Amer.

Bergquist, Patricia R. Sponges. LC 77-93644. 1978. 40.00x (ISBN 0-520-03658-1). U of Cal Pr.

Bergquist, Sidney R., ed. New Webster's Dictionary of the English Language (Handy School & Office Edition) LC 75-15424. 1975. 4.95 (ISBN 0-8326-0033-4, 6501). Delair.

--New Webster's Dictionary of the English Language (Modern Desk Edition) LC 76-3282. (Illus.). 1976. 8.95 (ISBN 0-8326-0040-7, 6603). Delair.

Bergqvist, D. Postoperative Thromboembolism: Frequency, Etiology, Prophylaxis. (Illus.). 248p. 1983. 38.50 (ISBN 0-387-12062-9). Springer-Verlag.

Bergreen, Laurence. Look Now Pay Later: The Rise of Network Broadcasting. LC 79-7859. (Illus.). 1980. 12.95 o.p. (ISBN 0-385-14465-2). Doubleday.

--Look Now, Pay Later: The Rise of Network Broadcasting. 1981. pap. 3.95 o.p. (ISBN 0-451-61966-8, ME1966, Ment). NAL.

Bergsma, Jurrit & Thomasma, David. Health Care: Its Psychosocial Dimensions. Orig. Title: The Other Side of Medicine. (Illus.). 225p. 1981. text ed. 15.50x (ISBN 0-391-01630-X). Duquesne.

Bergsman, Joel. Growth & Equity in Semi-Industrialized Countries. (Working Paper: No. 351). ii, 113p. 1979. 5.00 (ISBN 0-686-36050-8, WP-0351). World Bank.

Bergson & Levine. The Soviet Economy Towards the Year 2000. 37.50 (ISBN 0-04-335045-3). Allen Unwin.

Bergson, Anika & Tuchak, Vladimir. Shiatzu: Japanese Pressure Point Massage. (Illus.). 160p. (Orig.). 1980. pap. 1.95 (ISBN 0-523-41862-0). Pinnacle Bks.

Bergson, Anika, ed. Zone Therapy. Tuchak, Vladimir. (Illus.). 160p. 1980. pap. 2.25 (ISBN 0-523-41860-4). Pinnacle Bks.

Bergson, Henri. Dreams. Slosson, Edwin E., tr. 62p. 1982. Repr. of 1914 ed. lib. bdg. 35.00 (ISBN 0-89987-092-9). Darby Bks.

--Matter & Memory. (Muirhead Library of Philosophy). 1978. text ed. 19.50x (ISBN 0-391-00924-9). Humanities.

--Mind-Energy, Lectures & Essays. Carr, H. Wildon, tr. from Fr. LC 74-28922. 262p. 1975. Repr. of 1920 ed. lib. bdg. 21.25x (ISBN 0-8371-7931-9, BEEN). Greenwood.

--The Two Sources of Morality & Religion. LC 74-10373. 308p. 1974. Repr. of 1935 ed. lib. bdg. 25.00x (ISBN 0-8371-7679-4, BETS). Greenwood.

Bergson, Henri L. Creative Evolution. Mitchell, Arthur, tr. LC 74-28524. 453p. 1975. Repr. of 1944 ed. lib. bdg. 35.00x (ISBN 0-8371-7917-3, BECEV). Greenwood.

Bergsten, A. Fred & Krause, Lawrence B., eds. World Politics & International Economics. 1975. 24.95 (ISBN 0-8157-0916-1); pap. 9.95 (ISBN 0-8157-0915-3). Brookings.

Bergsten, C. F. The International Economic Policy of the United States: Selected Papers of C. Fred Bergsten, 1977-1979. LC 79-3040. 416p. 1980. 31.95x (ISBN 0-669-03314-6). Lexington Bks.

Bergsten, C. Fred. From Rambouillet to Versailles: A Symposium. (Princeton Studies in International Finance: No. 51). 1982. pap. text ed. 2.50x (ISBN 0-88165-056-0). Princeton U Int Finan Econ.

--Managing International Economic Interdependence: Selected Papers of C. Fred Bergsten. LC 77-2517. 1977. 24.95x o.p. (ISBN 0-669-01516-4). Lexington Bks.

--The World Economy in the Nineteen Eighties: Selected Papers of C. Fred Bergsten, 1980. 192p. 1981. 17.95x o.p. (ISBN 0-669-04658-2). Lexington Bks.

Bergsten, C. Fred & Cline, William R. Trade Policy in the 1980's. (Policy Analyses in International Economics Ser.: No. 3). 88p. 1982. 6.00 (ISBN 0-88132-002-1). Inst Intl Eco.

Bergsten, C. Fred & Williamson, John. The Multiple Reserve Currency System & International Monetary Reform. (Policy Analyses in International Economics Ser.: No. 4). 1983. 6.00 (ISBN 0-88132-003-X). Inst Intl Eco.

Bergsten, C. Fred, ed. Toward a New World: Trade Policy. LC 74-22304. 1975. 25.95x o.p. (ISBN 0-669-96743-2). Lexington Bks.

Bergsten, C. Fred, et al. American Multinationals & American Interests. LC 77-91786. 1978. 26.95 (ISBN 0-8157-0920-X); pap. 14.95 (ISBN 0-8157-0919-6). Brookings.

Bergsten, Fred & Cline, William R. Trade Policy in the 1980's. 600p. 1983. 35.00 (ISBN 0-88132-008-0). Inst Intl Eco.

Bergsten, Staffan. Osten Sjostrand. (World Authors Ser.: Spain: No. 309). 174p. 1974. lib. bdg. 12.50 o.p. (ISBN 0-8057-2844-9, Twayne). G K Hall.

Bergstom, Louise. Island Lovesong. 1980. pap. 1.50 o.s.i. (ISBN 0-440-13995-3). Dell.

Bergstrom. Teaching Young Children. 1977. text ed. 7.95 (ISBN 0-675-08455-5); 105.00 set (ISBN 0-675-08454-7). Additional supplements may be obtained from publisher. Merrill.

Bergstrom, A. R. Statistical Inference in Continuous Time Economic Models. (Contributions to Economic Analysis: Vol. 99). 1976. 68.00 (ISBN 0-444-10991-9, North-Holland). Elsevier.

Bergstrom, A. R., et al, eds. Stability & Inflation: Essays in Memory of A. W. Phillips. LC 77-4420. 323p. 1978. 69.95x (ISBN 0-471-99522-3, Pub. by Wiley-Interscience). Wiley.

Bergstrom, Harald. Weak Convergence of Measures. (Probability & Mathematical Statistics Ser.). 1982. 49.50 (ISBN 0-12-091080-2). Acad Pr.

Bergstrom, Louise. Claudia's Secret. (YA) 1969. 6.95 (ISBN 0-685-07426-9, Avalon). Bouregy.

--Dangerous Paradise. 192p. (YA) 1975. 6.95 (ISBN 0-685-52655-0, Avalon). Bouregy.

--The House of the Evening Star. 192p. (YA) 1976. 6.95 (ISBN 0-685-66574-7, Avalon). Bouregy.

--Pink Camellia. (YA) 1968. 6.95 (ISBN 0-685-07453-6, Avalon). Bouregy.

Bergstrom, Sune, jt. ed. see Vane, John R.

Bergveld, P. Electromedical Instrumentation: A Guide for Medical Personnel. LC 77-85711. (Techniques of Measurement in Medicine Ser.: No. 2). (Illus.). 1980. 32.50 (ISBN 0-521-21892-6); pap. 10.95 (ISBN 0-521-29305-7). Cambridge U Pr.

Berhens, D., ed. see Knapp, H. & Doring, R.

Beringause, Arthur, jt. auth. see Lieberman, Leo.

Beringer, Johann B. The Lying Stones of Johann Bartholomew Adam Beringer Being His Lithographiae Wirceburgensis. Jahn, Melvin E. & Woolf, Daniel J., trs. LC 63-8585. 1963. 37.50x (ISBN 0-520-00110-9). U of Cal Pr.

Beringer, Richard E. Historical Analysis: Contemporary Approaches to Clio's Craft. LC 77-10589. 317p. 1978. pap. text ed. 18.95x (ISBN 0-471-06996-5). Wiley.

Berington, Simon. Memoires de Gaudentio di Lucca, 2 vols. (Utopias in the Enlightenment Ser.). 544p. (Fr.). 1974. Repr. of 1746 ed. lib. bdg. 147.00x set o.p. (ISBN 0-8287-0082-6). Vol. 1 (019). Vol. 2 (020). Clearwater Pub.

Berk, Ann. Fast Forward. LC 82-45238. 264p. 1983. 14.95 (ISBN 0-385-17906-5). Doubleday.

Berk, Juliene. The Down Comforter. 1980. 10.95 o.p. (ISBN 0-312-21849-4). St Martin.

Berk, Richard A. & Rossi, Peter H. Prison Reform & State Elites. LC 76-21240. 224p. 1977. prof ref 19.50x (ISBN 0-88410-214-9). Ballinger Pub.

Berk, Z. Braverman's Introduction to the Biochemistry of Foods. 2nd ed. 1976. 41.50 (ISBN 0-444-41450-9, North Holland). Elsevier.

Berka, Karel. Measurement: Its Concepts, Theories & Problems. 1983. 49.50 (ISBN 90-277-1416-9, Pub. by Reidel Holland). Kluwer Boston.

Berke, Jacqueline. Twenty Questions for the Writer: A Rhetoric with Readings. 3rd ed. 597p. 1981. pap. text ed. 13.95 (ISBN 0-15-592401-X, HC); instr's. manual 1.50 (ISBN 0-15-592402-8). HarBraceJ.

Berke, Joel S. Answers to Educational Inequity. LC 73-7237. 1974. 22.00 (ISBN 0-685-42625-4); text ed. 20.20 (ISBN 0-685-42626-2). McCutchan.

Berke, Joel S., et al. Financing Equal Educational Opportunity: Alternatives for State Finance. LC 79-190059. 300p. 1972. 20.75x (ISBN 0-8211-0120-X); text ed. 18.60x (ISBN 0-685-24959-X). McCutchan.

Berke, Joseph, ed. Counter Culture: The Creation of an Alternative Society. (Illus.). 19.95x o.p. (ISBN 0-8464-0295-5). Beekman Pubs.

Berke, Melvyn & Grant, Joanne. Games Divorced People Play. (Illus.). 264p. 1980. 12.95 (ISBN 0-13-346205-6, Busn). P-H.

Berke, Roberta. Bounds Out of Bounds: A Compass for Recent American & British Poetry. 1981. 17.95 (ISBN 0-19-502872-4). Oxford U Pr.

Berke, Sally. When T V Began: The First TV Shows. LC 78-15168. (Famous Firsts Ser.). (Illus.). 1978. PLB 10.76 (ISBN 0-89547-060-8). Silver.

Berkebile, Don H. Carriage Terminology: An Historical Dictionary. (Illus.). 488p. 1978. 35.00 o.s.i. (ISBN 0-87474-166-1). Shumway.

Berkeley, A. Eliot & Barnes, Ann, eds. Labor Relations in Hospitals & Health Care Facilities. LC 75-45236. 110p. 1976. 10.00 o.p. (ISBN 0-87179-229-X). BNA.

Berkeley, G. The Administrative Revolution: Notes on the Passing of the Organization Man. 1971. 2.95 o.p. (ISBN 0-13-008532-4, S244, Spec). P-H.

Berkeley, George. Three Dialogues Between Hylas & Philonous. Adams, Robert M., ed. LC 79-65276. 1979. lib. bdg. 12.50 (ISBN 0-915144-62-X); pap. text ed. 2.95 (ISBN 0-915144-61-1). Hackett Pub.

--Three Dialogues Between Hylas & Philonous. McCormack, Thomas J., ed. vi, 144p. 1969. 12.00 (ISBN 0-87548-068-3); pap. 5.00 (ISBN 0-87548-069-1). Open Court.

--A Treatise Concerning the Principles of Human Knowledge. McCormack, Thomas J., ed. & pref. by. xv, 143p. 1963. 12.00 (ISBN 0-87548-071-3); pap. 5.00 (ISBN 0-87548-072-1). Open Court.

--A Treatise Concerning the Principles of Human Knowledge. Winkler, Kenneth, ed. & intro. by. LC 82-2876. (HPC Philosophical Classics Ser.). 160p. 1982. lib. bdg. 12.50 (ISBN 0-915145-40-5); pap. text ed. 3.45 (ISBN 0-915145-39-1). Hackett Pub.

--A Treatise Concerning the Principles of Human Knowledge: Text & Critical Essays. Turbayne, Colin M., ed. LC 69-16531. (Text & Critical Essays Ser). 1970. pap. 8.50 (ISBN 0-672-61115-5, TC2). Bobbs.

Berkeley, Henry R. Four Years in the Confederate Artillery: The Diary of Private Henry Robinson Berkeley. Runge, William, ed. (Virginia Historical Society Documents: No. 2). (Illus.). 1961. 11.95x o.p. (ISBN 0-8139-0026-3). U Pr of Va.

Berkeley, M. J. & Broome, C. E. Notices of British Fungi: 1841-45, 35 papers bd. in 1 vol. (Bibl. Myco.: Vol. 1). 1967. 56.00 (ISBN 3-7682-0456-1). Lubrecht & Cramer.

Berkeley Physics Laboratory. Laboratory Physics, 12 units. 2nd ed. Incl. Unit 5. Electrons & Fields. text ed. 1.40 o.p. (ISBN 0-07-050485-7); Unit 11. Nuclear Physics. text ed. o.p. (ISBN 0-07-050491-1). (Units 1-4, 6-10 & 12, o.p.). 1971 (C). McGraw.

Berkeley Planning Associates Inc. & Energyworks Inc. Energy Cost Control Guide for Multifamily Properties. Kirk, Nancye J., ed. (Illus.). 100p. (Orig.). 1982. pap. 19.95 (ISBN 0-912104-67-8). Inst Real Estate.

Berkeley, R. C., et al. Microbial Adhesion to Surfaces. LC 80-41358. 559p. 1981. 115.00 (ISBN 0-470-27083-7). Halsted Pr.

Berkeley, S. G. & Jackson, B. E. Your Career As a Medical Secretary-Transcriber. LC 74-34233. 194p. 1975. 14.95 o.p. (ISBN 0-471-07020-3, Pub. by Wiley Medical). Wiley.

Berkeley Symposia on Mathematical Statistics & Probability, 6th. Proceedings, Vols. 1-6. Le Cam, Lucien, et al, eds. Incl. Vol. 1. Theory of Statistics. 1972. 46.50 o.p. (ISBN 0-520-01964-4); Vol. 2. Probability Theory, Pt. 1. 1972. 67.50x (ISBN 0-520-02184-3); Vol. 3. Contributions to Probability Theory, Pt. 2. 1973. 38.50x o.p. (ISBN 0-520-02185-1); Vol. 4. Contributions to Biology & Problems of Health. 1973. 52.50x (ISBN 0-520-02187-8); Vol. 5. Darwinian, Neo-Darwinian, & Non-Darwinian Evolution. 23.50x o.p. (ISBN 0-520-02188-6); Vol. 6. Effects of Pollution on Health. 1972. 60.00x (ISBN 0-520-02189-4). U of Cal Pr.

Berkeley, William D. & Foster, Jerry. Long-Range Planning for Independent Schools. 1979. pap. 13.50 (ISBN 0-934338-36-1). NAIS.

Berket Habte Selassie. Conflict & Intervention in the Horn of Africa. LC 79-3868. (Illus.). 1982. pap. 6.50 (ISBN 0-85345-539-2, PB5392). Monthly Rev.

Berkey, Arthur L., ed. Teacher Education in Agriculture. 2nd ed. (Illus.). 350p. 1982. text ed. 14.75x (ISBN 0-8134-2217-5). Interstate.

Berkey, Ben B. Oscar, the Curious Ostrich. (Third Grade Bk.). (Illus.). (gr. 3-4). PLB 5.95 o.p. (ISBN 0-513-00387-8). Denison.

Berkey, Gordon, jt. auth. see Holloway, Gordon F.

Berkey, Rachel L. New Career Opportunities in the Paralegal Profession. LC 82-13929. (Illus.). 160p. 1983. 10.95 (ISBN 0-668-05478-6); pap. 5.95 (ISBN 0-668-05482-4). Arco.

Berkhof, Hendrikus. Doctrine of the Holy Spirit. LC 64-16279. 1976. pap. 5.95 (ISBN 0-8042-0551-5). John Knox.

Berkhof, Louis. The History of Christian Doctrine. 1978. 12.95 (ISBN 0-85151-005-1). Banner of Truth.

Berkhofer, Robert, ed. see Baker, M. Joyce.

Berkhofer, Robert, ed. see Biemer, Linda B.

Berkhofer, Robert, ed. see Blouin, Francis X., Jr.

Berkhofer, Robert, ed. see Conk, Margo A.

Berkhofer, Robert, ed. see Hanlan, James P.

Berkhofer, Robert, ed. see Hummer, Patricia M.

Berkhofer, Robert, ed. see Kanawada, Leo V., Jr.

Berkhofer, Robert, ed. see Selcraig, James T.

Berkhofer, Robert, ed. see Woods, Patricia D.

Berkhofer, Robert F. Salvation & the Savage: An Analysis of Protestant Missions & American Indian Response, 1787-1862. LC 77-22857. 1977. Repr. of 1965 ed. lib. bdg. 20.00x (ISBN 0-8371-9745-7, BESSA). Greenwood.

Berkhout, A. J. Seismic Migration: Imaging of Acoustic Energy by Wave Field Extrapolation. (Developments in Solid Earth Geophysics: Vol. 12). 1980. 56.00 o.p. (ISBN 0-444-41904-7). Elsevier.

--Seismic Migration: Imaging of Acoustic Energy by Wave Field Extrapolation; A Theoretical Aspects. 2nd rev. & enl. ed. (Developments in Solid Earth Geophysics Ser.: Vol. 14A). 352p. Date not set. 59.75 (ISBN 0-444-42130-0). Elsevier.

Berkhout, Carl T., jt. ed. see Gatch, Milton McC.

Berki, R. N., jt. ed. see Hayward, Jack.

Berki, S. E. & Heston, Alan W., eds. Nation's Health: Some Issues. LC 77-186411. (Annals of the American Academy of Political & Social Science Ser.: No. 399). 1972. pap. 7.95 (ISBN 0-87761-146-7). Am Acad Pol Soc Sci.

Berkin, Carol & Norton, Mary B. Women of America: A History. LC 78-69589. (Illus.). 1979. pap. text ed. 14.50 (ISBN 0-395-27067-7). HM.

Berklekamp, E. R., ed. Key Papers in the Development of Coding Theory. LC 73-87652. (Illus.). 1974. 23.95 (ISBN 0-87942-031-6). Inst Electrical.

Berkley, Sandra. Delta's Oral Placement Test Teacher's Manual. 16p. (Orig.). 1982. pap. text ed. 6.95 (ISBN 0-937354-04-X). Delta Systems.

Berkley, Sandra & Moore, Gary W. Delta's Oral Placement Test. 62p. (Orig.). 1982. pap. text ed. 18.95 (ISBN 0-937354-05-8). Delta Systems.

Berkman, Alexander. Prison Memoirs of an Anarchist. LC 77-130206. (Studies in the Libertarian and Utopian Tradition). (Illus.). 1970. pap. 4.95 o.p. (ISBN 0-8052-0267-6). Schocken.

--The Russian Tragedy. Nowlin, William G., Jr., ed. (Illus.). 1977. pap. 3.50 o.p. (ISBN 0-904564-11-8, Pub by Cienfuegos Pr). Carrier Pigeon.

Berkman, Eugene, ed. Granulocyte Physiology, Function & Dysfunction. 98p. 1979. 11.00 (ISBN 0-914404-50-4). Am Assn Blood.

Berkman, Eugene & Umlas, Joel, eds. Therapeutic Hemapheresis. 150p. 1980. 21.00 (ISBN 0-914404-54-7). Am Assn Blood.

Berkman, Eugene, jt. ed. see Nusbacher, Jacob.

Berkman, Harold W. & Gilson, Christopher. Consumer Behavior: Concepts & Strategies. 2nd ed. (Business Ser.). 483p. 1981. text ed. 23.95x (ISBN 0-534-00957-3). Kent Pub Co.

Berkman, Harold W. & Vernan, Ivan R. Contemporary Perspectives in International Business. 1979. 15.95 (ISBN 0-395-30562-4). HM.

Berkman, Harold W., jt. auth. see Gilson, Christopher.

Berkman, James L. Concerto for Knife & Axe. (Illus.). 28p. (Orig.). 1977. pap. 2.00 (ISBN 0-943662-00-1, 25-336). Runaway Pubns.

--Last of the Northside Cowboys & Other Smoke Rings. (Illus.). 40p. (Orig.). 1980. pap. 3.00 (ISBN 0-943662-01-X, 579-010). Runaway Pubns.

Berkman, Joyce. Olive Schreiner: Feminism on the Frontier. LC 78-74842. 1979. 11.95 (ISBN 0-88831-031-5). Eden Pr.

Berkman, Richard L. & Viscusi, W. Kip. Damming the West: The Report on the Bureau of Reclamation. LC 72-77707. (Ralph Nader Study Group Reports). 286p. 1973. 12.95 (ISBN 0-670-25460-6, Grossman). Viking Pr.

Berkman, Ronald. Opening the Gates: The Rise of the Prisoners Movement. 224p. 1979. 23.95x (ISBN 0-669-02828-2). Lexington Bks.

Berkman, Sue, et al. A Doctor Discusses Care of the Feet. (Illus.). 110p. 1979. pap. 2.50 o.p. (ISBN 0-685-46330-3). Budlong.

Berkner, Dimity S. & Sellen, Betty-Carol, eds. New Options for Librarians. 1983. pap. 19.95 (ISBN 0-918212-73-1). Neal-Schuman.

Berko, Roy M. & Bostwick, Fran. Basic-ly Communicating: An Activity Approach. 192p. 1982. pap. text ed. write for info. (ISBN 0-697-04208-1); inst. manual write for info. (ISBN 0-697-04222-7). Wm C Brown.

Berko, Roy M. & Wolvin, Andrew D. Communicating: A Social & Career Focus. 2nd ed. (Illus.). 432p. 1981. pap. text ed. 14.50 (ISBN 0-395-29170-4); instructor's manual with test options 1.00 (ISBN 0-395-29171-2). HM.

--This Business of Communicating. 2nd ed. 250p. 1983. pap. text ed. write for info. (ISBN 0-697-04227-8); instrs' manual avail. (ISBN 0-697-04232-4). Wm C Brown.

Berkofsky, Louis, et al, eds. Settling the Desert. 290p. 1981. 44.00 (ISBN 0-677-16280-4). Gordon.

Berkove, Laurence I. Ambrose Bierce: A Braver Man Than Anybody Knew. (Illus.). 1983. 22.00 (ISBN 0-88233-349-6). Ardis Pubs.

Berkow, Robert. The Merck Manual. 14th ed. 1982. 19.75 (ISBN 0-911910-03-4). Merck.

Berkow, Robert, ed. The Merck Manual, Vol. I: General Medicine. 14th ed. 1600p. 1982. pap. 11.95 (ISBN 0-911910-04-2). Merck.

--The Merck Manual, Vol. II: Obstetrics, Gynecology, Pediatrics, Genetics. 14th ed. 600p. 1982. pap. 6.95 (ISBN 0-911910-05-0). Merck.

Berkowitz, David S. & Thorne, Samuel E., eds. British Liberties. LC 77-89201. (Classics of English Legal History in the Modern Era Ser.: Vol. 57). 486p. 1979. lib. bdg. 55.00 (ISBN 0-8240-3156-3). Garland Pub.

Berkowitz, David S., ed. see Robinson, Henry, et al.

Berkowitz, Freda P. Popular Titles & Subtitles of Musical Compositions. 2nd ed. LC 75-4751. 217p. 1975. 11.00 o.p. (ISBN 0-8108-0806-4). Scarecrow.

Berkowitz, Gerald M. New Broadways: Theatre Across America 1950-1980. LC 81-21162. (Illus.). 208p. 1982. 19.50 (ISBN 0-8476-7031-7). Rowman.

Berkowitz, Gerald M. & Neimark, Paul. The Berkowitz Diet Switch. 288p. 1981. 10.95 o.p. (ISBN 0-87000-481-6, Arlington Hse). Crown.

Berkowitz, Henry. Fish Facts & Fancies. (Illus.). 32p. 1.95. Banyan Bks.

Berkowitz, Leonard. Social Psychology. 156p. 1972. pap. 10.95x (ISBN 0-673-07533-8). Scott F.

Berkowitz, Leonard, ed. Advances in Experimental Social Psychology, Vol. 13. (Serial Publication Ser.). 1980. 26.00 (ISBN 0-12-015213-4). Acad Pr.

--Advances in Experimental Social Psychology, Vol. 14. (Serial Publication Ser.). 1981. 34.00 (ISBN 0-12-015214-2); lib. ed. o.p. 44.50 (ISBN 0-12-015286-X); microfiche o.p. 24.00 (ISBN 0-12-015287-8). Acad Pr.

--Advances in Experimental Social Psychology, Vol. 15. 270p. 1982. 29.50 (ISBN 0-12-015215-0); lib. ed. 38.50 (ISBN 0-12-015288-6); microfiche 21.00 (ISBN 0-12-015289-4). Acad Pr.

Berkowitz, M., et al. The Politics of American Foreign Policy: The Social Contexts of Decisions. (Illus.). 1977. pap. text ed. 13.95 (ISBN 0-13-685073-1). P-H.

Berkowitz, Mildred N. & Owen, Jean. How to be Your Own Best Friend. 2.25 o.p. (ISBN 0-686-92345-6, 6465). Hazelden.

Berkowitz, Mona. How to Raise & Train an Old English Sheepdog. pap. 2.95 (ISBN 0-87666-344-7, DS1103). TFH Pubns.

Berkowitz, Monroe, et al. An Evaluation of Policy-Related Rehabilitation Research. LC 75-23957. (Illus.). 244p. 1975. text ed. 25.95 o.p. (ISBN 0-275-01260-3). Praeger.

Berkowitz, Raymond S. Modern Radar: Analysis, Evaluation & System Design. LC 65-21446. 660p. 1965. 60.00 o.s.i. (ISBN 0-471-07033-5, Pub by Wiley-Interscience). Wiley.

Berkowitz, Sol. Improvisation Through Keyboard Harmony. (Illus.). 288p. 1975. pap. 17.95 (ISBN 0-13-453472-7). P-H.

Berkowitz, Sol, et al. A New Approach to Sight Singing. rev ed. 346p. 1976. pap. text ed. 13.95x (ISBN 0-393-09194-5). Norton.

Berkowitz, Stanley. The Lowdown on Hemorrhoids, Piles & Other Lowdown Disorders. (Illus.). 1975. pap. 1.50 (ISBN 0-917746-01-5). A & B Pubs.

Berkson, Bill. Parts of the Body. 64p. (Orig.). 1980. pap. 5.00 o.p. (ISBN 0-931428-31-9). Vehicle Edns.

Berkson, Devaki. Foot Book. (Everyday Handbook). pap. 4.95 (ISBN 0-06-463474-4, EH 474, EH). B&N NY.

--The Foot Book: Healing with the Integrated Treatment of Foot Reflexology. LC 76-56733. (Funk & W Bk.). (Illus.). 1977. 11.49i (ISBN 0-308-10295-9). T Y Crowell.

Berkson, William. Fields of Force: The Development of a World View from Faraday to Einstein. 1974. 30.00 o.p. (ISBN 0-7100-7626-6). Routledge & Kegan.

Berkus, Rusty. Life Is a Gift. (Illus.). 32p. (Orig.). 1982. pap. 12.00 (ISBN 0-9609888-0-7). Red Rose Pr.

Berkwith, John, jt. ed. see Macmillan, Keith.

Berl, W. G. & Powell, W. R. Efficient Comfort Conditioning. 1979. lib. bdg. 27.50 (ISBN 0-89158-290-8). Westview.

Berlak, Ann & Berlak, Harold. Dilemmas of Schooling. 309p. 1981. 21.00x (ISBN 0-416-74140-1); pap. 8.95x (ISBN 0-416-74110-X). Methuen Inc.

Berlak, Harold, jt. auth. see Berlak, Ann.

Berland, Marshall. Cooking Without a Kitchen. (Illus.). 240p. 1978. 8.95 o.s.i. (ISBN 0-89479-019-6). A & W Pubs.

Berland, Ted. The Fitness Fact Book. 160p. 1980. pap. 2.25 o.p. (ISBN 0-915106-15-9). World Almanac.

Berland, Theodore. The Fitness Fact Book: A Guide to Diet, Exercise & Sport. 1981. pap. 1.95 o.p. (ISBN 0-686-69109-1, J9730, Sig). NAL.

--Rating the Diets. Consumer Guide Editors, ed. 1980. pap. 2.50 o.p. (ISBN 0-451-08940-5, E8940, Sig). NAL.

Berland, Theodore & Snider, Gordon. Living with Your Bronchitis & Emphysema. LC 72-89418. (Griffin Paperback Ser.). (Illus.). 197p. 1972. 5.95 o.p. (ISBN 0-312-49105-0, L61050); pap. 3.95 o.p. (ISBN 0-312-49140-9). St Martin.

Berland, Theodore, jt. auth. see Jordan, Henry A.

Berlant, Jeffrey L. Profession & Monopoly: A Study of Medicine in the United States & Great Britain. LC 74-76381. 1975. 30.00x (ISBN 0-520-02734-5). U of Cal Pr.

Berle, Adolf A. Power Without Property: A New Development in American Political Economy. LC 59-11771. 1962. pap. 1.65 o.p. (ISBN 0-15-673349-8, HB56, Harv). HarBraceJ.

Berle, Adolf A. & Means, Gardiner C. The Modern Corporation & Private Property. rev. ed. LC 68-28813. 1969. pap. 5.25 o.p. (ISBN 0-15-661176-7, HB152, Harv). HarBraceJ.

Berle, Adolf A., Jr. Tides of Crisis. LC 74-20074. 328p. 1975. Repr. of 1957 ed. lib. bdg. 17.50x o.p. (ISBN 0-8371-7844-4, BETC). Greenwood.

Berle, Adolf A., Jr. & Means, Gardiner C. The Modern Corporation & Private Property. xiii, 396p. 1982. Repr. of 1933 ed. lib. bdg. 30.00 (ISBN 0-89941-183-5). W S Hein.

Berle, Alf K. Inventions, Patents & Their Management. LC 59-13491. 602p. 1959. 25.50 (ISBN 0-442-00712-4, Pub. by Van Nos Reinhold). Krieger.

Berleant-Schiller, Riva & Shanklin, Eugenia, eds. The Keeping of Animals: Adaptation & Social Relations in Livestock Producing Communities. LC 81-65015. 170p. 1982. text ed. 23.95x (ISBN 0-86598-033-0). Allanheld.

Berlekamp, Elwyn R. Algebraic Coding Theory. (Series in Systems Science). 1968. text ed. 34.50 o.p. (ISBN 0-07-004903-3, C). McGraw.

Berlekamp, Elwyn R., et al. Winning Ways. LC 81-66678. 1982. Vol. 1: For Your Mathematical Plays: Games In General. 58.50 (ISBN 0-12-091150-7); Vol. 2: For Your Mathematical Plays: Games In Particular. pap. 22.50 (ISBN 0-12-091102-7); Set. 58.50 (ISBN 0-686-96644-9). Acad Pr.

Berlese, A. N. Icones Fungorum Omnium Hucusque Cognitorum: Ad usum sylloges Saccardianae accomodatae, 4 vols. 1968. 144.00 (ISBN 3-7682-0575-4). Lubrecht & Cramer.

Berley, Lawrence F. Holographic Mind, Holographic Vision: A New Theory of Vision in Art & Physics. LC 79-92384. (Illus.). 1980. 16.95 (ISBN 0-9603706-0-9); pap. 11.95 (ISBN 0-9603706-1-7). Lakstun Pr.

Berlin, Brent & Kay, Paul. Basic Color Terms: Their Universality & Evolution. LC 70-76541. (Illus.). 1969. 22.50x o.s.i. (ISBN 0-520-01442-1). U of Cal Pr.

Berlin, Helene, ed. see Anderson, Jerry D.

Berlin, Ira & Hoffman, Ronald, eds. Slavery & Freedom in the Age of the American Revolution. LC 82-8387. 368p. 1983. 15.95 (ISBN 0-8139-0969-4). U Pr of Va.

Berlin, Ira, et al. Freedom: The Black Military Experience, No. 2. LC 82-4446. (T). 784p. 1983. 37.50 (ISBN 0-521-22984-7). Cambridge U Pr.

Berlin, Irving, jt. auth. see French, Alfred.

Berlin, Isaiah. Hedgehog & the Fox. pap. 2.50 o.p. (ISBN 0-671-20709-1, Touchstone Bks). S&S.

--Personal Impressions. Hardy, Henry, ed. 1982. pap. 6.95 (ISBN 0-14-006313-7). Penguin.

Berlin, Isaiah, ed. Age of Enlightenment: The Eighteenth Century Philosophers. (Orig.). pap. 2.50 (ISBN 0-451-62003-8, ME2003, Ment). NAL.

Berlin, Isaiah, tr. see Turgenev, Ivan.

Berlin, Isaiah see Turgenev, Ivan.

Berlin, Isiah. Karl Marx: His Life & Environment. 4th ed. 1978. 17.50x (ISBN 0-19-219122-5); pap. 5.95 (ISBN 0-19-520052-7, GB 25, GB). Oxford U Pr.

Berlin, Louis, jt. auth. see Smith, Alexander B.

Berlin, Normand. Thomas Sackville. (English Authors Ser.: No. 165). 1974. lib. bdg. 10.95 o.p. (ISBN 0-8057-1471-5, Twayne). G K Hall.

Berlin, Sven. Amergin: An Enigma of the Forest. LC 77-91876. (Illus.). 1978. 6.50 o.p. (ISBN 0-7153-7447-8). David & Charles.

Berlin, William S. On the Edge of Politics: The Roots of Jewish Political Thought in America. (Contributions in Political Science: No. 14). 1978. lib. bdg. 25.95x (ISBN 0-313-20422-5, BEP/). Greenwood.

Berliner, Arthur K. Psychoanalysis & Society: The Social Thought of Sigmund Freud. LC 82-21932. 216p. (Orig.). 1983. lib. bdg. 20.75 (ISBN 0-8191-2893-7); pap. text ed. 10.50 (ISBN 0-8191-2894-5). U Pr of Amer.

Berliner, David C., jt. auth. see Gage, N. L.

Berliner, Don. Flying-Model Airplanes. LC 81-20720. (Superwheels & Thrills Sports Bks.). (Illus.). 48p. (gr. 4 up). 1982. PLB 7.95g (ISBN 0-8225-0449-9). Lerner Pubns.

--Helicopters. (Superwheels & Thrills Sports Bks.). (Illus.). 48p. (gr. 4 up). 1983. PLB 7.95g (ISBN 0-8225-0448-0). Lerner Pubns.

--Home-Built Airplanes. LC 79-1460. (Superwheels & Thrill Sports Bks.). (Illus.). (gr. 4 up). 1979. PLB 7.95g (ISBN 0-8225-0433-2). Lerner Pubns.

--Personal Airplanes. LC 81-15658. (Superwheels & Thrill Sports Bks.). (Illus.). (gr. 4 up). 1982. PLB 7.95g (ISBN 0-8225-0447-2). Lerner Pubns.

--Scale-Model Airplanes. LC 81-17120. (Superwheels & Thrill Sports Bks.). (Illus.). (gr. 4 up). 1982. PLB 7.95g (ISBN 0-8225-0446-4). Lerner Pubns.

Berliner, Donald L. Scale Reference Data: World War Two Jet Fighters. Angle, Burr, ed. (Illus.). 72p. (Orig.). 1982. pap. 8.50 (ISBN 0-89024-041-8). Kalmbach.

Berliner, Herman & Salvatore, Dominick. Economics. (College Outlines Ser.). pap. 4.95 o.p. (ISBN 0-671-08029-6, 08029). Monarch Pr.

--Statistics. (College Outlines Ser). pap. 4.95 o.p. (ISBN 0-671-08044-X). Monarch Pr.

Berliner, Paul F. The Soul of Mbira: Music & Tradition of the Shona People of Zimbabwe. LC 76-24578. (Perspectives on Southern Africa Ser.: No. 26). 1978. 29.50x (ISBN 0-520-03315-9); pap. 6.95 (ISBN 0-520-04268-9). U of Cal Pr.

Berliner, Ross. Manhood Ceremony. 1979. pap. 2.25 o.p. (ISBN 0-451-08509-4, E8509, Sig). NAL.

Berling, K., ed. Meissen China, an Illustrated History. 13.50 (ISBN 0-8446-4621-0). Peter Smith.

Berlinghoff, William P., et al. A Mathematical Panorama: Topics for the Liberal Arts. 1980. text ed. 19.95 (ISBN 0-669-02423-6). Heath.

Berlinski, David. On Systems Analysis: An Essay Concerning the Limitations of Some Mathematical Methods in the Social, Political, & Biological Sciences. 1976. pap. 4.95x (ISBN 0-262-52051-6). MIT Pr.

Berlinsky, Ellen B. & Biller, Henry B. Parental Death & Psychological Development. LC 82-48015. 176p. 1982. 21.95 (ISBN 0-669-05875-0). Lexington Bks.

Berlioz, Hector. New Letters of Berlioz, 1830-1868. Barzun, Jacques, tr. & intro. by. LC 75-100144. xxix, 322p. Repr. of 1954 ed. lib. bdg. 18.50x (ISBN 0-8371-3251-7, BENL). Greenwood.

Berlitz, Charles. The Bermuda Triangle. (General Ser.). 1975. lib. bdg. 12.50 (ISBN 0-8161-6283-2, Large Print Bks). G K Hall.
--French Step by Step. LC 78-73614. 1979. 10.95 (ISBN 0-89696-026-9, An Everest House Book). Dodd.
--German Step by Step. LC 78-73611. 1979. 10.95 (ISBN 0-89696-027-7, An Everest House Book). Dodd.
--Italian Step by Step. LC 78-73613. 1979. 10.95 (ISBN 0-89696-028-5, An Everest House Book). Dodd.
--Mysteries from Forgotten Worlds. LC 79-175360. 288p. 1972. 8.95 (ISBN 0-385-02965-9). Doubleday.
--Native Tongues: The Book of Language Facts. (Illus.). 352p. 1982. 14.95 (ISBN 0-448-12336-3, G&D). Putnam Pub Group.
--Passport to French. 1974. pap. 2.50 (ISBN 0-451-12171-6, AE2171, Sig). NAL.
--Passport to German. 1974. pap. 1.95 (ISBN 0-451-11328-4, AJ1328, Sig). NAL.
--Passport to Italian. 1974. pap. 2.25 (ISBN 0-451-12193-7, AE1717, Sig). NAL.
--Passport to Spanish. 224p. 1974. pap. 2.25 (ISBN 0-451-12193-7, AE2193, Sig). NAL.
--Spanish Step by Step. LC 78-73610. 1979. 10.95 (ISBN 0-89696-029-3, An Everest House Book). Dodd.
Berlitz, Charles & Moore, William L. The Roswell Incident. 1980. 10.00 (ISBN 0-448-21199-8, G&D). Putnam Pub Group.
Berlitz, Charles, jt. auth. see Moore, William.
Berlitz, Charles, ed. see Mawson, C. O.
Berlitz Editors. Arabic for Travel Cassettepack. 1983. 14.95 (ISBN 0-02-962780-X, Berlitz); cassette incl. Macmillan.
--Berlitz Arabic for Travellers. 192p. 1982. 8.95 (ISBN 0-02-964180-2, Berlitz); pap. 4.95. Macmillan.
--Berlitz Chinese for Travellers. 192p. 1982. pap. 4.95 (ISBN 0-686-93010-X, Berlitz); pap. 4.95 (ISBN 0-02-964210-8). Macmillan.
--Berlitz European Menu for Travellers. 192p. 1982. pap. 4.95 (ISBN 0-686-93020-7, Berlitz); pap. 4.95 (ISBN 0-02-964200-0). Macmillan.
--Berlitz French for Travellers. 192p. 1982. pap. 4.95 (ISBN 0-686-92978-0, Berlitz). Macmillan.
--Berlitz German for Travellers. 192p. 1982. pap. 4.95 (ISBN 0-686-92970-5, Berlitz); pap. 4.95 (ISBN 0-02-963930-1). Macmillan.
--Berlitz Greek for Travellers. 192p. 1982. pap. 4.95 (ISBN 0-686-92956-X, Berlitz); pap. 4.95 (ISBN 0-02-964040-7). Macmillan.
--Berlitz Hebrew for Travellers. 192p. 1982. pap. 4.95 (ISBN 0-02-964050-4, Berlitz). Macmillan.
--Berlitz Italian for Travellers. 192p. 1982. 8.95 (ISBN 0-02-965180-8, Berlitz); pap. 4.95 (ISBN 0-02-963940-9). Macmillan.
--Berlitz Japanese for Travellers. 192p. 1982. pap. 4.95 (ISBN 0-02-964070-9, Berlitz). Macmillan.
--Berlitz Latin-American Spanish for Travellers. 192p. 1982. 8.95 (ISBN 0-02-965510-2, Berlitz); pap. 4.95 (ISBN 0-02-963950-6). Macmillan.
--Berlitz Pocket Dictionaries: Danish-English. 300p. 1982. pap. 4.95 (ISBN 0-686-92980-2, Berlitz). Macmillan.
--Berlitz Pocket Dictionaries: Dutch-English. 300p. (Eng & Dutch.). 1982. pap. 4.95 (ISBN 0-686-92990-X, Berlitz). Macmillan.
--Berlitz Pocket Dictionaries: Finnish-English. 300p. (Eng & Finnish.). 1982. pap. 4.95 (ISBN 0-686-92984-5, Berlitz). Macmillan.
--Berlitz Pocket Dictionaries: French-English. 300p. (Eng. & Fr.). 1982. pap. 4.95 (ISBN 0-686-93004-5, Berlitz). Macmillan.
--Berlitz Pocket Dictionaries: German-English. 300p. (Eng. & Ger.). 1982. pap. 4.95 (ISBN 0-686-93007-X, Berlitz). Macmillan.
--Berlitz Pocket Dictionaries: Italian-English. 300p. (Eng. & Ital.). 1982. pap. 4.95 (ISBN 0-686-93001-0, Berlitz). Macmillan.
--Berlitz Pocket Dictionaries: Norwegian-English. 300p. (Eng & Norwegian.). 1982. pap. 4.95 (ISBN 0-686-92987-X, Berlitz). Macmillan.
--Berlitz Pocket Dictionaries: Spanish-English. 300p. (Eng. & Span.). 1982. pap. 4.95 (ISBN 0-686-92998-5, Berlitz). Macmillan.
--Berlitz Pocket Dictionaries: Swedish-English. 300p. (Eng & Swedish.). 1982. pap. 4.95 (ISBN 0-686-92996-9, Berlitz). Macmillan.
--Berlitz Portuguese for Travellers. 192p. 1982. pap. 4.95 (ISBN 0-02-963960-3, Berlitz). Macmillan.
--Berlitz Spanish for Travellers. 192p. 1982. 8.95 (ISBN 0-02-965190-5, Berlitz); pap. 4.95 (ISBN 0-02-963970-0). Macmillan.
--Berlitz Swedish for Travellers. 192p. 1982. pap. 4.95 (ISBN 0-02-963990-5, Berlitz). Macmillan.
--Berlitz Travel Guide: Egypt. (Illus.). 128p. 1982. pap. 4.95 (ISBN 0-02-969710-7, Berlitz). Macmillan.
--Berlitz Travel Guide: Hawaii. (Illus.). 128p. 1982. pap. 4.95 (ISBN 0-02-969770-0, Berlitz). Macmillan.
--Berlitz Travel Guide: Ireland. (Illus.). 128p. 1982. pap. 4.95 (ISBN 0-02-969190-7, Berlitz). Macmillan.
--Berlitz Travel Guide: Jerusalem. (Illus.). 128p. 1982. pap. 4.95 (ISBN 0-02-969250-4, Berlitz). Macmillan.
--Berlitz Travel Guide: London. (Illus.). 128p. 1982. pap. 4.95 (ISBN 0-02-969320-9, Berlitz). Macmillan.
--Berlitz Travel Guide: Mexico City. (Illus.). 128p. 1982. pap. 4.95 (ISBN 0-02-969660-7, Berlitz). Macmillan.
--Berlitz Travel Guide: New York. (Illus.). 128p. 1982. pap. 4.95 (ISBN 0-02-969400-0, Berlitz). Macmillan.
--Berlitz Travel Guide: Paris. (Illus.). 128p. 1982. pap. 4.95 (ISBN 0-02-969430-2, Berlitz). Macmillan.
--Berlitz Travel Guide: Rome. (Illus.). 128p. 1982. pap. 4.95 (ISBN 0-02-969470-1, Berlitz). Macmillan.
--Berlitz Travel Guide: Scotland. (Illus.). 128p. 1982. pap. 4.95 (ISBN 0-686-92937-3, Berlitz). Macmillan.
--Berlitz Travel Guide: Southern Caribbean. (Illus.). 128p. 1982. pap. 4.95 (ISBN 0-686-92930-6, Berlitz). Macmillan.
--Berlitz Travel Guide: Virgin Islands. (Illus.). 128p. 1982. pap. 4.95 (ISBN 0-686-92912-8, Berlitz). Macmillan.
--Chinese for Travel Cassettepack. 1983. 14.95 (ISBN 0-02-962210-7, Berlitz); cassette incl. Macmillan.
--Danish-English, English-Danish Pocket Dictionary. LC 74-1979. 1982. pap. 4.95 o.p. (ISBN 0-02-964300-7, Berlitz). Macmillan.
--Danish for Travel Cassettepack. 1983. 14.95 (ISBN 0-02-962970-5, Berlitz); cassette incl. Macmillan.
--Danish for Travellers. rev. ed. (Travellers Ser. for English Speakers). 1977. pap. 2.95 (ISBN 0-02-963890-9, Berlitz); cassettepak, 1973 14.95 (ISBN 0-02-962000-7, 96200). Macmillan.
--Dutch-English, English-Dutch Pocket Dictionary. LC 74-1988. 1974. pap. 4.95 o.p. (ISBN 0-02-964420-8, Berlitz). Macmillan.
--Dutch for Travel Cassettepack. 1983. 14.95 (ISBN 0-02-962950-0, Berlitz); cassette incl. Macmillan.
--Dutch for Travellers. rev. ed. (Travellers Ser. for English Speakers). 1977. pap. 4.95 (ISBN 0-02-964120-9, Berlitz); cassettepak, 1973 10.95 (ISBN 0-02-962120-8). Macmillan.
--English (British) for Italian Travellers. (Travellers Ser. for Non-English Speakers). 1971. pap. 4.95 (ISBN 0-02-965400-9, Berlitz). Macmillan.
--English (British) for Spanish Travellers. (Travellers Ser. for Non-English Speakers). 1971. pap. 4.95 (ISBN 0-02-966600-7, Berlitz). Macmillan.
--English for Arabic Phrasebook. 1982. pap. 4.95 (ISBN 0-02-965540-4, Berlitz). Macmillan.
--English for Danish Travellers. (Travellers Ser. for Non-English Speakers). 1971. pap. 4.95 o.p. (ISBN 0-02-966000-9, Berlitz). Macmillan.
--English for Dutch Travellers. (Travellers Series for Non-English Speakers). 1975. pap. 4.95 (ISBN 0-02-965600-1, Berlitz). Macmillan.
--English for Finnish Travellers. (Travellers Series for Non-English Speakers). 1971. pap. 4.95 o.p. (ISBN 0-02-966200-1, Berlitz). Macmillan.
--English for Japanese Travellers. Date not set. 4.95 (ISBN 0-02-966850-6, Berlitz). Macmillan.
--English for Norwegian Travellers. (Travellers Ser. for Non-English Speakers). 1971. pap. 4.95 o.p. (ISBN 0-02-965800-4, Berlitz). Macmillan.
--English (North American) for French Travellers. 1971. pap. 4.95 (ISBN 0-02-965050-X, Berlitz). Macmillan.
--English (North American) for German Travellers. 1974. pap. 4.95 (ISBN 0-02-965280-4, Berlitz, 96895). Macmillan.
--Finnish for Travel Cassettepack. 1983. 14.95 (ISBN 0-02-962960-8, Berlitz); cassette incl. Macmillan.
--French for Spanish Travellers. 1977. pap. 4.95 (ISBN 0-02-966610-4, Berlitz). Macmillan.
--French for Travel Cassettepack. 1983. 14.95 (ISBN 0-02-962190-9, Berlitz); cassette incl. Macmillan.
--German for Travel Cassettepack. 1983. 14.95 (ISBN 0-02-962200-X, Berlitz); cassette incl. Macmillan.
--Greek for Travel Cassettepack. 1983. 14.95 (ISBN 0-02-962940-3, Berlitz); cassette incl. Macmillan.
--Hebrew for Travel Cassettepack. 1983. 14.95 (ISBN 0-02-962890-3, Berlitz); cassette incl. Macmillan.
--Hungarian for Travellers. 1981. 4.95 (ISBN 0-02-964270-1, Berlitz). Macmillan.
--Japanese for Travel Cassettepack. 1983. 14.95 (ISBN 0-02-962850-4, Berlitz); cassette incl. Macmillan.
--Latin American Spanish for Travel Cassettepack. 1983. 14.95 (ISBN 0-02-962590-4, Berlitz); cassette incl. Macmillan.
--Norwegian-English, English-Norwegian Pocket Dictionary. rev ed. LC 74-1985. 1981. pap. 4.95 o.p. (ISBN 0-02-964380-5, Berlitz). Macmillan.
--Norwegian for Travel Cassettepack. 1983. 14.95 (ISBN 0-02-962870-9, Berlitz); cassette incl. Macmillan.
--Portuguese-English Dictionary. 1982. 4.95 (ISBN 0-02-964440-2, Berlitz). Macmillan.
--Portuguese for Travel Cassettepack. 1983. 14.95 (ISBN 0-02-962790-7, Berlitz); cassette incl. Macmillan.
--Russian for Travel Cassettepack. 1983. 14.95 (ISBN 0-02-962880-6, Berlitz); cassette incl. Macmillan.
--Serbo-Croatian for Travellers. LC 73-2272. (Travellers Ser. for English Speakers). (Illus.). 1973. pap. 4.95 (ISBN 0-02-964150-0, Berlitz); cassettepak, 1976 14.95 (ISBN 0-02-962150-X). Macmillan.
--Spanish-English Dictionary. 1979. 4.95 (ISBN 0-02-964510-7, Berlitz). Macmillan.
--Spanish for Travel Cassettepack. 1983. 14.95 (ISBN 0-02-962220-4, Berlitz); cassette incl. Macmillan.
--Swahili for Travellers. 1974. pap. 4.95 (ISBN 0-02-964220-5, Berlitz). Macmillan.
--Swedish for Travel Cassettepack. 1983. 14.95 (ISBN 0-02-962860-1, Berlitz); cassette incl. Macmillan.
--Turkish for Travellers. 1974. pap. 4.95 (ISBN 0-02-964230-2, Berlitz). Macmillan.
Berlitz Schools of Language. Berlitz Self-Teachers: French, Vol. 2. (Illus.). 300p. 1949. 8.95 (ISBN 0-448-01421-1, G&D). Putnam Pub Group.
--Berlitz Self-Teachers: German, Vol. 3. (Illus.). 300p. 1950. 8.95 (ISBN 0-448-01422-X, G&D). Putnam Pub Group.
--Berlitz Self-Teachers: Spanish, Vol. 1. (Illus.). 300p. 1950. 8.95 (ISBN 0-448-01427-0, G&D). Putnam Pub Group.
Berlitz Schools of Language. Berlitz Sin Maestro Ingles or, English for the Spanish-Speaking People, Vol. 5. (Span). 1960. 8.95 (ISBN 0-448-01428-9, G&D). Putnam Pub Group.
--Self-Teacher: French. 1958. 8.95 (ISBN 0-448-01421-1, G&D). Putnam Pub Group.
--Self-Teacher: German. 1958. 8.95 (ISBN 0-448-01422-X, G&D). Putnam Pub Group.
--Self-Teacher: Hebrew. 1963. 7.95 o.p. (ISBN 0-448-01423-8, G&D). Putnam Pub Group.
--Self-Teacher: Italian. 1958. 8.95 (ISBN 0-448-01424-6, G&D). Putnam Pub Group.
--Self-Teacher: Portuguese. 1963. 7.95 o.p. (ISBN 0-448-01425-4, G&D). Putnam Pub Group.
--Self-Teacher: Russian. 1958. 7.95 (ISBN 0-448-01426-2, G&D). Putnam Pub Group.
--Self-Teacher: Spanish. 1958. 8.95 (ISBN 0-448-01427-0, G&D). Putnam Pub Group.
Berlow, Lawrence H. Mexico in the Nineteen Eighties. (Library Research). (Illus.). 160p. 1983. 12.95 (ISBN 0-912526-23-8). Lib Res.
Berlye, Milton. Your Career in the World of Work. LC 75-12236. 1975. pap. 16.50 (ISBN 0-672-97534-3). Bobbs.
Berlye, Milton, jt. auth. see Conover, Hobart.
Berlye, Milton K. Encyclopedia of Working with Glass. 1967. cancelled o.p. (ISBN 0-89345-003-0, Freedeeds Bks). Garber Comm.
--Encyclopedia of Working with Glass. 1983. 29.95 (ISBN 0-89696-193-1). Dodd.
Berlyne, D. E. Structure & Direction in Thinking. LC 65-12720. (Illus.). 378p. 1965. text ed. 16.50 (ISBN 0-471-07035-1, Pub. by Wiley). Krieger.
Berman. The Glands Regulating Personality: A Study of the Glands of Internal Secretion in Relation to the Types of Human Nature. 341p. 1983. Repr. of 1933 ed. lib. bdg. 40.00 (ISBN 0-89760-051-7). Telegraph Bks.
Berman, A. Analysis of Drugs. 1977. 29.95 (ISBN 0-471-25650-1, Pub. by Wiley Heyden). Wiley.
Berman, A. & Hannibal, A. J., eds. Passenger Vibration in Transportation Vehicles-AMD, 1977, Vol. 24. 1977. pap. text ed. 15.00 o.p. (ISBN 0-685-86874-5, 100112). ASME.
Berman, Alvin L. Brain Stem of the Cat: A Cytoarchitectonic Atlas with Stereotaxic Coordinates. (Illus.). 192p. 1968. 250.00 (ISBN 0-299-04860-8). U of Wis Pr.
Berman, Barry, jt. auth. see Evans, Joel R.
Berman, Claire. Making It As a Stepparent: New Roles-New Rules. LC 78-22302. 1980. 8.95 o.p. (ISBN 0-385-13393-6). Doubleday.
Berman, Claire G. What Am I Doing in a Step-Family? 48p. 1982. 12.00 (ISBN 0-8184-0325-X). Lyle Stuart.
Berman, Connie. The Dolly Parton Scrapbook. LC 78-55621. (Illus.). 1978. 14.95 o.p. (ISBN 0-448-16176-1, G&D); pap. 5.95 o.p. (ISBN 0-448-16183-4, Today Pr). Putnam Pub Group.
Berman, Daniel, jt. ed. see Navarro, Vicente.
Berman, David R. American Government, Politics & Policymaking. 2nd ed. LC 82-61096. (Illus.). 1983. text ed. 13.95x (ISBN 0-913530-31-X). Palisades Pub.
Berman, Dorothy, jt. auth. see Matthews, Joseph.
Berman, E. Toxic Metals & Their Analysis. 304p. 1980. 42.95 (ISBN 0-471-25651-X, Wiley Heyden). Wiley.
Berman, Edgar. Hubert: The Triumph & Tragedy of the Humphrey I Knew. LC 79-4259. (Illus.). 1979. 10.95 o.p. (ISBN 0-399-12314-8). Putnam Pub Group.
Berman, Eleanor. Away for the Weekend: A Guide to Great Getaways Less Than 200 Miles from New York City for Every Season of the Year. (Illus.). 256p. 1982. pap. 7.95 (ISBN 0-517-54647-7, C N Potter Bks). Crown.
--Re-Entering: Successful Back-to-Work Strategies for Women Seeking a Fresh Start. 192p. 1980. 8.95 o.p. (ISBN 0-517-53943-8). Crown.
Berman, Filipp. Registrator. 140p. (Rus.). 1983. 16.00 (ISBN 0-88233-729-7); pap. 8.00 (ISBN 0-88233-730-0). Ardis Pubs.
Berman, Greta. The Lost Years: Mural Painting in New York City Under the Works Progress Administration's Federal Art Project 1935-1943. LC 77-94687. (Outstanding Dissertations in the Fine Arts Ser.). 1978. lib. bdg. 45.00 o.s.i. (ISBN 0-8240-3216-0). Garland Pub.
Berman, Harold. Encyclopedia of Bronzes, Sculptors & Founders: 1800-1930. LC 74-78612. (Abage Encyclopedia Ser.: Vols. 1-4). 1974-80. Set. lib. bdg. 210.00x (ISBN 0-917350-05-7); Vol. 1. lib. bdg. 45.00x (ISBN 0-917350-01-4); Vol. 2. lib. bdg. 50.00x (ISBN 0-917350-02-2); Vol. 3. lib. bdg. 55.00x (ISBN 0-917350-03-0); Vol. 4. lib. bdg. 60.00x (ISBN 0-917350-04-9). Abage.
Berman, Harold J. & Maggs, Peter B. Disarmament Inspection Under Soviet Law. LC 66-13368. 154p. 1967. 10.00 (ISBN 0-379-00293-0). Oceana.
Berman, Howard J. & Weeks, Lewis E., eds. Economics in Health Care. LC 77-10860. 402p. 1978. text ed. 34.00 (ISBN 0-89443-026-2). Aspen Systems.
Berman, Howard W. & Weeks, Lewis E. The Financial Management of Hospitals. 3rd ed. (Illus.). 585p. 1976. 17.50 (ISBN 0-686-68573-3, 1496). Healthcare Fin Man Assn.
Berman, Jan. Fiction Writing. (Learning Workbooks Language Arts). (gr. 4-6). pap. 1.50 (ISBN 0-8224-4182-9). Pitman.
--Nonfiction Writing. (Learning Workbooks Language Arts). (gr. 4-6). pap. 1.50 (ISBN 0-8224-4181-0). Pitman.
--Paragraph Writing. (Learning Workbooks Language Arts). (gr. 4-6). pap. 1.50 (ISBN 0-8224-4180-2). Pitman.
Berman, Jeffrey. Joseph Conrad: Writing As Rescue. LC 76-46909. 1977. 10.00 o.p. (ISBN 0-913994-30-8); pap. 5.95 o.p. (ISBN 0-913994-31-6). Hippocrene Bks.
Berman, L. I. & Sacco, W. J. Glyphs. (Cyometrics Math Enrichement Ser.). 26p. (Orig.). 1981. pap. text ed. 3.00 (ISBN 0-686-36282-9). Cyometrics.
Berman, Linda. The Goodbye Painting. LC 81-20217. 32p. 1982. 9.95 (ISBN 0-89885-074-6). Human Sci Pr.
Berman, Linda, et al. Tenth Year Mathematics. (Arco's Regents Review Ser.). 288p. (Orig.). 1982. pap. 3.95 o.p. (ISBN 0-668-05702-5, 5702). Arco.
Berman, Louise M. New Priorities in the Curriculum. LC 68-28703. (International Education Ser). 1968. text ed. 18.95 (ISBN 0-675-09612-X). Merrill.
Berman, Louise M. & Roderick, Jessie A. Curriculum: Teaching the What, How, & Why of Living. (Elementary Education Ser.). 1977. text ed. 17.95 (ISBN 0-675-08480-6). Merrill.
Berman, Marshall. All That is Solid Melts into Air. 1983. pap. 6.75 (ISBN 0-671-45700-4, Touchstone Bks). S&S.
Berman, Michael. Playing & Working with Words. LC 80-41911. (Materials for Language Practice Ser.). 96p. 1981. pap. 2.95 (ISBN 0-08-025352-0). Pergamon.
--Take Note: Materials for Listening Comprehension & Note Taking in English. 1980. pap. 3.95 (ISBN 0-08-025316-4). Pergamon.
Berman, Mones. Lipoprotein Kinetics & Modeling. LC 82-6749. 480p. 1982. 67.50 (ISBN 0-12-092480-3). Acad Pr.
Berman, Myron. Richmond's Jewry, Seventeen Sixty-Nine to Nineteen Seventy-Six. LC 78-6377. 438p. 1979. 14.95x (ISBN 0-8139-0743-8). U Pr of Va.
Berman, Neil D. Geriatric Cardiology. LC 81-70163. 256p. 1982. 25.95 (ISBN 0-669-04505-5). Heath.
Berman, Peter I. Inflation & the Money Supply in the United States, 1956-1977. LC 78-4344. 1978. 16.95x (ISBN 0-669-02346-9). Lexington Bks.
Berman, Robert P. Soviet Air Power in Transition. (Studies in Defense Policy). 1978. pap. 4.95 (ISBN 0-8157-0923-4). Brookings.
Berman, Robert P. & Baker, John C. Soviet Strategic Forces: Requirements & Responses. LC 82-70889. (Studies in Defense Policy). 240p. 1982. 22.95 (ISBN 0-8157-0926-9); pap. 8.95 (ISBN 0-8157-0925-0). Brookings.
Berman, Ronald. Reader's Guide to Shakespeare's Plays: A Discursive Bibliography. rev. ed. 1973. pap. 7.95x (ISBN 0-673-07878-7). Scott F.
Berman, Sanford. Joy of Cataloging: Essays, Letters, Reviews & Other Explosions. 240p. 1981. lib. bdg. 32.50x (ISBN 0-912700-51-3); pap. 25.00x (ISBN 0-912700-94-7). Oryx Pr.
Berman, Stephen. Pediatric Decision Making. 300p. 1983. text ed. 36.00 (ISBN 0-941158-17-9, D0640-3). Mosby.
Berman, Steve. How to Create Your Own Publicity for Names, Products or Services & Get It for Free. LC 77-2736. 128p. 1977. pap. 4.95 o.s.i. (ISBN 0-8119-0378-8). Fell.
Berman, Susan. Easy Street. 1983. pap. 2.95 (ISBN 0-553-22935-4). Bantam.
--Underground Guide to the College of Your Choice. (Orig.). 1971. pap. 1.95 o.p. (ISBN 0-451-07837-3, J7837, Sig). NAL.
--Your Career in Hotel Management. (Arco's Career Guidance Ser.). (Illus.). 128p. 1983. lib. bdg. 7.95 (ISBN 0-668-05501-4); pap. 4.50 (ISBN 0-668-05513-8). Arco.
--Your Career in the Foreign Service. (Arco's Career Guide Ser.). (Illus.). 128p. 1983. lib. bdg. 7.95 (ISBN 0-668-05510-3); pap. 4.50 (ISBN 0-668-05517-0). Arco.
Berman, Susan, ed. see Ninemeier, Jack D.
Berman, Susanna. Your Career in the International Field. (Arco's Career Guidance Ser.). (Illus.). 128p. 1983. lib. bdg. 7.95 (ISBN 0-668-05507-3); pap. 4.50 (ISBN 0-668-05515-4). Arco.

Bermant, Chaim. Belshazzar: A Cat's Story for Humans. 64p. 1982. pap. 2.95 (ISBN 0-380-58560-X, 58560, Bard). Avon.
Bermant, Gordon, ed. Perspectives on Animal Behavior: A First Course, Ten Original Essays. 1973. 19.95x (ISBN 0-673-07577-X). Scott F.
Bermant, Gordon, et al. Psychology & the Law. LC 75-40628. 1976. 23.95 (ISBN 0-669-00452-9). Lexington Bks.
Bermel, Albert. Farce. 1983. pap. 9.95 (ISBN 0-671-25149-X, Touchstone Bks). S&S.
--Six One-Act Farces. LC 82-81872. 75p. (Orig.). 1982. pap. 13.50 (ISBN 0-88127-005-9). Oracle Pr LA.
Bermingham, Jack, jt. auth. see Clausen, Edwin.
Bermont, Hubert, jt. auth. see Garvin, Andrew.
Bermont, Hubert, jt. auth. see Thomas, David S.
Bermont, John. How to Europe: The Complete Travelers Handbook. LC 82-170269. (Illus.). 332p. 1982. pap. 9.95 (ISBN 0-940792-01-X). Murphy & Broad.
Bermosk, Loretta S. & Mordan, Mary J. Interviewing in Nursing. (Illus.). 208p. 1973. pap. text ed. 9.95x (ISBN 0-02-308550-9, 30855). Macmillan.
Bermudez, Pedro P., et al. Fuentes para Conversacion y Composition. 1976. pap. 5.95 (ISBN 0-442-20689-5). Van Nos Reinhold.
Bernabe, Emma, et al. Ilokano Lessons. McKaughan, Howard P., ed. (PALI Language Texts: Philippines). (Orig.). 1971. pap. text ed. 8.00x o.p. (ISBN 0-87022-074-8). UH Pr.
Bernac, Pierre. The Interpretation of French Song. (Illus.). 1978. pap. 7.95x (ISBN 0-393-00878-9, N878, Norton Lib). Norton.
Bernacchi, Richard L. & Larsen, Gerald H. Data Processing Contracts & the Law. 1974. 35.00 (ISBN 0-316-09183-9). Little.
Bernal, jt. auth. see Ludwig.
Bernal, Ignacio. A History of Mexican Archaeology: The Vanished Civilizations of Middle America. (Illus.). 1983. pap. 9.95 (ISBN 0-500-79008-6). Thames Hudson.
Bernal, J. D. Science in History, 4 vols. Incl. Vol. 1. The Emergence of Science. pap. 7.95x (ISBN 0-262-52020-6); Vol. 2. The Scientific & Industrial Revolution. pap. 7.95x (ISBN 0-262-52021-4); Vol. 3. The Natural Sciences in Our Time. pap. 7.95x (ISBN 0-262-52022-2); Vol. 4. The Social Sciences: a Conclusion. pap. 7.95x (ISBN 0-262-52023-0). 1971. pap. 30.00x boxed set (ISBN 0-262-02142-0). MIT Pr.
Bernal, Louis C., jt. auth. see Martin, Patricia P.
Bernanos, Michel. The Other Side of the Mountain. LC 68-29550. 107p. 1973. Repr. of 1968 ed. 8.95 (ISBN 0-910220-47-6). Berg.
Bernard & Beuzamy. Introduction to Banach Spaces & Their Geometry. Date not set. 38.50 (ISBN 0-444-86416-4). Elsevier.
Bernard, Barbara. Fashion in the Sixties. LC 78-60788. (Illus.). 1978. pap. 4.95 o.p. (ISBN 0-312-28460-8). St Martin.
Bernard, C. H. & Epp, C. D. Laboratory Experiments in College Physics. 5th ed. 437p. 1980. 14.95 (ISBN 0-471-05441-0). Wiley.
Bernard, Carl & Norquay, Karen. Practical Effects in Photography. LC 80-40794. (Practical Photography Ser.). (Illus.). 168p. 1982. 22.95 (ISBN 0-240-51082-8). Focal Pr.
Bernard, Catherine, ed. see Pischel, Gina, et al.
Bernard, Dan, et al, eds. Charging for Computer Services: Principles & Guidelines. Emery, James C. & Nolan, Richard. LC 77-23811. (Computer & Data Processing Professionals Ser). 1977. text ed. 16.00 (ISBN 0-89433-055-1); pap. text ed. 12.00 (ISBN 0-89433-051-9). Petrocelli.
Bernard, Edward, pseud. The Name Changers. (Illus.). 528p. (Orig.). 1982. pap. 3.95 (ISBN 0-910797-00-5). Marketing Effect.
Bernard, Frank E. Recent Agricultural Change East of Mount Kenya. LC 79-630648. (Papers in International Studies: Africa: No. 4). (Illus.). 1969. pap. 4.00x (ISBN 0-89680-038-5, Ohio U Ctr Intl). Ohio U Pr.
Bernard, George & Cooke, John. Mosquito. (Illus.). 32p. 1982. 8.95 (ISBN 0-399-20905-0). Putnam Pub Group.
Bernard, George & Paling, John. Grey Squirrel. (Illus.). 32p. 1982. 8.95 (ISBN 0-399-20906-9). Putnam Pub Group.
Bernard, H. Russell. Human Way: Readings in Anthropology. 1975. pap. 14.95x (ISBN 0-02-308920-2, 30892). Macmillan.
Bernard, H. Russell & Pelto, Pertti J. Technology & Social Change. (Illus.). 352p. 1972. text ed. 24.95x (ISBN 0-02-309010-3, 30901). Macmillan.
Bernard, H. Y. Law of Death & Disposal of the Dead. 2nd ed. LC 79-19160. (Legal Almanac Ser.: No. 57). 114p. 1979. 5.95 (ISBN 0-379-11120-9). Oceana.
--Public Officials, Elected & Appointed. LC 68-54014. (Legal Almanac Ser.: No. 26). 119p. 1968. 5.95 (ISBN 0-379-11026-1). Oceana.
Bernard, Harold. The Greenhouse Effect. 208p. 1980. prof ref 18.00x (ISBN 0-88410-633-0). Ballinger Pub.
Bernard, Harold W., jt. auth. see Strom, Robert D.
Bernard, J. F. Talleyrand: A Biography. (Illus.). 1973. 12.95 o.p. (ISBN 0-399-11022-4). Putnam Pub Group.
Bernard, J. F., tr. see Lartigue, Jacques-Henri & Metral, Yvette.
Bernard, Jack, ed. see Hartmann, Sven & Hartner, Thoman.
Bernard, Jessie. The Future of Marriage. LC 82-6991. 384p. 1982. text ed. 25.00x (ISBN 0-300-02912-8); pap. 8.95 (ISBN 0-300-02853-9, Y-441). Yale U Pr.
Bernard, Luther L. War & Its Causes. LC 71-147465. (Library of War & Peace; the Character & Causes of War). lib. bdg. 38.00 o.s.i. (ISBN 0-8240-0256-3). Garland Pub.
Bernard, Marc, ed. see Zola, Emile.
Bernard, Michael M. Constitutions, Taxation, & Land Policy: Vol. II, Discussion & Analysis of Federal & State Constitutional Constraints on the Use of Taxation As an Instrument of Land-Planning Policy. LC 78-24792. (Lincoln Institute of Land Policy Bk). 144p. 1980. 18.95x (ISBN 0-669-03462-2). Lexington Bks.
--Constitutions, Taxations, & Land Policy: Vol. I, Abstract of Federal & State Constitutional Constraints on the Power of Taxation Relating to Land Planning Policy. (Lincoln Institute of Land Policy Book). (Illus.). 176p. 1979. 18.95x (ISBN 0-669-02823-1). Lexington Bks.
Bernard, Otis. Life With Yankee Wife. 120p. 1982. pap. 4.95 (ISBN 0-89221-093-1, Pub. by SonLife). New Leaf.
Bernard, Paul P. Jesuits & Jacobins: Enlightenment & Enlightened Despotism in Austria. LC 78-151997. 1971. 14.95 (ISBN 0-252-00180-X). U of Ill Pr.
Bernard, Paul P., II. Joseph II. (World Leaders Ser.). 12.95 (ISBN 0-8057-3052-4, Twayne). G K Hall.
Bernard, Robert. Death & the Princess. (Nightingale Series Paperbacks). 1983. pap. 9.95 (ISBN 0-8161-3520-7, Large Print Bks). G K Hall.
Bernard, Sidney. This Way to the Apocalypse: The Politics of the 1960's. LC 77-94632. 256p. 1969. 5.95 (ISBN 0-912292-09-1). The Smith.
Bernard, Thomas. Hindu Philosophy. 220p. Date not set. 10.00 (ISBN 0-89581-220-7); pap. 6.00 (ISBN 0-686-96768-2). Lancaster-Miller.
--The Progress of Doctrine in the New Testament. 1978. 9.00 (ISBN 0-86524-123-6, 8004). Klock & Klock.
Bernard, William S., ed. Americanization Studies: The Acculturation of Immigrant Groups into American Society, 10 vols. Incl. New Homes for Old. Breckinridge, S. P; Immigrant's Day in Court. Claghorn, K. H; America Via the Neighborhood. Daniels, J; Immigrant Health & the Community. Davis, M. M; Americans by Choice. Gavit, J. P; Adjusting Immigrant & Industry. Leiserson, W. M; Immigrant Press & Its Control. Park, R. E; Stake in the Land. Speek, P. A; Old World Traits Transplanted. Thomas, W. I., et al.; Schooling of the Immigrant. Thompson, F. V. LC 73-108242. (Criminology, Law Enforcement, & Social Problems Ser.: No. 125). (Illus., Repr. 1920-24 with intros. to all vols. & indexes added. Available in set only). 1971. Set. 200.00x (ISBN 0-87585-125-8). Patterson Smith.
Bernard de Clairvaux, St. On Loving God: Selections from Sermons by St. Bernard of Clairvaux. Martin, Hugh, ed. LC 79-8706. (A Treasury of Christian Books). 125p. 1981. Repr. of 1959 ed. lib. bdg. 19.25x (ISBN 0-313-20787-9, BEOL). Greenwood.
Bernardi, S. D. Bibliography of Schlicht Functions. 1983. 32.50 (ISBN 0-936166-09-6). Mariner Pub.
Bernardin. Women in the Work Force. 256p. 1982. 28.95 (ISBN 0-03-062471-1). Praeger.
Bernardin de Saint-Pierre, Jacques-Henri. Paul & Virginia. 110p. 1983. 14.95 (ISBN 0-7206-0598-9, Pub by Peter Owen). Merrimack Bk Serv.
Bernardo, Aldo S. Petrarch, Laura & the "Triumphs". LC 74-22084. 1974. 34.50x (ISBN 0-87395-289-8). State U NY Pr.
--Petrarch, Scipio & the "Africa". The Birth of Humanism's Dream. LC 78-19065. 1978. Repr. of 1962 ed. lib. bdg. 20.00x (ISBN 0-313-20535-3, BEPA). Greenwood.
Bernardo, Aldo S. & Mignani, Rigo. Ritratto Dell'Italia. 2nd ed. 1978. pap. text ed. 16.95x (ISBN 0-669-01157-6). Heath.
Bernardo, Aldo S. & Pellegrini, Anthony L., eds. Dante, Petrarch & Others: Studies in the Italian Trecento. 1983. write for info. (ISBN 0-86698-061-X). Medieval & Renaissance NY.
Bernardo, Roberto M. Popular Management & Pay in China. 1977. pap. text ed. 8.00x o.p. (ISBN 0-8248-0741-3). UH Pr.
Bernardo, Stephanie. The Ethnic Almanac. LC 80-14694. (Illus.). 576p. 1981. pap. 10.95 o.p. (ISBN 0-385-14144-0, Dolp). Doubleday.
--The Ultimate Checklist. LC 81-43589. 384p. 1982. pap. 9.95 (ISBN 0-385-17604-X, Dolp). Doubleday.
Bernard of Clairvaux & William of St. Thierry. The Love of God. Houston, James M., ed. (Classics of Faith & Devotion). Orig. Title: Life & Works of St. Bernard. 1983. 9.95 (ISBN 0-88070-017-3). Multnomah.
Bernards, Solomon S., ed. The Living Heritage of Passover: With an Abridged Passover Haggadah in English. 40p. 0.75 o.s.i. (ISBN 0-686-74965-0). ADL.
Bernart, Luelen. The Book of Luelen. Fischer, John L., et al, eds. LC 76-50497. (Pacific History Ser.: No. 8). 1977. text ed. 15.00x o.p. (ISBN 0-8248-0532-1). UH Pr.
Bernasconi, G. Creep of Engineering Materials & Structures. 1980. 65.75 (ISBN 0-85334-878-2, Pub. by Applied Sci England). Elsevier.
Bernasconi, J. R. Collector's Glossary of Antiques & Fine Arts. (Illus.). 1971. 17.50x (ISBN 0-900361-34-4). Intl Pubns Serv.
Bernath, Maria, ed. Pal Szinyei Merse. (Illus.). 155p. 1981. 30.00x (ISBN 0-686-81863-6). Intl Pubns Serv.
--Szinyei Merse. Horn, Susanna & West, Elizabeth, trs. from Eng., Fr., & Ger. (Illus.). 192p. 1982. 55.00 (ISBN 0-89893-177-0). CDP.
Bernath, Stefan. House Plants Coloring Book. (Illus.). 1976. pap. 2.00 (ISBN 0-486-23266-2). Dover.
--Trees of the Northeast Coloring Book. (Illus.). pap. 2.25 (ISBN 0-486-23734-6). Dover.
Bernath, Stefen. Common Weeds Coloring Book. (Illus.). pap. 2.25 (ISBN 0-486-23308-1). Dover.
--Tropical Fish Coloring Book. (Illus.). pap. 2.00 (ISBN 0-486-23620-X). Dover.
Bernath, Stuart L. Squall Across the Atlantic: American Civil War Prize Cases & Diplomacy. LC 76-79042. 1970. 28.50x (ISBN 0-520-01562-2). U of Cal Pr.
Bernatzky, A. Tree Ecology & Preservation. (Developments in Agricultural & Managed-Forest Ecology Ser.: Vol. 2). 1978. 68.00 (ISBN 0-444-41606-4). Elsevier.
Bernays, Anne. The School Book. LC 79-2643. 1980. 12.45i (ISBN 0-06-010332-9, HarpT). Har-Row.
Bernays, P. & Frankel, A. Axiomatic Set Theory. (Studies in Logic: Vol. 8). 1968. 24.50 (ISBN 0-7204-2202-7, North Holland). Elsevier.
Bernays, P., ed. see Symposium, Brussels.
Bernbaum, Edwin. The Way to Shambhala. LC 78-1234. (Illus.). 336p. (Orig.). 1980. pap. 8.95 (ISBN 0-385-12794-4, Anch). Doubleday.
Bernbaum, Ernest, ed. Anthology of Romanticism. 3rd enl. ed. 1948. 15.50 o.s.i. (ISBN 0-471-06954-X). Wiley.
Bernbaum, Gerald. Knowledge & Ideology in the Sociology of Education. (Studies in Sociology Ser.). 1977. pap. text ed. 6.25x (ISBN 0-333-15762-1). Humanities.
Bernd, Clifford A. German Poetic Realism. (World Authors Ser.). 1981. lib. bdg. 12.95 (ISBN 0-8057-6447-X, Twayne). G K Hall.
Bernd, Joseph L., jt. ed. see Havard, William C.
Berndt, Ernst R. & Field, Barry C., eds. Modeling & Measuring Natural Resource Substitution. 384p. 1982. text ed. 40.00x (ISBN 0-262-02174-9). MIT Pr.
Berndt, Harry E. New Rulers in the Ghetto: The Community Development Corporation & Urban Poverty. LC 76-47888. (Contributions in Afro-American & African Studies: No. 28). (Illus.). 1977. lib. bdg. 25.00 (ISBN 0-8371-9399-0, BNL/). Greenwood.
Berndt, Susan G. Berryman's Baedeker: The Epigraphs to the Dream Songs. LC 76-22155. 1976. pap. 2.50 o.p. (ISBN 0-916684-06-7). Rook Pr.
Berne, Bruce J. & Pecora, Robert. Dynamic Light Scattering: With Applications to Chemistry, Biology & Physics. LC 75-19140. 376p. 1976. 49.95x (ISBN 0-471-07100-5, Pub. by Wiley-Interscience). Wiley.
Berne, Patricia H. & Savary, Louis M. What Will the Neighbors Say? Facing the Fear of Disapproval. 176p. 1982. 10.95 (ISBN 0-8264-0196-1). Continuum.
Berne, R. M., et al, eds. Annual Review of Physiology, Vol. 45. LC 39-15404. (Illus.). 1983. text ed. 27.00 (ISBN 0-8243-0345-8). Annual Reviews.
Berne, Robert M. & Levy, Matthew N. Cardiovascular Physiology. 4th ed. LC 81-2039. (Illus.). 286p. 1981. pap. text ed. 18.95 (ISBN 0-8016-0655-1). Mosby.
Berne, Stanley. The Great American Empire. LC 81-85003. (Illus.). 232p. 1982. 17.95 (ISBN 0-686-82851-8); pap. 7.95 (ISBN 0-686-82850-X). Am Canadian.
--The Unconscious Victorious & Other Stories. LC 69-20442. (Archives of Post-Modern Literature). (Illus.). 1969. pap. 7.00 (ISBN 0-913844-04-7). Am Canadian.
Berner, Elsa R. Integrating Library Instruction with Classroom Teaching at Plainview Junior High School. LC 58-6978. 1958. pap. 5.00 (ISBN 0-8389-0040-2). ALA.
Berner, Jeff. The Foolproof Guide to SCRIPSIT. 225p. 1983. pap. text ed. 11.95 (ISBN 0-89588-098-9). Sybex.
--The Holography Book. 148p. 1980. pap. 5.95 o.p. (ISBN 0-380-75267-0, 75267). Avon.
Berner, R. A. Principles of Chemical Sedimentology. 1971. 43.50 (ISBN 0-07-004928-9, C). McGraw.
Berner, Richard C. Archival Theory & Practice in the United States: A Historical Analysis. LC 82-48869. 240p. 1983. 35.00 (ISBN 0-295-95992-4). U of Wash Pr.
Berner, Samuel, jt. ed. see Cantor, Norman F.
Berner, Wolfgang, et al. The Soviet Union 1973: Domestic Policy, Economics, Foreign Policy. LC 74-22285. 200p. 1975. text ed. 32.50x (ISBN 0-8419-0188-0). Holmes & Meier.
--The Soviet Union 1974-75: Domestic Policy, Economics, Foreign Policy. LC 74-22285. 1976. 32.50x (ISBN 0-8419-0216-X). Holmes & Meier.
Bernero, Jacqueline, jt. ed. see Wasserman, Paul.
Berners, Juliana. A Treatise on Fishing with a Hook. 9.95 o.p. (ISBN 0-88427-038-6). Green Hill.
--A Treatise on Fishing with a Hook. LC 79-20603. (Angling Classics Ser.). 1979. Repr. 15.00 (ISBN 0-88427-038-6). North River.
Bernfeld, Siegfried. Sisyphus; or, the Limits of Education. Lilge, Frederic, tr. from Ger. LC 77-84784. 1973. 21.50x (ISBN 0-520-01407-3). U of Cal Pr.
Bernfeld, Stephen R. & Lakshmikantham, V. An Introduction to Boundary Value Problems. (Mathematics in Science & Engineering: A Series of Monographs & Textbooks, Vol. 109). 1974. 43.50 (ISBN 0-12-093150-8). Acad Pr.
Bernhard, Buelow von see Von Bernhard, Buelow.
Bernhard, C. G. & Schade, J. Developmental Neurology. (Progress in Brain Research: Vol. 26). 1967. 65.75 (ISBN 0-444-40040-0, North Holland). Elsevier.
Bernhard, Edgar. Speakers on the Spot: A Treasury of Anecdotes for Coping with Sticky Situations. 1977. 12.95 o.p. (ISBN 0-13-824508-8, Parker). P-H.
Bernhard, Linda A. & Walsh, Michelle. Leadership: The Key to Professionalization of Nursing. (Illus.). 256p. 1981. pap. text ed. 13.50 (ISBN 0-07-004936-X, HP). McGraw.
Bernhard, Marcelle. Jamie's Magic Bullet. LC 68-11081. (Illus.). (ps-3). 1968. bds. 2.95 (ISBN 0-8048-0270-X). C E Tuttle.
Bernhard, Yetta. Self-Care. LC 75-9448. 1975. 11.95 o.p. (ISBN 0-89087-110-8); pap. 7.95 o.p. (ISBN 0-89087-111-6). Celestial Arts.
Bernhardt, Arthur D. Building Tomorrow: The Mobile-Manufactured Housing Industry. (Illus.). 1980. text ed. 50.00x (ISBN 0-262-02134-X). MIT Pr.
Bernhardt, Ernest C., ed. Processing of Thermoplastic Materials. LC 73-92132. 704p. 1974. Repr. of 1959 ed. 39.50 (ISBN 0-88275-145-X). Krieger.
Bernhardt, Frances S. Introduction to Library Technical Services. 322p. 1979. 18.00 (ISBN 0-8242-0637-1). Wilson.
Bernhardt, Kenneth L., jt. auth. see Kinnear, Thomas C.
Bernhardt, Roger & Martin, David. Self-Mastery Through Self-Hypnosis. 1978. pap. 2.25 (ISBN 0-451-12097-3, AE2097, Sig). NAL.
Bernhardt-Kabisch, Ernest. Robert Southey. (English Authors Ser.). 1977. lib. bdg. 13.95 (ISBN 0-8057-6692-8, Twayne). G K Hall.
Bernheim, Kayla F., et al. The Caring Family: Living with Chronic Mental Illness. LC 80-40248. 1982. 13.50 (ISBN 0-394-51028-3). Random.
Bernheimer, Alan W., ed. Perspectives in Toxicology. LC 80-11261. 218p. 1983. Repr. of 1977 ed. lib. bdg. write for info. (ISBN 0-89874-131-9). Krieger.
Bernheimer, Charles S., ed. The Russian Jew in the United States: Studies of Social Conditions in New York, Philadelphia, & Chicago, with a Description of Rural Settlements. LC 79-145470. (The American Immigration Library). 426p. 1971. Repr. of 1905 ed. lib. bdg. 16.50x (ISBN 0-89198-002-4). Ozer.
Bernholz, Peter. Flexible Exchange Rates in Historical Perspective. LC 82-6167. (Princeton Studies in International Finance Ser.: No. 49). 1982. pap. text ed. 4.50x (ISBN 0-88165-220-2). Princeton U Int Finan Econ.
Berni, Rosemarian & Fordyce, Wilbert E. Behavior Modification & the Nursing Process. 2nd ed. LC 76-57775. (Illus.). 160p. 1977. pap. text ed. 9.00 o.p. (ISBN 0-8016-0656-X). Mosby.
Bernice P. Bishop Museum - Honolulu. Dictionary Catalog of the Library of the Bernice P. Bishop Museum, 9 Vols. 1964. Set. lib. bdg. 660.00 (ISBN 0-8161-0679-7, Hall Library); lib. bdg. 115.00 1st suppl. 1967 (ISBN 0-8161-0722-X); lib. bdg. 40.00 2nd suppl. 1969 (ISBN 0-8161-0834-X). G K Hall.
Bernice Pauahi Bishop Museum, Honolulu. Museum of Polynesian Ethnology & Natural History: Honolulu Bulletins, Nos. 1-223. 1922-1961. 3741.00 set (ISBN 0-527-02103-2). Kraus Repr.
Bernier, Charles L. & Yerkey, A. Neil. Cogent Communication: Overcoming Reading Overload. LC 78-73794. (Contributions in Librarianship & Information Science: No. 26). (Illus.). 1979. lib. bdg. 29.95x (ISBN 0-313-20893-X, BEC/). Greenwood.
Bernier, Donald R., et al. Nuclear Medicine Technology & Techniques. LC 80-17455. (Illus.). 538p. 1981. pap. text ed. 42.50 (ISBN 0-8016-0662-4). Mosby.
Bernier, Joseph E., jt. ed. see Lifton, Walter M.
Bernier, Olivier. The Eighteenth-Century Women. Barnett, Mary, ed. LC 81-43302. (Illus.). 168p. 1982. 35.00 (ISBN 0-385-17875-1). Doubleday.
--Lafayette: Hero of Two Worlds. (Illus.). 320p. 1983. 17.50 (ISBN 0-525-24181-7, 01699-510). Dutton.
Bernier, Ronald M. Temple Arts of Kerala. (Illus.). 258p. 1982. 99.00x (ISBN 0-940500-79-5, Pub by S Chand India). Asia Bk Corp.

Bernikow, Louise. Among Women. 320p. 1980. 12.95 o.p. (ISBN 0-517-53843-1, Harmony). Crown.

--Among Women. LC 81-47083. 304p. 1981. pap. 4.95i (ISBN 0-06-090878-5, CN 878, CN). Har-Row.

Bernikow, Louise, ed. The World Split Open: Four Centuries of Women Poets in England & America, 1552-1950. LC 74-8582. 1974. pap. 4.95 (ISBN 0-394-71072-X, Vin). Random.

Berninghausen, David K. The Flight from Reason: Essays on Intellectual Freedom in the Academy, the Press, & the Library. LC 74-23236. 189p. 1975. pap. text ed. 9.00 (ISBN 0-8389-0192-1). ALA.

Berns, Gabriel, ed. & tr. see Alberti, Rafael.

Berns, Gabriel, tr. see De Ayala, Ramon P.

Berns, Joel M. What Is Periodontal Disease? (Illus.). 64p. (Orig.). 1982. pap. text ed. 18.00 (ISBN 0-86715-109-9). Quint Pub Co.

Bernstam, Mikhail, jt. auth. see Beichman, Arnold.

Bernstein, jt. auth. see Wong, H.

Bernstein, jt. auth. see Woodward.

Bernstein, Abraham. Education of Urban Populations. (Orig.). 1966. pap. text ed. 4.95x (ISBN 0-685-19721-2). Phila Bk Co.

--Teaching English in High School. 1961. 7.50x (ISBN 0-394-30056-4). Phila Bk Co.

Bernstein, Alan B. The Emergency Public Relations Manual. LC 82-80824. 94p. Repr. of 1982 ed. 75.00 (ISBN 0-686-38793-7). PASE.

Bernstein, Allen. Tax Guide for College Teachers, 1983. 352p. 1982. pap. 16.95 (ISBN 0-916018-21-0). Acad Info. Serv.

Bernstein, Alvin H., ed. see Polybius.

Bernstein, Barton J. & Matusow, Allen J., eds. Twentieth-Century America: Recent Interpretations. 2nd ed. (Orig.). 1972. pap. text ed. 14.95 (ISBN 0-15-592391-9, HC). HarBraceJ.

Bernstein, Basil. Class, Codes, & Control: Theoretical Studies Towards a Sociology of Language. LC 74-9130. 252p. 1975. pap. 4.95 o.p. (ISBN 0-8052-0458-X). Schocken.

Bernstein, Basil, jt. auth. see Brandis, Walter.

Bernstein, Bob. Monday Morning Magic. 64p. (gr. k-6). 1982. 5.95 (ISBN 0-86653-080-0, GA 425). Good Apple.

Bernstein, Bruce & Udell, James. Places & Spaces: The Nineteen Eighty-Two Housing Almanac. 256p. 1982. pap. 7.95 (ISBN 0-448-12335-5, G&D). Putnam Pub Group.

Bernstein, Bruce, jt. auth. see Udell, James.

Bernstein, Carl & Woodward, Bob. All the President's Men. (Illus.). 1976. pap. 3.95 (ISBN 0-446-30703-3). Warner Bks.

Bernstein, Carl, jt. auth. see Woodward, Bob.

Bernstein, Carol, jt. auth. see Bertherat, Therese.

Bernstein, Charles S., ed. Connecticut Real Estate Statutes. 480p. 1983. write for info. looseleaf binder (ISBN 0-88063-007-8). Butterworth Legal Pubs.

--Connecticut Time Limitations. LC 82-71705. 320p. 1982. loose leaf bdr. 39.95 (ISBN 0-88063-001-9). Butterworth Legal Pubs.

Bernstein, D. L. Existence Theorems in Partial Differential Equations. (Annals of Mathematic Studies: No. 23). 1950. pap. 20.00 (ISBN 0-527-02739-1). Kraus Repr.

Bernstein, Douglas A. & Nietzel, Michael T. Introduction to Clinical Psychology. (Psychology Ser.). (Illus.). 1980. text ed. 24.95 (ISBN 0-07-005016-3). McGraw.

Bernstein, Eckhard. German Humanism. (World Authors Ser.). 176p. 1983. lib. bdg. 18.95 (ISBN 0-8057-6537-9, Twayne). G K Hall.

Bernstein, Eduard. Evolutionary Socialism: A Criticism & Affirmation. 2nd ed. LC 61-16649. 1961. pap. 5.50 (ISBN 0-8052-0011-8). Schocken.

Bernstein, Eugene F. Noninvasive Diagnostic Techniques in Vascular Disease. 2nd ed. LC 81-14049. (Illus.). 626p. 1982. text ed. 79.50 (ISBN 0-8016-0807-4). Mosby.

Bernstein, Gail L. Haruko's World: A Japanese Farm Woman & Her Community. LC 82-61783. (Illus.). 192p. 1983. text ed. 19.50x (ISBN 0-8047-1174-7). Stanford U Pr.

Bernstein, George see Cordasco, Francesco.

Bernstein, I. M., jt. auth. see Peckner, Donald.

Bernstein, Ilene N. & Freeman, Howard E. Academic & Entreprenurial Research: The Consequences of Diversity in Federal Evaluation Studies. LC 74-83208. 108p. 1975. text ed. 9.95x (ISBN 0-87154-109-2). Russell Sage.

Bernstein, Irving. The New Deal Collective Bargaining Policy. LC 75-8997. (FDR & the Era of the New Deal Ser.). xi, 178p. 1975. Repr. of 1950 ed. lib. bdg. 27.50 (ISBN 0-306-70703-9). Da Capo.

Bernstein, J. L., jt. auth. see Elonka, Stephen M.

Bernstein, J. S., tr. see Garcia-Marquez, Gabriel.

Bernstein, Jacob. Handbook of Commodity Cycles: A Window on Time. 383p. 1982. 44.95x (ISBN 0-471-08197-3). Ronald Pr.

--The Investor's Quotient: The Psychology of Successful Investing in Commodities & Stock. LC 80-17127. 275p. 1980. 17.95 (ISBN 0-471-07849-2). Wiley.

Bernstein, James D., et al. Rural Health Centers in the United States. LC 79-903. (Rural Health Center Ser.: Vol. I). (Illus.). 1979. prof ref 18.50x (ISBN 0-88410-535-0); pap. 10.00x (ISBN 0-88410-541-5). Ballinger Pub.

Bernstein, Jay, jt. ed. see Rosenberg, Harvey S.

Bernstein, Jeremy. Einstein. (Modern Masters Ser.). 1976. pap. 4.95 (ISBN 0-14-004317-9). Penguin.

--Experiencing Science: Profiles in Discovery. 1980. pap. 5.95 o.p. (ISBN 0-525-47636-9). Dutton.

--Prophet of Energy: Han Bethe. 212p. 1981. pap. 7.25 o.p. (ISBN 0-525-47677-6, 0704-210). Dutton.

Bernstein, Jerrold G. Handbook of Drug Therapy in Psychiatry. (Illus.). 1983. 25.00 (ISBN 0-7236-7028-5). Wright-PSG.

Bernstein, Jerrold G., ed. Clinical Psychopharmacology. LC 76-15733. 166p. 1978. text ed. 19.50 (ISBN 0-7236-0563-7). Wright-PSG.

Bernstein, Joan Z. Health Maintenance Organizations: Opportunities & Problems. F & S Press Book, ed. 1982. 32.95x (ISBN 0-86621-004-0). Ballinger Pub.

Bernstein, Joanne. Fiddle with a Riddle: Write Your Own Riddles. LC 76-11391. (Illus.). (gr. 3-7). 1979. 9.25 (ISBN 0-525-29678-6, 0898-270). Dutton.

Bernstein, Joanne E. Books to Help Children Cope with Separation & Loss. 2nd ed. 304p. 1983. 24.95 (ISBN 0-8352-1484-2). Bowker.

Bernstein, Julian L. Audio Systems. LC 78-2563. 424p. 1978. Repr. of 1966 ed. lib. bdg. 22.00 (ISBN 0-88275-668-0). Krieger.

Bernstein, Kenneth. Music Lover's Europe: A Guidebook & Companion. (Illus.). 192p. 1983. 11.95 (ISBN 0-684-17770-6, ScribT). Scribner.

Bernstein, Leopold A. The Analysis of Financial Statements. LC 78-55533. 1978. 18.50 (ISBN 0-87094-164-X). Dow Jones-Irwin.

Bernstein, Lionel. Renal Function & Renal Failure. 208p. (Orig.). 1965. 8.50 o.p. (ISBN 0-683-00637-1, Pub. by Wiley). Krieger.

Bernstein, Louis. Challenge & Mission. LC 82-60203. 272p. 1982. 13.95 (ISBN 0-88400-081-8). Shengold.

Bernstein, M. H. John J. Chapman. (United States Authors Ser.). 13.95 (ISBN 0-8057-0136-2, Twayne). G K Hall.

Bernstein, Martin & Picker, Martin. Introduction to Music. 4th ed. LC 77-178158. (Illus.). 1972. text ed. 23.95 (ISBN 0-13-489559-2). P-H.

Bernstein, Marver H. Politics of Israel: The First Decade of Statehood. LC 69-13825. Repr. of 1957 ed. lib. bdg. 19.25x (ISBN 0-8371-2036-5, BEPI). Greenwood.

Bernstein, Melvin H., jt. ed. see Hoy, John C.

Bernstein, Merton C. Private Dispute Settlement. LC 68-17521. (Illus.). 1969. 20.95 (ISBN 0-02-903030-7); instr's manual avail. Free Pr.

Bernstein, Norman & Sussex, James, eds. Handbook of Child Psychiatry Consultation. 350p. 1983. text ed. 40.00 (ISBN 0-89335-188-1). SP Med & Sci Bks.

Bernstein, Paul & Green, Robert W. History of Civilization, Since Sixteen Forty-Eight. (Quality Paperback Ser.: No. 65). (Orig.). 1976. pap. 5.95 (ISBN 0-8226-0065-X). Littlefield.

--History of Civilization to Sixteen Forty-Eight. (Quality Paperback: No. 64). (Orig.). 1976. pap. 4.95 (ISBN 0-8226-0064-1). Littlefield.

Bernstein, Peter L. & Heilbroner, Robert L. A Primer on Government Spending. 1968. 3.95 (ISBN 0-394-30750-X). Random.

Bernstein, Philip, jt. auth. see Tsichritzis, Dionysios C.

Bernstein, R., ed. Digital Image Processing for Remote Sensing. LC 77-94520. 1978. 43.95 (ISBN 0-87942-105-3). Inst Electrical.

Bernstein, R. B. Chemical Dynamics Via Molecular & Laser Techniques. (Illus.). 1982. 49.00 (ISBN 0-19-855154-1); pap. 24.95 (ISBN 0-19-855169-X). Oxford U Pr.

Bernstein, Richard J. John Dewey. x, 214p. 1981. lib. bdg. 24.00 (ISBN 0-917930-35-5); pap. text ed. 8.50x (ISBN 0-917930-15-0). Ridgeview.

Bernstein, Richard J., ed. Perspectives on Peirce: Critical Essays on Charles Sanders Peirce. LC 80-13703. ix, 148p. 1980. Repr. of 1965 ed. lib. bdg. 17.50x (ISBN 0-313-22414-5, BEPP). Greenwood.

Bernstein, Robert A. & Dyer, James A. An Introduction to Political Science Methods. (Illus.). 1979. pap. 13.95 ref. ed. (ISBN 0-13-493304-4). P-H.

Bernstein, Rose. Helping Unmarried Mothers. Date not set. 6.95 o.s.i. (ISBN 0-8096-1782-X, Assn Pr). Follett.

Bernstein, Ruth & Bernstein, Stephen. Biology: The Study of Life. 672p. 1982. text ed. 24.95 (ISBN 0-15-505440-6, HC); instr's. manual 3.95 (ISBN 0-15-505441-4); study guide 8.95 (ISBN 0-15-505442-2). HarBraceJ.

Bernstein, Samuel J. The Strands Entwined. LC 80-12740. 171p. 1980. 20.95x (ISBN 0-930350-07-3). NE U Pr.

Bernstein, Serge & Poussin, Charles D. Approximation, 2 Vols. in 1. LC 69-16996. (Fr). 15.95 (ISBN 0-8284-0198-5). Chelsea Pub.

Bernstein, Seymour. With Your Own Two Hands: Self-Discovery Through Music. (Illus.). 320p. 1981. 16.95 (ISBN 0-02-870310-3). Schirmer Bks.

Bernstein, Stephen, jt. auth. see Bernstein, Ruth.

Bernstein, Susan, ed. Dog Digest. 2nd ed. (DBI Bks). (Illus.). 320p. 1975. pap. 7.95 o.s.i. (ISBN 0-695-80597-5). Follett.

Bernstein, Theodore M. Careful Writer: A Modern Guide to English Usage. LC 65-12404. 1965. o. p 14.95 (ISBN 0-689-10038-8); pap. 9.95 (ISBN 0-689-70555-7, 233). Atheneum.

--Dos, Don'ts & Maybes of the English Language. 1982. pap. 8.95 (ISBN 0-8129-6321-0). Times Bks.

Bernstein, William & Cawker, Ruth. Contemporary Canadian Architecture. (Illus.). 192p. 1983. 25.00 (ISBN 0-8038-1281-7). Architectural.

Bernstein-Tarrow, Norma, jt. auth. see Lundsteen, Sara.

Bernthal, John E. & Bankson, Nicholas W. Articulation Disorders. (Illus.). 352p. 1981. text ed. 23.95 (ISBN 0-13-049072-5). P-H.

Bernton, Hal, et al. The Forbidden Fuel: Power Alcohol in the Twentieth Century. LC 81-85112. (Illus.). 312p. 1982. 19.95 (ISBN 0-941726-00-2). Boyd Griffin.

Berntzen, Allen K., jt. auth. see Macy, Ralph W.

Bernussou, J. & Titli, A. Interconnected Dynamical Systems: Stability, Decomposition & Decentralisation. (North-Holland Systems & Control Ser.: Vol. 5). 330p. 1982. 59.50 (ISBN 0-444-86504-7, North Holland). Elsevier.

Bernzweig, Eli. The Nurse's Liability for Malpractice: A Programmed Course. 3rd ed. 368p. 1981. pap. text ed. 16.50 (ISBN 0-07-005058-9, HP); test bank 9.95 (ISBN 0-07-005059-7). McGraw.

Berolzheimer, Ruth, ed. The American Woman's Cook Book. rev ed. (Illus.). 960p. 1973. 19.95 (ISBN 0-385-00732-9). Doubleday.

--Encyclopedic Cookbook. 1962. 12.95 (ISBN 0-448-01366-5, G&D); bride's ed. 12.95 (ISBN 0-448-01367-3). Putnam Pub Group.

Berquist, Maurice. The Doctor Is In, 5 Vol. Set. (Wesleyan Theological Persective Ser.). 1983. write for info. Warner Pr.

Berrebi, E., jt. auth. see Abraham-Frois, Gilbert.

Berreman, Gerald D. Hindus of the Himalayas: Ethnography & Change. 2nd ed. LC 73-156468. (Center for South & Southeast Asia Studies, UC Berkeley). 1972. 34.50x (ISBN 0-520-01423-5); pap. 8.50x (ISBN 0-520-02035-9, CAMPUS66). U of Cal Pr.

Berreman, J. V. Tribal Distribution in Oregon. LC 37-20181. (American Anthropological Association Memoirs). Repr. of 1937 ed. pap. 8.00 (ISBN 0-527-00546-0). Kraus Repr.

Berreth, David, ed. American Paintings: 1830-1915. LC 82-61415. (Illus.). 40p. (Orig.). 1982. pap. 3.00 (ISBN 0-940784-03-3). Miami Univ Art.

Berrick, A. J. An Approach to Algebraic K-Theory. (Research Notes in Mathematics Ser.: No. 56). 120p. 1982. text ed. 16.50 (ISBN 0-273-08529-8). Pitman Pub MA.

Berridge, M. J. see Beament, J. W., et al.

Berrigan, Daniel. Beside the Sea of Glass: The Song of the Lamb. (Classic Prayer Ser.). (Illus.). 1978. pap. 2.50 (ISBN 0-8164-2174-9). Seabury.

--A Book of Parables. 1977. 3.00 (ISBN 0-8164-0328-7). Seabury.

--Prison Poems. 125p. 1982. pap. 6.00 (ISBN 0-686-81791-5). Unicorn Pr.

Berrigan, Sandy. Summer Sleeper. 43p. 1981. pap. 2.00 (ISBN 0-916382-24-9). Telephone Bks.

Berrigan, Ted, jt. auth. see Koch, Kenneth.

Berrill, K. Economic Development with Special Reference to East Asia. (International Economic Association Ser.). 1964. 32.00 (ISBN 0-312-23100-8). St Martin.

Berrill, N. J. Life of Sea Islands. (Our Living World of Nature Ser). (Illus.). 1969. 14.95 (ISBN 0-07-005026-0, P&RB); by subscription 3.95 (ISBN 0-07-046011-6). McGraw.

--Life of the Ocean. (Our Living World of Nature Ser). 1967. 14.95 (ISBN 0-07-005025-2, P&RB); by subscription 3.95 (ISBN 0-07-046007-8). McGraw.

Berrill, N. J., jt. auth. see Karp, Gerald.

Berriman, Algernon E. Historical Metrology. LC 70-91753. Repr. of 1953 ed. lib. bdg. 15.75x (ISBN 0-8371-2424-7, BEHM). Greenwood.

Berrin, Elliott R. Investigative Photography. Date not set. 3.25 (ISBN 0-686-22738-7, TR-77-1). Society Fire Protect.

Berrin, Kathleen & Seligman, Thomas K. The Bay Area Collects: Art from Africa, Oceania, & the Americas. LC 82-71433. (Illus.). 112p. 1982. pap. 7.95 (ISBN 0-88401-040-6). Fine Arts Mus.

Berrington, Hugh B. Backbench Opinion in the House of Commons, 1945-1955. 1974. text ed. write for info. (ISBN 0-08-016748-9). Pergamon.

Berrisford, Judith. Gardening on Chalk, Lime & Clay. 212p. 1979. pap. 6.95 (ISBN 0-571-11129-7). Faber & Faber.

--Rhododencrons & Azaleas. (Illus.). 1973. 17.95 o.p. (ISBN 0-571-04798-X). Faber & Faber.

Berrondo, Marie. Mathematical Games. Dax, Peter & Fitzpatrick, Mariana, trs. (Illus.). 192p. 1983. 15.95 (ISBN 0-13-561399-X); pap. 6.95 (ISBN 0-13-561381-7). P-H.

Berry, Albert. Essays on Industrialization in Colombia. 1983. write for info (ISBN 0-87918-053-6). ASU Lat Am St.

Berry, Ana M. Animals in Art. LC 79-162506. (Tower Bks.). (Illus.). 1971. Repr. of 1929 ed. 34.00x (ISBN 0-8103-3900-5). Gale.

Berry, B. J. City Classification Handbook: Methods & Applications. LC 71-171911. (Urban Research Ser.). 394p. 1972. 52.95 (ISBN 0-471-07115-3, Pub. by Wiley-Interscience). Wiley.

Berry, Bill. Water-Skiing. (Pelham Pictorial Sports Instruction Ser.). (Illus.). 1979. 12.50 o.p. (ISBN 0-7207-1067-7). Transatlantic.

Berry, Brewton. You & Your Superstitions. LC 78-174904. (Illus.). 249p. 1974. Repr. of 1940 ed. 34.00 o.p. (ISBN 0-8103-3985-4). Gale.

Berry, Brian. Geography of Market Centers & Retail Distribution. 1967. pap. 12.95 ref. ed. (ISBN 0-13-351304-1). P-H.

Berry, Brian J. Chicago: Transformations of an Urban System. LC 76-4790. (Contemporary Metropolitan Analysis Ser.). 120p. 1976. pap. 8.95x (ISBN 0-88410-435-4). Ballinger Pub.

--Essays on the Science of Geography: Reflections on a Revolution. cancelled o.s.i. (ISBN 0-88410-428-1). Ballinger Pub.

--Growth Centers in the American Urban System, 2 vols. Incl. Vol. 1. Community Development & Regional Growth in the Sixties & Seventies. LC 73-10362. 208p. text ed. 18.00 o.p. (ISBN 0-88410-400-1); Vol. 2. Working Materials on the U.S. Urban Hierachy. LC 73-10362. 600p. text ed. 25.00 o.p. (ISBN 0-88410-401-X). 1973. Ballinger Pub.

--The Human Consequences of Urbanization. LC 73-86361. (Making of the Twentieth Century Ser). 256p. 1974. pap. text ed. 8.95 o.p. (ISBN 0-312-39865-4). St Martin.

--The Open Housing Question: Race & Housing in Chicago 1966-1976. LC 79-14912. (Illus.). 544p. 1979. prof ref 35.00x (ISBN 0-88410-429-X). Ballinger Pub.

--Social Burdens of Environmental Pollution: Comparative Metropolitan Data Source. LC 76-40419. 624p. 1977. prof ref 29.00x (ISBN 0-88410-427-3). Ballinger Pub.

--Theories of Urban Location. LC 68-8949. (CCG Resource Papers Ser.: No. 1). (Illus.). 1968. pap. text ed. 4.00 o.p. (ISBN 0-89291-048-8). Assn Am Geographers.

Berry, Brian J. & Gillard, Quentin. The Changing Shape of Metropolitan America: Commuting Patterns, Urban Fields & Decentralization Processes, 1960-1970. 1977. prof ref 35.00x (ISBN 0-88410-424-9). Ballinger Pub.

Berry, Brian J. & Horton, Frank E. Urban Environmental Management: Planning for Pollution Control. (Illus.). 448p. 1974. 27.95 (ISBN 0-13-939611-X). P-H.

Berry, Brian J. & Kasarda, John D. Contemporary Urban Ecology. 1977. 26.95 (ISBN 0-02-309050-2, 30905). Macmillan.

Berry, Brian J. L. & Conkling, Edgar C. Geography of Economic Systems. ref. ed. 544p. 1976. 29.95 (ISBN 0-13-351296-7); wkbk. study guide 9.95 (ISBN 0-13-351338-6). P-H.

Berry, C. & Ferguson, J. G. Chapter Six - Discharge, Resist & Special Styles. 75.00x (ISBN 0-686-98198-7, Pub. by Soc Dyers & Colour); pap. 50.00x (ISBN 0-686-98199-5). State Mutual Bk.

Berry, C. L. The Effects of Estrogen Administration on the Male Breast. (Lectures in Toxicology Ser.: No. 15). (Illus.). 1982. 60.00 (ISBN 0-08-029791-9). Pergamon.

Berry, Caroline F., jt. auth. see Shaw, Diana.

Berry, Charles A., jt. ed. see Sells, Saul B.

Berry, Christopher J. Hume, Hegel & Human Nature. 1983. lib. bdg. 41.50 (ISBN 90-247-2682-4, Pub. by Martinus Nijhoff Netherlands). Kluwer Boston.

Berry, Cicely. Voice & the Actor. (Illus.). 149p. 1974. 12.95 (ISBN 0-02-510370-9). Macmillan.

Berry, D. B., jt. auth. see Smith, J. E.

Berry, D. R., jt. auth. see Smith, J. E.

Berry, D. R., ed. see Smith, J. E.

Berry, David, jt. ed. see Smith, John E.

Berry, David R. Biology of Yeast. (Studies in Biology: No. 140). 64p. 1982. pap. text ed. 8.95 (ISBN 0-7131-2838-0). E Arnold.

Berry, Donald, jt. auth. see Lindgren, Bernard.

Berry, Donald S. & Blomme, George W. The Technology of Urban Transportation. 145p. 1971. pap. 1.50 (ISBN 0-686-94040-7, Trans). Northwestern U Pr.

Berry, Dorothea M. & Martin, Gordon P. A Guide to Writing Research Papers. LC 70-139549. (Illus.). 176p. 1972. pap. text ed. 3.95 (ISBN 0-07-005029-5, SP). McGraw.

Berry, Eliot. A Poetry of Force & Darkness: The Fiction of John Hawkes. LC 79-282. (The Milford Ser.: Popular Writers of Today: Vol. 22). 1979. lib. bdg. 9.95x (ISBN 0-89370-132-7); pap. 3.95x (ISBN 0-89370-232-3). Borgo Pr.

Berry, Erick. When Wagon Trains Rolled to Santa Fe. LC 66-12813. (How They Lived Ser.). (Illus.). (gr. 3-6). 1966. PLB 7.12 (ISBN 0-8116-6902-5). Garrard.

Berry, Faith, ed. see Hughes, Langston.

Berry, Frederic A., et al. Handbook of Meteorology. 1947. 55.00 o.p. (ISBN 0-07-005030-9, P&RB). McGraw.

Berry, G. C. & Sroog, C. E. Rigid Chain Polymers: Synthesis & Properties. (Journal of Polymer Science Symposium Ser.: No. 65). 226p. 1979. 33.95x (ISBN 0-471-05802-5). Wiley.

Berry, George R. Interlinear Greek-English New Testament. LC 78-54242. 1978. pap. 13.95 (ISBN 0-8054-1372-3). Broadman.

Berry, Hedley, ed. Contemporary Topics in Pain Management: An Update on Zomepirac, No. 52. 1982. write for info. (ISBN 0-8089-1536-3). Grune.

Berry, I. William. The Great North American Ski Book. (Illus.). 512p. 1982. 24.95 (ISBN 0-684-17654-8, ScribT). Scribner.

--Kids on Skis. rev. ed. (Illus.). 240p. 1982. pap. 6.95 (ISBN 0-684-17782-X, ScribT). Scribner.

Berry, James. My Experiences As an Executioner. Ward, H. Snowden, ed. LC 70-170299. (Illus.). iv, 148p. Repr. of 1892 ed. 27.00 o.p. (ISBN 0-8103-3898-X). Gale.

Berry, James B. Western Forest Trees: A Guide to the Identification of Trees & Woods for Students, Teachers, Farmers & Woodsmen. (Illus.). 8.50 (ISBN 0-8446-1672-9). Peter Smith.

Berry, Jo, jt. auth. see Costales, Claire.

Berry, Joy W. What to Do When Your Mom Or Dad Says "Be Good While You're There!". LC 82-81202. (The Survival Series for Kids). (Illus.). 48p. (gr. 3 up). 1982. PLB 9.25 (ISBN 0-516-02570-8). Childrens.

--What To Do When Your Mom or Dad Says...Don't Hang Around with the Wrong Crowd. Kelly, Orly, ed. (Survival Series for Kids). (Illus.). 48p. (gr. k-6). 1982. 3.95 (ISBN 0-941510-10-7). Living Skills.

--What To Do When Your Mom or Dad Says...Help. Kelly, Orly, ed. (Survival Series for Kids). (Illus.). 48p. (gr. k-6). 1982. 3.95 (ISBN 0-941510-09-3). Living Skills.

--What to Do When Your Mom or Dad Says..."Be Kind to Your Guest!". LC 82-81203. (Survival Series for Kids). (gr. 3 up). 1982. 9.25 (ISBN 0-516-02571-6). Childrens.

--What To Do When Your Mom or Dad Says...Do Something Besides Watch TV. Kelly, Orly, et al, eds. (Survival Series for Kids). (Illus.). 48p. (gr. k-6). 1982. 3.95 (ISBN 0-941510-11-5). Living Skills.

--What to Do When Your Mom or Dad Says "Take Care of Your Clothes!". LC 82-81201. (The Surivial Series for Kids). (Illus.). 48p. (gr. 3 up). 1982. PLB 9.25 (ISBN 0-516-02573-2). Childrens.

--What To Do When Your Mom or Dad Says...Do Your Homework. (Survival Series for Kids). (Illus.). 48p. (gr. k-6). 1982. 3.95 (ISBN 0-941510-08-5). Living Skills.

--What to Do When Your Mom or Dad Says..."Clean Yourself Up!". LC 82-81200. (Survival Series for Kids). (gr. 3 up). 1982. 9.25 (ISBN 0-516-02572-4). Childrens.

Berry, Juliet. Daily Experience in Residential Life. (Library of Social Work). 1975. 18.95x o.p. (ISBN 0-7100-8115-4); pap. 7.95 o.p. (ISBN 0-7100-8116-2). Routledge & Kegan.

Berry, Ken. First Offender: Inside A New Zealand Prison. 192p. 1980. 13.95 (ISBN 0-00-222307-4, Pub. by W Collins Australia). Intl Schol Bk Serv.

Berry, L., ed. Tanzania in Maps. LC 70-654258. (Graphic Perspectives of Developing Countries Ser). (Illus.). 1972. text ed. 34.50x (ISBN 0-8419-0076-0, Africana). Holmes & Meier.

Berry, Leonidas H. I Wouldn't Take Nothin' for My Journey: Two Centuries of an American Minister's Family. 1981. 14.95 (ISBN 0-686-95206-5). Johnson Chi.

Berry, M. Black Resistance - White Law: A History of Institutional Racism in America. 1971. pap. text ed. 15.95 (ISBN 0-13-077735-8). P-H.

--Principles of Cosmology and Gravitation. LC 75-22559. (Illus.). 200p. 1976. 37.50 (ISBN 0-521-21061-5); pap. 12.95x (ISBN 0-521-29028-7). Cambridge U Pr.

Berry, M., ed. Growth & Regeneration of Axons in the Nervous System. (Bibliotheca Anatomica: No. 23). (Illus.). vi, 126p. 1982. pap. 68.50 (ISBN 3-8055-3528-7). S Karger.

Berry, Margaret. Introduction to Systemic Linguistics, Vol. 1. LC 74-83966. 224p. 1975. 21.00 (ISBN 0-312-43365-4). St Martin.

--Introduction to Systemic Linguistics: Levels & Links, Vol. 2. LC 74-83966. 1977. 21.00 (ISBN 0-312-43400-6). St Martin.

Berry, Mary E. Hideyoshi. (Harvard East Asian Ser.: No. 97). (Illus.). 320p. 1982. text ed. 30.00x (ISBN 0-674-39025-3). Harvard U Pr.

Berry, Mary F. Stability. Security & Continuity: Mr. Justice Burton & Decision-Making in the Supreme Court, 1945-1958. LC 77-84772. (Contributions in Legal Studies: No. 1). (Illus.). 1978. lib. bdg. 29.95x (ISBN 0-8371-9798-8, BSS/). Greenwood.

Berry, Mary F. & Blassingame, John W. Long Memory: The Black Experience in America. LC 80-24748. (Illus.). 512p. 1982. 19.95 (ISBN 0-19-502909-7); pap. 11.95 07/1982 (ISBN 0-19-502910-0). Oxford U Pr.

Berry, Michael S. Time: Space & Transition in Anasazi Prehistory. 112p. 1982. 20.00x (ISBN 0-87480-212-1). U of Utah Pr.

Berry, Mildred F. Language Disorders of Children: The Bases & Diagnoses. (Illus.). 1969. 24.95 (ISBN 0-13-522854-9). P-H.

--Teaching Linguistically Handicapped Children. 1980. text ed. 23.95 (ISBN 0-13-893545-9). P-H.

Berry, Newton & Drew, Christopher. The Best of Dial-an-Atheist, Vol. 1. 124p. (Orig.). 1982. pap. 4.00 (ISBN 0-910309-06-X). Am Atheist.

Berry, Patricia. Echo's Subtle Body: Contributions to an Archetypal Psychology. LC 82-19506. 198p. (Orig.). 1982. pap. 9.00 (ISBN 0-88214-313-1). Spring Pubns.

Berry, Paul. The Essential Self: An Introduction to Literature. (Illus.). 480p. 1975. pap. text ed. 14.95 (ISBN 0-07-005048-1, C); instructors' manual 9.95 (ISBN 0-07-005049-X). McGraw.

Berry, Paulette, jt. auth. see Warner, Laverne.

Berry, Philip A. A Review of the Mexican War on Christian Principles: And an Essay on the Means of Preventing War. LC 76-143427. (Peace Movement in America Ser). ix, 87p. 1972. Repr. of 1849 ed. lib. bdg. 9.95x (ISBN 0-89198-057-1). Ozer.

Berry, R. How to Write a Research Paper. 1974. pap. 7.00 (ISBN 0-08-006392-6). Pergamon.

Berry, R. E. Programming Language Translation. (Computers & Their Applications Ser.). 175p. 1981. 44.95 (ISBN 0-470-27305-4). Halsted Pr.

Berry, R. J. Darwin 1882. 12.50 (ISBN 0-12-093180-X). Acad Pr.

--Genetics. (Teach Yourself Ser.). 1973. pap. 2.95 o.p. (ISBN 0-679-10397-X). McKay.

--Neo-Darwinism. (Studies in Biology: No. 144). 72p. 1982. pap. text ed. 8.95 (ISBN 0-7131-2849-6). E Arnold.

Berry, R. Stephen, et al. Physical Chemistry. LC 79-790. 1281p. 1980. comb. text ed. 38.95x (ISBN 0-471-04829-1); solutions manual 10.95 (ISBN 0-471-04844-5). Wiley.

--Physical Chemistry, 3 pts. Incl. Pt. 1. The Structure of Matter. text ed. 22.50x (ISBN 0-471-05824-6); Pt. 2. Matter in Equilibrium Statistical Mechanics & Thermodynamics. text ed. 22.50x (ISBN 0-471-05825-4); Pt. 3. Physical & Chemical Kinetics. 281p. text ed. 18.50x (ISBN 0-471-05823-8). 1980. Wiley.

Berry, Roger L. God's World: His Story. 1980. 14.30 o.p. (ISBN 0-87813-914-1). Christian Light.

Berry, Roland. Berry's Book of How It Works. 1976. 5.95 o.p. (ISBN 0-7136-1585-0). Transatlantic.

Berry, Thomas. Religions of India: School Edition. 1971. pap. 5.95 o.p. (ISBN 0-02-811100-1). Glencoe.

--Tielherd in the Ecological Age. (Tielherd Studies). 1982. 2.00 (ISBN 0-89012-032-3). Anima Pubns.

Berry, Thomas E. The Craft of Writing. 1974. pap. text ed. 4.95 (ISBN 0-07-005051-1, SP). McGraw.

Berry, Wallace. Form in Music: An Examination of Traditional Techniques of Musical Structure & Their Application in Historical & Contemporary Styles. 1966. text ed. 24.95 (ISBN 0-13-329201-0). P-H.

Berry, Wallace & Chudacoff, Edward. Eighteenth Century Imitative Counterpoint: Music for Analysis. (Orig.). 1969. pap. 24.95 (ISBN 0-13-246843-3). P-H.

Berry, Wendell. Clearing. LC 76-27422. 1977. pap. 2.95 o.p. (ISBN 0-15-618051-0, Harv). HarBraceJ.

--The Gift of Good Land: Further Essays Cultural & Agricultural. LC 81-81507. 304p. 1981. 18.00 (ISBN 0-86547-051-0); pap. 9.50 (ISBN 0-86547-052-9). N Point Pr.

--The Memory of Old Jack. LC 75-6530. 223p. 1975. pap. 3.50 (ISBN 0-15-658670-3, Harv). HarBraceJ.

--November 26, 1963. LC 64-19345. (Illus.). 1964. 5.00 o.s.i. (ISBN 0-8076-0263-9). Braziller.

--Recollected Essays, Nineteen Sixty-Five to Nineteen Eighty. LC 80-28812. 352p. 1981. 18.00 (ISBN 0-86547-025-1); pap. 9.00 (ISBN 0-86547-026-X). N Point Pr.

Berry, William, et al. Master Production Scheduling: Principle & Practice. 184p. 1979. 29.00 (ISBN 0-935406-21-2). Am Prod & Inventory.

Berry, William H. Uncle Sam...You Must Be Born Again! 1978. 4.50 o.p. (ISBN 0-533-03106-0). Vantage.

Berry, William L., jt. ed. see Montgomery, Douglas C.

Berryman, Cynthia, ed. see Conference on Communication, Language & Sex, 1st Annual.

Berryman, Gregg. Designing Creative Resumes & Portfolios. (Illus.). 100p. 1983. pap. 7.95 (ISBN 0-86576-047-0). W Kaufmann.

Berryman, Gwen. Doris Archer's Farm Cookery. 12.50 (ISBN 0-392-05381-0, LTB). Sportshelf.

Berryman, John. Henry's Fate & Other Poems. Haffenden, John, selected by. 112p. 1977. 7.95 (ISBN 0-374-16950-0); pap. 3.95 o.p. (ISBN 0-374-51436-4). FS&G.

--Homage to Mistress Bradstreet & Other Poems. LC 68-24596. 1956. pap. 3.50 (ISBN 0-374-50660-4, N337). FS&G.

--Love & Fame. 96p. 1970. 12.95 (ISBN 0-374-19233-2); pap. 3.95 o.p. (ISBN 0-374-51031-8). FS&G.

--Stephen Crane: A Critical Biography. 1982. pap. 9.25 (ISBN 0-374-51732-0). FS&G.

Bers, L., et al. Contributions to the Theory of Partial Differential Equations. Repr. of 1954 ed. pap. 23.00 (ISBN 0-527-02749-9). Kraus Repr.

Bersani, Carl A. Crime & Delinquency: A Reader in Selected Areas. (Illus.). 1970. pap. 14.95 (ISBN 0-02-309100-2, 30910). Macmillan.

Bersani, Leo. Baudelaire & Freud. LC 76-55562. (Quantum Ser.). 1978. 15.95x (ISBN 0-520-03402-3); pap. 2.65 (ISBN 0-520-03535-6). U of Cal Pr.

--The Death of Stephane Mallarme. LC 81-3907. (Cambridge Studies in French). 140p. 1982. 19.95 (ISBN 0-521-23863-3). Cambridge U Pr.

Bersani, Leo, ed. see Flaubert, Gustave.

Bersoff, Edward, et al. Software Configuration Management: An Investment in Product Integrity. 1980. 29.95 (ISBN 0-13-821769-6). P-H.

Berson, Dvera & Roy, Sander. Pain-Free Arthritis. 1979. lib. bdg. 11.95 o.p. (ISBN 0-8161-6685-4, Large Print Bks). G K Hall.

Berson, Ginny. Making a Show of It: A Guide to Concert Production. Worley, Jo-Lynne, et al, eds. 100p. (Orig.). 1980. pap. text ed. 4.95 (ISBN 0-686-97699-1). Redwood Records.

Berson, Harold. Barrels to the Moon. (Illus.). 32p. 1982. 9.95 (ISBN 0-698-20551-0, Coward). Putnam Pub Group.

--Kassim's Shoes. LC 77-4688. (Illus.). (gr. k-3). 1977. reinforced lib. bdg. 5.95 o.p. (ISBN 0-517-53063-5). Crown.

--The Thief Who Hugged a Moonbeam. LC 70-190382. (Illus.). 40p. (ps-3). 1972. 7.95 (ISBN 0-395-28767-7, Clarion). HM.

Berson, Minnie, ed. Opening, Mixing, Matching. (Illus.). 44p. 1.50x (ISBN 0-87173-003-0). ACEI.

Berson, Misha, jt. ed. see Crane, Debra J.

Berson, S. A. & Yalow, R. S., eds. Peptide Hormones, 2 Vols. LC 72-93088. (Methods in Investigative & Diagnostic Endocrinology: Vol. 2). 1200p. 1973. Set. 285.00 (ISBN 0-444-10453-4, North-Holland). Elsevier.

Berssen, William. Pacific Boating Almanac 1983: Northern California & Nevada Edition. annual ed. 432p. 1982. pap. 8.95 (ISBN 0-930030-29-X). Western Marine Ent.

--Pacific Boating Almanac 1983: Oregon, Washington, British Columbia & Alaska Edition. annual ed. 432p. 1982. pap. 8.95 (ISBN 0-930030-30-3). Western Marine Ent.

--Pacific Boating Almanac 1983: Southern California, Arizona, Baja Edition. annual ed. 432p. 1982. pap. 8.95 (ISBN 0-930030-28-1). Western Marine Ent.

Berssenbrugge, Mei-Mei. The Heat Bird. (Burning Deck Poetry Ser.). 74p. 1983. 15.00 (ISBN 0-930901-02-9); pap. 4.00 (ISBN 0-930901-03-7). Burning Deck.

Berst, Charles A., ed. Shaw & Religion. LC 81-956. (Shaw: the Annual of Bernard Shaw Studies: Vol 1). 264p. 1981. 16.95x (ISBN 0-271-00280-8). Pa St U Pr.

Berst, Jesse, jt. auth. see Segal, Hillel.

Berstecher, Dieter, jt. auth. see Edding, Friedrich.

Berstein, Leonard. Findings. (Illus.). 1982. 17.95 (ISBN 0-671-42919-1). S&S.

Berstein, M. D. & Iotti, R. C., eds. Advances In Containment Design & Analysis. 127p. 1982. 30.00 (G00214). ASME.

Berstein, Richard K. Diabetes: The Glucograf Method for Normalizing Blood Sugar. (Illus.). 320p. 1981. 14.95 (ISBN 0-517-54155-6). Crown.

Berstein, Samuel. French Political & Intellectual History. 224p. 1983. pap. 24.95 (ISBN 0-87855-938-8). Transaction Bks.

Bertaccini, G., ed. Mediators & Drugs in Gastrointestinal Motility II: Endogenous & Exogenous Agents. (Handbook of Experimental Pharmacology: Vol. 59, II). (Illus.). 460p. 1982. 139.00 (ISBN 0-387-11333-9). Springer-Verlag.

Bertagnolli, Olivia & Rackham, Jeff, eds. Creativity & the Writing Process. 211p. 1982. pap. text ed. 8.95x (ISBN 0-673-15732-6). Scott F.

Bertaux, Daniel, ed. Biography & Society: The Life History Approach in the Social Sciences. (Sage Studies in International Sociology: Vol. 23). 308p. 1981. 25.00 (ISBN 0-8039-9800-7). Sage.

Berteaux, H. O. Buoy Engineering. LC 75-20046. (Ocean Engineering Ser). 336p. 1976. 49.95x (ISBN 0-471-07156-0, Pub. by Wiley-Interscience). Wiley.

Bertele, Umberto & Brioschi, Francesco. Nonserial Dynamic Programming. (Mathematics in Science & Engineering Ser.: Vol. 91). 1972. 43.50 (ISBN 0-12-093450-7). Acad Pr.

Bertensson, Sergei & Leyda, Jay. Sergei Rachmaninoff: A Lifetime in Music. LC 55-10065. (Illus.). 1956. 25.00x o.p. (ISBN 0-8147-0044-6). NYU Pr.

Bertensson, Sergei, jt. ed. see Leyda, Jay.

Bertherat, Therese & Bernstein, Carol. The Body Has Its Reasons. 1979. pap. 3.50 (ISBN 0-380-44321-X, 61788-9). Avon.

Berthet, P., jt. auth. see Lamy, A.

Berthiaume, Guy. Les Roles du Mageiros: Estudes sur la Boucherie la Cuisine et le Sacrifice dans la Grece Ancienne. (Mnemosyne Ser.: 70, Suppl.). (Illus.). xxvi, 141p. 1982. pap. write for info. (ISBN 90-04-06554-7). E J Brill.

Berthier, A. M. Spectral Theory & Wave Operators for the Schrodinger Equation. (Research Notes in Mathematics Ser.: No. 71). 256p. 1982. pap. text ed. 27.50 (ISBN 0-273-08562-X). Pitman Pub MA.

Berthier, P. Guillaume. Observations sur le Contrat Social de J. J. Rousseau. (Rousseauism, 1788-1797). 1978. Repr. lib. bdg. 88.00x o.p. (ISBN 0-8287-0084-2). Clearwater Pub.

Berthoff, Ann E. Forming-Thinking-Writing: The Composing Imagination. LC 78-3485. 248p. 1982. pap. text ed. 7.75x (ISBN 0-86709-027-8). Boynton Cook Pub.

--The Making of Meaning: Metaphors, Models, & Maxims for Writing Teachers. LC 81-9948. 224p. (Orig.). 1981. pap. text ed. 8.75x (ISBN 0-86709-003-0). Boynton Cook Pubs.

Berthoff, Warner. The Ferment of Realism: American Literature 1884-1919. LC 80-42335. 352p. 1981. 49.50 (ISBN 0-521-24092-1); pap. 13.95 (ISBN 0-521-28435-X). Cambridge U Pr.

Berthoff, Werner. A Literature Without Qualities: American Writing Since 1945. LC 78-57305. (Quantum Bks.). 1979. 13.95 (ISBN 0-520-03696-4). U of Cal Pr.

Berthold, Margot. A History of World Theater. Simmons, Edith, tr. LC 70-127203. (Illus.). 733p. 1972. 35.00 (ISBN 0-8044-2037-8); pap. 14.95 (ISBN 0-8044-6045-0). Ungar.

Bertholdi, Franz W. Von see Von Bertholdi, Franz W.

Bertholf, Robert. Robert Duncan: A Descriptive Bibliography. 1983. cancelled (ISBN 0-87338-268-4). Kent St U Pr.

Bertholf, Robert J. & Levitt, Annette S., eds. William Blake & the Moderns. 352p. 1982. 39.59x (ISBN 0-87395-615-X); pap. 14.95x (ISBN 0-87395-616-8). State U NY Pr.

Bertholle, Louisette. French Cuisine for All. Manheim, Mary, tr. LC 78-1235. (Illus.). 512p. 1981. 19.95 (ISBN 0-385-13087-2). Doubleday.

Berthollet, Claude-Louis. Elemens De L'art De la Teinture. Repr. of 1804 ed. 235.00 o.p. (ISBN 0-8287-0085-0). Clearwater Pub.

--Essai de Statique Chimique. Repr. of 1803 ed. 303.00 o.p. (ISBN 0-8287-0086-9). Clearwater Pub.

--Researches into the Laws of Chemical Affinity. 2nd ed. LC 65-23404. 1966. Repr. of 1809 ed. 27.50 (ISBN 0-306-70914-7). Da Capo.

Berthoud, Jacques. Joseph Conrad: The Major Phase. LC 77-8242. (British Authors Ser.). 1978. 27.95 (ISBN 0-521-21742-3); pap. 9.95x (ISBN 0-521-29273-5). Cambridge U Pr.

Berthoud, Richard & Brown, Joan C. Poverty & the Development of Anti-Poverty Policy in the U. K. (Policy Studies Institute). 288p. 1981. text ed. 27.00x (ISBN 0-435-83102-X). Heinemann Ed.

Berthouex, P. Mac & Rudd, Dale F. Strategy of Pollution Control. LC 76-29008. 579p. 1977. text ed. 39.95x (ISBN 0-471-74449-2). Wiley.

Berthrong, Donald J. Indians of Northern Indiana & Southwestern Michigan: An Historical Report on Indian Use & Occupancy of Northern Indiana & Southwestern Michigan. Horr, David A., ed. (North Central & Northeastern Indians - American Indian Ethnohistory Ser.). 1974. lib. bdg. 38.00 o.s.i. (ISBN 0-8240-0801-4). Garland Pub.

Berthrong, Donald J., ed. see Conner, Daniel E.

Berti. Florence. pap. 13.95 (ISBN 0-935748-36-9). ScalaBooks.

--Uffizzi. pap. 13.95 (ISBN 0-935748-40-7). ScalaBooks.

Berti, Luciano, intro. by. The Official Catalogue of the Uffizi. (Illus.). 1980. 530.00x (ISBN 88-7038-017-3, Centro Di). Gale.

Bertier de Sauvigny, G. de see De Bertier de Sauvigny, G. & Pinkney, David H.

Bertin, M. J., ed. Seminaire de Theorie des Nombres: Paris 1980-1982. (Progress in Mathematics Ser.: Vol. 22). 360p. 1982. text ed. 20.00 (ISBN 3-7643-3066-X). Birkhauser.

Bertin, P., jt. auth. see Pellerin, D.

Bertini, Aldo, ed. see Botticelli, Sandro.

Bertisch, Jan, ed. see Harvey, Bill.

Bertling, Ed, jt. auth. see Leen, Edie.

Berto, Giuseppe. Sky Is Red. Davidson, Angus, tr. from It. LC 76-138575. 1971. Repr. of 1948 ed. lib. bdg. 19.00x (ISBN 0-8371-5774-9, BESR). Greenwood.

Berto, Hazel. Cooking with Honey. (Illus.). 192p. 1972. 4.95 o.p. (ISBN 0-517-50115-5). Crown.

Bertocci, P. A. Empirical Argument for God in Late British Thought. Repr. of 1938 ed. 22.00 o.s.i. (ISBN 0-527-07300-8). Kraus Repr.

Bertocci, Peter A. The Goodness of God. LC 80-6094. (Illus.). 356p. (Orig.). 1981. lib. bdg. 22.25 (ISBN 0-8191-1636-X); pap. text ed. 12.75 (ISBN 0-8191-1637-8). U Pr of Amer.

Bertolet, Mary M. & Goldsmith, Lee S., eds. Hospital Liability: Law & Tactics. 4th ed. LC 79-92666. 789p. 1980. text ed. 35.00 (ISBN 0-686-65589-3). PLI.

Bertolino, James. Employed. 65p. 1972. 2.95 o.p. (ISBN 0-87886-019-3). Ithaca Hse.

--New & Selected Poems. LC 77-81274. (Poetry Ser). 1978. pap. 3.95 (ISBN 0-915604-14-0). Carnegie-Mellon.

--Precint Kali & the Gertruce Spicer Story. LC 81-80548. (Illus.). 108p. 1981. pap. 4.00 (ISBN 0-89823-034-9). New Rivers Pr.

Bertolotti, M., ed. Physical Processes in Laser-Materials Interactions. (NATO ASI Series B, Physics: Vol. 84). 535p. 1983. 69.50x (ISBN 0-306-41107-5, Plenum Pr). Plenum Pub.

Bertolucci, Michael D., jt. auth. see Harris, Daniel C.

Berton, Pierre. Klondike Fever: The Life & Death of the Last Great Stampede. (Illus.). 1958. 15.45 (ISBN 0-394-43206-1). Knopf.

Bertonasco, Marc F., jt. auth. see Miles, Robert.

Bertone, Pamela, et al. Introduction to American & Texas Government. (Illus.). 1979. pap. 10.95 o.p. (ISBN 0-88408-117-6); tchrs.' manual avail. o.p. Sterling Swift.

Bertotti-Scamozzi, Ottavio. The Buildings & Designs of Andrea Palladio, 2 vols. 1976. boxed o.p. 400.00x o.p. (ISBN 0-685-73875-2); Plates. boxed 200.00x o.p. (ISBN 0-8139-0932-5); 30 plates o.p. 30.00x o.p. (ISBN 0-686-67584-3); 10 plates 20.00x o.p. (ISBN 0-8139-0933-3); eng. trans. only 50.00x o.p. (ISBN 0-8139-0934-1). U Pr of Va.

Bertram & Kincade. Nuclear Proliferation in the 1980's. LC 82-42602. 290p. 1983. 27.50x (ISBN 0-312-57975-6). St Martin.

Bertram, Christoph, ed. Third-World Conflict & International Security. 128p. 1982. 49.00x (ISBN 0-333-32955-4, Pub. by Macmillan England). State Mutual Bk.

Bertram, Christopher. America's Security in the 1980's. LC 82-16814. 200p. 1982. 25.00x (ISBN 0-312-02199-2). St Martin.

Bertram, E. G. & Moore, Keith L. An Atlas of the Human Brain & Spinal Cord. (Illus.). 275p. 1982. text ed. 15.95 (ISBN 0-683-00610-X). Williams & Wilkins.

Bertram, G. L. Conservation of Sirenia: Current Status & Perspectives for Action. 1974. pap. 7.50 (ISBN 2-88032-023-2, IUCN35, IUCN). Unipub.

Bertram, James M. First Act in China: The Story of the Sian Mutiny. LC 74-31223. (China in the 20th Century Ser). Orig. Title: Crisis in China. (Illus.). xxii, 284p. 1975. Repr. of 1938 ed. lib. bdg. 35.00 (ISBN 0-306-70687-3). Da Capo.

--Unconquered: Journal of a Year's Adventure Among the Fighting Peasants of North China. (China in the 20th Century Ser). (Illus.). ix, 340p. 1975. Repr. of 1939 ed. lib. bdg. 39.50 (ISBN 0-306-70688-1). Da Capo.

Bertrand, A. R., jt. auth. see Kohnke, Helmut.

Bertrand, J. W. & Wortmann, J. C. Production Control & Information Systems for Component Manufacturing Shops. (Studies in Production & Engineering Economics: Vol. 1). 1981. 70.25 (ISBN 0-444-41964-0). Elsevier.

Bertrand, Joseph. Calcul Des Probabilites. 2nd ed. LC 78-113114. 389p. (Fr.). 1972. text ed. 13.95 (ISBN 0-8284-0262-0). Chelsea Pub.

Bertrand, Louis A. Gaspard De la Nuit: Fantasies in the Manner of Rembrandt & Callot. Wright, John, tr. from Fr. 1977. pap. text ed. 11.50 (ISBN 0-8191-0287-3). U Pr of Amer.

Bertrand, Trent. Thailand: Case Study of Agricultural Input & Output Pricing. (Working Paper: No. 385). ix, 134p. 1980. 5.00 (ISBN 0-686-36080-X, WP-0385). World Bank.

Bertsch, Gary, et al. Comparing Political System: Power & Policy in Three Worlds. 2nd ed. 548p. 1982. text ed. 19.95 (ISBN 0-471-08446-8); avail. tchrs.' manual (ISBN 0-471-86600-8). Wiley.

Bertsch, Gary K. Policy Making in Communist Party States. (CISE Learning Package Ser.: No. 10). (Illus.). 114p. (Orig.). 1975. pap. text ed. 4.00x (ISBN 0-936876-25-5). Learn Res Intl Stud.

--Power & Policy in Communist System. LC 77-26642. 177p. 1978. pap. text ed. 11.95 o.p. (ISBN 0-471-02709-X). Wiley.

--Power & Policy in Communist Systems. 2nd ed. LC 81-19715. 192p. 1982. text ed. 10.95 (ISBN 0-471-09005-0). Wiley.

Bertsch, Gary K., ed. Global Policy Studies. (Sage Focus Editions). (Illus.). 1982. 20.00 (ISBN 0-8039-0781-8); pap. 9.95 (ISBN 0-8039-0782-6). Sage.

Bertsch, Gary K. & McIntyre, John R., eds. National Security & Technology Transfer: The Strategic Dimensions of East-West Trade. 300p. 1983. price not set (ISBN 0-86531-614-7). Westview.

Bertsch, Gary K., et al. Comparing Political Systems: Power & Policy in Three Worlds. LC 77-27575. 515p. 1978. text ed. 21.95 (ISBN 0-471-02674-3). Wiley.

Bertsch, Judith, jt. ed. see Treacy, Margaret.

Bertsch, Lory. Willie Visits Tulip Time. 64p. 1983. 4.50 (ISBN 0-682-49980-3). Exposition.

Bertsekas, Dimitri P. Constrained Optimization & Lagrange Multipler Methods. (Computer Science & Applied Mathematics Ser.). 1982. 55.00 (ISBN 0-12-093480-9). Acad Pr.

Bertsekas, Dimitri P. & Shreve, Steven E. Stochastic Optimal Control: The Discrete Time Case. (Mathematics in Science & Engineering Ser.). 1978. 52.50 (ISBN 0-12-093260-1). Acad Pr.

Bertucci, Bob, jt. auth. see Siroky, Mike.

Bertucci, Bob, jt. auth. see Peterson, James A.

Berube, Maurice R. The Urban University in America. LC 77-87917. 1978. lib. bdg. 25.00x (ISBN 0-313-20031-9, BUU/). Greenwood.

Berulfsen, B. & Svenkerud, A. Norwegian Deluxe Dictionary: English-Norse. 1968. 100.00x (ISBN 82-02-06627-1, N461). Vanous.

Berven, Ken. Blest Be the Tie That Frees. LC 73-83784. 104p. 1973. pap. 2.95 o.p. (ISBN 0-8066-1337-8, 10-0775). Augsburg.

Berwanger, Eugene H. The Frontier Against Slavery: Western Anti-Negro Prejudice & the Slavery Extension Controversy. LC 67-21850. 1967. 10.00 o.p. (ISBN 0-252-74542-6); pap. 3.45 o.p. (ISBN 0-252-00158-3). U of Ill Pr.

Berwick, Donald M., et al. Cholesterol, Children, & Heart Disease: An Analysis of Alternatives. (Illus.). 416p. 1980. 39.50x (ISBN 0-19-502669-1). Oxford U Pr.

Berwitz, Clement J. The Job Analysis Approach to Affirmative Action. LC 75-11660. 327p. 1975. 39.95 o.p. (ISBN 0-471-07157-9, Pub. by Wiley-Interscience). Wiley.

Berzoa, Morton, jt. ed. see Leonbardt, Barbara A.

Berzonsky. Adolescent Development. 1981. 23.95 (ISBN 0-02-471360-0). Macmillan.

Bes & Geraud. Cerebral Circulation & Neurotransmitters: Proceedings. (International Congress Ser.: No. 507). 1980. 51.50 (ISBN 0-444-90129-9). Elsevier.

Besalel, Victoria A., jt. auth. see Azrin, Nathan H.

Besalel, Victoria B., jt. auth. see Azrin, Nathan.

Besant, Annie. From the Outer Court to the Inner Sanctum. Nicholson, Shirley, ed. LC 82-42703. 130p. 1983. pap. 4.50 (ISBN 0-8356-0574-4, Quest). Theos Pub Hse.

--Selection of the Social & Political Pamphlets of Annie Besant 1874-1890. LC 78-114024. 1970. 37.50x (ISBN 0-678-00638-5). Kelley.

Besant, C. B. Computer-Aided Design & Manufacture. 2nd ed. LC 79-40971. (Engineering Science Ser.). 228p. 1983. 54.95 (ISBN 0-470-27372-0); pap. 24.95 (ISBN 0-470-27373-9). Halsted Pr.

Besant, Walter. East London. LC 79-56945. (The English Working Class Ser.). 1980. lib. bdg. 32.00 o.s.i. (ISBN 0-8240-0100-1). Garland Pub.

Beschner & Friedman, eds. Youth Drug Abuse: Problems, Issues, & Treatment. LC 78-21197. 1979. 28.95x (ISBN 0-669-02804-5). Lexington Bks.

Besdime, Richard W., jt. auth. see Rowe, John W.

Besemeres, John. Socialist Population Politics: The Political Implications of Demographic Trends in the USSR & Eastern Europe. LC 80-65260. 1980. 30.00 (ISBN 0-87332-154-5). M E Sharpe.

Besford, Pat, compiled by. Encyclopaedia of Swimming. 2nd ed. LC 76-16687. 1977. 10.00 o.p. (ISBN 0-312-25060-6). St Martin.

Besharov, Douglas J. Protecting Abused & Neglected Children: Identification & Action. 1983. pap. text ed. price not set (ISBN 0-8391-1797-3, 17949). Univ Park.

Besier, Rudolf. The Barretts of Wimpole Street. (Illus.). 1930. 9.95 (ISBN 0-316-09223-1). Little.

Beskow, Elsa. Pelle's New Suit. (Illus.). (ps-1). 1929. PLB 12.89 (ISBN 0-06-020496-6, HarpJ). Har-Row.

--Peter's Adventures in Blueberry Land. La Farge, Sheila, tr. from Swedish. LC 74-22633. (Illus.). (ps-2). 1975. 6.95 o.s.i. (ISBN 0-440-04434-0, Sey Lawr); PLB 6.46 o.s.i. (ISBN 0-440-04435-9). Delacorte.

Beskow, Per. Strange Tales About Jesus: A Survey of Unfamiliar Gospels. LC 82-16001. 144p. 1983. pap. 6.95 (ISBN 0-8006-1686-3, 1-1686). Fortress.

Besmer, Fremont E. Horses, Musicians & Gods: The Hausa Cult of Spirit Possession. 272p. 1983. 35.00x (ISBN 0-89789-020-5). J F Bergin.

--Kidan Daran Salla: Music for the Eve of the Muslim Festivals of Id Al-Fitr & Id Al-Kabir in Kano, Nigeria. (African Humanities Ser.). (Illus.). 84p. (Orig.). 1974. pap. text ed. 4.00 (ISBN 0-941934-10-1). Ind U Afro-Amer Arts.

Besnard, M. & Coursodon, J. P. Ecritures: Techniques de Composition. 1972. 12.95 (ISBN 0-02-309150-9). Macmillan.

Besnard, Philippe, ed. The Sociological Domain: The Durkheimians & the Founding of French Sociology. LC 82-9485. (Illus.). 336p. Date not set. price not set (ISBN 0-521-23876-5). Cambridge U Pr.

Besner, Edward & Ferrigno, Peter. Practical Endodontics: A Clinical Guide. (Illus.). 184p. 1981. text ed. 22.00 (ISBN 0-683-00607-X). Williams & Wilkins.

Besner, Hilda F. & Robinson, Sandra J. Understanding & Solving your Police Marriage Problems. (Illus.). 174p. 1982. pap. 12.75x (ISBN 0-398-04707-3). C C Thomas.

Bespaloff, Alexis. The New Signet Book of Wine. 1980. pap. 3.50 (ISBN 0-451-12045-0, AE2045, Sig). NAL.

--New Signet Book of Wine. (Orig.). 1982. pap. 3.50 (ISBN 0-451-12045-0, AE2045, Sig). NAL.

Bess, C. W. Sparkling Object Sermons for Children. (Object Lesson Ser.). 120p. (Orig.). 1982. pap. 4.50 (ISBN 0-8010-0824-7). Baker Bk.

Bess, James L., ed. Motivating Professors to Teach Effectively. LC 81-48583. 1982. 7.95x (ISBN 0-87589-924-2, TL-10). Jossey-Bass.

Besselievre, Edmond & Schwartz, Max. The Treatment of Industrial Waste. 2nd ed. 1976. 36.50 (ISBN 0-07-005047-3, P&RB). McGraw.

Besser, G. M. & Martini, Luciano, eds. Clinical Neuroendocrinology, Vol. 2. 450p. 1982. 47.50 (ISBN 0-12-093602-X). Acad Pr.

Besser, Gretchen R. Nathalie Sarraute. (World Authors Ser.). 1979. lib. bdg. 13.95 (ISBN 0-8057-6376-7, Twayne). G K Hall.

Besserer, C. W. Missile Engineering Handbook. 600p. 1958. 27.50 o.p. (ISBN 0-442-00720-5, Pub. by Van Nos Reinhold). Krieger.

Bessick, Clarence E. Shifting Sands. 1978. 6.95 o.p. (ISBN 0-533-03482-5). Vantage.

Bessie, Alvah. Men in Battle. (Illus.). 352p. 1980. pap. 1.95 o.p. (ISBN 0-523-40037-3). Pinnacle Bks.

Besson, Pablo, tr. from Greek. Nuevo Testamento De Nuestro Senor Jesucristo. 576p. (Span.). 1981. pap. 6.50 cancelled (ISBN 0-311-48710-6, Edit Mundo). Casa Bautista.

Best & Ross. River Pollution Studies. 102p. 1982. 30.00x (ISBN 0-85323-363-2, Pub. by Liverpool Univ England). State Mutual Bk.

Best, Alan C. & Blij, Harm J. An African Survey. LC 76-44520. 626p. 1977. text ed. 32.95 (ISBN 0-471-20063-8). Wiley.

Best, Deborah L., jt. auth. see Williams, John E.

Best, Don & Freeman, Jim. Crystal Clarinets: A Coffee Table Book of Nice. LC 80-83629. (Illus.). 96p. (Orig.). pap. 10.00 (ISBN 0-938104-00-4). Cosmotic Concerns.

Best, E. & Wilson, R. McL., eds. Text & Interpretation. LC 78-2962. 1979. 44.50 (ISBN 0-521-22021-1). Cambridge U Pr.

Best, G. A. & Ross, S. L. River Pollution Studies. 92p. 1977. pap. 10.50x o.p. (ISBN 0-8476-2451-X). Rowman.

Best, Gary D. Herbert Hoover: The Postpresidential Years, 1933-1964, 2 Vols. 875p. 1983. Set. 75.00 (ISBN 0-8179-7761-9). Hoover Inst Pr.

--The Politics of American Individualism: Herbert Hoover in Transition, 1918-1921. LC 75-16960. 202p. 1975. lib. bdg. 25.00x (ISBN 0-8371-8160-7, BPA/). Greenwood.

--To Free a People: American Jewish Leaders & the Jewish Problem in Eastern Europe, 1890 to 1914. LC 81-4265. (Contributions in American History Ser.: No. 98). 240p. 1982. lib. bdg. 27.50 (ISBN 0-313-22532-X, BTO/). Greenwood.

Best, Geoffrey. Honour Among Men & Nations: Transformations of an Idea. 112p. 1982. 13.50x (ISBN 0-8020-2459-9); pap. 7.50 (ISBN 0-8020-6472-8). U of Toronto Pr.

--War & Society in Revolutionary Europe 1770-1870. LC 82-3261. 336p. 1982. 27.50x (ISBN 0-312-85551-6). St Martin.

Best, Joan & Erikson, Kate. Two Recipe Index, 1982. 250p. 1983. pap. text ed. 9.95 (ISBN 0-686-38724-4). Home Index Pubns.

Best, Joel, jt. auth. see Luckenbill, David F.

Best, John. Research in Education. 4th ed. (Illus.). 400p. 1981. text ed. 24.95 (ISBN 0-13-774026-3). P-H.

Best, John H., ed. Benjamin Franklin on Education. LC 62-20697. (Orig.). 1962. 10.00 (ISBN 0-686-82985-9); pap. text ed. 4.50x (ISBN 0-8077-1077-6). Tchrs Coll.

Best, Judith A. The Mainstream of Western Political Thought. LC 80-11042. 149p. 1980. text ed. 19.95 (ISBN 0-87705-271-9); pap. text ed. 9.95 (ISBN 0-87705-243-3). Human Sci Pr.

Best, Kenneth Y. Cultural Policy in Liberia. (Studies & Documents on Cultural Policies). (Illus.). 59p. 1974. pap. 5.00 o.p. (ISBN 92-3-101160-X, U132, UNESCO). Unipub.

Best, Leo, jt. auth. see Hein, Morris.

Best, Michael H. & Connolly, William E. The Politicized Economy. 2nd ed. 224p. 1982. pap. 8.95 (ISBN 0-669-04005-3). Heath.

Best, Michael R., ed. see Albertus Magnus.

Best, Otto F. Peter Weiss. Molinaro, Ursule, tr. from Ger. LC 75-10104. (Literature and Life Ser.). 170p. 1976. 11.95 (ISBN 0-8044-2038-6). Ungar.

Best Report Staff, ed. The Book of Bests. 1983. 14.95 (ISBN 0-89696-196-6). Dodd.

Best, Robert S. Faith, & Other Poems. 1983. 5.95 (ISBN 0-533-05536-9). Vantage.

Best, Robin H. Land Use & Living Space. 240p. 1981. 25.00x (ISBN 0-416-73760-9); pap. 12.95x (ISBN 0-416-73770-6). Methuen Inc.

Best, Robin H. & Rogers, Alan W. The Urban Countryside: The Land-Use Structure of Small Towns & Villages in England & Wales. 1973. 12.75x o.p. (ISBN 0-571-09961-0). Transatlantic.

Best, Simon & Kollerstrom, Nick. Planting by the Moon. 1982. pap. 3.95 (ISBN 0-917086-35-X, Pub. by Astro Comp Serv). Para Res.

Best, Thomas W. Jacob Bidermann. (World Authors Ser.). 1974. lib. bdg. 15.95 (ISBN 0-8057-2154-1, Twayne). G K Hall.

--Macropedius. (World Authors Ser.). lib. bdg. 15.95 (ISBN 0-8057-2560-1, Twayne). G K Hall.

--Reynard the Fox. (World Authors Ser.: No. 673). 170p. 1983. lib. bdg. 18.95 (ISBN 0-8057-6520-4, Twayne). G K Hall.

Best, W. E. God Forgives Sinners. 1978. pap. 2.95 o.p. (ISBN 0-8010-0720-8). Baker Bk.

Bester, Alfred. The Deceivers. 304p. 1982. pap. 2.50 (ISBN 0-523-48524-7). Pinnacle Bks.

--Golem One Hundred. (Illus.). 1980. 11.95 o.p. (ISBN 0-671-25321-2). S&S.

--The Stars My Destination. (Science Fiction Ser). 244p. 1975. Repr. of 1957 ed. lib. bdg. 12.50 o.p. (ISBN 0-8398-2300-2, Gregg). G K Hall.

Bester, Alred. Demolished Man. pap. 1.25 o.p. (ISBN 0-451-07585-4, Y7585, Sig). NAL.

Besterfield & O'Hagan. Technical Sketching for Engineers, Technologists & Technicians. 1983. text ed. 19.95 (ISBN 0-8359-7540-1). Reston.

Besterfield, Dale H. Quality Control: A Practical Approach. (Illus.). 1979. ref. 22.95 (ISBN 0-13-745232-2). P-H.

Besterman, Theodore. Voltaire Essays, & Another. LC 80-17075. (Illus.). 181p. 1980. Repr. of 1962 ed. lib. bdg. 20.50x (ISBN 0-313-22527-3, BEVO). Greenwood.

Besterman, Theodore, ed. see Crawley, Ernest.

Beston, Henry. The Outermost House. 1976. pap. 4.95 (ISBN 0-14-004315-2). Penguin.

Bestor, Dorothy K. Aside from Teaching, What in the World Can You Do? Career Strategies for Liberal Arts Graduates. LC 82-2009. 352p. (Orig.). 1982. 25.00 (ISBN 0-295-95960-6); pap. 9.95 (ISBN 0-295-95903-7). U of Wash Pr.

Bestor, William S., jt. ed. see Leakey, L. S.

Betancourt, Jeane. Am I Normal? 96p. 1983. pap. 1.95 (ISBN 0-380-82040-4, 82040-4, Flare). Avon.

--Dear Diary. 112p. 1983. pap. 1.95 o.p. (ISBN 0-380-82057-9, 82057-9, Flare). Avon.

Betancourt, Juan, ed. From the Palm Tree: The Cuban Revolution in Retrospect. 224p. 1983. 12.00 (ISBN 0-8184-0344-6). Lyle Stuart.

Betancourt, Roger & Clague, Christopher. Capacity Utilization: A Theoretical & Empirical Analysis. LC 80-22410. (Illus.). 320p. 1981. 49.50 (ISBN 0-521-23583-9). Cambridge U Pr.

Betcherman, Barbara. Suspicions. 1981. pap. 2.75 o.p. (ISBN 0-425-04839-X). Berkley Pub.

--Suspicions. 1980. 10.95 o.p. (ISBN 0-399-12439-X). Putnam Pub Group.

Beteille, Andre & Madan, T. N., eds. Encounter & Experience: Personal Accounts of Fieldwork. LC 74-84591. 235p. 1975. 10.00x o.p. (ISBN 0-8248-0351-5). UH Pr.

Beth, E. W. & Piaget, J. Mathematical Epistemology & Psychology. 348p. 1966. 62.00x (ISBN 0-677-01290-X). Gordon.

Beth Jacob Hebrew Teachers College. Deeds of the Righteous. (Illus.). 160p. 6.95 (ISBN 0-934390-00-2). B J Hebrew Tchrs.

--The Rebbe's Treasure. Date not set. price not set (ISBN 0-934390-01-0); pap. price not set (ISBN 0-934390-02-9). B J Hebrew Tchrs.

Beth, Loren P. Development of the American Constitution, 1877-1917. LC 79-138707. (New American Nation Ser). (Illus.). 1971. 16.30xi (ISBN 0-06-010314-0, HarpT). Har-Row.

Bethancourt, T. Ernesto. Doris Fein: Dead Heat at Long Beach. LC 82-48754. (Doris Fein Ser.). 160p. (YA) (gr. 9 up). 1983. 10.95 (ISBN 0-8234-0485-4). Holiday.

--Nightmare Town. LC 79-2091. 160p. (YA) 1979. 9.95 o.p. (ISBN 0-8234-0366-1). Holiday.

Bethea, David M. Khodasevich: His Life & Art. LC 82-61355. (Illus.). 424p. 1983. 35.00x (ISBN 0-691-06559-4). Princeton U Pr.

Bethel, A. C. Traditional Logic. 332p. (Orig.). 1982. pap. text ed. 12.75 (ISBN 0-8191-2616-0). U Pr of Amer.

Bethel, Dell. Coaching Winning Baseball. 1979. 14.95 o.p. (ISBN 0-8092-7460-4); pap. 8.95 (ISBN 0-8092-7459-0). Contemp Bks.

Bethel, Elizabeth R. Promise Land: A Century of Life in a Negro Community. 318p. 1981. 29.95 (ISBN 0-87722-211-8). Temple U Pr.

--Promised Land: A Century of Life in a Negro Community. 329p. 1982. pap. 5.95 (ISBN 0-87722-275-4). Temple U Pr.

Bethel, L., et al. Industrial Organization & Management. 5th ed. 1971. 19.50 o.p. (ISBN 0-07-005060-0, C); 5.50 o.p. solutions manual (ISBN 0-07-005061-9). McGraw.

Bethell, Leslie. Abolition of the Brazilian Slave Trade. (Latin American Studies). (Illus.). 1970. 42.50 (ISBN 0-521-07583-1). Cambridge U Pr.

Bethell, Nicholas. The Palestine Triangle: The Struggle for the Holy Land 1935-48. LC 79-50494. 1979. 12.95 o.p. (ISBN 0-399-12398-9). Putnam Pub Group.

--Russia Besieged. LC 77-77799. (World War II Ser.). (Illus.). (gr. 6 up). 1977. PLB 19.92 (ISBN 0-8094-2471-1, Pub. by Time-Life). Silver.

Bethemont, Jacques & Pelletier, Jean. Italy: A Geographical Introduction. King, Russel, ed. (Illus.). 224p. 1982. text ed. 28.00x (ISBN 0-582-30073-8). Longman.

Bethers. Language of Painting: Form & Content. (Pitman Art Ser.: Vol. 45). pap. 1.95 o.p. (ISBN 0-448-00554-9, G&D). Putnam Pub Group.

Bethke, Frederick J. Three Victorian Travel Writers: An Annotated Bibliography of Criticism on Mrs. Frances Milton Trollope, Samuel Butler, & Robert Louis Stevenson. 1977. lib. bdg. 25.00 (ISBN 0-8161-7852-6, Hall Reference). G K Hall.

Bethlem. Myopathies. 2nd ed. 1980. 73.75 (ISBN 0-444-80198-7). Elsevier.

Bethune, J. Essentials of Drafting. 416p. 1977. text ed. 21.95 (ISBN 0-13-284430-3). P-H.

Bethune, James D. Basic Electronic & Electrical Drafting. (Illus.). 1980. text ed. 20.95 (ISBN 0-13-060301-5). P-H.

--Technical Illustration. 237p. 1983. text ed. 22.95 (ISBN 0-471-05308-2). Wiley.

Betjeman, John. John Betjeman. (Pocket Poet Ser.). 1958. pap. 1.25 (ISBN 0-8023-9040-4). Dufour.

Betjeman, John, ed. Altar & Pew. (Pocket Poet Ser.). 1960. pap. 1.25 (ISBN 0-8023-9041-2). Dufour.

Betken, William T. The Other Shakespeare: Romeo & Juliet. 305p. (Orig.). 1983. 13.95. (ISBN 0-941672-04-2); pap. 7.95 (ISBN 0-941672-05-0). Valentine Pub.

--The Other Shakespeare: The Two Gentlemen of Verona. 215p. (Orig., Young People (Expurgated) Edition). Date not set. 13.95 (ISBN 0-941672-02-6); pap. 7.95 (ISBN 0-941672-03-4). Valentine Pub. Postponed.

Betlyon, John. The Coinage & Mints of Phoenicia: The Pre-Alexandrine Period. (Harvard Semitic Monographs). 184p. 1982. 18.75 (ISBN 0-686-42951-6, 04-00-26). Scholars Pr CA.

Betnun, Nathan S. Housing Finance Agencies: A Comparison Between State Agencies & Hud. LC 76-2899. 302p. 1976. 34.95 o.p. (ISBN 0-275-56660-9). Praeger.

Betourne, Henriette D., et al. Direct French Conversation, 2 Bks. (Orig., Fr.). (YA) (gr. 9 up). 1966. Bk. 1. pap. text ed. 2.95 (ISBN 0-88345-040-2, 17470); Bk. 2. pap. text ed. 2.95 (ISBN 0-88345-041-0, 17471). Regents Pub.

Betrock, Alan. Girl Groups: The Story of Sound. LC 81-71010. (Illus.). 176p. (Orig.). 1982. pap. 8.95 (ISBN 0-933328-25-7). Delilah Bks.

Bett, Henry. Games of Children, Their Origin & History. LC 68-31218. 1968. Repr. of 1929 ed. 27.00 o.p. (ISBN 0-8103-3473-9). Gale.

--Nursery Rhymes & Tales, Their Origin & History. LC 68-21756. 1968. Repr. of 1924 ed. 34.00x (ISBN 0-8103-3474-7). Gale.

Bett, K. E., et al. Thermodynamics for Chemical Engineers. LC 75-24573. 504p. 1975. text ed. 25.00x (ISBN 0-262-02119-6). MIT Pr.

Bettelheim, Bruno. Freud & Man's Soul. LC 82-47809. 112p. 1983. 11.95 (ISBN 0-394-52481-0). Knopf.

--Informed Heart. 1971. pap. 3.95 (ISBN 0-380-01302-9, 59246, Discus). Avon.

Bettelheim, Bruno & Zelan, Karen. On Learning to Read: The Child's Fascination with Meaning. 320p. 1983. pap. 5.95 (ISBN 0-394-71194-7, Vin). Random.

Bettelheim, Charles. Economic Calculation & Forms of Property. LC 74-21473. 1977. pap. 3.95 (ISBN 0-85345-427-2). Monthly Rev.

--Studies in the Theory of Planning. 1977. pap. text ed. 12.50 (ISBN 0-210-34019-3). Asia.

Bettelheim, R. & Takanishi, R. Early Schooling in Asia. 1976. 14.95 (ISBN 0-07-005127-5, P&RB). McGraw.

Bettencourt, Vladimir. New Discoveries in the Psychology of Management. (Research Center for Economic Psychology Library). (Illus.). 148p. 1983. 59.75 (ISBN 0-86654-061-X). Inst Econ Finan.

Bettenson, Henry, ed. Documents of the Christian Church. 2nd ed. 1963. 14.95x (ISBN 0-19-500388-8). Oxford U Pr.

--Documents of the Christian Church. 2nd ed. 1970. pap. 7.95 (ISBN 0-19-501293-3, GB). Oxford U Pr.

Better Business Bureau. Getting More for Your Money. LC 81-71070. Orig. Title: Guide to Wise Buying. 384p. 1982. pap. 7.95 (ISBN 0-448-16617-8, G&D). Putnam Pub Group.

Better Homes & Gardens Books, ed. Better Homes & Gardens Calorie Counter's Cook Book. rev. ed. LC 77-129266. (Illus.). 1970. text ed. 5.95 (ISBN 0-696-00493-3). BH&G.

Better Homes & Gardens Books editors, ed. Better Homes & Gardens All About Your House: Stretching your Living Space. (All About your House Ser.). (Illus.). 160p. 1983. 9.95 (ISBN 0-696-02162-5). Meredith Corp.

--Better Homes & Gardens All About Your House: Your Kitchen. (All About your House Ser.). 160p. 1983. 9.95 (ISBN 0-696-02161-7). Meredith Corp.

--Better Homes & Gardens All About Your House: Your Walls & Ceilings. (All About your House Ser.). (Illus.). 160p. 1983. 9.95 (ISBN 0-696-02163-3). Meredith Corp.

--Better Homes & Gardens Calorie-Counter's Cook Book. rev. ed. (Illus.). 96p. 1983. 5.95 (ISBN 0-696-00835-1). Meredith Corp.

--Better Homes & Gardens Christmas Crafts to Make Ahead. (Illus.). 80p. 1983. 5.95 (ISBN 0-696-00885-8). Meredith Corp.

--Better Homes & Gardens Cookies for Kids. (Illus.). 96p. 1983. pap. 4.95 (ISBN 0-696-00865-3). Meredith Corp.

Better Homes & Gardens Books Editors. Better Homes & Gardens Cooking for Two. rev ed. LC 73-185. (Illus.). 96p. 1982. 5.95 (ISBN 0-686-82871-2). BH&G.

Better Homes & Gardens Books editors, ed. Better Homes & Gardens Microwave Plus Cook Book. (Illus.). 96p. 1983. 5.95 (ISBN 0-696-00850-5). Meredith Corp.

--Better Homes & Gardens My Recipe Collection. (Illus.). 142p. 1983. 12.95 (ISBN 0-696-01070-4). Meredith Corp.

--Better Homes & Gardens My Turn to Cook. (Illus.). 96p. 1983. pap. 4.95 (ISBN 0-696-00875-0). Meredith Corp.

--Better Homes & Gardens Pasta Cook Book. (Illus.). 96p. 1983. 5.95 (ISBN 0-696-00855-6). Meredith Corp.

--Better Homes & Gardens Step-by-Step Cabinets & Shelves. (Illus.). 1983. pap. 5.95 (ISBN 0-696-01065-8). Meredith Corp.

Better Homes & Gardens Editors. Better Homes & Gardens New Cook Book. 960p. 1982. pap. 4.50 (ISBN 0-553-22528-6). Bantam.

Betteridge, Terry. An Algebraic Analysis of Storage Fragmentation. Stone, Harold, ed. LC 82-11194. (Computer Science: Systems Programming Ser.: No. 15). 232p. 1983. 44.95 (ISBN 0-8357-1364-4, Pub. by UMI Res Pr). Univ Microfilms.

Betteridge, W. Nickel & its Alloys. 160p. 1977. 29.00x (ISBN 0-686-81991-8, Pub. by Macdonald & Evans). State Mutual Bk.

Betteridge, W. & Krefeld, R., eds. Alloy Eight Hundred: Proceedings of the Petten International Conference, the Netherlands, 14-16 March, 1978. 1979. 83.00 (ISBN 0-444-85228-X, North Holland). Elsevier.

Betterley, Melvin. Sheet Metal Drafting. 2nd ed. (Illus.). 1977. pap. text ed. 19.95 (ISBN 0-07-005126-7, G). McGraw.

Bettey, J. H. & Taylor, C. W. Sacred & Satiric: Medieval Stone Carving in the West Country: With Illustrations from Churches in Avon, Gloucestershire, Somerset & Wiltshire. 1982. 39.00x (ISBN 0-686-82403-2, Pub. by Redcliffe England). State Mutual Bk.

Bettger, Frank. How I Raised Myself from Failure to Success in Selling. 1958. 8.95 (ISBN 0-13-399402-3). P-H.

--How I Raised Myself from Failure to Success in Selling. 192p. 1983. pap. 4.95 (ISBN 0-13-423970-9). P-H.

Betti, Liliana. Fellini: An Intimate Portrait. Nevgroschel, Joachim, tr. LC 79-12360. (Illus.). 1979. 9.95 o.p. (ISBN 0-316-09230-4). Little.

Bettman, James R. Information Processing Theory of Consumer Choice. LC 78-52496. (Advances in Marketing). 1979. text ed. 23.95 (ISBN 0-201-00834-3). A-W.

Bettoni, Efrem. Duns Scotus: The Basic Principles of His Philosophy. Bonansea, Berbardine, ed. LC 78-14031. 1979. Repr. of 1961 ed. lib. bdg. 18.75x (ISBN 0-313-21142-6, BEDS). Greenwood.

--Saint Bonaventure. Scuola, Editrice, Brescia, Italy, tr. from Ital. LC 81-13371. (The Notre Dame Pocket Library). 127p. 1982. Repr. of 1964 ed. lib. bdg. 19.25x (ISBN 0-313-23271-7, BESB). Greenwood.

Bettonica, Luis. Feast of Spain. (Illus.). 192p. 1982. 25.00 (ISBN 0-89479-128-1). A & W Pubs.

Betts. Patient Centred Multiple Choice Questions, Vol. 1. 96p. 1982. pap. text ed. 6.50 (ISBN 0-06-318231-9, Pub. by Har-Row Ltd England). Har-Row.

--Patient Centred Multiple Choice Questions, Vol. 2. 96p. 1982. pap. text ed. 6.50 (ISBN 0-06-318232-7, Pub. by Har-Row Ltd England). Har-Row.

Betts, C. J., tr. see Montesquieu.

Betts, D. S. Refrigeration & Thermometry Below One Kelvin. 40.00x (ISBN 0-686-97021-7, Pub. by Scottish Academic Pr Scotland). State Mutual Bk.

Betts, D. S., jt. auth. see Turner, R. E.

Betts, Doris. Heading West. 1982. pap. 3.50 (ISBN 0-451-11913-4, AE1913, Sig). NAL.

Betts, E. Outbreaks of the African Migratory Locust (Locusta Migratoria Migratoriodes R & F) Since 1871. 1961. 35.00x (ISBN 0-85135-005-4, Pub. by Centre Overseas Research). State Mutual Bk.

Betts, Edwin M., ed. Thomas Jefferson's Farm Book: With Commentary & Relevant Extracts from Other Writings. LC 52-13160. (Illus.). 552p. 1976. Repr. of 1953 ed. 20.00x (ISBN 0-8139-0705-5). U Pr of Va.

Betts, J. Signal Processing, Modulation & Noise. 1971. 23.95 (ISBN 0-444-19671-4). Elsevier.

Betts, Leonard C. Garden Pools. (Illus.). 1952. pap. 2.95 (ISBN 0-87666-077-4, M513). TFH Pubns.

Betts, R. R. Essays in Czech History. 1969. text ed. 26.75x o.p. (ISBN 0-485-11095-4, Athlone Pr). Humanities.

Betts, Raymond F. Europe in Retrospect: A Brief History of the Past Hundred Years. (Orig.). 1979. pap. 8.95 (ISBN 0-669-01366-8). Heath.

Betts, Richard. Cruise Missiles & U. S. Policy. LC 82-72704. 61p. 1982. pap. 5.95 (ISBN 0-8157-0933-1). Brookings.

Betts, Richard K., jt. auth. see Gelb, Leslie H.

Betts, Richard M. & Ely, Silas J. Basic Real Estate Appraisal. 367p. 1982. text ed. 21.95x (ISBN 0-471-87300-4); test 7.50x (ISBN 0-471-09293-2). Wiley.

Betts, Richard M., jt. auth. see McKenzie, Dennis J.

Betts, Robert B. Christians in the Arab East. LC 78-8674. 1981. 12.50 (ISBN 0-8042-0796-8). John Knox.

--In Search of York: The Black Member of the Lewis & Clark Expedition. 1982. 10.00 (ISBN 0-87081-144-4). Colo Assoc.

Betts, Wilbur, jt. auth. see Schultz, James W.

Bettsworth, Michael. Drownproofing: A Technique for Water Survival. LC 76-48762. 1977. 6.95x o.p. (ISBN 0-8052-3646-5); pap. 2.95 (ISBN 0-8052-0558-6). Schocken.

Betty, M. & Charter, D., eds. Marine Affairs Jounral, No. 3. 113p. 1975. 1.00 (ISBN 0-686-36973-4, P464). URI Mas.

Betz, Don. Cultivating Leadership: An Approach. LC 80-69039. 120p. (Orig.). 1981. pap. text ed. 5.75 (ISBN 0-8191-1441-3). U Pr of Amer.

Betz, H. D., ed. see Ebeling, Gerhard, et al.

Betz, Norm. AACC Technical Guide to Key Cereal & Making Ingredients. LC 80-68710. 138p. 1980. write for info. o.s.i. (ISBN 0-913250-19-8). Am Assn Cereal Chem.

Betz, Otto. Making Sense of Confession. LC 69-11225. 1969. 4.95 o.p. (ISBN 0-685-10970-4, L38410). Franciscan Herald.

Betzler, H., tr. see Von Mellenthin, F. W.

Beube, Douglas S. Manhattan Street Romance. (Artist Bk.). (Illus.). 40p. (Orig.). 1982. pap. text ed. 6.00 (ISBN 0-89822-027-0). Visual Studies.

Beulow, George, ed. see Grant, Kerry S.

Beum, Robert, ed. Classic European Short Stories. 276p. (Orig.). 1982. pap. 6.95 (ISBN 0-89385-025-X). Sugden.

Beumont & Burrows. Handbook of Psychiatry & Endocrinology. 1982. 109.00 (ISBN 0-444-80355-6). Elsevier.

Beutel, Frederick K. Bank Officer's Handbook of Commercial Banking Law. 5th ed. 1982. 48.00 (ISBN 0-88262-670-1). Warren.

Beutelspacher, H., jt. auth. see Van der Marel, R.

Beutler, Larry E. Eclectic Psychotherapy: A Systematic Approach. (General Psychology Ser.: No. 118). 270p. 1983. 26.00 (ISBN 0-08-028842-1). Pergamon.

Beutner, E. H., et al. Immunopathology of the Skin. 2nd ed. LC 78-24139. 496p. 1979. 69.50 o.p. (ISBN 0-471-03514-9, Pub. by Wiley Medical). Wiley.

Beuzamy, jt. auth. see Bernard.

Bevan, Bev. The Electric Light Orchestra Story. (Illus.). 176p. 1981. pap. 9.95 (ISBN 0-8256-3244-7, Quick Fox). Putnam Pub Group.

Bevan, Charles C. Women's Liberation & Chaos. 1982. 10.95 (ISBN 0-533-05328-5). Vantage.

Bevan, D. & Hagenmuller, P. Non-Stoichiometric Compounds: Tungsten Bronzes; Vanadium Bronzes; & Related Compounds. (Pergamon Texts in Inorganic Chemistry: Vol. 1). 154p. 1975. text ed. 29.00 o.p. (ISBN 0-08-018776-5); pap. text ed. 14.00 o.p. (ISBN 0-08-018775-7). Pergamon.

Bevan, David. Charles-Ferdinand Ramuz. (World Authors Ser.). 1979. lib. bdg. 15.95 (ISBN 0-8057-6353-8, Twayne). G K Hall.

Bevan, Elizabeth, jt. auth. see Weckselmann, David.

Bevan, G. A., ed. see University of Wales Press.

Bevan, John A. Fundamentos de Farmacologia. 2nd ed. (Span.). 1982. pap. text ed. 21.00 (ISBN 0-06-310065-7, Pub. by HarLA Mexico). Har-Row.

Bevan, John A., et al, eds. Vascular Neuroeffector Mechanisms: 4th International Symposium. Date not set. text ed. 47.00 (ISBN 0-89004-738-3). Raven.

--Vascular Neuroeffector Mechanisms. 429p. 1979. 47.00 (ISBN 0-89004-302-7). Raven.

Bevan, Ruth A. Marx & Burke: A Revisionist View. LC 73-79625. 208p. 1973. 16.00 (ISBN 0-87548-144-2). Open Court.

Bevan, S. C. A Concise Etymological Dictionary of Chemistry. 1976. 20.50 (ISBN 0-85334-653-4, Pub. by Applied Sci England). Elsevier.

Bevan, Stanley C., et al. A Concise Etymological Dictionary of Chemistry. ix, 140p. 1976. 20.50 (ISBN 0-85334-653-4, Pub. by Applied Sci England). Elsevier.

Bevelander, Gerrit. Outline of Histology. rev. ed. 7th ed. (Illus.). 297p. (Orig.). 1971. text ed. 12.95 o.p. (ISBN 0-8016-0680-2). Mosby.

Bevelander, Gerrit & Ramaley, Judith A. Essentials of Histology. 8th ed. LC 78-4847. 400p. 1979. text ed. 24.95 (ISBN 0-8016-0669-1). Mosby.

Beven, Annette. The Spade Sage. (Jataka Tales for Children). (Illus.). 24p. (gr. 1-8). 1975. 5.95 o.p. (ISBN 0-913546-24-0); pap. 4.95 o.p. (ISBN 0-913546-71-2). Dharma Pub.

Bevenot, Maurice. The Tradition of Manuscripts: A Study in the Transmission of St. Cyprian's Treatises. LC 78-14421. 1979. Repr. of 1961 ed. lib. bdg. 18.50x (ISBN 0-313-20622-8, BETM). Greenwood.

Beveridge, Albert J. The Life of John Marshall. 550.00 (ISBN 0-384-04088-8). Johnson Repr.

--Life of John Marshall: Unabridged, 4 vols. in 2. new ed. LC 34-7756. (Illus.). 2496p. 1974. lib. bdg. 99.95 set (ISBN 0-910220-65-4). Berg.

Beveridge, Annette S., tr. see Augustus, Frederick.

Beveridge, D. L., jt. auth. see Pople, J. A.

Beveridge, Michael, ed. Children Thinking Through Language. 280p. 1982. pap. text ed. 19.95 (ISBN 0-7131-6352-6). E Arnold.

Beveridge, S. G. & Schechter, Robert S. Optimization Theory & Practice. 1970. pap. text ed. 41.50 (ISBN 0-07-005128-3, C). McGraw.

Beveridge, W. H. Unemployment: A Problem of Industry. LC 79-59646. (The English Working Class Ser.). 1980. lib. bdg. 35.00 o.s.i. (ISBN 0-8240-0101-X). Garland Pub.

Beveridge, William H. Causes & Cures of Unemployment. LC 75-41030. (BCL Ser. II). 1976. Repr. of 1931 ed. 9.00 (ISBN 0-685-70886-1). AMS Pr.

Beveridge, William I. Art of Scientific Investigation. 1960. pap. 3.95 (ISBN 0-394-70129-1, V129, Vin). Random.

Beveridge-Wavering, Agnes & Seibert-Shook, Mavis. Reinforcing Home Activities: Program for Articulation Improvement. 2nd ed. 1981. pap. 9.00x (ISBN 0-8134-2158-6, 2158). Interstate.

Beverley, George H. Pioneer in the U. S. Air Corps: The Memoirs of Brigadier General George H. Beverley. 1982. pap. 9.95x (ISBN 0-89745-029-9). Sunflower U Pr.

Beverly, Farida, jt. auth. see Morris, Pauline.

Beverly Hills Bar Association & Barristers Committee for the Arts. Visual Artists Manual: A Practical Guide to Your Career. Grode, Susan A., ed. LC 82-45347. 320p. 1983. pap. 15.95 (ISBN 0-385-18251-1, Dolp). Doubleday.

Beverly Hills Bar Association. Barristers Committee for the Arts. The Actor's Manual: A Practical Legal Guide. Beil, Norman, et al, eds. 288p. 1981. o. p. 13.95 o.p. (ISBN 0-8015-0040-0, Hawthorn); pap. 9.95 o.p. (ISBN 0-8015-0041-9, Hawthorn). Dutton.

Bevier, Abraham G. The Indians: Or Narratives of Massacres & Depredations on the Frontier in Wawasink & Its Vicinity During the American Revolution. 1975. pap. 2.95 (ISBN 0-686-82641-8). Lib Res.

Bevier, Michael J. Politics Backstage: Inside the California Legislature. LC 79-1021. 293p. 1979. 29.95 (ISBN 0-87722-150-2). Temple U Pr.

Bevilacqua, Joseph J., ed. Changing Government Policies for the Mentally Disabled. 320p. 1982. prof ref 28.50x (ISBN 0-88410-384-6). Ballinger Pub.

Bevington, David. The Complete Works of Shakespeare. 3rd ed. 1980. text ed. 28.95x (ISBN 0-673-15193-X). Scott F.

--Medieval Drama. 1975. text ed. 26.50 (ISBN 0-395-13915-5). HM.

Bevington, David, jt. auth. see Craig, Hardin.

Bevington, David, compiled by. Shakespeare. LC 76-5220. (Goldentree Bibliographies in Language & Literature). 1978. text ed. 18.95 o.p. (ISBN 0-88295-556-X); pap. text ed. 13.95x (ISBN 0-88295-555-1). Harlan Davidson.

Bevington, Helen. The Journey Is Everything. 250p. Date not set. 14.95 (ISBN 0-8223-0553-4). Duke.

Bevington, Philip R. Data Reduction & Error Analysis for the Physical Sciences. LC 69-16942. 1969. pap. text ed. 17.95 (ISBN 0-07-005135-6, C). McGraw.

Bevington, S., ed. Twentieth Century Interpretations of Hamlet. (Orig.). (YA) (gr. 9-12). 1968. 8.95 o.p. (ISBN 0-13-372375-5, Spec); pap. 2.95 o.p. (ISBN 0-13-372367-4, Spec). P-H.

Bevis, Em O. Curriculum Building in Nursing: A Process. 3rd ed. LC 81-18888. (Illus.). 282p. 1982. pap. text ed. 16.95 (ISBN 0-8016-0667-5). Mosby.

Bevis, Richard, ed. Bibliotheca Cisorientalia: An Annotated Checklist of Early Travel Books on the Near & Middle East. 1973. lib. bdg. 33.50 (ISBN 0-8161-0969-9, Hall Reference). G K Hall.

Bew, P. & Gibbon, P. The State in Northern Ireland, 1921-72. 224p. 1982. pap. 8.50 (ISBN 0-7190-0814-X). Manchester.

Bew, Paul & Patterson, Henry. Sean Lemass & the Making of Modern Ireland, 1945-66. 1982. 70.00x (ISBN 0-7171-1260-8, Pub. by Gill & Macmillan Ireland). State Mutual Bk.

Bewick, Thomas. Eighteen Hundred Woodcuts by Thomas Bewick & His School. Cirker, Blanche, ed. pap. 7.95 (ISBN 0-486-20766-8). Dover.

--Memoir. Montague Weekley, ed. LC 62-52032. 1961. 8.95 (ISBN 0-248-98250-8). Dufour.

Bewley, Beulah R. & Day, Isobel. Smoking by Children in Great Britain. 21p. 20.00x (ISBN 0-686-98311-4, Pub. by Social Sci Res). State Mutual Bk.

Bewley, J. D., jt. auth. see Black, M.

Bewley, Marius, ed. English Romantic Poets: An Anthology with Commentaries. LC 69-16430. 1970. 5.95 o.s.i. (ISBN 0-394-60801-1, G101). Modern Lib.

Bexley, James B. Banking Management. 196p. 1978. 13.95 (ISBN 0-87201-054-6). Gulf Pub.

Beye, Charles R. Epic & Romance in the "Argonautica" of Apollonius. 1982. 22.50x (ISBN 0-8093-1020-1). S Ill U Pr.

Beyeler, Ernst. Picasso, Braque, Leger: Masterpieces from Swiss Collections. LC 75-34717. (Illus.). 1975. 6.00 o.p. (ISBN 0-912964-09-X). Minneapolis Inst Arts.

Beyer, Andrew. Picking Winners: A Horse Players Guide. LC 74-34311. 288p. 1975. 8.95 o.p. (ISBN 0-395-20424-0). HM.

Beyer, Barry K. Teaching Thinking in Social Studies: Using Inquiry in the Classroom. (General Education Ser.). 1979. pap. text ed. 14.95 (ISBN 0-675-08280-3). Additional supplements may be obtained from publisher. Merrill.

Beyer, Barry K. & Penna, Anthony N., eds. Concepts in the Social Studies. LC 76-150533. (Bulletin Ser.: No. 45). 96p. (Orig.). 1971. pap. 3.20 (ISBN 0-87986-016-2, 498-15248). Coun Soc Studies.

Beyer, Carlos, ed. Endocrine Control of Sexual Behavior. LC 78-24620. (Comprehensive Endocrinology Ser.). 424p. 1979. text ed. 43.00 (ISBN 0-89004-207-1). Raven.

Beyer, Jinny. Medallion Quilts: The Art & Techniques of Creating Medallion Quilts, Including a Rich Collection of Historic & Contemporary Examples. LC 82-13744. 188p. 1982. 29.95 (ISBN 0-914440-57-8). EPM Pubns.

Beyer, Monica M., ed. see International Society for Artificial Organs, 2nd, New York, April 18-19, 1979, et al.

Beyer, R. & Trawicki, D. J. Profitability Accounting: For Planning & Control. 2nd ed. 403p. 1972. 35.95 o.p. (ISBN 0-471-06523-4). Wiley.

Beyer, Robert & Trawicki, Donald. Profitability Accounting: For Planning & Control. 2d ed. LC 72-91123. 414p. Repr. of 1972 ed. text ed. 28.50 (ISBN 0-471-06523-4). Krieger.

Beyer, Werner W. The Enchanted Forest: Coleridge, Wordsworth. 273p. 1982. Repr. of 1963 ed. lib. bdg. 35.00 (ISBN 0-686-81684-6). Century Bookbindery.

Beyer, William, et al, eds. see Ulam, Stanislaw M.

Beyerle, Edith M., compiled by. Daily Meditations, 4 vols. 120p. Set. pap. 2.40 o.p. (ISBN 0-87509-073-7); Vol. 1. pap. 0.60 o.p. (ISBN 0-87509-074-5); Vol. 2. pap. 0.60 o.p. (ISBN 0-87509-075-3); Vol. 3. pap. 0.60 o.p. (ISBN 0-87509-076-1); Vol. 4. pap. 0.60 o.p. (ISBN 0-87509-077-X). Chr Pubns.

Beyerlin, Walter, ed. Near Eastern Religious Texts Relating to the Old Testament. Bowden, John, tr. (Old Testament Library). (Illus.). 1978. 22.00 (ISBN 0-664-21363-4). Westminster.

Beyer-Machule, Charles. Plastic & Reconstructive Surgery of the Eyelids. (Illus.). 128p. 1983. 21.00 (ISBN 0-86577-080-8). Thieme-Stratton.

Beyl, F. R. & Tappe, J. Group Extensions, Representations, & the Schur Multiplicator. (Lecture Notes in Mathematics Ser.: Vol. 958). 278p. 1983. pap. 13.50 (ISBN 0-387-11954-X). Springer-Verlag.

Beyle, Henri see Stendhal, pseud.

Beyle, Thad L. & Muchmore, Lynn, eds. Governorship: Views from the Office. (Duke Press Policy Studies). 220p. 1983. text ed. 25.00 (ISBN 0-8223-0506-2). Duke.

Beylsmit, J. J. Linguistic Bibliography for the Year Nineteen Seventy-Nine. 1982. 135.00 (ISBN 0-686-37163-1, Pub. by Martinus Nijhoff Netherlands). Kluwer Boston.

Beyme, Klaus von see Von Beyme, Klaus.

Beynon, J. H. & Williams, A. E. Mass & Abundance Tables for Use in Mass Spectrometry. 1963. 106.50 (ISBN 0-444-40044-3). Elsevier.

Beynon, J. H., ed. Recommendations for Symbolism & Nomenclature for Mass Spectroscopy. new ed. 1978. write for info. (ISBN 0-08-022368-0). Pergamon.

Beynon, J. H., et al. The Mass Spectra of Organic Molecules. (Illus.). 1968. 74.50 (ISBN 0-444-40046-X). Elsevier.

Beynon, L. R. & Cowell, E. B., eds. Ecological Aspects of the Toxicity Testing of Oils & Dispersants. (Illus.). viii, 149p. 1974. 33.00 (ISBN 0-85334-458-2, Pub. by Applied Sci England). Elsevier.

--Ecological Aspects of Toxicity Testing of Oils & Dispersants. 1974. 29.95 (ISBN 0-470-07190-7). Halsted Pr.

Beytagh, Francis, jt. auth. see Kauper, Paul.

Beytagh, Francis X. Constitutional Law, 1982 Supplement: Cases & Materials. 1982. pap. 8.95 (ISBN 0-316-48355-9). Little.

Bezauzee, N. Grammaire Generale, 2 vols. (Linguistics 13th-18th Centuries Ser.). (Fr.). 1974. Repr. of 1767 ed. Set. lib. bdg. 323.00x o.p. (ISBN 0-8287-0087-7). Vol. 1 (71-5025). Vol. 2 (71-5026). Clearwater Pub.

Bezdanov, Stevan. A Community School in Yugoslavia. (Experiments & Innovations in Education Ser., No. 6). 40p. (Orig.). 1974. pap. 2.50 o.p. (ISBN 92-3-101130-8, U92, UNESCO). Unipub.

Bezdechi, Adrian. Pianos & Player Pianos: An Informative Guide for Owners & Prospective Buyers. LC 79-318082. (Illus.). 63p. (Orig.). 1979. pap. 6.95 (ISBN 0-9604092-0-3). Interstate Piano.

Bezilla, Michael. Electric Traction on the Pennsylvania Railroad, 1895-1968. LC 79-65858. (Illus.). 1980. 17.95x (ISBN 0-271-00241-7). Pa St U Pr.

Bezold, C. The Future of Pharmaceuticals. LC 80-22603. 142p. 1981. 18.50 (ISBN 0-471-08343-7, Pub. by Wiley Med). Wiley.

Bezold, Clement, jt. auth. see Dator, James.

Bezuszka, Stanley, et al. Designs from Mathematical Patterns. Savage, Lyn, ed. (Illus.). (gr. 6-12). 1978. 9.50 (ISBN 0-88488-105-9). Creative Pubns.

--Tessellations: The Geometry of Patterns. (gr. 4-12). 1977. wkbk 10.25 (ISBN 0-88488-080-X). Creative Pubns.

Bhacca, Rosaria D. All'Italiana. Stevens, Cheryl J., ed. LC 81-84607. (Illus.). 133p. (Orig.). 1981. pap. 7.95 (ISBN 0-88127-001-6). Oracle Pr LA.

Bhaduri, R. K., jt. auth. see Preston, M. A.

Bhagavad-Gita. The Song of God. Prabhavananda, Swami & Isherwood, C., trs. pap. 2.50 (ISBN 0-451-62182-4, ME2182, Ment). NAL.

Bhagavan, M. R., jt. ed. see Arthurs, A. M.

Bhagwati, J. N. The Brain Drain & Taxation: Theory & Empirical Analysis. 1976. 44.00 o.p. (ISBN 0-444-11076-3, North-Holland); pap. 29.50 o.p. (ISBN 0-444-11090-9). Elsevier.

--Illegal Transactions in International Trade: Theory & Measurement. LC 73-88164. (Studies in International Economics Ser.: Vol. 1). 208p. 1974. 47.00 (ISBN 0-444-10581-6, North-Holland); pap. 17.00 (ISBN 0-444-10883-1). Elsevier.

Bhagwati, J. N. & Partington, M. Taxing the Brain Drain: A Proposal. 1976. 32.75 (ISBN 0-444-11027-5, North-Holland); pap. 22.00 (ISBN 0-444-11089-5). Elsevier.

Bhagwati, Jagdish. Foreign Trade Regimes & Economic Development: Anatomy & Consequences of Exchange Control Regimes, Vol. II. LC 78-18799. (Foreign Trade Regimes & Economic Development Ser.: Vol. XI). 256p. 1978. prof ref 27.50x (ISBN 0-88410-487-7). Ballinger Pub.

Bhagwati, Jagdish, ed. International Trade: Selected Readings. 456p. 1981. text ed. 27.50x (ISBN 0-262-02160-9); pap. text ed. 10.95x (ISBN 0-262-52060-5). MIT Pr.

Bhagwati, Jagdish N., ed. The New International Economic Order: The North-South Debate. 1977. text ed. 23.00x o.p. (ISBN 0-262-02126-9); pap. 12.00x (ISBN 0-262-52042-7). MIT Pr.

Bhajan, Yogi. The Golden Temple Cookbook. LC 78-52267. (Orig.). 1979. pap. 8.50 (ISBN 0-8015-3067-9, 0825-250, Hawthorn). Dutton.

Bhaktivedanta, Swami A. C. The Bhagavad-Gita As It Is. abr. ed. LC 75-34536. (Illus.). 330p. 1976. 7.95 (ISBN 0-912776-80-3); text ed. 3.95 (ISBN 0-686-96674-0); pap. write for info.; pap. text ed. 2.95 o.p. (ISBN 0-685-65674-8). Bhaktivedanta.

--Life Comes from Life. LC 75-39756. (Illus.). 1979. 5.95 (ISBN 0-89213-100-4); text ed. 1.95 (ISBN 0-686-96675-9). Bhaktivedanta.

Bhandari, J. R., jt. ed. see Singh, Bhupinder.

Bhappu, R. B., jt. ed. see Mular, A. L.

Bharadwaj, K. Production Conditions in Indian Agriculture. (Department of Applied Economics, Occasional Papers: No. 33). 175p. 1974. 27.50 (ISBN 0-521-08494-6); pap. 18.95 (ISBN 0-521-09862-9). Cambridge U Pr.

Bharati, Saroja & Lev, Maurice. Cardiac Surgery & the Conduction System. 108p. 1983. 59.50 (ISBN 0-471-08147-7, Pub. by Wiley Med). Wiley.

Bharati, Subramania. Poems of Subrarmania Bharati. Sundaram, P. S., tr. from Tamil. (Vikas Library of Modern Indian Writing: No. 25). 168p. 1982. text ed. 20.00x (ISBN 0-7069-2016-3, Pub. by Vikas India). Advent NY.

Bhardwaj, N., jt. auth. see Gopal, Brij.

Bhardwaj, Surinder M. Hindu Places of Pilgrimage in India: A Study in Cultural Geography. LC 73-174454. (Illus.). 1973. 36.50x (ISBN 0-520-02135-5). U of Cal Pr.

--Hindu Places of Pilgrimage in India: A Study in Cultural Geography. (Illus.). 278p. 1983. pap. 7.95 (ISBN 0-520-04951-9, CAL 621). U of Cal Pr.

Bhardwaj, V. B., ed. Self-Assessment of Current Knowledge in Internal Medicine. 4th ed. LC 79-91971. 1980. pap. 22.00 o.p. (ISBN 0-87488-257-5). Med Exam.

Bhargava, G. S. South Asian Security After Afghanistan. LC 82-47682. 208p. 1982. 23.95x (ISBN 0-669-05557-3). Lexington Bks.

Bhargava, V. K. & Haccoun, D. Digital Communications by Satellite: Modulation, Multiple Access & Coding. 569p. 1981. 45.00 (ISBN 0-686-98094-8). Telecom Lib.

Bhargava, Vijay K., et al. Digital Communications by Satellite: Modulaton, Multiple Access & Coding. LC 81-10276. 569p. 1981. 49.50x (ISBN 0-471-08316-X, Pub. by Wiley-Interscience). Wiley.

Bharti, Ma S., ed. see Rajneesh, Bhagwan S.

Bharucha-Reid, A. T., ed. Probabilistic Analysis & Related Topics, Vol. 3. LC 78-106053. 166p. 1983. price not set (ISBN 0-12-095603-9). Acad Pr.

Bhaskar, Roy. Philosophical Idealogies. 1983. text ed. write for info (ISBN 0-391-01773-X). Humanities.

Bhaskar, S. N. Radiographic Interpretation for the Dentist. 3rd ed. LC 78-31556. 296p. 1979. 34.50 o.p. (ISBN 0-8016-0690-X). Mosby.

--Synopsis of Oral Pathology. 6th ed. LC 80-39514. (Illus.). 732p. 1981. text ed. 32.95 (ISBN 0-8016-0685-3). Mosby.

Bhat, L. S. Micro-Level Planning: A Case Study of Karnal Area, Haryana, India. LC 76-900789. 1976. 11.00x o.p. (ISBN 0-88386-770-2). South Asia Bks.

Bhat, U. Narayan. Elements of Applied Stochastic Processes. LC 70-178140. (Probability & Mathematical Statistics Ser.). 368p. 1972. 42.95x (ISBN 0-471-07199-4, Pub. by Wiley-Interscience). Wiley.

Bhateja, Chander & Lindsay, Richard, eds. Grinding: Theory, Techniques & Trouble Shooting. LC 81-84502. (Manufacturing Update Ser.). (Illus.). 230p. 1982. 32.00 (ISBN 0-87263-077-3). SME.

Bhati, A., jt. ed. see Hamilton, R. J.

Bhatia, B., jt. ed. see Tajuddin, M.

Bhatia, B., et al, eds. Selected Topics in Environmental Biology. LC 76-47082. 1977. text ed. 200.00 (ISBN 0-08-021210-7). Pergamon.

Bhatia, H. L. Public Finance. 8th ed. 400p. 1982. text ed. 40.00x (ISBN 0-7069-2055-4, Pub. by Vikas India). Advent NY.

Bhatia, H. L., ed. Does Foreign Aid Help? 120p. 1981. 14.95x (ISBN 0-940500-84-1, Pub by Allied Pubs India). Asia Bk Corp.

Bhatia, H. S. Martial Law: Theory & Practice. 1979. text ed. 11.50x (ISBN 0-391-01039-5). Humanities.

--Military History of British India(1607-1947) 1977. pap. text ed. 15.25x (ISBN 0-391-02010-2). Humanities.

Bhatia, H. S., ed. International Law & Practice in Ancient India. 1977. text ed. 13.50x (ISBN 0-391-01081-6). Humanities.

--Legal & Political Systems in China, Vol. 1. 1974. text ed. 10.50x (ISBN 0-391-01084-0). Humanities.

--Origin & Development of Legal & Political System in India, Vol. 1. 1976. text ed. 9.50x (ISBN 0-391-01094-8). Humanities.

--Origin & Development of Legal & Political System in India, Vol. 2. 1978. text ed. 9.50x (ISBN 0-391-01095-6). Humanities.

--Origin & Development of Legal & Political System in India, Vol. 3. 1978. text ed. 9.50x (ISBN 0-391-01096-4). Humanities.

Bhatia, K. S., jt. auth. see Varute, A. T.

Bhatia, Prem. All My Yesterdays. (Illus.). 179p. 1972. 6.75x (ISBN 0-685-30444-2). Intl Pubns Serv.

Bhatnager, Rajendra S., ed. Molecular Basis of Environmental Toxicity. LC 79-88896. 1980. 49.95 (ISBN 0-250-40306-4). Ann Arbor Science.

Bhatt, Harasiddhiprasad D., jt. ed. see Sweeney, Thomas L.

Bhatt, Kiran V. Road Pricing Technologies: A Survey. 45p. 1974. pap. 3.00 o.p. (ISBN 0-87766-127-8, 85000). Urban Inst.

Bhatt, R. Kaladhar. The Vedanta of Pure Non-Dualism. Sharma, I. C., tr. LC 79-18019. 1979. pap. 4.95 o.p. (ISBN 0-915442-93-0, Unilaw). Donning Co.

Bhatt, S. Aviation, Environment & World Order. 196p. 1980. text ed. 15.75x (ISBN 0-391-01809-4). Humanities.

Bhatt, S. R. Studies in Ramanuja Vedanta. LC 75-908081. 1975. 8.00x o.p. (ISBN 0-88386-688-9). South Asia Bks.

Bhatt, Vinayak V. & Roe, Alan R. Capital Market Imperfections & Economic Development. (Working Paper: No. 338). 87p. 1979. 5.00 (ISBN 0-686-36170-9, WP-0338). World Bank.

Bhattacharajee. History of Ancient India. (Illus.). 1980. text ed. 20.00x (ISBN 0-391-01756-X). Humanities.

Bhattacharjee, J. B. The Garos & the English. 1978. 14.00x o.p. (ISBN 0-8364-0204-9). South Asia Bks.

Bhattacharjee, S. K., jt. auth. see Bosel, T. K.

Bhattacharrya, K. C. Search for the Absolute in Neo-Vedanta. Burch, George B., ed. LC 75-17740. 212p. 1976. text ed. 14.00x (ISBN 0-8248-0296-9). UH Pr.

Bhattacharya, A. N. & Vyas, R. N. Habitat, Economy & Society: A Study of the Dangis. 1979. text ed. 15.00x (ISBN 0-391-01818-3). Humanities.

Bhattacharya, Bhabani. Steel Hawk & Other Stories. 143p. 1968. pap. 2.95 (ISBN 0-88253-020-8). Ind-US Inc.

Bhattacharya, Bhabani, ed. Contemporary Indian Short Stories, 2 vols. 1967. Vol. 1. 3.50 (ISBN 0-88253-409-2); Vol. 2. 3.50 (ISBN 0-88253-327-4). Ind-US Inc.

Bhattacharya, Lokenath. The Virgin Fish of Babughat. Mukherjee, Meenakshi, tr. from Bengali. (Indian Novels Ser.). 160p. 1975. 5.95 (ISBN 0-89253-016-2). Ind-US Inc.

Bhattacharya, P. B. & Jain, S. K. First Course in Rings, Fields & Vector Spaces. 1977. 14.95 (ISBN 0-470-99047-3, 76-55303). Halsted Pr.

Bhattacharya, R. N. & Rao, R. Ranga. Normal Approximation & Asymptotic Expansions. LC 75-35876. (Probability & Mathematical Statistics Ser.). 274p. 1976. 46.95x (ISBN 0-471-07201-X, Pub. by Wiley-Interscience). Wiley.

Bhattacharya, Rameswar. Dynamics of Marine Vehicles. LC 78-950. (Ocean Engineering Ser.). 498p. 1978. text ed. 63.95x (ISBN 0-471-07206-0, Pub. by Wiley-Interscience). Wiley.

Bhattacharya, S. N. Rural Industrialisation in India. 387p. 1981. text ed. 26.00x (ISBN 0-391-02084-6, Pub. by Concept India). Humanities.

Bhattacharyya, et al, eds. The Cultural Heritage of India, 5 vols. Incl. Vol. 1. Early Phases. Radhakrishnan, S., intro. by. (ISBN 0-87481-560-6); Vol. 2. Itihasas, Puranas, Dharma & Other Shastras (ISBN 0-87481-561-4); Vol. 3. The Philosophies (ISBN 0-87481-562-2); Vol. 4. The Religions (ISBN 0-87481-563-0); Vol. 5: Languages & Literatures (ISBN 0-87481-564-9). (Illus.). 20.00x ea.; Set. 100.00x (ISBN 0-87481-558-4). Vedanta Pr.

Bhattacharyya, Ajit & Friedman, Gerald M., eds. Modern Carbonate Environments. LC 82-11816. (Benchmark Papers in Geology: Vol. 74). 400p. 1982. 50.00 (ISBN 0-87933-436-3). Hutchinson Ross.

Bhattacharyya, Amitabha, jt. auth. see Ham, Inyong.

Bhattacharyya, Arunodoy. The Sonnet & the Major English Romantic Poets. LC 77-900318. 1976. 8.00x o.p. (ISBN 0-88386-910-1). South Asia Bks.

Bhattacharyya, Asutosh. The Sun & the Serpent: Lore of Bengal. 1977. 11.50x o.p. (ISBN 0-8364-0087-9). South Asia Bks.

Bhattacharyya, B. K. Humour & Satire in Assame Literature. 263p. 1982. 39.95x (ISBN 0-940500-46-9, Pub. by Sterling India). Asia Bk Corp.

Bhattacharyya, Bhaskar. To Catch the Uncatchable: Baul Songs of Love & Ecstasy. Douglas, Nik, ed. (Illus.). 1983. 8.95 (ISBN 0-89281-019-X, Destiny Bks). Inner Tradit.

--To Catch the Uncatchable: Baul Songs of Love & Ecstasy. Douglas, Nik, ed. (Illus.). 192p. Date not set. pap. 8.95 (ISBN 0-89281-019-X). Destiny Bks. Postponed.

Bhattacharyya, D. K. Demand for Financial Assets. 200p. 1978. text ed. 30.25x (ISBN 0-566-00228-0). Gower Pub Ltd.

Bhattacharyya, Gouri K. & Johnson, Richard A. Statistical Concepts & Methods. LC 76-53783. (Probability & Mathematical Statistics). 639p. 1977. text ed. 27.95 (ISBN 0-471-07204-4). Wiley.

Bhattacharyya, N. N. History of the Tantric Religion. 1983. 34.00x (ISBN 0-8364-0942-6, Pub. by Manohar India); pap. 17.50x (ISBN 0-8364-0943-4). South Asia Bks.

Bhattacherje, M. M. Pictorial Poetry. 184p. Repr. of 1954 ed. lib. bdg. 35.00 (ISBN 0-89760-090-8). Telegraph Bks.

--Pictorial Poetry. 182p. 1983. Repr. of 1982 ed. lib. bdg. 40.00 (ISBN 0-686-42932-X). Century Bookbindery.

Bhattasali, B. N. Transfer of Technology Among the Developing Countries. LC 70-186286. 1972. 10.50 (ISBN 92-833-1013-6, APO4, APO). Unipub.

Bhave, Vinoba. Democratic Values & the Practice of Citizenship. Sykes, Marjorie, ed. & tr. from Hindi. 251p. 1980. pap. 4.75 (ISBN 0-934676-24-0). Greenlf Bks.

Bhavyananda, Swami, ed. see Monks of the Ramakrishna Order.

Bhebe, Ngwabi & Ngcongco, L. Junior Certificate History of Southern Africa, Bks 1 & 2. (Orig.). 1981. pap. text ed. 7.50x (ISBN 0-435-94160-7); pap. text ed. 7.50x (ISBN 0-686-98148-0). Heinemann Ed.

Bhikshu Heng Ching, et al, trs. see Ch'an Master Hua.

Bhikshu Heng Yo, et al, trs. see Ch'an Master Yung Chia & Ch'an Master Hua.

Bhikshu Hen Shun, et al, trs. see Ch'an Master Hua.

Bhikshun Heng Tao, tr. see Ch'an Master Hua.

Bhikshuni, Heng Tao, et al, trs. see Ch'an Master Hua.

Bhikshuni Heng Ch'ih, tr. see Ch'an Master Hua.

Bhikshuni Heng Hsien, tr. see Ch'an Master Hua.

Bhikshuni Heng Hsien, tr. see Master Ch'ing Liang.

Bhikshuni Heng Hsien, et al, trs. see Liang, Ch'ing.

Bhikshuni Heng Tao, et al, trs. see Ch'an Master Hua.

Bhikshuni Heng Tao, et al, trs. see Hui Seng, et al.

Bhikshuni Heng Yin, tr. see Ch'an Master Hua.

Bhikshuni Heng Yin, et al, trs. see Ch'an Master Hua.

Bhiksuni Heng Hsien, tr. see Master Hua, Ch'an.

Bhiksuni Heng Yin, tr. see Lien Ch'in & Ch'an Master Hua.

Bhuiyan, Abdul W. Emergence of Bangladesh & the Role of the Awami League. 275p. 1982. text ed. 32.50x (ISBN 0-7069-1773-1, Pub. by Vikas India). Advent NY.

--The Emergence of Bangladesh & the Role the Awami League. 1982. 45.00x (ISBN 0-686-94082-2, Pub. by Garlandfold England). State Mutual Bk.

Bhutto, Z. My Execution. 1980. 10.00x o.p. (ISBN 0-8364-0650-8, Pub. by Muswati India). South Asia Bks.

Bhutto, Zulfikar A. Myth of Independence. 1969. 12.50x (ISBN 0-19-215167-3). Oxford U Pr.

Bia, Fred & Lynch, R. Nihit Hahoodzoodoo-Diijjidi doo Adaadaa: Our Community-Today & Yesterday, Bk. 1. (Illus.). 98p. 1982. 10.00x (ISBN 0-936008-04-0). Navajo Curr.

Biagi, Adele, jt. ed. see Ragazzini, Giuseppe.

Bial, Raymond. Ivesdale: A Photographic Essay. LC 82-73325. (Champaign County Historical Archives Historical Publications Ser.: No. 5). (Illus.). 1982. 12.00 (ISBN 0-9609646-0-6). Champaign County.

Bialer, Irv., jt. ed. see Gadow, Kenneth D.

Bialer, Seweryn. Stalin's Successors: Leadership, Stability & Change in the Soviet Union. LC 80-12037. 416p. 1980. 24.95 (ISBN 0-521-23518-9); pap. 8.95 (ISBN 0-521-28906-8). Cambridge U Pr.

Bialer, Seweryn, ed. The Domestic Context of Soviet Foreign Policy. 500p. 1981. lib. bdg. 37.50 (ISBN 0-89158-783-7); pap. 15.00 (ISBN 0-89158-891-4). Westview.

--Stalin & His Generals: Soviet Military Memoirs of World War II. (Encore Edition). 650p. 1983. softcover 35.00x (ISBN 0-86531-610-4). Westview.

Bialer, Yehuda L. Jewish Life in Art & Tradition. LC 75-33424. (Illus.). 1976. 16.95 o.p. (ISBN 0-399-11695-8). Putnam Pub Group.

Bialers, Seweryn & Sluzar, Sophia, eds. Radicalism in the Contemporary Age: Vol. 1, Sources of Contemporary Radicalism. 396p. 1977. lib. bdg. 27.50 (ISBN 0-89158-130-8). Westview.

--Radicalism in the Contemporary Age: Vol. 2, Radical Visions of the Future. 197p. 1977. lib. bdg. 24.00 (ISBN 0-89158-131-6). Westview.

--Radicalism in the Contemporary Age: Vol. 3, Strategies & Impact of Contemporary Radicalism. 356p. 1977. lib. bdg. 27.50 (ISBN 0-89158-129-4). Westview.

Bialosky, Alan, jt. auth. see Bialosky, Peggy.

Bialosky, Peggy & Bialosky, Alan. Making Your Own Teddy Bear. LC 82-60061. (Illus.). 124p. 1983. pap. 7.95 (ISBN 0-89480-211-9). Workman Pub.

Bialystok, Ellen, jt. auth. see Olson, David R.

Biancani, Laurent. Nude Photography: The French Way. Orig. Title: Te Nu. (Illus.). 1980. 25.00 o.p. (ISBN 0-8174-5095-5, Amphoto); pap. 12.95 (ISBN 0-8174-5096-3). Watson-Guptill.

Bianchi, Donald E., ed. see Sheeler, Phillip.

Bianchi, Eugene C. Aging as a Spiritual Journey. 228p. 1982. 17.50 (ISBN 0-8245-0486-0). Crossroad NY.

Bianchi, G., et al, eds. Man Under Vibration: Suffering & Protection. (Studies in Environmental Science: Vol. 13). 1982. 74.50 (ISBN 0-444-99743-1). Elsevier.

Bianchi, G., jt. ed. see Morecki, A.

Bianchi, Herman, et al. Deviance & Control in Europe: (Papers from the European Group for the Study of Deviance & Social Control) LC 75-8747. 224p. 1975. 42.95x (ISBN 0-471-07207-9, Pub. by Wiley-Interscience). Wiley.

Bianchi, Ugo & Vermaseren, Maarten J. La Soteriologia dei Culti Orientali Nell' Impero Romano: Atti del Colloquio Internazionale su le Soteriologia dei Culti Nell' Impero Romano. (Etudes Preliminaires aux Religions Orientales dans l'Empire Romain Ser.: Wol. 92). (Illus.). xxii, 1025p. 1982. write for info. (ISBN 90-04-06501-6). E J Brill.

Bianchine, Joseph R., jt. auth. see Yetiv, Jack.

Bianchini, Francesco & Corbetta, Francesco. Health Plants of the World. LC 76-46692. (Illus.). 1977. 22.95 o.p. (ISBN 0-88225-250-X). Newsweek.

Bianco, David, compiled by. Who's New Wave in Music, 1976 to 1980: A Catalog & Directory. LC 80-21534. 300p. (Orig.). 1983. pap. 7.50 (ISBN 0-938136-00-3). Lunchroom Pr.

Bianco, Jose. Shadow Play & the Rats. Miller, Yvette E., ed. Balderston, Daniel, tr. 1982. pap. 9.50 (ISBN 0-935480-11-0). Lat Am Lit Rev Pr.

Bianco, Lucien. Origins of the Chinese Revolution, 1915-1949. Bell, Muriel, tr. from Fr. LC 75-150321. Orig. Title: Les Origines de la Revolution Chinoise, 1915-1949. xvii, 220p. 1971. 12.50x (ISBN 0-8047-0746-4); pap. 4.95 (ISBN 0-8047-0827-4, SP131). Stanford U Pr.

Bianco, Margery. The Skin Horse. (Illus.). pap. 4.95 (ISBN 0-914676-25-3). Green Tiger Pr.

Bianco, Margery W. The Hurdy-Gurdy Man. 1980. PLB 6.95 (ISBN 0-8398-2603-6, Gregg). G K Hall.

--A Street of Little Shops. 1981. 8.95 (ISBN 0-8398-2725-3, Gregg). G K Hall.

Biancolli, Louis, ed. The Mozart Handbook: A Guide to the Man & His Music. LC 75-32504. (Illus.). 629p. 1976. Repr. of 1954 ed. lib. bdg. 45.00x (ISBN 0-8371-8496-7, BIMH). Greenwood.

Biancolli, Louis L. & Peyser, Herbert F. Masters of the Orchestra from Bach to Prokofieff. LC 70-94578. Repr. of 1954 ed. lib. bdg. 19.75x (ISBN 0-8371-2545-6, BIMO). Greenwood.

Biasiny, Nan. Beautiful Baby Clothes: To Knit, Crochet & Embroider. LC 76-51753. 1977. 12.50 o.p. (ISBN 0-671-22467-0). S&S.

Biass-Ducroux, Francoise. Glossary of Genetics. (Eng., Fr., Span., Ital., Ger. & Rus.). 1970. 72.50 (ISBN 0-444-40712-X). Elsevier.

Biava, A. Dizionario Italiano-Portoghese, Portoghese-Italiano. 318p. (Ital. & Port.). 1980. leatherette 5.95 (ISBN 0-686-97345-3, M-9172). French & Eur.

Bibb, Elizabeth. Womb for Rent. 260p. 1982. cancelled (ISBN 0-86679-003-9). Oak Tree Pubns.

Bibb, John, jt. auth. see Graham, Lou.

Bibbero, Robert J. Microprocessors in Instruments & Control. LC 77-9929. 301p. 1977. 26.95x (ISBN 0-471-01595-4, Pub. by Wiley-Interscience). Wiley.

Bibbero, Robert J. & Stern, David. Microprocessor Systems: Interfacing & Applications. 224p. 1982. 20.00x (ISBN 0-471-05306-6, Pub. by Wiley-Interscience). Wiley.

Bibbesworth, Walter De. Le Traite de Walter de Bibbesworth Sur la Langue Francaise, Quatorzieme Siecle. (Linguistics, 13th-18th Centuries Ser.). 203p. (Fr.). 1974. Repr. of 1929 ed. lib. bdg. 58.00x o.p. (ISBN 0-8287-0088-5, 71-5001). Clearwater Pub.

Bibby, Basil G & Shern, Roald J, eds. Methods of Caries Prediction: Proceedings. LC 78-50300. 326p. 1978. 15.00 (ISBN 0-917000-05-6). IRL Pr.

Bibby, Cyril. Simple Experiments in Biology. 1950. pap. text ed. 4.95x o.p. (ISBN 0-435-59080-4). Heinemann Ed.

Bibby, Geoffrey. The Testimony of the Spade. 1974. pap. 2.50 o.p. (ISBN 0-451-61337-6, ME1337, Ment). NAL.

Bibby, John & Toutenburg, Helge. Prediction & Improved Estimation in Linear Models. (Probability & Mathematical Statistics Tracts: Probability & Statistic Section). 188p. 1977. 36.95x (ISBN 0-471-01656-X, Pub. by Wiley-Interscience). Wiley.

Bibby, John F., et al. Vital Statistics on Congress, 1980. 1980. 12.25 o.p. (ISBN 0-8447-3408-X); pap. 5.25 (ISBN 0-8447-3401-2). Am Enterprise.

Bibby, Violet. Many Waters Cannot Quench Love. LC 75-14446. 160p. (gr. 7 up). 1975. 8.95 (ISBN 0-688-22042-8); PLB 8.59 (ISBN 0-688-32042-2). Morrow.

Bibby, W. & Clare, E. N. Introduction to Latin Comprehension. 1971. pap. text ed. 3.00x o.p. (ISBN 0-435-36036-1). Heinemann Ed.

--New Latin Comprehension. 1970. pap. text ed. 3.00x o.p. (ISBN 0-435-36035-3). Heinemann Ed.

Bibeault, Donald. Corporate Turnaround: How Managers Turn Losers into Winners. 416p. 1982. 27.50 (ISBN 0-07-005190-9). McGraw.

Bibee, John. The Magic Bicycle. (Illus.). 220p. (Orig.). (gr. 4-9). 1983. pap. 5.95 (ISBN 0-87784-348-1). Inter-Varsity.

Bibliander. De Ratione Omnium Linguarum et Litterarum Commentarius. (Linguistics 13th-18th Centuries Ser.). 235p. (Fr.). 1974. Repr. of 1548 ed. lib. bdg. 65.00x o.p. (ISBN 0-8287-0089-3, 71-5004). Clearwater Pub.

Bibliographic Society of Northern Illinois. Index to Reviews of Bibliographical Publications, 1978, Vol. 3. Oggel, Terry, ed. 1979. lib. bdg. 26.00 (ISBN 0-8161-8477-1, Hall Reference). G K Hall.

Bibliotheca Press Educational Division. Small Press Publishers Workbook. 50p. 1983. wkbk. 19.95 (ISBN 0-939476-77-0). Biblio Pr GA.

Bibliotheca Press Research Dept. Almost Meat: Nutritional Foods that Can Be Prepared to Taste Like Meat. 50p. 1983. pap. 8.95 (ISBN 0-939476-60-6). Biblio Pr GA.

Bibliotheca Press Research Division, compiled by. The Baby Index. 300p. 1983. pap. 16.95 (ISBN 0-939476-66-5). Biblio Pr GA.

Bibliotheca Press Research Project. The Directory of Special Black Libraries, Museums, Halls of Fames, Colleges, Art Galleries, Etc. 300p. 1983. text ed. 39.95 (ISBN 0-939476-90-8). Biblio Pr GA.

--Selected Topics on Creative Ways to Recycle. (A Recycling Ser.). 1983. text ed. 79.95 (ISBN 0-939476-88-6); pap. text ed. 69.95 (ISBN 0-939476-89-4). Biblio Pr GA.

Bibliotheca Press Research Staff. An Unescorted Woman. Date not set. 12.95 (ISBN 0-939476-25-8); pap. 9.95 (ISBN 0-939476-26-6). Biblio Pr GA.

Bibliotheca Press Staff. Cookbooks & Recipes for Almost Nothing & More. 75p. 1983. pap. text ed. 9.95 (ISBN 0-939476-67-3). Biblio Pr GA.

--Directory of Vegetarian Cookbooks. 70p. 1983. pap. text ed. 9.95 (ISBN 0-939476-68-1). Biblio Pr GA.

Bibliotheca Press Staff, ed. The Cultural & Ethnic Cookbook Index. 60p. 1983. pap. 9.95 (ISBN 0-939476-69-X). Biblio Pr GA.

--Why Not an Answering Service? Telephone Answering Service Ideas. 50p. 1983. pap. text ed. 29.95 (ISBN 0-939476-65-7). Biblio Pr GA.

Bibliotheque du Musee de l'Homme, Paris. Catalogue Systematique De la Section Afrique (Classified Catalog of theAfrica Section, 2 Vols. 1970. Set. lib. bdg. 145.00 (ISBN 0-8161-0827-7, Hall Library). G K Hall.

Bibliotheque Forney. Davis Catalog of Periodical Articles-Decorative & Fine Arts, 4 vols. 1972. Set. lib. bdg. 380.00 (ISBN 0-8161-0965-6, Hall Library). G K Hall.

--Davis Catalog of the Catalogs of Sales of Art, 2 vols. 1972. Set. lib. bdg. 190.00 (ISBN 0-8161-0962-1, Hall Library). G K Hall.

Bibliotheque Imperiale Publique De St. Petersbourg. Catalogue De la Section Des Russica: Ecrits Sur la Russie En Langues Etrangere, 2 Vols. LC 72-115679. 1970. Repr. of 1873 ed. Set. lib. bdg. 125.00 (ISBN 0-306-71933-9). Da Capo.

Biblograph S.A., Spain. Larousse-Vox Concise Spanish-English, English-Spanish Dictionary. LC 75-13699. 981p. (Eng. & Span.). 1975. 7.95 o.p. (ISBN 0-88332-037-1, 23816). Larousse.

Bibo, Istvan. The Paralysis of International Institutions & the Remedies: A Study of Self-Determination, Concord Among the Major Powers & Political Arbitration. LC 75-17182. 152p. 1976. 34.95 (ISBN 0-470-07208-3). Halsted Pr.

--The Paralysis of International Institutions & the Remedies: A Study of Self-Determination, Concord Among the Major Powers, & Political Arbitration. LC 75-17182. 152p. 1976. 17.50 (ISBN 0-686-96767-4, Pub. by Wiley). Krieger.

Bic, Lubomir. Micos Handbook. 1983. text ed. price not set (ISBN 0-914894-76-5). Computer Sci.

Bicanic, R. Economic Policy in Socialist Yugoslavia. LC 72-80588. (Soviet & East European Studies). (Illus.). 270p. 1973. 47.50 (ISBN 0-521-08631-0). Cambridge U Pr.

Bicherx, Haim I. & Bruley, Duane F., eds. Hyperthermia. (Advances in Experimental Medicine & Biology: Vol. 157). 200p. 1982. 37.50 (ISBN 0-306-41172-5, Plenum Pr). Plenum Pub.

Bickart, T., jt. auth. see Balabanian, Norman.

Bickart, Theodore, jt. auth. see Balabanian, Norman.

Bickel, Alexander M. The Least Dangerous Branch: The Supreme Court at the Bar of Politics. LC 62-20685. (Orig.). 1962. pap. 8.50 o.p. (ISBN 0-672-60757-3). Bobbs.

--Politics & the Warren Court. LC 73-398. (American Constitutional & Legal History Ser.). 314p. 1973. Repr. of 1955 ed. lib. bdg. 35.00 (ISBN 0-306-70573-7). Da Capo.

Bickel, P. J. & Doksum, K. A. Mathematical Statistics: Basic Ideas & Selected Topics. LC 76-8724. 1977. 29.95x (ISBN 0-8162-0784-4). Holden-Day.

Bickel, Peter J. & Doksum, Kjell, eds. A Festschrift for Erich L. Lehmann. (Wadsworth Statistics-Probability Ser.). 461p. 1982. 39.95 (ISBN 0-534-98044-9). Wadsworth Pub.

Bickel, Robert D. & Young, Parker, eds. The College Administrator & the Courts. Date not set. price not set. Coll Admin Pubns.

Bickerman, Elias. From Ezra to the Last of the Maccabees: Foundations of Post-Biblical Judaism. 1962. pap. 4.95 (ISBN 0-8052-0036-3). Schocken.

Bickerman, Elias J., ed. see Rostovtzeff, Mikhail I.

Bickers, David, jt. auth. see Harber, Leonard C.

Bickers, David R., jt. auth. see Harber, Leonard C.

Bickerstaff, Edwin R. Neurological Complications of Oral Contraceptives. (Oxford Neurological Monographs). (Illus.). 1975. pap. text ed. 21.95x (ISBN 0-19-857207-7). Oxford U Pr.

Bickerton, D. Dynamics of a Creole System. LC 74-12971. (Illus.). 288p. 1975. 34.50 (ISBN 0-521-20514-X). Cambridge U Pr.

Bickerton, Derek. King of the Sea. 1981. pap. 2.50 o.p. (ISBN 0-425-04846-2). Berkley Pub.

Bickford, Christopher P. Farmington in Connecticut. LC 82-18575. (Illus.). 496p. 1982. 19.95 (ISBN 0-914016-92-X). Phoenix Pub.

Bickford, Elwood D. & Dunn, Stuart. Lighting for Plant Growth. LC 70-157464. (Illus.). 264p. 1972. 18.00x o.p. (ISBN 0-87338-116-5). Kent St U Pr.

Bickford, J. P. & Mullineux, N. Computation of Power-System Transients. (IEE Monograph Ser.: No. 18). 186p. 1980. pap. 27.50 (ISBN 0-906048-35-4). Inst Elect Eng.

Bickford, John H. Mechanisms for Internittent Motion. LC 75-184639. 272p. 1972. 28.50 (ISBN 0-8311-1091-0). Krieger.

Bickford, Paul. Poems & Other Stuff. (Illus.). 37p. 1982. pap. 4.95x (ISBN 0-910303-00-2). Writers Pub Serv.

Bickford, Ted, jt. ed. see Arnell, Peter.

Bickham, George. The Universal Penman. (Illus.). 1941. pap. 9.95 (ISBN 0-486-20616-5). Dover.

Bickham, Jack. All the Days Were Summer. 224p. 1982. pap. 2.25 (ISBN 0-448-16926-6, Pub. by Tempo). Ace Bks.

--Baker's Hawk. 240p. 1982. pap. 2.50 (ISBN 0-441-05723-3, Pub. by Tempo). Ace Bks.

Bickimer, David A. Christ the Placenta. LC 82-24097. 230p. (Orig.). 1983. pap. 12.95x (ISBN 0-89135-034-9). Religious Educ.

Bickley, A. C. see Gomme, George L., et al.

Bickley, Nora. Letters from & to Joseph Joachim. Bickley, Nora, tr. LC 70-183496. 470p. Date not set. Repr. of 1914 ed. price not set. Vienna Hse.

Bickley, R. Bruce, et al, eds. Joel Chandler Harris: A Reference Guide. 1978. lib. bdg. 35.00 (ISBN 0-8161-7873-9, Hall Reference). G K Hall.

Bickley, R. Bruce, Jr. Critical Essays on Joel Chandler Harris. (Critical Essays on American Literature). 1981. 25.00 (ISBN 0-8161-8381-3, Twayne). G K Hall.

--Joel Chandler Harris. (United States Authors Ser.). 1978. lib. bdg. 12.95 (ISBN 0-8057-7215-4, Twayne). G K Hall.

Bickman, Leonard, ed. Applied Social Psychology Annual, Vol. 3. (Illus.). 312p. 1982. 22.50 (ISBN 0-8039-0796-6); pap. 9.95 (ISBN 0-8039-0797-4). Sage.

Bickman, Leonard & Henchy, Thomas, eds. Beyond the Laboratory: Field Research in Social Psychology. 352p. 1971. text ed. 19.50 (ISBN 0-07-005192-5, C). McGraw.

Bicknell & Sines. Community Mental Handicap Nursing. 1983. pap. text ed. 12.95 (ISBN 0-06-318246-7, Pub. by Har-Row Ltd England). Har-Row.

Bicknell, A. J. Wooden & Brick Buildings with Details. (Architecture & Decorative Art Ser.). 1977. Repr. of 1875 ed. 85.00 (ISBN 0-306-70832-9). Da Capo.

Bicknell, Andrew, jt. auth. see Greenfingers, G.

Bicknell, D. J. Pica: A Childhood Symptom. 1975. 14.00 o.p. (ISBN 0-407-35858-7). Butterworth.

Bicknell, J. & McQuiston, L., eds. Design for Need. 1977. pap. write for info. o.p. (ISBN 0-08-021500-9). Pergamon.

Bicknese. Hier und Heute: Lesen Leicht Gemacht. 1983. pap. text ed. price not set. HM.

Bicknese, Gunther. Hier und Heute: Lessen Leicht Gemacht. LC 82-84304. 96p. 1983. pap. text ed. 7.95 (ISBN 0-395-33249-4). HM.

Bicksler, J. L., ed. Handbook of Financial Economics. 470p. 1980. 93.75 (ISBN 0-444-85224-7, North Holland). Elsevier.

Bicksler, James L. & Samuelson, Paul A., eds. Investment Portfolio Decision-Making. LC 73-1561. 1974. 22.95 (ISBN 0-669-86215-0). Lexington Bks.

Bickston, Diana. Street Birth. (Prison Writing Ser.). 36p. 1982. pap. 2.00 (ISBN 0-912678-52-6). Greenfld Rev Pr.

Bicudo, C. & Sormus, L. Desmidioflorula Paulista II: Genero Micrasterias C. Agardh ex Ralfs. (Bibliotheca Phycologica: No. 57). (Illus.). 230p. (Span.). 1982. pap. text ed. 36.00x (ISBN 0-686-36939-4). Lubrecht & Cramer.

Bicudo, C. E. & Azevedo, M. T. Desmidioflorula Paulista I: Genero Arthordesmus Ehr. ex Ralfs Emend. Arch. (Bibliotheca Phycologica Ser.: No. 36). (Illus., Port.). 1978. text ed. 16.00 (ISBN 3-7682-1156-8). Lubrecht & Cramer.

Bicudo, Carlos E., jt. auth. see Croasdale, Hannah.

Bicudo, Carlos E., jt. auth. see Prescott, G. W.

Bicudo, Carlos M. Contribution to the Knowledge of the Desmids of the State of Sao Paulo. (Illus.). 1969. 11.20 (ISBN 3-7682-0653-X). Lubrecht & Cramer.

Bicycling Magazine Editors. Basic Bicycle Repair. 96p. 1982. pap. 3.95 (ISBN 0-87857-315-1, 12-003-1). Rodale Pr Inc.

Biddle, Arthur W. & Eschholz, Paul A., eds. The Literature of Vermont: A Sampler. LC 73-76017. (Illus.). 390p. 1973. 25.00x (ISBN 0-87451-074-0). U Pr of New Eng.

Biddle, Bruce J., jt. auth. see Dunkin, Michael J.

Biddle, Bruce J., jt. auth. see Good, Thomas L.

Biddle, Edward & Fielding, Mantle. Life & Works of Thomas Sully. LC 74-77716. (Library of American Art Ser). 1970. Repr. of 1921 ed. lib. bdg. 42.50 (ISBN 0-306-71354-3). Da Capo.

Biddle, Francis. Fear of Freedom. LC 76-138496. (Civil Liberties in American History Ser). 1971. Repr. of 1951 ed. lib. bdg. 39.50 (ISBN 0-306-70073-5). Da Capo.

Biddle, Marcia. Tony Dorsett. LC 80-18302. (Illus.). 192p. (gr. 7 up). 1980. PLB 8.79 o.p. (ISBN 0-671-34040-9). Messner.

Biddulph, John. Tribes of the Hindoo Koosh. (Illus.). 352p. 1971. Repr. of 1880 ed. 45.00x (ISBN 0-8002-2109-5). Intl Pubns Serv.

Biddulph, M. W., jt. ed. see Henstock, M. E.

Bider, Djemma. The Buried Treasure. LC 81-43216. (Illus.). 32p. (gr. k-3). 1982. PLB 10.95 (ISBN 0-396-07991-1). Dodd.

Biderman, Bob. Letters to Nanette. LC 82-5180. (Contemporary Lit. Ser.). 256p. 1982. 11.95 (ISBN 0-915786-07-9); pap. 5.95 (ISBN 0-915786-08-7). Early Stages.

Biderman, Jaime, jt. auth. see Carnemark, Curt.

Bidwell, Bruce & Heffer, Linda. The Joycean Way: A Topographical Guide to "Dubliners" & "A Portrait of the Artist as a Young Man". LC 82-80660. 144p. 1982. 25.00x (ISBN 0-8018-2879-1). Johns Hopkins.

Bidwell, Charles, jt. ed. see Windham, Douglas.

Bidwell, John, ed. see Munsell, Joel.

Bidwell, John, ed. see R. Hoe & Co.

Bidwell, Percy W. Rural Economy in New England at the Beginning of the 19th Century. LC 68-55480. (Illus.). 1972. Repr. of 1916 ed. 19.50x (ISBN 0-678-00815-9). Kelley.

Bidwell, R. G. Plant Physiology. 2nd ed. 1979. text ed. 31.95 (ISBN 0-02-309430-3). Macmillan.

Bidwell, R. G., ed. Rusi & Brassey's Defense Yearbook 1976-77, Vol. 87. LC 76-29923. (Defense Publications Ser.). 1977. lib. bdg. 38.00 o.p. (ISBN 0-89158-630-X). Westview.

Bidwell, R. G., jt. ed. see Steward, F. C.

Bidwell, Robin. The Two Yemens. 250p. 1982. lib. bdg. 26.00X (ISBN 0-86531-295-8). Westview.

Bidwell, Shelford. Swords for Hire: European Mercenaries in Eighteenth Century India. (Illus.). 258p. 1972. 15.00x o.p. (ISBN 0-7195-2432-6). Transatlantic.

Bie, Oscar. History of the Pianoforte & Pianoforte Players. 2nd ed. LC 66-28445. 1966. Repr. of 1899 ed. lib. bdg. 27.50 (ISBN 0-306-70938-4). Da Capo.

Bie, S. W., ed. see ISSS Working Group on Soil Information Systems 2nd Varna-Sofia, Bulgaria, 30 May - 4 June, 1977.

Biebel, David B. Jonathan, You Left too Soon. 1982. pap. 2.95 (ISBN 0-451-11775-1, AE1775, Sig). NAL.

Biebel, P., ed. Desmid Research International Symposium, Second, Itasasca, Minnesota, 1976: Proceedings. (Beiheft Zur Nova Hedwigia 56 Ser.). lib. bdg. cancelled o.s.i. (ISBN 3-7682-5456-9). Lubrecht & Cramer.

Bieber, Konrad. Simone de Beauvoir. (World Authors Ser.). 1979. lib. bdg. 13.95 (ISBN 0-8057-6374-0, Twayne). G K Hall.

Bieberbach, Ludwig. Conformal Mapping. LC 53-7209. 7.95 (ISBN 0-8284-0090-3); pap. 2.95 o. p. (ISBN 0-8284-0176-4). Chelsea Pub.

Bieberstein, F. Marschall Von see Von Bieberstein, F. Marschall.

Biebuyck, Daniel. Lega Culture: Art, Initiation, & Moral Philosophy Among a Central African People. LC 71-165226. 1973. 40.00x o.p. (ISBN 0-520-02085-5). U of Cal Pr.

--Tradition & Creativity in Tribal Art. LC 69-12457. 1969. 44.00x (ISBN 0-520-01509-6); pap. 4.95 (ISBN 0-520-02487-7). U of Cal Pr.

Biebuyck, Daniel & Mateene, Kahombo C., eds. The Mwindo Epic from the Banyanga (Congo Republic) LC 68-28370. 1969. 30.00x (ISBN 0-520-01502-9); pap. 2.45 (ISBN 0-520-02049-9, CAL233). U of Cal Pr.

Biedenharn, L. C. & Louck, J. D. Racah-Wigner Algebra in Quantum Theory. (Encyclopedia of Mathematics & Its Applications Ser.: Vol. 9). (Illus.). 1980. text ed. 56.50 (ISBN 0-201-13508-6). A-W.

Biederman, Jerry, jt. auth. see Silberkleit, Tom.

Biederman-Thorson, M. A., tr. see Larcher, W.

Biederman-Thorson, M. A., tr. see Schmidt, R. F. & Thews, G.

Biederstadt, Lynn. The Eye of the Mind. LC 80-28717. 256p. 1981. 12.95 (ISBN 0-399-90108-6, Marek). Putnam Pub Group.

--Eye of the Mind. 1982. pap. 3.50 (ISBN 0-451-11736-0, AE1736, Sig). NAL.

Biefang, S., et al. Manual For the Planning & Implementation of Therapeutic Studies. (Lecture Notes in Medical Informatics Ser.: Vol. 20). 100p. 1983. pap. 12.00 (ISBN 0-387-11979-5). Springer-Verlag.

Biegal, Leonard. The Best Years Catalogue: A Source Book for Older Americans: Solving Problems & Living Fully. LC 77-24196. (Illus.). 1978. 12.95 o.p. (ISBN 0-399-11898-5); pap. 6.95 o.p. (ISBN 0-399-12093-9). Putnam Pub Group.

Biegel, David E. & Naparstek, Arthur J. Neighborhood Networks for Humane Mental Health Care. 238p. 1982. 24.50x (ISBN 0-306-41051-6, Plenum Pr). Plenum Pub.

Biegeleisen, J. I. Complete Book of Silk Screen Printing Production. (Illus., Orig.). 1963. pap. 4.00 (ISBN 0-486-21100-2). Dover.

Biegeleisen, Jacob I. Job Resumes. 112p. Date not set. pap. 4.95 (ISBN 0-448-00953-6, G&D). Putnam Pub Group.

--Job Resumes. rev. ed. 112p. 1976. pap. 3.95 (ISBN 0-448-00947-1, G&D). Putnam Pub Group.

Biegert, John E. Mirando Hacia Arriba en Medio de la Enfermedad. 24p. (Orig., Span.). 1983. pap. 1.25 (ISBN 0-8298-0663-6). Pilgrim NY.

Biehl, David L., jt. auth. see Bailard, Thomas E.

Biehler, Robert F. Child Development: An Introduction. 2nd ed. LC 80-82347. (Illus.). 704p. 1981. text ed. 23.50 (ISBN 0-395-29833-4); study guide 8.95 (ISBN 0-395-29835-0); instr's manual 1.00 (ISBN 0-395-29834-2). HM.

Biehler, Robert F. & Snowran, Jack. Psychology Applied to Teaching. 4th ed. LC 81-82572. 1982. 20.50 (ISBN 0-395-31681-2); Instr's man. & test 2.00; 9.95 (ISBN 0-395-31683-9). HM.

Biehler, Robert F., ed. Psychology Applied to Teaching: Selected Readings. LC 77-18726. (Illus., Orig.). 1972. pap. text ed. 5.95 (ISBN 0-395-13341-6). HM.

Bieker, Beverly, jt. auth. see Roth, Sandra.

Bielenstein, Hans. The Bureaucracy of Han Times. LC 78-72080. (Cambridge Studies in Chinese History, Literature & Institutions). (Illus.). 1980. 42.50 (ISBN 0-521-22510-8). Cambridge U Pr.

Bieler, Arthur, jt. auth. see Haac, Oscar A.

Bieler, Arthur, et al. Perspectives de France. 3rd ed. (Illus.). 576p. 1982. text ed. 21.95 (ISBN 0-13-660563-X). P-H.

Bieler, Henry G. Food Is Your Best Medicine. 256p. 1973. pap. 2.95 (ISBN 0-394-30190-0, V-837, Vin). Random.

Bielfeld, Horst & Heidenreich, Manfred. Handbook of Lovebirds: With Special Section on Diseases of Parrots. Arrens, Christa, tr. (Illus.). 111p. 1982. 16.95 (ISBN 0-87666-820-1, H-1040). TFH Pubns.

Bieliauskas, Linas A. Stress & Its Relationship to Health & Illness. (Behavioral Sciences for Health Care Professionals Ser.). 128p. (Orig.). 1982. 15.00 (ISBN 0-86531-002-5); pap. text ed. 6.75 (ISBN 0-86531-003-3). Westview.

Bielski, Nella. Oranges for the Son of Asher Levy. Berger, John & Appignanesi, Lisa, trs. (Fr.). 1982. 11.95 (ISBN 0-906495-70-9). Writers & Readers.

Biemel, Walter. Martin Heidegger. Mehta, J. L., tr. LC 76-21253. 1976. 6.95 (ISBN 0-15-657301-6, Harv). HarBraceJ.

Biemer, Linda B. Women & Property in Colonial New York: The Transition from Dutch to English Law, 1643-1727. Berkhofer, Robert, ed. LC 82-23701. (Studies in American History & Culture: No. 38). 1983. write for info. (ISBN 0-8357-1392-X). Univ Microfilms.

Biemiller, Carl, jt. auth. see Hill, Ivan.

Biemiller, Carl L. The Hydronaut Adventures. LC 80-2441. (Doubleday Fatback Ser.). (Illus.). 408p. (gr. 6-8). 1981. pap. 4.95 (ISBN 0-385-15536-0). Doubleday.

Bien, David D. The Calas Affair: Persecution, Toleration, & Heresy in Eighteenth-Century Toulouse. LC 78-12393. 1979. Repr. of 1960 ed. lib. bdg. 17.75x (ISBN 0-313-21206-6, BICA). Greenwood.

Bien, Joseph, ed. see Ricoeur, Paul.

Bien, Peter, et al. Demotic Greek II: The Flying Telephone Booth. LC 81-51609. (Illus.). 544p. (Orig.). 1982. pap. text ed. 12.50x (ISBN 0-87451-208-5); wkbk. 6.00x (ISBN 0-87451-209-3). U Pr of New Eng.

Biene, Susanna & Moneli, illus. Sing Through the Seasons: Ninety-Nine Songs for Children. LC 70-164916. (Illus.). 190p. 1972. 11.95 (ISBN 0-87486-006-7); l.p. record 6.00 (ISBN 0-87486-040-7). Plough.

Bienefeld, Manfred & Godfrey, Martin. The Struggle for Development: National Strategies in an International Contex. LC 81-19821. 352p. 1982. 29.95x (ISBN 0-471-10152-4). Wiley.

Bienenfeld, Florence. Child Custody. 1983. 9.95. Sci & Behavior.

Bienestock, Arthur, ed. Liquids & Amorphous Materials. pap. 7.50 (ISBN 0-686-60381-8). Polycrystal Bk Serv.

Bienkiewicz, Krzysztof J. Physical Chemistry of Leather Making. LC 80-27191. 1983. 34.50 (ISBN 0-89874-304-4). Krieger.

Bienvenue, Dudley. I'm an Alcoholic, What's Your Excuse? (Illus.). 1983. 7.95 (ISBN 0-533-05229-7). Vantage.

Bier, Norman & Lowther, Gerald. Contact Lens Correction. (Illus.). 1977. 74.95 (ISBN 0-407-00101-8). Butterworth.

Bierbrier, Doreen. Living with Tenants: How to Happily Share Your House with Renters for Profit & Security. 128p. (Orig.). 1983. pap. 7.00 (ISBN 0-9609586-0-6). Housing Connect.

Bierbrier, M. L. Hieroglyphic Texts from Egyptian Stelae etc. in the British Museum, Pt. X. 152p. 1982. 99.00x (ISBN 0-7141-0926-6, Pub. by Brot Mus Pubns England). State Mutual Bk.

Bierbrier, Morris. Tomb Builders of the Pharoahs. 160p. 1982. 75.00x (ISBN 0-7141-8044-0, Pub. by Brit Mus Pubns England). State Mutual Bk.

Bierce, Ambrose. Fantastic Fables. LC 73-92026. 1970. pap. 2.50 (ISBN 0-486-22225-X). Dover.

--For the Ahkoond. 1.00 o.p. (ISBN 0-686-31249-X). Necronomicon.

--An Occurrence at Owl Creek Bridge. (Creative's Classics Ser.). (Illus.). 40p. (gr. 4-9). 1980. PLB 7.95 (ISBN 0-87191-770-X). Creative Ed.

Bierhorst, John, ed. In the Trail of the Wind: American Indian Poems & Ritual Orations. LC 71-144822. (Illus.). (gr. 7 up). 1971. 6.95 (ISBN 0-374-33640-7); pap. 4.95 o.p. (ISBN 0-374-50901-8). FS&G.

Bieri, James, et al. Clinical & Social Judgment: The Discrimination of Behavioral Information. LC 75-11944. 288p. 1975. Repr. of 1966 ed. 17.50 (ISBN 0-88275-291-X). Krieger.

Bierley, Paul E. Hallelujah Trombone! The Story of Henry Fillmore. LC 82-90686. 1982. pap. 14.95 (ISBN 0-918048-03-6). Integrity.

--John Philip Sousa: American Phenomenon. 1973. 20.95 (ISBN 0-13-823534-1). P-H.

--The Music of Henry Fillmore & Will Huff. LC 82-81491. (Music Catalog Ser.). 1982. pap. 5.95 (ISBN 0-918048-02-8). Integrity.

Bierman, Arthur K. & Gould, James A. Philosophy for a New Generation. 4th ed. 1981. pap. 15.95 (ISBN 0-02-309640-3). Macmillan.

Bierman, Don E. The Oder River: Transport & Economic Development. 247p. 1973. pap. 2.50 (ISBN 0-686-94034-2, Trans). Northwestern U Pr.

Bierman, Edwin L., jt. ed. see Smith, David W.

Bierman, Harold, Jr. Decision Making & Planning for the Corporate Treasurer. LC 76-58435. (Systems & Controls for Financial Management Ser.). 1977. 39.95x (ISBN 0-471-07238-9). Ronald Pr.

Bierman, Harold, Jr. & Dyckman, Thomas R. Managerial Cost Accounting. 2nd ed. (Illus.). 480p. 1976. 29.95x (ISBN 0-02-309720-5, 30972). Macmillan.

Bierman, Harold, Jr. & Smidt, Seymour. The Capital Budgeting Decision: Economic Analysis of Investment Projects. 5th ed. (Illus.). 1980. text ed. 29.95 (ISBN 0-02-309480-X). Macmillan.

Bierman, John. Righteous Gentile: The Story of Raoul Wallenberg, Missing Hero of the Holocaust. 210p. Repr. 12.95 (ISBN 0-686-95084-4). ADL.

Biermann, J. H. Organographia Hildesiensis Specialis Hildesheim. (Bibliotheca Organologica Ser.: Vol. 29). 1980. Repr. of 1930 ed. 37.50 o.s.i. (ISBN 90-6027-167-X, Pub. by Frits Knuf Netherlands); wrappers 25.00 o.s.i. (ISBN 90-6027-166-1, Pub. by Frit Knuf Netherlands). Pendragon NY.

Biermann, June & Toohey, Barbara. The Diabetic's Sports & Exercise Book: How to Play Your Way to Better Health. LC 76-17894. (Illus.). 1977. 10.95 o.p. (ISBN 0-397-01115-6); pap. 5.95i (ISBN 0-397-01202-0, LP-114). Har-Row.

--The Woman's Holistic Headache Relief Book. 212p. Repr. of 1979 ed. 8.95 (ISBN 0-686-35967-4). Sugarfree.

Biers, Jane C. & Soren, David, eds. Studies in Cypriote Archaeology. (Monograph Ser.: No. XVIII). 190p. 1981. pap. 15.00 (ISBN 0-917956-23-0). UCLA Arch.

Bierstedt, Robert. The Social Order. 4th ed. (Illus.). 544p. 1974. text ed. 26.95 (ISBN 0-07-005253-0, C); instructor's manual by Hill 3.95 (ISBN 0-07-028815-1). McGraw.

Biersteker, Thomas J. Distortion or Development? Contending Perspectives on the Multinational Corporation. 1979. 22.50x (ISBN 0-262-02133-1); pap. 7.95x (ISBN 0-262-52065-6). MIT Pr.

Bierwag, G. O. The Primary Market for Municipal Debt: Bidding Rules & the Cost of Long-Term Borrowing, Vol. 29. Altman, Edward I. & Walter, Ingo, eds. LC 80-82480. (Contemporary Studies in Economic & Financial Analysis). 300p. 1981. 40.00 (ISBN 0-89232-167-9). Jai Pr.

Bies, John D. Architectural Drafting: Structure & Environment. (Illus.). 352p. 1983. pap. text ed. 15.95 (ISBN 0-686-82303-6). Bobbs.

Biesantz, Hagen & Klingborg, Arne. The Goetheanum: Rudolf Steiner's Architectural Impulse. Schmid, Jean, tr. from Ger. (Illus.). 131p. 1979. pap. 14.95 (ISBN 0-85440-355-8, Pub. by Steinerbooks). Anthroposophic.

Biesanz, John & Biesanz, Mavis. Modern Society with Revisions. 3rd ed. 1971. text ed. 22.95 (ISBN 0-13-597732-0). P-H.

Biesanz, John, jt. auth. see Biesanz, Mavis.

Biesanz, Mavis & Biesanz, John. Introduction to Sociology. 3rd ed. (Illus.). 1978. text ed. 22.95 (ISBN 0-13-497412-3); study guide 8.95 (ISBN 0-13-497404-2). P-H.

Biesanz, Mavis, jt. auth. see Biesanz, John.

Biesanz, Richard, et al. The Costa Ricans. (Illus.). 304p. 1982. pap. 17.95 reference (ISBN 0-13-179606-2). P-H.

Biever, Dale, et al. Four Pennsylvania German Studies, Vol. III. 1970. 15.00 (ISBN 0-911122-26-5). Penn German Soc.

Bigane, John E., III. Faith, Christ or Peter: Matthew Sixteen: Eighteen in Sixteenth Century Roman Catholic Exegesis. LC 80-6095. 247p. 1981. lib. bdg. 21.25 (ISBN 0-8191-1524-X); pap. text ed. 10.75 (ISBN 0-8191-1525-8). U Pr of Amer.

Bigazzi, Pierluigi E., jt. auth. see Rose, Noel.

Bigelow, Donald, ed. Schoolworlds 1976. LC 76-15293. 1976. 21.75x (ISBN 0-8211-0130-7); text ed. 19.50x ea. 10 or more copies. McCutchan.

Bigelow, Gordon E. & Monti, Laura V., eds. Selected Letters of Majorie Kinnan Rawlings. (Illus.). 384p. 1983. 30.00 (ISBN 0-8130-0728-3). U Presses Fla.

Bigelow, Howard E. North American Species of Clitocybe, Vol. I. (Nova Hedwigia Beiheft: No. 72). (Illus.). 500p. 1982. text ed. 54.00 (ISBN 3-7682-5472-0). Lubrecht & Cramer.

Bigelow, R. & Nycum, S. Your Computer & the Law. 1975. 24.95 (ISBN 0-13-977983-3). P-H.

Bigge, June L. Teaching Individuals with Physical & Multiple Disabilities. 2nd ed. 424p. 1982. text ed. 22.95 (ISBN 0-675-09928-5). Merrill.

Bigge, Morris L. & Reynolds, George W. Philosophies for Teachers. 240p. 1982. pap. text ed. 11.95 (ISBN 0-675-09839-4). Merrill.

Biggers, Earl D. The Agony Column. 1976. Repr. of 1916 ed. PLB 15.95 (ISBN 0-89966-074-6). Buccaneer Bks.

--Charlie Chan--Great Stories from the Saturday Evening Post. LC 77-90936. 320p. 1977. 5.95 o.p. (ISBN 0-89387-015-3, Co-Pub by Sat Eve Post). Curtis Pub Co.

--Fifty Candles. 1979. Repr. lib. bdg. 14.95 (ISBN 0-89966-079-7). Buccaneer Bks.

Biggs, A. K. Matrimonial Proceedings. 1980. 30.00x (ISBN 0-686-97103-5, Pub. by Fourmat England). State Mutual Bk.

Biggs, A. K. & Rogers, A. P. Probate Practice & Procedure. 1981. 40.00x (ISBN 0-686-97111-6, Pub. by Fourmat England). State Mutual Bk.

Biggs, Charles L., et al. Managing the Systems Development Process. 1980. text ed. 30.00 (ISBN 0-13-550830-4). P-H.

Biggs, Donald A., jt. auth. see Blocher, Donald H.

Biggs, Donald A., jt. auth. see Williamson, Edmund G.

Biggs, Donald A., jt. ed. see Giroux, Roy F.

Biggs, Donald C. Conquer & Colonize: Stevenson's Regiment & California. LC 77-73564. (Illus.). 1978. 12.95 o.p. (ISBN 0-89141-023-6). Presidio Pr.

Biggs, Howard. The River Medway. 160p. 1982. 35.00x (ISBN 0-86138-005-3, Pub. by Terence Dalton England). State Mutual Bk.

Biggs, J. B. Information & Human Learning. Lyman, John, adapted by. 1971. pap. 7.95x (ISBN 0-673-07555-9). Scott F.

--Mathematics & the Conditions of Learning: A Study of Arithmetic in the Primary School. (General Ser.). 1970. Repr. of 1967 ed. text ed. 24.75x o.p. (ISBN 0-901225-24-X, NFER). Humanities.

Biggs, John M. Introduction to Structural Dynamics. 1964. text ed. 36.50 (ISBN 0-07-005255-7, C). McGraw.

Biggs, Margaret K. Magnolias & Such. (Illus.). 1982. 2.00 (ISBN 0-943696-00-3). Red Key Pr.

--Petals from the Woman Flower. 20p. (Orig.). 1983. pap. 2.00 (ISBN 0-938566-14-8). Adastra Pr.

Biggs, Mouzon, Jr. Moments to Hold Close. 144p. 1983. 8.95 (ISBN 0-687-27147-9). Abingdon.

Biggs, N. L. Algebraic Graph Theory. LC 73-86042. (Tracts in Mathematics Ser.: No. 67). (Illus.). 180p. 1974. 29.95x (ISBN 0-521-20335-X). Cambridge U Pr.

--Interaction Models. LC 77-80827. (London Mathematical Society Lecture Ser.: No. 30). (Illus.). 1977. 18.95x (ISBN 0-521-21770-9). Cambridge U Pr.

Biggs, N. L. & White, A. T. Permutation Groups & Combinatorial Structures. LC 78-21485. (London Mathematical Society Lecture Note: No. 33). (Illus.). 1979. pap. 20.95x (ISBN 0-521-22287-7). Cambridge U Pr.

Biggs, P. & Dalwood, C. Les Orleanais ont la Parole. (Illus.). 1977. pap. text ed. 4.00x (ISBN 0-582-33121-8); tchr's ed. 4.50x (ISBN 0-582-33122-6); tapes 17.50x (ISBN 0-582-37885-0). Longman.

Biggs, Robert D. Inscriptions from Al-Hiba-Lagash: The First & Second Seasons. LC 76-47770. (Bibliotheca Mesopotamica: Vol.3). (Illus.). vi, 47p. 1976. 12.00x (ISBN 0-89003-018-9); pap. 6.50x o.p. (ISBN 0-89003-017-0). Undena Pubns.

Biggs, Shirley A., jt. auth. see Scales, Alice M.

Biggs, W. D. The Mechanical Behaviour of Engineering Materials. 1966. text ed. 12.75 (ISBN 0-08-011415-6); pap. text ed. 8.50 (ISBN 0-08-011414-8). Pergamon.

Bigl, Joseph H., et al. Blade Coating Technology. Clark, C. Wells, ed. (TAPPI PRESS Reports). (Illus.). 84p. (Orig.). 1978. pap. 24.95 (ISBN 0-89852-373-7, 01-01-R073). TAPPI.

Bigland, Eileen. In the Steps of George Borrow. 355p. 1982. Repr. of 1951 ed. lib. bdg. 50.00 (ISBN 0-89760-091-6). Telegraph Bks.

Bigler, Robert M. The Politics of German Protestantism: The Rise of the Protestant Church Elite in Prussia, 1815-1848. LC 77-142055. 1972. 36.50x (ISBN 0-520-01881-8). U of Cal Pr.

Bigliani, Raymond, jt. auth. see Nolan, Peter.

Biglieu, E. G., jt. auth. see Mantero, F.

Bigman, David. Coping with Hunger: Toward a System of Food Security & Price Stabilization. LC 81-22908. 384p. 1982. prof ref 35.00x (ISBN 0-88410-371-4). Ballinger Pub.

Bigman, David, ed. Floating Exchange Rates & the State of World Trade & Payments. Taya, Teizo. Date not set. price not set professional ref. (ISBN 0-88410-398-6). Ballinger Pub.

Bigman, David & Taya, Teizo, eds. Exchange Rate & Trade Instability: Causes, Consequences & Remedies. 320p. 1983. Prof. Ref. 35.00x (ISBN 0-88410-898-8). Ballinger Pub.

--The Functioning of Floating Exchange Rates: Theory, Evidence & Policy Implications. LC 79-21589. 448p. 1980. prof ref 39.50x (ISBN 0-88410-492-3). Ballinger Pub.

Bigmore, F. C. A Bibliography of Printing. 1982. 75.00x (ISBN 0-87556-157-8). Saifer.

Bignell, Merle. A Planet to Meet: A History of the Shire of Katanning Western Australia. 350p. 1983. 24.00 (ISBN 0-85564-202-5, Pub. by U of W Austral Pr). Intl Schol Bk Serv.

Bignell, Steven. Sex Education. Rev. ed. Hiatt, Jane & Nelson, Mary, eds. 227p. 1982. 20.00 o.p. (ISBN 0-941816-08-7); avail. tchr's guide o.p. (ISBN 0-941816-03-6). Network Pubns.

Bignell, Steven, jt. auth. see Abbey-Harris, Nancy.

Bignell, Steven, ed. Sex Education: Teacher's Guide & Resource Manual. 1977. 15.00 o.p. (ISBN 0-941816-03-6). Network Pubns.

Bigner, Jerry. Human Development: A Life-Span Approach. 688p. 1983. text ed. 19.95 (ISBN 0-02-309810-4). Macmillan.

Bigner, Jerry J. Parent-Child Relations: An Introduction to Parenting. (Illus.). 1979. text ed. 20.95 o.s.i. (ISBN 0-02-309820-1). Macmillan.

Bigner, Sandra H. & Johnston, William W. Cytopathology of the Central Nervous System. (Masson Monographs on Diagnostic Cytopathology, Vol. 3). 184p. 1983. price not set. Masson Pub.

Bigo, Pierre. The Church & Third World Revolution. Lyons, Jeanne Marie, tr. from Fr. LC 76-55388. 197p. (Orig.). 1977. 6.95x (ISBN 0-88344-071-7); pap. 4.95x o.p. (ISBN 0-686-82949-2). Orbis Bks.

Bigon, Mario & Regazzoni, Guido. Morrow's Guide to Knots. Lyman, Kennie, ed. Piotrowska, Maria, tr. from Ital. LC 82-6308. (Illus.). 258p. 1982. 15.00 (ISBN 0-688-01225-6); pap. 9.95 (ISBN 0-688-01226-4). Morrow.

Bigsby, C. Albee. (Writers & Critics Ser.). 120p. 1978. 19.75x (ISBN 0-912378-01-8). Chips.

Bigsby, C. W. A Critical Introduction to Twentieth Century American Drama: 1900-1940, Vol. 1. LC 81-18000. (Illus.). 340p. 1982. 39.50 (ISBN 0-521-24227-4); pap. 14.95 (ISBN 0-521-27116-9). Cambridge U Pr.

--The Second Black Renaissance: Essays in Black Literature. LC 79-7723. (Contributions in Afro-American & African Studies: No. 50). 1980. lib. bdg. 29.95x (ISBN 0-313-21304-6, BNB/). Greenwood.

Bigsby, Christopher W. Joe Orton. (Contemporary Writers Ser.). 1982. pap. 4.25 (ISBN 0-416-31690-5). Methuen Inc.

Bigsten, Arne. Regional Inequality & Development: A Case Study of Kenya. 191p. 1980. text ed. 44.00x (ISBN 0-566-00382-1). Gower Pub Ltd.

Bigwood, E. J. & Gerard, A. Fundamental Principles & Objectives of a Comparative Food Law, 4 vols. Incl. Vol. 1. General Introduction & Field of Application. xii, 128p. 1969. pap. 18.00 (ISBN 3-8055-0669-4); Vol. 2. Elements of Motivation & Elements of Qualification. (Illus.). xiv, 234p. 1968. pap. 35.50 (ISBN 3-8055-0670-8); Vol. 3. Elements of Structure & Institutional Elements. 240p. 1970. pap. text ed. 36.00 (ISBN 3-8055-0671-6); Vol. 4. Elements of Control & Sanction; Conclusion; Suggested Outline of a Modern Food Law. xiv, 329p. 1971. pap. text ed. 52.25 (ISBN 3-8055-1305-4). (Illus.). xxxviii, 803p. Set. pap. text ed. 96.00 (ISBN 3-8055-1332-1). S Karger.

Bigwood, E. J., et al, eds. Food Additives Tables, Parts 1-4. 1977. Set. 340.50 (ISBN 0-444-41181-X). Elsevier.

Bigwood, Jeremy, jt. ed. see Ott, Jonathan.

Bihalji-Merin, Oto. The Art of the Primitives. (Pocket Art Ser.). (Illus.). 1983. pap. 5.95 (ISBN 0-8120-2185-1). Barron.

Bikales, N. M., ed. Encyclopedia Reprints Series, 5 vols. LC 78-172950. 1239p. 1971. Set. pap. 95.00x (ISBN 0-471-07236-2, Pub. by Wiley-Interscience). Wiley.

Bikales, Norbert M., ed. Adhesion & Bonding. LC 78-172950. (Encyclopedia Reprints Ser). 208p. 1971. pap. 16.00 (ISBN 0-471-07230-3, Pub. by Wiley-Interscience). Wiley.

--Adhesion & Bonding. LC 78-172950. 220p. Repr. of 1971 ed. pap. text ed. 16.00 (ISBN 0-471-07230-3). Krieger.

--Characterization of Polymers. LC 78-172950. (Encyclopedia Reprints Ser). 264p. 1971. 16.00 o.p. (ISBN 0-471-07231-1, Pub. by Wiley-Interscience). Wiley.

--Extrusion & Other Plastics Operations. LC 78-172950. (Encyclopedia Reprints Ser). 281p. 1971. pap. 16.00 (ISBN 0-471-07232-X). Krieger.

--Mechanical Properties of Polymers. LC 78-172950. (Encyclopedia Reprints Ser). 268p. 1971. 16.00x (ISBN 0-471-07234-6, Pub. by Wiley-Interscience). Wiley.

--Mechanical Properties of Polymers. LC 78-172950. 280p. pap. text ed. 16.00 (ISBN 0-471-07234-6). Krieger.

--Molding of Plastics. LC 78-172950. (Encyclopedia Reprints Ser). 218p. 1971. 16.00x (ISBN 0-471-07233-8, Pub. by Wiley-Interscience). Wiley.

--Molding of Plastics. LC 78-172950. 230p. pap. text ed. 16.00 (ISBN 0-471-07233-8). Krieger.

Bikkal, Nicholas L. The Straight Man. 1983. 7.95 (ISBN 0-533-05041-3). Vantage.

Bikkie, J. A. General Business & Economic Foundations: Careers in Marketing. 1971. 6.56 (ISBN 0-07-005264-6, G). McGraw.

Bikkie, James A. Careers in Marketing. 2d ed. Dorr, Eugene, ed. LC 77-3865. (Occupational Manuals and Projects in Marketing). 1978. pap. text ed. 7.32 (ISBN 0-07-005236-0, G); teacher's manual & key 4.50 (ISBN 0-07-005237-9). McGraw.

Bikle, Nancy. Museum of Westward Expansion: A Photographic Collection. 126p. 1977. pap. 3.95 (ISBN 0-686-95748-2). Jefferson Natl.

Biklen, Douglas & Bailey, Lee, eds. Rudely Stamp'd: Imaginal Disability & Prejudice. LC 81-40278. (Illus.). 134p. (Orig.). 1982. lib. bdg. 19.25 (ISBN 0-8191-1982-2); pap. text ed. 8.25 (ISBN 0-8191-1983-0). U Pr of Amer.

Biklen, Douglas P. Community Organizing: Theory & Practice. 336p. 1983. text ed. 23.95 (ISBN 0-13-153676-1). P-H.

Biklen, Sari K. & Branningan, Marilyn. Women & Educational Leadership. LC 79-7748. 288p. 1980. 25.95x (ISBN 0-669-03216-6). Lexington Bks.

Bila, Dennis, et al. Arithmetic. LC 76-19446. 1976. 8.95x (ISBN 0-87901-058-4). Worth.

--Geometry & Measurement. LC 76-19445. 1976. 8.95x (ISBN 0-87901-059-2). Worth.

--Core Mathematics. LC 74-82696. (Illus.). ix, 603p. (Prog. Bk.). 1975. text ed. 18.95x (ISBN 0-87901-035-5). Worth.

--Intermediate Algebra. LC 74-84642. (Illus.). xvii, 625p. (Prog. Bk.). 1975. text ed. 18.95x (ISBN 0-87901-038-X). Worth.

--Introductory Algebra. LC 74-84641. (Illus.). xviii, 610p. (Prog. Bk.). 1975. text ed. 18.95x (ISBN 0-87901-037-1). Worth.

--Mathematics for Business Occupations. (Orig.). 1978. pap. text ed. 19.95 (ISBN 0-316-09475-7); tchr's. ed. avail. (ISBN 0-316-09477-3); test bank avail. (ISBN 0-316-09476-5). Little.

--Mathematics for Technical Occupations. (Orig.). 1978. pap. text ed. 19.95 (ISBN 0-316-09478-1). Little.

--Mathematics for the Health Occupations. (Orig.). 1978. pap. text ed. 19.95 (ISBN 0-316-09472-2); tchr's. manual avail. (ISBN 0-316-09474-9); test bank avail. (ISBN 0-316-09473-0). Little.

Bilai, V. I. Antibiotic Producing Microscopic Fungi. 1963. 19.50 (ISBN 0-444-40054-0). Elsevier.

Bilan, R. P. The Literary Criticism of F. R. Leavis. LC 78-18089. 1979. 37.50 (ISBN 0-521-22324-5). Cambridge U Pr.

Bilas, R. A. Microeconomic Theory. 2nd ed. 1971. 25.95 (ISBN 0-07-005258-1, C); instructors' manual 15.95 (ISBN 0-07-005272-7). McGraw.

Bild, Ian & Humphries, Stephen. Finding Out about Seaside Holidays. (Finding Out about Ser.). (Illus.). 48p. (gr. 5-8). 1983. 12.50 (ISBN 0-7134-4439-8, Pub. by Batsford England). David & Charles.

Bildarchiv Foto Marburg, ed. Photographic Index of Art in France. (Illus.). microfiche set 7700.00x (ISBN 0-686-75630-4, Pub. by K G Saur). Gale.

Bilder, Richard B. Managing the Risks of International Agreement. LC 80-52288. 320p. 1981. 25.00x (ISBN 0-299-08360-8). U of Wis Pr.

Biles, Blake A., jt. auth. see Denney, Richard J.

Biles, Fay, ed. TV: Production & Utilization in Physical Education. 1971. pap. 1.00x o.p. (ISBN 0-685-42442-1, 245-25136). AAHPERD.

Biles, William E. & Swain, James J. Optimization & Industrial Experimentation. LC 79-9516. 368p. 1980. 47.50x (ISBN 0-471-04244-7, Pub. by Wiley-Interscience). Wiley.

Biles, William E., jt. auth. see Gajda, Walter J., Jr.

Bilezikian, Gilbert. The Liberated Gospel: A Comparison of the Gospel of Mark & Greek Tragedy. LC 76-51082. (Baker Biblical Monographs). 1977. pap. 6.95 o.p. (ISBN 0-8010-0673-2). Baker Bk.

Bilhon, Jean F. Eloge De J. J. Rousseau. (Rousseauism, 1788-1797). 1978. Repr. lib. bdg. 27.00x o.p. (ISBN 0-8287-0090-7). Clearwater Pub.

Bilibin, Yu. A. see Alexandrov, Eugene.

Bilio, Beth De see De Bilio, Beth.

Bill, James A. The Politics of Iran: Groups, Classes & Modernization. LC 73-187714. 176p. 1972. pap. text ed. 9.95 (ISBN 0-675-09102-0). Merrill.

Bill, James A. & Leiden, Carl. Politics in the Middle East. 1979. 10.95 (ISBN 0-316-09505-2). Little.

Bill, Valentine T. The Forgotten Class. LC 75-25485. 1976. Repr. of 1959 ed. lib. bdg. 17.25x (ISBN 0-8371-8426-6, BIFOC). Greenwood.

Billard, Mary. All About Robots. LC 82-81328. (Platt & Munk Deluxe Illustrated Bks.). (Illus.). 48p. (gr. 2-8). 1982. 6.95 (ISBN 0-448-47493-X, G&D). Putnam Pub Group.

Billard-Dumineceau, E. Voltaire Apprecie: Comedie. 28.00 o.p. (ISBN 0-8287-0091-5). Clearwater Pub.

Billardiere, J. J. De La see De La Billardiere, J. J.

Billaud-Varenne, Jacques N. Les Elements Du Republicanisme. (Rousseauism, 1788-1797). 1978. Repr. lib. bdg. 44.00x o.p. (ISBN 0-8287-0092-3). Clearwater Pub.

--Principes Regenerateurs Du Systeme Social. (Rousseauism, 1788-1797). 1978. Repr. lib. bdg. 62.00x o.p. (ISBN 0-8287-0093-1). Clearwater Pub.

Billcliffe, Roger. Mackintosh Textile Designs. LC 82-60358. (Illus.). 80p. 1982. 25.00 (ISBN 0-8008-5059-9). Taplinger.

Bille, Donald. Staff Development: A Systems Approach. 1982. pap. 14.50 (ISBN 0-913590-85-1). Slack Inc.

Billeci, David A. The Year. LC 78-65690. 1979. 7.95 o.p. (ISBN 0-533-04114-7). Vantage.

Biller, Henry B. Paternal Deprivation: Family, School, Sexuality & Society. LC 74-928. 1974. pap. 10.95 (ISBN 0-669-02517-8). Lexington Bks.

Biller, Henry B., jt. auth. see Berlinsky, Ellen B.

Billerbeck, K. & Yasugi, Y. Private Direct Foreign Investment in Developing Countries. (Working Paper: No. 348). iv, 97p. 1979. 5.00 (ISBN 0-686-36174-1, WP-0348). World Bank.

Billeskov-Jansen, F. J. & Mitchell, P. M., eds. Anthology of Danish Literature: Middle Ages to Romanticism. bilingual ed. LC 72-5610. (Arcturus Books Paperbacks). 272p. 1972. pap. 7.95 (ISBN 0-8093-0596-8). S Ill U Pr.

--Anthology of Danish Literature: Realism to the Present. bilingual ed. LC 72-5610. (Arcturus Books Paperbacks). 349p. 1972. pap. 8.95 (ISBN 0-8093-0597-6). S Ill U Pr.

Billet, F., jt. auth. see Fouchier, J.

Billet, M. L. & Arndt, R. E., eds. International Symposium on Cavitation Noise. 1982. 30.00 (H00231). ASME.

Billett, F. S., jt. ed. see Balls, M.

Billheimer, Paul. The Mystery of God's Providence. 1983. pap. 3.95 (ISBN 0-8423-4664-3). Tyndale.

Billheimer, Paul E. Destined for the Cross. 1982. pap. 3.95 (ISBN 0-8423-0604-8). Tyndale.

Billias, George A., jt. auth. see Grob, Gerald N.

Billiet, Walter E. Do-It-Yourself Automotive Maintenance & Repair. LC 78-15055. (Illus.). 1979. 17.95 (ISBN 0-13-217190-2, Spec); pap. 7.95 (ISBN 0-13-217182-1). P-H.

Billig, Otto. Flying Saucers: Magic in the Skies. 256p. 1982. 16.95x (ISBN 0-87073-833-X). Schenkman.

Billigmeier, Jon C. Kadmos & Danaos: Possibility of a Semitic Presence in Halladic Greece. (No. 6). 1981. pap. text ed. price not set (ISBN 90-6032-110-3). Humanities.

Billing, D. E., ed. Aims, Methods & Assessment in Advanced Science Education. 1973. 29.95 (ISBN 0-471-25581-5, Pub. by Wiley Heyden). Wiley.

Billingham, J. & Pesek, R., eds. Communication with Extraterrestrial Intelligence. (Astronautica: Vol. 6, Nos. 1-2). 1979. 80.00 (ISBN 0-08-024727-X). Pergamon.

Billingham, John, et al, eds. Life in the Universe. 400p. 1982. text ed. 25.00 (ISBN 0-262-02155-2); pap. text ed. 12.50 (ISBN 0-262-52062-1). MIT Pr.

Billingham, Katherine A. Developmental Psychology for the Health Care Professions: Prenatal Through Adolescent Development, Pt. 1. (Behavioral Sciences for Health Care Professionals Ser.). 128p. (Orig.). 1981. lib. bdg. 16.50 (ISBN 0-86531-000-9); pap. 7.95 (ISBN 0-86531-001-7). Westview.

Billingham, R., jt. auth. see Fleischmajer, P.

Billingham, Richard & Goodkin, Marie. First Steps to Musicianship. 256p. 1980. pap. text ed. 11.50x (ISBN 0-917974-38-7). Waveland Pr.

Billings, Charlene W. Scorpions. LC 82-45994. (A Skylight Bk.). (Illus.). 48p. (gr. 2-5). 1983. PLB 7.95 (ISBN 0-396-08125-8). Dodd.

Billings, Diane, jt. auth. see Ellis, Patricia D.

Billings, Diane M. & Stokes, Lillian G. Medical-Surgical Nursing: Common Health Problems of Adults & Children Across the Life Span. LC 81-16856. (Illus.). 1440p. 1982. text ed. 36.95 (ISBN 0-8016-0736-1). Mosby.

Billings, Grace H. The Art of Transition in Plato. Taran, Leonardo, ed. LC 78-66578. (Ancient Philosophy Ser.: Vol. 2). 110p. 1979. lib. bdg. 13.00 o.s.i. (ISBN 0-8240-9609-6). Garland Pub.

Billings, Jeffrey D., jt. auth. see Larsen, James B.

Billings, John D. Hardtack & Coffee. LC 81-18207. (Collector's Library of the Civil War). 26.60 (ISBN 0-8094-4208-6). Silver.

Billings, K., jt. auth. see Angins, E.

Billings, Marland P. Structural Geology. 3rd ed. (Illus.). 1972. 32.95 (ISBN 0-13-853846-8). P-H.

Billings, Richard, jt. auth. see Donnelly, Honoria.

Billings, Roger D., Jr. Prepaid Legal Services. LC 79-92375. 1981. 65.00 (ISBN 0-686-35941-0). Lawyers Co-Op.

Billings, Rolland G. & Goldman, Errol. Professional Negotiations for Media-Library Professionals: District & School. LC 80-67724. 70p. 1980. pap. 8.50 (ISBN 0-89240-037-4). Assn Ed Comm T.

Billings, S. A., jt. auth. see Harris, C. J.

Billings, W. D. Plants, & the Ecosystem. 3rd ed. 1978. pap. 8.95x o.p. (ISBN 0-534-00571-3). Wadsworth Pub.

Billings, Warren M., ed. The Old Dominion in the Seventeenth Century: A Documentary History of Virginia, 1606-1689. LC 74-8302. (Institute of Early American History & Culture Ser.). xxiv, 352p. 1975. 21.00x (ISBN 0-8078-1234-X); pap. 7.00x (ISBN 0-8078-1237-4). U of NC Pr.

Billingsley, Andrew. Black Families in White America. LC 68-54602. 1968. pap. 4.95 (ISBN 0-13-077453-7, Spec). P-H.

Billingsley, Ed. Career Planning & Job Hunting for Today's Student: The Non-Job Interview. LC 77-17281. 1978. pap. 13.50x (ISBN 0-673-16076-9). Scott F.

Billingsley, P. Convergence of Probability Measures. (Probability & Mathematical Statistics Tracts: Probability & Statistics Section). 253p. 1968. 36.95x (ISBN 0-471-07242-7, Pub. by Wiley-Interscience). Wiley.

--Weak Convergence of Measures: Applications in Probability. (CBMS-NSF Regional Conference Ser.: No. 5). v, 31p. 1971. pap. 6.00 (ISBN 0-89871-176-2). Soc Indus-Appl Math.

Billingsley, Patrick. Probability & Measure. LC 78-25632. (Probability & Mathematical Statistics Ser.). 515p. 1979. 36.95x (ISBN 0-471-03173-9, Pub. by Wiley-Interscience). Wiley.

Billington, D. P. Thin Shell Concrete Structures. 1965. 45.50 (ISBN 0-07-005271-9, P&RB). McGraw.

Billington, David P. Thin-Shell Concrete Structures. 2nd ed. (Illus.). 432p. 1981. 44.50 (ISBN 0-07-005279-4). McGraw.

Billington, Dora & Colbeck, John. The Technique of Pottery. 1979. 24.00 (ISBN 0-7134-2836-8, Pub. by Batsford England). David & Charles.

Billington, E. J., et al, eds. Combinatorial Mathematics IX, Brisbane, Australia: Proceedings, 1981. (Lecture Notes in Mathematics Ser.: Vol. 952). 443p. 1983. pap. 23.00 (ISBN 0-387-11601-X). Springer-Verlag.

Billington, E. W. & Tate, A. The Physics of Deformation & Flow. 1981. 59.00 (ISBN 0-07-005285-9). McGraw.

Billington, James H. Fire in the Minds of Men. LC 79-2750. 677p. 1980. 26.50 (ISBN 0-465-02405-X); pap. 13.50 (ISBN 0-465-02407-6). Basic.

Billington, Michael. Theatre Facts & Feats. (Guinness Superlatives Ser.). (Illus.). 256p. 1982. 19.95 (ISBN 0-85112-239-6, Pub. by Guinness Superlatives England). Sterling.

Billington, Rachel. Occasion of Sin. 320p. 1983. 14.95 (ISBN 0-671-45938-4). Summit Bks.

Billington, Ray A. American History After Eighteen Sixty-Five. 8th ed. (Quality Paperback: No. 27). 364p. (Orig.). 1979. pap. 3.95 o.p. (ISBN 0-8226-0027-7). Littlefield.

--The Far Western Frontier: Far Western Frontier: Eighteen Thirty to Eighteen Sixty. LC 56-9665. (New American Nation Ser.). 1956. 16.30xi (ISBN 0-06-010330-2, HarpT); pap. 4.95xi (ISBN 0-06-133012-4, TB 3012). Har-Row.

--Frederick Jackson Turner. (Illus.). 1973. 29.95 (ISBN 0-19-501609-2). Oxford U Pr.

--People of the Plains & Mountains: Essays in the History of the West Dedicated to Everett Dick. LC 72-784. (Contr. in American History No. 25). (Illus.). 193p. 1973. lib. bdg. 25.00x (ISBN 0-8371-6358-7, BID/). Greenwood.

--Westward to the Pacific. 114p. 1979. pap. 3.95 (ISBN 0-931056-00-4). Jefferson Natl.

Billington, Ray A., jt. ed. see Ridge, Martin.

Billinton, R. Power System Reliability Evaluation. 310p. 1970. 50.00 (ISBN 0-677-02870-9). Gordon.

Billinton, Roy, et al. Power-System Reliability Calculations. (Modern Electrical Technology Ser.: No. 6). 195p. 1973. 25.00x (ISBN 0-262-02098-X). MIT Pr.

Billion, Anna. Kundalini: Secret of the Ancient Yogis. 1982. pap. 4.95 (ISBN 0-686-97516-2, Reward). P-H.

Billionis, Cynthia, jt. auth. see Foster, Sunny.

Billionis, Cynthia, jt. auth. see Horner, Don R.

Billipp, Betty. Please Pass the Salt. LC 74-84013. (Illus.). 64p. 1974. 4.00 (ISBN 0-911838-44-9). Windy Row.

Billis, David, et al. Organising Social Services Departments. 1981. text ed. 26.00x (ISBN 0-435-82085-0). Heinemann Ed.

Billmeyer, F. W., Jr. & Saltzman, M. Principles of Color Technology. LC 66-20386. 1966. 19.95 o.p. (ISBN 0-470-07290-3). Wiley.

Billmeyer, Fred W. & Kelley, Richard N. Entering Industry: A Guide for Young Professionals. LC 75-22283. 281p. 1975. 37.95x (ISBN 0-471-07285-0, Pub. by Wiley-Interscience). Wiley.

Billmeyer, Fred W., Jr. Textbook of Polymer Science. 2nd ed. LC 78-142713. 281p. 1971. 34.95x (ISBN 0-471-07296-6, Pub. by Wiley-Interscience). Wiley.

Billmeyer, Fred W., Jr. & Saltzman, Max. Principles of Color Technology. LC 80-21561. 272p. 1980. 33.95x (ISBN 0-471-03052-X, Pub. by Wiley-Interscience). Wiley.

Billout, Guy. By Camel or by Car. (Illus.). 32p. 1983. pap. 5.95 (ISBN 0-13-109595-1). P-H.

Billows, F. L. The Techniques of Language Teaching. (English As a Second Language Bk.). 1961. pap. text ed. 12.50x (ISBN 0-582-52505-5). Longman.

Bills, Scott, ed. see Aptheker, Bettina, et al.

Bills, Scott L., ed. Kent State-May Four: Echoes Through a Decade. LC 82-10102. (Illus.). 316p. 1982. 16.50 (ISBN 0-87338-278-1). Kent St U Pr.

Billson, Janet M., jt. ed. see Fritz, Jan.

Billstein, Richard, et al. A Problem-Solving Approach to Mathematics for Elementary School Teachers. 1981. 22.95 (ISBN 0-8053-0851-2). Benjamin-Cummings.

Bilmanis, Alfred. History of Latvia. LC 69-13827. Repr. of 1951 ed. lib. bdg. 35.00x (ISBN 0-8371-1446-2, BIHL). Greenwood.

Biloni, H., jt. auth. see Pampillo, C.

Biloon, F. Medical Equipment Service Manual: Theory & Maintenance Procedures. LC 77-513. 1978. 25.95 (ISBN 0-13-572644-1). P-H.

Bilotto, Gerardo & Washam, Veronica. Work Independence & the Severely Disabled: A Bibliography. LC 79-91351. 108p. 1980. 7.50 (ISBN 0-686-38821-6). Human Res Ctr.

Bilovsky, Frank. Lion Country: Inside Penn State Football. LC 82-81802. (Illus.). 192p. 1982. 12.95 (ISBN 0-88011-072-4). Leisure Pr.

Bilovsky, Frank & Westcott, Richard. The Phillies Encyclopedia. LC 82-83945. (Illus.). 500p. 1983. 29.95 (ISBN 0-88011-121-6). Leisure Pr.

Bilson, Elizabeth, jt. ed. see Terzian, Yervant.

Bilson, Frank. Crossbows. rev. ed. (Illus.). 186p. 1983. 14.95 (ISBN 0-88254-701-1). Hippocrene Bks.

Bilu, Dalya, tr. see Appelfeld, Aharon.

Bilyeu, Richard. The Tanelorn Archives: A Primary & Secondary Bibliography of the Works of Michael Moorcock,1949-1979. 160p. 1982. lib. bdg. 15.95x (ISBN 0-686-84015-1); pap. text ed. 7.95x (ISBN 0-686-84016-X). Borgo Pr.

Bimala dasi, ed. see Das Goswami, Satsvarupa.

Binchy, Maeve. Light a Penny Candle. 540p. 1983. 17.95 (ISBN 0-670-42827-2). Viking Pr.

Bindeman, Steven L. Heidegger & Wittgenstein: The Poetics of Silence. LC 80-6066. 159p. 1980. lib. bdg. 18.00 (ISBN 0-8191-1350-6); pap. text ed. 8.25 (ISBN 0-8191-1351-4). U Pr of Amer.

Binder, Abraham W. Studies in Jewish Music: The Collected Writings of the Noted Musicologist. Heskes, Irene, ed. LC 72-136423. 1971. 10.00x (ISBN 0-8197-0272-2). Bloch.

Binder, Arnold & Scharf, Peter. Police Use of Deadly Force. cancelled (ISBN 0-88410-885-6). Ballinger Pub.

Binder, Eando, et al. Missing World & Other Stories. Elwood, Roger, ed. LC 73-21481. (Science Fiction Bks). 48p. (gr. 4-8). 1974. PLB 3.95g (ISBN 0-8225-0955-5). Lerner Pubns.

Binder, Leonard. The Study of the Middle East: Research & Scholarship in the Humanities & Social Sciences. LC 76-7408. 648p. 1976. 59.95x (ISBN 0-471-07304-0, Pub. by Wiley-Interscience). Wiley.

Binder, Otto, ed. see Verne, Jules.

Binder, P. Cross Point System Esk 400e. 61.95 (ISBN 0-471-25585-8, Pub. by Wiley Heyden). Wiley.

Binder, Raymond C. Fluid Mechanics. 5th ed. (Illus.). 448p. 1973. ref. ed. 31.95 (ISBN 0-13-322594-1). P-H.

Binder, Raymond C., et al see Heat Transfer & Fluid Mechanics Institute.

Bindman, David. The Complete Graphic Work of William Blake. LC 77-92146. (Illus.). 1978. 45.00 o.p. (ISBN 0-399-12152-8). Putnam Pub Group.

--William Blake: His Art & Times. LC 82-80977. (Illus.). 192p. 1982. 22.50 (ISBN 0-500-23360-8). Thames Hudson.

Bindman, David, ed. John Flaxman. (Illus.). 1980. 24.95 o.p. (ISBN 0-500-09139-0). Thames Hudson.

Bindoff, S. T., ed. The House of Commons 1509-1558: The History of Parliament, 3-Vols. (Parliament Ser.). (700 Pgs. ea. vol.). 1983. Set. 250.00 (ISBN 0-436-04282-7, Pub by Secker & Warburg). David & Charles.

Bindon, Kathleen R. Inventories & Foreign Currency Translation Requirements. Farmer, Richard N., ed. LC 82-21729. (Research for Business Decisions Ser.). 1983. write for info. (ISBN 0-8357-1391-1). Univ Microfilms.

Bindra, Dalbir. A Theory of Intelligent Behavior. LC 75-46519. 447p. 1976. 30.50 o.p. (ISBN 0-471-07320-2, Pub. by Wiley-Interscience). Wiley.

Bindra, Jasjit S. & Lednicer, Daniel. Chronicles of Drug Discovery, Vol. 1. LC 81-11471. 283p. 1982. 32.50x (ISBN 0-471-06516-1, Pub. by Wiley-Interscience). Wiley.

--Chronicles of Drug Discovery, Vol. 2. 300p. 1983. 32.50 (ISBN 0-471-89135-5, Pub. by Wiley-Interscience). Wiley.

Bindseil, Kenneth R. & Dickey, Imogene B. Effective Writing: Methods & Examples. LC 77-72907. (Illus.). 1978. pap. text ed. 12.95 (ISBN 0-395-24950-3); instr's. manual & suppl. tests 0.50 (ISBN 0-395-24949-X). HM.

Bines, Harvey E. Law of Investment Management. 1977. 66.00 (ISBN 0-88262-150-5, 77-10130). Warren.

Binford, Charles M., et al. Loss Control in the OSHA Era. (Illus.). 288p. 1975. 26.50 o.p. (ISBN 0-07-005276-6, P&RB). McGraw.

Binford, Jesse S., Jr. Foundation of Chemistry. 1977. 22.95 (ISBN 0-02-309880-5, 30988). Macmillan.

Binford, Lewis R. In Pursuit of the Past: Decoding the Archaeological Record. (Illus.). 1983. 18.50 (ISBN 0-500-05042-2). Thames Hudson.

Binford, Lewis R., ed. Working at Archaeology. (Studies in Archaeology). Date not set. price not set Lib. ed. (ISBN 0-12-100060-5). Acad Pr.

Bing, Elisabeth. Moving Through Pregnancy. LC 74-17673. 144p. 1975. pap. 8.95 (ISBN 0-672-52095-8). Bobbs.

Bing, Elizabeth & Colman, Libby. Making Love During Pregnancy. (Orig.). 1982. pap. 2.95 (ISBN 0-553-14523-1). Bantam.

Bing, Elizabeth D. Adventure of Birth. 1970. 4.95 o.p. (ISBN 0-671-20486-6). S&S.

Bing, Gordon. Corporate Acquisitions. 248p. 1980. 19.95 (ISBN 0-87201-009-0). Gulf Pub.
--Corporate Divestment. 166p. 1978. 19.95 (ISBN 0-87201-141-0). Gulf Pub.
Bing, Rudolf. A Knight at the Opera. (Illus.). 1981. 14.95 (ISBN 0-399-12653-8). Putnam Pub Group.
Bing, Stephen & Brown, Larry. Standards Relating to Monitoring. LC 77-3939. (IJA-ABA Juvenile Justice Standards Project Ser.). 104p. 1980. prof ref 20.00x (ISBN 0-88410-753-1); pap. 10.00x (ISBN 0-88410-805-8). Ballinger Pub.
Bing, Valetyn & Braet Von Uberfeldt, Jan. Regional Costumes of the Netherlands. Wardle, Patricia, tr. from Dutch. (Illus.). 142p. 1978. 75.00 (ISBN 0-686-43013-1, Terra Netherlands). Heinman.
Binger. Lippincott's Guide to Nursing Literature. text ed. 11.50 (ISBN 0-397-54344-1, Lippincott Nursing). Lippincott.
Binger, Jane L., jt. auth. see Huntsman, Ann J.
Bingham, Bruce. The Sailor's Sketchbook. Gilbert, Jim, ed. 144p. 1983. pap. price not set (ISBN 0-915160-55-2). Seven Seas.
Bingham, Caroline. The Crowned Lions: The Early Plantagenet Kings. (Illus.). 192p. 1978. 16.00x o.p. (ISBN 0-8476-6095-8). Rowman.
--The Stewart Kingdom of Scotland. LC 74-81715. 1975. 12.50 o.p. (ISBN 0-312-76195-3). St Martin.
Bingham, Clifton, jt. auth. see Nister, Ernest.
Bingham, Colin. Wit & Wisdom: A Public Affairs Miscellany. 368p. 1982. 35.00 (ISBN 0-522-84241-0, Pub. by Melbourne U Pr); pap. 21.00 (ISBN 0-522-84255-0). Intl Schol Bk Serv.
Bingham, Earl. Pocketbook for Technical & Professional Writers. 304p. 1981. pap. text ed. 9.95x (ISBN 0-534-01004-0). Wadsworth Pub.
Bingham, Earl G. Pocketbook for Writers: A Guide to Writing & Revision. 416p. 1980. pap. text ed. 9.95x o.p. (ISBN 0-534-00773-2). Wadsworth Pub.
Bingham, Fred P. Practical Boat Joinery: Tools, Techniques, Tips. LC 81-81418. (Illus.). 320p. 1983. pap. 30.00 (ISBN 0-87742-140-4). Intl Marine.
Bingham, Hiram. Across South America. (Latin America in the 20th Century Ser.). 1976. Repr. of 1911 ed. lib. bdg. 45.00 (ISBN 0-306-70834-5). Da Capo.
--The Monroe Doctrine. (Latin America in the 20th Century Ser.). 1976. Repr. of 1913 ed. lib. bdg. 22.50 (ISBN 0-306-70833-7). Da Capo.
Bingham, Jane & Scholt, Grayce, eds. Fifteen Centuries of Children's Literature: An Annotated Chronology of British & American Works in Historical Context. LC 79-8584. (Illus.). l, 540p. 1980. lib. bdg. 39.95x (ISBN 0-313-22164-2, BCL/). Greenwood.
Bingham, Janet, jt. ed. see Bingham, Sam.
Bingham, Joan & Riccio, Dolores. The Energy Crunch Cookbook. LC 78-14632. 1979. 12.50 o.p. (ISBN 0-8019-6759-7); pap. 7.95 o.p. (ISBN 0-8019-6760-0). Chilton.
--Make It Yourself. LC 77-14689. (Illus.). 1978. 12.95 o.s.i. (ISBN 0-8019-6672-8); pap. 8.95 o.s.i. (ISBN 0-8019-6673-6). Chilton.
--The Smart Shopper's Guide to Food Buying & Preparation. 320p. 1983. pap. 6.95 (ISBN 0-686-83711-8, ScribT). Scribner.
Bingham, Joan, jt. auth. see Riccio, Dolores.
Bingham, Madeleine. Princess Lieven: Russian Intriguer. (Illus.). 288p. 1982. 35.00 (ISBN 0-241-10269-3, Pub by Hamish Hamilton England). David & Charles.
Bingham, Rebecca. Opals. (Illus.). 48p. 1982. 30.00 (ISBN 0-88014-042-9). Mosaic Pr OH.
Bingham, Richard, et al. Professional Associations & Municipal Innovation. 200p. 1981. 25.00 (ISBN 0-299-08330-6). U of Wis Pr.
Bingham, Richard D. Public Housing & Urban Renewal: An Analysis of Federal-Local Relations. LC 74-19822. (Illus.). 282p. 1975. text ed. 31.95 o.p. (ISBN 0-275-05810-7). Praeger.
Bingham, Richard D. & Ethridge, Marcus E. Reaching Decisions in Public Administration: Methods & Applications. LC 81-12427. (Illus.). 416p. 1982. pap. text ed. 17.95x (ISBN 0-582-28248-9). Longman.
Bingham, Sam & Bingham, Janet, eds. Between Sacred Mountains: Stories & Lessons from the Land. 296p. 1982. 30.00 (ISBN 0-910675-00-7); pap. 20.00 (ISBN 0-910675-01-5). Rock Point.
Bingham, William C. The Counselor & Youth Employment. LC 72-1843. 1973. pap. 2.40 o.p. (ISBN 0-395-14204-0). HM.
Bingley, William. Musical Biography, 2 vols. LC 70-127286. (Music Ser). 1971. Repr. of 1834 ed. Set. lib. bdg. 75.00 (ISBN 0-306-70032-8). Da Capo.
Bini, Elzio, jt. ed. see Bini, Luciano.
Bini, Luciano & Bini, Elzio, eds. Dolci Inizi. 1968. pap. text ed. 8.50x o.p. (ISBN 0-435-39630-7). Heinemann Ed.
Binkin, Martin. The Military Pay Muddle. (Studies in Defense Policy). 60p. 1975. pap. 4.95 (ISBN 0-8157-0961-7). Brookings.
--Shaping the Defense Civilian Work Force: Economics, Politics, & National Security. LC 78-14897. (Studies in Defense Policy). 1978. pap. 4.95 (ISBN 0-8157-0967-6). Brookings.
--Support Costs in the Defense Budget: The Submerged One-Third. (Studies in Defense Policy). 49p. 1972. pap. write for info (ISBN 0-8157-0957-9). Brookings.
--U. S. Reserve Forces: The Problem of the Weekend Warrior. (Studies in Defense Policy). 63p. 1974. pap. 4.95 (ISBN 0-8157-0959-5). Brookings.
Binkin, Martin & Bach, Shirley J. Women & the Military. (Studies in Defense Policy). 1977. 11.95 (ISBN 0-8157-0966-8); pap. 4.95 (ISBN 0-8157-0965-X). Brookings.
Binkin, Martin & Kyriakopoulos, Irene. Paying the Modern Military. LC 80-70080. (Studies in Defense Policy). 100p. 1981. pap. 4.95 (ISBN 0-8157-0971-4). Brookings.
--Youth or Experience? Manning the Modern Military. (Studies in Defense Policy). 1979. pap. 4.95 (ISBN 0-8157-0969-2). Brookings.
Binkin, Martin & Record, Jeffrey. Where Does the Marine Corps Go from Here? (Studies in Defense Policy). 1976. pap. 4.95 (ISBN 0-8157-0963-3). Brookings.
Binkley, Robert, et al, eds. see University of Western Ontario Philosophy Colloquim, 4th.
Binkley, Thomas, tr. see Winckel, Fritz.
Binkley, William C. The Expansionist Movement in Texas, 1836-1850. LC 71-77718. (American Scene Ser). 1970. Repr. of 1925 ed. lib. bdg. 35.00 (ISBN 0-306-71356-X). Da Capo.
Binks, R., et al. Tables for Use in High Resolution Mass Spectrometry: Incorporating Chemical Formulae from Mass Determinations. (Eng., Fr., & Ger.). 107.00 (ISBN 0-471-25593-9, Wiley Heyden). Wiley.
Binmore, K. G. Foundations of Analysis: A Straightforward Introduction: Bk. 1 Logic, Sets & Numbers. LC 79-41790. (Illus.). 200p. 1981. 26.95 (ISBN 0-521-23322-4); pap. 13.95 (ISBN 0-521-29915-2). Cambridge U Pr.
--Foundations of Analysis: A Straightforward Introduction: Bk. 2 Topological Ideas. LC 79-41790. (Illus.). 350p. 1981. 43.50 (ISBN 0-521-23350-X); pap. 17.95 (ISBN 0-521-29930-6). Cambridge U Pr.
Binner, Vinal O. American Folktales One: A Structured Reader. 1966. pap. text ed. 8.50 scp (ISBN 0-690-06704-6, HarpC). Har-Row.
Binney, Horace. An Enquiry into the Formation of Washington's Farewell Address. LC 74-98692. 1969. Repr. of 1859 ed. lib. bdg. 37.50 (ISBN 0-306-71840-5). Da Capo.
Binney, Marcus, jt. ed. see Lowenthal, David.
Binney, William R. The Architectural Characteristics & Types of Spanish Gardens. (The Masterpieces of World Architecture Library). (Illus.). 129p. 1983. 87.45 (ISBN 0-86650-045-6). Gloucester Art.
Binnick, Steven A. Skin Diseases: Diagnosis & Management in Clinical Practice. 1981. 29.95 (ISBN 0-201-03789-0, 03789, Med-Nurse). A-W.
Binnie & Partners. Islands for Offshore Nuclear Power Stations. 167p. 1982. pap. 40.00x (ISBN 0-8448-1423-7). Crane-Russak Co.
Binnie, William H. Oral Mucositis: Non-Infective Types. (Masson Monographs in Dentistry). (Illus.). 224p. 1983. write for info (ISBN 0-89352-169-8). Masson Pub.
Binnie-Clark, Georgina. Wheat & Woman. (Social History of Canada Ser.). 1979. 25.00x (ISBN 0-8020-2354-1); pap. 8.95 (ISBN 0-8020-6386-1). U of Toronto Pr.
Binns, David. Beyond the Sociology of Conflict. LC 77-82860. 1978. 25.00 (ISBN 0-312-07784-X). St Martin.
Binns, J. W., ed. Latin Literature of the Fourth Century. (Greek & Latin Studies). 1974. 18.95 (ISBN 0-7100-7796-3). Routledge & Kegan.
--The Latin Poetry of English Poets. 1974. 21.50 (ISBN 0-7100-7845-5). Routledge & Kegan.
Binns, Richard. Hidden France. (Illus.). 160p. 1983. 8.95 (ISBN 0-89919-157-6). Ticknor & Fields.
Bin-Nun, Judy & Cooper, Nancy. Pesach: A Holiday Funtext. (Illus.). 32p. (Orig.). (gr. 1-3). 1983. pap. text ed. 5.00 (ISBN 0-8074-0161-7, 101310). UAHC.
Binsack, R. see Soeder, C. J.
Binyon, Pamela M. The Concepts of Spirit & Demon: A Study in the Use of Different Languages Describing the Same Phenomena. (IC-Studies in the International History of Christianity: Vol. 8). 132p. 1977. pap. write for info. (ISBN 3-261-01787-2). P Lang Pubs.
Binzen, Bill. Miguel's Mountain. (Illus.). (gr. k-3). 1968. PLB 5.99 o.p. (ISBN 0-698-30235-4, Coward). Putnam Pub Group.
--The Walk. (Illus.). (gr. k-3). 1972. PLB 4.69 o.p. (ISBN 0-698-30417-9, Coward). Putnam Pub Group.
--Year After Year. (Illus.). (gr. k-3). 1976. 6.95 o.p. (ISBN 0-698-20361-5, Coward). Putnam Pub Group.
Biochemical Engineering Conference, 2nd, Henniker, New Hampshire, July 13-18, 1980. Biochemical Engineering II: Proceedings. Constantinides, A., et al, eds. (Annals of the New York Academy of Sciences Ser.: Vol. 369). 383p. 1981. 75.00 (ISBN 0-686-78146-5). NY Acad Sci.
Biochemical Societies of France, Great Britain, Italy, & the Netherlands. Joint Meeting, Venice, 1976. Phosphorylated Proteins & Related Enzymes: Proceedings. 121p. 8.00 (ISBN 0-686-70823-7). IRL Pr.
Bioff, Allan L., et al, eds. The Developing Labor Law: The Board, the Courts, & the National Labor Relations Act, 1977 Supplement. 340p. 1978. pap. 7.50 o.p. (ISBN 0-87179-286-9). BNA.
--The Developing Labor Law: The Board, the Courts, and the National Labor Relations Act, 1976 Supplement. 308p. 1977. pap. 5.00 o.p. (ISBN 0-87179-051-3). BNA.
--Developing Labor Law: The Board, the Courts, & the National Relations Act, 1971-75 Cumulative Supplement. LC 76-54726. 614p. 1976. 10.00 o.p. (ISBN 0-87179-240-0). BNA.
Bioler, I. & Sternlicht, M. The Psychology of Mental Retardation. LC 77-4137. 800p. 1977. 39.95 (ISBN 0-88437-013-5). Psych Dimensions.
Biological Laboratory, Imperial Household & Sakai, Tune, eds. The Crabs of Sagami Bay: Collected by His Majesty the Emperor of Japan. (Illus.). 1965. 40.00x (ISBN 0-8248-0033-8, Eastwest Ctr). UH Pr.
Biological Science Curriculum Study. Investigating Your Environment Ser. Incl. Bk. 1. The Environment: Some Viewpoints. pap. text ed. 5.16 (ISBN 0-201-00933-1); Bk. 2. The Price of Progress. pap. text ed. o.p. (ISBN 0-201-00934-X); Bk. 3. Food for Humanity. pap. text ed. o.p. (ISBN 0-201-00935-8); Bk. 4. Human Population. pap. text ed. 5.16 (ISBN 0-201-00936-6); Bk. 5. Solid Waste. pap. text ed. 5.16 (ISBN 0-201-00937-4); Bk. 6. Pesticides. pap. text ed. o.p. (ISBN 0-201-00938-2); Bk. 7. Land Use. pap. text ed. 5.16 (ISBN 0-201-00939-0); Bk. 8. Water Quality. pap. text ed. 5.16 (ISBN 0-201-00940-4). (gr. 9-12). 1975. pap. text ed. 10.08 student hndbk. (ISBN 0-201-00931-5, Sch Div); tchr's hndbk. 10.56 (ISBN 0-201-00932-3). A-W.
Biology Colloquium, 40th, Oregon State University, 1979. Forests: Fresh Perspectives from Ecosystems Analysis. Proceedings. Waring, Richard H., ed. LC 80-14883. (Illus.). 210p. 1979. pap. 14.50 (ISBN 0-87071-179-2). Oreg St U Pr.
Biomechanics Symposium, 1973. AMD: Proceedings, Vol. 2. Fung, Y. C. & Brighton, J. A., eds. 107p. pap. 12.00 o.p. (ISBN 0-685-38867-0, G00033). ASME.
Bion, W. R. Experiences in Groups. LC 61-7884. 1981. text ed. 12.95x o.s.i. (ISBN 0-465-02174-3). Basic.
Biondi, Angelo M., ed. The Creative Process. 72p. 1972. pap. 1.00 (ISBN 0-686-96455-1). DOK Pubs.
Biondi, F. J. Transistor Technology, Vol. 2. 1958. 27.50 (ISBN 0-442-00781-7, Pub. by Van Nos Reinhold). Krieger.
Biondo, Norma, jt. auth. see Woodward, Dan.
Bioy-Cesares, Adolfo, jt. auth. see Borges, Jorge L.
Biracree, Tom. The Red Berets. 352p. 1983. pap. 2.75 (ISBN 0-523-41704-7). Pinnacle Bks.
--The Torch. 240p. 1983. pap. 2.95 (ISBN 0-515-05622-7). Jove Pubns.
Biracree, Tom, jt. auth. see Coffey, Frank.
Birbari, Elizabeth. Dress in Italian Painting 1460-1500. (Illus.). 114p. 1976. 17.50 o.p. (ISBN 0-685-69162-4). Allanheld & Schram.
Birch. Nutritive Sweeteners. 1982. 59.50 (ISBN 0-85334-997-5, Pub. by Applied Sci England). Elsevier.
Birch, jt. auth. see Mauch.
Birch, A. & Tolmie, J. Anesthesia for the Uninterested. (Illus.). 200p. 1976. pap. text ed. 13.95 (ISBN 0-8391-0860-5). Univ Park.
Birch, A H. The British System of Government. 5th ed. (The Minerva Ser. of Students' Hand: No. 20). 1982. pap. text ed. 7.95x o.p. (ISBN 0-04-320149-0). Allen Unwin.
Birch, Alan & Cole, Martin. Captive Christmas: The Battle of Hong Kong December 1941. 179p. (Orig.). 1979. pap. text ed. 8.95 (ISBN 0-686-98158-8). Heinemann Ed.
Birch, Anthony H. The British System of Government. 6th ed. 298p. 1982. pap. text ed. 7.95x (ISBN 0-04-320154-7). Allen Unwin.
Birch, Austin. The Boy's Brigade. 9.50 (ISBN 0-392-07678-0, SpS). Sportshelf.
Birch, C. & Albrecht, P., eds. Genetics & the Quality of Life. 1976. text ed. 21.00 (ISBN 0-08-018210-0); pap. text ed. 16.50 (ISBN 0-08-019861-9). Pergamon.
Birch, Carol L., ed. see New American Foundation.
Birch, Clive. Book of Chesham. 1977. 20.00x o.p. (ISBN 0-86023-014-7). State Mutual Bk.
Birch, Clive & Armistead, John. Yesterday's Town: Chesham. 1981. 39.50x o.p. (ISBN 0-86023-049-X, Pub. by Barracuda England). State Mutual Bk.
Birch, Cyril, ed. & intro. by. Studies in Chinese Literary Genres. LC 77-157825. 1975. 27.50x (ISBN 0-520-02037-5). U of Cal Pr.
Birch, Cyril, tr. see Feng Meng-Lung.
Birch, D., jt. auth. see Rissover, F.
Birch, G. G. Vitamin C: Recent Aspects of Its Physiological & Technological Importance. 1974. 47.25 (ISBN 0-85334-606-2). Elsevier.
Birch, G. G. & Blakebrough. Enzymes & Food Processing: An Industry-University Co-Operation Symposium. Reading, England, April 1980. (Illus.). 295p. 1981. 49.25 (ISBN 0-85334-935-5, Pub. by Applied Sci England). Elsevier.
Birch, G. G., ed. Sweetness & Sweeteners. (Illus.). 1971. 26.75x (ISBN 0-85334-503-1, Pub. by Applied Sci England). Elsevier.
Birch, G. G. & Parker, K. J., eds. Food & Health: Science & Technology. (Illus.). xii, 521p. 1980. 78.00x (ISBN 0-85334-875-8, Pub. by Applied Sci England). Elsevier.
--Sugar: Science & Technology. (Illus.). 1979. 90.25x (ISBN 0-85334-805-7, Pub. by Applied Sci England). Elsevier.
Birch, G. G., et al, eds. Food from Waste. (Illus.). 1976. 71.75 (ISBN 0-85334-659-3, Pub. by Applied Sci England). Elsevier.
--Sensory Properties of Food. (Illus.). 1977. 55.50x (ISBN 0-85334-744-1, Pub. by Applied Sci England). Elsevier.
--Health & Food. (Illus.). xii, 224p. 1976. Repr. of 1972 ed. 24.75 (ISBN 0-85334-558-9, Pub. by Applied Sci England). Elsevier.
Birch, Herbert G. & Gussow, Joan D. Disadvantaged Children: Health, Nutrition & School Failure. LC 78-102443. (Illus.). 320p. 1970. 29.50 (ISBN 0-8089-0643-7). Grune.
Birch, Jack, jt. auth. see Sellin, Don.
Birch, L. C., jt. auth. see Andrewartha, H. G.
Birch, Martin C. & Haynes, Ken F. Insect Pheromones. (Studies in Biology: No. 147). 64p. 1982. pap. text ed. 8.95 (ISBN 0-7131-2852-6). E Arnold.
Birch, R. C. Seventeen Seventy-Six: The American Challenge. (Seminar Studies in History). 1976. pap. text ed. 5.95 (ISBN 0-582-35217-7). Longman.
--The Shaping of the Welfare State. (Seminar Studies in History Ser.). 126p. 1974. pap. text ed. 5.95x (ISBN 0-582-35200-2). Longman.
Birchall, Christopher, tr. see Holy Transfiguration Monastery.
Birchall, D. W. & Hammond, V. J. Tomorrow's Office Today: Managing Technological Change. 203p. 1981. 29.95 (ISBN 0-686-98084-0). Telecom Lib.
Birchall, M. Joyce. King Charles Spaniels. Foyle, Christina, ed. (Foyle's Handbks). (Illus.). 1973. 3.95 (ISBN 0-685-55788-X). Palmetto Pub.
Birchenall, Joan M. Care of the Older Adult. 2nd ed. (Illus.). 288p. 1982. text ed. 10.50 (ISBN 0-397-54271-2, Lippincott Nursing). Lippincott.
Bircher, Martin. Deutsch Drucke des Barock Sixteen Hundred to Seventeen Twenty, in der Herzog August Bibliothek Wolfenbuttel. 1977. Section A, 4 vols. Bibliotheca Augusta. lib. bdg. 420.00; Section B, 2 vols. Mittlere Aufstellung. lib. bdg. 210.00 (ISBN 3-262-00011-6); Section C, 1 Vol. Helmstedter Bestand. lib. bdg. 105.00. Kraus Intl.
Bird, Adren J., et al. The Craft of Hawaiian Lauhala Weaving. LC 82-4818. (Illus.). 163p. 1982. pap. 12.95 (ISBN 0-8248-0779-0). UH Pr.
Bird, Al. Murder So Real. LC 78-1968. 1978. 8.95 o.p. (ISBN 0-698-10891-4, Coward). Putnam Pub Group.
Bird, Anthony & Hallows, Ian, eds. The Rolls-Royce Motor Car. 3rd rev. ed. (Illus.). 327p. 1975. 25.00 o.p. (ISBN 0-517-52174-1). Crown.
Bird, B. M. & King, K. G. Power Electronics. 300p. 1983. price not set (ISBN 0-471-10430-2, Pub. by Wiley-Interscience); pap. price not set (ISBN 0-471-90051-6, Pub. by Wiley-Interscience). Wiley.
Bird, Byron R., et al. Dynamics of Polymeric Liquids, 2 vols. Incl. Vol. 1. Fluid Mechanics. 576p. 56.50 (ISBN 0-471-07375-X); Vol. 2. Kinetic Theory. 304p. 50.50x (ISBN 0-471-01596-2). LC 76-15408. 1977. Wiley.
Bird, C. L. & Boston, W. S. The Theory of Coloration of Textiles. 432p. 1975. 80.00x (ISBN 0-686-98192-8, Pub. by Soc Dyers & Colour). State Mutual Bk.
Bird, Caroline. Enterprising Women: Their Contribution to the American Economy, 1776-1976. 256p. 1976. 12.95 (ISBN 0-393-08724-7). Norton.
--The Good Years: Your Life in the 21st Century. 288p. 1983. 15.95 (01549-460). Dutton.
Bird, Charles & Koita, Mamadou. The Songs of Seydou Camara: Volume 1-Kambili. (Occasional Papers in Mande Studies). 120p. (Orig.). 1974. pap. text ed. 5.00 (ISBN 0-941934-12-8). Ind U Afro-Amer Arts.
Bird, Charles S., jt. auth. see Soumaoro, Bourama.
Bird, Christopher. The Divining Hand: The 500-Year-Old Mystery of Dowsing. (Illus.). 353p. 1983. pap. 13.50 (ISBN 0-525-48038-2, 01311-390). Dutton.
Bird, Christopher, jt. auth. see Tompkins, Peter.
Bird, David, jt. auth. see Reese, Terence.
Bird, E. C. Coasts. (Illus.). 1969. 19.50x (ISBN 0-262-02050-5). MIT Pr.
Bird, Francis A., ed. Accounting Theory: Selected Conceptual Readings. LC 81-66817. (Accounting Ser.). 450p. (Orig.). 1981. pap. 25.00 (ISBN 0-936328-09-6); pap. text ed. 14.50 (ISBN 0-686-94973-0). Dame Inc.
Bird, G., tr. see Wagner, Richard.
Bird, G. A. Molecular Gas Dynamics. (Oxford Engineering & Science Ser.). 1976. text ed. 69.00x (ISBN 0-19-856120-2). Oxford U Pr.
Bird, G. J. Radar Precision & Resolution. LC 74-8158. 151p. 1974. 29.95x o.p. (ISBN 0-470-07380-2). Halsted Pr.
Bird, George, et al, trs. see Dostoevsky, Fyodor.
Bird, H. A. & Wright, V. Applied Drug Therapy of the Rheumatic Diseases. (Illus.). 324p. 1982. pap. 30.00 (ISBN 0-7236-0658-7). Wright-PSG.

Bird, Isabelle. A Lady's Life in the Rocky Mountains. 298p. 1983. pap. 8.95 (ISBN 0-86068-267-6, Virago Pr). Merrimack Bk Serv.

Bird, James. Centrality & Cities. (Direct Editions Ser.). (Orig.). 1976. pap. 16.95 (ISBN 0-7100-8445-5). Routledge & Kegan.

Bird, Jean D. Factory Outlet Shopping Guide for New England: 1982 Edition. 1981. pap. 3.95 o.p. (ISBN 0-913464-60-0). FOSG Pubns.

--Factory Outlet Shopping Guide for New Jersey & Rockland County: 1982 Edition. 1981. pap. 3.95 o.p. (ISBN 0-913464-56-2). FOSG Pubns.

--Factory Outlet Shopping Guide for New York-Westchester-Long Island, 1982. 1981. pap. 3.95 o.p. (ISBN 0-913464-57-0). FOSG Pubns.

--Factory Outlet Shopping Guide for North & South Carolina, 1982. 1981. pap. 3.95 o.p. (ISBN 0-913464-61-9). FOSG Pubns.

--Factory Outlet Shopping Guide for Pennsylvania, 1982. 1981. pap. 3.95 o.p. (ISBN 0-913464-58-9). FOSG Pubns.

--Factory Outlet Shopping Guide for Washington D. C.-Maryland-Virginia-Delaware, 1982. 1981. pap. 3.95 o.p. (ISBN 0-913464-59-7). FOSG Pubns.

Bird, John. Science from Water Play. LC 77-82984. (Teaching Primary Science Ser.). (Illus.). 1977. pap. text ed. 9.85 (ISBN 0-356-05071-8). Raintree Pubs.

Bird, John & Catherall, Ed. Fibres & Fabrics. LC 77-82983. (Teaching Primary Science Ser.). (Illus.). 1977. pap. text ed. 9.85 (ISBN 0-356-05076-9). Raintree Pubs.

Bird, John & Diamond, Dorothy. Candles. LC 77-82987. (Teaching Primary Science Ser.). 1977. pap. text ed. 9.85 (ISBN 0-356-05070-X). Raintree Pubs.

Bird, John, ed. Plate Tectonics. rev. ed. 1980. pap. 25.00 (ISBN 0-87590-216-2, SP0026). Am Geophysical.

Bird, Joseph & Bird, Lois. Freedom to Live. 1979. 9.95 o.p. (ISBN 0-671-24699-2). S&S.

--To Live As Family: An Experience of Love & Bonding. LC 81-43392. (Illus.). 216p. 1981. 13.95 (ISBN 0-385-17492-6). Doubleday.

Bird, Joseph, jt. auth. see Bird, Lois.

Bird, Joseph W. & Bird, Lois F. Love Is All: Conversations of a Husband & Wife with God. LC 67-22453. 1968. pap. 3.50 (ISBN 0-385-00779-5, Im). Doubleday.

Bird, Lois & Bird, Joseph. To Live As a Family. LC 81-43392. 288p. 1983. pap. 5.50 (ISBN 0-385-19020-4, Im). Doubleday.

Bird, Lois, jt. auth. see Bird, Joseph.

Bird, Lois F., jt. auth. see Bird, Joseph W.

Bird, May. Electrical Principles Three Checkbook. text ed. 17.95 (ISBN 0-408-00636-6); pap. text ed. 9.95 (ISBN 0-408-00601-3). Butterworth.

--Electrical Science: No. 3-Checkbook. 1981. text ed. 18.95 (ISBN 0-408-00657-9); pap. text ed. 8.95 (ISBN 0-408-00626-9). Butterworth.

--Engineering Mathematics & Science 3 Checkbook. 1981. pap. text ed. 8.95 (ISBN 0-408-00625-0). Butterworth.

--Engineering Science Three Checkbook. 1983. text ed. price not set (ISBN 0-408-00624-2). Butterworth.

--Engineering Science Two Checkbook. 1982. text ed. 24.95 (ISBN 0-408-00691-9); pap. text ed. 12.50 (ISBN 0-408-00627-7). Butterworth.

Bird, Michael, jt. ed. see May, John R.

Bird, Pamela G., tr. see Veiga, Jose J.

Bird, Patricia. The Crystal Heart. 1982. 6.95 (ISBN 0-686-84157-3, Avalon). Bouregy.

--Golden Dream. (YA) 1979. 6.95 (ISBN 0-685-95873-6, Avalon). Bouregy.

--Shamrock in the Sun. (YA) 1980. 6.95 (ISBN 0-686-73921-3, Avalon). Bouregy.

--Sunshine Lost. (YA) 1979. 6.95 (ISBN 0-685-65276-9, Avalon). Bouregy.

Bird, Phyllis A. The Bible As the Church's Book. Date not set. write for info. Geneva Divinity.

--The Bible As the Church's Book, Vol. 5. LC 82-7049. (Library of Living Faith). 120p. 1982. pap. 5.95 (ISBN 0-664-24427-0). Westminster.

Bird, R. B. & Shetter, W. Z. Dutch: Een Goed Begin, a Contemporary Dutch Reader, 2 vols. Date not set. pap. price not set (ISBN 9-0247-2073-7). Vol. 1 (ISBN 9-0247-2071-0). Vol. 2 (ISBN 9-0247-2072-9). Heinman.

Bird, R. Byron, et al. Transport Phenomena. LC 60-11717. 780p. 1960. 40.95x (ISBN 0-471-07392-X). Wiley.

Bird, Roy D. & Wallace, Douglass W. Witness of the Times, a History of Shawnee County. Richmond, Robert W., ed. LC 76-4390. 376p. 1976. 7.95 (ISBN 0-685-72361-5); pap. 8.95 (ISBN 0-916934-03-9). Shawnee County Hist.

Bird, Vivian. Bird's Eye View: The Midlands. 1980. 9.00x o.p. (ISBN 0-900093-36-6, Pub. by Roundwood); pap. 3.00x o.p. (ISBN 0-900093-04-8). State Mutual Bk.

Birdahl, Paul, et al. California Solar Data Manual: 1977 Edition. Grether, Donald & Martin, Marlo, eds. LC 77-78409. 301p. 1977. pap. 20.00x (ISBN 0-930978-06-4, H-019). Solar Energy Info.

Birdsall. Plasma Physics via Computer. 1983. text ed. write for info. (ISBN 0-07-005371-5). McGraw.

Birdsall, Nancy. Population & Poverty in the Developing World. (Working Paper: No. 404). 96p. 1980. 5.00 (ISBN 0-686-36200-4, WP-0404). World Bank.

Birdsall, Stephen S. & Florin, John W. Regional Landscapes of the United States & Canada. LC 77-28103. 1978. text ed. 25.95 o.p. (ISBN 0-471-07397-0). Wiley.

Birdsell, J. B. Human Evolution. 3rd ed. 1981. 23.95 (ISBN 0-395-30784-8); instr's manual 1.50 (ISBN 0-395-30785-6). HM.

Birdseye, Clarence & Birdseye, Eleanor. Growing Woodland Plants. (Illus.). 1972. pap. 4.00 (ISBN 0-486-20661-0). Dover.

Birdseye, Eleanor, jt. auth. see Birdseye, Clarence.

Birdwell, Cleo. Amazons. 1981. pap. 2.95 o.p. (ISBN 0-425-05061-0). Berkley Pub.

Birdwell, Roger W. High-Tech Investing. 257p. 1983. 17.95 (ISBN 0-686-43181-2). Times Bks.

Birenbaum, Arnold. Health Care & Society. LC 80-67092. 272p. 1981. text ed. 28.50x (ISBN 0-916672-57-3). Allanheld.

Birenbaum, Harvey. Tragedy & Innocence. LC 82-23828. (Illus.). 176p. (Orig.). 1983. lib. bdg. 20.75 (ISBN 0-8191-2991-7); pap. text ed. 9.75 (ISBN 0-8191-2992-5). U Pr of Amer.

Birge, Edward B. History of Public School Music in the United States. 323p. Repr. of 1937 ed. 5.50 (ISBN 0-686-37916-0). Music Ed.

Birge, Lynn. Serving Adult Learners. (ALA Ser. in Librarianship). 230p. 1981. pap. text ed. 18.00 (ISBN 0-8389-0346-0). ALA.

Birk, Genevieve B., jt. auth. see Birk, Newman P.

Birk, Newman P. & Birk, Genevieve B. A Handbook of Grammar, Rhetoric, Mechanics & Usage. LC 71-179751. 148p. 1972. pap. text ed. 6.95 (ISBN 0-672-63275-6). Odyssey Pr.

--Practice for Understanding & Using English: Eighty Exercises. 2nd ed. LC 71-189751. 1972. pap. 5.95 (ISBN 0-672-63291-8). Odyssey Pr.

Birkbeck, Morris. Letters from Illinois. LC 68-8685. (American Scene Ser). 1970. Repr. of 1818 ed. lib. bdg. 24.50 (ISBN 0-306-71170-2). Da Capo.

--Letters from Illinois & Notes of a Journey in America. 3rd ed. LC 71-119545. Repr. of 1818 ed. 27.50x (ISBN 0-678-00686-5). Kelley.

Birkby, Elizabeth & Fitch, Canon J.compiled by. Suffolk Parochial Libraries: A Catalogue. 152p. 1977. lib. bdg. 24.00 o.p. (ISBN 0-7201-0704-0, Pub. by Mansell England). Wilson.

Birkby, Robert H. The Court & Public Policy. 435p. 1983. pap. 13.95 (ISBN 0-87187-248-X). Congr Quarterly.

Birke, Lynda & Gardner, Katy. Why Suffer? Periods & their Problems. 76p. 1983. pap. 3.95 (ISBN 0-86068-284-6, Virago Pr). Merrimack Bk Serv.

Birkeland, Joran, tr. see Undset, Sigrid.

Birkeland, Peter W. Pedology, Weathering & Geomorphological Research. (Illus.). 1974. text ed. 19.95x (ISBN 0-19-501730-7). Oxford U Pr.

Birken, Andrew. J. M. Barrie & the Lost Boys. (Illus.). 1979. 14.95 (ISBN 0-517-53873-3, C N Potter Bks). Crown.

Birkenhager, W. H. & De Leeuw, P. W., eds. Control Mechanisms in Essential Hypertension. 2nd, rev., enl. ed. 358p. 1982. 108.00 (ISBN 0-444-80405-6). Elsevier.

Birkett, Mary E. Lamartine & the Poetics of Landscape. LC 82-82427. (French Forum Monographs: No. 38). 105p. 1982. pap. 10.00x (ISBN 0-917058-37-2). French Forum.

Birkey, Verna & Turnquist, Jeanette. Building Happy Memories & Family Traditions. (Illus.). 128p. 1980. 7.95 (ISBN 0-8007-1126-2). Revell.

--A Mother's Problem Solver. 1979. pap. 5.95 (ISBN 0-8007-5050-0, Power Bks). Revell.

Birkhauser, Kaspar. Light from the Darkness: Paintings by Peter Birkhauser. Wertenschlag, Eva, ed. (Illus.). 80p. (English, German.). 1980. pap. 19.95x (ISBN 3-7643-1190-8, Dist. by Sigo Pr). Birkhauser.

Birkhimer, William E. Historical Sketch of the Organization, Administration, Materiel & Tactics of the Artillery, United States Army. LC 68-54788. Repr. of 1884 ed. lib. bdg. 17.00x (ISBN 0-8371-0314-2, BIAR). Greenwood.

Birkhoff, G. & Bartee, T. C. Modern Applied Algebra. 1970. text ed. 30.50 o.p. (ISBN 0-07-005381-2, C). McGraw.

Birkhoff, G., ed. see Symposia in Applied Mathematics-New York-1959.

Birkhoff, Garrett. The Numerical Solution of Elliptic Equations: Proceedings. (CBMS Conference Ser.: No. 1). xi, 82p. (Orig.). 1972. pap. text ed. 7.00 (ISBN 0-89871-001-4). Soc Indus-Appl Math.

Birkhoff, Garrett & Gian-Carlo Rota. Ordinary Differential Equations. 3rd ed. LC 78-8304. 350p. 1978. text ed. 31.95x (ISBN 0-471-07411-X). Wiley.

Birkhoff, Garrett & MacLane, Saunders. Survey of Modern Algebra. 4th ed. 1977. text ed. 29.95 (ISBN 0-02-310070-2, 31007). Macmillan.

Birkhoff, Garrett, jt. auth. see MacLane, Saunders.

Birkhoff, George D. Collected Mathematical Papers, 3 Vols. LC 66-23748. 1968. Repr. of 1950 ed. 12.50 ea. o.p.; Vol. 1. (ISBN 0-486-61955-9); Vol. 2. (ISBN 0-486-61956-7); Vol. 3. (ISBN 0-486-61957-5). Dover.

Birkin, Stanley J., jt. auth. see Richardson, Gary L.

Birkin, Stanley J., jt. auth. see Sanders, Donald H.

Birkin, Stanley J., jt. ed. see Walsh, Ruth M.

Birkland, Carol. Finding Home: A Guide to Solidarity with the World's Uprooted. (Orig.). 1983. pap. write for info. (ISBN 0-377-00129-5). Friend Pr.

Birkmayer, W. & Riederer, P. Parkinson's Disease: Biochemistry, Clinical Pathology, & Treatment. Reynolds, G., tr. from Ger. (Illus.). 240p. 1983. 39.00 (ISBN 0-387-81722-0). Springer-Verlag.

Birks, H. J., jt. auth. see Huntley, B.

Birks, J. B. & International Conference at the Calouste Gulbenkian Foundation Centre, Lisbon, Portugal, April 8-24, 1974. Excited States of Biological Molecules: Proceedings. LC 75-6985. 652p. 1976. 113.95 o.p. (ISBN 0-471-07413-6, Pub. by Wiley-Interscience). Wiley.

Birks, J. B., ed. Organic Molecular Photophysics, 2 vols. LC 74-8594. (Monographs in Chemical Physics Ser.). 600p. 1973. Vol. 1. 114.95x o.p. (ISBN 0-471-07415-2, Pub. by Wiley-Interscience); Vol. 2. 129.00x (ISBN 0-471-07421-7). Wiley.

Birks, J. S. & Sinclair, C. A. Arab Manpower. LC 80-12416. 450p. 1980. 50.00 (ISBN 0-312-04708-8). St Martin.

Birks, N. & Meier, G. H. An Introduction to High Temperature Oxidation of Metals. 208p. 1983. pap. text ed. 29.50 (ISBN 0-7131-3464-X). E Arnold.

Birla Institute of Scientific Research. Structural Transformation & Economic Development. 126p. 1980. text ed. 10.00x (ISBN 0-391-01790-X). Humanities.

Birley, Anthony. Lives of the Later Caesars. (Classics Ser.). 320p. 1976. pap. 4.95 (ISBN 0-14-044308-8). Penguin.

Birley, Anthony, tr. see Alfoldy, Geza.

Birley, Arthur W. & Scott, Martyn J. Plastic Materials. 1982. 43.00x (ISBN 0-412-00211-6, Pub. by Chapman & Hall); pap. 21.00x (ISBN 0-412-00221-3). Methuen Inc.

Birmingham, Frederic A. John--the Man Who Would Be President. Synhorst, Thomas J., ed. LC 79-93341. (Illus.). 128p. 1979. 9.95 (ISBN 0-89387-040-4, Co-Pub by Sat Eve Post). Curtis Pub Co.

Birmingham, Jacqueline. The Problem-Oriented Record: A Self-Learning Module. (Illus.). 1978. pap. text ed. 15.50 (ISBN 0-07-005385-5, HP). McGraw.

Birmingham, Jacqueline, jt. auth. see Carini, Geraldine.

Birmingham, Jacqueline J. Medical Terminology: A Self-Learning Module. (Illus.). 448p. 1981. pap. text ed. 15.50 (ISBN 0-07-005386-3, HP). McGraw.

Birmingham, Jacqueline J., jt. auth. see Hills, Sally W.

Birmingham, Jean. I Still Believe in Tomorrow. 62p. (Orig.). 1980. pap. 1.95 o.p. (ISBN 0-88347-120-5). Thomas More.

Birmingham, Nan T. Store: A Memoir of America's Great Department Stores. LC 78-14204. (Illus.). 1979. 12.50 o.p. (ISBN 0-399-11899-3). Putnam Pub Group.

Birmingham, Stephen. The Auerbach Will. 416p. 1983. 16.45 (ISBN 0-316-09646-6). Little.

--Certain People. 1977. 9.95 (ISBN 0-316-09642-3). Little.

--Duchess: The Story of Wallis Warfield Windsor. 1981. 15.00 (ISBN 0-316-09643-1). Little.

--The Grandes Dames. (General Ser.). 1983. lib. bdg. 18.95 (ISBN 0-8161-3498-7, Large Print Bks). G K Hall.

Birn, Herluf & Winther, Jens E. Manual of Minor Oral Surgery: A Step by Step Atlas. LC 75-18759. (Illus.). 1976. text ed. 15.00 (ISBN 0-7216-1705-0). Saunders.

Birn, Randi. Johan Borgen. (World Authors Ser.). 1974. lib. bdg. 15.95 (ISBN 0-8057-2167-3, Twayne). G K Hall.

Birnbach, Lisa, ed. Etiquette For the Preferred Lifestyle. LC 81-43784. (Illus.). 352p. 1983. pap. 6.95 (ISBN 0-89480-202-X). Workman Pub.

Birnbaum, George see Marton, L.

Birnbaum, H., et al, eds. Studia Linguistica Alexandro Vasilii Filio Issatschenko: A Collegis Amicusque Oblata. 517p. (Orig., Eng., Fr., Ger., Rus.). 1978. pap. 60.00 (ISBN 0-686-32343-2). Benjamins North Am.

Birnbaum, Henrik. Common Slavic Progress & Problems in Its Reconstruction. 1979. Repr. soft cover 16.95 (ISBN 0-89357-053-2). Slavica.

Birnbaum, Howard. The Cost of Catastrophic Illness. LC 77-9192. 1978. 16.95x (ISBN 0-669-01773-6). Lexington Bks.

Birnbaum, Hubert C. Amphoto's Guide to Cameras. (Illus.). 1978. 10.95 o.p. (ISBN 0-8174-2444-X, Amphoto); pap. 7.95 (ISBN 0-8174-2117-3). Watson-Guptill.

Birnbaum, Ian. An Introduction to Causal Analysis in Sociology. 1980. text ed. 37.50x (ISBN 0-333-26299-9); pap. text ed. 15.75x (ISBN 0-686-63378-4). Humanities.

Birnbaum, Jacob S. The Musculo-Skeletal Manual. LC 82-3878. 1982. 39.95 (ISBN 0-12-788075-5); pap. 19.95 (ISBN 0-12-788074-7). Acad Pr.

Birnbaum, Karl E. The Politics of East-West Communication in Europe. 180p. 1979. text ed. 31.25x (ISBN 0-566-00254-X). Gower Pub Ltd.

Birnbaum, Mark & Sickman, John. How to Choose Your Small Business Computer: Popular. LC 82-11665. (Microcomputer Bks.). 176p. 1982. pap. 9.95 (ISBN 0-201-10187-4). A-W.

Birnbaum, Martin. Functional Optometric Vision Care. LC 82-61251. 1983. write for info (ISBN 0-87873-032-X). Prof Press.

Birnbaum, Max, jt. auth. see Babad, Elisha Y.

Birnbaum, Michael, jt. auth. see Sonnenburg, David.

Birnbaum, Milton. Aldous Huxley's Quest for Values. LC 71-142146. 1971. 14.50x (ISBN 0-87049-127-X). U of Tenn Pr.

Birnbaum, Norman, ed. Beyond the Crisis. LC 16-42637. 1977. 18.95x (ISBN 0-19-502197-5). Oxford U Pr.

Birnbaum, Phyllis, ed. & tr. Rabbits, Crabs, Etc. LC 82-8365. 156p. 1982. text ed. 15.00x (ISBN 0-8248-0777-4); pap. 7.95 (ISBN 0-8248-0817-7). UH Pr.

Birnbaum, Pierre, jt. auth. see Badie, Bertrand.

Birnbaum, Robert. Creative Academic Bargaining: Managing Conflict in the Unionized College & University. LC 80-18806. 288p. 1980. text ed. 20.95 (ISBN 0-8077-2631-1). Tchrs Coll.

Birnbaum, Stephen. Canada, Nineteen Eighty-One. (Get 'em & Go Travel Guide Ser). 1980. pap. 9.95 o.p. (ISBN 0-395-29751-6). HM.

--Canada, Nineteen Eighty-Two. (The Get 'em & Go Travel Guide Ser.). 608p. 1981. pap. 10.95 o.p. (ISBN 0-395-31532-8). HM.

--Canada 1983. (The Get 'em & Go Travel Guide Ser.). 1982. 11.95 (ISBN 0-395-32868-3). HM.

--The Caribbean, Bermuda & the Bahamas. (Get 'em & Go Travel Guide Ser.). 1982. 11.95 (ISBN 0-686-84795-4). HM.

--The Caribbean, Bermuda & the Bahamas, Nineteen Eighty-Two. (The Get 'em & Go Travel Guide Ser.). 672p. 1981. pap. 10.95 o.p. (ISBN 0-395-31533-6). HM.

--Disneyland 1983. 1982. 4.95 (ISBN 0-395-32924-8). HM.

--Europe. (Get 'em & Go Travel Guide Ser.). 1982. 13.95 (ISBN 0-395-32870-5). HM.

--Europe, Nineteen Eight-Two. (The Get 'em & Go Travel Guide Ser.). 1232p. 1981. pap. 12.95 o.p. (ISBN 0-395-31534-4). HM.

--Great Britain & Ireland 1983. (Get 'em & Go Travel Guide Ser.). 1982. 11.95 (ISBN 0-395-32871-3). HM.

--Hawaii 1983. (Get 'em & Go Travel Guide Ser.). 1982. 11.95 (ISBN 0-395-32872-1). HM.

--Mexico, Nineteen Eighty-Two. (The Get 'em & Go Travel Guide Ser.). 704p. 1981. pap. 10.95 o.p. (ISBN 0-395-31536-0). HM.

--Mexico 1983. (Get 'em & Go Travel Guide Ser.). 1982. 11.95 (ISBN 0-395-32873-X). HM.

--South America, Nineteen Eighty-One. (Get 'em & Go Travel Guides). 1980. pap. 9.95 o.p. (ISBN 0-395-29757-5). HM.

--South America, Nineteen Eighty-Two. (The Get 'em & Go Travel Guide Ser.). 672p. 1981. pap. 10.95 o.p. (ISBN 0-395-31537-9). HM.

--United States, Nineteen Eighty-One. (Get 'em & Go Travel Guides). 1980. pap. 9.95 o.p. (ISBN 0-395-29753-2). HM.

--United States, Nineteen Eighty-Two. (The Get 'em & Go Travel Guide Ser.). 816p. 1981. pap. 10.95 o.p. (ISBN 0-395-31538-7). HM.

--United States 1983. (Get 'em & Go Travel Guide Ser.). 1982. 11.95 (ISBN 0-395-32875-6). HM.

--Walt Disney World. 1981. pap. 4.95 o.p. (ISBN 0-395-31792-4). HM.

--Walt Disney World 1983. rev. ed. 1982. 4.95 (ISBN 0-395-32952-3). HM.

Birney, Alice L. Satiric Catharsis in Shakespeare: A Theory of Dramatic Structure. LC 79-185976. 1973. 27.50x (ISBN 0-520-02214-9). U of Cal Pr.

Birnholz, Jason C. Clinical Diagnostic Pearls. 1971. spiral bdg. 8.50 o.p. (ISBN 0-87488-730-5). Med Exam.

Birnie, G. D. Subnuclear Components: Preparation & Fractionation. 160p. 1976. 31.50 o.p. (ISBN 0-408-70729-1). Butterworth.

Birnie, G. D. & Rickwood, D. Centrifugal Separations in Molecular & Cell Biology. (Illus.). 1978. 34.95 (ISBN 0-408-70803-4). Butterworth.

Birnie, Patricia, jt. ed. see Barston, R. P.

Biro, Yvette. Profane Mythology: The Savage Mind of the Cinema. Goldstein, Imre, tr. LC 82-48384. 160p. 1982. 22.50 (ISBN 0-253-18010-4); pap. 7.95 (ISBN 0-253-20293-0). Ind U Pr.

Birou see Schlegal, John P., et al.

Birr, C., ed. Methods of Peptide & Protein Sequence Analysis. 1980. 92.00 (ISBN 0-444-80218-5). Elsevier.

Birrell, Robert & Hill, Douglas, eds. Quarry Australia? Social & Environmental Perspectives on Managing the Nations Resources. (Illus.). 384p. 1982. text ed. 44.00x (ISBN 0-686-84066-6). Oxford U Pr.

Birren, J. E., ed. Aging: A Challenge to Science & Society; Vol. 3, Behavioral Sciences & Conclusions. (Illus.). 350p. 1983. text ed. 65.00x (ISBN 0-19-261256-5). Oxford U Pr.

Birren, James E. Psychology of Aging. 1964. text ed. 23.95 (ISBN 0-13-733428-1). P-H.

Birren, James E., jt. auth. see Woodruff, Diana S.

Birren, James E., et al. Developmental Psychology: A Life-Span Approach. LC 80-82839. (Illus.). 736p. 1981. text ed. 23.95 (ISBN 0-395-29717-6); instr's manual 1.00 (ISBN 0-395-29718-4); test-bank 1.75 (ISBN 0-395-29720-6); study guide 8.50 (ISBN 0-395-29719-2). HM.

Birrer, Christina D., jt. auth. see Birrer, Richard B.

Birrer, Richard B. & Birrer, Christina D. Medical Injuries in the Martial Arts. (Illus.). 240p. 1981. 18.75x (ISBN 0-398-04133-4); pap. 12.95x (ISBN 0-398-04134-2). C C Thomas.

Birt, David. The Black Death. (The Middle Ages, 1066-1485 Ser.). (Illus.). 24p. 1974. pap. text ed. 12.95 10 copies & tchr's guide (ISBN 0-582-39383-3). Longman.

--The Black Prince. (The Middle Ages, 1066-1485 Ser.). (Illus.). 24p. 1974. pap. text ed. 12.95 10 copies & tchr's guide (ISBN 0-582-39382-5). Longman.

--Knights & Tournaments. (The Middle Ages, 1066-1485 Ser.). (Illus.). 24p. 1974. pap. text ed. 12.95 10 copies & tchr's guide (ISBN 0-582-39374-4). Longman.

--The Medieval Town. (The Middle Ages, 1066-1485 Ser.). (Illus.). 24p. (Orig.). 1974. pap. text ed. 12.95 10 copies & tchr's guide (ISBN 0-582-39389-2). Longman.

--The Medieval Village. (The Middle Ages, 1066-1485 Ser.). (Illus.). 24p. 1974. pap. text ed. 12.95 10 copies & tchr's guide (ISBN 0-582-39373-6). Longman.

--The Monastery. (The Middle Ages, 1066-1485 Ser.). (Illus.). 1974. pap. text ed. 12.95 10 copies & tchr's guide (ISBN 0-582-39380-9). Longman.

--The Murder of Becket. (The Middle Ages, 1066-1485 Ser.). (Illus.). 24p. 1974. pap. text ed. 12.95 10 copies & tchr's guide (ISBN 0-582-39376-0). Longman.

--The Norman Conquest. (The Middle Ages, 1066-1485 Ser.). (Illus.). 24p. 1974. pap. text ed. 12.95 10 copies & tchr's guide (ISBN 0-582-39372-8). Longman.

--Peasants Revolt. (The Middle Ages, 1066-1485 Ser.). (Illus.). 24p. 1974. pap. text ed. 12.95 10 copies & tchr's guide (ISBN 0-582-39384-1). Longman.

--Stephen & Matilda. (The Middle Ages, 1066-1485 Ser.). (Illus.). 24p. 1974. pap. text ed. 12.95 10 copies & tchr's guide (ISBN 0-582-39375-2). Longman.

Birt, David & Carstairs, Ian. The Tudors Briefings Unit. (History Units Ser.). (Illus., Incl. 10 briefing, tchr's guide & ans. key). 1975. pap. text ed. 18.65 (ISBN 0-582-39616-6). Longman.

Birt, Mary, jt. auth. see Birt, Paul.

Birt, Paul & Birt, Mary. Living in Instant Forgiveness. 1979. pap. 1.25 o.s.i. (ISBN 0-89274-132-5). Harrison Hse.

--What Next? 32p. (Orig.). 1977. pap. 1.50 o.s.i. (ISBN 0-89274-053-1). Harrison Hse.

Birt, Robert F., jt. auth. see Morrison, Leger.

Birt, Robert F., jt. auth. see Morrison, Leger R.

Birtha, Becky. For Nights Like This One: Stories of Loving Women. 128p. (Orig.). 1983. pap. 4.75 (ISBN 0-9603628-4-3). Frog in Well.

Birtles, Philip. Mosquito. (Illus.). 192p. 1981. 19.95. Sci Bks Intl.

Birtles, T. G., jt. auth. see Menghetti, D.

Birzle, Hermann, et al. Radiology of Trauma. Kaufmann, Herbert, tr. LC 76-20070. 1978. text ed. 69.00 o.p. (ISBN 0-7216-1703-4). Saunders.

Bisagno, John R. Life Without Compromise. LC 81-71253. 1983. 3.25 (ISBN 0-8054-1503-3). Broadman.

Bisagno, Juan. El Poder De la Oracion Tenaz. De Lerin, Olivia S. D., tr. from Eng. Orig. Title: The Power of Positive Praying. 96p. (Span.). 1981. pap. 2.15 (ISBN 0-311-40029-9). Casa Bautista.

Bisaillon, Blaise. The Public Library: What Is Its Place & Function in the United States? (Vital Issues, Vol. XXIX 1979-80: No. 3). 0.60 (ISBN 0-686-81608-0). Ctr Info Am.

Bisanz, Rudolf. The Rene von Schleinitz Collection of the Milwaukee Art Center: Major Schools of German Nineteenth-Century Popular Painting. LC 78-53284. (Illus.). 256p. 1980. 37.50 (ISBN 0-299-07700-4). U of Wis Pr.

Bisbee, Gerald E., Jr. & Vraciu, Robert A., eds. Managing the Finances of Health Care Organizations. LC 80-17538. (Illus.). 549p. 1980. text ed. 21.00x (ISBN 0-914904-50-7); pap. text ed. o.s.i. (ISBN 0-914904-51-5). Health Admin Pr.

Bisch, Louis E. Be Glad You're Neurotic. 2nd ed. 1956. pap. 3.95 o.p. (ISBN 0-07-005390-1, SP). McGraw.

Bischel, Jon E., ed. Income Tax Treaties. LC 78-58373. 1978. text ed. 25.00 (ISBN 0-685-65701-9, J3-1412). PLI.

Bischel, Leonard. A Merry-Go-Round. (Illus.). 72p. (Orig.). (gr. 1-5). 1980. pap. 4.95 (ISBN 0-935110-01-1, 28711-TXU). Blackjack Ent.

Bischoff, David. Starfall. 1980. pap. 1.95 o.p. (ISBN 0-425-04524-2). Berkley Pub.

Bischoff, David, ed. Strange Encounters. LC 76-45662. (Illus.). (gr. 3-6). 1977. 10.65 o.p. (ISBN 0-8172-0525-X). Raintree Pubs.

Bischoff, David F. & Monteleone, Thomas F. Day of the Dragonstar. 352p. (Orig.). 1983. pap. 2.75 (ISBN 0-425-05932-4). Berkley Pub.

Bischoff, Kenneth B., jt. auth. see Froment, Gilbert F.

Bisconte, J. C., jt. ed. see Sklansky, J.

Bisen, Malini, tr. see Rajneesh, Acharya.

Biserte, G., et al, eds. Bronchoalveolar Lavage in Man. 544p. 1979. text ed. 24.00 o.s.i. (ISBN 0-686-74055-6). Masson Pub.

Bish, Robert & Nourse, Hugh. Urban Economics & Policy Analysis. (Illus.). 384p. 1975. text ed. 27.95 (ISBN 0-07-005388-X, C). McGraw.

Bish, Tommy. Home Gunsmithing Digest. 2nd ed. (DBI Bks). 1971. pap. 7.95 o.s.i. (ISBN 0-695-80212-2). Follett.

Bishay, A., ed. see Cairo International Workshop on Applications of Science & Technology for Desert Development September 9-15, 1978.

Bishirjian, Richard. The Nature of Public Philosophy. LC 82-20170. 62p. 1983. Repr. of 1978 ed. pap. text ed. 3.95 (ISBN 0-8191-2861-9). U Pr of Amer.

Bishirjian, Richard, ed. A Public Philosophy Reader. LC 78-23415. 1979. 9.95 o.p. (ISBN 0-87000-435-2, Arlington Hse). Crown.

Bishoff, David. War Games. (Orig.). 1983. pap. price not set (ISBN 0-440-19387-7). Dell.

Bishop. Altering Ready-to-Wear. (Illus.). 128p. 1976. pap. 3.44i (ISBN 0-397-40247-3). Har-Row.

Bishop, A. R. & Campbell, D. K. Nonlinear Problems: Present & Future. (Mathematical Studies Ser.). 1982. 64.00 (ISBN 0-444-86395-8). Elsevier.

Bishop, A. S. Rise of a Central Authority for English Education. LC 70-128634. (Cambridge Texts & Studies in the History of Education). (Illus.). 1971. 37.50 (ISBN 0-521-08023-1). Cambridge U Pr.

Bishop, A. W. & Henkel, D. J. Measurement of Soil Properties in the Triaxial Test. 2nd ed. (Illus.). 1962. 25.00 o.p. (ISBN 0-312-52430-7). St Martin.

Bishop, Alan, ed. see Brittain, Vera.

Bishop, Ann. Hello, Mr. Chips: Computer Jokes & Riddles. (Illus.). 64p. (YA) 1982. 8.95 (ISBN 0-525-66775-X); pap. 3.95 (ISBN 0-525-66782-2, 0383-120). Lodestar Bks.

--Noah Riddle? LC 71-115893. (Riddle Bk.). (gr. 1-3). 1970. 6.50g o.p. (ISBN 0-8075-5702-1). A Whitman.

Bishop, Arthur C. Outline of Crystal Morphology. 1970. pap. text ed. 9.50x (ISBN 0-09-079423-0). Humanities.

Bishop, Ashley, jt. auth. see Bean, Thomas W.

Bishop, Beata & McNeill, Pat. The Eggshell Ego: An Irreverent Look at Today's Male. LC 77-8249. 1978. 8.95 o.p. (ISBN 0-89490-002-1); pap. 7.95x o.p. (ISBN 0-89490-021-8). Enslow Pubs.

Bishop, Beverly & Craik, Rebecca L. Neural Plasticity. 1982. pap. 5.00 (ISBN 0-912452-38-2). Am Phys Therapy Assn.

Bishop, Bonnie. No One Noticed Ralph. LC 78-18555. (gr. k-3). 1979. 6.95a o.p. (ISBN 0-385-12158-X); PLB 6.95a (ISBN 0-385-12159-8). Doubleday.

--Ralph Rides Away. LC 78-20710. (Reading on My Own Bk.). (Illus.). (gr. 1). 1979. 6.95a o.p. (ISBN 0-385-14213-7); PLB 6.95a (ISBN 0-385-14214-5). Doubleday.

Bishop, C. James, jt. auth. see Kopf, David.

Bishop, Charles E. & Toussaint, W. D. Introduction to Agricultural Economic Analysis. LC 58-12715. (Illus.). 258p. 1958. 22.95x o.p. (ISBN 0-471-07557-4). Wiley.

Bishop, Claire H. The Five Chinese Brothers. (Illus.). (gr. k-3). 1938. 6.95 (ISBN 0-698-20044-6, Coward); gb 6.99 (ISBN 0-698-30089-0). Putnam Pub Group.

--Georgette. (Break-of-Day Ser.). (Illus.). 64p. (gr. k-3). 1974. PLB 4.69 o.p. (ISBN 0-698-30512-4, Coward). Putnam Pub Group.

--The Truffle Pig. (Break of Day Bk). (Illus.). (gr. k-3). 1971. PLB 4.99 o.p. (ISBN 0-698-30378-4, Coward). Putnam Pub Group.

Bishop, Curtis, et al. Trails to Texas. (Illus.). (gr. 7). 1965. text ed. 7.48 (ISBN 0-87443-039-9); tchrs' ed. 4.20 (ISBN 0-87443-040-2). Benson.

Bishop, D. F. & Desnick, R. J., eds. Assays of the Heme Biosynthetic Enzymes. (Journal: Enzyme: Vol. 28, No. 2-3). (Illus.). vi, 144p. 1982. pap. 58.25 (ISBN 3-8055-3573-2). S Karger.

Bishop, Dale, jt. ed. see Yarshater, Ehsan.

Bishop, Douglas & Carter, Lark P. Activity Guide for Crop Science & Food Production. 1983. 5.12 (ISBN 0-07-005432-0, G). McGraw.

Bishop, Douglas D. Working in Plant Science. Amberson, Max L. & Chapman, Stephen, eds. (Illus.). (gr. 9-10). 1978. pap. text ed. 9.96 (ISBN 0-07-000835-3, G). McGraw.

Bishop, E., jt. auth. see Oulton, A. J.

Bishop, Edward H. Perinatal Medicine: Practical Diagnosis & Management. 1981. 29.95 (ISBN 0-201-03887-0, 03887, Med-Nurse). A-W.

Bishop, Elizabeth. The Complete Poems Nineteen Twenty-Seven to Nineteen Seventy-Nine. 1983. 15.50 (ISBN 0-374-12747-6). FS&G.

Bishop, Eric. Dental Insurance: The What, the Why, & the How of Dental Benefits. 224p. 1983. 29.95 (ISBN 0-07-005471-1, P&RB). McGraw.

Bishop, Ferman. Henry Adams. (United States Authors Ser.: No. 293). 1979. lib. bdg. 11.95 o.p. (ISBN 0-8057-7257-X, Twayne). G K Hall.

Bishop, Gavin. Mrs. McGinty & the Bizarre Plant. (Illus.). 32p. (ps). 1983. bds. 9.95 (ISBN 0-19-558074-5, Pub by Oxford U Pr Childrens). Merrimack Bk Serv.

***Bishop, George.** The Encyclopedia of Motorcycling. 192p. 1980. 16.95 o.p. (ISBN 0-399-12557-4, Perige); pap. 8.95 o.p. (ISBN 0-399-50491-5). Putnam Pub Group.

Bishop Graphics, Inc. The Design & Drafting of Printed Circuits. 1979. 40.75 (ISBN 0-07-005430-4). McGraw.

Bishop, Hillman, jt. auth. see Hendel, Samuel.

Bishop, J. Dean, ed. see Burke, Kenneth, et al.

Bishop, Jim. The Day Christ Was Born. LC 60-13444. 1978. pap. 2.95i (ISBN 0-06-060785-8, HJ 37, HarpR). Har-Row.

Bishop, Joan S. Truth for Orange Trees. 1958. 2.50 o.p. (ISBN 0-8233-0007-2). Golden Quill.

Bishop, John. Confluence. Bd. with The Skirmishers. pap. 2.95 (ISBN 0-686-81619-6). Dramatists Play.

Bishop, John & Bishop, Naomi. An Ever-Changing Place. 1978. 8.95 o.p. (ISBN 0-671-22898-6). S&S.

Bishop, John A. & Rosenbloom, Arthur H. Federal Tax Valuation Digest Business Enterprises & Business Interests: Corporate Security Values As Determined by the Tax Court, 1977. 1982. pap. 85.00 (ISBN 0-88262-644-2). Warren.

Bishop, Jonathan. The Covenant: A Reading. 458p. (Orig.). 1983. pap. 9.95 (ISBN 0-87243-113-4). Templegate.

Bishop, Joseph P. The Eye of the Storm. 128p. (Orig.). 1983. pap. 3.95 (ISBN 0-87123-263-4). Bethany Hse.

--You Can Have a New Beginning. 123p. 1981. pap. 4.95 o.p. (ISBN 0-912376-72-4). Chosen Bks Pub.

Bishop, Joseph W., Jr. The Law of Corporate Officers & Directors: Indemnification & Insurance. LC 80-52859. 1981. 65.00 o.p. (ISBN 0-88262-504-7). Warren.

Bishop, Lee. Davy Crockett: Frontier Fighter. (American Explorer Ser.: No. 11). (Orig.). 1983. pap. 2.95 (ISBN 0-440-01695-9). Dell.

Bishop, Lloyd. In Search of Style: Essays in French Literary Stylistics. LC 82-13370. 224p. 1982. 14.95x (ISBN 0-8139-0957-0). U Pr of Va.

Bishop, Mary. Billy Graham: America's Evangelist. (Illus.). 1978. 10.95 o.p. (ISBN 0-448-14586-3, G&D); pap. 4.95 o.p. (ISBN 0-448-14587-1, Today Press). Putnam Pub Group.

Bishop, Maurice. Forward Ever! 280p. 1982. lib. bdg. 23.00 (ISBN 0-909196-16-8); pap. 6.95 (ISBN 0-909196-17-6). Path Pr NY.

Bishop, Michael. Catacomb Years. LC 78-18438. 1979. 10.95 (ISBN 0-399-12255-9, Pub. by Berkley). Putnam Pub Group.

--Transfigurations. 1980. pap. 2.25 o.p. (ISBN 0-425-04696-6). Berkley Pub.

--Transfigurations. LC 79-11025. 1979. 10.95 o.p. (ISBN 0-399-12379-2). Putnam Pub Group.

Bishop, Milo E. Mainstreaming: Practical Ideas for Educating Hearing-Impaired Students. 1979. 10.95 (ISBN 0-88200-126-4). Bell Assn Deaf.

Bishop, Morris. The Odyssey of Cabeza de Vaca. LC 70-139123. (Illus.). 306p. 1972. Repr. of 1933 ed. lib. bdg. 20.00x (ISBN 0-8371-5739-0, BICV). Greenwood.

--A Survey of French Literature, 2 vols. rev. ed. Incl. Vol. 1. The Middle Ages to 1800. 462p (ISBN 0-15-584963-8, HC); Vol. 2. The Nineteenth & Twentieth Centuries. 462p (ISBN 0-15-584964-6, HC). 1965. text ed. 20.95 ea. (HC). HarBraceJ.

Bishop, Morris, tr. see Moliere.

Bishop, Nan. Nan, Sarah & Clare: Letters Between Friends. 328p. 1980. pap. 4.95 o.p. (ISBN 0-380-75358-8, 75358). Avon.

Bishop, Naomi, jt. auth. see Bishop, John.

Bishop, Nathaniel Holmes. Four Months in a Sneak Box: A Boat Voyage of Twenty Six Hundred Miles Down the Ohio & Mississippi Rivers. LC 71-142572. (Illus.). xii, 322p. 1976. Repr. of 1879 ed. 45.00x (ISBN 0-8103-4170-0). Gale.

Bishop, Olga B. Bibliography of Ontario History, 1867-1976: Cultural, Economic, Political, Social, 2 vols. 1980. 85.00x set (ISBN 0-8020-2359-2). U of Toronto Pr.

--Canadian Official Publications. (Guides to Official Publications Ser.: Vol. 9). 308p. 1980. 44.00 (ISBN 0-08-024697-4). Pergamon.

Bishop, Paul L. Marine Pollution & Its Control. (Water Resource Engineering Ser.). (Illus.). 384p. 1982. text ed. 35.00 (ISBN 0-07-005482-7). McGraw.

Bishop, Peter. Comprehensive Computer Studies. 200p. 1981. pap. text ed. 12.95 (ISBN 0-7131-0371-X). E Arnold.

Bishop, R. E. Vibration. 2nd ed. LC 79-11172. (Illus.). 1979. 29.95 (ISBN 0-521-22779-8); pap. 11.95 (ISBN 0-521-29639-0). Cambridge U Pr.

Bishop, R. E. & Johnson, D. C. The Mechanics of Vibration. (Illus.). 1979. 110.00 (ISBN 0-521-04258-5). Cambridge U Pr.

Bishop, R. E., jt. auth. see Price, W. G.

Bishop, R. E., et al. The Matrix Analysis of Vibration. (Illus.). 1979. 89.50 (ISBN 0-521-04257-7). Cambridge U Pr.

Bishop, Robert. A Gallery of American Weathervanes & Whirligigs. (Illus.). 128p. 1981. pap. 16.95 (ISBN 0-525-47652-0). Dutton.

--New Discoveries in American Quilts. 128p. 1975. pap. 13.75 (ISBN 0-525-47410-2, 01335-400). Dutton.

--Quilts, Coverlets, Rugs & Samplers. LC 82-47848. (Collector's Guides to American Antiques Ser.). 1982. 13.95 (ISBN 0-394-71271-4). Knopf.

Bishop, Robert & Coblentz, Patricia. American Decorative Arts: 360 Years of Creative Design. (Illus.). 395p. 1982. 65.00 (ISBN 0-8109-0692-9). Abrams.

Bishop, Robert & Safanda, Elizabeth. A Gallery of Amish Quilts: Design Diversity from a Plain People. (Illus.). 1976. pap. 12.50 (ISBN 0-525-47444-7, 01214-360). Dutton.

Bishop, Robert & Weissman, Judith R. Folk Art: Painting, Sculpture & Country Objects. LC 82-48945. 13.95 (ISBN 0-394-71493-8). Knopf.

Bishop, Robert, jt. auth. see Safford, Carleton L.

Bishop, Ron, jt. auth. see Cannon, Bill.

Bishop, Russell H., jt. auth. see Miller, J. Dale.

Bishop, Ruth. Totonac: From Clause to Discourse. (Publications in Linguistics & Related Fields Ser.: No. 17). 185p. 1968. pap. 3.00 o. p. (ISBN 0-88312-019-4); microfiche 2.25 (ISBN 0-88312-599-4). Summer Inst Ling.

Bishop, Vaughn F. & Meszaros, J. William. Comparing Nations: The Developed & the Developing Worlds. 1980. text ed. 17.95 (ISBN 0-669-01142-8). Heath.

Bishop, Vernon S. Cardiac Performance, Vol. 1. Granger, Harris J., ed. (Annual Research Reviews). 1979. 18.00 (ISBN 0-88831-060-9). Eden Pr.

Bishop, Wiley L., jt. auth. see Weaver, Barbara N.

Bishop, William W., Jr. International Law: Cases & Materials. 3rd ed. 1122p. 1971. 27.50 (ISBN 0-316-09664-4). Little.

Bishop, Yvonne, et al. Discrete Multivariate Analysis: Theory & Practice. 1974. 47.50x (ISBN 0-262-02113-7); pap. 17.50x (ISBN 0-262-52040-0). MIT Pr.

Bisignani, J. D. Japan Handbook. (Illus.). 520p. (Orig.). 1983. pap. 12.95 (ISBN 0-9603322-2-7). Moon Pubns CA.

Bisignano, Alphonse. Cooking the Italian Way. LC 82-12641. (Easy Menu Ethnic Cookbooks Ser.). (Illus.). 48p. (gr. 5 up). 1982. PLB 7.95g (ISBN 0-8225-0906-7). Lerner Pubns.

Bisignano, Joseph & Bisignano, Judith. Creating Your Future: Level 3. (Illus.). 72p. 1982. workbook 6.95 (ISBN 0-9607366-9-7, KP109). Kino Pubns.

--Creating Your Future: Level 4. (Illus.). 64p. 1983. workbook 6.95 (ISBN 0-910141-01-0, KP115). Kino Pubns.

Bisignano, Judith, jt. auth. see Bisignano, Joseph.

Bisignano, Judith, jt. auth. see Cera, Mary J.

Bisignano, Judith, jt. auth. see Robinson, Marilyn.

Bisignano, Judith, jt. auth. see Bisignano, Joseph.

Bisio, Attilio. Encyclopedia of Energy Technology. 4000p. 1983. Set. 350.00 (ISBN 0-471-89039-1, Pub. by Wiley-Interscience). Wiley.

Biskind, Elliot L., ed. see Harvey, David C.

Biskind, Elliott L., ed. Boardman's Estate Management & Accounting, 2 Vols. 2nd ed. LC 64-8482. 1969. looseleaf with 1980 suppl. 110.00 (ISBN 0-87632-056-6). Boardman.

--Boardman's New York Family Law. rev. ed. LC 64-17549. 1981. 2 looseleaf vols. 110.00 (ISBN 0-87632-058-2). Boardman.

Biskind, Elliott L. & Barasch, Clarence S., eds. Law of Real Estate Brokers, N.Y. LC 70-83769. 1981. with 1979 suppl. 50.00 (ISBN 0-87632-050-7). Boardman.

Bisko, W. & Karolak, S. Beginner's Course in Polish. 1980. pap. 4.95 (ISBN 83-214-0089-2). Hippocrene Bks.

Biskup, Peter. Australian Libraries. 1982. 23.00 (ISBN 0-85157-326-6, Pub. by Bingley England). Shoe String.

Biskup, Peter, jt. auth. see Balnaves, John.

Biskup, Peter, ed. see Mouton, J. B.

Biskupski, Mieczyslaw B., jt. ed. see Blejwas, Stanislaus A.

Bismarck, Otto Von see Otto, Bismarck Von.

Bisplinghoff, Gretchen, jt. auth. see Wexman, Virginia W.

Bisplinghoff, Ross. Practical Wind Energy Applications. 1982. write for info. o.s.i. (ISBN 0-88410-901-1). Ballinger Pub.

Biss, Roderick, jt. auth. see Mitchell, Donald.

Bissainthe, Max. Dictionnaire De Bibliographie Haitienne: Premier Supplement. LC 51-12164. 1973. 11.00 o.p. (ISBN 0-8108-0667-3). Scarecrow.

Bissel, Richard E. & Crocker, Chester A., eds. South Africa into the Nineteen Eighties. (Special Studies on Africa). 1979. lib. bdg. 27.50 (ISBN 0-89158-373-4). Westview.

Bissell, Christa & Cohen, Leslie. The Good Food for You & Me Book. LC 81-86166. 48p. (Orig.). (gr. 1-5). 1982. pap. text ed. 3.95 (ISBN 0-937938-06-8). Gabriel Pr.

Bissell, LeClair & Watherwax, Richard. The Cat Who Drank Too Much. (Illus.). 48p. (gr. 4 up). 1982. pap. 4.00 (ISBN 0-911153-00-4). Bibliophile Pr.

Bissell, Richard E. Apartheid & International Organizations. 1977. lib. bdg. 22.00 o.p. (ISBN 0-89158-229-0). Westview.

Bissell, Richard E., jt. auth. see Ayubi, Shaheen.

Bisselle, Walter C., jt. auth. see Sanders, Irwin T.

Bisset, James & Stephensen, P. R. Sail Ho. LC 58-5447. (Illus.). 1958. 17.95 (ISBN 0-87599-015-0). S G Phillips.

--Tramps & Ladies. LC 59-12193. (Illus.). 1959. 17.95 (ISBN 0-87599-014-2). S G Phillips.

Bisset, Virgil, jt. ed. see Hunting, Constance.

Bisson, T. A. Yenan in June 1937: Talks with the Communist Leaders. LC 73-620023. (China Research Monographs: No. 11). 1973. pap. 5.00x (ISBN 0-912966-12-2). IEAS.

Bisson, Thomas A. Japan in China. LC 73-3920. (Illus.). 417p. 1973. Repr. of 1938 ed. lib. bdg. 21.00x (ISBN 0-8371-6858-9, BIJC). Greenwood.
Bisswanger, Hans & Schmincke-Ott, Eva, eds. Multifunctional Proteins. LC 79-16055. 333p. 1980. 66.50 (ISBN 0-471-04270-6, Pub. by Wiley-Interscience). Wiley.
Bistner, Stephen I., jt. auth. see Kirk, Robert W.
Bistner, Stephen I., et al. Atlas of Veterinary Ophthalmic Surgery. LC 76-58598. (Illus.). 1977. text ed. 32.00 o.p. (ISBN 0-7216-1699-2). Saunders.
Biswas, A. K., jt. ed. see Golubev, G. N.
Biswas, Amita, jt. auth. see Biswas, S. B.
Biswas, Asit K. History of Hydrology. 2nd ed. (Water Development, Supply & Management Ser.). 1984. price not set (ISBN 0-08-022433-4). Pergamon.
Biswas, Asit K., ed. Systems Approach to Water Management. (Illus.). 1976. text ed. 38.50 (ISBN 0-07-005480-0, C). McGraw.
Biswas, Asit K., jt. ed. see Biswas, Margaret R.
Biswas, D. C. Shakespeare in His Own Time. 1979. text ed. 12.50x (ISBN 0-391-01762-4). Humanities.
Biswas, Manju. Mentally Retarded & Normal Children: A Comparative Study of Their Family Conditions. 157p. 1980. 19.95x (ISBN 0-940500-50-7, Pub. by Sterling India). Asia Bk Corp.
Biswas, Margaret R. & Biswas, Asit K., eds. Food, Climate & Man. LC 78-15154. (Environmental Science & Technology Ser.: Texts & Monographs). 285p. 1979. 45.00 (ISBN 0-471-03240-9, Pub. by Wiley-Interscience). Wiley.
Biswas, S. B. & Biswas, Amita. An Introduction to Viruses. (Illus.). 200p. (Orig.). 1982. pap. text ed. 7.95x (ISBN 0-7069-1561-5, Pub. by Vikas India). Advent NY.
Bitman, Sam & Zalk, Sue R. Expectant Fathers. (Orig.). 1981. pap. 6.95 (ISBN 0-345-28746-0). Ballantine.
Bitsadze, A. V. Boundary Value Problems for Second Order Elliptic Equations. (Applied Mathematics & Mechanics Ser: Vol. 5). 1968. 38.50 (ISBN 0-444-10145-4, North-Holland). Elsevier.
Bitsilli, Peter. Chekhov's Art: A Stylistic Analysis. Clyman, Toby & Cruise, Edwina, trs. from Rus. 1983. 18.50 (ISBN 0-88233-100-0). Ardis Pubs.
Bittar, E. Edward. Membrane Structure & Function, 3 vols. LC 79-14969. (Membrane Structure & Function Ser.). 1980. Vol. 1. 37.95 (ISBN 0-471-03816-4, Pub. by Wiley-Interscience); Vol. 2. 59.95 (ISBN 0-471-03817-2); Vol. 3. 35.95 (ISBN 0-471-03818-0). Wiley.
--Membrane Structure & Function, Vol. 4. (Membrane Structure & Function Ser.). 246p. 1981. 47.95 (ISBN 0-471-08774-2, Pub. by Wiley-Interscience). Wiley.
Bittel, Lester R. Business in Action: An Introduction to Business. LC 79-9320. 1980. 21.90 (ISBN 0-07-079164-3); Course Management Guide & instructional resource bk. 6.75 (ISBN 0-07-005458-4); administrator's guide 3.10 (ISBN 0-07-005467-3); student bklet. 6.15 (ISBN 0-07-005464-9). McGraw.
--Encyclopedia of Professional Management. (Illus.). 1979. 42.50 (ISBN 0-07-005478-9, P&RB). McGraw.
--Essentials of Supervisory Management. LC 80-13784. (Illus.). 288p. 1980. softcover 14.50 (ISBN 0-07-005571-8, G); instrs'. manual & key 5.60 (ISBN 0-07-005572-6). McGraw.
--Improving Supervisory Performance. 1976. 17.10 (ISBN 0-07-005451-7, G); course management 7.30 (ISBN 0-07-005453-3); performance portfolio 7.85 (ISBN 0-07-005452-5). McGraw.
--The Nine Master Keys of Management. (Illus.). 256p. 1972. 23.50 (ISBN 0-07-005476-2, P&RB). McGraw.
--What Every Supervisor Should Know. 3rd ed. (Illus.). 544p. 1974. 19.95 (ISBN 0-07-005459-2, G); text ed. 20.80 (ISBN 0-07-005460-6); instructor's manual & key 8.75 (ISBN 0-07-005462-2). McGraw.
--What Every Supervisor Should Know: The Basics of Supervisory Management. 4th ed. LC 79-16387. 1980. 24.95x (ISBN 0-07-005573-4); text ed. 21.00x (ISBN 0-07-005561-0); Skills Development portfolio 8.20 (ISBN 0-07-005562-9); Course & Management key 6.30 (ISBN 0-07-005563-7). McGraw.
Bittel, Lester R., jt. auth. see Burke, Ronald S.
Bitter, et al. Classroom Management Guide, Grade 1. (McGraw-Hill Mathematics Ser.). 1981. 1.60 (ISBN 0-07-006091-6). McGraw.
--Classroom Management Guide, Grade 2. (McGraw-Hill Mathematics Ser.). 1981. 1.60 (ISBN 0-07-006092-4). McGraw.
--Classroom Management Guide, Grade 3. (McGraw-Hill Mathematics Ser.). 1981. 1.60 (ISBN 0-07-006093-2); 4 desktop duplicators 32.00 (ISBN 0-07-079023-X); duplicator 3A 9.96 (ISBN 0-07-006043-6); duplicator 3B 9.96 (ISBN 0-07-006053-3); duplicator 3C 9.96 (ISBN 0-07-006063-0); duplicator 3D 9.96 (ISBN 0-07-006073-8). McGraw.
--Classroom Management Guide, Grade 4. (McGraw-Hill Mathematics Ser.). 1981. Extra Practice Webstermasters 31.80 (ISBN 0-07-005744-3); Set. 4 desktop duplicators 32.00 (ISBN 0-07-079024-8); duplicator 4A 9.96 (ISBN 0-07-006044-4); duplicator 4B 9.96 (ISBN 0-07-006054-1); duplicator 4C 9.96 (ISBN 0-07-006064-9); duplicator 4D 9.96 (ISBN 0-07-006074-6). McGraw.
--Classroom Management Guide, Grade 5. (McGraw-Hill Mathematics Ser.). 1981. Set. 1.60 (ISBN 0-07-006095-9); 5 desktop duplicators 40.00 (ISBN 0-07-079025-6); duplicator 5A 9.96 (ISBN 0-07-006045-2); duplicator 5B 9.96 (ISBN 0-07-006055-X); duplicator 5C 9.96 (ISBN 0-07-006065-7); duplicator 5D 9.96 (ISBN 0-07-006075-4); duplicator 5E 9.96 (ISBN 0-07-006085-1). McGraw.
--Classroom Management Guide, Grade 6. (McGraw-Hill Mathematics Ser.). 1981. 1.60 (ISBN 0-07-006096-7); Extra Practice Webstermasters, level 6 31.80 (ISBN 0-07-005746-X); 5 desktop duplicators 40.00 (ISBN 0-07-079026-4); duplicator 6A 9.96 (ISBN 0-07-006046-0); duplicator 6B 9.96 (ISBN 0-07-006056-8); duplicator 6C 9.96 (ISBN 0-07-006066-5); duplicator 6D 9.96 (ISBN 0-07-006076-2); duplicator 6E 9.96 (ISBN 0-07-006086-X). McGraw.
--Classroom Management Guide, Grade 7. (McGraw-Hill Mathematics Ser.). 1981. 1.60 (ISBN 0-07-006097-5); Extra Practice Webster Masters, level 7 31.80 (ISBN 0-07-005747-8); Set. 5 desktop duplicators 40.00 (ISBN 0-07-079027-2); duplicator 7A 9.96 (ISBN 0-07-006047-9); duplicator 7B 9.96 (ISBN 0-07-006057-6); duplicator 7C 9.96 (ISBN 0-07-006067-3); duplicator 7D 9.96 (ISBN 0-07-006077-0); duplicator 7E 9.96 (ISBN 0-07-006087-8). McGraw.
--Classroom Management Guide, Grade 8. (McGraw-Hill Mathematics Ser.). 1981. 1.60 (ISBN 0-07-006098-3); Extra Practice Webstermasters, level 8 31.80 (ISBN 0-07-005748-6); Set. 5 desktop duplicators 40.00 (ISBN 0-07-079028-0); duplicator 8A 9.96 (ISBN 0-07-006048-7); duplicator 8B 9.96 (ISBN 0-07-006058-4); duplicator 8C 9.96 (ISBN 0-07-006068-1); duplicator 8D 9.96 (ISBN 0-07-006078-9); duplicator 8E 9.96 (ISBN 0-07-006088-6). McGraw.
--McGraw-Hill Mathematics, 8 levels. Incl. Level 1. text ed. 7.40 (ISBN 0-07-005761-3); tchr's ed. 21.40 (ISBN 0-07-005771-0); wkbk. 3.68 (ISBN 0-07-005781-8); Level 2. text ed. 7.40 (ISBN 0-07-005762-1); tchr's ed. 21.40 (ISBN 0-07-005772-9); wkbk 3.68 (ISBN 0-07-005782-6); Level 3. text ed. 12.08 (ISBN 0-07-005763-X); tchr's ed. 22.44 (ISBN 0-07-005773-7); wkbk. 4.08 (ISBN 0-07-005783-4); Level 4. text ed. 12.08 (ISBN 0-07-005764-8); tchr's ed. 22.44 (ISBN 0-07-005774-5); wkbk. 4.08 (ISBN 0-07-005784-2); Level 5. text ed. 12.08 (ISBN 0-07-005765-6); tchr's ed. 22.44 (ISBN 0-07-005775-3); wkbk. 4.08 (ISBN 0-07-005785-0); Level 6. text ed. 12.08 (ISBN 0-07-005766-4); tchr's ed. 22.44 (ISBN 0-07-005776-1); wkbk. 4.08 (ISBN 0-07-005786-9); Level 7. text ed. 14.56 (ISBN 0-07-005767-2); tchr's ed. 23.84 (ISBN 0-07-005777-X); wkbk. 4.08 (ISBN 0-07-005787-7); Level 8. text ed. 14.56 (ISBN 0-07-005768-0); tchr's ed. 23.84 (ISBN 0-07-005778-8); wkbk. 4.08 (ISBN 0-07-005788-5). 1981. write for info. supplementary materials. McGraw.
--McGraw-Hill Mathematics Parents Guide to Problem Solving. (McGraw-Hill Mathematics, Ser.). 16p. 1981. 0.92 (ISBN 0-07-005749-4, W). McGraw.
Bitter, G., et al. Discovering Metric Measure, Bk. 1. 1974. 5.48 (ISBN 0-07-005506-8, W). McGraw.
Bitter, Gary. Microcomputer Applications for Calculus. 256p. 1982. pap. text ed. write for info (ISBN 0-87150-378-6, 8010). Prindle.
Bitter, Gary G. & Gateley, Wilson Y. Basic for Beginners. 2nd ed. (Illus.). 1978. pap. text ed. 15.95 (ISBN 0-07-005492-4, C). McGraw.
Bitter, Gary G. & Metos, Thomas H. Exploring with Metrics. LC 75-25520. (Illus.). 64p. (gr. 3-5). 1975. PLB 6.29 o.p. (ISBN 0-671-32745-3). Messner.
Bitter, Gary G., et al. One Step at a Time. LC 77-82666. 1977. pap. text ed. 18.00 (ISBN 0-88436-419-4). EMC.
Bittiger, H. & Schnebli, H. P., eds. Concanavalin A As a Tool. LC 75-37841. 639p. 1976. 86.75 o.p. (ISBN 0-471-01350-1, Pub. by Wiley-Interscience). Wiley.
Bitting, Katherine G. Gastronomic Bibliography. LC 71-168559. (Illus.). 1971. Repr. of 1939 ed. 55.00 o.p. (ISBN 0-8103-3758-4). Gale.
Bittinger, Desmond. The Song of the Drums: African Life & Love Under the Monkey Bread Tree. 1978. 8.95 o.p. (ISBN 0-533-03111-7). Vantage.
Bittinger, M. L. Logic, Proof, & Sets. 2nd ed. LC 81-14913. 144p. 1982. pap. text ed. 7.95 (ISBN 0-201-10384-2). A-W.
Bittinger, M. L. & Crown, J. C. Mathematics for Business, Economics & Management. 1982. 26.95 (ISBN 0-201-10104-1); instrs' manual avail. (ISBN 0-201-10105-X). A-W.
Bittinger, M. L., jt. auth. see Keedy, M. L.
Bittinger, Marcin L., jt. auth. see Keedy, Mervin L.
Bittinger, Marvin L. Calculus: A Modeling Approach. 2nd ed. LC 79-18272. (Illus.). 1980. text ed. 24.95 (ISBN 0-201-01247-2); instrs' manual 4.00 (ISBN 0-201-01248-0). A-W.
Bittinger, Marvin L. & Crown, J. Conrad. Mathematics: A Modeling Approach. 1981. 24.95 (ISBN 0-201-03116-7); instrs' manual 2.50 (ISBN 0-201-03117-5). A-W.
Bittinger, Marvin L. & Rudolph, William B. Business Mathematics. (Illus.). 1980. text ed. 19.95 (ISBN 0-201-00283-3); instrs' manual with tests 3.00 (ISBN 0-201-00289-2). A-W.
Bittinger, Marvin L., jt. auth. see Crown, J. Conrad.
Bittinger, Marvin L., jt. auth. see Keedy, Mervin L.
Bittinger, Marvin L., ed. Living with Our Hyperactive Children: Parents' Own Stories. (Illus.). 1977. 8.95 o.p. (ISBN 0-8467-0275-4, Pub. by Two Continents). Hippocrene Bks.
Bittker, Boris & Stone, Lawrence. Federal Income Taxation 1981 Supplement. LC 79-89122. 90p. 1981. case book suppl. 5.95 o.p. (ISBN 0-316-09688-1, Law Division). Little.
Bittker, Boris & Stone, Lawrence M. Federal Income Taxation. 5th ed. 1196p. 1980. text ed. 26.50 (ISBN 0-316-09679-2). Little.
Bittker, Boris I. Federal Income Taxation of Corporations & Shareholders: Forms. 1975. 96.50 (ISBN 0-88262-822-4, 75-6129). Warren.
Bittker, Boris I. & Eustice, James S. Federal Income Taxation of Corporations & Shareholders. 4th. ed. 1979. 68.00 (ISBN 0-88262-288-9, 79-63336); pap. text ed. 22.50 (ISBN 0-686-96918-9). Warren.
Bittker, Boris I., jt. auth. see Goldstein, Gersham.
Bittleston, Adam. Meditative Prayers for Today. 6th ed. 1982. 3.75 o.p. (ISBN 0-900285-00-1, Pub. by Floris Books); pap. 4.95 (ISBN 0-903540-54-1). St George Bk Serv.
Bittleston, Adam, tr. see Von Goethe, Johann W. & Steiner, Rudolf.
Bittleston, R., jt. auth. see Weston, G. F.
Bittman, Sam, jt. auth. see Ubell, Alvin.
Bittman, Sam & Satullo, Steven A., eds. Berkshire Seasons of Celebration. (Illus.). 108p. 1982. 25.00 (ISBN 0-910931-01-1); pap. 15.00 (ISBN 0-910931-00-3). Either-Or Pr.
Bittner, Donald. The Lion & the White Falcon: Britain & Iceland in the World War II Era. (Illus.). 240p. 1983. 25.00 (ISBN 0-208-01956-1, Archon). Shoe String.
Bittner, Egon & Krantz, Sheldon. Standards Relating to Police Handling of Juvenile Problems. LC 77-3376. (IJA-ABA Juvenile Justice Standards Project Ser.). 168p. 1980. prof ref 20.00x (ISBN 0-88410-755-8); pap. 10.00x (ISBN 0-88410-806-6). Ballinger Pub.
Bittner, J. Broadcasting: An Introduction. 1980. 21.95 (ISBN 0-13-083535-8). P-H.
--Professional Broadcasting: A Brief Introduction. 1981. pap. 15.95 (ISBN 0-13-725465-2). P-H.
Bittner, John. Broadcast Law & Regulation. (Illus.). 464p. 1982. 25.95 (ISBN 0-13-083592-7). P-H.
Bittner, John R. Each Other: An Introduction to Interpersonal Communication. (Illus.). 368p. 1983. text ed. 16.95 (ISBN 0-13-222190-X). P-H.
--Mass Communication. 2nd ed. (Ser. in Speech Communication). (Illus.). 1980. pap. text ed. 18.95 (ISBN 0-13-559278-X). P-H.
Bitton, Davis, jt. auth. see Bunker, Gary L.
Bitton, Davis, ed. The Reminiscences & Civil War Letters of Levi Lamoni Wight: Life in a Mormon Splinter Colony on the Texas Frontier. LC 74-120412. (University of Utah Publications in the American West: Vol. 4). (Illus.). 1970. 15.00 o.p. (ISBN 0-87480-060-9). U of Utah Pr.
Bitton, G. Introduction to Environmental Virology. 326p. 1980. 30.50 (ISBN 0-471-04247-1; BG75, Pub. by Wiley-Interscience). Wiley.
Bitton, G., et al. Sludge: Health Risks of Land Application. LC 80-68822. (Illus.). 367p. 1980. 39.95 (ISBN 0-250-40374-9). Ann Arbor Science.
Bitton, Gabriel & Marshall, Kevin C., eds. Absorption of Micro-Organisms to Surfaces. LC 79-19482. 439p. 1979. 42.50x (ISBN 0-471-03157-7, Pub. by Wiley-Interscience). Wiley.
Bitton-Jackson, Livia. Madonna or Courtesan: The Jewish Woman in Christian Literature. 160p. 1983. pap. 7.95 (ISBN 0-8164-2440-3). Seabury.
Bitzer, Heinrich, ed. Light on the Path: Daily Scripture Readings in Hebrew & Greek. 400p. (Orig.). 1982. pap. 7.95 (ISBN 0-8010-0822-0). Baker Bk.
Bitzer, Lloyd & Rueter, Theodore. Carter Vs Ford: The Counterfeit Debates of Nineteen Seventy-Six. LC 80-5110. 444p. 1980. 35.00 (ISBN 0-299-08280-6); pap. 12.50 (ISBN 0-299-08284-9). U of Wis Pr.
Bitzer, Lloyd F., ed. see Campbell, George.
Bivon, R. Element Order. LC 72-134611. (Studies in the Modern Russian Language: No. 7). 1971. 16.95 (ISBN 0-521-08025-8). Cambridge U Pr.
Bixler, Herbert E. Railroads: Their Rise & Fall. 115p. (Orig.). 1982. pap. 7.95 (ISBN 0-9610066-0-9). H E Bixler.
Bixler, Russell. Learning To Know God As Provider. 96p. 1982. pap. 2.50 (ISBN 0-88368-120-X). Whitaker Hse.
Bizer, Linda & Nathan, Beverly. Discovering New Worlds. Lawrence, Leslie & Weingartner, Ronald, eds. (Bright Beginnings I). (Illus.). 48p. (Orig.). (gr. k-2). pap. 1.69 (ISBN 0-88049-023-3, 7386). Milton Bradley Co.
--Learning My Letters. Lawrence, Leslie & Weingartner, Ronald, eds. (Bright Beginnings I). (Illus.). 48p. (Orig.). (gr. k-2). pap. 1.69 (ISBN 0-88049-021-7, 7384). Milton Bradley Co.
--Learning My Numbers. Lawrence, Leslie & Weingartner, Ronald, eds. (Bright Beginnings I). (Illus.). 48p. (Orig.). (gr. k-2). pap. 1.69 (ISBN 0-88049-025-X, 7388). Milton Bradley Co.
--Letter Sounds. Lawrence, Leslie & Weingartner, Ronald, eds. (Bright Beginnings I Ser). (Illus.). 48p. (Orig.). (gr. k-2). pap. 1.69 (ISBN 0-88049-022-5, 7385). Milton Bradley Co.
--Put Together Take Away. Lawrence, Leslie & Weingartner, Ronald, eds. (Bright Beginnings I). (Illus.). 48p. (Orig.). (gr. k-2). pap. 1.69 (ISBN 0-88049-026-8, 7389). Milton Bradley Co.
--Spell Well. Lawrence, Leslie & Weingartner, Ronald, eds. (Bright Beginnings I). (Illus.). 48p. (Orig.). (gr. k-2). pap. 1.69 (ISBN 0-88049-028-4, 7391). Milton Bradley Co.
--Understanding What I Read. Lawrence, Leslie & Weingartner, Ronald, eds. (Bright Beginnings I). (Illus.). 48p. (Orig.). (gr. k-2). pap. 1.69 (ISBN 0-88049-024-1, 7387). Milton Bradley Co.
--Writing My Letters & Numbers. Lawrence, Leslie & Weingartner, Ronald, eds. (Bright Beginnings I). (Illus.). 48p. (Orig.). (gr. k-2). pap. 1.69 (ISBN 0-88049-027-6, 7390). Milton Bradley Co.
Bizer, Linda S. & Markel, Geraldine P. The ABC's of the SAT: A Parent's Guide to College Entrance Exams. LC 82-13858. (Illus.). 160p. (Orig.). 1983. pap. 3.95 (ISBN 0-668-05666-5, 5666). Arco.
Bizollon, C. A., ed. Physiological Peptides & New Trends in Radioimmunology. 1981. 59.25 (ISBN 0-444-80358-0). Elsevier.
Bizzaro, Patrick. Violence. (Orig.). 1979. pap. 2.00 (ISBN 0-918092-12-4). Tamarack Edns.
Bizzaro, Patrick & Dobrin, Arthur. The Man Who Eats Death for Breakfast. 48p. 1982. 5.00 (ISBN 0-943018-04-8). Backstreet.
Bizzozero, Julius. On a New Blood Particle & Its Role in Thrombosis & Blood Coagulation. Beck, Eugen A., tr. from Ger. (Illus.). 156p. 1982. pap. text ed. 16.50 (ISBN 3-456-81182-9, Pub. by Hans Huber Switzerland). J K Burgess.
Bjelica, Mihalo, jt. auth. see Lekovic, Zdravko.
Bjelland, Harley. Technical Writing: The Easy Way. LC 81-90026. (Illus.). 116p. (Orig.). 1981. pap. 9.95 (ISBN 0-939648-00-8). Norway Bks.
Bjerhammar, A. Theory of Errors & Generalized Matrix Inverses. LC 72-179998. 440p. 1973. 66.00 (ISBN 0-444-40981-5). Elsevier.
Bjerk, Irid. Boy Off the Farm. 272p. pap. 11.95 (ISBN 0-931170-18-4). Ctr Western Studies.
Bjerre, Andreas. The Psychology of Murder: A Study in Criminal Psychology. Classen, E., tr. from Swedish. (Historical Foundations of Forensic Psychiatry & Psychology Ser.). 164p. 1980. Repr. lib. bdg. 22.50 (ISBN 0-306-76067-3). Da Capo.
Bjorck, Margaret, et al. Now You Know about Animals, 5 bks. Incl. Animal Coverings. 32p; Animal Homes. 32p; How Animals Stay Alive. 32p; Many Animals. 32p (ISBN 0-87827-091-4); Where Animals Live. 32p (ISBN 0-87827-003-5). (Illus.). (gr. k-3). 1972. 99.00 (ISBN 0-87827-090-6); records, cassetts & tchr's guide avail. (ISBN 0-685-38373-3). Ency Brit Ed.
Bjorck, Svante. A Stratigraphic Study of Late Weichselian Delaciation, Shore Displacement, & Vegetation History in South-Eastern Sweden. 93p. (Orig.). 1982. pap. 22.00 (ISBN 82-00-09526-6). Universitet.
Bjorgum, Kenneth L. Bloodstone. 256p. (Orig.). 1980. pap. 2.25 o.p. (ISBN 0-515-05475-5). Jove Pubns.
--The Desert Sentinels. LC 79-6640. (Double D Western Ser.). 192p. 1980. 10.95 o.p. (ISBN 0-385-14752-X). Doubleday.
Bjork, Daniel W. The Compromised Scientist: William James in the Development of American Psychology. (Illus.). 224p. 1983. text ed. 25.00 (ISBN 0-231-05500-5); pap. 12.00 (ISBN 0-231-05501-3). Columbia U Pr.
--The Victorian Flight: Russell Conwell & the Crisis of American Individualism. LC 78-50767. 1978. pap. text ed. 7.75x o.p. (ISBN 0-8191-0464-7). U Pr of Amer.
Bjork, Gordon C. Life, Liberty & Property: The Economics & Politics of Land-Use Planning & Environmental Controls. LC 80-8038. 160p. 1980. 18.95x (ISBN 0-669-03952-7). Lexington Bks.
Bjork, J. E. Rings of Differential Operators. (Mathematical Library: Vol. 21). 360p. 1979. 66.00 (ISBN 0-444-85292-1, North Holland). Elsevier.
Bjork, Kenneth O., ed. Norwegian-American Studies, Vol. 26. LC 26-14503. 1974. lib. bdg. 8.95 (ISBN 0-8057-5722-8, Twayne). G K Hall.
Bjork, Lennart A. The Literary Notes of Thomas Hardy, Vol. 1 In 2 Pts. (Gothenburg Studies in English: No. 29). 479p. 1975. Set. text ed. 37.00x (ISBN 91-7346-002-8). Humanities.
Bjorkegren, Hans. Aleksandr Solzhenitsyn: A Biography. Eneberg, Kaa, tr. from Swed. LC 72-80185. 1973. pap. 4.95 (ISBN 0-89388-050-7). Okpaku Communications.
Bjorken, J. D., jt. auth. see Atwood, W. B.

Bjorken, James D. & Drell, S. D. Relativistic Quantum Fields. (International Pure & Applied Physics Ser.). 1965. text ed. 34.95 (ISBN 0-07-005494-0, C). McGraw.
--Relativistic Quantum Mechanics. (International Series in Pure & Applied Physics Ser.). 1964. text ed. 32.50 (ISBN 0-07-005493-2, C). McGraw.
Bjorklund, A. see Sjolund, B. H.
Bjorklund, Oddvar. Historical Atlas for the World. pap. 6.95 (ISBN 0-06-463249-0, EH 249, EH). B&N NY.
Bjorkman, Edwin, tr. see Christiansen, Sigurd.
Bjorkman, Edwin A. Voices of Tomorrow: Critical Studies of the New Spirit in Literature. LC 74-98818. Repr. of 1913 ed. lib. bdg. 15.75x (ISBN 0-8371-2962-1, BJVT). Greenwood.
Bjorkman, Erik. Scandinavian Loan-Words in Middle English. LC 69-13829. 1900-1902. Repr. lib. bdg. 17.50x (ISBN 0-8371-1803-4, BJLW). Greenwood.
Bjorkman, James W., jt. auth. see Altenstetter, Christa.
Bjorkman, Stig, et al. Bergman on Bergman. (Illus.). 288p. 1975. pap. 5.95 o.p. (ISBN 0-671-22157-4, Touchstone Bks). S&S.
Bjorn, Thyra F. The Home Has a Heart. (Orig.). pap. 1.75 o.s.i. Jove Pubns.
--This Is My Life. 1976. pap. 1.50 o.s.i. (ISBN 0-89129-137-7). Jove Pubns.
Bjorn, Thyre F. Dear Papa. 1976. pap. write for info (ISBN 0-515-09615-6). Jove Pubns.
Bjorn-Anderson, Neils, ed. Human Side of Information Processing. 1980. 36.25 (ISBN 0-444-85415-0). Elsevier.
Bjorndal, Karen A., ed. Biology & Conservation of Sea Turtles: Proceedings of the World Conference on Sea Turtle Conservation. (Illus.). 583p. 1982. pap. text ed. 25.00x (ISBN 0-87474-243-9). Smithsonian.
--Biology & Conservation of Sea Turtles: Proceedings of the World Conference on Sea Turtle Conservation. (Illus.). 480p. pap. text ed. 15.00x o.p. (ISBN 0-87474-242-0). Smithsonian.
Bjornson, Bjornstjerne. In God's Way. Carmichael, E., tr. from Swedish. LC 77-14542. 1983. Repr. of 1903 ed. 22.50 (ISBN 0-86527-261-1). Fertig.
--Three Dramas. Sharp, R. Farquharson, tr. LC 73-17654. 291p. 1974. Repr. of 1914 ed. lib. bdg. 17.25x (ISBN 0-8371-7260-8, BJTD). Greenwood.
Bjornson, Richard. The Picaresque Hero in European Fiction. LC 76-11312. (Illus.). 320p. 1977. 25.00x (ISBN 0-299-07100-6); pap. 9.95 (ISBN 0-299-07104-9). U of Wis Pr.
Bjornstad, James. Twentieth Century Prophecy. 1976. pap. 1.25 o.s.i. (ISBN 0-89129-150-4). Jove Pubns.
Bjorov, Malvin. Advances in Organic Geochemistry, 1981. 1000p. 1983. write for info. (ISBN 0-471-26229-3, Pub. by Wiley Heyden). Wiley.
Blaauw, Gerritt A. Digital System Implementation. (Illus.). 1976. 28.95 (ISBN 0-13-212241-3). P-H.
Blachford, G., jt. auth. see Divine, J. A.
Blachly, Paul H. Progress in Drug Abuse. (Illus.). 336p. 1972. photocopy ed. spiral 29.75x (ISBN 0-398-02233-X). C C Thomas.
Blachon, Roger, et al. Le Vin: French Wine Humor. 100p. 1982. 29.95 (ISBN 0-932664-28-8). Wine Appreciation.
Black, A. J. Monarchy & Community. LC 72-108101. (Studies in Medieval Life & Thought). 1970. 37.50 (ISBN 0-521-07739-7). Cambridge U Pr.
Black, Ann N. & Smith, Jo R. Ten Tools of Language - Written: Revised Edition II, Form B. rev. ed. 166p. 1983. pap. text ed. 12.60x (ISBN 0-910513-01-5). Mayfield Printing.
--Ten Tools of Language-Written. 2nd ed. (Illus.). 166p. (gr. 11-12). 1982. pap. text ed. 12.60x (ISBN 0-910513-00-7). Mayfield Printing.
Black, Arther. Freedom Poems. 1981. 4.95 (ISBN 0-8062-1807-X). Carlton.
Black, Austin I. The Aquarian Mandate. 1976. pap. 7.00 (ISBN 0-87613-046-5). Suratao.
Black, Bonnie L. Somewhere Child. 1983. pap. 3.50 (ISBN 0-553-22923-0). Bantam.
Black, C. A. Soil-Plant Relationships. 2nd ed. LC 67-28946. 792p. (Orig.). 1968. 49.95x (ISBN 0-471-07723-2). Wiley.
Black, Campbell. Asterisk Destiny. (YA) 1980. pap. 2.25 o.p. (ISBN 0-451-09246-5, E9246, Sig). NAL.
--Brainfire. 1980. pap. 2.50 o.p. (ISBN 0-451-09481-6, E9481, Sig). NAL.
Black, Charles. The Waking Passenger. Cassin, Maxine, ed. 80p. 1983. pap. 5.00 (ISBN 0-938498-03-7). New Orleans Poetry.
Black, Charles L., Jr. Capital Punishment: The Inevitability of Caprice & Mistake. Rev. ed. 1981. 12.95 (ISBN 0-393-01333-2); pap. 6.95 (ISBN 0-393-95289-4). Norton.
--Structure & Relationship in Constitutional Law. LC 69-17621. (Edward Douglass White Lectures). xii, 98p. 1969. 7.95x o.p. (ISBN 0-8071-0305-5). La State U Pr.
Black, Charles T. & Worden, Diane D., eds. Michigan Nature Centers & Other Environmental Education Facilities. 64p. 1982. pap. 6.50 (ISBN 0-939294-06-0, LB 1047). Beech Leaf.
Black, Claudia. My Dad Loves Me, My Dad Has a Disease: A Workbook for Children. 7.00 o.p. (ISBN 0-686-92100-3). Hazelden.
Black, Clayton C., jt. ed. see Burris, Robert H.
Black, D. S., jt. auth. see Swan, J. M.
Black, David. Animals in Danger. LC 80-50954. (New Reference Library). PLB 11.96 (ISBN 0-382-06399-6). Silver.
Black, Don. South African Bonsai Book. 93p. 1981. cloth 15.95x (ISBN 0-86978-136-7, Pub. by Timmins Africa). Intl Schol Bk Serv.
Black, Donald. The Behavior of Law. 1980. pap. 7.50 (ISBN 0-12-102652-3). Acad Pr.
Black, E. M. Simma & Other Stories. 1978. 4.95 o.p. (ISBN 0-533-03215-6). Vantage.
Black, Edwin. Rhetorical Criticism: A Study in Method. LC 77-91050. 1978. 20.00 (ISBN 0-299-07550-8); pap. text ed. 9.95 (ISBN 0-299-07554-0). U of Wis Pr.
Black, Elizabeth, jt. auth. see Fulton, James E.
Black, F. O., et al. Congenital Deafness: A New Approach to Early Detection of Deafness Through a High Risk Register. LC 76-135285. 1971. 12.50x (ISBN 0-87081-005-7). Colo Assoc.
Black, Frank G. & Black, Renee M., eds. Harney Papers. (Publications on Social History Ser: No. 5). 1969. text ed. 25.25x o.p. (ISBN 90-232-0270-8). Humanities.
Black, Gavin. The Eyes Around Me. LC 64-18085. 1980. pap. 1.95i o.p. (ISBN 0-06-080485-8, P 485, PL). Har-Row.
--You Want to Die, Johnny? LC 66-13934. 1979. pap. 1.95i o.p. (ISBN 0-06-080472-6, P 472, PL). Har-Row.
Black, George. Sales Engineering: An Emerging Profession. 2nd ed. (Illus.). 239p. 1979. 17.95 (ISBN 0-87201-799-0). Gulf Pub.
--Triumph of the People: The Sandinista Revolution in Nicaragua. 340p. 1981. 25.00 (ISBN 0-86232-092-5, Pub. by Zed Pr England); pap. 9.95 (ISBN 0-86232-036-4). Lawrence Hill.
Black, George F. Gypsy Bibliography. LC 74-149780. 1971. Repr. of 1914 ed. 34.00x (ISBN 0-8103-3708-8). Gale.
--Surnames of Scotland: Their Origin, Meaning & History. new, rev. ed. LC 47-1716. 1975. Repr. of 1946 ed. 25.00 (ISBN 0-87104-172-3). NY Pub Lib.
Black, George F., ed. Calendar of Cases of Witchcraft in Scotland, 1510-1727. LC 78-137707. 1971. Repr. of 1938 ed. 8.00 o.p. (ISBN 0-87104-501-X). NY Pub Lib.
Black, George W., Jr. American Science & Technology: A Bicentennial Bibliography. LC 78-15820. 172p. 1979. 15.95x (ISBN 0-8093-0898-3). S Ill U Pr.
Black, Gilbert J. Trends in Management, Development & Education: An Economic Study. LC 79-4435. (Communications Library). 1979. text ed. 29.95x (ISBN 0-914236-24-5). Knowledge Indus.
Black, H. L., jt. auth. see Hill, V. L.
Black, Hallie. Animal Cooperation: A Look at Sociobiology. LC 81-1355. (Illus.). 64p. (gr. 7-9). 1981. 8.95 (ISBN 0-688-00360-5); PLB 8.59 (ISBN 0-688-00361-3). Morrow.
--Dirt Cheap: Evolution of Renewable Resource Management. LC 79-11353. (Illus.). (gr. 4-6). 1979. 10.25 (ISBN 0-688-22184-X); PLB 9.84 (ISBN 0-688-32184-4). Morrow.
Black, Harry & Broadfoot, Patricia. Keeping Track of Teaching: Assessment in the Modern Classroom. (Education Bks.). 100p. (Orig.). 1982. pap. 11.95 (ISBN 0-7100-9017-X). Routledge & Kegan.
Black, Herbert. Doctor & Teacher, Hospital Chief: Dr. Samuel Proger & The New England Medical Center. LC 81-82605. (Illus.). 224p. 1982. 14.95 (ISBN 0-87106-960-1); pap. 9.95 (ISBN 0-87106-973-3). Globe Pequot.
Black, Hermina. Bitter Fruit. pap. 1.25 o.p. (ISBN 0-451-07720-2, Y7720, Sig). NAL.
--Who Is Lucinda. Bd. with Bitter Honey. 1977. pap. 2.95 (ISBN 0-451-11934-7, AE1934, Sig). NAL.
Black, Homer A. & Edwards, James D., eds. The Managerial & Cost Accountant's Handbook. LC 78-61201. 1979. 45.00 (ISBN 0-87094-173-9). Dow Jones-Irwin.
Black, Homer A., jt. ed. see Edwards, James D.
Black, Homer A., et al. Accounting in Business Decisions: Theory, Method, & Use. 3rd ed. (Illus.). 752p. 1973. 27.95x (ISBN 0-13-001545-8); accounting forms o.p 4.95x (ISBN 0-13-001644-6); practice case 4.95x (ISBN 0-13-001230-0). P-H.
Black, J. Liquid Fuels in Australia: A Social Science Research Perspective. 280p. 1983. 37.50 (ISBN 0-08-024834-9); 21.00 (ISBN 0-08-024833-0). Pergamon.
--Neonatal Emergencies & Other Problems. 288p. 1972. 29.95 (ISBN 0-407-32780-0). Butterworth.
Black, J. & Bradley, J. F. Essential Mathematics for Economists. 2nd ed. LC 79-40826. 316p. 1980. 59.95x (ISBN 0-471-27659-6, Pub. by Wiley-Interscience); pap. 13.95 o.p. (ISBN 0-471-07713-5). Wiley.
Black, J. M. How to Get Results from Interviewing: A Practical Guide for Operating Management. 1970. 31.00 (ISBN 0-07-005510-6, P&RB). McGraw.
Black, J. Thomas. Prospects for Rental Housing Production Under Rent: A Case Study of Washington, D.C. (Research Report Ser.: No. 24). 1976. pap. 4.00 o.p. (ISBN 0-87420-324-4). Urban Land.
Black, J. Thomas & Morina, Michael. Downtown Office Growth & the Role of Public Transit. LC 82-50921. (Illus.). 122p. (Orig.). 1982. pap. text ed. 26.00 (ISBN 0-87420-615-4, D31). Urban Land.
Black, Jackie. Autumn Fires. (Candlelight Ecstasy Ser.: No. 152). (Orig.). 1983. pap. 1.95 (ISBN 0-440-10272-3). Dell.
Black, James, jt. auth. see Jelen, Frederic C.
Black, James A. & Champion, Dean J. Methods & Issues in Social Research. LC 75-26659. 445p. 1975. 24.95 (ISBN 0-471-07705-4). Wiley.
Black, James M. & Black, Virginia T. The Front-Line Manager's Problem-Solver. LC 67-13509. 320p. 1967. 11.50 (ISBN 0-686-63921-9). Krieger.
Black, James M. & Ford, G. B. Front-Line Management: A Guide to Effective Supervisory Action. 1963. 29.95 (ISBN 0-07-005529-7, P&RB). McGraw.
Black, Jan K. Latin America: An Introduction. 450p. 1983. lib. bdg. price not set (ISBN 0-86531-212-5); pap. text ed. price not set (ISBN 0-86531-213-3). Westview.
Black, Jay & Whitney, Frederick C. Introduction to Mass Communications. 445p. 1983. pap. text ed. write for info (ISBN 0-697-04355-X); instrs.' manual avail. (ISBN 0-697-04360-6). Wm C Brown.
Black, John. The Economics of Modern Britain: An Introduction to Macroeconomics. 3rd ed. (Illus.). 304p. 1982. text ed. 27.50x (ISBN 0-85520-529-6, Pub. by Martin Robertson England). Biblio Dist.
Black, John, jt. auth. see Stanley, Del.
Black, John & Hindlin, Brian, eds. Current Issues in Commercial Policy & Diplomacy. 1980. 26.00 (ISBN 0-312-17926-X). St Martin.
Black, John D. Parity, Parity, Parity. LC 72-2364. (FDR & the Era of the New Deal Ser.). 367p. 1972. Repr. of 1942 ed. 45.00 (ISBN 0-306-70482-X). Da Capo.
Black, John D., et al. Provocative Perspectives: When We Were 20 & Now That We're 60. LC 82-60220. 137p. 1982. pap. 6.95 (ISBN 0-936988-07-X). Tompson & Rutter.
Black, John G. & Stanley, Delmar S. Practical Accounting. 3rd ed. LC 75-40983. 1980. pap. text ed. 12.95 (ISBN 0-673-16133-1); solutions manual avail. (ISBN 0-87620-730-1). Scott F.
Black, John W. American Speech for Foreign Students. 2nd ed. (Illus.). 408p. 1983. spiral 28.75x (ISBN 0-398-03999-2). C C Thomas.
Black, Jonathan. Dead Run. 256p. (Orig.). 1981. pap. write for info. o.s.i. (ISBN 0-515-05465-8). Jove Pubns.
Black, Kenneth, jt. auth. see Russell, Hugh.
Black, Kenneth, Jr. & Huebner, S. S. Life Insurance. 10th ed. (Illus.). 784p. 1982. 26.95 (ISBN 0-13-535799-3). P-H.
Black, Laura. Ravenburn. (General Ser.). 1980. lib. bdg. 16.95 (ISBN 0-8161-3129-5, Large Print Bks). G K Hall.
--Strathgallant. (General Ser.). 1982. lib. bdg. 15.95 (ISBN 0-8161-3361-1, Large Print Bks). G K Hall.
Black, Leo, tr. see Eimert, Herbert & Stockhausen, Karlheinz.
Black, Leo, tr. see Webern, Anton.
Black, M. & Bewley, J. D. Physiology & Biochemistry of Seeds in Relation to Germination: Viability, Dormancy, & Environmental Control, Vol. 2. (Illus.). 380p. 1982. 54.00 (ISBN 0-387-11656-7). Springer-Verlag.
Black, M. & Reed, J., eds. Perspectives on the American South: An Annual Review, Vol. 1. 424p. 1981. 35.00 (ISBN 0-677-16260-X). Gordon.
Black, Mary. American Advertising Posters of the Nineteenth Century. (Illus., Orig.). 1976. pap. 7.95 (ISBN 0-486-23356-1). Dover.
--What Is American in American Art? (Illus.). 80p. 1971. 9.50 o.p. (ISBN 0-517-50649-1, C N Potter Bks). Crown.
Black, Max. Critical Thinking. 2nd ed. 1952. text ed. 19.95 (ISBN 0-13-194092-9). P-H.
--Nature of Mathematics. (Quality Paperback: No. 201). 219p. 1965. pap. 3.95 (ISBN 0-8226-0201-6). Littlefield.
--Problems of Analysis: Philosophical Essays. LC 74-139124. 1971. Repr. of 1954 ed. lib. bdg. 16.25x (ISBN 0-8371-5740-4, BLPA). Greenwood.
Black, Max, ed. Importance of Language. 1968. pap. 5.95x (ISBN 0-8014-9077-4). Cornell U Pr.
Black, Nelson W., ed. see Huttman, Elizabeth D.
Black, Patsie. Tapestry: A Finespun Grace & Mercy. LC 82-8231. 1982. pap. 6.95 (ISBN 0-930014-92-8). Multnomah.
Black, Patti C., ed. Documentary Portrait of Mississippi: The Thirties. LC 82-4823. (Illus.). 128p. 1982. pap. text ed. 15.00 (ISBN 0-87805-166-X). U Pr of Miss.
Black, Paul H. & Adams, O. Eugene, Jr. Machine Design. 3rd ed. LC 68-13623. 1968. text ed. 38.50 (ISBN 0-07-005524-6, C). McGraw.
Black, Perry. Brain Dysfunction in Children: Etiology, Diagnosis & Management. 320p. 1981. text ed. 38.50 (ISBN 0-89004-022-2). Raven.
Black, Perry, ed. Physiological Correlates of Emotion: Based Upon a Symposium. 1970. 45.50 (ISBN 0-12-102850-X). Acad Pr.
Black, Perry O. & Scahill. Diesel Engine Manual. new ed. (Audel Ser.). 1983. 12.95 (ISBN 0-672-23371-1). Bobbs.
Black, Peter E. Conservation of Water & Related Resources. 234p. 1982. 25.95 (ISBN 0-03-060419-2). Praeger.
Black, R. L. Pastor, Why Can I Not Remarry. 1978. pap. 1.75 o.p. (ISBN 0-934942-12-9). White Wing Pub.
Black, Renee M., jt. ed. see Black, Frank G.
Black, Rhona M. Elements of Palaeontology. (Illus.). 1970. 59.50 (ISBN 0-521-07445-2); pap. 18.95x (ISBN 0-521-09615-4). Cambridge U Pr.
Black, Richard L., et al. Ninth Year Mathematics. (Arco's Regents Review Ser.). 288p. (Orig.). 1983. pap. 3.95 (ISBN 0-686-82195-5, 5701). Arco.
Black, Rita B., et al. Nursing Management of Epilepsy. LC 81-20524. 188p. 1982. text ed. 28.50 (ISBN 0-89443-675-9). Aspen Systems.
Black, Robert. A Limited Murder. 208p. (Orig.). Date not set. pap. price not set o.p. (ISBN 0-505-51837-6). Tower Bks.
--Nutrition of Finches & Other Cagebirds. 362p. 1981. 19.95 (ISBN 0-686-43316-5). Avian Pubns.
--Problems with Finches. (Illus.). 108p. 1980. pap. 9.95 (ISBN 0-686-43315-7). Avian Pubns.
Black, Robert E. The Books of Chronicles. (The Bible Study Textbook Ser.). (Illus.). 1973. 14.30 o.s.i. (ISBN 0-89900-013-4). College Pr Pub.
Black, Ronald E., jt. ed. see Schultz, Julius.
Black, Sam & Sharpe, Melvin A. Practical Public Relations: Common Sense Guidelines for Business & Professional People. 224p. 1983. 16.95 (ISBN 0-13-693531-1); pap. 8.95 (ISBN 0-13-693523-0). P-H.
Black, Sue, as told to see Posserello, Jodie A.
Black, Theodore M. Straight Talk About American Education. 307p. 1982. 14.95 (ISBN 0-15-185584-6). HarBraceJ.
Black, Thomas. Secured Transactions Handbook for the Texas Attorney. LC 81-85831. 171p. 1982. 30.00 (ISBN 0-938160-27-3, 6241). State Bar TX.
Black, Virginia T., jt. auth. see Black, James M.
Black, W. A. & Taylor, A. J., eds. Deviant Behavior: New Zealand Studies. 1980. pap. text ed. 24.50x o.p. (ISBN 0-86863-295-3, 00561). Heinemann Ed.
Black, William T. Mormon Athletes, Bk. 2. LC 82-14648. (Illus.). 285p. 1982. 7.95 (ISBN 0-87747-929-1). Deseret Bk.
Blackaby, F. T. British Economic Policy: Nineteen Sixty to Nineteen Seventy-Four. LC 77-28282. (NIESR Economic & Social Policy Studies: No. 31). (Illus.). 1979. 74.50 (ISBN 0-521-22042-4); pap. 19.95x (ISBN 0-521-29597-1). Cambridge U Pr.
Blackaby, Frank, ed. An Incomes Policy for Britain. 1972. text ed. 20.00x o.p. (ISBN 0-435-84075-4). Heinemann Ed.
Blackall, Eric A. Goethe & the Novel. LC 75-38426. 344p. 1976. 27.50x (ISBN 0-8014-0978-0). Cornell U Pr.
--The Novels of the German Romantics. LC 82-22104. (Illus.). 320p. 1983. 34.50x (ISBN 0-8014-1523-3); pap. 14.95 (ISBN 0-8014-9885-6). Cornell U Pr.
Blackard, M. Kay & Barsh, Elizabeth T. Reaching Out: Achieving Community Involvement with Developmentally Disabled Children. 72p. 1982. pap. text ed. 9.95 (ISBN 0-911227-00-8). Willoughby Wessington.
Blackbeard, Bill & Williams, Martin, eds. The Smithsonian Collection of Newspaper Comics. LC 77-608090. (Illus.). 336p. 1978. 29.95 (ISBN 0-686-77340-3); pap. 14.95 (ISBN 0-87474-167-X). Smithsonian.
Blackburn, Alex, ed. Writers Forum 8, 1982. LC 78-649046. pap. 8.95 (ISBN 0-9602992-2-X). U CO at Colorado Springs.
Blackburn, Alexander. The Cold War of Kitty Pentecost. 1979. 8.95 o.p. (ISBN 0-686-15536-X); pap. 4.50 o.p. (ISBN 0-686-15537-8). Writers West.
Blackburn, Emily, jt. auth. see Thomas, Art.
Blackburn, G. M, III see Brewton, John E.
Blackburn, Graham. An Illustrated Calendar of Home Repair. (Illus.). 192p. 1981. 15.00 (ISBN 0-399-90094-2, Marek); pap. 9.95 (ISBN 0-399-90115-9). Putnam Pub Group.
--The Illustrated Encyclopedia of Ships & Boats. LC 78-16565. (Illus.). 448p. 1982. pap. 12.95 (ISBN 0-87951-141-9). Overlook Pr.
--The Illustrated Encyclopedia of Ships, Boats & Vessels. LC 78-16565. (Illus.). 448p. 1978. 30.00 (ISBN 0-87951-082-X). Overlook Pr.
--Illustrated Housebuilding. LC 73-87998. (Illus.). 160p. 1977. pap. 6.95 (ISBN 0-87951-054-4). Overlook Pr.
--Illustrated Interior Carpentry. LC 77-12270. (Illus.). 1978. 11.95 o.p. (ISBN 0-672-52398-1). Bobbs.
--Illustrated Interior Carpentry. LC 77-12270. (Illus.). 192p. 1980. pap. 6.95 (ISBN 0-87951-092-7). Overlook Pr.
--The Parts of a House. (Illus.). 1981. pap. 9.95 o.s.i. (ISBN 0-399-90098-5, Marek). Putnam Pub Group.
--The Parts of a House. LC 80-382. (Illus.). 1980. 15.00 (ISBN 0-399-90074-8, Marek). Putnam Pub Group.
Blackburn, Henry. Randolph Caldecott. LC 68-21757. 1969. Repr. of 1886 ed. 30.00x (ISBN 0-8103-3490-9). Gale.

Blackburn, Jeanne M. & Seniz, Refah. Say It in Turkish. (Orig.). pap. 1.95 (ISBN 0-486-20821-4). Dover.

Blackburn, John D., jt. auth. see Getman, Julius G.

Blackburn, Kate & McDonald, Agnes. Four North Carolina Woman Poets. Bayes, Ronald H., ed. LC 82-62747. 84p. 1982. pap. 8.00 (ISBN 0-932662-42-0). St Andrews NC.

Blackburn, Lorraine see Brewton, John E.

Blackburn, Norma D. Legal Secretaryship. 2nd ed. (Illus.). 400p. 1981. text ed. 18.95 (ISBN 0-13-528927-0). P-H.

Blackburn, Paul, tr. Proensa: An Anthology of Troubador Poetry. LC 75-7466. 1978. 23.75x (ISBN 0-520-02985-2). U of Cal Pr.

Blackburn, R. M. & Mann, Michael. The Working Class in the Labour Market. (Cambridge Studies in Sociology). 1979. text ed. 25.00x o.p. (ISBN 0-333-24325-0). Humanities.

Blackburn, Roderic H. Cherry Hill: The History & Collections of a Van Rensselaer Family. LC 75-44844. (Illus.). 186p. 1976. 16.00x (ISBN 0-89062-098-9, Pub. by Historic Cherry); pap. 11.95x o.p. (ISBN 0-89062-099-7). Pub Ctr Cult Res.

--Cherry Hill: The History & Collections of a Van Rensselaer Family. LC 75-44844. (Illus.). 176p. 1976. 15.00 (ISBN 0-943366-00-3); pap. 9.00 (ISBN 0-943366-01-1). Hist-Cherry Hill.

Blackburn, S. Reason & Prediction. LC 72-83580. (Illus.). 192p. 1973. 27.95 (ISBN 0-521-08742-2). Cambridge U Pr.

Blackburn, Thomas C., jt. auth. see Hudson, Travis.

Blacker, Coit D., jt. ed. see Bellany, Ian.

Blacker, Harry see Nero, pseud.

Blacker, Irwin R. Cortes & the Aztec Conquest. LC 65-11533. (Horizon Caravel Bks.). 154p. (YA) (gr. 7 up). 1965. PLB 14.89 o.p. (ISBN 0-06-020531-8, HarpJ). Har-Row.

Blackett, D. W. Elementary Topology: A Combinatorial & Algebraic Approach. 1982. 14.50 (ISBN 0-12-103060-1). Acad Pr.

Blackett, R. J. Building an Antislavery Wall: Black Americans in the Atlantic Abolitionist Movement, 1830 to 1860. LC 82-21724. 264p. 1983. text ed. 25.00x (ISBN 0-8071-1082-5). La State U Pr.

Blackey, Robert. Revolutions & Revolutionists: A Comprehensive Guide to the Literature. Burns, Richard D., ed. LC 82-6653. (War-Peace Bibliography Ser.: No. 17). 488p. 1982. text ed. 55.75 (ISBN 0-87436-330-6). ABC-Clio.

Blackey, Robert, jt. ed. see Paynton, Clifford.

Blackford, Mansel G. A Portrait Cast in Steel: Buckeye International & Columbus, Ohio, 1881-1980. LC 82-6114. (Contributions in Economics & Economic History Ser.: No. 49). (Illus.). 248p. 1982. lib. bdg. 29.95 (ISBN 0-313-23393-4, BPC/). Greenwood.

Blackham, H. J. Six Existentialist Thinkers. 179p. 1965. pap. 7.95 (ISBN 0-7100-4611-1). Routledge & Kegan.

Blackhurst, Edward A. & Berdine, William H. An Introduction to Special Education. 1981. text ed. 20.95 (ISBN 0-316-09060-3); tchrs' manual avail. (ISBN 0-316-09061-1). Little.

Blackie And Son. Victorian Cabinet-Maker's Assistant. (Illus.). 1970. pap. 10.00 (ISBN 0-486-22353-1). Dover.

Blackie, C. Geographical Etymology: A Dictionary of Place-Names Giving Their Derivations. LC 68-17916. 1968. Repr. of 1887 ed. 30.00x (ISBN 0-8103-3882-3). Gale.

Blackie, John. Inside the Primary School. LC 71-163327. (Illus.). 1971. 4.95x o.p. (ISBN 0-8052-3427-6); pap. 2.25 (ISBN 0-8052-0311-7). Schocken.

--Inspecting & the Inspectorate. (Students Library of Education). 1970. 7.50x o.p. (ISBN 0-7100-6780-1). Routledge & Kegan.

Blackie, M. G. The Patient Not the Cure. 1978. 4.95x (ISBN 0-912800-49-6, Pub. by Woodbridge). Formur Intl.

Blackie, M. J., jt. auth. see Dent, J. B.

Blackie, M. J. & Dent, J. B., eds. Information Systems for Agriculture. (Illus.). 1979. 28.75 (ISBN 0-85334-829-4, Pub. by Applied Sci England). Elsevier.

Blacking, John. How Musical Is Man? LC 72-6710. (John Danz Lecture Ser). (Illus.). 132p. 1973. 11.95 (ISBN 0-295-95218-0, WP72); pap. 7.95 (ISBN 0-295-95338-1); tapes 17.50 (ISBN 0-295-75510-5); c-60 cassette 17.50 (ISBN 0-295-75517-2). U of Wash Pr.

Blackler, F. H. & Brown, C. A. Whatever Happened to Shell's New Philosophy of Management? 184p. 1980. text ed. 27.00x (ISBN 0-566-00306-6). Gower Pub Ltd.

Blackley, D. C. Emulsion Polymerisation: Theory & Practice. 1975. 49.25 (ISBN 0-85334-627-5, Pub. by Applied Sci England). Elsevier.

Blacklow, Robert S., et al, eds. MacBryde's Signs & Symptoms: Applied Pathologic Physiology & Clinical Interpretation. 6th ed. (Illus.). 864p. 1983. text ed. price not set (ISBN 0-397-52094-8, Lippincott Medical). Lippincott.

Blackman, Derek. Operant Conditioning: An Experimental Analysis of Behaviour. LC 74-18545. 247p. 1974. text ed. 13.95x o.p. (ISBN 0-416-13660-5); pap. 11.50 (ISBN 0-416-81480-8). Methuen Inc.

Blackman, Laura. Marina. 1981. pap. 2.95 o.p. (ISBN 0-451-09721-1, E9721, Sig). NAL.

Blackman, Margaret B. & Davidson, Florence E. During My Time: Florence Edenshaw Davidson, a Haida Woman. LC 82-8674. (Illus.). 192p. 1983. 18.95 (ISBN 0-295-95943-6). U of Wash Pr.

Blackman, Maurice. Design of Real Time Applications. LC 74-26960. 265p. 1975. 51.95x (ISBN 0-471-07770-4, Pub. by Wiley-Interscience). Wiley.

Blackman, Sheldon, jt. auth. see Goldstein, Kenneth M.

Blackmarr, Brian, et al. Syntopican X, Papers & Proceedings June 21 to 24, 1982 "The Informatio Manager in Focus". A Key Role Takes Shape". 340p. 1982. 40.00 (ISBN 0-935220-07-0). IIWPA.

Blackmer, Donald L. Unity in Diversity: Italian Communism & the Communist World. (Studies in Communism, Revisionism & Revolution). 1968. 25.00x (ISBN 0-262-02030-0). MIT Pr.

Blackmore, John. The Gibraltar Dialogues: A Philosophy for the Space Age. LC 80-5527. 249p. 1980. lib. bdg. 20.00 (ISBN 0-8191-1125-2); pap. text ed. 10.50 (ISBN 0-8191-1126-0). U Pr of Amer.

Blackmore, R. D. Lorna Doone. (Childrens Illustrated Classics Ser). (Illus.). 505p. 1974. Repr. of 1951 ed. 9.00x o.p. (ISBN 0-460-05022-2, Pub. by J. M. Dent England). Biblio Dist.

Blackmore, R. D see Swan, D. K.

Blackmore, Richard. Lorna Doone. 345p. 1981. Repr. PLB 17.95 (ISBN 0-89966-350-8). Buccaneer Bks.

--A Treatise of the Spleen & Vapours: Or, Hypocondriacal & Hysterical Affections. 320p. 1976. 40.00 (ISBN 0-686-84923-X, Oriel). Routledge & Kegan.

Blackmore, Susan J. Beyond the Body: An Investigation of Out-of-the-Body Experiences. 288p. 1982. 40.00x (ISBN 0-434-07470-5, Pub. by Heinemann England). State Mutual Bk.

Blackmur, R. P. Studies in Henry James. Makowsky, Veronica A., ed. LC 82-18911. 256p. 1983. 19.50 (ISBN 0-8112-0863-X); pap. 9.25 (ISBN 0-8112-0864-8, NDP 552). New Directions.

Blackmur, Richard P. Eleven Essays in the European Novel. LC 64-19367. (Orig.). 1964. pap. 2.95 o.p. (ISBN 0-15-628210-0, H036, Harv). HarBraceJ.

Blacksell, Mark. Post-War Europe: A Political Geography. LC 77-82814. (Illus.). 1978. lib. bdg. 24.50 o.p. (ISBN 0-89158-822-1). Westview.

Blackstock, Charity. Ghost Town. LC 76-6906. 224p. 1976. 7.95 o.p. (ISBN 0-698-10735-7, Coward). Putnam Pub Group.

--A House Possessed. 222p. 1976. Repr. of 1962 ed. lib. bdg. 16.95x (ISBN 0-89244-077-5). Queens Hse.

--People in Glass Houses. LC 74-30597. 256p. 1975. 7.95 o.p. (ISBN 0-698-10652-0, Coward). Putnam Pub Group.

--The Shirt Front. 1977. 7.95 o.p. (ISBN 0-698-10831-0, Coward). Putnam Pub Group.

Blackstock, Paul W. & Schaf, Frank, Jr. Intelligence, Espionage, Counterespionage & Covert Operations: A Guide to Information Sources. LC 74-11567. (International Relations Information Guide Ser.: Vol. 2). 1978. 42.00x (ISBN 0-8103-1323-5). Gale.

Blackstone, Tessa, jt. auth. see Lodge, Paul.

Blackstone, Tessa, jt. auth. see Mortimore, Jo.

Blackstone, W. Commentaries on the Law of England: First English Edition, Oxford, 1765-1769, 4 Vols. 1966. 150.00 (ISBN 0-379-00416-X). Oceana.

Blackstone, William. Commentaries on the Laws of England: A Facsimile of the First Edition of 1765-1769, 4 vols. LC 79-11753. 1979. Set. lib. bdg. 100.00x (ISBN 0-226-05536-1); pap. 12.00 ea. Vol. I (ISBN 0-226-05538-8). Vol. II (ISBN 0-226-05541-8). Vol. III (ISBN 0-226-05543-4). Vol. IV (ISBN 0-226-05545-0). U of Chicago Pr.

Blackton, Perter. The Mysterious Stranger Within Us. LC 79-17191. (Unsolved Mysteries of the World Ser.). PLB 11.96 (ISBN 0-89547-083-7). Silver.

Blackwelder, Boyce. The Four Gospels. 1980. padded gift box 9.95 (ISBN 0-87162-221-1, D3768). Warner Pr.

Blackwelder, Richard E. Taxonomy: A Text & Reference Book. LC 67-13520. 698p. 1967. 37.95 o.p. (ISBN 0-471-07800-X). Wiley.

Blackwell, Alice S. Lucy Stone: Pioneer of Woman's Rights. LC 77-164111. (Illus.). viii, 301p. 1971. Repr. of 1930 ed. 34.00x o.p. (ISBN 0-8103-3824-6). Gale.

Blackwell, Alice S., tr. Some Spanish-American Poets. LC 68-22694. (Eng. & Span.). 1968. Repr. of 1937 ed. 10.00x (ISBN 0-8196-0217-5). Biblo.

Blackwell, Earl, jt. auth. see Sheppard, Eugenia.

Blackwell, Gene. The Private Investigator. LC 79-4560. (Illus.). 1979. 18.95 (ISBN 0-913708-34-8). Butterworth.

Blackwell, Gordon W. Selected Addresses of Gordon W. Blackwell, the; President of Florida State University, Sept. 16, 1960 to Jan. 31, 1965. LC 65-64028. (Florida State U. Studies: No. 43). 1965. 6.95 (ISBN 0-8130-0481-0). U Presses Fla.

Blackwell, John, jt. auth. see Walton, Alan G.

Blackwell, Kate, jt. auth. see Nader, Ralph.

Blackwell, Marilyn J., ed. Structures of Influence: A Comparative Approach to August Strindberg. LC 80-29545. (Studies in the Germanic Languages & Literatures: No.98). xiv, 370p. 1982. 26.00x o.p. (ISBN 0-8078-8098-1). U of NC Pr.

Blackwell, Muriel F. Called to Teach Children. LC 82-82954. 1983. 5.95 (ISBN 0-8054-3233-7). Broadman.

Blackwell, Peter M., et al. Sentences & Other Systems: A Language & Learning Curriculum for Hearing-Impaired Children. LC 78-51922. 1978. pap. text ed. 14.50 (ISBN 0-88200-118-3, C2557). Alexander Graham.

Blackwell, Richard, tr. see Wolff, Christian.

Blackwell, Roger D. Living with Death. 1977. cancelled 6.95 o.p. (ISBN 0-8007-0919-5). Revell.

Blackwell, Russell T., jt. auth. see Todd, Charles L.

Blackwell, Thomas E., ed. College Law Digest, 1935-1970. xi, 256p. (Orig.). 1974. pap. text ed. 12.00x (ISBN 0-8377-0307-7). Rothman.

Blackwell, Wayne W. Chemical Process Design on a Programmable Calculator. (Illus.). 416p. 1983. 32.95 (ISBN 0-07-005545-9, P&RB). McGraw.

Blackwell, Will H., Jr. Guide to the Woody Plants of the Tri-State Area. (Illus.). 1976. pap. text ed. 6.95 (ISBN 0-8403-1581-3). Kendall-Hunt.

Blackwell, William L. The Industrialization of Russia. 2nd ed. (Europe Since 1500 Ser.). 216p. 1982. pap. 8.95x (ISBN 0-88295-813-5). Harlan Davidson.

Blackwood, A. W. La Preparacion de Sermones Biblicos. Crane, Santiago D., tr. 255p. (Span.). 1981. pap. 3.75 (ISBN 0-311-42030-3). Casa Bautista.

Blackwood, Alan. The Performing World of the Singer. LC 81-50926. (The Performing World Ser.). 15.20 (ISBN 0-382-06591-3). Silver.

Blackwood, Algernon. Tales of Terror & Darkness. 1978. 14.00 o.p. (ISBN 0-600-30347-0). Transatlantic.

Blackwood, Andrew W. Planning a Year's Pulpit Work. (Andrew W. Blackwood Library). 240p. 1975. pap. 4.50 o.p. (ISBN 0-8010-0640-6). Baker Bk.

Blackwood, B. G. The Lancashire Gentry & the Great Rebellion, 1640-60. 1978. 24.00 (ISBN 0-7190-1334-8). Manchester.

Blackwood, Cheryl P. A Bright-Shining Place. (Epiphany Ser.). 240p. 1983. pap. 2.75 (ISBN 0-345-30698-8). Ballantine.

Blackwood, Gary L. The Lion & the Unicorn. LC 82-90758. 291p. (Orig.). 1983. pap. 5.95 (ISBN 0-910971-00-5). Eagle Bks.

Blackwood, R. T., jt. ed. see Herman, A. L.

Blackwood, Robert. Thailand. (Illus.). 184p. 1983. pap. 9.95 (ISBN 0-686-42978-8). Hippocrene Bks.

Blackwood, W. Greenfield's Neuropathology. 3rd ed. (Illus.). 1976. 89.50 o.p. (ISBN 0-8151-0840-0). Year Bk Med.

Blade, Melinda K. Education of Italian Renaissance Women. rev. ed. LC 82-1190. (Woman in History Ser.: Vol. 21B). (Illus.). 86p. 1983. lib. bdg. 15.95 (ISBN 0-86663-070-8); pap. text ed. 8.95 (ISBN 0-86663-071-6). Ide Hse.

Bladen, Joan M. I Don't Remember If We Got a Spanking for That. 19p. (Orig.). (gr. k-12). 1981. 3.50 (ISBN 0-936412-03-8). Iota Pr.

Blades, James. Percussion Instruments & Their History. new ed. (Illus.). Date not set. 24.95 (ISBN 0-571-04832-3). Faber & Faber.

Blades, William. Books in Chains & Other Bibliographical Papers. LC 68-30610. 1968. Repr. of 1892 ed. 30.00x (ISBN 0-8103-3298-1). Gale.

Bladow, Suzanne W. The Midnight Flight of Moose, Mops, & Marvin. new ed. LC 75-10825. (Illus.). 48p. (ps-3). 1975. 5.95 o.p. (ISBN 0-07-005535-1, GB); PLB 6.95 o.p. (ISBN 0-07-005536-X). McGraw.

Blady, Michael. Children at Risk: Making a Difference Through the Court Appointed Special Advocate Project. (Illus.). 318p. 1982. wkbk 7.50 (ISBN 0-686-84113-1). NCJW.

Blagowidow, George. Operation Parterre. 286p. 1982. 10.95 (ISBN 0-88254-712-7). Hippocrene Bks.

Blahut, Richard E. Theory & Practice of Error Control Codes. LC 82-11441. (Illus.). 512p. Date not set. text ed. price not set (ISBN 0-201-10102-5). A-W.

Blaikie, W. G. & Law, R. The Inner Life of Christ. 459p. 1982. lib. bdg. 17.25 Smythe Sewn (ISBN 0-86524-156-2, 9515). Klock & Klock.

Blaikie, W. G. & Matthews, C. D. A Manual of Bible History. rev. ed. 432p. 1940. 17.95 o.p. (ISBN 0-471-07008-4). Wiley.

Blaikie, William G. David, King of Israel. 1981. 17.50 (ISBN 0-86524-054-X, 8401). Klock & Klock.

--Heroes of Israel. 1982. lib. bdg. 19.50 (ISBN 0-86524-082-5, 0102). Klock & Klock.

Blaiklock, E. M. Blaiklock's Handbook to the Bible. 1981. pap. 6.95 (ISBN 0-8007-5055-1, Power Bks). Revell.

--Letters to Children of Light: A Bible Commentary for Laymen in 1,2,3 John. 2nd ed. LC 75-14883. 1977. pap. 2.25 o.p. (ISBN 0-8307-0460-4, S293-1-29). Regal.

--The Pastoral Epistles. 128p. 1972. pap. 4.95 (ISBN 0-310-21233-2). Zondervan.

Blain, Beryl B., et al. A Complete Preparation for the New MCAT: Skills Development in Reading & Quantitative, Vol. II. (Illus.). 304p. (Orig.). 1982. pap. text ed. 12.50 (ISBN 0-941406-02-4). Betz Pub Co Inc.

Blain, Daniel & Barton, Michael, eds. The History of American Psychiatry: A Teaching & Research Guide. LC 78-78396. (Task Force Reports: 15). 44p. 1979. pap. 5.00 o.p. (ISBN 0-685-95863-9, P146-0). Am Psychiatric.

Blaine, Graham B. Are Parents Bad for Children? 1973. 5.95 o.p. (ISBN 0-698-10494-3, Coward). Putnam Pub Group.

Blaine, Lawrence. Grant Proposals: A Practical Guide to Planning, Funding & Managing. 105p. 1981. pap. text ed. 12.00 (ISBN 0-686-35865-1). Psyon Pubns.

Blainey, Geoffrey. Triumph of the Nomads: A History of Aboriginal Australia. LC 75-37122. 304p. 1976. 18.95 (ISBN 0-87951-043-9). Overlook Pr.

--Triumph of the Nomads: A History of the Aborigines. LC 75-37122. 304p. 1982. pap. 7.95 (ISBN 0-87951-084-6). Overlook Pr.

Blair & Rubin. Regulating the Professions: A Public-Policy Symposium. LC 79-2272. 336p. 1980. 29.95x (ISBN 0-669-03094-5). Lexington Bks.

Blair, jt. auth. see Rupley.

Blair, Alain, tr. see Lagerkvist, Par.

Blair, Alex. Blood Is Not Enough: Stories of One Sq. Mile. (Illus.). 172p. (Orig.). 1981. pap. 3.50 (ISBN 0-938918-00-1). Chong-Donnie.

Blair, Alex, ed. see Carleton, Bruce.

Blair, Alice C. No-Nonsense Principal Handbook for Educators. (Illus.). 112p. 1982. 10.95 (ISBN 0-941484-02-5). Urban Res Inst.

Blair, Anne Denton. Hurrah for Arthur: A Mount Vernon Birthday Party. LC 82-10636. (Illus.). (gr. k-3). 1983. 11.95 (ISBN 0-932020-15-1). Seven Locks Pr.

Blair, Charles & Sherrill, John. The Man Who Could Do No Wrong. 1982. pap. 3.50 (ISBN 0-8423-4002-5). Tyndale.

Blair, Claude, jt. ed. see Tarassuk, Leonid.

Blair, Clay. Beyond Courage. (War Library). 208p. 1983. pap. 2.50 (ISBN 0-345-30824-7). Ballantine.

Blair, Clay, jt. auth. see Blair, Joan.

Blair, Clay, jt. auth. see Bradley, Omar N.

Blair, Cynthia. Beautiful Dreamer. (Love & Life Romance Ser.). 176p. (Orig.). 1983. pap. 1.75 (ISBN 0-345-30794-1). Ballantine.

--Commitment. (Love & Life Romance Ser.). 176p. (Orig.). 1983. pap. 1.75 (ISBN 0-345-30795-X). Ballantine.

Blair, Edward P. Deuteronomy, Joshua. LC 59-10454. (Layman's Bible Commentary Ser: Vol. 5). 1964. pap. 3.25 (ISBN 0-8042-3065-X). John Knox.

Blair, Glenn M., et al. Educational Psychology. 4th ed. (Illus.). 672p. 1975. pap. text ed. 20.95 (ISBN 0-02-310500-3, 31050). Macmillan.

Blair, Graeme. Sulfur in the Tropics. (Technical Bulletin Ser.: T-12). (Illus.). 71p. (Orig.). 1979. pap. 4.00 (ISBN 0-88090-011-3). Intl Fertilizer.

Blair, Guillermo, tr. see Ford, LeRoy.

Blair, Gwenda. Laura Ingalls Wilder. (Beginning Biography Bk.). (Illus.). 64p. (gr. 1-4). 1981. lib. bdg. 5.99 (ISBN 0-399-61139-8). Putnam Pub Group.

Blair, H., ed. see Zoschenko, Mikhail.

Blair, J. A., jt. auth. see Johnson, R. H.

Blair, J. Allen. Jonah: Living Obediently. LC 63-18265. 1963. pap. 3.95 (ISBN 0-87213-050-9). Loizeaux.

--Profile of a Christian. 1982. pap. 2.50 (ISBN 0-89107-252-7). Good News.

Blair, J. W. Coleccion Navidena, No. 1. 1980. Repr. of 1977 ed. pap. 1.75 (ISBN 0-311-08201-7). Casa Bautista.

Blair, Jane N. The Gourmet's Bland Diet Cookbook. (Orig.). 1974. pap. 1.25 o.s.i. (ISBN 0-515-03306-5, V3306). Jove Pubns.

Blair, Joan & Blair, Clay. Return from the River Kwai. LC 79-531. 1979. 12.95 o.p. (ISBN 0-671-24278-4). S&S.

Blair, John. The Control of Oil. 1978. pap. 6.95 (ISBN 0-394-72532-8, V-532, Vin). Random.

--Illustrated Discography of Surf Music. (Illus.). 1983. price not set (ISBN 0-9601880-1-0). J Bee Prods.

Blair, John P., jt. auth. see Barrett, G. Vincent.

Blair, Karen. The Clubwoman As Feminist: True Womanhood Redefined, 1868 to 1914. LC 79-26390. 1980. text ed. 29.50x (ISBN 0-8419-0538-X). Holmes & Meier.

Blair, Karin. Cubal Analysis. 220p. Date not set. price not set (ISBN 0-913660-17-5); pap. price not set (ISBN 0-913660-18-3). Magic Circle Pr.

--Meaning in Star Trek. 1979. pap. 2.25 o.p. (ISBN 0-446-92095-9). Warner Bks.

Blair, Leona. A Woman's Place. 1983. pap. 3.95 (ISBN 0-440-19629-9). Dell.

Blair, Lowell, tr. see Dumas, Alexandre.

Blair, Lowell, tr. see Rostand, Edmond.

Blair, P. H. An Introduction to Anglo-Saxon England. 2nd ed. LC 77-71404. (Illus.). 1977. 54.50 (ISBN 0-521-21650-8); pap. 13.95x (ISBN 0-521-29219-0). Cambridge U Pr.

Blair, Patricia, jt. ed. see Ingle, John I.

Blair, Patricia W., ed. Health Needs of the World's Poor Women. 205p. pap. 17.50 (ISBN 0-941696-00-6). Equity Policy.

Blair, Perry. The Easter Rainbow. (Illus.). 24p. (Orig.). (gr. k-6). 1981. pap. 2.50x (ISBN 0-9607782-0-9). Blair Pub.

Blair, Peter, et al. Geothermal Energy: Prospects for Energy Production. LC 81-13139. (Wiley Alternate Energy Ser.). 184p. 1982. 32.95x (ISBN 0-471-08063-2, Pub. by Wiley-Interscience). Wiley.

Blair, Peter H. World of Bede. LC 73-135524. 1971. 12.95 o.p. (ISBN 0-312-89215-2, W59000). St Martin.

Blair, R. D. & Kenny, L. W. Microeconomics for Managerial Decision Making. 1982. 23.95 (ISBN 0-07-005800-8). McGraw.

Blair, Robert W., ed. Innovative Approaches to Language Teaching & Language Learning. 328p. 1982. pap. text ed. 19.95 (ISBN 0-88377-247-7). Newbury Hse.

Blair, Ruth. Van Ness, Mary's Monster. LC 74-16651. (A Science Discovery Book). (Illus.). 66p. (gr. 2-6). 1975. 5.95 o.p. (ISBN 0-698-20304-6, Coward). Putnam Pub Group.

Blair, Ruth V. Willa-Willa, the Wishful Witch. (Early Childhood Bk.). (Illus.). (ps-2). PLB 4.95 o.p. (ISBN 0-513-01224-9). Denison.

Blair, Ruth Van Ness see Blair, Ruth.

Blair, Sam, jt. auth. see Trevino, Lee.

Blair, T. & Fite, R. Weather Elements: Text in Elementary Meteorology. 5th ed. 1965. ref. ed. 27.95 (ISBN 0-13-947721-7). P-H.

Blair, Thomas. Oqua. LC 79-15861. 1983. 14.95 (ISBN 0-87949-163-9). Ashley Bks.

Blair, Timothy R., jt. auth. see Rupley, William H.

Blair, Valera G. The Cook's Idea Book: 1001 Imaginative Ideas for Those Who Love to Cook. 1977. 10.00 o.p. (ISBN 0-517-52740-5, C N Potter Bks). Crown.

Blair, W. F., et al. Vertebrates of the United States. 2nd ed. 1968. 31.00 o.p. (ISBN 0-07-005591-2, C). McGraw.

Blair, Walter. Mark Twain & Huck Finn: 1855-1873. Frank, Michael B. & Sanderson, Kenneth M, eds. (California Library Reprint). 1974. 34.50x (ISBN 0-520-02521-0). U of Cal Pr.

--Mike Fink, King of Mississippi Keelboatmen. LC 74-138143. (Illus.). 1971. Repr. of 1933 ed. lib. bdg. 17.00x (ISBN 0-8371-5600-9, BLMF). Greenwood.

--Tall Tale America. (Illus.). (gr. 4-9). 1944. PLB 6.99 (ISBN 0-698-30350-4, Coward). Putnam Pub Group.

Blair, Walter & Gerber, John. Repertory. rev. ed. 1967. text ed. 18.95x (ISBN 0-673-05240-0). Scott F.

Blair, Walter & Hill, Hamlin. America's Humor: From Poor Richard to Doonesbury. (Galaxy Bks.: No. 609). 1980. pap. 10.95 (ISBN 0-19-502756-6). Oxford U Pr.

Blair, Walter & McDavid, Raven I., Jr., eds. The Mirth of a Nation: America's Great Dialect. LC 81-16403. (Illus.). 336p. 1982. 35.00x (ISBN 0-8166-1022-3); pap. 12.95x (ISBN 0-8166-1168-8). U of Minn Pr.

Blair, Walter, ed. see Twain, Mark.

Blair, Walter, et al. The Literature of the United States, 2 vols. 3rd ed. (Heritage printing). 1970. text ed. 17.95x ea.; Vol. 1. (ISBN 0-673-07636-9); Vol. 2. (ISBN 0-673-07637-7). Scott F.

--Literature of the United States, Bk. 1. 3rd ed. 1969. pap. 12.50x (ISBN 0-673-05967-7). Scott F.

Blair, William. Fire! Survival & Prevention. (Illus.). 192p. (Orig.). 1983. pap. 2.84i (ISBN 0-06-465147-9, P-BN 5147). B&N NY.

Blaisdell, Donald C. Government & Agriculture: Growth of Federal Farm Aid. LC 72-2365. (FDR & the Era of the New Deal Ser.). 217p. 1974. Repr. of 1940 ed. lib. bdg. 32.50 (ISBN 0-306-70488-9). Da Capo.

Blaisdell, Gus, ed. see Connell, Evan S.

Blaisdell, Harold F. The Art of Fishing with Worms & Other Live Bait. 1978. 14.50 (ISBN 0-394-40039-9). Knopf.

Blaisdell, Paul H. Three Centuries on Winnipesaukee. LC 75-10740. (Illus.). 16p. 1975. 2.95 o.p. (ISBN 0-912274-96-4). Backcountry Pubns.

--Twenty-Five Walks in the Lakes Region of New Hampshire. LC 76-53697. (Twenty-Five Walks Ser.). (Illus.). 120p. 1977. 5.95 (ISBN 0-912274-68-9); pap. 4.95 (ISBN 0-912274-80-8). Backcountry Pubns.

Blake, Alexander. Design of Curved Members for Machines. LC 79-12202. 288p. 1979. Repr. of 1966 ed. lib. bdg. 18.50 (ISBN 0-88275-970-1). Krieger.

Blake, B. J., jt. ed. see Dixon, R. M.

Blake, C. Fred. Ethnic Groups & Social Change in a Chinese Market Town. LC 80-16978. (Asian Studies at Hawaii: No. 27). 192p. (Orig.). 1981. pap. 10.50x (ISBN 0-8248-0720-0). UH Pr.

Blake, Christina. Deadly Legacy. (Raven House Mysteries Ser.). 224p. 1982. pap. cancelled (ISBN 0-373-63045-X, Pub. by Worldwide). Harlequin Bks.

Blake, David, jt. auth. see Barnes, Charles.

Blake, David H. & Walters, Robert S. The Politics of Global Economic Relations. 2nd ed. (Illus.). 320p. 1983. pap. 13.95 (ISBN 0-13-684449-9). P-H.

Blake, David H. & Lambert, Richard D., eds. The Multinational Corporation. new ed. LC 72-85688. (The Annals of the American Academy of Political & Social Science: No. 403). 300p. 1972. 15.00 (ISBN 0-87761-154-8); pap. 7.95 (ISBN 0-87761-153-X). Am Acad Pol Soc Sci.

Blake, David H., et al. Social Auditing: Evaluating the Impact of Corporate Programs. LC 76-2901. (Illus.). 1976. pap. text ed. 11.95 (ISBN 0-275-85710-7). Praeger.

Blake, David P., et al. Making Seventy-Five Rugs by the Square. (Illus.). 1978. 10.95 (ISBN 0-517-52471-6); pap. 6.95 o.p. (ISBN 0-517-52472-4). Crown.

Blake, Donna J., jt. auth. see Glerum, Richard Z.

Blake, Duane L. Dynamics of Human Relations in Vocational Education: The Development of Self-Confidence & a Sense of Mastery. LC 77-9416. 152p. 1979. pap. 10.00x (ISBN 0-910328-26-9). Carroll Pr.

Blake, Frank R. Grammar of the Tagalog Language, the Chief Native Idiom of the Philippine Islands. 1925. pap. 28.00 (ISBN 0-527-02676-X). Kraus Repr.

Blake, Gary, jt. auth. see Bly, Robert W.

Blake, Howard E. Creating a Learning-Centered Classroom. 400p. (Orig.). 1977. pap. 8.95 o.s.i. (ISBN 0-89104-179-6, A & W Visual Library). A & W Pubs.

Blake, Ian F. Introduction to Applied Probability. LC 78-11360. 528p. 1979. text ed. 33.95x (ISBN 0-471-03210-7). Wiley.

Blake, Ian F., jt. auth. see Walker, B. J.

Blake, Ian F., ed. Algebraic Coding Theory: History & Development. LC 73-9627. (Benchmark Papers in Electrical Engineering & Computer Science: Vol. 3). 413p. 1973. 49.50 (ISBN 0-87933-038-4). Hutchinson Ross.

Blake, James Neal. ABC Phonics & Faces. (Illus.). 84p. 1972. photocopy ed. spiral 9.75x (ISBN 0-398-02528-2). C C Thomas.

Blake, Jane. How to Retouch Color Photographs for Fun & Profit. LC 77-20582. (Illus.). 78p. 1978. pap. 9.95 (ISBN 0-912760-57-5). Palmetto Pub.

Blake, Jeremy. La Falsa Prospettiva in Italian Renaissance Architecture. (Illus.). 1982. 250.00 (ISBN 0-85362-192-6). Routledge & Kegan.

Blake, Jill. Color & Pattern in the Home. (Illus.). 1978. pap. 7.95 o.p. (ISBN 0-8256-3137-8, Quick Fox). Putnam Pub Group.

Blake, John. All You Needed Was Love: The Beatles After the Beatles. (Illus.). 1981. pap. 7.95 (ISBN 0-399-50556-3, Perige). Putnam Pub Group.

Blake, Kathryn. Educating Exceptional Pupils: An Introduction to Contemporary Practices. LC 80-15222. (Illus.). 528p. 1981. text ed. 20.95 (ISBN 0-201-00083-0); instrs' manual 3.00 (ISBN 0-201-00084-9). A-W.

--The Mentally Retarded: An Educational Psychology. (Special Education Ser.). (Illus.). 416p. 1976. 24.95x (ISBN 0-13-576280-4). P-H.

--Teaching the Retarded. LC 73-13719. (Special Education Ser.). (Illus.). 384p. 1974. 23.95 (ISBN 0-13-895276-0). P-H.

Blake, Kathryn A. College Reading Skills. (Illus.). 304p. 1973. pap. text ed. 12.95 (ISBN 0-13-150003-1). P-H.

Blake, L. J. Antennas. (Electronic Technlogy Ser.). 415p. 1966. pap. 17.95 o.p. (ISBN 0-471-07928-6). Wiley.

Blake, Lamont V. Transmission Lines & Waveguides. LC 69-16039. (Electronic Engineering & Technology Ser). 1969. text ed. 19.95 o.p. (ISBN 0-471-07929-4). Wiley.

Blake, Laurel. Stormy Passage, No. 66. 1982. pap. 1.75 (ISBN 0-515-06677-X). Jove Pubns.

Blake, Marion E. Roman Construction in Italy from Tiberius Through Flavians. (Carnegie Institution Publication Ser: No. 616). (Illus.). Repr. of 1959 ed. 23.00 o.s.i. (ISBN 0-527-08870-6). Kraus Repr.

Blake, Michael, ed. see Dickson, Murray.

Blake, Michael J., jt. ed. see Kavass, Igor I.

Blake, Mindy. Golf: The Technique Barrier. (Illus.). 1979. 10.95 o.p. (ISBN 0-393-08825-1). Norton.

Blake, N. F. The Canterbury Tales. 720p. 1980. text ed. 98.50 (ISBN 0-7131-6217-1). E Arnold.

--The English Language in Medieval Literature. 1979. pap. 8.95x (ISBN 0-416-72470-1). Methuen Inc.

Blake, Nelson M. A History of American Life & Thought. 2nd ed. (Illus.). 781p. 1971. text ed. 25.00 (ISBN 0-07-005670-6, C). McGraw.

--Novelists' America: Fiction As History, 1910-1940. LC 68-31563. (Illus., Orig.). 1969. pap. 5.95x (ISBN 0-8156-2147-7). Syracuse U Pr.

Blake, Nelson M., jt. auth. see Barck, Oscar T.

Blake, Nelson M., jt. ed. see Rich, Jane K.

Blake, Nicholas. Minute for Murder. LC 75-44956. (Crime Fiction Ser). 1976. Repr. of 1947 ed. lib. bdg. 17.50 o.s.i. (ISBN 0-8240-2354-4). Garland Pub.

--Minute for Murder. 1977. Repr. pap. 1.95i o.p. (ISBN 0-06-080419-X, P418, PL). Har-Row.

Blake, Norman. Language Variety in English Literature. (The Language Library). 232p. 1982. lib. bdg. 18.00 o.p. (ISBN 0-686-78094-9). Westview.

Blake, O. & Walters, R. Politics of Global Economic Relations. (Illus.). 272p. 1976. pap. 13.95 (ISBN 0-13-684712-9). P-H.

Blake, P., ed. Advanced Manufacturing Technology: Programming Research & Operations Logistics. 1980. 59.75 (ISBN 0-444-85455-X). Elsevier.

Blake, Patricia, ed. see Hayward, Max.

Blake, Peter. Form Follows Fiasco: Why Modern Architecture Hasn't Worked. 1977. 13.95 (ISBN 0-316-09940-6, Pub. by Atlantic Monthly Pr); pap. 9.95 (ISBN 0-316-09939-2, Pub. by Atlantic Monthly Pr). Little.

--Harry Seidler: Australian Embassy, Paris. (Illus.). 56p. 1983. pap. 15.00 (ISBN 0-8390-0306-4). Allanheld & Schram.

Blake, Reed H. & Haroldsen, Edwin O. A Taxonomy of Concepts in Communication. (Humanistic Studies in the Communication Arts). (Illus.). 176p. 1975. 9.95 (ISBN 0-8038-7154-6); pap. text ed. 6.95x (ISBN 0-8038-7155-4). Hastings.

Blake, Richard. Water Treatment for HVAC & Potable Water Systems. (Illus.). 1979. 21.95 (ISBN 0-07-005840-7, P&RB). McGraw.

Blake, Robert. One Hundred & One Elephant Jokes. (Orig.). (YA) (gr. 7-12). 1964. pap. 0.95 o.p. (ISBN 0-515-01090-1, N1090). Jove Pubns.

Blake, Robert, ed. The English World: History, Character & People. LC 82-1788. (Illus.). 268p. 1982. 50.00 (ISBN 0-8109-0865-4). Abrams.

Blake, Robert R. & Mouton, Jane S. Consultation: A Comprehensive Approach to Individual & Organization Development. 2nd ed. LC 82-6746. (Illus.). 528p. 1983. pap. text ed. 25.00 (ISBN 0-201-10165-3). A-W.

--Corporate Excellence Through Grid Organization Development. (Illus.). 392p. 1968. 15.95 (ISBN 0-87201-331-6). Gulf Pub.

--Diary of an OD Man. 363p. 1976. 17.95 (ISBN 0-87201-169-0). Gulf Pub.

--Making Experience Work: The Grid Approach to Critique. (Illus.). 1977. 18.50 (ISBN 0-07-005675-7, P&RB). McGraw.

Blake, Robert R., et al. Managing Intergroup Conflict in Industry. 223p. 1964. 14.95 (ISBN 0-87201-375-8). Gulf Pub.

Blake, Roland P. Industrial Safety. 3rd ed. 1963. ref. ed. 19.95 (ISBN 0-13-463133-1). P-H.

Blake, S. F. Geographical Guide to Floras of the World: Annotated List with Special Reference to Useful Plants & Common Plant Names, Pt. II. LC 78-51431. (Landmark Reprints in Plant Science). 1978. Repr. of 1961 ed. text ed. 40.00x (ISBN 0-86598-006-3). Allanheld.

Blake, S. F. & Atwood, A. C. Geographical Guide to the Floras of the World: Western Europe, Finland, Sweden etc, Pt. 2. 742p. 1974. Repr. of 1961 ed. text ed. 56.00X (ISBN 3-87429-060-3). Lubrecht & Cramer.

Blake, Stephanie. A Glorious Passion. 1983. pap. 3.50 (ISBN 0-515-07071-8). Jove Pubns.

Blake, Sylvia & Kaufman, Sy. Practice Book for the Degrees of Reading Power Test. 1981. 4.50 (ISBN 0-9602800-6-5). Comp Pr.

--Practice Book for the Regents Comprehency Test in Reading. 103p. 1981. 4.50 (ISBN 0-9602800-0-6). Comp pr.

Blake, Viola, jt. auth. see Christenson, Evelyn.

Blake, William. Blake's Job: William Blake's Illustrations of the Book of Job. Damon, S. Foster, ed. LC 66-13155. (Illus.). 76p. 1982. pap. 8.95 (ISBN 0-87451-241-7, Pub. by Brown U Pr). U Pr of New Eng.

--Blake's Job: William Blake's Illustrations of the Book of Job. Damon, S. Foster, ed. LC 66-13155. (Illus.). 76p. 1966. 17.50x (ISBN 0-87057-096-X, Pub. by Brown U Pr). U Pr of New Eng.

--Choice of Blake's Verse. Raine, Kathleen, ed. 151p. 1970. pap. 6.95 (ISBN 0-571-09268-3). Faber & Faber.

--Complete Writings of William Blake, with Variant Readings. Keynes, Geoffrey, ed. (Oxford Standard Authors Ser.). 1966. 39.95 (ISBN 0-19-254157-9); pap. 9.95x (ISBN 0-19-281050-2). Oxford U Pr.

--Drawings of William Blake: Ninety-two Pencil Studies. Keynes, Geoffrey, intro. by. (Illus.). 10.50 (ISBN 0-8446-0033-4). Peter Smith.

--The Poems of William Blake. Yeats, W. B., ed. 277p. 1905. pap. 7.95 (ISBN 0-7100-0174-6). Routledge & Kegan.

--Selected Poems: William Blake. Butter, P. H., ed. (Everyman Library). 288p. 1983. pap. text ed. 6.00x (ISBN 0-460-01125-1, Evman). Biblio Dist.

--Selected Poetry & Prose of William Blake. Frye, Northrop, ed. (YA) 1966. pap. 3.95 (ISBN 0-394-30986-3, T86, Mod LibC). Modern Lib.

--William Blake's Works in Conventional Typography. LC 82-10815. 1983. write for info. (ISBN 0-8201-1388-3). Schol Facsimiles.

Blakeborough, Richard. Legends of Highwaymen & Others. LC 75-154493. (Illus.). 1971. Repr. of 1924 ed. 34.00x (ISBN 0-8103-3373-2). Gale.

Blakebrough, jt. auth. see Birch, G. G.

Blakebrough, N., ed. Biochemical & Biological Engineering Science, 2 Vols. Vol. 1. 1967. o. p. 32.00 (ISBN 0-12-103601-4); Vol. 2. 1969. 56.00 (ISBN 0-12-103602-2). Acad Pr.

Blakeley, Brian L. & Collins, Jacquelin. Documents in English History: Early Times to the Present. LC 74-18264. 467p. 1975. pap. text ed. 16.50x (ISBN 0-471-07946-4). Wiley.

Blakeley, Edward, ed. Community Development Research: Concepts, Issues & Strategies. LC 78-11568. 224p. 1979. text ed. 24.95 (ISBN 0-87705-334-0); pap. text ed. 11.95 (ISBN 0-87705-348-0). Human Sci Pr.

Blakeley, Walter R. Calculus for Engineering Technology. LC 67-29017. 441p. 1968. text ed. 23.95 (ISBN 0-471-07931-6). Wiley.

Blakelock, John H. Automatic Control of Aircraft & Missiles. LC 65-16402. 1965. 54.95x (ISBN 0-471-07930-8, Pub. by Wiley-Interscience). Wiley.

Blakely & Bade. Science of Animal Husbandry. 3rd ed. 544p. 1982. text ed. 18.95 (ISBN 0-8359-6978-9); instr's. manual free (ISBN 0-8359-6979-7). Reston.

Blakely, B. E. Alumni Administration at State Colleges & Universities. 30p. 1979. 10.50 (ISBN 0-89964-000-1). CASE.

Blakely, Jeffry A. & Toombs, Lawrence E. The Tell el-Hesi Field Manual. LC 80-21724. (Joint Archaeological Expedition to Tell el-Hesi: Vol. 1). 134p. 1981. text ed. 15.00x (ISBN 0-89757-205-X, Am Sch Orient Res); pap. text ed. 12.00x (ISBN 0-89757-203-3). Eisenbrauns.

Blakely, Mary K., jt. ed. see Kaufman, Gloria.

Blakely, Pat. What's Skin for? (Creative Question & Answer Library). 32p. (gr. 3-4). 1981. PLB 5.95 (ISBN 0-87191-745-9). Creative Ed.

Blakely, Peggy, tr. see Kobayashi, Kenzo.

Blakely, Roger. North From Duluth: Tourist & Hiking Guide for Minnesota's North Shore. LC 81-83882. (Illus.). 96p. 1981. pap. 10.00. New Rivers Pr.

Blakely, W. A., ed. American State Papers Bearing on Sunday Legislation. LC 79-122165. (Civil Liberties in American History Ser.). 1970. Repr. of 1911 ed. lib. bdg. 95.00 (ISBN 0-306-71973-8). Da Capo.

Blakemore, Colin. Mechanics of the Mind. LC 76-53515. (BBC Reith Lectures: 1976). 1977. 39.95 (ISBN 0-521-21559-5); pap. 11.95x (ISBN 0-521-29185-2). Cambridge U Pr.

Blakemore, Colin, jt. ed. see Gazzaniga, Michael S.

Blakemore, Harold & Smith, Clifford T., eds. Latin America: Geographical Perspectives. (Illus.). 1971. 42.00x (ISBN 0-416-10820-2); pap. 19.95x (ISBN 0-416-80500-0). Methuen Inc.

Blakeney, E. H., ed. see Smith, William.

Blaker. Japan's National Security. 128p. 1983. 6.96 (ISBN 0-03-062003-1). Praeger.

Blakeslee, et al. Tunnel Diode Interconnect Junctions for Cascade Solar Cells: Progess in Solar Energy Supplements. (SERI Ser.). 50p. 1983. pap. text ed. 7.50x (ISBN 0-89553-078-3). Am Solar Energy.

Blakeslee, A. F. Sexual Reproduction in the Mucorinaeae. (Biblioteca Mycologica Ser: No. 48). 1976. Repr. of 1904 ed. text ed. 16.00 (ISBN 3-7682-1064-2). Lubrecht & Cramer.

Blakeslee, Berton, ed. The Limb-Deficient Child. (Illus.). 1963. 44.00x (ISBN 0-520-00125-7). U of Cal Pr.

Blakeslee, David W. & Chinn, William G. Introductory Statistics & Probability: A Basis for Decision-Making. (gr. 11-12). 1975. text ed. 18.36 o.p. (ISBN 0-395-19992-1); instrs' guide 5.44 o.p. (ISBN 0-395-19991-3). HM.

Blakeslee, Thomas R. Digital Design with Standard MSI & LSI: Design Techniques for the Microcomputer Age. 2nd ed. LC 78-24201. 1979. 24.95 (ISBN 0-471-05222-1, Pub. by Wiley-Interscience). Wiley.

--The Right Brain. LC 82-60690. 288p. 1983. pap. 3.50 (ISBN 0-86721-233-0). Playboy Pbks.

Blakeway, M. G., jt. auth. see Derry, T. K.

Blakey, T. N., ed. English for Maritime Studies Book. (Materials for Language Practice (ESP)). 192p. 1982. pap. 9.95 (ISBN 0-08-028636-4). Pergamon.

Blakey, Walker, jt. auth. see Howe, Joseph.

Blakiston. Blakiston's Gould Medical Dictionary. 4th ed. (Illus.). 1979. Trade ed. 35.00 (ISBN 0-07-005703-6, HP); text ed. 32.00 (ISBN 0-07-005700-1). McGraw.

--Blakiston's Pocket Medical Dictionary. 4th ed. Gennaro, Alphonso R., ed. 1979. 19.95 (ISBN 0-07-005715-X, SP); text ed. 17.95 (ISBN 0-07-005714-1). McGraw.

Blakney, R. B., tr. see Lao Tzu.

Blalock, A., jt. auth. see Blalock, Hubert M.

Blalock, H., Jr. Theory Construction: From Verbal to Mathematical Formulations. LC 69-17478. 1969. pap. text ed. 14.95 (ISBN 0-13-913343-7). P-H.

Blalock, H. M. Social Statistics. 2nd ed. 1979. 22.95 (ISBN 0-07-005752-4); instr's manual 9.95 (ISBN 0-07-005753-2). McGraw.

Blalock, Hubert M. Social Statistics. 2nd ed. (Sociology Ser.). (Illus.). 512p. 1972. text ed. 18.00 o.p. (ISBN 0-07-005751-6, C). McGraw.

Blalock, Hubert M. & Blalock, A. Methodology in Social Research. (Sociology Ser). 1968. text ed. 18.50 o.p. (ISBN 0-07-005705-2, C). McGraw.

Blaman, Anna. A Matter of Life & Death. (International Studies & Translations Ser.). 1974. lib. bdg. 9.95 o.p. (ISBN 0-8057-3441-4, Twayne). G K Hall.

Blamey, jt. auth. see Fitter.

Blamey, jt. auth. see Grey-Wilson.

Blamires, D. David Jones: Artist & Writer. 1978. pap. 8.50 (ISBN 0-7190-0730-5). Manchester.

Blamires, D. M., ed. see Rothwell, W. & Barron, W. R.

Blamires, Harry. The Bloomsday Book: A Guide Through Joyce's Ulysses. (Orig.). 1966. pap. 10.95x (ISBN 0-416-69500-0). Methuen Inc.

--On Christian Truth. 168p. (Orig.). 1983. pap. 4.95 (ISBN 0-89283-130-8). Servant.

--Twentieth-Century English Literature. Jeffares, A. Norman, ed. LC 82-5749. (History of Literature Ser.). (Illus.). 312p. 1982. 28.50x (ISBN 0-8052-3827-1). Schocken.

Blanc, Albert D. So You Have Asthma! (Illus.). 280p. 1966. photocopy ed. spiral 28.75x (ISBN 0-398-00168-5). C C Thomas.

Blanc, Charles. Art in Ornament & Dress. LC 77-156923. (Tower Bks). (Illus.). 1971. Repr. of 1876 ed. 37.00x (ISBN 0-8103-3922-6). Gale.

Blanc, Elsie T. The Cooperative Movement in Russia. LC 75-37206. (Russia Studies: Perspectives on the Revolution Ser). 324p. 1977. Repr. of 1924 ed. lib. bdg. 23.50 (ISBN 0-88355-425-9). Hyperion-Conn.

Blanc, L. Le see Le Blanc, L.

Blanc, Robert P. & Cotton, Ira W., eds. Computer Networking. LC 75-36308. 1976. 25.95 o.p. (ISBN 0-87942-071-5). Inst Electrical.

Blance & Cook. Monstruo, 12 bks, Set 1. Incl. Monstruo busca un amigo (ISBN 0-8372-1163-8); Monstruo busca una Casa (ISBN 0-8372-1161-1); Monstruo conoce a la Senorita Monstruo (ISBN 0-8372-1164-6); Monstruo da una Fiesta (ISBN 0-8372-1170-0); Monstruo en la Escuela (ISBN 0-8372-1169-7); Monstruo en el Autobus; Monstruo limpia su Casa (ISBN 0-8372-1162-X); Monstruo va a la Escuela; Monstruo va al Museo (ISBN 0-8372-1166-2); Monstruo va al Zoologico (ISBN 0-8372-1171-9); Monstruo viene a la Ciudad (ISBN 0-8372-1160-3); Monstruo y la Sombrilla Magica (ISBN 0-8372-1165-4). (gr. k-4). pap. 1.74 ea.; pap. 19.50 1 of ea. title with tchr's. guide (ISBN 0-8372-1173-5); tchr's. guide 1.50 (ISBN 0-8372-0707-X); filmstrips & tapes avail. Bowmar-Noble.

--Monstruo, 12 bks, Set 2. Incl. Monstruo Compre un Animalito (ISBN 0-8372-3482-4); Monstruo Encuentra Trabajo (ISBN 0-8372-3485-9); Monstruo, la Senorita Monstruo y el Paseo en bicicleta (ISBN 0-8372-3488-3); Monstruo Recorre la Ciudad (ISBN 0-8372-3490-5); Monstruo va al Circo (ISBN 0-8372-3483-2); Monstruo va al Hospital (ISBN 0-8372-3489-1); Monstruo va a la Playa (ISBN 0-8372-3479-4); Monstruo y la Galleta de Sorpresa (ISBN 0-8372-3486-7); Monstruo y la Liquidacion de Juguetes (ISBN 0-8372-3480-8); Monstruo y el Muro (ISBN 0-8372-3487-5); El Plan de la Senorita Monstruo (ISBN 0-8372-3481-6); La Senorita Monstruo (ISBN 0-8372-3484-0). (gr. k-4). pap. 1.77 ea.; pap. 19.95 1 of ea. title with tchr's. guide (ISBN 0-8372-3491-3); tchr's. guide 1.50 (ISBN 0-8372-9175-5); filmstrips & tapes avail. Bowmar-Noble.

Blance, Ellen, et al. Monster Books: Set 1, 12 bks. Incl. Monster Comes to the City (ISBN 0-8372-0826-2); Monster Looks for a House (ISBN 0-8372-0827-0); Monster Cleans His House (ISBN 0-8372-0828-9); Monster Looks for a Friend (ISBN 0-8372-0829-7); Monster on the Bus (ISBN 0-8372-0830-0); Monster Meets Lady Monster (ISBN 0-8372-0831-9); Monster Goes to the Museum (ISBN 0-8372-0832-7); Monster Goes to School (ISBN 0-8372-0833-5); Monster at School (ISBN 0-8372-0834-3); Monster & the Magic Umbrella (ISBN 0-8372-0835-1); Monster Has a Party (ISBN 0-8372-0836-X); Monster Goes to the Zoo (ISBN 0-8372-0837-8); Monster & the Toy Sale (ISBN 0-8372-2133-1). (Illus., Avail. in Spanish). (ps-3). 1973. pap. 1.50 ea.; pap. 169.95 set of 10 ea. of 12 titles & tchr's. guide (ISBN 0-8372-0300-7, 300); pap. 17.85 set of monster bks. 1 ea. title & tchr's. guide (ISBN 0-8372-0301-5, 301). Bowmar-Noble.

--More Monster Books: Set 2, 12 bks. Incl. Monster & the Mural (ISBN 0-8372-2124-2); Monster, Lady Monster & the Bike Ride (ISBN 0-8372-2125-0); Lady Monster Helps Out (ISBN 0-8372-2126-9); Monster Goes to the Circus (ISBN 0-8372-2127-7); Monster Goes to the Hospital (ISBN 0-8372-2128-5); Monster Goes to the Beach (ISBN 0-8372-2129-3); Monster Gets a Job (ISBN 0-8372-2130-7); Monster & the Surprise Cookie (ISBN 0-8372-2131-5); Monster Goes Around the Town (ISBN 0-8372-2132-3); Monster Buys a Pet (ISBN 0-8372-2134-X); Lady Monster Has a Plan (ISBN 0-8372-2135-8). (Illus., Avail. in Span.). (ps-3). 1976. pap. 1.50 ea.; pap. text ed. 17.85 12 bks. 1 of ea. & tchr's guide (ISBN 0-8372-2122-6, 2122); pap. text ed. 169.95 120 bks 10 of ea. & tchr's guide (ISBN 0-8372-2123-4, 2123). Bowmar-Noble.

Blanch, Jose M., tr. see Lebar, Lois & Berg, Miguel.

Blanch, Leslie. Wilder Shores of Love. 1970. pap. 3.95 o.p. (ISBN 0-671-20508-0, Touchstone Bks). S&S.

Blanch, Michael. Soldiers. LC 82-50400. (History Eye Witness Ser.). PLB 15.96 (ISBN 0-382-06663-4). Silver.

Blanch, Stuart. For All Mankind: A New Approach to the Old Testament. 10.95 o.p. (ISBN 0-19-520024-1, GB 546); pap. 3.95 (ISBN 0-19-520025-X). Oxford U Pr.

Blanchard, Adele B. Quickscript: The Fast & Simple Shorthand Method. LC 82-67031. 160p. 1982. pap. 4.95 (ISBN 0-668-05572-3, 5572). Arco.

Blanchard, Alain A. Phase-Locked Loops: Application to Coherent Receiver Design. LC 75-30941. 1976. 41.50x (ISBN 0-471-07941-3, Pub. by Wiley-Interscience). Wiley.

Blanchard, B. & Fabrycky, W. Systems Engineering & Analysis. 1981. 29.95 (ISBN 0-13-881631-X). P-H.

Blanchard, Benjamin S. Engineering Organization & Management. (P-H International Industrial & System Engineering Ser.). (Illus.). 544p. 1976. 25.95 (ISBN 0-13-279430-6). P-H.

--Logistics Engineering & Management. (Int'l. Series in Industrial Systems Engr.). (Illus.). 416p. 1974. ref. ed. 29.95 o.p. (ISBN 0-13-540047-3). P-H.

--Logistics Engineering & Management. 2nd ed. (P-H Ser. in Industrial & Systems Engineering). (Illus.). 464p. 1981. text ed. 29.95 (ISBN 0-13-540088-0). P-H.

Blanchard, Caroline, jt. ed. see Blanchard, Robert J.

Blanchard, Fessenden, jt. auth. see Stone, William T.

Blanchard, Fessenden S., jt. auth. see Stone, William T.

Blanchard, Homer D., tr. see Lindow, Ch. W.

Blanchard, J. M. & Gavronsky, S. La Litterature Francaise: Le Milieu et le Moment, Vol. 1: Le Moyen Age. 1972. pap. 8.95 (ISBN 0-02-310680-8). Macmillan.

Blanchard, John. Right with God. LC 78-6809. 1978. pap. 2.95 (ISBN 0-8024-7357-1). Moody.

Blanchard, Kenneth & Johnson, Spencer. The One Minute Manager. Golbitz, Pat, ed. LC 82-8106. 112p. 1982. 15.00 (ISBN 0-688-01429-1). Morrow.

Blanchard, Kenneth H., jt. auth. see Hersey, Paul.

Blanchard, Leslie. Leslie Blanchard's Hair Coloring Book. Hanle, Zack, as told to. LC 78-1181. (Illus.). 128p. 1982. 17.95 (ISBN 0-385-12484-8). Doubleday.

Blanchard, Nina. How to Break into Motion Pictures, Television Commercials & Modeling. 1980. pap. 2.50 o.p. (ISBN 0-380-47118-3, 47118). Avon.

--How to Break into Motion Pictures, Television, Commercials & Modeling. LC 77-14890. 1978. 11.95 (ISBN 0-385-14109-2). Doubleday.

Blanchard, Paula. Margaret Fuller: From Transcendentalist to Revolution. (Radcliffe Biography Ser.). 1978. 11.95 o.s.i. (ISBN 0-440-05314-5, Sey Lawr). Delacorte.

--Margaret Fuller: From Transcendentalism to Revolution. 1979. pap. 5.95 o.s.i. (ISBN 0-440-56242-2, Delta). Dell.

Blanchard, Peter. The Origins of the Peruvian Labor Movement, 1883-1919. LC 81-23102. (Pitt Latin American Ser.). xx, 214p. 1982. 23.95 (ISBN 0-8229-3455-8). U of Pittsburgh Pr.

Blanchard, Robert J. & Blanchard, Caroline, eds. Advances in the Study of Aggression, Vol. 1. (Serial Publication). 238p. 1983. price not set (ISBN 0-12-037701-2). Acad Pr.

Blanchard, William. Aggression: American Style. LC 77-28051. 1978. pap. 12.50x (ISBN 0-673-16254-0). Scott F.

Blanchard, William H. Revolutionary Morality: Psychosexual Analysis of Twelve Revolutionists. c, 400p. (Orig.). (gr. 12). 1983. lib. bdg. 24.75 (ISBN 0-87436-032-3); pap. 14.75 (ISBN 0-87436-039-0). ABC Clio.

Blanche, Ella. Searching the Shadows. (Contemporary Poets Ser.: No. 1). 48p. (Orig.). 1983. pap. 3.95 (ISBN 0-916982-26-2, RL226). Realities.

Blanchfield, William C., jt. auth. see Oser, Jacob.

Blanchflower, Danny. Soccer My Way. pap. 5.00x (ISBN 0-392-07454-0, SpS). Sportshelf.

Blanchi, D. E., jt. auth. see Sheeler, P.

Blanchot, Maurice. Death Sentence. Davis, Lydia, tr. from French. LC 78-59907. Orig. Title: L'Arret De Mort. 88p. 1978. 10.00 (ISBN 0-930794-05-2); pap. 4.95 (ISBN 0-930794-04-4). Station Hill Pr.

--The Madness of the Day: La Folie du Jour. Davis, Lydia, tr. Orig. Title: La Folie Du Jour. 32p. (Eng. & Fr.). 1981. 8.50 (ISBN 0-930794-39-7); pap. 3.95 (ISBN 0-930794-36-2). Station Hill Pr.

--The Space of Literature: A Translation of "L'Espace Litteraire". Smock, Ann, tr. from Fr. LC 82-2062. vii, 276p. 1982. 23.50x (ISBN 0-8032-1166-X). U of Nebr Pr.

Blanck, Jacob, compiled by. Bibliographyoff American Literature, 7 vols. Incl. Vol. 1. Henry Adams to Donn Byrne. xlix, 474p. 1955. 50.00x (ISBN 0-300-00310-2); Vol. 2. George W. Cable to Timothy Dwight. xix, 534p. 1957. 50.00x (ISBN 0-300-00311-0); Vol. 3. Edward Eggleston to Bret Harte. xxi, 482p. 1959. 50.00x (ISBN 0-300-00312-9); Vol. 4. Nathaniel Hawthorne to Joseph Holt Ingraham. xxii, 495p. 1963. 50.00x (ISBN 0-300-00313-7); Vol. 5. Washington Irving to Henry Wadsworth Longfellow. xxii, 1969p. 1969. 60.00x (ISBN 0-300-01099-0); Vol. 6. Augustus Baldwin Longstreet to Thomas William Parsons. LC 54-5283. 608p. 1973. 50.00x (ISBN 0-300-01618-2); Vol. 7. James Kirke Paulding to Frank Richard Stockton. 700p. text ed. 75.00x (ISBN 0-300-02636-6). LC 54-5283. (Illus.). Yale U Pr.

Blanc-LaPierre, A. Mankind & Energy: Needs, Resources, Hopes. (Studies in Environmental Science: Vol. 16). 1982. 149.00 (ISBN 0-444-99715-6). Elsevier.

Blanco, L., jt. auth. see Bassols, C.

Blanco, Miquel A., jt. auth. see Watson, E. W.

Blanco, Ralph F. & Rosenfeld, Joseph G. Case Studies in Clinical & School Psychology. 2nd ed. (Illus.). 256p. 1982. 17.75x (ISBN 0-398-03807-4). C C Thomas.

Blancq, Charles. Sonny Rollins: The Journey of a Jazzman. (Music Ser.). 160p. (gr. 10-12). 1982. pap. 18.95 (ISBN 0-8057-9460-3, Twayne). G K Hall.

Bland, Alexander. Men Dancing. (Illus.). 192p. 1983. 35.00 (ISBN 0-686-97321-6). Macmillan.

Bland, D. S. Three Revels from the Inns of the Court. 1981. 45.00x o.p. (ISBN 0-86127-402-4, Pub. by Avebury Pub England). State Mutual Bk.

Bland, Glenn. Success: The Glenn Bland Method. 1983. pap. 2.95 (ISBN 0-8423-6689-X). Tyndale.

Bland, Jeffrey. Choline, Lecithin Inositol. Passwater, Richard, ed. (Good Health Guide Ser.). 1983. pap. 1.45 (ISBN 0-87983-277-0). Keats.

--Octacosanol & Glucamannan. Passwater, Richard A. & Mindell, Earl, eds. (Good Health Guide Ser.). 36p. 1982. pap. text ed. 1.45 (ISBN 0-87983-316-5). Keats.

--Your Health under Siege. 256p. 1982. pap. 8.50 (ISBN 0-8289-0416-2). Greene.

--Your Health Under Siege: Using Nutrition to Fight Back. 224p. 1981. 12.95 o.p. (ISBN 0-8289-0415-4). Greene.

Bland, Jeffrey, ed. Medical Applications of Clinical Nutrition. LC 82-84365. 250p. 1983. 25.00 (ISBN 0-87983-327-0). Keats.

Bland, Margaret. Shadows of Things Past. 1982. 5.95 (ISBN 0-686-84431-9). Vantage.

Bland, Michael. The Executive's Guide to TV & Radio Appearances. LC 79-9607. (Video Bookshelf Ser.). 138p. 1980. text ed. 14.95 (ISBN 0-914236-53-9). Knowledge Indus.

Bland, Robert. The Four Slaves of Cythera, a Romance in Ten Cantos. Reiman, Donald H., ed. LC 75-31160. (Romantic Context Ser.: Poetry 1789-1830: Vol. 15). 1978. Repr. of 1809 ed. lib. bdg. 47.00 o.s.i. (ISBN 0-8240-2114-2). Garland Pub.

Bland, Roger G. & Jaques, H. E. How to Know the Insects. 3rd ed. (Pictured Key Nature Ser.). 400p. 1978. text ed. o.p. (ISBN 0-697-04753-9); wire coil avail. (ISBN 0-697-04752-0). Wm C Brown.

Bland, William F. & Davidson, R. L. Petroleum Processing Handbook. 1967. 76.50 (ISBN 0-07-005860-1, P&RB). McGraw.

Blanda, George & Herskowitz, Mickey. Over Forty Feeling Great & Looking Good. 1978. 9.95 o.p. (ISBN 0-671-22472-7). S&S.

Blandford. The Master Handbook of Sheetmetalwork--with Projects. 378p. 1981. 16.95 (ISBN 0-8306-9644-X); pap. 9.95 (ISBN 0-8306-1257-2, 1257). TAB Bks.

Blandford, Linda, jt. auth. see Evans, Patricia.

Blandford, Percy. The Upholsterer's Bible. 1978. 14.95 o.p. (ISBN 0-8306-9986-4); pap. 9.95 (ISBN 0-8306-1004-9, 1004). TAB Bks.

--The Woodworker's Bible. LC 76-8647. (Illus.). 1976. pap. 8.95 o.p. (ISBN 0-8306-5860-2, 860). TAB Bks.

Blandford, Percy W. Country Craft Tools. LC 73-22569. (Illus.). 240p. 1974. 30.00x (ISBN 0-8103-2011-8). Gale.

--Old Farm Tools & Machinery: An Illustrated History. LC 75-44376. 1976. 36.00x (ISBN 0-8103-2019-3). Gale.

Blandy, John. Lecture Notes on Urology. (Illus.). 192p. 1975. 10.00 o.p. (ISBN 0-685-59087-9, 08899, Blackwell). Mosby.

Blaney, Harry C. Global Challenges. 1979. 12.95 o.p. (ISBN 0-531-05408-X); pap. 6.95 o.p. (ISBN 0-531-05619-8). Watts.

Blank, Chotsie. California Artists Cookbook. LC 82-6798. (Illus.). 216p. 1982. 25.00 (ISBN 0-89659-246-4). Abbeville Pr.

Blank, David. Ancient Philosophy & Grammar: The Syntax of Apollonius Dyscolus. LC 82-5751. (American Philological Association, American Classical Studies). 136p. 1982. pap. 11.25 (ISBN 0-89130-580-7, 40 04 10). Scholars Pr CA.

Blank, H., ed. see International Conference, 5th, Baden-Baden, Sep. 10-13, 1975.

Blank, H., jt. ed. see Muller, W.

Blank, Hannah I. Mastering Micros. (Illus.). 250p. 1983. 24.95x (ISBN 0-89433-207-4). Petrocelli.

Blank, Joan. Laugh Lines. (Illus.). 96p. (Orig.). 1982. pap. 4.95 (ISBN 0-941374-01-7). Grapetree Prods.

Blank, Joani. Good Vibrations: The Complete Guide to Vibrators. 52p. 1982. pap. 4.50 (ISBN 0-940208-05-9). Down There Pr.

Blank, Joseph P. Nineteen Steps up the Mountain: The Story of the DeBolt Family. LC 76-22659. (Illus.). 1976. 11.49i (ISBN 0-397-01155-5). Har-Row.

Blank, Leland T. Statistical Procedures for Engineering, Management & Science. (Industrial Engineering & Management Science Ser.). (Illus.). 1980. text ed. 29.95 (ISBN 0-07-005851-2). McGraw.

Blank, Leland T. & Tarquin, Anthony J. Engineering Economy. (Illus.). 1975. text ed. 29.95 (ISBN 0-07-062934-X, C); solutions manual 25.00 (ISBN 0-07-062935-8). McGraw.

--Engineering Economy. 2nd ed. (Illus.). 496p. 1983. text ed. 26.50 (ISBN 0-07-062961-7); write for info solutions manual (ISBN 0-07-062962-5). McGraw.

Blank, Marion S., compiled by. Working with People: A Selected Social Casework Bibliography. 2nd ed. 94p. 1981. pap. 7.95 o.p. (ISBN 0-87304-161-5). Family Serv.

--Working with People: A Selected Social Casework Bibliography. 2nd ed. LC 81-43789. 126p. 1982. 7.95 (ISBN 0-87304-193-3). Family Serv.

Blank, Nina, et al, eds. see Rama, Frederick Lenz.

Blank, R. Political Parties: An Introduction. 1980. 22.95 (ISBN 0-13-684761-7). P-H.

Blank, Robert H. The Political Implications of Human Genetic Technology. (Special Studies in Science, Technology, & Public Policy). 209p. (Orig.). 1981. lib. bdg. 26.50 (ISBN 0-89158-975-9); pap. text ed. 12.00 (ISBN 0-86531-193-5). Westview.

--Regional Diversity of Political Values: Idaho Political Culture. LC 78-62742. 1978. pap. text ed. 9.50 (ISBN 0-8191-0590-2). U Pr of Amer.

Blank, Robert H., jt. ed. see Darrough, Masako N.

Blank, S., et al see Blom, G. M.

Blank, S. J., jt. auth. see Hobbs, D. A.

Blank, Thomas O. A Social Psychology of Developing Adults. LC 81-19835. (Personality Processes Ser.). 325p. 1982. 31.95 (ISBN 0-471-08787-4, Pub. by Wiley-Interscience). Wiley.

Blank, William E. Handbook for Developing Competency-Based Training Programs. (Illus.). 352p. 1982. 19.95 (ISBN 0-13-377416-3). P-H.

Blankenbaker, E. Keith. Modern Plumbing. rev. ed. LC 81-4114. (Illus.). 300p. 1981. text ed. 15.00 (ISBN 0-87006-325-1). Goodheart.

Blankenburg, Quirinus Van. Elementa Musica...'s. (Early Music Theory in the Low Countries Ser.: Vol. 4). 1973. Repr. of 1739 ed. wrappers 37.50 o.s.i. (ISBN 0-686-30910-3, Pub. by Frits Knuf Netherlands). Pendragon NY.

Blankenship, A. B. Professional Telephone Surveys. LC 77-7023. (Illus.). 1977. 27.50 (ISBN 0-07-005862-8, P&RB). McGraw.

Blankert, Albert, et al. Gods, Saints & Heroes: Dutch Painting in the Age of Rembrandt. LC 80-20371. (Illus.). pap. 14.00 (ISBN 0-89468-039-0). Natl Gallery Art.

Blanning, T. C. Reform & Revolution in Mainz, 1743-1803. (Studies in Early Modern History). 384p. 1974. 44.50 (ISBN 0-521-20418-6). Cambridge U Pr.

Blanpain, Jan & Delesie, Luk. Community Health Investment: Health Services Research in Belgium, France, Federal German Republic & the Netherlands. McLachlan, Gordon, ed. (Nuffield Publications Ser). 1976. 24.50x o.p. (ISBN 0-19-721391-X). Oxford U Pr.

Blanpain, Roger, ed. Comparative Labour Law & Industrial Relations. 416p. 1983. text ed. 30.00 (ISBN 0-87179-396-2). BNA.

Blanpied, Pamela W. Dragons: An Introduction to the Modern Infestation. LC 79-26465. (Illus.). 224p. (Orig.). 1981. 9.95 (ISBN 0-446-51205-2); pap. 2.75, 208p. (ISBN 0-446-90481-3). Warner Bks.

Blanqui, Adolphe. Des Classes Ouvrieres En France Pendant L'annee 1848. (Conditions in the 19th Century French Working Class Ser.). 255p. (Fr.). 1974. Repr. of 1849 ed. lib. bdg. 73.75x o.p. (ISBN 0-8287-0096-6, 1117). Clearwater Pub.

Blanshard, Brand. Nature of Thought, 2 Vols. (Muirhead Library of Philosophy). 1964. Set. text ed. 37.50x o.p. (ISBN 0-391-00923-0); Vol. 1. text ed. (ISBN 0-685-92789-X); Vol. 2. text ed. (ISBN 0-685-92790-3); pap. text ed. 42.50x o.p. (ISBN 0-391-00923-0). Humanities.

--Reason & Analysis. 2nd ed. LC 62-9576. (Paul Carus Lectures Ser.). 505p. 1962. 27.00 (ISBN 0-87548-104-3). Open Court.

--The Uses of a Liberal Education, & Other Talks to Students. 436p. 1974. 24.50 (ISBN 0-87548-122-1). Open Court.

Blanshard, J. M. & Mitchell, J. R. Polysaccharides in Food. new ed. LC 79-40370. (Studies in the Agricultural & Food Sciences). (Illus.). 1979. text ed. 67.95 (ISBN 0-408-10618-2). Butterworth.

Blanshard, Paul. Communism, Democracy, & Catholic Power. LC 75-156175. 340p. 1972. Repr. of 1952 ed. lib. bdg. 18.50x (ISBN 0-8371-6118-5, BLCD). Greenwood.

--The Irish & Catholic Power: An American Interpretation. LC 70-112321. 375p. 1972. Repr. of 1953 ed. lib. bdg. 18.50x (ISBN 0-8371-4708-5, BLIC). Greenwood.

--Some of My Best Friends Are Christians. LC 74-744. 200p. 1974. 15.50x (ISBN 0-87548-149-3). Open Court.

Blanshard, Paul, ed. Classics of Free Thought. LC 77-73846. (Skeptic's Bookshelf Ser.). 190p. 1977. 12.95 (ISBN 0-87975-071-5); pap. 5.95 o.p. (ISBN 0-87975-079-0). Prometheus Bks.

Blansitt, E., jt. auth. see Lado, Robert.

Blansitt, Edward L., Jr., ed. A Festschrift for Jacob Ornstein: Studies in General Linguistics & Sociolinguistics. Teschner, Richard V. (Orig.). 1980. pap. text ed. 17.95 (ISBN 0-88377-172-1). Newbury Hse.

Blanton, Linda L. Elementary Composition Practice Book 1. 1978. pap. text ed. 7.95 (ISBN 0-88377-112-8). Newbury Hse.

--Intermediate Composition Practice, Bk I. (Illus., Orig.). (gr. 7-12). 1981. pap. text ed. 7.95 (ISBN 0-88377-194-2). Newbury Hse.

Blaquier, Jorge A., jt. auth. see DeNicola, Alejandro F.

Blaquiere, A., jt. auth. see Avez, A.

Blaquiere, Austin, ed. Topics in Differential Games. LC 73-75528. 460p. 1973. 42.75 (ISBN 0-444-10467-4, North-Holland). Elsevier.

Blasberg, Robert W. & Bohdan, Carol L. Fulper Art Pottery: An Aesthetic Appreciation 1909-1929. (Illus.). 88p. pap. 15.00 (ISBN 0-942410-00-9). Jordan-Volpe Gall.

Blaschke, W. S. & McGill, J. The Control of Industrial Processes by Digital Techniques: The Organization, Design & Construction of Digital Control Systems. 1976. 47.00 (ISBN 0-444-41493-2). Elsevier.
Blaschke, Wilhelm. Differentialgeometrie, 2 Vols. in 1. LC 62-11596. (Ger). 35.00 (ISBN 0-8284-0202-7). Chelsea Pub.
Blase, Melvin G., ed. Institutions in Agricultural Development. LC 72-137088. 1971. 8.95x (ISBN 0-8138-0855-3). Iowa St U Pr.
Blaser, Werner. Filigree Architecture: Metal & Glass Construction. (Illus.). 216p. (Eng. Fr. & Ger.). 1980. pap. 19.00 o.p. (ISBN 0-89192-298-9). Transbooks.
--Folding Chairs, Klappstuehle. 110p. 1982. 17.95 (ISBN 3-7643-1357-9). Birkhauser.
--The Rock Is My Home: Structures in Stone. (Illus.). 224p. (Eng., Fr. & Ger.). 1976. pap. 15.00 o.p. (ISBN 0-89192-299-7). Transbooks.
--Wood Houses: Form in Rural Architecture. (Illus.). 216p. (Eng., Fr. & Ger.). 1980. pap. 19.00 o.p. (ISBN 0-89192-300-4). Transbooks.
--Wooden Bridges in Switzerland (Ponts de Bois en Suisse; Schweizer Holzbrucken) 184p. 1982. 49.95 (ISBN 3-7643-1334-X). Birkhauser.
Blasewitz, A. G. & Davis, John M., eds. Treatment & Handling of Radioactive Wastes. LC 82-22695. 672p. 1983. 65.00 (ISBN 0-935470-14-X). Battelle.
Blashford-Snell, John & Ballantine, Alistair, eds. Expeditions: The Experts' Way. (Illus.). 256p. 1977. pap. 7.50 (ISBN 0-571-11116-5). Faber & Faber.
Blasi, Anthony J. Segregationist Violence & Civil Rights Movements in Tuscaloosa. LC 79-3714. 1980. text ed. 17.75 o.p. (ISBN 0-8191-0913-4); pap. text ed. 9.50 o.p. (ISBN 0-8191-0914-2). U Pr of Amer.
Blasi, Anthony J., et al. Toward an Interpretive Sociology. 1978. pap. text ed. 15.25 (ISBN 0-8191-0382-9). U Pr of Amer.
Blasier, Cole, ed. Constructive Change in Latin America. LC 68-12724. (Pitt Latin American Ser.). 1968. 12.95 (ISBN 0-8229-3145-1). U of Pittsburgh Pr.
Blasing, Randy. To Continue. 75p. (Orig.). 1983. cancelled 10.95 (ISBN 0-89255-070-8); pap. 5.95 (ISBN 0-89255-071-6). Persea Bks.
Blasing, Randy, tr. see Hiket, Nazim.
Blasing, Randy, tr. see Hikmet, Nazim.
Blasio, Jose L. Maximilian, Emperor of Mexico. 1934. text ed. 42.50x (ISBN 0-686-83620-0). Elliots Bks.
Blasis, Celeste De see De Blasis, Celeste.
Blass, Bill, jt. auth. see Molinsky, Steven J.
Blass, Thomas. Contemporary Social Psychology: Representative Readings. LC 75-17318. 1976. pap. text ed. 12.95 (ISBN 0-87581-190-6, 190). Peacock Pubs.
Blassingame, jt. auth. see Cottman.
Blassingame, John W. The Slave Community: Plantation Life in the Ante-Bellum South. 2nd rev. enl. ed. (Illus.). 1979. 18.95x (ISBN 0-19-502562-8); pap. text ed. 7.95x (ISBN 0-19-502563-6). Oxford U Pr.
Blassingame, John W. & Henderson, Mae G. Anti-Slavery Newspapers & Periodicals: An Annotated Index of Letters in the Philanthropist Emancipator, Genius of Universal Emancipation, Abolition Intelligencer, African Observer & the Liberator, 1817-1845. 1980. lib. bdg. 70.00 (ISBN 0-8161-8163-2, Hall Reference). G K Hall.
--Antislavery Newspapers & Periodicals: Annotated Index of Letters, 1817 - 1871, Vol. III: 1836-1854. 1981. lib. bdg. 80.00 (ISBN 0-8161-8558-1, Hall Reference). G K Hall.
--Antislavery Newspapers & Periodicals, Vol. II: Annotated Index of Letters in the "Liberator, Anti-Slavery Record, Human Rights & Observer, 1846-1865. 1980. lib. bdg. 70.00 (ISBN 0-8161-8434-8, Hall Reference). G K Hall.
Blassingame, John W., jt. auth. see Berry, Mary F.
Blassingame, Wyatt. Bent's Fort: Crossroads of the Great West. LC 67-10020. (How They Lived Ser). (Illus.). (gr. 3-6). 1967. PLB 6.48 o.p. (ISBN 0-8116-6906-8). Garrard.
--Bowleg Bill: Seagoing Cowboy. LC 75-22230. (American Folktales Ser.). (Illus.). 48p. (gr. 2-5). 1976. PLB 6.09 o.p. (ISBN 0-8116-4044-2). Garrard.
--Dan Beard: Scoutmaster of America. LC 72-76325. (Illus.). (gr. 2-5). 1972. PLB 3.98 (ISBN 0-8116-6754-5). Garrard.
--The Everglades: From Yesterday to Tomorrow. (Illus.). 128p. (gr. 6 up). 1974. PLB 5.29 o.p. (ISBN 0-399-60866-4). Putnam Pub Group.
--Franklin D. Roosevelt: Four Times President. LC 66-10024. (Discovery Books Ser.). (Illus.). (gr. 2-5). 1966. PLB 6.69 (ISBN 0-8116-6294-2). Garrard.
--How Davy Crockett Got a Bearskin Coat. LC 74-180783. (American Folktales). (Illus.). 36p. (gr. 2-5). 1972. PLB 6.69 (ISBN 0-8116-4035-3). Garrard.
--Jim Beckwourth: Black Trapper & Indian Chief. LC 73-5698. (Discovery Ser). (Illus.). 80p. (gr. 2-5). 1973. PLB 6.69 (ISBN 0-8116-6314-0). Garrard.
--John Henry & Paul Bunyan Play Baseball. LC 72-151138. (American Folktales Ser.). (Illus.). (gr. 2-5). 1971. PLB 6.69 (ISBN 0-8116-4027-2). Garrard.
--Joseph Stalin & Communist Russia. LC 70-153153. (Century Biographies Ser.). (Illus.). (gr. 4-8). 1971. PLB 3.98 (ISBN 0-8116-4753-6). Garrard.
--The Little Killers: Fleas, Lice & Mosquitoes. 128p. (gr. 5 up). 1975. 5.95 o.p. (ISBN 0-399-20466-0). Putnam Pub Group.
--Paul Bunyan Fights the Monster Plants. LC 73-16032. (American Folktales Ser.). (Illus.). 40p. (gr. 2-5). 1974. PLB 6.69 (ISBN 0-8116-4039-6). Garrard.
--Pecos Bill & the Wonderful Clothesline Snake. LC 77-17972. (American Folktales Ser.). (Illus.). (gr. 2-5). 1978. PLB 6.69 (ISBN 0-8116-4046-9). Garrard.
--Pecos Bill Catches a Hidebehind. LC 76-23336. (American Folktales Ser.). (Illus.). (gr. 2-5). 1977. lib. bdg. 6.69 (ISBN 0-8116-4045-0). Garrard.
--Pecos Bill Rides a Tornado. LC 73-5894. (American Folktales Ser.). (Illus.). (gr. 2-5). 1973. PLB 6.69 (ISBN 0-8116-4038-8). Garrard.
--Porcupines. LC 82-7379. (Skylight Bk.). (Illus.). 64p. (gr. 2-5). 1982. PLB 7.95 (ISBN 0-396-08074-X). Dodd.
--Story of the Boy Scouts. LC 68-13593. (American Democracy Ser). (Illus.). (gr. 3-6). 1968. PLB 7.12 (ISBN 0-8116-6500-3). Garrard.
--Story of the United States Flag. LC 68-10030. (American Democracy Ser). (Illus.). (gr. 3-6). 1969. PLB 7.12 (ISBN 0-8116-6502-X). Garrard.
--The U. S. Frogmen of World War II. (Landmark Ser.: No. 106). (gr. 5-9). 1964. 2.95 (ISBN 0-394-80406-6); PLB 4.39 (ISBN 0-394-90406-0). Random.
--William Beebe: Underwater Explorer. LC 75-29069. (Americans All Ser). (Illus.). 96p. (gr. 3-6). 1976. PLB 7.12 (ISBN 0-8116-4584-3). Garrard.
Blatch, Harriot S. Mobilizing Woman-Power. LC 74-75231. (The United States in World War 1 Ser). (Illus.). iv, 195p. 1974. Repr. of 1918 ed. lib. bdg. 13.95x (ISBN 0-89198-094-6). Ozer.
Blatchford, William, ed. see Pearl, Cora.
Blate, Michael. First-Aid Using Simple Remedies. (The G-Jo Institute Self-Health Ser.). (Illus.). 196p. (Orig.). 1983. pap. 8.95 (ISBN 0-916878-17-1). Falkynor Bks.
--The G-Jo Institute Manual of Medicinal Herbs. (The G-Jo Institute Self-Health Ser.). (Illus.). 96p. (Orig.). 1983. pap. 6.95 (ISBN 0-916878-19-8). Falkynor Bks.
--How to Heal Yourself Using Foot Acupressure (Foot Reflexology) (The G-Jo Institute Self-Health Ser.). (Illus.). 185p. (Orig.). 1982. pap. 8.95 (ISBN 0-916878-22-8). Falkynor Bks.
--How to Heal Yourself Using Hand Acupressure (Hand Reflexology) (The G-Jo Institute Self-Health Ser.). (Illus.). 195p. (Orig.). 1982. pap. 8.95 (ISBN 0-916878-21-X). Falkynor Bks.
--The Natural Healer's Acupressure Handbook: Advanced G-Jo, Vol. 2. (The G-Jo Institute Self-Health Ser.). (Illus.). 272p. 1982. case 12.95 (ISBN 0-916878-14-7). Falkynor Bks.
--The Natural Healer's Acupressure Handbook, Vol. 1, revised: Basic G-Jo. (The G-Jo Institute Self-Health Ser.). (Illus.). 224p. 1982. case 12.95 (ISBN 0-686-37114-3). Falkynor Bks.
Blatt, A. H. Organic Synthesis Collective Volumes, Vol. 2. 654p. 1943. 35.95 (ISBN 0-471-07986-3). Wiley.
Blatt, Burton. In & Out of the University. LC 81-1652. 224p. 1982. pap. text ed. 21.95 (ISBN 0-8391-1734-5, 18333). Univ Park.
--Revolt of the Idiots. 1976. 10.95 (ISBN 0-686-84868-3). Exceptional Pr Inc.
Blatt, H., et al. Origin of Sedimentary Rock. 2nd ed. 1980. 37.95 (ISBN 0-13-642710-3). P-H.
Blatt, Max, compiled by. Index to Monthly Review: May 1949-April 1981. LC 81-85233. 1982. 25.00 (ISBN 0-85345-585-6, CL5856). Monthly Rev.
Blattner, Barbara. Holistic Nursing. (Illus.). 400p. 1981. text ed. 20.95 (ISBN 0-13-392563-3); pap. text ed. 16.95 (ISBN 0-686-68605-5). P-H.
Blatz, Hanson. Introduction to Radiological Health. 1964. text ed. 27.50 o.p. (ISBN 0-07-005884-9, P&RB). McGraw.
Blau, Esther, ed. The Spice & Spirit of Kosher-Jewish Cooking. LC 77-72116. (Illus.). 1977. 14.95 (ISBN 0-8197-0455-5). Bloch.
Blau, Herbert. Blooded Thought: Occasions of Theatre. LC 82-81976. 1982. 18.95 (ISBN 0-933826-38-9); pap. 6.95 (ISBN 0-933826-39-7). Performing Arts.
Blau, J. L. Pragmatism & Other Essays. 1983. pap. 3.95 (ISBN 0-686-37708-7). WSP.
Blau, J. L., ed. see James, William.
Blau, Joshua. The Renaissance of Modern Hebrew & Modern Standard Arabic: Parallels & Differences in the Revival of Two Semitic Languages. (Publications in Near East Studies: Vol. 18). 1982. 21.00 (ISBN 0-520-09548-0). U of Cal Pr.
Blau, Judith H. & Dean, L. The Bagel Baker of Mulliner Lane. (Illus.). (ps-5). 1976. 7.95 (ISBN 0-07-005882-2, GB); PLB 7.95 o.p. (ISBN 0-07-005883-0). McGraw.
Blau, K., ed. Handbook of Derivatives for Chromatography. King, G. 99.95 (ISBN 0-471-25597-1, Pub. by Wiley Heyden). Wiley.
Blau, Melinda. First Over the Oceans. LC 78-12960. (Famous Firsts Ser.). (Illus.). 1978. PLB 10.76 (ISBN 0-89547-050-0). Silver.
Blau, Peter M. Exchange & Power in Social Life. LC 64-23827. 352p. 1964. 29.95x (ISBN 0-471-08030-6). Wiley.
--On the Nature of Organizations. LC 81-19330. 368p. 1983. write for info. (ISBN 0-89874-463-6). Krieger.
--On the Nature of Organizations. LC 74-7392. 358p. 1974. 31.95 o.p. (ISBN 0-471-08037-3, Pub. by Wiley-Interscience). Wiley.
--The Organization of Academic Work. LC 73-6992. 310p. 1973. 25.50 o.p. (ISBN 0-471-08025-X, Pub. by Wiley-Interscience). Wiley.
Blauch, Lloyd E., ed. see U. S. Office Of Education.
Blauer, Stephen. The Miracle of Sprouting. 80p. (Orig.). 1982. pap. 3.95 (ISBN 0-89529-177-0). Avery Pub.
--Rejuvenation: Dr. Ann Wigmore's Complete Diet & Health Program. 280p. (Orig.). 1982. pap. 4.95 (ISBN 0-89529-178-9). Avery Pub.
Blaufox, M. Donald, jt. ed. see Freeman, Leonard M.
Blaug, M. Economic Theory in Retrospect. LC 77-7899. 1978. 27.95x (ISBN 0-521-21733-4). Cambridge U Pr.
--Methodology of Appraisal of Marxian Economics. (Lectures in Economics Ser.: Vol. 3). 1980. 27.75 (ISBN 0-444-85424-X). Elsevier.
Blaug, Mark. Education & the Employment Problem in Developing Countries. 3rd ed. 1978. 6.85 (ISBN 92-2-101005-8). Intl Labour Office.
--The Methodology of Economics: Or How Economists Explain. LC 80-13802. (Cambridge Surveys of Economic Literature). 325p. 1980. 37.50 (ISBN 0-521-22288-5); pap. 12.95 (ISBN 0-521-29437-1). Cambridge U Pr.
--Ricardian Economics. LC 73-9208. 269p. 1973. Repr. of 1958 ed. lib. bdg. 17.75x (ISBN 0-8371-6982-8, BLRE). Greenwood.
Blaug, Mark, ed. The Economics of the Arts. LC 76-5889. 1976. 28.75 (ISBN 0-89158-613-X). Westview.
Blaug, Mark & Sturges, Paul, eds. Who's Who in Economics: A Biographical Dictionary of Major Economics, 1700-1981. 416p. 1983. 65.00x (ISBN 0-262-02188-9). MIT Pr.
Blaukopf, K., ed. The Phonogram in Cultural Communications. (Illus.). 180p. 1983. pap. 24.00 (ISBN 0-387-81725-5). Springer-Verlag.
Blaukopf, Kurt & Desmont, Mark, eds. The Cultural Behaviour of Youth: Towards a Cross-Cultural Survey in Europe & Asia. 1976. pap. 25.00 (ISBN 3-7024-0114-8, 51-26247). Eur-Am Music.
Blaukopf, Kurt, ed. see Bontinck-Kueffel, Irmgard.
Blauner, Robert. Alienation & Freedom: The Factory Worker & His Industry. LC 64-15820. 1967. pap. 3.45 (ISBN 0-226-05811-5, P271, Phoen). U of Chicago Pr.
Blaustein, Albert P. & Blaustien, Eric B., eds. Constitutions of Dependencies & Special Sovereignties, 6 vols. plus yearly supplements. LC 75-21651. 1977. Suppl. 75.00x ea.; Set. 600.00 (ISBN 0-379-00278-7). Oceana.
Blaustein, Albert P. & Flanz, Gisbert H., eds. Constitutions of the Countries of the World: Supplement Binder, 15 vols. plus 3-4 supplements a year. LC 76-141327. 1976. 75.00 ea. (ISBN 0-379-00467-4); Set. 1300.00 (ISBN 0-686-66329-2). Oceana.
Blaustein, Albert P., et al. Independence Documents of the World, 2 vols. LC 77-7333. 1977. Set. 85.00. Vol. 1 (ISBN 0-379-00794-0). Vol. 2 (ISBN 0-379-00795-9). Oceana.
Blaustein, Ancel. Interpretation of Biopsy of Endometrium. (Biopsy Interpretation Ser.). 207p. 1979. text ed. 30.00 (ISBN 0-89004-370-1). Raven.
Blaustein, Ancel U., et al. Pathology of the Ovary. 189p. 1974. pap. 147.50 o.p. (ISBN 0-7216-9858-1); cassette & filmstrips avail. o.p. (ISBN 0-7216-9815-8). Saunders.
Blaustein, Bernard D. & Bockrath, Bradley C., eds. New Approaches in Coal Chemistry. (ACS Symposium Ser.: No. 169). 1981. write for info. (ISBN 0-8412-0659-7). Am Chemical.
Blaustein, Randy B. How to Do Business with the IRS. LC 82-5319. 342p. 39.95 (ISBN 0-13-396168-0, Busn). P-H.
Blaustien, Eric B., jt. ed. see Blaustein, Albert P.
Blauvelt, Carolyn T. & Nelson, Fred. A Manual of Orthopaedic Terminology. 2nd ed. LC 81-4029. (Illus.). 257p. 1981. pap. text ed. 22.95 (ISBN 0-8016-0752-3). Mosby.
Blauvelt, Evan & Durlacher, Jennifer, eds. Sources of European Economic Information. 4th ed. 656p. 1983. ref 95.00x (ISBN 0-88410-888-0). Ballinger Pub.
Blauvelt, Evan, et al, eds. World Sources of Market Information: Vol. 3, Europe. Grindlays Bank Economics Dept. 360p. 1983. ref 95.00x (ISBN 0-88410-863-5). Ballinger Pub.
--World Sources of Market Information: Vol. 1, Asia & Pacific. Grindlays Bank Economics Dept. 352p. 1982. ref 95.00x (ISBN 0-88410-861-9). Ballinger Pub.
--World Sources of Market Information, Vol. 2: Africa-Middle East. Grindlays Bank Economics Dept. 304p. 1982. ref 95.00x (ISBN 0-88410-862-7). Ballinger Pub.
Blavatsky, H. P. Collected Writings of H. P. Blavatsky, Vol. 13. De Zirkoff, Boris, ed. LC 75-10528. (Illus.). 465p. 1983. 16.50 (ISBN 0-8356-0229-X). Theos Pub Hse.
Blavatsky, Helena P. Collected Writings of H. P. Blavatsky, Vols. 1-11. Incl. Vol. 1. 1874-1878. rev. ed. 14.50 (ISBN 0-8356-0082-3); Vol. 2. 1879-1880 (ISBN 0-8356-0091-2); Vol. 3. 1881-1882 (ISBN 0-8356-0099-8); Vol. 4. 1882-1883 (ISBN 0-8356-0106-4); Vol. 5. 1883 (ISBN 0-8356-0117-X); Vol. 6. 1883-1884-1885 (ISBN 0-8356-0125-0); Vol. 7. 1886-1887 (ISBN 0-8356-0222-2); Vol. 8. 1887 (ISBN 0-8356-7166-6); Vol. 9. 1888 (ISBN 0-8356-0217-6); Vol. 10. 1888-1889 (ISBN 0-8356-0218-4); Vol. 11. 1889. 14.50 (ISBN 0-686-86789-0). (Illus.). 16.50 ea. Theos Pub Hse.
--H. P. Blavatsky Collected Writings, Vol. XII. De Zirkoff, Boris, ed. LC 80-53953. (Illus.). 849p. 1981. cloth 16.50 (ISBN 0-8356-0228-1). Theos Pub Hse.
Blavatsky, Helene P. Theosophical Glossary. LC 74-142546. 1971. Repr. of 1892 ed. 40.00x (ISBN 0-8103-3679-0). Gale.
Blaxland, Gregory. J. H. Thomas: A Life for Unity. 17.50x (ISBN 0-392-07986-0, SpS). Sportshelf.
Blaxter, J. H., et al. Advances in Marine Biology, Vol. 20. (Serial Publication). 65.00 (ISBN 0-12-026120-0). Acad Pr.
Blaxter, K. Food Chains & Human Nutrition. 1980. 65.75 (ISBN 0-85334-863-4, Pub. by Applied Sci England). Elsevier.
Blaxter, K. L., ed. see Symposium On Energy Metabolism, Troon Scotland, 3d, 1964.
Blaxter, Mildred. The Health of the Children. (SSRC-DHSS Studies in Deprivation & Disadvantages: No. 3). 1982. text ed. 30.00x (ISBN 0-435-82034-6). Heinemann Ed.
Blaydes, Sophia B., jt. auth. see Bordinat, Philip.
Blaylock, James P. The Disappearing Dwarf. 288p. (Orig.). 1983. pap. 2.75 (ISBN 0-345-30376-8, Del Rey). Ballantine.
Blayne, Diana. White Sand, Wild Sea. (Candlelight Ecstasy Ser.: No. 138). (Orig.). 1983. pap. 1.95 (ISBN 0-440-19627-2). Dell.
Blaysek, J., jt. auth. see Balaz, S.
Blazek, Ron. Influencing Students Toward Media Center Use. LC 75-26769. (Studies in Librarianship Ser: No. 5). 238p. 1976. pap. text ed. 9.00 (ISBN 0-8389-0201-4). ALA.
Blazek, Ron, ed. Achieving Accountability. 280p. 1982. pap. text ed. 14.50 (ISBN 0-8389-0349-5). ALA.
Blazer, Don. Horses Don't Care About Women's Lib. LC 78-53437. 1978. 9.95 (ISBN 0-89325-010-4). Joyce Pr.
Blazier, Kenneth D. & Huber, Evelyn M. Planning Christian Education in Your Church. LC 73-19585. 32p. (Orig.). 1974. pap. 1.00 (ISBN 0-8170-0633-8); pap. 2.95 spanish ed (ISBN 0-8170-0685-0). Judson.
Bleakly, Kenneth, jt. auth. see Hughes, James.
Bleaney, Michael F. Underconsumption Theories. LC 76-26935. 1977. pap. 3.95 (ISBN 0-7178-0476-3). Intl Pub Co.
Bleau, Barbara L. Forgotten Algebra: A Refresher Course. (Barron's Educational Ser.). 1983. pap. text ed. 8.95 (ISBN 0-8120-2438-9). Barron.
Bleazard, G. B. Program Design Methods: Results of an NCC Study. LC 78-314354. 1976. pap. 15.50x (ISBN 0-85012-164-7). Intl Pubns Serv.
--Teleprocessing Monitor Packages for ICL 2903-04. 1978. pap. 34.50x (ISBN 0-85012-197-3). Intl Pubns Serv.
--Why Packet Switching. (Illus.). 174p. (Orig.). 1979. pap. 32.50x (ISBN 0-85012-194-9). Intl Pubns Serv.
Blecha, Diane, jt. auth. see Timmermann, Tim.
Blecher, George, tr. see Kullman, Harry.
Blecher, Lone T., tr. see Kullman, Harry.
Blecher, Marc J. & White, Gordon. Micropolitics in Contemporary China: A Technical Unit During & After the Cultural Revolution. LC 79-67176. 1980. 22.50 (ISBN 0-87332-136-7). M E Sharpe.
Blecher, Melvin & Barr, Robert S. Receptors & Human Disease. (Illus.). 332p. 1981. 50.00 (ISBN 0-686-77753-0, 0609-6). Williams & Wilkins.
Blechman, Barry M. The Changing Soviet Navy. (Studies in Defense Policy). 1973. pap. 4.95 (ISBN 0-8157-0995-1). Brookings.
--The Control of Naval Armaments: Prospects & Possibilities. (Studies in Defense Policy). 1975. 4.95 (ISBN 0-8157-0987-0). Brookings.
Blechman, Barry M. & Kaplan, Stephen S. Force Without War: U. S. Armed Forces As a Political Instrument. 1978. 28.95 (ISBN 0-8157-0986-2); pap. 14.95 (ISBN 0-8157-0985-4). Brookings.
Blechman, Barry M., jt. auth. see Quanbeck, Alton H.
Blechman, Barry M., ed. Rethinking the U. S. Strategic Posture. 320p. 1982. prof ref 28.00x (ISBN 0-88410-874-0); pap. 14.95x prof ref (ISBN 0-88410-910-0). Ballinger Pub.
Blechman, Barry M., et al. Setting National Priorities: The 1976 Budget. 200p. 1975. 14.95 (ISBN 0-8157-0992-7); pap. 5.95 (ISBN 0-8157-0991-9). Brookings.
--The Soviet Military Buildup & U. S. Defense Spending. (Studies in Defense Policy). 1977. pap. 4.95 (ISBN 0-8157-0989-7). Brookings.
--Setting National Priorities: The 1975 Budget. LC 74-282. 1974. 14.95 (ISBN 0-8157-0994-3); pap. 5.95 (ISBN 0-8157-0993-5). Brookings.
Bleck, Robert T., jt. auth. see Araoz, Daniel L.

Blecka, Lawernce J. Concise Medical Parasitology. LC 79-9452. 1980. pap. 19.95 (ISBN 0-686-96631-7, Med-Nurse). A-W.

Bleckman, Isaac A. Death & Dying A to Z. LC 80-65302. 1982. 69.00 (ISBN 0-87514-007-6). Croner.

Bledsoe, Dennis, jt. ed. see Cutino, Peter.

Bledsoe, Jerry. Where's Mark Twain When We Really Need Him? 183p. 1982. 9.95 (ISBN 0-9610320-0-6). Grape Hill Pr.

Bledsoe, John, tr. see Steiner, Rudolf.

Bledsoe, Marvin. Thunderbolt: Memoirs of a World War II Fighter Pilot. 282p. 1982. 15.95 (ISBN 0-442-21355-7). Van Nos Reinhold.

Bledsoe, Shirley, jt. auth. see MacKenzie, Joy.

Bledsoe, Thomas. Meanwhile Back at the Henhouse: A Novel. LC 82-71306. 185p. 1966. 4.95 (ISBN 0-8040-0197-9). Swallow.

Blee, Ben W. Battleship North Carolina. Conlon, Frank S. & Judd, Amos F., eds. (Illus.). 100p. 1982. 14.95 (ISBN 0-9608538-0-4); pap. 8.95 (ISBN 0-9608538-1-2). USS North Car.

Bleeck, Oliver. The Brass Go-Between. LC 82-48806. 224p. 1983. pap. 2.84i (ISBN 0-06-080645-1, P 645, PL). Har-Row.

--Protocol for a Kidnapping. LC 82-48807. 256p. 1983. pap. 2.84i (ISBN 0-06-080646-X, P 646, PL). Har-Row.

Bleehan & Glatstein. Radiation Therapy Planning, Vol. 1. (Fundamentals of Cancer Management). 792p. 1983. 69.75 (ISBN 0-8247-1830-5). Dekker.

Bleek, Wilhelm, jt. auth. see Sontheimer, Kurt.

Bleeker, P. & Healy, P. A. Analytical Data of Papua New Guinea Soils, 2 vols. 1982. 40.00x (ISBN 0-686-97924-9, Pub. by CSIRO Australia). State Mutual Bk.

Bleeker, Pieter. Atlas Ichtyologique Indes Orientales Neerlandaises, Vols. 11-14. (Atlas of Fishes of the Dutch East Indies). (Illus.). 200p. 1983. text ed. 250.00x (ISBN 0-87474-240-4). Smithsonian.

Bleeker, Sonia. The Apache Indians: Raiders of the Southwest. (Illus.). (gr. 4-7). 1951. PLB 8.16 (ISBN 0-688-31046-X). Morrow.

--The Ashanti of Ghana. (Illus.). (gr. 4-7). 1966. PLB 8.40 (ISBN 0-688-31052-4). Morrow.

--The Aztec: Indians of Mexico. (Illus.). (gr. 4-7). 1963. PLB 8.40 (ISBN 0-688-31057-5). Morrow.

--The Cherokee: Indians of the Mountains. (Illus.). (gr. 3-6). 1952. PLB 8.40 (ISBN 0-688-31160-1). Morrow.

--The Chippewa Indians: Rice Gatherers of the Great Lakes. (Illus.). (gr. 3-6). 1955. PLB 8.40 (ISBN 0-688-31167-9). Morrow.

--The Delaware Indians: Eastern Fishermen & Farmers. (Illus.). (gr. 3-6). 1953. PLB 8.40 (ISBN 0-688-31230-6). Morrow.

--The Eskimo: Arctic Hunters & Trappers. (Illus.). (gr. 3-6). 1959. PLB 8.40 (ISBN 0-688-31275-6). Morrow.

--The Inca: Indians of the Andes. (Illus.). (gr. 3-6). 1960. PLB 8.40 (ISBN 0-688-31417-1). Morrow.

--Indians of the Longhouse. (Illus.). (gr. 3-6). 1950. PLB 8.40 (ISBN 0-688-31453-8). Morrow.

--The Masai: Herders of East Africa. (Illus.). (gr. 3-6). 1963. PLB 8.40 (ISBN 0-688-31460-0). Morrow.

--The Maya: Indians of Central America. (Illus.). (gr. 3-6). 1961. PLB 8.40 (ISBN 0-688-31461-9). Morrow.

--The Navajo: Herders, Weavers & Silversmiths. (Illus.). (gr. 3-6). 1958. PLB 8.40 (ISBN 0-688-31456-2). Morrow.

--The Pygmies: Africans of the Congo Forest. LC 68-25481. (Illus.). (gr. 3-6). 1968. PLB 8.40 (ISBN 0-688-31462-7). Morrow.

--The Sea Hunters: Indians of the Northwestern Coast. (Illus.). (gr. 3-6). 1951. PLB 8.40 (ISBN 0-688-31458-9). Morrow.

--The Sioux Indians: Hunters & Warriors of the Plains. (Illus.). (gr. 3-6). 1962. PLB 8.40 (ISBN 0-688-31457-0). Morrow.

--The Zulu of South Africa, Cattlemen, Farmers, & Warriors. (Illus.). (gr. 3-6). 1970. PLB 8.40 (ISBN 0-688-31451-1). Morrow.

Blegen, Theodore C. The Land Lies Open. LC 74-27727. 246p. 1975. Repr. of 1949 ed. lib. bdg. 17.00x (ISBN 0-8371-7912-2, BLLO). Greenwood.

--The Voyageurs & Their Songs. 24p. 1966. pap. 1.75 (ISBN 0-87351-029-1). Minn Hist.

Blegvad, Erik, jt. auth. see Blegvad, Lenore.

Blegvad, Lenore & Blegvad, Erik. One Is for the Sun. LC 67-17151. (Illus.). (gr. k-3). 1968. 5.50 o.p. (ISBN 0-15-258685-7, HJ). HarBraceJ.

Bleher, Petra, jt. auth. see Vriends, Matthew M.

Bleher, Petra, tr. see Nicolai, Jurgen.

Blehl, Vincent & Connolly, Francis X., eds. Newman's Apologia: A Classic Reconsidered. LC 64-18283. 1964. 4.50 o.p. (ISBN 0-15-165204-X). HarBraceJ.

Blei, Norbert. Adventures in an American's Literature. 224p. (Orig.). 1982. pap. 5.95 (ISBN 0-933180-41-1). Ellis Pr.

--Dear Light. 240p. 1983. price not set (ISBN 0-933180-44-6). Ellis Pr.

Bleich, Arthur H. & McCullough, Jerry. The Photojournalists Guide: Keep the Sun at Your Back. Cryer, Gene, ed. (Illus.). 170p. (Orig.). 1980. pap. 8.95 (ISBN 0-937816-04-3). Tech Data.

Bleicher, F., et al. Highlights of Pewabic Pottery. LC 77-92628. 1977. pap. 8.50 (ISBN 0-89344-015-9). ARS Ceramica.

Bleicher, Josef. The Hermeneutic Imagination: Outline of a Positive Critique of Scientism & Sociology. 240p. 1982. 19.95x (ISBN 0-7100-9256-3); pap. 9.95 (ISBN 0-7100-9257-1). Routledge & Kegan.

Bleicher, Sheldon, jt. auth. see Brodoff, Bernard N.

Bleier, Inge J. Workbook in Bedside Maternity Nursing. 2nd ed. LC 71-151675. (Illus.). 175p. 1974. pap. text ed. 8.95 o.p. (ISBN 0-7216-1746-8). Saunders.

Bleifeld, Maurice. Barron's How to Prepare for the College Board Achievement Tests - Biology. 7th ed. LC 81-3892. 352p. 1981. 9.50 (ISBN 0-8120-5416-4); pap. 7.95 (ISBN 0-8120-2345-5). Barron.

Bleikasten, Andre. William Faulkner's The Sound & the Fury: Selected Criticism. LC 81-43365. 242p. 1982. lib. bdg. 30.00 (ISBN 0-8240-9269-4). Garland Pub.

Bleiler, E. F., ed. Three Supernatural Novels of the Victorian Period. Incl. The Haunted Hotel. Collins, Wilkie. Repr. of 1889 ed; The Haunted House at Latchford. Riddell. Orig. Title: Fairy Water. Repr. of 1878 ed; The Lost Stradivarius. Falkner, Meade. Repr. of 1896 ed. LC 74-82204. (Illus.). 352p. 1975. pap. 4.00 o.p. (ISBN 0-486-22571-2). Dover.

Bleiler, E. F., ed. see Futrelle, Jacques.

Bleiler, E. F., ed. see Meyrink, Gustav & Busson, Paul.

Bleiler, E. F., ed. see Mother Goose.

Bleiler, Ellen, tr. see Puccini, Giacomo.

Bleiler, Ellen, tr. see Verdi, Giuseppe.

Bleiler, Everett. A Treasury of Victorian Ghost Stories. 368p. 1983. pap. 7.95 (ISBN 0-686-83713-4, ScribT). Scribner.

Bleiler, Everett F. The Guide to Supernatural Fiction. 736p. 1983. 55.00X (ISBN 0-87338-288-9). Kent St U Pr.

Blejwas, Stanislaus A. & Biskupski, Mieczyslaw B., eds. Pastor of the Poles: Polish American Essays Presented to Right Reverend Monsignor John P. Wodarski. LC 82-72307. (Polish Studies Program Monographs: I). (Illus.). 223p. 1982. 15.00 (ISBN 0-910179-00-X). Polish Stud Prog.

Blendermann, Louis. Controlled Storm Water Drainage. LC 78-15080. (Illus.). 200p. 1979. 29.95 o.p. (ISBN 0-8311-1123-2). Indus Pr.

--Design of Plumbing & Drainage Systems. 3rd ed. (Illus.). 450p. 1982. write for info. o.p. (ISBN 0-8311-1142-9). Indus Pr.

Blendon, E. G. & Nalepa, B. H. Quick Survey Course in Forms Typing. 1967. standard ed. 4.96 (ISBN 0-07-005892-X, G); facsimile ed. 4.96 (ISBN 0-07-005891-1). McGraw.

Blendon, Robert J. & Moloney, Thomas W., eds. New Approaches to the Medicaid Crisis. (Health Care Economics & Technology Ser.). 480p. 1983. 33.95 (ISBN 0-86621-007-5). F&S Pr.

Blenkin & Kelly. Primary Curriculum in Action. 1983. text ed. 21.00 (ISBN 0-06-318223-8, Pub. by Har-Row Ltd England); pap. text ed. 10.50 (Pub. by Har-Row Ltd England). Har-Row.

Blenkin, Geva & Kelly, A. V. The Primary Curriculum. 1981. text ed. 19.95 (ISBN 0-06-318121-5, IntlDept); pap. text ed. 10.50 (ISBN 0-686-96732-1). Har-Row.

Blenkinsopp, J. Gibeon & Israel: The Role of Gibeon & the Gibeonites in the Political and Religious History of Early Israel. LC 74-171672. (Society for Old Testament Studies Monographs). 1972. 32.50 (ISBN 0-521-08368-0). Cambridge U Pr.

Blenkinsopp, Joseph. Deuteronomy. (Scripture Discussion Outlines Ser). 1968. pap. 0.75 o.p. (ISBN 0-685-07627-X, 80044). Glencoe.

--Genesis One-Eleven. 1969. pap. 0.75 o.p. (ISBN 0-685-07638-5, 80045). Glencoe.

--Prophecy & Canon: A Contribution to the Study of Jewish Origins. LC 76-22411. 1977. text ed. 14.95 o.p. (ISBN 0-268-01522-8). U of Notre Dame Pr.

Blensly, Douglas L. & Plank, Tom M. Accounting Desk Book. 7th ed. LC 82-6231. 472p. 1982. text ed. 54.50 (ISBN 0-87624-010-4). Inst Busn Plan.

Blesh, Rudi. Classic Piano Rags. (Orig.). 1973. pap. 10.95 (ISBN 0-486-20469-3). Dover.

--Combo, U.S.A. Eight Lives in Jazz. (The Roots of Jazz Ser.). 1979. Repr. of 1971 ed. 25.00 (ISBN 0-306-79568-X). Da Capo.

--Shining Trumpets: A History of Jazz. rev. 2nd ed. LC 75-31664. (Roots of Jazz Ser). (Illus.). xxxii, 412p. 1975. lib. bdg. 32.50 (ISBN 0-306-70658-X); pap. 7.95 (ISBN 0-306-80029-2). Da Capo.

Blesser, William B. Systems Approach to Bio-Medicine. LC 68-8658. (Illus.). 1969. text ed. 29.95 o.p. (ISBN 0-07-005893-8, C). McGraw.

--A Systems Approach to Biomedicine. LC 80-11717. 632p. 1981. Repr. of 1969 ed. lib. bdg. 31.00 (ISBN 0-89874-146-7). Krieger.

Blessing, Richard. A Passing Season. LC 82-47912. 228p. (gr. 6 up). 1982. 11.95 (ISBN 0-316-09957-0). Little.

--Poems & Stories. 88p. 1983. 13.00 (ISBN 0-937872-12-1); pap. 6.00 (ISBN 0-937872-13-X). Dragon Gate.

Blessington, Francis C. & Rotella, Guy, eds. Motive for Metaphor. 192p. 1983. 18.95x (ISBN 0-930350-38-3). NE U Pr.

Blessitt, Arthur. Tell them I Am Coming: A Jesus People Manual. LC 78-177397. (Spire Bk). 64p. (Orig.). 1973. pap. 0.95 o.p. (ISBN 0-8007-8113-9). Revell.

Blevins, Dorothy. The Diabetic & Nursing Care. (Illus.). 1979. text ed. 23.95 (ISBN 0-07-005902-0, HP). McGraw.

Blevins, James L. The Messianic Secret in Markan Research, 1901-1976. LC 80-69035. 233p. 1981. lib. bdg. 19.75 (ISBN 0-8191-1606-8); pap. text ed. 10.25 (ISBN 0-8191-1607-6). U Pr of Amer.

Blevins, Winfred. Give Your Heart to the Hawks: A Tribute to the Mountain Men. 328p. 1983. pap. 3.75 (ISBN 0-380-00694-4, 61770-6, Discus). Avon.

Blewett, George J. The Christian View of the World. 1912. 39.50x (ISBN 0-685-89741-9). Elliots Bks.

Blewett, Mary H., intro. by. Handbook for the Visiter to Lowell. 46p. 1982. pap. 3.50 (ISBN 0-943730-01-5). Lowell Pub.

Blewitt, Mary. Navigation for Yachtsmen. 10.50 (ISBN 0-392-14436-0, SpS). Sportshelf.

Bley, Edgar S. Best Singing Games for Children of All Ages. rev. ed. LC 57-1014. (Illus.). (gr. k-6). 1959. 10.95 (ISBN 0-8069-4450-1); PLB 13.29 (ISBN 0-8069-4451-X). Sterling.

Bley, Nancy S. & Thornton, Carol A. Teaching Mathematics to the Learning Disabled. LC 81-3569. 421p. 1981. text ed. 28.75 (ISBN 0-89443-357-1). Aspen Systems.

Bleyer, Willard G. Main Currents in the History of American Journalism. LC 70-77720. (American Scene Ser). (Illus.). v, 464p. 1973. Repr. of 1927 ed. lib. bdg. 59.50 (ISBN 0-306-71358-6). Da Capo.

Bleyhl, Norris A., compiled by. Indian-White Relationships in Northern California 1849-1920 in the Congressional Set of U.S. Public Documents. 109p. 1978. 12.00 (ISBN 0-686-38930-1). Assn NC Records.

--Some Newspaper References Concerning Indian-White Relationships in Northeastern California 1850-1920. 209p. 1979. 9.00 (ISBN 0-686-38929-8). Assn NC Records.

Bleything, Dennis & Hawkins, Susan. Getting off on Ninety-Six & Other Less Traveled Roads. LC 75-9248. (Illus.). 1975. pap. 4.95 (ISBN 0-911518-32-0). Touchstone Pr Ore.

Bleznick, Donald W. A Sourcebook for Hispanic Literature & Language: A Selected, Annotated Guide to Spanish American Bibliography, Literature, Linguistics, Journals, & Other Source Material. LC 74-77776. 192p. 1974. 14.95 (ISBN 0-87722-036-0). Temple U Pr.

Bleznick, Donald W., jt. ed. see Pattison, Walter T.

Blicher, S. S. Twelve Stories. Repr. of 1945 ed. 21.00 o.s.i. (ISBN 0-527-08950-8). Kraus Repr.

Blickle, Margaret D., jt. auth. see Andrews, Deborah C.

Blicq, R. On the Move: Communication for Employees. 1976. pap. 12.95 (ISBN 0-13-634212-4). P-H.

Bliese, Loren. A Generative Grammar of Afar. (SIL Publications on Linguistics Ser. No. 65). 306p. 1981. 10.00x (ISBN 0-88312-083-6); microfiche 3.75x (ISBN 0-88312-483-1). Summer Inst Ling.

Bligh, A. S., et al. Radioisotopes in Radiodiagnosis. 256p. 1975. 29.95 o.p. (ISBN 0-407-00036-4). Butterworth.

Bligh, William. An Account of the Mutiny on H. M. S. Bounty. Bowman, Robert, ed. 224p. 1980. text ed. 23.50x (ISBN 0-391-02095-1). Humanities.

Bligh, William, ed. A Book of the "Bounty". William Bligh & Others. Mackaness, George, ed. 1982. 12.95x (ISBN 0-460-00950-8, Evman). Biblio Dist.

Bliitchington, W. Peter. Sex Roles & the Christian Family. 1983. pap. 5.95 (ISBN 0-8423-5896-X); wkbk. 2.95 (ISBN 0-8423-5897-8). Tyndale.

Blij, Harm J., jt. auth. see Best, Alan C.

Blilz, Michael. Partitions. 50p. (Orig.). 1982. 11.00 (ISBN 0-916258-13-0); pap. 7.50 (ISBN 0-916258-12-2). Volaphon Bks.

Blin, Jean, et al. Flexible Exchange Rates & International Business. LC 81-85396. (British-North American Committee Ser.). 112p. 1981. pap. 8.00 (ISBN 0-89068-058-2). Natl Planning.

Blinchikoff, Herman J. & Zverev, Anatol I. Filtering in the Time & Frequency Domains. LC 76-120. 1976. 52.50x (ISBN 0-471-98679-8, Pub. by Wiley-Interscience). Wiley.

Blinder, Alan S. Toward an Economic Theory of Income Distribution. LC 74-5417. 1975. 20.00x (ISBN 0-262-02114-5). MIT Pr.

Blinder, Alan S., et al. The Economics of Public Finance. (Studies of Government Finance). 22.95 (ISBN 0-8157-0998-6); pap. 8.95 (ISBN 0-8157-0997-8). Brookings.

Blinder, Henriette, jt. auth. see Osman, Betty.

Blinderman, Abraham. American Writers on Education After 1865. (World Leader Ser.: No. 54). 1976. lib. bdg. 12.95 (ISBN 0-8057-7654-0, Twayne). G K Hall.

--American Writers on Education Before 1865. (World Leaders Ser). 1975. lib. bdg. 8.95 o.p. (ISBN 0-8057-3503-8, Twayne). G K Hall.

Bling, M. see Von Wiesner, J. & Von Regel, C.

Blinick, Augusta. Joanna's People. LC 82-61565. 260p. 1983. pap. 9.95 (ISBN 0-910873-00-3). Springtide.

Blinkenberg, C. The Thunderweapon in Religion & Folklore. xii, 122p. 1983. Repr. of 1911 ed. lib. bdg. 20.00x (ISBN 0-89241-205-4). Caratzas Bros.

Blinkhorn, M. Carlism & Crisis in Spain: 1931-1939. LC 75-2727. (Illus.). 408p. 1975. 57.50 (ISBN 0-521-20729-0). Cambridge U Pr.

Blinn, D. W., jt. auth. see Czarnecki, D. B.

Blinn, Lynn. Making Decisions. LC 79-54910. 1980. pap. 8.00 (ISBN 0-8273-1712-3); instr's. guide 2.75 (ISBN 0-8273-1711-5). Delmar.

Blish, James. Black Easter - The Day after Judgement. (Science Fiction Ser.). 1980. lib. bdg. 16.95 o.p. (ISBN 0-8398-2644-3, Gregg). G K Hall.

--A Case of Conscience: Science Fiction Ser. 1981. lib. bdg. cancelled o.s.i. (ISBN 0-8398-2673-7, Gregg). G K Hall.

--The Day After Judgement. 1982. pap. 2.50 (ISBN 0-380-59527-3, 59527). Avon.

--Fallen Star. 192p. 1983. pap. 2.50 (ISBN 0-380-62463-X, 62463). Avon.

--Galactic Cluster. 176p. 1972. pap. 0.95 o.p. (ISBN 0-451-05441-5, Q5441, Sig). NAL.

--Jack of Eagles. 208p. 1982. pap. 2.75 (ISBN 0-380-61150-3, 61150). Avon.

--Welcome to Mars. 160p. 1983. pap. 2.50 (ISBN 0-380-63347-7). Avon.

Blish, James, Jr. And All the Stars a Stage. 1982. pap. 2.25 (ISBN 0-380-00013-X, 617390). Avon.

Blish, Nelson A. Some Times. 1978. 4.95 o.p. (ISBN 0-533-03536-8). Vantage.

Blishen, Edward. A Back-Handed War. 224p. 1983. pap. 14.95 (ISBN 0-241-10919-1, Pub. by Hamish Hamilton England). David & Charles.

--A Cackhanded War: Memoirs of a Conscientious Objector. 230p. 1972. 8.75 o.p. (ISBN 0-500-01082-X). Transatlantic.

--Uncommon Entrance. 192p. 1983. pap. 14.95 (ISBN 0-241-10920-5, Pub. by Hamish Hamilton England). David & Charles.

Bliss. Bliss Bibliography, Second Class H: Anthropology, Human Biology & Health Sciences. 1981. 67.95 o.p. (ISBN 0-408-70828-X). Butterworth.

--Zero-Base Budgeting: A Management Tool for School Districts. 1978. 5.95 (ISBN 0-910170-04-5). Assn Sch Busn.

Bliss, A. J. A Dictionary of Foreign Words & Phrases in Current English. 400p. 1983. 18.00 (ISBN 0-7100-1092-3); pap. 9.95 (ISBN 0-7100-9521-X). Routledge & Kegan.

Bliss, Anne. A Handbook of Dyes from Natural Materials. (Illus.). 192p. 1983. pap. 9.95 (ISBN 0-686-83790-8, ScribT). Scribner.

Bliss, Betsy L., jt. auth. see Brody, Eugene D.

Bliss, Bill, jt. auth. see Molinsky, Steven J.

Bliss, Chester I. Statistics in Biology, 2 Vols. (Illus.). 1967. Vol. 1. text ed. 49.95 (ISBN 0-07-005895-4, 07-005894-6, C); Vol. 2. text ed. 49.95 (ISBN 0-07-005894-6). McGraw.

Bliss, Corinne D. Daffodils or the Death of Love: Short Fiction. LC 82-11048. (Breakthrough Bks.: No.39). 128p. (Orig.). 1983. pap. 6.95 (ISBN 0-8262-0385-X). U of Mo Pr.

--The Same River Twice. LC 82-45169. 288p. 1982. 13.95 (ISBN 0-689-11296-3). Atheneum.

Bliss, Dorothy, ed. The Biology of Crustacea: Vol. 7: Behavior & Ecology of Crustacea. Date not set. price not set (ISBN 0-12-106407-7). Acad Pr.

Bliss, Dorothy & Abele, Lawrence, eds. Biology of Crustacea: Vols. 1 & 2: Systematic Fossil & Biogeo graphy Record. 1982. Vol. 1. 38.50 (ISBN 0-12-106401-8); Vol. 2: Embryology, Morphology, & Genetics. 49.50 (ISBN 0-12-106402-6). Acad Pr.

Bliss, Dorothy & Atwood, H. L., eds. The Biology of Crustacea: Vol. 3, Structure & Function. 1982. 59.00 (ISBN 0-12-106403-4). Acad Pr.

Bliss, Dorothy E., ed. The Biology of Crustacea: Environmental Adaptations, Vol. 8. Date not set. price not set (ISBN 0-12-106408-5). Acad Pr.

Bliss, Dorothy E. & Provenzano, J., eds. Biology of the Crustacea: Vol. 6, Economic Aspects: Pathobiology, Culture & Fisheries. LC 82-4058. Date not set. 39.00 (ISBN 0-12-106406-9). Acad Pr.

Bliss, Dorothy E., jt. ed. see Mantel, Linda H.

Bliss, I. St. John. Edward Young. (English Authors Ser.). lib. bdg. 14.95 (ISBN 0-8057-1588-6, Twayne). G K Hall.

Bliss, James & Morella, Joseph. The Left Handers' Handbook. LC 78-71038. 160p. 1980. 12.95 (ISBN 0-89104-134-6, A & W Visual Library); pap. 6.95 (ISBN 0-89104-133-8, A & W Visual Library). A & W Pubs.

Bliss, Jane, jt. auth. see Lerch, Constance.

Bliss, Lee. The World's Perspective: John Webster & the Jacobean Drama. 239p. Date not set. 20.00x (ISBN 0-8135-0967-X). Rutgers U Pr.

Bliss, Lynn S. & Allen, Doris V. SKOLD: Screening Kit of Language Development. (Illus.). 1982. write for info. (19488). Univ Park.

Bliss, Mark. Abstractions in a Park. 1979. 4.95 o.p. (ISBN 0-533-03758-1). Vantage.

Bliss, Michael. Confederation: A New Nationality. 1981. lib. bdg. 8.40 (ISBN 0-531-02074-6). Watts.

--The Discovery of Insulin. (Illus.). 304p. 1982. lib. bdg. 20.00 (ISBN 0-226-05897-2). U of Chicago Pr.

Bliss, Richard. Origins: Two Models. Gish, Duane T. & Moore, John N., eds. LC 76-20178. (Illus.). 1976. 4.95 (ISBN 0-89051-027-X); tchr's guide avail. CLP Pubs.

Bliss, Richard, et al. Fossils: Key to the Present. 1980. pap. 4.95 (ISBN 0-89051-058-X). CLP Pubs.
Bliss, Richard B. & Parker, Gary E. Origin of Life. LC 78-58477. (Illus.). 1978. pap. 4.95 (ISBN 0-89051-053-9). CLP Pubs.
Bliss, Virginia, jt. auth. see Lerch, Constance.
Bliss, William R. Side Glimpses from the Colonial Meeting House. LC 70-140410. 1970. Repr. of 1894 ed. 34.00x (ISBN 0-8103-3594-8). Gale.
Blitchington, Peter & Cruise, Robert J. Understanding Your Temperament: A Self-Analysis with a Christian Viewpoint. 38p. (Orig.). 1979. pap. 2.95 (ISBN 0-943872-67-7). Andrews Univ Pr.
Blitchington, W. Peter. The Christian Woman's Search for Self-Esteem. LC 81-18963. 168p. 1982. 8.95 (ISBN 0-8407-5251-2). Nelson.
Blitsten, Dorothy. The World of the Family: A Comparative Study of Family Organization in Their Social & Cultural Settings. 1963. text ed. 6.95x (ISBN 0-685-77219-5, 0-394-30072). Phila Bk Co.
Blitt, jt. auth. see Adair, J.
Blitz, J. Electrical, Magnetic & Visual Methods, of Testing Materials. 1969. text ed. 7.95 o.p. (ISBN 0-408-18350-0). Butterworth.
Blitz, Marcia. Donald Duck. (Illus.). 1979. 12.95 o.p. (ISBN 0-517-52961-0, Harmony). Crown.
Blitzer, Charles. Age of Kings. LC 67-23412. (Great Ages of Man). (Illus.). (gr. 6 up). 1967. PLB 19.96 (ISBN 0-8094-0376-5, Pub. by Time-Life). Silver.
Blitzer, Richard. Basic Electricity for Electronics. LC 73-20102. 727p. 1974. text ed. 25.95x (ISBN 0-471-08160-4). Wiley.
--Basic Pulse Circuits. 1964. text ed. 25.95 (ISBN 0-07-005896-2, G). McGraw.
Blitzer, Robert & Gill, Jack C. College Mathematics Review. (Illus.). 238p. (Orig.). 1982. pap. text ed. 12.95x (ISBN 0-943202-03-5). H & H Pub.
Blitzer, Robert, jt. auth. see Gill, Jack C.
Bliven, Bruce, Jr. From Casablanca to Berlin. (Landmark Ser, No. 112). (gr. 5-9). 1965. 2.95 o.p. (ISBN 0-394-80412-0, BYR); PLB 5.99 (ISBN 0-394-90412-5). Random.
--Story of D-Day: June 6, 1944. (Landmark Ser.: No. 94). (Illus.). (gr. 6-8). 1956. 2.95 o.p. (ISBN 0-394-80362-0, BYR); PLB 5.99 (ISBN 0-394-90362-5). Random.
Bliven, Lorayne. Read English, Bk. 5. (Speak English Ser.). (Illus.). 80p. (Orig.). 1983. pap. text ed. 4.95 (ISBN 0-88499-679-4). Inst Mod Lang.
Blizard, David, jt. ed. see Dimond, Stuart J.
Blizek, William L., jt. ed. see Cederblom, J. B.
Bloch, Alexander, ed. Chemistry, Biology, & Clinical Uses of Nucleoside Analogs, Vol. 255. (Annals of the New York Academy of Sciences). 610p. 1975. 71.00x (ISBN 0-89072-009-6). NY Acad Sci.
Bloch, Alice. The Law of Return. 300p. (Orig.). 1983. pap. price not set (ISBN 0-930436-19-9). Persephone.
Bloch, Barbara. If It Doesn't Pan Out: How to Cope With Cooking Disasters. LC 80-26508. 1981. 10.95 (ISBN 0-934878-02-1); pap. 7.95 (ISBN 0-934878-19-6). Dembner Bks.
--Meat Board Meat Book. (Illus.). 1977. 12.95 (ISBN 0-07-005908-X, GB); pap. 4.95 (ISBN 0-07-005909-8). McGraw.
Bloch, Bobbie, jt. auth. see Orque, Modesta S.
Bloch, Carl, illus. Jesus, the Son of Man. (Illus.). 80p. 1983. pap. 12.95 (ISBN 0-87973-652-6, 652). Our Sunday Visitor.
Bloch, Cheree, jt. auth. see Putterill, Martin.
Bloch, Donald & Simon, Robert, eds. The Strength of Family Therapy: Selected Papers of Nathan W. Ackerman. LC 82-4285. 480p. 1982. 39.95 (ISBN 0-87630-271-1). Brunner-Mazel.
Bloch, E. M. Systema Ichthyologiae: Post Obitum Auctoris Opus Inchoatum Absolvit, J. G. Schneider, 2 vols. in 1. (Illus.). 1967. Repr. of 1801 ed. 80.00 (ISBN 3-7682-7191-9). Lubrecht & Cramer.
Bloch, Ernest & Schwartz, Robert A. Impending Changes for Securities Markets: What Role for the Exchanges? Altman, Edward I. & Walter, Ingo, eds. LC 77-7784. (Contemporary Studies in Economic & Financial Analysis: Vol. 14). lib. bdg. 34.50 (ISBN 0-89232-081-8). Jai Pr.
Bloch, Ernst, et al. Aesthetics & Politics. 1979. 19.25 (ISBN 0-8052-7062-0, Pub. by NLB). Schocken.
Bloch, Farrell, ed. Research in Labor Economics, Supplement 1: Evaluating Manpower Training Programs. 1979. lib. bdg. 42.50 (ISBN 0-89232-046-X). Jai Pr.
Bloch, H. P. & Geitner, F. K. Failure Analysis & Troubleshooting. (Practical Machinery Management for Process Plants Ser.). 1983. text ed. 59.95x (ISBN 0-87201-872-5). Gulf Pub.
Bloch, Herbert A. & Niederhoffer, Arthur. The Gang: A Study in Adolescent Behavior. LC 76-6517. 1976. Repr. of 1958 ed. lib. bdg. 17.50x (ISBN 0-8371-8865-2, BLTG). Greenwood.
Bloch, Herbert A. & Prince, Melvin. Social Crisis & Deviance: Theoretical Foundations. 1967. pap. text ed. 3.95 (ISBN 0-685-19767-0). Phila Bk Co.
Bloch, Howard R. Etymologies & Genealogies: A Literary Anthropology of the French Middle Ages. LC 82-20036. 296p. 1983. lib. bdg. 29.00x (ISBN 0-226-05981-2). U of Chicago Pr.
Bloch, J. The Formation of the Marathi Language. Chanana, D. R., tr. 1970. 10.95 (ISBN 0-89684-206-1). Orient Bk Dist.
Bloch, M. The Historian's Craft. 1954. pap. 7.00 (ISBN 0-7190-0664-3). Manchester.
Bloch, Marc. Feudal Society, 2 Vols. Manyon, L. A., tr. LC 61-4322. 1961. Vol. 1. pap. 3.45 (ISBN 0-226-05978-2, P156, Phoen); Vol. 2. pap. 5.95 (ISBN 0-226-05979-0, P157, Phoen). U of Chicago Pr.
--French Rural History: An Essay on Its Basic Characteristics. Sondheimer, Janet, tr. LC 66-15483. (Illus.). 1966. 34.50x (ISBN 0-520-00127-3); pap. 8.95x (ISBN 0-520-01660-2, CAMPUS28). U of Cal Pr.
--Strange Defeat: A Statement of Evidence Written in 1940. Hopkins, Gerard M., tr. 1968. pap. 5.95 (ISBN 0-393-00371-X, Norton Lib). Norton.
Bloch, Marie H. Dinosaurs. (Illus.). (gr. 3-6). 1955. PLB 5.99 (ISBN 0-698-30062-9, Coward). Putnam Pub Group.
Bloch, Mark. Slavery & Serfdom in the Middle Ages: Selected Papers by Marc Bloch. Beer, William R., tr. LC 79-123627. 320p. 1975. 38.00x (ISBN 0-520-01767-6). U of Cal Pr.
Bloch, Maurice. Marxism & Anthropology. (Illus.). 1982. 18.95x (ISBN 0-19-876091-4). Oxford U Pr.
Bloch, Maurice & Parry, Jonathan, eds. Death & the Regeneration of Life. LC 82-9467. 256p. 1982. 29.50 (ISBN 0-521-24875-2); pap. 8.95 (ISBN 0-521-27037-5). Cambridge U Pr.
Bloch, Max. Lecture Notes for American Pension Fund Actuaries. LC 77-77007. 1977. 25.00x (ISBN 0-9601248-1-0). Johnson Higgins.
Bloch, Michael. The Duke of Windsor's War: The Windsors in the Bahamas, 1940-1945. 388p. 1983. 16.95 (ISBN 0-698-11177-X, Coward). Putnam Pub Group.
Bloch, N. J., jt. auth. see Michaels, J. G.
Bloch, Norman J. & Michaels, John G. Linear Algebra. (Illus.). 1976. text ed. 24.95 (ISBN 0-07-005906-3, C); instr's manual 9.95 (ISBN 0-07-005907-1). McGraw.
Bloch, R. Howard. Medieval French Literature & Law. LC 76-7754. 1977. 30.00x (ISBN 0-520-03230-6). U of Cal Pr.
Bloch, Richard I. & Zack, Arnold. The Labor Agreement in Negotiation & Arbitration. 200p. 1983. text ed. 20.00 (ISBN 0-87179-398-9). BNA.
Bloch, Robert. Cold Chills. 224p. 1982. pap. 2.50 o.p. (ISBN 0-505-51863-5). Tower Bks.
--Psycho II. 224p. 1982. 16.00 (ISBN 0-918372-09-7); signed & slipcased 36.00x (ISBN 0-918372-08-9). Whispers.
Bloch, Sidney. What is Psychotherapy? 208p. 1983. text ed. 18.95x (ISBN 0-19-219154-3). Oxford U Pr.
--What is Psychotherapy? 208p. 1983. pap. 7.95 (ISBN 0-19-289142-1, GB 734, GB). Oxford U Pr.
Bloch, Sidney, ed. An Introduction to the Psychotherapies. 1979. pap. text ed. 14.95x (ISBN 0-19-261217-4). Oxford U Pr.
Bloch, Sidney & Chodoff, Paul, eds. Psychiatric Ethics. 1981. text ed. 32.50x (ISBN 0-19-261182-8). Oxford U Pr.
Bloch, Stuart M., ed. see Burlingame, et al.
Bloch, Thomas. Orbit. 1982. 13.95 (ISBN 0-698-11153-2, Coward). Putnam Pub Group.
Blocher, Donald H. & Biggs, Donald A. Counseling Psychology in Community Settings. 304p. 1983. text ed. 23.95 (ISBN 0-8261-3680-X). Springer Pub.
Block, A. The Changing World in Plays & Theatre. LC 73-77721. 448p. 1971. Repr. of 1939 ed. lib. bdg. 42.50 (ISBN 0-306-71359-4). Da Capo.
Block, Abby & Margie, Joyce D. Nutrition & the Cancer Patient. LC 81-70351. 224p. 1982. 10.95 (ISBN 0-8019-7120-9). Chilton.
Block, Adrienne F. The Early French Parody Noel. Buelow, George, ed. (Studies in Musicology: No. 36). 430p. 1983. write for info (ISBN 0-8357-1123-4, Pub. by UMI Res Pr). Univ Microfilms.
Block, Adrienne F. & Neuls-Bates, Carol, eds. Women in American Music: A Bibliography of Music & Literature. LC 79-7722. (Illus.). 1979. lib. bdg. 35.95x (ISBN 0-313-21410-7, NBW/). Greenwood.
Block, Alan. East Side - West Side: Organizing Crime in New York, 1930-1950. 280p. 1983. pap. 9.95 (ISBN 0-87855-931-0). Transaction Bks.
Block, Andrew. English Novel, Seventeen Forty to Eighteen Fifty: A Catalogue Including Prose Romances, Short Stories & Translations of Foreign Fiction. LC 62-3325. 349p. 1968. 32.00 (ISBN 0-379-00028-8). Oceana.
Block, Bob. The Politics of Projects. (Illus.). 160p. 1983. pap. 19.00 (ISBN 0-917072-35-9). Yourdon.
Block, Davida. A Guide to Effective Real Estate Advertising. LC 79-27219. (Illus.). 192p. 1980. 19.95 (ISBN 0-07-005930-6). McGraw.
Block, Gertrude. Effective Legal Writing: A Style Book for Law Students & Lawyers. 2nd ed. 205p. 1983. pap. text ed. write for info. (ISBN 0-88277-109-4). Foundation Pr.
Block, H. & Block, R. H&R Block Income Tax Workbook 1981. 1980. 3.95 (ISBN 0-02-511890-0); prepack avail. (ISBN 0-02-511840-4). Macmillan.
Block, H. & Holliday, A. K. Modern Physical Chemistry: An Introductory Text. (Illus.). 311p. 1973. pap. text ed. 12.50 (ISBN 0-408-70378-4). Butterworth.
Block, Haskell & Shedd, Robert, eds. Masters of Modern Drama. 1962. 35.00 (ISBN 0-394-40625-7); text ed. 28.00 (ISBN 0-394-30084-X). Random.
Block, Haskell M. Naturalistic Triptych: The Fictive & the Real in Zola, Mann & Dreiser. 1970. pap. text ed. 2.95 (ISBN 0-685-19749-2). Phila Bk Co.
Block, Haskell M., ed. see Voltaire, Francois M.
Block, I. E., et al, eds. Studies in Approximation & Analysis. (Illus.). 195p. 1966. text ed. 15.50 (ISBN 0-89871-156-8). Soc Indus-Appl Math.
Block, Ira, jt. auth. see Smith, Betty.
Block, Irving, ed. Perspectives on the Philosophy of Wittgenstein. (Studies in Contemporary German Social Thought). 224p. 1982. text ed. 25.50x (ISBN 0-262-02173-0). MIT Pr.
Block, J. & Labonville, J. English Skills for Technicians. 1971. 15.25 (ISBN 0-07-005910-1, G); instructor's guide 1.29 (ISBN 0-07-005911-X). McGraw.
Block, J. Richard, jt. auth. see Yuker, Harold E.
Block, Jack. The Q-Sort Method in Personality Assessment & Psychiatric Research. Harrower, Molly, ed. LC 61-10370. 161p. 1978. pap. 12.50x (ISBN 0-89106-000-6, 0791). Consulting Psychol.
Block, James H. & Anderson, Lorin W. Mastery Learning & Classroom Instruction. 1975. pap. 7.95x (ISBN 0-02-311000-7, 31100). Macmillan.
Block, Jean L., jt. auth. see Mansfield, Irving.
Block, Jerome B. Oncology: Internal Medicine Today: Comprehensive Postgraduate Library. LC 81-318. 350p. 1982. 40.00 (ISBN 0-471-09511-7, Pub. by Wiley Med). Wiley.
--Oncology: UCLA Postgraduate Medicine for the Internist. (Illus.). 1981. write for info. (ISBN 0-89289-376-1). Wiley.
Block, Joel. The Other Men, the Other Women. LC 77-87790. 1978. 8.95 o.p. (ISBN 0-448-14568-5, G&D). Putnam Pub Group.
Block, Joel D. Lasting Love: How to Give It, How to Get It, How to Keep It. 256p. 1982. 13.50 (ISBN 0-02-511800-5). Macmillan.
--To Marry Again. LC 78-60461. 1979. 10.00 o.p. (ISBN 0-448-16420-5, G&D). Putnam Pub Group.
Block, Judy R. The First Woman in Congress: Jeanette Rankin. LC 78-14490. (Famous Firsts Ser.). (Illus.). 1978. PLB 10.76 (ISBN 0-89547-053-5). Silver.
--The World's First Police Detective. LC 78-16169. (Famous Firsts Ser.). (Illus.). 1978. PLB 10.76 (ISBN 0-686-51116-6). Silver.
Block, Lawrence. A.K.A. Chip Harrison. 380p. 1983. pap. 5.95 (ISBN 0-686-84719-9, Foul Play Pr). Countryman.
--The Burglar Who Studied Spinoza. LC 80-5288. 1981. 8.95 o.p. (ISBN 0-394-51065-8). Random.
--The Burglar Who Studied Spinoza. 1982. pap. 2.75 (ISBN 0-686-83023-7). PB.
--Eight Million Ways to Die. Date not set. pap. price not set. Jove Pubns.
--In the Midst of Death. 192p. 1982. pap. 2.75 (ISBN 0-515-06731-8). Jove Pubns.
--Sometimes They Bite. 1983. 14.50 (ISBN 0-87795-485-2). Arbor Hse.
--A Stab in the Dark. 192p. 1982. pap. 2.75 (ISBN 0-515-06717-2). Jove Pubns.
--Time to Murder & Create. 192p. 1983. pap. 2.95 (ISBN 0-515-06801-2). Jove Pubns.
Block, Michael, compiled by. Letters to Michael: How Women in the Seventies Really Feel, As Revealed in Their Letters to the Man Who Advertised for Wife. LC 78-11128. 1979. 8.95 o.p. (ISBN 0-698-10932-5, Coward). Putnam Pub Group.
Block, Ned, ed. Readings in Philosophy of Psychology, Vol. I. (Language & Thought Ser.). 320p. 1983. pap. text ed. 8.95x (ISBN 0-674-74876-X). Harvard U Pr.
Block, Ned J., ed. Imagery. LC 81-24732. 192p. 1981. text ed. 16.50x (ISBN 0-262-02168-4, Pub. by Bradford); pap. text ed. 7.50x (ISBN 0-262-52072-9). MIT Pr.
Block, R., jt. auth. see Block, H.
Block, Richard A. New-Unified Navigation Rules for International & Inland Waters Including the Great Lakes & Western Rivers: R.B.-169. (Illus.). 131p. (Orig.). 1981. pap. text ed. 10.00 (ISBN 0-934114-32-3). Marine Educ.
Block, Richard A., ed. Master & Mate License Preparation Course. (Illus., Orig.). 1979. 27.00 o.p. (ISBN 0-934114-18-8). Marine Educ.
--Tankerman: All Grades. rev. ed. (Illus.). 250p. 1981. pap. 21.00 o.p. (ISBN 0-934114-30-7). Marine Educ.
Block, Richard A. & Hall, Daniel W., eds. Able Seaman & Lifeboatman: All Grades. rev. "E" ed. (Illus.). 528p. 1981. pap. 30.00 (ISBN 0-934114-40-4). Marine Educ.
Block, Seymor S., ed. Disinfection, Sterilization & Preservation. 3rd ed. LC 82-24002. (Illus.). 1500p. 1983. text ed. price not set (ISBN 0-8121-0863-9). Lea & Febiger.
Block, Stanley & Correnti, Samuel. Psyche, Sex & Stocks. 1973. 9.95 o.s.i. (ISBN 0-685-40602-4). Windsor.
Block, Stanley, ed. Mechanisms of Phase Transitions. pap. 5.00 (ISBN 0-686-60378-8). Polycrystal Bk Serv.
Block, Stanley B. & Hirt, Geoffrey A. Introduction to Finance. 1980. write for info. o.p. (CPCU 8). IIA.
--Introduction to Finance. LC 80-69851. Orig. Title: Foundation of Financial Management. 289p. 1980. Repr. of 1978 ed. text ed. 14.00 (ISBN 0-89463-030-X). Am Inst Property.
Block, Thomas. Mayday. LC 79-16933. 1980. 10.95 (ISBN 0-399-90057-8, Marek). Putnam Pub Group.
--Orbit. 320p. 1983. pap. 3.50 (ISBN 0-425-05740-2). Berkley Pub.
Block, Walter. Defending the Undefendables: The Pimp, Prostitute, Scab, Usurer, Libeler, & Other Scapegoats in the Rogue's Gallery of American Society. new ed. LC 74-21359. 1976. 10.95 (ISBN 0-8303-0136-4); pap. 6.95 (ISBN 0-8303-0183-6). Fleet.
Blockcolsky, V. D., et al. Peel & Put Manual for Speech & Language Development. rev. ed. 88p. 1977. pap. 8.00 (ISBN 0-88450-173-6, 2040-B). Communication Skill.
Blockcolsky, Valeda & Frazer, Joan. Peel & Put Reading Manual. 84p. 1980. pap. text ed. 8.00 (ISBN 0-88450-180-9, 3122-B). Communication Skill.
--Star Trails, "CH". 1980. 20.00 (ISBN 0-88450-726-2, 3150-B). Communication Skill.
--Star Trails, "L". 1978. 20.00 (ISBN 0-88450-793-9, 3070-B). Communication Skill.
--Star Trails, "R". 1978. 20.00 (ISBN 0-88450-791-2, 3050-B). Communication Skill.
--Star Trails, "S". 1978. 20.00 (ISBN 0-88450-792-0, 3060-B). Communication Skill.
--Star Trails,"SH". 1980. 20.00 (ISBN 0-88450-727-0, 3140-B). Communication Skill.
--Star Trails,"TH". 1980. 20.00 (ISBN 0-686-85812-3, 3131-B). Communication Skill.
Blocker, Gene & Hannaford, William. Introduction to Philosophy. 350p. 1974. pap. text ed. 8.95x (ISBN 0-442-20827-8). Van Nos Reinhold.
Blocker, H. Gene. The Metaphysics of Absurdity. LC 78-78399. 1979. pap. text ed. 9.75 (ISBN 0-8191-0712-3). U Pr of Amer.
Blocker, H. Gene, jt. auth. see Stewart, David.
Blocker, H. Gene & Smith, Elizabeth H., eds. John Rawls' Theory of Social Justice: An Introduction. LC 80-11272. xxiv, 520p. 1980. 26.95x (ISBN 0-8214-0445-8, 82-83368); pap. text ed. 11.95 (ISBN 0-8214-0593-4, 82-83376). Ohio U Pr.
Blocker, Jack S., Jr. Retreat from Reform: The Prohibition Movement in the United States, 1890-1913. LC 76-5325. (Contributions in American History: No. 51). 288p. 1976. lib. bdg. 29.95x (ISBN 0-8371-8899-7, BRR/). Greenwood.
Blocker, Jack S., Jr., ed. Alcohol, Reform & Society: The Liquor Issue in Social Context. LC 78-73800. (Contributions in American History: No. 83). (Illus.). 1979. lib. bdg. 27.50x (ISBN 0-313-20889-1, BLA/). Greenwood.
Blocker, Joel, ed. Israeli Stories: A Selection of the Best Contemporary Hebrew Writing. LC 61-14918. 1965. 8.00x o.p. (ISBN 0-8052-3119-6); pap. 5.95 (ISBN 0-8052-0108-4). Schocken.
Blocker, William, Jr. & Cardus, David, eds. Rehabilitation in Ischemic Heart Disease. LC 80-22840. (Illus.). 500p. 1983. text ed. 80.00 (ISBN 0-89335-096-6). SP Med & Sci Bks.
Blockey, Harry & Paz, Jaime. Great Western Recipes from Texas. 48p. 1983. pap. 8.95 (ISBN 0-88409-086-8). Creative Bk Co.
Blockhus, Wanda A., jt. auth. see Stewart, Jeffrey R., Jr.
Blockley, John. How To Paint with Pastels. 64p. 1982. pap. 5.95 (ISBN 0-89586-159-3). H P Bks.
Blodgett, Diane E., ed. Manual of Respiratory Care Procedures. (Illus.). 239p. 1980. pap. text ed. 11.75 (ISBN 0-397-50434-9, Lippincott Medical). Lippincott.
Blodgett, George B. Early Settlers of Rowley MA. 472p. 1981. Repr. of 1933 ed. 45.00x (ISBN 0-89725-027-3). NH Pub Co.
Blodgett, Harold W., ed. see Whitman, Walt.
Blodgett, O. W. Design for Welding. 2.50 o.p. (ISBN 0-685-65958-5). Am Welding.
Blodgett, Richard. The Merrill Lynch Guide to Financial Planning. 1983. 17.50 (ISBN 0-671-45695-4). S&S.
Blodinger. Formulation of Veterinary Dosage Forms. (Drugs & the Pharmaceutical Sciences Ser.). 454p. 1983. 48.50 (ISBN 0-8247-1730-9). Dekker.
Bloedow, Edmund, tr. see Bengtson, Hermann.
Bloem, Diane B. Challenging Bible Crossword Puzzles, No. 2. (Fun to Learn Ser.). 1979. pap. 2.50 (ISBN 0-310-21382-7). Zondervan.
Bloem, Diane B. & Bloem, Robert C. A Women's Workshop on Bible Marriages. (Woman's Workshop Series of Study Books). 128p. (Orig.). 1980. pap. 3.95 (ISBN 0-310-21391-6); pap. 2.50 leader's manual (ISBN 0-310-21401-7). Zondervan.
Bloem, Robert C., jt. auth. see Bloem, Diane B.
Bloembergen, N., ed. see Enrico Fermi Course 64, Vareno, Italy, 1975.
Bloemendal, H., ed. Cell Separation Methods. 1977. 57.50 (ISBN 0-7204-0649-8, North Holland). Elsevier.
Bloemendal, Hans. Molecular & Cellular Biology of the Eye Lens. LC 80-26815. 469p. 1981. 86.50 (ISBN 0-471-05171-3, Pub. by Wiley-Interscience). Wiley.

Bloesch, Donald G. Essentials of Evangelical Theology, Vol. I: God, Authority, Salvation. LC 77-15872. 288p. 1982. pap. 9.57i (ISBN 0-686-81487-8, RD 386, HarpR). Har-Row.

--Essentials of Evangelical Theology, Vol. II: Life, Ministry, & Hope. LC 78-3140. 352p. 1982. pap. 10.53i (ISBN 0-06-060803-X, RD 387, HarpR). Har-Row.

Blofeld, J. Bangkok. (The Great Cities Ser.). (Illus.). 1979. lib. bdg. 12.00 (ISBN 0-8094-3101-7); kivar bdg. 12.00 (ISBN 0-8094-3102-5). Silver.

Blofeld, John. The Wheel of Life: The Autobiography of a Western Buddhist. LC 78-58185. (Illus.). 1978. pap. 5.95 o.p. (ISBN 0-394-73548-X). Shambhala Pubns.

Blofeld, John, tr. I Ching, the Book of Change. 1968. pap. 4.25 (ISBN 0-525-47212-6, 0413-120). Dutton.

Blofeld, John, tr. see Huang Po.

Blogg, J. Rowan. The Eye in Veterinary Practice. LC 76-54038. (Illus.). 1980. text ed. 70.00 (ISBN 0-7216-1751-4). Saunders.

Blois, Keith, et al. Case Studies in Competition Policy. 1975. pap. text ed. 5.00x o.p. (ISBN 0-435-84469-5); tchr's guide 8.50x o.p. (ISBN 0-435-84470-9). Heinemann Ed.

Bloker, Richard A., ed. Tankerman-All Grades: B Edition. (Illus.). 353p. pap. 14.00 (ISBN 0-934114-41-2). Marine Educ.

Blom, Benjamin. New York: Photographs 1850-1950. 432p. (800 photographs). 1983. 65.00 (ISBN 0-943276-00-4, Pub. by Amaryllis Press Inc.). Dutton.

Blom, Eric. Beethoven's Pianoforte Sonatas Discussed. LC 68-21092. (Music Ser). 1968. Repr. of 1938 ed. 25.00 (ISBN 0-306-71059-5). Da Capo.

--Classics: Major & Minor. LC 74-166098. 212p. 1972. Repr. of 1958 ed. lib. bdg. 22.50 (ISBN 0-306-70293-2). Da Capo.

--A General Index to Modern Musical Literature in the English Language: Including Periodicals for the Years 1915-1926. LC 71-108736. (Music Ser). 1970. Repr. of 1927 ed. lib. bdg. 19.50 (ISBN 0-306-71898-7). Da Capo.

--Romance of the Piano. LC 69-15608. (Music Ser). (Illus.). 1969. Repr. of 1928 ed. 25.00 (ISBN 0-306-71060-9). Da Capo.

Blom, G. M., ed. Liquid Phase Epitaxy (From J. Crystal Growth, Vol. 27, 1974) Blank, S., et al. 332p. 1975. Repr. 68.00 (ISBN 0-444-10821-1, North-Holland). Elsevier.

Blom, Lynne A. & Chaplin, L. Tarin. The Intimate Act of Choreography. LC 82-2056. (Illus.). xx, 230p. 1982. 17.95 (ISBN 0-8229-3463-9); pap. 7.95x (ISBN 0-8229-5342-0). U of Pittsburgh Pr.

Blom, Margaret. Charlotte Bronte. (English Authors Ser.). 1977. lib. bdg. 11.95 (ISBN 0-8057-6673-1, Twayne). G K Hall.

Blombach, Birger & Hanson, Lars A., eds. Plasma Proteins. LC 78-102126. 1979. 87.00x (ISBN 0-471-99730-7, Pub. by Wiley-Interscience). Wiley.

Blomberg, Thomas G. Juvenile Court Reform & the Widening Social Control Net. 256p. 1982. text ed. cancelled (ISBN 0-89946-087-9). Oelgeschlager.

Blomfield, Reginald T. History of French Architecture from the Reign of Charles 8th till the Death of Mazarin 1494-1661 & History of French Architecture from the Death of Mazarin till the Death of Louis 15th 1661-1774, 4 vols. in 2. LC 77-143339. (Illus.). 1974. Repr. of 1921 ed. 60.00 o.s.i. (ISBN 0-87817-059-6). Hacker.

Blomjous, Joseph J. Priesthood in Crisis. 1969. 5.95 o.p. (ISBN 0-685-07661-X, 80048). Glencoe.

Blomme, George W., jt. auth. see Berry, Donald S.

Blomstrom, Robert L., ed. Strategic Marketing Planning in the Hospitality Industry: A Book of Readings. 1983. pap. 23.95 (ISBN 0-86612-013-0). Educ Inst Am Hotel.

Blond, Anthony. Family Business. LC 77-3784. 1978. 13.41i (ISBN 0-06-010364-7, HarpT). Har-Row.

Blondal, S. The Varangians of Byzantium. Benedikz, S., tr. LC 77-82486. (Illus.). 1979. 54.50 (ISBN 0-521-21745-8). Cambridge U Pr.

Blonde, Allan. The Complete Guide to Researching & Writing the English Term Paper. LC 78-63036. (Orig.). 1978. pap. text ed. 4.95x (ISBN 0-87936-013-5). Scholium Intl.

Blondel, J., jt. auth. see Ridley, F.

Blondel, Jean. Comparative Legislatures. (Contemporary Comparative Politics Ser.). (Illus.). 176p. 1973. ref. ed. o.p. 7.95 (ISBN 0-13-153874-8); pap. text ed. 10.95 (ISBN 0-13-153866-7). P-H.

--Contemporary France. 1974. pap. 6.95x o.p. (ISBN 0-416-81610-X). Methuen Inc.

--The Organization of Governments: A Comparative Analysis of Governmental Structures. LC 82-80523. (Political Executives in Comparative Perspective: A Cross-National Empirical Study: Vol. 2). (Illus.). 248p. 1982. 25.00 (ISBN 0-8039-9776-0); pap. 12.50 (ISBN 0-8039-9777-9). Sage.

--Political Parties. 1977. 15.00 o.p. (ISBN 0-686-23782-X). State Mutual Bk.

Blondin, Antoine. To Live in Paris. 264p. 1981. 60.00 (ISBN 0-686-98225-8). Edns Vilo.

Blondis, Marion N. & Jackson, Barbara. Nonverbal Communication with Patients: Back to the Human Touch. LC 76-30732. 1977. 9.95 o.p. (ISBN 0-471-01753-1, Pub. by Wiley Med). Wiley.

Blondis, Marion N. & Jackson, Barbara E. Nonverbal Communication with Patients: Back to the Human Touch. 2nd ed. LC 81-16261. 260p. 1982. pap. 11.95 (ISBN 0-471-08217-1, Pub. by Wiley Med). Wiley.

Blonien, Rodney & Greenfield, Joel I. California Law Manual for the Administration of Justice. (Criminal Justice Ser.). 1979. pap. text ed. 22.50 (ISBN 0-8299-0252-X). West Pub.

Blonk, W. A. Transport & Regional Development. 1979. text ed. 47.50x (ISBN 0-566-00285-X). Gower Pub Ltd.

Blood, Benjamin P. The Poetical Alphabet. (Surrealist Research & Development Monograph). 24p. 1972. pap. 2.50. Black Swan Pr.

Blood, Henry F. A Reconstruction of Proto-Mnong. 110p. 1968. pap. 4.00x o. p. (ISBN 0-88312-641-9); microfiche 2.25 (ISBN 0-88312-493-9). Summer Inst Ling.

Blood-Horse. Thoroughbred Broodmare Records, 1982: Annual Edition. 2724p. 1983. 87.50 (ISBN 0-936032-59-6); leather binding 102.50 (ISBN 0-936032-60-X). Blood-Horse.

Blood-Horse, ed. Stake Winners of 1982. (Annual Supplement to the Blood-Horse). 900p. 1983. 30.00 (ISBN 0-936032-61-8); pap. 20.00 (ISBN 0-936032-62-6). Blood-Horse.

--Stakes Winners of 1979. (Annual Supplement, the Blood-Horse). 1980. lib. bdg. 20.00 o.p. (ISBN 0-936032-23-5); pap. 10.00 o.p. (ISBN 0-936032-24-3). Blood-Horse.

Blood-Horse-Thoroughbred Owners & Breeders Assn. The Breeder's Guide of 1982, 1 vol. (Bound Supplements of the Blood-Horse). 1983. 47.50 (ISBN 0-936032-58-8). Blood-Horse.

Bloodgood, Lida. Saddle of the Queens. (Illus.). 15.00x o.p. (ISBN 0-87556-028-8). Saifer.

Bloodstein, Oliver. Speech Pathology: An Introduction. LC 78-69600. (Illus.). 1979. text ed. 21.50 (ISBN 0-395-27048-0); 20 35mm slides 15.50 (ISBN 0-395-27057-X). HM.

Bloodworth, Dennis. Crosstalk. LC 77-20044. 1978. 8.95 o.p. (ISBN 0-698-10872-8, Coward). Putnam Pub Group.

--The Messiah & the Mandarins. LC 82-45182. 384p. 1982. 15.95 (ISBN 0-689-11297-1). Atheneum.

Bloodworth, Dennis & Ching Ping. Heirs Apparent: What Happens When Mao Dies? 272p. 1973. 7.95 o.p. (ISBN 0-374-16898-9). FS&G.

Bloodworth, William, Jr. Upton Sinclair. (United States Authors Ser.). 1977. lib. bdg. 12.95 (ISBN 0-8057-7197-2, Twayne). G K Hall.

Bloom, A. Diabetes Explained. (Illus.). 160p. 1975. text ed. 13.95 (ISBN 0-8391-0577-0). Univ Park.

Bloom, A., ed. Whittington Postgraduate Medicine. 1974. Repr. of 1975 ed. 13.95 o.p. (ISBN 0-407-93500-2). Butterworth.

Bloom, A. L. Surface of the Earth. (gr. 10 up). pap. text ed. 11.95 (ISBN 0-13-877944-9). P-H.

Bloom, Alan. Two Hundred & Fifty Years of Steam. 1981. 24.95 (ISBN 0-437-01400-2, Pub. by World's Work). David & Charles.

Bloom, Alfred. Tannisho: A Resource for Modern Living. LC 80-39523. 112p. (Orig.). 1981. pap. 5.95 (ISBN 0-938474-00-6). Buddhist Study.

Bloom, Allan, tr. see Rousseau, Jean-Jacques.

Bloom, Allen & Jaffa, Harry V. Shakespeare's Politics. LC 81-10342. 160p. 1981. pap. 6.00 (ISBN 0-226-06041-1). U of Chicago Pr.

Bloom, Andy. Snow Sport. LC 80-53609. (Intersport Ser.). 13.00 (ISBN 0-382-06517-4). Silver.

Bloom, Anthony. Beginning to Pray. LC 70-169613. 96p. 1982. pap. 3.95 (ISBN 0-8091-1509-3). Paulist Pr.

--God & Man. LC 75-34845. 128p. 1976. pap. 2.45 o.p. (ISBN 0-8091-1923-4). Paulist Pr.

Bloom, Arnold L. Gas Lasers. LC 77-28278. 184p. 1978. Repr. of 1968 ed. lib. bdg. 14.50 (ISBN 0-88275-659-1). Krieger.

Bloom, Arthur D. & James, L. S., eds. The Fetus & the Newborn. (Alan R. Less, Inc. Ser.: Vol. 17, No.1). 1981. 36.00 (ISBN 0-686-37765-6). March of Dimes.

Bloom, Arthur L. Geomorphology: A Systematic Analysis of Late Cenozoic Landforms. LC 77-25816. (Illus.). 1978. ref. ed. 33.95 (ISBN 0-13-353086-8). P-H.

Bloom, Benjamin S. All Our Children Learning: A Primer for Parents, Teachers & Other Educators. 256p. 1980. 17.95 (ISBN 0-07-006120-3). McGraw.

--Human Characteristics & School Learning. 1976. 19.95 (ISBN 0-07-006117-3, P&RB). McGraw.

Bloom, Benjamin S. & Madaus, George F. Evaluation of Student Learning. 1981. 16.95 (ISBN 0-07-006109-2). McGraw.

Bloom, Benjamin S., et al. Handbook on Formative & Summative Evaluation of Student Learning. 1971. text ed. 39.95 o.p. (ISBN 0-07-006114-9, C). McGraw.

Bloom, Bernard L. Community Mental Health: A General Introduction. LC 77-419. 1977. text ed. 19.95 (ISBN 0-8185-0215-0). Brooks-Cole.

Bloom, Bernard L. & Asher, Shirley J., eds. Psychiatric Patient Rights & Patient Advocacy: Issues & Evidence. LC 81-13165. (Community Psychology Ser.: Vol. VII). 287p. 1982. 29.95 (ISBN 0-89885-056-8). Human Sci Pr.

Bloom, Clare T. Dreams & Memories. (Illus.). 45p. 1976. pap. 2.25 (ISBN 0-913270-56-3). Sunstone Pr.

Bloom, D. M. Linear Algebra & Geometry. LC 77-26666. 1979. 41.50 (ISBN 0-521-21959-0); pap. 26.95x (ISBN 0-521-29324-3). Cambridge U Pr.

Bloom, Edward A., et al, eds. see Burney, Fanny.

Bloom, Floyd, jt. auth. see Symposium of Beta-Carbolines & Tetrahydroisoquinolines, La Jolla, Ca., December, 12-13, 1981.

Bloom, Floyd E., ed. Peptides: Integrators of Cell & Tissue Function, Vol. 35. (Society of General Physiologists Ser.). 274p. 1980. text ed. 27.50 (ISBN 0-89004-485-6). Raven.

Bloom, Floyd E., jt. auth. see Cooper, Jack R.

Bloom, George, et al. Real Estate. 8th ed. LC 81-15933. 738p. 1982. text ed. 30.95 (ISBN 0-471-09398-X); tchrs. manual 16.00 (ISBN 0-471-86234-7). Wiley.

Bloom, Gordon F. Productivity in the Food Industry: Problems & Potential. 240p. 1972. 20.00x (ISBN 0-262-02088-2). MIT Pr.

Bloom, Harold. Agon: Towards a Theory of Revisionism. 1982. 22.50x (ISBN 0-19-502945-3). Oxford U Pr.

--An American Gnosis. 160p. 1981. cancelled 9.95 o.p. (ISBN 0-8164-9307-3). Continuum.

--The Anxiety of Influence: A Theory of Poetry. 176p. 1973. 14.95x (ISBN 0-19-501613-0). Oxford U Pr.

--Anxiety of Influence: A Theory of Poetry. 165p. 1975. pap. 5.95 (ISBN 0-19-501896-6, GB426, GB). Oxford U Pr.

--The Breaking of the Vessels. LC 81-12975. (Wellek Library Lectures). 1982. 10.00 (ISBN 0-226-06043-8). U of Chicago Pr.

--The Breaking of the Vessels. LC 81-12975. xiv, 108p. 1982. pap. 4.95 (ISBN 0-226-06044-6). U of Chicago Pr.

--Kabbalah & Criticism. 126p. Date not set. pap. 6.95 (ISBN 0-8245-0487-9). Crossroad NY.

--A Map of Misreading. 1975. 16.95x (ISBN 0-19-501874-5). Oxford U Pr.

--A Map of Misreading. pap. 6.95 (ISBN 0-19-502809-0, GB 623). Oxford U Pr.

--Poetry & Repression: Revisionism from Blake to Stevens. LC 75-18165. 304p. 1976. 22.50x (ISBN 0-300-01923-8, Y-378); pap. 6.95x (ISBN 0-300-02604-8). Yale U Pr.

--Visionary Company: A Reading of English Romantic Poetry. rev. ed. LC 73-144032. 506p. 1971. pap. 7.95x (ISBN 0-8014-9117-7, CP117). Cornell U Pr.

--Yeats. 1972. pap. 8.95 (ISBN 0-19-501603-3, 378, GB). Oxford U Pr.

Bloom, Harold, ed. see Pater, Walter.

Bloom, Herbert I. Economic Activities of the Jews of Amsterdam in the Seventeenth & Eighteenth Centuries. LC 70-91036. 1969. Repr. of 1937 ed. 15.00 o.p. (ISBN 0-8046-0646-3). Kennikat.

Bloom, J. Harvey. Folk Lore, Old Customs & Superstitions in Shakespeare Land. LC 73-2830. viii, 167p. 1973. Repr. of 1930 ed. 31.00x (ISBN 0-8103-3269-8). Gale.

--Shakespeare's Garden: Being a Compendium of Quotations & References from the Bard to All Manner of Flower, Tree, Bush, Vine & Herb. LC 78-77000. (Tower Bks). (Illus.). 1971. Repr. of 1903 ed. 37.00 o.p. (ISBN 0-8103-3916-1). Gale.

Bloom, Joel A., jt. auth. see Fleming, A. William.

Bloom, John P., ed. The American Territorial System. LC 72-96397. (National Archives Conferences Ser.: Vol. 5). xv, 248p. 1973. 15.00x (ISBN 0-8214-0130-0, 82-81339). Ohio U Pr.

Bloom, Ken. American Song: The Complete Stage Musical, Vol. I. (Illus.). 500p. 1983. 24.95 (ISBN 0-918432-48-0). NY Zoetrope.

Bloom, Lois. Language Development: Form & Function in Emerging Grammars. 1970. 17.50x (ISBN 0-262-02056-4). MIT Pr.

Bloom, Lois & Lahey, Margaret. Language Development & Language Disorders. LC 77-21482. (Communication Disorders Ser.). 506p. 1978. text ed. 29.50 (ISBN 0-471-08220-1). Wiley.

Bloom, Lois, ed. Readings in Language Development. LC 77-10717. (Communications Disorders Ser.). 506p. 1978. text ed. 26.50x (ISBN 0-471-08221-X). Wiley.

Bloom, Mark, jt. auth. see Barley, Elizabeth G.

Bloom, Martin. Life Span Development: Bases for Preventative & Interventive Helping. (Illus.). 1980. pap. text ed. 18.95 (ISBN 0-02-311020-1). Macmillan.

--The Paradox of Helping: Introduction to the Philosophy of Scientific Practice. LC 74-13524. 283p. 1975. text ed. 25.95x (ISBN 0-471-08235-X). Wiley.

--Primary Prevention: The Possible Science. (P-H Ser. in Social Work). (Illus.). 288p. 1981. pap. text ed. 13.95 (ISBN 0-13-700062-6). P-H.

Bloom, Martin & Fischer, Joel. Evaluating Practice: Guidelines for the Accountable Professional. (Prentice Hall Series in Sociology Work Practice). (Illus.). 512p. 1982. reference 25.95 (ISBN 0-13-292318-1). P-H.

Bloom, Martin, ed. Single-System Research Designs. (Journal of Social Service Research Ser.: Vol. 3, No. 1). 189p. (Orig.). 1979. pap. text ed. 10.00 (ISBN 0-917724-70-4, B70). Haworth Pr.

Bloom, Mortimer, jt. auth. see Booth, Verne H.

Bloom, Murray T. The Brotherhood of Money. 302p. 1983. 17.95 (ISBN 0-931960-12-6). BNR Pr.

--Money of Their Own. 2nd ed. (Illus.). 320p. 1983. 17.95 (ISBN 0-931960-09-6). BNR Pr.

Bloom, Naomi. Contributions of Women: Religion. LC 77-20034. (Contributions of Women Ser.). (Illus.). (gr. 6 up). 1978. PLB 8.95 o.p. (ISBN 0-87518-123-6). Dillon.

Bloom, Paul N. Advertising, Competition & Public Policy: A Simulation Study. LC 75-37590. 168p. 1976. prof ref 17.50 (ISBN 0-88410-280-7). Ballinger Pub.

Bloom, Robert & Elgers, Pieter T. Accounting Theory & Policy: A Reader. 529p. 1981. pap. text ed. 14.95 (ISBN 0-15-500477-8, HC). HarBraceJ.

Bloom, Stephen R. & Long, R. G. Radioimmunoassay Of Gut Regulatory Peptides. 256p. 1982. 31.95 (ISBN 0-03-062116-X). Praeger.

Bloom, Ursula. The Magnificent Courtesan. 1979. pap. 2.25 o.p. (ISBN 0-523-40542-1). Pinnacle Bks.

Bloom, William L., Jr., et al. Medical Radiographic Technic. 3rd ed. (Illus.). 368p. 1979. pap. 18.75x (ISBN 0-398-00171-5). C C Thomas.

Bloomberg, Hans & Ylinen, R., eds. Algebraic Theory for Multivariable Linear Systems. (Math Science Engineering Ser.). Date not set. price not set (ISBN 0-12-107150-2). Acad Pr.

Bloomberg, Marty. Introduction to Public Services for Library Technicians. 3rd ed. LC 81-8210. (Library Science Text Ser.). (Illus.). 323p. 1981. text ed. 28.00 (ISBN 0-87287-257-2); pap. text ed. 20.00 (ISBN 0-87287-263-7). Libs Unl.

--The Jewish Holocaust: An Annotated Guide to Books in English. LC 81-21605. (Borgo Reference Library: Vol. 13). 192p. 1983. lib. bdg. 19.95x (ISBN 0-89370-160-2); pap. 9.95x (ISBN 0-89370-260-9). Borgo Pr.

Bloomberg, Marty & Evans, G. Edward. Introduction to Technical Services for Library Technicians. 4th ed. LC 81-798. (Library Science Text Ser.). (Illus.). 363p. 1981. lib. bdg. 28.00 (ISBN 0-87287-228-9); pap. text ed. 20.00 (ISBN 0-87287-248-3). Libs Unl.

Bloomberg, Marty & Weber, Hans. An Introduction to Classification & Number Building in Dewey. Immroth, John P., ed. LC 76-26975. 199p. 1976. lib. bdg. 18.50x o.p. (ISBN 0-87287-115-0). Libs Unl.

Bloome, Enid. Dogs Don't Belong on Beds. LC 79-139337. (gr. k-1). 1971. 6.95 o.p. (ISBN 0-385-08033-6). Doubleday.

Bloomenthal, Harold. Securities & Federal Corporate Law, 3 vols. LC 72-90956. 1972. Set. looseleaf with 1981 rev. pages 310.00 (ISBN 0-87632-086-8). Boardman.

Bloomenthal, Harold S. Securities Law Handbook. 1981. pap. 26.50 (ISBN 0-87632-351-4). Boardman.

--Securities Law in Perspective. 1977. pap. text ed. 7.95 (ISBN 0-316-09988-0). Little.

Bloomer, D. C. Life & Writings of Amelia Bloomer. LC 76-26848. 1975. pap. 4.95 (ISBN 0-8052-0483-0). Schocken.

Bloomfield. Dye Curves. 48.00 o.p. (ISBN 0-85602-038-9). Wiley.

Bloomfield, Arthur. The Changing Climate. LC 77-80427. 1977. pap. 1.95 (ISBN 0-87123-060-7, 200060). Bethany Hse.

Bloomfield, Arthur E. Antes de la Ultima Batalla-Armagedon. 192p. Date not set. 2.95 (ISBN 0-88113-003-6). Edit Betania.

Bloomfield, B. C., ed. Acquisition & Provision of Foreign Books by National & University Libraries in the United Kingdom. 1972. 10.00 o.p. (ISBN 0-7201-0299-5, Pub. by Mansell England). Wilson.

Bloomfield, C. D. Adult Leukemias. 1982. 69.50 (ISBN 90-247-2478-3, Pub. by Martinus Nijhoff Netherlands). Kluwer Boston.

Bloomfield, Dennis A., jt. auth. see Simon, Hansjorg.

Bloomfield, Derek. From Arithmetic to Algebra. 2nd ed. (Illus.). 1976. pap. 18.95 (ISBN 0-8359-2110-7); instrs'. manual avail. (ISBN 0-8359-2111-5). Reston.

Bloomfield, Edward H. The Opposition to the English Separatists, Fifteen Seventy to Sixteen Twenty-Five: A Survey of the Polemical Literature Written by the Opponents to Separatism. LC 81-40172. 206p. (Orig.). 1982. lib. bdg. 21.75 (ISBN 0-8191-1853-2); pap. text ed. 10.75 (ISBN 0-8191-1854-0). U Pr of Amer.

Bloomfield, Horace R. Female Executives & the Degeneration of Management. (Illus.). 129p. 1983. 59.85 (ISBN 0-86654-063-6). Inst Econ Finan.

Bloomfield, J. A., ed. The Lakes of New York State, 2 vols. Incl. Vol. 1. Ecology of the Finger Lakes. 39.50, by subscription 32.00 (ISBN 0-12-107301-7); Vol. 2: The Lakes of Western New York. 35.50, by subscription 31.00 (ISBN 0-12-107302-5). 1978. Acad Pr.

Bloomfield, Jonathan. The Passive Revolution: Politics & the Czechoslovak Working Class 1945-48. LC 78-25922. 1979. 26.00x (ISBN 0-312-59788-6). St Martin.

Bloomfield, Julia, ed. Oppositions, Vol. 27-28: Double Issue. (Illus.). 288p. 1983. pap. 30.00 (ISBN 0-686-83765-7). Rizzoli Intl.

Bloomfield, Leonard. Introduction to the Study of Language. (Classics in Psycholinguistics: 3). x, 355p. 1982. 40.00 (ISBN 90-272-1891-9); pap. 25.00 (ISBN 0-686-37774-5). Benjamins North Am.
--The Menominio Language. 1962. 49.50x (ISBN 0-686-50049-0). Elliots Bks.
Bloomfield, Lincoln P. & Yost, Charles W. What Future for the U. N.? 40p. pap. 2.00 (ISBN 0-87855-741-5). Transaction Bks.
Bloomfield, Lincoln P., et al. Khrushchev & the Arms Race: Soviet Interests in Arms Control & Disarmament 1954-1964. (Illus.). 1966. 20.00x (ISBN 0-262-02017-3). MIT Pr.
Bloomfield, Louis M. & FitzGerald, Gerald F. Crimes Against Internationally Protected Persons: Prevention & Punishment - an Analysis of the UN Convention. LC 74-33031. 296p. 1975. 31.95 o.p. (ISBN 0-275-05350-4). Praeger.
Bloomfield, M. M. Chemistry & the Organism. 599p. 25.95x (ISBN 0-471-04754-6). Wiley.
Bloomfield, Meyer, ed. Readings in Vocational Guidance. 723p. 1982. Repr. of 1915 ed. lib. bdg. 65.00 (ISBN 0-89987-090-2). Darby Bks.
Bloomfield, Morton W. & Newmark, Leonard. Linguistic Introduction to the History of English. LC 79-4563. (Illus.). 1979. Repr. of 1963 ed. lib. bdg. 35.00x (ISBN 0-313-20936-7, BLLI). Greenwood.
Bloomfield, Peter. Fourier Analysis of Time Series: An Introduction. LC 75-34294. (Probability & Mathematical Statistics Ser.). 258p. 1976. 31.95x (ISBN 0-471-08256-2, Pub. by Wiley-Interscience); pap. 14.50 (ISBN 0-471-05587-5). Wiley.
Bloomfield, Robert. Collected Poems, 1800-1822, 5 vols. in 1. Lawson, Jonathan N., ed. & intro. by. LC 79-161927. 704p. 1971. 70.00x (ISBN 0-8201-1088-4). Schol Facsimiles.
Bloomfield, Stephen, jt. auth. see Theordore, Frederick.
Bloomfield, Valerie. Commonwealth Elections, 1945-1970: A Bibliography. LC 76-24992. 1977. lib. bdg. 45.00x (ISBN 0-8371-9067-3, BCE/). Greenwood.
Bloomingdale, Teresa. Murphy Must Have Been a Mother. (General Ser.). 1983. lib. bdg. 13.95 (ISBN 0-8161-3505-3, Large Print Bks). G K Hall.
--Up a Family Tree. 1983. pap. 2.95 (ISBN 0-686-43063-8). Bantam.
Bloomquist, R., et al. Number-Key Practice for Use on Typewriter, Ten-Key & Keypunch Keyboards. 1975. 6.96 (ISBN 0-07-006105-X, G). McGraw.
Bloor, David. Knowledge & Social Imagery. (Routledge Direct Editions). 168p. 1976. 16.50 (ISBN 0-7100-8377-7). Routledge & Kegan.
Bloss, Donald F. The Spindle Stage: Principles & Practice. LC 80-21488. (Illus.). 416p. 1981. 76.50 (ISBN 0-521-23292-9). Cambridge U Pr.
Bloss, Margaret V. & Bramall, Norman. Squash Racquets. (Physical Education Activities Ser.). 80p. 1967. pap. text ed. write for info (ISBN 0-697-07027-1); tchrs.' man. avail. (ISBN 0-697-07224-X). Wm C Brown.
Bloss, W. H. & Grassi, G., eds. E. C. Photovoltaic Solar Energy Conference, 4th. 1982. 96.00 (ISBN 90-277-1463-0, Pub. by Reidel Holland). Kluwer Boston.
Blossom, Barbara C., jt. auth. see Sites, W. Kilmer.
Blossom, F. A. La Composition de Salammbo, d'Apres la Correspondance de Flaubert, 1857-62. (Elliott Monographs: Vol. 3.). 1914. pap. 12.00 (ISBN 0-527-02607-7). Kraus Repr.
Blot, David & Davidson, David. Put It in Writing: Writing Activities for Students of ESL. (Illus.). 96p. (Orig.). 1981. pap. text ed. 5.95 (ISBN 0-88377-175-6). Newbury Hse.
Blotner, Joseph, ed. Selected Letters of William Faulkner. 1977. 15.00 o.p. (ISBN 0-394-49485-7). Random.
Blotner, Joseph L. The Political Novel. LC 78-9868. 1979. Repr. of 1955 ed. lib. bdg. 16.25x (ISBN 0-313-21228-7, BLPN). Greenwood.
Blotner, Joseph L., jt. ed. see Gwynn, Frederick L.
Blotnick, Srully. Career Crises. 1983. 11.95 o.p. (ISBN 0-517-54904-2). Crown.
--Winning: The Psychology of Successful Investing. 1978. 24.95 (ISBN 0-07-006119-X, P&RB). McGraw.
Blotter, P. Thomas. Introduction to Engineering. LC 80-25375. 289p. 1981. 24.95x (ISBN 0-471-04935-2); solutions 10.00 (ISBN 0-471-09947-3). Wiley.
Blouch, Ralph I., ed. see International Association of Fish & Wildlife Agencies.
Blough, Glenn O. Discovering Cycles. LC 73-6622. (Illus.). 48p. (gr. 3-7). 1978. PLB 5.72 o.p. (ISBN 0-07-006165-3, GB). McGraw.
Blouin, Andree & MacKellar, Jean. My Country, Africa: The Autobiography of the Black Passionaria. 302p. 1983. 19.95 (ISBN 0-03-062759-1). Praeger.
Blouin, Francis X., Jr. The Boston Region, 1810-1850: A Study of Urbanization. Berkhofer, Robert, ed. LC 79-28080. (Studies in American History & Culture: No. 10). 234p. 1980. 39.95 (ISBN 0-8357-1077-7, Pub. by UMI Res Pr). Univ Microfilms.
Blount, Ben G. Language, Culture & Society: A Book of Readings. (Orig.). 1974. pap. text ed. 10.95 (ISBN 0-316-10007-2). Little.
Blount, Ben G., jt. auth. see Sanches, Mary.
Blount, George. Peace Through World Government. 1974. pap. 5.00 (ISBN 0-87716-055-4, Pub. by Moore Pub Co). F Apple.
Blount, Roy J. One Fell Soup: or I'm Just a Bug on the Windshield of Life. 255p. 1982. 12.95 (ISBN 0-316-10005-6, Pub. by Atlantic Monthly Pr). Little.
Blount, W. P. Fractures in Children. LC 76-11. 294p. 1977. Repr. of 1972 ed. 19.50 (ISBN 0-88275-392-4). Krieger.
Blount, Walter P. & Moe, John H. The Milwaukee Brace. 2nd ed. 272p. 1980. lib. bdg. 22.00 (ISBN 0-683-00871-4). Williams & Wilkins.
Blout, E. R., et al. Peptides, Polypeptides & Proteins. LC 74-22202. 656p. 1974. 36.00 (ISBN 0-471-08387-9). Krieger.
Blow, D. M., jt. auth. see Holmes, K. C.
Blower, G. J. Plumbing. (Illus.). 208p. 1982. pap. text ed. 13.95x (ISBN 0-7121-1750-4). Intl Ideas.
Blowers, Andrew. The Limits of Power: The Politics of Local Planning Policy. (Urban & Regional Planning Ser.: Vol. 21). (Illus.). 1980. 25.00 (ISBN 0-08-023016-4). Pergamon.
Blu, Karen. The Lumbee Problem. LC 79-12908. (Cambridge Studies of Cultural Systems). (Illus.). 1980. 29.95 (ISBN 0-521-22525-6); pap. 8.95 (ISBN 0-521-29542-4). Cambridge U Pr.
Blucher, Judy, jt. auth. see Llewellyn, Jack H.
Blue, Betty. Authentic Mexican Cooking. LC 77-23355. 1977. 11.95o.p. (ISBN 0-13-054106-0, Spec); pap. 5.95 (ISBN 0-13-054098-6, Spec). P-H.
Blue, Frederick J. The Free Soilers: Third Party Politics, 1848-54. LC 72-86408. 384p. 1973. 21.95 (ISBN 0-252-00308-X). U of Ill Pr.
Blue, Jane. The Madeleine Poems. (Illus.). 55p. 1982. pap. 4.00 (ISBN 0-686-36921-1). Trill Pr.
Blue Lake-Deerhaven Cookbook Staff. A Texas Hill Country Cookbook. 8th ed. (Illus.). 406p. 1982. pap. 10.95 (ISBN 0-9609210-0-1). Blue Haven.
Blue, Lionel. To Heaven with Scribes & Pharisees. 1976. 8.95 o.p. (ISBN 0-19-519831-X). Oxford U Pr.
Blue Ribbon Commission of the World Jewish Congress. Issues Facing World Jewry. LC 81-53025. Orig. Title: The Implications of Israel-Arab Peace for World Jewry. (Illus.). 144p. 1982. pap. 6.95 (ISBN 0-9607092-0-7). Hershel Shanks Pubs.
Blue, Rose. Grandma Didn't Wave Back. LC 79-189568. 64p. (gr. 3-5). 1972. PLB 8.90 (ISBN 0-531-02557-8). Watts.
--Wishful Lying. LC 79-20622. 32p. 1980. 9.95 o.p. (ISBN 0-87705-473-8). Human Sci Pr.
Blue, William F., Jr., jt. auth. see Moore, Charles B.
Blue, William R. The Development of Imagery in Calderons Comedias. 220p. 1983. 18.00 (ISBN 0-938972-05-7). Spanish Lit Pubns.
Bluem, William A. Documentary in American Television. (Communication Arts Bks.). (Illus.). 1964. 10.50 o.s.i. (ISBN 0-8038-1527-1). Hastings.
Blues, Suzie. Scurrying in Rhythm. 64p. 1982. pap. 6.00 (ISBN 0-9604198-2-9). Three Tree Pr.
--South of Summer. 28p. 1979. pap. 2.50 (ISBN 0-9604198-1-0). Three Tree Pr.
Bluestein, Bernard R. & Hilton, Clifford L., eds. Amphoteric Surfactants. (Surfactant Science Ser.: Vol. 12). (Illus.). 352p. 1982. 55.00 (ISBN 0-8247-1277-3). Dekker.
Blueston, Barry & Harrison, Bennett. The Deindustrialization of America. 1982. 19.95 (ISBN 0-465-01590-5). Basic.
Bluestone, Rodney. Diagnosis & Management of Rheumatic Diseases. LC 79-25718. 1980. 29.95 (ISBN 0-201-00094-6, Med-Nurse). A-W.
Bluestone, Rodney, ed. Rheumatology. (UCLA Postgraduate Medicine Ser.). 1980. 40.00 (ISBN 0-471-09475-7, Pub. by Wiley Med). Wiley.
Bluffield, Bob. The Focalguide to Weddings & Special Occasions. (Focalguide Ser.). (Illus.). 1979. pap. 7.95 (ISBN 0-240-51000-3). Focal Pr.
Bluffield, Robert. Making & Managing a Photographic Studio in Britain. (Illus.). 144p. 1982. 17.95 (ISBN 0-7153-8245-4). David & Charles.
Bluhm, William T. Theories of the Political System: Classics of Political Thought & Modern Political Analysis. 3rd ed. 1978. ref. ed. 22.95 (ISBN 0-13-913327-5). P-H.
Bluhm, William T., ed. The Paradigm Problem in Political Science: Perspectives from Philosophy & from Practice. LC 81-70433. 224p. 1982. 19.95 (ISBN 0-89089-218-0); pap. 9.95 (ISBN 0-89089-219-9). Carolina Acad Pr.
Blum, Albert & Estey, Martin. White Collar Workers. 1971. text ed. 9.50x (ISBN 0-685-77218-7, 0-394-30111). Phila Bk Co.
Blum, Albert A., ed. International Handbook of Industrial Relations: Contemporary Developments & Research. LC 79-8586. (Illus.). xiv, 698p. 1981. 55.00 (ISBN 0-313-21303-8, BLH/). Greenwood.
Blum, Barbara L. Psychological Aspects of Pregnancy, Birthing, & Bonding. LC 80-14227. (New Directions in Psychotherapy Ser.: Vol. IV). 380p. (Series editor Paul T. Olsen). 1980. 29.95 (ISBN 0-87705-210-7). Human Sci Pr.
Blum, Daniel. A New Pictorial History of the Talkies. 1982. 9.95 (ISBN 0-686-83117-9, Perige). Putnam Pub Group.
--Pictorial History of the Silent Screen. 1955. 7.95 o.p. (ISBN 0-448-01477-7, G&D). Putnam Pub Group.
--A Pictorial History of the Silent Screen. (Illus.). 1972. pap. 6.95 o.p. (ISBN 0-399-11098-4). Putnam Pub Group.
--A Pictorial History of the Silent Screen. 1982. 9.95 (ISBN 0-686-83116-0, Perige). Putnam Pub Group.
Blum, Daniel & Kobal, John. A New Pictorial History of the Talkies. rev. ed. (Illus.). 384p. 1973. pap. 7.95 o.p. (ISBN 0-399-11231-6). Putnam Pub Group.
Blum, Ethel. The Total Traveller by Ship. rev. ed. 400p. 1983. pap. 12.95 (ISBN 0-88254-738-0). Hippocrene Bks.
Blum, Etta. The Space My Body Fills. LC 80-26565. 68p. (Orig.). 1980. pap. 4.95 (ISBN 0-913270-93-8). Sunstone Pr.
Blum, Henrik L. Planning for Health. LC 74-722. 622p. 1974. 29.95 o.p. (ISBN 0-87705-149-6). Human Sci Pr.
--Planning for Health: Generics for the Eighties. 2nd ed. LC 80-23461. 1981. 34.95 (ISBN 0-89885-013-4). Human Sci Pr.
Blum, John M. The Progressive Presidents: Theodore Roosevelt, Woodrow Wilson, Franklin D. Roosevelt, Lyndon B. Johnson. 224p. 1982. pap. 5.95x (ISBN 0-393-00063-X). Norton.
--Woodrow Wilson & the Politics of Morality. (Library of American Biography). 1962. pap. 5.95 (ISBN 0-316-10021-8). Little.
Blum, John M. & Morgan, Edmund S. The National Experience: A History of the United States, Two Part Paperbound Format. 5th ed. 1981. Vol. 1 to 1977, 473p. pap. text ed. 14.95 (ISBN 0-15-565673-2, HC); Vol. 2 since 1865, 583p. pap. text ed. 14.95 (ISBN 0-15-565674-0); test manual 3.95 (ISBN 0-15-565675-9). HarBraceJ.
Blum, John M., jt. auth. see Cole, Donald B.
Blum, John M., et al. The National Experience: A History of the United States. 5th ed. 970p. 1981. text ed. 23.95 (ISBN 0-15-565672-4, HC); Learning History Vol.1. student's guide 6.95 (ISBN 0-15-565676-7); Learning History Vol. 2. student's guide 6.95 (ISBN 0-15-565677-5); test manual 3.95 (ISBN 0-15-565675-9). HarBraceJ.
--The National Experience: Part 2: A History of the United States Since 1865. 583p. 1981. pap. text ed. 14.95 (ISBN 0-15-565674-0, HC). HarBraceJ.
Blum, Kenneth. Handbook of Abusable Drugs. 1983. 79.95 (ISBN 0-89876-036-4). Gardner Pr.
Blum, Leonor, tr. see Fraginals, Manuel M.
Blum, R. L. Discovery & Representation of Causal Relationships from a Large Time-Oriented Clinical Database: The RX Project. (Lecture Notes in Medical Informatics Ser.: Vol. 19). 242p. 1983. pap. 18.00 (ISBN 0-387-11962-0). Springer-Verlag.
Blum, Richard H. Deceivers & Deceived: Observations on Confidence Men & Their Victims, Informants & Their Quarry, Political & Industrial Spies & Ordinary Citizens. (Illus.). 340p. 1972. photocopy ed. spiral 34.75x (ISBN 0-398-02235-6). C C Thomas.
Blum, Robert. Drawing the Line: The Origin of the American Containment Policy in South Asia. 1982. 22.95 (ISBN 0-393-01565-3). Norton.
Blum, Ronald & Roller, Duane. Physics: Electricity, Magnetism & Light, Vol. 2. (Illus.). 1800p. 1981. text ed. 28.95; write for info. solutions manual. Holden-Day.
Blum, Ronald, jt. auth. see Roller, Duane.
Blum, Shirley N. Early Netherlandish Triptychs: A Study in Patronage. LC 68-10902. (California Studies in the History of Art: No. XIII). (Illus.). 1969. 90.00x (ISBN 0-520-01444-8). U of Cal Pr.
Blum, Stella, ed. see Ackermann, Rudolph.
Blum, Virgil C. Freedom of Choice in Education. LC 77-8086. 1977. Repr. of 1958 ed. lib. bdg. 19.25x (ISBN 0-8371-9677-9, BLFC). Greenwood.
Blumberg, A. A. & Stanley, J. Form & Function: Science in a Technological Society. text ed. 18.50 o.p. (ISBN 0-07-006186-6, C); 1.50 o.p. instructor's manual (ISBN 0-07-006188-2). McGraw.
Blumberg, Abraham S. Current Perspectives on Criminal Behavior. 2nd ed. 442p. 1981. pap. text ed. 12.00 (ISBN 0-394-32156-1). Knopf.
Blumberg, Abraham S., ed. Law & Order: The Scales of Justice. rev. 2nd. ed. LC 72-87667. 188p. 1970. pap. text ed. 4.95 (ISBN 0-87855-543-9). Transaction Bks.
Blumberg, Arthur. Supervisors & Teachers: A Private Cold War. 2nd ed. LC 79-89771. 1980. 20.75 (ISBN 0-8211-0133-1); text ed. 18.60 in copies of 10 (ISBN 0-686-66218-0). McCutchan.
Blumberg, Herbert H. & Hare, A. Paul. Small Groups & Social Interaction, Vol. 1. 750p. 1983. write for info. (ISBN 0-471-10242-3, Pub. by Wiley-Interscience). Wiley.
--Small Groups & Social Interactions, Vol. 2. 750p. 1983. write for info. (ISBN 0-471-90091-5, Pub. by Wiley-Interscience). Wiley.
Blumberg, Leonard, et al. Skid Row & Its Alternatives: Research & Recommendations from Philadelphia. LC 72-92877. 350p. 1973. 29.95 (ISBN 0-87722-055-7). Temple U Pr.
Blumberg, Paul. Industrial Democracy: The Sociology of Participation. LC 69-12382. 288p. 1974. pap. 4.95 o.p. (ISBN 0-8052-0414-8). Schocken.
--Inequality in an Age of Decline. (Illus.). 1981. pap. 6.95 (ISBN 0-19-502967-4, GB 649). Oxford U Pr.
Blumberg, Phillip I. The Megacorporation in American Society: The Scope of Corporate Power. LC 75-6667. 1975. pap. text ed. 12.95 (ISBN 0-13-574053-3). P-H.
Blumberg, Rena. Headstrong: My Story of Conquest & Celebrations... Living With Chemotherapy. 1982. 10.95 (ISBN 0-517-54723-6). Crown.
Blumberg, Rhoda. Backyard Bestiary. LC 78-6755. (Illus.). (gr. 2-6). 1979. 7.50 o.p. (ISBN 0-698-20444-1, Coward). Putnam Pub Group.
--Famine. LC 78-6837. (Impact Bks.). (Illus.). (gr. 9 up). 1978. PLB 8.90 s&l (ISBN 0-531-02201-3). Watts.
--First Ladies. LC 77-2617. (First Books About Washington Ser.). (gr. 4 up). 1981. PLB 7.90 o.p. (ISBN 0-531-01286-7). Watts.
--The First Travel Guide to the Bottom of the Sea. LC 82-17938. (Illus.). 96p. (gr. 4 up). 1983. 9.00 (ISBN 0-688-01692-8). Lothrop.
--Sharks. (First Bks.). (Illus.). 72p. (gr. 4 up). 1976. PLB 8.90 (ISBN 0-531-00846-0). Watts.
--Witches. (First Bks.). (Illus.). (gr. 4 up). 1979. PLB 8.90 s&l (ISBN 0-531-02948-4). Watts.
Blumberg, Richard E. & Grow, James R. The Rights of Tenants. 1979. pap. 2.50 o.p. (ISBN 0-380-41780-4, 56739). Avon.
Blumberg, Stanley & Owens, Gwinn. Energy & Conflict: The Life & Times of Edward Teller. LC 75-43812. 1976. 12.95 o.p. (ISBN 0-399-11551-X). Putnam Pub Group.
Blumberg, Stanley A. & Owens, Gwinn. The Survival Factor: Israeli Intelligence from World War I to the Present. (Illus.). 320p. 1982. 15.95 (ISBN 0-399-12646-5). Putnam Pub Group.
Blume, Bernhard & Schmidt, Henry J. German Literature: Texts & Contexts. 416p. 1973. text ed. 13.95 o.p. (ISBN 0-07-006187-4, C). McGraw.
Blume, Dieter. The Sculpture of Anthony Caro, 1942-1980: A Catalogue Raisonne, 4 Vols. (Illus.). 736p. (Orig.). 1983. Set. pap. 85.00 (ISBN 0-8390-0299-8). Allanheld & Schram.
Blume, Friedrich. Two Centuries of Bach. Godman, Stanley, tr. (Music Reprint Ser.). 1978. Repr. of 1950 ed. lib. bdg. 16.50 (ISBN 0-306-77567-0). Da Capo.
Blume, Judy. Are You There God? It's Me, Margaret. LC 79-122741. 160p. (gr. 5-7). 1970. 9.95 (ISBN 0-02-710990-9). Bradbury Pr.
--Are You There God? It's Me, Margaret. 1974. pap. 1.95 (ISBN 0-440-90419-6, LFL). Dell.
--La Ballena. Ada, Alma F., tr. 160p. (gr. 3-5). 1983. 9.95 (ISBN 0-02-710940-2). Bradbury Pr.
--Blubber. LC 73-94116. 160p. (gr. 4-6). 1974. 9.95 (ISBN 0-02-711010-9). Bradbury Pr.
--Blubber. 160p. 1976. pap. 2.50 (ISBN 0-440-40707-9, YB). Dell.
--Deenie. LC 73-80197. 192p. (gr. 6-8). 1973. 9.95 (ISBN 0-02-711020-6). Bradbury Pr.
--Deenie. 1974. pap. 2.25 (ISBN 0-440-93259-9, LFL). Dell.
--Estas ahi Dios? Soy yo Margaret. Ada, Alma F., tr. 160p. (gr. 5-7). 1983. 9.95 (ISBN 0-02-710950-X). Bradbury Pr.
--Forever. LC 74-22850. 216p. 1975. 9.95 (ISBN 0-02-711030-3). Bradbury Pr.
--Freckle Juice. 1978. pap. 1.75 (ISBN 0-440-42813-0, YB). Dell.
--Iggie's House. LC 70-104340. 128p. (gr. 4-7). 1970. 9.95 (ISBN 0-02-711040-0). Bradbury Pr.
--Iggie's House. (gr. k-6). 1981. pap. 2.50 (ISBN 0-440-44062-9, YB). Dell.
--It's Not the End of the World. LC 70-181739. 176p. (gr. 5-7). 1972. 9.95 (ISBN 0-02-711050-8). Bradbury Pr.
--The One in the Middle Is the Green Kangaroo. LC 80-29664. (Illus.). 40p. (gr. k-3). 1981. 8.95 (ISBN 0-02-711060-5). Bradbury Pr.
--Otherwise Known As Sheila the Great. (gr. 3-6). 1972. 9.25 (ISBN 0-525-36455-2, 0898-270). Dutton.
--Otherwise Known as Shelia the Great. (gr. k-6). 1981. pap. 2.25 (ISBN 0-440-46701-2, YB). Dell.
--Starring Sally J. Freedman As Herself. LC 76-57805. 296p. (gr. 4-7). 1977. 10.95 (ISBN 0-02-711070-2). Bradbury Pr.
--Superfudge. LC 80-10439. 176p. (gr. 3-6). 1980. 9.25 (ISBN 0-525-40522-4, 0898-270). Dutton.
--Tales of a Fourth Grade Nothing. (gr. 3-7). 1981. pap. 2.25 (ISBN 0-440-48474-X, YB). Dell.
--Tales of a Fourth Grade Nothing. LC 70-179050. (Illus.). 128p. (gr. 2-5). 1972. 9.25 (ISBN 0-525-40720-0, 0898-270). Dutton.
--Then Again, Maybe I Won't. LC 77-156548. 176p. (gr. 5-7). 1971. 9.95 (ISBN 0-02-711090-7). Bradbury Pr.
--Then Again, Maybe I Won't. pap. 1.95 (ISBN 0-440-98659-1, LFL). Dell.
--Then Again, Maybe I Won't. (gr. k-6). Date not set. pap. 2.25 (ISBN 0-440-48659-9, YB). Dell.
--Tiger Eyes. LC 81-6152. 256p. (gr. 7 up). 1981. 10.95 (ISBN 0-02-711080-X). Bradbury Pr.
--Wifey. LC 78-6145. 1978. 8.95 o.s.i. (ISBN 0-399-12241-9). Putnam Pub Group.
Blume, Marshall E. & Friend, Irwin. The Changing Role of the Individual Investor: A Twentieth Century Fund Report. LC 78-18303. 1978. 29.95 o.p. (ISBN 0-471-04547-0, Pub. by Wiley-Interscience). Wiley.

Blume, Marshall E., et al, eds. Economic Activity & Finance. 288p. 1982. prof ref 35.00x (ISBN 0-88410-858-9). Ballinger Pub.

Blume, Stuart S. Perspectives in the Sociology of Science. LC 76-30827. 1977. 48.95 (ISBN 0-471-99480-4, Pub. by Wiley-Interscience). Wiley.

Blume, Warren T. Atlas of Pediatric Electroencephalography. 344p. 1982. text ed. 93.50 (ISBN 0-89004-564-X). Raven.

Blumenfeld, Hans. Metropolis...& Beyond: Selected Essays. LC 78-17955. 1979. 48.50 (ISBN 0-471-04281-1, Pub. by Wiley-Interscience). Wiley.

Blumenfeld, Harold, tr. see Praetorius, Michael.

Blumenfeld, Milton J. Careers in Photography. LC 79-16299. (Early Career Bks.). (Illus.). (gr. 2-5). 1979. PLB 5.95g (ISBN 0-8225-0338-7). Lerner Pubns.

Blumenfeld, Ralph & Staff & Editors of the New York Post. Henry Kissinger: The Private & Public Story. (Illus., Orig.). 1974. pap. 1.75 o.p. (ISBN 0-451-06343-0, E6343, Sig). NAL.

Blumenfeld, Samuel, ed. Property in a Humane Economy. LC 74-22455. 294p. 1974. pap. 9.00 (ISBN 0-87548-340-2). Open Court.

Blumenfeld, Samuel L. Alpha-Phonics: A Primer for Beginning Readers. 160p. (Orig.). 1983. pap. 19.95 (ISBN 0-686-83942-0); 19.95 (ISBN 0-8159-6916-3). Devin.

--Teach Them to Read: A Step-by-Step Primer. 1982. pap. 19.95 spiral bdg. (ISBN 0-686-81779-6). Devin.

Blumenfeld, Yorick. Jenny. 1982. 5.95 (ISBN 0-316-10032-3). Little.

Blumenfield, Thomas, jt. ed. see Slockbower, Jean.

Blumenschein, Marian. Home in Honduras. LC 74-82186. 1975. 7.50 o.p. (ISBN 0-8309-0125-6). Herald Hse.

Blumensen, Martin. Patton Papers, Nineteen Forty to Nineteen Forty-Five, Vol. 2. LC 74-156490. 912p. 1974. 39.50 (ISBN 0-395-18498-9). HM.

Blumenson, Martin. Kasserine Pass. LC 82-60693. 351p. 1983. pap. 3.15 (ISBN 0-86721-238-1). Playboy Pbks.

--Liberation. LC 78-21967. (World War II Ser.). (Illus.). 1979. lib. bdg. 19.92 (ISBN 0-8094-2511-4). Silver.

Blumensow, John J. Identifying American Architecture: A Pictorial Guide to Styles & Terms, 1600-1945. Rev. ed. LC 80-28103. (Illus.). 1981. pap. 7.95 (ISBN 0-910050-50-3). AASLH.

Blumenthal. The Art of Letter Writing. Date not set. pap. price not set (ISBN 0-448-12040-2, G&D). Putnam Pub Group.

Blumenthal, Arthur. Process of Cognition. (Illus.). 1977. ref. ed. 23.95 (ISBN 0-13-722983-6). P-H.

Blumenthal, Arthur R. Theater Art of the Medici. LC 80-22452. (Illus.). 248p. 1980. pap. 20.00x (ISBN 0-87451-191-7). U Pr of New Eng.

Blumenthal, David R., intro. by see Seventy First Infantry Division, U.S. Army.

Blumenthal, Henry. American & French Culture, 1800 to 1900: Interchanges in Art, Science, Literature & Society. LC 74-27187. xv, 554p. 1976. 37.50x (ISBN 0-8071-0155-9). La State U Pr.

Blumenthal, Herman T., ed. Handbook of the Diseases of Aging. 512p. 1983. text ed. 36.50 (ISBN 0-442-21566-5). Van Nos Reinhold.

Blumenthal, Howard J. Everyone's Guide to Personal Computers. (Orig.). 1983. pap. 5.95 (ISBN 0-345-30218-4). Ballantine.

--The Media Room: Creating Your Own Home Entertainment & Information Center. (Orig.). 1983. pap. 8.95 (ISBN 0-14-046538-3). Penguin.

Blumenthal, Joseph. Art of the Printed Book, Fourteen Fifty-Five to Nineteen Fifty-Five. LC 73-82830. (Illus.). 212p. 1973. 30.00 (ISBN 0-87923-082-7). Godine.

--Art of the Printed Book, Fourteen Fifty-Five to Nineteen Fifty-Five. LC 73-82830. (Illus.). 1974. pap. 15.00 (ISBN 0-87923-259-5). Godine.

Blumenthal, Joseph C. English Thirty-Two Hundred. 3rd ed. 550p. 1981. pap. text ed. 10.95 (ISBN 0-15-522711-4, HC); tests 1.50 (ISBN 0-15-522712-2); answer key to tests 0.95 (ISBN 0-15-522713-0); alternate tests 1.50 (ISBN 0-15-522714-9); answer key to alternate tests 0.95 (ISBN 0-15-522715-7). HarBraceJ.

--English Twenty-Six Hundred. 5th ed. 448p. 1981. pap. text ed. 9.95 (ISBN 0-15-522716-5, HC); tests 1.50 (ISBN 0-15-522717-3); answer key to tests 0.95 (ISBN 0-15-522718-1). HarBraceJ.

--English Twenty-Two Hundred. 3rd ed. 383p. 1981. pap. text ed. 9.95 (ISBN 0-15-522719-X, HC); tests 1.50 (ISBN 0-15-522720-3); answer key to tests 0.95 (ISBN 0-15-522721-1). HarBraceJ.

Blumenthal, Lassor A. Successful Business Writing: How to Write Successful Letters, Proposals, Resumes, & Speeches. 80p. 1976. pap. 2.95 (ISBN 0-448-12042-9, G&D). Putnam Pub Group.

Blumenthal, Leonard M. Theory & Applications of Distance Geometry. 2nd ed. LC 79-113117. 1970. text ed. 16.95 (ISBN 0-8284-0242-6). Chelsea Pub.

Blumenthal, Michael. Sympathetic Magic. LC 80-50812. (Illus.). 96p. (Orig.). 1980. 25.00 o.p. (ISBN 0-931956-04-8); pap. 6.50 (ISBN 0-931956-03-X); handbound o.p. 60.00 (ISBN 0-686-70197-6). Water Mark.

Blumenthal, Monica D., et al. Justifying Violence: Attitudes of American Men. LC 74-169101. 380p. 1972. 18.00x (ISBN 0-87944-005-8); pap. 12.00x (ISBN 0-87944-004-X). Inst Soc Res.

--More About Justifying Violence: Methodological Studies of Attitudes & Behavior. LC 74-620136. 416p. 1975. 20.00x (ISBN 0-87944-192-5); pap. 12.00 (ISBN 0-87944-191-7). Inst Soc Res.

Blumenthal, P. J. Slow Train to Cincinnati. 1975. pap. 3.00 (ISBN 0-915572-51-6, Pub by Black Dragon Bks). Panjandrum.

Blumenthal, S., jt. auth. see Yazijian, H.

Blumenthal, Sherman S. Management Information Systems: A Framework for Planning & Development. 1969. ref. ed. 21.95 (ISBN 0-13-548636-X). P-H.

Blumenthal, Sidney. The Permanent Campaign. 1982. pap. 6.95 (ISBN 0-671-45341-6, Touchstone Bks). S&S.

Blumenthal, Susan. Understanding & Buying a Small Business Computer. Date not set. pap. 8.95 (ISBN 0-672-21890-9). Sams.

Blumenthal, W. B. The Chemical Behavior of Zirconium. 398p. 1958. 23.50 (ISBN 0-442-00832-5, Pub. by Van Nos Reinhold). Krieger.

Blumenthal, Warren B. The Creator & Man. LC 80-5843. 139p. 1980. lib. bdg. 18.00 (ISBN 0-8191-1340-9); pap. text ed. 8.25 (ISBN 0-8191-1341-7). U Pr of Amer.

Blumer, Diedrich, jt. ed. see Benson, Frank.

Blumer, Erna. Ring Tail Tooter. new ed. (Illus.). 350p. 1975. 9.95 (ISBN 0-89121-000-8); pap. 5.95 (ISBN 0-89121-001-6). Westland Pub Co.

Blumer, Herbert. Appraisal of Thomas & Znaniecki's the Polish Peasant in Europe & America. LC 40-4813. 1939. pap. 4.50 o.s.i. (ISBN 0-527-03278-6). Kraus Repr.

--Symbolic Interactionism: Perspective & Method. 1969. text ed. 18.95 (ISBN 0-13-879924-5). P-H.

Blumhagen, Kathleen O. & Johnson, Walter D., eds. Women's Studies: An Interdisciplinary Collection. (Contributions in Women's Studies: No. 2). 1978. lib. bdg. 22.50 (ISBN 0-313-20028-9, SJW/). Greenwood.

Blumhardt, Christoph. Evening Prayers for Every Day in the Year. Society Of Brothers, ed. LC 73-141948. 1971. 3.50 (ISBN 0-87486-204-3). Plough.

Blundell. A Guide to the Flowers of Kenya. 34.95 (ISBN 0-686-42770-X, Collins Pub England). Greene.

Blundell, Alan. Bond Graphs for Modelling Engineering Systems. (Electrical & Electronic Engineering Ser.). 151p. 1982. 44.95x (ISBN 0-470-27546-4). Halsted Pr.

Blundell, T. L., jt. ed. see Noble, D.

Blunden, E. Shelley & Keats As They Struck Their Contemporaries. LC 70-174689. (English Literature Ser., No. 33). 1971. Repr. of 1925 ed. lib. bdg. 32.95x (ISBN 0-8383-1341-8). Haskell.

Blunden, Edmund. Selected Poems-Blunden. Marsack, Robyn, ed. 107p. 1982. pap. text ed. 10.50x (ISBN 0-85635-425-2, 80639, Pub. by Carcanet New Pr England). Humanities.

--Undertones of War. LC 66-12379. 1966. pap. 1.85 o.p. (ISBN 0-15-692821-3, Harv). HarBraceJ.

Blunden, R. Social Development. (Studies in Developmental Paediatrics). (Illus.). 160p. 1982. text ed. 25.00 (ISBN 0-85200-304-8, Pub. by MTP Pr England). Kluwer Boston.

Blunt, Anthony. Artistic Theory in Italy, 1450-1600. 1956. 22.50x (ISBN 0-19-817106-4); pap. 6.95x (ISBN 0-19-881050-4, OPB). Oxford U Pr.

--Guide to Baroque Rome. LC 82-47546. (Icon Editions). (Illus.). 256p. 1982. 33.65i (ISBN 0-06-430395-0, HarpT). Har-Row.

--Picasso's Guernica. (Whidden Lectures Ser). 1969. pap. 8.95 (ISBN 0-19-500135-4). Oxford U Pr.

Blunt, Anthony & Lockspeiser, Edward. French Art & Music Since Fifteen Hundred. 1974. pap. 4.95x (ISBN 0-416-81650-9). Methuen Inc.

Blunt, Jerry. Composite Art of Acting. 1966. text ed. 20.95 (ISBN 0-02-311150-X, 31115). Macmillan.

--More Stage Dialects. (Illus.). 1980. text ed. 20.95 scp (ISBN 0-06-040784-0, HarpC); scp cassettes to accompany text 26.50 (ISBN 0-06-040796-4). Har-Row.

Blunt, John H. Dictionary of Sects, Heresies, Ecclesiastical Parties & Schools of Religious Thought. LC 74-9653. 1974. Repr. of 1874 ed. 68.00x (ISBN 0-8103-3751-7). Gale.

Blunt, M. A New Approach to Teaching & Learning Anatomy: Objectives & Learning Activities for the Anatomy Course. 1976. 12.95 (ISBN 0-407-00098-4). Butterworth.

Blunt, Michael J. & Girgis, M. Multiple Choice Questions in Anatomy & Neurobiology for Undergraduates. (Illus.). 1979. pap. 8.50 o.p. (ISBN 0-407-00153-0). Butterworth.

Blust, Robert A. The Proto-Oceanic Palatals. 1979. pap. text ed. 15.00x (ISBN 0-8248-0684-0, Pub. by Polynesian Soc). UH Pr.

Blustein, Jeffrey. Parents & Children: The Ethics of the Family. 1982. text ed. 19.95x (ISBN 0-19-503072-9); pap. text ed. 9.95x (ISBN 0-19-503073-7). Oxford U Pr.

Bly, Coletta B. The Figleaf Collection. (Illus.). (gr. 5 up). 1977. 4.50 o.p. (ISBN 0-533-02501-X). Vantage.

Bly, J. Hall Marks on English Silver. (Illus.). 1975. pap. 2.25 o.p. (ISBN 0-912728-87-6). Newbury Bks.

Bly, Janet, jt. auth. see Bly, Stephen.

Bly, Robert. The Eight Stages of Translation. (Poetic Ser.: No. 2). 64p. 1983. pap. text ed. 5.95 (ISBN 0-937672-10-6). Rowan Tree.

--Four Ramages. (Illus.). 12p. (Orig.). 1983. pap. 3.95 (ISBN 0-935306-11-0). Barnwood Pr.

--The Man in the Black Coat Turns: Poems. 76p. 1983. pap. 5.95 (ISBN 0-14-042303-6). Penguin.

--Talking All Morning. (Poets on Poetry Ser.). 316p. 1980. pap. 7.95 (ISBN 0-472-15760-4). U of Mich Pr.

Bly, Robert, ed. Neruda & Vallejo: Selected Poems. 1971. pap. 5.95 (ISBN 0-8070-6421-1, BP376). Beacon Pr.

Bly, Robert, intro. by see Sonnevi, Goran.

Bly, Robert, tr. Times Alone: Selected Poems of Antonio Machado. 176p. 1983. 17.95 (ISBN 0-8195-5087-6); pap. 8.95 (ISBN 0-8195-6081-2). Wesleyan U Pr.

Bly, Robert, tr. see Hamsun, Knut.

Bly, Robert, tr. see Machado, Antonio.

Bly, Robert, tr. see Rumi.

Bly, Robert W. & Blake, Gary. Technical Writing: Structure, Standards & Style. LC 82-15223. 160p. 1982. 11.95 (ISBN 0-07-006174-2); pap. 6.95 (ISBN 0-07-006173-4). McGraw.

Bly, Stephen. Radical Discipleship. 128p. (Orig.). 1981. pap. 5.95 (ISBN 0-8024-8219-8). Moody.

Bly, Stephen & Bly, Janet. Devotions with a Difference. LC 82-8304. 128p. (gr. 3 up). 1982. pap. 5.95 (ISBN 0-8024-1789-2). Moody.

--Questions I'd Like to Ask. LC 82-2252. 1982. 2.95 (ISBN 0-8024-7058-0). Moody.

Bly, Stephen A. God's Angry Side. LC 82-12411. 1982. pap. 5.95 (ISBN 0-8024-4918-2). Moody.

--The President Is Stuck in the Mud. (Making Choices Ser.: No. 4). (Orig.). (gr. 3-8). 1982. pap. 2.50 (ISBN 0-89191-661-X, 56614). Cook.

Blyden, Edward W. From West Africa to Palestine. LC 74-155376. Repr. of 1873 ed. cancelled (ISBN 0-8371-1407-1, Pub. by Negro U Pr). Greenwood.

Blyn, Martin R. & Krooss, Herman E. History of Financial Intermediaries. 1971. text ed. 7.95x (ISBN 0-685-47982-X). Phila Bk Co.

Blyth, Alan. Opera on Record. LC 81-47801. 688p. 1982. pap. 11.06i (ISBN 0-06-090910-2, CN 910, CN). Har-Row.

Blyth, F. G. Geological Maps & Their Interpretation. 48p. 1976. pap. text ed. 6.95 (ISBN 0-7131-2568-3). E Arnold.

Blyth, Hugh F., jt. auth. see Stevenson, Don.

Blyth, John A. English University Adult Education 1908-1958. 384p. 1982. 20.00 (ISBN 0-7190-0903-0). Manchester.

Blyth, R. H. History of Haiku, Vol. 1. (Illus.). 1963. pap. 19.95 o.p. (ISBN 0-89346-066-4, Pub. by Hokuseido Pr). Heian Intl.

--History of Haiku, Vols. 1 & 2. (Illus.). 1964. Set. 42.45 o.p. (ISBN 0-89346-068-0, Pub. by Hokuseido Pr). Heian Intl.

--History of Haiku, Vol. 2. (Illus.). 1964. 22.50 o.p. (ISBN 0-89346-067-2, Pub. by Hokuseido Pr). Heian Intl.

--Zen & Zen Classics, 5 vols. Incl. Vol. 1. 1960. pap. 7.95 o.p. (ISBN 0-89346-048-6); Vol. 2. 1964. 11.95 o.p. (ISBN 0-89346-049-4); Vol. 3. 1970. 11.95 o.p. (ISBN 0-89346-050-8); Vol. 4. 1966. pap. 17.50 o.p. (ISBN 0-89346-051-6); Vol. 5. 1962. 11.95 o.p. (ISBN 0-89346-052-4). ISBN 0-89346-053-2, Pub. by Hokuseido Pr). Heian Intl.

--Zen in English Literature & Oriental Classics. (Illus.). 460p. Date not set. pap. price not set (ISBN 0-89346-207-1). Heian Intl.

Blyth, R. H., jt. auth. see Eun, Lee.

Blyth, W. A. & Derricott, R. The Social Significance of Middle Schools. 1977. 31.50 (ISBN 0-7134-0488-4, Pub. by Batsford England); pap. 17.50 (ISBN 0-686-82894-1). David & Charles.

Blythe, Bruce T., jt. auth. see Garcia, Edward J.

Blythe, Hal T., et al. Competencies in Materials Development & Machine Operation, Self Directive Activities: A Functional Approach. 2nd ed. (Illus.). 173p. 1982. pap. text ed. 6.95x (ISBN 0-686-43235-5). American Pr.

--Competencies in Materials Development & Machine Operation: Self-Directive Activities, a Functional Approach. (Illus.). 173p. (Orig.). 1979. pap. 4.95x o.p. (ISBN 0-89641-019-6). American Pr.

Blythe, Myrna. For Better & for Worse. LC 78-16874. 1979. 9.95 o.p. (ISBN 0-399-12166-8). Putnam Pub Group.

Blythe, Richard. The Dinosaurs Footprint. LC 80-52533. (Starters Ser.). PLB 8.00 (ISBN 0-382-06503-4). Silver.

--Dragons & Other Fabulous Beasts. LC 79-51211. (Illus.). (gr. 3-7). 1980. 5.95 (ISBN 0-448-16561-9, G&D); PLB 11.85 (ISBN 0-448-13611-2). Putnam Pub Group.

Blythe, William, ed. see Hazlitt, William.

Blyton, Enid see Swan, D. K.

BNA Editorial Staff. The Comparable Worth Issue. LC 81-18103. 144p. 1981. pap. text ed. 12.00 (ISBN 0-87179-372-5). BNA.

--Highlights of the New Pension Reform Law. 372p. 1974. pap. 12.50 o.p. (ISBN 0-87179-250-8). BNA.

--The New Federal Rules of Evidence, Annotated, with Analysis. LC 75-10794. 100p. 1975. pap. 4.00 o.p. (ISBN 0-87179-218-4). BNA.

BNA Editorial Staff, ed. Equal Employment Opportunity Act of 1972. LC 72-93800. 432p. 1973. 18.50 (ISBN 0-87179-171-4). BNA.

Boa, Kenneth. Cults, World Religions, & You. 1977. pap. 5.95 (ISBN 0-88207-752-X). Victor Bks.

--God I Don't Understand. 156p. 1975. pap. 4.95 (ISBN 0-88207-722-8). Victor Bks.

Boa, Kenneth & Moody, Larry. I'm Glad You Asked. 1982. pap. 5.95 (ISBN 0-88207-354-0). Victor Bks.

Boa, Kenneth & Proctor, William. Return of the Star of Bethlehem. LC 79-8548. 216p. 1980. 8.95 o.p. (ISBN 0-385-15454-2, Galilee). Doubleday.

Boa, Kenneth, jt. auth. see Livgren, Kerry.

Boa, Kenneth, jt. auth. see Wilkinson, Bruce.

Boaden, Noel T. Urban Policy-Making: Influences on County Boroughs in England & Wales. LC 71-158554. 1971. 22.95 (ISBN 0-521-08208-0). Cambridge U Pr.

Boadt, Lawrence. Jeremiah 1-25, Vol. 9. 1982. 12.95 (ISBN 0-89453-244-8); pap. 7.95 (ISBN 0-686-32764-0). M Glazier.

Boadt, Lawrence & Croner, Helga, eds. Biblical Studies: Meeting Ground of Jews & Christians. 220p. pap. 7.95 (ISBN 0-686-95166-2). ADL.

Boag, P., ed. see Lack, David.

Boahen, A. A., jt. auth. see Webster, J. B.

Boahen, Adu. Topics in West African History. (Africana Forum Ser.). (Orig.). 1977. pap. text ed. 4.50x (ISBN 0-582-64502-6). Humanities.

Boak, Arthur E., jt. auth. see Sinnigen, William G.

Boal, Augusto. Theater of the Oppressed. 200p. 1982. cancelled 8.95 (ISBN 0-8264-0197-X). Continuum.

Boalt, Gunnar, et al. European Orders of Chivalry. LC 70-151002. 153p. 1971. 7.50x o.p. (ISBN 0-8093-0506-2). S Ill U Pr.

Boar, B. H. Abend Debugging for Cobol Programmers. LC 75-42457. 321p. 1976. 32.50x (ISBN 0-471-08413-1, Pub. by Wiley-Interscience). Wiley.

Board, Christopher & Chorley, Richard J., eds. Progress in Geography, Vol. 8. LC 75-37304. 240p. 1976. 25.00 o.p. (ISBN 0-312-65065-5). St Martin.

Board, Christopher, et al, eds. Progress in Geography, Vols. 1-5. LC 74-94756. (International Reviews of Current Research Ser.). 1970. 22.50 ea. o.p. Vol. 1 (ISBN 0-312-64820-0). Vol. 2 (ISBN 0-312-64855-3). Vol. 3 (ISBN 0-312-64890-1). Vol. 4 (ISBN 0-312-64925-8). Vol. 5 (ISBN 0-312-64960-6). St Martin.

--Progress in Geography, Vol. 6. LC 74-94756. (Progress in Geography Ser). 320p. 1975. 25.00 o.p. (ISBN 0-312-64995-9). St Martin.

--Progress in Geography, Vol. 7. LC 74-22664. 320p. 1975. 25.00 o.p. (ISBN 0-312-65030-2). St Martin.

--Progress in Geography, Vol. 9. LC 76-14514. 1976. 25.00x o.p. (ISBN 0-312-65100-7). St Martin.

Board, Evelyn. Right Way to His Heart Cookbook. 9.50 (ISBN 0-392-05459-0, LTB). Sportshelf.

Board of Cooperative Education Services, Nassau County. Two Hundred Ways to Help Children Learn While You're at It. 1976. 16.00 (ISBN 0-87909-845-7). Reston.

Board of Education & Training. Bringing Life to Microbiology. 1979. 7.00 (ISBN 0-686-95719-9). Am Soc Microbio.

--Directory of Colleges & Universities Granting Degrees in Microbiology Nineteen Eighty. 1980. 5.00 (ISBN 0-686-95711-3). Am Soc Microbio.

--EleSec. subscription, quarterly 15.00 (ISBN 0-686-95724-5). Am Soc Microbio.

--Highlights in Microbiology Nineteen Seventy-Nine to Eighty, Vol. 3. (Highlights Ser.). 1981. 5.00 (ISBN 0-686-95718-0). Am Soc Microbio.

--Identification of Aerobic Gram-Positive & Gram-Negative Cocci. 3rd ed. (Continuing Education Manual Ser.). 1981. 7.00 (ISBN 0-686-95651-6). Am Soc Microbio.

--Identification of Glucose-Nonfermenting Gram-Negative Rods. (Continuing Education Manual Ser.). 1977. 7.00 (ISBN 0-686-95697-4). Am Soc Microbio.

--Identification of Saprophytic Fungi Commonly Encountered in a Clinical Environment. (Continuing Education Manual Ser.). (Illus.). 1979. 10.00 (ISBN 0-686-95686-9). Am Soc Microbio.

--Pathogenesis of Microbial Infections. (Illus.). 1981. 8.50 (ISBN 0-686-95662-1). Am Soc Microbio.

--Topic Outlines in Microbiology. 1980. 20.00 (ISBN 0-686-95715-6). Am Soc Microbio.

Board of Music Trade of the USA. Complete Catalogue of Sheet Music & Musical Works. LC 69-1666. 575p. 1973. Repr. of 1871 ed. lib. bdg. 55.00 o.p. (ISBN 0-306-71401-9). Da Capo.

Board, Tessa. Birds. (Insight Ser.). (gr. 4 up). 1983. PLB 8.90 (ISBN 0-531-03472-0). Watts.

--Mammals. (Insight Ser.). (Illus.). 40p. (gr. 4 up). 1983. PLB 8.90 (ISBN 0-531-03473-9). Watts.

Boardman, A. D. Electromagnetic Surface Modes. 816p. 1982. 83.00 (ISBN 0-471-10077-3, Pub. by Wiley-Interscience); pap. 72.00 (ISBN 0-471-27674-X). Wiley.

--Physics Programs. Incl. Applied Physics. LC 80-40121. 136p. 1980 (ISBN 0-471-27740-1); Magnetism. LC 80-40124. 219p (ISBN 0-471-27733-9); Optics. LC 80-40123. 123p (ISBN 0-471-27729-0); Solid State Physics. LC 80-40125. 353p (ISBN 0-471-27734-7). 1980. 13.95x ea. Wiley.

Boardman, David. Graphicacy & Geography Teaching. 208p. 1983. pap. text ed. 19.50x (ISBN 0-7099-0644-7, Pub. by Croom Helm Ltd England). Biblio Dist.

Boardman, Helen E, et al. The Neglected Battered Child Syndrome: Role Reversal in Parents. LC 63-21525. 1963. pap. 3.15 (ISBN 0-87868-074-8, G-17). Child Welfare.

Boardman, John. Greek Sculpture: The Archaic Period. LC 77-25202. (World of Art Ser.). (Illus.). 1978. 22.50x (ISBN 0-19-520046-2); pap. 9.95 (ISBN 0-19-520047-0). Oxford U Pr.

Boardman, John & La Rocca, Eugenio. Eros in Greece. LC 77-94381. (Illus.). 1978. write for info. o.s.i. (ISBN 0-913568-25-2). Avant-Garde.

Boardman, John, ed. see Dunbabin, Thomas J.

Boardman, Michael. Defoe & the Usage of Narrative. 195p. 1982. text ed. 22.50x (ISBN 0-8135-0961-0). Rutgers U Pr.

Boardman, Peter. Sacred Summits. (Illus.). 264p. 1983. 20.00 (ISBN 0-89886-045-8). Mountaineers.

Boardman, Peter & Tasker, Joe. The Shining Mountain. (Illus.). 192p. 1983. 14.95 (ISBN 0-525-24186-8, 01451-440); pap. 7.95 (ISBN 0-525-48053-6, 0772-230). Dutton.

Boardman, R. S. Roger Sherman: Signer & Statesman. LC 75-168671. (Era of the American Revolution Ser.). 396p. 1971. Repr. of 1938 ed. lib. bdg. 45.00 (ISBN 0-306-70412-9). Da Capo.

Boardman, Richard S., et al. Animal Colonies: Development & Function Through Time. 624p. 1973. 60.00 o.s.i. (ISBN 0-12-786175-0). Acad Pr.

Boardman, Robert & Keeley, James. Nuclear Exports & World Politics. LC 82-10779. 272p. 1982. 26.00x (ISBN 0-312-57976-4). St Martin.

Boardroom Reports, Editors & Experts. Encyclopedia of Practical Business. rev. ed. 400p. 1983. 50.00 (ISBN 0-932648-37-1). Boardroom.

Boarman, Patrick M. & Mugar, Jayson. Trade with China: Assessments by Leading Businessmen & Scholars. LC 74-1727. 208p. 1974. text ed. 23.95 o.p. (ISBN 0-275-08830-8). Praeger.

Boarman, Patrick M., tr. see Ropke, Wilhelm T.

Boas, F. Shakespeare & His Predecessors. LC 68-24898. (Studies in Shakespeare, No. 24). 1969. Repr. of 1904 ed. lib. bdg. 53.95x (ISBN 0-8383-0914-3). Haskell.

Boas, Mrs. F. Rossetti & His Poetry. LC 75-22072. (English Literature Ser., No. 33). 1975. lib. bdg. 31.95x (ISBN 0-8383-2074-0). Haskell.

Boas, F. S., ed. see Fletcher, Giles & Fletcher, Phineas.

Boas, Franz. Primitive Art. (Illus.). 1962. 9.50 (ISBN 0-8446-1695-8). Peter Smith.

--Race & Democratic Society. LC 70-86641. 1969. Repr. of 1945 ed. 10.00x (ISBN 0-8196-0248-5). Biblo.

Boas, Frederick S., ed. Songs & Lyrics from the English Masques & Light Operas. LC 77-14508. 1977. Repr. of 1949 ed. lib. bdg. 17.00x (ISBN 0-8371-9842-9, BOMO). Greenwood.

Boas, George. Inquiring Mind: An Introduction to Epistemology. LC 58-6815. (Paul Carus Lectures Ser.). vi, 437p. 1959. 23.50 (ISBN 0-87548-099-3). Open Court.

Boas, George & Wrenn, Harold H. What Is a Picture? LC 66-14867. (Illus.). (YA) (gr. 9 up). 1966. 6.50x o.p. (ISBN 0-8052-3284-2). Schocken.

Boas, Mary L. Mathematical Methods in Physical Sciences. LC 66-17646. 778p. 1966. 29.95x (ISBN 0-471-08417-4). Wiley.

--Mathematical Methods in the Physical Sciences. 2nd ed. 800p. 1983. text ed. write for info (ISBN 0-471-04409-1); solutions manual avail. Wiley.

Boas, Max & Chain, Steve. Big Mac: The Unauthorized Story of McDonald's. (RL 10). 1977. pap. 2.95 (ISBN 0-451-62227-8, ME2227, Ment). NAL.

Boas, Ralph, ed. see Polya, George.

Boas, Ralph P. & Smith, Edwin. An Introduction to the Study of Literature. 454p. 1982. Repr. of 1933 ed. lib. bdg. 30.00 (ISBN 0-89760-097-5). Telegraph Bks.

Boas, Ralph P., Jr. A Primer of Real Functions. 3rd ed. LC 81-82669. (Carus Monograph: No. 13). 196p. 1981. 16.50 (ISBN 0-88385-022-2). Math Assn.

Boas, Robert, jt. ed. see Stanton-Hicks, Michael.

Boase, Paul H., jt. auth. see Eisenson, Jon.

Boase, Paul H., jt. auth. see Whitman, Richard F.

Boase, Paul H., ed. The Rhetoric of Protest & Reform, 1878-1898. LC 80-11631. viii, 354p. 1980. 18.95x (ISBN 0-8214-0421-0, 82-83137). Ohio U Pr.

Boase, T. S. Death in the Middle Ages: Mortality, Judgment & Remembrance. LC 74-39152. (Illus.). 144p. 1972. pap. 3.95 o.p. (ISBN 0-07-006204-8, SP). McGraw.

Boase, T. S., ed. Cilician Kingdom of Armenia. LC 74-22291. 1979. text ed. 25.00 (ISBN 0-312-13895-4). St Martin.

Boase, Wendy. Early China. LC 77-12606. (Civilization Library). (Illus.). (gr. 5-8). 1978. PLB 9.40 s&l (ISBN 0-531-01426-6, Gloucester). Watts.

Boat, Jaydee. Dining In: Denver. (Dining in Ser.). (Orig.). 1981. pap. 7.95 (ISBN 0-89716-036-3). Peanut Butter.

Boateng, E. A. A Political Geography of Africa. LC 77-80828. 1978. 42.50 (ISBN 0-521-21764-4); pap. 15.95x (ISBN 0-521-29269-7). Cambridge U Pr.

Boater, Debbie, jt. auth. see Saint-Pierre, Gaston.

Boatman, Don E. Helps from Hebrews. LC 75-1066. (The Bible Study Textbook Ser.). (Illus.). 1960. 14.30 (ISBN 0-89900-044-4). College Pr Pub.

Boatman, Don E., ed. Out of My Treasure, 4 vols. Incl. Vol. I. White, Willie, ed. 1964 (ISBN 0-89900-117-3); Vol. II. 1965. o.p. (ISBN 0-89900-118-1); Vol. III. 1967 (ISBN 0-89900-119-X); Vol. IV. 1968. o.p. (ISBN 0-89900-120-3). pap. 4.95 ea. College Pr Pub.

--Out of My Treasure: Special Alumni Edition, Vol. V. LC 80-71104. (Out of My Treasure Ser.). 260p. 1981. pap. 4.95 o.p. (ISBN 0-89900-121-1). College Pr Pub.

Boatman, Russel. What the Bible Says about the End Time. LC 79-56542. (What the Bible Says Ser.). 1980. 13.50 o.s.i. (ISBN 0-89900-075-4). College Pr Pub.

Boatright, Kevin, ed. see Stetson, Daniel E.

Boatwright, Victor T., jt. ed. see Sheets, Herman E.

Boaz, Martha. Strategies for Meeting the Information Needs of Society in the Year 2000. LC 81-11751. 197p. 1981. lib. bdg. 23.50 (ISBN 0-87287-249-1). Libs Unl.

Bobak, Irene, jt. auth. see Jensen, Margaret.

Bobak, Irene M. & Jensen, Margaret D. A Modular Study Guide to Maternity Care. LC 82-7911. (Illus.). 229p. 1982. pap. text ed. 11.95 (ISBN 0-8016-0738-8). Mosby.

Bobart, Henry H. Basketwork Through the Ages. LC 72-171354. 188p. 1971. Repr. of 1936 ed. 30.00x (ISBN 0-8103-3400-3). Gale.

Bobbitt. Indiana Appellate Practice & Procedure, 2 vols. 1972. 59.50, with 1981 cum. (ISBN 0-672-81526-5, Bobbs-Merrill Law); 1981 cum. 15.00 (ISBN 0-672-82813-8). Michie-Bobbs.

Bober, G. F. Protection & the Law. (Contemporary Consumer Ser.). text ed. 6.68 (ISBN 0-07-006210-2, G); tchr's. manual & key 6.50 (ISBN 0-07-006211-0). McGraw.

Bober, Phyllis P. & Rubenstein, Ruth. Renaissance Artists & Antique Sculpture: A Handbook of Sources. (A Harvey Miller Publication). (Illus.). 1982. 45.00x (ISBN 0-19-921029-2). Oxford U Pr.

Bober, Stanley. Capital, Distribution & Growth: A Look at Neo-Keynesian Economics. LC 80-5861. 229p. 1980. lib. bdg. 20.00 (ISBN 0-8191-1263-1); pap. 10.25 (ISBN 0-8191-1264-X). U Pr of Amer.

Bober, William & Kenyon, Richard A. Fluid Mechanics. LC 79-12977. 558p. 1980. 34.95x (ISBN 0-471-04886-0); solutions manual avail. (ISBN 0-471-04999-9). Wiley.

Bobet, Bonnie, ed. see Reynolds, Maureen.

Bobillier, Marie see Brenet, Michel, pseud.

Bobillier, P. A., et al. Simulation with Gpss & Gpssv. LC 75-40316. 1976. 29.95 (ISBN 0-13-810549-9). P-H.

Bobinski, George S. Carnegie Libraries: Their History & Impact on American Public Library Developments. LC 68-54216. (Illus.). 1969. 10.00 (ISBN 0-8389-0022-4). ALA.

Bobker, Lee R. The Unicorn Group. LC 78-23545. 1979. pap. 9.95 (ISBN 0-688-03395-4). Morrow.

Bobo, Benjamin F., et al. No Land Is an Island: Individual Rights & Government Control of Land Use. LC 75-38415. (Illus.). 1975. pap. 5.95 o.p. (ISBN 0-917616-03-0). ICS Pr.

Bobon, D., ed. AMDP System in Psychopharmacology. (Modern Problems of Pharmacopsychiatry: Vol. 20). (Illus.). viii, 240p. 1983. 96.00 (ISBN 3-8055-3637-2). S Karger.

Bobrow, Edwin E. How to Sell Your Way Into Your Own Business. 1977. text ed. 24.95 (ISBN 0-686-98284-3). Sales & Mktg.

--Selling the Volume Retailer: A Practical Plan for Success. LC 75-1168. 126p. 1975. 15.95 (ISBN 0-86730-511-8). Lebhar Friedman.

Bobrow, Edwin E. & Wizenberg, Larry, eds. Sales Manager's Handbook. LC 82-71068. 576p. 1983. 45.00 (ISBN 0-87094-240-9). Dow Jones-Irwin.

Bobrow, J. Barron's New Guide to the Law School Admission Test (LSAT) Rev. ed. 640p. 1982. 17.95 (ISBN 0-8120-5420-2); pap. 7.95 (ISBN 0-8120-2362-5). Barron.

Bobrow, Jerry. Barron's How to Prepare for the Law School Admission Test (LSAT) LC 79-12930. 1982. 18.00 o.p. (ISBN 0-8120-5337-0); pap. 7.95 (ISBN 0-8120-2035-9). Barron.

Bobrow, Jerry & Covino, William A. GMAT (Graduate Management Admissions Test) Preparation Guide. (Cliffs Test Preparation Ser.). (Illus.). 1982. pap. text ed. 5.95 (ISBN 0-8220-2006-8). Cliffs.

--PSAT (Preliminary Scholastic Aptitude Test) Preparation Guide. (Cliffs Test Preparation Ser.). (Illus.). (gr. 10-11). 1982. pap. 3.25 (ISBN 0-8220-2002-5). Cliffs.

--SAT (Scholastic Aptitude Test) Preparation Guide. (Cliffs Test Preparation Ser.). (Illus.). (gr. 11-12). 1982. pap. 4.95 wkbk. (ISBN 0-8220-2000-9). Cliffs.

Bobrow, Jerry, et al. ACT (American College Testing Preparation Guide) (Cliffs Test Preparation Ser.). (Illus.). (gr. 10-12). 1982. pap. 4.95 wkbk. (ISBN 0-8220-2004-1). Cliffs.

Bobrow, Jill & Jinkins, Dana. Classic Yacht Interiors. (Illus.). 1982. 40.00 (ISBN 0-393-03274-4). Norton.

Bocca, Geoffrey. Amanda in Germany. (Commander Amanda). 208p. (Orig.). 1976. pap. 1.50 o.s.i. (ISBN 0-89083-156-4). Zebra.

Boccaccio. Andreuccio de Perugia. (Easy Reader, A). pap. 2.95 (ISBN 0-88436-049-0, 55250). EMC.

Boccaccio, G. The Decameron. 1982. pap. 5.95 (ISBN 0-451-62134-4, ME2134, Ment). NAL.

Boccaccio, Giovanni. Amorous Fiammetta. LC 76-98821. Repr. of 1926 ed. lib. bdg. 17.00x (ISBN 0-8371-3026-3, BOAF). Greenwood.

--Genealogia. LC 75-27843. (Renaissance & the Gods Ser.: Vol. 2). (Illus.). 1976. Repr. of 1494 ed. lib. bdg. 73.00 o.s.i. (ISBN 0-8240-2051-0). Garland Pub.

--Genealogie. LC 75-27847. (Renaissance & the Gods Ser.: Vol. 5). (Illus., Fr.). 1976. Repr. of 1531 ed. lib. bdg. 73.00 o.s.i. (ISBN 0-8240-2054-5). Garland Pub.

Bocchicchio, Lucille & Castle, Sue. Our Child's Medical History. LC 82-71745. 288p. 1982. 14.95 (ISBN 0-8119-0472-5). Fell.

Bocchino, Anthony J. & Tanford, J. Alexander. North Carolina Trial Evidence Manual. LC 76-29099. 1976. with 1978 suppl 25.00 (ISBN 0-87215-188-3); 1978 suppl. 7.50 (ISBN 0-87215-277-4). Michie-Bobbs.

Bocchino, William A. Management Information Systems: Tools & Techniques. LC 73-38416. (Illus.). 384p. 1972. ref. ed. 22.95 (ISBN 0-13-548693-9). P-H.

--Simplified Guide to Microcomputers with Practical Programs & Applications. LC 82-3671. 256p. 1982. 19.95 (ISBN 0-13-810085-3, Busn). P-H.

Boccio, Karen C. Inner Sanctions. rev. ed. 35p. (Orig.). 1980. pap. 3.50 (ISBN 0-910829-01-2). First East.

Bochenski, I. Ancient Formal Logic. (Studies in Logic & the Foundations of Mathematics: Vol. 10). 1968. Repr. of 1951 ed. 22.00 (ISBN 0-7204-2204-3, North Holland). Elsevier.

Bochenski, Innocenty M. History of Formal Logic. 2nd ed. LC 72-113118. 1970. text ed. 24.95 (ISBN 0-8284-0238-8). Chelsea Pub.

Bochenski, Joseph M., et al, eds. Guide to Marxist Philosophy: An Introductory Bibliography. LC 82-72940. 81p. 1972. pap. 4.95x (ISBN 0-8040-0561-3). Swallow.

Bochkor, Jeno, tr. see Ban, Jeno.

Bochner, S. & Chandrasekharan, K. Fourier Transforms. 1949. pap. 16.00 (ISBN 0-527-02735-9). Kraus Repr.

Bochner, S., jt. auth. see Yano, K.

Bochner, Salomon. Fouriersche Integrale. LC 49-22695. (Ger). 9.95 (ISBN 0-8284-0042-3). Chelsea Pub.

Bochner, Stephen, ed. The Meditating Person: Bridges Between Cultures. 380p. 1982. text ed. 22.50x (ISBN 0-686-64398-4); pap. text ed. 13.95x (ISBN 0-87073-893-3). Schenkman.

Bochnovic, John. The Inventive Step: Its Evolution in Canada, the United Kingdom, & the United States. Beier, Freidrich & Schricker, Gerhard, eds. (I I C Studies, Vol. 5). 128p. pap. write for info. (ISBN 0-89573-058-8). Verlag Chemie.

Bochroch, Albert R. American Automobile Racing: An Illustrated History. (Illus.). 1974. 16.95 o.p. (ISBN 0-670-11686-6, Studio). Viking Pr.

Bock, Audie E., tr. see Kurosawa, Akira.

Bock, C. V. & Riley, V. J. Theses in Germanic Studies, 1972-1977. 57p. 1980. 35.00x (ISBN 0-85457-081-0, Pub. by Inst Germanic Stud England). State Mutual Bk.

Bock, Darrell. Multivariate Statistical Methods in Behavioral Research. LC 74-8618. (Psychology Ser.). (Illus.). 640p. 1975. text ed. 40.50 (ISBN 0-07-006305-2, C). McGraw.

Bock, Edward C. Wilhelm Von Ketteler, Bishop of Mainz: His Life, Times & Ideas. 287p. 1977. pap. text ed. 10.75 (ISBN 0-8191-0270-9). U Pr of Amer.

Bock, Emil & Goebel, R. The Catacombs. Heidenreich, Alfred, ed. (Illus.). 1962. Repr. of 1931 ed. 13.50 (ISBN 0-900285-03-6, Pub by Floris Books). St George Bk Serv.

Bock, Felicia G. Classical Learning & Taoist Practices in Early Japan, with Translation of Books XVI & XX of the Engi-Shiki. Bock, Felicia G., tr. from Japanese. & intro. by. (Occasional Paper Arizona State Univ., Center for Asian Studies Ser.: No. 17). 100p. 1983. pap. 4.00. ASU Ctr Asian.

Bock, Fred G., jt. ed. see Gori, Gio B.

Bock, Glenn H., ed. see Haensel, Phyllis C.

Bock, H., jt. auth. see Heilbronner, E.

Bock, Hal, jt. auth. see Albert, Marv.

Bock, Joanne. Pop Wiener: Naive Painter. LC 72-90409. (Illus.). 178p. 1974. lib. bdg. 20.00 (ISBN 0-87023-122-7). U of Mass Pr.

Bock, Kenneth. Human Nature & History: A Response to Sociobiology. 192p. 1980. 20.00x (ISBN 0-231-05078-X); pap. 9.95 (ISBN 0-231-05079-8). Columbia U Pr.

Bock, M. E., jt. auth. see Judge, G. G.

Bock, Maria P. Von see Von Bock, Maria P.

Bock, R. Heavy Ion Collisions, Vol. 3. Date not set. 132.00 (ISBN 0-444-85352-9). Elsevier.

--Heavy Ion Collsision, Vol. 2: Heavy Ion Reactors & Microscopic Properties of Nuclear States. 1980. 95.75 (ISBN 0-444-85295-6). Elsevier.

Bock, R., ed. Heavy Ion Collisions, Vol. 1: Heavy Ion Reactors & Microscopic Properties of Nuclear States. 1979. 113.00 (ISBN 0-7204-0738-9, North Holland). Elsevier.

Bock, R. Darrell & Kolakowski, Donald. Logog: Maximum Likelihood Item Analysis & Test Scoring-Logical Model for Multiple Item Responses. pap. 3.25 (ISBN 0-89498-005-X). Natl Ed Res.

Bock, R. Darrell & Yates, George R. Multiqual: Log-linear Analysis of Nominal or Ordinal Qualitative Data by the Method of Maximum Likelihood. pap. 3.00 (ISBN 0-89498-008-4). Natl Ed Res.

Bock, Walter J., jt. auth. see Richards, Lawrence P.

Bockar, J. A. Primer for the Psychotherapist. 2nd. ed. 149p. 1981. text ed. 16.95 (ISBN 0-89335-127-X). SP Med & Sci Bks.

Bockeria, L. A., jt. auth. see Burakovsky, V. I.

Bockhoff, Frank J. Elements of Quantum Theory. rev. enl. 2nd ed. LC 76-41769. 1976. text ed. 29.50 (ISBN 0-201-00799-1, Adv Bk Prog). A-W.

Bockhoot, Robert. Social Action & the Law. pap. 2.50 (ISBN 0-686-37042-2). Ctr Respon Psych.

Bockl, George. Recycling Real Estate: The Number One Way to Make Money in the 80's. LC 82-12244. 237p. 1983. 19.95 (ISBN 0-13-768804-0, Busn). P-H.

Bockle, Franz. Fundamental Moral Theology. Smith, N. D., tr. from Ger. (Orig.). 1980. pap. 19.50 (ISBN 0-916134-42-3). Pueblo Pub Co.

Bocknek, Gene. The Young Adult: Development After Adolescence. LC 80-15148. 250p. 1980. text ed. 13.95 (ISBN 0-8185-0387-4). Brooks-Cole.

Bocknis, J. O'M. Energy Options Real Economics & the Solar-Hydrogen System. 441p. 1980. write for info. (ISBN 0-85066-204-4, Pub. by Taylor & Francis). Intl Pubns Serv.

Bockrath, Bradley C., jt. ed. see Blaustein, Bernard D.

Bockris, J. O'M & Conway, Brian E., eds. Comprehensive Treatise in Electrochemistry, Vol. 6: Electrodiscs-Transport. LC 82-13144. 546p. 1982. 67.50x (ISBN 0-306-40942-9, Plenum Pr). Plenum Pub.

Bockus, H. William. Designer's Notebook. 1977. 18.95 (ISBN 0-02-311520-3, 31152). Macmillan.

Bockus, H. William, Jr. Advertising Graphics. 3rd ed. 1979. pap. 17.95 (ISBN 0-02-311490-8). Macmillan.

Boclima, E. & Rumke, Ph, eds. Tumour Markers: Impact & Prospects. (Applied Methods in Oncologyy Ser.: Vol. 2). 346p. 1979. 69.00 (ISBN 0-686-63097-1, North Holland). Elsevier.

Bocquet, Gilbert. Revisio Physolychnidum: Silene Subg. Physolychnis. (Phanero Gamarum Monographiae: Vol. 1). (Illus.). 1969. 60.00 (ISBN 3-7682-0624-6). Lubrecht & Cramer.

Boda, Yang, jt. auth. see Wan-go Weng.

Bodaken, Edward, jt. auth. see Sereno, Kenneth.

Bodak-Gyovai, Levente Z. & Manzione, James V., Jr. Oral Medicine: Patient Evaluation & Management. (Illus.). 202p. 1980. soft cover 18.95 (ISBN 0-683-00901-X). Williams & Wilkins.

Bodansky, Oscar see Sobotka, Harry & Stewart, C. P.

Bodanza, Mary R. Clinical & Laboratory Procedures in the Physicians Office. LC 81-11573. 313p. 1982. 17.95 (ISBN 0-471-06497-1, Pub. by Wiley Med). Wiley.

Bodanzky, Miklos, et al. Peptide Synthesis. 2nd ed. LC 76-16099. (Interscience Monographs on Organic Chemistry). 208p. 1976. 40.50x (ISBN 0-471-08451-4, Pub. by Wiley-Interscience). Wiley.

Bodart, Joni. Booktalk! 246p. 1980. 10.00 (ISBN 0-8242-0650-9). Wilson.

Bodde, D., tr. see Ssu-Ma, Ch'Ien.

Boddewyn, J. J., ed. European Industrial Managers: West & East. LC 76-10916. 560p. 1976. 30.00 (ISBN 0-87332-085-9). M E Sharpe.

Boddy, John. Brain Systems & Psychological Concepts. LC 77-21203. 461p. 1978. 48.00 (ISBN 0-471-99601-7); pap. 21.95x (ISBN 0-471-99600-9, Pub. by Wiley-Interscience). Wiley.

Boddy, William. The History of Motor Racing. LC 77-2499. (Illus.). 1977. 17.95 o.p. (ISBN 0-399-12026-2). Putnam Pub Group.

Bode, B. H., ed. see John Dewey Society.

Bode, Carl. Practical Magic: Poems. LC 80-75091. viii, 54p. 1981. 11.95x (ISBN 0-8040-0362-9); pap. 6.95 (ISBN 0-8040-0373-4). Swallow.

Bode, Carl, ed. see Emerson, Ralph W.

Bode, Carl, ed. see Thoreau, Henry D.

Bode, Elroy. To Be Alive. 1979. 10.00 (ISBN 0-87404-064-7). Tex Western.

Bode, Frances. New Structures in Flower Arrangement. (Illus.). 1968. 5.95 (ISBN 0-8208-0050-3). Hearthside.

Bode, Frederick A. Protestantism & the New South: North Carolina Baptists & Methodists in Political Crisis, 1894-1903. LC 75-1289. 171p. 1975. 10.95x (ISBN 0-8139-0597-4). U Pr of Va.

Bode, Hans. Lead Acid Batteries. LC 76-58418. (The Electrochemical Society Ser). 1977. 49.95x (ISBN 0-471-08455-7, Pub. by Wiley-Interscience). Wiley.

Bode, Janet. Kids Having Kids. (gr. 9 up). 1980. PLB 8.90 (ISBN 0-531-02882-8, B19). Watts.

--Rape: Preventing It; Coping with the Legal, Medical, & Emotional Aftermath. (Impact Ser.). (gr. 7 up). 1979. PLB 8.90 s&l (ISBN 0-531-02289-7). Watts.

Bode, Sharon, et al. Listening in & Speaking Out: Advanced. (English As a Second Language Bk.). 1981. pap. text ed. 4.95x (ISBN 0-582-79737-3); cassette 10.95 (ISBN 0-582-79738-1); cassette & bk. in plastic tote 13.95x (ISBN 0-686-31604-5). Longman.

--Listening in & Speaking Out: Intermediate. (Listening in & Speaking Out Ser.). (Illus.). 128p. (Orig.). 1980. pap. 4.95x (ISBN 0-582-79735-7); cassette 10.95x (ISBN 0-582-79736-5); bk. & cassette in tote 13.95 (ISBN 0-582-79770-5). Longman.

Bodea, Cornelia & Candea, Virgil. Heritage & Continuity in Eastern Europe: The Transylvanian Legacy in the History of the Romanians. (East European Monographs: No. 117). 160p. 1982. 17.50x (ISBN 0-88033-010-4). East Eur Quarterly.

Bodecker, N. M. Pigeon Cubes & Other Verse. LC 82-3954. (Illus.). 80p. 1982. 9.95 (ISBN 0-689-50235-4, McElderry). Atheneum.

--Snowman Sniffles. LC 82-13927. (Illus.). 80p. (gr. 4-7). 1983. 8.95 (ISBN 0-689-50263-X, McElderry Bk). Atheneum.

Bodel, John. Brick Stamps in the Kelsey Museum. (Illus.). 112p. 1982. 22.50x (ISBN 0-472-10030-0). U of Mich Pr.

--Roman Brick Stamps in the Kelsey Museum. (Kelsey Museum Ser.). (Illus.). 1983. pap. text ed. 22.50 (ISBN 0-472-08039-3). U of Mich Pr.

Boden, Margaret A. Jean Piaget. (Modern Masters Ser.). 171p. 1980. 11.95 o.p. (ISBN 0-670-40632-5). Viking Pr.

--Minds & Mechanism: Philosophical Psychology & Computational Models. 256p. 1981. 29.50x (ISBN 0-8014-1431-8). Cornell U Pr.

Boden, Robert. Teen Talks with God. 1980. pap. 2.95 (ISBN 0-570-03812-X, 12-2921). Concordia.

Bodenhamer, Greg. Back in Control: How to Get Your Children to Behave. 144p. 1983. 9.95 (ISBN 0-13-055871-0). P-H.

Bodha, Daji, ed. see Da Free, John.

Bodian, Nat G. Book Marketing Handbook, Vol. II. 2nd ed. 525p. 1983. 60.00 (ISBN 0-8352-1685-3). Bowker.

Bodie, Idella. The Secret of Telfair Inn. LC 79-177909. (Illus.). 112p. (gr. 5-9). 1971. 3.95 o.p. (ISBN 0-87844-015-1). Sandlapper Pub Co.

Bodie, Idella F. A Hunt for Life's Extras, the Story of Archibald Rutledge. LC 80-50789. (Illus.). 176p. 1982. 11.95 (ISBN 0-87844-046-1). Sandlapper Pub Co.

Bodin, Fredrick D. How to Get the Best Travel Photographs. 220p. 1982. pap. 14.95 (ISBN 0-930764-40-4). Van Nos Reinhold.

Bodin, Fredrik D. How to Get the Best Travel Photographs. (Illus.). 150p. 1982. pap. 14.95 (ISBN 0-930764-40-4). Curtin & London.

Bodin, Jeanne & Mitelman, Bonnie. Mothers Who Work: Strategies for Coping. 320p. (Orig.). 1983. pap. 5.95 (ISBN 0-345-30140-4). Ballantine.

Bodin, Jeanne, jt. auth. see Millstein, Beth.

Bodin, L. D., jt. auth. see Golden, B. L.

Bodine, A. Aubrey. Chesapeake Bay & Tidewater. LC 67-70707. (Illus.). 1969. 22.50 o.p. (ISBN 0-910254-02-8). Bodine.

--Chesapeake Bay & Tidewater. (Illus.). 160p. 1980. Repr. 10.00 (ISBN 0-686-36505-4). Md Hist.

Bodine, Jay F., jt. ed. see Probst, Gerhard F.

Bodine, Walter R. The Greek Text of Judges: Recensional Developments. LC 80-12578. (Harvard Semitic Monographs: No. 23). 15.00x (ISBN 0-89130-400-2, 04-00-23). Scholars Pr CA.

Bodington, Stephen. Science & Social Action. 192p. 1980. 14.00x (Pub. by Allison & Busby England); pap. 7.95 (ISBN 0-8052-8026-X, Pub. by Allison & Busby England). Schocken.

Bodinski, Lois H. The Nurse's Guide to Diet Therapy. LC 82-6954. 381p. 1982. pap. 16.95 (ISBN 0-471-08167-1, Pub. by Wiley Med). Wiley.

Bodker, Cecil. Silas & Ben-Godik. La Farge, Sheila, tr. from Danish. LC 78-50459. (gr. 5-9). 1978. 7.95 o.s.i. (ISBN 0-440-07923-3, Sey Lawr); PLB 7.45 o.s.i. (ISBN 0-440-07924-1). Delacorte.

--Silas & the Black Mare. La Farge, Sheila, tr. LC 77-86303. (gr. 5-9). 1978. 7.95 o.s.i. (ISBN 0-440-07921-7, Sey Lawr); PLB 7.45 o.s.i. (ISBN 0-440-07922-5). Delacorte.

--Silas & the Runaway Coach. LC 78-50465. (gr. 5-9). 1978. 7.95 o.s.i. (ISBN 0-440-07953-5, Sey Lawr); PLB 7.45 o.s.i. (ISBN 0-440-07954-3). Delacorte.

Bodkin, Cora, et al. Crafts for Your Leisure Years. 1976. 14.95 o.s.i. (ISBN 0-395-24767-5); pap. 7.95 o.s.i. (ISBN 0-395-24837-X). HM.

Bodle, Marie, tr. see Armstrong, Virginia W.

Bodle, Yvonne & Corey, Joseph. Retail Selling. 2nd ed. McGarry, Mary A., ed. (Illus.). (gr. 10-12). 1976. text ed. 15.48 (ISBN 0-07-006371-0, G); teacher's manual & key 5.50 (ISBN 0-07-006372-9); lab manual 7.80 (ISBN 0-07-006373-7). McGraw.

Bodley, John H. Victims of Progress. LC 74-84817. 1975. pap. text ed. 10.95 o.p. (ISBN 0-8465-0540-1). Benjamin-Cummings.

--Victims of Progress. 2nd ed. (Illus.). 264p. 1982. pap. 9.95 (ISBN 0-87484-593-9). Mayfield Pub.

Bodley, Ronald V. Messenger: The Life of Mohammed. LC 70-92296. Repr. of 1946 ed. lib. bdg. 20.25x (ISBN 0-8371-2423-9, BOTM). Greenwood.

Bodman, Nicholas C. Spoken Amoy Hokkien: Units 1-30. (Spoken Language Series). 450p. (Amoy Hokkien.). 1983. pap. text ed. 15.00x (ISBN 0-87950-450-1); cassettes, 16 dual track 120.00x (ISBN 0-87950-451-X); bk. & cassettes combined 130.00x (ISBN 0-87950-452-8). Spoken Lang Serv.

Bodnar, John. Immigration & Industrialization: Ethnicity in an American Mill Town, 1870-1940. LC 77-74549. 1977. 11.95 o.p. (ISBN 0-8229-3348-9). U of Pittsburgh Pr.

--Workers' World: Kinship, Community & Protest in an Industrial Society, 1900-1940. LC 82-6626. (Illus.). 256p. 1982. 19.50x (ISBN 0-8018-2785-X). Johns Hopkins.

Bodnar, M. J. Durability of Adhesive Bonded Structures: Journal of Applied Polymer Science. (Applied Polymer Symposium: No. 32). 1977. 42.00 o.p. (ISBN 0-471-04564-0, Pub. by Wiley-Interscience). Wiley.

Bodo, G., jt. ed. see Surjan, L.

Bodo, John R. A Gallery of New Testament Rogues: From Herod to Satan. LC 78-13984. 1979. pap. 6.95 (ISBN 0-664-24227-8). Westminster.

Bodo, Murray. Francis: The Journey & the Dream. (Illus.). 1972. pap. 2.95 (ISBN 0-912228-07-5). St Anthony Mess Pr.

Bodo, Peter. Soccer: America's New Sport. LC 77-93732. (Gallery Format Ser.). (Illus.). 1978. 12.95 o.s.i. (ISBN 0-8027-0599-5); pap. 6.95 o.s.i. (ISBN 0-8027-7131-9). Walker & Co.

Bodoczky, Caroline, tr. see Feher, Zsuzsa D.

Bodoczky, Caroline, tr. see Solymar, Istvan.

Bodoczky, Istvan, tr. see Feher, Zsuzsa D.

Bodoczky, Istvan, tr. see Solymar, Istvan.

Bodoni, Giambattista. Manuale Typografia, 2 Vols. 20.00x (ISBN 0-87556-035-0). Saifer.

Bodor, G. B. Orientation Effects in Solid Polymers. (Journal of Polymer Science Symposium: No. 58). 1978. 44.95 (ISBN 0-471-04658-2, Pub. by Wiley-Interscience). Wiley.

Bodwell, C. E. & Adkins, J. S. Protein Quality In Humans: Assessment & in Vitro Estimation. (Illus.). 1981. lib. bdg. 49.50 (ISBN 0-87055-388-7). AVI.

Body, George. The Mystery of Suffering. LC 82-80697. (A Shepherd Illustrated Classic Ser.). Date not set. pap. 6.95 o.p. (ISBN 0-87983-292-4). Keats. Postponed.

Boe, Alf. From Gothic Revival to Functional Form. (Architecture & Decorative Art Ser.). 1979. Repr. of 1957 ed. 25.00 (ISBN 0-306-77544-1). Da Capo.

Boe, Beverly, jt. auth. see Philcox, Phil.

Boece De Boodt, Anselme. Le Parfaict Joallier, Ou Histoire Des Pierreries. Repr. of 1644 ed. 207.00 o.p. (ISBN 0-8287-0099-0). Clearwater Pub.

Boeck, Alvord L. The Economic Essentials of World Peace. LC 36-4173. 45p. 1982. lib. bdg. 19.95x (ISBN 0-89370-710-4). Borgo Pr.

Boeckmann, J., tr. see Schill, Gottfried.

Boeder, Robert B. Malawi. (World Bibliographical Ser.: No. 8). 165p. 1979. 28.50 (ISBN 0-903450-22-4). ABC Clio.

Boegehold, Betty. Bear Underground. LC 79-7683. (Illus.). (gr. k-3). 1980. 8.95a o.p. (ISBN 0-385-15062-8); PLB 8.95a (ISBN 0-385-15063-6). Doubleday.

--Chipper's Choices. (Illus.). 64p. (gr. 6-9). 1981. PLB 6.99 (ISBN 0-698-30725-9, Coward). Putnam Pub Group.

--Education Before Five. 1978. pap. 8.50x (ISBN 0-8077-2557-9). Tchrs Coll.

--Small Deer's Magic Tricks. (Break-of-Day Bk.). (Illus.). 64p. (gr. k-3). 1977. PLB 6.59 o.p. (ISBN 0-698-30659-7, Coward). Putnam Pub Group.

Boehlke, Neal. Jesus & Bartimaeus. 1982. pap. 0.89 (ISBN 0-570-06156-3, 59-1270). Concordia.

--Zacchaeus Meets the Savior. 1980. pap. 0.89 (ISBN 0-570-06132-6, 59-1250, Arch Bk). Concordia.

Boehlke, Neal A. Man Who Met Jesus at Bethesda. (Arch Bk.). (gr. k-4). 1981. pap. 0.89 (ISBN 0-570-06143-1, 59-1260). Concordia.

Boehm, B. W. & Brown, J. R. Characteristics of Software Quality. (TRW Ser. on Software Technology: Vol. 1). 1978. 53.25 (ISBN 0-444-85105-4, North-Holland). Elsevier.

Boehm, Barry W. Software Engineering Economics. (Illus.). 768p. 1981. text ed. 35.00 (ISBN 0-13-822122-7). P-H.

Boehm, Barry W., jt. ed. see Sackman, Harold.

Boehm, Ellen, jt. auth. see Toole, Amy L.

Boehm, Eric, jt. ed. see Hodl, Gunther.

Boehm, Eric H. & Hodl, Guenther, eds. Austrian Historical Bibliography: Annual, 1979. LC 68-19156. 203p. 1981. 49.50 ea. (ISBN 0-87436-255-5). ABC-Clio.

Boehm, Eric H., et al, eds. Historical Periodicals Directory. LC 81-12892. (Clio Periodicals Directories Ser.). 1982. lib. bdg. 87.50 ea. Vol. 1:U. S. A. & Canada 180 p (ISBN 0-87436-018-8). Vol. 2:Europe: West, North Central & South 600p (ISBN 0-87436-019-6). ABC-Clio.

Boehm, K. H. & Silberston, A. British Patent System. (Cambridge Dept. of Applied Economics Monographs: No. 13). 1967. 34.50 (ISBN 0-521-04274-7). Cambridge U Pr.

Boehm, Klaus & Wellings, Nick, eds. The Student Book 1979-80: The Discriminating Students' Guide to Uk Colleges, Polytechnics & Universities. (Littlefield, Adams Quality Paperback Ser.: No. 354). (Illus.). 424p. (Orig.). 1979. pap. 7.95 o.p. (ISBN 0-8226-0354-3). Littlefield.

Boehm, Sylvia L., ed. After-Dinner Laughter. LC 76-51166. 1977. 7.95 o.p. (ISBN 0-8069-0102-0); lib. bdg. 7.49 o.p. (ISBN 0-8069-0103-9). Sterling.

Boehm, Theobald. Flute & Flute-Playing: In Acoustal, Technical & Artistic Aspects. (Illus.). 9.00 (ISBN 0-8446-1697-4). Peter Smith.

--Uber den Flotenbau. (The Flute Library: Vol. 16). (Ger. & Eng.). 1981. 35.00 o.s.i. (ISBN 90-6027-169-6, Pub. by Frits Knuf Netherlands). Pendragon NY.

Boehm, W. M., tr. see Kautzky, R.

Boehme, Jacob. Signature of All Things: & Other Writings. 1968. pap. 12.95 (ISBN 0-227-67733-1). Attic Pr.

Boehme, S., et al. Astronomy & Astrophysics Abstracts, Vol. 31: Literature 1982, Pt. 1. 776p. 1983. 66.00 (ISBN 0-387-12072-6). Springer-Verlag.

Boehmer, Raquel. A Foraging Vacation: Edibles from Maine's Sea & Shore. (Illus.). 150p. (Orig.). 1982. pap. 7.95 (ISBN 0-89272-139-1, PIC488). Down East.

Boehne, Patricia J. J. V. Foix. (World Authors Ser.). 1980. 15.95 (ISBN 0-8057-6412-7, Twayne). G K Hall.

Boekholt, Albert. Puppets & Masks. LC 81-8572. (Illus.). 112p. (gr. 4 up). 1981. 10.95 (ISBN 0-8069-7042-1); PLB 13.29 (ISBN 0-8069-7043-X). Sterling.

Boekman. Surviving Your Parent's Divorce. (gr. 7 up). 1980. PLB 8.90 (ISBN 0-531-02869-0, B51). Watts.

Boelhower, William Q., tr. see Goldmann, Lucien.

Boelt, Martha M. Recipes & Revelry: Celebrations from the Colonial South. Hartwiger, Sidney M., ed. 320p. 1983. 12.95 (ISBN 0-932298-31-1). Copple Hse.

Boeman, John. Morotai: A Memoir of War. LC 80-697. 288p. 1981. 12.95 o.p. (ISBN 0-385-15586-7). Doubleday.

Boen, James R. & Zahn, Douglas A. The Human Side of Statistical Consulting. (Research Methods Ser.). 208p. 1981. 14.95 (ISBN 0-534-97949-1). Lifetime Learn.

Boenisch, Edmond W., Jr., jt. auth. see Haney, C. Michele.

Boer, ed. see International Solar Energy Society.

Boer, Bertil H. van see Bengtsson, Ingmar & Van Boer, Bertil H., Jr.

Boer, Charles, tr. from Gr. The Homeric Hymns. rev. ed. (Dunquin Ser.: No. 10). 182p. 1982. pap. text ed. 9.50 o.p. (ISBN 0-88214-210-0). Spring Pubns.

Boer, Germain B. Direct Cost & Contribution Accounting: An Integrated Management Accounting System. LC 73-17324. (Systems & Controls for Financial Managment Ser.). 256p. 1974. 39.95 (ISBN 0-471-08505-7, Pub. by Wiley-Interscience). Wiley.

Boer, H. J., jt. auth. see McConnell, P. S.

Boer, Harry R. The Doctrine of Reprobation in the Christian Reformed Church. 104p. 1983. pap. 6.95 (ISBN 0-8028-1952-4). Eerdmans.

Boer, John J. De see De Boer, John J.

Boer, K. W., ed. Sharing the Sun, Vols. 1-10. Incl. Vol. 1. International & US Programs Solar Flux. pap. text ed. 33.00 (ISBN 0-08-021686-2); Vol. 2. Solar Collectors. pap. text ed. 33.00 (ISBN 0-08-021687-0); Vol. 3. Solar Heating & Cooling Buildings. pap. text ed. 33.00 (ISBN 0-08-021688-9); Vol. 4. Solar System, Simulation, Design. pap. text ed. 38.50 (ISBN 0-08-021689-7); Vol. 5. Solar Thermal & Ocean Thermal. pap. text ed. 44.00 (ISBN 0-08-021690-0); Vol. 6. Photovoltaics & Materials. pap. text ed. 33.00 (ISBN 0-08-021691-9); Vol. 7. Agriculture, Biomass, Wind, New Developments. pap. text ed. 33.00 (ISBN 0-08-021692-7); Vol. 8. Storage, Water Heater, Data Communication, Education. pap. text ed. 33.00 (ISBN 0-08-021693-5); Vol. 9. Socio - Economics & Cultural. pap. text ed. 27.50 (ISBN 0-08-021694-3); Vol. 10. Business & Commercial Implications. pap. text ed. 22.00 (ISBN 0-08-021695-1). 1977. Set. pap. text ed. 375.00 (ISBN 0-08-021696-X). Pergamon.

Boer, Karl W. & Duffie, John A., eds. Advances in Solar Energy: An Annual Review of Research & Development in 1981, Vol. I. (Illus.). 1982. pap. text ed. 75.00x (ISBN 0-89553-040-6). Am Solar Energy.

Boer, Karl W., ed. see International Solar Energy Society, American Section.

Boer, Karl W., ed. see International Solar Energy Society, American Section, Annual Meeting, Denver, 1978.

Boer, P. A. H. de see De Boer, P. A. H.

Boer, S. P. De see De Boer, S. P. & Driessen, E. J.

Boer, Theo de see De Boer, Theo.

Boer-Hoff, Louise E., tr. see Schuurman, C. J.

Boericke, Arthur, jt. auth. see Shapiro, Barry.

Boericke, William. Materia Medica with Repertory. 1982. 20.00x (ISBN 0-685-76567-9, Pub. by Boericke & Tafel). Formur Intl.

Boericke, William F. Prospecting & Operating Small Gold Placers. 2nd ed. 1936. 14.95 (ISBN 0-471-08514-6, Pub. by Wiley-Interscience). Wiley.

Boeringa, R. Alternative Methods of Agriculture. (Developments in Agricultural & Managed-Forest Ecology Ser.: Vol. 10). 1980. 51.00 (ISBN 0-444-41893-8). Elsevier.

Boersner, Demetrio. The Bolsheviks & the National & Colonial Question, 1917-1928. LC 79-2894. 285p. 1981. Repr. of 1957 ed. 36.50 (ISBN 0-8305-0062-6). Hyperion Conn.

Boes, D., et al, eds. Public Production: International Seminar in Public Economics, Bonn, FRG 1981. (Journal of Economics Supplementum: Vol. 2). (Illus.). 222p. 1983. pap. 62.00 (ISBN 0-387-81726-3). Springer-Verlag.

Boesak, Allan. Farewell to Innocence. LC 77-5578. Orig. Title: X. 197p. 1977. pap. 6.95x (ISBN 0-88344-130-6). Orbis Bks.

--The Finger of God: Sermons on Faith & Socio-Political Responsibility. Randall, Peter, tr. from Afrikaans. LC 81-16943. 112p. (Orig.). 1982. pap. 5.95 (ISBN 0-88344-135-7). Orbis Bks.

Boesch, Francis T. Large-Scale Networks: Theory & Design. LC 75-25324. (IEEE Press Selected Reprint Ser.). 483p. 1976. 31.95x (ISBN 0-471-01616-0); pap. 20.95x o.p. (ISBN 0-471-01617-9, Pub. by Wiley-Interscience). Wiley.

Boesch, Francis T., ed. Large-Scale Networks: Theory & Design. LC 75-25324. 1976. 31.95 (ISBN 0-87942-063-4). Inst Electrical.

Boeschen, John. The Build-a-Bed Book. (Illus.). 160p. 1982. 19.95 (ISBN 0-312-10766-8); pap. 10.95 (ISBN 0-312-10767-6). St Martin.

Boeschen, John, jt. auth. see Schram, Joseph.

Boeschenstein, Hermann. German Literature in the Nineteenth Century. LC 70-76383. 1969. 18.95 (ISBN 0-312-32585-1). St Martin.

Boese, A., ed. Search for the Cause of Multiple Sclerosis & Other Chronic Diseases of the Central Nervous System. (Illus.). 516p. (Orig.). 1980. pap. 60.00x (ISBN 3-527-25875-2). Verlag Chemie.

Boesen, Victor. Doing Something About the Weather. (Illus.). 128p. (gr. 7 up). 1975. 6.95 o.p. (ISBN 0-399-20465-2). Putnam Pub Group.

--Storm: Irving Krick vs. The U. S. Weather Bureaucracy. LC 77-26726. (Illus.). (gr. 6-8). 1978. 7.95 o.p. (ISBN 0-399-20636-1). Putnam Pub Group.

Boesiger, Willy see Le Corbusier.

Boesiger, Wlly see Le Corbusier.

Boestamam, Ahmad. Carving the Path to the Summit. Roff, William R., tr. from Malayan. LC 79-11174. (Southeast Asia Translation Ser.: Vol. 2). xxxii, 149p. 1980. 13.95x (ISBN 0-8214-0397-4, 82-82881); pap. 6.50x (ISBN 0-8214-0409-1, 82-82899). Ohio U Pr.

Boethius. On the Consolation of Philosophy. LC 81-52212. 128p. 1981. pap. 3.95 (ISBN 0-89526-885-X). Regnery-Gateway.

Boetner, Maxine & Gates, John E. A Dictionary of American Idioms. rev. ed. Makkai, Adam, ed. LC 75-42110. 1984. 14.95 (ISBN 0-8120-5102-5); pap. 9.95 (ISBN 0-8120-0612-7). Barron.

Boettcher, Jurgen. Coffee Houses of Europe. (Illus.). 1983. 29.95 (ISBN 0-500-54063-2). Thames Hudson.

Boeynaems, J. J. & Dumont, J. E., eds. Outlines of Receptor Theory. 1980. 67.00 (ISBN 0-444-80131-6). Elsevier.

Boff, Leonardo. The Lord's Prayer: The Prayer of Integral Liberation. Morrow, Theodore, tr. LC 82-18811. Orig. Title: Portugese. 144p. (Orig.). 1983. pap. 6.95 (ISBN 0-88344-299-X). Orbis Bks.

--The Way of the Cross: Way of Justice. Drury, John, tr. LC 79-23776. Orig. Title: Via-Sacra Da Justica. 144p. (Orig.). 1980. pap. 4.95 (ISBN 0-686-82950-6). Orbis Bks.

Boffa, M., et al, eds. Logic Colloquium 1978. (Studies in Logic & the Foundations of Mathematics: Vol. 97). 550p. 1979. 64.00 (ISBN 0-444-85378-2, North Holland). Elsevier.

Bogan, Louise. The Blue Estuaries: Poems, 1923-1968. LC 76-46175. (American Poetry Ser: Vol. 11). 1977. pap. 7.95 (ISBN 0-912946-37-7). Ecco Pr.

--What the Woman Lived: Selected Letters of Louise Bogan, 1920-1970. Limmer, Ruth, ed. LC 73-9737. 1973. 14.50 o.p. (ISBN 0-15-195878-5). HarBraceJ.

Bogan, Louise, tr. see Goethe, Johann W.

Bogard, Larry. Bad Apple. 176p. 1982. 10.95 (ISBN 0-374-30472-6). FS&G.

Bogard, Travis, ed. see O'Neill, Eugene.

Bogard, Travis, et al. Revels History of Drama in English, Vol. 8: American Drama. (Illus.). 1978. 53.00x (ISBN 0-416-13090-9); pap. 18.95x (ISBN 0-416-81400-X). Methuen Inc.

Bogart, Bonnie. The Ewoks Join the Fight. LC 82-62834. (Illus.). 32p. (ps-4). 1983. PLB 4.99 (ISBN 0-394-95858-6); pap. 1.95 (ISBN 0-394-85858-1). Random.

Bogart, Ernest L. Peacham: The Story of a Vermont Hill Town. LC 81-40567. (Illus.). 510p. 1982. lib. bdg. 30.75 (ISBN 0-8191-1990-3); pap. text ed. 19.75 (ISBN 0-8191-1991-1). U Pr of Amer.

--War Costs & Their Financing: A Study of the Financing of the War & the After-War Problems of Debt & Taxation. LC 74-75232. (The United States in World War 1 Ser). xxiv, 510p. 1974. Repr. of 1921 ed. lib. bdg. 23.95x (ISBN 0-89198-095-4). Ozer.

Bogart, Gary L. see Cook, Dorothy E. & Monro, Isabel S.

Bogart, Kenneth P. Introductory Combinatorics. 400p. 1983. text ed. 24.95 (ISBN 0-273-01923-6). Pitman Pub MA.

Bogart, Marcel J. Ammonia Absorption Refrigeration in Industrial Processes. 470p. 1981. 59.95x (ISBN 0-87201-027-9). Gulf Pub.

Bogart, Theodore F. Laplace Transforms & Control Systems Theory for Technology: Including Microprocessor Based Control System. LC 81-14708. 541p. 1982. text ed. 26.95 (ISBN 0-471-09044-1); write for info solns. manual (ISBN 0-471-86325-4). Wiley.

Bogdan, jt. auth. see Skalimierski, B.

Bogdan, Robert & Taylor, Steven J. An Introduction to Qualitative Research Methods: A Phenomenological Approach to the Social Sciences. LC 75-19407. 266p. 1975. 27.95x (ISBN 0-471-08571-5, Pub. by Wiley-Interscience). Wiley.

Bogdanor, Vernon. The People & the Party System: The Referendum & Electoral Reform in British Politics. LC 81-3895. 280p. 1981. 42.50 (ISBN 0-521-24207-X); pap. 15.95 (ISBN 0-521-28525-9). Cambridge U Pr.

Bogdonoff, Morton D. Forever Fit: The Exercise Program for Men & Women Over Forty. (Illus.). 224p. 1983. 22.00i (ISBN 0-316-10085-4); pap. 10.45i (ISBN 0-316-10086-2). Little.

Bogdonoff, Nancy D., ed. Handwoven Textiles of Early New England. LC 75-5582. (Illus.). 192p. 1975. pap. 9.95 (ISBN 0-8117-2069-1). Stackpole.

Bogdonovich, Peter. Fritz Lang in America. (Belvedere Bk.). (Illus.). 144p. Date not set. pap. 5.95 (ISBN 0-686-97283-X). Chelsea Hse. Postponed.

Bogen, Boris D. Jewish Philanthropy: An Exposition of Principles & Methods of Jewish Social Service in the United States. LC 69-16225. (Criminology, Law Enforcement, & Social Problems Ser.: No. 86). (With a new intro. by Harry Lurie). 1969. Repr. of 1917 ed. 17.00x (ISBN 0-87585-086-3). Patterson Smith.

Bogen, J. I. & Shipman, S. S. Financial Handbook. 4th ed. 1208p. 1968. 44.50x o.p. (ISBN 0-471-06556-0). Wiley.

Bogen, Lester, ed. see Lootens, J. Ghislain.

Bogen, M. Arthur. Double Dealing. 160p. 1983. pap. 2.25 (ISBN 0-380-83394-8, Flare). Avon.

Bogenschneider, Duane, ed. A Directory to Collective Bargaining Agreements: Private Sector, 1981. 275p. 1982. reference bk. 100.00 (ISBN 0-667-00643-5). Microfilming Corp.

Boger, Jan. To Live in the Fire. Seaton, Lionel, tr. from Ger. Orig. Title: Im Feuer Zu Leben. (Illus.). 1978. 9.95 o.p. (ISBN 0-89149-036-1); pap. 6.95 o.p. (ISBN 0-89149-035-3). Jolex.

Boger, Louise A. House & Garden's Antiques: Questions & Answers. 1973. 12.95 o.p. (ISBN 0-671-21506-X). S&S.

Boggan, Louise. The Ivory Cup. LC 76-4739. 1976. 4.95 o.p. (ISBN 0-87397-095-0). Strode.

Boggess, Bill & Boggess, Louise. American Brilliant Cut Glass. 1977. 16.95 (ISBN 0-517-52525-9). Crown.

Boggess, Louise. How to Write Fillers & Short Features that Sell. (EH 546). 192p. (Orig.). pap. 5.72i (ISBN 0-686-37128-3). B&N NY.

Boggess, Louise, jt. auth. see Boggess, Bill.

Boggio, G. & Gallimore, R., eds. Evaluation of Research & Development. 1982. lib. bdg. 24.50 (ISBN 90-277-1425-8, Pub. by Reidel Holland). Kluwer Boston.

Boggis, J. G., jt. auth. see Forde, M. J.

Boggs, Bill. At First Sight. LC 78-67235. 1980. 10.95 o.p. (ISBN 0-448-15778-0, G&D). Putnam Pub Group.

Boggs, Carl. The Impasse of European Communism. 1981. lib. bdg. 23.50 (ISBN 0-89158-784-5); pap. 10.75 o.p. (ISBN 0-86531-285-0). Westview.

Boggs, Dane R. & Winkelstein, Alan. White Cell Manual. 4th ed. (Illus.). 130p. 1983. pap. text ed. 6.95 (ISBN 0-8036-0961-2, 0961-2). Davis Co.

Boggs, Donald L. & Merkel, Robert A. Live Animal Carcass Evaluation & Selection Manual. 208p. (Orig.). 1979. pap. text ed. 11.95 (ISBN 0-8403-2036-1). Kendall-Hunt.

Boggs, James D. To Challenge & to Write. LC 75-84738. 96p. 1969. 3.50 o.p. (ISBN 0-89227-013-6). Commonwealth Pr.

Boggs, Juanita, jt. auth. see Strand, Julie.

Boggs, Ralph S. Basic Spanish Pronunciation. (Orig., Span.). (gr. 9-11). 1969. pap. 3.25 (ISBN 0-88345-012-7, 17442); 40.00 o.p. tapes (ISBN 0-685-19784-0); cassettes 60.00 (ISBN 0-685-19785-9). Regents Pub.

Boggs, S. A., et al, eds. Underground Cable Thermal Backfill: Proceedings of the Symposium on Underground Cable Thermal Backfill, Sept. 17-18, 1981, Toronto, Canada. (Illus.). 248p. 1982. 40.00 (ISBN 0-08-025387-3); 30.00 o.p. (ISBN 0-08-025393-8). Pergamon.

Boggs, Sue H. Is a Job Really Worth It? 1979. pap. 2.95 (ISBN 0-89137-522-8). Quality Pubns.

--The Secret of Hind's Feet. write for info. (ISBN 0-89137-537-6). Quality Pubns.

Boggs, Vernon, et al, eds. The Apple Sliced: The Sociology of New York City. (Illus.). 352p. 1983. text ed. 29.95x; pap. text ed. 12.95x (ISBN 0-89789-016-7). J F Bergin.

Boggs, Winthrop S. Postage Stamps & Postal History of Newfoundland. LC 75-1791. (Illus.). 288p. 1975. Repr. 35.00x o.p. (ISBN 0-88000-066-X). Quarterman.

Bogle, Irma, jt. auth. see Adams, Carolyn E.

Bogle, Margaret L., jt. auth. see Alford, Betty B.

Bognar, Desi K., ed. Hungarians in America: A Biographical Directory of Professionals of Hungarian Origin. rev. ed. LC 81-71176. (East Central European Biographies & Studies Ser.: Nos. 4 & 5). xiiii, 369p. 1981. 25.00 (ISBN 0-912460-04-0). AFI Pubns.

Bogner, R. E. & Constantinides, A. G., eds. Introduction to Digital Filtering. LC 74-4924. 1975. 39.95 (ISBN 0-471-08590-1, Pub. by Wiley-Interscience). Wiley.

Bogod. The Role of Computing in Developing Countries. 1979. 11.95 (ISBN 0-471-25599-8, Wiley Heyden). Wiley.

Bogojavlensky, Ann, et al. The Great Learning Book. new ed. 1977. pap. text ed. 12.15 (ISBN 0-201-00844-0, Sch Div). A-W.

Bogoliubov, N. M. & Mitropolsky, Y. A. Asymptotic Methods in the Theory of Non-Linear Oscillations. 548p. 1961. write for info. (ISBN 0-677-20050-1). Gordon.

Bogoliubov, N. N. Lectures on Quantum Statistics, 2 vols. 240p. 1967. Vol. 1. 60.00x (ISBN 0-677-20030-7); Vol. 2. 44.00x (ISBN 0-677-20570-8). Gordon.

Bogoliubov, N. N. & Shirkov, D. V. Introduction to the Theory of Quantized Fields. 3rd ed. LC 79-17919. 1980. 73.95 (ISBN 0-471-04223-4, Pub. by Wiley-Interscience). Wiley.

Bogoliubov, N. N., ed. The Theory of Superconductivity. (International Science Review Ser.). (Illus.). 1968. 49.00x (ISBN 0-677-00080-4). Gordon.

Bogomolov, Yu. G. & Zhabin, V. F., eds. Effect of Reclamation on Hydrogeological Conditions. Erastov, Konstantin, tr. from Rus. 300p. 1983. 97.00 (ISBN 0-677-06070-X). Gordon.

Bogot, Howard. Yoni. 1982. pap. 4.00 (ISBN 0-686-82564-0). UAHC.

Bogot, Howard, jt. auth. see Syme, Daniel.

Bograd, Larry. The Kolokol Papers. (YA) (gr. 7-12). 1983. pap. 2.25 (ISBN 0-440-94552-6, LFL). Dell.

Bogue, Allan G. & Taylor, Robert, eds. The University of Wisconsin: One Hundred & Twenty-Five Years. LC 74-27306. (Illus.). 302p. 1975. 15.00 (ISBN 0-299-06840-4). U of Wis Pr.

Bogue, Grant. Basic Sociological Research Design. 1981. pap. text ed. 9.95x o.p. (ISBN 0-673-15349-5). Scott F.

Bogue, Margaret B. & Palmer, Virginia A. Around the Shores of Lake Superior: A Guide to Historic Sites. LC 79-65184. (Illus.). 186p. 1979. pap. 7.95 (ISBN 0-299-97013-2). U of Wis Pr.

Bogue, Robert H. There Is a Time: The Downbeat of Pristine Christianity. 1983. 11.95 (ISBN 0-533-05592-X). Vantage.

Bogue, Ted. How to Compile a Consumer's Directory of Doctors & their Fee. 69p. 1982. 3.50 (ISBN 0-686-96311-3). Pub Citizen Health.

Bogus, Donald, jt. auth. see Landau, Sidney.

Bogus, Ronald, jt. ed. see Landau, Sidney.

Bogus, Sdiane. Her Poems: An Anniversaric Chronology. (Illus., Orig.). 1980. 2.00 (ISBN 0-934172-02-1). WIM Pubns.

--I'm Off to See the Goddamn Wizard, Alright! 1980. pap. 4.00 (ISBN 0-934172-00-5). WIM Pubns.

--Sapphire's Sampler. (Illus.). 228p. (Orig.). 1982. 10.00 (ISBN 0-934172-07-2); pap. 7.00 (ISBN 0-934172-06-4). WIM Pubns.

--Woman in the Moon. (Illus.). 1979. pap. 6.00 (ISBN 0-934172-01-3). WIM Pubns.

Boguslavsky, Boris. Elementary Computer Programming in FORTRAN IV. 2nd ed. (Illus.). 1980. pap. text ed. 21.95 (ISBN 0-8359-1648-0). Reston.

Boguslawski, Dorothy B. Guide for Establishing & Operating Day Care Centers for Young Children. LC 66-18695. 1966. pap. 5.70 (ISBN 0-87868-032-2, J-52). Child Welfare.

Bohachevska-Chomiak, Martha, tr. see Struk, Danylo S.

Bohannan, Paul & Glazer, Mark. High Points in Anthropology. 1973. text ed. 13.00 (ISBN 0-394-31672-X). Knopf.

Bohart, R. M. & Menke, A. S. Sphecid Wasps of the World: A Generic Revision. 1976. 87.50x (ISBN 0-520-02318-8). U of Cal Pr.

Bohdan, Carol L., jt. auth. see Blasberg, Robert W.

Bohdanecky, M. & Kovar, J. Viscosity of Polymer Solutions: Polymer Science Library, No. 2. 286p. 1982. 76.75 (ISBN 0-444-42066-5). Elsevier.

Bohen, Halcyone H. & Viveros-Long, Anamaria. Balancing Jobs & Family Life: Do Flexible Work Schedules Help? (Illus.). 360p. 1981. 27.95 (ISBN 0-87722-199-5). Temple U Pr.

Bohensky, Fred. Photo Manual & Disection Guide of the Rat. (Avery's Anatomy Ser.). (Illus.). 140p. (Orig.). 1983. lab manual 5.95 (ISBN 0-89529-213-0). Avery Pub.

--Photo Manual & Dissection Guide of the Frog. (Avery's Anatomy Ser.). (Illus.). 88p. (Orig.). 1982. lab manual 4.95x (ISBN 0-89529-162-2). Avery Pub.

Bohigian, Haig. Track & Field Masters Ranking Book 1982: Men & Women Ages 30-89, U.S.A., Canada Mexico. 96p. (Orig.). 1981. pap. 10.00 (ISBN 0-686-91816-9). Gazette Pr.

--Track & Field Masters Ranking Book 1981: Men & Women Ages 30-89; U.S.A., Canada & Mexico. 104p. (Orig.). 1980. pap. 6.00 (ISBN 0-933390-06-8). Gazette Pr.

Bohl, Marilyn. Computer Concepts. LC 75-101499. (Illus.). 1970. text ed. 20.95 (ISBN 0-574-16080-9, 13-0751); instr's guide avail. (ISBN 0-574-16082-5, 13-0753); problems & exercises 7.95 (ISBN 0-574-16081-7, 13-0752); transparency masters 33.00 (ISBN 0-574-16083-3, 13-0754); problem-set master tape 57.50 (ISBN 0-574-16084-1, 13-0755). SRA.

--Flowcharting Techniques. 208p. 1971. pap. text ed. 9.95 (ISBN 0-574-16096-5, 13-1440). SRA.

--A Guide for Programmers. LC 77-14982. (Illus.). 1978. ref. 17.95x (ISBN 0-13-370551-X); pap. text ed. 12.95 (ISBN 0-13-370544-7). P-H.

--Information Processing. 3rd ed. 1980. pap. text ed. 16.95 (ISBN 0-574-21265-5, 13-4265); instr's. guide avail. (ISBN 0-574-21266-3, 13-4266); study guide 7.75 (ISBN 0-574-21267-1, 13-4267). SRA.

--Information Processing: With BASIC. 3rd ed. 575p. 1982. text ed. 17.95 (ISBN 0-574-21350-3, 13-4350); instr. guide avail. (ISBN 0-574-21351-1, 13-4351). SRA.

--Information Processing: With Pascal. 3rd ed. 1982. text ed. 18.95 (ISBN 0-574-21390-2, 13-4390). supp. instr. guide avail. (ISBN 0-574-21391-0, 13-4391). SRA.

--Tools for Structured Design. LC 77-13704. 1978. pap. text ed. 9.95 (ISBN 0-574-21170-5, 13-4170). SRA.

Bohl, Marilyn & Walter, Arline. Introduction to PL-I Programming & PL-C. LC 72-92560. (Computer Science Ser.). (Illus.). 280p. 1973. pap. text ed. 14.95 (ISBN 0-574-17075-8, 13-0075). SRA.

Bohl, Marilyn, jt. auth. see Parker, James L.

Bohlen, John R. How to Rule the World: Seek First the Kingdom of God. LC 81-90513. (Illus.). 271p. 1982. pap. 3.95 (ISBN 0-9607702-0-8). Kingdom God.

Bohler, Lorenz, et al. The Treatment of Fractures. LC 55-5445. (Illus.). 1956-58. Vol. 1. o.p. (ISBN 0-8089-0064-1); Vol. 2, 450pps. 1957. 63.00 o.p. (ISBN 0-8089-0065-X); Vol. 3, 816pps, 1958. 77.50 (ISBN 0-8089-0066-8). Grune.

Bohlin, Diane D. Prints & Related Drawings by the Carracci Family. LC 78-31551. (Illus.). pap. 8.00 (ISBN 0-89468-047-1). Natl Gallery Art.

Bohlinger, Maryanne Smith. Merchandise Buying: A Practical Guide. 2nd ed. 570p. 1982. pap. text ed. write for info. (ISBN 0-697-08086-2). Wm C Brown.

Bohlmann, Otto. Yeats & Nietzsche: An Exploration of Major Nietzschean Echoes in the Writings of William Butler Yeats. 240p. 1981. 39.00x (ISBN 0-333-27601-9, Pub. by Macmillan England). State Mutual Bk.

Bohm & MacDonald. Power: Mechanics of Energy Control. 2nd ed. 1983. 18.64 (ISBN 0-686-38845-3). McKnight.

Bohm, Bob. Notes on India. 220p. (Orig.). 1982. 20.00 (ISBN 0-89608-126-5); pap. 7.50 (ISBN 0-686-96888-3). South End Pr.

Bohm, David. Quantum Theory. 1951. ref. ed. 31.95 (ISBN 0-13-747873-9). P-H.

Bohm, J. Electrostatic Precipitators. (Chemical Engineering Monographs: Vol. 14). 1982. 78.75 (ISBN 0-444-99764-4). Elsevier.

Bohm, Peter & Kneese, Allen V. The Economics of Environment: Papers from Four Nations. LC 73-178244. 1972. 22.50 (ISBN 0-312-23240-3). St Martin.

Bohm, Robert A., et al, eds. Improving World Energy Production & Productivity. Energy, Environment, & Resources Center, the University of Tennessee. (International Energy Symposia Ser.: Vol. II). 1982. prof ref 35.00x (ISBN 0-88410-877-5). Ballinger Pub.

--Toward an Efficient Energy Future: Proceedings of the III International Energy Symposium III-May 23-27, 1982. Energy, Environment, & Resources Center,the University of Tennessee. (International Energy Symposia Ser.). 352p. 1983. prof ref 35.00x (ISBN 0-88410-878-3). Ballinger Pub.

--World Energy Production & Productivity: Proceedings of the International Energy Symposium I-October 14, 1980. Energy, Environment, & Resource Center, the University of Tennessee. (International Energy Symposia Ser.). 448p. 1981. prof ref 28.50x (ISBN 0-88410-698-5). Ballinger Pub.

Bohm-Bawerk, Eugen Von. Capital & Interest, 3 vols. Incl. Vol. 1. History & Critique of Interest Theories. 512p (ISBN 0-910884-09-9); Vol. 2. Positive Theory of Capital. 480p (ISBN 0-910884-10-2); Vol. 3. Further Essays on Capital & Interest. 256p (ISBN 0-910884-11-0). LC 58-5555. 1959. 3 vols. 47.50 (ISBN 0-910884-07-2). Libertarian Press.

Bohme, Gunther. Urbanitat. 116p. (Ger.). 1982. write for info. (ISBN 3-8204-7025-5). P Lang Pubs.

Bohme, H. & Viehe, H. G. Imminium Salts in Organic Chemistry. LC 76-16155. (Advances in Organic Chemistry Ser.: Vol. 9, Pt. 2). 1979. 123.00 (ISBN 0-471-90693-X, Pub. by Wiley-Interscience). Wiley.

Bohme, H. & Viehe, H. G., eds. Iminium Salts in Organic Chemistry. LC 76-16155. (Advances in Organic Chemistry Ser: Vol. 9, Pt. 1). 544p. 1976. 100.00 (ISBN 0-471-90692-1, Pub. by Wiley-Interscience). Wiley.

Bohmer, M., jt. auth. see Kuzvart, M.

Bohn, Dave & Petschek, Rodolfo. Kinsey, Photographer. LC 78-1029. (Illus.). 1978. Repr. 45.00 (ISBN 0-87701-107-9). Chronicle Bks.

Bohn, Henry G., ed. Hand-Book of Games. LC 73-84610. 1969. Repr. of 1850 ed. 37.00x (ISBN 0-8103-3570-0). Gale.

--Polyglot of Foreign Proverbs - with English Translations. LC 67-23915. (Polyglot). 1968. Repr. of 1857 ed. 40.00x (ISBN 0-8103-3197-7). Gale.

Bohn, Hinrich, et al. Soil Chemistry. LC 79-14515. 1979. 26.50x (ISBN 0-471-04082-7, Pub. by Wiley-Interscience). Wiley.

Bohn, M., jt. auth. see Masterson, K.

Bohn, Ralph C., jt. auth. see Silvius, G. Harold.

Bohn, Raymond J. & Wool, John D. Useful Arithmetic, Vol. 1. rev. ed. 1981. pap. 2.75x (ISBN 0-88323-164-6, 251); tchr's. key 1.00x (ISBN 0-88323-167-0, 252). Richards Pub.

Bohn, Raymond J., jt. auth. see Wool, John D.

Bohner, Charles. Robert Penn Warren. rev. ed. (United States Authors Ser.). 1981. lib. bdg. 12.95 (ISBN 0-8057-7345-2, Twayne). G K Hall.

Bohner, Charles H. Robert Penn Warren. (U. S. Authors Ser.: No. 69). 1964. lib. bdg. 9.95 o.p. (ISBN 0-8057-0772-7, Twayne). G K Hall.

Bohnert, Herbert G. Logic: Its Use & Basis. 1977. pap. text ed. 12.25 (ISBN 0-8191-0265-2). U Pr of Amer.

Bohning, I., ed. Autonome Architekur und Partizipatorisches Bauen. 356p. (Ger.). 1981. text ed. 27.50x (ISBN 3-7643-1260-2). Birkhauser.

Bohr, Harald. Almost Periodic Functions. LC 47-5500. 1980. 9.95 (ISBN 0-8284-0027-X). Chelsea Pub.

Bohr, Niels. Niels Bohr Collected Works, Vol. 1: Early Work, 1905-1911. 1973. 117.00 (ISBN 0-444-10003-2, North-Holland). Elsevier.

--Niels Bohr Collected Works, Vol 2: Work on Atomic Physics, 1912-1917. Hoyer, V., ed. 1982. 117.00 (ISBN 0-444-86132-7, North Holland). Elsevier.

Bohr, Peter. The Money-Wise Guide to Sports Cars. LC 82-47678. (Illus.). 240p. 1982. 19.95 (ISBN 0-15-162052-0); pap. 9.95 (ISBN 0-15-661956-3, Harv). HarBraceJ.

Bohren, Craig F. & Huffman, Donald R. Absorption & Scattering of Light by Small Particles. 550p. 1983. 44.95 (ISBN 0-471-05772-X, Pub. by Wiley-Interscience). Wiley.

Bohrer, Dick. They Called Him Shifta. LC 95-28. 320p. 1981. pap. 4.95 (ISBN 0-8024-7910-3). Moody.

Bohrnstedt, George W. & Knoke, David. Statistics for Social Data Analysis. LC 81-82889. 544p. 1982. text ed. 23.95 (ISBN 0-87581-275-9). Peacock Pubs.

Bohrod, Aaron. Decade of Still Life. (Illus.). 312p. 1966. 45.00 (ISBN 0-299-04121-2). U of Wis Pr.

Bohstedt, John. Riots & Community Politics in England & Wales, 1790-1810. (Illus.). 336p. 1983. text ed. 30.00x (ISBN 0-674-77120-6). Harvard U Pr.

Bohus, B., tr. see Gispen, W. H. & Van Wimersma, Greidanus.

Bohuslov, Ronald L. Analytic Geometry: A Precalculus Approach. (Illus.). 1970. text ed. 18.95 (ISBN 0-02-311810-5, 31181). Macmillan.

--Basic Mathematics for Technical Occupations. (Illus.). 480p. 1976. 21.95 (ISBN 0-13-063396-8). P-H.

Boice, James M. Does Inerrancy Matter. 1980. pap. 2.95 (ISBN 0-8423-0653-6). Tyndale.

--The Epistles of John. 224p. 1983. pap. 6.95 (ISBN 0-310-21531-5). Zondervan.

--The Gospel of John, Vol.V. 416p. 1982. pap. 12.95 o.p. (ISBN 0-310-21471-8). Zondervan.

--The Gospel of John: Peace in Storm, Vol. IV. 496p. 1983. pap. 9.95 (ISBN 0-310-21461-0). Zondervan.

--How to Live the Christian Life. LC 81-18839. 128p. 1982. pap. 5.95 (ISBN 0-8024-3666-8). Moody.

--The Parables of Jesus. 1983. pap. 6.95 (ISBN 0-8024-0163-5). Moody.

--Witness & the Revelation in the Gospel of John. 1970. pap. 5.75 (ISBN 0-85364-099-8). Attic Pr.

Boies, Jack J. The Lost Domain: Avatars of the Earthly Paradise in Western Literature. LC 81-40923. 244p. (Orig.). 1982. lib. bdg. 21.75 (ISBN 0-8191-2387-0); pap. text ed. 10.75 (ISBN 0-8191-2388-9). U Pr of Amer.

Boikess, Robert S. & Edelson, Edward. Chemical Principles. 2nd ed. (Illus.). 1981. text ed. 30.95 (ISBN 0-06-040808-1, HarpC); scp lab manual 15.50 (ISBN 0-06-040811-1); study guide scp 7.50 (ISBN 0-06-040809-X); scp solutions manual 6.50 (ISBN 0-06-040812-X); instr. manual avail. (ISBN 0-06-360792-1); ans. bk. avail. (ISBN 0-06-360793-X). Har-Row.

Boikess, Robert S. & Sorum, C. Harvey. How to Solve General Chemistry Problems. 6th ed. (Illus.). 1981. pap. text ed. 13.95 (ISBN 0-13-434126-0). P-H.

Boiko, Claire. Plays & Programs for Girls & Boys. (gr. 3-6). 1972. 12.00 (ISBN 0-8238-0134-9). Plays.

Boillot, Michael H., et al. Essentials of Flowcharting. 3rd ed. 125p. 1982. pap. text ed. write for info. (ISBN 0-697-08151-6). Wm C Brown.

Boillot, Michel. Understanding Basic in Business. 1978. pap. text ed. 14.95 (ISBN 0-8299-0206-6). West Pub.

--Understanding FORTRAN. (Illus.). 1978. pap. text ed. 12.50 o.s.i. (ISBN 0-8299-0205-8). West Pub.

--Understanding FORTRAN. 2nd ed. (Illus.). 520p. 1981. pap. text ed. 17.95 (ISBN 0-8299-0355-0). West Pub.

Boillot, Michel & Boillot, Mona. Understanding Structured COBOL. (Illus.). 600p. 1982. pap. text ed. 18.50 (ISBN 0-314-63161-5). West Pub.

Boillot, Michel & Horn, L. Wayne. BASIC. 3rd ed. (Illus.). 375p. 1983. pap. text ed. 13.95 (ISBN 0-314-69636-9). West Pub.

Boillot, Mona, jt. auth. see Boillot, Michel.

Bois, Edward Du see Du Bois, Edward.

Bois, Pene du. Lion. reissue ed. 1981. 12.95 (ISBN 0-670-42950-3). Viking Pr.

Bois, W. E. B. Du see Du Bois, W. E. B.

Bois, William E. Du see Du Bois, William E.

Bois, William Pene Du see Du Bois, William P.

Bois, William Pene Du see Pene du Bois, William.

Bois, William Pene Du see Pene Du Bois, William.

Boisard, Marcel. The Humanism of Islam. Quinlan, Hamid, ed. Al-Jarrahi, Abdussamad, tr. from Fr. LC 82-70456. 200p. (Orig.). 1983. pap. 8.00 (ISBN 0-89259-035-1). Am Trust Pubns.

Boiselle, Arthur H., et al. Using Mathematics in Business. LC 80-16710. (Illus.). 384p. 1981. pap. 17.95 (ISBN 0-201-00098-9); tests 3.00 (ISBN 0-201-00041-5); instrs' manual 9.95 (ISBN 0-201-00099-7). A-W.

Boisen, Monte B., Jr. & Larsen, Max D. Understanding Basic Calculus: With Application from the Managerial, Social & Life Sciences. (Mathematics Ser.). 1978. text ed. 21.95 (ISBN 0-675-08430-X). Additional supplements may be obtained from publisher. Merrill.

Boisgontier, Jacques. BASIC & Its Files, Vol. 1. Ropiequet, Suzanne, tr. from Fr. 170p. Date not set. pap. 8.95 (ISBN 0-88056-065-7). Dilithium Pr. Postponed.

Boisselier, Jean. Ceylon. (Archaeologia Mundi Ser.). 1975. 29.50x o.s.i. (ISBN 0-88254-329-6). Hippocrene Bks.

Boisson, Claude. Contribution a l'Etude Biologique du Leptoporus Lignosus. (Black Africa Ser.). 101p. (Fr.). 1974. Repr. lib. bdg. 35.50 o.p. (ISBN 0-8287-0103-2, 71-2014). Clearwater Pub.

Boisson, M., jt. ed. see Chalazonitis, N.

Boissonnade, Prosper. Life & Work in Medieval Europe: The Evolution of Medieval Economy from the Fifth to the Fifteenth Century. Power, Eileen, tr. from Fr. LC 82-11818. (Illus.). 395p. 1982. Repr. of 1964 ed. lib. bdg. 37.75x (ISBN 0-313-23566-X, BOLW). Greenwood.

Boitani, Piero. English Medieval Narrative in the Thirteenth & Fourteenth Centuries. Hall, Joan, tr. LC 81-17081. 328p. 1982. 42.50 (ISBN 0-521-23562-6). Cambridge U Pr.

Boite, R. & De Wilde, P. Circuit Theory & Design. 1982. 117.00 (ISBN 0-444-86307-9). Elsevier.

Bojars, Nick. The Struggle in the Kremlin. 1978. 8.95 o.p. (ISBN 0-533-03071-4). Vantage.

Bojer, Johan. The Emigrants. Jayne, A. G., tr. from Norwegian. LC 78-9813. xviii, 355p. 1978. pap. 8.95 (ISBN 0-8032-6051-2, BB 673, Bison). U of Nebr Pr.

Bojtar, Endre. Slavic Structuralism in Literary Science. (Linguistic & Literary Studies in Eastern Europe: 11). 150p. 1983. 24.00 (ISBN 90-272-1507-3). Benjamins North Am.

Bok, Derek C. & Dunlop, John T. Labor & the American Community. 1970. pap. 6.95 o.p. (ISBN 0-671-20415-7, Touchstone Bks). S&S.

Bok, Sissela. Secrets: On the Ethics of Concealment & Revelation. 1983. 16.95 (ISBN 0-394-51581-1). Pantheon.

Boker, Carlos. Joris Ivens, Film-maker: Facing Reality. Kirkpatrick, Diane, ed. LC 81-4697. (Studies in Cinema: No. 1). 222p. 1981. 39.95 (ISBN 0-8357-1182-X, Pub. by UMI Res Pr). Univ Microfilms.

Boklage, Cecilia, jt. auth. see Veitch, Carol.

Boklund, Gunnar. Sources of the White Devil, John Webster. LC 68-1396. (Studies in Comparative Literature, No. 35). 1969. Repr. of 1957 ed. lib. bdg. 49.95x o.p. (ISBN 0-8383-0648-9). Haskell.

Bokor-Szego, H. The Role of the United States in International Legislation. 1979. 47.00 (ISBN 0-444-85041-4, North Holland). Elsevier.

Bokser, Baruch M. History of Judaism: The Next Ten Years. Neusner, Jacob, ed. LC 80-25501. (Brown Judaic Studies). 1980. 15.00 (ISBN 0-89130-450-9, 14-00-21); pap. 10.50 (ISBN 0-89130-451-7). Scholars Pr CA.

Bola Publications. Bola Glossary of Civil Procedural Law: Spanish-English & English-Spanish. LC 82-72320. (Bola Glossary Ser.: Vol. 2). 100p. (Orig.). pap. 19.95 (ISBN 0-943118-01-8). Bola Pubns.

Bolam, Ray, ed. School-Focused in-Service Training. (Heinemann Organization in Schools Ser.). x, 246p. 1983. pap. text ed. 25.00x (ISBN 0-435-80090-6). Heinemann Ed.

Boland, Bill, ed. Annals Index, Vol. 289. (Annals of the New York Academy of Sciences). 581p. 1977. 47.00x (ISBN 0-89072-035-5). NY Acad Sci.

Boland, Bill M. & Cullinan, Justine, eds. Annals Index (1975-1977) (Annals of the New York Academy of Sciences: Vol. 331). 226p. 1979. 41.00x (ISBN 0-89766-041-2). NY Acad Sci.

Boland, D. J., et al. Eucalyptus Seed. (Illus.). 191p. 1980. pap. 25.00 (ISBN 0-643-02586-3). Sabbot-Natural Hist Bks.

--Eucalyptus Seed. (Illus.). 191p. 1980. 25.00x (ISBN 0-643-02586-3). Timber.

Boland, Richard, jt. auth. see Tricker, R. I.

Bolande, Robert P., jt. ed. see Rosenberg, Harvey S.

Bolandis, Jerry. Hospital Finance: A Comprehensive Approach. LC 81-20506. 284p. 1982. text ed. 32.50 (ISBN 0-89443-377-6). Aspen Systems.

Bolce, William J., ed. see Hysom, John L.

Bold, Alan. The Ballad. (Critical Idiom Ser.). 1979. 19.95x (ISBN 0-416-70890-0); pap. 4.95x (ISBN 0-416-70900-1). Methuen Inc.

--Scots Football: A Celebration in Verse & Pictures. (Illus.). 1978. text ed. 10.95x o.p. (ISBN 0-8464-0824-4); pap. 5.95x o.p. (ISBN 0-686-77126-5). Beekman Pubs.

--The Sexual Dimension in Literature. LC 82-13894. (Critical Studies Ser.). 224p. 1982. text ed. 28.50x (ISBN 0-389-20314-9). B&N Imports.

Bold, G. H., ed. Soil Chemistry, Pt. B: Physico-Chemical Models. 2nd ed. (Developments in Soil Science Ser.: Vol. 5B). 1982. 76.75 (ISBN 0-444-42060-6). Elsevier.

Bold, H. C., jt. auth. see Cox, E. R.

Bold, Harold C. & Wynne, Michael J. Introduction to the Algae: Structure & Reproduction. (P-H Biology Ser.). (Illus.). 1978. ref. ed. 32.95 (ISBN 0-13-477786-7). P-H.

Bold, Harold C., jt. auth. see Alexopoulos, Constantine J.

Boldan, Ruth I. Freddy Frog Wakes up. 1981. 4.75 (ISBN 0-8062-1750-2). Carlton.

Boldea, I., jt. auth. see Nasar, S. A.

Bolden, Theodore E., et al. Dental Hygiene Examination Review, Vol. 1. 4th ed. 1982. pap. 17.50 (ISBN 0-87488-461-6). Med Exam.

Bolding, Amy. I'll Be Glad to Give a Devotion. (Paperback Program Ser). 1978. pap. 3.95 (ISBN 0-8010-0709-7). Baker Bk.

--Please Give a Devotion: For Women's Groups. (Paperback Program Ser.). 108p. 1976. pap. 3.95 (ISBN 0-8010-0583-3). Baker Bk.

--Simple Welcome Speeches & Other Helps. (Pocket Pulpit Library). 1973. pap. 4.50 (ISBN 0-8010-0612-0). Baker Bk.

--A Sourcebook of Comfort. (Pocket Pulpit Library Ser). 1979. pap. 1.95 o.p. (ISBN 0-8010-0520-5). Baker Bk.

Boldman, Craig & Boldman, Craig. Comic Characters. (How to Draw Ser.: No. 2152). (Illus.). 48p. 1983. pap. 0.99 (ISBN 0-307-20152-X). Western Pub.

Boldt, Marjorie A. Acute Coronary Care. LC 81-67663. (Series in Critical Care Nursing). (Illus.). 175p. (Orig.). 1982. pap. text ed. 12.95. Wiley.

Boldy & Heuman. Housing For the Elderly: Planning & Policy Formation in Western Europe & North America. LC 82-10684. 224p. 1982. 25.00x (ISBN 0-312-39349-0). St Martin.

Boldy, Duncan, ed. Operational Research Applied to Health Services. 1981. 32.50x (ISBN 0-312-58682-5). St Martin.

Boldy, Stephen. The Novels of Julio Cortazar. LC 79-41579. (Cambridge Iberian & Latin American Studies). 320p. 1980. 29.95 (ISBN 0-521-23097-7). Cambridge U Pr.

Boldyrev, V. V., et al, eds. Control of the Reactivity of Solids. (Studies in Surface Science & Catalysts: Vol. 2). 1979. 57.50 (ISBN 0-444-41800-8). Elsevier.

Bole, A. G. & Jones, K. D. Automatic Radar Plotting Aids Manual. 160p. 1982. 49.00x (ISBN 0-434-90160-1, Pub. by Heinemann England). State Mutual Bk.

Boleach, Jim, jt. auth. see Fobel, Jim.

Bolen, William H. Advertising. LC 80-18915. (Marketing Ser.). 504p. 1981. text ed. 25.95 (ISBN 0-471-03486-X); avail. tchrs. manual (ISBN 0-471-08937-0). Wiley.

--Contemporary Retailing. (Illus.). 1978. ref. ed. 21.00 o.p. (ISBN 0-13-170290-4). P-H.

Boler, Deetje. Psyche in the Mouth of the Dragon. (Illus.). 1978. pap. 4.00 (ISBN 0-686-14354-X). Cassandra Pubns.

Boles, Donald E. Two Swords: Commentaries & Cases in Religion & Education. 1967. 10.95x o.p. (ISBN 0-8138-1707-2). Iowa St U Pr.

Boles, H. Leo. The Holy Spirit. 8.95 (ISBN 0-89225-102-6). Gospel Advocate.

Boles, H. Leo see Gospel Advocate.

Boley, B. A., jt. ed. see Rastoin, J.

Boley, Bruno A. & Weiner, Jerome H. Theory of Thermal Stresses. LC 60-6446. 1960. 45.50x (ISBN 0-685-22215-2, 471-08679-7, Pub. by Wiley-Interscience). Wiley.

Boley, Jack. A Guide to Effective Industrial Safety. 120p. 1977. 12.95 (ISBN 0-87201-798-2). Gulf Pub.

Boley, Robert E., ed. Land: Recreation & Leisure. LC 78-123466. (Special Report Ser). (Orig.). 1970. pap. 5.00 o.p. (ISBN 0-87420-554-9). Urban Land.

Bolge, Richard, jt. auth. see Gerlach, Joel.

Bolger, ed. see British European Centre, Paris.

Bolger, Philip C. Thirty-Odd Boats. LC 82-80403. (Illus.). 224p. 1982. 22.50 (ISBN 0-87742-152-8). Intl Marine.

Bolger, William F., intro. by. All about Letters. Rev. ed. LC 82-600601. (Illus.). 64p. (gr. 9-12). 1982. pap. 2.50x (ISBN 0-8141-0113-5, 01135). USPS.

--P. S. Write Soon! All about Letters. LC 82-600641. (Illus.). 64p. (Orig.). (gr. 4-8). 1982. pap. 2.50x (ISBN 0-8141-3796-2, 37962). USPS.

Bolian. Growing Up Slim. 1971. 5.95 o.p. (ISBN 0-07-006380-X, GB). McGraw.

Bolian, Polly, jt. auth. see Schima, Marilyn.

Bolick, James H. Sermons for Revival Preaching. (Pocket Pulpit Library Ser). pap. 2.25 o.p. (ISBN 0-8010-0551-5). Baker Bk.

Bolin, B., et al. The Global Carbon Cycle: Scope Report 13. (Scientific Committee on Problems of the Environment Ser). 491p. 1979. pap. 52.95x (ISBN 0-471-99710-2, Pub. by Wiley-Interscience). Wiley.

Bolin, Bert. Carbon Cycle Modelling. (Scientific Committee on Problems of the Environment Scope Ser.). 408p. 1981. 44.95x (ISBN 0-471-10051-X, Pub. by Wiley-Interscience). Wiley.

Bolin, T. D., jt. auth. see Davis, A. E.

Boling, Edwin T. & Vrooman, David M. Nursing Home Management: A Humanistic Approach. (Illus.). 403p. 1983. text ed. price not set (ISBN 0-398-04823-1). C C Thomas.

Boling, Robert, jt. ed. see Campbell, Edward F., Jr.

Boling, Robert G. & Wright, Ernest. Joshua, Vol. 6. LC 79-6583. (Anchor Bible Ser.). (Illus.). 432p. 1982. 18.00 (ISBN 0-385-00034-0). Doubleday.

Boling, T. Edwin. Managemet: Making Organizations Perform, Study Guide. (Illus.). 1980. pap. text ed. 9.95 (ISBN 0-02-311870-9). Macmillan.

Bolingbroke, J. M., jt. auth. see Victoria And Albert Museum.

Bolinger, Dwight & Sears, Donald A. Aspects of Language. 3rd ed. 352p. (Orig.). 1981. pap. text ed. 12.95 (ISBN 0-15-503872-9, HC). HarBraceJ.

Bolinger, Robert E. Endocrinology: New Directions in Therapy. 2nd ed. 1982. write for info. (ISBN 0-87488-678-3). Med Exam.

Bolino, August C. Ellis Island Source Book. (Illus.). 224p. 1983. 15.00 (ISBN 0-89962-331-X). Todd & Honeywell.

Bolis, C. L., jt. ed. see Refsum, S.

Bolis, Lian, jt. ed. see Karnovsky, Manfred L.

Bolis, Liana, et al, eds. Membranes & Disease. LC 75-30235. 424p. 1976. 43.00 (ISBN 0-89004-082-6). Raven.

Bolitho, A. R. & Sandler, P. L. Learn English for Science. (English As a Second Language Bk.). 108p. 1977. pap. text ed. 4.50x student bk. (ISBN 0-582-55247-8); pap. text ed. 2.95x tchr's bk. (ISBN 0-582-55482-9). Longman.

--Study English for Science. (English As a Second Language Bk.). 104p. 1980. pap. text ed. 4.50x (ISBN 0-582-55248-6); tchr's ed. 2.95x (ISBN 0-582-74821-6). Longman.

Bolitho, Harold. Meiji Japan. LC 80-7448. (Cambridge Topic Bks.). (Illus.). (gr. 5-10). 1980. PLB 6.95g (ISBN 0-8225-1219-X). Lerner Pubns.

Bolitho, William. Murder for Profit. 407p. 1982. 14.95 (ISBN 0-910395-02-0); pap. 7.95 (ISBN 0-910395-03-9). Marlboro Pr.

Bolkosky, Sidney, jt. auth. see Lipson, Greta.

Bolkstein. Modern Liberalism. 1982. 19.25 (ISBN 0-444-86484-9). Elsevier.

Boll. Erzahlungen. (Easy Reader, D). pap. 3.95 (ISBN 0-88436-108-X, 45275). EMC.

Boll, Carl R. Executive Jobs Unlimited: Updated Edition. 1980. 11.95 (ISBN 0-02-512790-X). Macmillan.

Boll, Eleanor. Man That You Marry. (gr. 9 up). 1963. 6.25 (ISBN 0-8255-1700-1). Macrae.

Boll, Eleanor, jt. auth. see Bossard, James.

Boll, Eleanor S., jt. auth. see Bossard, James.

Boll, Eleanor S., jt. auth. see Bossard, James H.

Boll, Heinrich. Billiards at Half-Past Nine. 1975. pap. 3.95 (ISBN 0-380-00280-9, 62471-0, Bard). Avon.

--The Clown. 1975. pap. 3.50 (ISBN 0-380-00333-3, 61622X, Bard). Avon.

--Eighteen Stories. Vennewitz, Leila, tr. from Ger. 1966. 6.95 o.p. (ISBN 0-07-006403-2, GB); pap. 4.95 o.p. (ISBN 0-07-006416-4). McGraw.

--The Safety Net. Vennewitz, Leila, tr. from Ger. 1983. pap. 4.95 (ISBN 0-14-006468-0). Penguin.

Boll, John J. Introduction to Cataloging, Vol. 1: Descriptive Cataloging. (Library Education Ser). 1970. 25.95 (ISBN 0-07-006411-3, C). McGraw.

--Introduction to Cataloging, Vol. 2: Entry Headings with Emphasis on Cataloging Process & Personal Names. new ed. (Library Education Ser). (Illus.). 448p. 1974. 25.95 (ISBN 0-07-006412-1, C). McGraw.

Boll, Michael M. The Petrograd Armed Workers Movement in the February Revolution (February July, 1917) A Study in the Radicalization of the Petrograd Proletariat. LC 79-66232. 1979. pap. text ed. 10.25 (ISBN 0-8191-0806-5). U Pr of Amer.

Boll, R. Soft Magnetic Materials. 41.00 (ISBN 0-471-25600-5, Wiley Heyden). Wiley.

Boll, Thomas J., jt. auth. see Filskov, Susan B.

Boll, Thomas J., jt. ed. see Alpern, Gerald D.

Boll, Tom. Teach Me Tonight. 64p. Date not set. pap. 5.95 (ISBN 0-686-38774-0). Mercury Pr.

Bollabas, B., ed. Graph Theory: Proceedings of the Conference on Graph Theory, Cambridge. (North-Holland Mathematics Studies: Vol. 62). 202p. 1982. 42.75 (ISBN 0-444-86449-0, North Holland). Elsevier.

Bollan, William. The Freedom of Speech & Writing upon Public Affairs Considered. LC 75-107346. (Civil Liberties in American History Ser). 1970. Repr. of 1766 ed. lib. bdg. 25.00 (ISBN 0-306-71878-2). Da Capo.

Boller, Francois & Frank, Ellen. Sexual Dysfunction in Neurological Disorders: Diagnosis Management & Rehabilitation. 104p. 1982. text ed. 12.50 (ISBN 0-89004-500-3). Raven.

Boller, Paul F., Jr. American Thought in Transition: The Impact of Evolutionary Naturalism, 1865-1900. LC 80-6210. 285p. 1981. lib. bdg. 21.75 (ISBN 0-8191-1550-9); pap. text ed. 11.25 (ISBN 0-8191-1551-7). U Pr of Amer.

Bolles, Richard N. Quick Job-Hunting Map for Beginners. 1977. pap. 1.25x (ISBN 0-913668-59-1). Ten Speed Pr.

--The Three Boxes of Life. LC 78-17000. (Illus.). 466p. 1981. 14.95 (ISBN 0-913668-52-4); pap. 8.95 (ISBN 0-913668-58-3). Ten Speed Pr.

--What Color Is Your Parachute? rev. ed. LC 81-50471. 352p. 1982. 14.95 (ISBN 0-89815-068-X); pap. 7.95 (ISBN 0-89815-067-1). Ten Speed Pr.

--What Color is Your Parachute? 1983. rev. ed. (Illus.). 320p. 1983. 14.95 (ISBN 0-89815-092-2); pap. 7.95 (ISBN 0-89815-091-4). Ten Speed Pr.

Bollet, A. J. Harrison's Principles of Internal Medicine Patient Management Problems: PreTest Self-Assessment & Review, Vol. 2. 276p. 1983. 32.00 (ISBN 0-07-051929-3). McGraw-Pretest.

Bollettieri, Nick, jt. auth. see Anthony, Julie.

Bollier, David. How to Appraise & Improve Your Daily Newspaper. 1980. pap. 5.00 (ISBN 0-686-36550-X). Ctr Responsive Law.

--Liberty & Justice for Some: Defending a Free Society from the Radical Right's Holy War on Democracy. LC 82-51019. 336p. (Orig.). 1982. pap. 8.95 (ISBN 0-8044-6060-4). Ungar.

--Liberty & Justice for Some: Defending a Free Society from the Radical Right's Holy War on Democracy. LC 82-51019. 336p. (Orig.). 1982. pap. 8.95 (ISBN 0-8044-6060-4, Co-pub. by People for Amer Way). Ungar.

Bolliger, Markus. Die Gattung Pulmonaria in Westeuropa. (Phanerogamarum Monographiae VIII). 250p. (Orig., Ger.). 1982. text ed. 54.00x (ISBN 3-7682-1338-2). Lubrecht & Cramer.

Bolling, Landrum R. & Smith, Craig. Private Foreign Aid: U. S. Philanthropy in Relief & Development. (Illus.). 240p. 1982. lib. bdg. 25.00 (ISBN 0-86531-393-8). Westview.

Bolling, R. & Bowles, J. America's Competitive Edge: How to Get Our Country Moving Again. 1982. 16.50 (ISBN 0-07-006438-5). McGraw.

Bollinger, Edward E. The Cross & the Floating Dragon: The Gospel in Ryukyu. (Illus.). 368p. 1983. pap. 10.95 (ISBN 0-87808-190-9). William Carey Lib.

Bollinger, Edward T. & Bauer, Frederick. The Moffat Road. LC 82-84341. (Illus.). 359p. 1981. Repr. of 1967 ed. 39.95 (ISBN 0-8214-0665-5). Swallow.

Bollinger, William H., et al. Project Design & Recommendations for Watershed Reforestation & Fuelwood Development in Sri Lanka. (Illus.). 122p. 1979. pap. 20.00 (ISBN 0-936130-03-2). Intl Sci Tech.

Bollmann, Willi E. Kamuti: A New Way in Bonsai. LC 75-821. (Illus.). 1977. pap. 7.95 o.p. (ISBN 0-88254-445-4). Hippocrene Bks.

Bollobas, B., ed. Advances in Graph Theory. (Annals of Discrete Mathematics Ser.: Vol. 3). 1978. 64.00 (ISBN 0-444-85075-9, North-Holland). Elsevier.

Bollobas, Bella, ed. Survey in Combinatorics. LC 79-51596. (London Mathematical Society Lecture Note Ser.: No. 38). 1979. pap. 25.95x (ISBN 0-521-22846-8). Cambridge U Pr.

Bolloten, Burnett. The Spanish Revolution: The Left & the Struggle for Power During the Civil War. LC 78-5011. xxvi, 665p. 1980. O.P. (ISBN 0-8078-1297-8); pap. 14.00x (ISBN 0-8078-4077-7). U of NC Pr.

Bolmeier, Edward C. Landmark Supreme Court Decisions on Public School Issues. 233p. 1973. 12.50 o.p. (ISBN 0-87215-160-3). Michie-Bobbs.

Bologna, G. & Vincelli, M., eds. Data Acquisition in High Physics: Proceedings of the International School of Physics "Enrico Fermi," Course LXXXIV, Varenna, Italy, July 28-Aug. 7, 1981. (Enrico Fermi International Summer School of Physics Ser.: Vol. 84). 400p. 1982. 83.00 (ISBN 0-444-86520-9, North Holland). Elsevier.

Bologna, Gianfranco. The World of Birds. Pleasance, Simon, tr. LC 79-1190. (Abbeville Press Encyclopedia of Natural Science). (Illus.). 256p. 1979. 13.95 (ISBN 0-89659-034-8); pap. 7.95 o. p. (ISBN 0-89659-028-3). Abbeville Pr.

Bolognese, Don, jt. auth. see Raphael, Elaine.

Bolognese, Ronald J. & Schwarz, R. H. Perinatal Medicine: Clinical Management of the High Risk Fetus & Neonate. 332p. 1977. 33.00 o.p. (ISBN 0-683-00907-9). Williams & Wilkins.

Bolognese, Ronald J. & Schwarz, Richard H. Perinatal Medicine: Management of the High Risk Fetus & Neonate. 2nd ed. (Illus.). 546p. 1981. lib. bdg. 58.00 (ISBN 0-683-00908-7). Williams & Wilkins.

Bolooki, H. Thoracic Surgery. 3rd ed. (Medical Examination Review Book: Vol. 18). 1981. pap. 26.00 (ISBN 0-87488-118-8). Med Exam.

Bolooki, Hooshang, ed. Clinical Application of Intra-Aortic Balloon Pump. LC 77-84351. (Illus.). 512p. 1977. 34.50 o.p. (ISBN 0-87993-104-3). Futura Pub.

--Clinical Application of Intra-Aortic Balloon Pump. 1983. write for info (ISBN 0-87993-184-1). Futura Pub.

Bols, Jan. Hondred Vlaamsche Liederen, met woorden en zangwijzen, voor de eerste maal aan het licht gebracht. (Facsimile of Dutch Songbks.: Vol. 5). 1979. Repr. of 1897 ed. 36.00 o.s.i. (ISBN 90-6027-171-8, Pub. by Frits Knuf Netherlands); wrappers 24.00 o.s.i. (ISBN 90-6027-170-X, Pub. by Frtis Knuf Netherlands). Pendragon NY.

Bolsterli, Margaret J. The Early Community at Bedford Park: The Pursuit of "Corporate Happiness" in the First Garden Suburb. LC 76-8299. (Illus.). xii, 133p. 1977. 14.00x (ISBN 0-8214-0224-2, 82-82295). Ohio U Pr.

Bolsterli, Margaret J., ed. Vinegar Pie & Chicken Bread: A Woman's Diary of Life in the Rural South, 1890-1891. LC 82-4922. 144p. 1982. 14.00 (ISBN 0-938626-10-8). U of Ark Pr.

Bolt, Albert B. & Wardle, M. E. Communicating with a Computer. LC 73-85713. (Illus.). 1970. 12.95 (ISBN 0-521-07633-1); pap. 6.95x (ISBN 0-521-09587-5). Cambridge U Pr.

Bolt, Christine, jt. auth. see Barbrook, Alec.

Bolt, David. Samson. 322p. 1980. 12.95 o.p. (ISBN 0-312-69848-8). St Martin.

Bolt, G. H. & Bruggenwert, M. G. Soil Chemistry, Pt. A: Basic Elements. (Developments in Soil Science: Vol. 5A). 1976. 25.75 (ISBN 0-444-41435-5). Elsevier.

Bolt, Robert J. & Palmer, Philip E. The Digestive System. LC 82-10906. 429p. 1983. pap. 24.95x (ISBN 0-471-92207-2, Pub. by Wiley Med). Wiley.

Boltax, Robert S., jt. auth. see Krat, Siegfried J.

Bolten, Steven E. Managerial Finance: Principles & Practice. LC 75-31036. (Illus.). 896p. 1976. text ed. 26.95 (ISBN 0-395-20462-3); instr's. manual 2.15 (ISBN 0-395-20461-5). HM.

Bolten, Steven E. & Conn, Robert L. Essentials of Managerial Finance: Principles & Practice. LC 80-80961. (Illus.). 800p. 1981. text ed. 24.95 (ISBN 0-395-29638-2); instr's manual 2.00 (ISBN 0-395-29639-0); test-bank 1.50 (ISBN 0-395-30359-1); study guide 10.50 (ISBN 0-395-30089-4). HM.

Boltho, Andrea. The European Economy: Growth & Crisis. (Illus.). 650p. 1982. 49.00 (ISBN 0-19-877119-3); pap. 19.95 (ISBN 0-19-877118-5). Oxford U Pr.

--Foreign Trade Criteria in Socialist Economies. LC 78-121366. (Soviet & East European Studies). 1970. 27.50 (ISBN 0-521-07883-0). Cambridge U Pr.

Boltman, Brigid. Cook-Freeze Catering Systems. (Illus.). 1978. text ed. 39.00x (ISBN 0-85334-768-9, Pub. by Applied Sci England). Elsevier.

Bolton. General & Communications Studies, No. I, II. 1983. No. I. text ed. write for info. (ISBN 0-408-01195-5); No. II. text ed. write for info. (ISBN 0-408-01197-1). Butterworth.

--Vocational Adjustment of Disabled Persons. 272p. 1982. pap. text ed. 16.95 (ISBN 0-8391-1722-1). Univ Park.

Bolton, Brian. Introduction to Rehabilitation Research. (Illus.). 146p. 1974. 18.50x o.p. (ISBN 0-398-03109-6). C C Thomas.

--Rehabilitation Counseling Research. 323p. 1979. pap. text ed. 14.95 (ISBN 0-8391-1434-6). Univ Park.

Bolton, Brian & Cook, Daniel W. Rehabilitation Client Assessment. 336p. 1980. pap. text ed. 14.95 (ISBN 0-8391-1546-6). Univ Park.

Bolton, Brian, ed. Rehabilitation Counseling: Theory & Practice. LC 77-18287. 303p. 1978. pap. 12.95 (ISBN 0-8391-1199-1). Univ Park.

Bolton, Carole. The Good-Bye Year. 192p. (gr. 5-9). 1982. 10.95 (ISBN 0-525-66787-3, 01063-320). Lodestar Bks.

Bolton, Charles S. Southern Anglicanism: The Church of England in Colonial South Carolina. LC 81-6669. (Contribution to the Study of Religion: No. 5). (Illus.). 248p. 1982. lib. bdg. 29.95 (ISBN 0-313-23090-0, BOS/). Greenwood.

Bolton, Clyde. Alabama Football. (College Sports Ser.: Football). 1981. 10.95 o.p. (ISBN 0-87397-020-9). Strode.

Bolton, Dale. Selection & Evaluation of Teachers. LC 72-10648. 260p. 1973. 19.95x (ISBN 0-8211-0123-4); text ed. 17.95x (ISBN 0-685-28805-6). McCutchan.

Bolton, Ethel S. Wax Portraits & Silhouettes. LC 71-164115. 88p. 1974. Repr. of 1914 ed. 34.00x (ISBN 0-8103-3168-3). Gale.

Bolton, Ethel S. & Coe, Eva J. American Samplers. (Illus.). 12.50 o.p. (ISBN 0-8446-4713-6). Peter Smith.

Bolton, Evelyn. Dream Dancer. LC 74-9571. (Evelyn Bolton's Horse Stories Ser). (Illus.). 32p. (gr. 3-7). 1974. PLB 6.95 (ISBN 0-87191-371-2); pap. 3.25 (ISBN 0-89812-128-0). Creative Ed.

--Goodbye Charlie. LC 74-9572. (Evelyn Bolton's Horse Stories Ser). (Illus.). 32p. (gr. 2-6). 1974. PLB 6.95 (ISBN 0-87191-369-0); pap. 3.25 (ISBN 0-89812-127-2). Creative Ed.

--Lady's Girl. LC 74-9528. (Evelyn Bolton's Horse Stories Ser). (Illus.). 32p. (gr. 3-7). 1974. PLB 6.95 (ISBN 0-87191-372-0); pap. 3.25 (ISBN 0-89812-125-6). Creative Ed.

--Ride When You're Ready. LC 74-9763. (Evelyn Bolton's Horse Stories Ser). (Illus.). 32p. (gr. 3-7). 1974. PLB 6.95 (ISBN 0-87191-373-9); pap. 3.25 (ISBN 0-89812-130-2). Creative Ed.

--Stable of Fear. LC 74-9704. (Evelyn Bolton's Horse Stories Ser). (Illus.). 32p. (gr. 3-7). 1974. PLB 6.95 (ISBN 0-87191-370-4); pap. 2.95 (ISBN 0-89812-129-9). Creative Ed.

--The Wild Horses. LC 74-9530. (Evelyn Bolton's Horse Stories Ser). (Illus.). 32p. (gr. 3-7). 1974. PLB 6.95 (ISBN 0-87191-374-7); pap. 3.25 (ISBN 0-89812-126-4). Creative Ed.

Bolton, Gary R. Handbook of Canine Electrocardiography. LC 74-17749. (Illus.). 1975. 32.00 o.p. (ISBN 0-7216-1838-3). Saunders.

Bolton, Geoffrey. Spoils & Spoilers: Australians Make their Environment 1788-1980. (Australian Experience Ser.: No. 3). (Illus.). 200p. 1982. pap. text ed. 12.50 (ISBN 0-86861-226-X). Allen Unwin.

Bolton, Henry C. Counting-Out Rhymes of Children. LC 68-23139. 1969. Repr. of 1888 ed. 30.00x (ISBN 0-8103-3475-5). Gale.

Bolton, Herbert E. Guide to Materials for the History of the United States in the Principal Archives of Mexico. 1913. pap. 45.00 (ISBN 0-527-00698-X). Kraus Repr.

--Spanish Borderlands. 1921. text ed. 8.50x (ISBN 0-686-83780-0). Elliots Bks.

--Texas in the Middle Eighteenth Century: Studies in Spanish Colonial History & Administration. 1977. Repr. of 1915 ed. 48.00 (ISBN 0-527-00941-5). Kraus Repr.

--Texas in the Middle Eighteenth Century: Studies in Spanish Colonial History & Administration. (Texas History Paperbacks Ser.: No. 8). 511p. 1970. 0.00 o.p.; pap. 8.95x (ISBN 0-292-70034-2). U of Tex Pr.

Bolton, J. L. The Medieval English Economy: Eleven Fifty to Fifteen Hundred. LC 80-503599. (Rowman & Littlefield University Library). (Illus.). 400p. 1980. 25.00x (ISBN 0-8476-6234-9); pap. 16.00x (ISBN 0-8476-6235-7). Rowman.

Bolton, James. Ancient Crete & Mycenae. Reeves, Marjorie, ed. (Then & There Ser.). (Illus.). 96p. (gr. 7-12). 1968. pap. text ed. 3.10 (ISBN 0-582-20415-1). Longman.

Bolton, James R. Biological & Chemical Energy Conversion, 4 vols. (Illus.). 1983. Set. lib. bdg. 220.00x (ISBN 0-89553-039-2). Am Solar Energy.

Bolton, James R., jt. auth. see Wertz, John E.

Bolton, James R. & Connolly, John S., eds. Photochemical Solar Energy Conversion. (Biological & Chemical Energy Conversion). (Illus.). 1983. lib. bdg. 55.00x (ISBN 0-89553-041-4). Am Solar Energy.

Bolton, James R., jt. ed. see Seibert, Michael.

Bolton, Kathleen, ed. Current Accounting Literature 1972. new ed. 256p. 1974. 19.00x o.p. (ISBN 0-7201-0372-X, Pub. by Mansell England). Wilson.

Bolton, Kathleen M., ed. Current Accounting Literature 1973: Supplement to Current Accounting Literature 1971. 290p. 1975. 26.00 o.p. (ISBN 0-7201-0455-6, Pub. by Mansell England). Wilson.

--Historical Accounting Literature. LC 75-328383. 386p. 1975. 72.00 o.p. (ISBN 0-7201-0519-6, Pub. by Mansell England). Wilson.

Bolton, Neil, ed. Philosophical Problems in Psychology. (Psychology in Progress Ser.). 1979. 27.00x (ISBN 0-416-70980-X); pap. 12.50x (ISBN 0-416-70990-7). Methuen Inc.

Bolton, R., jt. auth. see De la Mare, P. D.

Bolton, R. & Mayer, E., eds. Andean Kinship & Marriage. 1977. 7.50 (ISBN 0-686-36559-3). Am Anthro Assn.

Bolton, Reginald P. Indian Life of Long Ago in the City of New York. LC 72-89363. (Illus.). 193p. 1972. 4.95 o.p. (ISBN 0-517-50155-4, Harmony). Crown.

Bolton, Theodore. Early American Portrait Draughtsmen in Crayons. LC 74-77724. (Library of American Art Ser). (Illus.). 1970. Repr. of 1923 ed. lib. bdg. 27.50 (ISBN 0-306-71362-4). Da Capo.

Bolton, W. Atoms, Nuclei, & Electrons, Book 7. LC 80-41395. (Study Topics in Physics Ser.). 96p. 1981. pap. text ed. 4.95 (ISBN 0-408-10658-1). Butterworth.

--Electronic Systems, Bk. 8. LC 80-41394. (Study Topics in Physics Ser.). 96p. 1981. pap. text ed. 4.95 (ISBN 0-408-10659-X). Butterworth.

--Engineering Instrumentation & Control. 9th ed. (Technicians Ser.). (Illus.). 120p. 1980. pap. 15.95 (ISBN 0-408-00462-2). Butterworth.

--Fields, Bk. 5. LC 80-41166. (Study Topics in Physics Ser.). 96p. 1981. pap. text ed. 4.95 (ISBN 0-408-10656-5). Butterworth.

Bolton, W. F. Alcuin & Beowulf: An Eighth-Century View. 1978. 18.00 (ISBN 0-8135-0865-7). Rutgers U Pr.

Bolton, W. F. & Crystal, D. J. English Language, 2 vols. Incl. Vol. 1. 1490-1839. 43.50 (ISBN 0-521-04280-1); pap. 13.95x (ISBN 0-521-09379-1); Vol. 2. 1858-1964. 1965. 54.50 (ISBN 0-521-07325-1); pap. 16.95x (ISBN 0-521-09545-X). 1966. Cambridge U Pr.

Bolton, Whitney F. A Living Language: The History & Structure of English. 512p. 1982. 20.00 (ISBN 0-394-32280-0). Random.

Boltz, Carol & Seyler, Dorothy. Language Power. 303p. 1982. pap. text ed. 10.50 (ISBN 0-394-32715-2). Random.

Boltz, David F. & Howell, James A., eds. Colorimetric Determination of Nonmetals. 2nd ed. LC 77-12398. (Chemical Analysis Ser.: Vol. 8). 1978. 71.50 (ISBN 0-471-08750-5, Pub by Wiley-Interscience). Wiley.

Boltzmann, Ludwig. Wissenschaftliche Abhandlungen, 3 Vols. Hasenohrl, Fritz, ed. LC 66-26524. (Ger). 1969. Set. 99.50 (ISBN 0-8284-0215-9). Chelsea Pub.

Bolz, Harold A., et al, eds. Materials Handling Handbook. LC 57-11291. 1958. 75.95x o.p. (ISBN 0-8260-1175-6, Pub. by Wiley-Interscience). Wiley.

Bolz, Roger W., jt. auth. see Tuer, David F.

Bolza, Eleanor, jt. auth. see Keating, W. G.

Bolza, Eleanor, jt. auth. see Benni, C. A.

Bolza, Oskar. Lectures on the Calculus of Variations. 3rd ed. LC 73-16324. 11.95 (ISBN 0-8284-0145-4). Chelsea Pub.

--Vorlesungen Ueber Variationsrechnung. LC 62-8228. 23.95 (ISBN 0-8284-0160-8). Chelsea Pub.

Bolza, Oskar, et al. Festschrift Schwarz. LC 73-20209. Orig. Title: Mathematische Abhandlungen. viii, 451p. 1974. Repr. text ed. 25.00 (ISBN 0-8284-0275-2). Chelsea Pub.

Bolzano, Bernhard. The Theory of Science, (Die Wissenschaftslehre Oder Versuch Einer Neuen Darstellung der Logik) George, Rolf, ed. & tr. LC 71-126765. 1972. 42.50x (ISBN 0-520-01787-0). U of Cal Pr.

Bom, N. New Concepts in Echocardiography. 1972. lib. bdg. 21.00 o.p. (ISBN 90-207-0346-3, Pub. by Martinus Nijhoff Netherlands). Kluwer Boston.

Bomar, jt. auth. see Sager.

Bomar, George W. Texas Weather. (Illus.). 256p. 1983. 22.50 (ISBN 0-292-78052-4); pap. 9.95 (ISBN 0-292-78053-2). U of Tex Pr.

Bomar, Suzanne K., jt. auth. see Sager, Diane P.

Bombal, Maria L. New Islands: And Other Stories. Cunningham, Richard, tr. from Span. 1982. 12.95 (ISBN 0-374-22118-9). FS&G.

Bombaugh, Charles C. Gleanings for the Curious from the Harvest Fields of Literature: A Melange of Excerpta. LC 68-23465. 1970. Repr. of 1875 ed. 54.00x (ISBN 0-8103-3086-5). Gale.

--Oddities & Curiosities of Words & Literature. Gardner, M., ed. Orig. Title: Gleanings for the Curious. 1961. pap. 5.95 (ISBN 0-486-20759-5). Dover.

Bombaugh, Charles C., ed. Facts & Fancies for the Curious from the Harvest-Fields of Literature. LC 68-23464. 1968. Repr. of 1905 ed. 38.00x (ISBN 0-8103-3085-7). Gale.

Bombeck, Erma. Erma Bombeck Giant Economy Size. LC 82-45557. (Illus.). 540p. 1983. price not set (ISBN 0-385-18394-1). Doubleday.

--I Lost Everything in the Post-Natal Depression. LC 72-97269. 168p. 1973. 8.95 (ISBN 0-385-02904-7). Doubleday.

Bombelli, R. Osteoarthritis of the Hip: Classification & Pathogenesis-The Role of Osteotomy as Consequent Therapy. 2nd, rev. & enl ed. (Illus.). 386p. 1983. 165.00 (ISBN 0-387-11422-X). Springer-Verlag.

Bombieri, Enrico. Seminar on Minimal Submanifolds. LC 82-61356. (Annals of Mathematics Studies, 103). 500p. 1983. 45.00 (ISBN 0-686-38855-0); pap. 15.00 (ISBN 0-691-08319-3). Princeton U Pr.

Bombwall, K. R. Foundations of Indian Federalism. 1967. 10.00x o.p. (ISBN 0-210-22721-4). Asia.

Bomhoff. Inflation: The Quantity Theory & Rational Expectations. (Studies in Monetary Economics: Vol. 5). 1980. 42.75 (ISBN 0-444-85472-X). Elsevier.

Bommarito, James W. Preventive & Clinical Management of Troubled Children. 301p. 1977. pap. text ed. 12.50 (ISBN 0-8191-0180-X). U Pr of Amer.

Bommer, Michael R. W. & Chorba, Ronald W. Decision Making for Library Management. LC 81-17160. (Professional Librarian). 180p. 1982. text ed. 34.50 (ISBN 0-86729-001-3); pap. text ed. 27.50 (ISBN 0-86729-000-5). Knowledge Indus.

Bon Appetit Magazine Editors, ed. The Best of Bon Appetit. LC 79-2384. (Illus.). 1979. 19.95 (ISBN 0-89535-008-4). Knapp Pr.

Bon, Gustave Le see Le Bon, Gustave.

Bona, Constantin & Cazenave, Pierre-Andre. Lymphocytic Regulation by Antibodies. LC 80-17399. 324p. 1981. 62.50 (ISBN 0-471-05693-6, Pub. by Wiley-Interscience). Wiley.

Bonachea, Ramon L. & Martin, Marta S. The Cuban Insurrection, 1952-1959. LC 72-94546. (Social History Ser). 450p. 1974. text ed. 14.95 o.p. (ISBN 0-87855-074-7); pap. 7.95 (ISBN 0-87855-576-5). Transaction Bks.

Bonachea, Rolando, ed. see Castro, Fidel.

Bonafous, Louis-Abel De see De Bonafous, Louis-Abel.

Bonanno, Ellen, jt. auth. see Mechlin, Stuart.

Bonansea, Berbardine, ed. see Bettoni, Efrem.

Bonaparte, Louis-Napoleon. Extinction du Pauperisme. (Conditions of the 19th Century French Working Class Ser.). 31p. (Fr.). 1974. Repr. of 1848 ed. 22.50x o.p. (ISBN 0-8287-1375-8, 1116). Clearwater Pub.

Bonaparte, Marie, et al, eds. see Freud, Sigmund.

Bonaparte, T. H. & Franzen, William L. Instructional Innovations: Ideals, Issues, Impediments. 165p. 1977. 7.50 (ISBN 0-686-38272-2, 16-1687). Natl League Nurse.

Bonar, Andrew. The Life of R. M. M'Cheyne. 1978. pap. 3.45 (ISBN 0-85151-085-X). Banner of Truth.

Bonar, Andrew A. Memoir & Remains of R. M. M'cheyne. 1978. 15.95 (ISBN 0-85151-084-1). Banner of Truth.

--Memoirs of McCheyne. (Wycliffe Classic Ser.). 1978. pap. 9.95 (ISBN 0-8024-5241-8). Moody.

Bonar, Ann. How to Book of Basic Gardening. Daniels, Gilbert, ed. (How to Bks.). (Illus.). 96p. 1982. pap. 3.95 (ISBN 0-7137-1287-2, Pub. by Blandford Pr England). Sterling.

--How to Book of Flower Gardening. Daniels, Gilbert, ed. (How to Bks.). (Illus.). 96p. (Orig.). Date not set. pap. 3.95 (ISBN 0-7137-1289-9, Pub. by Blandford Pr England). Sterling.

--How to Book of Vegetable Gardening. (How to Bks.). (Illus.). 96p. (Orig.). 1982. pap. 3.95 (ISBN 0-7137-1288-0, Pub. by Blandford Pr England). Sterling.

--Shrubs for All Seasons. (Leisure Plan Books in Color). pap. 2.95 o.p. (ISBN 0-600-44175-X). Transatlantic.

Bonar, Jeanne R. Diabetes: A Clinical Guide. 2nd ed. (Medical Outline Ser.). 1980. pap. 25.00 (ISBN 0-87488-710-0). Med Exam.

Bonarius, Han, et al, eds. Personal Construct Psychology. 300p. 1981. 32.50x (ISBN 0-312-60228-6). St Martin.

Bonavia, David. The Chinese. LC 80-7873. (Illus.). 288p. 1980. 14.37i (ISBN 0-690-01996-3). Har-Row.

--The Chinese. rev. ed. 1983. pap. 4.95 (ISBN 0-14-022394-0, Pelican). Penguin.

--Vienna. (The Great Cities Ser.). (Illus.). 1978. lib. bdg. 12.00 (ISBN 0-686-51009-7). Silver.

Bonavia, Michael R. British Rail: The First Twenty-Five Years. LC 80-68687. (Illus.). 208p. 1981. 21.00 (ISBN 0-7153-8002-8). David & Charles.

--Railway Policy Between the Wars. 160p. 1982. 15.00 (ISBN 0-7190-0826-3). Manchester.

Bonavia-Hunt, Noel A. Modern Organ Stops: A Practical Guide to Their Nomenclature, Construction, Voicing & Artistic Use. (Bibliotheca Organologica Ser.: Vol. 52). 1974. Repr. of 1923 ed. wrappers 15.00 o.s.i. (ISBN 90-6027-172-6, Pub. by Frits Knuf Netherlands). Pendragon NY.

Bonazza, Blaze O., et al. Studies in Fiction. enl. 3rd ed. 880p. 1982. pap. text ed. 9.50 scp (ISBN 0-06-040832-4, HarpC); instructors manual avail. (ISBN 0-06-360849-9); scp wkbk. 6.50 (ISBN 0-06-040842-1); instr's manual for workers avail. (ISBN 0-06-360851-0). Har-Row.

Bonbright, James C. Public Utilities & the National Power Policies. LC 73-172007. (FDR & the Era of the New Deal Ser.). 1972. Repr. of 1940 ed. lib. bdg. 19.50 (ISBN 0-306-70424-2). Da Capo.

--Valuation of Property, 2 Vols. 1965. Repr. 60.00 (ISBN 0-87215-014-3). Michie-Bobbs.

Bonbright, James C. & Means, Gardiner C. Holding Company: Its Public Significance & Its Regulation. LC 68-55486. Repr. of 1932 ed. 27.50x (ISBN 0-678-00502-8). Kelley.

Boncerf, Pierre-Francois. Les Inconveniens Des Droits Feodaux. Repr. of 1776 ed. 18.50 o.p. (ISBN 0-8287-0105-9). Clearwater Pub.

Boncompagno, Signa Da see Boncompagno da Signa.

Boncompagno da Signa. Rota Veneris. Purkart, Josef, ed. LC 74-18250. 128p. 1975. Repr. of 1474 ed. lib. bdg. 25.00x (ISBN 0-8201-1137-6). Schol Facsimiles.

Bond, jt. auth. see Hughes.

Bond, A. M. & Hefter, G. T., eds. Critical Survey of Stability Constants & Related Thermodynamic Data of Flouride Complexes in Aqueous Solution. (Chemical Data Ser.: No. 27). 80p. 1980. pap. text ed. 29.00 (ISBN 0-08-022377-X). Pergamon.

Bond, Alec. Poems for an Only Daughter. 24p. 1982. pap. 2.50 (ISBN 0-933180-39-X). Spoon Riv Poetry.

Bond, Alison. The Glove Compartment Book. LC 79-51119. 1979. paper over board ed. 4.95 o.p. (ISBN 0-448-15701-2, G&D). Putnam Pub Group.

Bond, Ann S. Adam & Noah & the Cops. LC 82-21181. (Illus.). 160p. (gr. 3-6). 1983. 8.95 (ISBN 0-395-33225-7). HM.

Bond, Bob. Cruising Boat Sailing: The Basic Guide. LC 82-48882. 1982. 14.95 (ISBN 0-394-52447-0). Knopf.

--The Handbook of Sailing. LC 79-3496. (Illus.). 1980. 22.50 (ISBN 0-394-50838-6). Knopf.

--Small Boat Sailing: The Basic Guide. LC 82-48883. 1983. 14.95 (ISBN 0-394-52446-2). Knopf.

Bond, Clara-Beth Young, et al. Low Fat, Low Cholesterol Diet. rev. ed. LC 76-103741. 1971. 17.95 (ISBN 0-385-03905-0). Doubleday.

Bond, David. The Fiction of Andre Pieyre de Mandiargues. LC 82-5894. 176p. 1982. text ed. 22.00x (ISBN 0-8156-2265-1); pap. text ed. 12.95x (ISBN 0-8156-2283-X). Syracuse U Pr.

Bond, E. J. Reason & Value. LC 82-4564. (Cambridge Studies in Philosophy). 220p. Date not set. p.n.s. (ISBN 0-521-24571-0); pap. p.n.s. (ISBN 0-521-27079-0). Cambridge U Pr.

Bond, Edward. A-A-America! & Stone. Rev. ed. 115p. 1981. pap. 6.50 (ISBN 0-413-48320-7). Methuen Inc.

--Narrow Road to the Deep North. 59p. 1969. pap. 1.50 o.p. (ISBN 0-8090-1219-7, New Mermaid). Hill & Wang.

--Restoration & the Cat. 1982. pap. 7.95 (ISBN 0-413-49920-0). Methuen Inc.

--Summer. 1982. pap. 5.95 (ISBN 0-413-49320-2). Methuen Inc.

Bond, Edward, jt. auth. see Corrace, Douglas.

Bond, Felicia. Four Valentines in a Rainstorm. (Illus.). (ps-3). 4.95 (ISBN 0-686-43187-1, TYC-J). Har-Row.

--Mary Betty Lizzie McNutt's Birthday. (Illus.). (ps-3). Date not set. 4.95 (ISBN 0-690-04255-8, TYC-J). Har-Row.

Bond, George D., jt. auth. see Carter, John R.

Bond, Godfrey W., ed. see Euripides.

Bond, Guy L., et al. Reading Difficulties: Their Diagnosis & Correction. 4th ed. (Illus.). 1979. ref. 24.95 (ISBN 0-13-754978-4). P-H.

Bond, Harold, ed. see Shoehmelian, O.

Bond, James. Birds of the West Indies. (Illus.). 1971. 14.95 (ISBN 0-395-07431-2). HM.

Bond, James E. Plea Bargaining & Guilty Pleas. 2nd ed. LC 82-4125. 1982. looseleaf 55.00 (ISBN 0-87632-105-8). Boardman.

Bond, James O. We Held Hands Within the Dark. Bond, Lydia S., ed. LC 82-90272. 182p. (Orig.). 1982. pap. 5.95 (ISBN 0-9608520-0-X). J O Bond.

Bond, John J. Handy-Book of Rules & Tables for Verifying Dates with the Christian Era. LC 66-29473. 1966. Repr. of 1889 ed. 10.00x (ISBN 0-8462-1795-3). Russell.

Bond, Julian. A Time to Speak, a Time to Act. 1972. pap. 1.95 o.p. (ISBN 0-671-21345-8, Touchstone Bks). S&S.

Bond, Lydia S., ed. see Bond, James O.

Bond, Lynne A. & Joffe, Justin M., eds. Facilitating Infant & Early Childhood Development. LC 81-69944. (Primary Prevention of Psychopathology Ser.: Vol. 6). (Illus.). 586p. 1982. 35.00x (ISBN 0-87451-205-0). U Pr of New Eng.

Bond, Lynne A. & Rosen, James C., eds. Competence & Coping During Adulthood. LC 79-56776. (Primary Prevention of Psychopathology Ser.: Vol. 4). (Illus.). 400p. 1980. text ed. 27.50x (ISBN 0-87451-159-3). U Pr of New Eng.

Bond, M. G., et al, eds. Clinical Diagnosis of Atherosclerosis: Quantitative Methods of Evaluation. (Illus.). 544p. 1983. 19.50 (ISBN 0-387-90780-7). Springer-Verlag.

Bond, Michael. Bear Called Paddington. LC 60-9096. (Illus.). (gr. 3-7). 1968. pap. 1.95 (ISBN 0-440-40483-5, YB). Dell.

--The Complete Adventures of Olga da Polga. LC 82-72753. (Illus.). 512p. (gr. 3-6). 1983. 16.95 (ISBN 0-440-00981-2). Delacorte.

--More About Paddington. (Illus.). (gr. 3-7). 1970. pap. 1.75 (ISBN 0-440-45825-0, YB). Dell.

--Olga Carries On. (Orig.). (gr. k-6). 1983. pap. 2.25 (ISBN 0-440-46541-9, YB). Dell.

--Olga Counts Her Blessings. LC 77-10685. (Olga Da Polga Ser.). (Illus.). (gr. k-3). 1977. pap. text ed. 1.45 (ISBN 0-88436-458-5). EMC.

--Olga Makes a Friend. LC 77-10684. (Olga Da Polga Ser.). (Illus.). (gr. k-3). 1977. pap. text ed. 1.45 (ISBN 0-88436-462-3). EMC.

--Olga Makes a Wish. LC 77-10683. (Olga Da Polga). (Illus.). (gr. k-3). 1977. pap. text ed. 1.45 (ISBN 0-88436-456-9). EMC.

--Olga Makes Her Mark. LC 77-10713. (Olga Da Polga). (Illus.). (gr. k-3). 1977. pap. text ed. 1.45 (ISBN 0-88436-459-3). EMC.

--Olga Meets Her Match. (Orig.). (gr. k-6). 1983. pap. 2.25 (ISBN 0-440-46622-9, YB). Dell.

--Olga Takes a Bite. LC 77-21321. (Olga Da Polga Ser.). (Illus.). (gr. k-3). 1977. pap. text ed. 1.45 (ISBN 0-88436-460-7). EMC.

--Olga Takes Charge. (Orig.). (gr. k-6). 1983. pap. 2.25 (ISBN 0-440-46620-2, YB). Dell.

--Olga's New Home. LC 77-10476. (Olga Da Polga Ser.). (Illus.). (gr. k-3). 1977. pap. text ed. 1.45 (ISBN 0-88436-457-7). EMC.

--Olga's Second Home. LC 77-10477. (Olga Da Polga Ser.). (Illus.). (gr. k-3). 1977. pap. text ed. 1.45 (ISBN 0-88436-461-5). EMC.

--Olga's Special Day. LC 77-10714. (Olga Da Polga Ser.). (Illus.). (gr. k-3). 1977. pap. text ed. 1.45 (ISBN 0-88436-463-1). EMC.

--Paddington at Large. (Illus.). (gr. 3-7). 1970. pap. 1.75 (ISBN 0-440-46801-9, YB). Dell.

--Paddington on Screen. (gr. 2-5). 1982. PLB 8.95 (ISBN 0-395-32950-7); 8.70. HM.

--Paddington Takes the Test. (gr. k-6). 1982. pap. 1.95 (ISBN 0-440-47021-8, YB). Dell.

--Paddington's Lucky Day. LC 74-5007. (The Paddington Picture Bks). (Illus.). 36p. (ps-2). 1974. 3.95 (ISBN 0-394-82919-0, BYR); PLB 4.99 o.p. (ISBN 0-394-92919-5). Random.

--The Tales of Olga da Polga. (Orig.). (gr. k-6). 1983. pap. 2.25 (ISBN 0-440-48818-4, YB). Dell.

Bond, Otto F., jt. auth. see Bauer, Camille.

Bond, Otto F., jt. auth. see Castillo, Carlos.

Bond, Otto F., et al, eds. Graded Russian Readers, 5 bks. Incl. Bk. 1. Taman. Lermontov, Mihail L. pap. text ed. o.p. (ISBN 0-669-30619-3); Bk. 2. Two Stories. Pushkin, Alexander. pap. text ed. o.p. (ISBN 0-669-30627-4); Bk. 3. Lermontov's Bela. Lermonton, Mihail. o. p. (ISBN 0-685-24361-3); Bk. 4. Three Short Stories. Turgenev, Ivan. pap. text ed. o.p. (ISBN 0-669-30643-6); Bk. 5. The Provincial Lady. Turgenev, Ivan. pap. text ed. 2.95x o.p. (ISBN 0-669-30650-9). 1961. pap. text ed. 9.95x five vols. in one (ISBN 0-669-30676-2). Heath.

Bond, P. S., jt. auth. see Garber, Max B.

Bond, R. Warwick, ed. see Lyly, John.

Bond, Richmond P., ed. Studies in the Early English Periodical. LC 77-8233. 1977. Repr. of 1957 ed. lib. bdg. 17.50x (ISBN 0-8371-9683-3, BOEE). Greenwood.

Bond, Robert J. Getting Started in California Real Estate. 2nd ed. LC 74-82673. (Kendall Hunt Real Estate Ser.). 1977. pap. text ed. 12.95 (ISBN 0-8403-0988-0). Kendall-Hunt.

Bond, Robert J. & Bowman, Arthur G. California Real Estate Practice. 2nd ed. LC 73-86436. 480p. 1981. text ed. 27.95x (ISBN 0-673-16474-8). Scott F.

--California Real Estate Principles. 3rd ed. 1982. text ed. 27.50x (ISBN 0-673-16010-6). Scott F.

Bond, Robert J., et al. California Real Estate Finance. 2nd ed. LC 79-3850. (California Real Estate Ser.). 330p. 1980. text ed. 21.95x (ISBN 0-471-06230-8); avail. questions (ISBN 0-471-86103-0). Wiley.

Bond, Ruskin. Flames in the Forest. LC 80-83009. (Julia MacRae Bks.). (gr. k-3). 1981. PLB 5.95 (ISBN 0-531-04282-0). Watts.

--The Road to the Bazaar. (gr. 2-6). 1980. PLB 9.90 o.s.i. (ISBN 0-531-04181-6, Julia Macrae). Watts.

Bond, Serena K. Basic Skills School Newspaper Workbook. (Basic Skills Workbooks). 32p. (gr. 8-12). 1983. 0.99 (ISBN 0-8209-0553-4, SNW-1). ESP.

--The School Newspaper. (Language Arts Ser.). 24p. (gr. 8-12). 1982. wkbk. 5.00 (ISBN 0-8209-0328-0, J-1). ESP.

Bond, Simon. Bizarre Sights & Odd Visions. 1983. pap. 2.95 (ISBN 0-517-54605-1, C N Potter Bks). Crown.

--One Hundred & One Uses for a Dead Cat. 1981. pap. 2.95 (ISBN 0-517-54516-0, C N Potter Bks). Crown.

Bond, Susan. Ride with Me Through ABC. LC 67-19376. (Illus.). 32p. (ps-k). 5.95 (ISBN 0-87592-043-8). Scroll Pr.

Bond, Thomas, jt. auth. see Albanese, Joseph.

Bond, W. L. Crystal Technology. LC 75-23364. (Pure & Applied Optics Ser). 342p. 1976. 47.95x (ISBN 0-471-08765-3, Pub. by Wiley-Interscience). Wiley.

Bond, William J. One Thousand One Ways to Beat the Time Trap. LC 81-68915. 192p. 1982. 14.95 (ISBN 0-8119-0441-5). Fell.

Bondanella, Julia C., ed. see Bondanella, Peter.

Bondanella, Peter. Dictionary of Italian Literature. Bondanella, Julia C., ed. LC 78-4022. 1978. lib. bdg. 45.00x (ISBN 0-313-20421-7, BDI/). Greenwood.

--Italian Cinema: From Neorealism to the Present. LC 82-40255. (Ungar Film Library). (Illus.). 400p. 1983. 17.95 (ISBN 0-8044-2064-5); pap. 10.95 (ISBN 0-8044-6061-2). Ungar.

Bondanella, Peter, ed. Federico Fellini: Essays in Criticism. (Illus.). 1978. pap. 7.95 (ISBN 0-19-502274-2, GB515, GB). Oxford U Pr.

Bondanella, Peter E. Francesco Guicciardini. (World Authors Ser.). 1976. lib. bdg. 15.95 (ISBN 0-8057-6231-0, Twayne). G K Hall.

Bonderoff, Jason. Alan Alda: An Unauthorized Biography. 1982. pap. 2.95 (ISBN 0-451-12030-2, AE2030, Sig). NAL.

--The Soap Opera Trivia Quiz Book. 1982. pap. 2.95 (ISBN 0-451-11750-6, AE1750, Sig). NAL.

Bondi, H. Assumption & Myth in Physical Theory. 1967. 13.95 (ISBN 0-521-04282-8). Cambridge U Pr.

Bondi, Joseph, jt. auth. see Wiles, Jon.

Bondi, Joseph, Jr., jt. auth. see Wiles, Jon W.

Bonds, Parris A. Stardust. 256p. (Orig.). 1983. pap. 2.95 (ISBN 0-449-12539-4, GM). Fawcett.

Bondurant, Joan V. Conquest of Violence: The Gandhian Philosophy of Conflict. rev. ed. LC 65-23153. (gr. 9 up). 1965. 24.50x (ISBN 0-520-00143-5); pap. 6.95x (ISBN 0-520-00145-1, CAMPUS243). U of Cal Pr.

Bondy, Jeffrey S., jt. auth. see Guzzo, Richard A.

Bondy, Philip K. & Rosenberg, Leon E. Diseases of Metabolism. 8th ed. LC 78-52722. (Illus.). 1980. text ed. 95.00 (ISBN 0-7216-1844-8). Saunders.

Bondy, Susan. Other People's Money. LC 81-18185. 1982. 12.95 o.p. (ISBN 0-672-52702-2). Bobbs.

Bone, Barry & Donsky, Joanne. La Creme de la Creme: A Guide to the Very Best Restaurants of France. (Illus.). 216p. (Orig.). 1982. 10.95 (ISBN 0-9608070-0-4). Epicurean.

Bone, Hugh A. & Ranney, Austin. Politics & Voters. 5th ed. Munson, Eric M., ed. (Harris Ser.). 144p. 1981. pap. text ed. 9.95 (ISBN 0-07-006492-X, C). McGraw.

Bone, J. F. Confederation Matador. Freas, Polly & Freas, Kelly, eds. LC 78-2196. (Illus.). 1978. pap. 4.95 o.p. (ISBN 0-915442-53-1, Starblaze). Donning Co.

Bone, Jan, jt. auth. see Johnson, Ron.

Bone, Jesse F. Animal Anatomy & Physiology. 2nd ed. 1981. text ed. 21.95 (ISBN 0-8359-0216-1). Reston.

--Animal Anatomy & Physiology. (Illus.). 1979. ref. 20.00 o.p. (ISBN 0-8359-0220-X); instrs'. manual avail. o.p. (ISBN 0-8359-0221-8). Reston.

Bone, Philip J. The Guitar & Mandolin, Biographies of Celebrated Players & Composers. LC 75-329. (Illus.). 1972. 53.00 (ISBN 0-901938-02-5, 75 A11329). Eur-Am Music.

Bone, Robert C. American Government. LC 76-52828. 306p. 1977. pap. 5.50 (ISBN 0-06-460170-6, CO 170, COS). B&N NY.

Bone, Robert W. The Maverick Guide to Australia 1983 Edition. (Maverick Guide Ser.). (Illus.). 324p. (Orig.). 1982. pap. 10.95 (ISBN 0-88289-337-8). Pelican.

--The Maverick Guide to Hawaii 1983 Edition. Rev. ed. (Maverick Guide Ser.). (Illus.). 437p. (Orig.). 1983. pap. 9.95 (ISBN 0-88289-371-8). Pelican.

--The Maverick Guide to New Zealand 1983 Edition. (Maverick Guide Ser.). (Illus.). 305p. (Orig.). 1983. pap. 10.95 (ISBN 0-88289-370-X). Pelican.

Bone, Roger C. Pulmonary Disease Review, Vol. 1. (Pulmonary Disease Review Ser.). 581p. 1980. 45.00 (ISBN 0-471-05736-3, Pub. by Wiley Med). Wiley.

--Pulmonary Disease Review, Vol. 2. 642p. 1981. 49.95x (ISBN 0-471-09047-6, Pub. by Wiley Med). Wiley.

Bone, Woutrina A. Children's Stories & How to Tell Them. LC 75-28363. (Illus.). xviii, 200p. 1975. Repr. of 1924 ed. 34.00x (ISBN 0-8103-3747-9). Gale.

Bonebreak, Robert L. Practical Techniques of Electronic Circuit Design. LC 81-11394. 306p. 1982. 34.95 (ISBN 0-471-09612-1, Pub. by Wiley Interscience). Wiley.

Bones, Jim, Jr. & Graves, John. Texas Heartland: A Hill Country Year. LC 75-16352. (Illus.). 104p. 1975. 24.95 (ISBN 0-89096-002-X). Tex A&M Univ Pr.

Bones, R. Concise Encyclopedia Dictionary of Telecommunications. Date not set. 15.00 (ISBN 0-444-99955-8). Elsevier.

Bonett, Emery, jt. auth. see Bonett, John.

Bonett, John & Bonett, Emery. A Banner for Pegasus. LC 81-47806. 240p. 1982. pap. 2.40i (ISBN 0-06-080554-4, P 554, PL). Har-Row.

--The Sound of Murder. LC 82-48809. 224p. 1983. pap. 2.84i (ISBN 0-06-080642-7, P 642, PL). Har-Row.

Boney, A. D. Phytoplankton. (Studies in Biology: No. 52). 124p. 1975. pap. text ed. 8.95 (ISBN 0-7131-2476-8). E Arnold.

Bonfante, Larissa & Bonfante-Warren, Alexandra, trs. from Lat. The Plays of Hrotswitha of Gandersheim. LC 79-90053. (Illus.). 206p. (Orig.). 1979. pap. 16.75 (ISBN 0-8147-1028-X, IS-00094, Pub. by NYU Pr). Univ Microfilms.

Bonfante-Warren, Alexandra, jt. tr. see Bonfante, Larissa.

Bonfiglio, Thomas A. Cytopathologic Interpretation of Transthoracic Fine-Needle Biopsies. (Masspn Monographs in Diagnostic Cytopathology, Vol. 4). 208p. 1983. write for info. (ISBN 0-89352-197-3). Masson Pub.

Bonfils, S., et al, eds. Hormonal Receptors in Digestive Tract Physiology. (INSERM Symposium: No. 3). 1977. 64.50 (ISBN 0-7204-0618-8, North-Holland). Elsevier.

Bonforte, Lisa, illus. Baby Animals. (Sturdy Shape Bks.). (Illus.). 14p. (ps). 1980. 2.95 (ISBN 0-307-12250-6, Golden Pr). Western Pub.

--Farm Animals. LC 80-53106. (Board Bks.). (Illus.). 14p. (ps). 1981. boards 3.50 (ISBN 0-394-84767-9). Random.

Bongaarts, John & Potter, Robert G., eds. Fertility, Biology & Behavior: An Analysis of the Proximate Determinants (Monograph) (Studies in Population). 216p. 1983. price not set (ISBN 0-12-114380-5). Acad Pr.

Bonger, Willem A. Race & Crime. Hordyk, Margaret M., tr. LC 69-14912. (Criminology, Law Enforcement, & Social Problems Ser.: No. 34). 1969. 10.00x (ISBN 0-87585-034-0); pap. 5.00x (ISBN 0-87585-907-0). Patterson Smith.

Bongiovanni, Alfred M., ed. Adolescent Gynecology: A Guide for Clinicians. 275p. 1983. 32.50x (ISBN 0-306-41203-9, Plenum Pr). Plenum Pub.

Bongiovanni, G. Manual of Clinical Gastroenterology. 598p. 1982. 13.95 (ISBN 0-07-006471-7). McGraw.

Bongiovanni, Gail. Manual of Clinical Gastroenterology. (PreTest Manuals of Clinical Medicine Ser.). 400p. (Orig.). 1982. manual 14.95 (ISBN 0-07-019901-9, HP). McGraw.

--Medical Spanish. 1977. pap. text ed. 11.95 (ISBN 0-07-006470-9, HP). McGraw.

Bongo, Ali. Be a Magician. LC 80-50949. (Whizz Kids Ser.). 8.00 (ISBN 0-382-06439-9). Silver.

Bongo, Joseph, jt. auth. see Hillson, Maurie.

Bonham, Frank. Bold Passage. 192p. 1982. pap. 2.25 o.p. (ISBN 0-425-05754-2). Berkley Pub.

--Cast a Long Shadow. (Orig.). 1980. pap. 1.75 o.p. (ISBN 0-425-04465-3). Berkley Pub.

--Cool Cat. 1972. pap. 1.50 o.p. (ISBN 0-440-91520-1, LFL). Dell.

--Durango Street. 192p. 1972. pap. 2.25 (ISBN 0-440-92183-X, LFL). Dell.

--Fort Hogan. (Orig.). 1980. pap. 1.75 o.p. (ISBN 0-425-04562-5). Berkley Pub.

--Hardrock. 1979. pap. 1.75 o.p. (ISBN 0-425-04087-9). Berkley Pub.

--The Nitty Gritty. 160p. 1971. pap. 1.75 o.p. (ISBN 0-440-96416-4, LFL). Dell.

--Nitty Gritty. LC 68-24719. (Illus.). (gr. 5 up). 1968. 8.95 o.p. (ISBN 0-525-35957-5). Dutton.

--The Rascals from Haskell's Gym. (gr. 4-6). 1977. 9.95 (ISBN 0-525-38070-1, 0966-290). Dutton.

--Snaketrack. 176p. 1982. pap. 2.25 (ISBN 0-425-05886-7). Berkley Pub.

--Viva Chicano. (gr. 5-8). 1971. pap. 1.95 (ISBN 0-440-99400-4, LFL). Dell.

Bonhan, Frank, ed. Snaketrack. 176p. (Orig.). 1981. pap. 1.75 o.p. (ISBN 0-425-04812-8). Berkley Pub.

Bonheur, Gaston. To Live in France. 272p. 1981. 60.00 (ISBN 0-686-98224-X). Edns Vilo.

Bonhoeffer, Dietrich. Cost of Discipleship. 1963. pap. 4.95 (ISBN 0-02-083850-6, Collier). Macmillan.

--Creation & Fall. Bd. with Temptation. 1965. pap. 2.95 (ISBN 0-02-083890-5, 08389). Macmillan.

--Letters & Papers from Prison. enl. ed. 448p. 1972. 17.95 (ISBN 0-02-513110-9); pap. 5.95. Macmillan.

--The Martyred Christian: 160 Readings. Brown, Joan W., ed. 256p. 1983. 14.95 (ISBN 0-02-513120-6). Macmillan.

Boni, Ada. Talisman Italian Cook Book. La Rosa, Mathilde, tr. (International Cook Book Ser). 1955. 8.95 (ISBN 0-517-50387-5, Harmony). Crown.

Boni, Margaret & Lloyd, Norman. Fireside Book of Favorite American Songs. (Illus.). (gr. 3 up). 1963. 15.95 o.p. (ISBN 0-671-24771-9). S&S.

--Fireside Book of Favorite American Songs. (Illus.). 360p. 1975. pap. 9.95 o.p. (ISBN 0-671-22061-6, Fireside). S&S.

--Fireside Book of Folk Songs. (Illus., New edition with guitar chords). (gr. 5 up). 1966. 22.95 o.p. (ISBN 0-671-25836-2). S&S.

Boni, Sylvain. The Self & the Other in the Ontologies of Sartre & Buber. LC 82-20130. 202p. (Orig.). 1983. lib. bdg. 21.75 (ISBN 0-8191-2852-X); pap. text ed. 10.75 (ISBN 0-8191-2853-8). U Pr of Amer.

Bonica, John J., ed. Pain. (Association for Research in Nervous & Mental Disease Publications Ser.: Vol. 58). 424p. 1979. text ed. 42.00 (ISBN 0-89004-376-0). Raven.

Bonica, John J. & Ventafridda, Vittorio, eds. International Symposium on Pain of Advanced Cancer. LC 78-55811. (Advances in Pain Research & Therapy Ser.: Vol. 2). 734p. 1979. text ed. 81.00 (ISBN 0-89004-271-3). Raven.

Bonica, John J., ed. see World Congress on Pain, 1st, Florence, 1975.

Bonica, John J., et al, eds. Management of the Superior Pulmonary Sulcus Syndrome. (Advances in Pain Research & Therapy Ser.: Vol. 4). 256p. 1982. text ed. 39.00 (ISBN 0-89004-770-7). Raven.

Bonica, John J., et al, eds. see World Congress on Pain, 2nd, Montreal, Aug. 1978.

Bonifazi, Conrad. The Soul of the World: An Account of Inwardness of Things. LC 78-64826. 1978. pap. text ed. 11.50 (ISBN 0-8191-0638-0). U Pr of Amer.

--A Theology of Things. LC 76-7549. 1976. Repr. of 1967 ed. lib. bdg. 17.00x (ISBN 0-8371-8838-5, BOTT). Greenwood.

Bonifer, Michael. The Making of Tron. (Illus.). 96p. (Orig.). (gr. 1-4). 1982. pap. 7.95 (ISBN 0-671-45575-3, Little Simon). S&S.

Bonilla, Frank & Silva-Michelena, Jose A. The Politics of Change in Venezuela, 3 vols. Incl. Vol. 1. A Strategy for Research on Social Policy. 1967. o.p. (ISBN 0-262-02028-9); Vol. 2. The Failure of Elites. 1970. 25.00x (ISBN 0-262-02058-0); Vol. 3. The Illusion of Democracy in Dependent Nations. 1971. 22.50x (ISBN 0-262-19069-9). MIT Pr.

Bonime, Walter. The Clinical Use of Dreams. (Psychoanalysis Examined & Re-Examined Ser.). 343p. 1982. Repr. of 1962 ed. lib. bdg. 27.50 (ISBN 0-306-79710-0). Da Capo.

Bonin, Gerhardt Von. The Evolution of the Human Brain. LC 63-13062. (Midway Reprint Ser.). 1975. pap. 6.95x (ISBN 0-226-06436-0). U of Chicago Pr.

Bonin, Helene, tr. see Champsaur, Paul & Milleron, Jean-Claude.

Bonin, Jane. Mario Fratti. (World Authors Ser.). 1982. lib. bdg. 17.95 (ISBN 0-8057-6498-4, Twayne). G K Hall.

Bonin, John P., tr. see Champsaur, Paul & Milleron, Jean-Claude.

Bonine, Michael E. & Keddie, Nikki R., eds. Modern Iran: The Dialectics of Continuity & Change. LC 80-19463. 400p. 1981. 39.50x (ISBN 0-686-72180-2); pap. 12.95x (ISBN 0-87395-641-9). State U NY Pr.

Bonington, Chris. Annapurna South Face. (Illus.). 1978. 12.50 o.p. (ISBN 0-07-006490-3, GB). McGraw.

--Quest for Adventure. (Illus.). 448p. Date not set. 30.00 (ISBN 0-686-82352-4). Crown.

Bonington, Chris see Allen, W. S.

Bonini, Charles P. Computer Models for Decision Analysis. (Illus.). 148p. (Orig.). 1980. pap. text ed. 15.00x (ISBN 0-89426-042-1); tchrs'. ed. 15.00x (ISBN 0-89426-043-X). Scientific Pr.

Bonino, Jose M. Toward a Christian Political Ethics. LC 82-48541. 144p. 1983. pap. 5.95 (ISBN 0-8006-1697-9, 1-1697). Fortress.

Bonjean, C., jt. ed. see Schneider, L.

Bonk, U. E. Biopsie und Operationspraeparat. (Illus.). viii, 140p. 1983. pap. 13.25 (ISBN 3-8055-3702-6). S Karger.

Bonn, Franz. The Children's Theatre. (Illus.). 1978. 7.95 (ISBN 0-686-36721-9). Md Hist.

Bonn, George S., ed. Library Education & Training in Developing Countries. 1966. pap. 5.50x o.p. (ISBN 0-8248-0052-4, Eastwest Ctr). UH Pr.

Bonn, George S. & Faibisoff, Sylvia G., eds. Changing Times: Changing Libraries. LC 78-1283. (Allerton Part Institutes Ser.: No. 22). 166p. 1978. 8.00x (ISBN 0-87845-047-5). U of Ill Lib Info Sci.

Bonnard, H., et al. Modern French Usage: A Student Guide. 1971. 9.95 (ISBN 0-02-312100-9). Macmillan.

Bonnat, Yves, jt. ed. see Hainaux, Rene.

Bonneau, B. Lee & Smith, Billy A., eds. Astronomy Illustrated. 3rd ed. 1980. pap. text ed. 15.95 (ISBN 0-8403-2168-6). Kendall-Hunt.

Bonneau, M & Hennessen, W., eds. Herpes Virus of Man & Animal: Standardization of Immunological Procedures. (Developments in Biological Standardization Ser.: Vol. 52). (Illus.). x, 574p. 1983. pap. 78.00 (ISBN 3-8055-3636-4). S Karger.

Bonnefond, Th. Esquisse Bibliographique Recente en Sciences Humaines du Departement du Centre de la Cote d'Ivoire. (Black Africa Ser.). 50p. (Fr.). 1974. Repr. of 1968 ed. 29.00x o.p. (ISBN 0-8287-0106-7, 71-2072). Clearwater Pub.

Bonnefoy, Claude, et al. Dictionaire De Literature Contemporaire. 22.50 o.p. (ISBN 2-7113-0077-3). Gaylord Prof Pubns.

Bonnefoy, Yves. Words in Stone: Pierre Ecrite. Lang, Susanna, tr. LC 75-32481. 160p. (Eng. & Fr.). 1976. lib. bdg. 10.00x (ISBN 0-87023-203-7). U of Mass Pr.

Bonnell, F. C. & Bonnell, F. W. Conrad Aiken: A Bibliography. LC 82-9241. 291p. 1983. 45.00 (ISBN 0-87328-118-7). Huntington Lib.

Bonnell, F. W., jt. auth. see Bonnell, F. C.

Bonnell, Peter & Sedwick, Frank. Conversation in French: Points of Departure. 3rd ed. (Orig.). 1981. pap. text ed. write for info. (ISBN 0-442-24468-1). Van Nos Reinhold.

--Conversation in German: Points of Departure. 3rd ed. (Orig.). 1981. pap. text ed. write for info. (ISBN 0-442-24466-5). Van Nos Reinhold.

--German for Careers: Conversational Perspectives. (Orig.). 1980. pap. text ed. 8.95 (ISBN 0-442-20563-5). Van Nos Reinhold.

Bonnelle, C. & Mande, C., eds. Advances in X-Ray Spectroscopy: A Reference Text in Honour of Professor Y Cauchois. (Illus.). 400p. 1982. 80.00 (ISBN 0-08-025266-4). Pergamon.

Bonnemann, K. H., et al, eds. Ionic Liquids, Molten Salts, & Polyelectrolytes: Berlin (West), 1982 Proceedings. (Lecture Notes in Physics Ser.: Vol. 172). 253p. 1983. pap. 14.50 (ISBN 0-387-11952-3). Springer-Verlag.

Bonner, Anthony, ed. & tr. from Fr. Songs of the Troubadours. LC 72-80034. 320p. 1974. 7.95 o.p. (ISBN 0-8052-3459-4); pap. 3.95 o.p. (ISBN 0-8052-0448-2). Schocken.

Bonner, Anthony, tr. see Verne, Jules.

Bonner, C. E. Index Hepaticarum: An Index to the Liverworts of the World. Incl. Pt. 2. Achiton to Balantiopsis. 30.00 (ISBN 3-7682-0092-2); Pt. 3. Barbilophozia to Ceranthus. 30.00 (ISBN 3-7682-0093-0); Pt. 4. Ceratolejeunea to Crystolejeunea. 30.00 (ISBN 3-7682-0094-9); Pt. 5. Delavayella to Geothallus. 40.00 (ISBN 3-7682-0095-7); Pt. 6. Goebelliella to Jubula. 30.00 (ISBN 3-7682-0096-5). 1963-66. Lubrecht & Cramer.

--Index Hepaticarum, Index to the Liverworts of the World Part 7A: Supplement, Additions & Corrections to Parts 2-4. 1977. pap. text ed. 24.00 (ISBN 3-7682-0097-3). Lubrecht & Cramer.

--Index Hepaticarum. Index to the Liverworts of the World Part 8: Jungermannia. 1976. pap. text ed. 48.00. Lubrecht & Cramer.

--Index Hepaticarum. Part 9: Jungermanniopsis-Lejeunea. 1978. pap. 40.00x. Lubrecht & Cramer.

Bonner, Deborah, tr. see Manila, Gabriel J.

Bonner, James. The World's People & the World's Food Supply. Head, J. J., ed. (Carolina Biology Readers Ser.). (Illus.). 16p. (gr. 11 up). 1980. pap. 1.60 (ISBN 0-89278-322-2, 45-9722). Carolina Biological.

Bonner, John T., ed. see Thompson, D'Arcy W.

Bonner, Mary G. Mystery at Lake Ashburn. (gr. 6-8). 1962. PLB 6.19 o.p. (ISBN 0-8313-0012-4). Lantern.

Bonner, Patricia A., jt. auth. see Coate, L. Edwin.

Bonner, Stanley F. Education in Ancient Rome: From the Older Cato to the Younger Pliny. LC 76-52023. (Illus.). 1977. 36.50x (ISBN 0-520-03439-2); pap. 11.95x (ISBN 0-520-03501-1). U of Cal Pr.

Bonner, Terry N. The Free Woman. (The Australians Ser.: No. 3). 352p. (Orig.). 1983. pap. 3.50 (ISBN 0-440-01072-1, Emerald). Dell.

--The Pioneers. (New South Wales Ser.: No. 4). (Orig.). 1983. pap. 3.50 (ISBN 0-440-07166-6). Dell.

Bonner, Thomas N., ed. see Schiel, Jacob H.

Bonner, William H. Communicating Clearly: The Effective Message. 384p. 1980. pap. text ed. 11.95 (ISBN 0-574-20605-1, 13-3605); instr's. guide avail. (ISBN 0-574-20606-X, 13-3606). SRA.

Bonner, William H. & Voyles, Jean. Communicating in Business: Key to Success, Vol. 1. 3rd. ed. LC 82-71522. (Illus.). 551p. 1983. text ed. 20.95x (ISBN 0-931920-42-6); study guide 5.95 (ISBN 0-686-63215-X); letter writing wkbk. o.p. 4.50 (ISBN 0-686-63216-8); report writing wkbk. o.p. 3.95 (ISBN 0-686-63217-6). Dame Pubns.

Bonnerjea, Biren. Dictionary of Superstitions & Mythology. LC 69-17755. 1969. Repr. of 1927 ed. 37.00x (ISBN 0-8103-3572-7). Gale.

Bonnet, Charles. Considerations sur les Corps Organises. Repr. of 1761 ed. 190.00 o.p. (ISBN 0-8287-0107-5). Clearwater Pub.

--Palingenesie Philosophique. Repr. of 1770 ed. 251.00 o.p. (ISBN 0-8287-0108-3). Clearwater Pub.

Bonnet, L., jt. auth. see Schroeder, A.

Bonnet, Marguerite & Chenieux-Gendron, Jacqueline. Revues Surrealistes Francaises Autour d'Andre Breton, 1948-1972. LC 82-14045. 294p. (Orig.). 1982. lib. bdg. 35.00 (ISBN 0-527-09750-0). Kraus Intl.

Bonnet, Mireille. Microsurgery of Retinal Detachment. (Illus.). 1980. text ed. 31.25x (ISBN 0-89352-067-5). Masson Pub.

Bonne-Tamir, Batsheva & Cohen, Tirza, eds. Human Genetics, Part A: The Unfolding Genome. LC 82-17230. (Progress in Clinical & Biological Research Ser.: Vol. 103A). 531p. 1982. 88.00 (ISBN 0-8451-0168-4). A R Liss.

--Human Genetics, Part B: Medical Aspects. LC 82-17230. (Progress in Clinical & Biological Research Ser.: Vol. 103B). 619p. 1982. 98.00 (ISBN 0-8451-0169-2). A R Liss.

Bonnett, Aubrey W. Institutional Adaptation of West Indian Immigrants to America: An Analysis of Rotating Credit Associations. LC 80-69054. 160p. 1981. lib. bdg. 18.75 (ISBN 0-8191-1500-2); pap. text ed. 8.50 (ISBN 0-8191-1501-0). U Pr of Amer.

Bonnette, Jeanne. Three Friends. (Read-to-Me Coloring Bks.). (ps-2). 1982. pap. 1.95 (ISBN 0-89992-066-7). MT Coun Indian.

Bonneville, Nicolas De, ed. Le Tribun Du Peuple. (Le Cercle Social). (Fr.). 1978. lib. bdg. 65.00x o.p. (ISBN 0-8287-1425-8). Clearwater Pub.

--Le Vieux Tribun Du Peuple. (Le Cercle Social). (Fr.). 1978. lib. bdg. 79.00x o.p. (ISBN 0-8287-1431-2). Clearwater Pub.

--Le Vieux Tribun Du Peuple et Sa Bouche De Fer. (Le Cercle Social). (Fr.). 1978. lib. bdg. 145.00x o.p. (ISBN 0-8287-1430-4). Clearwater Pub.

Bonneville, Nicolas De, jt. ed. see Fauchet, Claude.

Bonney, Lorraine, jt. auth. see Bonney, Orin H.

Bonney, Lorraine, jt. auth. see Bonney, Orrin H.

Bonney, Orin H. & Bonney, Lorraine. Guide to the Wyoming Mountains & Wilderness Areas. 3rd ed. LC 82-72734. 701p. 1977. 24.95 (ISBN 0-8040-0537-0, SB). Swallow.

Bonney, Orrin H. & Bonney, Lorraine. Field Book. Incl. The Teton Range & the Gros Ventre Range: Climbing Routes & Back Country. rev., 2nd ed. LC 82-73096. 263p (ISBN 0-8040-0578-8); Yellowstone Park: Absaroka Range. rev. 2nd ed. LC 82-73104. 162p (ISBN 0-8040-0579-6); Big Horn Range. LC 82-72726. 172p (ISBN 0-8040-0536-2). (Illus.). 1977. pap. 7.95 ea. (SB). Swallow.

--Field Book: Wind River Range. 3rd rev. ed. LC 82-70688. (No. 1). (Illus., Orig.). 1977. pap. 5.95 (ISBN 0-8040-0113-8, SB). Swallow.

Bonney, William W. AUA Courses in Urology 1979, Vol. 1. 1979. 23.00 o.p. (ISBN 0-683-00918-4). Williams & Wilkins.

Bonney, William W. & Prout, George R., Jr. Bladder Cancer: AUA Monograph, Vol. 1. (Illus.). 398p. 1981. text ed. 29.95 (ISBN 0-683-00919-2). Williams & Wilkins.

Bonnice, J. G. & Rosenberg, R. Business Law Thirty. 3rd. ed. 1982. 8.64 (ISBN 0-07-006472-5). McGraw.

Bonnice, Joseph G., jt. auth. see Rosenberg, R. Robert.

Bonnici, Roberta. I'm Scared to Witness! (Discovery Bks.). (Illus.). 48p. (Orig.). (YA) (gr. 9-12). 1979. pap. 1.35 (ISBN 0-88243-931-6, 02-0931). Gospel Pub.

--Your Right to Be Different. (Discovery Bks.). 48p. (YA) (gr. 9-12). pap. text ed. 1.35 (ISBN 0-88243-842-5, 02-0842). Gospel Pub.

Bonnicksen, Andrea L. Civil Rights & Liberties: Principles of Interpretation. LC 81-81279. 311p. 1981. pap. 9.95 (ISBN 0-87484-476-2). Mayfield Pub.

Bonnifield, Mathew P. Oklahoma Innovator: The Life of Virgil Browne. LC 75-41452. (Oklahoma Trackmaker Ser: Vol. 2). (Illus.). 190p. 1976. 13.95 (ISBN 0-8061-1326-X). U of Okla Pr.

Bonnington, S. T., jt. auth. see Bain, A. G.

Bonnot De Condillac, Etienne see Condillac, Etienne Bonnot de.

Bonnyns, M., jt. ed. see Bastenie, P. A.

Bono, E. De see De Bono, E.

Bono, Edward De see De Bono, Edward.

Bonoma, Thomas V. & Zaltman, Gerald. Psychology for Management. (Business Ser.). 337p. 1981. text ed. 12.95x (ISBN 0-534-00904-2). Kent Pub Co.

Bonomo, Joe. Improve Your Dancing. (Illus.). 1963. pap. 2.95x (ISBN 0-685-21989-5). Wehman.

Bonotto, S., et al, eds. Developmental Biology of Acetabularia. (Developments in Cell Biology: Vol. 3). 1979. 73.75 (ISBN 0-444-80098-0, Biomedical Pr). Elsevier.

Bonsall, Crosby N. Case of the Dumb Bells. LC 66-8267. (I Can Read Mystery Books). (Illus.). (gr. k-3). 1966. 7.64i (ISBN 0-06-020623-3, HarpJ); PLB 8.89 (ISBN 0-06-020624-1). Har-Row.

--Case of the Hungry Stranger. LC 63-17947. (I Can Read Mystery Books). (Illus.). (gr. k-3). 1963. PLB 8.89 (ISBN 0-06-020571-7, HarpJ). Har-Row.

Bonsall, F. F. & Duncan, J. Numerical Ranges, No. 2. (London Mathematical Society Lecture Note Ser.: No. 10). (Illus.). 192p. 1973. pap. text ed. 21.95x (ISBN 0-521-20227-2). Cambridge U Pr.

Bonsall, Thomas E. Mercury & Edsel 1939-1969. (Identification Guide Ser.). (Illus.). 96p. 1982. pap. 8.95 (ISBN 0-934780-15-3). Bookman Dan.

--Pontiac 1926-1966. (Identification Guide Ser.). (Illus.). 96p. (Orig.). 1982. pap. 8.95 (ISBN 0-934780-14-5). Bookman Dan.

Bonsignore, John J., et al. Before the Law: An Introduction to the Legal Process. 2nd ed. LC 78-69606. (Illus.). 1979. pap. text ed. 15.50 (ISBN 0-395-27514-8). HM.

Bontecou, Eleanor. The Federal Loyalty-Security Program. LC 73-17628. 377p. 1974. Repr. of 1953 ed. lib. bdg. 18.75x (ISBN 0-8371-7256-X, BOFL). Greenwood.

Bontemps, Arna, ed. American Negro Poetry. rev. ed. 1974. 6.95 o.p. (ISBN 0-8090-2521-3); pap. 6.25 o.p. (ISBN 0-8090-0108-X). Hill & Wang.

--Black Thunder. LC 68-31383. 1968. pap. 4.95x (ISBN 0-8070-6429-7, BP305). Beacon Pr.

Bontinck, Irmgard, ed. New Patterns of Musical Behaviour of the Young Generation in Industrial Societies. 1974. 34.00 (ISBN 3-7024-0057-5, 51-26246). Eur-Am Music.

Bontinck-Kueffel, Irmgard. Opern Auf Schallplatten Nineteen Hundred to Nineteen Sixty-Two. Blaukopf, Kurt & Wagner, Manfred, eds. (Ger.). 1974. pap. 18.75 (ISBN 3-7024-0014-1, 51-26205). Eur-Am Music.

Bonting, S. L. & De Pont, J. J., eds. Membrane Transport. (New Comprehensive Biochemistry Ser.: Vol. 2). 1981. 64.25 (ISBN 0-444-80307-6). Elsevier.

Bontly, Thomas. Adventures of a Young Outlaw. 320p. 1974. 6.95 o.p. (ISBN 0-399-11248-0). Putnam Pub Group.

Bontrager, Kenneth L. & Anthony, Barry T. Textbook of Radiographic Positioning & Related Anatomy. LC 81-82006. (Illus.). 560p. (Orig.). 1982. text ed. 49.95x (ISBN 0-940122-01-4). Multi Media CO.

Bonvallet, des Brosses. Richesses et Resources De la France... 305p. 1981. Repr. of 1789 ed. lib. bdg. 120.00 o.p. (ISBN 0-8287-1575-0). Clearwater Pub.

Bonwick, G. Automation on Shipboard. 1967. 35.00 (ISBN 0-312-06195-1). St Martin.

Boockholdt, James L., jt. auth. see Liad, Woody M.

Boocock, Sarane S. Sociology of Education: An Introduction. 2nd ed. LC 79-88445. (Illus.). 1980. text ed. 23.50 (ISBN 0-395-28524-0). HM.

Boodberg, Peter A. Selected Works of Peter A. Boodberg. Cohen, Alvin P., ed. LC 76-24580. 1979. 33.00x (ISBN 0-520-03314-0). U of Cal Pr.

Boodley, James W. The Commercial Greenhouse. LC 78-74806. (Agriculture Ser.). 568p. 1981. 18.80 (ISBN 0-8273-1719-0); instr's. guide 3.25 (ISBN 0-8273-1718-2). Delmar.

Boodman, D. M., jt. auth. see Magee, John R.

Boodt, M. De see De Boodt, M.

Boohe, John P. Quest for the Dream. 308p. 1.00 o.p. (ISBN 0-686-74924-3). ADL.

Booher, Dianna. Would You Put That in Writing? How to Write Your Way to Success in Business. LC 82-1529. 224p. 1983. 12.95 (ISBN 0-87196-650-6). Facts on File.

Booher, Dianna D. Making Friends With Yourself & Other Strangers. 192p. (gr. 9 up). 1982. PLB 9.29g (ISBN 0-686-97686-X). Messner.

Booij, G. E. Dutch Morphology: A Study of Word Formation in Generative Grammar. (Illus.). x, 181p. (Orig.). 1977. pap. 14.00 (ISBN 90-316-0150-0). Benjamins North Am.

--Dutch Morphology: A Study of Word Formation in Generative Grammar. (PdR Press Dutch: No. 2). (Illus.). 1977. pap. text ed. 14.25x o.p. (ISBN 90-316-0150-0). Humanities.

Book, Albert C. & Cary, Norman D. The Radio & Television Commercial. LC 78-529597. 1978. 8.95x (ISBN 0-87251-038-7). Crain Bks.

Book, Albert C., jt. auth. see Schick, C. Dennis.

Book, Stephen A. Essentials of Statistics. (Illus.). 1977. text ed. 23.95 (ISBN 0-07-006464-4, C); instructor's manual 14.95 (ISBN 0-07-006465-2); wkbk. 8.95 (ISBN 0-07-006466-0). McGraw.

--Statistics: Basic Techniques for Solving Problems. new ed. (Illus.). 1976. text ed. 23.95 (ISBN 0-07-006493-8, C); instrs manual 9.95 (ISBN 0-07-006494-6). McGraw.

Book, Stephen A. & Epstein, Marc J. Statistical Analysis. 1982. text ed. 27.50x (ISBN 0-673-16002-5). Scott F.

Book, W. J., ed. Robotics Research & Advanced Applications. 1982. 50.00 (H00236). ASME.

Bookbinder, Albert I. IBM Personal Computer Guide. (Illus.). 1983. pap. 14.95 (ISBN 0-916106-05-5). Prog Pr.

Bookbinder, Albert I. A. Computer-Assisted Investment Handbook. (Illus.). 1983. pap. text ed. 19.95 (ISBN 0-916106-03-9). Prog Pr.

--Investment Decision Making. LC 67-29760. (Illus.). 145p. 1968. 9.95 (ISBN 0-916106-00-4). Prog Pr.

Bookbinder, David. What Folk Music Is All About. LC 79-229. (Illus.). 320p. (gr. 7 up). 1979. PLB 9.29 o.p. (ISBN 0-671-32893-X). Messner.

Bookchin, Murray. The Ecology of Freedom: The Emergence & Dissolution of Hierarchy. LC 81-21745. 1982. 19.95 (ISBN 0-917352-09-2); pap. 11.50 (ISBN 0-917352-10-6). Cheshire.

--Post-Scarcity Anarchism. rev. ed. Date not set. 15.00 o.p. (ISBN 0-87867-081-5); pap. 6.95 o.p. (ISBN 0-87867-004-1). Ramparts. Postponed.

Booker, Christopher. Neophiliacs. LC 76-112442. 1970. 8.95 o.p. (ISBN 0-87645-000-1). Gambit.

Booker, John M. The Wiston Archives. 541p. 1975. 65.00x (ISBN 0-900801-35-2). State Mutual Bk.

Booker, P. J. Three Dimensional Projection Drawing. (Illus.). 64p. 5.00x (ISBN 0-85344-082-4). Intl Pubns Serv.

Booker, P. J., et al. Project Apollo: The Way to the Moon. 1970. 28.95 (ISBN 0-444-19705-2). Elsevier.

Booker, Stephen T. Waves & License. (Prison Writing Ser.). write for info. Greenfld Rev Pr.

Bookspan, Martin & Yockey, Ross. Andre Previn: A Biography. LC 80-2746. (Illus.). 408p. 1981. 15.95 o.p. (ISBN 0-385-15157-8). Doubleday.

Bookstaber, Philip D. Judaism & the American Mind: In Theory & Practice. LC 78-26404. 1979. Repr. of 1939 ed. lib. bdg. 20.75x (ISBN 0-313-20875-1, BOJU). Greenwood.

Boole, George. Laws of Thought. 1953. pap. 6.95 (ISBN 0-486-60028-9). Dover.

--Logical Works, 2 vols. Incl. Vol. 1. Studies in Logic & Probability. 500p. 27.50 (ISBN 0-87548-038-1); Vol. 2. Laws of Thought. xvi, 464p. 27.50 (ISBN 0-87548-039-X). 1952. Open Court.

--Treatise on Differential Equations. 5th ed. LC 59-9980. 25.00 o.p. (ISBN 0-8284-0128-4). Chelsea Pub.

--Treatise on the Calculus of Finite Differences. 5th ed. LC 76-119364. text ed. 12.95 (ISBN 0-8284-1121-2). Chelsea Pub.

Boole, Mary E. The Preparation of the Child for Science. 1983. 5.00 (ISBN 0-686-84073-9). Intl Gen Semantics.

Boolootian, Richard A. Zoology: An Introduction to the Study of Animals. (Illus.). 1979. text ed. 23.95 (ISBN 0-02-312030-4); student study guide avail.; instrs'. manual avail.; lab. manual avail. Macmillan.

Boolootian, Richard A. & Stiles, Karl A. College Zoology. 10th ed. (Illus.). 768p. 1981. text ed. 26.95 (ISBN 0-02-311990-X). Macmillan.

Boolos, G. The Unprovability of Consistency. LC 77-85710. (Illus.). 1979. 32.50 (ISBN 0-521-21879-9). Cambridge U Pr.

Boolos, G. S. & Jeffrey, R. C. Computability & Logic. 2nd ed. LC 77-85710. (Illus.). 280p. 1981. 43.50 (ISBN 0-521-23479-4); pap. 14.95 (ISBN 0-521-29967-5). Cambridge U Pr.

Boom, B. K., jt. auth. see Ouden, P. den.

Boom, Corrie T. Amazing Love. 1982. pap. 2.50 (ISBN 0-515-06735-0). Jove Pubns.

--Amor, Asombroso Amor. Orig. Title: Amazing Love. 112p. 1980. pap. 2.25 (ISBN 0-311-40035-3, Edit Mundo). Casa Bautista.

--Hiding Place. 219p. 1971. PLB 7.95 o.p. (ISBN 0-912376-01-5); pap. 3.95 o.p. (ISBN 0-912376-05-8). Chosen Bks Pub.

--A Prisoner & Yet. (Orig.). 1982. pap. 2.50 (ISBN 0-515-06736-9). Jove Pubns.

--This Day is the Lord's. 1982. pap. 2.75 (ISBN 0-515-06734-2). Jove Pubns.

--Tramp for the Lord. 1976. pap. 2.50 (ISBN 0-515-06486-6). Jove Pubns.

Boom, Corrie ten. Prayers & Promises for Every Day: With Corrie ten Boom. Shaw, Luci, ed. LC 77-92352. (Day Star Devotional Ser). 1977. pap. 2.95 (ISBN 0-87788-689-X). Shaw Pubs.

Boom, Corrie Ten see Ten Boom, Corrie.

Boon, J. A. The Anthropological Romance of Bali 1597-1972. LC 76-19626. (Geertz Ser.). (Illus.). 1977. 37.50 (ISBN 0-521-21398-3); pap. 10.95 (ISBN 0-521-29226-3). Cambridge U Pr.

Boon, James A. Other Tribes, Other Scribes: Symbolic Anthropology in the Comparative Study of Cultures, Histories, Religions & Texts. LC 82-9516. (Illus.). 320p. 1983. 27.50 (ISBN 0-521-25081-1); pap. 9.95 (ISBN 0-521-27197-5). Cambridge U Pr.

Boon, Jean P. & Yip, Sidney. Molecular Hydrodynamics. (Illus.). 440p. 1979. text ed. 67.50 (ISBN 0-07-006560-8). McGraw.

Boon, Louis P. Chapel Road. Dixon, Adrienne, tr. from Flem. 338p. 1972. pap. 3.95 o.p. (ISBN 0-88254-004-1). Hippocrene Bks.
--Chapel Road. Dixon, Adrienne, tr. (International Studies & Translations Ser.). lib. bdg. 7.95 o.p. (ISBN 0-8057-3410-4, Twayne). G K Hall.
--Minuet. Dixon, Adrienne, tr. from Flemish. LC 78-61063. 1980. 8.95 o.p. (ISBN 0-89255-039-2). Persea Bks.
Boone & Kurtz. Sales Management Game. 2nd ed. (Orig.). 1978. pap. 11.95 (ISBN 0-686-28581-6). Pennwell Pub.
Boone, Bruce, jt. tr. see Gluck, Robert.
Boone, Cheri, ed. see International Conference on Underwater Education, 11th.
Boone, Daniel. Cerebral Palsy. LC 76-190708. (Studies in Communicative Disorders). 1972. pap. text ed. 2.95 o.p. (ISBN 0-672-61290-9). Bobbs.
Boone, Daniel R. The Voice & Voice Therapy. 2nd ed. (Illus.). 1977. 23.95 (ISBN 0-13-943100-4). P-H.
Boone, Debby & Baker, Dennis. Debby Boone--So Far. LC 81-11037. (Illus.). 208p. 1980. 9.95 (ISBN 0-8407-4092-1). Nelson.
--So Far. 224p. 1982. pap. 2.95 (ISBN 0-515-06323-1). Jove Pubns.
Boone, Debby, et al. Debby Boone -- So Far. cancelled (ISBN 0-8407-4092-1). Warner Bks.
Boone, Elizabeth H., jt. auth. see Nuttal, Zelia.
Boone, Gene. Classics in Consumer Behavior. new ed. (Orig.). 1977. pap. 13.95 (ISBN 0-87814-092-1). Pennwell Books Division.
Boone, Hubert. De Hommel in de Lage Landen: L'epinette aus Pays Bas. (Illus.). 188p. 1976. 37.50 o.s.i. (ISBN 90-6027-174-2, Pub. by Frits Knuf Netherlands); wrappers 25.00 o.s.i. (ISBN 90-6027-173-4, Pub. by Frits Knuf Netherlands). Pendragon NY.
Boone, L. V., et al, eds. Producing Farm Crops. 3rd ed. 1981. 17.30 (ISBN 0-8134-2151-9); text ed. 13.00x. Interstate.
Boone, Louis E. & Bowen, Donald. Great Writings in Management & Organizational Behavior. 475p. 1980. pap. text ed. 13.95 (ISBN 0-87814-097-2). Pennwell Pub.
Boone, Louis E. & Hackleman, Edwin C. Marketing Strategy: A Marketing Decision Game. 2nd ed. LC 74-27870. (Illus.). 224p. 1975. pap. text ed. 12.95 (ISBN 0-675-08713-9). Additional supplements may be obtained from publisher. Merrill.
Boone, Louis E. & Kurtz, David L. Comtemporary Marketing. 4th ed. 1983. text ed. 24.95x; 4.50 o.p. (ISBN 0-03-019011-8); readings 9.95x (ISBN 0-03-062641-2). Dryden Pr.
Boone, Louis E., jt. auth. see Kurtz, David L.
Boone, Pat. My Brothers Keeper? Orig. Title: Dr. Balaam's Talking Mule. 1975. pap. write for info (ISBN 0-515-09524-9). Jove Pubns.
--My Brothers Keeper. LC 75-7829. 1975. pap. 2.95 (ISBN 0-686-95481-5). Omega Pubns Or.
--Pray to Win: God Wants You to Succeed. 1980. 8.95 o.p. (ISBN 0-399-12494-2). Putnam Pub Group.
Boone, Robert, jt. ed. see McGee, Leo.
Boone, Robert S., jt. auth. see Flanigan, Michael G.
Boone, W., et al, eds. Word Problems I. (Studies in Logic: Vol. 71). 1973. 63.50 (ISBN 0-7204-2271-X, North Holland). Elsevier.
Boonin, Joseph M. An Index to the Solo Songs of Robert Franz. (Music Indexes & Bibliographies: No. 4). 1970. pap. 1.75 (ISBN 0-913574-04-X). Eur-Am Music.
Boor, Jacklyn, jt. auth. see Collins, Dennis.
Boorer, Michael. The Life of Monkeys & Apes. LC 78-56603. (Easy Reading Edition of Introduction to Nature Ser.). (Illus.). 1978. PLB 12.68 (ISBN 0-382-06188-8). Silver.
--The Life of Strange Mammals. LC 78-56571. (Easy Reading Edition of Introduction to Nature Ser.). (Illus.). 1978. PLB 12.68 (ISBN 0-686-51147-6). Silver.
Boorman, John T. & Havrilesky, Thomas M. Money Supply, Money Demand & Macroeconomic Models. LC 79-167998. 1972. pap. 13.95x o.p. (ISBN 0-88295-400-8). Harlan Davidson.
Boorman, John T., jt. auth. see Havrilesky, Thomas M.
Boorman, Scott A. Protracted Game: A Wei-Ch'i Interpretation of Maoist Revolutionary Strategy. (Illus.). 1971. pap. 6.95 (ISBN 0-19-501493-6, GB). Oxford U Pr.
Boorstin, Daniel J. Decline of Radicalism: Reflections of America Today. 192p. 1969. 5.95 (ISBN 0-394-42184-1, Vin). Random.
--Genius of American Politics, Nineteen Fifty-eight. (Walgreen Foundation Lectures). 10.50x (ISBN 0-226-06490-5, Phoen). U of Chicago Pr.
--Image: A Guide to Pseudo-Events in America. LC 62-7936. Orig. Title: What Happened to the American Dream. 1962. pap. text ed. 4.95x (ISBN 0-689-70280-9, 173). Atheneum.
Boorstin, Daniel J., ed. American Primer. pap. 4.95 (ISBN 0-451-62201-4, ME2201, Ment). NAL.
Boorstin, Paul. Savage. 304p. 1981. pap. 2.95 o.p. (ISBN 0-425-04938-8). Berkley Pub.
--Savage. LC 79-28636. 320p. 1980. 12.95 o.s.i. (ISBN 0-399-90037-3, Marek). Putnam Pub Group.
Boorstin, Paul & Boorstin, Sharon. The Glory Hand. 320p. 1981. cancelled o.s.i. (ISBN 0-399-90100-0, Marek). Putnam Pub Group.
--The Glory Hand. 288p. (Orig.). pap. 2.95 (ISBN 0-425-05861-1). Berkley Pub.
Boorstin, Sharon. Keep on Rollin' The Complete Guide to Roller Skating in America. (Illus., Orig.). 1978. pap. 5.95 o.p. (ISBN 0-446-87811-1). Warner Bks.
Boorstin, Sharon, jt. auth. see Boorstin, Paul.
Boos-Hamberger, Hilde. The Nine Training Sketches for the Painter (Nature's Moods) by Rudolf Steiner. Fletcher, John, ed. Frommer, E., tr. from Ger. 23p. 1982. pap. 1.95 (ISBN 0-88010-058-3, Pub. by Steinerbooks). Anthroposophic.
Boot, Adrian & Thomas, Michael. Jamaica: Babylon on a Thin Wire. LC 76-41756. (Illus.). 1977. pap. 6.95 o.p. (ISBN 0-8052-0556-X). Schocken.
Boot, F. Illustrations of the Genus Carex: 1858-1867, 4 pts. in 1. (Illus.). 1968. 128.00 (ISBN 3-7682-0553-3). Lubrecht & Cramer.
Boot, John C. & Cox, Edwin. Statistical Analysis for Managerial Decisions. 2nd ed. (Illus.). 672p. 1973. text ed. 24.95 (ISBN 0-07-006518-7, C); instructor's manual 4.95 (ISBN 0-07-006519-5). McGraw.
Booth. Basic Elememts of Landscape Architectural Design. Date not set. price not set (ISBN 0-444-00766-0). Elsevier.
--Nurses Handbook of Investigations. 224p. 1982. pap. text ed. 10.50 (ISBN 0-06-318235-1, Pub. by Har-Row Ltd England). Har-Row.
Booth, A. E. Ministry of Peter, John & Paul. Date not set. pap. 0.95 (ISBN 0-88172-004-6). Believers Bkshelf.
Booth, Anne & McCawley, Peter, eds. The Indonesian Economy During the Soeharto Era. (East Asian Social Science Monographs). (Illus.). 356p. 1981. text ed. 42.00x (ISBN 0-19-580477-5). Oxford U Pr.
Booth, Arthur H. Sir Christopher Wren. 11.75x o.p. (ISBN 0-392-09883-0, SpS). Sportshelf.
Booth, Basil & Fitch, Frank. Earthshock. LC 77-90487. (Illus.). 1979. 14.95 o.s.i. (ISBN 0-8027-0593-6). Walker & Co.
Booth, David. Eura & Zephyra...with Poetical Pieces, Repr. Of 1816. Bd. with Elizabeth Hitchener (1783?-1822) The Fire-Side Bagatelle, Containing Enigmas on the Chief Towns of England & Wales. Hitchener, Elizabeth. Repr. of 1818 ed; The Weald of Sussex, a Poem. Repr. of 1822 ed. LC 75-31163. (Romantic Context Ser.: Poetry 1789-1830: Vol. 18). 1978. lib. bdg. 47.00 o.s.i. (ISBN 0-8240-2117-7). Garland Pub.
Booth, Don & Booth, Jonathan. Building for Energy Independence With Sun Earth Buffering & Superinsulation. (Orig.). 1983. 25.00 (ISBN 0-686-37853-9); pap. 20.00 (ISBN 0-9604422-3-5). Community Builders.
--Building for Energy Independence with Sun-Earth Buffering & Superinsulation. 1983. pap. 17.95 (ISBN 0-9604422-3-5). Comm Builders.
Booth, E. Donald, jt. ed. see Locke, William N.
Booth, Edwin. The Colt-Packin' Parson. 192p. (YA) 1976. 6.95 (ISBN 0-685-57546-2, Avalon). Bouregy.
Booth, Ernest S. Field Record for Birds. (YA) (gr. 7 up). 1960. pap. 2.00 (ISBN 0-911080-03-1). Outdoor Pict.
--How to Know the Mammals. 4th ed. (Picture Key Nature Ser.). 220p. 1982. wire coil write for info. (ISBN 0-697-04781-4). Wm C Brown.
--Life List for Birds. (YA) (gr. 7 up). 1969. pap. 2.00 (ISBN 0-911080-04-X). Outdoor Pict.
Booth, Eugene. At the Beach. LC 77-7659. (A Raintree Spotlight Book). (Illus.). (gr. k-3). 1977. PLB 11.55 (ISBN 0-8393-0111-1). Raintree Pubs.
--At the Circus. LC 77-7946. (A Raintree Spotlight Book). (Illus.). (gr. k-3). 1977. PLB 11.55 (ISBN 0-8393-0112-X). Raintree Pubs.
--At the Fair. LC 77-7961. (A Raintree Spotlight Book). (Illus.). (gr. k-3). 1977. PLB 11.55 (ISBN 0-8393-0114-6). Raintree Pubs.
--At the Zoo. LC 77-7627. (A Raintree Spotlight Book). (Illus.). (gr. k-3). 1977. PLB 11.55 (ISBN 0-8393-0107-3). Raintree Pubs.
--In the Air. LC 77-7984. (A Raintree Spotlight Book). (Illus.). (gr. k-3). 1977. PLB 11.55 (ISBN 0-8393-0105-7). Raintree Pubs.
--In the City. LC 77-7949. (A Raintree Spotlight Book). (Illus.). (gr. k-3). 1977. PLB 11.55 (ISBN 0-8393-0109-X). Raintree Pubs.
--In the Garden. LC 77-7628. (A Raintree Spotlight Book). (Illus.). (gr. k-3). 1977. PLB 11.55 (ISBN 0-8393-0115-4). Raintree Pubs.
--In the Jungle. LC 77-7947. (A Raintree Spotlight Book). (Illus.). (gr. k-3). 1977. PLB 11.55 (ISBN 0-8393-0104-9). Raintree Pubs.
--In the Park. LC 77-7622. (A Raintree Spotlight Book). (Illus.). (gr. k-3). 1977. PLB 11.55 (ISBN 0-8393-0106-5). Raintree Pubs.
--On the Farm. LC 77-7965. (A Raintree Spotlight Book). (Illus.). (gr. k-3). 1977. PLB 11.55 (ISBN 0-8393-0113-8). Raintree Pubs.
--Under the Ground. LC 77-8037. (A Raintree Spotlight Book). (Illus.). (gr. k-3). 1977. PLB 11.55 (ISBN 0-8393-0110-3). Raintree Pubs.
--Under the Ocean. LC 77-7983. (A Raintree Spotlight Book). (Illus.). (gr. k-3). 1977. PLB 11.55 (ISBN 0-8393-0108-1). Raintree Pubs.
Booth, Franklin. The Art of Franklin Booth. (Illus.). 76p. 1976. pap. 8.95 o.p. (ISBN 0-517-52808-8). Crown.
Booth, George. Pussycats Need Love, Too. 128p. 1981. pap. 6.95 (ISBN 0-380-55533-6, 55533-6). Avon.
Booth, George C. The Food & Drink of Mexico. 8.50 (ISBN 0-8446-5481-7). Peter Smith.
Booth, Gotthard. The Cancer Epidemic: Shadow of the Conquest of Nature. (Illus.). 277p. (A-597362). 1980. 29.95 (ISBN 0-88946-625-4). E Mellen.
Booth, Grayce M. The Design of Complex Information Systems: Common Sense Methods for Success. (Illus.). 288p. 1983. 29.95 (ISBN 0-07-006506-3, P&RB). McGraw.
--The Distributed System Environment. (Illus.). 288p. 1980. 26.95 (ISBN 0-07-006507-1, P&RB). McGraw.
--Functional Analysis of Information Processing. LC 80-11247. 288p. 1983. Repr. of 1973 ed. lib. bdg. write for info. (ISBN 0-89874-135-1). Krieger.
Booth, J. E. Principles of Textile Testing. 3rd ed. text ed. 39.95x (ISBN 0-592-06325-9). Butterworth.
--Textile Mathematics, Vol. 1. 1975. 26.00x (ISBN 0-87245-586-6). Textile Bk.
--Textile Mathematics, Vol. 2. 1976. 28.00x (ISBN 0-87245-587-4). Textile Bk.
--Textile Mathematics, Vol. 3. 22.00x (ISBN 0-87245-588-2). Textile Bk.
Booth, Janine, tr. see Scheller, William G.
Booth, Joan, tr. Ovid: Amores, Bk. II. 220p. 1983. text ed. 14.50x (ISBN 0-85668-174-1, 41067, Pub. by Aris & Phillips England). Humanities.
Booth, John A. The End & the Beginning: The Nicaraguan Revolution. LC 82-2690. (Latin America & the Caribbean Special Studies). 277p. 1982. 25.00 (ISBN 0-89158-939-2); pap. 11.50 (ISBN 0-86531-148-X). Westview.
Booth, John N. Booths in History: Their Roots & Lives, Encounters & Achievements. LC 82-5421. (Illus.). 242p. 1982. text ed. 38.95 (ISBN 0-943230-00-4); pap. text ed. 28.95 (ISBN 0-943230-01-2). Ridgeway Pr.
Booth, Jonathan, jt. auth. see Booth, Don.
Booth, Julianne. Books of the New Testament. (Arch Book Supplement Ser.). 1981. pap. 0.89 (ISBN 0-570-06150-4, 59-1305). Concordia.
--Books of the Old Testament. (Arch Book Supplement Ser.). 1981. pap. 0.89 (ISBN 0-570-06151-2, 59-1306). Concordia.
--Parables of Jesus. (Arch Bks.). 1982. pap. 0.89 (ISBN 0-570-06163-6, 59-1309). Concordia.
Booth, Larry, jt. auth. see Weinstein, Robert A.
Booth, M. R., et al. Revels History of Drama in English, Vol. 6: 1750-1880. LC 74-15178. (Illus.). 250p. 1975. 53.00x (ISBN 0-416-13070-4); pap. 18.95x (ISBN 0-416-81380-1). Methuen Inc.
Booth, Martin. Devils' Wine. 112p. 1980. text ed. 16.25x (ISBN 0-86140-044-5); pap. text ed. 8.50x (ISBN 0-686-96742-9). Humanities.
Booth, Martin, et al. Bismarck. Yapp, Martin & Killingray, Margaret, eds. (Greenhaven World History Ser.). (Illus.). 32p. (gr. 10). 1980. lib. bdg. 6.95 (ISBN 0-89908-048-0); pap. text ed. 2.25 (ISBN 0-89908-023-5). Greenhaven.
Booth, P. H. W. The Financial Administration of the Lordship & Country of Chester, 1272-1377. 192p. 1982. 20.00 (ISBN 0-7190-1337-2). Manchester.
Booth, R. G., jt. auth. see Herzka, A.
Booth, Sally S. The Witches of Early America. new ed. 256p. 1975. 10.50 o.s.i. (ISBN 0-8038-8072-3). Hastings.
Booth, Stephen, commentary by. Shakespeare's Sonnets. LC 76-56161. 1977. 37.50x (ISBN 0-300-01959-9); pap. 12.95 (ISBN 0-300-02495-9). Yale U Pr.
Booth, Sterling R., Jr. Allergy Cures Your Allergist Never Mentioned. LC 80-20698. 1983. 15.95 (ISBN 0-87949-191-4). Ashley Bks.
Booth, Taylor L. Digital Network & Computer Systems. 2nd ed. LC 77-10832. 592p. 1978. text ed. 30.95 (ISBN 0-471-08842-0); tchrs. manual avail. (ISBN 0-471-03049-X). Wiley.
--Sequential Machines & Automata Theory. LC 80-24620. 608p. 1983. Repr. of 1967 ed. text ed. write for info. (ISBN 0-89874-269-2). Krieger.
Booth, Taylor L. & Chien, Yi-Tzuu. Computing: Fundamentals & Applications. LC 73-20157. 497p. 1974. 29.95x (ISBN 0-471-08847-1). Wiley.
Booth, Tony. Growing Up in Society. (Essential Psychology Ser.). 1975. pap. 4.50x (ISBN 0-416-81900-1). Methuen Inc.
Booth, Verne H. & Bloom, Mortimer. Physical Science: A Study of Matter & Energy. 3rd ed. (Illus.). 800p. 1972. text ed. 22.95 (ISBN 0-02-312280-3, 31228). Macmillan.
Booth, Wayne C. Critical Understanding: The Powers & Limits of Pluralism. LC 78-15107. 1979. 20.00 (ISBN 0-226-06554-5, Phoen); pap. 8.95 (ISBN 0-226-06555-3). U of Chicago Pr.
--Now Don't Try to Reason with Me: Essays & Ironies for a Credulous Age. LC 73-12359. 1970. 9.50x (ISBN 0-226-06579-0, Phoen); pap. 2.95 (ISBN 0-226-06580-4, P461). U of Chicago Pr.
--Rhetoric of Fiction. LC 61-14947. 1961. pap. 6.50 (ISBN 0-226-06578-2, P267, Phoen). U of Chicago Pr.
--The Rhetoric of Film. Rev. ed. 576p. 1982. pap. 9.95 (ISBN 0-226-06558-8). U of Chicago Pr.
Booth, William. In Darkest England & the Way Out. LC 76-108240. (Criminology, Law Enforcement, & Social Problems Ser.: No. 142). 10.00x (ISBN 0-87585-142-8). Patterson Smith.
Booth-Clibborn, Edward, ed. European Photography 1982: European Photography & European Illustration. (Illus.). 240p. 1982. 40.00 (ISBN 0-8109-0866-2). Abrams.
Boothe, Joan N., jt. auth. see Council on Economic Priorities.
Boothroyd, Arthur. Hearing Impairments in Young Children. (Illus.). 266p. 1982. 21.95 (ISBN 0-13-384701-2). P-H.
Boothroyd, Geoffrey. Fundamentals of Metal Machining & Machine Tools. (Illus.). 350p. 1975. text ed. 36.00 (ISBN 0-07-006498-9, C); solutions manual 4.50 (ISBN 0-07-006502-0). McGraw.
Boothroyd, R. G. Flowing Gas-Solids Suspensions. 289p. 1971. 40.00x (ISBN 0-412-09660-9, Pub. by Chapman & Hall England). Methuen Inc.
Booton, Harold W. Architecture of Spain. 1966. 5.95 o.p. (ISBN 0-85362-020-2, Oriel). Routledge & Kegan.
Boots, B., jt. auth. see Getis, A.
Bootsma, G. A., ed. see Symposium on Surface Physics, 3rd, June 26-28,1974.
Booty, John E. The Church in History. (Church's Teaching Ser.: Vol. 3). 320p. 1979. 5.95 (ISBN 0-8164-0420-8); pap. 3.95 (ISBN 0-8164-2216-8); user guide 0.95 (ISBN 0-8164-2223-0). Seabury.
Bootzin, Richard R. Behavior Modification & Therapy: An Introduction. (Orig.). 1975. pap. text ed. 9.95 (ISBN 0-316-10260-1). Little.
Bootzin, Richard R. & Acocella, Joan. Abnormal Psychology: Current Perspectives. 3rd ed. 608p. 1980. text ed. 23.00 (ISBN 0-394-32281-9); wkbk. 8.00 (ISBN 0-394-32507-9). Random.
Booz & Allen. Coping with Inflation: Experiences of Financial Executives in the U. K., West Germany & Brazil. LC 81-706. 1982. 4.00. Finan Exec.
Bopp, Steven, jt. auth. see Zaccaria, Joseph.
Boppart, H., jt. ed. see Wachter, P.
Bor, N. L. Grasses of Ihdia, Burma & Ceylon: Excluding Bambuseae. (Illus.). 1973. Repr. of 1960 ed. 88.00 (ISBN 3-87429-043-3). Lubrecht & Cramer.
Bora, Ben. Voyagers. 400p. 1982. pap. 3.50 (ISBN 0-553-22522-7). Bantam.
Bora, K. C., et al, eds. Chemical Mutagenesis: Progress in Mutation Research, Vol. 3. 360p. 1982. 87.25 (ISBN 0-444-80352-1). Elsevier.
Borah, Woodrow, jt. auth. see Cook, Sherburne F.
Boraks, Jagna, tr. see Busza, Andrzej.
Boram, Clifford. How to Get Parts Cast for Your Antique Stove. 5.00 (ISBN 0-686-38103-3). Autonomy Hse.
Boraston, J. H., ed. Sir Douglas Haig's Despatches. (Illus.). 371p. 1979. Repr. of 1919 ed. 25.00x o.p. (ISBN 0-460-04371-4, Pub by J. M. Dent England). Biblio Dist.
Borba, Michele & Ungaro, Dan. Bookends. (gr. 1-4). 1982. 8.95 (ISBN 0-86653-065-7, GA 432). Good Apple.
Borch, C. & Mossiv, Jan, eds. Risk & Uncertainty. LC 68-29940. (International Economic Assn. Ser). (Illus.). 1969. 32.50 (ISBN 0-312-68460-6). St Martin.
Borch, Karl. The Mathematical Theory of Insurance. LC 73-11670. 352p. 1974. 26.95x (ISBN 0-669-86942-2). Lexington Bks.
Borchard, Edwin M. Convicting the Innocent: Errors of Criminal Justice. LC 74-107406. (Civil Liberties in American History Ser). 1970. Repr. of 1932 ed. lib. bdg. 39.50 (ISBN 0-306-71886-3). Da Capo.
Borchard, Franz. The Adrenergic Nerves of the Normal & Atrophied Heart. Bergmann, Wolfgang & Doerr, Wilhelm, eds. Hirsch, H. J., tr. from Ger. LC 77-92112. (Normal & Pathologic Anatomy Ser.). (Illus.). 72p. 1978. pap. 24.50 o.p. (ISBN 0-88416-240-0). Wright-PSG.
Borchardt, D. H. Australian Bibliography: A Guide to Printed Sources of Information. 284p. 1976. text ed. 38.00 (ISBN 0-08-020551-8); pap. text ed. 15.75 (ISBN 0-08-020550-X). Pergamon.
Borchardt, D. H. & Horacek, J. Librarianship in Australia, New Zealand & Oceania. Date not set. 16.50 (ISBN 0-08-019920-8); pap. text ed. write for info. (ISBN 0-08-019752-3). Pergamon.
Borchardt, Gordon C., jt. auth. see Beighey, Clyde.
Borchardt, Jack A., et al, eds. Sludge & Its Ultimate Disposal. Jones & Redman. LC 80-68821. 286p. 1981. text ed. 37.50 (ISBN 0-250-40386-2). Ann Arbor Science.
Borchardt, Marguerite, tr. see Brunner, Heinrich.
Borchers, jt. auth. see Oppenheimer, S. L.
Borchgrave, Arnaud de see Moss, Robert & De Borchgrave, Arnaud.
Borchgrevink, Hans, jt. auth. see Butenschon, Sine.
Borck, Leslie E. & Fawcett, Stephen B. Learning Counseling & Problem-Solving Skills. LC 82-2916. 172p. (Orig.). 1982. text ed. 26.00 (ISBN 0-917724-30-5, B30); pap. text ed. 13.95 (ISBN 0-917724-35-6, B35). Haworth Pr.
Bord, Colin, jt. auth. see Bord, Janet.
Bord, Janet & Bord, Colin. Mysterious Britain. (Illus.). 1978. pap. text ed. 5.95x o.p. (ISBN 0-8464-0663-2). Beekman Pubs.

Borde, Charles. Le Catechumene. (Holbach & His Friends Ser). 27p. (Fr.). 1974. Repr. of 1768 ed. lib. bdg. 23.00 o.p. (ISBN 0-8287-0117-2, 1532). Clearwater Pub.
--Tableau Philosophique du Genre Humain. (Holbach & His Friends Ser). 228p. (Fr.). 1974. Repr. of 1767 ed. lib. bdg. 64.00x o.p. (ISBN 0-8287-0118-0, 1585). Clearwater Pub.
Bordeau, Elvi L., tr. see Cancrinus, Franz L.
Bordeau, Kenneth V., tr. see Cancrinus, Franz L.
Bordeaux, Norma N. Dewdrops on A Lotus Leaf. (Illus.). 28p. 1974. pap. 2.75 (ISBN 0-89564-076-7). IBS Intl.
Bordeaux, Norma N., jt. auth. see Szekely, Edmond B.
Borden. A Course in Advanced Calculus. 1982. 29.50 (ISBN 0-444-00638-9). Elsevier.
Borden, Arthur R., Jr. A Comprehensive Old-English Dictionary. LC 81-40837. 1612p. 1982. lib. bdg. 101.75 (ISBN 0-8191-2254-8). U Pr of Amer.
Borden, Carla M., jt. ed. see Jackman, Jarrell C.
Borden, Morton. Parties & Politics in the Early Republic, 1789-1815. LC 67-14298. (American History Ser.). (Orig.). 1967. pap. 5.95x (ISBN 0-88295-704-X). Harlan Davidson.
Borden, Morton & Graham, Otis. The American Profile. 2nd ed. 1978. pap. text ed. 17.95x (ISBN 0-669-84822-0); instr's. manual 1.95 (ISBN 0-669-99994-6). Heath.
Borden, Morton & Graham, Otis L. Speculations on American History. 1977. pap. text ed. 7.95x (ISBN 0-669-00488-X). Heath.
Borden, Morton & Borden, Penn, eds. The American Tory. LC 73-168739. (Great Lives Observed). 160p. 1972. 8.95 (ISBN 0-13-031385-8, Spec); pap. 2.45 o.p. (ISBN 0-686-96840-9, Spec). P-H.
Borden, Neil H., Jr. Acceptance of New Food Products by Supermarkets. LC 68-15544. 248p. 1969. pap. 3.00 o.p. (ISBN 0-87005-000-1). Fairchild.
Borden, Penn, jt. ed. see Borden, Morton.
Borden, Rose M. Glad Tidings: A Treasury of Inspiring Quotations. 192p. 1983. 8.95 (ISBN 0-89479-111-7). A & W Pubs.
Borden, Thomas A. see Crawford, E. David.
Borden, Weston T. Diradicals. LC 82-8604. 343p. 1982. 44.95 (ISBN 0-471-08661-4, Pub. by Wiley-Interscience). Wiley.
Border, Barbara. Food Safety & Sanitation. (Careers in Home Economics Ser.). (Illus.). 1979. pap. text ed. 10.96 (ISBN 0-07-006511-X, G); tchr's manual & key 4.00 (ISBN 0-07-006516-0); wkbk 5.96 (ISBN 0-07-006512-8). McGraw.
Border, Rosy. Nuka's Tale. LC 81-52497. (Starters Ser.). PLB 8.00 (ISBN 0-382-06510-7). Silver.
Bordes, Charles, ed. Anthologie Des Maitres Religieux Primirties Des XV, XVI & XVII Siecles, 6 vols. (Music Ser.). 1981. Repr. of 1893 ed. Set. lib. bdg. 225.00 (ISBN 0-306-76089-4); Vol. 1; IV, 184 Pp. lib. bdg. 42.50 (ISBN 0-306-76114-9); Vol. 2; VIII, 194 Pp. lib. bdg. 42.50 (ISBN 0-306-76115-7); Vol. 3; IV, 184 Pp. lib. bdg. 42.50 (ISBN 0-306-76116-5); Vol. 4; IV, 190 Pp. lib. bdg. 42.50 (ISBN 0-306-76117-3); Vol. 5; II, 190 Pp. lib. bdg. 42.50 (ISBN 0-306-76118-1); Vol. 6; II, 202 Pp. lib. bdg. 42.50 (ISBN 0-306-76119-X). Da Capo.
Bordewijk, P., jt. auth. see Bottcher, C. J.
Bordewijk, P., ed. see Bottcher, C. J., et al.
Bordewyk, H. W., et al. Netherlands & the World War: Studies in the War History of a Neutral: Volume 4-Effect of the War upon Banking & Currency-War Finances in the Netherlands, 1918-1922-Costs of the War. (Economic & Social History of the World War Ser.). 1928. text ed. 75.00x (ISBN 0-686-83642-1). Elliots Bks.
Bordicks, Katherine J. Patterns of Shock: Implications for Nursing Care. 2nd ed. (Illus.). 1980. text ed. 29.95 (ISBN 0-02-312450-4). Macmillan.
Bordignon Favero, Giampaolo. The Villa Emo at Fanzolo. LC 73-139113. (Corpus Palladianum, Vol. 5). (Illus.). 42.50x (ISBN 0-271-01153-X). Pa St U Pr.
Bordin, Ruth. Woman & Temperance: The Quest for Power & Liberty, 1873 to 1900. Davis, Allen F., ed. LC 80-21140. (American Civilization Ser.). 225p. 1980. 24.95 (ISBN 0-87722-157-X). Temple U Pr.
Bordinat, Philip & Blaydes, Sophia B. Sir William Davenant. (English Authors Ser.). 1981. lib. bdg. 13.95 (ISBN 0-8057-6795-9, Twayne). G K Hall.
Bordman, Gerald. American Operetta: From H.M.S. Pinafore to Sweeney Todd. (Illus.). 1981. 17.95 (ISBN 0-19-502869-4). Oxford U Pr.
--Jerome Kern: His Life & Music. (Illus.). 1980. 25.00x (ISBN 0-19-502649-7). Oxford U Pr.
Bordogna, J., jt. auth. see Ruston, H.
Bordwell, David & Thompson, Kristin. Film Art: An Introduction. LC 78-18633. (Illus.). 1979. pap. text ed. 15.95 (ISBN 0-201-00566-2). A-W.
Borek, Carmia & Williams, Gary M., eds. Differentiation & Carcinogenesis in Liver Cell Cultures. LC 80-20918. (Annals of the New York Academy of Sciences: Vol. 349). 429p. 1980. 85.00x (ISBN 0-89766-087-0); pap. 85.00x (ISBN 0-89766-088-9). NY Acad Sci.
Boreman, Thomas. Gigantick Histories of the Two Famous Giants of Guildhall. Lurie, Alison & Schiller, Justin G., eds. LC 75-32140. (Classics of Children's Literature Ser.: 1621-1932). PLB 38.00 o.s.i. (ISBN 0-8240-2256-4). Garland Pub.
Boren, jt. auth. see Hook.
Boren, Robert. R, jt. auth. see Pace, R. Wayne.
Boren, Sharon. An Apple in the Classroom. 170p. (gr. 3-8). 1983. pap. 7.95 (ISBN 0-88056-119-X). Dilithium Pr.
--A Pet for Kids. (Illus.). 1983. pap. 7.95 (ISBN 0-88056-106-8). Dilithium Pr.
Boren, Tinka, jt. auth. see Hook, Martha.
Borenstein, Audrey. Older Women in Twentieth Century America: A Selected Annotated Bibliography. LC 82-6082. (Women Studies, Facts & Issues: Vol. 3). 351p. 1982. 40.00 (ISBN 0-8240-9396-8). Garland Pub.
Borer, J. R. Design & Control of Chemical Process Systems. 1976. 28.50 o.p. (ISBN 0-07-084447-X, P&RB). McGraw.
Borer, Mary C. Background to Archaeology. 172p. 1975. 12.00 o.p. (ISBN 0-7207-0744-7). Transatlantic.
--Mayfair: The Years of Grandeur. (Illus.). 308p. 1976. 15.00 o.p. (ISBN 0-491-01645-X). Transatlantic.
Boresi, Arthur P. & Lynn, Paul P. Elasticity in Engineering Mechanics. (Civil Engineering & Engineering Mechanics Ser.). 1974. 38.95 (ISBN 0-13-247080-2). P-H.
Boresi, Arthur P., et al. Advanced Mechanics of Materials. 3rd ed. LC 77-28283. 696p. 1978. text ed. 38.95x (ISBN 0-471-08892-7). Wiley.
Boreta, Anne & Cashel, Sue. Gummy Bear Goes to Camp. LC 82-50668. (Illus.). 48p. (Orig.). 1982. pap. 3.95 (ISBN 0-89815-075-2). Ten Speed Pr.
Boretz, Benjamin & Cone, Edward T., eds. Perspectives on Contemporary Music Theory. 304p. (Orig.). 1972. pap. 5.95 (ISBN 0-393-00548-8, Norton Lib). Norton.
--Perspectives on Notation & Performance. (Illus.). 1976. 10.00x o.p. (ISBN 0-393-02190-4, Norton Lib); pap. 3.95 o.p. (ISBN 0-393-00809-6). Norton.
Boreus, Lars O. Fetal Pharmacology. 445p. 1973. text ed. 33.00 (ISBN 0-911216-32-4). Raven.
Borg, Alan. Architectural Sculpture in Romanesque Provence. (Oxford Studies in the History of Art & Architecture). 1972. 39.00x o.p. (ISBN 0-19-817192-7). Oxford U Pr.
Borg, Albert J. & De Waard, Jan. A Study of Aspect in Maltese. xvi, 188p. 1981. 15.50 (ISBN 0-89720-042-X); pap. 10.50 (ISBN 0-89720-043-8). Karoma.
Borg, Bjorn. Bjorn Borg: My Life & Game. 1980. 11.95 o.p. (ISBN 0-671-41207-8). S&S.
Borg, I. Y. & Smith, D. K. Calculated X-Ray Powder Patterns for Silicate Minerals. LC 72-110814. (Memoir Ser.: No. 122). (Illus.). 1970. 10.00x (ISBN 0-8137-1122-3). Geol Soc.
Borg, John. Descriptive Flora of the Maltese Islands Including the Ferns & Flowering Plants. 846p. 1976. pap. text ed. 79.20 (ISBN 3-87429-104-9). Lubrecht & Cramer.
Borg, Nan, ed. see American Association of Critical Care Nurses.
Borg, Nicholas & David, Leonard. Arson: A Multi-Dimensional Problem. 1976. 2.50 (ISBN 0-686-17606-5, TR 76-4). Society Fire Protect.
Borg, S. F. Fundamentals of Engineering Elasticity. LC 62-1352. 288p. 1973. Repr. of 1962 ed. lib. bdg. 16.50 (ISBN 0-88275-089-5). Krieger.
Borgatta, Edgar F., et al. Social Workers' Perceptions of Clients: A Study of the Caseload of a Social Agency. LC 80-27204. 92p. 1981. Repr. of 1960 ed. lib. bdg. 19.25x (ISBN 0-313-22812-4, BOSW). Greenwood.
Borge, Victor & Sherman, Robert. Borge's Musical Briefs. 1982. pap. write for info. o.p. (ISBN 0-417-07500-6). Methuen Inc.
Borgen, C. Winston, jt. auth. see Miller, Gary A.
Borger, R. & Cioffi, F., eds. Explanation in the Behavioural Sciences. LC 71-105497. 1970. 60.00 (ISBN 0-521-07820-2); pap. 22.95 (ISBN 0-521-09905-6). Cambridge U Pr.
Borger, Robert & Seaborne, A. E. The Psychology of Learning. rev. ed. 1982. pap. 5.95 (ISBN 0-14-080443-9, Pelican). Penguin.
Borgers, M., ed. see International Symposium on Microtubule Inhibitors, Belgium, 1975.
Borges, J. L. Irish Strategies. (Dolmen Editions: No. XXI). (Illus.). 87p. 1975. text ed. 39.00x o.p. (ISBN 0-85105-277-0, Dolmen Pr). Humanities.
Borges, Jorge L. The Aleph & Other Stories Nineteen Thirty-Three to Nineteen Sixty-Nine. 1979. pap. 5.95 (ISBN 0-525-45037-8, 0578-170). Dutton.
--Ficciones. Kerrigan, Anthony, ed. & intro. by. 1962. pap. 4.95 (ISBN 0-394-17244-2, E368, Ever). Grove.
--Six Problems for Don Isidro Parodi. 160p. 1981. 13.95 (ISBN 0-525-20480-6, 01354-410). Dutton.
Borges, Jorge L. & Bioy-Cesares, Adolfo. Six Problems for Don Isidro Parodi. Di Giovanni, Norman T., tr. 160p. 1983. pap. 6.95 (ISBN 0-525-48035-8, 0481-140). Dutton.
Borges, Jorge L. & De Torres, Esther Z. An Introduction to American Literature. Keating, L. Clark & Evans, Robert O., eds. Keating, L. Clark & Evans, Robert O., trs. from Sp. LC 73-147854. 1973. pap. 2.25 o.p. (ISBN 0-8052-0403-2). Schocken.
Borges, Jorge L., et al. Dante Studies, Vol. I: Dante in the Twentieth Century. Date not set. 15.00; lea. 25.00; leather ltd. ed. 50.00. Branden.
Borgese, Elisabeth M. & Ginsburg, Norton. Ocean Yearbook, No. 3. LC 79-642855. 672p. 1982. lib. bdg. 49.00x (ISBN 0-226-06604-5). U of Chicago Pr.
Borgese, Elisabeth M. & Ginsburg, Norton, eds. Ocean Yearbook Two. LC 79-642855. 1981. 40.00x (ISBN 0-226-06603-7). U of Chicago Pr.
Borgese, Elizabeth M. & Ginsburg, Norton, eds. Ocean Yearbook One Nineteen Seventy-Seven. 1979. 30.00x (ISBN 0-226-06602-9). U of Chicago Pr.
Borgeson, Bet. The Colored Pencil: Key Concepts for Handling the Medium. (Illus.). 144p. 1983. 22.50 (ISBN 0-8230-0742-1). Watson-Guptill.
Borghetty, H. C., jt. tr. see Edelstein, Sidney M.
Borgman, Albert S. The Life & Death of William Mountfort. (Harvard Studies in English Ser: Vol. 15). Repr. of 1935 ed. 23.00 (ISBN 0-384-05135-9). Johnson Repr.
Borgman, Harry. Advertising Layout: A Step-by-Step Guide for Print & T.V. (Illus.). 160p. 1983. 22.50 (ISBN 0-8230-0154-7). Watson-Guptill.
Borgman, Jim. Smorgasborgman. Borgman, Lynn G., ed. (Illus.). 160p. (Orig.). 1982. pap. 6.95 (ISBN 0-9609632-0-0). Armadillo Pr.
Borgman, Lynn G., ed. see Borgman, Jim.
Borgo, Ludovico. The Works of Mariotto Abertinelli. LC 75-23781. (Outstanding Dissertations in the Fine Arts - 16th Century). (Illus.). 1976. lib. bdg. 60.50 o.s.i. (ISBN 0-8240-1978-4). Garland Pub.
Borgstedt, Doug & Borgstedt, Jean. The Pet Set, Bk II. 1979. pap. 2.00 o.p. (ISBN 0-87666-637-3, PS-766). TFH Pubns.
Borgstedt, Jean, jt. auth. see Borgstedt, Doug.
Borgstrom, G. Harvesting the Earth. (Illus.). 1973. 11.49i (ISBN 0-200-71974-2). Har-Row.
Borhek, James T. & Curtis, Richard F. A Sociology of Belief. LC 80-12472. 216p. 1983. Repr. of 1975 ed. lib. bdg. write for info. (ISBN 0-89874-177-7). Krieger.
Borich, Gary D., jt. auth. see Kash, Marilynn M.
Borick, Paul M., ed. Chemical Sterilization. LC 73-4967. (Benchmark Papers in Microbiology Ser.). 368p. 1973. 46.50 o.s.i. (ISBN 0-12-786180-7). Acad Pr.
Boring, Edwin G. History of Experimental Psychology. 2nd ed. 1950. 29.95 (ISBN 0-13-390039-8). P-H.
Boring, M. Eugene. Sayings of the Risen Jesus: Christian Prophecy in the Synoptic Tradition. LC 81-18022. (Society for New Testament Studies Monograph: No. 46). (Illus.). 310p. 1981. 39.50 (ISBN 0-521-24117-0). Cambridge U Pr.
Boring, Phyllis Z. Elena Quiroga. (World Authors Ser.). 1977. lib. bdg. 15.95 (ISBN 0-8057-6296-5, Twayne). G K Hall.
--Victor Ruiz Iriarte. (World Authors Ser.). 1980. lib. bdg. 15.95 (ISBN 0-8057-6382-1, Twayne). G K Hall.
Borins, Sandford F. The Language of the Skies: The Bilingual Air Traffic Control Conflict in Canada. (Canadian Public Administration Series: IPAC). 352p. 1983. 30.00x (ISBN 0-7735-0402-8); pap. 12.95 (ISBN 0-7735-0403-6). McGill-Queens U Pr.
Boris, Martin. Woodridge, Nineteen Forty-Six. 352p. 1980. 11.95 o.p. (ISBN 0-517-54109-2). Crown.
Borisov, C. B. & Dubinin, Y. V. Modern Diplomacy of Capitalist Powers. (World Leaders Speeches & Writings Ser.). 396p. 1983. 50.00 (ISBN 0-08-028173-7). Pergamon.
Boritt, Gabor S. Lincoln & the Economics of the American Dream. LC 78-2926. 1978. 16.95x o.p. (ISBN 0-87870-043-9). Memphis St Univ.
Borjas, George J. Union Control of Pension Funds: Will the North Rise Again? LC 79-66581. 41p. 1979. pap. 2.00 (ISBN 0-917616-36-7). ICS Pr.
--Wage Policy in the Federal Bureaucracy. 1980. pap. 4.25 (ISBN 0-8447-3410-1). Am Enterprise.
Bork, A. Computer Assisted Learning in Physics Education. (Illus.). 90p. 1980. 33.00 (ISBN 0-08-025812-3). Pergamon.
Bork, Robert H. The Antitrust Paradox: A Policy at War with Itself. LC 77-74573. 462p. 1980. pap. 9.50 (ISBN 0-465-00370-2). Basic.
Borka, H., jt. ed. see Slamecka, V.
Borkat, Roberta F. & Backscheider, P. R., eds. The Plays of Richard Cumberland: Eighteenth Century English Drama Ser, 3 Vols. LC 78-66651. lib. bdg. 50.00 (ISBN 0-8240-3587-9). Garland Pub.
Borkin, Ann. Form & Function. Ross, John R. & Lakoff, George, eds. (Language & Being Ser.). 232p. 1983. 17.50 (ISBN 0-89391-116-X). Ablex Pub.
Borkin, Sheldon A. Data Models: A Semantic Approach for Database Systems. (Illus.). 275p. 1980. 30.00x (ISBN 0-262-02151-X). MIT Pr.
Borklund, C. W. The Department of Defense. 2nd rev. ed. (Illus.). 400p. 1983. lib. bdg. 27.50x (ISBN 0-86531-384-9). Westview.
Borkowski, John G. & Anderson, D. Chris. Experimental Psychology: Tactics of Behavioral Research. 1977. pap. 15.50x (ISBN 0-673-15085-2). Scott F.
Borkowski, John G., jt. auth. see Anderson, D. Chris.
Borkowski, Pioter. English-Polish Dictionary of Idioms & Phrases. 244p. (Orig.). 1983. pap. 6.95. Hippocrene Bks.
Borland, Douglas. Homeopathy in Practice. reprint ed. LC 82-84366. 1983. pap. 9.95 (ISBN 0-87983-326-2). Keats.
Borland, Hal. The Golden Circle: A Book of Months. LC 77-23560. (Illus.). (gr. 5 up). 1977. 12.45i (ISBN 0-690-03803-8, TYC-J). Har-Row.
--Hal Borland's Book of Days. 1976. 12.95 (ISBN 0-394-40187-5). Knopf.
--The History of Wildlife in America. Bourne, Russell & MacConomy, Alma D., eds. LC 75-15494. (Illus.). 208p. 1975. 14.95 o.p. (ISBN 0-912186-20-8). Natl Wildlife.
--How to Write & Sell Non-Fiction. LC 72-7972. 223p. 1973. Repr. of 1956 ed. lib. bdg. 17.50x (ISBN 0-8371-6558-X, BONF). Greenwood.
Borland, Harold, tr. see Engstrom, Albert.
Borland, James A. Christ in the Old Testament. 1978. pap. 4.95 o.p. (ISBN 0-8024-1391-9). Moody.
Borlaug, Norman, jt. auth. see Hanson, Haldore.
Borlick, Martha M., et al. Community Health Nursing. 2nd ed. (Nursing Examination Bk.: Vol. 9). 1974. pap. 7.50 (ISBN 0-87488-509-4). Med Exam.
Borman, Ernest, et al. Interpersonal Communication in the Modern Organization. 2nd ed. (Illus.). 304p. 1982. text ed. 21.95 (ISBN 0-13-475061-6). P-H.
Borman, K. M. The Social Life of Children in a Changing Society. (Illus.). 320p. 1982. text ed. 29.95 (ISBN 0-89859-187-2). L Erlbaum Assoc.
Borman, Kathryn M., ed. The Social Life of Children in a Changing Society. 320p. 1982. text ed. 29.95 (ISBN 0-89391-165-8). Ablex Pub.
Bormann, E., et al. Interpersonal Communication in the Modern Organization. 1969. text ed. 19.95 o.p. (ISBN 0-13-475038-1). P-H.
Bormuth, Robert, jt. auth. see Usher, Michael.
Born, Ann R., tr. see Brandt, Frithiof.
Born, Dorothy. Diabetes in the Family. (Illus.). 1982. 12.95 (ISBN 0-89303-067-8); pap. 9.95 (ISBN 0-89303-075-9). R J Brady.
Born, G. V., jt. auth. see Bagge, U.
Born, Juergen, ed. see Kafka, Franz.
Born, Karl B. International Banking in the 19th & 20th Centuries. Berghahn, Volker R., tr. LC 82-42715. 360p. 1983. 30.00x (ISBN 0-312-41975-9). St Martin.
Born, Max. The Restless Universe. LC 51-13192. 1951. lib. bdg. 13.50x (ISBN 0-88307-609-8). Gannon.
Born, Nicolas. The Deception. Vennewitz, Leila, tr. 1983. 15.00i (ISBN 0-316-10273-3). Little.
Bornand, Odette, ed. see Rossetti, W. M.
Bornemann, Bernd. A. Paul Weber. 229p. (Ger.). 1982. write for info. (ISBN 3-8204-6952-4). P Lang Pubs.
Bornet, E. & Flahault, C. Revision Des Noostocacees Heterocystees: Contocacees Dans les Principaux Herbiers De France, Vol. 1. 1969. 24.00 (ISBN 3-7682-0002-7). Lubrecht & Cramer.
Bornet, E. & Thuret, G. Notes Algologiques: Recueil D'observation Sur les Algues, 2 parts in 1 vol. (Bibl. Phyco.: Vol. 9). (Illus.). 1969. 80.00 (ISBN 3-7682-0601-7). Lubrecht & Cramer.
Bornkamm, Gunther, et al. Tradition & Interpretation in Matthew. LC 63-10495. 1963. 13.95 (ISBN 0-664-20453-8). Westminster.
Bornkamm, Heinrich. Luther in Mid-Career 1521-1530. Bachmann, E. Theodore, tr. from German. LC 82-48591. 736p. 1983. 36.95 (ISBN 0-8006-0692-2, 1-692). Fortress.
Bornoff, Jack, ed. Music Theatre in a Changing Society: The Influence of the Technical Media. 1968. pap. 6.00 o.p. (ISBN 92-3-100709-2, U397, UNESCO). Unipub.
Borns, Steven. People of Plains, Ga. (Illus.). 1978. pap. 7.95 o.p. (ISBN 0-07-006535-7, SP). McGraw.
Bornschlegel, Ruth. More Fast & Fresh. LC 82-824814. (Illus.). 240p. 1983. pap. 14.95 (ISBN 0-686-42800-5, HarpT). Har-Row.
Bornstein, Diane. The Lady in the Tower: Medieval Courtesy. (Literature For Women Ser.). 1983. lib. bdg. 15.00 (ISBN 0-208-01995-2, Archon). Shoe String.
Bornstein, Diane, ed. Distaves & Dames: Renaissance Treatises for & About Women. LC 78-15069. 1978. 85.00x (ISBN 0-8201-1317-4). Schol Facsimiles.
Bornstein, Diane D. An Introduction to Transformational Grammar. (Orig.). 1977. text ed. 15.95 (ISBN 0-316-10277-6); pap. text ed. 9.95 (ISBN 0-316-10278-4). Little.
Bornstein, Harry & Saulnier, Karen L., eds. The Comprehensive Signed English Dictionary. LC 82-21044. (Illus.). x, 454p. 1983. 27.95 (ISBN 0-913580-81-3). Gallaudet Coll.
Bornstein, Morris, ed. Economic Planning, East & West. LC 75-20470. 416p. 1975. prof ref 25.00x (ISBN 0-88410-283-1). Ballinger Pub.
--The Soviet Economy: Continuity & Change. 532p. (Orig.). 1981. lib. bdg. 34.50 (ISBN 0-89158-958-9); pap. text ed. 12.95 (ISBN 0-89158-959-7). Westview.
Bornstein, Ruth. Annabelle. LC 77-20059. (Illus.). (gr. k-1). 1978. o. p. 4.95i (ISBN 0-690-03804-6, TYC-J); PLB 7.89 (ISBN 0-690-03810-0). Har-Row.
--Of Course a Goat. LC 79-2015. (Illus.). (ps-3). 1980. 7.95 o.p. (ISBN 0-06-020608-X, HarpJ); PLB 8.89 (ISBN 0-06-020609-8). Har-Row.
Bornstein, Scott. Vocabulary Mastery. (Illus.). 272p. (YA) (gr. 9-12). 1982. 19.95 (ISBN 0-9602610-1-X). Bornstein Memory.

Boroch, Rose M. Elements of Rehabilitation in Nursing: An Introduction. LC 76-4590. (Illus.). 1976. pap. text ed. 13.95 o.p. (ISBN 0-8016-1425-2). Mosby.

Borochov, Ber. Class Struggle & the Jewish Nation: Selected Essays in Marxist Zionism. Cohen, Mitchell, ed. 358p. 1983. 29.95 (ISBN 0-87855-479-3). Transaction Bks.

Borodin, A. & Munn, I. Computational Complexity of Algebraic & Numeric Problems. (Theory of Computation Ser.: Vol. 1). 1975. 16.95 (ISBN 0-444-00168-9, North Holland); pap. 14.50 (ISBN 0-444-00156-5). Elsevier.

Borodin, A., jt. auth. see Gotlieb, C. C.

Boroffka, Alexander. Benedict Nta Tanka's Commentary & Dramatized Ideas on Disease & Witchcraft in Our Society: A Schreber Case from Cameroon African on His Mental Illness. (Medical Care in Developing Countries Ser.: Vol. 7). 150p. 1980. write for info. (ISBN 3-8204-6901-X). P Lang Pubs.

Boros, Ladislaus. God's Image & Faith. Cunningham, Robert, tr. 1983. 6.00 (ISBN 0-8199-0858-4). Franciscan Herald.

--Meeting God in Man. 1971. pap. 1.45 o.p. (ISBN 0-385-05377-0, Im). Doubleday.

Boros, Laszlo, tr. see Detshy, Mihaly.

Boroson, Warren. How to Buy or Sell Your Home in a Changing Market. 250p. 1983. softcover 15.95 (ISBN 0-87489-278-3). Med Economics.

Boross, L., jt. auth. see Kremmer, T.

Borovits, Israel & Seev, Neumann. Computer Systems Performance Evaluation: Criteria, Measurement, Techniques, & Costs. (Illus.). 160p. 1979. 17.95x (ISBN 0-669-02802-9). Lexington Bks.

Borow, Henry, et al. Career Guidance for a New Age. (Illus.). 336p. 1973. text ed. 21.95 o.p. (ISBN 0-395-14362-4, 3-05191). HM.

Borow, Lawrence S., ed. see Semm, K.

Borow, Maxwell. Body Function in Health & Disease. 3rd ed. 1982. pap. text ed. 22.50 (ISBN 0-87488-758-5). Med Exam.

Borowiec, Andrew. The Mediterranean Feud. 206p. 1983. 28.95 (ISBN 0-03-061847-9). Praeger.

Borowitz, Albert. A Gallery of Sinister Perspectives: Ten Crimes & a Scandal. LC 81-19352. 250p. 1982. 0.00 o.p. (ISBN 0-87338-264-1); pap. 5.75 (ISBN 0-87338-271-4). Kent St U Pr.

Borowitz, Eugene B. Choices in Modern Jewish Thought. 352p. 1983. pap. text ed. 9.95x (ISBN 0-87441-343-5). Behrman.

--Pondering God: The Jewish Way. LC 82-6702. 250p. Date not set. 20.00 (ISBN 0-87668-600-5). Aronson.

--Reform Judaism Today. 800p. 1983. pap. text ed. 9.95x (ISBN 0-87441-364-8). Behrman.

--Reform Judaism Today: How We Live, Bk. 3. LC 78-24676. 1978. pap. text ed. 2.50x o.p. (ISBN 0-87441-273-0). Behrman.

--Reform Judaism Today: Reform in the Process of Change, Bk. 1. LC 78-24676. 1978. pap. text ed. 2.50x o.p. (ISBN 0-87441-271-4). Behrman.

--Reform Judaism Today: What We Believe, Bk. 2. LC 77-24676. 1977. pap. text ed. 2.50x o.p. (ISBN 0-87441-272-2). Behrman.

Borowitz, Eugene B., ed. see Rosner, Joseph.

Borradaile, B. & Borradaile, R. Strasburg Manuscript: A Medieval Painters Handbook. 10.00 o.s.i. (ISBN 0-685-20636-X). Transatlantic.

Borradaile, L. A. & Potts, F. A. Invertebrata. 4th ed. 1961. text ed. 39.50x (ISBN 0-521-04285-2). Cambridge U Pr.

Borradaile, R., jt. auth. see Borradaile, B.

Borras, A. A., ed. The Theatre & Hispanic Life: Essays in Honour of Neale H. Taylor. 97p. 1982. text ed. 11.50x (ISBN 0-88920-129-3, Pub. by Wilfred Laurier U Pr Canada). Humanities.

Borrego, John. Space Grid Structures: Skeletal Frameworks & Stressed Skin Systems. (Report Ser.: No. 11). 1968. pap. 7.95x (ISBN 0-262-52009-5). MIT Pr.

Borrell, Alexander. Mamiya M645 Book. 128p. 1983. pap. 9.95 (ISBN 0-240-51197-2). Focal Pr.

Borrell, Clive & Cashinella, Brian. Crime in Britain Today. (Illus.). 232p. 1975. 17.95 o.p. (ISBN 0-7100-8232-0). Routledge & Kegan.

Borrello, Alfred. Gabriel Fielding. (English Authors Ser.): 1974. lib. bdg. 14.95 (ISBN 0-8057-1194-5, Twayne). G K Hall.

Borren, Charles V. Sources of Keyboard Music in England. Matthew, James E., tr. LC 78-106714 Repr. of 1914 ed. lib. bdg. 18.00x (ISBN 0-8371-3444-7, BOKM). Greenwood.

Borresen, Kari E. Subordination & Equivalence: The Nature & Role of Women in Augustine & Thomas Aquinas. Talbot, Charles H., tr. from Fr. & Ital. LC 80-67199. 390p. 1981. lib. bdg. 23.25 (ISBN 0-8191-1681-5); pap. text ed. 13.50 (ISBN 0-8191-1682-3). U Pr of Amer.

Borreson, Mary Jo. Let's Go to Colonial Williamsburg. (Building America Ser.). (Illus.). (gr. 4-6). 1962. PLB 4.29 o.p. (ISBN 0-399-60360-3). Putnam Pub Group.

--Let's Go to Plymouth with the Pilgrims. (Building America Ser.). (Illus.). (gr. 4-6). 1963. PLB 4.29 o.p. (ISBN 0-399-60391-3). Putnam Pub Group.

Borrie, W. D. Population, Environment, & Society. (Illus.). 1974. pap. 4.95x o.p. (ISBN 0-19-647730-1). Oxford U Pr.

Borrie, Y. M., jt. auth. see Burghes, D. N.

Borroff, Edith. Music in Europe & the United States: A History. (Illus.). 1971. text ed. 24.95 (ISBN 0-13-608083-9). P-H.

--The Music of the Baroque. LC 77-17401. (Music Reprint Ser.: 1978). (Illus.). 1978. Repr. of 1970 ed. lib. bdg. 22.50 (ISBN 0-306-77438-0). Da Capo.

Borroff, Edith & Irvin, Marjory. Music in Perspective. (Illus.). 310p. (Orig.). 1976. pap. text ed. 13.95 (ISBN 0-15-564883-7, HC); 6 record set 19.95 (ISBN 0-15-564884-5). HarBraceJ.

Borroff, Edith, ed. see De Mondonville, Jean-Joseph C.

Borror, Donald J. Songs of Western Birds. 1970. pap. 4.95 booklet with record (ISBN 0-486-22765-0). Dover.

Borrow, George. Romano Lavo-Lil: A Book of the Gypsy. 192p. 1982. pap. text ed. 6.25x (ISBN 0-86299-024-6, Pub. by Alan Sutton England). Humanities.

--Romany Rye. 1948. 7.00 o.p. (ISBN 0-248-98251-6). Dufour.

Borsch, Frederick H. Coming Together in the Spirit. 1981. pap. 1.10 (ISBN 0-8358-0426-7). Upper Room.

Borsch-Supan, Helmut. Caspar David Friedrich. LC 73-93687. (Illus.). 184p. 1974. 35.00 o.s.i. (ISBN 0-8076-0747-9). Braziller.

Borsenik, Frank D. The Management of Maintenance & Engineering Systems in Hospitality Industries. LC 78-13677. (Service Management Ser.). 494p. 1979. text ed. 27.95 (ISBN 0-471-03213-1). Wiley.

Borsh, Frederick H. Power in Weakness: New Hearing for Gospel Stories of Healing & Discipleship. LC 82-15997. 160p. 1983. pap. 8.95 (ISBN 0-8006-1703-7, 1-1703). Fortress.

Borsody, Stephen, tr. from Hungar see Janics, Kalman.

Borsook, Eve. Companion Guide to Florence. (Illus.). 432p. 1983. 16.95 (ISBN 0-13-154484-5); pap. 8.95 (ISBN 0-13-154476-4). P-H.

--The Mural Painters of Tuscany: From Cimabue to Andrea Del Sarto. (Oxford Studies in the History of Art & Architecture Ser.). (Illus.). 1981. 150.00x (ISBN 0-19-817301-6). Oxford U Pr.

Borssuck, B. Ninety-Seven Needlepoint Alphabets. LC 74-19792. (Illus.). 128p. 1975. lib. bdg. 7.95 o.p. (ISBN 0-668-03723-7); pap. 6.95 (ISBN 0-668-03655-9). Arco.

Borst, Bill. Baseball Through a Knothole. (Orig.). 1980. pap. 5.95 (ISBN 0-940056-05-4). Chapter & Cask.

--A Fan's Memoir: The Brooklyn Dodgers 1953-1957. 106p. (Orig.). 1982. pap. 5.95 (ISBN 0-940056-09-7). Chapter & Cask.

Borsy, J. Symposium on Gastrin & It's Antagonists, Vol. 3. (Hungarian Pharmacological Society, First Congress Ser.). (Illus.). 153p. 1973. 10.00 (ISBN 0-8002-3045-0). Intl Pubns Serv.

Bort, Barry D., jt. auth. see Marks, Alfred H.

Borten, Helen. Halloween. LC 65-16184. (Holiday Ser.). (Illus.). (gr. 1-3). 1965. PLB 9.89 (ISBN 0-690-36314-1, TYC-J). Har-Row.

Borthwick, Bruce M. Comparative Politics of the Middle East: An Introduction. 1980. pap. text ed. 13.95 (ISBN 0-13-154088-2). P-H.

Borthwick, J. S. The Case of the Hook-Billed Kites. 256p. 1982. 12.95 (ISBN 0-312-12335-3). St Martin.

Borthwick, Sally. Education & Social Change in China: The Beginning of the Modern Era, No. 268. LC 81-83853. (Publication Ser.). (Illus.). 250p. 1983. lib. bdg. 21.95 (ISBN 0-8179-7681-7). Hoover Inst Pr.

Bortin, Mortimer, ed. Alien Histocompatibility Antigens on Cancer Cells: Biologic Significance & Potential Usefulness in Prevention, Diagnosis, & Treatment, Vol. 2. (A "Transplantation Proceedings" Reprint Ser.). 244p. 1982. 49.50 (ISBN 0-8089-1492-8, 79045). Grune.

Bortner, Doyle M. Public Relations for Public Schools. LC 79-183947. 400p. 1983. text ed. 18.95 (ISBN 0-87073-508-X); pap. text ed. 8.95 (ISBN 0-87073-509-8). Schenkman.

Bortner, M. A. Inside a Juvenile Court: The Tarnished Ideal of Individualized Justice. 328p. 1982. 42.50 (ISBN 0-8147-1041-7). NYU Pr.

Borton, Hugh. Japan's Modern Century--from Perry to 1970. 2nd ed. 610p. 1970. 25.50x (ISBN 0-471-07032-7). Wiley.

Bortz, John, jt. auth. see Mader, Chris.

Boruch, Robert F. & Cecil, Joe S., eds. Solutions to Ethical & Legal Problems in Social Research: Symposuim. (Quantitative Studies in Social Relations). Date not set. 27.5007615723x (ISBN 0-12-118680-6). Acad Pr.

Boruch, Robert F., ed. see Social Science Research Council Conference on Social Experiments.

Borus, Michael E., ed. Tomorrow's Workers. 208p. 1982. 25.95 (ISBN 0-669-06090-9). Lexington Bks.

Borwick, John. The Gramophone Guide to Hi-Fi. (Illus.). 260p. 1982. 31.50 (ISBN 0-7153-8231-4). David & Charles.

Borys, Jurij. The Russian Communist Party & the Sovietization of Ukraine: A Study in the Communist Doctrine of the Self-Determination of Nations. LC 79-2895. 374p. 1981. Repr. of 1960 ed. 37.50 (ISBN 0-8305-0063-4). Hyperion Conn.

Borza, Eugene, et al. Studies in the History of Art 1982, Vol. 10. LC 72-600309. (Illus.). pap. 18.95 (ISBN 0-89468-005-6). Natl Gallery Art.

Borza, Eugene N., jt. ed. see Adams, W. Lindsay.

Borzaga, Reynold. In Pursuit of Religion. pap. 4.95 (ISBN 0-941850-01-3). Sunday Pubn.

Bos, H. C., ed. Towards Balanced International Growth. 1969. 30.25 (ISBN 0-444-10153-5, North-Holland). Elsevier.

Bos, L. Symptoms of Virus Diseases in Plants. 3rd ed. (Illus.). 225p. 1978. 25.00 (ISBN 0-686-93182-3, PDC6, Pudoc). Unipub.

Bos, V. T., jt. ed. see Hajnal, A.

Bosanquet, B. Meeting of Extremes in Contemporary Philosophy. Repr. of 1921 ed. 12.00 o.p. (ISBN 0-527-10030-7). Kraus Repr.

Bosanquet, Bernard. Philosophical Theory of the State. 4th ed. 1899. 8.95 o.p. (ISBN 0-312-60550-1). St Martin.

Bosanquet, E. F. English Printed Almanacks & Prognostications: A Bibliographical History to Sixteen Hundred. Repr. of 1917 ed. lib. bdg. 27.50x (ISBN 0-87991-961-2). Porcupine Pr.

Bosanquet, Helen. The Strength of the People: A Study in Social Economics. 2nd ed. LC 79-56950. (The English Working Class Ser.). 1980. lib. bdg. 30.00 o.s.i. (ISBN 0-8240-0104-4). Garland Pub.

Bosanquet, N. & Townsend, P. Labour & Equality. 1980. text ed. 22.00x (ISBN 0-435-83105-4). Heinemann Ed.

Bosanquet, T. Henry James at Work. (Studies in Henry James, No. 17). 1970. pap. 11.95x (ISBN 0-8383-0009-X). Haskell.

Bosar, Gary J. Mechanical End Face Seals-Guidelines for the Pulp & Paper Industry. (Illus.). 21p. 1981. 24.95 (ISBN 0-89852-392-3, 01-01-R092). TAPPI.

Bosch, David J. Witness to the World: The Christian Mission in Theological Perspective. LC 79-91241. (New Foundations Theological Library). 285p. (Series editors Peter Toon & Ralph Martin). 1980. 12.95 (ISBN 0-8042-3706-9, 3706-9). John Knox.

Bosch, Donald & Bosch, Eloise. Seashells of Oman. LC 81-14236. (Illus.). 1982. text ed. 35.00x (ISBN 0-582-78309-7). Longman.

Bosch, Eloise, jt. auth. see Bosch, Donald.

Boschke, F., ed. Inorganic & Analytical Chemistry. LC 51-5497. (Topics in Current Chemistry: Vol. 26). (Illus.). 125p. 1972. pap. 26.00 o.p. (ISBN 0-387-05589-4). Springer-Verlag.

--Reactive Intermediates. LC 51-5497. (Topics in Current Chemistry: Vol. 16, Pt. 1). (Illus.). 1970. pap. 48.40 o.p. (ISBN 0-387-05103-1). Springer-Verlag.

Boschman, Roger. Hong Kong by Night. (Asia by Night Ser.). (Illus.). 64p. (Orig.). 1981. pap. 4.95 (ISBN 962-7031-07-0, Pub. by CFW Pubns Hong Kong). C E Tuttle.

Boschmann, Erwin. Dear Chris: A Letter of Advice on How to Study in College. (Illus.). 1981. write for info. (ISBN 0-930116-04-6). Sci Ent.

Bosco, Dominick. The People's Guide to Vitamins & Minerals: From A to Zinc. 1980. 12.95 o.p. (ISBN 0-8092-7140-0); pap. 7.95 (ISBN 0-8092-7139-7). Contemp Bks.

Bosco, F. J. & Lolli, F. Incontro Con l'Italiano: Primo Corso. 403p. 1967. text ed. 18.95 o.p. (ISBN 0-471-00040-X); tapes o.p. (ISBN 0-471-00041-8). Wiley.

Bosco, James J. & Robin, Stanley S. The Hyperactive Child & Stimulant Drugs. LC 76-57934. 1977. 14.00x (ISBN 0-226-06661-4). U of Chicago Pr.

Bosco, James S. & Gustafson, William F. Measurement & Evaluation in Physical Education, Fitness & Sports. (Illus.). 384p. 1983. 21.95 (ISBN 0-13-568352-1). P-H.

Bosco, Ronald A., ed. Lessons for the Children of Godly Ancestors. LC 82-5444. 1983. 50.00 (ISBN 0-8201-1381-6). Schol Facsimiles.

Bosco, Ronald A., ed. see Mather, Cotton.

Bose, A. N. Calcutta & Rural Bengal: Small Sector Symbiosis. 1978. 17.50x o.p. (ISBN 0-8364-0305-3). South Asia Bks.

Bose, Arun. Political Paradoxes & Puzzles. (Illus.). 1978. pap. text ed. 5.50x o.p. (ISBN 0-19-827417-3). Oxford U Pr.

Bose, Ashish, et al, eds. Social Statistics: Health & Education. 375p. 1982. text ed. 37.50 (ISBN 0-7069-1083-4, Pub. by Vikas India). Advent NY.

Bose, M. L. British Policy in the North-East Frontier Agency. 1980. text ed. 23.50x (ISBN 0-391-01833-7). Humanities.

Bose, M. L., ed. Historical & Constitutional Documents of North Eastern India. 1980. text ed. 20.50x (ISBN 0-391-01867-1). Humanities.

Bose, N. K. Adjustable Speed AC Drive Systems. LC 80-27789. 449p. 1981. 39.50 (ISBN 0-471-09395-5, Pub. by Wiley-Interscience); pap. 25.95 (ISBN 0-471-09396-3, Pub. by Wiley-Interscience). Wiley.

--Multidimensional Systems: Theory & Applications. (IEEE Reprint Ser.). 295p. 1979. 35.95x (ISBN 0-471-05214-0); pap. 21.50 (ISBN 0-471-05215-9, Pub. by Wiley-Interscience). Wiley.

Bose, Nirmal K., ed. Multidimensional Systems: Theory & Applications. LC 78-55096. 1979. 35.95 (ISBN 0-87942-109-6). Inst Electrical.

Bose, Prabodh C. Introduction to Juristic Psychology. (Historical Foundations of Forensic Psychiatry & Psychology Ser.). 426p. 1980. Repr. of 1917 ed. lib. bdg. 42.50 (ISBN 0-686-68561-X). Da Capo.

Bosel, T. K. & Bhattacharjee, S. K. Garden Plants. 282p. 1980. 50.00x (ISBN 0-686-84453-X, Pub. by Oxford & I B H India). State Mutual Bk.

Boseman, G., jt. auth. see Schellenberger, R.

Boseman, Glenn, jt. auth. see Schellenberger, Robert E.

Boserup, A., jt. ed. see Barnaby, C. F.

Boserup, Ester. Population & Technological Change: A Study of Long-Term Trends. LC 80-21116. (Illus.). 256p. 1981. lib. bdg. 17.50x (ISBN 0-226-06673-8); pap. 7.95 (ISBN 0-226-06674-6). U of Chicago Pr.

Bosha, Francis J. John Cheever: A Reference Guide. (Reference Books Ser.). 1981. 22.00 (ISBN 0-8161-8447-X, Hall Reference). G K Hall.

Bosha, Francis J., ed. William Faulkner's Soldier's Pay: A Bibliographical Study. LC 80-54205. 542p. 1982. 42.50x (ISBN 0-87875-211-0). Whitston Pub.

Boshear, Walton C. & Albrecht, Karl G. Understanding People: Models & Concepts. LC 75-41686. (Illus.). 275p. 1977. pap. 17.50 (ISBN 0-88390-115-3). Univ Assocs.

Boshell, Gordon. The Plot Against Buster the Dog. LC 75-186885. (Illus.). 64p. (gr. 3-5). 1972. 3.50 (ISBN 0-87955-201-8). O'Hara.

Bosi, Roberto. The Lapps. Cadell, James, tr. LC 75-32455. 1976. Repr. of 1960 ed. lib. bdg. 20.25x (ISBN 0-8371-8545-9, BOTL). Greenwood.

Bosker, Gideon, jt. auth. see Brooks, Karen.

Boskey, James B. & Hughes, Susan C. Teaching about Aging: Religious & Advocacy Perspectives. LC 82-17589. 184p. (Orig.). 1983. lib. bdg. 20.75 (ISBN 0-8191-2802-3); pap. text ed. 10.00 (ISBN 0-8191-2803-1). U Pr of Amer.

Boskin, Joseph. Into Slavery: Racial Decisions in the Virginia Colony. LC 79-5347. 1979. pap. text ed. 8.25 (ISBN 0-8191-0868-5). U Pr of Amer.

--Issues in American Society. 1978. pap. text ed. 11.95 (ISBN 0-02-472330-4). Macmillan.

--Opposition Politics: The Anti-New Deal Tradition. (Insight Series: Studies in Contemporary Issues). 1968. pap. text ed. 6.95 (ISBN 0-02-473770-4). Macmillan.

--Urban Racial Violence, in the Twentieth Century. 2nd ed. 1976. pap. 7.95x (ISBN 0-02-470890-9). Macmillan.

Boskin, Joseph & Rosenstone, Robert A., eds. Seasons of Rebellion: Protest & Radicalism in Recent America. LC 79-9678. 349p. 1980. text ed. 21.75 (ISBN 0-8191-0976-2); pap. text ed. 11.50 (ISBN 0-8191-0977-0). U Pr of Amer.

Boskin, Michael J., ed. The Crisis in Social Security: Problems & Prospects. 2nd ed. LC 77-72542. 222p. 1978. pap. text ed. 6.95 (ISBN 0-917616-25-1). ICS Pr.

--The Economy in the 1980s: A Program for Growth & Stability. LC 80-80647. 462p. (Orig.). 1980. text ed. 17.95 (ISBN 0-87855-399-1); pap. text ed. 7.95 (ISBN 0-917616-39-1). Transaction Bks.

--Federal Tax Reform: Myths & Realities. LC 78-61661. 270p. 1978. pap. 5.95 o.p. (ISBN 0-917616-32-4). ICS Pr.

Boskin, Michael J. & Wildavsky, Aaron, eds. The Federal Budget, Economics & Politics. LC 81-86378. 416p. 1982. text ed. 19.95 (ISBN 0-917616-49-9); pap. text ed. 8.95 (ISBN 0-917616-48-0). ICS Pr.

Boskin, Michael J., jt. ed. see Aaron, Henry J.

Boskind-White, Marlene & White, William C. Bulimarexia: The Binge-Purge Cycle. 1983. 15.00 (ISBN 0-393-01650-1). Norton.

Boskoff, Alvin. Sociology of Urban Regions. 2nd ed. (Illus.). 1970. pap. text ed. 23.95 (ISBN 0-13-821751-3). P-H.

Boskovic, Rudzer J. De Continuitatis Lege et Ejus Consectariis Pertinentibus Ad Prima Materiae Elementa Eorumque Vires. Repr. of 1754 ed. 33.00 (ISBN 0-8287-0121-0). Clearwater Pub.

Bosler, Raymond T. What They Ask About Marriage. LC 75-11019. 288p. 1975. pap. 3.50 o.p. (ISBN 0-87793-096-1). Ave Maria.

Bosley, Keith, tr. see De la Ceppede, Jean.

Bosley, Keith, tr. see Jouve, Pierre J.

Bosley, Richard. On Truth: A Neo-Pragmatist Treatise in Logic, Metaphysics & Epistemology. LC 81-43800. 244p. (Orig.). 1982. lib. bdg. 22.00 (ISBN 0-8191-2568-7); pap. text ed. 10.75 (ISBN 0-8191-2569-5). U Pr of Amer.

Bosmajian, C. Perry & Bosmajian, Linda S. Personalized Guide to Stress Evaluation. Snyder, Thomas L. & Felmeister, Charles J., eds. LC 82-8182. (Dental Practice Management Ser.). (Illus.). 103p. 1983. pap. text ed. 12.95 (ISBN 0-8016-4724-X). Mosby.

Bosmajian, Haig. The Rhetoric of Nonverbal Communication: Readings. 1971. pap. 7.95x (ISBN 0-673-07608-3). Scott F.

Bosmajian, Haig A. The Principles & Practice of Freedom of Speech. 2nd ed. LC 82-23739. 424p. 1983. pap. text ed. 15.75 (ISBN 0-8191-2962-3). U Pr of Amer.

Bosmajian, Haig A. & Bosmajian, Hamida. Rhetoric of the Civil Rights Movement. 1969. pap. text ed. 2.95 (ISBN 0-685-19763-8). Phila Bk Co.

Bosmajian, Haig A., compiled by. Censorship, Libraries, & the Law. 1983. 22.95 (ISBN 0-918212-54-5). Neal-Schuman.

Bosmajian, Hamida, jt. auth. see Bosmajian, Haig A.

Bosmajian, Linda S., jt. auth. see Bosmajian, C. Perry.

Bosman, Willem. Voyage de Guinee Contenant une Description Nouvelle et Tres Exacte de Cette Cote. (Bibliotheque Africaine Ser.). 565p. (Fr.). 1974. Repr. of 1705 ed. lib. bdg. 138.00x o.p. (ISBN 0-8287-0122-9, 72-2117). Clearwater Pub.

Bosniak, Stephen L., jt. ed. see Smith, Byron C.

Bosquet, Alain. Selected Poems. Beckett, Samuel, et al, trs. from Fr. & Eng. LC 71-181687. 189p. 1972. 12.95 (ISBN 0-8214-0111-4, 82-81149); pap. 7.95 (ISBN 0-8214-0112-2, 82-81156). Ohio U Pr.

--Speech Is Plurality. Yoken, Melvin B. & Lapointe, Juliet G., trs. from Fr. LC 78-61914. 1978. pap. text ed. 8.25 (ISBN 0-8191-0626-7). U Pr of Amer.

Bosqui & Co. Grapes & Grapevines of California. LC 81-4775. (Illus.). 64p. 1981. 29.95 (ISBN 0-15-136786-8). HarBraceJ.

Boss, Allan. Family Therapy. LC 82-15555. (Family Therapy Ser.). 253p. 1983. 20.00x (ISBN 0-89862-045-7). Guilford Pr.

Boss, Judith A. Newport: A Pictorial History. Friedman, Donna R., ed. LC 80-22896. (Illus.). 208p. 1981. pap. 12.95 o.p. (ISBN 0-89865-097-6). Donning Co.

Boss, Judy. In Silence They Return. 1972. pap. 5.00 (ISBN 0-87542-080-X). Llewellyn Pubns.

Boss, Richard W. Automating Library Acquisitions: Issues & Outlook. LC 82-8941. (Professional Librarian Ser.). 139p. 1982. pap. text ed. 27.50 (ISBN 0-86729-006-4). Knowledge Indus.

--The Library Manager's Guide to Automation. LC 79-3057. (Professional Librarian Ser.). 1979. text ed. 29.50x (ISBN 0-914236-33-4); text ed. 24.50x softcover (ISBN 0-914236-38-5). Knowledge Indus.

--The Library Manager's Guide to Automation. 165p. 1983. 36.50 (ISBN 0-86729-052-8); pap. 27.50 (ISBN 0-86729-051-X). Knowledge Indus.

Bossard, James & Boll, Eleanor. Ritual in Family Living. LC 75-45454. 228p. 1976. Repr. of 1950 ed. lib. bdg. 19.75x (ISBN 0-8371-8678-1, BORF). Greenwood.

Bossard, James & Boll, Eleanor S. Girl That You Marry. (Illus.). (gr. 9 up). 1960. 6.25 (ISBN 0-8255-1725-7). Macrae.

Bossard, James H. & Boll, Eleanor S. Family Situations: An Introduction to the Study of Child Behavior. LC 69-10071. 1969. Repr. of 1943 ed. lib. bdg. 15.50x (ISBN 0-8371-0024-0, BOCB). Greenwood.

Bossard, Samuel B., ed. see Yandell, Keith E.

Bossard, Sebastien De see De Brossard, Sebastien.

Bosscher, Marcia V., jt. auth. see Grills, Norma J.

Bosse, Abraham. Sentimens sur la distinction des manieres de peinture, dessein et graveure. (Documents of Art & Architectural History Series 2: Vol. 5). 142p. (Fr.). 1981. Repr. of 1649 ed. 27.50x (ISBN 0-89371-205-1). Broude Intl Edns.

Bosse, Malcolm. The Warlords. 1983. price not set (ISBN 0-671-44332-1). S&S.

Bosse, Malcolm J. The Barracuda Gang. 192p. (YA) 1982. 9.95 (ISBN 0-525-66737-7, 0966-290). Lodestar Bks.

Bosserman, Lorelei, jt. auth. see Simon, Kia.

Bosserman, R. W., jt. ed. see Mitsch, W. J.

Bossert, Helmuth T. Peasant Art of Europe & Asia. (Illus.). 1977. 29.50 (ISBN 0-8038-5818-3). Hastings.

Bossert, Steven T. Tasks & Social Relationships in the Classroom. LC 78-67260. (American Sociological Association Rose Monograph Ser.). 1979. 21.95 (ISBN 0-521-22445-4); pap. 7.95x (ISBN 0-521-29505-X). Cambridge U Pr.

Bossevain, Jeremy. Friends of Friends: Networks, Manipulators, & Coalitions. LC 74-83521. 288p. 1975. 19.95 o.p. (ISBN 0-312-30590-7). St Martin.

Bosshard, B. Holzkunde: Mikroskopie und Makroskopie des Holzes, Vol. 1. 225p. Date not set. 26.95 (ISBN 3-7643-1328-5). Birkhauser.

Bossi, E., ed. Praktische Neonatologie. (Paediatrische Fortbildungskurse fuer die Praxis Ser.: Vol. 57). (Illus.). viii, 150p. 1983. pap. 72.00 (ISBN 3-8055-3657-7). S Karger.

Bossone, Richard M. English Proficiency: Developing Your Reading & Writing Power, Bk. 2. (gr. 10-12). 1979. pap. text ed. 8.84 (ISBN 0-07-006591-8, W); tchrs' manual 7.76 (ISBN 0-07-006592-6). McGraw.

Bossone, Richard M. & Ashe, Amy E. English Proficiency: Developing Your Reading & Writing Power, Bk. 1. 320p. (gr. 7-9). 1980. 12.60 (ISBN 0-07-006589-6, W); tchrs. manual 7.76 (ISBN 0-07-006590-X). McGraw.

Bossone, Richard M. & Reid, James M. Handbook of Basic English Skills. 2nd ed. 1977. pap. text ed. 14.50x (ISBN 0-673-15654-0). Scott F.

Bossone, Richard M. & Reid, James M., Jr. Handbook of Basic English Skills. 2nd ed. LC 77-20017. 1977. pap. text ed. 12.95 o.p. (ISBN 0-471-02196-2). Wiley.

Bossong, Ken & Pilarski, Jan. National Passive Solar Directory. (Illus.). 100p. 1983. pap. text ed. 7.50 (ISBN 0-89988-100-9). Citizens Energy.

Bossong, Ken & Simpson, Jan. Appropriate Community Technologies Sourcebook. (Illus.). 180p. (Orig.). 1983. pap. text ed. 7.50 (ISBN 0-89988-055-X). Citizens Energy.

Bossong, Ken, et al. Solar Energy & Big Business (A Compendium of Studies) (Illus.). 50p. (Orig.). 1983. pap. text ed. 4.00 (ISBN 0-89988-082-7). Citizens Energy.

Bosstick, Maurice & Cable, John L. Patterns in the Sand: An Exploration in Mathematics. 2nd ed. (Illus.). 1975. text ed. 18.95 (ISBN 0-02-471960-9); ans. bk free (ISBN 0-02-471970-6). Macmillan.

Bostaph, Charles, jt. auth. see Moore, Marti.

Bostetter, Edward E., ed. Twentieth Century Interpretations of Don Juan. LC 76-79452. 1969. pap. 1.25 o.p. (ISBN 0-13-218693-4, Spec). P-H.

Bostian, C. W., jt. auth. see Krauss, H. L.

Bostock, Anna, tr. see Kataev, Valentin.

Bostock, Anna, tr. see Lukacs, Georg.

Bostock, David. Logic & Arithmetic, Vol. I: Natural Numbers. 1974. 45.00x (ISBN 0-19-824366-9). Oxford U Pr.

Bostok, Anna, tr. see Ehrenburg, Ilya.

Boston Athenaeum. Index of Obituaries in Boston Newspapers, 1704-1800, 3 Vols. 1968. Set. 150.00 (ISBN 0-8161-0761-0, Hall Library). G K Hall.

Boston, Bernard. History of the Three Hundred Ninety-Eighth Infantry Regiment in World War II. (Combat Arms Ser.: No. 7). (Illus.). 208p. 1982. 20.00x (ISBN 0-89839-063-X). Battery Pr.

Boston Children's Medical Center. Pregnancy, Birth & the Newborn Baby. 1972. 15.95 o.s.i. (ISBN 0-440-07088-0, Sey Lawr). Delacorte.

Boston, L. M. Adventures at Green Knowe, 5 vols. Incl. The Children of Green Knowe. Repr. of 1955 ed; Treasure of Green Knowe. Repr. of 1958 ed; The River at Green Knowe. Repr. of 1959 ed; Stranger at Green Knowe. Repr. of 1961 ed; An Enemy at Green Knowe. Repr. of 1964 ed. (Illus.). (gr. 4-7). 1979. Boxed Set. pap. text ed. 9.95 (ISBN 0-15-603246-5, VoyB). HarBraceJ.

--The Children of Green Knowe. LC 77-4506. (Illus.). (gr. 4-7). 1977. pap. 2.95 (ISBN 0-15-616870-7, VoyB). HarBraceJ.

--An Enemy at Green Knowe. LC 78-71151. (Illus.). (gr. 4-7). 1979. pap. 1.95 (ISBN 0-15-628792-7, VoyB). HarBraceJ.

--Perverse & Foolish. LC 78-71593. 180p. 1979. 8.95 o.p. (ISBN 0-689-50136-6, McElderry Bk). Atheneum.

--River at Green Knowe. LC 59-8950. (Illus.). (gr. 4-7). 1966. pap. 2.95 (ISBN 0-15-677701-0, VoyB). HarBraceJ.

--A Stranger at Green Knowe. LC 78-71150. (Illus.). (gr. 4-7). 1979. pap. 1.95 (ISBN 0-15-685657-3, VoyB). HarBraceJ.

--The Treasure of Green Knowe. LC 77-16689. (Illus.). (gr. 4-7). 1978. pap. 1.95 (ISBN 0-15-691302-X, VoyB). HarBraceJ.

Boston, Lucy M. River at Green Knowe. LC 57-8950. (Illus.). (gr. 4-7). 1959. 5.95 o.p. (ISBN 0-15-267446-2, HJ). HarBraceJ.

--Sea Egg. LC 67-10200. (Illus.). (gr. 2-5). 1967. 8.95 (ISBN 0-15-271050-7, HJ). HarBraceJ.

Boston, Mary. Child Psychotherapist. 25.00 o.p. (ISBN 0-7045-0273-9). State Mutual Bk.

Boston Medical Library, jt. auth. see Harvard Medical Library.

Boston Public Library. Canadian Manuscripts in the Boston Public Library: A Descriptive Catalog. 1971. lib. bdg. 65.00 (ISBN 0-8161-0930-3, Hall Library). G K Hall.

--Catalog of the Defoe Collection in the Boston Public Library. 1966. 65.00 (ISBN 0-8161-0731-9, Hall Library). G K Hall.

--Catalogue of the Spanish Library, & of the Portuguese Books Bequeathed by George Ticknor to the Boston Public Library. 1970. lib. bdg. 75.00 (ISBN 0-8161-0865-X, Hall Library). G K Hall.

--Dictionary Catalog of the Music Collection, Boston Public Library, 20 vols. 15617p. 1972. Set. lib. bdg. 1900.00 (ISBN 0-8161-0956-7, Hall Library); lib. bdg. 420.00 1st suppl., 4 vols. 1977 (ISBN 0-8161-1014-X). G K Hall.

--Manuscripts of the American Revolution in the Boston Public Library: A Descriptive Catalog. 1968. 65.00 (ISBN 0-8161-0825-0, Hall Library). G K Hall.

--Young Adult Catalog of the Boston Public Library, 2 vols. 1112p. 1972. Set. lib. bdg. 190.00 (ISBN 0-8161-1028-X, Hall Library). G K Hall.

Boston Society of Architects. Architecture Boston. (Illus.). 1976. 12.95 (ISBN 0-517-52501-1, C N Potter Bks); pap. 7.95 (ISBN 0-517-52502-X). Crown.

Boston, Thomas. Human Nature in Its Fourfold State. 1964. pap. 4.95 (ISBN 0-686-12519-3). Banner of Truth.

Boston University Center for Banking Law Studies, ed. Annual Review of Banking Law. 1982. 42.00 (ISBN 0-88262-818-6). Warren.

Boston University Libraries. Index to the Classed Catalog of the Boston University Libraries, 2 vols. 3rd. rev ed. 1187p. 1972. Set. lib. bdg. 190.00 (ISBN 0-8161-1029-8, Hall Library). G K Hall.

--List of French Doctoral Dissertations on Africa, 1884-1961. 1966. 65.00 (ISBN 0-8161-0742-4, Hall Library). G K Hall.

Boston University Library. Catalog of African Government Documents. 3rd, rev. ed. 1976. lib. bdg. 70.00 (ISBN 0-8161-0036-5, Hall Library). G K Hall.

Boston University School of Medicine see Shapiro, Eileen C. & Lowenstein, Leah M.

Boston Urban Gardeners. A Handbook of Community Gardening. (Illus.). 192p. 1983. pap. 7.95 (ISBN 0-686-37894-6). CribT.

Boston, W. S., jt. auth. see Bird, C. L.

Boston Women's Health Book Collective. Our Bodies, Ourselves. rev. 2nd ed. (Illus.). 352p. 1976. 14.95 o.p. (ISBN 0-671-22145-0); pap. 8.95 (ISBN 0-671-22146-9). S&S.

Bostrom, Alice. Search the Word Bible Puzzles. (Illus.). 48p. 1983. pap. 1.50 (ISBN 0-87239-589-8, 2787). Standard Pub.

Bostrom, Christopher J. Philosophy of Religion. 1962. 34.50x (ISBN 0-685-69791-6). Elliots Bks.

Bostrom, Robert N. Persuasion. (Illus.). 320p. 1983. text ed. 20.95 o.p. (ISBN 0-13-661157-5). P-H.

Bostwick, Burdette. One Hundred Eleven Proven Techniques & Strategies: Getting the Job Interview. LC 80-26454. 285p. 1981. 14.95 (ISBN 0-471-07762-3, Pub. by Wiley-Interscience). Wiley.

Bostwick, Burdette E. Finding the Job You've Always Wanted. 2nd ed. LC 79-15567. 292p. 1980. 12.50 (ISBN 0-471-05281-7, Pub. by Wiley-Interscience). Wiley.

--How to Find the Job You've Always Wanted. 2nd ed. 288p. 1982. pap. 9.95 (ISBN 0-471-87116-8). Wiley.

--Resume Writing: A Comprehensive How-to-Do-It Guide. 2nd ed. LC 80-18100. 314p. 1982. pap. 7.95 (ISBN 0-471-09943-0, Pub. by Wiley-Interscience). Wiley.

Bostwick, Fran, jt. auth. see Berko, Roy M.

Bostwick, Harold S., et al. Auto Mechanics, Standard Practice Job Sheets: The Engine. 1964. pap. text ed. 2.50 o.p. (ISBN 0-02-811400-0). Glencoe.

--Auto Mechanics Standard Practice Job Sheets: The Fuel & Electrical Systems. 1964. pap. text ed. 2.50 o.p. (ISBN 0-02-811410-8). Glencoe.

--Auto Mechanics Standard Practice Job Sheets: The Power Flow. 1964. pap. text ed. 2.50 o.p. (ISBN 0-02-811420-5). Glencoe.

Bostwick, John, III. Aesthetic & Reconstructive Breast Surgery. (Illus.). 748p. 1983. text ed. 155.00 (ISBN 0-8016-0731-0). Mosby.

Boswell, James. Boswell for the Defense. Wimsatt & Pottle, Frederick A., eds. 1959. 19.95 (ISBN 0-07-070965-3, P&RB). McGraw.

--Boswell in Extremes: 1776-1778. Weis, Charles M. & Pottle, Frederick A., eds. 1970. 21.95 (ISBN 0-07-069059-6, P&RB). McGraw.

--Boswell's Journal of a Tour to the Hebrides with Samuel Johnson. Bd. with Johnson's Journey to the Western Islands of Scotland. Johnson, Samuel. (Oxford Standard Authors Ser.). 1930. 22.50 (ISBN 0-19-254131-5). Oxford U Pr.

--Boswell's London. 1978. 25.00 o.p. (ISBN 0-7045-0259-3). State Mutual Bk.

--Correspondence of James Boswell & John Johnston of Grange, Vol. 1. (Research ed). 1966. 12.50 (ISBN 0-07-006610-8, P&RB). McGraw.

--Dorando: A Spanish Tale, 1767. Shugrue, Michael F., ed. Bd. with The History of Nourjahad, 1767. Sheridan, Frances. LC 74-17301. (The Flowering of the Novel, 1740-1775 Ser: Vol. 78). 1974. lib. bdg. 50.00 o.s.i. (ISBN 0-8240-1177-5). Garland Pub.

--Everybody's Boswell: Being the Life of Samuel Johnson. abr. ed. Morley, Frank, ed. (Illus.). xvii, 665p. 1981. 24.95x (ISBN 0-7135-1237-7, 82-87708). Ohio U Pr.

--Life of Samuel Johnson. abr. ed. Brady, Frank, ed. 1968. pap. 3.50 (ISBN 0-451-51507-2, CE1507, Sig Classics). NAL.

--Ominous Years. Ryskamp, C. A. & Pottle, Frederick A., eds. 1963. 4.75 o.p. (ISBN 0-07-054367-4, P&RB). McGraw.

Boswell, John. Christianity, Social Tolerance, & Homosexuality: Gay People in Western Europe from the Beginning of the Christian Era to the Fourteenth Century. LC 79-11171. (Illus.). xviii, 424p. 1980. 27.50x (ISBN 0-226-06710-6); pap. 9.95 (ISBN 0-226-06711-4). U of Chicago Pr.

Boswell, John, ed. The First Family Paper Doll Book. (Illus.). 1982. pap. 14.95 o.p. (ISBN 0-393-01531-9). Norton.

Boswell, Kathryn, jt. auth. see O'Connor, Francine M.

Boswell, Thomas. How Life Imitates the World Series. (Penguin Sports Library). 1983. pap. 4.95 (ISBN 0-14-006469-9). Penguin.

Boswell, Thomas D. & Curtis, James R. The Cuban-American Experience: Culture, Images and Perspectives. 250p. 1983. text ed. 29.50x (ISBN 0-86598-116-7). Allanheld.

Bosworth. Codes, Ciphers, & Computers: An Introduction to Information Security. Date not set. 13.95 (ISBN 0-686-82006-1, 5149). Hayden.

Bosworth, Barry, et al. Capital Needs in the Seventies. 70p. 1975. pap. 4.95 (ISBN 0-8157-1031-3). Brookings.

Bosworth, Bruce & Nagel, Harry. Programming in BASIC for Business. 2nd ed. 256p. 1981. text ed. 14.95 (ISBN 0-574-21325-2, 13-4325); instr's. guide avail. (ISBN 0-574-21326-0, 13-4326). SRA.

Bosworth, Bruce & Nagel, Harry L. Programming in BASIC for Business. LC 76-48291. 1977. pap. text ed. 9.95 o.s.i. (ISBN 0-574-21090-3, 13-4090); solutions manual 2.25 o.s.i. (ISBN 0-574-21091-1, 13-4091). SRA.

Bosworth, C. E. The Islamic Dynasties. 245p. 1980. pap. 9.00x (ISBN 0-85224-402-9, Pub. by Edinburgh U Pr Scotland). Columbia U Pr.

Bosworth, C. E., jt. ed. see Schacht, Joseph.

Bosworth, Derek L. & Dawkins, Peter J. Work Patterns: An Economic Analysis. 271p. 1981. text ed. 47.50x (ISBN 0-566-00310-4). Gower Pub Ltd.

Bosworth, F. F. Christ the Healer. pap. 5.95 (ISBN 0-8007-0647-1). Revell.

Bosworth, J. Allan. A Darkness of Giants. LC 79-180062. 168p. (gr. 6-9). 1972. PLB 7.95 (ISBN 0-385-00776-0). Doubleday.

Bosworth, R. J. Italy, the Least of the Great Powers. LC 78-18090. (Illus.). 532p. 1980. 74.50 (ISBN 0-521-22366-0). Cambridge U Pr.

Boszormenyi-Nagy, Ivan, jt. ed. see Zuk, Gerald H.

Botein, Bernard. Trial Judge: The Candid, Behind the Bench Story of Justice Bernard Botein. (American Constitutional & Legal History Ser.). 337p. 1974. Repr. of 1952 ed. lib. bdg. 39.50 (ISBN 0-306-70630-X). Da Capo.

Botein, Michael & Rice, David, eds. Network Television & the Public Interest: A Preliminary Inquiry. LC 79-1751. 320p. 1980. 23.95x (ISBN 0-669-02927-0). Lexington Bks.

Botel, Morton, jt. auth. see Preston, Ralph C.

Botella-Llusia, Jose. Obstetrical Endocrinology. (Illus.). 140p. 1961. photocopy ed. spiral 14.50x (ISBN 0-398-00199-5). C C Thomas.

Botez, M. I. & Reynolds, E. H., eds. Folic Acid in Neurology, Psychiatry, & Internal Medicine. LC 78-57243. 550p. 1979. text ed. 54.50 (ISBN 0-89004-338-8). Raven.

Botfield, Beriah. Notes on the Cathedral Libraries of England. LC 68-23138. 1969. Repr. of 1849 ed. 56.00x (ISBN 0-8103-3174-8). Gale.

Botham, C. N. Audio-Visual Aids for Cooperative Education & Training. (FAO Agricultural Development Papers Ser., No. 86). (Orig.). 1969. pap. 11.00 (ISBN 0-685-02451-2, F52, FAO). Unipub.

Botham, Mary & Sharrad, L. Manual of Wigmaking. (Illus.). 112p. 1983. 12.50 (ISBN 0-434-90164-4, Pub. by Heinemann England). David & Charles.

Bothe, M. & Partsch, K. J. New Rules for Victims of Armed Conflict. 1982. lib. bdg. 145.00 (ISBN 90-247-2537-2, Pub. by Martinus Nijhoff Netherlands). Kluwer Boston.

Bothmer, Bernard, ed. see Holz, R., et al.

Bothmer, Dietrich von see Von Bothmer, Dietrich & Mertens, Joan R.

Bothwell, Jean. India. 2nd rev. ed. Whipple, Jane, ed. LC 78-2511. (First Bks). (Illus.). (gr. 4-6). 1978. PLB 8.90 s&l (ISBN 0-531-02229-3). Watts.

Bothwell, Lin K. The Art of Leadership: Skill-Building Techniques that Produce Results. (Illus.). 272p. 1983. 18.95 (ISBN 0-13-047100-3); pap. 9.95 (ISBN 0-13-047092-9). P-H.

Botjer, George F. Short History of Nationalist China, Nineteen Nineteen to Nineteen Forty-Nine. LC 79-10525. 1980. 15.95 o.p. (ISBN 0-399-12382-2). Putnam Pub Group.

Botkin, B. A. A Treasury of New England Folklore. 1947. 9.98 (ISBN 0-517-10918-2). Crown.

Botkin, Benjamin A., ed. Civil War Treasury of Tales, Legends, & Folklore. (Illus.). 1966. 22.00 (ISBN 0-394-44943-6). Random.

Botkin, Daniel B. & Keller, Edward A. Environmental Studies. 480p. 1982. text ed. 23.95 (ISBN 0-675-09813-0). Additional supplements may be obtained from publisher. Merrill.

Botkin, James & Dimancescu, Dan. Global Stakes: The Future of High Technology in America. LC 82-8747. 248p. 1982. prof ref 17.50 (ISBN 0-88410-886-4). Ballinger Pub.

Botsford, Keith, jt. auth. see Jones, Alan.

Bott. Interior of the Earth. 1982. 35.00 (ISBN 0-444-00723-7). Elsevier.

Bott, Elizabeth. Tongan Society at the Time of Captain Cook's Visits: Discussions with Her Majesty Queen Salote Tupou. 187p. 1983. pap. text ed. 15.00x (ISBN 0-8248-0864-9). UH Pr.

Bott, J. F., jt. auth. see Gross, R. W.

Bott, Martin H. & Saxov, Svend, eds. Structure & Development of Greenland-Scotland Ridge: New Methods & Concepts. (NATO Conference Ser.: IV-Marine Sciences, Vol.8). 675p. 1982. 85.00x (ISBN 0-306-41019-2, Plenum Pr). Plenum Pub.

Bott, R., et al. Lectures on Algebraic & Differential Topology: Delivered at the II. ELAM. LC 72-86695. (Lecture Notes in Mathematics: Vol. 279). v, 174p. 1972. pap. 7.00 o.p. (ISBN 0-387-05944-X). Springer-Verlag.

Bott, Raymond & Morrison, Stanley. Junior Chess Puzzles. (Illus.). 104p. (Orig.). 1975. pap. 3.95 o.p. (ISBN 0-571-10688-9). Faber & Faber.

--Your Book of Chess. (gr. 7 up). 1968. 6.25 o.p. (ISBN 0-571-08112-6). Transatlantic.

Bottaccini, M. R. Instruments & Measurement. LC 73-85467. 384p. 1975. text ed. 28.95 (ISBN 0-675-08889-5). Merrill.

Bottcher, C. J. & Bordewijk, P. Theory of Electric Polarization, Vol. 2: Dielectrics in Time Dependent Fields. 2nd ed. 1978. 127.75 (ISBN 0-444-41579-3). Elsevier.

Bottcher, C. J., et al. Theory of Electric Polarization, Vol. 1: Dielectrics in Static Fields. 2nd ed. Van Belle, O.. C. & Bordewijk, P., eds. LC 72-83198. 396p. 1973. 95.75 (ISBN 0-444-41019-8). Elsevier.

Bottcher, Cordelia. Felix Finestitch. (Illus.). 1982. 14.95 (ISBN 0-903540-52-5, Pub. by Floris Bks). St George Bk Serv.

Botteghe Oscure. Anthology of New Italian Writers. Caetani, Marquerite, ed. LC 72-110822. Repr. of 1950 ed. lib. bdg. 20.75x (ISBN 0-8371-3211-8, BOIW). Greenwood.

Botterill, G. S., ed. British Chess. (Chess Ser.). (Illus.). 300p. 1983. 30.01 (ISBN 0-08-024134-4). Pergamon.

Botterweck, C. Michael. A Test of Faith: Challenges of Modern Day Christians. 304p. (Orig.). 1983. pap. 8.95 (ISBN 0-686-37684-6). Gregory Pub.

Botticelli, Sandro. Drawings. Bertini, Aldo, ed. Phillips, Florence H., tr. (Great Masters of Drawing Ser.). (Illus.). 1968. pap. 2.50 o.p. (ISBN 0-486-21946-1). Dover.

Botting, C. G., jt. auth. see Hillard, A. E.

Botting, Douglas. The Aftermath: Europe. (World War II Ser.). 1983. lib. bdg. 19.92 (ISBN 0-8094-3412-1, Pub. by Time-Life). Silver.

--The Giant Airships. LC 80-12128. (Epic of Flight Ser.). PLB 19.96 (ISBN 0-8094-3271-4). Silver.

--The Pirates. LC 77-91928. (The Seafarers Ser.). (Illus.). 1978. lib. bdg. 19.92 (ISBN 0-8094-2651-X). Silver.

--Rio. (The Great Cities Ser.). (Illus.). 1978. lib. bdg. 12.00 (ISBN 0-8094-2295-6). Silver.

--The Second Front. LC 78-3405. (World War II Ser.). (Illus.). 1978. lib. bdg. 19.92 (ISBN 0-8094-2499-1). Silver.

--Wilderness Europe. (The World's Wild Places Ser.). (Illus.). 1976. lib. bdg. 15.96 (ISBN 0-8094-2064-3). Silver.

Bottke, K. Brief Oral French Review. 3rd ed. 1964. pap. 10.95 o.p. (ISBN 0-13-082040-7). P-H.

Bottle, R. T. Use of Biological Literature. 2nd ed. 1972. 39.95 o.p. (ISBN 0-408-38411-5). Butterworth.

--Use of Chemical Literature. 3rd ed. LC 79-41061. 1979. 39.95 (ISBN 0-408-38452-2). Butterworth.

Bottner, Barbara. Dumb Old Casey Is a Fat Tree. LC 78-19474. (Illus.). (gr. 1-4). 1979. 8.95 o.p. (ISBN 0-06-020616-0, HarpJ); PLB 9.89 (ISBN 0-06-020617-9). Har-Row.

--Messy. LC 78-50420. (Illus.). (gr. k-2). 1979. 6.95 o.s.i. (ISBN 0-440-05492-3); PLB 6.46 o.s.i. (ISBN 0-440-05493-1). Delacorte.

--What Would You Do with a Giant? (Illus.). 32p. (ps-3). 1972. PLB 4.79 o.p. (ISBN 0-399-60738-2). Putnam Pub Group.

Bottom Line Personal, Experts, ed. The Book of Inside Information. 500p. 1982. 50.00 (ISBN 0-932648-50-9). Boardroom.

Bottom, Norman R. & Kostanoski, John. Security & Loss Control. 1st ed. 352p. 1983. 22.95 (ISBN 0-02-312700-7). Macmillan.

Bottomley, Denys, ed. see Rosenberg, Isaac.

Bottomley, Jim. Paper Projects for Creative Kids of All Ages. 160p. 1983. 12.45i (ISBN 0-316-10348-9); pap. 8.70i (ISBN 0-316-10349-7). Little.

Bottomley, Tom. Cruising for Fun. (Illus.). 1977. 8.95 o.s.i. (ISBN 0-8096-1913-X, Assn Pr); pap. 4.95 o.s.i. (ISBN 0-8096-1908-3). Follett.

Bottomley, Tom, jt. auth. see Whiting, John.

Bottomly, Heath. Prodigal Father. LC 75-14884. 144p. 1976. pap. 4.95 o.p. (ISBN 0-8307-0431-0, 54-038-04). Regal.

Bottomore, Tom. Political Sociology. LC 79-3043. 176p. 1980. 14.37i (ISBN 0-06-010438-4, HarpT); pap. 3.95i (ISBN 0-06-090751-7, CN-751, HarpT). Har-Row.

Bottomore, Tom, ed. Karl Marx. 194p. 1979. 29.00x o.p. (ISBN 0-631-10961-7, Pub. by Basil Blackwell); pap. 10.50x (ISBN 0-631-11061-5). Biblio Dist.

Bottomore, Tom & Goode, Patrick, eds. Austro-Marxism. 1978. text ed. 37.50x (ISBN 0-19-827229-4); pap. text ed. 9.95x (ISBN 0-19-827230-8). Oxford U Pr.

Bottomore, Tom & Nowak, Stefan, eds. Sociology: The State of the Art. 382p. 1982. 27.50 (ISBN 0-8039-9790-6); pap. 12.95 (ISBN 0-8039-9791-4). Sage.

Bottomore, Tom, tr. see Simmel, Georg.

Bottoms, A. E. & McClean, J. D. Defendants in the Criminal Process. (International Library of Social Policy). 250p. 1975. 25.75x (ISBN 0-7100-8274-6). Routledge & Kegan.

Bottoms, David. In a U-Haul North of Damascus. 59p. 1983. 8.95 (ISBN 0-688-02067-4). Morrow.

--In a U-Haul North of Damascus. 59p. 1983. pap. 3.95 (ISBN 0-688-01743-6). Quill NY.

--Shooting Rats at the Bibb Co. Dump. 64p. 1980. pap. 3.95 (ISBN 0-688-08609-8). Quill NY.

Bottoms, Lawrence. Ecclesiastes Speaks to Us Today. LC 78-71053. (The Bible Speaks to Us Today). 1979. pap. 1.99 (ISBN 0-8042-0104-8). John Knox.

Bottorff, Leslie. A Thin Volume of Hate. 1973. pap. 2.95 (ISBN 0-913270-15-6). Sunstone Pr.

Bottorff, William K. James Lane Allen. (United States Authors Ser.: No. 56). 13.95 o.p. (ISBN 0-8057-0016-1, Twayne). G K Hall.

--Thomas Jefferson. (United States Authors Ser.). 1979. lib. bdg. 11.95 (ISBN 0-8057-7260-X, Twayne). G K Hall.

Botts, Linda. Loose Talk: The Book of Quotes from the Pages of Rolling Stone Magazine. (Illus.). 220p. 1981. pap. 6.95 (ISBN 0-8256-3168-8, Quick Fox). Putnam Pub Group.

Botvinick & Shames. Nuclear Cardiology: Clinical Applications. (Illus.). 1979. 28.00 o.p. (ISBN 0-683-00943-5). Williams & Wilkins.

Botvinnik, M. M. Achieving the Aim. LC 80-40437. (Pergamon Russian Chess Ser.). (Illus.). 230p. 1981. text ed. 19.00 (ISBN 0-08-024120-4). Pergamon.

--Computers, Chess & Long-Range Planning. Brown, A., tr. LC 75-85203. (Heidelberg Science Library: Vol. 11). (Illus.). 1970. pap. 6.50 o.p. (ISBN 0-387-90012-8). Springer-Verlag.

Botwin, Carol. Love Lives: Why Women Behave the Way They Do in Relationships. 1983. pap. 3.50 (ISBN 0-686-43066-2). Bantam.

Botwinick, Aryeh. Ethics, Politics & Epistemology: A Study in the Unity of Hume's Thought. LC 80-5809. 197p. 1980. lib. bdg. 19.75 (ISBN 0-8191-1288-7); pap. text ed. 9.75 (ISBN 0-8191-1289-5). U Pr of Amer.

--Wittgenstein & Historical Understanding. LC 80-5968. 65p. (Orig.). 1981. pap. text ed. 5.25 (ISBN 0-8191-1431-6). U Pr of Amer.

Botwinick, Jack. Aging & Behavior. 2nd ed. LC 78-8535. 1978. text ed. 19.95 (ISBN 0-8261-1441-5). Springer Pub.

Botwinick, Jack & Storandt, Martha. Memory, Related Functions & Age. (Illus.). 208p. 1974. photocopy ed. spiral 21.50x (ISBN 0-398-03143-6). C C Thomas.

Boua, Chanthou, jt. ed. see Kiernan, Ben.

Boublik, et al. Statistical Thermodynamics of Simple Liquids & Their Mixtures. (Studies in Physical & Chemistry: Vol. 2). 1980. 40.50 (ISBN 0-444-99784-9). Elsevier.

Boublik, T., et al. The Vapour Pressures of Pure Substances. 634p. 1973. 106.50 (ISBN 0-444-41097-X). Elsevier.

Bouce, Paul-Gabriel, ed. Sexuality in Eighteenth-Century Britain. LC 82-8785. (Illus.). 274p. 1982. text ed. 25.00x (ISBN 0-389-20313-0). B&N Imports.

Bouchard, Eric. Radiology Management: An Introduction. LC 82-22355. (Illus.). 310p. (Orig.). 1983. pap. 18.95X (ISBN 0-940122-04-9). Multi Media CO.

Bouchard, Harry, jt. auth. see Moffitt, Francis H.

Bouchard, Robert F., jt. ed. see Franklin, Justin D.

Bouchard, Sharon, jt. auth. see Fruehling, Rosemary T.

Boucher, Anthony. The Case of the Baker Street Irregulars. 1980. lib. bdg. 11.95 (ISBN 0-8398-2655-9, Gregg). G K Hall.

Boucher, Carl O., ed. Current Clinical Dental Terminology: A Glossary of Accepted Terms in All Disciplines of Dentistry. 2nd ed. LC 73-4651. 1974. 27.50 o.p. (ISBN 0-8016-0719-1). Mosby.

Boucher, Chauncey S. Nullification Controversy in South Carolina. LC 18-1105. (Illus.). 1969. Repr. of 1916 ed. lib. bdg. 18.00x o.p. (ISBN 0-8371-0321-5, BONU). Greenwood.

Boucher, E. A., jt. auth. see Murrell, J. N.

Boucher, H. J., ed. How-to-Live-&-Die-with California Probate. (Probate Ser.). (Illus.). 171p. 1970. 6.95 o.p. (ISBN 0-87201-094-5). Gulf Pub.

Boucher, Louis J. & Renner, Robert P. Treatment of Partially Edentulous Patients. LC 81-19016. (Illus.). 352p. 1982. pap. text ed. 37.95 (ISBN 0-8016-0821-X). Mosby.

Boucher, Sandy. The Notebooks of Leni Clare & Other Short Stories. LC 82-2542. 136p. (Orig.). 1982. 15.95 (ISBN 0-89594-077-9); pap. 6.95 (ISBN 0-89594-076-0). Crossing Pr.

Bouchier, David. Idealism & Revolution: New Ideologies of Liberation in Britain & the United States. LC 78-17007. 1979. 25.00 (ISBN 0-312-40439-5). St Martin.

Bouchier, I. A. & Morris, J. S., eds. Clinical Skills: A System of Clinical Examinations. LC 76-8568. 1976. text ed. 19.95 o.p. (ISBN 0-7216-1892-8). Saunders.

Bouchner, Miroslav. Birds of Prey of Britain & Europe. (Concise Guides Ser.). (Illus.). 1979. 7.95 o.p. (ISBN 0-600-31291-7). Transatlantic.

Bouchot, Henri. Book: Its Printers, Illustrators, & Binders, from Gutenberg to the Present Time. Grevel, H., ed. LC 77-155741. (Illus.). 1971. Repr. of 1890 ed. 42.00 o.p. (ISBN 0-8103-3392-9). Gale.

Boucot, A. J. Evolution & Extinction Rate Controls. (Developments in Palaeontology & Stratigraphy Ser.: Vol. 1). 350p. 1975. 89.50 (ISBN 0-444-41182-8). Elsevier.

Boudart, M., jt. ed. see Anderson, J. R.

Boudewyns, P. & Keefe, J. F. Behavioral Medicine in General Medical Practice. 1982. 26.95 (ISBN 0-201-10173-4, Med-Nurse). A-W.

Boudinot, Elias. The Life & Public Services, Addresses & Letters of Elias Boudinot, President of the Continental Congress, 2 Vols. Boudinot, Jane J., ed. LC 72-119059. (Era of the American Revolution Ser). 1971. Repr. of 1896 ed. Set. lib. bdg. 95.00 (ISBN 0-306-71946-0). Da Capo.

Boudinot, Jane J., ed. see Boudinot, Elias.

Boudon, Philippe. Lived-In Architecture: Le Corbusier's Pessac Revisited. Onn, Gerald, tr. (Illus.). 1972. pap. 5.95x (ISBN 0-262-52053-2). MIT Pr.

Boudon, Raymond, ed. see Wiggins, Lee M.

Boudreau, Albert. The Born-Again Catholic. (Illus., Orig.). 1979. pap. 4.50 (ISBN 0-914544-26-8). Living Flame Pr.

Boudreau, Eugene H., ed. see Grisby, Robert F.

Boudreaux, E. A. & Mulay, L. N. Theory & Applications of Molecular Paramagnetism. LC 75-28418. 1976. 62.50 o.p. (ISBN 0-471-09106-5, Pub. by Wiley-Interscience). Wiley.

Boudreaux, H. Bruce. Arthropod Phylogeny with Special Reference to Insects. LC 78-16638. 1979. 32.95x (ISBN 0-471-04290-0, Pub. by Wiley-Interscience). Wiley.

Bouet-Willaumez, E. Commerce et Traite des Noirs aux Cotes Occidentales d'Afrique. (Slave Trade in France, 1744-1848, Ser.). 240p. (Fr.). 1974. Repr. of 1848 ed. lib. bdg. 66.00 o.p. (ISBN 0-8287-0123-7, 2221). Clearwater Pub.

Bougeant, R. P. Amusement Philosophique sur le Langage des Betes. (Linguistics 13th-18th Centuries Ser). 160p. (Fr.). 1974. Repr. of 1739 ed. lib. bdg. 48.50 o.p. (ISBN 0-8287-0124-5, 71-5027). Clearwater Pub.

Boughey, Arthur S. Ecology of Populations. 2nd ed. (Illus.). 192p. 1973. pap. text ed. 13.95 (ISBN 0-02-312730-9, 31273). Macmillan.

--Fundamental Ecology. 222p. 1971. pap. text ed. 12.50 scp o.p. (ISBN 0-7002-2363-0, HarpC). Har-Row.

--Man & the Environment. 2nd ed. (Illus.). 480p. pap. text ed. 15.95 (ISBN 0-02-312770-8, 31277). Macmillan.

Boughner. Posters. (Grosset Art Instruction Ser.: Vol. 38). pap. 2.95 (ISBN 0-448-00547-6, G&D). Putnam Pub Group.

Boughner, Daniel C. The Devil's Disciple: Ben Jonson's Debt to Machiavelli. LC 73-16606. 264p. 1975. Repr. of 1968 ed. lib. bdg. 16.00x (ISBN 0-8371-7183-0, BODD). Greenwood.

Boughner, Howard. Dictionary of Things to Draw. (gr. 1-7). 1979. PLB 3.99 (ISBN 0-448-13125-0, G&D); pap. 1.50 (ISBN 0-448-14991-5). Putnam Pub Group.

Boughton, Robert, jt. auth. see Cromer, Alan.

Boughton, Terrence. Story of the British Light Aeroplane. (Illus.). 11.50 o.p. (ISBN 0-685-20635-1). Transatlantic.

Bouhours, Dominique. Art of Criticism. LC 81-8900. 1981. Repr. of 1705 ed. 40.00x (ISBN 0-8201-1364-6). Schol Facsimiles.

Bouillon, Antoine, jt. auth. see Archer, Robert.

Bouilly, J. N. Fidelio, or Wedded Love. Dent, Edward J., tr. (Musical Score by Ludwig Van Beethoven). 1938. 2.50 o.p. (ISBN 0-19-313302-4). Oxford U Pr.

Bouis, Antonina W., tr. see Beliaev, Alexander.

Bouis, Antonina W., tr. see Tolstoy, Alexei.

Bouis, Antonina W., tr. see Troyepolsky, Gavriil.

Boukema, H. J. Good Law: Toward a Rational Lawmaking Process. 156p. 1982. write for info. (ISBN 3-8204-7020-4). P Lang Pubs.

Boukli, Noureddine. Mostaganem Institute of Agricultural Technology: An Educational Innovation. (Experiments & Innovations in Education Ser.: No. 19). 46p. 1975. pap. 2.75 (ISBN 92-3-101309-2, U391, UNESCO). Unipub.

Boulanger, Ghislaine, tr. see Jurgensen, Genevieve.

Boulanger, Nadia & Britten, Benjamin. Mozart & His World. LC 80-68213. (Great Masters Ser.). 13.00 (ISBN 0-382-06377-5). Silver.

Boulanger, Nicolas A. L' Antiquite Devoilee par ses Usages ou Examen Critique. (Holbach & His Friends Ser.). 420p. (Fr.). 1974. Repr. of 1766 ed. lib. bdg. 106.00 o.p. (ISBN 0-8287-0126-1, 1594). Clearwater Pub.

--Recherches sur l'Origine du Despotisme Oriental. (Holbach & His Friends Ser.). 467p. (Fr.). 1974. Repr. of 1761 ed. lib. bdg. 117.00 o.p. (ISBN 0-8287-0127-X, 1537). Clearwater Pub.

Boulard, jt. auth. see Doten.

Boulay, G. H. Du see Du Boulay, G. H.

Boulby, Mark. Uwe Johnson. LC 73-82315. (Literature and Life Ser.). 1974. 11.95 (ISBN 0-8044-2062-9). Ungar.

Boulden, James B. Computer-Assisted Planning Systems: Management Concept, Application & Implementation. 1975. 26.50 (ISBN 0-07-006657-4, P&RB). McGraw.

Boulder Conference on High Energy Physics. Proceedings. Mahanthappa, K. T., et al, eds. LC 71-115692. (Illus.). 1970. 17.50x (ISBN 0-87081-002-2). Colo Assoc.

Boulding, Elise. From a Monastery Kitchen. LC 76-9973. (Illus.). 128p. 1976. pap. 9.57i (ISBN 0-06-060980-X, RD173, HarpR). Har-Row.

--The Underside of History: A View of Women Through Time. LC 75-30558. 750p. 1976. lib. bdg. 33.75 (ISBN 0-89158-009-3); pap. 18.50 (ISBN 0-89158-056-5). Westview.

Boulding, K. E. Economics As a Science. 1970. pap. text ed. 9.95 o.p. (ISBN 0-07-006670-1, C). McGraw.

--Primer on Social Dynamics. LC 70-123192. 1970. pap. 3.50 (ISBN 0-02-904570-3). Free Pr.

Boulding, Kenneth E. Beyond Economics: Essays on Society, Religion & Ethics. LC 68-29259. 1968. 15.00 o.p. (ISBN 0-472-16800-2). U of Mich Pr.

--Collected Papers of Kenneth E. Boulding, Vol. 3: Political Economy. Singell, Larry D., ed. LC 77-135288. 465p. 1973. text ed. 15.95x (ISBN 0-87081-046-4). Colo Assoc.

--Collected Papers of Kenneth E. Boulding, Vol. 4: Toward a General Social Science. Singell, Larry D., ed. LC 77-135288. 1974. text ed. 15.95x (ISBN 0-87081-053-7). Colo Assoc.

--Collected Papers of Kenneth E. Boulding, Vol. 5: International Systems. Singell, Larry D., ed. LC 77-135288. 500p. 1975. 15.95x (ISBN 0-87081-062-6). Colo Assoc.

--Sonnets from the Interior Life & Other Autobiographical Verse. LC 75-289. 176p. 1975. pap. 10.00x (ISBN 0-87081-064-2). Colo Assoc.

Boulding, Kenneth E., ed. see Senesh, Lawrence.

Boulding, Maria. The Coming of God. 224p. 1982. pap. text ed. 9.00 (ISBN 0-8146-1278-4). Liturgical Pr.

Boulenger, G. A. Catalogue of the Batrachia Gradienta S. Caudata & Batrachia Apoda: Collection of the British Museum. 2nd ed. (Illus.). 1966. 16.00 (ISBN 3-7682-0289-5). Lubrecht & Cramer.

--Catalogue of the Batrachia Salienta S. Ecaudata: Collection of the British Museum. (Illus.). 1966. 54.40 (ISBN 3-7682-0291-7). Lubrecht & Cramer.

--Catalogue of the Chelonians, Rhynchocephalians, & Crocodiles in the British Museum. new ed. (Illus.). 1966. 30.40 (ISBN 3-7682-0443-X). Lubrecht & Cramer.

--Catalogue of the Lizards in the British Museum, 3 vols. in 2. (Illus.). 1964. 192.00 (ISBN 3-7682-0239-9). Lubrecht & Cramer.

--Fishes of the Nile. 1964. Repr. of 1907 ed. 148.00 (ISBN 3-7682-0241-0). Lubrecht & Cramer.

Boulle, Pierre. Le Bon Leviathan. 224p. 1978. 14.95 (ISBN 0-686-54097-2). French & Eur.

--Ears of the Jungle. LC 72-83350. 230p. 1972. 10.95 o.s.i. (ISBN 0-8149-0720-2). Vanguard.

--Face of a Hero. LC 56-12030. 1956. 10.95 o.s.i. (ISBN 0-8149-0070-4). Vanguard.

--Other Side of the Coin. LC 58-13675. 1958. 8.95 o.s.i. (ISBN 0-8149-0068-2). Vanguard.

--Planet of the Apes. (RL 7). 1968. pap. 1.95 (ISBN 0-451-12318-2, AJ2318, Sig). NAL.

--S. O. P. H. I. A. LC 59-12392. 1959. 10.95 o.s.i. (ISBN 0-8149-0067-4). Vanguard.

--Time Out of Mind. 280p. (Fr.). 1974. pap. 1.25 o.p. (ISBN 0-451-05871-2, Y5871, Sig). NAL.

Boullin, David J. Cerebral Vasospasm. LC 79-40735. 1980. 61.95 (ISBN 0-471-27639-1, Pub. by Wiley-Interscience). Wiley.

--Serotonin in Mental Abnormalities. LC 77-1828. 1978. 51.95 o.p. (ISBN 0-471-99501-0, Pub. by Wiley-Interscience). Wiley.

Boulos, Loutfy. Medicinal Plants of North Africa. Ayensu, Edward S., ed. LC 82-20412. (Medicinal Plants of the World Ser.: No. 3). (Illus.). 300p. 1983. 29.95 (ISBN 0-917256-16-6). Ref Pubns.

Boulougouris, John C. Learning Theory Approaches to Psychiatry. 256p. 1981. 57.00x (ISBN 0-471-28042-9, Wiley-Interscience, Pub. by Wiley-Interscience). Wiley.

Boult, Pamela, ed. see Newhouse, Flower A.

Boulter, C. G., et al, eds. Lectures in Memory of Louise Taft Semple: Classical Studies, Second Series, 1966-1970. LC 72-9256. (Illus.). 350p. 1974. 15.95x (ISBN 0-8061-1062-7); pap. 11.95x (ISBN 0-8061-1178-X). U of Okla Pr.

Boulter, D., jt. ed. see Parthier, B.

Boulter, Eric, jt. auth. see Dobree, John H.

Boulton, A. J., jt. ed. see Katritzky, A. R.

Boulton, J. T., ed. The Letters of D. H. Lawrence, 2Vols. LC 78-7531. (Illus.). 1979. Vol. 1. 39.95 (ISBN 0-521-22147-1); Vol. 2. 39.95 (ISBN 0-521-23111-6). Cambridge U Pr.

Boulton, James T. The Language of Politics in the Age of Wilkes & Burke. LC 74-33503. 282p. 1975. Repr. of 1963 ed. lib. bdg. 18.25x (ISBN 0-8371-7969-6, BOLP). Greenwood.

Boulton, Majorie. The Anatomy of Poetry. Rev. ed. 1982. pap. 7.95 (ISBN 0-7100-9087-0). Routledge & Kegan.

Boulton, Marjorie. The Anatomy of Poetry. 1970. pap. 7.95 o.p. (ISBN 0-7100-6091-2). Routledge & Kegan.

Boulton, Roger, et al. Canada Coast to Coast. (Illus.). 1982. 29.95 (ISBN 0-19-540388-6). Oxford U Pr.

Boulton-Jones, J. M., et al. Diagnosis & Management of Renal & Urinary Disorders. (Illus.). 312p. 1982. pap. text ed. 21.95 (ISBN 0-632-00677-3, B0895-3). Mosby.

Boulware, Marcus H. Oratory of Negro Leaders: Nineteen Hunderd - Nineteen Sixty-Eight. LC 72-90794. 1969. lib. bdg. 29.95 (ISBN 0-8371-1849-2, BOO); pap. 4.95 (ISBN 0-8371-7353-1, BOO). Greenwood.

Bouma, J. J., jt. ed. see Tromp, S. W.

Bouma, P. J. Physical Aspects of Colour. LC 70-143101. (Illus.). 1971. text ed. 20.00 o.p. (ISBN 0-312-60865-9, P19000). St Martin.

Bouman, Helen H., tr. see Chander, Krishan.

Bouman, Herbert, tr. see Schlink, Edmund.

Bounds, Barbara, jt. auth. see Robertson, Patricia.

Bounds, E. M. The Essentials of Prayer. (E. M. Bounds Ser. on Prayer). 144p. 1980. pap. 2.50 o.p. (ISBN 0-8024-6723-7). Moody.

--The Necessity of Prayer. (Direction Bks). 144p. 1976. pap. 2.45 (ISBN 0-8010-0659-7). Baker Bk.

--The Possibilities of Prayer. (E. M. Bounds Series on Prayer). 160p. 1980. pap. 2.50 o.p. (ISBN 0-8024-6724-5). Moody.

--Power Through Prayer. 128p. 1983. pap. text ed. 2.50 (ISBN 0-88368-117-X). Whitaker Hse.

--Prayer & Praying Men. (E. M. Bounds Ser.). 160p. 1980. pap. 2.95 (ISBN 0-8024-6725-3). Moody.
--Reality of Prayer. (Direction Bks). 1978. pap. 3.50 (ISBN 0-8010-0739-9). Baker Bk.
--The Reality of Prayer. (E. M. Bounds Ser.). 160p. 1980. pap. 2.95 (ISBN 0-8024-6726-1). Moody.
--The Weapon of Prayer. (E. M. Bounds Ser. on Prayer). 160p. 1980. pap. 2.50 o.p. (ISBN 0-8024-6727-X). Moody.

Bounds, Edward M. Purpose in Prayer. (E.M. Bound Ser.). pap. 2.95 (ISBN 0-8024-6949-3). Moody.

Bounds, Edward M., ed. Power Through Prayer. 1979. pap. 2.95 (ISBN 0-8024-6722-9). Moody.

Bouquet, Louis. Le Travail des Enfants et des Filles Mineures dans l'Industrie. (Conditions of the 19th Century French Working Class Ser.). 356p. (Fr.). 1974. Repr. of 1885 ed. lib. bdg. 93.50x o.p. (ISBN 0-8287-0129-6, 1106). Clearwater Pub.

Bourbaki, N. Elements of Mathematics: Commutative Algebra. 1972. 59.50 (ISBN 0-201-00644-8, Adv Bk Prog). A-W.

Bourbaki, Nicholas. Algebra, Part One: Elements of Mathematics. (Chapters 1-3). 1973. 59.50 (ISBN 0-201-00639-1, Adv Bk Prog). A-W.

Bourbaki, Nicolas. Elements of Mathematics, 3 vols. Incl. Vol. 1. General Topology: Part 1. 1966. text ed. 42.50 (ISBN 0-201-00636-7); Vol. 2. General Topology: Part 2. 1967. text ed. 39.50 (ISBN 0-201-00637-5); Vol. 3. Theory of Sets. 1968. text ed. 42.50 (ISBN 0-201-00634-0). A-W.

Bourbaki, Nocolas. Elements of Mathematics: Lie Groups & Lie Algebras, Part 1. 1975. pap. 59.50 (ISBN 0-201-00643-X, Adv Bk Prog). A-W.

Bourbousson & Ashworth. Electrical & Electronic Principles for Craft Studies. 1974. text ed. 13.95 (ISBN 0-408-00121-6). Butterworth.

Bourdeaux, Kenneth J. & Long, Hugh W. The Basic Theory of Corporate Finance. LC 76-27895. (Illus.). 1977. pap. text ed. 25.95 (ISBN 0-13-069435-5). P-H.

Bourdieu, P. Algeria Nineteen Sixty. LC 78-4237. (Studies in Modern Capitalism). (Illus.). 1979. 24.95 (ISBN 0-521-22090-4). Cambridge U Pr.
--Outline of a Theory of Practice. LC 76-11073. (Studies in Social Anthropology: No. 16). (Illus.). 1977. 37.50 (ISBN 0-521-21178-6); pap. 11.95x (ISBN 0-521-29164-X). Cambridge U Pr.

Bourdin, Janine, jt. ed. see Remond, Rene.

Bourdon, Clinton C. & Levitt, Raymond E. Union & Open-Shop Construction: Compensation, Work Practices, & Labor Markets. LC 79-1724. (Illus.). 176p. 1980. 22.95x (ISBN 0-669-02918-1). Lexington Bks.

Bourdon, David see Robbins, Daniel.

Bourdon, J. Growth & Properties of Metal Clusters: Application to Catalysis & the Photographic Process. (Studies in Surface Science & Catalysis: Vol. 4). 1980. 85.00 (ISBN 0-444-41877-6). Elsevier.

Bourdot, H. & Galzin, A. Hymenomycetes De France: Heterobasidies-Homobasidies Gymnocarpes. (Biblio. Myco. Ser.: No.23). 1969. Repr. of 1927 ed. 48.00 (ISBN 3-7682-0655-6). Lubrecht & Cramer.

Bourgault, Priscilla, jt. auth. see Ciancio, Sebastian.

Bourgeacq, Jacques A., jt. auth. see Limouzy, Pierre.

Bourgeois, G. Patrick, et al. Walker's Quantity Surveying & Basic Construction Estimating. Frank R. Walker Company, ed. (Illus.). 128p. 1981. pap. 12.95 (ISBN 0-911592-75-X). F R Walker.

Bourgeois, J., jt. ed. see Fairbridge, R. W.

Bourgeois, Jean-Francois. Los Ninos de la Biblia. Maecha, Alberto, ed. Orig. Title: Les Enfants de la Bible. 40p. (Span.). (gr. 3-5). 1982. pap. write for info. (ISBN 0-942504-11-9). Overcomer Pr.

Bourgin, H. DeJaures a Blum: L'ecole Normale et la Republique. 524p. (Fr.). 1970. 74.00x (ISBN 0-677-50375-X). Gordon.

Bourgoin, J. Design Discovery Coloring Book. (Illus.). 1976. pap. 2.25 (ISBN 0-486-23390-1). Dover.

Bourgoing, Jean De see Franz Joseph, I.

Bourgue, R., jt. auth. see Green, C.

Bourguignon, Erika, ed. A World of Women: Anthropological Studies of Women in the Societies of the World. 364p. 1980. 27.95x (ISBN 0-686-92297-2); pap. 12.95x (ISBN 0-686-98501-X). J F Bergin.

Bourke, John G. MacKenzie's Last Fight with the Cheyennes. (Illus.). 1970. 7.95 (ISBN 0-88342-009-0). Old Army.
--The Medicine Men of the Apache. LC 71-175003. (Illus.). 150p. 13.50 (ISBN 0-87026-049-9). Westernlore.
--The Medicine Men of the Apache. LC 77-135517. (A Paper from the Nineth Annual Report (1887, 1888) of the B.A.E.). (Illus.). 196p. 1983. Repr. of 1970 ed. casebound 20.00 (ISBN 0-87380-050-8); lib. bdg. 17.50. Rio Grande.
--On the Border with Crook. Repr. of 1891 ed. lib. bdg. 17.75x (ISBN 0-8371-5002-7, BOOB). Greenwood.
--On the Border with Crook. (Classics of the Old West Ser.). 1980. lib. bdg. 17.28 (ISBN 0-8094-3584-5). Silver.

Bourke, Vernon J. Saint Thomas & the Greek Moralists. 1947. 7.95 (ISBN 0-87462-111-9). Marquette.

Bourke, Vernon J., commentary by see Augustine, Saint.

Bourke-White, M. & Caldwell, E. Say, Is This the U. S. A. LC 77-9598. (Photography Ser.). (Illus.). 1977. lib. bdg. 29.50 (ISBN 0-306-77434-8); pap. 6.95 (ISBN 0-306-80071-3). Da Capo.

Bourke-White, Margaret, jt. auth. see Caldwell, Erskine.

Bourland, Gary N. An Executive Primer: The Management Club. 15p. 1983. spiral 5.95x (ISBN 0-9609350-0-2). Management Club.

Bourland, W. George. Who Gets the Antelope's Liver? 12.95 (ISBN 0-686-37633-1). Harp & Thistle.

Bourliere, F. Tropical Savannas. (Ecosystems of the World Ser.: Vol. 13). Date not set. 198.00 (ISBN 0-444-42035-5). Elsevier.

Bourliere, Francois. The Land & Wildlife of Eurasia. rev. ed. LC 80-52603. (Life Nature Library). PLB 13.40 (ISBN 0-8094-3911-5). Silver.

Bourman, Anatole. Tragedy of Nijinsky. LC 70-98822. Repr. of 1936 ed. lib. bdg. 18.25x (ISBN 0-8371-2965-6, BOTN). Greenwood.

Bourne, A. J., jt. auth. see Green, A. E.

Bourne, Eleanor. The Heritage of Flowers. (The Leprechaun Library). (Illus.). 64p. 1980. 3.95 o.p. (ISBN 0-399-12544-2). Putnam Pub Group.

Bourne, Frank C. History of the Romans. 1966. text ed. 20.95 (ISBN 0-669-22483-9). Heath.

Bourne, G. H. & Danielli, J. F. International Review of Cytology, Vol. 69. (Serial Publications Ser.). 1981. 43.50 (ISBN 0-12-364469-0). Acad Pr.

Bourne, G. H., ed. Aspects of Human & National Nutrition. (World Review of Nutrition & Dietetics Ser.: Vol. 41). (Illus.). xii, 260p. 1982. 140.75 (ISBN 3-8055-3591-0). S Karger.
--Nutrition Education & Modern Concepts of Food Assimilation. (World Review of Nutrition & Dietetics: Vol. 40). (Illus.). xii, 192p. 1982. 97.75 (ISBN 3-8055-3519-8). S Karger.
--World Review of Nutrition & Dietetics, Vol. 37: Human Nutrition & Animal Feeding. (Illus.). xii, 292p. 1981. 148.00 (ISBN 3-8055-2143-X). S Karger.
--World Review of Nutrition & Dietetics, Vol. 38: Physiology & Social Nutrition & Nutritional Education. (Illus.). x, 230p. 1981. 97.75 (ISBN 3-8055-3048-X). S Karger.

Bourne, G. H. & Danielli, J. F., eds. International Review of Cytology, Vol. 78. 360p. 1982. 49.50 (ISBN 0-12-364478-X). Acad Pr.
--International Review of Cytology, Vol. 79. 315p. 1982. 42.00 (ISBN 0-12-364479-8). Acad Pr.
--International Review of Cytology, Vol. 80. 322p. 1982. 42.00 (ISBN 0-12-364480-1). Acad Pr.

Bourne, Geoffrey & Danielli, James, eds. International Review of Cytology. LC 52-5203. (Serial Publication). 1982. 37.00 ea. Vol. 74 (ISBN 0-12-364474-7). Vol. 75 (ISBN 0-12-364475-5). Acad Pr.
--International Review of Cytology Supplement, No. 14. (Serial Publication). Date not set. 44.00 (ISBN 0-12-364375-9). Acad Pr.

Bourne, Geoffrey H. Primate Odyssey. LC 73-78596. (Illus.). 384p. 1974. 9.95 o.p. (ISBN 0-399-11200-6). Putnam Pub Group.
--The Structure & Function of Muscle. 2nd ed. Vol. 1, 1972. 87.50 o.p. (ISBN 0-12-119101-X); Vol. 2, 1973. 95.00 o.p. (ISBN 0-12-119102-8); Vol. 3, 1973. 87.50 o.p. (ISBN 0-12-119103-6); Vol. 4, 1974. 87.50 o.p. (ISBN 0-12-119104-4); 290.50 set o.p. (ISBN 0-685-36103-9). Acad Pr.

Bourne, Geoffrey H. & Cohen, Maury. The Gentle Giants: The Gorilla Story. (Illus.). 1975. 12.50 o.p. (ISBN 0-399-11528-5). Putnam Pub Group.

Bourne, Geoffrey H., ed. Hearts & Heart-Like Organs: Vol. 3, Physiology. 1980. subscription 51.50 60.50 (ISBN 0-12-119403-5) (ISBN 0-686-77476-0). Acad Pr.

Bourne, Geoffrey H. & Danielli, James F., eds. International Review of Cytology, Vol. 77. 284p. 1982. 38.00 (ISBN 0-12-364477-1). Acad Pr.

Bourne, Geoffrey H., jt. ed. see Sandler, Maurice.

Bourne, Joanna W. Her Ladyship's Companion. (Regency Romance Ser.). 224p. 1983. pap. 2.75 (ISBN 0-380-81596-6). Avon.

Bourne, K. Palmerston. (Illus.). 750p. 1982. 24.95 (ISBN 0-02-903740-9). Macmillan.

Bourne, Kenneth. Britain & the Balance of Power in North America, 1815-1908. LC 67-26632. 1967. 38.50x (ISBN 0-520-00153-2). U of Cal Pr.

Bourne, Larry S., ed. Internal Structure of the City: Readings on Space & Environment. 1971. pap. text ed. 8.95x o.p. (ISBN 0-19-501321-2). Oxford U Pr.

Bourne, Lyle E., Jr., et al. Psychology of Thinking. LC 79-135409. 1971. ref. ed. 23.95 (ISBN 0-13-736702-3). P-H.

Bourne, Malcolm. Food Texture Seven Viscosity: Concepts & Measurement. (Food Science & Technology). 312p. 1982. 36.00 (ISBN 0-12-119060-9). Acad Pr.

Bourne, Michael & Weeks, Christopher. Inventory of Historic Sites in Caroline County. (Illus.). 80p. 1980. pap. 7.95 (ISBN 0-686-36798-7). Md Hist.

Bourne, Miriam A. Bright Lights to See by. LC 75-2540. (Break of Day Bk). (Illus.). 48p. (gr. k-3). 1975. PLB 6.59 o.p. (ISBN 0-698-30580-9, Coward). Putnam Pub Group.
--Emilio's Summer Day. LC 66-7089. (Illus.). (gr. k-3). 1966. 10.89 (ISBN 0-06-020626-8, HarpJ). Har-Row.
--Four-Ring Three. (Break-of-Day Bk.). (Illus.). 48p. (gr. k-3). 1973. PLB 4.99 o.p. (ISBN 0-698-30483-7, Coward). Putnam Pub Group.
--Nabby Adams' Diary. LC 74-83017. (Illus.). 128p. (gr. 5-11). 1975. 7.95 o.p. (ISBN 0-698-20312-7, Coward). Putnam Pub Group.
--Patsy Jefferson's Diary. LC 75-23371. (Illus.). 96p. (gr. 5-11). 1976. 5.95 o.p. (ISBN 0-698-20352-6, Coward). Putnam Pub Group.
--The Second Car in Town. (Break of Day Bk). (Illus.). (gr. k-3). 1972. PLB 6.99 o.p. (ISBN 0-698-30306-7, Coward). Putnam Pub Group.
--What Is Papa up to Now? (Break-of-Day Ser.). (Illus.). 64p. (gr. k-3). 1977. PLB 6.99 (ISBN 0-698-30658-9, Coward). Putnam Pub Group.

Bourne, Richard & Levin, Jack. Social Problems: Causes, Consequences, Interventions. (Illus.). 500p. 1983. text ed. 12.95 (ISBN 0-314-69661-X); tchrs.' manual avail. (ISBN 0-314-71081-7). West Pub.

Bourne, Richard & Newberger, Eli H., eds. Critical Perspectives on Child Abuse. LC 77-18565. (Illus.). 1978. 21.95x (ISBN 0-669-02109-1). Lexington Bks.

Bourne, Ross, ed. Serials Librarianship. 258p. 1981. 25.00x (ISBN 0-85365-631-2, Pub. by Lib Assn England); pap. text ed. o.p. Oryx Pr.

Bourne, Russell, ed. see Borland, Hal.

Bourne, Russell, ed. see Peterson, Roger T., et al.

Bourne, Stanford. Under the Doctor: Studies in the Psychological Problems of Physiotherapists, Patients & Doctors. 1981. 50.00x o.p. (ISBN 0-686-75432-8, Pub. by Avebury Pub England). State Mutual Bk.
--Under the Doctor: Studies in the Psychological Problems of Physiotherapists, Patients & Doctors. 1981. 50.00x o.p. (ISBN 0-86127-601-9, Pub. by Avebury Pub England). State Mutual Bk.

Bourne, Stephen R. The Unix System. 320p. 1982. pap. text ed. 25.00 (ISBN 0-201-13791-7, Adv Bk Prog). A-W.

Bournett, Ruth. Nurse Maggie's Dream. 1982. 6.95 (ISBN 0-686-84156-5, Avalon). Bouregy.

Bournot, K. see Von Wiesner, J. & Von Regel, C.

Bournoutian, George A. Eastern Armenia in the Last Decade of Persian Rule, 1807-1828, Vol. 5. (Studies in Near Eastern Culture & Society Ser., Vol. 5). 315p. 1982. 34.00x (ISBN 0-89003-123-1); pap. 29.00x (ISBN 0-89003-122-3). Undena Pubns.

Bourns Inc. The Pontentiometer Handbook. 1975. 29.50 (ISBN 0-07-006690-6, P&RB). McGraw.

Bourrelly, P. Recherches Sur les Chrysophycees: Morphologie, Phylogenie, Systematique. (Illus.). 1971. Repr. of 1957 ed. 32.00 (ISBN 3-7682-0703-X). Lubrecht & Cramer.

Bourricaud, Francois. The Sociology of Talcott Parsons. Goldhammer, Arthur, tr. LC 81-1348. 336p. 1981. lib. bdg. 20.00x (ISBN 0-226-06755-6). U of Chicago Pr.

Bouscaren, Anthony T. Government in American Society. LC 78-62171. 1978. pap. text ed. 10.75 o.p. (ISBN 0-8191-0506-6). U Pr of Amer.
--Government in American Society. Rev. ed. LC 82-11006. 402p. 1982. pap. text ed. 14.50 (ISBN 0-8191-2615-2). U Pr of Amer.
--Textbook on Communism. (Orig.). 1965. pap. 2.96 o.p. (ISBN 0-02-811670-4). Glencoe.

Bouska, V. Geochemistry of Coal: Coal Science & Technology Ser. (Vol. 1). 1982. 55.50 (ISBN 0-444-99738-5). Elsevier.

Boussel. History of Pharmacy. 1983. 75.00 (ISBN 0-686-43177-4). Thieme-Stratton.

Boutas, V., ed. Women in Islam: Social Attitudes & Historical Perspectives. 224p. 1983. 30.00x (ISBN 0-7007-0154-0, Pub. by Curzon England). State Mutual Bk.

Boutell, Charles. Boutell's Heraldry. rev. ed. LC 73-75030. (Illus.). 368p. 1982. 30.00 (ISBN 0-7232-3093-5). Warne.

Boutell, Wayne S. Accounting for Everyone. (Illus.). 240p. 1982. pap. 12.95 (ISBN 0-13-001602-0). P-H.

Boutflower, Charles. In & Around the Book of Daniel. LC 77-7648. (Kregel Reprint Library). 1977. 9.95 (ISBN 0-8254-2229-9). Kregel.

Bouthillier, Patrick H. Hydraulic Tables for Water Supply & Drainage. LC 81-69115. (Illus.). 150p. 1981. pap. text ed. 12.95 (ISBN 0-250-40517-2). Ann Arbor Science.

Boutilier, Mary A. & SanGiovanni, Lucinda F. The Sporting Woman. LC 82-83147. 300p. 1983. text ed. 21.95x (ISBN 0-931250-35-8). Human Kinetics.

Boutin, Henri & Yip, Sidney. Molecular Spectroscopy with Neutrons. LC 68-22823. 1968. 22.50x (ISBN 0-262-02042-4). MIT Pr.

Boutmy, Emile. Studies in Constitutional Law: France-England-United States. 2nd ed. Dicey, E. M., tr. xiv, 183p. 1982. Repr. of 1891 ed. lib. bdg. 22.50x (ISBN 0-8377-0332-8). Rothman.

Bouton, Bobbie & Marshall, Nancy. Home Games: Two Baseball Wives Speak Out. 1983. 12.95 (ISBN 0-312-38846-2, Pub. by Marek). St Martin.

Bouton, Jim. Ball Four Plus Ball Five: An Update, 1970-1980. LC 80-6165. (Illus.). 489p. 1982. pap. 10.95 (ISBN 0-8128-6146-9). Stein & Day.

Bouvier, Jean. The Innocent Years. 99p. 1981. 6.95 (ISBN 0-86666-034-8). GWP.

Bouvier, Leon & Rao, Sethu. Socioreligious Factors in Fertility Decline. LC 75-26602. 224p. 1975. text ed. 20.00x prof ref (ISBN 0-88410-352-8). Ballinger Pub.

Bouvier, Leon F. Illegal Immigration: What Can We Do About It? (Vital Issues, Vol. XXVIII 1978-79). 0.50 (ISBN 0-686-81621-8). Ctr Info Am.

Bouvier, Virginia. Alliance or Compliance: Implications of the Chilean Experience for the Catholic Church in Latin America. (Foreign & Comparative Studies Program, Latin American Ser.: No. 3). (Orig.). 1983. pap. text ed. write for info. (ISBN 0-915984-94-6). Syracuse U Foreign Comp.

Bouwer, Herman. Groundwater Hydrology. (Environment Water & Resources Ser). (Illus.). 1978. text ed. 34.50x (ISBN 0-07-006715-5, C); solution manual 7.95 (ISBN 0-07-006716-3). McGraw.

Bouwmeester, H. Winning Chess Combinations. 1977. 17.95 o.p. (ISBN 0-7134-0419-1, Pub. by Batsford England); pap. 11.50 (ISBN 0-7134-0420-5). David & Charles.

Bouwsma, O. K. Philosophical Essays. Landmark, ed. LC 82-7001. (Landmark Ed. Ser.). x, 209p. 1982. Repr. of 1965 ed. 18.95x (ISBN 0-8032-1179-1). U of Nebr Pr.

Bouwsma, William J. Venice & the Defense of Republican Liberty: Renaissance Values in the Age of the Counter Reformation. LC 68-14642. (Illus.). 1968. 44.00x (ISBN 0-520-00151-6). U of Cal Pr.

Bouyer, Louis. A History of Christian Spirituality, 3 vols. 1977. Set. 52.50 (ISBN 0-8164-0349-X); Vol. 1. 17.50 (ISBN 0-8164-0325-2); Vol. 2. 19.50 (ISBN 0-8164-0326-0); Vol. 3. 12.50 (ISBN 0-8164-0327-9). Seabury.

Bova, Ben. Vision of the Future: The Art of Robert McCall. LC 81-20542. (Illus.). 192p. 1982. 25.00 (ISBN 0-686-83927-7). Abrams.

Bova, Ben, ed. Analog Science Fact Reader. LC 73-87398. 1976. pap. 7.95 o.p. (ISBN 0-312-03220-X). St Martin.
--Close up New Worlds: Galaxy-Shaking Modern Views of the Solar System. 1977. 15.00 o.p. (ISBN 0-312-14490-3); pap. write for info. o.p. (ISBN 0-312-14491-1). St Martin.
--Exiles. LC 78-3974. 1978. 7.95 o.p. (ISBN 0-312-27493-9). St Martin.
--The Science Fiction Hall of Fame, Vol. 2B. 1974. pap. 3.95 (ISBN 0-380-00054-7, 60194-X). Avon.

Bovay, H. E., Jr., ed. Handbook of Mechanical & Electrical Systems for Buildings. (Illus.). 864p. 1981. 54.50 (ISBN 0-07-006718-X). McGraw.

Bovbjerg, Dana, jt. auth. see Iggers, Jeremy.

Bovbjerg, Randall R. & Holahan, John. Medicaid in the Reagan Era: Federal Policy & State Choices. LC 82-83893. (Changing Domestic Priorities Ser.). 72p. (Orig.). 1982. pap. 7.95 (ISBN 0-87766-319-X, 34500). Urban Inst.

Bove, Alfred A., jt. ed. see Santamore, William P.

Bove, Tony & Finkel, LeRoy. The TRS-80 TM Model III User's Guide. 252p. 1983. pap. 12.95 (ISBN 0-471-86242-8). Wiley.

Bovet, David & Unnevehr, Laurian. Agricultural Pricing in Togo. (Working Paper: No. 467). 76p. 1981. 5.00 (ISBN 0-686-36094-X, WP-0467). World Bank.

Bovet, Eric D. Stagflation: The Penalty of Speculative Production in a Multi-Stage Economy. LC 82-48021. 1983. price not set (ISBN 0-669-05883-1). Lexington Bks.

Bovey, F. A. & Winslow, F. H., eds. Macromolecules: Student Edition. 576p. 1982. pap. 23.00 (ISBN 0-12-119756-5). Acad Pr.

Bovey, Frank A. NMR Data Tables for Organic Compounds, Vol. 1. LC 67-20258. 1967. 165.00 o.p. (ISBN 0-470-09210-6, Pub. by Wiley-Interscience). Wiley.
--Polymer Conformation & Configuration. (Current Chemical Concepts Monographs). 1969. 39.00 (ISBN 0-12-119760-3). Acad Pr.

Bovey, Frank A. & Jelinski, Lynn W., eds. Chain Structure & Conformation of Macromolecules. LC 82-20779. (Monograph). 1982. 19.50 (ISBN 0-12-119780-8). Acad Pr.

Bovey, Rodney W. & Young, Alvin L. The Science of Two, Four, Five-T & Associated Phenoxy Herbicides. 462p. 1980. 47.95x (ISBN 0-471-05134-9, Pub. by Wiley-Interscience). Wiley.

Bovie, Palmer, ed. & frwd. by. The Complete Comedies of Terrence: Modern Verse Translations. Parker, Douglass & Carrier, Constance, trs. 420p. 1975. pap. 12.50x (ISBN 0-8135-0805-3). Rutgers U Pr.

Bovill, Diana. Tutorial Therapy: Teaching Neurotics to Treat Themselves. (Illus.). 200p. 1982. text ed. 25.00 (ISBN 0-85200-451-6, Pub. by MTP Pr England). Kluwer Boston.

Bow, Paul, et al. The State in Northern Ireland: Political Forces & Social Classes. LC 79-13020. 1980. 25.00x (ISBN 0-312-75608-9). St Martin.

Bowcock, Philip & Rose, J. J. Valuing with a Pocket Calculator. 160p. 1981. 35.00x (ISBN 0-686-99796-4, Pub. by Tech Pr). State Mutual Bk.

Bowden, Charles & Burstein, Alvin. Psychosocial Basis of Medical Practice: An Introduction to Human Behavior. 3rd ed. 1979. pap. 17.00 o.p. (ISBN 0-683-00992-3). Williams & Wilkins.

Bowden, D. M., tr. see Startsev, V. G.

Bowden, David K. The Execution of Isaac Hayne. new ed. LC 76-20850. (Illus.). 1977. 5.95 (ISBN 0-87844-037-2); ltd signed ed o.p. 12.95 (ISBN 0-87844-014-3). Sandlapper Store.

Bowden, Elbert. Economics Through the Looking Glass. LC 74-11179. 1974. pap. 10.95 o.p. (ISBN 0-06-380850-1, HarpC). Har-Row.

Bowden, Elbert V. Revolution Banking. LC 80-67370. 203p. (Orig.). Date not set. pap. 15.00 (ISBN 0-936328-01-0); pap. text ed. 9.95 (ISBN 0-686-83171-3). Dame Inc.

Bowden, Henry L. Boards of Trustees: Their Organization & Operation at Private Colleges & Universities. LC 82-7991. 60p. 1982. 8.95x (ISBN 0-86554-040-3). Mercer Univ Pr.

Bowden, Henry W. Dictionary of American Religious Biography. Gaustad, Edwin S., ed. LC 76-5258. (Orig.). 1976. lib. bdg. 45.00x (ISBN 0-8371-8906-3, BAR/). Greenwood.

Bowden, Henry W., ed. see Eliot, John.

Bowden, J. H. Peter De Vries. (United States Authors Ser.). 177p. 1983. lib. bdg. 15.95 (ISBN 0-8057-7388-6, Twayne). G K Hall.

Bowden, John. Archeology & the Bible. 24p. 1982. pap. 3.00 (ISBN 0-910309-00-0). Am Atheist.

--The Bible Contradicts Itself. 36p. 1982. pap. 3.00 (ISBN 0-686-81732-X). Am Atheist.

--Herbert Armstrong & His Worldwide Church of God: An Exposure & an Indictment. 64p. 1982. pap. 3.00 (ISBN 0-686-97500-6). Am Atheist.

--Karl Barth. (Student Christian Movement Press Ser.). (Orig.). 1971. pap. 3.95x (ISBN 0-19-520308-9). Oxford U Pr.

Bowden, John, tr. see Beyerlin, Walter.

Bowden, John, tr. see Gunneweg, A. H.

Bowden, John, tr. see Hengel, Martin.

Bowden, John, tr. see Herrmann, Siegfried.

Bowden, John, tr. see Jagersma, Henk.

Bowden, John, tr. see Soggin, J. Alberto.

Bowden, John, tr. see Theissen, Gerd.

Bowden, Jon G. Bible Absurdities. 20p. 1982. pap. 1.50 (ISBN 0-911826-45-9). Am Atheist.

Bowden, Ken, jt. auth. see Jacobs, John.

Bowden, Ken, jt. auth. see Nicklaus, Jack.

Bowden, Leon, jt. auth. see Shiffer, M. M.

Bowden, Liz. Mysterious Doubles. LC 79-19034. (Unsolved Mysteries of the World Ser.). PLB 11.96 (ISBN 0-89547-080-2). Silver.

Bowden, Malcolm. Ape-Men. 1979. pap. 8.95 (ISBN 0-9506042-0-8). CLP Pubs.

Bowden, Mary W. Philip Freneau. (United States Authors Ser.). 1976. lib. bdg. 12.95 (ISBN 0-8057-7161-1, Twayne). G K Hall.

--Washington Irving. (United States Authors Ser.). 1981. lib. bdg. 10.95 (ISBN 0-8057-7314-2, Twayne). G K Hall.

Bowden, R. The Econometrics of Disequalibrium. (Studies in Mathematical & Managerial Economics: Vol. 26). 1978. 51.00 (ISBN 0-444-85251-4, North Holland). Elsevier.

Bowden, Robert. Get That Picture. (Illus.). 1977. 13.95 o.p. (ISBN 0-8174-2430-X, Amphoto); pap. 8.95 o.p. (ISBN 0-8174-2111-4). Watson-Guptill.

Bowden, Russell, ed. Library Education Programmes in Developing Countries with Special Reference to Asia. (IFLA Publications: No. 20). 208p. 1983. price not set (ISBN 3-598-20383-7, Pub. by K G Saur). Shoe String.

Bowder, Diana, ed. Biographical Dictionary of the Greek World. 256p. 1982. 29.95 (ISBN 0-8014-1538-1). Cornell U Pr.

Bowditch, James L., jt. auth. see Huse, Edgar F.

Bowditch, John & Ramsland, Clement, eds. Voices of the Industrial Revolution: Selected Readings from the Liberal Economists & Their Critics. 1961. pap. 6.50 (ISBN 0-472-06053-8, 53, AA). U of Mich Pr.

Bowditch, Nathaniel. Bowditch for Yachtsmen: Piloting. abridged ed. (Illus.). 270p. 1976. 9.95 o.s.i. (ISBN 0-679-50603-9). McKay.

--Waves, Wind & Weather: Selected from American Practical Navigator. (Nautical Ser.). (Illus.). 1977. 7.95 o.p. (ISBN 0-679-50753-1). McKay.

Bowdle, Donald, ed. see Ellicott, Charles J.

Bowdler, George A., jt. auth. see Cotter, Patrick.

Bowdler, Lucy. Nurse Sandra's Choice. (YA) 1978. 6.95 (ISBN 0-685-85781-6, Avalon). Bouregy.

Bowdler, Sandra, ed. Coastal Archaeology in Eastern Australia. 151p. (Orig.). 1982. pap. text ed. 17.95 (ISBN 0-86784-015-3, 1185, Pub. by ANUP Australia). Bks Australia.

Bowe, Frank. Handicapping America: Barriers to Disabled People. LC 77-11816. 1978. 15.34i (ISBN 0-06-010422-8, HarpT). Har-Row.

--Rehabilitating America: Toward Independence for Disabled & Elderly People. LC 79-1654. 1980. 12.45i (ISBN 0-06-010436-8, HarpT). Har-Row.

Bowe, William J. & Parker, Douglas H. Page on the Law of Wills: Bowe-Parker Revision, Vols. 1-6, Vol. 7 Parts 1, 2, 3, Vol. 8 Parts 1 & 2 With 1981-82 Supplements. 1981. text ed. 425.00 (ISBN 0-87084-682-5). Anderson Pub Co.

Bowen & Behr. The Logical Design of Multiple Microprocessor Systems. (Illus.). 272p. 1980. text ed. 27.95 (ISBN 0-13-539908-4). P-H.

Bowen, Angela. The Diabetic Gourmet. rev. ed. (Illus.). 196p. 1981. pap. 4.76i (ISBN 0-06-463526-0, EH 526, EH). B&N NY.

--The Diabetic Gourmet. rev ed. LC 79-1655. (Illus.). 1980. 12.45i (ISBN 0-06-010437-6, HarpT). Har-Row.

Bowen, B. A. & Brown, W. R. VLSI Systems Design for Digital Signal Processing, Vol. 1: Signal Processing & Signal Processors. (Illus.). 256p. 1982. text ed. 32.95 (ISBN 0-13-942706-6). P-H.

Bowen, Barbara C. Words & the Man in French Renaissance Literature. LC 83-80027. (French Forum Monographs: No. 45). (Orig.). 1983. pap. 12.50 (ISBN 0-917058-45-3). French Forum.

Bowen, Catherine. Biography: The Craft & the Calling. LC 77-19110. 1978. Repr. of 1969 ed. lib. bdg. 21.00x (ISBN 0-313-20219-2, BOBI). Greenwood.

Bowen, Desmond. The Protestant Crusade in Ireland, 1800-70: A Study of Protestant-Catholic Relations Between the Act of Union & Disestablishment. 1978. 27.50x (ISBN 0-7735-0295-5). McGill-Queens U Pr.

Bowen, Donald, jt. auth. see Boone, Louis E.

Bowen, E. K. & Starr, M. K. Basic Statistics for Business & Economics. 1982. 26.95x (ISBN 0-07-006725-2); pap. 9.95x (ISBN 0-07-006727-9). McGraw.

Bowen, Elbert R., et al. Communicative Reading. 4th ed. (Illus.). 1978. 21.95x (ISBN 0-02-313000-8). Macmillan.

Bowen, Elizabeth. The Death of the Heart. 1979. pap. 2.25 o.s.i. (ISBN 0-380-43604-3, 43604). Avon.

--The Death of the Heart. 352p. Date not set. 11.95 (ISBN 0-394-42172-8, Vin). Random.

--Heat of the Day. 258p. 1981. Repr. lib. bdg. 16.95 (ISBN 0-89966-259-5). Buccaneer Bks.

--The Hotel. LC 73-141416. 294p. 1972. Repr. of 1928 ed. lib. bdg. 15.50x (ISBN 0-8371-4685-2, BOHO). Greenwood.

Bowen, Elizabeth, ed. see Mansfield, Katherine.

Bowen, Ezra. The High Sierra. (American Wilderness Ser.). (Illus.). (gr. 6 up). 1972. lib. bdg. 15.96 (ISBN 0-8094-1141-5, Pub. by Time-Life). Silver.

--Knights of the Air. LC 79-9398. (Epic of Flight Ser.). 19.96 (ISBN 0-686-79794-9). Silver.

Bowen, Glen. Collectible Fountain Pens: Parker, Sheaffer, Wahl-Eversharp, Waterman. LC 82-90494. (Illus.). 320p. (Orig.). 1982. pap. 16.95 (ISBN 0-910173-00-1). G Bowen Comm.

Bowen, Howard. Toward Social Economy. LC 76-43973. (Political & Social Economy Ser.). 367p. 1977. Repr. of 1948 ed. 22.50x (ISBN 0-8093-0813-4). S Ill U Pr.

Bowen, Howard R. The Business Enterprise As a Subject for Research. LC 55-8373. 1955. pap. 2.50 o.s.i. (ISBN 0-527-03299-9). Kraus Repr.

Bowen, I. & Lockshin, R. Cell Death in Biology & Pathology. (Illus.). 450p. 1981. 69.00x (ISBN 0-412-16010-2, Pub. by Chapman & Hall). Methuen Inc.

Bowen, J. Donald. Patterns of English Pronunciation. LC 75-24702. 1975. pap. 10.95 (ISBN 0-88377-044-X). Newbury Hse.

--Spoken Tagalog. (Spoken Language Ser.). 1982. bk. & Cassettes I 100.00x (ISBN 0-686-97804-8). Spoken Lang Serv.

--Spoken Tagalog. LC 65-25321. (Spoken Language Ser.). 551p. (Orig.). 1982. pap. text ed. 20.00x (ISBN 0-87950-465-X); Cassettes I, Units 1-12. 6 dual trk. cass. 90.00x (ISBN 0-87950-466-8); Cassettes II, Units 13-25. 22 dual trk. cass. 130.00x (ISBN 0-686-97805-6); Book & Cassettes I & II 220.00x (ISBN 0-87950-469-2). Spoken Lang Serv.

Bowen, J. Donald, jt. auth. see Madsen, Harold S.

Bowen, J. Donald, tr. see Cabrera, Neonetta C. & Cunanan, Augustina S.

Bowen, James. A History of Western Education, Vol. 1. LC 79-185251. 1972. 27.50 (ISBN 0-312-38710-5). St Martin.

--A History of Western Education: Civilization of Europe Sixth to Sixteenth Century, Vol. 2. LC 79-185251. (Illus.). 536p. 1975. 27.50 (ISBN 0-312-38745-8). St Martin.

Bowen, John. Little Boxes. 110p. 1968. pap. 7.95 o.p. (ISBN 0-686-86356-9, Pub. by Eyre Methuen England). Methuen Inc.

--A Ship Model Maker's Manual. 192p. 1982. 42.00x (ISBN 0-85177-235-8, Pub. by Conway Maritime England). State Mutual Bk.

Bowen, Kurt. Protestants in a Catholic State: Ireland's Privileged Minority. 240p. 1983. 25.00x (ISBN 0-7735-0412-5). McGill-Queens U Pr.

Bowen, Leslie. The Art & Craft of Growing Orchids. LC 75-39781. (Illus.). 1976. 10.95 o.p. (ISBN 0-399-11736-9). Putnam Pub Group.

Bowen, Majorie. Peter Porcupine. LC 78-145715. 1971. Repr. of 1935 ed. 34.00 o.p. (ISBN 0-8103-3677-4). Gale.

Bowen, Margarita. Empiricism & Geographical Thought: From Francis Bacon to Alexander von Humboldt. LC 80-42058. (Cambridge Geographical Studies: No. 15). 336p. 1981. 52.50 (ISBN 0-521-23653-3). Cambridge U Pr.

Bowen, Michael. Journey to Nepal. 1970. pap. 2.50 o.p. (ISBN 0-87286-003-5). City Lights.

Bowen, Oliver E., Jr. Rocks & Minerals of the San Francisco Bay Region. (California Natural History Guides: No. 5). (Illus.). 1962. 14.95x o.p. (ISBN 0-520-03244-6); pap. 2.85 (ISBN 0-520-00158-3). U of Cal Pr.

Bowen, R. L. The Early Arabian Necropolis of Ain Jawan: A Pre-Islamic & Early Islamic Site on the Persian Gulf. (American Schools of Oriental Research, Supplementary Studies: Vols. 7-9). 70p. 1950. text ed. 3.50x (ISBN 0-89757-309-9, Am Sch Orient Res). Eisenbrauns.

Bowen, Robert. Grouting in Engineering Practice. 2nd ed. LC 81-1015. 240p. 1981. 44.95x o.p. (ISBN 0-470-27147-7). Halsted Pr.

--Paleotemperature Analysis. (Methods in Geochemistry & Geophysics: Vol. 2). 1966. 68.00 (ISBN 0-444-40074-5). Elsevier.

--Surface Water. 290p. 1982. 49.95x (ISBN 0-471-87418-3, Pub. by Wiley-Interscience). Wiley.

Bowen, Robert G., Jr. My Philosophy: Why My Paintings are Signed "A Friend of Civilization". LC 81-69045. (Orig.). 1982. black & white ed. 30.00 (ISBN 0-9607512-1-1); color ed. 30.00 (ISBN 0-9607512-3-8); pap. 4.00 black & white ed. (ISBN 0-9607512-0-3); pap. 6.00 color ed. (ISBN 0-9607512-2-X). R G Bowen.

Bowen, Roger W. Rebellion & Democracy in Meiji Japan: A Study of Commoners in the Popular Rights Movement. LC 78-51755. 450p. 1980. 32.50x (ISBN 0-520-03665-4). U of Cal Pr.

Bowen, Van. Vestryman's Guide. pap. 2.95 (ISBN 0-8164-2136-6). Seabury.

Bowen, Van S. A Vestry Member's Guide. rev. ed. 80p. 1983. pap. 3.95 (ISBN 0-8164-2464-0). Seabury.

Bowen, W. H., et al, eds. Immunologic Aspects of Dental Caries. (Illus.). 1976. pap. text ed. 10.00 o.p. (ISBN 0-917000-00-5). IRL Pr.

Bowen, William R. & Baxter, William D. Experimental Cell Biology: An Integrated Laboratory Guide & Text. 2nd ed. (Illus.). 1980. pap. text ed. 15.95 (ISBN 0-02-312940-9). Macmillan.

Bowen Jones, John, jt. auth. see Evans, D. MacLean.

Bower, B. M. Border Vengeance. (YA) 1971. 6.95 (ISBN 0-685-03333-3, Avalon). Bouregy.

Bower, Blair T., jt. ed. see Basta, Daniel J.

Bower, Carol E. The Basic Marine Aquarium: A Simplified, Modern Approach to the Care of Saltwater Fishes. (Illus.). 264p. 1982. pap. 14.95x (ISBN 0-398-04736-7). C C Thomas.

Bower, Cynthia E. & Rhoads, Mary L. EPA Index: A Key to U. S. Environmental Protection Agency Reports & Superintendent of Documents & NTIS Numbers. 1983. lib. bdg. 27.50 (ISBN 0-89774-032-7). Oryx Pr.

Bower, Eli M. Early Identification of Emotionally Handicapped Children in School. 2nd ed. (Illus.). 276p. 1974. photocopy ed. spiral 18.50x o.p. (ISBN 0-398-00202-9). C C Thomas.

Bower, F. L. Foundations of Pharmacologic Therapy. LC 77-3582. (Nursing Concept Modulas Ser.). 1977. 15.95x o.p. (ISBN 0-471-02168-7, Pub. by Wiley Med). Wiley.

--Nursing & the Concept of Loss. (Nursing Concept Modules Ser.). 214p. 1980. 15.95 (ISBN 0-471-04790-2). Wiley.

Bower, Fay L. Health Maintenance. LC 79-25269. (Wiley Nursing Concept Module Ser.). 1980. pap. 18.50x (ISBN 0-471-03782-6, Pub. by Wiley Med). Wiley.

--Health Screening. LC 80-10197. (Nursing Concept Modules Ser.). 1980. pap. 16.95 o.p. (ISBN 0-471-03781-8, Pub. by Wiley Med). Wiley.

--Nutrition in Nursing. LC 79-10562. (Nursing Concept Modules Ser.). 1979. pap. 15.95 o.p. (ISBN 0-471-04124-6, Pub. by Wiley Med). Wiley.

--The Process of Planning Nursing Care: Nursing Practice Models. 3rd ed. LC 81-14164. (Illus.). 207p. 1982. pap. text ed. 11.95 (ISBN 0-8016-0721-3). Mosby.

Bower, Fay L., ed. Distortions in Body Image in Illness & Disability. LC 77-4429. (Nursing Concept Modules Ser.). 1977. pap. 15.95 o.p. (ISBN 0-471-02169-5, Pub. by Wiley Med). Wiley.

--Normal Development of Body Image. LC 77-3487. (Nursing Concept Modules Ser.). 1977. pap. 15.95 (ISBN 0-471-02170-9, Pub. by Wiley Med). Wiley.

Bower, Fay L. & Wheeler, Robinetta T., eds. The Nursing Assessment. LC 77-5160. (Wiley Nursing Concept Modules). 1977. pap. 18.50x (ISBN 0-471-02167-9, Pub. by Wiley Med). Wiley.

Bower, G. H. see Spence, Kenneth W., et al.

Bower, Gordon H. & Hilgard, Ernest J. Theories of Learning. 5th ed. (Illus.). 640p. 1981. text ed. 26.95 (ISBN 0-13-914432-3). P-H.

Bower, Gordon H., jt. auth. see Bower, Sharon A.

Bower, Kathleen A., jt. ed. see Zander, Karen S.

Bower, Marvin. Will to Manage: Corporate Success Through Programmed Management. 1966. 29.95 (ISBN 0-07-006735-X, P&RB). McGraw.

Bower, Robert T. & De Gasparis, Priscilla. Ethics in Social Research: Protecting the Interests of Human Subjects. LC 78-19452. 240p. 1978. 26.95 o.p. (ISBN 0-03-046406-4). Praeger.

Bower, Sharon A. Painless Public Speaking. (Illus.). 272p. 1981. 12.95 (ISBN 0-13-647933-2, Spec); pap. 6.95 (ISBN 0-13-647925-1). P-H.

Bower, Sharon A. & Bower, Gordon H. Asserting Yourself: A Practical Guide for Positive Change. 6.95 o.p. (ISBN 0-686-92299-9, 6348). Hazelden.

Bowerman, Bill, jt. auth. see Moore, Bobbie.

Bowerman, Guy E. The Compensations of War: The Diary of an Ambulance Driver During the Great War. Carnes, Mark C., ed. 200p. 1983. 9.95 (ISBN 0-292-71074-7). U of Tex Pr.

Bowerman, Melissa. Early Syntactic Development: A Cross Linguistic Study with Special Reference to Finnish. (Cambridge Studies in Linguistics: No. 11). 49.50 (ISBN 0-521-20019-9); pap. 15.95 (ISBN 0-521-09797-5). Cambridge U Pr.

Bowers, Arden C., jt. auth. see Thompson, June M.

Bowers, B. A History of Electric Light & Power. (IEE History of Technology Ser.: No. 3). 304p. 1982. 71.00 (ISBN 0-906048-68-0); pap. 43.50 (ISBN 0-906048-71-0). Inst Elect Eng.

Bowers, C. A. Progressive Educator & the Depression: The Radical Years. (Western Educational Tradition Ser). (Orig.). 1968. pap. text ed. 3.95 (ISBN 0-685-19757-3). Phila Bk Co.

Bowers, C. A., et al, eds. Education & Social Policy: Local Control of Education. (Orig.). 1970. pap. text ed. 4.75x (ISBN 0-685-19689-5). Phila Bk Co.

Bowers, Carolyn O., et al. Judging & Coaching Women's Gymnastics. 2nd ed. (Illus.). 363p. 1981. text ed. 19.95 (ISBN 0-87484-391-X). Mayfield Pub.

Bowers, Claude G. & Browder, Earl. The Heritage of Jefferson. Franklin, Francis, ed. LC 82-24251. 48p. 1983. Repr. of 1944 ed. lib. bdg. 19.75x (ISBN 0-313-23839-1, BOHE). Greenwood.

Bowers, Cyril Y., et al. Endocrine-Metabolic Drugs. LC 74-21392. (Principles & Techniques of Human Research & Therapeutics Ser.: Vol. 6). (Illus.). 224p. 1975. 14.75 o.p. (ISBN 0-87993-050-0). Futura Pub.

Bowers, D., jt. auth. see Bennet, S.

Bowers, David G. & Franklin, Jerome L. Survey-Guided Development I: Data-Based Organizational Change. rev. ed. LC 77-75523. 145p. 1977. pap. 11.50 (ISBN 0-88390-137-4). Univ Assocs.

Bowers, David G., jt. auth. see Taylor, James C.

Bowers, David Q. United States Gold Coins: An Illustrated History. (Illus.). 415p. 1982. 35.00 (ISBN 0-914490-21-4). Bowers & Ruddy.

Bowers, Dennis. Records Management Projects. 1982. pap. text ed. 11.00 (ISBN 0-8359-6613-5). Reston.

Bowers, Edgar. Living Together: New & Selected Poems. LC 73-81061. 88p. 1973. pap. 5.95 (ISBN 0-87923-104-1). Godine.

Bowers, Fredson. Textual & Literary Criticism. 1959. 29.95 (ISBN 0-521-04290-9); pap. 6.95x o.p. (ISBN 0-521-09407-0, 407). Cambridge U Pr.

Bowers, Fredson, ed. The Red Badge of Courage: A Facsimile of the Manuscript. 1973. deluxe ed. 150.00 boxed (ISBN 0-89723-035-3). Bruccoli.

Bowers, Fredson, ed. see Beaumont, Francis & Fletcher, John.

Bowers, Fredson, ed. see Crane, Stephen.

Bowers, Fredson, ed. see Dryden, John.

Bowers, Fredson, ed. see Hoy, Cyrus.

Bowers, Fredson, ed. see Nabokov, Vladimir.

Bowers, Fredson, ed. see James, William.

Bowers, Joan S. Psychopharmacology for Non-Medical Therapists: A Manual for Psychologists, Social Workers, Counselors & Nurses. 53p. 1981. pap. write for info. Ohio Psych Pub.

Bowers, John & Deaton, David. Labour Hoarding in British Industry. (Warwick Studies in Industrial Relations). (Illus.). 176p. 1982. text ed. 29.50x (ISBN 0-631-13128-0, Pub. by Basil Blackwell England). Biblio Dist.

Bowers, John B. The Midwife Murder Case: The Rosalie Tarpening Story. (Illus.). 300p. (Orig.). 1983. pap. 7.95 (ISBN 0-917982-24-X). Cougar Bks.

Bowers, John Z. & Purcell, Elizabeth, eds. National Health Services: Their Impact on Medical Education & Their Role in Prevention. LC 73-77541. (Illus.). 168p. 1973. pap. 7.50 o.p. (ISBN 0-914362-03-8). J Macy Foun.

Bowers, John Z. & Purcell, Elizabeth F., eds. Aspects of the History of Medicine in Latin America. LC 79-91586. (Illus.). 196p. pap. 4.00 o.p. (ISBN 0-914362-29-1). J Macy Foun.

Bowers, Kathleen R. At This Very Minute. (Illus.). 32p. (gr. k-3). 1983. 12.00i (ISBN 0-316-10400-0); pap. 5.70i (ISBN 0-316-10401-9). Little.

Bowers, Larry D., jt. auth. see Carr, Peter.

Bowers, Mary C. Best Nurse in Missouri. 1982. 6.95 (ISBN 0-686-84167-0, Avalon). Bouregy.

--The Loves of Nurse Rachel. (YA) 1981. 6.95 (ISBN 0-686-74797-6, Avalon). Bouregy.

--Nurse Beckie's New World. 1982. 6.95 (ISBN 0-686-84184-0, Avalon). Bouregy.

--Nurse Charly's New Love. 1982. pap. 6.95 (ISBN 0-686-84742-3, Avalon). Bouregy.

--Nurse in Australia. 1981. pap. 6.95 (ISBN 0-686-84704-0, Avalon). Bouregy.

--Nurse in Peru. 1981. pap. 6.95 (ISBN 0-686-84689-3, Avalon). Bouregy.

--Nurse Jamie's Surprise. 1982. 6.95 (ISBN 0-686-84172-7, Avalon). Bouregy.

--Nurse Karen's Masquerade. 1982. pap. 6.95 (ISBN 0-686-84724-5, Avalon). Bouregy.

Bowers, Peter M. Forgotten Fighters & Experimental Aircraft of the U. S. Army, 1918-1941. LC 70-124505. (Illus.). 80p. (Orig.). 1971. pap. 3.95 o.p. (ISBN 0-668-02403-8). Arco.

--Yesterday's Wings: Eighty-Two Historical Aircraft. pap. 8.95x o.p. (ISBN 0-911720-87-1). Aviation.

Bowers, Redson, ed. see James, William.

Bowers, Terrell L. Avery's Vengeance. 1982. 6.95 (ISBN 0-686-84166-2, Avalon). Bouregy.
--Banyon's War. 1982. 6.95 (ISBN 0-686-84177-8, Avalon). Bouregy.
--Chase into Mexico. 1982. pap. 6.95 (ISBN 0-686-84734-2, Avalon). Bouregy.
--Crossfire at Twin Forks. (YA) 1980. 6.95 (ISBN 0-686-73938-8, Avalon). Bouregy.
--Frozen Trail. (YA) 1981. 6.95 (ISBN 0-686-74796-8, Avalon). Bouregy.
--Gunfire at Flintlock. (YA) 1981. 6.95 (ISBN 0-686-73952-3, Avalon). Bouregy.
--Last Stand at Rio Blanco. 1981. pap. 6.95 (ISBN 0-686-84703-2, Avalon). Bouregy.
--Maverick Raid. 1982. 6.95 (ISBN 0-686-84188-3, Avalon). Bouregy.
--Rio Grande Death Ride. (YA) 1980. 6.95 (ISBN 0-686-73924-8, Avalon). Bouregy.
Bowers, Terry. Dance of Love. 1981. pap. 6.95 (ISBN 0-686-84679-6, Avalon). Bouregy.
Bowers, Thomas A., jt. auth. see Fletcher, Alan D.
Bowers, Warner F & Dimendberg, David C. Emergency Medical Technician Examination Review, Vol. 2. 1972. spiral bdg. 12.00 o.p. (ISBN 0-87488-466-7). Med Exam.
Bowers, Warner F., et al. ECFMG Examination Review. 4th ed. LC 76-9880. 1976. Pt. 1. pap. 15.50 (ISBN 0-87488-120-X); Pt. 2. pap. 15.50 (ISBN 0-87488-121-8). Med Exam.
Bowers, William J. Executions in America. LC 81-11309. 489p. 1983. Repr. of 1974 ed. 35.00x (ISBN 0-930350-25-1). NE U Pr.
Bowersox, Donald J. Logistical Management: A System Integration of Physical Distribution Management, & Materials Management. 2nd ed. (Illus.). 512p. 1978. text ed. 26.95 (ISBN 0-02-313110-1, 31311). Macmillan.
Bowersox, Donald J., et al. Management in Marketing Channels. (Illus.). 1979. text ed. 24.95 (ISBN 0-07-006740-6). McGraw.
--Introduction to Transportation. 1980. text ed. 21.95 (ISBN 0-02-313030-X). Macmillan.
Bowes, Betty. Ministry of the Cradle Roll. (Orig.). 1970. pap. 1.50 (ISBN 0-8341-0190-4). Beacon Hill.
--Planning Church Time for Children. 1969. pap. 1.50 (ISBN 0-8341-0153-X). Beacon Hill.
Bowes, Clare. Man from Inverness. LC 68-31508. (Foreign Lands Bks). (Illus.). (gr. k-5). 1968. PLB 3.95g (ISBN 0-8225-0361-1). Lerner Pubns.
Bowes, D. R. & Leake, B. E. Crustal Evolution in Northwestern Britain & Adjacent Regions: Geological Journal Special Issue, No. 10. (Liverpool Geological Society & the Manchester Geological Association). 508p. 1980. 114.95x (ISBN 0-471-27757-6, Pub. by Wiley-Interscience). Wiley.
Bowes, Edwin E., jt. auth. see Pottenger, Francis M.
Bowes, Florence. Beauchamp. LC 82-45142. (Starlight Romance Ser.). 192p. 1983. 11.95 (ISBN 0-385-18076-4). Doubleday.
--The Macorvan Curse. LC 79-48086. (Romantic Suspense Ser.). 192p. 1980. 10.95 o.p. (ISBN 0-385-15844-0). Doubleday.
--Web of Solitude. (Orig.). 1980. pap. 1.95 o.p. (ISBN 0-523-40561-8). Pinnacle Bks.
Bowes, Frederick P. The Culture of Early Charleston. LC 78-897. (Illus.). 1978. Repr. of 1942 ed. lib. bdg. 17.50x (ISBN 0-313-20278-8, BOCE). Greenwood.
Bowes, W. H. & Russell, Leslie T. Stress Analysis by the Finite Element Method for Practically Engineers. 128p. 1975. 24.95x (ISBN 0-669-99903-2). Lexington Bks.
Bowett, Derek. The Legal Regime of Islands in International Law. LC 78-23571. 337p. 1979. lib. bdg. 32.50 (ISBN 0-379-20346-4). Oceana.
Bowey, Angela M., ed. Handbook of Salary & Wage Systems. 2nd ed. 446p. 1982. text ed. 47.50 (ISBN 0-566-02261-3). Gower Pub Ltd.
Bowie, Gary W., jt. auth. see Zeigler, Earle F.
Bowie, Henry P. On the Laws of Japanese Painting. (Illus.). 1911. pap. 6.00 (ISBN 0-486-20030-2). Dover.
--On the Laws of Japanese Painting. (Illus.). 9.50 (ISBN 0-8446-0504-2). Peter Smith.
Bowie, Leland. The Impact of the Protege System in Morocco: 1880-1912. LC 79-633875. (Papers in International Studies: Africa: No. 11). 1970. pap. 2.75x (ISBN 0-89680-044-X, Ohio U Ctr Intl). Ohio U Pr.
Bowie, Malcolm. Mallarme & the Art of Being Difficult. LC 77-82488. 1978. 29.95 (ISBN 0-521-21813-6). Cambridge U Pr.
Bowie, Malcolm, et al, eds. Baudelaire, Mallarme, Valery: New Essays in Honour of Lloyd Austin. LC 81-12239. 300p. 1982. 57.50 (ISBN 0-521-23443-3). Cambridge U Pr.
Bowie, Norman. Business Ethics. (Illus.). 176p. 1982. pap. 10.50 (ISBN 0-13-095901-4). P-H.
Bowie, Norman E. & Simon, R. L. The Individual & the Political Order: An Introduction to Social & Political Philosophy. 1977. pap. text ed. 15.95 (ISBN 0-13-457143-6). P-H.
Bowie, Norman E., jt. auth. see Beauchamp, Tom L.
Bowie, Norman E., ed. Ethical Issues in Government. 251p. 1981. 27.95 (ISBN 0-87722-165-0). Temple U Pr.
--Ethical Theory in the Last Quarter of the Twentieth Century. LC 82-1006. 180p. 1982. text ed. 19.50 (ISBN 0-915145-34-0). Hackett Pub.
Bowie, Norman E., jt. ed. see Beauchamp, Tom L.
Bowie, Norman E., jt. ed. see Elliston, Frederick A.
Bowie, Robert, tr. see Bunin, Ivan.
Bowie, Sam. Canyon War. 128p. (gr. 8 up). 1980. pap. 1.50 (ISBN 0-448-17224-0, G&D). Putnam Pub Group.
Bowie, Theodore, ed. see De Honnecourt, Villard.
Bowker, Albert & Lieberman, Gerald. Engineering Statistics. 2nd ed. (Illus.). 608p. 1972. ref. ed. 28.95 (ISBN 0-13-279455-1). P-H.
Bowker, John. Jesus & the Pharisees. 240p. 1973. 37.50 (ISBN 0-521-20055-5). Cambridge U Pr.
--Problems of Suffering in the Religions of the World. LC 77-93706. 1975. 44.50 (ISBN 0-521-07412-6); pap. 10.95x (ISBN 0-521-09903-X). Cambridge U Pr.
--Targums & Rabbinic Literature. LC 71-80817. 1969. 54.50 (ISBN 0-521-07415-0). Cambridge U Pr.
Bowker, Lee H. Beating Wife-Beating. LC 82-48603. 176p. 1983. 21.95x (ISBN 0-669-06345-2). Lexington Bks.
--Humanizing Institutions for the Aged. LC 81-47977. (Illus.). 128p. 1982. 16.95x (ISBN 0-669-05209-4). Lexington Bks.
--Women & Crime in America. 1981. pap. text ed. 13.95x (ISBN 0-02-476830-8). Macmillan.
--Women, Crime, & the Criminal Justice System. LC 78-57180. (Illus.). 1978. 25.95x (ISBN 0-669-02374-4). Lexington Bks.
Bowker, Margaret. The Henrician Reformation: The Diocese of Lincoln Under John Longland 1521-1547. LC 80-41655. (Illus.). 256p. 1981. 44.50 (ISBN 0-521-23639-8). Cambridge U Pr.
Bowker, R. M. & Budd, S. A. Make Your Own Sails. rev. ed. LC 61-3835. (Illus.). 1976. pap. 3.95 o.p. (ISBN 0-312-50540-X). St Martin.
Bowlby, John. Loss. LC 79-2759. 1982. pap. 9.30 (ISBN 0-465-04238-4). Basic.
--The Making & Breaking of Affectional Bonds. 1979. 29.95x (ISBN 0-422-76850-2, Pub. by Tavistock England); pap. 7.95x (ISBN 0-422-76860-X). Methuen Inc.
Bowle, John. Man Through the Ages. LC 76-30532. 1977. 13.95 o.p. (ISBN 0-689-10797-8). Atheneum.
Bowler, K., jt. auth. see Hollingsworth, M. J.
Bowler, M. G. Nuclear Physics. 444p. 1973. text ed. write for info. (ISBN 0-08-016983-X); pap. text ed. write for info. (ISBN 0-08-018990-3). Pergamon.
Bowler, Marion. The Odd One. Ashton, Sylvia, ed. LC 77-86486. 1979. 13.95 o.s.i. (ISBN 0-87949-092-6). Ashley Bks.
Bowler, Peter, jt. auth. see Hughes, Denis.
Bowles, D. Richard. Make Way for Metrication. LC 72-13331. (Math Concepts Bks.). (Illus.). 56p. (gr. 6-10). 1975. PLB 4.95g (ISBN 0-8225-0583-5). Lerner Pubns.
Bowles, Ella S. About Antiques. LC 70-174011. (Tower Bks). (Illus.). 1971. Repr. of 1929 ed. 34.00x (ISBN 0-8103-3921-8). Gale.
Bowles, Gloria & Duelli-Klein, Renata, eds. Theories of Women's Studies. 270p. (Orig.). 1982. pap. 10.95 (ISBN 0-7100-9488-4). Routledge & Kegan.
Bowles, J. Foundation Analysis & Design. 3rd ed. 1982. 36.50x (ISBN 0-07-006770-8). McGraw.
Bowles, J., jt. auth. see Bolling, R.
Bowles, J. B., jt. auth. see Vichnevetsky, R.
Bowles, J. E. Foundation Analysis & Design. 2nd ed. 1977. text ed. 34.50 (ISBN 0-07-006750-3). McGraw.
Bowles, Jane. My Sister's Hand in Mine: An Expanded Edition of the Collected Works of Jane Bowles. LC 77-71329. (Neglected Books of the Twentieth Century). 1978. pap. 9.95 (ISBN 0-912946-44-X). Ecco Pr.
Bowles, Jerry. A Thousand Sundays: The Story of the Ed Sullivan Show. (Illus.). 192p. 1980. 9.95 o.p. (ISBN 0-399-12493-4). Putnam Pub Group.
Bowles, Joseph E. Analytic & Computer Methods in Foundation Engineering. (Illus.). 480p. 1973. text ed. 30.50 (ISBN 0-07-006753-8, C). McGraw.
--Engineering Properties of Soils & Their Measurements. 2nd ed. (Illus.). 1978. pap. text ed. 32.50 (ISBN 0-07-006752-X, C). McGraw.
--Physical & Geotechnical Properties of Soils. (Illus.). 1979. text ed. 37.95x (ISBN 0-07-006760-0, C); solutions manual 25.00 (ISBN 0-07-006761-9). McGraw.
--Structural Steel Design. (Illus.). 1980. text ed. 36.95 (ISBN 0-07-006765-1); data manual 18.00 (ISBN 0-07-006766-X). McGraw.
Bowles, Ken. The Beginner's Manual for the Pascal System. (Orig.). 1980. pap. 11.95 (ISBN 0-07-006745-7, BYTE Bks). McGraw.
Bowles, Michael. The Art of Conducting. LC 74-23419. (Music Ser.). 210p. 1975. Repr. of 1959 ed. lib. bdg. 22.50 (ISBN 0-306-70718-7). Da Capo.
Bowles, Norma & Hynds, Fran. PSI Search: The Comprehensive Guide to Psychic Phenomena. LC 77-7847. 1978. 6.95i o.p. (ISBN 0-06-064083-9, RD 234, HarpR). Har-Row.
Bowles, Paul. Midnight Mass. 176p. 1983. 14.00 (ISBN 0-87685-477-3); pap. 7.50 (ISBN 0-87685-476-5). Black Sparrow.
Bowles, Paul, tr. see Choukri, Mohamed.
Bowles, Paul, tr. see Eberhardt, Isabelle.
Bowles, Robert N. How to Buy Gold for Thirty Percent Below Market: And to Avoid Confiscation by the Government. 1981. 45.00 (ISBN 0-940372-00-2). Berot Bk.
Bowles, Roger. Law & the Economy. 256p. 1983. text ed. 29.50x (ISBN 0-85520-465-6, Pub. by Martin Robertson England). Biblio Dist.
Bowles, Roger A., jt. auth. see Whynes, David K.
Bowles, Samuel. Life & Times of Samuel Bowles, 2 Vols. Merriam, George S., ed. LC 75-87417. (American Scene Ser). 1970. Repr. of 1885 ed. Set. lib. bdg. 95.00 (ISBN 0-306-71562-7). Da Capo.
Bowles, Samuel & Gintis, Herbert. Schooling in Capitalist America: Educational Reform & the Contradictions of Economic Life. LC 75-7267. 320p. 1976. 15.00x o.s.i. (ISBN 0-465-07230-5); pap. 6.95x o.s.i. (ISBN 0-465-09718-9, CN-5018). Basic.
Bowles, Samuel, et al. Beyond the Wasteland: A Democratic Alternative to Economic Decline. LC 82-45514. 432p. 1983. 17.95 (ISBN 0-385-18345-3, Anchor Pr). Doubleday.
Bowles, Stephen E. Sidney Lumet: A Guide to References & Resources. (Reference Books). 1979. lib. bdg. 17.50 (ISBN 0-8161-7938-7, Hall Reference). G K Hall.
Bowlin, Oswald D., et al. Guide to Financial Analysis. LC 78-27412. (Illus.). 1979. 19.95 (ISBN 0-07-006781-3, C); pap. 14.95 (ISBN 0-07-006780-5). McGraw.
Bowling, W Kerby & Loving, Waldon. Management Fumbles & Union Recoveries. 232p. 1982. pap. text ed. 12.95 (ISBN 0-8403-2775-7). Kendall-Hunt.
Bowman, Alfred C. Zones of Strain: A Memoir of the Early Cold War. (Publications Ser.: P-273). 175p. 1982. 19.95 (ISBN 0-8179-7731-7). Hoover Inst Pr.
Bowman, Ann, jt. ed. see Lester, James P.
Bowman, Arthur G. & Milligan, W. D. Real Estate Law in California. new, 6th ed. (Illus.). 368p. 1982. 24.95 (ISBN 0-13-764035-8). P-H.
--Real Estate Law in California. 5th ed. 1978. ref. ed. 23.95 (ISBN 0-13-764043-9). P-H.
Bowman, Arthur G., jt. auth. see Bond, Robert J.
Bowman, Bruce. Toothpick Sculpture & Ice-Cream Stick Art. LC 76-19808. (Illus.). (gr. 5 up). 1976. 8.95 (ISBN 0-8069-5372-1); PLB 10.99 (ISBN 0-8069-5373-X). Sterling.
Bowman, Clell. Bold Steer. LC 73-92508. 250p. 1974. 8.95 o.s.i. (ISBN 0-8283-1540-X). Branden.
Bowman, Dee. Southwestern Cooking Recipes. 16p. pap. 2.00x (ISBN 0-943462-05-3). CaseCo.
Bowman, Derek. Life into Autobiography: A Study of Goethe's "Dichtung und Wahrheit". (Germanic Studies in America: Vol. 5). 162p. 1971. write for info. (ISBN 3-261-00311-1). P Lang Pubs.
Bowman, Derek, ed. The Diary of Dawid Rubinowicz. 80p. 1981. 15.00x o.p. (ISBN 0-85158-157-9, Pub. by Blackwood & Sons Scotland). State Mutual Bk.
--The Diary of Dawid Rubinowicz. 128p. 1982. 10.95 (ISBN 0-938106-03-1); limited ed.-o.p. 19.95 (ISBN 0-938106-04-X). Creative Options.
Bowman, Derek, ed. see Bassin, Ethel.
Bowman, Eldon. A Guide to the General Crook Trail. (Illus.). 1978. pap. 2.00 (ISBN 0-89734-045-0). Mus Northern Ariz.
Bowman, Elizabeth. Minor & Fragmentary Sentences of a Corpus of Spoken English. LC 66-63898. (General Publications Ser: Vol. 42). (Orig.). 1966. pap. text ed. 4.00x o.p. (ISBN 0-87750-130-0). Res Ctr Lang Semiotic.
Bowman, Ethel, jt. auth. see Palmer, Marjorie.
Bowman, Forest J. The Complete Retirement Handbook. LC 82-82307. 320p. (Orig.). pap. 8.95 (ISBN 0-448-16810-3, G&D). Putnam Pub Group.
Bowman, Frank. New Horizons Beyond the World. 5.95 o.p. (ISBN 0-87516-006-9). De Vorss.
Bowman, G. With Lewis & Clark Through the Rockies. (Illus.). (gr. 7 up). 12.75x (ISBN 0-392-01900-0, LTB). Sportshelf.
Bowman, George M. How to Succeed with Your Money. pap. 3.95 (ISBN 0-8024-3656-0). Moody.
--How to Succeed with Your Money. study ed 7.95 (ISBN 0-8024-3662-5). Moody.
Bowman, Gerald. With Amundsen at the North Pole. (Illus.). (gr. 7 up). 12.75x (ISBN 0-392-01847-0, LTB). Sportshelf.
Bowman, H. B. Handbook of Percision Sheet, Strip & Foil. 1980. 90.00 (ISBN 0-87170-091-3). ASM.
Bowman, Henry A. Marriage for Moderns. 7th ed. (Illus.). 576p. 1974. text ed. 18.95 (ISBN 0-07-006800-3, C); 9.95 (ISBN 0-07-006801-1). McGraw.
Bowman, Henry A. & Spanier, Graham B. Modern Marriage. 8th ed. 1977. text ed. 27.00 (ISBN 0-07-006802-X, C); instructor's manual 8.50 (ISBN 0-07-006803-8). McGraw.
Bowman, J. M., ed. Molecular Collision Dynamics. (Topics in Current Physics Ser.: Vol. 33). (Illus.). 180p. 1983. 19.00 (ISBN 0-387-12014-9). Springer-Verlag.
Bowman, Jayne, compiled by. Dear Mother: Words of Thanks & Thoughts of Love. (Illus.). 1979. boxed 5.50 (ISBN 0-8378-1703-X). Gibson.
--God, Grant Me Serenity. 1982. 3.95 (ISBN 0-8378-2030-8). Gibson.
--Messages of Faith from the Bible. 1982. 3.95 (ISBN 0-8378-2029-4). Gibson.
Bowman, Joel P. & Branchaw, Bernadine B. Effective Business Correspondence. 1978. pap. text ed. 12.50 scp (ISBN 0-06-453713-7, HarpC); instructors manual avail. (ISBN 0-06-453734-X). Har-Row.
Bowman, John. De Valera & the Ulster Question, Nineteen Seventeen to Nineteen Seventy-three. 384p. 1983. 39.00 (ISBN 0-19-822681-0). Oxford U Pr.
Bowman, John & O'Donoghue, Ronan. Portraits: Belvedere College, 1832-1982. 1982. 75.00x (ISBN 0-7171-1235-7, Pub. by Gill & Macmillan Ireland). State Mutual Bk.
Bowman, John, ed. see Ivanoff, Pierre.
Bowman, John, ed. see Laroche, Lucienne.
Bowman, John, ed. see Tamburello, Adolfo.
Bowman, John C. Animals for Man. (Studies in Biology: No. 78). 72p. 1977. pap. text ed. 8.95 (ISBN 0-7131-2629-9). E Arnold.
Bowman, John J., jt. auth. see Hardy, R. Allen.
Bowman, John W. Hebrews-Second Peter. LC 59-10454. (Layman's Bible Commentary Ser: Vol. 24). 1962. pap. 3.95 (ISBN 0-8042-3084-6). John Knox.
Bowman, Larry G. Captive Americans: Prisoners During the American Revolution. LC 75-36984. viii, 146p. 1976. 9.00x (ISBN 0-8214-0215-3, 82-82204); pap. 4.50x (ISBN 0-8214-0229-3, 82-82212). Ohio U Pr.
Bowman, Larry W. South Africa's Outward Strategy: A Foreign Policy Dilemma for the United States. LC 72-183388. (Papers in International Studies: Africa: No. 13). (Illus.). 32p. 1971. pap. 3.25x (ISBN 0-89680-046-6, Ohio U Ctr Intl). Ohio U Pr.
Bowman, Larry W. & Clark, Ian, eds. The Indian Ocean in Global Politics. (Westview Special Studies in International Relations). 270p. 1980. lib. bdg. 27.50 (ISBN 0-86531-038-6); pap. 12.00 (ISBN 0-86531-191-9). Westview.
Bowman, Mary A., compiled by. Western Mysticism: A Guide to the Basic Sources. LC 78-18311. 1978. pap. 9.00 (ISBN 0-8389-0266-9). ALA.
Bowman, Ned A., jt. auth. see Silverman, Maxwell.
Bowman, Norman H., et al. The Grandparenting Book. LC 82-72106. (Illus.). 128p. (Orig.). 1982. pap. 6.95 (ISBN 0-939894-01-7). Blossom Valley.
Bowman, Peter Boyd. Lexico Hispanicoamericano del siglo XVIII. (Spanish Ser.: No. 5). 1982. Hispanic Seminary.
Bowman, Ray, ed. Church Building Sourcebook, No. 2. 264p. 1982. 39.95 (ISBN 0-8341-0759-7). Beacon Hill.
Bowman, Richard E., jt. auth. see Kircher, John F.
Bowman, Robert, ed. see Bligh, William.
Bowman, Ruth. Murals Without Walls: Arshile Gorky's Aviation Murals Rediscovered. LC 78-13898. 1978. soft cover 7.95 (ISBN 0-932828-01-9). Newark Mus.
Bowman, Sarah & Vardey, Lucinda. Pigs: A Troughful of Treasures. Date not set. 7.95 (ISBN 0-02-040340-2). Macmillan.
Bowman, Stanley F. & Cox, Harold E. Trolleys of Chester County, Pennsylvania. (Illus.). 68p. (Orig.). 1975. pap. 9.00 (ISBN 0-911940-22-7). Cox.
Bowman, Thomas, et al. Finding Your Best Place to Live in America. 416p. 1983. pap. 3.95 (ISBN 0-446-30586-3). Warner Bks.
Bowman, W. C. Pharmacology of Neuromuscular Function. 200p. 1981. text ed. 19.95 (ISBN 0-8391-4144-0). Univ Park.
Bowman, W. Dodgson. Charlie Chaplin: His Life & Art. LC 74-1090. (American Biography Ser., No. 32). 1974. lib. bdg. 49.95x o.p. (ISBN 0-8383-1841-X). Haskell.
Bowman, William D. Story of Surnames. LC 68-8906. 1968. Repr. of 1932 ed. 33.00x (ISBN 0-8103-3110-1). Gale.
Bownas, Geoffrey & Thwaite, Anthony, trs. The Penguin Book of Japanese Verse. (Orig.). 1982. pap. 5.95 (ISBN 0-14-042077-0). Penguin.
Bowra, C. M. Classical Greece. LC 65-17305. (Great Ages of Man). (Illus.). (gr. 6 up). 1965. PLB 11.97 o.p. (ISBN 0-8094-0363-3, Pub. by Time-Life). Silver.
Bowra, C. M., tr. see Pindar.
Bowra, Cecil M. From Virgil to Milton. 1945. 17.95 o.p. (ISBN 0-312-30835-3). St Martin.
--Greek Experience. pap. 3.50 (ISBN 0-451-62041-0, ME2041, Ment). NAL.
--Heritage of Symbolism. 1943. 17.95 o.p. (ISBN 0-312-36995-6). St Martin.
--Memories, 1898-1939. LC 67-27994. (Illus.). 1966. 15.00 o.p. (ISBN 0-674-56650-5). Harvard U Pr.
Bowring, C. S. Radionuclide Tracer Techniques in Hematology. 1981. text ed. 19.95 (ISBN 0-407-00183-2). Butterworth.
Bowring, Jean. New Cake Decorating Book. LC 76-113947. (Illus.). 1977. 10.95 (ISBN 0-668-04343-1, 4343). Arco.
Bowring, Mary. The Animals Come First. 1978. 8.95 o.p. (ISBN 0-671-22440-9). S&S.
Bowron, Bernard R., Jr. Henry B. Fuller of Chicago. LC 70-140915. (Contributions in American Studies, No. 11). (Illus.). 1974. lib. bdg. 25.00x (ISBN 0-8371-5820-6, BHF/). Greenwood.
Bowron, Edgar P., ed. The North Carolina Museum of Art: Introduction to the Collection. LC 82-21982. (Illus.). 320p. 1983. pap. 19.95 (ISBN 0-8078-4097-1). U of NC Pr.

Bowron, P. & Stephenson, F. W. Active Filters for Communication & Instrumentation. (Illus.). 320p. 1979. text ed. 27.00 (ISBN 0-07-084086-5) (ISBN 0-07-084085-7). McGraw.

Bowry, T. R. Immunology Simplified. (Illus.). 1978. pap. text ed. 9.95x (ISBN 0-19-261148-8). Oxford U Pr.

Bowser, et al. Performing Arts Resources Two. Perry, Ted, ed. LC 75-646287. 144p. 1976. text ed. 10.00x (ISBN 0-910482-73-X). Drama Bk.

Bowskill, Derek. All About Cinema. 1976. 7.50 o.p. (ISBN 0-491-01716-2). Transatlantic.

Bowsky, William M., ed. The Black Death: A Turning Point in History? LC 77-21196. (European Problem Studies). 134p. 1978. pap. text ed. 5.95 (ISBN 0-88275-636-2). Krieger.

Bowyer, Chaz. The Age of the Biplane. (Illus.). 192p. 1981. 24.95 o.p. (ISBN 0-13-018713-5). P-H.

--History of the RAF. (Illus.). 224p. 1982. 11.98 (ISBN 0-8119-0519-5, Pub. by Bison Bks.). Fell.

Bowyer, Jack. Building Technology Three. (Newnes-Butterworths Technician Ser.). 96p. 1980. pap. 12.50 (ISBN 0-408-00411-8). Butterworth.

Bowyer, John W. Celebrated Mrs. Centlivre. LC 68-9539. (Illus.). 1968. Repr. of 1952 ed. lib. bdg. 16.25x (ISBN 0-8371-0026-7, BOCC). Greenwood.

Bowyer, John W. & Brooks, John L., eds. Victorian Age: Prose, Poetry & Drama. 2nd ed. 1954. text ed. 28.95 (ISBN 0-13-941724-9). P-H.

Bowyer, Michael J. Action Stations: Wartime Military Airfields of East Anglia 1939-45. (Illus.). 1979. 24.95 (ISBN 0-85059-335-2). Aztex.

--Aviation Photo Album. (Illus.). 1978. pap. 9.95 (ISBN 0-85059-297-6). Aztex.

--Aviation Photo Album 2. 1980. 9.95 (ISBN 0-85059-410-3). Aztex.

--Two Group R.A.F. LC 74-180641. (Illus.). 532p. 1979. pap. 9.95 (ISBN 0-571-11460-1). Faber & Faber.

Bowyer, P. J. Boat Engines: A Manual for Work & Pleasure Boats. LC 79-5369. (Illus.). 1979. 21.50 (ISBN 0-7153-7776-0). David & Charles.

Box, Doris. The Church Kitchen. LC 76-1001. 1977. bds. 10.95 (ISBN 0-8054-3701-0). Broadman.

Box, G. E. & Leonard, Chien-Fu-Wu, eds. Scientific Inference: Data Analysis & Robustiness (Symposium) LC 82-22755. Date not set. price not set (ISBN 0-12-121160-6). Acad Pr.

Box, George E. & Draper, Norman R. Evolutionary Operation: A Statistical Method for Process Improvement. LC 68-56159. (Applied Probability & Mathematical Statistics Ser). 1969. 34.95x (ISBN 0-471-09305-X, Pub. by Wiley-Interscience). Wiley.

Box, George E. & Jenkins, Gwilym. Time Series Analysis, Forecasting & Control. rev. ed. LC 76-8713. 500p. 1976. text ed. 40.50x (ISBN 0-8162-1104-3). Holden-Day.

Box, George E., et al. Statistics for Experimenters: An Introduction to Design, Data Analysis & Model Building. LC 77-15087. (Wiley Ser. in Probability & Mathematical Statistics). 1978. 35.95x (ISBN 0-471-09315-7, Pub. by Wiley-Inerscience). Wiley.

Box, Joan F. R. A. Fisher: The Life of a Scientist. LC 78-1668. (Probability & Mathematical Statistics Ser.). 1978. 43.50x (ISBN 0-471-09300-9, Pub. by Wiley-Interscience). Wiley.

Box, Sue, jt. auth. see Gibson, Michael.

Boxer, Arabella. Mediterranean Cookbook. (Illus.). 200p. 1983. 21.95x (ISBN 0-460-04442-7, Pub. by J. M. Dent England). Biblio Dist.

Boxer, Bruce H. The Solstice Cipher. 1979. 11.53i (ISBN 0-397-01346-9). Har-Row.

Boxer, C. Solving Life's Problems: Government & Law, Level 1. 1980. pap. 4.95 (ISBN 0-07-006851-8). McGraw.

Boxer, C. R. The Christian Century in Japan: Fifteen forty-Nine to Sixteen-Fifty. (Library Reprint Ser.: No. 51). (Illus.). 552p. 1974. Repr. of 1967 ed. 47.50x (ISBN 0-520-02702-7). U of Cal Pr.

--The Golden Age of Brazil, 1695-1750: Growing Pains of a Colonial Society. LC 62-11583. 1962. 27.50x (ISBN 0-520-00162-1); pap. 9.50x (ISBN 0-520-01550-9, CAMPUS78). U of Cal Pr.

--Jan Compagnie in War & Peace. (Orig.). 1980. pap. text ed. 10.95x o.p. (ISBN 0-686-71777-5, 00133). Heinemann Ed.

--Joao De Barros. (XCHR Studies Ser.: No. 1). 159p. 1981. text ed. 14.25x (ISBN 0-686-73708-3, Pub. by Concept India). Humanities.

Boxshall, G. A., jt. auth. see Lincoln, R. J.

Boyadjian, Knarig. In Search of Life. Kegham-Keghag, tr. 1978. 4.50 o.p. (ISBN 0-533-03143-5). Vantage.

Boyajian, Dickran H. Armenia: The Case for a Forgotten Genocide. LC 73-188056. (Illus.). 512p. 1972. 17.50 (ISBN 0-912826-01-0); lib. bdg. 17.50 (ISBN 0-685-23984-5). Ed Bk Crafters.

Boyajian, James C. Portuguese Bankers at the Court of Spain 1626-1650. 300p. Date not set. 35.00 (ISBN 0-8135-0962-9). Rutgers U Pr.

Boyan. Institute Supervision Training Program. 1978. text ed. 10.95 o.s.i. (ISBN 0-675-08415-6); video 695.00 o.s.i. (ISBN 0-675-08350-8); 16 mm film 395.00 o.s.i. (ISBN 0-675-08414-8). Merrill.

Boyan, A. Stephen, Jr., ed. Constitutional Aspects of Watergate: Documents & Materials, 5 vols & index. LC 75-45440. 1977. 45.00 ea. (ISBN 0-379-10069-X); Set. 225.00. Oceana.

Boyan, Douglas R., ed. Open Doors: Report on International Educational Exchange, 1981-82. rev. ed. LC 55-4544. 157p. 1982. 22.95 (ISBN 0-87206-117-5). Inst Intl Educ.

--Profiles: The Foreign Student in the United States. rev. ed. 128p. (Orig.). 1981. pap. 22.95 (ISBN 0-87206-111-6). Inst Intl Educ.

--Profiles: The Foreign Student in the United States, 1983. rev. ed. 140p. 1983. pap. text ed. 22.95 (ISBN 0-87206-118-3). Inst Intl Educ.

Boyan, Norman & Copeland, Willis. Instructional Supervision Training Program. 1978. text ed. 8.50 (ISBN 0-675-08415-6). Additional supplements may be obtained from publisher. Merrill.

Boyars, Arthur, tr. see Daniel, Yuli.

Boyatzis, Richard E. The Competent Manager: A Model for Effective Performance. LC 81-13113. 308p. 1982. 29.50x (ISBN 0-471-09031-X, Pub. by Wiley-Interscience). Wiley.

Boyce, jt. auth. see Bacon.

Boyce, A. J. Chromosome Variation in Human Evolution: Symposia of the Institute of Biology Ser, Vol. 14. 131p. 1975. 29.95 (ISBN 0-470-09330-7). Wiley.

Boyce, A. J., jt. ed. see Harrison, G. A.

Boyce, B. Mercury Systems Inc. Practice Set in Word-Information Processing for Conventional & Text-Editing Typewriters. 1981. tchr's manual & key 6.72 (ISBN 0-07-006901-8). McGraw.

Boyce, B. & Popyk, M. K. Developing Concepts for Word Processing. 192p. 1983. 7.50 (ISBN 0-07-006921-2, Gregg). McGraw.

Boyce, Bryl N. Industrial Real Estate Student's Manual. 5.00 (ISBN 0-686-37025-2). Soc Industrial Realtors.

Boyce, Byrl N., ed. Real Estate Appraisal Terminology. 2nd ed. 384p. 1981. 18.00 (ISBN 0-88410-597-0). Ballinger Pub.

Boyce, D. George. Nationalism in Ireland. 1982. 70.00x (ISBN 0-7171-1219-5, Pub. by Gill & Macmillan Ireland). State Mutual Bk.

Boyce, Jean. What Every Mother Knows. 1982. 5.50 (ISBN 0-686-84484-X). Gibson.

Boyce, Jefferson. Digital Logic: Operation & Analysis. 2nd ed. (Illus.). 464p. 1982. 26.95 (ISBN 0-13-214619-3). P-H.

Boyce, Jefferson C. Modern Electronics: A Survey of the New Technology. Zuredjian, George Z., ed. (Illus.). 256p. 1982. pap. 12.95x (ISBN 0-07-006915-8). McGraw.

--Operational Amplifiers for Technicians. 1983. text ed. 25.95 (ISBN 0-534-01243-4, Pub. by Breton Pubs). Wadsworth Pubs.

Boyce, Jefferson C., jt. auth. see Shrader, Robert L.

Boyce, John, illus. Aphrodisiac. (Illus.). 1976. pap. 4.95 o.p. (ISBN 0-517-52679-4). Crown.

Boyce, John, et al. Mathematics for Technical & Vocational Students. 7th ed. LC 81-2686. 576p. 1982. text ed. 19.95x (ISBN 0-471-05182-9); students solutions 7.95 (ISBN 0-471-09266-5). Wiley.

Boyce, John S. Forest Pathology. 3rd ed. (American Forestry Ser.). (Illus.). 1961. text ed. 38.50 (ISBN 0-07-006898-4, C). McGraw.

Boyce, Mary. A History of Zorastrianism, Vol. 2: Under the Achaemenians. (Handbuch der Orientalistik, I Abt Ser.: Vol. VII). xvi, 306p. 1982. pap. write for info. (ISBN 90-04-06506-7). E J Brill.

Boyce, Meherwan P. Gas Turbine Engineering Handbook. 616p. 1982. 65.95x (ISBN 0-87201-878-4). Gulf Pub.

Boyce, Nancy L. & Larson, Vicki L. Adolescents' Communication: Development & Disorders. 250p. 1983. three-ring binder 15.95 (ISBN 0-9610370-0-8). Thinking Ink Pr.

Boyce, P. J. Foreign Affairs for New States: Some Questions of Credentials. LC 77-87169. 1978. 26.00x (ISBN 0-312-29837-4). St Martin.

Boyce, Ronald N., jt. auth. see Perkins, Rollin M.

Boyce, Terry. Car Interior Restoration. 1975. 7.95 o.p. (ISBN 0-8306-9989-9); pap. 5.95 o.p. (ISBN 0-8306-2002-8, 2002). TAB Bks.

Boyce, W. E., ed. Case Studies in Mathematical Modelling. LC 80-14252. (Applicable Mathematics Ser.). 432p. 1980. text ed. 47.50 (ISBN 0-273-08486-0). Pitman Pub MA.

Boyce, William E. & Di Prima, Richard C. Elementary Differential Equations. 3rd ed. LC 75-35565. 497p. 1977. text ed. 26.50 (ISBN 0-471-09339-4). Wiley.

Boyce, William E. & DiPrima, Richard C. Elementary Differential Equations & Boundary Value Problems. 3rd ed. LC 75-45093. 638p. 1977. 26.50 (ISBN 0-471-09334-3). Wiley.

--Introduction to Differential Equations. 310p. 1970. text ed. 22.95x (ISBN 0-471-09338-6). Wiley.

Boycott, J. A. Natural History of Infectious Disease. LC 73-161616. (Studies in Biology). 1971. 17.95 (ISBN 0-312-56070-2). St Martin.

Boyd, jt. auth. see Garrard.

Boyd & Ransauer, eds. Career Connections: A Guide to Career Planning Throughout Massachusetts. 200p. (Orig.). 1983. pap. 9.95 (ISBN 0-937860-32-8). Adams Inc MA.

Boyd, Alvin A., ed. The Narrative Bible: Edited & Condensed for Easy Reading. LC 80-29302. 324p. 1982. pap. 7.95 (ISBN 0-89490-047-1). Enslow Pubs.

Boyd, Anne. Life in a Fifteenth Century Monastery. LC 76-22452. (Cambridge Topic Bks). (Illus.). (gr. 5-10). 1978. PLB 6.95g (ISBN 0-8225-1208-4). Lerner Pubns.

Boyd, Bradford B. Management-Minded Supervision. 2nd ed. 1976. text ed. 16.60 (ISBN 0-07-006941-7, G); instructor's manual & key 7.90 (ISBN 0-07-006942-5). McGraw.

--Management-Minded Supervision: A Self-Study Training Program. (Illus.). 1979. 41.00 (ISBN 0-07-006943-3, G); manager's guide 58.25 (ISBN 0-07-006944-1). McGraw.

Boyd, Brendan & Engel, Louis. How to Buy Stocks. 1983. 14.00i (ISBN 0-316-10439-6). Little.

Boyd, C. E. Water Quality Management for Pond Fish Culture. (Developments in Aquaculture & Fisheries Science Ser.: Vol. 9). 318p. 1982. 64.00 (ISBN 0-444-42054-1). Elsevier.

Boyd, Carl. The Extraordinary Envoy: General Hiroshi Oshima & Diplomacy in the Third Reich 1934-1939. LC 79-9600. 246p. 1980. text ed. 20.75 (ISBN 0-8191-0957-6); pap. text ed. 10.75 (ISBN 0-8191-0958-4). U Pr of Amer.

Boyd, Don, jt. auth. see Sork, David.

Boyd, Doug. Rolling Thunder. 1976. pap. 6.95 (ISBN 0-440-57435-8, Delta). Dell.

Boyd, Douglas. Broadcasting in the Arab World: A Survey of Radio & Television in the Middle East. (International & Comparative Broadcasting Ser.). 306p. 1982. 32.95 (ISBN 0-87722-237-1). Temple U Pr.

Boyd, Elizabeth. The Happy-Unfortunate: or the Female-Page. LC 76-170583. (Foundations of the Novel Ser.: Vol. 56). lib. bdg. 50.00 o.s.i. (ISBN 0-8240-0568-6). Garland Pub.

Boyd, Ernest, tr. see Verneuil, Louis.

Boyd, Ernest A. Studies from Ten Literatures. (English Literary Reference Ser.). Repr. of 1927 ed. 17.00 (ISBN 0-384-05330-0). Johnson Repr.

Boyd, Ester. Bali Breezes. (Orig.). 1980. pap. 1.50 o.s.i. (ISBN 0-440-10404-1). Dell.

--Omen for Love. (Orig.). 1980. pap. 1.25 o.s.i. (ISBN 0-440-16108-8). Dell.

Boyd, Esther. Precious Pirate. (Orig.). 1980. pap. 1.25 o.s.i. (ISBN 0-440-17004-4). Dell.

Boyd, Eve, et al. Language for Learning. omnibus ed. pap. text ed. 48.50x o.p. (ISBN 0-435-01923-6). Heinemann Ed.

Boyd, F. R., ed. Kimberlites, Diatremes, & Diamonds: Their Geology, Petrology & Geochemistry. LC 78-72025. 1979. 25.00 (ISBN 0-87590-212-X, SP0024). Am Geophysical.

--The Mantle Sample: Inclusions in Kimberlites & Other Volcanics. 1979. 25.00 (ISBN 0-87590-213-8, SP0025). Am Geophysical.

Boyd, George A. Elias Boudinot, Patriot & Statesman, Seventeen Forty to Eighteen Twenty-One. LC 69-13835. Repr. of 1952 ed. lib. bdg. 17.75x o.p. (ISBN 0-8371-1345-8, BOEB). Greenwood.

Boyd, Gertrude A. Linguistics in the Elementary School. LC 75-17319. 1976. pap. text ed. 8.50 (ISBN 0-87581-154-X). Peacock Pubs.

Boyd, Hamish. Introduction to Homeopathic Medicine. LC 82-84367. 1983. pap. 12.95 (ISBN 0-87983-324-6). Keats.

Boyd, Harper W., jt. auth. see Britt, Steuart H.

Boyd, Harper W., Jr. & Levy, Sidney J. Promotion: A Behavioral View. 1967. pap. 10.95 ref. ed. (ISBN 0-13-730846-9). P-H.

Boyd, Herb. Former Portugese Colonies. LC 80-24752. (First Bks.). (gr. 4 up). 1981. PLB 8.90 (ISBN 0-531-04273-1). Watts.

Boyd, Ina C. Cocktails & Hors D'Oeuvres. Walsh, Jackie, ed. LC 77-93841. (Illus.). 1978. pap. 5.95 (ISBN 0-911954-45-7). Nitty Gritty.

Boyd, J., jt. auth. see O'Connor, J. J.

Boyd, Jack. Rehearsal Guide for the Choral Director. LC 77-2051. 1977. pap. text ed. 9.95 (ISBN 0-916656-03-9, MF278). Mark Foster Mus.

--Teaching Choral Sight Reading. LC 75-12658. 210p. 1982. pap. text ed. 10.95 (ISBN 0-916656-17-9). Mark Foster Mus.

Boyd, James, jt. auth. see Anderson, Jack.

Boyd, James R., jt. ed. see Kastrup, Erwin K.

Boyd, James S. Building for Small Acreages. LC 77-80716. 1978. 13.35 (ISBN 0-8134-1966-2); text ed. 10.00x. Interstate.

--Practical Farm Buildings: A Text & Handbook. 2nd ed. LC 78-179872. 1979. 11.95 (ISBN 0-8134-2054-7, 2054); text ed. 8.95x. Interstate.

Boyd, James W., jt. auth. see Kotwal, Firoze M.

Boyd, John, jt. auth. see Grieger, Russell.

Boyd, K. T. ATP-FAR 135: Airline Transport Pilot. (Illus.). 96p. 1983. pap. 9.25 (ISBN 0-8138-0510-4). Iowa St U Pr.

Boyd, L. M. Boyd's Book of Odd Facts. 1980. pap. 3.50 (ISBN 0-451-11966-5, AE1966, Sig). NAL.

Boyd, Lawrence H. & Iversen, Gudmund R. Contextual Analysis: Concepts & Statistical Techniques. 1979. text ed. 38.95x (ISBN 0-534-00693-0). Wadsworth Pub.

Boyd, Linn J., tr. see Zdansky, Erick.

Boyd, Lizzie, ed. British Cookery: A Complete Guide to Culinary Practice in England, Scotland, Ireland & Wales. LC 78-60775. (Illus.). 640p. 1979. 35.00 (ISBN 0-87951-087-0). Overlook Pr.

Boyd, Lois A. & Brackenridge, Douglas. Presbyterian Women in America: Two Centuries of a Quest for Status. LC 82-15845. (Contributions to the Study of Religion: No. 9). 416p. 1983. lib. bdg. 35.00 (ISBN 0-313-23678-X, BOY/). Greenwood.

Boyd, Malcolm. Human Like Me, Jesus. 1973. pap. 1.25 o.s.i. (ISBN 0-89129-148-2). Jove Pubns.

Boyd, Marcia. Curriculum Guide for Nuclear Medicine Technologists. McKeown, Joan A., et al, eds. LC 82-50338. 336p. 1982. 60.00 (ISBN 0-932004-12-1). Soc Nuclear Med.

Boyd, Marion. Say It Graciously. 1982. Repr. of 1976 ed. s.p. soft cover 2.50 (ISBN 0-88053-321-8). Macoy Pub.

Boyd, Maurice. Kiowa Voices: Ceremonial Dance, Ritual & Song, Vol. 1. Worcester, Donald, ed. LC 81-50977. (Illus.). 165p. (gr. 3 up). 1981. text ed. 29.95 (ISBN 0-912646-67-5). Tex Christian.

--Tarascan Myths & Legends. LC 68-59408. (History & Culture Monograph Ser. No. 4). 1969. 4.50 o.p. (ISBN 0-912646-09-8). Tex Christian.

Boyd, Patricia R. The Furry Wind. (Illus.). 28p. (gr. 2-3). 1982. pap. 2.25 (ISBN 0-9603840-4-9). Andrew Mtn Pr.

Boyd, Pauline, jt. auth. see Boyd, Selma.

Boyd, Preston, jt. auth. see Babcock, Dennis.

Boyd, Robert, jt. auth. see Modell, Michael.

Boyd, Robert F. & Hoerl, Bryan G. Basic Medical Microbiology. 2nd ed. 1981. text ed. 21.95 (ISBN 0-316-10433-7); lab manual 7.95 (ISBN 0-316-10434-5). Little.

Boyd, Robert T. Boyd's Bible Handbook. LC 82-81088. 800p. 1983. 24.95 (ISBN 0-89081-352-3, 3523). Harvest Hse.

Boyd, Robert W. Radiometry & the Detection of Optical Radiation. (Pure & Applied Optics Ser.). 325p. 1983. 34.95x (ISBN 0-471-86188-X, Pub. by Wiley-Interscience). Wiley.

Boyd, Rosalind E., ed. see Bacchus, M. K.

Boyd, Rosalind E., jt. ed. see Barrett, Stanley R.

Boyd, Rosamonde R. & McConatha, Douglas, eds. Gerontological Practice: Issues & Perspectives. LC 81-40706. 242p. (Orig.). 1982. lib. bdg. 22.00 (ISBN 0-8191-2110-X); pap. text ed. 10.75 (ISBN 0-8191-2111-8). U Pr of Amer.

Boyd, Selma & Boyd, Pauline. Footprints in the Refrigerator. LC 82-7112. (Easy-Read Story Bks.). (Illus.). (gr. k-3). 1982. 3.95 (ISBN 0-531-03554-9); PLB 8.60 (ISBN 0-531-04450-5). Watts.

--The How: Making the Best of a Mistake. LC 80-13513. (Illus.). 32p. 1981. 9.95 (ISBN 0-87705-176-3). Human Sci Pr.

Boyd, Steven R. The Politics of Opposition: Antifederalists & the Acceptance of the Constitution. LC 79-14640. (KTO Studies in American History Ser.). 1979. lib. bdg. 25.00 (ISBN 0-527-10465-5). Kraus Intl.

Boyd, T. Gardner, jt. auth. see Miller, W. R.

Boyd, T. Munford & Graves, Edward S. Virginia Civil Procedure. 700p. 1982. 65.00 (ISBN 0-87215-424-6). Michie-Bobbs.

Boyd, Thomas, jt. auth. see Korn, S. Winton.

Boyd, W. Harland & Ludeke, John, eds. Inside Historic Kern. (Illus.). 1982. 16.95 (ISBN 0-943500-09-5). Kern Historical.

Boyd, W. T. Fiber Optics Communications: Experiments & Projects. Date not set. pap. 15.95 (ISBN 0-672-21834-8). Sams.

Boyd, Waldo T. The World of Energy Storage. LC 76-39936. (Illus.). (gr. 6-8). 1977. PLB 5.29 o.p. (ISBN 0-399-61058-8). Putnam Pub Group.

Boyd, William. Emile of Jean Jacques Rousseau. (No. 11). 1962. text ed. 10.00 (ISBN 0-8077-1110-1); pap. text ed. 5.00x (ISBN 0-8077-1107-1). Tchrs Coll.

--A Good Man in Africa. 1983. pap. 3.95 (ISBN 0-14-005887-7). Penguin.

--An Ice-Cream War. 352p. 1983. 13.95 (ISBN 0-688-01904-8). Morrow.

Boyd, William C. Fundamentals of Immunology. 4th ed. LC 66-20389. 1967. 45.00 o.p. (ISBN 0-470-09342-0, Pub. by Wiley-Interscience). Wiley.

Boyd, William H., ed. Minor Educational Writings of Jean-Jacques Rousseau. LC 62-21561. 1962. pap. text ed. 4.50x (ISBN 0-8077-1113-6); 9.50 (ISBN 0-686-86787-4). Tchrs Coll.

Boyd, William L., jt. ed. see Immegart, Glenn L.

Boyd-Bowman, Peter. Lexico hispanoamericano del siglo XVIII. (Spanish Ser.: No. 5). 1982. 10.00 (ISBN 0-942260-21-X). Hispanic Seminary.

--Self-Instructional Language Programs. (Occasional Publication). 1973. pap. 1.50 o.p. (ISBN 0-89192-139-7). Interbk Inc.

Boyde, Patrick. Dante Philomythes & Philosopher: Man in the Cosmos. LC 80-40551. (Cambridge Paperback Library). 408p. Date not set. pap. 17.95 (ISBN 0-521-27390-0). Cambridge U Pr.

Boydell, Barra. The Crumhorn. 1981. write for info. o.s.i. (ISBN 90-6027-176-9, Pub. by Frits Knuf Netherlands). Pendragon NY.

Boydell, Tom & Pedler, Mike, eds. Management Self-Development: Concepts & Practices. 272p. 1981. text ed. 41.00x (ISBN 0-566-02194-3). Gower Pub Ltd.

Boydson, Jo Ann, intro. by see Dewey, John.

Boydston, Jo Ann, ed. see Dewey, John.

Boydston, Jo Ann, intro. by see Dewey, John.

Boydston, Jo Ann, ed. see Dewey, John.

Boydstun, J. B. On the Wings of Truth. 1978. 6.50 o.p. (ISBN 0-533-03261-X). Vantage.

Boye, Fred, jt. auth. see Louden, Louise.
Boyen, John L. Thermal Energy Recovery. 2nd ed. LC 79-19704. 1980. 37.95x (ISBN 0-471-04981-6, Pub. by Wiley-Interscience). Wiley.
Boyenga, Kirk W. & O'Dell, Gene J. Marketing Your Services to Business & Industry: Fundamentals for Winning Revenues. (Illus.). 80p. 1982. wkbk. 93.00 (ISBN 0-9606362-1-8). Burrell Comm Mental.
Boyer. Accident Kids. LC 73-93019. (Oddo Safety Ser.). (Illus.). (gr. 2-5). 1974. 6.75x (ISBN 0-87783-119-X); pap. 2.99 deluxe ed. (ISBN 0-87783-120-3). cassettes 5.95 (ISBN 0-87783-175-0). Oddo.
--Let's Walk Safely. LC 80-82953. (Oddo Safety Ser.). (Illus.). (gr. 1-6). PLB 6.75x (ISBN 0-87783-159-9). Oddo.
--Lucky Bus. LC 73-87801. (Oddo Safety Ser.). (Illus.). (gr. k-2). 1974. PLB 7.99x prebound (ISBN 0-87783-131-9); pap. 2.95x deluxe ed. (ISBN 0-87783-132-7); cassette 5.95x (ISBN 0-87783-193-9). Oddo.
--Safety on Wheels. LC 73-87802. (Oddo Safety Ser.). (Illus.). (gr. k-5). 1974. prebound 7.99x (ISBN 0-87783-133-5); pap. 2.95x deluxe ed. (ISBN 0-87783-134-3); cassette 5.95x (ISBN 0-87783-199-8). Oddo.
Boyer & Kihlstrom. Bayesian Models in Economic Theory, Vol. 5. Date not set. price not set (ISBN 0-444-86502-0). Elsevier.
Boyer, Adolphe. De l'Etat des Ouvriers et de Son Amelioration par l'Organisation du Travail. (Conditions of the 19th Century French Working Class Ser.). 141p. (Fr.). 1974. Repr. of 1841 ed. lib. bdg. 44.50x o.p. (ISBN 0-8287-0133-4, 1105). Clearwater Pub.
Boyer, Blanche, ed. see Abailard, P.
Boyer, Bryce L., jt. ed. see Muensterberger, Werner.
Boyer, Carl B. History of Mathematics. LC 68-16506. 717p. 1968. 29.95x (ISBN 0-471-09374-2). Wiley.
Boyer, Carl, III. How to Publish & Market Your Family History. LC 82-70972. 160p. 1982. 12.50 (ISBN 0-936124-06-7). C Boyer.
Boyer, Carl, 3rd. Ship Passenger Lists: National & New England (1600-1825) LC 76-37355. 270p. 1977. text ed. 20.00 (ISBN 0-936124-00-8). C Boyer.
--Ship Passenger Lists: New York & New Jersey (1600-1825) LC 78-52617. 333p. 1978. text ed. 18.35 o.s.i. (ISBN 0-936124-01-6). C Boyer.
--Ship Passenger Lists: Pennsylvania & Delaware (1641-1825) LC 79-57204. 289p. 1980. text ed. 20.00 (ISBN 0-936124-02-4). C Boyer.
--Ship Passenger Lists: The South (1538-1825) LC 78-52618. 314p. 1979. text ed. 18.35 o.s.i. (ISBN 0-936124-03-2). C Boyer.
Boyer, Carl, 3rd, et al. Brown Families of Bristol Counties, Massachusetts & Rhode Island & Descendants of Jared Talbot. LC 80-68755. (New England Colonial Families Ser.: Vol. 1). 219p. 1982. 18.35 (ISBN 0-936124-04-0). C Boyer.
Boyer, Dale, ed. see Crews, Judson.
Boyer, David L., et al, eds. The Philosopher's Annual, 1981, Vol. IV. xii, 250p. (Orig.). 1981. lib. bdg. 24.00 (ISBN 0-917930-75-4); pap. 8.50x (ISBN 0-917930-61-4). Ridgeview.
--The Philosopher's Annual 1980, Vol. III. xii, 225p. (Orig.). 1980. lib. bdg. 24.00 (ISBN 0-917930-38-X); pap. text ed. 8.50x (ISBN 0-917930-18-5). Ridgeview.
Boyer, Dean. Computer Word Processing: Do You Want It? 148p. 1981. pap. 14.95 (ISBN 0-88022-000-7, 81-52571). Que Corp.
Boyer, Elizabeth. A Colony of One. (Illus.). 1983. write for info. Veritie Pr.
--Freydis & Gudrid. LC 76-23353. (Illus., Orig.). 1976. 9.95 (ISBN 0-915964-02-3). Veritie Pr.
Boyer, G. G. Morgette in the Yukon. 1983. 11.95 (ISBN 0-8027-4020-0). Walker & Co.
Boyer, Glenn C. The Guns of Morgette. LC 81-71192. 197p. 1982. 11.95 (ISBN 0-8027-4007-3). Walker & Co.
Boyer, Glenn G., ed. see Earp, Wyatt S.
Boyer, John L., jt. auth. see Kasch, Fred W.
Boyer, L. Bryce, jt. ed. see Giovacchini, Peter.
Boyer, Linda. God Made Me. LC 81-50677. (A Happy Day Bk.). (Illus.). 24p. (Orig.). (ps-1). 1981. pap. 1.29 (ISBN 0-87239-464-6, 3597). Standard Pub.
Boyer, Mary G. Arizona in Literature. LC 74-145714. 1971. Repr. of 1935 ed. 56.00x (ISBN 0-8103-3703-7). Gale.
Boyer, Mildred, ed. The Texas Collection of Comedias Sueltas: A Descriptive Bibliography. (Reference Publications Ser.). 1978. lib. bdg. 65.00 (ISBN 0-8161-8117-9, Hall Reference). G K Hall.
BOyer, Orlando. Biografias de Grandes Cristianos: Tomo 1. Carrodeguas, Andy & Marosi, Esteban, eds. Kjellgreen, Shily, tr. 160p. (Span.). 1983. pap. 2.00 (ISBN 0-8297-1342-5). Life Pubs Intl.
--Biografias de Grandes Cristianos: Tomo 2. Carrodeguas, Andy & Marosi, Esteban, eds. Kjellgreen, Shily, tr. 176p. (Span.). 1983. pap. 2.00 (ISBN 0-8297-1343-3). Life Pubs Intl.
Boyer, Paul & Nissenbaum, Stephen, eds. The Salem Witchcraft Papers: Verbatim Transcripts, 3 vols. (Civil Liberties in American History Ser.). 1977. Set. lib. bdg. 145.00 (ISBN 0-306-70655-5). Da Capo.
Boyer, Robert D., ed. Realism in European Theater & Drama, Eighteen Seventy to Nineteen Twenty: A Bibliography. LC 78-19934. Orig. Title: Compiled by. 1979. lib. bdg. 29.95x (ISBN 0-313-20607-4, BOR/). Greenwood.
Boyer, Walter E., et al. Songs Along the Mahantonga: Pennsylvania Dutch Folksongs. 231p. 1964. Repr. of 1951 ed. 30.00x (ISBN 0-8103-5002-5). Gale.
Boyer, William W. America's Virgin Islands: A History of Human Rights & Wrongs. 425p. 1982. lib. bdg. 34.95 (ISBN 0-89089-239-3); pap. text ed. 14.95 (ISBN 0-89089-240-7). Carolina Acad Pr.
Boyes, R. G. Structural & Cut-off Diaphragm Walls. (Illus.). ix, 181p. 1975. 41.00 (ISBN 0-85334-607-0, Pub. by Applied Sci England). Elsevier.
Boyes, William E., ed. Jigs & Fixtures. LC 79-64915. (Manufacturing Update Ser.). (Illus.). 1979. 29.00 o.p. (ISBN 0-87263-051-X). SME.
Boyett, Rose-Marie. The Adventures of Tiger. (Illus.). 36p. 1982. pap. 4.95 (ISBN 0-9609566-0-3). Ro-Mar.
Boykin, A. Wade, et al, eds. Research Directions of Black Psychologists. Franklin, Anderson J. & Yates, J. Frank. LC 79-7348. 440p. 1980. 20.00x (ISBN 0-87154-254-4). Russell Sage.
Boykin, James H. Financing Real Estate. LC 77-205. (Special Ser. in Real Estate & Urban Land Economics). (Illus.). 1979. 31.95x (ISBN 0-669-01449-4); instr's manual avail. (ISBN 0-669-03998-5). Lexington Bks.
Boylan, Brian. Benedict Arnold: The Dark Eagle. (Illus.). 266p. 1973. 7.95 o.p. (ISBN 0-393-07471-4). Norton.
Boylan, Brian R., jt. auth. see Weller, Charles.
Boylan, M. Eugene. This Tremendous Lover. 1957. pap. 4.95 (ISBN 0-8091-1702-9). Paulist Pr.
Boylan, Michael. Method & Practice in Aristotle's Biology. LC 82-23708. (Illus.). 300p. (Orig.). 1983. lib. bdg. 22.50 (ISBN 0-8191-2952-6); pap. text ed. 11.75 (ISBN 0-8191-2953-4). U Pr of Amer.
Boyle, Ann. Veil of Sand. (YA) 1977. 6.95 (ISBN 0-685-81425-4, Avalon). Bouregy.
Boyle, Charles. House of Cards. 64p. 1982. pap. text ed. 7.00x (ISBN 0-85635-426-0, 61049, Pub. by Carcanet New Pr England). Humanities.
Boyle, David H. How to Succeed in Big Time Trucking. LC 77-70986. (Orig.). 1977. pap. 6.95 (ISBN 0-913668-97-4). Ten Speed Pr.
Boyle, Deidre, et al, eds. Children's Media Market Place. 1978. pap. 16.95 o.p. (ISBN 0-915794-17-9, 9325/78). Gaylord Prof Pubns.
Boyle, Denis & Bradick, Bill. The Challenge of Change: Developing Business Leaders for the 1980s. 45p. 1961. pap. text ed. 10.00x (ISBN 0-566-02283-4). Gower Pub Ltd.
Boyle, Desmond. Energy. LC 82-50390. (Visual Science Ser.). PLB 13.00 (ISBN 0-382-06658-8). Silver.
Boyle, Donzella C. Quest of a Hemisphere. LC 71-113036. (Illus.). (gr. 7 up). 1970. PLB 18.00 (ISBN 0-88279-218-0). Western Islands.
Boyle, Jack. Boston Blackie. 1979. lib. bdg. 9.95 (ISBN 0-8398-2536-6, Gregg). G K Hall.
Boyle, Joe, intro. by. The Federal Way with Words. 1982. 15.00 (ISBN 0-9609194-0-6). Twain Pub.
Boyle, John E. Graffiti on the Wall of Time: Thirty Poems Celebrating the Triumph of Heresy in our Day. 1983. 5.00 (ISBN 0-686-86890-0). Wheat Forders.
--The Indra Web: The Renewal of Ancient Oriental Concepts in Modern Western Thought. 1982. 10.00 (ISBN 0-686-86891-9). Wheat Forders.
Boyle, John H. China & Japan at War, 1939-1945: The Politics of Collaboration. LC 76-183886. (Illus.). 456p. 1972. 25.00x (ISBN 0-8047-0800-2). Stanford U Pr.
Boyle, John P. The Sterilization Controversy: A New Crisis for Catholic Hospitals. LC 77-73978. 112p. 1977. pap. 3.95 o.p. (ISBN 0-8091-2016-X). Paulist Pr.
Boyle, Kay. Monday Night. 1977. Repr. of 1938 ed. 10.00x (ISBN 0-911858-35-0). Appel.
Boyle, Kay see Bush, George, et al.
Boyle, Kevin, et al. Law & State: The Case of Northern Ireland. LC 75-10914. 206p. 1975. lib. bdg. 12.50x (ISBN 0-87023-197-9). U of Mass Pr.
Boyle, Michael J., ed. Boyle's Connecticut Almanac & Guide: 1983. (Illus.). 96p. (Orig.). 1982. pap. 2.95 (ISBN 0-911097-00-7). M Boyle Pub.
Boyle, P. R. Molluscs & Man. (Studies in Biology: No. 134). 64p. 1981. pap. text ed. 8.95 (ISBN 0-7131-2824-0). E Arnold.
Boyle, Pat. Graph Gallery. 1971. pap. 5.75 wkbk. (ISBN 0-88488-028-1). Creative Pubns.
Boyle, Pat & Juarez, Bill. Accent on Algebra. rev. ed. 1972. wkbk. 8.95 (ISBN 0-88488-046-X). Creative Pubns.
Boyle, Patrick G. Planning Better Programs. Pardoen, Alan & Seaman, Don, eds. (Adult Education Association Professional Development Ser.). (Illus.). 272p. 1980. text ed. 14.95 (ISBN 0-07-000552-4, C). McGraw.
Boyle, Patrick J. Trigonometry with Applications. 448p. 1983. text ed. 19.50 scp (ISBN 0-06-040898-7, HarpC); instr's. manual avail. (ISBN 0-06-360869-3). Har-Row.
Boyle, Patrick J., jt. auth. see Smith, Karl J.
Boyle, R. Alexander, jt. auth. see Boyle, Robert H.
Boyle, R. W. Geochemical Prospecting for Thorium & Uranium. (Developments in Economic Geology Ser.: Vol. 16). 498p. Date not set. 85.00 (ISBN 0-444-42070-3). Elsevier.
Boyle, Rena F., jt. auth. see Raff, Beverly.
Boyle, Robert. James Joyce's Pauline Vision: A Catholic Exposition. LC 78-18901. 133p. 1978. 9.95x (ISBN 0-8093-0861-4). S Ill U Pr.
Boyle, Robert, jt. ed. see Whitlock, Dave.
Boyle, Robert H. AT the Top of Their Game: Profiles from Sports Illustrated. 224p. 1983. 12.95 (ISBN 0-8329-0274-8); pap. 8.95 (ISBN 0-8329-0283-7). Winchester Pr.
--The Hudson River: A Natural & Unnatural History. LC 68-10877. (Illus.). 1969 o.p. 7.95 (ISBN 0-393-05379-2, N844, Norton Lib); pap. 6.95 1979 (ISBN 0-393-00844-4). Norton.
Boyle, Robert H. & Boyle, R. Alexander. Acid Rain. LC 82-21410. 128p. (Orig.). 1983. 14.95 (ISBN 0-8052-3854-9); pap. 8.95 (ISBN 0-8052-0746-5). Schocken.
Boyle, T. Coraghessan. Water Music. 1983. pap. 6.95 (ISBN 0-14-006550-4). Penguin.
Boyle, Ted E. Brendan Behan. (English Authors Ser.: No. 91). lib. bdg. 10.95 o.p. (ISBN 0-8057-1036-1, Twayne). G K Hall.
Boyle, William C. Design Production Safety Systems. 264p. 1979. 42.95x (ISBN 0-87814-096-4). Pennwell Books Division.
Boyles, Marcia V., et al. The Health Professions. LC 77-11331. (Illus.). 465p. 1982. 16.50 (ISBN 0-7216-1904-5). Saunders.
Boyles, Margaret. The Margaret Boyles Book of Crewel Embroidery. 1979. 12.95 o.p. (ISBN 0-671-24616-X). S&S.
--Margaret Boyles' Craft Designs for Babies. 1983. write for info (ISBN 0-671-43902-2). S&S.
--Margaret Boyles' Needlework Gifts for Special Occasions. (Illus.). 1981. 15.95 o.p. (ISBN 0-671-25322-0). S&S.
Boylestad, Robert & Nashelsky, Louis. Electricity, Electronics, & Electromagnetics: Principles & Applications. 2nd ed. (Illus.). 544p. 1983. 21.95 (ISBN 0-13-248146-4). P-H.
--Electronic Devices & Circuit Theory. 3rd ed. (Illus.). 768p. 1982. 26.95 (ISBN 0-13-250324-7). P-H.
Boylestad, Robert L. Introductory Circuit Analysis. 3rd ed. (Electronics Technology Ser.). 1977. text ed. 26.95 (ISBN 0-675-08559-4); student guide 8.95 (ISBN 0-675-08542-X). Additional supplements may be obtained from publisher. Merrill.
--Introductory Circuit Analysis. 4th ed. 800p. 1982. text ed. 26.95 (ISBN 0-675-09938-2); student guide 9.95x (ISBN 0-675-09856-4); experiments 11.95x (ISBN 0-675-09858-0). Additional supplements may be obtained from publisher. Merrill.
Boylestad, Robert L. & Nashelsky, L. Electricity, Electronics & Electromagnetics: Principles & Applications. (Illus.). 1977. text ed. 21.95 o.p. (ISBN 0-13-248310-6). P-H.
Boyle-Turner, Caroline. Paul Serusier. Foster, Stephen, ed. LC 82-21783. (Studies in Fine Arts: The Avant-Garde: No. 37). 1983. write for info. (ISBN 0-8357-1388-1). Univ Microfilms.
Boylston, Helen D., jt. auth. see Lane, Rose W.
Boyne, D. A. & Wright, Lance, eds. Architect's Working Details, 15 vols. Incl. Repr. of 1953 ed. Vol. 1 (ISBN 0-85139-022-6); Repr. of 1954 ed. Vol. 2 (ISBN 0-85139-023-4); Repr. of 1955 ed. Vol. 3 (ISBN 0-85139-024-2); Repr. of 1957 ed. Vol. 4 (ISBN 0-85139-025-0); Repr. of 1958 ed. Vol. 5 (ISBN 0-85139-026-9); Repr. of 1959 ed. Vol. 6; Repr. of 1960 ed. Vol. 7 (ISBN 0-85139-028-5); Vol. 8. Repr. of 1961 ed (ISBN 0-85139-029-3); Repr. of 1962 ed. Vol. 9 (ISBN 0-85139-030-7); Repr. of 1954 ed. Vol. 10 (ISBN 0-85139-031-5); Repr. of 1965 ed. Vol. 11 (ISBN 0-85139-032-3); Repr. of 1965 ed. Vol. 12 (ISBN 0-85139-033-1); Repr. of 1969 ed. Vol. 13 (ISBN 0-85139-034-X); Repr. of 1971 ed. Vol. 14 (ISBN 0-85139-035-8); Repr. of 1973 ed. Vol. 15. 17.50 o.p. (ISBN 0-85139-036-6). 1978. o.p. 275.00 set o.p. (ISBN 0-685-38821-2, Pub. by Architectural); o.p. 25.00 ea. o.p. Nichols Pub.
Boyne, Gil, ed. Hypnosis; New Tool in Nursing Practice. 197p. 1982. 20.00 (ISBN 0-930298-12-8). Westwood Pub Co.
Boyne, Harry. The Houses of Parliament. LC 81-81038. (Illus.). 96p. 1981. 17.95 o.p. (ISBN 0-88332-259-5, 8185). Larousse.
Boyne, Walter. Boeing B-52: A Documentary History. (Illus.). 160p. 1982. 19.95 (ISBN 0-86720-550-4). Sci Bks Intl.
Boyne, Walter J. The Messerschmitt ME 262: Arrow to the Future. LC 80-607090. (Illus.). 192p. (Orig.). 1980. 19.95 (ISBN 0-87474-276-5); pap. 10.95 (ISBN 0-87474-275-7). Smithsonian.
Boynton, Alton L. & McKeehan, Wallace L., eds. Ions, Cell Proliferation, & Cancer. LC 82-20786. 1982. 39.50 (ISBN 0-12-123050-3). Acad Pr.
Boynton, Edward C., ed. see United States Army, Continental Army.
Boynton, John. Nuclear War: Can You Survive? (Illus.). 64p. pap. 4.95 (ISBN 0-917814-05-3). Astroart Ent.
Boynton, Percy H. Some Contemporary Americans. LC 66-23516. 1924. 9.00x (ISBN 0-8196-0181-0). Biblo.
Boynton, Richard W., tr. see Loisy, Alfred F.
Boynton, Robert S. Chemistry & Technology of Lime & Limestone. 2nd ed. LC 79-16140. 1980. 77.95 (ISBN 0-471-02771-5, Pub. by Wiley-Interscience). Wiley.
Boynton, Robert W., ed. see Shakespeare, William.
Boynton, Sandra. But not the Hippopotamus. Klimo, Kate, ed. (Sandra Boynton Board Bks.). (Illus.). 14p. (ps-k). 1982. bds. 3.50 (ISBN 0-671-44904-4, Little Simon). S&S.
--Chocolate: The Consuming Passion. LC 81-43781. (Illus.). 112p. 1982. 8.95 (ISBN 0-89480-197-X); pap. 5.95 (ISBN 0-89480-199-6). Workman Pub.
--Chocolate: The Consuming Passion. 1982. pap. 0.00 o.p. (ISBN 0-413-51170-7). Methuen Inc.
--The Compleat Turkey. (Illus.). 1980. 4.95 (ISBN 0-316-10484-1). Little.
--The Going to Bed Book. Klimo, Kate, ed. (Sandra Boynton Board Bks.). (Illus.). 14p. (ps-k). 1982. bds. 3.50 (ISBN 0-671-44902-8, Little Simon). S&S.
--Hester in the Wild. LC 78-67026. (Illus.). 1979. 9.57i (ISBN 0-06-020631-4, HarpJ); PLB 10.89 (ISBN 0-06-020654-3). Har-Row.
--If at First... (Illus.). 32p. (ps-1). 1980. 7.95 (ISBN 0-316-10487-6); pap. 3.95 (ISBN 0-316-10486-8). Little.
--Moo Baa La La La. Klimo, Kate, ed. (Boynton Board Bks.). (Illus.). 14p. 1982. 3.50 (ISBN 0-671-44901-X, Little Simon). S&S.
--Opposites. Klimo, Kate, ed. (Sandra Boynton Board Bks.). (Illus.). (ps-k). 1982. bds. 3.50 (ISBN 0-671-44903-6, Little Simon). S&S.
Boys, J. V., jt. auth. see Prendergast, E. D.
Boys' Life Magazine Editors, ed. Best Jokes from Boys' Life. LC 74-104392. (Illus.). (gr. 4 up). 1970. 6.95 o.p. (ISBN 0-399-20014-2). Putnam Pub Group.
Boyson, Rhodes, ed. Goodbye to Nationalization. pap. 3.50 o.p. (ISBN 0-902782-05-3). Transatlantic.
Boyson, Rhodes, jt. ed. see Cox, C. B.
Boyt, David, jt. ed. see Talbot, Mike.
Boyte, Harry C. The Backyard Revolution: Understanding the New Citizen Movement. 288p. 1980. 27.95 (ISBN 0-87722-192-8). Temple U Pr.
Boytinck, Paul. C. P. Snow: A Reference Guide. 1980. lib. bdg. 27.00 (ISBN 0-8161-8357-0, Hall Reference). G K Hall.
Bozak, Richard E. Solving Organic Chemistry Problems. LC 73-86758. 320p. 1974. pap. text ed. 9.95 (ISBN 0-675-08925-5). Merrill.
Bozanic, Nick. Wood, Birds, Water, Stone. 8p. (Orig.). 1983. pap. 2.95 (ISBN 0-935306-20-X). Barnwood Pr.
Bozarth, J. & Rubin, S. Facilitative Management in Rehabilitation Counseling. 1972. pap. 8.40x (ISBN 0-87563-053-7). Stipes.
Bozeat, Nicholas, jt. auth. see Rose, Edgar.
Bozeman, Adda B. Future of Law in a Multicultural World. LC 78-131127. 1971. 21.00x (ISBN 0-691-05643-9); pap. 6.95 o.p. (ISBN 0-691-01060-9). Princeton U Pr.
Bozie, S. M. & Cheng, R. M. Electronic & Switching Circuits. 392p. 1979. pap. text ed. 19.95 (ISBN 0-7131-3338-4). E Arnold.
Bozimo, Henry T. & Weiss, Louis. Chemistry: Advanced Test for the G. R. E. (Orig.). 1967. lib. bdg. 5.50 (ISBN 0-668-01571-3); pap. 6.95 (ISBN 0-668-01069-X). Arco.
Bozza, Linda. Ready, Willing & Able: What You Should Know About Workers With Disabilities. Lindberg, Charles A., ed. LC 79-118229. (Illus.). 44p. 1979. 3.25 (ISBN 0-686-42977-X). Humana.
Bozzi, jt. auth. see Bent, Bob.
Bozzini, Yvette M., jt. auth. see Hudson, William R.
Bozzo, Maxine Z. Toby in the Country, Toby in the City. (Illus.). (ps-1). 1982. 9.50 (ISBN 0-688-00916-6); PLB 8.59 (ISBN 0-688-00917-4). Morrow.
Braae, R. Matrix Algebra for Electrical Engineers. (Illus.). 1965. 6.50 o.p. (ISBN 0-201-00651-0, Adv Bk Prog). A-W.
Braaten, Carl E. The Flaming Center: A Theology of the Christian Mission. LC 76-62605. 176p. 1977. 4.25 o.p. (ISBN 0-8006-0490-3, 1-490). Fortress.
--Principles of Lutheran Theology. LC 82-16542. 160p. 1983. pap. 8.95 (ISBN 0-8006-1689-8). Fortress.
--Stewards of the Mysteries: Sermons for Festivals & Special Occasions. LC 82-72639. 128p. (Orig.). 1983. pap. 5.95 (ISBN 0-8066-1945-7, 10-6004). Augsburg.
Brabander, M. De see International Symposium on Microtubule Inhibitors, Belgium, 1975.
Brabant, J. M. Van see Van Brabant, J. M.
Brabazon, James. Albert Schweitzer: A Biography. LC 74-30545. (Illus.). 1975. 12.95 o.p. (ISBN 0-399-11421-1). Putnam Pub Group.
Brabb, George. Computers & Information Systems in Business. 2nd ed. LC 79-88716. (Illus.). 1980. text ed. 22.95 (ISBN 0-395-28671-9); instr's. manual 1.00 (ISBN 0-395-28670-0). HM.

Brabb, George J. & McKean, Gerald. Business Data Processing: Concepts & Practices. LC 81-82556. 1982. 22.95 (ISBN 0-395-31684-7); 1.50 (ISBN 0-395-31685-5); study guide 9.50 (ISBN 0-686-97247-3); test bank 1.50 (ISBN 0-395-31687-1); practice set 1.00 (ISBN 0-395-32018-6); practice set II o.p. 0.00 (ISBN 0-395-32024-0). HM.

Bracanga, Aquino de see De Branganca, Aquino.

Braccio, M. Basic Electrical & Electronic Tests & Measurement. 1979. 18.95 (ISBN 0-8359-0589-6); instrs'. manual avail. (ISBN 0-8359-0590-X). Reston.

Bracco. Stratified Charge Engines, Vol. 2. 112p. 1976. pap. 49.00x (ISBN 0-677-05355-X). Gordon.

Bracco, F. V. Stratified Charge Engines. 104p. 1973. 40.00x (ISBN 0-677-05165-4). Gordon.

Bracco, Patrick & Lebovici, Elisabeth. Fireworks: Feux d' Artifices. Breitenbach, Mrs. Edgar, tr. (Illus.). 1976. soft bdg. 1.75 (ISBN 0-88397-024-4). Intl Exhibit Foun.

Brace, Betty L. & Croghan, Tonita. Understanding Adolescents & Safety at Home & on the Job. LC 79-21803. (Lifeworks Ser.). (Illus.). 1980. pap. text ed. 6.40 (ISBN 0-07-060912-8). McGraw.

Brace, C. The Stages of Human Evolution. 2nd ed. 1979. 9.95 (ISBN 0-13-840157-8); pap. 9.95 (ISBN 0-13-840140-3). P-H.

Brace, Charles L. The Dangerous Classes of New York. LC 73-84256. (NASW Classics Ser). (Illus.). 448p. 1973. pap. text ed. 6.50x (ISBN 0-87101-061-5, CBC-061-I). Natl Assn Soc Wkrs.

--Dangerous Classes of New York & Twenty Years's Work Among Them. 3rd ed. LC 67-26666. (Criminology, Law Enforcement, & Social Problems Ser.: No. 3). 1967. Repr. of 1880 ed. 17.00x (ISBN 0-87585-003-0). Patterson Smith.

Brace, Geoffrey. Something to Play. (Resources of Music Ser). 4.95 (ISBN 0-521-07753-2). Cambridge U Pr.

--Something to Sing, 4 Bks. Bk. 1 Piano Ed. 8.95 (ISBN 0-521-04296-8); Bk. 1 Melody Ed. text ed. 3.95 (ISBN 0-521-04295-X); Bk. 2 Piano. 8.95 (ISBN 0-521-04298-4); Bk. 2 Melody Ed. 3.95 (ISBN 0-521-04297-6); Bk. 3. 4.95 (ISBN 0-521-04299-2); Bk. 4. 4.95 (ISBN 0-521-04300-X). Cambridge U Pr.

--Something to Sing at Assembly. (Resources of Music Ser). Music. 4.95 (ISBN 0-521-07570-X); Words. 3.95 (ISBN 0-521-07573-4). Cambridge U Pr.

Brace, Geoffrey & Burton, I. Listen! Music & Nature. (Illus.). (gr. 5-8). 1976. pap. 6.95 (ISBN 0-521-20706-1). Cambridge U Pr.

Brace, Gerald W. The Department. (Phoenix Fiction Ser.). 290p. 1968. pap. 6.95 (ISBN 0-226-06968-0). U of Chicago Pr.

Bracegirdle, Brian, jt. auth. see Freeman, W. H.

Bracewell, R. The Fourier Transform & Its Applications. 2nd ed. (Electrical Engineering Ser.). (Illus.). 1978. text ed. 39.50 (ISBN 0-07-007013-X, C); solutions manual 25.00 (ISBN 0-07-007014-8). McGraw.

Bracewell-Milnes, Barry. Eastern & Western European Economic Integration. LC 76-6671. (Illus.). 300p. 1976. text ed. 26.00 (ISBN 0-312-22470-2). St Martin.

Bracey, Audrey. Resolution of the Dominican Crisis, 1965: A Study in Mediation. LC 80-27239. 64p. 1980. 3.50 (ISBN 0-934742-04-9, Inst Study Diplomacy). Geo U Sch For Serv.

Bracey, Dorothy H., intro. by see Letman, Sloan T.

Bracey, Lucius H. & Rogers, Walter R. Wills: A Virginia Law Practice System. 305p. 1982. looseleaf with forms 75.00 (ISBN 0-686-84233-2). Michie-Bobbs.

Bracher, Frederick, ed. see Etherege, Sir George.

Bracher, Frederick G. The Novels of James Gould Cozzens. LC 72-6187. 306p. 1972. Repr. of 1959 ed. lib. bdg. 19.25x (ISBN 0-8371-6448-6, BRJC). Greenwood.

Brachet, J. Biological Role of Ribonuclear Acids. 1961. 11.50 (ISBN 0-444-40075-3). Elsevier.

--Introduction to Molecular Embryology. LC 73-12632. (Heidelberg Science Library: Vol. 19). (Illus.). 180p. 1974. pap. 10.00 o.p. (ISBN 0-387-90077-2). Springer-Verlag.

Brachet, J., jt. ed. see Abercrombie, M.

Brachet, Jean & Mirsky, A. E., eds. The Cell: Biochemistry, Physiology, Morphology, 6 vols. Incl. Vol. 1. Methods: Problems of Cell Biology. 1959. 81.00 (ISBN 0-12-123301-4); Vol. 2. Cells & Their Component Parts. 1961. 81.00 (ISBN 0-12-123302-2); Vol. 3. Meiosis & Mitosis. 1961. 62.00 (ISBN 0-12-123303-0); Vol. 4. Specialized Cells, Part 1. 1960. 67.00 (ISBN 0-12-123304-9); Vol. 5. Specialized Cells, Part 2. 1961. 72.50 (ISBN 0-12-123305-7); Vol. 6. Supplementary Volume. 1964. 72.50 (ISBN 0-12-123306-5). Set. 352.00 (ISBN 0-685-23120-8). Acad Pr.

Bracht, Neil F. Social Work in Health Care: A Guide to Professional Practice. LC 78-7881. 1978. 24.95 (ISBN 0-917724-04-6, B4); pap. 14.95 (ISBN 0-917724-05-4, B5). Haworth Pr.

Brackbill, Yvonne & Thompson, G. G. Behavior in Infancy & Early Childhood. LC 67-15056. 1967. text ed. 16.95 (ISBN 0-02-904530-4). Free Pr.

Bracken, Bruce A., jt. ed. see Paget, Kathleen D.

Bracken, Carolyn. Little Simon Says I Can, Can You? (Illus.). 6p. (ps). 1981. deluxe ed. 6.95 deluxe cloth ed. (ISBN 0-671-44425-5, Little Simon). S&S.

--Little Teddy Bear. (Shaggies Ser.). (Illus.). 12p. (ps-2). 1982. board 3.95 (ISBN 0-671-42550-1, Little Simon). S&S.

--Peter Rabbit's Pockets. (Illus.). 8p. (ps). 1982. 3.95 (ISBN 0-671-44528-6, Little Simon). S&S.

--Super Stickers for Kids: One Hundred & Twenty-Eight Fun Labels. (Illus.). 16p. (Orig.). 1981. pap. 2.50 (ISBN 0-486-24092-4). Dover.

Bracken, Carolyn, illus. Bunny. (Floppies Ser.). (Illus.). 6p. (ps-k). 1981. cloth ed. 2.50 (ISBN 0-671-42531-5, Little Simon). S&S.

--Panda. (Floppies Ser.). (Illus.). 6p. (ps-k). 1981. 2.50 (ISBN 0-671-42530-7, Little Simon). S&S.

--You Can Fly a Jet Plane. LC 82-83118. (A Golden Drive Away Bk.). (Illus.). 12p. (ps-5). 1983. 3.95 (ISBN 0-307-10760-4, Golden Pr). Western Pub.

--You Can Pilot a Submarine. LC 82-83115. (A Golden Drive Away Bk.). (Illus.). 12p. (ps-5). 1983. 3.95 (ISBN 0-307-10763-9, Golden Pr). Western Pub.

Bracken, Harry M. Berkeley. LC 74-15569. 176p. 1975. 17.95 (ISBN 0-312-07595-2). St Martin.

Bracken, Ian. Urban Planning Methods: Research & Policy Analysis. LC 81-13013. 420p. 1981. 29.95x (ISBN 0-416-74860-0); pap. 15.95 (ISBN 0-416-74870-8). Methuen Inc.

Bracken, Jeanne, et al. Books for Today's Young Readers: An Annotated Bibliography of Recommended Fiction for Ages 10-14. 64p. (Orig.). (gr. 4-7). 1981. 4.95 (ISBN 0-935312-03-X). Feminist Pr.

Bracken, John. Great Plants for Cool Places. LC 80-5406. (Illus.). 192p. (Orig.). 1980. 12.95 (ISBN 0-8128-2721-X); pap. 8.95 (ISBN 0-8128-6064-0). Stein & Day.

Bracken, Peg. A Window over the Sink. 256p. 1982. pap. 2.95 (ISBN 0-380-58149-3, 58149). Avon.

Brackenbury, Alison. Dreams of Power & Other Poems. 128p. (Orig.). 1981. pap. text ed. 6.25x (ISBN 0-85635-352-3, Pub. by Carcanet New Pr England). Humanities.

Brackenridge, Douglas, jt. auth. see Boyd, Lois A.

Brackenridge, R. Douglas. Eugene Carson Blake: Prophet with Portfolio. LC 77-25281. (Illus.). 1978. 3.00 (ISBN 0-8164-0383-X). Seabury.

Brackenridge, W. D. see Wilkes, Charles.

Bracker, jt. auth. see Henderson.

Bracker, Jon, jt. auth. see Wallach, Mark I.

Bracker, William & Nabors, James J. The Third National Cone Box Show Catalog. (Illus.). 64p. (Orig.). 1980. pap. text ed. 9.95 (ISBN 0-8403-2181-3). Kendall-Hunt.

Brackett, Babette & Lash, MaryAnn. The Wild Gourmet. LC 74-25953. (Illus.). 144p. 1975. 17.95 (ISBN 0-87923-132-7); pap. 6.95 (ISBN 0-87923-142-4). Godine.

Brackett, Bruce, jt. ed. see Paget, Kathleen.

Brackett, Leigh. The Sword of Rhiannon. 1979. lib. bdg. 9.95 (ISBN 0-8398-2522-6, Gregg). G K Hall.

Brackett, Michael H. Developing Data Structured Information Systems. (Illus.). 250p. (Orig.). 1983. pap. 20.00 (ISBN 0-9605884-1-8). Orr & Assocs.

Brackman, Agnes D. Cook Indonesian. (Golden Asia Cookbooks Ser.). 128p. 1982. pap. 21.95 (ISBN 9971-65-077-0). Hippocrene Bks.

Brackman, Arnold C. The Luck of Nineveh. LC 78-1893. 1978. 14.95 o.p. (ISBN 0-07-007030-X, GB). McGraw.

Brackman, Henrietta. The Perfect Portfolio: Guidelines for Creating a Portfolio That Sells. 192p. 1983. price not set (Amphoto). Watson-Guptill.

Brackmann, Derald E., ed. Neurological Surgery of the Ear & Skull Base. 424p. 1982. text ed. 68.00 (ISBN 0-89004-691-3). Raven.

Brackt, F. & Delanghe, R. Clifford Analysis. (Research Notes in Mathematics Ser.: No. 76). 200p. 1982. pap. text ed. 23.95 (ISBN 0-273-08535-2). Pitman Pub MA.

Bracton, Henry De. De Legibus et Consuetudinibus Angliae. Woodbine, G. E., ed. 1942. Vol. 4. 100.00x (ISBN 0-686-51370-3). Elliots Bks.

Bracy, Jane & McClintock, Marian. Read to Succeed. (gr. 9-12). 1975. 45.00 o.p. (ISBN 0-07-007031-8, C). McGraw.

Bracy, Jane, et al. Read to Succeed. 2nd ed. (Illus.). 192p. 1980. pap. text ed. 13.95x (ISBN 0-07-007035-0); cassettes & tapes 69.95 (ISBN 0-07-007037-7); instr's manual 13.50. McGraw.

Bradac, G. B. & Oberson, R. Angiography & Computed Tomography in Cerebroarterial Occlusive Diseases. (Illus.). 290p. 1982. 68.00 (ISBN 0-387-11453-X). Springer-Verlag.

Bradac, James J., jt. auth. see Berger, Charles R.

Bradach, Wilfrid, tr. see Johnson, Thomas M.

Bradbeer, Robin. The Personal Computer Book. 2nd ed. 240p. 1982. text ed. 23.50x (ISBN 0-566-03445-X). Gower Pub Ltd.

Bradbeer, Robin & Allason, Julian. Choosing & Using a Business Microcomputer. 172p. 1982. text ed. 32.50x (ISBN 0-566-03405-0). Gower Pub Ltd.

Bradbeer, Robin & DeBono, Peter. The Beginners Guide to Computers: Everything you Need to Know About the New Technology. (Illus.). 208p. 1982. 19.95 (ISBN 0-201-11208-6); pap. 9.95 (ISBN 0-201-11209-4). A-W.

Bradbrook, M. C. The Living Monument: Shakespeare & the Theatre of His Time. LC 79-2317. (History of Elizabethan Drama Ser.: Vol. 6). (Illus.). 1976. 39.50 (ISBN 0-521-21255-3); pap. 11.95 (ISBN 0-521-29530-0). Cambridge U Pr.

Bradbrook, Muriel. Women & Literature Seventeen Seventy-Nine to Nineteen Eighty-Two: The Collected Papers of Muriel Bradbrook, Vol. II. LC 82-13914. 180p. 1983. text ed. 24.95x (ISBN 0-389-20295-9). B&N Imports.

Bradbrook, Muriel C. The Growth & Structure of Elizabethan Comedy. LC 79-2313. (History of Elizabethan Drama Ser.: Vol. 2). 1979. pap. 11.95 (ISBN 0-521-29526-2). Cambridge U Pr.

--Malcolm Lowry: His Art & Early Life. (Illus.). 170p. 1975. 29.95 (ISBN 0-521-20473-9); pap. 8.95x (ISBN 0-521-09985-4). Cambridge U Pr.

--The Rise of the Common Player. LC 79-2314. (History of Elizabethan Drama Ser.: Vol. 3). (Illus.). 1979. pap. 11.95 (ISBN 0-521-29527-0). Cambridge U Pr.

--Shakespeare & the Elizabethan Poetry. LC 79-2315. (History of Elizabethan Drama Ser.: Vol. 4). (Illus.). 1979. pap. 11.95 (ISBN 0-521-29528-9). Cambridge U Pr.

--Shakespeare the Craftsman. LC 79-2316. (History of Elizabethan Drama Ser.: Vol. 5). (Illus.). 1979. pap. 9.95 (ISBN 0-521-29529-7). Cambridge U Pr.

Bradburn, Norman M., jt. auth. see Sudman, Seymour.

Bradbury, D. E., jt. ed. see Thrower, Norman J.

Bradbury, Ellen & Flory, E. I Wear the Morning Star. (Illus.). 1976. 7.50 o.p. (ISBN 0-912964-06-5). Minneapolis Inst Arts.

Bradbury, Frederick. Bradbury's Book of Hallmarks. Rev. ed. 108p. (Orig.). pap. 3.95 (ISBN 0-686-36223-3, Pub by JW Northend England). Seven Hills Bks.

Bradbury, Jim. Shakespeare & His Theatre. Reeves, Marjorie, ed. (Then & There Ser.). (Illus.). 95p. (Orig.). (gr. 7-12). 1977. pap. text ed. 3.10 (ISBN 0-582-20539-5). Longman.

Bradbury, Katharine L. & Downs, Anthony. Housing & Energy in the Nineteen Eighties. new ed. 320p. 1983. 28.95 (ISBN 0-8157-1050-X); pap. 10.95 (ISBN 0-8157-1049-6). Brookings.

Bradbury, Katharine L. & Downs, Anthony, eds. Do Housing Allowances Work? LC 81-6689. (Studies in Social Experimentation). 430p. 1981. 27.95 (ISBN 0-8157-1052-6); pap. 11.95 (ISBN 0-8157-1051-8). Brookings.

Bradbury, L. J., et al. Turbulent Shear Flow 3rd: University of California, Selected Papers, 1981. (Illus.). 321p. 1983. 64.00 (ISBN 0-387-11817-9). Springer-Verlag.

Bradbury, Malcolm. Saul Bellow. (Contemporary Writers Ser.). 1982. pap. 4.25 (ISBN 0-416-31650-6). Methuen Inc.

Bradbury, Margaret. The Shepherd's Guidebook: Raising Sheep for Meat, Wool, & Hides. LC 76-30713. 1977. 12.95 o.p. (ISBN 0-87857-159-0). Rodale Pr Inc.

Bradbury, Michael. The Concept of a Blood-Brain Barrier. LC 79-16764. 1979. 84.95x (ISBN 0-471-99688-2, Pub. by Wiley-Interscience). Wiley.

Bradbury, Peggy. The Snake That Couldn't Slither. LC 76-3633. (See & Read Storybooks). (Illus.). (gr. k-3). 1976. PLB 6.29 o.p. (ISBN 0-399-61015-4). Putnam Pub Group.

Bradbury, Ray. The Halloween Tree. 192p. (gr. 7 up). 1982. pap. 2.25 (ISBN 0-553-20064-X). Bantam.

--The Halloween Tree. (Illus.). (gr. 5 up). 1972. 4.50 (ISBN 0-394-82409-1); PLB 7.99 (ISBN 0-394-92409-6). Knopf.

--I Sing the Body Electric. LC 75-88745. (YA) 1969. 13.50 (ISBN 0-394-42985-0). Knopf.

--The Love Affair. 40p. DEC Limited signed ed. 35.00 (ISBN 0-935716-17-3). Lord John.

--Machineries of Joy. 1963. 6.95 o.p. (ISBN 0-671-43830-1). S&S.

--The Martian Chronicles. LC 58-8207. (Science Fiction Ser.). 1958. 12.95 (ISBN 0-385-05060-7). Doubleday.

--October Country. (YA) 1970. 12.50 (ISBN 0-394-43892-2). Knopf.

--Something Wicked This Way Comes. LC 82-48732. 1983. 13.95 (ISBN 0-394-53041-1). Knopf.

--Twice Twenty-Two. LC 66-10615. (Science Fiction Ser.). 1966. 14.95 (ISBN 0-385-05594-3). Doubleday.

--Vintage Bradbury. 1965. pap. 1.95 (ISBN 0-394-74059-9, Vin, V294). Random.

Bradbury, Samuel, ed. Source Book on Powder Metallurgy. 1979. 46.00 (ISBN 0-87170-030-1). ASM.

Bradbury, Savile. Optical Microscope in Biology. (Studies in Biology: No. 59). 80p. 1976. pap. text ed. 8.95 (ISBN 0-7131-2533-0). E Arnold.

Bradbury, Wilbur. The Adult Years. LC 75-18649. (Human Behavior). (Illus.). (gr. 5 up). 1975. lib. bdg. 13.28 (ISBN 0-8094-1942-4, Pub. by Time-Life). Silver.

Bradbury, Will. The God Cell. LC 76-14786. 1976. 7.95 o.p. (ISBN 0-399-11757-1). Putnam Pub Group.

Braddon, Russell. The Naked Island. LC 82-13375. (Illus.). 288p. 1982. pap. 8.95 (ISBN 0-689-70629-4, 282). Atheneum.

Brade, W., ed. Tegafur-Ftorafur. (Beitraege zur Onkologie-Contributions to Oncology Ser.: Vol. 14). viii, 200p. 1983. pap. 39.00 (ISBN 3-8055-3653-4). S Karger.

Braden, Irene A. Undergraduate Library. LC 75-80834. (A.C.R.L. Monograph Ser: No. 31). (Orig.). 1970. pap. 10.00 o.p. (ISBN 0-8389-3097-2). ALA.

Braden, Su. Artists & People. (Illus.). 1978. pap. 12.95 (ISBN 0-7100-8920-1). Routledge & Kegan.

Braden, Waldo see Braden, Waldo W. & Peterson, Owen.

Braden, Waldo W. The Oral Tradition in the South. LC 82-20827. 152p. 1983. text ed. 17.50x (ISBN 0-8071-1093-0). La State U Pr.

Braden, Waldo W. & Peterson, Owen, eds. Representative American Speeches. Incl. 1966-1967. Thonssen, Lester, ed. 197p. 1969. o.p. (ISBN 0-8242-0098-5); 1968-1969. Thonssen, Lester, ed. 200p. 1969 (ISBN 0-8242-0109-4); 1969-1970 up to 1979-1989. Braden, Waldo, ed. 1970 (ISBN 0-8242-0412-3); 1970-1971. Braden, Waldo W., ed. 200p. 1971 (ISBN 0-8242-0449-2); 1971-1972. 200p. 1972 (ISBN 0-8242-0467-0); 1972-1973. 1973 (ISBN 0-8242-0507-3); 1973-1974. 1974 (ISBN 0-8242-0524-3); 1974-1975. 1975 (ISBN 0-8242-0572-3); 1975-1976. 1976 (ISBN 0-8242-0598-7); 1976-1977. 1977 (ISBN 0-8242-0606-1); 1977-78. 1978 (ISBN 0-8242-0625-8); 1978-1979. 1979 (ISBN 0-8242-0634-7); 1979-1980. 1980 (ISBN 0-8242-0648-7); 1980-1981. Peterson, Owen, ed. 1981 (ISBN 0-8242-0657-6); 1981-1982. Peterson, Owen, ed. 1982 (ISBN 0-8242-0669-X). (Reference Shelf Ser). 6.25 ea. Wilson.

Bradfield, Cecil D. Neo-Pentecostalism: A Sociological Assessment. LC 79-66228. 1979. pap. text ed. 7.00 (ISBN 0-8191-0809-X). U Pr of Amer.

Bradfield, D. J. Guide to Extension Training. (Orig.). 1966. pap. 12.25 o.p. (ISBN 0-685-02452-0, F218, FAO). Unipub.

Bradfield, E. G., ed. Franklin in Numismatics: An Anthology. 1982. pap. 8.00 (ISBN 0-942666-05-4). S J Durst.

Bradfield, R. The Changing Pattern of Hopi Agriculture. 1971. 40.00x (ISBN 0-686-98307-6, Pub. by Royal Anthro Ireland). State Mutual Bk.

Bradfield, Roger. Jolly Roger Bradfield Storybooks. Incl. Flying Hockey Stock (ISBN 0-528-82415-5); Giants Come in Different Sizes (ISBN 0-528-82414-7); Benjamin Dilley's Thirsty Camel (ISBN 0-528-82417-1); Pickle-Chiffon Pie (ISBN 0-528-82416-3). (Illus.). 64p. (gr. 4-7). 7.95 ea. Rand.

Bradford, Alden. Speeches of the Governors of Massachusetts from 1765 to 1775. LC 71-119048. (Era of the American Revolution Ser). 1971. Repr. of 1818 ed. 59.50 (ISBN 0-306-71947-9). Da Capo.

Bradford, Ann & Gezi, Kal. The Mystery at Misty Falls. LC 80-15708. (The Maple Street Five Ser.). (Illus.). 32p. (gr. 3-6). 1980. 8.65g (ISBN 0-516-06491-6). Childrens.

--The Mystery at the Tree House. LC 80-15654. (The Maple Street Five Ser.). (Illus.). 32p. (gr. 3-6). 1980. 8.65g (ISBN 0-516-06494-0). Childrens.

--The Mystery of the Blind Writer. LC 80-12395. (The Maple Street Five Ser.). (Illus.). 32p. (gr. 3-6). 1980. 8.65g (ISBN 0-516-06493-2). Childrens.

--The Mystery of the Midget Clown. LC 80-12513. (The Maple Street Five Ser.). (Illus.). 32p. (gr. 3-6). 1980. 8.65g (ISBN 0-516-06495-9). Childrens.

--The Mystery of the Missing Dogs. LC 80-10437. (The Maple Street Five Ser.). (Illus.). 32p. (gr. 3-6). 1980. 8.65g (ISBN 0-516-06492-4). Childrens.

--The Mystery of the Square Footprints. LC 80-10437. (The Maple Street Five Ser.). (Illus.). 32p. (gr. 3-6). 1980. 8.65g (ISBN 0-516-06496-7). Childrens.

Bradford, Ann L. & Murai, Harold M. Pocket Patches. 2nd ed. (New Cornerstone Ser.). (gr. 1). 1978. pap. text ed. 5.32 (ISBN 0-201-41020-6, Sch Div); tchr's. ed. 6.76 (ISBN 0-201-41021-4). A-W.

Bradford, Barbara T. Designs for Casual Living. (Illus.). 1977. 16.95 o.p. (ISBN 0-671-21969-3). S&S.

--Voice of the Heart. LC 81-47863. 744p. 1983. 17.95 (ISBN 0-385-15323-6). Doubleday.

--A Woman of Substance. 832p. 1983. pap. 3.95 (ISBN 0-380-49163-X, 61986-5). Avon.

Bradford, Curtis. Yeats's Last Poems Again. (Yeats Cent. Papers: Vol. 8). 1966. pap. text ed. 1.75x o.p. (ISBN 0-85105-471-4, Dolmen Pr). Humanities.

Bradford, Dennis E. The Concept of Existence: A Study of Nonexistent Particulars. LC 80-5526. 142p. 1980. lib. bdg. 19.00 (ISBN 0-8191-1124-4); pap. text ed. 8.25 (ISBN 0-8191-1127-9). U Pr of Amer.

Bradford, Elizabeth A., ed. see Pick, Michael R.

Bradford, Ernle. Companion Guide to the Greek Islands. (Illus.). 336p. 1983. 15.95 (ISBN 0-13-154500-0); pap. 7.95 (ISBN 0-13-154492-6). P-H.

--The Story of the Mary Rose. (Illus.). 1982. 24.95 (ISBN 0-393-01620-X). Norton.

--The Sword & the Scimitar: The Saga of the Crusades. (Illus.). 264p. 1974. 15.95 o.p. (ISBN 0-399-11375-4). Putnam Pub Group.

Bradford, G. Eric, jt. ed. see Fitzhugh, Hank A.

Bradford, Gamaliel. Life & I, an Autobiography of Humanity. LC 68-54987. (Illus.). 1968. Repr. of 1928 ed. lib. bdg. 16.00x (ISBN 0-8371-0324-X, BRLI). Greenwood.

Bradford, George. Great Tank Battles of World War 2. LC 77-106482. (Illus.). 1970. pap. 3.95 o.p. (ISBN 0-668-02288-4). Arco.

Bradford, George & Morgan, Len. Fifty Famous Tanks. 2nd ed. LC 74-80997. (Illus.). 1974. pap. 2.95 o.p. (ISBN 0-668-01583-7). Arco.

Bradford, James N. Escape Route: Surviving the Earth Changes. 120p. 1983. pap. 6.50 (ISBN 0-89540-135-5, SB-135). Sun Pub.

Bradford, John. Writings of Bradford. 1979. Set. 29.95 (ISBN 0-686-70955-1). Vol. 1 (ISBN 0-85151-283-6). Vol. 2 (ISBN 0-85151-284-4). Banner of Truth.

Bradford, Leland P. Making Meetings Work: A Guide for Leaders & Group Members. LC 76-16886. 121p. 1976. pap. 13.95 (ISBN 0-88390-122-6). Univ Assocs.

--Preparing for Retirement: A Program for Survival-A Trainers Kit. LC 80-52897. 124p. 1981. looseleaf notebook & wkbk. 45.00 (ISBN 0-88390-161-7). Univ Assocs.

Bradford, Leland P., ed. Group Development. 2nd, rev, enl. ed. LC 78-51283. 234p. 1978. pap. 14.50 (ISBN 0-88390-144-7). Univ Assocs.

Bradford, Leland P., et al, eds. T-Group Theory & Laboratory Method: Innovation in Re-Education. LC 64-11499. 498p. 1964. 32.95x (ISBN 0-471-09510-9). Wiley.

Bradford, M. E. Generations of the Faithful Heart: On the Literature of the South. 216p. (Orig.). 1982. text ed. 14.95 (ISBN 0-89385-024-1); pap. 5.95 (ISBN 0-89385-023-3). Sugden.

Bradford, Mary L., ed. Mormon Women Speak. LC 82-62366. 1982. 9.95 (ISBN 0-913420-94-8). Olympus Pub Co.

Bradford, Ned & Bradford, Pam. Boston's Locke-Ober Cafe. LC 77-15871. (Illus.). 1978. 12.95 o.p. (ISBN 0-689-10865-6). Atheneum.

Bradford, Pam, jt. auth. see Bradford, Ned.

Bradford, Richard. Red Sky at Morning. LC 68-11272. 1968. 12.45i (ISBN 0-397-00549-0). Har-Row.

Bradford, Richard H. The Virginius Affair. LC 20-520000. 1980. 13.50x (ISBN 0-87081-080-4). Colo Assoc.

Bradford, Robert. Mathematics for Carpenters. LC 75-19525. 1975. pap. 13.00 (ISBN 0-8273-1116-8); instructor's guide 3.75 (ISBN 0-8273-1117-6). Delmar.

Bradford, S. S. Liberty's Road: A Guide to Revolutionary War Sites, 2 vols. 1976. Vol. 1. pap. 5.95 (ISBN 0-07-007060-1); Vol. 2. pap. 5.95 (ISBN 0-07-007061-X). McGraw.

Bradford, S. Sydney. Liberty's Road: A Guide to Revolutionary War Sites, 2 vols. Incl. Vol. 1. Conn., Maine, Mass, N.H., N.J., N.Y., Pa., R.I., & Vt. pap. 5.95 (ISBN 0-07-007060-1); Vol. 2. Del., Ga., Md., N.C., S.C., Va., & W. Va. pap. 5.95 (ISBN 0-07-007061-X). LC 75-38695. (Illus.). 1976 (P&RB). McGraw.

Bradford, Sarah. Disraeli. LC 82-42728. 464p. 1983. 19.95 (ISBN 0-8128-2899-2). Stein & Day.

Bradford, Thomas L. Bibliographer's Manual of American History, 5 Vols. Henkels, Stan V., ed. LC 67-14023. 1968. Repr. of 1907 ed. 134.00x (ISBN 0-8103-3319-8). Gale.

Bradford, William. The Encyclopedia of Strength Training. LC 82-81810. (Illus.). 224p. (Orig.). Date not set. pap. 11.95 (ISBN 0-88011-054-6). Leisure Pr. Postponed.

--Of Plymouth Plantation: 1620-1647. Morison, Samuel E., ed. (The American Past Ser). (Illus.). (YA) 1952. 17.95 (ISBN 0-394-43895-7). Knopf.

Bradick, Bill, jt. auth. see Boyle, Denis.

Brading, D. A. Haciendas & Ranchos in the Mexican Bajio Leon 1700-1860. LC 77-90203. (Cambridge Latin American Studies: No. 32). (Illus.). 1979. 47.50 (ISBN 0-521-22200-1). Cambridge U Pr.

--Miners & Merchants in Bourbon Mexico, 1763-1810. LC 74-123666. (Cambridge Latin American Studies: No. 10). (Illus.). 1971. 49.50 (ISBN 0-521-07874-1). Cambridge U Pr.

Brading, D. A., ed. Caudillo & Peasant in the Mexican Revolution. LC 79-16593. (Cambridge Latin American Studies: No. 38). 1980. 47.50 (ISBN 0-521-22997-9). Cambridge U Pr.

Bradlee, Ben, Jr. & Van Atta, Dale. Prophet of Blood: The Story of the "Mormon Manson". (Illus.). 384p. 1981. 15.95 (ISBN 0-399-12371-7). Putnam Pub Group.

Bradley, Andrew C. Shakespearean Tragedy: Lectures on Hamlet, Othello, King Lear & Macbeth. 2nd ed. 432p. 1905. 22.50 (ISBN 0-312-71470-X). St Martin.

Bradley, Anne. Take Note of College Study Skills. 1983. pap. text ed. 10.95x (ISBN 0-673-15578-1). Scott F.

Bradley, Anthony. William Butler Yeats. LC 77-6953. (Literature and Life Ser.). 1980. 18.50 (ISBN 0-8044-2068-8). Ungar.

Bradley, Ardyth. Inside the Bones Is Flesh. LC 78-20985. 45p. 1978. 3.50 (ISBN 0-87886-103-3). Ithaca Hse.

Bradley, Barbara, ed. Proceeding of the National Passive Solar Energy Conference, 1-6, 1976-1981: Index & Supplement. 1983. pap. text ed. 10.00x (ISBN 0-89553-109-7). Am Solar Energy.

Bradley, Bill, jt. auth. see Vital Issues Editor.

Bradley, Bill, ed. see Steinheimer, Richard & Sims, Donald.

Bradley, C. Henry. A Linguistic Sketch of Jicaltepec Mixtec. (Publications in Linguistics & Related Fields Ser.: No. 25). 97p. 1970. pap. 3.00x (ISBN 0-88312-027-5); microfiche 2.25x (ISBN 0-686-66936-3). Summer Inst Ling.

Bradley, C. Paul. Recent United States Policy in the Persian Gulf (1971-82) LC 82-16049. 128p. (Orig.). 1982. pap. text ed. 6.95 (ISBN 0-936988-08-8). Tompson & Rutter.

Bradley, Carol. Music Collections in American Libraries: A Chronology. LC 81-2907. (Detroit Studies in Music Bibliography Ser.: No. 46). 1981. 18.50 (ISBN 0-89990-002-X). Info Coord.

Bradley, Curtis H. & Friedenberg, Joan E. Foundations & Strategies for Bilingual Vocational Education. 128p. 1982. pap. 9.95x (ISBN 0-87281-311-8). Ctr Appl Ling.

Bradley, David. South Street. 1977. pap. 1.95 o.p. (ISBN 0-451-07355-X, J7355, Sig). NAL.

Bradley, David J., jt. auth. see Feachem, Richard G.

Bradley, Donald. The Parallax Problem in Astrology. 60p. 1983. soft cover 4.00 (ISBN 0-87542-042-7, L-042). Llewellyn Pubns.

Bradley, E. F. & Denmead, O. T. The Collection & Processing of Field Data. LC 67-20259. 597p. 1967. text ed. 29.50 (ISBN 0-470-09517-2, Pub. by Wiley). Krieger.

Bradley, Edward S., jt. auth. see Teweles, Richard J.

Bradley, Francis H. Collected Essays. 1935. 49.00x (ISBN 0-19-824341-3). Oxford U Pr.

--Ethical Studies: Selected Essays. 1951. pap. 5.95 o.p. (ISBN 0-672-60189-3, LLA28). Bobbs.

Bradley, Fred O. & Stone, Lloyd A. Parenting Without Hassles: Children as Partners. LC 82-62365. 170p. 1983. 8.95 (ISBN 0-913420-14-X). Olympus Pub Co.

Bradley, Gerald L. A Primer of Linear Algebra. (Illus.). 448p. 1975. text ed. 21.95 (ISBN 0-13-700328-5). P-H.

Bradley, Gerard T. Face the Light. 1982. 8.95 (ISBN 0-533-05448-6). Vantage.

Bradley, Glenn D. The Story of the Pony Express. LC 75-141793. 1974. Repr. of 1913 ed. 27.00 o.p. (ISBN 0-8103-3632-4). Gale.

Bradley, Hila M., jt. auth. see Kinn, Mary E.

Bradley, Ian. Annotated Gilbert & Sullivan. 1983. pap. 7.95 (ISBN 0-14-070848-0). Penguin.

--Shaping Machine & Lathe Tools. rev. ed. LC 77-371812. (Illus.). 74p. 1976. pap. 6.50x (ISBN 0-85242-485-X). Intl Pubns Serv.

--Sharpening Small Tools. LC 79-91402. (Home Craftsman Bk.). (Illus.). 128p. 1980. pap. 5.95 (ISBN 0-8069-8922-X). Sterling.

Bradley, Ian, jt. ed. see Simon, Brian.

Bradley, J. E., tr. see Nikolskii, G. V.

Bradley, J. F. Politics in Czechoslovakia, Nineteen Forty-Five to Nineteen Seventy-One. LC 80-5632. 231p. 1981. lib. bdg. 20.00 (ISBN 0-8191-1582-7); pap. text ed. 10.25 (ISBN 0-8191-1583-5). U Pr of Amer.

Bradley, J. F., jt. auth. see Black, J.

Bradley, Jack I. & McClelland, James N. Basic Statistical Concepts: A Self-Instructional Text. 2nd ed. 1978. pap. 8.95x (ISBN 0-673-15075-5). Scott F.

Bradley, James V. Elementary Microstudies of Human Tissues. (Illus.). 376p. 1972. 36.50x o.p. (ISBN 0-398-02240-2). C C Thomas.

Bradley, James W. & Korn, Donald H. Acquisition & Corporate Development: A Contemporary Perspective for the Manager. LC 79-7719. (An Arthur D. Little Bk.). (Illus.). 272p. 1981. 28.95x (ISBN 0-669-03170-4). Lexington Bks.

Bradley, Jeff. A Young Person's Guide to Military Service. 160p. 1983. 11.95 (ISBN 0-916782-31-X); pap. 5.95 (ISBN 0-916782-32-8). Harvard Common Pr.

Bradley, Jessica. Canada-Paterson Ewen-XL Biennale Di Venezia. Trilingual ed. (Illus.). 32p. (Eng., Fr. & Ital.). 1982. 4.95 (ISBN 0-686-97831-5, 56294-8, Pub. by Natl Mus Canada). U of Chicago Pr.

Bradley, John. Civil War in Russia, 1917-20. LC 75-18594. 200p. 1975. 19.95 o.p. (ISBN 0-312-14140-8). St Martin.

--Illustrated History of the Third Reich. LC 77-87811. (Illus.). 1978. 14.95 o.s.i. (ISBN 0-448-14628-2, G&D). Putnam Pub Group.

Bradley, Johnson T. The Foundation of Maryland & the Origin of the Act Concerning Religion. 210p. 1883. 9.50 (ISBN 0-686-36846-0). Md Hist.

Bradley, Joseph F. Role of Trade Associations & Professional Business Societies in America. LC 64-8082. 1965. 17.50x (ISBN 0-271-73097-8). Pa St U Pr.

Bradley, Loretta D. Career Education & Biological Sciences. 1975. pap. 2.40 o.p. (ISBN 0-395-20047-4). HM.

Bradley, Marion. The Complete Darkover Series. (Science Fiction Ser.). 1979. 120.00 o.p. (ISBN 0-686-74240-0, Gregg). G K Hall.

--Hunters of the Red Moon. (Science Fiction Ser). pap. 1.95 (ISBN 0-87997-713-2, UE1713). DAW Bks.

Bradley, Marion Z. The Bloody Sun. 1979. lib. bdg. 12.00 (ISBN 0-8398-2513-7, Gregg). G K Hall.

--The Colors of Space. Rev. ed. Stine, Hank, ed. LC 82-5008. (Illus.). 146p. 1983. pap. 5.95 (ISBN 0-89865-191-3, AACR2, Starblaze). Donning Co.

--Darkover Landfall. (Science Fiction Ser.). (Orig.). 1972. pap. 2.25 (ISBN 0-87997-806-6, UE1806). DAW Bks.

--Darkover Landfall. (Darkover Ser.). 1978. lib. bdg. 10.95 o.p. (ISBN 0-8398-2404-1, Gregg). G K Hall.

--The Forbidden Tower. (Darkover Ser.). (Orig.). 1977. pap. 2.95 (ISBN 0-87997-752-3, UE1752). DAW Bks.

--The Forbidden Tower. 1979. lib. bdg. 14.00 o.p. (ISBN 0-8398-2405-X, Gregg). G K Hall.

--The Heritage of Hastur. (Science Fiction Ser). 1975. pap. 2.95 (ISBN 0-87997-744-2, UE1744). DAW Bks.

--The Heritage of Hastur. (Science Fiction Ser.). 1977. Repr. of 1975 ed. lib. bdg. 14.00 o.p. (ISBN 0-8398-2363-0, Gregg). G K Hall.

--The Keeper's Price. (Science Fiction Ser.). 1980. pap. 2.50 (ISBN 0-87997-837-6, UE1837). DAW Bks.

--The Mists of Avalon. 1983. 17.50 (ISBN 0-394-52406-3). Knopf.

--The Planet Savers. 1979. lib. bdg. 9.95 (ISBN 0-8398-2514-5, Gregg). G K Hall.

--The Ruins of Isis. Freas, Polly & Freas, Kelly, eds. LC 78-14268. (Illus.). 1978. pap. 5.95 (ISBN 0-915442-60-4, Starblaze). Donning Co.

--The Shattered Chain. 1979. lib. bdg. 12.00 (ISBN 0-8398-2502-1, Gregg). G K Hall.

--The Spell Sword. 1979. lib. bdg. 9.95 (ISBN 0-8398-2503-X, Gregg). G K Hall.

--Star of Danger. 1979. lib. bdg. 9.95 (ISBN 0-8398-2512-9, Gregg). G K Hall.

--Stormqueen! 1979. lib. bdg. 9.95 (ISBN 0-8398-2504-8, Gregg). G K Hall.

--The Sword of Aldones. LC 77-4513. (Darkover Ser.). 1977. Repr. of 1962 ed. lib. bdg. 10.95 o.p. (ISBN 0-8398-2367-3, Gregg). G K Hall.

--Sword of Chaos. 1982. pap. 2.95 (ISBN 0-87997-722-1, UE1722). DAW Bks.

--The Web of Darkness. LC 80-22995. 1983. pap. 5.95 (ISBN 0-89865-032-1, Starblaze). Donning Co.

--The Winds of Darkover. (Darkover Ser.). 1979. lib. bdg. 9.95 o.p. (ISBN 0-8398-2511-0, Gregg). G K Hall.

--The World Wreckers. 1979. lib. bdg. 10.95 (ISBN 0-8398-2515-3, Gregg). G K Hall.

Bradley, Martin. The Coordination of Services for Children under Five. (NFER General Ser.). 172p. 1982. pap. text ed. 15.25x (ISBN 0-7005-0507-5, NFER). Humanities.

Bradley, Martin A., jt. auth. see McWhinney, Edward.

Bradley, Melvin. Horses: A Practical & Scientific Approach. (Illus.). 560p. 1980. text ed. 25.50x (ISBN 0-07-007065-2). McGraw.

Bradley, Michael. The Black Discovery of America. 224p. 1981. 12.95 (ISBN 0-920510-36-1, Pub. by Personal Lib). Dodd.

--The Iceman Inheritance. 256p. (Orig.). 1981. pap. 2.95 o.p. (ISBN 0-446-93506-9). Warner Bks.

Bradley, Michael E. Economics. 1980. text ed. 24.50x (ISBN 0-673-15231-6). Scott F.

--Macroeconomics. 1980. pap. text ed. 15.50x (ISBN 0-673-15336-3); study guide 7.95x (ISBN 0-673-15423-8). Scott F.

--Microeconomics. 1980. pap. text ed. 15.50x (ISBN 0-673-15335-5); study guide 7.95x (ISBN 0-673-15286-3). Scott F.

Bradley, Omar N. & Blair, Clay. A General's Life. (Illus.). 540p. 1983. 19.95 (ISBN 0-671-41023-7). S&S.

Bradley, P. B. & Brimblecombe, R. W. Biochemical & Pharmacological Mechanisms Underlying Behavior. (Progress in Brain Research Ser.: Vol. 36). 1972. 53.00 (ISBN 0-444-40992-0). Elsevier.

Bradley, P. B., ed. Methods in Brain Research. LC 74-404. 557p. 1975. 104.95 (ISBN 0-471-09514-1, Pub. by Wiley-Interscience). Wiley.

Bradley, P. B., ed. see Symposium on Anticholinergic Drugs & Brain Functions in Animals & Man - 6th - Washington D. C., 1968.

Bradley, Patricia H. & Baird, John E., Jr. Communication for Business & the Professions. 300p. 1980. pap. text ed. write for info. o.p. (ISBN 0-697-04166-2); instrs' manual o.p. (ISBN 0-697-04169-7). Wm C Brown.

--Communication for Business & the Professions. 2nd ed. 360p. 1983. pap. text ed. Write for info. (ISBN 0-697-04223-5); instrs.' manual avail. (ISBN 0-697-04233-2). Wm C Brown.

Bradley, Phillips, ed. see Tocqueville, Alexis De.

Bradley, Raymond & Swartz, Norman. Possible Worlds: An Introduction to Logic & Its Philosophy. LC 79-51037. (Illus.). 1979. lib. bdg. 25.00 (ISBN 0-915144-60-3); pap. text ed. 14.50 (ISBN 0-915144-59-X). Hackett Pub.

Bradley, Robert A. Husband Coached Childbirth. 3rd ed. LC 80-8683. (Illus.). 256p. 1981. 10.53i (ISBN 0-06-014850-0, HarpT). Har-Row.

Bradley, Ronald, jt. ed. see Smythies, John.

Bradley, S. E. & Purcell, E. F., eds. The Parcellular Pathway. LC 82-81100. (Illus.). 382p. 1982. pap. 15.00 (ISBN 0-914362-38-0). J Macy Foun.

Bradley, Sam. Men, in Good Measure. 1966. 3.00 o.p. (ISBN 0-8233-0009-9). Golden Quill.

Bradley, Sculley, ed. see Whitman, Walt.

Bradley, Stanley E. & Purcell, Elizabeth F., eds. The Paracellular Pathway. (Illus.). 382p. 1982. pap. 15.00 (ISBN 0-914362-37-2). J Macy Foun.

Bradley, Stephen P. & Crane, Dwight B. Management of Bank Portfolios. LC 75-23030. 299p. 1975. 43.95 (ISBN 0-471-09522-2, Pub. by Wiley-Interscience). Wiley.

Bradley, Stephen P., et al. Applied Mathematical Programming. LC 76-10426. (Illus.). 1977. text ed. 29.95 (ISBN 0-201-00464-X). A-W.

Bradley, Susannah. How to Be a Cook. LC 80-50948. (Whizz Kids Ser.). 8.00 (ISBN 0-382-06441-0). Silver.

Bradley, T. J. Hospital Pharmacy & the Patient. 250p. 1983. text ed. 25.00 (ISBN 0-85200-485-0, Pub. by MTP Pr England). Kluwer Boston.

Bradley, Van A. The Book Collectors Handbook of Values: 1978-1979 Values. 3rd rev. ed. LC 75-13906. (Illus.). 1978. 25.00 o.p. (ISBN 0-399-12110-2). Putnam Pub Group.

Bradley, Van Allen. The Book Collector's Handbook of Values: 1982-1983 Edition. Rev. ed. LC 81-10610. 624p. 1982. 29.95 (ISBN 0-399-12629-5). Putnam Pub Group.

Bradley, W. F. & Hanson, Harold P., eds. Machine Interpretations of Patterson Functions & Alternative Direct Approaches & the Austin Symposium on Gas Phase Molecular Structure. pap. 5.00 (ISBN 0-686-60373-7). Polycrystal Bk Serv.

Bradley, William, et al. Thailand, Domino by Default? The 1976 Coup & Implications for U. S. Policy, with an Epilogue on the October 1977 Coup. LC 77-620050. (Papers in International Studies: Southeast Asia: No. 46). 1977. pap. 6.00 (ISBN 0-89680-032-6, Ohio U Ctr Intl). Ohio U Pr.

Bradley, William A. Dutch Landscape Etchers of the Seventeenth Century. (Illus.). 1919. 29.50x (ISBN 0-685-89748-6). Elliots Bks.

Bradley, William E., jt. auth. see Hald, Tage.

Bradley, William J. Citizen's Band Radio Digest: A Complete Guide to Personal Communications. (Illus.). 192p. (Orig.). 1976. pap. 5.95 o.s.i. (ISBN 0-695-80677-7). Follett.

Bradshaw, A. D. & McNeilly, D. T. Evolution & Pollution. (Studies in Biology: No. 130). 80p. 1981. pap. text ed. 8.95 (ISBN 0-7131-2818-6). E Arnold.

Bradshaw, Barbara, jt. auth. see Faderman, Lillian.

Bradshaw, Brendan. The Dissolution of the Religious Orders in Ireland Under Henry Eighth. LC 73-83104. (Illus.). 248p. 1974. 47.50 (ISBN 0-521-20342-2). Cambridge U Pr.

--The Irish Constitutional Revolution in the Sixteenth Century. LC 78-58785. 1979. 44.50 (ISBN 0-521-22206-0). Cambridge U Pr.

Bradshaw, C. M., et al, eds. Quantification of Steady State Operant Behaviour. 1981. 70.25 (ISBN 0-444-80298-3). Elsevier.

Bradshaw, George. Bradshaw's General Railway & Steam Navigation Guide: Great Britain & Ireland. LC 68-24743. (Illus.). Repr. of 1910 ed. 22.50x (ISBN 0-678-05550-5). Kelley.

--Bradshaw's July 1938 Railway Guide. LC 68-24743. (Illus.). Repr. of 1938 ed. 25.00x (ISBN 0-678-05750-8). Kelley.

Bradshaw, Gillian. Hawk of May. 1980. 10.95 o.p. (ISBN 0-671-25093-0). S&S.

--Kingdom of Summer. 1982. pap. 2.75 (ISBN 0-451-11550-3, AE1550, Sig). NAL.

Bradshaw, J., ed. The Women's Liberation Movement: Europe & North America. 100p. 1982. 19.00 (ISBN 0-08-028932-0). Pergamon.

Bradshaw, L. Jack. Introduction to Molecular Biological Techniques. 1966. pap. 12.95x ref. ed. (ISBN 0-13-489187-2). P-H.

Bradshaw, M. E. & Garstang, B. M. Word Processing: An Elementary Workbook for Students. 48p. 1982. pap. text ed. 8.95 (ISBN 0-7131-0803-7). E Arnold.

--Word Processing: An Intermediate, Advanced Workbook for Students. 80p. 1982. pap. text ed. 9.95 (ISBN 0-7131-0815-0). E Arnold.

Bradshaw, P. Conceptual Models in Exploration Geochemistry. 1975. 19.00 (ISBN 0-444-41314-6). Elsevier.

--An Introduction to Turbulance & Its Measurements. Woods, W. A., ed. 218p. 1971. text ed. 27.00 o.s.i. (ISBN 0-08-016620-2); pap. text ed. 13.25 (ISBN 0-08-016621-0). Pergamon.

Bradshaw, P., jt. auth. see Cebeci, T.

Bradshaw, P., ed. Turbulence. (Topics in Applied Physics: Vol. 12). 1976. 24.00 (ISBN 0-387-08864-4). Springer-Verlag.

Bradshaw, Paul F. Daily Prayer in the Early Church: A Study of the Origins & Early Development of the Divine Office. 202p. 1982. 24.50x (ISBN 0-19-520394-1); pap. 8.85x (ISBN 0-19-520395-X). Oxford U Pr.

Bradshaw, Ralph & Schneider, Diana, eds. Proteins of the Nervous System. 2nd ed. 407p. 1980. 49.50 (ISBN 0-89004-327-2). Raven.

Bradshaw, Ralph A., et al, eds. Proteins in Biology & Medicine. 1983. 31.50 (ISBN 0-12-124580-2). Acad Pr.

Bradshaw, Thorton & Vogel, David. Corporations & Their Critics: Issues & Answers to the Problems of Corporate Social Responsibility. LC 80-11393. (Illus.). 288p. 1980. 19.95 (ISBN 0-07-007075-X, P&RB). McGraw.

Bradsher, Frances, jt. auth. see Parker, Cherry.

Bradsher, Henry S. Afghanistan & the Soviet Union. (Duke Press Policy Studies). (Illus.). 350p. 1983. 35.00 (ISBN 0-8223-0496-1); pap. 12.75 (ISBN 0-8223-0563-1). Duke.

Bradsma, L. & Verkruijsse, H. D. Synthesis of Acetylenes, Allenes & Cumulenes: A Laboratory Manual. (Studies in Organic Chemistry: No. 8). 1981. 70.25 (ISBN 0-444-42009-6). Elsevier.

Bradt, George. South America River Trips, Vol. I. LC 80-69523. (Illus.). 108p. (Orig.). 1981. pap. 8.95 (ISBN 0-933982-13-5). Bradt Ent.

Bradt, George, jt. auth. see Bradt, Hilary.

Bradt, Hilary. Backpacker's Africa. 2nd ed. (Backpacker's Guide Ser.). (Illus.). 150p. 1983. pap. 11.95 (ISBN 0-9505797-9-3). Bradt Ent.

Bradt, Hilary & Bradt, George. Backpacking in Mexico & Central America: Nicaragua, Colombia, Costa Rica, Panama, Mexico, Guatemala, El Salvador, Honduras. new ed. (Backpacker Guide Ser.). (Illus.). 247p. 1982. pap. 9.95 (ISBN 0-9505797-8-5). Bradt Ent.

Bradt, Hilary & Pilkington, John. Backpacking & Trekking in Chile & Argentina. LC 80-68116. (Backpacker Guide Ser.). (Illus.). 144p. 1980. pap. 7.95 (ISBN 0-9505797-7-7). Bradt Ent.

Bradway, John S. Progress in Family Law. Lambert, Richard D., ed. LC 71-81088. (Annals Ser.: No. 383). 1969. 15.00 (ISBN 0-87761-116-5); pap. 7.95 (ISBN 0-87761-115-7). Am Acad Pol Soc Sci.

Brady. Biological Clocks. (Studies in Biology: No. 104). 1979. 5.95 o.p. (ISBN 0-8391-0254-2). Univ Park.

Brady, Charles. Paints & Materials. LC 77-82985. (Teaching Primary Science Ser.). (Illus.). 1977. pap. text ed. 9.85 (ISBN 0-356-05075-0). Raintree Pubs.

--A Spark of Godness. LC 82-11949. 372p. 1983. 14.95 (ISBN 0-395-31257-4). HM.

Brady, Christine. Home Entertaining. 5.50x o.p. (ISBN 0-392-06160-0, LTB). Sportshelf.

Brady, Constance. Right Where You Live. LC 78-73550. (Illus.). 1979. pap. 9.95 o.p. (ISBN 0-89087-242-2). Celestial Arts.

--Right Where You Live. (Illus.). 188p. (Orig.). 1982. pap. 9.95 (ISBN 0-686-35975-5). Conarc.

Brady, Darlene & Serban, William, eds. Stained Glass: A Guide to Information Sources. LC 79-23712. (Art & Architecture Information Guide Ser.: Vol. 10). 1980. 42.00x (ISBN 0-8103-1445-2). Gale.

Brady, Donald, ed. Green Words: A Handbook. LC 79-92506. 91p. 1980. pap. text ed. 2.75 o.p. (ISBN 0-8191-0965-7). U Pr of Amer.

Brady, Frank. Barbra: An Illustrated Biography. LC 78-73322. (Illus.). 1979. pap. 8.95 (ISBN 0-448-16534-1, G&D). Putnam Pub Group.

Brady, Frank & Wimsatt, W. K., eds. Samuel Johnson: Selected Poetry & Prose. 1978. 38.50x (ISBN 0-520-02929-1); pap. 6.95 (ISBN 0-520-03552-6). U of Cal Pr.

Brady, Frank, ed. see Boswell, James.

Brady, Frank, ed. see Kupferberg, Tuli & Topp, Sylvia.

Brady, G. S. & Clauser, H. Materials Handbook. 11th ed. 1977. 46.75 (ISBN 0-07-007069-5). McGraw.

Brady, Gerald P., jt. auth. see Thompson, George C.

Brady, Ignatius C., jt. ed. see Armstrong, Regis J.

Brady, Ivan A., ed. Transactions in Kinship: Adoption & Fosterage in Oceania. LC 76-10342. (Association for Social Anthropology in Oceania Monograph: No.4). 320p. 1976. text ed. 20.00x (ISBN 0-8248-0478-3). UH Pr.

Brady, J. & Nauta, W. J. Principles, Practices & Positions in Neuropsychiatric Research. 320p. 1972. text ed. 72.00 (ISBN 0-08-017007-2). Pergamon.

Brady, J. E. & Humiston, G. E. General Chemistry: Principles & Structure. 2nd ed. LC 80-14887. 779p. 1980. 27.95 (ISBN 0-471-06315-0). Wiley.

Brady, J. E., jt. auth. see Beran, J. A.

Brady, J. M. The Theory of Computer Science: A Programming Approach. 1977. pap. 17.50x (ISBN 0-412-15040-9, Pub. by Chapman & Hall). Methuen Inc.

Brady, J. P., ed. Justice & Politics in People's China: Legal Order of Continuing Revolution. Date not set. 33.00 (ISBN 0-12-124750-3). Acad Pr.

Brady, James. Holy Wars. 1983. price not set (ISBN 0-671-42589-7). S&S.

--Nielsen's Children. LC 78-7058. 1978. 10.95 o.p. (ISBN 0-399-12165-X). Putnam Pub Group.

--The Press Lord. 1983. pap. 3.95 (ISBN 0-440-17080-X). Dell.

Brady, James E. & Holum, John R. Fundamentals of Chemistry. 797p. 1981. text ed. 27.95 (ISBN 0-471-05816-5); study guide avail. Wiley.

Brady, James E. & Humiston, Gerard E. General Chemistry: Principles & Structure. 3rd ed. 831p. 1982. 29.95x (ISBN 0-471-07806-9); study guide avail. Wiley.

--General Chemistry: Principles & Structure. 2nd ed. LC 77-11045. 800p. 1978. text ed. 25.95 (ISBN 0-471-01910-0). wkbk. 8.25x (ISBN 0-471-03498-3). Wiley.

Brady, Jayne, et al. The Literature of Aging: A Decade Review (1969-1979) 127p. 1980. softcover 7.95 (ISBN 0-932930-22-0). Pilgrimage Inc.

Brady, John. The Unmaking of a Dancer: An Unconventional Life. 1983. pap. 3.95 (ISBN 0-686-37706-0). WSP.

Brady, John & White, Brian. Fifty Hikes in Massachusetts: Hikes & Walks from the Top of the Berkshires to the Tip of Cape Cod. LC 74-33817. (Fifty Hikes Ser.). (Illus.). 224p. 1983. pap. 8.95 (ISBN 0-942440-11-0). Backcountry Pubns.

Brady, John & Hall, James, eds. Sports Literature. (Patterns in Literary Art Ser). 276p. (gr. 9-12). 1974. pap. text ed. 9.16 (ISBN 0-07-007085-7, W). McGraw.

Brady, John P., jt. auth. see Pomerleau, Ovide F.

Brady, Jules M. A Philosopher's Search for the Infinite. 96p. 1983. 10.00 (ISBN 0-8022-2410-5). Philos Lib.

Brady, Katherine. Father's Days. 1981. pap. 3.25 (ISBN 0-440-12475-1). Dell.

Brady, Kathleen. Inside Out. 1979. 8.95 o.p. (ISBN 0-393-08843-X). Norton.

Brady, Luther W., ed. Radiation Sensitizers: Their Use in the Clinical Management of Cancer. LC 80-81987. (Masson Cancer Management Ser.: Vol. 5). (Illus.). 544p. 1980. 67.25x (ISBN 0-89352-112-4). Masson Pub.

Brady, M., ed. Computer Vision. 508p. 1982. Repr. 64.00 (ISBN 0-444-86343-5). Elsevier.

Brady, Margaret. Having a Baby Easily. (Illus.). 144p. (Orig.). 1983. pap. 6.95 (ISBN 0-7225-0668-6, Pub. by Thorsons Pubs England). Sterling.

Brady, Maureen. Folly. LC 82-17235. 250p. 1982. 15.95 (ISBN 0-89594-091-4); pap. 7.95 (ISBN 0-89594-090-6). Crossing Pr.

Brady, Michael & Hollerbach, John. Robot Motion: Planning & Control. 1982. 37.50 (ISBN 0-262-02182-X). MIT Pr.

Brady, Michael, ed. Computation Aspects of Discourse. 1982. 25.00 (ISBN 0-262-02183-8). MIT Pr.

Brady, N. C., ed. Advances in Agronomy, Vol. 35. (Serial Publication). 1982. 35.00 (ISBN 0-12-000735-5); 45.50 (ISBN 0-12-000790-8); 24.50 (ISBN 0-12-000791-6). Acad Pr.

Brady, N. C. see Norman, A. G.

Brady, Nyle C. The Nature & Properties of Soils. 8th ed. (Illus.). 672p. 1974. text ed. 29.95 (ISBN 0-02-313350-3, 31335). Macmillan.

Brady, Patrick. Marcel Proust. (World Authors Ser.). 1977. lib. bdg. 12.95 (ISBN 0-8057-6307-4, Twayne). G K Hall.

Brady, Peggy, jt. auth. see Martin, Paul.

Brady, R. J. Microbiology: A Programmed Introduction to. (Illus.). 1969. pap. 10.95 o.p. (ISBN 0-87618-075-6). R J Brady.

--On the Job Training: A Practical Guide for Food Service Supervisors. (Illus.). 1975. pap. 8.95 o.p. (ISBN 0-87618-655-X). R J Brady.

Brady, Terence & Jones, Evan. The Fight Against Slavery. (Illus.). 1977. 7.95 o.p. (ISBN 0-393-05659-7). Norton.

Braeman, Shirley. Fold, Tie, Dip & Dye. LC 76-12062. (Early Craft Books). (Illus.). (gr. k-3). 1976. PLB 3.95g (ISBN 0-8225-0877-X). Lerner Pubns.

Braestrup, Peter. How the American Press & Television Reported & Interpreted the Crisis of Tet 1968 in Vietnam & Washington. LC 82-11041. 632p. 1983. text ed. 25.00x (ISBN 0-300-02953-5); pap. 9.95 (ISBN 0-300-02807-5, Y-446). Yale U Pr.

Braet Von Uberfeldt, Jan, jt. auth. see Bing, Valetyn.

Braeutigam, Ronald, jt. auth. see Owen, Bruce M.

Braeutigam, Ronald R. & Baesemann, Robert. On the Economics of Motor Carrier Regulation: Proceedings. 42p. 1977. pap. 2.50 (ISBN 0-686-94045-8, Trans). Northwestern U Pr.

Brafield. Life in Sandy Shores. (Studies in Biology: No. 89). 1978. 5.95 o.p. (ISBN 0-7131-2682-5). Univ Park.

Brafield, Alan E. Life in Sandy Shores. (Studies in Biology: No. 89). 64p. 1978. pap. text ed. 8.95 (ISBN 0-686-43115-4). E Arnold.

Brafield, Alan E. & Llewellyn, Michael J. Animal Energetics. (Tertiary Level Biology Ser.). 1982. 38.00x (ISBN 0-412-00021-0, Pub. by Chapman & Hall); pap. 18.95x (ISBN 0-412-00031-8). Methuen Inc.

Braford, Leroy. Staying Awake: More Fun Than Sleeping. LC 81-90342. 54p. (Orig.). 1981. 12.50 (ISBN 0-686-32459-5); pap. 9.00x (ISBN 0-686-36897-5). L Bradford.

Braga, Joseph & Braga, Laurie. Children & Adults: Activities for Growing Together. (Human Development Bks.). (Illus.). 1976. 12.95 (ISBN 0-13-130351-1, Spec); pap. 10.95 (ISBN 0-13-130344-9). P-H.

Braga, Joseph, jt. auth. see Braga, Laurie.

Braga, Laurie & Braga, Joseph. Learning & Growing: A Guide to Child Development. 192p. 1975. 8.95 o.p. (ISBN 0-13-527614-4, Spec); pap. 3.95 o.p. (ISBN 0-13-527606-3, Spec). P-H.

Braga, Laurie, jt. auth. see Braga, Joseph.

Braga, Meg. Make & Tell: A Christmas Holiday Book of Family Fun & Crafts, Bk. 2. (Illus.). 1978. Repr. of 1974 ed. saddlestitched 1.95 (ISBN 0-87788-535-4). Shaw Pubs.

Braga de Macedo, Jorge. Portugal Since the Revolution: Economic & Political Perspectives. Serfaty, Simon, ed. (Westview Special Studies in West European Politics & Society). 128p. 1981. lib. bdg. 18.50 (ISBN 0-89158-972-4). Westview.

Braganca, Aquino de see De Braganca, Aquino.

Bragantini, Irene, jt. ed. see Einaudi, Karen.

Bragaw, Louis K., jt. auth. see Allen, William R.

Bragdon, Allen & Fellows, Len. Diabolical Diversions. LC 79-7487. (Illus.). 1980. 9.95 (ISBN 0-385-15152-7). Doubleday.

Bragdon, Allen D., ed. The Homeowner's Complete Manual of Repair & Improvement. LC 82-18184. (Illus.). 576p. 1983. 19.95 (ISBN 0-668-05737-8, 5737). Arco.

Bragdon, Charles R. Metal Decorating from Start to Finishes. LC 61-17350. (Illus.). 1969. 5.95 (ISBN 0-87027-065-6). Cumberland Pr.

Bragdon, Clifford R. Municipal Noise Legislation. text ed. 45.00 (ISBN 0-89671-018-1). Southeast Acoustics.

Bragdon, Clifford R., ed. Noise Pollution: A Guide to Information Sources. LC 73-17535. (Man & the Environment Information Guide Ser.: Vol. 5). 600p. 1979. 42.00x (ISBN 0-8103-1345-6). Gale.

Bragg, Gordon M. Principles of Experimentation & Measurement. (Illus.). 192p. 1974. 23.95 (ISBN 0-13-701169-5). P-H.

Bragg, Gordon M. & Strauss, Jennifer. Air Pollution Control, Pt. 4. LC 79-28773. (Environmental Science & Technology Ser.). 356p. 1981. 43.95x (ISBN 0-471-07957-X, Pub. by Wiley-Interscience). Wiley.

Bragg, Gordon M., jt. auth. see Rajhans, Gyan S.

Bragg, Melvyn. Hired Man. 1969. 14.95 (ISBN 0-436-06705-6, Pub. by Secker & Warburg). David & Charles.

--Kingdom Come. 1980. 16.50 (ISBN 0-436-06714-5, Pub. by Secker & Warburg). David & Charles.

--Second Inheritance. 1966. 13.95 (ISBN 0-436-06701-3, Pub. by Secker & Warburg). David & Charles.

--Without a City Wall. 1973. 9.95 (ISBN 0-436-06702-1, Pub. by Secker & Warburg). David & Charles.

Bragg, Patricia, jt. auth. see Bragg, Paul C.

Bragg, Patricia, jt. auth. see Johnson, Bob.

Bragg, Paul. Health Food Cookbook. 6.95x (ISBN 0-87790-001-9). Cancer Control Soc.

Bragg, Paul C. & Bragg, Patricia. How to Keep the Heart Healthy Fit. 10th ed. LC 68-24215. pap. 4.95 (ISBN 0-87790-004-3). Health Sci.

--Shocking Truth About Water. 23rd ed. LC 77-101348. pap. 4.95 (ISBN 0-87790-000-0). Health Sci.

Bragg, S. L., frwd. by. Engineering Challenges in the 1980's, Vol. 2. (Proceedings of the Engineering Section of the British Association for the Advancement of Science Ser.). 103p. 1982. text ed. 60.00 (ISBN 0-89116-349-2, Pub. by Cambridge Info & Res Serv England). Hemisphere Pub.

Bragg, W. L., ed. see Royal Institution Library of Science.

Bragg, Wayne G., jt. ed. see Ingerson, Earl.

Bragg, William L., ed. The Royal Institution Library of Science: Physical Sciences, 11 vols. (Illus.). 5300p. 1974. Set. 295.00x o.p. (ISBN 0-444-20048-7). Intl Pubns Serv.

Bragg, William L. & Porter, George, eds. Physical Sciences: The Royal Institution Library of Science, 10 vols. plus index. (Illus.). 1969. Set. 205.00 (ISBN 0-444-20048-7, Pub. by Applied Sci England); Set. pap. 82.00 (ISBN 0-85334-615-1). Elsevier.

Bragg, Yana, ed. see Harvey, Bill.

Bragger, Jeanette D. & Shupp, Robert P. Chere Francoise: Revision de la Grammaire Francaise. 477p. 1978. 19.95 (ISBN 0-395-30960-3); Le Monde Francais (Reader) 10.50 (ISBN 0-395-30962-X); Instr's. manual 2.00 (ISBN 0-395-30963-8); wkbk. 8.50 (ISBN 0-395-30961-1); recordings 200.00 (ISBN 0-395-30964-6). HM.

Bragin, Joan. The Weekend Connoisseur: The Antique Collector's Guide to the Best in Antiquing, Dining, Regional Museums & Just Plain Lovely Things to Do When Touring. LC 78-1187. 1979. 5.95 o.p. (ISBN 0-385-13465-7, Dolp). Doubleday.

Braginsky, Benjamin M., et al. Methods of Madness: The Mental Hospital as a Last Resort. LC 81-40099. (Illus.). 238p. 1982. pap. text ed. 10.75 (ISBN 0-8191-2400-1). U Pr of Amer.

Bragonier, Reg, jt. auth. see Fisher, David.

Bragt, Jan Van, tr. see Nishitani, Keiji.

Braham, Mark. Aspects of Education. LC 80-42315. 215p. 1982. 59.95x (ISBN 0-471-28019-4, Pub. by Wiley Interscience); pap. 19.95x (ISBN 0-471-28022-4). Wiley.

Braham, Randolph L. Perspectives on the Holocaust. (Holocaust Studies). 1983. lib. bdg. 20.00 (ISBN 0-89838-124-X). Kluwer Nijhoff.

Brahmachari, Dhirendra. Yogasana Vijnana: The Science of Yoga. (Illus.). 1970. 18.75x o.p. (ISBN 0-210-98161-X). Asia.

Brahms, Johannes. Complete Chamber Music for Strings & Clarinet Quintet. Gal, Hans, ed. (Vienna Gesellscaft der Musikfreunde Ed.). 6.00 (ISBN 0-8446-1724-5). Peter Smith.

--Complete Shorter Works for Piano. Mandyczewski, Eusebius, ed. LC 70-116828. 1970. pap. 6.00 (ISBN 0-486-22651-4). Dover.

--Complete Symphonies; in Full Orchestral Score. Gal, Hans, ed. LC 73-92635. 352p. 1974. pap. 9.95 (ISBN 0-486-23053-8). Dover.

Braider, Donald. The Life, History & Magic of the Horse. LC 72-77107. 256p. 1973. Repr. 8.95 o.p. (ISBN 0-448-02169-2, G&D). Putnam Pub Group.

Braidfoot, Larry. The Bible & America. LC 82-73371. 1983. 3.25 (ISBN 0-8054-5519-1). Broadman.

Braidwood, Robert J. Prehistoric Men. 8th ed. 213p. 1975. pap. 10.95x o.p. (ISBN 0-673-07851-5). Scott F.

Braiker, Harriet B., ed. see Polich, J. Michael & Armor, David J.

Brailsford, D. F. & Walker, A. N. Introductory ALGOL Sixty-Eight Programming. LC 79-40241. (Computers & Their Applications Ser.). 1979. 54.95x (ISBN 0-470-26746-1); pap. text ed. 24.95x (ISBN 0-470-26799-2). Halsted Pr.

Braimbridge, M. V. Postoperative Cardiac Intensive Care. 3rd. ed. (Illus.). 240p. 1981. pap. text ed. 24.95 (ISBN 0-632-00233-6, B 0781-7). Mosby.

Brain, Jeffrey P., jt. auth. see Williams, Stephen.

Brain, Joseph L. Poetry & Prose. (Blue Book Ser). pap. text ed. 1.00 o.p. (ISBN 0-671-17504-1). Monarch Pr.

Brain, Joy. Christian Indians in Natal, 1860-1911. (Illus.). 272p. 1982. 18.95x (ISBN 0-19-570297-2). Oxford U Pr.

Brain, Michael C. & McCulloch, Peter B. Current Therapy in Hematology-Oncology. 400p. 1983. text ed. 44.00 (ISBN 0-941158-05-5, D07809). Mosby.

Brain, P. F. & Denton, D., eds. Multidisciplinary Approaches to Aggression Research. 1981. 135.75 (ISBN 0-444-80317-3). Elsevier.

Brain, R., tr. see Godelier, M.

Brain, R. L. & Norris, F. H., Jr., eds. Remote Effects of Cancer on the Nervous System. LC 65-21048. (Contemporary Neurology Symposia: Vol. 1). 240p. 1965. 64.50 o.s.i. (ISBN 0-8089-0070-6). Grune.

Brain, Robert. Bangwa Kinship & Marriage. LC 70-166945. (Illus.). 1972. 29.95 (ISBN 0-521-08311-7). Cambridge U Pr.

Brainard, Joe. I Remember. LC 75-23153. 1975. 17.95 (ISBN 0-916190-02-1); pap. 6.95 (ISBN 0-916190-03-X). Full Court NY.

Brainard, Kathy, jt. auth. see Lott, Johnny.

Brainbridge, Beryl. Sweet William. 1977. pap. 1.50 o.p. (ISBN 0-451-07525-0, W7525, Sig). NAL.

Braine, John. Writing a Novel. 224p. 1975. pap. 5.95 (ISBN 0-07-007112-8, SP). McGraw.

Brainerd Art Gallery. V. I. P. (Vogels in Potsdam) Selections from the Collection of Dorothy & Herbert Vogel. (Illus.). 60p. (Orig.). 1982. pap. 12.50 (ISBN 0-942746-03-1). Brainerd.

Brainerd, Charles J. Piaget's Theory of Intelligence. (Illus.). 1978. 23.95 (ISBN 0-13-675108-3). P-H.

Brainerd, Charles J., ed. Recent Advances in Cognitive-Developmental Theory. Progress in Cognitive Developmental Research. (Springer Series in Cognitive Development). (Illus.). 288p. 1983. 29.95 (ISBN 0-387-90767-X). Springer-Verlag.

Brainerd, John W. Working with Nature: A Practical Guide. (Illus.). 550p. 1973. 29.50x (ISBN 0-19-501667-X). Oxford U Pr.

Brainerd, Walter S., jt. auth. see Gross, Jonathan L.

Brainina, K. Z. Stripping Voltammetry in Chemical Analysis. Shelnitz, P., tr. from Rus. LC 74-13974. 222p. 1974. 39.95 o.p. (ISBN 0-470-09590-3). Halsted Pr.

Braisted, William R. Meiroku: Journal of the Japanese Enlightenment. 1976. 27.50x (ISBN 0-674-54670-9). Harvard U Pr.

Braithewaite, Walter. A Book of Songs. Vaughan, Michael, ed. 29p. (gr. 5-7). 1978. pap. 4.00 (ISBN 0-88010-036-2, Pub. by Steinerbooks). Anthroposophic.

Braithwaite, David. Savage of King's Lynn: Inventor of Machines & Merry-Go-Rounds. (Illus.). 1978. pap. 11.95 (ISBN 0-85059-333-6). Aztex.

Braithwaite, E. R. To Sir, with Love. (gr. 9-12). 1973. pap. 2.25 (ISBN 0-515-06968-X). Jove Pubns.

--To Sir With Love. 1982. pap. 1.75 (ISBN 0-451-11533-3, AE1533, Sig). NAL.

Braithwaite, Errol. Companion Guide to Westland. (Illus.). 1982. pap. 12.95 (ISBN 0-00-216967-3, Pub. by W Collins Australia). Intl Schol Bk Serv.

Braithwaite, Henry W. The Conductor's Art. (Illus.). 1978. Repr. of 1952 ed. lib. bdg. 19.75x (ISBN 0-313-20058-0, BRCAR). Greenwood.

Braitta, Louis, Jr. The Audit Director's Guide: How to Serve Effectively on the Corporate Audit Committee. LC 80-23989. 303p. 1981. 39.50x (ISBN 0-471-05866-1). Ronald Pr.

Brake, B. J., jt. auth. see Mallinson, G.

Brake, Brian & Shadbolt, Maurice. New Zealand, Gift of the Sea. (Illus.). 1964. 12.00 o.p. (ISBN 0-8248-0009-5, Eastwest Ctr). UH Pr.

Brakefield, Tom. Big Game Hunter's Digest. (DBI Bks). (Illus.). 288p. (Orig.). 1977. pap. 7.95 o.s.i. (ISBN 0-695-80685-8). Follett.

Brakeley, George A., Jr. Tested Ways to Successful Fund Raising. 19.95 (ISBN 0-686-38896-8). Public Serv Materials.

Brakeman, Louis, jt. auth. see Baldwin, Roger.

Braley, Russell. Bad News. 1983. 14.95 (ISBN 0-89526-627-X). Regnery-Gateway.

Braly, Malcolm. On the Yard. 1977. pap. 3.95 (ISBN 0-14-004455-8). Penguin.

--The Protector. (Orig.). 1979. pap. 2.25 o.s.i. (ISBN 0-515-05178-0). Jove Pubns.

Bram, Elizabeth. The Man on the Unicycle & Other Stories. LC 76-22666. (Greenwillow Read-Alone Bks.). (Illus.). (gr. 1-4). 1977. 5.95 o.p. (ISBN 0-688-80059-9); PLB 7.44 (ISBN 0-688-84059-0). Greenwillow.

Bramall, Norman, jt. auth. see Bloss, Margaret V.

Braman, O. Randall. The Oppositional Child. LC 82-80895. (Illus.). 121p. (Orig.). 1982. text ed. 12.95 (ISBN 0-942780-01-9); pap. 7.95 (ISBN 0-942780-00-0). Isle of Guam.

Braman, Sandra & Woolf, Douglas, eds. Vital Statistics, Vol. 1. 1978. pap. 3.00 (ISBN 0-942296-04-4). Wolf Run Bks.

--Vital Statistics, Vol. 2. 1978. pap. 3.00 (ISBN 0-942296-05-2). Wolf Run Bks.

--Vital Statistics, Vol. 3. 1980. pap. 3.00 (ISBN 0-942296-06-0). Wolf Run Bks.

Brambilla & Racagni. Progress in Psychoneuroendocrinology. (Grovanni Lorrenzini Foundation Symposia Ser.: Vol. 8). 1980. 105.75 (ISBN 0-444-80294-0). Elsevier.

Brambilla, Robert & Longo, Gianni. For Pedestrians Only: Planning, Design & Management of Traffic-Free Zones. (Illus.). 1977. 24.95 (ISBN 0-8230-7174-X, Whitney Lib). Watson-Guptill.

Brambilla, Roberto & Longo, Gianni. Learning from Atlanta. (Learning from the USA Ser.). (Illus.). 150p. Date not set. pap. price not set (ISBN 0-936020-04-0). Inst for Environ Action. Postponed.

--Learning from Minneapolis, St. Paul. (Learning from the USA Ser.). (Illus.). 150p. (Orig.). Date not set. pap. price not set (ISBN 0-936020-03-2). Inst for Environ Action. Postponed.

Bramble, Forbes. Fools. 192p. 1983. 16.95 (ISBN 0-241-10895-0, Pub. by Hamish Hamilton England). David & Charles.

--Regent Square. 1977. 9.95 o.p. (ISBN 0-698-10836-1, Coward). Putnam Pub Group.

Bramble, William J., jt. auth. see Mason, Emanuel J.

Bramblett, Claud A. Patterns of Primate Behavior. LC 75-44695. (Illus.). 320p. 1976. text ed. 15.95 o.p. (ISBN 0-87484-327-8); pap. text ed. 9.95 (ISBN 0-87484-326-X). Mayfield Pub.

Brame, Michael K. Base Generated Syntax. LC 78-70404. (Linguistics Research Monograph Ser.). 1978. text ed. 28.00x (ISBN 0-932998-00-3). Noit Amrofer.

--Essays Toward Realistic Syntax. new ed. LC 79-67347. (Linguistics Research Monograph: Vol. 2). 1979. text ed. 38.00x (ISBN 0-932998-01-1). Noit Amrofer.

Brameld, Theodore. Tourism As Cultural Learning: Two Controversial Case Studies in Educational Anthropology. 1977. pap. text ed. 10.50 (ISBN 0-8191-0293-8). U Pr of Amer.

Bramer, George R. Process One: A Multi-Media College Writing Program. 1976. pap. text ed. 12.95 (ISBN 0-675-08682-5); cassettes & filmstrips o.s.i. 495.00 (ISBN 0-686-86340-2). Additional supplements may be obtained from publisher. Merrill.

Bramer, George R. & Sedley, Dorothy. Writing for Readers. (Illus.). 500p. 1981. text ed. 13.95 (ISBN 0-675-08045-2); tchr's ed. 13.95 (ISBN 0-675-08038-X). Additional supplements may be obtained from publisher. Merrill.

Bramer, T. C., et al. Basic Vibration Control. 1978. pap. 19.95x (ISBN 0-419-11440-8, Pub. by E & FN Spon England). Methuen Inc.

Bramesco, Norton, jt. auth. see Donner, Michael.

Bramhall, David F., jt. ed. see Karaska, Gerald J.

Bramham, Peter. How Staff Rule: Structures of Authority in Two Community Schools. 213p. 1980. text ed. 29.50x (ISBN 0-566-00321-X). Gower Pub Ltd.

Bramly, Serge. Macumba: The Teachings of Maria Jose, Mother of the Gods. LC 77-76628. 1977. 10.95 o.p. (ISBN 0-312-50338-5). St Martin.

Brammer, Lawrence M. & Shostrum, Everett L. Therapeutic Psychology: Fundamentals of Counseling & Psychotherapy. 4th ed. (Illus.). 480p. 1982. 23.95 (ISBN 0-13-914614-8). P-H.

Bramnick, Lea & Simon, Anita. The Parents' Solution Book. 320p. 1983. 14.95 (ISBN 0-531-09881-8). Watts.

Brams, Steven J. Biblical Games: A Strategic Analysis of Stories in the Old Testament. 1980. text ed. 16.50x (ISBN 0-262-02144-7); pap. 5.95 (ISBN 0-262-52074-5). MIT Pr.

Brams, Steven J., et al, eds. Applied Game Theory. 447p. 1979. text ed. 80.00x (ISBN 3-7908-0208-5). Birkhauser.

Bramscher, Cynthia S. Holiday Music Activities for the Entire School Year. LC 82-6414. 224p. 1982. 13.50 (ISBN 0-13-392613-3). P-H.

--Treasury of Musical Motivators for the Elementary Classroom. (Illus.). 1979. 13.95 o.p. (ISBN 0-13-930610-2, Parker). P-H.

Bramson, Ann. Soap. 2nd ed. LC 75-7286. 1975. pap. 4.95 (ISBN 0-911104-57-7). Workman Pub.

Bramson, Leon & Goethals, George W., eds. War. rev ed. LC 68-24485. 1968. pap. text ed. 8.95x o.s.i. (ISBN 0-465-09071-0). Basic.

Bramson, Morris. Math Review for All State High School Competency & Proficiency Tests. 256p. Date not set. 5.95 o.p. (ISBN 0-15-600041-5). HarBraceJ. Postponed.

Bramwell, David & Bramwell, Zoe. Flores Silvestres de las Islas Canarias. 364p. 1977. 50.00x (ISBN 0-686-99797-2, Pub. by Thornes England). State Mutual Bk.

Bramwell, Fitzgerald B., et al. Investigations in General Chemistry: Quantitative Techniques and Basic Principles. 1977. spiral bdg. 12.95x (ISBN 0-8087-2803-2). Burgess.

Bramwell, Zoe, jt. auth. see Bramwell, David.

Branann, J., et al, eds. see Brown, Oskar.

Brana-Shute, G. On the Corner: Male Social Life in a Paramaribo Creole Neighborhood. (Studies of Developing Countries: No. 21). 1979. pap. text ed. 13.50x (ISBN 90-232-1605-9). Humanities.

Branca, Patricia. Women in Modern Europe Since Seventeen Fifty. LC 77-20202. 1978. 22.50x (ISBN 0-312-88739-6). St Martin.

Brancaforte, Benito. Guzman de Alfarache: conversion o proceso de degradacion? vi, 230p. 1980. 11.00 (ISBN 0-942260-14-7). Hispanic Seminary.

Brancas-Villeneuve, Andre F. Histoire Ou Police du Royaume de Gala. (Utopias in the Enlightenment Ser.). 187p. (Fr.). 1974. Repr. of 1754 ed. lib. bdg. 54.50x o.p. (ISBN 0-8287-0135-0, 014). Clearwater Pub.

Branch & Swann. The Wage & Hour Law Handbook for the Lodging & Food Service Industry. LC 80-65115. 1980. 34.95 (ISBN 0-86730-236-4). Lebhar Friedman.

Branch, Alan E. Economics of Shipping Practice & Management. 1982. 27.00x (ISBN 0-412-23580-3, Pub. By Chapman & Hall England); pap. 12.95x (ISBN 0-412-16350-0). Methuen Inc.

--Elements of Export Practice. 400p. 1977. pap. 14.95x (ISBN 0-412-15610-5, Pub. by Chapman & Hall England). Methuen Inc.

--Elements of Shipping. 5th ed. 238p. 1982. 28.00x (ISBN 0-412-23700-8, Pub. by Chapman & Hall England); pap. 14.95x (ISBN 0-412-23710-5). Methuen Inc.

Branch, Ben. Fundamentals of Investing. LC 75-26703. 301p. 1976. 29.95x (ISBN 0-471-09650-4). Wiley.

Branch, Edgar M., ed. Clemens of the Call: Mark Twain in San Francisco. 1969. 29.95x (ISBN 0-520-01385-9). U of Cal Pr.

Branch, Kip. Gnawing at My Soul. 320p. 1981. 11.95 (ISBN 0-399-90123-X, Marek). Putnam Pub Group.

Branch, Mary. Tell Me a Story 2. (Outreach Ser.). 31p. (ps-4). 1982. pap. 0.95 (ISBN 0-8163-0477-7). Pacific Pr Pub Assn.

Branch, Melville C. Comprehensive Planning: General Theory & Principles. LC 83-61680. (Illus.). 1983. text ed. 12.95x (ISBN 0-913530-32-8). Palisades Pub.

--Continuous City Planning: Integrating Municipal & City Planning. 181p. 1980. 24.95x (ISBN 0-471-08943-5, Pub. by Wiley-Interscience). Wiley.

Branch, Rene O., Jr., jt. auth. see Stigum, Marcia.

Branch, Taylor, jt. auth. see Propper, Eugene M.

Branch, Tom. The Photographer's Build-It-Yourself Book. (Illus.). 160p. (Orig.). 1982. 16.95 (ISBN 0-8174-5406-3, Amphoto); pap. text ed. 9.95 (ISBN 0-8174-5407-1). Watson-Guptill.

Branch, William T. Office Practice of Medicine. (Illus.). 1318p. 1982. 69.00 (ISBN 0-7216-1914-2). Saunders.

Branchaw, Bernadine B., jt. auth. see Bowman, Joel P.

Branchaw, Bernadine P. English Made Easy. (gr. 9-12). 1979. pap. 6.96 (ISBN 0-07-007171-3, G); teacher's manual & key 6.40 (ISBN 0-07-007173-X). McGraw.

Brand, Alice G. Therapy in Writing: A Psycho-Educational Enterprise. LC 79-2790. (Illus.). 240p. 1980. 24.95x (ISBN 0-669-03232-8). Lexington Bks.

Brand, C. Starrbelow. 1977. 15.00 (ISBN 0-86025-065-2). State Mutual Bk.

Brand, Christianna. Fog of Doubt. 1979. lib. bdg. 9.95 (ISBN 0-8398-2535-8, Gregg). G K Hall.

--Nurse Matilda. 1980. lib. bdg. 7.95 (ISBN 0-8398-2604-4, Gregg). G K Hall.

Brand, Dennis J., Jr., tr. from Span. The Book of Causes. 56p. Date not set. pap. 7.95 (ISBN 0-87462-225-5). Marquette.

Brand, E. W. & Brenner, R. P., eds. Soft Clay Engineering. (Developments in Geotechnical Engineering: Vol. 20). 1982. 134.00 (ISBN 0-444-41784-2). Elsevier.

Brand, Edward A. Modern Supermarket Operation. 2nd ed. LC 62-19750. (Illus.). 1965. 15.00 o.p. (ISBN 0-87005-047-8). Fairchild.

Brand, Geoffrey, jt. auth. see Brand, Violet.

Brand, Gordon. Industrial Buying Decision: Implications for the Sales Approach in Industrial Marketing. 134p. 1965. 15.00x o.p. (ISBN 0-304-29078-5). Intl Pubns Serv.

Brand, Jeanne L., jt. auth. see Mora, George.

Brand, John. Observations on the Popular Antiquities of Great Britain: Chiefly Illustrating the Origin of Our Vulgar & Provincial Customs, Ceremonies & Superstitions, 3 vols. LC 67-23896. 1969. Repr. of 1849 ed. Set. 68.00x (ISBN 0-8103-3256-6). Gale.

Brand, Katarzyna Mroczkowska see Kapuscinski, Ryszard.

Brand, L., jt. auth. see Morse, P.

Brand, Max. Bull Hunter. 192p. 1982. pap. 1.95 (ISBN 0-446-30231-7). Warner Bks.

--Destry Rides Again. 1979. lib. bdg. 9.95 (ISBN 0-8398-2583-8, Gregg). G K Hall.

--The Dude. 208p. 1971. pap. 1.95 (ISBN 0-446-90313-2). Warner Bks.

--Frontier Feud. 192p. 1976. pap. 1.95 o.s.i. (ISBN 0-446-30168-X). Warner Bks.

--The Gentle Desperado. (Max Brand Popular Classics Ser.). 160p. (Orig.). Date not set. cancelled o.p. (ISBN 0-88496-180-X). Capra Pr.

--Gunfighter's Return. 192p. 1982. pap. 2.25 o.s.i. (ISBN 0-446-30362-3). Warner Bks.

--Happy Jack. large print ed. 1981. cancelled 18.00x o.p. (ISBN 0-89340-277-X, Pub. by Curley Assoc England). State Mutual Bk.

--The Making of a Gunman. LC 82-19940. 1983. 10.95 (ISBN 0-396-08128-2). Dodd.

--Max Brand's Best Western Stories. 240p. 1983. pap. 2.25 (ISBN 0-446-30232-5). Warner Bks.

--Ride the Wild Trail. (General Ser.). 1983. lib. bdg. 13.95 (ISBN 0-8161-3435-9, Large Print Bks). G K Hall.

--Rider of the High Hill. 240p. 1983. pap. 1.95 (ISBN 0-446-30607-X). Warner Bks.

--Rider of the High Hills. 1978. lib. bdg. 11.95 o.p. (ISBN 0-8161-6545-9, Large Print Bks). G K Hall.

--Steve Train's Ordeal. large print ed. LC 82-859. 341p. 1982. Repr. of 1924 ed. 10.95 (ISBN 0-89621-351-X). Thorndike Pr.

--Thunder Moon. 1975. pap. 1.25 o.s.i. (ISBN 0-671-80102-3). PB.

--Thunder Moon. 160p. 1982. pap. 1.95 (ISBN 0-671-41567-0). PB.

--Thunder Moon Strikes. LC 82-5087. (Silver Star Western Ser.). 1982. 12.95 (ISBN 0-396-08081-2). Dodd.

--Thunder Moon's Challenge. LC 82-5023. (Silver Star Western Ser.). 1982. 11.95 (ISBN 0-396-08077-4). Dodd.

--The Untamed. (Western Fiction Ser.). 1978. lib. bdg. 10.95 (ISBN 0-8398-2462-9, Gregg). G K Hall.

--Wild Freedom. 240p. 1983. pap. 2.25 (ISBN 0-446-30230-9). Warner Bks.

Brand, Mildred. Candy & Candy Molding. (Illus.). 64p. 1982. pap. 3.25 (ISBN 0-686-83999-4). Ideals.

Brand, Millen. Local Lives: Poems About the Pennsylvania Dutch. 576p. 1975. 12.50 o.p. (ISBN 0-517-51998-4, C N Potter Bks). Crown.

Brand, Oscar. When I First Came to This Land. LC 74-77596. (Illus.). 48p. (gr. k-4). 1974. 5.95 o.p. (ISBN 0-399-20415-6). Putnam Pub Group.

Brand, Richard W. & Isselhard, Donald E. Anatomy of Orofacial Structures. 2nd ed. LC 81-14103. (Illus.). 405p. 1982. pap. text ed. 20.95 (ISBN 0-8016-0857-0). Mosby.

Brand, Sandra. I Dared to Live. LC 78-52142. 1978. 8.95 o.p. (ISBN 0-88400-058-3). Shengold.

Brand, Stewart. Two Cybernetic Frontiers. 1974. 6.00 (ISBN 0-394-49283-8); pap. 2.00 (ISBN 0-394-70689-7). Random.

Brand, Violet & Brand, Geoffrey. Brass Bands in the 20th Century. 239p. 1979. 34.75x o.p. (ISBN 0-905858-12-3, Pub. by Egon England). State Mutual Bk.

Brand, William R., tr. see Kapuscinski, Ryszard.

Brandauer, Frederick P. Tung Yueh. (World Authors Ser.). 1978. 15.95 (ISBN 0-8057-6339-2, Twayne). G K Hall.

Brandeis, Irma, tr. see Rostand, Jean.

Brandejs, Jan F. & Pace, Graham. Physician's Primer on Computers: Private Practice. LC 75-39315. (Illus.). 1979. 21.95x (ISBN 0-669-00431-6). Lexington Bks.

Brandel, Marc. The Hand. 1981. pap. 2.50 o.p. (ISBN 0-425-04838-1). Berkley Pub.

--Lizard's Tail. 1979. 9.95 o.p. (ISBN 0-671-22475-1). S&S.

Branden, Nathaniel. If You Could Hear What I Cannot Say: Learning to Communicate with the Ones You Love. 1983. pap. 8.95 (ISBN 0-686-82126-2). Bantam.

Brandenberg, Franz. Leo & Emily's Big Ideas. (Illus.). (gr. 1-3). 1982. 6.50 (ISBN 0-688-00754-6); PLB 5.71 (ISBN 0-688-00755-4). Morrow.

--A Robber! a Robber! LC 75-26999. (Illus.). 32p. (gr. k-3). 1976. 9.55 o.p. (ISBN 0-688-80027-0); PLB 9.55 (ISBN 0-688-84027-2). Greenwillow.

Brandenburg, Hans. The Meek & the Mighty. Matchett, Kathy, tr. (Eng.). 1977. 13.95x (ISBN 0-19-519914-6). Oxford U Pr.

Brandenburg, M. M., tr. see Baegert, Johann J.

Brandenburger, Nelda H. Interpretive Flower Arrangements: How to Express Yourself with Plant Materials, Including Designs to Fit Holiday Occasions, Themes, Moods & Seasons. (Illus.). 1969. 6.95 (ISBN 0-8208-0059-7). Hearthside.

Brandenstein, C. G. Von see Von Brandenstein, C. G. & Thomas, A. P.

Brander, George C., et al. Veterinary Applied Pharmacology & Therapeutics. 4th ed. 540p. 1982. text ed. write for info. o.p. (ISBN 0-8121-0808-6). Lea & Febiger.

Brander, Harry. What Rhymes With Cancer? LC 82-81363. (Illus.). 54p. 1982. pap. 3.00 (ISBN 0-89823-038-1). New Rivers Pr.

Brander, Laurence, ed. Aldous Huxley: A Critical Study. 1979. pap. 9.95 o.s.i. (ISBN 0-8464-0082-0). Beekman Pubs.

Brander, Michael. Scottish & Border Battles & Ballads. 1976. 10.00 o.p. (ISBN 0-517-52500-3, C N Potter Bks). Crown.

Brandes, Joseph. Herbert Hoover & Economic Diplomacy. LC 75-26622. (Illus.). 237p. 1975. Repr. of 1962 ed. lib. bdg. 17.25x (ISBN 0-8371-8362-6, BRHH). Greenwood.

Brandewyne, Rebecca. Forever My Love. 560p. (Orig.). 1983. pap. 2.95 (ISBN 0-446-90981-5). Warner Bks.

--Love, Cherish Me. 576p. 1983. pap. 3.95 (ISBN 0-446-30039-X). Warner Bks.

--No Gentle Love. 592p. (Orig.). 1983. pap. 3.95 (ISBN 0-446-30619-3). Warner Bks.

Brandi, John. Rite for the Beautification of All Beings. (Illus.). 24p. 1983. deluxe ed. 20.00 (ISBN 0-915124-64-5); pap. 5.00 (ISBN 0-915124-65-3). Toothpaste.

Brandis, Henry. Brandis on North Carolina Evidence, 2 vols. 1982. 80.00 (ISBN 0-87215-447-5). Michie-Bobbs.

--Stansbury's North Carolina Evidence: Brandis Revision, 2 vols. rev. ed. LC 72-97320. 1038p. 1973. with 1979 suppl 75.00 o.p. (ISBN 0-87215-159-X); 1979 suppl. separately 25.00 o.p. (ISBN 0-87215-278-2). Michie-Bobbs.

Brandis, Walter & Bernstein, Basil. Selection & Control: Teacher's Ratings of Children in the Infant School. (Primary Socialization, Language & Education Ser). 1974. 17.50x (ISBN 0-7100-7729-7). Routledge & Kegan.

Brandly, C. A. & Jungherr, E. L., eds. Advances in Veterinary Science, Vol. 26. 332p. 1982. 45.00 (ISBN 0-12-039226-7); lib ed 58.50 (ISBN 0-12-039288-7); microfiche 31.50 (ISBN 0-12-039289-5). Acad Pr.

--Advances in VEterinary Science & Comparative Medicine. Incl. Vol. 13. 1969. 59.50 (ISBN 0-12-039213-5); Vol. 14. 1970. 59.50 (ISBN 0-12-039214-3); Vol. 15. 1971. 59.50 (ISBN 0-12-039215-1); Vol. 16. 1972. 60.00 (ISBN 0-12-039216-X); Vol. 17. 1973. 63.50 (ISBN 0-12-039217-8); Vol. 18. 1974. 54.00 (ISBN 0-12-039218-6); Vol. 19. 1976. 55.00 (ISBN 0-12-039219-4); lib. ed. 70.50 (ISBN 0-12-039274-7); microfiche 39.50 (ISBN 0-12-039275-5); Vol. 20. 1976. 54.00 (ISBN 0-12-039220-8); lib ed. 69.00 (ISBN 0-12-039276-3); microfiche 39.00 (ISBN 0-12-039277-1); Vol. 21. 1977. 60.50 (ISBN 0-12-039221-6); lib ed. 77.50 (ISBN 0-12-039278-X); microfiche 43.50 (ISBN 0-12-039279-8); Vol. 22. 1978. 50.00 (ISBN 0-12-039222-4); lib ed. 57.00 (ISBN 0-12-039280-1); microfiche 36.00 (ISBN 0-12-039281-X). LC 53-7098. Acad Pr.

Brandner, Gary. Offshore. (Orig.). 1978. pap. 1.95 o.p. (ISBN 0-523-40198-1). Pinnacle Bks.

Brandner, John H. Mammoth Vehicles of the World: Land-Sea-Air. (Illus.). 1982. pap. 15.95 (ISBN 0-89404-009-X). Aztex.

Brandom, Robert, jt. auth. see Rescher, Nicholas.

Brandon, Beatrice. The Cliffs of Night. 1975. pap. 1.50 o.p. (ISBN 0-451-06575-1, W6575, Sig). NAL.

Brandon, Belinda B., ed. Effect of the Demographics of Individual Households on Their Telphone Usage. 432p. 1981. prof ref 45.00x (ISBN 0-88410-695-0). Ballinger Pub.

Brandon, David. Zen in the Art of Helping. 1978. pap. 5.95 (ISBN 0-440-59897-4, Delta). Dell.

Brandon, James R. Brandon's Guide to Theater in Asia. LC 75-37506. 178p. 1976. pap. 3.95 (ISBN 0-8248-0369-8). UH Pr.

--Theatre in Southeast Asia. LC 67-14338. (Illus.). 1967. 15.00x o.p. (ISBN 0-674-87585-0). Harvard U Pr.

Brandon, James R., jt. auth. see Baumer, Rachel.

Brandon, James R., ed. Chushingura: Studies in Kabuki & the Puppet Theatre. LC 82-1921. (Illus.). 243p. 1982. text ed. 30.00x (ISBN 0-8248-0793-6). UH Pr.

--The Performing Arts in Asia. 168p. 1972. pap. 6.00 o.p. (ISBN 92-3-100902-8, U445, UNESCO). Unipub.

Brandon, James R., et al. Studies in Kabuki: Its Acting, Music, & Historical Context. LC 77-5336. 1978. pap. 7.50x (ISBN 0-8248-0452-X, Eastwest Ctr). UH Pr.

Brandon, P. F. & Millman, R. N. Recording Historic Landscapes: Principles & Practice. 1981p. 1981. 60.00x o.p. (ISBN 0-86127-305-2, Pub. by Avebury Pub England). State Mutual Bk.

Brandon, P. F. & Millman, R. N., eds. Historic Landscapes: Observer's & Recorder's Handbook. 1981. 40.00x o.p. (ISBN 0-86127-306-0, Pub. by Avebury Pub England). State Mutual Bk.

Brandon, Peter S. & Moore, Geoffrey. Microcomputers in Building Appraisal. 320p. 1983. pap. 25.95 (ISBN 0-89397-147-2). Nichols Pub.

Brandon, William. The Last American: The Indian in American Culture. LC 73-6956. 564p. 1973. 15.00 o.p. (ISBN 0-07-007201-9, GB). McGraw.

--The Men & the Mountain: Fremont's Fourth Expedition. LC 73-20901. (Illus.). 337p. 1974. Repr. of 1955 ed. lib. bdg. 18.25x (ISBN 0-8371-5873-7, BRME). Greenwood.

Brandon, William, ed. American Heritage Book of the Indians. 1964. pap. 1.75 o.p. (ISBN 0-440-30113-0, LFL). Dell.
Brandreth, Gyles. The Biggest Tongue-Twister Book in the World. LC 78-57784. (Illus.). (gr. 2 up). 1978. 6.95 (ISBN 0-8069-4594-X); PLB 9.99 (ISBN 0-8069-4595-8). Sterling.
--Brain-Teasers & Mind-Benders. LC 78-66297. (Illus.). (gr. 3 up). 1979. 7.95 (ISBN 0-8069-4596-6); PLB 9.99 (ISBN 0-8069-4597-4). Sterling.
--The Complete Puzzler. 192p. 1983. pap. 6.95 (ISBN 0-312-15839-4). St Martin.
--Game a Day Book. LC 79-91386. (Illus.). 192p. (gr. 2-12). 1980. 7.95 (ISBN 0-8069-4610-5); PLB 9.99 (ISBN 0-8069-4611-3). Sterling.
--A Joke-a-Day Book. LC 78-66298. (Illus.). (gr. 3 up). 1979. 7.95 (ISBN 0-8069-4598-2); PLB 9.99 (ISBN 0-8069-4599-0). Sterling.
--The Joy of Lex. LC 80-82360. (Illus.). 288p. 1980. 12.45 (ISBN 0-688-03709-7). Morrow.
--The Joy of Lex. 320p. 1983. pap. 6.95 (ISBN 0-686-84858-6). Quill NY.
--The Last Word. LC 79-65075. 1979. 7.95 o.p. (ISBN 0-8069-0172-1); lib. bdg. 7.49 o.p. (ISBN 0-8069-0173-X). Sterling.
--Pears Family Quiz Book. 1977. pap. 5.25 o.p. (ISBN 0-7207-0907-5). Transatlantic.
--Pranks, Tricks & Practical Jokes. LC 79-65291. (Illus.). (gr. 3 up). 1979. 6.95 o.p. (ISBN 0-8069-4606-7); PLB 7.49 o.p. (ISBN 0-8069-4607-5). Sterling.
--Seeing Is Not Believing. LC 79-91401. (Illus.). 96p. (gr. 3-12). 1980. 7.95 (ISBN 0-8069-4615-6); PLB 9.99. Sterling.
--The Super Joke Book. LC 83-397. (Illus.). 128p. (gr. 3 up). 1983. 7.95 (ISBN 0-8069-4672-5); PLB 9.99 (ISBN 0-8069-4673-3). Sterling.
--This Is Your Body. LC 79-65078. (Illus.). (gr. 3-7). 1979. 6.95 o.p. (ISBN 0-8069-3112-4); PLB 7.49 o.p. (ISBN 0-8069-3113-2). Sterling.
--Total Nonsense Z to A. LC 80-54349. (Illus.). 96p. (gr. 4 up). 1981. 7.95 (ISBN 0-8069-4644-X); lib. bdg. 9.99 (ISBN 0-8069-4645-8). Sterling.
Brandreth, Gyles & Moran, George. More Joy of Lex: An Amusing & Amazing Z to A & A to Z of Words. LC 82-8127. (Illus.). 310p. 1982. 13.00 (ISBN 0-688-01338-4). Morrow.
Brandreth, Gyles & Morley, John. The Magic of Houdini. (Illus.). 1979. 18.00 o.p. (ISBN 0-7207-1114-2). Transatlantic.
Brandreth, Gyles, ed. The Puzzle Mountain. LC 81-4003. (Illus.). 256p. (Orig.). 1981. pap. 7.95 (ISBN 0-688-00686-8). Quill NY.
Brandrup, Johannes & Immergut, E. H., eds. Polymer Handbook. 2nd ed. LC 74-11381. 1408p. 1975. 79.50x (ISBN 0-471-09804-3, Pub. by Wiley-Interscience). Wiley.
Brandsma, Jeffrey M. Outpatient Treatment of Alcoholism. 224p. 1979. pap. text ed. 19.95 (ISBN 0-8391-1393-5). Univ Park.
Brandstatter, A. F. & Hyman, A. A. Fundamentals of Law Enforcement. (Criminal Justice Ser). 1972. text ed. 21.95 (ISBN 0-02-473740-2). Macmillan.
Brandstatter, Julius J., tr. see Caratheodory, Constantin.
Brandstein, C. G. Von see Von Brandenstein, C. G.
Brandt, Andres von. Fish Catching Methods of the World. 2nd ed. (Illus.). 256p. 19.50 o.p. (ISBN 0-85238-026-7, FNB). Unipub.
Brandt, Andres von see Von Brandt, Andres.
Brandt, Anne, jt. auth. see Trussel, Patricia.
Brandt, Bill. Shadow of Light. LC 76-52463. (Quality Paperback Ser.). (Illus.). 1977. lib. bdg. 29.50 o. p. (ISBN 0-306-70858-2); pap. 14.50 (ISBN 0-306-80066-7). Da Capo.
Brandt, Bill & Haworth-Booth, Mark, eds. The Land: Twentieth Century Landscape Photographs. LC 75-30640. 1976. 17.50 (ISBN 0-306-70753-5); pap. 7.95 o. p. (ISBN 0-306-80026-8). Da Capo.
Brandt, Catharine. Forgotten People. 1978. pap. 3.95 o.p. (ISBN 0-8024-2832-0). Moody.
--Still Time to Pray. LC 82-72648. 96p. (Orig.). 1983. pap. 4.95 (ISBN 0-8066-1955-4, 10-6007). Augsburg.
Brandt, Frans M. A Guide to Rational Weight Control. LC 79-63237. 320p. 1979. pap. 8.95 (ISBN 0-941954-00-5). Wesselhoeft Assoc.
Brandt, Frithiof. Soren Kierkegaard His Life - His Works. Born, Ann R., tr. (Danes of the Present & Past). (Illus.). 117p. (Danish.). 1983. pap. text ed. 7.95 (ISBN 0-933748-05-1). Nordic Bks.
Brandt, G. W., tr. see Calderon.
Brandt, George, ed. British Television Drama. LC 80-41031. (Illus.). 300p. 1981. 49.50 (ISBN 0-521-22186-2); pap. 15.95 (ISBN 0-521-29384-7). Cambridge U Pr.
Brandt, Harry, ed. see Dyer, Lorna.
Brandt, Henry & Landrum, Phil. I Want My Marriage to Be Better. 1976. 4.95 o.p. (ISBN 0-310-21620-6); pap. 4.95 (ISBN 0-310-21621-4). Zondervan.
Brandt, Jane. Grogs, Granites, Slushes & Flings: Drinks Without Liquor. LC 82-40504. (Illus.). 192p. 1983. pap. 4.95 (ISBN 0-89480-358-1). Workman Pub.
Brandt, Jane L. La Chingada. LC 79-4360. 1979. 12.95 (ISBN 0-07-007216-7, GB). McGraw.
Brandt, John C. Our Changing Universe. (Physical Science Ser.). 1976. pap. text ed. 7.95 (ISBN 0-675-08574-8); cassettes & filmstrips o.s.i. avail. Additional supplements may be obtained from publisher. Merrill.
Brandt, John C. & Chapman, Robert C. Introduction to Comets. LC 76-47207. (Illus.). 256p. 1981. 47.50 (ISBN 0-521-23906-0). Cambridge U Pr.
Brandt, John C. & Chapman, Robert D. Introduction to Comets. LC 76-47207. 256p. 1982. pap. 11.95 (ISBN 0-521-27218-1). Cambridge U Pr.
Brandt, K. & Apstein, C., eds. Nordisches Plankton: 1911-42, 7 vols. 1964. 480.00 (ISBN 90-6123-110-8). Lubrecht & Cramer.
Brandt, Keith. Daniel Boone: Frontier Adventures. LC 82-15915. (Illus.). 48p. (gr. 4-6). 1983. PLB 6.89 (ISBN 0-89375-843-4); pap. text ed. 1.95 (ISBN 0-89375-844-2). Troll Assocs.
--John Paul Jones: Hero of the Seas. LC 82-16045. (Illus.). 48p. (gr. 4-6). 1983. PLB 6.89 (ISBN 0-89375-849-3); pap. text ed. 1.95 (ISBN 0-89375-850-7). Troll Assocs.
--Marie Curie: Brave Scientist. LC 82-16092. (Illus.). 48p. (gr. 4-6). 1983. PLB 6.89 (ISBN 0-89375-855-8); pap. text ed. 1.95 (ISBN 0-89375-856-6). Troll Assocs.
--Pete Rose: Mr. 300. LC 76-54137. (Putnam Sports Shelf). (Illus.). (gr. 6-8). 1977. PLB 5.29 o.p. (ISBN 0-399-61071-5). Putnam Pub Group.
Brandt, L. Meditations on a Loving God. 1983. 9.95 (ISBN 0-570-03858-8). Concordia.
Brandt, Leonore. Raccoon Family Pets. pap. 2.95 (ISBN 0-87666-216-5, AP7500). TFH Pubns.
Brandt, Louis, jt. auth. see Love, W. W.
Brandt, Louis W. Psychologists Caught: A Psycho-Logic of Psychology. 248p. 1982. 40.00x (ISBN 0-8020-5539-7); pap. 14.95. U of Toronto Pr.
Brandt, Lucile. The Flame Tree. new ed. 96p. 1973. pap. 2.95 o.p. (ISBN 0-87178-275-8). Brethren.
Brandt, Patricia, et al. Current Practice in Pediatric Nursing, Vol. 2. LC 75-22183. (Current Practice Ser.). 1978. 12.50 o.p. (ISBN 0-8016-0750-7); pap. 9.50 o.p. (ISBN 0-8016-0751-5). Mosby.
Brandt, R. L. Charasmatics: Are We Missing Something? 1981. pap. 4.95 (ISBN 0-686-38055-X). Bridge Pub.
Brandt, Rhonda O., jt. auth. see Reece, Barry.
Brandt, Richard B. Philosophy of Schleiermacher: The Development of His Theory of Scientific & Religious Knowledge. LC 68-19265. 1968. Repr. of 1941 ed. lib. bdg. 18.50x (ISBN 0-8371-0027-5, BRPS). Greenwood.
Brandt, Richard M. Public Education Under Scrutiny. LC 80-6080. 197p. 1981. lib. bdg. 20.00 (ISBN 0-8191-1566-5); pap. text ed. 9.50 (ISBN 0-8191-1567-3). U Pr of Amer.
--Studying Behavior in Natural Settings. LC 81-40189. (Illus.). 416p. 1981. lib. bdg. 27.00 (ISBN 0-8191-1829-X); pap. text ed. 15.50 (ISBN 0-8191-1830-3). U Pr of Amer.
Brandt, Siegmund. Statistical & Computational Methods in Data Analysis. 2nd ed. 1976. 51.00 (ISBN 0-444-10893-9, North-Holland). Elsevier.
Brandt, Sue R. First Book of How to Write a Report. LC 68-17702. (First Bks). (Illus.). (gr. 4-6). 1968. PLB 7.90 (ISBN 0-531-00554-2); pap. 0.95 (ISBN 0-685-21862-7). Watts.
Brandt, Vincent S. A Korean Village: Between Farm & Sea. LC 73-162857. (East Asian Ser: No. 65). (Illus.). 224p. 1972. 16.00x o.p. (ISBN 0-674-50565-4). Harvard U Pr.
Brandt, W., et al. Craft of Writing. 1969. pap. text ed. 10.95 (ISBN 0-13-188797-1). P-H.
Brandt, William, et al. The Comprehensive Study of Music: Piano Reductions for Harmonic Music. 1979. pap. text ed. 13.50 scp o.p. (ISBN 0-06-161421-1, HarpC). Har-Row.
Brandt, Willy & Sampson, Anthony, eds. North-South: A Program for Survival (The Brandt Report) 320p. (Orig.). 1980. pap. text ed. 5.95 (ISBN 0-262-52059-1). MIT Pr.
Brandt-Zawadzki, Michael, jt. auth. see Federle, Michael P.
Brandvold, D. C. Water Treatment: Industrial-Commercial-Municipal. 2nd ed. (Illus.). 1982. pap. 5.00 (ISBN 0-9610178-0-5). Branchemco.
Brandwein & MacNiece. The Complete Group House Handbook: How to Live with others (and love it). 1982. pap. 6.95 (ISBN 0-87491-090-0). Acropolis.
Brandwein, Paul F. Memorandum: On Renewing Schooling & Education. Jovanovich, William, intro. by. LC 81-47301. 320p. 1981. 14.95 (ISBN 0-15-158857-0). HarBraceJ.
Brandywine Conservancy, Inc. Historic Preservation in the Lower Delaware Valley. 150p. 1983. write for info. Brandywine Conserv.
Brandzel, Rose, jt. auth. see Siemens, Sydney.
Branfield, John. The Fox in Winter. LC 81-10793. (gr. 7 up). 1982. PLB 9.95 (ISBN 0-689-50219-2, McElderry Bk). Atheneum.
Brang, Peter & Zullig, Monika. Kommentierte Bibliographie Zur Slavischen Soziolinguistik. 1639p. (Ger.). 1982. write for info. (ISBN 3-261-04958-8). P Lang Pubs.
Brangham, A. N. Auvergne: History, People & Places. (Illus.). 1978. pap. 6.95 o.p. (ISBN 0-904978-63-X). Hippocrene Bks.
Brangwyn, Frank & Preston, Hayter. Windmills. LC 70-176821. (Illus.). 126p. 1975. Repr. of 1923 ed. 37.00x (ISBN 0-8103-4077-1). Gale.
Branick, Vincent P. Wonder in a Technical World: An Introduction to the Method & Writers of Philosophy. LC 80-67205. 256p. 1980. lib. bdg. 10.75 (ISBN 0-8191-1248-8). U Pr of Amer.
Branigan, Keith, ed. The Atlas of Archaeology. (Illus.). 240p. 1982. 25.00 (ISBN 0-312-05957-4). St Martin.
Branks, Judith & Sanchez, Juan B. The Drama of Life: Guambino Life Cycle. (Museum of Anthropology Publications: No. 4). 1978. pap. 5.00x (ISBN 0-88312-153-0); microfiche 2.25x (ISBN 0-88312-239-1). Summer Inst Ling.
Branley, F., et al. Astronomy. 1975. text ed. 22.50 scp (ISBN 0-690-00760-4, HarpC). Har-Row.
Branley, Franklyn. Air Is All Around You. LC 62-7738. (A Let's-Read-& Find-Out Science Bk). (Illus.). (gr. k-3). 1962. PLB 10.89 (ISBN 0-690-05356-8, TYC-J). Har-Row.
--Saturn. LC 81-43890. (Illus.). 64p. (gr. 3-6). 1983. 11.49i (ISBN 0-690-04213-2, TYC-J); PLB 11.89g (ISBN 0-690-04214-0). Har-Row.
Branley, Franklyn M. The Beginning of the Earth. LC 79-184979. (A Let's-Read-&-Find-Out Science Bk.). (Illus.). (gr. k-3). 1972. 6.95 o.p. (ISBN 0-690-12987-4, TYC-J); PLB 10.89 (ISBN 0-690-12988-2). Har-Row.
--Big Dipper. LC 62-10999. (A Let's-Read-&-Find-Out Science Bk). (Illus.). (gr. k-3). 1962. PLB 10.89 (ISBN 0-690-01116-4, TYC-J). Har-Row.
--Big Tracks, Little Tracks. LC 60-6251. (A Let's-Read-&-Find-Out Science Bk). (Illus.). (gr. k-3). 1960. PLB 10.89 (ISBN 0-690-14371-0, TYC-J). Har-Row.
--Book of Outer Space for You. LC 71-94790. (Illus.). (gr. 2-5). 1970. PLB 9.89 o.p. (ISBN 0-690-15474-7, TYC-J). Har-Row.
--Book of Planets for You. rev. ed. LC 66-16919. (Illus.). (gr. 3-6). 1966. PLB 10.89 (ISBN 0-690-15509-3, TYC-J). Har-Row.
--Book of Stars for You. LC 67-18509. (Illus.). (gr. 3-6). 1967. 8.95 o.p. (ISBN 0-690-15721-5, TYC-J); PLB 9.89 o.p. (ISBN 0-690-15722-3). Har-Row.
--Book of Venus for You. LC 73-78256. (Illus.). (gr. 3-6). 1969. 9.95 o.p. (ISBN 0-690-15792-4, TYC-J); PLB 9.89 o.p. (ISBN 0-690-15793-2). Har-Row.
--Columbia & Beyond: The Story of the Space Shuttle. (Illus.). (gr. 4 up). 1979. 13.95 o.p. (ISBN 0-399-20844-5, Philomel). Putnam Pub Group.
--Eclipse: Darkness in Daytime. LC 73-3492. (A Let's-Read-&-Find-Out Science Bk). (Illus.). (gr. k-3). 1973. PLB 10.89 (ISBN 0-690-25414-8, TYC-J). Har-Row.
--Experiments in the Principles of Space Travel. rev. ed. LC 72-7543. (Illus.). (gr. 6 up). 1973. 10.53i o.p. (ISBN 0-690-27792-X, TYC-J). Har-Row.
--Flash, Crash, Rumble, & Roll. LC 64-18161. (A Let's-Read-&-Find-Out Science Bk). (Illus.). (gr. k-3). 1964. PLB 10.89 (ISBN 0-690-30563-X, TYC-J). Har-Row.
--Floating & Sinking. LC 67-15396. (A Let's-Read-&-Find-Out Science Bk). (Illus.). (gr. k-3). 1967. bds. 9.89 o.p. (ISBN 0-690-30917-1, TYC-J); PLB 10.89 (ISBN 0-690-30918-X). Har-Row.
--Gravity Is a Mystery. LC 70-101922. (A Let's-Read-and-Find-Out Science Bk). (Illus.). (gr. k-3). 1970. 10.53i (ISBN 0-690-35071-6, TYC-J); PLB 10.89 (ISBN 0-690-35072-4). Har-Row.
--Halley: Comet 1986. (Illus.). 96p. (gr. 7 up). 1983. 10.95 (ISBN 0-525-66780-6, 01063-280). Lodestar Bks.
--High Sounds, Low Sounds. LC 67-23662. (A Let's-Read-&-Find-Out Science Bk). (Illus.). (gr. k-3). 1967. 6.95 o.p. (ISBN 0-690-38017-8, TYC-J); PLB 10.89 (ISBN 0-690-38018-6). Har-Row.
--How Little, & How Much: A Book About Scales. LC 75-43643. (Young Math Ser.). (Illus.). 40p. (gr. k-3). 1976. PLB 9.89 o.p. (ISBN 0-690-01058-3, TYC-J). Har-Row.
--Jupiter: King of the Gods, Giant of the Planets. (Illus.). 96p. (gr. 7 up). 1981. 10.95 (ISBN 0-525-66739-3, 01063-320). Lodestar Bks.
--Light & Darkness. LC 74-23938. (A Let's Read & Find Out Science Bk). (Illus.). 40p. (gr. k-3). 1975. 9.89 o.p. (ISBN 0-690-00704-3, TYC-J); PLB 10.89 (ISBN 0-690-01122-9). Har-Row.
--Moon Seems to Change. LC 60-8796. (A Let's-Read-&-Find-Out Science Bk). (Illus.). (gr. k-3). 1960. PLB 10.89 (ISBN 0-690-55485-0, TYC-J). Har-Row.
--North, South, East, & West. LC 66-14486. (A Let's-Read-&-Find-Out Science Bk). (Illus.). (gr. k-3). 1966. PLB 10.89 (ISBN 0-690-58609-4, TYC-J). Har-Row.
--Oxygen Keeps You Alive. LC 73-139093. (A Let's-Read-&-Find-Out Science Bk). (Illus.). (gr. k-3). 1971. 10.53i (ISBN 0-690-60702-4, TYC-J); PLB 10.89 (ISBN 0-690-60703-2). Har-Row.
--The Planets in Our Solar System. LC 79-7894. (A Let's Read & Find Out Science Bk.). (Illus.). 40p. (gr. k-3). 1981. 10.53 (ISBN 0-690-04025-3, TYC-J); PLB 10.89 (ISBN 0-690-04026-1). Har-Row.
--The Planets in Our Solar System. LC 79-7894. (A Trophy Let's-Read-and-Find-out Science Bk.). (Illus.). 40p. (gr. k-3). 1983. pap. 3.80i (ISBN 0-06-445001-5, Trophy). Har-Row.
--Roots Are Food Finders. LC 74-23924. (A Let's Read & Find Out Bk). (Illus.). 40p. (gr. k-3). 1975. PLB 10.89 (ISBN 0-690-00703-5, TYC-J). Har-Row.
--Secret Three. LC 81-43037. (A Trophy Let's Read-&-Find-Out Science Bk). (Illus.). 40p. (gr. k-3). 1983. pap. 3.80i (ISBN 0-06-445002-3, Trophy). Har-Row.
--Shakes, Quakes & Shifts: Earth Tectonics. LC 73-18059. 40p. (gr. 5 up). 1974. o. p. 8.95 (ISBN 0-690-00422-2, TYC-J); PLB 10.89 (ISBN 0-690-00423-0). Har-Row.
--Sun: Our Nearest Star. LC 60-13241. (A Let's-Read-&-Find-Out Science Bk). (Illus.). (gr. k-3). 1961. PLB 10.89 (ISBN 0-690-79483-5, TYC-J). Har-Row.
--Sunshine Makes the Seasons. LC 73-19694. (A Let's Read & Find Out Science Bk). (Illus.). 40p. (ps-3). 1974. PLB 10.89 (ISBN 0-690-00438-9, TYC-J). Har-Row.
--Think Metric! LC 72-78279. (Illus.). (gr. 3-6). 1973. 9.57i o.p. (ISBN 0-690-81861-0, TYC-J); PLB 10.89 (ISBN 0-690-81862-9). Har-Row.
--Weight & Weightlessness. LC 70-132292. (Let's-Read-&-Find-Out Science Bks.). (Illus.). (gr. k-3). 1972. PLB 10.89 (ISBN 0-690-87329-8, TYC-J). Har-Row.
--What Makes Day & Night. LC 60-8258. (A Let's-Read-&-Find-Out Science Bks.). (Illus.). (gr. k-3). 1961. PLB 10.89 (ISBN 0-690-87790-0, TYC-J). Har-Row.
--What the Moon Is Like. LC 63-8479. (A Let's-Read-&-Find-Out Science Bk). (Illus.). (gr. k-3). 1963. pap. 2.95 (ISBN 0-690-00203-3, TYC-J); lib. bdg. 10.89 (ISBN 0-690-87860-5). Har-Row.
Brann, Donald R. Bricklaying Simplified. LC 77-140968. 1979. pap. 6.95 (ISBN 0-87733-668-7). Easi-Bild.
--Carpeting Simplified. LC 72-91055. (Illus.). 1980. pap. 6.95 (ISBN 0-87733-683-0). Easi-Bild.
--How to Add an Extra Bathroom. rev. ed. LC 68-18108. 1976. lib. bdg. 5.95 (ISBN 0-87733-082-4); pap. 6.95 (ISBN 0-87733-682-2). Easi-Bild.
--How to Build a One Car Garage-Carport-Stable. rev. ed. LC 72-88709. 1973. lib. bdg. 5.95 (ISBN 0-87733-800-0); pap. 6.95 (ISBN 0-87733-680-6). Easi-Bild.
--How to Build a Two Bedroom Ranch House. LC 82-90748. 224p. 1983. pap. 6.95 (ISBN 0-87733-831-0). Easi-Bild.
--How to Build a Two Car Garage, Lean-to Porch Cabana. LC 65-27707. 1979. pap. 6.95 (ISBN 0-87733-663-6). Easi-Bild.
--How to Build an Addition. rev. ed. LC 63-16211. Orig. Title: How to Add-a-Room. 1978. lib. bdg. 5.95 (ISBN 0-87733-009-3); pap. 6.95 (ISBN 0-87733-609-1). Easi-Bild.
--How to Build Bars. LC 67-15263. 1979. pap. 6.95 (ISBN 0-87733-690-3). Easi-Bild.
--How to Build Outdoor Furniture. LC 76-14045. 1978. pap. 6.95 (ISBN 0-87733-754-3). Easi-Bild.
--How to Build Pet Housing, Bk. 751. LC 75-269. 1978. lib. bdg. 5.95 o.p. (ISBN 0-87733-051-4); pap. 6.95 (ISBN 0-87733-751-9). Easi-Bild.
--How to Build Workbenches. LC 66-30452. 1979. pap. 6.95 (ISBN 0-87733-672-5). Easi-Bild.
--How to Install Paneling, Make Valances, Cornices. LC 65-25756. 1979. pap. 6.95 (ISBN 0-87733-605-9). Easi-Bild.
--How to Transform a Garage into Living Space, Bk. 684. LC 72-92125. (Illus.). 128p. 1974. lib. bdg. 5.95 (ISBN 0-87733-084-0); pap. 6.95 (ISBN 0-87733-684-9). Easi-Bild.
--Roofing Simplified. LC 81-65487. 176p. 1983. pap. 6.95 (ISBN 0-87733-896-5). Easi-Bild.
Brannan, Carl. Process Systems Development. (The Process Engineer's Handbook Ser.). 1938. pap. text ed. 9.95x (ISBN 0-87201-713-3). Gulf Pub.
Brannen, Noah, tr. see Fujiwara, Yoichi.
Branner, Robert. Manuscript Painting in Paris During the Reign of St. Louis. LC 73-78514. (Studies in the History of Art). (Illus.). 1977. 87.50x (ISBN 0-520-02462-1). U of Cal Pr.
Brannigan, Augustine. The Social Basis of Scientific Discoveries. 228p. 1981. 27.95 (ISBN 0-521-23695-9); pap. 10.95 (ISBN 0-521-28163-6). Cambridge U Pr.
Brannigan, Francis L. Building Construction for the Fire Service. 2nd ed. McKinnon, Gordon P. & Matson, Debra, eds. LC 78-178805. (Illus.). 392p. 1982. text ed. 20.00 (ISBN 0-87765-227-9, FSP-33A). Natl Fire Prot.
Brannin, Marilyn. Your Body in Mind. 192p. 1983. pap. 2.95 (ISBN 0-345-29787-3). Ballantine.
Branningan, Marilyn, jt. auth. see Biklen, Sari K.
Brannon, Gerard M. Energy Taxes & Subsidies. LC 74-9645. (Ford Foundation Energy Policy Project Ser.). 160p. 1974. prof ref 19.50 (ISBN 0-88410-308-0); pap. text ed. 9.95 (ISBN 0-88410-329-3). Ballinger Pub.
Brannon, Lil & Knight, Melinda. Writers Writing. LC 82-14587. 192p. (Orig.). 1982. pap. text ed. 7.75 (ISBN 0-86709-045-6). Boynton Cook Pubs.
Branquart, P., et al. An Analytical Description of CHILL, the CCITT High Level Language. (Lectur Notes in Computer Science Ser.: Vol. 128). 277p. 1982. pap. 16.80 (ISBN 0-387-11196-4). Springer-Verlag.
Brans, J. P., ed. Operational Research, 1981. 1982. 127.75 (ISBN 0-444-86223-4). Elsevier.
Branscomb, Lewis C. Case for the Faculty Status for Academic Librarians. LC 75-118198. (A.C.R.L. Monograph: No. 33). 1970. pap. 6.00 o.p. (ISBN 0-8389-3114-6). ALA.

Branscombe, Peter, jt. ed. see Badura-Skoda, Eva.
Branscum, Robbie. The Murder of Hound Dog Bates. LC 82-1911. 96p. (gr. 3-7). 1982. 9.95 (ISBN 0-670-49521-2). Viking Pr.
--The Saving of P.S. LC 76-2757. (gr. 5-7). 1977. 5.95a o.p. (ISBN 0-385-11270-X); PLB 5.95a (ISBN 0-385-11271-8). Doubleday.
--Spud Tackett & the Angel of Doom. 128p. (gr. 3-8). 1983. 10.50 (ISBN 0-670-66582-7). Viking Pr.
--To the Tune of a Hickory Stick. LC 77-12844. (gr. 3-7). 1978. 7.95a (ISBN 0-686-85899-9); PLB 7.95a (ISBN 0-385-13038-4). Doubleday.
--Toby Alone. LC 78-22152. (gr. 5). 1979. 7.95a o.p. (ISBN 0-686-85900-6); PLB (ISBN 0-385-14018-5). Doubleday.
--Toby & Johnny Joe. LC 78-22153. (gr. 5). 1979. 7.95a o.p. (ISBN 0-686-85901-4); PLB (ISBN 0-385-13036-8). Doubleday.
--Toby, Granny & George. LC 75-21211. 112p. (gr. 3-9). 1976. 7.95a o.p. (ISBN 0-686-85902-2); PLB 7.95a (ISBN 0-385-11269-6). Doubleday.
Bransden, B. H. Atomic Collision Theory. 2nd ed. (Illus.). 500p. 1970. text ed. 29.95 (ISBN 0-8053-1181-5). Benjamin-Cummings.
Bransford, Kent. The No-Nonsense Guide to Get You into Medical School. LC 78-11160. 1979. 8.95 o.p. (ISBN 0-671-18412-1); pap. write for info. Sovereign Bks.
Branson. Macroeconomica. 2nd ed. 436p. (Span.). 1981. pap. text ed. write for info. (Pub. by HarLA Mexico). Har-Row.
Branson, D. The Deformation of Concrete Structures. 1977. pap. 5.95 (ISBN 0-07-007240-X). McGraw.
Branson, Karen. The Potato Eaters. LC 78-24330. (Illus.). (gr. 6-8). 1979. 8.95 (ISBN 0-399-20678-7). Putnam Pub Group.
--Streets of Gold. 160p. (gr. 10 up). 1981. 9.95 (ISBN 0-399-20791-0). Putnam Pub Group.
Branson, Margaret S. & Torney-Purta, Judith, eds. International Human Rights, Society, & the Schools. LC 82-60695. (Illus.). 100p. (Orig.). pap. 7.25 (ISBN 0-87986-044-8). Coun Soc Studies.
Branson, Mark L., ed. The Reader's Guide to the Best Evangelical Books. LC 82-48205. 224p. (Orig.). 1982. pap. 6.68i (ISBN 0-06-061046-8, HarpR). Har-Row.
Branson, Mark L., ed. see Aune, David E.
Branson, Mark L., ed. see Goldingay, John.
Branson, Robert E. & Norvell, Douglas G. Introduction to Agricultural Marketing. (Illus.). 544p. 1983. text ed. 28.95x (ISBN 0-07-007241-8, C); write for info instr's manual (ISBN 0-07-007242-6). McGraw.
Branson, Roy, jt. ed. see Veatch, Robert M.
Branson, William H. & Litvack, James M. Macroeconomics. 2nd ed. 407p. 1981. text ed. 22.95 scp (ISBN 0-06-040937-1, HarpC); Instr's. manual avail. (ISBN 0-06-360895-2). Har-Row.
Branson, William H. & Litvak, James. Macroeconomia. (Span.). 1979. 15.40 o.p. (ISBN 0-06-310059-2, Pub. by HarLA Mexico). Har-Row.
Branstatter, jt. auth. see Hiebsch.
Bransten, Richard, jt. auth. see McKenney, Ruth.
Branston, Frank. Sergeant Ritchie's Conscience. LC 77-9171. 1978. 8.95 o.p. (ISBN 0-312-71307-X). St Martin.
Brant, Carroll A. Electronics for Communication. 800p. 1983. text ed. write for info. (ISBN 0-574-21575-1, 13-4575); write for info. instr's. guide (ISBN 0-574-21576-X, 13-4576). SRA.
Brant, Charles. Jim Whitewolf: The Life of a Kiowa Apache. 1969. pap. 2.25 (ISBN 0-686-95783-0). Jefferson Natl.
Brant, Michelle. Timeless Walks in San Francisco: A Historical Walking Guide to the City. 3rd ed. (Illus.). 70p. 1982. Repr. of 1976 ed. 3.50 (ISBN 0-686-35807-4). M J B CA.
Brant, Roxanne. From Decision to Discipleship. 68p. (Orig.). 1975. pap. text ed. 1.50 (ISBN 0-89228-033-6). Impact Bks MO.
--Ministering to the Lord. 80p. (Orig.). 1973. pap. 3.50 (ISBN 0-89228-031-X). Impact Bks MO.
Brant, Russell A. Coal Resources of the Princess District, Kentucky. Pettit, Rhonda & Cobb, James, eds. (Energy Resource Ser.). (Illus.). 50p. (Orig.). 1982. pap. text ed. 10.00 (ISBN 0-86607-011-7). Inst Mining & Minerals.
Brantingham, Paul J., jt. auth. see Faust, Frederic L.
Brantley, Jill, jt. ed. see Maiolo, Joseph.
Brantley, William H., ed. see Soldano, B. A.
Branyan, Robert L. The Eisenhower Administration, Nineteen Fifty-Three to Nineteen Sixty-One: A Documentary History, 2 vols. LC 71-164935. 1971. Set. lib. bdg. 95.00 (ISBN 0-313-20126-9). Greenwood.
Branzuela, Len B., ed. see Martinez, Maria.
Braque, Georges. Illustrated Notebooks, 1917-1955. Appelbaum, Stanley, tr. Orig. Title: Cahier De Georges Braque. (Illus., Fr.). 1971. pap. 4.00 (ISBN 0-486-20232-1). Dover.
Bras, Monique. Your Guide to French Pronunciation. (Illus.). 231p. 1975. pap. text ed. 17.50 (ISBN 2-03-043101-X, 3819). Larousse.
Brasch, Walter M. Columbia County Place Names. (Illus.). 232p. (Orig.). 1982. 15.00 (ISBN 0-88023-028-2). Columbia County Hist Soc.
Brasch, Wayne. Real Estate By the Numbers. LC 81-6779. 230p. 1981. 24.50 (ISBN 0-87624-479-7). Inst Busn Plan.
Brascho, Donn J. & Shawker, Thomas H. Abdominal Ultrasound in the Cancer Patient. LC 80-15838. (Diagnostic & Therapeutic Radiology Ser.). 414p. 1980. 55.00 (ISBN 0-471-01742-6, Pub. by Wiley Med). Wiley.
Brase, Charles & Brase, Corrinne. Understandable Statistics: Concepts & Methods. 1983. text ed. 21.95 (ISBN 0-669-05387-2); instrs'. manual with tests 1.95 (ISBN 0-669-01013-8). Heath.
Brase, Charles H. & Brase, Corrine P. College Algebra. 544p. 1982. text ed. 20.95 (ISBN 0-669-02432-5); 1.95 (ISBN 0-669-02433-3). Heath.
Brase, Charles H., jt. auth. see Brase, Corrinne P.
Brase, Corrine P., jt. auth. see Brase, Charles H.
Brase, Corrinne, jt. auth. see Brase, Charles.
Brase, Corrinne P. & Brase, Charles H. Basic Algebra for College Students. LC 75-26093. (Illus.). 480p. 1976. text ed. 18.95 (ISBN 0-395-20656-1); instructional options guide & solutions manual 1.90 (ISBN 0-395-20655-3). HM.
Brasel, jt. auth. see Kretchmer.
Brasfield, Philip & Elliot, Jeffrey M. Deathman Pass Me by: Two Years on Death Row. LC 82-4126. (Borgo Bioviews Ser.: No. 3). 96p. 1983. lib. bdg. 10.95x (ISBN 0-89370-164-5); pap. text ed. 4.95x (ISBN 0-89370-264-1). Borgo Pr.
Brashear, H. Robert & Raney, R. Beverly. Shands' Handbook of Orthopaedic Surgery. 9th ed. LC 78-65. 548p. 1978. text ed. 39.95 (ISBN 0-8016-4082-2). Mosby.
Brashear, Richard E. & Rhodes, Mitchell L. Chronic Obstructive Lung Disease: Clinical Treatment & Management. new ed. LC 77-18551. (Illus.). 264p. 1978. text ed. 39.50 o.p. (ISBN 0-8016-0753-1). Mosby.
Brashear, Richard E., jt. auth. see Mishkin, Fred S.
Brasher, N. H. Arguments in History: Britain in the 19th Century. LC 68-10753. (Illus.). 1969. 15.95 o.p. (ISBN 0-312-04900-5). St Martin.
Brashers, Charles. Creative Writing Handbook. 1982. pap. 3.95 (ISBN 0-933362-04-8). Assoc Creative Writers.
Brashers, H. C. Other Side of Love: Two Novellas. LC 82-71611. 88p. (Orig.). 1963. pap. 3.50 (ISBN 0-8040-0237-1). Swallow.
Brashler, William. The Bingo Long Traveling All-Stars and Motor Kings. (RL 7). 1976. pap. 1.50 o.p. (ISBN 0-451-06833-5, W6833, Sig). NAL.
--The Chosen Prey. 1983. pap. 3.50 (ISBN 0-440-11216-8). Dell.
Brasier, M. D. Microfossils. (Illus., Orig.). 1980. text ed. 30.00x (ISBN 0-04-562001-6); pap. text ed. 15.95x (ISBN 0-04-562002-4). Allen Unwin.
Brasier, Virginia. Survival of the Unicorn. (Orig.). pap. 3.50 (ISBN 0-685-08706-9). Creative Pr.
Brasil, Emanuel, ed. Brazilian Poetry, 1950-1980. Smith, William J. 160p. 25.00x (ISBN 0-686-43258-4); pap. 9.95x. Wesleyan U Pr.
Brasnett, Clive. English for Medical Students. 1976. pap. 6.95x (ISBN 0-423-49760-X). Methuen Inc.
Brasol, Boris. Elements of Crime: Psycho-Social Interpretation. 2nd ed. LC 69-16226. (Criminology, Law Enforcement, & Social Problems Ser.: No. 93). 1969. Repr. of 1931 ed. 20.00x (ISBN 0-87585-093-6). Patterson Smith.
Brass, ed. see Mendenhall, J. Howard.
Brass, George A., jt. auth. see Castaldi, C. R.
Brass, P. R. Language, Religion & Politics in North India. LC 73-82453. (Illus.). 400p. 1974. 54.50 (ISBN 0-521-20324-4). Cambridge U Pr.
Brass, Paul R. & Franda, Marcus F., eds. Radical Politics in South Asia. (Studies in Communism, Revisionism, & Revolution, No. 19). 475p. 1973. 25.00x (ISBN 0-262-02099-8). MIT Pr.
Brassai. The Artists of My Life. Miller, Richard, tr. from Fr. LC 82-70182. 224p. (Fr.). 1982. 45.00 (ISBN 0-670-13648-4, Studio). Viking Pr.
Brasseaux, Carl A., jt. auth. see Conrad, Glenn R.
Brasseaux, Carl A., ed. see De Villiers du Terrage, Marc.
Brassil, James. And I Will Fill This House with Glory: Renewal Within a Suburban Parish. (Orig.). 1977. pap. 1.50 o.p. (ISBN 0-914544-19-5). Living Flame Pr.
Brassley, P., jt. auth. see Hopkins, A.
Brassy, Thomas. Jack Gould. (Claredon Biography Ser.). (Illus.). pap. 3.50 (ISBN 0-912729-15-5). Newbury Bk.
Braswell, George W., Jr. To Ride a Magic Carpet. LC 77-78472. 1977. 3.95 o.p. (ISBN 0-8054-6308-9). Broadman.
--Understanding World Religions. LC 81-65828. (Orig.). 1983. pap. 7.50 (ISBN 0-8054-6605-3). Broadman.
Braswell, Laurel N. Western Manuscripts from Classical Antiquity to the Renaissance: A Handbook. 1981. lib. bdg. 50.00 o.s.i. (ISBN 0-8240-9541-3). Garland Pub.
Braswell, Michael, jt. auth. see Taylor, William.
Braswell, Michael, et al, eds. Approaches to Counseling & Psychotherapy: A Brief Overview of Issues, Systems, & Applications. LC 79-6845. 154p. 1980. pap. text ed. 8.50 o.p. (ISBN 0-8191-0964-9). U Pr of Amer.
Braswell, Michael C. & Fletcher, Tyler. Cases in Corrections. 1980. text ed. 8.95x o.p. (ISBN 0-673-16295-8). Scott F.
Braswell, Michael C., jt. auth. see Miller, Larry S.
Bratchell, D. F. The Impact of Darwinism: Texts & Commentary Illustrating Nineteenth Century Religious, Scientific & Literary Attitudes. 1980. 40.00x o.p. (ISBN 0-86127-204-8, Pub. by Avebury Pub England). State Mutual Bk.
--Robert Greene's Planetomachia & the Text of the Third Tragedy: A Bibliographical Explanation & a New Edition of the Text. 1979. 40.00x o.p. (ISBN 0-86127-201-3, Pub. by Avebury Pub England). State Mutual Bk.
Bratcher, R. G. Translator's Guide to Paul's First Letter to the Corinthians. (Helps for Translators Ser.). 1982. pap. 2.55 (ISBN 0-8267-0185-X, 08566). Am Bible.
--Translator's Guide to the Gospel of Luke. (Helps for Translators Ser.). 1982. pap. 3.95 (ISBN 0-8267-0181-7, 08712). Am Bible.
Bratcher, R. G. & Nida, E. A. Translator's Handbook on Mark. (Helps for Translators Ser.). 1980. Repr. of 1961 ed. soft cover 4.60x (ISBN 0-8267-0135-3, 08501). United Bible.
Bratcher, R. G. & Thompson, J. A., eds. Bible Index. 1970. pap. 2.00x (ISBN 0-8267-0005-5, 08511). United Bible.
--A Short Index to the Bible. 1973. pap. 0.50x (ISBN 0-8267-0007-1, 08519). United Bible.
Bratcher, Robert G. & Nida, Eugene A. A Translator's Handbook on Paul's Letters to the Colossians & to Philemon. (Helps for Translators Ser.). 1981. Repr. of 1977 ed. softcover 2.40x (ISBN 0-8267-0145-0, 08529). United Bible.
Brater, Craig. Drug Use in Renal Disease. (Illus.). 250p. 1982. text ed. write for info. (ISBN 0-86792-005-X, Pub by Adis Pr Australia). Wright-PSG.
Brater, E. F. Handbook of Hydraulics. 6th ed. (Handbook Ser.). 1976. 42.50 (ISBN 0-07-007243-4, P&RB). McGraw.
Brater, E. F., jt. auth. see Wisler, Chester O.
Bratt, David. Tom Stoppard: A Reference Guide. 1982. lib. bdg. 35.00 (ISBN 0-8161-8576-X, Hall Reference). G K Hall.
Bratteli, O. & Robinson, D. W., eds. Operators Algebra & Quantum Statistical Mechanics, Vol. II: Equilibrium States; Models. (Texts & Monographs in Physics Ser.). 496p. 1981. 42.00 (ISBN 0-387-09187-4). Springer-Verlag.
Bratter, Thomas E., jt. auth. see Bassin, Alexander.
Brattgard, Helge. God's Stewards. LC 63-16594. (Orig.). 1963. pap. 3.95 (ISBN 0-8066-0317-8, 10-2710). Augsburg.
Bratton, Esther C., jt. auth. see Steidl, Rose E.
Bratton, Michael. The Local Politics of Rural Development: Peasant & Party-State in Zambia. LC 79-56775. (Illus.). 350p. 1980. text ed. 25.00x (ISBN 0-87451-178-X). U Pr of New Eng.
Brau, Jean-Louis & Weaver, Helen. Larousse Encyclopedia of Astrology. LC 80-14845. (Illus.). 320p. 1980. 16.95 o.p. (ISBN 0-07-007244-2). McGraw.
Brauch, Hans G. & Clarke, Duncan L., eds. DecisionMaking for Arms Limitation in the 1980's: Assessments & Prospects. 384p. 1983. prof ref 35.00x (ISBN 0-88410-864-3). Ballinger Pub.
Braude, jt. auth. see Vesell.
Braude, Abraham I. Medical Microbiology & Infectious Diseases. Samiy, A. H., et al, eds. (International System of Medicine Ser.: Vol. 2). 2000p. 1981. text ed. 70.00 (ISBN 0-7216-1919-3). Saunders.
--Microbiology. LC 81-40588. (Illus.). 845p. 1982. pap. text ed. 22.50 (ISBN 0-7216-1920-7). Saunders.
Braude, Beatrice & Coste, Brigitte. Engagements: Prises de Positions Litteraires et Culturelles. 299p. 1981. pap. text ed. 9.95 (ISBN 0-15-522604-5, HC). HarBraceJ.
Braude, Benjamin & Lewis, Bernard, eds. Christians & Jews in the Ottoman Empire: The Functioning of a Plural Society, 2 vols. LC 80-11337. 1982. Set. text ed. 85.00x (ISBN 0-686-86059-4); Vol. 2, The Arabic-speaking Lands, 350p. text ed. 30.00x (ISBN 0-8419-0520-7). Holmes & Meier.
Braude, Jacob M. Braude's Handbook of Stories for Toastmasters & Speakers. 1967. 16.95 (ISBN 0-13-081315-X, Reward); pap. 6.95 (ISBN 0-13-081323-0). P-H.
--Braude's Treasury of Wit & Humor. 1964. 14.95 (ISBN 0-13-081448-2, Reward); pap. 4.95 (ISBN 0-13-081380-X). P-H.
Braude, Lee. Work & Workers: A Sociological Analysis. rev. ed. LC 79-20996. 240p. 1983. Repr. of 1975 ed. lib. bdg. write for info. (ISBN 0-89874-017-7). Krieger.
Braude, M. C., et al, eds. Narcotic Antagonists. LC 73-84113. (Advances in Biochemical Psychopharmacology Ser.: Vol. 8). (Illus.). 580p. 1974. 53.00 (ISBN 0-911216-55-3). Raven.
Braude, Michael. Andy Learns about Advertising. (Career Guidance Ser.). (Illus.). (gr. 3-6). PLB 2.00 o.p. (ISBN 0-513-00295-2). Denison.
--Danny Graham, Banker. (Career Guidance Ser.). (Illus.). (gr. 3-6). PLB 2.00 o.p. (ISBN 0-513-00319-3). Denison.
--Larry Learns About Computers. (Career Guidance Ser.). (Illus.). (gr. 3-6). PLB 2.00 o.p. (ISBN 0-513-00486-6). Denison.
--Peter Enters the Jet Age. (Career Guidance Ser.). (Illus.). (gr. 3-6). PLB 2.00 o.p. (ISBN 0-513-00390-8). Denison.
--Richard Learns About Railroading. (Career Guidance Ser.). (Illus.). (gr. 3-6). PLB 2.00 o.p. (ISBN 0-513-00450-5). Denison.
--Ronald Learns about College Teaching. (Career Guidance Ser.). (Illus.). (gr. 3-6). PLB 2.00 o.p. (ISBN 0-513-00449-1). Denison.
--Shelby Goes to Wall Street. (Career Guidance Ser.). (Illus.). (gr. 3-6). PLB 2.00 o.p. (ISBN 0-513-00407-6). Denison.
--Tim Learns About Mutual Funds. (Career Guidance Ser.). (Illus.). (gr. 3-6). PLB 2.00 o.p. (ISBN 0-513-00448-3). Denison.
Braude, Monique C. & Szara, Stephen, eds. Pharmacology of Marihuana, 2 vols. LC 75-14562. (National Institute on Drug Abuse Monograph). 901p. 1976. Set. 75.50 (ISBN 0-89004-067-2). Raven.
Braude, Stephen E. ESP & Psychokinesis: A Philosophical Examination. Margolis, Joseph, ed. (Philosophical Monographs: 3rd Ser.). 300p. 1979. 27.95 (ISBN 0-87722-163-4). Temple U Pr.
Braudel, Fernand. Capitalism & Material Life, 1400-1800. (Illus.). 1974. pap. 8.95xi (ISBN 0-06-131836-1, TB1836, Torch). Har-Row.
--The Mediterranean & the Mediterranean World in the Age of Philip Second, 2 vols. rev. 2nd ed. Reynolds, Sian, tr. from Fr. (Illus.). 1418p. 1976. Vol. 1. pap. 10.95i (ISBN 0-06-090566-2, CN566, CN); Vol. 2. pap. 11.06i (ISBN 0-06-090567-0, CN567, CN). Har-Row.
--The Wheels of Commerce: Civilization & Capitalism, 15th-18th Century Vol. 2. Reynolds, Sian, tr. from Fr. LC 82-48109. (Illus.). 720p. 1983. 33.65i (ISBN 0-06-015091-2, HarpT). Har-Row.
Braue, Frederick, jt. auth. see Hugard, Jean.
Brauer, A. Die Suesswasserfauna Deutchlands. (Illus.). 1961. Repr. of 1909 ed. 140.00 (ISBN 3-7682-0045-0). Lubrecht & Cramer.
Brauer, Alan P., et al. ESO: How You & Your Lover Can Give Each Other Hours of Extended Sexual Orgasm. (Illus.). 192p. 1983. pap. 13.50 (ISBN 0-446-51270-2). Warner Bks.
Brauer, D. R. Harold, the Easter Rat. 1981. 4.95 o.p. (ISBN 0-8062-1631-X). Carlton.
Brauer, Jerald C. Images of Religion in America. Wolf, Richard C., ed. LC 67-22984. (Facet Bks). 48p. 1967. pap. 0.50 o.p. (ISBN 0-8006-3040-8, 1-3040). Fortress.
--Protestantism in America: A Narrative History. rev. ed. 1972. pap. 5.95 (ISBN 0-664-24956-6). Westminster.
Brauer, Karl O. Handbook of Pyrotechnics. (Illus.). 1974. 37.00 o.p. (ISBN 0-8206-0220-5). Chem Pub.
Brauer, Richard. Richard Brauer: Collected Papers, 3 vols. Wong, Warren J. & Fong, Paul, eds. 1980. Vol. 1. 60.00x (ISBN 0-262-02135-8); Vol. 2. 60.00x (ISBN 0-262-02148-X); Vol. 3. 60.00x (ISBN 0-262-02149-8). MIT Pr.
Brauers, W. K. Systems Analysis Planning & Decision Models. 1976. 30.25 (ISBN 0-444-41433-9). Elsevier.
Brault, Gerard J. Eight Thirteenth-Century Rolls of Arms in French & Anglo-Norman Blazon. LC 72-1065. 148p. 1973. 18.75x (ISBN 0-271-01115-7). Pa St U Pr.
Braumbaugh, James. Welders Guide. new ed. (Audel Ser.). 1983. 19.95 (ISBN 0-672-23374-6). Bobbs.
Braun, Armin C. Biology of Cancer. LC 74-20895. 169p. 1974. text ed. 11.50 o.p. (ISBN 0-201-00764-9). A-W.
--The Biology of Cancer. 169p. 26.50 (ISBN 0-201-00318-X); pap. 19.50 (ISBN 0-201-00319-8). A-W.
Braun, Aurel. Romain Foreign Policy Since 1965: The Political & Military Limits of Autonomy. LC 78-9516. (Praeger Special Studies). 1978. 27.95 o.p. (ISBN 0-03-043471-8). Praeger.
Braun, D., et al. Practical Macromolecular Organic Chemistry. Ivin, Kenneth J., tr. from Ger. (MMI Press Polymer Monograph: Vol. 4). 300p. Date not set. 70.00 (ISBN 3-7186-0059-5). Harwood Academic Pubs.
Braun, Dietrich. Identification of Plastics. 1982. pap. text ed. 14.95x (ISBN 0-686-97711-4). Macmillan.
Braun, Ernest & Cavagnaro, David. Living Water. LC 75-142443. (Images of America Ser.). (Illus.). 184p. 1974. pap. 5.95 o.p. (ISBN 0-517-52702-2). Crown.
Braun, Ernest & Macdonald, Stuart. Revolution in Miniature: The History & Impact of Semiconductor Electronics Re-Explored. 2nd ed. LC 82-1117. (Illus.). 250p. 1982. 24.95 (ISBN 0-521-24701-2); pap. 9.95 (ISBN 0-521-28903-3). Cambridge U Pr.
Braun, Frederick G., jt. auth. see Whitman, Nancy C.
Braun, Gerhard. Planning & Engineering of Shortwave Links. 252p. 1982. 39.95 (ISBN 0-471-26213-7, Pub. by Wiley Heyden). Wiley.
Braun, Hugh. Parish Churches: Their Architectural Development in England. 1970. 12.50 o.s.i. (ISBN 0-571-09045-1). Transatlantic.
Braun, Isabella. The Little Actor's Theater. Didriksen, Paula, tr. (Illus.). 10p. 1981. 10.95 (ISBN 0-399-20846-1, Philomel). Putnam Pub Group.
Braun, Jack, jt. auth. see Becker, Nancy.

Braun, K., et al. Deutsch Als Fremdsprache: Ein Unterrichtswerk Fuer Auslaender. Incl. Pt. 1. Grundkurs. text ed. 11.50x lehrbuch (ISBN 3-12-554100-X); strukturuebungen und tests 8.95x (ISBN 3-12-554150-6); dialogische uebungen 10.25x (ISBN 3-12-554160-3); glossar deutsch-englisch 2.75x (ISBN 3-12-556110-8); sprechuebungen fuer das elektronische klassenzimmer, textband. 8.60x, 8 tonbaender, 9.5 cm/s, tapes, 405.00x (ISBN 3-12-554120-4); 4 schallplatten, lektion 1-19 des grundkurses, 17 cm, 33 1/3 rpm, records 16.95x (ISBN 3-12-554110-7); compact-cassette, lektion 1-19 des grundkurses 16.65x (ISBN 0-685-47448-8); 16 tonba 200.00x (ISBN 0-685-47449-6); Pt. 1B. Ergaenzungskurs. text ed. 11.50x lehrbuch (ISBN 3-12-554500-5); glossar deutsch-englisch 2.75x (ISBN 3-12-556510-3); schallplatten, records 16.65x (ISBN 0-685-47450-X); Pt. 2. Aufbaukurs. text ed. 9.25x lehrbuch (ISBN 3-12-554200-6); strukturuebungen und tests 7.25x (ISBN 0-686-66995-9); dialogische uebungen 8.60x (ISBN 0-686-66996-7); **glossar deutsch-englisch 2.20x (ISBN 3-12-556210-4); 3 schallplatten, lektion 1-17 des aufbaukurses,17 cm, 33 1/3 rpm, records 16.65x (ISBN 3-12-554210-3); compact-cassette, lektion 1-17 des aufbaukurses 16.65x (ISBN 0-685-47451-8); 12 tonbaender, dialoge und hoer-sprechuebungen, 9.5 cm/s, tapes 221.00x (ISBN 3-12-990430-1). Schoenhof.**

Braun, Kurt. Labor Disputes & Their Settlement. LC 73-13320. 343p. 1974. Repr. of 1955 ed. lib. bdg. 18.25x (ISBN 0-8371-7121-0, BRDS). Greenwood.

Braun, Louis & Diez, W. Costumes Through the Ages. LC 82-60208. (Illus.). 256p. 1982. 45.00. Rizzoli Intl.

Braun, M. Differential Equations & Their Applications: An Introduction to Applied Mathematics. LC 74-31123. (Applied Mathematics Sciences Ser.: Vol. 15). (Illus.). xiv, 718p. 1975. pap. 18.00 (ISBN 0-387-90266-X). Springer-Verlag.

Braun, Matthew. The Kincaids. LC 75-34224. 1976. 10.00 o.p. (ISBN 0-399-11585-4). Putnam Pub Group.

--The Stuart Women. LC 79-17245. 1980. 11.95 o.p. (ISBN 0-399-12050-5). Putnam Pub Group.

Braun, Otto. A Comintern Agent in China, 1932-1939. Moore, Jeanne, tr. from Ger. LC 81-85452. (Illus.). 304p. 1982. 25.00x (ISBN 0-8047-1138-0). Stanford U Pr.

Braun, Peter, ed. Interpretation of Prostate Biopsies. (Biopsy Interpretation Ser.). 1982. text ed. write for info. (ISBN 0-89004-864-9). Raven.

Braun, R. D. Introduction to Chemical Analysis. 544p. 1982. 25.50x (ISBN 0-07-007280-9). McGraw.

Braun, Richard E. Bad Land. LC 70-79736. 1971. pap. 4.00 (ISBN 0-912330-08-2, Dist. by Inland Bk). Jargon Soc.

Braun, Robert J. Dentist's Manual of Emergency Medical Treatment. (Illus.). 1979. text ed. 15.95 (ISBN 0-8359-1263-9). Reston.

--Teachers & Power. 1973. pap. 2.95 o.p. (ISBN 0-671-21615-5, Touchstone Bks). S&S.

Braun, Sidney D. Andre Suares: Hero among Heroes. 11.00 (ISBN 0-686-38460-1). French Lit.

Braun, Sidney D. & Lainoff, Seymour, eds. Transatlantic Mirrors: Essays in Franco-American Literary Relations. (United States Authors Ser.). 1978. lib. bdg. 25.00 (ISBN 0-8057-9008-X, Twayne). G K Hall.

Braun, T. & Ghersini, G., eds. Extraction Chromatography. (Journal of Chromatography Library: Vol. 2). 592p. 1975. 68.00 (ISBN 0-444-99878-0). Elsevier.

Braun, Theodore, jt. auth. see Barrette, Paul.

Braun, Thomas, ed. see Rosenthal-Schneider, Ilse.

Braun, W., jt. ed. see Landy, Maurice.

Braun, Werner, jt. auth. see Avi-Yonah, Michael.

Braun, Wernher Von see Von Braun, Wernher & Ordway, Frederick I., 3rd.

Braun, Wolfgang. Die Kalkflachmoore. (Illus.). 1968. 16.00 (ISBN 3-7682-0580-0). Lubrecht & Cramer.

Braunberg, Rudolf & Brownjohn, John M. Betrayed Skies. LC 79-7860. 384p. 1980. 12.95 o.p. (ISBN 0-385-15183-7). Doubleday.

Braund, H. E., ed. Calling to Mind: An Account of the First Hundred Years of Steel Brothers & Company Ltd. (Illus.). 1975. 27.00 (ISBN 0-08-017415-9). Pergamon.

Braun-Falco, O., jt. auth. see Burg, G.

Braunlich, Tom. The Official Book of Penter: The Classic Game of Skill. 128p. (Orig.). 1983. pap. 7.95 (ISBN 0-8092-5522-7). Contemp Bks.

--Pente Strategy Book I. Date not set. pap. 3.50 (ISBN 0-9609414-0-1). Pente Games.

--Pente Strategy Book II. Date not set. pap. 4.00 (ISBN 0-9609414-1-X). Pente Games.

Braun-Ronsdorf, M. History of the Handkerchief. 33.50x (ISBN 0-87245-499-1). Textile Bk.

Brauns, Robert & Slater, Sarah W. Bankers Desk Reference. 1978. 42.00 (ISBN 0-88262-196-3, 78-50154). Warren.

Braunstein & Copenhaver. Environmental, Health & Control Aspects of Coal Conversion: An Information Overview, 2 vols. LC 81-65350. 1338p. 1981. Set. text ed. 130.00 (ISBN 0-250-40445-1). Ann Arbor Science.

Braunstein, Daniel N., jt. auth. see Ungson, Gerardo R.

Braunstein, H. Terry. Windows. LC 82-4292. (Artist Bk.). (Illus.). 32p. 1982. 25.00 (ISBN 0-942868-01-3). Visual Studies.

Braunstein, Herbert. Outlines of Pathology. 1st ed. LC 81-14145. (Illus.). 605p. 1982. pap. text ed. 18.95 (ISBN 0-8016-0869-4). Mosby.

Braunstein, Joseph. Musica Aeterna: Program Notes, 1961-1967. LC 72-8420. (Music Ser). 332p. 1973. Repr. of 1968 ed. lib. bdg. 37.50 (ISBN 0-306-70554-0). Da Capo.

Braunthal, Gerard. The West German Social Democrats, 1969-1982: Profile of a Party in Power. (Replica Edition Ser.). 400p. 1983. softcover 25.00x (ISBN 0-86531-958-8). Westview.

Braunthal, Julius. History of the International: World Socialism Nineteen Forty-Three to Nineteen Sixty-Eight. LC 67-17667. 656p. 1980. lib. bdg. 45.00 (ISBN 0-89158-369-6). Westview.

Braunwald. Beta Andrenergic Blockade. (International Congress Ser.: No. 446). 1979. 53.00 (ISBN 0-444-90038-1). Elsevier.

Braunwald, Eugene & Mock, Michael B., eds. Congestive Heart Failure: Current Research & Clinical Applications. LC 82-908. 400p. 1982. 34.50 (ISBN 0-8089-1469-3, 790657). Grune.

Brautigan, Richard. The Abortion. 1971. pap. 2.95 o.p. (ISBN 0-671-20873-X, Touchstone Bks). S&S.

--A Confederate General from Big Sur. 1979. 8.95 o.s.i. (ISBN 0-440-01692-4, Sey Lawr). Delacorte.

--A Confederate General from Big Sur. 1979. pap. 3.95 o.s.i. (ISBN 0-440-51693-5, Delta). Dell.

--Dreaming of Babylon. 1978. pap. 6.95 (ISBN 0-440-52059-2, Delta). Dell.

--In Watermelon Sugar. 1969. pap. 3.95 o.s.i. (ISBN 0-440-54026-7, Delta). Dell.

--June Thirtieth, June Thirtieth. 1977. 6.95 o.s.i. (ISBN 0-440-04295-X, Sey Lawr). Delacorte.

--June Thirtieth, June Thirtieth. 1978. pap. 3.95 o.s.i. (ISBN 0-440-54265-0, Delta). Dell.

--Pill Versus the Springhill Mine Disaster. 1969. pap. 2.50 o.s.i. (ISBN 0-440-56956-7, Delta). Dell.

--Revenge of the Lawn. 1971. pap. 2.95 o.p. (ISBN 0-671-20961-2, Touchstone Bks). S&S.

--Rommel Drives on Deep into Egypt. 1970. pap. 2.50 o.s.i. (ISBN 0-440-57496-X, Delta). Dell.

--So the Wind Won't Blow It All Away. 160p. 1982. 12.95 (ISBN 0-440-08195-5, Sey Lawr). Delacorte.

--The Tokyo-Montana Express. 1981. pap. 5.95 (ISBN 0-440-58679-8, Delta). Dell.

--The Toyko-Montana Express. 1980. 10.95 o.s.i. (ISBN 0-440-08770-8, Sey Lawr); pap. 2.50 o.s.i. (ISBN 0-440-03725-5). Delacorte.

--Trout Fishing in America. Bd. with The Pill Versus the Springhill Mine Disaster; In Watermelon Sugar. (Illus.). 156p. 1968. 14.95 o.s.i. (ISBN 0-440-07436-3, Sey Lawr). Delacorte.

--Trout Fishing in America. 1969. pap. 3.95 o.s.i. (ISBN 0-440-59126-0, Delta). Dell.

--Willard & His Bowling Trophies. 1977. pap. 2.95 o.p. (ISBN 0-671-22745-9, Touchstone Bks). S&S.

Bravais, A. On the Systems Formed by Points Regularly Distributed on a Plane or in Space. pap. 3.00 (ISBN 0-686-60370-2). Polycrystal Bk Serv.

Bravard, Robert S., jt. auth. see Peplow, Michael W.

Brave, John R. Uncle John's Original Bread Book. 1976. pap. 2.25 o.s.i. (ISBN 0-515-05830-0). Jove Pubns.

Braveboy-Wagner, Jacqueline A. The Venezuela-Guyana Border Dispute: Britain's Colonial Legacy in Latin America. (Replica Edition Ser.). 200p. 1983. softcover 20.00x (ISBN 0-86531-953-7). Westview.

Bravenec, Lorence C. Taxation of Subchapter S Corporations & Shareholders: Including 1979 Supplement. (Incl. a 1979 suppl.). 1978. text ed. 30.00 (ISBN 0-685-59690-7, J6-1429). PLI.

Braverman, H. Precalculus Mathematics: Algebra, Trigonometry & Analytical Geometry. LC 74-13571. 533p. 1975. 16.50 (ISBN 0-683-01013-1, Pub. by W & W). Krieger.

Braverman, Jack R., ed. see Educational Research Council of America.

Braverman, Libbie L. & Silver, Samuel M. Six-Day Warriors: An Introduction to Those Who Gave Israel Its Vigor and Its Victories. LC 75-78093. (Illus.). (gr. 5-10). 1969. 4.95 o.p. (ISBN 0-8197-0199-8). Bloch.

Braverman, Miriam. Youth, Society & the Public Library. LC 78-17267. 1979. 20.00 (ISBN 0-8389-0260-X). ALA.

Braverman, Robert & Neumann, Bill. Here Is Your Hobby: Slot Car Racing. (Here Is Your Hobby Ser.). (Illus.). (gr. 6-9). 1969. PLB 5.29 o.p. (ISBN 0-399-60254-2). Putnam Pub Group.

Braverman, Sydell, jt. auth. see Chevigny, Hector.

Bravmann, A. Rene. The Poetry of Form: Hans & Thelma Lehmann Collection of African Art. LC 82-83027. (Illus.). 80p. (Orig.). 1982. 14.95 (ISBN 0-935558-09-8); pap. 9.95 (ISBN 0-935558-12-8). Henry Art.

Bravmann, R. A. Islam & Tribal Art in West Africa. (African Studies: No. 11). (Illus.). 180p. 1974. 39.50 (ISBN 0-521-20192-6). Cambridge U Pr.

Brawley, Benjamin. Early American Negro Writers. Foner, Philip S., ed. (Black Rediscovery Ser). 1970. pap. 6.95 (ISBN 0-486-22623-9). Dover.

--Early Negro American Writers: Selections with Biographical & Critical Introductions. 9.50 (ISBN 0-8446-0509-3). Peter Smith.

Brawley, Benjamin G. Negro Genius. LC 66-17517. 1966. Repr. of 1937 ed. 10.00x (ISBN 0-8196-0184-5). Biblo.

Brawley, Ernest. Selena. 1980. pap. 2.75 o.p. (ISBN 0-451-09242-2, E9242, Sig). NAL.

Brawley-Martinez, Emilia E. Rural Social & Community Work in the U. S. & U. K. A Cross-Cultural Perspective. 304p. 1982. 27.95 (ISBN 0-03-060433-8). Praeger.

Brawne, Michael. The Museum Interior: Temporary & Permanent Display Techniques. (Illus.). 1982. 33.95 (ISBN 0-8038-9500-3). Architectural.

Brawner, C. O., ed. Stability in Surface Mining, Vol. 3. LC 81-70690. 872p. 1982. 39.00x (ISBN 0-89520-292-1). Soc Mining Eng.

Brawner, Carroll O., ed. First International Conference on Uranium Mine Waste Disposal. LC 80-69552. (Illus.). 626p. 1980. 25.00x (ISBN 0-89520-279-4). Soc Mining Eng.

Brawner, Darnell L. The Clarence Chronicle. 1981. 4.95 (ISBN 0-8062-1754-5). Carlton.

Brawner, Julianne R., et al. The Kudzu-Ivy Guide to Southern Colleges. LC 81-82293. 580p. (Orig.). 1982. pap. 10.95 (ISBN 0-9605142-1-X). Kudzu-Ivy.

Bray & Trump. Dictionary of Archaeology. rev. ed. 1982. pap. 6.95 (ISBN 0-14-051116-4). Penguin.

Bray, Alan. Homosexuality in Renaissance England. 132p. (Orig.). 1982. pap. 7.50 (ISBN 0-907040-13-6). Gay Mens Pr.

Bray, Barbara, tr. see Crebillon, Claude P.

Bray, Barbara, tr. see Nadeau, Maurice.

Bray, Barbara, tr. see Orieux, Jean.

Bray, Barbara, tr. see Starobinski, Jean.

Bray, Charles W. Psychology & Military Proficiency. LC 69-13837. Repr. of 1948 ed. lib. bdg. 15.75x (ISBN 0-8371-1444-6, BRMI). Greenwood.

Bray, Dennis, jt. auth. see Alberts, Bruce.

Bray, F. E., jt. ed. see Hurst, C. V.

Bray, F. Sewell. The Interpretation of Accounts. LC 79-22380. 232p. 1979. Repr. of 1957 ed. text ed. 13.00 (ISBN 0-914348-29-9). Scholars Bk.

Bray, Frank S. The Accounting Mission. LC 73-84525. 1973. Repr. of 1951 ed. text ed. 13.00 (ISBN 0-914348-01-9). Scholars Bk.

Bray, Frank T. & Moodie, Michael. Defense Technology & the Atlantic Alliance: Competition or Collaboration? LC 77-80297. (Foreign Policy Report Ser.). 42p. 1977. 5.00 (ISBN 0-89549-000-5). Inst Foreign Policy Anal.

Bray, George A. The Obese Patient. LC 75-20798. (Major Problems in Internal Medicine Ser.: Vol. 9). (Illus.). 480p. 1976. 25.00 o.p. (ISBN 0-7216-1931-2). Saunders.

Bray, Gerald L. Holiness & the Will of God: Perspectives on the Theology of Tertullian. LC 79-5211. (New Foundations Theological Library). (Peter Toon & Ralph Martin series editors). 1980. 12.95 (ISBN 0-8042-3705-0). John Knox.

Bray, Helen, jt. auth. see Guttentag, Marcia.

Bray, J. & Sanchez, Gomez. Spanish in the Office. 128p. (Span.). 1980. pap. text ed. 6.25x (ISBN 0-582-35236-3). Longman.

Bray, J. W., jt. auth. see Hoek, E.

Bray, Jacqueline H., jt. auth. see Cohen, Theodore J.

Bray, Jeremy. Production, Purpose & Structure. LC 82-42603. 1982. 19.95x (ISBN 0-312-64778-6). St Martin.

Bray, John, jt. auth. see Barker, John N.

Bray, K. M. & Croxton, P. C. Matrix Analysis of Structures. 160p. 1976. pap. text ed. 14.95 (ISBN 0-7131-3373-2). E Arnold.

Bray, Mark. Universal Primary Education in Nigeria: A Study of Kano State. 272p. (Orig.). 1982. pap. write for info. (ISBN 0-7100-0933-X). Routledge & Kegan.

Bray, Olin H. Distributed Database Management Systems. LC 79-3185. 176p. 1981. 20.95x (ISBN 0-669-03396-0). Lexington Bks.

Bray, Olin H. & Freeman, Harvey A. Data-Base Computers. LC 78-24765. 192p. 1979. 23.95x (ISBN 0-669-02834-7). Lexington Bks.

Bray, R. N. Dredging: A Handbook for Engineers. 288p. 1979. pap. text ed. 65.00 (ISBN 0-686-43106-5). E Arnold.

Bray, Reginald A. Boy Labour & Apprenticeship. LC 79-56952. (The English Working Class Ser.). 1980. lib. bdg. 22.00 o.s.i. (ISBN 0-8240-0106-0). Garland Pub.

Bray, Robert C. & Bushnell, Paul E., eds. Diary of a Common Soldier in the American Revolution, 1775-1783: An Annotated Edition of the Military Journal of Jeremiah Greenman. LC 77-18528. (Revolutionary Heritage Ser.: Vol. 3). (Illus.). 1978. 5.00 (ISBN 0-917012-04-6). RI Pubns Soc.

Bray, Rodney A., jt. auth. see Prudhoe, Stephen.

Bray, Ruth G. De, tr. see Reymond, Arnold.

Bray, Sewell F. Four Essays in Accounting Theory bound with Some Accounting Terms & Concepts. LC 82-48352. (Accountancy in Transition Ser.). 160p. 1982. lib. bdg. 20.00 (ISBN 0-8240-5305-2). Garland Pub.

Bray, Warwick. Everyday Life of the Aztecs. (Everyday Life Ser). (Illus.). (gr. 7-11). 1969. 6.75 o.p. (ISBN 0-399-20053-3). Putnam Pub Group.

Braybrooke, David. Ethics in the World of Business. LC 82-18547. (Philosophy & Society Ser.). 512p. 1983. text ed. 32.50x (ISBN 0-8476-7069-4); pap. text ed. 13.95x (ISBN 0-8476-7107-0). Rowman.

Braybrooke, Susan, ed. see American Institute of Architects.

Brayer, K. Data Communications Via Fading Channels. LC 74-33060. (IEEE Press Selected Reprint Ser.). 1975. 23.95 o.p. (ISBN 0-471-09815-9, Pub. by Wiley-Interscience); pap. text ed. 20.95 (ISBN 0-471-09816-7). Wiley.

Brayer, K, ed. Data Communications Via Fading Channels. LC 74-33060. 1975. 31.95 (ISBN 0-87942-047-2). Inst Electrical.

Brayer, Yves & Faxon, Alicia. Jean-Louis Forain: Artist, Realist, Humanist. Walker, Janet, ed. Grasselli, Margaret M., tr. from Fr. LC 82-82968. (Illus.). 60p. (Orig.). 1982. pap. 10.00 (ISBN 0-88397-042-2). Intl Exhibit Foun.

Brayman, Harold. Corporative Management in a World of Politics: The Public, Political & Governmental Problems of Business. 1967. 21.95 o.p. (ISBN 0-07-007350-3, P&RB). McGraw.

Braymer, Daniel H. & Roe, A. C. Rewinding Small Motors. 3rd ed. LC 80-29580. 432p. 1983. Repr. of 1949 ed. lib. bdg. write for info. (ISBN 0-89874-291-9). Krieger.

Braymer, Marjorie. Atlantis: The Biography of a Legend. LC 82-16727. (Illus.). 256p. (gr. 7 up). 1983. 12.95 (ISBN 0-689-50264-8, McElderry Bk). Atheneum.

--Walls of Windy Troy: A Biography of Heinrich Schliemann. LC 60-6207. (gr. 7 up). 1966. pap. 1.45 (ISBN 0-15-694201-1, VoyB). HarBraceJ.

Braynard, Frank O. Lives of the Liners. LC 48-304. (Illus.). 1947. pap. 4.00 o.p. (ISBN 0-87033-041-1). Cornell Maritime.

Brayton, Abbott A. & Landwehr, Stephana J. The Politics of War & Peace: A Survey of Thought. LC 80-67206. 320p. (Orig.). 1981. lib. bdg. 22.00 (ISBN 0-8191-1726-9); pap. text ed. 12.00 (ISBN 0-8191-1727-7). U Pr of Amer.

Brayton, R., jt. auth. see Spence, R.

Brazell, Karen, tr. from Jap. The Confessions of Lady Nijo. 320p. 1973. 15.00x (ISBN 0-8047-0929-7); pap. 6.95 (ISBN 0-8047-0930-0, SP 140). Stanford U Pr.

Brazelton, T. Berry. Doctor & Child. 1976. 8.95 o.s.i. (ISBN 0-440-02074-3, Sey Lawr). Delacorte.

--Infants & Mothers. 1972. pap. 9.95 (ISBN 0-440-54076-3, Delta). Dell.

--Infants & Mothers: Differences in Development. rev. ed. 1983. pap. 9.95 (ISBN 0-440-54010-0, Delta). Dell.

--Infants & Mothers: Differences in Development. rev. ed. 1983. 16.95 (ISBN 0-440-04259-3, Sey Lawr). Delacorte.

--Infants & Mothers: Individual Differences in Development. (Illus.). 1969. 13.95 o.s.i. (ISBN 0-440-04045-0, Sey Lawr). Delacorte.

--Neonatal Behavioral Assessment Scale. (Illus.). 1974. 13.00 (ISBN 0-433-04030-0). Intl Ideas.

--Neonatal Behavioural Assessment Scale. (Clinics in Developmental Medicine Ser.: Vol. 50). 88p. 1973. text ed. 13.00 (ISBN 0-433-04030-0, Pub. by Spastics Intl England); pap. text ed. 4.95 (ISBN 0-686-96929-4). Lippincott.

--Toddlers & Parents: A Declaration of Independence. 1974. 14.95 o.s.i. (ISBN 0-440-08750-3, Sey Lawr). Delacorte.

Brazer, Clarence. Essays of U. S. Adhesive Postage Stamps. LC 75-40503. 1977. 35.00x o.p. (ISBN 0-88000-081-3). Quarterman.

Brazier, M. Bibliography of Electroencephalography, Vol. 1. 1950. 12.25 (ISBN 0-444-40081-8). Elsevier.

Brazier, M., jt. ed. see Walter, D.

Brazier, M. A., ed. Growth & Development of the Brain: Nutritional, Genetic, & Environmental Factors. LC 75-14565. (International Brain Research Organization Ser.: Vol. 1). 412p. 1975. 43.00 (ISBN 0-89004-037-0). Raven.

Brazier, Mary, jt. ed. see Honrubia, Vicente.

Brazier, Mary, jt. ed. see Sigman, David S.

Brazier, Mary A. & Coceani, Flavio. Brain Dysfunction in Infantile Febrile Convulsions. LC 75-14564. (International Brain Research Organization Monograph: Vol. 2). 384p. 1976. 41.50 (ISBN 0-89004-068-0). Raven.

Brazier, Mary A., jt. auth. see Meisami, Esmail.

Brazier, Mary A. & Petsche, Hellmuth, eds. Architectonics of the Cerebral Cortex. LC 77-83694. (International Brain Research Organization (IBRO) Monograph Ser.: Vol. 3). 502p. 1978. 52.00 (ISBN 0-89004-140-7). Raven.

Brazier, Mary A., jt. ed. see Hobson, J. Allan.

Brazil. Commissao de Linhas Telegraphicas Estrategieas de Matto-Grosso ao Amazonas. Lectures Delivered by Colonel Candido Mariano da Silva Rondon on the 5th, 7th, & 9th of Oct, 1915. LC 68-55215. 1968. Repr. of 1916 ed. lib. bdg. 23.50x o.p. (ISBN 0-8371-1088-2, ROLO). Greenwood.

Brazil, Harold E. A World Apart: American Military Diplomacy in Southeast Asia. 1976. pap. text ed. 7.00 (ISBN 0-8191-0058-7). U Pr of Amer.

Braziller, Karen, jt. ed. see Braziller, Michael.

Braziller, Michael & Braziller, Karen, eds. Persea I: An International Review. 1977. pap. 3.95 o.p. (ISBN 0-89255-020-1). Persea Bks.

--Persea Three. 152p. (Orig.). 1982. pap. 3.95 o.p. (ISBN 0-89255-057-0). Persea Bks.

--Persea Two: An International Review. 1978. pap. 3.95 o.p. (ISBN 0-89255-028-7). Persea Bks.

Brazini, Luigi. The Europeans. 1983. price not set (ISBN 0-671-24578-3). S&S.

Brazleton, T. Berry. Toddlers & Parents. 1976. pap. 8.95 (ISBN 0-440-58772-7, Delta). Dell.

Brcher, Charles & Horton, Raymond, eds. Setting Municipal Priorities 1983. 200p. 1982. 25.00 (ISBN 0-8147-1042-5). Columbia U Pr.

Breach, jt. auth. see Gordon.

Breach, N., jt. auth. see Fishman, W. J.

Break, George F. Financing Government in a Federal System. (Studies of Government Finance). 1980. 22.95 (ISBN 0-8157-1068-2); pap. 8.95 (ISBN 0-8157-1067-4). Brookings.

Break, George F.. & Break, George F. Federal Tax Reform: The Impossible Dream? (Studies of Government Finance). 142p. 1975. 12.95 (ISBN 0-8157-1072-0); pap. 5.95 (ISBN 0-8157-1071-2). Brookings.

Break, George F., jt. auth. see Break, George F..

Breakey, Gail F. & Voulgaropoulos, Emmanuel. Laos Health Survey: Mekong Valley, 1968-1969. LC 76-14. 140p. 1976. pap. text ed. 7.50x (ISBN 0-8248-0378-7). UH Pr.

Breakwell, Glynis M. Threatened Identities. 270p. 1983. 34.95x (ISBN 0-471-10233-4, Pub. by Wiley-Interscience). Wiley.

Brealey, L., jt. auth. see Energlyn, L.

Brealey, Richard & Myers, Stewart C. Principles of Corporate Finance. (Finance Ser.). (Illus.). 1980. text ed. 26.95x (ISBN 0-07-007380-5, C); study guide 9.95 (ISBN 0-07-007381-3); instructor's manual 30.00 (ISBN 0-07-007382-1). McGraw.

Brealey, Richard A. Introduction to Risk & Return from Common Stocks. 1969. 15.00x (ISBN 0-262-02047-5). MIT Pr.

--Security Prices in a Competitive Market: More About Risk & Return from Common Stocks. 1971. 16.00x (ISBN 0-262-02077-7). MIT Pr.

Brealy, jt. auth. see Lorie.

Brealy, John, jt. auth. see Ainworth, Maryan W.

Bream, Howard N., et al, eds. A Light unto My Path: Old Testament Studies in Honor of Jacob M. Myers. LC 73-85042. (Gettysburg Theological Studies, No. 4). 576p. 1974. 27.95 (ISBN 0-87722-026-3). Temple U Pr.

Brearley, A., et al. An Outline of Statistical Methods for Use in the Textile Industry. 1975. 8.95 o.s.i. (ISBN 0-87245-605-6). Textile Bk.

Brearley, Alan & Treadle, John. The Worsted Industry. 198p. 1982. 59.00x (ISBN 0-686-87182-0). State Mutual Bk.

Brearley, C. Residential Work with the Elderly. (Library of Social Work Ser.). 1977. 14.95x (ISBN 0-7100-8587-7); pap. 7.95 (ISBN 0-7100-8588-5). Routledge & Kegan.

Brearley, C. Paul. Risk & Social Work. (Hazards & Helping Ser.). 224p. (Orig.). 1982. pap. 9.95 (ISBN 0-7100-0999-2). Routledge & Kegan.

--Social Work, Aging & Society. (Library of Social Work Ser.). 1975. 14.50x (ISBN 0-7100-8184-7); pap. 7.95 (ISBN 0-7100-8185-5). Routledge & Kegan.

Brearley, H. C. Homicide in the United States. LC 69-14913. (Criminology, Law Enforcement, & Social Problems Ser.: No. 36). 1969. Repr. of 1932 ed. 15.00x (ISBN 0-87585-036-7). Patterson Smith.

Brearley, Joan. Ibizan Hounds. (Illus.). 128p. 1980. 4.95 (ISBN 0-87666-694-2, KW-060). TFH Pubns.

Brearley, Joan M. All About Himalayan Cats. (Illus.). 96p. (Orig.). 1976. 6.95 (ISBN 0-87666-756-6, PS736). TFH Pubns.

--Book of the Afghan Hound. (Illus.). 1978. 20.00 (ISBN 0-87666-665-9, H-991). TFH Pubns.

--The Book of the Cocker Spaniel. (Illus.). 300p. 1982. 29.95 (ISBN 0-87666-737-X, H-1034). TFH Pubns.

--The Book of the Doberman Pinscher. (Illus.). 1976. 17.95 (ISBN 0-87666-658-6, H-968). TFH Pubns.

--The Book of the Pug. (Illus.). 320p. 1980. 24.95 (ISBN 0-87666-683-7, H-1021). TFH Pubns.

--This Is the Afghan Hound. (Illus.). 1965. 12.95 (ISBN 0-87666-231-9, PS639). TFH Pubns.

--This Is the Alaskan Malamute. (Illus.). 415p. 1975. 19.95 (ISBN 0-87666-650-0, PS-737). TFH Pubns.

--This Is the Irish Setter. (Illus.). 480p. 1975. 19.95 (ISBN 0-87666-655-1, H-952). TFH Pubns.

--This Is the Lhasa Apso. (Illus.). 1977. text ed. 14.95 (ISBN 0-87666-663-2, PS-744). TFH Pubns.

--This Is the Samoyed. (Illus.). 384p. 1975. 17.95 (ISBN 0-87666-379-X, H-954). TFH Pubns.

Brearley, Joan M. & Easton, Allen. Book of the Shih Tzu. (Illus.). 304p. 1980. 34.95 (ISBN 0-87666-664-0, H-996). TFH Pubns.

Brearley, Joan M. & Nicholas, Anna K. The Book of the Boxer. (Illus.). 1977. 24.95 (ISBN 0-87666-652-7, H-959). TFH Pubns.

--This Is the Skye Terrier. (Illus.). 560p. 1975. 19.95 (ISBN 0-87666-396-X, PS-708). TFH Pubns.

Brearley, Joan M., jt. auth. see Anderson, Marlene.

Brearley, Joan M., jt. auth. see Nicholas, Anna K.

Brearley, Molly & Hitchfield, Elizabeth. Guide to Reading Piaget. LC 67-25234. 1969. 8.00x o.p. (ISBN 0-8052-3092-0); pap. 3.45 (ISBN 0-8052-0222-6). Schocken.

Brearley, Molly, ed. The Teaching of Young Children: Some Applications of Piaget's Learning Theory. LC 70-98939. (Illus.). 1978. pap. 5.50 o.p. (ISBN 0-8052-0597-7). Schocken.

Brearley, Paul, et al. Leaving Residential Care. 1982. 15.00x o.p. (ISBN 0-422-77920-2, Pub. by Tavistock); pap. 7.95x (ISBN 0-422-77930-X). Methuen Inc.

Brearly, Joan M. This Is the Siberian Husky. (Illus.). 543p. 1974. 17.95 (ISBN 0-87666-392-7, PS-707). TFH Pubns.

Brearly, Joan M. & Nicholas, Anna K. This Is the Bichon Frise. (Illus.). 1973. 14.95 (ISBN 0-87666-247-5, PS-700). TFH Pubns.

Breasted, Mary. I Shouldn't Be Telling You This. LC 82-48141. 384p. 1983. 15.95 (ISBN 0-06-015092-0, HarpT). Har-Row.

Breathed, Berke. Bloom County: American Tails. (Illus.). 160p. (Orig.). 1983. pap. 6.70i (ISBN 0-316-10710-7). Little.

Breault, Joseph. Seeking Purity of Heart: The Gift of Ourselves to God. (Illus.). 96p. (Orig.). 1975. pap. 2.50 (ISBN 0-914544-07-1). Living Flame Pr.

Brebbia. Computational Hydraulics. 1982. text ed. 39.95. Butterworth.

Brebbia, C. A. Dynamic Analysis of Offshore Structures. (Illus.). 1979. 69.95 (ISBN 0-408-00393-6). Butterworth.

Brebbia, C. A., ed. Boundary Element Methods in Engineering, Southampton, England 1982: Proceedings. (Illus.). 649p. 1982. 59.00 (ISBN 0-387-11819-5). Springer-Verlag.

Brebner, J. Environmental Psychology in Building Design. (Illus.). x, 213p. 1982. 37.00 (ISBN 0-85334-969-X, Pub. by Applied Sci England). Elsevier.

Brechbuhl, E. Conversation Handbook for Policeman. 128p. 1977. 35.00x (ISBN 0-7121-5619-4, Pub. by Macdonald & Evans). State Mutual Bk.

Brecheen, Joel. Tennis Made Easy. 1971. pap. 3.00 (ISBN 0-87980-160-3). Wilshire.

Brecher, Charles, jt. auth. see Ostow, Miriam.

Brecher, Charles & Horton, Raymond D., eds. Setting Municipal Priorities, 1982. LC 81-66978. 464p. 1981. text ed. 29.95x (ISBN 0-87154-137-8). Russell Sage.

Brecher, Charles, jt. ed. see Horton, Raymond D.

Brecher, Irving & Abbas, S. A. Foreign Aid & Industrial Development in Pakistan. (Perspectives on Development Ser.: No. 1). 1971. 37.50 (ISBN 0-521-08339-7). Cambridge U Pr.

Brecher, Jeremy, et al, eds. Brass Valley: The Story of Working People's Lives & Struggles in an American Industrial Region. 340p. 1982. 29.95 (ISBN 0-87722-271-1); pap. 14.95 (ISBN 0-87722-272-X). Temple U Pr.

Brecher, Kenneth & Setti, Ginancarlo. High Energy Astrophysics & Its Relation to Elementary Particle Physics. LC 74-19794. 1974. 37.50x; pap. 12.50x o.p. (ISBN 0-686-96797-6). MIT Pr.

Brecher, Kenneth & Feirtag, Michael, eds. Astronomy of the Ancients. (Illus.). 1979. 16.50 (ISBN 0-262-02137-4); pap. 7.95 (ISBN 0-262-52070-2). MIT Pr.

Brecher, Michael. Nehru's Mantle: The Politics of Succession in India. LC 75-32653. 1976. Repr. of 1966 ed. lib. bdg. 19.75x (ISBN 0-8371-8553-X, BRNM). Greenwood.

Brechling, F. P., ed. see International Economic Association.

Brechner, Irv. Getting into Computers: A Career Guide to Today's Hottest New Field. 224p. (Orig.). 1983. pap. 4.95 (ISBN 0-345-30172-2). Ballantine.

Brechner, Irv, jt. auth. see Schwartz, Lester.

Brecht, Bertolt. Brecht: Mutter Courage und Ihre Kinder. Sander, Volkmar, ed. (Illus., Ger.). (gr. 9-12). 1964. pap. text ed. 7.95x (ISBN 0-19-500835-9). Oxford U Pr.

--Manual of Piety (Die Hauspostille) Bentley, Eric, tr. (Bilingual ed.). 1966. pap. 2.45 o.s.i. (ISBN 0-394-17436-4, B129, BC). Grove.

--The Rise & Fall of the City of Mahagonny. Auden, W. H. & Kallman, Chester, trs. LC 75-11466. 1976. 12.95 (ISBN 0-87923-149-1); pap. 6.95 (ISBN 0-87923-205-6). Godine.

Brecht, George. Chance Imagery. (Orig.). 1965. pap. 3.50 o.p. (ISBN 0-89366-069-8). Ultramarine Pub.

Brecht, Richard D., jt. ed. see Chvany, Catherine V.

Breck & Brown. Chemistry for Science & Engineering. 450p. Date not set. 29.95 (ISBN 0-07-092372-8). McGraw.

Breck, Donald W. Zeolite Molecular Sieves: Structure, Chemistry & Use. LC 73-11028. 1974. 82.00 (ISBN 0-471-09985-6, Pub. by Wiley-Interscience). Wiley.

Breckenridge, Adam C. Executive Privilege: Presidential Control over Information. LC 73-82011. x, 188p. 1974. 13.50x o.p. (ISBN 0-8032-0835-9). U of Nebr Pr.

Breckenridge, James F. The Theological Self-Understanding of the Catholic Charismatic Movement. LC 79-6198. 154p. 1980. pap. text ed. 9.25 (ISBN 0-8191-1006-X). U Pr of Amer.

Breckenridge, Muriel. Lap Quilting: How to Make Beautiful Quilted Projects - Large & Small. LC 81-50545. (Illus.). 96p. 1981. 14.95 (ISBN 0-8069-5446-9); lib. bdg. 17.79 (ISBN 0-8069-5447-7); pap. 6.95 (ISBN 0-8069-7522-9). Sterling.

Breckinridge, John, jt. auth. see Hughes, John.

Breckinridge, S. P; see Bernard, William S.

Brecknock, Albert. Byron: A Study of the Poet in the Light of New Discoveries. LC 67-30808. (Studies in Byron, No. 5). (Illus.). 1969. Repr. of 1926 ed. lib. bdg. 27.95x o.p. (ISBN 0-8383-0708-6). Haskell.

Bredehoeft, John. Groundwater Management: The Use of Numerical Models. (Water Resources Monograph). 1980. pap. 10.00 (ISBN 0-87590-306-1, WR0500). Am Geophysical.

Breder, Charles M., Jr. Field Book of Marine Fishes of the Atlantic Coast. (Putnam Nature Field Bks.). (Illus.). 1948. 7.95 o.p. (ISBN 0-399-10524-7). Putnam Pub Group.

Brederlow, G., et al. The High-Power Iodine Laser. (Springer Ser. in Optical Sciences: Vol. 34). (Illus.). 182p. 1983. 35.00 (ISBN 0-387-11792-X). Springer-Verlag.

Brederoo, P. F., et al, eds. Electron Microscopy, 4 vols. Incl. Vol. 1: Physics. 106.50 (ISBN 0-444-86179-3); Vol. 2: Biology. 159.75 (ISBN 0-444-86180-7); 1vol. 3: Analysis. 85.00 (ISBN 0-444-86181-5); Vol. 4: High Voltage. 64.00 (ISBN 0-444-86182-3). 1981. Set. 340.50 (ISBN 0-444-86183-1, Pub. by Applied Sci England). Elsevier.

Bredes, Don. Hard Feelings. LC 76-42213. 1977. 8.95 o.p. (ISBN 0-689-10745-5). Atheneum.

Bredimas, A. E. Methods of Interpretation & Community Law. (European Studies in Law Ser: Vol. 6). 1978. 51.00 (ISBN 0-444-85081-3, North-Holland). Elsevier.

Bredo, Eric & Feinberg, Walter, eds. Knowledge & Values in Social & Educational Research. LC 82-10371. 456p. 1982. 29.95 (ISBN 0-87722-242-8); pap. 12.95 (ISBN 0-87722-245-2). Temple U Pr.

Bredow, Miriam. Medical Office Procedures. (Illus.). 416p. 1973. pap. text ed. 17.05 (ISBN 0-07-007425-9, G); instructor's manual & key 8.20 (ISBN 0-07-007426-7). McGraw.

Bredow, Miriam, jt. auth. see Cooper, Marian.

Bredow, Miriam, et al. Medical Office Procedures. 2nd ed. (Illus.). 480p. 1981. pap. text ed. 16.40 (ISBN 0-07-007441-0, G); simulation recordings, non-steno 115.00 (ISBN 0-07-087647-9); simulation recordings, steno 115.00 (ISBN 0-07-087646-0); instr's manual 7.30 (ISBN 0-07-007442-9). McGraw.

Bredsdorff, Elias. Danish: An Elementary Grammar & Reader. 1959. 17.95x (ISBN 0-521-09821-1). Cambridge U Pr.

Bredsdorff, Elias, tr. Contemporary Danish Prose. LC 74-41. 375p. 1974. Repr. of 1958 ed. lib. bdg. 19.25x (ISBN 0-8371-7358-2, BRDP). Greenwood.

Bredvold, L. I., ed. The Best of Dryden. 1933. 17.95 o.p. (ISBN 0-471-06965-5). Wiley.

Bredvold, L. I., et al, eds. Eighteenth Century Poetry & Prose. 3rd ed. 1493p. 1973. text ed. 25.95 o.p. (ISBN 0-471-06957-4). Wiley.

Bredvold, Louis I., ed. The Best of Dryden. 1933. text ed. 21.95x (ISBN 0-673-15655-9). Scott F.

Bree, G. & Kroff, A. Y. Twentieth Century French Drama. 1969. text ed. 22.95 (ISBN 0-02-313820-3). Macmillan.

Bree, Germaine. Camus & Sartre. 288p. 1972. pap. 3.95 o.s.i. (ISBN 0-440-51003-1, Delta). Dell.

Bree, Germaine, ed. see Beckett, Samuel.

Bree, Germine. Twentieth-Century French Literature, 1920-1970. Guiney, Louise, tr. LC 82-15980. (Illus.). 352p. 1983. lib. bdg. 25.00x (ISBN 0-226-07195-2). U of Chicago Pr.

Bree, M. Groundwork of the Leschetizky Method. LC 68-25284. (Studies in Music, No. 42). (Illus.). 1969. Repr. of 1902 ed. lib. bdg. 36.95x (ISBN 0-8383-0290-4). Haskell.

Bree, Marlin, jt. auth. see Spiess, Gerry.

Breed, C. B. Surveying. 3rd ed. 495p. 1971. 31.95x (ISBN 0-471-10070-6). Wiley.

Breed, C. B. & Hosmer, G. L. Principles & Practice of Surveying, 2 vols. Incl. Vol. 1. Elementary Surveying. 11th ed. 717p. 1977. 35.95x (ISBN 0-471-02979-3); Vol. 2. Higher Surveying. 8th ed. 543p. 1962. 35.95 (ISBN 0-471-10164-8). Wiley.

Breed, Paul F & Sniderman, Florence M. Dramatic Criticism Index: Bibliography of Commentaries on Playwrights from Ibsen to the Avant-Garde. LC 79-127598. 1972. 52.00x (ISBN 0-8103-1090-2). Gale.

Breeden, James O., ed. Advice Among Masters: The Ideal in Slave Management in the Old South. LC 79-54054. (Contributions in Afro-American & African Studies: No. 51). (Illus.). xxvi, 350p. 1980. lib. bdg. 29.95 (ISBN 0-313-20658-9, BRS/). Greenwood.

Breeden, Maurice J. The Intimate Love Story of Anthony & Cleopatra. (Great Love Stories of History Library). (Illus.). 83p. 1983. 16.75 (ISBN 0-86650-056-1). Gloucester Art.

Breem, Wallace. The Leopard & the Cliff. LC 78-71884. 1979. 10.95 o.p. (ISBN 0-312-48008-3). St Martin.

Breemen, Peter G. van see Van Breemen, Peter G.

Breen, David H. The Canadian Prairie West & the Ranching Frontier. 312p. 1983. 28.95x (ISBN 0-8020-5548-6). U of Toronto Pr.

Breen, Eileen, compiled by. Mary the Second Eve. 40p. 1977. pap. 1.25 (ISBN 0-686-81627-7). TAN Bks Pubs.

Breen, George E. Do-It-Yourself Marketing Research. (Illus.). 1977. 28.95 (ISBN 0-07-007445-3, P&RB). McGraw.

Breen, John F. Encyclopedia of Reptiles & Amphibians. (Illus.). 576p. 1974. text ed. 24.95 (ISBN 0-87666-220-3, H935). TFH Pubns.

Breen, John J., jt. auth. see Hill, Evan.

Breen, Jon L. Listen for the Click. 192p. 1983. 12.95 (ISBN 0-8027-5492-9). Walker & Co.

--Listen for the Clock. 200p. 1983. 12.95 (ISBN 0-686-38883-6). Walker.

Breen, Robert S. Chamber Theater. (P-H Series in Theatre & Drama). 1978. pap. 13.95 ref. ed. (ISBN 0-13-125211-9). P-H.

Breen, T. H. Puritans & Adventurers: Change & Persistence in Early America. 1982. pap. 8.95 (ISBN 0-19-503207-1). Oxford U Pr.

Breen, T. H. & Innes, Stephen. Myne Owne Ground: Race & Freedom on Virginia's Eastern Shore, 1640-1676. (Illus.). 1980. 17.95x (ISBN 0-19-502727-2). Oxford U Pr.

--Myne Owne Ground: Race & Freedom on Virginia's Eastern Shore, 1640-1676. 152p. 1982. pap. 5.95x (ISBN 0-19-503206-3). Oxford U Pr.

Breen, T. H., ed. Shaping Southern Society: The Colonial Experience. 1976. pap. text ed. 7.95x (ISBN 0-19-502078-2). Oxford U Pr.

Breen, W. Proof Coins Struck at the U.S. Mints: Updated. 1983. Repr. of 1953 ed. softcover 10.00 (ISBN 0-915262-94-0). S J Durst.

Breene, R. G., Jr. Theories of Spectral Line Shape. LC 80-20664. 344p. 1981. 39.95x (ISBN 0-471-08361-5, Pub. by Wiley-Interscience). Wiley.

Breese, Burtis B. & Hall, Caroline. Beta Hemolytic Streptococcal Diseases. (Illus.). 287p. 1978. 50.00 (ISBN 0-471-09476-5, Pub. by Wiley Med). Wiley.

Breese, Dave. Know the Marks of Cults. LC 74-21907. 128p. 1975. pap. 3.95 (ISBN 0-88207-704-X). Victor Bks.

Breese, Gerald. Urbanization in Newly Developing Countries. (Illus., Orig.). 1966. pap. 11.95 ref. ed. (ISBN 0-13-939181-9). P-H.

Breeze, Katie. Nekkid Cowboy. 288p. 1982. 11.95 (ISBN 0-931722-17-9). Corona Pub.

Breffny, Brian De see De Breffny, Brian.

Breffny, Brian de see De Breffny, Brian.

Bregenzer, John. Tryin' to Make It: Adapting to the Bahamas. (Illus.). 96p. (Orig.). 1982. lib. bdg. 18.00 (ISBN 0-8191-2621-7); pap. text ed. 7.00 (ISBN 0-8191-2622-5). U Pr of Amer.

Breger, Louis. From Instinct to Identity: The Development of Personality. LC 73-5766. (P-H Personality Ser). (Illus.). 400p. 1974. ref. ed. 23.95 (ISBN 0-13-331637-8). P-H.

Breggin, Peter R. Psychiatric Drugs: Hazards to the Brain. 352p. 1983. text ed. 24.95 (ISBN 0-8261-2930-7). Springer Pub.

Bregman, Allyn A. Laboratory Investigations in Cell Biology. 250p. 1982. pap. text ed. 14.95 (ISBN 0-471-86241-X). Wiley.

Bregman, Douglas M. & Miller, Peter G., eds. Model Contingencies for Real Estate Sales. 9.50 (ISBN 0-943954-00-2). Tremont Pr.

Bregman, Jacob I., jt. auth. see Gehm, Harry W.

Bregy, Katherine. Queen of Paradox: A Stuart Tragedy (Mary Stuart, Queen of Scots) 221p. 1982. Repr. of 1950 ed. lib. bdg. 35.00 (ISBN 0-8495-0612-3). Arden Lib.

--The Story of Saint Francis de Sales: Patron of Catholic Writers. 108p. 1982. Repr. of 1958 ed. lib. bdg. 35.00 (ISBN 0-686-81682-X). Century Bookbindery.

Bregy, Katherine M. From Dante to Jeanne D'Arc: Adventures in Medieval Life & Letters. LC 78-774. (Science & Culture Ser.). 1978. Repr. of 1933 ed. lib. bdg. 16.00x (ISBN 0-313-20290-7, BRFD). Greenwood.

Brehaut, Roger N. Ecology of Rocky Shores. (Studies in Biology: No. 139). 64p. 1982. pap. text ed. 8.95 (ISBN 0-7131-2839-9). E Arnold.

Breheny, Michael J., ed. Development in Urban & Regional Analysis. (London Papers in Regional Science). 162p. 1979. pap. 14.00x (ISBN 0-85086-078-4, Pub. by Pion England). Methuen Inc.

Brehier, Emile. History of Philosophy, 7 vols. Incl. Vol. 1. The Hellenic Age. Thomas, Joseph, tr. LC 63-20912. 1963. pap. text ed. 5.00x (ISBN 0-226-07217-7); Vol. 2. The Hellenistic & Roman Age. Baskin, Wade, tr. LC 63-20913. 1965. pap. text ed. 7.00x (ISBN 0-226-07221-5, P199); Vol. 3. The Middle Ages & the Renaissance. Baskin, Wade, tr. LC 63-20912. 1965. pap. text ed. 5.00x (ISBN 0-226-07219-3); Vol. 4. The Seventeenth Century. Baskin, Wade, tr. LC 63-20912. 1966. pap. text ed. 5.00x (ISBN 0-226-07225-8); Vol. 5. The Eighteenth Century. Baskin, Wade, tr. LC 63-20912. 1971. pap. text ed. 5.00x o.p. (ISBN 0-226-07227-4); Vol. 6. The Nineteenth Century: Period of Systems 1800-1850. Baskin, Wade, tr. LC 63-20912. 1973. pap. text ed. 5.00x (ISBN 0-226-07229-0); Vol. 7. Contemporary Philosophy - Since 1850. Baskin, Wade, tr. LC 63-20912. 1973. pap. text ed. 5.00x (ISBN 0-226-07231-2, P538). Phoen). U of Chicago Pr.

Brehier, L. The Life & Death of Byzantium. (Europe in the Middle Ages Selected Studies: Vol. 5). 1977. 57.50 (ISBN 0-444-11128-X, North-Holland). Elsevier.

Brehm, Henry P., jt. auth. see Lopata, Helena Z.

Brehm, J. W., jt. auth. see Wicklund, R. A.

Brehm, Sharon S., et al, eds. Developmental Social Psychology: Theory & Research. (Illus.). 384p. 1981. text ed. 24.00x (ISBN 0-19-502840-6); pap. text ed. 13.95x (ISBN 0-19-502841-4). Oxford U Pr.

Breide, Ole. Three Weeks On - Three Weeks Off. LC 80-52960. 1982. 9.95 (ISBN 0-533-04801-X). Vantage.

Breidenbach, Monica E., jt. auth. see Hover, Margot K.

Breig, Alf. Adverse Mechanical Tension of the Central Nervous System: An Analysis of Cause & Effect. LC 77-88852. 1978. 84.50 o.p. (ISBN 0-471-04137-8, Pub. by Wiley Medical). Wiley.

Breihan, Carl W. The Day Jesse James Was Killed. (Illus.). 1979. pap. 1.75 o.p. (ISBN 0-451-08611-2, E8611, Sig). NAL.

--Great Gunfighters of the West. 1977. pap. 1.50 o.p. (ISBN 0-451-07434-3, W7434, Sig). NAL.

--Gunslingers. (Illus.). 300p. 1983. 12.95 (ISBN 0-89769-076-1); pap. 6.95 (ISBN 0-89769-048-6). Pine Mntn.

--Outlaws of the Old West. (Illus.). 1980. pap. 1.75 o.p. (ISBN 0-451-09172-8, E9172, Sig). NAL.

--Wild Women of the West. 1982. pap. 2.50 (ISBN 0-451-11951-7, AE1951, Sig). NAL.

Breiman, Leo. Statistics: With a View Toward Applications. LC 72-3131. 480p. 1973. text ed. 29.95 (ISBN 0-395-04232-1, 3-05972). HM.

Breimer & Speiser, eds. Topics in Pharmaceutical Sciences. 1982. 64.00 (ISBN 0-444-80403-X). Elsevier.

Breimer, D. D., ed. Towards Better Safety of Drugs & Pharmaceutical Products. 1980. 59.75 (ISBN 0-444-80216-9). Elsevier.

Breimer, T. Environmental Factors & Cultural Measures Affecting the Nitrate of Spinach. 1982. pap. text ed. 22.00 (ISBN 90-247-3053-8, Pub. by Martinus Nijhoff Netherlands). Kluwer Boston.

Breinburg, Petronella. Doctor Shawn. LC 74-15265. (Illus.). 32p. (gr. k-2). 1975. 10.53i (ISBN 0-690-00721-3, TYC-J); PLB 10.89 (ISBN 0-690-00722-1). Har-Row.

--Shawn Goes to School. LC 73-8003. (Illus.). 32p. (ps-2). 1974. PLB 10.89 (ISBN 0-690-00277-7, TYC-J). Har-Row.

Breines, Wini. Community & Organization in the New Left 1962-1968: The Great Refusal. 224p. 1982. 26.95 (ISBN 0-03-060099-5). Praeger.

Breinhost, Willy. Cheer up! Things Might Get Worse. 8.50 (ISBN 0-392-08393-0, SpS). Sportshelf.

Breining, Greg. Boundary Waters. (Illus.). 96p. 1983. 19.95X (ISBN 0-931714-20-6). Nodin Pr.

Breipohl, Arthur M. Probabilistic System Analysis: An Introduction to Probabilistic Models, Decisions & Applications of Random Processes. LC 77-94920. 352p. 1970. 33.95 (ISBN 0-471-10181-8). Wiley.

Breipohl, W., ed. Olfaction & Endocrine Regulation: Proceedings of the Fourth European Chemoreception Research Organization Mini-Symposium & the Second International Laboratory Workshop on Olfaction, Essen FRC, 1981. 460p. 1982. pap. 26.00 (ISBN 0-904147-35-5). IRL Pr.

Breisach, Ernst. Caterina Sforza: A Renaissance Virago. LC 67-25511. (Illus.). 1967. 15.00x o.s.i. (ISBN 0-226-07271-1). U of Chicago Pr.

--Historiography: Ancient, Medieval, & Modern. LC 82-20246. 416p. 1983. pap. 12.50 (ISBN 0-226-07275-4). U of Chicago Pr.

Breisacher, E. H., ed. Last Resting Places, Being a Compendium of Fact Pertaining to the Mortal Remains of the Famous & Infamous. LC 79-52704. (Illus.). 320p. 1983. 19.95 (ISBN 0-87850-032-4). Darwin Pr.

Breit, William & Elzinga, Kenneth G. The Antitrust Casebook. 400p. 1982. text ed. 16.95 (ISBN 0-03-060147-9). Dryden Pr.

Breitenbach, Mrs. Edgar, tr. see Bracco, Patrick & Lebovici, Elisabeth.

Breitenlohner, Peter & Duerr, Hans-Peter. Unified Theories of Elementary Particles: Proceedings. (Lecture Notes in Physics Ser.: Vol. 160). 217p. 1982. pap. 12.50 (ISBN 0-387-11560-9). Springer-Verlag.

Breiter, Herta S. Fuel & Energy. LC 77-18560. (Read About Science Ser.). (Illus.). (gr. k-3). 1978. PLB 13.30 (ISBN 0-8393-0083-2). Raintree Pubs.

--Pollution. LC 77-26886. (Read About Science Ser.). (Illus.). (gr. k-3). 1978. PLB 13.30 (ISBN 0-8393-0081-6). Raintree Pubs.

--Time & Clocks. LC 77-19007. (Read About Science Ser.). (Illus.). (gr. k-3). 1978. PLB 13.30 (ISBN 0-8393-0088-3). Raintree Pubs.

--Weather. LC 77-27239. (Read About Science Ser.). (Illus.). (gr. k-3). 1978. PLB 13.30 (ISBN 0-8393-0079-4). Raintree Pubs.

Breithaupt, S. & Agnew, H. W. The Dallas Doctors' Diet. 208p. 1983. 12.95 (ISBN 0-07-007447-X, GB). McGraw.

Breitmaier, E., et al. Atlas of Carbon-13 NMR Data, 2 vols. Set. casebound 285.00 (ISBN 0-471-25582-3, Pub. by Wiley Heyden). Wiley.

Breitmaier, Eberhard & Bauer, Gerhard. Thirteen C-NMR Spectroscopy: A Working Manual with Exercises. Cassels, Bruce K., tr. from Ger. (MMI Press Polymer Monographs). 600p. write for info. (ISBN 3-7186-0022-6). Harwood Academic.

Breitman, George, ed. see Trotsky, Leon.

Breitman, George, et al. The Assassination of Malcolm X. Miah, Malik, ed. (Illus.). 1977. cloth o. p. 9.00 (ISBN 0-87348-472-X); pap. 2.95 (ISBN 0-87348-473-8). Path Pr NY.

Breitner, Bina, jt. auth. see Perry, Henry B.

Breitowicz, Jakob. Through Hell to Life. LC 82-61793. (Illus.). 1983. 10.00 (ISBN 0-88400-091-5). Shengold.

Breivik, Patricia S. Open Admissions & the Academic Library. LC 77-5816. 1977. pap. 10.00 (ISBN 0-8389-3195-2). ALA.

--Planning the Library Instruction Program. 156p. (Orig.). 1982. pap. text ed. 10.00 (ISBN 0-8389-0358-4). ALA.

Brejcha, M. F. & Samuels, C. L. Automotive Chassis & Accessory Circuits. LC 76-14835. (Illus.). 1977 19.95 (ISBN 0-13-055475-8). P-H.

Brekhman, I. I. & Nesterenko, I. F. Brown Sugar & Health. (Illus.). 104p. 1982. 20.00 (ISBN 0-08-026837-4). Pergamon.

Brekhovskikh, L. M. Waves in Layered Media. 2nd ed. LC 79-51695. (Applied Mathematics & Mechanics Ser.). 1980. 66.50 o.p. (ISBN 0-12-130560-0). Acad Pr.

Brekke, Jerald. An Assessment of the Bloc Grant Provisions of the Omnibus Crime Control & Safe Streets Act of 1968: The Missouri Experience. 1977. pap. text ed. 7.25 o.p. (ISBN 0-8191-0254-7). U Pr of Amer.

Breland, O. P., jt. auth. see Barker, Kenneth.

Breland, Osmond P. Manual of Comparative Anatomy. 2nd ed. (Zoological Sciences Ser.). (Illus.). 1953. text ed. 13.95 o.p. (ISBN 0-07-007449-6, C). McGraw.

Brelsford, William M., jt. auth. see Levenbach, Hans.

Brem, M. M. The Man Caught by a Fish. (Arch Bks: Set 4). 1967. laminated bdg. 0.89 (ISBN 0-570-06025-7, 59-1136). Concordia.

--Mary's Story. (Arch Bks: Set 4). 1967. laminated bdg. 0.89 (ISBN 0-570-06029-X, 59-1140). Concordia.

Breman, Jan. Patronage & Exploitation: Changing Agrarian Relations in South Gujarat, India. LC 73-186114. 1974. 33.00x (ISBN 0-520-02197-5). U of Cal Pr.

Breman, von L. see Von Breman, L., et al.

Brembeck, Winston L. & Howell, William S. Persuasion: A Means of Social Influence. 2nd ed. (Illus.). 384p. 1976. 19.95 (ISBN 0-13-661090-0). P-H.

Bremer, Gerry, jt. auth. see Mackie, Bob.

Bremer, Hans J., et al. Disturbances of Amino Acid Metabolism: Clinical Chemistry & Diagnosis. LC 78-31995. (Illus.). 536p. 1980. text ed. 57.00 (ISBN 0-8067-0251-6). Urban & S.

Bremer, James, jt. auth. see Zaritsky, Howard M.

Bremer, Jan M., jt. auth. see Mastronarde, Donald J.

Bremmel, J. H. Van see IFPtC4 Working Conference, Amsterdam, 1976.

Bremner, Robert H. & Reichard, Gary W., eds. Reshaping America: Society & Institutions, 1945-1960. LC 82-3409. (U.S.A. 20-21: Studies in Recent American History: No. 1). 415p. 1982. 22.50x (ISBN 0-8142-0308-6). Ohio St U Pr.

Bremner, W. Fraser. The Hyperlipoproteinaemias & Atherosclerosis: Current Understanding of Their Inter-Relationships, Vol. 1. Horrobin, D. F., ed. (Annual Research Reviews). 1979. 26.00 (ISBN 0-88831-056-0). Eden Pr.

Brems, Hans. Fiscal Theory: Government, Inflation, & Growth. LC 82-47905. 1983. price not set (ISBN 0-669-05688-X). Lexington Bks.

--Inflation, Interest, & Growth: A Synthesis. LC 78-19226. 192p. 1980. 21.95x (ISBN 0-669-02466-X). Lexington Bks.

--Labor, Capital & Growth. LC 72-7015. (Illus.). 160p. 1973. 16.95x o.p. (ISBN 0-669-84905-7). Lexington Bks.

--Output, Employment, Capital, & Growth: A Quantitative Analysis. LC 73-7071. (Illus.). 349p. 1973. Repr. of 1959 ed. lib. bdg. 19.75x (ISBN 0-8371-6906-2, BROE). Greenwood.

Bremser, W., et al. Chemical Shift Ranges in Carbon-13 NMR Spectroscopy. vvii, 891p. 1982. 137.50X (ISBN 0-89573-053-7). Verlag Chemie.

Bren, Carol. I Love You, Dear. 32p. 1979. pap. 0.75 o.p. (ISBN 0-930756-44-4). Women's Aglow.

Brena. La Ley Federal del Trabajo. 250p. (Span.). 1983. pap. text ed. write for info. (ISBN 0-06-310067-3, Pub. by HarLA Mexico). Har-Row.

Brena, Steven & Chapman, Stanley, eds. Management of Chronic Pain. 326p. 1983. text ed. 40.00 (ISBN 0-89335-165-2). SP Med & Sci Bks.

Brena, Steven F. Chronic Pain. LC 77-15888. 1978. 8.95 o.p. (ISBN 0-689-10874-5). Atheneum.

Brenan, Gerald. A Life of One's Own, Vol. 1. 1979. pap. 9.95 (ISBN 0-521-29734-6). Cambridge U Pr.

--Personal Record Nineteen Twenty to Nineteen Seventy-Two, Vol. 2. 1979. pap. 9.95 (ISBN 0-521-29735-4). Cambridge U Pr.

--St. John of the Cross: His Life & Poetry. Nicholson, Lynda, tr. LC 72-83577. (Illus.). 224p. 1973. 39.50 (ISBN 0-521-20006-7); pap. 10.95x (ISBN 0-521-09953-6). Cambridge U Pr.

--South from Granada. LC 80-40376. (Illus.). 282p. 1980. pap. 10.95 (ISBN 0-521-28029-X). Cambridge U Pr.

--Spanish Labyrinth. 2nd ed. 1950-1960. pap. 44.50 (ISBN 0-521-04314-X); pap. 11.95 (ISBN 0-521-09107-1, 107). Cambridge U Pr.

--Thoughts in a Dry Season. LC 78-4508. 1978. 21.95 (ISBN 0-521-22006-8). Cambridge U Pr.

Brenan, J. P. see Jackson, B. D., et al.

Brenchley, David L. & Turley, C. David, eds. Industrial Source Sampling. LC 72-96908. 300p. 1973. 39.95 (ISBN 0-250-40012-X). Ann Arbor Science.

Brend. Advances in Tagmemics. LC 73-81526. (North Holland Linguistic Ser.: Vol. 9). 600p. 1974. pap. 30.25 (ISBN 0-444-10534-4, North-Holland). Elsevier.

Brenda see Avery, Gillian.

Brendel, LeRoy A. & Leffingwell, Elsie. English Usage Drills & Exercises: Programmed for the Typewriter. 1968. 5.12 o.p. (ISBN 0-07-007472-0, G). McGraw.

--English Usage Drills & Exercises: Programmed for the Typewriter. 2nd ed. (gr. 10-11). 1977. pap. 7.64 (ISBN 0-07-007485-2, G). McGraw.

Brendel, LeRoy A. & Near, D. Punctuation Drills & Exercises: Programmed for the Typewriter. 1970. pap. text ed. 6.64 (ISBN 0-07-007478-X, G). McGraw.

Brendel, LeRoy A. & Near, Doris. Punctuation Drills & Exercises. 2nd ed. (gr. 9-12). 1978. pap. text ed. 7.64 (ISBN 0-07-007479-8, G). McGraw.

--Spelling Drills & Exercises: Programmed for the Typewriter. 3rd ed. (Illus.). 1979. pap. text ed. 7.64 (ISBN 0-07-007491-7, G). McGraw.

Brendel, LeRoy A., et al. Communication Word Power: Vocabulary & Spelling Master, a Text-Workbook for College. 1968. 11.60 (ISBN 0-07-007471-2, G); instructor's guide & key 7.95 (ISBN 0-07-007473-9). McGraw.

Brendel, W. & Zink, R. A., eds. High Altitude Physiology & Medicine I: Physiology of Adaptation. (Topics in Environmental Physiology & Medicine Ser.). (Illus.). 190p. 1981. 65.00 (ISBN 0-387-90482-4). Springer-Verlag.

Brendon, Piers. The Life & Death of the Press Barons. LC 82-73017. 288p. 1983. 14.95 (ISBN 0-689-11341-2). Atheneum.

Brenellerie, Paul P. De La. Supplement Au Contrat Social. (Rousseausim, 1788-1797). 1978. Repr. lib. bdg. 115.00x o.p. (ISBN 0-8287-1421-5). Clearwater Pub.

Breneman, David W. & Finn, Chester E., eds. Public Policy & Private Higher Education. (Studies in Higher Education Policy). 1978. 24.95 (ISBN 0-8157-1066-6); pap. 10.95 (ISBN 0-8157-1065-8). Brookings.

Breneman, John W. Mathematics. 2nd ed. (Illus.). 1944. text ed. 22.95 (ISBN 0-07-007480-1, G). McGraw.

--Mechanics. 3rd ed. (Illus.). 1960. 20.95 (ISBN 0-07-007538-7, G); answers to odd-numbered problems 1.00 (ISBN 0-07-007543-3). McGraw.

--Strength of Materials. 3rd ed. 1965. 20.95 (ISBN 0-07-007536-0, G); answers key 1.00 (ISBN 0-07-007537-9). McGraw.

Brenenstuhl, Daniel C., jt. auth. see Certo, Samuel C.

Brenenstuhl, Daniel L., jt. auth. see Certo, Samuel.

Brener, Etta R., jt. auth. see Harrington, Joan.

Brenet, Michel, pseud. Bibliographie des Bibliographies Musicales. LC 73-125065. (Music Ser). 1971. Repr. of 1913 ed. lib. bdg. 22.50 (ISBN 0-306-70002-6). Da Capo.

Brenet, Michel. Les Concerts en France Sous l'Ancien Regime. LC 68-16224. (Music Ser). 1970. Repr. of 1900 ed. lib. bdg. 45.00 (ISBN 0-306-71061-7). Da Capo.

Brengelmann, J. C., ed. Progress in Behaviour Therapy. LC 75-5542. (Illus.). 340p. 1975. 39.40 o.p. (ISBN 0-387-07224-1). Springer-Verlag.

Brenig, W., jt. ed. see Stuke, J.

Brenkert, K. Elementary Theoretical Fluid Mechanics. LC 60-11718. 348p. 1960. 16.50 (ISBN 0-471-10197-4, Pub by Wiley). Krieger.

Brenman-Gibson, Margaret. Clifford Odets: American Playwright. LC 80-7927. (Illus.). 1981. 30.00 (ISBN 0-689-11160-6). Atheneum.

Brennan, Andrew, ed. Worksite Health Promotion. 96p. 1982. pap. text ed. 9.95 (ISBN 0-89885-142-4). Human Sci Pr.

Brennan, Andrew, ed. see Elder, Crawford.

Brennan, Bernard P. William James. (U. S. Authors Ser.: No. 131). 1968. lib. bdg. 10.95 o.p. (ISBN 0-8057-0408-6, Twayne). G K Hall.

Brennan, Frank E. Personal Selling: A Professional Approach. 448p. 1983. text ed. write for info. (ISBN 0-574-20685-X, 13-3685); write for info. instr's. guide (ISBN 0-574-20686-8, 13-3686). SRA.

Brennan, G. & Buchanan, J. The Power to Tax. LC 79-56862. (Illus.). 300p. 1980. 27.95 (ISBN 0-521-23329-1). Cambridge U Pr.

Brennan, Gale. What If.... (Illus.). 32p. (Orig.). (ps-2). 1980. pap. 1.95 o.p. (ISBN 0-89542-932-2). Ideals.

Brennan, J. Applications of Critical Path Techniques. 1968. 22.50 (ISBN 0-444-19976-4). Elsevier.

Brennan, J. G., et al. Food Engineering Operations. 2nd ed. (Illus.). 1976. 45.00x (ISBN 0-85334-694-1, Pub. by Applied Sci England). Elsevier.

--Food Engineering Operations. 2nd ed. (Illus.). xiv, 532p. 1981. Repr. 45.00 (ISBN 0-85334-694-1, Pub. by Applied Sci England). Elsevier.

Brennan, Jan. Dream of Destiny. LC 79-8555. 1980. 10.95 o.p. (ISBN 0-385-14983-2). Doubleday.

Brennan, Jennifer. The Original Thai Cookbook. (Illus.). 276p. 1981. 12.95 (ISBN 0-399-90110-8, Marek). Putnam Pub Group.

Brennan, Joseph P. Evil Always Ends. (Illus.). 128p. 1983. 15.00 (ISBN 0-937986-53-4). D M Grant.

Brennan, Lawrence. Freshman English One (Grammar) (Monarch College Outlines). pap. 4.95 o.p. (ISBN 0-671-08025-3). Monarch Pr.

--Freshman English Two (Composition) (Monarch College Outlines). pap. 4.95 o.p. (ISBN 0-671-08043-1). Monarch Pr.

Brennan, M. Theory of Economic Statics. 2nd ed. 1970. 21.00 (ISBN 0-13-913624-X). P-H.

Brennan, Mary, ed. Employer Contributions & Delinquencies Under Erisa Institute, Las Vegas, Nov. 12-15, 1978. (Orig.). 1979. pap. 7.50 (ISBN 0-89154-097-0). Intl Found Employ.

Brennan, Mary E., ed. Canadian Conference, 13th Annual, Oct. 4-8, 1980: Proceedings. 145p. (Orig.). 1981. pap. 11.00 (ISBN 0-89154-145-4). Intl Found Employ.

--Canadian Conference, 14th Annual Nov. 23-27, 1981 Proceedings. 280p. (Orig.). 1982. pap. 14.00 (ISBN 0-89154-177-2). Intl Found Employ.

Brennan, Mary E. & Hieb, Elizabeth A., eds. Investments Institute, Hollywood, Florida, April 27 to 30, 1980: Proceedings. 137p. 1980. pap. 10.00 (ISBN 0-89154-134-9). Intl Found Employ.

Brennan, Michael. The War in Clare Nineteen Eleven-Nineteen Twenty-One: Personal Memoirs of the Irish War of Independence. 112p. 1980. 25.00x (ISBN 0-7165-0125-2, Pub. by Irish Academic Pr Ireland). Biblio Dist.

Brennan, Neil. Anthony Powell. (English Authors Ser.: No. 158). 1974. lib. bdg. 11.95 o.p. (ISBN 0-8057-1454-5, Twayne). G K Hall.

Brennan, Peter, jt. auth. see Handman, Heidi.

Brennan, R. O. Nutrigenetics: New Concepts for Relieving Hypoglycemia. 1977. pap. 2.25 (ISBN 0-451-09392-5, E9392, Sig). NAL.

Brennan, R. O., ed. see Addanki, Sam & Kindrick, Shirley A.

Brennan, Richard D. Dr. Brennan's Diet Menus. rev. ed. LC 79-91110. 1980. pap. 2.50 o.p. (ISBN 0-89081-218-7). Harvest Hse.

Brennan, Steve, ed. Photo Lab Index: Compact Three. 3rd, rev. ed. 725p. (Orig.). 1982. pap. text ed. 13.95 (ISBN 0-87100-185-3, 2185). Morgan.

Brennan, T. Politics & Government in Britain. LC 78-171673. 10.95x (ISBN 0-521-08366-4). Cambridge U Pr.

Brennan, Tim, et al. The Social Psychology of Runaways. LC 75-42947. 1978. 28.95x (ISBN 0-669-00565-7). Lexington Bks.

Brennan, Tom. Politics & Government in Britain. 2nd ed. LC 82-4145. (Illus.). 352p. 1982. pap. 14.95 (ISBN 0-521-28600-X). Cambridge U Pr.

Brennan, W. K. Shaping the Education of Slow Learners. (Special Needs in Education Ser.). 1974. 14.95 (ISBN 0-7100-7984-2); pap. 4.95 (ISBN 0-7100-7985-0). Routledge & Kegan.

Brennan, William T. & Crowe, James W. Guide to Problems & Practices in First Aid & Emergency Care. 4th ed. 208p. 1981. wire coil (ISBN 0-697-07390-4); instr's manual avail. (ISBN 0-697-07396-3). Wm C Brown.

Brennecke, John & Amick, Robert. Psychology: Understanding Yourself. 1975. text ed. 7.04 o.p. (ISBN 0-02-640170-3, 64017); tchr's manual 1.44 o.p. (ISBN 0-02-640180-0, 64018). Glencoe.

Brennecke, John H. & Amick, Robert G. Psychology & Human Experience. 2nd ed. 1978. pap. text ed. 20.95x (ISBN 0-02-471030-X); wkbk 8.95 (ISBN 0-02-471060-1); readings to accompany 9.95x (ISBN 0-02-471050-4). Macmillan.

--Significance: The Struggle We Share: Book of Readings. 1971. pap. text ed. 3.95x o.p. (ISBN 0-02-473370-9). Glencoe.

Brennecke, John J. & Amick, Robert G. Psychology & Human Experience. LC 73-7373. (Illus.). 320p. 1974. pap. text ed. 10.95x o.p. (ISBN 0-02-473210-9, 47321); wkbk 3.95x o.p. (ISBN 0-02-473230-3, 47323); readings 6.95x o.p. (ISBN 0-02-473220-6, 47322). Glencoe.

Brenneman, H. G. Meditaciones Para la Nueva Madre. 80p. 1982. Repr. of 1978 ed. 2.75 (ISBN 0-311-40032-9). Casa Bautista.

Brenneman, Walter L., Jr. Spirals: A Study in Symbol, Myth & Ritual. LC 77-26365. 1978. pap. text ed. 8.25 (ISBN 0-8191-0463-9). U Pr of Amer.

Brenneman, Walter L., Jr., et al. The Seeing Eye: Hermeneutical Phenomenology in the Study of Religion. LC 81-47174. 168p. 1982. 15.95x (ISBN 0-271-00291-3). Pa St U Pr.

Brennenstuhl, Waltraud. Control & Ability: Towards a Biocybernetics of Language. (Pragmatics & Beyond Ser.: III: 4). 120p. (Orig.). 1982. pap. 16.00 (ISBN 90-272-2522-2). Benjamins North Am.

Brenner, Barbara. Beware! These Animals Are Poison. LC 77-27591. (Illus.). (gr. 2-6). 1979. 8.95 (ISBN 0-698-20438-7, Coward). Putnam Pub Group.

--Bodies. (Illus.). 48p. (ps-3). 1973. 9.95 (ISBN 0-525-26770-0, 0966-290). Dutton.

--A Dog I Know. LC 82-47572. (Illus.). 32p. (gr. k-4). 1983. 8.61i (ISBN 0-06-020684-5, HarpJ); PLB 8.89g (ISBN 0-06-020685-3). Har-Row.

--Faces. (Illus.). (ps-1). 1970. 10.95 (ISBN 0-525-29518-6, 01064-310). Dutton.

--Have You Ever Heard of a Kangaroo Bird? (Illus.). 48p. (gr. 3-5). 1980. 7.95 (ISBN 0-698-20446-8, Coward). Putnam Pub Group.

--Little One Inch. (Illus.). 32p. (ps-3). 1977. 6.95 o.p. (ISBN 0-698-20408-5, Coward). Putnam Pub Group.

--On the Frontier with Mr. Audubon. (Illus.). (gr. 3-6). 1977. 7.95 (ISBN 0-698-20385-2, Coward). Putnam Pub Group.

--Walt Disney's The Penguin That Hated the Cold. (Disney's Wonderful World of Reading Ser.: No. 7). (Illus.). (ps-3). 1973. 4.95 (ISBN 0-394-82628-0, BYR); PLB 4.99 (ISBN 0-394-92628-5). Random.

--Walt Disney's The Three Little Pigs. (Disney's Wonderful World of Reading Ser.: No. 6). (Illus.). (ps-3). 1974. 4.95 (ISBN 0-394-82522-5, BYR); PLB 4.99 (ISBN 0-394-92522-X). Random.

Brenner, Barbara & Bank Street College of Education. Love & Discipline. 224p. (Orig.). 1983. pap. 5.95 (ISBN 0-345-30520-5). Ballantine.

Brenner, Barry E., jt. auth. see Simon, Robert.

Brenner, Barry M. & Rector, Floyd C., eds. The Kidney, 2 vols. LC 74-25474. (Illus.). 2708p. 1981. Set. text ed. 145.00 (ISBN 0-7216-1969-X); Vol. 1. 75.00 (ISBN 0-7216-1968-1). Saunders.

Brenner, Charles. An Elementary Textbook of Psychoanalysis. rev. ed. 280p. 1974. pap. 4.95 (ISBN 0-385-09884-7, Anch). Doubleday.

Brenner, Daniel & Rivers, William, eds. Free but Regulated: Conflicting Traditions in Media Law. 320p. 1982. text ed. 24.95x (ISBN 0-8138-0756-5). Iowa St U Pr.

Brenner, David. Hot Pretzels With Mustard: And Other Revelations of a South Philadelphia Boychik. LC 82-72575. 300p. 1982. 14.95 (ISBN 0-87795-442-9). Arbor Hse.

--Soft Pretzels with Mustard. (Illus.). 1983. 14.95 (ISBN 0-87795-442-9). Arbor Hse.

Brenner, Donald J., jt. ed. see Brown, Steven R.

Brenner, Egon & Javid, M. Analysis of Electric Circuits. 2nd ed. (Electrical & Electronic Engineering Ser.). 1967. text ed. 32.50 (ISBN 0-07-007630-8, C). McGraw.

Brenner, Egon, jt. auth. see Javid, Mansour.

Brenner, Everett, ed. The Information Age in Perspective: Proceedings of the ASIS Annual Meeting, 1978, Vol. 15. LC 64-8303. 1978. pap. 17.50x o.s.i. (ISBN 0-914236-22-9). Knowledge Indus.

Brenner, Gerry. Concealments in Hemingway's Works. 300p. 1983. 22.50 (ISBN 0-8142-0338-8). Ohio St U Pr.

Brenner, H. Transport Processes in Porous Media. Date not set. price not set (ISBN 0-07-007645-6). McGraw.

Brenner, Lenni. Zionism in the Age of the Dictators. 256p. 1983. 16.95 (ISBN 0-88208-163-2); pap. 8.95 (ISBN 0-88208-164-0). Lawrence Hill.

Brenner, Martha. Fireworks! (Illus.). 128p. (gr. 3-7). 1983. PLB 9.95 (ISBN 0-8038-2400-9). Hastings.

Brenner, Menachem. Option Pricing: Theory & Applications. (Salomon Brothers Center Bks.). 1983. write for info. (ISBN 0-669-05714-2). Lexington Bks.

Brenner, Michael. The Structure of Action. LC 80-16125. 1980. 27.50 (ISBN 0-312-76710-2). St Martin.

Brenner, Michael, et al, eds. The Social Contexts of Method. LC 77-17903. 1978. 25.00x (ISBN 0-312-73165-5). St Martin.

Brenner, R. P., jt. ed. see Brand, E. W.

Brenner, Shauna C. & Smoot, Shields. The Vegetable Lover's Cookbook. (Illus.). 128p. (Orig.). 1983. pap. 7.95 (ISBN 0-8092-5642-8). Contemp Bks.

Brenner, Vincent C. & Davies, Jonathan. West's Intermediate Accounting. (Illus.). 1100p. 1983. text ed. 24.95 (ISBN 0-314-63307-3); instrs.' manual avail. (ISBN 0-314-63310-3); Working Papers, Pt. I avail. (ISBN 0-314-72286-6); Working Papers, Pt. II avail. (ISBN 0-314-72287-4); student guide avail. (ISBN 0-314-63308-1); solutions manual avail. (ISBN 0-314-63309-X). West Pub.

Brenni, Vito J., compiled by. Book Illustration & Decoration: A Guide to Research. LC 80-1701. (Art Reference Collection Ser.: No. 1). viii, 191p. 1980. lib. bdg. 29.95 (ISBN 0-313-22340-8, BBI/). Greenwood.

--Bookbinding: A Guide to the Literature. LC 82-15810. 200p. 1983. lib. bdg. 35.00 (ISBN 0-313-23718-2, BBB/). Greenwood.

Brent, Allen. Philosophical Foundations for the Curriculum. (Unwin Education Books). 1978. text ed. 22.50x (ISBN 0-04-370084-5); pap. text ed. 8.95x (ISBN 0-04-370085-3). Allen Unwin.

Brent, Bill. Unto Perfection. 90p. 1983. pap. 6.95 (ISBN 0-913408-82-4). Friends United.

Brent, Eva. Nature in Needlepoint. (Illus.). 128p. 1975. 12.95 o.p. (ISBN 0-671-22081-0). S&S.

Brent, Harry & Lutz, William. Rhetorical Considerations: Essays for Analysis. 3rd ed. 1980. pap. text ed. 10.95 (ISBN 0-316-10781-6); tchr's ed. avail. (ISBN 0-316-10782-4). Little.

Brent, Linda, pseud. Incidents in the Life of a Slave Girl. Child, L. Maria, ed. LC 72-90506. (Illus.). 1973. pap. 4.95 o.p. (ISBN 0-15-644350-3, HB245, Harv). HarBraceJ.

Brent, Madeleine. Moonraker's Bride. LC 73-79649. 360p. 1973. 8.95 o.p. (ISBN 0-385-06445-4). Doubleday.

Brent, Peter. Charles Darwin: A Man of Enlarged Curiosity. (Illus.). 560p. 1983. pap. 9.25x (ISBN 0-393-30109-5). Norton.

--T. E. Lawrence. LC 74-32436. (Illus.). 232p. 1975. 12.95 o.p. (ISBN 0-399-11584-6). Putnam Pub Group.

--The Viking Saga. LC 74-28550. (Illus.). 264p. 1975. 16.95 o.p. (ISBN 0-399-11521-8). Putnam Pub Group.

Brent, Ruth H. The Earthquake Survival Handbook: How to Prepare for the Coming Earthquake. (Illus.). 128p. (Orig.). 1983. text ed. 9.95 (ISBN 0-915520-59-1); pap. 6.95 (ISBN 0-915520-58-3). Ross Erikson.

Brent, Stuart. The Seven Stairs. LC 73-4748. 224p. 1973. pap. 3.50 cancelled o.p. (ISBN 0-87955-307-3). O'Hara.

Brentano, Franz. Aristotle & His World View. George, Rolf & Chisholm, Roderick, trs. from Ger. LC 76-50245. 1978. 21.50x (ISBN 0-520-03390-6). U of Cal Pr.

--The Foundation & Construction of Ethics, Compiled from His Lectures on Practical Philosophy by Franziska Mayer-Hillebrand. Schneewind, Elizabeth H., tr. from Ger. (International Library of Philosophy & Scientific Method). 381p. (Orig.). 1973. text ed. 26.95x (ISBN 0-391-00254-6). Humanities.

--The Psychology of Aristotle: In Particular His Doctrine of the Active Intellect with an Appendix Concerning the Activity of Aristotle's God. George, Rolf, tr. LC 75-17303. 1977. 23.00x (ISBN 0-520-03081-8). U of Cal Pr.

--Sensory & Noetic Consciousness: Psychology from an Empirical Standpoint -Three. Kraus, Oskar, ed. McAlister, Linda & Schattle, M., trs. from Ger. 139p. 1981. text ed. 22.75x (ISBN 0-391-01175-8, Pub. by Routledge England). Humanities.

Brentano, Ron B. Historic Wagons in Miniature: The Genius of Ivan Collins. (Illus.). 160p. (Orig.). 1983. price not set (ISBN 0-87595-112-0, Western Imprints); pap. price not set (ISBN 0-87595-072-8, Western Imprints). Oreg Hist Soc.

Brenton, Howard. Revenge. 2nd ed. 1982. 6.95 (ISBN 0-413-50010-1). Methuen Inc.

--The Romans in Britain: A Play. 3rd ed. 112p. 1982. pap. 3.95 (ISBN 0-413-46590-X). Methuen Inc.

--Sore Throats & Sonnets of Love & Opposition. 47p. 1979. pap. 4.95 (ISBN 0-413-46580-2). Methuen Inc.

--Weapons of Happiness. 79p. 1976. pap. 6.95 (ISBN 0-413-36650-2). Methuen Inc.

Brenton, Thaddeus R. Bahia: Ensenada & It's Bay; Farce, Fiesta & Frustration in a Small Mexican City. LC 77-26758. (Illus.). 1978. Repr. of 1961 ed. lib. bdg. 16.00x (ISBN 0-313-20173-0, BRBA). Greenwood.

Brents, T. W. The Gospel Plan of Salvation. 12.95 (ISBN 0-89225-095-X). Gospel Advocate.

Breo, Dennis L., jt. auth. see Keane, Noel P.

Brereton, Bridget. Race Relations in Colonial Trinidad 1870-1900. LC 78-72081. (Illus.). 1980. 47.50 (ISBN 0-521-22428-4). Cambridge U Pr.

Brereton, Geoffrey. French Comic Drama from the Sixteenth to the Eighteenth Century. 1977. 29.95x (ISBN 0-416-78220-5); pap. 15.95x (ISBN 0-416-80710-0). Methuen Inc.

Brereton, Joel P. The Rigvedic Adityas. (American Oriental Ser.: Vol. 63). 1981. pap. 17.00 (ISBN 0-940490-63-3). Am Orient Soc.

Brereton, Lewis. The Brereton Diaries. (Politics & Strategy of World War II Ser.). 1976. Repr. of 1946 ed. lib. bdg. 45.00 (ISBN 0-306-70766-7). Da Capo.

Bres, Pieter H. de see De Bres, Pieter H.

Brescia, Frank, et al. Fundamentals of Chemistry: A Modern Introduction. 3rd ed. 1975. 7.50 (ISBN 0-12-132332-3); tchr's manual 1976 o.p. 1.00 (ISBN 0-12-132373-0). Acad Pr.

Bresciani, Francesco, ed. Perspectives in Steroid Receptor Research. 334p. 1980. text ed. 33.00 (ISBN 0-89004-490-2). Raven.

Bresciani-Turroni, Constantino. Economics of Inflation. Savers, Millicent E., tr. LC 68-6120. (Illus.). Repr. of 1937 ed. 27.50x (ISBN 0-678-06030-4). Kelley.

Breskin, Myrna, ed. see Burke, Ronald & Kramer, Arthur.

Breskin, Myrna, ed. see Jensen, et al.

Breslau, Lawrence & Haug, Marie. Depression & Aging: Causes, Care & Consequences. 1983. text ed. 24.95 (ISBN 0-8261-3710-5). Springer Pub.

Breslauer, George, jt. auth. see Rothman, Stanley.

Bresler, B., et al. Design of Steel Structures. 2nd ed. 352p. 1968. 37.95 o.p. (ISBN 0-471-10297-0). Wiley.

Bresler, Boris. Reinforced Concrete Engineering, Vol. 1. LC 73-19862. 576p. 1974. 35.00 o.p. (ISBN 0-471-10279-2, Pub. by Wiley-Interscience). Wiley.

Bresler, David. Free Yourself from Pain. 15.95x (ISBN 0-686-29877-2); pap. 9.95x (ISBN 0-671-42500-5). Cancer Control Soc.

Breslich, Ernest R. The Technique of Teaching Secondary School Mathematics. 239p. 1982. Repr. of 1930 ed. lib. bdg. 45.00 (ISBN 0-89984-089-2). Century Bookbindery.

Breslin, Catherine. Unholy Child. 1980. pap. 3.95 (ISBN 0-451-12378-6, AE2378, Sig). NAL.

Breslin, Cormick & Troxel, Terrie E. Property-Liability Insurance Accounting & Finance. LC 78-67500. 349p. 1980. text ed. 16.00 (ISBN 0-89463-015-6). Am Inst Property.

Breslin, Cormick L. & Troxel, Terrie E. Property-Liability Insurance Accounting & Finance. 1978. write for info. o.p. (CPCU 8). IIA.

Breslin, Donald J., et al. Renovascular Hypertension. (Illus.). 210p. 1981. lib. bdg. 30.00 (ISBN 0-683-01075-1). Williams & Wilkins.

Breslin, Jimmy. Forsaking All Others. 448p. 1983. pap. 3.95 (ISBN 0-449-20250-X, Crest). Fawcett.

Breslin, Jimmy & Schaap, Dick. Forty-Four Caliber. 1979. pap. 2.50 o.p. (ISBN 0-451-08459-4, E8459, Sig). NAL.

Breslin, Thomas A. China, American Catholicism, & the Missionary. LC 79-27857. (Illus.). 1980. text ed. 16.50x (ISBN 0-271-00259-X). Pa St U Pr.

Breslow, Aron. Hello Equal Rights! 1983. 2.00 (ISBN 0-918430-01-1). Happy History.

--Nothing Stops a Determined Being! 1983. 4.00t (ISBN 0-918430-03-8). Happy History.

Breslow, Kay & Breslow, Paul. Charles Gwathmey & Robert Siegel: Residential Works Nineteen Sixty-Six to Nineteen Seventy-Seven. (Illus.). 172p. 1980. 49.95 o.s.i. (ISBN 0-8038-0045-2). Architectural.

Breslow, Lester, et al, eds. Annual Review of Public Health, Vol. 4. 1983. text ed. 27.00 (ISBN 0-8243-2704-7). Annual Reviews.

Breslow, Lori, ed. see Jankowiak, James.

Breslow, N. E. & Whittemore, A. S., eds. Energy & Health: Proceedings. LC 79-63265. (SIAM-SIMS Conference Ser.: No. 6). xii, 340p. 1979. pap. 18.00 (ISBN 0-89871-000-6). Soc Indus-Appl Math.

Breslow, Paul. Romance of the Buyer. 180p. Date not set. 11.95 (ISBN 0-8180-0637-4). Horizon. Postponed.

Breslow, Paul, jt. auth. see Breslow, Kay.

Bresnick, David A. Public Organizations & Policy. 1982. pap. text ed. 13.50x (ISBN 0-673-16054-8). Scott F.

Bressand, Albert, ed. The RAMSES Nineteen Eighty-Two: State of the World Economy: A Report of the French Institute for International Relations. 384p. 1982. prof ref 32.00 (ISBN 0-88410-897-X). Ballinger Pub.

Bresser Pereira, Luis C. Development & Crisis in Brazil, 1930-1982. 275p. 1983. lib. bdg. 25.00x (ISBN 0-86531-559-0). Westview.

Bressers, J., ed. Creep & Fatigue in High Temperature Alloys: Proceedings of a Course Held at the Joint Research Centre of the Commission of the European Communities Petten Establishment, the Netherlands. (Illus.). 190p. 1981. 47.25 (ISBN 0-85334-947-9, Pub. by Applied Sci England). Elsevier.

Bressett, Ken. Prices for Buying & Selling United States Coins, 1983. Rev. ed. (Illus.). 192p. 1982. pap. 2.50 (ISBN 0-307-90520-9, Pub. by Whitman Coin Products). Western Pub.

Bressett, Ken & Kosoff, A., eds. The Official American Numismatic Association Grading Standards for United States Coins. 2nd ed. (Illus.). 352p. 1981. 6.95 (ISBN 0-307-09095-7). Western Pub.

Bressett, Kenneth, jt. auth. see Newman, Eric P.

Bressett, Kenneth E., ed. see Yeoman, R. S.

Bressler, M. H., et al. Criteria for Nuclear Safety Related Piping & Component Support Snubbers. (PVP: No. 45). 40p. 1980. 6.00 (ISBN 0-686-69846-0, H00172). ASME.

Bressler, Marvin & Lambert, Richard D., eds. American Higher Education: Prospects & Choices. new ed. LC 72-85689. (Annals Ser.: 404). 300p. 1972. 15.00 (ISBN 0-87761-156-4); pap. 7.95 (ISBN 0-87761-155-6). Am Acad Pol Soc Sci.

Bressler, R., jt. ed. see Brodie, Bernard B.

Bressler, Rubin, jt. auth. see Conrad, Kenneth.

Bressler, Rubin & Johnson, David G., eds. Management of Diabetes Mellitus. LC 80-10866. 328p. 1982. 32.00 (ISBN 0-88416-259-1). Wright-PSG.

Bressler, Stacey E., jt. auth. see Chen, Ching-chih.

Bresson, D., jt. ed. see Berge, C.

Brest, Albert, ed. Congestive Heart Failure. 157p. 1975. pap. 15.00 o.p. (ISBN 0-683-01054-9, Pub. by W & W). Krieger.

Brest, Levinson. Processes of Constitutional Decisionmaking. 2nd ed. LC 81-86686. 1983. text ed. cancelled (ISBN 0-316-10794-8). Little.

Brest, Paul. Processes of Constitutional Decisionmaking: Cases & Materials. 1375p. 1975. 28.50 o.p. (ISBN 0-316-10790-5); Suppl., 1980. pap. 8.95 o.p. (ISBN 0-316-10791-3). Little.

Brestensky, Dennis F., et al. Patch-Work Voices: The Culture & Lore of a Mining People. LC 78-23824. (Orig.). 1978. pap. text ed. 4.95 (ISBN 0-8229-8255-2, Pub. by U Ctr Intl St). U of Pittsburgh Pr.

Brestin, Dee. Finders Keepers: Small Group Evangelism. 1983. 8.95 (ISBN 0-87788-259-2); pap. 5.95. Shaw Pubs.

Brestin, Dee & Brestin, Steve. Higher Ground: For the Believer Who Seeks Joy & Victory. (Fisherman Bible Studyguides Ser.). 1978. saddle-stitched 2.50 (ISBN 0-87788-345-9). Shaw Pubs.

Brestin, Dee, jt. auth. see Brestin, Steve.

Brestin, Steve & Brestin, Dee. Building Your House on the Lord: Marriage & Parenthood. rev. ed. (Fisherman Bible Studyguides). 78p. 1979. saddle stitch 2.50 (ISBN 0-87788-099-9). Shaw Pubs.

Brestin, Steve, jt. auth. see Brestin, Dee.

Bretano, ed. see International Society for Artificial Organs.

Bretherick, L. Handbook of Reactive Chemical Hazards. 2nd ed. 1979. text ed. 149.00 (ISBN 0-408-70927-8). Butterworth.

Brethern House Team. Hunger Activities for Children. 5.00 (ISBN 0-686-95928-0). Alternatives.

Bretland. Essentials of Radiology. new ed. 1978. 27.95 (ISBN 0-407-00067-4). Butterworth.

Bretnor, Reginald, ed. Craft of Science Fiction. pap. 4.95 o.p. (ISBN 0-06-463457-4, BN). B&N NY.

--The Craft of Science Fiction: A Symposium on Writing Science Fiction & Science Fantasy. LC 75-23872. 288p. (YA) 1976. 12.45i (ISBN 0-06-010461-9, HarpT). Har-Row.

Breton, Albert & Breton, Raymond. Why Disunity? 83p. 1980. pap. text ed. 6.95x (ISBN 0-920380-70-0, Inst Res Pub Canada). Renouf.

Breton, Albert & Wintrobe, Ronald. The Logic of Bureaucratic Conduct. LC 81-21722. (Illus.). 208p. 1982. 29.95 (ISBN 0-521-24589-3). Cambridge U Pr.

Breton, Andre. Fata Morgana & Other Poems. Mills, Clark, tr. (Illus.). 48p. (Fr.). 1982. pap. 4.95 (ISBN 0-941194-01-9). Black Swan Pr.

--Poems of Andre Breton: A Bilingual Anthology. Cauvin, Jean-Pierre, ed. Caws, Mary A. & Cauvin, Jean-Pierre, trs. 298p. 1982. text ed. 27.50x (ISBN 0-292-76476-6); pap. 12.95 (ISBN 0-292-76477-4). U of Tex Pr.

--Surrealism & Painting. Taylor, Simon W., tr. from Fr. LC 70-188930. (Icon Editions Ser.). (Illus.). 428p. 1973. pap. 8.95xi o.p. (ISBN 0-06-430024-2, IN-24, HarpT). Har-Row.

Breton, Anne-Marie. To Flee from Eagles. 288p. (Orig.). 1981. pap. 2.75 o.p. (ISBN 0-523-40405-0). Pinnacle Bks.

Breton, Denise. This Lie Called Evil. LC 82-80906. 130p. (Orig.). 1983. pap. 8.50 (ISBN 0-942958-02-0). Kappeler Inst Pub.

Breton, Myron. Lasting Relationships: How to Recognize the Man or Woman Who's Right for You. 204p. 1983. pap. 5.95 (ISBN 0-89104-333-0, A & W Visual Library). A & W Pubs.

Breton, Raymond, jt. auth. see Breton, Albert.

Breton de Nijs, E. Faded Portraits. Beekman, E M., ed. Sturtevant, Donald & Sturtevant, Elsje, trs. from Dutch. LC 81-19653. (Library of the Indies). Orig. Title: Vergeelde Portretten Uit Een Indisch Familie-Album. 192p. 1982. lib. bdg. 12.50x (ISBN 0-87023-363-7). U of Mass Pr.

Bretschneider, Charles L. Topics in Ocean Engineering, Vol. 3. 339p. 1976. 26.50x o.p. (ISBN 0-87201-600-5). Gulf Pub.

Bretschneider, Charles L., ed. Topics in Ocean Engineering. Incl. Vol. 1. 428p. 1969. (ISBN 0-87201-598-X); Vol. 2. (Illus.). 229p. 1970 (ISBN 0-87201-599-8). 26.50x ea. o.p. Gulf Pub.

Brett, Barbara. Love After Hours. 352p. 1981. pap. 2.50 o.p. (ISBN 0-380-76257-9, 76257). Avon.

Brett, Bernard. Ghosts. (Chiller Ser.). 128p. (gr. 8-12). 1983. PLB 8.79 (ISBN 0-686-84204-9). Messner.

--Monsters. (Chiller Ser.). 128p. 1983. PLB 8.79 (ISBN 0-671-46745-X). Messner.

Brett, Bernard see Allen, W. S.

Brett, James. Looking into Houses. (Illus.). 192p. 1979. pap. 9.95 (ISBN 0-8230-7359-9, Whitney Lib). Watson-Guptill.

Brett, John. Who'd Hire John Brett. LC 80-29008. 176p. 1981. 9.95 o.p. (ISBN 0-312-87038-8). St Martin.

Brett, Lionel. Architecture in a Crowded World: Vision & Reality in Planning. LC 73-148713. 1971. 6.50x o.p. (ISBN 0-8052-3392-X). Schocken.

Brett, Martin, jt. auth. see Whitlock, Dorothy.

Brett, Michael, jt. auth. see Toma, David.

Brett, Patricia, jt. auth. see Brett, Robert.

Brett, Philip. Benjamin Britten: Peter Grimes. LC 82-14627. (Cambridge Opera Handbooks). (Illus.). 180p. Date not set. price not set (ISBN 0-521-22916-2); pap. price not set (ISBN 0-521-29716-8). Cambridge U Pr.

Brett, Robert & Brett, Patricia. Hispanoamerica One: Al Sur Del Ecuador. LC 78-15378. 1978. pap. 4.95 (ISBN 0-88436-496-8, 70252). EMC.

Brett, Simon. The Faber Book of Useful Verse. 254p. 1982. pap. 7.95 (ISBN 0-571-11782-1). Faber & Faber.

--Murder in the Title: A Charles Paris Mystery. 192p. 1982. 12.95 (ISBN 0-686-83677-4, ScribT). Scribner.

--Situation Tragedy. 1983. pap. 2.50 (ISBN 0-440-18792-3). Dell.

Brett, Vanessa. Phaidon Guide to Pewter. (Illus.). 256p. 1983. 12.95 (ISBN 0-13-662049-3); pap. 6.95 (ISBN 0-13-662031-0). P-H.

Brett, William & Sentlowitz, Michael. Elementary Algebra by Example. LC 76-11979. (Illus.). 1977. pap. text ed. 19.95 (ISBN 0-395-24425-0); instr's. manual 1.90 (ISBN 0-395-24426-9). HM.

Brett, William F., et al. Contemporary College Mathematics. 320p. 1975. text ed. 20.95 (ISBN 0-8299-0038-1). West Pub.

Brett, William J. Biological Explorations I: Laboratory Manual. 1978. pap. text ed. 9.95 (ISBN 0-8403-1925-8). Kendall-Hunt.

--Biological Explorations II: Laboratory Manual. 1979. pap. text ed. 11.95 (ISBN 0-8403-1938-X, 40193801). Kendall-Hunt.

Brettell, Richard R. Historic Denver: The Architects & the Architecture, 1858-1893. 1979. pap. 14.95 (ISBN 0-914248-00-6). Hist Denver.

Bretton, Barbara. Love Changes. (American Romance Ser.). 192p. 1983. pap. 2.25 (ISBN 0-686-38729-5). Harlequin Bks.

Brett-Smith, Richard. Hitler's Generals. LC 77-85481. (Illus.). 1978. Repr. 12.95 o.p. (ISBN 0-89141-044-9). Presidio Pr.

Bretz, Mary L. Concha Espina. (World Authors Ser.). 1980. lib. bdg. 15.95 (ISBN 0-8057-6401-1, Twayne). G K Hall.

Bretz, Rudy. Techniques of Television Production. 2nd ed. (Television Ser). (Illus.). 1962. text ed. 27.50 (ISBN 0-07-007664-2, C). McGraw.

Breuer, Georg. Air in Danger: Ecological Perspectives of the Atmosphere. Fabian, P., tr. from Ger. LC 79-18820. (Illus.). 180p. 1980. 27.95 (ISBN 0-521-22417-9); pap. 9.95 (ISBN 0-521-29483-5). Cambridge U Pr.

--Weather Modification, Prospect & Problems. Morth, H. T., tr. from Ger. LC 79-73236. (Illus.). 1980. 32.50 (ISBN 0-521-22453-5); pap. 10.95 (ISBN 0-521-29577-7). Cambridge U Pr.

Breuer, Josef & Freud, Sigmund. Studies on Hysteria. LC 57-12310. 1982. 16.35 (ISBN 0-465-08274-2); pap. 6.95 (ISBN 0-465-08275-0). Basic.

Breuer, Joseph A. A Handbook of Assistive Devices for the Handicapped Elderly: New Help for Independent Living. LC 81-20270. (Physical & Occupational Therapy in Geriatrics: Vol. 1, No. 2). (Illus.). 87p. 1982. text ed. 20.00 (ISBN 0-86656-152-8, B152). Haworth Pr.

Breuer, Lee. Animations: A Trilogy for Mabou Mines. Marranca, Bonnie & Dasgupta, Gautam, eds. LC 79-84185. 1979. 16.95 (ISBN 0-933826-01-X); signed ltd. ed. 25.00 (ISBN 0-686-31924-9); pap. 8.95 (ISBN 0-933826-03-6). Performing Arts.

Breuer, M. & Hartenstein, R., eds. Computer Hardware Description Languages & Their Applications. 1982. 39.75 (ISBN 0-444-86279-X). Elsevier.

Breuer, Melvin A. & Friedman, Arthur D. Diagnosis & Reliable Design of Digital Systems. LC 76-19081. (Illus.). 300p. 1976. text ed. 28.95x (ISBN 0-914894-57-9). Computer Sci.

Breuer, Reinhard & Lechleitner, Hans. The EMP Factor: The Twenty-Minute War. Orig. Title: Der Lautlose Schlag. (Illus.). 150p. (Orig.). 1983. pap. 6.95 (ISBN 0-914842-99-4). Madrona Pubs.

Breugelmans, Rene. Jacques Perk. (World Authors Ser.). 1974. lib. bdg. 15.95 (ISBN 0-8057-2688-8, Twayne). G K Hall.

Breuilly, John. Nationalism & the State. 366p. 1982. 25.00x (ISBN 0-312-56005-2). St Martin.

Breva-Claramonte, Manuel. Sanctius' Theory of Language: A Contribution to the History of Renaissance Linguistics. (Studies in the History of Linguistics Ser.: 27). 350p. 1983. 36.00x (ISBN 90-272-4505-3). Benjamins North Am.

Brevard, C. & Granger, P. Handbook of High Resolution Multinuclear NMR. LC 81-8603. 229p. 1981. 24.50x o.p. (ISBN 0-471-06323-1, Pub. by Wiley-Interscience). Wiley.

Brewer. Cellular Pathology. (Postgraduate Pathology Ser.). 1982. cancelled o.p. (ISBN 0-407-00050-X). Butterworth.

Brewer, jt. auth. see Pitzer.

Brewer, Allen A. & Morrow, Robert M. Overdentures. 2nd ed. LC 80-19356. (Illus.). 426p. 1980. text ed. 64.50 (ISBN 0-8016-0785-X). Mosby.

Brewer, Allen F. Effective Lubrication. LC 72-87324. 366p. 1974. lib. bdg. 20.50 (ISBN 0-88275-083-6). Krieger.

Brewer, Annie, ed. Abbreviations, Acronyms, Ciphers & Signs:...A Reference Source for Identifying Books in Many Languages Which Concern Themselves with Short Forms of Comunications. 315p. 1981. 60.00x (ISBN 0-8103-0529-1). Gale.

--Biography Almanac: A Comprehensive Reference Guide to More Than 20,000 Famous & Infamous Newsmakers from Biblical Times to the Present. LC 80-19504. 1100p. 1981. 46.00x (ISBN 0-8103-1076-7). Gale.

Brewer, Annie M. Biography Almanac: Supplement. 181p. 1982. pap. 30.00x (ISBN 0-8103-1141-0). Gale.

--Indexes, Abstracts & Digests. 801p. 1982. 150.00x (ISBN 0-8103-1686-2). Gale.

Brewer, Annie M., ed. Dictionaries, Encyclopedias, & Other Word-Related Books, 3 vols. 3rd ed. LC 81-20247. 1982. Vol. 1: English. 100.00x (ISBN 0-8103-1191-7); Vol. 2: Polyglot. 150.00x (ISBN 0-8103-1192-5); Vol. 3: Foreign. 150.00x (ISBN 0-8103-1193-3). Gale.

--Youth-Serving Organizations Directory. 2nd ed. 1980. 56.00x (ISBN 0-8103-0238-1). Gale.

Brewer, Bryan, jt. auth. see Hester, Debbie.

Brewer, D. Tradition & Innovation in Chaucer. 256p. 1982. text ed. 37.00x (ISBN 0-333-28427-5, 50794, Pub. by Macmillan England). Humanities.

Brewer, D. F. Progress in Low Temperature Physics, 2 vols, Vol. 7. 1979. Set. 81.00 (ISBN 0-444-85210-7, North Holland); Vol. 7a. 138.50 (ISBN 0-444-85177-1); Vol. 7b. 81.00 (ISBN 0-444-85209-3). Elsevier.

Brewer, D. F., ed. Progress in Low Temperature Physics, Vol. 8. Date not set. 64.00 (ISBN 0-444-86228-5). Elsevier.

Brewer, Derek S., ed. Writers & Their Background: Geoffrey Chaucer. LC 74-84295. (Writers & Their Background Ser.). xiv, 401p. 1975. 17.00x (ISBN 0-8214-0183-1, 82-81834); pap. 8.50x (ISBN 0-8214-0184-X, 82-81842). Ohio U Pr.

Brewer, Donald J. George Cohen, Paintings & Constructions. (Illus.). 24p. 1965. 1.00 o.p. (ISBN 0-686-99841-3). La Jolla Mus Contemp Art.

--Hans Hofmann Paintings. (Illus.). 16p. 1968. 7.00x (ISBN 0-686-99836-7). La Jolla Mus Contemp Art.

--Louis & Charlotte Bergman Collection. (Illus.). 60p. 1967. 5.00x (ISBN 0-686-99837-5). La Jolla Mus Contemp Art.

--New Modes in California: Paintings & Sculpture. (Illus.). 32p. 1966. 2.00x (ISBN 0-686-99838-3). La Jolla Mus Contemp Art.

--Twentieth Century Latin American Naive Art. (Illus.). 24p. 1964. 0.50x (ISBN 0-686-99842-1). La Jolla Mus Contemp Art.

Brewer, Donald J. & Kirby, Sheldon. A Survey 1957-1968 Sheldon Kirby. 24p. 1968. 1.00x (ISBN 0-686-99835-9). La Jolla Mus Contemp Art.

Brewer, Donald J. & Reich, Sheldon. Marsden Hartley-John Marin. (Illus.). 48p. 1966. 3.00x (ISBN 0-686-99839-1). La Jolla Mus Contemp Art.

Brewer, E. Cobham. Authors & Their Works, with Dates. LC 71-134907. (Readers Handbook Ser.: Vol. 3). 1970. Repr. of 1898 ed. 47.00x (ISBN 0-8103-3025-3). Gale.

--A Dictionary of Miracles, Imitative, Realistic, & Dogmatic. LC 66-29783. 1966. Repr. of 1885 ed. 42.00 (ISBN 0-8103-3000-8). Gale.

--Reader's Handbook: Famous Names in Fiction, Allusions, References, Proverbs, Plots, Stories, & Poems, 3 vols. LC 71-134907. 1966. Repr. of 1899 ed. Set. 105.00x (ISBN 0-8103-0153-9). Gale.

Brewer, Earl D. Continuation or Transformation? The Involvement of United Methodism in Social Movements & Issues. (Into our Third Century Ser.). 128p. (Orig.). 1982. pap. 4.25 (ISBN 0-687-09623-5). Abingdon.

Brewer, Earl J. Juvenile Rheumatoid Arthritis. 2nd ed. LC 78-64701. (MPCP-VI). 1982. text ed. 48.00 (ISBN 0-7216-1986-X). Saunders.

Brewer, Earl J., Jr. Juvenile Rheumatoid Arthritis. LC 69-12875. (Major Problems in Clinical Pediatrics: Vol. 6). 1970. 11.50 o.p. (ISBN 0-7216-1985-1). Saunders.

Brewer, Edward S. Cruising Designs. (Illus.). 144p. 1976. 4.00 (ISBN 0-915160-15-3). Seven Seas.

Brewer, Forrest & Brewer, Jean. Vocabulario Mexicano de Tetelcingo. (Vocabularios Indigenas Ser.: No. 8). 274p. 1962. pap. 4.00x (ISBN 0-88312-658-3); microfiche 3.00x (ISBN 0-88312-363-0). Summer Inst Ling.

Brewer, Gail S., jt. auth. see Presser, Janice.

Brewer, Garry D. & Kakalik, James S. Handicapped Children: Strategies for Improving Services. (Illus.). 1978. 29.95 (ISBN 0-07-007680-4, P&RB). McGraw.

Brewer, George J. & Sing, Charles F. Genetics. (Biology Ser.). (Illus.). 575p. 1983. text ed. 24.95 (ISBN 0-201-10138-6); Courseware avail.; Solutions Manual avail. A-W.

Brewer, J. E. Distance: A New, Yet Old Approach to Art. Barrett, Benjamin & Young, Madilyn, eds. (Illus.). 142p. 1983. pap. 6.95 (ISBN 0-939502-03-8); 15.95 (ISBN 0-939502-05-4). St Luke Pub.

--Handbook of Style for Art History. Barrett, Benjamin & Schaefer, V. A., eds. (Illus.). 127p. (Orig.). 1983. pap. 6.95 (ISBN 0-939502-02-X); 15.95 (ISBN 0-939502-04-6). St Luke Pub.

Brewer, J. M., et al. Experimental Techniques in Biochemistry. (Foundations of Modern Biochemistry Ser). (Illus.). 384p. 1974. ref. ed. 20.95 (ISBN 0-13-295071-5). P-H.

Brewer, J. S. & Wace, Henry. English Studies, or Essays in English History & Literature. 448p. 1982. Repr. of 1881 ed. lib. bdg. 75.00 (ISBN 0-8495-0611-5). Arden Lib.

Brewer, Jean, jt. auth. see Brewer, Forrest.

Brewer, John. Party Ideology & Popular Politics at the Accession of George Third. (Illus.). 400p. 44.50 (ISBN 0-521-21049-6); pap. 19.95 (ISBN 0-521-28701-4). Cambridge U Pr.

Brewer, John, jt. auth. see McKendrick, Neil.

Brewer, John C., jt. ed. see Rea, Kenneth W.

Brewer, John E., ed. see Salinger, John. P.

Brewer, K. R. & Hanif, M. Sampling with Unequal Probabilities. (Lecture Notes in Statistics Ser.: Vol. 15). (Illus.). 164p. 1983. pap. 12.80 (ISBN 0-387-90807-2). Springer-Verlag.

Brewer, Kenneth W. To Remember What is Lost. 59p. 1982. 9.50x (ISBN 0-87421-114-X). Utah St U Pr.

Brewer, Lucy. The Female Marine: Adventures of Miss Lucy Brewer. 2nd ed. LC 65-23390. 1966. Repr. of 1817 ed. 19.50 (ISBN 0-306-70913-9). Da Capo.

Brewer, Lyman A., jt. auth. see Beijing Symposium on Cardiothoracic Surgery.

Brewer, Marilyn B., jt. auth. see Crano, William D.

Brewer, Marilynn B. & Campbell, Donald T. Ethnocentrism & Intergroup Attitudes: East African Evidence. LC 75-26930. 218p. 1976. 15.95 o.p. (ISBN 0-470-10330-2, Pub. by Wiley). Krieger.

Brewer, P. G. Oceanography: The Present & the Future. (Illus.). 392p. 1983. 39.80 (ISBN 0-387-90720-3). Springer-Verlag.

Brewer, Robert N., et al. Solar Applications in Agriculture. 143p. 1981. 20.00 (ISBN 0-89168-034-9). Franklin Inst Pr.

Brewer, Robert S., jt. auth. see Curtis, Dan B.

Brewer, Stephen. Solving Problems in Analytical Chemistry. LC 79-17164. 528p. 1980. pap. text ed. 13.95x (ISBN 0-471-04098-3). Wiley.

Brewer, Thomas H. Metabolic Toxemia of Late Pregnancy. Rev. ed. 1982. pap. 7.95 (ISBN 0-87983-308-4). Keats.

Brewer, Thomas L. American Foreign Policy: A Contemporary Introduction. (Illus.). 1980. pap. text ed. 14.95 (ISBN 0-13-026740-6). P-H.

Brewer, W., jt. auth. see Rowe, R. G.

Brewer, Walter V. Victor Cousin As a Comparative Educator. LC 75-148593. 1971. text ed. 10.95x (ISBN 0-8077-1117-9). Tchrs Coll.

Brewer, William H. Up & Down California in Eighteen Sixty to Eighteen Sixty-Four: The Journal of William H. Brewer. Farquhar, Francis P., ed. LC 66-26246. (California Library Reprint Ser: No. 59). (Illus.). 1974. 32.50x (ISBN 0-520-02803-1); pap. 10.95 (ISBN 0-520-02762-0). U of Cal Pr.

Brewin, Chris, jt. ed. see Antaki, Charles.

Brewin, Robert, jt. auth. see Hughes, Richard.

Brewington, Dorothy, jt. auth. see Brewington, M. V.

Brewington, M. V. Check List of the Paintings, Drawings & Prints at the Kendall Whaling Museum. (Illus.). 74p. 1957. pap. 2.00 (ISBN 0-686-83951-X). Kendall Whaling.

--Chesapeake Bay Log Canoes & Bugeyes. rev. ed. (Illus.). 171p. 1963. 10.00 (ISBN 0-686-36507-0). Md Hist.

Brewington, M. V. & Brewington, Dorothy. Kendall Whaling Museum Paintings. LC 65-28071. (Illus.). 137p. 1965. 23.50 (ISBN 0-686-83944-7). Kendall Whaling.

--Kendall Whaling Museum Prints. LC 70-107611. (Illus.). 209p. 1969. 37.50 (ISBN 0-686-83946-3). Kendall Whaling.

Brews, J. R., jt. auth. see Nicollian, E. H.

Brewster, Ben, tr. see Althusser, Louis.

Brewster, Benjamin. First Book of Baseball. rev. ed. LC 78-24230. (First Bks). (Illus.). (gr. 4-6). 1979. PLB 7.90 (ISBN 0-531-02932-8). Watts.

Brewster, Charles. Rambles About Portsmouth, Vol. 2. LC 70-181350. 445p. 1972. Repr. 22.50x o.p. (ISBN 0-912274-21-2); 55.00x set o.p. NH Pub Co.

Brewster, Charles W. Rambles About Portsmouth, Vol. I. LC 70-181350. 1971. Repr. 22.50x o.p. (ISBN 0-912274-12-3); 55.00x set o.p. NH Pub Co.

Brewster, Dave. Graduate School, USDA: Sixty Years of Continuing Education. 1982p. pap. write for info. o.p. (ISBN 0-87771-029-5). Grad School.

Brewster, David. The Best Places. 4th ed. 192p. (Orig.). 1982. pap. 9.95 (ISBN 0-914842-76-5). Sasquatch Pub.

--Conversations with Henry Moore. 1978. 3.00 (ISBN 0-686-63617-1). Jawbone Pr.

--A Poultice for Each Season. 1979. 2.50 (ISBN 0-918116-16-3). Jawbone Pr.

Brewster, David & Watson, Emmett. Seattle: The Best Places. 192p. (Orig.). 1983. pap. 5.95 (ISBN 0-914842-94-3). Madrona Pubs.

Brewster, David C., jt. auth. see Hallett, John W., Jr.

Brewster, David E. & Rasmussen, Wayne D., eds. Farms in Transition: Interdisciplinary Perspective on farm Structure. 136p. 1982. pap. 8.25 (ISBN 0-8138-0636-4). Iowa St U Pr.

Brewster, E. Thomas & Brewster, Elizabeth S. Language Acquisition Made Practical (LAMP) new ed. LC 75-43377. (Illus.). 1976. 12.00 (ISBN 0-916636-00-3); tape 3.50x (ISBN 0-686-96771-2); bk. & tape 15.00x (ISBN 0-685-63930-4). Lingua Hse.

Brewster, Elizabeth S., jt. auth. see Brewster, E. Thomas.

Brewster, Ellis W. Plymouth in My Father's Time. 1968. 2.50 o.p. (ISBN 0-686-33122-2). Pilgrim Hall.

Brewster, Jennifer, tr. see Fujiwara no Nagako.

Brewster, Kingman, et al. The Tanner Lectures on Human Values: Vol. IV, 1983. 300p. 1983. 20.00x (ISBN 0-87480-216-4). U of Utah Pr.

Brewster, Marge A. Self-Assessment of Current Knowledge in Clinical Biochemistry. 2nd ed. 1976. 13.00 (ISBN 0-87488-266-4). Med Exam.

Brewster, Mela S. A Practical Study of the Use of the Natural Vegetable Dyes in New Mexico. LC 38-28365. 1982. lib. bdg. 19.95x (ISBN 0-89370-726-0). Borgo Pr.

Brewster, Patience, illus. Dame Wiggins of Lee & Her Seven Wonderful Cats. LC 79-7901. (Illus.). 32p. (gr. k-4). 1980. 8.61i o.p. (ISBN 0-690-03915-8, TYC-J); PLB 8.89 (ISBN 0-690-03916-6). Har-Row.

Brewster, Ray O., et al. Brief Course in Experimental Organic Chemistry. 1972. text ed. 8.95x (ISBN 0-442-31054-4). Van Nos Reinhold.

Brewton, John E. & Brewton, Sara W. Index to Children's Poetry. 966p. 1942. 26.00 (ISBN 0-8242-0021-7); first suppl. 1954, 405 p. 16.00 (ISBN 0-8242-0022-5); second suppl. 1965, 453 p. 16.00 (ISBN 0-8242-0023-3). Wilson.

Brewton, John E., ed. Index to Poetry for Children & Young People: 1970-1975. Blackburn, G. M, III & Blackburn, Lorraine. 471p. 1978. 23.00 (ISBN 0-8242-0618-5). Wilson.

Brewton, Sara W., jt. auth. see Brewton, John E.

Breyer, Betty J., ed. The Christmas Stories. LC 79-15520. (Anthony Trollope; The Complete Short Stories Ser.: Vol. I). 1979. 17.50 (ISBN 0-912646-56-X). Tex Christian.

--Editors & Writers. LC 79-19986. (Anthony Trollope; The Complete Short Stories Ser.: Vol. II). 1979. 17.50 (ISBN 0-912646-57-8). Tex Christian.

--Tourists & Colonials. LC 80-54162. (Anthony Trollope: the Complete Short Stories: Vol. III). 260p. 1981. 17.50 (ISBN 0-912646-62-4). Tex Christian.

Breyer, Donald E. & Ank, John A. Design of Wood Structures. (Illus.). 1980. 35.95 (ISBN 0-07-007671-5). McGraw.

Breyer, Stephen & Stewart, Richard. Administrative Law & Regulatory Policy. 1979. text ed. 27.50 (ISBN 0-316-10796-4). Little.

--Administrative Law & Regulatory Policy, 1982 Supplement. 1982. pap. 6.95 (ISBN 0-316-10802-2). Little.

Breyer, Stephen G. & MacAvoy, Paul W. Energy Regulation by the Federal Power Commission. LC 74-273. (Studies in the Regulation of Economic Activity). 163p. 1974. 13.95 (ISBN 0-8157-1076-3). Brookings.

Breyfogle, Newell D. The Common Sense Medical Guide & Outdoor Reference. McGraw, Robert P., ed. (Illus.). 416p. 1981. text ed. 13.95 (ISBN 0-07-007672-3, HP); pap. text ed. 6.95 (ISBN 0-07-007673-1). McGraw.

Brezhnev, L. I. We Are Optimists: Report of the Central Committee of the Communist of the Soviet Union to the 26th Congress of the CPSU. LC 81-6304. 96p. (Orig.). 1981. pap. 1.00 (ISBN 0-7178-0586-7). Intl Pub Co.

Brezhnev, Leonid I. Selected Speeches & Writings on Foreign Affairs. LC 78-40614. 1979. text ed. 48.00 (ISBN 0-08-023569-7). Pergamon.

Brezik, Victor B. One Hundred Years of Thomism. 210p. 1981. 7.00 (ISBN 0-9605456-0-3). Lumen Christi.

Brezis, H. & Lions, J. L. Nonlinear Partial Differential Equations & Their Applications: College de France Seminar Vol. 1. (Research Notes in Mathematics Ser.: No. 53). 350p. 1981. pap. text ed. 27.50 (ISBN 0-273-08491-7). Pitman Pub MA.

Brezis, H., jt. auth. see Berestyci, H.

Brezis, H. & Lions, J. L., eds. Nonlinear Partial Differential Equations & Their Applications, Vol. 3. (Research Notes in Mathematics: No. 70). 350p. 1982. pap. text ed. 27.50 (ISBN 0-273-08568-9). Pitman Pub MA.

--Nonlinear Partial Differential Equations & Their Applications: College de France Seminar, Vol. 2. (Research Notes in Mathematics Ser.: No. 60). 250p. 1982. pap. text ed. 27.50 (ISBN 0-273-08541-7). Pitman Pub MA.

Brezis, Haim. Operateurs Maximaux Monotones: Et Semi-Groupes de Contractions dans les Espaces de Hilbert. LC 72-95271. (North-Holland Mathematics Studies: Vol. 5). 132p. 1973. pap. 40.50 (ISBN 0-444-10430-5, North-Holland). Elsevier.

Breznitz, Shlomo. Stress in Israel. 304p. 1982. text ed. 19.95 (ISBN 0-442-24422-3). Van Nos Reinhold.

Breznitz, Shlomo, jt. auth. see Goldberger, Leo.

Breznitz, Shlomo, jt. ed. see Goldberger, Leo.

Brian, George C. & Smith, Bessie G. Stage Makeup for the Dark Complexioned Actor. (Illus.). 100p. (Orig.). 1983. pap. write for info. (ISBN 0-88127-012-1). Oracle Pr LA.

Brian, P. L. Staged Cascades in Chemical Processing. (International Ser. in the Physical & Chemical Engineering Sciences). (Illus.). 272p. 1972. ref. ed. 33.95 (ISBN 0-13-840280-9). P-H.

Briandet, Philippe A., jt. auth. see Goris, Michael L.

Briarpatch. The Briarpatch Book: Experiences in Right Livelihood & Simple Living. LC 78-5990. 1978. 15.00 (ISBN 0-912078-63-4); pap. 8.00 (ISBN 0-912078-60-X). Reed Bks.

Bricaire De La Dixmerie, N. Eloge De Voltaire, Prononce das la Maconnique Des Neufs Soeurs. Repr. of 1779 ed. 42.00 o.p. (ISBN 0-8287-0136-9). Clearwater Pub.

Bricas, E., ed. see European Peptide Symposium, 9th, France, 1968.

Brice, Donna. Step-by-Step Guide For: Making Busts & Masks (Cold-Cast Bronze or Plaster Hydrocal) LC 82-15703. (Illus.). 52p. 1983. 18.95 (ISBN 0-910733-00-7); pap. 10.95 (ISBN 0-910733-01-5). ICTL Pubns.

Brice, James C. & Levin, Harold L. Laboratory Studies in Earth History. 3rd ed. 190p. 1982. wire coil write for info. (ISBN 0-697-05057-2); instrs.' manual (ISBN 0-697-05058-0). Wm C Brown.

Brice, Martin. Axis Blockade Runners of World War II. LC 81-80883. 300p. 1981. 18.95 (ISBN 0-87021-908-1). Naval Inst Pr.

Brice, Pat, ed. see Hubbard, L. Ron.

Briceno, Guillermo. Como Amar Al Projimo-Concepto Transferible. 59p. 1982. pap. 0.65 (ISBN 0-8297-1381-6). Life Pubs Intl.

Brichant, Colette. La France Au Cours Des Ages. (Illus.). 480p. 1972. text ed. 37.95 (ISBN 0-07-007712-6, C). McGraw.

Brichant, Colette D. Premier Guide de France: The First Year Reader. (Illus.). 1978. pap. text ed. 14.95 (ISBN 0-13-695460-X). P-H.

Brichant, Collette. French Grammar: The Key to Reading. (Orig.). 1968. pap. text ed. 12.95 (ISBN 0-13-331264-X). P-H.

Brichant, Collette, ed. French for the Humanities. 1968. pap. text ed. 11.50 (ISBN 0-13-331199-6). P-H.

Brichard, Pierre. Fishes of Lake Tanganyika. (Illus.). 1978. 29.95 (ISBN 0-87666-464-8, H-972). TFH Pubns.

Brick, jt. auth. see Pohorecky.

Brick, James, jt. auth. see Mick, John.

Brick, John R., ed. Bank Management: Concepts & Issues. LC 80-68804. (Banking Ser.). 551p. (Orig.). 1980. pap. 22.50 (ISBN 0-936328-00-2); pap. text ed. 14.50 (ISBN 0-686-94976-5). Dame Inc.

Brick, R. M., et al. Structure & Properties of Engineering Materials. 4th ed. (McGraw-Hill Ser. in Materials Science & Engineering). (Illus.). 1977. text ed. 32.50 (ISBN 0-07-007721-5, C). McGraw.

Brickbauer, Elwood A. & Mortenson, William P. Approved Practices in Crop Production. 2nd ed. LC 77-89853. (Illus.). (gr. 9-12). 1978. 16.50 (ISBN 0-8134-1975-1, 1975); text ed. 12.50x. Interstate.

Bricker, Dianne D., jt. ed. see Schiefelbusch, Richard L.

Bricker, George W., jt. ed. see Pond, Samuel A.

Bricker, Neal S. & Kirschenbaum, Michael. The Kidney: Diagnosis & Management. 525p. 1983. 29.95 (ISBN 0-471-09572-9, Pub. by Wiley Med). Wiley.

Bricker, Victoria R. & Sabloff, Jeremy A., eds. Supplement to the Handbook of Middle American Indians: Vol. 1,Archaeology. (Illus.). 475p. 1981. text ed. 55.00x (ISBN 0-292-77556-3). U of Tex Pr.

Bricker, William R. Breaking the Youth Unemployment Cycle: The Boys Clubs of America Approach. (Vital Issues Ser.: Vol. XXXI, No. 6). 0.80 (ISBN 0-686-84144-1). Ctr Info Am.

Brickford, Maynard. National Catalog of Sources for the History of Librarianship. 12p. 1982. pap. text ed. 10.00 (ISBN 0-686-37932-2); write for info. Microfiche. ALA.

Brickham, Jack M. I Still Dream about Columbus. LC 82-5742. 240p. 1982. 13.95 (ISBN 0-312-40276-7). St Martin.

Brickley, David. Shooting Star. 224p. 1983. 11.95 (ISBN 0-686-83655-3, ScribT). Scribner.

Brickman. Solving the Computer Contract Dilemma: A How-To Book for Decision Makers. Date not set. 20.00 (ISBN 0-686-82000-2, 6259). Hayden.

Brickman, Richard, jt. auth. see Irwin, Robert.

Brickman, William W. & Lehrer, Stanley. A Century of Higher Education: Classical Citadel to Collegiate Colossus. LC 73-17857. 293p. 1974. Repr. of 1962 ed. lib. bdg. 17.25x (ISBN 0-8371-7267-5, BCHE). Greenwood.

Brickner, William H. & Cope, Donald M. The Planning Process. 1977. pap. text ed. 7.95 (ISBN 0-316-10798-0). Little.

Bricktop & Haskins, James. Bricktop. LC 82-73006. 320p. 1983. 14.95 (ISBN 0-689-11349-8). Atheneum.

Bricq, Ron S. Technically Write! Communicating in a Technological Era. 2nd ed. (Illus.). 448p. 1981. pap. text ed. 14.95 (ISBN 0-13-898700-9). P-H.

Bricta, Ira, jt. auth. see Margolin, Victor.

Bridaham, Lester B. Gargoyles, Chimeres, & the Grotesque in French Gothic Sculpture. enl. & 2nd ed. LC 68-27724. (Architecture & Decorative Art Ser.: Vol. 22). (Illus.). 1969. Repr. of 1930 ed. lib. bdg. 55.00 o.p. (ISBN 0-306-71152-4). Da Capo.

Bridbury, A. R. Historian's & the Open Society. 1972. 14.95x (ISBN 0-7100-7337-2). Routledge & Kegan.

--Medieval English Clothmaking: An Economic Survey. 160p. 1982. 75.00x (ISBN 0-435-32138-2). State Mutual Bk.

--Medieval English Clothmaking: An Economic Survey. (Pasold Studies in Textile History). 160p. 1982. text ed. 27.50x (ISBN 0-435-32138-2). Heinemann Ed.

Briden, J. C., jt. auth. see Smith, A. G.

Bridenbaugh, Carl. Cities in Revolt: Urban Life in America, 1743-1776. (Illus.). 1970. pap. 9.95 (ISBN 0-19-501362-X, GB). Oxford U Pr.

--Jamestown, Fifteen Forty-Four to Sixteen Ninity-Nine. (Illus.). 1980. 22.50x (ISBN 0-19-502650-0). Oxford U Pr.

--Silas Downer - Forgotten Patriot: His Life & Writings. LC 74-83462. (Rhode Island Revolutionary Heritage Ser.: Vol. 1). (Illus.). 1974. 3.75 (ISBN 0-917012-01-1). Ri Pubns Soc.

--Spirit of Seventy-Six: The Growth of American Patriotism Before Independence, 1607-1776. LC 75-4323. 1977. pap. 4.95 (ISBN 0-19-502179-7, 488, GB). Oxford U Pr.

--Vexed & Troubled Englishmen, 1590-1642. 1968. 25.00x (ISBN 0-19-500493-0). Oxford U Pr.

Bridenbaugh, Carl, ed. & intro. by see Hamilton, Alexander.

Bridenbaugh, Phillip O., jt. auth. see Cousins, Michael J.

Bridenthal, Renate & Koonz, Claudia. Becoming Visible: Women in European History. LC 76-11978. 1977. pap. text ed. 12.50 (ISBN 0-395-24477-3). HM.

Bride's Magazine Editors. Bride's Book of Etiquette. (Illus.). 144p. 1976. pap. 2.95 (ISBN 0-448-12487-4, G&D). Putnam Pub Group.

--The Bride's Wedding Planner. Date not set. pap. 6.95 (ISBN 0-449-90005-3, Columbine). Fawcett.

--The New Bride's Book of Etiquette. rev. ed. Conde Nast, ed. LC 80-84126. (Illus.). 1981. 10.00 (ISBN 0-448-01560-9, G&D); pap. 4.95 (ISBN 0-448-01115-8). Putnam Pub Group.

Bridge. Communication in Nursing Care. 9.95 (ISBN 0-471-25604-8, Pub. by Wiley Heyden). Wiley.

Bridge, Donald & Phypers, David. Communion: The Meal That Unites? 192p. 1983. pap. 5.95 (ISBN 0-87788-160-X). Shaw Pubs.

--The Water That Divides: The Baptism Debate. (Orig.). 1977. pap. 3.95 o.p. (ISBN 0-87784-787-8). Inter-Varsity.

Bridge, F. R. From Sadowa to Sarajevo: The Foreign Policy of Austria-Hungary 1866-1914. (Foreign Policies of Great Powers Ser.). (Illus.). 496p. 1972. 33.50x (ISBN 0-7100-7269-4). Routledge & Kegan.

Bridge, Frederick. Twelve Good Musicians: From John Bull to Henry Purcell. 152p. 1983. pap. 6.50 (ISBN 0-88072-001-8). Tanager Bks.

Bridge, J. Applied Econometrics. 1971. 29.50 (ISBN 0-444-10098-9). Elsevier.

Bridge, Jane. Beginning Model Theory: The Completeness Theorem & Some Consequences. (Oxford Logic Guides Ser.). 1977. 23.50x (ISBN 0-19-853157-5). Oxford U Pr.

Bridge, R. Gary, et al. The Determinants of Educational Outcomes: Impact of Families, Peers, Teachers & Schools. LC 78-26467. 384p. 1979. prof ref 22.50x (ISBN 0-88410-182-7). Ballinger Pub.

Bridgeman, Bruce & Bridgeman, Dinae, eds. Readings on Fundamental Issues on Learning & Memory. 343p. 1977. pap. text ed. 14.95x (ISBN 0-8422-0548-9). Irvington.

Bridgeman, Dinae, jt. ed. see Bridgeman, Bruce.

Bridgeman, Harriet & Drury, Elizabeth, eds. The British Eccentric. (Illus.). 1976. 12.50 o.p. (ISBN 0-517-52499-6, C N Potter Bks). Crown.

Bridger, J. P., et al. Glossary of United Kingdom Fishing Gear Terms. 128p. 1981. 55.00x o.p. (ISBN 0-85238-119-0, Pub. by A Hilger). State Mutual Bk.

Bridger, William A. & Hendessen, J. Frank. Cell ATP. (Transport in Life Science Ser.). 200p. 1983. 39.50 (ISBN 0-471-08507-3, Pub. by Wiley-Interscience). Wiley.

Bridgers, Sue E. All Together Now. (YA) 1979. 7.95 o.p. (ISBN 0-394-84098-4); PLB 7.99 (ISBN 0-394-94098-9). Knopf.

--Notes for Another Life. LC 81-1673. 256p. (YA) 1981. 9.95 (ISBN 0-394-84889-6); PLB 9.99 (ISBN 0-394-94889-0). Knopf.

Bridgers, Sue Ellen. Notes for Another Life. (gr. 7 up). 1982. pap. 2.25 (ISBN 0-553-22605-3). Bantam.

Bridges, B. A. & Harnden, D. G. Ataxia Telangietasia: A Cellular & Molecular Link Between Cancer, Neuropathology & Immune Deficiency. LC 81-13146. 424p. 1982. 46.95 (ISBN 0-471-10055-2, Pub. by Wiley Med). Wiley.

Bridges, Bryn A., et al, eds. Banbury Report 13: Indicators of Genotoxic Exposure. LC 82-1972. (Banbury Report Ser.: Vol. 13). 500p. 1982. 62.50X (ISBN 0-87969-212-X). Cold Spring Harbor.

Bridges, Charles. The Christian Ministry. 1980. 13.95 (ISBN 0-85151-087-6). Banner of Truth.

--Ecclesiastes. 319p. 1981. Repr. 10.95 (ISBN 0-85151-322-0). Banner of Truth.

Bridges, Douglas S. Constructive Functional Analysis. (Research Notes in Mathematics Ser.: No. 28). 203p. (Orig.). 1979. pap. text ed. 21.95 (ISBN 0-273-08418-6). Pitman Pub MA.

Bridges, E. M. World Soils. 2nd ed. LC 77-90204. (Illus.). 1979. 27.95 (ISBN 0-521-21956-6); pap. 9.95x (ISBN 0-521-29339-1). Cambridge U Pr.

Bridges, J. W. & Chasseaud, L. F. Progress in Drug Metabolism, Vol. 6. LC 80-42314. (Progress in Drug Metabolism Ser.). 321p. 1981. 59.00x (ISBN 0-471-28023-2, Pub. by Wiley Interscience). Wiley.

Bridges, J. W. & Chasseaud, L. F., eds. Progress in Drug Metabolism, Vols. 1-4. Incl. Vol. 1. 1977. 55.95x (ISBN 0-471-10370-5); Vol. 2. 1977. 67.00 (ISBN 0-471-99442-1); Vol. 3. LC 75-19446. 1979. 74.95x (ISBN 0-471-99711-0); Vol. 4. LC 79-42723. 304p. 1980. 75.95x (ISBN 0-471-27702-9). Pub. by Wiley-Interscience). Wiley.

Bridges, Julian C. Guia De Estudios Sobre Bases Biblicas De la Etica. 96p. Repr. of 1973 ed. 4.50 (ISBN 0-311-43505-X). Casa Bautista.

Bridges, Kent W. see Mueller-Dombois, Dieter.

Bridges, Robert. Influence of the Audience on Shakespeare's Drama. (Studies in Shakespeare, No. 24). 1970. pap. 12.95x o.p. (ISBN 0-8383-0085-5). Haskell.

--Selected Poems. Stanford, Donald, ed. (Fyfield). 1979. 7.95 o.p. (ISBN 0-85635-087-7, Pub. by Carcanet New Pr England). Humanities.

Bridges, Robert S. Three Friends. LC 75-3863. (Illus.). 243p. Repr. of 1932 ed. lib. bdg. 16.25x (ISBN 0-8371-8094-5, BRTFR). Greenwood.

Bridges, William. Zoo Doctor. (Illus.). (gr. 3-6). 1957. 8.95 (ISBN 0-688-21499-1). Morrow.

Bridgid & Bruce. How to Do Sex Properly. (Illus.). 64p. (Orig.). 1982. pap. 5.95 (ISBN 0-89104-303-9, A & W Visual Library). A & W Pubs.

Bridgman, George B. Book of One-Hundred Hands. (Illus.). 1972. pap. 4.00 (ISBN 0-486-22709-X). Dover.

--Bridgman's Complete Guide to Drawing from Life. (Illus.). 1970. 20.00 (ISBN 0-8069-5000-5); lib. bdg. 17.59 o.p. (ISBN 0-8069-5001-3). Sterling.

--Constructive Anatomy. (Illus.). 160p. 1973. pap. 3.95 (ISBN 0-486-21104-5). Dover.

--Heads, Features, & Faces. LC 74-78681. (Illus.). 64p. 1974. pap. 2.50 (ISBN 0-486-22708-1). Dover.

--The Human Machine: The Anatomical Structure & Mechanism of the Human Body. LC 70-187018. (Illus.). 160p. 1972. pap. 3.95 (ISBN 0-486-22707-3). Dover.

Bridgman, J. Camping. (Illustrated Guides Ser). (Illus., Orig.). 1977. pap. 2.95 o.p. (ISBN 0-671-18764-3). Monarch Pr.

Bridgman, Richard. Gertrude Stein in Pieces. 1970. 25.00x (ISBN 0-19-501280-1). Oxford U Pr.

Bridwell, Randall & Whitten, Ralph U. The Constitution & the Common Law. LC 77-5281. 1977. 23.95x (ISBN 0-669-01601-2). Lexington Bks.

Brie, G. A. De see De Brie, G. A.

Brief, Arthur, jt. auth. see Aldag, Ramon.

Brief, Arthur P., jt. auth. see Aldag, Ramon J.

Brief, Richard P., ed. Four Classics on the Theory of Double Entry Bookkeeping. LC 82-82949. (Accountancy in Transition Ser.). 90p. 1982. lib. bdg. 20.00 (ISBN 0-8240-5333-8). Garland Pub.

Brieland, Donald, et al. Contemporary Social Work: An Introduction to Social Work & Social Welfare. 2nd ed. Munson, Eric M., ed. (Illus.). 1980. 23.95x (ISBN 0-07-007767-3). McGraw.

Brien, David M. O' see O'Brien, David M.

Brien, Mimi. Moneywise. 1982. pap. 3.50 (ISBN 0-686-82381-8). Bantam.

Brienes, Wini. Community & Organization in the New Left, 1962-1968: The Great Refusal. (Illus.). 224p. 1982. text ed. 22.95x (ISBN 0-686-78909-1). J F Bergin.

Brier, Bob. Ancient Egyptian Magic. LC 81-11224. (Illus.). 1981. pap. 7.95 (ISBN 0-688-00796-1). Quill NY.

Brier, Peter A. & Arthur, Anthony, eds. American Prose & Criticism, Nineteen Hundred to Nineteen Fifty: A Guide to Information Sources. (American Literature, English Literature & World Literatures in English Information Guide Ser.: Vol. 35). 260p. 1981. 42.00x (ISBN 0-8103-1214-X). Gale.

Briere, Eloise, et al. A French Cultural Reader. Date not set. pap. price not set (ISBN 0-394-32642-3). Random.

Briere, O. Fifty Years of Chinese Philosophy: Eighteen Ninety-Eight to Nineteen Fifty. Thompson, Laurence G., tr. LC 78-31391. 1979. Repr. of 1956 ed. lib. bdg. 17.50x (ISBN 0-313-20650-3, BRFY). Greenwood.

Brierly, James L. Law of Nations: An Introduction to the International Law of Peace. new ed. Waldock, Humphrey, ed. 1978. 13.95x (ISBN 0-19-825105-X). Oxford U Pr.

Brierly, John E., jt. auth. see David, Rene.

Briffault, Herma, tr. see Colette.

Briffault, R. Sin & Sex. LC 72-6300. (Studies in Philosophy, No. 40). 228p. 1972. Repr. of 1931 ed. lib. bdg. 49.95x (ISBN 0-8383-1634-X). Haskell.

Briffault, Robert. The Mothers: A Study of the Origins of Sentiments & Institutions, 3 vols. (Anthropology Ser). Repr. of 1927 ed. Set. 150.00 (ISBN 0-384-05800-0). Johnson Repr.

Brigadier, Anne. Collage: A Complete Guide for Artists. (Illus.). 192p. 1978. pap. 9.95 o.p. (ISBN 0-8230-0651-4). Watson-Guptill.

Brigance, William N. Jeremiah Sullivan Black, a Defender of the Constitution & the Ten Commandments. LC 72-139196. (American Scene Ser). (Illus.). 1971. Repr. of 1934 ed. lib. bdg. 39.50 (ISBN 0-306-70078-6). Da Capo.

Brigermann, Chuck. Record Collector's Fact Book, Vol. I. LC 82-73474. (Illus.). 96p. 1983. pap. 7.95 (ISBN 0-89709-037-3). Liberty Pub.

Briggaman, Joan. Practical Problems in Mathematics for Office Workers. LC 76-54051. 1977. pap. text ed. 7.00 (ISBN 0-8273-1612-7); instr.'s guide 4.25 (ISBN 0-8273-1613-5). Delmar.

--Small Business Recordkeeping. LC 81-68212. (Management Ser.). (Illus.). 256p. (Orig.). 1983. pap. text ed. 11.80 (ISBN 0-8273-1861-8); instructor's guide 5.25 (ISBN 0-8273-1862-6). Delmar.

Briggs. Soils. (Sources & Methods in Geography). 1977. pap. 9.95 (ISBN 0-408-70911-1). Butterworth.

Briggs, A. D. Alexander Pushkin: A Critical Study. LC 82-16242. 258p. 1983. text ed. 26.50x (ISBN 0-389-20340-8). B&N Imports.

Briggs, A. D., tr. see Medvedev, Roy A.

Briggs Amasco Ltd. Flat Roofing: A Guide to Good Practice. (Illus.). 216p. 1982. pap. 33.95 (ISBN 0-9507919-0-3, Pub. by RIBA). Intl Schol Bk Serv.

Briggs, Anne K. & Agrin, Alice R., eds. Crossroads: A Reader for Psychosocial Occupational Therapy. 2nd ed. 215p. 1982. pap. text ed. 15.00 (ISBN 0-910317-04-6). Am Occup Therapy.

Briggs, Asa. The Power of Steam: An Illustrated History of the World's Steam Age. LC 82-40321. (Illus.). 208p. 1982. pap. 22.50 (ISBN 0-226-07495-1). U of Chicago Pr.

--Social Thought & Social Action. LC 73-17859. (Illus.). 371p. 1974. Repr. of 1961 ed. lib. bdg. 19.00x (ISBN 0-8371-7269-1, BSOT). Greenwood.

Briggs, Asa & Dekker, John. Marx in London. 96p. 1982. 25.00x (ISBN 0-563-20076-6, BBC Pubns). State Mutual Bk.

Briggs, Barry. Trackin' with Briggo. (Briggo Motorcycle Racing Library: No. 4). (Illus.). 128p. 1975. 15.95 (ISBN 0-285-62206-4, Pub. by Souvenir). Scholium Intl.

Briggs, Carol S. Sport Diving. LC 82-35. (Superwheels & Thrill Sports Bks.). (Illus.). (gr. 4 up). 1982. PLB 7.95g (ISBN 0-8225-0503-7). Lerner Pubns.

Briggs, Carole S. Diving Is for Me. LC 82-17242. (Sports for Me Bks.). (Illus.). 48p. (gr. 2-5). 1983. PLB 6.95g (ISBN 0-8225-1135-5). Lerner Pubns.

--Skin Diving is for Me. LC 80-27409. (Sports for Me Bks.). (Illus.). (gr. 2-5). 1981. PLB 6.95g (ISBN 0-8225-1132-0, AACR1). Lerner Pubns.

Briggs, Charles L. The Wood Carvers of Cordova, New Mexico: Social Dimensions of an Artistic "Revival". LC 79-20883. 1980. 21.95x (ISBN 0-87049-275-6). U of Tenn Pr.

Briggs, D., ed. Handbook of X-Ray & Ultraviolet Photoelectron Spectroscopy. 1977. 99.95 (ISBN 0-471-25605-6, Pub. by Wiley Heyden). Wiley.

Briggs, D., jt. ed. see Morgan, Michael.

Briggs, D. E. Barley. 1978. 82.00x (ISBN 0-412-11870-X, Pub. by Chapman & Hall). Methuen Inc.

Briggs, Dinus M., jt. auth. see Briggs, Hilton M.

Briggs, Dorothy C. Your Child's Self-Esteem: The Key to His Life. LC 70-121948. 360p. 1970. pap. 6.95 (ISBN 0-385-04020-2, Dolp). Doubleday.

Briggs, Enang, jt. auth. see Ojo, O. A.

Briggs, Frances. Handbook of English Grammar. LC 75-99290. (gr. 8-12). 1970. text ed. 8.95 (ISBN 0-87716-023-6, Pub. by Moore Pub Co). F Apple.

Briggs, G. A. Plume Rise. LC 77-603261. (AEC Critical Review Ser.). 81p. 1969. pap. 10.00 (ISBN 0-87079-304-7, TID-25075); microfiche 4.50 (ISBN 0-87079-305-5, TID-25075). DOE.

Briggs, Geoffrey, ed. Civic & Corporate Heraldry: A Dictionary of Impersonal Arms of England, Wales, & Northern Ireland. (Illus.). 432p. 1971. 32.00x (ISBN 0-685-29194-4). Gale.

Briggs, Geoffrey A. & Taylor, Frederick W. The Cambridge Photographic Atlas of the Planets. LC 81-38529. (Illus.). 224p. 1982. 24.95 (ISBN 0-521-23976-1). Cambridge U Pr.

Briggs, George M. & Weininger, Jean. Nutrition Update, Vol. 1. 350p. 1982. 45.00 (ISBN 0-471-09607-5, Pub. by Wiley-Interscience). Wiley.

Briggs, Gerald G. Teratogenic Drugs in Clinical Practice. 400p. 1983. price not set (ISBN 0-683-01057-3). Williams & Wilkins.

Briggs, Gordon, jt. auth. see Goldsmith, John.

Briggs, Hazel F. I'll Tell You Tomorrow. 98p. 1983. pap. 5.95 (ISBN 0-942802-01-2). Northword.

Briggs, Hilton M. & Briggs, Dinus M. Modern Breeds of Livestock. 4th ed. (Illus.). 1980. text ed. 29.95 (ISBN 0-02-314730-X). Macmillan.

Briggs, J. H. & Sellers, I., eds. Victorian Nonconformity. LC 73-89997. (Documents of Modern History Ser.). 192p. 1974. 15.95 o.p. (ISBN 0-312-84315-1). St Martin.

Briggs, Jeanine & Crean, John E. Alles Gute! Basic German for Communication. 350p. 1982. 18.00 (ISBN 0-394-32872-8); wkbk. 7.95 (ISBN 0-394-32873-6); lab manual 7.95 (ISBN 0-394-33028-5); Cultural Reader by Lalande 7.95 (ISBN 0-394-33013-7). Random.

Briggs, John. The Collector's Beethoven. LC 77-28258. (Keystone Books in English Ser.). 1978. Repr. of 1962 ed. lib. bdg. 15.50x (ISBN 0-313-20243-5, BRBE). Greenwood.

Briggs, K. M. Hobberdy Dick. LC 76-39896. (gr. 5-9). 1977. 9.95 (ISBN 0-688-80079-3); PLB 8.55 (ISBN 0-688-84079-5). Greenwillow.

Briggs, Katharine M. Personnel of Fairyland: A Short Account of the Fairy People of Great Britain for Those Who Tell Stories to Children. LC 70-147084. (Illus.). 1971. Repr. of 1953 ed. 30.00x (ISBN 0-8103-3372-4). Gale.

Briggs, L. Vernon. The Manner of Man that Kills. (Historical Foundations of Forensic Psychiatry & Psychology Ser.). (Illus.). 444p. 1983. Repr. of 1921 ed. lib. bdg. 45.00 (ISBN 0-306-76182-3). Da Capo.

Briggs, Martin S. The Architect in History. LC 69-15613. (Architecture & Decorative Art Ser.). (Illus.). 400p. 1974. Repr. of 1927 ed. lib. bdg. 35.00 (ISBN 0-306-70584-2). Da Capo.

--Baroque Architecture. LC 67-23634. (Architecture & Decorative Art Ser.). 1967. Repr. of 1913 ed. 35.00 (ISBN 0-306-70960-0). Da Capo.

--Muhammadan Architecture in Egypt & Palestine. LC 74-1287. (Architecture & Decorative Arts Ser.). (Illus.). 255p. 1974. Repr. of 1924 ed. lib. bdg. 32.50 (ISBN 0-306-70590-7). Da Capo.

Briggs, Maxine, jt. auth. see Briggs, Michael.

Briggs, Michael & Briggs, Maxine. Oral Contraceptives, Vol. 1. LC 77-670169. (Annual Research Reviews Ser.). 1977. 14.40 (ISBN 0-88831-005-6). Eden Pr.

--Oral Contraceptives, Vol. 2. LC 77-670169. (Annual Research Reviews Ser.). 1978. 19.20 (ISBN 0-88831-020-X). Eden Pr.

--Oral Contraceptives, Vol. 3. LC 77-670169. (Annual Research Reviews Ser.). 1979. 26.00 (ISBN 0-88831-053-6). Eden Pr.

--Oral Contraceptives, Vol. 4. Horrobin, D. F., ed. (Annual Research Reviews Ser.). 232p. 1980. 30.00 (ISBN 0-88831-078-1). Eden Pr.

Briggs, Michael & Corbin, Alan, eds. Progress in Hormone Biochemistry & Pharmacology, Vol. 1. (Endocrinology Ser.). (Illus.). 300p. 1980. 34.95 (ISBN 0-88831-076-5). Eden Pr.

Briggs, Michael, ed. see Elstein, Max & Sparks, Richard.

Briggs, Michael, et al. Oral Contraceptives, Vol. 5. (Annual Research Reviews Ser.). 331p. 1981. 36.00 (ISBN 0-88831-096-X). Eden Pr.

Briggs, R. C. Interpreting the New Testament Today. rev. ed. LC 73-8024. 288p. (Orig.). 1973. pap. 9.95 o.p. (ISBN 0-687-19327-3). Abingdon.

Briggs, R. T. Plymouth Rock. 1968. 1.50 (ISBN 0-686-30041-6). Pilgrim Hall.

Briggs, Raymond. Father Christmas. (Illus.). 32p. (gr. k-3). 1973. 9.95 (ISBN 0-698-20272-4, Coward). Putnam Pub Group.

--Father Christmas Goes on Holiday. LC 75-2541. (Illus.). (gr. 5 up). 1975. 6.95 o.p. (ISBN 0-698-20331-3, Coward). Putnam Pub Group.

--Jim & the Beanstalk. LC 77-111062. (Illus.). (gr. k-3). 1980. PLB 5.99 (ISBN 0-698-30203-6, Coward); pap. 2.95 (ISBN 0-698-20510-3). Putnam Pub Group.

--The Snowman. LC 78-55904. (Illus.). (ps-2). 1978. 4.95 (ISBN 0-394-83973-0, BYR); PLB 5.99 o.p. (ISBN 0-394-93973-5). Random.

Briggs, Raymond, ed. & illus. Mother Goose Treasury. (Illus.). (ps-3). 1966. PLB 9.99 o.p. (ISBN 0-698-30243-5, Coward). Putnam Pub Group.

Briggs, Raymond, illus. The Mother Goose Treasury. (Illus.). 224p. 1980. 16.95 (ISBN 0-698-20094-2, Coward). Putnam Pub Group.

Briggs, S., jt. auth. see Freedland, R. A.

Briggs, Steven. The Municipal Grievance Process. (Monograph & Research Ser.: No. 34). 350p. 1983. price not set (ISBN 0-89215-118-8). U Cal LA Indus Rel.

Briggs, Vernon M., Jr. & Foltman, Felician F., eds. Apprenticeship Research: Emerging Findings & Future Trends. LC 81-1434. 232p. 1981. pap. 7.50 (ISBN 0-87546-085-2). ILR Pr.

Briggs, W. R., et al, eds. Annual Review of Plant Physiology, Vol. 31. LC 51-1660. (Illus.). 1980. text ed. 17.00 (ISBN 0-8243-0631-7). Annual Reviews.

--Annual Review of Plant Physiology, Vol. 34. (Illus.). 510p. 1983. text ed. 27.00 (ISBN 0-8243-0634-1). Annual Reviews.

Briggs, Wallace A. & Benet, William R., eds. Great Poems of the English Language, 2 vols. enl. ed. LC 79-51965. (Granger Poetry Library). 1983. Repr. of 1941 ed. Set. 98.50x (ISBN 0-89609-178-3). Granger Bk.

Briggum, Sue M. & Bender, Todd K. A Concordance to Conrad's Almayer's Folly. (Reference Library in the Humanities: Vol. 101). (LC 77-083408). 1978. lib. bdg. 40.00 o.s.i. (ISBN 0-8240-9843-9). Garland Pub.

Brigham, jt. auth. see Weston.

Brigham, Amariah. Observations on the Influence of Religion upon the Health & Physical Welfare of Mankind, 1835: Remarks on the Influence of Mental Cultivation & Mental Excitement Upon Health, 2 vols. in 1. LC 73-17271. (Hist. of Psych. Ser.). 1973. 53.00x (ISBN 0-8201-1125-2). Schol Facsimiles.

Brigham, Eugene, jt. auth. see Pappas, James L.

Brigham, Eugene F. Financial Management. 3rd ed. LC 78-56209. 1982. text ed. 26.95. Dryden Pr.

--Fundamentals of Financial Management. 3rd ed. 627p. 1983. 26.95 (ISBN 0-03-054771-7). Dryden Pr.

Brigham, John. Constitutional Language: An Interpretation of Judicial Decision. LC 78-4020. (Contribution in Political Science: No. 17). 1978. lib. bdg. 25.00 (ISBN 0-313-20420-9, BCO/). Greenwood.

--Making Public Policy: Studies in American Politics. 1977. pap. text ed. 11.95 (ISBN 0-669-00225-9). Heath.

Bright, Bill. A Movement of Miracles. LC 77-80071. (Illus.). 1977. pap. 2.95 o.p. (ISBN 0-918956-38-2). Campus Crusade.

Bright, Chuck. University of Iowa Football: The Hawkeyes. (College Sports Ser.). 1982. 10.95 (ISBN 0-87397-233-3). Strode.

Bright, Freda. Futures. 1983. 15.95 (ISBN 0-671-44114-0, Pub by Poseidon). S&S.

Bright, Hazel M. Some Remediation Suggestions for Concepts of Boehm Test of Basic Concepts, Bk. 1, Form A Or B. rev. ed. (Illus.). (gr. k-3). 1979. pap. 5.00 (ISBN 0-686-26609-9). Redwood Pub Co.

--Some Remediation Suggestions for Concepts of Boehm Test of Basic Concepts, Bk. 2, Form A Or B. (Illus.). (gr. k-3). 1979. pap. 6.00 (ISBN 0-686-26608-0). Redwood Pub Co.

Bright, James R. Automation & Management. 1958. 30.00 o.p. (ISBN 0-08-022293-5). Pergamon.

Bright, John & McGregor, Gordon. Teaching English As a Second Language. (English As a Second Language Bk.). 1975. text ed. 10.75x (ISBN 0-582-54003-8). Longman.

Bright, Joyce. The Passion Season. LC 78-31894. 1981. 12.95 (ISBN 0-87949-144-2). Ashley Bks.

Bright, Laurence. First Corinthians. (Scripture Discussion Outlines Ser.). 1968. pap. 0.75 o.p. (ISBN 0-685-07625-3, 80078). Glencoe.

Bright, Robert. Georgie & the Magician. LC 66-10822. (ps-1). 1966. 7.95 o.p. (ISBN 0-385-04824-6); PLB 7.95 (ISBN 0-385-05948-5); Softbound 2.50 (ISBN 0-385-01021-4). Doubleday.

--Georgie Goes West. LC 73-79650. 48p. (gr. k-3). 1973. 7.95a (ISBN 0-686-85895-6); PLB (ISBN 0-385-05277-4). Doubleday.

--Georgie to the Rescue. LC 56-5582. (ps-1). 7.95a (ISBN 0-385-07308-9); PLB (ISBN 0-385-07613-4); 2.50 o.p. softbound (ISBN 0-385-08067-0). Doubleday.

--Jorgito. LC 76-23789. (ps-k). 1977. PLB 5.95 o.p. (ISBN 0-385-12005-2). Doubleday.

--My Red Umbrella. (Illus.). (ps-1). 1959. PLB 8.16 (ISBN 0-688-31619-0). Morrow.

Bright, Susan. Occasional Poems, Vol. 1. (Illus.). 80p. (Orig.). 1982. pap. 4.95 (ISBN 0-911051-01-5). Plain View.

Brightbill, Charles K. & Mobley, Tony A. Educating for Leisure-Centered Living. 2nd ed. LC 76-47010. 1977. pap. text ed. 15.95x (ISBN 0-471-94914-0). Wiley.

Brightfield, Glory, jt. auth. see Brightfield, Rick.

Brightfield, Myron F. Issue in Literary Criticism. LC 68-23278. 1968. Repr. of 1932 ed. lib. bdg. 18.50x (ISBN 0-8371-0029-1, BRLC). Greenwood.

Brightfield, Rick & Brightfield, Glory. Outer Space Mazes. (Orig.). 1978. pap. 2.95i o.p. (ISBN 0-06-090588-3, CN 588, CN). Har-Row.

Bright-Holmes, John, ed. see Muggeridge, Malcolm.

Brightman, Alan. Like Me. (Illus.). 48p. (gr. k-3). 1976. PLB 8.95 (ISBN 0-316-10808-1); pap. 6.95 (ISBN 0-316-10807-3). Little.

Brightman, Alan J., ed. Negotiating the Mainstream: Personal Accounts of the Disabled Experience in Contemporary Society. (Illus.). 1983. pap. text ed. price not set (ISBN 0-8391-1791-4, 17981). Univ Park.

Brightman, Carol, jt. auth. see Rivers, Larry.

Brightman, Edgar S. Studies in Personalism. Steinkraus, Warren & Beck, Robert, eds. (Signature Series of Philosophy & Religion). Date not set. 16.00 (ISBN 0-86610-067-9). Meridian Pub.

Brightman, Frank H. Oxford Book of Flowerless Plants: Ferns, Fungi, Mosses, & Liverworts, Lichens, & Seaweeds. Nicholson, B. E., ed. (Illus.). 1966. 29.95x (ISBN 0-19-910004-7). Oxford U Pr.

Brightman, Robert. The Home Owner Handbook of Carpentry & Woodworking. (Illus.). 124p. 1974. 1.98 o.p. (ISBN 0-517-51443-5). Crown.

--One-Hundred One Practical Uses for Propane Torches. (Illus.). 1978. 6.95 o.p. (ISBN 0-8306-9976-7); pap. 5.95 (ISBN 0-8306-1030-8, 1030). TAB Bks.

Brighton, C. A., et al. Styrene Polymers: Technology & Environmental Aspects. (Illus.). 1979. 45.00x (ISBN 0-85334-810-3, Pub. by Applied Sci England). Elsevier.

Brighton, J. A., jt. auth. see Hughes, W. F.

Brighton, J. A., ed. see Biomechanics Symposium, 1973.

Brighton, Trevor. Buildings of Britain, 1550-1750: North Midlands. 160p. 1982. 50.00x (ISBN 0-86190-059-6, Pub. by Moorland). State Mutual Bk.

Brights, Bill. Manual del Maestro. Carrodeguas, Andy & Marosi, Estenan, eds. 533p. (Span.). 1982. Repr. text ed. 6.25 (ISBN 0-8297-1395-6). Life Pubs Intl.

Brignac, Margie. Southern Spice a la Microwave. LC 81-19241. (Illus.). 224p. (Orig.). 1982. spiral bound 8.95 (ISBN 0-88289-318-1). Pelican.

Brignal, T. J., jt. auth. see Bryer, R. A.

Brignano, Russell. Black Americans in Autobiography: An Annotated Bibliography of Autobiographies & Autobiographical Books Written Since the Civil War. 180p. Date not set. text ed. 25.00x (ISBN 0-8223-0559-3). Duke.

Brignano, Russell C. Richard Wright: An Introduction to the Man & His Works. LC 72-81667. (Critical Essays in Modern Literature Ser). 1970. pap. 5.95 (ISBN 0-8229-5211-4). U of Pittsburgh Pr.

Brik, Lily, jt. auth. see Mayakovsky, Vladimir.

Briley, John. Gandhi: Screenplay for the Film by Richard Attenborough. 192p. 1983. 6.95 (ISBN 0-394-62471-8, E856, Ever). Grove.

Briley, Michael, jt. auth. see Devries, Herbert.

Brilhart, John K., jt. auth. see Edwards, Barbara J.

Brill, A. Right to Financial Privacy Act: A Compliance Guide for Financial Institutions. 1979. 39.95 (ISBN 0-13-781161-6). P-H.

Brill, A. A., ed. & intro. by see Freud, Sigmund.

Brill, A. A., tr. see Freud, Sigmund.

Brill, Alan E. Building Controls into Structured Systems. (Illus.). 256p. (Orig.). 1983. pap. 19.00 (ISBN 0-917072-27-8). Yourdon.

Brill, Alida, jt. auth. see McClosky, Herbert.

Brill, Allen & Torbet, Laura. The Complete Book of Skateboarding. LC 76-26710. (Funk & W Bk.). (Illus.). 1976. 9.95i (ISBN 0-308-10266-5). T y Crowell.

Brill, Bertrand. Low Level Radiation Fact Book. Adelstein, James, et al, eds. 156p. 1982. 25.00 (ISBN 0-932004-14-8). Soc Nuclear Med.

Brill, Chip, ed. N. Y. C. Casting Survival Guide & Datebook 1983. 3rd ed. 300p. 10.00 (ISBN 0-87314-038-9). Peter Glenn.

Brill, Earl H. The Christain Moral Vision. (Church's Teaching Ser.: Vol. 6). 254p. 1979. 5.95 (ISBN 0-8164-0423-2); pap. 3.95 (ISBN 0-8164-2219-2). Seabury.

Brill, Edith. Old Cotswold. LC 68-23829. 1968. 12.95x (ISBN 0-678-05584-X). Kelley.

Brill, Harry. Why Organizers Fail: The Story of a Rent Strike. LC 76-104103. 1971. 21.00x (ISBN 0-520-01672-6). U of Cal Pr.

Brill, James E., ed. see State Bar of Texas Professional Efficiency & Economic Research Committee.

Brill, Naomi I. Working with People: The Helping Process. 2nd ed. 1978. pap. text ed. 8.95 sep o.p. (ISBN 0-397-47382-6, HarpC). Har-Row.

Brill, Peter L. & Hayes, John P. Taming Your Turmoil: Managing the Transitions of Adult Life. (Illus.). 256p. 1981. 15.95 (ISBN 0-13-884445-3, Spectrum); pap. 6.95 (ISBN 0-13-884437-2). P-H.

Brill, Robert H., ed. Science & Archaeology. 1971. 50.00x (ISBN 0-262-02061-0). MIT Pr.

Brill, Steven. The American Lawyer Guide to Leading Law Firms, 1983-1984, 2 vols. Kenyon, Joan, ed. 1000p. 1983. 475.00 ea. Vol. 1 (ISBN 0-9606682-2-5). Vol. 2 (ISBN 0-9606682-3-3). Set. write for info. (ISBN 0-9606682-1-7). Am Law Pub.

--The Teamsters. 1978. 11.95 o.s.i. (ISBN 0-671-22771-8). S&S.

Brillat-Savarin. The Physiology of Taste. Fisher, M. F., tr. LC 78-7199. 1978. pap. 7.95 (ISBN 0-15-671770-0, Harv). HarBraceJ.

Briller, Sarah W., jt. auth. see Gold, Anne.

Brilliant, Richard. Arts of the Ancient Greeks. (Illus.). 416p. 1973. text ed. 35.00 o.p. (ISBN 0-07-007850-5, C). McGraw.

--Pompeii Ad Seventy-Nine. (Illus.). 1979. 25.00 o.p. (ISBN 0-517-53859-8, C N Potter Bks). Crown.

Brillinger, David R. Time Series: Data Analysis & Theory. enl. ed. LC 80-84117. (Illus.). 552p. 1980. Repr. of 1975 ed. 36.00x (ISBN 0-8162-1150-7); text ed. 29.50 foreign ed. (ISBN 0-686-69028-1). Holden-Day.

Brillinger, Peter C., jt. auth. see Cohen, Doron J.

Briloff, Abraham J. More Debits Than Credits: The Burnt Investor's Guide to Financial Statements. LC 74-15812. (Illus.). 448p. 1976. 16.30i (ISBN 0-06-010476-7, HarpT). Har-Row.

--Unaccountable Accounting. LC 71-156509. 1972. 16.30i (ISBN 0-06-010471-6, HarpT). Har-Row.

Brim, Orville G., Jr. & Kagan, Jerome, eds. Constancy & Change in Human Development. (Illus.). 760p. 1980. 29.50x (ISBN 0-674-16625-6). Harvard U Pr.

Brim, Orville G., Jr., et al. American Beliefs & Attitudes About Intelligence. LC 75-76746. 292p. 1969. 9.95x (ISBN 0-87154-152-1). Russell Sage.

Brim, Orville G., Jr., et al, eds. The Dying Patient. Freeman, Howard E. LC 77-104181. 1970. 12.95x (ISBN 0-87154-155-6). Russell Sage.

Brim, Q. G. & Wheeler, S. Socialization after Childhood: Two Essays. 1966. pap. text ed. 15.50 (ISBN 0-471-10418-3). Wiley.

Brimah, K. Farouk, jt. auth. see Hudlin, Richard A.

Brimblecombe, R. W., jt. auth. see Bradley, P. B.

Brimer, M. A. & Pauli, L. Wastage in Education: A World Problem. (Studies & Surveys in Comparative Education). 155p. (Orig.). 1972. pap. 5.25 (ISBN 92-3-100934-6, U713, UNESCO). Unipub.

Brin, Ruth. Butterflies Are Beautiful. LC 73-21359. (Nature Bks. for Young Readers). 32p. (gr. 4-8). 1974. PLB 4.95g (ISBN 0-8225-0290-9). Lerner Pubns.

Brin, Ruth F. David & Goliath. (Foreign Lands Bks). (Illus.). 32p. (gr. k-5). 1977. PLB 5.95g (ISBN 0-8225-0365-4). Lerner Pubns.

--The Story of Esther. LC 75-743. (Outstanding Books from Foreign Lands Ser.). 32p. (gr. 1-4). 1976. PLB 5.95g (ISBN 0-8225-0364-6). Lerner Pubns.

Brin, Ruth F. & Stalland, Mary K. Wildflowers to Color. (Illus.). 36p. 1982. pap. 5.95 (ISBN 0-686-83871-8). Nodin Pr.

Brinberg, David & Kidder, Louise H., eds. Forms of Validity in Research. LC 81-48577. 1982. 7.95x (ISBN 0-87589-912-9, MSBS-12). Jossey-Bass.

Brincat, Matthew De. Salt & Light. 56p. (gr. 6up). 1983. pap. 3.00 (ISBN 0-911423-00-1). Bible-Speak.

Brinch-Hanson, P. Architecture of Concurrent Programs. 1977. 28.95 (ISBN 0-13-044628-9). P-H.

Brinckle, Gertrude, jt. auth. see Morse, Willard S.

Brincklow, William D., jt. auth. see Deep, Samuel D.

Brindle, John & Secrist, Sally. American Cornucopia, Nineteenth Century Still Lifes & Studies. (Illus.). 48p. 1976. pap. 2.00 (ISBN 0-913196-18-5). Hunt Inst Botanical.

Brindle, Reginald S. The New Music. (Illus.). 1975. pap. 11.75x (ISBN 0-19-315424-2). Oxford U Pr.

--Serial Composition. (YA) (gr. 9 up). 1966. 12.50x (ISBN 0-19-311906-4). Oxford U Pr.

Brindze, Ruth. Investing Money: The Facts about Stocks & Bonds. LC 68-28801. (Illus.). (gr. 7 up). 1968. 5.50 o.p. (ISBN 0-15-238828-1, HJ). HarBraceJ.

--Not to Be Broadcast: The Truth About the Radio. LC 73-19802. (Civil Liberties in American History Ser.). 310p. 1974. Repr. of 1937 ed. lib. bdg. 37.50 (ISBN 0-306-70598-2). Da Capo.

Brinegar, Bonnie C. & Skates, Craig B. Technical Writing: A Guide with Models. 1982. text ed. 13.95x (ISBN 0-673-15410-6). Scott F.

Bring, Mitchell & Wayembergh, Josse. Design & Meaning in Japanese Gardens. (Illus.). 1981. 27.50 (ISBN 0-07-007825-4). McGraw.

Bringas, Ernie. The Astrolabe Mind. Horwege, Richard A., ed. LC 82-9758. 164p. (Orig.). 1983. pap. 6.95 (ISBN 0-89865-143-3). Donning Co.

Bringhurst, Bruce. Antitrust & Oil Monopoly: The Standard Oil Cases, 1890-1911. LC 78-67908. (Contributions in Legal Studies: No. 8). (Illus.). 1979. lib. bdg. 29.95 (ISBN 0-313-20642-2, BRA/). Greenwood.

Bringhurst, Newell G. Saints, Slaves, & Blacks: The Changing Place of Black People Within Mormonism. LC 81-1093. (Contributions to the Study of Religion Ser.: No. 4). (Illus.). 256p. 1981. lib. bdg. 29.95 (ISBN 0-313-22752-7, BSB/). Greenwood.

Bringle, Jerald, ed. see Shaw, George B.

Bringle, Mary. Fortunes. 1980. 11.95 o.p. (ISBN 0-399-12458-6). Putnam Pub Group.

--Open Heart. 1982. 14.95 (ISBN 0-453-00423-7, H423). NAL.

Brininstool, E. A., ed. see Standing Bear, Luther.

Brink, A. B. & Partridge, T. C. Soil Survey for Engineering. (Monographs on Soil Survey). 1982. text ed. 74.00x (ISBN 0-19-854537-1). Oxford U Pr.

Brink, Andre. A Chain of Voices. 1983. pap. 5.95 (ISBN 0-14-006538-5). Penguin.

Brink, B. Language of Metre of Chaucer. LC 68-24899. (Studies in Chaucer, No. 6). 1969. Repr. of 1901 ed. lib. bdg. 49.95x (ISBN 0-8383-0917-8). Haskell.

Brink, Carol. Harps in the Wind: The Story of The Singing Hutchinsons. (The Story of the Singing Hutchinsons). (Illus.). v, 312p. 1980. Repr. of 1947 ed. lib. bdg. 32.50 (ISBN 0-306-76024-X). Da Capo.

Brink, Carol R. Caddie Woodlawn. rev. ed. (gr. 4-6). 1970. pap. 2.95 (ISBN 0-02-041880-9). Macmillan.

--Snow in the River. 1964. 12.95 o.p. (ISBN 0-02-515890-2). Macmillan.

Brink, Charles O. Horace on Poetry: Epistles Book II: The Letters to Augustus & Florus, Vol. 3. LC 63-4908. 656p. 1982. 99.50 (ISBN 0-521-20069-5). Cambridge U Pr.

Brink, Jeanie R., ed. Female Scholars: A Tradition of Learned Women Before 1800. (Illus.). 1980. 17.95 (ISBN 0-920792-02-2). Eden Pr.

Brink, Joseph, jt. auth. see Shreve, R. Norris.

Brink, P. J. Transcultural Nursing: A Book of Readings. (Illus.). 320p. 1976. pap. 15.95 (ISBN 0-13-928101-0). P-H.

Brink, Pamela J. & Wood, Marilynn T. Basic Steps in Planning Nursing Research. 2nd ed. LC 82-17426. 304p. 1983. pap. text ed. 15.95 (ISBN 0-534-01241-8). Brooks-Cole.

Brink, Terry L. Geriatric Psychotherapy. LC 78-26232. 318p. 1979. text ed. 32.95 (ISBN 0-87705-344-8); pap. text ed. 12.95 (ISBN 0-87705-346-4). Human Sci Pr.

Brink, V. Z., et al. Modern Internal Auditing: An Operational Approach. 3rd ed. 795p. 1973. 49.95 (ISBN 0-471-06524-2). Wiley.

Brink, Victor Z. & Witt, Herbert. Modern Internal Auditing: Appraising Operations & Controls. 4th ed. 792p. 1982. 49.95x (ISBN 0-471-08097-7). Ronald Pr.

Brink, Vonder Marylou. Seventeen Blocks from the River. Ashton, Sylvia, ed. LC 75-16568. 1976. 8.95 o.p. (ISBN 0-87949-046-2). Ashley Bks.

Brink, William & Harris, Louis. Negro Revolution in America. 1963. pap. 2.25 o.p. (ISBN 0-671-20419-X, Touchstone Bks). S&S.

Brinkerhoff, Dericksen M. Hellenistic Statues of Aphrodite: Studies in the History of Their Stylistic Development. LC 77-94688. (Outstanding Dissertations in the Fine Arts Ser.). 1978. lib. bdg. 24.00 o.s.i. (ISBN 0-8240-3217-9). Garland Pub.

Brinkerhoff, Donna & Rippy, Susan. The Cupboard Cookbook. (Illus.). 155p. (Orig.). 1981. pap. 11.95 (ISBN 0-686-37044-9). Brinkerhoff & Rippy.

Brinkerhoff, Robert O., et al. Program Evaluation: A Design Manual. (Evaluation in Education & Human Services Ser.). 1983. lib. bdg. 14.95 (ISBN 0-89838-122-3). Kluwer Nijhoff.

--Program Evaluation: A Sourcebook. (Evaluation in Education & Human Services). 1983. lib. bdg. 24.95 (ISBN 0-89838-120-7). Kluwer Nijhoff.

--Program Evaluation: A Sourcebook & Casebook. (Evaluation in Education & Human Services Ser.). (a). 1983. lib. bdg. 35.95 (ISBN 0-89838-121-5). Kluwer Nijhoff.

Brinkernoff, Sidney, jt. ed. see Crowe, Rosalie.

Brinkhous, Kenneth M., ed. Year Book of Pathology & Clinical Pathology, 1983. 1983. 44.00 (ISBN 0-8151-1238-6). Year Bk Med.

Brinkhurst, R. O. The Benthos of Lakes. LC 74-16826. 192p. 1975. text ed. 29.95 o.p. (ISBN 0-312-07525-1). St Martin.

Brinkley. A Family Is... (gr. 9-12). 1981. text ed. 10.12 (ISBN 0-87002-320-9). Bennett IL.

Brinkley, jt. auth. see Lyle.

Brinkley, Christie. Beauty & the Beach. 1983. price not set (ISBN 0-671-46190-7). S&S.

Brinkley, Ginny, jt. auth. see Childbirth Education Association of Jacksonville, Fla., Inc.

Brinkley, J. H., et al. Teen Guide to Homemaking. 4th ed. 1976. 21.28 (ISBN 0-07-007840-8, W); ans. key 4.20 (ISBN 0-07-007841-6). McGraw.

Brinkley, Jeanne, jt. auth. see Aletti, Ann.

Brinkman, Carl. Recent Theories of Citizenship. 1927. 24.50x (ISBN 0-686-51297-9). Elliots Bks.

Brinkman, Grover. Night of the Blood Moon. 200p. (gr. 4-6). 1976. 8.00 o.p. (ISBN 0-8309-0149-3). Ind Pr MO.

Brinkman, Marilyn S. & Morgan, William T. Light from the Hearth. (Illus.). 144p. (Orig.). 1983. pap. 12.00 (ISBN 0-87839-038-3). North Star.

Brinkman, Michael W. Sonnets: In Pursuit of Life. LC 78-71813. (Illus.). 1978. pap. 3.95 (ISBN 0-932996-01-9). Mich Muse.

Brinkman, Robert N. Twenty Million Volts. 1978. 5.95 o.p. (ISBN 0-533-03595-3). Vantage.

Brinkmann, R. Geology of Turkey. 1976. 57.50 (ISBN 0-444-99833-0). Elsevier.

Brinks, Glenn. Ultralight Propulsion: The Basic Handbook of Ultralight Engines, Drives & Propellers. LC 82-60020. (Ultralight Aviation Ser.: No. 4). (Illus.). 192p. (Orig.). 1983. 20.95 (ISBN 0-938716-05-0); pap. 13.95 (ISBN 0-938716-04-2). Ultralight Pubns.

Brinks, Herbert & Heynen, A. James. A Time to Keep: A History of the Christian Reformed Church. 1982. text ed. 12.95 (ISBN 0-933140-44-4); leader's guide 5.95 (ISBN 0-933140-45-2). Bd of Pubns CRC.

Brinkworth, B. J. An Introduction to Experimentation. 2nd ed. LC 74-19568. 183p. 1975. text ed. 13.50 (ISBN 0-444-19517-3). Elsevier.

--Solar Energy for Man. LC 73-549. 264p. 1972. 18.95x o.p. (ISBN 0-470-10425-2). Halsted Pr.

Brinley, Bertrand R. The Big Chunk of Ice. LC 74-7665. 176p. (gr. 4 up). Date not set. cancelled (ISBN 0-8255-1836-9). Macrae.

--The Big Kerplop. 192p. (gr. 4 up). 1974. 6.25 (ISBN 0-8255-1834-2). Macrae.

--Mad Scientists' Club. (Illus.). (gr. 9 up). 1964. 6.25 (ISBN 0-8255-1830-X). Macrae.

--New Adventures of the Mad Scientists' Club. LC 68-31487. (Illus.). (gr. 4-6). 1968. 6.25 (ISBN 0-8255-1832-6). Macrae.

Brinley, Maryann B., jt. auth. see Matthews, Sanford J.

Brinn, Ruth E. Lets Celebrate: Fifty-Seven Jewish Holiday Crafts for Young Children. (Illus.). (ps-2). 1977. pap. 4.95 (ISBN 0-930494-02-4). Kar Ben.

Brinnin, J. M. & Read, B. Modern Poets. 2nd ed. (gr. 11-12). 1970. text ed. 16.95 (ISBN 0-07-007908-0, C). McGraw.

Brinnin, John M. Sextet: T. S. Eliot & Truman Capote & Others. 1982. pap. 7.95 (ISBN 0-440-57785-3, Delta). Dell.

--Sextet: T. S. Eliot & Truman Capote & Others. 1981. 15.95 o.s.i. (ISBN 0-440-07785-0, Sey Lawr). Delacorte.

Brino, Nicholas Di see Di Brino, Nicholas.

Brinser, A. The Respectability of Mr. Bernard Shaw. LC 75-22167. (Studies in George Bernard Shaw., No. 92). 1975. lib. bdg. 40.95x (ISBN 0-8383-2082-1). Haskell.

Brinser, Marlin. Dictionary of Twentieth Century Italian Violin Makers & Import Dealers Scrapbook. 1978. pap. 14.00 (ISBN 0-9602298-1-7). M Brinser.

Brinsmead, Edgar. History of the Pianoforte. LC 79-76136. (Music Story Ser.). (Illus.). 1969. Repr. of 1879 ed. 34.00x (ISBN 0-8103-3559-X). Gale.

--History of the Pianoforte. 120p. Date not set. pap. 17.50 (ISBN 0-87556-489-5). Saifer.

Brinson, Bonne, jt. auth. see Romo, Richard.

Brintnall, Douglas, jt. auth. see Roberts, Ron E.

Brinton, et al. History of Civilization: Vol. 1, Prehistory to 1715. 5th ed. 1976. pap. 17.95 (ISBN 0-13-389007-4); study guide 5.95 (ISBN 0-13-389833-4). P-H.

Brinton, C., et al. A History of Civilization: Prehistory to 1300. 5th ed. (Illus.). 352p. 1976. pap. text ed. 15.95 (ISBN 0-13-389791-5). P-H.

--A History of Civilization: Thirteen Hundred to Eighteen-Fifteen. 5th ed. (Illus.). 288p. 1976. pap. text ed. 15.95 (ISBN 0-13-389817-2). P-H.

--A History of Civilization: 1715 to Present. 5th ed. (Illus.). 528p. 1976. pap. text ed. 17.95 (ISBN 0-13-389809-1). P-H.

Brinton, Crane. Anatomy of Revolution. 8.50 (ISBN 0-8446-1740-7). Peter Smith.

Brinton, Daniel G. The Myths of the New World: A Treatise on the Symbolism & Mythology of the Red Race in America. LC 74-1038. 360p. 1974. Repr. of 1896 ed. 30.00x (ISBN 0-8103-3959-5). Gale.

--Myths of the New World Indians. LC 72-81594. (Illus.). 334p. 1976. pap. 8.50 (ISBN 0-89345-207-6, Steinerbks). Garber Comm.

Brinton, Henry, jt. auth. see Moore, Patrick.

Brinton, William, Jr., ed. see Schmid, Otto & Klay, Ruedi.

Brion, John M. Corporate Marketing Planning. LC 67-19446. (Marketing Ser.). 577p. 1967. 32.50 o.p. (ISBN 0-471-10440-X). Wiley.

Brion De Latour, Louis. Tableau De la Population De la France. Repr. of 1789 ed. 11.50 o.p. (ISBN 0-8287-0139-3). Clearwater Pub.

Brioschi, Francesco, jt. auth. see Bertele, Umberto.

Brisbane. Developing Child. rev. ed. (gr. 9-12). 1980. text ed. 16.40 (ISBN 0-87002-312-8); tchr's guide 10.00 (ISBN 0-87002-324-1); student guide 3.96 (ISBN 0-87002-325-X). Bennett IL.

Brisbin, I. Lehr, jt. ed. see Adriano, Domy C.

Brisbin, James S., ed. Belden, the White Chief: Or, Twelve Years Among the Wild Indians of the Plains from the Diaries & Manuscripts of George P. Belden. facsimile ed. LC 73-92900. (Illus.). xxvi, 513p. 1974. Repr. of 1870 ed. 15.00 (ISBN 0-8214-0150-5, 82-81537). Ohio U Pr.

Brisbin, Richard A., Jr., jt. auth. see Buell, Emmett H., Jr.

Briscall, C. M. & Farrell, Gordon H. Canadian Hardware Supplied Ltd: Four Parts. (Illus.). 1982. pap. text ed. 15.50 (ISBN 0-8403-2613-0). Kendall-Hunt.

Brisco, et al. Gold Dust Books, 2 Libraries. Incl. Library I (ISBN 0-8372-3579-0). tchr's. guide 2.79 (ISBN 0-8372-3534-0); Big Bad Ernie (ISBN 0-8372-3533-2); The Big Find (ISBN 0-8372-3530-8); Crazy Minnie (ISBN 0-8372-3531-6); Mystery at Beach Bay (ISBN 0-8372-3528-6); No Place to Hide (ISBN 0-8372-3529-4); Ride to Win (ISBN 0-8372-3532-4); Library II (ISBN 0-8372-3580-4). tchr's. guide 2.79 (ISBN 0-8372-3541-3); Calling Earth (ISBN 0-8372-3537-5); The Champion's Jacket (ISBN 0-8372-3540-5); Escape from the Tower (ISBN 0-8372-3538-3); The Full of the Moon (ISBN 0-8372-3539-1); Nightmare Nina (ISBN 0-8372-3535-9); Raging Rapids (ISBN 0-8372-3536-7). (Ea. Library contains 3 copies of 6 titles). (gr. 4-6). Libraries I & II. pap. 97.50 (ISBN 0-8372-3581-2); Libraries I & II. pap. 48.75 ea.; pap. 2.79 ea. title. Bowmar-Noble.

Brisco, Patty. Merry's Treasure. (YA) 1970. 6.95 (ISBN 0-685-07447-1, Avalon). Bouregy.

Briscoe, Anne & Pfafflin, Sheila M., eds. Expanding the Role of Women in the Sciences. (Annals of the New York Academy of Sciences: Vol. 323). 344p. (Orig.). 1979. 47.00x (ISBN 0-89766-014-5); pap. 47.00x (ISBN 0-686-77682-8). NY Acad Sci.

Briscoe, D. Stuart. What Works When Life Doesn't. 144p. 1976. pap. 4.50 (ISBN 0-88207-725-2). Victor Bks.

--When the Going Gets Tough. LC 82-11205. 1982. 5.95 (ISBN 0-8307-0802-2, 5417507). Regal.

Briscoe, Jill. Here I Am--Send Aaron. 1978. pap. 4.50 (ISBN 0-88207-767-8). Victor Bks.

--Jonah & Little Worm. 120p. 1983. 6.95 (ISBN 0-8407-5289-X). Nelson.

Briscoe, Laurel. Lectura y Lengua: Curso Intermedio. LC 77-83324. (Illus.). 1978. text ed. 20.95 (ISBN 0-395-25545-7); write for info. instrs' annotated ed. (ISBN 0-395-25539-2). HM.

Briscoe, Leonard R., jt. auth. see Briscoe, W. S.

Briscoe, Mary L., et al. A Bibliography of American Autobiography, 1945-1980. LC 82-70547. 384p. 1982. text ed. 30.00 (ISBN 0-299-09090-6). U of Wis Pr.

Briscoe, Melbourne, ed. Oceanic Internal Waves. 1976. pap. 15.00 o.p. (ISBN 0-87590-222-7). Am Geophysical.

Briscoe, Stuart. All Things Weird & Wonderful. 1977. pap. text ed. 4.95 (ISBN 0-88207-749-X). Victor Bks.

Briscoe, W. S. & Briscoe, Leonard R. Wildlife Adventure Ser, 8 vols. (gr. 3-7). 1966. pap. text ed. 6.52 ea. o.p. (Sch Div); tchr's. manual 4.52 o.p. (ISBN 0-201-40712-4). A-W.

Briseno, Gillermo. Como Experimentar-Amor-Poder. 54p. 1982. pap. 0.65 (ISBN 0-686-37071-6). Life Pubs Intl.

Briseno, Guillermo. Como Ayudar Cristianizacion. 77p. 1982. pap. 0.65 (ISBN 0-8297-1380-8). Life Pubs Intl.

--Como Caminar En El Espiritu. 70p. 1982. pap. 0.55 (ISBN 0-8297-1381-6). Life Pubs Intl.

--Como Comunicar El Evangelio. 75p. 1982. pap. 0.65 (ISBN 0-8297-1378-6). Life Pubs Intl.

--Como Dirigir A Otros A Cristo. 66p. 1982. pap. 0.65 (ISBN 0-686-37083-X). Life Pubs Intl.

--Como Estar Seguro-Conocer A Dios. 64p. 1982. pap. 0.65 (ISBN 0-8297-1374-3). Life Pubs Intl.

--Como Hablar Con Dios. 58p. 1982. pap. 0.65 (ISBN 0-8297-1382-4). Life Pubs Intl.

Brisk, Maria E., et al. Working with the Bilingual Community. LC 79-84372. 96p. (Orig.). 1979. pap. 6.75 (ISBN 0-89763-013-0). Natl Clearinghse Bilingual Ed.

Brisk, William J., tr. see Campos, German J.

Briskin, Jacqueline. The Onyx. 1983. pap. 3.95 (ISBN 0-440-16667-5). Dell.

--Paloverde. 624p. 1983. pap. 3.95 o.p. (ISBN 0-446-30345-3). Warner Bks.

--Rich Friends. 1983. pap. 3.95 (ISBN 0-440-17380-9). Dell.

Brisley, Chester L., ed. Fixed Interval Work Sampling. 1969. pap. text ed. 12.00 (ISBN 0-89806-025-7, 147); pap. text ed. 6.00 members. Inst Indus Eng.

Brislin, R. W., et al. Cross-Cultural Research Methods. 351p. 1973. 36.95x o.p. (ISBN 0-471-10470-1). Halsted Pr.

Brislin, R. W., et al, eds. Cross Cultural Perspectives in Learning. LC 73-91353. (Cross Cultural Research & Methodology Ser.). 366p. 1975. 18.95x o.p. (ISBN 0-470-10471-6). Halsted Pr.

Brislin, Richard W. see Hamnett, Michael P.

Brislin, Richard W., ed. Culture Learning: Concepts, Applications, & Research. 1977. pap. text ed. 12.00x (ISBN 0-8248-0544-5, Eastwest Ctr). UH Pr.

Brislin, Richard W., jt. ed. see Landis, Dan.

Brislin, Richard W., et al. Cross-Cultural Research Methods. LC 73-772. (Comparative Studies in Behavioral Sciences). 1973. 41.50 (ISBN 0-471-10470-1, Pub. by Wiley-Interscience). Wiley.

Brissenden, Alan, ed. Portable Rolf Boldrewood. (Portable Australian Authors Ser.). 1979. 30.00x (ISBN 0-7022-1288-1); pap. 12.95x (ISBN 0-7022-1277-6). U of Queensland Pr.

Brissenden, R. F., ed. see Fielding, Henry.

Brisson, P. R. de. Histoire du Naufrage et de la Captivite de M. de Brisson. (Bibliotheque Africaine Ser.). 200p. (Fr.). 1974. Repr. of 1789 ed. lib. bdg. 57.00x o.p. (ISBN 0-8287-0142-3, 72-2109). Clearwater Pub.

Bristal, Joanna. Fortunes of Evie. (Orig.). 1978. pap. 1.50 o.p. (ISBN 0-451-07982-5, W7982, Sig). NAL.

Brister, C. W. El Cuidado Pastoral De la Iglesia. Tinao, D., et al, trs. Orig. Title: Pastoral Care in the Church. 226p. (Span.). 1980. pap. 5.50 (ISBN 0-311-42040-0). Casa Bautista.

--Pastoral Care in the Church. LC 64-19497. 1977. pap. 6.68i (ISBN 0-06-061051-4, RD 222, HarpR). Har-Row.

--The Promise of Counseling. LC 77-20453. 1978. 9.95i o.p. (ISBN 0-06-061052-2, HarpR). Har-Row.

Brister, Judith, tr. see Galeano, Eduardo.

Bristol (England) Women's Studies Group. Half the Sky: Introduction to Women's Studies. 306p. 1983. pap. 9.95 (ISBN 0-86068-086-X, Virago Pr). Merrimack Bk Serv.

Bristol, Evelyn, ed. & intro. by. East European Literature: Papers from the Second World Congress for Soviet & East European Studies. 106p. 1982. pap. 8.00 (ISBN 0-933884-26-5). Berkeley Slavic.

Bristol, James. Nonviolence: Not First for Export. 1972. pap. 0.30 (ISBN 0-686-95383-5). Am Fr Serv Comm.

Bristol, Joanna. Evie's Fortune in Paris. (Orig.). 1978. pap. 1.50 o.p. (ISBN 0-451-08267-2, W8267, Sig). NAL.

--Evie's Roman Fortune. 1979. pap. 1.50 o.p. (ISBN 0-451-08616-3, W8616, Sig). NAL.

Bristol, Marc. Homegrown Music. LC 82-17217. (Illus.). 144p. (Orig.). 1983. pap. 8.95 (ISBN 0-914842-91-9). Madrona Pubs.

Briston, J. H. & Neill, T. J. Packaging Management. 1973. 23.00x o.p. (ISBN 0-8464-0700-0). Beekman Pubs.

Briston, R. J., jt. auth. see Paish, F. W.

Bristow, Alec. The Easy Garden. LC 78-65630. (Illus.). 1979. 11.95 o.p. (ISBN 0-690-01802-9); pap. 5.95i (ISBN 0-690-01822-3, TYC-T). T Y Crowell.

--Grow Your Own. LC 78-65629. (Illus.). 1979. 11.95 o.p. (ISBN 0-690-01803-7); pap. 5.95 (ISBN 0-690-01821-5, TYC-T). T Y Crowell.

Bristow, Camille & Cohn, Marian R. Services for Sexually Active, Pregnant, & Parenting Adolescents in New York City: Planning for the Future, Vol. 1. LC 82-71262. (Illus.). 140p. (Orig.). 1982. pap. write for info. (ISBN 0-943138-01-9). Ctr Pub.

Bristow, Eugene K., ed. see Chekhov, Anton.

Bristow, George. Rip Van Winkle. (Early American Music Ser.: No. 25). 297p. 1983. 39.50 (ISBN 0-306-76124-6). Da Capo.

Bristow, Gwen. Calico Palace. LC 72-106584. 1970. 12.45i (ISBN 0-690-16608-7). T Y Crowell.

--Deep Summer. LC 37-1118. 1964. 12.45 (ISBN 0-690-23318-3). T Y Crowell.

--Golden Dreams. (Illus.). 1980. 12.45i (ISBN 0-690-01678-6). T Y Crowell.

--Handsome Road. 320p. 1979. Repr. lib. bdg. 16.95 (ISBN 0-89966-028-2). Buccaneer Bks.

--This Side of Glory. 278p. 1979. Repr. lib. bdg. 16.95x (ISBN 0-89966-026-6). Buccaneer Bks.

Bristow, Linda. Bed & Breakfast: California. (Illus.). 180p. 1983. pap. 7.95 (ISBN 0-87701-196-6). Chronicle Bks.

Bristow, M. R., ed. Drug-Induced Heart Disease. (Drug Induced Diseases Ser.: Vol. 5). 1981. 101.50 (ISBN 0-444-80206-1). Elsevier.

Bristow, Opal & Stickney, Carol. Discharge Planning for Continuity of Care. (League Exchange Ser.: No. 112). 144p. 1976. 5.95 (ISBN 0-686-38206-4, 21-1604). Natl League Nurse.

Britan, Halbert H., tr. see De Spinoza, Benedictus.

Britch, Carroll, et al. Speech Acts: Hints & Samples. 112p. (Orig.). 1983. pap. text ed. 6.95x (ISBN 0-88133-016-7). Waveland Pr.

Britchky, Seymour. The Restaurants of New York, 1980-1981. 4th ed. 352p. 1980. 7.95 o.p. (ISBN 0-394-73758-X). Random.

--Seymour Britchky's New Revised Guide to the Restaurants of New York: An Irreverent Appraisal of the Best, Most Interesting, Most Famous, Most Underated or Worst Restaurants in New York City. 1976. pap. 8.95 (ISBN 0-394-74863-8). Random.

Brite, Robert L. Business Statistics. LC 79-25657. 1980. text ed. 19.95 (ISBN 0-201-00561-1); solutions manual 2.95 (ISBN 0-201-00562-X). A-W.

--Introduction to Business Statistics. LC 76-17717. (Illus.). 1977. text ed. 17.95 (ISBN 0-201-00593-X). A-W.

British Association For The Advancement Of Science - Committee On Local Industries. Resources, Products & Industrial History of Birmingham & the Midland Hardware Districts. Timmins, Samuel, ed. LC 68-103772. (Illus.). Repr. of 1866 ed. lib. bdg. 32.50x o.p. (ISBN 0-678-05205-0). Kelley.

British Association of Illustrators Staff. Images: The British Association of Illustrators Sixth Annual 1981-82. (Illus.). 1983. 35.00 (ISBN 0-393-50001-2). Norton.

British Astronomical Association. Observing the Moon. (Illus.). 64p. 1983. pap. text ed. 10.95 (ISBN 0-89490-085-4). Enslow Pubs.

British Australian & New Zealand Antarctic Research Expedition-1929-1931. Winning of Australian Antarctica, Mawson's B.A.N.Z.A.R.E. Voyages, 1929-32: Based on the Mawson Papers. Price, A. Grenfell, tr. LC 63-196. (Illus.). 1968. Repr. of 1962 ed. lib. bdg. 19.00x (ISBN 0-8371-5030-2, PRWA). Greenwood.

British Combinatorial Conference, Sixth. Combinatorial Surveys: Proceedings. Cameron, Peter, ed. 1977. 36.50 (ISBN 0-12-157150-5). Acad Pr.

British Computer Society. Algol Sixty Booklet. 1978. 11.95 o.p. (ISBN 0-471-25606-4, Pub. by Wiley Heyden). Wiley.

--Data Dictionary Systems Working Party Report. 1977. 19.95 o.p. (ISBN 0-471-25609-9, Pub by Wiley Heyden). Wiley.

--Minicomputers: Proceedings of the Nottingham Branch Winter School. 1975. 17.50 o.p. (ISBN 0-85501-425-3). Wiley.

--Privacy & the Computer: Steps to Practicality. 1972. 11.95 o.p. (ISBN 0-471-25610-2, Wiley Heyden). Wiley.

--Simplicity of Comp-Proc. Microform Specialist Group Seminar. 1976. 19.95 o.p. (ISBN 0-471-25611-0, Wiley Heyden). Wiley.

--User Requirements for Data Processing. 1978. 42.95 o.p. (ISBN 0-471-25612-9, Wiley Heyden). Wiley.

--Weekly Wages by Direct Credit. 1979. 42.95 o.p. (ISBN 0-471-25613-7, Wiley Heyden). Wiley.

British Computer Society & Salter, J. Query Languages: A Unified Approach. 88p. 1980. 29.95 (ISBN 0-471-26012-6). Wiley.

British European Centre, Paris. Explorations: The English Language Course of the British European Centre. Bolger, ed. (Pergamon Institute of English Courses). (Illus.). 160p. 1981. pap. 6.95 (ISBN 0-08-025358-X). Pergamon.

British Family Research Committee. Families in Britain. 350p. 1983. pap. 25.00 (ISBN 0-7100-9236-9). Routledge & Kegan.

British Film Institute, London. Catalogue of the Book Library of the British Film Institute, 3 vols. 1975. Set. lib. bdg. 285.00 (ISBN 0-8161-0004-7, Hall Library). G K Hall.

British Horse Society & Pony Club. Aids & Their Application. 1976. pap. 3.95 (ISBN 0-8120-0760-3). Barron.

--The Foot & Shoeing. LC 76-55015. 1976. pap. 2.95 (ISBN 0-8120-0758-1). Barron.

--A Guide to the Purchase of Children's Ponies. 1979. pap. 2.95 (ISBN 0-8120-0786-7). Barron.

--The Instructors' Handbook. LC 76-55317. 1977. 7.75 (ISBN 0-8120-5125-4). Barron.

--Keeping a Pony at Grass. LC 76-54872. 1977. 5.95 (ISBN 0-8120-5126-2). Barron.

--The Manual of Horsemanship. (Illus.). Repr. of 1950 ed. text ed. 8.95 (ISBN 0-8120-5462-8). Barron.

--Mounted Games & Gymkhanas. LC 76-56448. 1977. 6.95 (ISBN 0-8120-5124-6). Barron.

--Polo for the Pony Club. LC 76-54905. 1977. pap. 2.95 (ISBN 0-8120-0785-9). Barron.

--Riding to Hounds. 1976. pap. 2.95 (ISBN 0-8120-0756-5). Barron.

--Training the Young Horse & Pony. LC 76-41140. 1977. text ed. 5.95 (ISBN 0-8120-5106-8). Barron.

British Hotels, Restaurants & Caterers Association. Hotels & Restaurants in Britain 1983. (Illus.). 550p. 1983. pap. 12.95 (ISBN 0-13-394916-8). P-H.

British Institute of International & Comparative Law. Selected Documents on International Environmental Law. LC 75-15273. 197p. 1975. 15.00 (ISBN 0-379-00348-1). Oceana.

British Museum. Dinosaurs & Their Living Relatives. LC 79-14504. (Natural History Ser.). 1980. 21.95 (ISBN 0-521-22887-5); pap. 7.95 (ISBN 0-521-29698-6). Cambridge U Pr.

--Life Before Birth. LC 78-60029. (Natural History Ser.). (Illus.). 1979. 7.95 (ISBN 0-521-22382-2); pap. 4.95 (ISBN 0-521-29464-9). Cambridge U Pr.

--Man's Place in Evolution. (Natural History Ser.). (Illus.). 120p. 1981. 22.95 (ISBN 0-521-23177-9); pap. 8.95 (ISBN 0-521-29849-0). Cambridge U Pr.

--Nature at Work. LC 78-66795. (Natural History Ser.). (Illus.). 1978. 18.95 (ISBN 0-521-22390-3); pap. 7.95 (ISBN 0-521-29469-X). Cambridge U Pr.

--Origin of Species. LC 80-42170. (Natural History Ser.). 120p. 1981. 24.95 (ISBN 0-521-23878-1); pap. 9.95 (ISBN 0-521-28276-4). Cambridge U Pr.

British Museum & Metropolitan Museum of Art. The Vikings. LC 79-25486. (Illus.). 192p. 1980. 22.95 o.p. (ISBN 0-688-03603-1). Morrow.

British Museum (Natural History) Nature Stored, Nature Studied: Collections, Conservation & Allied Research at the British Museum (Natural History) (Illus.). 64p. 1981. pap. 6.50x (ISBN 0-565-00835-8, Pub. by Brit Mus Nat Hist England). Sabbot-Natural Hist Bks.

British Tourist Authority. AA Greater London Street Atlas. 1982. 39.95 o.p. (ISBN 0-86145-070-1, Pub. by B T A). Merrimack Bk Serv.

--AA Touring Map of South-East Europe. 1982. 3.95 o.p. (ISBN 0-86145-072-8, Pub. by B T A). Merrimack Bk Serv.

--Britain: Commended Country Hotels. (Illus.). 120p. 1982. pap. 6.95 o.p. (ISBN 0-7095-0899-9, Pub. by Auto Assn-British Tourist Authority England). Merrimack Bk Serv.

--Country Life Living History of Britain. 1982. 39.95 (ISBN 0-600-36783-5, Pub. by B T A). Merrimack Bk Serv.

--Discovering Cathedrals. (Illus.). 80p. 1981. pap. 2.95 o.p. (ISBN 0-85263-472-2, Pub. by Auto Assn-British Tourist Authority England). Merrimack Bk Serv.

--Discovering English Customs & Traditions. (Illus.). 80p. 1981. pap. 2.95 o.p. (ISBN 0-686-34422-7, Pub. by Auto Assn-British Tourist Authority). Merrimack Bk Serv.

--Discovering Gardens in Britain. (Illus.). 80p. 1981. pap. 2.95 o.p. (ISBN 0-85263-456-0, Pub. by Auto Assn-British Tourist Authority England). Merrimack Bk Serv.

--Discovering Kings & Queens. (Illus.). 88p. 1981. pap. 2.95 o.p. (ISBN 0-85263-439-0, Pub. by Auto Assn-British Tourist Authority England). Merrimack Bk Serv.

--Discovering London's Villages. (Illus.). 72p. 1981. pap. 2.95 o.p. (ISBN 0-85263-451-X, Pub. by Auto Assn-British Tourist Authority England). Merrimack Bk Serv.

--Discovering Preserved Railways. (Illus.). 72p. 1981. pap. cancelled o.p. (ISBN 0-85263-515-X, Pub. by Auto Assn-British Tourist Authority England). Merrimack Bk Serv.

--East Anglia. (Illus.). 130p. 1982. pap. 3.25 o.p. (ISBN 0-86143-064-6, Pub. by Auto Assn-British Tourist Authority England). Merrimack Bk Serv.

--East Midlands. (Illus.). 82p. 1982. pap. 3.25 o.p. (ISBN 0-86143-062-X, Pub. by Auto Assn-British Tourist Authority England). Merrimack Bk Serv.

--Egon Ronay's Pub Guide, 1982. 384p. 1982. pap. 4.95 o.p. (ISBN 0-14-006114-2, Pub. by Auto Assn-British Tourist Authority England). Merrimack Bk Serv.

--English Lakeland-Cumbria. (Illus.). 186p. 1982. pap. 3.25 o.p. (ISBN 0-86143-057-3, Pub. by Auto Assn-British Tourist Authority England). Merrimack Bk Serv.

--English Lakeland: Cumbria. rev. ed. (Illus.). 114p. 1981. pap. 3.25 o.p. (ISBN 0-86143-037-9, Pub. by Auto Assn-British Tourist Authority England). Merrimack Bk Serv.

--Heart of England. (Illus.). 122p. 1982. pap. 3.25 o.p. (ISBN 0-86143-061-1, Pub. by Auto Assn-British Tourist Authority England). Merrimack Bk Serv.

--Hotels & Restaurants in Britain, 1982-3. LC 52-21171. (Illus.). 600p. 1982. pap. 10.00x (ISBN 0-7095-0897-2). Intl Pubns Serv.

--London: Hotels & Restaurants. (Illus.). 138p. 1982. pap. 3.95 o.p. (ISBN 0-7095-0904-9, Pub. by Auto Assn-British Tourist Authority England). Merrimack Bk Serv.

--North-West England. (Illus.). 82p. 1982. pap. 3.25 o.p. (ISBN 0-86143-059-X, Pub. by Auto Assn-British Tourist Authority England). Merrimack Bk Serv.

--North West England. rev. ed. (Illus.). 74p. 1981. pap. 3.25 o.p. (ISBN 0-86143-039-5, Pub. by Auto Assn-British Tourist Authority England). Merrimack Bk Serv.

--Northumbria. (Illus.). 82p. 1982. pap. 3.25 o.p. (ISBN 0-86143-058-1, Pub. by Auto Assn-British Tourist Authority England). Merrimack Bk Serv.

British Tourist Authority, jt. auth. see Automobile Association.

Britnieva, Mary, tr. see Benois, Alexandre.

Britt, George, jt. auth. see Broun, Heywood.

Britt, Steuart, ed. Consumer Behavior & the Behavioral Sciences: Theories & Applications. LC 78-9748. 624p. 1979. Repr. of 1966 ed. lib. bdg. 28.50 (ISBN 0-88275-704-0). Krieger.

Britt, Steuart H. Marketing Manager's Handbook. 1983. 57.50 (ISBN 0-85013-135-9). Dartnell Corp.

Britt, Steuart H. & Boyd, Harper W. Marketing Management & Administrative Action. 4th ed. (Illus.). 1978. pap. text ed. 16.95 (ISBN 0-07-007923-4, C). McGraw.

--Marketing Management & Administrative Action. 5th ed. (Illus.). 496p. 1983. text ed. 16.95 (ISBN 0-07-006949-2, C). McGraw.

Britt, Stewart H. Psychological Principles of Marketing & Consumer Behavior. LC 77-75658. 1978. 33.95x (ISBN 0-669-01513-X). Lexington Bks.

Brittain, Bill. The Wish Giver. LC 82-48264. (Illus.). 192p. (gr. 3-7). 1983. 9.57i (ISBN 0-06-020686-1, HarpJ); PLB 9.89g (ISBN 0-06-020687-X). Har-Row.

Brittain, Frederick. A History of Jesus College, Cambridge. 1979. text ed. 19.95x o.p. (ISBN 0-435-32141-2). Heinemann Ed.

Brittain, J., jt. auth. see Keith, L.

Brittain, James E., ed. Turning Points in American Electrical History. LC 76-18433. (Illus.). 1977. 36.95 (ISBN 0-87942-081-2). Inst Electrical.

Brittain, Joan T. Laurence Stallings. LC 74-23831. (United States Authors Ser.). 1975. lib. bdg. 13.95 (ISBN 0-8057-0686-0, Twayne). G K Hall.

Brittain, John A. Inheritance & the Inequality of Material Wealth. LC 77-91814. (Studies in Social Economics). 1978. 11.95 (ISBN 0-8157-1084-4); pap. 4.95 (ISBN 0-8157-1083-6). Brookings.

--The Inheritance of Economic Status. LC 76-56369. (Studies in Social Economics). 1977. 15.95 (ISBN 0-8157-1082-8); pap. 5.95 (ISBN 0-8157-1081-X). Brookings.

Brittain, Robert. Punctuation the Easy Way. 85p. (gr. 10-12). 1983. pap. text ed. 1.95 (ISBN 0-8120-2426-5). Barron.

Brittain, Robert, ed. The Booklover's Almanac. 432p. 1982. 39.00x (ISBN 0-284-79527-5, Pub. by C Skilton Scotland). State Mutual Bk.

Brittain, Vera. Account Rendered. 340p. 1983. pap. 7.95 (ISBN 0-86068-268-4, Virago Pr). Merrimack Bk Serv.

--Born Nineteen Twenty-Five. 384p. 1983. pap. 7.95 (ISBN 0-86068-270-6, Virago Pr). Merrimack Bk Serv.

--Chronicle of Youth: The War Diary 1913-1917. Bishop, Alan, ed. LC 82-6340. 1982. 15.50 (ISBN 0-688-01523-9). Morrow.

Brittain, W. Bruce, jt. auth. see Cleveland, Harold Van B.

Brittain, W. Lambert. Creativity, Art, & the Young Child. (Illus.). 1979. text ed. 17.95 (ISBN 0-02-314990-6). Macmillan.

Brittain, W. Lambert, jt. auth. see Lowenfeld, Viktor.

Brittain, William. Survival Outdoors. (Monarch Illustrated Guide Ser.). (Illus.). 1977. pap. 2.95 o.p. (ISBN 0-671-18763-5). Monarch Pr.

Brittan, Arthur. Meanings & Situations. (International Library of Sociology). 222p. 1973. 18.50 (ISBN 0-7100-7509-X); pap. 6.00 o.p. (ISBN 0-7100-7551-0). Routledge & Kegan.

Brittan, Gordon G., Jr., jt. auth. see Lambert, Karel.

Brittan, Martin. Rasbora. (Illus.). 1972. 19.95 (ISBN 0-87666-136-3, PS-681). TFH Pubns.

Brittan, Samuel. Price of Economic Freedom. LC 73-130745. 1971. 8.95 o.p. (ISBN 0-312-64225-3, P39970). St Martin.

--Steering the Economy: The British Experiment. LC 71-152814. 504p. 1971. 27.50x (ISBN 0-912050-05-5, Library Pr). Open Court.

Brittan, Samuel & Lilley, Peter. Delusion of Incomes Policy. 1977. pap. 13.50x (ISBN 0-8419-6900-0). Holmes & Meier.

Britten, Anthony F., jt. ed. see Kolins, Jerry.

Britten, Benjamin, jt. auth. see Boulanger, Nadia.

Britter, R. E. & Griffiths, R. F. Dense Gas Dispersion. (Chemical Engineering Monographs: Vol. 16). 1982. Repr. 68.00 (ISBN 0-444-42095-9). Elsevier.

Brittin, Norman A. Edna St. Vincent Millay. (U. S. Authors Ser.: No. 116). 1967. lib. bdg. 10.95 o.p. (ISBN 0-8057-0496-5, Twayne). G K Hall.

--Edna St. Vincent Millay. Rev. ed. (United States Authors Ser.). 1982. lib. bdg. 12.95 (ISBN 0-8057-7362-2, Twayne). G K Hall.

--Thomas Middleton. (English Authors Ser.). lib. bdg. 14.95 (ISBN 0-8057-1388-3, Twayne). G K Hall.

Brittin, W., ed. Lectures in Theoretical Physics. Vol. 14 B: Mathematical Methods in Theoretical Physics. LC 59-13034. (Illus.). 520p. 1973. 19.50x (ISBN 0-87081-047-2). Colo Assoc.

Brittin, Wesley E. & Odabasi, Halis, eds. Topics in Modern Physics: Tribute to E. U. Condon. LC 70-135286. 1971. 18.50x (ISBN 0-87081-010-3). Colo Assoc.

Brittin, Wesley E., jt. ed. see Barut, A. O.

Brittin, Wesley E., jt. ed. see Barut, Asim O.

Brittin, Wesley E., et al. Air & Water Pollution. LC 72-165367. 1971. 17.95x (ISBN 0-87081-024-3); pap. 4.95x (ISBN 0-87081-040-5). Colo Assoc.

Britting, Kenneth R. Inertial Navigation Systems Analysis. LC 70-168635. 1971. 37.50 (ISBN 0-471-10485-X, Pub. by Wiley-Interscience). Wiley.

Brittingham, Barbara E., jt. auth. see Pezzullo, Thomas R.

Britto, Rudolf, jt. auth. see Asselmann, Teresa.

Britton, Anna. Fike's Point. LC 78-11281. (gr. 6-12). 1979. 7.95 o.p. (ISBN 0-698-20474-3, Coward). Putnam Pub Group.

Britton, Bryce. The Love Muscle: Every Woman's Guide to Intensifying Sexual Pleasure. (Illus.). 1982. pap. 7.95 (ISBN 0-452-25382-9, Plume). NAL.

Britton, Coburn. Second Seasons. (Illus.). 80p. (Orig.). 1982. pap. 6.95 (ISBN 0-8180-1584-5). Horizon.

Britton, D. K. Cereals in the United Kingdom. 1969. inquire for price o.p. (ISBN 0-08-013896-9). Pergamon.

Britton, Frank. English Delftware in the Bristol Collection. (Illus.). 336p. 1982. 100.00x (ISBN 0-85667-152-5, Pub. by Sotheby Pubns England). Biblio Dist.

Britton, Jack L. Nazi Belt Buckles. (Illus.). 1983. pap. 7.95 (ISBN 0-912958-07-3). MCN Pr.

--Nazi Dagger I.D. (Illus.). 1983. pap. 7.95 (ISBN 0-912958-08-1). MCN Pr.

Britton, Jack R. & Bello, Ignacio. Contemporary College Algebra & Trigonometry. 581p. 1982. text ed. 21.50 scp (ISBN 0-06-040989-4, HarpC); instr. manual avail.; chapter test avail. (ISBN 0-06-360923-1). Har-Row.

Britton, James. Language & Learning. 304p. (Orig.). 1972. pap. text ed. 7.00 (ISBN 0-14-021456-9). Boynton Cook Pubs.

--Prospect & Retrospect: Selected Essays of James Britton. Pradl, Gordon M., ed. LC 82-14608. 224p. 1982. pap. text ed. 9.00 (ISBN 0-686-38081-9). Boynton Cook Pubs.

Britton, James, jt. auth. see Barnes, Douglas.

Britton, James A., Jr. & Kerwood, Lewis O., eds. Financing Income-Producing Real Estate. (Illus.). 1977. text ed. 34.95 (ISBN 0-07-007926-9, T&D); case solutions manual 1.95 (ISBN 0-07-007927-7). McGraw.

Britton, Phil, jt. auth. see Daniel, Joe.

Britton, Raymond L. The Arbitration Guide. (Illus.). 304p. 1982. three-ring binder 45.00 (ISBN 0-13-043984-3). P-H.

Britton, Scott G. Practical Coal Mine Management. LC 81-11426. 233p. 1981. 32.95 (ISBN 0-471-09035-2, Pub. by Wiley-Interscience). Wiley.

Britz-Crecelius, Heidi. Children at Play. (Illus.). 1979. 16.50 (ISBN 0-903540-24-X, Pub. by Floris Books); pap. 9.50 (ISBN 0-903540-27-4, Pub. by Floris Books). St George Bk Serv.

Briusov, Valery. Complete Short Stories. Gilbert, Gail & Hart, Pierre, trs. from Rus. 200p. 1983. 20.00 (ISBN 0-88233-790-4); pap. 5.00 (ISBN 0-88233-791-2). Ardis Pubs.

Brix, Dale, jt. auth. see Wimer, Arthur.

Brix, V. H. You Are a Computer: Cybernetics in Everyday Life. (gr. 9 up). 1970. 8.95 (ISBN 0-87523-169-1). Emerson.

Brizendine, Nancy H. & Thomas, James L. Learning Through Dramatics: Ideas for Teachers & Librarians. LC 82-2239. 1982. pap. text ed. 18.50x (ISBN 0-89774-005-X). Oryx Pr.

Brizzee, Ken, jt. ed. see Ordy, J. Mark.

Brizzolara, Andrew, compiled by. A Directory of Italian & Italian American Organizations & Community Services in the Metropolitan Area of Greater New York: in the Metropolitan Area of Greater New York, Vol. II. rev. ed. 1980. 9.95x (ISBN 0-913256-44-7, Dist. by Ozer). Ctr Migration.

Brkic, S. Serbocroatian-English Dictionary. 416p. (Serbocroatian & Eng.). 1980. pap. 14.95 (ISBN 0-686-97436-0, M-9631). French & Eur.

Bro, Bernard. Happy Those Who Believe. rev. 2nd ed. Morriss, John M., tr. from Fr. (Illus.). 142p. (Eng.). 1973. pap. 0.95 o.p. (ISBN 0-8189-1105-0, Pub. by Alba Bks). Alba.

--The Little Way. pap. 5.95 o.p. (ISBN 0-87061-052-X). Chr Classics.

--The Rediscovery of Prayer. Morriss, John, tr. from Fr. LC 72-9578. Orig. Title: Learning to Pray. 220p. (Eng.). 1973. pap. 1.25 o.p. (ISBN 0-8189-1110-7, Pub. by Alba Bks.). Alba.

Broad, C. D. Religion, Philosophy & Psychical Research. (International Library of Psychology, Philosophy & Scientific Method Ser.). 1969. Repr. of 1953 ed. text ed. 15.00x (ISBN 0-391-00441-7). Humanities.

Broad, C. D. & Lewy, C. Leibniz: An Introduction. LC 74-31784. 192p. 1975. 29.95 (ISBN 0-521-20691-X); pap. 9.95 (ISBN 0-521-09925-0). Cambridge U Pr.

Broad, Charles D. Scientific Thought. (Quality Paperback: No. 208). 555p. 1959. pap. 4.95 (ISBN 0-8226-0208-3). Littlefield.

Broad, Delia. Space Adventures Reading Series Sampler. 1980. pap. 24.00 (ISBN 0-88450-723-8, 4520-B). Communication Skill.

Broad, Laura P. & Butterworth, Nancy T. The Playgroup Handbook. LC 73-87399. (Griffin Ser.). (Illus.). 1974. 10.00 (ISBN 0-312-61565-5); pap. 6.95 (ISBN 0-312-61600-7). St Martin.

Broad, O. D. Kant: An Introduction. Lewy, C., ed. LC 77-80829. 1978. 47.50 (ISBN 0-521-21755-5); pap. 12.95 (ISBN 0-521-29265-4). Cambridge U Pr.

Broad, William & Wade, Nicholas. Betrayers of the Truth. LC 82-10583. 1983. 14.95 (ISBN 0-671-44769-6). S&S.

Broadbent, et al, eds. see Milton, John.

Broadbent, D. E. & Weiskrantz, L., eds. The Neuropsychology of Cognitive Function: Proceedings of a Royal Society Discussion Meeting, November 18-19, 1981. (RSL Philosophical Transcriptions of the Royal Society of London, Ser. B: Vol. 298, No. 1089). (Illus.). 230p. 1982. text ed. 68.00x (ISBN 0-85403-190-1, Pub. by Royal Soc London). Scholium Intl.

Broadbent, Geoffrey. Design in Architecture: Architecture & the Human Sciences. LC 71-39233. 504p. 1978. pap. 23.95x (ISBN 0-471-99527-4). Wiley.

Broadbent, Geoffrey, et al. Signs, Symbols & Architecture. LC 78-13557. 1980. 59.95x (ISBN 0-471-99718-8, Pub. by Wiley-Interscience). Wiley.

Broadbent, Geoffrey, et al, eds. Meaning & Behaviour in the Built Environment. LC 79-41490. 372p. 1980. 57.00x (ISBN 0-471-27708-8, Pub. by Wiley-Interscience). Wiley.

Broadbent, John. Introduction to Paradise Lost. (Milton for Schools & Colleges Ser.). (Illus.). 1971. 29.95 (ISBN 0-521-08068-1); pap. 9.50 (ISBN 0-521-09639-1). Cambridge U Pr.

Broadbent, John, ed. see Milton, John.

Broadbent, John J. Signet Classic Poets of the Seventeenth Century, 2 vols. (Orig.). 1974. Vol. 1. pap. 2.25 o.p. (ISBN 0-685-50245-7, CE728, Sig Classics); Vol. 2. pap. 2.25 o.p. (ISBN 0-685-50246-5, CE729). NAL.

Broadbent, Michael. Michael Broadbent's Pocket Guide to Wine Tasting. (Illus.). 1982. 5.95 (ISBN 0-671-45235-5). S&S.

--Wine Tasting: Enjoying & Understanding. 6th ed. (Christie Wine Publications). 68p. 1979. 15.00x o.p. (ISBN 0-304-30277-5). Intl Pubns Serv.

Broadbent, T. A. Planning & Profit in the Urban Economy. 1977. 12.95x (ISBN 0-416-56320-1); pap. 12.95x (ISBN 0-416-56330-9). Methuen Inc.

Broadbent, W. W. How to be Loved. 208p. 1977. pap. 2.95 (ISBN 0-446-30024-1). Warner Bks.

Broadcast Information Bureau, Inc. The Radio Programs Source Book. Doris, Liz, ed. 100p. (Orig.). 1982. pap. 62.95 (ISBN 0-943174-01-5). Broadcast Info.

Broadfoot, Patricia, jt. auth. see Black, Harry.

Broadhead, Robert S. The Private Lives of Medical Students. 200p. 1983. 24.95 (ISBN 0-87855-478-5). Transaction Bks.

Broadhouse, John, tr. see Anbele, H. & Niederheitmann, F.

Broadhurst, R. J. A History of the Ayyubid Sultans of Egypt. (International Studies & Translations Program). 1980. lib. bdg. 25.00 (ISBN 0-8057-8168-4, Twayne). G K Hall.

Broadhurst, V. A. The Health & Safety at Work Act in Practice. 1978. 28.95 (ISBN 0-471-25614-5, Pub. by Wiley Heyden). Wiley.

Broadribb, Violet. Introductory Pediatric Nursing. 3rd ed. (Illus.). 392p. 1982. pap. text ed. 13.50 (ISBN 0-397-54330-1, Lippincott Nursing). Lippincott.

Broadus, J. A. Tratado Sobre la Predicacion. Barocio, Ernesto, tr. Orig. Title: On the Preparation & Delivery of Sermons. 336p. 1981. pap. 5.25 (ISBN 0-311-42034-6). Casa Bautista.

Broadus, Loren. How to Stop Procrastinating & Start Living. LC 82-72641. 128p. 1983. pap. 4.95 (ISBN 0-8066-1947-3, 10-3178). Augsburg.

Broadus, Robert N. Selecting Materials for Libraries. 2nd ed. xiv, 464p. 1981. 18.00 (ISBN 0-8242-0659-2). Wilson.

Broadwell, Bruce, jt. auth. see Edwards, Perry.

Broadwell, Lucile & Milutinovic, Barbara. Medical-Surgical Nursing Procedures. LC 76-4305. 1977. pap. text ed. 16.60 (ISBN 0-8273-0353-X); instructor's guide 2.50 (ISBN 0-8273-0354-8). Delmar.

Brobeck, John R. Neural Control Systems. LC 72-85159. 108p. 1973. pap. 9.50 o.p. (ISBN 0-686-65351-3, Pub. by Williams & Wilkens). Krieger.

Brobst, Bob & Bush, Ronald F. Marketing Simulation: Analysis for Decision Making. 2nd ed. 152p. 1983. pap. text ed. 10.95 scp (ISBN 0-06-041104-X, HarpC); instr. manual avail. (ISBN 0-06-361069-8); write for info. deck or tape (ISBN 0-686-82911-5). Har-Row.

Brocardo, G. Minerals & Gemstones: An Identification Guide. (Illus.). 220p. (gr. 6 up). 1983. 12.95 (ISBN 0-88254-756-9). Hippocrene Bks.

Brocas, J. & Gielen, M. Permutational Approach to Dynamic Stereochemistry. 720p. 69.50 (ISBN 0-07-007971-4). McGraw.

Broccoletti, Pete. Prime Cut: Total Fitness for Men 18-34. (Illus.). 1983. 16.95 (ISBN 0-89651-604-0); wire bdg. 10.95 (ISBN 0-89651-605-9). Icarus.

Broccoletti, Peter P. & Scanlon, Pat. The Notre Dame Weight Training Program for Football. LC 78-20947. (Illus.). 1979. 12.95 o.s.i. (ISBN 0-89651-502-8). Icarus.

Broce, Thomas E. & Junkin, Daniel P. Directory of Oklahoma Foundations. Rev., 2nd ed. 304p. 1982. 22.50x (ISBN 0-8061-1827-X). U of Okla Pr.

Broch, Hermann. The Death of Virgil. Untermeyer, Jean S., tr. LC 82-73718. 496p. 1983. pap. 15.50 (ISBN 0-86547-115-0). N Point Pr.

Brochard, Phillippe. Castles of the Middle Ages. LC 81-51439. (Picture Histories Ser.). PLB 12.68 (ISBN 0-382-06610-3). Silver.

--Days of Knights & Castles. LC 81-51439. (Picture Histories Ser.). 12.68 (ISBN 0-382-06472-0). Silver.

Broch De Rothermann, H. F., tr. see Brunner, Heinrich.

Brochmann-Hanssen, E., jt. ed. see Higuchi, T.

Brochner, Jessie, tr. see Lagerlof, Selma O.

Brochner, Jessie, tr. see Reumert, Elith.

Brock, A. A. van Den see Nieuwenhuis, Paul & Van den Brock, A. A.

Brock, Bernard L., et al. Public Policy Decision-Making: Systems Analysis & Comparative Advantages Debate. (Aver Ser.). 1973. pap. text ed. 10.50 scp o.p. (ISBN 0-06-040963-0, HarpC). Har-Row.

Brock, Betty. No Flying in the House. LC 79-104755. (A Trophy Bk.). (Illus.). 144p. (gr. 3-6). 1982. pap. 2.84i (ISBN 0-06-440130-8, Trophy). Har-Row.

Brock, Bill, ed. see Schiller, Donald.

Brock, C. Control of Restrictive Practices from 1956. 1969. 6.95 o.p. (ISBN 0-07-094038-X, P&RB). McGraw.

Brock, D. Heyward. A Ben Jonson Companion. LC 81-48383. 320p. 1983. 25.00x (ISBN 0-253-31159-4). Ind U Pr.

Brock, Dee & Howard, C. Jeriel. Writing for a Reason. LC 77-12617. 1978. pap. text ed. 10.95 o.p. (ISBN 0-471-03017-1); instrs.' manual 1.40 o.p. (ISBN 0-471-04052-5). Scott F.

--Writing for a Reason. 1978. pap. text ed. 13.50x (ISBN 0-673-15657-5). Scott F.

Brock, Eleanor, jt. ed. see Brock, Michael.

Brock, Gerald W. The Telecommunications Industry: The Dynamics of Market Structure. 336p. 1981. 25.00 (ISBN 0-686-98080-8). Telecom Lib.

--The United States Computer Industry: A Study of Market Power. LC 74-22441. 1975. prof ref 22.50x (ISBN 0-88410-261-0). Ballinger Pub.

Brock, Horace, et al. Cost Accounting: Principles & Applications. 3rd ed. (Accounting Instructional System). (Illus.). 1978. text ed. 15.75 (ISBN 0-07-008051-8, G); course management manual 12.40 (ISBN 0-07-008054-2); individualized performance guide 7.85 (ISBN 0-07-008052-6). McGraw.

Brock, Horace R. & Klingstedt, John P. Accounting for Oil & Gas Producing Companies: Pt. 2: Amortization, Conveyances, Full Costing & Disclosures. LC 81-82890. 384p. 1982. pap. text ed. 22.50 (ISBN 0-940966-02-6). N Texas St U Pro Devel Inst.

Brock, Horace R. & Palmer, Charles E. Individualized Performance Guide for Accounting: Principles & Applications, Fourth Edition, Part I. (College Accounting Instructional System). (Illus.). 160p. wkbk. 7.35 (ISBN 0-07-008095-X, C). McGraw.

--Sole Proprietorship Merchandising Business Practice Set: Schier Furniture Company. 2nd ed. (College Accounting Instructional System Ser.). (Illus.). 120p. 1981. 8.35x (ISBN 0-07-008106-9, G). McGraw.

--Sole Proprietorship Service Business Practice Set: Garden Real Estate. (College Accounting Instructional System Ser.). (Illus.). 232p. 1981. 7.80 (ISBN 0-07-008104-2, G); solutions manual 5.05 (ISBN 0-07-008109-3). McGraw.

Brock, Horace R., et al. Accounting: Basic Principles. 3rd ed. 1974. 13.50 o.p. (ISBN 0-07-008024-0, G); individualized performance guide 6.90 o.p. (ISBN 0-07-008022-4); course management & solutions manual for units 1-28 17.95 o.p. (ISBN 0-07-008033-X); test, set 1, units 1-28 free o.p. (ISBN 0-07-008031-3). McGraw.

--College Accounting for Secretaries. 1971. 22.45 (ISBN 0-07-007853-X, G); solutions manual 11.75 (ISBN 0-07-007854-8). McGraw.

--Accounting, Principles & Applications. 3rd ed. 320p. 1974. text ed. 21.35 (ISBN 0-07-008021-6, G); individualized performance guide 8.95 (ISBN 0-07-008023-2); course management & solutions manual for units 29-57 7.95 (ISBN 0-07-008034-8). McGraw.

Brock, Jim & Gilmartin, Joe. The Devils' Coach. LC 77-87255. (Illus.). 1977. 6.95 o.p. (ISBN 0-89191-103-0). Cook.

Brock, Katherine M., jt. auth. see Brock, Thomas D.

Brock, Luther A. How to Communicate by Letter & Memo. (Illus.). 304p. 1974. text ed. 16.95 (ISBN 0-07-008043-7, G); instructor's manual & key 9.40 (ISBN 0-07-008044-5). McGraw.

Brock, M., jt. ed. see Hartmann, A.

Brock, Michael & Brock, Eleanor, eds. H. H. Asquith: Letters to Venetia Stanley. (Illus.). 672p. 1983. 29.95 (ISBN 0-19-212200-2). Oxford U Pr.

Brock, Para L. Sahani. LC 81-10611. (Illus.). (gr. 6-8). 1981. 8.95 (ISBN 0-931948-19-3). Peachtree Pubs.

Brock, Raymond, jt. auth. see Schmidt, Jerry.

Brock, Raymond T. Dating & Waiting for Marriage. LC 81-84763. 1982. pap. 2.50 (ISBN 0-88243-881-6, 02-0881); teacher's ed. 3.95 (ISBN 0-88243-192-7, 32-0190). Gospel Pub.

Brock, Stuart. Double-Cross Ranch. 256p. (YA) 1974. 6.95 (ISBN 0-685-49064-5, Avalon). Bouregy.

Brock, Thomas D. Biology of Microorganisms. 3rd ed. LC 78-13707. 1979. text ed. 31.95 (ISBN 0-13-076778-6). P-H.

--Membrane Filtration: A User's Guide & Reference Manual. (Illus.). 1983. 29.95 (ISBN 0-910239-00-2). Sci Tech Inc.

Brock, Thomas D. & Brock, Katherine M. Basic Microbiology with Applications. 2nd ed. (Illus.). 1978. 26.95 (ISBN 0-13-065284-9). P-H.

Brock, Van K., ed. The Space Behind the Clock. pap. 3.00 o.s.i. (ISBN 0-686-81803-2). Anhinga Pr.

Brock, Van K. & Jordan, David, eds. Cafe at St. Marks. pap. 3.50 (ISBN 0-686-81804-0). Anhinga Pr.

Brock, Van K. & Poole, Francis, eds. Lime Tree Prison. pap. 3.00 (ISBN 0-938078-00-3). Anhinga Pr.

--A Spot of Purple is Deaf. pap. 3.50 (ISBN 0-686-81801-6). Anhinga Pr.

Brock, Vernon E., jt. auth. see Gosline, William A.

Brock, W. H., ed. H. E. Armstrong & the Teaching of Science 1880-1930. LC 72-87179. (Cambridge Texts & Studies in the History of Education: No. 14). 168p. 1973. 25.95 (ISBN 0-521-08679-5). Cambridge U Pr.

Brock, W. R. Character of American History. 2nd ed. (Illus.). 1965. 22.50 (ISBN 0-312-12985-8). St Martin.

--The United States 1789-1890. (Sources of History Ser.). 352p. 1975. 24.50x (ISBN 0-8014-0723-0). Cornell U Pr.

Brock, William. Parties & Political Conscience: American Dilemmas, 1840-1850. LC 78-32174. (KTO Studies in American History). 1979. lib. bdg. 25.00 (ISBN 0-527-11800-1). Kraus Intl.

Brockbank, Phillip, ed. see Shakespeare, William.

Brockelman, Paul T. Existential Phenomenology & the World of Ordinary Experience: An Introduction. LC 80-67208. 83p. 1980. lib. bdg. 16.75 (ISBN 0-8191-1191-0); pap. text ed. 7.25 (ISBN 0-8191-1192-9). U Pr of Amer.

Brocker, T. H. Differentiable Germs & Catastrophes. Lander, L., tr. from Ger. LC 74-17000. (London Mathematical Society Lecture Note Ser.: No. 17). 160p. (Eng.). 1975. pap. text ed. 21.95 (ISBN 0-521-20681-2). Cambridge U Pr.

Brocker, Theodor & Janich, Klaus. Introduction to Differential Topology. LC 81-21591. (Illus.). 150p. 1982. 27.50 (ISBN 0-521-24135-9); pap. 11.95 (ISBN 0-521-28470-8). Cambridge U Pr.

Brockerhoff, Hans & Jensen, Robert G. Lipolytic Enzymes. 1974. 51.00 (ISBN 0-12-134550-5). Acad Pr.

Brocket, E. Old European Fairy Tales. (gr. 1-4). 1971. 8.50 o.p. (ISBN 0-584-62385-2). Transatlantic.

Brockett, Eleanor, tr. see Rebuffat, Gaston.

Brockett, Henry E. Christian & Romans 7. 1972. 1.95 o.p. (ISBN 0-8341-0281-1). Beacon Hill.

Brockett, O. & Findlay, R. Century of Innovation: A History of European & American Theatre & Drama, 1870-1970. (Theater & Drama Ser.). 1973. 29.95 (ISBN 0-13-122747-5). P-H.

Brockett, Paul. Bibliography of Aeronautics. LC 66-25692. 1966. Repr. of 1910 ed. 74.00x (ISBN 0-8103-3320-1). Gale.

Brockhuizen, S., jt. ed. see Thran, P.

Brockington, Dave, jt. auth. see White, Roger.

Brockington, I. F. & Kumar, R., eds. Motherhood & Mental Illness. 1982. 31.00 (ISBN 0-8089-1481-2, 790666). Grune.

Brockington, L. H. Ezra, Nehemiah & Esther. (New Century Bible Ser). 1969. text ed. 12.95 (ISBN 0-551-00530-0). Attic Pr.

Brockington, L. H., jt. ed. see Robinson, T. H.

Brockington, N. R. Computer Modelling in Agriculture. (Illus.). 1979. 35.00x (ISBN 0-19-854523-1). Oxford U Pr.

Brockis, J. G. The Scientific Fundamentals of Surgery. (Illus.). 1972. 38.00 o.p. (ISBN 0-407-39000-6). Butterworth.

Brockman, Bennett see Butler, Francelia, et al.

Brockman, C. Frank & Merriam, Lawrence C., Jr. Recreational Use of Wild Lands. 3rd ed. (M-H Series in Forest Resources). (Illus.). 1979. text ed. 27.50 (ISBN 0-07-007982-X, C). McGraw.

--Recreational Use of Wildlands. 2nd ed. (American Forestry Ser.). (Illus.). 336p. 1972. text ed. 17.00 o.p. (ISBN 0-07-007981-1, C). McGraw.

Brockman, H. L. Theory of Fashion Design. 1965. 25.50 o.p. (ISBN 0-87245-041-4). Textile Bk.

Brockman, Helen L. Theory of Fashion Design. LC 65-25852. 268p. 1965. 26.50x (ISBN 0-471-10586-4). Wiley.

Brockman, James R. The Word Remains: A Life of Oscar Romero. LC 82-3607. (Illus.). 256p. (Orig.). 1982. pap. 12.95 (ISBN 0-88344-364-3). Orbis Bks.

Brockman, John, jt. auth. see Schlossberg, Edwin.

Brockman, John, ed. About Bateson: An Introduction to Gregory Bateson. LC 77-4971. 1977. pap. 4.95 o.p. (ISBN 0-525-47469-2). Dutton.

Brockmann, John, jt. ed. see Anderson, Paul.

Brockmeyer, Lloyd & Collison, Kathleen. New Beginnings: A Confirmation Resource. 96p. (Orig.). (gr. 7-8). pap. text ed. 4.00 (ISBN 0-941988-00-7); 3.00 (ISBN 0-941988-01-5). K Q Assocs.

Brockreide, Wayne & Scott, Robert L. Moments in the Rhetoric of the Cold War. (Orig.). 1970. pap. text ed. 3.50 (ISBN 0-685-04767-9). Phila Bk Co.

Brockriede, W., jt. auth. see Darnell, D. K.

Brockriede, Wayne, jt. ed. see Scott, Robert L.

Brockris, J. Energy: The Solar Hydrogen Alternative. LC 75-19125. 365p. Repr. of 1975 ed. 29.50 o.p. (ISBN 0-470-08429-4). Krieger.

Brockway, Earl, jt. auth. see Tuggy, David H.

Brockway, Fenner. The Colonial Revolution. LC 74-77269. 650p. 1974. 29.95 o.p. (ISBN 0-312-15050-4). St Martin.

Brockway, L. O., ed. Fifty Years of Electron Diffraction. pap. 7.50 (ISBN 0-686-60383-4). Polycrystal Bk Serv.

Brockway, Maureen. Clay Projects. LC 72-13337. (Early Craft Bks). (Illus.). 36p. (gr. 1-4). 1973. PLB 3.95g (ISBN 0-8225-0853-2). Lerner Pubns.

Brockway, Zebulon R. Fifty Years of Prison Service: An Autobiography. LC 69-14914. (Criminology, Law Enforcement, & Social Problems Ser.: No. 61). (Illus.). 1969. Repr. of 1912 ed. 17.00x (ISBN 0-87585-061-8). Patterson Smith.

Brod, J. The Kidney. (Illus.). 750p. 1973. 75.00 o.p. (ISBN 0-407-23900-6). Butterworth.

Brod, J. & Knell, A. J. Diagnose in der Inneren Medizin. (Illus.). xiv, 362p. 1982. pap. 28.75 (ISBN 3-8055-3483-3). S Karger.

Brod, Max. Franz Kafka: A Biography. 2nd ed. LC 60-14601. (gr. 7-12). 1963. pap. 5.95 (ISBN 0-8052-0047-9). Schocken.

Brod, Max, ed. see Kafka, Franz.

Brod, Ruth H., jt. auth. see Reilly, Harold J.

Broda, E. Evolution of Bioenergetic Processes. LC 75-6847. 220p. 1978. pap. text ed. 18.00 (ISBN 0-08-022651-5). Pergamon.

--Ludwig Boltzmann: Man, Physicist, Philosopher. LC 82-80707. (Illus.). 179p. 1983. 22.50 (ISBN 0-918024-24-2). Ox Bow.

Brodal, A. & Pompeiano, O. Basic Aspects of Central Vestibular Mechanisms. (Progress in Brain Research Ser: Vol. 37). 1972. 164.25 (ISBN 0-444-41048-1, North Holland). Elsevier.

Brodatz, Phil. PhotoGRAPHICS: A Workshop in High-Contrast Techniques. (Illus.). 96p. 1981. 10.95 (ISBN 0-8174-5417-9, Amphoto). Watson-Guptill.

Broder, Bill, jt. auth. see Broder, Gloria K.

Broder, David S. Changing of the Guard. 1980. 14.95 o.p. (ISBN 0-671-24566-X). S&S.

--The Party's Over: The Failure of Politics in America. 265p. 1972. pap. 5.95xi o.p. (ISBN 0-06-131919-8, TB1919, Torch). Har-Row.

Broder, Gloria K. & Broder, Bill. Remember This Time. 380p. 1983. 14.95 (ISBN 0-937858-23-4). Newmarket.

Broder, Nathan. The Collector's Bach. LC 77-28265. (Keystone Books in English Ser.). 1978. Repr. of 1958 ed. lib. bdg. 18.25x (ISBN 0-313-20240-0, BRBAC). Greenwood.

Broderick, Carlfred. Couples. 1981. pap. 6.75 (ISBN 0-671-43827-1, Touchstone Bks). S&S.

--Couples: How to Confront Problems & Maintain Loving Relationships. 1979. 13.95 o.s.i. (ISBN 0-671-24246-6). S&S.

Broderick, Carlfred B. The Theraputic Triangle: A Sourcebook on Marital Therapy. (Illus.). 200p. 1983. 20.00 (ISBN 0-8039-1943-3). Sage.

Broderick, Dorothy M., ed. Library Work with Children. 197p. 1977. 12.00 (ISBN 0-8242-0620-7). Wilson.

Broderick, Mary E., jt. auth. see Peterson, Carol J.

Broderick, Richard. Night Sale. LC 82-61652. (Minnesota Voices Project Ser.: No. 8). (Illus.). 135p. 1982. pap. 5.00 (ISBN 0-89823-040-3). New Rivers Pr.

Brodeur, Armand E. & Silberstein, Michael J. Fundamentals of Radiologic Pathology. (Illus.). 1983. write for info. (ISBN 0-8391-1803-1, 15636). Univ Park.

Brodey, Jean L. Mid-Life Careers. LC 82-24478. 244p. 1983. price not set (ISBN 0-664-27003-4, Bridgebooks Publications). Westminster.

Brodhage, H. & Hormuth, W. Planning & Engineering of Radio Relay Links. 1977. 116.95 o.p. (ISBN 0-471-25615-3, Wiley Heyden). Wiley.

Brodhead, Richard H. Hawthorne, Melville & the Novel. LC 75-5071. (Midway Reprint Ser.). 1982. pap. o.p. (ISBN 0-226-07523-0); 8.00 (ISBN 0-226-07524-9). U of Chicago Pr.

Brodie, Bernard. Sea Power in the Machine Age. LC 69-13840. Repr. of 1943 ed. lib. bdg. 20.50x (ISBN 0-8371-1445-4, BRSP). Greenwood.

--War & Politics. 514p. 1973. 13.95 (ISBN 0-02-315020-3); pap. 7.75 (ISBN 0-685-28575-8). Macmillan.

Brodie, Bernard & Intriligator, Michael D., eds. National Security & International Stability. LC 82-18913. 368p. 1983. text ed. 27.50 (ISBN 0-89946-172-7). Oelgeschlager.

Brodie, Bernard B. & Bressler, R., eds. Minireviews of the Neurosciences from Life Sciences, Vols. 13-15. LC 75-8733. 493p. 1975. text ed. 34.00 (ISBN 0-08-019724-8); pap. text ed. write for info. (ISBN 0-08-019723-X). Pergamon.

Brodie, Edmund D., Jr., jt. auth. see Nussbaum, Ronald A.

Brodie, Fawn M., ed. see Piercy, Frederick.

Brodie, Iain. Ferrets & Ferreting. (Illus.). 1979. 9.95 o.p. (ISBN 0-7137-0903-0, Pub. by Blandford Pr England). Sterling.

Brodie, K. Mathematical Methods in Computer Graphics & Design. LC 79-50302. 1980. 26.00 o.s.i. (ISBN 0-12-134880-6). Acad Pr.

Brodie, Keith H., jt. ed. see Cavenar, Jesse O.

Brodie, Keith H., jt. ed. see Cavenar, Jesse O., Jr.

Brodie, Leo, jt. auth. see Forth, Inc.

Brodie, M. L., jt. ed. see Schmidt, J. W.

Brodkey, Robert S., ed. see Symposium at Pittsburgh, Penn., June, 1974.

Brodoff, Bernard N. & Bleicher, Sheldon. Diabetes Mellitus & Obesity. (Illus.). 1020p. 1982. lib. bdg. 60.00 (ISBN 0-683-01071-9). Williams & Wilkins.

Brodrick, Alan H. Father of Prehistory: The Abbe Henri Breuil. LC 73-2342. (Illus.). 306p. 1973. Repr. of 1963 ed. lib. bdg. 17.75x (ISBN 0-8371-6840-6, BRFP). Greenwood.

Brodrith, Gerald. Hit for Six. 9.50x o.p. (ISBN 0-392-07129-0, SpS). Sportshelf.

Brodsky, Annette M. & Hare-Mustin, Rachel, eds. Women & Psychotherapy. LC 80-14842. 428p. 1980. 25.00 (ISBN 0-89862-605-6). Guilford Pr.

Brodsky, Archie, jt. auth. see Edelwich, Jerry.

Brodsky, Archie, jt. auth. see Peele, Stanton.

Brodsky, B. The Treasures from Moscow Museums. 374p. 1980. 85.00x (ISBN 0-686-97673-8, Pub. by Collet's). State Mutual Bk.

Brodsky, Carroll M. The Harassed Worker. LC 76-43115. 1976. 19.95x (ISBN 0-669-01041-3). Lexington Bks.

Brodsky, Carroll M. & Platt, Robert T. Rehabilitation Environment. LC 77-26370. 1978. 18.95 (ISBN 0-669-02168-7). Lexington Bks.

Brodsky, Joseph. Less Than One. 256p. 1983. 12.50 (ISBN 0-374-18503-4). FS&G.

--Rimskie Elegii. 20p. (Rus.). 1982. pap. 5.00 (ISBN 0-89830-062-2). Russica Pubs.

Brodsky, Louis D. Mississippi Vistas. LC 82-20065. (Center for the Study of Southern Culture Ser.). 80p. 1983. 10.00 (ISBN 0-87805-173-2). U Pr of Miss.

Brodsky, Louis D. & Hamlin, Robert W. Faulkner: A Comprehensive Guide to the Brodsky Collection. (Illus.). 440p. 1983. 35.00 (ISBN 0-87805-159-7). U Pr of Miss.

Brodsky, Louis D., jt. auth. see Hamblin, Robert W.

Brodsky, Stanley L. Psychologists in the Criminal Justice System. LC 72-87472. 183p. 1973. pap. 5.95 (ISBN 0-252-00432-9). U of Ill Pr.

Brodsky, Stanley L., jt. ed. see Walker, Marcia J.

Brodsky, William A., ed. Anion & Proton Transport, Vol. 341. new ed. LC 80-15917. (Annals of the New York Academy of Sciences). 570p. 1980. 109.00x (ISBN 0-89766-070-6); pap. 107.00x (ISBN 0-89766-071-4). NY Acad Sci.

Brodsly, David. L. A. Freeway: An Appreciative Essay. (Illus.). 188p. 1983. pap. 8.95 (ISBN 0-520-04546-7, CAL 535). U of Cal Pr.

Brody, Baruch, ed. Readings in the Philosophy of Religion: An Analytic Approach. LC 73-20485. 608p. 1974. text ed. 26.95 (ISBN 0-13-759340-6). P-H.

Brody, Baruch A. Beginning Philosophy. 1977. pap. text ed. 13.95 (ISBN 0-13-073882-4). P-H.

Brody, Boruch. Readings in the Philosophy of Science. LC 71-98091. (Philosophy Ser). 1970. text ed. 27.95 (ISBN 0-13-760702-4). P-H.

Brody, David. Labor in Crisis: The Steel Strike of 1919. LC 82-11746. (Critical Periods of History Ser.). 208p. 1982. Repr. lib. bdg. 25.00x (ISBN 0-313-23499-X, BROL). Greenwood.

--Workers in Industrial America: Essays on the 20th Century Struggle. 1979. text ed. 17.95x (ISBN 0-19-502490-7); pap. text ed. 5.95x (ISBN 0-19-502491-5). Oxford U Pr.

Brody, Eugene B. Minority Group Adolescents in the United States. LC 78-20769. 256p. 1979. Repr. of 1968 ed. lib. bdg. 13.00 (ISBN 0-88275-849-7). Krieger.

Brody, Eugene D. & Bliss, Betsy L. Odds on Investing: Survival & Success in the New Stock Market. LC 78-18222. 1978. 32.95 o.p. (ISBN 0-471-04478-4, Pub. by Wiley-Interscience). Wiley.

Brody, Garry S., jt. ed. see Fredricks, Simon.

Brody, Jane. Jane Brody's Nutrition Book. 1982. pap. 8.95 (ISBN 0-686-82120-3). Bantam.

Brody, Jean & Osborne, Gail B. The Twenty Year Phenomenon. 1980. 11.95 o.p. (ISBN 0-671-25042-6). S&S.

Brody, Jerome. The Grand Central Oyster Bar & Restaurant Seafood Cookbook: Compiled & Edited from 64 Years of Recipes & Recollections. 1977. 12.95 o.p. (ISBN 0-517-52829-0). Crown.

Brody, Jules. Lectures de Montaigne. LC 82-42428. (French Forum Monographs: No. 39). 181p. (Orig.). 1982. pap. 15.00x (ISBN 0-917058-38-0). French Forum.

Brody, Jules, jt. auth. see Spitzer, Leo.

Brody, Marvin D., jt. auth. see Berger, Jordan C.

Brody, Nathan, ed. Motivation. LC 82-22654. Date not set. price not set (ISBN 0-12-134840-7). Acad Pr.

Brody, Ralph. Problem Solving: Concepts & Methods for Community Organizations. LC 81-7221. 240p. 1982. 29.95x (ISBN 0-89885-078-9); pap. 14.95x (ISBN 0-89885-079-7). Human Sci Pr.

Brody, Steve. How to Break Ninety Before You Reach It. 3rd ed. LC 80-10704. 1980. pap. 6.95 (ISBN 0-88427-040-8). North River.

Broed, Paul. Accounting the Easy Way. (Easy Way Ser.). 320p. 1983. pap. 5.95 (ISBN 0-8120-2623-3). Barron.

Broek, C. M. & Webb, John W. A Geography of Mankind. 3rd ed. (Illus.). 1978. text ed. 32.50 (ISBN 0-07-008012-7, C); instructors manual 15.00 (ISBN 0-07-008013-5). McGraw.

Broek, David. Elementary Engineering Fracture Mechanics. 1982. lib. bdg. 69.00 (ISBN 90-247-2580-1, Pub. by Martinus Nijhoff Netherlands); pap. 29.50 (ISBN 90-247-2656-5, Pub. by Martinus Nijhoff Netherlands). Kluwer Boston.

Broek, den van Silvere O. F., jt. ed. see Broek, van den Silvere O. F.

Broek, Jacobus ten see Ten Broek, Jacobus.

Broek, Jan O., et al. The Study & Teaching of Geography. 2nd ed. (Social Science Seminar, Secondary Education Ser.: No. C28). 120p. 1980. pap. text ed. 7.95 (ISBN 0-675-08163-7). Merrill.

Broek, van den Silvere O. F. & Broek, den van Silvere O. F., eds. The Spiritual Legacy of Sister Mary of the Holy Trinity. 364p. 1950. pap. 5.00 (ISBN 0-686-81630-7). TAN Bks Pubs.

Broekel, Ray. Aquariums & Terrariums. LC 82-4428. (New True Bks.). (gr. k-4). 1982. 9.25 (ISBN 0-516-01660-1). Childrens.

--Dangerous Fish. LC 82-4464. (New True Bks.). (gr. k-4). 1982. 9.25 (ISBN 0-516-01635-0). Childrens.

--Football. LC 81-15484. (New True Bks.). (Illus.). 48p. (gr. k-4). 1982. PLB 9.25 (ISBN 0-686-97367-4). Childrens.

--Police. LC 81-7693. (The New True Books). (Illus.). 48p. (gr. k-4). 1981. PLB 9.25 (ISBN 0-516-01643-1). Childrens.

Broekel, Ray, jt. auth. see White, Lawrence B., Jr.

Broekema, Andrew J. The Music Listener. 500p. 1978. text ed. write for info. (ISBN 0-697-03400-3); instr's manual avail. (ISBN 0-697-03570-0); 8 records avail. (ISBN 0-697-03416-X); student study guide avail. (ISBN 0-697-03415-1). Wm C Brown.

Broekhuizen, Richard. Graphic Communications. 380p. 1979. text ed. 17.28 (ISBN 0-87345-246-1); study guide 6.00 (ISBN 0-87345-247-X); ans. key free (ISBN 0-87345-248-8). McKnight.

Broekhuizen, S. & Thran, P., eds. Atlas of Cereal Growing in Europe. (Agro-Ecological Atlas Ser.: Vol. 2). 1970. 138.50 (ISBN 0-444-40819-3). Elsevier.

Broennimann, P. Auca on the Cononaco: Indians of the Ecuadorian Rain Forest. 184p. 1981. 29.95x (ISBN 3-7643-1226-2). Birkhauser.

Broer, M. R. & Wilson, R. M. Fundamentals of Marching. (Illus.). 122p. 1965. 13.50 o.p. (ISBN 0-471-07068-8). Wiley.

Broertjes, C. & Van Harten, A. M. The Application of Mutation Breeding Methods in the Improvement of Vegetatively Propagated Crops. (Developments in Crop Science: Vol. 2). 1978. 70.25 (ISBN 0-444-41618-8, DIC 2). Elsevier.

Brof, Janet, tr. see Slote, Alfred.

Brog, Molly J., jt. auth. see Hafen, Brent Q.

Brogan, Denis W. America in the Modern World. LC 79-25851. 117p. 1980. Repr. of 1960 ed. lib. bdg. 16.25x (ISBN 0-313-22254-1, BRAW). Greenwood.

--Era of Franklin D. Roosevelt. 1951. text ed. 8.50x (ISBN 0-686-83537-9). Elliots Bks.

Brogan, Frankie. The Snare of the Fowler. 208p. 1983. 11.95 (ISBN 0-310-60280-7). Chosen Bks Pub.

Brogan, John A. Clear Technical Writing. new ed. 1973. 15.15 (ISBN 0-07-007974-9, G). McGraw.

Brogan, Peggy & Fox, Lorene. Helping Children Read: Some Proven Approaches. LC 77-840. 334p. 1979. Repr. of 1961 ed. 9.95 (ISBN 0-88275-533-1). Krieger.

Brogdon, Byron G. Opinions, Comments & Reflections on Radiology. LC 82-82972. (Illus.). 249p. 1982. 27.95 (ISBN 0-939442-01-9). Brentwood Pub.

Broger, Achim. Bruno. Van Stockum, Hilda, tr. from Ger. LC 75-15800. (Illus.). 160p. (gr. 3-6). 1975. 7.95 (ISBN 0-688-22051-7); PLB 7.63 (ISBN 0-688-32051-1). Morrow.

--Bruno Takes a Trip. Gueritz, Caroline, tr. from Ger. LC 78-3878. (Illus.). (gr. k-3). 1978. 9.25 (ISBN 0-688-22138-6); PLB 8.88 (ISBN 0-688-32138-0). Morrow.

--Little Harry. Crawford, Elizabeth D., tr. from Ger. LC 78-26028. (Illus.). (gr. 4-6). 1979. 9.25 (ISBN 0-688-22185-8); PLB 8.88 (ISBN 0-688-32185-2). Morrow.

--Outrageous Kasimir. Van Stockum, Hilda, tr. (Illus.). (gr. 5-9). 1976. 9.95 (ISBN 0-688-22085-1); PLB 9.55 (ISBN 0-688-32085-6). Morrow.

--Running in Circles. Crampton, Patricia, tr. from Germ. (gr. 7 up). 1977. 9.95 (ISBN 0-688-22119-X); PLB 9.55 (ISBN 0-688-32119-4). Morrow.

Broglia, R. A. & Ricci, R. A. Nuclear Structure & Heavy Ion Collisions. (Enrico Fermi Summer School Ser.: Vol. 77). 1982. 142.75 (ISBN 0-444-85462-2). Elsevier.

Brogyanyi, Bela, jt. ed. see Untermann, Juergen.

Broida, Patricia see Colgate, Craig, Jr.

Broili, June. Nevada Cookery: Table Traditions & Tales of the Sagebrush State. Browder, Robyn, ed. LC 82-14771. (Regional Cookbook Ser.). (Illus.). 300p. (Orig.). 1983. pap. 8.95 (ISBN 0-89865-255-3). Donning Co.

Broinowski, Alison, ed. Understanding ASEAN. LC 81-9036. 320p. 1982. 27.50x (ISBN 0-312-83076-9). St Martin.

Brokensha, David, et al, eds. Indigenous Knowledge Systems & Development. LC 80-5481. 474p. 1980. lib. bdg. 28.50 (ISBN 0-8191-1102-3); pap. text ed. 17.25 (ISBN 0-8191-1103-1). U Pr of Amer.

Brokering, Herb & Bainton, Roland. Pilgrimage to Luther's Germany. 80p. 1983. 14.95 (ISBN 0-86683-629-2). Winston Pr.

Brokering, Herbert F. In Due Season. LC 66-22563. (Illus.). 1966. 6.50 o.p. (ISBN 0-8066-0620-7, 10-3209). Augsburg.

Brokering, L. Thirty Six Creative Ideas for Children in the Church School. LC 12-2958. 1982. pap. 4.50 (ISBN 0-570-03865-0). Concordia.

Brokke, Harold J. Salvados por Su Vida. 224p. Date not set. 2.25 (ISBN 0-88113-317-5). Edit Betania.

--Ten Steps to the Good Life. LC 75-44926. 1976. pap. 1.95 (ISBN 0-87123-332-0, 200332). Bethany Hse.

Brolin, Don E. & Brolin, James C. Vocational Preparation of Handicapped Individuals. 2nd ed. 368p. 1982. pap. text ed. 18.95 (ISBN 0-675-09878-5). Merrill.

Brolin, Donn E. & Kokaska, Charles J. Career Education for Handicapped Children & Youth. (Special Education Ser.). 1979. text ed. 23.95 (ISBN 0-675-08278-1). Merrill.

Brolin, James C., jt. auth. see Brolin, Don E.

Bromage, B. Occult Arts in Ancient Egypt. pap. 4.95 o.p. (ISBN 0-87728-041-X). Weiser.

Bromage, Mary C. De Valera & the March of a Nation. LC 75-389. (Illus.). 328p. 1975. Repr. of 1956 ed. lib. bdg. 17.00x (ISBN 0-8371-8022-8, BRDV). Greenwood.

Bromage, Philip R. Epidural Analgesia. LC 79-9389. (Illus.). 1978. text ed. 47.50 (ISBN 0-7216-2005-1). Saunders.

Broman, Betty. The Early Years in Childhood Education. 2nd ed. LC 81-82557. 1982. 21.95 (ISBN 0-395-31803-3); instr's manual 1.00 (ISBN 0-395-31804-1). HM.

Broman, Betty, jt. auth. see Burns, Paul C.

Broman, Betty L. The Early Years in Childhood Education. 1978. 19.95 o.p. (ISBN 0-395-30565-9); Instr's. manual 1.10 o.p. (ISBN 0-395-30566-7). HM.

Broman, Sven, jt. auth. see Sands, Frederick.

Bromberg, et al. English Now. 1984. 5.95 (ISBN 0-8120-2407-9). Barron.

Bromberg, A. Securities Law: Fraud, SEC 10b-5. 1967. pap. text ed. 160.00 o.p. (ISBN 0-07-007998-6, P&RB). McGraw.

Bromberg, Andrew. Computer Overbyte & Other Stories. LC 82-81248. (Illus.). 48p. (gr. 2-6). 1982. pap. 4.45 (ISBN 0-688-00943-3). Greenwillow.

--Flute Revenge. LC 82-81246. (Hidden Clue Mystery Ser.). (Illus.). 48p. (gr. 2-6). 1982. pap. 4.45 (ISBN 0-688-00942-5). Greenwillow.

--The House on Blackthorn Hill: A Hidden Clue Mystery. LC 82-81245. 48p. (Orig.). (gr. 2-6). 1982. pap. 4.45 (ISBN 0-688-00941-7). Greenwillow.

--Rubik's Ruse & Other Stories. LC 82-81247. (Hidden Clue Codebreaker Ser.). (Illus.). 48p. (gr. 2-6). 1982. pap. 4.45 (ISBN 0-686-97200-7). Greenwillow.

Bromberg, Charles M. The Meeting Will Come to Order. LC 81-43862. 74p. (Orig.). 1982. pap. text ed. 4.75 (ISBN 0-8191-2328-5). U Pr of Amer.

Bromberg, Murray & Gordon, Melvin. Eleven Hundred Words You Need to Know. LC 70-12919. 1971. pap. 5.50 (ISBN 0-8120-0405-1). Barron.

Bromberg, Murray & Katz, Milton. Getting Your Words Across. 256p. (gr. 7-12). 1983. pap. text ed. 3.95 (ISBN 0-8120-2082-0). Barron.

Bromberg, Murray, ed. see Drabkin, Marjorie.

Bromberg, Murray, et al. Five Hundred & Four Absolutely Essential Words. rev. ed. LC 74-5052. 1975. pap. 4.25 (ISBN 0-8120-0525-2). Barron.

Bromberg, Walter. The Uses of Psychiatry in the Law: A Clinical View of Forensic Psychiatry. LC 78-22724. (Illus.). 1979. lib. bdg. 29.95 (ISBN 0-89930-000-6, BRP, Quorum). Greenwood.

Brombert, Beth A. Cristina: Portraits of a Princess. (Illus.). xii, 402p. 1977. pap. 10.95 (ISBN 0-226-07551-6). U of Chicago Pr.

Brombert, Victor. Stendhal: Fiction & the Themes of Freedom. LC 75-37057. (Midway Reprint Ser). xii, 210p. 1976. pap. 4.95x o.s.i. (ISBN 0-226-07548-6). U of Chicago Pr.

Brome, Vincent. The Ambassador & the Spy. 1973. 6.95 o.p. (ISBN 0-517-51115-0). Crown.

--Aneurin Bevan: A Biography. (Illus.). 1953. 5.95 o.s.i. (ISBN 0-686-00952-5). Wellington.

--Ernest Jones: A Biography. (Illus.). 1983. 19.50 (ISBN 0-393-01594-7). Norton.

--Jung: Man & Myth. LC 77-14736. 1978. 11.95 (ISBN 0-689-10853-2); pap. 6.95 (ISBN 0-689-70588-3, 262). Atheneum.

Bromell, Henry. I Know Your Heart, Marco Polo. LC 78-3580. 1979. 7.95 o.p. (ISBN 0-394-50116-0). Knopf.

Bromhall, A. J. Hudson Taylor & China's Open Century: Bk. II; Over the Treaty Wall. 1981. pap. 9.95 (ISBN 0-340-27561-8). OMF Bks.

Bromhead, P. A. The House of Lords & Contemporary Politics: 1911-1957. LC 75-27676. 283p. 1976. Repr. of 1958 ed. lib. bdg. 18.50x (ISBN 0-8371-8458-4, BRHL). Greenwood.

--Private Members' Bills in the British Parliament. LC 75-27677. 216p. 1976. Repr. of 1956 ed. lib. bdg. 15.50x (ISBN 0-8371-8462-2, BRPM). Greenwood.

Bromhead, Peter. Britain's Developing Constitution. LC 74-82270. 227p. 1974. 20.00 o.p. (ISBN 0-312-09905-3). St Martin.

Bromige, Iris. A Distant Song. (Aston Hall Romances Ser.: No. 105). 192p. (Orig.). 1980. pap. 1.50 o.p. (ISBN 0-523-41117-0). Pinnacle Bks.

--Rough Weather. (Aston Hall Romances Ser.). 192p. (Orig.). 1981. pap. 1.75 o.p. (ISBN 0-523-41133-2). Pinnacle Bks.

Bromiley, G. W. see Barth, Karl.

Bromiley, Geoffrey W., tr. see Barth, Karl.

Bromiley, Geoffrey W., tr. see Barth, Karl & Zuckmayer, Carl.

Bromiley, Geoffrey W., tr. see Thielicke, Helmut.

Bromke, Adam. Poland's Politics: Idealism vs. Realism. LC 66-21331. (Russian Research Center Studies: No. 51). 1967. 18.50x o.p. (ISBN 0-674-68200-9). Harvard U Pr.

Bromley, D. A., ed. Large Electrostatic Accelerators - from J. Nuclear Instruments & Methods, Vol. 122, 1974. LC 74-84732. 288p. 1975. Repr. 59.75 (ISBN 0-444-10787-8, North-Holland). Elsevier.

Bromley, D. B. Personality Description in Ordinary Language. 1977. 42.95x o.p. (ISBN 0-471-99443-X, Pub. by Wiley-Interscience). Wiley.

Bromley, D. B., jt. auth. see Livesley, W. J.

Bromley, David & Shupe, Anson. Strange Gods: The Great American Cult Scare. LC 81-65763. 192p. 1981. 12.98 (ISBN 0-8070-3256-5). Beacon Pr.

--Strange Gods: The Great American Cult Scare. LC 81-65763. 270p. 1982. pap. 6.68 (ISBN 0-8070-1109-6, BP641). Beacon Pr.

Bromley, Dudley. Bedford Fever. LC 81-82039. (Doomsday Journals). 80p. (gr. 6-12). 1982. lib. bdg. 8.65 (ISBN 0-516-02241-5). Childrens.

--Comet! LC 81-82040. (Doomsday Journals). (gr. 6-12). 1982. 8.65 (ISBN 0-516-02242-3). Childrens.

--Final Warning. LC 81-82037. (Doomsday Journals). 80p. (gr. 6-12). 1982. lib. bdg. 8.65 (ISBN 0-516-02243-1). Childrens.

--Fireball. LC 81-82035. (Doomsday Journals). 80p. (gr. 6-12). 1982. lib. bdg. 8.65 (ISBN 0-516-02244-X). Childrens.

--Lost Valley. LC 81-82036. (Doomsday Journals). 80p. (gr. 6-12). 1982. lib. bdg. 8.65 (ISBN 0-516-02245-8). Childrens.

--North to Oak Island. LC 77-82062. (Pacesetters Ser.). (Illus.). 64p. (gr. 4 up). 1978. PLB 8.65 (ISBN 0-516-02171-0). Childrens.

--The Seep. LC 81-82038. (Doomsday Journals). 80p. (gr. 6-12). 1982. lib. bdg. 8.65 (ISBN 0-516-02245-8). Childrens.

Bromley, Lynn. Monkeys, Apes & Other Primates. (Illus.). 64p. 1981. pap. 3.95 (ISBN 0-686-80426-0). Bellerophon Bks.

Bromley, Ray. The Urban Informal Sector: Critical Perspectives. (Illus.). 1979. 40.00 (ISBN 0-08-024270-7). Pergamon.

Bromley, Ray, jt. auth. see Bromley, Rosemary.

Bromley, Ray & Gerry, Chris, eds. Casual Work & Poverty in Third World Cities. LC 78-11329. 1979. 54.95 (ISBN 0-471-99731-5, Pub. by Wiley-Interscience). Wiley.

Bromley, Rosemary & Bromley, Ray. South American Development: A Geographical Introduction. 2nd ed. LC 82-1171. (Cambridge Topics in Geography Ser.: No. 2). (Illus.). 112p. 1982. 12.95 (ISBN 0-521-23496-4); pap. 6.95 (ISBN 0-521-28008-7). Cambridge U Pr.

Bromley, S. C., jt. ed. see Thornton, C. S.

Brommel, Bernard J., jt. auth. see Galvin, Kathleen M.

Brommer, Frank. The Twelve Labors of the Hero in Ancient Art & Literature. Schwarz, S. J., tr. (Illus.). 128p. lib. bdg. 20.00x (ISBN 0-89241-375-1). Caratzas Bros.

Brommer, Gerald F. Movement & Rhythm: A Design Principle. LC 75-21111. (Concepts of Design Ser.). (Illus.). 80p. (gr. 7-12). 1975. 9.95 (ISBN 0-87192-076-X). Davis Mass.

--Space: A Design Element. LC 74-82680. (Concepts of Design Ser). (Illus.). 80p. (gr. 7up). 1974. ref. ed. 9.95 (ISBN 0-87192-062-X). Davis Mass.

Bromwell, C. David. India Emerges. (Asia Emerges Ser.). 1975. pap. 4.80 o.p. (ISBN 0-02-648230-4, 64823); tchr's guide 1.36 o.p. (ISBN 0-02-648240-1, 64824). Glencoe.

--Japan Emerges. (Asia Emerges Ser.). 1975. pap. 4.80 o.p. (ISBN 0-02-648300-9, 64830); tchr's guide 1.36 o.p. (ISBN 0-02-648310-6, 64831). Glencoe.

Bromwell, C. David, et al. China Emerges. (Asia Emerges Ser.). 1974. pap. 4.80 o.p. (ISBN 0-02-648820-5, 64882); tchr's guide 1.36 o.p. (ISBN 0-02-648830-2, 64883). Glencoe.

Bronaugh, Richard, ed. Philosophical Law: Authority, Equality, Adjudication, Privacy. (Contributions in Legal Studies: No. 2). 1978. lib. bdg. 25.00 (ISBN 0-8371-9809-7, BPL/). Greenwood.

Bronder, Saul E. Social Justice & Church Authority: The Public Life of Archbishop Robert E. Lucey. 215p. 1982. 27.95 (ISBN 0-87722-239-8). Temple U Pr.

Brondfield, Jerry. The Great NFL Funbook II. (Illus.). (gr. 3-7). Date not set. pap. 1.95 (ISBN 0-686-97339-9). Schol Bk Serv.

--Roberto Clemente: Pride of the Pirates. LC 75-22145. (Sports Library Ser). (Illus.). 96p. (gr. 3-6). 1976. PLB 7.12 (ISBN 0-8116-6675-1). Garrard.

Brondsted, Johannes. The Vikings. lib. bdg. 11.50x (ISBN 0-88307-040-5). Gannon.

Brondum, Jack, tr. see Ditlevsen, Tove.

Brondum, Jack, tr. see Scherfig, Hans.

Bronfenbrenner, Martin. Macroeconomic Alternatives. LC 79-50880. (Illus.). 1979. text ed. 24.95x (ISBN 0-88295-404-0). Harlan Davidson.

Bronfenbrenner, Urie. Two Worlds of Childhood. 1972. pap. 8.50 (ISBN 0-671-21238-9, Touchstone Bks). S&S.

--Two Worlds of Childhood: U. S. & U. S. S. R. LC 71-104182. (Illus.). 190p. 1970. 10.00x (ISBN 0-87154-168-8). Russell Sage.

Bronin, Andrew. The Cave: What Lives There. (What Lives There Ser.). (Illus.). 32p. (gr. 3-5). 1972. PLB 4.99 o.p. (ISBN 0-698-30437-3, Coward). Putnam Pub Group.

--The Desert: What Lives There. (What Lives There Ser.). (Illus.). 32p. (gr. 1-3). 1972. PLB 5.49 o.p. (ISBN 0-698-30440-3, Coward). Putnam Pub Group.

--Gus & Buster Work Things Out. (Break-of-Day Bk). (Illus.). 64p. (gr. k-3). 1975. PLB 6.59 o.p. (ISBN 0-698-30561-2, Coward). Putnam Pub Group.

--I Know a Football Player. (Community Helper Bks.). (Illus.). 48p. (gr. 1-3). 1973. PLB 4.29 o.p. (ISBN 0-399-60810-9). Putnam Pub Group.

Bronk, Detev W., ed. see Rockefeller University & State University of New York, Nov. 26-27, 1965.

Bronner, Augusta F., jt. auth. see Healy, William.

Bronner, Edwin B. William Penn: Seventeenth Century Founding Father. LC 75-32728. (Illus.). 36p. (Orig.). 1975. pap. 1.50 (ISBN 0-87574-204-1). Pendle Hill.

Bronner, Felix & Coburn, Jack, eds. Disorders of Mineral Metabolism: Pathophysiology of Calcium, Phosphorus & Magnesium, Vol. 3. LC 81-12713. 1981. 62.00 (ISBN 0-12-135303-6); Set. 53.00 (ISBN 0-686-85519-1). Acad Pr.

Bronner, Felix & Kleinzeller, Annost, eds. Current Topics in Membranes & Transport, Vols. 1-9, 11. Incl. Vol. 1. 1970. 38.00 (ISBN 0-12-153301-8); Vol. 2. 1971. 38.00 (ISBN 0-12-153302-6); Vol. 3. 1972. 56.00 (ISBN 0-12-153303-4); Vol. 4. 1974. 55.00 (ISBN 0-12-153304-2); Vol. 5. 1974. 55.00 (ISBN 0-12-153305-0); Vol. 6. 1975. 52.50 (ISBN 0-12-153306-9); Vol. 7. 1975. 52.50 (ISBN 0-12-153307-7); Vol. 8. 1976. 54.00 (ISBN 0-12-153308-5); Vol. 9. 1977. 59.00 (ISBN 0-12-153309-3); Vol. 11. 1978. 59.50 (ISBN 0-12-153311-5). Acad Pr.

Bronner, Felix & Kleinzeller, Arnost, eds. Current Topics in Membranes & Transport, Vol. 18. (Serial Publication). Date not set. price not set (ISBN 0-12-153318-2). Acad Pr.

Bronner, Felix & Miller, William, eds. Current Topics in Membranes & Tranport: Vol. 15, Molecular Mechanisms of Photo-Receptor Transduction. LC 70-117091. 1981. 54.50 o.s.i. (ISBN 0-12-153315-8). Acad Pr.

Bronner, Felix & Peterlik, Meindrad, eds. Calcium & Phosphate Transport Across Biomembranes. LC 81-17617. 1981. 28.00 (ISBN 0-12-135280-3). Acad Pr.

Bronner, Leah. Biblical Personalities & Archaeology. (Illus.). 216p. 1975. 7.95x (ISBN 0-685-58308-2). Bloch.

Bronner, Stephen, ed. The Letters of Rosa Luxemburg. 1979. lib. bdg. 26.50 (ISBN 0-89158-186-3); pap. text ed. 10.00 (ISBN 0-89158-188-X). Westview.

Bronner, Stephen & Kellner, Douglas, eds. Passion & Rebellion: The Expressionist Heritage. 480p. 1983. 29.95x (ISBN 0-686-86220-1); pap. 16.95x (ISBN 0-89789-017-5). J F Bergin.

--Passion & Rebellion: The Expressionist Heritage. LC 81-40492. (Illus.). 448p. 1983. text ed. 35.00x (ISBN 0-87663-356-4). Universe.

Bronosted, A. An Introduction to Convex Polytopes. (Graduate Texts in Mathematics Ser.: Vol. 90). (Illus.). 160p. 1983. 28.00 (ISBN 0-387-90722-X). Springer-Verlag.

Bronowski, Jacob. The Origins of Knowledge & Imagination. LC 77-13209. (Silliman Lectures Ser.). 1978. 15.00x (ISBN 0-300-02192-5); pap. 4.45 (ISBN 0-300-02409-6). Yale U Pr.

--Science & Human Values. enl. ed. pap. 4.95xi (ISBN 0-06-130505-7, TB505, TB). Har-Row.

--A Sense of the Future: Essays in Natural Philosophy. Ariotti, Piero & Bronowski, Rita, eds. LC 77-9292. 1977. 20.00x (ISBN 0-262-02128-5); pap. 6.95 (ISBN 0-262-52050-8). MIT Pr.

--The Visionary Eye: Essays in the Arts, Literature, & Science. Ariotti, Piero & Bronowski, Rita, eds. 1978. 17.50x (ISBN 0-262-52068-0); pap. 4.95 (ISBN 0-686-96799-2). MIT Pr.

Bronowski, Rita, ed. see Bronowski, Jacob.

Bronson, Anita. Lucy Emmett, or a Lady of Quality. LC 78-481. (Fic). 1978. 10.95 o.p. (ISBN 0-698-10887-6, Coward). Putnam Pub Group.

Bronson, Bertrand H. The Ballad as Song. LC 74-84045. (Illus.). 1969. 33.00x (ISBN 0-520-01399-9). U of Cal Pr.

--Facets of the Enlightenment: Studies in English Literature & Its Contexts. LC 68-56074. 1968. 31.00x (ISBN 0-520-00176-1). U of Cal Pr.

--Printing As an Index of Taste in Eighteenth-Century England. rev. ed. (Illus.). 1963. pap. 4.00 o.p. (ISBN 0-87104-146-4). NY Pub Lib.

Bronson, C. & Bronson, Gary J. Mathemathics for Management. 1977. text ed. 26.50 scp (ISBN 0-7002-2503-X, HarpC); solutions manual avail. (ISBN 0-7002-2505-6). Har-Row.

Bronson, Gary J., jt. auth. see Bronson, C.

Bronson, Gordon. The Scanning Patterns of Human Infants: Implications for Visual Learning. (Monographs on Infancy: Vol. 2). 1982. 16.50 (ISBN 0-89391-114-3). Ablex Pub.

Bronson, R. Matrix Methods: An Introduction. 1970. text ed. 17.00 (ISBN 0-12-135250-1). Acad Pr.

Bronson, Richard. Modern Introductory Differential Equations. (Schaum Outline Ser.). 1973. pap. text ed. 6.95 (ISBN 0-07-008009-7, SP). McGraw.

Bronson, Richard A., frwd. by see Barker, Graham H.

Bronson, Wanda C. Toddler's Behaviors with Age Mates: Issues of Interaction, Cognition & Affect. (Monographs on Infancy: Vol. 1). 100p. 1981. text ed. 16.50 (ISBN 0-89391-080-5). Ablex Pub.

Bronson, Wilfrid S. Cats. LC 50-9467. (Illus.). (gr. 4-6). 1950. 5.50 (ISBN 0-15-215357-8, HJ). HarBraceJ.

--Dogs: Best Breeds for Young People. LC 69-11594. (Illus.). (gr. 5-8). 1969. prepub. 6.50 o.p. (ISBN 0-15-223935-9, HJ). HarBraceJ.

Bronson, William. Earth Shook, the Sky Burned. LC 59-6893. 1959. 24.95 (ISBN 0-385-05379-7). Doubleday.

Bronstein, Alvin J. Representing Prisoners: A Course Handbook. (Litigation & Adminstrative Practice Ser.). 973p. 1981. softcover 35.00 (ISBN 0-686-79681-0, C4-4154). PLI.

Bronstein, Alvin J. & Hirschkop, Philip J. Prisoner's Rights Nineteen Seventy-Nine, 2 vols. (Litigation & Administrative Practice Course Handbook Ser 1978-79: Vols. 105 & 106). 1979. pap. 30.00 (ISBN 0-685-94312-7, C6-4133). PLI.

Bronstein, Arthur J. Pronunciation of American English. (Illus.). 1960. 17.95 (ISBN 0-13-730887-6). P-H.

Bronstein, Audrey. The Triple Struggle: Latin American Peasant Women. 268p. Date not set. 20.00 (ISBN 0-89608-180-X); pap. 7.50 (ISBN 0-89608-179-6). South End Pr.

Bronstein, Daniel J., et al. Basic Problems of Philosophy. 4th ed. LC 79-179449. 656p. 1972. text ed. 22.95 (ISBN 0-13-067637-3). P-H.

Bronstein, E. Graphing Equations. (Finite Math Text Ser.). write for info. (ISBN 0-685-84472-2). J W Wills.

--Lines & Half Planes. (Finite Math Text Ser.). write for info. (ISBN 0-685-84473-0). J W Wills.

Bronstein, Edwin S. Laparoscopy for Sterilization. (Illus.). 221p. 1975. pap. 21.50 o.p. (ISBN 0-8151-1275-0). Year Bk Med.

Bronstein, Eugene, jt. auth. see Hisrich, Bob.

Bronstein, Herbert, ed. A Passover Haggadah. (Illus.). 1974. 60.00 set (ISBN 0-916694-66-6); 5.95 (ISBN 0-916694-71-2); lib. bdg. 27.50 (ISBN 0-916694-06-2); pap. 5.00 (ISBN 0-916694-05-4). Central Conf.

Bronstein, Herbert, ed. see Central Conference of American Rabbis.

Bronstein, Leo. Five Variations on the Theme of Japanese Painting. LC 65-27614. (Illus.). 1969. 25.00 (ISBN 0-87027-105-9). Cumberland Pr.

--Kabbalah & Art. LC 78-63585. (Illus.). 146p. 1980. 22.50x (ISBN 0-87451-163-1). U Pr of New Eng.

Bronstein, Raphael. Science of Violin Playing. 2nd ed. 288p. 1981. 25.00 (ISBN 0-87666-601-2, Z-10). Paganiniana Pubns.

Bronstein, Ricki A., et al. Teleconferencing: A Practical Guide to Teaching by Telephone. LC 82-11534. (Illus.). 150p. 1982. pap. text ed. 15.00 (ISBN 0-89189-150-1, 45-9-014-00). Am Soc Clinical.

Bronstein, Russell, jt. auth. see Maidment, Robert.

Bronte, Anne. The Tenant of Wildfell Hall. 1982. pap. 4.75x (ISBN 0-460-11685-1, Evman). Biblio Dist.

Bronte, Charlotte. Emma. 224p. 1981. 11.95 (ISBN 0-89696-114-1, An Everest House Book). Dodd.

--Jane Eyre. (Bantam Classics Ser.). 433p. (gr. 7-12). 1981. pap. 1.75 (ISBN 0-553-21020-3). Bantam.

--Jane Eyre. 1928. 3.95 o.s.i. (ISBN 0-394-60064-9, M64). Modern Lib.

--Jane Eyre. LC 78-3388. (Raintree's Illustrated Classics). (Illus.). (gr. 5-8). 1978. PLB 13.30 (ISBN 0-8393-6202-1). Raintree Pubs.

--Jane Eyre. 560p. 1982. pap. 3.95 (ISBN 0-671-45996-1). WSP.

--Shirley. 1975. Repr. of 1908 ed. 9.95x (ISBN 0-460-00288-0, Evman). Biblio Dist.

--Shirley. (Clarendon Edition of the Novels of Brontes). (Illus.). 1979. text ed. 79.00x (ISBN 0-19-812565-8). Oxford U Pr.

--Villette. 1974. 9.95x (ISBN 0-460-00351-8, Evman); pap. 2.75x (ISBN 0-460-01351-3, Evman). Biblio Dist.

Bronte, Charlotte see Eyre, A. G.

Bronte, Charlotte see Swan, D. K.

Bronte, Charlotte, et al. Poems by the Bronte Sisters. 165p. 1978. Repr. of 1846 ed. 8.75x o.p. (ISBN 0-8476-6101-6). Rowman.

Bronte, Emily. Wuthering Heights. (Bantam Classics Ser.). 320p. (gr. 7-12). 1981. pap. 1.75 (ISBN 0-553-21021-1). Bantam.

--Wuthering Heights. 1950. pap. 3.95 (ISBN 0-394-30904-9, T4, Mod LibC). Modern Lib.

--Wuthering Heights. 320p. (RL 10). 1973. pap. 1.75 (ISBN 0-451-51650-8, CE1650, Sig Classics). NAL.

--Wuthering Heights. Marsden, Hilda & Jack, Ion, eds. (Clarendon Edition of the Novels of the Brontes Ser.). 1976. 49.00x (ISBN 0-19-812511-9). Oxford U Pr.

--Wuthering Heights. 1977. pap. 1.95 o.p. (ISBN 0-523-40126-4). Pinnacle Bks.

--Wuthering Heights. LC 78-4049. (Raintree's Illustrated Classics). (Illus.). (gr. 5-8). 1978. PLB 13.85 (ISBN 0-8172-1128-4). Raintree Pubs.

--Wuthering Heights. (Illus.). 8.95 (ISBN 0-394-60458-X). Modern Lib.

Bronte, Emily see Eyre, A. G.

Bronte, Patrick. Cottage Poems: A Miscellany of Descriptive Poems, Repr. Of 1811 Ed. Bd. with The Rural Minstrel: A Miscellany of Descriptive Poems. Repr. of 1813 ed. LC 75-31169. (Romantic Context Ser.: Poetry 1789-1830: Vol. 23). 1977. lib. bdg. 47.00 o.s.i. (ISBN 0-8240-2122-3). Garland Pub.

Bronthon & McLaughlin. Heating Service Design. 1981. text ed. 54.00 (ISBN 0-408-00380-4). Butterworth.

Brontman, Lazar K. On the Top of the World: The Soviet Expedition to the North Pole, 1937. Schmidt, O. J., ed. LC 68-55180. 1968. Repr. of 1938 ed. lib. bdg. 18.50x (ISBN 0-8371-0326-6, BRTW). Greenwood.

Bronwell, Arthur B. Science & Technology in the World of the Future. LC 74-114914. 1970. 22.50 (ISBN 0-471-10594-5, Pub. by Wiley). Krieger.

Bronwing, Iain. Petra. (Illus.). 256p. 1982. 27.50 (ISBN 0-7011-2622-1, Pub. by Chatto-Bodley-Jonathan). Merrimack Bk Serv.

Bronzan, Robert T. Public Relations, Promotions, & Fund-Raising for Athletic & Physical Education Programs. LC 76-10950. 268p. 1977. text ed. 26.50 o.p. (ISBN 0-471-01540-7). Wiley.

Bronzino, Joseph D. Computer Applications for Patient Care. 1982. 24.95 (ISBN 0-201-10156-4, 10156, Pub. by Med-Nurse); Soft Bdg. 17.95 (ISBN 0-686-97450-6, Pub. by Med-Nurse). A-W.

Brook, Charles G. Clinical Pediatric Endocrinology. (Illus.). 704p. 1981. text ed. 108.00 (ISBN 0-632-00698-6, B 0888-0). Mosby.

Brook, Christopher. Saxon & Norman Kings. 1978. 25.00 o.p. (ISBN 0-7134-1534-7, Pub. by Batsford England). David & Charles.

Brook, Danae, jt. auth. see Redgrave, Deirdre.

Brook, G. L. Books & Book-Collecting. 176p. 1980. 17.00 (ISBN 0-233-97154-8, 05772-X, Pub. by Gower Pub Co England). Lexington Bks.

--English Dialects. (Andre Deutsch Language Library). 1972. PLB 13.50 o.p. (ISBN 0-233-95641-7). Westview.

--English Sound Changes. 175p. 19.50x (ISBN 0-7190-0111-0, Pub. by Manchester U Pr England). State Mutual Bk.

--English Sound Changes. 1935. 3.00 (ISBN 0-7190-0111-0). Manchester.

Brook, George L., ed. see Layamon.

Brook, K. M., jt. auth. see Murdock, L. J.

Brook, M., jt. auth. see Ager, D. V.

Brooke. The Other Side of Death. 1979. pap. 3.95 (ISBN 0-8423-4759-3). Tyndale.

Brooke, Avery. As Never Before. 1976. pap. 2.00 (ISBN 0-8164-0905-6, Vineyard). Seabury.

--Doorway to Meditation. 1976. pap. 6.95 (ISBN 0-8164-0903-X, Vineyard). Seabury.

--Hidden in Plain Sight: The Practice of Christian Meditation. LC 77-17548. (Illus., Orig.). 1978. pap. 3.50 (ISBN 0-8164-2176-5, Vineyard). Seabury.

--How to Meditate Without Leaving the World. 1976. pap. 3.00 (ISBN 0-8164-0906-4, Vineyard). Seabury.

--Plain Prayers for a Complicated World. 124p. 1983. 5.95 (ISBN 0-8164-0501-8, Vineyard); pap. 2.95 (ISBN 0-8164-2428-4). Seabury.

Brooke, B. N., et al. Crohn's Disease. (Illus.). 1977. text ed. 29.50x (ISBN 0-19-519975-8). Oxford U Pr.

Brooke, C., et al, eds. Church & Government in the Middle Ages. LC 75-41614. (Illus.). 1977. 59.50 (ISBN 0-521-21172-7). Cambridge U Pr.

Brooke, C. N. & Postan, M. M. Carte Nativorum: A Peterborough Cartulary of the 14th Century. 1960. 48.00x (ISBN 0-686-87138-3, Pub. by Northamptonshire). State Mutual Bk.

Brooke, C. N., jt. auth. see Morey, Adrian.

Brooke, Charles F. & Paradise, Nathaniel B. English Drama, 1580-1642. 1933. text ed. 24.95x (ISBN 0-669-21105-2). Heath.

Brooke, Charlotte, ed. Reliques of Irish Poetry, 1789. Bd. with A Memoir of Miss Brooke, 1816. Seymour, A. C. LC 76-133327. 544p. 1970. 55.00x (ISBN 0-8201-1082-5). Schol Facsimiles.

Brooke, Christopher. From Alfred to Henry the Third, Eight Hundred Seventy-One to Twelve Seventy-Two. (Illus.). 1966. pap. 5.95x (ISBN 0-393-00362-0, Norton Lib). Norton.

--London, Eight Hundred to Twelve Sixteen: The Shaping of a City. LC 73-92620. (The History of London Ser). (Illus.). 1975. 42.50x (ISBN 0-520-02686-1). U of Cal Pr.

--Structure of Medieval Society. (Illus.). 1971. pap. 4.95 o.p. (ISBN 0-07-008061-5, SP). McGraw.

Brooke, I. English Costume of the Seventeenth Century. 2nd ed. (English Costume Ser.). (Illus.). 1977. Repr. of 1950 ed. text ed. 8.50x (ISBN 0-7136-0157-4). Humanities.

Brooke, Iris. Dress & Undress, the Restoration & Eighteenth Century. LC 73-3011. (Illus.). 161p. 1973. Repr. of 1958 ed. lib. bdg. 19.75x (ISBN 0-8371-6829-5, BRDU). Greenwood.

Brooke, James W. Disability Reporting. 1983. 20.00 (ISBN 0-87527-262-2). Green.

Brooke, Michael H. A Clinician's View of Neuromuscular Diseases. 1977. 27.00 o.p. (ISBN 0-683-01063-8). Williams & Wilkins.

Brooke, Michael Z. & Remers, H. Lee. The Strategy of Multinational Enterprise. 277p. 1979. text ed. 28.95 (ISBN 0-273-01178-2). Pitman Pub MA.

Brooke, Michael Z. & Remmers, H. Lee. International Management & Business Policy. LC 78-69612. (Illus.). 1978. Repr. of 1977 ed. text ed. 26.95 (ISBN 0-395-26505-3). HM.

Brooke, Rupert. Rupert Brooke. (Pocket Poet Ser.). 1968. pap. 1.25 (ISBN 0-8023-9042-0). Dufour.

Brooke, Stopford A. The Poetry of Robert Browning. 461p. 1982. Repr. 40.00 (ISBN 0-8495-0633-6). Arden Lib.

Brooke-Little, John. The British Monarchy in Color. (Color Ser.). (Illus.). 1976. 9.95 o.p. (ISBN 0-7137-0774-7, Pub by Blandford Pr England). Sterling.

Brooker, et al, eds. Current Methodology. LC 78-55806. (Advances in Cyclic Nucleotide Research Ser.: Vol. 10). 271p. 1979. 31.00 (ISBN 0-89004-265-9). Raven.

Brooker, Andrew F. & Cooney, William P., 3rd. Prinicples of External Fixation. 300p. 1983. lib. bdg. price not set (ISBN 0-683-01065-4). Williams & Wilkins.

Brooker, M. P., jt. auth. see Edwards, R. W.

Brooker, Nancy J., ed. John Schlesinger: A Guide to References & Resources. 1978. lib. bdg. 17.50 (ISBN 0-8161-8024-5, Hall Reference). G K Hall.

Brooker, R. E., Jr. British Military Pistols 1603-1888. 22.95 (ISBN 0-686-43082-4). Gun Room.

Brooker, S. G. & Cambie, R. C. New Zealand Medicinal Plants. (Illus.). 117p. 1983. 36.95 (ISBN 0-86863-382-8, Pub. by Heinemann Pubs New Zealand). Intl Schol Bk Serv.

Brooker, Stanley & Cambie, Conrad. New Zealand Medicinal Plants. (Illus.). 117p. 1981. 32.50 (ISBN 0-86863-382-8, Pub. by Heinemann New Zealand). Smithsonian.

Brookes, Andrew. V Force: The History of Britain's Airborne Deterrent. (Illus.). 173p. 1983. 19.95 (ISBN 0-86720-639-X). Sci Bks Intl.

Brookes, C. J., et al. Fundamentals of Mathematics: For Students of Chemistry & Allied Subjects. LC 78-26110. 496p. 1979. 67.00 (ISBN 0-471-99733-1); pap. 27.95x (ISBN 0-471-99732-3, Pub. by Wiley-Interscience). Wiley.

Brookes, Cyril & Grouse, Phil. Information Systems Design & Analysis. 488p. 1983. 24.00 (ISBN 0-13-464685-1). P-H.

Brookes, Edgar H. Three Letters from Africa. LC 65-12948. (Orig.). 1965. pap. 1.50 o.p. (ISBN 0-87574-139-8). Pendle Hill.

Brookes, Gerry H. The Rhetorical Form of Carlyle's Sartor Resartus. LC 71-185974. 208p. 1972. 26.00x (ISBN 0-520-02213-0). U of Cal Pr.

Brookes, H. F., ed. see Grass, Gunter.

Brookes, Ivan S. The Lower St. Lawrence. (Illus.). 1974. 9.75 (ISBN 0-685-41361-6). Freshwater.

Brookes, N. & Koullis, L., eds. Andy & Anna (Pupil's Book) A Coursebook for English Courses Ser.). 128p. (Pergamon Institute of English Courses Ser.). 128p. 1983. 3.95 (ISBN 0-08-025341-5). Pergamon.

Brookes, Vincent J. & Jacobs, Morris B. Poisons: Properties, Chemical Identification Origin & Use - Signs Symptoms & Emergency Treatment. 3rd ed. LC 74-9601. 318p. 1975. Repr. of 1958 ed. 18.00 (ISBN 0-88275-148-4). Krieger.

Brookesmith, Frank. I Remember the Tall Ships. (Illus.). 270p. Repr. 20.00 (ISBN 0-87556-543-3). Saifer.

Brookfield, Charles & Glover, J. M. The Poet & the Puppets: A Travestie Suggested by "Lady Windermere's Fan". Fletcher, Ian & Stokes, John, eds. Bd. with Aristophanes at Oxford. LC 76-20012. (Decadent Consciousness Ser.). 1978. lib. bdg. 38.00 o.s.i. (ISBN 0-8240-2784-1). Garland Pub.

Brookhart, C. E., ed. Graduate Music Teacher Education Report: A Final Report by the MENC Commission on Graduate Music Teacher Education. 25p. 6.00 (ISBN 0-686-37915-2). Music Ed.

Brooking, Walter J., ed. Career Opportunities-Engineering Technicians. 1970. 14.95 (ISBN 0-385-03181-5). Doubleday.

Brookings, Ernest N. We Did Not Plummet into Space. (Illus.). 1982. pap. text ed. 7.50 (ISBN 0-911623-01-9). I Klang.

Brookins, Dana. Who Killed Sack Annie? 160p. (gr. 4-7). 1983. 9.95 (ISBN 0-89919-137-1, Clarion). HM.

Brookins, Douglas G. Earth Resources, Energy & the Environment. (Illus.). 160p. (Orig.). 1981. pap. text ed. 10.95 (ISBN 0-675-08113-0). Merrill.

Brookner, Anita. The Debut. 1981. 11.95 o.p. (ISBN 0-671-42626-5, Linden). S&S.

Brookov, Wilbur, ed. School Social Systems & Student Achievement: Schools Can Make a Difference. 239p. 1979. 24.95x (ISBN 0-686-92315-4). J F Bergin.

Brooks & Brooks. The Human Body: Structure & Function in Health & Disease. 2nd ed. LC 79-24085. (Illus.). 1980. pap. text ed. 21.95 (ISBN 0-8016-0808-2). Mosby.

Brooks, jt. auth. see Pratt.

Brooks, A. Russell. James Boswell. (English Authors Ser.: No. 122). lib. bdg. 10.95 o.p. (ISBN 0-8057-1048-5, Twayne). G K Hall.

Brooks, Alexander D. Law, Psychiatry & the Mental Health System. 1974. 27.50 (ISBN 0-316-10970-3); Suppl., 1980. pap. 8.95 (ISBN 0-316-10971-1). Little.

Brooks, Alfred. From Holbein to Whistler: Notes on Drawing & Engraving. (Illus.). 1920. 87.50x (ISBN 0-685-69792-4). Elliots Bks.

Brooks, Aubrey J., ed. see Clark, Walter.

Brooks, Audrey W. Foundations of Instruction. 1977. pap. text ed. 12.00 o.p. (ISBN 0-8191-0024-2). U Pr of Amer.

Brooks, Barbara, ed. see Reynolds, Lloyd G.

Brooks, Bearl. Alphabet. (Early Education Ser.). 26p. (ps-1). 1979. wkbk. 5.00 (ISBN 0-8209-0199-7, K-1). ESP.

--American Indians. (Social Studies). 24p. (gr. 4-6). 1977. wkbk. 5.00 (ISBN 0-8209-0239-X, SS-6). ESP.

--Basic Cursive Handwriting. (Handwriting Ser.). 24p. (gr. 2-3). 1979. wkbk. 5.00 (ISBN 0-8209-0270-5, W-2). ESP.

--Basic Manuscript Handwriting. (Handwriting Ser.). 24p. (gr. 1-2). 1978. wkbk. 5.00 (ISBN 0-8209-0269-1, W-1). ESP.

--Basic Reading Comprehension: Grade Eight. (Reading Ser.). 24p. 1979. wkbk. 5.00 (ISBN 0-8209-0194-6, R-8). ESP.

--Basic Reading Comprehension: Grade Five. (Reading Ser.). 24p. 1977. wkbk. 5.00 (ISBN 0-8209-0191-1, R-5). ESP.

--Basic Reading Comprehension: Grade Four. (Reading Ser.). 24p. 1980. wkbk. 5.00 (ISBN 0-8209-0190-3, R-4). ESP.

--Basic Reading Comprehension: Grade One. (Reading Ser.). 24p. 1980. wkbk. 5.00 (ISBN 0-8209-0187-3, R-1). ESP.

--Basic Reading Comprehension: Grade Seven. (Reading Ser.). 24p. 1977. wkbk. 5.00 (ISBN 0-8209-0193-8, R-7). ESP.

--Basic Reading Comprehension: Grade Six. (Reading Ser.). 24p. 1979. wkbk. 5.00 (ISBN 0-8209-0192-X, R-6). ESP.

--Basic Reading Comprehension: Grade Three. (Reading Ser.). 24p. 1976. wkbk. 5.00 (ISBN 0-8209-0189-X, R-3). ESP.

--Basic Reading Comprehension: Grade Two. (Reading Ser.). 24p. 1977. wkbk. 5.00 (ISBN 0-8209-0188-1, R-2). ESP.

--Basic Skills Beginning Sounds Workbook. (Basic Skills Workbooks). 32p. (gr. k-1). 1983. 0.99 (ISBN 0-8209-0562-3, EEW-3). ESP.

--Basic Skills Following Directions Workbook. (Basic Skills Workbooks). 32p. (ps-1). 1983. 0.99 (ISBN 0-8209-0586-0, EEW-9). ESP.

--Basic Skills Healthy Body Workbook. (Basic Skills Workbooks). 32p. (gr. 6-7). 1983. 0.99 (ISBN 0-8209-0575-5, HW-2). ESP.

--Basic Skills Learning to Think Workbook. (Basic Skills Workbooks). 32p. (ps-1). 1983. 0.99 (ISBN 0-8209-0587-9, EEW-10). ESP.

--Basic Skills Listening for Sounds Workbook. (Basic Skills Workbooks). 32p. (gr. 2-3). 1983. 0.99 (ISBN 0-8209-0546-1, PW-6). ESP.

--Basic Skills Phonics Workbook: Part I. (Basic Skills Workbooks). 32p. (gr. 1-3). 1982. tchrs' ed. 0.99 (ISBN 0-8209-0385-X, PW-1). ESP.

--Basic Skills Phonics Workbook: Part II. (Basic Skills Workbooks). 32p. (gr. 1-3). 1982. tchrs' ed. 0.99 (ISBN 0-8209-0386-8, PW-2). ESP.

--Basic Skills Phonics Workbook: Part III. (Basic Skills Workbooks). 32p. (gr. 1-3). 1982. tchrs' ed. 0.99 (ISBN 0-8209-0387-6, PW-3). ESP.

--Basic Skills Punctuation Workbook. (Basic Skills Workbooks). 32p. (gr. 4-7). 1983. 0.99 (ISBN 0-8209-0548-8, EW-4). ESP.

--Basic Skills Reading Comprehension Workbook. (Basic Skills Workbooks). 32p. (gr. 1-2). 1982. 0.99 (ISBN 0-8209-0554-2, RCW-1). ESP.

--Basic Skills Reading Comprehension Workbooks. (Basic Skills Workbooks). 32p. (gr. 3-4). 1983. 0.99 (ISBN 0-8209-0555-0, RCW-2). ESP.

--Basic Skills Reading Comprehension Workbook. (Basic Skills Workbooks). 32p. (gr. 5-6). 1983. 0.99 (ISBN 0-8209-0556-9, RCW-3). ESP.

--Basic Skills Reading Comprehension Workbook. (Basic Skills Workbooks). 32p. (gr. 7-8). 1983. 0.99 (ISBN 0-8209-0557-7, RCW-4). ESP.

--Basic Skills Reading Workbook: Grade 8. (Basic Skills Workbooks). 32p. (gr. 8). 1982. wkbk. 0.99 (ISBN 0-8209-0362-0, RW-A). ESP.

--Basic Skills Telling Time Workbook. (Basic Skills Workbooks). 32p. (gr. 2-3). 1983. 0.99 (ISBN 0-8209-0552-6, EEW-13). ESP.

--Basic Skills World Neighbors Workbook. (Basic Skills Workbooks). 32p. (gr. 4-7). 1983. 0.99 (ISBN 0-8209-0558-5, SSW-6). ESP.

--Basic Spelling: Grade One. (Spelling Ser.). 24p. 1979. wkbk. 5.00 (ISBN 0-8209-0165-2, SP-1). ESP.
--Basic Spelling: Grade Three. (Spelling Ser.). 24p. 1977. wkbk. 5.00 (ISBN 0-8209-0167-9, SP-3). ESP.
--Basic Spelling: Grade Two. (Spelling Ser.). 24p. 1979. wkbk. 5.00 (ISBN 0-8209-0166-0, SP-2). ESP.
--Beginning Phonics. (Phonics Ser.). 24p. (gr. 1). 1979. wkbk. 5.00 (ISBN 0-8209-0329-9, P-1). ESP.
--Beginning Science. (Science Ser.). 24p. (gr. 1). 1979. wkbk. 5.00 (ISBN 0-8209-0139-3, S-1). ESP.
--Beginning Sounds. (Early Education Ser.). 24p. (ps-1). 1978. wkbk. 5.00 (ISBN 0-8209-0204-7, K-6). ESP.
--Bilingual Mathematics: Grade Four. (Math Ser.). 24p. 1977. wkbk. 5.00 (ISBN 0-8209-0137-7, BLM-3). ESP.
--Bilingual Mathematics: Grade Three. (Math Ser.). 24p. 1977. wkbk. 5.00 (ISBN 0-8209-0136-9, BLM-2). ESP.
--Bilingual Mathematics: Grade Two. (Math Ser.). 24p. 1977. wkbk. 5.00 (ISBN 0-8209-0135-0, BLM-1). ESP.
--Bilingual Reading: Level One. (Reading Ser.). 24p. 1979. wkbk. 5.00 (ISBN 0-8209-0196-2, BLR-1). ESP.
--Bilingual Reading: Level Three. (Reading Ser.). 24p. 1981. wkbk. 5.00 (ISBN 0-8209-0198-9, BLR-3). ESP.
--Bilingual Reading: Level Two. (Reading Ser.). 24p. 1981. wkbk. 5.00 (ISBN 0-8209-0197-0, BLR-2). ESP.
--Cursive Practice. (Handwriting Ser.). 24p. (gr. 2-3). 1979. wkbk. 5.00 (ISBN 0-8209-0271-3, W-3). ESP.
--Famous American Indian Leaders. (Social Studies). 24p. (gr. 4-6). 1979. wkbk. 5.00 (ISBN 0-8209-0243-8, SS-10). ESP.
--Following Directions. (Early Education Ser.). 24p. (ps-3). 1980. wkbk. 5.00 (ISBN 0-8209-0208-X, K-10). ESP.
--Health & Fun. (Health Ser.). 24p. (gr. 2-4). 1979. wkbk. 5.00 (ISBN 0-8209-0343-4, H-4). ESP.
--Health & Good Manners. (Health Ser.). 24p. (gr. 2-3). 1979. wkbk. 5.00 (ISBN 0-8209-0342-6, H-3). ESP.
--Health & Safety. (Health Ser.). 24p. (gr. 1-2). 1979. wkbk. 5.00 (ISBN 0-8209-0341-8, H-2). ESP.
--Health Habits. (Health Ser.). 24p. (gr. 1-2). 1980. wkbk. 5.00 (ISBN 0-8209-0340-X, H-1). ESP.
--The Healthy Body. (Health Ser.). 24p. (gr. 4-6). 1977. wkbk. 5.00 (ISBN 0-8209-0345-0, H-6). ESP.
--Jumbo Cursive Handwriting Yearbook. (Jumbo Handwriting Ser.). 96p. (gr. 3). 1978. wkbk. 14.00 (ISBN 0-8209-0019-2, JHWY-3). ESP.
--Jumbo Phonics Yearbook. (Jumbo Phonics Ser.). 96p. (gr. 1-3). 1977. 14.00 (ISBN 0-8209-0049-4, JPY 1). ESP.
--Jumbo Reading Yearbook: Kindergarten. (Jumbo Reading Ser.). 96p. (gr. k). 1980. 14.00 (ISBN 0-8209-0011-7, JRY R). ESP.
--Learning Phonics: Grade 1. (Phonics Ser.). 24p. 1979. wkbk. 5.00 (ISBN 0-8209-0330-2, P-2). ESP.
--Learning Phonics: Grade 3. (Phonics Ser.). 24p. 1977. wkbk. 5.00 (ISBN 0-8209-0333-7, P-5). ESP.
--Learning to Tell Time. (Early Education Ser.). 24p. (ps-2). 1979. wkbk. 5.00 (ISBN 0-8209-0207-1, K-9). ESP.
--Learning to Think. (Early Education Ser.). 24p. (gr. k). 1979. wkbk. 5.00 (ISBN 0-8209-0205-5, K-7). ESP.
--Listening for Sounds. (Phonics Ser.). 24p. (gr. 2). 1977. wkbk. 5.00 (ISBN 0-8209-0332-9, P-4). ESP.
--My Fifth Grade Yearbook. (My Yearbook Ser.). 832p. (gr. 5). 1981. 14.00 (ISBN 0-8209-0085-0, MFG-5). ESP.
--My First Grade Yearbook. (My Yearbook Ser.). 544p. (gr. 1). 1979. 14.00 (ISBN 0-8209-0081-8, MFG-1). ESP.
--My Kindergarten Yearbook. (My Yearbook Ser.). 544p. (gr. k). 1980. 14.00 (ISBN 0-8209-0080-X, MKY K). ESP.
--My Second Grade Yearbook. (My Yearbook Ser.). 640p. (gr. 2). 1979. 14.00 (ISBN 0-8209-0082-6, MSG-2). ESP.
--My Sixth Grade Yearbook. (My Yearbook Ser.). 832p. 1981. 14.00 (ISBN 0-8209-0086-9, MSG-6). ESP.
--My Third Grade Yearbook. (My Yearbook Ser.). 768p. (gr. 3). 1979. 14.00 (ISBN 0-8209-0083-4, MTG-3). ESP.
--Nonreading Exercises. (Early Education Ser.). 24p. (ps-1). 1975. wkbk. 5.00 (ISBN 0-8209-0202-0, K-4). ESP.
--Our Community. (Social Studies Ser.). 24p. (gr. 2-3). 1979. wkbk. 5.00 (ISBN 0-8209-0236-5, SS-3). ESP.
--Our Home. (Social Studies Ser.). 24p. (gr. 1). 1979. wkbk. 5.00 (ISBN 0-8209-0234-9, SS-1). ESP.
--Our Neighborhood. (Social Studies Ser.). 24p. (gr. 2). 1979. wkbk. 5.00 (ISBN 0-8209-0235-7, SS-2). ESP.
--Our World Neighbors. (Social Studies Ser.). 24p. (gr. 5-6). 1979. wkbk. 5.00 (ISBN 0-8209-0242-X, SS-9). ESP.
--Phonetic Sounds. (Phonics Ser.). 24p. (gr. 2). 1979. wkbk. 5.00 (ISBN 0-8209-0331-0, P-3). ESP.
--Phonetic Sounds & Symbols: Part 1. (Phonics Ser.). 24p. (gr. 1). 1978. wkbk. 5.00 (ISBN 0-8209-0335-3, P-7). ESP.
--Phonetic Sounds & Symbols: Part 2. (Phonics Ser.). 24p. (gr. 1). 1978. wkbk. 5.00 (ISBN 0-8209-0336-1, P-8). ESP.
--Phonics for Reading & Spelling: Grade 2. (Phonics Ser.). 24p. 1978. wkbk. 5.00 (ISBN 0-8209-0337-X, P-9). ESP.
--Phonics for Reading & Spelling: Grade 3. (Phonics Ser.). 24p. 1978. wkbk. 5.00 (ISBN 0-8209-0338-8, P-10). ESP.
--Phonics for Reading & Spelling: Grade 4. (Phonics Ser.). 24p. 1978. wkbk. 5.00 (ISBN 0-8209-0339-6, P-11). ESP.
--Shelter & the Family. (Social Studies Ser.). 24p. (gr. 4-6). 1976. wkbk. 5.00 (ISBN 0-8209-0249-7, SS-16). ESP.
--Understanding Punctuation: Grades 4-7. (English Ser.). 24p. (gr. 4-7). 1979. wkbk. 5.00 (ISBN 0-8209-0186-5, E-15). ESP.
--Using Phonics. (Phonics Ser.). 24p. (gr. 1-4). 1978. wkbk. 5.00 (ISBN 0-8209-0334-5, P-6). ESP.
--Writing Letters & Words. (Handwriting). 24p. (gr. k-1). 1980. wkbk. 5.00 (ISBN 0-8209-0268-3, W-0). ESP.
Brooks, Bearl, jt. auth. see Taylor, Ralph.
Brooks, Bearl, et al. Jumbo Word Games Yearbook. (Jumbo Vocabulary Ser.). 96p. (gr. 3). 1980. 14.00 (ISBN 0-8209-0059-1, JWG 1). ESP.
Brooks, Brian S., et al. News Reporting & Writing. 542p. (Orig.). 1980. text ed. 18.95x (ISBN 0-312-57201-8); pap. text ed. 14.95x (ISBN 0-312-57202-6); instructor's manual available (ISBN 0-312-57203-4). St Martin.
Brooks Bright Foundation. Aspects of Anglo-American Relations. 1928. 24.50x (ISBN 0-685-69830-0). Elliots Bks.
Brooks, C. M., et al, eds. Integrative Functions of the Autonomic Nervous System. 1979. 104.00 (ISBN 0-444-80140-5, North Holland). Elsevier.
Brooks, Chandler McC., et al, eds. The Life & Contributions of Walter Bradford Cannon, 1871-1945. LC 74-20825. 1975. 39.50x (ISBN 0-87395-261-8). State U NY Pr.
Brooks, Charles, ed. Best Editorial Cartoons of the Year: 1972 Edition. (Best Editorial Cartoon Ser.). (Illus.). 160p. 1973. 13.95 (ISBN 0-911116-95-8). Pelican.
--Best Editorial Cartoons of the Year: 1974 Edition. LC 74-3807. (Best Editorial Cartoon Ser.). (Illus.). 160p. 1974. 13.95 (ISBN 0-88289-027-1). Pelican.
--Best Editorial Cartoons of the Year: 1975 Edition. LC 74-29707. (Best Editorial Cartoon Ser.). (Illus.). 160p. 1975. 13.95 (ISBN 0-88289-077-8). Pelican.
--Best Editorial Cartoons of the Year: 1976 Edition. LC 74-29707. (Best Editorial Cartoon Ser.). (Illus.). 160p. 1976. 13.95 (ISBN 0-88289-122-7). Pelican.
--Best Editorial Cartoons of the Year: 1977 Edition. LC 74-29707. (Best Editorial Cartoon Ser.). (Illus.). 1977. 13.95 (ISBN 0-88289-170-7); pap. 9.95 (ISBN 0-88289-171-5). Pelican.
--Best Editorial Cartoons of the Year: 1978 Edition. LC 73-643645. (Best Editorial Cartoon Ser.). (Illus.). 1978. 12.95 o.p. (ISBN 0-88289-192-8); pap. 9.95 (ISBN 0-88289-193-6). Pelican.
--Best Editorial Cartoons of the Year: 1979 Edition. (Best Editorial Cartoon Ser.). (Illus.). 1979. 13.95 (ISBN 0-88289-229-0); pap. 8.95 o.p. (ISBN 0-88289-230-4). Pelican.
--Best Editorial Cartoons of the Year: 1980 Edition. LC 73-643645. (Illus.). 160p. (Orig.). 1980. 13.95 (ISBN 0-88289-264-9); pap. 9.95 (ISBN 0-88289-265-7). Pelican.
--Best Editorial Cartoons of the Year: 1981 Edition. LC 73-643645. (Best Editorial Cartoons of the Year Ser.: Vol. 9). (Illus.). 160p. 1981. pap. 9.95 (ISBN 0-88289-281-9). Pelican.
--Best Editorial Cartoons of the Year: 1982 Edition. LC 73-643645. (Illus.). 160p. (Orig.). 1982. pap. 9.95 (ISBN 0-88289-319-X). Pelican.
--Best Editorial Cartoons of the Year: 1983 Edition. LC 73-643645. 160p. 1983. pap. 9.95 (ISBN 0-88289-406-4). Pelican.
Brooks, Charles E. Climate in Everyday Life. LC 75-36507. (Illus.). 314p. 1976. Repr. of 1950 ed. lib. bdg. 19.25x (ISBN 0-8371-8647-1, BRCEL). Greenwood.
--Nymph Fishing for Larger Trout. 1976. 10.95 o.p. (ISBN 0-517-52551-8). Crown.
Brooks, Charles V. Sensory Awareness: The Rediscovery of Experiencing. 2nd ed. (Illus.). 260p. 1982. pap. 8.95 (ISBN 0-915520-56-7). Ross Erikson.
Brooks, Charlie R. Heat Treatment of Ferrous Alloys. (Illus.). 1979. text ed. 39.00x (ISBN 0-07-008076-3). McGraw.
Brooks, Cleanth. The Well Wrought Urn: Studies in the Structure of Poetry. LC 47-3143. (Orig.). (YA) 1956. pap. 4.95 (ISBN 0-15-695705-1, Harv). HarBraceJ.
Brooks, Cleanth & Warren, Robert P. Modern Rhetoric. 4th ed. 401p. 1979. pap. text ed. 13.95 (ISBN 0-15-562815-1, HC); instructor's manual avail. (ISBN 0-15-562816-X). HarBraceJ.
--Scope of Fiction. 1960. text ed. 14.50 (ISBN 0-13-796656-3). P-H.
Brooks, Cleanth, jt. auth. see Warren, Robert P.
Brooks, Cleanth, et al. An Approach to Literature. 5th ed. 832p. 1975. ref. ed. 22.95x (ISBN 0-13-043802-2). P-H.
Brooks, Courtaney. Plays & Puppets et Cetera. LC 81-68933. (Illus.). 100p. (Orig.). 1981. pap. 9.00x (ISBN 0-941274-00-4). Belnice Bks.
Brooks, Daniel T., ed. Computer Law 1982: Acquiring Computer Goods & Services. (Nineteen Eighty-Two to Nineteen Eighty-Three Commercial Law & Practice Course Handbook Ser.). 1000p. 1982. pap. 30.00 (ISBN 0-686-69165-2, A6-4041). PLI.
Brooks, Daniel T., et al. Computer Law 1982: Acquiring Computer Goods & Services, 2 vols. LC 82-61508. (Commercial Law & Practice Course Handbook Ser.). 1370p. 1982. 30.00 (A6-4041). PLI.
Brooks, David K., Jr., jt. ed. see Warner, Richard, Jr.
Brooks, Dennis L. & Henley, Arthur. Don't be Afraid of Cataracts. 128p. 1983. pap. 5.95 (ISBN 0-8065-0823-X). Citadel Pr.
Brooks, Don. Washington Rock: A Climbing Guide. (Illus., Orig.). 1982. pap. 7.95 (ISBN 0-89886-046-6). Mountaineers.
Brooks, Douglas. Number & Pattern in the Eighteen-Century Novel: Defoe, Fielding, Smollett & Sterne. 208p. 1973. 18.95x (ISBN 0-7100-7598-7). Routledge & Kegan.
Brooks, Douglas M. Common Sense in Teaching & Supervising. 1977. pap. text ed. 7.00 (ISBN 0-8191-0271-7). U Pr of Amer.
Brooks, Douglas M. & Van Cleaf, David W. Pupil Evaluation in the Classroom: An All Level Guide to Practice. LC 82-13650. (Illus.). 170p. 1983. lib. bdg. 22.00 (ISBN 0-8191-2736-1); pap. text ed. 10.00 (ISBN 0-8191-2737-X). U Pr of Amer.
Brooks, Edward. The Bessie Smith Companion. (Roots of Jazz Ser.). xx, 250p. 1983. lib. bdg. 22.50 (ISBN 0-306-76202-1). Da Capo.
Brooks, Edward F. & Wade, Torlen L. Planning & Managing Rural Health Centers. LC 78-27667. (Rural Health Center Ser.). (Illus.). 192p. 1979. prof ref 20.00x (ISBN 0-88410-536-9); pap. 12.95 (ISBN 0-88410-542-3). Ballinger Pub.
Brooks, Frank P., ed. Gastrointestinal Pathophysiology. 2nd ed. (Pathophysiology Ser.). 1978. text ed. 24.95x (ISBN 0-19-502330-7); pap. text ed. 15.95x (ISBN 0-19-502331-5). Oxford U Pr.
Brooks, Frederick P., Jr. The Mythical Man-Month: Essays on Software Engineering. (Illus.). 200p. 1974. pap. text ed. 12.95 (ISBN 0-201-00650-2). A-W.
Brooks, G. L. An Introduction of Old English. 1955. pap. 5.50 (ISBN 0-7190-0569-8). Manchester.
Brooks, George, jt. auth. see Orloff, Neil.
Brooks, George E., Jr. Themes in African & World History: A Schema for Integrating Africa into World History; Tropical Africa: The Colonial Heritage; The African Heritage & the Slave Trade. (African Humanities Ser.). 45p. (Orig.). 1973. pap. text ed. 2.00 (ISBN 0-941934-06-3). Ind U Afro-Amer Arts.
Brooks, Gregory. Monroe's Island. LC 79-1568. (Illus.). (ps-1). 1979. 7.95 (ISBN 0-02-714810-6). Bradbury Pr.
Brooks, Gwendolyn. Bronzeville Boys & Girls. LC 56-8152. (Illus.). (gr. 3-6). 1956. 7.95 o.p. (ISBN 0-06-020650-0, HarpJ); PLB 9.89 (ISBN 0-06-020651-9). Har-Row.
--Selected Poems. 1963. 11.49i (ISBN 0-06-010535-6, HarpT); pap. 4.50 o. p. (ISBN 0-06-010536-4, TD-137, HarpT). Har-Row.
Brooks, Harold F., ed. A Midsummer Night's Dream. 3rd ed. (The Arden Shakespeare Ser.). 1979. 30.00x (ISBN 0-416-17930-4); pap. 5.95 (ISBN 0-416-17940-1). Methuen Inc.
Brooks, Hugh, ed. Illustrated Encyclopedic Dictionary of Building & Construction Terms. (Illus.). 1975. 29.95 o.p. (ISBN 0-13-451013-5, Busn). P-H.
Brooks, Hugh C., jt. auth. see Lees, Francis.
Brooks, J. & Shaw, G. Origin & Development of Living Systems. 1973. 61.00 (ISBN 0-12-135740-6). Acad Pr.
Brooks, J. L., ed. Benito Perez Galdos: Torquemada en la Hoguera. 100p. 1973. text ed. 5.90 o.s.i. (ISBN 0-08-016917-1); pap. text ed. 4.80 (ISBN 0-08-016918-X). Pergamon.
Brooks, Jack. Front Row Center: Southern California. (Illus.). 216p. (Orig.). 1983. pap. 6.95 (ISBN 0-89286-205-X). One Hund One Prods.
Brooks, James A. & Winbery, Carlton L. Syntax of New Testament Greek. LC 78-51150. 1978. pap. text ed. 8.00 (ISBN 0-8191-0473-6). U Pr of Amer.
Brooks, Janice Y. Kings & Queens: The Plantagenets of England. LC 75-17843. 160p. (gr. 6 up). 1975. 7.95 o.p. (ISBN 0-525-66438-6). Lodestar Bks.
--Still the Mighty Waters. (Orig.). 1983. pap. 3.95 (ISBN 0-440-17630-1). Dell.
Brooks, Jerome. Make Me a Hero. LC 79-20269. 176p. (gr. 5-9). 1980. 9.95 (ISBN 0-525-34475-6, 0966-290). Dutton.
Brooks, Joa G., et al. No More Diapers. (Illus.). (ps). 1977. pap. 6.95 (ISBN 0-440-06508-9, Sey Lawr). Delacorte.
Brooks, John, ed. South American Handbook 1981. 57th ed. LC 25-514. (Illus.). 1306p. 1979. 30.00x o.p. (ISBN 0-900751-17-7). Intl Pubns Serv.
--South American Handbook, 1982. 58th ed. LC 25-514. (Illus.). 1341p. 1981. 25.00 (ISBN 0-900751-18-5). Intl Pubns Serv.
--South American Handbook, 1983. (Illus.). 29.95 (ISBN 0-528-84618-3). Rand.
Brooks, John G. American Syndicalism: The I.W.W. LC 78-107407. (Civil Liberties in American History Ser). 1970. Repr. of 1913 ed. lib. bdg. 32.50 (ISBN 0-306-71887-1). Da Capo.
Brooks, John L., jt. ed. see Bowyer, John W.
Brooks, Juanita, ed. On the Mormon Frontier: The Diary of Hosea Stout, 2 Vols. 832p. 1982. Repr. of 1964 ed. 40.00 (ISBN 0-87480-214-8, SET). U of Utah Pr.
Brooks, Karen. Forget about Meat Cookbook. 1978. pap. 7.95 o.p. (ISBN 0-87857-218-X). Rodale Pr Inc.
Brooks, Karen & Bosker, Gideon. Showcase Portland Restaurants. (Illus.). 288p. (Orig.). 1982. 4.95 (ISBN 0-942098-01-3). Class Media Prod.
Brooks, Karen M., jt. auth. see Johnson, D. Gale.
Brooks, Keith L. Acts, Adventures of the Early Church. (Teach Yourself the Bible Ser). 1961. pap. 2.25 (ISBN 0-8024-0125-2). Moody.
--Basic Bible Study for New Christians. (Teach Yourself the Bible Ser). 1961. pap. 2.25 (ISBN 0-8024-0478-2). Moody.
--Ephesians, the Epistle of Christian Maturity. (Teach Yourself the Bible Ser.). 1944. pap. 2.25 (ISBN 0-8024-2333-7). Moody.
Brooks, L. D. ConsultaMation, Inc. An Applications Program for Word Processing. 192p. 1982. 10.00x (ISBN 0-07-008081-X, G). McGraw.
Brooks, Leroy D. Financial Management Decision Game (Fingame) rev. ed. 1982. pap. 12.95x (ISBN 0-256-02622-X). Irwin.
Brooks, Louise. Early History of Divine Science. 1963. 5.95 (ISBN 0-686-24363-3). Divine Sci Fed.
Brooks, Lucy. The Nurse Assistant. LC 77-73939. 1978. pap. text ed. 9.80 (ISBN 0-8273-1620-8); instr.'s guide 2.75 (ISBN 0-8273-1621-6). Delmar.
Brooks, Marie E. The Little Red Schoolhouse: Ain't What It Used to Be. Young, Billie, ed. LC 73-76539. 1974. 8.95 o.p. (ISBN 0-87949-010-1). Ashley Bks.
Brooks, Martin. The Dream Weaver. LC 77-94412. 1978. 10.95 o.p. (ISBN 0-89662-000-X, Mecox Bks). Atheneum.
Brooks, Maurice. Life of the Mountains. (Our Living World of Nature Ser). (Illus.). (gr. 7 up). 1968. 14.95 (ISBN 0-07-008075-5, P&RB); by subscription. 3.95 (ISBN 0-07-046010-8). McGraw.
Brooks, Nancy A., jt. auth. see Riemer, Jeffrey W.
Brooks, Natalie A., jt. auth. see Brooks, Stewart M.
Brooks, Neal A. & Rockel, Eric G. A History of Baltimore County. (Illus.). 555p. 1979. 20.00 (ISBN 0-686-36504-6). Md Hist.
Brooks, Nicholas, ed. Latin & the Vernacular Languages in Early Medieval Britain. (Studies in the Early History of Britain Ser.: Vol. 1). 200p. 1982. text ed. 52.50x (ISBN 0-7185-1209-X, Leicester). Humanities.
Brooks, Noah. Henry Knox, a Soldier of the Revolution. LC 74-8496. (Era of the American Revolution Ser.). (Illus.). xiv, 286p. 1974. Repr. of 1900 ed. lib. bdg. 32.50 (ISBN 0-306-70617-2). Da Capo.
Brooks, Noel. Let There Be Life. 3.95 (ISBN 0-911866-71-X); pap. 3.95 (ISBN 0-911866-88-4). Advocate.
Brooks, Nona L. Mysteries. 1977. 6.95 (ISBN 0-686-24364-1); pap. 4.50 (ISBN 0-686-24365-X). Divine Sci Fed.
--Short Lessons in Divine Science. 1973. pap. 4.95 (ISBN 0-686-24348-X). Divine Sci Fed.
Brooks, Patricia. Best Restaurants New England. LC 80-16277. 211p. (Orig.). 1980. pap. write for info. o.p. One Hund One Prods.
--Best Restaurants Southern New England. (Best Restaurants Ser.). (Illus.). 200p. 1983. pap. 4.95 (ISBN 0-89286-214-9). One Hund One Prods.
Brooks, Pearl. Basic Skills Handwriting Workbook: Grade 1. (Basic Skills Workbooks). 32p. 1982. tchrs' ed. 0.99 (ISBN 0-8209-0370-1, CHW-1). ESP.
--Basic Skills Handwriting Workbook: Grade 2. (Basic Skills Workbooks). 32p. 1982. tchr's ed. 0.99 (ISBN 0-8209-0371-X, CHW-2). ESP.
--Basic Skills Handwriting Workbook: Grade 3. (Basic Skills Workbooks). 32p. 1982. tchr's ed. 0.99 (ISBN 0-8209-0372-8, CHW-3). ESP.
Brooks, Peter see Giamatti, A. Bartlett.
Brooks, Philip C. Research in Archives: The Use of Unpublished Primary Sources. LC 69-19273. 1969. 7.50x o.s.i. (ISBN 0-226-07575-3). U of Chicago Pr.
--Research in Archives: The Use of Unpublished Primary Sources. LC 69-19273. (Midway Reprint Ser.). xii, 128p. 1982. pap. text ed. 8.00x (ISBN 0-226-07576-1). U of Chicago Pr.
Brooks, R. A., ed. see Floy, Michael.
Brooks, R. R. Biological Methods of Prospecting for Minerals. 325p. 1983. price not set (ISBN 0-471-87470-0, Pub. by Wiley-Interscience). Wiley.
Brooks, R. R., jt. auth. see Reeves, R. D.
Brooks, R. T. A Place to Start: The Bible as a Guide for Today. 120p. 1983. pap. 4.95 (ISBN 0-86683-708-6). Winston Pr.

Brooks, Reid M. & Olmo, Harold P. Register of New Fruit & Nut Varieties. 2nd rev. & enl. ed. LC 76-100017. 512p. 1972. 33.00x (ISBN 0-520-01638-6). U of Cal Pr.

Brooks, Richard A., ed. The Selected Letters of Voltaire. LC 72-96429. 349p. 1973. 17.50x o.p. (ISBN 0-8147-0972-9). NYU Pr.

Brooks, Richard A., jt. ed. see Hall, H. Gaston.

Brooks, Robert. So That's How I Was Born! (Illus.). 48p. (ps-3). Date not set. 5.95 (ISBN 0-671-44501-4, Little Simon). S&S.

Brooks, Ron. Annie's Rainbow. LC 76-8840. (Illus.). 32p. (gr. k-4). 1976. 5.95 o.p. (ISBN 0-529-05290-3, Philomel). Putnam Pub Group.

--Timothy & Gramps. LC 78-17389. (ps-2). 1979. 7.95 (ISBN 0-02-714790-8). Bradbury Pr.

Brooks, Rose-Marie. Sunbeam Great Crepe Recipes. cancelled o.p. (ISBN 0-916752-03-8). Green Hill.

Brooks, Sandra. I Can Pray to God. Mahany, Patricia, ed. LC 82-80031. (Happy Day Bks.). (Illus.). 24p. (Orig.). (ps-3). 1982. pap. 1.29 (ISBN 0-87239-540-5, 3586). Standard Pub.

Brooks, Shirley J. Stories for Fun: Four Delightful Stories for Children. 1978. 4.50 o.p. (ISBN 0-533-02990-2). Vantage.

Brooks, Shirley M. Instrumentation for the Operating Room: A Photographic Manual. 2nd ed. LC 82-2225. (Illus.). 476p. 1982. pap. text ed. 22.95 (ISBN 0-8016-0817-1). Mosby.

Brooks, Steve. Phillip Blanc in San Francisco. (Illus.). 1972. pap. 3.00 (ISBN 0-915572-12-5). Panjandrum.

Brooks, Stewart M. Integrated Basic Science. 4th ed. LC 78-24430. (Illus.). 556p. 1979. 21.95 (ISBN 0-8016-0805-8). Mosby.

Brooks, Stewart M. & Brooks, Natalie A. Turner's Personal & Community Health. 16th ed. (Illus.). 540p. 1983. pap. text ed. 20.95 (ISBN 0-8016-5128-X). Mosby.

Brooks, Susan, ed. see Chamness, Danford.

Brooks, Svevo & Burkhart, John. A Guide to Political Fasting. LC 82-13008. 56p. (Orig.). 1982. pap. 3.95 (ISBN 0-943726-01-8). Langdon Pubns.

Brooks, Terrance V. & Stewart, Tamara A., eds. Judicial Discipline & Disability Digest: 1980 Supplement. LC 81-65601. 256p. 1983. 95.00 (ISBN 0-938870-29-7); lib. bdg. 50.00. Am Judicature.

Brooks, Thomas. Toil & Trouble. 2nd ed. 1971. 10.95 o.s.i. (ISBN 0-440-08975-1). Delacorte.

Brooks, Thomas R. Clint: Biography of a Labor Intellectual Clinton S. Golden. LC 77-3152. 1978. 14.95 o.p. (ISBN 0-689-10923-7). Atheneum.

--Toil & Trouble: A History of American Labor. rev ed. 432p. 1972. pap. 9.95 (ISBN 0-440-59016-7, Delta). Dell.

Brooks, Tommy C. The Flip-Flop Spy. 1983. 10.95 (ISBN 0-533-05251-3). Vantage.

Brooks, Valrie, ed. see Hill, Douglas.

Brooks, Virginia R. Minority Stress & Lesbian Women. LC 80-8116. 240p. 1981. 24.95x (ISBN 0-669-03953-5). Lexington Bks.

Brooks, W. D. & Vogel, R. A., eds. Business Communication. LC 76-44138. (Series in Speech Communication). 1977. pap. text ed. 9.95 (ISBN 0-8465-7600-7); instr's guide 4.95 (ISBN 0-8465-7607-4). Benjamin-Cummings.

Brooks, W. D., ed. see Leth, Pamela C. & Leth, Steven A.

Brooks, William D. & Scafe, Marla G. Verbal Language & Communication. (Comm Comp Ser.). (Illus.). 32p. 1980. pap. text ed. 2.95 (ISBN 0-686-84490-4). Gorsuch Scarisbrick.

Brooks, William E. Grant of Appomattox, a Study of the Man. LC 73-138577. (Illus.). 1971. Repr. of 1942 ed. lib. bdg. 16.25x (ISBN 0-8371-5776-5, BRGR). Greenwood.

Brook-Smith, John, et al, trs. see Macedo, Helder & De Melo e Castro, E. M.

Broom, Leonard & Kitsuse, John L. The Managed Casualty: The Japanese-American Family in World War II. (Library Reprint Ser.: No. 40). 1974. Repr. 21.00x (ISBN 0-520-02523-7). U of Cal Pr.

Broome, C. E., jt. auth. see Berkeley, M. J.

Broome, P. & Chesters, G. The Appreciation of Modern French Poetry: 1850 to 1950. LC 75-40768. 176p. 1976. 29.95 (ISBN 0-521-20792-4); pap. 9.95 (ISBN 0-521-20930-7). Cambridge U Pr.

Broome, P. & Chesters, G., eds. An Anthology of Modern French Poetry. LC 75-40769. 224p. 1976. 37.50 (ISBN 0-521-20793-2); pap. 11.95 (ISBN 0-521-20929-3). Cambridge U Pr.

Broome, Peter. Henri Michaux. (Athlone French Poets Ser.). 1977. text ed. 19.75x o.p. (ISBN 0-485-14605-3, Athlone Pr); pap. text ed. 11.75x o.p. (ISBN 0-485-12205-7). Humanities.

Broome, Peter, ed. see Michaux, Henri.

Broome, Richard. Aboriginal Australians: Black Response to White Dominance 1788-1980. (The Australian Experience Ser.). 1982. text ed. 25.00x (ISBN 0-86861-043-7); pap. 12.50x (ISBN 0-86861-051-8). Allen Unwin.

Broome, Susannah. The Amulet of Fortune. 1980. pap. 1.95 o.p. (ISBN 0-451-09134-5, J9134, Sig). NAL.

Broomfield, J. H. Elite Conflict in a Plural Society: Twentieth-Century Bengal. LC 68-13822. 1968. 30.00x (ISBN 0-520-00179-6). U of Cal Pr.

Broomfield, Robert. Baby Animal ABC. (Picture Ser). (Orig.). 1968. pap. 2.95 (ISBN 0-14-050006-5, Puffin). Penguin.

Broomhall, A. J. Hudson Taylor & China's Open Century: Bk. I, Barbarians at the Gates. 1981. pap. 7.95 (ISBN 0-340-26210-9). OMF Bks.

--Hudson Taylor & China's Open Century: Bk. III, If I Had A Thousand Lives. 1983. pap. 10.95 (ISBN 0-340-32392-2). OMF Bks.

Brooner, Ernie. Microcomputer Data-Base Management. Date not set. pap. 12.95 (ISBN 0-672-21875-5). Sams.

Brooten & Hayman. Leadership for Change: A Guide for the Frustrated Nurse. text ed. 9.00 (ISBN 0-686-97985-0, Lippincott Nursing). Lippincott.

Brooten, Bernadette J. Women Leaders in the Ancient Synagogue: Inscriptional Evidence & Background Issues. LC 82-10658. (Brown Judaic Studies). 292p. 1982. pap. 20.00 (ISBN 0-89130-587-4, 14 00 36). Scholars Pr CA.

Brophy, Brigid. Hackenfeller's Ape. 128p. 1980. 12.95 (ISBN 0-8052-8009-X, Pub. by Allison & Busby England); pap. 4.95 (ISBN 0-8052-8008-1, Pub. by Allison & Busby England). Schocken.

--Palace Without Chairs. LC 77-18387. 1978. 9.95 o.p. (ISBN 0-689-10883-4). Atheneum.

--The Prince & the Wild Geese. (Illus.). 64p. 1983. 10.95 (ISBN 0-312-64551-1). St Martin.

--The Snow Ball. 144p. 1980. 12.95 (Pub. by Allison & Busby England); pap. 4.95 (ISBN 0-8052-8006-5, Pub. by Allison & Busby England). Schocken.

Brophy, Elizabeth B. Samuel Richardson: The Triumph of Craft. LC 74-3248. 1974. 11.50x (ISBN 0-87049-153-9). U of Tenn Pr.

Brophy, J. H., et al. Thermodynamics of Structure. (Structure & Properties of Materials Ser: Vol. 2). 216p. 1964. pap. text ed. 17.50x (ISBN 0-471-10610-0). Wiley.

Brophy, J. J., jt. auth. see Azaroff, Leonid V.

Brophy, James D. & Porter, Raymond J., eds. Modern Irish Literature: Essays in Honor of William York Tyndall. lib. bdg. 9.95 o.p. (ISBN 0-8057-5717-1, Twayne). G K Hall.

Brophy, James J. Basic Electronics for Scientists. 3rd ed. (Illus.). 1977. text ed. 31.50 (ISBN 0-07-008107-7, C); solutions manual 9.95 (ISBN 0-07-008108-5). McGraw.

--Basic Electronics for Scientists. 4th ed. (Illus.). 464p. 1982. text ed. 34.95x (ISBN 0-07-008133-6, C); instructor's manual avail. (ISBN 0-07-008134-4). McGraw.

Brophy, Peter. Cobol Programming: An Introduction for Librarians. 153p. 1976. 13.50 o.p. (ISBN 0-208-01527-2, Linnet). Shoe String.

Brophy, William S. The Krag Rifle. 29.95 (ISBN 0-686-43084-0). Gun Room.

--L. C. Smith Shotguns. 29.95 (ISBN 0-686-43085-9). Gun Room.

Brosche, F. & Suendermann, J., eds. Tidal Friction & the Earth's Rotation, Bielefeld, FRG, 1981: Proceedings. (Illus.). 345p. 1983. pap. 28.00 (ISBN 0-387-12011-4). Springer-Verlag.

Brose, Olive J. Frederick Denison Maurice: Rebellious Conformist, 1805-1872. LC 74-141380. xxiii, 308p. 1971. 16.00x (ISBN 0-8214-0092-4, 82-80976). Ohio U Pr.

Brosheer, J. C., ed. see Munson, Robert D.

Broskii, Iosif. Novye Stansy K. Avguste: Stikhotvoreniia K. M. B. 136p. (Russian.). 1983. 17.00 (ISBN 0-686-79333-1). Ardis Pubs.

Brosnac, Donald. Guitar Electronics: A Work Book. (Illus.). 150p. (Orig.). 1980. lib. bdg. 12.00 (ISBN 0-942760-00-X); 12.00 (ISBN 0-686-36861-4). DB Music.

Brosnahan, Jo A. & Milne, Barbara. A Calendar of Home-School Activities. 1979. text ed. 13.95x (ISBN 0-673-16345-8); pap. text ed. 11.95x (ISBN 0-673-16346-6). Scott F.

Brosnan, Jim. Ron Santo: 3 B. new ed. (Putnam Sports Shelf). 144p. (gr. 5 up). 1974. PLB 5.29 o.p. (ISBN 0-399-60875-3). Putnam Pub Group.

--The Ted Simmons Story. LC 76-30443. (Putnam Sports Shelf). (Illus.). (gr. 6-8). 1977. PLB 6.29 o.p. (ISBN 0-399-61075-8). Putnam Pub Group.

Brosnan, John. Movie Magic: The Story of Special Effects in the Cinema. 304p. (RL 8). 1976. pap. 6.95 (ISBN 0-452-25355-1, Z5355, Plume). NAL.

Bross, Theodore D. Anton. 8.95 (ISBN 0-533-05669-1). Vantage.

Brosses. Traite de la Formation Mecanique des Langues, 2 vols. (Linguistics 13th-18th Centuries Ser.). (Fr.). 1974. Repr. of 1765 ed. Set. lib. bdg. 269.50x o.p. (ISBN 0-8287-0146-6). Vol. 1 (71-5028). Vol. 2 (71-5029). Clearwater Pub.

Brossi, A. Organic Synthesis. LC 21-17747. (Organic Synthesis Ser.: Vol. 53). 193p. 1973. 15.95 (ISBN 0-471-10615-1). Wiley.

Brossi, Arnold, ed. The Alkaloids: Chemistry & Pharmacology, Vol. 21. Date not set. price not set (ISBN 0-12-469521-3). Acad Pr.

Brossman, Mark E., jt. auth. see Levin, Noel A.

Broster, W. H. & Swan, Henry. Feeding Strategy for the High Yielding Dairy Cow. 432p. 1979. text ed. 45.00x (ISBN 0-258-97126-6, Pub. by Granada England). Renouf.

Brosterman, Robert. The Complete Estate Planning Guide. rev. ed. 1981. pap. 3.95 (ISBN 0-451-62126-3, ME1692, Ment). NAL.

Brostow, Witold. Science of Materials. LC 78-5983. 1979. 49.95 (ISBN 0-471-01885-6, Pub. by Wiley-Interscience). Wiley.

Brother Aloysius. Comfort to the Sick: A Recipe Book of Medicinal Herbs. 416p. Date not set. pap. write for info. (ISBN 0-87728-525-X). Weiser.

Brother Andrew. Building in a Broken World. 144p. 1981. pap. 4.95 (ISBN 0-8423-0184-4). Tyndale.

Brother Lawerance & Laubach, Frank. Practicing His Presence. 3rd ed. Edwards, Gene, ed. 1973. pap. 4.95 (ISBN 0-940232-01-4). Christian Bks.

Brother Lawrence Of The Resurrection, see Delaney, John J.

Brothers, Church & School. 196p. 1982. 39.00x (ISBN 0-85323-021-8, Pub. by Liverpool Univ England). State Mutual Bk.

Brothers Grimm. Fairy Tales. Barish, Wendy, ed. (Illus.). 304p. 1982. 14.95 (ISBN 0-671-43792-5). Wanderer Bks.

--Snow White. Heins, Paul, tr. LC 73-13585. (Illus.). (gr. k-3). 1979. pap. 4.95 o.p. (ISBN 0-316-35451-1, Pub. by Atlantic-Little Brown); 8.95 o.p. (ISBN 0-316-35450-3). Little.

Brothers, Joyce. What Every Woman Should Know About Men. 288p. 1983. pap. 2.95 (ISBN 0-345-30848-4). Ballantine.

Brothers, Milton J. Diabetes: A New Approach. LC 72-90859. 1978. pap. 5.95 o.p. (ISBN 0-448-12237-5, G&D). Putnam Pub Group.

Brothers Grimm. The Devil with the Three Golden Hairs. LC 82-12735. (Illus.). 40p. (gr. k-3). 1983. 10.95 (ISBN 0-394-85560-4); lib. bdg. 10.99 (ISBN 0-394-95560-9). Knopf.

--Favorite Tales from Grimm. (Illus.). (gr. 1 up). 1982. 15.95 (ISBN 0-590-07791-0, Four Winds). Schol Bk Serv.

--Little Red Riding Hood. Hyman, Trina S., retold by. & illus. LC 82-7700. (Illus.). 32p. (ps-3). 1982. reinforced binding 13.95 (ISBN 0-8234-0470-6). Holiday.

--Snow White. LC 82-20960. (Illus.). 24p. (ps-3). 1983. PLB 11.95 (ISBN 0-571-12518-2). Faber & Faber.

--Three Grimms' Fairy Tales: The Fox & the Geese, The Magic Porridge Pot, The Silver Pennies. (Illus.). (ps-3). 1981. boxed set 7.95 (ISBN 0-316-32885-5). Little.

--Wanda Gag's the Six Swans. (Illus.). 48p. 1982. 8.95 (ISBN 0-698-20552-9, Coward). Putnam Pub Group.

Brotherston, Gordon. The Emergence of the Latin American Novel. LC 76-40834. 1977. 27.50 (ISBN 0-521-21478-5); pap. text ed. 9.95 (ISBN 0-521-29565-3). Cambridge U Pr.

--Image of the New World: The American Continent Portrayed in Native Texts. 1982. pap. 9.95x (ISBN 0-500-27232-8). Thames Hudson.

--Manuel Machado: A Revaluation. LC 68-11281. (Illus.). 1968. 37.50 (ISBN 0-521-04334-4). Cambridge U Pr.

Brotherton, Christopher J., jt. auth. see Stephenson, Geoffrey M.

Brotherton, Jack. The Annals of Stanislaus County California. (Illus.). 260p. 1982. 22.95 (ISBN 0-934136-29-7). Western Tanager.

Brotherus, V. F. Die Laubmoose Fennoskandias. (Flora Fennica Ser.: Vol. 1). (Illus.). 635p. (Ger.). 1974. Repr. of 1923 ed. lib. bdg. 79.20x (ISBN 3-87429-078-6). Lubrecht & Cramer.

Brothwell, D. R. Digging up Bones: The Excavation, Treatment, & Study of Human Skeletal Remains. 3rd rev. ed. LC 80-66914. (Illus.). 224p. pap. 14.95x (ISBN 0-8014-9875-9). Cornell U Pr.

Brothwell, Don & Sandison, A. T. Diseases in Antiquity: A Survey of the Diseases, Injuries & Surgery of Early Populations. (Illus.). 792p. 1967. photocopy ed. spiral 79.25x (ISBN 0-398-00233-9). C C Thomas.

Broude, Norma, ed. Seurat in Perspective. LC 78-1600. (Artists in Perspective Ser.). (Illus.). 1979. 12.95 (ISBN 0-13-807115-2, Spec); pap. 5.95 (ISBN 0-13-807107-1). P-H.

Broudy, Harry S., et al, eds. Philosophy of Educational Research. LC 72-2332. (Readings in Educational Research Ser.). 1973. 30.75 (ISBN 0-471-10625-9); text ed. 28.00 10 or more copies (ISBN 0-686-67151-1). McCutchan.

Broue, Pierre & Temime, Emile. Revolution & the Civil War in Spain. White, Tony, tr. from Fr. 612p. 1973. 25.00x o.p. (ISBN 0-262-02067-X). MIT Pr.

Brough, James. Consuelo: Portrait of an American Heiress. LC 78-21244. (Illus.). 1979. 14.95 o.p. (ISBN 0-698-10782-9, Coward). Putnam Pub Group.

--Margaret: The Tragic Princess. 1979. pap. 2.25 o.p. (ISBN 0-380-44206-X, 44206). Avon.

--Margaret: The Tragic Princess. LC 77-21635. (Illus.). 1978. 9.95 o.p. (ISBN 0-399-12051-3). Putnam Pub Group.

--The Vixens. 1981. 12.95 o.p. (ISBN 0-671-22688-6). S&S.

Brough, James, jt. auth. see Roosevelt, Elliott.

Brough, James H. Miss Lillian Russell: A Novel Memoir. 1978. 11.95 o.p. (ISBN 0-07-008120-4, GB). McGraw.

Brough, John, tr. Poems from the Sanskrit. 1982. pap. 4.95 (ISBN 0-14-044198-0). Penguin.

Brougham, Eleanor M. Corn from Olde Fieldes: An Anthology of English Poems from the 14th to the 17th Century with Biographical Notes. 294p. 1982. Repr. of 1918 ed. lib. bdg. 40.00 (ISBN 0-89760-095-9). Telegraph Bks.

Brougher, Toni. A Way with Words: How to Improve Your Relationships Through Better Communications. LC 81-18841. 352p. 1982. text ed. 22.95x (ISBN 0-88229-645-0); pap. text ed. 11.95x (ISBN 0-88229-810-0). Nelson-Hall.

Broughton, jt. auth. see Mills.

Broughton, Jacqueline P. Garden Flowers to Color. (Illus.). 32p. (ps-2). 1972. pap. 1.25 (ISBN 0-913456-51-9). Transbooks.

Broughton, James. High Kukus. LC 68-58535. 1968. 4.95 (ISBN 0-912330-09-0, Dist. by Inland Bk). Jargon Soc.

--Long Undressing: Collected Poems 1949-69. LC 74-137209. 1971. 10.00 (ISBN 0-912330-10-4, Dist. by Inland Bk); ltd. ed. o.p. 25.00x (ISBN 0-912330-11-2); pap. 7.50 (ISBN 0-912330-24-4). Jargon Soc.

--Shaman Psalm. Date not set. price not set (ISBN 0-9608372-0-5). Syzygy Pr.

Broughton, John. The Wild Man of the Four Winds. (Illus.). 32p. (gr. 1-3). 1983. 10.95 (ISBN 0-241-10816-0, Pub. by Hamish Hamilton England). David & Charles.

Broughton, John M. & Freeman-Moir, John D. The Cognitive Developmental Psychology of James Mark Baldwin: Current Theory & Research in Genetic Epistemology. (Publications for the Advancement of Theory & History in Psychology (PATH) Ser.). 480p. 1982. 39.50x (ISBN 0-89391-043-0). Ablex Pub.

Broughton, R. J., ed. Henri Gastaut & the Marseilles School's Contribution to the Neurosciences: Proceedings of the 25th & Final Colloque de Marseille. (Electroencephalography & Clinical Neurophysiology Ser.: Suppl. No. 35). 448p. 1982. 130.25 (ISBN 0-444-80363-7, Biomedical Pr). Elsevier.

Broughton, Rhoda. Not Wisely, but Too Well. Van Thal, Herbert, ed. 1867-1967. 7.95 (ISBN 0-304-92524-1); pap. 4.95 (ISBN 0-8023-9053-6). Dufour.

Broughton, Robert. Measures of Property Rights. (Orig.). 1977. pap. 5.95 o.p. (ISBN 0-910286-51-5). Boxwood.

Broughton, T. A. Winter Journey. 1980. 10.95 o.p. (ISBN 0-525-23515-9). Dutton.

Broughton, T. Alan. Far from Home. LC 78-74989. (Poetry Ser.). 1979. 8.95 o.p. (ISBN 0-915604-25-6); pap. 4.50 (ISBN 0-915604-26-4). Carnegie-Mellon.

--In the Face of Descent. LC 75-4386. (Poetry Ser.). 1975. pap. 3.50 o.p. (ISBN 0-915604-02-7). Carnegie-Mellon.

Broughton, T. Allan. Dreams Before Sleep. LC 81-71589. 1982. 13.95 (ISBN 0-915604-68-X); pap. 5.95 (ISBN 0-915604-69-8). Carnegie-Mellon.

Broughton, Thomas R. Romanization of Africa Proconsularis. LC 68-23279. 1968. Repr. of 1929 ed. lib. bdg. 19.00x (ISBN 0-8371-0030-5, BRAD). Greenwood.

Broughton, V., jt. auth. see Mills, J.

Broughton, V., jt. ed. see Mills, J.

Broughton, W. J., ed. Nitrogen Fixation: Rhizobium, Vol. 2 & Vol. 3. (Illus.). 1982. Vol. 2 63.00x, (ISBN 0-19-854552-5); Vol. 3, 1983 74.00x, (ISBN 0-19-854555-X). Oxford U Pr.

Brouillard, F., ed. Physics of Ion-Ion & Electron-Ion Collisions. (NATO ASI Series B, Physics: Vol. 83). 535p. 1983. 69.50x (ISBN 0-306-41105-9, Plenum Pr). Plenum Pub.

Broul, M. & Hyvit, J. Solubility in Inorganic Two-Component Systems. (Physical Sciences Data Ser.: Vol. 6). 1981. 85.00 (ISBN 0-444-99763-6). Elsevier.

Broun, Heywood & Britt, George. Christians Only: A Study in Prejudice. LC 73-19688. (Civil Liberties in American History Ser). 333p. 1974. Repr. of 1931 ed. lib. bdg. 39.50 (ISBN 0-306-70599-0). Da Capo.

Broun, Heywood H. A Studied Madness. LC 79-84436. 298p. 1983. pap. 4.95 (ISBN 0-933256-40-X). Second Chance.

--Tumultuous Merriment. 1979. 8.95 o.s.i. (ISBN 0-399-90047-0, Marek). Putnam Pub Group.

--Whose Little Boy Are You? A Memoir of the Broun Family. (Illus.). 1983. 13.95 (ISBN 0-312-87765-X, Pub. by Marek). St Martin.

Broun, Hob. Odditorium. LC 82-48101. 228p. 1983. 14.37i (ISBN 0-06-015027-0, HarpT). Har-Row.

Broun, Kenneth S. & Meisenholder, Robert. Problems in Evidence. 2nd ed. LC 80-28083. (American Casebook Ser.). 304p. 1981. pap. text ed. 7.50 (ISBN 0-8299-2125-7); tchr's manual avail. (ISBN 0-314-60971-7). West Pub.

Broussard, E. Joseph & Holgate, Jack F. Writing & Reporting Broadcast News. 1982. text ed. 16.95 (ISBN 0-02-315270-2). Macmillan.

Broussard, Sharon, jt. auth. see Alexander, Stan.

Broutman, Lawrence J., jt. auth. see Agarwal, B. D.

Brouwer, L. & Heyting, A. L. E. J. Brouwer Collected Works, Vol. 1. 1975. 127.75 (ISBN 0-444-10474-7). Elsevier.

Brouwer, L. E. L. E. J. Brouwer-Collected Works, Vol. 2. Heyting, A., ed. LC 73-75529. 628p. 1976. 127.75 (ISBN 0-444-10643-X, North-Holland). Elsevier.

Brouws, Jeffrey T. & Hill, Ronald C. Railroading West: A Contemporary Glimpse. (Illus.). 12.95 o.s.i. (ISBN 0-933506-02-3). Darwin Pubns.

Brovald, Ken C. Alaska's Wilderness Rails: From the Taiga to the Tundra. LC 82-80963. (Illus.). 104p. 1982. pap. text ed. 8.95 (ISBN 0-933126-21-2). Pictorial Hist.

Broven, John. South To Louisiana: The Music of the Cajun Bayous. LC 82-11247. 1983. 19.95 (ISBN 0-88289-300-9). Pelican.

Brow. Collage. (The Grosset Art Instruction Ser.: No. 46). (Illus.). 48p. Date not set. pap. price not set (ISBN 0-448-00555-7, G&D). Putnam Pub Group.

Brow, Dix. Sea of Cortez Guide: For Fishermen, Cruisers, Trailerboaters & Cartoppers in Mexico's Gulf of California. New ed. LC 82-15877. (Illus.). 272p. (Orig.). 1982. pap. 19.95 (ISBN 0-930030-26-5). Western Marine Ent.

Browder, Earl, jt. auth. see Bowers, Claude G.

Browder, Robyn, ed. see Broili, June.

Browder, Robyn, ed. see DeBolt, Margaret W.

Browder, Robyn, ed. see DuSablon, Mary Anna.

Browder, Robyn, ed. see Nusom, Lynn.

Browder, Robyn, ed. see Weiner, Melissa R. & Ruffner, Budge.

Browder, Robyn S., ed. see Clifford, Sally A.

Browder, Sue. The New Age Baby Name Book. 272p. 1974. pap. 3.50 (ISBN 0-446-30824-2). Warner Bks.

Browdy, Jerad D. Health Care Executive Compensation: Principles & Strategies. LC 82-11384. 214p. 1982. 28.50 (ISBN 0-89443-827-1). Aspen Systems.

Brower, David J., jt. auth. see Godschalk, David R.

Brower, David J., et al. Urban Growth Management Through Development Timing. LC 75-19766. 172p. 1976. text ed. 23.95 o.p. (ISBN 0-275-55530-5). Praeger.

Brower, James E. & Zar, Jerrold H. Field & Laboratory Methods for General Ecology. 208p. 1977. wire coil write for info. (ISBN 0-697-04545-5). Wm C Brown.

Brower, Kenneth. A Song For Satawal: A Magical Passage to a Faraway Eden. LC 82-48110. 224p. 1983. 13.41i (ISBN 0-06-015093-9, HarpT). Har-Row.

--The Starship & the Canoe. LC 82-48519. 256p. 1983. pap. 4.76i (ISBN 0-06-091030-5, CN 1030, CN). Har-Row.

Brower, Kenneth, jt. auth. see Curtsinger, William R.

Brower, R. H., tr. see Teika, Fujiwara.

Brower, Reuben, ed. see Shakespeare, William.

Brower, W. A., jt. auth. see Lee, D. E.

Brower, Walter A., jt. auth. see Lee, Dorothy E.

Brown. Questions & Answers: Hi-Fi. (Illus.). 1974. pap. 4.95 (ISBN 0-408-00151-8). Focal Pr.

Brown & Brown. Consulting with Parents & Teachers. LC 81-10100. 1982. 20.00x (ISBN 0-910328-35-8); pap. 15.00x (ISBN 0-910328-36-6). Carroll Pr.

Brown & Dorweiler. CB Radio Operator's Guide. 2nd ed. LC 75-31462. 256p. 1975. 8.95 o.p. (ISBN 0-8306-5799-1); pap. 5.95 o.p. (ISBN 0-8306-4799-6, 799). TAB Bks.

Brown & Watson. Talking of Gandiji: BBC Programs. 159p. Cloth 7.50 o.p. (ISBN 0-686-96941-3). Greenlf Bks.

Brown, jt. auth. see Grill.

Brown, jt. auth. see Schmitz, J. V.

Brown, jt. auth. see Breck.

Brown, jt. auth. see Cargill.

Brown, jt. auth. see Goldmann.

Brown, A., tr. see Botvinnik, M. M.

Brown, A. A. & Davis, Kenneth P. Forest Fire: Control & Use. 2nd ed. (Forest Resources Ser.). (Illus.). 544p. 1973. text ed. 33.50 (ISBN 0-07-008205-7, C). McGraw.

Brown, A. A. & Neuberger, E. Perspectives in Economics. 1971. text ed. 16.95 (ISBN 0-07-008311-8, C). McGraw.

Brown, A. G., et al. An Introduction to Subject Indexing, Vol. 1: Subject Analysis & Practical Classification. (Programmed Texts in Library & Information Science Ser.). 144p. 1976. 13.50 o.p. (ISBN 0-208-01524-8, Linnet). Shoe String.

Brown, A. H. Soviet Politics & Political Science. LC 75-29858. 128p. 1976. 20.00 (ISBN 0-312-74865-5). St Martin.

Brown, A. H., ed. see C.O.S.P.A.R International Space Science Symposium, 7th, Vienna, 1966.

Brown, A. Lee. Rules & Conflicts: An Introduction to Political Life & Its Study. (Illus.). 384p. 1981. pap. text ed. 14.95 (ISBN 0-13-783738-0). P-H.

Brown, A. R. Optimum Packing & Depletion. (Computer Monograph Ser: No. 14). 1972. 14.95 (ISBN 0-444-19588-2). Elsevier.

Brown, A. W. Ecology of Pesticides. LC 77-11730. 1978. 40.50x (ISBN 0-471-10790-5, Pub by Wiley-Interscience). Wiley.

Brown, A. W., jt. ed. see Watson, David L.

Brown, Aggrey, jt. ed. see Stone, Carl.

Brown, Aileen, jt. ed. see Shaw, Stephen M.

Brown, Aileen, ed. see Shaw, Stephen M.

Brown, Alan. An Introduction to Subject Indexing. 240p. 1982. 17.50 o.p. (ISBN 0-208-01937-5, Pub. by Bingley England). Shoe String.

--Invitation to Sailboat Racing. LC 70-154095. 1972. 12.95 o.p. (ISBN 0-671-20987-6). S&S.

--Invitation to Sailing. 1962. Repr. of 1962 ed. 9.95 o.p. (ISBN 0-671-38350-7). S&S.

Brown, Alan R., ed. Prejudice in Children. 224p. 1972. 17.50x (ISBN 0-398-02247-X); pap. 11.50 o.p. (ISBN 0-398-02478-2). C C Thomas.

Brown, Albert J., Jr. Branch Manager's Workbook. LC 75-36011. 1975. plastic comb 15.00 o.p. (ISBN 0-87267-023-6). Bankers.

Brown, Alec, tr. see Leonov, Leonid M.

Brown, Alex. Making Books Work. 11.50x (ISBN 0-392-16526-0, ABC). Sportshelf.

Brown, Alexander C. Steam Packets on the Chesapeake: A History of the Old Bay Line Since Eighteen Forty. (Illus.). 192p. 1961. 6.00 (ISBN 0-686-36508-9). Md Hist.

Brown, Allen, jt. auth. see Teller, Edward.

Brown, Allen R. English Castles. 1976. 31.50 (ISBN 0-7134-3119-9, Pub. by Batsford England). David & Charles.

Brown, Alpha. One Hundred & One Practical Activities for Use in Classes of Pupils Who Are Retarded. 1970. pap. 3.25x (ISBN 0-88323-058-5, 156). Richards Pub.

Brown, Andrew J. Community Health: An Introduction for the Health Professional. LC 80-67481. 255p. (Orig.). 1981. 14.95x (ISBN 0-8087-4040-7). Burgess.

Brown, Ann L., jt. ed. see Lamb, Michael E.

Brown, Annice H. Thank You, Lord, for Little Things. LC 72-11166. (Illus.). 1973. 3.25 (ISBN 0-8042-2580-X). John Knox.

Brown, Anthony C. & MacDonald, Charles B. On a Field of Red: The Communist International & the Coming of World War II. 800p. 1981. 19.95 o.p. (ISBN 0-399-12542-6). Putnam Pub Group.

Brown, Archie & Kaser, Michael, eds. Soviet Policy for the Nineteen Eighties. LC 82-48593. 296p. 1983. 19.50x (ISBN 0-253-35412-9). Ind U Pr.

Brown, Arlen D. & Strickland, R. Mack. Tractor & Small Engine Maintenance. 5th ed. 350p. 1983. 15.65 (ISBN 0-8134-2258-2); text ed. 11.75x (ISBN 0-686-83991-9). Interstate.

Brown, Arthur W. Margaret Fuller. (United States Authors Ser.). 13.95 (ISBN 0-8057-0304-7, Twayne). G K Hall.

Brown, Arthur W., et al, eds. see Kiraly, Bela.

Brown, Ashley & Kimmey, John L. Comedy. LC 69-10745. 1968. pap. text ed. 3.95 (ISBN 0-675-09591-3). Merrill.

--Romance. LC 69-10742. 1968. pap. text ed. 3.95 (ISBN 0-675-09587-5). Merrill.

Brown, Ashley, ed. see Tate, Allen.

Brown, Aubrey I. & Marco, S. M. Introduction to Heat Transfer. 3rd ed. 1958. text ed. 37.95 (ISBN 0-07-008458-0, C). McGraw.

Brown, Audrey K., jt. ed. see Aladjem, Silvio.

Brown, Austin R., Jr. Arbplot: A Computer Graphics Utility for Calculus. (A Software Microcomputer Program Ser.). 1982. scp Users manual 5.95 (ISBN 0-06-041027-2, HarpC); scp computer package 125.00 (ISBN 0-06-041026-4). Har-Row.

Brown, Barbara. Stress & the Art of Biofeedback. LC 76-5115. (Illus.). 1977. 14.37i (ISBN 0-06-010544-5, HarpT). Har-Row.

Brown, Barbara B. The Biofeedback Syllabus: A Handbook for the Psychophysiologic Study of Biofeedback. 516p. 1975. 45.50x (ISBN 0-398-03268-8); pap. 31.75x. C C Thomas.

--Supermind: The Ultimate Energy. LC 79-2614. (Illus.). 1980. 12.45i (ISBN 0-06-010518-6, HarpT). Har-Row.

Brown, Barbara B. & Klug, Jay, eds. The Alpha Syllabus: A Handbook of Human EEG Alpha Activity. 368p. 1974. 34.50x (ISBN 0-398-03020-0); 28.50x (ISBN 0-398-03021-9). C C Thomas.

Brown, Barbara J. Perspectives in Primary Nursing: Professional Practice Environments. LC 81-20579. 366p. 1982. text ed. 26.50 (ISBN 0-89443-683-X). Aspen Systems.

Brown, Barbara J. & Chinn, Peggy L., eds. Nursing Education: Practical Methods & Models. LC 82-11370. 297p. 1982. 27.50 (ISBN 0-89443-807-7). Aspen Systems.

Brown, Benjamin F., ed. Scritti e Discorsi Extraparlamiatari, 2 vols. (Ital.). 1973. Vol. Primo, 1870-1902, xxii, 932p. (ISBN 0-7006-0119-8); Vol. Secondo, 1903-1920, xv, 774p. Set. 45.00 (ISBN 0-686-84039-9). Univ Pr KS.

Brown, Bernard, ed. Found: Long-Term Gains from Early Intervention. LC 78-3120. (AAAS Selected Symposium Ser.: No. 8). 1978. lib. bdg. 24.00 o.p. (ISBN 0-89158-436-6). Westview.

Brown, Bernard E. Socialism of a Different Kind: Reshaping the Left in France. LC 82-6125. (Contributions in Political Science Ser.: No. 85). 248p. 1982. lib. bdg. 29.95 (ISBN 0-313-23377-2, BFL/). Greenwood.

Brown, Bernard E., jt. ed. see Christoph, James B.

Brown, Beth, jt. auth. see Thackeray, Helen.

Brown, Beverly S. Erica the Ecologist. LC 81-71554. (Illus.). 60p. (Orig.). (gr. 3-5). 1982. pap. 2.50x (ISBN 0-943864-01-1). Davenport.

--Erica the Ecologist. (Illus.). 60p. 1982. 2.50 (ISBN 0-943864-01-1). MD Bks.

Brown, Bob. How to Fool Your Friends. (Kids Paperbacks). (gr. 3 up). 1978. PLB 10.69 (ISBN 0-307-63435-3, Golden Pr); pap. 1.95 (ISBN 0-307-12082-1). Western Pub.

Brown, Bob, et al. South American Cook Book; Including Central America, Mexico & the West Indies. LC 72-166427. 1971. pap. 4.95 (ISBN 0-486-20190-2). Dover.

Brown, Brendan. The Dollar-Mark Axis: On Currency Power. LC 79-5354. 1979. 25.00 (ISBN 0-312-21623-8). St Martin.

Brown, Brendan F., ed. The Natural Law Reader. LC 59-8601. (Docket Ser.: Vol. 13). 230p. 1960. pap. 2.50 (ISBN 0-379-11313-9). Oceana.

Brown, Brendon. The Futures Market in Foreign Exchange. LC 82-42562. 240p. 1982. 25.00x o.p. (ISBN 0-312-31473-6). St Martin.

--A Theory of Hedge Investment. LC 82-5651. 240p. 1982. 25.00 (ISBN 0-312-79783-4). St Martin.

Brown, Bryan. The England of Henry Taunt: Victorian Photographer. (Illus.). 1980. pap. 8.95 (ISBN 0-7100-0557-1). Routledge & Kegan.

Brown, Burnell R., Jr. Fluid & Blood Therapy in Anesthesia. LC 82-10075. (Contemporary Anesthesia Practice Ser.: Vol. 6). 187p. 1983. 26.00 (ISBN 0-8036-1273-7). Davis Co.

Brown, Byron W., Jr. & Hollander, Myles. Statistics: A Biomedical Introduction. LC 77-396. (Probability & Mathematical Statistics Ser). 1977. 30.50 (ISBN 0-471-11240-2, Pub. by Wiley-Interscience). Wiley.

Brown, C. A., jt. auth. see Blackler, F. H.

Brown, C. Christopher. Introduction to Maryland Civil Litigation. 258p. 1982. 30.00 (ISBN 0-87215-528-5). Michie-Bobbs.

Brown, C. M., jt. ed. see Nedwell, D. B.

Brown, C. V. & Jackson, P. M. Public Sector Economics. 2nd ed. (Illus.). 512p. 1982. text ed. 37.50x (ISBN 0-85520-525-3, Pub. by Martin Robertson England). Biblio Dist.

Brown, Calvin S. A Glossary of Faulkner's South. LC 75-43308. (Illus.). 1976. 22.50x (ISBN 0-300-01944-0); pap. 5.95 (ISBN 0-300-02240-9). Yale U Pr.

Brown, Carl F. & Brown, Mac H. Handbook of Reading Activities: From Teacher to Parent to Child. 162p. (Orig.). 1982. pap. 12.95 (ISBN 0-89334-036-7). Humanics Ltd.

Brown, Carter. The Aseptic Murders. Bd. with Night Wheeler. 1979. pap. 2.50 (ISBN 0-451-11701-8, AE1701, Sig). NAL.

--The Blonde. Bd. with Girl in a Shroud. 1979. pap. 2.50 (ISBN 0-451-11703-4, AE1703, Sig). NAL.

--The Brazen. Bd. with The Stripper. pap. 2.50 (ISBN 0-451-11704-2, AE1704, Sig). NAL.

--Catch Me a Phoenix-Nymph to the Slaughter. 1979. pap. 2.50 (ISBN 0-451-11702-6, AE1702, Sig). NAL.

--The Coven. Bd. with The Creative Murders. 1978. pap. 2.50 (ISBN 0-451-11697-6, AE1697, Sig). NAL.

--The Dance of Death. Bd. with A Corpse for Christmas. 1982. pap. 2.75 (ISBN 0-451-11926-6, AE1926, Sig). NAL.

--The DumDum Murder. Bd. with The Hellcat. 1982. pap. 2.75 (ISBN 0-451-11873-1, AE1873, Sig). NAL.

--Ice-Cold Nude: The Lover Don't Come Back. 1982. pap. 2.75 (ISBN 0-451-11780-8, AE1780, Sig). NAL.

--The Lover. Bd. with The Bombshell. 1980. pap. 1.75 (ISBN 0-451-09121-3, E9121, Sig). NAL.

--Mini-Murders. pap. 1.25 o.p. (ISBN 0-451-07263-4, Y7263, Sig). NAL.

--Negative in Blue. (Orig.). 1974. pap. 0.95 o.p. (ISBN 0-451-06220-5, Q6220, Sig). NAL.

--The Sad-Eyed Seductress. Bd. with The Ever-Loving Blues. 1982. pap. 2.50 (ISBN 0-451-11520-1, AE1520, Sig). NAL.

--Sex Clinic. Bd. with W.H.O.R.E. 1978. pap. 2.50 (ISBN 0-451-11698-4, AE1698, Sig). NAL.

--The Tigress. Bd. with Angeli. 1981. pap. write for info. o.p. (ISBN 0-451-11027-7, AE1027, Sig). NAL.

--Zelda: The Wind-Up Doll. 1982. pap. 2.75 (ISBN 0-451-11629-1, AE1629, Sig). NAL.

Brown, Cassie. Standing into Danger: A Dramatic Story of Shipwreck & Rescue. LC 78-1236. (Illus.). 1979. 15.95 o.p. (ISBN 0-385-13681-1). Doubleday.

Brown, Charlene, et al. The Media & the People. LC 78-8375. 480p. 1978. Repr. lib. bdg. 18.50 (ISBN 0-88275-689-3). Krieger.

Brown, Charles & Kreta, Eleanor. Introduction to Data Entry Devices with a Subset of BASIC. 1979. pap. text ed. 6.25 (ISBN 0-8403-1952-5, 40195201). Kendall-Hunt.

Brown, Charles B. Ormond, or the Secret Witness. Krause, Sydney & Reid, S. W., eds. LC 82-14904. (The Novels & Related Works of Charles Brockden Brown: Vol. 2). 500p. 1983. 30.00X (ISBN 0-87338-277-3). Kent St U Pr.

--Wieland: Or, the Transformation. pap. 4.95 (ISBN 0-385-03100-9, Anch). Doubleday.

--Wieland or the Transformation. Pattee, F. L., ed. LC 58-13328. 1969. pap. 5.95 (ISBN 0-15-696680-8, Harv). HarBraceJ.

Brown, Charles N. & Brown, Dena, eds. Locus: The Newspaper of the Science Fiction Field, 1968-1977. (Science Fiction Ser.). 1978. lib. bdg. 95.00 o.p. (ISBN 0-8398-2443-2, Gregg). G K Hall.

Brown, Charles R. Education for Christian Service. 1922. 37.50x (ISBN 0-685-89749-4). Elliots Bks.

--Yale Talks. 1919. 22.50x (ISBN 0-686-51327-4). Elliots Bks.

Brown, Charles T. & Keller, Paul T. Monologue to Dialogue: An Exploration of Interpersonal Communication. 2nd ed. LC 78-16541. (Special Communication Ser.). 1979. pap. 17.95 (ISBN 0-13-600825-9). P-H.

Brown, Charlotte & Hyman, Paula. The Jewish Woman in America. 1977. pap. 5.95 (ISBN 0-452-25282-2, Z5282, Plume). NAL.

Brown, Cheever M. God As Mother: A Feminine Theology in India, an Historical & Theological Study of the Brahmavaivarta Purana. LC 74-76006. (God Ser.: No. 106). 1974. 15.00 (ISBN 0-89007-004-0). C Stark.

Brown, Christopher. The Paintings of Carel Fabritius: Complete Edition with a Catalogue Raisonne. LC 80-69741. (Illus.). 1981. 75.00x (ISBN 0-8014-1394-X, Cornell Phaidon Books). Cornell U Pr.

--Van Dyck. LC 82-72566. (Illus.). 240p. 1982. 48.50x (ISBN 0-8014-1537-3). Cornell U Pr.

Brown, Christopher & Dunham, Judith. New Bay Area Painting & Sculpture. LC 82-80488. 1982. pap. 7.50 (ISBN 0-9608270-0-5). Squeezer.

Brown, Christopher, jt. auth. see Turner, Anthony.

Brown, Christy. Collected Poems. 216p. 1983. 18.95 (ISBN 0-436-07089-8, Pub. by Secker & Warburg). David & Charles.

--A Promising Career. 248p. 1983. 16.95 (ISBN 0-436-07097-9, Pub. by Secker & Warburg). David & Charles.

Brown, Claude. Manchild in the Promised Land. (RL 7). 1971. pap. 2.95 (AE1251, Sig). NAL.

Brown, Clifton F., compiled by. Ethiopian Perspectives: A Bibliographical Guide to the History of Ethiopia. LC 77-89111. (African Bibliographic Center, Special Bibliographic Series, New Series: No. 5). lib. bdg. 35.00 (ISBN 0-8371-9850-X, BET/). Greenwood.

Brown, Craig & Cunliffe, Lesley. The Book of Royal Lists. 292p. (Orig.). 1983. 15.95 (ISBN 0-671-46507-4); pap. 7.95 (ISBN 0-671-47282-8). Summit Bks.

Brown, Curtis F. Star-Spangled Kitsch. LC 75-1139. (Illus.). 204p. 1976. pap. 4.95 o.s.i. (ISBN 0-87663-948-1). Universe.

Brown, Curtis M. Boundary Control & Legal Principles. 2nd ed. LC 68-8712. 1969. 36.95 (ISBN 0-471-10660-7, Pub. by Wiley-Interscience). Wiley.

Brown, Curtis M. & Eldridge, Winfield H. Evidence & Procedures for Boundary Location. LC 62-18988. (Illus.). 1962. 39.95 o.p. (ISBN 0-471-10663-1, Pub. by Wiley-Interscience). Wiley.

Brown, Curtis M., et al. Evidence & Procedures for Boundary Location. 2nd ed. LC 81-11440. 450p. 1981. 42.50x (ISBN 0-471-08382-8, Pub. by Wiley-Interscience). Wiley.

Brown, D. Systems Analysis & Design for Safety. 399p. 1976. text ed. 31.95 (ISBN 0-13-881177-6). P-H.

Brown, D. B. Samuel Palmer: Paintings, Drawings & Prints in the Ashmolean Museum, Oxford. 50.00x (ISBN 0-900090-95-2, Pub. by Ashmolean Mus Oxford). State Mutual Bk.

Brown, D. Clayton. Electricity for Rural America: The Fight for the REA. LC 79-8287. (Contributions in Economics & Economic History: No. 29). (Illus.). 1980. lib. bdg. 25.00 (ISBN 0-313-21478-6, BEF/). Greenwood.

Brown, D. E. Principles of Social Structure: Southeast Asia. LC 76-25889. 1977. lib. bdg. 26.75 o.p. (ISBN 0-89158-643-1). Westview.

Brown, D. F. A Monographic Study of Thr Fern Genus Woodsia. (Illus.). 1964. 24.00 (ISBN 3-7682-5416-X). Lubrecht & Cramer.

Brown, D. S. W., et al. The Geological Evolution of Australia & New Zealand. 1968. 28.00 o.s.i. (ISBN 0-08-012278-7); pap. 15.50 (ISBN 0-08-012277-9). Pergamon.

Brown, D. W. Reinforced Concrete Design Charts for Beams & Slabs in 30 Grade Concrete. 1979. pap. 35.00x (ISBN 0-419-11600-1, Pub. by E & FN Spon). Methuen Inc.

Brown, Dale. Cooking of Scandinavia. LC 68-21587. (Foods of the World Ser.). (Illus.). (gr. 6 up). 1968. PLB 17.28 (ISBN 0-8094-0058-8, Pub. by Time-Life). Silver.

--Wild Alaska. LC 74-190658. (American Wilderness Ser.). (Illus.). (gr. 6 up). 1972. lib. bdg. 15.96 (ISBN 0-8094-1153-9, Pub. by Time-Life). Silver.

--World of Velazquez. LC 77-84575. (Library of Art Ser.). (Illus.). (gr. 6 up). 1969. 19.92 (ISBN 0-8094-0281-5, Pub. by Time-Life). Silver.

Brown, Dale, jt. auth. see Peterson, James A.

Brown, Dale, et al. American Cooking: The Melting Pot. LC 76-173191. (Foods of the World Ser.). (Illus.). (gr. 6 up). 1971. lib. bdg. 17.28 (ISBN 0-8094-0082-0, Pub. by Time-Life). Silver.

Brown, Daniel P. The Protectorate & The Northumberland Conspiracy: Political Intrigue in the Reign of Edward VI. LC 80-65156. (European History: Ser. I-1001). (Illus.). 74p. (Orig.). 1982. pap. 3.15 (ISBN 0-930860-02-0). Golden West Hist.

Brown, Daphne M. Mother Tongue in English. LC 77-83987. 1979. 26.50 (ISBN 0-521-21873-X); pap. 9.95 (ISBN 0-521-29299-9). Cambridge U Pr.

Brown, David. Christ's Second Coming. 1983. pap. 10.95 (ISBN 0-8010-0833-6). Baker Bk.

--Tchaikovsky: The Crisis Years (1874-1878) (Illus.). 1983. 25.00 (ISBN 0-393-01707-9). Norton.

Brown, David A. The Tertiary Cheilostomatous Polyzoa of New Zealand. (Illus.). 406p. 1952. 44.00x (ISBN 0-565-00064-0, Pub. by Brit Mus Nat Hist England). Sabbot-Natural Hist Bks.

--The Young Correggio & His Leonardesque Sources. LC 79-57510. (Outstanding Dissertations in the Fine Arts Ser.: No. 5). 390p. 1982. lib. bdg. 44.00 (ISBN 0-8240-3928-9). Garland Pub.

Brown, David A., tr. see Sobolev, N. V.

Brown, David B., ed. Catalogue of the Collection of Drawings in the Ashmolean Museum: Earlier British Drawings, Vol. IV. (Illus.). 1982. 110.00x (ISBN 0-19-817375-X). Oxford U Pr.

Brown, David E., ed. The Wolf in the Southwest: The Making of an Endangered Species. 200p. 1983. 19.95x (ISBN 0-8165-0782-1); pap. 9.95 (ISBN 0-8165-0796-1). U of Ariz Pr.

Brown, David S. Managing the Large Organization: Issues, Ideals, Precepts, Innovations. 307p. 1982. 27.50x (ISBN 0-912338-31-8). Lomond.

Brown, David T. Hawaii Recalls. (Illus.). 130p. (Orig.). 1982. 19.95 (ISBN 0-9607938-3-6); pap. 9.95 (ISBN 0-9607938-2-8). Editions Ltd.

Brown, Dean. Photographers of the American Wilderness. (Illus.). 1977. 13.95 o.p. (ISBN 0-8174-2413-X, Amphoto). Watson-Guptill.

Brown, Deborah, jt. auth. see Fawdry, Marguerite.

Brown, Dee. Andrew Jackson & the Battle of New Orleans. (American Battles & Campaigns Ser.). (gr. 6 up). 1972. PLB 4.49 o.p. (ISBN 0-399-60024-8). Putnam Pub Group.

--Killdeer Mountain. LC 82-15460. 256p. 1983. 10.95 (ISBN 0-03-040691-9). HR&W.

--Tales of the Warrior Ants. 128p. (gr. 6 up). 1973. PLB 4.29 o.p. (ISBN 0-399-60804-4). Putnam Pub Group.

Brown, Dena, jt. ed. see Brown, Charles N.

Brown, Dennis, jt. ed. see Wright, Michael.

Brown, Dennis G. & Pedder, Jonathan R. Introduction to Psychotherapy: An Outline to Psychodynamic Principles & Practice. 1979. 10.95x (ISBN 0-422-76670-4, Pub by Tavistock England); pap. 10.95x (ISBN 0-422-76680-1). Methuen Inc.

Brown, Diana. A Debt of Honor. 1982. pap. 2.25 (ISBN 0-451-11417-5, AE1417, Sig). NAL.

--The Emerald Necklace. 1981. pap. 1.95 o.p. (ISBN 0-451-09727-0, J9727, Sig). NAL.

--The Emerald Necklace. 1980. 10.95 o.p. (ISBN 0-312-24385-5). St Martin.

--St. Martin's Summer. 1982. pap. 2.25 (ISBN 0-451-11624-0, AE1624, Sig). NAL.

Brown, Diane. Notemaking. 245p. 1977. text ed. 9.28x (ISBN 0-7715-0858-1); tchr's. manual 11.96x (ISBN 0-7715-0859-X). Forkner.

Brown, Dick. Hot Air Ballooning. (Modern Aviation Ser.). (Illus.). 1979. 8.95 (ISBN 0-8306-9817-5); pap. 5.95 o.p. (ISBN 0-8306-2249-7, 2249). TAB Bks.

Brown, Dik. Hagar the Horrible. 128p. 1983. pap. 1.75 (ISBN 0-523-49039-9). Pinnacle Bks.

Brown, Dik, jt. auth. see Walker, Mort.

Brown, Don A. Reading Diagnosis & Remediation. (Illus.). 384p. 1982. 23.95 (ISBN 0-13-754952-0). P-H.

Brown, Donald, et al. Role & Status of Women in the Soviet Union. LC 68-27326. 1968. text ed. 11.50x (ISBN 0-8077-1128-4); pap. 6.95x (ISBN 0-8077-2466-1). Tchrs Coll.

Brown, Donald D. & Clary, Chanda. Sexuality in America: Contemporary Perspectives on Sexual Identity, Dysfunction & Treatment. LC 81-81824. 1981. 12.95 (ISBN 0-686-97769-6). Pierian.

Brown, Donald R., jt. auth. see Harvey, D.

Brown, Donald R., jt. auth. see Harvey, Donald F.

Brown, Douglas. Doomsday Nineteen Seventeen: The Destruction of Russia's Ruling Class. LC 75-256p. 1976. 7.95 o.p. (ISBN 0-399-11615-X). Putnam Pub Group.

--Flyers. LC 82-50397. (History Eye Witness Ser.). PLB 15.96 (ISBN 0-382-06667-7). Silver.

--Thomas Hardy. LC 79-19057. (Illus.). 1980. Repr. of 1954 ed. lib. bdg. 20.25x (ISBN 0-313-22105-7, BRTH). Greenwood.

Brown, Douglas M. Introduction to Urban Economics. 301p. 1974. tchrs' ed. 14.50 (ISBN 0-12-136650-2). Acad Pr.

Brown, Douglas R. The Restaurant Managers Handbook: How to Set up, Operate, & Manage a Finacially Successful Resturant. Montgomery, Robert, ed. LC 82-72992. (Illus.). 326p. text ed. 49.95 (ISBN 0-910627-00-2). Atlantic Pub FL.

Brown, Douglas T., jt. auth. see Prout, H. Thompson.

Brown, Douglas V., et al. The Economics of the Recovery Program. LC 70-163644. (FDR & the Era of the New Deal Ser). 1971. Repr. of 1934 ed. lib. bdg. 27.50 (ISBN 0-306-70197-9). Da Capo.

Brown, Duane. Students' Vocational Choices: A Review & Critique. (Guidance Monograph). 1970. pap. 2.40 o.p. (ISBN 0-395-09936-6, 9-78836). HM.

Brown, E. Carey, jt. ed. see Solow, Robert.

Brown, E. D., jt. auth. see Schwarzenberger, Georg.

Brown, E. Evan. World Fish Farming Cultivation & Economics. (Illus.). 1977. lib. bdg. 22.50 o.p. (ISBN 0-87055-234-1). AVI.

--World Fish Farming: Cultivation & Economics. 2nd ed. (Illus.). 1983. text ed. 27.00 (ISBN 0-87055-427-1). AVI.

Brown, E. K. & Miller, J. E. Syntax: A Linguistic Introduction to Sentence Structure. 394p. 1981. text ed. 33.75x (ISBN 0-09-138620-9, Hutchinson U Lib); pap. text ed. 15.50x (ISBN 0-09-138621-7). Humanities.

--Syntax: Generative Grammar. 240p. 1982. text ed. 28.50x (ISBN 0-09-144110-2, Hutchinson U Lib); pap. text ed. 17.00x (ISBN 0-09-144111-0). Humanities.

Brown, E. K., ed. Victorian Poetry. 2nd ed. 1962. text ed. 28.95x (ISBN 0-673-15659-1). Scott F.

Brown, E. K., ed. see Arnold, Matthew.

Brown, E. Richard. Rockefeller Medicine Men: Medicine & Capitalism in America. LC 78-65461. (Illus.). 295p. 1979. 14.95 (ISBN 0-520-03817-7); pap. 5.95 (ISBN 0-520-04269-7, CAL 467). U of Cal Pr.

Brown, E. T., jt. auth. see Hoek, E.

Brown, Ed. A History of Voter Education Project. 1979. 2.00 (ISBN 0-686-36622-0). Voter Ed Proj.

--Race & Class in Southern Politics. 1979. 2.00 (ISBN 0-686-36620-4). Voter Ed Proj.

--Race & Class in Southern Politics & a History of Voter Education Project. 1979. 2.00 (ISBN 0-686-38003-7). Voter Ed Proj.

Brown, Edmund R. & Very, Alice. How to Use Peat Moss. (Orig.). 1953. pap. 1.00 (ISBN 0-8283-1162-5). Branden.

Brown, Edmund R., ed. Five Modern Plays. Incl. Dreamy Kig. O'Neill, Eugene; Farewell Supper. Schnitzler, Arthur; Lost Silk Hat. Dunsany, Edward; Sisters Tragedy. Hughes, Richard; Intruder. Maeterlinck, Maurice. pap. 3.00 (ISBN 0-8283-1435-7). Branden.

--Modern Essays. Incl. Civil Disobedience. Thoreau, Henry D; Religion of the Future. Eliot, Charles; On Going to Church. Shaw, George B. pap. 3.00 (ISBN 0-8283-1449-7). Branden.

Brown, Edmund R., ed. see Dunsany, Lord.

Brown, Edmund R., ed. see Eliot, Charles W.

Brown, Edmund R., ed. see Hughes, Richard.

Brown, Edmund R., ed. see Maeterlinck, Maurice.

Brown, Edmund R., ed. see O'Neill, Eugene.

Brown, Edmund R., ed. see Schnitzler, Arthur.

Brown, Edmund R., ed. see Shaw, George B.

Brown, Edmund R., ed. see Thoreau, Henry D.

Brown, Edward J. Russian Literature since the Revolution. Rev. & Enl. ed. (Illus.). 400p. 1982. text ed. 25.00x (ISBN 0-674-78203-8); pap. text ed. 9.95x (ISBN 0-674-78204-6). Harvard U Pr.

Brown, Edward K. & Bailey, J. O., eds. Victorian Poetry. 2nd ed. 1962. 21.95 o.p. (ISBN 0-8260-1400-3). Wiley.

Brown, Elaine K. Mobile Intensive Care Manual. 176p. 1982. pap. text ed. 7.95 (ISBN 0-397-54379-4, Lippincott Nursing). Lippincott.

Brown, Elizabeth G. British Statutes in American Law. LC 73-21605. (American Constitutional & Legal History Ser). 1974. Repr. of 1964 ed. lib. bdg. 42.50 (ISBN 0-306-70610-5). Da Capo.

Brown, Elsa L., jt. auth. see Lyons, John M.

Brown, Emily C. Soviet Trade Unions & Labor Relations. LC 66-21332. 1966. 22.50x o.p. (ISBN 0-674-82905-0). Harvard U Pr.

Brown, Eric. Wings of the Navy. Green, William, ed. (Illus.). 192p. 1980. 19.95 (ISBN 0-86720-579-2). Sci Bks Intl.

Brown, Erica. Sixty Years of Interior Design: The World of McMillen. LC 82-70185. (Illus.). 320p. 1982. 50.00 (ISBN 0-670-64775-6, Studio). Viking Pr.

Brown, Erik. Seat in a Wild Place. LC 81-15017. (Illus.). 128p. 1983. 8.95 (ISBN 0-87233-059-1). Bauhan.

Brown, Ernest & Hedrick, Henry B. Tables of the Motion of the Moon, 3 vols. 1920. pap. 250.00x set (ISBN 0-685-89789-3). Elliots Bks.

Brown, Ernest F. Raymond of the Times. LC 79-100216. Repr. of 1951 ed. lib. bdg. 18.00x (ISBN 0-8371-3256-8, BRRT). Greenwood.

Brown, Esther L. Newer Dimensions of Patient Care, 3 pts. Incl. Pt. 1. The Use of the Physical & Social Environment of the General Hospital for Therapeutic Purposes. LC 61-13217. 160p. 1961. pap. 4.95x (ISBN 0-87154-183-1); Pt. 2. Improving Staff Motivation & Competence in the General Hospital. LC 62-18147. 194p. 1962. pap. 4.95x (ISBN 0-87154-184-X); Pt. 3. Patients As People. LC 64-17897. 164p. 1964. pap. 4.95x (ISBN 0-87154-185-8). 160p. pap. 4.95x ea.; Three Vol. Set. (ISBN 0-87154-182-3). Russell Sage.

Brown, Everett S. Ratification of the Twenty-First Amendment to the Constitution of the United States. LC 78-114757. (American Constitutional & Legal History Ser). 1970. Repr. of 1938 ed. 85.00 (ISBN 0-306-71928-2). Da Capo.

Brown, Everett S., ed. William Plumer's Memorandum of Proceedings in the United States Senate 1803-1807. LC 74-94626. (Law, Politics & History Ser). 1969. Repr. of 1923 ed. 85.00 (ISBN 0-306-71823-5). Da Capo.

Brown, Everett S., ed. see Plumer, William, Jr.

Brown, F. C. & Noriaki Itoh, eds. Recombination-Induced Defect Formation in Crystals. (Semiconductors & Insulators Ser.: Special Issue). 300p. 1983. write for info. (ISBN 0-677-40365-8). Gordon.

Brown, F. Martin & Bailey, Wayne. Earth Science. 1978. text ed. 21.95x (ISBN 0-673-15311-8). Scott F.

Brown, Fern G. Valentine's Day. (First Bks.). (Illus.). 72p. (gr. 4 up). 1983. PLB 8.90 (ISBN 0-531-04533-1). Watts.

Brown, Fletch. Street Boy. LC 82-8221. 152p. (gr. 6-9). 1980. pap. 2.95 (ISBN 0-8024-8365-8). Moody.

--Street Boy Returns. pap. 2.95 (ISBN 0-8024-8366-6). Moody.

Brown, Frances A. Comprehensive Forkner Shorthand Dictionary. rev. ed. LC 81-66122. 297p. (gr. 10-12). 1982. text ed. 11.84x (ISBN 0-912036-37-0). Forkner.

Brown, Frances A. & Forkner, Hamden L. Instructor's Manual for Correlated Dictation & Transcription. 2nd. ed. 1974. pap. 5.84x (ISBN 0-912036-20-6). Forkner.

Brown, Francis, et al, eds. see Gesenius, William.

Brown, Francis A. & Forkner, Hamden L. Correlated Dictation & Transcription. 2nd. ed. (Forkner Shorthand). 1974. 11.40x (ISBN 0-912036-15-X); pap. 8.88x (ISBN 0-912036-16-8); tape library (18 cassettes) 240.00x (ISBN 0-912036-42-7). Forkner.

Brown, Frank A. Selected Invertebrate Types. 1950. 27.50 o.p. (ISBN 0-471-10857-X). Wiley.

Brown, Frank B. The Transition of Youth to Adulthood: A Bridge Too Long. 1980. lib. bdg. 26.50 (ISBN 0-89158-675-X); pap. text ed. 11.50 (ISBN 0-89158-756-X). Westview.

Brown, Frank E. The House in Block E4, Block F3, the Roman Baths, Discoveries in the Temple of Artemis-Manaia, Arms & Armor, New & Revised Material from the Temple of Azzanathkona. (Illus.). 1936. pap. 59.50x (ISBN 0-686-52157-9). Elliots Bks.

--Roman Architecture. LC 61-13688. (Great Ages of World Architecture Ser). (Illus.). 1961. pap. 7.95 (ISBN 0-8076-0331-7). Braziller.

Brown, Fred & Kempton, Rudolf T. Sex Questions & Answers. 2nd ed. 1970. pap. 2.95 o.p. (ISBN 0-07-008354-1, SP). McGraw.

Brown, Fredric. The Fabulous Clipjoint. 1979. lib. bdg. 9.95 (ISBN 0-8398-2541-2, Gregg). G K Hall.

Brown, G. Phonological Rules & Dialect Variation: A Study of the Phonology of Lumasaaba. LC 70-184904. (Studies in Linguistics: No. 7). (Illus.). 200p. 1972. 32.50 (ISBN 0-521-08485-7); pap. 12.95 (ISBN 0-521-29063-5). Cambridge U Pr.

Brown, G. C. & Mussett, A. E. The Inaccessible Earth. (Illus.). 272p. 1981. text ed. 45.00x (ISBN 0-04-550027-4); pap. text ed. 22.50x (ISBN 0-04-550028-2). Allen Unwin.

Brown, G. E. Many Body Problems. 1972. pap. text ed. 46.50 (ISBN 0-444-10420-8, North-Holland). Elsevier.

Brown, G. E. & Jackson, A. D. The Nucleon-Nucleon Interaction. LC 75-37972. 242p. 1976. 34.00 (ISBN 0-444-10894-7, North-Holland); pap. 46.50 (ISBN 0-444-11064-X). Elsevier.

Brown, G. H. see Weissberger, A.

Brown, G. M. Ionosphere. (Progress in Radio Science Ser.: Vol. 3). 1965. 17.00 (ISBN 0-444-40087-7). Elsevier.

Brown, G. Spencer. Laws of Form. LC 72-80668. (Illus.). 176p. 1973. 9.00 o.p. (ISBN 0-517-52776-6). Crown.

Brown, G. Thompson. Christianity in the People's Republic of China. LC 82-49018. 240p. 1983. pap. 6.95 (ISBN 0-8042-1484-0). John Knox.

Brown, G. W., jt. auth. see Wing, J. K.

Brown, G. W. see Halpenny, Francess.

Brown, Gar, jt. auth. see Spence, Jim.

Brown, Gardner M., jt. auth. see Johnson, Ralph W.

Brown, Gardner M., Jr. & Crutchfield, James, eds. Economics of Ocean Resources: A Research Agenda. LC 82-17471. 242p. (Orig.). 1983. pap. 12.00 (ISBN 0-295-95982-7, Pub. by Wash Sea Grant). U of Wash Pr.

Brown, Gary & Tasman, William, eds. Congenital Anomalies of the Optic Disc. Date not set. price not set (ISBN 0-8089-1515-0). Grune.

Brown, Gary D. Advanced ANS Cobol: With Structured Programming. LC 76-55706. 1977. 31.50x (ISBN 0-471-10642-9, Pub. by Wiley-Interscience). Wiley.

--Beyond COBOL: Survival in Business Applications Programming. LC 80-28650. 200p. 1981. 18.95 (ISBN 0-471-09030-1, Pub. by Wiley-Interscience); pap. 15.00 (ISBN 0-471-09949-X). Wiley.

--FORTRAN to PL-I Dictionary: PL-I to FORTRAN Dictionary. LC 82-21283. 218p. 1983. Repr. of 1975 ed. lib. bdg. write for info. (ISBN 0-89874-587-X). Krieger.

--Fortran to PL-One Dictionary, PL-One to Fortran Dictionary. LC 74-30147. 288p. 1975. 21.95x o.p. (ISBN 0-471-10796-4, Pub. by Wiley-Interscience). Wiley.

--System-360 Job-Control Language. 1970. pap. 19.95 (ISBN 0-471-10870-7, Pub. by Wiley-Interscience). Wiley.

--System-370 Job Control Language. LC 77-24901. 1977. 18.95x (ISBN 0-471-03155-0, Pub. by Wiley-Interscience). Wiley.

Brown, Gary D. & Sefton, Donald. Surviving with Packaged Systems. 250p. 1983. 25.00 (ISBN 0-471-87065-X, Pub. by Wiley-Interscience). Wiley.

Brown, Gene, jt. auth. see Suares, J. C.

Brown, Geoff. Diana Ross. (Illus.). 144p. 1983. pap. 8.95 (ISBN 0-312-19932-5). St Martin.

Brown, George. Lecturing & Explaining. 1978. 25.00x o.p. (ISBN 0-416-70910-9); pap. 11.95 (ISBN 0-416-70920-6). Methuen Inc.

--Microteaching. 1975. 14.95x o.p. (ISBN 0-416-83010-2); pap. 13.95x (ISBN 0-416-83020-X). Methuen Inc.

Brown, George, jt. auth. see Flanders, Helen H.

Brown, George D. & Ladd, George T. Excursions in Historical Geology: A Modular Approach. 1973. 11.95 o.p. (ISBN 0-395-16830-9); Instr's. manual 8.05 o.p. (ISBN 0-395-16733-7); Student's manual avail. o.p. HM.

--Excursions in Historical Geology: A Modular Approach, Units 1-12. 1977. 11.95 o.p. (ISBN 0-395-24243-6); Instr's. manual 5.75 o.p. (ISBN 0-686-97245-7); Student's manual avail. o.p. HM.

Brown, George D., Jr. & Ladd, George T. The Earth: Man's Geologic Environment. new ed. (Physical Science Ser.). 1976. pap. text ed. 7.95 (ISBN 0-675-08578-0); cassettes & filmstrips o.s.i. 230.00 (ISBN 0-686-86334-8). Merrill.

Brown, George E. The Pruning of Trees, Shrubs & Conifers. 1977. pap. 13.95 (ISBN 0-571-11084-3). Faber & Faber.

Brown, George I., jt. auth. see Shiflett, John M.

Brown, George M. An Orkney Tapestry. 1969. 16.95 o.p. (ISBN 0-575-00318-9, Pub. by Gollancz England). David & Charles.

Brown, Gilbert, jt. auth. see Gotsch, Carl.

Brown, Glenn. History of the United States Capitol, 2 Vols. in 1. LC 71-77734. (Architecture & Decorative Art Ser.: Vol. 34). (Illus.). 1970. Repr. of 1903 ed. lib. bdg. 85.00 (ISBN 0-306-71372-1). Da Capo.

Brown, Glenn H., ed. Advances in Liquid Crystals, Vol. 5. Date not set. price not set (ISBN 0-12-025005-5); price not set lib. ed. (ISBN 0-12-025082-9); price not set microfiche (ISBN 0-12-025083-7). Acad Pr.

Brown, Goold. The Institutes of English Grammar. LC 81-18517. 1982. Repr. of 1853 ed. 45.00 (ISBN 0-8201-1372-7). Schol Facsimiles.

Brown, Gordon & McGraw, Marsha, eds. The Role of the Academy in Addressing the Issues of Nuclear War. 138p. 1982. pap. text ed. write for info. (ISBN 0-910969-00-0). Hobart & Wm Smith.

Brown, Gordon H. & Hamish, Keith. An Introduction to New Zealand Painting, 1839-1930. (Illus.). 256p. 1982. 29.95 (ISBN 0-00-216989-4, Pub. by W Collins Australia). Intl Schol Bk Serv.

Brown, Gordon W. & Rosenberg, R. Robert. Performance Guide for Understanding Business & Personal Law. 7th ed. (Illus.). 144p. Date not set. pap. text ed. 5.80 (ISBN 0-07-053636-8, G). McGraw.

Brown, Gwen, et al. Educating Adolescents with Behavior Disorders. (Special Education Ser.). 448p. 1981. text ed. 21.95 (ISBN 0-675-08056-8). Merrill.

Brown, H. Douglas. Principles of Language Learning & Teaching. (Illus.). 1980. pap. text ed. 12.95 (ISBN 0-13-709295-4). P-H.

Brown, H. Douglas, jt. ed. see Wardhaugh, Ronald.

Brown, H. Glenn & Brown, Maude O. Directory of Printing, Publishing, Bookselling & Allied Trades in Rhode Island to 1865. LC 58-13176. (Orig.). 1958. pap. 12.00 o.p. (ISBN 0-87104-062-X). NY Pub Lib.

Brown, H. U. Telecommunications for Health Care. 112p. 1982. 42.50 (ISBN 0-8493-5588-5). CRC Pr.

Brown, Hamish, selected by. Poems of the Scottish Hills: An Anthology. 216p. 1982. 19.00 (ISBN 0-08-028476-0); pap. 10.35 (ISBN 0-08-028477-9). Pergamon.

Brown, Hanbury. Man & the Stars. (Illus.). 1978. 19.95x (ISBN 0-19-851001-2). Oxford U Pr.

Brown, Harold. Thinking About Defense: National Security in a Dangerous World. 280p. 1983. 16.95 (ISBN 0-86531-548-5). Westview.

Brown, Harold, et al. Crystallographic Groups of Four-Dimensional Space. (Wiley Monographs in Crystallography). 1978. 86.00 (ISBN 0-471-03095-3, Pub. by Wiley-Interscience). Wiley.

Brown, Harold I. Perception, Theory & Committment: A New Philosophy of Science. LC 76-22991. 1979. pap. 5.50 (ISBN 0-226-07618-0, P812, Phoen). U of Chicago Pr.

Brown, Harrison, ed. China Among the Nations of the Pacific. (Special Study on China & East Asia). 125p. (Orig.). 1982. lib. bdg. 15.00 (ISBN 0-86531-260-5); pap. 8.50 (ISBN 0-86531-279-6). Westview.

Brown, Harry J. & Williams, Frederick D., eds. Diary of James A. Garfield: Vol. I, 1848-1871, Vol. II, 1872-1874, 2 vols. 1967. Set. 30.00x (ISBN 0-87013-111-7). Mich St U Pr.

--The Diary of James A. Garfield, Vol. IV: 1878-1881. 1982. 40.00 (ISBN 0-87013-221-0). Mich St U Pr.

Brown, Harry J., jt. ed. see Williams, Frederick D.

Brown, Hazel E. Grant Wood & Marvin Cone: Artists of an Era. 1972. 7.50 (ISBN 0-8138-1775-7). Iowa St U Pr.

Brown, Helen G. Having it All: Love Success Sex-Money. 1982. 17.50 (ISBN 0-671-45813-2, Linden). S&S.

Brown, Helene. Yesterday's Child. 1977. pap. 2.50 (ISBN 0-451-11300-4, AE1300, Sig). NAL.

Brown, Henry C., Jr., et al. Steps to the Sermon. LC 63-19068. 1963. 10.95 (ISBN 0-8054-2103-3). Broadman.

Brown, Henry P. & Hopkins, Sheila V. Perspectives of Wages & Prices. 256p. 1981. 27.00x (ISBN 0-416-31950-5). Methuen Inc.

Brown, Herbert C. Explorations in the Nonclassical Ion Area. 1976. pap. text ed. 12.75 o.p. (ISBN 0-08-020488-0). Pergamon.

--Organic Syntheses Via Boranes. LC 74-20520. 320p. 1975. 36.50 (ISBN 0-471-11280-1, Pub. by Wiley-Interscience). Wiley.

Brown, Herbert P. & Schanzer, Stephan N. Female Sterilization. 122p. 1982. text ed. 16.50 (ISBN 0-88416-356-3). Wright-PSG.

Brown, Homer E. Solution of Large Networks by Matrix Methods. LC 74-34159. 256p. 1975. 32.50x (ISBN 0-471-11045-0, Pub. by Wiley-Interscience). Wiley.

Brown, Howard, jt. auth. see Keim, Curtis A.

Brown, Howard M. Music in the Renaissance. (History of Music Ser.). (Illus.). 368p. 1976. pap. text ed. 14.95 (ISBN 0-13-608497-4). P-H.

Brown, Howard M., ed. A Florentine Chansonnier from the Time of Lorenzo the Magnificent: Monuments of Renaissance Music Ser, Vol. VII. LC 81-16515. 1983. Vol. 1 (Text), 328 p. lib. bdg. 150.00x 2 vol. set (ISBN 0-226-07623-7). Vol. 2 (Music), 656 p. U of Chicago Pr.

Brown, Hudson. The First Official Gay Handbook. (Illus.). 160p. (Orig.). 1983. pap. 5.95 (ISBN 0-943084-03-2). Print Mat.

Brown, Hugh A. Cataclysms of the Earth. (Illus.). 288p. 14.00 (ISBN 0-89345-005-7, Freedeeds Bks). Garber Comm.

Brown, Ian W. The Southeastern Check Stamped Pottery Tradition: A View from Louisiana, Vol. 4. (MCJA Special Papers Ser.). (Illus.). 112p. 1982. pap. text ed. 6.25x (ISBN 0-87338-272-2). Kent St U Pr.

Brown, Irene B. Before the Lark. LC 82-1729. 204p. (gr. 4-7). 1982. 10.95 (ISBN 0-689-30920-1). Atheneum.

--Morning Glory Afternoon. LC 80-18495. 224p. (gr. 5-9). 1981. PLB 10.95 (ISBN 0-689-30802-7). Atheneum.

--Willow Whip. LC 79-11725. (gr. 4-6). 1979. 10.95 (ISBN 0-689-30703-9). Atheneum.

Brown, Irving H. Gypsy Fires in America. LC 74-1035. Repr. of 1924 ed. 34.00x (ISBN 0-8103-3942-0). Gale.

Brown, Ivor. A Rhapsody of Words. 1972. 5.95 o.p. (ISBN 0-370-00333-0). Transatlantic.

--A Ring of Words. 1972. 5.95 o.p. (ISBN 0-370-00426-4). Transatlantic.

--Shakespeare in His Time. 238p. 1982. Repr. of 1960 ed. lib. bdg. 40.00 (ISBN 0-89984-090-6). Century Bookbindery.

--Words on the Level. 126p. 1974. 5.95 o.p. (ISBN 0-370-10241-X). Transatlantic.

Brown, Ivor J. & Fearon, George. This Shakespeare Industry: Amazing Monument. LC 77-98824. Repr. of 1939 ed. lib. bdg. 16.25x (ISBN 0-8371-2850-1, BRSI). Greenwood.

Brown, J. Recall & Recognition. LC 75-8770. 1976. 55.95 (ISBN 0-471-11229-1, Pub. by Wiley-Interscience). Wiley.

--A Socioeconomic History of Argentina: Seventeen Seventy-Six to Eighteen Sixty. LC 78-6800. (Latin American Studies: No. 35). (Illus.). 1979. 39.50 (ISBN 0-521-22219-2). Cambridge U Pr.

Brown, J., ed. Modern British Dramatists: A Collection of Critical Essays. 1968. 12.95t (ISBN 0-13-588053-X, S-TC-74, Spec). P-H.

Brown, J., ed. see Cheldelin, Larry V.

Brown, J., et al, eds. An Arctic Ecosystem: The Coastal Tundra at Barrow, Alaska. (US-IBP Synthesis Ser.). 571p. 1981. 34.00 o.s.i. (ISBN 0-12-786185-8). Acad Pr.

Brown, J. A., jt. auth. see Aitchison, John.

Brown, J. C. Gastric Inhibitory Polypetide. (Monographs on Endocrinology: Vol. 24). (Illus.). 200p. 1982. 32.00 (ISBN 0-387-11271-5). Springer-Verlag.

Brown, J. H. U. The Politics of Health Care. LC 78-13755. 184p. 1978. prof ref 25.00x (ISBN 0-88410-531-8). Ballinger Pub.

Brown, J. Lewis & Howard, Leslie R. Managerial Accounting & Finance. 4th ed. 896p. 1982. pap. text ed. 29.95x (ISBN 0-7121-1751-2). Intl Ideas.

Brown, J. M. & Jaros, G. G. Elementary Medical Biochemistry. 1978. 19.95 o.p. (ISBN 0-409-08268-6). Butterworth.

Brown, J. Marvin, jt. auth. see Hsu Ying.

Brown, J. R., jt. auth. see Boehm, B. W.

Brown, James. The Everywhere Landscape. 1982. 27.50x (ISBN 0-686-98445-5, Pub. by Wildwood House). State Mutual Bk.

--Kierkegaard, Heidegger, Buber & Barth. Orig. Title: Subject & Object in Modern Theology. 1962. pap. 1.25 o.p. (ISBN 0-02-064550-3, Collier). Macmillan.

Brown, James, jt. auth. see Margiotta, Franklin D.

Brown, James, et al. AV Instruction: Technology, Media & Methods. 6th ed. (Illus.). 512p. 1983. text ed. 24.95 (ISBN 0-07-008176-X, C). McGraw.

Brown, James A., jt. auth. see Phillips, Philip.

Brown, James D. & Stratton, Stephen S. British Musical Biography: A Dictionary of Musical Artists, Authors & Composers, Born in Britain & Its Colonies. LC 76-139197. (Music Ser). 1971. Repr. of 1897 ed. lib. bdg. 47.50 (ISBN 0-306-70076-X). Da Capo.

Brown, James F. Affectivity: Its Language & Meaning. 280p. (Orig.). 1982. lib. bdg. 24.00 (ISBN 0-8191-2613-6); pap. text ed. 11.75 (ISBN 0-8191-2614-4). U Pr of Amer.

Brown, James F., jt. ed. see King, Robert R.

Brown, James H. & Gibson, Arthur C. Biogeography. (Illus.). 992p. 1983. text ed. 32.95 (ISBN 0-8016-0824-4). Mosby.

Brown, James H., ed. The Hostile Shore: & Other Writings from American Prisons. 112p. 1983. 13.95 (ISBN 0-87073-582-9); pap. 6.95 (ISBN 0-87073-583-7). Schenkman.

Brown, James I. Efficient Reading, Form B. rev. ed. 320p. 1976. pap. text ed. 12.95x (ISBN 0-669-94466-1). Heath.

--Efficient Reading Instructors Manual. 5th ed ed. 75p. 1982. pap. text ed. 19.95 (ISBN 0-943000-07-6). Telstar Inc.

--Efficient Reading Revised, Form A. pap. text ed. 12.95x 1972 ed. (ISBN 0-669-61036-4); pap. text ed. 12.95x 1962 ed. (ISBN 0-669-20370-X). Heath.

--Programmed Vocabulary. 3rd ed. (The CPD Approach). 1980. pap. text ed. 11.95 (ISBN 0-13-729707-6). P-H.

--Reading Power. 1975. pap. 12.95x (ISBN 0-669-85571-5). Heath.

--Reading Power. 2nd ed. 400p. 1982. pap. text ed. 10.95 (ISBN 0-669-05318-X). Heath.

Brown, James I. & Pearsall, Thomas E. Better Spelling. 2nd ed. 1978. pap. text ed. 7.95x (ISBN 0-669-01904-6). Heath.

Brown, James R. & Wardell, David B. Teaching & Coaching Gymnastics for Men & Women. 441p. 1980. text ed. 23.95x (ISBN 0-471-10798-0). Wiley.

Brown, James S. The Motivation of Behavior. (Psychology Ser.). 1961. text ed. 25.00 (ISBN 0-07-008305-3, C). McGraw.

Brown, James W. Heriberto Frias. (World Authors Ser.). 1978. lib. bdg. 15.95 (ISBN 0-8057-6327-9, Twayne). G K Hall.

--New Media in Public Libraries: A Survey of Current Practices. pap. 12.50 o.p. (ISBN 0-88432-003-0). Gaylord Prof Pubns.

Brown, James W. & Lewis, Richard B. AV Instructional Technology Manual for Independent Study. 5th ed. (Illus.). 208p. 1982. pap. text ed. 15.00 (ISBN 0-07-008170-0, C). McGraw.

Brown, James W. & Norberg, Kenneth. Administering Educational Media: Instructional Technology & Library Services. 2nd ed. (Illus.). 384p. 1972. text ed. 29.95 (ISBN 0-07-008326-6, C). McGraw.

Brown, James W., jt. auth. see Churchill, Ruel V.

Brown, James W. & Brown, Shirley N., eds. Educational Media Yearbook 1980. 6th ed. LC 73-4891. 445p. 1980. lib. bdg. 30.00 (ISBN 0-87287-223-8). Libs Unl.

Brown, James W. & Lewis, Richard B., eds. Audio-Visual Instruction: Technology, Media & Methods. 5th ed. (Illus.). 1976. text ed. 25.50x (ISBN 0-07-008165-4, C); instructor's manual o.p. 15.95 (ISBN 0-07-008171-9); transparencies 35.00 (ISBN 0-07-008172-7). McGraw.

Brown, Jamieson-Fausett. Comentario Exegetico y Explicativo De la Biblia Tomo I. 982p. 1981. 12.95 (ISBN 0-311-03002-5); pap. 12.95 (ISBN 0-311-03003-3). Casa Bautista.

--Comentario Exegetico y Explicativo De la Biblia Tomo II. Quarles, Jaime C. & Quarles, Lemuel C., trs. from Eng. 382p. 1981. pap. 12.95 (ISBN 0-311-03005-X). Casa Bautista.

Brown, Jan. Buy It Right. LC 73-81039. pap. 3.45 o.p. (ISBN 0-911744-14-2). Career Inst.

Brown, Jan & Kmetz, Yoko Sakakibara. Exploring Tohoku: A Guide to Japan's Back Country. LC 82-17467. (Illus.). 312p. (Orig.). 1983. pap. 9.95 (ISBN 0-8348-0177-9). Weatherhill.

Brown, Jane. Gardens of a Golden Afternoon: The Story of a Partnership: Gertrude Jekyll & Sir Edwin Lutyens. 208p. 1982. 40.00x o.p. (ISBN 0-7139-1440-8, Pub. by Penguin Bks). State Mutual Bk.

Brown, Janet F., ed. Curriculum Planning for Young Children. 267p. 1982. pap. text ed. 5.50 (ISBN 0-912674-83-0). Natl Assn Child Ed.

Brown, Jean M., ed. The Vision of Modern Dance. LC 79-88382. (Illus.). 208p. 1979. pap. text ed. 7.95 (ISBN 0-916622-12-6). Princeton Bk Co.

Brown, Jeannette A. & Pate, Robert H., Jr. Being a Counselor: Directions & Challenges. LC 82-20764. (Psychology Ser.). 450p. 1983. text ed. 20.95. (ISBN 0-534-01261-2). Brooks-Cole.

Brown, Jeff. Flat Stanley. LC 63-17525. (Illus.). (gr. 1-5). 1964. PLB 10.89 (ISBN 0-06-020681-0, HarpJ). Har-Row.

Brown, Jeffrey L. The Complete Parents' Guide to Telephone Medicine: How, When & Why to Call Your Child's Doctor. 224p. 1982. pap. 6.95 (ISBN 0-399-50582-2, Perige). Putnam Pub Group.

--The Complete Parent's Guide to Telephone Medicine: How, When & Why to Call Your Child's Doctor. 304p. 1983. pap. 3.50 (ISBN 0-425-05496-9). Berkley Pub.

--Telephone Medicine: A Practical Guide to Pediatric Telephone Advice. LC 80-16674. (Illus.). 154p. 1980. pap. text ed. 16.50 (ISBN 0-8016-0856-2). Mosby.

Brown, Jennifer. Scottish Society in the Fifteenth Century. LC 77-81309. 1978. 25.00 (ISBN 0-312-70539-5). St Martin.

Brown, Jerald R. & Finkel, LeRoy. BASIC for the Apple II. LC 82-10962. (Self-Teaching Guide). 410p. 1982. pap. 12.95 (ISBN 0-471-86596-6). Wiley.

Brown, Jerald R., jt. auth. see Finkel, Leroy.

Brown, Jerald R., jt. auth. see Finkel, LeRoy.

Brown, Jim. Tennis: Strokes, Strategy, & Programs. (Illus.). 1980. text ed. 17.95 (ISBN 0-13-903351-3). P-H.

--Tennis: Teaching, Coaching, & Directing Programs. (Illus.). 256p. 1976. 17.95 (ISBN 0-13-903344-0). P-H.

--Tennis Without Lessons. (Illus.). 1977. 13.95 (ISBN 0-13-903252-5); pap. 7.95 (ISBN 0-13-903245-2). P-H.

Brown, Joan C., jt. auth. see Berthoud, Richard.

Brown, Joan W. Christmas Joys. LC 81-43454. (Illus.). 192p. 1982. 10.95 (ISBN 0-385-17440-3, Galilee). Doubleday.

--Every Knee Shall Bow. 192p. 1978. 11.95 (ISBN 0-8007-0941-1). Revell.

--Joy in His Presence. New ed. LC 82-60307. 300p. 1982. 10.95 (ISBN 0-89066-041-7). World Wide Pubs.

Brown, Joan W., compiled by. Dia-Tras-Dia Con Billy Graham. Orig. Title: Day by Day with Billy Graham. 192p. 1982. Repr. of 1978 ed. 3.95 (ISBN 0-311-40039-6, Edit Mundo). Casa Bautista.

Brown, Joan W., ed. see Bonhoeffer, Dietrich.

Brown, Jody. The Best Little Rivalry in Town: A Game by Game History of the USC-UCLA Football Rivalry 1929 to 1981. LC 82-81806. (Great Rivalry Ser.). (Illus.). 400p. 1982. 10.95 (ISBN 0-88011-069-4). Leisure Pr.

Brown, John. Brief Sketch of the First Settlement of the County of Schoharie by the Germans. 1981. pap. 2.00 (ISBN 0-686-97285-6). Hope Farm.

--Galatians. 1982. lib. bdg. 16.00 (ISBN 0-86524-083-3, 4802). Klock & Klock.

--The Intercessory Prayer of Our Lord Jesus Christ. 1978. 11.50 (ISBN 0-86524-104-X, 4301). Klock & Klock.

--Life, Trial & Execution of Captain John Brown, Known As "Old Brown of Ossawatomie". LC 69-18827. (Law, Politics & History Ser). 1969. Repr. of 1859 ed. lib. bdg. 22.50 (ISBN 0-306-71250-4). Da Capo.

--New Ways in Worship for Youth. LC 68-20435. (YA) 1969. pap. 5.95 o.p. (ISBN 0-8170-0405-X). Judson.

--Parting Counsels: Exposition of II Peter 1. (Banner of Truth Geneva Series Commentaries). 1980. 12.95 (ISBN 0-85151-301-8). Banner of Truth.

--Rab & His Friends & Other Papers. 1970. 7.95x (ISBN 0-460-00116-7, Evman); pap. 2.95x (ISBN 0-460-01116-2, Evman). Biblio Dist.

--The Resurrection of Life. 1978. 15.50 (ISBN 0-86524-962-8, 4601). Klock & Klock.

Brown, John, jt. auth. see Jones, Kathleen.

Brown, John C. Ethics of George Eliot's Works. LC 73-91037. 1969. Repr. of 1879 ed. 12.00 o.p. (ISBN 0-8046-0647-1). Kennikat.

Brown, John H. & Grant, Steven A. The Russian Empire & Soviet Union: A Guide to Manuscripts & Archival Materials in the United States. 1981. lib. bdg. 95.00 (ISBN 0-8161-1300-9, Hall Library). G K Hall.

Brown, John L. Valery Larbaud. (World Authors Ser.). 14.95 (ISBN 0-8057-6439-9, Twayne). G K Hall.

Brown, John M. Daniel Boone. (Landmark Ser.: No. 21). (Illus.). (gr. 7-9). 1952. 1.95 (ISBN 0-394-80643-3, BYR); PLB 4.39 (ISBN 0-394-90643-8). Random.

--Seeing Things. LC 75-138209. viii, 341p. Repr. of 1946 ed. lib. bdg. 17.50x (ISBN 0-8371-5564-9, BRST). Greenwood.

--Still Seeing Things. LC 79-156176. 1971. Repr. of 1950 ed. lib. bdg. 17.00x (ISBN 0-8371-6119-3, BRSS). Greenwood.

Brown, John M., jt. auth. see Carr, Joseph J.

Brown, John M., ed. see Lamb, Charles.

Brown, John P. & York, Richard L. Covenant of Peace: A Liberation Prayer Book. 1971. pap. 4.50 o.p. (ISBN 0-8192-1115-X). Morehouse.

Brown, John R. Shakespeare & His Theatre. (gr. 7 up). 1982. 12.50 (ISBN 0-686-96945-6). Morrow.

--A Short Guide to Modern British Drama. LC 82-22699. 150p. 1983. pap. text ed. 7.95x (ISBN 0-389-20353-X). B&N Imports.

Brown, John R., ed. Drama & the Theatre: With Radio, Film & Television; an Outline for the Student. (Outlines Ser). 1971. 15.95x (ISBN 0-7100-6971-5); pap. 7.95 (ISBN 0-7100-7053-5). Routledge & Kegan.

Brown, John R. & Harris, Bernard, eds. Hamlet: A Reading & Playing Guide. LC 66-16311. 1966. pap. 1.95 o.p. (ISBN 0-8052-0120-3). Schocken.

Brown, John R., ed. see Shakespeare, William.

Brown, Jonathan, jt. auth. see Enggass, Robert.

Brown, Jonathan, et al. Studies in the History of Art 1982, Vol. 11. (Illus.). pap. 8.95 (ISBN 0-89468-058-7). Natl Gallery Art.

Brown, Jonathan, et al, eds. El Greco of Toledo. (Illus.). 272p. 35.00 (ISBN 0-8212-1501-9, 233846). NYGS.

Brown, Joseph E. Wonders of Seals & Sea Lions. (Wonders Ser.). (gr. 4 up). 1976. 7.95 (ISBN 0-396-07344-1). Dodd.

Brown, Joseph E., jt. auth. see Drysdale, Vera L.

Brown, Joseph E., ed. The Sacred Pipe: Black Elk's Account of the Seven Rites of Oglala Sioux. (Civilization of the American Indian Ser.: No. 36). (Illus.). 1953. 12.95 (ISBN 0-8061-0272-1). U of Okla Pr.

Brown, Judith E. Nutrition for Your Pregnancy: The University of Minnesota Guide. LC 82-21852. (Illus.). 140p. 1983. 12.95 (ISBN 0-8166-1151-3). U of Minn Pr.

Brown, Judith M. Gandhi & Civil Disobedience. LC 76-10407. (Illus.). 1977. 47.50 (ISBN 0-521-21279-0). Cambridge U Pr.

--Gandhi's Rise to Power: Indian Politics 1915-1922. LC 71-171674. (Cambridge South Asian Studies: No. 11). (Illus.). 460p. 1972. 42.50 (ISBN 0-521-08353-2); pap. 11.95 (ISBN 0-521-09873-4). Cambridge U Pr.

--Men & Gods in a Changing World: Some Themes in Religious Experience of Twentieth-Century Hindus & Christians. (Student Christian Movement Press). 192p. (Orig.). 1980. pap. 14.95x (ISBN 0-19-520310-0). Oxford U Pr.

Brown, June H., et al. Child, Family, Neighborhood: A Master Plan for Social Service Delivery. 1981. 5.95 (ISBN 0-87868-209-0, CW-34). Child Welfare.

Brown, K. W. & Warner, A. R. Free Enterprise: Fundamentals of the American System. 1981. 14.80 (ISBN 0-07-067501-5). McGraw.

Brown, Karen A. French Country Inns & Chateau Hotels. LC 77-82024. (Illus., Orig.). 1977. pap. 7.95 o.p. (ISBN 0-930328-01-9). Travel Pr.

--French Country Inns & Chateau Hotels. 2nd ed. LC 77-32024. (Illus., Orig.). 1982. pap. 9.95 (ISBN 0-930328-03-5). Travel Pr.

Brown, Karl. Adventures with D. W. Griffith. Brownlow, Kevin, ed. LC 75-31755. 1976. pap. 6.95 (ISBN 0-306-80032-2). Da Capo.

Brown, Karl & Haskell, Daniel C., eds. Shorthand Collection in the New York Public Library. LC 77-137704. 1971. Repr. of 1935 ed. 35.00 o.p. (ISBN 0-87104-507-9). NY Pub Lib.

Brown, Katherine. Commentary: Nineteen Forty to Nineteen Eighty. 1983. 5.95 (ISBN 0-533-05473-7). Vantage.

Brown, Kenneth A., tr. see Perelman, Charles.

Brown, Kenneth D. The English Labour Movement, 1700-1951. 280p. 1982. 45.00x (ISBN 0-7171-0870-8, Pub. by Macmillan England). State Mutual Bk.

Brown, Kenneth S. & ReVelle, Jack B. Quantitative Methods for Managerial Decisions. LC 76-10408. (Illus.). 1978. text ed. 25.95 (ISBN 0-201-06448-0). A-W.

Brown, Kermit. Technology of Artificial Lift Methods, Vols. 2a & 2b. 1980. 69.95x ea. Vol. 2a, 736 P (ISBN 0-87814-031-X). Vol. 2b, 607 P (ISBN 0-87814-133-2). Pennwell Book Division.

Brown, L. & Urban, E. K., eds. The Birds of Africa. LC 81-69594. 1982. Vol. 1. 99.00 (ISBN 0-12-137301-0); Vol. 2: 256 pgs. 42.50 (ISBN 0-12-200102-8). Acad Pr.

Brown, L. Dave. Managing Conflict at Organizational Interfaces. LC 82-6762. (Managing Human Resources Ser.). 250p. 1983. pap. text ed. 8.95 (ISBN 0-201-00884-X). A-W.

Brown, L. F., Jr., jt. auth. see Galloway, W. E.

Brown, Larry, jt. auth. see Bing, Stephen.

Brown, Lauren. Weeds in Winter. LC 77-4712. 1977. pap. 7.95 (ISBN 0-395-25785-9). HM.

Brown, Lauren R. The Point Loma Theosophical Society: A List of Publications, 1898-1942. (Illus.). 1977. pap. 4.50 (ISBN 0-930730-00-3). Friends UCSD Lib.

Brown, Laverne K. The Year of Birth: A Guide for Expectant Parents. (Illus.). 215p. (Orig.). 1982. pap. 5.95 (ISBN 0-9608446-0-0). Lake Pr.

Brown, Lawrence. British Historical Medals Seventeen Sixty - Nineteen Sixty: The Accession of George III to the Death of William IV, Vol. 1. 1980. 112.50. Numismatic Fine Arts.

--Might of the West. 1962. 19.95 (ISBN 0-8392-1069-8). Astor-Honor.

Brown, Lawrence D. New Politics, New Policies: Government's Response to Government's Growth. 100p. 1983. pap. 5.95 (ISBN 0-8157-1165-4, 82-45979). Brookings.

--The Political Structure of the Federal Health Planning Program. LC 81-70468. 70p. 1982. pap. 5.95 (ISBN 0-8157-1159-X). Brookings.

--Politics & Health Care Organization: HMO as Federal Policy. LC 81-70466. 600p. 1983. 33.95 (ISBN 0-8157-1158-1); pap. 16.95 (ISBN 0-8157-1157-3). Brookings.

Brown, Lee, jt. ed. see Weatherford, Gary.

Brown, Leland. Communicating Facts & Ideas in Business. 3rd ed. (Illus.). 496p. 1982. reference 20.95 (ISBN 0-13-153403-3). P-H.

--Effective Business Report Writing. 3rd ed. (Illus.). 448p. (Reference ed.). 1973. 20.95 (ISBN 0-13-241653-0). P-H.

Brown, Len, intro. by. Great Old Bubble Gum Cards & Some Cigarette Cards. 1977. 6.95 o.p. (ISBN 0-517-53240-9). Crown.

Brown, Lena M., ed. see Brown, Lewis S.

Brown, Lennox see Harrison, Paul C.

Brown, Leroy, jt. auth. see Marcus, Michael.

Brown, Les & Channels Magazine. Fast Forward: The New Television & American Society. 264p. 1982. pap. 8.95 (ISBN 0-8362-6208-5). Andrews & McMeel.

Brown, Leslie. The Indian Christians of St. Thomas: An Account of the Ancient Syrian Church of Malabar. LC 81-21766. (Illus.). 330p. 1982. 34.50 (ISBN 0-521-21258-8). Cambridge U Pr.

--The Life of the African Plains. (Our Living World of Nature Ser). (Illus.). 1972. 14.95 o.p. (ISBN 0-07-008245-6, P&RB); by subscription 12.95 o.p. (ISBN 0-07-046013-2). McGraw.

--Three Worlds: One Word; Account of a Mission. 278p. 1981. text ed. 22.50x (ISBN 0-8476-4740-4). Rowman.

Brown, Lester. U. S. & Soviet Agriculture: The Shifting Balance of Power. LC 82-61876. (Worldwatch Papers). 1982. pap. 2.00 (ISBN 0-916468-51-8). Worldwatch Inst.

Brown, Lester R. Our Daily Bread. LC 75-851. (Headline Ser.: No. 225). (Illus.). 1975. pap. 3.00 (ISBN 0-87124-030-0). Foreign Policy.

Brown, Lewis S. Yes, Helen, there were Dinosaurs. Brown, Lena M., ed. (Illus.). 152p. (Orig.). 1982. pap. 7.95 (ISBN 0-9608542-0-7). L S Brown Pub.

Brown, Lewis S., ed. see Muybridge, Eadweard.

Brown, Lionel H. Victor Trumper & the 1922 Australians. 1981. 24.95 (ISBN 0-436-07107-X, Pub. by Secker & Warburg). David & Charles.

Brown, Lloyd A. & Peckham, Howard H., eds. Revolutionary War Journals of Henry Dearborn, 1775-1783. LC 74-146143. (Era of the American Revolution Ser). 1971. Repr. of 1939 ed. lib. bdg. 37.50 (ISBN 0-306-70107-3). Da Capo.

Brown, Lloyd W. Amiri Baraka (LeRoi Jones) (United States Authors Ser.). 1980. lib. bdg. 11.95 (ISBN 0-8057-7317-7, Twayne). G K Hall.

--West Indian Poetry. (World Authors Ser.). 1978. lib. bdg. 13.95 (ISBN 0-8057-6262-0, Twayne). G K Hall.

--Women Writers in Black Africa. LC 80-1710. (Contributions in Women's Studies: No. 21). vii, 204p. 1981. lib. bdg. 29.95 (ISBN 0-313-22540-0, BRW/). Greenwood.

Brown, Lorraine, jt. auth. see O'Connor, John.

Brown, Louis J., jt. ed. see Haring, Norris G.

Brown, Louis M. Preventive Law. LC 72-97326. Repr. of 1950 ed. lib. bdg. 17.50x (ISBN 0-8371-3077-8, BRPL). Greenwood.

Brown, Lucy M. & Christie, Ian R. Bibliography of British History Seventeen Eighty-Nine to Eighteen Fifty-One. 1977. 110.00x (ISBN 0-19-822390-0). Oxford U Pr.

Brown, Lyle C., jt. auth. see Jones, Eugene W.

Brown, M., et al. American Art: Painting, Sculpture, Architecture, Decorative Arts, Photography. 1979. 27.95 (ISBN 0-13-024653-0). P-H.

Brown, M. H., ed. Meat Microbiology. (Applied Science Publications). (Illus.). 576p. 1982. 94.50 (ISBN 0-85334-138-9, Pub. by Applied Sci England). Elsevier.

Brown, M. J., jt. ed. see Hall, J. L.

Brown, M. Ralph. Legal Psychology. (Historical Foundations of Forensic Psychiatry & Psychology Ser.). (Illus.). 346p. 1980. Repr. of 1926 ed. lib. bdg. 39.50 (ISBN 0-306-76065-7). Da Capo.

Brown, Mac H., jt. auth. see Brown, Carl F.

Brown, MacAlister, jt. auth. see Zasloff, Joseph J.

Brown, Malcolm & Webb, John N. Seven Stranded Coal Towns: A Study of an American Depressed Area. LC 76-165680. (Research Monograph: Vol. 23). 1971. Repr. of 1941 ed. lib. bdg. 25.00 (ISBN 0-306-70355-6). Da Capo.

Brown, Malcolm, jt. auth. see Webb, John N.

Brown, Malcolm, ed. see Asafiev.

Brown, Malcolm, ed. see Orlova, Alexandra.

Brown, Marc. Arthur's April Fool. LC 82-20368. (Illus.). 32p. (gr. 1-3). 1983. 10.45i (ISBN 0-316-11196-1, Pub. by Atlantic Monthly Pr.). Little.

--Arthur's Eyes. LC 79-11734. (Illus.). (gr. k-3). 1979. 8.95 (ISBN 0-316-11063-9, Pub. by Atlantic-Little Brown). Little.

--Finger Rhymes. LC 80-10173. (Illus.). 32p. (ps-2). 1980. 9.95 (ISBN 0-525-29732-4, 0966-290, Unicorn Bk). Dutton.

--One Two Three: An Animal Counting Book. 32p. (gr. k-3). 1976. PLB 5.95 (ISBN 0-316-11064-7, Pub. by Atlantic Monthly Pr). Little.

--What Do You Call a Dumb Bunny? & Other Rabbit Riddles, Games, Jokes, & Cartoons. (Illus.). 32p. (gr. 1-3). 1983. 9.70i (ISBN 0-316-11117-1, Pub. by Atlantic Monthly Pr); pap. 3.70i (ISBN 0-316-11119-8, Pub. by Atlantic Monthly Pr); 10-copy counter display 37.00i (ISBN 0-316-11192-9). Little.

Brown, Marc, ed. see Thompson, George A.

Brown, Marcia. Bun: A Tale from Russia. LC 75-167832. (Illus.). 32p. (gr. k-3). 1972. 6.95 o.p. (ISBN 0-15-213450-6, HJ). HarBraceJ.

--Listen to a Shape. (Marcia Brown Concept Library). (gr. 1-4). 1979. 4.95 o.p. (ISBN 0-531-02383-4); PLB 8.90 s&l (ISBN 0-531-02930-1). Watts.

--The Three Billy Goats Gruff. LC 57-5265. (Illus.). (gr. 1-4). 1972. pap. 2.95 (ISBN 0-15-690150-1, VoyB). HarBraceJ.

--Touch Will Tell. (Marcia Brown Concept Library Ser.). (Illus.). (gr. 1-4). 1979. 4.95 (ISBN 0-531-02384-2); PLB 8.90 s&l (ISBN 0-531-02931-X). Watts.

Brown, Marcia, ed. & illus. Three Billy Goats Gruff. LC 57-5265. (Illus.). (gr. k-3). 1957. 10.95 (ISBN 0-15-286399-0, HJ). HarBraceJ.

Brown, Margaret D. Shepherdess of Elk River Valley. 2nd ed. (Illus.). 1967. 5.50x (ISBN 0-87315-037-6). Golden Bell.

Brown, Margaret W. Country Noisy Book. LC 40-32066. (Illus.). (ps-1). 1940. PLB 10.89 (ISBN 0-06-020811-2, HarpJ). Har-Row.

--Indoor Noisy Book. LC 42-23589. (Illus.). (ps-1). 1942. PLB 10.89 (ISBN 0-06-020821-X, HarpJ). Har-Row.

--Little Chicken. LC 43-16942. (Illus.). 32p. (gr. k-3). 1982. 7.64i o.p. (ISBN 0-06-020739-6, HarpJ); PLB 7.89g (ISBN 0-06-020740-X). Har-Row.

--Noisy Book (City) LC 39-31264. Orig. Title: City Noisy Book. (Illus.). (ps-1). 1939. 7.95 o.p. (ISBN 0-06-020830-9, HarpJ); PLB 10.89 (ISBN 0-06-020831-7). Har-Row.

--Quiet Noisy Book. LC 50-9797. (Illus.). (ps-1). 1950. 10.53i (ISBN 0-06-020845-7, HarpJ). Har-Row.

--Seashore Noisy Book. LC 41-13238. (Illus.). (ps-1). 1941. PLB 9.89 o.p. (ISBN 0-06-020841-4, HarpJ). Har-Row.

--Summer Noisy Book. LC 51-8509. (Illus.). (ps-1). 1951. PLB 10.89 (ISBN 0-06-020856-2, HarpJ). Har-Row.

--Where Have You Been? (Illus.). 32p. (ps-1). 1981. PLB 5.95 o.s.i. (ISBN 0-8038-8018-9). Hastings.

Brown, Margaret W., adapted by. Brer Rabbit: Stories from Uncle Remus. LC 41-24406. (Illus.). (gr. 1-5). 1941. PLB 8.79 o.p. (ISBN 0-06-020876-7, HarpJ). Har-Row.

Brown, Margery. Cane & Rush Seating. (Craft Ser). (Illus.). (gr. 7). 1977. 10.95 (ISBN 0-88332-049-5); pap. 8.95 (ISBN 0-88332-075-4, 8096). Larousse.

Brown, Margery W. Animals Made by Me. (Illus.). (gr. 2-5). 1970. PLB 5.29 o.p. (ISBN 0-399-60029-9). Putnam Pub Group.

--The Second Stone. LC 73-76131. (Illus.). 128p. (gr. 4-7). 1974. PLB 4.99 o.p. (ISBN 0-399-60848-6). Putnam Pub Group.

--Yesterday I Climbed a Mountain. (Illus.). (gr. k-3). 1977. PLB 4.69 o.p. (ISBN 0-399-61040-5). Putnam Pub Group.

Brown, Margie. The Stick Stories. (Illus., Orig.). 1982. pap. 5.56 (ISBN 0-89390-035-4); pap. text ed. 6.95 (ISBN 0-686-83133-0). Resource Pubns.

Brown, Marie & Murphy, Mary A. Ambulatory Pediatrics for Nurses. 2nd ed. (Illus.). 624p. 1980. text ed. 22.95 (ISBN 0-07-008291-X, HP). McGraw.

Brown, Marie S., jt. auth. see Alexander, Mary M.

Brown, Marion M. & Leech, Jane K. Dreamcatcher: The Life of John Neihardt. 144p. (Orig.). Date not set. pap. 6.95 (ISBN 0-687-11174-9). Abingdon.

Brown, Marshall. Wit & Humor of Well-Known Quotations. LC 70-146919. 1971. Repr. of 1905 ed. 34.00 o.p. (ISBN 0-8103-3644-8). Gale.

Brown, Martin B. Compendium & Communication & Broadcast Satellites 1958-1981. LC 81-81858. 375p. 1981. 34.95x (ISBN 0-471-86198-7, Pub. by Wiley Interscience). Wiley.

Brown, Martin P. Jr., ed. Compendium of Communication & Broadcast Satellites. LC 81-81858. 1981. 34.95 (ISBN 0-87942-153-3). Inst Electrical.

Brown, Marvin L., jt. auth. see Parker, Harold T.

Brown, Marvin L., Jr. Louis Veuillot. LC 77-82882. 1977. 15.00 (ISBN 0-87716-070-8, Pub. by Moore Pub Co). F Apple.

--The Wisdom of Christendom. 131p. 1982. pap. 5.95. Edenwood Hse.

Brown, Mary K. Aunt Mary's Kitchen Cookbook. (Illus.). 224p. 1983. pap. 6.95 (ISBN 0-02-009320-9, Collier). Macmillan.

Brown, Maude O., jt. auth. see Brown, H. Glenn.

Brown, Maurice J. Chopin: An Index of His Works in Chronological Order. 2nd ed. LC 70-39498. (Music Ser.). 1972. Repr. of 1960 ed. 25.00 (ISBN 0-306-70500-1). Da Capo.

--Essays on Schubert. LC 77-22216. (Music Reprint Ser.). (Illus.). 1978. Repr. of 1966 ed. lib. bdg. 29.50 (ISBN 0-306-77439-9). Da Capo.

--Schubert: A Critical Biography. LC 77-4160. (Music Reprint Ser., 1977). (Illus.). 1977. Repr. of 1958 ed. lib. bdg. 35.00 (ISBN 0-306-77409-7). Da Capo.

--Schubert Symphonies. LC 70-127653. (BBC Music Guides Ser.: No. 13). (Illus.). 64p. 1971. pap. 1.95 o.p. (ISBN 0-295-95106-0). U of Wash Pr.

Brown, Maurice J. & Sams, Eric. The New Grove Schubert. (The New Grove Composer Biography Ser.). (Illus.). 1983. 16.50 (ISBN 0-393-01683-8); pap. 7.95 (ISBN 0-393-30087-0). Norton.

Brown, Mervyn. Madagascar Rediscovered: A History from Early Times to Independence. 1979. pap. text ed. cancelled o.p. (ISBN 0-9506284-0-9). Humanities.

Brown, Meta & Mulholland, Joyce. Basic Drug Calculations. LC 79-10785. 190p. 1979. pap. 10.95 (ISBN 0-8016-4488-7). Mosby.

Brown, Michael. Laying Waste: The Poisoning of America by Toxic Chemicals. 384p. 1981. pap. 3.95 (ISBN 0-671-45359-9). WSP.

--Santa Mouse. (Illus.). (gr. k-3). 1966. 1.95 (ISBN 0-448-04213-4). Putnam Pub Group.

--Santa Mouse Meets Marmaduke. Duenewald, Doris, ed. LC 74-92384. (Elephant Books Ser.). (Illus.). (gr. k-7). 1978. pap. 1.50 (ISBN 0-448-14749-1, G&D). Putnam Pub Group.

Brown, Michael D. Resource Recovery Project Studies. (Illus.). 169p. 1983. 29.95 (ISBN 0-250-40611-X). Ann Arbor Science.

Brown, Michael D. & Reilly, Thomas C. Solid Waste Transfer Fundamentals. LC 81-66617. (Illus.). 1981. 19.95 (ISBN 0-250-40426-5). Ann Arbor Science.

Brown, Michael H. PK: A Report on the Power of Psychokinesis; Mental Energy That Moves Matter. LC 76-21121. (Rudolf Steiner Publications Ser.). (Illus.). 320p. 1976. 12.00 (ISBN 0-89345-013-8); pap. 6.00 (ISBN 0-89345-200-9). Garber Comm.

Brown, Mike. P. K. A Report on the Power of Psychokinesis, Mental Energy That Moves Matter. LC 76-21121. (Illus.). 320p. 1976. pap. 6.00 (ISBN 0-89345-200-9, Steinerbks). Garber Comm.

Brown, Mollie, ed. Readings in Gerontology. 2nd ed. LC 77-14088. (Illus.). 126p. 1978. pap. text ed. 8.00 o.p. (ISBN 0-8016-0734-5). Mosby.

Brown, Montague & McCool, Barbara P. Multihospital Systems: Strategies for Organization & Management. LC 79-23439. 564p. 1980. text ed. 48.50 (ISBN 0-89443-169-2). Aspen Systems.

Brown, Montague, ed. Health Care Management Review. LC 75-45767. annual subscription 55.00 (ISBN 0-912862-50-5). Aspen Systems.

Brown, Montague, jt. ed. see Shortell, Stephen M.

Brown, Muriel & Madge, Nicola. Despite the Welfare State. (SSRC-DHSS Studies in Deprivation & Disadvantage). xii, 388p. 1982. text ed. 29.00x (ISBN 0-435-82095-8). Heinemann Ed.

Brown, Muriel J., jt. auth. see Farmer, Geraldine M.

Brown, Myrtle L., jt. auth. see Pike, Ruth L.

Brown, Nina W., jt. ed. see Grob, Paul.

Brown, Norman D., ed. Journey to Pleasant Hill: The Civil War Letters of Captain Elijah P. Petty. (Illus.). 504p. 1982. 35.00 (ISBN 0-933164-94-7); deluxe ed. 75.00 (ISBN 0-686-82617-5). U of Tex Inst Tex Culture.

Brown, Norman L., ed. Renewable Energy Resources & Rural Applications in the Developing World. (AAAS Selected Symposium Ser: No. 6). (Illus.). 1978. lib. bdg. 22.00 o.p. (ISBN 0-89158-433-1). Westview.

Brown, O. Phelps. The Complete Herbalist or the People Their Own Physicians. 504p. Date not set. pap. 18.00 (ISBN 0-89540-118-5, SB-118). Sun Pub.

Brown, Oliver B. Vital Records of Falmouth, Mass. to 1850. LC 76-3955. 1976. 8.00 o.p. (ISBN 0-930272-01-3). RI Mayflower.

Brown, Opal. Fun with Handcraft. 1973. pap. 1.00 (ISBN 0-8341-0250-1). Beacon Hill.

Brown, Osa. The Metropolitan Museum of Art Activity Book. (Illus.). 96p. (gr. 5-9). 1983. 6.95 (ISBN 0-394-85241-9). Random.

Brown, Oscar C., Sr. By a Thread. 1982. 8.95 (ISBN 0-533-05464-8). Vantage.

Brown, Oskar. The Songs of Kicks & Co. Branann, J., et al, eds. 42p. (Orig.). 1982. pap. 2.50 o.p. (ISBN 0-941452-00-X). Allen Unwin.

Brown, Otis S. One Day Celestial Navigation. 132p. 1981. perfect bdg. 7.00 (ISBN 0-686-94857-2). Maryland Hist Pr.

Brown, P. Chathamites. (Illus.). 1967. 25.00 (ISBN 0-312-13160-7). St Martin.

Brown, P. J. Macroprocessors: And Techniques for Portable Software. LC 3-17597. (Computing Ser.). 244p. 1974. 46.95 (ISBN 0-471-11005-1, Pub. by Wiley-Interscience). Wiley.

--Writing Interactive Compilers & Interpreters. LC 79-40513. (Computing Ser.). 265p. 1981. pap. 14.50x (ISBN 0-471-10072-2, Pub. by Wiley-Interscience). Wiley.

--Writing Interactive Compilers & Interpreters. LC 79-40513. (Wiley Series in Computing). 1979. 38.95 (ISBN 0-471-27609-X, Pub. by Wiley-Interscience). Wiley.

Brown, P. J., ed. Software Portability. LC 76-40835. (Illus.). 1977. 44.50 (ISBN 0-521-21485-8); pap. 13.95x (ISBN 0-521-29725-7). Cambridge U Pr.

Brown, P. Jane & Forsyth, J. B. The Crystal Structure of Solids. (Structures & Properties of Solids Ser.). 184p. 1973. pap. text ed. write for info (ISBN 0-7131-2388-5). E Arnold.

Brown, Patricia, et al. Energy Information Resources: An Inventory of Energy Research & Development Information Resources in the Continental U.S., Hawaii, & Alaska. LC 75-13917. 207p. 1975. lexhide 18.50 (ISBN 0-87715-111-3). Am Soc Info Sci.

Brown, Paul B., et al. Electronics for Neurobiologists. 525p. 1973. 37.50x o.p. (ISBN 0-262-02094-7). MIT Pr.

Brown, Paul L. Managing Behavior on the Job. LC 81-23063. (Self-Teaching Guide Ser.). 190p. 1982. pap. text ed. 9.95 (ISBN 0-471-86516-8). Wiley.

Brown, Paula. Highland Peoples of New Guinea. LC 77-80830. (Illus.). 1978. 32.50 (ISBN 0-521-21748-2); pap. 9.95 (ISBN 0-521-29249-2). Cambridge U Pr.

Brown, Peter. Augustine of Hippo: A Biography. 1967. 15.00 o.p. (ISBN 0-520-00186-9); pap. 5.95 (ISBN 0-520-01411-1, CAL179). U of Cal Pr.

--The Real Oscar. (Illus.). 256p. 1981. 15.95 o.p. (ISBN 0-87000-498-0, Arlington Hse). Crown.

Brown, Peter G. & MacLean, Douglas, eds. Human Rights & U. S. Foreign Policy: Principles & Applications. Principles & Applications. 1979. 21.95x (ISBN 0-669-02807-X); pap. 10.95x (ISBN 0-669-04326-5). Lexington Bks.

Brown, Peter G. & Shue, Henry, eds. The Border That Joins: Mexican Migrants & U.S. Responsibility. LC 82-7526. (Maryland Studies in Public Philosophy). 264p. 1982. text ed. 26.50x (ISBN 0-8476-7072-4); pap. text ed. 17.95x (ISBN 0-8476-7206-9). Rowman.

Brown, Peter G., jt. ed. see MacLean, Douglas.

Brown, Philip. Uncle Whiskers. 1976. pap. 2.95 (ISBN 0-446-87108-7). Warner Bks.

Brown, Philomena. A Basic Dictionary of Home Economics. 64p. 1982. 25.00x (ISBN 0-7135-1317-9, Pub. by Bell & Hyman England). State Mutual Bk.

Brown, Phyllis R., jt. auth. see Krstulovic, Ante M.

Brown, R. Elements of Modern Topology. 1968. text ed. 16.50 o.p. (ISBN 0-07-094059-2, C). McGraw.

--Prodromus Flora Novae-Hollandiae et Insulae Van Dieman (Now Australia & Tasmania) 1960. Repr. of 1830 ed. 56.00 (ISBN 3-7682-0033-7). Lubrecht & Cramer.

Brown, R., et al. Settlement in North America. 1974. pap. text ed. 3.95x o.p. (ISBN 0-435-34066-2). Heinemann Ed.

--Agricultural Mid-West. 1975. pap. text ed. 3.95x o.p. (ISBN 0-435-34065-4). Heinemann Ed.

Brown, R. A. Analytica Methods in Planetary Bondaryj-Layer Modeling. 1974. 43.95x o.p. (ISBN 0-470-11160-7). Halsted Pr.

--The Brown Book. (Illus.). 11.95 o.p. (ISBN 0-933506-04-X). Darwin Pubns.

Brown, R. Allen, ed. Battle Conference on Anglo-Norman Studies IV: Proceedings 1981. (Illus.). 248p. 1982. text ed. 49.50x (ISBN 0-85115-161-2, Pub. by Boydell & Brewer). Biblio Dist.

--Castles: A History & Guide. (Illus.). 196p. 1981. 19.95 o.p. (ISBN 0-7137-1100-0, Pub. by Blandford Pr England). Sterling.

--Proceedings of the Battle Conference on Anglo-Norman Studies II: 1979. (Illus.). 210p. 1979. 49.50x (ISBN 0-8476-3455-8). Rowman.

Brown, R. Don & Daigneault, Ernest A. Pharmacology of Hearing: Experimental & Clinical Bases. 376p. 1980. 60.50 (ISBN 0-471-05074-1, Pub. by Wiley-Interscience). Wiley.

Brown, R. G. The Changing National Health Service. 2nd ed. (Library of Social Policy & Administration). 1978. pap. 8.95 (ISBN 0-7100-8898-1). Routledge & Kegan.

Brown, R. G., et al. Lines, Waves & Antennas: The Transmission of Electric Energy. 2nd ed. (Illus.). 471p. 1973. text ed. 22.50 (ISBN 0-8260-1431-3). Wiley.

Brown, R. H. A Poetics for Sociology. LC 75-35454. (Illus.). 1977. 39.50 (ISBN 0-521-21121-2); pap. 10.95 (ISBN 0-521-29391-X). Cambridge U Pr.

Brown, R. H. & Lyman, S. M., eds. Structure, Consciousness, & History. LC 77-90212. (Illus.). 1978. 34.50 (ISBN 0-521-22047-5); pap. 10.95x (ISBN 0-521-29340-5). Cambridge U Pr.

Brown, R. Hanbury. The Intensity Interferometer: Its Application to Astronomy. LC 74-14878. 184p. 1974. 33.95x o.p. (ISBN 0-470-10797-9). Halsted Pr.

Brown, R. J. Windmills of England. (Illus.). 1977. 12.75 o.p. (ISBN 0-7091-5641-3). Transatlantic.

Brown, R. P. Physical Testing of Rubbers. 1979. 45.00 (ISBN 0-85334-788-3, Pub. by Applied Sci England). Elsevier.

Brown, R. S., Jr., ed. see Walpole, Horace.

Brown, Ralph H. Historical Geography of the United States. (Illus.). 596p. 1948. text ed. 24.95 (ISBN 0-15-539194-1, HC). HarBraceJ.

--Mirror for Americans: Likeness of the Eastern Seaboard, 1810. LC 67-27449. (American Scene Ser). 1968. Repr. of 1943 ed. 45.00 (ISBN 0-306-70974-0). Da Capo.

Brown, Ralph S., Jr. Loyalty & Security: Employment Tests in the United States. LC 79-151417. (Civil Liberties in American History Ser). 522p. 1972. Repr. of 1958 ed. lib. bdg. 59.50 (ISBN 0-306-70218-5). Da Capo.

Brown, Ray. The Brown Book: The Complete Guide to Buying & Selling HO Brass Locomotives. 2nd ed. (Illus.). 160p. 1982. pap. 13.95 (ISBN 0-933506-10-4). Darwin Pubns.

--Characteristics of Local Media Audiences. 1978. text ed. 28.00x (ISBN 0-566-00218-3). Gower Pub Ltd.

Brown, Ray E. Judgement in Administration. LC 82-82148. 248p. 1982. Repr. of 1966 ed. 25.00 (ISBN 0-931028-31-0). Pluribus Pr.

Brown, Raymond. The Community of the Beloved Disciple. LC 78-65894. 204p. 1979. 6.95 (ISBN 0-8091-0274-9); pap. 4.50. Paulist Pr.

Brown, Raymond & Meier, John. Antioch & Rome. 256p. 1983. 8.95 (ISBN 0-8091-0339-7); pap. 4.95 (ISBN 0-8091-2532-3). Paulist Pr.

Brown, Raymond, et al, eds. Mary in the New Testament. LC 78-8797. 336p. 1978. pap. 4.95 (ISBN 0-8091-2168-9). Paulist Pr.

Brown, Raymond B. Marcos Presenta Al Salvador. Lerin, Olivia Y Alfredo, tr. Orig. Title: Mark - the Saviour for Sinners. 160p. 1982. pap. 4.25 (ISBN 0-311-04346-1). Casa Bautista.

Brown, Raymond E. The Birth of the Messiah: A Commentary on the Infancy Narratives in Matthew & Luke. LC 76-56271. 1977. pap. 7.95 (ISBN 0-385-05405-X, Im). Doubleday.

--New Testament Essays. 1968. pap. 1.95 (ISBN 0-385-05276-6, Im). Doubleday.

--New Testament Essays. pap. 4.95 (ISBN 0-8091-2470-X). Paulist Pr.

--Priest & Bishop. LC 78-139594. 96p. 1970. pap. 2.95 o.p. (ISBN 0-8091-1661-8). Paulist Pr.

Brown, Raymond E., et al. Peter in the New Testament. LC 73-84424. (Orig.). 1973. pap. 4.95 (ISBN 0-8091-1790-8). Paulist Pr.

Brown, Raymond K. Reach Out to Singles: A Challenge to Ministry. LC 79-15495. 1979. pap. 7.95 (ISBN 0-664-24270-7). Westminster.

Brown, Richard & Cook, Melva. Special Occasion Cookbook. 1983. 9.95 (ISBN 0-8054-7001-8). Broadman.

Brown, Richard & Robbins, David. Advanced Mathematics: An Introductory Course. (gr. 11-12). 1981. text ed. 18.56 (ISBN 0-395-29335-9); instrs.' guide & solns. 10.72 (ISBN 0-395-29336-7). HM.

Brown, Richard, jt. auth. see Leiff, Jonathan D.

Brown, Richard D. & Ouellette, Robert P. Pollution Control at Electric Power Stations: Comparisons for U. S. & Europe. 110p. 1983. 29.95 (ISBN 0-250-40618-7). Ann Arbor Science.

Brown, Richard D. & Petrello, George J. Introduction to Business. 2nd ed. 622p. 1979. text ed. 21.95 (ISBN 0-02-471310-4). Macmillan.

Brown, Richard D. & Rabe, Steven G., eds. Slavery in American Society. 2nd ed. (Problems in American Civilization Ser.). 1977. pap. text ed. 5.95 (ISBN 0-669-00073-6). Heath.

Brown, Richard E. The GAO: Untapped Source of Congressional Power. LC 78-111049. 1970. 11.50x (ISBN 0-87049-120-2). U of Tenn Pr.

Brown, Richard H., ed. see Bennett, P.

Brown, Richard H., ed. see Casey, Dayle A.

Brown, Richard H., ed. see Guttmann, Allen.

Brown, Richard H., ed. see Harris, Jonathan.

Brown, Richard H., jt. ed. see Winston, Patrik H.

Brown, Richard M. Strain of Violence: Historical Studies of American Violence & Vigilantism. LC 75-7351. 1977. pap. 9.95 (ISBN 0-19-502247-5, GB513, GB). Oxford U Pr.

Brown, Richard M., jt. ed. see Olson, Alison G.

Brown, Rita Mae. Sudden Death. 1983. 12.95 (ISBN 0-553-05037-0). Bantam.

Brown, Robert. Art Deco Internationale. LC 77-78540. (Illus.). 1977. pap. 7.95 (ISBN 0-8256-3070-3, 030070, Quick Fox). Putnam Pub Group.

--Beyond the Cape of Hope. 7.50 o.p. (ISBN 0-685-20563-0). Transatlantic.

Brown, Robert & Reinhold, Susan. The Poster Art of A. M. Cassandre. (Illus.). 1980. 19.95 o.p. (ISBN 0-525-18175-X); pap. 10.95 o.p. (ISBN 0-525-47602-4). Dutton.

Brown, Robert, ed. Boater's Safety Handbook. (Illus.). 52p. (Orig.). 1982. pap. 2.95 (ISBN 0-89886-072-5). Mountaineers.

Brown, Robert B., jt. auth. see Bell, Irene W.

Brown, Robert D. & DeCoster, David A., eds. Mentoring-Transcript Systems for Promoting Student Growth. LC 81-48581. 1982. 7.95x (ISBN 0-87589-921-8, SS-19). Jossey-Bass.

Brown, Robert E. Charles Beard & the Constitution. A Critical Analysis of "An Economic Interpretation of the Constitution". LC 78-14426. 1979. Repr. of 1956 ed. lib. bdg. 18.75x (ISBN 0-313-21048-9, BRBC). Greenwood.

Brown, Robert F. The Lefschetz Fixed Point Theorem. 1970. text ed. 27.95x (ISBN 0-673-05395-4). Scott F.

Brown, Robert G. Introduction to Random Signal Analysis & Kalman Filtering. 416p. 1983. text ed. price not set (ISBN 0-471-08732-7). Wiley.

Brown, Robert H. Farm Electrification. (Agricultural Engineering Ser). 1956. 32.50 (ISBN 0-07-008462-9, C). McGraw.

--Wyoming: A Geography. (Geographies of the United States Ser.). (Illus.). 375p. 1980. lib. bdg. 36.25x (ISBN 0-89158-560-5); text ed. 20.00 (ISBN 0-686-96923-5). Westview.

Brown, Robert K. Essentials of Real Estate. LC 75-92119. 1969. pap. text ed. 12.95 o.p. (ISBN 0-13-287474-1). P-H.

Brown, Robert L. Jeep Trails to Colorado Ghost Towns. LC 63-7443. (Illus.). 1963. pap. 7.95 (ISBN 0-87004-021-9). Caxton.

Brown, Robert M. The Bible Speaks to You. LC 55-7089. 1978. pap. 5.95 (ISBN 0-664-24193-X). Westminster.

--Gustavo Gutierrez. LC 80-82185. (Makers of Contemporary Theology Ser.). 89p. 1981. pap. 3.95 (ISBN 0-8042-0651-1). John Knox.

--One Hundred & Four Easy Transistor Projects You Can Build. LC 68-29177. (Illus.). (YA) 1968. pap. 7.95 o.p. (ISBN 0-8306-7462-4, 462). TAB Bks.

--Spirit of Protestantism. (YA) (gr. 9 up). 1965. pap. 7.95 (ISBN 0-19-500724-7, GB). Oxford U Pr.

Brown, Robert M. & Lawrence, Paul. How to Read Electronic Circuit Diagrams. LC 72-105970. 1970. 13.95 (ISBN 0-8306-0510-X); pap. 7.95 (ISBN 0-8306-9510-9, 510). TAB Bks.

Brown, Robert M., tr. see Casalis, George.

Brown, Robert M., tr. see De Dietrich, Suzanne.

Brown, Robin. Jet Cutting Technology: 1971-1980, A Review & Bibliography. 1982. 90.00x (ISBN 0-686-97018-7, Pub. by BHRA Fluid England). State Mutual BK.

--Megalodon. 1981. 13.95 (ISBN 0-698-11078-1, Coward). Putnam Pub Group.

Brown, Roger, jt. auth. see Mason, Linda.

Brown, Ronald & Oren, John W. Physical Distribution in Agribusiness: Activity Guide. Lee, Jasper S., ed. (Career Preparation for Agriculture-Agribusiness). 1980. pap. text ed. 8.96 (ISBN 0-07-008181-6, G); tchr's manual & key 3.00 (ISBN 0-07-008183-2); activity guide 5.96 (ISBN 0-07-008182-4). McGraw.

Brown, Rosellen. Street Games. 224p. 1983. pap. 2.75 (ISBN 0-345-28739-8). Ballantine.

Brown, Rosellen, et al. Banquet: 5 Short Stories. LC 78-56621. (Illus.). 1978. 12.00x (ISBN 0-915778-24-6); pap. 5.00 (ISBN 0-915778-25-4); deluxe ed 175.00x deluxe ed (ISBN 0-915778-23-8). Penmaen Pr.

Brown, Rosemary S., jt. auth. see Savicki, Victor.

Brown, Ross F. Basic Arithmetic. 1979. pap. 14.50x (ISBN 0-673-15106-9). Scott F.

Brown, Roy I. Psychology & Education of Slow Learners. (Students Library of Education). 1976. 10.00x o.p. (ISBN 0-7100-8410-2). Routledge & Kegan.

Brown, Roy M., jt. auth. see Steiner, Jesse F.

Brown, Ruth. If at First You Do Not See. LC 82-15527. (Illus.). 24p. 1983. 11.95 (ISBN 0-03-063521-7). HR&W.

Brown, S. F., et al, eds. Chemical Diagnosis & Disease. 1374p. 1979. 78.50 (ISBN 0-444-80089-1, North Holland). Elsevier.

Brown, S. S., ed. Clinical Chemistry & Chemical Toxicology. 1977. 47.00 (ISBN 0-444-41601-3). Elsevier.

Brown, Sam E. Activities for Teaching Metrics in Kindergarden. LC 77-95155. 1978. pap. text ed. 7.25 (ISBN 0-8191-0462-0). U Pr of Amer.

Brown, Sanborn C. Benjamin Thompson, Count Rumford. (Illus.). 1979. 25.00 (ISBN 0-262-02138-2); pap. 9.95 (ISBN 0-262-52069-9). MIT Pr.

--Count Rumford, Physicist Extraordinary. LC 78-25712. (Illus.). 1979. Repr. of 1962 ed. lib. bdg. 20.25x (ISBN 0-313-20772-0, BRCR). Greenwood.

--Electron Molecule Scattering. LC 79-12705. (Wiley Series in Plasma Physics). 1980. 34.95 o.p. (ISBN 0-471-05205-1, Pub. by Wiley-Interscience). Wiley.

--Wines & Beers of Old New England: A How-to-Do-It History. LC 77-72519. (Illus.). 187p. 1978. text ed. 12.50x (ISBN 0-87451-144-5); pap. text ed. 5.95 (ISBN 0-87451-148-8). U Pr of New Eng.

Brown, Sanborn C. & Clarke, Norman, eds. International Education in Physics. (Illus.). 1959. 12.50x o.p. (ISBN 0-262-02005-X). MIT Pr.

Brown, Sanborn C., ed. see Rumford, Benjamin T.

Brown, Sandra. Heaven's Price. (Loveswept Ser.: No. 1). 1983. pap. 1.95 (ISBN 0-686-43202-9). Bantam.

--Relentless Desire. (Second Chance at Love Ser.: No. 106). 1.75 (ISBN 0-515-06870-5). Jove Pubns.

--Tomorrow's Promise. (American Romance Ser.). 192p. 1983. pap. 2.25 (ISBN 0-686-38744-9). Harlequin Bks.

Brown, Sanford J. Getting into Medical School. 6th ed. 256p. 1983. pap. price not set (ISBN 0-8120-2542-3). Barron.

Brown, Seyom. New Forces in World Politics. LC 74-912. 200p. 1974. 18.95 (ISBN 0-8157-1118-2); pap. 7.95 (ISBN 0-8157-1117-4). Brookings.

Brown, Seyom, et al. Regimes for the Ocean, Outer Space, & Weather. 1977. 22.95 (ISBN 0-8157-1156-5); pap. 8.95 (ISBN 0-8157-1155-7). Brookings.

Brown, Shelagh. Someone There. 96p. (Orig.). 1982. pap. 1.70 (ISBN 0-88028-019-0). Forward Movement.

Brown, Sheldon S. A Guide to Study Children & Adolescents. 2nd ed. 1978. pap. text ed. 8.95 (ISBN 0-8403-1304-7). Kendall-Hunt.

--Your Career in Court Administration. LC 79-13488. (Arco's Career Guidance Ser.). 1979. lib. bdg. 7.95 (ISBN 0-668-04448-9, 4448-9); pap. 4.50 (ISBN 0-668-04452-7, 4452-7). Arco.

Brown, Shirley N., jt. ed. see Brown, James W.

Brown, Shiron L. Expressions from the Heart. Cherry, Annie, ed. 44p. (Orig.). 1982. pap. 4.95 (ISBN 0-910515-00-X). Brown Cherry Pub.

Brown, Skip & Graham, John. Target Twenty Six: A Practical Guide to the Marathon. 1979. pap. 6.95 (ISBN 0-02-028820-4, Collier); pap. 59.40 prepack(12). Macmillan.

Brown, Slater. Ethan Allen & the Green Mountain Boys. (Landmark Ser.: No. 66). (Illus.). (gr. 4-6). 1956. PLB 5.99 o.s.i. (ISBN 0-394-90366-8). Random.

Brown, Stanley C. God's Plan for Marriage. LC 77-6674. 1977. 10.00 o.s.i. (ISBN 0-664-24758-X). Westminster.

Brown, Stanley H. A Tale of Two Cities: Houston & Detroit. (Illus.). 1983. 16.95 (ISBN 0-87795-486-0). Arbor Hse.

Brown, Stanley H., jt. auth. see Girard, Joe.

Brown, Stephen. If God Is In Charge. 180p. 1983. pap. 4.95 (ISBN 0-8407-5844-8). Nelson.

Brown, Stephen D. Places to Visit Near Harpers Ferry. 3rd rev. ed. (Illus.). 1982. pap. 2.50 o.p. (ISBN 0-685-93630-9). The Little Brown House.

--Ralph's Nadir: What Went Wrong with the Nader Congress Project. (Illus.). 1976. 8.95 (ISBN 0-686-16898-4). Bookhaus.

Brown, Stephen G. & DiSaisa, Philip J. Cancer of the Cervix. (Oncologic Ser.: Vol. 14). (Illus.). 308p. 1981. pap. 100.00 (ISBN 0-08-027465-X). Pergamon.

Brown, Stephen I., jt. auth. see Walter, Marion I.

Brown, Sterling A. The Collected Poems of Sterling A. Brown. LC 79-5221. (National Poetry Ser.). 1980. 13.41i (ISBN 0-06-010517-8, HarpT). Har-Row.

--The Collected Poems of Sterling A. Brown. Harper, Michael S., selected by. LC 82-48230. 270p. 1983. pap. 5.72i (ISBN 0-06-091016-X, CN 1016, CN). Har-Row.

Brown, Steven F., ed. see Doty, M. R.

Brown, Steven R. & Brenner, Donald J., eds. Science, Psychology, & Communication: Essays Honoring William Stephenson. LC 73-165607. (Illus.). 1972. text ed. 17.95x (ISBN 0-8077-1132-2). Tchrs Coll.

Brown, Stewart J. Thomas Chalmers & Godly Commonwealth in Scotland. (Illus.). 368p. 1983. 55.00 (ISBN 0-19-213114-1). Oxford U Pr.

Brown, Stuart G. Conscience in Politics: Adlai E. Stevenson in the 1950's. 1961. 16.95x (ISBN 0-8156-0022-4). Syracuse U Pr.

--The First Republicans: Political Philosophy & Public Policy in the Party of Jefferson & Madison. LC 76-48247. 1977. Repr. of 1954 ed. lib. bdg. 10.00x (ISBN 0-8371-9339-7, BRFR). Greenwood.

--Presidency on Trial: Robert Kennedy's 1968 Campaign & Afterwards. 1972. 10.00x (ISBN 0-8248-0202-0). UH Pr.

Brown, Stuart G., ed. see Royce, Josiah.

Brown, T. Freeze Branding. (Orig.). 1982. pap. 3.50 (ISBN 0-911217-00-2). SW Amer Pub Co.

Brown, T. A., ed. see Piaget, Jean.

Brown, T. C., jt. auth. see Hunter, R. H.

Brown, T. Merritt. Specification & Uses of Econometric Models. LC 70-88172. 1970. 26.00 (ISBN 0-312-75110-9). St Martin.

Brown, T. Nigel, ed. Brown's Nautical Almanac, 1983. 106th ed. LC 32-280. (Illus.). 946p. 1982. 37.50x (ISBN 0-8002-3066-3). Intl Pubns Serv.

Brown, Terry & Hunter, Rob. Parallel Skiing. (Venture Guides Ser.). (Illus.). 1978. pap. 2.95 o.p. (ISBN 0-904978-82-6). Hippocrene Bks.

--Skiing. (Venture Guides). (Illus.). 1978. pap. 2.95 o.p. (ISBN 0-904978-77-X). Hippocrene Bks.

Brown, Theodore & Le May, Eugene. Qualitative Inorganic Analysis. (Illus.). 160p. 1983. pap. 4.95 (ISBN 0-686-38828-3). P H.

Brown, Theodore L. & LeMay, H. Eugene. Chemistry: The Central Science. 2nd ed. 832p. 1981. text ed. 30.95 (ISBN 0-13-128504-1); lab experiments 16.95 (ISBN 0-13-128520-3); solution manual 7.95 (ISBN 0-13-128538-6); student guide 10.95 (ISBN 0-13-128512-2). P-H.

Brown, Thomas. Inquiry into the Relation of Cause & Effect. 4th ed. LC 77-16224. 1977. Repr. of 1835 ed. lib. bdg. 55.00x (ISBN 0-8201-1301-8). Schol Facsimiles.

--Letter to a Friend. Keynes, Geoffrey, ed. LC 71-143387. 1971. 50.00 (ISBN 0-87923-035-5). Godine.

Brown, Thomas, jt. auth. see Holladay, Sylvia.

Brown, Thomas, jt. auth. see Smith, Mickey.

Brown, Thomas, et al. Teaching Secondary English: Alternative Approaches. LC 74-78738. 448p. 1975. text ed. 15.95x (ISBN 0-675-08788-0). Merrill.

Brown, Thomas H. French: Listening, Speaking, Reading, Writing. 3rd ed. (Illus., Fr.). 1977. text ed. 24.00 (ISBN 0-07-008396-7, C); instructor's manual 15.00 (ISBN 0-07-008397-5); cahier d'exercises 11.95 (ISBN 0-07-008398-3); tapes 495.00 (ISBN 0-07-008399-1). McGraw.

--Langue et Litterature: A Second Course in French. 2nd ed. (Illus.). 448p. 1974. text ed. 27.50x (ISBN 0-07-008400-9, C); instructor's manual 15.00 (ISBN 0-07-008401-7); workbook 15.00 (ISBN 0-07-008402-5). McGraw.

--Themes et Discussions. 240p. 1981. pap. text ed. 9.95 (ISBN 0-669-02844-4). Heath.

Brown, Thomas H. & Sandberg, Karl C. Conversational English. LC 69-12073. 1969. pap. text ed. 11.95x o.p. (ISBN 0-471-00050-7). tapes avail. o.p. (ISBN 0-471-00052-3). Scott F.

--Conversational English. 1969. pap. text ed. 14.50x (ISBN 0-673-15658-3). Scott F.

Brown, Thomas K., tr. see Jorns, Auguste.

Brown, Thomas N. Irish-American Nationalism, Eighteen Seventy to Eighteen Ninety. LC 80-11094. (Critical Periods of History Ser.). xvii, 206p. 1980. Repr. of 1966 ed. lib. bdg. 21.00x (ISBN 0-313-22204-5, BRIA). Greenwood.

Brown, Thomas S. & Wallace, Patricia. Physiological Psychology. 1980. tchrs' ed. 23.00 (ISBN 0-12-136660-X); study guide 7.75 (ISBN 0-12-136663-4). Acad Pr.

Brown, Tom, Jr. & Morgan, Brandt. Tom Brown's Guide to Wilderness Survival. 240p. (Orig.). 1983. pap. 6.95 (ISBN 0-425-05876-X). Berkley Pub.

Brown, Tom, Jr. & Owen, William. The Search: The Continuing Story of the Tracker. LC 80-20588. 1980. 10.95 o.p. (ISBN 0-13-796953-8). P-H.

Brown University. Dictionary Catalog of the Harris Collection of American Poetry & Plays, Brown University, 13 vols. 1972. Set. lib. bdg. 1620.00 (ISBN 0-8161-0974-5, Hall Library). G K Hall.

Brown University - John Carter Brown Library. Bibliotheca Americana, Books to Sixteen Seventy Four, 3 Vols. 3rd ed. 1919-1931. Set. 117.00 o.s.i. (ISBN 0-527-46200-4). Kraus Repr.

--Bibliotheca Americana, Catalogue of Books of North & South America, 2 Vols. 1870-1871. Set. 69.00 o.s.i. (ISBN 0-527-46210-1). Kraus Repr.

Brown, V. Backyard Wild Birds of the Pacific Northwest & California. pap. 3.95 (ISBN 0-87666-411-7, M521). TFH Pubns.

Brown, V. K. Acute Toxicity in Theory & Practice: With Special Reference to the Toxicoloty of Pesticides. LC 79-42905. (Monographs in Toxicology; Environmental & Safety Aspects). 159p. 1980. 35.95 (ISBN 0-471-27690-1, Pub. by Wiley-Interscience). Wiley.

Brown, Vinson. The Amateur Naturalist's Diary. (Illus.). 192p. 1983. 15.95 (ISBN 0-13-023689-6); pap. 8.95 (ISBN 0-13-023671-3). P-H.

--The Amateur Naturalists's Handbook. (Illus.). 448p. 1980. 15.95 (ISBN 0-13-023739-6, Spec); pap. 7.95 (ISBN 0-13-023721-3). P-H.

--Peoples of the Sea Wind. 250p. 1983. price not set. Naturegraph.

Brown, Vinson, et al. Prevent Doomsday! new ed. (Illus.). 96p. 1983. pap. 4.95 (ISBN 0-8283-1875-1). Branden.

Brown, Virginia P. & Akens, Helen M. Alabama Heritage. LC 67-28403. (Illus.). 1967. 15.95 (ISBN 0-87397-001-2). Strode.

--Alabama Mounds to Missiles. LC 66-23127. (Illus.). 1966. pap. 5.95 (ISBN 0-87397-002-0). Strode.

Brown, Virginia P., ed. see Legislative Wives Club.

Brown, W. Psychological Care During Pregnancy & the Postpartum Period. 171p. 1979. 20.00 (ISBN 0-89004-371-X); pap. 12.00 (ISBN 0-686-66187-7). Raven.

Brown, W. D. Welcome Stress, It Can Help You Be Your Best. 150p. (Orig.). 1983. pap. 8.95 (ISBN 0-89638-067-X). CompCare.

Brown, W. Norman. Manuscript Illustrations of the Uttaradhyayana Sutra. (American Oriental Ser.: Vol. 21). (Illus.). 1941. 8.00x o.p. (ISBN 0-940490-21-8). Kraus Repr.

Brown, W. R., jt. auth. see Bowen, B. A.

Brown, Wallace C. The Triumph of Form. LC 73-13452. 212p. 1973. Repr. of 1948 ed. lib. bdg. 19.25x (ISBN 0-8371-7135-0, BRTF). Greenwood.

Brown, Walter, jt. auth. see Anderson, Norman.

Brown, Walter C. Basic Mathematics. 128p. 1981. pap. text ed. 5.60 (ISBN 0-87006-315-4). Goodheart.

--Blueprint Reading for Industry. Rev. ed. LC 82-20949. 345p. 1983. spiral bdg. 14.00 (ISBN 0-87006-429-0). Goodheart.

--Drafting. LC 81-20004. (Illus.). 128p. 1982. text ed. 5.80 (ISBN 0-87006-405-3). Goodheart.

--Drafting for Industry: 1981 Ed. LC 80-28657. (Illus.). 616p. 18.64 (ISBN 0-87006-320-0); wkbk. 4.96 (ISBN 0-87006-306-5). Goodheart.

Brown, Walter R., jt. auth. see Anderson, Norman D.

Brown, Warren B. & Moberg, Dennis G. Organization & Management. LC 79-18709. (Management Ser.). 685p. 1980. text ed. 27.95 (ISBN 0-471-02023-0). Wiley.

Brown, Wayne S., et al, eds. Monograph on Rock Mechanics Applications in Mining. LC 76-45924. 1977. pap. text ed. 18.00x (ISBN 0-89520-046-5). Soc Mining Eng.

Brown, William D. Families Under Stress. 154p. 1977. pap. text ed. 7.95 o.p. (ISBN 0-87619-844-2). R J Brady.

Brown, William E. Alaska National Parklands: This Last Treasure. LC 82-71677. (Illus.). 128p. (Orig.). 1982. 25.00; pap. 10.95 (ISBN 0-9602876-5-5). Alaska Natural.

--Hydraulics for Operators. LC 81-68896. (Illus.). 145p. 1981. pap. text ed. 16.95 (ISBN 0-250-40503-2). Ann Arbor Science.

Brown, William E. & Sacks, Richard S. Review Manual for Operators. LC 81-68888. (Illus.). 182p. 1981. pap. text ed. 16.95 (ISBN 0-250-40501-6). Ann Arbor Science.

Brown, William E., ed. Testing of Polymers. LC 65-14733. (Testing of Polymers Ser.: Vol. 4). 1969. 46.00 o.p. (ISBN 0-470-11175-5, Pub. by Wiley-Interscience). Wiley.

Brown, William G. Life of Oliver Ellsworth. LC 76-118028. (American Constitutional & Legal History Ser). 1970. Repr. of 1905 ed. lib. bdg. 45.00 (ISBN 0-306-71940-1). Da Capo.

Brown, William H. & McClarin, Judith A. Introduction to Organic & Biochemistry. 3rd ed. 524p. 1981. text ed. write for info. (ISBN 0-87150-738-2, 4282); pap. text ed. write for info. study guide (ISBN 0-87150-739-0, 4286). Grant Pr.

Brown, William H. & Rogers, Elizabeth P. General, Organic & Biochemistry. 2nd ed. 900p. 1983. text ed. write for info (ISBN 0-87150-762-5, 4461). Grant Pr.

Brown, William R. Academic Politics. LC 81-23100. 202p. 1982. text ed. 17.50 (ISBN 0-8173-0116-X). U of Ala Pr.

Brown, Wilmore, ed. Legal Architect. 1959. 12.50 (ISBN 0-87215-015-1). Michie-Bobbs.

Brown, Wilmore, ed. see Musmanno, Michael A.

Brown, Wm. A., Jr. Groping Giant: Russia. 1920. 29.50x (ISBN 0-685-69793-2). Elliots Bks.

Brown-Azarowicz, Marjory F. Individual & Group Procedures in Reading: For the Classroom Teacher in Grades 4-7. LC 81-40095. (Illus.). 310p. (Orig.). 1982. pap. text ed. 12.75 (ISBN 0-8191-2264-5). U Pr of Amer.

Brownback, Paul. Danger of Self-Love. LC 82-12543. 1982. pap. 4.95 (ISBN 0-8024-2068-0). Moody.

Browne. Look What I've Got. (gr. k-3). 1980. PLB 8.90 (ISBN 0-531-04118-2). Watts.

Browne, Cynthia, compiled by. State Constitutional Conventions Bibliography. LC 73-9327. 1973. lib. bdg. 35.00 (ISBN 0-8371-7005-2, SCB/). Greenwood.

Browne, Dan. The Housebuilding Book. (Illus.). 192p. 1974. 17.95 (ISBN 0-07-008486-6, GB); pap. 6.95 (ISBN 0-07-008487-4). McGraw.

--Multiply Your Living Space: How to Put an Addition on Your Home at a Cost You Can Afford. (Illus.). 1978. 12.95 o.p. (ISBN 0-07-008485-8, GB). McGraw.

Browne, Dik. Hagar the Horrible, No. 1. 128p. 1982. pap. 1.75 (ISBN 0-448-16883-9, Pub. by Tempo). Ace Bks.

--Hagar the Horrible Puzzlers. 128p. (gr. 5 up). 1982. pap. 1.75 (ISBN 0-686-81832-6, Pub. by Tempo). Ace Bks.

Browne, Edward G. Literary History of Persia, 4 Vols. 1928. 65.00 ea. Vol. 1 (ISBN 0-521-04344-1). Vol. 2 (ISBN 0-521-04345-X). Vol. 3 (ISBN 0-521-04346-8). Vol. 4. Cambridge U Pr.

--The Press & Poetry of Modern Persia. (Illus.). xi, 357p. 1983. Repr. of 1914 ed. 30.00 (ISBN 0-933770-39-1). Kalimat.

Browne, Edward G., tr. see Abdu'l-Baha.

Browne, Edward G., tr. see Isfandiyar, Ibn & Ibn-al-Hasan, Muhammad.

Browne, Eric C. & Dreijmanis, John, eds. Government Coalitions in Western Democracies. LC 81-8241. (Professional Studies Ser.). (Illus.). 384p. (Orig.). 1982. text ed. 30.00x (ISBN 0-582-28218-7); pap. text ed. 17.50x (ISBN 0-582-28219-5). Longman.

Browne, Gary. Baltimore in the Nation. 349p. 1980. 20.00 (ISBN 0-686-36490-2). Md Hist.

Browne, Gerald A. Nineteen Purchase Street. 1983. pap. 3.50 (ISBN 0-425-06154-X). Berkley Pub.

Browne, H. Joseph Chamberlain. (Seminar Studies in History Ser.). 164p. 1974. pap. text ed. 6.95x (ISBN 0-582-35214-2). Longman.

Browne, Irving. Elements of the Law of Domestic Relations & of Employer & Employed. xxi, 162p. 1981. Repr. of 1883 ed. lib. bdg. 22.50x (ISBN 0-8377-0321-2). Rothman.

--Law & Lawyers in Literature. LC 82-82459. 413p. 1982. Repr. of 1883 ed. lib. bdg. 45.00x (ISBN 0-912004-22-3). W W Gaunt.

--Short Studies of Great Lawyers. iv, 382p. 1982. Repr. of 1878 ed. lib. bdg. 30.00x (ISBN 0-8377-0330-1). Rothman.

Browne, J. A. & Kirlin, Betty A. Rehabilitation Services & the Social Work Role: Challenge for Change. (Rehabilitation Medicine Library). 362p. 1981. lib. bdg. 25.00 (ISBN 0-683-01091-3). Williams & Wilkins.

Browne, J. S. Basic Theory of Structures. 1966. 27.00 o.p. (ISBN 0-08-011654-X); pap. 12.75 o.p. (ISBN 0-08-011653-1). Pergamon.

Browne, Janet. The Secular Ark: Studies in the History of Biogeography. LC 82-17497. (Illus.). 272p. 1983. text ed. 27.50x (ISBN 0-300-02460-6). Yale U Pr.

Browne, Joseph W. Personal Dignity. LC 82-18944. 1983. 15.00 (ISBN 0-8022-2409-1). Philos Lib.

Browne, Louis & Romero, Adrian. Manual de Investigaciones Biologicas. (Span.). 1979. pap. text ed. 6.50 (ISBN 0-8403-1949-5, 40194901). Kendall-Hunt.

Browne, M. Neil & Keely, Stuart M. Asking the Right Questions. 224p. 1981. pap. text ed. 9.50 (ISBN 0-13-049395-3). P-H.

Browne, Muriel. The Messiah Comes. (Christmas Programs Ser.). 1977. pap. 1.95 o.p. (ISBN 0-8024-5256-6). Moody.

Browne, Patrick S. Basic Facts in Orthopaedics. (Illus.). 352p. 1981. pap. text ed. 15.95 (ISBN 0-632-00718-4, B 0877-5). Mosby.

Browne, Peter S. Security: Checklist for Computer Center Self-Audits. LC 79-56012. (Illus.). 189p. 1979. pap. 40.25 (ISBN 0-88283-024-4). AFIPS Pr.

Browne, Ray B., ed. Lincoln-Lore: Lincoln in the Popular Mind. 500p. 1975. 20.00 o.p. (ISBN 0-87972-035-2). Bowling Green Univ.

Browne, Roland A. The Rose-Lover's Guide: A Practical Handbook for Rose Gardening. LC 73-92067. (Illus.). 256p. 1983. pap. 9.95 (ISBN 0-689-70642-1, 291). Atheneum.

Browne, Steven E. The Video Tape Post-Production Primer. (Illus.). 218p. 1982. 25.00 (ISBN 0-686-37656-0). Wilton Place.

Browne, Thomas. Hydriotaphia (Urn Burial) Huntley, Frank L., ed. Bd. with The Garden of Cyrus. LC 66-16496. (Crofts Classics Ser.). 1966. pap. text ed. 3.25x (ISBN 0-88295-017-7). Harlan Davidson.

Browne, Tom. Rivers & People. LC 79-21943. (Nature's Landscape Ser.). PLB 15.96 (ISBN 0-382-06671-5). Silver.

Browne, Turner & Partnow, Elaine. Photographic Artists & Innovators. (Illus.). 896p. 1983. 39.95 (ISBN 0-02-517500-9). Macmillan.

Browne, William & Hadwiger, Don, eds. Rural Policy. (Orig.). 1982. pap. 6.00 (ISBN 0-918592-55-0). Policy Studies.

Browne, William P. & Hadwiger, Don F., eds. Rural Policy Problems: Changing Dimensions. LC 81-48069. (A Policy Studies Organization Book). (Illus.). 272p. 1982. 29.95 (ISBN 0-669-05242-6). Lexington Bks.

Browne, William P. & Olson, Laura K., eds. Aging & Public Policy: The Politics of Growing Old in America. LC 82-6138. (Contributions in Political Science Ser.: No. 83). (Illus.). 304p. 1983. lib. bdg. 35.00 (ISBN 0-313-22855-8, BAG/). Greenwood.

Brownell, Blaine A., jt. auth. see Goldfield, David R.

Brownell, Blaine A. & Stickle, Warren E., eds. Bosses & Reformers: Urban Politics in America, 1880-1920. LC 72-4798. (New Perspectives in History Ser.). 250p. (Orig.). 1973. pap. text ed. 9.50 o.p. (ISBN 0-395-14050-1, 3-41025). HM.

Brownell, David W., ed. Vintage Auto Almanac. 4th ed. LC 76-649715. 288p. 1981. pap. 7.95 o.p. (ISBN 0-917808-04-5). Hemmings.

Brownell, John A. A Directory of Selected Resources for the Study of English in Japan. LC 76-10955. 1976. pap. text ed. 3.95x (ISBN 0-8248-0463-5). UH Pr.

Brownell, Joseph W. Census Statistics in Geography: A Manual for New York State. (Illus.). 1975. pap. 3.50x o.p. (ISBN 0-910042-23-3). Allegheny.

Brownell, Lloyd E. & Young, Edwin H. Process Equipment Design: Vessel Design. LC 59-5882. 1959. 59.95 (ISBN 0-471-11319-0, Pub by Wiley-Interscience). Wiley.

Brownhill, R. J. Education & the Nature of Knowledge. (New Patterns of Learning Ser.). 144p. 1983. text ed. 27.25x (ISBN 0-7099-0654-4, Pub. by Croom Helm Ltd England). Biblio Dist.

Browning, Charles H. Private Practice Handbook: The Tools, Tactics & Techniques for Successful Practice Development. 2nd ed. 238p. 1982. 24.95 (ISBN 0-911663-02-9); pap. 21.95 (ISBN 0-911663-01-0). Duncliffs Intl.

Browning, D. R. Chromatography. 1970. 17.50 o.p. (ISBN 0-07-094096-7, P&RB). McGraw.

Browning, D. S. Everyman's Dictionary of Literary Biography. 3th ed. (Everyman's Reference Library). 812p. 1969. 13.50x (ISBN 0-460-03008-6, Pub. by J. M. Dent England). Biblio Dist.

Browning, Don S. Generative Man. 272p. 1975. pap. 2.95 o.s.i. (ISBN 0-440-54403-3, Delta). Dell.

--The Moral Context of Pastoral Care. LC 76-5858. 1976. 10.00 (ISBN 0-664-20742-1). Westminster.

Browning, Don S., ed. Practical Theology: The Emerging Field in Theology, Chruch & World. LC 82-47739. 128p. (Orig.). 1982. pap. 7.64i (ISBN 0-06-061153-7, HarpR). Har-Row.

Browning, Edgar K. & Browning, Jacquelene M. Public Finance & the Price System. 1979. text ed. 25.95 (ISBN 0-02-315650-3). Macmillan.

Browning, Edgar K. & Browning, Jacqueline M. Public Finance & the Price System. 2nd ed. 500p. 1983. text ed. 24.95 (ISBN 0-686-84132-8). Macmillan.

Browning, Elizabeth B. Sonnets from the Portuguese, 2 vols. Peterson, William S., ed. (Illus.). 1977. 45.00 o.s.i. (ISBN 0-517-53167-4); sonnets 7.95 (ISBN 0-517-53178-X). Crown.

--Sonnets from the Portuguese. 1932. 10.53i (ISBN 0-06-010555-0, HarpT). Har-Row.

Browning, Frank, jt. auth. see Gerassi, John.

Browning, Gordon, jt. auth. see Bach, Bert C.

Browning, Iain. Jerash & the Decapolis. (Illus.). 224p. 1983. 22.95 (ISBN 0-7011-2591-8, Pub by Chatto & Windus). Merrimack Bk Serv.

Browning, J. D. Biography in the Eighteenth Century: Publications of the McMaster University Association for 18th Century Studies. LC 80-14652. (Vol. 8). 207p. 1980. 27.50 o.s.i. (ISBN 0-8240-4007-4). Garland Pub.

Browning, Jacquelene M., jt. auth. see Browning, Edgar K.

Browning, Jacqueline M., jt. auth. see Browning, Edgar K.

Browning, John. Tarantulas. (Illus.). 96p. 1981. 4.95 (ISBN 0-87666-931-3, KW-075). TFH Pubns.

Browning, John, ed. Education in the Eighteenth Century. LC 79-18182. (The Eighteenth Century Ser.). 145p. 1979. lib. bdg. 27.50 o.s.i. (ISBN 0-8240-4006-6). Garland Pub.

Browning, John & Morton, Richard, eds. Religion in the Eighteenth Century. LC 79-17715. (The Eighteenth Century Ser.). 145p. 1979. lib. bdg. 20.00 o.s.i. (ISBN 0-8240-4005-8). Garland Pub.

Browning, Jon E. & Roberson, James O. How to Relocate or Expand Your Business: The Executive's Guide to Managing a Move. 1980. 21.00 (ISBN 0-07-008495-5). McGraw.

Browning, K. A., ed. Nowcasting. LC 82-45030. 1982. 45.00 (ISBN 0-12-137760-1). Acad Pr.

Browning, Martha, ed. see Mayfield, Peggy, et al.

Browning, Mary H. & Lewis, Ruth P., eds. Maternal & Newborn Care: Nursing Interventions. 258p. 1973. 6.50 o.s.i. (ISBN 0-686-11198-2, C07). Am Journal Nurse.

Browning, Oscar. Life of George Eliot. Robertson, Eric S., ed. 174p. 1982. Repr. of 1892 ed. lib. bdg. 20.00 (ISBN 0-89984-087-6). Century Bookbindery.

Browning, Peter. Fell's International Directory of Stamp-Auction Houses. LC 82-71749. 336p. 1982. 24.95 (ISBN 0-8119-0452-0). Fell.

Browning, Robert. Byzantium & Bulgaria: A Comparative Study Across the Early Medieval Frontier. LC 73-91665. (Illus.). 1975. 31.50x (ISBN 0-520-02670-5). U of Cal Pr.

--A Choice of Browning's Verse. Lucie-Smith, Edward, ed. 1967. pap. 4.95 (ISBN 0-571-08170-3). Faber & Faber.

--The Complete Works of Robert Browning, with Variant Readings & Annotations, 4 vols. King, Roma A., Jr., et al, eds. Incl. Vol. 1. xx, 306p. 1969 (ISBN 0-8214-0049-5, 82-80547); Vol. 2. xx, 422p. 1970 (ISBN 0-8214-0074-6, 82-80794); Vol. 3. xxviii, 397p. 1971 (ISBN 0-8214-0084-3, 82-80885); Vol. 4. xxviii, 404p. 1973 (ISBN 0-8214-0115-7, 82-81180). LC 68-18389. 30.00x ea. Ohio U Pr.

--The Complete Works of Robert Browning: With Variant Readings & Annotations, Vol. V. King, Roma A., Jr., et al, eds. LC 68-18389. (Illus.). xxiv, 395p. 1981. 35.00x (ISBN 0-8214-0220-X, 82-82261). Ohio U Pr.

--Dearest Isa: Robert Browning's Letters to Isabella Blagden. McAleer, Edward C., ed. LC 76-100218. Repr. of 1951 ed. lib. bdg. 18.75x (ISBN 0-8371-3036-0, BRDI). Greenwood.

--The Pied Piper of Hamelin. (Illus.). (gr. 3 up). 1971. PLB 5.29 o.p. (ISBN 0-698-30280-X, Coward). Putnam Pub Group.

--Pied Piper of Hamelin. (gr. 2-5). 1889. 9.95 (ISBN 0-7232-0586-8). Warne.

--Poems, Eighteen Thirty-Five to Eighteen Eighty-Nine. Milford, Humphrey, ed. (World's Classics Ser.). 1954. 12.95 (ISBN 0-19-250513-0). Oxford U Pr.

--Selected Poetry of Browning. Ridenour, George, ed. pap. 3.50 (ISBN 0-451-51599-4, CE1599, Sig Classics). NAL.

--Selected Poetry of Robert Browning. Knickerbocker, K. L., ed. (YA) 1951. pap. 4.95x (ISBN 0-394-30943-X, T43, Mod LibC). Modern Lib.

Browning, Robert & Holleuffer, Carol. Roaming the Back Roads. rev. ed. LC 78-27569. (Illus.). 175p. (Orig.). 1981. pap. 6.95 (ISBN 0-87701-235-0). Chronicle Bks.

Browning, Robert M. German Baroque Poetry, Sixteen Eighteen to Seventeen Twenty-Three. LC 77-136959. 1971. 18.95x (ISBN 0-271-01146-7). Pa St U Pr.

Browning, W. R. The Gospel According to St. Luke. (Student Christian Movement Press Torch Bible Ser.). (Orig.). 1972. pap. 7.95x (ISBN 0-19-520293-7). Oxford U Pr.

Brownjohn, J. Maxwell, tr. see Gregor-Dellin, Martin.

Brownjohn, John M., jt. auth. see Braunberg, Rudolf.

Brownlee, jt. auth. see Coleman.

Brownlee, G. G. Determination of Sequences in RNA, Vol. 3, Pt. 1. (Laboratory Techniques in Biochemistry & Molecular Biology Ser.). 1973. Repr. 21.75 (ISBN 0-444-10102-0, North-Hollnd). Elsevier.

Brownlee, Kenneth A. Statistical Theory & Methodology in Science & Engineering. 2nd ed. 590p. 1965. 39.95x (ISBN 0-471-11355-7). Wiley.

Brownlee, W. D. The First Ships Around the World. LC 76-22430. (Cambridge Topic Bks). (Illus.). (gr. 5-10). 1977. PLB 6.95g (ISBN 0-8225-1204-1). Lerner Pubns.

Brownlee, Walter. The Navy That Beat Napoleon. LC 81-13733. (Cambridge Topic Bks.). (Illus.). 52p. (gr. 6 up). 1982. PLB 6.95g (ISBN 0-8225-1226-2). Lerner Pubns.

Brownleigh, Eleanora. Heirloom. 1983. pap. 3.95 (ISBN 0-8217-1200-4). Zebra.

Brownlie, G. The Pteridophyte Flora of Fiji. (Beihefte Zur Nova Hedwigia 55). 1977. lib. bdg. 80.00x (ISBN 3-7682-5455-0). Lubrecht & Cramer.

Brownlie, Ian, ed. Basic Documents of Human Rights. 2nd ed. 1981. 65.00x (ISBN 0-19-876124-4); pap. 28.95x (ISBN 0-19-876125-2). Oxford U Pr.

Brownlie, Ian, jt. ed. see Jennings, R. Y.

Brownlie, William H., ed. Basic Documents in International Law. 2nd ed. 1972. 22.00x (ISBN 0-19-876023-X); pap. 14.95x (ISBN 0-19-876024-8). Oxford U Pr.

Brownlow, Arthur H. Geochemistry. (Illus.). 1979. text ed. 30.95 (ISBN 0-13-351064-6). P-H.

Brownlow, Kevin, ed. see Brown, Karl.

Brownlow, Leroy. Today Is Mine. 5.95 o.p. (ISBN 0-686-92410-X, 6283). Hazelden.

Brownlow, Margaret. Herbs & the Fragrant Garden. 1980. 30.00x o.p. (ISBN 0-232-51396-1, Pub. by Darton-Longman-Todd England). State Mutual Bk.

Brownlow, William G. Sketches of the Rise, Progress, & Decline of Secession. 2nd ed. LC 68-23813. (American Scene Ser). 1968. Repr. of 1862 ed. 55.00 (ISBN 0-306-71137-0). Da Capo.

Brownmiller, Susan. Against Our Will. LC 75-12705. 480p. 1975. 12.95 o.p. (ISBN 0-671-22062-4). S&S.

Brownridge, Linda, jt. auth. see Thorne-Thomsen, Kathleen.

Brownrigg, Ronald. Who's Who in the New Testament. 1977. pap. 2.45 (ISBN 0-687-45352-6, Festival). Abingdon.

Brownrigg, W. G. Out of the Red: Strategies for Effective Corporate Fundraising. (Illus.). 176p. 1983. pap. 12.95 (ISBN 0-915400-43-X). Am Council Arts.

Brownsberger, Susan, tr. see Iskander, Fazil.

Brownson, Anna L., jt. auth. see Brownson, Charles.

Brownson, Anna L., jt. auth. see Brownson, Charles B.

Brownson, Anna L., ed. C. S. D. Election Index, 1982. 560p. 1982. pap. 10.00 (ISBN 0-686-97314-3). Congr Staff.

Brownson, Charles & Brownson, Anna L. Advance Locator for Capitol Hill. 19th ed. 520p. 1983. 10.00 (ISBN 0-87289-054-6). Congr Staff.

Brownson, Charles B. C. S. D. Advance Locator, 1982. 20th ed. 544p. 1982. pap. 10.00 (ISBN 0-686-97317-8). Congr Staff.

--Congressional Staff Directory, 1982. 24th ed. 1198p. 1982. 30.00 (ISBN 0-686-97320-8). Congr Staff.

--Federal Staff Directory, 1982-1983. 2nd ed. 1032p. 1982. 30.00 (ISBN 0-686-97316-X). Congr Staff.

Brownson, Charles B. & Brownson, Anna L. Congressional Staff Directory: 1983. 24th ed. 1064p. 1983. 30.00 (ISBN 0-87289-055-4). Congr Staff.

Brownson, Orestes A. The Laboring Classes. LC 78-17952. 1978. Repr. of 1840 ed. 25.00 (ISBN 0-8201-1314-X). Schol Facsimiles.

--Literary Scientific & Political Views of Oresets A. Brownson. 1893. 45.00 (ISBN 0-8414-2513-2). Folcroft.

Brownstein. Mathematics Workbook for College Entrance Examinations. rev. ed. (gr. 10-12). 1976. pap. text ed. 6.95 (ISBN 0-8120-0654-2). Barron.

Brownstein & Weiner. Barron's Basic Word List. 1984. pap. 2.50 (ISBN 0-8120-2300-5). Barron.

--Barron's How to Prepare for the College Entrance Examinations: (SAT) 11th ed. LC 80-330. 704p. (gr. 11-12). 1982. 19.00 o.p. (ISBN 0-8120-5323-0); pap. 7.95 (ISBN 0-8120-2445-1). Barron.

--Barron's How to Prepare for the Preliminary Scholastic Aptitude Test - National Merit Scholarship Q Test (PSAT - NMSQT) 5th ed. 336p. 1982. pap. 5.95 (ISBN 0-8120-2336-6). Barron.

--Barron's How to Prepare for the Preliminary Scholastic Aptitude Test - National Merit Scholarship Qalifying Test (PSAT-NMSQT) rev. ed. LC 76-22169. (gr. 10-12). 1976. pap. text ed. 4.95 o.p. (ISBN 0-8120-0633-X). Barron.

--Basic Word List. 1977. pap. 2.75 (ISBN 0-8120-0709-3). Barron.

Brownstein, A. M. U. S. Petrochemicals: Technologies, Markets & Economics. LC 77-184571. 1972. 25.50 o.p. (ISBN 0-87814-008-5). Pennwell Book Division.

Brownstein, I. & Lerner, N. Guidelines for Evaluating Software Packages. 1982. 75.00 (ISBN 0-444-00767-9). Elsevier.

Brownstein, Karen. Memorial Day. LC 82-45594. 240p. 1983. 14.95 (ISBN 0-385-18427-1). Doubleday.

Brownstein, Michael. Strange Days Ahead. LC 75-26450. (Illus.). 98p. (Orig.). 1976. pap. 5.00 (ISBN 0-915990-01-6). Z Pr.

Brownstein, Michael, ed. see Jacob, Max.

Brownstein, Rachel M. Becoming A Heroine: Reading About Women in Novels. LC 81-24021. 320p. 1982. 17.95 (ISBN 0-670-15443-1). Viking Pr.

Brownstein, Ronald & Easton, Nina, eds. Reagan's Ruling Class: Portraits of the President's Top 100 Officials. LC 82-60917. 747p. 1982. 24.50 (ISBN 0-936486-03-1). Presidential Acct.

Brownstein, S. & Weiner, M. How to Prepare for the College Entrance Examination. Rev. ed. 705p. (gr. 10-12). 1982. 21.95 (ISBN 0-8120-5448-2); pap. 7.95 (ISBN 0-8120-2445-1). Barron.

Brownstein, Samuel C. & Weiner, Mitchel. Barron's Vocabulary Builder: A Systematic Plan for Building a Vocabulary, Testing Progress & Applying Knowledge. rev. ed. LC 75-14340. (Orig.). (gr. 9-12). 1982. pap. 3.95 (ISBN 0-8120-2449-4). Barron.

--You Can Win a Scholarship. 5th ed. (gr. 10-12). Date not set. pap. text ed. cancelled o.p. (ISBN 0-8120-2073-1). Barron.

Brownstein, Weiner. Basic Tips on the SAT. rev. ed. 306p. (gr. 10-12). 1982. pap. text ed. 2.95 (ISBN 0-8120-2463-X). Barron.

Brownstone, David, ed. see Doyle, Dennis M.

Brownstone, David M. & Carruth, Gorton. Where to Find Business Information: A Worldwide Guide for Everyone Who Needs the Answers to Business Questions. 2nd ed. LC 81-16439. 632p. 1982. Set. 49.50 (ISBN 0-471-08736-X, Pub. by Wiley-Interscience). Wiley.

--Where to Find Business Information: A Worldwide Guide for Everyone Who Needs the Answers to Business Questions. LC 79-15799. 1979. 38.50 o.p. (ISBN 0-471-03919-5, Pub. by Wiley-Interscience). Wiley.

Brownstone, David M. & Sartisky, Jacques. Personal Financial Survival: A Guide for the 1980's & Beyond. LC 81-1796. 364p. 1981. 19.95 (ISBN 0-471-05588-3, Pub. by Wiley-Interscience). Wiley.

Brownstone, Meyer & Plunkett, T. J. Politics & the Reform of Local Government in Metropolitan Winnipeg. LC 81-19658. (Lane Ser. in Regional Government). 240p. 1983. 35.00x (ISBN 0-520-04197-6). U of Cal Pr.

Broxup, Marie, jt. auth. see Bennigsen, Alexandre.

Broy, M. & Schmidt, G., eds. Theoretical Foundations of Programming Methodology. 1982. lib. bdg. 78.50 (ISBN 90-277-1460-6, Pub. by Reidel Holland); pap. 39.50 (ISBN 90-277-1462-2). Kluwer Boston.

Broyles, J. E., jt. auth. see Franks, J. R.

Broyles, J. Frank & Hay, Robert D. Administration of Athletic Programs: A Managerial Approach. (Illus.). 1979. ref. ed. 23.95 (ISBN 0-13-005249-3). P-H.

Broze, Matt C. Freestyle Skiing. rev. ed. LC 76-25013. (Illus.). 1978. lib. bdg. 7.95 o.p. (ISBN 0-668-04091-2); pap. 3.95 o.p. (ISBN 0-668-04083-1). Arco.

Brozen, Yale. Concentration, Mergers & Public Policy. (Illus.). 496p. 1982. text ed. 29.95 (ISBN 0-02-904270-4). Free Pr.

--Mergers in Perspective. 1982. 14.95 (ISBN 0-8447-3489-6); pap. 6.95 (ISBN 0-8447-3483-7). Am Enterprise.

Brubacher, John S. History of the Problems of Education. 2nd ed. (Foundations in Education Ser.). 1966. text ed. 17.95 o.p. (ISBN 0-07-008542-0, C). McGraw.

--On the Philosophy of Higher Education. LC 82-48076. (Higher Education Ser.). 160p. 1982. Repr. of 1977 ed. text ed. 15.95x (ISBN 0-87589-536-0). Jossey-Bass.

Brubacher, John S. & Rudy, Willis. Higher Education in Transition: A History of American Colleges & Universities, 1636-1976. 3rd, rev. ed. LC 75-6331. 546p. 1976. 23.99xi (ISBN 0-06-010548-8, HarpT). Har-Row.

Brubacher, Lewis J., jt. auth. see Bender, Myron L.

Brubaker, Dale. Who's Teaching? Who's Learning? Active Learning in Elementary Schools. LC 77-20894. 1979. pap. text ed. 11.95x (ISBN 0-673-16152-8). Scott F.

Brubaker, Darrel J., jt. ed. see Sider, Ronald J.

Brubaker, J. Lester. Personnel Administration in the Christian School. 168p. (Orig.). 1980. pap. 6.95 (ISBN 0-88469-130-6). BMH Bks.

Brubaker, J. Omar & Clark, Robert E. Understanding People: Children, Youth, Adults. LC 75-172116. 96p. 1981. pap. text ed. 4.25 (ISBN 0-910566-15-1); Perfect bdg. instr's. guide 4.25 (ISBN 0-910566-25-9). Evang Tchr.

Brubaker, Susan H. Sourcebook for Aphasia: A Guide to Family Activities & Community Resources. 206p. 1982. pap. 12.00 (ISBN 0-8143-1697-2). Wayne St U Pr.

Brubeck, William H. The American National Interest & Middle East Peace. (Seven Springs Studies). 1981. pap. 3.00 (ISBN 0-943006-03-1). Seven Springs.

--Israelis & Palestinians: The Need for an Alliance of Moderates. (Seven Springs Studies). 43p. 1982. pap. 3.00 (ISBN 0-943006-14-7). Seven Springs.

--Reflections on the Path to Middle East Peace. (Seven Springs Studies). 1982. pap. 3.00 (ISBN 0-943006-00-7). Seven Springs.

Bruccoli, Mary, ed. Dictionary of Literary Biography Documentary Series: An Illustrated Chronicle, Vol. 3. 450p. 1983. 74.00x (ISBN 0-8103-1115-1, Pub. by K G Saur). Gale.

Bruccoli, Matthew J. James Gould Cozzens: A Life Apart. 384p. 19.95 (ISBN 0-15-146048-5). HarBraceJ.

--Profile of F. Scott Fitzgerald. LC 75-139588. 1971. pap. text ed. 3.50x (ISBN 0-675-09263-9). Merrill.

Bruccoli, Matthew J., ed. Fitzgerald-Hemingway Annual 1976. 1978. 25.00 (ISBN 0-910972-62-1). Bruccoli.

--The Great Gatsby a Facsimile of the Manuscript. 1973. deluxe ed. 100.00 boxed (ISBN 0-89723-032-9). Bruccoli.

--Kenneth Millar-Ross Macdonald: A Checklist. LC 77-39690. (Modern Authors Checklist Ser.). (Illus.). 86p. 1971. 20.00x (ISBN 0-8103-0901-7, Bruccoli Clark Book). Gale.

Bruccoli, Matthew J. & Clark, C. E., eds. Fitzgerald-Hemingway Annual 1970. 1970. 25.00 (ISBN 0-910972-03-6). Bruccoli.

Bruccoli, Matthew J. & Clark, C. E., Jr., eds. First Printings of American Authors, 4 vols. LC 74-11756. (Illus.). 1978. 72.00x (ISBN 0-8103-0933-5). Gale.

--First Printings of American Authors: Supplement, Vol. 5. (Illus.). Date not set. 72.00x (ISBN 0-8103-0934-3, Bruccoli Clark Bk). Gale.

--Fitzgerald-Hemingway Annual 1971. 1971. 25.00 (ISBN 0-910972-12-5). Bruccoli.

--Fitzgerald-Hemingway Annual 1972. 1973. 25.00 (ISBN 0-910972-12-5). Bruccoli.

Bruccoli, Matthew J. & Layman, Richard, eds. Fitzgerald-Hemingway Annual, 3 vols. Incl. 1977 Annual. 1978 (ISBN 0-8103-0909-2); 1978 Annual. 1979 (ISBN 0-8103-0910-6); 1979 Annual. 1980 (ISBN 0-8103-0911-4). LC 75-83781. (Illus.). 54.00x ea. (Bruccoli Clark). Gale.

Bruccoli, Matthew J., jt. ed. see Clark, C. E., Jr.

Bruccoli, Matthew J., ed. see Schulberg, Budd.

Bruccoli, Matthew J., et al, eds. Conversations with Jazz Musicians. LC 77-9143. (Conversations Ser.: Vol. 2). 1977. 40.00x (ISBN 0-8103-0944-0, A Bruccoli Clark Book). Gale.

--Conversations with Writers. LC 77-9142. (Conversations Ser.: Vol. 1). 1977. 40.00x (ISBN 0-8103-0943-2, Bruccoli Clark Book). Gale.

--Conversations with Writers II. LC 77-27992. (Conversations Ser.: Vol. 3). 1978. 40.00x (ISBN 0-8103-0945-9, Bruccoli Clark Book). Gale.

Bruce, jt. auth. see Bridgid.

Bruce, jt. auth. see Brudenell.

Bruce, A. B. The Epistle to the Hebrews. 1980. 17.25 (ISBN 0-86524-027-2, 5802). Klock & Klock.

--The Miracles of Christ. 1980. 20.00 (ISBN 0-86524-060-4, 9504). Klock & Klock.

--The Parables of Christ. 1980. 15.50 (ISBN 0-86524-059-0, 9503). Klock & Klock.

Bruce, A. D. & Cowley, R. A. Structural Phase Transitions. 325p. 1981. 35.00x (ISBN 0-85066-206-0, Pub by Pion England). Methuen Inc.

--Structural Phase Transitions. 326p. 1981. write for info. (ISBN 0-85066-206-0, Pub. by Taylor & Francis). Intl Pubns Serv.

Bruce, Alexander B. Training of the Twelve. LC 73-129738. 1974. 9.95 (ISBN 0-8254-2212-4); pap. 6.95 (ISBN 0-8254-2236-1). Kregel.

Bruce, Andrew A., et al. Workings of the Indeterminate-Sentence Law & the Parole System in Illinois. LC 68-19466. (Criminology, Law Enforcement, & Social Problems Ser.: No. 5). 1968. Repr. of 1928 ed. 15.00x (ISBN 0-87585-005-7). Patterson Smith.

Bruce, Colin. Social Cost-Benefit Analysis: A Guide for Country & Project Economists to the Derivation & Application of Economic & Social Accounting Prices. (Working Paper: No. 239). iii, 143p. 1976. 5.00 (ISBN 0-686-36092-3, WP-0239). World Bank.

Bruce, Colin, jt. auth. see Scanduzzo, Pasquale L.

Bruce, Colin, ed. see Pick, Albert.

Bruce, Derek A., jt. auth. see Ivan, Leslie P.

Bruce, Dickson D., Jr. The Rhetoric of Conservatism: The Virginia Convention of 1829-30 & the Conservative Tradition in the South. LC 82-9224. 218p. 1982. 18.00 (ISBN 0-87328-121-7). Huntington Lib.

Bruce, Donald. Topics of Restoration Comedy. LC 74-80652. 224p. 1974. 22.50 (ISBN 0-312-80920-4). St Martin.

Bruce, F. F. History of the Bible in English. 3rd ed. 1978. 15.95x (ISBN 0-19-520087-X). Oxford U Pr.

--History of the Bible in English. 3rd ed. 1978. pap. 6.95 (ISBN 0-19-520088-8, GB542, GB). Oxford U Pr.

--Jesus & Christian Origins Outside the New Testament. 1974. pap. 5.95 (ISBN 0-8028-1575-8). Eerdmans.

--Jesus & Paul: Places They Knew. 128p. 1983. Repr. of 1981 ed. 12.95 (ISBN 0-8407-5281-4). Nelson.

--Paul & Jesus. (Orig.). 1974. pap. 4.50 (ISBN 0-8010-0631-7). Baker Bk.

Bruce, Frederick F. The Books & the Parchments. rev. ed. (Illus.). 304p. 13.95 (ISBN 0-8007-0032-5). Revell.

Bruce, Gail C., jt. auth. see Harper, Frederick D.

Bruce, Gustav M. Luther As an Educator. LC 77-114482. (Illus.). 318p. Repr. of 1928 ed. lib. bdg. 20.50x (ISBN 0-8371-4771-9, BRLD). Greenwood.

Bruce, H. William Blake in This World. LC 73-18085. (Studies in Blake, No. 3). 1974. Repr. of 1925 ed. lib. bdg. 49.95x (ISBN 0-8383-1732-4). Haskell.

Bruce, Harold L. Voltaire on the English Stage. (Studies in Comparative Literature: No. 1). 152p. Repr. of 1918 ed. lib. bdg. 17.50x (ISBN 0-87991-500-5). Porcupine Pr.

Bruce, I. A. Historical Commentary on the Hellenica Oxyrhynchia. (Cambridge Classical Studies). 1967. 22.50 (ISBN 0-521-04352-2). Cambridge U Pr.

Bruce, J. M. Spad Scouts S7-S13. LC 77-93931. (Aircam Aviation Ser. No. 9). (Illus., Orig.). 1969. pap. 2.95 o.p. (ISBN 0-668-02110-1). Arco.

Bruce, John C. & Stokoe, John. Northumbrian Minstrelsy: A Collection of the Ballads, Melodies, & Small-Pipe Tunes of Northumbria. LC 65-4143. xxxiv, 197p. 1965. Repr. of 1882 ed. 10.00 o.p. (ISBN 0-8103-5042-4). Gale.

Bruce, Leo. Case for Sergeant Beef. 198p. 1980. 14.95 (ISBN 0-89733-037-4); pap. 4.50 (ISBN 0-89733-036-6). Academy Chi Ltd.

--Case for Three Detectives. 240p. 1980. 14.95 (ISBN 0-89733-032-3); pap. 4.50 (ISBN 0-89733-033-1). Academy Chi Ltd.

--Case with Ropes & Rings. 192p. 1980. 14.95 (ISBN 0-89733-034-X); pap. 4.50 (ISBN 0-89733-035-8). Academy Chi Ltd.

--Case Without a Corpse. (Sgt. Beef Mysteries). 284p. 1982. Repr. of 1937 ed. 14.95 (ISBN 0-89733-052-8); pap. 4.50 (ISBN 0-89733-051-X). Academy Chi Ltd.

--Cold Blood. 205p. 1980. Repr. of 1952 ed. 14.95 (ISBN 0-89733-039-0). Academy Chi Ltd.

--Neck & Neck. 224p. 1980. Repr. of 1951 ed. 14.95 (ISBN 0-89733-041-2). Academy Chi Ltd.

Bruce, Marie L. The Making of Henry VIII. (Illus.). 1977. 9.95 o.p. (ISBN 0-698-10714-4, Coward). Putnam Pub Group.

Bruce, Marjory. The Book of Craftsmen: The Story of Man's Handiwork Through the Ages. LC 70-185352. (Illus.). 283p. 1974. Repr. of 1937 ed. 34.00x (ISBN 0-8103-3960-9). Gale.

Bruce, Nigel. Teamwork for Preventive Care, Vol. 1. LC 80-41095. (Social Policy Research Monographs). 241p. 1980. 58.95 (ISBN 0-471-27883-1, Pub. by Res Stud Pr). Wiley.

Bruce, Peter H. Memoirs of Peter Henry Bruce: A Military Officer in the Services of Prussia, Russia, & Great Britian. (Russia Through European Eyes Ser). 1970. Repr. of 1782 ed. 59.50 (ISBN 0-306-77029-6). Da Capo.

Bruce, Phillip & Pederson, Sam. The Software Development Project: Planning & Management. LC 81-10457. 210p. 1982. 22.50x (ISBN 0-471-06269-3, Pub. by Wiley-Interscience). Wiley.

Bruce, Preston. From the Door of the White House. LC 81-23672. (Illus.). 160p. (gr. 6 up). 1983. 10.00 (ISBN 0-688-00883-6). Lothrop.

Bruce, Robert. Software Debugging for Microcomputers. (Illus.). 1980. text ed. 20.95 (ISBN 0-8359-7021-3); pap. text ed. 14.95 (ISBN 0-8359-7020-5). Reston.

Bruce, Robert V. Lincoln & the Tools of War. LC 73-15241. (Illus.). 368p. 1974. Repr. of 1956 ed. lib. bdg. 19.00x (ISBN 0-8371-7167-9, BRLS). Greenwood.

Bruce-Briggs, B., et al. The Politics of Planning: A Review & Critique of Centralized Economic Planning. LC 76-7714. (Illus.). 1976. pap. 5.95 o.p. (ISBN 0-917616-05-7). ICS Pr.

Bruce-Mitford, R. L., tr. see Glob, P. V.

Bruce-Novoa. Chicano Poetry: A Response to Chaos. 246p. 1982. text ed. 25.00x (ISBN 0-292-71075-5). U of Tex Pr.

Bruch, Catherine B., jt. auth. see Gowan, John C.

Bruch, Charles D. Mechanics for Technology. LC 75-31719. 386p. 1976. text ed. 24.95x (ISBN 0-471-11369-7). Wiley.

--Strength of Materials for Technology. LC 77-27629. 376p. 1978. text ed. 24.95x (ISBN 0-471-11372-7); solutions manual avail. (ISBN 0-471-04513-6). Wiley.

Bruchac, Joseph. Indian Mountain & Other Poems. 1971. 2.95 o.p. (ISBN 0-87886-010-X). Ithaca Hse.

--Stone Giants & Flying Heads, Adventure Stories from the Iroquois. LC 78-15556. (Children's Stories Ser.). (Illus.). (gr. 5-12). 1979. 9.95 (ISBN 0-89594-006-X); pap. 3.95 (ISBN 0-89594-007-8). Crossing Pr.

Bruchac, Joseph, ed. The Next World: Poems by Third World Americans. LC 78-1923. 1978. 18.95 (ISBN 0-89594-008-6); pap. 8.95 (ISBN 0-89594-009-4). Crossing Pr.

Bruchey, Stuart. Roots of American Economic Growth, 1607-1861: An Essay in Social Causation. 1968. pap. 4.50xi o.p. (ISBN 0-06-131350-5, TB1350, Torch). Har-Row.

Bruchey, Stuart, jt. ed. see Hull, Walter.

Bruchey, Stuart, ed. see Preston, Howard H.

Bruchey, Stuart, ed. see Scott, William A.

Bruchey, Stuart, ed. see Wright, Benjamin C.

Bruchis, Michael. One Step Back, Two Steps Forward: On the Language Policy of the Communist Party of the Soviet Union in the National Republics. (East European Monographs: No. 109). 320p. 1982. 25.00x (ISBN 0-88033-002-3). East Eur Quarterly.

Bruck. Capital Markets under Inflation. 456p. 1982. 29.95 (ISBN 0-03-063249-8). Praeger.

Bruck & Corke, eds. Who's Who in Latin America: Government & Politics. 300p. (Span. & Eng.). 1983. 65.00 (ISBN 0-910365-02-4). Decade Media.

Bruck, Axel. Practical Close-Up Photography. (Practical Ser.). (Illus.). write for info. (ISBN 0-240-51190-5). Focal Pr.

--Practical Composition in Photography. LC 80-40759. (Practical Photography Ser.). (Illus.). 164p. 1981. 19.95 (ISBN 0-240-51060-7). Focal Pr.

--Practical Landscape Photography. (Practical Ser.). (Illus.). 1983. write for info. (ISBN 0-240-51080-1). Focal Pr.

Bruck, Charlott M. Discovery Through Guidance, Group Guidancefor Elementary Schools: Search. 1969. pap. text ed. 2.48 o.p. (ISBN 0-02-811720-4); teachers manual 3.52 o.p. (ISBN 0-02-811730-1). Glencoe.

--Discovery Through Guidance, Group Guidance for Elementary Schools: Alive Student Activity Book. 1971. pap. 2.48 o.p. (ISBN 0-02-811810-3); teachers guide 3.52 o.p. (ISBN 0-685-65901-1). Glencoe.

--Discovery Through Guidance, Group Guidance for Elementary Schools: Build. 1969. pap. text ed. 2.48 o.p. (ISBN 0-02-811770-0); teachers manual 3.52 o.p. (ISBN 0-02-811780-8). Glencoe.

--Discovery Through Guidance, Group Guidance for Elementary Schools: Quest. 1968. pap. text ed. 2.48 o.p. (ISBN 0-02-811740-9); teacher's manual 3.52 o.p. (ISBN 0-02-811760-3). Glencoe.

Bruck, Charlotte M. Discovery Through Guidance, Group Guidance for Elementary Schools: Focus. 1968. pap. text ed. 2.48 o.p. (ISBN 0-02-812000-0); teachers' manual 3.52 o.p. (ISBN 0-02-812020-5). Glencoe.

Bruck, Nicholas, ed. Mercados de Capitales Bajo Inflacion. (Illus.). 496p. 1982. 24.95 (ISBN 0-910365-00-8). Decade Media.

Bruck, P. & Karrer, W., eds. The Afro-American Novel Since Nineteen Sixty. 325p. 1982. pap. text ed. 27.75x (ISBN 90-6032-219-3, Pub. by B R Gruner Netherlands). Humanities.

Bruckberger, R. L. God & Politics. LC 78-190754. (Howard Greenfield Bk.). 1971. 7.95 (ISBN 0-87955-302-2). O'Hara.

Brucker, Gene A. Renaissance Florence. LC 74-10921. 320p. 1975. Repr. of 1969 ed. lib. bdg. 16.50 (ISBN 0-88275-184-0). Krieger.

--Renaissance Florence. (New Dimensions in History-Historical Cities Ser.). 306p. 1969. pap. text ed. 14.50 (ISBN 0-471-11371-9). Wiley.

--Renaissance Florence. rev. ed. LC 82-40097. (Illus.). 320p. 1983. text ed. 25.00x (ISBN 0-520-04919-5); pap. 7.95x (ISBN 0-520-04695-1). U of Cal Pr.

Brucker, Herbert. Communication Is Power: Unchanging Values in a Changing Journalism. 1973. 16.95 (ISBN 0-19-501599-1). Oxford U Pr.

Brucker, Meredith B., ed. One Love Forever. 1978. pap. 1.25 o.s.i. (ISBN 0-440-19302-8). Dell.

Brucker, Roger & Murray, Robert. Trapped! (Illus.). 1979. 12.50 o.p. (ISBN 0-399-12373-3). Putnam Pub Group.

Brucker, Roger W., jt. auth. see Murray, Robert K.

Bruckner, Christine. Flight of Cranes. Hein, Ruth, tr. from Ger. LC 81-22176. Orig. Title: Nirgendwo ist Poenichen. 372p. 1982. 14.95 (ISBN 0-88064-001-4). Fromm Intl Pub.

--Gillyflower Kid. Hein, Ruth, tr. from Ger. LC 82-13531. Orig. Title: Jauche und Levkojen. 360p. 1982. 14.95 (ISBN 0-88064-006-5). Fromm Intl Pub.

Bruckner, Matilda T. Narrative Invention in Twelfth-Century French Romance: The Convention of Hospitality (1160-1200) LC 79-53400. (French Forum Monographs: No. 17). 232p. 1980. pap. 12.50x (ISBN 0-917058-16-X). French Forum.

Bruckner, Steven, jt. auth. see Bergman, Samuel.

Bruckner-Bigenwald, Martha. Die Anfange der Liepzieger Allgemeinen Musiualischen Zeitung. 1965. Repr. of 1938 ed. wrappers 20.00 o.s.i. (ISBN 90-6027-018-5, Pub. by Frits Knuf Netherlands). Pendragon NY.

Brucknet, A. P. & Hertzberg, A. High Temperature Integrated Thermal Energy Storage for Solar Thermal Applications. (Progress in Solar Energy Ser.: Suppl.). 115p. 1983. pap. text ed. 13.00x (ISBN 0-89553-135-6). Am Solar Energy.

Brudenell & Bruce. The Birds of New Province & the Bahama Islands. 19.95 (ISBN 0-686-42758-0, Collins Pub England). Greene.

Bruder, Roy. Discovering Natural Foods. LC 82-2705. (Illus.). 288p. (Orig.). 1982. pap. 7.95 (ISBN 0-912800-86-0). Woodbridge Pr.

Brudigan, Nancy A. Training of Caged Birds. (Illus.). 96p. 1982. 8.95 (ISBN 0-87666-827-9, PS-788). TFH Pubns.

Brudney, Victor & Chirelstein, Marvin A. Cases & Materials in Corporate Finance, 1982: New Developments Supplement. 2nd ed. (University Casebook Ser.). 154p. 1982. pap. text ed. write for info. (ISBN 0-88277-094-2). Foundation Pr.

Brue, Stanley L. & Wentworth, Donald R. Economic Scenes: Theory in Today's World. 2nd ed. (Illus.). 1980. text ed. 15.95 (ISBN 0-13-233510-7). P-H.

Bruegel, J. W. Czechoslovakia Before Munich: The German Minority Problem & British Appeasement Policy. 47.50 (ISBN 0-521-08687-6). Cambridge U Pr.

Brueggemann, Doris. From Life to Life. 1971. pap. 0.95 (ISBN 0-8100-0063-6, 16N1619). Northwest Pub.

Brueggemann, Walter. The Bible Makes Sense. LC 76-29883. 1977. pap. 4.95 (ISBN 0-88489-087-2). St Mary's.

--Kings I. (Knox Preaching Guide Ser.). 132p. 1983. pap. 4.95 (ISBN 0-8042-3212-1). John Knox.

--Living Toward a Vision: Biblical Reflections on Shalom. rev. ed. LC 76-22172. (Shalom Resource Ser.). 1982. pap. 6.95 (ISBN 0-8298-0613-X). Pilgrim NY.

Brueggemann, Walter & Wolff, Hans W. The Vitality Old Testament Traditions. 2nd ed. LC 82-7141. pap. 6.95 (ISBN 0-8042-0112-9). John Knox.

Brueggemann, Walter, ed. see Zimmerli, Walther.

Bruel, J. M., jt. auth. see Lammarque, J. L.

Bruell, Steven C., jt. auth. see Schneider, Michael G.

Bruemmer, S. Suzanne, jt. auth. see Tiedt, Iris M.

Bruening, William H. Introduction to the Philosophy of Law. LC 78-62249. 1978. pap. text ed. 9.75 (ISBN 0-8191-0570-8). U Pr of Amer.

--The Is-Ought Problem: Its History, Analysis, & Dissolution. LC 77-18569. 1978. pap. text ed. 9.50 (ISBN 0-8191-0364-0). U Pr of Amer.

--Wittgenstein. 1977. pap. text ed. 9.75 (ISBN 0-8191-0289-X). U Pr of Amer.

Bruening, William H., jt. ed. see Durland, William R.

Brues, Alice M. People & Races. 1977. 14.95x (ISBN 0-02-315670-8, 31567). Macmillan.

Bruess, Clint E. & Gay, John E. Implementing Comprehensive School Health. (Illus.). 1978. text ed. 18.95 (ISBN 0-02-315690-2). Macmillan.

Bruette, William A. & Donnelly, Kerry V. The Original Complete Dog Book. (Illus.). 1979. 8.95 (ISBN 0-87666-667-5, H-989). TFH Pubns.

Bruffee, Kenneth A. A Short Course in Writing. 2nd ed. 1980. pap. text ed. 10.95 (ISBN 0-316-11241-0). Little.

Bruford, Walter H. Germany in the Eighteenth Century. 1935. 44.50 (ISBN 0-521-04354-9); pap. 13.95 (ISBN 0-521-09259-0, 259). Cambridge U Pr.

Brugel, W., ed. Handbook of NMR Spectral Parameters, 3 vols. casebound set 546.00 (ISBN 0-471-25617-X, Pub. by Wiley Heyden). Wiley.

Bruggee, David M. & Frisbie, Charlotte J., eds. Navajo Religion & Culture: Selected Views Papers in Honor of Leland C. Wyman. (Orig.). 1982. pap. text ed. 14.95 (ISBN 0-89013-138-4). Museum NM Pr.

Bruggeling, Ir A. Prestressed Concrete for the Storage of Liquefied Gas. Van Amerongen, C., tr. from Dutch. (Viewpoint Ser.). (Illus.). 111p. 1981. pap. text ed. 47.50x (ISBN 0-7210-1187-X, Pub. by C & CA London). Scholium Intl.

Bruggen, Theodore Van see Van Bruggen, Theodore.

Bruggencate, K. Ten. Dutch-English, English-Dutch Dictionary, 2 vols. Set. 50.00 (ISBN 9-0019-6819-8). Dutch-Eng. Eng.-Dutch (ISBN 90-01-96818-X). Heinman.

Bruggenwert, M. G., jt. auth. see Bolt, G. H.

Brugger, Bill, ed. China Since the Gang of Four. LC 80-10251. 288p. 1980. 30.00 (ISBN 0-312-13323-5). St Martin.

Brugger, W. Democracy & Organization in the Chinese Industrial Enterprise: 1948-1953. LC 75-9284. (Contemporary China Institute Publications Ser.). (Illus.). 300p. 1975. 49.50 (ISBN 0-521-20790-8). Cambridge U Pr.

Brugmans, Linette F., ed. see Gide, Andre & Gosse, Edmund.

Brugnoli, Maria V., ed. see Michelangelo.

Bruguera, Miquel, et al. Atlas of Laparoscopy & Biopsy of the Liver. Galambos, Joht T. & Jinich, Horacio, trs. LC 78-64703. (Illus.). 1979. text ed. 60.00 o.p. (ISBN 0-7216-2182-1). Saunders.

Bruhn, W. & Tilke, M. A Pictorial History of Costume. 1976. 67.50 o.s.i. (ISBN 0-8038-5801-9). Hastings.

Bruhns. New Manual of Logarithms. 634p. 1941. 17.50 (ISBN 0-442-01145-8, Pub. by Van Nos Reinhold). Krieger.

Bruin, A. De see De Bruin, A.

Bruins, Elton J. Americanization of a Congregation. LC 63-11498. pap. 3.95 (ISBN 0-8028-1330-5). Eerdmans.

Bruins, Paul F., ed. Packaging with Plastics. new ed. LC 72-78922. 220p. 1974. 42.00x (ISBN 0-677-12200-4). Gordon.

--Polyurethane Technology. LC 68-54598. (Polymer Engineering & Technology Ser.). 1969. 44.50x (ISBN 0-471-11395-6, Pub by Wiley-Interscience). Wiley.

Bruinsma, Sheryl. Easy-to-Use Object Lessons. (Object Lesson Ser.). 96p. (Orig.). 1983. pap. 3.95 (ISBN 0-8010-0832-8). Baker Bk.

Brukner, Ira. Hardon. LC 80-18377. (Illus.). 1980. cloth 13.00 (ISBN 0-916906-30-2); pap. 7.50 (ISBN 0-686-86245-7). Konglomerati.

Bruley, Duane F., jt. ed. see Bicherx, Haim I.

Brulin, O. & Hsieh, R. K., eds. Continuum Models of Discrete Systems. 1981. 72.50 (ISBN 0-444-86309-5). Elsevier.

Brumat, ed. see CEDEP-INSEAD Conference, Jun. 1976.

Brumbaugh, J. Frank. Mail Order Make Easy. Date not set. pap. 10.00 (ISBN 0-87980-394-0). Wilshire.

Brumbaugh, James. UPholstering. new ed. (Audel Ser.). 1983. 12.95 (ISBN 0-672-23372-X). Bobbs.

Brumbaugh, Robert S. The Philosophers of Greece. LC 81-9120. (Illus.). 274p. 1981. 27.50x (ISBN 0-87395-550-1); pap. 8.95x (ISBN 0-87395-551-X). State U NY Pr.

--Whitehead, Process Philosophy, & Education. LC 81-14329. 144p. 1982. 30.50x (ISBN 0-87395-574-9); pap. 9.95x (ISBN 0-87395-575-7). State U NY Pr.

Brumbaugh, Robert S., jt. auth. see Stallknecht, Newton P.

Brumberg, Abraham, ed. Poland: Genesis of a Revolution. LC 82-40137. 320p. 1982. pap. 7.95 (ISBN 0-394-71025-8). Random.

Brumblay, Ray U. Quantitative Analysis. 2nd ed. (Orig.). 1972. pap. 4.95 (ISBN 0-06-460050-5, CO 50, COS). B&N NY.

Brumfiel, Charles & Krause, Eugene. Mathematics I & II: Grade 8 Mathematics, 2 bks. 1974. Bk. 1. text ed. cancelled o.p. (ISBN 0-201-00603-0, Sch Div); Bk. 2. text ed. cancelled o.p. (ISBN 0-201-00605-7); Bk. 1. cancelled tchr's. ed. o.p. (ISBN 0-201-00604-9); Bk. 2. cancelled tchr's. ed. o.p. (ISBN 0-201-00606-5). A-W.

Brumfield, Gregory W. Partially Ordered Rings & Semi-Algebraic Geometry. (London Mathematical Society Lecture Note Ser.: No. 37). 1980. pap. 25.95x (ISBN 0-521-22845-X). Cambridge U Pr.

Brumfield, J. C. Comfort for Troubled Christians. (Moody Acorn Ser.). 1975. pap. 5.95 package of 10 (ISBN 0-8024-1400-1). Moody.

Brumfield, William C. Gold in Azure. (Illus.). 290p. 1983. 60.00 (ISBN 0-87923-436-9). Godine.

Brumfit, Christopher, jt. auth. see Finocchiaro, Mary.

Brumgardt, John R., ed. Civil War Nurse: The Diary & Letters of Hannah Ropes. LC 79-28372. 200p. 1980. 13.50x (ISBN 0-87049-280-2). U of Tenn Pr.

Brumlik, Joel & Chong-Bun Yap. Normal Tremor: A Comparative Study. (Illus.). 112p. 1970. photocopy ed. spiral 14.50x (ISBN 0-398-00244-4). C C Thomas.

Brumlik, Joel, jt. auth. see Cohen, Hyman L.

Brumm, Barbara. Marxismus und Realismus Am Beispiel Balzac. 153p. (Ger.). 1982. write for info. (ISBN 3-8204-5784-4). P Lang Pubs.

Brummett, Wyatt. Photography Is... 2nd ed. (Illus.). 1977. 12.95 o.p. (ISBN 0-8174-2428-8, Amphoto). Watson-Guptill.

Brummitt, Wyatt. Kites. (Golden Guide Ser). (Illus.). 1971. PLB 11.54 (ISBN 0-307-24344-3, 64344, Golden Pr); pap. 1.95 (ISBN 0-686-76849-3). Western Pub.

Brun & Olsen. Atlas of Renal Biopsy. (Illus.). 266p. 1981. text ed. 40.00 (ISBN 0-7216-2164-3). Saunders.

Brun, Kim, ed. see Federico, Pat A., et al.

Bruna, Dick. Another Story to Tell. LC 77-17742. (Bruna Books). (Illus.). 1976. 3.50 (ISBN 0-416-30241-6). Methuen Inc.

--The Apple. (Bruna Books). (Illus.). 28p. (ps-2). 1965. 3.50 (ISBN 0-416-30381-1). Methuen Inc.

--The Circus. (Bruna Books). (Illus.). 28p. (ps-2). 1963. 3.50 (ISBN 0-416-30361-7). Methuen Inc.

--The Egg. (Bruna Books). (Illus.). 28p. (ps-2). 1964. 3.50 (ISBN 0-416-30351-X). Methuen Inc.

--Poppy Pig's Garden. (Bruna Bks). 1982. 3.50 (ISBN 0-416-86430-9). Methuen Inc.

--Word Book. (Bruna Bks.). 1982. 5.50 (ISBN 0-416-21560-2). Methuen Inc.

Brundage, Burr C. The Phoenix of the Western World: Quetzalcoatl & the Sky Religion. LC 81-40278. (The Civilization of the American Indian Ser.: Vol. 160). (Illus.). 320p. 1982. 19.50 (ISBN 0-8061-1773-7). U of Okla Pr.

--Two Earths, Two Heavens: An Essay Contrasting the Aztecs & the Incas. LC 75-17372. 128p. 1975. 7.95x o.p. (ISBN 0-8263-0392-7). U of NM Pr.

Brundage, Dorothy J. Nursing Management of Renal Problems. LC 75-22149. (Illus.). 204p. 1976. pap. text ed. 13.95 o.p. (ISBN 0-8016-0850-3). Mosby.

Brundage, James, jt. ed. see Bullough, Vern.

Brundage, James A. Crusades: A Documentary Survey. 1962. 14.95 (ISBN 0-87462-423-1). Marquette.

Brundage, James A., ed. Medieval Canon Law & the Crusader. Brundage, James A., tr. 1969. 17.50 o.p. (ISBN 0-299-05480-2). U of Wis Pr.

Brundage, Percival F. Changing Concepts of Business Income. LC 75-21163. 1975. Repr. of 1952 ed. text ed. 13.00 (ISBN 0-914348-18-3). Scholars Bk.

Brundenius, Claes. Revolutionary Cuba: Economic Growth, Income Distribution, & Basic Needs. (WVSS on Latin America & the Caribbean). 160p. 1983. lib. bdg. 30.00 (ISBN 0-86531-355-5). Westview.

Brundin, C. L. see Von Mises, Richard & Von Karman, Theodore.

Brundza, Paul, jt. auth. see Starck, Walter A.

Brune, K., jt. ed. see Rainsford, K. D.

Bruneau, T. C. The Political Transformation of the Brazilian Catholic Church. LC 73-79318. (Perspectives on Development Ser.: No. 2). 302p. 1974. 47.50 (ISBN 0-521-20256-6); pap. 13.95 (ISBN 0-521-09848-3). Cambridge U Pr.

Bruneau, Thomas C. & Faucher, Philippe. Authoritarian Capitalism: Brazil's Contemporary Economic & Political Development. (A Westview Special Study). 225p. 1981. lib. bdg. 27.00 (ISBN 0-86531-220-6); pap. 12.50 (ISBN 0-86531-284-2). Westview.

Brunell, Lillian F. & Young, Wayne D. Multimodal Handbook for a Mental Hospital: Designing Specific Treatments for Specific Problems. (Springer Series on Behavior Therapy & Behavioral Medicine: Vol. 7). 383p. 1982. text ed. 34.95 (ISBN 0-8261-3700-8). Springer Pub.

Brunelle, Jim, ed. see Clark, William.

Brunelli, B. Driven Magnetic Fusion Reactors: Proceedings. (Commission of the European Communities Ser.: EUR 6146). (Illus.). 1979. pap. 88.00 (ISBN 0-08-024459-9). Pergamon.

Bruner, Edward M. & Becker, Judith O., eds. Art, Ritual & Society in Indonesia. LC 79-11667. (Papers in International Studies: Southeast Asia: No. 53). (Orig.). 1979. pap. 13.00 (ISBN 0-89680-080-6, Ohio U Ctr Intl). Ohio U Pr.

Bruner, Jerome S. The Relevance of Education. LC 74-139376. 192p. 1971. 5.95x (ISBN 0-393-04334-7, Norton Lib.); pap. 4.95x (ISBN 0-393-00690-5, Norton Lib). Norton.

Bruner, Jerome S. & Krech, David, eds. Perception & Personality: A Symposium. LC 68-21325. (Illus.). 1968. Repr. of 1950 ed. lib. bdg. 17.25x (ISBN 0-8371-0031-3, BRPP). Greenwood.

Brunet, Jacques, ed. Oriental Music: A Selected Discography. (Occasional Publication). 1971. pap. 3.00 o.p. (ISBN 0-89192-148-6). Interbk Inc.

Brunetti, Mendor T., tr. see Verne, Jules.

Brungardt, Terrence, jt. auth. see Arnold, William.

Brunhammer, Yvonne. Art Deco Style. LC 80-51498. (Illus.). 176p. 1983. pap. 19.95 (ISBN 0-8478-0332-5). Rizzoli Intl.

Brunhoff, Jean De see De Brunhoff, Jean.

Brunhoff, Laurent De see De Brunhoff, Laurent.

Brunhoff, Laurent de see De Brunhoff, Laurent.

Brunhoff, Laurent De see De Brunhoff, Laurent.

Brunhoff, Laurent De see De Brunhoff, Sean & De Brunhoff, Laurent.

Brunhoff, Sean de see De Brunhoff, Sean & De Brunhoff, Laurent.

Bruni, J. Edward, jt. auth. see Montemurro, Donald G.

Bruni, Joseph, jt. auth. see Wilder, B. Joseph.

Bruning, James L. & Kintz, B. L. Computational Handbook of Statistics. 2nd ed. 1977. pap. 16.95x (ISBN 0-673-15014-3). Scott F.

Bruning, Nancy P., jt. auth. see Katz, Jane.

Bruning, Ted & Paulin, Keith. The David & Charles Book of Historic English Inns. (Illus.). 256p. 1982. 23.95 (ISBN 0-7153-8178-4). David & Charles.

Brunk, Gregory G., ed. World Countermarks on Medieval & Modern Coins. LC 75-39496. (Gleanings from the Numismatist Ser.: Vol. 8). (Illus.). 1976. 30.00x o.p. (ISBN 0-88000-074-0). Quarterman.

Brunk, H. D. Introduction to Mathematical Statistics. 3rd ed. LC 74-82348. 400p. 1975. text ed. 27.50 (ISBN 0-471-00834-6). Wiley.

Brunk, J. D., ed. Church & Sunday School Hymnal with Supplement. (532 hymns & songs, & 50 german songs, words only, 1902; supplement 1911). 1902. 6.95x (ISBN 0-8361-1110-9). Herald Pr.

Brunk, M. J. Fulfilled Prophecies. 160p. 6.00 (ISBN 0-686-05601-9). Rod & Staff.

Brunke, Ottillie. O.E.S. Floor Work. 18p. 1977. Repr. of 1960 ed. pap. 1.25 (ISBN 0-88053-331-5, S-241). Macoy Pub.

Brunkow, Robert, ed. Religion & Society in North America: An Annotated Bibliography. (Clio Bibliography Ser.: No. 12). 514p. 1983. lib. bdg. 60.00 (ISBN 0-87436-042-0). ABC-Clio.

Brunn, H. H. Science, Value & Politics in Max Webers Methodology. 1972. pap. text ed. 12.50x o.p. (ISBN 87-16009-93-2). Humanities.

Brunn, H. O. The Story of the Original Dixieland Jazz Band. LC 77-3791. (Roots of Jazz Ser.). (Illus.). 1977. Repr. of 1960 ed. lib. bdg. 27.50 (ISBN 0-306-70892-2). Da Capo.

Brunn, Robert. The Initiation. (Twilight Ser.). (gr. 5 up). 1982. pap. 1.95 (ISBN 0-440-94047-8, LFL). Dell.

Brunn, Stanley & Williams, Jack. Cities of the World: World Regional Urban Development. 506p. 1983. pap. text ed. 18.95 scp (ISBN 0-06-381225-8, HarpC). Har-Row.

Brunn, Stanley D. & Wheeler, James O. The American Metropolitan Systems: Present & Future. LC 80-36824. (Scripta Series in Geography). 216p. 1980. 29.95x o.p. (ISBN 0-470-27018-7, Pub. by Halsted Pr). Wiley.

Brunn, Stanley D., jt. auth. see Harries, Keith D.

Brunner & Suddarth. Lippincott Manual of Medical Surgical Nursing, Vol. 1. 512p. 1982. pap. text ed. 15.50 (ISBN 0-06-318207-6, Pub. by Har-Row Ltd England). Har-Row.

--Lippincott Manual of Medical Surgical Nursing, Vol. 2. 512p. 1982. pap. text ed. 18.50 (ISBN 0-06-318208-4, Pub. by Har-Row Ltd England). Har-Row.

--Lippincott Manual of Medical Surgical Nursing, Vol. 3. 512p. 1982. pap. text ed. 15.50 (ISBN 0-06-318209-2, Pub. by Har-Row Ltd England). Har-Row.

Brunner, Calvin. Incineration Systems Course Notebook. 411p. 1982. Wkbk. 85.00 (ISBN 0-86587-111-6). Gov Insts.

Brunner, Edmund & Kolb, John H. Rural Social Trends. LC 70-98825. Repr. of 1933 ed. lib. bdg. 20.75x (ISBN 0-8371-2889-7, BRRS). Greenwood.

Brunner, Emil. The Christian Doctrine of God. Wyon, Olive, tr. LC 50-6821. (Dogmatics Ser.: Vol. 1). 1980. soft cover 9.95 (ISBN 0-664-24304-5). Westminster.

--The Christian Doctrine of the Church Faith & the Consummation. LC 50-6821. (Dogmatic Ser., Vol. 3). 1978. softcover 9.95 (ISBN 0-664-24218-9). Westminster.

--The Divine-Human Encounter. Loos, Amandus W., tr. from Ger. 207p. 1980. Repr. of 1943 ed. lib. bdg. 19.00x (ISBN 0-313-22398-X, BRDH). Greenwood.

Brunner, Francis A., tr. see Fellerer, Karl G.

Brunner, Gerhard. Aquarium Plants. Vevers, Gwynne, tr. from Ger. 1973. pap. 6.95 o.p. (ISBN 0-87666-026-X, PS-692). TFH Pubns.

Brunner, Heinrich. Cuban Sugar Policy from 1963 to 1970. Borchardt, Marguerite & Broch De Rothermann, H. F., trs. LC 76-50883. (Pitt Latin American Ser.). 1977. 9.95x o.p. (ISBN 0-8229-3342-X). U of Pittsburgh Pr.

Brunner, Heinrich E. Eternal Hope. Knight, Harold, tr. LC 72-6930. 232p. 1973. Repr. of 1954 ed. lib. bdg. 20.50x (ISBN 0-8371-6508-3, BREH). Greenwood.

Brunner, Herb. Introduction to Microprocessors. 1982. text ed. 23.95 (ISBN 0-8359-3247-8); instr's. manual free (ISBN 0-8359-3248-6). Reston.

Brunner, John. The Avengers of Carrig. (Science Fiction Ser.). 1980. pap. 1.75 o.p. (ISBN 0-87997-509-1, UE1509). DAW Bks.

--The Dramaturges of Yan. 208p. 1982. pap. 2.50 (ISBN 0-345-30677-5, Del Rey). Ballantine.

--Foreign Constellations. LC 79-92183. 1980. 8.95x (ISBN 0-89696-094-3, An Everest House Book). Dodd.

--Galactic Bodies, Strange Stars: The Fantastic Worlds of John Brunner. Date not set. 8.95 o.p. (ISBN 0-89696-094-3, An Everest House Book). Dodd.

--The Great Steamboat Race. LC 82-90222. (Illus.). 592p. 1983. pap. 7.95 (ISBN 0-345-25853-3). Ballantine.

--Interstellar Empire. (Science Fiction Ser.). 1978. pap. 2.50 (ISBN 0-87997-668-3, UE1668). DAW Bks.

--Times Without Number. 224p. 1983. pap. 2.50 (ISBN 0-345-30679-1, Del Rey). Ballantine.

--To Conquer Chaos. 1981. pap. 1.95 (ISBN 0-87997-596-2, UJ1596). DAW Bks.

--The Webs of Everywhere. 192p. 1983. pap. 2.25 (ISBN 0-345-30680-5, Del Rey). Ballantine.

Brunner, Joseph F. & Campbell, John J. Participating in Secondary Reading: A Practical Approach. (Illus.). 1978. ref. 22.95 (ISBN 0-13-651323-9). P-H.

Brunner, K. & Meltzer, A. International Organization, National Policies & Economic Development. (Carnegie-Rochester Conference Ser. on Public Policy: Vol. 6). 1977. 18.75 (ISBN 0-7204-0744-3, North-Holland). Elsevier.

Brunner, K. & Meltzer, A. H., eds. The Problem of Inflation. (Carnegie-Rochester Conference Ser. on Public Policy: Vol. 8). 1978. pap. 32.00 (ISBN 0-444-85147-X, North-Holland). Elsevier.

--Public Policies in Open Economies. (Carnegie-Rochester Conference on Public Policy Ser.: Vol. 9). 1978. 23.25 (ISBN 0-444-85213-1, North Holland). Elsevier.

--Three Aspects of Policy & Policy-Making: Knowledge, Data & Institutions. LC 79-12445. (Carnegie-Rochester Conference Ser. on Public Policy: Vol. 10). 362p. 1979. 27.75 (ISBN 0-444-85331-6, North Holland). Elsevier.

Brunner, K. & Metlyer, A. H., eds. Policies for Employment, Prices, & Exchange Rates. (Carnegie-Rochester Conference Ser. on Public Policy: Vol. 11). 252p. 1979. 19.75 (ISBN 0-444-85392-8). Elsevier.

Brunner, Karl & Meltzer, A. H., eds. Institutional Policies & Economic Performance. (Carnegie-Rochester Conference Series on Public Policy: Vol. 4). 1976. pap. text ed. 23.50 (ISBN 0-7204-0564-5, North-Holland). Elsevier.

Brunner, Lillian & Suddarth, Doris. The Lippincott Manual of Nursing Practice. 3rd ed. text ed. 37.50 (ISBN 0-397-54352-2, Lippincott Nursing). Lippincott.

Brunner, Nancy A. Orthopedic Nursing: A Programmed Approach. 4th ed. (Illus.). 288p. 1983. spiral 14.95 (ISBN 0-8016-0839-2). Mosby.

Bruno. Haircutting the Professional Way. (Everyday Handbook Ser.). pap. 2.95 (ISBN 0-06-463459-0, EH 459, EH). B&N NY.

Bruno, Angela & Jessie, Karen. Hands-On Activities for Children's Writing. (Illus.). 256p. 1983. pap. 14.95 (ISBN 0-13-383596-0). P-H.

Bruno, Carole. Paralegal's Litigation Handbook. LC 79-19960. 544p. 1980. 45.00 (ISBN 0-87624-425-8). Inst Busn Plan.

Bruno, E. J., ed. High-Velocity Forming of Metals. rev. ed. LC 68-23027. (Manufacturing Data Ser.). 1968. pap. 10.75 (ISBN 0-87263-009-9). SME.

Bruno, Frank J. Adjustment & Personal Growth: Seven Pathways. 2nd ed. LC 82-8520. 466p. 1983. text ed. 22.95 (ISBN 0-471-09296-7); tchr's manual 20.00 (ISBN 0-471-87195-8). Wiley.

--Behavior & Life: An Introduction to Psychology. 660p. 1980. text ed. 21.95 (ISBN 0-471-02191-1); study guide 8.95 (ISBN 0-471-06340-1). Wiley.

--Human Adjustment & Personal Growth: Seven Pathways. Vol. 1. LC 76-54654. 499p. 1977. text ed. 21.95 (ISBN 0-471-11435-9). Wiley.

--Think Yourself Thin. 272p. 1975. pap. 4.95 (ISBN 0-06-465025-1, EH 348, EH). B&N NY.

--Think Yourself Thin. (PBN Ser.). 265p. 1974. pap. 2.25 (ISBN 0-06-465024-3, 5024). B&N NY.

Bruno, Giordano. Cause, Principle & Unity: Five Dialogues. Lindsay, Jack, tr. LC 76-28448. 1976. Repr. of 1962 ed. lib. bdg. 17.00x (ISBN 0-8371-9040-1, BRCP). Greenwood.

Brunoff, Laurent De see De Brunoff, Laurent.

Brunori, M., jt. auth. see Antonini, E.

Bruns, Bill, jt. auth. see Sorenson, Jacki.

Brunskill, R. W. Vernacular Architecture of the Lake Countries: A Field Handbook. 1974. 16.95 o.p. (ISBN 0-571-09460-0). Faber & Faber.

Brunson, Marion B. Our Bailey & Staggers History & Genealogy. 1980. 10.00 o.p. (ISBN 0-916620-51-4). Portals Pr.

--Pea River Reflections. LC 74-28559. (Illus.). 1975. 7.50 o.s.i. (ISBN 0-916620-01-8). Portals Pr.

Brunt & Rowen, eds. Feminism, Culture & Politics. 190p. 1982. text ed. 21.00x (ISBN 0-85315-543-7, Pub. by Lawrence & Wishart Ltd England). Humanities.

Brunt, H. L. Van see Van Brunt, H. L.

Brunt, P. A. Italian Manpower 225 B.C.-A.D. 14. 1971. 65.00x o.p. (ISBN 0-19-814283-8). Oxford U Pr.

--Social Conflicts in the Roman Republic. (Illus.). 176p. 1972 6.00 o.s.i. (ISBN 0-393-04335-5, Norton Lib); pap. 4.95x 1974 o.s.i. (ISBN 0-393-00586-0). Norton.

Bruntjien, Scott, jt. auth. see Carter, Ruth C.

Brunton, Charles, et al, eds. British Brachiopods. LC 79-40899. (Synopses of the British Fauna Ser.). 1980. 13.00 o.s.i. (ISBN 0-12-137960-4). Acad Pr.

Brunton, David W., ed. Index to the Contemporary Scene, Vol. 1. LC 73-645955. 122p. 1973. 38.00x (ISBN 0-8103-1056-2). Gale.

--Index to the Contemporary Scene, Vol. 2. xvi, 120p. 1975. 38.00x (ISBN 0-8103-1057-0). Gale.

Brunton, Mary. Self-Control: A Novel, 2 vols. Luria, Gina, ed. (The Feminist Controversy in England, 1788-1810 Ser.). 1974. Set. lib. bdg. 50.00 ea. o.s.i. (ISBN 0-8240-0852-9). Garland Pub.

Bruntz, George G. The History of Los Gatos: Gem of the Foothills. LC 79-174678. xii, 173p. Date not set. Repr. of 1971 ed. cancelled (ISBN 0-939224-05-4). Western Tanager. Postponed.

Brunvand, Jan H. Guide for Collectors of Folklore in Utah. LC 73-168609. (University of Utah Publications in the American West: Vol. 7). 1971. pap. 10.00 o.p. (ISBN 0-87480-084-6). U of Utah Pr.

Brunworth & Rigdon. Patient Education for the Family. (Illus.). 109p. 1979. text ed. 40.00x (Harper Medical). Lippincott.

Brusatti, Otto, jt. ed. see Hilmar, Ernst.

Brusaw, Charles, et al. The Business Writer's Handbook: 2nd ed. LC 81-51835. 650p. 1982. 19.95 (ISBN 0-312-10994-6); pap. 9.95 (ISBN 0-312-10993-8). St Martin.

Brusca, Richard C. Handbook to the Common Intertidal Invertebrates of the Gulf of California. LC 72-76901. (Illus.). 1973. pap. 10.95x o.p. (ISBN 0-8165-0356-7). U of Ariz Pr.

Brusewitz, Gunnar. Wings & Seasons. Wheeler, Walston, tr. from Swedish. (Illus.). 119p. 1983. 20.00 (ISBN 0-88072-029-8). Tanager Bks.

Brush, Bill. Flowers & Plants. LC 12-2710. (A Nice Place to Live Ser.). 1978. pap. 2.25 o.p. (ISBN 0-570-07751-6, 12-2710). Concordia.

Brush, Don O. & Almroth, B. Buckling of Bars, Plates, Shells. (Illus.). 379p. 1974. text ed. 38.50 (ISBN 0-07-008593-5, C). McGraw.

Brush, Elizabeth P. Guizot in the Early Years of the Orleanist Monarchy. LC 74-2319. (University of Illinois Studies in the Social Sciences). 236p. 1975. Repr. of 1929 ed. 22.50x (ISBN 0-86527-090-2). Fertig.

Brush, Michael G., jt. auth. see Lever, Judy.

Brush, S. G. The Kind of Motion We Call Heat: A History of the Kinetic Theory of Gases in the Nineteenth Century, 2 bks. 1976. Bk. 1. 53.25 (ISBN 0-7204-0370-7, North-Holland); Bk. 2. 93.75 (ISBN 0-7204-0482-7); Set. 121.50 (ISBN 0-686-67836-2). Elsevier.

Brusilov, Aleksiei A. Soldiers Note-Book, 1914-1918. LC 75-84265. Repr. of 1930 ed. lib. bdg. 19.75x (ISBN 0-8371-5003-5, BRSN). Greenwood.

Bruss, Robert. The Smart Investor's Guide to Real Estate: Big Profits from Small Investors. 224p. 1981. 13.95 (ISBN 0-517-54232-3). Crown.

Brusselmans, C., ed. Jesus Loves Children. 5.95 (ISBN 0-8215-9889-9). Sadlier.

Brusselmans, Christiane. I Go to Mass with God's Family. rev. ed. 1970. 1.95 o.p. (ISBN 0-685-01123-2, 80926). Glencoe.

Brust, Steven. Jhereg. 1983. pap. 2.50 (ISBN 0-441-38551-6, Pub. by Ace Science Fiction). Ace Bks.

Brustein, Robert. Third Theatre. 1970. pap. 2.95 o.p. (ISBN 0-671-20537-4, Touchstone Bks). S&S.

Bruster, Bill G. & Dale, Robert D. How to Encourage Others. LC 82-70868. (Orig.). 1983. pap. 6.95 (ISBN 0-8054-2247-1). Broadman.

Brustman, Barbara & Kastenbaum, Roberts. Condemned to Life. (Cushing Hospital Ser. on Aging & Terminal Care). 1983. prof ref 25.00x (ISBN 0-88410-715-9). Ballinger Pub.

Bruton, Henry J. The Promise of Peace: Economic Cooperation between Egypt & Israel. 29p. 1981. 3.95 (ISBN 0-8157-1125-5). Brookings.

Bruton, Len T. RC-Active Networks: Theory & Design. (Ser. in Electrical & Computer Engineering). (Illus.). 1980. text ed. 36.00 (ISBN 0-13-753467-1). P-H.

Bruun, Geoffrey, jt. auth. see Ferguson, Wallace K.

Bruun, K., et al. Alcohol Control Policies in Public Health Perspective. (The Finnish Foundation for Alcohol Studies: Vol. 25). (Illus.). 1975. 8.00 o.p. (ISBN 951-9191-29-1). Rutgers Ctr Alcohol.

Bruun, Kettil & Hauge, Ragnar. Drinking Habits Among Northern Youth: A Cross-National Study in the Scandinavian Capitals. (The Finnish Foundation for Alcohol Studies: Vol. 12). 1963. 4.00x. Rutgers Ctr Alcohol.

Bruun, P. & Mehta, A. J. Stability of Tidal Inlets. (Developments in Geotechnical Engineering Ser.: Vol. 23). 1978. 70.25 (ISBN 0-444-41728-1). Elsevier.

Bruun-Rasmussen, Ole & Petersen, Grete. Make-up, Costumes & Masks for the Stage. LC 76-19803. (Illus.). 96p. (gr. 4-12). 1981. pap. 7.95 (ISBN 0-8069-8992-0). Sterling.

--Make up, Costumes & Masks for the Stage. LC 76-19803. (Illus.). (gr. 5 up). 1976. 12.95 (ISBN 0-8069-7024-3); PLB 15.69 (ISBN 0-8069-7025-1). Sterling.

Bruxner, Mervyn. Mastering the Piano: A Guide for the Amateur. 1972. 6.95 o.p. (ISBN 0-312-52115-4, M18500). St Martin.

Bruyere, Christian & Inwood, Robert. Country Comforts. (Illus.). 224p. 1979. pap. 8.95 (ISBN 0-8069-8270-5). Sterling.

Bruyere, Christian, jt. auth. see Inwood, Robert.

Bruyn, G. W., jt. ed. see Vinken, P. J.

Bruyn, J. A Corpus of Rembrandt Paintings, Vol. 1. 1983. lib. bdg. 325.00 (ISBN 90-247-2614-X, Pub. by Martinus Nijhoff). Kluwer Boston.

Bruyn, Monica G. De see De Bruyn, Monica G.

Bruyn, S. T. The Social Economy: People Transforming Modern Business. 392p. 1977. 34.95 o.p. (ISBN 0-471-01985-2). Wiley.

Bry, Adelaide. EST. 1976. pap. 2.50 (ISBN 0-380-00697-9, 50401). Avon.

--Friendship: How to Have a Friend & Be a Friend. 1979. 10.00 o.p. (ISBN 0-448-15494-3, G&D). Putnam Pub Group.

--How to Get Angry Without Feeling Guilty. 1977. pap. 2.25 (ISBN 0-451-11517-1, AE1517, Sig). NAL.

Bry, Adelaide & Bair, Marjorie. Directing the Movies of Your Mind: Visualization for Health & Insight. LC 77-3741. 1978. 12.45i (ISBN 0-06-010528-3, HarpT). Har-Row.

--Visualization: Directing the Movies of Your Mind. LC 77-3741. (Illus.). 192p. 1979. pap. 4.95 (ISBN 0-06-464033-7, BN4033, BN). B&N NY.

Bry, Doris. Alfred Stieglitz: Photographer. LC 65-24359. (Illus.). 1965. bds. 14.95 o.p. (ISBN 0-87846-133-7, Pub. by Boston Museum of Fine Arts). NYGS.

Bryan, Anne-Marie & Duche, Jean. Pour Parler: Manual De Conversation Francaise. 2nd ed. (Illus.). 1977. text ed. 17.95 (ISBN 0-13-686386-8); exercises de laboratoire 8.50 (ISBN 0-13-686394-9); tapes 100.00 (ISBN 0-13-686378-7). P-H.

Bryan, Ashley. I'm Going to Sing: Black American Spirituals, Vol. II. (Illus.). 64p. 1982. 10.95 (ISBN 0-689-30915-5). Atheneum.

Bryan, C. D. Beautiful Women, Ugly Scenes. 1982. 15.95. Doubleday.

--Friendly Fire. LC 76-1335. 1976. 10.95 o.s.i. (ISBN 0-399-11688-5). Putnam Pub Group.

--National Air & Space Museum. (Illus.). 1979. 60.00 (ISBN 0-8109-0666-X). Abrams.

--National Air & Space Museum. 160p. 1982. 12.95 ea. Vol. I (ISBN 0-553-01384-X). Vol. II (ISBN 0-553-01385-8). Bantam.

Bryan, Eileen. Loving Adversaries. (Candlelight Ecstasy Ser.: No. 155). (Orig.). 1983. pap. 1.95 (ISBN 0-440-14885-5). Dell.

Bryan, Frank L., jt. ed. see Riemann, Hans.

Bryan, Frank M. Politics in Rural America: People, Parties, & Policy. (Special Study Ser.). 320p. (Orig.). lib. bdg. 29.50 (ISBN 0-89158-561-3); pap. text ed. 10.95 (ISBN 0-89158-984-8). Westview.

--Yankee Politics in Rural Vermont. LC 73-78913. (Illus.). 334p. 1974. text ed. 22.50x (ISBN 0-87451-082-1). U Pr of New Eng.

Bryan, George T., ed. Nitrofurans. LC 77-72824. (Carcinogenesis-A Comprehensive Survey Ser.: Vol. 4). 243p. 1978. 27.50 (ISBN 0-89004-250-0). Raven.

Bryan, Greyson. Taxing Unfair International Trade Practices: A Study of the U. S. Antidumping & Countervailing Duty Law. LC 80-7571. 1980. 36.95x (ISBN 0-669-03752-4). Lexington Bks.

Bryan, J., jt. auth. see Halsey, William.

Bryan, J., jt. auth. see Murphy, Charles J., III.

Bryan, J. W. Development of the English Law of Conspiracy. LC 72-77737. (Law, Politics, & History Ser). 1970. Repr. of 1909 ed. lib. bdg. 25.00 (ISBN 0-306-71375-6). Da Capo.

Bryan, John & Castle, Coralie. Edible Ornamental Garden. LC 73-91941. (Illus.). 192p. (Orig.). 1974. pap. 4.95 o.s.i. (ISBN 0-686-76998-8). One Hund One Prods.

Bryan, John L. Fire Suppression & Detections Systems. 2nd ed. 464p. 1982. text ed. 23.95 (ISBN 0-02-471300-7). Macmillan.

Bryan, John L. & Picard, Raymond C., eds. Managing Fire Services. LC 79-10067. (Municipal Management Ser.). (Illus.). 1979. text ed. 37.00 (ISBN 0-87326-018-X). Intl City Mgt.

Bryan, John R. Managing Restaurant Personnel: A Handbook for Food Service Operators. LC 73-94217. (Illus.). 192p. 1974. 15.95 (ISBN 0-86730-217-8). Lebhar Friedman.

Bryan, Liz. British Columbia: This Favoured Land. (Illus.). 160p. 1982. 29.95 (ISBN 0-295-95952-5, Pub. by Douglas & McIntyre Canada). U of Wash Pr.

Bryan, M. Leonard, ed. Remote Sensing of Earth Resources: A Guide to Information Sources. LC 79-22792. (Geography & Travel Information Guide Ser.: Vol. 1). (Illus.). 1979. 42.00x (ISBN 0-8103-1413-4). Gale.

Bryan, Mary. Forrest Reid. (English Author Ser.). 1976. lib. bdg. 14.95 (ISBN 0-8057-6661-8, Twayne). G K Hall.

Bryan, Robert, jt. auth. see Dodge, Marshall.

Bryan, Sharon. Salt Air. (New Poets Ser.). 64p. 1983. 15.00x (ISBN 0-8195-2111-6); pap. 6.95x (ISBN 0-8195-1111-0). Wesleyan U Pr.

Bryan, T. Avril. Censorship & Social Conflict in the Spanish Theatre: The Case of Alfonso Sastre. LC 82-17445. 156p. (Orig.). 1983. lib. bdg. 19.25 (ISBN 0-8191-2829-5); pap. text ed. 8.75 (ISBN 0-8191-2830-9). U Pr of Amer.

Bryan, William L. Wars of Families of Minds. 1940. 29.50x (ISBN 0-686-51324-X). Elliots Bks.

Bryant. Perception & Understanding in Young Children. LC 73-92722. 1974. 10.00x o.s.i. (ISBN 0-465-05488-9); pap. 4.95x o.s.i. (ISBN 0-465-09520-8, TB5021). Basic.

Bryant, Al. New Compact Bible Dictionary. 1967. 8.95 (ISBN 0-310-22080-7); pap. 4.95 (ISBN 0-310-22082-3). Zondervan.

Bryant, Al, ed. Climbing Higher. LC 77-24978. 1978. 9.95 (ISBN 0-87123-052-6, 230052); pap. 5.95 (ISBN 0-87123-054-2, 210054). Bethany Hse.

--Poems That Bless. 96p. 1972. pap. 2.50 o.p. (ISBN 0-310-22092-0). Zondervan.

Bryant, Alan. Second Chance: The Story of the New Quay Hospital. (Illus.). 208p. 1982. 11.95 (ISBN 0-312-70828-9). St Martin.

Bryant, Arthur. Age of Chivalry. 3.95 o.s.i. (ISBN 0-452-25002-1, Z5002, Plume). NAL.

Bryant, Arthur, ed. Postman's Horn: An Anthology of Letters of Latter Seventeenth Century England. LC 77-109713. Repr. of 1936 ed. lib. bdg. 15.75x o.p. (ISBN 0-8371-4203-2). Greenwood.

Bryant, B. & Bryant, R. Change & Conflict: A Study of Community Work in Glasgow. 250p. 1983. 21.00 (ISBN 0-08-028475-2); pap. 11.50 (ISBN 0-08-028480-9). Pergamon.

Bryant, Bill. The Armadillo Book. 1983. pap. 4.95 (ISBN 0-88289-383-1). Pelican.

Bryant, Brad. Special Foster Care: A History & Rationale. 50p. 1980. 4.85 (ISBN 0-9604068-0-8, KGH-150). Child Welfare.

Bryant, Bunyan, jt. auth. see Crowfoot, James.

Bryant, Christopher R. The City's Countryside. 1983. pap. 15.95x (ISBN 0-582-30045-2). Longman.

Bryant, Clifton D. Deviancy & the Family. LC 72-77588. pap. 12.95x (ISBN 0-88295-201-3). Harlan Davidson.

Bryant, Coralie & White, Louise G. Managing Rural Development: Peasant Participation in Rural Development. 3rd ed. LC 80-80681. (Kumarian Press Development Monographs, No. 1). 56p. (Orig.). 1981. pap. 4.95x (ISBN 0-931816-50-5). Kumarian Pr.

Bryant, Donald C. & Wallace, Karl R. Fundamentals of Public Speaking. 5th ed. (Illus.). 640p. 1976. pap. 18.95 (ISBN 0-13-342725-0). P-H.

Bryant, Donald C., et al. Oral Communication: A Short Course in Speaking. 5th ed. (Illus.). 288p. 1982. 14.95 (ISBN 0-13-638437-4). P-H.

Bryant, Dorothy. Day in San Francisco. LC 82-73209. 144p. 1983. 12.00 (ISBN 0-931688-09-4); pap. 6.00 (ISBN 0-931688-10-8). Ata Bks.

--Ella Price's Journal. 192p. 1973. pap. 1.50 o.p. (ISBN 0-451-07040-2, W7040, Sig). NAL.

--Ella Price's Journal. LC 75-39758. 227p. 1982. pap. text ed. 6.00 (ISBN 0-931688-08-6). Ata Bks.

Bryant, Edward. Wyoming Sun. (Illus.). 132p. 1980. deluxe ed. 15.50 signed (ISBN 0-936204-15-X); pap. 6.00 (ISBN 0-936204-12-5). Jelm Mtn.

Bryant, Eric T. Collecting Gramophone Records. LC 77-28263. (Illus.). 1978. Repr. of 1962 ed. lib. bdg. 18.50x (ISBN 0-313-20258-3, BRCGR). Greenwood.

Bryant, Gerald R., Jr., jt. auth. see Hogins, James B.

Bryant, Hannah, tr. see Kalbeck, Max.

Bryant, Henry A., ed. Black Politics & Race: A Contemporary Reader of Racism & Black Politics. 1976. pap. text ed. 6.75. (ISBN 0-8191-0003-X). U Pr of Amer.

Bryant, Ina. Foot Reflexology. LC 81-11016. 1981. pap. 4.95 (ISBN 0-89019-076-3). O'Sullivan Woodside.

Bryant, James C. Charlie Brown Remembers Atlanta: Memoirs of a Public Man. LC 82-71963. 370p. 1982. 12.95 (ISBN 0-934870-07-1). R L Bryan.

Bryant, James W. Financial Modelling in Corporate Management. 448p. 1983. 49.25x (ISBN 0-471-10021-8, Pub. by Wiley-Interscience). Wiley.

Bryant, Jennings & Anderson, Daniel, eds. Understanding TV: Research in Children's Attention & Comprehension. LC 82-16280. 320p. Date not set. 29.50 (ISBN 0-12-138160-9). Acad Pr.

Bryant, John H., et al. Community Hospitals & Primary Care. LC 76-14833. 1976. prof ref 20.00 (ISBN 0-88410-121-5). Ballinger Pub.

Bryant, Joseph, ed. see Shakespeare, William.

Bryant, Keith L., Jr. & Dethloff, Henry C. A History of American Business. (Illus.). 368p. 1983. pap. 15.95 (ISBN 0-13-389247-6). P-H.

Bryant, Lee. The Magic Bottle. LC 78-16132. 1982. pap. 4.95 o.p. (ISBN 0-8054-5905-7). Broadman.

Bryant, Lee, jt. auth. see Pask, Raymond.

Bryant, Louise. Six Red Months in Russia. pap. 5.00 o.p. (ISBN 0-904526-03-8, Journeyman Press). Carrier Pigeon.

Bryant, M. Darrol & Dayton, Donald, eds. The Coming Kingdom: Essays in American Millennialism & Eschatology. (Conference Ser.: No. 16). 1983. pap. text ed. write for info. (ISBN 0-932894-16-X). Unif Theol Seminary.

Bryant, M. Darrol, jt. ed. see Sontag, Frederick.

Bryant, Margaret M., ed. Current American Usage: How Americans Say It & Write It. LC 62-9735. (Funk & W Bk.). 1965. 11.49 (ISBN 0-308-40056-9). T Y Crowell.

Bryant, Neville J. An Introduction to Immunohematology. LC 75-25269. (Illus.). 320p. 1976. text ed. 18.95 o.p. (ISBN 0-7216-2170-8). Saunders.

Bryant, Nigel, tr. see De Troyes, Chretien.

Bryant, Paul T. H. L. Davis. (United States Authors Ser.). 1978. lib. bdg. 13.95 (ISBN 0-8057-7211-1, Twayne). G K Hall.

Bryant, R., jt. auth. see Bryant, B.

Bryant, Ralph C. Controlling Money: The Federal Reserve & Its Critics. LC 82-45983. 150p. 1983. 18.95 (ISBN 0-8157-1136-0); pap. 7.95 (ISBN 0-8157-1135-2). Brookings.

--Financial Interdependence & Variability in Exchange Rates. 1980. pap. 4.95 (ISBN 0-8157-1127-1). Brookings.

--Notes on the Analysis of Capital Flows to Developing Nations & the "Recycling" Problem. (Working Paper: No. 476). 67p. 1981. 5.00 (ISBN 0-686-36165-2, WP-0476). World Bank.

Bryant, Raymond C. & McGorray, J. J. Managing Energy for Buildings: Mid-Atlantic Energy Conference Proceedings. LC 82-84596. 400p. 1983. text ed. 40.00 (ISBN 0-86587-109-4). Gov Insts.

Bryant, Raymond C. & McGorray, J. J., eds. Managing Energy for Industry: Mid-Atlantic Energy Conference Proceedings. LC 82-84596. (Illus.). 270p. 1983. 40.00 (ISBN 0-86587-108-6). Gov Insts.

Bryant, Rosalie & Oliver, Eloise M. Complete Elementary Physical Education Guide. 1974. 15.50 (ISBN 0-13-159939-9, Parker). P-H.

Bryant, Sandra, jt. auth. see Tucker, Susan M.

Bryant, Sara C. How to Tell Stories to Children. LC 72-12693. 1973. Repr. of 1924 ed. 34.00x (ISBN 0-8103-3740-1). Gale.

Bryant, Steve J., et al. College Algebra & Trigonometry. LC 73-81071. 465p. 1974. 23.50x (ISBN 0-673-16228-1); o.p. instructor's manual (ISBN 0-87620-170-2); o.p. study guide & involvement manual (ISBN 0-685-39069-1). Scott F.

Bryant, Steven & Saltz, Daniel. Precalculus & Mathematics: Algebra & Trigonometry. (Illus.). 1980. 23.50x (ISBN 0-673-16242-7). Scott F.

Bryant, Steven, jt. ed. see Chapman, Gary.

Bryant, Willis R. Mortgage Lending: Fundamentals & Practices. 2nd ed. 1962. text ed. 29.95 (ISBN 0-07-008609-5, C); instructors' handbook 5.50 (ISBN 0-07-008608-7). McGraw.

Bryce, Felicia. Portia in Distress. (YA) 1977. 6.95 (ISBN 0-685-74267-9, Avalon). Bouregy.

Bryce, Herrington J. Planning Smaller Cities. LC 78-14154. (Urban Round Table Ser.: No. 1). 1979. 25.95x (ISBN 0-669-02680-8). Lexington Bks.

Bryce, Herrington J., ed. Cities & Firms. LC 80-8367. (The Urban Roundtable Ser.). 272p. 1980. 21.95x (ISBN 0-669-04042-8). Lexington Bks.

--Revitalizing Cities. (Urban Round Table Ser.: No. 2). (Illus.). 320p. 1979. 26.95x (ISBN 0-669-02846-0). Lexington Bks.

--Small Cities in Transition: The Dynamics of Growth & Decline. LC 77-9629. (A Joint Center for Political Studies). 488p. 1977. prof ref 25.00x (ISBN 0-88410-473-7). Ballinger Pub.

Bryce, Iris. Canals Are My Life. (Illus.). 104p. 1982. 14.50 (ISBN 0-85937-277-4). Sheridan.

Bryce, J. C., ed. see Smith, Adam.

Bryce, James. The Hindrances to Good Citizenship. 1909. 24.50x (ISBN 0-686-51399-1). Elliots Bks.

--Public Opinion in the American Commonwealth. Nisbet, Robert, ed. 1981. cancelled 18.95 (ISBN 0-87923-370-2); pap. 8.95 cancelled (ISBN 0-87923-371-0). Godine.

--South America: Observations & Impressions. (Latin America in the 20th Century Ser.). 1977. Repr. of 1912 ed. lib. bdg. 69.50 (ISBN 0-306-70835-3). Da Capo.

Bryce, James R. Basic Finance: An Introduction to Financial Theory, Practices & Institutions. 158p. 1980. pap. text ed. 6.95x (ISBN 0-89641-038-2). American Pr.

Bryce-Smith, D. & Dickerson, J. W. Environmental Influences on Pre & Postnatal Development. 104p. 1981. Write for Info. (ISBN 0-677-05990-6). Gordon.

Brycha, M. Automatic Transmissions. 2nd ed. 1982. 18.95 (ISBN 0-13-054577-5). P-H.

Bryd, L. G., ed. see Baker, Robert F.

Bryden, Bill see Goldoni, Carolo.

Bryden, J. M. Tourism & Development: A Case Study of the Commonwealth Caribbean. (Illus.). 280p. 1973. 44.50 (ISBN 0-521-20263-9). Cambridge U Pr.

Bryden, James D. Your Child's Experience in Speech Correction. (Illus.). 1966. pap. text ed. 0.30x (ISBN 0-8134-0851-2, 851). Interstate.

Bryden, M. P. Laterality, Functional Asymetry in the Intact Brain. (Perspectives in Neurolinguistics, Neuropsychology & Psycholinguisitcs Ser.). 315p. (gr. 2-5). 1982. 29.50 (ISBN 0-12-138180-3). Acad Pr.

Brydges, Samuel E. & Quillinan, Edward. Bertram, a Poetical Tale, Repr. Of 1814. Bd. with Occasional Poems, Written in the Year 1811. Repr. of 1814 ed; Select Poems. Repr. of 1814 ed; Five Sonnets Addressed to Wootton, the Spot of the Author's Nativity. Repr. of 1819 ed; Edward Quillian: Dunluce Castle, a Poem, 4 pts. Repr. of 1814 ed. LC 75-31171. (Romantic Context Ser.: Poetry 1789-1830: Vol. 25). 1978. lib. bdg. 47.00 o.s.i. (ISBN 0-8240-2124-X). Garland Pub.

Brydson, J. Rubber Chemistry. (Illus.). 1978. text ed. 90.25x (ISBN 0-85334-779-4, Pub. by Applied Sci England). Elsevier.

Brydson, J. A., ed. Developments with Natural Rubber. (Illus.). 1967. 16.50 (ISBN 0-85334-062-5, Pub. by Applied Sci England). Elsevier.

Brydson, J. A., jt. ed. see Whelan, A.

Brye, David L., ed. European Immigration & Ethnicity in the United States & Canada: A Bibliography. LC 82-24306. (Clio Bibliography Ser.: No. 7). 457p. 1982. 55.00 (ISBN 0-87436-258-X). ABC Clio.

Brye, Joseph. Basic Principles of Music Theory. (Illus.). 278p. 1965. 25.50x (ISBN 0-8260-1460-7). Wiley.

Bryer, Jackson & Hatem, Mary B. William Styron: A Reference Guide. 1978. lib. bdg. 21.00 (ISBN 0-8161-8042-3, Hall Reference). G K Hall.

Bryer, Jackson R. The Critical Reputation of F. Scott Fitzgerald: Supplement I through 1981. 2nd ed. 464p. 1983. price not set (ISBN 0-208-01489-6, Archon). Shoe String.

--Louis Auchincloss & His Critics: A Bibliographical Record. 1977. lib. bdg. 22.00 (ISBN 0-8161-7965-4, Hall Reference). G K Hall.

Bryer, Jackson R., ed. The Short Stories of F. Scott Fitzgerald: New Approaches in Criticism. 416p. 1982. text ed. 30.00 (ISBN 0-299-09080-9); pap. text ed. 7.95 (ISBN 0-299-09084-1). U of Wis Pr.

Bryer, Jackson R., jt. ed. see Duke, Maurice.

Bryer, R. A. & Brignal, T. J. Accounting for British Steel: A Financial Analysis of the Failure of BSC. 303p. 1982. text ed. 37.50x (ISBN 0-686-82418-0). Gower Pub Ltd.

Bryer, Robin. Jolie Brise: A Tall Ship's Tale. (Illus.). 256p. 1983. 24.95 (ISBN 0-436-07181-9, Pub by Secker & Warburg). David & Charles.

Bryfonski, Dedria, ed. Contemporary Issues Criticism: Excerpts from Criticism of Contemporary Writings in Sociology, Politics, Psychology, Anthropology, Education, History, Law, Biography, & Related Fields, Vol. 1. 600p. 1982. 62.00x (ISBN 0-8103-1550-5). Gale.

Brykczynski, Terry. Caged. 256p. 1980. 9.95 o.p. (ISBN 0-517-53995-0). Crown.

Brym, Robert J. Intellectuals & Politics. (Controversies in Sociology Ser.: No. 9). (Orig.). 1980. text ed. 19.95x (ISBN 0-04-322005-3); pap. text ed. 6.95x (ISBN 0-04-322006-1). Allen Unwin.

Brymer, Robert A. Introduction to Hotel & Restaurant Management: A Book of Readings. 3rd ed. 1981. pap. text ed. 13.95 (ISBN 0-8403-2478-2, 40247802). Kendall-Hunt.

Bryngelson, Bryng & Mikalson, Elaine. Speech Correction Through Listening. 1959. pap. 7.95x (ISBN 0-673-05618-X). Scott F.

Brynger, Hans. Clinical Kidney Transplant. 240p. 1982. 44.50 (ISBN 0-8089-1523-1). Grune.

Brynildsen, Ken. School's Out. 160p. 1982. 9.95 (ISBN 0-698-20537-5, Coward). Putnam Pub Group.

Brynner, Joseph F., jt. ed. see Schantz, Maria E.

Bryson, Gladys. Man & Society: The Scottish Inquiry of the Eighteenth Century. LC 66-21657. Repr. of 1945 ed. 25.00x (ISBN 0-678-00373-4). Kelley.

Bryson, Harold T. Increasing the Joy: Studies in I John. LC 81-67200. 1982. pap. 5.95 (ISBN 0-8054-1390-1). Broadman.

Bryson, John. Whoring Around. 1983. pap. 4.95 (ISBN 0-14-005906-7). Penguin.

Bryson, Joseph E. & Detty, Elizabeth W. The Legal Aspects of Censorship of Public School Library & Instructional Materials. 247p. 1982. 20.00 (ISBN 0-87215-556-0). Michie-Bobbs.

Bryson, Norman, jt. ed. see Kappeler, Susanne.

Bryson, R. A. & Hare, F., eds. Climates of North America. LC 74-477739. (World Survey of Climatology Ser.: Vol. 11). 1974. 102.25 (ISBN 0-444-41062-7). Elsevier.

Bryson, Reid A. & Murray, Thomas J. Climates of Hunger: Mankind & the World's Changing Weather. LC 76-53649. (Illus.). 190p. 1977. 25.00 (ISBN 0-299-07370-X); pap. 8.95 (ISBN 0-299-07374-2). U of Wis Pr.

Bryson, William H., ed. The Virginia Law Reporters Before 1880. LC 77-21451. 130p. 1977. 9.75x (ISBN 0-8139-0747-0). U Pr of Va.

Brzezinski, Zbiegniew. The Relevance of Liberalism. LC 77-8202. (Studies of the Research Institute on International Change, Columbia University: Vol. 2). 1978. lib. bdg. 25.00 o.p. (ISBN 0-89158-134-0). Westview.

Brzezinski, Zbigniew. Between Two Ages: America's Role in the Technetronic Era. LC 82-15867. xvii, 334p. 1982. Repr. of 1970 ed. lib. bdg. 35.00x (ISBN 0-313-23498-1, BRZB). Greenwood.

--Power & Principle: Memoirs of the National Security Advisor, 1977-1981. 1983. 22.50 (ISBN 0-374-23663-1). FS&G.

Brzezinski, Zbigniew K. Ideology & Power in Soviet Politics. LC 76-6571. 1976. Repr. of 1962 ed. lib. bdg. 19.75x (ISBN 0-8371-8880-6, BRIP). Greenwood.

Brzozowski, J. A. & Yoeli, M. Digital Networks. (Illus.). 416p. 1976. ref. ed. 29.95 (ISBN 0-13-214189-2). P-H.

Buban, P., et al. Understanding Electricity & Electronics. 4th ed. 1981. text ed. 19.20 (ISBN 0-07-008678-8, W); lab manual 6.64 (ISBN 0-07-008681-8); tchr's. resource guide 6.64 (ISBN 0-07-008679-6). McGraw.

Buban, Peter & Schmitt, Marshall L. Technical Electricity & Electronics. 2nd ed. (Illus.). (gr. 11-12). 1976. text ed. 20.88 (ISBN 0-07-008643-5, W). McGraw.

--Understanding Electricity & Electronics. 2nd ed. 1969. 14.12 o.p. (ISBN 0-07-008640-0, W). McGraw.

--Understanding Electricity & Electronics. 3rd ed. 1974. 19.20 (ISBN 0-07-008675-3, W); study guide 5.68 (ISBN 0-07-008676-1). McGraw.

Bubani, Pietro. Flora Virgiliana. 134p. 1974. Repr. of 1869 ed. lib. bdg. 20.00x (ISBN 3-87429-075-1). Lubrecht & Cramer.

Bube, Richard, jt. auth. see Fahrenbruch, Alan.

Bubeck, Mark I. The Adversary. 1975. pap. 5.95 (ISBN 0-8024-0143-0). Moody.

Bubel, Nancy. The Country Journal Book of Vegetable Gardening. (Illus.). 256p. (Orig.). 1983. pap. 10.95 (ISBN 0-918678-03-X). Country Journ.

Bubel, Nancy W. Vegetables Money Can't Buy But You Can Grow. LC 76-57875. 1977. 15.00 (ISBN 0-87923-202-1); pap. 6.95 (ISBN 0-87923-203-X). Godine.

Buber, Martin. Eclipse of God: Studies in the Relation Between Religion & Philosophy. LC 77-10030. 1977. Repr. of 1952 ed. lib. bdg. 16.25x (ISBN 0-8371-9718-X, BUEG). Greenwood.

--The Legend of the Baal-Shem. LC 76-86849. 1969. pap. 5.95 (ISBN 0-8052-0233-1). Schocken.

--Meetings. Friedman, Maurice, ed. & tr. from Ger. LC 73-82780. 123p. 1973. Repr. 12.00 (ISBN 0-87548-085-3). Open Court.

--On Judaism. Glatzer, Nahum, ed. LC 67-28091. 256p. 1972. 8.00x o.p. (ISBN 0-8052-3186-2); pap. 6.95 (ISBN 0-8052-0343-5). Schocken.

--On the Bible: Eighteen Studies. Glatzer, Nahum N., ed. LC 68-16653. 1968. 8.00x o.p. (ISBN 0-8052-3188-9). Schocken.

--On Zion: The History of an Idea. LC 72-88533. 1973. 7.00x o.p. (ISBN 0-8052-3485-3). Schocken.

--Pointing the Way. Friedman, Maurice S., ed. & tr. LC 74-10148. 249p. 1974. pap. 2.95 o.p. (ISBN 0-8052-0461-X). Schocken.

--The Prophetic Faith. 1977. pap. 4.95xi (ISBN 0-06-130073-X, TB 73, Torch). Har-Row.

--Tales of the Hasidim, 2 vols. Incl. The Early Masters. pap. 6.95 (ISBN 0-8052-0001-0); The Later Masters. pap. 5.95 (ISBN 0-8052-0002-9). LC 47-2952. 1961. Schocken.

--Ten Rungs: Hasidic Sayings. LC 62-13135. 1962. pap. 3.95 (ISBN 0-8052-0018-5). Schocken.

--Way of Man. 1966. pap. 2.95 (ISBN 0-8065-0024-7, 219). Citadel Pr.

--The Way of Response: Selections from His Writings. Glatzer, Nahum N., ed. LC 66-26977. 1971. pap. 5.95 (ISBN 0-8052-0292-7). Schocken.

--Writings of Martin Buber. Herberg, Will, ed. (Orig.). pap. 8.95 (ISBN 0-452-00616-3, F616, Mer). NAL.

--The Writings of Martin Buber. Herberg, Will, ed. 8.50 (ISBN 0-8446-5837-5). Peter Smith.

Bubis, Gerald B. & Wasserman, Harry. Synagogue Havurot: A Comparative Study. LC 82-23912. 160p. (Orig.). 1983. lib. bdg. 21.50 (ISBN 0-8191-2969-0, Co-pub. by Ctr Jewish Comm Studies); pap. text ed. 10.00 (ISBN 0-8191-2970-4). U Pr of Amer.

Bubna, Donald. Como Edificar Otros. 160p. Date not set. 2.50 (ISBN 0-88113-038-9). Edit Betania.

Bubna, Donald & Ricketts, Sarah. Building People. 1978. pap. 4.95 (ISBN 0-8423-0185-2). Tyndale.

Bubna, Paul, frwd. by see Schroeder, David.

Bubnicki, J. Identification of Control Plants. (Studies in Automation & Control: Vol. 3). 1980. 59.75 (ISBN 0-444-99767-9). Elsevier.

Bubnov, Yu N., jt. auth. see Mikhailov, B. M.

Bucalossi, P., ed. see International Cancer Congress, 11th, October 1974.

Buccellati, Giorgio. Terqa Preliminary Reports, No. 10: The Fourth Season, Introduction & the Stratigraphic Record. (Bibliotheca Mesopotamica Ser.: Vol. 10). (Illus.). 150p. 1979. 28.50x (ISBN 0-89003-042-1); pap. 23.50x (ISBN 0-89003-043-X). Undena Pubns.

Bucchieri, Theresa F. Keep You Old Folks at Home. LC 75-9276. 183p. 1975. pap. 1.65 o.p. (ISBN 0-8189-1126-3, Pub. by Alba Bks). Alba.

Bucci, A., ed. The Bay Bib: Vol. I, Rhode Island Marine Bibliography. (Technical Report Ser.: No. 70). 282p. 1979. 5.00 o.p. (ISBN 0-686-36970-X, P778). URI Mas.

--The Bay Bib: Vol. II, Rhode Island Marine Bibliography. (Technical Report Ser.: No. 71). 123p. 1979. 2.00 o.p. (ISBN 0-686-36971-8, P779). URI Mas.

Bucco, Martin. Rene Wellek. (United States Authors Ser.). 1981. lib. bdg. 13.95 (ISBN 0-8057-7339-8, Twayne). G K Hall.

--Wilbur Daniel Steele. (United States Author Ser.). lib. bdg. 13.95 (ISBN 0-8057-0688-7, Twayne). G K Hall.

Buchan, Alastair. Change Without War: The Shifting Structure of World Power. LC 74-19962. 112p. 1975. 22.50 (ISBN 0-312-12880-0). St Martin.

Buchan, David, ed. Scottish Ballad Book. 244p. 1973. 18.95 (ISBN 0-7100-7566-9). Routledge & Kegan.

Buchan, John. Huntingtower. LC 73-106682. 316p. 1972. Repr. of 1932 ed. lib. bdg. 15.50x (ISBN 0-8371-3353-X, BUHU). Greenwood.

--Julius Caesar. LC 75-11491. 170p. 1975. Repr. of 1938 ed. lib. bdg. 15.50x (ISBN 0-8371-8203-4, BUJC). Greenwood.

--The Magic Walking Stick. LC 75-32205. (Classics of Children's Literature, 1621-1932: Vol. 66). (Illus.). 1976. Repr. of 1932 ed. PLB 38.00 o.s.i. (ISBN 0-8240-2315-3). Garland Pub.

Buchan, John see Eyre, A. G.

Buchan, John, ed. A History of English Literature: From Chaucer to the end of the 19th Century. 675p. 1982. Repr. of 1923 ed. lib. bdg. 45.00 (ISBN 0-686-81843-1). Darby Bks.

Buchan, Robert J. & Johnston, C. Christopher. Telecommunications Regulation & the Constitution. 276p. (Orig.). 1982. pap. text ed. 18.95x (ISBN 0-920380-69-7, Pub. by Inst Res Pub Canada). Renouf.

Buchan, William. John Buchan: A Memoir. 288p. 1982. 42.50x (ISBN 0-907675-03-4, Pub. by Muller Ltd). State Mutual Bk.

Buchanan, A. Russell. United States & World War Two, Vol. 2. (New American Nation Ser). (Illus.). (YA) 1964. 17.50i (ISBN 0-06-010571-2, HarpT). Har-Row.

--The United States in World War II, Vol. I. LC 63-20287. (Illus.). 1964. 17.50xi (ISBN 0-06-010570-4, HarpT); Vol. 2. 19.18xi (ISBN 0-06-010571-2). Har-Row.

Buchanan, Cynthia D. Programed Introduction to Linguistics: Phonetics & Phonemics. 1963. pap. text ed. 17.95x o.p. (ISBN 0-669-20453-6). Heath.

Buchanan, Daniel, tr. One Hundred Famous Haiku. LC 72-95667. 1977. pap. 5.95 o.p. (ISBN 0-87040-222-6). Japan Pubns.

Buchanan, David. Greek Athletics. McLeish, Kenneth & McLeish, Valerie, eds. (Aspects of Greek Life Ser.). (Illus.). 48p. (gr. 7-12). 1976. pap. text ed. 3.50 (ISBN 0-582-20059-8). Longman.

--Roman Sport & Entertainment. Hodge, Peter, ed. (Aspects of Roman Life Ser.). (Illus.). 64p. (Orig.). (gr. 7-12). 1976. pap. text ed. 3.50 (ISBN 0-582-31415-1). Longman.

--The Treasure of Auchinleck: The Story of the Boswell Papers. LC 73-18422. (Illus.). 394p. 1974. 15.95 o.p. (ISBN 0-07-008710-5, P&RB). McGraw.

Buchanan, Diane E., jt. auth. see Clements, Imelda W.

Buchanan, Edward A. Broken Jars & Empty Cisterns: Studies in Jeremiah. 36p. 1982. pap. 3.50 (ISBN 0-939298-09-0). J M Prods.

Buchanan, George. Possible Being. (Carcanet New Poetry Ser.). 63p. (Orig.). 1981. pap. 8.95 o.p. (ISBN 0-85635-312-4, Pub. by Carcanet New Pr England). Humanities.

Buchanan, George W. The Prophet's Mantle in the Nation's Capital. LC 78-59167. 1978. pap. text ed. 6.50 (ISBN 0-8191-0545-7). U Pr of Amer.

Buchanan, J. Consumers Guide to Mobile Home Living. 1982. pap. 3.50 (ISBN 0-918734-32-0). Reymont.

Buchanan, J., jt. auth. see Brennan, G.

Buchanan, J. E. Phoenix: A Chronological & Documentary History, 1865-1976. LC 77-26763. (American Cities Chronology Ser.). 149p. 1978. 8.50 (ISBN 0-379-00617-0). Oceana.

Buchanan, James. Miami: A Chronological & Documentary History, 1513-1977. LC 77-27462. (American Cities Chronology Ser.). 155p. 1978. 8.50 (ISBN 0-379-00616-2). Oceana.

Buchanan, James, jt. auth. see Gilbert, Robert P.

Buchanan, James W. Minnesota Walk Book: A Guide to Hiking & Cross-Country Skiing In the Viking-Land Region, Vol. VI. (Walk Book Ser.). (Illus.). 64p. 1982. pap. 4.50 (ISBN 0-931714-19-2). Nodin Pr.

Buchanan, John G. Thomas Paine: American Revolutionary Writer. Rahmas, D. Steve, ed. (Outstanding Personalities Ser.: No. 85). 1976. lib. bdg. 2.95 incl. catalog cards (ISBN 0-87157-585-X); pap. 1.95 vinyl laminated covers (ISBN 0-87157-085-8). SamHar Pr.

Buchanan, Lamont. A Pictorial History of the Confederacy. (Illus.). 1951. 10.00 o.p. (ISBN 0-517-00621-9). Crown.

Buchanan, Lea C. A Modern Princess & Her World. 160p. 1983. 8.50 (ISBN 0-682-49984-6). Exposition.

Buchanan, Malcolm, et al. Transport Planning for Greater London. 315p. 1980. text ed. 42.75x (ISBN 0-566-00314-7). Gower Pub Ltd.

Buchanan, O. Lexton, Jr. Limits: A Transition to Calculus. Meder, Albert E., Jr., ed. (Modern Mathematics Ser). (gr. 9 up). 1974. pap. 6.96 (ISBN 0-395-17941-6); instr's. guide & solution key 3.56 (ISBN 0-395-17942-4). HM.

Buchanan, R. A. History & Industrial Civilization. LC 79-14550. 1979. 20.00x (ISBN 0-312-37401-1). St Martin.

Buchanan, R. H., et al. Man & His Habitat: Essays Presented to Emyr Estyn Evans. 1971. 26.50 o.p. (ISBN 0-7100-6908-1). Routledge & Kegan.

Buchanan, Robert J. Health-Care Finance: An Analysis of Cost & Utilization Issues. LC 80-8362. 1981. 23.95x (ISBN 0-669-04035-5). Lexington Bks.

Buchanan, William. A Shining Season. LC 78-11303. (Illus.). 1978. 8.95 o.s.i. (ISBN 0-698-10888-4, Coward). Putnam Pub Group.

Buchanek & Bergin. Piloting-Navigation with the Pocket Calculator. LC 76-23228. (Illus.). 1976. 14.95 (ISBN 0-8306-6853-5); pap. 8.95 o.p. (ISBN 0-8306-5853-X, 853). TAB Bks.

Buchard, O. Photochemistry of Heterocyclic Compounds. LC 75-33855. 622p. 1976. 97.50x (ISBN 0-471-11510-X). Wiley.

Buchbaum, W. H. & Mauro, R. Microprocessor-Based Electronic Games. 304p. 1983. 9.95 (ISBN 0-07-008722-9). McGraw.

Buchberger, B., et al, eds. Computer Algebra, Symbolic & Algebraic Computation. (Computing Supplementum Ser.: No. 4). (Illus.). 300p. 1982. pap. 49.00 (ISBN 0-387-81684-4). Springer-Verlag.

Buchdahl, H. A. Seventeen Simple Lectures on General Relativity Theory. LC 81-11376. 174p. 1981. 23.95x (ISBN 0-471-09684-9, Pub. by Wiley-Interscience). Wiley.

--Twenty Lectures on Thermodynamics. 1975. text ed. 23.00 (ISBN 0-08-018299-2); pap. text ed. 16.00 (ISBN 0-08-018951-2). Pergamon.

Buchdahl, Hans A. Concepts of Classical Thermodynamics. (Cambridge Monograph on Physics). 1966. 44.50 (ISBN 0-521-04359-X). Cambridge U Pr.

--Introduction to Hamiltonian Optics. LC 69-19372. (Cambridge Monographs on Physics). (Illus.). 1970. 47.50 (ISBN 0-521-07516-5). Cambridge U Pr.

Buchel, K. H. Chemistry of Pesticides. (Environmental Science & Technology Ser.). 300p. 1982. write for info (ISBN 0-471-05682-0, Pub. by Wiley-Interscience). Wiley.

Buchele, Robert & Cohen, Howard. Equity & Efficiency in Public Policy. (Learning Packages in the Policy Sciences Ser.: No. 15). (Illus.). 30p. (Orig.). 1978. pap. text ed. 1.50x (ISBN 0-936826-04-5). Pol Stud Assocs.

Buchele, Robert B. The Management of Business & Public Organizations. new ed. (Management Ser.). (Illus.). 1976. text ed. 25.95 (ISBN 0-07-008697-4, C); instructor's manual 15.95 (ISBN 0-07-008698-2). McGraw.

Bucheli, Fausto & Maxson, Robin. Hostage. 208p. (Orig.). 1982. pap. 6.95 (ISBN 0-310-45631-2). Zondervan.

Bucher, Bernadette & Sturtevant, William C., eds. Guide to the Grands Voyages. LC 81-67814. 160p. 1982. lib. bdg. cancelled o.p. (ISBN 0-88354-222-6). Clearwater Pub.

Bucher, Charles & Olsen, Einar. Foundations of Health. 2nd ed. (Illus.). 448p. 1976. Ref. Ed. 19.95 (ISBN 0-13-329896-5). P-H.

Bucher, Charles A. Administration of Physical Education & Athletic Programs. 8th ed. LC 82-6479. (Illus.). 632p. 1983. pap. text ed. 21.95 (ISBN 0-8016-0852-X). Mosby.

--Foundations of Physical Education & Sport. 9th ed. LC 82-3495. (Illus.). 642p. 1983. pap. text ed. 19.95 (ISBN 0-8016-0868-6). Mosby.

Bucher, Charles A. & Bucher, Richard D. Recreation for Today's Society. (Illus.). 224p. 1974. 17.95 (ISBN 0-13-768721-4). P-H.

Bucher, Charles A. & Koenig, Constance R. Methods & Materials for Secondary School Physical Education. 6th ed. (Illus.). 454p. 1983. pap. text ed. 20.95 (ISBN 0-8016-0874-0). Mosby.

Bucher, Charles A. & Thaxton, Nolan A. Physical Education & Sport: Change & Challenge. LC 80-25237. (Illus.). 243p. 1981. 13.95 (ISBN 0-8016-0876-7). Mosby.

Bucher, Charles A. & Thaxton, Nolan A., eds. Physical Education for Children: Movement Foundations & Experiences. 21.95x (ISBN 0-02-316300-3). Macmillan.

Bucher, Dorothy, tr. see Bailey, Keith M.

Bucher, Dorothy, tr. see Simpson, A. B.

Bucher, Francois, jt. auth. see Albers, Josef.

Bucher, Glenn R., ed. Straight-White-Male. LC 75-13039. 160p. 1976. pap. 1.00 o.p. (ISBN 0-8006-1209-4, 1-1209). Fortress.

Bucher, Richard D., jt. auth. see Bucher, Charles A.

Buchheimer, Arnold, jt. auth. see Buchheimer, Naomi.

Buchheimer, Naomi. Let's Go to a Bakery. (Let's Go Ser.). (Illus.). (gr. 2-4). 1956. PLB 4.29 o.p. (ISBN 0-399-60351-4). Putnam Pub Group.

--Let's Go to a Post Office. (Lets Go Ser.). (Illus.). (gr. 2-4). 1964. PLB 4.29 o.p. (ISBN 0-399-60393-X). Putnam Pub Group.

Buchheimer, Naomi & Buchheimer, Arnold. Equality Through Integration. 70p. 1.50 o.p. (ISBN 0-686-74893-X). ADL.

Buchheit, William & Truex, Raymond C., eds. Surgery of the Posterior Fossa. LC 78-73554. (Seminars in Neurological Surgery: Vol. 3). 197p. 1979. text ed. 26.50 (ISBN 0-89004-256-X). Raven.

Buchholz, Arnold, ed. Soviet & East European Studies in the International Framework. LC 82-62037. 96p. 1982. 15.00 (ISBN 0-941320-08-1). Transnatl Pubs.

Buchholz, Barbara. The Aviator's Source Book. (Illus.). 512p. 1982. 24.95 (ISBN 0-312-06251-6); pap. 16.95 (ISBN 0-312-06252-4). St Martin.

Buchholz, Ester S. & Mishne, Judith M. Ego & Self Psychology: Interventions with Children, Adolescents, & Parents. LC 81-22806. 284p. 1983. 25.00 (ISBN 0-87668-487-8). Aronson.

Buchi, George H. Organic Synthesis, Vol. 56. LC 22-17747. (Organic Synthesis Ser.). 157p. 1977. 18.95 (ISBN 0-471-02218-7, Pub. by Wiley-Interscience). Wiley.

Buchin, Su. Affine Differential Geometry. 1982. write for info. (ISBN 0-677-31060-9). Gordon.

Buchler, Justus, jt. auth. see Randall, John H., Jr.

Buchman, Tom, jt. auth. see Goeldner, C. R.

Buchner, Georg. Danton's Death. Rappolt, Hedwig, tr. from Ger. LC 82-51254. 96p. (Orig.). 1983. pap. text ed. 4.00 (ISBN 0-939858-02-9). Time & Space.

--Lenz. Rappolt, Hedwig, tr. from Ger. 96p. (Orig.). 1983. pap. text ed. 4.00 (ISBN 0-939858-04-5). Time & Space.

--Leonce & Lena. Rappolt, Hedwig, tr. from Ger. 96p. (Orig.). 1983. pap. text ed. 4.00 (ISBN 0-939858-03-7). Time & Space.

Bucholz, Robert W. & Wenger, Dennis R. Orthopaedic Decision Making. 300p. 1983. text ed. 36.00 (ISBN 0-941158-10-1, D0798-1). Mosby.

Buchsbaum, Ralph. Animals Without Backbones. rev., 2nd ed. LC 48-9508. (Illus.). 405p. 1975. pap. 10.50 (ISBN 0-226-07870-1). U of Chicago Pr.

--Animals Without Backbones: An Introduction to the Invertebrates. rev. ed. LC 48-9508. (Illus.). (gr. 9 up). 1948. text ed. 17.00x (ISBN 0-226-07869-8). U of Chicago Pr.

Buchsbaum, W. H. & Mauro, R. Electronic Games: Design, Programming, Troubleshooting. 1979. 26.95 (ISBN 0-07-008721-0). McGraw.

Buchter, H. H. Industrial Sealing Technology. 441p. 1979. 49.95 (ISBN 0-471-03184-4, EM20, Pub. by Wiley-Interscience). Wiley.

Buchthal, Hugo. Art of the Mediterranean World: 100-1400 A. D. Folda, Jaroslav, et al, eds. (Art History Ser.: No. V.). (Illus.). 207p. 1983. 75.00 (ISBN 0-916276-11-2). Decatur Hse.

Buchwald, Ann. Seems Like Yesterday. 288p. 1980. 10.95 o.p. (ISBN 0-399-12440-3). Putnam Pub Group.

Buchwald, Ann, jt. auth. see Young, Marjabelle.

Buchwald, Art. The Buchwald Stops Here. LC 78-18919. 1978. 9.95 (ISBN 0-399-12168-4). Putnam Pub Group.

--Down the Seine & up the Potomac with Art Buchwald. LC 77-24466. (Illus.). 1977. 10.95 o.s.i. (ISBN 0-399-12019-X). Putnam Pub Group.

--I Am Not a Crook. LC 74-40134. 288p. 1974. 6.95 o.s.i. (ISBN 0-399-11413-0). Putnam Pub Group.

--Laid Back in Washington. 1981. 12.95 (ISBN 0-399-12648-1). Putnam Pub Group.

--Laid Back in Washington. 384p. 1983. pap. 3.25 (ISBN 0-425-05779-8). Berkley Pub.

--Washington Is Leaking. LC 76-8197. 1976. 8.95 (ISBN 0-399-11758-X). Putnam Pub Group.

Buchwald, Edith. Physical Rehabilitation for Daily Living. (Illus.). 1952. 34.95 (ISBN 0-07-008735-0, HP). McGraw.

Buck, Anne. Dress in Eighteenth Century England. (Illus.). 224p. 1979. 38.00 o.p. (ISBN 0-7134-0415-9, Pub. by Batsford England). David & Charles.

--Thomas Lester: His Lace & the East Midlands Industry. 29.95 (ISBN 0-903585-09-X). Robin & Russ.

Buck, Babs F., ed. see Hoffman, Emanuel.

Buck, Barbara D. The Enchanted Heart. 416p. (Orig.). 1980. pap. 2.50 o.p. (ISBN 0-523-40520-0). Pinnacle Bks.

Buck, Edith V. Treasure in Golden Canyon. 120p. (gr. 2-6). 1983. pap. 2.95 (ISBN 0-88207-494-6). Victor Bks.

Buck, Ellen, jt. auth. see Buck, R. Creighton.

Buck, George. The History of King Richard the Third (1619) Kincaid, A. N., ed. 512p. 1982. text ed. 60.50x (ISBN 0-904387-26-7); pap. text ed. 34.00x (ISBN 0-86299-008-4). Humanities.

Buck, Irving A. Cleburne & His Command. 396p. 1982. 27.50 (ISBN 0-686-97669-X). Pr of Morningside.

Buck, Kathryn, et al, eds. Teaching Business & Technical German: Problems & Prospects. (Illus.). 56p. (Orig., Ger. & Eng.). Date not set. 7.50 (ISBN 0-686-32878-7). C Duisberg Soc. Postponed.

Buck, P. American Science & Modern China, 1876-1936. LC 79-19190. (Illus.). 1980. 32.50 (ISBN 0-521-22744-5). Cambridge U Pr.

Buck, Pearl S. East Wind: West Wind. (John Day Bk.). 1973. 14.37i (ISBN 0-381-98026-X, A21660). T Y Crowell.

--The Good Earth. Shefter, Harry, ed. (Enriched Classics Edition Ser.). 320p. pap. 3.50 (ISBN 0-671-47226-7). WSP.

--The Joy of Children. new ed. LC 74-84887. 1974. 10.00 (ISBN 0-914242-01-6); pap. 7.95 (ISBN 0-686-96679-1). Bookworld Comm.

--The Lovers & Other Stories. LC 76-56819. (John Day Bk.). 1977. 14.37 (ISBN 0-381-97109-0). T Y Crowell.

--Man Who Changed China: The Story of Sun Yat-Sen. (World Landmark Ser.: No. 9). (Illus.). (gr. 7-9). 1953. PLB 5.99 o.s.i. (ISBN 0-394-90509-1). Random.

--The Old Demon. (Creative's Classics Ser.). (Illus.). 40p. (gr. 6-12). 1982. lib. bdg. 7.95 (ISBN 0-87191-828-5). Creative Ed.

--Secrets of the Heart. LC 76-6550. (John Day Bk.). 1965. 14.37i (ISBN 0-381-98287-4). T Y Crowell.

--The Story Bible: Old Testament, Vol. 1. 1972. pap. 2.95 (ISBN 0-451-11946-0, AE1946, Sig). NAL.

--The Woman Who Was Changed & Other Stories. LC 78-69522. 1979. 11.49 (ISBN 0-690-01789-8). T Y Crowell.

Buck, Pearl S., ed. Pearl S. Buck's Book of Christmas. 1974. 12.95 o.p. (ISBN 0-671-21868-9). S&S.

Buck, Pearl S., tr. All Men Are Brothers - Shui Huchuan, Vol. I. (John Day Bk.). 1968. Repr. of 1933 ed. 10.00i (ISBN 0-381-98017-0, A2000, TYC-T). T Y Crowell.

Buck, Peter. Arts & Crafts of Hawaii: Canoes, Sec. VI. (Special Pulbication Ser.: No. 45). (Illus.). 41p. 1957. pap. 3.00 (ISBN 0-910240-39-6). Bishop Mus.

--Arts & Crafts of Hawaii: Clothing, Sec. V. (Special Publication Ser.: No. 45). (Illus.). 97p. 1957. pap. 3.00 (ISBN 0-910240-38-8). Bishop Mus.

--Arts & Crafts of Hawaii: Death & Burial, Sec. XIII. (Special Publication Ser.: No. 45). (Illus.). 26p. 1957. pap. 2.00 (ISBN 0-910240-46-9). Bishop Mus.

--Arts & Crafts of Hawaii: Fishing, Sec. VII. (Special Publication Ser.: No. 45). (Illus.). 78p. 1957. pap. 4.50 (ISBN 0-910240-40-X). Bishop Mus.

--Arts & Crafts of Hawaii: Food, Sec. I. (Special Publication Ser.: No. 45). (Illus.). 83p. 1957. pap. 4.50 (ISBN 0-910240-34-5). Bishop Mus.

--Arts & Crafts of Hawaii: Games & Recreation, VIII. (Special Publication Ser.: No. 45). (Illus.). 32p. 1957. pap. 3.00 (ISBN 0-910240-41-8). Bishop Mus.

--Arts & Crafts of Hawaii: Houses, Sec. II. (Special Publication Ser.: No. 45). (Illus.). 52p. 1957. pap. 3.00 (ISBN 0-910240-35-3). Bishop Mus.

--Arts & Crafts of Hawaii: Index, Sec. XIV. (Special Publication Ser.: No. 45). 19p. 1957. pap. 1.50 (ISBN 0-910240-47-7). Bishop Mus.

--Arts & Crafts of Hawaii: Musical Instruments, Sec. IX. (Special Publication Ser.: No. 45). 39p. 1957. pap. 3.00 (ISBN 0-910240-42-6). Bishop Mus.

--Arts & Crafts of Hawaii: Ornaments & Personal Adornment, Sec. XII. (Special Publication Ser.: No. 45). (Illus.). 40p. 1957. pap. 3.50 (ISBN 0-910240-45-0). Bishop Mus.

--Arts & Crafts of Hawaii: Plaiting, Sec. III. (Special Publication Ser.: No. 43). (Illus.). 39p. 1957. pap. 3.00 (ISBN 0-910240-36-1). Bishop Mus.

--Arts & Crafts of Hawaii: Religion, Sec. XI. (Special Publication Ser.: No. 45). (Illus.). 77p. 1957. pap. 4.50 (ISBN 0-910240-44-2). Bishop Mus.

--Arts & Crafts of Hawaii: Twined Baskets, Sec. IV. (Special Publication Ser.: No. 45). (Illus.). 33p. 1957. pap. 3.00 (ISBN 0-910240-37-X). Bishop Mus.

--Arts & Crafts of Hawaii: War & Weapons, Sec. X. (Special Publication Ser.: No. 45). (Illus.). 57p. 1957. pap. 3.00 (ISBN 0-910240-43-4). Bishop Mus.

--Marc Dean, Mercenary, No. 5: School for Slaughter. 1982. pap. 2.25 (ISBN 0-451-11457-4, AE1457, Sig). NAL.

--Marc Dean, Mercenary, No. 6: Ready, Aim, Die. Date not set. pap. 2.25 (ISBN 0-451-11619-4, Sig). NAL.

--Marc Dean, Mercenary, No. 7: The Black Gold Briefing. 224p. 1982. pap. 2.50 (ISBN 0-451-11824-3, Sig). NAL.

--Operation Icicle. (Marc Dean, Mercenary Ser.: No. 4). (Orig.). 1982. pap. 2.50 (ISBN 0-451-11269-5, AE1269, Sig). NAL.

Buck, Peter H. Anthropology & Religion. 1939. text ed. 11.50x (ISBN 0-686-83471-2). Elliots Bks.

Buck, R. Creighton. Advanced Calculus. 3rd ed. LC 77-2859. (McGraw-Hill Intl. Ser. in Pure & Applied Mathematics). (Illus.). 1978. text ed. 29.00 (ISBN 0-07-008728-8, C); instructor's manual 9.95 (ISBN 0-07-008729-6). McGraw.

Buck, R. Creighton & Buck, Ellen. An Introduction to Differential Equations. LC 75-25009. (Illus.). 416p. 1976. text ed. 26.95 (ISBN 0-395-20654-5). HM.

Buck, Robert N. Weather Flying. rev. ed. (Illus.). 1978. 14.95 (ISBN 0-02-518020-7). Macmillan.

Buck, Ross W. Human Motivation & Emotion. LC 75-37893. 529p. 1976. text ed. 26.95x (ISBN 0-471-11570-3). Wiley.

Buck, Solon J. Agrarian Crusade. 1920. text ed. 8.50x (ISBN 0-686-83457-7). Elliots Bks.

Buck, Stratton. Gustave Flaubert. (World Authors Ser.). 1966. pap. 12.95 (ISBN 0-8057-2312-9, Twayne). G K Hall.

Buck, William. Mahabharata. (Illus.). 1974. 16.95 o.p. (ISBN 0-520-02017-0); pap. 7.95 (ISBN 0-520-04393-6). U of Cal Pr.

Buckberrough, Sherry A. Robert Delaunay: The Discovery of Simultaneity. Foster, Stephen, ed. LC 82-1869. (Studies in Fine Arts: The Avant-Garde: No. 21). 416p. 1982. 44.95 (ISBN 0-8357-1297-4, Pub. by UMI Res Pr). Univ Microfilms.

Buckby, M. see Allen, W. S.

Bucke, Richard M. Cosmic Consciousness. rev. ed. pap. 6.25 (ISBN 0-525-47245-2, 0607-180). Dutton.

Bucker, Bradley, jt. auth. see Lovaas, Ivar.

Buckingham, A. D., et al. Organic Liquids: Structure, Dynamics & Chemical Properties. LC 78-8462. 1978. 69.00x (ISBN 0-471-99673-4, Pub. by Wiley-Interscience). Wiley.

Buckingham, Jamie. Hija del Destino. 288p. Date not set. 3.50 (ISBN 0-88113-098-2). Edit Betania.

--The Last Word. 1978. pap. 4.95 (ISBN 0-88270-404-4, Pub. by Logos). Bridge Pub.

--Risky Living: The Key to Inner Healing. LC 76-12033. 1976. 5.95 o.p. (ISBN 0-88270-175-4, Pub. by Logos); pap. 4.95 (ISBN 0-88270-177-0). Bridge Pub.

Buckingham, Jamie, jt. auth. see Cruz, Nicky.

Buckingham, Jamie, jt. auth. see Riley, Jeannie C.

Buckingham, P. D., jt. auth. see Clark, J. C.

Buckingham, R. A., ed. Education & Large Information Systems: Proceedings of the IFIP TC3-TC8 Working Conference, The Hague, The Netherlands, April 1977. 1978. 38.50 (ISBN 0-444-85047-3, North-Holland). Elsevier.

Buckingham, Robert W. A Special Kind of Love: Care for the Dying Child. 192p. 1983. 12.95 (ISBN 0-8264-0229-1). Continuum.

Buckland, Charles E. Dictionary of Indian Biography. LC 68-23140. 1968. Repr. of 1906 ed. 58.00x (ISBN 0-8103-3156-X). Gale.

Buckland, Gail. Cecil Beaton War Photographs Nineteen Thirty-Nine to Nineteen Forty-Five. (Illus.). 192p. 1982. 24.95. Sci Bks Intl.

Buckland, Raymond. Color Magick Rituals. 1983. 6.95 (ISBN 0-87542-047-8). Llewellyn Pubns.

--The Tree: The Complete Book of Saxon Witchcraft. LC 74-79397. (Illus.). 158p. 1981. pap. 4.95 (ISBN 0-87728-258-7). Weiser.

Buckland, Raymond & Carrington, Hereward. Amazing Secrets of the Psychic World. 1976. 4.95 (ISBN 0-13-024059-1, Reward); pap. 3.95 o.p. (ISBN 0-686-96839-5). P-H.

Buckland, Richard. Palace of Snow. LC 80-83200. (Starters Ser.). PLB 8.00 (ISBN 0-382-06504-2). Silver.

Buckle, Eileen. Birdwatching. LC 80-50946. (Whizz Kids Ser.). 8.00 (ISBN 0-382-06442-9). Silver.

Buckle, I., ed. see Morgan, William.

Buckle, Joanna. Intake Teams. (Tavistock Library of Social Work Practice). 213p. 1981. 24.00x (ISBN 0-422-77300-X, Pub. by Tavistock England); pap. 10.95x (ISBN 0-422-77310-7). Methuen Inc.

Buckle, Leonard & Buckle, Suzann. Standards Relating to Planning for Juvenile Justice. LC 77-3938. (IJA-ABA Juvenile Justice Standards Project Ser.). 132p. 1980. prof ref 20.00x (ISBN 0-88410-754-X); pap. 10.00x (ISBN 0-88410-807-4). Ballinger Pub.

Buckle, Mary, jt. auth. see Day, Lewis F.

Buckle, Richard. Diaghilev. LC 78-73084. 1979. 22.50 o.p. (ISBN 0-689-10952-0). Atheneum.

--In the Wake of Diaghilev. LC 82-12096. (Illus.). 400p. 1983. 19.95 (ISBN 0-03-062493-2). HR&W.

Buckle, Suzann, jt. auth. see Buckle, Leonard.

Buckler, William E. On the Poetry of Matthew Arnold. (The Gotham Library Ser.). 228p. 1982. 27.50 (ISBN 0-8147-1039-5). NYU Pr.

Buckler, William E., jt. auth. see Anderson, George K.

Buckles, Mary P. Animals of the World. LC 78-66401. 1978. 25.00 o.p. (ISBN 0-448-16451-5, G&D). Putnam Pub Group.

Buckley, A. & Swain, C. Retail Trade Developments in Great Britain. 4th ed. 1979. text ed. 82.25x (ISBN 0-566-02152-8). Gower Pub Ltd.

Buckley, A., jt. ed. see Hartley, M. G.

Buckley, A. G. & Goffin, J. L. Algorithms for Constrained Minimumization of South Nonlinear Functions. (Mathematical Programming Studies: Vol. 16). 1982. 25.75 (ISBN 0-444-86390-7). Elsevier.

Buckley, Ann, tr. see Baker, Theodore.

Buckley, Anne, jt. ed. see Hartley, Michael G.

Buckley, Barbara E., jt. auth. see Abel, Ernest L.

Buckley, Christopher. Last Rites. LC 80-12937. 92p. 1980. 4.50 (ISBN 0-87886-109-2). Ithaca Hse.

Buckley, D. H. Surface Effects in Adhesion, Friction, Wear & Lubrication. (Tribiology Ser.: Vol. 5). 1981. 100.00 (ISBN 0-444-41966-7). Elsevier.

Buckley, David G., ed. Archaeology in Sussex to AD Fifteen Hundred. (CBA Research Report Ser.: No. 34). 101p. 1980. pap. text ed. 27.95x (ISBN 0-900312-83-1, Pub. by Coun Brit Archaeology). Humanities.

Buckley, Earle A. How to Write Better Business Letters. 4th ed. (Illus.). 1957. 10.95 o.p. (ISBN 0-07-008778-4, P&RB); pap. 4.95 (ISBN 0-07-008779-2). McGraw.

Buckley, Harry E. Guillaume Apollinaire as an Art Critic. Kuspit, Donald, ed. LC 80-28095. (Studies in Fine Arts. Criticism: No. 11). 354p. 1981. 49.95 (ISBN 0-8357-1164-1, Pub. by UMI Res Pr). Univ Microfilms.

Buckley, J. P. & Ferrario, C. M. Central Actions of Antiotensin & Related Hormones. 1977. text ed. write for info. (ISBN 0-08-020933-5). Pergamon.

Buckley, J. W., et al. SEC Accounting. 484p. 1980. text ed. 27.95 (ISBN 0-471-01861-9); avail. tchrs. manual (ISBN 0-471-07778-X). Wiley.

Buckley, James L. If Men Were Angels: A View from the Senate. LC 75-27407. 320p. 1975. 8.95 o.p. (ISBN 0-399-11589-7). Putnam Pub Group.

Buckley, Jerome H. The Victorian Temper: A Study in Literary Culture. LC 81-6142. (Illus.). 282p. 1981. pap. 10.95 (ISBN 0-521-28448-1). Cambridge U Pr.

Buckley, Jerome H. & Woods, George B. Poetry of the Victorian Period. 3rd ed. 1965. text ed. 21.95x (ISBN 0-673-05630-9). Scott F.

Buckley, John W., ed. see UCLA Extension.

Buckley, John W., ed. see Walton, Thomas F.

Buckley, John W., et al. Research Methodology & Business Decisions. 89p. 1976. 7.95 (ISBN 0-86641-039-2, 7581). Natl Assn Accts.

Buckley, Joseph C. Retirement Handbook. pap. 4.25 o.p. (ISBN 0-06-463366-7, EH 366, EH). B&N NY.

--The Retirement Handbook: A Complete Guide to Planning Your Future. 6th ed. Schmidt, Henry, ed. LC 78-138712. (Illus.). 1977. 12.45i (ISBN 0-06-010568-2, HarpT). Har-Row.

Buckley, Joseph P. & Ferrario, Carlos, eds. Central Nervous System Mechanisms in Hypertension. (Perspectives in Cardiovascular Research Ser.: Vol. 6). 434p. 1981. 43.50 (ISBN 0-89004-545-3). Raven.

Buckley, Kathleen & Kulb, Nancy. Handbook of Maternal-Newborn Nursing. LC 82-20048. 654p. 1983. 17.50x (ISBN 0-471-86984-8, Pub. by Wiley Med). Wiley.

Buckley, Marie. Breaking into Prison: A Citizen Guide to Volunteer Action. LC 74-206. 192p. 1974. 7.93 (ISBN 0-8070-0876-1). Beacon Pr.

Buckley, Mary & Baum, David, eds. Color Theory: A Guide to Information Sources. LC 73-17517. (Art & Architecture Information Guide Ser.: Vol. 2). x, 173p. 1975. 42.00x (ISBN 0-8103-1275-1). Gale.

Buckley, P. M., jt. auth. see Hoskyns, A. H.

Buckley, Peter, jt. auth. see Mack, Walter S.

Buckley, Peter J. & Roberts, Brian R. European Direct Investment in the U. S. A. Before World War I. 200p. 1981. 49.00x (ISBN 0-333-29079-8, Pub. by Macmillan England). State Mutual Bk.

Buckley, R. Ant-Plant Interactions in Australia. 1982. text ed. 54.50 (ISBN 90-6193-684-5, Pub. by Junk Pubs Netherlands). Kluwer Boston.

Buckley, Robert H., et al, eds. Capital Markets & the Housing Sector: Perspectives on Financial Reform. LC 77-5117. 416p. 1977. prof ref 22.50x (ISBN 0-88410-658-6). Ballinger Pub.

Buckley, Roger. Occupation Diplomacy: Britain, the United States & Japan, 1945-1952. LC 82-4147. (International Studies). (Illus.). 296p. 1982. 39.50 (ISBN 0-521-23567-7). Cambridge U Pr.

Buckley, William F. Who's on First. LC 79-55374. 1980. 13.95 (ISBN 0-385-14681-7). Doubleday.

Buckley, William F., Jr. Atlantic High: A Celebration. LC 81-43455. (Illus.). 280p. 1982. 22.50 (ISBN 0-385-15233-7); 150.00 o.p. limited ed. (ISBN 0-385-18298-8). Doubleday.

--Cruising Speed: A Documentary. 1971. 6.95 o.p. (ISBN 0-399-10181-0). Putnam Pub Group.

--Execution Eve & Other Contemporary Ballads. LC 75-17593. 512p. 9.95 o.p. (ISBN 0-399-11531-5). Putnam Pub Group.

--A Hymnal: The Controversial Arts. LC 78-18892. 1978. 12.95 o.s.i. (ISBN 0-399-12227-3). Putnam Pub Group.

--Marco Polo, If You Can. 1983. pap. 3.50 (ISBN 0-380-61424-3, 61424-3). Avon.

--Marco Polo, If You Can. large print ed. LC 82-5470. 414p. 1982. Repr. of 1982 ed. 13.95 (ISBN 0-89621-361-7). Thorndike Pr.

--Overdrive: A Personal Documentary. 1982. 16.95. Doubleday.

--Saving the Queen. LC 75-17405. 1976. 13.95 (ISBN 0-385-03800-3). Doubleday.

--Stained Glass. 352p. 1981. pap. 2.95 (ISBN 0-380-54791-0, 61481-2). Avon.

--Stained Glass. LC 77-91557. 1978. 13.95 (ISBN 0-385-12542-9). Doubleday.

--The Unmaking of a Mayor. (Illus.). 1977. Repr. of 1966 ed. 9.95 o.p. (ISBN 0-87000-391-7, Arlington Hse). Crown.

Buckman, David. James Bolivar Manson: An English Impressionist. 56p. 1981. 19.00x (ISBN 0-686-97684-3, Pub. by Redcliffe England). State Mutual Bk.

Buckman, David L. Old Steamboat Days on the Hudson River: Tales & Reminiscences of the Stirring Times That Followed the Introduction of Steam Navigation. LC 77-156931. (Illus.). 1971. Repr. of 1909 ed. 34.00x o.p. (ISBN 0-8103-3737-1). Gale.

Buckman, Peter. The Rothschild Conversion. LC 79-9108. 1980. 10.95 o.p. (ISBN 0-07-008795-4). McGraw.

Buckman, William. Physics: Principles & Life Science Applications. Date not set. text ed. price not set o.s.i. (ISBN 0-442-20844-8). Van Nos Reinhold.

Buckmaster, Henrietta. Flight to Freedom: The Story of the Underground Railroad. LC 58-9731. (gr. 7 up). 1958. 12.45i o.p. (ISBN 0-690-30846-9, TYC-J). Har-Row.

Buckmaster, J. D. & Ludford, G. S. S. Theory of Laminar Flames. LC 81-21573. (Cambridge Monographs on Mechanics & Applied Mathematics Ser.). (Illus.). 250p. 1982. 49.50 (ISBN 0-521-23929-X). Cambridge U Pr.

Buckmaster, J. D., ed. Fluid Mechanics in Energy Conversion: Proceedings. LC 80-65817. (SIAM-SIMS Conference Ser.: No. 7). ix, 315p. 1980. pap. 31.00 (ISBN 0-89871-165-7). Soc Indus-Appl Math.

Buckminster Staff. Synergetic Stew: Explorations in Dymaxion Dining. 120p. (Orig.). 1982. 6.95 (ISBN 0-911573-00-3). Buckminster Fuller.

Bucknall, Barbara J. Ursula K. LeGuin. LC 81-10371. (Recognitions). 186p. 1981. 11.95 (ISBN 0-8044-2085-8); pap. 5.95 (ISBN 0-8044-6063-9). Ungar.

Bucknall, C. B. Toughened Plastics. (Illus.). 1977. 57.50x (ISBN 0-85334-695-X, Pub. by Applied Sci England). Elsevier.

Bucknell, Howard, III. Energy & the National Defense. Davis, Vincent, ed. LC 79-57566. (Essays for the Third Century). 256p. (General editor, Vincent Davis). 1981. 19.50x (ISBN 0-8131-0402-5). U Pr of Ky.

Bucknell, Howard, 3rd, ed. see Cope, Harley F.

Bucknell, Peter A., jt. auth. see Hill, Margot H.

Buckner, Leroy M. Customer Services. (Occupational Manuals & Projects in Marketing). (Illus.). 1978. pap. text ed. 7.32 (ISBN 0-07-008823-3, G); teacher's manual & key 4.50 (ISBN 0-07-008824-1). McGraw.

Buckner, Michael D., jt. auth. see Abrams, Natalie.

Bucknill, John C. & Hammond, William. Insanity & the Law: Two Nineteenth Century Classics. LC 81-916. (The Historical Foundations of Forensic Psychiatry & Psychology Ser.). 145p. 1981. Repr. of 1856 ed. lib. bdg. 29.50 (ISBN 0-306-76066-5). Da Capo.

BUCOP, ed. World List Scientific Periodicals, 1980, Vol. 17: Scientific Annual. 1981. text ed. write for info. o.p. (ISBN 0-408-70862-X). Butterworth.

Buczacki, S. T., ed. Zoosporic Plant Pathogens. Date not set. price not set (ISBN 0-12-139180-9). Acad Pr.

Budak, Aram. Circuit Theory Fundamentals & Applications. LC 77-22344. (Illus.). 1978. 32.95 (ISBN 0-13-133975-3). P-H.

--Passive & Active Network Analysis & Synthesis. 600p. 1974. text ed. 24.95 (ISBN 0-395-17203-9); solutions manual 5.50 (ISBN 0-395-17835-5). HM.

Budassi, Susan, jt. ed. see Auerbach, Paul.

Buday, George. The History of the Christmas Card. LC 74-174012. (Tower Bks). (Illus.). xxiii, 304p. 1972. Repr. of 1954 ed. 42.00x (ISBN 0-8103-3931-5). Gale.

Budd, D. A. & Loucks, R. G. Report of Investigations No. One Hundred Twelve: Smackover & Lower Buckner Formations, Jurassic, South Texas-Depositional Systems on a Carbonate Ramp, No. 112. (Illus.). 38p. 1981. 2.25 (ISBN 0-686-36601-8). Bur Econ Geology.

--Smackover & Lower Buckner Formations, Jurassic, South Texas: Depositional Systems on a Carbonate Ramp. (Report of Investigations: No. 112). (Illus.). 38p. 2.25 (ISBN 0-686-36593-3). Bur Econ Geology.

Budd, Elaine, jt. auth. see Place, Stan.

Budd, John, compiled by. Eight Scandanavian Novelists: Criticism & Reviews in English. LC 80-24895. viii, 180p. 1981. lib. bdg. 29.95 (ISBN 0-313-22869-8, BSN/). Greenwood.

--Henry James: A Bibliography of Criticism, 1975-1981. LC 82-21463. 216p. 1983. lib. bdg. 35.00 (ISBN 0-313-23515-5, BHJ/). Greenwood.

Budd, John F. Corporate Video in Focus: A Management Guide to Private TV. (Illus.). 224p. 1983. 21.95 (ISBN 0-13-176206-0); pap. 10.95 (ISBN 0-13-176198-6). P-H.

Budd, Lillian. April Harvest. 304p. 1980. pap. 2.25 o.s.i. (ISBN 0-380-49593-7, 49593). Avon.

--Land of Strangers. 1979. pap. 2.25 o.p. (ISBN 0-380-48314-9, 48314). Avon.

Budd, Louis J. Critical Essays on Mark Twain, 1867-1910. (Critical Essays on American Literature). 1982. lib. bdg. 28.50 (ISBN 0-8161-8619-7, Twayne). G K Hall.

Budd, Mavis. So Beautiful: My Grandmother's Natural Beauty Creams, Lotions, & Remedies. (Illus.). 64p. 1982. 7.95 (ISBN 0-7188-2511-X, Pub. by Salem Hse Ltd.). Merrimack Bk Serv.

Budd, S. A., jt. auth. see Bowker, R. M.

Budde, William L. & Eichelberger, James W., eds. Organics Analysis Using Gas Chromatography-Mass Spectrometry: A Techniques & Procedures Manual. LC 79-88484. (Illus.). 1979. 29.95 (ISBN 0-250-40318-8). Ann Arbor Science.

Budden, Julian. Operas of Verdi: From Il Trovatore to la Forza Del Destino, Vol. 2. (The Operas of Verdi Ser). (Illus.). 1978. 39.95x (ISBN 0-19-520068-3). Oxford U Pr.

Buddha, Gautama. Dhammapada. Babbitt, Irving, tr. LC 64-23655. 1965. pap. 4.95 (ISBN 0-8112-0004-3, NDP188). New Directions.

Buddhist Association of the United States, tr. see Chang, Garma C.

Buddhist Books International, tr. see Yamaguchi, Susumu.

Buddhist Rext Translation Society, tr. see Ch'an Master Hua.

Buddhist Text Translation Society, tr. see Ch'an Master Hua.

Buder, Stanley. Pullman: An Experiment in Industrial Order & Community Planning, 1880-1930. (Urban Life in America). 1967. pap. 6.95x (ISBN 0-19-500838-3). Oxford U Pr.

Budge, E. A. The Gods of the Egyptians: Studies in Egyptian Mythology, 2 Vols. LC 67-28633. (Illus.). 1969. pap. 10.00 ea.; Vol. 1. pap. (ISBN 0-486-22055-9); Vol. 2. pap. (ISBN 0-486-22056-7). Dover.

Budge, E. A. Wallis. Amulets & Superstitions. 10.00 (ISBN 0-8446-5676-3). Peter Smith.

--Divine Origin of the Craft of the Herbalist. LC 78-174013. (Illus.). 1971. Repr. of 1928 ed. 34.00x (ISBN 0-8103-3794-0). Gale.

--Egyptian Book of the Dead: The Papyrus of Ani in the British Museum. 1967. pap. 6.95 (ISBN 0-486-21866-X). Dover.

Budge, E. Wallis. The Dwellers on the Nile: The Life, History, Religion, & Literature of the Ancient Egyptians. (Illus.). 1977. pap. 5.50 (ISBN 0-486-23501-7). Dover.

--Egyptian Magic. 1971. pap. 4.00 (ISBN 0-486-22681-6). Dover.

--Osiris & the Egyptian Resurrection, 2 vols. LC 72-81534. (Illus.). 906p. 1973. Vol. 1. pap. 7.50 (ISBN 0-486-22780-4); Vol. 2. pap. 6.00 (ISBN 0-486-22781-2). Dover.

Budge, Ernest A. The Egyptian Heaven & Hell. (Illus.). 200p. 1974. lib. bdg. 15.50 (ISBN 0-87548-311-9); pap. 6.00 (ISBN 0-87548-298-8). Open Court.

Budge, Ernest A., tr. The History of the Blessed Virgin Mary & the History of the Likeness of Christ Which the Jews of Tiberius Made to Mock At, 2 vols. LC 73-18848. (Luzac's Semitic Text & Translation Ser.: Nos. 4-5). Repr. of 1899 ed. 32.50 set (ISBN 0-404-11341-9). AMS Pr.

Budge, Ian & Farlie, Dennis. Voting & Party Competition: A Theoretical Critique & Synthesis Applied to Surveys from Ten Democracies. LC 76-44456. 1977. 74.95 (ISBN 0-471-99454-5, Pub. by Wiley-Interscience). Wiley.

Budge, Ian & O'Leary, Cornelius. Belfast: Approach to Crisis. LC 72-85194. 1973. 18.95 o.p. (ISBN 0-312-07420-4). St Martin.

Budge, Ian, et al, eds. Party Identification & Beyond: Representatives of Voting & Party Competition. LC 74-35615. 358p. 1976. 55.95 (ISBN 0-471-01355-2, Pub. by Wiley-Interscience). Wiley.

Budgett, Winifred, tr. see Steiner, Rudolf & Steiner Von Sivers, Marie.

Budinger, Thomas F., et al, eds. Noninvasive Techniques for Assessment of Atherosclerosis in Peripheral, Carotid, & Coronary Arteries. 235p. 1982. text ed. 49.00 (ISBN 0-89004-679-4). Raven.

Budinski, Kenneth G. Engineering Materials: Properties & Selection. (Illus.). 1979. text ed. 23.95 (ISBN 0-8359-1693-6); students manual avail. (ISBN 0-8359-1694-4). Reston.

Budlong, Ware & Fleitzer, Mark H. Experimenting with Seeds & Plants. LC 74-77775. (Illus.). (gr. 3-7). 1970. PLB 5.29 o.p. (ISBN 0-399-60157-0). Putnam Pub Group.

Budnick, Frank S. Applied Mathematics for Business, Economics, & the Social Sciences. (Illus.). 1979. text ed. 23.95 (ISBN 0-07-008851-9, C); wkbk o.p. 6.96 (ISBN 0-07-008854-3); instructor's manual 7.95 (ISBN 0-07-008852-7). McGraw.

--Applied Mathematics for Business, Economics & the Social Sciences. 2nd ed. 842p. 1983. 26.50x (ISBN 0-07-008858-6); write for info. (ISBN 0-07-008859-4). McGraw.

Budny, Mildred, tr. see Tammuz, Benjamin.

Budoff, Penny W. No More Menstrual Cramps & Other Good News. 384p. 1980. 11.95 (ISBN 0-399-12519-1). Putnam Pub Group.

Budreckis, Algirdas, ed. The Lithuanians in America, 1651-1975: A Chronology & Fact Book. LC 76-6680. (Ethnic Chronology Ser: No. 21). 174p. 1976. lib. bdg. 8.50 (ISBN 0-379-00517-4). Oceana.

Budrow, Nancy, jt. auth. see Hartline, Jane.

Budrow, Nancy S., jt. auth. see Hartline, Jane.

Budrys, Algis. Rogue Moon. (Science Fiction). 1977. Repr. of 1960 ed. lib. bdg. 11.00 o.p. (ISBN 0-8398-2369-X, Gregg). G K Hall.

--Some Will Not Die. Freas, Polly & Freas, Kelly, eds. LC 78-2193. (Illus.). 1978. pap. 5.95 (ISBN 0-915442-52-3, Starblaze). Donning Co.

--Who? 1979. lib. bdg. 10.95 (ISBN 0-8398-2492-0, Gregg). G K Hall.

Budson, R. D., jt. ed. see Barofsky, I.

Budy, A. M., ed. see Interdisciplinary Conference - 1st.

Budy, A. M., ed. see Interdisciplinary Conference - 3rd.

Budy, Andrea H. Living on the Cusp. Hettich, M. & Ahern, Colleen, eds. 35p. 1980. 3.00 (ISBN 0-686-38059-2). Moons Quilt Pr.

Budyko, M. I. Climate Changes. Zolina, R., tr. from Rus. 1977. 24.00 (ISBN 0-87590-206-5). Am Geophysical.

Budynas, Richard G. Advanced Strength & Applied Stress Analysis. (Illus.). 1977. text ed. 37.50 (ISBN 0-07-008828-4, C); solutions manual 7.95 (ISBN 0-07-008829-2). McGraw.

Budzik, Janet K., jt. auth. see Budzik, Richard S.

Budzik, Richard S. Fittings Used Today That Require Triangulation Including the Theory of Triangulation. 2nd ed. LC 75-182389. (Illus.). 1982. 17.95 (ISBN 0-912914-21-1). Practical Pubns.

--Practical Sheet Metal Projects-130 Graded Projects with Drawings, Forming Information & Sequences. LC 79-93132. (Illus.). (gr. 7-12). 1979. 14.95 (ISBN 0-912914-06-8). Practical Pubns.

--Precision Sheet Metal Blueprint Reading. LC 75-86373. (Illus.). 127p. 1969. text ed. 17.95 (ISBN 0-912914-11-4); tchr's materials 24.95 (ISBN 0-912914-13-0); wkbk 17.95 (ISBN 0-912914-12-2). Practical Pubns.

--Precision Sheet Metal Mathematics. LC 71-83129. (Illus.). 349p. 1969. text ed. 17.95 (ISBN 0-912914-14-9); instr's guide 24.95 (ISBN 0-912914-16-5); wkbk 17.95 (ISBN 0-912914-15-7). Practical Pubns.

--Precision Sheet Metal Shop Practice. LC 78-97566. (Illus.). 96p. 1969. 11.95 (ISBN 0-912914-17-3); tchrs' materials 24.95 (ISBN 0-912914-19-X); wkbk 17.95 (ISBN 0-912914-18-1). Practical Pubns.

--Precision Sheet Metal Shop Theory. LC 79-77566. (Illus.). 334p. 1969. 17.95 (ISBN 0-912914-08-4); tchrs' materials 24.95 (ISBN 0-912914-10-6); wkbk 17.95 (ISBN 0-912914-09-2). Practical Pubns.

--Round Fittings Used Today Including Methods & Techniques of Fabricating Round Work. 2nd ed. LC 71-182388. (Illus.). 1982. 17.95 (ISBN 0-912914-20-3). Practical Pubns.

--Sheet Metal Shop Fabrication Projects Including Over Three Hundred Fifty Graded Parts. LC 80-84009. (Illus.). (gr. 7-12). 1980. 17.95 (ISBN 0-912914-07-6). Practical Pubns.

--Short Course in Sheet Metal Shop Theory: Including 25 Practical Projects. LC 79-93131. (Illus.). (gr. 7-12). 1979. 12.50 (ISBN 0-912914-05-X). Practical Pubns.

--Specialty Items Used Today (Sheet Metal) Including Methods of Design & Fabrication & Important Trade Topics. LC 74-79537. (Illus.). 1979. 35.95 (ISBN 0-912914-04-1). Practical Pubns.

--Today's Forty Most Frequently-Used Fittings. 2nd ed. LC 73-188876. (Illus.). 184p. 1983. 17.95 (ISBN 0-912914-22-X). Practical Pubns.

Budzik, Richard S. & Budzik, Janet K. Today's Practical Guide to Increasing Profits for Contractors with Easy-to-Use Suggestions & Aids. LC 74-79535. (Illus.). 1974. 39.95 (ISBN 0-912914-03-3). Practical Pubns.

Bueche, Frederick. Introduction to Physics for Scientists & Engineers. 3rd ed. (Illus.). 1980. text ed. 32.50 (ISBN 0-07-008875-6); wkbk. 11.95 (ISBN 0-07-008878-0). McGraw.

--Principles of Physics. 4th ed. (Illus.). 864p. 1982. 27.50x (ISBN 0-07-008867-5); wkbk. 10.95 (ISBN 0-07-008868-3); solutions manual 15.95. McGraw.

--Principles of Physics. 3rd ed. (Illus.). 1977. text ed. 25.50 (ISBN 0-07-008848-9, C); workbook 10.95 (ISBN 0-07-008849-7); instructor's manual 14.95 (ISBN 0-07-008850-0). McGraw.

--Schaum's Outline of College Physics. 7th ed. (Schaum's Outline Ser.). (Illus.). 1979. pap. 6.95 (ISBN 0-07-008857-8, SP). McGraw.

--Understanding the World of Physics. (Illus.). 752p. 1981. text ed. 22.50 (ISBN 0-07-008863-2, C); instructor's manual 15.95 (ISBN 0-07-008864-0). McGraw.

Bueche, Frederick J. Introduction to Physics for Scientists & Engineers. 2nd ed. (Illus.). 960p. 1975. text ed. 26.50 (ISBN 0-07-008836-5, C). McGraw.

Buechler, John. Correspondence of Francis Parkman & Henry Stevens. LC 67-27070. (Transactions Ser.: Vol. 57, Pt. 6). (Illus.). 1967. pap. 0.50 o.p. (ISBN 0-87169-576-6). Am Philos.

Buechler, Sandra. Sesquicentennial of Effingham County. (Illus.). 808p. 1982. 75.00 (ISBN 0-9609598-0-7). Banbury Pub Co.

Buechner, Frederick. The Alphabet of Grace. (Orig.). 1977. pap. 4.95 (ISBN 0-8164-2163-3). Seabury.

--The Book of Bebb. LC 79-63795. 512p. 1979. 14.95 (ISBN 0-689-10986-5). Atheneum.

--The Final Beast. LC 81-47438. 1982. 10.53i (ISBN 0-686-97205-8, HarpR). Har-Row.

--Magnificent Defeat. 1968. pap. 5.95 (ISBN 0-8164-2045-9, SP44). Seabury.

Buechner, Katy. File Folder Math, Set D. (gr. 4-6). 1978. pap. 16.25 (ISBN 0-88488-113-X). Creative Pubns.

--File Folder Math, Set E. (gr. 5-7). 1978. pap. 16.25 (ISBN 0-88488-114-8). Creative Pubns.

Buechner, Katy & Lowell. File Folder Math: Sets A-C, 3 bks. 1977. pap. 18.25 ea.; Set. pap. 48.50 (ISBN 0-88488-153-9); Set A. pap. (ISBN 0-88488-141-5); Set B. pap. (ISBN 0-88488-142-3); Set C. pap. (ISBN 0-88488-143-1). Creative Pubns.

Buechner, Robert. Prosper Through Tax Planning. (Illus.). 288p. 1983. 17.95 (ISBN 0-698-11196-6, Coward). Putnam Pub Group.

Buechner, Robert & Manzler, David. Accumulating Wealth with Before Tax Dollars. LC 79-88648. 44p. 1979. looseleaf 35.00 o.p. (ISBN 0-87218-403-X); Desk Bk. 78p. 20.00 o.p. (ISBN 0-87218-404-8). Natl Underwriter.

Buechner, Robert W. & Manzler, David L. Accumulating Wealth with Before Tax Dollars (Desk Book) LC 81-86381. (Illus.). 1982. write for info. looseleaf (ISBN 0-87218-417-X); write for info. visual, 48 p. (ISBN 0-87218-416-1). Natl Underwriter.

Buechner, Thomas & Warmus, William. Czechoslovakia Diary. 16p. 1980. pap. 3.00 (ISBN 0-87290-102-5). Corning.

Buegler, Joseph. God's Love Machine. 160p. 1983. 7.95 (ISBN 0-89962-305-0). Todd & Honeywell.

Buehler, Ezra C. & Johannesen, Richard L. Building the Contest Oration. 202p. 1965. 8.00 (ISBN 0-8242-0008-X). Wilson.

Buehler, Janice A. Nurses & Physicians in Transition. Kalisch, Philip & Kalisch, Beatrice, eds. LC 82-10940. (Studies in Nursing Management: No. 10). 164p. 1982. 39.95 (ISBN 0-8357-1379-2). Univ Microfilms.

Buehr, Walter. Chivalry & the Mailed Knight. (Illus.). (gr. 3 up). 1963. PLB 5.29 o.p. (ISBN 0-399-60094-9). Putnam Pub Group.

--The Crusaders. (Illus.). (gr. 4-6). 1959. PLB 5.79 o.p. (ISBN 0-399-60113-9). Putnam Pub Group.

--Freight Trains of the Sky. (gr. 3-7). 1969. PLB 4.79 o.p. (ISBN 0-399-60188-0). Putnam Pub Group.

--French Explorers in America. (Illus.). (gr. 4-6). 1961. PLB 5.29 o.p. (ISBN 0-399-60189-9). Putnam Pub Group.

--Knights, Castles & Feudal Life. (Illus.). (gr. 4-6). 1957. PLB 5.29 o.p. (ISBN 0-399-60341-7). Putnam Pub Group.

--Meat, from Ranch to Table. (Illus.). (gr. 5-9). 1956. PLB 8.59 (ISBN 0-688-31557-7). Morrow.

--The Portuguese Explorers. (Illus.). (gr. 3-7). 1966. PLB 5.29 o.p. (ISBN 0-399-60518-5). Putnam Pub Group.

--The Spanish Conquistadores. (Illus.). (gr. 3-7). 1962. PLB 5.29 o.p. (ISBN 0-399-60595-9). Putnam Pub Group.

--Viking Explorers. (Illus.). (gr. 3-7). 1967. PLB 5.29 o.p. (ISBN 0-399-60654-8). Putnam Pub Group.

Buel, Larry V., jt. ed. see Hanrieder, Wolfram F.

Bueler, William. Mountains of the World. LC 74-87796. (Illus.). 1977. pap. 5.95 o.p. (ISBN 0-916890-49-X). Mountaineers.

Bueler, William M. U. S. China Policy & the Problem of Taiwan. LC 79-25371. 143p. 1980. Repr. of 1971 ed. lib. bdg. 17.00x (ISBN 0-313-22153-7, BUUS). Greenwood.

Buelke-Sam, Judith, jt. ed. see Kimmel, Carole A.

Buell, Charles E. Physical Education for Blind Children. (Illus.). 232p. 1983. pap. text ed. 16.50x (ISBN 0-398-04816-9). C C Thomas.

Buell, Edith M. Outline of Language for Deaf Children: Book I. 1952. pap. text ed. 3.50 o.p. (ISBN 0-88200-101-9, C1569). Alexander Graham.

Buell, Ellen L., ed. Treasury of Little Golden Books. Rev. ed. 96p. (ps-2). 1982. 6.95 (ISBN 0-307-96540-6). Western Pub.

Buell, Emmett H., Jr. & Brisbin, Richard A., Jr. School Desegregation & Defended Neighborhoods: The Boston Controversy. LC 78-19598. (Illus.). 208p. 1981. 23.95x (ISBN 0-669-02646-8). Lexington Bks.

Buell, Frederick. Theseus & Other Poems. 89p. 1971. 2.95 (ISBN 0-87886-003-7). Ithaca Hse.

Buell, Hal. World of Red China. LC 67-10548. (Illus.). (gr. 5 up). 1967. PLB 5.95 o.p. (ISBN 0-396-06467-1). Dodd.

Buell, Lawrence. Design of Literature. new ed. LC 73-75452. (gr. 7-12). 1973. pap. text ed. 1.45 o.p. (ISBN 0-88301-078-X). Pendulum Pr.

Buell, Lawrence, ed. see Longsworth, Robert.

Buell, Lawrence, ed. see Olmstead, John.

Buell, Lawrence, ed. see Pierce, Barbara B., et al.

Buell, Lawrence, ed. see Whitman, Walt.

Buell, Lillian P. How to Raise & Train a Saint Bernard. (Orig.). pap. 2.95 (ISBN 0-87666-374-9, DS1125). TFH Pubns.

Buell, Murray F., jt. auth. see Robichaud, Beryl.

Buell, Raymond L. Liberia: A Century of Survival, Eighteen Forty-Seven to Nineteen Forty-Seven. (African Handbooks Ser.: Vol. 7). (Illus.). 1947. 3.00x (ISBN 0-686-24090-1). Univ Mus of U.

Buell, Victor P., et al, eds. Handbook of Modern Marketing. LC 78-96238. (Illus.). 1504p. 1970. 74.95 (ISBN 0-07-008838-1). McGraw.

Buelow, George, ed. see Berger, Karol.

Buelow, George, ed. see Block, Adrienne F.

Buelow, George, ed. see Daniel, Keith W.

Buelow, George, ed. see Friedland, Bea.

Buelow, George, ed. see Harriss, Ernest C.

Buelow, George, ed. see Hill, John.

Buelow, George, ed. see Hosler, Bellamy.

Buelow, George, ed. see McCreless, Patrick P.

Buelow, George, ed. see Mead, Rita.

Buelow, George, ed. see Neumann, Frederick.

Buelow, George, ed. see Nicolaisen, Jay.

Buelow, George, ed. see Palmer, A. Dean.

Buelow, George, ed. see Pennington, Neil D.

Buelow, George, ed. see Petty, Fred C.

Buelow, George, ed. see Samuel, Harold E.

Buelow, George, ed. see Silbiger, Alexander.

Buelow, George, ed. see Tick, Judith.

Buelow, George, ed. see Virga, Patricia H.

Buelow, George, ed. see Witherell, Anne L.

Buelow, George J. Thorough Bass Accompaniment According to Johann David Heinichen. LC 65-12891. 1966. 35.00x o.p. (ISBN 0-520-00188-5). U of Cal Pr.

Buelow, George J., jt. auth. see Daviau, Donald G.

Buenker, John, et al, eds. Urban History: a Guide to Information Sources. LC 80-19643. (American Government & History Ser., Part of the Gale Information Guide Library: Vol. 9). 400p. 1981. 42.00x (ISBN 0-8103-1479-7). Gale.

Buenker, John D. & Burckel, Nicholas C. Immigration & Ethnicity: A Guide to Information Sources. LC 74-11515. (American Government & History Information Guide Ser.: Vol. 1). 1977. 42.00x (ISBN 0-8103-1202-6). Gale.

Buenker, John D. & Burckel, Nicholas C., eds. Progressive Reform: A Guide to Information Sources. (The American Government & History Information Guide Ser.: Vol. 8). 300p. 1981. 42.00x (ISBN 0-8103-1485-1). Gale.

Bueno, Dorothy Del see Del Bueno, Dorothy.

Bueno, Julian A. La Sotana De Juan Ruiz -Elementos Eclesiasticos En el Libro De Buen Amor. 200p. 1983. 17.00 (ISBN 0-938972-02-2). Spanish Lit Pubns.

Bueno de Mesquita, B. Strategy, Risk & Personality in Coalition Politics. LC 75-3853. (Illus.). 224p. 1976. 29.95 (ISBN 0-521-20874-2). Cambridge U Pr.

Bueno De Mesquita, Bruce & Park, Richard L. India's Political System. 2nd ed. (Illus.). 1979. pap. 11.95 ref. (ISBN 0-13-456921-0). P-H.

Buergenthal, Thomas & Norris, Robert. Human Rights: The Inter-American System. LC 82-81889. (Human Rights Ser.). 1982. loose-leaf 85.00 (ISBN 0-379-20723-0). Oceana.

Buerger, Jane. Obedience. LC 80-39520. (Values to Live by). (Illus.). 32p. (ps-3). 1981. PLB 8.65 (ISBN 0-516-06526-2). Childrens.

Buerger, Jane, ed. see Baker, Eugene.

Buerger, Jane, ed. see Moncure, Jane B.

Buerger, Jane, ed. see Odor, Ruth.

Buerger, Janet E. The Era of the French Calotype. LC 82-82296. (Illus.). 64p. (Orig.). 1982. pap. 15.00 (ISBN 0-935398-07-4). Intl Mus Photo.

Buerger, M. J. Contemporary Crystallography. 1970. text ed. 26.00 (ISBN 0-07-008840-3, C). McGraw.

Buerger, M. L., jt. auth. see Azaroff, Leonid V.

Buerger, Martin J. Crystal-Structure Analysis. LC 79-1407. 690p. 1979. Repr. of 1960 ed. lib. bdg. 37.50 (ISBN 0-88275-900-0). Krieger.

--X-Ray Crystallography. LC 80-12459. 564p. 1980. Repr. of 1942 ed. lib. bdg. 34.00 (ISBN 0-89874-176-9). Krieger.

--X-Ray Crystallography. 1942. 32.00 o.p. (ISBN 0-471-11781-1, Pub. by Wiley-Interscience). Wiley.

Buerger, Martin J., jt. auth. see Azaroff, Leonid V.

Buerk, Charles A., jt. auth. see Van Way, Charles W.

Buerki, F. A. Stagecraft for Nonprofessionals. 3rd ed. (Illus.). 144p. (Orig.). 1972. pap. 6.95 (ISBN 0-299-06234-1). U of Wis Pr.

Buerkle, Jack V. & Barker, Danny. Bourbon Street Black: The New Orleans Black Jazzman. LC 73-77926. (Illus.). 1974. pap. 5.95 (ISBN 0-19-501832-X, GB415, GB). Oxford U Pr.

Bueso, Alberto T., jt. auth. see O'Connor, Dennis J.

Buess, Bob. Favor the Road to Success. 1982. Repr. of 1975 ed. 1.95 (ISBN 0-934244-17-0). Sweeter Than Honey.

--Favor, the Road to Success. 110p. 1980. pap. 1.50 (ISBN 0-934244-15-4, 317). Sweeter Than Honey.

Buess, Lynn M. The Tarot & Transformation. LC 73-77608. (Illus.). 1977. pap. 6.50 (ISBN 0-87516-238-X). De Vorss.

Buetow, Harole A. The Scabbardless Sword: Criminal Justice & the Quality of Mercy. LC 82-71695. (New Studies on Law & Society). 390p. (Orig.). 1982. text ed. 37.50x (ISBN 0-86733-022-8). Assoc Faculty Pr.

Buettner, Stewart. American Art Theory, 1945-1970. Kuspit, Donald, ed. LC 81-1812. (Studies in Fine Arts: Art Theory, No. 1). 226p. 1981. 39.95 (ISBN 0-8357-1178-1, Pub. by UMI Res Pr). Univ Microfilms.

Bufalini, Joseph J. & Arnts, Robt R. Atmospheric Biogenic Hydrocarbons, 2 vols. LC 81-52298. (Illus.). 181p. 1981. Vol. 1, Emissions. text ed. 25.95 (ISBN 0-250-40497-4); Vol. 2, Ambient Concentrations & Atmospheric Chemistry. text ed. 25.95 (ISBN 0-250-40498-2); Set. text ed. 51.90 (ISBN 0-250-40499-0). Ann Arbor Science.

Buferd, Norma B., jt. auth. see Cooper, Patricia.

Buff, Iva M. A Thematic Catalog of the Sacred Works of Giacomo Carissimi. LC 80-142011. 157p. 1979. 39.00 (ISBN 0-913574-15-5). Eur Am Music.

Buffa & Newman. Plaid for Production & Operations Management. rev. ed. 1981. 7.95 (ISBN 0-256-02222-4). Dow Jones-Irwin.

Buffa, Elwood S. Basic Production Management. 2nd ed. LC 74-28396. (Management & Administration Ser.). 683p. 1975. text ed. 29.95x o.p. (ISBN 0-471-11801-X). Wiley.

--Basic Production Management, 2 vols. Incl. Vol. 1. A Short Course in Managing Day-to-Day Operations. LC 75-27388. 24.95x (ISBN 0-471-11830-3); Vol. 2. A Short Course in Planning & Designing Productive Systems. LC 75-27389. 39.95 (ISBN 0-471-11831-1). (Business Administration Ser.). 1975. Set. text ed. 49.90x (ISBN 0-471-11832-X, Pub. by Wiley-Interscience). Wiley.

--Modern Production-Operations Management. 6th ed. LC 79-17788. (Wiley Ser. in Management). 673p. 1980. text ed. 32.95x (ISBN 0-471-05672-3). Wiley.

--Operations Management: Problems & Models. 3rd ed. LC 78-37167. (Management & Administration Ser). 762p. 1972. 33.95 (ISBN 0-471-11867-2). Wiley.

--Operations Management: The Management of Productive Systems. LC 75-33179. (Management & Administration Ser.). 686p. 1976. text ed. 35.95 (ISBN 0-471-11890-7). Wiley.

Buffa, Elwood S. & Dyer, James S. Essentials of Management Science-Operations Research. LC 77-23799. (Manangement & Administration Ser.). 528p. 1978. text ed. 33.95x (ISBN 0-471-02003-6). Wiley.

--Management Science-Operations Research: Formulation & Solution Methods. 2nd ed. LC 80-18082. 718p. 1981. text ed. 32.95 (ISBN 0-471-05851-3). Wiley.

Buffa, Sebastian, ed. Italian Artists of the Sixteenth Century, Vols. 34-38. (Illus.). Date not set. 120.00 (ISBN 0-89835-034-4). Abaris Bks.

Buffalo Fine Arts Academy & Cranbook Academy of Art-Museum. Donald Blumberg. LC 79-50455. (Illus.). 1983. pap. 8.95 (ISBN 0-914782-24-X). Buffalo Acad.

Buffaloe, Neal D. & Ferguson, Dale V. Microbiology. 2nd ed. LC 80-82842. (Illus.). 752p. 1981. text ed. 27.95 (ISBN 0-395-29649-8); lab manual 9.95 (ISBN 0-395-29652-8); instr's manual 1.00 (ISBN 0-395-29650-1); study guide 8.95 (ISBN 0-395-29651-X). HM.

Buffart, H. F., jt. auth. see Leeuwenberg, E. L.

Buffier. Grammaire Francaise sur un Plan Nouveau. (Linguistics 13th-18th Centuries Ser.). 494p. (Fr.). 1974. Repr. of 1709 ed. lib. bdg. 123.50 o.p. (ISBN 0-8287-0149-0, 71-5030). Clearwater Pub.

--Suite de la Grammaire Francaise sur un Plan Nouveau. (Linguistics 13th-18th Centuries Ser.). 608p. (Fr.). 1974. Repr. of 1728 ed. lib. bdg. 148.00x o.p. (ISBN 0-8287-0150-4, 71-5031). Clearwater Pub.

Buffington, jt. auth. see Graham, Frank.

Buffington, Albert F. Dutchified German Spirituals, Vol. 62. 1963. 15.00 o.p. (ISBN 0-911122-16-8). Penn German Soc.

--Pennsylvania German Secular Folk Songs, Vol. VIII. LC 74-78062. 1974. 15.00 (ISBN 0-911122-30-3). Penn German Soc.

Buffum, Imbrie. Studies in the Baroque From Montaigne to Rotrov. 1957. text ed. 47.50x (ISBN 0-686-83793-2). Elliots Bks.

Bufhanan, James W. Minnesota Walk Book: A Guide to Backpacking & Hiking in the Arrowhead & Isle Royale, Vol. 1. Reprint ed. 105p. 1982. pap. 4.50 (ISBN 0-931714-02-8). Nodin Pr.

Bufithis, Philip H. Norman Mailer. LC 74-78438. (Literature and Life Ser.). 1978. 11.95 (ISBN 0-8044-2097-1); pap. 4.95 (ISBN 0-8044-6064-7). Ungar.

Bufkin, E. C. P. H. Newby. (English Authors Ser.). 1975. lib. bdg. 13.95 (ISBN 0-8057-1414-6, Twayne). G K Hall.

Buford, Lolah. Alyx. 1977. pap. 1.95 o.p. (ISBN 0-451-07640-0, J7640, Sig). NAL.

Buford, Thomas O. Philosophy for Adults. LC 80-5524. 639p. 1980. pap. text ed. 18.50 (ISBN 0-8191-1118-X). U Pr of Amer.

Buford, Thomas O., ed. Essays on Other Minds. LC 73-122911. 1971. 25.95 (ISBN 0-252-00123-0). U of Ill Pr.

Buford, Thomas O., jt. ed. see Howie, John.

Bugat, Paul, jt. auth. see Healy, Bruce.

Bugday, M. Celalettin. Dizionario Italiano-Turco, Turco-Italiano. 410p. (Ital. & Turkish.). 1979. leatherette 5.95 (ISBN 0-686-97351-8, M-9178). French & Eur.

Bugental, James T. The Search for Authenticity. 477p. 1982. pap. text ed. 12.95x (ISBN 0-8290-1298-2). Irvington.

Bugg, Charles B. Things My Children Are Teaching Me. LC 81-70409. 1982. pap. 3.95 (ISBN 0-8054-5650-3). Broadman.

Bugialli, Giuliano. Giuliano Bugialli's Classic Techniques of Italian Cooking. LC 82-10753. 526p. 1982. 19.95 (ISBN 0-671-25218-6). S&S.

Bugliarello, George & Simon, H. A., eds. Technology, the University, & the Community. 1976. 45.00 (ISBN 0-08-017872-3). Pergamon.

Bugliosi, Vincent. Shadow of Cain. 1981. 12.95 (ISBN 0-393-01466-5). Norton.

Bugliosi, Vincent & Hurwitz, Ken. Shadow of Cain. 304p. 1982. 3.95 (ISBN 0-553-20922-1). Bantam.

Bugner, Ladislas, ed. see Devisse, Jean & Courtes, Jean Marie.

Bugner, Ladislas, ed. see Devisse, Jean & Mollat, Michel.

Bugner, Ladislas, ed. see M'Bow, Amadou-Mahtar & Vercoutter, Jean.

Bugnet, Nicolas, jt. auth. see Jaunez-Sponville, Pierre-Ignace.

Bugrov, Y. S. & Nikolsky, S. M. Fundamentals of Linear Algebra & Analytical Geometry. 189p. 1982. pap. 3.45 (ISBN 0-8285-2445-9, Pub. by Mir Pubs USSR). Imported Pubns.

Buheiry, Leila G., jt. ed. see Buheiry, Marwan R.

Buheiry, Marwan R. & Buheiry, Leila G., eds. The Splendor of Lebanon. LC 77-13169. 1977. deluxe ed. 400.00x (ISBN 0-88206-018-X). Caravan Bks.

Buhiery, Marwan, ed. The Splendor of the Holy Land. LC 77-5503. 1979. deluxe ed. 400.00x (ISBN 0-88206-019-8). Caravan Bks.

Buhite, Russell D. Soviet-American Relations in Asia, 1945-1954. LC 81-40285. (Illus.). 256p. 1981. 17.95 (ISBN 0-8061-1729-X). U of Okla Pr.

Buhl, Harold R. Creative Engineering Design. facsimile ed. (Illus.). 1960. pap. 9.45x o.p. (ISBN 0-8138-2215-7). Iowa St U Pr.

Buhle, Mari J. & Buhle, Paul, eds. The Concise History of Woman Suffrage: Selections from the Classic Work of Stanton, Anthony, Gage, & Harper. LC 78-1733. 1978. 25.95 (ISBN 0-252-00669-0); pap. 9.95 (ISBN 0-252-00691-7). U of Ill Pr.

Buhle, Paul, jt. ed. see Buhle, Mari J.

Buhler, Charlotte. The First Year of Life. Greenberg, Pearl & Ripin, Rowena, trs. LC 73-16646. 281p. 1974. Repr. of 1930 ed. lib. bdg. 15.50x o.p. (ISBN 0-8371-7214-4, BUFY). Greenwood.

--From Birth to Maturity. 1968. text ed. 11.25x o.p. (ISBN 0-7100-6244-3). Humanities.

Buhler, Charlotte, et al. Childhood Problems & the Teacher. LC 70-95114. Repr. of 1952 ed. lib. bdg. 16.25x o.p. (ISBN 0-8371-2496-4, BUCP). Greenwood.

Buhler, Fritz R., ed. Alpha-Adrenoceptors in Cardiovascular Regulation. 192p. 1982. text ed. 19.00 (ISBN 0-89004-858-4). Raven.

Buhler, Georg, ed. The Sacred Laws of the Aryas. (Sacred Bks. of the East: Vols. 2 & 14). both vols. 22.00 (ISBN 0-686-97474-3); 11.00 ea. Lancaster-Miller.

Buhler, Kathryn C. American Silver Sixteen Fifty-Five to Eighteen Twenty-Five, 2 vols. (Illus.). 740p. 1972. cloth, boxed 45.00 (ISBN 0-87846-064-0); pap. 22.00 (ISBN 0-87846-148-5). Mus Fine Arts Boston.

--American Silver Sixteen Fifty-Five to Eighteen Twenty-Five in the Museum of Fine Arts, Boston. LC 75-190547. (Illus.). 740p. 1972. slipcase 45.00 o.p. (ISBN 0-87846-064-0, Pub. by Boston Museum of Fine Arts). NYGS.

--Paul Revere, Goldsmith: 1735-1818. rev. ed. (Illus.). 56p. 1975. pap. 1.95 (ISBN 0-87846-219-8). Mus Fine Arts Boston.

Buhler, Michael. Tin Toys. 1978. pap. 6.95 (ISBN 0-8256-3119-X, Quick Fox). Putnam Pub Group.

Buhler, Walther. Living with Your Body. Maloney, L., tr. from Ger. 117p. (Orig.). 1979. pap. 9.95 (ISBN 0-85440-345-0, Pub. by Steinerbooks). Anthroposophic.

Buhlmann, Walbert. God's Chosen Peoples. Barr, Robert R., tr. from Ger. LC 82-12635. Orig. Title: Die Auserwahlten Volker. 320p. (Orig.). 1982. pap. 8.95 (ISBN 0-88344-150-0). Orbis Bks.

Building Cost File, compiled by. The Berger Building Cost File 1981: General Construction Trades with Comparative Building Systems & Costs, 4 editions. Incl. Eastern Edition (ISBN 0-442-21240-2); Western Edition (ISBN 0-442-21238-0); Central Edition (ISBN 0-442-21237-2); Southern Edition (ISBN 0-442-21236-4). 210p. 1980. pap. text ed. 34.95 ea. o.p. Van Nos Reinhold.

Buist, Charlotte A. & Schulman, Jerome L. Toys & Games for Educationally Handicapped Children. 240p. 1976. pap. 18.75x (ISBN 0-398-00250-9). C C Thomas.

Buist, J. M. Developments in Polyurethane, Vol. 1. 1978. 51.25 (ISBN 0-85334-756-5, Pub. by Applied Sci England). Elsevier.

Buitenen, J. A. van see Dimmitt, Cornelia.

Buj, Moira, illus. Mother Goose. (Illus.). 12p. 1977. pap. 2.00 (ISBN 0-85953-080-9, Pub. by Child's Play England). Playspaces.

Bukalski, Peter J., compiled by. Film Research: A Critical Bibliography with Annotations & Essay. 1972. lib. bdg. 20.00 (ISBN 0-8161-0971-0, Hall Reference). G K Hall.

Bukhari, Emil. Napoleon's Guards Cavalry. (Men-at-Arms Ser.). (Illus.). 48p. 1979. pap. 7.95 o.p. (ISBN 0-85045-288-0). Hippocrene Bks.

Bukhari, Emir. Napoleon's Dragoons & Lancers. (Men-at-Arms Ser.). (Illus.). 40p. 1976. pap. 7.95 o.p. (ISBN 0-85045-088-8). Hippocrene Bks.

--Napoleon's Line Chasseurs. (Men-at-Arms Ser.). (Illus.). 48p. 1977. pap. 7.95 o.p. (ISBN 0-85045-269-4). Hippocrene Bks.

Bukharin, Nikolai, jt. auth. see Luxemburg, Rosa.

Bukhsh, S. K. The Renaissance of Islam. 1981. 29.00 (ISBN 0-686-97863-3). Kazi Pubns.

Bukkila, Laura, jt. auth. see Sandhu, Harpreet.

Bukofzer, M. Geschichte des emglischen Diskants und des Fauxbourdons nach den Theoretischen Quellen. (Sammlung Mw. Abh. 21-1936 Ser.). 184p. 35.00 o.s.i. (ISBN 90-6027-178-5, Pub. by Frits Knuf Netherlands). Pendragon NY.

Bukofzer, Manfred, et al, eds. The Place of Musicology in American Institutions of Higher Learning, 2 vols. in one. Incl. Some Aspects of Musicology. LC 77-4226. (Music Reprint Ser.). 1977. Repr. of 1957 ed. lib. bdg. 22.50 (ISBN 0-306-77407-0). Da Capo.

Bukofzer, Manfred F. Music in the Baroque Era. (Illus.). 1947. 18.95x (ISBN 0-393-09745-5, NortonC). Norton.

Bukowski see Stafford, William.

Bukowski, Charles. Burning in Water, Drowning in Flame. 232p. (Orig.). 1981. 14.00 (ISBN 0-87685-192-8); pap. 6.00 (ISBN 0-87685-191-X). Black Sparrow.

--Dangling in the Tournefortia. 285p. (Orig.). 1981. 14.00 (ISBN 0-87685-526-5). pap. 7.50 (ISBN 0-87685-525-7). Black Sparrow.

--Erections, Ejaculations, Exhibitions, & Other Tales of Ordinary Madness. LC 75-164498. 1972. pap. 7.50 (ISBN 0-87286-061-2). City Lights.

--Factotum. 212p. 1982. 14.00 (ISBN 0-87685-264-9); pap. 6.00 (ISBN 0-87685-263-0). Black Sparrow.

--Ham on Rye. 288p. 1982. 14.00 (ISBN 0-87685-558-3); pap. 8.50 (ISBN 0-87685-557-5). Black Sparrow.

--Legs, Hips, & Behind. 40p. 1978. pap. 2.00 o.p. (ISBN 0-935390-03-0). Wormwood Rev.

--Love Is a Dog from Hell: Poems 1974-1977. 312p. (Orig.). 1982. 14.00 (ISBN 0-87685-363-7); pap. 7.50 (ISBN 0-87685-362-9). Black Sparrow.

--Poems Written Before Jumping Out of an Eight Story Window. LC 74-26231. (Illus.). 50p. 1975. perfect bdg. 3.00 o.p. (ISBN 0-915214-00-8). Litmus.

--Post Office. 115p. (Orig.). 1982. 14.00 (ISBN 0-87685-087-5); pap. 5.00 (ISBN 0-87685-086-7). Black Sparrow.

--Women. 296p. 1982. 14.00 (ISBN 0-87685-391-2); pap. 7.50 (ISBN 0-87685-390-4). Black Sparrow.

Bulatao, Rodolfo A. see Arnold, Fred, et al.

Bulbring, E. & Shuba, M. F., eds. Physiology of Smooth Muscle. LC 75-14566. 448p. 1976. 45.50 (ISBN 0-89004-051-6). Raven.

Bulcke, J. A. & Baert, A. L. Clinical & Radiological Aspects of Myopathies: CT Scanning-EMG-Radio-Isotopes. (Illus.). 187p. 1983. 56.00 (ISBN 0-387-11443-2). Springer-Verlag.

Buley, Jerry L. Relationships & Communication: A Book for Friends, Co-Workers & Lovers. 2nd ed. 1979. pap. text ed. 10.95 (ISBN 0-8403-2041-8). Kendall-Hunt.

Bulfinch, Thomas. Bulfinch's Mythology, 3 vols. Incl. Vol. 1. The Age of Fable. pap. 2.95 (ISBN 0-451-62230-8, ME2230); Vols 2 & 3. The Age of Chivalry & Legends of Charlemagne. pap. 3.50 (ISBN 0-451-62024-0, ME2024). (RL 7, Ment). NAL.

--Bulfinch's Mythology. 7.95 (ISBN 0-394-60437-7). Modern Lib.

Bulgakov, M. Master & Margarita. pap. 4.95 (ISBN 0-451-51701-6, CE1701, Sig Classics). NAL.

Bulgakov, Mikhail. D'iavoliada Rasskazy. LC 79-92495. 160p. 1979. pap. 5.95 o.p. (ISBN 0-89830-013-4). Russica Pubs.

--Heart of a Dog. Ginsburg, Mirra, tr. from Russian. 1968. pap. 2.95 (ISBN 0-394-17442-9, E841, BC). Grove.

--Sobranie Sochinenii, Vol. 3. 202p. (Rus.). 1983. 25.00 (ISBN 0-88233-698-3). Ardis Pubs.

--The White Guard. Glenny, Michael, tr. from Rus. 320p. 1975. pap. 3.95 o.p. (ISBN 0-07-008853-5). McGraw.

Bulgarian Academy of Sciences. International Conference on Chemistry & Biotechnology of Biologically Active Natural Products: First, Varna, Bulgaria, September, 21 to 26, 1981. 1982. pap. 34.50 (ISBN 0-686-37434-7, Pub. by Reidel Holland). Kluwer Boston.

Bulgin, Gwen. The Yorkshire Terrier. 1977. pap. 2.50 (ISBN 0-7028-1084-3). Palmetto Pub.

Bulgren, William. Discrete System Simulation. (Illus.). 224p. 1982. text ed. 22.95 (ISBN 0-13-215764-0). P-H.

Bulick, Stephen. Structure & Subject Interaction: Toward a Sociology of Knowledge in the Social Sciences. (Bks in Library & Information Science: Vol. 41). (Illus.). 256p. 1982. 35.00 (ISBN 0-8247-1847-X). Dekker.

Bulka, Reuven P., ed. Holocaust Aftermath: Continuing Impact on the Generations. LC 81-84341. (A Special Issue of Journal of School Psychology & Judaism: Vol. 6). 76p. 1982. pap. 8.95 (ISBN 0-89885-127-0). Human Sci Pr.

Bulka, Rueven P. Dimensions of American Orthodox Judaism. 1983. 20.00x (ISBN 0-87068-894-4). Ktav.

Bulkin, Elly, ed. Lesbian Fiction: An Anthology. LC 81-12194. 336p. (Orig.). 1981. pap. 8.95 (ISBN 0-930436-11-3). Persephone.

Bulkin, Elly & Larkin, Joan, eds. Lesbian Poetry: An Anthology. LC 81-2607. 336p. (Orig.). 1981. pap. 10.95 (ISBN 0-930436-08-3). Persephone.

Bulkley, Mildred E. Bibliographical Survey of Contemporary Sources for the Economic & Social History of the World War. 1922. text ed. 75.00x (ISBN 0-686-83490-9). Elliots Bks.

Bull, A. T., jt. ed. see Quayle, J. R.

Bull, A. T., et al. Microbial Technology: Society for General Microbiology Symposium 29. LC 78-12206. (Illus.). 1979. 65.00 (ISBN 0-521-22500-0). Cambridge U Pr.

Bull, Alan T. & Holt, Geoffrey. Biotechnology: International Trends & Perspectives. 86p. 1982. 5.50 (ISBN 92-64-12362-8). OECD.

Bull, Alvin & Runkel, Sylvian. Wildflowers of Illinois Woodlands. pap. 14.95 (ISBN 0-87069-310-7). Wallace-Homestead.

--Wildflowers of Indiana Woodlands. pap. 14.95 (ISBN 0-87069-309-3). Wallace-Homestead.

Bull, Alvin & Runkle, Sylvian. Wildflowers of Iowa Woodlands. pap. 14.95 (ISBN 0-686-97921-4). Wallace-Homestead.

Bull, Angela. The Accidental Twins. (Illus.). 63p. 1983. 6.95 (ISBN 0-571-11761-9). Faber & Faber.

Bull, Deborah, jt. auth. see Lorimar, Donald.

Bull, G. M. Dartmouth Time-Sharing System. LC 80-41327. (Computers & Their Applications Ser.). 240p. 1980. 87.95 (ISBN 0-470-27082-9). Halsted Pr.

Bull, George. Industrial Relations: The Boardroom Viewpoint. 208p. 1972. 8.75 o.p. (ISBN 0-370-01387-5). Transatlantic.

--Inside the Vatican. 294p. 1983. 13.95 (ISBN 0-312-41884-1). St Martin.

Bull, Gordon, jt. auth. see Bull, Jean.

Bull, Hedley, et al. Greece & the European Community. 172p. 1979. text ed. 27.25x (ISBN 0-566-00232-9). Gower Pub Ltd.

Bull, Jean & Bull, Gordon. Questions in Hotel Reception. 96p. 1981. 25.00x (ISBN 0-85950-310-0, Pub. by Thornes England). State Mutual Bk.

Bull, John. Birds of the New York Area. (Illus.). 11.00 (ISBN 0-8446-5167-2). Peter Smith.

Bull, John & Farrand, John. The Audubon Society Guides to North American Birds: Eastern Region. 1977. 12.50 (ISBN 0-394-41405-5). Knopf.

Bull, M. J. Progress in Industrial Microbiology, Vol. 14. 1978. 59.75 (ISBN 0-444-41665-X). Elsevier.

Bull, M. J., ed. Progress in Industrial Microbiology, Vol. 15. 1979. 64.00 (ISBN 0-444-41815-6, North Holland). Elsevier.

--Progress in Industrial Microbiology, Vol. 16. 1982. 74.50 (ISBN 0-444-42037-1). Elsevier.

Bull, Norman. The Story of Jesus. 160p. 1983. 13.95 (ISBN 0-687-39659-X). Abingdon.

Bull, Odd. War & Peace in the Middle East: The Experiences & Views of a U. N. Observer. (Illus., Stickered only). 1977. lib. bdg. 22.00 o.p. (ISBN 0-89158-706-3). Westview.

Bull, R. J. Accounting in Business. 4th ed. LC 80-49870. (Illus.). 448p. 1980. text ed. 32.50 o.p. (ISBN 0-408-10669-7); pap. text ed. 19.95 o.p. (ISBN 0-408-10670-0). Butterworth.

Bull, Richard H. & Ide, Sachiko. English Made Polite. 2nd ed. (Illus.). 264p. (Orig.). 1981. pap. text ed. 6.50x (ISBN 0-19-581710-9). Oxford U Pr.

Bull, T. R. & Cook, Joyce L. Speech Theraphy & ENT Surgery. (Blackwell Scientific Pubns.). (Illus.). 1976. 13.95 (ISBN 0-632-09410-9, B0883X). Mosby.

Bull, Vivien & Guillet-Rydell, Mireille. A Vous de Choisir: Traditional & Self-Paced Learning in French. LC 82-23781. (Illus.). 342p. (Orig.). 1983. pap. text ed. 13.50 (ISBN 0-8191-2915-1). U Pr of Amer.

Bull, William E. Spanish for Communication. 1972. visual grammar of spanish 187.28 (ISBN 0-395-12445-X). flash cards 42.68 (ISBN 0-395-12447-6); verb slot charts 32.68 (ISBN 0-685-39915-X). HM.

--Spanish for Communication, Level 2. 1975. text ed. 18.52; wkbk. o.p. 4.76; dupl. masters 36.60 (ISBN 0-395-19947-6); recordings 182.92 (ISBN 0-395-12470-0); daily lesson plans 121-244 o.p. 19.36. HM.

--Spanish for Teachers: Applied Linguistics. 306p. 1965. 20.95 (ISBN 0-471-06858-6). Wiley.

Bull, William E., et al. Spanish for Communication, Level 1. 1972. Pt. A. text ed. 10.28 o.p. (ISBN 0-395-12449-2, 2-53531); Pt. B. text ed. 10.28 o.p. (ISBN 0-395-12450-6, 2-53532); Combined Ed. text ed. 17.72 (ISBN 0-395-19942-5); wkbk. o.p. 4.20; dupl. masters, set of 45 33.56 (ISBN 0-395-19944-1). HM.

Bulla & Cheng. Pathobiology of Invertebrate Vectors of Disease, Vol. 266. 1975. 64.00 (ISBN 0-89072-020-7). NY Acad Sci.

Bulla, Clyde R. Charlie's House. LC 82-45576. (Illus.). 128p. (gr. 2-5). 1983. 10.10i (ISBN 0-690-04259-0, TYC-J); PLB 10.89g (ISBN 0-690-04260-4). Har-Row.

--What Makes a Shadow. LC 62-11001. (A Let's-Read-&-Find-Out Science Bks.). (Illus.). (gr. k-3). 1962. PLB 10.89 (ISBN 0-690-87648-3, TYC-J). Har-Row.

Bulla, Monika, ed. Renal Insufficiency in Children, Cologne, Germany, 1981: Proceedings. (Illus.). 280p. 1982. pap. 38.00 (ISBN 0-387-10902-1). Springer-Verlag.

Bullard, Brian & Charlsen, David. I Can Dance. LC 79-13759. (Illus.). 1979. 10.95 o.p. (ISBN 0-399-12383-0). Putnam Pub Group.

--I Can Dance. (Illus.). 128p. 1981. pap. 5.95 (ISBN 0-399-50571-7, Perige). Putnam Pub Group.

Bullard, David G. & Knight, Susan E. Sexuality & Physical Disability: Personal Perspectives. LC 81-11008. 318p. 1981. pap. text ed. 18.95 (ISBN 0-8016-0861-9). Mosby.

Bullard, Harvelene. The Curious Princess & Harry, the Sad Easter Bunny. 1978. 3.75 o.p. (ISBN 0-533-01720-3). Vantage.

Bullard, Melissa M. Filippo Strozzi & the Medici: Favour & Finance in Sixteenth-Century Florence & Rome. LC 79-51822. (Cambridge Studies in Early Modern History). 216p. 1980. 32.50 (ISBN 0-521-22301-6). Cambridge U Pr.

Bullaty, Sonja. Sudek. (Illus.). 1978. 25.00 (ISBN 0-517-53294-8, C N Potter Bks). Crown.

Bulle, Florence. God Wants You Rich: And Other Enticing Doctrines. 192p. (Orig.). 1983. pap. 4.95 (ISBN 0-87123-264-2). Bethany Hse.

Bullen, F. T. The Distribution of the Damage Potential of the Desert Locust (Schistocerca Gregaria Forskal) 1969. 35.00x (ISBN 0-85135-045-3, Pub. by Centre Overseas Research). State Mutual Bk.

Bullen, J. B., ed. see Fry, Roger.

Bullen, K. E. The Earth's Density. 1975. 46.00x (ISBN 0-412-10860-7, Pub. by Chapman & Hall). Methuen Inc.

--Introduction to the Theory of Mechanics. 8th ed. 1971. 37.50 (ISBN 0-521-08291-9). Cambridge U Pr.

--An Introduction to the Theory of Seismology. 3rd ed. LC 79-7707. (Illus.). 1979. 49.50 (ISBN 0-521-04367-0); pap. 17.95x (ISBN 0-521-29686-2). Cambridge U Pr.

Bullen, Mary S. L., ed. see Legare, H. S.

Buller, Jon. Buller's Professional Course in Bartending for Home Study. (Illus.). 128p. 1983. 11.95 (ISBN 0-916782-34-4); pap. 6.95 comb. binding (ISBN 0-916782-33-6). Harvard Common Pr.

Buller, Walter L. Buller's Birds of New Zealand: A History of the Birds of New Zealand. Turbott, E. G., ed. LC 67-20253. 1967. 35.00 (ISBN 0-8248-0064-8, Eastwest Ctr). UH Pr.

Bullert, Gary. The Politics of John Dewey. 275p. 1983. 19.95 (ISBN 0-87975-208-4). Prometheus Bks.

Bullett, Gerald W. George Eliot: Her Life & Books. LC 76-156178. 273p. 1972. Repr. of 1948 ed. lib. bdg. 15.75x (ISBN 0-8371-6121-5, BUGE). Greenwood.

--Sydney Smith: A Biography & a Selection. LC 77-138578. (Illus.). 1971. Repr. of 1951 ed. lib. bdg. 16.25x (ISBN 0-8371-5777-3, BUSS). Greenwood.

Bullied, H. A. The Aspinall Era. 22.50x (ISBN 0-392-07597-0, SpS). Sportshelf.

Bullins, Ed. The Duplex: A Black Love Fable in Four Movements. LC 70-132162. 1971. 5.95 o.p. (ISBN 0-686-82941-7). Morrow.

Bullion, John L. A Great & Necessary Measure: George Grenville & the Genesis of the Stamp Act 1763-1765. 360p. 1983. 24.00 (ISBN 0-8262-0375-2). U of MO Pr.

Bullions, Peter. The Principles of English Grammar. LC 82-10418. (American Linguistics Ser.). 1983. 30.00x (ISBN 0-8201-1386-7). Schol Facsimiles.

Bullis, Jerald. Adorning the Buckhorn Helmet. 58p. 1976. 3.50 (ISBN 0-87886-069-X). Ithaca Hse.

--Taking up the Serpent. 1973. 2.95 (ISBN 0-87886-025-8). Ithaca Hse.

Bullis, Mary A. Mary, Come Home! LC 82-71445. (Orig.). 1982. pap. 4.95 (ISBN 0-8054-6330-5). Broadman.

Bullitt, Stimson. To Be a Politician. rev. ed. LC 75-43310. 1977. 22.50x (ISBN 0-300-02009-0); pap. 6.95x (ISBN 0-300-02013-9). Yale U Pr.

Bullivant, K., jt. auth. see Thomas, R. H.

Bullivant, Keith, ed. Culture & Society in the Weimar Republic. 205p. 1977. 19.50x o.p. (ISBN 0-8476-6012-5). Rowman.

Bulloch, James, et al. Accountant's Cost Handbook. 3rd ed. 870p. write for info (ISBN 0-471-05352-X). Ronald Pr.

Bullock, Alan. Hitler, a Study in Tyranny. abr. ed. 1971. pap. 3.71i (ISBN 0-06-080216-2, P216, PL). Har-Row.

Bullock, Alice. Living Legends. LC 72-90383. (Illus.). 1978. pap. 4.25 (ISBN 0-913270-06-7). Sunstone Pr.

--Mountain Villages. (Illus.). 1973. pap. 5.95 (ISBN 0-913270-13-X). Sunstone Pr.

Bullock, Barbara, jt. auth. see Kernicki, Jeannette.

Bullock, Charles J. Essays on the Monetary History of the United States. LC 69-18301. Repr. of 1900 ed. lib. bdg. 18.50x (ISBN 0-8371-0332-0, BUMH). Greenwood.

Bullock, Charles S., jt. auth. see Rodgers, Harrell R.

Bullock, Charles S., III & Lamb, Charles M. Implementation of Civil Rights Policy. (Political Science Ser.). 250p. 1983. pap. text ed. 12.95 (ISBN 0-534-01259-0). Brooks-Cole.

Bullock, Charles S., 3rd, jt. auth. see Rodgers, Harrell R., Jr.

Bullock, Dorothy. Give Your Child Permission to Unfold. LC 80-70509. 64p. (Orig.). 1981. pap. 2.95 o.p. (ISBN 0-87516-438-2). De Vorss.

Bullock, G. R. & Petrusz, P., eds. Techniques in Immunocytochemistry, Vol. 1. 1982. 44.50 (ISBN 0-12-140401-3). Acad Pr.

Bullock, G. William, Jr. & Conrad, Clifton F. Management: Perspectives from the Social Sciences. LC 80-6097. 343p. 1981. lib. bdg. 22.25 (ISBN 0-8191-1466-9); pap. text ed. 11.50 (ISBN 0-8191-1467-7). U Pr of Amer.

Bullock, Henry M. A History of Emory University. 391p. 1972. Repr. of 1936 ed. bds. 12.00 (ISBN 0-87797-019-X). Cherokee.

Bullock, James H. Maintenance Planning & Control. 146p. pap. 12.95 (ISBN 0-86641-026-0, 79113). Natl Assn Accts.

Bullock, Mary B. An American Transplant: The Rockefeller Foundation & Peking Union Medical College. LC 77-83098. 280p. 1981. 21.50x (ISBN 0-520-03559-3). U of Cal Pr.

Bullock, Michael, tr. see Frisch, Max.

Bullock, Micheal, tr. see Busza, Andrzej.

Bullock, Nadine. The Open Door, Bk. 2. LC 78-56655. (Illus.). 57p. (Orig.). 1982. pap. 11.95 (ISBN 0-911335-02-1). Open Door Foun.

Bullock, Paul. Executive Wealth-Building Plans. 1983. 24.95 (ISBN 0-910580-35-9). Farnswth Pub.

Bullock, R. L. & Jacoby, H. J., eds. RETC Proceedings, 1981, 2 vols. LC 81-65517. (Illus.). 1759p. Set. 70.00x (ISBN 0-686-79141-X). Soc Mining Eng.

Bullock, Spencer M. & Hosie, Kenneth. Learning to Care: The Training of Staff for Residential Social Work with Young People. 136p. 1980. text ed. 24.00x (ISBN 0-566-00400-3). Gower Pub Ltd.

Bullock, Waneta B. & Meister, Barbara. Ann Arbor Learning Inventory Grades Two to Four Manual. (Ann Arbor Learning Inventory Ser.). (Illus.). 56p. (gr. 2-4). 1977. 4.00 (ISBN 0-89039-225-0); wkbk. 0.50 (ISBN 0-89039-227-7). Ann Arbor Pubs.

--Ann Arbor Learning Inventory K-1 Manual. (Ann Arbor Learning Inventory Ser.). (Illus.). 64p. (gr. k-1). 1978. 4.00 (ISBN 0-89039-246-3); wkbk. 0.50 (ISBN 0-89039-248-X). Ann Arbor Pubs.

Bullough, Bonnie & Bullough, Vern. Nursing Issues & Nursing Strategies for the Eighties. 1983. pap. 17.95 (ISBN 0-8261-4441-1). Springer Pub.

Bullough, Bonnie, et al. Nursing: A Historical Bibliography. LC 80-836. 500p. 1981. lib. bdg. 50.00 o.s.i. (ISBN 0-8240-9511-1). Garland Pub.

Bullough, Edward. Aesthetics: Lectures & Essays. Wilkinson, Elizabeth M., ed. LC 77-21814. 1977. Repr. of 1957 ed. lib. bdg. 18.00x (ISBN 0-8371-9789-9, WIAE). Greenwood.

Bullough, Vern & Brundage, James, eds. Sexual Practices & the Medieval Church. LC 80-85227. (New Concepts in Human Sexuality Ser.). 289p. 1982. 22.95 (ISBN 0-87975-141-X); pap. 9.95 o.p. (ISBN 0-87975-151-7). Prometheus Bks.

Bullough, Vern, jt. auth. see Bullough, Bonnie.

Bullough, Vern L. & Elcano, Barrett W. A Bibliography of Prostitution. LC 75-42891. (Reference Library of Social Science). lib. bdg. 43.00 o.s.i. (ISBN 0-8240-9947-8). Garland Pub.

Bullough, William S. Practical Invertebrate Anatomy. 2nd ed. 1958. 17.95 o.p. (ISBN 0-312-63490-0). St Martin.

Bullowa, Margaret, ed. Before Speech. LC 78-51671. (Illus.). 1979. 49.50 (ISBN 0-521-22031-9); pap. 14.95 (ISBN 0-521-29522-X). Cambridge U Pr.

Bullrich, Kurt. Die Farbigen Dammerungserscheinngen. 100p. 1982. 17.95 (ISBN 3-7643-1355-2). Birkhauser.

Bullwinkle, Alice & Galloway, Howard P. Finding Summer Staff. 1979. pap. 6.85 (ISBN 0-87874-016-3). Galloway.

Bulmer, Charles & Carmichael, John L. Employment & Labor-Relations Policy. LC 79-3145. (Policy Studies Book). 1980. 26.95x (ISBN 0-669-03388-X). Lexington Bks.

Bulmer, Charles, jt. auth. see Carmichael, John, Jr.

Bulmer, M. G. Principles of Statistics. LC 78-72991. 1979. pap. 4.00 (ISBN 0-486-63760-3). Dover.

Bulmer, Martin. Censuses, Surveys & Privacy. LC 79-9292. 320p. 1979. text ed. 27.50 (ISBN 0-686-97571-5). Holmes & Meier.

--Sociological Research Methods: An Introduction. 1977. text ed. 31.25x o.p. (ISBN 0-333-21252-5); pap. text ed. 13.00x o.p. (ISBN 0-333-21273-8). Humanities.

Bulmer, Martin, ed. Social Research Ethics. LC 81-4250. 304p. 1982. text ed. 39.50x (ISBN 0-8419-0713-7); pap. text ed. 14.50x (ISBN 0-8419-0780-3). Holmes & Meier.

Bulnheim, H. P., jt. auth. see Kinne, O.

Bulow, Marie von see Von Bulow, Marie.

Bulson, P. S., jt. auth. see Allen, H. G.

Bulter, Paul T. Twenty-Six Lessons on Revelation, Pt. 1. LC 82-71688. (Bible Student Study Guide Ser.). 133p. 1982. pap. 2.95 (ISBN 0-89900-173-4). College Pr Pub.

--Twenty-Six Lessons on Revelations, Pt. 2. LC 82-71688. (Bible Student study Guide Ser.). 284p. 1982. pap. 4.95 (ISBN 0-89900-176-9). College Pr Pub.

Bultmann, Rudolf. History of the Synoptic Tradition. LC 62-7282. 1963. pap. 6.95xi (ISBN 0-06-061172-3, RD 187, HarpR). Har-Row.

Bulwer-Lytton, E. Zanoni: A Rosicrucian Tale. LC 78-157505. (Spiritual Science Library). 416p. 1971. 15.00 (ISBN 0-89345-014-6, Steinerbks); pap. 10.00 (ISBN 0-89345-015-4). Garber Comm.

Bulwer-Lytton, Edward. G. E. Falkland. Thal, Herbert V., ed. (First Novel Library). 1967. 7.95 (ISBN 0-304-92027-4); pap. 4.95 (ISBN 0-8023-9054-4). Dufour.

--Zanoni: A Rosicrucian Tale. 3rd ed. (Steiner Books Spiritual Science Library). 416p. 1982. lib. bdg. 15.00; pap. 10.00. Garber Comm.

--Zanoni: A Rosicrucian Tale. LC 78-157505. 416p. 1982. pap. 10.00 (ISBN 0-8334-1723-1, Steinerbks). Garber Comm.

Bulychev, Kirill. Gusliar Wonders. DeGaris, Roger, tr. 320p. 1983. 16.95 (ISBN 0-02-518010-X). Macmillan.

Bumagin, Victoria E. & Hirn, Kathryn F. Aging Is a Family Affair. LC 78-22459. 1979. 12.45i (ISBN 0-690-01823-1). T Y Crowell.

Bumb, Balu. A Survey of the Fertilizer Sector in India. (Working Paper: No. 331). iv, 216p. 1979. 5.00 (ISBN 0-686-36189-X, WP-0331). World Bank.

Bumba, V., jt. auth. see Howard, Robert.

Bumbalough, Marine. Puppet Pillows. (Illus.). 18p. 1982. pap. 4.00 (ISBN 0-943574-13-7). That Patchwork.

Bumgarner, Norma J. Mothering Your Nursing Toddler. 2nd ed. LC 82-84383. 210p. 1982. pap. 6.50 (ISBN 0-912500-12-3). La Leche.

Bumke, Joachim. The Concept of Knighthood in the Middle Ages. Jackson, Erika, tr. from Ger. LC 79-8840. (AMS Studies in the Middle Ages Ser.: No. 2). 278p. 1981. 29.50 (ISBN 0-404-18034-5). AMS Pr.

Bumli, George R., ed. Principles of Project Formulation for Irrigation & Drainage Projects. LC 82-73505. 132p. 1982. pap. text ed. 15.75 (ISBN 0-87262-345-9). Am Soc Civil Eng.

Bump, Jerome. Gerard Manley Hopkins. (English Authors Ser.). 1982. lib. bdg. 12.95 (ISBN 0-8057-6819-X, Twayne). G K Hall.

Bumpus, Jerry. Special Offer. LC 80-20671. 1981. pap. 5.95x (ISBN 0-914140-08-6). Carpenter Pr.

Bumpus, John S. Dictionary of Ecclesiastical Terms: Being a History & Explanation of Certain Terms Used in Architecture, Ecclesiology, Liturgiology, Music, Ritual, Cathedral, Constitution, Etc. LC 68-30653. 1969. Repr. of 1910 ed. 30.00x (ISBN 0-8103-3321-X). Gale.

Bumsted, J. M., ed. Documentary Problems in Canadian History, 2 Vols. 1969. pap. text ed. 11.95x ea. o.p.; Vol. I. pap. Pre-Confederation o.p. (ISBN 0-256-01061-7); Vol. II. pap. Post-Confederation o.p. (ISBN 0-256-01066-8). Dorsey.

Bumsted, J. M., ed. see Walker, Alexander.

Bunce, Arthur C. Economic Nationalism & the Farmer. LC 73-17655. 232p. 1975. Repr. of 1938 ed. lib. bdg. 15.50x (ISBN 0-8371-7257-8, BUEN). Greenwood.

BUncel & Lee. Isotopes in Cationic Reactions. (Isotopes in Organic Chemistry Ser.: Vol. 5). 1980. 64.00 (ISBN 0-444-41927-6). Elsevier.

Buncel, E. Carbanions: Mechanistic & Isotopic Aspects. (Reaction Mechanisms in Organic Chemistry Ser.: Vol. 9). 1974. 59.75 (ISBN 0-444-41190-9). Elsevier.

--Tritium in Organic Chemistry, Vol. 4. (Isotopes in Organic Chemistry Ser.). 1978. 64.00 (ISBN 0-444-41741-9). Elsevier.

Buncel, E. & Durst, T., eds. Comprehensive Carbanion Chemistry. (Studies in Organic Chemistry: Vol. 5, Pt. A). 1980. 78.75 (ISBN 0-444-41913-6). Elsevier.

Buncel, E. & Lee, C. C., eds. Carbon-Thirteen in Organic Chemistry. (Isotopes in Organic Chemistry Ser.: Vol. 3). 1977. 64.00 (ISBN 0-444-41472-X). Elsevier.

--Isotopes in Hydrogen Transfer Processes. (Isotopes in Organic Chemistry: Vol. 2). 1976. 64.00 (ISBN 0-444-41352-9). Elsevier.

--Isotopes in Molecular Rearrangements. (Isotopes in Organic Chemistry Ser.: Vol. 1). 320p. 1975. 64.00 (ISBN 0-444-41223-9). Elsevier.

Bunch, Clarence, ed. Art Education: A Guide to Information Sources. LC 73-17518. (Art & Architecture Information Guide Ser: Vol. 6). 1977. 42.00x (ISBN 0-8103-1272-7). Gale.

Bunch, William A. Jean Mairet. (World Authors Ser.: France: No. 358). 1975. lib. bdg. 10.95 o.p. (ISBN 0-8057-2565-2, Twayne). G K Hall.

Bunch, Wilton H. & Keagy, Robert D. Principles of Orthotic Treatment. LC 76-10467. (Illus.). 144p. (Orig.). 1976. 24.95 o.p. (ISBN 0-8016-0880-5). Mosby.

Buncher, Judith, ed. CIA & the Security Debate, 1971-76, Vol. 2. new ed. LC 75-18070. 240p. 1977. lib. bdg. 19.95 (ISBN 0-87196-364-7). Facts on File.

Buncke, Harry, jt. auth. see Serafin, Donald.

Bund, J. W. The Civil War in Worchestershire Sixteen Forty-Two to Sixteen Forty-Six & the Scotch Invasion of 1651. 267p. 1979. Repr. of 1905 ed. text ed. 15.75x (ISBN 0-904387-32-1, Pub. by Alan Sutton England). Humanities.

Bunday, B. D. & Mulholland, H. Pure Mathematics for Advanced Level. 538p. 1967. 13.95 (ISBN 0-408-70032-7). Butterworth.

Bundesinstitut Fur Ostwissenschaftliche und Internationale Studien. The Soviet Union, Nineteen Seventy-Eight to Nineteen Seventy-Nine. (The Soviet Union Ser.: Vol. 5). 220p. 1981. text ed. 35.00x (ISBN 0-8419-0632-7). Holmes & Meier.

Bundesverband der Pharmzeutischen Industrie, ed. Rote Liste, 1981. 1138p. (Ger.). 1981. 35.00x o.p. (ISBN 3-87193-055-5). Intl Pubns Serv.

--Rote Liste 1982. 1167p. (Ger.). 1982. 35.00x (ISBN 3-87193-063-6). Intl Pubns Serv.

Bundt, Nancy. The Fire Station Book. LC 80-16617. (Illus.). 32p. (ps-3). 1981. PLB 7.95g (ISBN 0-87614-126-2). Carolrhoda Bks.

Bundy, Alan. The Computer Modelling of Mathematical Reasoning. Date not set. price not set (ISBN 0-12-141252-0). Acad Pr.

Bundy, Carol, jt. ed. see Zell, Hans.

Bundy, Colin. The Rise & Fall of South African Peasantry. LC 79-62841. (Perspectives on Southern Africa Ser.: No. 28). 1979. 30.00x (ISBN 0-520-03754-5). U of Cal Pr.

Bundy, William P., jt. ed. see Foreign Affairs.

Bunge, M., ed. Studies in the Foundations, Methodology & Philosophy of Science, 4 vols. Incl. Vol. 1. Delaware Seminar in the Foundations of Physics. (Illus.). 26.30 (ISBN 0-387-03992-9); Vol. 2. Quantum Theory & Reality. 1967. o.p. (ISBN 0-387-03993-7); Vol. 3, Pt. 1. The Search for System. (Illus.). xii, 536p. 1967. 53.30 (ISBN 0-387-03994-5); Vol. 3, Pt. 2. The Search for Truth. (Illus.). viii, 374p. 1967. 44.70 (ISBN 0-387-03995-3); Vol. 4. Problems in the Foundations of Physics. (Illus.). 1972. 26.00 (ISBN 0-387-05490-1). LC 71-163433. Springer-Verlag.

Bunge, Mario. Causality & Modern Science. (Illus.). 1979. pap. 6.95 (ISBN 0-486-23728-1). Dover.

Bunger, William B. see Weissberger, A.

Bungey, J. H., jt. auth. see Mosley, W. H.

Bungey, John H. Testing of Concrete in Structures. 1982. 39.00X (ISBN 0-412-00231-0, Pub. by Chapman & Hall England). Methuen Inc.

Bunin, Greta & Jacobson, Michael. Does Everything Cause Cancer? 1979. pap. 1.50 (ISBN 0-89329-026-2). Ctr Sci Public.

Bunin, I. Stories & Poems. 515p. 1979. 8.95 (ISBN 0-686-98357-2, Pub. by Progress Pubs USSR). Imported Pubns.

Bunin, Ivan. In a Far Distant Land. Bowie, Robert, tr. from Rus. 1983. pap. 8.50 (ISBN 0-938920-27-8). Hermitage MI.

Buning, W. De Cock & Alting, J. H. Netherlands & the World War: Studies in the War HIstory of a Neutral: Volume 3-Effect of the War Upon the Colonies. (Economic & Social History of the World War Ser.). 1928. text ed. 49.50x (ISBN 0-686-83636-7). Elliots Bks.

Bunis, Al & Williams, Roger. Tennis with the Grand Masters. LC 82-80145. (Illus.). 160p. cancelled (ISBN 0-914178-53-9, 43766). Golf Digest.

Bunke, Joan, ed. see Mills, George.

Bunker, Andrew F. & Chaffee, Margaret. Tropical Indian Ocean Clouds. LC 69-17882. (International Indian Ocean Expedition Meteorological Monographs: No. 4). (Illus.). 1970. 20.00x (ISBN 0-8248-0083-4, Eastwest Ctr). UH Pr.

Bunker, Gary L. & Bitton, Davis. The Mormon Graphic Image, Eighteen Thirty-Four to Nineteen Fourteen: Cartoons, Caricatures, & Illustrations. (Publications in the American West: Vol. 16). (Illus.). 140p. 1983. 20.00 (ISBN 0-87480-218-0). U of Utah Pr.

Bunker, R., jt. auth. see Thorp, R.

Bunn, D. S. & Warburton, A. B. The Barn Owl. (Illus.). 264p. 1982. 32.50 (ISBN 0-931130-09-3). Buteo.

Bunn, Derek W. Analysis for Optimal Decisions. LC 81-19698. 275p. 1982. 39.95 (ISBN 0-471-10132-X, Pub. by Wiley-Interscience); pap. 19.95 (ISBN 0-471-10133-8, Pub. by Wiley-Interscience). Wiley.

Bunn, John. Scientific Principles of Coaching. 2nd ed. LC 70-159445. (Illus.). 1972. 19.95 (ISBN 0-13-796177-4). P-H.

Bunn, Thomas. Closet Bones. LC 76-49788. 1977. 8.95 o.p. (ISBN 0-399-11874-8). Putnam Pub Group.

Bunnag, C., jt. ed. see Prasansuk, S.

Bunnag, Jane. Buddhist Monk, Buddhist Layman: A Study of Urban Monastic Organisation in Central Thailand. LC 72-86420. (Cambridge Studies in Social Anthropology: No. 6). (Illus.). 230p. 1973. 29.95 (ISBN 0-521-08591-8). Cambridge U Pr.

Bunnag, Tej. The Provincial Administration of Siam 1892-1915. (East Asian Historical Monographs). 1978. 29.95x o.p. (ISBN 0-19-580343-4). Oxford U Pr.

Bunnell, C. A., jt. auth. see Fuchs, P. L.

Bunnell, David, jt. auth. see Osborne, Adam.

Bunnell, F., tr. see Ziswiler, V.

Bunnell, Fredrick. American Reactions to Indonesia's Role in the Belgrade Conference. 86p. 1964. pap. 2.00 o.p. (ISBN 0-87763-026-7). Cornell Mod Indo.

Bunnell, P., tr. see Ziswiler, V.

Bunney, William E., jt. auth. see Usdin, Earl.

Bunney, William E., Jr. see Usdin, Earl, et al.

Bunshah, R. F., ed. Techniques of Metals Research. 802p. 1968. Vol. 1, Pt. 2. 51.00 (ISBN 0-470-12197-1, Pub. by Wiley). Krieger.

--Techniques of Metals Research, Vol. 2, Pt. 2. 502p. 1983. Repr. of 1968 ed. write for info. (ISBN 0-89874-306-0). Krieger.

--Techniques of Metals Research, Vol. 5, Pt. 2. 1983. Repr. of 1970 ed. write for info. (ISBN 0-89874-308-7). Krieger.

--Techniques of Metals Research: Techniques for the Direct Observation of Structure & Imperfections, Vol. 2, Pt. 1. LC 80-27162. 497p. 1983. Repr. of 1968 ed. write for info. (ISBN 0-89874-305-2). Krieger.

Bunshah, Rointan F., et al. Deposition Technologies for Films & Coatings: Developments & Applications. LC 82-7862. (Illus.). 585p. 1983. 69.00 (ISBN 0-8155-0906-5). Noyes.

Bunshaw, R. F., ed. Techniques of Metals Research: Measurement of Mechanical Properties, Vol. 5, Pt. 1. LC 80-26986. 474p. 1983. Repr. of 1970 ed. write for info. (ISBN 0-89874-307-9). Krieger.

Bunstock, Richard L. A High Plains Legacy. (Jelm Press Poets Ser.). 1982. pap. 6.95 (ISBN 0-936204-43-5). Jelm Mtn.

Bunt, C., ed. Sicilian & Lucchese Fabrics. (The World's Heritage of Woven Fabrics Ser.). (Illus.). 1961. text ed. 15.00x (ISBN 0-686-86110-8, Pub. by A & C Black England). Humanities.

Bunt, C. G., ed. Byzantine Fabrics. (Worlds Heritage of Woven Fabrics Ser.). 22.50 o.p. (ISBN 0-87245-390-1). Textile Bk.

--Florentine Fabrics. (World's Heritage of Woven Fabrics). 1961. 22.50x (ISBN 0-87245-393-6). Textile Bk.

Bunt, Cyril G., ed. Sicilian & Lucchese Fabrics. (World's Heritage of Woven Fabrics). 1961. 22.50x (ISBN 0-87245-397-9). Textile Bk.

--Silks of Lyons & Philippe De la Salle. (World's Heritage of Woven Fabrics). 1960. 22.50x (ISBN 0-87245-398-7). Textile Bk.

Bunt, Richard B., jt. auth. see Tremblay, Jean P.

Bunt, Richard B., jt. auth. see Tremblay, Jean-Paul.

Buntain, Mark, et al. Miracle in the Mirror. (Illus.). 155p. 1982. pap. 2.95 (ISBN 0-87123-352-5, 210352). Bethany Hse.

Buntain, Ruth J. Children in the Shadows. 78p. pap. 4.95 (ISBN 0-686-82632-9). Review & Herald.

Bunter, Bill M. J., et al. Djugurba: Tales from the Spirit Time. LC 76-12381. (Illus.). 64p. (gr. 1-6). 1976. 6.95x o.p. (ISBN 0-253-31808-4). Ind U Pr.

Bunting, David. Statistical View of the Trusts: A Manual of Large American Industrial & Mining Corporations Active Around 1900. LC 72-9824. (Contributions in Economics & Economic History: No. 9). 311p. 1974. lib. bdg. 29.95 (ISBN 0-8371-6624-1, BOM/). Greenwood.

Bunting, Eve. The Big Red Barn. LC 78-12186. (Let Me Read Ser.). (Illus.). (gr. k-3). 1979. pap. 1.95 (ISBN 0-15-611938-2, VoyB). HarBraceJ.

--The Cloverdale Switch. LC 79-2404. (gr. 7 up). 1979. 7.95 (ISBN 0-397-31866-9, JBL-J); PLB 8.89 (ISBN 0-397-31867-7). Har-Row.

--The Creature of Cranberry Cove. LC 76-18124. (No Such Things.. Ser.). (Illus.). (gr. 2-6). 1976. PLB 6.95 (ISBN 0-88436-300-7); pap. 3.95 (ISBN 0-88436-301-5). EMC.

--The Day of the Dinosaur. LC 75-19023. (The Dinosaur Machine Ser.). (Illus.). 40p. (gr. 7 up). 1975. PLB 6.95 (ISBN 0-88436-193-4); pap. 3.95 (ISBN 0-88436-194-2). EMC.

--The Day of the Earthlings. (Science Fiction Ser.). (Illus.). 32p. (gr. 3-9). 1978. PLB 6.95 (ISBN 0-87191-621-5); pap. 3.25 (ISBN 0-89812-054-3). Creative Ed.

--Death of a Dinosaur. LC 75-17926. (The Dinosaur Machine Ser.). (Illus.). 40p. (gr. 7 up). 1975. PLB 6.95 (ISBN 0-88436-199-3); pap. 3.95 (ISBN 0-88436-200-0). EMC.

--Demetrius & the Golden Goblet. LC 79-14865. (Illus.). (gr. k-4). 1980. pap. 3.95 (ISBN 0-15-625282-1, VoyB). HarBraceJ.

--The Demon. LC 76-18125. (No Such Things Ser.). (Illus.). 1976. 6.95 (ISBN 0-88436-273-6); pap. 3.95 (ISBN 0-88436-274-4). EMC.

--The Dinosaur Trap. LC 75-17909. (The Dinosaur Machine Ser.). (Illus.). 40p. (gr. 7 up). 1975. PLB 6.95 (ISBN 0-88436-197-7); pap. 3.95 (ISBN 0-88436-198-5). EMC.

--Escape from Tyrannosaurus. LC 75-19024. (The Dinosaur Machine Ser.). (Illus.). 40p. (gr. 7 up). 1975. PLB 6.95 (ISBN 0-88436-195-0); pap. 3.95 (ISBN 0-88436-196-9). EMC.

--Fifteen. (Young Romance Ser.). (Illus.). (gr. 3-9). 1978. PLB 6.95 (ISBN 0-87191-632-0); pap. 3.25 (ISBN 0-89812-064-0). Creative Ed.

--For Always. (Young Romance Ser.). (Illus.). (gr. 3-9). 1978. PLB 6.95 (ISBN 0-87191-636-3); pap. 3.25 (ISBN 0-89812-068-3). Creative Ed.

--The Ghost. LC 76-18131. (No Such Things.. Ser.). (Illus.). (gr. 2-6). 1976. PLB 6.95 (ISBN 0-88436-271-X); pap. 3.95 (ISBN 0-88436-272-8). EMC.

--The Girl in the Painting. (Young Romance Ser.). (Illus.). (gr. 3-9). 1978. PLB 6.95 (ISBN 0-87191-639-8); pap. 3.25 (ISBN 0-89812-069-1). Creative Ed.

--Goose Dinner. LC 80-39747. (A Let Me Read Bk.). (Illus.). 32p. (gr. 6-10). 1981. 7.95 (ISBN 0-15-232224-8, HJ); pap. 2.95 (ISBN 0-15-232225-6, VoyB). HarBraceJ.

--Island of One. (Science Fiction Ser.). (Illus.). (gr. 3-9). 1978. PLB 6.95 (ISBN 0-87191-626-6); pap. 3.25 (ISBN 0-89812-058-6). Creative Ed.

--Josefina Finds the Prince. LC 76-16063. (For Real Books). (Illus.). 64p. (gr. 2-6). 1976. PLB 6.69 (ISBN 0-8116-4300-X). Garrard.

--Just Like Everyone Else. (Young Romance Ser.). (Illus.). (gr. 3-9). 1978. PLB 6.95 (ISBN 0-87191-630-4); pap. 3.25 (ISBN 0-89812-062-4). Creative Ed.

--Maggie the Freak. (Young Romance Ser.). (Illus.). (gr. 3-9). 1978. PLB 6.95 (ISBN 0-87191-633-9); pap. 3.25 (ISBN 0-685-59452-1). Creative Ed.

--The Mask. (Science Fiction Ser.). (Illus.). (gr. 3-9). 1978. PLB 6.95 (ISBN 0-87191-625-8); pap. 3.25 (ISBN 0-89812-056-X). Creative Ed.

--The Mirror Planet. (Science Fiction Ser.). (Illus.). (gr. 3-9). 1978. PLB 6.95 (ISBN 0-87191-628-2); pap. 3.25 (ISBN 0-89812-057-8). Creative Ed.

--Oh, Rick. (Young Romance Ser.). (Illus.). (gr. 3-9). 1978. PLB 6.95 (ISBN 0-87191-634-7); pap. 3.25 (ISBN 0-89812-061-6). Creative Ed.

--A Part of the Dream. (Young Romance Ser.). (Illus.). (gr. 3-9). 1978. PLB 6.95 (ISBN 0-87191-638-X); pap. 3.25 (ISBN 0-89812-066-7). Creative Ed.

--The Robot People. (Science Fiction Ser.). (Illus.). (gr. 3-9). 1978. PLB 6.95 (ISBN 0-87191-622-3); pap. 3.25 (ISBN 0-89812-051-9). Creative Ed.

--St. Patrick's Day in the Morning. (Illus.). 32p. (gr. 3). 1983. pap. 3.45 (ISBN 0-89919-162-2, Clarion). HM.

--The Sea World Book of Sharks. LC 79-63920. (Sea World Press Ser.). (Illus.). 80p. (gr. 4-6). 1980. 9.95 (ISBN 0-15-271948-2, HJ). HarBraceJ.

--The Space People. (Science Fiction Ser.). (Illus.). (gr. 3-9). 1978. PLB 6.95 (ISBN 0-87191-623-1); pap. 3.25 (ISBN 0-89812-053-5). Creative Ed.

--Survival Camp. (Young Romance Ser.). (Illus.). (gr. 3-9). 1978. PLB 6.95 (ISBN 0-87191-631-2); pap. 3.25 (ISBN 0-89812-063-2). Creative Ed.

--Terrible Things. LC 79-2692. (Illus.). (gr. k-3). 1980. PLB 7.89 o.p. (ISBN 0-06-020903-8, HarpJ); PLB 7.95 o.p. (ISBN 0-06-020904-6). Har-Row.

--The Tongue of the Ocean. LC 76-17624. (No Such Things..Ser.). (Illus.). 1976. PLB 6.95 (ISBN 0-88436-302-3); pap. 3.95 (ISBN 0-88436-303-1). EMC.

--The Traveling Men of Ballycoo. LC 82-15799. (Illus.). 32p. (gr. 4-8). 12.95 (ISBN 0-15-289792-5, HJ). HarBraceJ.

--Two Different Girls. (Young Romance Ser.). (Illus.). (gr. 3-9). 1978. PLB 6.95 (ISBN 0-87191-637-1); pap. 3.25 (ISBN 0-89812-067-5). Creative Ed.

--The Undersea People. (Science Fiction Ser.). (Illus.). (gr. 3-9). 1978. PLB 6.95 (ISBN 0-87191-624-X); pap. 3.25 (ISBN 0-89812-052-7). Creative Ed.

--The Valentine Bears. (Illus.). 32p. (gr. 3). 1983. 9.95 (ISBN 0-89919-138-X, Clarion). HM.

--Winter's Coming. LC 76-28321. (Illus.). (gr. 1-3). 1977. 4.95 (ISBN 0-15-298036-9, HJ); pap. 1.65 (ISBN 0-15-298037-7, VoyB). HarBraceJ.

--Winter's Coming. LC 76-28321. (Let Me Read Ser.). (Illus.). (gr. 1-3). 1977. pap. 1.65 (ISBN 0-15-298037-7, VoyB). HarBraceJ.

Bunting, G. R. & Lee, M. J. Evolution of the United Nations. 1964. pap. 4.20 o.p. (ISBN 0-08-010922-5). Pergamon.

Bunting, James. The Protection of Property Against Crime. LC 76-352875. (Illus.). 1975. 8.50x o.p. (ISBN 0-561-00224-X). Intl Pubns Serv.

Bunting, Richard L., jt. auth. see Benton, Allen H.

Bunting, Sharon. Preparing Students for Mainstreaming. 80p. (Orig.). 1982. pap. 8.90 (ISBN 0-936326-02-6). Cedars Pr.

Bunton, John, jt. auth. see Hall, James J.

Bunuel. Las Tres de la Madrugada. (Easy Reader, A). 1972. pap. 2.95 (ISBN 0-88436-061-X, 70265). EMC.

Bunuel, Luis. L' Age Dor: Un Chien Andalou. Bd. with Chien Andalou. LC 68-27591. (Classic Film Scripts). 1968. pap. 1.95 o.p. (ISBN 0-671-20086-0, Touchstone Bks). S&S.

--Belle De Jour. (Film Scripts Modern Ser). 1970. 2.95 o.p. (ISBN 0-671-20793-8, Touchstone Bks). S&S.

--Exterminating Angel. Bd. with Los Olvidados; Nazarin. LC 79-119354. (Modern Film Scripts Ser.). 1972. pap. 4.95 o.p. (ISBN 0-671-21276-1, Touchstone Bks). S&S.

--Tristana. (Film Scripts-Modern Ser.). 1971. pap. 2.95 o.p. (ISBN 0-671-21078-5, Touchstone Bks). S&S.

Bunyan, John. Christiana's Journey. Rev. ed. Wright, Christopher, ed. 1982. pap. 4.95 (ISBN 0-88270-533-4). Bridge Pub.

--Grace Abounding to the Chief of Sinners & the Life & Death of Mr. Badman. 1979. pap. 3.95x (ISBN 0-460-11815-3, Evman). Biblio Dist.

--Grace Abounding to the Chief of Sinners. Sharrock, Roger, ed. & intro. by. Bd. with The Pilgrim's Progress from This World to That Which Is to Come. (Oxford Standard Authors Ser). 1966. 29.95 (ISBN 0-19-254159-5). Oxford U Pr.

--The Miscellaneous Works of John Bunyan, Vols. 8 & 9. Greaves, Richard L., ed. (Oxford English Texts). 1979. 74.00x (ISBN 0-19-812736-7); Vol. 9, 1981 89.00x, (ISBN 0-19-812737-5). Oxford U Pr.

--The Miscellaneous Works of John Bunyan: The Poems, Vol. VI. Midgley, E. G., ed. (Oxford English Text Ser.). (Illus.). 1980. 74.00x (ISBN 0-19-812734-0). Oxford U Pr.

--Pictorial Pilgrim's Progress. 1960. pap. 3.95 (ISBN 0-8024-0019-1). Moody.

--Pilgrim's Progress. pap. 3.95 (ISBN 0-8024-0012-4). Moody.

--Pilgrim's Progress. (RL 10). pap. 2.25 (ISBN 0-451-51643-5, CE1643, Sig Classics). NAL.

--Pilgrim's Progress. Helms, Hal M., ed. (Illus.). 1982. 4.95 (ISBN 0-941478-02-5). Paraclete Pr.

--Pilgrim's Progress in Today's English. LC 64-25255. 1964. pap. 5.95 (ISBN 0-8024-6520-X). Moody.

--Progreso Del Peregrino Ilustrado. Orig. Title: Pictorial Pilgrim's Progress. (Span). 1960. pap. 3.95 (ISBN 0-8024-1750-7). Moody.

--Young Christian's Pilgrimage. Rev. ed. Wright, Christopher, ed. 1982. pap. 4.95 (ISBN 0-88270-534-2). Bridge Pub.

Bunyan, John A., et al. Practical Video: The Manager's Guide to Applications. LC 78-23533. 1978. pap. text ed. 17.95 (ISBN 0-914236-20-2). Knowledge Indus.

Bunyan, Juan & Leavell, L. P. El Progreso Del Peregrino. Duffer, Hiram F., Jr., tr. from Eng. (Span.). 1980. pap. 2.20 (ISBN 0-311-37006-3). Casa Bautista.

Bunyan, Tony. The Political Police in Britain. LC 75-45815. (Illus.). 304p. 1976. 22.50 (ISBN 0-312-62405-0). St Martin.

Bunyard, R. S. Police: Organization & Command. 400p. 1978. 39.00x (ISBN 0-7121-1671-0, Pub. by Macdonald & Evans). State Mutual Bk.

Bunye, Maria V. & Yap, Elsa P. Cebuano for Beginners. McKaughan, Howard P., ed. (PALI Language Texts: Philippines). (Orig.). 1971. pap. text ed. 14.00x (ISBN 0-87022-091-8). UH Pr.

--Cebuano Grammar Notes. McKaughan, Howard P., ed. LC 70-152460. (PALI Language Texts: Philippines). (Orig.). 1971. pap. text ed. 5.50x (ISBN 0-87022-092-6). UH Pr.

Bunye, Maria V., jt. auth. see Yap, Elsa P.

Bunzel, John H. New Force on the Left: Tom Hayden & the Campaign Against Corporate America. (Publication Ser.: No. 280). 131p. 1983. pap. 6.95 (ISBN 0-8179-7802-X). Hoover Inst Pr.

Bunzel, Ruth L. Suni Katcinas. LC 72-13917. Repr. of 1932 ed. lib. bdg. 27.50 (ISBN 0-686-84607-9). Rio Grande.

Buonarroti, Philippe, ed. Giornale Patriottico Di Corsica: April to November, 1790. (Babeuf & Babouvism Ser.). 1976. Repr. lib. bdg. 72.00x o.p. (ISBN 0-8287-1377-4). Clearwater Pub.

Buonassisi, Vincenzo & Razzoli, Guido. The Italian Gourmet Diet: A Seven Week Plan for Wine & Pasta Lovers. 224p. 1983. 14.95 (ISBN 0-02-518080-0). Macmillan.

Buoncristiano, S., et al. A Geometric Approach to Homology Theory. LC 75-22980. (London Mathematical Society Lecture Note Ser.: No. 18). (Illus.). 216p. 1976. pap. text ed. 19.95x (ISBN 0-521-20940-4). Cambridge U Pr.

Buonicore, Anthony J., jt. ed. see Theodore, Louis.

Bupp, Irvin C. & Derian, Claude. Light Water: How the Nuclear Dream Dissolved. LC 77-20419. 1978. 13.95x o.s.i. (ISBN 0-465-04107-8). Basic.

Burack, Elmer H. Human Resource Planning Approaches: A Managerial Summary. 150p. (Orig.). 1983. pap. 13.00 (ISBN 0-942560-09-4); pap. text ed. 10.95 (ISBN 0-686-38254-4). Brace-Park.

--Managing Careers in Organizations: A Managerial Summary. 150p. (Orig.). 1983. pap. 13.00 (ISBN 0-942560-07-8); pap. text ed. 10.95 (ISBN 0-686-38251-X). Brace-Park.

--Personnel Management: Cases & Exercises. (Illus.). 1978. pap. text ed. 15.50 (ISBN 0-8299-0203-1); IM avail. (ISBN 0-8299-0461-1); exam questions avail. (ISBN 0-8299-0463-8). West Pub.

Burack, Elmer H. & Smith, Robert D. Personnel Management: A Human Resource Systems Approach. 500p. 1977. text ed. 22.95 o.s.i. (ISBN 0-8299-0130-2); IM avail. o.s.i. (ISBN 0-8299-0462-X). West Pub.

--Personnel Management: A Human Resource System Approach. (Management Ser.). 609p. 1982. text ed. 28.95x (ISBN 0-471-09283-5); tchrs.' manual 9.00 (ISBN 0-471-86236-3). Wiley.

Burack, Elmer H., et al. Growing: A Woman's Guide to Career Satisfaction. LC 80-11990. 295p. (Orig.). 1980. pap. 7.95 (ISBN 0-534-97990-4). Lifetime Learn.

Burago, Alla, jt. ed. see Raffel, Burton.

Burakovsky, V. I. & Bockeria, L. A. Hyperbaric Oxygenation & Its Value in Cardiovascular Surgery. 343p. 1981. 11.50 (ISBN 0-8285-2282-0, Pub. by Mir Pubs USSR). Imported Pubns.

Buranelli, Vincent. Edgar Allan Poe. 2nd ed. (United States Authors Ser.). 1977. lib. bdg. 10.95 (ISBN 0-8057-7189-1, Twayne). G K Hall.

--The Wizard from Vienna: Franz Anton Mesmer. LC 75-24072. (Illus.). 256p. 1975. 8.95 o.p. (ISBN 0-698-10697-0, Coward). Putnam Pub Group.

Burawoy, Michael & Shocpol, Theda, eds. Marxian Inquiries: Studies of Labor, Class, & States (Supplement to the American Journal of Sociology) 1983. lib. bdg. 25.00x (08039-0); pap. 12.50 (08040-4). U of Chicago Pr.

Burba, Linda. Ben's Blanket & the Baby Jesus. 1980. pap. 0.89 (ISBN 0-570-06137-7, 59-1255, Arch Bk). Concordia.

Burbach, Hal. Especially for Him. LC 82-50937. (Illus.). 236p. (Orig.). 1982. pap. 7.95 (ISBN 0-942320-03-4). WRC Pub.

Burbach, Harold J., ed. Mainstreaming: A Book of Readings & Resources for the Classroom Teacher. LC 80-81281. 224p. 1980. pap. text ed. 13.95 (ISBN 0-8403-2208-9). Kendall-Hunt.

Burbach, Roger & Flynn, Patricia. Agribusiness in the Americas: The Political Economy of Corporate Agriculture. LC 80-17114. 314p. 1980. 16.00 (ISBN 0-85345-535-X); pap. 6.50 (ISBN 0-85345-536-8). Monthly Rev.

Burbank. Literature of Early America. 1967. pap. text ed. 6.95 (ISBN 0-675-09753-3, 9753). Merrill.

Burbank, Garin. When Farmers Voted Red: The Gospel of Socialism in the Oklahoma Countryside, 1910-1924. LC 76-5259. (Contributions in American History Ser.: No. 53). (Illus.). 1976. lib. bdg. 27.50 (ISBN 0-8371-8903-9, BSO/). Greenwood.

Burbank, Rex. Sherwood Anderson. (United States Authors Ser.). 1964. lib. bdg. 11.95 (ISBN 0-8057-0020-X, Twayne). G K Hall.

Burbank, Rex & Moore, Jack. Literature of the American Renaissance. 1969. pap. text ed. 5.95x o.p. (ISBN 0-675-09586-7). Merrill.

Burbank, Rex J. Thornton Wilder. 2nd ed. (United States Authors Ser.). 1978. lib. bdg. 11.95 (ISBN 0-8057-7223-5). G K Hall.

Burberry, Peter. Building for Energy Conservation. LC 77-17943. 1978. 19.95x o.s.i. (ISBN 0-470-99350-2). Halsted Pr.

--Environment & Services. 2nd ed. (Mitchell's Building Construction Ser.). 1978. pap. 19.95x o.p. (ISBN 0-470-26352-0). Halsted Pr.

Burbidge, Geoffrey, et al, eds. Annual Review of Astronomy & Astrophysics, Vol. 20. LC 63-8846. (Illus.). 1982. text ed. 22.00 (ISBN 0-8243-0920-0). Annual Reviews.

Burbidge, Peter & Sutton, Richard, eds. The Wagner Companion. LC 79-50099. 1979. 42.50 (ISBN 0-521-22787-9); pap. 10.95 (ISBN 0-521-29657-9). Cambridge U Pr.

Burbridge, Paul & Watts, Murray. Time to Act. 128p. (Orig.). 1980. pap. 3.95 o.p. (ISBN 0-87784-404-6). Inter-Varsity.

Burby, Raymond & Bell, A. Fleming, eds. Energy & the Community. LC 78-15760. 160p. 1979. prof ref 24.00x (ISBN 0-88410-083-9). Ballinger Pub.

Burby, Raymond J., 3rd. Recreation & Leisure in New Communities. LC 76-17871. (New Communities Research Ser.). 400p. 1976. prof ref 22.50x (ISBN 0-88410-448-6). Ballinger Pub.

Burby, Raymond J., 3rd, jt. ed. see Loewenthal, Norman H.

Burcaw, G. Ellis. Introduction to Museum Work. LC 74-32248. (Illus.). 200p. 1975. pap. text ed. 9.75x (ISBN 0-910050-14-7). AASLH.

Burch, Buford H. & Miller, Arthur C. Atlas of Pulmonary Resections. (Illus.). 176p. 1964. photocopy ed. spiral 24.50x (ISBN 0-398-00253-3). C C Thomas.

Burch, Ernest S., Jr. Eskimo Kinsmen: Changing Family Relationships in Northwest Alaska. LC 75-4972. (AES Ser). (Illus.). 352p. 1975. text ed. 23.95 (ISBN 0-8299-0049-7). West Pub.

Burch, George B., ed. see Bhattacharrya, K. C.

Burch, George E., et al, eds. General Considerations & Principles. (Principles & Techniques of Human Research & Therapeutics Ser: Vol. 1). (Illus.). 256p. 1974. 16.00 o.p. (ISBN 0-87993-039-X). Futura Pub.

Burch, J., jt. auth. see Gerrard, A.

Burch, J. G., et al. Information Systems: Theory & Practice. 3rd ed. 1983. 29.95 (ISBN 0-471-06211-1). Wiley.

--Information Systems: Theory & Practice. 2nd ed. 571p. 1979. 33.95x (ISBN 0-471-12322-6). Wiley.

Burch, James. Lubyanka. LC 82-73022. 256p. 1983. 12.95 (ISBN 0-689-11342-0). Atheneum.

Burch, John G., jt. auth. see Sardinas, Joseph.

Burch, John G., Jr. & Sardinas, Joseph L., Jr. Computer Control & Audit: A Total Systems Approach. 492p. 1978. 35.95 (ISBN 0-471-03491-6). Wiley.

Burch, Martin, jt. auth. see Balsom, Denis.

Burch, Monte. Building & Equipping the Garden & Small Farm Workshop. LC 79-20721. (Illus.). 1979. pap. 5.95 o.p. (ISBN 0-88266-156-6). Garden Way Pub.

--Waterfowling. LC 74-1795. (Illus.). 1978. 15.34i (ISBN 0-06-010572-0, HarpT). Har-Row.

Burch, Noel. To the Distant Observer: Form & Meaning in Japanese Cinema. LC 77-20316. 1979. 29.75x (ISBN 0-520-03605-0); pap. 9.75 (ISBN 0-520-03877-0). U of Cal Pr.

Burch, Noel, tr. see Hodeir, Andre.

Burch, Philip H. Elites in American History: The Civil War to the New Deal. 300p. 1981. text ed. 38.50x (ISBN 0-8419-0595-9); pap. 19.75x (ISBN 0-8419-0705-6). Holmes & Meier.

Burch, Robert. Ida Early Comes Over the Mountain. LC 79-20532. (gr. 5-9). 1980. 10.95 (ISBN 0-670-39169-7). Viking Pr.

Burchard, John. Bernini Is Dead? Architecture & the Social Purpose. (Illus.). 1976. 12.50 o.p. (ISBN 0-07-008922-1, P&RB). McGraw.

Burchard, John, jt. ed. see Handlin, Oscar.

Burchard, Marshall. Sports Hero: Bill Walton. LC 78-17442. (Sports Hero Ser.). (Illus.). (gr. 3-5). 1978. PLB 6.29 o.p. (ISBN 0-399-61128-2). Putnam Pub Group.

--Sports Hero: Dr. J: the Story of Julius Irving. LC 75-58689. (Sports Hero Ser.). (Illus.). 96p. (gr. 3-5). 1976. PLB 6.99 (ISBN 0-399-60985-7). Putnam Pub Group.

--Sports Hero: Fran Tarkenton. LC 77-7393. (Sports Hero Ser.). (Illus.). (gr. 3-5). 1977. pap. 6.99 (ISBN 0-399-61096-0). Putnam Pub Group.

--Sports Hero: Fred Lynn. LC 76-19043. (Sports Hero Ser.). (Illus.). 96p. (gr. 3-5). 1976. PLB 6.29 o.p. (ISBN 0-399-61008-1). Putnam Pub Group.

--Sports Hero: Jimmy Connors. new ed. LC 76-6148. (Sports Hero Ser.). (Illus.). 96p. (gr. 3-5). 1976. PLB 6.29 o.p. (ISBN 0-399-60993-8). Putnam Pub Group.

--Sports Hero: Joe Morgan. LC 77-15509. (Sports Hero Ser.). (Illus.). (gr. 3-5). 1978. PLB 6.29 o.p. (ISBN 0-399-61095-2). Putnam Pub Group.

--Sports Hero: Larry Bird. (Sports Hero Ser.). (Illus.). 96p. (gr. 2-5). 1982. PLB 6.99 (ISBN 0-399-61197-5); pap. 3.95 (ISBN 0-399-20874-7). Putnam Pub Group.

--Sports Hero: Magic Johnson. (Sports Hero Ser.). (Illus.). 96p. (gr. 2-5). 1981. lib. bdg. 6.99 (ISBN 0-399-61187-8); pap. 3.95 (ISBN 0-399-20839-9). Putnam Pub Group.

--Sports Hero: Mario Andretti. LC 76-56764. (Sports Hero Ser.). (Illus.). (gr. 3-5). 1977. PLB 6.99 (ISBN 0-399-61077-4). Putnam Pub Group.

--Sports Hero: Muhammad Ali. (Sports Hero Ser.). (Illus.). 96p. (gr. 3-5). 1975. PLB 6.99 (ISBN 0-399-61013-8). Putnam Pub Group.

--Sports Hero: Pete Rose. (Sports Hero Ser.). (Illus.). 1976. PLB 6.99 (ISBN 0-399-61038-3). Putnam Pub Group.

--Sports Hero: Reggie Jackson. (Sports Hero Ser.). (Illus.). 1975. PLB 6.29 o.p. (ISBN 0-399-61014-6). Putnam Pub Group.

--Sports Hero: Rick Barry. LC 76-43964. (Sports Hero Ser.). (Illus.). (gr. 3-5). 1977. PLB 6.29 o.p. (ISBN 0-399-61064-2). Putnam Pub Group.

--Sports Hero: Rod Carew. LC 78-738. (Sports Hero Ser.). (Illus.). (gr. 3-5). PLB 6.99 (ISBN 0-399-61120-7). Putnam Pub Group.

--Sports Hero: Ron Guidry. (Sports Hero Ser.). (Illus.). 96p. (gr. 7-10). 1981. PLB 6.99 (ISBN 0-399-61178-9); pap. 2.95 (ISBN 0-399-20821-6). Putnam Pub Group.

--Sports Hero: Ron le Flore. (Sports Hero Ser.). (Illus.). (gr. 3-5). 1979. PLB 6.99 (ISBN 0-399-61134-7). Putnam Pub Group.

--Sports Hero: Terry Bradshaw. (Sports Hero Ser.). (Illus.). (gr. 6-8). 1980. PLB 6.99 (ISBN 0-399-61133-9). Putnam Pub Group.

Burchard, Marshall & Burchard, Sue. Auto Racing Highlights. LC 75-6692. (Sports Ser.). (Illus.). 96p. (gr. 3-6). 1975. PLB 7.12 (ISBN 0-8116-6673-5). Garrard.

--I Know a Baseball Player. LC 73-82026. (Community Helper Bks.). (Illus.). (gr. k-3). 1975. PLB 4.29 o.p. (ISBN 0-399-60867-2). Putnam Pub Group.

--Sports Hero: Billie Jean King. LC 74-16623. (Sports Hero Ser.). 96p. (gr. 3-5). 1975. PLB 6.29 o.p. (ISBN 0-399-60907-5). Putnam Pub Group.

--Sports Hero: Bobby Orr. (Sports Hero Ser.). (Illus.). 96p. (gr. 3-5). 1973. PLB 6.29 o.p. (ISBN 0-399-60795-1). Putnam Pub Group.

--Sports Hero: Brooks Robinson. (Sports Hero Ser.). (Illus.). (gr. 3-5). 1971. PLB 5.49 o.p. (ISBN 0-399-60077-9). Putnam Pub Group.

--Sports Hero: Henry Aaron. LC 74-76359. (Sports Hero Ser.). (Illus.). 96p. (gr. 3-5). 1974. PLB 6.29 o.p. (ISBN 0-399-60903-2). Putnam Pub Group.

--Sports Hero: Joe Namath. (Sports Hero Ser.). (Illus.). (gr. 3-5). 1971. PLB 6.29 o.p. (ISBN 0-399-60601-7). Putnam Pub Group.

--Sports Hero: Johnny Bench. (Sports Hero Ser.). (Illus.). (gr. 3-5). 1973. PLB 6.99 o.p. (ISBN 0-399-60739-0). Putnam Pub Group.

--Sports Hero: Kareem Abdul Jabbar. (Sports Hero Ser.). (Illus.). 96p. (gr. 3-5). 1972. PLB 5.49 o.p. (ISBN 0-399-60699-8). Putnam Pub Group.

--Sports Hero: Larry Csonka. (Sports Hero Ser.). (Illus.). 96p. (gr. 3-5). 1975. PLB 6.29 o.p. (ISBN 0-399-60938-5). Putnam Pub Group.

--Sports Hero: O. J. Simpson. LC 74-21082. (Sports Hero Ser.). (Illus.). (gr. 3-5). 1975. PLB 6.29 o.p. (ISBN 0-399-60940-7). Putnam Pub Group.

--Sports Hero: Phil Esposito. LC 74-21083. (Sports Hero Ser.). (Illus.). 96p. (gr. 3-5). 1975. PLB 5.49 o.p. (ISBN 0-399-60941-5). Putnam Pub Group.

--Sports Hero: Richard Petty. LC 74-77296. (Sports Hero Ser.). (Illus.). 96p. (gr. 3-5). 1974. PLB 6.29 o.p. (ISBN 0-399-60899-0). Putnam Pub Group.

--Sports Hero: Roger Staubach. (Sports Hero Ser.). (Illus.). 96p. (gr. 3-5). 1973. PLB 6.99 (ISBN 0-399-60829-X). Putnam Pub Group.

--Sports Star: Tom Seaver. LC 74-7265. (Sports Star Ser.). (Illus.). (gr. 1-5). 1976. pap. 3.95 (ISBN 0-15-278011-4, VoyB). HarBraceJ.

Burchard, Peter. Bimby. (Illus.). (gr. 3-7). 1968. 6.95 o.p. (ISBN 0-698-20012-8, Coward). Putnam Pub Group.

--Chinwe. (Illus.). (gr. 6-8). 1979. 6.95 (ISBN 0-399-20667-1). Putnam Pub Group.

--The Deserter: A Spy Story of the Civil War. (Illus.). 96p. (gr. 4-7). 1974. 5.95 o.p. (ISBN 0-698-20266-X, Coward). Putnam Pub Group.

--Digger. 128p. (gr. 5-12). 1980. 8.95 (ISBN 0-399-20717-1). Putnam Pub Group.

--Harbor Tug. LC 75-18884. (Illus.). (gr. 5 up). 1975. 6.95 o.p. (ISBN 0-399-20479-2). Putnam Pub Group.

--Ocean Race: A Sea Venture. LC 77-11034. (Illus.). (gr. 5-8). 1978. 7.95 o.p. (ISBN 0-399-20580-2). Putnam Pub Group.

--A Quiet Place. 96p. (gr. 4-8). 1972. 5.95 o.p. (ISBN 0-698-20191-4, Coward). Putnam Pub Group.

--Whaleboat Raid. (Illus.). 96p. (gr. 3-6). 1977. 7.95 o.p. (ISBN 0-698-20412-3, Coward). Putnam Pub Group.

Burchard, S. H. Sports Star: Brad Park. LC 75-11778. (Sports Star Ser.). (Illus.). (gr. 1-5). 1975. pap. 2.95 (ISBN 0-15-278003-3, VoyB). HarBraceJ.

--Sports Star: Chris Evert Lloyd. LC 76-18156. (Sports Star Ser.). (Illus.). (gr. 1-5). 1976. pap. 3.95 (ISBN 0-15-278008-4, VoyB). HarBraceJ.

--Sports Star: Elvin Hayes. LC 79-24286. (Sports Star Ser.). (Illus.). 64p. (gr. 1-5). 1980. 5.95 (ISBN 0-15-278018-1, HJ); pap. 2.50 (ISBN 0-15-684828-7). HarBraceJ.

--Sports Star: Franco Harris. LC 75-35527. (Sports Star Ser). (Illus.). (gr. 1-5). 1976. pap. 3.95 (ISBN 0-15-278005-X, VoyB). HarBraceJ.

--Sports Star: Jim "Catfish" Hunter. LC 75-35525. (Sports Star Ser). (Illus.). (gr. 1-5). 1976. pap. 2.50 (ISBN 0-15-278031-9, VoyB). HarBraceJ.

--Sports Star: John McEnroe. LC 79-87509. (Sports Star Ser.). (Illus.). (gr. 1-5). 1979. pap. 2.25 (ISBN 0-15-684787-6, VoyB). HarBraceJ.

--Sports Star: Mark "The Bird" Fidrych. LC 77-4685. (Sports Star Ser.). (Illus.). (gr. 1-5). 1977. pap. 2.95 (ISBN 0-15-684826-0, VoyB). HarBraceJ.

--Sports Star: Nadia Comaneci. LC 77-3967. (Sports Star Ser.). (Illus.). (gr. 1-5). 1977. pap. 2.95 (ISBN 0-15-684827-9, VoyB). HarBraceJ.

--Sports Star: Pele. LC 75-33707. (Sports Star Ser). (Illus.). (gr. 1-5). 1976. pap. 2.50 (ISBN 0-15-278006-8, VoyB). HarBraceJ.

--Sports Star: Reggie Jackson. LC 78-20567. (Sports Star Ser.). (Illus.). 64p. (gr. 1-4). 1979. 6.95 (ISBN 0-15-278016-5, HJ). HarBraceJ.

--Sports Star: Reggie Jackson. LC 78-20567. (Sports Star Ser). (Illus.). (gr. 1-5). 1979. pap. 2.95 (ISBN 0-15-684791-4, VoyB). HarBraceJ.

--Sports Star: Sugar Ray Leonard. LC 82-48764. 64p. (gr. 6-10). 10.95 (ISBN 0-15-278048-3, HJ). HarBraceJ.

--Sports Star: Sugar Ray Leonard. LC 82-48764. (Illus.). 64p. (gr. 6-10). pap. 4.95 (ISBN 0-15-278049-1, VoyB). HarBraceJ.

--Sports Star: The Book of Baseball Greats. LC 82-48763. 64p. (gr. 6-10). 10.95 (ISBN 0-15-278060-2, HJ). HarBraceJ.

--Sports Star: The Book of Baseball Greats. LC 82-48763. 64p. (gr. 6-10). pap. 4.95 (ISBN 0-15-278061-0, VoyB). HarBraceJ.

--Sports Star: Tony Dorsett. LC 78-52808. (Sports Star Ser). (Illus.). (gr. 1-5). 1978. pap. 3.95 (ISBN 0-15-684792-2, VoyB). HarBraceJ.

--Sports Star: Walt Frazier. LC 75-11781. (Sports Star Ser.). (Illus.). (gr. 1-5). 1975. pap. 3.95 (ISBN 0-15-278004-1, VoyB). HarBraceJ.

Burchard, Sue, jt. auth. see Burchard, Marshall.

Burchardt, Bill. The Lighthorseman. 192p. 1982. pap. 1.95 (ISBN 0-441-48316-X, Pub. by Charter Bks). Ace Bks.

Burcheil, Scott W., et al, eds. Tumor Imaging: The Radioimmunochemical Detection of Cancer. (Illus.). 272p. 1981. 41.50x (ISBN 0-89352-156-6). Masson Pub.

Burchell, G., ed. Ideology & Consciousness: Life, Labour & Insecurity, Vol. 9. 122p. 1981. pap. text ed. 4.00x (Pub. by I & C England). Humanities.

Burchell, Mary. Masquerade with Music. (Harlequin Romances Ser.). 192p. 1983. pap. 1.50 (ISBN 0-373-02528-9). Harlequin Bks.

Burchell, Robert W. Frontiers of Planned Unit Development. 300p. 1973. text ed. 15.00 o.p. (ISBN 0-87855-095-X). Transaction Bks.

Burchell, Robert W. & Carr, James H. The Rise & Fall of the Intergovernmental City. 480p. 1983. pap. text ed. 27.50x (ISBN 0-88285-091-1, Dist. by Transaction Bks). Ctr Urban Pol Res.

Burchell, Robert W. & Sternlieb, George, eds. Planning Theory in the Nineteen Eighties: A Search for Future Directions. LC 78-12929. 1978. pap. text ed. 12.95 (ISBN 0-88285-048-2). Ctr Urban Pol Res.

Burchell, Samuel C. Age of Progress. LC 66-22782. (Great Ages of Man Ser.). PLB 19.96 (ISBN 0-8094-0373-0). Silver.

Burchfiel, B. Clark, et al. Physical Geology: The Structure & Processes of the Earth. 496p. 1982. text ed. 25.95 (ISBN 0-675-09913-7). Additional Supplement May Be Obtained From Publisher. Merrill.

Burchfield, Robert W. The Spoken Word. 40p. 1981. 20.00x (ISBN 0-563-17979-1, BBC PUbns). State Mutual Bk.

Burchfield, Robert W., ed. A Supplement to the Oxford English Dictionary, Vol. 3. 1982. 125.00 (ISBN 0-19-861124-2). Oxford U Pr.

Burchfield, Susan R., ed. Stress: Physiological & Psychological Interactions. (Clinical & Community Psychology Ser.). 450p. Date not set. text ed. 32.00 (ISBN 0-89116-267-4). Hemisphere Pub.

Burchsted, C. A., et al. Nuclear Air Cleaning Handbook. LC 76-52974. (ERDA Technical Information Center). 302p. 1976. pap. 23.50 (ISBN 0-87079-103-6, ERDA-76-21); microfiche 4.50 (ISBN 0-87079-296-2, ERDA-76-21). DOE.

Burck, H. D., et al. Counseling & Accountability: Methods & Critique. 224p. 1974. text ed. 29.00 (ISBN 0-08-017029-3); pap. text ed. 12.75 (ISBN 0-08-017684-4). Pergamon.

Burckel, Nicholas C., jt. auth. see Buenker, John D.

Burckel, Nicholas C., jt. ed. see Buenker, John D.

Burckhalter, Joseph H., jt. auth. see Korolkovas, Andrejus.

Burckhardt, J. K., tr. Arabic Proverbs: Or the Manners & Customs of the Modern Egyptian Illustrated from Their Proverbial Sayings Current at Cairo. 1972. Repr. text ed. 12.50x o.p. (ISBN 0-7007-0019-6). Humanities.

Burckhardt, Jacob. The Civilization of the Renaissance in Italy. LC 54-6894. 6.95 (ISBN 0-394-60497-0). Modern Lib.

--The Civilization of the Renaissance in Italy. (Illus.). 486p. 1983. 13.95 (ISBN 0-7148-2140-3, Pub by Salem Hse Ltd). Merrimack Bk Serv.

Burckhardt, Rudy. Mobile Homes. Elmslie, Kenward, ed. LC 79-90670. (Illus.). 1980. 15.00 (ISBN 0-915990-18-0); pap. 7.50 (ISBN 0-915990-19-9). Z Pr.

Burckle, L. H., jt. ed. see Saito, T.

Burd, Van Akin, ed. see LaTouche, Rose.

Burda, R. W. Clinemark's Tale. LC 79-51199. 1980. 10.95 o.p. (ISBN 0-89696-066-8, An Everest House Book). Dodd.

Burdekin, D. A., jt. auth. see Phillips, D. H.

Burden, E. E. Architectural Delineation: A Photographic Approach to Presentation. 1971. 42.50 (ISBN 0-07-008924-8, P&RB). McGraw.

Burden, Ernest. Entourage: A Tracing File for Architecture & Interior Design Drawing. (Illus.). 256p. 1981. pap. 19.95 (ISBN 0-07-008930-2). McGraw.

Burden, Ernest E. Design Presentation: Techniques for Marketing & Project Presentation. (Illus.). 256p. 1983. 34.95 (ISBN 0-07-008931-0, P&RB). McGraw.

--Visual Presentation. 1978. 21.95 o.p. (ISBN 0-07-008926-4, P&RB). McGraw.

Burden, Jean. The Woman's Day Book of Hints for Cat-Owners. Date not set. pap. 5.95 (ISBN 0-686-82631-0, Columbine). Fawcett.

Burder, John. Work of the Industrial Film Maker. (Library of Film & Television Practice). 1974. 22.95 o.s.i. (ISBN 0-240-50762-2). Focal Pr.

Burdett, Harold N. Yesteryear In Annapolis. (Illus.). 90p. 1974. pap. 4.00 (ISBN 0-686-36488-0). Md Hist.

Burdett, Jeremy K. Molecular Shapes: Theoretical Models of Inorganic Stereochemistry. LC 80-15463. 287p. 1980. 39.95 (ISBN 0-471-07860-3, Pub. by Wiley-Interscience). Wiley.

Burdett, O. William Blake. LC 74-1127. (Studies in Blake, No. 3). 1974. lib. bdg. 32.95x (ISBN 0-8383-2021-X). Haskell.

Burdette, Kay. Fabric Painting in Tole, Bk. 1. (Illus., Orig.). 1982. pap. 7.95 (ISBN 0-941284-16-6). Deco Design Studio.

Burdge, Rabel J., jt. auth. see Rogers, Everett M.

Burdick, Arthur J. Prospectors' Manual. (Shorey Prospecting Ser.). (Illus.). 160p. pap. 8.95 (ISBN 0-8466-6018-0, SJU18). Shorey.

Burdick, C. R., jt. ed. see Kruse, E. G.

Burdick, Charles B. Germany's Military Strategy & Spain in World War Two. LC 68-26994. (Illus.). 1968. 16.95x (ISBN 0-8156-2122-1). Syracuse U Pr.

Burdick, Charles B., jt. ed. see Detwiler, Donald S.

Burdick, Donald. Epistles of John. (Everyman's Bible Commentary Ser.). 1970. pap. 4.50 (ISBN 0-8024-2062-1). Moody.

Burdick, Donald L. & Leffler, William L. Petrochemicals for the Nontechnical Person. 224p. 1983. 37.50x (ISBN 0-87814-207-X). Pennwell Books Division.

Burdick, Eugene & Wheeler, Harvey. Fail-Safe. 1962. 10.95 (ISBN 0-07-008927-2, GB). McGraw.

Burdick, Eugene, jt. auth. see Lederer, William J.

Burdick, Francis M. The Law of Partnership, Including Limited Partnerships. lii, 422p. 1983. Repr. of 1899 ed. lib. bdg. 37.50x (ISBN 0-8377-0333-6). Rothman.

Burdick, G. R., jt. ed. see Fussell, J. B.

Burdick, Jacques. Theater. (World of Culture Ser.). (Illus.). 192p. 1974. 12.95 o.p. (ISBN 0-88225-103-1). Newsweek.

Burdick, Loraine. The Shirley Temple Scrapbook. 1982. pap. 8.95 (ISBN 0-8246-0277-3). Jonathan David.

Burdick, William L. The Bench & Bar of Other Lands. LC 39-32691. xii, 652p. 1982. Repr. of 1939 ed. lib. bdg. 32.00 (ISBN 0-89941-163-0). W S Hein.

Burdon, jt. auth. see Work, T.

Burdon, Roy M. RNA Biosynthesis. (Outline Studies in Biology Ser.). 1976. pap. 6.50x (ISBN 0-412-14050-0, Pub. by Chapman & Hall). Methuen Inc.

Bureau of Social Science Research. International Communication & Political Opinion. Smith, B. L. & Smith, C. M., eds. LC 72-1108. 325p. 1972. Repr. of 1956 ed. lib. bdg. 18.50x (ISBN 0-8371-6007-3, INCO). Greenwood.

Bureau of Statistics-Australia. Yearbook Australia, Nineteen-Eighty. 64th ed. LC 9-6317. (Illus.). 834p. (Orig.). 1980. pap. 30.00x o.p. (ISBN 0-8002-0496-4). Intl Pubns Serv.

Bureloff, Morris. De Code Puzzles - Math. Laycock, Mary, ed. (Illus.). 64p. pap. text ed. 4.95 (ISBN 0-918932-79-3). Activity Resources.

Buren, Martin Van see Van Buren, Martin.

Bures, Jan & Krekule, Ivan. Practical Guide to Computer Applications in Neurosciences. 1983. 42.95 (ISBN 0-471-10012-9, Pub. by Wiley-Interscience). Wiley.

Bures, Jan, et al. Techniques & Basic Experiments for the Study of Brain & Behavior. 1976. 41.50 (ISBN 0-444-41502-5, North Holland). Elsevier.

Bures, Ruth A. Here Comes Christmas. 40p. (gr. k-8). 1982. pap. write for info. (ISBN 0-86704-008-4). Clarus Music.

Buresch, M. Photovoltaic Energy Systems: Design & Installation. 352p. 1983. 24.50 (ISBN 0-07-008952-3, P&RB). McGraw.

Buret, Eugene. De la Misere des Classes Laborieuses en Angleterre et en France, 2 vols. (Conditions of the 19th Century French Working Class Ser.). 924p. (Fr.). 1974. Repr. of 1840 ed. lib. bdg. 234.00x set o.p. (ISBN 0-8287-0152-0). Vol. 1 (1170). Vol. 2 (1171). Clearwater Pub.

Burford. The Greek Temple Builders at Epidauros. 274p. 1982. 50.00x (ISBN 0-85323-080-3, Pub. by Liverpool Univ England). State Mutual Bk.

Burford, E. J., ed. Bawdy Verse: A Pleasant Collection. 1983. pap. 3.95 (ISBN 0-14-042297-8). Penguin.

Burford Mason, Roger. Up at the Big House. (Illus.). 32p. 1981. 22.00 (ISBN 0-930126-08-4). Typographeum.

Burg, B. Richard. Richard Mather. (United States Authors Ser.). 1982. lib. bdg. 15.50 (ISBN 0-8057-7364-9, Twayne). G K Hall.

Burg, David, tr. see Daniel, Yuli.

Burg, G. & Braun-Falco, O. Cutaneous Lymphomas, Pseudolymphomas, & Related Disorders. (Illus.). 550p. 1983. 135.00 (ISBN 0-387-10467-4). Springer-Verlag.

Burg, Leslie, et al. The Complete Reading Supervisor: Task & Roles. 1978. text ed. 18.95 (ISBN 0-675-08481-4). Additional supplements may be obtained from publisher. Merrill.

Burg, Steven. Conflict & Cohesion in Socialist Yugoslavia: Political Decision Making since 1966. LC 82-61358. 456p. 1983. 37.50x (ISBN 0-691-07651-0). Princeton U Pr.

Burgard, Andrea, ed. Directory of Educational Programs in Information Science: Supplement for 1972/1973. LC 70-179373. 38p. 1972. pap. 3.00 (ISBN 0-87715-601-8). Am Soc Info Sci.

Burgdorf, Robert L., Jr., ed. The Legal Rights of Handicapped Persons: Cases, Materials, & Text. LC 79-26311. 1178p. 1980. text ed. 29.95 (ISBN 0-933716-01-X). P H Brookes.

Burgdorf, Shirley M. Who Am I. pap. 1.50 o.p. (ISBN 0-686-12937-7). Pyramid Iowa.

Burge, David A. Patent & Trademark Tactics & Practice. LC 79-16835. 186p. 1979. 21.95 (ISBN 0-471-04937-9, Pub. by Wiley-Interscience). Wiley.

Burge, David L. Perfect Pitch: Color Hearing for Expanded Musical Awareness. LC 81-85963. 60p. 1983. pap. 5.95 (ISBN 0-942542-97-5). Innersphere.

Burge, William. Commentaries on Colonial & Foreign Laws Generally & in Their Conflict with Each Other & with the Law of England, 4 bks. in 5 vols., bk. 21-25. Renton, Alexander W., et al, eds. LC 80-84956. (Historical Writings in Law & Jurisprudence Ser.: No. 17). 1981. Repr. of 1907 ed. Set. lib. bdg. 240.00 (ISBN 0-89941-186-X). Vol. 1 (ISBN 0-89941-073-1). Vol. 2 (ISBN 0-89941-074-X). Vol. 3 (ISBN 0-89941-075-8). Vol. 4, Pt. 1 (ISBN 0-89941-076-6). Vol. 4, Pt. 2. W S Hein.

--Commentaries on the Law of Suretyship, & the Rights & Obligations of Parties Thereto. Helmholz, R. H. & Reams, Bernard D., Jr., eds. (Historical Writings in Law & Jurisprudence Ser.). 616p. 1981. Repr. of 1847 ed. PLB 38.50 (ISBN 0-89941-078-2). W S HEIN.

Burge, William H. Recursive Programming Techniques. LC 74-28812. (IBM Systems Programming Ser.). (Illus.). 280p. 1975. text ed. 23.95 (ISBN 0-201-14450-6). A-W.

Burgen, A. S. & Roberts, G. C., eds. Topics in Molecular Pharmacology, Vol. 1. 1982. 68.00 (ISBN 0-444-80354-8, Biomedical Bks). Elsevier.

Burgen, A. S., ed. see Gaddum, John.

Burger, A. W. Laboratory Exercises in Field Crop Science. 1977. spiral bdg. 7.60x (ISBN 0-87563-031-6). Stipes.

Burger, Angela S. Opposition in a Dominant-Party System: A Study of the Jan Sangh, the Praja Socialist & Socialist Parties in Uttar Pradesh, India. LC 77-76540. (Center for South & Southeast Asia Studies, UC Berkeley). 1969. 27.50x (ISBN 0-520-01428-6). U of Cal Pr.

Burger, Dionys. Sphereland. Rheinboldt, Cornelie J., tr. from Fr. (Illus.). 224p. 1983. pap. 4.76i (ISBN 0-06-463574-0, EH 574). B&N NY.

Burger, Douglas C. Bibliotheca Chrysostomica, Bibliographia Analytica Corporis Chrysostomici, Volumen 2: Index Initiorvm Latinorvm Opervm Chrysostomo Adscriptorvm. (Illus.). vix, 464p. (Lat. & Gr.). 1982. 69.00 (ISBN 0-943684-04-8). Bibliotheca Chrysostomica.

--Bibliotheca Chrysostomica, Bibliographia Analytica Corporis Chrysostomici, Volumen 1: Index Initiorvm Graecorvm Opervm Chrysostomo Adscriptorvm. (Illus.). xiv, 586p. (Lat. & Gr.). 1982. 69.00 (ISBN 0-943684-00-5). Bibliotheca Chrysostomica.

Burger, G., et al. Radiation Protection Quantities for External Exposure. (European Applied Reports Special Topics Ser.). 268p. 1981. 56.00 (ISBN 3-7186-0063-3). Harwood Academic.

Burger, Henry & Dekretser, David, eds. The Testis. (Comprehensive Endocrinology Ser.). 454p. 1981. text ed. 54.50 (ISBN 0-89004-247-0). Raven.

Burger, Henry G. Wordtree: A Transitive Cladistic for Solving Physical & Social Problems. 1st ed. 360p. 1983. 149.00t (ISBN 0-936312-00-9). Wordtree.

Burger, Joanne. SF Published in Nineteen Seventy-Seven. (Orig.). 1978. pap. 4.00x (ISBN 0-916188-08-6). J Burger.

Burger, John R. & Gardner, Lewis. Children of the Wild. LC 78-4627. (Illus.). 128p. (gr. 7 up). 1978. PLB 7.29 o.p. (ISBN 0-671-32879-4). Messner.

Burger, Max M., jt. ed. see Lash, James.

Burger, Neal, jt. auth. see Simpson, George.

Burger, Neal R., jt. auth. see Simpson, George E.

Burger, Peter C. & Vogel, F. Stephen. Surgical Pathology of the Nervous System & Its Coverings. 2nd ed. LC 81-16250. 739p. 1982. 75.00x (ISBN 0-471-05876-9, Pub. by Wiley Med). Wiley.

--Surgical Pathology of the Nervous System & Its Coverings. 2nd ed. LC 76-6492. 1976. 80.00x o.p. (ISBN 0-471-12347-1, Pub. by Wiley Med); pap. 65.00 o.p. (ISBN 0-471-05876-9). Wiley.

Burger, Pixie. A Woman of Two Continents. 1982. pap. 3.50 (ISBN 0-553-20833-0). Bantam.

Burger, Robert, jt. auth. see Morton, Craig.

Burger, Robert M., et al. Independence Training, 5 bks. Incl. Bk. 1. Underwear & Footwear. 8.10 (ISBN 0-685-55874-6); Bk. 2. Indoor & Outdoor Clothing. 8.10 (ISBN 0-685-55875-4); Bk. 3. Fastenings. 7.40 (ISBN 0-685-55876-2); Bk. 4. Grooming & Self-Care Skills. 8.90 (ISBN 0-685-55877-0); Bk. 5. Parent's Guide. 7.40 (ISBN 0-685-55878-9). LC 77-85435. 1977. pap. (ISBN 0-685-55873-8). Western Psych.

Burgess & Latham. Elementary Reaction Kinetics. 3rd ed. 1977. 9.95x o.p. (ISBN 0-408-46102-0). Butterworth.

Burgess, A. W. & Lazare. Community Mental Health: Target Population. LC 75-37561. 256p. 1976. 21.95x (ISBN 0-13-153148-4). P-H.

Burgess, Alan, jt. auth. see Bergman, Ingrid.

Burgess, Ann W. & Lazare, Aaron. Psychiatric Nursing in the Hospital & the Community. 3rd ed. (Illus.). 736p. 1981. text ed. 24.95 (ISBN 0-13-731927-4). P-H.

Burgess, Ann W., jt. auth. see Holmstrom, Lynda L.

Burgess, Ann W., et al. Sexual Assault of Children & Adolescents. LC 77-10217. 1978. 24.95x (ISBN 0-669-01890-2); pap. 10.95x (ISBN 0-669-01892-9). Lexington Bks.

Burgess, Ann Wolbert, jt. auth. see Holmstrom, Lynda Lytle.

Burgess, Anthony. Earthly Powers. 1980. 16.95 o.p. (ISBN 0-686-85722-4). Bobbs.

--Earthly Powers: A Novel. 1980. 16.95 o.s.i. (ISBN 0-671-41490-9). S&S.

--End of the World News. 388p. 1983. 15.95 (ISBN 0-07-008965-5). McGraw.

--Jesus of Nazareth. 1979. 10.95 (ISBN 0-07-008962-0, GB). McGraw.

--New York. (The Great Cities Ser.). (Illus.). (gr. 6 up). 1977. PLB 14.94 o.p. (ISBN 0-8094-2271-9, Pub. by Time-Life). Silver.

--Nothing Like the Sun. 240p. 1975. pap. 5.95 (ISBN 0-393-00795-2, N795, Norton Lib). Norton.

--Puma. Date not set. price not set (ISBN 0-07-008963-9). McGraw.

--Tremor of Intent. 1977. 4.95 (ISBN 0-393-08539-2, Norton Lib); pap. 4.95 1977 (ISBN 0-393-00416-3). Norton.

Burgess, Anthony, jt. auth. see Testa, Fulvio.

Burgess, Audrey. The Nurse's Guide to Fluid & Electrolyte Balance. 2nd ed. (Illus.). 1979. pap. text ed. 19.95 (ISBN 0-07-008955-8, HP). McGraw.

Burgess, Beverly. Three Bears in the Ministry. 28p. (Orig.). (ps). 1982. pap. 3.50 (ISBN 0-89274-252-6). Harrison Hse.

--Three Little Pigs: Build Your House Upon the Rock. (Orig.). (ps). 1983. pap. write for info. (ISBN 0-89274-283-6). Harrison Hse.

Burgess, C. & Knowles, A. Standards in Absorption Spectrometry. (Techniques in Visible & Ultraviolet Spectrometry Ser.). 1981. 22.00x (ISBN 0-412-22470-4, Pub. by Chapman & Hall). Methuen Inc.

Burgess, C., jt. ed. see Strickland, C. E.

Burgess, C. R. Meteorology for Seamen. 4th ed. 251p. 1982. text ed. 25.00x (ISBN 0-85174-315-3). Sheridan.

Burgess, Carol, et al. Understanding Children Writing. 192p. (Orig.). 1973. pap. 7.00 (ISBN 0-14-080700-4). Boynton Cook Pubs.

Burgess, Charles. In Care & into Work. LC 80-42289. (Residential Social Work Ser.). 160p. 1981. 21.00x (ISBN 0-422-77640-8, Pub by Tavistock England). Methuen Inc.

Burgess, Ebeneezer, tr. from Sanscrit. Surya Siddhanta. LC 74-78001. (Secret Doctrine Reference Ser.). 368p. 1977. Repr. of 1860 ed. 17.50 (ISBN 0-913510-13-0). Wizards.

Burgess, Eric. Celestial Basic: Astronomy on Your Computer. LC 82-60187. (Illus.). 300p. 1982. pap. text ed. 13.95 (ISBN 0-89588-087-3). Sybex.

Burgess, Ernest W., et al. The Family: From Traditional to Companionship. 4th ed. 1971. 12.95x (ISBN 0-442-20893-6); instructor's manual 1.50x (ISBN 0-442-20894-4). Van Nos Reinhold.

Burgess, Frederick W. Antique Jewelry & Trinkets. LC 74-178622. (Illus.). xvi, 399p. 1972. Repr. of 1919 ed. 35.00 o.p. (ISBN 0-8103-3863-7). Gale.

Burgess, Gelett. Goops & How to Be Them: A Manual of Manners for Polite Infants. LC 68-55630. (Illus.). (ps-4). 1968. pap. 2.75 (ISBN 0-486-22233-0). Dover.

Burgess, Harold W. An Invitation to Religious Education. LC 75-14980. 190p. 1975. lib. bdg. 12.95 (ISBN 0-89135-004-7); pap. 9.95 (ISBN 0-89135-019-5). Religious Educ.

Burgess, Hovey. Circus Techniques. (Illus.). 1977. 11.95i (ISBN 0-690-01463-5, TYC-T); pap. 7.95 o.p. (ISBN 0-690-01464-3, TYC-T). T Y Crowell.

Burgess, Hugh. Dwell With These Distances, Vol. 10. 50p. 1982. pap. 2.95 (ISBN 0-932616-08-9). New Poets.

Burgess, Jacquelin, ed. see Gold, John.

Burgess, James Z. Burgess History: The Tennessee Pioneer. 300p. 1982. lib. bdg. 49.95x (ISBN 0-89370-740-6). Borgo Pr.

Burgess, John. Connoisseurs' Choice: Racing, Sports & Touring Cars. LC 77-93729. (Illus.). 1978. 11.95 o.s.i. (ISBN 0-8027-0601-0); pap. 6.95 o.s.i. (ISBN 0-8027-7133-5). Walker & Co.

Burgess, John W. Reconstruction & the Constitution, 1866-1876. LC 70-99479. (American Constitutional & Legal History Ser.: Americana Ser). 1970. Repr. of 1902 ed. lib. bdg. 42.50 (ISBN 0-306-71849-9). Da Capo.

Burgess, Keith. The Challenge of Labour: Shaping British Society, 1850-1930. LC 80-10251. 224p. 1980. 25.00 (ISBN 0-312-12805-3). St Martin.

Burgess, Linda C. The Art of Adoption. 176p. 1981. pap. 4.95 (ISBN 0-393-00036-2). Norton.

Burgess, Lorraine M. The Garden Maker's Answer Book. (Illus.). 1975 (Assn Pr). pap. 6.95 o.s.i. (ISBN 0-686-67236-4). Follett.

Burgess, Lourdes, jt. auth. see Axelrod, Herbert R.

Burgess, M. R. The House of the Burgesses. LC 80-10759. (Borgo Family Histories: No. 1). 168p. 1983. lib. bdg. 14.95x (ISBN 0-89370-801-1); pap. 6.95x (ISBN 0-89370-901-8). Borgo Pr.

Burgess, M. R., jt. ed. see Reginald, Robert.

Burgess, Mary A. The Wickizer Annals. LC 80-11075. (Borgo Family Histories Ser.: No. 2). 144p. 1983. lib. bdg. 14.95x (ISBN 0-89370-802-X); pap. 6.95x (ISBN 0-89370-902-6). Borgo Pr.

Burgess, Mary A., jt. auth. see Clarke, Boden.

Burgess, Mary A., jt. auth. see Reginald, R.

Burgess, P., tr. see Frobel, Folker, et al.

Burgess, Patricia S. My Name Is Ruth: The Story of a Pastor's Wife. 1979. 5.95 o.p. (ISBN 0-533-03723-9). Vantage.

Burgess, Robert H. Chesapeake Circle. (Illus.). 211p. 1965. 15.00 (ISBN 0-686-36510-0). Md Hist.

--This Was Chesapeake Bay. (Illus.). 210p. 1963. 11.00 (ISBN 0-686-36511-9). Md Hist.

Burgess, Thornton. The Dear Old Briar-Patch. 192p. 1982. pap. 7.25i (ISBN 0-316-11654-8). Little.

Burgess, Thornton W. Adventures of Bob White. (Bedtime Story Bks.: Vol. 19). (Illus.). (gr. 2-5). 1956. 2.95 o.s.i. (ISBN 0-448-02719-4, G&D). Putnam Pub Group.

--Adventures of Bobby Coon. (Bedtime Story Bks.: Vol. 17). (gr. 2-5). 1954. 2.95 o.p. (ISBN 0-448-02717-8, G&D). Putnam Pub Group.

--Adventures of Buster Bear. (Bedtime Story Bks.). (gr. 2-5). 1950. 2.95 (ISBN 0-448-02701-1, G&D); PLB 6.75 (ISBN 0-448-13701-1). Putnam Pub Group.

--Adventures of Chatterer the Red Squirrel. (Bedtime Story Bks.: Vol. 2). (gr. 2-5). 1949. 2.95 (ISBN 0-448-02702-X, G&D). Putnam Pub Group.

--Adventures of Danny Meadow Mouse. (Bedtime Story Bks.). (gr. 2-5). 1950. 2.95 (ISBN 0-448-02703-8, G&D); PLB 6.75 (ISBN 0-448-13703-8). Putnam Pub Group.

--Adventures of Grandfather Frog. (Thornton W. Burgess Storybks.). (gr. 2-5). 1952. 2.95 (ISBN 0-448-02704-6, G&D); PLB 6.75 (ISBN 0-448-13704-6). Putnam Pub Group.

--Adventures of Jerry Muskrat. (Thornton W. Burgess Storybks.). (gr. 2-5). 1951. 2.95 (ISBN 0-448-02705-4, G&D); PLB 6.75 (ISBN 0-448-13705-4). Putnam Pub Group.

--Adventures of Jimmy Skunk. (Bedtime Story Bks.: Vol. 18). (gr. 2-5). 1954. 2.95 o.p. (ISBN 0-448-02718-6, G&D). Putnam Pub Group.

--Adventures of Johnny Chuck. (Thornton W. Burgess Storybks.). (gr. 2-5). 1952. 2.95 (ISBN 0-448-02706-2, G&D); PLB 6.75 (ISBN 0-448-13706-2). Putnam Pub Group.

--Adventures of Lightfoot the Deer. (Green Forest Ser.: Vol. 1). (gr. k-3). 1944. 2.95 o.p. (ISBN 0-448-02741-0, G&D). Putnam Pub Group.

--Adventures of Ol' Mistah Buzzard. (Bedtime Story Bks.: Vol. 20). (Illus.). (gr. 2-5). 1957. 2.95 o.p. (ISBN 0-448-02720-8, G&D). Putnam Pub Group.

--Adventures of Old Granny Fox. (Green Forest Ser.: Vol. 4). (gr. k-3). 1943. 2.95 o.p. (ISBN 0-448-02784-4, G&D). Putnam Pub Group.

--Adventures of Old Man Coyote. (Thornton W. Burgess Storybks.). (gr. 2-5). 1952. 2.95 (ISBN 0-448-02708-9, G&D); PLB 6.75 (ISBN 0-448-13708-9). Putnam Pub Group.

--Adventures of Old Mr. Toad. (Thornton W. Burgess Storybks.). (gr. 2-5). 1949. 2.95 (ISBN 0-448-02709-7, G&D); PLB 6.75 (ISBN 0-448-13709-7). Putnam Pub Group.

--Adventures of Paddy the Beaver. (Thornton W. Burgess Storybks.). (gr. 2-5). 1953. 2.95 (ISBN 0-448-02710-0, 2710, G&D); PLB 6.75 (ISBN 0-448-13710-0). Putnam Pub Group.

--Adventures of Peter Cottontail. (Bedtime Story Bks.: Vol. 11). (gr. k-3). 1950. 2.95 o.s.i. (ISBN 0-448-02711-9, G&D). Putnam Pub Group.

--Adventures of Peter Cottontail. (Grow-up Books Ser.). (Illus.). (gr. k-3). 1970. 1.95 o.s.i. (ISBN 0-448-02246-X, G&D). Putnam Pub Group.

--Adventures of Poor Mrs. Quack. (gr. 2-5). 1953. 2.95 o.p. (ISBN 0-448-02712-7, G&D). Putnam Pub Group.

--Adventures of Prickly Porky. (Thornton W. Burgess Storybks.). (gr. 2-5). 1949. 2.95 (ISBN 0-448-02713-5, G&D); PLB 6.75 (ISBN 0-448-13713-5). Putnam Pub Group.

--Adventures of Ready Fox. (Thornton W. Burgess Storybks.). (gr. 2-5). 1950. 2.95 (ISBN 0-448-02714-3, G&D); PLB 6.75 (ISBN 0-448-13714-3). Putnam Pub Group.

--Adventures of Sammy Jay. (Thornton W. Burgess Storybks.). (gr. 2-5). 1949. 2.95 (ISBN 0-448-02715-1, G&D); PLB 6.75 (ISBN 0-448-13715-1). Putnam Pub Group.

--Adventures of Unc' Billy Possum. (Bedtime Story Bks.: Vol. 16). (gr. 2-5). 1951. 2.95 o.p. (ISBN 0-448-02716-X, G&D); PLB 6.75 (ISBN 0-448-13723-2). Putnam Pub Group.

--Adventures of Whitefoot the Woodmouse. (Green Forest Ser.: Vol. 3). (gr. k-3). 1944. 2.95 o.p. (ISBN 0-448-02743-7, G&D). Putnam Pub Group.

--Burgess Bedtime Stories. LC 76-14691. (Elephant Books). (Illus.). (ps-5). 1976. pap. 3.95 (ISBN 0-448-12690-7, G&D). Putnam Pub Group.

--Mother West Wind's Animal Friends. (Mother West Wind Ser.: Vol. 3). (gr. k-3). 1940. 2.95 o.s.i. (ISBN 0-448-02763-1, G&D). Putnam Pub Group.

--Mother West Wind's Children. (Mother West Wind Ser.: Vol. 2). (gr. k-3). 1940. 2.95 (ISBN 0-448-02762-3, G&D); PLB 6.75 (ISBN 0-448-13726-7). Putnam Pub Group.

--Mother West Wind's Children. new ed. (Nature Story Bks). (Illus.). (gr. 1-3). 1962. 11.95 (ISBN 0-316-11645-9). Little.

--Mother West Wind's "How" Stories. (Mother West Wind Ser.: Vol. 6). (gr. k-3). 1941. 2.95 (ISBN 0-448-02766-6, G&D); PLB 6.75 (ISBN 0-448-13730-5). Putnam Pub Group.

--Mother West Wind's Neighbors. (Mother West Wind Ser.: Vol. 4). (gr. k-3). 1940. 2.95 o.p. (ISBN 0-448-02764-X, G&D); PLB 6.75 o.p. (ISBN 0-448-13728-3). Putnam Pub Group.

--Mother West Wind's "When" Stories. (Mother West Wind Ser.: Vol. 7). (gr. k-3). 1941. 2.95 (ISBN 0-448-02767-4, G&D); PLB 6.75 (ISBN 0-448-13731-3). Putnam Pub Group.

--Mother West Wind's "Why" Stories. (Mother West Wind Ser.: Vol. 5). (gr. k-3). 1941. 2.95 (ISBN 0-448-02765-8, G&D); PLB 6.75 (ISBN 0-448-13729-1). Putnam Pub Group.

--Old Mother West Wind. (Mother West Wind Ser.: Vol. 1). (gr. k-3). 1940. 2.95 o.s.i. (ISBN 0-448-02761-5, G&D). Putnam Pub Group.

--Old Mother West Wind. golden anniversary ed. (Nature-Story Books). (Illus.). (gr. 1 up). 1960. 9.95 (ISBN 0-316-11648-3). Little.

Burgess, Thorton. Favorite Tales by Thorton Burgess. (Platt & Munk Pandabacks Ser.). (Illus.). 24p. (ps-3). Date not set. pap. price not set (ISBN 0-448-49613-5, G&D). Putnam Pub Group.

Burgess, Thorton W. Thorton W. Burgess Bedtime Stories. (Illus.). 108p. Date not set. pap. price not set (ISBN 0-448-12690-7, G&D). Putnam Pub Group.

Burgess, Tom, jt. ed. see McBee, Robert.

Burgess, Warren, jt. auth. see Axelrod, Herbert R.

Burgess, Dr. Warren, jt. auth. see Axelrod, Herbert R.

Burgess, Warren E. Butterflyfishes of the World. (Illus.). 1979. 29.95 (ISBN 0-87666-470-2, H-988). TFH Pubns.

--Corals. (Illus.). 1979. 4.95 (ISBN 0-87666-521-0, KW-053). TFH Pubns.

--Marine Aquaria. (Illus.). 96p. text ed. 4.95 (ISBN 0-87666-533-4, KW-088). TFH Pubns.

Burgess, Warren E. & Axelrod, Herbert R. Pacific Marine Fishes, Bk. 3. (Illus.). 272p. 1973. 29.95 (ISBN 0-87666-125-8, PS-719). TFH Pubns.

--Pacific Marine Fishes, Bk. 4. (Illus.). 272p. 1974. 29.95 (ISBN 0-87666-126-6, PS-720). TFH Pubns.

--Pacific Marine Fishes, Bk. 5. (Illus.). 271p. 1975. 29.95 (ISBN 0-87666-127-4, PS-721). TFH Pubns.

Burgess, Warren E., jt. auth. see Axelrod, Herbert R.

Burgess, William A. Recognition of Health Hazards in Industry: A Review of Materials & Processes. LC 81-2132. 275p. 1981. 30.95x (ISBN 0-471-06339-8, Pub. by Wiley-Interscience). Wiley.

Burgess Wise, David. The Motor Car: An Illustrated International History. LC 77-2500. (Illus.). 1979. 25.00 o.p. (ISBN 0-399-12388-1). Putnam Pub Group.

Burgest, David R. Social Work Practice with Minorities. LC 81-14461. 322p. 1982. text ed. 16.50 (ISBN 0-8108-1476-5). Scarecrow.

Burgett, Gordon L. How To Produce & Market Your Own Audio Cassettes. 100p. 1983. pap. 7.95 (ISBN 0-9605078-3-3). Successful Sem.

--How To Set Up & Market Your Own Seminar or Workshop. (Illus.). 120p. 1983. 19.95 (ISBN 0-9605078-4-1). Successful Sem.

Burgh, Edward M. Mortgage Investing by Life Insurance Companies. LC 80-80943. (FLMI Insurance Education Program Ser.). (Illus.). 202p. (Orig.). 1980. pap. text ed. 13.00 (ISBN 0-915322-36-6). LOMA.

Burgh, James. Political Disquisitions, 3 Vols. LC 78-146144. (American Constitutional & Legal History Ser). 1971. Repr. of 1775 ed. Set. lib. bdg. 175.00 (ISBN 0-306-70101-4). Da Capo.

Burghard, August. Half a Century in Florida. (Illus.). 263p. Date not set. 25.00 (ISBN 0-686-84226-X). Banyan Bks.

Burghardt. Ingenieria Termodinamica. 2nd ed. 600p. (Span.). 1983. pap. text ed. write for info. (ISBN 0-06-310071-1, Pub. by HarLA Mexico). Har-Row.

Burghardt & Axelrod. Machine Tool Operation, Pts. 1-2. (gr. 10-12). 1959-60. Pt. 1, 5th Ed. text ed. 20.65 (ISBN 0-07-008961-2, W); Pt. 2, 4th Ed o.p. text ed. 14.45 (ISBN 0-07-008966-3). McGraw.

Burghardt, E., et al. Cervical Pathology & Colopscopy. LC 77-99150. 160p. 1978. 24.50 o.p. (ISBN 0-88416-241-9). Wright-PSG.

Burghardt, Erich. Early Histological Diagnosis of Cervical Cancer. LC 79-176203. (Major Problem in Obstetrics & Gynecology Ser.: Vol. 6). (Illus.). 1973. text ed. 10.00 (ISBN 0-7216-2175-9). Saunders.

Burghardt, Gordon M., ed. Iguanas of the World: Their Behavior, Ecology & Conservation. Rand, A. Stanley. LC 82-7932. (Animal Behavior, Ecology, Conservation & Management Ser.). (Illus.). 472p. 1983. 55.00 (ISBN 0-8155-0917-0). Noyes.

Burghardt, Steven. Organizing for Community Action. (Sage Human Services Guides: Vol. 27). 120p. 1982. pap. 7.00 (ISBN 0-8039-0206-9). Sage.

Burghardt, Walter, ed. Why the Church. LC 77-74583. 1977. pap. 4.95 o.p. (ISBN 0-8091-2028-3). Paulist Pr.

Burghardt, Walter J. Sir, We Would Like to See Jesus: Homilies from a Hilltop. LC 82-60589. 1983. 12.95 (ISBN 0-8091-0338-9); pap. 8.95 (ISBN 0-8091-2490-4). Paulist Pr.

Burghardt, Walter J., ed. see Lawler, Thomas C.

Burgher, Peter H. Changement: Understanding & Managing Business. 1979. 18.95x (ISBN 0-669-02569-0). Lexington Bks.

Burghes, D. N. & Borrie, Y. M. Modelling with Differential Equations. LC 80-41936. (Mathematics & Its Applications Ser.). 172p. 1981. 34.95x o.p. (ISBN 0-470-27101-9). Halsted Pr.

Burghes, D. N., et al. Applying Mathematics: A Course in Mathematical. (Mathematics & its Applications Harwood Ser.). 194p. 1982. 44.95X (ISBN 0-470-27523-5). Halsted Pr.

Burgin, Diana, ed. see Chukovsky, Kornei.

Burgin, James. Guide Book for the Family with Alcohol Problems. 3.95 (ISBN 0-89486-155-7). Hazelden.

Burgoon, Judee K. & Saine, Thomas. The Unspoken Dialogue: An Introduction to Nonverbal Communication. (Illus., LC 77-078913). 1978. text ed. 17.50 (ISBN 0-395-25792-1); pap. 1.00 instrs.' manual (ISBN 0-395-25793-X). HM.

Burgoon, Michael, ed. Communication Yearbook Six: An Annual Review Published for the International Commucation Association. LC 76-45943. (Communication Yearbook Ser.: Vol. 6). 968p. 1982. 45.00 (ISBN 0-8039-1862-3). Sage.

Burgoyne, Arthur G. Homestead. LC 68-55495. Repr. of 1893 ed. 25.00x (ISBN 0-678-00872-8). Kelley.

Burgoyne, Edward E. A Short Course in Organic Chemistry. (Illus.). 1979. text ed. 23.95 o.p. (ISBN 0-07-009171-4, C); instructor's manual 9.95 o.p. (ISBN 0-07-009174-9); study guide & solution manual 11.50 o.p. (ISBN 0-07-009173-0). McGraw.

Burgoyne, J. & Stuart, R., eds. Management Development: Context & Strategies. text ed. 29.00x (ISBN 0-566-02101-3). Gower Pub Ltd.

Burgoyne, John. The Dramatic & Poetical Works of the Late Lieut. Gen. J. Burgoyne. LC 77-2932. 1977. Repr. of 1808 ed. 57.00x (ISBN 0-8201-1285-2). Schol Facsimiles.

Burgum, Thomas & Anderson, Scott. The Counselor & the Law. 1975. 9.75 (ISBN 0-686-36428-7, 72005); nonmembers 13.50 (ISBN 0-686-37315-4). Am Personnel.

Burgwyn, Diana. Marriage Without Children. LC 80-8197. 256p. 1982. pap. 4.76i (ISBN 0-06-090940-4, CN940, CN). Har-Row.

Burhenne, H. Joachim, jt. auth. see Margulis, Alexander R.

Burhenne, H. Joachim, jt. ed. see Margulis, Alexander R.

Burhop, E. H. see Massey, H. S.

Burian, Barbara J. A Simplified Approach to S-370 Assembly Language Programming. (Illus.). 1977. 21.95 (ISBN 0-13-810119-1); self study guide 7.50 (ISBN 0-13-810101-9). P-H.

Burian, Jiri & Shvidkovsky, Oleg A. The Kremlin of Moscow. LC 74-21650. (Illus.). 25.00 o.p. (ISBN 0-312-46095-3). St Martin.

Burickson, Sherwin, ed. Concise Dictionary of Contemporary History. 1959. 4.75 o.p. (ISBN 0-8022-0196-2). Philos Lib.

Buridan, John. John Buridan on Self-Reference: Chapter Eight of Buridan's Sophismata, with a Translation, an Introduction, & a Philosophical Commentary. Hughes, G. E., ed. LC 81-15465. 272p. 1982. 39.50 (ISBN 0-521-24086-7); pap. 12.95 (ISBN 0-521-28864-9). Cambridge U Pr.

Burigny, Jean-Levesque De see De Burigny, Jean-Levesque.

Buringh, P. Introduction to the Study of Soils in Tropical & Subtropical Regions. 3rd ed. (Illus.). 146p. 1979. pap. 15.00 (ISBN 0-686-93167-X, PDC146, Pudoc). Unipub.

Burington, Richard S. Handbook of Mathematical Tables & Formulas. 5th ed. LC 78-39634. (Illus.). 480p. 1973. text ed. 21.00 (ISBN 0-07-009015-7, C). McGraw.

Burington, Richard S. & May, Donald C., Jr. Handbook of Probability & Statistics with Tables. 2nd ed. 1970. 28.50 (ISBN 0-07-009030-0, P&RB). McGraw.

Buripakdi, Chalio. The Value of Children: a Cross-National Study: Thailand, Vol. 4. 1977. pap. 3.00x o.p. (ISBN 0-8248-0385-X, Eastwest Ctr). UH Pr.

Burk, Dale A. A Brush with the West. (Illus.). 256p. 1980. 19.95 o.p. (ISBN 0-87842-133-5); limited ed. 60.00 o.p. (ISBN 0-87842-134-3). Mountain Pr.

Burk, John N., ed. Letters of Richard Wagner: The Burrell Collection. LC 78-183325. 665p. Date not set. Repr. of 1950 ed. price not set. Vienna Hse.

Burk, John N., ed. see Hale, Philip.

Burk, John N., ed. see Howe, Mark A.

Burk, W. R. A Bibliography of North American Gasteromycetes I: Phalales. 200p. 1981. pap. text ed. 16.00x (ISBN 3-7682-1262-9). Lubrecht & Cramer.

Burkatt, Leonard, tr. see Munch, Charles.

Burke. Burke's Introduction to Irish Ancestry. pap. 5.95 (ISBN 0-8277-7206-8). British Bk Ctr.

--Burke's Irish Family Records: American Edition. 110.00 (ISBN 0-8277-7205-X). British Bk Ctr.

--Burke's Presidential Families of the USA: Standard Edition. rev ed. 1981. 69.95x (ISBN 0-8277-7209-2); deluxe ed. 250.00x deluxe ed. (ISBN 0-8277-7210-6). British Bk Ctr.

--Cell Biology. 343p. 1970. 16.00 (ISBN 0-683-01212-6). Krieger.

Burke, jt. auth. see Comoss.

Burke, Albert L. He That Hath an Ear. 101p. (Orig.). 1982. pap. 3.50 (ISBN 0-9608662-0-5). Eleventh Hour.

Burke, Anna M. Are You Ready? A Survival Manual for Women Returning to School. 160p. 1980. text ed. 9.95 o.p. (ISBN 0-13-045617-9, Spec); pap. text ed. 4.95 o.p. (ISBN 0-13-045609-8). P-H.

Burke, Carol. Close Quarters. 52p. 1975. 3.50 (ISBN 0-87886-066-5). Ithaca Hse.

Burke, Carol, ed. Plain Talk. LC 82-81678. (Illus.). 160p. (Orig.). 1983. pap. 3.50 (ISBN 0-911198-67-9). Purdue.

Burke, Catherine G. Innovation & Public Policy: The Case of Personal Rapid Transit. LC 79-2410. (Illus.). 416p. 1979. 25.95x (ISBN 0-669-03167-4). Lexington Bks.

Burke, Charles J., jt. auth. see Barnett, Raymond A.

Burke, Clifford. A Rainy Day Guide to Seattle. (Orig.). 1983. pap. 6.95 (ISBN 0-87701-290-3). Chronicle Bks.

Burke, Daniel. Notes on Literary Stucture. LC 81-40645. 280p. (Orig.). 1982. lib. bdg. 22.75 (ISBN 0-8191-2119-3); pap. text ed. 11.50 (ISBN 0-8191-2120-7). U Pr of Amer.

Burke, David G., ed. The Poetry of Baruch: A Reconstruction & Analysis of the Original Hebrew Text of Baruch 3: 9-5: 9. LC 80-10271. (Society of Biblical Literature, Septuagint & Cognate Studies: No. 10). pap. 15.95 (ISBN 0-89130-382-0, 06-04-10). Scholars Pr CA.

Burke, Dennis. Understanding the Fear of the Lord. 1982. pap. 1.50 (ISBN 0-686-83915-3). Harrison Hse.

Burke, Edmond & Paine, Thomas. Reflections on the Revolution in France (Burke) Bd. with The Rights of Man (Paine) Doubleday. pap. 7.50 (ISBN 0-385-08190-1, Anch). Doubleday.

Burke, Edmund. Selected Writings & Speeches. Stanlis, J. P., ed. 12.50 (ISBN 0-8446-1094-1). Peter Smith.

--Speeches. Selby, F. G., ed. LC 73-9127. 328p. 1974. Repr. of 1956 ed. lib. bdg. 19.00x (ISBN 0-8371-6984-4, BUSP). Greenwood.

--A Vindication of Natural Society. LC 81-84826. (Illus.). 130p. 1982. 8.50 (ISBN 0-86597-009-2); pap. text ed. 4.50 (ISBN 0-86597-010-6). Liberty Fund.

Burke, Edmund H. History of Archery. LC 70-138579. 1971. Repr. of 1957 ed. lib. bdg. 17.50x (ISBN 0-8371-5778-1, BUHA). Greenwood.

Burke, Edmund J., tr. see Klausen, Klaus & Hemmingsen, Ib.

Burke, Edward. Reflections on Revolution in France. 1982. pap. 3.50 (ISBN 0-14-043204-3). Penguin.

Burke, Fielding, tr. Call Home the Heart: A Novel of the Thirties. 448p. 1983. pap. 8.95 (ISBN 0-935312-11-0). Feminist Pr.

Burke, J., jt. ed. see Auriche, M.

Burke, J. D. Advertising in the Marketplace. 1980. text ed. 17.60 (ISBN 0-07-009035-1); instr's manual & key 4.55 (ISBN 0-07-009036-X). McGraw.

Burke, James. Connections. (Illus.). 312p. 1979. pap. 14.25 (ISBN 0-316-11685-8). Little.

Burke, James L. Gathering of Horsemen. (Orig.). 1982. pap. write for info o.p. (ISBN 0-671-44112-4). PB.

Burke, John. The Black Charade. 1977. 7.95 o.p. (ISBN 0-698-10847-7, Coward). Putnam Pub Group.

--Buffalo Bill: The Noblest Whiteskin. LC 72-87607. (Illus.). 352p. 1973. 7.95 o.p. (ISBN 0-399-11060-7). Putnam Pub Group.

--Ladygrove: The Third Adventure of Dr. Caspian & Bronwen. LC 78-14539. 1978. 8.95 o.p. (ISBN 0-698-10933-3, Coward). Putnam Pub Group.

--Origins of the Science of Crystals. LC 66-13584. 1966. 32.50x (ISBN 0-520-00198-2). U of Cal Pr.

Burke, John, jt. ed. see Mathieu, Alix.

Burke, John C. The Value of a Woman. 100p. (Orig.). 1983. pap. 9.95 (ISBN 0-931494-39-7). Brunswick Pub.

Burke, John D. Advertising in the Marketplace. (Illus.). 454p. 1973. text ed. 16.95 o.p. (ISBN 0-07-009031-9, G); instructors' manual & key 4.00 o.p. (ISBN 0-07-009032-7). McGraw.

Burke, John D. & Cruikshank, Warren L. Real Estate Sales & Brokerage. 1975. pap. 17.85 (ISBN 0-07-009040-8, G); instructor's guide 4.50 (ISBN 0-07-009041-6). McGraw.

Burke, John G. & Reddig, Jill S. Guide to Ecology Information & Organizations. 292p. 1976. 15.00 (ISBN 0-8242-0567-7). Wilson.

Burke, John G. & Wilson, Carol D. The Monthly Catalog of United States Government Publications: An Introduction to Its Use. vi, 113p. 1973. 14.50 o.p. (ISBN 0-208-01287-7, Linnet). Shoe String.

Burke, John J. The Writer in Pennsylvania, 1681-1981. LC 81-85496. 93p. 1982. pap. 5.95 (ISBN 0-686-36440-6). St Joseph.

--The Writer in Philadelphia, 1682-1982. LC 81-51298. 84p. 1981. pap. 5.95 (ISBN 0-686-36439-2). St Joseph.

Burke, John J. & Weiss, Volker, eds. Fatigue: Environment & Temperature Effect, Vol. 27. (Sagamore Army Materials Research Conference Ser.). 425p. 1983. 59.50x (ISBN 0-306-41101-6, Plenum Pr). Plenum Pub.

Burke, John J., Jr. & Kay, Donald, eds. The Unknown Samuel Johnson. (Illus.). 200p. 1983. 30.00 (ISBN 0-299-09150-3). U of Wis Pr.

Burke, Ken, ed. see Ortho Books Staff.

Burke, Ken, ed. see Sinnes, A. Cort.

Burke, Kenneth. Collected Poems, 1915-1967. LC 67-29786. 1968. 23.50x (ISBN 0-520-00195-8). U of Cal Pr.

--A Rhetoric of Motives. LC 69-16742. 1969. 19.50x o.p. (ISBN 0-520-01545-2); pap. 8.95x (ISBN 0-520-01546-0, CAL178). U of Cal Pr.

--Towards a Better Life: Being a Series of Epistles, or Declamations. 1966. 21.50x (ISBN 0-520-00193-1). U of Cal Pr.

Burke, Kenneth, et al. Rhetoric in Change. Tanner, William E. & Bishop, J. Dean, eds. 217p. (Orig.). 1982. 16.95 (ISBN 0-86663-900-4); 10.95 (ISBN 0-86663-901-2). Ide Hse.

Burke, Lew. Lew Burke's Dog Training. (Illus.). 1976. 12.95 (ISBN 0-87666-656-X, H962). TFH Pubns.

Burke, Mary Alice H. Elizabeth Nourse, Eighteen Fifty-Nine to Nineteen Thirty-Eight: A Salon Career. (Illus.). 280p. 1983. text ed. 47.50x (ISBN 0-87474-298-6). Smithsonian.

Burke, Owen. The Figurehead. LC 78-11784. 1979. 10.95 o.p. (ISBN 0-698-10958-9, Coward). Putnam Pub Group.

Burke, P. G. & Eissner, W. B., eds. Atoms in Astrophysics. (Physics of Atoms & Molecules Ser.). 350p. 1983. 49.50x (ISBN 0-306-41097-4, Plenum Pr). Plenum Pub.

Burke, Peter. Montaigne. Thomas, Keith, ed. (Past Masters Ser.). 1982. 8.95 (ISBN 0-8090-7001-4); pap. 3.25 (ISBN 0-8090-1424-6). Hill & Wang.

--Sociology & History. (Controversies in Sociology Ser.: No. 10). 128p. (Orig.). 1980. text ed. 17.95x (ISBN 0-04-301114-4); pap. text ed. 5.95x (ISBN 0-04-301115-2). Allen Unwin.

Burke, Péter, ed. Renaissance Sense of the Past. (Documents of Modern History Ser). 1970. 18.95 (ISBN 0-312-67375-2); pap. 8.95 (ISBN 0-312-67340-X). St Martin.

Burke, Robert E. & Lowitt, Richard, eds. The New Era & the New Deal, 1920-1940. (Goldentree Bibliography in American History Ser.). 240p. 1981. text ed. 24.95x (ISBN 0-88295-537-3); pap. text ed. 18.95x (ISBN 0-88295-581-0). Harlan Davidson.

Burke, Robert L. CAI Sourcebook. (Illus.). 160p. 1982. text ed. 18.95 (ISBN 0-13-110155-2). P-H.

Burke, Ronald & Kramer, Arthur. Workbook for Microcomputer Courseware for Technical Mathematics. Breskin, Myrna, ed. 96p. 1982. 6.95 (ISBN 0-07-009049-1, G). McGraw.

Burke, Ronald S. Administrative Skills for the Manager. LC 82-72868. 275p. 1982. ringed binder 29.95x (ISBN 0-87094-348-0). Dow Jones-Irwin.

Burke, Ronald S. & Bittel, Lester R. Introduction to Management Practice. LC 80-19088. (Illus.). 608p. 1981. text ed. 19.95x (ISBN 0-07-009042-4); self study guide 7.05 (ISBN 0-07-009044-0). McGraw.

Burke, S. M. Pakistan's Foreign Policy: An Historical Analysis. 1973. 20.25x o.p. (ISBN 0-19-215179-7). Oxford U Pr.

Burke, Shirley R. The Composition & Function of Body Fluids. 3rd ed. LC 80-17952. (Illus.). 208p. 1980. pap. text ed. 11.95 (ISBN 0-8016-0903-8). Mosby.

Burke, Susan. The Island Bike Business. (Illus.). 80p. (gr. 3-7). 1983. bds. 10.95 (ISBN 0-19-554297-5, Pub by Oxford U Pr Childrens). Merrimack Bk Serv.

Burke, Tom. Burke's Steerage. LC 75-34992. 1976. 10.00 o.p. (ISBN 0-399-11662-1). Putnam Pub Group.

Burke, W. J. & Howe, W. D. American Authors & Book. 3rd. rev. ed. 960p. 1972. 12.50 o.p. (ISBN 0-517-50139-2). Crown.

Burke, W. Warner. Organization Development: Principles & Practices. 1982. pap. text ed. 20.95 (ISBN 0-316-11686-6). Little.

Burke, W. Warner & Beckhard, Richard, eds. Conference Planning. 2nd ed. LC 76-124090. 174p. 1970. pap. 10.00 o.p. (ISBN 0-88390-118-8). Univ Assocs.

Burke, W. Warner & Goodstein, Leonard D., eds. Trends & Issues in OD: Current Theory & Practice. LC 80-52929. 351p. (Orig.). 1980. pap. 16.50 (ISBN 0-88390-162-5). Univ Assocs.

Burke, W. Warner, jt. ed. see Eddy, William B.

Burke, Walter. Complete Book of Colon Self-Care. (Illus., Orig.). 1982. pap. 6.95 o.p. (ISBN 0-939472-01-5). Thalassa Pr.

Burke, William J. Literature of Slang. LC 67-982. 1965. Repr. of 1939 ed. 30.00x (ISBN 0-8103-3243-4). Gale.

Burkert, Walter. Structure & History in Greek Mythology & Ritual. LC 78-62856. (Sather Classical Lectures: Vol. 47). 1982. 23.50x (ISBN 0-520-03771-5); pap. 7.95 (ISBN 0-520-04770-2). U of Cal Pr.

Burkes, Joyce M. The Math Machine Book for Addition. LC 81-90590. (The Word Machine & Math Machine Books). (Illus.). 48p. (gr. 1-5). 1983. pap. write for info. (ISBN 0-931218-13-6). Joybug.

--The Math Machine Book for Subtraction. LC 81-90590. (The Word Machine & Math Machine Books). (Illus.). 48p. (gr. 1-3). 1983. pap. write for info. (ISBN 0-931218-14-4). Joybug.

Burkett, David. Very Good Management: A Guide to Managing-by-Communication. 146p. 1983. 12.95 (ISBN 0-13-941377-4); pap. 6.95 (ISBN 0-13-941369-3). P-H.

Burkett, David & Narcisco, John. Declare Yourself: Discovering the Me in Relationships. LC 75-11802. (Illus.). 1975. 11.95 (ISBN 0-13-197582-X, Spec); pap. 5.95 (ISBN 0-13-197574-9, Spec). P-H.

Burkett, J., ed. Agricultural Research Index: A Guide to Agricultural Research Including Dairy Farming, Fisheries, Food, Forestry, Horticulture, & Veterinary Science, 2vols. 6th ed. LC 78-40700. 1020p. Set. 210.00x (ISBN 0-686-75635-5, Pub. by Longman). Gale.

--Directory of Scientific Directories: A World Guide to Scientific Directories Including Medicine, Agriculture, Engineering, Manufacturing, & Industrial Directories. 3rd ed. LC 79-40288. 649p. 95.00x (ISBN 0-686-75636-3, Pub. by Longman). Gale.

Burkett, Larry. The Financial Planning Workbook. LC 82-7877. (Christian Financial Concepts Ser.). 1982. pap. 6.95 (ISBN 0-8024-2546-1). Moody.

--How to Manage Your Money. LC 82-7904. (Christian Financial Concepts Ser.). 1982. pap. 7.95 (ISBN 0-8024-2547-X). Moody.

--What Husbands Wish Their Wives Knew about Money. 1977. pap. 3.95 (ISBN 0-88207-758-9). Victor Bks.

Burkett, Randall K. & Newman, Richard. Black Apostles: Afro-American Clergy Confront the Twentieth Century. 1978. lib. bdg. 27.00 (ISBN 0-8161-8137-3, Hall Reference). G K Hall.

Burkett, Randall K., ed. Black Redemption: Churchmen Speak for the Garvey Movement. LC 77-81332. 207p. 1978. 24.95 (ISBN 0-87722-116-2). Temple U Pr.

Burkett, Tony. Parties & Elections in West Germany: The Search for Stability. LC 75-6051. 200p. 1975. 22.50 (ISBN 0-312-59745-2). St Martin.

Burkhalter, Pamela & Donley, Diana, eds. Dynamics of Oncology Nursing. (Illus.). 1977. text ed. 21.95 (ISBN 0-07-009052-1, HP). McGraw.

Burkhalter, Pamela K. Nursing Care of the Alcoholic & Drug Abuser. (Illus.). 384p. 1975. pap. text ed. 17.50 (ISBN 0-07-009051-3, HP). McGraw.

Burkhard, Marianne. Conrad Ferdinand Meyer. (World Authors Ser.). 1978. 15.95 (ISBN 0-8057-6321-X, Twayne). G K Hall.

Burkhard, Ursula. Farbvostellungen blinder Menschen. 56p. (Ger.). 1981. pap. text ed. 5.95x (ISBN 3-7643-1266-1). Birkhauser.

Burkhardt, A., jt. auth. see Gebbers, J. O.

Burkhardt, Charles H. Domestic & Commercial Oil Burners. 3rd ed. LC 68-31659. (Illus.). 1969. text ed. 23.95 (ISBN 0-07-009039-4, G). McGraw.

Burkhardt, Frederick, ed. see James, William.

Burkhart, Harold E., jt. auth. see Avery, Thomas E.

Burkhart, James L., et al. The Clash of Issues: Readings & Problems in American Government. 7th ed. 352p. 1981. pap. text ed. 12.95 (ISBN 0-13-135087-0). P-H.

Burkhart, John, jt. auth. see Brooks, Svevo.

Burkhart, Kathryn W. Growing into Love: Teenagers Talk Candidly About Sex in the 1980's. 336p. 1981. 14.95 (ISBN 0-399-12640-6). Putnam Pub Group.

Burkhauser, Richard V. & Haveman, Robert. Disability & Work: The Economics of American Policy. LC 82-113. (Policy Studies in Employment & Welfare Ser.: No. 38). 144p. 1982. text ed. 14.00x (ISBN 0-8018-2834-1). Johns Hopkins.

Burkhauser, Richard V., ed. A Challenge to Social Security. LC 82-1596. (Research on Poverty Monograph). 282p. 1982. 27.50 (ISBN 0-12-144680-8). Acad Pr.

Burkhauser, Richard V., ed. see Conference on Income Support Policies for the Aging-University of Chicago.

Burkhead, Jesse. Governmental Budgeting. LC 56-8000. 498p. 1956. 39.95 (ISBN 0-471-12375-7). Wiley.

Burkhead, Jesse, jt. ed. see Bahl, Roy W.

Burkhill, H., jt. auth. see Burkhill, John C.

Burkhill, John C. & Burkhill, H. Second Course in Mathematical Analysis. LC 69-16278. (Illus.). 1970. text ed. 43.50 (ISBN 0-521-07519-X); pap. 26.95 (ISBN 0-521-28061-3). Cambridge U Pr.

Burkholder, Clyde. The Ox-Bow Incident Notes. 55p. (Orig.). 1974. pap. text ed. 2.50 (ISBN 0-8220-0971-4). Cliffs.

Burkholder, Lloyd K. Basic Pipe Estimating. 224p. (Orig.). 1981. pap. 15.50 o.p. (ISBN 0-910460-84-1). Zondervan.

Burkholder, Mark A. & Chandler, D. S. Biographical Dictionary of Audiencia Ministers in the Americas, 1687-1821. LC 82-925. 480p. 1982. lib. bdg. 49.95 (ISBN 0-313-22038-7, BBD/). Greenwood.

Burkholder, Robert E. & Myerson, Joel, eds. Critical Essays on Ralph Waldo Emerson. (Critical Essays in American Literature Ser.). 618p. 1983. lib. bdg. 60.00 (ISBN 0-8161-8305-8). G K Hall.

Burki, Shahid J. Pakistan: A Nation in the Making. (Nations of Contemporary Asia). 128p. 1983. lib. bdg. 16.00 (ISBN 0-86531-353-9). Westview.

Burkill, John C. First Course in Mathematical Analysis. 1962. 25.95x (ISBN 0-521-04381-6); pap. 14.95x (ISBN 0-521-29468-1). Cambridge U Pr.

--Lebesgue Integral. (Cambridge Tracts in Mathematics & Mathematical Physics). 1951. 15.95 (ISBN 0-521-04382-4). Cambridge U Pr.

Burkin, A. R., ed. Leaching & Reduction in Hydrometallurgy. 109p. (Orig.). 1975. pap. text ed. 40.25x (ISBN 0-900488-27-1). IMM North Am.

Burkitt, Denis. Eat Right--To Keep Healthy & Enjoy Life More. LC 78-24492. (Positive Health Guides). (Illus.). 1979. 8.95 (ISBN 0-668-04676-7); pap. 5.95 (ISBN 0-668-04682-1). Arco.

Burkitt, Dennis. Eat Right to Stay Healthy. 1979. 5.95x (ISBN 0-668-04682-1). Cancer Control Soc.

Burkman, Katherine, jt. auth. see Auburn, Mark.

Burkman, Katherine H. Literature Through Performance: "Shakespeare's Mirror" & "A Canterbury Caper". LC 76-25615. (Illus.). xxviii, 104p. 1978. 10.00x (ISBN 0-8214-0365-6, 82-82568); pap. 3.95x (ISBN 0-8214-0384-2, 82-82576). Ohio U Pr.

Burkowsky, Mitchell. Teaching American Pronunciation to Foreign Students. LC 73-84897. 134p. 1969. 10.00 o.s.i. (ISBN 0-87527-027-1). Green.

Burks, A. W. see Peirce, Charles S.

Burks, Ardath W. Japan: Profile of a Postindustrial Power. (Nations of Contemporary Asia Ser.). (Illus.). 250p. 1980. lib. bdg. 26.00 (ISBN 0-89158-786-1); pap. 9.50 (ISBN 0-86531-040-8). Westview.

Burks, Ardath W., jt. auth. see Beck, Clark L.

Burks, David R., jt. auth. see Griffin, Gerald.

Burks, Herbert M., Jr. & Stefflre, Buford. Theories of Counseling. 3rd. ed. (Illus.). 1979. text ed. 24.00 (ISBN 0-07-009061-0, C). McGraw.

Burks, John, jt. auth. see Hall, George.

Burl. The Stone Circles of the British Isles. 1976. 40.00X (ISBN 0-300-01972-6); pap. 14.95x (ISBN 0-300-02398-7, Y-341). Yale U Pr.

Burl, Aubrey. Rites of the Gods. (Illus.). 272p. 1981. text ed. 26.50x (ISBN 0-460-04313-7, Pub. by J M Dent England). Biblio Dist.

Burlace, C. J. & Whalley, L. Waste Plastics & Their Potential for Recycle, 1977. 1981. 40.00x (ISBN 0-686-97166-3, Pub. by W Spring England). State Mutual Bk.

Burland, C. A. The Gods & Heroes of War. new ed. LC 73-88518. (Illus.). 96p. (gr. 6 up). 1974. PLB 4.99 o.p. (ISBN 0-399-60873-7). Putnam Pub Group.

Burland, Cottie. The Incas. LC 78-61225. (Peoples of the Past Ser.). (Illus.). 1979. lib. bdg. 12.68 (ISBN 0-382-06193-4). Silver.

--See Inside an Aztec Town. (gr. 5 up). 1980. PLB 9.40 (ISBN 0-531-09173-2, G18, Warwick Press). Watts.

Burleigh, John H. Church History of Scotland. (Illus.). 1960. 16.95x o.p. (ISBN 0-19-213921-5). Oxford U Pr.

Burleson, Donald R. Elementary Statistics. 1980. 19.95 (ISBN 0-316-11696-3); teachers manual avail. (ISBN 0-316-11697-1). Little.

--Topics in Precalculus Mathematics. (Illus.). 544p. 1974. text ed. 23.95 (ISBN 0-13-925461-7); study guide o.p. 1.95 (ISBN 0-13-925214-2). P-H.

Burley, Gertrude S., jt. auth. see Gard, Robert E.

Burley, W. J. Death in Willow Pattern. 192p. 1983. pap. 2.95 (ISBN 0-8027-3025-6). Walker & Co.

Burley-Allen, Madelyn. Assertive Supervision. 1982. pap. 9.95 (ISBN 0-471-09750-0). Wiley.

Burling, Robbins. Sounding Right. 160p. 1982. pap. text ed. 12.95 (ISBN 0-88377-216-7). Newbury Hse.

Burlingame, et al. Timesharing Two. Bloch, Stuart M. & Ingersoll, William B., eds. LC 82-60331. (Illus.). 200p. (Orig.). 1982. pap. 32.00 (ISBN 0-87420-611-1, TO4). Urban Land.

Burlingame, Hardin J. Leaves from Conjurors' Scrap Books, Or, Modern Magicians & Their Works. LC 74-148349. 1971. Repr. of 1891 ed. 34.00x (ISBN 0-8103-3371-6). Gale.

Burlingame, Roger. Don't Let Them Scare You. LC 73-21284. (Illus.). 352p. 1974. Repr. of 1961 ed. lib. bdg. 19.25x (ISBN 0-8371-6146-0, BUSY). Greenwood.

Burman, C. R. How to Find Out in Chemistry. 2nd ed. 1967. 16.25 o.s.i. (ISBN 0-08-011881-X); pap. 7.00 o.p. (ISBN 0-08-011880-1). Pergamon.

Burman, Margaret. The Eternal Eye. (Orig.). (gr. 7-12). 1982. pap. write for info (ISBN 0-440-92099-X, LFL). Dell.

--How Do You Say Goodby. 1982. pap. 1.95 (ISBN 0-553-22517-0). Bantam.

Burman, Sandra, ed. Fit Work for Women. LC 78-25895. 1979. 22.50x (ISBN 0-312-29417-4). St Martin.

Burmaster, Orvis C., ed. see Ferril, Thomas H.

Burme, Marshall E. & Friend, Irwin. The Changing Role of the Individual Investor: A Twentieth Century Fund Report. LC 78-18303. 256p. Repr. of 1978 ed. pap. text ed. 15.95 (ISBN 0-471-04547-0). Krieger.

Burmeister, E. Capital Theory & Dynamics. LC 79-28412. (Cambridge Surveys of Economic Literature Ser.). 224p. 1980. 42.50 (ISBN 0-521-22889-1); pap. 16.95 (ISBN 0-521-29703-6). Cambridge U Pr.

Burmeister, Eva, et al. Training for Child Care Staff. LC 63-18016. 1963. pap. 5.15 (ISBN 0-87868-065-9, I-27). Child Welfare.

Burmeister, Jill & Hutchinson, Rosemary, eds. Better Homes & Gardens Complete Quick & Easy Cook Book. 1983. 24.95 (ISBN 0-696-00725-8). Meredith Corp.

Burmeister, Jon. The Protector Conclusion. LC 76-62750. 1977. 7.95 o.p. (ISBN 0-312-65222-4). St Martin.

Burmeister, Lou E. Reading Strategies for Middle & Secondary School Teaching. 2nd ed. LC 77-88054. (Education Ser.). (Illus.). 1978. text ed. 18.95 (ISBN 0-201-00316-3). A-W.

Burmeister, Walter F. Appalachian Waters, I: The Delaware River & Its Tributaries. LC 74-80983. 1974. 10.00 (ISBN 0-912660-19-8); pap. 6.95 (ISBN 0-686-96660-0). Appalachian Bks.

Burn, A. R. Romans in Britain: An Anthology of Inscriptions. 2nd ed. LC 77-75795. (Illus.). xvi, 206p. 1969. 14.95x o.s.i. (ISBN 0-87249-142-0). U of SC Pr.

Burn, Andrew R. Persia & the Greeks: The Defence of the West, 546-478 B. C. (Illus.). 1962. 25.00 o.p. (ISBN 0-312-60165-4). St Martin.

Burn, Barbara, jt. auth. see Dolensek, Nancy.

Burn, Barbara B., ed. Higher Education Reform: Implications for Foreign Students. LC 78-58811. 1978. pap. text ed. 11.95 (ISBN 0-87206-089-6). Inst Intl Educ.

Burn, David. The Bushrangers. (Australian Theatre Workshop Ser.). 1971. pap. 4.50x o.p. (ISBN 0-85859-120-0, 00523). Heinemann Ed.

Burn, Doris. Andrew-Henry's Meadow. (Illus.). (gr. k-3). 1965. PLB 4.99 o.p. (ISBN 0-698-30011-4, Coward). Putnam Pub Group.

--The Tale of Lazy Lizard Canyon. LC 75-42251. (Illus.). (gr. 3-5). 1977. PLB 5.29 o.p. (ISBN 0-399-61012-X). Putnam Pub Group.

Burn, June. Living High. rev. ed. (Illus.). 1962. 10.00 o.s.i. (ISBN 0-686-00955-X). Wellington.

Burn, R. P. Deductive Transformation Geometry. LC 74-82223. (Illus.). 152p. 1975. 21.95 (ISBN 0-521-20565-4). Cambridge U Pr.

Burn, Samuel C. Jonah. 1981. lib. bdg. 11.25 (ISBN 0-86524-071-X, 3201). Klock & Klock.

Burnam, Tom. Dictionary of Misinformation. LC 75-15651. 352p. 1975. 14.37i (ISBN 0-690-00147-9). T Y Crowell.

Burnap, jt. auth. see Edmundson.

Burnchurch, Richard de. An Outline of Dutch History. (Illus.). 128p. (Orig.). 1980. pap. 10.00 (ISBN 0-686-43014-X, Wouter Wagner Netherlands). Heinman.

Burne, Glenn S. Julian Green. (World Authors Ser.). lib. bdg. 15.95 (ISBN 0-8057-2404-4, Twayne). G K Hall.

Burne, J. R. Caisse De Joseph. 1966. text ed. 2.50x (ISBN 0-521-04388-3). Cambridge U Pr.

Burne, Kevin G., et al. Functional English for Writers. 2nd ed. 1978. pap. 12.50x (ISBN 0-673-15105-0). Scott F.

Burnel, F. Changing Patterns: An Atypical Autobiography. 1970. 9.50 (ISBN 0-444-19703-6). Elsevier.

Burner, David. Herbert Hoover: A Public Life. 2nd ed. LC 78-54912. (Illus.). xii, 434p. Date not set. pap. cancelled (ISBN 0-934136-24-6). Western Tanager. Postponed.

Burner, David, jt. auth. see Marcus, Robert.

Burner, Victor B. A. The Noblest Form. LC 81-80167. (Illus.). 64p. 1983. pap. 5.95 (ISBN 0-86666-020-8). GWP.

Burness, Taqd. Pickup & Van Spotter's Guide, 1945-1982. (Illus.). 160p. 1982. pap. 9.95 (ISBN 0-87938-156-6). Motorbooks Intl.

Burnet, F. M. & Stanley, W. M., eds. The Viruses: Biochemical, Biological & Biophysical Properties, 3 vols. Incl. Vol. 1. General Virology. 1959. o.p. (ISBN 0-12-145601-3); Vol. 2. Plant & Bacterial Viruses. 1959. 55.00 (ISBN 0-12-145602-1); Vol. 3. Animal Viruses. 1959. o.p. (ISBN 0-12-145603-X). Acad Pr.

Burnet, F. Macfarlane. Cellular Immunology: Book One, Self & Not Self. (Illus.). 1969. 34.50 (ISBN 0-521-07521-1); pap. 15.95x (ISBN 0-521-09558-1). Cambridge U Pr.

--Cellular Immunology: Books One & Two. LC 69-12162. (Illus.). 1969. 75.00 (ISBN 0-521-07217-4). Cambridge U Pr.

--Endurance of Life. (Illus.). 1980. pap. 10.95 (ISBN 0-521-29783-4). Cambridge U Pr.

--Endurance of Life. LC 78-54323. (Illus.). 1978. 32.50 (ISBN 0-521-22114-5). Cambridge U Pr.

Burnet, F. Macfarlane & White, D. O. Natural History of Infectious Disease. 4th ed. LC 74-174264. (Illus.). 400p. 1972. 42.50 (ISBN 0-521-08389-3); pap. 15.95 (ISBN 0-521-09688-X). Cambridge U Pr.

Burnet, Gilbert. History of His Own Time. 1979. Repr. of 1906 ed. 12.95x (ISBN 0-460-00085-3, Evman). Biblio Dist.

Burnet, James L. Origin & Progress of Language, 6 vols. (Linguistics 13th-18th Century Ser.). (Fr.). 1974. Repr. of 1792 ed. lib. bdg. 792.50x set, order nos. are 71-5032 to 71-5037 o.p. (ISBN 0-8287-0154-7). Clearwater Pub.

Burnet, Macfarlane. Intrinsic Mutagenesis: A Genetic Approach to Aging. LC 74-6978. 236p. 1974. 50.00 o.p. (ISBN 0-471-12440-0, Pub. by Wiley Med). Wiley.

Burnet, Mary. The Mass Media in a Violent World. (Reports & Papers on Mass Communication: No. 63). 44p. 1971. pap. 2.50 (ISBN 92-3-100904-4, U371, UNESCO). Unipub.

Burnet, Sir Thomas & Duckett, George. Second Tale of a Tub, or, the History of Robert Powel the Puppet-Show-Man. Shugrue, Michael, ed. LC 71-170539. (Foundations of the Novel Ser: Vol. 26). iv, 219p. 1973. Repr. of 1715 ed. lib. bdg. 50.00 o.s.i. (ISBN 0-8240-0538-4). Garland Pub.

Burnett, Alan D. & Taylor, Peter J. Political Studies from Spatial Perspectives: Anglo-American Essays on Political Geography. LC 80-41384. 1981. 57.95x (ISBN 0-471-27909-9, Pub. by Wiley-Interscience); pap. 21.95 (ISBN 0-471-27910-2). Wiley.

Burnett, Clyde W. My Return to New Caledonia. 1978. 5.95 o.p. (ISBN 0-533-03298-9). Vantage.

Burnett, Constance B. Five for Freedom: Lucretia Mott, Elizabeth Cady Stanton, Lucy Stone, Susan B. Anthony, Carrie Chapman Catt. LC 68-8734. (Illus.). 1968. Repr. of 1953 ed. lib. bdg. 19.25x (ISBN 0-8371-0034-8, BUFF). Greenwood.

Burnett, Dale. LOGO: An Introduction. LC 82-73547. (Illus.). 56p. 1983. pap. 7.95 (ISBN 0-916688-39-9). Creative Comp.

Burnett, David, jt. ed. see Foley, Martha.

Burnett, Frances H. Little Lord Fauntleroy. LC 75-32191. (Classics of Children's Literature, 1621-1932: Vol. 53). (Illus.). 1976. Repr. of 1886 ed. PLB 38.00 o.s.i. (ISBN 0-8240-2302-1). Garland Pub.

--A Little Princess. 232p. 1981. Repr. PLB 16.95 (ISBN 0-89966-327-3). Buccaneer Bks.

--A Little Princess. (Illus.). 288p. (gr. 3-7). 1981. 7.95 (ISBN 0-448-40083-9, G&D). Putnam Pub Group.

--Secret Garden. (gr. 4 up). 1971. pap. 2.95 (ISBN 0-440-47706-9, YB). Dell.

--The Secret Garden. LC 78-2914. (Raintree's Illustrated Classics). (Illus.). (gr. 5-8). 1978. PLB 13.30 (ISBN 0-8172-1129-2). Raintree Pubs.

Burnett, Frances H; see Avery, Gillian.

Burnett, Frances H see Swan, D. K.

Burnett, Francis, ed. The School Counselor's Involvement in Career Education. 1980. members 7.50 (ISBN 0-686-36400-7); non-members 9.00 (ISBN 0-686-37307-3). Am Personnel.

Burnett, Fred W. The Testament of Jesus-Sophia: A Redaction-Critical Study of the Eschatological Discourse in Matthew. LC 80-67211. 491p. (Orig.). 1981. lib. bdg. 28.50 (ISBN 0-8191-1743-9); pap. text ed. 17.50 (ISBN 0-8191-1744-7). U Pr of Amer.

Burnett, G. F. Field Observations on the Behavior of the Red Locust (Nomadacris Septemfasciata Serville) in the Solitary Phase. 1951. 35.00x (ISBN 0-85135-006-2, Pub. by Centre Overseas Research). State Mutual Bk.

Burnett, G. M., et al. Transfer & Storage of Energy by Molecules, Vol. 4. LC 77-78048. 612p. 1969. 128.00x o.p. (ISBN 0-471-12433-8, Pub. by Wiley-Interscience). Wiley.

Burnett, George W. & Burnett, George W. Oral Microbiology & Infectious Disease. 4th ed. (Illus.). 784p. 1976. 79.00 (ISBN 0-683-01225-8); student ed. 26.00 (ISBN 0-683-01226-6). Williams & Wilkins.

Burnett, Hallie & Burnett, Whit. Fiction Writer's Handbook. LC 74-1797. 1979. pap. 4.95 (ISBN 0-06-463492-2, EH 492, EH). B&N NY.

Burnett, J. H. Fundamentals of Mycology. 2nd ed. 688p. 1980. pap. text ed. 45.00 (ISBN 0-7131-2778-3). Univ Park.

--Fundamentals of Mycology. 688p. 1976. pap. text ed. 45.00 (ISBN 0-7131-2617-5). E Arnold.

--Mycogenetics: An Introduction to the General Genetics of Fungi. LC 74-13143. 375p. 1975. 62.95 (ISBN 0-471-12445-1, Pub. by Wiley-Interscience); pap. 18.95 (ISBN 0-471-12446-X). Wiley.

Burnett, J. H. & Trinci, A. P., eds. Fungal Walls & Hyphal Growth. LC 78-72082. (Illus.). 1980. 75.00 (ISBN 0-521-22499-3). Cambridge U Pr.

Burnett, Janet, jt. auth. see Burnett, Laurence.

Burnett, John, jt. auth. see Pryor, Sam.

Burnett, John H., jt. auth. see Mayer, Lawrence C.

Burnett, Laurence & Burnett, Janet. Picture Framer's Handbook. (Illus.). 256p. 1973. 7.95 o.p. (ISBN 0-517-50058-2, C N Potter Bks). Crown.

Burnett, Neil. Turning Assets into Prosperity: How to Trade Your Way to Financial Success. 206p. 1982. pap. 6.95 (ISBN 0-940986-03-5). ValuWrite.

Burnett, Peter H. Recollections & Opinions of an Old Pioneer. LC 76-87661. (American Scene Ser.). 1969. Repr. of 1880 ed. lib. bdg. 55.00 (ISBN 0-306-71765-4). Da Capo.

Burnett, R. T. Concertos for Violin & Viola. 1000p. (Orig.). 1982. pap. 48.00 (ISBN 0-9601054-8-4). Cleaning Consul.

Burnett, Ruth. April Games. (YA) 1981. 6.95 (ISBN 0-686-74798-4, Avalon). Bouregy.

--The Captain's Nurse. (YA) 1980. 6.95 (ISBN 0-686-73920-5, Avalon). Bouregy.

--Lord of the Island. 1981. pap. 6.95 (ISBN 0-686-84686-9, Avalon). Bouregy.

--Love Star. 1983. 6.95 (ISBN 0-686-84190-5, Avalon). Bouregy.

--The Picolata Treasure. 192p. (YA) 1974. 6.95 (ISBN 0-685-50326-7, Avalon). Bouregy.

--The Sweetest Treasure. 1981. pap. 6.95 (ISBN 0-686-84691-5, Avalon). Bouregy.

--To Love a Mermaid. (YA) 1979. 6.95 (ISBN 0-685-65277-7, Avalon). Bouregy.

--When Lily Smiles. 1982. pap. 6.95 (ISBN 0-686-84731-8, Avalon). Bouregy.

Burnett, W. R. Good-Bye Chicago. 182p. 1981. 9.95 o.p. (ISBN 0-312-33851-1). St Martin.

Burnett, Whit, jt. auth. see Burnett, Hallie.

Burnett, Yumiko M., tr. see Rodieck, Jorma.

Burney, Charles. Catalogue of the Valuable Collection of Music. (Auction Catalogues of Music Ser.: Vol. 2). 1973. Repr. of 1814 ed. 22.50 o.s.i. (ISBN 90-6027-188-2, Pub. by Frits Knuf Netherlands). Pendragon NY.

Burney, Eugenia. Colonial North Carolina. LC 75-20192. (Colonial History Ser.). (Illus.). 160p. (gr. 5 up). 1975. 7.95 o.p. (ISBN 0-525-67134-X). Lodestar Bks.

--Fort Sumter. LC 74-28435. (Cornerstones of Freedom). (Illus.). 32p. (gr. 3-6). 1975. 7.95 (ISBN 0-516-04611-X). Childrens.

Burney, Eugenia, jt. auth. see Capps, Clifford S.

Burney, Fanny. The Journals & Letters of Fanny Burney (Madame D'Arblay), Eighteen Twelve to Eighteen Fourteen: Vol. VII, Letters 632-834. Bloom, Edward A., et al, eds. (Illus.). 1978. 85.00x (ISBN 0-19-812468-6). Oxford U Pr.

Burney, William. Wallace Stevens. (U. S. Authors Ser.: No. 127). 1968. lib. bdg. 10.95 o.p. (ISBN 0-8057-0696-8, Twayne). G K Hall.

Burnford, J. F., jt. auth. see Chenault, Joann.

Burnford, Sheila E. Bel Ria. LC 77-21082. 215p. (YA) (gr. 6 up). 1978. 7.95 o.p. (ISBN 0-316-77139-2). Little.

Burnham, Betsy. When Your Friend is Dying. 96p. 1983. pap. 4.95 (ISBN 0-310-60341-2). Chosen Bks Pub.

Burnham, C. P., jt. auth. see McRae, S. G.

Burnham, Daniel H. & Bennett, Edward H. Plan of Chicago Prepared Under the Direction of the Commercial Club During the Years 1906, 1907, 1908. Moore, Charles, ed. LC 71-75303. (Architecture & Decorative Art Ser.: Vol. 29). (Illus.). 1970. Repr. of 1909 ed. lib. bdg. 85.00 (ISBN 0-306-71261-X). Da Capo.

Burnham, James. Coming Defeat of Communism. LC 68-8735. (Illus.). 1968. Repr. of 1950 ed. lib. bdg. 15.75x (ISBN 0-8371-0035-6, BUDC). Greenwood.

--Machiavellians: Defenders of Freedom. 1962. pap. 2.95 o.p. (ISBN 0-89526-946-5). Regnery-Gateway.

--The Managerial Revolution: What Is Happening in the World. LC 71-138102. 285p. 1972. Repr. of 1960 ed. lib. bdg. 17.50x (ISBN 0-8371-5678-5, BUMR). Greenwood.

--Suicide of the West. LC 64-14211. 1970. Repr. of 1964 ed. 10.00 o.p. (ISBN 0-87000-056-X, Arlington Hse). Crown.

Burnham, Patricia M. & Price, Martin. John Trumbull: The Hand & Spirit of a Painter. Cooper, Helen, ed. (Illus.). 308p. 1982. write for info. (ISBN 0-89467-024-7); pap. write for info. Yale Art Gallery.

Burnham, Paul S., jt. auth. see Crawford, Albert B.

Burnham, Robert, Jr. Burnham's Celestial Handbook: An Observer's Guide to the Universe Beyond the Solar System, 3 vols. rev. ed. (Illus.). 2000p. 1980. 20.00 ea. o.p. Vol. 1 (ISBN 0-486-24063-0). Vol. 2 (ISBN 0-486-24064-9). Vol. 3 (ISBN 0-486-24065-7). Dover.

Burnham, Sophy. The Landed Gentry: Passions & Personalities Inside Americas' Propertied Class. LC 78-1464. 1978. 10.00 o.p. (ISBN 0-399-11968-X). Putnam Pub Group.

Burnham, Walter D. The Current Crisis in American Politics. (Illus.). 1983. 29.95 (ISBN 0-19-503219-5). Oxford U Pr.

--Democracy in the Making: American Government & Politics. 640p. 1983. text ed. 22.95 (ISBN 0-13-198366-0); study guide 6.95 (ISBN 0-13-198382-2). P-H.

--Politics in America: The Cutting Edge of Change. (Transaction Ser). 1973. pap. text ed. 8.95x (ISBN 0-442-21188-0). Van Nos Reinhold.

Burnham, Walter D. & Weinberg, Martha W., eds. American Politics & Public Policy. (MIT Studies in American Politics & Public Policy: 4th). 1978. 22.50x (ISBN 0-262-02132-3); pap. text ed. 9.95x (ISBN 0-262-52061-3). MIT Pr.

Burnham, Walter D., jt. ed. see Chambers, W. N.

Burningham, Robin. Illustrated Hawaiian Word Book. (Illus.). 104p. (Orig.). 1982. pap. 5.95 (ISBN 0-935848-12-6). Bess Pr.

Burnite, Alvena. Tips for Teens on Love, Sex & Marriage. rev. ed. 1968. pap. 1.25 o.p. (ISBN 0-685-07669-5, 80098). Glencoe.

Burnley, I. H. Urbanization in Australia: The Post-War Experience. LC 73-77261. (Illus.). 1973. 34.50 (ISBN 0-521-20250-7). Cambridge U Pr.

Burnley, Judith. Unrepentant Women. LC 82-42836. 210p. 1983. 14.95 (ISBN 0-8128-2914-X). Stein & Day.

Burns & Sorsabal. A Handbook for In-Service Training of Classified Employees. (Research Bulletin: No. 11). pap. 0.69 (ISBN 0-685-57179-3). Assn Sch Busn.

Burns, A., jt. auth. see Goodnow, J.

Burns, Alexander. Australian Butterflies in Colour. (Illus.). 112p. 1969. 10.25 o.p. (ISBN 0-589-07007-X, Pub. by Reed Books Australia). C E Tuttle.

Burns, Alice, et al. Child Abuse & Neglect in Suffolk County. 1973. pap. 2.00 (ISBN 0-912954-12-4). Edmond Pub Co.

Burns, Allan F., tr. An Epoch of Miracles: Oral Literature of the Yucatec Maya. (Texas Pan American Ser.). (Illus.). 282p. 1983. text ed. 24.50x (ISBN 0-292-72037-8). U of Tex Pr.

Burns, Arthur & Williams, Edward. Federal Work, Security, & Relief Programs. LC 71-166956. (Research Monograph: Vol. 24). 1971. Repr. of 1941 ed. lib. bdg. 19.50 (ISBN 0-306-70356-4). Da Capo.

Burns, Arthur E. & Watson, Donald S. Government Spending & Economic Expansion. LC 75-173452. (FDR & the Era of the New Deal Ser.). 174p. 1972. Repr. of 1940 ed. lib. bdg. 27.50 (ISBN 0-306-70368-8). Da Capo.

Burns, Arthur L. & Heathcote, Nina. Peace-Keeping by U. N. Forces, from Suez to the Congo. LC 75-27678. (Princeton Studies in World Politics Ser.: No. 4). 256p. 1976. Repr. of 1963 ed. lib. bdg. 17.50x (ISBN 0-8371-8452-5, BUPK). Greenwood.

Burns, D. T., et al. Inorganic Reaction Chemistry: Reactions of the Elements & Their Compounds, Vol. 2A. (Analytical Chemistry Ser.). 410p. 1981. 79.95x (ISBN 0-686-36895-9). Halsted Pr.

Burns, David. Feeling Good: The New Mood Therapy. pap. 3.95 (ISBN 0-686-36693-X). Inst Rat Liv.

Burns, Donald & Alcocer, Pablo H. Un Analisis Perliminar del Discurso En Quechua. (Documentos Del Trabajo: No. 6). 1975. 1.50 (ISBN 0-88312-737-7). Summer Inst Ling.

Burns, Donald H., jt. auth. see Guacho, Juan N.

Burns, Donald J. An Introduction to Karate for Student & Teacher. 1977. pap. text ed. 7.95 (ISBN 0-8403-1692-5). Kendall-Hunt.

Burns, E. Bradford. Latin America: A Concise Interpretive History. 3rd ed. (Illus.). 352p. 1982. pap. 15.95 (ISBN 0-13-524322-X). P-H.

Burns, Edward, ed. see Toklas, Alice B.

Burns, Edward M. & Ralph, Philip L. World Civilizations, 2 vols. 5th ed. (Illus.). 1974. 19.95x (ISBN 0-393-09276-3); Vol. 1. pap. text ed. 13.95x (ISBN 0-393-09266-6); Vol. 2. pap. text ed. 13.95x (ISBN 0-393-09272-0); Vol. 1. study guide o.p. 5.95x (ISBN 0-393-09277-1); Vol. 2. study guide 5.95x (ISBN 0-393-09285-2). Norton.

--World Civilizations. 6th ed. (Illus.). 1981. Two Vols. In 1. 23.95x (ISBN 0-393-95077-8); Vol. 1. pap. 16.95x (ISBN 0-393-95083-2); Vol. 2. pap. 16.95x (ISBN 0-393-95095-6); instr's manual avail. (ISBN 0-393-95089-1); Vol. 1. study guide 5.95x (ISBN 0-393-95103-0); Vol. 2. 5.95x (ISBN 0-393-95107-3). Norton.

--World Civilizations, 2 vols. 4th ed. 1968. Vol. 1. pap. 8.95x ea (ISBN 0-393-09828-1); Vol. 2. pap. 8.95 o.p.; Vol. 1. study guide 2.50 (ISBN 0-393-09836-2); Vol. 2. study guide 2.50 (ISBN 0-393-09849-4); instrs'. manual free (ISBN 0-393-09833-8). Norton.

--World Civilizations, 2 Vols. 4th ed. (Illus.). 1968. 8.95x ea. (NortonC). Vol. 1 (ISBN 0-393-09828-1). Vol. 2. study guide 2.50x ea. (ISBN 0-393-09844-3). Vol. 1 (ISBN 0-393-09836-2). Vol. 2 (ISBN 0-393-09849-4). free tchr'. manual (ISBN 0-393-09833-8). Norton.

Burns, Edward M., et al. Western Civilizations, 2 vols. 9th ed. (Illus.). 1980. text ed. 20.95x one vol. ed. (ISBN 0-393-95074-3); Vol. 1. pap. text ed. 16.95x (ISBN 0-393-95080-8); Vol. 2. pap. text ed. 16.95x (ISBN 0-393-95087-5); instr's manual pap. 2.95x (ISBN 0-393-95099-9); study guide 7.95x (ISBN 0-393-95091-3). Norton.

Burns, G. Frank & Corlew, Robert E. Wilson County, No. 95. (Tennessee County History Ser.). (Illus.). 144p. 1983. 12.50x (ISBN 0-87870-190-7). Memphis St Univ.

Burns, Gary, jt. auth. see Sobey, Edwin J.

Burns, George. Living It Up; or, They Still Love Me in Altoona! LC 76-16059. (Illus.). 1976. 8.95 o.p. (ISBN 0-399-11636-2). Putnam Pub Group.

--The Third Time Around: Confessions of a Happy Hoofer. LC 79-15370. (Illus.). 1980. 10.95 o.p. (ISBN 0-399-12169-2). Putnam Pub Group.

Burns, George S. The Strange Adventures of Roger Ward. (Illus.). 48p. (gr. 9-12). 1981. 7.95 (ISBN 0-698-20495-6). Putnam Pub Group.

Burns, George W. Plant Kingdom. (Illus.). 640p. 1974. text ed. 26.95x (ISBN 0-02-317200-2, 31720). Macmillan.

--The Science of Genetics. 4th ed. (Illus.). 1980. text ed. 26.95x (ISBN 0-02-317140-5). Macmillan.

Burns, George W. & Tullis, James E. Solutions Manual for Burns: The Science of Genetics- an Inttroduction to Heredity. 4th ed. 1980. 1.95x (ISBN 0-02-317150-2). Macmillan.

Burns, Helen. The American Banking Community & New Deal Banking Reforms: 1933-1935. LC 72-789. (Contributions in Economics & Economic History: No. 11). 203p. 1974. lib. bdg. 25.00 (ISBN 0-8371-6362-5, BAB). Greenwood.

Burns, Henry. Corrections: Organization & Administration. (Criminal Justice Ser.). 1975. text ed. 20.95 (ISBN 0-8299-0606-1); pap. instrs. manual avail. (ISBN 0-8299-0610-X); instrs. manual avail. West Pub.

Burns, Hugh J. The Parents Guide to Teenage Drug Abuse. 1983. pap. 3.95 (ISBN 0-932972-02-0). Sprout Pubns.

Burns, J. H., ed. see Bentham, Jeremy.

Burns, J. K. Life Science & Religions. (Illus.). 1983. 25.00 (ISBN 0-8022-2415-6). Philos Lib.

Burns, James J. The Colonial Agents of New England. LC 75-29253. (Perspectives in American History Ser., No. 26). 156p. 1975. Repr. of 1935 ed. lib. bdg. 17.50x (ISBN 0-87991-350-9). Porcupine Pr.

Burns, James M. Edward Kennedy & the Camelot Legacy. (Illus.). 384p. 1976. 11.95 o.p. (ISBN 0-393-07501-X). Norton.

--Leadership. LC 76-5117. 1979. pap. 8.95xi (ISBN 0-06-131975-9, TB 1975, TB). Har-Row.

--Roosevelt: The Lion & the Fox. LC 56-7920. 15.00 o.p. (ISBN 0-15-178869-3). HarBraceJ.

--Roosevelt: The Soldier of Freedom. LC 71-95877. 1970. 15.00 o.p. (ISBN 0-15-178871-5). HarBraceJ.

--Roosevelt: The Soldier of Freedom. LC 71-95877. (Illus.). 722p. 1973. pap. 9.95 (ISBN 0-15-678875-6, HB247, Harv). HarBraceJ.

--The Vineyard of Liberty. (American Experiment Ser.: Bk. 1). 1982. 22.45 (ISBN 0-394-50546-8). Knopf.

Burns, James M., et al. Government by the People, 3 pts. 11th ed. Incl. National, State, Local. 800p. text ed. 23.95 (ISBN 0-13-361253-8); wkbk. 8.50 (ISBN 0-13-361295-3); Basic. 480p. text ed. 21.95 (ISBN 0-13-361238-4); National. 640p. text ed. 22.95 (ISBN 0-13-361246-5); study guide 7.95 (ISBN 0-13-361287-2). (Illus.). 1981. study guide 7.95 (ISBN 0-13-361279-1). P-H.

--State & Local Politics: Government by the People. 3rd ed. (Illus.). 1981. 12.95 (ISBN 0-13-843516-2). P-H.

Burns, Jim. Putting God First. (Illus.). 64p. (gr. 7-10). 1983. wkbk. 3.95 (ISBN 0-89081-366-3). Harvest Hse.

Burns, John. Answer to Addiction. (Rudolf Steiner Publications). 232p. 1980. 10.00 (ISBN 0-89345-006-5). Garber Comm.

Burns, Kathryn A. Managing the Burn Patient: A Guide for Nurses. LC 82-62402. 1983. write for info. (ISBN 0-913590-97-5). Slack Inc.

Burns, Kenneth R. & Johnson, Patricia J. Health Assessment in Clinical Practice. (Illus.). 1980. text ed. 29.95 (ISBN 0-13-385054-4). P-H.

Burns, L. S. & Grebler, L. The Housing of Nations: Analysis & Policy in a Comparative Framework. LC 76-43023. 1977. 41.95x o.s.i. (ISBN 0-470-98970-X). Halsted Pr.

Burns, Laurence E., jt. auth. see Thorpe, Geoffrey L.

Burns, Lawrence D. Transportation, Temporal & Spatial Components of Accessibility. LC 79-1725. (Illus.). 176p. 1979. 21.95x o.p. (ISBN 0-669-02916-5). Lexington Bks.

Burns, Linda, jt. ed. see Meshenberg, Kathryn.

Burns, M. A., et al. Lingua Latina: Liber Alter. 1965. 7.45 o.p. (ISBN 0-02-812760-9); manual & key o. p. o.p. (ISBN 0-02-812780-3); Italian tapes o.p. (ISBN 0-02-812800-1); classical tapes 60.00 o.p. (ISBN 0-685-38291-5, 81282). Glencoe.

--Lingua Latina: Liber Primus. 1964. 7.45 o.p. (ISBN 0-02-812720-X); manual & key o. p. o.p. (ISBN 0-02-812740-4); Italian tapes o.p. (ISBN 0-685-38292-3); classical tapes 138.00 o.p. (ISBN 0-685-38293-1, 81286). Glencoe.

Burns, Margaret A. & Morrissy, Lois E. Self-Assessment of Current Knowledge for the Operating Room Technician. 2nd ed. 1976. pap. 12.75 (ISBN 0-87488-474-8). Med Exam.

Burns, Marilyn. Good for Me! All About Food in 32 Bites. LC 78-6727. (Brown Paper School Book). (Illus.). (gr. 5 up). 1978. 9.95 (ISBN 0-316-11749-8); pap. 5.95 (ISBN 0-316-11747-1). Little.

--The Good Time Math Event Book. (Illus.). (gr. 4-6). 1977. wkbk. 9.50 (ISBN 0-88488-059-1). Creative Pubns.

Burns, N. D., jt. auth. see Kochar, A. K.

Burns, Ned H., jt. auth. see Lin, T. Y.

Burns, Norman T. & Reagan, Christopher J., eds. The Concepts of the Hero in the Middle Ages & the Renaissance. LC 74-34081. (Illus.). 1975. 22.00 o.s.i. (ISBN 0-87395-276-6); microfiche 22.00 o.s.i. (ISBN 0-87395-277-4). State U NY Pr.

Burns, Paul, jt. ed. see Cumming, John.

Burns, Paul C. & Broman, Betty. The Language Arts in Childhood Education. 5th ed. LC 82-83367. 560p. 1982. text ed. 22.95 (ISBN 0-395-32756-3, EA92); write for info. instr's manual (ISBN 0-395-32757-1, EA93). HM.

Burns, Paul C. & Roe, Betty D. Informal Reading Assessment. 1980. pap. 7.50 (ISBN 0-395-30574-8). HM.

--Reading Activities for Today's Elementary Schools. 1979. pap. 12.50 (ISBN 0-395-30573-X). HM.

--Teaching Reading in Today's Elementary Schools. 2nd ed. LC 81-80804. 544p. 1980. text ed. 21.95 (ISBN 0-395-30568-3); instr's. manual 1.10 (ISBN 0-395-30569-1). HM.

Burns, R. B. Experimental Psychology. 452p. 1981. text ed. 27.95 (ISBN 0-8391-1646-2). Univ Park.

Burns, R. C. & Kaufman, S. H. Actions Styles & Symbols in Kinetic Family Drawings: An Interpretative Manual. LC 70-186854. 1972. pap. 15.95 (ISBN 0-87630-228-2). Brunner-Mazel.

Burns, Rex. The Avenging Angel. (Gabe Wager Mystery Ser.). 240p. 1983. 12.50 (ISBN 0-670-14317-0). Viking Pr.

Burns, Richard. Roots-Routes. (Illus.). 44p. (Orig.). 1982. pap. 8.00 (ISBN 0-914946-32-3). Cleveland St Univ Poetry Ctr.

Burns, Richard, ed. see Carroll, Berenice, et al.

Burns, Richard C., jt. auth. see Cohen, Stephen.

Burns, Richard D. Arms Control & Disarmament: A Bibliography. LC 77-24931. (War-Peace Bibliography Ser.: No. 6). 430p. 1978. text ed. 62.50 o.s.i. (ISBN 0-87436-245-8). ABC-Clio.

Burns, Richard D. & Leitenberg, Milton. The Wars in Vietnam, Cambodia, & Laos, 1945-1982: A Bibliographic Guide. LC 80-13246. (War & Peace Bibliography Ser.: No. 3). 1983. write for info (ISBN 0-87436-310-1). ABC-Clio.

Burns, Richard D. & Society for Historians of American Foreign Relations. Guide to American Foreign Relations Since 1700. LC 82-13905. 1311p. 1982. text ed. 135.00 (ISBN 0-87436-323-3). ABC-Clio.

Burns, Richard D. & Bennett, Edward M., eds. Diplomats in Crisis: United States-Chinese-Japanese Relations, 1919-1941. LC 74-76444. 346p. 1974. text ed. 34.75 o.s.i. (ISBN 0-87436-135-4). ABC-Clio.

--Diplomats in Crisis: United States-Chinese-Japanese Relations, 1919-1941. 345p. 1974. 15.95 (ISBN 0-686-84012-7); text ed. 6.95 (ISBN 0-686-84013-5). Regina Bks.

Burns, Richard D., ed. see Blackey, Robert.

Burns, Richard D., ed. see Lewis, John R.

Burns, Richard D., ed. see Schaffer, Ronald.

Burns, Richard D., ed. see Smith, Myron J., Jr.

Burns, Robert. Choice of Burns's Poems & Songs. 156p. 1966. pap. 6.95 (ISBN 0-571-06835-9). Faber & Faber.

--Poems & Songs. 1978. 9.95x o.p. (ISBN 0-8464-0728-0). Beekman Pubs.

--Poems & Songs. Kinsley, James, ed. (Oxford Standard Authors Ser). 1969. 35.00 (ISBN 0-19-254164-1); pap. 11.50x (ISBN 0-19-281114-2). Oxford U Pr.

--Twenty Favorite Songs & Poems of Robert Burns. 45p. 1982. 3.95 (ISBN 0-85683-040-2, Pub by Shepheard-Walwyn England). Flatiron Book.

Burns, Robert C. Self-Growth in Families: Kinetic Family Drawings (K-F-D Research & Application) LC 81-21659. (Illus.). 220p. 1982. 25.00 (ISBN 0-87630-291-6); pap. 16.95 (ISBN 0-87630-305-X). Brunner-Mazel.

Burns, Robert D. & Stiles, Karl A. Laboratory Explorations in General Zoology. 6th ed. 1977. 12.95 (ISBN 0-02-317160-X, 31716). Macmillan.

Burns, Robert E. Catholics on the Cutting Edge. 1983. 9.95 (ISBN 0-88347-151-5); pap. 5.95 (ISBN 0-686-83925-0). Thomas More.

--I Am a Fugitive from a Georgia Chain Gang. LC 76-164143. 257p. 1972. Repr. of 1932 ed. 37.00x (ISBN 0-8103-3016-4). Gale.

Burns, Robert P., jt. ed. see Leopold, Irving H.

Burns, Tom & Stalker, G. M. Management of Innovation. (Orig.). 1961. pap. 13.95x (ISBN 0-422-72050-X, 6, Pub. by Tavistock England). Methuen Inc.

Burns, Wayne. Journey Through the Dark Woods. LC 82-15822. 230p. (Orig.). 1982. pap. 6.95 (ISBN 0-686-42801-3). Howe St Pr.

Burns, William C. Revival Sermons. 205p. 1981. pap. 4.45 (ISBN 0-85151-316-6). Banner of Truth.

Burns, William H. The Voices of Negro Protest in Amercia. LC 80-21197. 88p. 1980. Repr. of 1963 ed. lib. bdg. 19.25x (ISBN 0-313-22219-3, BUVN). Greenwood.

Burns Florey, Kitty. Family Matters. 1981. pap. 2.50 o.p. (ISBN 0-451-09667-3, E9667, Sig). NAL.

Burnside, Irene & Ebersole, Priscilla. Psychosocial Caring Throughout the Life Span. (Illus.). 1979. text ed. 24.00 (ISBN 0-07-009213-3, HP). McGraw.

Burnside, Irene M. Nursing & the Aged. 1976. 16.95 o.p. (ISBN 0-07-009209-5, HP); instr's manual 3.00 o.p. (ISBN 0-07-042705-4). McGraw.

--Nursing & the Aged. 2nd ed. (Illus.). 736p. 1980. text ed. 25.00 (ISBN 0-07-009211-7, HP). McGraw.

--Psychosocial Nursing Care of the Aged. 2nd ed. (Illus.). 1981. text ed. 15.00 (ISBN 0-07-009210-9). McGraw.

Burnside, Irving L. The First American Circus Ever. LC 78-15552. (Famous Firsts Ser.). (Illus.). 1978. PLB 10.76 (ISBN 0-89547-040-3). Silver.

Burnside, John, jt. auth. see Harron, Frank.

Burnside, John A. Physical Diagnosis. 16th ed. (Illus.). 260p. 1981. 17.50 (ISBN 0-686-77738-7, 1137-5). Williams & Wilkins.

Burnstein, M. L. New Directions in Economic Policy. LC 78-3104. (Illus.). 1978. 26.00x (ISBN 0-312-56620-4). St Martin.

Burnstein, Susan. The Digest Book of Dog Care. (Sports & Leisure Library). (Illus.). 1979. pap. 2.95 o.s.i. (ISBN 0-695-81289-0). Follett.

Burnstock, G., ed. Purinergic Receptors. (Receptors & Recognition Series B: Vol. 12). 49.95x (ISBN 0-412-15840-X, Pub by Chapman & Hall England). Methuen Inc.

Burnyeat, Myles, ed. The Skeptical Tradition. LC 78-62833. (Major Thinkers Ser.). 536p. 1983. text ed. 38.50x (ISBN 0-520-03747-2); pap. text ed. 10.95x (ISBN 0-520-04795-8). U of Cal Pr.

Buros, Oscar K., ed. English Tests & Reviews. LC 75-8109. xxiii, 395p. 1975. 30.00x (ISBN 0-910674-15-9). U of Nebr Pr.

--Foreign Language Tests & Reviews. LC 75-8110. xxiii, 312p. 1975. 25.00x (ISBN 0-910674-16-7). U of Nebr Pr.

--Intelligence Tests & Reviews. LC 75-8112. xxvii, 1129p. 1975. 70.00x (ISBN 0-8032-1163-5). U of Nebr Pr.

--Mathematics Tests & Reviews. LC 75-8113. xxv, 435p. 1975. 25.00x (ISBN 0-910674-18-3). U of Nebr Pr.

--Mental Measurements Yearbook. Incl. 1st. xv, 415p. 1938. 25.00x (ISBN 0-910674-12-4); 2nd. xxi, 674p. 1941. 30.00x (ISBN 0-910674-13-2); 3rd. 1949. xiv, 1047p. 35.00x (ISBN 0-910674-03-5); 4th. 1953. xxvi, 1163p. 40.00x (ISBN 0-910674-04-3); 5th. xxvii, 1292p. 1959. 45.00x (ISBN 0-8032-1164-3); 6th. xxxvi, 1714p. 1965. 60.00x (ISBN 0-910674-06-X); 7th, 2 vols. xl, 1986p. 1972. Set. 95.00x (ISBN 0-8032-1160-0); 8th, 2 vols. xliv, 2182p. 1978. Set. 120.00x (ISBN 0-910674-24-8). LC 39-3422. U of Nebr Pr.

--Personality Tests & Reviews, Vol. 1. xxxi, 1659p. 1970. 50.00x (ISBN 0-910674-10-8). U of Nebr Pr.

--Personality Tests & Reviews, Vol. 2. LC 74-13192. xxxi, 841p. 1975. 50.00x (ISBN 0-910674-19-1). U of Nebr Pr.

--Reading Tests & Reviews-One. xxii, 520p. 1968. 20.00x (ISBN 0-910674-09-4). U of Nebr Pr.

--Reading Tests & Reviews 2. LC 70-13495. xxvi, 257p. 1975. 20.00x (ISBN 0-910674-20-5). U of Nebr Pr.

--Science Tests & Reviews. LC 75-8114. xxiii, 296p. 1975. 25.00x (ISBN 0-910674-21-3). U of Nebr Pr.

--Social Studies Tests & Reviews. LC 75-8115. xxiii, 227p. 1975. 25.00x (ISBN 0-910674-22-1). U of Nebr Pr.

--Tests in Print-One. xxix, 479p. 1961. 25.00x (ISBN 0-910674-08-6). U of Nebr Pr.

--Tests in Print-Two. LC 74-24605. xxxix, 1107p. 1974. 80.00x (ISBN 0-910674-14-0). U of Nebr Pr.

Burow, Daniel R. I Meet God Through the Strangest People: 110 Devotions for the 9 to 13 Generation. LC 77-98299. (gr. 9 up). 1970. 5.95 o.p. (ISBN 0-570-03002-1, 6-1138); pap. 5.95 (ISBN 0-570-03793-X, 12-2756). Concordia.

Burpee, Lois. Lois Burpee's Gardener's Companion & Cookbook. LC 82-47736. (Illus.). 256p. 1983. 14.37i (ISBN 0-06-038021-7, HarpT). Har-Row.

Burquest, D. A. A Preliminary Study of Angas Phonology. (Language Data, African Ser.: No. 1). 52p. 1971. pap. 2.75x (ISBN 0-88312-601-X); microfiche 1.50x (ISBN 0-88312-701-6). Summer Inst Ling.

Burr. Elementary Statistical Quality Control. (Statistics; Textbooks & Monograph Ser.: Vol. 25). 1978. 22.50 (ISBN 0-8247-6686-5). Dekker.

Burr, Aaron. Reports of the Trials of Colonel Aaron Burr, 2 Vols. LC 69-11321. (Law, Politics & History Ser). 1969. Repr. of 1808 ed. lib. bdg. 89.50 (ISBN 0-306-71182-6). Da Capo.

Burr, Elisha W. Diseases of Parrots. (Illus.). 318p. 1982. 24.95 (ISBN 0-87666-843-0, H-1037). TFH Pubns.

Burr, John R., ed. Handbook of World Philosophy: Contemporary Developments Since 1945. LC 80-539. (Illus.). xxii, 639p. 1980. lib. bdg. 55.00 (ISBN 0-313-22381-5, BCD/). Greenwood.

Burr, Samuel E., Jr. China A.P.O. More than Experience. LC 82-72321. (Illus.). 209p. 1982. soft cover & supplement 5.00 (ISBN 0-911994-07-6). Burr Pubns.

Burr, Stefan A., ed. The Mathematics of Networks. LC 82-18469. 16.00 (ISBN 0-8218-0031-0, PSAPM-26). Am Math.

Burr, Tim. Old Nick: The Secret from an Old Wooden Box. (Illus.). 16p. 1981. pap. 6.95 (ISBN 0-686-96019-X). Dill Ent.

Burra, P. Wordsworth. LC 72-2096. (Studies in Wordsworth, No. 29). 1972. Repr. of 1935 ed. lib. bdg. 31.95x (ISBN 0-8383-1486-4). Haskell.

Burrell, jt. auth. see Feder.

Burrell, Arthur. Guide to Story Telling. LC 74-23577. 1971. Repr. of 1926 ed. 37.00x (ISBN 0-8103-3764-9). Gale.

Burrell, Berkeley G., jt. auth. see Seder, John.

Burrell, Brian. Combat Weapons: Handguns & Shoulder Arms of World War 2. (Illus.). 112p. 1974. 9.50 o.s.i. (ISBN 0-902875-35-3). Transatlantic.

Burrell, Craig D. & Sheps, Cecil G., eds. Primary Health Care in Industrialized Nations. (Annals of the New York Academy of Sciences: Vol. 310). 274p. 1978. pap. 42.00x professional (ISBN 0-89072-066-5). NY Acad Sci.

Burrell, D. C. Marine Environmental Studies in Boca de Quadra & Smeaton Bay: Chemical & Geochemical. (IMS Report Ser.: No. R82-2). 1980. write for info. (ISBN 0-914500-16-3). U of AK Inst Marine.

Burrell, David C. Atomic Spectrometric Analysis of Heavy-Metal Pollutants in Water. LC 73-92513. (Illus.). 1974. 49.95 (ISBN 0-250-40052-9). Ann Arbor Science.

Burrell, Jill & Burrell, Maurice. Arctic Mission. 1974. 1.55 (ISBN 0-08-017621-6). Pergamon.

Burrell, Lenette O. & Burrell, Zeb L., Jr. Critical Care. 4th ed. LC 81-9544. (Illus.). 622p. 1982. text ed. 24.95 (ISBN 0-8016-0906-2). Mosby.

Burrell, Leon F., jt. auth. see Clements, Zacharie J.

Burrell, Leonard F. Beginner's Guide to Home Coarse Tacklemaking. (Illus.). 134p. 1973. 12.95 o.p. (ISBN 0-7207-0548-7). Transatlantic.

Burrell, Maurice, jt. auth. see Burrell, Jill.

Burrell, Randal C., ed. see Capek, Karel.

Burrell, Sidney A. Handbook of Western Civilization: Beginnings to 1700. 2nd ed. LC 76-37642. 1972. pap. text ed. 5.75x o.p. (ISBN 0-471-12515-6). Wiley.

--Handbook of Western Civilization: 1700 to Present. 2nd ed. LC 76-37642. 262p. 1972. pap. text ed. 15.50 o.p. (ISBN 0-471-12516-4). Wiley.

Burrell, Zeb L., Jr., jt. auth. see Burrell, Lenette O.

Burrello, Leonard C. & Sage, Daniel D. Leadership & Change in Special Education. (P-H Ser. in Special Education). 1979. 23.95 (ISBN 0-13-526921-0). P-H.

Burridge, Shirley, ed. Oxford Elementary Learner's Dictionary of English. (Illus.). 304p. (Orig.). 1981. pap. text ed. 9.95x (ISBN 0-19-431253-4). Oxford U Pr.

Burril, Claude W. & Ellsworth, Leon W. Quality Data Processing. LC 79-9623. (Data Processing Handbook). (Illus.). 208p. 1982. text ed. 25.00 (ISBN 0-935310-01-0). Burrill-Ellsworth.

Burrington, John D. Pediatric Surgery Continuing Education Review. 1976. spiral bdg. 18.50 o.p. (ISBN 0-87488-332-6). Med Exam.

Burris. No Room at the Top. 352p. 1983. 32.50 (ISBN 0-03-061923-8). Praeger.

Burris, Robert H. & Black, Clayton C., eds. Carbon Dioxide Metabolism & Plant Productivity. (Harry Steenbock Symposia Ser). 446p. 1976. text ed. 59.50 o.p. (ISBN 0-8391-0849-4). Univ Park.

Burris, Russel W., et al. Teaching Law with Computers. (EDUCOM Series in Computing & Telecommunications in Higher Education). 1979. lib. bdg. 22.00 (ISBN 0-89158-193-6). Westview.

Burris-Meyer, Harold & Goodfriend, Lewis S. Acoustics for the Architect. 2nd ed. 1983. price not set (ISBN 0-89874-421-0). Krieger.

Burriss, Eli E. & Casson, Lionel. Latin & Greek in Current Use. 2nd ed. 1949. text ed. 16.95 (ISBN 0-13-524991-0). P-H.

Burritt, Elihu. Walks in the Black Country & Its Green Borderland. 1980. 15.00x o.p. (ISBN 0-900093-48-X, Pub. by Peter Dix). State Mutual Bk.

Burron, Arnold & Claybaugh, Amos L. Basic Concepts in Reading Instruction. 2nd ed. (Elementary Education Ser.). 1977. pap. text ed. 11.95 (ISBN 0-675-08539-X). Merrill.

--Using Reading to Teach Subject Matter: Fundamentals for Content Teachers. new ed. LC 73-90572. (Education - Elementary Ser). 128p. 1974. pap. text ed. 7.95 o.p. (ISBN 0-675-08838-0). Merrill.

Burros, Marian & Levine, Lois. Freeze with Ease. LC 65-21466. 1968. pap. 3.95 (ISBN 0-02-009280-6, Collier). Macmillan.

Burroughs, Alan. Art Criticism from a Laboratory. LC 70-110267. Repr. lib. bdg. 18.50x (ISBN 0-8371-4493-0, BUAC). Greenwood.

Burroughs, Ben. New Sketches. LC 61-11605. 172p. 1982. 8.50 o.p. (ISBN 0-8303-0049-X). Fleet.

Burroughs Corporation. Digital Computer Principles. 2nd ed. 1969. text ed. 17.95 o.p. (ISBN 0-07-009232-X, G). McGraw.

Burroughs, Edgar R. Apache Devil. 1978. lib. bdg. 9.95 (ISBN 0-8398-2454-8, Gregg). G K Hall.

--The Bandit of Hell's Bend. 1979. lib. bdg. 9.95 (ISBN 0-8398-2577-3, Gregg). G K Hall.

--The Deputy Sheriff of Comanche County. 1979. lib. bdg. 9.95 (ISBN 0-8398-2578-1, Gregg). G K Hall.

--The Oakdale Affair. 1976. Repr. of 1937 ed. lib. bdg. 14.95 (ISBN 0-89966-041-X). Buccaneer Bks.

--Out of the Time's Abyss. 144p. 1982. pap. 1.95 (ISBN 0-441-64485-6, Pub. by Ace Science Fiction). Ace Bks.

--The People That Time Forgot. 160p. 1982. pap. 2.25 (ISBN 0-441-65945-4, Pub. by Ace Science Fiction). Ace Bks.

--Tarzan & the Castaways. 1980. pap. 1.95 (ISBN 0-686-82860-7). Ballantine.

--The War Chief. 1978. lib. bdg. 9.95 (ISBN 0-8398-2453-X, Gregg). G K Hall.

Burroughs, Edgar Rice. The Land of the Hidden Men. 1982. pap. 2.25 (ISBN 0-686-97606-1). Ace Bks.

--The Land That Time Forgot. 192p. 1982. pap. 2.25 (ISBN 0-441-47026-2, Pub. by Ace Science Fiction). Ace Bks.

Burroughs, Jean M. Children of Destiny. (Illus.). 1975. pap. 4.95 (ISBN 0-913270-75-X). Sunstone Pr.

Burroughs, John. In the Catskills. LC 10-21755. (Illus.). 263p. (Orig.). 1974. pap. 10.95 o.p. (ISBN 0-910220-58-1). Berg.

--Return of the Birds: Selected Nature Essays of John Burroughs, Vol. 1. Bergon, Frank, ed. (Literature of the American Wilderness). 320p. Date not set. cancelled (ISBN 0-87905-081-0). Peregrine Smith.

--A River View & Other Hudson Valley Essays. LC 81-16945. 224p. 1981. 11.95 (ISBN 0-88427-049-1). North River.

--A Sharp Lookout: Nature Essays of John Burroughs, Vol. II. Bergone, Frank, ed. (Literature of the American Wilderness). 320p. Date not set. cancelled (ISBN 0-87905-082-9). Peregrine Smith.

--Writings of John Burroughs, 23 vols. Incl. Vol. 1. Wake Robin (ISBN 0-8462-1434-2); Vol. 2. Winter Sunshine (ISBN 0-8462-1435-0); Vol. 3. Birds & Poets (ISBN 0-8462-1436-9); Vol. 4. Locusts & Wild Honey (ISBN 0-8462-1437-7); Vol. 5. Pepacton (ISBN 0-8462-1438-5); Vol. 6. Fresh Fields (ISBN 0-8462-1439-3); Vol. 7. Signs & Seasons (ISBN 0-8462-1440-7); Vol. 8. Indoor Studies (ISBN 0-8462-1441-5); Vol. 9. Riverby (ISBN 0-8462-1442-3); Vol. 10. Literary Values (ISBN 0-8462-1443-1); Vol. 11. Far & Near (ISBN 0-8462-1444-X); Vol. 12. Ways of Nature (ISBN 0-8462-1445-8); Vol. 13. Leaf & Tendril (ISBN 0-8462-1446-6); Vol. 14. Time & Change (ISBN 0-8462-1447-4); Vol. 15. Summit of the Years (ISBN 0-8462-1448-2); Vol. 16. Whitman-A Study (ISBN 0-8462-1449-0); Vol. 17. Light of Day (ISBN 0-8462-1450-4); Vol. 18. Breath of Life (ISBN 0-8462-1451-2); Vol. 19. Under the Apple Trees (ISBN 0-8462-1452-0); Vol. 20. Field & Study (ISBN 0-8462-1453-9); Vol. 21. Accepting the Universe (ISBN 0-8462-1454-7); Vol. 22. Under the Maples (ISBN 0-8462-1455-5); Vol. 23. Last Harvest (ISBN 0-8462-1456-3). LC 68-15108. (Illus., Repr. of 1871-1922 ed.). 1968. 7.50x ea; 150.00x set (ISBN 0-8462-1087-8). Russell.

Burroughs, Lou. Microphones: Design & Application. LC 73-87056. (Illus.). 250p. 1976. 20.00 o.p. (ISBN 0-914130-00-5). pap. 12.95 o.p. (ISBN 0-914130-02-1). Elar Pub Co.

Burroughs, Polly. Exploring Martha's Vineyard. LC 72-93259. (Illustrated Guide Ser.). 1973. pap. 4.95 (ISBN 0-85699-064-7). Chatham Pr.

--Nantucket: A Guide with Tours. LC 74-76535. (Illus.). 64p. (Orig.). 1974. pap. 4.95 o.p. (ISBN 0-87106-144-9). Globe Pequot.

--Thomas Hart Benton: A Portrait. LC 77-16903. (Illus.). 208p. 1981. 29.95 o.p. (ISBN 0-385-12342-6). Doubleday.

--Zeb: A Celebrated Schooner Life. LC 72-80278. (Illus.). 160p. 1979. pap. 7.95 o.p. (ISBN 0-87106-023-X). Globe Pequot.

Burroughs, William. Early Routines. LC 79-54919. 80p. 1981. signed ltd. ed. 40.00 o.p. (ISBN 0-932274-03-X); pap. 10.00 o.p. (ISBN 0-932274-02-1). Cadmus Eds.

Burroughs, William S. Ah Pook is Here. 1982. pap. 8.95 (ISBN 0-7145-3683-0). Riverrun NY.

--Blade Runner: A Movie. LC 78-21584. 1979. 8.95 (ISBN 0-912652-45-4, Dynamite Bks); pap. 3.95 o.s.i. (ISBN 0-912652-46-2); signed ed. o.p. 20.00 (ISBN 0-912652-47-0). Blue Wind.

--Letters to Allen Ginsberg, 1953-1957. 210p. 1982. 17.95 (ISBN 0-916190-16-1); pap. 8.95 (ISBN 0-916190-17-X). Full Court NY.

--Port of Saints. LC 80-10309. 1980. 15.95 o.s.i. (ISBN 0-912652-64-0); signed, numbered & boxed 39.95x (ISBN 0-912652-66-7); pap. 5.95 (ISBN 0-912652-65-9). Blue Wind.

Burrous, Clifford N., jt. auth. see Deboo, Gordon J.

Burrow, G. N., jt. ed. see Fisher, D. A.

Burrow, Gerard N. & Ferris, Thomas F. Medical Complications During Pregnancy. LC 74-11685. (Illus.). 845p. 1975. text ed. 40.00 o.p. (ISBN 0-7216-2186-4). Saunders.

Burrow, Gerard N. & Dussault, Jean H., eds. Neonatal Thyroid Screening. 336p. 1980. text ed. 35.00 (ISBN 0-89004-483-X). Raven.

Burrow, J. A., ed. Sir Cawain & the Green Knight: Pearl Poet. (English Poets Ser.: No. 13). 176p. 1982. text ed. 15.00x (ISBN 0-300-02906-3); pap. 4.95x (ISBN 0-300-02907-1, YEP-13). Yale U Pr.

Burrow, J. W. A Liberal Descent: Victorian Historians & the English Past. LC 81-3912. 318p. Date not set. pap. 14.95 (ISBN 0-521-27482-6). Cambridge U Pr.

Burrow, J. W., ed. see Von Humboldt, Wilhelm.

Burrow, John W. Evolution & Society: A Study in Victorian Social Theory. 1966. 32.50 (ISBN 0-521-04393-X); pap. 10.95x (ISBN 0-521-09600-6). Cambridge U Pr.

Burrow, Roy D. Mind Hunger. 1975. 5.00 o.p. (ISBN 0-8233-0208-3). Golden Quill.

Burrow, Thomas. The Problem of Shwa in Sanskrit. 1979. 22.00x o.p. (ISBN 0-19-815452-6). Oxford U Pr.

Burrow, Trigant. Social Consciousness & Human Survival. Galt, Alfreda S., ed. 250p. 1983. 15.95 (ISBN 0-8180-1450-4). Horizon.

Burrowes, George. Song of Solomon. (Geneva Commentaries Ser.). 1977. 12.95 (ISBN 0-85151-157-0). Banner of Truth.

Burrowes, Reynold. Politics, Personalities, & Parties in Guyana. 256p. 1983. 16.95 (ISBN 0-87073-037-1). Schenkman.

Burrows & Davier. Handbook of Studies in Anxiety. 1981. 85.00 (ISBN 0-444-80224-X). Elsevier.

Burrows, jt. auth. see Beumont.

Burrows, Bernard, et al, eds. Federal Solutions to European Issues. LC 78-8066. 1978. 26.00x (ISBN 0-312-28546-9). St Martin.

Burrows, David L., ed. see Gasparini, Francesco.

Burrows, E. G. Kiva. 56p. 1976. 3.50 (ISBN 0-87886-077-0). Ithaca Hse.

Burrows, G. D., ed. Handbook of Studies on Depression. 1977. 96.75 (ISBN 90-219-2108-1, North Holland). Elsevier.

Burrows, G. D., et al, eds. Hypnosis Nineteen Hundred Seventy-Nine. LC 79-16095. 354p. 1979. 73.75 (ISBN 0-444-80142-1, North Holland). Elsevier.

Burrows, Graham D. & Werry, John S., eds. Advances in Human Psychopharmacology, Vol. 2. 375p. 1981. 45.00 (ISBN 0-89232-193-8). Jai Pr.

Burrows, Graham D., jt. ed. see Werry, John S.

Burrows, Paul. Economic Theory of Pollution Control. 240p. 1980. 27.50x (ISBN 0-262-02150-1); pap. text ed. 8.95x (ISBN 0-262-52056-7). MIT Pr.

Burrows, Paul & Hitiris, Theodore. Macroeconomic Theory: A Mathematical Introduction. LC 73-2779. 1974. text ed. 23.95x (ISBN 0-471-12525-3, Pub. by Wiley-Interscience). Wiley.

Burrows, Susan G. & Gassert, Carole A. Moving Right Along after Open Heart Surgery. Hull, Nancy R., ed. (Illus.). 52p. (Orig.). (gr. 8-10). 1979. pap. text ed. 5.00 o.p. (ISBN 0-939838-03-6). Pritchett & Hull.

Burrus, Bernie R. Administrative Law & Local Government. LC 63-63661. (Michigan Legal Publications Ser.). 139p. 1982. Repr. of 1963 ed. lib. bdg. 30.00 (ISBN 0-89941-170-3). W S Hein.

Burrus, Ernest J., tr. see De Salvatierra, Juan M.

Burrus, Victoria. A Procedural Manual for Entry Establishment in the Dictionary of the Old Spanish Language. 1982. pap. 10.00 (ISBN 0-942260-24-4). Hispanic Seminary.

Burry, J. H., jt. ed. see Singh, S. P.

Bursak, Laura Z., jt. auth. see Ives, Josephine.

Bursch, J. H., jt. ed. see Heintzen, Paul H.

Bursill, Henry. More Hand Shadows to Be Thrown Upon a Wall. (Illus.). (gr. 1-6). 1971. pap. 1.95 (ISBN 0-486-21384-6). Dover.

Bursk, Edward C. & Grayser, Stephen A. Advanced Cases in Marketing Management. LC 68-24633. (Foundations of Marketing Ser). (Orig.). 1968. pap. 11.95 ref. ed. (ISBN 0-13-011320-4). P-H.

Bursk, Edward C. & Chapman, John F., eds. New Decision-Making Tools for Managers: Mathematical Programing As an Aid in the Solving of Business Problems. LC 63-11416. (Illus.). 1963. 22.50x o.p. (ISBN 0-674-61050-4). Harvard U Pr.

--New Decision Making Tools for Managers. 1971. pap. 1.25 o.p. (ISBN 0-451-61017-2, MY1017, Ment). NAL.

Bursk, Edward C. & Greyset, Stephen A., eds. Cases in Marketing Management. 2nd ed. (Foundations of Marketing Ser.). (Illus.). 240p. 1975. pap. 11.95 ref. ed. (ISBN 0-13-118893-3). P-H.

Burssens, Gaston. From the Flemish of Gaston Burssens. Wade, John S., tr. from Flemish. LC 82-8756. 21p. (Orig.). 1982. o.s.i 10.00 (ISBN 0-933292-11-2); pap. 2.50 (ISBN 0-933292-10-4). Arts End.

Burstall, Tim. Sebastian & the Sausages. (Illus.). (gr. 4 up). 11.50x (ISBN 0-392-04506-0, ABC). Sportshelf.

Burstein. The Get Well Hotel. 113p. 1980. 4.95 (ISBN 0-07-009244-3). McGraw.

Burstein, Alvin, jt. auth. see Bowden, Charles.

Burstein, Chaya M. The Jewish Kids' Catalog. (Illus.). 224p. (gr. 3-7). 1983. pap. 10.95 (ISBN 0-8276-0215-4). Jewish Pubn.

Burstein, David, jt. auth. see Stasiowski, Frank.

Burstein, E., ed. see U. S.-Japan Seminar or Inelastic Light Scattering, Santa Monica, California. January 22-25, 1979.

Burstein, Elias & De Martini, Francesco, eds. Polaritons: Proceedings, Taormina Research Conference on the Structure of Matter, 1st, Taormina, Italy, Oct, 1972. LC 73-12845. 1975. text ed. 48.00 (ISBN 0-08-017825-1). Pergamon.

Burstein, H. Attribute Sampling: Tables & Explanations. 1971. 29.50 (ISBN 0-07-009250-8, P&RB). McGraw.

Burstein, John. Slim Goodbody: What Can Go Wrong & How to Be Strong. (Illus.). (gr. k-6). 1978. 8.95 (ISBN 0-07-009242-7, GB). McGraw.

Burstein, Joseph. Blackout in Mathematical Manuals. (Illus.). 70p. 1983. 12.00 (ISBN 0-9607126-0-7). Metrics Pr.

Burstein, Jules Q. Conjugal Visits in Prison: Psychological & Social Consequences. LC 76-50485. (Illus.). 1977. 17.95x o.p. (ISBN 0-669-01287-4). Lexington Bks.

Burstein, M. & Legmann, P. Lipoprotein Precipitation. (Monographs on Atherosclerosis: Vol. 11). (Illus.). viii, 132p. 1982. 58.25 (ISBN 3-8055-3512-0). S Karger.

Burstein, Milton B. What You Should Know About Acquisitions & Mergers. LC 72-5483. (Business Almanac Ser: No. 19). 128p. 1973. lib. bdg. 5.95 o.p. (ISBN 0-379-11219-1). Oceana.

Bursten, Martin A. Escape from Fear. LC 73-8563. (Illus.). 224p. 1973. Repr. of 1958 ed. lib. bdg. 15.75x (ISBN 0-8371-6961-5, BUEF). Greenwood.

Burstiner, Irving. Small Business Handbook: Comprehensive Guide to Starting & Running Your Own Business. (Illus.). 1979. text ed. 22.95 o.p. (ISBN 0-13-814202-5, Spec); pap. text ed. 14.95 (ISBN 0-13-814194-0). P-H.

Burstinger, Irving. Run Your Own Retail Store: From Raising the Money to Counting the Profits. (Illus.). 304p. 1981. 19.95 (ISBN 0-13-784017-9, Spec); pap. 22.95 (ISBN 0-13-784009-8). P-H.

Burston, W. H., ed. James Mill on Education. LC 69-11268. (Cambridge Texts & Studies in Education: No. 6). 1969. 24.95 (ISBN 0-521-07414-2). Cambridge U Pr.

Burston, W. H., et al, eds. Handbook for History Teachers. 2nd ed. 1972. 39.95x (ISBN 0-423-49060-5). Methuen Inc.

Burstyn, Ben. Bicycle Repair & Maintenance. LC 72-86242. (Illus.). 224p. 1974. 6.95 o.p. (ISBN 0-668-02706-1); pap. 2.95 (ISBN 0-668-02708-8). Arco.

Bursztayn, Harold. Medical Choices, Medical Chances. 480p. (Orig.). 1983. pap. 10.95 (ISBN 0-440-55750-X, Delta). Dell.

Bursztyn, Sylvia & Tunick, Barry. The Los Angeles Times Crossword Puzzle Collection. 1982. 4.95 (ISBN 0-399-50664-0, Perige). Putnam Pub Group.

Burt, Alison. Fondue Cookery. 1971. 10.00x (ISBN 0-600-33465-1). Intl Pubns Serv.

Burt, Barbara J., jt. ed. see Nax, Beunab.

Burt, C. ESP & Psychology. LC 75-16165. 179p. Repr. of 1975 ed. 13.50 o.p. (ISBN 0-470-12531-4). Krieger.

Burt, Catherine N. Snow Blind. Bd. with The Tall Ladder. 1979. pap. 1.75 o.p. (ISBN 0-451-08477-2, E8477, Sig). NAL.

Burt, Cyril. E.S.P. & Psychology. LC 75-16165. 179p. 1975. 24.95x o.s.i. (ISBN 0-470-12531-4). Halsted Pr.

Burt, D. R. Platyhelminthes & Parasitism: An Introduction to Parasitology. 1970. 17.95 o.p. (ISBN 0-444-19697-8). Elsevier.

Burt, Daniel S., jt. auth. see Bader, William.

Burt, Edward A. Telephoraceae of North America, 15 Pts. (Illus.). 900p. 1966. Repr. of 1926 ed. lib. bdg. 25.00x (ISBN 0-02-842320-8). Lubrecht & Cramert.

Burt, Forest D. & Want, E. Cleve. Invention & Design: Rhetorical Reader. 3rd ed. 406p. 1981. pap. text ed. 11.00 (ISBN 0-394-32557-5). Random.

Burt, Forrest D. The Effective Writer. 1978. pap. text ed. 3.25x o.p. (ISBN 0-89641-005-6). American Pr.

Burt, John J., et al. Toward a Healthy Lifestyle: Through Elementary Education. 608p. 1980. text ed. 20.95x (ISBN 0-534-00776-7). Wadsworth Pub.

Burt, John R. From Phonology to Philology: An Outline of Descriptive & Historical Spanish Linguistics. LC 80-67212. 208p. 1980. lib. bdg. 19.75 (ISBN 0-8191-1310-7); pap. text ed. 10.00 (ISBN 0-8191-1311-5). U Pr of Amer.

Burt, Katharine N. Red Lady. Bd. with Hidden Creek. 1979. pap. 2.50 (ISBN 0-451-11596-1, AE1596, Sig). NAL.

Burt, Larry W. Tribalism in Crisis: Federal Indian Policy, 1953-1961. 192p. 1982. 17.50 (ISBN 0-8263-0633-0). U of NM Pr.

Burt, Mala S. & Burt, Roger B. What's Special About Our Stepfamily? A Participation Book for Children. LC 81-43287. (Illus.). 160p. (gr. 3-7). 1983. pap. 9.95 (ISBN 0-385-17808-5, Dolp). Doubleday.

Burt, Marina K. & Kiparsky, Carol. The Gooficon: A Repair Manual for English. 1972. pap. 6.95 (ISBN 0-912066-07-5). Newbury Hse.

Burt, Martha R., jt. auth. see Moore, Kristin A.

Burt, Marvin R., jt. auth. see Sowder, Barbara J.

Burt, Olive W. Black Sunshine: The Story of Coal. LC 77-10874. (Illus.). 64p. (gr. 3 up). 1977. PLB 6.97 o.p. (ISBN 0-671-32847-6). Messner.

Burt, Philip B. Quantum Mechanics & Nonlinear Waves. 331p. 1981. 75.00 (ISBN 3-7186-0072-2). Harwood Academic Pubs.

Burt, Rob. Rockerama: Twenty-Five Years of Teen Screen Idols. (Illus.). 208p. (Orig.). 1982. pap. 9.95 cancelled (ISBN 0-89104-310-1, A & W Visual Library). A & W Pubs.

Burt, Robert, et al, eds. The Role of Centrosema, Desmodium & Stylosanthes in Improved Tropical Pastures. (Tropical Agriculture Ser.). (Illus.). 315p. 1982. lib. bdg. 23.50 (ISBN 0-86531-401-2). Westview.

Burt, Robert A. & Wald, Michael. Standards Relating to Abuse & Neglect. LC 77-3279. (IJA-ABA Juvenile Justice Standards Project Ser.). 224p. 1981. pref ref 22.50x (ISBN 0-88410-242-4); pap. 10.00x (ISBN 0-88410-830-9). Ballinger Pub.

Burt, Roger B., jt. auth. see Burt, Mala S.

Burt, Ronald. Toward a Structural Theory of Action: Network Models of Social Structure, Perception & Action. (Quantitative Studies in Social Relations). 1982. 29.50 (ISBN 0-12-147150-0). Acad Pr.

Burt, Ronald S. & Minor, Michael J. Applied Network Analysis: A Methodological Introduction. 352p. 1982. 25.00 (ISBN 0-8039-1906-9); pap. 12.50 (ISBN 0-8039-1907-7). Sage.

Burt, William H., ed. Antarctic Pinnipedia. LC 76-182566. (Antarctic Research Ser.: Vol. 18). (Illus.). 1971. 32.00 (ISBN 0-87590-118-2). Am Geophysical.

Burtenshaw, D. The City in West Europe. LC 80-41589. 320p. 1981. 43.95 (ISBN 0-471-27929-3, Pub. by Wiley-Interscience). Wiley.

--Saar-Lorraine. (Problem Regions of Europe). (Illus., Orig.). 1976. pap. text ed. 7.95x o.p. (ISBN 0-19-913193-7). Oxford U Pr.

Burthogge, Richard. The Philosophical Writings of Richard Burthogge. Landes, Margaret W., ed. xxi, 266p. 1921. 17.00 (ISBN 0-87548-048-9). Open Court.

Burtle, Vasanti. Women Who Drink: Alchoholic Experience & Psychotherapy. (Illus.). 304p. 1979. 21.00x (ISBN 0-398-03854-6). C C Thomas.

Burtle, Vasanti, jt. ed. see Franks, Violet.

Burton, jt. auth. see Arnold.

Burton, Andrew, jt. auth. see Radford, John.

Burton, Anne. Worse Than a Crime. (Raven House Mysteries Ser.). 224p. 1982. pap. cancelled (ISBN 0-373-63046-8, Pub. by Worldwide). Harlequin Bks.

Burton, Anthony. The Canal Builders. LC 80-85493. (Illus.). 256p. 1981. 23.50 (ISBN 0-7153-8120-2). David & Charles.

--Canals in Color. (Illus.). 176p. 1975. 8.50 o.p. (ISBN 0-7137-0715-1). Transatlantic.

--The Coventry Option. 1976. 7.95 o.p. (ISBN 0-399-11740-7). Putnam Pub Group.

--Embrace of the Butcher. LC 82-5068. 225p. 1982. 12.95 (ISBN 0-396-08059-6). Dodd.

Burton, Anthony & Burton, Pip. Green Bag Travellers: Britain's First Tourists. (Illus.). 1979. 10.95 o.p. (ISBN 0-233-96761-3). Transatlantic.

Burton, Arthur, ed. Psychotherapy of the Psychoses: Perspectives on Current Techiques of Treatment. LC 76-13507. 396p. 1976. Repr. of 1961 ed. 20.50 (ISBN 0-88275-413-0). Krieger.

Burton, Asa. Essays on Some of the First Principles of Metaphysicks, Ethicks, & Theology. LC 73-4839. (History of Psychology Ser). 440p. 1973. Repr. of 1824 ed. lib. bdg. 45.00x (ISBN 0-8201-1114-7). Schol Facsimiles.

Burton, B. T. Human Nutrition. 3rd ed. Orig. Title: Heinz Handbook of Nutrition. (Illus.). 1975. 30.00 (ISBN 0-07-009282-6, HP); pap. 21.50 (ISBN 0-07-009281-8). McGraw.

Burton, Charles & Nida, Gail. Be Good to Your Back. Rev. ed. 57p. 6.00 (ISBN 0-686-95712-1, 738). Sis Kenny Inst.

--Revised Gravity Lumbar Reduction Therapy Program. 48p. 1982. 6.25 (ISBN 0-88440-026-3). Sis Kenny Inst.

Burton, D. & Wohl, Gary S. Joy of Quitting: How to Help Young People Stop Smoking. 1979. 8.95 o.s.i. (ISBN 0-686-67546-0). Macmillan.

Burton, D. M. First Course in Rings & Ideals. LC 73-100855. 1970. text ed. 19.50 (ISBN 0-201-00731-2, Adv Bk Prog). A-W.

Burton, David. Oliver Wendell Holmes, Jr. What Manner of Liberal? LC 78-23645. (American Problem Ser.). 168p. 1979. pap. 5.95 (ISBN 0-88275-793-8). Krieger.

Burton, David H. Oliver Wendell Holmes, Jr. (United States Authors Ser.). 1980. lib. bdg. 10.95 (ISBN 0-8057-7262-6, Twayne). G K Hall.

--Theodore Roosevelt. (World Leaders Ser). 1973. lib. bdg. 11.95 (ISBN 0-8057-3709-X, Twayne). G K Hall.

Burton, Deirdrie, jt. auth. see Carter, Ronald.

Burton, Dolores M., jt. auth. see Bailey, Richard W.

Burton, Dwight L., et al. Teaching English Today. 1975. text ed. 21.95 o.p. (ISBN 0-395-18616-1). HM.

Burton, Elsie, jt. auth. see Werner, Peter H.

Burton, Elsie C. The New Physical Education for Elementary School Children. LC 76-11981. (Illus.). 1977. text ed. 21.95 (ISBN 0-395-20658-8). HM.

--Physical Activities for the Developing Child. (Illus.). 304p. 1980. 14.95x (ISBN 0-398-03939-9). C C Thomas.

Burton, Eva, et al see Linguistic Circle of Saigon & Summer Institute of Linguistics.

Burton, Gary. A Musician's Guide to the Road. 164p. 1981. pap. 7.95 (ISBN 0-8230-7583-4, Billboard Bks). Watson-Guptill.

Burton, H., et al. Milk Sterilization. (FAO Agricultural Studies: No. 65). (Orig.). 1969. pap. 7.25 (ISBN 0-685-02454-7, F279, FAO). Unipub.

Burton, I., jt. auth. see Brace, Geoffrey.

Burton, Ian & Kates, Robert W. The Environment As Hazard. (Illus.). 1978. text ed. 15.95x (ISBN 0-19-502221-1); pap. text ed. 12.95x (ISBN 0-19-502222-X). Oxford U Pr.

Burton, Ian, jt. auth. see Whyte, Ann V.

Burton, Ian J. Out of Season. 192p. 1981. 9.95 o.p. (ISBN 0-517-54334-6). Crown.

Burton, Ivor & Drewry, Gavin. Legislation & Public Policy: Public Bills in the 1970-74 Parliament. 300p. 1981. text ed. 47.50x (ISBN 0-8419-5065-2). Holmes & Meier.

Burton, J. M. Honore De Balzac & His Figures of Speech. (Elliott Monographs: Vol. 8). 1921. pap. 12.00 (ISBN 0-527-02612-3). Kraus Repr.

Burton, Jane, jt. auth. see Burton, Maurice.

Burton, Jimalee. Indian Heritage, Indian Pride: Stories That Touched My Life. LC 73-7426. (Illus.). 1981. pap. 11.95 (ISBN 0-8061-1707-9). U of Okla Pr.

Burton, John. The Collection of the Qur'an. LC 76-27899. 1977. 42.50 (ISBN 0-521-21439-4); pap. 13.95 (ISBN 0-521-29652-8). Cambridge U Pr.

--Dear Survivors. 160p. 1982. lib. bdg. 17.50x (ISBN 0-86531-455-1); pap. text ed. 8.50x (ISBN 0-86531-456-X). Westview.

--Deviance, Terrorism & War: The Process of Solving Unsolved Social & Political Problems. LC 79-16484. 1979. 26.00x (ISBN 0-312-19753-5). St Martin.

Burton, John, ed. Owls of the World. 1973. 19.95 o.p. (ISBN 0-525-17432-X). Dutton.

Burton, John A. Birds of the Tropics. (World of Nature Ser.). (Illus.). 128p. 1973. 3.98 o.p. (ISBN 0-517-12036-4). Crown.

Burton, John H. Book Hunter. Slater, Herbert J., ed. LC 79-78122. 1971. Repr. of 1895 ed. 34.00 o.p. (ISBN 0-8103-3607-3). Gale.

Burton, John W. Systems, States, Diplomacy & Rules. 256p. 1968. 32.50 (ISBN 0-521-07316-2). Cambridge U Pr.

--World Society. LC 71-176252. (Illus.). 250p. 1972. 29.95 (ISBN 0-521-08425-3); pap. 9.95 (ISBN 0-521-09694-4). Cambridge U Pr.

Burton, Julianne, ed. The New Latin American Cinema: An Annotated Bibliography of English-Languages Sources, 1960-1980. (Orig.). 1983. pap. 4.00 (ISBN 0-918266-17-3). Smyrna.

Burton, Leon, jt. auth. see University of Hawaii Music Project.

Burton, Leon, ed. see Gillett, Dorothy.

Burton, Leon, ed. see Tait, Malcolm.

Burton, Linda. Stories from Tennessee. LC 82-16016. 488p. 1983. text ed. 27.95x (ISBN 0-87049-376-0); pap. 12.95 (ISBN 0-87049-377-9). U of Tenn Pr.

Burton, Lindy. Vulnerable Children. (International Library of Sociology). 272p. 1968. 18.00 (ISBN 0-7100-3500-4). Routledge & Kegan.

--Vulnerable Children: Three Studies of Children in Conflict: Accident Involved Children, Sexually Assaulted Children & Children with Asthma. LC 68-21683. 1968. 6.50x o.p. (ISBN 0-8052-3276-1). Schocken.

Burton, Lloyd E., et al. Public Health & Community Medicine. 3rd ed. (Illus.). 616p. 1980. softcover 31.00 (ISBN 0-683-01236-3). Williams & Wilkins.

Burton, Malcolm S. Applied Metallurgy for Engineers. 1956. text ed. 21.95 o.p. (ISBN 0-07-009292-3, C). McGraw.

Burton, Marilee R. Aaron Awoke. LC 81-48638. (Illus.). 40p. (ps-k). 1982. 8.61i (ISBN 0-06-020891-0, HarpJ); PLB 8.89g (ISBN 0-06-020892-9). Har-Row.

Burton, Maurice. Deserts. (Illus.). 119p. (gr. 4 up). 1975. 8.50 o.p. (ISBN 0-584-62047-0). Transatlantic.

--The Life of Birds. LC 77-88440. (Easy Reading Edition of Introduction to Nature Ser.). (Illus.). 1978. PLB 12.68 (ISBN 0-382-06126-8). Silver.

--The Life of Fishes. LC 77-88434. (Easy Reading Edition of Introduction to Nature Ser.). (Illus.). 1978. PLB 12.68 (ISBN 0-686-51140-9). Silver.

--The Life of Insects. LC 78-56576. (Easy Reading Edition of Introduction to Nature Ser.). (Illus.). 1979. PLB 12.68 (ISBN 0-382-06185-3). Silver.

--The Life of Reptiles & Amphibians. LC 77-88437. (Easy Reading Edition of Introduction to Nature Ser.). (Illus.). 1978. PLB 12.68 (ISBN 0-382-06131-4). Silver.

--A Revision of the Classification of the Calcarous Sponges: With a Catalogue of the Specimens in the British Museum (Natural History) (Illus.). 693p. 1963. 70.00x (ISBN 0-565-00698-3, Pub. by Brit Mus Nat Hist England). Sabbot-Natural Hist Bks.

--True Book About Animals. 12.75x (ISBN 0-392-08507-0, SpS). Sportshelf.

Burton, Maurice & Burton, Jane. The Family of Animals. LC 78-17855. 1978. 12.95 o.p. (ISBN 0-668-04662-7). Arco.

Burton, Maurice & Burton, Robert. The Life of Meat Eaters. LC 77-88439. (Easy Reading Edition of Introduction to Nature Ser.). (Illus.). 1978. PLB 12.68 (ISBN 0-686-51142-5). Silver.

Burton, P. J. Feeding & the Feeding Apparatus in Waders. (Illus.). 1974. text ed. 20.75x (ISBN 0-565-00719-X, Pub. by Brit Mus Nat Hist). Sabbot-Natural Hist Bks.

Burton, Peter, ed. see Maugham, Robin.

Burton, Philip E., ed. A Dictionary of Microcomputing. LC 76-24762. (Reference Library of Science & Technology Ser.: Vol. 5). 1980. lib. bdg. 19.50 o.s.i. (ISBN 0-8240-9930-3). Garland Pub.

Burton, Philip W. Advertising Copywriting. 5th ed. LC 82-9319. (Grid Series in Advertising & Journalism). 320p. 1983. text ed. 27.95 (ISBN 0-88244-254-6). Grid Pub.

--Which Ad Pulled Best? 4th ed. LC 80-70202. 136p. 1981. pap. text ed. 9.95x (ISBN 0-87251-060-3). Crain Bks.

Burton, Phillip E. A Dictionary of Minicomputing & Microcomputing. LC 80-28272. 368p. 1981. lib. bdg. 42.50 o.s.i. (ISBN 0-8240-7263-4). Garland Pub.

Burton, Pip, jt. auth. see Burton, Anthony.

Burton, Richard. Ultima Thule. LC 82-73425. 788p. Repr. of 1875 ed. lib. bdg. 65.00 (ISBN 0-88116-001-6). Brenner Bks.

Burton, Richard F. The Gold Mines of Midian. Ward, Philip, ed. (Arabia Past & Present Ser.: Vol. 8). (Illus.). 1979. 35.00 (ISBN 0-900891-50-5). Oleander Pr.

--The Land of Midian, 2 vols. (Arabia Past & Present Ser.: Vol. 11). (Illus.). 1983. Set. cancelled (ISBN 0-900891-55-6). Oleander Pr.

--Nile Basin. 2nd ed. LC 65-23403. 1967. Repr. of 1864 ed. 25.00 (ISBN 0-306-70926-0). Da Capo.

Burton, Richard F., tr. see Da Gama, Jose B.

Burton, Richard M. & Chandler, John S. Management Science: Quantitative Approaches to Business Decision Making. 512p. Date not set. text ed. 23.50 scp (ISBN 0-06-041086-8, HarpC); instr's manual avail. (ISBN 0-06-361067-1). Har-Row. Postponed.

Burton, Sir Richard, tr. see Vatsyayana.

Burton, Robert. The Cat Family. LC 78-64654. (Fact Finders Ser.). (Illus.). 1979. lib. bdg. 8.00 (ISBN 0-382-06235-3). Silver.

--The Language of Smell. (Illus.). 1976. 16.95 (ISBN 0-7100-8429-3). Routledge & Kegan.

--The Seashore. LC 76-28656. (Illus.). 1977. 14.95 o.p. (ISBN 0-399-11886-1). Putnam Pub Group.

Burton, Robert, jt. auth. see Burton, Maurice.

Burton, Robert A., et al. Key Issues in Health. (Illus.). 369p. 1978. pap. text ed. 11.95 o.p. (ISBN 0-15-548368-4, HC); instructor's manual avail. o.p. (ISBN 0-15-548369-2). HarBraceJ.

Burton, Robert E., ed. Travel in Oceania, Australia & New Zealand: A Guide to Information Sources. LC 80-15333. (Geography & Travel Information Guide Ser.: Vol. 2). 150p. 1980. 42.00x (ISBN 0-8103-1421-5). Gale.

Burton, Robert H. & Petrello, George J. Personal Finance. (Illus.). 1978. text ed. 22.95 (ISBN 0-02-317350-5). Macmillan.

Burton, S. H see Allen, W. S.

Burton, Steven D. Orchestration. 500p. 1982. 23.95 (ISBN 0-13-639500-7); wkbk. 10.95 (ISBN 0-13-639526-0). P-H.

Burton, T. A., ed. Volterra Integral & Differential Equations. LC 82-18932. (Mathematics in Science & Engineering Ser.). Date not set. price not set (ISBN 0-12-147380-5). Acad Pr.

Burton, Theodore E. The Constitution of the United States. 1923. 14.50x o.p. (ISBN 0-685-89744-3). Elliots Bks.

--Financial Crises & Periods of Industrial & Commercial Depressions. 1983. Repr. of 1902 ed. flexible cover 12.00 (ISBN 0-87034-021-2). Fraser Pub Co.

Burton, Virginia L. Little House. (Illus.). (gr. k-3). 1942. reinforced ed. 10.89 (ISBN 0-395-18156-9). HM.

Burton, W. G. Post-Harvest Physiology of Food Crops. (Illus.). 320p. 1982. 32.00x (ISBN 0-582-46038-7). Longman.

Burton, William C. Legal Thesaurus. 1983. 19.95 (ISBN 0-02-691020-9). Macmillan.

Burton, William H. Supervision & the Improvement of Teaching. 510p. 1982. Repr. of 1927 ed. lib. bdg. 35.00 (ISBN 0-89760-098-3). Telegraph Bks.

Burton, William H., et al. Developmental Reading Text Workbooks. Incl. Ready to Read. (readiness). text ed. 1.60 o.p. (ISBN 0-672-70588-5); Play Time. (primer). text ed. o.p. (ISBN 0-672-71285-7); Up & Away. (gr. 1). text ed. 2.00 o.p. (ISBN 0-672-71287-3); Animal Parade. (gr. 2). text ed. 2.00 o.p. (ISBN 0-672-71289-X); Picnic Basket. (gr. 3). text ed. 2.00 o.p. (ISBN 0-672-71291-1); Blazing New Trails. (gr. 6). text ed. 2.24 o.p. (ISBN 0-672-71293-8); Flying High. (gr. 5). text ed. 2.24 o.p. (ISBN 0-672-71295-4); Shooting Stars. (gr. 6). text ed. 2.24 o.p. (ISBN 0-672-71297-0). (readiness-6). 1975. tchrs' ed. 2.40 ea. o.p. Bobbs.

Burtschi, Mary. European Journey. (Illus.). 93p. pap. 5.95 (ISBN 0-686-84842-X). Little Brick Hse.

Burtt, Edwin A. Metaphysical Foundations of Modern Physical Science. 2nd ed. (International Library of Psychology, Philosophy & Scientific Method). 1967. Repr. of 1932 ed. text ed. 27.50x (ISBN 0-7100-3032-0); pap. text ed. 6.95x (ISBN 0-391-01633-4). Humanities.

Burtt, Edwin A., ed. The English Philosophers from Bacon to Mill. 9.95 (ISBN 0-394-60411-3). Modern Lib.

--Teachings of the Compassionate Buddha. (Orig.). 1955. pap. 2.50 (ISBN 0-451-62185-9, ME2185, Ment). NAL.

Burtt, Everett J. Social Perspectives in the History of Economic Theory. 1972. pap. 12.95 (ISBN 0-312-73325-9). St Martin.

Burtt, George. The Barter Way to Beat Inflation. LC 79-51192. 1980. 10.95 (ISBN 0-89696-053-6, An Everest House Book); pap. 6.95 (ISBN 0-686-65978-3). Dodd.

Burwash, Peter & Tullius, John. Peter Burwash's Vegetarian Primer. LC 82-45165. (Illus.). 192p. 1983. 14.95 (ISBN 0-689-11299-8). Atheneum.

Burwick, Ray. Anger: Defusing the Bomb. 128p. 1981. pap. 2.95 (ISBN 0-8423-0053-8). Tyndale.

--Self Esteem: You're Better than You Think. 1983. pap. 4.95 (ISBN 0-686-82695-7, 75-5865-X). Tyndale.

Bury, B. R. Sodomy & the Perception of Evil: English Sea Rovers in the Seventeenth Century Caribbean. 300p. 1982. 19.50 (ISBN 0-8147-1040-9). NYU Pr.

Bury, Charles. Telephone Techniques That Sell. 148p. 1980. 4.95 (ISBN 0-686-98048-4). Telecom Lib.

Bury, J. B. History of the Later Roman Empire from the Death of Theodosius Eight to the Death of Justinian, 2 vols. 12.00 ea. (ISBN 0-8446-1785-7). Peter Smith.

Bury, John B. A History of Freedom of Thought. LC 74-30844. 246p. 1975. Repr. of 1952 ed. lib. bdg. 17.00x (ISBN 0-8371-7935-1, BUHF). Greenwood.

--The Idea of Progress: An Inquiry into Its Origin & Growth. LC 82-6261. xl, 357p. 1982. Repr. of 1932 ed. lib. bdg. 39.75x (ISBN 0-313-23374-8, BUIP). Greenwood.

Bury, John P. Gambetta-the National Defence: A Republican Dictatorship in France. LC 77-114490. (Illus.). 1971. Repr. of 1936 ed. lib. bdg. 17.00x (ISBN 0-8371-4818-9, BUGN). Greenwood.

Bury, Karl V. Statistical Models in Applied Science. LC 74-23834. (Probability & Mathematical Statistics Ser.). 640p. 1975. 51.95 (ISBN 0-471-12590-3, Pub. by Wiley-Interscience). Wiley.

Bury, Shirley. Victorian Electroplate. (Country Life Collectors Guides Ser). 1972. 4.95 o.p. (ISBN 0-600-43501-6). Transatlantic.

Buryn, Ed. Vagabonding in the U. S. A. A Guide to Independent Travel. LC 82-83637. (Illus.). 432p. 1982. pap. 10.95 (ISBN 0-916804-02-X). ExPress CA.

Busacker, Robert G. & Saaty, T. Finite Graphs & Networks: An Introduction with Applications. (International Pure & Applied Mathematics Ser). 1965. text ed. 18.95 o.p. (ISBN 0-07-009305-9, C). McGraw.

Busald, Gerald. An Introduction to Computer Terminals. 64p. 1982. pap. text ed. 4.50 (ISBN 0-8403-2788-9). Kendall-Hunt.

Busbee, Shirlee. Gyspy Lady. 1977. pap. 3.50 (ISBN 0-380-01824-1, 82859-6). Avon.

--While Passion Sleeps. 3.95 (ISBN 0-380-82297-0). Avon.

Busby, Thomas. General History of Music from the Earliest Times, 2 vols. LC 68-21091. (Music Ser). 1968. Repr. of 1819 ed. Set. 65.00 (ISBN 0-306-71063-3). Da Capo.

--A Grammar of Music. LC 76-20711. (Music Reprint Ser). 1976. Repr. of 1818 ed. lib. bdg. 39.50 (ISBN 0-306-70789-6). Da Capo.

--A Musical Manual, or Technical Directory. LC 76-20708. (Music Reprint Ser). 1976. Repr. of 1828 ed. lib. bdg. 25.00 (ISBN 0-306-70788-8). Da Capo.

Buscaglia, Leo. Living, Learning & Loving. 288p. 1983. pap. 5.95 (ISBN 0-449-90024-X, Columbine). Fawcett.

--Living, Loving & Learning. 264p. 1982. 13.50 (ISBN 0-686-84812-8). Slack Inc.

--Love. 2.95 o.p. (ISBN 0-686-92373-1, 6488). Hazelden.

--The Way of the Bull. 192p. 1983. pap. 2.95 (ISBN 0-449-20090-6, Crest). Fawcett.

Buscaglia, Leo F. Because I Am Human. LC 72-92809. 72p. 1972. 5.95 (ISBN 0-913590-06-1). Slack Inc.

--Love. LC 72-92810. 147p. 1972. 9.95 (ISBN 0-913590-07-X). Slack Inc.

--Personhood. LC 78-66423. 1978. 9.95 (ISBN 0-913590-63-0). Slack Inc.

--The Way of the Bull. LC 73-83777. 176p. 1974. 9.95 (ISBN 0-913590-08-8). Slack Inc.

Buscema, John, jt. auth. see Lee, Stan.

Busch & Wilkie Bros. Foundation. Fundamentals of Dimensional Metrology. LC 64-12593. 428p. 1966. 17.00 (ISBN 0-8273-0193-6); instr.'s guide 3.25 (ISBN 0-8273-0197-9). Delmar.

Busch, Arthur W. Aerobic Biological Treatment of Waste Waters. 418p. 1971. 35.00x (ISBN 0-87201-008-2). Gulf Pub.

Busch, Briton C. Britain & the Persian Gulf, 1894-1914. LC 67-24120. 1967. 32.50x (ISBN 0-520-00200-8). U of Cal Pr.

--Britain, India, & the Arabs, 1914-1921. LC 71-132421. 1971. 37.50x (ISBN 0-520-01821-4). U of Cal Pr.

Busch, Briton C, ed. see Phelps, William D.

Busch, Frederick. Take This Man. 224p. 1983. pap. 2.95 (ISBN 0-345-30548-5). Ballantine.

Busch, Harris & Rothblum, Lawrence. The Cell Nucleus: DNA, Vol. 12. 248p. 1982. 42.00 (ISBN 0-12-147612-X). Acad Pr.

Busch, Harris, ed. The Cell Nucleus: DNA, Vol. 10. 408p. 1982. 57.00 (ISBN 0-12-147610-3). Acad Pr.

--Methods in Cancer Research, Vol. 20. (Serial Publication). 1982. 48.50 (ISBN 0-12-147680-4). Acad Pr.

Busch, Harris & Rothblum, Lawrence, eds. The Cell Nucleus, Vol. 11. 310p. 1982. 45.00 (ISBN 0-12-147611-1). Acad Pr.

Busch, Harris & Yeoman, Lynn, eds. Methods in Cancer Research: Vol. 19, Tumor Markers. LC 66-29495. 464p. 1982. 56.00 (ISBN 0-12-147679-0); subscription 48.00 (ISBN 0-686-81714-1). Acad Pr.
Busch, John C., jt. ed. see Goldman, Bert A.
Busch, Kenneth W., jt. auth. see Kenner, Charles T.
Busch, Lawerence & Lacy, William B. Science, Agriculture, & Government: The Politics of Research. (WVSS in Agriculture Aquaculture Science & Policy Ser.). (Illus.). 325p. (Orig.). 1982. lib. bdg. 30.00 (ISBN 0-86531-225-7); pap. text ed. 12.95 (ISBN 0-86531-230-3). Westview.
Busch, Noel F. Briton Hadden: A Biography of the Co-Founder of Time. LC 75-25253. 236p. 1975. Repr. of 1949 ed. lib. bdg. 16.25x (ISBN 0-8371-8395-2, BUBH). Greenwood.
Busch, Phyllis. Cactus in the Desert. LC 78-4771. (A Let's-Read-&-Find-Out Science Bk.). (Illus.). (gr. k-3). 1979 (ISBN 0-690-00292-0, TYC-J). PLB 10.89 (ISBN 0-690-01336-1). Har-Row.
Busch, Walter. Casarismuskritik und Epische Historik. xv, 415p. (Ger.). 1982. write for info. (ISBN 3-8204-6266-X). P Lang Pubs.
Busch, William. The Genius of Wilhelm Busch. Arndt, Walter, ed. LC 79-63545. (Illus.). 450p. 1981. 39.95 (ISBN 0-520-03897-5). U of Cal Pr.
Buschardt, A. Zur Fletchtenflora der Inneralpinen Trockentaeler unter Besonderer Beruecksichtinhung des Vinschgaus. (Bibliotheca Lichenologica 10). 1979. lib. bdg. 32.00x (ISBN 3-7682-1226-2). Lubrecht & Cramer.
Buschkens, W. & Slikkerveer, L. Health Care in East Africa. (Studies in Developing Countries: No. 28). 144p. 1982. text ed. 10.50x (ISBN 0-686-82311-7, 41379, Pub. by Van Gorcum Holland). Humanities.
Buschkuhl, Matthias. Great Britain & the Holy See. 220p. 1983. text ed. 35.00x (ISBN 0-7165-0290-9, Pub. by Irish Academic Pr Ireland). Biblio Dist.
Buschle, K. B., jt. auth. see Narrow, B. W.
Buschman, R. G., jt. auth. see Srivastava, H. M.
Buscombe, Ed, ed. & intro. by. MGM. (BFI Dossiers Ser.: No. 1). (Orig.). 1980. pap. 6.00 o.p. (ISBN 0-918432-33-2). NY Zoetrope.
Buscombe, W. New Catalogues of Stellar Data. (Illus.). (1974 ed.) 10.00 (ISBN 0-939160-00-5); (1977 ed.) 15.00 (ISBN 0-939160-01-3); (1980 ed.) 15.00 (ISBN 0-939160-02-1); (1981 ed.) 15.00 (ISBN 0-939160-03-X). NWU Astro.
Buscombe, William. MK Spectral Classification: Fourth General Catalogue. 1980. pap. text ed. 15.00x (ISBN 0-939160-02-1). Buscombe.
Buse, Melanie R. Drug Store Market Guide, 1983. 540p. (Orig.). 1982. pap. 149.00x (ISBN 0-9606064-2-4). Drug Store Mkt.
Buseman, Herbert H. Metric Methods in Finsler Spaces. (Annals of Mathematics Studies: No. 8). 1942. pap. 20.00 (ISBN 0-527-02724-3). Kraus Repr.
Busenbark, R., jt. auth. see Bates, Henry.
Busenbark, Robert, jt. auth. see Bates, Henry.
Busenbark, Robert I., jt. auth. see Bates, Henry J.
Busenkell, Richard L. Jaguar: Since 1945. (North Automobile Ser.). (Illus.). 1982. 19.95 (ISBN 0-393-01566-1). Norton.
Buser, P., jt. ed. see Pfurtscheller, G.
Buser, P. A. & Rougeul-Buser, A. Cerebral Correlates of Conscious Experience. (INSERM Symposium Ser.: Vol. 6). 1978. 71.00 (ISBN 0-7204-0659-5, North-Holland). Elsevier.
Busey, James L. Latin America: Political Institutions & Processes. (Orig.). 1964. pap. text ed. 3.95 (ISBN 0-685-19741-7). Phila Bk Co.
Busfield, Joan & Paddon, M. Thinking About Children. LC 76-22986. (Illus.). 1977. 32.50 (ISBN 0-521-21402-5). Cambridge U Pr.
Busfield, Roger M. Playwright's Art: Stage, Radio, Television, Motion Pictures. LC 78-139125. 1971. Repr. of 1958 ed. lib. bdg. 17.50x (ISBN 0-8371-5741-2, BUPA). Greenwood.
Bush, Archie C. Studies in Roman Social Structure. LC 81-40816. (Illus.). 266p. (Orig.). 1982. lib. bdg. 23.00 (ISBN 0-8191-2337-4); pap. text ed. 11.50 (ISBN 0-8191-2338-2). U Pr of Amer.
Bush, B. M., jt. ed. see Roberts, A.
Bush, Barbara. Walking in Wisdom: A Woman's Workshop on Ecclesiastes. (Woman's Workshop Ser.). 128p. (Orig.). 1982. pap. 2.95 (ISBN 0-310-43041-0). Zondervan.
Bush, Barbara J. Ask Adam. 160p. 1978. 6.95 o.p. (ISBN 0-8007-0942-X). Revell.
Bush, Barney. Petroglyphs. LC 82-82422. (Illus.). 84p. (Orig.). 1982. pap. 6.00 (ISBN 0-912678-54-2). Greenfld Rev Pr.
Bush, Carol, jt. auth. see Garland, LaRetta.
Bush, Catherine S. Language Remediation & Expansion: One Hundred Skill-Building Reference Lists. (Illus.). 216p. 1979. pap. text ed. 15.95 (ISBN 0-88450-797-1, 3052-B). Communication Skill.
--Language Remediation & Expansion: School & Home Program. 1980. pap. 15.95 (ISBN 0-88450-711-4, 3063-B). Communication Skill.
--Language Remediation & Expansion Workshops for Parents & Teachers. 1981. 15.95 (ISBN 0-88450-738-6, 3134-B). Communication Skill.
Bush, Chan, jt. auth. see Olney, Ross R.
Bush, Clifford L. & Huebner, Mildred H. Strategies for Reading in the Elementary School. 2nd ed. (Illus.). 1979. text ed. 22.95 (ISBN 0-02-317510-9); instrs'. manual avail. Macmillan.
Bush, Clive. The Dream of Reason: American Consciousness & Cultural Achievement from Independence to the Civil War. LC 77-93574. (Illus.). 1978. 29.95x o.p. (ISBN 0-312-21960-1). St Martin.
Bush, Douglas. English Literature in the Earlier Seventeenth Century, 1600-1660. 2nd ed. (Oxford Paperbacks Ser: No. 299). 1975. pap. 6.95x (ISBN 0-19-881299-X, OPB299). Oxford U Pr.
--Prefaces to Renaissance Literature. LC 65-13837. 1965. 7.95x o.p. (ISBN 0-674-70000-7). Harvard U Pr.
--Science & English Poetry: A Historical Sketch, 1590-1950. LC 80-18161. (The Patten Lectures Ser., 1949, Indiana Univ.). viii, 166p. 1980. Repr. of 1950 ed. lib. bdg. 20.75x (ISBN 0-313-22654-7, BUSC). Greenwood.
Bush, Douglas, ed. see Baptista Mantuanus.
Bush, Douglas, ed. see Shakespeare, William.
Bush, Elsie. The Big Creek Album: Yesterday & Today. (Illus.). 132p. 1982. 25.00 (ISBN 0-9609440-0-1). D & E Bush.
Bush, Fred W., ed. The Centennial Atlas of Athens County, Ohio 1905. LC 75-23393. (Illus.). 168p. (Facsimile Ed., reduced). 1975. 20.00 (ISBN 0-8214-0203-X, 82-82105). Ohio U Pr.
Bush, Frederic W. & Hubbard, David A. Old Testament Survey: The Message, Form, & Background of the Old Testament. 688p. 1982. 24.95 (ISBN 0-8028-3556-2). Eerdmans.
Bush, George. Exodus. 1981. 22.50 (ISBN 0-86524-097-3, 0202). Klock & Klock.
--Genesis, 2 vols. 1981. 29.95 (ISBN 0-86524-094-9, 0103). Klock & Klock.
--Joshua & Judges. 1981. 17.95 (ISBN 0-86524-100-7, 0602). Klock & Klock.
--Leviticus. 1981. 10.50 (ISBN 0-86524-098-1, 0302). Klock & Klock.
--Numbers. 1981. 17.75 (ISBN 0-86524-099-X, 0401). Klock & Klock.
--The Strange World of Insects. (Illus.). (gr. 6-11). 1968. PLB 6.29 o.p. (ISBN 0-399-60616-5). Putnam Pub Group.
Bush, George, et al, eds. Windfall Poems Nineteen Seventy-Seven to Nineteen Seventy-Eight: A Special Collection. Fuller, Buckminster & Boyle, Kay. 1977. text ed. 5.00 (ISBN 0-9610536-0-7). Mainespring.
Bush, George P., ed. Technology & Copyright: Annotated Bibliography & Source Materials. LC 72-87129. 454p. 1972. 28.50 (ISBN 0-912338-03-2); microfiche 9.50 (ISBN 0-912338-04-0). Lomond.
Bush, George S. An American Harvest: The Story of Weil Brothers-Cotton. LC 82-9797. 495p. 25.00 (ISBN 0-13-027458-5, Busn). P-H.
Bush, Grace & Young, John. The Mathematics of Business. LC 73-93624. (Illus.). 384p. 1974. pap. text ed. 15.95 wkbk (ISBN 0-574-19105-4, 13-2105); instr's guide avail. (ISBN 0-574-19106-2, 13-2106). SRA.
Bush, Grace A., jt. auth. see Young, John E.
Bush, I. E., et al. The Chromatography of Steroids. 1961. 41.00 o.p. (ISBN 0-08-009544-5). Pergamon.
Bush, Ian. The Siberian Reservoir. 1983. 16.95 (ISBN 0-395-32560-9). HM.
Bush, James. The Handyman's Handbook. LC 78-50817. 1978. 14.95 o.p. (ISBN 0-528-81038-3); pap. 8.95 (ISBN 0-528-88197-3). Rand.
Bush, K. J; see Eisen, G.
Bush, Keith, tr. see Wadekin, Karl-Eugen.
Bush, Lawrence. Bessie. LC 82-80372. 448p. 1983. 16.95 (ISBN 0-399-31001-0). Seaview Bks.
Bush, Lee, ed. see Munch, Richard W.
Bush, Lee O. & Chukayne, Edward C. Euclid Beach Park: A Second Look. (Illus.). 229p. 1979. 12.95 (ISBN 0-935408-01-0). Amusement Pk Bks.
--Euclid Beach Park is Closed for the Season. (Illus.). 331p. 1977. 19.95 (ISBN 0-913228-22-2); pap. 12.95 (ISBN 0-686-43325-4). Amusement Pk Bks.
Bush, Monroe, Jr. Adventure Called Death. 1950. 2.95 o.s.i. (ISBN 0-87027-049-4). Cumberland Pr.
Bush, Patricia J. Drugs, Alcohol, & Sex. 352p. 1980. 12.95 o.s.i. (ISBN 0-399-90080-2, Marek). Putnam Pub Group.
Bush, R. H., jt. ed. see Sanders, C. L.
Bush, Richard. China Briefing, 1982. 125p. 1982. lib. bdg. 14.50x (ISBN 0-86531-516-7); pap. text ed. 6.95x (ISBN 0-86531-517-5). Westview.
Bush, Richard C. The Politics of Cotton Textiles in Kuomintang China, 1927-1937: China During the Interregnum 1911-1949, the Economy & Society. Myers, Ramon H., ed. LC 80-8836. 360p. 1982. lib. bdg. 30.00 (ISBN 0-8240-4691-9). Garland Pub.
Bush, Richard C. & Townsend, James R. The People's Republic of China: A Basic Handbook. 3rd, rev. ed. (Illus.). 114p. (Orig.). 1982. pap. text ed. 4.50x (ISBN 0-936876-16-6). Learn Res Intl Stud.
Bush, Richard C., jt. ed. see Townsend, James R.
Bush, Richard C., et al. Religious Word. 1982. text ed. 21.95 (ISBN 0-02-317480-3). Macmillan.
Bush, Richardc., jt. ed. see Oxnam, Robert B.
Bush, Robin. The Book of Wellington. 1981. 39.50x o.p. (ISBN 0-686-79154-1, Pub. by Barracuda England). State Mutual Bk.
Bush, Ronald F. Retailing Simulation. 160p. 1983. pap. text ed. 8.50 scp (ISBN 0-06-041105-8, HarpC); instr's. manual avail. (ISBN 0-06-361070-1); tape or deck avail. Har-Row.
Bush, Ronald F., jt. auth. see Brobst, Bob.
Bush, Ronald F. & Hunt, Shelby D., eds. Marketing Theory: Philosophy of Science Perspectives Proceedings. LC 82-6747. (Illus.). 315p. (Orig.). 1982. pap. text ed. 24.00 (ISBN 0-87757-159-7). Am Mktg.
Bush, Russ & Nettles, Tom. Baptists & the Bible. LC 80-11694. 1980. 14.95 (ISBN 0-8024-0466-9). Moody.
Bush, Sargent, Jr. The Writings of Thomas Hooker: Spiritual Adventure in Two Worlds. LC 79-5404. 400p. 1980. 25.00 (ISBN 0-299-08070-6). U of Wis Pr.
Bush, Wilma J. & Giles, Marian T. Aids to Psycholinguistic Teaching. 2nd ed. (Special Education Ser.). 1977. text ed. 22.95 (ISBN 0-675-08525-X). Merrill.
Bush, Wilma J. & Waugh, Kenneth. Diagnosing Learning Disabilities. (Illus.). 448p. 1976. text ed. 19.50 (ISBN 0-675-08612-4). Merrill.
Bush, Wilma J. & Waugh, Kenneth W. Diagnosing Learning Problems. 3rd ed. 480p. 1982. pap. text ed. 20.95 (ISBN 0-675-09822-X). Additional Supplements May Be Obtained From Publisher. Merrill.
Busha, Charles H., ed. A Library Science Research Reader & Bibliographic Guide. LC 80-22507. 201p. 1981. lib. bdg. 23.50 (ISBN 0-87287-237-8). Libs Unl.
Bush-Brown, Albert. Skidmore, Owings & Merrill: Architecture & Urbanism, 1974-1982. (Illus.). 400p. 1983. 49.95 (ISBN 0-8038-0401-6). Architectural.
Bushey, Jerry. The Barge Book. (Illus.). 32p. (gr. 1-4). 1983. lib. bdg. 7.95g (ISBN 0-87614-205-6). Carolrhoda Bks.
--Building a Fire Truck. LC 81-6182. (Illus.). 32p. (gr. k-4). 1981. PLB 7.95g (ISBN 0-87614-170-X, AACR2). Carolrhoda Bks.
Bushkovitch, Paul. The Merchants of Moscow, Fifteen Eighty to Sixteen Fifty. LC 79-14491. (Illus.). 1980. 29.95 (ISBN 0-521-22589-2). Cambridge U Pr.
Bushman, Ann S. & Bushman, Robert W. Your Weight Problem Solved Forever: A Powerful New Method of Weight Control. LC 82-4858. 150p. 1982. pap. 9.85 (ISBN 0-9608232-1-2). Weight Control.
Bushman, Claudia L. A Good Poor Man's Wife: Being a Chronicle of Harriet Hanson Robinson & Her Family in Nineteenth Century New England. LC 80-54470. 292p. 1981. 18.00x (ISBN 0-87451-193-3). U Pr of New Eng.
Bushman, John C., et al, eds. Read & Write. 3rd ed. 1972. pap. text ed. 12.50 scp o.p. (ISBN 0-06-041101-5, HarpC); ans. bklet avail. o.p. (ISBN 0-06-361071-X). Har-Row.
Bushman, Robert W., jt. auth. see Bushman, Ann S.
Bushman, Tanisse, ed. see Leonard, Anne & Terrell, John.
Bushnell, David. Santander Regime in Gran Colombia. LC 78-100248. Repr. of 1954 ed. lib. bdg. 18.00x (ISBN 0-8371-2981-8, BUSR). Greenwood.
Bushnell, David S. Priorities for Community Colleges: Organizing for Change. 1973. 14.95 o.p. (ISBN 0-07-009311-3, G). McGraw.
--Training for New Technology. (Work in America Institute Studies in Productivity). 1983. 35.00 (ISBN 0-08-029508-8). Pergamon.
Bushnell, Horace. Views of Christian Nurture & Subjects Related Thereto. LC 74-23297. 260p. 1975. Repr. of 1847 ed. lib. bdg. 32.00x (ISBN 0-8201-1147-3). Schol Facsimiles.
Bushnell, O. A. Ka'a'awa: A Novel About Hawaii in the 1850's. LC 72-83490. 350p. 1972. 10.00 (ISBN 0-8248-0206-3). UH Pr.
--Ka'a'awa: A Novel About Hawaii in the 1850s. LC 72-83490. (Pacific Classics Ser.: No. 7). 506p. 1980. pap. 6.95 (ISBN 0-8248-0729-4). UH Pr.
--Molokai. LC 74-31402. (Pacific Classics Ser.: No. 4). 544p. 1975. pap. 8.95 (ISBN 0-8248-0287-X). UH Pr.
--Return of Lono. (Pacific Classics Ser.: No. 1). 1971. pap. 4.95 (ISBN 0-87022-931-1). UH Pr.
--The Stone of Kannon. LC 79-2563. 1979. 12.95 (ISBN 0-8248-0663-8). UH Pr.
--The Water of Kane. LC 80-5463. 472p. 1980. 12.95 (ISBN 0-8248-0714-6). UH Pr.
Bushnell, Paul E., jt. ed. see Bray, Robert C.
Bushnell, Rick B. Northwest Waters: Harbors. (Illus.). 122p. pap. write for info. (ISBN 0-941368-01-7). Pub Enterprises.
Bushong, Ann B. A Guide to the Lectionary. 1978. pap. 3.00 (ISBN 0-8164-2156-0). Seabury.
Bushong, Stewart C. Radiologic Science for Technologists: Physics, Biology & Protection. 2nd ed. LC 80-19. (Illus.). 504p. 1980. 28.95 (ISBN 0-8016-0928-3). Mosby.
Bushrui, S., ed. Essays & Studies,1982. (Essays & Studies: No. 35). 123p. 1982. text ed. 18.00x (ISBN 0-391-02622-4, 20098). Humanities.
Bushrui, S. B. & Munro, J. M., eds. Images & Memories: A Pictorial Record of the Life & Work of W. B. Yeats. (Illus.). 180p. 1970. text ed. 30.00x (ISBN 0-8156-6063-4, Am U Beirut). Syracuse U Pr.
Bushrui, Suheil. Gibran of Lebanon. 12.00x (ISBN 0-86685-008-2). Intl Bk Ctr.
Busi, F., jt. auth. see Baxendale, J.
Busignani, Alberto, ed. Botticelli. (Art Library Ser.: Vol. 7). (Illus., Orig.). 1968. pap. 2.95 o.s.i. (ISBN 0-448-00450-X, G&D). Putnam Pub Group.
Businer, Joost A., ed. see Lettau, H., et al.
Business Communicaions Staff. Piezo Electricity, GB-064. Date not set. 1100.00 (ISBN 0-89336-324-3). BCC.
Business Communications, ed. Engergy Efficient Reactive Cure Systems, C-026. 1982. 950.00 (ISBN 0-89336-213-1, C-026). BCC.
--Fermentation Products & Processes, C-018R. 1983. 750.00 (ISBN 0-89336-222-0). BCC.
--Industrial Coatings: New Trends, Markets, C-017. 1982. 950.00 (ISBN 0-89336-221-2). BCC.
--Inks & Printing Chemicals: New Developments, C-025. 1982. 975.00 (ISBN 0-89336-212-3). BCC.
--Markets for Desk Top Computers, G-055. 1981. 750.00 (ISBN 0-89336-220-4, G-055). BCC.
--Polishes & Waxes: Shifts & Changes, C-024. Date not set. 950.00 (ISBN 0-89336-211-5). BCC.
--Roadway Maintenance, E-027. 1982. 1000.00 (ISBN 0-89336-224-7). BCC.
Business Communications Co. Plastics vs. Other Pipes, P-043R. 1980. 750.00 (ISBN 0-89336-270-0). BCC.
--Sulfur Specialty Chemicals, C-031. 1983. 1250.00 (ISBN 0-89336-272-7). BCC.
Business Communications Co. Staff. Synfuels: Equipment, Technology, Supplies, Money, People. 1982. 975.00 (ISBN 0-89336-281-6, E-042). BCC.
--Total Energy Systems, E-021. Date not set. 950.00 (ISBN 0-89336-282-4). BCC.
Business Communications Staff. CAD-CAM, GB-063. 1982. 975.00 (ISBN 0-89336-323-5). BCC.
--Commercial Data Base Industry, G-068. 1983. 1500.00 (ISBN 0-89336-320-0). BCC.
--Dynamics of the Financial Information Revolution, G-066. 1983. 1500.00 (ISBN 0-89336-316-2). BCC.
--Electrically Conductive Plastics, P-067. 1982. 1250.00 (ISBN 0-89336-325-1). BCC.
--Electronic Sensors. 1983. 1250.00 (ISBN 0-89336-354-5, G-076). BCC.
--Emerging Local Area Network Business. 1983. 1250.00 (ISBN 0-89336-349-9, G-074). BCC.
--Food Additives: Markets, GA-040. 1983. 1250.00 (ISBN 0-89336-331-6). BCC.
--High Temperature Thermoplastics: P-051. 1983. 1500.00 (ISBN 0-89336-175-5). BCC.
--Mail Delivery: Viable Alternatives, G-015R. 1983. 975.00 (ISBN 0-89336-328-6). BCC.
--Medical Diagnostic Reagents & O Products. 1983. 1250.00 (ISBN 0-89336-352-9, C-045). BCC.
--New Commercial Opportunities in Electrochemistry. 1983. 1500.00 (ISBN 0-89336-351-0, C-044). BCC.
--New Diet, Meal Replacement & Substitute Foods. 1983. 1250.00 (ISBN 0-89336-353-7, GA-052). BCC.
--New Sterilized Foods Markets & Packages, GA-050. 1983. 1250.00 (ISBN 0-89336-322-7). BCC.
--Office of the Future, G-057. 1982. 1250.00 (ISBN 0-89336-321-9). BCC.
--Oil & Gas Field Equipment & Supplies: E-045. 1983. 1250.00 (ISBN 0-89336-295-6). BCC.
--Oil Field Drilling Chemicals: C-034. 1982. cancelled (ISBN 0-89336-297-2). BCC.
--The Plastics Closure Market: P-062. Date not set. 1500.00 (ISBN 0-89336-291-3). BCC.
--Plastics Conference Proceedings, 1982. 1983. 125.00 (ISBN 0-686-84693-1). BCC.
--Plastics in Transportation. 1983. 1000.00 (ISBN 0-686-84702-4, P-069). BCC.
--Plastics Scrap & Regrind. 1983. 1500.00 (ISBN 0-686-84700-8, P-070). BCC.
--Specialty Natural & Health Food Market, GA-037. 1983. 1250.00 (ISBN 0-89336-330-8). BCC.
--Speech Synthesis & Recognition Equipment: G-056. 1982. 975.00 (ISBN 0-89336-299-9). BCC.
--Strategic Materials, GB-062. Date not set. 1250.00 (ISBN 0-89336-332-4, AB-062). BCC.
--Structural Foam. 1982. 1750.00 (ISBN 0-686-84696-6, P-006). BCC.
--Sugar, Sweeteners & Substitutes. 1982. 1250.00 (ISBN 0-89336-091-0, C-005). BCC.
--Synthetic Crystals. 1983. 1250.00 (ISBN 0-89336-350-2, C-039). BCC.
--Tamperproof Packaging. 1983. 1500.00 (ISBN 0-89336-355-3, GB-067). BCC.
--Water Recycling Equipment, Systems: GB-055. Date not set. 950.00 (ISBN 0-89336-303-0). BCC.
Business-Higher Education Forum. Agenda for Business & Higher Education. 1980. 10.50 o.p. (ISBN 0-8268-1443-3). ACE.
Business Week Magazine. The Reindustrialization of America. 1982. 16.50 (ISBN 0-07-009324-5). McGraw.
Business Week Team. The Reindustrialization of America. 1983. pap. 5.95 (ISBN 0-671-45617-2). WSP.
Busing, William R., ed. Intermolecular Forces & Packing in Crystals. pap. 5.00 (ISBN 0-686-60377-X). Polycrystal Bk Serv.
Businger, J. A., jt. auth. see Fleagle, Robert G.
Businger, Joost A., ed. see Dalrymple, Paul, et al.
Businger, Joost A., ed. see Kuhn, M., et al.
Buske, Dorothea. The Last Romantic. LC 78-3966. 1979. 8.95 o.p. (ISBN 0-312-47135-1). St Martin.

Buskirk, Bruce, jt. auth. see Buskirk, Richard.

Buskirk, Kenneth M. Hear Me. LC 79-54949. 102p. (Orig.). 1980. 12.95 (ISBN 0-9603522-1-X); pap. 4.95 (ISBN 0-9603522-0-1). KMB Pubns.

Buskirk, Richard. Your Career: How to Plan It, How to Manage It, How to Change It. 1977. pap. 2.50 (ISBN 0-451-62059-3, ME2059, Ment). NAL.

Buskirk, Richard & Buskirk, Bruce. Retailing. (Marketing Ser.). (Illus.). 1979. text ed. 23.95 (ISBN 0-07-009318-0, C); manual 20.00instr's. (ISBN 0-07-009319-9); wkbk. 8.95 (ISBN 0-07-009323-7). McGraw.

Buskirk, Richard H. Business & Administrative Policy. LC 75-137106. 528p. 1971. 24.00 (ISBN 0-471-12638-1, Pub. by Wiley). Krieger.

Buskirk, Richard H. & Vaughn, Percy J. Managing New Enterprises. LC 75-37999. (Illus.). 400p. 1976. text ed. 15.50 (ISBN 0-8299-0071-3). West Pub.

Buskirk, Robert Van see Van Buskirk, Robert & Bauer, Fred.

Busoni, Ferruccio. Letters to His Wife. Ley, Rosamond, tr. LC 74-34378. (Music Reprint Ser). (Illus.). 319p. 1975. Repr. of 1938 ed. lib. bdg. 29.50 (ISBN 0-306-70732-2). Da Capo.

Busool, A. N. Forty Ahadith: Asqalani. 1981. 4.50 (ISBN 0-686-97860-9). Kazi Pubns.

Buss, Arnold H. Psychology: Behavior in Perspective. 2nd ed. LC 77-11676. 575p. 1978. text ed. 26.50 (ISBN 0-471-12646-2). study guide, 174 p. 11.95x (ISBN 0-471-03060-0). Wiley.

--Psychopathology. 483p. 1966. text ed. 35.95 (ISBN 0-471-12642-X). Wiley.

Buss, Arnold H. & Plomin, Robert. A Temperament Theory of Personality Development. LC 80-11395. 268p. 1983. Repr. of 1975 ed. lib. bdg. write for info. (ISBN 0-89874-138-6). Krieger.

Buss, Arnold M. & Plomin, Robert. A Temperament Theory of Personality Development. LC 74-32442. (Behavior Ser.). 256p. 1975. 24.95 o.p. (ISBN 0-471-12649-7, Pub. by Wiley-Interscience). Wiley.

Buss, D., jt. auth. see Melen, R.

Buss, Dennis, jt. ed. see Melen, Roger.

Buss, Philip H. & Mollo, Andrew. Hitler's Germanic Legions: Illustrated History of Western European Legions with the SS, 1941-3. (Illus.). 1978. 26.95x o.p. (ISBN 0-8464-0486-9). Beekman Pubs.

Buss, Reinhard J. The Klabautermann of the Northern Seas: An Analysis of the Protective Spirit of Ships & Sailors in the Context of Popular Belief, Christian Legend & Indo-European Mythology. (U. C. Publ. in Folklore Studies: Vol. 25). pap. 13.00x (ISBN 0-520-09399-2). U of Cal Pr.

Buss, Terry, jt. auth. see Redburn, F. Stevens.

Buss, Terry F. & Redburn, F. Stevens. Shutdown at Youngstown: Public Policy for Mass Unemployment. (Urban Public Policy Ser.). 176p. 1982. 39.50x (ISBN 0-87395-646-X); pap. 10.95 (ISBN 0-87395-647-8). State U NY Pr.

Buss, Terry F., jt. ed. see Redburn, F. Stevens.

Buss, William G. & Goldstein, Stephen R. Standards Relating to Schools & Education. LC 77-1741. (IJA-ABA Juvenile Justice Standards Project Ser.). 182p. 1982. prof ref 20.00x (ISBN 0-88410-241-6); pap. 10.00x (ISBN 0-88410-841-4). Ballinger Pub.

Bussabarger, Robert F. & Stack, Frank, eds. Selection of Etchings by John Sloan. LC 67-22228. (Illus.). 62p. 1967. pap. 12.00x (ISBN 0-8262-0059-1). U of Mo Pr.

Bussagli, Mario. Indian Minatures. 1976. 8.50x o.p. (ISBN 0-333-90152-5). South Asia Bks.

Bussard, R. W. & De Lauer, R. D. Fundamentals of Nuclear Flight. 1965. text ed. 26.95 o.p. (ISBN 0-07-009300-8, C). McGraw.

Busse, Ewald & Sussex, James N., eds. The Working Papers of the 1975 Conference on Education of Psychiatrists. 432p. 1976. 12.50 o.p. (ISBN 0-685-83185-X, P236-0). Am Psychiatric.

Busse, Ewald E. Cerebral Manifestations of Episodic Cardiac Dyserythmias. (International Congress Ser.: No. 489). (Proceedings). 1979. 47.75 (ISBN 0-444-90098-5). Elsevier.

Busse, Ewald W. & Pfeiffer, Eric. Mental Illness in Later Life. 301p. 1973. casebound 12.00 o.p. (ISBN 0-685-38355-5, P188-1); pap. 9.00 o.p. (ISBN 0-685-38356-3, 188). Am Psychiatric.

Busse, Ewald W., et al, eds. see Rosenfeld, Anne H.

Bussell, Harold L. Unholy Devotion: Why Cults Lure Christians. 160p. 1983. pap. 4.95 (ISBN 0-310-37251-8). Zondervan.

Busselle, Michael. The Complete Book of Photographing People. 1980. 19.95 o.p. (ISBN 0-671-41257-4). S&S.

--The Photographer's Weekend Book: One Hundred One Creative Projects for the Amateur Photographer. (Illus.). 224p. 1982. 14.50 (ISBN 0-8174-5408-X, Amphoto). Watson-Guptill.

Bussey, Lynn E. The Economic Analysis of Industrial Projects. (International Ser. in Industrial & System Engineering). (Illus.). 1978. ref. 29.95 (ISBN 0-13-223388-6). P-H.

Busshoff, Ludger. Das Zehn Bildungsjahr Unter Bildungspolitischem Aspekt. 234p. (Ger.). 1982. write for info. (ISBN 3-8204-7044-1). P Lang Pubs.

Bussi, F. L' Antifonario Graduale della Basilica di S. Antonio in Piacenza: Saggio Storico Critico, Sec. XII. (Illus.). 1977. Repr. of 1956 ed. 28.00 o.s.i. (ISBN 90-6027-189-0, Pub. by Frits Knuf Netherlands). Pendragon NY.

--Catalogo del Fondo Musicale dell'Archivo del Duomo di Piacenza. 1967. wrappers 31.00 o.s.i. (ISBN 90-6027-191-2, Pub. by Frits Knuf Netherlands). Pendragon NY.

--Umanita e Arte di Gerolamo Parabosco: Madrigalista, Organista e Poligrafo, 2 vols. (Illus.). 278p. 1961. 34.00 o.s.i. (ISBN 90-6027-190-4, Pub. by Frits Knuf Netherlands). Pendragon NY.

Bussink, Willem & Davies, David. Poverty & the Development of Human Resources: Regional Perspective. (Working Paper: No. 406). iii, 193p. 1980. 5.00 (ISBN 0-686-36133-4, WP-0406). World Bank.

Bussmann, W. D., jt. ed. see Just, H.

Busson, Paul, jt. auth. see Meyrink, Gustav.

Bussy, Carvel De. Conferences De Litterature Francaise: XVIIIe Siecle. LC 78-66098. (Fr.). 1979. pap. text ed. 15.00 (ISBN 0-9602260-0-1). C de Bussy.

Bustad, Leo K., jt. ed. see Goldman, Marvin.

Bustanoby, Andre. The Readymade Family: How to be a Stepparent & Survive. 160p. (Orig.). 1982. pap. 5.95 (ISBN 0-310-45361-5). Zondervan.

Busteed, Mervyn, ed. Developments in Political Geography. Date not set. price not set (ISBN 0-12-148420-3). Acad Pr.

Bustin, Dillon. If You Don't Outdie Me: The Legacy of Brown County. LC 82-47784. (Midland Bks.: No. 305). 160p. (Orig.). 1983. 20.00 (ISBN 0-253-13916-3); pap. 12.95 (ISBN 0-253-20305-8). Ind U Pr.

Bustos-Fernandez, Luis, ed. Colon: Structure & Function. (Topics in Gastroenterology Ser.). 326p. 1983. 39.50x (ISBN 0-306-41056-7, Plenum Pr). Plenum Pub.

Busu, Fatimah. Ombak Bukan Biru. (Karyawan Malaysia Ser.). (Malay.). 1979. pap. text ed. 5.50x o.p. (ISBN 0-686-60457-1, 00350). Heinemann Ed.

Busvine, J. R. Anthropod Vectors of Diseases. (Studies in Biology: No. 55). 72p. 1975. pap. text ed. 8.95 (ISBN 0-7131-2501-2). E Arnold.

Busvine, James R. Insects & Hygiene. 3rd ed. 420p. 1980. 58.00x (ISBN 0-412-15910-4, Pub. by Chapman & Hall England). Methuen Inc.

Buswell, Robert E., Jr. The Korean Approach to Zen: The Collected Works of Chinul. LC 82-23873. 540p. 1983. text ed. 29.95x (ISBN 0-8248-0785-5). UH Pr.

Busza, Andrzej. Astrologer in the Underground. Boraks, Jagna & Bullock, Micheal, trs. from Polish & Eng. LC 70-108331. 61p. 1970. 6.95 o.p. (ISBN 0-8214-0073-8). Ohio U Pr.

Butch, Suzanna, ed. Clinically Significant & Insignificant Antibodies. 70p. 1979. 11.00 (ISBN 0-914404-49-0). Am Assn Blood.

Butchart, Ian, jt. auth. see Fothergill, Richard.

Butchart, Ronald E. Northern Schools, Southern Blacks, & Reconstruction: Freedmen's Education, 1862-1875. LC 79-8949. (Contributions in American History: No. 87). (Illus.). xiv, 309p. 1980. lib. bdg. 29.95 (ISBN 0-313-22073-5, BNS/). Greenwood.

Butcher, D. G. & Parnell, A. C. Smoke Control in Fire Safety Design. 1979. 39.95x (ISBN 0-419-11190-5, Pub. by E & FN Spon). Methuen Inc.

Butcher, David. Official Publications in Britain. 160p. 1983. 18.50 (ISBN 0-85157-351-7, Pub. by Bingley England). Shoe String.

Butcher, Grace. Rumors of Ecstasy, Rumors of Death. 64p. (Orig.). 1981. pap. 6.95 (ISBN 0-935306-13-7). Barnwood Pr.

Butcher, H. J. & Lomax, D. E., eds. Readings in Human Intelligence. 1972. 13.95x o.p. (ISBN 0-416-60260-6); pap. 12.95x. Methuen Inc.

Butcher, Irene, jt. ed. see Rudkin, Anthony.

Butcher, James N., jt. auth. see Kendall, Philip C.

Butcher, James N. & Spielberger, Charles D., eds. Advances in Personality Assesment, Vol. 2. 256p. 1982. text ed. 24.95 (ISBN 0-89859-216-X). L Erlbaum Assocs.

Butcher, Philip, ed. The Ethnic Image of Modern American Literature: 1900-1950, Vols. 1 & 2. 1983. 14.95 ea.; Set. 27.50 (ISBN 0-88258-110-4). Vol. 1 (ISBN 0-88258-119-8). Vol. 2 (ISBN 0-88258-120-1). Howard U Pr.

--The Minority Presence in American Literature 1600-1900, 2 vols. LC 77-5687. 1977. Vol. 1. 12.95 (ISBN 0-88258-101-5); Vol. 2. 11.95 (ISBN 0-88258-102-3); Vol. 1. pap. 7.95 (ISBN 0-88258-061-2); Vol. 2. pap. 6.95 (ISBN 0-88258-100-7). Howard U Pr.

Butcher, Phillip A., ed. see Wiener, Harvey S.

Butcher, S. H. see Demosthenes.

Butcher, S. H., tr. see Aristotle.

Buteaux, Paul. Strategy, Doctrine, & the Politcs of Alliance: Theatre Nuclear Force Modernization in NATO. Replica ed. 150p. 1982. softcover 17.00 (ISBN 0-86531-940-5). Westview.

Butel, Jane. Chili Madness. LC 80-51617. (Passionate Cookbook Ser.). 96p. 1980. 7.95 (ISBN 0-89480-135-X); pap. 4.95 (ISBN 0-89480-134-1). Workman Pub.

--Finger Lickin', Rib Stickin', Great Tastin' Hot & Spicy Barbecue. LC 81-43785. (Passionate Cookbook Ser.). (Illus.). 96p. 1982. 8.95 (ISBN 0-89480-207-0); pap. 4.95 (ISBN 0-89480-208-9). Workman Pub.

--Jane Butel's Freezer Cookbook: How to Use Your Freezer for All It's Worth. 256p. 1977. 8.95 o.p. (ISBN 0-698-10727-6, Coward). Putnam Pub Group.

Butenandt, O., jt. ed. see Laron, Z.

Butenschon, Sine & Borchgrevink, Hans. Voice & Song. LC 81-38464. 80p. 1982. 19.95 (ISBN 0-521-28011-7). Cambridge U Pr.

Butera, M. C., et al. College English: Grammar & Style. 1967. text ed. 16.35 (ISBN 0-07-009320-2, G); instructor's key 8.75 (ISBN 0-07-009321-0); test free (ISBN 0-07-009322-9). McGraw.

Butikov, Georgy, compiled by. St. Isacc's Cathedral, Leningrad. Andrews, Daniel & Andrews, Judith, trs. (Illus.). 164p. 1981. 14.95 (ISBN 0-89893-078-2). CDP.

Butkovsky-Hewitt, Anna. With Gurdjieff in St. Petersburg. 1978. 8.95 (ISBN 0-87728-387-7). Weiser.

Butler, A. R. & Perkins, J. M., eds. Organic Reaction Mechanism. Incl. Vol. 9. 1973. 96.95 o.p. (ISBN 0-471-12690-X); Vol. 10. 1974. 131.95 o.p. (ISBN 0-471-12693-4); Reprint A. o. p. 7.50 o.p. (ISBN 0-471-01531-8); Reprint B. o. p. 8.95 o.p. (ISBN 0-471-01532-6); Vol. 11. 1975. 127.50 o.p. (ISBN 0-471-01864-3); Vol. 12. 1976. 125.50 o.p. (ISBN 0-471-99523-1). LC 66-23143. 1975-1978 (Pub. by Wiley-Interscience). Wiley.

Butler, Alan & Stem, Thad, Jr. Senator Sam Ervin's Best Stories. LC 73-86470. 1973. 8.95 (ISBN 0-87716-052-X, Pub. by Moore Pub Co); pap. 5.50 (ISBN 0-686-66961-4). F Apple.

Butler, Annie L. Early Childhood Education: Planning & Administering Programs. 249p. 1974. pap. text ed. 6.95x (ISBN 0-442-20897-9). Van Nos Reinhold.

Butler, Barbara M. The Evolution of the Black Nurse Midwife. 64p. 1983. 5.50 (ISBN 0-682-49966-8). Exposition.

Butler, Beverly. The Wind & Me. LC 70-162612. (Illus.). (gr. 1 up). 1971. 4.95 o.p. (ISBN 0-396-06380-2). Dodd.

Butler, Bill. Dictionary of the Tarot. LC 74-9230. (Illus.). 1977. 7.95 (ISBN 0-8052-3557-4); pap. 6.50 (ISBN 0-8052-0559-4). Schocken.

Butler, Blaine, jt. auth. see Smith, Ralph.

Butler, Brett & Martin, Susan K., eds. Library Automation Two. LC 75-20168. 200p. 1975. pap. text ed. 9.00 (ISBN 0-8389-3152-9). ALA.

Butler, Charles. Principles of Musik, in Singing & Setting. LC 68-13273. (Music Ser). 1970. Repr. of 1636 ed. lib. bdg. 19.50 (ISBN 0-306-70939-2). Da Capo.

Butler, Clark. G. W. F. Hegel. (World Authors Ser.). 1977. lib. bdg. 15.95 (ISBN 0-8057-6298-1, Twayne). G K Hall.

Butler, D. H. & Wren, F. L. Teaching of Secondary Mathematics. 5th ed. (Curriculum & Methods in Education). 1970. text ed. 17.95 o.p. (ISBN 0-07-009330-X, C). McGraw.

Butler, David. Lusitania. 576p. Date not set. 17.95 (ISBN 0-394-52809-3). Random.

Butler, David & Kavanagh, Dennis. The British General Election of October 1974. LC 75-21706. 350p. 1975. 27.50 (ISBN 0-312-10255-0). St Martin.

--The British General Elections of 1979. 1982. text ed. 50.00x (ISBN 0-8419-5081-4). Holmes & Meier.

Butler, David & Kitzinger, Uwe. The Nineteen Seventy-Five Referendum. LC 76-16701. 1976. 27.50x (ISBN 0-312-57435-5). St Martin.

Butler, David & Stokes, Donald. Political Change in Britain: The Evolution of Electoral Choice. 2nd ed. LC 75-29935. 300p. 1976. 27.50 (ISBN 0-312-62160-4); pap. 8.95 (ISBN 0-312-62195-7). St Martin.

Butler, David, jt. auth. see Miles, Keith.

Butler, David, ed. Coalitions in British Politics. LC 77-17791. 1978. 22.50 (ISBN 0-312-14503-9). St Martin.

Butler, David E. & King, A. British General Election of 1966. 1966. 25.00 o.p. (ISBN 0-312-10150-3). St Martin.

--British General Election of 1970. 350p. 1971. 25.00 o.p. (ISBN 0-312-10185-6). St Martin.

Butler, David E. & Sloman, Anne, eds. British Political Facts: Nineteen-Hundred to Nineteen Seventy-Four. 4th rev. ed. LC 74-24816. 352p. 1975. 35.00 (ISBN 0-312-10465-0). St Martin.

Butler, Dorothy. Cushla & Her Books. LC 79-25695. (Illus.). 128p. 1980. 15.00 (ISBN 0-87675-279-2); pap. 12.50 (ISBN 0-87675-283-0). Horn Bk.

Butler, Dorothy & Clay, Marie. Reading Begins at Home: Preparing Children for Reading Before They Go to School. LC 82-6172. (Illus.). 44p. 1982. pap. text ed. 6.00x. Heinemann Ed.

Butler, Dougal & Tengrove, Chris. Full Moon: The Amazing Rock & Roll Life of the Late Keith Moon. 269p. 1981. pap. 6.95 (ISBN 0-688-00759-7). Quill NY.

Butler, E. M. The Fortunes of Faust. 1979. 49.50 (ISBN 0-521-22562-0); pap. 12.95 (ISBN 0-521-29552-1). Cambridge U Pr.

--The Myth of the Magus. LC 78-73950. 1979. 39.50 (ISBN 0-521-22564-7); pap. 11.95 (ISBN 0-521-29554-8). Cambridge U Pr.

--The Myth of the Magus. 283p. 1982. Repr. of 1948 ed. lib. bdg. 65.00 (ISBN 0-89984-084-1). Century Bookbindery.

--Ritual Magic. LC 80-19324. 329p. 1980. Repr. of 1971 ed. lib. bdg. 12.95x (ISBN 0-89370-601-9). Borgo Pr.

--Ritual Magic. LC 78-73949. 1979. 39.50 (ISBN 0-521-22563-9); pap. 11.95 (ISBN 0-521-29553-X). Cambridge U Pr.

Butler, Edgar. An Industry Survey of the Need for a Federal Grant-Assisted Geothermal Demonstration Power Plant. (Illus.). 36p. 1978. pap. 3.50 o.p. (ISBN 0-934412-75-8). Geothermal.

Butler, Eliza M. Heinrich Heine: A Biography. LC 70-106684. Repr. of 1956 ed. lib. bdg. 15.75x (ISBN 0-8371-3607-5, BUHH). Greenwood.

Butler, Eric, jt. auth. see Mills, Roger.

Butler, Eugenia, et al. An Auto-Instructional Text in Correct Writing, Form B. 2nd ed. 1980. pap. text ed. 11.95x (ISBN 0-669-02484-8); answer key 1.95 (ISBN 0-669-02486-4). Heath.

--Correct Writing, Form Three. 3rd ed. 1983. pap. text ed. 11.95x (ISBN 0-669-02487-2); answer key 1.95 (ISBN 0-669-02488-0). Heath.

--Correct Writing, Form Two. 2nd ed. 1978. pap. text ed. 11.95 (ISBN 0-669-01627-6); answer key 1.95 (ISBN 0-669-01629-2). Heath.

--An Auto-Intructional Text in Correct Writing, Form A. 2nd ed. 416p. 1976. pap. text ed. 11.95 (ISBN 0-669-95844-1); answer key 1.95 (ISBN 0-669-96511-1). Heath.

--Correct Writing Form. 2nd ed. 384p. 1976. pap. text ed. 11.95 (ISBN 0-669-99655-6); answers 1.95 (ISBN 0-669-99663-7). Heath.

Butler, Eugenia W. & Hickman, Mary A. Correct Writing. 3rd ed. 384p. 1983. pap. 11.95 (ISBN 0-669-05437-2). Heath.

Butler, Francelia. Strange Critical Fortunes of Shakespeare's Timon of Athens. (Illus.). 1966. 5.50x o.p. (ISBN 0-8138-1706-4). Iowa St U Pr.

Butler, Francelia & Pickering, Samuel, Jr. Children's Literature: Annual of the Modern Language Association Division on Children's Literature & the Children's Literature Association, No. 11. LC 79-66588. (Illus.). 224p. 1983. text ed. 20.00x (ISBN 0-300-02991-8); pap. text ed. 8.95x (ISBN 0-300-02992-6). Yale U Pr.

Butler, Francelia, et al, eds. Children's Literature, 6 vols. Brockman, Bennett & Sheidley, William E. Incl. Vol. 1. 1972. (ISBN 0-87722-082-4); pap. (ISBN 0-87722-081-6); Vol. 2. 1973. (ISBN 0-87722-080-8); pap. (ISBN 0-87722-079-4); Vol. 3. 1974. (ISBN 0-87722-078-6); pap. (ISBN 0-87722-077-8); Vol. 4. 1975. (ISBN 0-87722-042-5); pap. (ISBN 0-87722-076-X); Vol. 5. 1976. (ISBN 0-87722-069-7); pap. (ISBN 0-87722-070-0); Vol. 6. 1977. (ISBN 0-87722-104-9); pap. (ISBN 0-87722-105-7). LC 75-21550. 17.95 ea.; pap. 10.95 ea. Temple U Pr.

--Annual of the Modern Language Association Group on Children's Literature & the Children's Literature Association, Vol. 8. (Illus.). vi, 212p. 1980. 30.00x (ISBN 0-300-02452-5); pap. 9.95x (ISBN 0-300-02491-6). Yale U Pr.

Butler, G. & Ison, H. C. Corrosion & Its Prevention in Waters. LC 76-30515. 310p. 1978. Repr. of 1966 ed. 18.00 (ISBN 0-88275-515-3). Krieger.

Butler, G. C., ed. Principles of Ecotoxicology. LC 78-4045. (Scope Reports Ser.: No. 12). 350p. 1978. 42.00 o.p. (ISBN 0-471-99638-6, Pub. by Wiley-Interscience). Wiley.

Butler, G. D. Introduction to Community Recreation. 5th ed. 1975. text ed. 28.00 (ISBN 0-07-009361-X, C). McGraw.

Butler, George, jt. auth. see Gaines, Charles.

Butler, George D. Playgrounds: Their Administration & Operation. 3rd ed. (Illus.). 513p. 1960. 30.95 (ISBN 0-471-07086-6). Wiley.

--Recreation Areas, Their Design & Equipment. 2nd ed. (Illus.). 174p. 1958. 29.95 (ISBN 0-471-07087-4). Wiley.

Butler, Gwendoline. Albion Walk. 336p. 1982. 14.95 (ISBN 0-698-11172-9, Coward). Putnam Pub Group.

--Meadowsweet. LC 77-1726. 1977. 8.95 o.p. (ISBN 0-698-10824-8, Coward). Putnam Pub Group.

--The Red Staircase. LC 78-31665. 1979. 11.95 o.p. (ISBN 0-698-10981-3, Coward). Putnam Pub Group.

Butler, H. E., ed. see Suetonius.

Butler, Herbert J., ed. Antique Auto Body Leather Work for the Restorer. LC 82-62713. (Vintage Craft Ser.: No. 3). (Illus.). 1969. pap. 6.00 (ISBN 0-911160-03-5). Post-Era.

Butler, Ian S. & Grosse, Arthur E. Relevant Problems for Chemical Principles. 3rd ed. 1979. text ed. 13.95 (ISBN 0-8053-1587-X). Benjamin-Cummings.

Butler, Ira. The Little Lost Reindeer. 1982. 5.95 (ISBN 0-533-05469-9). Vantage.

Butler, Ivan. Trials of Brian Donald Hume. LC 76-4366. (Celebrated Trials Ser.). 1977. 5.95 o.p. (ISBN 0-7153-7118-5). David & Charles.

Butler, J. K., ed. Semiconductor Injection Lasers. LC 79-79615. 1980. 40.95 (ISBN 0-87942-129-0). Inst Electrical.

Butler, Jack. Hawk Gumbo & Other Stories. LC 82-70167. (Illus.). 1983. 14.95 (ISBN 0-935304-34-7); pap. 6.95 (ISBN 0-935304-35-5). August Hse.

Butler, James L. The Master. 1982. 9.95 (ISBN 0-8062-1899-1). Carlton.

Butler, Jeffrey E., jt. auth. see Martello, William E.

Butler, Jerry. Swift to Hear, Slow to Speak. 1975. pap. 4.75 (ISBN 0-89137-511-2). Quality Pubns.

Butler, Jim. There is a Time. 1982. 6.95 (ISBN 0-533-05294-7). Vantage.

Butler, Joan & Walker, Katherine S. Ballet for Boys & Girls. (Illus.). (gr. 3-7). 1979. 9.95x (ISBN 0-13-055574-6). P-H.

Butler, John. Family Doctors & Public Policy: A Study of Manpower Distribution. (International Library of Social Policy). 1973. 22.95x (ISBN 0-7100-7640-1). Routledge & Kegan.

Butler, John T. Elements of Administration for Building Students. new ed. (Illus.). 221p. 1971. pap. text ed. 19.50x (ISBN 0-392-01119-0, LTB). Sportshelf.

Butler, Joseph. Five Sermons. Darwell, Stephen, ed. (HPC Philosophical Classics Ser.). 88p. 1983. pap. text ed. 3.95 (ISBN 0-915145-61-8). Hackett Pub.

Butler, Joseph H. Economic Geography: Spatial & Environmental Aspects of Economic Activity. LC 80-14542. 402p. 1980. 27.95 (ISBN 0-471-12681-0). Wiley.

Butler, Katherine G. & Wallach, Geraldine P. Language Disorders & Learning Disabilities, Topics in Language Disorders; Vol. 1, No.1. LC 82-1665. 118p. 1982. 17.50 (ISBN 0-89443-688-0). Aspen Systems.

Butler, L. D. Exercises in English for the Spanish Speaker. 1972. 3.20 o.p. (ISBN 0-07-090852-4, W). McGraw.

Butler, L. J. Thomas Hardy. LC 77-23532. (British Authors Ser.). 1978. 24.95 (ISBN 0-521-21743-1); pap. 9.50 (ISBN 0-521-29271-9). Cambridge U Pr.

Butler, Lance S., ed. Thomas Hardy: After Fifty Years. LC 77-3057. 153p. 1977. 19.50x o.p. (ISBN 0-87471-980-1). Rowman.

Butler, Lindley S. Rockingham County: A Brief History. 92p. 1982. pap. 2.00 (ISBN 0-86526-198-9). NC Archives.

Butler, Lord. Jawaharlal Nehru. 1967. 1.95 (ISBN 0-521-04404-9). Cambridge U Pr.

Butler, Lucy. Diana: The Fairy Tale Princess. (YA) (gr. 5-12). 1983. 8.95. Summit Bks.

Butler, M. C. Esperanto-English. 10.00 o.p. (ISBN 0-685-85558-9). Heinman.

Butler, Margaret. The Lion of Christ. LC 76-58024. 320p. 1977. 9.95 o.p. (ISBN 0-698-10820-5, Coward). Putnam Pub Group.

Butler, Marylin. Half Past Sunset. 78p. (Orig.). 1983. 12.95 (ISBN 0-939208-00-8); pap. 7.95 (ISBN 0-939208-01-6). Horizon.

Butler, Matilda & Paisley, William J. Knowledge Utilization Systems in Education. (Illus.). 320p. 1983. 27.50 (ISBN 0-8039-1944-1). Sage.

Butler, Matilda & Paisley, William, eds. Women & the Mass Media: Sourcebook for Research & Action. LC 79-16271. 432p. 1980. text ed. 34.95 (ISBN 0-87705-409-6); pap. text ed. 14.95 (ISBN 0-87705-419-3). Human Sci Pr.

Butler, Maureen, ed. see Emig, Janet.

Butler, Natalie S. Dwight C. Sturges: Etcher of an Era. LC 74-20198. 1974. 12.95 (ISBN 0-87027-154-7); pap. 7.95 (ISBN 0-87027-155-5). Cumberland Pr.

Butler, Pamela E. Self-Assertion for Women. rev. ed. LC 80-8904. (Illus.). 320p. (Orig.). 1981. pap. 7.64i (ISBN 0-06-250121-6, CN4011, HarpR). Har-Row.

Butler, Paul. Isaiah, Vol. III. (The Bible Study Textbook Ser.). (Illus.). 1978. 14.30 o.s.i. (ISBN 0-89900-022-3). College Pr Pub.

--Luke. LC 81-68817. (Bible Study Textbook Ser.). 512p. 1981. 17.50 (ISBN 0-89900-062-2). College Pr Pub.

Butler, Perry. Gladstone: Church, State & Tractarianism, a Study of His Religious Ideas & Attitudes, 1809-1859. (Oxford Historical Monographs). 1982. 42.00x (ISBN 0-19-821890-7). Oxford U Pr.

Butler, Pierce. Laurel Hill & Later: The Record of a Teacher. (Illus.). 10.00 (ISBN 0-88289-386-6). Pelican.

--A Malady. 106p. 1982. pap. 5.95 (ISBN 0-905441-48-6, Pub. by Salem Hse Ltd.). Merrimack Bk Serv.

--Origin of Printing in Europe. 1940. 10.00x o.s.i. (ISBN 0-226-08605-4). U of Chicago Pr.

Butler, R., ed. Rodin in Perspective. 1980. 12.95 (ISBN 0-13-782326-6, Spec); pap. 5.95 (ISBN 0-13-782318-5, Spec). P-H.

Butler, R. A. The Art of the Possible. (Illus.). 288p. 1983. Repr. of 1971 ed. 24.95 (ISBN 0-241-10896-9, Pub. by Hamish Hamilton England). David & Charles.

Butler, R. R., jt. auth. see Higgins, P. C.

Butler, Robert A. Handbook of Practical Writing. (Orig.). 1978. pap. text ed. 7.20 (ISBN 0-07-009341-5, G). McGraw.

Butler, Robert B. Architectural & Engineering Calculations Manual. (Illus.). 384p. 1983. 19.95 (ISBN 0-07-009363-6, P&RB). McGraw.

Butler, Robert E., jt. auth. see Rappaport, Donald.

Butler, Robert N. & Lewis, Myrna I. Aging & Mental Health. (Medical Library). (Illus.). 400p. 1983. pap. price not set (ISBN 0-452-25405-1, 1002-8). Mosby.

--Love & Sex After Sixty: A Guide for Men & Women in Their Later Years. 1977. pap. 2.95i (ISBN 0-06-080423-5, P423, PL). Har-Row.

--Sex After Sixty: A Guide for Men & Women for Their Later Years. 1977. lib. bdg. 9.95 o.p. (ISBN 0-8161-6507-6, Large Print Bks). G K Hall.

Butler, Robert O. The Alleys of Eden. 256p. 1983. pap. 2.95 (ISBN 0-345-30774-7). Ballantine.

Butler, Rohan. Choiseul: Vol. 1; Father & Son, 1719-1754. (Illus.). 1981. 125.00x (ISBN 0-19-822509-1). Oxford U Pr.

Butler, Ruth L., ed. Guide to the Hispanic American Historical Review, 1918-1945. pap. 14.00 o.s.i. (ISBN 0-527-36700-1). Kraus Repr.

Butler, Samuel. Erewhon. (English Library). 272p. 1970. pap. 3.95 (ISBN 0-14-043057-1). Penguin.

--Life & Habit. 320p. 1982. 30.00x (ISBN 0-7045-0425-1, Pub. by Wildwood House). State Mutual Bk.

--Prose Observations. De Quehen, Hugh, ed. (English Texts Ser.). (Illus.). 1979. text ed. 74.00x (ISBN 0-19-812728-6). Oxford U Pr.

--Way of All Flesh. pap. 2.95 (ISBN 0-451-51695-8, CE1695, Sig Classics). NAL.

Butler, Trent C. Layman's Bible Book Commentary: Isaiah, Vol. 10. LC 80-68890. 1983. 4.75 (ISBN 0-8054-1180-1). Broadman.

Butler, W. E. Collected Legislation of the U. S. S. R, 7 binders. Incl. Union Republic Legislation, 1 binder; Constitutions, 2 binders; U. S. S. R, 4 binders. LC 78-24391. 1980. Set. 680.00 (ISBN 0-379-20450-9). Oceana.

--The Soviet Legal System: Selected Contemporary Legislation & Documents. LC 78-2419. (Parker School Studies in Foreign & Comparative Law). 733p. 1978. 45.00 (ISBN 0-379-00791-6). Oceana.

Butler, W. H., jt. ed. see Newberne, Paul M.

Butler, William. How to Read the Aura, Practice Psychometry, Telepathy, & Clairvoyancy. 335p. 2.95 (ISBN 0-446-82751-7). Inner Tradit.

--How to Read the Aura, Practice Psychometry, Telepathy & Clairvoyance. (Warner Destiny Book). (Orig.). 1978. pap. 3.50 (ISBN 0-446-30708-4). Warner Bks.

Butler, William E. The Mongolian Legal System. 1982. lib. bdg. 195.00 (ISBN 90-247-2685-9, Pub. by Martinus Nijhoff Netherlands). Kluwer Boston.

Butler, William E., ed. Anglo-Polish Legal Essays. LC 81-16259. (Transnational Studies in East-West Relations). 272p. 1981. lib. bdg. 19.50x (ISBN 0-941320-00-6). Transnatl Pubs.

--International Commercial Arbitration: Soviet Commercial & Maritime Arbitration. LC 80-10606. 1980. 75.00 (ISBN 0-686-84383-5). Oceana.

Butler, Winifred. Needlework. 1982. pap. 13.00 (ISBN 0-686-98219-3, Pub. by Pan Bks). State Mutual Bk.

Butlin, J. A., ed. The Economics of Environmental & Natural Resources Policy. 200p. 1981. lib. bdg. 30.00 (ISBN 0-86531-190-0); pap. 14.00 (ISBN 0-86531-196-X). Westview.

Butlin, Martin. Water Colors from the Turner Bequest. (Tate Gallery Art Ser.). 1977. 17.95 o.p. (ISBN 0-8120-5195-5). Barron.

--William Blake. (Tate Gallery: Little Art Book Ser.). (Illus.). 1977. 21.95 (ISBN 0-686-85703-8); pap. 1.95 (ISBN 0-686-91509-7); pap. 15.95 full size ed. (ISBN 0-686-91509-7). Barron.

Butlin, R. A., jt. ed. see Baker, Alan R.

Butnarescu, G. F., et al. Perinatal Nursing: Vol. II, Reproductive Risk. 553p. 1980. 33.50 (ISBN 0-471-04445-8). Wiley.

Butnarescu, Glenda F. & Tillotson, Delight M. Maternity Nursing: Theory to Practice. 700p. 1983. 28.95x (ISBN 0-471-07793-3, Pub. by Wiley Med); tchr's. manual avail. (ISBN 0-471-87070-6). Wiley.

Butnaurescu, Glenda F. Perinatal Nursing: Reproductive Health, Vol. 1. LC 77-25924. 1978. 33.50 (ISBN 0-471-04361-3, Pub. by Wiley Med). Wiley.

Butner, Alfred N. Textbook Study Guide of Surgery. 2nd ed. (Medical Examination Review Book: Vol. 5A). 1975. pap. 12.95 o.p. (ISBN 0-87488-150-1). Med Exam.

Butor, Michel. Letters from the Antipodes. Spencer, Michael, tr. from Fr. xii, 177p. 1981. lib. bdg. 21.95x (ISBN 0-8214-0659-0, 82-84291). Ohio U Pr.

Butrick, Richard. Deduction & Analysis. rev. ed. LC 80-6177. 121p. 1981. lib. bdg. 16.75 (ISBN 0-8191-1410-3); pap. text ed. 7.00 (ISBN 0-8191-1411-1). U Pr of Amer.

Butrym, Zofia & Horder, John. Health, Doctors, & Social Workers. (Library of Social Work). 192p. (Orig.). 1983. price not set. Routledge & Kegan.

Butscher, Edward. Adelaide Crapsey. (United States Authors Ser.). 1979. lib. bdg. 13.95 (ISBN 0-8057-7273-1, Twayne). G K Hall.

Butscher, Edward, ed. Sylvia Plath: The Woman & the Work. LC 77-24700. 1977. 8.95 o.p. (ISBN 0-396-07497-9). Dodd.

Butt, C. R. & Smith, R. E., eds. Conceptual Models in Exploration Geochemistry: Australia. (Developments in Economic Geology: Vol. 13). 1980. 61.75 (ISBN 0-444-41902-0). Elsevier.

Butt, Dorcas S. Psychology of Sport. LC 82-12661. 208p. 1982. Repr. of 1976 ed. lib. bdg. 14.95 (ISBN 0-89874-535-7). Krieger.

Butt, Howard & Wright, Elliott. At the Edge of Hope: Christain Laity in Paradox. 223p. 1979. 3.00 (ISBN 0-8164-0414-3); pap. 1.00 (ISBN 0-8164-2614-7). Seabury.

Butt, J. Reaction Kinetic & Reactor Design. 1980. 33.95 (ISBN 0-13-753335-7). P-H.

Butt, John. The Mid-Eighteenth Century. Carnall, Geoffrey, ed. (Oxford History of English Literature Ser.). 1979. text ed. 44.00x (ISBN 0-19-812212-8). Oxford U Pr.

Butt, John, ed. see Pope, Alexander.

Buttel, Frederick H. & Newby, Howard, eds. The Rural Sociology of the Advanced Societies: Critical Perspectives. LC 79-5177. 538p. 1980. text ed. 20.50x (ISBN 0-916672-30-1); pap. text ed. 9.50x (ISBN 0-916672-34-4). Allanheld.

Butter, P. H., ed. Shelley-Alastor & Other Poems, Prometheus Unbound with Other Poems, Adonais. 368p. 1981. 29.00x (ISBN 0-7121-0145-4, Pub. by Macdonald & Evans). State Mutual Bk.

Butter, P. H., ed. see Blake, William.

Butterfield, Arthur, et al. Europe & the Americas. (World of Knowledge Ser.). 16.72 (ISBN 0-382-06412-7). Silver.

Butterfield, B. G. & Meylan, B. Three-Dimensional Structure of Wood. 1980. 39.95x (ISBN 0-412-16320-9, Pub by Chapman & Hall England). Methuen Inc.

Butterfield, Herbert. Man on His Past. 37.50 (ISBN 0-521-07265-4); pap. 9.95 (ISBN 0-521-09567-0). Cambridge U Pr.

Butterfield, Jan. Frog Raising. 1983. pap. 2.95 (ISBN 0-440-52866-6, Dell Trade Pbks). Dell.

Butterfield, Jan, jt. auth. see Albright, Thomas.

Butterfield, John H. & Siegel, Robert. The Extraterrestrial Report. (Illus.). 160p. 1978. 15.00 o.s.i. (ISBN 0-89104-107-9, A & W Visual Library); pap. 7.95 o.s.i. (ISBN 0-89104-093-5). A & W Pubs.

Butterfield, R., jt. auth. see Banerjee, P. K.

Butterfield, Rex M., jt. auth. see Berg, Roy T.

Butterfield, Roger, ed. American Past. 2nd rev. ed. (Illus.). 1966. 15.95 o.p. (ISBN 0-671-02611-9). S&S.

Butterfield, S. M. The Wonderful World of Soccer. (Illus.). 64p. (gr. 3-10). 1982. pap. 3.95 (ISBN 0-448-15461-7, G&D). Putnam Pub Group.

Butterick. Vogue Sewing. LC 81-48031. (Illus.). 568p. 1982. 23.99i (ISBN 0-06-015001-7, HarpT). Har-Row.

Butterick, George F. A Guide to the Maximus Poems of Charles Olson. LC 75-27921. 1978. 47.50x (ISBN 0-520-03140-7); pap. 14.95 (ISBN 0-520-04270-0). U of Cal Pr.

Butterick, George F., ed. see Olson, Charles.

Butterick, George F., ed. see Olson, Charles & Creeley, Robert.

Butters, G., ed. Particulate Nature of PVC. (Illus.). xv, 240p. 1982. 41.00 (ISBN 0-85334-120-6, Pub. by Applied Sci England). Elsevier.

Butters, Gordon, ed. Plastics Pneumatic Conveying & Bulk Storage. (Illus.). 296p. 1981. 59.50 (ISBN 0-85334-983-5, Pub. by Applied Sci England). Elsevier.

Butterton, Meredith L. Metric Sixteen. LC 72-90711. (Illus.). 496p. 1973. 15.00 (ISBN 0-87716-038-4, Pub. by Moore Pub Co). F Apple.

Butterworth, Bill. Materials Handling in Farm Production: A Guide to the Control of Handling Costs on the Farm. LC 78-21166. 1979. pap. 16.95x o.p. (ISBN 0-470-26589-2). Halsted Pr.

Butterworth, Charles E., tr. Averroe's Middle Commentaries on Aristotle's Categories & De Interpretations. LC 82-61359. 192p. 1983. 17.50 (ISBN 0-691-07276-0). Princeton U Pr.

Butterworth, Douglas & Chance, John K. Latin American Urbanization. LC 80-18486. (Urbanization in Developing Countries Ser.). (Illus.). 320p. 1981. text ed. 37.50 (ISBN 0-521-23713-0); pap. text ed. 10.95 (ISBN 0-521-28175-X). Cambridge U Pr.

Butterworth, Eric. In the Flow of Life. LC 82-50121. 181p. 1982. Repr. 4.95 (ISBN 0-87159-065-4). Unity Bks.

--Life Is for Loving. LC 73-6326. 128p. 1974. 9.95i (ISBN 0-06-061268-1, HarpR). Har-Row.

--Spiritual Economics--the Prosperity Process. 220p. 1983. 4.95 (ISBN 0-87159-142-1). Unity Bks.

Butterworth, F. Edward. Secrets of the Mighty Sioux. 1982. pap. 11.00 (ISBN 0-8309-0352-6). Ind Pr MO.

--White Shadows Among the Mighty Sioux, Vol. 1. (Illus.). 1977. 10.00 o.p. (ISBN 0-685-80867-X). Ind Pr MO.

Butterworth, Hezekiah. In Old New England. LC 73-19716. 1974. Repr. of 1895 ed. 30.00x (ISBN 0-8103-3686-3). Gale.

Butterworth, Keen & Kibler, James E., Jr. William Gilmore Simms: A Reference Guide. 1980. lib. bdg. 27.00 (ISBN 0-8161-1059-X, Hall Reference). G K Hall.

Butterworth, Michael. The Man Who Broke the Bank at Monte Carlo. LC 82-48705. (Crime Club Ser.). 192p. 1983. 11.95 (ISBN 0-385-18751-3). Doubleday.

Butterworth, Nancy T., jt. auth. see Broad, Laura P.

Butterworth, Neal. Dvorak: His Life & Times. Eden, William, ed. (Composers-Their Life & Times Ser.). (Illus.). 144p. 1982. 16.95 o.s.i. (ISBN 0-8467-0583-4, Pub. by Midas England); pap. cancelled o.s.i. (ISBN 0-8467-0584-2, Pub. by Midas England). Hippocrene Bks.

Butterworth, Neil. A Dictionary of American Composers. LC 81-43331. 600p. 1983. lib. bdg. 75.00 (ISBN 0-8240-9311-9). Garland Pub.

--Dvorak: His Life & Times. expanded ed. (Life & Times Ser.). (Illus.). 176p. 1981. Repr. of 1980 ed. 12.95 (ISBN 0-87666-580-6, Z-49). Paganiniana Pubns.

--Haydn: His Life & Times. expanded ed. (Life & Times Ser.). (Illus.). 176p. 1980. Repr. of 1977 ed. 12.95 (ISBN 0-87666-645-4, Z-44). Paganiniana Pubns.

Butterworth, Nick, illus. B. B. Blacksheep. LC 82-80874. (Illus.). 48p. (gr. k-2). 1982. 5.95 (ISBN 0-448-16577-5, G&D). Putnam Pub Group.

Butterworth, Oliver. The Enormous Egg. 1978. pap. 2.25 (ISBN 0-440-42337-6, YB). Dell.

--The Enormous Egg. (gr. 4-6). 1956. 9.95 (ISBN 0-316-11904-0, Pub. by Atlantic Monthly Pr). Little.

Butterworth, William. Moose, the Thing, & Me. (gr. 5 up). 1982. PLB 9.95 (ISBN 0-395-32077-1); 9.70. HM.

--Next Stop, Earth. LC 77-18346. (Illus.). (gr. 2-4). 1978. 5.95 (ISBN 0-8027-6322-7); PLB 5.85 (ISBN 0-8027-6323-5). Walker & Co.

Buttery, P. J. & Lindsay, D. B. Protein Deposition in Animals. 29th ed. LC 80-49869. (Nottingham Easter School Ser.). (Illus.). 320p. 1980. text ed. 69.95 (ISBN 0-408-10676-X). Butterworth.

Buttimer, Anne & Seaman, David. The Human Experience of Space & Place. LC 80-12173. (Illus.). 1980. 29.00 (ISBN 0-312-39910-3). St Martin.

Buttlar, Johannes von see Von Buttlar, Johannes.

Buttlar, Lois, jt. auth. see Wynar, Lubomyr R.

Buttle, Bernard, jt. auth. see Kemp, Fred.

Buttle, J. W. Chemistry: A Unified Approach. 3rd ed. Daniels, D. J. & Beckett, P. J., eds. 608p. 1974. 12.95 o.p. (ISBN 0-408-70541-8). Butterworth.

Buttle, J. W., et al. Chemistry: A Unified Approach. 4th ed. 1981. text ed. 18.95 (ISBN 0-408-70938-3). Butterworth.

Buttner, Horst & Meissner, Gunter. Town Houses of Europe. (Illus.). 351p. 1982. 45.00 (ISBN 0-312-81157-8). St Martin.

Button, H. Warren & Provenzo, Eugene F., Jr. History of Education & Culture in America. (Illus.). 400p. 1983. 21.95 (ISBN 0-13-390237-4, Busn). P-H.

Button, James E. Communications Research in Learning Disabilities & Mental Retardation. 368p. 1979. pap. text ed. 27.95 (ISBN 0-8391-1262-9). Univ Park.

Button, K. J. Transport Economics. viii, 295p. (Orig.). 1982. pap. text ed. 15.00 (ISBN 0-435-84093-2). Heinemann Ed.

Button, K. J., et al. Car Ownership Modelling & Forecasting. 157p. 1982. text ed. 47.50x (ISBN 0-566-00320-1). Gower Pub Ltd.

Button, Kenneth. The Economics of Urban Transport. (Illus.). 1977. 23.95x o.p. (ISBN 0-566-00148-9, 00720-X, Pub. by Saxon Hse). Lexington Bks.

Button, Kenneth & Gillingwater, David. Case Studies in Regional Economics. Maunder, Peter, ed. (Case Studies in Economic Analysis). 1976. 5.00x o.p. (ISBN 0-435-84090-8); tchr's ed. 8.50x o.p. (ISBN 0-435-84091-6). Heinemann Ed.

Button, Kenneth, jt. auth. see Barker, Peter.

Button, Kenneth J., ed. Infrared & Millimeter Waves: Electromagnetic Waves in Matter, Vol. 8. LC 79-6949. Date not set. price not set (ISBN 0-12-147708-8). Acad Pr.

Button, Phelps. Why Things Are As They Are. 1979. 6.95 o.p. (ISBN 0-533-04223-2). Vantage.

Buttress, F. A., ed. World Guide to Abbreviations of Organizations. 6th ed. 500p. 1980. 115.00x (ISBN 0-8103-2024-X). Gale.

Buttrey, D. N., ed. Plastics in Furniture. (Illus.). 1976. 24.75 (ISBN 0-85334-647-X, Pub. by Applied Sci England). Elsevier.

Buttrick, George A. The Interpreter's Bible, 12 vols. Incl. Vol. 1. General Articles, Genesis, Exodus. 1952 (ISBN 0-687-19207-2); Vol. 2. Leviticus - Samuel. 1953 (ISBN 0-687-19208-0); Vol. 3. Kings - Job. 1954 (ISBN 0-687-19209-9); Vol. 4. Psalms, Proverbs. 1955 (ISBN 0-687-19210-2); Vol. 5. Ecclesiates - Jeremiah. 1956 (ISBN 0-687-19211-0); Vol. 6. Lamentations - Malachi. 1956 (ISBN 0-687-19212-9); Vol. 7. General Articles, Matthew, Mark. 1951 (ISBN 0-687-19213-7); Vol. 8. Luke, John. 1952 (ISBN 0-687-19214-5); Vol. 9. The Acts, Romans. 1954 (ISBN 0-687-19215-3); Vol. 10. Corinthians, Ephesians. 1953 (ISBN 0-687-19216-1); Vol. 11. Philippians - Hebrews. 1955 (ISBN 0-687-19217-X); Vol. 12. James - Revelation. 1957 (ISBN 0-687-19218-8). LC 51-12276. 1957. 18.95 (ISBN 0-686-76914-7); 210.00 (ISBN 0-687-19206-4). Abingdon.

Buttrick, George A. & Crim, Keith R., eds. The Interpreter's Dictionary of the Bible, 5 vols. LC 62-9387. 1976. Set. 99.50 (ISBN 0-687-19268-4). Abingdon.

Butts, Allison. Metallurgical Problems. 2nd ed. (Metallurgy & Metallurgical Engineering Ser.). 1943. text ed. 20.50 o.p. (ISBN 0-07-009420-9, C); answers 1.50 o.p. (ISBN 0-07-009450-0). McGraw.

Butts, David, jt. auth. see Peterson, Rita W.

Butts, Karen R. Breathing Exercises for Asthma. (Illus.). 66p. 1980. spiral 11.75x (ISBN 0-398-04104-0). C C Thomas.

Butts, Robert F., jt. auth. see Roberts, Jane.

Butturff, Diane & Coffman, Mary. French: Language & Life Styles. new ed. (Illus.). 512p. 1975. text ed. 25.00 (ISBN 0-07-009455-1, C); manual 10.00instructor's (ISBN 0-07-009456-X); d'exercises 16.00cahier (ISBN 0-07-009457-8). McGraw.

Butwin, Frances, jt. auth. see Butwin, Joseph.

Butwin, Joseph & Butwin, Frances. Sholom Aleichem. (World Authors Ser.: No. 460). 1977. lib. bdg. 12.95 o.p. (ISBN 0-8057-6297-3, Twayne). G K Hall.

Butwin, Miriam & Chaffin, Lillie. America's First Ladies, 2 vols. Incl. Vol. 1. 1789-1865 (ISBN 0-8225-0455-3); Vol. 2. 1865 to the Present Day (ISBN 0-8225-0456-1). LC 68-31499. (Pull-Ahead Bks). (Illus.). (gr. 5 up). PLB 4.95g ea. Lerner Pubns.

Butwin, Miriam & Pirmantgen, Pat. Protest I. LC 76-128798. (Real World: Crisis & Conflict Bks). (Illus.). (gr. 5-11). 1972. PLB 4.95g (ISBN 0-8225-0623-8). Lerner Pubns.

--Protest II. LC 76-128798. (Real World: Crisis & Conflict Bks). (Illus.). (gr. 5-11). 1972. PLB 4.95g (ISBN 0-8225-0626-2). Lerner Pubns.

Butz, Arthur R. The Hoax of the Twentieth Century. LC 77-78964. 12.00 (ISBN 0-911038-23-X); pap. 8.00 (ISBN 0-911038-00-0). Inst Hist Rev.

Butzer, Karl & Freeman, Leslie G., eds. Early Hydraulic Civilization in Egypt. LC 75-36398. (Prehistoric Archaelogy & Ecology Ser). (Illus.). 1976. 5.00x (ISBN 0-226-08634-8); pap. 3.25x o.s. (ISBN 0-226-08635-6). U of Chicago Pr.

Butzer, Karl W. & Hansen, Carl L. Desert & River in Nubia: Geomorphology & Prehistoric Environments at the Aswan Reservoir. LC 67-20761. (Illus.). 1968. 40.00 (ISBN 0-299-04770-9); Set Of 15 Maps. 20.00x (ISBN 0-685-20706-4). U of Wis Pr.

Buuren, Catherine Van see Van Buuren, Catherine.

Buvet, R. & Ponnamperuma, C., eds. Chemical Evolution & the Origin of Life. LC 75-146189. (Molecular Evolution Ser.: Vol. 1). (Illus.). 571p. 1971. 34.00 (ISBN 0-444-10093-8, North-Holland). Elsevier.

Buvinic, Mayra, jt. ed. see Tinker, Irene.

Bux, William E. & Cunningham, Edward G. RPG and RPG II Programming: Applied Fundamentals. (Illus.). 1979. pap. text ed. 19.95 (ISBN 0-13-783423-3). P-H.

Buxbaum, David C., et al, eds. China Trade: Prospects & Perspectives. 448p. 1982. 41.95 (ISBN 0-03-056687-8). Praeger.

Buxbaum, James M. The Corporate Politeia: A Conceptual Approach to Business, Government & Society. LC 81-40313. (Illus.). 96p. (Orig.). 1981. text ed. 18.00 (ISBN 0-8191-1763-3); pap. text ed. 7.50 (ISBN 0-8191-1764-1). U Pr of Amer.

Buxbaum, Melvin H. Benjamin Franklin, 1721-1906: A Reference Guide. 334p. 1983. 35.00 (ISBN 0-8161-7985-9, Hall Reference). G K Hall.

Buxbaum, Susan K., jt. auth. see Gelman, Rita G.

Buxton, Angela, jt. auth. see Jones, C. M.

Buxton, D. R., jt. auth. see Johnston, H. B.

Buxton, David, tr. see Mattelart, Armand.

Buxton, Graham. Effective Marketing Logistics: The Analysis Planning & Control of Distribution Operations. 1975. 45.00x (ISBN 0-8419-5007-5). Holmes & Meier.

Buxton, John, ed. see Walton, Izaak & Cotton, Charles.

Buxton, Virginia H. Roseville Pottery for Love or Money. (Illus.). 19.95 (ISBN 0-686-51526-9, 99051). Wallace-Homestead.

Buyers, Rebecca. The Marvelous Macadamia Nut. LC 82-73616. (Illus.). 84p. (Orig.). 1982. pap. write for info. (ISBN 0-941034-74-7). I Chalmers.

Buysse, James L. The Definitive Guide on How Not to Quit Smoking. (Illus.). 63p. (Orig.). 1982. pap. 3.95 (ISBN 0-911435-00-X). King Freedom.

Buzan, Norma & Howell, Bert. Bed & Breakfast in Michigan. (Illus.). 50p. 1983. pap. 3.50 (ISBN 0-943232-02-3). Betsy Ross Pub.

Buzan, Norma S. Bed & Breakfast North America: A Directory of Agencies & Small Inns. 1983 ed. LC 82-138156. (Illus.). 250p. 1983. pap. 6.95 (ISBN 0-943232-01-5). Betsy Ross Pub.

Buzan, Tony. The Brain User's Guide. (Illus.). 144p. 1983. pap. 7.95 (0772-230). Dutton.

--The Brain User's Guide: A Handbook for Sorting out Your Life. (Illus.). 128p. 1983. pap. 7.95 (ISBN 0-525-48045-5, 0772-230). Dutton.

--Use Both Sides of Your Brain. rev. ed. (Illus.). 160p. 1983. pap. 7.25 (ISBN 0-525-48011-0, 0704-210). Dutton.

Buzas, jt. auth. see ICTA Conference, 4th.

Buzas, I., jt. ed. see Pungor, E.

Buzby, Beth. Data Entry: Concepts & Applications. 480p. 1980. pap. text ed. 16.95 (ISBN 0-574-21255-8, 13-4255); instructor's guide avail. (ISBN 0-574-21256-6, 13-4256). SRA.

Buzby, Walter J. & Paine, David. Hotel & Motel Security Management. LC 76-12555. 256p. 1976. 18.95 (ISBN 0-913708-24-0). Butterworth.

Buziak, Ed. The Focalguide to Selling Photographs. (Focalguide Ser.). (Illus.). 1979. pap. 7.95 (ISBN 0-240-51012-7). Focal Pr.

Buzzard, Lynn. Schools: They Haven't Got a Prayer. (Issues & Insights Ser.). 1982. pap. 5.95 (ISBN 0-89191-713-6). Cook.

Buzzard, Lynn & Eck, Laurence. Tell It to the Church: Reconciling Out of Court. 1982. 9.95 o.p. (ISBN 0-89191-551-6); pap. 5.95 (ISBN 0-89191-630-X). Cook.

Buzzard, Lynn & Ericcson, Samuel. The Battle for Religious Liberty. (Issues & Insight Ser.). (Orig.). 1982. pap. 6.95 (ISBN 0-89191-552-4, 55525). Cook.

Buzzati, Dino. Restless Nights. Venuti, Lawrence, tr. & intro. by. LC 82-73713. 176p. 1983. pap. 12.00 (ISBN 0-86547-100-2). N Point Pr.

Buzzell, R. D., et al. Marketing Research & Information Systems: Text & Cases. 1969. text ed. 25.50 o.p. (ISBN 0-07-009475-6, C); instructor's manual 4.95 o.p. (ISBN 0-07-009476-4). tapes 325.00 o.p. (ISBN 0-07-097280-X). McGraw.

Buzzotta, V. R., et al. Effective Motivation Through Performance Appraisal. 360p. 1980. Repr. of 1977 ed. prof ref 20.00x (ISBN 0-88410-499-0). Ballinger Pub.

--Effective Selling Through Psychology: Dimensional Sales Management Strategies. 2nd ed. 400p. 1980. prof ref 25.00x (ISBN 0-88410-393-5). Ballinger Pub.

Byalin, Joan. Women's Energy Tool Kit. Katz, Rita E. & Tinsley, Elizabeth, eds. LC 82-82705. pap. 9.95 o.s.i. (ISBN 0-316-15343-5). Consumer Act.

Byant, Edward. Cinnabar. 1983. pap. 2.50 (ISBN 0-553-22855-2). Bantam.

Byars, Betsy. The Cartoonist. (gr. k-6). 1981. pap. 1.95 (ISBN 0-440-41046-0, YB). Dell.

--The Eighteenth Emergency. (gr. 4-6). 1974. pap. 1.75 o.p. (ISBN 0-380-00099-7, 51367, Camelot). Avon.

--Go & Hush the Baby. (Illus.). (ps-3). 1982. pap. 2.95 (ISBN 0-14-050396-X, Puffin). Penguin.

--The Summer of the Swans. 1974. pap. 1.75 o.p. (ISBN 0-380-00098-9, 50526, Camelot). Avon.

Byars, Betsy C. After the Goat Man. (Illus.). 128p. (gr. 5-9). 1974. 10.95 (ISBN 0-670-10908-8). Viking Pr.

--After the Goat Man. (Illus.). (gr. 3-7). 1982. pap. 2.95 (ISBN 0-14-031533-0, Puffin). Penguin.

--The Cybil War. LC 80-26912. (Illus.). 144p. (gr. 8-12). 1981. 9.95 (ISBN 0-670-25248-4). Viking Pr.

--The Summer of the Swans. 144p. 1981. pap. 2.95 (ISBN 0-14-031420-2, Puffin). Penguin.

Byars, E. F. & Snyder, R. D. Engineering Mechanics of Deformable Bodies. 3rd ed. 1974. text ed. 32.50 scp o.p. (ISBN 0-7002-2460-2, HarpC). Har-Row.

Byars, Edward F. Engineering Mechanics of Deformable Bodies. 4th ed. 528p. 1983. text ed. 29.50 scp (ISBN 0-06-041109-0, HarpC); solution manual avail. (ISBN 0-06-361100-7). Har-Row.

Bybee, Roger & Sund. Piaget for Educators. 2nd ed. 288p. 1982. pap. text ed. 11.95 (ISBN 0-675-09838-6). Merrill.

Byde, Alan. Beginner's Guide to Canoeing. 184p. 1973. 14.00 o.p. (ISBN 0-7207-0628-9). Transatlantic.

--Canoe Design & Construction. (Illus.). 176p. 1976. 16.50 o.p. (ISBN 0-7207-0862-1). Transatlantic.

Bye, A. E. Art into Landscape, Landscape into Art. LC 82-22406. (Illus.). 178p. 1983. 26.00 (ISBN 0-914886-19-3); pap. 19.75 (ISBN 0-914886-20-7). PDA Pubs.

Byer, Norman. The Peripheral Retina in Profile. (Illus.). 159p. 1982. incl. cassettes 295.00 (ISBN 0-9609428-0-7). Criterion Pr.

Byer, Trevor A., jt. auth. see Fallen-Bailey, Darrel G.

Byerly, Greg & Rubin, Rick. Pornography: The Conflict Over Sexually Explicit Materials in the United States. An Annotated Bibliography. LC 80-14336. (Garland Reference Library of Social Science). 162p. 1980. 20.00 o.s.i. (ISBN 0-8240-9514-6). Garland Pub.

Byerly, R. T. & Kimbark, E. W., eds. Stability of Large Electric Power Systems. LC 74-81759. (Illus.). 1974. 28.95 o.p. (ISBN 0-87942-037-5). Inst Electrical.

Byerly, Richard T. & Kimbark, Edward W., eds. Stability of Large Electric Power Systems. LC 74-81759. (IEEE Press Selected Reprint Ser). 560p. 1974. 31.95x (ISBN 0-471-12887-2, Pub. by Wiley-Interscience). Wiley.

Byers, David & Quinn, Bernard. New Directions for the Rural Church. LC 77-14799. 192p. 1978. pap. 3.95 o.p. (ISBN 0-8091-2085-2). Paulist Pr.

Byers, Douglas S. & MacNeish, R. S., eds. Prehistory of the Tehuacan Valley. Incl. Vol. 1. Environment & Subsistence. (Illus.). 339p. 1968. 35.00x (ISBN 0-292-73683-5); Vol. 2. The Non-Ceramic Artifacts. (Illus.). 272p. 1968. 30.00x (ISBN 0-292-73684-3). (Illus.). 1968. U of Tex Pr.

Byers, E. E., jt. auth. see Root, Kathleen B.

Byers, Edward E. Gregg Medical Shorthand Dictionary. 1975. 19.60 (ISBN 0-07-009504-3, G). McGraw.

--Ten Thousand Medical Words, Spelled & Divided for Quick Reference. 128p. 1972. text ed. 6.40 (ISBN 0-07-009503-5, G). McGraw.

Byers, Edward E., jt. auth. see Place, Irene.

Byers, Edward E., ed. see Rosenberg, R. Robert, et al.

Byers, Horace R. General Meteorology. 4th ed. (Illus.). 550p. 1974. text ed. 38.00 (ISBN 0-07-009500-0, C). McGraw.

Byers, Mary, et al. Rural Roots: Pre-Confederation Buildings of the York Region of Ontario. LC 76-26867. (Illus.). 1976. 25.00 (ISBN 0-8020-2230-8); pap. 8.50 o.p. (ISBN 0-8020-6287-3). U of Toronto Pr.

Byers, Patricia & Preston, Julia. The Kid's Money Book. LC 82-184275. (Illus.). 120p. 1983. pap. 4.95 (ISBN 0-89709-041-1). Liberty Pub.

Byers, R. B., ed. Canadian Annual Review of Politics & Public Affairs, 1981. 400p. 1983. 50.00x (ISBN 0-8020-2500-5). U of Toronto Pr.

Byers, T. J. Microprocessor Support Chips: Theory, Design, & Applications. (Illus.). 300p. 1983. 38.00 (ISBN 0-07-009518-3, P&RB). McGraw.

Byers, Tracy. Martha Berry, the Sunday Lady of Possum Trot. LC 72-159905. 1971. Repr. of 1932 ed. 34.00x (ISBN 0-8103-3783-5). Gale.

Byfield, Barbara N. A Parcel of Their Fortunes. LC 79-7565. (Crime Club Ser.). 192p. 1979. 10.95 o.p. (ISBN 0-385-14611-6). Doubleday.

Byfield, Magdelina. In a Miniature Garden. 64p. pap. 6.95 (ISBN 0-87588-175-0). Hobby Hse.

Byfield, Sue. To Be or Not to Be. (Harlequin Romances Ser.). 192p. 1983. pap. 1.50 (ISBN 0-373-02529-7). Harlequin Bks.

Bygrave, Mike & Dowdall, Jim. Motorcycle. (Illus.). (gr. 5 up). 1978. 7.90 (ISBN 0-531-02484-9). Watts.

Byham, William C., jt. ed. see Moses, Joseph L.

Byington, Margaret. Homestead: The Households of a Milltown. (Illus.). 1974. text ed. 14.95 (ISBN 0-8229-4200-3); pap. text ed. 6.95 (ISBN 0-8229-8250-1). U of Pittsburgh Pr.

Byington, Steven, tr. see Stirner, Max.

Byington, Steven T., tr. see Stirner, Max.

Bykhovskii, B. E., ed. Bird Migrations: Ecological & Physiological Factors. Gordon, E. D., tr. from Rus. 298p. 1974. 49.95 o.p. (ISBN 0-470-12890-9). Halsted Pr.

Bykhovsky, Isidor I. Fundamentals of Vibration Engineering. 2nd ed. Zhitomirsky, V., tr. from Russ. LC 77-20089. 384p. 1980. lib. bdg. 23.50 (ISBN 0-88275-550-1). Krieger.

Bylander, E. G. Electronic Displays. LC 78-31849. (Illus.). 1979. 31.50 (ISBN 0-07-009510-8). McGraw.

Bylaws, jt. auth. see Carter.

Byles, Anthea & Morris, Pauline. Unmet Need: The Case of the Neighborhood Law Center. (Direct Editions Ser). 1978. pap. 9.95 o.p. (ISBN 0-7100-8649-0). Routledge & Kegan.

Byles, Mather. The Works of Mather Byles. LC 78-6439. 1978. 60.00x (ISBN 0-8201-1309-3). Schol Facsimiles.

Bynner, Wittter. Selected Letters. Kraft, James, ed. 328p. 1981. 30.00 (ISBN 0-374-18504-2). FS&G.

Bynon, Theodora. Historical Linguistics. LC 76-62588. (Cambridge Textbooks in Linguistics Ser.). (Illus.). 1977. 44.50 (ISBN 0-521-21582-X); pap. 12.95 (ISBN 0-521-29188-7). Cambridge U Pr.

Bynum, W. F., jt. ed. see Rose, Clifford F.

Byock, Jesse. Feud in the Icelandic Saga. LC 82-40098. (Illus.). 300p. 1982. 22.50x (ISBN 0-520-04564-5). U of Cal Pr.

Byram, M. S. Tom Kristensen. (World Authors Ser.). 1982. lib. bdg. 17.50 (ISBN 0-8057-6491-7, Twayne). G K Hall.

Byrd, Anne. Omelettes & Souffles. LC 82-47860. (Great American Cooking Schools Ser.). (Illus.). 84p. 1982. 8.61i (ISBN 0-06-015065-3, HarpT). Har-Row.

Byrd, Doris Elaine. Organizational Constraints on Psychiatric Treatment. Roth, Julius A., ed. (Research in the Sociology of Health Care: Supplement No. 1). 285p. 1981. 40.00 (ISBN 0-89232-176-8). Jai Pr.

Byrd, Elizabeth. It Had to Be You. LC 82-2604. 180p. (gr. 7 up). 1982. 11.95 (ISBN 0-670-40306-7). Viking Pr.

Byrd, Harold E. The Black Experience in Big Business. (Illus.). 1977. 6.50 o.p. (ISBN 0-682-48901-8). Exposition.

Byrd, Larry, jt. auth. see Henrickson, Charles.

Byrd, Max. Visits to Bedlam: Madness & Literature in the Eighteenth Century. LC 73-19855. (Illus.). xx, 210p. 1974. 14.95x o.s.i. (ISBN 0-87249-312-1). U of SC Pr.

Byrd, P., et al. Guide to Academic Libraries in the United States. 1981. pap. 10.95 (ISBN 0-13-367979-9). P-H.

Byrd, Richard E. Discovery: The Story of the Second Byrd Antarctic Expedition. LC 76-159906. (Tower Bks). (Illus.). 1971. Repr. of 1935 ed. 47.00x (ISBN 0-8103-3904-8). Gale.

Byrd, William. China's Financial System: The Changing Role of Banks. (Replica Edition Ser.). 150p. 1982. softcover 17.00x (ISBN 0-86531-943-X). Westview.

Byres, Terence. Adam Smith, Malthus & Marx. Yapp, Malcolm, et al, eds. (World History Ser.). (Illus.). 32p. (gr. 10). 1980. Repr. of 1977 ed. lib. bdg. 6.95 (ISBN 0-89908-046-4); pap. text ed. 2.25 (ISBN 0-89908-021-9). Greenhaven.

Byrkit & Shamma. Calculus for Business & Economics. 1981. text ed. write for info. (ISBN 0-442-21305-0). Van Nos Reinhold.

Byrkit, Donald R. Elements of Statistics. 3rd ed. 1980. text ed. 16.95x (ISBN 0-442-25771-6); instructor's manual 2.50x (ISBN 0-442-25772-4). Van Nos Reinhold.

Byrkit, James W. Forging the Copper Collar: Arizona's Labor-Management War, 1901-1921. 440p. 1982. 24.95 (ISBN 0-8165-0745-7). U of Ariz Pr.

Byrn, Stephen. Solid State Chemistry of Drugs. LC 82-13950. 349p. 1982. 55.00 (ISBN 0-12-148620-6). Acad Pr.

Byrne, Claire J., et al. Laboratory Tests: Implications for Nurses & Allied Health Professionals. 1981. 16.95 (ISBN 0-201-00088-1, Med-Nurse). A-W.

Byrne, D. & Wright, A. What Do You Think? (English As a Second Language Bk.). (Illus.). 1974. pap. text ed. 3.50x student bk. 1 (ISBN 0-582-52269-2); pap. text ed. 3.50x student bk. 2 (ISBN 0-582-52271-4); tchr's bk. 1 3.25x (ISBN 0-582-52270-6); pap. text ed. 3.25x tchr's bk. 2 (ISBN 0-582-52272-2). Longman.

Byrne, Donn. English Teaching Perspectives. (English As a Second Language Bk.). 1980. pap. text ed. 9.25x (ISBN 0-582-74604-3). Longman.

--Listening Comprehension Practice. 1978. student bk. 2.25x (ISBN 0-582-55295-8); tchr's bk. 3.50 (ISBN 0-582-55297-4). Longman.

--Messer Marco Polo. 151p. 1982. Repr. of 1892 ed. lib. bdg. 30.00 (ISBN 0-686-94649-9). Century Bookbindery.

--Teaching Oral English. (Longman Handbooks for Language Teachers Ser.). (Illus.). 192p. 1976. pap. text ed. 8.95x (ISBN 0-582-55081-5). Longman.

--Teaching Writing Skills. (Longman Handbooks for Language Teachers). (Illus.). 1980. pap. text ed. 8.95x (ISBN 0-582-74602-7). Longman.

Byrne, Donn & Cornelius, Edwin T. Thirty Passages: Comprehension Practice for High Intermediate & Advanced Students. (English As a Second Language Bk.). (Illus.). 1978. pap. text ed. 3.55x (ISBN 0-582-79704-7). Longman.

Byrne, Donn & Kelly, Kathryn. An Introduction to Personality. 3rd ed. (Illus.). 576p. 1981. text ed. 24.95 (ISBN 0-13-491605-0). P-H.

Byrne, Donn see Allen, W. S.

Byrne, Donn, jt. auth. see Lindgren, Henry C.

Byrne, H. W. Improving Church Education. LC 79-10852. 352p. (Orig.). 1979. pap. 12.95 (ISBN 0-89135-017-9). Religious Educ.

Byrne, Jack. Salmon Country. (Illus.). 224p. 1982. 15.95 (ISBN 0-00-216975-4, Pub. by W Collins Australia). Intl Schol Bk Serv.

Byrne, James. Living in the Spirit: A Handbook on Catholic Charismatic Christianity. LC 75-28628. 1976. pap. 3.50 o.p. (ISBN 0-8091-1902-1). Paulist Pr.

Byrne, John H. & Koester, John, eds. Molluscan Nerve Cells: From Biophysics to Behavior. LC 80-39967. (Cold Spring Harbor Reports in the Neurosciences Ser.: Vol. 1). 230p. 1980. 32.00x (ISBN 0-87969-135-2). Cold Spring Harbor.

Byrne, Julia. Curiosities of the Search-Room. LC 70-78117. 1969. Repr. of 1880 ed. 34.00x (ISBN 0-8103-3573-5). Gale.

Byrne, Kathleen D. & Snyder, Richard C. Chrysalis: Willa Cather in Pittsburgh, 1896-1906. LC 80-80284. (Illus.). 160p. 1982. 14.95 o.p. (ISBN 0-936340-00-2). Hist Soc West Pa.

Byrne, L. S. & Churchill, E. L. A Comprehensive French Grammar: With Classified Vocabularies. 515p. (Orig.). 1980. pap. 15.95x o.p. (ISBN 0-631-12594-9, Pub. by Basil Blackwell England). Biblio Dist.

Byrne, Liam. History of Aviation in Ireland. 1981. 30.00 (ISBN 0-686-96953-7, Pub. by Blackwater Pr Ireland). State Mutual Bk.

Byrne, M. St. Clare, ed. see Massinger, Philip.

Byrne, Majorie L. & Thompson, Lida F. Key Concepts for the Study & Practice of Nursing. 2nd ed. LC 77-26957. (Illus.). 1978. pap. text ed. 10.95 (ISBN 0-8016-0920-8). Mosby.

Byrne, Muriel S., ed. The Lisle Letters, 6 vols. LC 80-12019. 1981. Set. 300.00x (ISBN 0-226-08801-4). U of Chicago Pr.

Byrne, Robert. Always a Catholic. 192p. (Orig.). 1981. pap. 2.50 (ISBN 0-523-42035-8). Pinnacle Bks.

--Byrne's Treasury of Trick Shots in Pool & Billiards. LC 82-47676. (Illus.). 320p. 1982. 15.95 o.p. (ISBN 0-15-115224-1). HarBraceJ.

--Byrne's Treasury of Trick Shots in Pool & Billiards. LC 82-47676. (Illus.). 320p. 1982. 19.95 (ISBN 0-15-115224-1). HarBraceJ.

--The Six Hundred Thirty-Seven Best Things Anybody Ever Said. LC 82-45172. 192p. 1982. 10.95 (ISBN 0-689-11300-5). Atheneum.

Byrnes, Dennis L., jt. auth. see Wingfield, Arthur.

Byrnes, Heidi, ed. Georgetown University Round Table on Languages & Linguistics 1982: Contemporary Perceptions of Language: Interdisciplinary Dimensions. LC 58-31607. (Georgetown University Round Table on Languages and Linguistics (GURT) Ser.). 262p. (Orig.). 1983. pap. text ed. 8.95 (ISBN 0-87840-117-2). Georgetown U Pr.

Byrnes, Laurence. History of the Ninety-Fourth Infantry Division in World War II. (Divisional Ser.: No. 22). (Illus.). 534p. 1982. Repr. of 1948 ed. 25.00x (ISBN 0-89839-064-8). Battery Pr.

Byrnes, Patricia & Krenz, Nancy. Southwestern Arts & Crafts Projects. Smith, James C., Jr., ed. LC 77-18988. (Illus.). (gr. 1-8). 1979. pap. 12.95 (ISBN 0-913270-62-8). Sunstone Pr.

Byrnes, Robert F. Awakening American Education to the World: The Role of Archibald Cary Coolidge, 1866-1928. LC 81-40451. 256p. 1982. 21.95 (ISBN 0-268-00599-0). U of Notre Dame Pr.

Byrnes, Robert F., ed. After Brezhnev: Sources of Soviet Conduct in the 1980's. LC 82-24614. (Midland Bks.: No. 306). 512p. 1983. 25.00x (ISBN 0-253-35392-0); pap. 12.50x (ISBN 0-253-20306-6). Ind U Pr.

--The United States & Eastern Europe. LC 67-23502. 1967. pap. 1.95 o.p. (ISBN 0-936904-04-6). Am Assembly.

Byrns & Stone. Great Ideas for Teaching Economics. 846p. 1981. pap. 10.95x (ISBN 0-673-16163-3). Scott F.

Byrns, James H. Speak for Yourself. 329p. 1981. pap. text ed. 12.00 (ISBN 0-394-32410-2). Random.

Byrns, Ralph T. & Stone, Gerald W. An Economics Casebook: Applications from the Law. 1980. 9.95x (ISBN 0-673-16162-5). Scott F.

Byrns, Ralph T. & Stone, Gerald W., Jr. Macroeconomics. 1981. pap. text ed. 16.50x (ISBN 0-673-16015-7). Scott F.

--Microeconomics. 1981. pap. text ed. 16.50x (ISBN 0-673-16016-5). Scott F.

Byron. Byron: Poetical Works. rev. ed. Page, Frederick & Jump, John, eds. (Oxford Standard Author Ser.). (Illus.). 1979. Leatherbound 60.00x (ISBN 0-19-192822-4). Oxford U Pr.

--Byron's Letters & Journals, Volume 12: The Trouble of an Index. LC 73-81853. 176p. 1982. 15.00 (ISBN 0-674-08954-5, Belknap Pr). Harvard U Pr.

--Lord Byron: Selected Prose. Gunn, Peter, ed. (Penguin English Library). 1982. pap. 5.95 (ISBN 0-14-043080-6). Penguin.

Byron, ed. Lord Byron: Selected Letters & Journals. 416p. 1982. 17.50 (ISBN 0-674-53915-X, Belknap Pr). Harvard U Pr.

Byron, D. The Firearms Price Guide. (Illus.). 1977. pap. 9.95 o.p. (ISBN 0-517-53113-5). Crown.

Byron, David. The Firearms Price Guide. rev. ed. (Illus.). 416p. 1980. pap. 9.95 o.p. (ISBN 0-517-54065-7, Michelman Books). Crown.

--Gunmarks. (Illus.). 1979. 10.00 o.p. (ISBN 0-517-53848-2). Crown.

--Official Price Guide to Antique & Modern Firearms. LC 81-81803. (Collector Ser.). (Illus.). 500p. 1982. pap. 9.95 (ISBN 0-87637-363-5, 190-0X). Hse of Collectibles.

Byron, George G. Byron: Childe Harold's Pilgrimage & Other Romantic Poems. Jump, John D., ed. (Rowman & Littlefield University Library). 233p. 1975. 11.50x o.p. (ISBN 0-87471-626-8). Rowman.

--Byron's Letters & Journals, 12 vols. Marchand, Leslie A., ed. Incl. Vol. 1. In My Hot Youth: Seventeen Ninety-Eight to Eighteen Ten. 288p. 1973. 15.00x (ISBN 0-674-08940-5); Vol. II. Famous in My Time: Eighteen Ten to Eighteen Twelve. 298p. 1974. 15.00x (ISBN 0-674-08941-3); Vol. III. Alas! the Love of Women: Eighteen Thirteen to Eighteen Fourteen. 285p. 1974. 15.00x (ISBN 0-674-08942-1); Vol. IV. Wedlock's the Devil: Eighteen Fourteen to Eighteen Fifteen. 369p. 1975. 16.50x (ISBN 0-674-08944-8); Vol. V. So Late into the Night. 320p. 1976. 15.00x (ISBN 0-674-08945-6); Vol. VI. The Flesh Is Frail: Eighteen Eighteen to Eighteen Nineteen. 289p. 1976. 15.00x (ISBN 0-674-08946-4); Vol. VII. Between Two Worlds: Eighteen Twenty. 282p. 1977. 15.00x (ISBN 0-674-08947-2); Vol. VIII. Born for Opposition: Eighteen Twenty-One. 384p. 1978. 16.50x (ISBN 0-674-08948-0); Vol. 9. In the Wind's Eye: 1821-1822. 248p. 1979. 15.00x (ISBN 0-674-08949-9); Vol. 10. A Heart for Every Fate: 1822-1823. 239p. 1980. 15.00x (ISBN 0-674-08952-9); Vol. 11. For Freedom's Battle. 256p. 15.00 (ISBN 0-674-08953-7). Harvard U Pr.

--Lord Byron: Don Juan. Steffan, T. G., et al, eds. LC 81-3011. (Yale English Poets Ser.: No. 10). 760p. 1982. text ed. 25.00x (ISBN 0-300-02678-1); pap. 8.95x (ISBN 0-300-02686-2, YEP-10). Yale U Pr.

--Selected Poems & Letters. Marshall, William H., ed. LC 77-76594. (Gotham Library). 536p. 1977. 22.50x o.p. (ISBN 0-8147-5417-1); pap. 12.50x o.p. (ISBN 0-8147-5418-X). NYU Pr.

--Selected Poetry of Byron. Auden, W. H., ed. (Orig.). 1966. pap. 2.95 (ISBN 0-451-51559-5, CE1559, Sig Classics). NAL.

Byron, Gilbert. Chesapeake Duke. 163p. 1975. pap. 5.00 (ISBN 0-686-36629-8). Md Hist.

--The Lord's Oysters. LC 74-9246. xiv, 330p. 1967. Repr. of 1957 ed. 30.00x (ISBN 0-8103-5032-7). Gale.

--The War of Eighteen-Twelve on the Chesapeake Bay. (Illus.). 94p. 1964. 5.00 (ISBN 0-686-36633-6). Md Hist.

Byron, James. Or Be He Dead. LC 81-48169. 224p. 1982. pap. 2.84i (ISBN 0-06-080585-4, P585, PL). Har-Row.

Byron, Joseph. New York Interiors at the Turn of the Century. (Illus.). 192p. (Orig.). 1976. pap. 6.95 (ISBN 0-486-23359-6). Dover.

Byron, Stuart & Weis, Elisabeth, eds. Movie Comedy. 1977. pap. 5.95 (ISBN 0-14-004578-3). Penguin.

Byron, William, ed. The Causes of World Hunger. LC 82-60591. 1983. pap. 8.95 (ISBN 0-8091-2483-1). Paulist Pr.

Byron, William, tr. see Le Vot, Andre.

Byrum, C. Stephen. The Value Structure of Theology. 1978. pap. text ed. 7.50 o.p. (ISBN 0-8191-0391-8). U Pr of Amer.

Byrum, Douglas. Practical Drilling & Production Design. 528p. 1982. 49.95x (ISBN 0-87814-180-4). Pennwell Books Division.

Byrum, Isabel. Harry the Newsboy & Other Stories. 32p. 1982. pap. 0.35 (ISBN 0-686-36266-7). Faith Pub Hse.

Byse, Clark, jt. auth. see Gellhorn, Walter.

Byskov, A. G. & Peters, H., eds. Development & Function of Reproductive Organs: Proceedings of the Workshop on the Development & Function of the Reproduction Organs, 5th, Copenhagen, Jul. 6-9, 1981. (International Congress Ser.: No. 559). 450p. 1981. 73.75 (ISBN 0-444-90230-9). Elsevier.

Bystrom, Marcia, jt. auth. see Hauck, Roland D.

Bythell, Duncan. Handloom Weavers. LC 69-10487. (Illus.). 1969. 59.50 (ISBN 0-521-07580-7). Cambridge U Pr.

--The Sweated Trade: Outwork in Nineteenth Century Britain. LC 78-451. 1979. 26.00 (ISBN 0-312-77999-2). St Martin.

--The Sweated Trades: Outwork in the Nineteenth Century. 1978. 42.50 o.p. (ISBN 0-7134-1259-3, Pub. by Batsford England). David & Charles.

Bytheriver, Marylee. A Short Dictionary of Astrology. (Illus.). 1978. pap. 2.95i o.p. (ISBN 0-06-090629-4, CN 629, CN). Har-Row.

Bytwerk, Randall L. Julius Streicher: The Man Who Persuaded a Nation to Hate Jews. LC 81-40814. (Illus.). 208p. 1982. 18.95 (ISBN 0-8128-2834-8). Stein & Day.

Bywater, H. E. Dogs: Their Care, Training & Health. 1969. 1.00 (ISBN 0-7137-0113-7). Palmetto Pub.

Bywater, Ingram, tr. see Aristotle.

Bywater, R. Hardware-Software Design of Digital Systems. 1981. 27.95 (ISBN 0-13-383950-8). P-H.

Bzoch, K. Assessing Language Skills in Infancy. 68p. 1978. pap. text ed. 16.95 (ISBN 0-8391-1240-8). Univ Park.

C

C. & Chia, L. S. Developing Economies & the Environment: The Southeast Asia Experience. 1982. 13.00x (ISBN 0-07-099458-7). McGraw.

C, Chester, jt. auth. see O'Brien, Bonnie B.

Caballero, Cesar. Chicano Organizations Directory. (Orig.). 1983. pap. 24.95 (ISBN 0-918212-65-0). Neal-Schuman.

Caballero, Jane A. Art Projects for Young Children. LC 79-65813. (Illus.). 142p. (Orig.). pap. 14.95 (ISBN 0-89334-051-0). Humanics Ltd.

Caballero, Jane A. & Whordley, Derek. Children Around the World. 172p. (Orig.). 1982. pap. 12.95 (ISBN 0-89334-033-2). Humanics Ltd.

Cabaniss, Allen, ed. Son of Charlemagne: A Contemporary Life of Louis the Pious. LC 61-1398. 1961. 16.95x (ISBN 0-8156-2031-4). Syracuse U Pr.

Cabanne, Pierre. Pablo Picasso: His Life & Times. 2nd ed. Salemson, Harold J., tr. from Fr. LC 77-4984. (Illus.). 1979. pap. 6.95 (ISBN 0-688-08232-7). Quill NY.

Cabannes, Henri. Theoretical Magneto Fluid-Dynamics. LC 75-117095. (Applied Mathematics & Mechanics Ser.: Vol. 13). 1970. 48.00 (ISBN 0-12-153750-1). Acad Pr.

Cabarga, Leslie. The Fleischer Story. 1976. 12.50 o.p. (ISBN 0-517-52580-1). Crown.

Cabat, Louis, jt. auth. see Lopez, Juan E.

Cabeceiras, James. The Multimedia Library: Materials Selection & Use. 275p. 1978. tchrs' ed. 14.50 (ISBN 0-12-153950-4). Acad Pr.

--The Multimedia Library: Materials Selection & Use. (Library & Information Science). 1982. 19.50 (ISBN 0-12-153952-0). Acad Pr.

Cabeen, David C. & Holmes, Urban T., eds. Critical Bibliography of French Literature, Vol. 1: The Medieval Period. LC 47-3282. 1952. 34.95x o.p. (ISBN 0-8156-2005-5). Syracuse U Pr.

Cabeen, Richard M. Standard Handbook of Stamp Collecting. 3rd ed. LC 78-3297. (Illus.). 1979. 15.34i (ISBN 0-690-01773-1). T Y Crowell.

Cabelka, J., jt. auth. see Novak, P.

Cabell, Harriet W., jt. auth. see Willimon, William H.

Cabell, James B. Jurgen. (Illus.). 9.50 (ISBN 0-8446-5561-9). Peter Smith.

Cabellero, Nicolas. The Way to Freedom: Oriental & Christian Approaches to Meditation. LC 82-60852. 160p. 1982. pap. 7.95 (ISBN 0-8091-2476-9). Paulist Pr.

Cabibi, John F. Copy Preparation for Printing. Cleverdon, Ardelle, ed. (Illus.). 144p. 1973. pap. text ed. 18.05 (ISBN 0-07-009524-8, G). McGraw.

Cable, George W. Silent South: Including the Freedman's Case in Equity, the Convict Lease System & to Which Has Been Added Eight Hitherto Uncollected Essays by Cable on Prison & Asylum Reform & an Essay on Cable by Arlin Turner. LC 69-14915. (Criminology, Law Enforcement, & Social Problems Ser.: No. 57). 1969. 10.00x (ISBN 0-87585-057-X). Patterson Smith.

Cable, James. Gunboat Diplomacy. 2nd ed. 260p. 1981. 26.00 (ISBN 0-312-35346-4). St Martin.

Cable, Sir James. The Royal Navy & the Siege of Bilbao. LC 78-73238. (Illus.). 1980. 24.95 (ISBN 0-521-22516-7). Cambridge U Pr.

Cable, John L., jt. auth. see Bosstick, Maurice.

Cable, Mary. Avery's Knot. 248p. 1981. 12.95 (ISBN 0-399-12569-8). Putnam Pub Group.

Cable, Thomas. The Meter & Melody of Beowulf. LC 72-97683. (Studies in Language & Literature Ser: No. 64). 144p. 1974. 10.00 o.p. (ISBN 0-252-00348-9). U of Ill Pr.

Cable, Thomas, jt. auth. see Baugh, Albert C.

Cable, Vincent & Rebelo, Ivonia. Britain's Pattern of Specialization in Manufactured Goods with Developing Countries & Trade Protection. (Working Paper: No. 425). 61p. 1980. 3.00 (ISBN 0-686-36204-7, WP-0425). World Bank.

Cabot, A. Victor & Hartnett, Donald L. Introduction to Management Science. LC 76-20024. (Illus.). 1977. text ed. 27.95 (ISBN 0-201-02746-1). A-W.

Cabot, George. Life & Letters of George Cabot. Lodge, Henry C., ed. LC 71-124902. (American Public Figures Ser). xi, 617p. 1974. Repr. of 1877 ed. lib. bdg. 79.50 (ISBN 0-306-71001-3). Da Capo.

Cabot, Isabel. Enchanted Carousel. (YA) 1981. 6.95 (ISBN 0-686-74794-1, Avalon). Bouregy.

--Love Finds Dr. Shelly. (YA) 1978. 6.95 (ISBN 0-685-05590-6, Avalon). Bouregy.

--Share of Danger. (YA) 1980. 6.95 (ISBN 0-686-59801-6, Avalon). Bouregy.

--Summer of Discovery. (YA) 1980. 6.95 (ISBN 0-686-73940-X, Avalon). Bouregy.

Cabot, Philippe S., ed. Juvenile Delinquency: A Critical Annotated Bibliography. LC 75-138580. 1971. Repr. of 1946 ed. lib. bdg. 17.50x (ISBN 0-8371-5779-X, CAJD). Greenwood.

Cabot, Richard C. Social Service & the Art of Healing. LC 73-84257. (NASW Classics Ser). 192p. 1973. pap. text ed. 5.00 (ISBN 0-87101-062-3, CBC-062-1). Natl Assn Soc Wkrs.

Cabot, Stephen J. Labor Management Relations Act Manual. 1st ed. 1978. 48.00 (ISBN 0-88262-208-0, 78-60446). Warren.

Cabot, Tracy, jt. auth. see Wanderer, Zev.

Cabot, Tracy, jt. auth. see Wanderer, Dr. Zev.

Cabral, Amilcar. Unity & Struggle: Speeches & Writings. LC 79-2337. 1979. 16.50 (ISBN 0-85345-510-4, CL5104); pap. 10.00 (ISBN 0-85345-625-9, PB6259). Monthly Rev.

Cabral, J. Religiones, Sectas y Herejias. Carrodeguas, Andy & Marosi, Esteban, eds. Marosi, Antonio, tr. 176p. (Span.). 1982. pap. 3.00 (ISBN 0-8297-1282-8). Life Pubs Intl.

Cabrera, Neonetta C. & Cunanan, Augustina S. Tagalog Beginning Course. Bowen, J. Donald, tr. 526p. Date not set. with 33 audio cassettes 295.00x (ISBN 0-88432-103-7). J Norton Pubs.

Cabrera, Roberto & Meyers, Patricia. Classic Tailoring Techniques: A Construction Guide for Men's Wear. (Illus.). 260p. 1983. text ed. 18.50 (ISBN 0-87005-431-7). Fairchild.

Cabrera, Vicente. Juan Benet. (World Authors Ser.). 176p. 1983. lib. bdg. 17.95 (ISBN 0-8057-6532-8, Twayne). G K Hall.

Cabrera, Victor J. El Diacono un Enfoque Biblico. 64p. (Span.). Date not set. pap. cancelled (ISBN 0-311-17021-8, Edit Mundo). Casa Bautista.

Cabrera, Y. Arturo. Emerging Faces: The Mexican-Americans. LC 79-135153. 1978. pap. 5.95x (ISBN 0-932848-02-8). Sierra Pubns Co.

--Minorities in Higher Education. LC 78-68819. 1978. pap. 6.95x (ISBN 0-932848-01-X). Sierra Pubns Co.

Cabrera, Y. Arturo & Perea, Jose A. Community College Conflict: Chicano Under Fire. LC 78-56755. (Illus.). 1979. pap. 4.95x (ISBN 0-932848-03-6). Sierra Pubns Co.

Cabrera, Y. Arturo, ed. Strategies for the Education of Chicanos. LC 78-52129. 1978. pap. 5.95x (ISBN 0-932848-00-1). Sierra Pubns Co.

Cabrera-Infante, G. Three Trapped Tigers. 1978. pap. 5.95i o.p. (ISBN 0-06-090636-7, CN 636, CN). Har-Row.

Caccamise, Frank & Garritson, Mervin, eds. Teaching ASL as a Second-Foreign Language: Proceedings of National Symposium on Sign Language Research & Teaching. 240p. (Orig.). 1982. pap. text ed. 15.95 (ISBN 0-913072-49-4). Natl Assn Deaf.

Cachiaras, Dot. I'm Glad God Thought of Mothers. (Happy Day Bks.). (Illus.). 24p. (gr. k-3). 1979. 1.29 (ISBN 0-87239-360-7, 3630). Standard Pub.

--Sharing Makes Me Happy. Mahany, Patricia, ed. LC 82-80030. (Happy Day Bks.). (Illus.). 24p. (Orig.). (ps-3). 1982. pap. 1.29 (ISBN 0-87239-543-X, 3589). Standard Pub.

Cacioppo, John T. & Petty, Richard E., eds. Perspectives in Cardiovascular Psychophysiology. LC 81-6766. 392p. 1982. 34.50 (ISBN 0-89862-613-7). Guilford Pr.

Cacoyannis, Michael, tr. see Euripides.

Cada, Lawrence, et al. Shaping the Coming Age of Religious Life. 1979. 10.95x (ISBN 0-8164-0425-9); pap. 4.95 (ISBN 0-8164-2207-9). Seabury.

Cadbury, William & Poague, Leland. Film Criticism: A Counter Theory. 330p. 1983. 23.50x (ISBN 0-8138-0352-7). Iowa St U Pr.

Caddell, Gloria M., et al see Oakley, Carey.

Caddell, Laurie. Modern Motor Bikes. (Illus.). 1979. 12.50 o.p. (ISBN 0-7137-0989-8, Pub by Blandford Pr England). Sterling.

Caddell, Robert M. Deformation & Fracture of Solids. (Illus.). 1980. text ed. 32.00 (ISBN 0-13-198309-1). P-H.

Caddell, Robert M. & Hosford, William F. Metal Forming: Mechanics & Metallurgy. (Illus.). 352p. 1983. text ed. 30.00 (ISBN 0-13-577700-3). P-H.

Cade, C. Maxwell & Coxhead, Nona. The Awakened Mind. 1980. pap. 4.95 o.s.i. (ISBN 0-440-50303-5, Delta). Dell.

Cade, Laurie. Sports Cars. 5.50x (ISBN 0-392-06000-0, SpS). Sportshelf.

Cade, Toni, ed. The Black Woman: An Anthology. 256p. 1974. pap. 2.50 (ISBN 0-451-62068-2, ME2068, Ment). NAL.

Cadell, Elizabeth. The Cuckoo in Spring. 214p. 1976. Repr. of 1954 ed. lib. bdg. 15.95x (ISBN 0-89244-067-8). Queens Hse.

--A Lion in the Way. 330p. 1982. 13.50 (ISBN 0-688-01098-9). Morrow.

--Parson's House. 1977. lib. bdg. 11.95 o.p. (ISBN 0-8161-6528-9, Large Print Bks). G K Hall.

--Return Match. (General Ser.). 1979. lib. bdg. 13.95 (ISBN 0-8161-6757-5, Large Print Bks). G K Hall.

Cadell, James, tr. see Bosi, Roberto.

Cadenet, J. J. De see Castro, R. & De Cadenet, J. J.

Cadenhead, Ivie E., Jr. Jesus Gonzalez Ortega & Mexican National Politics. Worcester, Donald E., ed. LC 73-161482. (History & Culture Monograph Ser.: No. 9). 161p. 1972. pap. 6.00x (ISBN 0-912646-05-5). Tex Christian.

Cadieux, Charles L. Coyotes: Predators & Survivors. (Illus.). 224p. 1983. 16.95 (ISBN 0-913276-42-1). Stone Wall Pr.

Cadiz, Luis M. de see De Cesarea, Eusebio.

Cadnum, Michael. The Morning of the Massacre. 1982. 25.00 (ISBN 0-931460-19-0). Bieler.

Cadogan, Mary & Craig, Patricia. Women & Children First. 1978. 18.95 o.p. (ISBN 0-575-02418-6, Pub. by Gollancz England). David & Charles.

Cadogan, Peter. The Moon-Our Sister Planet. LC 80-41564. (Illus.). 400p. 1981. 64.50 (ISBN 0-521-23684-3); pap. 27.95 (ISBN 0-521-28152-0). Cambridge U Pr.

Cadoux, R. Envolee. college ed. 1973. 13.95 (ISBN 0-02-318020-X). Macmillan.

Cadow, Harry W. Punched-Card Data Processing. LC 72-95421. (Illus.). 344p. 1973. pap. text ed. 16.95 (ISBN 0-574-18485-6, 13-1485); instr's guide avail. (ISBN 0-574-18486-4, 13-1486). SRA.

Cadwallader, Sharon. Cooking Adventures for Kids. LC 74-9544. (A San Francisco Ser.). 101p. 1974. 8.95 o.s.i. (ISBN 0-395-19976-X); pap. 6.95 (ISBN 0-395-19980-8). HM.

--The Living Kitchen. LC 82-10763. (Tools for Today Ser.). (Illus.). 128p. (Orig.). 1983. pap. 7.95 (ISBN 0-87156-326-6). Sierra.

--The Living Kitchen. (Tools for Today Ser.). 1983. pap. 6.95 (ISBN 0-686-84928-0). Sierra.

Cadwell, Jerry J. Nuclear Facility Treat Analysis & Tactical Response Procedures. (Illus.). 120p. 1983. 22.50x (ISBN 0-398-04778-2). C C Thomas.

Cady, Edwin H. Stephen Crane. (U. S. Authors Ser.: No. 23). 1962. lib. bdg. 9.95 o.p. (ISBN 0-8057-0168-0, Twayne). G K Hall.

--Stephen Crane. rev. ed. (United States Author Ser.). 1980. lib. bdg. 10.95 (ISBN 0-8057-7299-5, Twayne). G K Hall.

Cady, Edwin H., ed. W. D. Howells a Critic. (Routledge Critic Ser). 510p. 1973. 30.00x o.p. (ISBN 0-7100-7676-2). Routledge & Kegan.

Cady, Edwin H., ed. see Howells, William D.

Cady, Jack. The Jonah Watch. 224p. 1983. pap. 2.75 (ISBN 0-380-62828-7, 62828). Avon.

--Singleton. LC 81-8117. 288p. 1981. 13.95 (ISBN 0-914842-63-3). Madrona Pubs.

Cady, John F. The History of Post War Southeast Asia: Independence Problems. LC 74-82497. xxii, 720p. 1974. 26.00x (ISBN 0-8214-0160-2, 82-81594); pap. 12.00x (ISBN 0-8214-0175-0, 82-81602). Ohio U Pr.

--Southeast Asia: Its Historical Development. 1964. 28.95 (ISBN 0-07-009530-2, C). McGraw.

--The Southeast Asian World. LC 76-53353. (World of Asia Ser). (Illus.). 1977. pap. text ed. 4.25x (ISBN 0-88273-502-0). Forum Pr IL.

Cady, Leo & Rotherham, Edward R. Australian Native Orchids in Colour. LC 70-138063. (Illus.). 1971. 10.25 (ISBN 0-589-07011-8, Pub. by Reed Books Australia). C E Tuttle.

Cadzow, James A. Discrete Time Systems: An Introduction with Interdisciplinary Applications. (Computer Applications in Electrical Engineering Ser.). (Illus.). 448p. 1973. ref. ed. 31.95 (ISBN 0-13-215996-1). P-H.

Cadzow, James A. & Martens, Hinrich R. Discrete Time & Computer Control Systems. (Electrical Engineering Ser). 1970. ref. ed. 31.95 (ISBN 0-13-216036-6). P-H.

Cadzow, John F. & Ludanyi, Andrew, eds. Transylvania: The Roots of Ethnic Conflict. LC 82-23354. (Illus.). 360p. 1983. 32.50 (ISBN 0-87338-283-8). Kent St U Pr.

Caemmerer, H. Paul. Life of Pierre Charles l'Enfant. LC 71-87546. (Architecture & Decorative Art Ser.: Vol. 33). 1970. Repr. of 1950 ed. lib. bdg. 55.00 (ISBN 0-306-71381-0). Da Capo.

Caen, Herb. The Cable Car & the Dragon. LC 77-157151. 32p. (gr. 1-3). 1972. 7.95a o.p. (ISBN 0-385-05643-5); PLB (ISBN 0-385-06672-4). Doubleday.

Caenegem, R. C. Van see Van Caenegem, R. C.

Caes, Charles J. Introduction to the Arguments for God. 1983. 8.95 (ISBN 0-686-97926-5). Libra.

Caesar, A. D., jt. auth. see Rivise, Charles W.

Caesar, Clifford, compiled by. Stravinsky: A Complete Catalogue. LC 81-51157. (Illus.). 1982. pap. 7.50 (ISBN 0-911302-41-7). San Francisco Pr.

Caesar, Irving. Sing a Song of Friendship. Repr. 1.95 (ISBN 0-686-95023-2). ADL.

Caesar, Julius. The Civil War. Mitchell, Jane F., tr. (Classics Ser.). 1976. pap. 3.95 (ISBN 0-14-044187-5). Penguin.

--The Conquest of Gaul. rev. ed. Handford, S. A., tr. 1983. pap. 3.95 (ISBN 0-14-044433-5). Penguin.

Caesar, Sid & Davidson, Bill. Where Have I Been? An Autobiography. 288p. 1982. 12.95 (ISBN 0-517-54794-5). Crown.

Caesarius Of Arles, St. Sermons, Nos. 187-238. (Fathers of the Church Ser.: Vol. 66). 1973. 14.95 (ISBN 0-8132-0066-0). Cath U Pr.

--Sermons-One to Eighty. (Fathers of the Church Ser.: Vol. 31). 1956. 20.00 (ISBN 0-8132-0031-8). Cath U Pr.

Caetani, Marguerite, ed. see Botteghe Oscure.

Cafarelli, Eugene J. Developing New Products & Repositing Mature Brands: A Risk-Reduction System That Produces Investment Alternatives. (Marketing Management Ser.). 253p. 1980. 29.95 (ISBN 0-471-04634-5, Pub by Ronald Pr). Wiley.

Cafferata, John. Rites. LC 73-19686. (Illus.). 544p. 1974. pap. text ed. 12.95 o.p. (ISBN 0-07-009561-2, C). McGraw.

Cafferty, B., jt. auth. see Lisitsyn, G. M.

Cafferty, Pastora S. & Chestang, Leon W., eds. The Diverse Society: Implications for Social Policy. LC 76-43633. 176p. 1976. pap. 8.50x (ISBN 0-87101-072-0, CBC-072-C). Natl Assn Soc Wkrs.

Caffin, Caroline & Caffin, Charles H. Dancing & Dancers of Today. (Series in Dance). (Illus.). 1978. Repr. of 1912 ed. lib. bdg. 27.50 (ISBN 0-306-77579-4). Da Capo.

Caffin, Charles H. Photography as a Fine Art. facsimile ed. LC 73-167715. 192p. 1981. Repr. of 1901 ed. pap. 12.95 (ISBN 0-87100-019-9). Morgan.

Caffin, Charles H., jt. auth. see Caffin, Caroline.

Cagan, Carl. Data Management Systems. LC 73-11036. 141p. 1973. 29.95 o.p. (ISBN 0-471-12915-1, Pub. by Wiley-Interscience). Wiley.

Cagan, Phillip & Lipsey, Robert. The Financial Effects of Inflation. LC 78-13124. (National Bureau of Economic Research General Studies: No. 103). 112p. 1978. prof ref 18.50x (ISBN 0-88410-486-9). Ballinger Pub.

Cage, John M., jt. auth. see Oliver, Bernard M.

Cagle, Charles V. Handbook of Adhesive Bonding. 1973. 55.00 (ISBN 0-07-009588-4, P&RB). McGraw.

Cagle, James V. The Story of Santa Claus, Junior. (Illus.). 1979. 5.00 o.p. (ISBN 0-682-49464-X). Exposition.

Caglioti, G. & Milone, A. F., eds. Mechanical & Thermal Behaviour of Metallic Materials: Proceedings of the International School of Physics, "Enrico Fermi," Course LXXXII, Varenna, Italy, 30 June-10 July, 1981. (Enrico Fermi International Summer School of Physics Ser.: Vol. 82). 500p. 1982. 99.75 (ISBN 0-444-86500-4, North Holland). Elsevier.

Caglioti, G., ed. see International School of Physics "Enrico Fermi" Course LXI, Varenna, July 8-20, 1974.

Caglioti, Luciano & Giacconi, Mirella. The Two Faces of Chemistry: The Benefits & the Risks of Chemical Technology. LC 82-12706. 230p. 1983. 17.50 (ISBN 0-262-03088-8). MIT Pr.

Cagnacci & Schwicker, A. International Dictionary of Metallurgy, Mineralogy, Geology & the Mining Oil Industries. (Eng, Ger, Fr, Ital.). 1970. 54.50 o.p. (ISBN 0-07-009580-9, P&RB). McGraw.

Cagnoa, B. & Pebay-Peyroula, J. C. Modern Atomic Physics: Quantum Theory & Its Application, Vol. 2. LC 74-26875. 253p. Repr. of 1975 ed. 19.25 (ISBN 0-470-12921-2). Krieger.

Cahalan, Don & Cisin, Ira H. American Drinking Practices. 9.50 o.p. (ISBN 0-686-92179-8, 4225). Hazelden.

Cahalan, M. J., intro. by. Advances in Extractive Metallurgy. 1023p. 1968. text ed. 40.25x (ISBN 0-686-32508-7). IMM North Am.

Cahill, Daniel J. Harriet Monroe. (U. S. Authors Ser.: No. 222). 1973. lib. bdg. 10.95 o.p. (ISBN 0-8057-0515-5, Twayne). G K Hall.

Cahill, George F., Jr., ed. see American Physiological Society.

Cahill, George F., Jr., jt. ed. see Renold, Albert E.

Cahill, George F., Jr., ed. see Wechsler, Henry, et al.

Cahill, James. Sakaki Hyakusen & Early Nanga Painting. (Japan Research Monograph: No. 3). (Illus.). 100p. (Orig.). 1983. pap. 8.00x (ISBN 0-912966-58-0). IEAS.

Cahill, James, compiled by. An Index of Early Chinese Painters & Painting: T'ang, Sung & Yuan. LC 77-85755. 1980. 32.50x (ISBN 0-520-03576-3). U of Cal Pr.

Cahill, P. Joseph, tr. see Leon-Dufour, Xavier.

Cahill, Robert B. & Herbic, Herbert J. Fan the Deck. rev. ed. 1980. pap. text ed. 4.50 (ISBN 0-933282-02-8). Stack the Deck.

Cahill, Robert B. & Hrebic, Herbert J. Cut the Deck. rev. ed. (Illus., Orig.). (gr. 7-8). 1979. pap. 4.50 (ISBN 0-933282-01-X). Stack the Deck.

Cahill, Susan. Women & Fiction, Vol. 2. (Orig.). 1978. pap. 3.95 (ISBN 0-451-62156-5, ME2156, Ment). NAL.

Cahill, Susan & Cooper, Michele. Urban Reader. LC 75-137898. (Illus.). 1971. pap. text ed. 13.95 (ISBN 0-13-939041-3). P-H.

Cahn, Anne, et al. Controlling Future Arms Trade. (Nineteen Eighties Project, Council on Foreign Relations Ser.). 1977. text ed. 13.95 o.p. (ISBN 0-07-009589-2, P&RB); pap. 5.95 o.p. (ISBN 0-07-009590-6). McGraw.

Cahn, Cynthia. The Day the Sun Split. pap. 3.00 (ISBN 0-686-81815-6). Anhinga Pr.

Cahn, Edmond, ed. Supreme Court & Supreme Law. 1971. pap. 2.95 o.p. (ISBN 0-671-21067-X, Touchstone Bks). S&S.

Cahn, Edmond N. The Predicament of Democratic Man. LC 78-16399. 1979. Repr. of 1961 ed. lib. bdg. 18.75x (ISBN 0-313-20597-3, CAPR). Greenwood.

Cahn, Julie. The Dating Book. Schneider, Meg, ed. (Just For Teens). 160p. 1983. pap. 3.50 (ISBN 0-671-46277-6). Wanderer Bks.

--The Dating Book. (Teen Survival Library). 160p. (gr. 9-12). 1983. PLB 9.29 (ISBN 0-671-46742-5). Messner.

--Holiday Romance. Schnedier, Meg & Schwartz, Betty, eds. (Dream Your Own Romance Ser.). 128p. (Orig.). (gr. 4-5). 1983. pap. 2.95 (ISBN 0-671-46450-7). Wanderer Bks.

Cahn, L. R., ed. see International Academy of Oral Pathology.

Cahn, R. W., ed. Physical Metallurgy. 2nd rev. ed. 1971. 127.75 (ISBN 0-444-10063-6, North-Holland). Elsevier.

Cahn, Rhoda, jt. auth. see Cahn, William.

Cahn, Robert. The Fight to Save Wild Alaska. (Illus.). 34p. 1982. pap. write for info. (ISBN 0-930698-14-2). Natl Audubon.

Cahn, Steven M., ed. Classics of Western Philosophy. LC 76-54500. (Illus.). 1977. 30.00 (ISBN 0-915144-29-8); pap. text ed. 17.50 (ISBN 0-915144-28-X). Hackett Pub.

--New Studies in the Philosophy of John Dewey. LC 76-62914. 227p. 1977. text ed. 12.00 o.p. (ISBN 0-87451-140-2); pap. 8.00x (ISBN 0-87451-219-0). U Pr of New Eng.

Cahn, Walter. Romanesque Bible Illumination. LC 82-71593. 308p. 1982. 95.00x (ISBN 0-8014-1446-6). Cornell U Pr.

Cahn, William. A Pictorial History of American Labor. (Illus.). 12.50 o.p. (ISBN 0-517-50040-X). Crown.

Cahn, William & Cahn, Rhoda. The Great American Comedy Scene. LC 77-21676. (Illus.). 192p. (gr. 7 up). 1978. PLB 7.79 o.p. (ISBN 0-671-32835-2). Messner.

Cahoon, Herbert. Thomas Lange & Charles Ryskamp: American Literary Autographs from Washington Irving to Henry James. 15.00 o.p. (ISBN 0-8446-5655-0). Peter Smith.

Cahoon, N. Corey & Heise, Eorge W. The Primary Battery, Vol. 2. LC 73-121906. (Electrochemical Society Ser.). 528p. 1976. 71.50x (ISBN 0-471-12923-2, Pub. by Wiley-Interscience). Wiley.

Caiden, Gerald, ed. Public Policy & Administrative Reform. (Orig.). 1981. pap. 6.00 (ISBN 0-918592-46-1). Policy Studies.

Caiden, Gerald E. & Siedentopf, Heinrich. Strategies for Administrative Reform. LC 81-48070. (A Policy Studies Organization Bk.). 272p. 1982. 26.95x (ISBN 0-669-05241-8). Lexington Bks.

Caiden, Gerald E., ed. International Handbook of the Ombudsman: Country Surveys. LC 81-20190. (Illus.). 1983. lib. bdg. 75.00 (ISBN 0-313-23716-6, COM/02). Greenwood.

--International Handbook of the Ombudsman: Evolution & Present Function, Vol II of II. LC 81-20190. (Illus.). 1983. lib. bdg. 45.00 (ISBN 0-313-23715-8, COM/01). Greenwood.

Caiden, Naomi & Wildavsky, Aaron. Planning & Budgeting in Poor Countries. 371p. (Orig.). 1980. pap. text ed. 14.95 (ISBN 0-87855-707-5). Transaction Bks.

--Planning & Budgeting in Poor Countries. LC 73-12312. (Comparative Studies in Behavioral Science). 416p. 1974. 35.95x (ISBN 0-471-12925-9, Pub. by Wiley-Interscience). Wiley.

Caidin, Martin. Deathmate. 240p. 1982. pap. 2.95 (ISBN 0-553-20355-X). Bantam.

--The Tigers Are Burning. (Illus.). 1980. pap. 2.75 (ISBN 0-523-41816-7). Pinnacle Bks.

Caillat, Collette. Jain Cosmology. (Illus.). 192p. 1982. 55.00 (ISBN 0-517-54662-0, Harmony). Crown.

Cailler, Bernadette, et al see Johnson & Lemuel, A.

Cailleux, jt. auth. see Tricart, J.

Cailliet, Emile. Pascal: The Emergence of Genius. 2nd ed. LC 75-94602. 383p. Repr. of 1961 ed. lib. bdg. 18.75x (ISBN 0-8371-2537-5, CAP). Greenwood.

Cailliet, Gregor M., jt. ed. see Love, Milton.

Cailliet, Rene. Foot & Ankle Pain. (Illus.). 1968. pap. 8.95x o.p. (ISBN 0-8036-1600-7). Davis Co.

--Foot & Ankle Pain. 2nd ed. LC 82-9967. (The Pain Ser.). (Illus.). 200p. 1982. pap. text ed. 11.95 (ISBN 0-8036-1601-5). Davis Co.

--Hand Pain & Impairment. 2nd ed. LC 75-6660. (Illus.). 170p. 1975. pap. text ed. 7.95x o.p. (ISBN 0-8036-1617-1). Davis Co.

--Knee Pain & Disability. 2nd ed. LC 82-17296. (Pain Ser.). (Illus.). 220p. 1983. pap. text ed. 11.95 (ISBN 0-8036-1621-X, 1621-X). Davis Co.

Caillois, Roger. Man & the Sacred. Barash, Meyer, tr. from Fr. LC 79-8709. 190p. 1980. Repr. of 1959 ed. lib. bdg. 19.00x (ISBN 0-313-22196-0, CAMS). Greenwood.

Caillot, Simonne, jt. auth. see Nail, Simonne.

Caillou, Alan. Afghan Assault. (Tobin's War Ser.: No. 4). 192p. 1980. pap. 1.95 o.p. (ISBN 0-523-41052-2). Pinnacle Bks.

--Congo War Cry. (Tobin's War Ser.: No. 3). 192p. (Orig.). 1980. pap. 1.95 o.p. (ISBN 0-523-41029-8). Pinnacle Bks.

--Dead Sea Submarine. (Tobin's War Ser.: No. 1). 192p. (Orig.). 1980. pap. 1.75 o.p. (ISBN 0-523-40958-3). Pinnacle Bks.

--Terror in Rio. (Tobin's War Ser.: No. 2). 192p. 1980. pap. 2.25 o.p. (ISBN 0-523-41028-X). Pinnacle Bks.

Cai Longyun & Shao Shankang. Zuijiuquan: A Drunkard's Boxing. (Chinese Kung-Fu Ser.). (Illus.). 155p. 1982. pap. 6.95 (ISBN 0-686-42862-5). China Bks.

Cain, Albert C., ed. Survivors of Suicide. (Illus.). 324p. 1972. photocopy ed. spiral 26.75x (ISBN 0-398-02252-6). C C Thomas.

Cain, Arthur H. Young People & Health. LC 72-12083. (John Day Bk.). 160p. 1973. 8.61i (ISBN 0-381-98241-6). T Y Crowell.

Cain, C. K., ed. Annual Reports in Medicinal Chemistry, Vol. 17. (Serial Publication). 400p. 1982. 32.00 (ISBN 0-12-040517-2); membership Price 4.00 (ISBN 0-686-82449-0). Acad Pr.

Cain, Cornelius K., ed. Annual Reports in Medicinal Chemistry. 37.00 ea. Vol. 1 1966 (ISBN 0-12-040501-6). Vol. 2 1967 (ISBN 0-12-040502-4). Vol. 3 1968 (ISBN 0-12-040503-2). Vol. 4 1969 (ISBN 0-12-040504-0). Vol. 5 1970 (ISBN 0-12-040505-9). Vol. 6 1971 (ISBN 0-12-040506-7). Vol. 7 1972 (ISBN 0-12-040507-5). Acad Pr.

Cain, Errol Le see Le Cain, Errol.

Cain, Harvey D., jt. auth. see Flint, Thomas, Jr.

Cain, Jack & Carman, Robert A. Mathematics for Business Careers. LC 79-21747. 616p. 1981. pap. text ed. 19.95x (ISBN 0-471-03163-1); tchrs. manual 8.00 (ISBN 0-471-09086-7). Wiley.

Cain, James M. Hard Cain. 13.95 (ISBN 0-8398-2656-7, Gregg). G K hall.

--Love's Lovely Counterfeit. LC 79-10778. 1979. pap. 2.95 (ISBN 0-394-74213-3, Vin). Random.

--The Postman Always Rings Twice. 1978. pap. 2.25 (ISBN 0-394-74545-0, Vin). Random.

Cain, Maureen E. Society & the Policeman's Role. (International Library of Sociology). (Illus.). 326p. 1973. 26.50x (ISBN 0-7100-7490-5). Routledge & Kegan.

Cain, Melinda, jt. ed. see Dauber, Roslyn.

Cain, Roy L. Studies of Coprophilous Sphaeriales in Ontario. (Illus.). 1968. Repr. of 1934 ed. 16.00 (ISBN 3-7682-0531-2). Lubrecht & Cramer.

Cain, Sandra E. & Evans, Jack M. Sciencing: An Involvement Approach to Elementary Science Methods. 350p. 1983. pap. text ed. 16.95 (ISBN 0-675-20055-5). Additional supplements may be obtained from publisher. Merrill.

Cain, Sandra G. & Evans, Jack M. Sciencing: An Involvement Approach to Elementary Science Methods. 1979. 16.95 (ISBN 0-675-08364-8). Additional supplements may be obtained from publisher. Merrill.

Cain, T. G., ed. Jacobean & Caroline Poetry: An Anthology. LC 80-42217. 352p. 1982. 22.00x (ISBN 0-416-31060-5); pap. 10.95x (ISBN 0-416-31070-2). Methuen Inc.

Cain, William, ed. see Clark, Michael P.

Cain, William, ed. see Young, Thomas D.

Caine, Nancy, jt. ed. see Reite, Martin.

Caines, Jeanette. Window Wishing. LC 79-2698. (Illus.). 32p. (gr. k-3). 1980. 8.61 (ISBN 0-06-020933-X, HarpJ); PLB 8.89 (ISBN 0-06-020934-8). Har-Row.

Caines, Jeannette. Abby. LC 73-5480. (Illus.). 32p. (ps-3). 1973. 9.57i (ISBN 0-06-020921-6, HarpJ); PLB 9.89 (ISBN 0-06-020922-4). Har-Row.

Cairas, David, tr. see Althaus, Paul.

Caird, Edward. Critical Philosophy of Immanuel Kant, 2 Vols. LC 4-196. 1968. Repr. of 1889 ed. Set. 72.00 o.s.i. (ISBN 0-527-14100-3). Kraus Repr.

Caird, F. I. & Evans, J. Grimley, eds. Advanced Geriatric Medicine, No. 2. 192p. 1982. 27.95 (ISBN 0-272-79670-0). Pitman Pub MA.

Caird, G. B. The Revelation of St. John the Divine. LC 66-20774. (New Testament Commentaries Ser.). 1966. 14.95i (ISBN 0-06-061296-7, HarpR). Har-Row.

--Saint Luke. LC 77-81622. (Westminster Pelican Commentaries Ser.). 1978. 10.95 (ISBN 0-664-21345-6). Westminster.

Caird, George B. Pelican Gospel Commentaries: The Gospel of St. Luke. (Orig.). 1964. pap. 6.95 (ISBN 0-14-020490-3, Pelican). Penguin.

Caird, James. English Agriculture in Eighteen Fifty & Eighteen Fifty-One. LC 67-16347. Repr. of 1852 ed. 30.00x (ISBN 0-678-05033-3). Kelley.

Cairncoss, Alexander K. Home & Foreign Investment, 1870-1913. LC 74-17410. 251p. Repr. of 1953 ed. lib. bdg. 25.00x (ISBN 0-678-01023-4). Kelley.

Cairncross, Alec, ed. see Singer, H. W.

Cairncross, Alec, et al. Economic Policy for the European Community. LC 74-22006. 304p. 1975. text ed. 39.50x (ISBN 0-8419-0189-9). Holmes & Meier.

Cairncross, Andrew S., ed. see Kyd, Thomas.

Cairncross, Andrew S., ed. see Shakespeare, William.

Cairncross, John. After Polygamy Was Made a Sin: The Social History of Christian Polygamy. 1974. 19.95x (ISBN 0-7100-7730-0). Routledge & Kegan.

Cairncross, Sandy, et al. Evaluation for Village Water Supply Planning. 1980. 26.95 (ISBN 0-471-27662-6, Pub. by Wiley-Interscience). Wiley.

Cairnes, J. E. The Slave Power: Its Character, Career, & Probable Designs. 8.00 (ISBN 0-8446-0434-8). Peter Smith.

Cairns & Oswin. Packaging for Climatic Protection. 1975. text ed. 19.95 o.p. (ISBN 0-408-00146-1). Butterworth.

Cairns, David, tr. see Gollwitzer, Helmut.

Cairns, Huntington. Law & the Social Sciences. LC 69-18855. Repr. of 1935 ed. lib. bdg. 12.00x o.p. (ISBN 0-678-04536-4). Kelley.

Cairns, Huntington, ed. see Mencken, Henry L.

Cairns, Huntington, ed. see Saintsbury, George E.

Cairns, J. F. The Eagle & the Lotus: Western Intervention in Vietnam. pap. 7.95x o.p. (ISBN 0-7018-0160-3, ABC). Sportshelf.

Cairns, J., Jr. Biological Monitoring in Water Pollution. (Illus.). 144p. 1982. 30.00 (ISBN 0-08-028730-1). Pergamon.

Cairns, John, Jr., ed. Aquatic Microbial Communities. (LC 76-052711). 1977. lib. bdg. 70.00 o.s.i. (ISBN 0-8240-9860-9, Garland STPM Pr). Garland Pub.

--Artificial Substrates. LC 81-69073. (Illus.). 279p. 1982. text ed. 29.50 (ISBN 0-250-40404-4). Ann Arbor Science.

Cairns, L. G., jt. auth. see Turney, C.

Cairns, Trevor. Europe Around the World. LC 81-13719. (Cambridge Introduction to History Ser.). (Illus.). 104p. (gr. 6 up). 1982. PLB 8.95g (ISBN 0-8225-0809-5). Lerner Pubns.

Cairns, Trevor, ed. Europe & the World. new, rev. ed. LC 73-22523. (The Cambridge Introduction to History). Orig. Title: Europe Finds the World. (Illus.). 104p. (gr. 6-10). 1975. PLB 8.95g (ISBN 0-8225-0805-2). Lerner Pubns.

Cairns, W. J. On-Shore Impacts of Off-Shore Oil. 1981. 53.50 (ISBN 0-85334-974-6, Pub. by Applied Sci England). Elsevier.

Cairns-Smith, A. G. Genetic Takeover & the Mineral Origins of Life. LC 81-17070. (Illus.). 1982. 29.95 (ISBN 0-521-23312-7). Cambridge U Pr.

Cairo International Workshop on Applications of Science & Technology for Desert Development September 9-15, 1978. Proceedings. Bishay, A. & McGinnies, W. B., eds. (Advances in Desert & Arid Land Technology & Development: Vol. 1). 630p. 1979. lib. bdg. 89.00 (ISBN 3-7186-0002-1). Harwood Academic.

Cairoli, Oscar & Voyce, Pamela. Memory Bank for Hemodialysis. (Memory Banks Ser.). (Illus., Orig.). 1982. pap. 10.95 (ISBN 0-935236-19-8). Nurseco.

Cais, Michael, ed. Progress in Coordination Chemistry. 1969. 59.75 (ISBN 0-444-40746-4). Elsevier.

Cajal, Santiago Ramon Y see Ramon Y Cajal, Santiago.

Cajori, F; see Ball, W. Rouse, et al.

Cajori, Florian. History of Mathematical Notations, 2 vols. Incl. Vol. 1. Notations in Elementary Mathematics. xvi, 467p. 1951. pap. 10.00 (ISBN 0-87548-154-X); Vol. 2. Notations Mainly in Higher Mathematics. xviii, 384p. 1952. 24.50 (ISBN 0-87548-172-8). (Illus.). Open Court.

--William Oughtred: A Great Seventeenth-Century Teacher of Mathematics. vi, 106p. 1916. 12.00 (ISBN 0-87548-174-4). Open Court.

Cakir, A., et al. Visual Display Terminals: A Manual Covering Ergonomics, Workplace Design, Health & Safety, Task Organization. LC 80-40070. 328p. 1980. 58.95x (ISBN 0-471-27793-2, Pub. by Wiley-Interscience). Wiley.

Calabrese, E. J. Methodological Approaches to Deriving Environmental & Occupational Health Standards. 402p. 1978. 70.00 (ISBN 0-471-04544-6, Pub. by Wiley-Interscience). Wiley.

Calabrese, Edward J. Nutrition & Environmental Health: The Influence of Nutritional Status on Pollutant Toxicity & Carcinogenicity, 2 vols. Incl. Vol. 1. The Vitamins. 77.50 (ISBN 0-471-04833-X); Vol. 2. Minerals & Macronutrients. 544p. 54.95 (ISBN 0-471-08207-4). LC 9-21089. (Environmental Science & Technology Ser.). 1980 (Pub. by Wiley-Interscience). Wiley.

--Pollutants & High Risk Groups: The Biological Basis of Increased Human Susceptibility to Environmental & Occupational Pollutants. LC 77-13957. (Environmental Science & Technology: Wiley-Interscience Series of Texts & Monographs). 266p. 1977. 45.00 (ISBN 0-471-02940-8, Pub. by Wiley-Inerscience). Wiley.

Calabro, John J., jt. auth. see Calin, Andrei.

Calabro, S. R. Reliability Principles & Practices. 1962. 43.50 (ISBN 0-07-009600-7, P&RB). McGraw.

Calahan, Donald. Computer Aided Network Design. rev. ed. (Illus.). 368p. 1972. text ed. 26.95 o.p. (ISBN 0-07-009601-5, C). McGraw.

Calan, Pierre De see De Calan, Pierre.

Calandra, Denis. Comedy of Errors Notes. Bd. with Love's Labour's Lost & The Two Gentlemen of Verona Notes. 88p. (Orig.). 1982. pap. 2.75 (ISBN 0-8220-0010-5). Cliffs.

Calandra, Denis M. Crucible Notes. (Orig.). 1968. pap. 2.50 (ISBN 0-8220-0337-6). Cliffs.

--Lord of the Flies Notes. (Orig.). 1971. pap. 2.95 (ISBN 0-8220-0754-1). Cliffs.

Calandra, Denis M., jt. auth. see Roberts, James L.

Calbally, E. I. & Freney, J. R., eds. The Cycling of Carbon, Nitrogen, Sulfur, & Phosphorus in Terrestrial & Aquatic Ecosystems. 230p. 1982. 26.00 (ISBN 0-387-11272-3). Springer-Verlag.

Calbeto, G. Eight Reales Compendium, 2 Vols. (Illus.). 1983. Repr. of 1970 ed. Set. lib. bdg. 140.00 (ISBN 0-942666-14-3). S J Durst.

Caldarera, Claudio M., et al, eds. Advances in Polyamine Research, Vol. 3. 512p. 1981. 60.50 (ISBN 0-89004-621-2). Raven.

Calde, Mark. Shadowboxer. LC 76-8278. 1976. 7.95 o.p. (ISBN 0-399-11799-7). Putnam Pub Group.

Calde, Mark A. Conquest. 1980. 12.95 o.p. (ISBN 0-312-16257-X). St Martin.

Calder, Angus. Revolutionary Empire: The Rise of the English-Speaking Empires from the 15th Century to the 1780's. 900p. 1981. 36.00 o.p. (ISBN 0-525-19080-5, 03495-105). Dutton.

Calder, Angus, ed. see Scott, Walter.

Calder, Bruce J. The Impact of Intervention: The Dominican Republic During the U. S. Occupation of 1916-1924. (Texas Pan American Ser.). (Illus.). 352p. 1983. text ed. 22.50x (ISBN 0-292-73830-7). U of Tex Pr.

Calder, Clarence R., jt. auth. see Shivers, Jay S.

Calder, Daniel C., ed. Old English Poetry: Essays on Style. (Contributions of the Center for Medieval & Renaissance Studies, UCLA: No. 10). 1979. 24.50x (ISBN 0-520-03830-4). U of Cal Pr.

Calder, Daniel G. Cynewulf. (English Authors Ser.). 1981. lib. bdg. 13.95 (ISBN 0-8057-6814-9, Twayne). G K Hall.

Calder, George, ed. see MacDougall, James.

Calder, Isabel M., ed. see Davenport, John.

Calder, Jenni. Chronicles of Conscience: A Study of George Orwell & Arthur Koestler. LC 69-12146. (Critical Essays in Modern Literature Ser.). 1969. pap. 5.95 o.p. (ISBN 0-8229-5205-X). U of Pittsburgh Pr.

Calder, John, intro. by. A Nouveau Roman Reader. 1983. 11.95 (ISBN 0-7145-3719-5); pap. 5.95 cancelled (ISBN 0-7145-3720-9). Riverrun NY.

Calder, Julian & Garrett, John. The Thirty-Five MM Photographer's Handbook. (Illus.). 1979. 14.95 (ISBN 0-517-53917-9); pap. 11.95 (ISBN 0-517-53918-7). Crown.

Calder, K. J. Britain & the Origins of the New Europe, 1914-1918. LC 75-12161. (International Studies Ser.). 282p. 1976. 37.50 (ISBN 0-521-20897-1). Cambridge U Pr.

Calder, L., et al. The Correspondence of Lu: Samarin & Baroness Rahden (1861-1876) 267p. 1974. text ed. 9.25x (ISBN 0-88920-005-X, Pub. by Wilfrid Laurier U Pr Canada); pap. 5.75x (ISBN 0-88920-004-1). Humanities.

Calder, Nigel. The Comet Is Coming: The Ferverish Legacy of Mr. Halley. (Illus.). 1982. pap. 6.95 (ISBN 0-14-006069-3). Penguin.

--Technopolis. LC 79-101867. 1960. pap. 3.95 o.p. (ISBN 0-671-21062-9, Touchstone Bks). S&S.

Calder, Robert. Best Offer. 288p. (Orig.). 1981. pap. 2.95 (ISBN 0-515-04759-7). Jove Pubns.

Calderelli, David D. Pediatric Otolaryngology. (New Directions in Therapy Ser.). 1982. 32.50 (ISBN 0-87488-695-3). Med Exam.

Calderon. The Great Stage of the World. Brandt, G. W., tr. from Span. (Classics of Drama in English Translation Ser.). 1976. pap. 6.50 (ISBN 0-7190-0571-X). Manchester.

Calderon, Erma & Teel, Leonard R. ERMA. 11.95 (ISBN 0-394-51743-1). Random.

Calderon, Wilfredo. Administracion-Iglesia Cristiana. Carrodeguas, Andy, et al, eds. Orig. Title: Liderazgo y Administracion en la Iglesia. 1982. pap. 3.25 (ISBN 0-8297-1354-9). Life Pubs Intl.

Calderon, Wilfredo, tr. see Lockyer, Herbert, Sr.

Calderon, Wilfredo, tr. see Petersen, William J.

Calderone, Mary S. & Ramey, James W. Talking with Your Child About Sex: Questions & Answers for Children from Birth to Puberty. LC 84-48319. 256p. 1983. 14.95 (ISBN 0-394-52124-2). Random.

Calderone, Mary S., ed. Sexuality & Human Values. 160p. 1975. 7.95 o.s.i. (ISBN 0-8096-1891-5, Assn Pr). Follett.

Calderwood, Ann, jt. ed. see Rossi, Alice S.

Calderwood, James L. Metadrama in Shakespeare's Henriad: Richard II to Henry V. LC 77-93467. 1979. 21.50x (ISBN 0-520-03652-2). U of Cal Pr.

Caldicott, C. E. Marcel Pagnol. (World Author Ser.). 1977. lib. bdg. 15.95 (ISBN 0-8057-6233-7, Twayne). G K Hall.

Caldie, Roberta W. Dominance & Language: A New Perspective on Sexism. LC 81-40141. (Illus.). 130p. (Orig.). 1982. lib. bdg. 19.00 (ISBN 0-8191-1966-0); pap. text ed. 8.25 (ISBN 0-8191-1967-9). U Pr of Amer.

Caldin, E. F. & Gold, V., eds. Proton Transfer Reactions. 1975. 66.00x (ISBN 0-412-12700-8, Pub. by Chapman & Hall). Methuen Inc.

Caldwell & Hegner. Health Assistant. 3rd ed. LC 79-50661. (Illus.). 1980. pap. 12.00 (ISBN 0-8273-1337-3); instr's. guide 2.50 (ISBN 0-8273-1338-1). Delmar.

Caldwell, jt. ed. see Mulder.

Caldwell, Bettye & Ricciuti, Henry N. Review of Child Development Research, Vol. 3. 1974. 25.00x o.s.i. (ISBN 0-226-09045-0); pap. 7.95 (ISBN 0-226-09044-2, P680, Phoen). U of Chicago Pr.

Caldwell, Bill. Islands of Maine: Where America Really Began. LC 81-81541. (Illus.). 240p. 1981. 12.95 (ISBN 0-930096-17-7). G Gannett.

Caldwell, Bruce. Beyond Positivism: Economic Methodology in the Twentieth Century. 260p. 1982. text ed. 29.00x (ISBN 0-04-330327-7). Allen Unwin.

Caldwell, Charles. Autobiography of Charles Caldwell, M. D. LC 67-27450. (Science & Medicine Ser.). 1968. Repr. of 1855 ed. 55.00 (ISBN 0-306-70978-3). Da Capo.

Caldwell, D. K., et al, eds. Progress in Simulation, 2 vols. 1971. Vol. 1,382. 92.00x (ISBN 0-677-14890-9); Vol. 2. 40.00 (ISBN 0-677-00110-X). Gordon.

Caldwell, Dan. American-Soviet Relations: From Nineteen Forty-Seven to the Nixon-Kissinger Grand Design. LC 80-27333. (Contributions in Political Science Ser.: No. 69). (Illus.). 288p. 1981. lib. bdg. 29.95 (ISBN 0-313-22538-9, CCC/). Greenwood.

Caldwell, Dan, ed. Henry Kissinger: His Personality & Policies. (Duke Press Policy Studies). 300p. 1983. text ed. 27.00x (ISBN 0-8223-0485-6). Duke.

Caldwell, E., jt. auth. see Bourke-White, M.

Caldwell, E. S. Bautismo Pentecostal. Carrodeguas, Andy & Marosi, Esteban, eds. 108p. 1982. pap. 1.75 (ISBN 0-8297-1324-7). Life Pubs Intl.

Caldwell, Erskin. Close to Home. pap. 1.25 o.p. (ISBN 0-451-07445-9, Y7445, Sig). NAL.

Caldwell, Erskine. God's Little Acre. 1976. 6.95 o.p. (ISBN 0-453-00367-2, H367); pap. 2.95 (ISBN 0-451-12155-4). NAL.

--God's Little Acre. pap. 2.95 (ISBN 0-451-12155-4, AE1255, Sig). NAL.

--Stories of Life, North & South. LC 82-9922. 1983. 14.95 (ISBN 0-396-08133-9). Dodd.

--Tobacco Road. 1970. pap. 2.95 (ISBN 0-451-12156-2, AE2156, Sig). NAL.

--Tragic Ground. Bd. with Trouble in July. 1979. pap. 4.95 o.p. (ISBN 0-452-25204-0, Z5204, Plume). NAL.

--Trouble in July. pap. 1.25 o.p. (ISBN 0-451-06527-1, Y6527, Sig). NAL.

Caldwell, Erskine & Bourke-White, Margaret. North of the Danube. LC 77-1494. (Photography Ser.). (Illus.). 1977. Repr. of 1939 ed. lib. bdg. 32.50 (ISBN 0-306-70877-9). Da Capo.

Caldwell, Esther & Hegner, Barbara. Geriatrics: A Study of Maturity. 3rd ed. LC 79-55313. (Practical Nursing Ser.). (Illus.). 288p. 1981. pap. text ed. 12.00 (ISBN 0-8273-1935-5); instr's. guide 2.75 (ISBN 0-8273-1934-7). Delmar.

Caldwell, Esther & Hegner, Barbara R. Foundation for Medical Communication. (Illus.). 1978. text ed. 18.95 (ISBN 0-87909-299-8); pap. text ed. 14.95 (ISBN 0-87909-298-X); instrs'. manual o.p. avail. (ISBN 0-8359-2080-1). Reston.

Caldwell, Francis E. Pacific Troller: Life on the Northwest Fishing Grounds. LC 77-10324. (Illus.). 1978. pap. 5.95 (ISBN 0-88240-099-1). Alaska Northwest.

Caldwell, Guy A. Early History of the Ochsner Medical Center: The First Twenty-Two Years. (Illus.). 128p. 1965. photocopy ed. spiral 14.75x (ISBN 0-398-00272-X). C C Thomas.

Caldwell, H. M. History of the Elyton Land Company & Birmingham, Ala. The Origin & Development of an American City. pap. 3.00 (ISBN 0-686-92272-7). Southern U Pr.

Caldwell, Helen. Machado de Assis: The Brazilian Master & His Novels. LC 76-89891. 1970. 23.50x (ISBN 0-520-01608-4). U of Cal Pr.

--Michio Ito: The Dancer & His Dances. LC 76-7756. (Illus.). 1977. 27.50 (ISBN 0-520-03219-5). U of Cal Pr.

Caldwell, Helen, tr. see Machado de Assis, Joaquim M.

Caldwell, John & Jakoby, William B., eds. Biological Basis of Detoxification. LC 82-18933. (Biochemical Pharmacology & Toxicology). Date not set. price not set (ISBN 0-12-155060-5). Acad Pr.

Caldwell, John C. Let's Visit China. LC 80-54760. cancelled (ISBN 0-89526-096-4). Regnery-Gateway.

--Let's Visit the Middle East. LC 80-54761. cancelled (ISBN 0-89526-096-4). Regnery-Gateway.

Caldwell, Lawrence & Diebold, William, Jr. Soviet-American Relations in the 1980's: Super-Power Politics & East-West Trade. (Illus.). 1980. 14.95 (ISBN 0-07-009615-5); pap. 9.95 (ISBN 0-07-009616-3). McGraw.

Caldwell, Lawrence T. Soviet-American Relations: One-half Decade of Detente Problems & Issues. (The Atlantic Papers: No. 75/5). (Orig.). 1976. pap. text ed. 4.75x (ISBN 0-686-83640-5). Allanheld.

Caldwell, Lesley, jt. ed. see Robbins, David.

Caldwell, Lisley, jt. ed. see Day, Graham.

Caldwell, Louis O. Cogradulations: A Graduation Remembrance. (Ultra Books). 64p. 1982. 4.95 (ISBN 0-8010-2485-4). Baker Bk.

--When Partners Become Parents. (Ultra Bks Ser). 3.95 o.p. (ISBN 0-8010-2317-3). Baker Bk.

Caldwell, Lynton K. Science & the National Environmental Policy Act: Redirecting Policy Through Procedural Reform. 1982. 17.75 (ISBN 0-8173-0111-9); pap. 7.95 (ISBN 0-8173-0112-7). U of Ala Pr.

Caldwell, Patsy, jt. auth. see Weinberg, Robert.

Caldwell, R. L., jt. ed. see Lidicker, W. Z., Jr.

Caldwell, Robert C. & Stallard, Richard E. A Textbook of Preventive Dentistry. LC 73-76184. (Illus.). 1977. text ed. 27.50 o.p. (ISBN 0-7216-2239-9). Saunders.

Caldwell, Robert G. Criminology. 2nd ed. 773p. 1965. 26.95 (ISBN 0-471-06933-7). Wiley.

Caldwell, Ronald C. Softly We Lay & Other Poems. 1979. 4.95 o.p. (ISBN 0-533-03491-4). Vantage.

Caldwell, Taylor. Answer As a Man. 464p. 1981. 12.95 (ISBN 0-399-12566-3). Putnam Pub Group.

--The Balance Wheel. 512p. 1980. pap. 3.50 (ISBN 0-515-06631-1). Jove Pubns.

--Dialogues with the Devil. LC 67-11736. 1967. 4.95 (ISBN 0-385-04573-5). Doubleday.

--Dynasty of Death. 1970. 7.95 (ISBN 0-385-01066-4). Doubleday.

--The Eagles Gather. 1979. pap. 3.50. Jove Pubns.

--A Prologue to Love. LC 61-12500. 1961. 5.95 (ISBN 0-385-03269-2). Doubleday.

--There Was a Time. 1979. pap. 3.50 o.s.i. (ISBN 0-515-06170-0). Jove Pubns.

--Time No Longer. 1980. pap. 2.75 o.p. (ISBN 0-515-05441-0). Putnam Pub Group.

--The Turnbulls. (Orig.). 1981. pap. 3.50 (ISBN 0-515-06327-4). Jove Pubns.

--The Turnbulls. pap. 2.75 (ISBN 0-515-05291-4). Jove Pubns.

--The Wide House. 1979. pap. 3.50 o.s.i. (ISBN 0-515-06092-5). Jove Pubns.

Caldwell, Taylor & Stearn, Jess. I, Judas. LC 77-5518. 1977. 10.95 o.p. (ISBN 0-689-10806-0). Atheneum.

--I, Judas. 1978. pap. 3.50 (ISBN 0-451-12038-8, AE2038, Sig). NAL.

Caldwell, Thomas, et al. An Akkadian Grammar: A Translation of Lehrbuch Des Akkadischen. 3rd ed. 1978. 29.95 (ISBN 0-87462-445-2); pap. 19.95 (ISBN 0-87462-444-4). Marquette.

Caldwell, Thomas D., ed. see Helsel, James L.

Caldwell, William E., jt. auth. see King, G. Brooks.

Caldwell, William L. Cancer of the Urinary Bladder: With Emphasis on Treatment by Irradiation. LC 72-96980. (Illus.). 128p. 1970. 12.50 o.s.i. (ISBN 0-87527-003-4). Green.

Cale, David Lee. The Basics of Consequentialism. 2nd ed. LC 80-82228. (Illus.). 170p. 1981. 12.95 (ISBN 0-940284-00-6, Pub. by Philosophy Press); pap. 7.95 (ISBN 0-940284-01-4). Philos Pr.

Calenoff, Leonid. Radiology of Spinal Cord Injury. LC 80-27532. (Illus.). 573p. 1981. text ed. 89.50 (ISBN 0-8016-1114-8). Mosby.

Calero, Henry H. Winning the Negotiation. LC 79-84208. 1979. 12.50 o.p. (ISBN 0-8015-3680-4, Hawthorn). Dutton.

Calero, Henry H. & Nierenberg, Gerald I. How to Read a Person Like a Book. (Illus.). 192p. 1982. pap. 2.95 (ISBN 0-671-45664-4). PB.

Calero, Henry H., jt. auth. see Nierenberg, Gerard I.

Caleron, Eduardo, et al. Eduardo el Curandero: The Words of a Peruvian Healer. (Illus.). 200p. 1982. 17.95 (ISBN 0-913028-94-0); pap. 7.95 (ISBN 0-913028-95-9). North Atlantic.

Calhoun, Calfrey C. Managing the Learning Process in Business Education. 624p. 1980. text ed. 22.95x (ISBN 0-534-00834-8). Wadsworth Pub.

Calhoun, Catherine. Egyptian Designs. (The International Design Library). (Illus.). 48p. 1983. pap. 2.95 (ISBN 0-88045-012-6). Stemmer Hse.

Calhoun, Craig. The Question of Class Struggle: The Social Foundation of Popular Radicalism During the Industrial Revolution. LC 81-2018. xiv, 322p. 1982. lib. bdg. 25.00x (ISBN 0-226-09090-6, PHOEN); pap. 8.95 (ISBN 0-226-09091-4). U of Chicago Pr.

Calhoun, D. F. The United Front: The TUC & the Russians 1923-1928. (Soviet & East European Studies). 432p. 1976. 54.50 (ISBN 0-521-21056-9). Cambridge U Pr.

Calhoun, Daniel H. Professional Lives in America: Structure & Aspiration, 1750-1850. LC 65-22042. (Center for the Study of the History of Liberty in America Ser). (Illus.). 1965. 14.00x o.p. (ISBN 0-674-71250-1). Harvard U Pr.

Calhoun, Don. The Oceanic Quest: Toward a Religion Beyond Illusion. 1983. 10.95 (ISBN 0-533-05591-1). Vantage.

Calhoun, G. M & Delamere, C. A Working Bibliography of Greek Law. 1968. Repr. of 1927 ed. text ed. 23.00x o.p. (ISBN 90-6032-051-4). Humanities.

Calhoun, James F., jt. auth. see Goodstein, Leonard D.

Calhoun, John C. Calhoun: Basic Documents. Anderson, John M., ed. 330p. 18.75x (ISBN 0-271-00322-7, Pub. by Bald Eagle). Pa St U Pr.

Calhoun, Mary. Audubon Cat. LC 80-16278. (Illus.). 32p. (gr. k-3). 1981. 8.95 (ISBN 0-688-22253-6); PLB 8.59 (ISBN 0-688-32253-0). Morrow.

--The Battle of Reuben Robin & Kite Uncle John. LC 72-12949. (Illus.). 32p. (gr. k-3). 1973. PLB 9.55 (ISBN 0-688-30075-8). Morrow.

--Camels Are Meaner Than Mules. LC 72-141255. (Regional American Stories Ser). (Illus.). 64p. (gr. 3-6). 1971. PLB 6.69 (ISBN 0-8116-4250-X). Garrard.

--Cross-Country Cat. (Illus.). (gr. k-3). 1979. 9.25 (ISBN 0-688-22186-6); PLB 8.88 (ISBN 0-688-32186-0). Morrow.

--Hot-Air Henry. LC 80-26189. (Illus.). 40p. (gr. k-3). 1981. 8.95 (ISBN 0-688-00501-2); PLB 8.59 (ISBN 0-688-00502-0). Morrow.

--Houn' Dog. (Illus.). (gr. k-3). 1959. 7.95 (ISBN 0-688-21406-1). Morrow.

--The House of Thirty Cats. (Illus.). (gr. 4-6). 1970. pap. 1.95 (ISBN 0-671-42064-X). Archway.

--Hungry Leprechaun. (Illus.). (gr. k-3). 1962. PLB 9.12 (ISBN 0-688-31713-8). Morrow.

--Jack the Wise & the Cornish Cuckoos. LC 77-22714. (Illus.). (gr. k-3). 1978. 9.75 (ISBN 0-688-22132-7); PLB 9.36 (ISBN 0-688-32132-1). Morrow.

--Katie John & Heathcliff. LC 80-7770. 160p. (gr. 3-6). 1980. 8.95 o.p. (ISBN 0-06-020931-3, HarpJ); PLB 9.89 (ISBN 0-06-020932-1). Har-Row.

--Mermaid of Storms. LC 71-118059. (Illus.). (gr. k-3). 1970. PLB 8.59 (ISBN 0-688-31884-3). Morrow.

--The Witch of Hissing Hill. (Illus.). (gr. k-3). 1964. PLB 9.12 (ISBN 0-688-31762-6). Morrow.

--The Witch Who Lost Her Shadow. (Illus.). (gr. k-3). 1979. 9.57i o.p. (ISBN 0-06-020946-1, HarpJ); PLB 10.89 (ISBN 0-06-020947-X). Har-Row.

--The Witch's Pig: A Cornish Folktale. (gr. k-3). 1977. 9.55 (ISBN 0-688-32092-9). Morrow.

--Wobble the Witch Cat. (Illus.). (gr. k-3). 1958. PLB 8.16 (ISBN 0-688-31621-2). Morrow.

Calhoun, Mary L. & Hawisher, Margaret. Teaching & Learnning Strategies for Physically Handicapped Students. 384p. 1979. pap. text ed. 19.95 (ISBN 0-8391-1394-3). Univ Park.

Calhoun, Mary L., jt. auth. see Hawisher, Margaret F.

Cali, J. P., ed. Trace Analysis of Semiconductor Materials. 1964. 37.00 (ISBN 0-08-010031-7). Pergamon.

Cali, Vincent M. The New Lower-Cost Way to End Gum Trouble Without Surgery. LC 81-14702. (Illus.). 206p. 1982. pap. 6.95 (ISBN 0-446-37348-6). Warner Bks.

Calian, C. S. For All Your Seasons. LC 78-71050. 1979. 7.95 (ISBN 0-8042-2084-0). John Knox.

Calian, Carnegie S. Today's Pastor in Tomorrow's World. Rev. ed. LC 82-7114. 1982. pap. 8.95 (ISBN 0-664-24426-2). Westminster.

Caliendo, Mary A. Nutrition & Preventative Health Care. (Illus.). 1981. text ed. 24.95x (ISBN 0-02-318330-6). Macmillan.

--The Nutrition Crisis: Alternatives for Change. (Illus.). 1979. pap. text ed. 13.95x (ISBN 0-02-318340-3). Macmillan.

Califana, Anthony & Levkov, Jerome S. Criminalistics for the Law Enforcement Officer. (Illus.). 1978. text ed. 21.50 (ISBN 0-07-009620-1, G); ans. key & resource guide 4.50 (ISBN 0-07-009622-8); student wkbk. 7.95 (ISBN 0-07-009621-X). McGraw.

Califano, Joseph A., Jr. Report on Drug Abuse & Alcoholism, 1982. (Illus.). 312p. (Orig.). pap. 3.95 (ISBN 0-446-30625-8). Warner Bks.

Califano, S. Vibrational States. 335p. 1976. 87.95 (ISBN 0-471-12996-8). Wiley.

California Academy of Sciences see Washburn, Dorothy.

California Coastal Commission. The California Coastal Access Guide: Anniversary Ed. LC 82-45905. (Illus.). 285p. 25.00 (ISBN 0-520-04984-5). U of Cal Pr.

California Critic Editors, ed. Best Restaurants of Los Angeles & Southern California. LC 78-18227. (Best Restaurants Ser.). (Illus.). 1978. pap. write for info. o.p. One Hund One Prods.

California Fertilizer Association. Western Fertilizer Handbook. 6th ed. 252p. 1980. pap. text ed. 5.50x (ISBN 0-8134-2122-5). Interstate.

California Governor's Office of Planning & Research. The California Water Atlas. Kahrl, William L., ed. LC 78-620062. (Illus.). 124p. 1979. 37.50x (ISBN 0-913232-68-8). W Kaufmann.

California Institute of Public Affairs. Academic Research & Public Service Centers in California: A Guide. LC 82-70806. (California Information Guides Ser.). 50p. (Orig.). 1983. pap. 18.50x (ISBN 0-912102-61-6). Cal Inst Public.

California Institute of Public Affairs Staff. Ethnic Groups in California: A Guide to Organizations & Information Resources. LC 81-67062. (California Information Guides Ser.). 58p. 1981. pap. 16.50x (ISBN 0-912102-56-X). Cal Inst Public.

California State Library Sutro Branch San Francisco. Catalogue of Mexican Pamphlets in the Sutro Collection 1623-1888. Radin, P. & Gans, A. I., eds. 1939-1941. 90.00 o.s.i. (ISBN 0-527-14400-2). Kraus Repr.

California University at Los Angeles African Studies Center, jt. ed. see Kuper, Hilda.

Calin, Andre. Diagnosis & Management of Rheumatoid Arthritis in Primary Care. Date not set. 24.95 (ISBN 0-201-10810-0, Med-Nurse). A-W.

Calin, Andrei & Calabro, John J. Sulindac - A Five-Year Perspective: Proceedings of an International Symposium. Language Center, Inc., tr. 128p. 1982. write for info. (ISBN 0-911910-20-4). Merck.

Calin, Harold. Attack In the Forest. 288p. 1982. pap. 2.75 o.s.i. (ISBN 0-8439-1176-X, Leisure Bks). Nordon Pubns.

--White Forest Battle. (Inflation Fighter). 208p. 1982. pap. 1.50 o.s.i. (ISBN 0-8439-1150-6, Leisure Bks). Nordon Pubns.

Calin, William. A Muse for Heroes: Nine Centuries of the Epic in France. (Romance Ser.). 504p. 1983. 47.50x (ISBN 0-8020-5599-0). U of Toronto Pr.

Calingaert, Efrem F. & Serwer, Jacquelyn D. Pasta & Rice Italian Style. (Illus.). 256p. 1983. 12.95 (ISBN 0-686-83859-9, ScribT). Scribner.

Calingaert, Peter. Assemblers, Compilers, & Program Translation. LC 78-21905. 1979. text ed. 24.95x (ISBN 0-914894-23-4). Computer Sci.

Calinger, Ronald, ed. Classics of Mathematics. LC 80-15567. (Classics Ser.). (Orig.). 1982. pap. 18.00x (ISBN 0-935610-13-8). Moore Pub IL.

Calisca, Claude, jt. auth. see Grout, Donald J.

Calisher, Hortense. Mysteries of Motion. 1982. 22.50. Doubleday.

Calistro, Paddy. Edith Head's Hollywood. 1983. write for info. Dutton.

Calkin, Ruth H. Lord, Could You Hurry a Little. 1983. pap. 2.50 r (ISBN 0-686-82690-6, 07-3816-0). Tyndale.

Calkins, Carroll C., jt. auth. see Eaton, Jerome A.

Calkins, Earnest E. Louder Please: The Autobiography of a Deaf Man. LC 74-164148. 1971. Repr. of 1924 ed. 34.00x (ISBN 0-8103-3792-4). Gale.

Calkins, Fay G. My Samoan Chief. (Pacific Classics Ser.: No. 2). (Illus.). 1971. pap. 5.95 (ISBN 0-87022-932-X). UH Pr.

Calkins, Mary W., ed. see Hume, David.

Calkins, Peter H. & DiPietre, Dennis D. Farm Business Management: Successful Decisions in a Changing Environment. 464p. 1983. text ed. 24.95 (ISBN 0-02-364050-2). Macmillan.

Call, Dwight M. Tales by Paw Paw, Bk. 1. 1978. 5.95 o.p. (ISBN 0-533-03483-3). Vantage.

Call, Frances & Dowd, Merle E. The Practical Book of Bicycling. rev. ed. (Illus.). 256p. 1981. pap. 7.75 (ISBN 0-525-93203-8, 0752-230). Dutton.

Call, Justin D., jt. ed. see Galenson, Eleanor.

Call, Max. Deadline in Rome. 220p. 1980. PLB 8.95 o.p. (ISBN 0-912376-54-6). Chosen Bks Pub.

Call, Vaughn R. & Otto, Luther B. Tracking Respondents: A Multi-Method Approach, Vol. II. LC 79-48034. (Entry into Careers Ser.). 176p. 1982. 20.95x (ISBN 0-669-03644-7). Lexington Bks.

Calladine, Andrew & Calladine, Carol. Raising Siblings. 1979. 8.95 o.s.i. (ISBN 0-440-07314-6). Delacorte.

Calladine, C. R. Theory of Shell Structures. LC 82-4255. 700p. Date not set. price not set (ISBN 0-521-23835-8). Cambridge U Pr.

Calladine, Carol, jt. auth. see Calladine, Andrew.

Callaghan, Barry. Black Queen Stories. 224p. 1982. 13.95 (ISBN 0-86538-017-1); pap. 7.95 (ISBN 0-86538-018-X). Ontario Rev NJ.

Callaghan, Christopher T., jt. ed. see Connors, Tracy D.

Callaghan, Dennis W., jt. auth. see Elkins, Arthur.

Callaghy, Thomas M., jt. ed. see Rosberg, Carl G.

Callaham, Ludmilla I. Russian-English Chemical & Polytechnical Dictionary. 3rd ed. LC 75-5982. 852p. 1975. 58.50x (ISBN 0-471-12998-4, Pub. by Wiley-Interscience). Wiley.

Callahan, Daniel & Jennings, Bruce, eds. Ethics, The Social Sciences & Policy Analysis. (The Hastings Center Series in Ethics). 370p. 1983. 29.50x (ISBN 0-306-41143-1, Plenum Pr). Plenum Pub.

Callahan, Ed. Charcoal Cookbook. LC 73-21244. (Illus., Orig.). 1970. pap. 4.95 o.p. (ISBN 0-911954-10-4). Nitty Gritty.

Callahan, Edward J. & McCluskey, Kathleen, eds. Life-Span Development Psychology: Non-Normative-Life Events. LC 82-22784. Date not set. price not set (ISBN 0-12-155140-7). Acad Pr.

Callahan, James M. Diplomatic History of the Southern Confederacy. LC 69-13849. Repr. of 1901 ed. lib. bdg. 15.75x (ISBN 0-8371-0336-3, CADH). Greenwood.

Callahan, John J. Needed: Professional Management in Data Processing. (Illus.). 240p. 1983. 25.00 (ISBN 0-13-610956-X). P-H.

Callahan, John W. & Lowden, J. Alexander, eds. Lysosomes & Lysosomal Storage Diseases. 455p. 1981. text ed. 55.00 (ISBN 0-89004-476-7). Raven.

Callahan, Joseph F. & Clark, Leonard H. Foundations of Education: Planning for Competence 1977. 1977. 14.95x o.p. (ISBN 0-02-318200-8). Macmillan.

--Innovations & Issues in Education: Planning for Competence. 1977. 15.95x (ISBN 0-02-318050-1, 31805). Macmillan.

--Introduction to American Education. 2nd ed. 352p. 1983. pap. text ed. 16.95 (ISBN 0-02-318240-7). Macmillan.

--Introduction to American Education: Planning for Competence. 1977. 10.95 o.p. (ISBN 0-02-318230-X). Macmillan.

--Teaching in the Elementary School: Planning for Competence. 1977. 14.95x (ISBN 0-02-318070-6, 31807). Macmillan.

--Teaching in the Middle & Secondary School. 2nd ed. 1982. text ed. 16.95 (ISBN 0-02-318260-1). Macmillan.

Callahan, Leroy G., jt. auth. see Riedesel, C. Alan.

Callahan, North. Flight from the Republic: The Tories of the American Revolution. LC 75-42359. (Illus.). 208p. 1976. Repr. of 1967 ed. lib. bdg. 17.00x (ISBN 0-8371-7428-7, CAFR). Greenwood.

Callahan, North see Weaver, Glenn.

Callahan, P. J. How to Make a Will, How to Use Trusts. 4th ed. LC 78-7913. (Legal Almanac Ser.: No. 2). Orig. Title: How to Make a Will Simplified. 119p. 1978. 5.95 (ISBN 0-379-11109-8). Oceana.

--Law of Real Estate. 2nd ed. (Legal Almanac Ser.: No. 4). 1960. 4.95 o.p. (ISBN 0-379-11004-0). Oceana.

Callahan, Parnell J. How to Serve on a Jury. 2nd ed. LC 79-19272. (Legal Almanac Ser: No. 31). 120p. (Orig.). 1979. 5.95 (ISBN 0-379-11122-5). Oceana.

--Law of Separation & Divorce. 4th ed. LC 78-25547. (Legal Almanac Ser.: No. 1). 123p. 1979. 5.95 (ISBN 0-379-11108-X). Oceana.

--Legal Status of Women. 2nd ed. LC 78-3469. (Legal Almanac Ser.: No. 53). 122p. 1978. 5.95 (ISBN 0-379-11115-2). Oceana.

--Protection Through the Law. 2nd ed. LC 78-808956. (Legal Almanac Ser.: No. 55). 122p. (Orig.). 1978. 5.95 (ISBN 0-379-11055-5). Oceana.

Callahan, Parnell J. & Nussbaum, Louis M. Real Estate Law for the Homeowner & Broker. Sloan, Irving J., ed. LC 79-28178. (Legal Almanac Ser.: No. 4). 120p. 1980. lib. bdg. 5.95 (ISBN 0-379-11121-7). Oceana.

Callahan, Philip S. Tuning into Nature. (Illus.). 240p. 1976. 10.00 (ISBN 0-8159-6309-2). Devin.

Callahan, Raymond, jt. auth. see Payne, Howard E.

Callahan, Sean. Photographs of Margaret Bourke-White. LC 72-80415. (Illus.). 1975. pap. 11.95 (ISBN 0-8212-0656-7, 706655). NYGS.

Callahan, Sterling G. Successful Teaching in Secondary Schools: A Guide for Student & In-Service Teachers. rev. ed. 1971. text ed. 18.95x (ISBN 0-673-07720-9). Scott F.

Callahan, Timothy R. Callahan's Compact College Guide to Athletics & Academics in America. LC 82-73347. 264p. 1982. 12.95 (ISBN 0-910967-00-8). Callahan's Guides.

--The College Guide to Athletics & Academics in the Northeast. Date not set. write for info. o.p. Callahan's Guides.

Callahan, W. J. & Higgs, D. Church & Society in Catholic Europe of the Eighteenth Century. LC 78-12165. 1979. 24.95 (ISBN 0-521-22424-1). Cambridge U Pr.

Callahan, William E., et al. The Continuing Quest: Introductory Readings in Philosophy. 1979. pap. text ed. 10.95 (ISBN 0-8403-2075-2). Kendall-Hunt.

Callahan, William J. Honor, Commerce & Industry in Eighteenth-Century Spain. (Kress Library of Business & Economics: No. 22). 1972. pap. 5.00x o.p. (ISBN 0-678-09916-2, Baker Lib). Kelley.

Callan, Edward. Alan Paton. LC 67-25207. (World Authors Ser.: South Africa: No. 40). 1968. lib. bdg. 10.95 o.p. (ISBN 0-8057-2686-1, Twayne). G K Hall.

--Alan Paton. Rev. ed. (Twayne's World Authors Ser.). 1982. lib. bdg. 13.95 (ISBN 0-8057-6512-3, Twayne). G K Hall.

Callan, John P. Your Guide to Mental Help. (People's Health Library). 200p. 1982. 12.50 (ISBN 0-89313-059-1). G F Stickley.

Callan, Mallory. Jaws 2 Activity Book. Duenewald, Doris, ed. (Illus.). (gr. 1-7). 1978. pap. 1.50 o.s.i. (ISBN 0-448-16338-1, G&D). Putnam Pub Group.

--Jaws 2 Adventure Activity Book. Duenewald, Doris, ed. (Illus.). (gr. 1-7). 1978. pap. 1.50 o.s.i. (ISBN 0-448-16339-X, G&D). Putnam Pub Group.

Callan, Richard J. Miguel Angel Asturias. (World Authors Ser.: Guatemala: No. 122). lib. bdg. 9.95 o.p. (ISBN 0-8057-2072-3, Twayne). G K Hall.

Callander, Lee A., jt. auth. see Fawcett, David M.

Callander, R. A., jt. auth. see Stephenson, J.

Callaway, Cason J., Jr. & Flowers, Charles M., eds. A Southern Collection. LC 81-68298. (Illus.). 318p. (Orig.). 1979. pap. 10.00 (ISBN 0-9606300-0-7). Jr League Columbus.

Callaway, Frank, ed. Australian Composition in the Twentieth Century. Tunley, David. 1979. 49.95x (ISBN 0-19-550522-0). Oxford U Pr.

Callaway, Joseph A. The Early Bronze Age Citadel & Lower City at Ai. LC 79-23011. (Report of the Joint Archaeological Expedition to Ai Ser: Vol. 2). 295p. 1981. text ed. 25.00x (ISBN 0-89757-202-5, Am Sch Orient Res). Eisenbrauns.

Callaway, Joseph A. & Adams, J. McKee, eds. Biblical Backgrounds. rev. ed. 1966. 12.95 (ISBN 0-8054-1113-5). Broadman.

Callaway, Morgan. The Consecutive Subjunctive in Old English. LC 73-9714. 1973. Repr. of 1933 ed. 7.00 o.s.i. (ISBN 0-527-14450-9). Kraus Repr.

Callaway, Tucker N. Zen Way - Jesus Way. LC 76-6032. 1976. 11.00 (ISBN 0-8048-1190-3). C E Tuttle.

Callaway, William J., jt. auth. see Gurley, LaVerne T.

Callcott, George H. A History of the University of Maryland. (Illus.). 422p. 1966. 9.50 (ISBN 0-686-36824-X). Md Hist.

Callcott, George H., jt. auth. see Elkins, Wilson H.

Callcott, M. V. & Peters, Terry, eds. Mr. George, 2 pts. Incl. Pt. 1. In Victorian England; Pt. 2. In Pioneer Texas. (National History Ser.). (Illus.). 1983. 16.95 (ISBN 0-89482-046-X); ltd. ed. 39.95 (ISBN 0-89482-048-6); pap. 8.95 (ISBN 0-89482-047-8); video cassette of Frank Callcott 165.00 (ISBN 0-89482-022-2). Stevenson Pr. Postponed.

Callcott, Margaret L. The Negro in Maryland Politics 1870-1912. 199p. 1969. 20.00 (ISBN 0-686-36826-6). Md Hist.

Calleley, A. & Forster, C. Treatment of Industrial Effluents. LC 76-54909. 1977. 39.95x o.s.i. (ISBN 0-470-98934-3). Halsted Pr.

Callen, Donald M., ed. see Beardsley, Monroe C.

Callen, Herbert B. Thermodynamics: An Introduction to the Physical Theories of Equilibrium Thermostatics & Irreversible Thermodynamics. LC 60-5597. (Illus.). 376p. 1960. text ed. 27.50 (ISBN 0-471-13035-4). Wiley.

Callen, Larry. Pinch. (Illus.). 1976. 8.95 (ISBN 0-316-12495-8, Pub.by Atlantic Monthly Pr). Little.

Callender, J. Time-Saver Standards for Architectural Design Data. 6th ed. 1982. 82.50 (ISBN 0-07-009663-5). McGraw.

Callender, John. Middle Egyptian. LC 74-21132. (AfroAsiatic Dialects Ser.: Vol. 2). (Illus.). 143p. 1975. pap. 11.50x o.p. (ISBN 0-89003-006-5). Undena Pubns.

Callender, John, jt. auth. see De Chiara, Joseph.

Callender, John H. Time-Saver Standards for Architectural Design Data. 5th ed. 1974. 53.50 (ISBN 0-07-009647-3, P&RB). McGraw.

Calleo, David. The German Problem Reconsidered. LC 78-9683. 1978. 24.95 (ISBN 0-521-22309-1). Cambridge U Pr.

--The German Problem Reconsidered. LC 78-9683. 208p. 1980. pap. 8.95 (ISBN 0-521-29966-7). Cambridge U Pr.

Callewaert, Denis M. & Genyea, Julien. Basic Chemistry: General, Organic, Biological. 1980. text ed. 25.95x (ISBN 0-87901-130-0). Worth.

--Fundamentals of College Chemistry. 1980. text ed. 22.95x (ISBN 0-87901-125-4). Worth.

--Fundamentals of Organic & Biological Chemistry. 1980. text ed. 23.95x (ISBN 0-87901-129-7). Worth.

Callicutt, James W. & Lecca, Pedro J., eds. Social Work & Mental Health. LC 82-71734. 245p. 1983. 22.95 (ISBN 0-02-905830-9); pap. text ed. write for info. Free Pr.

Callier, F. M. & Desoer, C. A. Multivariable Feedback Systems. (Springer Texts in Electrical Engineering). (Illus.). 275p. 1983. 36.00 (ISBN 0-387-90768-8); pap. 19.50 (ISBN 0-387-90759-9). Springer-Verlag.

Callies, Fritz A. God's Animals. (gr. 2-6). 1966. pap. 2.25 (ISBN 0-8100-0062-8, 16N1615). Northwest Pub.

Callihan, Jeanne. Our Mexican Ancestors, Vol. I. (The Institute's Stories for Young Readers Ser.). (Illus.). 124p. 8.95 (ISBN 0-686-97532-4); pap. 5.95 (ISBN 0-686-97533-2). U of Tex Inst Tex Culture.

Callinicos, Luli. Gold & Workers: A People's History of South Africa, Pt. 2. (Illus.). 120p. Date not set. pap. 0.00 (ISBN 0-86232-061-5, Pub. by Zed Pr). Lawrence Hill. Postponed.

Callison, C. H., ed. America's Natural Resources. rev. ed. 1967. 14.95 o.p. (ISBN 0-8260-1685-5, Pub. by Wiley-Interscience). Wiley.

Callison, C. Stuart. The Land-to-the-Tiller Program & Rural Resource Mobilization in the Mekong Delta of South Vietnam. LC 74-620183. (Papers in International Studies: Southeast Asia: No. 34). (Illus.). 1974. pap. 4.50x (ISBN 0-89680-020-2, Ohio U Ctr Intl). Ohio U Pr.

Callison, Herbert G. Introduction to Community-Based Corrections. (McGraw-Hill Ser. in Criminology & Criminal Justice). (Illus.). 384p. 1982. text ed. 19.95x (ISBN 0-07-009637-6, C). McGraw.

Calloud, Jean. Structural Analysis of Narrative. Beardslee, William A., ed. Patte, Daniel, tr. from Fr. LC 75-37158. (Semeia Studies). 128p. 1976. pap. 3.95 o.p. (ISBN 0-8006-1503-4, 1-1503). Fortress.

Callow, Alexander B., Jr., ed. The City Boss in America: An Interpretive Reader. 1976. pap. text ed. 9.95x (ISBN 0-19-501975-X). Oxford U Pr.

Calloway, Barbara & Stone, Alan, eds. Turmoil & Consensus: A Reader in Basic Political Issues. 300p. 1983. 14.50 (ISBN 0-87073-868-2); pap. 8.95x (ISBN 0-87073-867-4). Schenkman.

Calloway, Bill, jt. auth. see Ecker, Tom.

Calloway, Jo. Dawn's Promise. (Candlelight Ecstasy Ser.: No. 121). (Orig.). 1983. pap. 1.95 (ISBN 0-440-11619-8). Dell.

--One of a Kind. (Candlelight Ecstasy Ser.: No. 150). (Orig.). 1983. pap. 1.95 (ISBN 0-440-16689-6). Dell.

Calloway, Northern J. & Hall, Carol. Super-Vroomer. LC 77-26512. (gr. k-3). 1978. PLB 7.95 o.p. (ISBN 0-385-14178-5). Doubleday.

Callson, Oliver G., jt. auth. see Flood, Kenneth U.

Callus, D. A., ed. Robert Grosseteste: Scholar & Bishop. 1955. 22.50x o.p. (ISBN 0-19-821387-5). Oxford U Pr.

Callwell, C. E. Small Wars: Their Principles & Practice. 3rd ed. (Illus.). 559p. 1976. Repr. of 1906 ed. 26.50x o.p. (ISBN 0-8476-6064-8). Rowman.

Callwood, June. Love, Hate, Fear, Anger, & the Other Lively Emotions. LC 80-19320. 168p. 1980. Repr. of 1971 ed. lib. bdg. 12.95x (ISBN 0-89370-602-7). Borgo Pr.

--Love, Hate, Fear, Anger, & the Other Lively Emotions. 1971. pap. 4.95 o.p. (ISBN 0-87877-002-X, S-2). Newcastle Pub.

--Portrait of Canada. LC 77-25579. 1981. 14.95 (ISBN 0-385-05746-6). Doubleday.

Calmenson, Stephanie. Barney's Sandcastle. LC 81-86492. (First Little Golden Bks.). (Illus.). (ps). 1983. 0.69 (ISBN 0-307-11136-9, Golden Pr); PLB price not set (ISBN 0-307-68130-0). Western Pub.

Calmes, Robert B. & Lillich, Thomas T. Disinfection & Sterilization in Dental Practice. (Illus.). 1978. pap. text ed. 14.95 (ISBN 0-07-009661-9, HP). McGraw.

Calmet, J., ed. Computer Algebra: EUROCAM 82, Marseille, France 1982. (Lecture Notes in Computer Science: Vol. 144). 301p. 1983. pap. 14.00 (ISBN 0-387-11607-9). Springer-Verlag.

Calmfors, Lars. Long-Run Effects of Short-Run Stabilization Policy. 276p. 1983. text ed. 30.75x (ISBN 0-333-33172-9, Pub. by Macmillan England). Humanities.

Calmus, Thomas W., jt. auth. see Sampson, Roy J.

Calne, D. B., et al, eds. Dopaminergic Mechanisms. LC 74-13904. (Advances in Neurology Ser: Vol. 9). 445p. 1975. 45.50 (ISBN 0-911216-93-6). Raven.

Calne, Donald B., et al. Lisuride. 1982. text ed. write for info. (ISBN 0-89004-867-3). Raven.

Calne, Roy Y., ed. Liver Transplant. write for info. (ISBN 0-12-790767-X). Grune.

Calogero, F., ed. Nonlinear Evolution Equations Solvable by the Spectral Transform. (Research Notes in Mathematics Ser.: No. 26). 257p. (Orig.). 1978. pap. text ed. 25.00 (ISBN 0-273-08402-X). Pitman Pub MA.

Calogers, F. & Degasperis, A. Special Transform & Solutions: Tools to Solve & Investigate Evolution Equations. (Studies in Applied Mechanics: Vol. 13). Date not set. 102.25 (ISBN 0-444-86368-0). Elsevier.

Calow, Peter. Life Cycles: An Evolutionary Approach to the Physiology of Reproduction. 1978. 17.95x (ISBN 0-412-21510-1, Pub. by Chapman & Hall). Methuen Inc.

Calter, Paul. Problem Solving with Computers. 1972. pap. text ed. 19.95 (ISBN 0-07-009648-1, G); instructor's manual 4.00 (ISBN 0-07-009649-X). McGraw.

--Schaum's Outline of Technical Mathematics. (Schaum's Outline Ser). (Illus.). 1979. pap. 7.95 (ISBN 0-07-009651-1, SP). McGraw.

Calusaru, Auralian. Electrodeposition of Metal Powders. (Materials Science Monographs: Vol. 3). 1980. 83.00 (ISBN 0-444-99781-4). Elsevier.

Calverley, E. E. The Mysteries of Worship in Islam. 1981. 5.50 (ISBN 0-686-97865-X). Kazi Pubns.

Calvert. Introduction to Building Management. 4th ed. 1981. text ed. 24.95 (ISBN 0-408-00520-3). Butterworth.

Calvert, Barbara. Role of the Pupil. (Students Library of Education Ser.). 1975. 13.95x (ISBN 0-7100-8065-4); pap. 6.95 (ISBN 0-7100-8066-2). Routledge & Kegan.

Calvert, Donald R. & Silverman, S. Richard. Speech & Deafness. LC 75-22602. 1975. pap. text ed. 9.95 (ISBN 0-88200-070-5, A1215). Alexander Graham.

Calvert, E. Roy. Capital Punishment in the Twentieth Century. 5th, rev. ed. Bd. with The Death Penalty Enquiry. 1931. LC 73-172571. (Criminology, Law Enforcement, & Social Problems Ser., No. 153). (Intro. added). 1973. Repr. 13.50x (ISBN 0-87585-153-3). Patterson Smith.

Calvert, G. H. Cortina Handy Spanish-English, English-Spanish Dictionary. LC 81-47221. 546p. 1982. 7.95 (ISBN 0-06-464800-1, PBN-4800). B&N NY.

Calvert, J. M. & McCausland, M. A. Electronics. LC 78-4113. (Manchester Physics Ser.). 615p. 1978. 76.95x (ISBN 0-471-99640-8); pap. 33.95 (ISBN 0-471-99639-4, Pub. by Wiley-Interscience). Wiley.

Calvert, Mary. Maine Captured in Color. (Illus.). 120p. 1982. 12.95 (ISBN 0-9609914-0-9). M Calvert.

Calvert, Patricia. The Money Creek Mare. 1983. pap. 2.25 (ISBN 0-686-43401-3, Sig Vista). NAL.

Calvert, Peter. The Concept of Class. LC 82-10617. 256p. 1982. 22.50x (ISBN 0-312-15918-8). St Martin.

--The Falklands Crisis. LC 82-42611. 1982. 20.00x (ISBN 0-312-27964-7). St Martin.

--Mexican Revolution Nineteen Ten - Nineteen Fourteen: The Diplomacy of Anglo-American Conflict. (Cambridge Latin American Studies: No. 3). (Illus.). 1968. 47.50 (ISBN 0-521-04423-5). Cambridge U Pr.

--Politics, Power & Revolution: A Comparative Analysis of Contemporary Gov't. LC 82-16879. 208p. 1982. 22.50x (ISBN 0-312-62954-0). St Martin.

Calvert, Robert A., jt. auth. see Barr, Alwyn.

Calvert, Robert A., jt. auth. see Rosaldo, Renato.

Calvert, Robert, Jr. Career Patterns of Liberal Arts Graduates. LC 73-84568. (gr. 12). 1973. 10.00x o.s.i. (ISBN 0-910328-00-5). Carroll Pr.

Calvert, Robert, Jr. & Steel, John E. Planning Your Career. 1963. pap. 3.95 (ISBN 0-07-009658-9, SP). McGraw.

Calvert, Stephen, ed. Information Industry Market Place, 1982: An International Directory of Information Products & Services. 266p. 1981. pap. 37.50 o.p. (ISBN 0-8352-1364-1). Bowker.

Calvin, Clyde L. & Knutson, Donald. Modern Home Gardening. 544p. 1983. text ed. price not set (ISBN 0-471-02486-4). Wiley.

Calvin, Henry. It's Different Abroad. LC 82-48241. 192p. 1983. pap. 2.84i (ISBN 0-06-080640-0, P 640, PL). Har-Row.

Calvin Institutes of the Christian Religion, jt. ed. see McNeill, John T.

Calvin, Jack, jt. auth. see Ricketts, Edward F.

Calvin, John. Calvin: Institutes of the Christian Religion, 2 Vols. McNeill, John T., ed. (Library of Christian Classics). 1960. Set. 27.95; (ISBN 0-664-22020-7). Westminster.

--Calvin's Letters. pap. 5.45 (ISBN 0-85151-323-9). Banner of Truth.

--Concerning the Eternal Predestination of God. Reid, J. K., tr. 1961. pap. 12.50 (ISBN 0-227-67438-3). Attic Pr.

--Golden Booklet of the True Christian Life: Devotional Classic. (Summit Books). 1975. pap. 2.95 (ISBN 0-8010-2366-1). Baker Bk.

--Sermons on Isaiah's Prophecy of the Death & Passion of Christ. Parker, T. H., tr. cancelled o.p. (ISBN 0-227-67427-8). Attic Pr.

Calvin, Melvin, ed. Organic Chemistry of Life: Readings from Scientific American. LC 73-12475. (Illus.). 452p. 1973. text ed. 22.00x (ISBN 0-7167-0884-1); pap. text ed. 10.95x (ISBN 0-7167-0883-3). W H Freeman.

Calvin, William H. & Ojemann, George A. Inside the Brain. (Illus., Orig.). 1980. pap. 2.95 (ISBN 0-451-62171-9, ME2171, Ment). NAL.

Calvino, Italo. The Baron in the Trees. Colquhoun, Archibald, tr. LC 76-39704. 1977. pap. 3.50 (ISBN 0-15-610680-9, Harv). HarBraceJ.

--Cosmicomics. Weaver, William, tr. LC 76-14795. 1976. pap. 2.95 (ISBN 0-15-622600-6, Harv). HarBraceJ.

--Italian Folktales. Martin, George, tr. from Italian. LC 80-11879. (Helen & Kurt Woolf Bk.). (Illus.). 800p. 1980. Repr. of 1956 ed. 27.50 (ISBN 0-15-145770-0). HarBraceJ.

--The Nonexistent Knight & the Cloven Viscount. Ferrone, J. & Wolff, H., eds. LC 76-39699. 1977. pap. 4.95 (ISBN 0-15-665975-1, Harv). HarBraceJ.

--Saul Steinberg: Still Life & Architecture. (Illus.). 40p. (Orig.). 1982. pap. 15.00 (ISBN 0-938608-07-X). Pace Gallery Pubns.

--T Zero. Weaver, William, tr. LC 76-14789. (A Helen & Kurt Wolff Bk.). 1976. pap. 2.95 (ISBN 0-15-692400-5, Harv). HarBraceJ.

--The Watcher & Other Stories. Weaver, William & Colquhoun, Archibald, trs. from It. LC 75-9829. 181p. 1975. pap. 3.95 (ISBN 0-15-694952-0, Harv). HarBraceJ.

Calvo, Zoraida, jt. auth. see Acosta, Antonio A.

Calvocoressi, M. D. Mussorgsky. rev. ed. (Master Musicians Ser). (Illus.). 224p. 1974. 11.00x (ISBN 0-460-03152-X, Pub. by J. M. Dent England). Biblio Dist.

Calvocoressi, M. D., tr. see Bartok, Bela.

Calwallader, S. Sharing in the Kitchen. 1979. pap. 5.95 (ISBN 0-07-009528-0). McGraw.

Cam, Gilbert A. Survey of the Literature on Investment Companies, 1864-1957. 1964. pap. 3.00 o.p. (ISBN 0-87104-173-1). NY Pub Lib.

Cam, Lucien Le see Berkeley Symposia on Mathematical Statistics & Probability, 6th.

Camacho, Oliver, jt. auth. see Roth, Audrey.

Camaione, David N. & Tillman, Kenneth G. Teaching & Coaching Wrestling: A Scientific Approach. 2nd ed. LC 79-18686. 373p. 1980. text ed. 28.50 (ISBN 0-471-05032-6). Wiley.

Camara, Dom H. Desert Is Fertile. 1976. pap. write for info (ISBN 0-515-09572-9). Jove Pubns.

--Desert Is Fertile. McDonagh, Francis, tr. from Fr. LC 73-89315. (Illus.). 80p. 1974. 4.95x o.p. (ISBN 0-88344-078-4); pap. 1.50x o.p. (ISBN 0-88344-077-6). Orbis Bks.

--Desert is Fertile. McDonagh, tr. from Fr. LC 73-89315. (Illus.). 86p. 1981. pap. 4.95 (ISBN 0-88344-093-8). Orbis Bks.

Camarao, P. C. & Serra, M. A. Great Technical Dictionary: Dicionario Tecnico English-Portuguese. 462p. (Eng. & Portuguese.). 1979. pap. 39.95 (ISBN 0-686-97435-2, M-9214). French & Eur.

Camarillo, Leo. Team Roping. Witte, Randy, tr. (Illus.). 144p. (Orig.). 1982. 7.95 (ISBN 0-911647-00-7). Western Horseman.

Camaro editors. Old California: Almanac of Fairs & Festivals. (Old California Ser.: No. 1). (Illus.). 1983. pap. 3.95 (ISBN 0-913290-43-2). Camaro Pub.

--Old California: Art, Theater, & Museums. (Old California Ser.: No. 10). (Illus.). 1983. pap. 3.95 (ISBN 0-913290-51-3). Camaro Pub.

--Old California: Camping Sites, Campgrounds, & Recreation Areas. (Old California Ser.: No. 7). (Illus.). 1983. pap. 3.95 (ISBN 0-913290-48-3). Camaro Pub.

--Old California: Christmastime, Mountain Recreation, & Romantic Hide-a-Ways. (Old California Ser.: No. 12). (Illus.). 1983. pap. 3.95 (ISBN 0-913290-53-X). Camaro Pub.

--Old California: Cooking, Recipes, & Menus. (Old California Ser.: No. 11). (Illus.). 1983. pap. 3.95 (ISBN 0-913290-52-1). Camaro Pub.

--Old California: Country Inns & Historic Hotels. (Old California Ser.: No. 4). (Illus.). 1983. pap. 3.95 (ISBN 0-913290-45-9). Camaro Pub.

--Old California for Children: Picnic Spots, Haunted Houses, & Ghost Towns. (Old California Ser.: No. 6). (Illus.). 1983. pap. 3.95 (ISBN 0-913290-47-5). Camaro Pub.

--Old California: Gold Mines, Gold Mining Towns, & Country Stores. (Old California Ser.: No. 8). (Illus.). 1983. pap. 3.95 (ISBN 0-913290-49-1). Camaro Pub.

--Old California: Historical Restaurants, Wineries, & Wine Tasting. (Old California Ser.: No. 3). (Illus.). 1983. pap. 3.95 (ISBN 0-913290-44-0). Camaro Pub.

--Old California: Historical Sights & Scenic Backroads. (Old California Ser.: No. 9). (Illus.). 1983. pap. 3.95 (ISBN 0-913290-50-5). Camaro Pub.

--Old California: Visitors Guide. (Old California Ser.: No. 5). (Illus.). 1983. pap. 3.95 (ISBN 0-913290-46-7). Camaro Pub.

Cambell, Andrew & Martine, Roddy. The Swinging Sporran: A Lighthearted Guide to the Basic Steps of Scottish Reels & Country Dances. (Illus.). 120p. 1982. 10.95 (ISBN 0-904505-88-X, Pub. by Salem Hse Ltd.). Merrimack Bk Serv.

Cambie, Conrad, jt. auth. see Brooker, Stanley.

Cambie, R. C., jt. auth. see Brooker, S. G.

Cambitoglou, A., jt. auth. see Trendall, A. D.

Camblos, Ruth & Winger, Virginia. North Carolina Round the Mountains Guide Book. 3rd, rev. ed. (Round the Mountains Ser.). (Illus., Orig.). 1978. pap. 3.50x perfect bdg. (ISBN 0-9602706-0-4). Camblos-Winger.

Cambon, Glauco. Eugenio Montale's Poetry: A Dream in Reason's Presence. 270p. 1982. 22.50 (ISBN 0-691-06520-9). Princeton U Pr.

Cambrensis, Giraldus. History & Topography of Ireland. O'Meara, John J., tr. (Dolmen Texts Ser.: No. 4). 1982. text ed. 21.00x (ISBN 0-391-01166-9, Dolmen Pr). Humanities.

Cambridge Book Editors. Increase Your Vocabulary, 2 Bks. (Illus.). pap. text ed. 4.00 ea.; Bk. 1. pap. text ed. (ISBN 0-8428-0008-5); Bk. 2. pap. text ed. (ISBN 0-8428-0009-3); Bk. 1. key 1.13 (ISBN 0-8428-0028-X); Bk. 2. key 1.13 (ISBN 0-8428-0029-8). Cambridge Bk.

--Spelling. (Illus.). (gr. 7-12). pap. text ed. 4.66 (ISBN 0-8428-0076-X); key 2.00 (ISBN 0-8428-0027-1). Cambridge Bk.

Cambridge Consultants Training Ltd. Programmed Introduction to Critical Path Methods. 1967. pap. 6.25 o.p. (ISBN 0-08-014027-0). Pergamon.

Cambridge Historical Commission. Survey of Architectural History in Cambridge. Incl. Report One: East Cambridge. pap. o.p. (ISBN 0-685-27127-7); Report Two: Mid Cambridge. 1967. pap. 8.95 (ISBN 0-262-53012-0); Report Three: Cambridgeport. 1971. pap. 8.95 (ISBN 0-262-53013-9); Report Four: Old Cambridge. 1973. pap. 8.95 o.p. (ISBN 0-262-75001-5); Report Five: Northwest Cambridge. 1977. pap. 9.95 (ISBN 0-262-53032-5). MIT Pr.

Cambridge Research Institute. Omnibus Copyright Revision: Comparative Analysis of the Issues. LC 73-84952. 1973. 48.00 (ISBN 0-87715-103-2). Am Soc Info Sci.

Cambridge School Classics Project. Cambridge Latin Course, 5 units. Incl. Unit 1. text ed. 7.95 (ISBN 0-521-07922-5); tchr's handbk. 7.95x (ISBN 0-521-07902-0); tape recording 18.50x (ISBN 0-521-08036-3); slides 45.00x (ISBN 0-521-08009-6); Unit 2. text ed. 7.95x (ISBN 0-521-08043-6); tchr's handbk. 7.50 (ISBN 0-521-08157-2); tape recording 18.50x (ISBN 0-521-08158-0); slides 45.00x (ISBN 0-521-08159-9); Unit 3. text ed. 8.95x (ISBN 0-521-08515-2); tchr's handbk. 7.50x (ISBN 0-521-08539-X); slides 49.00x (ISBN 0-521-08541-1); tape recording 18.50x (ISBN 0-521-08540-3); Unit 4. text ed. 7.50x (ISBN 0-521-08542-X); tchr's handbk. 9.50x (ISBN 0-521-08543-8); tape recordings 18.50x (ISBN 0-521-20231-0); limp bdg. 9.50x (ISBN 0-686-82874-7); Unit 5. 1977. tchr's handbk. 6.95x (ISBN 0-521-08544-6). LC 72-132282. (gr. 9-12). 1971-73. Cambridge U Pr.

Cambridge Women's Study Group. Women in Society: Interdisciplinary Essays. 314p. 1983. pap. 9.95 (ISBN 0-86068-083-5, Virago Pr). Merrimack Bk Serv.

Cambron-McCabe, Nelda H., ed. The Changing Politics of School Finance. (American Education Finance Association). 312p. 1982. prof ref 29.00x (ISBN 0-88410-896-1). Ballinger Pub.

Camburn, K. E., et al. The Haptobenthic Diatom Flora of Long Branch Creek, South Carolina. (Offprint from Nova Hedwigia Ser.: No. 30). (Illus.). 1979. pap. text ed. 24.00x (ISBN 3-7682-1197-5). Lubrecht & Cramer.

Camden, Archie. Blow by Blow: The Memories of a Musical Rogue & Vagabond. (Illus.). 208p. 1983. text ed. 15.00x (ISBN 0-87663-421-8). Universe.

Camden, K. R. A Revision Course in School Certificate Mathematics. pap. 6.50x (ISBN 0-392-08359-0, SpS). Sportshelf.

Camden, Kenneth. Graphical Work. pap. 7.50x (ISBN 0-392-08412-0, ABC). Sportshelf.

Camden, Thomas M. & Schwartz, Susan H. How to Get a Job in Chicago: The Insider's Guide. LC 82-99938. (Illus.). 440p. 1983. pap. 10.95 (ISBN 0-9609516-0-1). Surrey Bks.

Camehl, Ada W. Blue-China Book: Early American Scenes & History Pictured in the Pottery of the Time. (Illus.). pap. 5.00 o.p. (ISBN 0-486-22749-9). Dover.

Camejo, Peter, et al. The Lesser Evil? The Left Debates the Democratic Party & Social Change. 1978. cloth 12.00 (ISBN 0-87348-517-3). Path Pr NY.

Cameli, Louis. Mary's Journey. 5.95 (ISBN 0-8215-9911-9). Sadlier.

Cameli, Louis J. Stories of Paradise. pap. 3.50 o.p. (ISBN 0-8091-2130-1). Paulist Pr.

Camerini-Davalos, Rafael A., et al, eds. Atherogenesis, Vol. 275. (Annals of the New York Academy of Sciences). 1976. 40.00x (ISBN 0-89072-054-1). NY Acad Sci.

Cameron. How to Buy & Install Your Hi-Fi Stereo System. (Illus.). 112p. 1980. pap. 6.95 (ISBN 0-8359-2921-3). Reston.

Cameron, jt. auth. see Field.

Cameron, jt. auth. see Kerney.

Cameron, A. Living under the Normans. (Exploring History Ser.). (Illus.). 48p. 1978. wkbk. 3.15 (ISBN 0-05-003123-6). Longman.

Cameron, A., ed. Basic Lubrication Theory. 3rd ed. (Series in Engineering Science: Civil Engineering). 256p. 1981. 34.95x o.p. (ISBN 0-470-27187-6). Halsted Pr.

Cameron, A. E., ed. Determination of the Isotopic Composition of Uranium. (National Nuclear Energy Ser.: Div. I, Vol. 13). 173p. 1950. pap. 15.00 (ISBN 0-87079-177-X, TID-5213); microfilm 4.50 (ISBN 0-87079-452-3, TID-5213). DOE.

Cameron, A. G. W., jt. ed. see Ponnamperuma, Cyril.

Cameron, Allan G., jt. auth. see Fox, Brian A.

Cameron, Angus & Kingsmill, Allison, eds. Old English Word Studies: A Preliminary Word & Author List. (Old English Ser.). 208p. 1983. 60.00x (ISBN 0-8020-5526-5); fiche incl. U of Toronto Pr.

Cameron, Angus, intro. by. The Magic of Owls. LC 77-78130. 1977. 11.95 (ISBN 0-8027-0578-2); pap. 6.95 (ISBN 0-8027-7117-3). Walker & Co.

Cameron, Ann. The Journey. 336p. 1982. pap. 5.95 (ISBN 0-380-79087-4, 79087). Avon.

Cameron, Averil, ed. Flavius Cresconius Corippus: In Laudem Lustini Augusti Minoris. (Illus.). 235p. 1976. text ed. 52.00x o.p. (ISBN 0-485-11157-8, Athlone Pr). Humanities.

Cameron, Barbara. An Affair to Remember. (Candlelight Ecstasy Ser.: No. 124). (Orig.). 1983. pap. 1.95 (ISBN 0-440-11405-5). Dell.

Cameron, Betsy. Lisanne: A Young Model. (Illus.). 1979. 10.95 o.p. (ISBN 0-517-53866-0, C N Potter Bks). Crown.

Cameron, Catherine. The Name Givers: How They Influence Your Life. 230p. 1983. 13.95 (ISBN 0-13-609495-3); pap. 6.95 (ISBN 0-13-609487-2). P-H.

Cameron, Claire. Amethyst Summer. (Adventures in Love Ser.: No. 21). 1982. pap. 1.75 (ISBN 0-451-11469-8, AE1469, Sig). NAL.

Cameron, Derek. Advanced Electronic Troubleshooting. (Illus.). 1977. 21.95 (ISBN 0-87909-002-2). Reston.

--Audio Technology Systems: Principles, Applications & Troubleshooting. (Illus.). 1978. text ed. 21.95 (ISBN 0-87909-050-2). Reston.

--Hi-Fi Stereo Installation Simplified. (Illus.). 1978. 19.00 (ISBN 0-8359-2842-X). Reston.

Cameron, E. Hyaluronidase & Cancer. 1966. inquire for price o.p. (ISBN 0-08-011480-6). Pergamon.

Cameron, Eleanor. The Court of the Stone Children. (gr. 5-10). 1976. pap. 1.75 o.p. (ISBN 0-380-00681-2, 48942). Avon.

--The Court of the Stone Children. 208p. (gr. 5 up). 1973. 11.50 (ISBN 0-525-28350-1, 01117-330). Dutton.

--Stowaway to the Mushroom Planet. (gr. 3-7). 1956. 11.95 (ISBN 0-316-12534-2, Atlantic-Little, Brown). Little.

Cameron, Elizabeth. Big Book of Real Trucks. (Grosset Picture Bks.). (gr. 1-5). 1970. 2.95 (ISBN 0-448-02240-0, G&D). Putnam Pub Group.

--A Floral ABC. (Illus.). 64p. 1983. 7.95 (ISBN 0-688-01821-1). Morrow.

Cameron, Frank & Campione, Frank. Micro Guns. (Illus.). 48p. 1982. 24.00 (ISBN 0-88014-049-6). Mosaic Pr OH.

Cameron, Helen, jt. auth. see Henderson, William C.

Cameron, I. R. Nuclear Fission Reactors. 410p. 1982. 42.50x (ISBN 0-306-41073-7, Plenum Pr). PLenum Pub.

Cameron, Iain. Scientific Images & Their Social Uses. (Science in a Social Context Ser.). 1979. pap. text ed. 3.95 o.p. (ISBN 0-408-71309-7). Butterworth.

Cameron, Iain A. Crime & Represssion in the Auvergne & Guyenne, 1720-1790. LC 80-41953. (Illus.). 256p. 1982. 39.50 (ISBN 0-521-23882-X). Cambridge U Pr.

Cameron, Ian. To the Farthest Ends of the Earth: One Hundred Fifty Years of World Exploration by the Royal Geographical Society. (Illus.). 304p. 1980. 27.00 o.p. (ISBN 0-525-22065-8). Dutton.

Cameron, J. & Dodd, W. A. Society, Schools & Progress in Tanzania. 1970. 24.00 o.s.i. (ISBN 0-08-015564-2); pap. 12.00 (ISBN 0-08-015563-4). Pergamon.

Cameron, J. M. R. Ambition's Fire: The Agricultural Colonization of Pre-Convict Western Australia. 238p. 1982. pap. 27.00 (ISBN 0-85564-196-7, Pub. by U of W Austral Pr). Intl Schol Bk Serv.

Cameron, James B., et al. Advanced Accounting: Theory & Practice. LC 78-69529. (Illus.). 1979. text ed. 28.95 (ISBN 0-395-27446-X); solutions manual 3.50 (ISBN 0-395-27447-8); student check sheets. set of 100 2.50 (ISBN 0-395-27497-4). HM.

Cameron, James R. Frederick William Maitland & the History of English Law. LC 77-677. 1977. Repr. of 1961 ed. lib. bdg. 19.75x (ISBN 0-8371-9499-7, CAFWM). Greenwood.

Cameron, Janet E. Double Crostics. No 18. 1982. 5.00 (ISBN 0-918684-17-X). Cameron & Co.

Cameron, Jean. For All That Has Been: Time to Live & Time to Die. 120p. 1982. pap. 9.50 (ISBN 0-02-521980-4). Macmillan.

Cameron, Jenks. The Development of Governmental Forest Control in the United States. LC 79-38096. (Law, Politics, & History Ser.). 484p. 1972. Repr. of 1928 ed. lib. bdg. 55.00 (ISBN 0-306-70440-4). Da Capo.

Cameron, John. Development of Education in East Africa. LC 68-9320. (Illus.). 1970. pap. text ed. 6.95x (ISBN 0-8077-1137-3). Tchrs Coll.

--Space Travel. LC 80-52519. (Starters Ser.). PLB 8.00 (ISBN 0-382-06483-6). Silver.

Cameron, John R. & Skofronick, James G. Medical Physics. LC 77-26909. 1978. 38.50 (ISBN 0-471-13131-8, Pub. by Wiley-Interscience). Wiley.

Cameron, Keith. Agrippa d'Aubigne. (World Authors Ser.). 1977. lib. bdg. 15.95 (ISBN 0-8057-6280-9, Twayne). G K Hall.

--A Concordance of Agrippa d'Aubigne's "Les Traigques". 400p. 1982. 95.00x (ISBN 0-85989-143-7, Pub. by Exeter Univ England). State Mutual Bk.

Cameron, Kenneth. English Place-Names. 1977. 22.50 (ISBN 0-7134-0841-3, Pub by Batsford, England). David & Charles.

Cameron, Kenneth M. & Gillespie, Patti P. The Enjoyment of Theatre. (Illus.). 1980. pap. text ed. 15.95 (ISBN 0-02-318360-8). Macmillan.

Cameron, Kenneth M. & Hoffman, Theodore J. Guide to Theatre Study. 2nd ed. (Illus.). 384p. 1974. text ed. 19.95 (ISBN 0-02-318350-0, 31835). Macmillan.

Cameron, Kenneth W. Thoreau Discovers Emerson: A College Reading Record. 1953. pap. 3.00 o.p. (ISBN 0-87104-176-6). NY Pub Lib.

Cameron, Kim S. & Whetten, David A., eds. Organizational Effectiveness: A Comparison of Multiple Models. 320p. 1982. 29.50 (ISBN 0-12-157180-7). Acad Pr.

Cameron, Lewis. Opportunity My Ally. (Illus.). 1965. 10.95 (ISBN 0-227-67706-4). Attic Pr.

Cameron, Lou. The Hot Car. 208p. (Orig.). 1981. pap. 2.25 o.p. (ISBN 0-380-78949-3, 78949). Avon.

Cameron, Mabel W., ed. The Biographical Cyclopaedia of American Women, 2 vols. LC 24-7615. 408p. 1975. Repr. of 1924 ed. 94.00x (ISBN 0-8103-3990-0). Gale.

Cameron, Margaret & Hofvander, Tngve. Manual on Feeding Infants & Young Children. 3rd ed. (Illus.). 240p. 1983. pap. 9.95 (ISBN 0-19-261403-7). Oxford U Pr.

Cameron, Norman. Personality Development & Psychopathology: A Dynamic Approach. LC 63-6438. 1963. text ed. 26.95 (ISBN 0-395-04251-8); tchr's. manual by K.E. Renner 1.90 (ISBN 0-395-04252-6). HM.

Cameron, P. J. Parallelisms of Complete Designs. LC 75-32912. (London Mathematical Society Lecture Note Ser.: No. 23). (Illus.). 1976. 19.95 (ISBN 0-521-21160-3). Cambridge U Pr.

Cameron, P. J. & Van Lint, J. H. Graphs, Codes & Designs. (London Mathematical Society Lecture Notes Ser.: No. 43). 180p. 1980. 21.95x (ISBN 0-521-23141-8). Cambridge U Pr.

Cameron, Peter, ed. see British Combinatorial Conference, Sixth.

Cameron, Polly. The Cat Who Thought He Was a Tiger. (Illus.). (gr. k-3). 1956. PLB 4.99 o.p. (ISBN 0-698-30039-4). Putnam Pub Group.

--Green Machine. (Illus.). (ps-3). 1969. PLB 5.39 o.p. (ISBN 0-698-30181-1, Coward). Putnam Pub Group.

--I Can't Said the Ant. (Illus.). (gr. k-3). 1961. PLB 5.99 (ISBN 0-698-30197-8, Coward). Putnam Pub Group.

--The Two-Ton Canary & Other Nonsense Riddles. LC 65-20387. (Illus.). (gr. k-2). 1978. pap. 1.95 (ISBN 0-698-20471-9, Coward). Putnam Pub Group.

Cameron, Ron, ed. The Other Gospels: Non-Canonical Gospel Texts. LC 82-8662. 192p. 1982. pap. 11.95 (ISBN 0-664-24428-9). Westminster.

Cameron, Rondo, ed. Civilization Since Waterloo: A Book of Source Readings. LC 75-108872. 1971. text ed. 23.95x (ISBN 0-88295-778-3); pap. text ed. 13.95x (ISBN 0-88295-779-1). Harlan Davidson.

Cameron, Sean, ed. Working Together: New Developments Incorporating the Portage Teaching Model. (NFER General Ser.). 172p. 1982. pap. text ed. 12.50x (ISBN 0-85633-241-0, 51732, NFER). Humanities.

Cameron, Sheila M. More of the Best From New Mexico Kitchens. King, Scottie, ed. LC 82-62076. (Illus.). 160p. (Orig.). 1982. pap. 5.95 (ISBN 0-937206-02-4, Pub. by NM Magazine). U of NM Pr.

Cameron, Stewart. Kidney Disease: The Facts. (The Facts Ser.). (Illus.). 1981. text ed. 18.95x (ISBN 0-19-261329-4). Oxford U Pr.

Cameron, William B. Informal Sociology: A Casual Introduction to Sociological Thinking. (Orig.). 1963. pap. text ed. 2.95x (ISBN 0-685-19735-2). Phila Bk Co.

Cameron, William E. Great Dramas of the Bible. LC 81-71560. 305p. 1982. 4.95 (ISBN 0-87159-047-6). Unity Bks.

Camerron, Donald. My Tanganyika Service: And Some Nigeria. Huessler, Robert, ed. LC 82-8666. (Illus.). 308p. 1982. lib. bdg. 24.00 (ISBN 0-8191-2441-9); pap. text ed. 13.25 (ISBN 0-8191-2442-7) U Pr of Amer.

Camesasca. Mantegna. pap. 12.50 (ISBN 0-935748-11-3). ScalaBooks.

Camille, A. & Johnson, R. Dinner on a Toothpick. 1971. 3.95 o.p. (ISBN 0-685-01124-0, 80102). Glencoe.

Camilleri, J. A. Civilization in Crisis. LC 76-4240. (Illus.). 1977. 32.50 (ISBN 0-521-21248-0); pap. 12.95 (ISBN 0-521-29078-3). Cambridge U Pr.

Camilli, M. Camillo, tr. see Huarte de San Juan, Juan.

Camilli, Thomas. Make It Metric. (Illus.). 72p. (Orig.). 1982. 6.95 (ISBN 0-9607366-7-0, KP111). Kino Pubns.

Camillus, John C. The Practice of Strategic Planning. (League Exchange Ser.: No. 124). 79p. 1980. 5.95 (ISBN 0-686-38163-7, 21-1803). Natl League Nurse.

Caminha, Adolfo. Bom-Crioulo: The Black Man & the Cabin Boy. Lacey, E. A., tr. from Portuguese. 144p. 1982. 20.00 (ISBN 0-917342-87-9); pap. 7.95 (ISBN 0-917342-88-7). Gay Sunshine.

Caminos, Horacio & Goethert, Reinhard. Urbanization Primer: Project Assessment, Site Analysis, Design Criteria for Site & Services & Similar Dwelling Environments in Developing Areas, with a Documentary Collection of Photographs on Urbanization. (Illus.). 1978. text ed. 35.00x (ISBN 0-262-03066-7). MIT Pr.

Camner, James. Great Conductors in Historic Photographs: 193 Portraits. (Music Ser.). (Illus.). 96p. (Orig.). 1983. pap. 7.95 (ISBN 0-486-24397-4). Dover.

Camoin, Francois. The End of the World Is Los Angeles: Stories. LC 81-69838. 112p. 1982. pap. 6.95 (ISBN 0-8262-0365-5). U of Mo Pr.

Camotta, Sharon. Susie's Wish. 35p. (Orig.). 1982. pap. 4.95 (ISBN 0-931494-31-1). Brunswick Pub.

Camougis, G. Environmental Biology for Engineers: A Guide to Environmental Assessment. 1980. 24.50 (ISBN 0-07-009677-5). McGraw.

Camp, Bonnie W., ed. Advances in Behavioral Pediatrics, Vol. 1. 266p. 1980. 40.00 (ISBN 0-89232-076-1). Jai Pr.

--Advances in Behavioral Pediatrics, Vol. 2. 232p. 1981. 40.00 (ISBN 0-89232-185-7). Jai Pr.

Camp, Dennis, ed. see Lindsay, Vachel.

Camp, Diana Van. Basic Skills Human Body Workbook: Grade 5. (Basic Skills Workbooks). 32p. 1982. tchrs' ed. 0.99 (ISBN 0-8209-0420-1, HBW-F). ESP.

--Basic Skills Human Body Workbook: Grade 8. (Basic Skills Workbook). 32p. 1982. tchrs' ed. 0.99 (ISBN 0-8209-0423-6, HBW-I). ESP.

--Basic Skills Human Workbook: Grade 7. (Basic Skills Workbook). 32p. 1982. tchrs' ed. 0.99 (ISBN 0-8209-0422-8, HBW-H). ESP.

--Basic Skills Human Workbooks: Grade 6. (Basic Skills Workbooks). 32p. 1982. tchrs' ed. 0.99 (ISBN 0-8209-0421-X, HBW-G). ESP.

Camp, Diana van see Van Camp, Diana.

Camp, Gerald, ed. Teaching Writing: Essays from the Bay Area Writing Project. 336p. (Orig.). 1983. pap. text ed. 7.80x (ISBN 0-86709-081-2). Boynton Cook Pubs.

Camp, James, et al. Three Tenors, One Vehicle: A Book of Songs. LC 74-28757. (Open Places Poets Ser.: No. 2). 1975. pap. 2.50x (ISBN 0-913398-01-2). Open Places.

Camp, John. One Hundred Years of Medical Murder. 224p. 1983. 12.95 (ISBN 0-370-30354-7, Pub by The Bodley Head). Merrimack Bk Serv.

Camp, L. Sprague De see De Camp, L. Sprague.

Camp, L. Sprague de see De Camp, L. Sprague.

Camp, L. Sprague De see De Camp, L. Sprague.

Camp, L. Sprague de see De Camp, L. Sprague.

Camp, L. Sprague De see De Camp, L. Sprague.

Camp, L. Sprague De see De Camp, L. Sprague & Howard, Robert E.

Camp, L. Sprague de see Howard, Robert E.

Camp, L. Sprague De see Sprague De Camp, L.

Camp, Norman. Pensando Con Dios. 128p. (Span.). 1981. pap. 2.95 (ISBN 0-8024-6593-5). Moody.

Camp, Roderic A. Mexican Political Biographies, Nineteen Thirty-Five to Nineteen Eighty. 2nd, rev., exp. ed. 1982. 35.00x (ISBN 0-8165-0743-0). U of Ariz Pr.

Camp, Sue C. Developing Proofreading Skill. Tinervia, Joseph, ed. LC 80-12596. (Illus.). 128p. (gr. 11-12). 1980. pap. text ed. 3.96 (ISBN 0-07-009635-X). McGraw.

Camp, Thomas & Maserve, Robert L. Water & Its Impurities. LC 74-7012. (Illus.). 384p. 1974. text ed. 48.50 (ISBN 0-87933-112-7). Hutchinson Ross.

Camp, Wesley D. Roots of Western Civilization: From Ancient Times to 1715, Vol. 1. LC 82-13576. 230p. 1983. pap. text ed. 11.95x (ISBN 0-471-87642-9). Wiley.

--Roots of Western Civilization: From the Enlightment to the 1980's, Vol. 2. LC 82-13576. 299p. 1983. pap. text ed. 11.95x (ISBN 0-471-87641-0). Wiley.

Camp, William L. & Schwark, Bryan L. Guide to Periodicals in Education & Its Academic Disciplines. 2nd ed. LC 75-6784. 568p. 1975. 25.50 (ISBN 0-8108-0814-5). Scarecrow.

Campaign for Political Rights. U.S. Covert Operations Against Nicaragua: A Public Forum. (Illus.). 95p. pap. 5.00 (ISBN 0-910175-02-0). Campaign Political.

Campanella, Tommaso. The City of the Sun: A Poetical Dialogue of Tommaso Campanella. Donno, Daniel J., ed. LC 80-20133. (Biblioteca Italiana Ser.). 1981. 17.50 (ISBN 0-520-04034-1); pap. 3.95x (ISBN 0-520-04036-8). U of Cal Pr.

Campanis, Al. Play Ball with Roger the Dodger. (Illus.). 80p. (gr. 1-5). 1980. 7.95 (ISBN 0-399-20710-4); pap. 3.95 (ISBN 0-399-20711-2, Peppercorn). Putnam Pub Group.

Campannella, Thomas. The City of the Sun. Elliott, A. M. & Millner, R., trs. from Ital. 64p. 1982. pap. 4.50 (ISBN 0-904526-16-X, Pub. by Journeyman England). Lawrence Hill.

Campardon, Emile. L'Academie Royale de Musique au 18 Siecle, 2 Vols. LC 73-141152. (Music Ser). 1971. Repr. of 1884 ed. Set. lib. bdg. 95.00 (ISBN 0-306-70090-5). Da Capo.

Campbel, S. L. Singular Systems of Differential Equations. LC 79-20908. (Reserach Notes in Mathematics Ser.: No. 40). 176p. (Orig.). 1980. pap. text ed. 20.95 (ISBN 0-273-08438-0). Pitman Pub MA.

Campbell. EEC Competition Law: A Practitioner's Textbook. 1980. 64.00 (ISBN 0-444-85496-7). Elsevier.

Campbell & Fields. Introduction to Health Assessment. 1982. text ed. 27.95 (ISBN 0-8359-3191-9). Reston.

Campbell, A. B. Queer Shipmates. (Illus.). (gr. 9 up). 10.00 (ISBN 0-392-04313-0, SpS). Sportshelf.

Campbell, A. H., ed. see Vecchio, Giorgio del.

Campbell, A. K., jt. auth. see Ashley, C. C.

Campbell, Alan. Common Market Law, Vol. 3. 2nd ed. 1973. 65.00 (ISBN 0-379-16063-5). Oceana.

Campbell, Alexander. Christian System. 9.95 (ISBN 0-89225-064-X). Gospel Advocate.

--Heroes Then, Heroes Now. (Illus.). 89p. (Orig.). 1981. pap. 12.95 (ISBN 0-940754-08-8). Ed Ministries.

--Live with Moses. 90p. (Orig.). 1982. pap. 12.95 (ISBN 0-940754-13-4). Ed Ministries.

--Stories of Jesus, Stories of Now. 80p. (Orig.). (gr. 1-6). 1980. pap. 12.95 (ISBN 0-940754-04-5). Ed Ministries.

Campbell, Alexander, tr. from Gk. Living Oracles. 1975. Repr. 12.00 (ISBN 0-89225-216-2); kivar 9.50 (ISBN 0-89225-217-0). Gospel Advocate.

Campbell, Andrew C. Coral Seas. LC 76-6036. (Illus.). 1976. 12.95 o.p. (ISBN 0-399-11778-4). Putnam Pub Group.

Campbell, Angus. The Sense of Well Being in America: Recent Patterns & Trends. 256p. 1980. 17.95 (ISBN 0-07-009683-X). McGraw.

--White Attitudes Toward Black People. LC 74-161548. 177p. 1971. 12.00x (ISBN 0-87944-007-4); pap. 8.00x (ISBN 0-87944-006-6). Inst Soc Res.

Campbell, Angus & Converse, Phillip E. Quality of American Life, Nineteen Seventy-Eight. LC 80-84081. 1980. write for info (ISBN 0-89138-951-2). ICPSR.

Campbell, Angus & Converse, Philip E., eds. Human Meaning of Social Change. LC 75-169837. 548p. 1972. 16.00x (ISBN 0-87154-193-9). Russell Sage.

Campbell, Angus, et al. American Voter: An Abridgement. LC 64-20076. (Illus.). 302p. 1964. pap. text ed. 17.95 (ISBN 0-471-13335-3). Wiley.

--The Quality of American Life: Perceptions, Evaluations & Satisfactions. LC 75-7176. 600p. 1976. 16.95x (ISBN 0-87154-194-7). Russell Sage.

--The Voter Decides. LC 73-138211. 242p. 1972. Repr. of 1954 ed. lib. bdg. 17.75x (ISBN 0-8371-5566-5, CAVD). Greenwood.

Campbell, Ann O. Archibald the Horse: A Children's Illustrated Story Book. (Illus.). 1982. 4.95 (ISBN 0-938686-25-9). H Spriggle.

Campbell, Anthony. Seven States of Consciousness: Vision of Possibilities Suggested by the Teaching of Maharishi Mahesh Yogi. LC 73-9078. (Orig.). 1974. pap. 2.50i o.p. (ISBN 0-06-080289-8, P289, PL). Har-Row.

Campbell, Anthony K. Intracellular Calcium: Its Universal Role As Regulator. (Monographs in Molecular Biophysics & Biochemistry). 540p. 1982. write for info. (ISBN 0-471-10488-4, Pub. by Wiley-Interscience). Wiley.

Campbell, Archibald. Scottish Swords from the Battlefield at Culloden. Mowbray, Andrew, ed. (Illus.). 1971. 5.00 (ISBN 0-917218-04-3). Mowbray Co.

--Voyage Around the World from 1806 to 1812. (Fasc, of 1822 Ed). 1967. Repr. 7.95 (ISBN 0-87022-100-0). UH Pr.

Campbell, Archibald Y. Horace, a New Interpretation. LC 70-109714. Repr. of 1924 ed. lib. bdg. 17.00x (ISBN 0-8371-4204-0, CAHO). Greenwood.

Campbell, Ashley S. Thermodynamic Analysis of Combustion Engines. LC 78-16181. 366p. 1979. text ed. 40.95x (ISBN 0-471-03751-6). Wiley.

Campbell, Barbara K. The Liberated Woman of 1914: Prominent Women in the Progressive Era. LC 78-27703. (Studies in American History & Culture: No. 6). 220p. 1979. 39.95 (ISBN 0-8357-0980-9, Pub. by UMI Res Pr); pap. 20.95 o.p. (ISBN 0-8357-0981-7). Univ Microfilms.

Campbell, Bernard G. Humankind Emerging. 3rd ed. 1982. pap. text ed. 17.95 (ISBN 0-316-12622-5); tchrs.' manual avail. (ISBN 0-316-12623-3). Little.

Campbell, Bernard G., ed. Humankind Emerging. 2nd ed. 1979. 15.95 o.p. (ISBN 0-316-12601-2); training manual free o.p. (ISBN 0-316-12621-7). Little.

Campbell, Bonita J. Understanding Information Systems: Foundations for Control. (Orig.). 1977. pap. text ed. 7.95 (ISBN 0-316-12624-1). Little.

Campbell, Bonnie, jt. auth. see Campbell, Will.

Campbell, Bruce, ed. see Hanzak, J.

Campbell, Bryn. Exploring Photography. LC 79-13440. (Illus.). 1979. 20.00 o.s.i. (ISBN 0-933920-01-6); pap. 9.95 o.s.i. (ISBN 0-933920-02-4). Hudson Hills.

Campbell, Burt L. Marine Badges & Insignia of the World: Including Marines, Commandos & Navel Infantrymen. (Illus.). 160p. 1983. 16.95 (ISBN 0-7137-1138-8, Pub. by Blandford Pr England). Sterling.

Campbell, C. D., tr. see Ibanez, V. Blasco.

Campbell, C. Lee. The Fischer-Smith Controversy: Are There Bacterial Diseases of Plants. LC 80-85458. (Phytopathology Classic Ser.: No. 13). (Illus.). 65p. 1981. 8.50 (ISBN 0-89054-014-4). Am Phytopathol Soc.

Campbell, C. M. & Robertson, E. F., eds. Groups: St. Andrew's 1981. LC 82-4427. (London Mathematical Society Lecture Note Ser.: No. 71). 360p. 1982. pap. 34.50 (ISBN 0-521-28974-2). Cambridge U Pr.

Campbell, Carlos C., et al. Great Smoky Mountains Wildflowers. 4th ed. LC 77-126938. (Illus.). 1977. spiral bdg. 4.75 (ISBN 0-87049-124-5). U of Tenn Pr.

Campbell, Claire. Nursing Diagnosis & Intervention in Nursing Practice. LC 77-17095. 1978. text ed. 37.50x (ISBN 0-471-13307-8, Pub. by Wiley Medical). Wiley.

Campbell, Colin. Governments under Stress: Political Executives & Key Bureaucrats in Washington, London, & Ottawa. 384p. 1983. 25.00 (ISBN 0-8020-5622-9). U of Toronto Pr.

--Tuning for Economy. (Illus.). 160p. 1981. 17.95x (ISBN 0-412-23480-7, Pub by Chapman & Hall England); pap. 9.95 (ISBN 0-412-23490-4). Methuen Inc.

Campbell, Colin & Murphy, Allan. Things We Said Today: The Complete Lyrics & a Concordance to the Beatles' Songs, 1962-1970. (Rock & Roll Reference Ser.: No. 4). 1980. individuals 27.50 (ISBN 0-87650-104-8); institutions 35.00. Pierian.

Campbell, Colin A., ed. see Weaver, Betsy & Frederick, Gary E.

Campbell, Colin D., ed. Financing Social Security. 1979. 16.25 (ISBN 0-8447-2140-9); pap. 8.25 (ISBN 0-8447-2139-5). Am Enterprise.

Campbell, D. K., jt. auth. see Bishop, A. R.

Campbell, D. Ross. How to Really Love Your Child. 1977. 9.95 (ISBN 0-686-86856-0); pap. 4.50 (ISBN 0-88207-751-1). Victor Bks.

Campbell, Diana. Lord Margrave's Deception. 1982. pap. 2.25 (ISBN 0-451-11460-4, AE1460, Sig). NAL.

--A Marriage of Inconvenience. 1982. pap. 2.25 (ISBN 0-451-11867-7, AE1867, Sig). NAL.

Campbell, Diane. Step-by-Step to Natural Food. 224p. comb bdg. 7.95 (ISBN 0-686-97060-8). C C Pubs.

Campbell, Doak S. El Maestro Eficiente. Rodriguez, Jose M., tr. from Eng. Orig. Title: When Do Teachers Teach. 160p. (Span.). 1980. pap. 2.50 (ISBN 0-311-11029-0). Casa Bautista.

Campbell, Don. Police: The Exercise of Power. 128p. 1978. 30.00x (ISBN 0-7121-1678-8, Pub. by Macdonald & Evans). State Mutual Bk.

Campbell, Donald K. Daniel: Decoder of Dreams. 1977. pap. 4.50 (ISBN 0-88207-747-3). Victor Bks.

--No Time for Neutrality. 144p. 1981. pap. 4.50 (ISBN 0-88207-337-0). Victor Bks.

Campbell, Donald K., ed. Walvoord: A Tribute. LC 81-16888. 396p. 1982. 12.95 (ISBN 0-8024-9227-4). Moody.

Campbell, Donald T., jt. auth. see Brewer, Marilynn B.

Campbell, Donald T., jt. auth. see Cook, Thomas.

Campbell, Donald T., jt. auth. see Webb, Eugene J.

Campbell, Dorothy W. Index to Black American Authors in Collective Biographies. 162p. 1983. lib. bdg. 27.50 (ISBN 0-87287-349-8). Libs Unl.

Campbell, Duncan C. & Rowan, Richard L. Multinational Corporations & the OECD Industrial Relations Guidelines. (Multinational Industrial Relations Ser.: No. 11). (Illus.). 250p. (Orig.). 1983. pap. 22.00 (ISBN 0-89546-039-4). Indus Res Unit-Wharton.

Campbell, Ed, jt. ed. see Wilkinson, Sylvia.

Campbell, Edward F. Ruth. LC 74-18785. (Anchor Bible Ser.: Vol. 7). (Illus.). 216p. 1975. 14.00 (ISBN 0-385-05316-9). Doubleday.

Campbell, Edward F., jt. ed. see Freedman, David N.

Campbell, Edward F., Jr. & Boling, Robert, eds. Essays in Honor of George Ernest Wright. 177p. 1976. text ed. 10.00x (ISBN 0-89757-003-0, Am Sch Orient Res). Eisenbrauns.

Campbell, Elizabeth. Jamestown: The Beginning. (Illus.). 96p. (gr. 4-6). 1974. 8.95 (ISBN 0-316-12599-7). Little.

Campbell, Ernest T. Where Cross the Crowded Ways: Prayers of a City Pastor. 1973. pap. 2.95 o.s.i. (ISBN 0-8096-1861-3, Assn Pr). Follett.

Campbell, Evelyn, jt. auth. see Schambach, Mardel C.

Campbell, Ferdinand. A Profile of Love. LC 78-62758. 96p. Repr. of 1978 ed. 5.00 (ISBN 0-912444-16-9). Gaus.

Campbell, Frank & Sinaer, George. Brain & Behaviour: Psychobiology of Everyday Life. (Illus.). 168p. 1980. 24.00 (ISBN 0-08-024788-1); pap. 13.50 (ISBN 0-08-024787-3). Pergamon.

Campbell, Frank D. John D. MacDonald & the Colorful World of Travis McGee. LC 77-773. (Milford Series Popular Writers of Today: Vol. 5). 1977. lib. bdg. 9.95x (ISBN 0-89370-108-4); pap. 3.95x (ISBN 0-89370-208-0). Borgo Pr.

Campbell, G. Doctor's Proven Home Cure for Arthritis. 3.95x (ISBN 0-13-217034-5). Cancer Control Soc.

Campbell, Gail. Salt-Water Tropical Fish in Your Home. LC 76-1175. (Illus.). 160p. (YA) 1976. 11.95 (ISBN 0-8069-3730-0); PLB 14.49 (ISBN 0-8069-3731-9). Sterling.

Campbell, George. Philosophy of Rhetoric. Bitzer, Lloyd F., ed. LC 63-14291. (Landmarks in Rhetoric & Public Address Ser.). 476p. 1963. 12.95x o.p. (ISBN 0-8093-0100-8). S Ill U Pr.

Campbell, George E. Model Sailing Ships. (Illus.). 1978. pap. 5.00x o.p. (ISBN 0-85242-662-3). Intl Pubns Serv.

Campbell, Greg. The Joy of Jumping: A Complete Jump-Rope Program for Health, Looks & Fun. (Illus.). 1978. 8.95 o.p. (ISBN 0-399-90015-2, Marek); pap. 3.50 (ISBN 0-399-90010-1). Putnam Pub Group.

Campbell, Helen. Darkness & Daylight: Or, Lights & Shadows of New York Life: A Pictorial Record of Personal Experiences by Day & Night in the Great Metropolis with Hundreds of Thrilling Anecdotes & Incidents. LC 76-81511. 1969. Repr. of 1895 ed. 42.00x (ISBN 0-8103-3566-2). Gale.

Campbell, Hilbert H. James Thomson. (English Authors Ser.). 1979. lib. bdg. 14.95 (ISBN 0-8057-6715-0, Twayne). G K Hall.

Campbell, Howard E. & Dierker, Paul F. Student Supplement to Accompany Calculus with Analytic Geometry. 3rd ed. (Math Ser.). 341p. 1982. pap. text ed. write for info. (ISBN 0-87150-353-0, 2646). Prindle.

Campbell, Hugh G. Introduction to Matrices, Vectors & Linear Programming. 2nd ed. LC 76-22757. (Illus.). 1977. text ed. 21.95 (ISBN 0-13-487439-0). P-H.

--Matrices with Applications. (Illus.). 1968. pap. text ed. 13.95 (ISBN 0-13-565424-6). P-H.

Campbell, Hugh G. & Spencer, Robert E. A Short Course in Calculus with Application. (Illus.). 352p. 1975. text ed. 23.95x (ISBN 0-02-318590-2, 31859). Macmillan.

Campbell, J. K. Honour, Family & Patronage: A Study of Institutions & Moral Values in a Greek Mountain Community. (Illus.). 406p. 1973. 34.95x (ISBN 0-19-823122-9); pap. text ed. 8.95x (ISBN 0-19-519756-9). Oxford U Pr.

Campbell, J. L. & Zimmerman, Lance. Programming the Apple: A Structured Approach. (Illus.). 544p. 1982. pap. 19.95 (ISBN 0-89303-267-0); casebound 24.95 (ISBN 0-89303-269-7). R J Brady.

Campbell, J. R. & Marshall, R. T. The Science of Providing Milk for Man. (Agricultural Sciences Ser). 1975. 33.00 (ISBN 0-07-009690-2, C). McGraw.

Campbell, James. Language of Religion. 1971. pap. 4.95 o.p. (ISBN 0-02-813310-2). Glencoe.

--New Morality or No Morality? 1969. 6.95 o.p. (ISBN 0-685-15632-X, 80119). Glencoe.

Campbell, James, ed. The Anglo-Saxons. LC 81-70710. 272p. 1982. 39.95x (ISBN 0-8014-1482-2). Cornell U Pr.

Campbell, James E., ed. Pottery & Ceramics: A Guide to Information Sources. LC 74-11545. (Art & Architecture Information Guide Ser.: Vol. 7). 1978. 42.00x (ISBN 0-8103-1274-3). Gale.

Campbell, James W. America in Her Centennial Year 1876. LC 79-6757. 272p. 1980. pap. text ed. 11.50 (ISBN 0-8191-0947-9). U Pr of Amer.

Campbell, Jane. The Retrospective Review (1820-1828) & the Revival of Seventeenth-Century Poetry. 76p. pap. text ed. 5.75x (ISBN 0-88920-001-7, Pub. by Wilfred Laurier U Pr Canada). Humanities.

Campbell, Jane & Doyle, James, eds. The Practical Vision: Essays in Honour of Flora Roy. xvi, 163p. 1978. text ed. 9.80x (ISBN 0-88920-066-1, Pub. by Wilfred Laurier U Pr Canada). Humanities.

Campbell, Jean, ed. see Ridley, Gustave.

Campbell, Jeffrey. The Homing. LC 79-17477. 1980. 9.95 o.p. (ISBN 0-399-12487-X). Putnam Pub Group.

Campbell, Jeremy. Grammatical Man: Information, Entropy, Language, & Life. 320p. 1982. 15.50 (ISBN 0-671-44061-6). S&S.

Campbell, Jim. The Second Offical NFL Trivia Book. 1982. pap. 2.25 (ISBN 0-451-11789-1, AE1789, Sig). NAL.

Campbell, Joanna. Secret Identity. 1982. pap. 1.95 (ISBN 0-553-22683-5). Bantam.

Campbell, Joe B., jt. auth. see Campbell, June.

Campbell, John A. Adding Logic to Fire Prevention Systems. Date not set. 4.65 (ISBN 0-686-37669-2, TR 82-5). Society Fire Protect.

--Speech Preparation. rev. ed. Applbaum, Ronald & Hart, Roderick, eds. LC 13-5567. (Modcom, Modules in Speech Communication Ser.). 1980. pap. text ed. 2.75 (ISBN 0-574-22567-6, 13-5567). SRA.

Campbell, John B., jt. auth. see Willson, James D.

Campbell, John C. Contemporary Japanese Budget Politics. LC 73-85782. 1977. 30.00x (ISBN 0-520-02573-3); pap. 8.95x (ISBN 0-520-04087-2, CAMPUS NO. 253). U of Cal Pr.

Campbell, John F. Popular Tales of the West Highlands, 4 Vols. LC 67-23921. 1969. Repr. of 1890 ed. 134.00x (ISBN 0-8103-3458-5). Gale.

Campbell, John G. Superstitions of the Highlands & Islands of Scotland. 1970. 37.00x (ISBN 0-8103-3589-1). Gale.

Campbell, John J., jt. auth. see Brunner, Joseph F.

Campbell, John L. Hebridean Folksongs, Vol. 2. 1977. 39.50x o.p. (ISBN 0-19-815214-0). Oxford U Pr.

Campbell, John L. & Collinson, Francis, eds. Hebridean Folksongs, Vol. 3. 1981. 69.00 (ISBN 0-19-815215-9). Oxford U Pr.

Campbell, John P. & Daft, Richard L. What to Study: Generating & Developing Research Questions. (Studying Organizations: Innovations in Methodology). 168p. 1982. 17.95 (ISBN 0-8039-1871-2); pap. 7.95 (ISBN 0-8039-1872-0). Sage.

Campbell, John R. Introductory Treatise on Lie's Theory. LC 65-28441. 16.95 (ISBN 0-8284-0183-7). Chelsea Pub.

Campbell, John R. & Lasley, John F. The Science of Animals That Serve Mankind. 2nd ed. (Agricultural Science Ser.). (Illus.). 736p. 1975. text ed. 32.00 (ISBN 0-07-009696-1, C). McGraw.

Campbell, John S. Improve Your Technical Communication. LC 76-8493. 216p. 1976. pap. text ed. 9.95x (ISBN 0-915668-26-2). G S E Pubns.

Campbell, Joseph. The Flight of the Wild Gander. LC 70-183820. 256p. 1972. pap. 6.95 (ISBN 0-89526-914-7). Regnery-Gateway.

Campbell, Joseph, ed. Myths, Dreams, & Religion. 1970. pap. 6.50 (ISBN 0-525-47255-X, 0631-190). Dutton.

Campbell, Judith. Queen Elizabeth Two. (Illus.). 192p. 1980. 12.95 o.p. (ISBN 0-517-53974-8). Crown.

--The World of the Horse. LC 76-49701. 1977. pap. 7.95 o.s.i. (ISBN 0-89104-056-0). A & W Pubs.

Campbell, Julie & Kenny, Katherine. Mystery of the Midnight Marauder. (Trixie Belden Mystery Ser.). 236p. (gr. 4-6). 1980. PLB 5.52 (ISBN 0-307-61552-9, Golden Pr); pap. 1.50 (ISBN 0-307-21551-2). Western Pub.

Campbell, June & Campbell, Joe B. Laboratory Mathematics: Medical & Biological Applications. 2nd ed. LC 79-24996. (Illus.). 290p. 1980. pap. text ed. 15.95 (ISBN 0-8016-0702-7). Mosby.

Campbell, Karel. Blue Jay & the Monster. LC 67-14952. (General Juvenile Bks). (Illus.). (gr. k-5). 1967. PLB 3.95g (ISBN 0-8225-0258-5). Lerner Pubns.

Campbell, Karlyn K., jt. auth. see Jamieson, Kathleen H.

Campbell, Keith O. Food for the Future: How Agriculture Can Meet the Challenge. LC 78-23982. xii, 178p. 1979. 14.50 (ISBN 0-8032-0965-7). U of Nebr Pr.

Campbell, Ken. Caribbean. LC 80-54668. (Countries Ser.). PLB 12.68 (ISBN 0-382-06415-1). Silver.

Campbell, L. J. & Carlton, R. J. Atoms & Waves: Physics, Bk.2. (Secondary Science Ser.). (Illus., Orig.). (gr. 8-11). 1975. pap. text ed. 8.95 (ISBN 0-7100-7740-8). Routledge & Kegan.

--Force & Energy: Physics, Bk. 1. (Secondary Science Ser.). (Illus., Orig.). (gr. 8-11). 1974. pap. text ed. 8.95 (ISBN 0-7100-7739-4). Routledge & Kegan.

--Foundation Science. (Secondary Science Ser). (Illus., Orig.). (gr. 6-8). 1969. pap. text ed. 9.95 (ISBN 0-7100-0020-0). Routledge & Kegan.

Campbell, L. J. & Carlton, R. J., eds. Science: The Basic Skills. (Secondary Science Ser.). (Illus., Orig.). (gr. 6-7). 1978. pap. text ed. 10.95 (ISBN 0-7100-8808-6). Routledge & Kegan.

Campbell, Liberty. Haiku of Old Japan. 1983. 6.95 (ISBN 0-533-05185-1). Vantage.

Campbell, Lyle. Quichean Linguistic Pre-History. (Publications in Linguistics: Vol. 81). 1977. 15.50x (ISBN 0-520-09531-6). U of Cal Pr.

Campbell, Malcolm J. Case Studies in Business Information Provision. 204p. 1983. price not set (ISBN 0-85157-353-3, Pub. by Bingley England). Shoe String.

Campbell, Margaret. The Spectral Bride. 1975. pap. 1.25 o.p. (ISBN 0-451-06431-3, Y6431, Sig). NAL.

Campbell, Marian. An Introduction to Medieval Enamels. (The Victoria & Albert Museum Introductions to the Decorative Arts). (Illus.). 48p. 9.95 (ISBN 0-88045-021-5). Stemmer Hse.

Campbell, Marie. Tales from the Cloud Walking Country. LC 76-14944. (Illus.). 1976. Repr. of 1958 ed. lib. bdg. 19.25x (ISBN 0-8371-8607-2, CATC). Greenwood.

Campbell, Mary C. & Stewart, Joyce L. The Medical Mycology Handbook. LC 80-11935. 436p. 1980. pap. 30.00x (ISBN 0-471-04728-7, Pub. by Wiley Med). Wiley.

Campbell, Mary M. & Greely, Deborah W., eds. A Basket of Herbs. (Illus.). 1983. text ed. 10.95 (ISBN 0-8289-0500-2). Greene.

Campbell, Moran, jt. auth. see Jones, Norman L.

Campbell, N. J. Battlecruisers. 72p. 1980. 11.50x o.p. (ISBN 0-85177-130-0, Pub. by Cornell England). State Mutual Bk.

Campbell, Oscar J., et al. Studies in Shakespeare, Milton & Donne. McCartney, Eugene S., ed. LC 78-93244. (University of Michigan Publications: Vol. 1). 1970. Repr. of 1925 ed. 10.00x (ISBN 0-87753-020-3). Phaeton.

Campbell, P. J. The Ebb & Flow of Battle. LC 77-83846. 1978. 8.95 o.p. (ISBN 0-312-22518-0). St Martin.

Campbell, P. N., ed. Biology in Profile: An Introduction to the Many Branches of Biology. (Illus.). 148p. 1981. 19.50 (ISBN 0-08-026846-3); pap. 9.50 (ISBN 0-08-026845-5). Pergamon.

Campbell, Paul, ed. see Hopkins, Stephen.

Campbell, R., tr. see Taleghani, Sayyid M.

Campbell, R. C. Statistics for Biologists. 2nd ed. (Illus.). 300p. 1974. 52.50 (ISBN 0-521-20381-3); pap. 13.95 (ISBN 0-521-09836-X). Cambridge U Pr.

Campbell, R. E. Microbial Ecology. 148p. 17.95x o.p. (ISBN 0-470-99164-X). Halsted Pr.

Campbell, R. H. & Skinner, A. The Origins & Nature of the Scottish Enlightenment. 240p. 1982. text ed. 31.50x (ISBN 0-85976-076-6, Pub. by John Donald). Humanities.

Campbell, R. H. & Skinner, A. S. Adam Smith. LC 82-3308. 231p. 1982. 25.00x (ISBN 0-312-00423-0). St Martin.

Campbell, R. K. The Christian Home. 3.50 (ISBN 0-88172-005-4); pap. 3.75 (ISBN 0-88172-006-2). Believers Bkshelf.

--The Church of the Living God. 5.95 (ISBN 0-88172-007-0); pap. 3.50.o.p. (ISBN 0-686-13515-6). Believers Bkshelf.

--Essentials of the Christian Life. 46p. pap. 0.40 (ISBN 0-88172-008-9). Believers Bkshelf.

--Moses, the Man of God. tchr's lesson outline 0.50 o.p. (ISBN 0-686-13893-7); primary companion wkbk 0.40 o.p. (ISBN 0-686-13894-5); jr. companion wkbk 0.40 o.p. (ISBN 0-686-13895-3); intermediate companion wkbk 0.40 o.p. (ISBN 0-686-13896-1). Believers Bkshelf.

--Our Wonderful Bible. 417p. 15.95 (ISBN 0-88172-009-7); pap. 11.95 (ISBN 0-88172-010-0). Believers Bkshelf.

--Parables in Matthew's Gospel: Matthew 13. tchr's lesson outline 2.25 (ISBN 0-88172-011-9); primary companion wkbk o.p. 0.40; jr. companion wkbk o.p. 0.40; sr. companion wkbk o.p. 0.40. Believers Bkshelf.

--Prophetic History of Christendom. 5.25 (ISBN 0-88172-012-7). Believers Bkshelf.

--Things That Accompany Salvation. 40p. pap. 0.35 (ISBN 0-88172-013-5). Believers Bkshelf.

--Woman's Place. 32p. pap. 0.40 (ISBN 0-88172-014-3). Believers Bkshelf.

Campbell, R. N., jt. auth. see Allen, H. B.

Campbell, R. Wright. Circus Couronne. LC 77-22232. 1977. 8.95 o.p. (ISBN 0-399-11706-7). Putnam Pub Group.

--Fat Tuesday. LC 82-19264. 384p. 1983. 15.95 (ISBN 0-89919-158-4). Ticknor & Fields.

--The Spy Who Sat & Waited. LC 74-16580. 384p. 1975. 7.95 o.p. (ISBN 0-399-11424-6). Putnam Pub Group.

Campbell, Ramsey. Dark Companions. 258p. 1982. 13.95 (ISBN 0-02-521090-4). Macmillan.

Campbell, Reginald J. Livingstone. LC 77-138212. (Illus.). 295p. 1972. Repr. of 1930 ed. lib. bdg. 17.75x (ISBN 0-8371-5567-3, CALI). Greenwood.

Campbell, Roald F. & Mazzoni, Tim L., Jr. State Policy Making for the Public Schools. new ed. LC 75-31311. 476p. 1976. 24.75 (ISBN 0-8211-0224-9); pap. text ed. 22.25x (ISBN 0-685-61059-4). McCutchan.

Campbell, Robert. The Enigma of the Mind. LC 75-39976. (Human Behavior). (Illus.). (gr. 5 up). 1976. PLB 13.28 (ISBN 0-8094-1946-7, Pub. by Time-Life). Silver.

Campbell, Robert, jt. auth. see Delany, M. R.

Campbell, Robert, ed. Spectrum of Catholic Attitudes. 1969. 4.95 o.p. (ISBN 0-685-07666-0, 80115). Glencoe.

Campbell, Robert A., et al, eds. Advances in Polyamine Research. LC 77-83687. 1978. 45.00 (ISBN 0-89004-194-6). Raven.

Campbell, Robert B., jt. auth. see Remmling, Gunter W.

Campbell, Robert J. Psychiatric Education & the Primary Physician. (Task Force Report: No. 2). 74p. 1970. pap. 5.00 o.p. (ISBN 0-685-24864-X, P241-0). Am Psychiatric.

Campbell, Robert W. Soviet-Type Economies: Performance & Evolution. 3rd ed. 272p. 1974. pap. text ed. 13.50 (ISBN 0-395-17231-4). HM.

Campbell, Roderick. Israel & the New Covenant. LC 54-8387. 364p. 1982. Repr. of 1954 ed. 12.95 (ISBN 0-939404-01-X). Geneva Divinity.

Campbell, Rodney. The Luciano Project: The Secret Wartime Collaboration of the Mafia & the U.S. Navy. 1977. 9.95 o.p. (ISBN 0-07-009674-0, GB). McGraw.

Campbell, Roger. Weight! A Better Way to Lose. 128p. 1976. pap. 3.95 (ISBN 0-88207-735-X). Victor Bks.

Campbell, Roger F. A Place to Hide. 108p. 1983. pap. 3.95 (ISBN 0-88207-383-4). Victor Bks.

Campbell, Ronald F., et al. The Organization & Control of American Schools. 4th ed. (Educational Administration Ser.: No. C21). 520p. 1980. text ed. 24.95 (ISBN 0-675-08164-5). Merrill.

Campbell, Ross. How to Really Love Your Child. 1982. pap. 2.75 (ISBN 0-451-11871-5, AE1871, Sig). NAL.

--How to Really Love Your Teenager. 1981. 9.95 (ISBN 0-88207-341-9); pap. 4.50 (ISBN 0-88207-341-9). Victor Bks.

Campbell, Roy J. Peggy. 208p. 1983. 10.00 (ISBN 0-682-49952-8). Exposition.

Campbell, Russell N. & Lindfors, Judith W. Insights into English Structure: A Programmed Course. 1969. pap. text ed. 10.95 (ISBN 0-13-467571-1). P-H.

Campbell, Russell N., jt. auth. see King, Harold V.

Campbell, S. F. Piaget Sampler: An Introduction to Jean Piaget Through His Own Words. LC 75-34129. 154p. 1976. pap. text ed. 13.95 (ISBN 0-471-13344-2). Wiley.

Campbell, S. L. Singular Systems of Differential Equations, Vol. 2. (Research Notes in Mathematics Ser.: No. 61). 200p. 1982. pap. text ed. 21.95 (ISBN 0-273-08516-6). Pitman Pub MA.

Campbell, S. L. & Meyer, C. D. Generalized Inverses of Linear Transformations. (Surveys & References Ser.: No. 4). 284p. 1979. text ed. 49.50 (ISBN 0-273-08422-4). Pitman Pub MA.

Campbell, S. L., ed. Recent Applications of Generalized Inverses. (Research Notes in Mathematics Ser.: No. 66). 300p. 1982. pap. text ed. 26.50 (ISBN 0-273-08550-6). Pitman Pub MA.

Campbell, Sally R. The Confident Consumer. LC 81-20013. (Illus.). 368p. 1982. text ed. 14.64 (ISBN 0-87006-403-7). Goodheart.

Campbell, Scott D. The Complete Book of Birdhouse Construction for Woodworkers. (Crafts Ser.). 48p. (Orig.). Date not set. pap. 2.50 (ISBN 0-486-24407-5). Dover. Postponed.

Campbell, Sid & Logsdon, Jim. This Book Could Save Your Life. (Illus.). 16p. pap. 1.80x (ISBN 0-686-36029-X). Self Defense.

Campbell, Stephanie, ed. As We Seek God: International Reflections on Contemporary Benedictine Monasticism. (Cistercian Studies Ser.: No. 52). (Orig.). 1983. pap. write for info. (ISBN 0-87907-752-2). Cistercian Pubns.

Campbell, Stephen K. Flaws & Fallacies in Statistical Thinking. LC 73-5655. (Illus.). 192p. 1974. pap. 12.95 (ISBN 0-13-322214-4). P-H.

Campbell, Stu. Home Water Supply: How to Find, Filter, Store & Conserve It. Griffith, Roger, ed. (Illus.). 280p. (Orig.). 1983. pap. 10.95 (ISBN 0-88266-324-0). Garden Way Pub.

Campbell, T. R., jt. auth. see Paterson, W. E.

Campbell, T. S. Financial Institutions, Markets & Economic Activity. 1982. 23.95x (ISBN 0-07-009691-0). McGraw.

Campbell, Tessa. Children's Picture Atlas. LC 77-17968. (Children's Guides Ser.). (Illus.). (gr. 3 up). 1978. PLB 7.95 (ISBN 0-88436-465-8). EMC.

Campbell, Tom. The Contemplative Stroller. (Illus.). 96p. 1982. pap. 4.95 (ISBN 0-9607506-1-4). News Rev Pub.

--The Left & Rights: A Conceptual Analysis of the Idea of Socialist Rights. (International Library of Welfare & Philosophy). 296p. (Orig.). 1983. pap. 11.95 (ISBN 0-7100-9085-4). Routledge & Kegan.

--Seven Theories of Human Society. 1981. text ed. 19.95x (ISBN 0-19-876104-X); pap. text ed. 8.95x (ISBN 0-19-876105-8). Oxford U Pr.

Campbell, Viola, ed. Programas Para Reuniones Sociales y Banquetes. (Illus.). 1979. pap. 1.80 (ISBN 0-311-11011-8). Casa Bautista.

Campbell, Viola D. Juguemos. (Illus.). 199p. 1981. pap. 2.75 (ISBN 0-311-11006-1). Casa Bautista.

--Recreacion Cristiana. (Illus.). 160p. (Span.). 1981. pap. 4.25 (ISBN 0-311-11037-1). Casa Bautista.

Campbell, Viola D., tr. see Ford, LeRoy.

Campbell, W. Reason. Dead Man Walking: Teaching in a Maximum-Security Prison. LC 78-4868. 1978. 9.95 o.p. (ISBN 0-399-90008-X, Marek). Putnam Pub Group.

Campbell, Will & Campbell, Bonnie. God on Earth: The Lord's Prayer for Our Time. (Illus.). 128p. 1983. 11.95 (ISBN 0-8245-0550-6). Crossroad NY.

Campbell, William. Villi the Clown. 272p. 1983. 15.95 (ISBN 0-571-11794-5). Faber & Faber.

Campbell, William G., et al. Form & Style: Theses, Reports, Term Papers. 6th ed. LC 81-82571. 1981. pap. 7.16 (ISBN 0-395-31689-8). HM.

Campbell-Johnson, Alan. Eden: The Making of a Statesman. LC 76-6056. (Illus.). 306p. 1976. Repr. of 1955 ed. lib. bdg. 21.00x (ISBN 0-8371-8813-X, CAED). Greenwood.

Campbell-Kelly, Martin. The Charles Babbage Institute Reprint Series for the History of Computing. 1982. write for info. limited edition (ISBN 0-938228-01-3). Tomash Pubs.

Campderros, Daniel. Bosquejos Biblicos, Tomo III. 96p. 1981. pap. 2.50 (ISBN 0-311-43033-3). Casa Bautista.

--Bosquejos Biblicos Tomo I: Antiguo Testamento. 1981. pap. 2.50 (ISBN 0-311-43025-2). Casa Bautista.

--Bosquejos Biblicos Tomo II. 1981. Repr. of 1979 ed. pap. 2.50 (ISBN 0-311-43026-0). Casa Bautista.

Campe, J. H. The New Robinson Crusoe, 4 vols. in 2. LC 75-32148. (Classics of Children's Literature, 1621-1932: Vol. 14). 1976. Repr. of 1788 ed. Set. PLB 70.00 o.s.i. (ISBN 0-8240-2262-9); PLB 38.00 ea. o.s.i. Garland Pub.

Campen. The Selection Administration & Content of Health Insurance Plans for Public School District Personnel. (Research Bulletin: No. 23). pap. 0.69 (ISBN 0-685-57186-6). Assn Sch Busn.

Campen, Richard N. Sanibel & Captiva-Enchanting Islands. 3rd ed. LC 77-76136. (Illus.). 96p. 1982. 8.95 (ISBN 0-686-91787-1). West Summit.

Campen, Shirley Van see Van Campen, Shirley.

Campese, V. M. & Hsueh, W. A., eds. The Kidney in Hypertension. 120p. 1983. pap. price not set (ISBN 3-8055-3648-8). S Karger.

Campion, Gilbert F. European Parliamentary Procedure: A Comparative Handbook. LC 78-59009. (Illus.). 1981. Repr. of 1953 ed. cancelled o.p. (ISBN 0-88355-684-7). Hyperion Conn.

Campion, Kathy, jt. auth. see Campion, Mike.

Campion, Mike & Campion, Kathy. The Very Special Stone. (Andrew Ser.: No. 4). 1982. pap. 3.95 (ISBN 0-8024-9449-8). Moody.

--Where Does the White Go When the Snow Melts? (Andrew Ser.: No. 1). 1982. 3.95 (ISBN 0-8024-9446-3). Moody.

Campion, Thomas. Ayres & Observations: Selected Poems of Thomas Campion. Hart, Joan, ed. (Fyfield Ser.). 1979. 7.95 o.p. (ISBN 0-85635-099-0, Pub. by Carcanet New Pr England); pap. 4.95 o.p. (ISBN 0-85635-100-8). Humanities.

--The Selected Songs of Thomas Campion. Auden, W. H., ed. LC 71-152794. (Illus.). 168p. 1972. 15.00x (ISBN 0-87923-037-1); ltd. ed. 40.00 (ISBN 0-87923-036-3); pap. 10.00. Godine.

Campione, Frank, jt. auth. see Cameron, Frank.

Campling, Jo, ed. see Smith, Carole R.

Campo, Michael R., ed. Pirandello, Moravia & Italian Poetry: Intermediate Readings in Italian. (It). 1968. text ed. 9.95 (ISBN 0-02-318750-6). Macmillan.

Campo-Flores, Filemon, jt. auth. see Chang, Y. N.

Campolo, Anthony. A Reasonable Faith: Responding to Secularism. 1983. 8.95 (ISBN 0-686-84760-1). Word Bks.

--The Success Fantasy. 1980. pap. 4.50 (ISBN 0-88207-796-1). Victor Bks.

Campos, German J. The Argentine Supreme Court: The Court of Constitutional Guarantees. Brisk, William J., tr. from Span. viii, 143p. 1982. pap. 15.00x (ISBN 9-500621-14-2). Rothman.

Camp-Randolph, I. Lillian. I, Lillian, Here. 40p. (Orig.). 1983. pap. 4.00 (ISBN 0-934172-09-9). WIM Pubns.

Camps, jt. auth. see Gree.

Camps, Arnulf. Partners in Dialogue: Christianity & Other World Religions. Drury, John, tr. from Dutch. LC 82-18798. 272p. (Orig.). 1983. pap. 10.95 (ISBN 0-88344-378-3). Orbis Bks.

Camps, Luis, jt. auth. see Gree, Alain.

Camps, Miriam. First World Relationships: The Role of the OECD. 56p. (Orig.). 1975. pap. text ed. 4.75x (ISBN 0-686-83638-3). Allanheld.

Camps, Miriam & Gwin, Catherine. Collective Management: The Reform of Global Economic Organizations. 371p. 1982. 17.95 (ISBN 0-07-009708-9); pap. 10.95 (ISBN 0-07-009709-7). McGraw.

Camps, W. A., ed. see Propertius.

Camus, Albert. Caligula & Three Other Plays. Gilbert, Stuart, tr. Incl. Misunderstanding; State of Siege; Just Assassin. 1962. pap. 3.95 (ISBN 0-394-70207-7, V-207, Vin). Random.

--Exile & the Kingdom. 1965. pap. 3.95 (ISBN 0-394-70281-6, V281, Vin). Random.

--Fall. 1957. 10.95 (ISBN 0-394-42424-7). Knopf.

--Fall, Exile & the Kingdom. 1964. 3.95 o.s.i. (ISBN 0-394-60352-4, M352). Modern Lib.

--A Happy Death: A Novel. LC 72-8028. 224p. 1973. pap. 3.95 (ISBN 0-394-71865-8, V865, Vin). Random.

--Lyrical & Critical Essays. LC 67-18621. 1970. pap. 3.95 (ISBN 0-394-70852-0, V626, Vin). Random.

--Malentendu. Hardre, Jacques & Daniel, George, eds. (Orig., Fr.). 1964. pap. text ed. 7.95 (ISBN 0-02-318800-6). Macmillan.

--Notebooks: 1935-1942. 1965. 3.95 o.p. (ISBN 0-394-60349-4, M349). Modern Lib.

--Plague. Gilbert, Stuart, tr. 1967. 3.95 o.s.i. (ISBN 0-394-60109-2, M109). Modern Lib.

--Plague. Gilbert, Stuart, tr. 1965. pap. 1.95 (ISBN 0-394-30969-3, T69, Mod LibC). Modern Lib.

--Rebel. 1954. 13.50 (ISBN 0-394-44232-6). Knopf.

--Resistance, Rebellion & Death. 1963. 3.95 o.s.i. (ISBN 0-394-60339-7, M339). Modern Lib.

--The Stranger. Griffith, Kate, tr. from Fr. LC 81-40927. 110p. (Orig.). 1982. lib. bdg. 19.00 (ISBN 0-8191-2141-X); pap. text ed. 8.00 (ISBN 0-8191-2142-8). U Pr of Amer.

Camus, Renaud. Tricks: Twenty-Five Encounters. 252p. 1981. pap. 11.95 (ISBN 0-312-81823-8). St Martin.

Cana Conference of Chicago. Pre-Cana Packet. 1973. pap. 1.75 (ISBN 0-915388-08-1). Delaney.

Cana, Proinsias Mac see Mac Cana, Proinsias.

Canada, et al. Surviving the First Year of Law School. 1979. pap. 7.95 o.s.i. (ISBN 0-930204-03-4). Lord Pub.

Canada, John R. Intermediate Economic Analysis for Management & Engineering. (Illus.). 1971. ref. ed. 28.95 (ISBN 0-13-469916-5). P-H.

Canada, Lena. To Elvis, with Love. LC 78-57566. 1978. 6.95 (ISBN 0-89696-009-9, An Everest House Book). Dodd.

Canaday, John. Mainstreams of Modern Art: David to Picasso. (Illus.). 1959. 29.95 o.p. (ISBN 0-671-44020-9). S&S.

--What Is Art? An Introduction to Painting, Sculpture, & Architecture. LC 79-23256. (Illus.). 1980. 30.00 (ISBN 0-394-50320-1); pap. text ed. 20.00 (ISBN 0-394-32450-1). Knopf.

Canaday, Nicholas, Jr. Melville & Authority. LC 68-65060. (U of Fla. Humanities Monographs: No. 28). 1968. pap. 3.50 o.p. (ISBN 0-8130-0041-6). U Presses Fla.

Canadian-American Conference on Parkinson's Disease, 2nd. Parkinson's Disease: Advances in Neurology, Vol. 5. McDowell, F. & Barbeau, A., eds. LC 72-93317. (Advances in Neurology Ser.: Vol. 5). 527p. 1974. 41.50 (ISBN 0-911216-63-4). Raven.

Canadian Association of Oilwell Drilling Contractors. Drilling Rig Task Details & Performance Standards for the Driller. (Drilling-Servicing Rig Task Details & Performance Standards Ser.). 1982. pap. text ed. 9.95x (ISBN 0-87201-930-6). Gulf Pub.

Canadian Association of Oilwell Drilling Contractors. Drilling Rig Task Details & Performance Standards for the Derrickhand. (Drilling-Servicing Rig Task Details & Performance Standards Ser.). 1982. pap. 9.95 (ISBN 0-87201-931-4). Gulf Pub.

--Drilling Rig Task Manual & Performance Standards for the Floorhand. (Drilling-Servicing Rig Details & Performance Standards Ser.). 1982. pap. text ed. 9.95x (ISBN 0-87201-933-0). Gulf Pub.

--Drilling Task Details & Performance Standards for the Motorhand. (Drilling-Servicing Rig Task Details & Performance Standards Ser.). 1982. pap. 9.95x (ISBN 0-87201-932-2). Gulf Pub.

--Drilling Task Details for the Rig Manager. (Drilling-Servicing Rig Task Details & Performance Standards Ser.). 1982. pap. 9.95x (ISBN 0-87201-929-2). Gulf Pub.

--An Introduction to Oilwell Drilling & Servicing. 1982. pap. 6.95x (ISBN 0-87201-202-6). Gulf Pub.

--Servicing Rig Task Details & Performance Standards for the Derrickhand. (Drilling-Servicing Rig Task Details & Performance Standards Ser.). 1982. pap. text ed. 9.95x (ISBN 0-87201-936-5). Gulf Pub.

--Servicing Rig Task Details & Performance Standards for the Floorhand. (Drilling-Servicing Rig Task Details & Performance Standards Ser.). 1982. pap. text ed. 9.95x (ISBN 0-87201-937-3). Gulf Pub.

--Servicing Rig Task Details & Performance Standards for the Rig Operator. (Drilling-Servicing Rig Task Details & Performance Standards Ser.). 1982. pap. 9.95x (ISBN 0-87201-935-7). Gulf Pub.

Canadian Association of Oilwell Drilling Contractor. SI Drilling Manual. 1983. text ed. 175.00 (ISBN 0-87201-211-5). Gulf Pub.

Canadian Association of Oilwell Performance Standards Ser. Servicing Rig Task Details & Performance Standards for the Rig Manager. (Drilling-Servicing Rig Task Details & Performance Standards Ser.). 1982. pap. text ed. 9.95x (ISBN 0-87201-934-9). Gulf Pub.

Canadian Government. Winning Low Energy Building Designs. 651p. 1980. text ed. 35.00x (ISBN 0-660-50675-0, Pub. by Inst Engineering Australia). Renouf.

Canadian Solar Energy Society. Energex 82 Technical Conference: Proceedings. 500p. 1983. pap. text ed. 70.00 (ISBN 0-89553-120-8). Am Solar Energy.

Canal Zone Library-Museum. Panama Subject Catalog of the Special Panama Collection of the Canal Zone Library-Museum. 1964. lib. bdg. 75.00 (ISBN 0-8161-0675-4, Hall Library). G K Hall.

Canale, Andrew. Masters of the Heart. pap. 9.95 o.p. (ISBN 0-8091-0271-4). Paulist Pr.

Canan, Craig T. Southern Progressive Periodicals Directory. LC 80-644934. 1982. 4.00 (ISBN 0-935396-01-2). Prog Educ.

--U. S. Progressive Periodicals Directory. LC 81-85888. 1982. 8.00 (ISBN 0-935396-02-0). Prog Educ.

Canan, James. War in Space. LC 81-48032. 192p. 1982. 13.41i (ISBN 0-06-038022-5, HarpT). Har-Row.

Canart, Paul. Studies in Comparative Semantics. 1979. 19.95x (ISBN 0-312-77087-1). St Martin.

Canary, Branda B. Home to the Mountain. 224p. 1982. pap. 2.75 (ISBN 0-380-61127-9, 61127). Avon.

Canary, Robert H. George Bancroft. (United States Authors Ser.). 1974. lib. bdg. 12.95 (ISBN 0-8057-0034-X, Twayne). G K Hall.

--Robert Graves. (English Authors Ser.). 1980. lib. bdg. 8.95 (ISBN 0-8057-6720-7, Twayne). G K Hall.

--William Dunlap. (United States Authors Ser.). 13.95 (ISBN 0-686-75278-3, Twayne). G K Hall.

Canavan, Francis S. & Cole, R. T., eds. The Ethical Dimensions of Political Life: Essays in Honor of John H. Hallowell. 250p. 1983. 20.00 (ISBN 0-8223-0490-2). Duke.

Canavan, P J. Paragraphs & Themes. 4th ed. 510p. 1983. pap. text ed. 12.95 (ISBN 0-669-05273-6). Heath.

Canavan, P. Joseph. The Effective Writer's Companion. 1981. pap. text ed. 12.50x (ISBN 0-673-15449-1). Scott F.

--Paragraphs & Themes. 3rd ed. 1979. pap. text ed. 12.95x (ISBN 0-669-01695-0); instructor's manual free (ISBN 0-669-01905-4). Heath.

--Rhetoric & Literature. 352p. (Orig.). 1974. text ed. 13.95 (ISBN 0-07-009705-4, C). McGraw.

Canavan-Gumpert, Donnah, et al. The Success Fearing Personality. LC 76-42853. 1978. 22.95x (ISBN 0-669-01075-8). Lexington Bks.

Canavor, Natalie. Sell Your Photographs: The Complete Marketing Strategy for the Freelancer. LC 79-18958. 320p. 1979. 17.95 (ISBN 0-914842-40-4). Madrona Pubs.

--Sell Your Photographs: The Complete Marketing Strategy for the Freelancer. 1982. pap. 6.95 (ISBN 0-452-25362-4, Z5362, Plume). NAL.

Canby, Henry S. Walt Whitman: An American. LC 72-106663. Repr. of 1943 ed. lib. bdg. 18.75x (ISBN 0-8371-3421-8, CAWW). Greenwood.

Cancer Care, Inc. & the National Cancer Foundation, Inc. The Impact, Costs & Consequences of Catastrophic Illness on Patients & Families: A Report of a Social Research Study of Selected Families Stricken by Advanced Cancer. LC 73-175425. 1973. 3.50 (ISBN 0-9606494-3-3). Cancer Care.

Cancian, F. What Are Norms? A Study of Beliefs & Action in a Maya Community. LC 74-77833. 256p. 1975. 27.95 (ISBN 0-521-20536-0). Cambridge U Pr.

Canclini, Arnoldo, tr. see McNeely, Edwin.

Canclini, Arnoldo, tr. see Stagg, Frank.

Cancrinus, Franz L. First Principles of the Science of Mining & Salt Mining. Bordeau, Kenneth V. & Bordeau, Elvi L., trs. LC 80-65488. (Microform Publication: No. 10). 1980. 4.00x (ISBN 0-8137-6010-0). Geol Soc.

Cancro, Robert, ed. Annual Review of the Schizophrenic Syndrome, 5 vols. Incl. Vol. 1. 1971 (ISBN 0-87630-043-3); Vol. 2. 1972 (ISBN 0-87630-058-1); Vol. 3. 1973; Vol. 4. 1974-75 (ISBN 0-87630-108-1); Vol. 5. 1976-77 (ISBN 0-87630-160-X). LC 76-156466. Orig. Title: Schizophrenic Syndrome. 35.00 ea. Brunner-Mazel.

Candea, Virgil, jt. auth. see Bodea, Cornelia.

Candler, Teresa. The Northern Italian Cookbook. LC 76-30450. (Illus.). 1977. 14.95 (ISBN 0-07-009721-6, GB). McGraw.

C&MA Home Department Board. The Pastor's Handbook. 102p. pap. 4.95 (ISBN 0-87509-118-0). Chr Pubns.

Candolle, A. De. Memoires Sur la Famille Des Legumineuses. (Illus.). 1966. Repr. of 1825 ed. 89.60 (ISBN 3-7682-0299-2). Lubrecht & Cramer.

Candolle, A. P. de see De Candolle, A. P.

Candy, D. J. & Kilby, B. A., eds. Insect Biochemistry & Function. 1975. 29.95x (ISBN 0-412-21530-6, Pub. by Chapman & Hall). Methuen Inc.

Candy, Edward. Bones of Contention. LC 82-45964. (Crime Club Ser.). 192p. 1983. 11.95 (ISBN 0-385-18804-8). Doubleday.

Candy, Robert. Getting the Most from Game & Fish. Hard, Walter, ed. LC 78-1777. (Illus.). 1978. pap. 12.95 o.p. (ISBN 0-88266-113-2). Garden Way Pub.

Canemaker, John, jt. auth. see Abrams, Robert E.

Canes, Michael, ed. see Markun, Patricia M.

Canetti, Elias. Comedy of Vanities & Life-Terms. Honegger, Gitta, tr. LC 82-62100. 1983. 18.95 (ISBN 0-933826-30-3); pap. 7.95 (ISBN 0-933826-31-1). Performing Arts.

--The Torch in My Ear. Neugroschel, Joachim, tr. from Ger. 500p. 1982. 16.50 (ISBN 0-374-27847-4). FS&G.

Caneva-Decevska, N., ed. see Stamov, Stefan & Angreova, R.

Caney, Steven. Steven Caney's Invention Book. LC 78-73723. (Illus.). 256p. (Orig.). (gr. 4-6). 1983. 12.95 (ISBN 0-89480-077-9); pap. 6.95 (ISBN 0-89480-076-0). Workman Pub.

Canfield, Carolyn. One Vision Only. 1959. pap. 3.50 o.p. (ISBN 0-340-24607-3). OMF Bks.

Canfield, Cass. The Iron Will of Jefferson Davis. LC 78-53908. (Illus.). 1978. 7.95 o.p. (ISBN 0-15-145642-9). HarBraceJ.

--Up & Down & Around: A Publisher Recollects the Time of His Life. LC 73-156512. (Illus.). 228p. 1971. 10.00i o.p. (ISBN 0-06-121540-6). Har-Row.

Canfield, Gae W. Sarah Winnemucca of the Northern Paiutes. LC 82-40448. (Illus.). 336p. 1983. 19.95 (ISBN 0-8061-1814-8). U of Okla Pr.

Canfield, George L. & Dalzell, George W. The Law of the Sea: A Manual of the Principles of Admiralty Law for Students, Mariners & Ship Operators. xvi, 315p. 1983. Repr. of 1926 ed. lib. bdg. 35.00x (ISBN 0-8377-0442-1). Rothman.

Canfield, John V. Wittgenstein: Language & World. LC 81-4522. 240p. 1981. lib. bdg. 17.50x (ISBN 0-87023-318-1); pap. 8.00x (ISBN 0-87023-319-X). U of Mass Pr.

Canfield, Michael & Weberman, Alan J. Coup d'etat in America: The CIA & the Assassination of John F. Kennedy. LC 75-4360. (Illus.). 340p. 1975. 12.95 (ISBN 0-89388-204-6). Okpaku Communications.

Canfield, Muriel. I Wish I Could Say, "I Love You". 224p. (Orig.). 1983. pap. 4.95 (ISBN 0-87123-265-0). Bethany Hse.

Canfield Press - Chek-Chart. Automatic Transmissions, 2 vols. 1979. pap. text ed. 20.50 scp (ISBN 0-06-454001-4, HarpC); instructors manual avail. (ISBN 0-06-454007-3). Har-Row.

Cangelosi, Vincent E. & Taylor, Phillip H. Basic Statistics: A Real World Approach. 3rd ed. (Illus.). 550p. 1983. text ed. 19.95 (ISBN 0-314-69637-7); study guide avail. (ISBN 0-314-71082-5); solutions manual avail. (ISBN 0-314-71083-3). West Pub.

Cangelosi, Vincent E., et al. Basic Statistics: A Real World Approach. 2nd ed. (Illus.). 1979. text ed. 22.95 (ISBN 0-8299-0194-9); pap. study guide 8.95 (ISBN 0-8299-0245-7); wkbk avail. (ISBN 0-8299-0464-6). West Pub.

Cangemi, Joseph & Kowalski, Casimir. Perspectives in Higher Education. LC 80-81695. 128p. 1983. 9.95 (ISBN 0-8022-2369-9). Philos Lib.

Cangemi, Joseph P., jt. auth. see Kowalski, Casimir.

Canger, Raffaele, ed. see Epilepsy International Symposium, 11th., et al.

Canini, A. see Caninius.

Caninius. Institutiones...Linguae Syriacae, Assyriacae. (Linguistics 13th-18th Centuries Ser.). 93p. (Fr.). 1974. Repr. of 1554 ed. lib. bdg. 34.00x o.p. (ISBN 0-8287-0158-X, 71-5005). Clearwater Pub.

Canipe, Bonnie. Sneaky Christians. 1981. cancelled 3.95 (ISBN 0-8062-1010-9). Carlton.

Canjar, Lawrence & Manning, Francis. Thermodynamic Properties & Reduced Correlations for Gases. 222p. 1967. 21.95x o.p. (ISBN 0-87201-867-9); pap. text ed. 4.95x o.p. (ISBN 0-87201-868-7). Gulf Pub.

Cannadine, David, ed. Patricians, Power & Politics in Nineteenth Century Towns. LC 82-42544. 240p. 1982. 35.00x (ISBN 0-312-59803-3). St Martin.

Cannadine, David, ed. see Dyos, H. J.

Cannan, Edwin, ed. & intro. by see Smith, Adam.

Cannan, Edwin, ed. see Smith, Adam.

Cannan, G. Samuel Butler: A Critical Study. LC 70-133284. (English Biography Ser., No. 31). 1970. Repr. of 1925 ed. lib. bdg. 33.95x (ISBN 0-8383-1183-0). Haskell.

Cannan, May W. Grey Ghosts & Voices. 1980. 12.00x o.p. (ISBN 0-900093-50-1, Pub. by Roundwood). State Mutual Bk.

Cannavale, Frank J. & Falcon, William D. Witness Cooperation. 1978. pap. text ed. 8.95x (ISBN 0-669-01063-4). Heath.

Cannell, C. F., jt. auth. see Kahn, R. L.

Cannell, Charles F. Experiments in Interviewing Techniques: Field Experiments in Health Reporting, 1971-1977. 446p. 1979. pap. 18.00x (ISBN 0-87944-247-6). Inst Soc Res.

Cannell, Charles F., jt. auth. see Kahn, Robert L.

Cannell, Charles F., et al. A Technique for Evaluating Interviewer Performance. LC 74-620203. 138p. 1975. pap. 10.00x (ISBN 0-87944-174-7). Inst Soc Res.

Cannell, J. C. Secrets of Houdini. LC 74-10523. (Illus.). 1974. Repr. of 1931 ed. 39.00 o.p. (ISBN 0-8103-3725-8). Gale.

Cannell, M. G., ed. World Forest Biomass & Primary Production Data. 1982. 50.00 (ISBN 0-12-158780-0). Acad Pr.

Canney, M., et al, eds. The Catalogue of the Goldsmiths' Library of Economic Literature, Vol. 1. 838p. 1970. Repr. of 1967 ed. text ed. 100.00x (ISBN 0-485-15014-X, Athlone Pr). Humanities.

--The Catalogue of the Goldsmiths' Library of Economic Literature, Vol. 2. 772p. 1975. text ed. 100.00x (ISBN 0-485-15015-8, Athlone Pr). Humanities.

--The Catalogue of the Goldsmiths' Library of Economic Literature, Vol. 3. 336p. 1982. text ed. 120.00x (ISBN 0-485-15012-3, Athlone Pr). Humanities.

Canning, Connie, compiled by. State Constitutional Conventions, Revisions & Amendments, 1959-1976: A Bibliography, Supplement One. LC 76-57843. 1977. lib. bdg. 22.50 (ISBN 0-8371-9487-3, CSC/). Greenwood.

Canning House Library. Catalogues of the Canning House Library: Author & Subject Catalogues, 2 pts. Incl. Pt. 1. Hispanic Catalogues, 4 vols. Hispanic Council. 1967. 310.00 (ISBN 0-8161-0741-6); First Supplement, 1973. 110.00 (ISBN 0-8161-1125-1); Pt. 2. Luso-Brazilian Catalogues. Luso-Brazilian Council. 1967. 65.00 (ISBN 0-8161-0126-4); First Supplement, 1973. lib. bdg. 105.00 (ISBN 0-8161-1100-6). Hall Library). G K Hall.

Canning, R. G. & Leeper, N. C. So You Are Thinking About A Small Business Computer. 203p. 1982. 18.95 (ISBN 0-13-823625-9); pap. 10.95 (ISBN 0-13-823617-8). P-H.

Canning, Victor. Vanishing Point. LC 82-18845. 224p. 1983. 10.95 (ISBN 0-688-01107-1). Morrow.

Cannizarro, Marilyn. Cooking with Abstinence: An Inspirational Cookbook for the Compulsive Overeater. LC 81-43898. (Illus.). 96p. 1983. pap. 5.95 (ISBN 0-385-18140-X, Dolp). Doubleday.

Cannon, Ann. My Home Has One Parent. LC 81-86637. (gr. 7-12). 1983. pap. 4.95 (ISBN 0-8054-5337-7). Broadman.

Cannon, Bill & Bishop, Ron. One Hundred One Tips & Tricks for Car Restorers. (Modern Automotive Ser.). (Illus.). 1979. 7.95 o.p. (ISBN 0-8306-9819-1); pap. 4.95 (ISBN 0-8306-2054-0, 2054). TAB Bks.

Cannon, Calvin & Wickens, Elaine. Kirt's New House. (Illus.). 48p. (gr. k-3). 1972. PLB 4.99 o.p. (ISBN 0-698-30419-5, Coward). Putnam Pub Group.

Cannon, Calvin, ed. Modern Spanish Poems. 1965. 7.95x (ISBN 0-02-318870-7). Macmillan.

Cannon, Chapman R. & Cannon, Donnie. How We Made Millions & Never Left the Ghetto. 1983. 6.95 (ISBN 0-8062-1956-4). Carlton.

Cannon, Don L. Fundamentals of Microcomputer Design. LC 81-51951. (Illus.). 560p. 1981. pap. 15.00 (ISBN 0-89512-050-X). Tex Instr Inc.

--Understanding Electronic Control of Energy Systems. LC 79-65510. (Understanding Ser.). (Illus.). 256p. 1982. pap. 6.95 (ISBN 0-89512-051-8). Tex Instr Inc.

Cannon, Don L. & Luecke, Gerald. Understanding Communications Systems. LC 79-92683. (Understanding Ser.). (Illus.). 288p. (Orig.). 1980. pap. 6.95 (ISBN 0-89512-035-6, LCB4521). Tex Instr Inc.

--Understanding Microprocessors. LC 78-57029. (Understanding Ser.). (Illus.). 288p. (Orig.). 1979. pap. 6.95 (ISBN 0-89512-021-6, LCB 4023). Tex Instr Inc.

Cannon, Donald Q. & Cook, Lyndon W., eds. Far West Record. LC 82-23476. 318p. 1983. 10.95 (ISBN 0-87747-901-1). Deseret Bk.

Cannon, Donald W., jt. auth. see Cook, Lyndon W.

Cannon, Donnie, jt. auth. see Cannon, Chapman R.

Cannon, Garland. Sir William Jones: A Bibliography of Primary & Secondary Sources. (Library & Information Sources in Linguistics Ser.). xiv, 73p. 1979. 14.00 (ISBN 90-272-0998-7, 7). Benjamins North Am.

Cannon, Gwenda L. Financial & Estate Planning Applications, 2 Vols. (Huebner School Ser.). (Illus.). 463p. (Orig.). 1983. Vol. 1. pap. text ed. 32.00 (ISBN 0-943590-05-1); Vol. 2. pap. text ed. 32.00 (ISBN 0-943590-06-X). E Mellen.

Cannon, H. Graham. Lamarck & Modern Genetics. LC 75-10211. 152p. 1975. Repr. of 1959 ed. lib. bdg. 25.00x (ISBN 0-8371-8173-9, CALA). Greenwood.

Cannon, Helen. Seasons Change. 320p. 1981. pap. 2.50 o.p. (ISBN 0-380-77164-0, 77164). Avon.

Cannon, J. Parliamentary Reform: 1640-1832. LC 72-83588. (Illus.). 288p. 1973. 37.95 (ISBN 0-521-08697-3); pap. 14.95 (ISBN 0-521-09736-3). Cambridge U Pr.

Cannon, Jack, ed. see Cannon, Jimmy.

Cannon, James P. Letters from Prison. Lavan, George, ed. LC 73-79781. 1968. cloth 23.00 (ISBN 0-87348-006-6). Path Pr NY.

--Socialism on Trial. LC 73-86630. 1969. cloth 15.00 (ISBN 0-87348-009-0). Path Pr NY.

Cannon, Jim, et al. The Contemporary World: Conflict or Co-Operation? (Illus.). 128p. (Orig.). (gr. 9-12). 1979. pap. text ed. 8.75 (ISBN 0-05-003159-7); resource bk. 3.95 (ISBN 0-686-32526-5). Longman.

Cannon, Jimmy. Nobody Asked Me but... The World of Jimmy Cannon. Cannon, Jack & Cannon, Tom, eds. (Penguin Sports Library). 1983. pap. 5.95 (ISBN 0-14-006617-9). Penguin.

Cannon, Joan B. & Smith, Ed. Resources for Affirmative Action: An Annotated Directory of Books, Periodicals, Films, Training Aids, & Consultants on Equal Opportunity. LC 82-83304. 190p. (Orig.). 1982. pap. 12.95 (ISBN 0-912048-32-8). Garrett Pk.

Cannon, John, ed. The Historian at Work. 216p. (Orig.). 1980. text ed. 25.00x (ISBN 0-04-901025-5); pap. text ed. 7.95x (ISBN 0-04-901026-3). Allen Unwin.

Cannon, Lou. Reagan. (Illus.). 432p. 1982. 18.95 (ISBN 0-399-12756-9). Putnam Pub Group.

Cannon, Raymond. How to Fish the Pacific Coast. 3rd ed. LC 67-15740. (Illus.). 160p. 1967. pap. 5.95 o.p. (ISBN 0-376-06362-9, Sunset Bks.). Sunset-Lane.

Cannon, Robert H. Dynamics of Physical Systems. 1967. text ed. 39.50 (ISBN 0-07-009754-2, C). McGraw.

Cannon, Tom, ed. see Cannon, Jimmy.

Cannon, William R. A Disciple's Profile of Jesus. LC 75-2956. 1975. 2.95x (ISBN 0-8358-0322-8). Upper Room.

--The Gospel of Matthew. 128p. (Orig.). 1983. pap. 4.95 (ISBN 0-8358-0450-X). Upper Room.

Canny, J. R., jt. auth. see Heartman, C. F.

Canny, Nicholas. The Upstart Earl: A Study of the Social & Mental World of Richard Boyle, First Earl of Cork, 1566-1643. LC 81-21687. 208p. 1982. 34.50 (ISBN 0-521-24416-1). Cambridge U Pr.

Canobbio, Mary M., jt. auth. see Pollack-Latham, Christine L.

Canon, Claudia Von see Von Canon, Claudia.

Canon, Jack. Sable & Gold. 288p. (Orig.). 1981. pap. 2.50 o.p. (ISBN 0-523-41105-7). Pinnacle Bks.

Canon Law Society of America Staff. Canon Law Society of America, Forty-Second Annual Convention: Proceedings. 252p. (Orig.). 1981. pap. 5.00x (ISBN 0-943616-06-9). Canon Law Soc.

--Canon Law Society of America, Forty-Third Annual Convention: Proceedings. 332p. (Orig.). 1982. pap. 6.50x (ISBN 0-943616-08-5). Canon Law Soc.

--Proceedings of the Forty-Fourth Annual Convention. (Orig.). 1983. pap. 6.00x (ISBN 0-943616-14-X). Canon Law Soc.

Canon, M., et al. Theory of Optimal Control & Mathematical Programming. 1970. text ed. 22.50 o.p. (ISBN 0-07-009760-7, C). McGraw.

Canon, Michael J., ed. Texas Legislative Highlights 1981. LC 81-52623. 388p. 1981. pap. 35.00 (ISBN 0-938160-26-5, 6209). State Bar TX.

Canonico, P. G., jt. ed. see Powanda, M. C.

Canright, D. M. El Adventismo Del Septimo Dia. Correa, F. G., tr. 1977. pap. 1.50 (ISBN 0-311-05601-6). Casa Bautista.

--Seventh Day Adventism Renounced. 1982. 9.50 (ISBN 0-89225-163-8); pap. 4.95. Gospel Advocate.

Cantelon, Philip L. & Williams, Robert C. Crisis Contained: The Department of Energy at Three Mile Island. (Science & International Affairs Ser.). (Illus.). 213p. 1982. 17.50 (ISBN 0-8093-1079-1). S Ill U Pr.

Cantelon, Willard. The Day the Dollar Dies: Biblical Prophecy of a New World System in the End Times. LC 72-94186. 190p. 1973. 4.95 o.p. (ISBN 0-912106-92-1, Pub. by Logos); pap. 2.95 (ISBN 0-88270-170-3). Bridge Pub.

Cantelon, Willard, tr. Le Bapteme Dans le Saint-Esprit. (French Bks.). (Fr.). 1979. 1.30 (ISBN 0-8297-0913-4). Life Pubs Intl.

Canter, D. Psychology for Architects. 1982. 26.75 (ISBN 0-85334-115-X, Pub. by Applied Sci England). Elsevier.

Canter, David. Fires & Human Behaviour. LC 79-41489. 338p. 1980. 35.95 (ISBN 0-471-27709-6, Pub. by Wiley-Interscience). Wiley.

--The Psychology of Place. LC 77-73621. (Illus.). 1977. 20.00 (ISBN 0-312-65322-0). St Martin.

Canter, David & Canter, Sandra. Designing for Therapeutic Environments: A Review of Research. LC 79-40510. 1979. 52.95 (ISBN 0-471-27569-7, Pub. by Wiley-Interscience). Wiley.

Canter, David, jt. auth. see Canter, Sandra.

Canter, Larry. Environmental Impact Assessment. (McGraw-Hill Ser. in Environmental Engineering & Water Resources). (Illus.). 1977. text ed. 36.50 (ISBN 0-07-009764-X, C). McGraw.

Canter, Larry W. Water Resources Assessment: Methodology & Technology Sourcebook. LC 79-88942. (Illus.). 1979. 29.50 o.p. (ISBN 0-250-40320-X). Ann Arbor Science.

Canter, Lee & Canter, Marlene. Assertive Discipline for Parents. LC 82-74174. 206p. 1982. 12.95 (ISBN 0-06-859835-1). Canter & Assoc.

Canter, Marlene, jt. auth. see Canter, Lee.

Canter, Sandra & Canter, David. Perspectives on Professional Psychology. 300p. 1983. 22.95 (ISBN 0-471-10411-6, Pub. by Wiley-Interscience). Wiley.

Canter, Sandra, jt. auth. see Canter, David.

Canter, Sandra, jt. auth. see Wilkinson, Jill.

Canterbery, Ray, jt. auth. see Bell, Frederick.

Cantilli, Edmund J., jt. auth. see Horodniceanu, Michael.

Cantin, Eileen. Mounier: A Personalist View of History. LC 73-87031. 184p. (Orig.). 1974. pap. 4.95 o.p. (ISBN 0-8091-1801-7). Paulist Pr.

Cantin, M., ed. The Secretory Process. (Illus.). x, 490p. 1983. 178.50 (ISBN 3-8055-3619-4). S Karger.

Cantle, J. E. Atomic Absorption Spectrometry: Techniques & Instrumetation in Analytical Chemistry. 1982. 89.50 (ISBN 0-444-42015-0). Elsevier.

Cantlie, Audrey. The Assamese: Religion, Caste & Sect in an Indian Village. 240p. 1983. 39.00x (ISBN 0-7007-0149-4, Pub. by Curzon England). State Mutual Bk.

Canto, Victor. Foundations of Supply-Side Economics: Theory & Evidence. 284p. 1982. write for info. (ISBN 0-12-158820-3). Acad Pr.

Canton, Alan N. Computermoney: How to Make It in Data Processing Consulting. Kent, Richard S., ed. 189p. 1981. pap. 25.00 (ISBN 0-935730-00-1). Computer Prog Assocs.

Cantoni, Lea. Mood Signs. LC 79-93257. (Illus.). 1980. pap. 3.95 o.p. (ISBN 0-8069-8898-3). Sterling.

Cantor, Alfred J. Doctor Cantor's Longevity Diet. 1982. pap. 4.95 (ISBN 0-13-216549-X, Reward). P-H.

Cantor, Alfred U. Doctor Cantor's Longevity Diet: How to Slow Down Aging & Prolong Youth & Vigor. 1967. 14.95 (ISBN 0-13-216267-9, Parker). P-H.

Cantor, D., et al, eds. Selected Papers of Theodore S. Motzkin. Date not set. text ed. price not set (ISBN 3-7643-3087-2). Birkhauser.

Cantor, Dorothy W. & Drake, Ellen A. Divorced Parents & Their Children: A Guide for Mental Health Professionals. 1983. text ed. 19.95 (ISBN 0-8261-3560-9). Springer Pub.

Cantor, Edward B. Female Urinary Stress Incontinence. (Illus.). 360p. 1979. 30.25x (ISBN 0-398-03819-8). C C Thomas.

Cantor, G. N. & Hodge, M. J. Conceptions of Ether: Studies in the History of Ether Theories 1740 to 1900. LC 80-21174. (Illus.). 350p. 1981. 60.00 (ISBN 0-521-22430-6). Cambridge U Pr.

Cantor, Georg. Acta Matematica, Memoires De la Societe Des Sciences Physiques et Naturelles De Bordeaux. Repr. of 1889 ed. 67.00 o.p. (ISBN 0-8287-0159-8). Clearwater Pub.

--Contributions to the Founding of the Theory of Transfinite Numbers. Jourdain, Philip E., tr. pap. 4.00 (ISBN 0-486-60045-9). Dover.

--Contributions to the Founding of the Theory of Transfinite Numbers. Jourdain, P. E., tr. ix, 220p. 1952. 15.50 (ISBN 0-87548-157-4). Open Court.

Cantor, Leonard M. & Roberts, I. F. Further Education in England & Wales. 2nd rev. ed. (Illus.). 348p. 1972. 27.50x (ISBN 0-7100-7358-5). Routledge & Kegan.

--Further Education Today: A Critical Review. 1979. 25.00x (ISBN 0-7100-0412-5); pap. 12.95 (ISBN 0-7100-0413-3). Routledge & Kegan.

Cantor, Milton, ed. American Workingclass Culture: Explorations in American Labor & Social History. LC 78-59260. (Contributions in Labor History: No. 7). 1979. lib. bdg. 35.00 (ISBN 0-313-20611-2, CAW/). Greenwood.

--Black Labor in America. LC 74-111265. (Contributions in Afro-American & African Studies, No. 2). 1969. 25.00 (ISBN 0-8371-4667-4, Pub. by Negro U Pr). Greenwood.

Cantor, Milton & Laurie, Bruce, eds. Class, Sex, & the Woman Worker. LC 76-15304. (Contributions in Labor History Ser.: No. 1). 1977. lib. bdg. 25.00 (ISBN 0-8371-9032-0, CCS/). Greenwood.

--Class, Sex, & the Woman Worker. LC 76-15304. (Contributions in Labor History Ser.: No. 1). ix, 253p. 1980. pap. text ed. 7.95 (ISBN 0-313-22733-0, CSS/). Greenwood.

Cantor, Milton, jt. ed. see Fink, Gary M.

Cantor, Norman F. Medieval History: The Life & Death of a Civilization. 2nd ed. 1975. pap. 17.95 (ISBN 0-02-319020-5). Macmillan.

--Medieval World: Three Hundred to Thirteen Hundred. 2nd ed. (Orig.). 1968. pap. text ed. 13.95x (ISBN 0-02-319110-4, 31911). Macmillan.

--Perspectives on the European Past: Conversations with Historians. 1971. combined ed. 18.95x (ISBN 0-02-319180-5); pap. 7.50 ea. o.p.; Vol. 1. pap. (ISBN 0-02-319050-7); Vol. 2. pap. (ISBN 0-685-01461-4). Macmillan.

--Western Civilization: Its Genesis & Destiny, 2 bks. Incl. Bk. 2 (ISBN 0-673-07574-5); Bk. 3 (ISBN 0-673-07575-3). 1970. pap. 12.50x ea. Scott F.

--Western Civilization: Its Genesis & Destiny, Vol. 2. 1969. text ed. 18.95x (ISBN 0-673-05583-3). Scott F.

--Western Civilization: The Modern Heritage, 1500-Present. 1971. text ed. 19.95x (ISBN 0-673-07654-7). Scott F.

Cantor, Norman F. & Berner, Samuel, eds. Early Modern Europe: Fifteen Hundred to Eighteen Fifteen. LC 70-101941. (AHM Problems in European History Ser.: Vol. 2). 1970. pap. 11.95x o.p. (ISBN 0-88295-707-4). Harlan Davidson.

Cantor, P. Understanding a Child's World: Readings in Infancy Through Adolescence. 1977. 15.95 (ISBN 0-07-009766-6). McGraw.

Cantor, Shelia. The Schizophrenic Child: A Primer for Parents & Professionals. 130p. 1982. pap. 6.95 (ISBN 0-920792-13-8). Eden Pr.

Cantow, H. J., et al. Light Scattering from Polymers. (Advances in Polymer Science: Vol. 48). (Illus.). 167p. 1983. 39.50 (ISBN 0-387-12030-0). Springer-Verlag.

--Unusual Properties of New Polymers. (Advances in Polymer Science: Vol. 50). (Illus.). 149p. 1983. 37.00 (ISBN 0-387-12048-3). Springer-Verlag.

Cantow, H. J., et al, eds. Synthesis & Degradation-Rheology & Extrusion. (Advances in Polymer Science: Vol. 47). (Illus.). 170p. 1982. 37.00 (ISBN 0-387-11774-1). Springer-Verlag.

Cantraine, G. & Destine, J., eds. New Systems & Services in Telecommunications. 1981. 64.00 (ISBN 0-444-86206-4). Elsevier.

Cantrell, Ray. Alpha Motivation. (Illus.). 120p. 1982. 5.00 (ISBN 0-940178-13-3). Sitare Inc.

Cantril, Hadley, jt. auth. see Free, Lloyd A.

Cantu, Robert. Toward Fitness: Guided Exercise for Those with Health Problems. LC 79-27686. 258p. 1980. 19.95 (ISBN 0-87705-496-7). Human Sci Pr.

Cantu, Robert C. Sports Medicine for the Primary Care Physician. LC 81-70166. 240p. 1982. write for info. (ISBN 0-669-05429-1, Collamore); pap. write for info. (ISBN 0-669-04593-4). Heath.

Cantu, Robert C. & Gillespie, W. Jay. Sports Medicine, Sports Science: Bridging the Gap. LC 81-70165. 252p. 1982. 18.95 (ISBN 0-669-05226-4, Collamore). Heath.

Cantwell & Svajian. Adolescence. LC 73-85769. 1974. pap. text ed. 10.50 (ISBN 0-87581-165-5). Peacock Pubs.

Cantwell, Aileen, jt. auth. see Polon, Linda.

Cantwell, Aston. Double Delight. (Erotica Ser.). 256p. (Orig.). 1983. pap. 2.75 (ISBN 0-446-30298-8). Warner Bks.

--Tease for Two. 240p. (Orig.). 1983. pap. 2.75 (ISBN 0-446-30293-7). Warner Bks.

Cantwell, Donald W., jt. auth. see Isakson, Hans R.

Cantwell, Peter. Counseling Today's Youth. (Synthesis Ser.). 1976. pap. 1.95 o.p. (ISBN 0-685-71936-7). Franciscan Herald.

Canty, Donald, ed. The Annual of American Architecture, 1980. (Annual of American Architecture). (Illus.). 124p. 1980. 21.95x (ISBN 0-913962-30-9). Am Inst Arch.

Canudo, Eugene R. New York Corporations. 112p. 1969. pap. text ed. 5.50x (ISBN 0-87526-215-5). Gould.

--New York Criminal Law. 600p. (Supplemented annually). looseleaf 20.00 (ISBN 0-87526-201-5). Gould.

--New York Evidence Laws. 260p. (Supplemented annually). looseleaf 12.00 (ISBN 0-87526-175-2). Gould.

Canuto, V., ed. Role of Magnetic Fields in Physics & Astrophysics, Vol. 257. (Annals of the New York Academy of Sciences). 226p. 1975. 38.00x (ISBN 0-89072-012-6). NY Acad Sci.

Canzano, Dorthea & Canzano, Phyllis. A Practical Guide to Multi-Level Modular ESL. 1975. pap. 12.95 o.p. (ISBN 0-87789-130-3); cassettes intermediate 70.00 o.p. (ISBN 0-87789-133-8); cassettes advanced 75.00 o.p. (ISBN 0-87789-136-2). Eng Language.

Canzano, Phyllis, jt. auth. see Canzano, Dorthea.

Cao, Antonio & Carcassi, Ugo, eds. Thalassemia: Recent Advances in Detection & Treatment. LC 82-16179. (Birth Defects: Original Article Ser.: Vol. 18, No. 7). 230p. 1982. 74.00 (ISBN 0-8451-1051-9). A R Liss.

Cao, Xueqin. The Story of the Stone (The Dream of the Red Chamber) The Warning Voice, Vol. 3. Hawkes, David, tr. LC 78-20279. (Chinese Literature in Translation Ser.). 640p. 1981. 35.00x (ISBN 0-253-19263-3). Ind U Pr.

--The Story of the Stone (The Dream of the Red Chamber), Vol. 1: The Golden Days. Hawkes, David, tr. from Chinese. LC 78-20279. (Chinese Literature in Translation Ser.). 544p. 1979. 25.00x (ISBN 0-253-19261-7). Ind U Pr.

--The Story of the Stone (The Dream of the Red Chamber), Vol. 2: The Crab-Flower Club. Hawkes, David, tr. from Chinese. LC 78-20279. (Chinese Literature in Translation Ser.). 608p. 1979. 25.00x (ISBN 0-253-19262-5). Ind U Pr.

--The Story of the Stone (The Dream of the Red Chamber), Vol. 4: The Debt of Tears. Gao, E., ed. Minford, John, tr. LC 78-20279. (Chinese Literature in Translation Ser.). 400p. (Chinese.). 1983. 30.00X (ISBN 0-253-19264-1). Ind U Pr.

Caoursin, Guillaume see Aesopus.

Cao Xuequin. The Story of the Stone, Vol. 1: The Golden Days. Hawkes, David, tr. (Classics Ser.). 1974. pap. 6.95 (ISBN 0-14-044293-6). Penguin.

--The Story of the Stone, Vol. 2: The Crab-Flower Club. Hawks, David, tr. (Classics Ser.). 1977. pap. 8.95 (ISBN 0-14-044326-6). Penguin.

--The Story of the Stone, Vol. 3: The Warning Voice. Hawkes, David, tr. 1981. pap. 8.95 (ISBN 0-14-044370-3). Penguin.

Cao Xuequin & Gao E. The Story of the Stone, Vol. 4: The Debt of Tears. Minford, John, tr. 1982. pap. 8.95 (ISBN 0-14-044371-1). Penguin.

Cap, Ferdinand, tr. see Karpman, V. I.

Capa, Cornell. Lewis W. Hine. LC 72-11010. (Library of Photographers Ser.). (Illus.). 96p. 1974. 14.95 (ISBN 0-670-42742-X, Grossman). Viking Pr.

Capa, Cornell, ed. Concerned Photographer No. 2. LC 68-31898. (Illus.). 1972. 19.95 (ISBN 0-670-23556-3, Grossman). Viking Pr.

Capablanca, Jose R. Primer of Chess. LC 35-3374. (Illus.). 7.95 (ISBN 0-15-174039-9, Harv); pap. 3.95 (ISBN 0-15-673900-3). HarBraceJ.

Capacchione, Lucia. The Creative Journal: The Art of Finding Yourself. LC 82-79527. (Illus.). 180p. 1979. pap. 11.95 (ISBN 0-8040-0798-5). Swallow.

Capaldi, Nicholas. The Art of Deception. 2nd ed. LC 75-21077. 200p. 1979. pap. text ed. 6.95 (ISBN 0-87975-046-4). Prometheus Bks.

--David Hume. LC 74-20931. (World Leaders Ser.: No. 48). 1975. lib. bdg. 9.95 o.p. (ISBN 0-8057-3685-9, Twayne). G K Hall.

Capaldi, Nicholas, et al, eds. An Invitation to Philosophy. Kelly, Eugene & Navia, Luis E. LC 81-81131. 295p. (Orig.). 1981. pap. text ed. 13.95 (ISBN 0-87975-162-2). Prometheus Bks.

Capano, Carmela, ed. see Gansert, Robert.

Cape, Peter. Please Touch: A Srvey of the Three-Dimensional Arts in New Zealand. (Illus.). 160p. 1980. 29.95 (ISBN 0-00-216957-6, Pub. by W Collins Australia). Intl Schol Bk Serv.

Cape, Peter, jt. auth. see Reid, J. C.

Cape, Ronald D. Aging: Its Complex Management. 1978. text ed. 19.75x (ISBN 0-06-140622-8, Harper Medical). Lippincott.

Capece, Raymond P., ed. see Electronics Magazine.

Capeci, Dominic J., Jr. The Harlem Riot of 1943. LC 77-70328. 278p. 1977. 29.95 (ISBN 0-87722-094-8). Temple U Pr.

Capek, Josef & Capek, Karel. R.U.R. Bd. with The Insect Play. 1961. pap. 5.95x (ISBN 0-19-281010-3). Oxford U Pr.

Capek, Karel. Makropoulos Secret. Burrell, Randal C., ed. (Orig.). 1925. pap. 2.50 (ISBN 0-8283-1447-0, 41). Branden.

--War with the Newts. (Science Fiction Ser). 368p. 1975. Repr. of 1937 ed. lib. bdg. 15.00 o.p. (ISBN 0-8398-2301-0, Gregg). G K Hall.

Capek, Karel, jt. auth. see Capek, Josef.

Capek, Karel see Dent, Anthony.

Capek, Leslie. Transforming Your Office. LC 81-68395. (Illus.). 220p. (Orig.). 1981. pap. 6.95 (ISBN 0-89708-080-7). And Bks.

Capek, Thomas. The Cechs (Bohemian) in America. LC 74-109715. Repr. of 1920 ed. lib. bdg. 19.00x o.p. (ISBN 0-8371-4205-9, CACA). Greenwood.

Capel, Vivian. Public Address Handbook. (Illus.). 238p. 1981. 16.50x (ISBN 0-907266-02-9). Intl Pubns Serv.

--Public Address Handbook. 2nd ed. 182p. 1980. 25.00x o.p. (ISBN 0-686-87320-3, Pub. by Dickson England). State Mutual Bk.

Capell, Richard. Schubert's Songs. LC 77-5524. (Music Reprint Ser.). 1977. Repr. of 1928 ed. lib. bdg. 29.50 (ISBN 0-306-77422-4). Da Capo.

Capellan, Angel. El Viejo y el Mar, Hemingway. (Portico Ser.). 1976. pap. 1.50 o.p. (ISBN 0-671-08080-6). Monarch Pr.

Capelle, Friedrich W. Professional Perspective Drawing for Architects & Engineers. LC 69-12407. (Illus.). 1969. text ed. 39.50 (ISBN 0-07-009776-3, P&RB). McGraw.

Capelle, Ronald G. Changing Human Systems. 1979. 16.95x (ISBN 0-9690171-0-3). New Comm Pr.

Capers, Gerald M. Stephen A. Douglas: Defender of the Union. (The Library of American Biography). 239p. 1972. pap. 5.95 (ISBN 0-316-12814-7). Little.

Capetanos, Leon, jt. auth. see Mazursky, Paul.

Capie, Forrest & Collins, Michael. The Inter-War Economy: A Statistical Abstract. 200p. 1983. 24.00 (ISBN 0-7190-0901-4). Manchester.

Capildeo, Rudy, jt. auth. see Rose, Clifford.

Capildeo, Rudy, jt. ed. see Rose, F. Clifford.

Capirola, Vincenzo. Vincenzo Capirola Lute Book. Gombosi, Otto, ed. (Music Ser.). 236p. 1982. Repr. of 1955 ed. lib. bdg. 65.00 (ISBN 0-306-76100-9). Da Capo.

Capitol Childrens Museum. Paint. 1982. lib. bdg. 39.95 (ISBN 0-8359-5425-0). Reston.

Capizzi, Joseph, jt. auth. see Larew, Hiram.

Caplan, Ann P. Choice & Constraint in a Swahili Community: Property Hierarchy & Cognatic Descent on the East African Coast. (International African Institute Ser.). (Illus.). 1975. 29.95x (ISBN 0-19-724195-6). Oxford U Pr.

Caplan, Arnold I., jt. ed. see Fallon, John F.

Caplan, Arthur L., et al. Concepts of Health & Disease: Interdisciplinary Perspectives. 608p. 1981. pap. text ed. 32.50 (ISBN 0-201-00973-0). A-W.

Caplan, David, ed. Biological Studies of Mental Processes. (Illus.). 1980. 27.50x (ISBN 0-262-03061-6). MIT Pr.

Caplan, Edwin H. & Champoux, Joseph E. Cases in Management Accounting: Context & Behavior. 88p. pap. 12.95 (ISBN 0-686-37886-5, 78101). Natl Assn Accts.

Caplan, Edwin H. & Landekich, Stephen. Human Resource Accounting: Past, Present, & Future. 256p. 14.95 (ISBN 0-86641-055-4, 7465). Natl Assn Accts.

Caplan, Frank & Caplan, Theresa. The Second Twelve Months of Life. LC 77-78748. (Illus.). 1979. pap. 9.95 (ISBN 0-448-16533-3, G&D). Putnam Pub Group.

--The Second Twelve Months of Life: A Kaleidoscope of Growth. (Illus.). 1979. 14.95 o.s.i. (ISBN 0-448-14420-4, G&D). Putnam Pub Group.

Caplan, H. H., ed. Classified Directory of Artists' Signatures, Symbols & Monograms. 2nd ed. 850p. 1982. 185.00x (ISBN 0-8103-0977-7). Gale.

Caplan, Neil. Futile Diplomacy: Early Arab-Zionist Negotiation Attempts, 1913-1931, Vol. 1. 250p. 1983. text ed. 32.00x (ISBN 0-7146-3214-7, F Cass Co). Biblio Dist.

Caplan, Paula. Between Women: Lowering the Barriers. 216p. 1981. 12.95 (ISBN 0-920510-20-5, Pub. by Personal Lib). Dodd.

Caplan, Ralph. By Design: Why There are No Locks on the Bathroom Doors in the Hotel Louis XIV & Other Object Lessons. (Illus.). 192p. 1982. 16.95 (ISBN 0-312-11085-5). St Martin.

Caplan, Robert D., et al. Adhering to Medical Regimens: Pilot Experiments in Patient Education & Social Support. LC 76-620035. 284p. 1976. pap. 14.00x (ISBN 0-87944-207-7). Inst Soc Res.

--Social Support & Patient Adherence: Experimental Survey Findings. 284p. 1980. pap. 16.00x (ISBN 0-87944-260-3). Inst Soc Res.

Caplan, Ronald M. Principles of Obstetrics. (Illus.). 321p. 1982. pap. text ed. 19.95 (ISBN 0-683-01436-6). Williams & Wilkins.

Caplan, Ronald M. & Sweeney, Wm. J., III. Advances in Obstetrics & Gynecology. 710p. 1978. lib. bdg. 53.00 (ISBN 0-683-01435-8). Williams & Wilkins.

Caplan, S. Roy & Essig, Alvin. Bioenergetics & Linear Nonequilibrium Thermodynamics: The Steady State. (Harvard Books in Biophysics: No. 3). (Illus.). 448p. 1983. text ed. 37.50x (ISBN 0-674-07352-5). Harvard U Pr.

Caplan, Theresa, jt. auth. see Caplan, Frank.

Caplen, R. H. A Practical Approach to Quality Control. 4th ed. 326p. 1982. pap. text ed. 14.50x (ISBN 0-09-147451-5, Pub. by Busn Bks England). Renouf.

Caples, J. Tested Advertising Methods. 4th ed. 256p. 1974. 14.95 (ISBN 0-13-906909-7, Busn). P-H.

Capley, M. J. More Bible Puzzles & Games. 128p. 1978. pap. 1.95 o.p. (ISBN 0-8007-8320-4, Spire Bks). Revell.

Caplin, A. D. Electronic Structure of Solids. (Structure & Properties of Solids Ser.). 148p. 1976. pap. text ed. 16.95 (ISBN 0-7131-2527-6). E Arnold.

Caplin, Lee E., ed. The Business of Art. 1982. 20.00 (ISBN 0-13-106518-1, Busn); pap. 9.95 (ISBN 0-13-106500-9). P-H.

Caplovitz, David. The Working Addict. LC 77-94070. 1978. 22.50 (ISBN 0-87332-116-2). M E Sharpe.

Caplow, Theodore. Sociology. 2nd ed. LC 74-22417. (Illus.). 448p. 1975. text ed. 22.95 (ISBN 0-13-821363-1); study guide 8.95 (ISBN 0-13-821090-X). P-H.

Capon, Edmund. The Art & Archaeology in China. 1977. 32.50 (ISBN 0-262-03060-8); deluxe ed. 55.00 o.p. (ISBN 0-262-03064-0); pap. 9.95 (ISBN 0-262-53034-1). MIT Pr.

Capon, Paul, tr. see Duplessis, Yves.

Capon, Robert F. Between Noon & Three: A Parable of Romance, Law, & the Outrage of Grace. LC 81-47832. 192p. 1982. 11.49i (ISBN 0-06-061308-4, HarpR). Har-Row.

--Hunting the Divine Fox. 1977. pap. 5.95 (ISBN 0-8164-2137-4). Seabury.

--The Youngest Day: Nature & Grace on Shelter Island. LC 82-48414. (Illus.). 160p. 1983. 11.49i (ISBN 0-06-061309-2, HarpR). Har-Row.

Capon Springs Public Policy Conference, No. 1. Key Issues in Population: Problems, Options, & Recommendations for Action. Glassheim, Eliot, et al, eds. LC 78-50770. 1978. pap. text ed. 15.50 o.p. (ISBN 0-8191-0467-1). U Pr of Amer.

Capone, Donald, jt. auth. see Cheyney, Arnold.

Caponi, Anthony. Boulders & Pebbles of Poetry & Prose. (Illus.). 96p. 1972. 2.50 o.p. (ISBN 0-8309-0085-3). Ind Pr MO.

Caporale, Rocco & Grumelli, Antonio, eds. The Culture of Unbelief: Studies & Proceedings from the First International Symposium on Belief, Held in Rome, March 22-27, 1969. LC 75-138513. 1971. 30.00x (ISBN 0-520-01856-7). U of Cal Pr.

Capossela, Jim. Fifty Secrets of Success: A Common Sense Approach. 24p. 1982. pap. 1.95 (ISBN 0-942990-03-X). Northeast Sportsmans.

--How to Catch Crabs by the Bushel: The Manual of Sport Crabbing. LC 82-90080. (Illus.). 64p. 1982. pap. 3.95 (ISBN 0-942990-01-3). Northeast Sportsman.

--How to Turn Your Fishing-Hunting Experiences into Cash: Twenty-Five Ways to Earn Cash from Your Hobbies. LC 82-80911. 52p. (Orig.). 1982. pap. 2.50 (ISBN 0-942990-02-1). Northeast Sportsmans.

Capossela, Jim & Capossela, Josephine. Festive Christmas Recipes. 36p. 1982. pap. 1.95 (ISBN 0-942990-04-8). Northeast Sportsmans.

Capossela, Josephine, jt. auth. see Capossela, Jim.

Capostosto, John. Basic Carpentry. 2nd ed. (Illus.). 1980. text ed. 20.95 (ISBN 0-8359-0368-0). Reston.

Capotasto, John. Residential Carpentry for the 1980's. 1982. text ed. 22.95 (ISBN 0-8359-6648-8); solutions manual o.p. free (ISBN 0-8359-6649-6). Reston.

Capote, Truman. Breakfast at Tiffany's. 1959. pap. 2.50 (ISBN 0-451-12042-6, AE2402, Sig). NAL.

--The Dogs Bark: Public People & Private Places. 1977. pap. 8.95 (ISBN 0-452-25389-6, Z5389, Plume). NAL.

--The Grass Harp, & A Tree of Night & Other Short Stories. pap. 2.75 (ISBN 0-451-12043-4, AE2043, Sig). NAL.

--In Cold Blood. 1971. pap. 3.95 (ISBN 0-451-12198-8, AE2198, Sig). NAL.

--Miriam. (Creative's Classics Ser.). (Illus.). 40p. (gr. 6-12). 1982. lib. bdg. 7.95 (ISBN 0-87191-829-3). Creative Ed.

--The Muses Are Heard. pap. 1.25 (ISBN 0-394-70148-8, V-148, Vin). Random.

--Selected Writings of Truman Capote. 6.95 (ISBN 0-394-60495-4). Modern Lib.

Capotosto, Rosario. Capotosto's Woodworking Techniques & Projects. (Popular Science Bk). 480p. 1982. 29.95 (ISBN 0-442-21497-9). Van Nos Reinhold.

Capouya, Emile & Tompkins, Keitha, eds. The Essential Kropotkin. 296p. 1975. 12.50x o.s.i. (ISBN 0-87140-591-1); pap. 3.95x o.s.i. (ISBN 0-87140-400-1). Liveright.

Capp, Glenn R., et al. Basic Oral Communication. 3rd ed. (Illus.). 416p. 1981. pap. text ed. 16.95 (ISBN 0-13-065979-7). P-H.

Cappadona, Diane A., ed. The Sacred Play of Children. 160p. 1983. pap. 9.95 (ISBN 0-8164-2427-6). Seabury.

Cappelletti, M. Procedure Orale et Procedure Ecrite: Oral & Written Procedure in Civil Litigation. (Studi di Diritto Comparato: No. 4). 968p. 1971. 12.00 (ISBN 0-379-00032-6). Oceana.

Cappelletti, Mauro, et al. Toward Equal Justice: A Comparative Study of Legal Aid in Modern Societies. LC 75-18519. (Studies in Comparative Law: No. 13). 756p. 1975. text ed. 30.00x (ISBN 0-379-00213-2). Oceana.

Cappelluzzo, Emma. Guidance & the Migrant Child. (Guidance Monograph). 1971. pap. 2.40 o.p. (ISBN 0-395-12436-0, 9-78860). HM.

Capper, P. L. & Cassie, W. F. Mechanics of Engineering Soils: SI Version. 6th ed. 1976. pap. 14.95x (ISBN 0-419-10990-0, Pub. by E & FN Spon). Methuen Inc.

Cappon, Alexander P. Aspects of Wordsworth & Whitehead. 1983. 19.95 (ISBN 0-8022-2412-1). Philos Lib.

Cappon, Lester J. American Genealogical Periodicals: A Bibliography with a Chronological Finding-List. LC 61-18771. 1964. pap. 4.00 o.p. (ISBN 0-87104-000-X). NY Pub Lib.

Cappon, Lester J., ed. Adams-Jefferson Letters. 1971. pap. 5.95 o.p. (ISBN 0-671-21063-7, Touchstone Bks). S&S.

Cappon, Rene J & Associated Press. The Associated Press Guide to Newswriting. 196p. 1982. pap. 7.95 (ISBN 0-201-10320-6). A-W.

Capps, Alton C., ed. Bible As Literature. (Patterns in Literary Art Ser.). 1971. 9.16 (ISBN 0-07-009782-8, W). McGraw.

Capps, B. The Indians. LC 72-93991. (Old West Ser). (Illus.). (gr. 5 up). 1973. 17.28 (ISBN 0-8094-1455-4, Pub. by Time-Life). Silver.

Capps, Benjamin. The Great Chiefs. LC 75-744. (The Old West). (Illus.). (gr. 5 up). 1975. 17.28 (ISBN 0-8094-1494-5, Pub. by Time-Life). Silver.

Capps, Charles. Changing the Seen & Shaping the Unseen. 1980. pap. 1.75 o.s.i. (ISBN 0-89274-165-1). Harrison Hse.

--The Tongue-a Creative Force. rev. ed. 1976. pocket size 2.95 (ISBN 0-89274-061-2). Harrison Hse.

Capps, Clifford S. & Burney, Eugenia. Colonial Georgia. LC 73-181674. (Colonial History Books). (Illus.). (gr. 5 up). 1972. 7.95 o.p. (ISBN 0-525-67112-9). Lodestar Bks.

Capps, Donald, et al, eds. Psychology of Religion: A Guide to Information Sources. LC 73-17530. (Philosophy & Religion Information Guide Ser.: Vol. 1). vii, 380p. 1976. 42.00x (ISBN 0-8103-1356-1). Gale.

Capps, Mary J. Yellow Leaf. LC 73-11874. (Illus.). (gr. 5 up). 1974. pap. 2.95 o.p. (ISBN 0-570-03603-8, 39-1028). Concordia.

Capps, Walter H., ed. Seeing with the Native Eye: Contributions to the Study of Native American Religion. LC 76-9980. 1976. pap. 5.95xi (ISBN 0-06-061312-2, RD-177, HarpR). Har-Row.

Cappuccinelli, P. Motility of Living Cells. 80p. 1980. pap. 6.50x (ISBN 0-412-15770-5, Pub. by Chapman & Hall England). Methuen Inc.

Cappucino, James C. & Sherman, Natalie. Microciology. (Biology Ser.). (Illus.). 400p. 1982. pap. text ed. 12.95 (ISBN 0-201-11160-8). A-W.

Cappuzzello, Paul & Schlesinger, Mark. Recent Trends in History Curricula & Pedagogy: A Bibliographic Study. Woditsch, Gary, ed. LC 76-22292. (CUE Project Technical Paper Ser.: No. 1). 1976. pap. 4.95 (ISBN 0-89372-000-3). General Stud Res.

Capranica, Robert & Ewert, Jorg-Peter, eds. Advances in Vertebrate Neuroethology. (NATO ASI Ser.A, Life Sciences: Vol. 56). 1238p. 1983. 150.00x (ISBN 0-306-41197-0, Plenum Pr). Plenum Pub.

Caprentier, L. J., ed. New Developments in Phosphate Fertilizer Technology: Proceedings of the 1976 Technical Conference, The Hague, Sept. 1976. 1977. 91.50 (ISBN 0-444-41535-1). Elsevier.

Capri, Antonio. Il Settecento Musicale in Europa. LC 77-5523. (Music Reprint Ser). 1977. Repr. of 1936 ed. lib. bdg. 39.50 (ISBN 0-306-77413-5). Da Capo.

Capri-Karka, C. Love & the Symbolic Journey in the Poetry of Cavafy, Eliot, & Seferis. LC 82-81629. 1982. 22.00 (ISBN 0-918618-21-5); pap. 9.95 (ISBN 0-686-97762-9). Pella Pub.

Caprio, Anthony, jt. auth. see Carton, Dana.

Caprio, Betsy. The Woman Sealed in the Tower: A Psychological Approach to Feminine Spirituality. 1983. pap. 5.95 (ISBN 0-8091-2486-6). Paulist Pr.

Caprio, Dennis. Appliance Repair. (Illus.). 1979. 19.95 (ISBN 0-8359-0244-7). Reston.

Caprio, Frank S. & Berger, Joseph R. Helping Yourself with Self-Hypnosis. 1983. pap. 3.50 o.p. (ISBN 0-446-30598-7). Warner Bks.

Capron & Williams. Computers & Data Processing. 1982. 23.95 (ISBN 0-8053-2201-9, 32201); study guide 6.95 (ISBN 0-8053-2209-4); instr's guide avail. (ISBN 0-8053-2202-7); test items 4.95 (ISBN 0-8053-2210-8); suppl. sampler avail. (ISBN 0-8053-2205-1); programs in BASIC 4.95 (32211). Benjamin-Cummings.

Capron, Alexander M., jt. auth. see Katz, Jay.

Capron, J. Hugh. Wood Laminating. rev. ed. (gr. 11-12). 1972. 16.64 (ISBN 0-87345-046-9). McKnight.

Capstick, M. Economics of Agriculture. 672p. 1971. 20.00 (ISBN 0-312-22645-4). St Martin.

Capstick, Peter H. Death in the Dark Continent. (Illus.). 1983. 14.95 (ISBN 0-312-18615-0). St Martin.

--Death in the Long Grass. LC 77-9224. (Illus.). 1978. 12.95 (ISBN 0-312-18613-4). St Martin.

Capt, E. Raymond. The Glory of the Stars. LC 79-116390. (Illus.). 144p. (Orig.). 1976. pap. 4.00 (ISBN 0-934666-02-4). Artisan Sales.

--The Great Pyramid Decoded. rev. ed. LC 78-101677. (Illus.). 96p. 1978. pap. 3.00 (ISBN 0-934666-01-6). Artisan Sales.

--Jacob's Pillar. LC 79-116385. (Illus.). 96p. 1977. pap. 3.00 (ISBN 0-934666-03-2). Artisan Sales.

Capt, Raymond E. Scottish Declaration of Independence. (Illus.). 32p. 1983. pap. 2.00 (ISBN 0-934666-11-3). Artisan Sales.

--The Traditions of Glastonbury. LC 82-72525. (Illus.). 128p. 1983. pap. 5.00 (ISBN 0-934666-10-5). Artisan Sales.

Captain Marryat, see Marryat, Captain.

Captor, Renee S. Library Research for the Analysis of Public Policy. (Learning Packages in the Policy Sciences Ser.: No. 19). 36p. (Orig.). 1979. pap. text ed. 2.50x (ISBN 0-936826-08-8). Pol Stud Assocs.

Capurro, L. R. & Reid, Joseph L., eds. Contributions on the Physical Oceanography of the Gulf of Mexico. LC 71-135998. (Texas A&M University Oceanographic Studies on the Gulf of Mexico: Vol. 2). 288p. 1972. 29.95x (ISBN 0-87201-347-2). Gulf Pub.

Capute, Arnold J., et al. Primitive Reflex Profile. LC 77-27294. 114p. 1977. text ed. 19.95 (ISBN 0-8391-1181-9). Univ Park.

Caputo, John D. The Mystical Element in Heidegger's Thought. LC 77-92251. xvi, 292p. 1978. 20.00x (ISBN 0-8214-0372-9, 82-82667). Ohio U Pr.

Caputo, Luciano V. Questioned Document Case Studies. LC 82-3563. (Illus.). 100p. 1982. text ed. 38.95x (ISBN 0-88229-259-5). Nelson-Hall.

Caputo, Robert. More Than Just Pets: Why People Study Animals. LC 79-11493. (Illus.). (gr. 3-5). 1980. 7.95 o.p. (ISBN 0-698-20460-3, Coward). Putnam Pub Group.

Caputo, Robert & Hsia, Miriam. Hyena Day. (Illus.). (gr. 2-6). 1978. 7.95 o.p. (ISBN 0-698-20428-X, Coward). Putnam Pub Group.

Caputo, William V. How to Stop Being Insurance Poor. 1979. 5.95 o.p. (ISBN 0-533-03891-X). Vantage.

Caputto, R. & Marsan, C. Ajmone, eds. Molecular Aspects of Nervous Stimulation, Transmission, & Learning & Memory. (International Brain Research Organization (IBRO) Monograph Ser.: Vol. 10). 305p. 1983. text ed. write for info. (ISBN 0-89004-860-6). Raven.

Capuzzi, Dave, ed. Family Counseling: The School Counseling Role. 1981. 3.00 (ISBN 0-686-36366-3); nonmembers 3.50 (ISBN 0-686-37291-3). Am Personnel.

--Family Counseling: The School Counselor's Role. 1981. 3.00 (ISBN 0-686-36449-X, 70405); nonmembers 3.50 (ISBN 0-686-37322-7). Am Personnel.

Capuzzi, Frank, tr. see Heidegger, Martin.

Caraboolad, Clemens J. Mysticism & Zen: An Introduction. LC 77-18492. 1978. pap. text ed. 8.00 (ISBN 0-8191-0422-1). U Pr of Amer.

Caradon & Goldberg, Arthur J. U. N. Security Council Resolution 242: A Case Study in Diplomatic Ambiguity. LC 81-1671. 64p. 1981. 4.00 (ISBN 0-934742-11-1, Inst Study Diplomacy). Geo U Sch For Serv.

Caraeff, Ed. Dolly: Close Up. (Illus.). 96p. (Orig.). 1982. pap. 9.95 (ISBN 0-933328-58-3). Delilah Bks.

Caraeff, Eddie J. The Gourmet Cabbie. (Illus.). 144p. (Orig.). 1983. pap. 5.95 (ISBN 0-933328-26-5). Delilah Bks.

Carafiol, Peter C. Transcendent Reason: James Marsh & the Forms of Romantic Thought. 1982. write for info. (ISBN 0-8130-0732-1). U Presses Fla.

Carafoli, E., et al, eds. Calcium Transport in Contractions & Secretion. (Proceedings). 1975. 70.00 (ISBN 0-444-10917-X). Elsevier.

Carafoli, Ernesto, jt. ed. see Scarpa, Antonio.

Carafoli, John. The Cookie Cookbook. (Beginning-to-Read Ser.). (Illus.). (gr. 2-4). 1977. pap. 1.95 o.s.i. (ISBN 0-695-30742-8); PLB 4.39 o.s.i. (ISBN 0-695-40742-2). Follett.

Carafoli, John & Carafoli, Marci. Look Who's Cooking. LC 73-93550. (Beginning-to-Read Bks). (Illus.). 32p. (gr. 2-4). 1974. 2.50 o.s.i. (ISBN 0-695-80475-8); lib. bdg. 3.39 o.s.i. (ISBN 0-695-40475-X); pap. 1.50 o.s.i. (ISBN 0-685-50751-3). Follett.

Carafoli, Marci, jt. auth. see Carafoli, John.

Caraion, Ion. Ion Caraion: Poems. Dorian, Marguerite & Urdang, Elliott B., trs. from Romanian. LC 81-4847. vii, 112p. 1981. 17.95x (ISBN 0-8214-0608-6, 82-83947); pap. 8.95 (ISBN 0-8214-0620-5, 82-83954). Ohio U Pr.

Caraley, Demetrios. City Governments & Urban Problems: A New Introduction to Urban Politics. LC 76-28327. (Illus.). 1977. 22.95 (ISBN 0-13-134973-2). P-H.

Caralieri, Grace. Creature Comforts. LC 82-51068. 56p. 1982. pap. text ed. 5.95 (ISBN 0-915380-16-1). Word Works.

Caraman, Phillip, ed. Saints & Ourselves: A Selection of Saints Lives. 226p. 1982. pap. 6.95 (ISBN 0-89283-123-5). Servant.

Caramello, Charles, jt. ed. see Benamou, Michel.

Caran, S. C., et al. Geological Circular 82-1: Lineament Analysis & Inference of Geologic Structure-Examples from the Balcones-Ouachita Trend of Texas. 11p. 1982. Repr. 1.00 (ISBN 0-686-37545-9). U of Tex Econ Geology.

Caran, S. Christopher, jt. auth. see Kutac, Edward A.

Carano, Paul & Sanchez, Pedro C. A Complete History of Guam. LC 64-21619. (Illus.). 1964. 20.50 (ISBN 0-8048-0114-2). C E Tuttle.

Caras, Roger. A Celebration of Dogs. 1982. 14.95 (ISBN 0-8129-1029-X). Times Bks.

--Dangerous to Man. (Stoeger Bks). (Illus.). 1977. pap. 7.95 o.s.i. (ISBN 0-695-80738-2). Follett.

--The Private Lives of Animals. (Illus.). 224p. 1982. pap. 12.95 (ISBN 0-448-12694-X, G&D). Putnam Pub Group.

--The Private Lives of Animals. LC 73-21217. (Illus.). 224p. 1974. 3.95 (ISBN 0-448-11802-5, G&D). Putnam Pub Group.

--A Zoo in Your Room. LC 74-24322. (Illus.). 96p. (gr. 7-11). 1975. 5.95 o.p. (ISBN 0-15-299968-X, HJ). HarBraceJ.

Caras, Roger, ed. Dog Owner's Bible. 1978. pap. 7.95 o.s.i. (ISBN 0-685-89386-3). Follett.

Caras, Roger A. Yankee: The Inside Story of a Champion Bloodhound. LC 79-12133. (Illus.). (gr. 7-12). 1979. 8.95 o.p. (ISBN 0-399-20688-4). Putnam Pub Group.

Carasso, Alfred & Stone, Alex P., eds. Improperly Posed Boundary Value Problems. (Research Notes in Mathematics Ser.: No. 1). 157p. 1975. pap. text ed. 18.95 (ISBN 0-273-00105-1). Pitman Pub MA.

Caratheodory, Constantin. Calculus of Variations & Partial Differential Equations of the First Order. 2nd ed. Brandstatter, Julius J., tr. from Ger. LC 81-71519. (Illus.). 421p. 1982. text ed. 25.00 (ISBN 0-8284-0318-X). Chelsea Pub.

--Theory of Functions. 2nd ed. LC 60-16838. Vol. 1. 14.95 (ISBN 0-8284-0097-0); Vol. 2. 14.95 (ISBN 0-8284-0106-3). Chelsea Pub.

--Vorlesungen Ueber Reelle Funktionen. 3rd ed. LC 63-11321. (Ger). 1968. 29.95 (ISBN 0-8284-0038-5). Chelsea Pub.

Caraway. The Beginner's Guide to Quilting: Easy-to-Make Coverlets, Pillows, & Hangings. 1980. 8.95 o.p. (ISBN 0-679-20532-2). McKay.

Caraway, Caren. Applique Quilts to Color. 1980. 48p. pap. 2.95 (ISBN 0-686-81961-6). Stemmer Hse.

--Beginners's Guide to Quilting. (gr. 7 up). 1980. 8.95 o.p. (ISBN 0-679-20532-2). McKay.

--Hansel & Gretel. 32p. (ps up). 1982. pap. 2.95 (ISBN 0-88045-017-7). Stemmer Hse.

--Peruvian Textile Designs. (The International Design Library). (Illus.). 1983. pap. 2.95 (ISBN 0-88045-026-6). Stemmer Hse.

Caraway, Hattie W. Silent Hattie Speaks: The Personal Journal of Senator Hattie Caraway. Kincaid, Diane D., ed. LC 78-22136. (Contributions in Women's Studies: No. 9). (Illus.). 1979. lib. bdg. 25.00 (ISBN 0-313-20820-4, KSI/). Greenwood.

Caraway, James E. God As Dynamic Actuality: A Preliminary Study of the Process Theologies of John B. Cobb, Jr. & Schubert M. Ogden. LC 78-61388. 1978. pap. text ed. 11.25 (ISBN 0-8191-0485-X). U Pr of Amer.

Carballido, Emilio. The Golden Thread & Other Plays. Peden, Margaret S., tr. from Sp. (Texas Pan American Ser). 255p. 1970. 11.95 (ISBN 0-292-70039-3). U of Tex Pr.

Carberry, James J. Chemistry & Catalytic Reaction Engineering. (Chemical Engineering Ser.). (Illus.). 1976. 36.50 (ISBN 0-07-009790-9, C); solutions manual 11.00 (ISBN 0-07-009791-7). McGraw.

Carberry, M., et al. Foundations of Computer Science. LC 78-27891. 1979. text ed. 23.95x (ISBN 0-914894-18-8). Computer Sci.

Carberry, M. S., jt. auth. see Khalil, H. M.

Carbino, Rosemarie. Foster Parenting: An Updated Review of the Literature. (Orig.). 1980. pap. text ed. 4.95 (ISBN 0-87868-178-7, F-56). Child Welfare.

Carbo. Current Aspects of Quantum Chemistry, 1981. (Studies in Physical & Theoretical Chemistry: Vol. 21). 1982. 106.50 (ISBN 0-444-42119-X). Elsevier.

Carbonell, Jaime G., jt. ed. see Michalski, Ryszard S.

Carby, Keith & Thakur, Manab. No Problems Here? Management & the Multi-Racial Workforce Including a Guide to the Race Relations Act 1976. 1977. pap. 9.00x (ISBN 0-85292-151-9). Intl Pubns Serv.

Carcamo, L. Dictionnaire pour Ingenieurs et Techniciens: Francais-Espagnol, Espagnol-Francais. 1106p. 1981. 95.00 (ISBN 0-686-92423-1, M-7669). French & Eur.

Carcassi, Ugo, jt. ed. see Cao, Antonio.

Carcasson. The Butterflies of Africa. 29.95 (ISBN 0-686-42747-5, Collins Pub England). Greene.

Carchedi, Guglielmo. Problems in Class Analysis. 300p. (Orig.). 1983. pap. price not set (ISBN 0-7100-9426-4). Routledge & Kegan.

Carchmichael, Carrie, jt. auth. see Storch, Marcia L.

Carcione, Joe & Lucas, Bob. The Greengrocer. LC 72-85171. (Illus.). 1978. pap. 6.95 (ISBN 0-87701-113-3). Chronicle Bks.

Carcopino, Jerome. Daily Life in Ancient Rome: The People & the City at the Height of the Empire. Rowell, Henry T., ed. Lorimer, E. O., tr. (Illus., Fr.). 1940. 27.50x (ISBN 0-300-00344-7); pap. 6.95x 1960 (ISBN 0-300-00031-6, Y28). Yale U Pr.

Carcow Museum Curatorial Staff. Carcow Museum. LaFarge, Henry A, ed. LC 82-48023. (Great Museums of the World Ser.). 176p. 1982. 19.95x (ISBN 0-88225-245-3). Newsweek.

Card, Josefina J. Lives after Vietnam: The Personal Impact of Military Service. 1983. price not set (ISBN 0-669-06420-3). Lexington Bks.

Card, Maura, jt. auth. see Lappen, Lee E.

Card, Orson S. Hart's Hope. 272p. 1983. pap. 2.75 (ISBN 0-425-05819-0). Berkley Pub.

Card, Stuart K. & Moran, Thomas P. The Psychology of Human-Computer Interaction. 464p. 1983. text ed. write for info. (ISBN 0-89859-243-7). L Erlbaum Assocs.

Cardamone, Tom. Advertising Agency & Studio Skills: A Guide to the Preparation of Art & Mechanicals for Reproduction. rev. ed. (Illus.). 1970. 12.95 o.p. (ISBN 0-8230-0151-2). Watson-Guptill.

Cardelle, Gustavo. Reflejos Sobre la Nieve. LC 78-59838. (Senda Poetica Ser.). (Span.). 1978. pap. 3.95 (ISBN 0-918454-07-7). Senda Nueva.

Carden, Maren L. The New Feminist Movement. LC 73-83889. 226p. 1974. 9.95x (ISBN 0-87154-196-3). Russell Sage.

Cardenas, Alfonso F., et al. Computer Science. LC 71-169162. 1972. 45.00x o.p. (ISBN 0-471-13468-6, Pub. by Wiley-Interscience). Wiley.

Cardenas, Anthony & Gilkison, Jean. Bibliography of Old Spanish Texts. 2nd ed. (Literary Texts Ser.). x, 128p. 1977. pap. 7.50 (ISBN 0-942260-08-2). Hispanic Seminary.

Cardenas, Reyes. Survivors of the Chicano Titanic. 80p. 1982. 16.00 (ISBN 0-916908-20-8); pap. 6.00 (ISBN 0-916908-15-1). Place Herons.

Carder, Mary E., et al. Productive Reading & Study Skills: A Student's Guide. 1979. pap. text ed. 10.95 (ISBN 0-8403-1997-5). Kendall-Hunt.

Carder, Polly, jt. auth. see Landis, Beth.

Cardew, Cornelius, tr. see Eimert, Herbert & Stockhausen, Karlheinz.

Cardew, Cornelius, tr. see Webern, Anton.

Cardew, Richard V. & Langdale, John V., eds. Why Cities Change: Urban Development & Economic Change in Sydney. 304p. 1983. text ed. 37.50x (ISBN 0-86861-252-9). Allen Unwin.

Cardiff, Gray E. & English, John W. The Coming Real Estate Crash. (Illus.). 1979. 12.95 o.p. (ISBN 0-87000-415-8, Arlington Hse). Crown.

Cardinal, Andre. Etude Sur les Ectocarpacees de la Manche. (Illus.). 1965. pap. 24.00 (ISBN 3-7682-5415-1). Lubrecht & Cramer.

Cardinal, Marie. Cul-De-Sac: A Personal Account. Goodheart, Pat, tr. from Fr. 320p. 1983. 14.95 (ISBN 0-941324-02-8). Van Vactor & Goodheart.

Cardinale, Hyginus E. The Holy See & the International Order. (Illus.). 1976. text ed. 36.75x (ISBN 0-686-86092-6). Humanities.

Cardona, Elizabeth, ed. see Henderson, Thomas.

Cardona, George. Studies in Indian Grammarians: One. LC 69-18745. (Transactions Ser.: Vol. 59, Pt. 1). 1969. pap. 1.00 o.p. (ISBN 0-87169-591-X). Am Philos.

Cardona, M., ed. Light Scattering in Solids I. 2nd ed. (Topics in Applied Physics Ser.: Vol. 8). (Illus.). 363p. 1983. pap. 29.00 (ISBN 0-387-11913-2). Springer-Verlag.

Cardona-Hine, Alvaro. When I Was A Father. LC 82-80604. (Minnesota Voices Project Ser.: No. 7). (Illus.). 73p. 1982. pap. 4.00 (ISBN 0-89823-036-5). New Rivers Pr.

Cardoso, Fernando E. & Faletto, Enzo. Dependency & Development in Latin America. Urquidi, Marjory M., tr. LC 75-46033. 1979. 30.00x (ISBN 0-520-03193-8); pap. 5.95x (ISBN 0-520-03527-5). U of Cal Pr.

Cardoso, Gerald. Negro Slavery in the Sugar Plantations of Veracruz & Pernambuco, 1550-1680: A Comparative Study. LC 82-21731. 224p. (Orig.). 1983. lib. bdg. 21.50 (ISBN 0-8191-2926-7); pap. text ed. 10.75 (ISBN 0-8191-2927-5). U Pr of Amer.

Cardozo, Benjamin N. Paradoxes of Legal Science. LC 76-104241. Repr. of 1928 ed. lib. bdg. 16.50x (ISBN 0-8371-3263-0, CALS). Greenwood.

Cardozo, Manoel D. The Portuguese in America, 590 BC-1974: A Chronology & Fact Book. LC 75-45203. (Ethnic Chronology Ser.: No. 22). 154p. 1976. lib. bdg. 8.50 (ISBN 0-379-00520-4). Oceana.

Cardozo, Richard N. Product Policy: Cases & Concepts. LC 78-67939. 1979. text ed. 23.95 (ISBN 0-201-00888-2). A-W.

Carducci, Joshua. The Inspired Poetry by Joshua Carducci. Corradini, V., tr. (The Most Meaningful Classics in the World Culture Ser.). (Illus.). 137p. 1982. Repr. of 1916 ed. 110.00 (ISBN 0-89901-074-1). Found Class Reprints.

Carduner, Jean & Carduner, Sylvie. Contextes: A French College Reader. 1975. pap. text ed. 9.95x o.p. (ISBN 0-669-73627-9). Heath.

Carduner, Jean, jt. auth. see Benamou, Michel.

Carduner, Sylvie & Hagiwara, Peter M. D'Accord: La Prononciation Du Francais International: Acquisition et Perfectionnement. LC 81-13123. 304p. 1982. text ed. 19.95x (ISBN 0-471-09729-2); tapes 76.00 (ISBN 0-471-86551-6); cassettes avail. (ISBN 0-471-86757-8). Wiley.

Carduner, Sylvie, jt. auth. see Carduner, Jean.

Cardus, David, jt. ed. see Blocker, William, Jr.

Cardus, Neville. Autobiography. LC 75-37825. (Illus.). 288p. 1976. Repr. of 1947 ed. lib. bdg. 19.25x (ISBN 0-8371-8577-7, CAAU). Greenwood.

--Talking of Music. LC 74-14112. 320p. 1975. Repr. of 1957 ed. lib. bdg. 18.00x (ISBN 0-8371-7786-3, CAMU). Greenwood.

Cardwell, Charles E. Argument & Inference: An Introduction to Symbolic Logic. (Philosophy Ser.). 1978. pap. text ed. 12.95 (ISBN 0-675-08368-0). Additional supplements may be obtained from publisher. Merrill.

Cardwell, D. S., ed. Artisan to Graduate. 1974. 23.50 (ISBN 0-7190-1272-4). Manchester.

Cardwell, Guy, ed. see Twain, Mark.

Cardwell, Jerry D. The Social Context of Religiosity. LC 80-67216. 174p. 1980. lib. bdg. 19.75 (ISBN 0-8191-1135-X); pap. text ed. 9.50 (ISBN 0-8191-1136-8). U Pr of Amer.

--Social Psychology: A Symbolic Interaction Perspective. LC 75-158650. pap. 6.75x (ISBN 0-88295-203-X). Harlan Davidson.

Cardwell, Jerry D., jt. auth. see Vernon, Glenn M.

Cardwell, Julia C. The Moonshine Special. (Illus.). 1983. 5.75 (ISBN 0-8062-1908-4). Carlton.

Cardwell, Kenneth. Bernard Maybeck: Artisan, Architect, Artist. LC 77-13773. (Illus.). 1977. 29.95 o.p. (ISBN 0-87905-022-5); pap. 19.95 o.p. (ISBN 0-87905-148-5). Peregrine Smith.

Cardy, Lynn & Dart, Alan. Maternity Clothes: Simple Patterns to Make while You Wait. 128p. 1982. 30.00x (ISBN 0-7135-1312-8, Pub. by Bell & Hyman England). State Mutual Bk.

Cardy, Wayne C., jt. auth. see Arnold, Wesley F.

Care, R. A. Fire & Fuels. (Illus.). 176p. (gr. 5-8). 1975. 12.50 o.p. (ISBN 0-263-05593-0). Transatlantic.

Careers Research & Advisory Centre, ed. Graduate Studies 1982-83: The Guide to Postgraduate Study in the UK. 1013p. 1982. 150.00x (ISBN 0-86021-343-9). Intl Pubns Serv.

Carello, Claudia A., jt. auth. see Michaels, Claire F.

Carelman. The Catalog of Unfindable Objects: Everything You've Always Wanted & Can't Get. Orig. Title: Catalogue d'Objects Introuvables. (Illus.). 240p. Date not set. pap. 14.95 cancelled (ISBN 0-89104-311-X, A & W Visual Library). A & W Pubs. Postponed.

Carelse, Xavier. Making Science Laboratory Equipment: A Manual for Students & Teachers in Developing Countries. 240p. 1983. pap. price not set (ISBN 0-471-10353-5, Pub. by Wiley-Interscience). Wiley.

Careme, Maurice. The Peace. Neumeyer, Helen, tr. (Illus.). 8p. (Orig.). 1982. pap. 2.50 (ISBN 0-914676-68-7, Pub. by Envelope Bks). Green Tiger Pr.

Carenza, L., et al, eds. Clinical Psychoneuroendocrinology in Reproduction. (Proceedings of the Serono Symposia). 1979. 49.50 (ISBN 0-12-159450-5). Acad Pr.

Caret, jt. auth. see Wingrove.

Caret, Robert L., jt. auth. see Wingrove, Alan S.

Carew, Anthony. The Lower Deck of the Royal Navy, 1900-39: The Invergordon Mutiny in Perspective. 256p. 1982. 25.00 (ISBN 0-7190-0841-7). Manchester.

Carew, Jan. Black Midas. 2nd ed. 184p. 1981. cancelled o.s.i. (ISBN 0-89410-124-2); pap. 5.00x o.s.i. (ISBN 0-89410-125-0). Three Continents.

Carew, Richard. Richard Carew's Survey of Cornwall. Halliday, F. E., ed. LC 76-93273. Repr. of 1953 ed. lib. bdg. 25.00x o.p. (ISBN 0-678-07504-2). Kelley.

Carew, Richard, tr. see Huarte de San Juan, Juan.

Carey, A. G., jt. auth. see Benson, John H.

Carey, Anne. The Children's Pharmacy. new ed. 192p. 1983. 11.95 (ISBN 0-672-52727-8). Bobbs.

Carey, Betsy, ed. WomanSource: A Guide to Women's Resources in Metropolitan Denver. LC 81-71997. (Illus.). 184p. (Orig.). 1982. pap. 4.95 (ISBN 0-9608012-0-0). WomanSource.

Carey, Bonnie, tr. from Rus. Grasshopper to the Rescue. (Illus.). (gr. k-3). 1979. 9.25 (ISBN 0-688-22172-6); PLB 8.88 (ISBN 0-688-32172-0). Morrow.

Carey, Bonnie, tr. see Aleksin, Anatoli.

Carey, Clarence B. Business Speller & Vocabulary Builder. 3rd ed. 1978. 002 o.p. (ISBN 0-8224-0177-0). Pitman Learning.

Carey, Ernestine G., jt. auth. see Gilbreth, Frank B.

Carey, G. F., jt. auth. see Martin, Harold C.

Carey, Gary. Brothers Karamazov Notes. (Orig.). 1967. pap. 2.95 (ISBN 0-8220-0265-5). Cliffs.

--Mrs. Dalloway Notes. (Orig.). 1969. pap. 2.95 (ISBN 0-8220-0855-6). Cliffs.

--Sun Also Rises Notes. (Orig.). 1968. pap. 2.95 (ISBN 0-8220-1237-5). Cliffs.

Carey, Gary & Jorgenson, Paul A. Othello Notes. (Orig.). 1980. pap. 2.50 (ISBN 0-8220-0063-6). Cliffs.

Carey, George g. Maryland Folk Legends & Folk Songs. 120p. 1971. pap. 4.00 (ISBN 0-686-36827-4). Md Hist.

Carey, George G., ed. A Sailor's Songbag: An American Rebel in an English Prison,1777-1779. LC 75-32483. (Illus.). 176p. 1976. lib. bdg. 10.00x (ISBN 0-87023-200-2). U of Mass Pr.

Carey, George W. A Vignette of the New York-New Jersey Metropolitan Region. LC 76-4796. (Contemporary Metropolitan Analysis Ser.). (Illus.). 96p. 1976. pap. 8.95x prof ref (ISBN 0-88410-436-2). Ballinger Pub.

Carey, Graham F., jt. auth. see Oden, J. Tinsley.

Carey, H. M. Clinical Use of Female Sex Steroids. (Illus.). 1978. pap. text ed. 9.95 o.p. (ISBN 0-409-33750-1). Butterworth.

Carey, Hugh. Duet for Two Voices. LC 78-62115. (Illus.). 1980. 29.95 (ISBN 0-521-22312-1). Cambridge U Pr.

Carey, J., jt. auth. see Franck, T. M.

Carey, J. R., tr. see Becquer, G. A.

Carey, James. When the Doors Break. 1982. 7.75 (ISBN 0-8062-1870-3). Carlton.

Carey, James T. Introduction to Criminology. 1978. ref. ed. 23.95 (ISBN 0-13-481143-7). P-H.

Carey, John. John Donne: Life, Mind & Art. 1981. 22.50x (ISBN 0-19-520242-2). Oxford U Pr.

Carey, John, ed. see Levie, H. S.

Carey, John, ed. see Thomas, Aaron J. & Thomas, Ann.

Carey, John see Milton, John.

Carey, John L. Rise of the Accounting Profession, 2 Vols. 1969. Set. 36.50 (ISBN 0-685-05617-1). Am Inst CPA.

Carey, Jonathan S., jt. ed. see Ahlstrom, Sydney E.

Carey, Lou, jt. auth. see Dick, Walter.

Carey, M. V. Alfred Hitchcock & the Three Investigators in the Mystery of the Magic Circle. LC 78-55915. (Alfred Hitchcock & the Three Investigators Ser.: No. 27). (Illus.). (gr. 4-7). 1978. 2.95 o.p. (ISBN 0-394-83607-3, BYR); PLB 5.39 (ISBN 0-394-93607-8); pap. 1.95 (ISBN 0-394-84490-4). Random.

--Alfred Hitchcock & the Three Investigators in the Mystery of the Invisible Dog. LC 75-8073. (Three Investigators Ser.: No. 23). (Illus.). 160p. (gr. 4-7). 1975. 2.95 o.p. (ISBN 0-394-83105-5, BYR); PLB 5.39 (ISBN 0-394-93105-X); pap. 1.95 o.p. (ISBN 0-394-84492-0). Random.

--Alfred Hitchcock & the Three Investigators in the Mystery of Death Trap Mine. LC 76-8135. (Illus.). (gr. 4-7). 1976. o. p. 2.95 (ISBN 0-394-83321-X, BYR); PLB 5.39 (ISBN 0-394-93321-4); pap. 1.95 o.p. (ISBN 0-394-84449-1). Random.

--Alfred Hitchcock & the Three Investigators in the Mystery of the Flaming Footprints. Hitchcock, Alfred, ed. (Three Investigators Ser.: No. 15). (Illus.). (gr. 4-7). 1971. 2.95 o.s.i. (ISBN 0-394-82296-X, BYR); PLB 5.39 (ISBN 0-394-92296-4); pap. 1.95 o.p. (ISBN 0-394-83776-2). Random.

--Alfred Hitchcock & the Three Investigators in the Mystery of the Singing Serpent. Hitchcock, Alfred, ed. (Three Investigators Ser.: No. 17). (Illus.). (gr. 4-7). 1972. 2.95 o.p. (ISBN 0-394-82408-3, BYR); PLB 5.39 (ISBN 0-394-92408-8). Random.

--Alfred Hitchcock & the Three Investigators in the Mystery of Monster Mountain. Hitchcock, Alfred, ed. (Three Investigators Ser.: No. 20). (Illus.). (gr. 4-7). 1973. 2.95 o.p. (ISBN 0-394-82664-7, BYR); PLB 5.39 (ISBN 0-394-92664-1); pap. 1.95 o.p. (ISBN 0-394-84259-6). Random.

--Alfred Hitchcock & the Three Investigators in the Secret of the Haunted Mirror. LC 74-5750. (Alfred Hitchcock & the Three Investigators). (Illus.). 160p. (gr. 4-7). 1974. 2.95 o.p. (ISBN 0-394-82820-8, BYR); PLB 5.39 (ISBN 0-394-92820-2); pap. 1.95 o.p. (ISBN 0-394-84450-5). Random.

Carey, MacDonald. A Day in the Life. (Illus.). 1982. 7.95 (ISBN 0-698-11165-6, Coward). Putnam Pub Group.

Carey, Margaret S. & Hainline, Patricia H. Shedd, Linn County's Early Dairy Center & Memories of Boston. (Illus.). 64p. (Orig.). 1978. pap. 3.95 (ISBN 0-934784-03-5). Calapooia Pubns.

Carey, Mary. Happy, Healthy Pooh Book. (Look-Look Ser.). (Illus.). 1977. PLB 5.38 o.p. (ISBN 0-307-61832-3, Golden Pr); pap. 1.25 (ISBN 0-307-11832-0). Western Pub.

Carey, Mary, compiled by. Grandmothers Are Very Special People. (Illus.). 1977. boxed 5.50 (ISBN 0-8378-1735-8). Gibson.

Carey, P. R. Biochemical Applications of Raman & Resonance Raman Spectroscopies. (Molecular Biology Ser.). 1982. 34.00 (ISBN 0-12-159650-8). Acad Pr.

Carey, Raymond G., jt. auth. see Posavac, Emile J.

Carey, Robert J., jt. auth. see Coulacos, Spero.

Carey, W. S. The Expanding Earth. (Developments in Geotectonics Ser.: Vol. 10). 1976. 55.50 (ISBN 0-444-41485-1). Elsevier.

Cargas, Harry J. David's Decision: Betrayal or Trust? 1979. pap. 2.25 (ISBN 0-570-07978-0, 39-1118). Concordia.

--Encountering Myself: Contemporary Christian Meditations. LC 76-56519. 1977. 1.00 (ISBN 0-8164-0372-4). Seabury.

Cargas, Harry J., ed. Responses to Elie Wiesel. LC 77-94055. 1978. o. p. 15.00 (ISBN 0-89255-031-7); pap. 5.95 (ISBN 0-89255-032-5). Persea Bks.

--Responses to Elie Wiesel. 286p. 15.00 (ISBN 0-686-95081-X); pap. 5.95 (ISBN 0-686-99458-2). ADL.

Cargile, J. Paradoxes. LC 78-67299. (Cambridge Studies in Philosophy). 1979. 37.50 (ISBN 0-521-22475-6). Cambridge U Pr.

Cargill & Brown. Signos Para el Ingles Exacto: A Book for Spanish-Speaking Families of Deaf Children in Schools Using Signing Exact English. LC 82-61647. (Illus.). 152p. Date not set. pap. 10.95 (ISBN 0-916708-06-3). Modern Signs.

Cargill, Burton F., jt. auth. see O'Brien, Michael.

Cargill, Jennifer S., jt. auth. see Alley, Brian.

Cargille, Charles, jt. ed. see Glassheim, Eliot.

Cargo, David M., jt. auth. see Mallory, Bob F.

Carhart, Jane M., jt. ed. see Kline, Linda J.

Carico, Charles C. College Algebra & Trigonometry. 512p. 1983. text ed. 19.95x (ISBN 0-471-07700-3); student supplement avail. (ISBN 0-471-09269-X). Wiley.

Carico, Charles C. & Drooyan, Irving. Analytic Geometry. LC 79-21633. 310p. 1980. 23.95x (ISBN 0-471-06435-1); student supplement, 175 p. 9.95 (ISBN 0-471-06378-9). Wiley.

Caridi, R. Twentieth Century American Foreign Policy, Security, & Self Interest. 1974. 15.95 o.p. (ISBN 0-13-934935-9); pap. 12.95 o.p. (ISBN 0-13-934927-8). P-H.

Carim, Enver, ed. Africa Guide: 1983. (World of Information Ser.). pap. 24.95 (ISBN 0-911818-31-6). World Almanac.

--Asia & Pacific: 1983. (World of Information Ser.). 328p. 1983. pap. 24.95 (ISBN 0-911818-34-0). World Almanac.

--Latin America & Caribbean: 1982-83. (World of Information Ser.). 256p. pap. 24.95 (ISBN 0-911818-32-4). World Almanac.

--Middle East Review: 1983. (World of Information Ser.). 350p. 1983. pap. 24.95 (ISBN 0-911818-33-2). World Almanac.

Carin. Creative Questioning & Sensitivity: Listening Techniques. 2nd ed. 1978. text ed. 10.95x (ISBN 0-675-08421-0). Merrill.

Carin, Arthur A. & Sund, Robert B. Discovery Activities for Elementary Science. (Elementary Education Ser.: No. C22). 296p. 1980. pap. text ed. 12.95 (ISBN 0-675-08089-4). Merrill.

--Teaching Modern Science. 3rd ed. (Elementary Education Ser.: No. C22). 352p. 1980. pap. text ed. 16.95 (ISBN 0-675-08193-9). Merrill.

--Teaching Science Through Discovery. 4th ed. (Elementary Education Ser.: No. C22). 512p. 1980. text ed. 22.95 (ISBN 0-675-08157-2). Additional supplements may be obtained from publisher. Merrill.

Carini, Anselmo, tr. see Goguel, Catherine M. & Viatte, Francoise.

Carini, Geraldine & Birmingham, Jacqueline. Traction Made Manageable: A Self Learning Module. (Illus.). 1980. pap. text ed. 16.50 (ISBN 0-07-009841-7). McGraw.

Carl, Angela, jt. auth. see Lang, June.

Carl, Mary K. & Kramer, Marlene. Curriculum in Graduate Education in Nursing: Part I-Factors Influencing Curriculum in Graduate Education in Nursing. 61p. 1975. 4.95 (ISBN 0-686-38253-6, 15-1596). Natl League Nurse.

Carlaw, Raymond W., ed. Perspectives on Community Health Education: A Series of Case Studies. LC 80-54741. 224p. 1982. pap. text ed. 7.95 (ISBN 0-89914-007-6). Third Party Pub.

Carlberg, Bo Casten. The Creative Cooperation Movement: The Swedish Cutting Edge to Productivity & Quality Work Life. LC 82-60736. 120p. 1982. softcover 8.95 (ISBN 0-913420-13-1). Olympus Pub Co.

Carlbom, Hans. Horseshoe-Nail Crafting. LC 73-83450. (Little Craft Book Ser.). 48p. (gr. 7 up). 1973. 6.95 (ISBN 0-8069-5280-6); PLB 8.99 (ISBN 0-8069-5281-4). Sterling.

Carle, Don De see DeCarle, Don.

Carle, Eric. Catch the Ball. 10p. 1982. 4.95 (ISBN 0-399-20885-2, Philomel). Putnam Pub Group.

--The Grouchy Ladybug. LC 77-3170. (Illus.). (ps). 1977. 9.57i (ISBN 0-690-01391-4, TYC-J); PLB 10.89 (ISBN 0-690-01392-2). Har-Row.

--The Honeybee & the Robber: A Moving Picture Book. (Illus.). 16p. (gr. 4-8). 1981. 10.95 (ISBN 0-399-20767-8, Philomel). Putnam Pub Group.

--Let's Paint a Rainbow. 10p. 1982. 4.95 (ISBN 0-399-20881-X, Philomel). Putnam Pub Group.

--One, Two, Three to the Zoo. LC 68-26967. (Illus.). (ps-2). 1968. 8.99 (ISBN 0-399-61172-X, Philomel); pap. 4.95 (ISBN 0-399-20847-X). Putnam Pub Group.

--Very Hungry Caterpillar. LC 70-82764. (Ger). (ps-2). 1969. 9.95 o.p. (ISBN 0-399-20853-4, Philomel); PLB 9.99 o.p. (ISBN 0-399-61193-2). Putnam Pub Group.

--Watch Out, a Giant! LC 78-8244. (Illus.). (ps-3). 1978. 8.95 (ISBN 0-529-05455-8, Philomel); PLB 8.99 (ISBN 0-529-05456-6, 05456). Putnam Pub Group.

--What's for Lunch? 10p. 1982. 4.95 (ISBN 0-399-20897-6, Philomel). Putnam Pub Group.

Carle, Eric, retold by. & illus. Twelve Tales from Aesop. LC 80-17824. (Illus.). 32p. (gr. 1 up). 1980. 9.95 (ISBN 0-399-20753-8, Philomel); PLB 9.99 (ISBN 0-399-61163-0). Putnam Pub Group.

Carles, A. B. Sheep Production in the Tropics. (Tropical Handbooks). (Illus.). 200p. 1982. 29.00x (ISBN 0-19-859449-6). Oxford U Pr.

Carleson, Lennart, jt. auth. see Salem, Raphael.

Carleton, A. J. Absorption of Odours: Summary Report, 1979. 1981. 65.00x (ISBN 0-686-97007-1, Pub. by W Spring England). State Mutual Bk.

--Odour Control by Thermal Incineration, 1978. 1981. 75.00x (ISBN 0-686-97130-2, Pub. by W Spring England). State Mutual Bk.

Carleton, A. J. & French, R. J. Hydraulic Transport of Limestone Aggregates & Colliery Spoil, 1978. 1981. 80.00x (ISBN 0-686-97086-1, Pub. by W Spring England). State Mutual Bk.

Carleton, Bruce. Fun Is Sick, Vol. 1. Blair, Alex, ed. (Illus.). 64p. (Orig.). 1982. pap. 10.00 (ISBN 0-938918-02-8). Chong-Donnie.

Carleton, J. Henry. The Prarie Logbooks: Dragoon Campaigns to the Pawnee Villages in 1844, & to the Rocky Mountains in 1845. Pelzer, Louis, ed. (Illus.). xviii, 295p. 1983. 19.95x (ISBN 0-8032-1422-7); pap. 7.50 (ISBN 0-8032-6314-7, BB 845, Bison). U of Nebr Pr.

Carleton, Nancy G., ed. see Dukes, Hubert N.

Carley, Eliane. Classics from a French Kitchen: Delicious Recipes, both Ancient & Modern, Together with Savory History & Gastronomic Lore in the Grand Tradition of the Cuisine of France. 1983. 14.95 (ISBN 0-517-54919-0). Crown.

Carley, Isabel M. Simple Settings of American Folk Songs: For Orff Ensemble Book 2. 1981. pap. 1.75 (ISBN 0-918812-07-0). Magnamusic.

Carley, James. The Medieval & the Modern. 127p. 1983. 9.95 (ISBN 0-8180-2302-3). Horizon.

Carley, Kenneth. Minnesota in the Civil War. 6.95 (ISBN 0-87018-006-1). Ross.

Carley, Michael J. & Derow, Ellan O. Social Impact Assessment: A Cross-Disciplinary Guide to the Literature. (Social Impact Assessment Ser.). 250p. 1983. lib. bdg. 22.50 (ISBN 0-86531-529-9). Westview.

Carley, Royal V., compiled by. & Lord's Prayer for Today. LC 73-86686. 30p. 1974. 3.95 (ISBN 0-8378-2005-7). Gibson.

Carley, Royal V., ed. Twenty-Third Psalm for Today. LC 73-101450. (Illus.). 1971. 3.95 (ISBN 0-8378-2001-4). Gibson.

Carley, Wayne. Alone Is No Fun. LC 72-1921. (Venture Ser.). (Illus.). 64p. (gr. 2). 1972. PLB 6.89 (ISBN 0-8116-6966-1). Garrard.

--Charley the Mouse Finds Christmas. LC 72-1770. (Venture Ser). (Illus.). 64p. (gr. 2). 1972. PLB 6.89 (ISBN 0-8116-6953-X). Garrard.

--Color My World. LC 73-21584. (Easy Venture Ser). (Illus.). 32p. (gr. k-2). 1974. PLB 6.69 (ISBN 0-8116-6056-7). Garrard.

--Here Comes Mirium the Mixed-up Witch. LC 72-1771. (Venture Ser). (Illus.). 64p. (gr. 2). 1972. PLB 6.27 o.p. (ISBN 0-8116-6959-9). Garrard.

--Mixed-up Magic. LC 70-157999. (Venture Ser). (Illus.). (gr. 1). 1971. PLB 6.69 (ISBN 0-8116-6711-1). Garrard.

--Percy the Parrot Passes the Puck. LC 72-1925. (Venture Ser). (Illus.). 64p. (gr. 2). 1972. PLB 6.89 (ISBN 0-8116-6969-6). Garrard.

--Percy the Parrot Strikes Out. LC 77-157998. (Venture Ser). (Illus.). (gr. 1). 1971. PLB 6.69 (ISBN 0-8116-6710-3). Garrard.

--Percy the Parrot Yelled Quiet! LC 73-21585. (Easy Venture Ser). (Illus.). 32p. (gr. k-2). 1974. PLB 6.69 (ISBN 0-8116-6058-3). Garrard.

--Puppy Love. LC 75-161027. (Venture Ser). (Illus.). (gr. 1). 1971. PLB 6.69 (ISBN 0-8116-6716-2). Garrard.

--Unlucky Day at Camp How-Ja-Do. LC 72-1075. (Venture Ser). (Illus.). 64p. (gr. 2). 1972. PLB 6.89 (ISBN 0-8116-6955-6). Garrard.

--The Witch Who Forgot. LC 73-21729. (Easy Venture Ser). (Illus.). 32p. (gr. k-2). 1974. PLB 6.69 (ISBN 0-8116-6057-5). Garrard.

Carlgren, M. W. Swedish Foreign Policy During the Second World War. LC 77-78681. (Illus.). 1977. 22.50x (ISBN 0-312-78058-3). St Martin.

Carli, Franco De see De Carli, Franco.

Carlile, Clancy. Honkytonk Man. 320p. Date not set. pap. 2.95 (ISBN 0-515-07125-0). Jove Pubns.

--Spore Seven. 288p. 1979. pap. 2.25 o.p. (ISBN 0-380-49031-5, 49031). Avon.

Carlile, Clark S. Thirty-Eight Basic Speech Experiences. rev. ed. 1977. lib. bdg. 6.75 o.p. (ISBN 0-931054-03-6). Clark Pub.

--Thirty Eighty Basic Speech Experiences. 7th ed. 235p. 1982. pap. text ed. 6.75 (ISBN 0-931054-07-9). Clark Pub.

Carlile, M. J., et al. Molecular & Cellular Aspects of Microbial Evolution. LC 80-42172. (Society for General Microbiology Ser.: Symposium 32). (Illus.). 400p. 1981. 69.50 (ISBN 0-521-24108-1). Cambridge U Pr.

Carlile, R. E. & Gillett, B. E. Fortran & Computer Mathematics. LC 72-95446. 520p. 1974. 37.95x (ISBN 0-87814-016-6). Pennwell Pub.

Carlin, Harriette L. Medical Secretary Medispeller: A Transcription Aid. 260p. 1973. pap. 11.50x (ISBN 0-398-02579-7). C C Thomas.

Carling & Moore. Language Understanding. LC 82-10568. 240p. 1982. 22.50x (ISBN 0-312-46922-5). St Martin.

Carlino, Lawrence L. The Proto-Spin Theory of the Universe. (Illus.). 1983. 10.95 (ISBN 0-533-05344-7). Vantage.

Carlinsky, Dan. Celebrity Yearbook. 96p. (Orig.). 1982. pap. 5.95 (ISBN 0-8431-0619-0). Price Stern.

--The Great Nineteen Sixties Quiz. LC 77-11817. (Illus., Orig.). 1978. pap. 4.95i o.p. (ISBN 0-06-090646-4, CN 646, CN). Har-Row.

Carlinsky, Dan & Heim, David. Bicycle Tours in & Around New York. LC 75-4036. 1975. pap. 2.95 (ISBN 0-02-938850-3). Hagstrom Map.

Carlinsky, Dan, ed. College Humor. (Illus.). 228p. 1982. pap. 9.57i (ISBN 0-06-464052-3, BN 4052). B&N NY.

Carlisle, Douglas H. Venezuelan Foreign Policy: Its Organization & Beginning. LC 78-57979. 1978. pap. text ed. 10.50 (ISBN 0-8191-0317-9). U Pr of Amer.

Carlisle, E. Dialogues on "MAC" Management Organization. (New Press Ser.). 112p. 1983. 10.95 (ISBN 0-07-009843-3). McGraw.

Carlisle, E. Fred. Loren Eiseley: The Development of a Writer. LC 82-8459. 216p. 1983. 18.95 (ISBN 0-252-00987-8). U of Ill Pr.

Carlisle, Howard M. Management: Concepts & Situations. LC 75-29382. (Illus.). 608p. 1976. text ed. 22.95 (ISBN 0-574-19230-1, 13-2230); instr's guide avail. (ISBN 0-574-19231-X, 13-2231). SRA.

--Management Essentials: Concepts & Applications. LC 78-16303. 1979. text ed. 17.95 o.s.i. (ISBN 0-574-19370-7, 13-2370); instr's guide avail. o.s.i. (ISBN 0-574-19371-5, 13-2371); study guide 6.95 o.s.i. (ISBN 0-574-19372-3, 13-2372); lecture suppl. 2.95 o.s.i. (ISBN 0-574-19373-1, 13-2373). SRA.

Carlisle, Norman. Satellites: Servants of Man. LC 72-141456. 96p. (gr. 4-6). 1971. 8.95i o.p. (ISBN 0-397-31367-5, JBL-J). Har-Row.

Carlisle, Olga A. & Styron, Rose, trs. Modern Russian Poetry. 224p. (gr. 7 up). 1972. 9.95 o.p. (ISBN 0-670-48387-7). Viking Pr.

Carlisle, Rodney P. Hearst & the New Deal - The Progressive As Reactionary. Freidel, Frank, ed. LC 78-62378. (Modern American History Ser.: Vol. 4). 1979. lib. bdg. 28.00 o.s.i. (ISBN 0-8240-3628-X). Garland Pub.

Carll, Barbara & Richard, Nancy. One Piece of the Puzzle: A School Readiness Manual. rev. ed. LC 77-76434. (Illus.). 1977. pap. text ed. 6.70x (ISBN 0-932950-00-0). Athena Pubns.

Carlo & Murphy. Merchandising Mathmematics. 179p. 1981. pap. 10.00 (ISBN 0-8273-1416-7); instructor's guide 3.25 (ISBN 0-8273-1417-5). Delmar.

Carlo, Mona, jt. auth. see Scott, Gwendolyn D.

Carlock, Charlene, jt. auth. see Frey, Diane.

Carlon, Patricia, et al. Illinois Supplement for Real Estate Principles & Practices. (Business & Economics Ser.). 112p. 1976. 4.95 o.p. (ISBN 0-675-08583-7). Merrill.

Carlos, Alberto J., ed. see Hernandez, Jose.

Carlquist, Sherwin. Ecological Strategies of Xylem Evolution. LC 74-76382. (Illus.). 1975. 30.00x (ISBN 0-520-02730-2). U of Cal Pr.

Carlsen, Darvey. Graphic Arts. new ed. (gr. 7-12). 1977. text ed. 12.28 (ISBN 0-87002-177-X); tchr's guide free. Bennett IL.

Carlsen, Fran, jt. ed. see Lace, Vivian.

Carlsen, G. R. & Gilbert, Miriam. British & Western Literature. 3rd ed. (Themes & Writers Ser.). (Illus.). 1979. text ed. 21.52 (ISBN 0-07-009871-9); tchr's resource guide 17.76 (ISBN 0-07-009872-7); tests 98.76 (ISBN 0-07-009873-5). McGraw.

Carlsen, G. R., et al. Focus: Themes in Literature. 2nd ed. 1975. 18.20 (ISBN 0-07-009907-3, W); tchr's. resource guide 8.96 (ISBN 0-07-009913-8). McGraw.

--Perception: Themes in Literature. 2nd ed. 1975. 18.20 (ISBN 0-07-009908-1, W); tchr's resource guide 8.96 (ISBN 0-07-009914-6). McGraw.

Carlsen, G. Robert. Books & the Teenage Reader: A Guide for Teachers, Librarians & Parents. 2nd, rev. ed. LC 78-2117. 1980. 12.45i (ISBN 0-06-010626-3, HarpT). Har-Row.

--Encounters: Themes in Literature. 3rd ed. (Themes & Writers Ser.). (Illus.). (gr. 10). 1979. text ed. 19.96 (ISBN 0-07-009863-8, W); tchr's. resource guide 17.76 (ISBN 0-07-009864-6); tests 87.52 (ISBN 0-07-009865-4). McGraw.

--Focus: Themes in Literature. 3rd ed. (Themes & Writers Ser.). (Illus.). (gr. 7). 1979. text ed. 18.20 (ISBN 0-07-009851-4, W); tchr's. resource guide 16.44 (ISBN 0-07-009852-2); tests 86.56 (ISBN 0-07-009853-0). McGraw.

--Perception: Themes in Literature. 3rd ed. Rothermich, John A., ed. (Themes & Writers Ser.). (Illus.). (gr. 8). 1979. text ed. 18.20 (ISBN 0-07-009855-7, W); resource guide 16.44 (ISBN 0-07-009856-5); tests 86.56 (ISBN 0-07-009857-3). McGraw.

Carlsen, G. Robert & Tovatt, A. Insights: Themes in Literature. 3rd ed. (Themes & Writers Ser). (Illus.). 1979. pap. text ed. 19.96 (ISBN 0-07-009859-X, W); tchr's. resource guide 17.76 (ISBN 0-07-009860-3); tests 87.52 (ISBN 0-07-009861-1). McGraw.

Carlsen, G. Robert, et al. Western Literature: Themes & Writers. 2nd ed. (Themes & Writers Ser.). (Illus.). 768p. (gr. 12). 1975. text ed. 21.52 (ISBN 0-07-009906-5, W); tchr's. resource guide 8.96 (ISBN 0-07-009912-X). McGraw.

--American Literature: Themes & Writers. 3rd ed. (Illus.). (gr. 11). 1979. text ed. 21.08 (ISBN 0-07-009867-0); tchr's resource guide 17.76 (ISBN 0-07-009868-9); tests 98.76 (ISBN 0-07-009869-7). McGraw.

Carlsen, G. Robert, et al, eds. Encounters: Themes in Literature. 2nd ed. Tovatt. (Themes & Writers Ser). (Illus.). 768p. (gr. 10). 1972. text ed. 20.68 (ISBN 0-07-009904-9, W); tchr's. resource guide 8.96 (ISBN 0-07-009910-3). McGraw.

--American Literature: Themes & Writers. 2nd ed. (Illus.). 768p. (gr. 11). 1972. text ed. 21.84 (ISBN 0-07-009905-7, W); tchr's resource guide 8.96 (ISBN 0-07-009911-1). McGraw.

Carlsen, James C. Melodic Perception: A Program for Self-Instruction. 1965. text ed. 22.00 (ISBN 0-07-009975-8, C); instructor's manual 7.95 (ISBN 0-07-009977-4); tapes 249.00 (ISBN 0-07-009976-6). McGraw.

Carlsen, Martin, et al. Student Workbook for Introduction to the Administration of Justice. 1978. pap. text ed. 10.95 (ISBN 0-8403-1921-5). Kendall-Hunt.

Carlsen, Peter & Wilson, William. Manstyle: The GQ Guide to Fashion, Fitness, & Grooming. (Illus.). 1977. 14.95 (ISBN 0-517-53076-7, C N Potter Bks); pap. 8.95 (ISBN 0-517-53077-5, C N Potter). Crown.

Carlsen, Robert & McHugh, James. Handbook of Research & Development Forms & Formats. (Illus.). 1978. pap. 39.95 (ISBN 0-13-380766-5, Busn). P-H.

Carlsen, Robert D. Handbook & Portfolio of Successful Sales Proposals. LC 82-15085. 506p. looseleaf bdg. 125.00 (ISBN 0-13-380808-4, Busn). P-H.

Carlsen, Robert D. & Lewis, James A. The Systems Analysis Workbook: A Complete Guide to Project Implementation & Control. 2nd ed. 288p. 1979. 45.00 (ISBN 0-686-98491-9). P-H.

Carlsen, Robert D. & McHugh, James F. Handbook of Sales & Marketing Forms & Formats. (Illus.). 1978. 54.95 (ISBN 0-13-380857-2, Busn). P-H.

Carlsen-Jones, M. Introduction to Logic. 624p. 1983. 22.95 (ISBN 0-07-032890-0). McGraw.

Carlson. Spring Manufacturing Handbook. (Mechanical Engineering Ser.). 344p. 1982. 45.00 (ISBN 0-8247-1678-7). Dekker.

Carlson & Lassey. Rural Society & Environment in America. (Agricultural Science Ser.). (Illus.). 448p. 1981. text ed. 23.50x (ISBN 0-07-009959-6, C). McGraw.

Carlson, A. B. Communications Systems. 2nd ed. (Electrical & Electronic Engineering Ser.). 1974. text ed. 37.50 (ISBN 0-07-009957-X, C); manual 20.00solutions (ISBN 0-07-009958-8). McGraw.

Carlson, A. Bruce & Gisser, David G. Electrical Engineering: Concepts & Applications. LC 80-21519. (Electrical Engineering Ser.). 640p. 1981. text ed. 32.95 (ISBN 0-201-03940-0); solutions manual 4.00 (ISBN 0-201-03941-9). A-W.

Carlson, A. Bruce, jt. auth. see Frederick, Dean K.

Carlson, Albert D., jt. auth. see Soucek, Branko.

Carlson, Betty, jt. auth. see Smith, Jane S.

Carlson, Bruce M. Patten's Foundations of Embryology. 4th, rev. ed. (Organismal Biology Ser.). (Illus.). 608p. 1981. text ed. 29.95 (ISBN 0-07-009875-1, C). McGraw.

Carlson, C. Lennart. The First Magazine. LC 74-3762. 281p. 1975. Repr. of 1938 ed. lib. bdg. 18.25x (ISBN 0-8371-7464-3, CAFM). Greenwood.

Carlson, Carole, jt. auth. see Ross, Skip.

Carlson, Carole C. Corrie Ten Boom: Her Life, Her Faith. (Illus.). 224p. 1982. 12.95 (ISBN 0-8007-1293-5). Revell.

Carlson, Carole C., jt. auth. see Rogers, Dale E.

Carlson, Chas., tr. see Mihaly, Ida F.

Carlson, D. & Shield, R., eds. Finite Elasticity. 1982. lib. bdg. 79.00 (ISBN 90-247-2629-8, Pub. by Martinus Nijhoff Netherlands). Kluwer Boston.

Carlson, Dale. The Frog People. (Illus.). 80p. (gr. 7 up). 1982. 8.95 (ISBN 0-525-45107-2, 0869-260, Skinny Bk). Dutton.

--The Plant People. (YA) 1979. pap. 1.75 (ISBN 0-440-96959-X, LFL). Dell.

Carlson, Dale & Fitzgibbon, Dan. Manners That Matter: For People Under Twenty-One. LC 82-9761. 144p. (gr. 7-12). 1983. 8.95 (ISBN 0-525-44008-9, 0869-260). Dutton.

Carlson, Delbert G. & Giffin, James M. Cat Owner's Home Veterinary Handbook. LC 82-23383. (Illus.). 392p. 1983. 17.95 (ISBN 0-87605-814-4). Howell Bk.

Carlson, Diane. You Can't Tell Me What to Do! Uhlich, Richard, ed. (Bluejeans Paperback Ser.). (Illus., Orig.). (gr. 7-12). 1978. pap. text ed. 1.25 o.p. (ISBN 0-8374-0041-4). Xerox Ed Pubns.

Carlson, Edgar M. The Church & the Public Conscience. LC 79-8710. xii, 104p. 1981. Repr. of 1956 ed. lib. bdg. 19.25x (ISBN 0-313-22195-2, CACH). Greenwood.

Carlson, Elof A., ed. see Muller, Hermann J.

Carlson, Faith. Alternate Methods of Communication. 1981. pap. text ed. 3.95x (ISBN 0-8134-2237-X). Interstate.

Carlson, G. R. Comment Etudier et Enselgner la Parole de Dieu. Cosson, Annie, ed. Orig. Title: Preparing to Teach God's Word. (Fr.). 1982. pap. 2.00 (ISBN 0-8297-1235-6). Life Pubs Intl.

Carlson, G. Raymond. La Palabra Viva Y Eficaz. Marosi, Esteban & Carrodeguas, Andy, eds. Powell, David, tr. 176p. (Span.). 1982. pap. 2.00 (ISBN 0-8297-1254-2). Life Pubs Intl.

--Prayer & the Christian's Devotional Life. LC 80-83522. (Radiant Life Ser.). 128p. (Orig.). 1981. 1.95 (ISBN 0-88243-878-6, 02-0878); teacher's ed. 3.95 (ISBN 0-88243-190-0, 32-0190). Gospel Pub.

--Spiritual Dynamics. (Radiant Life Ser). 1976. pap. 1.95 (ISBN 0-88243-894-8, 02-0894); teacher's ed 3.95 (ISBN 0-88243-168-4, 32-0168). Gospel Pub.

Carlson, Glenn. Airplane Talk. 276p. 1982. pap. 16.95 (ISBN 0-686-43398-X, Pub. by Watosh Pub). Aviation.

Carlson, Gordon. Get Me Out of Here! Uhlich, Richard, ed. (Bluejeans Paperbacks Ser.). (Illus., Orig.). (gr. 7-12). 1978. pap. text ed. 1.25- o.p. (ISBN 0-8374-0040-6). Xerox Ed Pubns.

Carlson, Harold E. Endocrinology. (UCLA Series of Internal Medicine Today: A Comprehensive Postgraduate Library). 328p. 1983. 35.00 (ISBN 0-471-09553-2, Pub. By Wiley Med). Wiley.

Carlson, Harry G. Strindberg & the Poetry of Myth. 252p. 1982. 22.50x (ISBN 0-520-04442-8). U of Cal Pr.

Carlson, Harry G., tr. see Strindberg, August.

Carlson, Jon, jt. auth. see Hendricks, Gay.

Carlson, Karen & Meyers, Alan. Speaking with Confidence. 1977. pap. 12.50x (ISBN 0-673-15022-4). Scott F.

Carlson, Katherine. Casualties. LC 82-61652. (Minnesota Voices Project Ser.: No. 9). (Illus.). 124p. 1982. pap. 5.00. New Rivers Pr.

Carlson, Kurt. The Law of the Sea Treaty: Current Choices. 64p. 1981. 2.50 (ISBN 0-686-81729-X). World Without War.

Carlson, Lars A. & Pernow, Bengt, eds. Metabolic Risk Factors in Ischemic Cardiovascular Disease. 264p. 1982. text ed. 32.50 (ISBN 0-89004-614-X). Raven.

Carlson, Lars A., et al, eds. see International Conference on Atherosclerosis, Milan, November 1977.

Carlson, Loraine. The TraveLeer Guide to Yucatan. rev. ed. LC 82-17449. (Illus.). 208p. (Orig.). 1982. pap. 6.95 (ISBN 0-932554-04-0). Upland Pr.

Carlson, Lucile. Africa's Lands & Nations. 1967. 17.95 o.p. (ISBN 0-07-009950-2, C). McGraw.

Carlson, Margaret B. & Shafer, Ronald G. How to Get Your Car Repaired Without Getting Gypped. LC 72-11811. (Illus.). 288p. 1973. 11.49i (ISBN 0-06-010612-3, HarpT). Har-Row.

Carlson, Nancy. Harriet & the Garden. LC 81-18136. (Illus.). 32p. (ps-3). 1982. lib. bdg. 6.95g (ISBN 0-87614-184-X). Carolrhoda Bks.

--Harriet & the Roller Coaster. LC 81-18138. (Illus.). 32p. (ps-3). 1982. lib. bdg. 6.95g (ISBN 0-87614-183-1). Carolrhoda Bks.

--Harriet & Walt. LC 81-18137. (Illus.). 32p. (ps-3). 1982. lib. bdg. 6.95g (ISBN 0-87614-185-8). Carolrhoda Bks.

--Harriet's Halloween Candy. LC 81-18140. (Illus.). 32p. (ps-3). 1982. lib. bdg. 6.95g (ISBN 0-87614-182-3). Carolrhoda Bks.

--Harriet's Recital. LC 81-18135. (Illus.). 32p. (ps-3). 1982. lib. bdg. 6.95g (ISBN 0-87614-181-5). Carolrhoda Bks.

Carlson, Nancy, ed. see Pederson, Rolf A.

Carlson, Natalie S. Alphonse, That Bearded One. LC 54-5151. (Illus.). (gr. k-3). 1954. 7.95 (ISBN 0-15-202648-7, HJ). HarBraceJ.

--Brother for the Orphelines. LC 59-5313. (Illus.). (gr. 2-6). 1959. PLB 10.89 o.p. (ISBN 0-06-020961-5, HarpJ). Har-Row.

--Carnival in Paris. LC 62-13319. (Illus.). (gr. 2-6). PLB 12.89 (ISBN 0-06-020971-2, HarpJ). Har-Row.

--Family Under the Bridge. LC 58-5292. (Illus.). (gr. 3-7). 1958. PLB 12.89 (ISBN 0-06-020991-7, HarpJ). Har-Row.

--Happy Orpheline. LC 57-9260. (Illus.). (gr. 3-6). 1957. PLB 12.89 (ISBN 0-06-021007-9, HarpJ). Har-Row.

--Luvvy & the Girls. LC 77-145999. (Illus.). (gr. 4-8). 1971. 5.95 o.p. (ISBN 0-06-020968-2, HarpJ); PLB 9.89 (ISBN 0-06-020969-0). Har-Row.

--Luvvy & the Girls. LC 77-145999. (Illus.). 176p. (gr. 4-8). 1975. pap. 1.50 o.p. (ISBN 0-06-440071-9, Trophy). Har-Row.

--Orphelines in the Enchanted Castle. LC 63-14368. (Illus.). (gr. 3-7). 1964. PLB 10.89 o.p. (ISBN 0-06-021046-X, HarpJ). Har-Row.

--Pet for the Orphelines. LC 62-7947. (Illus.). (gr. 3-7). 1962. PLB 10.89 o.p. (ISBN 0-06-021056-7, HarpJ). Har-Row.

--Talking Cat & Other Stories of French Canada. LC 52-5429. (Illus.). (gr. 3-6). 1952. PLB 9.89 (ISBN 0-06-021081-8, HarpJ). Har-Row.

Carlson, Norman & Keevil, Walter, eds. Chicago's Rapid Transit: Rolling Stock, 1947-1976, Vol. 2, Bulletin No. 115. LC 72-96588. (Illus.). 1976. 23.00 (ISBN 0-915348-15-2). Central Electric.

Carlson, Oliver. Brisbane: A Candid Biography. LC 75-98829. Repr. of 1937 ed. lib. bdg. 16.25x (ISBN 0-8371-2980-X, CABR). Greenwood.

Carlson, Paul H. Texas Woolybacks: The Range Sheep & Goat Industry. LC 82-40311. (Illus.). 272p. 1982. 17.50x (ISBN 0-89096-133-6). Tex A&M Univ Pr.

Carlson, Peter. Roughneck: The Life & Times of Big Bill Haywood. (Illus.). 1983. 17.00x (ISBN 0-393-01621-8). Norton.

Carlson, R. & Granstrom, B., eds. The Representation of Speech in the Peripheral Auditory System: Proceedings of the Symposium, Stockholm, Sweden, May, 1982. 294p. 1982. 63.00 (ISBN 0-444-80447-1, Biomedical Pr). Elsevier.

Carlson, R. W., ed. see Vollrath, H. K.

Carlson, R. W., ed. see Wood, S. R. & Nichols, H. E.

Carlson, Richard O. School Superintendents: Careers & Performance. LC 72-175818. 172p. 1972. text ed. 9.95x (ISBN 0-675-09165-9). Merrill.

Carlson, Rick J. The End of Medicine. LC 75-6856. (Health, Medicine & Society Ser). 1975. pap. 33.95x (ISBN 0-471-13494-5, Pub. by Wiley-Interscience). Wiley.

Carlson, Rick J. & Cunningham, Robert, eds. Future Directions in Health Care: A New Public Policy. LC 78-9568. 272p. 1978. prof ref 20.00x (ISBN 0-88410-519-9). Ballinger Pub.

Carlson, Rodger D. The Economics for the Profitable Mining & Marketing of Gold, Silver, Copper, Lead & Zinc Ores. LC 81-40818. (Illus.). 88p. (Orig.). 1982. lib. bdg. 18.25 (ISBN 0-8191-2021-9); pap. text ed. 7.00 (ISBN 0-8191-2022-7). U Pr of Amer.

Carlson, Sevinc. Indonesia's Oil. LC 76-30852. (Westview Special Studies in Natural Resources Management). (Illus.). 1977. lib. bdg. 30.00 o.p. (ISBN 0-89158-202-9). Westview.

Carlson, Sylvia, jt. auth. see Carlson, Verne.

Carlson, Sylvia, jt. auth. see Stanton, Marjorie.

Carlson, T. A. X-Ray Photoelectron Spectroscopy. LC 77-28499. (Benchmark Papers in Physical Chemistry & Chemical Physics: Vol. 2). 341p. 1978. 51.00 (ISBN 0-87933-325-1). Hutchinson Ross.

Carlson, Verne. The Cowboy Cookbook. LC 80-68342. (Illus.). 186p. 1981. 10.95 o.p. (ISBN 0-937844-00-4); pap. 6.95 o.p. (ISBN 0-937844-01-2). Double C Inc.

--Translation of Film-Video Terms, 5 bks. 160p. 1983. pap. 50.00 set (ISBN 0-943288-05-3). Double C Inc.

--Translation of Film-Video Terms into French. 160p. 1983. pap. 10.95 (ISBN 0-943288-00-2). Double C Inc.

--Translation of Film-Video Terms into: German. 160p. 1983. pap. 10.95 (ISBN 0-943288-01-0). Double C Inc.

--Translation of Film-Video Terms into: Italian. 160p. 1983. pap. 10.95 (ISBN 0-943288-02-9). Double C Inc.

--Translation of Film-Video Terms into: Japanese. 160p. 1983. pap. 10.95 (ISBN 0-943288-04-5). Double C Inc.

--Translation of Film-Video Terms Into Series, 5 Bks. Incl. French (ISBN 0-943288-00-2); German (ISBN 0-943288-01-0); Italian (ISBN 0-943288-02-9); Spanish (ISBN 0-943288-03-7); Japanese (ISBN 0-943288-04-5). 1982. pap. 10.95 ea.; 50.00 set (ISBN 0-686-36361-2). Double C Inc.

--Translation of Film-Video Terms into: Spanish. 160p. 1983. pap. 10.95 (ISBN 0-943288-03-7). Double C Inc.

Carlson, Verne & Carlson, Sylvia. Professional Camerman's Handbook. rev ed. (Illus.). 575p. 1981. 24.95 (ISBN 0-8174-5548-5, Amphoto). Waston-Guptill.

--Professional Sixteen & Thirty-Five Millimeter Camerman's Handbook. 2nd ed. (Illus.). 416p. 1974. 19.95 o.p. (ISBN 0-8174-0528-3, Amphoto). Watson-Guptill.

Carlson, Victor. Hubert Robert: Drawings & Watercolors. LC 78-22022. (Illus.). pap. 5.00 (ISBN 0-89468-040-4). Natl Gallery Art.

Carlson, Victor I. Picasso Drawings & Watercolors, 1899-1907 in the Collection of the Baltimore Museum of Art. LC 76-41022. 1977. pap. 25.00 (ISBN 0-912298-43-X); pap. 17.50 (ISBN 0-912298-42-1). Baltimore Mus.

Carlson, William. Sunrise West. LC 79-7043. (Science Fiction Ser.). 192p. 1981. 9.95 o.p. (ISBN 0-385-14498-9). Doubleday.

Carlson, William K. Elysium. LC 81-43542. (Science Fiction Ser.). 192p. 1982. 10.95 (ISBN 0-385-17273-7). Doubleday.

Carlsson, Erik, jt. ed. see Higgins, Charles B.

Carlstedt, G., jt. ed. see Tiberghien, J.

Carlstein, Tommy. Time Resources, Society & Ecology. (Preindustrial Society Ser.: Vol. 1). (Illus.). 300p. 1983. text ed. 30.00x (ISBN 0-04-300082-7); pap. text ed. 14.95x (ISBN 0-04-300083-5). Allen Unwin.

Carlstein, Tommy, et al, eds. Timing Space & Spacing Time, 3 vols. Incl. Vol. I. Making Sense of Time. 29.95x o.s.i. (ISBN 0-470-26511-6); Vol. II. Human Activity & Time Geography. 49.95x o.s.i. (ISBN 0-470-26513-2); Vol. III. Time & Regional Dynamics. 29.95x o.s.i. (ISBN 0-470-26512-4). 1979. Halsted Pr.

Carlton, Charles. Charles the First: The Personal Monarch. (Illus.). 432p. 1983. price not set (ISBN 0-7100-9485-X). Routledge & Kegan.

Carlton, David. Mill & Town in South Carolina, 1880-1920. 336p. 1982. text ed. 32.50x (ISBN 0-8071-1042-6); pap. text ed. 14.95x (ISBN 0-8071-1059-0). La State U Pr.

Carlton, David & Schaerf, Carlo, eds. The Arms Race in the Nineteen Eighties. LC 81-21303. 256p. 1982. 27.50x (ISBN 0-312-04946-3). St Martin.

--Contemporary Terror: Studies in Sub-State Violence. 1981. 27.50 (ISBN 0-312-16841-1). St Martin.

--The Dynamics of the Arms Race. LC 74-20106. 244p. 1975. 33.95x o.s.i. (ISBN 0-470-13480-1). Halsted Pr.

Carlton, Doren van see Van Carlton, Doren, et al.

Carlton, Eric. Patterns of Belief, 2 vols. Incl. Vol. 1. Peoples & Religion. 130p (ISBN 0-04-377004-5); Vol. 2. Religions in Society. 140p. pap. 6.95 2 vols. (ISBN 0-04-377005-3). 1973. pap. 6.95 ea. Attic Pr.

Carlton, Frank T. Economic Influences Upon Educational Progress in the United States 1820-1850. LC 66-11657. (Orig.). 1966. text ed. 5.00xo.p. (ISBN 0-8077-1143-8); pap. text ed. 4.50x o.p. (ISBN 0-8077-1140-3). Tchrs Coll.

Carlton, James T., ed. see Light.

Carlton, R. J., jt. auth. see Campbell, L. J.

Carlton, R. J., jt. ed. see Campbell, L. J.

Carlton, William M. Laboratory Studies in General Botany. (Illus.). 426p. (Orig.). 1961. pap. 17.50 (ISBN 0-471-06806-3). Wiley.

Carlucci, Rocco, jt. auth. see Gargiulo, Albert F.

Carlwright, jt. auth. see Rawson.

Carlyle, Ken. Challenging & Highly Profitable Business Careers for the New College Graduate Eager for Success & Adventure. (Illus.). 1977. 47.50 (ISBN 0-89266-078-3). Am Classical Coll Pr.

Carlyle, Thomas. The French Revolution, 2 vols. in 1. 1980. Repr. of 1906 ed. 15.95x o.p. (ISBN 0-460-10031-9, Evman). Biblio Dist.

--On Heroes, Hero-Worship & the Heroic in History. (World's Classics Ser: No. 62). 1975. 12.95 (ISBN 0-19-250062-7). Oxford U Pr.

--On Heroes, Hero-Worship & the Heroic in History. Niemeyer, Carl, ed. LC 66-12130. (Illus.). xxviii, 255p. 1966. pap. 6.95x (ISBN 0-8032-5030-4, BB 334, Bison). U of Nebr Pr.

--The Psychological Theory of the Hero in History & in Politics. (The Essential Library of the Great Philosophers Ser.). (Illus.). 121p. 1983. 61.85 (ISBN 0-686-82208-0). Am Inst Psych.

Carlyle, Thomas, tr. see Von Goethe, Johann W. & Steiner, Rudolf.

Carlyle, William. A Comprehensive Outline Guide to Ancient Empires. 1983. 8.95 (ISBN 0-533-05166-5). Vantage.

Carmack, Robert M. Quichean Civilization: The Ethnohistoric, Ethnographic & Archaelogical Sources. LC 70-149948. (Illus.). 1973. 37.50x (ISBN 0-520-01963-6). U of Cal Pr.

Carman, Bliss, ed. The World's Best Poetry, Vol. I: Home & Friendship. LC 80-84498. (The Granger Anthology Ser.: Ser. I). 480p. 1981. Repr. of 1904 ed. lib. bdg. 39.95x (ISBN 0-89609-202-X). Granger Bk.

--The World's Best Poetry: Vol. IX-Tragedy & Humor. LC 81-83524. (The Granger Anthology, Series I). 494p. 1982. Repr. of 1904 ed. lib. bdg. 39.95x (ISBN 0-89609-210-0). Granger Bk.

--The World's Best Poetry: Vol. VI-Fancy & Sentiment. LC 81-83521. (The Granger Anthology, Series I). 486p. 1982. Repr. of 1904 ed. lib. bdg. 39.95x (ISBN 0-89609-207-0). Granger Bk.

--The World's Best Poetry: Vol. VII-Descriptive & Narrative. LC 81-83522. (The Grannger Anthology, Series I). 474p. 1982. Repr. of 1904 ed. lib. bdg. 39.95 (ISBN 0-89609-208-9). Granger Bk.

--The World's Best Poetry: Vol. VIII-National Spirit. new ed. LC 81-83523. (The Granger Anthology, Series I). 498p. 1982. Repr. of 1904 ed. lib. bdg. 39.95x (ISBN 0-89609-209-7). Granger Bk.

--The World's Best Poetry: Vol. X-Poetical Quotations, General Indexes. new ed. LC 81-83525. (The Granger Anthology, Series I). 538p. 1983. Repr. of 1904 ed. lib. bdg. 39.95x (ISBN 0-89609-211-9). Granger Bk.

--The World's Best Poetry: Vol. 2-Love. LC 80-84498. (The Granger Anthology Ser.: Ser. I). 504p. 1981. Repr. of 1904 ed. lib. bdg. 39.95x (ISBN 0-89609-203-8). Granger Bk.

--The World's Best Poetry: Vol. 3, Sorrow - Consolation. LC 80-84498. (The Granger Anthology: Ser. I). 512p. 1981. Repr. of 1904 ed. lib. bdg. 39.95 (ISBN 0-89609-204-6). Granger Bk.

--The World's Best Poetry: Vol. 4, The Higher Life. LC 80-84498. (The Granger Anthology: Ser. I). 482p. 1981. Repr. of 1904 ed. lib. bdg. 39.95x (ISBN 0-89609-205-4). Granger Bk.

Carman, Harry, et al. History of American People: To 1877, Vol. 1. 1967. pap. text ed. 6.95x (ISBN 0-394-30106-4). Phila Bk Co.

Carman, J. Neale. A Study of the Pseudo-Map Cycle of Arthurian Romance to Investigate Its Historico-Geographic Background & to Provide a Hypothesis As to Its Fabrication. LC 72-88008. 144p. 1973. 14.95x (ISBN 0-7006-0100-7). Univ Pr KS.

Carman, Marilyn J., jt. auth. see Carman, Robert A.

Carman, Robert A. & Adams, W. Royce, Jr. Study Skills: A Student's Guide for Survival. LC 72-4506. (Wiley-Self Teaching Guides). 256p. 1972. 6.95x (ISBN 0-471-13491-0). Wiley.

Carman, Robert A. & Carman, Marilyn J. Basic Mathematical Skills: A Guided Approach. 2nd ed. LC 80-19121. 576p. 1981. pap. text ed. 21.95x (ISBN 0-471-03608-0). Wiley.

--Intermediate Algebra: A Guided Approach. 571p. 1980. text ed. 23.95x (ISBN 0-471-02104-0). Wiley.

Carman, Robert A. & Saunders, Hal M. Mathematics for the Trades: A Guided Approach. LC 79-11491. 580p. 1981. pap. text ed. 19.95x (ISBN 0-471-13481-3); tchr's manual 7.00 (ISBN 0-471-07791-7). Wiley.

Carman, Robert A., jt. auth. see Cain, Jack.

Carman, W. Y. The Royal Artillery. (Men-at-Arms Ser.). (Illus.). 40p. 1976. pap. 7.95 o.p. (ISBN 0-85045-140-X). Hippocrene Bks.

Carmean, E. A. Bellows: The Boxing Pictures. (Illus.). 1982. pap. 9.50 (ISBN 0-89468-028-5). Natl Gallery Art.

Carmean, E. A., jt. auth. see Mond-Fontaine, Isabelle.

Carmean, E. A., Jr. The Morton G. Neumann Family Collection: Picasso Prints & Drawings, III. LC 81-14151. (Illus.). pap. 2.00 (ISBN 0-89468-042-0). Natl Gallery Art.

Carmean, E. A., Jr. & Clark, Trinkett. The Morton G. Neumann Family Collection: Selected Works, Vol. 2. LC 80-20844. (Illus.). pap. 5.00 (ISBN 0-89468-045-5). Natl Gallery Art.

Carmean, E. A., Jr. & Hunter, Sam. The Morton G. Neumann Family Collection: Selected Works, Vol. 1. LC 80-20844. (Illus.). pap. 2.00 (ISBN 0-89468-044-7). Natl Gallery Art.

Carmean, E. R. David Smith. 1982. pap. 17.50 (ISBN 0-89468-061-7). Natl Gallery Art.

Carmel, Peter W. Congress of Neurological Surgeons: Clinical Neurosurgery, Vol. 27. (CNS Ser.). (Illus.). 624p. 1981. lib. bdg. 44.00 (ISBN 0-683-02022-6). Williams & Wilkins.

Carmel, Peter W., ed. Clinical Neurosurgery, Vol. 28. (Congress of Neurological Surgeons Ser.). (Illus.). 534p. 1981. lib. bdg. 48.00 (ISBN 0-683-02023-4). Williams & Wilkins.

Carmel, Peter W., ed. see Congress of Neurological Surgeons.

Carmeli. Statical Theory & Random Matrices. (Pure & Applied Mathematics Ser.). 184p. 1983. 35.00 (ISBN 0-8247-1779-1). Dekker.

Carmeli, Moshe. Classical Fields: General Relativity & Gauge Theory. LC 82-2704. 650p. 1982. 44.95 (ISBN 0-471-86437-4, Pub. by Wiley-Interscience). Wiley.

--Group Theory & General Relativity. (Pure & Applied Physics Ser.). (Illus.). 1977. text ed. 45.00x (ISBN 0-07-009986-3, C). McGraw.

Carmen, Rolando Del see Del Carmen, Rolando.

Carmer, Carl, jt. auth. see Carmer, Elizabeth.

Carmer, Elizabeth & Carmer, Carl. Captain Abner & Henry Q. LC 65-10059. (American Folktales Ser). (gr. 2-5). 1965. PLB 6.69 (ISBN 0-8116-4001-9). Garrard.

--The Susquehanna: From New York to the Chesapeake. LC 64-10245. (Rivers of the World Ser.). (Illus.). (gr. 4-7). 1964. PLB 3.98 (ISBN 0-8116-6360-4). Garrard.

Carmi, S., jt. ed. see Peterson, F.

Carmi, T. At the Stone of Losses. Schulman, Grace, tr. from Hebrew. (Jewish Poetry Ser.). 192p. (Orig.). 1983. 13.95 (ISBN 0-8276-0218-9); pap. 8.95 (ISBN 0-8276-0219-7). Jewish Pubn.

Carmichael, Ann, jt. auth. see Sparkman, Brandon.

Carmichael, C. see Kent, R. T.

Carmichael, D. R. & Willingham, John J. Perspectives in Auditing. 3rd ed. 1979. pap. text ed. 16.95 (ISBN 0-07-009991-X). McGraw.

Carmichael, D. R., jt. auth. see Seidler, L. J.

Carmichael, D. R., jt. auth. see Willingham, John.

Carmichael, Douglas R., jt. auth. see Seidler, Lee J.

Carmichael, E., tr. see Bjornson, Bjornstjerne.

Carmichael, Fitzhugh L. & Nassimbene, Raymond. Changing Aspects of Urban Relief. LC 72-173446. (FDR & the Era of the New Deal Ser.). 94p. 1971. Repr. of 1939 ed. lib. bdg. 19.50 (ISBN 0-306-70370-X). Da Capo.

Carmichael, Hoagy. Stardust Road. LC 79-94603. Repr. of 1948 ed. lib. bdg. 19.00x (ISBN 0-8371-2451-4, CASR). Greenwood.

--The Stardust Road. LC 82-48583. (Midland Bks.). (Illus.). 160p. 1983. pap. 6.95 (ISBN 0-253-20269-8). Ind U Pr.

Carmichael, Hoagy & Longstreet, Stephen. Sometimes I Wonder. LC 76-7577. (Roots of Jazz Ser.). 1976. Repr. of 1965 ed. lib. bdg. 27.50 (ISBN 0-306-70809-4). Da Capo.

Carmichael, Ian S., et al. Igneous Petrology. (International Series in the Earth & Planetary Sciences). (Illus.). 704p. 1974. text ed. 45.00 (ISBN 0-07-009987-1, C). McGraw.

Carmichael, Jim. The Modern Rifle. (Stoeger Bks). (Illus.). 352p. 1976. pap. 5.95 o.s.i. (ISBN 0-695-80686-6). Follett.

Carmichael, Joel, tr. see Aldanov, Mark.

Carmichael, Joel, tr. see Tolstoy, Leo.

Carmichael, John, Jr. & Bulmer, Charles. Labor & Employment Policy. (Orig.). 1979. pap. 6.00 (ISBN 0-918592-35-6). Policy Studies.

Carmichael, John L. His Many Mansions: A Christian Physician's View of Humanity's Quest for the Divine. LC 76-3323. 1977. 7.50 o.p. (ISBN 0-916620-04-2). Portals Pr.

Carmichael, John L., jt. auth. see Bulmer, Charles.

Carmichael, John P., jt. ed. see Griesbach, Marc F.

Carmichael, Oliver C. Graduate Education: A Critique & a Program. LC 77-4229. 1977. Repr. of 1961 ed. lib. bdg. 18.50x (ISBN 0-8371-9585-3, CAGE). Greenwood.

Carmichael, Patrick H., ed. Understanding the Books of the New Testament. rev. ed. LC 61-9583. 1961. pap. 5.95 (ISBN 0-8042-3304-7). John Knox.

--Understanding the Books of the Old Testament. rev. ed. LC 61-9223. 1961. pap. 5.95 (ISBN 0-8042-3316-0). John Knox.

Carmichael, Robert D. & Smith, Edwin R. Mathematical Tables & Formulas. 1931. pap. 3.75 (ISBN 0-486-60111-0). Dover.

Carmichael, Rodick, jt. auth. see Nuttall, Jeff.

Carmichael, Ronald L., jt. auth. see Eckles, Robert W.

Carmichael, Standrod, ed. see Knight, Tanis & Lewin, Larry.

Carmichael, Stephen. The Adrenal Medulla, Vol. 1. Horrobin, D. F., ed. (Annual Research Reviews). 1979. 20.00 (ISBN 0-88831-051-X). Eden Pr.

Carmichael, Stephen W. The Adrenal Medulla, Vol. 2. Horrobin, David F., ed. (Annual Research Reviews). 118p. 1981. 18.00 (ISBN 0-88831-108-7). Eden Pr.

Carmicharl, D. R., jt. auth. see Willingham, John J.

Carmichel, Jim. The Women's Guide to Handguns: A Guide to Safe Self-Defense. 1982. 11.95 (ISBN 0-672-52714-6). Bobbs.

Carmines, E. G., jt. auth. see Zeller, R. A.

Carmines, Edward G., jt. auth. see Zeller, Richard A.

Carmo, Manfredo Do see Do Carmo, Manfredo.

Carmo, Pamela B. Do. see Do Carmo, Pamela B. & Patterson, Angelo T.

Carmody, Denise L. & Carmody, John T. Christianity: An Introduction. 288p. 1982. pap. text ed. 11.95x (ISBN 0-534-01181-0). Wadsworth Pub.

Carmody, Denise L., jt. auth. see Carmody, John.

Carmody, Dennis L. & Carmody, John T. Ways to the Center: An Introduction to World Religions. 432p. 1981. text ed. 21.95x (ISBN 0-534-00890-9). Wadsworth Pub.

Carmody, John. Ecology & Religion: Toward a New Christian Theology of Nature. LC 82-62412. 1983. pap. 6.95 (ISBN 0-8091-2526-9). Paulist Pr.

--The Heart of the Christian Matter: An Ecumenical Approach. 304p. (Orig.). 1983. pap. 11.95 (ISBN 0-687-16765-5). Abingdon.

--Reexamining Conscience. 144p. (Orig.). 1982. pap. 8.95 (ISBN 0-8164-2405-5). Seabury.

Carmody, John & Carmody, Denise L. Religion: The Great Questions. 160p. 1983. pap. price not set. Seabury.
Carmody, John T., jt. auth. see Carmody, Denise L.
Carmody, John T., jt. auth. see Carmody, Dennis L.
Carn, Neil, jt. auth. see Hinds, Dudley.
Carnahan, Brice & Wilkes, James O. Digital Computing & Numerical Methods with Fortran LV Watfor & Watfiv Programming. LC 72-13010. 477p. 1973. text ed. 35.95 (ISBN 0-471-13500-3). Wiley.
Carnahan, Brice, et al. Applied Numerical Methods. LC 67-27555. 604p. 1969. 37.95 (ISBN 0-471-13507-0). Wiley.
Carnall, C. A. The Evaluation of Organisational Change. 130p. 1982. text ed. 31.00x (ISBN 0-566-00519-0). Gower Pub Ltd.
Carnall, Geoffrey, ed. see Butt, John.
Carnap, Rudolf. Two Essays on Entropy. Shimony, Abner, ed. LC 73-94444. 1978. 24.50x (ISBN 0-520-02715-9). U of Cal Pr.
Carnduff, John. An Introduction to Organic Chemistry. LC 78-16664. 194p. 1978. 33.95 (ISBN 0-471-99647-5, Pub. by Wiley-Interscience). Wiley.
Carne, Marcel, jt. auth. see Prevert, Jacques.
Carnegie, Andrew. Empire of Business. LC 68-23280. 1968. Repr. of 1933 ed. lib. bdg. 20.00x (ISBN 0-8371-0037-2, CAEB). Greenwood.
Carnegie Commission on Higher Education. Credit for College: Public Policy for Student Loans. 1971. 7.50 o.p. (ISBN 0-07-010030-6, P&RB). McGraw.
--Reports, 21 vols. 1974. Set. 40.00 o.p. (ISBN 0-07-079384-0, P&RB). McGraw.
Carnegie Council on Policy Studies in Higher Education. Giving Youth a Better Chance: Options for Education, Work, & Service. LC 79-90851. (Carnegie Council Ser.). 1980. 17.95x (ISBN 0-87589-441-0). Jossey-Bass.
Carnegie, Dale. How to Help Your Husband Get Ahead. 192p. 1982. pap. 2.75 (ISBN 0-515-06895-0). Jove Pubns.
--How to Stop Worrying & Start Living. 1948. 9.95 o.p. (ISBN 0-671-34900-7). S&S.
--How to Win Friends & Influence People. rev. & updated ed. 1982. pap. 3.50 (ISBN 0-671-45086-7). PB.
--How to Win Friends & Influence People. 1937. 9.95 o.s.i. (ISBN 0-671-35500-7). S&S.
--Quick & Easy Way to Effective Speaking. Carnegie, Dorothy, ed. 1962. 6.95 o.s.i. (ISBN 0-8096-1470-7, Assn Pr). Follett.
Carnegie, Dorothy, ed. Dale Carnegie's Scrapbook. 1959. 9.95 o.p. (ISBN 0-671-18950-6). S&S.
Carnegie, Dorothy, ed. see Carnegie, Dale.
Carnegie Endowment for International Peace. A Repertoire of League of Nations Documents, 1919-1947, 2 vols. Ghebali, Victor-Yves, ed. LC 73-7839. 773p. 1973. lib. bdg. 85.00 (ISBN 0-379-00371-6); lib. bdg. 42.50 ea. Oceana.
Carnegie Foundation for the Advancement of Teaching Staff. The Control of the Campus: A Report on the Governance of Higher Education. LC 82-18772. 128p. 1982. pap. text ed. 6.95 (ISBN 0-931050-21-9). Carnegie Found Adv Teach.
Carnegie, Mary E. Disadvantaged Students in R.N. Programs. (League Exchange Ser.: No. 100). 118p. 1974. 6.95 (ISBN 0-686-38365-6, 14-1471). Natl League Nurse.
Carneiro, Cecilio J. The Bonfire: A Fogueira. Poore, Dudley, tr. from Port. LC 75-139127. 334p. 1972. Repr. of 1944 ed. lib. bdg. 17.00x (ISBN 0-8371-5743-9, CABF). Greenwood.
Carneiro, F. L., et al. Offshore Structures Engineering, Vol. 1. (Offshore Structures Engineering Ser.). 424p. 1979. 42.50x (ISBN 0-87201-608-0). Gulf Pub.
Carnell, Corbin S., ed. see Twain, Mark.
Carnell, Hilary, jt. auth. see Eagle, Dorothy.
Carnemark, Curt & Biderman, Jaime. The Economic Analysis of Rural Road Projects. (Working Paper: No. 241). 92p. 1976. 5.00 (ISBN 0-686-36217-9, WP-0241). World Bank.
Carner, Mosco. Alban Berg. 2nd rev. ed. (Illus.). 255p. 1983. text ed. 35.00x (ISBN 0-8419-0841-9). Holmes & Meier.
--Hugo Wolf Songs. LC 81-71301. (BBC Music Guides Ser.). 72p. (Orig.). 1983. pap. 4.95 (ISBN 0-295-95851-0). U of Wash Pr.
--Madam Butterfly. LC 79-67164. (Masterworks of Opera Ser.). 15.96 (ISBN 0-382-06313-9). Silver.
--Wolf Songs: BBC. 1983. write for info. U of Wash Pr.
Carner, Mosco, jt. auth. see Lenormand, Rene.
Carne-Ross, D. S. Instaurations: Essays in & Out of Literature, Pindar to Pound. LC 77-91772. 1979. 27.50x (ISBN 0-520-03619-0). U of Cal Pr.
Carne-Ross, Luna. Emergency First Aid. (Illus.). 24p. 1981. spiral bound, vinyl slipcase 3.95 (ISBN 0-8256-3241-2, Quick Fox). Putnam Pub group.
Carnes, Conrad D., jt. auth. see Church, Gene.
Carnes, Mark C., ed. see Bowerman, Guy E.
Carnes, Patrick J. Counseling the Sexual Addict. 150p. 1983. 9.95 (ISBN 0-89638-059-9). CompCare.
--Sexual Addiction. 215p. 1983. 12.95 (ISBN 0-89638-058-0); pap. 8.95 (ISBN 0-89638-066-1). CompCare.
Carnes, Ralph & Carnes, Valerie. Sportspower. (Illus.). 256p. 1982. 14.95 (ISBN 0-312-75344-6). St Martin.
Carnes, Ralph, jt. auth. see Carnes, Valerie.
Carnes, Valerie & Carnes, Ralph. Bodysculpture: Weight Training for Women. (Illus.). 1979. 9.95 o.p. (ISBN 0-671-23058-1). S&S.
Carnes, Valerie, jt. auth. see Carnes, Ralph.
Carnes, William T. Effective Meetings for Busy People: Let's Decide It & Go Home. 368p. 1983. pap. 9.95 (ISBN 0-07-010118-3, P&RB). McGraw.
Carnevale, Thomas & Shloming, Robert. Encounters with Algebra. 480p. 1981. pap. text ed. 17.95 (ISBN 0-15-522593-6, HC); instr's. manual 3.50 (ISBN 0-15-522594-4). HarBraceJ.
--Encounters with Arithmetic. 449p. 1979. pap. text ed. 17.95 (ISBN 0-15-522596-0, HC); instructor's manual avail. (ISBN 0-15-522597-9). HarBraceJ.
Carnevali, jt. auth. see Little.
Carney, et al. Career Planning: Skills to Build Your Future. (Orig.). 1980. 8.95 (ISBN 0-442-23350-7); instr's. manual 2.50 (ISBN 0-442-25860-7). Van Nos Reinhold.
Carney, Andrew L. & Anderson, Evelyn M., eds. Diagnosis & Treatment of Brain Ischemia, Vol. 30. (Advances in Neurology). (Illus.). 424p. 1981. 54.50 (ISBN 0-89004-529-1). Raven.
Carney, Ann. No More Here & There. Adopting the Older Child. LC 76-4535. vii, 88p. 1976. pap. 5.95 (ISBN 0-8078-1278-1). U of NC Pr.
Carney, Clarke G. & McMahon, Sarah Lynne, eds. Exploring Contemporary Male-Female Roles: A Facilitator's Guide. LC 76-58237. 276p. 1977. pap. 15.50 (ISBN 0-88390-135-8). Univ Assocs.
Carney, Daniel. Under a Raging Sky. 322p. 1981. 10.95 o.p. (ISBN 0-312-83013-0). St Martin.
Carney, George O. The Sounds of People & Places: Readings in the Geography of Music. 1978. pap. text ed. 13.25 (ISBN 0-8191-0394-2). U Pr of Amer.
Carney, J., et al, eds. Regions in Crisis: New Perspectives in European Regional Theory. 1980. 26.00 (ISBN 0-312-66944-5). St Martin.
Carney, James D. & Scheer, Richard K. Fundamentals of Logic. 3rd ed. (Illus.). 1980. text ed. 21.95x (ISBN 0-02-319480-4). Macmillan.
Carney, Jo & Clemente, Vince. Kon Kon's Grand Daughter. 48p. 1982. limited ed. 5.00x (ISBN 0-943018-03-X). Backstreet.
Carney, Louis P. Introduction to Correctional Science. 2nd ed. (Illus.). 1978. text ed. 21.50 (ISBN 0-07-010077-2, G). McGraw.
--Probation & Parole: Legal & Social Dimensions. (Illus.). 1976. text ed. 21.50 (ISBN 0-07-010126-4, G); instructor's manual & key 4.50 (ISBN 0-07-010127-2). McGraw.
Carney, Thomas. Daylight Moon. (Orig.). 1979. pap. 1.95 o.p. (ISBN 0-451-08755-0, J8755, Sig). NAL.
Carney, William. The Rose Exterminator. 320p. 1983. 13.95 (ISBN 0-89696-177-X, An Everest House Book). Dodd.
Carney, William J., ed. see Pashigian, B. P.
Carnine, Douglas & Elkind, David. Interdisciplinary Voices in Learning Disabilities & Remedial Education. (Illus.). 196p. (Orig.). 1982. pap. text ed. 15.00x (ISBN 0-936104-27-9). Pro-Ed.
Carnine, Douglas & Silbert, Jerry. Direct Instruction Reading. (Illus.). 560p. 1979. text ed. 24.95 (ISBN 0-675-08277-3). Additional supplements may be obtained from publisher. Merrill.
Carnochan, W. B. Confinement & Flight: An Essay on English Literature of the Eighteenth Century. 1977. 21.50x (ISBN 0-520-03188-1). U of Cal Pr.
Carnoy, Albert J; see Keith, A. Berriedale.
Carnoy, Martin, et al. Can Educational Policy Equalise Income Distribution in Latin America. 1979. text ed. 22.00x (ISBN 0-566-00255-8). Gower Pub Ltd.
Caro, Annibal. The Scruffy Scoundrels (Gli Straccioni) Ciavolella, M. & Beecher, Donald, trs. from Ital. 95p. 1980. pap. text ed. 3.50x (ISBN 0-88920-103-X, Pub. by Wilfred Laurier U Pr Canada). Humanities.
Caro, C. G., et al. Mechanics of the Circulation. (Illus.). 1978. text ed. 39.50x (ISBN 0-19-263323-6). Oxford U Pr.
Caro, Francis G., ed. Readings in Evaluation Research. 2nd ed. LC 76-12706. 436p. 1976. 15.95 (ISBN 0-87154-201-3). Russell Sage.
Caro, Mike. Caro's Book of Tells: Poker Body Language. 275p. 1983. 16.95 (ISBN 0-914314-04-1). Gambling Times.
Caro, Robert A. The Power Broker: Robert Moses & the Fall of New York. 1975. 13.95 (ISBN 0-394-72024-5, Vin). Random.
Caro-Costas, Aida R. Antologia de Lecturas de Historia de Puerto Rico, Siglos XV-XVIII. LC 77-10947. Date not set. pap. cancelled (ISBN 0-8477-0849-7). U of PR Pr.
Caroe, Gwendolen M. William Henry Bragg, Eighteen Sixty-Two to Nineteen Forty-Two. LC 77-84799. (Illus.). 1978. 32.50 (ISBN 0-521-21839-X). Cambridge U Pr.
Caroe, Laurence C. Probate Guide for Ontario. 2nd ed. 118p. 1979. 9.95 (ISBN 0-88908-323-1); forms 11.50 (ISBN 0-686-35993-3). Self Counsel Pr.
Caroe, Olaf. Wells of Power: The Oil Fields of South-Western Asia. (Middle East in the 20th Century Ser.). 1976. Repr. of 1951 ed. lib. bdg. 29.50 (ISBN 0-306-70825-6). Da Capo.
Caroe, Olaf K. Soviet Empire: The Turks of Central Asia & Stalinism. 2nd ed. 1967. 25.00 (ISBN 0-312-74795-0). St Martin.
Caroff, Phyllis, ed. Treatments Formulations & Clinical Social Work. LC 82-62378. 52p. (Orig.). 1982. pap. text ed. 6.95 (ISBN 0-87101-118-2). Natl Assn Soc Wkrs.
Carol, Juniper. De Corredemptione Beatae Virginis Mariae. (Theology Ser). 1950. 7.00 o.p. (ISBN 0-686-11586-4). Franciscan Inst.
Carol, M. Chesterton G. K. The Dynamic Classicist. 1971. 8.50 (ISBN 0-89684-185-5). Orient Bk Dist.
Carola, Robert, jt. auth. see Ritchie, Donald.
Carola, Robert, jt. auth. see Ritchie, Donald D.
Carole, Julia. Un Jour...Une Autre Chance. (Collection Colombine Ser.). 192p. 1983. pap. 1.95 (ISBN 0-373-48067-9). Harlequin Bks.
--Pour une Seule Valse. (Collection Colombine). 192p. 1983. pap. 1.95 (ISBN 0-373-48057-1). Harlequin Bks.
Caroli, Betty B., jt. auth. see Kessner, Thomas.
Caroline, John, jt. auth. see Gooch, Ken.
Caroline, Nancy. Emergency Care in the Streets. 1979. 13.95 o.p. (ISBN 0-316-12870-8). Little.
Caroline, Nancy L. Emergency Care in the Streets. 1983. pap. write for info. (ISBN 0-316-12875-9). Little.
--Emergency Medical Treatment: A Text for EMT-As & EMT-Intermediates. 1982. pap. text ed. 13.95 (ISBN 0-316-12872-4); wkbk. 8.95 (ISBN 0-316-12873-2); answer 3.95 (ISBN 0-316-12874-0). Little.
--Workbook in Emergency Treatment: Review Problem for EMT's. 1982. 8.95 o.p. (ISBN 0-316-12873-2). Little.
Caroll, S. J. & Park, R. E. The Search for Equity in School Finance. 200p. 1983. prof ref 19.50x (ISBN 0-88410-840-6). Ballinger Pub.
Caron, Denis R. Connecticut Foreclosures: An Attorney's Manual of Practice & Procedure. 2nd ed. 229p. 1982. 35.00 (ISBN 0-910051-00-3). CT Law Trib.
Caron, Fabien, ed. see Universite Laval,Centre d'Etudes Nordiques, Quebec.
Caron, Louis. The Draft Dodger. Homel, David T., tr. from Fr. (Fiction Ser: No. 42). 150p. (Orig.). 1980. pap. 8.95 (ISBN 0-88784-085-X, Pub. by Anansi Pr Canada). U of Toronto Pr.
Carona, Philip. Basic Science Skills. (Pre-GED Basic Skills Ser.). 1979. pap. 5.95 (ISBN 0-07-010138-8, Trafalgar Hse Pub). McGraw.
--Numbers. LC 82-4455. (New True Bks.). (gr. k-4). 1982. 9.25 (ISBN 0-516-01634-2). Childrens.
Carona, Philip B. Earth Through the Ages. (Beginning Science Ser.). (Illus.). (gr. 2-4). 1968. lib. ed. 2.97 o.s.i. (ISBN 0-695-42136-0). Follett.
--Water. (Beginning Science Ser.). (Illus.). (gr. 2-4). 1966. 2.50 o.s.i. (ISBN 0-695-89180-4). Follett.
Carone, Pasquale, ed. Addictive Disorders Update: Alcoholism, Drug Abuse, Gambling. Kieffer, Sherman, et al. LC 81-6880. (Problems of Industrial Psychiatric Medicine Ser.: Vol. VII). 192p. 1982. 24.95 (ISBN 0-89885-034-7). Human Sci Pr.
Carone, Pasquale, et al, eds. The Emotionally Troubled Employee: A Challenge to Industry. LC 76-26603. 1976. 24.50x (ISBN 0-87395-801-2). State U NY Pr.
Caroselli, Remus F. The Mystery Cottage in Left Field. LC 78-24368. (gr. 5 up). 1979. 7.95 o.p. (ISBN 0-399-20672-8). Putnam Pub Group.
Carosso, Vincent P. The California Wine Industry: A Study of the Formative Years, 1830-1895. (California Library Reprint). 1976. 27.50x (ISBN 0-520-03178-4). U of Cal Pr.
--More Than a Century of Investment Banking: The Didder, Peabody & Co. Story. (Illus.). 1979. 19.95 (ISBN 0-07-010136-1, P&RB). McGraw.
Carothers, Diane F. Self-Instruction Manual for Filing Catalog Cards. LC 81-3606. 128p. 1981. pap. 9.00 (ISBN 0-8389-0326-6). ALA.
Carothers, Doris. Chronology of the Federal Emergency Relief Administration: May 12, 1933 to December 31, 1935. LC 70-165681. (Research Monograph: Vol. 6). 1971. Repr. of 1937 ed. lib. bdg. 19.50 (ISBN 0-306-70338-6). Da Capo.
Carothers, Gibson & Lacey, James. Slanguage: America's Second Language. LC 79-65076. (Illus.). 1979. 5.95 o.p. (ISBN 0-8069-4602-4); lib. bdg. 6.69 o.p. (ISBN 0-8069-4603-2). Sterling.
Carothers, James E. & Gasten, Ruth S. Helping Children to Like Themselves: Activities for Building Self-Esteem. 1978. pap. 4.95 (ISBN 0-9602090-1-8). RJ Assocs.
Carothers, Merlin. Praise Works! LC 73-84414. 161p. 1973. pap. 4.95 (ISBN 0-88270-060-X, Pub. by Logos). Bridge Pub.
--Walking & Leaping. LC 74-79173. 1974. 4.95 o.p. (ISBN 0-88270-102-9, Pub. by Logos); pap. 4.95 (ISBN 0-88270-104-5). Bridge Pub.
Carothers, Merlin R. Power in Praise: Sequel to Prison to Praise. 115p. 1972. pap. 4.95 (ISBN 0-912106-26-3, Pub. by Logos). Bridge Pub.
Carothers, Robert. John Calvin's Favorite Son. (Illus.). 24p. (Orig.). 1980. pap. 3.95 (ISBN 0-935306-07-2). Barnwood Pr.
Carovillano, R. L., et al, eds. see Air Force Cambridge Research Laboratories - Boston College - 1967.
Carovillano, Robert L. & Skehan, James W., eds. Science & the Future of Man. 1st u.s. ed. 1971. 17.50x (ISBN 0-262-03031-4). MIT Pr.
Carozzi, Albert V. Microscopic Sedimentary Petrography. LC 60-6447. 498p. 1972. Repr. of 1960 ed. 26.50 (ISBN 0-88275-061-5). Krieger.
Carp, Robert A. & Rowland, C. K. Policymaking & Politics in the Federal District Courts. LC 82-13462. (Illus.). 256p. 1983. text ed. 17.95x (ISBN 0-87049-369-8). U of Tenn Pr.
Carpenter, et al. The Economics of Long-Distance Transportation: Proceedings of a Conference Held by the International Economic Association in Moscow. LC 82-791. 280p. 1982. 32.50x (ISBN 0-312-23439-2). St Martin.
Carpenter, Allan. Cameroon. LC 77-670. (Enchantment of Africa Ser.). (Illus.). 96p. (gr. 5 up). 1977. PLB 10.60 (ISBN 0-516-04555-5). Childrens.
--Central African Republic. LC 77-668. (Enchantment of Africa Ser.). (Illus.). 96p. (gr. 5 up). 1977. 10.60 (ISBN 0-516-04556-3). Childrens.
--Iowa. new ed. LC 79-11802. (New Enchantment of America State Bks.). (Illus.). 96p. (gr. 4 up). 1979. PLB 10.60 (ISBN 0-516-04115-0). Childrens.
Carpenter, Allan & Baker, Janice. Upper Volta. LC 74-10957. (Enchantment of Africa Ser.). (Illus.). 96p. (gr. 5 up). 1974. PLB 10.60 (ISBN 0-516-04592-X). Childrens.
Carpenter, Allan & Chourou, Bechir. Tunisia. LC 73-8872. (Enchantment of Africa Ser.). (Illus.). 96p. (gr. 5 up). 1973. PLB 10.60 o.p. (ISBN 0-516-04590-3). Childrens.
Carpenter, Allan, et al. Gambia. LC 76-52910. (Enchantment of Africa Ser.). (Illus.). 96p. (gr. 4 up). 1977. 10.60 (ISBN 0-516-04564-4). Childrens.
--Mali. LC 75-2269. (Enchantment of Africa Ser.). (Illus.). 96p. (gr. 5 up). 1975. 10.60 (ISBN 0-516-04574-1). Childrens.
Carpenter, Alton E. The Infinite Thought Projections of Jesus. 1975. 10.00 o.p. (ISBN 0-682-48356-7). Exposition.
--Twenty-One Keys to a Beautiful Life. 1976. 7.50 o.p. (ISBN 0-682-48357-5). Exposition.
--Twenty-Three Keys to Inner Peace from the 23rd Psalm. 1974. 7.50 o.p. (ISBN 0-682-48058-4). Exposition.
Carpenter, B. Stephen, ed. Computers in Activation Analysis & Gamma-Ray Spectroscopy: Proceedings. LC 79-19600. (DOE Symposium Ser.). 904p. 1979. pap. 30.50 (ISBN 0-87079-117-6, CONF-780421); microfiche 4.50 (ISBN 0-87079-169-9, CONF-780421). DOE.
Carpenter, Bogdana. The Poetic Avant-Garde in Poland: 1918-1939. LC 82-48870. (Publications on Russia & Eastern Europe of the School of International Studies: No. 11). (Illus.). 300p. 1983. 22.50 (ISBN 0-295-95996-7). U of Wash Pr.
Carpenter, Cal. The Walton War & Tales of the Great Smoky Mts. 96p. 1980. pap. 5.95 (ISBN 0-932298-03-6). Copple Hse.
Carpenter, Carol B. & Rakow, Sue F. Say it in Sign: A Workbook of Sign Language Exercises. (Illus.). 112p. 1983. pap. 14.75x spiral (ISBN 0-398-04779-0). C C Thomas.
Carpenter, Charles A. Modern British Drama. LC 76-4654. (Goldentree Bibliographies in Language & Literature). 1979. text ed. 22.50x (ISBN 0-88295-568-3); pap. text ed. 13.95x (ISBN 0-88295-559-4). Harlan Davidson.
Carpenter, Charles H., Jr. Gorham Silver. LC 82-2359. 1983. 34.95 (ISBN 0-396-08068-5). Dodd.
Carpenter, David O. Cellular Pacemakers: Function in Normal & Diseased States, Vol. 1. LC 81-11711. 352p. 1982. 50.50 (ISBN 0-471-06509-9, Pub. by Wiley-Interscience). Wiley.
Carpenter, Delores B., ed. The Life of Lidian Jackson Emerson by Ellen Tucker Emerson. (American Literary Manuscripts Ser.). 1980. lib. bdg. 25.00 (ISBN 0-8057-9651-7, Twayne). G K Hall.
Carpenter, Don. A Couple of Comedians. 1980. 9.95 o.p. (ISBN 0-671-22839-0). S&S.
--Turnaround. 1981. 13.95 o.s.i. (ISBN 0-671-25353-0). S&S.
Carpenter, Edward. Iolaus: An Anthology of Friendship. 3rd ed. LC 76-174018. 1971. Repr. of 1920 ed. 30.00x (ISBN 0-8103-3790-8). Gale.
Carpenter, Edward K. Thirty-Seven Design & Environment Projects: First Annual Review. (Illus.). 96p. 1976. 13.95 (ISBN 0-8230-7456-0, Whitney Lib). Watson-Guptill.
Carpenter, Frances. Tales of a Chinese Grandmother. LC 72-77514. (Illus.). 302p. (gr. 3-8). 1972. pap. 6.95 (ISBN 0-8048-1042-7). C E Tuttle.
Carpenter, Francis R. The Old China Trade: Americans in Canton 1784-1843. LC 75-30985. (Illus.). 160p. (gr. 6-8). 1976. 7.95 o.p. (ISBN 0-698-20358-5, Coward). Putnam Pub Group.
Carpenter, Frederic I. Eugene O'Neill. (U. S. Authors Ser.: No. 66). 1964. lib. bdg. 8.50 o.p. (ISBN 0-8057-0572-4, Twayne). G K Hall.
--Eugene O'Neill. rev. ed. (United States Authors Ser.). 1979. lib. bdg. 10.95 (ISBN 0-8057-7267-7, Twayne). G K Hall.
--Robinson Jeffers. (U. S. Authors Ser.: No. 22). lib. bdg. 10.95 o.p. (ISBN 0-8057-0412-4, Twayne). G K Hall.
Carpenter, G. Russell, jt. auth. see Gove, Walter R.

Carpenter, H. J. Popular Christianity & the Early Theologians. Lee, Clarence L., ed. LC 66-12387. (Orig.). 1966. pap. 0.50 o.p. (ISBN 0-8006-3025-4, 1-3025). Fortress.

Carpenter, Humphrey. Jesus. Thomas, Keith, ed. (Past Masters Ser.). 1980. 7.95 o.p. (ISBN 0-8090-6082-5); pap. 2.95 (ISBN 0-8090-1410-6). Hill & Wang.

Carpenter, J. Estlin. The Life and Work of Mary Carpenter. 2nd ed. LC 77-172564. (Criminology, Law Enforcement & Social Problems Ser.: No. 145). (Illus.). 420p. (Index added). 1974. Repr. of 1881 ed. lib. bdg. 20.00x (ISBN 0-87585-145-2). Patterson Smith.

--Theism in Medieval India. 1977. Repr. of 1921 ed. 22.50x (ISBN 0-8002-0231-7). Intl Pubns Serv.

Carpenter, James M. Visual Art: A Critical Introduction. 289p. 1982. pap. text ed. 19.95 (ISBN 0-15-594935-7, HC). HarBraceJ.

Carpenter, Jesse T. Competition & Collective Bargaining in the Needle Trades, 1910-1967. LC 79-630987. (Cornell Studies in Industrial & Labor Relations: No. 17). 936p. 1972. 17.50 (ISBN 0-87546-035-6). ILR Pr.

Carpenter, John. Poetry & Space. 1983. write for info. U of Wash Pr.

Carpenter, Johonet H. The Well of Understanding. LC 82-61176. (Illus.). 136p. 1982. 13.00 (ISBN 0-9609378-0-3). Sophia Pr.

Carpenter, Juliet W., tr. see Abe, Kobo.

Carpenter, Juliet W., tr. see Enchi, Fumiko.

Carpenter, Kenneth, ed. Pellagra. LC 81-6514. (Benchmark Papers in Biochemistry Ser.: Vol. 2). 416p. 1981. 48.00 (ISBN 0-87933-364-2). Hutchinson Ross.

Carpenter, Kenneth E. Books & Society in History. 300p. 1983. 29.95 (ISBN 0-8352-1675-6). Bowker.

Carpenter, L. Vacuum Technology. 1970. 15.00 (ISBN 0-444-19670-6). Elsevier.

Carpenter, M. B., jt. auth. see Truex, R. C.

Carpenter, Malcolm B. & Sutin, J. Human Neuroanatomy. 7th ed. 741p. 1976. 39.95 o.p. (ISBN 0-683-01460-9). Williams & Wilkins.

Carpenter, Malcolm B. & Sutin, Jerome. Human Neuroanatomy. 8th ed. (Illus.). 906p. 1982. text ed. 44.00 (ISBN 0-683-01461-7). Williams & Wilkins.

Carpenter, Mary. Juvenile Delinquents, Their Condition & Treatment. LC 76-108224. (Criminology, Law Enforcement, & Social Problems Ser.: No. 107). (With essay by Katharine Lenroot & index added). 1970. Repr. of 1953 ed. lib. bdg. 15.00x (ISBN 0-87585-107-X). Patterson Smith.

--Our Convicts, 2 vols. in 1. LC 69-16229. (Criminology, Law Enforcement, & Social Problems Ser.: No. 88). 1969. Repr. of 1864 ed. 25.00x (ISBN 0-87585-080-4). Patterson Smith.

--Reformatory Prison Discipline As Developed by the Rt. Hon. Sir Walter Crofton in the Irish Convict Prisons. LC 67-26667. (Criminology, Law Enforcement, & Social Problems Ser.: No. 2). 1967. Repr. of 1872 ed. 10.00x (ISBN 0-87585-002-2). Patterson Smith.

--Reformatory Schools for the Children of the Perishing & Dangerous Classes & for Juvenile Offenders. LC 72-108223. (Criminology, Law Enforcement, & Social Problems Ser.: No. 106). 1970. Repr. of 1851 ed. lib. bdg. 15.00x (ISBN 0-87585-106-1). Patterson Smith.

Carpenter, Nan Cooke. Music in the Medieval & Renaissance Universities. LC 70-171380. (Music Ser). (Illus.). 394p. 1972. Repr. of 1958 ed. lib. bdg. 35.00 (ISBN 0-306-70453-6). Da Capo.

Carpenter, Philip P. Catalogue of the Collection of Mazatlan Shells in the British Museum. 1967. Repr. of 1857 ed. 8.00 o.p. (ISBN 0-87710-371-2). Paleo Res.

Carpenter, R. H. Movements of the Eyes. 420p. 1977. 38.50x (ISBN 0-85086-063-6, Pub. by Pion England). Methuen Inc.

Carpenter, Ray L. Statistical Methods for Librarians. LC 78-3476. 1978. 15.00 (ISBN 0-8389-0256-1). ALA.

Carpenter, Rhys. Folk Tale, Fiction & Saga in the Homeric Epics. LC 55-7555. (Sather Classical Lectures Ser.: No. 20). 1974. 26.50x (ISBN 0-520-02808-2). U of Cal Pr.

Carpenter, Richard C. Thomas Hardy. (English Authors Ser.). 1964. lib. bdg. 11.95 (ISBN 0-8057-1244-5, Twayne). G K Hall.

Carpenter, Ronald H. The Eloquence of Frederick Jackson Turner. 275p. 1983. price not set (ISBN 0-87328-078-4). Huntington Lib.

Carpenter, Samuel T. Structural Mechanics. LC 75-31671. 550p. 1976. Repr. of 1966 ed. 30.50 (ISBN 0-88275-363-0). Krieger.

Carpenter, Stanley J. & Lacasse, Walter J. Mosquitoes of North America. (California Library Reprint Ser.). (Illus.). 1974. Repr. 57.50x (ISBN 0-520-02638-1). U of Cal Pr.

Carpenter, Steven E. Monograph of Crocicreas: Ascomycetes, Helotiales, Helotiaceae, Vol. 33. (Memoirs of the New York Botanical Garden). (Illus.). 1981. pap. 35.00 (ISBN 0-89327-230-2). NY Botanical.

Carpenter, Thomas, et al. Results from the First Mathematics Assessment of the National Assessment of Educational Progress. LC 78-2345. 144p. 1978. pap. 9.00 (ISBN 0-87353-123-X). NCTM.

Carpenter, V. A. Ulysses S. Grant. (World Leaders Ser.). 12.50 (ISBN 0-8057-3040-0, Twayne). G K Hall.

Carpenter, William S. The Unfinished Business of Civil Service Reform. LC 79-16863. 1980. Repr. of 1952 ed. lib. bdg. 16.25x (ISBN 0-313-22051-4, CACS). Greenwood.

Carpenter-Huffman, P., et al. Change in Education: Insights from Performance Contracting. LC 74-13457. (Rand Educational Policy Ser). 200p. 1974. prof ref 18.50 (ISBN 0-88410-158-4). Ballinger Pub.

Carpentier, Alejo. Explosion in a Cathedral. Sturrock, John, tr. from Span. 1979. pap. 4.95i o.p. (ISBN 0-06-090651-0, CN 651, CN). Har-Row.

Carpentier, Hortense, tr. see Skarmeta, Antonio.

Carper, Dean. Sound of Drums. LC 73-87638. 1975. 6.00 o.p. (ISBN 0-8309-0110-8). Herald Hse.

Carper, Janice M. Between the Bays: Somerset, Wicomico & Worcester Counties Maryland. LC 78-71245. (Illus.). 86p. 1979. pap. 13.00 (ISBN 0-935968-05-9). EPM Pubns.

Carpinisan, Mariana, tr. see Stanescu, Nichita.

Carqou, J. M. Paris. Henderson, S. D., tr. (Illus.). 144p. (French.). 1982. 30.00 o.p. (ISBN 2-03-523102-7). Larousse.

Carque, Otto. Vital Facts About Foods. LC 75-18697. 240p. 1975. pap. 3.50 o.p. (ISBN 0-87983-113-8). Keats.

Carr, A., jt. ed. see Hails, J.

Carr, Anna. Gardening in Containers. Halpin, Anne, ed. (Rodale's Grow-It Guides Ser.). (Illus.). 128p. Date not set. pap. 6.95 (ISBN 0-87857-425-5, 01-126-1). Rodale Pr Inc. Postponed.

--Rodale's Color Handbook of Garden Insects. (Illus.). 256p. 1983. pap. 10.95 (ISBN 0-87857-460-3, 01-637-1). Rodale Pr Inc.

Carr, Anna & Olkowski, William. Rodale's Color Handbook of Garden Insects. (Illus.). 1979. 14.95 o.p. (ISBN 0-87857-250-3). Rodale Pr Inc.

Carr, Anne, et al. Academic Study of Religion: Nineteen Seventy-Five: Public Schools Religion-Studies: 1975. LC 75-26653. (American Academy of Religion. Section Papers). 1975. pap. 9.95 (ISBN 0-89130-023-6, 01-09-17). Scholars Pr Ca.

Carr, Archie. The Everglades. LC 72-96548. (American Wilderness Ser). (Illus.). 1973. lib. bdg. 15.96 (ISBN 0-8094-1173-3, Pub. by Time-Life). Silver.

--The Land & Wildlife of Africa. rev. ed. LC 80-52260. (Life Nature Library). PLB 13.40 (ISBN 0-8094-3903-4). Silver.

--The Reptiles. rev. ed. LC 80-52122. (Life Nature Library). PLB 13.40 (ISBN 0-8094-3875-5). Silver.

--The Reptiles. (Young Readers Library). (Illus.). 1977. PLB 6.80 (ISBN 0-8094-1389-2). Silver.

Carr, Arthur C., et al, eds. Grief: Selected Readings. 155p. 1974. pap. 7.50 (ISBN 0-930194-76-4). Ctr Thanatology.

Carr, Audrey, jt. auth. see Sohl, Robert.

Carr, Audrey, jt. ed. see Sohl, Robert.

Carr, Benjamin. Musical Miscellany in Occasional Numbers. (Early American Music Ser.: No. 21). 1982. Repr. of 1825 ed. 47.50 (ISBN 0-306-79547-7). Da Capo.

Carr, Clare, ed. The Gathering of Souls. Freelander, Iris. LC 81-69576. (Illus.). 240p. 1981. pap. 10.00 (ISBN 0-910378-17-7). Christward.

Carr, David, jt. auth. see Beckett, Kenneth A.

Carr, David W. Foreign Investment & Development in the Southwest Pacific: With Special Reference to Austrailia & Indonesia. LC 78-8598. (Praeger Special Studies). 224p. 1978. 28.95 o.p. (ISBN 0-03-042271-X). Praeger.

Carr, Donald E. The Deadly Feast of Life. LC 75-135712. 1971. 8.95 (ISBN 0-385-01406-6). Doubleday.

Carr, E. H. From Napoleon to Stalin & Other Essays. 1980. 25.00 (ISBN 0-312-30774-8). St Martin.

--The Twenty Years' Crisis Nineteen Nineteen to Nineteen Thirty-Nine. 244p. 1981. Repr. of 1939 ed. text ed. 18.95x (ISBN 0-333-06913-7, Pub. by Macmillan England). Humanities.

Carr, E. W. Short Term Trusts. 2nd ed. 208p. 1979. 29.95 (ISBN 0-686-92109-7). P-H.

Carr, Edward H. International Relations Between the Two World Wars: 1919-1939. (Illus.). 1969. 22.50 (ISBN 0-312-42315-2). St Martin.

--Nationalism & After. 1945. 9.95 o.p. (ISBN 0-312-56000-1). St Martin.

--Twilight of the Comintern, 1930-1935. 436p. 1983. 22.50 (ISBN 0-394-52512-4). Pantheon.

Carr, Elizabeth B. Da Kine Talk: From Pidgin to Standard English in Hawaii. LC 70-151455. 240p. 1972. 10.00x (ISBN 0-8248-0209-8). UH Pr.

Carr, Frank C. The Medley of Mast & Sail: a Camera Record, Vol. 1. LC 76-62879. 330p. 1977. 23.95 (ISBN 0-87021-939-1). Naval Inst Pr.

Carr, Gerald F., jt. ed. see Rauch, Irmangard.

Carr, H. Wildon, tr. see Bergson, Henri.

Carr, Herman Y. & Weidner, Richard T. Physics from the Ground Up, Pt. 1, 2, 3. LC 78-22000. 296p. 1979. Repr. Pt. 1. lib. bdg. 9.95 (ISBN 0-88275-791-1); Pt. 2. lib. bdg. 9.95 (ISBN 0-89874-021-5); Pt. 3. lib. bdg. 9.95 (ISBN 0-89874-213-7). Krieger.

Carr, Hugh. Encounter in the Wilderness. (Irish Play Ser.). pap. 2.95x (ISBN 0-912262-65-6). Proscenium.

Carr, Ian. Miles Davis: A Critical Biography. LC 82-6469. (Illus.). 324p. 1982. 14.95 (ISBN 0-688-01321-X). Morrow.

Carr, J. G. Biological Principles in Fermentation. 1968. pap. text ed. 3.50x o.p. (ISBN 0-435-61152-6). Heinemann Ed.

Carr, Jacquelyn B. Communicating & Relating. LC 78-58969. 1979. pap. text ed. 15.95 (ISBN 0-8053-1820-8); instr's guide 4.95 (ISBN 0-8053-1821-6). Benjamin-Cummings.

Carr, James G. The Law of Electronic Surveillance. LC 76-56748. 1977. 55.00 (ISBN 0-87632-108-2). Boardman.

Carr, James G., ed. Criminal Law Review - 1981. 1981. 42.50 (ISBN 0-87632-284-4). Boardman.

Carr, James H. Crisis & Constraints in Municipal Finance: Local Fiscal Prospects in a Period of Uncertainty. 256p. 1983. pap. text ed. 12.95x (ISBN 0-88285-092-X, Dist. by Transaction Bks). Ctr Urban Pol Res.

Carr, James H., jt. auth. see Burchell, Robert W.

Carr, Janet H. & Shepherd, Roberta B. Early Care of the Stroke Patient: A Positive Approach. 55p. Repr. of 1979 ed. 8.50 (ISBN 0-89443-812-3, Pub. by W Heinemann). Aspen Systems.

--A Motor Relearning Programme for Stroke. 175p. 1983. 24.50 (ISBN 0-89443-931-6). Aspen Systems.

--Physiotheraphy in Pediatrics. 2nd ed. 524p. Repr. of 1980 ed. 29.50 (ISBN 0-89443-813-1, Pub. by W Heinemann). Aspen Systems.

--Physiotherapy in Disorders of the Brain. 408p. Date not set. Repr. of 1980 ed. 28.50 (ISBN 0-89443-656-2). Aspen Systems.

Carr, Jayge. Navigator's Syndrome. LC 81-43446. (Science Fiction Ser.). 192p. 1983. 11.95 (ISBN 0-385-17221-4). Doubleday.

Carr, Jean F., ed. see Emerson, Ralph W.

Carr, Jess. The Falls of Rabbor. LC 73-75340. 1973. 10.95 (ISBN 0-87716-042-2, Pub. by Moore Pub Co). F Apple.

--The Frost of Summer. LC 75-4257. 244p. 1975. 8.95 (ISBN 0-686-77195-8, Pub. by Moore Pub Co). F Apple.

--Frost of Summer. LC 75-4257. 248p. 1975. 7.95 (ISBN 0-89227-046-2). Commonwealth Pr.

--How a Book Is Born. LC 78-59112. 1978. 10.95 (ISBN 0-89227-041-1). Commonwealth Pr.

--How a Book Is Born. LC 78-59112. 1978. pap. 12.95 (ISBN 0-87716-088-0, Pub. by Moore Pub Co). F Apple.

--The Moonshiners. LC 77-71601. 1977. 9.95 (ISBN 0-89227-042-X). Commonwealth Pr.

--Ship Ride Down the Spring Branch. LC 78-60480. 200p. 1978. 8.95 (ISBN 0-89227-048-9). Commonwealth Pr.

--Ship Ride Down the Spring Branch & Other Stories. LC 78-60480. 1978. 9.95 (ISBN 0-87716-092-9, Pub. by Moore Pub Co). F Apple.

Carr, Jo & Cash, Donna. Advent: A Calendar of Devotions, 1982. 48p. 1982. pap. 22.00 per 100 o.p. (ISBN 0-687-00881-6). Abingdon.

Carr, Jo & Sorley, Imogene. Bless This Mess. 1976. pap. 1.50 o.s.i. (ISBN 0-89129-130-X). Jove Pubns.

--Plum Jelly & Stained Glass & Other Prayers. LC 72-14163. 112p. 1973. 4.95 o.p. (ISBN 0-687-31659-6). Abingdon.

--Plum Jelly & Stained Glass & Other Prayers. 1981. pap. 1.95 o.p. (ISBN 0-687-31660-X, Festival). Abingdon.

--Too Busy Not to Pray. (Festival Books). 1978. pap. 2.25 (ISBN 0-687-42380-5). Abingdon.

Carr, Jo, jt. auth. see Norwood, Frederick A.

Carr, John D. The Dead Sleep Lightly. LC 82-45870. (Crime Club Ser.). 192p. 1983. 11.95 (ISBN 0-385-18714-9). Doubleday.

--The Murder of Sir Edmund Godfrey. LC 74-10426. (Classics of Crime & Criminology Ser). (Illus.). 352p. 1975. Repr. of 1936 ed. 26.50 (ISBN 0-88355-193-4). Hyperion Conn.

--The Three Coffins. 1979. lib. bdg. 9.95 (ISBN 0-8398-2533-1, Gregg). G K Hall.

Carr, John F. Carnifex Mardi Gras. (Illus.). 218p. 1982. 12.00 (ISBN 0-937912-00-X). Pequod Press.

Carr, John F., ed. The Worlds of H. Beam Piper. 1983. pap. 2.95 (ISBN 0-686-43005-0). Ace Bks.

Carr, Joseph. Digital Interfacing with an Analog World. (Illus.). 1978. 16.95 (ISBN 0-8306-9886-8); pap. 10.95 (ISBN 0-8306-1070-7, 1070). TAB Bks.

--Elements of Electronic Instrumentation & Measurement. (Illus.). 1979. text ed. 19.95 (ISBN 0-8359-1650-2); students manual o.p. avail. (ISBN 0-8359-1651-0). Reston.

--Op Amp Circuit Design & Applications. LC 75-41721. (Illus.). 1976. 9.95 o.p. (ISBN 0-8306-6787-3); pap. 6.95 o.p. (ISBN 0-8306-5787-8, 787). TAB Bks.

--Servicing Medical & Bio-Electronic Equipment. LC 77-73. (Illus.). 1977. 10.95 o.p. (ISBN 0-8306-7930-8); pap. 8.95 o.p. (ISBN 0-8306-6930-2, 930). TAB Bks.

Carr, Joseph J. Antenna Data Reference Manual-Including Dimension Tables. (Illus.). 1979. 13.95 (ISBN 0-8306-9738-1); pap. 7.95 o.p. (ISBN 0-8306-1152-5, 1152). TAB Bks.

--The Complete Handbook of Amplifiers, Oscillators & Multivibrators. (Illus.). 364p. 1981. 15.95 o.p. (ISBN 0-8306-9653-9, 1230); pap. 10.95 (ISBN 0-8306-1230-0, 1230). TAB Bks.

--How to Design & Build Electronic Instrumentation. (Illus.). 1978. 14.95 o.p. (ISBN 0-8306-9910-4); pap. 9.95 (ISBN 0-8306-1012-X, 1012). TAB Bks.

Carr, Joseph J. & Brown, John M. Introduction to Biomedical Equipment Technology. LC 80-6218. (Electronic Technology Ser.). 430p. 1981. text ed. 29.95x (ISBN 0-471-04143-2); tchr's manual avail. (ISBN 0-471-04144-0). Wiley.

Carr, Josephine. No Regrets. LC 82-70194. 192p. (gr. 7 up). 1982. 10.95 (ISBN 0-8037-6721-8). Dial.

Carr, Marilyn. Developing Small Scale Industries in India: An Integrated Approach. (Illus.). 87p. (Orig.). 1981. pap. 10.50x (ISBN 0-903031-81-7, Pub. by Intermediate Tech England). Intermediate Tech.

Carr, Martha, jt. auth. see Bannon, Lois.

Carr, Mary J. Children of the Covered Wagon. rev. ed. LC 56-13460. (Illus.). (gr. 3-7). 1957. 12.95i o.p. (ISBN 0-690-18987-7, TYC-J). Har-Row.

Carr, Micheline, jt. auth. see Crouch, James.

Carr, N. G. & Whitton, B. A. Biology of Cyanobacteria. LC 82-1906. (Botanical Monographs: Vol. 19). (Illus.). 700p. 1982. 70.00x (ISBN 0-520-04717-6). U of Cal Pr.

Carr, N. G. & Whitton, B. A., eds. Biology of Blue-Green Algae. LC 72-89785. (Botanical Monographs: Vol. 9). 1973. 50.00x o.s.i. (ISBN 0-520-02344-7). U of Cal Pr.

Carr, Pat & Tracey, Steve. Enchantments. (Mindstrechers Level Two). (gr. 4-6). pap. 4.95 (ISBN 0-8224-4508-5). Pitman.

--Great Explorations. (Mindstrechers Level Two). (gr. 4-6). pap. 4.95 (ISBN 0-8224-4507-7). Pitman.

--Star Gazing. (Mindstrechers Level Two). (gr. 4-6). 4.95 (ISBN 0-8224-4505-0). Pitman.

--Who Done It? (Mindstrechers: Level Two). (gr. 4-6). pap. 4.95 (ISBN 0-8224-4506-9). Pitman.

Carr, Pat M. Bernard Shaw. LC 75-37263. (Literature and Life Ser.). 1976. 13.00 (ISBN 0-8044-2112-9). Ungar.

Carr, Patrick. Word Trip Games for the (l), (r), & (s) Sounds. 1974. text ed. 10.50x (ISBN 0-8134-1603-5). Interstate.

Carr, Patrick & Country Music Magazine, eds. The Illustrated History of Country Music. (Illus.). 368p. 1980. pap. 9.95 o.p. (ISBN 0-385-15385-6, Dolp). Doubleday.

Carr, Peter & Bowers, Larry D. Immobilized Enzymes in Analytical & Clinical Chemistry: Fundamentals & Applications. LC 80-13694. (Chemical Analysis: A Series of Monographs on Analytical Chemistry & Its Applications). 460p. 1980. 59.95 (ISBN 0-471-04919-0, Pub. by Wiley-Interscience). Wiley.

Carr, Philippa. The Adultress. 336p. 1982. 12.95 (ISBN 0-399-12680-5). Putnam Pub Group.

--Lament for a Lost Lover. LC 77-9497. 1977. 8.95 (ISBN 0-399-12021-1). Putnam Pub Group.

--The Lion Triumphant. 384p. 1974. 7.95 (ISBN 0-399-11135-2). Putnam Pub Group.

--The Love Child. LC 78-16708. 1978. 9.95 (ISBN 0-399-12302-4). Putnam Pub Group.

--Saraband for Two Sisters. LC 75-45062. 384p. 1976. 8.95 o.p. (ISBN 0-399-11746-6). Putnam Pub Group.

--The Song of the Siren. LC 79-10124. 1980. 10.95 (ISBN 0-399-12426-8). Putnam Pub Group.

--Will You Love Me in September. LC 80-24326. 324p. 1981. 11.95 (ISBN 0-399-12590-6). Putnam Pub Group.

--The Witch from the Sea. LC 74-16582. 384p. 1975. 7.95 o.p. (ISBN 0-399-11427-0). Putnam Pub Group.

Carr, Philippa see Holt, Victoria, pseud.

Carr, Rachel. Arthritis: Relief Beyond Drugs. (Illus.). 160p. 1983. pap. 6.68i (ISBN 0-06-464054-X, BN 4054). B&N NY.

--Be a Frog, a Bird, or a Tree. LC 72-92198. (Illus.). 1977. pap. 5.95i (ISBN 0-06-090570-0, CN 570, CN). Har-Row.

--Safari to Ngorongoro. LC 75-44152. (Illus.). 48p. (gr. 3-6). 1976. 6.95 o.p. (ISBN 0-698-20351-8, Coward). Putnam Pub Group.

--The Yoga Way to Release Tension: Techniques for Relaxation & Mind Control. (Illus.). 1974. 7.95 o.p. (ISBN 0-698-10611-3, Coward). Putnam Pub Group.

Carr, Rachel E. Be a Frog, a Bird, or a Tree: Rachel Carr's Creative Yoga Exercises for Children. LC 72-92198. 96p. (gr. 4-7). 1973. 8.95a o.p. (ISBN 0-686-85888-3); PLB 8.95a (ISBN 0-385-02358-8). Doubleday.

Carr, Raymond. Spain, Eighteen Eight to Nineteen Seventy-Five. 2nd ed. (Oxford History of Modern Europe Ser.). 800p. 1982. 44.00x (ISBN 0-19-822127-4); pap. 13.95x (ISBN 0-19-822128-2). Oxford U Pr.

--Spain 1808-1939. (Oxford History of Modern Europe Ser.). 1966. 32.50x o.p. (ISBN 0-19-822102-9). Oxford U Pr.

Carr, Richard & O'Con, Robert. Welding Practices & Procedures. (Illus.). 416p. 1983. text ed. 17.95 (ISBN 0-13-948059-5). P-H.

Carr, Robert F. & Hazard, James E. Tikal Reports No. 11: Map of the Ruins of Tikal, El Peten, Guatemala. (Museum Monograph: No. 11). (Illus.). iv, 24p. 1961. pap. 15.00x (ISBN 0-934718-13-X). Univ Mus of U PA.

Carr, Robert K. & Van Eyke, Daniel K. Collective Bargaining Comes to the Campus. 1973. 10.50 o.p. (ISBN 0-8268-1401-8). ACE.

Carr, Ronald E. & Siegel, Irwin M. Visual Electrodiagnostic Testing: A Practical Guide for the Clinician. (Illus.). 137p. 1982. text ed. 32.00 (ISBN 0-683-01462-5). Williams & Wilkins.

Carr, Roy. The Rolling Stones: An Illustrated Record. (Illus.). 1976. pap. 6.95 o.p. (ISBN 0-517-52641-7, Harmony). Crown.

Carr, Roy & Farren, Fick. Elvis Presley: The Completed Illustrated Record. LC 79-17184. (Illus.). 192p. 1982. 27.00 (ISBN 0-517-53978-0, Harmony); pap. 12.95 (ISBN 0-517-53979-9). Crown.

Carr, Roy & Murray, Charles S. David Bowie: An Illustrated Record. 120p. 1981. pap. 9.95 (ISBN 0-380-77966-8, 77966). Avon.

Carr, Sally B., ed. see Fisher, Terry.

Carr, Stephen. City Signs & Lights: Prepared for the Boston Redevelopment Authority & U.S. Dept. of Housing & Urban Development paper. 1973. 16.50 (ISBN 0-262-02087-4). MIT Pr.

Carr, Terry. Fantasy Annual V. 1982. pap. 2.95 (Timescape). PB.

Carr, Terry, ed. Universe, No. 10. 1982. pap. 2.50 (ISBN 0-8217-1114-8). Zebra.

--Universe, No. 11. 1983. pap. 2.50 (ISBN 0-8217-1143-1). Zebra.

--Universe Thirteen. LC 82-45351. (Science Fiction Ser.). (Illus.). 192p. 1983. 11.95 (ISBN 0-385-18288-0). Doubleday.

Carr, W. J., Jr. AC Loss & Macroscopic Theory of Superconductors. 1982. write for info. (ISBN 0-677-05700-8). Gordon.

Carr, Walter H. The World & William Walker. LC 75-18354. (Illus.). 289p. 1975. Repr. of 1963 ed. lib. bdg. 20.75x (ISBN 0-8371-8328-6, CAWWW). Greenwood.

Carr, William. A History of Germany Eighteen Fifteen to Nineteen Forty-Five. 2nd ed. LC 79-20108. (Illus.). 1979. 22.50x (ISBN 0-312-37871-8); pap. 10.95 (ISBN 0-312-37872-6). St Martin.

--Hitler: A Study in Personality & Politics. 1979. 25.00x (ISBN 0-312-38818-7). St Martin.

Carr, William N. & Mize, Jack P. MOS-LSI Design & Application. LC 72-7407. (Texas Instruments Electronics Ser.). (Illus.). 320p. 1972. 49.00 (ISBN 0-07-010081-0, P&RB). McGraw.

Carrabis, Joseph D. Mainely Bread. (Illus.). 1983. pap. 7.95 (ISBN 0-89272-161-8). Down East.

Carrada-Bravo, Francisco. Oil, Money, & the Mexican Economy: A Macroeconometric Analysis. (Replica Edition Ser.). 135p. 1982. softcover 17.50 (ISBN 0-86531-902-2). Westview.

Carraher, Charles E., Jr. & Gebelein, Charles G., eds. Biological Activities of Polymers. (ACS Symposium Ser.: No. 186). 1982. write for info. (ISBN 0-8412-0719-4). Am Chemical.

Carraher, Charles E., Jr. & Preston, Jack, eds. Interfacial Synthesis: Vol. III: Recent Advances. (Illus.). 408p. 1982. 65.00 (ISBN 0-686-82218-8). Dekker.

Carraher, Charles E., Jr. & Sheats, John E., eds. Advances in Organometallic & Inorganic Polymer Science. (Illus.). 472p. 1982. 67.50 (ISBN 0-686-82220-X). Dekker.

Carranco, Lynwood. The Redwood Lumber Industry of Northern California. (Illus.). 250p. 35.95 (ISBN 0-87095-084-3). Golden West.

Carranco, Lynwood & Beard, Estle. Genocide & Vendetta: The Round Valley Wars in Northern California. LC 81-40279. (Illus.). 384p. 1981. 22.50 (ISBN 0-8061-1549-1). U of Okla Pr.

Carranza, Fermin A. Glickman's Clinical Periodontology: Prevention, Diagnosis & Treatment of Periodonal Disease in the Practice of General Dentistry. 5th ed. LC 77-16991. (Illus.). 1979. text ed. 49.00 (ISBN 0-7216-2440-5). Saunders.

Carrara, Antonio, jt. auth. see Frassica, Pietro.

Carras, Mary C. Indira Gandhi in the Crucible of Leadership. LC 78-19598. 1979. 13.94 (ISBN 0-8070-0242-9). Beacon Pr.

Carrasco, David. Quetzalcoatl & the Irony of Empire: Myth & Prophecies in the Aztec Tradition. (Illus.). 224p. 1983. lib. bdg. 20.00x (ISBN 0-226-09487-1). U of Chicago Pr.

Carrasco-Urgoiti, Maria S. The Moorish Novel: "El Abencerraje" & Gines Perez de Hita. (World Authors Ser.). 1976. lib. bdg. 15.95 (ISBN 0-8057-6178-0, Twayne). G K Hall.

Carre, John Le see Le Carre, John.

Carre, John le see Le Carre, John.

Carre, John Le see Le Carre, John.

Carre, Meyrick H. Phases of Thought in England. LC 72-7858. 392p. 1973. Repr. of 1949 ed. lib. bdg. 19.25x (ISBN 0-8371-6537-7, CAPT). Greenwood.

Carrea, R., jt. auth. see De Robertis, E. D.

Carreira, Antonio. The People of the Cape Verde Islands. 1982. 21.50 (ISBN 0-208-01988-X, Archon Bks). Shoe String.

Carrell, A. Super Handyman's Encyclopedia of Home Repair Hints: Better, Faster, Cheaper, & Easier Ideas for House & Workshop. 1971. o. p. 8.95 (ISBN 0-13-875922-7); pap. 4.95 (ISBN 0-13-875914-6). P-H.

Carrell, Al. The Superhandyman's Fix & Finish Furniture Guide. 180p. 1982. pap. 5.95 (ISBN 0-13-875971-5); 7.95 (ISBN 0-13-875997-9). P-H.

Carrell, J. B., ed. Group Actions & Vector Fields: Vancouver, Canada, 1981, Proceedings. (Lecture Notes in Mathematics: Vol. 956). 144p. 1983. pap. 8.00 (ISBN 0-387-11946-9). Springer-Verlag.

Carrell, James. Disorders of Articulation. 1968. ref. ed. 16.95 (ISBN 0-13-216168-0). P-H.

Carrell, James, jt. auth. see Tiffany, William R.

Carrell, James B., et al. Topics in the Theory of Algebraic Groups. LC 82-17329. (Notre Dame Mathematical Lectures Ser.: No. 10a). 192p. (Orig.). 1982. pap. text ed. 9.95x (ISBN 0-268-01843-X, 85-18433). U of Notre Dame Pr.

Carrell, Mary J. Learning Math Skills. 1978. pap. text ed. 2.75x (ISBN 0-88323-139-5, 228). Richards Pub.

--Understanding the Metric System. 1978. pap. text ed. 2.75x (ISBN 0-88323-140-9, 229). Richards Pub.

Carrell, Mary Jane. Understanding English. rev. ed. 1982. pap. 2.75x (ISBN 0-88323-093-3, 197). Richards Pub.

Carreno, Teresa. Selected Piano Music. (Women Composers Ser.: No. 15). 235p. 1983. Repr. lib. bdg. 32.50 (ISBN 0-306-76193-9). Da Capo.

Carrett, Philip L. The Art of Speculation. 1979. Repr. of 1930 ed. flexible cover 12.00 (ISBN 0-87034-050-6). Fraser Pub Co.

Carretto, Carlo. Blessed Are You Who Believed. Wall, Barbara, tr. from Ital. LC 82-22504. (Illus.). 96p. (Orig.). 1983. 8.95 (ISBN 0-88344-040-7); pap. 4.95 (ISBN 0-88344-038-5). Orbis Bks.

--God Who Comes. 1976. pap. 1.50 o.s.i. (ISBN 0-89129-062-1). Jove Pubns.

--The God Who Comes. Hancock, Rose M., tr. from It. LC 73-89358. (Illus.). 160p. (Orig.). 1974. 6.95x o.p. (ISBN 0-88344-160-8). Orbis Bks.

--I, Francis. Barr, Robert R., tr. from Ital. LC 81-16913. Orig. Title: Io Francesco. 144p. (Orig.). 1982. 9.95 (ISBN 0-88344-201-9); pap. 5.95 (ISBN 0-88344-200-0). Orbis Bks.

--Letters from the Desert. 1976. pap. write for info (ISBN 0-515-09573-7). Jove Pubns.

--Letters from the Desert. Hancock, Rose, tr. from Ital. LC 72-85791. Orig. Title: Lettres dal deserts. 146p. (Orig.). 1982. pap. 4.95 (ISBN 0-88344-280-9). Orbis Bks.

Carr-Gregg, Charlotte. Japanese Prisoners of War in Revolt: The Outbreaks at Featherston & Cowra During World War II. LC 78-2103. (Illus.). 1978. 22.50x (ISBN 0-312-44060-X). St Martin.

Carriazo, Eduardo, tr. see Kaufmann, William J., 3rd.

Carrick, A. Computers & Instrumentation. Thomas, L. C., ed. 1979. casebound 42.95 (ISBN 0-471-25624-2, Pub. by Wiley Heyden). Wiley.

Carrick, Alice V. & Robinson, Kenneth A. A Mother Goose for Antique Collectors. LC 74-17746. (Illus.). 64p. 1975. pap. 1.50 o.p. (ISBN 0-486-23166-6). Dover.

Carrick, Carol. Sand Tiger Shark. LC 76-40206. (gr. 1-5). 1976. 9.95 (ISBN 0-395-28779-0, Clarion). HM.

--What a Whip! (Illus.). 96p. (gr. 3-6). 1983. 9.25 (ISBN 0-89919-139-8, Clarion). HM.

Carrick, Malcolm. Tramp. LC 76-58723. (gr. 2-5). 1977. 5.95 o.p. (ISBN 0-06-021117-2, HarpJ); PLB 5.79 o.p. (ISBN 0-06-021118-0). Har-Row.

Carrick, Peter. All Hell & Autocross-More Hell & Rallycross. 1972. 10.00 o.p. (ISBN 0-7207-0463-4). Transatlantic.

--Great Moments in Sport: Motor Cycle Racing. (Illus.). 1977. 16.95 o.p. (ISBN 0-7207-0972-5). Transatlantic.

--Hell Raisers. (Illus.). 173p. 1974. 8.75 o.p. (ISBN 0-7207-0668-8). Transatlantic.

Carrick, Peter, compiled by. Encyclopedia of Motor Cycle Sport. Rev. ed. (Illus.). 240p. 1982. 14.95 (ISBN 0-312-24868-7). St Martin.

Carrick, R. J. East-West Technology Transfer in Perspective. LC 78-78134. (Policy Papers in International Affairs Ser.: No. 9). 1978. pap. 5.50x (ISBN 0-87725-509-1). U of Cal Intl St.

Carrick, Robert & Henderson, Richard. John Alden's Yacht Designs. LC 77-85407. (Illus.). 320p. 1983. 35.00 (ISBN 0-87742-089-0). Intl Marine.

Carrie, Christopher. Adventure at the Pirates' Cave. (Crayola Activity Storybooks). (Illus.). 48p. (Orig.). (gr. k-4). 1980. pap. 1.32 (ISBN 0-86696-025-2). Binney & Smith.

--Adventure of the Haunted Mansion. (Crayola Activity Storybooks). (Illus.). 48p. (Orig.). (gr. k-4). 1980. pap. 1.32 (ISBN 0-86696-030-9). Binney & Smith.

--Adventure of the Space Robots. (Crayola Activity Storybooks). (Illus.). 48p. (Orig.). (gr. k-4). 1980. pap. 1.32 (ISBN 0-86696-027-9). Binney & Smith.

--Amazing Cars. (Crayola Laugh & Play Bks.). (Illus.). 48p. (Orig.) (gr. k-4). 1981. pap. 1.32 (ISBN 0-86696-033-3). Binney & Smith.

--Astounding Animals. (Crayola Laugh & Play Bks.). (Illus.). 48p. (Orig.). (gr. k-4). 1981. pap. 1.32 (ISBN 0-86696-032-5). Binney & Smith.

--Exciting Outer Space. (Crayola Laugh & Play Books). (Illus.). 48p. (Orig.). (gr. k-4). 1981. pap. 1.32 (ISBN 0-86696-036-8). Binney & Smith.

--Fantastic Airplanes. (Crayola Laugh & Play Bks.). (Illus.). 48p. (Orig.). (gr. k-4). 1981. pap. 1.32 (ISBN 0-86696-035-X). Binney & Smith.

--Friendly Monsters. (Crayola Laugh & Play Bks.). (Illus.). 48p. (Orig.). (gr. k-4). 1981. pap. 1.32 (ISBN 0-86696-034-1). Binney & Smith.

--Mystery of Dinosaur Island. (Crayola Activity Storybooks). (Illus.). 48p. (Orig.). (gr. k-4). 1980. pap. 1.32 (ISBN 0-86696-029-5). Binney & Smith.

--Mystery of the Missing Wand. (Crayola Activity Storybooks). (Illus.). 48p. (Orig.). (gr. k-4). 1980. pap. 1.32 (ISBN 0-86696-028-7). Binney & Smith.

--Mystery of the Stolen Gold. (Crayola Activity Storybooks). (Illus.). 48p. (Orig.). (gr. k-4). 1980. pap. 1.32 (ISBN 0-86696-026-0). Binney & Smith.

--Surprising People. (Crayola Laugh & Play Bks.). (Illus.). 48p. (Orig.). (gr. k-4). 1981. pap. 1.32 (ISBN 0-86696-031-7). Binney & Smith.

Carrie, Jacques. Intrepid Visions. LC 81-67260. (Illus.). 138p. (Orig.). 1982. pap. 4.95 (ISBN 0-937578-01-0). Fablewaves.

Carrier Air Conditioning Co. Handbook of Air Conditioning System Design. 1965. 59.50 (ISBN 0-07-010090-X, P&RB). McGraw.

Carrier, Constance, tr. see Bovie, Palmer.

Carrier, George F., et al. Functions of a Complex Variable: Theory & Technique. 1966. 34.95 (ISBN 0-07-010089-6, C). McGraw.

Carrier, Lois, jt. auth. see Gooch, Bill.

Carrier, Lyman. Agriculture in Virginia, Sixteen Hundred & Seven to Sixteen Ninety-Nine. (Illus.). 41p. 1957. pap. 2.95 (ISBN 0-8139-0138-3). U Pr of Va.

Carrier, Robert. Entertaining. LC 78-58768. (Illus.). 1978. 16.95 o.s.i. (ISBN 0-89479-034-X). A & W Pubs.

Carrier, Roch. La Guerre, Yes Sir! Fischman, Sheila, tr. from Fr. (Anansi Fiction Ser.: No. 10). 113p. 1970. 9.95 (ISBN 0-88784-410-3, Pub. by Hse Anansi Pr Canada); pap. 4.95 (ISBN 0-88784-310-7); study guide by Peter Carver 1.00x (ISBN 0-88784-068-X). U of Toronto Pr.

--The Hockey Sweater & Other Stories. Fischman, Sheila, tr. from Fr. (Anansi Fiction Ser.: No. 40). 160p. (Orig.). 1979. pap. 6.95 (ISBN 0-88784-078-7, Pub. by Hse Anansi Pr Canada). U of Toronto Pr.

--They Won't Demolish Me! Fischman, Sheila, tr. from Fr. (Anansi Fiction Ser.: No. 30). 134p. (Orig.). 1974. pap. 6.95 (ISBN 0-88784-328-X, Pub. by Hse Anansi Pr Canada). U of Toronto Pr.

Carrigan, Arnold. How to Get the Most from Your IRA. 1982. 9.95 o.p. (ISBN 0-517-54917-4, Harmony Bks); pap. 3.95 o.p. (ISBN 0-517-54918-2). Crown.

Carrigan, R. A., et al, eds. see AIP Conference, 87th, Fermilab School, 1981.

Carrigan, R. A., Jr. & Huson, F. R., eds. The State of Particle Accelerators & High Energy (Fermilab Summer School, 1981) LC 82-73861. (AIP Conference Proceedings Ser.: No.92). 337p. 1982. lib. bdg. 33.75 (ISBN 0-88318-191-6). Am Inst Physics.

Carril, Bonifacio Del see Saint-Exupery, Antone De.

Carrillo, Santiago. Eurocommunism & the State. Green, Nan & Elliott, A. M., trs. LC 78-51455. 180p. 1978. 8.95 (ISBN 0-88208-093-8); pap. 4.95 o.s.i. (ISBN 0-88208-094-6). Lawrence Hill.

Carrilo, Salvador. Power from on High: The Holy Spirit in the Gospels & the Acts. Mishler, Carolyn, tr. from Sp. 1978. pap. 2.95 (ISBN 0-89283-060-3). Servant.

Carringer, Robert L., ed. The Jazz Singer. LC 78-53295. (Screenplay Ser.). (Illus.). 1979. 17.50 (ISBN 0-299-07660-1); pap. 6.95 (ISBN 0-299-07664-4). U of Wis Pr.

Carringer, Robert L. & Sabath, Barry, eds. Ernst Lubitsch: A Guide to References & Resources. 1978. lib. bdg. 25.00 (ISBN 0-8161-7895-X, Hall Reference). G K Hall.

Carrington. Ab-Sa-Ra-Ka, Land of Massacre. (Classics of the Old West Ser.). 1983. lib. bdg. 17.28 (ISBN 0-686-42740-8). Silver.

Carrington, A. & McLachlan, A. D. Introduction to Magnetic Resonance: With Applications to Chemistry & Chemical Physics. 1979. pap. 19.50x (ISBN 0-412-21700-7, Pub. by Chapman & Hall). Methuen Inc.

Carrington, Charles E. British Overseas. 2nd ed. LC 68-23176. (Illus.). 1968. 62.50 (ISBN 0-521-07174-7). Cambridge U Pr.

Carrington, Elsie R., jt. auth. see Willson, J. Robert.

Carrington, Frank G. Neither Cruel nor Unusual: The Case for Capital Punishment. 1978. 9.95 o.p. (ISBN 0-87000-405-0, Arlington Hse). Crown.

Carrington, Grant. Time's Fool. LC 79-8558. (Science Fiction Ser.). 192p. 1981. 10.95 o.p. (ISBN 0-385-15288-4). Doubleday.

Carrington, Hereward, jt. auth. see Buckland, Raymond.

Carrington, Hereward, jt. auth. see Muldoon, Sylvan.

Carrington, John F. Talking Drums of Africa. (Illus.). 96p. 1949. 14.00. G Vanderstoel.

Carrington, Paul & Babcock, Barbara A. Civil Procedure: Cases & Comments on the Process of Adjudication. 2nd ed. 1977. text ed. 28.00 (ISBN 0-316-12984-4); pap. 6.95 (ISBN 0-316-12987-9). Little.

Carrington, R. & Bellairs. World of Reptiles. 1966. 5.50 (ISBN 0-444-19969-1). Elsevier.

Carrington, R. A. Computers for Spectroscopists. LC 74-12526. 275p. 27.50 (ISBN 0-470-13581-6). Krieger.

Carrington, Richard. The Mammals. rev. ed. LC 80-52257. (Life Nature Library). 13.40 (ISBN 0-8094-3907-7). Silver.

--The Mammals. (Young Readers Library). (Illus.). 1977. PLB 6.80 (ISBN 0-8094-1381-7). Silver.

Carrino, Frank G., ed. see Hernandez, Jose.

Carrion, Arturo M., et al. Puerto Rico: A Political & Cultural Odyssey. (Illus.). 1983. 19.50 (ISBN 0-393-01740-0). Norton.

Carris, William. Inside Atari Basic: A Fast, Fun & Friendly Approach. 1982. text ed. 17.95 (ISBN 0-8359-3083-1); pap. text ed. 12.95 (ISBN 0-8359-3082-3). Reston.

Carrithers, David W., ed. see Montesquieu.

Carrodeguas, Andy, ed. see Barber, Cyril J.

Carrodeguas, Andy, ed. see BOyer, Orlando.

Carrodeguas, Andy, ed. see Boyer, Orlando.

Carrodeguas, Andy, ed. see Brights, Bill.

Carrodeguas, Andy, ed. see Cabral, J.

Carrodeguas, Andy, ed. see Caldwell, E. S.

Carrodeguas, Andy, ed. see Carlson, G. Raymond.

Carrodeguas, Andy, ed. see Charles, J. Norman & Charles, Sharon.

Carrodeguas, Andy, ed. see Cho, Paul Y.

Carrodeguas, Andy, ed. see Coleman, William L.

Carrodeguas, Andy, ed. see Cornwall, Judson.

Carrodeguas, Andy, ed. see Ekvall, Robert B.

Carrodeguas, Andy, ed. see Henrichsen, Walter A.

Carrodeguas, Andy, ed. see Hook & Boren.

Carrodeguas, Andy, ed. see Hutchison, Becky & Farish, Kay.

Carrodeguas, Andy, ed. see Kerstan, Reinhold.

Carrodeguas, Andy, ed. see Lin, Yi.

Carrodeguas, Andy, ed. see Lockyer, Herbert, Sr.

Carrodeguas, Andy, ed. see McManus, Una & Cooper, John C.

Carrodeguas, Andy, ed. see Mayhall, Jack & Mayhall, Carole.

Carrodeguas, Andy, ed. see Nee, T. S.

Carrodeguas, Andy, ed. see Petersen, William J.

Carrodeguas, Andy, ed. see Strauss, Richard.

Carrodeguas, Andy, ed. see Tenney, Merrill C.

Carrodeguas, Andy, et al, eds. see Calderon, Wilfredo.

Carrodeguas, Andy, et al, eds. see Cook, Jerry.

Carrodeguas, Andy, et al, eds. see Getz, Gene.

Carrodeguas, Andy, et al, eds. see Raburn, Terry.

Carrol, F. Nosie the Research Hound. 50p. Date not set. pap. 7.95. Biblio Pr GA.

Carrol, Frieda. Creative Financing for Education, Housing, Automobiles, Vacations, Medical Care Etc. 60p. 1983. pap. text ed. 29.95 (ISBN 0-939476-58-4). Biblio Pr GA.

--Directory of Factory Outlet Directories. 50p. 1983. pap. text ed. 12.95 (ISBN 0-939476-91-6). Biblio Pr GA.

--Unemployment Challenge Log Workbook. 60p. 1983. pap. 9.95 (ISBN 0-939476-86-X). Biblio Pr GA.

Carrol, Frieda, compiled by. Directory of Registering Agents Services for Delaware Incorporators. 150p. 1983. pap. text ed. 19.95 (ISBN 0-939476-87-8). Biblio Pr GA.

Carrol, Frieda. Boom Businesses U. S. A. 50p. 1983. 8.95 (ISBN 0-939476-75-4). Biblio Pr GA.

--Boom Cities & Towns: U. S. A. Workbook. 50p. 1983. 8.95 (ISBN 0-939476-51-7). Biblio Pr GA.

--Boom Towns U. S. A. LC 81-68664. 50p. 1981. pap. text ed. 7.95 (ISBN 0-939476-31-2). Biblio Pr GA.

--Continuing Education Alternatives. LC 80-68549. 1981. 49.95 (ISBN 0-939476-14-2); pap. 39.95 (ISBN 0-939476-15-0). Biblio Pr GA.

--Continuing Education Alternatives Workbook. 50p. 1983. 8.95. Biblio Pr GA.

--Creative Uses for the Barter Card. 16p. 1983. pap. 4.95 (ISBN 0-911617-56-6). Barter Pub.

--Directory of Farmer's Markets in the U. S. & Some Other Countries. 60p. Date not set. pap. text ed. 10.95 (ISBN 0-939476-78-9). Biblio Pr GA.

--Guide for the Unemployed Workbook. 60p. Date not set. 9.95 (ISBN 0-939476-80-0). Biblio Pr GA.

--New & Useful Forms, Stationery, & Greetings To Duplicate & Use. 50p. Date not set. pap. text ed. 10.95 (ISBN 0-939476-84-3). Biblio Pr GA.

--People's Money Pages. 1st ed. LC 80-70419. 50p. 1981. 16.50 (ISBN 0-9605246-3-0); pap. 9.95 (ISBN 0-686-96676-7). Biblio Pr GA.

--Pick Your Own Fruits & Vegetables & More. LC 80-70861. 1981. 14.95 (ISBN 0-939476-12-6); pap. 9.95 (ISBN 0-939476-11-8); wkbk. 8.95 (ISBN 0-939476-82-7). Biblio Pr GA.

--Prescriptions for Survival. LC 78-72312. 148p. 1981. pap. text ed. 21.95 (ISBN 0-9605246-1-4). Biblio Pr GA.

--Recycling Suggestions For Home, Business, Associations, Government etc. 60p. Date not set. pap. text ed. 17.95 (ISBN 0-939476-83-5). Biblio Pr GA.

--Smorgasboard U. S. A. 150p. (Orig.). 1982. pap. text ed. 9.95 (ISBN 0-939476-49-5). Biblio Pr GA.

--Survival Handbook for Small Business. LC 80-70496. 73p. 1981. 16.95 (ISBN 0-9605246-4-9); pap. 12.95 (ISBN 0-686-96677-5); 8.95 (ISBN 0-939476-79-7). Biblio Pr GA.

--The Traveler's Workbook: Based on the People's Travel Book Index. 50p. 1983. 7.95 (ISBN 0-939476-52-5). Biblio Pr GA.

Carrol, Frieda, compiled by. Bibliotheca Press Subject Notebook with Bibliographic Information. 300p. 1983. notebook 35.00 (ISBN 0-939476-64-9). Biblio Pr GA.

--Directory of Barter Directories. 100p. 1983. pap. 19.95 (ISBN 0-911617-55-8). Barter Pub.

--International Directory of Barter Associations & Organizations. 200p. 1983. pap. 19.95 (ISBN 0-911617-54-X). Barter Pub.
--The People's Travel Book. LC 80-70869. 115p. 1981. 39.95 (ISBN 0-939476-05-3); pap. 29.95 (ISBN 0-939476-06-1). Biblio Pr Ga.
Carroll. Handbook for Schoolbook & Supply Store Management. (Bulletin 24). 1977. 5.00 (ISBN 0-910170-02-9). Assn Sch Busn.
--White Collar Crime. 1982. text ed. 21.95 (ISBN 0-409-95065-3). Butterworth.
Carroll, ed. see McMahon, Ed.
Carroll, Alan. Pirate Subdivisions & the Market for Residential Lots in Bogota. (Working Paper: No. 435). 116p. 1980. 5.00 (ISBN 0-686-36229-2, WP-0435). World Bank.
Carroll, Albert. Crosswords for the Connoisseur, 4 Vols. (Illus., Orig.). 1955-69. Series 1. pap. 2.95 (ISBN 0-448-01558-7, G&D); Series 2. pap. 2.95 (ISBN 0-448-01559-5); Series 3. pap. 2.95 (ISBN 0-448-01577-3); Series 4. pap. 2.95 (ISBN 0-448-01588-9). Putnam Pub Group.
Carroll, Alice M., abridged by see Morris, Milton D. & Mayio, Albert.
Carroll, Anne K., jt. auth. see Cooper, Darien.
Carroll, Anne K., jt. auth. see Cooper, Darien B.
Carroll, Anne Kristin. Together Forever: For Healthy Marriages, or for Strained, or Broken Ones. 256p. (Orig.). 1982. pap. 7.95 (ISBN 0-310-45021-7). Zondervan.
Carroll, Archie B. Business & Society: Managing Corporate Social Performance. text ed. 18.95 (ISBN 0-316-13010-9); tchr's manual avail. (ISBN 0-316-13011-7). Little.
Carroll, Archie B., ed. Managing Corporate Social Responsibility. pap. text ed. 11.95 (ISBN 0-316-13008-7). Little.
Carroll, B. J. General English Tests Elementary One Pack. (Illus.). 8p. 1982. pap. 100.00 (ISBN 0-08-029432-4). Pergamon.
Carroll, Berenice, et al. Peace & War: A Guide to Bibliographies. Burns, Richard, ed. LC 81-4980. (War-Peace Bibliography Ser.: No.16). 1983. text ed. 42.50 (ISBN 0-87436-322-5). ABC-Clio.
Carroll, Bonnie. Job Satisfaction. rev. ed. (Key Issues Ser.: No. 3). 60p. 1973. pap. 2.00 (ISBN 0-87546-206-5). ILR Pr.
Carroll, Charles. Journal of Charles Carroll of Carrollton. 110p. 20.00 (ISBN 0-686-36706-5). Md Hist.
Carroll, D., jt. auth. see Baxter, R. R.
Carroll, D. Allen, ed. see Guilpin, Everard.
Carroll, D. M., ed. Euroanalysis III. (Illus.). 1979. 92.25x (ISBN 0-85334-847-2, Pub. by Applied Sci England). Elsevier.
Carroll, David. Chinua Achebe. (World Authors Ser.: Nigeria: No. 101). lib. bdg. 9.95 o.p. (ISBN 0-8057-2004-9, Twayne). G K Hall.
--Playboy's Illustrated Treasury of Gambling. (Illus.). 1977. 19.95 o.p. (ISBN 0-517-53050-3). Crown.
--The Subject in Question: The Languages of Theory & the Strategies of Fiction. LC 82-1995. 240p. (Orig.). 1982. lib. bdg. 26.00x (ISBN 0-226-09493-6); pap. 12.95x (ISBN 0-226-09494-4). U of Chicago Pr.
Carroll, Dennis, ed. Kumu Kahua Plays. LC 82-23724. (Orig.). 1983. pap. text ed. 10.95x (ISBN 0-8248-0805-3). UH Pr.
Carroll, Don & Carroll, Marie. Focus on Special Effects: Locating Pictures That Exist Only in Your Mind. (Illus.). 184p. 1982. 24.95 (ISBN 0-8174-3885-8, Amphoto). Watson-Guptill.
Carroll, Donald C. see Sheppard, C. Stewart.
Carroll, Elizabeth. Summer Love, No. 1. (Dream your own Romance Ser.). 128p. (gr. 3-7). 1983. pap. 2.95 (ISBN 0-671-46449-3). Wanderer Bks.
Carroll, Francis M. American Opinion & the Irish Question: 1910-1923. LC 78-58897. 1978. 26.00x (ISBN 0-312-02890-3). St Martin.
Carroll, Harold. OS Data Processing with Review of OS-VS. LC 74-2047. 28p. 1974. 27.50 o.p. (ISBN 0-471-13600-X, Pub. by Wiley-Interscience). Wiley.
Carroll, Harry J., Jr., et al. The Development of Civilization: A Documentary History of Politics, Society & Thought, 2 vols. rev. ed. 1969. pap. 12.50x ea.; Vol. 1. (ISBN 0-673-05784-4); Vol.2. (ISBN 0-673-05785-2). Scott F.
Carroll, Herbert A. Mental Hygiene: Dynamics of Adjustment. 5th ed. 1969. text ed. 23.95x (ISBN 0-13-576314-2). P-H.
Carroll, Jackson W. & Hargrove, Barbara J. Women of the Cloth: New Opportunity for the Churches. LC 82-47740. 288p. 1983. 12.95 (ISBN 0-06-061321-1, HarpR). Har-Row.
Carroll, James. Family Trade. (General Ser.). 1983. lib. bdg. 18.95 (ISBN 0-8161-3483-9, Large Print Bks). G K Hall.
--Forbidden Disappointments. 6.95 o.p. (ISBN 0-8091-1842-4); pap. 3.95 o.p. (ISBN 0-686-82952-2). Paulist Pr.
--Tender of Wishes. (Illus.). 1974. pap. 1.95 o.p. (ISBN 0-8091-1836-X). Paulist Pr.
--A Terrible Beauty: Conversions in Prayers, Politics & Imagination. LC 72-97400. 1973. 4.95 o.p. (ISBN 0-8091-0182-3). Paulist Pr.
--Utopia Now. 160p. 1977. pap. 1.95 (ISBN 0-89826-001-9). Natl Paperback.
Carroll, James & Overton, Barbara. Be Sure Your Child Learns to Read. 160p. 1976. pap. 1.95 (ISBN 0-89826-000-0). Natl Paperback.
Carroll, James, ed. see Hartmann, Frederick H.
Carroll, James J., ed. see Hartmann, Frederick H.
Carroll, Jane, tr. see Baccheschi, Edi.
Carroll, Jean & Lofthouse, Peter. Creative Dance for Boys. (Illus.). 1979. Repr. of 1969 ed. 12.50 (ISBN 0-7121-0318-X). Dufour.
Carroll, Jean G. Patient Care Audit Criteria: Standards for Hospital Quality Assurance. LC 82-72867. 250p. 1983. 49.50 (ISBN 0-87094-392-8). Dow Jones-Irwin.
Carroll, Joan & Lofthouse, Peter. Creative Dance for Boys. 72p. 1972. 30.00x (ISBN 0-7121-0318-X, Pub. by Macdonald & Evans). State Mutual Bk.
Carroll, Joellyn. A Flight of Splendor. (Candlelight Ecstasy Ser.: No. 159). (Orig.). 1983. pap. 1.95 (ISBN 0-440-12858-7). Dell.
--Run Before the Wind. (Candlelight Ecstasy Ser.: No. 131). (Orig.). 1983. pap. 1.95 (ISBN 0-440-17880-0). Dell.
Carroll, John. Break-Out from the Crystal Palace: The Anarcho-Psychological Critique-Stirner, Nietzsche, Dostoevsky. (International Library of Sociology). 1974. 19.95x (ISBN 0-7100-7750-5). Routledge & Kegan.
--Home Study Darkroom Course. (Illus.). 1980. 17.95 o.p. (ISBN 0-8174-3687-1, Amphoto). Watson-Guptill.
--How to Handicap the Claiming Races Professionally. 1983. 10.00 (ISBN 0-533-05233-5). Vantage.
--Intruders in the Bush: The Australian Quest for Identity. 1982. pap. 11.95 (ISBN 0-19-554308-4). Oxford U Pr.
--Photographic Lab Handbook. 5th ed. (Amphoto Ser.). (Illus.). 1979. text ed. 24.95 o.p. (ISBN 0-13-665422-3, Spec). P-H.
--Puritan, Paranoid, Remissive: A Sociology of Modern Culture. 1977. 16.95x (ISBN 0-7100-8622-9). Routledge & Kegan.
Carroll, John, ed. Computer Simulation in Emergency Planning. (Simulation Series: Vol. 11, No. 2). 30.00 (ISBN 0-686-38791-0). Soc Computer Sim.
--Samuel Richardson: A Collection of Critical Essays. LC 69-17372. (Twentieth Century Views Ser). 1969. 12.95t (ISBN 0-13-791160-2, Spec); pap. 1.95 o.p. (ISBN 0-13-791152-1, STC85, Spec). P-H.
Carroll, John B. Language & Thought. (Orig.). 1964. pap. 9.95 ref. ed. (ISBN 0-13-522706-2). P-H.
--The Teaching of French As a Foreign Language in Eight Countries. LC 75-17945. (International Studies in Evaluation, Vol. 5). 281p. 1975. 19.95x o.p. (ISBN 0-470-13602-2); pap. write for info o.p. Halsted Pr.
Carroll, John B., ed. Language, Thought & Reality: Selected Writings of Benjamin Lee Whorf. 1956. 18.00x (ISBN 0-262-23003-8); pap. 5.95 (ISBN 0-262-73006-5). MIT Pr.
Carroll, John B. & Chall, Jeanne, eds. Toward a Literate Society: A Report from the National Academy of Education. 352p. 1975. 21.95 (ISBN 0-07-010130-2, P&RB). McGraw.
Carroll, John E. Acid Rain: An Issue in Canadian-American Relations. LC 82-82205. (Canadian-American Committee). 98p. (Orig.). 1982. pap. 6.00 (ISBN 0-89068-064-7). Natl Planning.
--Environmental Diplomacy: An Examination & a Perspective of Canadian-U. S. Transboundary Environmental Relations. 402p. 1983. text ed. 22.50x (ISBN 0-472-10029-7). U of Mich Pr.
Carroll, John M. Computer Security. LC 77-10615. (Illus.). 1977. 21.95 (ISBN 0-913708-28-3). Butterworth.
--Confidential Information Sources: Public & Private. LC 74-20177. (Illus.). 320p. 1975. 19.95 (ISBN 0-913708-19-4). Butterworth.
--Custer in Periodicals: A Bibliographic Checklist. (Source Custeriana Ser.: No. 5). 1975. 27.50 (ISBN 0-88342-043-0). Old Army.
--Mechanical Design for Electronics Production. 1956. 30.00 o.p. (ISBN 0-07-010110-8, P&RB). McGraw.
--Modern Transistor Circuits. 1959. 27.50 o.p. (ISBN 0-07-010141-8, P&RB). McGraw.
Carroll, John M., jt. auth. see Varnum, Charles.
Carroll, John M., ed. Custer in the Civil War: His Unfinished Memoirs. LC 77-85602. (Illus.). 1978. 27.50 o.p. (ISBN 0-89141-049-X). Presidio Pr.
--Design Manual for Transistor Circuits. (Illus.). 1961. 36.00 (ISBN 0-07-010144-2, P&RB). McGraw.
--General Custer & the Battle of the Little Big Horn: The Federal View. LC 76-11331. (Illus.). 1978. 19.50 o.p. (ISBN 0-686-77344-6). Presidio Pr.
--The Two Battles of the Little Big Horn. (Illus.). 1974. 35.00 o.s.i. (ISBN 0-87140-586-5). Liveright.
Carroll, John R. Physical & Technical Aspects of Fire & Arson Investigation. (Illus.). 470p. 1979. 44.50x (ISBN 0-398-03785-X). C C Thomas.
Carroll, John S. Photographic Facts & Formulas. (Illus.). 1975. 22.50 o.p. (ISBN 0-8174-0580-1, Amphoto); pap. 12.95 o.p. (ISBN 0-8174-2193-9). Watson-Guptill.
--Photographic Lab Handbook. 5th ed. (Illus.). 1979. pap. 14.95 (ISBN 0-8174-2158-0, Amphoto). Watson-Guptill.
--Photographic Lab Handbook. 4th ed. 1977. pap. 10.95 o.p. (ISBN 0-8174-2109-2, Amphoto). Watson-Guptill.
Carroll, Jonathan. The Voice of Our Shadow. LC 82-70560. 168p. 1983. 13.50 (ISBN 0-670-49240-X). Viking Pr.
Carroll, Joseph. Ireland in the War Years: 1939-1945. LC 74-16547. 192p. 1975. 14.50x o.s.i. (ISBN 0-8448-0607-2). Crane-Russak Co.
Carroll, L. Alice's Adventures in Wonderland. (Illus.). 285p. (gr. 4 up). 1969. pap. 2.25 (ISBN 0-312-01821-5, Papermac). St Martin.
Carroll, L. Patrick, jt. auth. see Dyckman, Katherine M.
Carroll, Lewis. Alice in Wonderland. 1977. pap. 1.95x o.p. (ISBN 0-460-01836-1, Evman). Biblio Dist.
--Alice in Wonderland. (Illus.). 108p. 1973. o. p 7.95 (ISBN 0-517-50857-5, C N Potter Bks); pap. 3.95 (ISBN 0-517-50858-3, C N Potter). Crown.
--Alice in Wonderland. (gr. 3 up). 1979. pap. 1.50 (ISBN 0-307-21616-0, Golden Pr). Western Pub.
--Alice in Wonderland & Other Favorites. 288p. 1983. pap. 2.95 (ISBN 0-671-46688-7). WSP.
--Alice in Wonderland & Through the Looking Glass. (Illus.). (gr. 4-6). 1946-63. companion lib. ed. 2.95 (ISBN 0-448-05454-X, G&D); il. jr. lib. ed. 5.95 (ISBN 0-448-05804-9); deluxe ed. 8.95 (ISBN 0-448-06004-3). Putnam Pub Group.
--Alice Through the Looking Glass & What Alice Found There. (Illus.). 144p. 1973. 7.95 o.p. (ISBN 0-517-50857-5, C N Potter); pap. 3.95 (ISBN 0-517-50858-3, C N Potter Bks). Crown.
--Alice's Adventures in Wonderland. LC 77-72625. (Illus.). 1977. 7.95 o.s.i. (ISBN 0-440-00069-6, Sey Lawr); PLB 7.45 o.s.i. (ISBN 0-440-00075-0). Delacorte.
--Alice's Adventures in Wonderland. Bd. with Through the Looking Glass. 1950. pap. 2.25 (ISBN 0-14-030169-0, Puffin). Penguin.
--Alice's Adventures in Wonderland. Bd. with Through the Looking Glass: And What Alice Found There; The Hunting of the Snark: An Agony in Eight Fits. LC 77-17651. (Illus.). 1978. pap. 4.95 (ISBN 0-8052-0594-2). Schocken.
--Alice's Adventures in Wonderland, No. I. Pennyroyal ed. (Illus.). 148p. 1982. 19.95 (ISBN 0-520-04815-6); deluxe ed. 195.00 (ISBN 0-520-04820-2). U of Cal Pr.
--Alice's Adventures in Wonderland. Bd. with Through the Looking Glass. (Bantam Classics Ser.). (Illus.). 256p. (gr. 6-12). 1981. pap. 1.75 (ISBN 0-553-21052-1). Bantam.
--Alice's Adventures in Wonderland & Through the Looking Glass. LC 78-3389. (Raintree's Illustrated Classics). (Illus.). (gr. 5-8). 1978. PLB 13.30 (ISBN 0-8172-1133-0). Raintree Pubs.
--Alice's Adventures in Wonderland & Through the Looking Glass. Barish, Wendy, ed. (Illus.). 256p. 1982. 14.95 (ISBN 0-671-43788-7). Wanderer Bks.
--Alice's Adventures in Wonderland & Through the Looking-Glass. Green, Roger L., ed. (World's Classics Ser.). (Illus.). 1983. pap. 4.95 (ISBN 0-19-281620-9). Oxford U Pr.
--The Annotated Alice. 352p. 1962. 10.00 o.p. (ISBN 0-517-02962-6, C N Potter Bks). Crown.
--Le Avventure D'alice Nel Paese Della Meraviglie. Pietrocola-Rossetti, T., tr. from Italian. (Illus.). 1978. pap. 3.50 o.p. (ISBN 0-486-23277-8). Dover.
--Complete Works. 1976. pap. 9.95 (ISBN 0-394-71661-2, Vin). Random.
--The Complete Works of Lewis Carroll. 10.95 (ISBN 0-394-60485-7). Modern Lib.
--Humorous Verse of Lewis Carroll. Orig. Title: Collected Verse of Lewis Carroll. (Illus.). (gr. 1 up). 1933. pap. 6.50 (ISBN 0-486-20654-8). Dover.
--The Hunting of the Snark. (Illus.). 96p. (YA) 1975. pap. 4.95 o.p. (ISBN 0-517-52399-X, C N Potter Bks). Crown.
--The Letters of Lewis Carroll, 2 vols. Cohen, Morton H. & Green, Roger L., eds. (Illus.). 1979. Set. 65.00x (ISBN 0-19-520090-X). Oxford U Pr.
--Lewis Carroll's Symbolic Logic: Part I & Part II. Bartley, W. W., ed. 1977. pap. 6.95 (ISBN 0-517-53363-4, C N Potter Bks). Crown.
--The Nursery Alice. (gr. 4-9). pap. 3.95 (ISBN 0-486-21610-1). Dover.
--The Philosopher's Alice: Alice's Adventures in Wonderland & Through the Looking-Glass. (Illus.). 256p. 1983. pap. 7.95 (ISBN 0-312-60518-8). St Martin.
--The Pig-Tale. (Illus.). 32p. (gr. 4-6). 1975. 7.95 (ISBN 0-316-13006-0). Little.
--Poems of Lewis Carroll. Livingston, Myra C., compiled by. LC 73-7914. (Poets Ser.). (Illus.). (gr. 6 up). 1973. 10.53i o.p. (ISBN 0-690-00178-9, TYC-J). Har-Row.
--A Tangled Tale. LC 74-82735. 1975. 4.95 o.s.i. (ISBN 0-89388-181-3). Okpaku Communications.
--Through the Looking Glass. 1979. pap. 1.95x (ISBN 0-460-01018-2, Evman). Biblio Dist.
--The Wasp in a Wig. (Illus.). 1978. pap. 4.95 o.p. (ISBN 0-517-53266-2, C N Potter Bks). Crown.
Carroll, Lewis see Swan, D. K.
Carroll, Malcolm E. Origins of the Whig Party: A Dissertation. LC 72-112705. (Law, Politics & History Ser). 1970. Repr. of 1925 ed. lib. bdg. 37.50 (ISBN 0-306-71917-7). Da Capo.
Carroll, Margaret D. & Abraham, Sidney. Dietary Intake Source Data: United States, 1976-80. Olmstead, Mary, ed. (Ser. 11: No. 231). 50p. 1982. pap. text ed. 1.75 (ISBN 0-8406-0265-0). Natl Ctr Health Stats.
Carroll, Marie, jt. auth. see Carroll, Don.
Carroll, Mary A. & Humphrey, Richard A. Moral Problems in Nursing: Case Studies. 1979. pap. text ed. 10.50 (ISBN 0-8191-0705-0). U Pr of Amer.
Carroll, Noel. Sport in Ireland. (Aspects of Ireland Ser.: Vol. 6). (Illus.). 105p. Date not set. pap. 5.95 (ISBN 0-906404-06-1, Pub. by Dept Foreign Ireland). Irish Bks Media.
Carroll, Peter & Noble, David W. The Restless Centuries: A History of the American People. 2nd ed. LC 78-67974. 1979. pap. text ed. 12.95x (ISBN 0-8087-2920-9). Burgess.
Carroll, R. Transmutation, Scattering Theory & Special Functions. (North-Holland Mathematics Studies: Vol. 69). 458p. 1982. 64.00 (ISBN 0-444-86426-1, North Holland). Elsevier.
Carroll, R. W. Transmutation & Operator Differential Equations. (Mathematics Studies: Vol. 37). 1979. 40.50 (ISBN 0-444-85328-6, North Holland). Elsevier.
Carroll, Raymond. The Palestine Question. (Impact Ser.). 96p. (gr. 7 up). 1983. PLB 8.90 (ISBN 0-531-04549-8). Watts.
Carroll, Robert & Gaskill, Pamela. The Order Microsauria. LC 78-56735. (Memoirs Ser.: Vol. 126). (Illus.). pap. 20.00 (ISBN 0-87169-126-4). Am Philos.
Carroll, Shana. Paxton Pride. (Orig.). 1976. pap. 1.95 o.p. (ISBN 0-515-04019-3). Jove Pubns.
Carroll, Stephen J. & Schneier, Craig E. Performance Appraisal & Review Systems. (The Scott, Foresman Series in Management & Organizations). 1982. pap. text ed. 10.95x (ISBN 0-673-16006-8). Scott F.
Carroll, Stephen J. & Tosi, Henry L. Organizational Behavior. (Illus.). 590p. 1977. 29.95 (ISBN 0-471-06234-0). Wiley.
Carroll, Stephen J., jt. auth. see Tosi, Henry L.
Carroll, Stephen J., Jr. & Paine, Frank T. Management Process: Cases & Readings. 2nd ed. 448p. 1977. pap. text ed. 14.95x (ISBN 0-02-319520-7, 31952). Macmillan.
Carroll, Stephen J., Jr. & Schuler, Randall S. Human Resources Management in the 1980s. 250p. 1983. pap. text ed. 15.00 (ISBN 0-87179-401-2). BNA.
Carroll, Susanne, jt. auth. see Gregory, Michael.
Carroll, Theodus. Firsts Under the Wire: The World's Fastest Horses (1900-1950) LC 78-11476. (Famous Firsts Ser.). (Illus.). 1978. PLB 10.76 (ISBN 0-89547-062-4). Silver.
--The Mystery of Body Clocks. LC 79-17622. (Unsolved Mysteries of the World Ser.). PLB 11.96 (ISBN 0-89547-078-0). Silver.
Carroll, Theodus C. The Lost Christmas Star. (Mystery Ser.: Gr. 3). (Illus., Based on a story by Elizabeth Yates). (gr. 3-6). 1979. PLB 6.89 (ISBN 0-8116-6409-0, 79-12224). Garrard.
Carroll, Vern & Soulik, Tobias. Nukuoro Lexicon. LC 73-78975. (PALI Language Texts: Polynesia). 859p. (Orig.). 1973. pap. text ed. 17.50x (ISBN 0-8248-0250-0). UH Pr.
Carroll, Vern, ed. Adoption in Eastern Oceania. LC 77-89650. (Association for Social Anthropology in Oceania Monographs: No. 1). (Illus.). 1970. text ed. 15.00x (ISBN 0-87022-110-8). UH Pr.
--Pacific Atoll Populations. LC 75-1264. (Asao Monograph Ser.: No. 3). (Illus.). 550p. 1975. text ed. 22.50x (ISBN 0-8248-0354-X, Eastwest Ctr). UH Pr.
Carroll, W. E., jt. auth. see Krider, J. L.
Carroll, W. H., et al. Reasons for Hope. rev. ed. 264p. 1982. pap. 5.95 (ISBN 0-931888-07-7, Chris. Coll. Pr.). Christendom Pubns.
Carroll, Walter J., ed. The Education Media Handbook, 1983. 1983. 26.00 (ISBN 0-88367-475-0). Olympic Media.
--Educational Media Catalogs on Microfiche: 1981-82. 175.00x set (ISBN 0-88367-301-0). Olympic Media.
--Educational Media Catalogs on Microfiche. 1983. 87.50x (ISBN 0-88367-304-5). Olympic Media.
--Media Profiles: The Audiovisual Marketing Newsletter, 1983, Vol. 1. 1983. 48.00x (ISBN 0-88367-450-5). Olympic Media.
--Media Profiles: The Career Development Edition, 1983, Vol. 15. 1983. 185.00 (ISBN 0-88367-350-9). Olympic Media.
--Media Profiles: The Career Development Edition, 1968-1981, Vols. 1-14. abr. ed. 1981. 496.00x set (ISBN 0-88367-000-3). Olympic Media.
--Media Profiles: The Health Science Edition, Vols. 3-9. 1981. 496.00x set (ISBN 0-88367-200-6). Olympic Media.
--Media Profiles: The Health Science Edition, 1983, Vol. 10. 1983. 87.50 (ISBN 0-88367-210-3). Olympic Media.
--Media Profiles: The Whole Earth Edition, 1983, Vol. 1. 1983. 18.00x. Olympic Media.
--Olympic's Film Finder: 1983-Business Edition. 1983. 24.00x (ISBN 0-88367-601-X). Olympic Media.
--The Salestrainer's Media Handbook. 1983. 24.00 (ISBN 0-88367-375-4). Olympic Media.
--Training Film Profiles, Vol. 14. 1981. 175.00 o.p. (ISBN 0-88367-014-3). Olympic Media.

Carron, Alan J., jt. auth. see Packard, Sidney.

Carron, Andrew S. The Plight of the Thrift Institutions. LC 81-71434. (Regulation of Economic Activity Ser.). 120p. 1982. 12.95 (ISBN 0-8157-1299-5); pap. 5.95 (ISBN 0-8157-1300-2). Brookings.

--Transition to a Free Market: Deregulation of the Air Cargo Industry. LC 81-10244. (Studies in the Regulation of Economic Activity). 73p. 1981. pap. 4.95 (ISBN 0-8157-1297-9). Brookings.

Carron, Harold & McLaughlin, Robert E. Management of Low Back Pain. (Illus.). 256p. 1982. 32.00 (ISBN 0-7236-7001-3). Wright-PSG.

Carron, L P. How to Break into the Computer Field. LC 81-69763. (Illus.). 140p. 1981. pap. 7.95 (ISBN 0-686-32449-8). Carron Pubs.

Carrott, Richard G. The Egyptian Revival: Its Sources, Monuments, & Meaning, 1808-1858. LC 76-24579. (Illus.). 1978. 37.50x (ISBN 0-520-03324-8). U of Cal Pr.

Carrow, Milton M., jt. ed. see Nyhart, J. D.

Carrozza-Martin, Fay, jt. ed. see Hauser-Cram, Penny.

Carr-Ruffino, N. Writing Short Business Reports. 1979. pap. text ed. 10.70 (ISBN 0-07-010155-8, G); instructor's manual & key 6.00 (ISBN 0-07-010156-6). McGraw.

Carr-Saunders, Alexander M. World Population. (Illus.). 336p. 1964. 32.50x (ISBN 0-7146-1283-9, F Cass Co). Biblio Dist.

Carrubba, Eugene R., et al. Assuring Product Integrity. 160p. 1975. 23.95x o.p. (ISBN 0-669-00088-4). Lexington Bks.

Carruth & Hildebrandt. The Theory of Topological Semigroups. (Monographs & Textbooks in Pure & Applied Mathematics). 408p. 1983. 34.75 (ISBN 0-8247-1795-3). Dekker.

Carruth, Gorton, jt. auth. see Brownstone, David M.

Carruth, Gorton, jt. auth. see Ehrlich, Eugene.

Carruth, Hayden. Brothers, I Loved You All. 100p. 1982. pap. 7.95 (ISBN 0-935296-35-2). Sheep Meadow.

--From Snow & Rock, from Chaos. LC 72-93973. 1973. pap. 2.95 (ISBN 0-8112-0469-3, NDP 349). New Directions.

--The Mythology of Dark & Light. (Illus.). 28p. 1982. 12.00 (ISBN 0-918092-33-7); pap. 5.00 (ISBN 0-918092-34-5); signed 35.00 (ISBN 0-918092-32-9). Tamarack Edns.

--The Sleeping Beauty. LC 82-47518. 144p. 1982. 11.49i (ISBN 0-06-015021-1, HarpT); pap. 6.68i (ISBN 0-06-090973-0, CN973). Har-Row.

Carruthers, Mary J. & Kirk, Elizabeth D., eds. Acts of Interpretation: The Text in Its Context. 1982. 32.95 (ISBN 0-937664-60-X). Pilgrim Bks OK.

Carruthers, N. B., jt. auth. see Houghton, E. I.

Carruthers, P., ed. The Coming Age of Psychosomatics: Proceedings of the 21st Annual Conference of the Society of Psychosomatic Research, November 21-22 1977, Royal College of Physicians. (Illus.). 163p. 1979. 29.50 (ISBN 0-08-023736-3). Pergamon.

Carruthers, Peter A. Spin & Isospin in Particle Physics. LC 72-160021. (Illus.). 268p. 1971. 60.00x (ISBN 0-677-02580-7). Gordon.

Carse, Adam. Musical Wind Instruments: A History of the Wind Instruments Used in European Orchestras & Wind Bands, from the Later Middle Ages up to the Present Time. 2nd ed. LC 65-18502. (Music Ser.). 1965. Repr. of 1939 ed. 35.00 (ISBN 0-306-70906-6). Da Capo.

Carse, Adam V. Eighteenth Century Symphonies: A Short History of the Symphony in the 18th Century. LC 78-66900. (Encore Music Editions Ser.). (Illus.). 1979. Repr. of 1951 ed. 12.00 (ISBN 0-88355-731-2). Hyperion Conn.

Carse, James P. Death & Existence: A Conceptual History of Human Mortality. LC 79-24830. (Contemporary Religious Movements: a Wiley-Interscience Ser.). 1980. 31.95 (ISBN 0-471-13704-9, Pub. by Wiley-Interscience). Wiley.

Carse, Stephen, et al. The Financing Procedures of British Foreign Trade. LC 79-18146. 160p. 1980. 29.95 (ISBN 0-521-22534-5). Cambridge U Pr.

Carslaw, Horatio S; see Ball, W. Rouse, et al.

Carson, Ada & Carson, Herbert. Royall Tyler. (United States Authors Ser.). 1979. lib. bdg. 13.95 (ISBN 0-8057-7281-2, Twayne). G K Hall.

Carson, Arthur B. Foundation Construction. 1965. 32.50 o.p. (ISBN 0-07-010167-1, P&RB). McGraw.

Carson, Barbara. A Basis for Composition. 416p. 1982. pap. text ed. 10.95 (ISBN 0-675-09848-3). Additional Supplements May Be Obtained From Publisher. Merrill.

Carson, Ben, ed. see Martin, Betty.

Carson, Bonnie, jt. auth. see Smith, Ivan C.

Carson, Bonnie L., jt. auth. see Smith, Ivan C.

Carson, Bonnie L., jt. ed. see Smith, Ivan C.

Carson, Byrta, et al. How You Plan & Prepare Meals. 3rd ed. (Illus.). 1980. text ed. 18.64 (ISBN 0-07-010162-0). McGraw.

Carson, Byrta R. How You Look & Dress. 4th ed. (American Home & Family Ser). (gr. 7-9). 1969. text ed. 15.80 (ISBN 0-07-010174-4, W). McGraw.

Carson, Byrta R. & Ramee, Marue C. How You Plan & Prepare Meals. 2nd ed. (gr. 7-12). 1968. text ed. 19.16 (ISBN 0-07-010161-2, W). McGraw.

Carson, C. Deane. Money & Finance: Readings in Theory, Policy & Institutions. 2nd ed. LC 70-37643. 492p. 1972. text ed. 25.95x o.p. (ISBN 0-471-13712-X). Wiley.

Carson, Charles R. Managing Employee Honesty. LC 76-51836. (Illus.). 1977. 19.95 (ISBN 0-913708-27-5). Butterworth.

Carson, Clarence B. The World in the Grip of an Idea. 1980. 14.95 o.p. (ISBN 0-87000-456-5, Arlington Hse). Crown.

Carson, Clayborne. In Struggle: SNCC & the Black Awakening of the Nineteen Sixties. LC 80-16540. (Illus.). 384p. 1981. text ed. 22.00x (ISBN 0-674-44725-5); pap. text ed. 8.95 (ISBN 0-674-44726-3). Harvard U Pr.

Carson, D. A. Divine Sovereignty & Human Responsibility: Biblical Perspectives in Tension. Toon, Peter & Martin, Ralph, eds. LC 79-27589. (New Foundations Theological Library). 228p. 1981. 12.95 (ISBN 0-8042-3707-7); pap. 11.95 (ISBN 0-8042-3727-1). John Knox.

Carson, E. R., jt. auth. see Finkelstein, L.

Carson, E. W., Jr., ed. The Plant Root & Its Environment. LC 72-92877. (Illus.). xxiii, 425p. 1974. 17.50x (ISBN 0-8139-0411-0). U Pr of Va.

Carson, H. Glenn. Coinshooting II: Digging Deeper Coins. (Illus.). 106p. (Orig.). 1982. pap. 5.95 (ISBN 0-941620-17-4). H G Carson Ent.

--Treasure Hunting: A Modern Search for Adventure. (Illus.). 82p. 1981. pap. 4.00 (ISBN 0-941620-05-0). H G Carson Ent.

Carson, H. L., jt. ed. see Ashburner, M.

Carson, Hampton L. see Mueller-Dombois, Dieter.

Carson, Herbert, jt. auth. see Carson, Ada.

Carson, J. W. & Rickards, T. Industrial New Product Development: A Manual for the 1980's. LC 79-65781. 166p. 1979. 44.95 (ISBN 0-470-26821-2). Halsted Pr.

Carson, James. Desert & People. LC 82-50396. (Nature's Landscape Ser.). PLB 15.96 (ISBN 0-382-06669-3). Silver.

Carson, Jo. X-Ray Diganosis Positioning Manual. 1971. pap. text ed. 6.95x (ISBN 0-02-473270-2, 47327). Macmillan.

Carson, M. A. The Mechanics of Erosion. (Monographs in Spatial & Environmental Systems Analysis). (Illus.). 174p. 1971. 14.00x (ISBN 0-85086-029-6, Pub. by Pion England). Methuen Inc.

Carson, M. A. & Kirkby, M. J. Hillslope Form & Process. (Cambridge Geographical Studies). 59.50 (ISBN 0-521-08234-X). Cambridge U Pr.

Carson, Mary B., ed. Womanly Art of Breastfeeding. 2nd ed. LC 63-14460. (Illus.). 1963. 6.95 o.p. (ISBN 0-912500-00-X); pap. 3.95 o.p. (ISBN 0-912500-01-8). La Leche.

Carson, Michael. Pain. 1982. pap. 2.95 (ISBN 0-451-11732-8, AE1732, Sig). NAL.

Carson, R. A., jt. auth. see Sutherland, C. H.

Carson, Rachel. Silent Spring. 2.50x o.p. (ISBN 0-449-23871-7). Cancer Control Soc.

Carson, Rachel L. Sea Around Us. 1954. pap. 3.95 (ISBN 0-451-62164-6, ME2164, Ment). NAL.

Carson, Ralph S. High-Frequency Amplifiers. 2nd ed. LC 75-8780. 225p. 1975. 28.50x (ISBN 0-471-13705-7, Pub. by Wiley-Interscience); 29.95 (ISBN 0-471-86832-9). Wiley.

Carson, Robert B. American Economy in Conflict. LC 74-135858. 415p. 1971. pap. text ed. 7.95x o.p. (ISBN 0-669-50815-2). Heath.

--Economic Issues Today: Alternative Approaches. 2nd ed. 342p. 1980. text ed. 15.95x (ISBN 0-312-23424-4); pap. text ed. 8.95x (ISBN 0-312-23425-2); inst. manual avail. St Martin.

--Macroeconomic Issues Today. 182p. (Orig.). 1980. text ed. 14.95 (ISBN 0-312-50324-5); pap. text ed. 7.50 (ISBN 0-312-50325-3); instructor's manual available (ISBN 0-312-50326-1). St Martin.

--Microeconomic Issues Today. 182p. (Orig.). 1980. text ed. 14.95 (ISBN 0-312-53175-3); pap. text ed. 7.50 (ISBN 0-312-53176-1); instructor's manual available (ISBN 0-312-53177-X). St Martin.

--Whatever Happened to the Trolley? 1977. pap. text ed. 8.25 (ISBN 0-8191-0330-6). U Pr of Amer.

Carson, Robert B. & Friesen, John W. Teacher Participation: A Second Look. LC 78-64522. 1978. pap. text ed. 7.25 o.p. (ISBN 0-8191-0634-8). U Pr of Amer.

Carson, Robert R., jt. auth. see Rose, Elizabeth A.

Carson, Robert R., ed. see Rose, Elizabeth A.

Carson, Tom. Twisted Kicks. LC 81-67560. 264p. 1981. 12.95 (ISBN 0-934558-03-5); pap. 5.95 (ISBN 0-934558-05-1). Entwhistle Bks.

Carstairs, G. M. & Kapur, R. L. The Great Universe of Kota: Stress, Change & Mental Disorder in an Indian Village. LC 75-13151. 1976. 27.50x (ISBN 0-520-03024-9). U of Cal Pr.

Carstairs, G. Morris. The Twice-Born: A Study of a Community of High-Caste Hindus. LC 58-9003. (Midland Bks.: No. 108). 344p. 1957. pap. 3.95x o.p. (ISBN 0-253-20108-X). Ind U Pr.

Carstairs, Ian, jt. auth. see Birt, David.

Carstarphen. Windjammer World. 1979. pap. 4.95 (ISBN 0-89272-066-2). Down East.

Carstarphen, Dee. The Conch Book. LC 81-9632. (Illus.). 80p. Date not set. pap. 6.95 (ISBN 0-686-84296-0). Banyan Bks.

--Maverick Sea Fare, A Caribbean Cook Book. LC 78-107177. 60p. Date not set. pap. 5.95 (ISBN 0-686-84293-6). Banyan Bks.

Carsten, F. L. Revolution in Central Europe, 1918-1919. LC 78-165225. 1972. 35.75x (ISBN 0-520-02084-7). U of Cal Pr.

Carstens, W. Peter. The Social Structure of a Cape Coloured Reserve. LC 75-3985. (Illus.). 264p. 1975. Repr. of 1966 ed. lib. bdg. 17.75x (ISBN 0-8371-7431-7, CACR). Greenwood.

Carstensen, Fred V., jt. auth. see Guroff, Gregory.

Carstensen, Jens T. Pharmaceutics of Solids & Solid Dosage Forms. LC 76-22754. 1977. 38.50 (ISBN 0-471-13726-X, Pub. by Wiley-Interscience). Wiley.

Carswell, Catherine. Life of Robert Burns. LC 78-164157. (Illus.). 1971. Repr. of 1931 ed. 42.00x (ISBN 0-8103-3788-6). Gale.

--The Savage Pilgrimage: A Narrative of D. H. Lawrence. LC 81-3891. 330p. 1981. 37.50 (ISBN 0-521-23975-3); pap. 11.95 (ISBN 0-521-28386-8). Cambridge U Pr.

Carta. Israel Motor Atlas. rev. ed. (Illus.). 1978. pap. 9.75 (ISBN 0-930038-06-1). Arbit.

Cartan, Henri. Elementary Theory of Analytic Functions of One or Several Complex Variables. rev. ed. 1963. 26.50 (ISBN 0-201-00901-3, Adv Bk Prog). A-W.

Carte, Elaine A., jt. auth. see Carte, Gene E.

Carte, Gene E. & Carte, Elaine A. Police Reform in the United States: The Era of August Vollmer, 1905-1932. LC 73-87248. 390p. 1976. 21.00x (ISBN 0-520-02599-7). U of Cal Pr.

Carter. Chemotherapy of Cancer. 2nd ed. LC 80-24450. 379p. 1981. 24.00x (ISBN 0-471-08045-4, Pub. by Wiley Medical). Wiley.

--Corrosion Testing for Metal Finishing. 1982. text ed. 24.95 (ISBN 0-408-01194-7). Butterworth.

--Discovery of Tutankhamun's Tomb. 6.95 o.p. (ISBN 0-448-14546-4, G&D). Putnam Pub Group.

--Metallic Coatings for Corrosion Control. 1977. text ed. 39.95 (ISBN 0-408-00270-0). Butterworth.

--South East Africa. 1972. 8.90 (ISBN 0-531-00794-4). Watts.

Carter & Bylaws. Library Association Yearbooks. 1982. pap. 33.00 (ISBN 0-686-94482-8). Oryx Pr.

Carter, jt. auth. see Hubert, J. J.

Carter, jt. auth. see Srivastava.

Carter, A. E. Charles Baudelaire. (World Authors Ser.). 1977. lib. bdg. 12.95 (ISBN 0-8057-6269-8, Twayne). G K Hall.

--Paul Verlaine. (World Authors Ser.). lib. bdg. 12.95 (ISBN 0-8057-2944-5, Twayne). G K Hall.

Carter, A. T. Elite Politics in Rural India. LC 73-86043. (Studies in Social Anthropology: No. 9). (Illus.). 224p. 1974. 24.95 (ISBN 0-521-20366-X). Cambridge U Pr.

Carter, Angela. The Bloody Chamber. LC 79-2645. 1980. 9.57i (ISBN 0-06-010708-1, HarpT). Har-Row.

--Comic & Curious Cats. 1979. 7.95 o.p. (ISBN 0-517-53753-2, Harmony). Crown.

--Fireworks: Nine Stories in Various Disguises. LC 80-8706. 144p. 1981. 10.53i (ISBN 0-06-014852-7, HarpT). Har-Row.

--The War of Dreams. LC 74-1157. 288p. 1974. 6.95 o.p. (ISBN 0-15-144375-0). HarBraceJ.

Carter, Anne P., ed. Energy & the Environment: A Structural Analysis. LC 74-15447. (Illus.). 280p. 1976. text ed. 20.00x (ISBN 0-87451-112-7). U Pr of New Eng.

Carter, Ashley. Rogue of Falconhurst. 448p. 1983. pap. 3.50 (ISBN 0-449-12514-9, GM). Fawcett.

Carter, Avis M. One Day in Shakespeare's England. LC 73-21097. (Day Book Ser). (Illus.). 48p. (gr. 3 up). 1974. 12.45i (ISBN 0-200-00135-3, AbS-J). Har-Row.

Carter, Bruce. Buzzbugs. LC 77-75044. (gr. 5-8). 1977. 6.95 o.p. (ISBN 0-7232-6148-2). Warne.

Carter, Burnham, Jr., et al. Writing Laboratory. 1964. pap. 8.95x (ISBN 0-673-05218-4). Scott F.

Carter, C. E. Case Studies in East African Geography. 96p. 1974. pap. 6.50 o.s.i. (ISBN 0-7179-1577-8). Transatlantic.

--Zodiac & the Soul. 4th ed. 1968. 9.75 o.p. (ISBN 0-8356-5098-7). Theos Pub Hse.

Carter, Candy & Committee on Classroom Practices, eds. Non-Native & Nonstandard Dialect Students: Classroom Practices in Teaching English, 1982-1983. LC 82-14502. (Classroom Practices in Teaching English Ser.). 112p. 1982. pap. 7.00 (ISBN 0-8141-3351-7, 33517). NCTE.

Carter, Carrol J. Pike in Colorado. LC 78-60399. (Illus.). 1978. 12.95 (ISBN 0-88342-058-9); pap. 4.95 (ISBN 0-88342-241-7). Old Army.

Carter, Charles F. The Wedding Day in Literature & Art: A Collection of the Best Descriptions of Wedding from the Works of the World's Leading Novelists & Poets. LC 74-86598. 1969. Repr. of 1900 ed. 30.00x (ISBN 0-8103-0154-7). Gale.

Carter, Charles F., jt. auth. see Barroitt, Denis P.

Carter, Charles W. Person & Ministry of the Holy Spirit: A Wesleyan-Perspective. 1974. pap. 4.95 o.p. (ISBN 0-8010-2401-3). Baker Bk.

Carter, Clarence E., ed. see Gage, Thomas.

Carter, Codell K. A Contemporary Introduction to Logic with Applications. 1977. text ed. 11.95 (ISBN 0-02-471500-X). Macmillan.

Carter, Colin A., ed. see Schmitz, Andrew, et al.

Carter, Dagny. China Magnificent: Five Thousand Years of Chinese Art. LC 78-114493. (Illus.). 225p. 1973. Repr. of 1935 ed. lib. bdg. 18.25x (ISBN 0-8371-4777-8, CACM). Greenwood.

Carter, Dan T. Scottsboro: A Tragedy of the American South. LC 79-1090. (Illus.). 512p. 1979. 35.00x (ISBN 0-8071-0568-6); pap. 7.95x (ISBN 0-8071-0498-1). La State U Pr.

Carter, David. Build It Underground: A Guide for the Self-Builder & Building Professional. LC 81-85021. (Illus.). 224p. 1982. 14.95 (ISBN 0-8069-5454-X); lib. bdg. 17.79 (ISBN 0-8069-5455-8); pap. 7.95 (ISBN 0-8069-7582-2). Sterling.

Carter, David E., ed. Corporate Identity Manuals. new ed. LC 75-44679. (Illus.). 460p. 1978. Repr. of 1976 ed. 32.50 (ISBN 0-910158-33-9). Art Dir.

Carter, E. Eugene. College Financial Management: Basics for Administrators. LC 80-7465. 1980. 20.95x (ISBN 0-669-03700-1). Lexington Bks.

Carter, E. Eugene & Rodriguez, Rita M. International Financial Management. 2nd ed. (Illus.). 1979. text ed. 25.95 (ISBN 0-13-472977-3). P-H.

Carter, Edith. Records in Review Nineteen Eighty, Vol. 25. (Records in Review Nineteen Eighty). 1980. 15.95 (ISBN 0-911656-09-X). Wyeth Pr.

Carter, Edith, ed. Records in Review 1975. LC 55-10600. 1975. 14.95 (ISBN 0-911656-02-2). Wyeth Pr.

--Records in Review 1976. LC 55-10600. 1976. 16.95 (ISBN 0-911656-03-0). Wyeth Pr.

--Records in Review 1977. LC 55-10600. 1977. 14.95 (ISBN 0-911656-04-9). Wyeth Pr.

--Records in Review 1978, Vol. 23. LC 55-10600. 1978. 15.95 (ISBN 0-911656-05-7). Wyeth Pr.

--Records in Review 1979, Vol. 24. 1979. 15.95 (ISBN 0-911656-06-5). Wyeth Pr.

Carter, Edward. The Jesus Experience. LC 76-6701. (Illus.). 1976. pap. 1.75 o.p. (ISBN 0-8189-1131-X, Pub. by Alba Bks). Alba.

--Now Is the Time: Christian Reflections. LC 74-27609. 128p. 1975. pap. 1.45 o.p. (ISBN 0-8189-1121-2, Pub. by Alba Bks). Alba.

--Response in Christ: A Study of the Christian Life. 2nd rev. ed. LC 72-85215. 272p. 1972. pap. 1.45 o.p. (ISBN 0-8189-1103-4, Pub. by Alba Bks). Alba.

--The Spirit Is Present. LC 72-9577. 140p. 1973. pap. 1.25 o.p. (ISBN 0-8189-1109-3, Pub. by Alba Bks). Alba.

Carter, Elizabeth. The Marriage Mart. 256p. (Orig.). 1983. pap. 2.25 (ISBN 0-449-20082-5, Crest). Fawcett.

Carter, Ernest. British Steam Locomotives. pap. 5.50x (ISBN 0-392-08880-0, SpS). Sportshelf.

Carter, Ernestine. The Changing World of Fashion: 1900 to the Present. LC 77-309. (Illus.). 1977. 25.00 o.p. (ISBN 0-399-11969-8). Putnam Pub Group.

Carter, Everett & Homburger, Wolfgang S. Introduction to Transportation Engineering: Highways & Transit. (Illus.). 1978. ref. ed. 23.95 (ISBN 0-87909-388-9). Reston.

Carter, F. D. H. Lawrence & the Body Mystical. LC 68-910. (Studies in D. H. Lawrence, No. 20). 1969. Repr. of 1932 ed. lib. bdg. 22.95x (ISBN 0-8383-0653-5). Haskell.

Carter, F. T., jt. ed. see Leschonski, K.

Carter, Forrest. The Education of Little Tree. 1976. 9.95 o.s.i. (ISBN 0-440-02319-X). Delacorte.

--The Education of Little Tree. (gr. 7-12). 1981. pap. 1.50 o.p. (ISBN 0-440-92200-3, LE). Dell.

--Gone to Texas. 1975. 9.95 o.s.i. (ISBN 0-440-04565-7). Delacorte.

--Watch for Me on the Mountain. 1978. 9.95 o.s.i. (ISBN 0-440-02202-9, E Friede). Delacorte.

--Watch for Me on the Mountain. 1983. pap. 3.95 (ISBN 0-440-39065-6, LE). Dell.

Carter, Forrest L., ed. Molecular Electronic Devices. 424p. 1982. 65.00 (ISBN 0-8247-1676-0). Dekker.

Carter, Frances M. Psychosocial Nursing. 3rd ed. 1981. text ed. 25.95 (ISBN 0-02-319660-2). Macmillan.

Carter, G. A. J. L. Hobb's Local History & the Library. (Grafton Books on Library Science). (Illus.). 1977. lib. bdg. 18.50 o.p. (ISBN 0-233-95615-8). Westview.

--J. L. Hobbs' Local History & the Library. 2nd, rev. ed. 352p. 1973. 20.00 (ISBN 0-233-95615-8, 05773-8, Pub. by Gower Pub Co England). Lexington Bks.

Carter, G. W. & Richardson, A. Techniques of Circuit Analysis. LC 79-183222. (Illus.). 544p. 1972. 42.50x (ISBN 0-521-08435-0). Cambridge U Pr.

Carter, Genevieve W., jt. auth. see Steinberg, Raymond M.

Carter, George R. Twilight of the Jackass Prospector: Death Valley Area Portraits of the 1930's. (Illus.). 1982. 10.00 (ISBN 0-930704-13-4). Sagebrush Pr.

Carter, Germaine. The Home Book of French Cookery. 288p. (Orig.). 1973. pap. 3.95 o.p. (ISBN 0-571-10415-0). Faber & Faber.

Carter, Giles F. Principles of Physical & Chemical Metallurgy. 1979. 51.00 (ISBN 0-87170-080-8). ASM.

Carter, Gwendolen M. & O'Meara, Patrick, eds. Southern Africa: The Continuing Crisis. 2nd ed. LC 81-48324. (Midland Bks.: No. 280). 416p. 1982. 35.00x (ISBN 0-253-35400-5); pap. 9.95x (ISBN 0-253-20280-9). Ind U Pr.

Carter, Gwendolen M., ed. see Le Vine, Victor T.

Carter, H. & Partington, I. Applied Economics in Banking & Finance. 2nd ed. 1981. 34.50x (ISBN 0-19-877171-1). Oxford U Pr.

Carter, Harold. An Introduction to Urban Historical Geography. 320p. 1983. pap. text ed. price not set (ISBN 0-7131-6386-0). E Arnold.

--The Study of Urban Geography. 2nd ed. LC 76-22730. 398p. 1976. pap. text ed. 21.95x o.s.i. (ISBN 0-470-98911-4). Halsted Pr.

--The Study of Urban Geography. 434p. 1981. pap. text ed. 14.95 (ISBN 0-7131-6235-X). E Arnold.

Carter, Hodding. Doomed Road of Empire: The Spanish Trail of Conquest. (American Trails Library Ser). (Illus.). 1963. 5.25 (ISBN 0-07-010182-5, P&RB). McGraw.

--First Person Rural. LC 77-10014. 1977. Repr. lib. bdg. 20.00x (ISBN 0-8371-9727-9, CAFI). Greenwood.

Carter, Howard. Questions & Answers on Spiritual Gifts. 127p. 1976. pocket bk. 2.95 (ISBN 0-89274-007-8). Harrison Hse.

Carter, Howard & Mace, A. C. The Discovery of the Tomb of Tutankhamen. LC 77-71042. (Illus.). 1977. pap. 5.50 (ISBN 0-486-23500-9). Dover.

Carter, I. R. Alien Blossom: A Japanese-Australian Love Story. 14.50x (ISBN 0-686-30459-4, ABC). Sportshelf.

Carter, Ian, ed. Aberdeenshire Peasant Life: William Alexander-Scottish Peasant Life. (Library of Peasant Studies: No. 5). 1983. 28.00x (ISBN 0-7146-3087-X, F Cass Co). Biblio Dist.

Carter, J. R. Leading Merchant Families of Saudi Arabia. 190p. 1980. 99.00x (ISBN 0-905906-22-5, Pub. by Scorpion England). State Mutual Bk.

Carter, J. R., ed. see Desikachar, T. K.

Carter, James. Law: Its Origin, Growth & Function. LC 74-6413. (American Constitutional & Legal History Ser.). 1974. Repr. of 1907 ed. lib. bdg. 42.50 (ISBN 0-306-70631-8). Da Capo.

Carter, James L., ed. see Van-Riper, Charles.

Carter, Jared. Early Warning. 16p. (Orig.). 1979. pap. 2.95 (ISBN 0-935306-06-4). Barnwood Pr.

Carter, Jenny & Hardley, Dennis. The Highlands & Islands of Scotland in Colour. (Illus.). 64p. 1983. 12.50 (ISBN 0-7134-3825-8, Pub. by Batsford England). David & Charles.

Carter, Jimmy. Keeping Faith: Memories of a President. LC 82-90323. (Illus.). 640p. 1982. 22.50 (ISBN 0-553-05023-0). Bantam.

Carter, John F. Layman's Harmony of the Gospel. 1961. 10.95 (ISBN 0-8054-1326-X). Broadman.

--The New Dealers: By the Unofficial Observer. LC 74-23461. (Fdr & the Era of the New Deal Ser.). ix, 414p. 1975. Repr. of 1934 ed. lib. bdg. 45.00 (ISBN 0-306-70710-1). Da Capo.

Carter, John M. All the Lovely Ladies. 1982. cancelled (ISBN 0-698-11073-0, Coward). Putnam Pub Group.

Carter, John R. & Bond, George D. The Threefold Refuge in the Theravada Buddhist Tradition. 1982. 3.95 (ISBN 0-89012-030-7). Anima Pubns.

Carter, Juanita E. & Young, Darroch. Electronic Calculators: A Mastery Approach Year. 1981. 12.50 (ISBN 0-395-29621-8); instr's manual 1.00 (ISBN 0-686-97252-X). HM.

Carter, Juanita E. & Young, Darroch F. Calculating Machines: A Ten-Key Approach. 1975. pap. text ed. 16.95 (ISBN 0-395-18594-7); instrs.' manual 1.15 (ISBN 0-395-18805-9). HM.

Carter, Katherine. Houses. LC 82-4431. (New True Bks.). (Illus.). (gr. k-4). 1982. PLB 9.25g (ISBN 0-516-01672-5). Childrens.

--Ships & Seaports. LC 82-4463. (New True Bks.). (Illus.). (gr. k-4). 1982. PLB 9.25g (ISBN 0-516-01656-3). Childrens.

Carter, Kennard, Jr. Love Poems. Bk. 1. pap. 3.95 (ISBN 0-686-26432-0); Bk. 2. pap. 5.95 (ISBN 0-686-26433-9). Kennard Carter.

Carter, Kenneth J. I Was a Giant Last Night, Mom. (Illus.). 44p. (gr. k-5). 1983. PLB price not set (ISBN 0-911247-00-9). Calif Cam.

Carter, L. R. & Huzan, E. A Practical Approach to Computer Simulation in Business. LC 73-11017. 298p. 1973. 32.95x o.p. (ISBN 0-470-13729-0). Halsted Pr.

Carter, Lark, et al. Working in Plant Science: Activity Guide. Aaberson, Max, ed. (Illus.). (gr. 9-10). 1978. pap. text ed. 6.96 (ISBN 0-07-000836-1); tchr's manual 4.95 (ISBN 0-07-000837-X). McGraw.

Carter, Lark P., jt. auth. see Bishop, Douglas.

Carter, Les. Good 'n Angry. 128p. 1983. 8.95 (ISBN 0-8010-2481-1); pap. 5.95 (ISBN 0-686-83175-6). Baker Bk.

Carter, Lief H. Reason in Law. 1979. pap. text ed. 9.95 (ISBN 0-316-13045-1). Little.

Carter, Lin. As the Green Star Rises. (Science Fiction Ser). 1975. pap. 1.25 o.p. (ISBN 0-87997-156-8, UY1156). DAW Bks.

--The Barbarian of World's End. (Science Fiction Ser.). 1977. pap. 1.50 o.p. (ISBN 0-87997-300-5, UW1300). DAW Bks.

--By the Light of the Green Star. (Science Fiction Ser.). 1974. pap. 2.25 (ISBN 0-87997-742-6, UE1742). DAW Bks.

--Darya of the Bronze Age. (Science Fiction Ser.). 1981. pap. 1.95 o.p. (ISBN 0-87997-655-1, UJ1655). DAW Bks.

--The Immortal of World's End. (Science Fiction Ser.). 1976. pap. 1.25 o.p. (ISBN 0-87997-254-8, UY1254). DAW Bks.

--Journey to the Underground World. (Science Fiction Ser.). (Orig.). 1979. pap. 1.75 (ISBN 0-87997-499-0, UE1499). Daw Bks.

--Kesrick. 1982. pap. 2.25 (ISBN 0-87997-779-5, UE1779). DAW Bks.

--Lost Worlds. (Science Fiction Ser.). 1980. pap. 1.95 o.p. (ISBN 0-87997-556-3, UJ1556). Daw Bks.

Carter, Lin, jt. auth. see DeCamp, L. Sprague.

Carter, Linda & Culinary Arts Institute Staff. The Food Processor Cookbook. Finnegan, Edward G., ed. LC 78-54620. (Adventures in Cooking Ser). (Illus.). 1980. pap. write for info (ISBN 0-8326-0607-3, 2517). Delair.

Carter, Lynn R. An Analysis of Pascal Programs. Stone, Harold, ed. LC 82-4925. (Computer Science: Systems Programming: No. 6). 203p. 1982. 44.95 (ISBN 0-8357-1331-8). Univ Microfilms.

Carter, Mary E. Edgar Cayce on Prophecy. 208p. 1968. pap. 2.95 (ISBN 0-446-30611-8). Warner Bks.

Carter, Michael. Archaeology. (Illus.). 176p. 1980. 12.95 o.p. (ISBN 0-7137-0861-1, Pub. by Blandford Pr England); pap. 6.95 o.p. (ISBN 0-7137-1067-5, Pub. by Blandford Pr England). Sterling.

Carter, N. F. History of Pembroke, 2 Vols. 1976. Repr. of 1895 ed. 45.00X (ISBN 0-89725-032-X). NH Pub Co.

Carter, Nick. Doctor Dna. 224p. 1982. pap. 2.50 (ISBN 0-441-15676-2, Pub. by Charter Bks). Ace Bks.

--Turkish Bloodbath. (Nick Carter Ser.). 224p. (Orig.). 1982. pap. 2.25 (ISBN 0-441-82726-8, Pub. by Charter Bks). Ace Bks.

Carter, Noel V. Miss Hungerford's Handsome Hero. (Orig.). 1981. pap. 1.50 o.s.i. (ISBN 0-440-15312-3). Dell.

--This Band of Spirits. (Orig.). 1980. pap. 2.25 o.p. (ISBN 0-451-09069-1, E9069, Sig). NAL.

Carter, P. B., jt. auth. see Cowen, Zelman.

Carter, Pat H. Vivamos En el Espiritu Cada Dia. 160p. 1979. pap. 3.25 (ISBN 0-311-09089-3). Casa Bautista.

Carter, Paul A. Idea of Progress in Recent American Protestant Thought, 1930-1960. Wolf, Richard C., ed. LC 69-14621. (Facet Bks). 1969. pap. 0.50 o.p. (ISBN 0-8006-3052-1, 1-3052). Fortress.

Carter, R. J. Stores Management. 250p. 1982. pap. text ed. 12.95x (ISBN 0-7121-1979-5). Intl Ideas.

Carter, R. W. Simple Groups of Lie Type. LC 72-39228. (Pure & Applied Mathematics Ser.). 280p. 1972. 53.95x o.s.i. (ISBN 0-471-13735-9, Pub. by Wiley-Interscience). Wiley.

Carter, Robert. Carter's Coast of New England. Ford, Daniel, ed. LC 75-18528. (Illus.). 1977. pap. 15.00 (ISBN 0-912274-53-0). NH Pub Co.

Carter, Robert A., ed. Trade Marketing Handbook. 320p. 1983. 29.95 (ISBN 0-8352-1692-6); pap. 19.95 (ISBN 0-8352-1693-4). Bowker.

Carter, Robert E. Arson Investigation. 1978. text ed. 22.95x (ISBN 0-02-472400-9). Macmillan.

Carter, Robert L. Systematic Thinking Curriculum: Language Analysis & Composition. (Orig.). 1980. pap. text ed. 8.95 (ISBN 0-8403-2145-7). Kendall-Hunt.

Carter, Robert M., ed. Communication in Organizations: An Annotated Bibliography & Sourcebook. LC 73-161194. (Management Information Guide Ser.: No. 25). 1972. 42.00x (ISBN 0-8103-0825-8). Gale.

Carter, Robert M. & Wilkins, Leslie T., eds. Probation, Parole, & Community Corrections. 2nd ed. LC 75-44332. 874p. 1976. text ed. 32.95 (ISBN 0-471-13845-2). Wiley.

Carter, Roger. Business Administration. 224p. 1982. pap. 50.00x (ISBN 0-434-90219-5, Pub. by Heinemann England). State Mutual Bk.

Carter, Ron. Early Civilizations. LC 80-50339. (World of Knowledge Ser.). PLB 16.72 (ISBN 0-382-06407-0). Silver.

--The Spread of Civilization. LC 80-50335. (World of Knowledge Ser.). 16.72 (ISBN 0-382-06408-9). Silver.

Carter, Ron & Way, Peter. Asia, Africa, & Oceania. (World of Knowledge Ser.). PLB 16.72 (ISBN 0-382-06411-9). Silver.

Carter, Ronald & Burton, Deirdre. Literary Text & Language Study. 128p. 1982. pap. text ed. 9.95 (ISBN 0-7131-6263-5). E Arnold.

Carter, Ronald, ed. Linguistics & the Teacher. (Language, Education & Society Ser.). 208p. (Orig.). 1983. pap. 12.50 (ISBN 0-7100-9193-1). Routledge & Kegan.

Carter, Rosemary. Master of Tinarua. (Harlequin Presents Ser.). 192p. 1983. pap. 1.95 (ISBN 0-373-10575-4). Harlequin Bks.

Carter, Ruth C. & Bruntjien, Scott. Data Conversion. 130p. 1983. 34.50 (ISBN 0-86729-047-1); pap. 27.50 (ISBN 0-86729-046-3). Knowledge Indus.

Carter, Stephen K., et al. Chemotherapy of Cancer. LC 77-8142. 1977. 20.00 o.p. (ISBN 0-471-02935-1, Pub. by Wiley Med). Wiley.

--Principles of Cancer Treatment. (Illus.). 1312p. 1982. 85.00 (ISBN 0-07-010183-3). McGraw.

Carter, Thomas P., jt. ed. see Willey, Ann M.

Carter, Timothy J., et al, eds. Rural Crime: Integrating Research & Prevention. LC 81-65018. 284p. 1982. text ed. 29.95x (ISBN 0-86598-023-3). Allanheld.

Carter, Virginia L., compiled by. How to Survey Your Readers. 48p. 1981. 10.50 (ISBN 0-89964-189-X). CASE.

Carter, W. Horace, jt. auth. see Faircloth, Rudy.

Carter, Walter. Insects in Relation to Plant Disease. 2nd ed. LC 73-4362. 72.95x (ISBN 0-471-13849-5, Pub. by Wiley-Interscience). Wiley.

Carter, William C. & Vines, Robert F., eds. A Concordance to the Oeuvres Completes of Arthur Rimbaud. LC 75-36985. xiv, 810p. 1978. 40.00x (ISBN 0-8214-0216-1, 82-82220). Ohio U Pr.

Carter, William E. South America. rev. ed. (First Bks.). (Illus.). 72p. (gr. 4 up). 1983. PLB 8.90 (ISBN 0-531-04531-5). Watts.

Carterette, Edward C. & Jones, Margaret H. Informal Speech: Alphabetic & Phonemic Text. LC 73-92376. 1975. 57.50x (ISBN 0-520-01476-6). U of Cal Pr.

Carterette, Edward C. & Friedman, Morton P., eds. Handbook of Perception. Incl. Vol. 1. 1974. 49.00 (ISBN 0-12-161901-X); Vol. 2. 1974. 59.00 (ISBN 0-12-161902-8); Vol. 4. Hearing. 1978. 62.50 (ISBN 0-12-161904-4); Vol. 5. 1975. 59.00 (ISBN 0-12-161905-2); Vol. 6, 2 pts. 1978. Pt. A, Testing & Smelling. 37.50 (ISBN 0-12-161906-0); Pt. B, Feeling & Hurting. 37.50 (ISBN 0-12-161922-2); Vol. 7. 1975. 59.00 (ISBN 0-12-161907-9); Vol. 8. Perceptual Coding. 1978. 49.00, by subscription 42.00 (ISBN 0-12-161908-7); Vol. 9. Perceptual Processing. 1978. 36.00, by subscription 42.50 (ISBN 0-12-161909-5); Vol. 10. Perceptual Ecology. 1978. 54.50, by subscription 43.50 (ISBN 0-12-161910-9). Acad Pr.

Carteris, Ernest, et al. Cookbook for Lovers: Menus, Recipes & Treats for Two. (Illus.). 1970. 5.95 (ISBN 0-8208-0223-9). Hearthside.

Cartey, Tom. I Am God. 112p. 1977. write for info. (ISBN 0-89452-001-6). Dunhere.

Cartey, Wilfred. Black Images. LC 75-113096. 1970. text ed. 9.40x o.p. (ISBN 0-8077-1145-4); pap. 8.95x (ISBN 0-8077-1144-6). Tchrs Coll.

Carthy, Mary P. Old St. Patrick's: New York's First Cathedral. (Monograph Ser.: No. 23). (Illus.). 1947. 10.00x (ISBN 0-930060-05-9). US Cath Hist.

Cartier, Francis A. & Todaro, Martin T. The Phonetic Alphabet. 2nd ed. 94p. 1971. pap. text ed. write for info. o.p. (ISBN 0-697-04170-0); instrs.' guide ans. key avail. o.p. Wm C Brown.

--The Phonetic Alphabet. 3rd ed. 110p. 1982. pap. text ed. write for info. (ISBN 0-697-04218-9); avail. instr's. guide & answer key (ISBN 0-697-04231-6). Wm C Brown.

Cartin, Hazel. Elijah. 322p. 1981. 13.95 o.p. (ISBN 0-312-24239-5). St Martin.

Cartland, Barbara. Again this Rapture. 240p. 1982. pap. 1.95 (ISBN 0-515-06385-1). Jove Pubns.

--The Audacious Adventuress. (Barbara Cartland Romance Ser.: No. 41). 240p. 1982. pap. 1.95 o.s.i. (ISBN 0-515-06212-X). Jove Pubns.

--Barbara Cartland's Book of Celebrities. (Illus.). 176p. 1983. pap. 9.95 (ISBN 0-7043-3395-3, Pub. by Quartet Bks). Merrimack Bk Serv.

--The Captive Heart. pap. 1.75 o.s.i. (ISBN 0-515-05566-2). Jove Pubns.

--The Coin of Love. pap. 1.75 o.s.i. (ISBN 0-515-05560-3). Jove Pubns.

--Desire of the Heart. 224p. 1980. pap. 1.75 o.s.i. (ISBN 0-515-05497-6). Jove Pubns.

--For All Eternity. (Barbara Cartland Romance Ser.: No. 93). 192p. (Orig.). 1981. pap. 1.95 o.s.i. (ISBN 0-515-05964-1). Jove Pubns.

--A Ghost in Monte Carlo. (The Barbara Cartland Ser.: No. 48). 336p. 1981. pap. write for info o.s.i. (ISBN 0-515-05097-0). Jove Pubns.

--The Golden Gondola. (Barbara Cartland Ser.). (Orig.). pap. 1.75 o.s.i. (ISBN 0-515-05509-3). Jove Pubns.

--A Heart is Broken. (Romance Ser.: No. 20). 288p. 1983. pap. 2.25 (ISBN 0-515-06392-4). Jove Pubns.

--The Innocent Heiress, No. 15. 1979. pap. 1.50 o.s.i. (ISBN 0-685-63662-3, 04880-1). Jove Pubns.

--A King in Love. 150p. 1982. 10.95 (ISBN 0-89696-166-4, An Everest House Book). Dodd.

--The Kiss of Paris. 224p. pap. 2.25 (ISBN 0-515-06391-6). Jove Pubns.

--The Kiss of the Devil. (Barbara Cartland Ser.: No. 32). 224p. 1981. pap. 1.95 o.s.i. (ISBN 0-515-05957-9). Jove Pubns.

--Light of the Gods. (Camfield Ser.: No. 6). 192p. 1982. pap. 1.95 (ISBN 0-515-06297-9). Jove Pubns.

--A Light to the Heart, No. 56. 256p. 1982. pap. 1.95 (ISBN 0-515-06387-8). Jove Pubns.

--Lost Enchantment. (Barbara Cartland Ser.: No. 15). 256p. 1981. pap. 1.75 o.s.i. (ISBN 0-515-05942-0). Jove Pubns.

--Love & the Marquis. (Camfield Romance Ser.: No. 4). 192p. 1982. pap. 1.95 (ISBN 0-515-06295-2). Jove Pubns.

--Love at the Helm. 224p. 1981. 9.95 (ISBN 0-89696-126-5, An Everest House Book). Dodd.

--Love is Dangerous. (Barbara Cartland Ser.: No. 31). 208p. 1981. pap. 1.95 o.s.i. (ISBN 0-515-05960-9). Jove Pubns.

--Love on the Run. (Barbara Cartland Ser.: No. 50). 256p. 1981. pap. 1.75 o.s.i. (ISBN 0-515-05956-0). Jove Pubns.

--Love Under Fire. (Barbara Cartland Romance Ser.: No.39). 224p. 1981. pap. 1.95 o.s.i. (ISBN 0-515-05965-X). Jove Pubns.

--A Marriage Made in Heaven. (Romance Ser.: No. 165). 160p. 1982. pap. 2.25 (ISBN 0-553-22918-4). Bantam.

--A Miracle in Music. (Camfield Romance Ser.: No. 5). 192p. 1982. pap. 1.95 o.s.i. (ISBN 0-515-06296-0). Jove Pubns.

--Open Wings, No. 37. 256p. 1982. pap. 1.95 (ISBN 0-515-06388-6). Jove Pubns.

--Pure & Untouched. 224p. 1981. 10.95 (ISBN 0-686-30965-0, An Everest House Book). Dodd.

--Riding to the Moon. 150p. 1982. 10.95 (ISBN 0-89696-174-5, An Everest House Book). Dodd.

--The Runaway Heart, No. 69. 224p. 1983. pap. 2.25 (ISBN 0-515-06389-4). Jove Pubns.

--The Secret Fear. (Barbara Cartland Ser.: No. 23). 240p. 1981. pap. 1.95 o.s.i. (ISBN 0-515-05962-5). Jove Pubns.

--Sweet Adventure, No. 17. 1978. pap. 2.25 o.s.i. (ISBN 0-515-06390-8). Jove Pubns.

--A Virgin in Paris. (Barbara Cartland Ser.: No. 14). 208p. 1981. pap. 1.75 o.s.i. (ISBN 0-515-05571-9). Jove Pubns.

Cartland, Barbara, ed. see Wynne, Pamela.

Cartledge, T. M., ed. see Shaw, Martin & Coleman, Henry.

Cartlidge, David R. & Dungan, David L. Documents for the Study of the Gospels. LC 79-21341. 300p. (Orig.). 1980. 14.95 (ISBN 0-8006-0640-X, 1-640); pap. 8.95 (ISBN -08006-1640-5, 1-1640). Fortress.

Cartlidge, Niall & Shaw, David. Head Injury. (Major Problems in Neurosurgery Ser.: Vol. III). 1981. text ed. 35.00 (ISBN 0-7216-2443-X). Saunders.

Cartmell & Fowles. Valency & Molecular Structure. 4th ed. 1977. 18.95 (ISBN 0-408-70809-3). Butterworth.

Cartmell, ed. see Henry, O.

Cartner, William. Fun with Geology. (Learning with Fun Ser.). (Illus.). (gr. 5 up). 1971. 13.50x o.p. (ISBN 0-7182-0076-4, SpS). Sportshelf.

Carto, W. Profiles in Populism. 1982. 12.95 (ISBN 0-8159-6518-4); pap. 7.95 (ISBN 0-8159-6519-2). Devin.

Cartographic Dept. of the Clarendon Pr. Oxford Economic Atlas of the World. 4th ed. (Illus.). 1972. 37.50 (ISBN 0-19-894106-4); pap. 12.95x (ISBN 0-19-894107-2). Oxford U Pr.

Cartographic Publishing House Staff, ed. Map of the People's Republic of China-Relief. 1981. pap. 3.95 (ISBN 0-8351-1035-4). China Bks.

Carton, Dana & Caprio, Anthony. En Francais: Practical Conversational French. 2nd ed. 1980. text ed. write for info. (ISBN 0-442-21215-1); write for info. instr's. manual (ISBN 0-442-21218-6); write for info. tape (ISBN 0-442-21219-4); write for info. cassette (ISBN 0-442-21220-8). Van Nos Reinhold.

--En Francais: Practical Conversational French. 1976. pap. 11.95 (ISBN 0-442-21468-5); tapes 85.00 (ISBN 0-442-21467-7); cassettes 54.95 (ISBN 0-442-21469-3). Van Nos Reinhold.

Carton, Jane. A Child's Garland. 1942. 6.95 o.p. (ISBN 0-571-05352-1). Faber & Faber.

Carton, Lonnie. Raise Your Kids Right: Candid Advice to Parents on How to Say No. LC 79-20646. 1980. 9.95 o.p. (ISBN 0-399-12468-3). Putnam Pub Group.

Cartoun, Susan. The Complete New York Guide for Singles. 256p. 1983. pap. 7.95 (ISBN 0-02-097360-8). Macmillan.

Cartter, Allan M. Theory of Wages & Employment. LC 75-31357. (Illus.). 193p. 1976. Repr. of 1959 ed. lib. bdg. 17.00x (ISBN 0-8371-8512-2, CATW). Greenwood.

Cartwright & Rawson. Wizards. (Story Books). (gr. k-4). 1980. 5.95 (ISBN 0-86020-381-6, Usborne-Hayes); PLB 8.95 (ISBN 0-88110-052-8); pap. 2.95 (ISBN 0-86020-380-8). EDC.

Cartwright, Ann. The Dignity of Labour? A Study of Childbearing & Induction. 1979. 29.95x (ISBN 0-422-76690-9, Pub by Tavistock England). Methuen Inc.

--How Many Children? (Direct Editions Ser.). (Orig.). 1976. pap. 117.50 (ISBN 0-7100-8341-6). Routledge & Kegan.

--Patients & Their Doctors: A Study of General Practice. (Reports of the Institute of Community Studies). 1967. 25.00x (ISBN 0-7100-3919-0). Routledge & Kegan.

Cartwright, Ann, jt. auth. see Dunnell, Karen.

Cartwright, Ann, et al. Life Before Death. (Social Studies in Medical Care). 310p. 1973. 26.50x (ISBN 0-7100-7540-5). Routledge & Kegan.

Cartwright, Carol A. & Cartwright, G. Phillip. Developing Observation Skills. (Illus.). 180p. 1974. pap. text ed. 14.50 (ISBN 0-07-010184-1, C). McGraw.

Cartwright, D. E., tr. see Marchuk, G. I. & Kagan, B. A.

Cartwright, Desmond S. Introduction to Personality. 1974. 24.50 (ISBN 0-395-30788-0). HM.

Cartwright, Dorwin, ed. Studies in Social Power. LC 59-63036. 225p. 1959. 12.00x (ISBN 0-87944-230-1). Inst Soc Res.

Cartwright, G. Philip, et al. Educating Special Learners. 496p. 1981. text ed. 21.95x (ISBN 0-534-00939-5). Wadsworth Pub.

Cartwright, G. Phillip, jt. auth. see Cartwright, Carol A.
Cartwright, John R. Politics in Sierra Leone, Nineteen Forty-Seven to Nineteen Sixty-Seven. (Scholarly Reprint Ser.). 35.00x o.p. (ISBN 0-8020-7103-1). U of Toronto Pr.
Cartwright, Mary. ABC. (Illus.). 40p. (ps-1). 1981. 5.95 o.p. (ISBN 0-528-82405-8). Rand.
--One Two Three. (Illus.). 40p. (ps-1). 1981. 5.95 o.p. (ISBN 0-528-82406-6). Rand.
Cartwright, Sally. Animal Homes. (Science Is What & Why Ser.). (Illus.). 48p. (gr. k-3). 1973. PLB 5.99 o.p. (ISBN 0-698-30492-6, Coward). Putnam Pub Group.
--Sand. LC 74-83011. (Illus.). 32p. (gr. k-3). 1975. PLB 4.97 o.p. (ISBN 0-698-30562-0, Coward). Putnam Pub Group.
--Sunlight. LC 73-88022. (Illus.). 32p. (gr. k-3). 1974. PLB 5.99 (ISBN 0-698-30540-X, Coward). Putnam Pub Group.
--The Tide. LC 79-127949. (Science Is What & Why Ser). (Illus.). (gr. k-3). 1971. PLB 4.49 o.p. (ISBN 0-698-30367-9, Coward). Putnam Pub Group.
--Water Is Wet. (Illus.). 32p. (gr. k-3). 1973. PLB 5.49 o.p. (ISBN 0-698-30491-8, Coward). Putnam Pub Group.
--What's in a Map? LC 76-10694. (Illus.). (gr. k-3). 1976. PLB 5.29 (ISBN 0-698-30635-X, Coward). Putnam Pub Group.
Carty, Charles M. Stigmata & Modern Science. 31p. 1958. pap. 0.65 (ISBN 0-686-81641-2). TAN Bks Pubs.
Carty, Richard. Visual Merchandising -- Principles & Practice. 1978. text ed. 9.92 (ISBN 0-87350-255-8); wkbk. 5.35 (ISBN 0-87350-256-6). Milady.
Carty, Tony & Smith, Alexander M. Power & Manoeuvrability. 1978. 30.00x o.p. (ISBN 0-905470-04-4, Pub. by Q Press). State Mutual Bk.
Caruana, Russell A. A Guide to Organizing a Health Care Fiscal Services Division with Job Descriptions for Key Functions. 2nd ed. 94p. 1981. pap. 8.50 (ISBN 0-930228-13-8). Healthcare Fin Man Assn.
Caruba, Rebecca. Cooking with Wine & Higher Spirits. (Illus.). 3.00 o.p. (ISBN 0-517-07069-3). Crown.
Carus, Paul. Chinese Astrology. LC 73-20411. (Illus.). 114p. 1974. pap. 5.00 (ISBN 0-87548-155-8). Open Court.
--God: An Enquiry & a Solution. iv, 253p. 1943. 17.00 (ISBN 0-87548-223-6); pap. 7.50 (ISBN 0-87548-224-4). Open Court.
--Gospel of Buddha. rev. & enl. ed. LC 17-29837. (Illus.). 331p. 1973. deluxe ed. 21.00 (ISBN 0-87548-226-0); pap. 9.00 (ISBN 0-87548-228-7). Open Court.
--History of the Devil & the Idea of Evil. (Illus.). 496p. 1974. 27.50 (ISBN 0-87548-356-9); pap. 11.00x (ISBN 0-87548-307-0). Open Court.
--Karma; Nirvana: Two Buddhist Tales. LC 73-82781. (Illus.). 160p. 1973. 15.50 (ISBN 0-87548-249-X); pap. 6.00 (ISBN 0-87548-359-3). Open Court.
--Point of View. Cook, Catherine E., ed. (Illus.). xvi, 227p. 1927. 16.00 (ISBN 0-87548-268-6). Open Court.
Carus, Paul, ed. Yin Chih Wen: The Tract of the Quiet Way. Suzuki, Teitaro & Carus, Paul, trs. from Chinese. 52p. 1906. pap. 4.00 (ISBN 0-87548-245-7). Open Court.
Carus, Paul, ed. see Lao-Tze.
Carus, Paul, tr. see Carus, Paul.
Carus, Paul, tr. see Kant, Immanuel.
Carus, Paul, tr. see Lao Tze.
Carus, Victor. Histoire De la Zoologie Depuis L'antiquite Jusqu'au XIXe Siecle. Repr. of 1880 ed. 168.00 o.p. (ISBN 0-8287-0163-6). Clearwater Pub.
Caruso, Enrico & Tetrazzini, Louisa. The Art of Singing: How to Sing, 2 vols. in 1. LC 74-23417. (Music Reprint Ser.). 1975. Repr. of 1909 ed. lib. bdg. 22.50 (ISBN 0-306-70674-1). Da Capo.
Caruso, Luis, ed. see Bennett, Rita & Bennett, Dennis.
Caruso, Luis, ed. see Hutchison, Becky & Farish, Kay.
Caruso, Luis, ed. see Williams, Moris.
Caruso, Luis, tr. see Williams, Moris.
Caruthers, J. W. Fundamentals of Marine Acoustics. (Elsevier Oceanography Ser.: Vol. 18). 1977. 42.75 (ISBN 0-444-41552-1). Elsevier.
Caruthers, Madeline, jt. auth. see Tucker, Dennis.
Carvainis, Maria & Lax, Roger. The Moustache Book. 1978. pap. 6.95 (ISBN 0-8256-3144-0, Quick Fox). Putnam Pub Group.
Carvell, Fred J. Human Relations in Business. 3rd ed. (Illus.). 1980. text ed. 20.95 (ISBN 0-02-319840-0). Macmillan.
Carver, D. K. Introduction to Business Data Processing: With Basic, Fortran & Cobol Programming. 2nd ed. LC 78-19131. 366p. 1979. text ed. 26.95 (ISBN 0-471-03091-0). wkbk. 11.50 (ISBN 0-471-03998-5). Wiley.
Carver, D. Keith. Beginning BASIC. LC 79-20457. 1980. pap. text ed. 17.95 (ISBN 0-8185-0368-8). Brooks-Cole.
--Structured COBOL for Microcomputers. LC 82-20573. (Computer Science Ser.). 418p. 1983. pap. text ed. 17.95 (ISBN 0-534-01421-6). Brooks-Cole.
Carver, Frank. Peter the Rock-Man. 1973. pap. 1.50 o.p. (ISBN 0-8341-0156-4). Beacon Hill.
Carver, Fred D. & Sergiovanni, Thomas J. Organizations & Human Behavior: Focus on Schools. LC 69-13215. (Illus.). 1969. pap. text ed. 21.00 (ISBN 0-07-010191-4, C). McGraw.
Carver, Joyce S. Jonny Lincoln & His Three Dogs. (Illus.). 48p. 1982. 5.50 (ISBN 0-682-49920-X). Exposition.
Carver, Leona P., ed. You Can't Get the Coons All Up One Tree: True Life Story of John N. Jones. 244p. (Orig.). 1980. pap. 7.95x (ISBN 0-686-36932-7). Coltharp Pub.
Carver, M. O. H. Two Town Houses in Medieval Shrewsbury. 144p. 1982. pap. text ed. 25.25x (ISBN 0-86299-023-8, Pub. by Alan Sutton England). Humanities.
Carver, Michael. Painting in Oil by the Five-Color Method: A Course of Lessons by Michael Carver. (Illus.). 1961. 14.95 o.p. (ISBN 0-07-010190-6, GB). McGraw.
--War Since Nineteen Forty-Five. 1981. 14.95 (ISBN 0-399-12594-9). Putnam Pub Group.
Carver, Norman F., Jr. Italian Hilltowns. 2nd ed. (Illus.). 1979. 24.95 (ISBN 0-932076-00-9); pap. 17.95 (ISBN 0-932076-01-7). Documan Pr.
Carver, Raymond. Fires: Essays, Poems, Stories 1966-1982. LC 82-22210. 196p. 1983. text ed. 25.00 (ISBN 0-88496-195-8); pap. 8.95 (ISBN 0-88496-196-6). Capra Pr.
--Furious Seasons & Other Stories. (Noel Young Bks.). 1977. pap. 3.95 o.p. (ISBN 0-88496-113-3). Capra Pr.
--The Pheasant. (Metacom Limited Edition Ser.: No. 7). 24p. 1982. ltd. 37.50x (ISBN 0-911381-06-6). Metacom Pr.
--Will You Please Be Quiet, Please? (McGraw-Hill Paperbacks Ser.). 1978. pap. 4.95 (ISBN 0-07-010194-9, SP). McGraw.
Carver, Robert E., ed. Procedures in Sedimentary Petrology. LC 75-138907. 1971. 71.95 (ISBN 0-471-13855-X, Pub. by Wiley-Interscience). Wiley.
Carver, Sally S. The American Postcard Guide to Tuck. rev. ed. (Illus.). 7.95 (ISBN 0-686-51576-5). Wallace-Homestead.
--American Postcard Guide to Tuck: 1983-84. rev. ed. pap. 8.95 (ISBN 0-686-38919-0). Carves.
Carver, Terrel. Marx's Social Theory. 128p. 1983. 17.95 (ISBN 0-19-219170-5); pap. 6.95 (ISBN 0-19-289158-8). Oxford U Pr.
Carver, Terrell, ed. & tr. see Zeleny, Jindrich.
Carver, W. O. Ephesians: The Glory of God in the Christian Calling. LC 78-74597. 1979. pap. 4.50 o.p. (ISBN 0-8054-1313-8). Broadman.
Carvey, Davis W., jt. auth. see Barndt, Stephen E.
Carvill. Famous Names in Engineering. 1981. text ed. 23.95 o.p. (ISBN 0-408-00539-4). Butterworth.
Carvill, Barbara M. Der Verfuhrte Leser J.K.A. Musaus' Romane und Romankritiken. LC 81-69879. (Studies in German Literature, Linguistics & Culture: Vol. 12). (Illus.). 275p. 1983. 24.00x (ISBN 0-938100-13-0). Camden Hse.
Carvill, J. Student Engineer's Companion: A Handbook for Engineers, Draftsmen & Students. (Illus.). 1980. pap. 13.95 (ISBN 0-408-00438-X). Butterworth.
Carville, Geraldine. The Occupation of Celtic Sites in Medieval Ireland by the Canons Regular of St Augustine & the Cistercians. (Cistercian Studies Ser.: Nbr. 56). (Illus.). 1982. write for info. (ISBN 0-87907-856-1). Cistercian Pubns.
Carwardine, Richard. Transatlantic Revivalism: Popular Evangelicalism in Britain & America, 1790-1865. LC 77-94740. (Contributions in American History Ser.: No. 75). 1978. lib. bdg. 29.95 (ISBN 0-313-20308-3, CTR/). Greenwood.
Carwile, Ruth, ed. see Gold, David T.
Carwile, Ruth H., ed. see Karter, Michael J.
Carwin, Merle A. Supervised Occupational Experience Manual. 2nd ed. 242p. 1982. pap. text ed. 4.50x (ISBN 0-8134-2228-0, 2228). Interstate.
Cary, Barbara. Meet Abraham Lincoln. (Step-up-Books Ser.). (Illus.). (gr. 2-6). 1965. 4.95 (ISBN 0-394-80057-5, BYR); PLB 5.99 (ISBN 0-394-90057-X). Random.
Cary, Bob. Winter Camping. LC 78-58680. (An Environmental Sport Book). 1979. 10.95 (ISBN 0-8289-0339-5); pap. 6.95 (ISBN 0-8289-0340-9). Greene.
Cary, Edward. George William Curtis. LC 69-13851. Repr. of 1894 ed. lib. bdg. 17.50x o.p. (ISBN 0-8371-1624-4, CAGC). Greenwood.
Cary, Emily. The Ghost of Whitaker Mountain. (YA) 1979. 6.95 (ISBN 0-685-65270-X, Avalon). Bouregy.
Cary, Howard B. Modern Welding Technology. LC 78-2966. (Illus.). 1979. 24.00 (ISBN 0-13-599290-7); text ed. 34.00 (ISBN 0-686-67267-4). P-H.
Cary, Jere. Building Your Own Kitchen Cabinets. (Illus.). 1983. pap. 11.95 (ISBN 0-918804-15-9). Taunton.
Cary, Joyce. A Fearful Joy, a Novel. LC 73-428. 343p. 1973. Repr. of 1949 ed. lib. bdg. 17.50x (ISBN 0-8371-6777-9, CAFJ). Greenwood.
--Herself Surprised. 275p. 1976. Repr. of 1948 ed. lib. bdg. 16.95x (ISBN 0-89244-070-8). Queens Hse.
--The Horse's Mouth. 1965. pap. 2.95i (ISBN 0-06-080046-1, P46, PL). Har-Row.
--Prisoner of Grace. 301p. 1976. Repr. of 1952 ed. lib. bdg. 16.95x (ISBN 0-89244-072-4). Queens Hse.
Cary, M., ed. see Suetonius.
Cary, Mara. Basic Baskets. LC 75-14222. 127p. 1975. 7.95 o.p. (ISBN 0-395-21626-5); pap. 7.95 (ISBN 0-395-21989-2). HM.
Cary, Norman D., jt. auth. see Book, Albert C.
Cary, Otis. A History of Christianity in Japan: Roman Catholic & Greek Orthodox Missions, 2 vols. LC 75-28972. (Illus.). 1975. Repr. of 1909 ed. boxed 32.50 (ISBN 0-8048-1177-6). C E Tuttle.
Cary, Patrick. The Poems of Patrick Cary. Delany, Veronica, ed. 1978. 36.95x (ISBN 0-19-812566-6). Oxford U Pr.
Cary, R., jt. auth. see Roberts, G.
Cary, Richard. Mary N. Murfree. (United States Authors Ser.). 12.50 (ISBN 0-8057-0540-6, Twayne). G K Hall.
Cary, Willie M. Worse Than Silence: The Black Child's Dilemma. 5.95 o.p. (ISBN 0-533-01641-X). Vantage.
Carylon, Richard. A Guide to the Gods. 1982. 16.95 (ISBN 0-688-01332-5); pap. 8.00 (ISBN 0-688-01333-3). Morrow.
Casad, Dede, jt. auth. see Driskill, Frank A.
Casad, Eugene. Dialect Intelligibility Tests. (Publications in Linguistics & Related Fields Ser.: No. 38). 1974. pap. 8.00x (ISBN 0-88312-040-2); microfiche 3.00 (ISBN 0-88312-440-8). Summer Inst Ling.
Casady, Edwin E. Henry Howard, Earl of Surrey. (MLA Rev. Fund Ser.). 1938. 24.00 (ISBN 0-527-15250-1). Kraus Repr.
Casagrande, Richard, jt. ed. see Lashomb, James.
Casale, Michael see Lion, Eugene & Ball, David.
Casalis, George. Portrait of Karl Barth. Brown, Robert M., tr. LC 80-25829. viii, 135p. 1981. Repr. of 1963 ed. lib. bdg. 19.25x (ISBN 0-313-22775-6, CAKB). Greenwood.
Casals, Felipe G. The Syncretic Society. Meyer, Alfred G., ed. Daniels, Guy, tr. from Fr. LC 80-5455. 100p. 1980. 20.00 (ISBN 0-87332-176-6). M E Sharpe.
Casamassa, J. V. & Bent, R. D. Jet Aircraft Power Systems. 3rd ed. 1965. text ed. 22.50 (ISBN 0-07-010199-X, G). McGraw.
Casanova, P. Gonzales, jt. ed. see De Vries, Egbert.
Casanova, Richard L. & Ratkevich, Ronald P. Illustrated Guide to Fossil Collecting. rev., 3rd ed. (Illus.). 240p. 1981. lib. bdg. 11.95 (ISBN 0-87961-112-X); pap. 6.95 (ISBN 0-87961-113-8). Naturegraph.
Casarett, Alison P. Radiation Biology. (Illus.). 1968. 22.95 (ISBN 0-13-750356-3). P-H.
Casas, Celso A. De see De Casas, Celso A.
Casas, Penelope. Foods & Wines of Spain. LC 82-47830. 1982. 17.95 (ISBN 0-394-51348-7). Knopf.
Casaubon, Isaac. De Satyrica Graecorum Poesi & Romanorum Satira. LC 72-13784. 392p. (Lat.). 1973. Repr. of 1605 ed. lib. bdg. 45.00x (ISBN 0-8201-1115-5). Schol Facsimiles.
Casaubon, Meric. A Letter of Meric Casaubon to Peter du Moulin Concerning Natural Experimental Philosophie. LC 76-47045. 1976. Repr. of 1669 ed. 65.00x (ISBN 0-8201-1284-4). Schol Facsimiles.
--Treatise Concerning Enthusiasme. LC 77-119864. 1970. Repr. of 1656 ed. 37.00x (ISBN 0-8201-1077-9). Schol Facsimiles.
Casavant & Infanger. Agricultural Economics. 1981. text ed. 18.95 (ISBN 0-8359-0185-8); instr's. manual free (ISBN 0-8359-0184-X). Reston.
Casavis, James N. The Chalk Line: A Study in Continuous Progress Education. 211p. 1973. 5.95 o.p. (ISBN 0-685-41036-6). Gaus.
--A First Year Principal Remembers. LC 73-89726. 36p. 1973. 2.50 o.p. (ISBN 0-685-41035-8). Gaus.
Casazza, John A. Condominium Conversions. LC 82-70139. (Illus.). 157p. 1982. pap. text ed. 26.00 (ISBN 0-87420-606-5, C19). Urban Land.
Casazza, John A., jt. auth. see O'Mara, W. Paul.
Casberg, Melvin A. Five Rivers to Death. LC 82-5814. (Illus.). 240p. (Orig.). 1982. pap. 6.95 (ISBN 0-89407-051-7). Strawberry Hill.
Casciani, Patricia N. The Lizards of Trianada. 1983. 10.00 (ISBN 0-533-05500-8). Vantage.
Casciano-Savignano, C. Jennie. Systems Approach to Curriculum & Instructional Improvement. (Secondary Education Ser.). (gr. 6-12). 1978. pap. text ed. 14.95 (ISBN 0-675-08394-X). Merrill.
Casciero, Albert J. & Roney, Raymond G. Introduction to AV for Technical Assistants. LC 81-13690. (Library Science Text). (Illus.). 250p. 1981. lib. bdg. 28.00 (ISBN 0-87287-232-7); pap. 20.00 (ISBN 0-87287-281-5). Libs Unl.
Cascio, Wayne F. & Awad, Elias M. Human Resources Management: An Information Systems Approach. 450p. 1981. text ed. 27.95 (ISBN 0-8359-3008-4); student activities guide o.p. 7.95 (ISBN 0-8359-3010-6); instr's. manual o.p. avail. (ISBN 0-8359-3009-2). Reston.
Casclato, Arthur D. & West, James L., III, eds. Critical Essays on William Styron. (Critical Essays On American Literature Ser.). 1982. lib. bdg. 32.50 (ISBN 0-8161-8261-2). G K Hall.
Cascone, Gina. Pagan Babies & Other Catholic Memories. 160p. 1983. pap. 4.95 (ISBN 0-312-59419-4). St Martin.
Casdia, Maria I. The Homecoming. (Readers' Theatre Exercise Ser: No. 2). (Illus.). 1978. pap. text ed. 2.95 o.p. (ISBN 0-912484-12-8). Joseph Nichols.
Case, Charles C. Culture, the Human Plan: Essays in the Anthropological Interpretation of Human Behavior. 186p. (Orig.). 1977. pap. text ed. 10.00 (ISBN 0-8191-0268-7). U Pr of Amer.
--The Yankee Generations: A History of the Case Family in America. LC 81-40638. (Illus.). 338p. (Orig.). 1982. lib. bdg. 25.25 (ISBN 0-8191-1947-4); pap. text ed. 14.25 (ISBN 0-8191-1948-2). U Pr of Amer.
Case, Clarence M. Non-Violent Coercion: A Study in Methods of Social Pressure. LC 78-137530. (Peace Movement in America Ser). viii, 423p. 1972. Repr. of 1923 ed. lib. bdg. 22.95x (ISBN 0-89198-058-X). Ozer.
Case, Doug & Davey, John. Developing Writing Skills in English. 1982. pap. text ed. 4.00x (ISBN 0-435-28021-X); tchr's. ed. 6.00x (ISBN 0-435-28022-8); wkbk. 2.00x (ISBN 0-435-28023-6). Heinemann Ed.
Case, Fred E. Professional Real Estate Investing: How to Evaluate Complex Investment Alternatives. 326p. 1983. 22.95 (ISBN 0-13-725861-5); pap. 12.95 (ISBN 0-13-725853-4). P-H.
--Real Estate Brokerage: A System's Approach. 2nd ed. (Illus.). 416p. 1982. 24.95 (ISBN 0-13-762344-5). P-H.
Case, Frederick E. & Clapp, John M. Real Estate Financing. LC 77-27938. 417p. 1978. text ed. 31.95 (ISBN 0-471-07248-6); tchrs. manual 8.00 (ISBN 0-471-04411-3). Wiley.
Case, Frederick E., jt. auth. see Kahn, Sanders A.
Case, H. J. & Whittle, A. W., eds. Settlement Patterns in the Oxford Region: The Abingdon Causewayed Enclosure & Other Sites. (CBA Research Report: No. 44). 170p. 1982. pap. text ed. 38.00x (ISBN 0-906780-14-4, 41438, Pub. by Coun Brit Archaeology England). Humanities.
Case, James F. Biology: Observation & Concept. 2nd ed. (Illus.). 1979. 23.95 (ISBN 0-02-319980-6). Macmillan.
Case, John, jt. auth. see Sevareid, Eric.
Case, Karl E. Property Taxation: The Need for Reform. LC 78-9850. 144p. 1978. prof ref 22.00x (ISBN 0-88410-485-0). Ballinger Pub.
Case, Kenneth E. & Jones, Lynn L. Profit Through Quality: Quality Assurance Programs for Manufacturers. 1978. pap. text ed. 14.00 (ISBN 0-89806-005-2, 124); pap. text ed. 7.00 members. Inst Indus Eng.
Case, L. C. Water Problems in Oil Production: An Operator's Manual. 2nd ed. LC 75-118940. 168p. 1977. 37.95 (ISBN 0-87814-001-8). Pennwell Book Division.
Case, Laurel, ed. Guide to the Management of Infectious Diseases. X ed. (Mongraphs in Family Medicine). Date not set. price not set (ISBN 0-8089-1506-1). Grune.
Case, Maynard, et al, eds. Electrolyte & Water Transport Across Gastrointestinal Epithelia. 335p. 1982. text ed. 44.00 (ISBN 0-89004-765-0). Raven.
Case, Patricia A. How to Write Your Autobiography: Preserving Your Family Heritage. LC 77-72670. (Orig.). 1977. pap. 4.95 (ISBN 0-912800-38-0). Woodbridge Pr.
Case, Paul F. The Magical Language. 320p. Date not set. pap. write for info. (ISBN 0-87728-526-8). Weiser.
--The Name of Names. 1981. 2.00 (ISBN 0-686-38082-7). Builders of Adytum.
Case, Paul Foster. Tarot: A Key to the Wisdom of the Ages. 1981. Repr. of 1977 ed. 6.95 (ISBN 0-686-43319-X). Macoy Pub.
Case, Project N. & Lowry, Anna M. Evaluation of Alternative Curricula: Approaches to School Library Media Education. 1975. pap. text ed. 12.50 o.p. (ISBN 0-8389-3165-0). ALA.
Case, Shirley J. Jesus: A New Biography. LC 68-57594. 1968. Repr. of 1927 ed. lib. bdg. 20.50x (ISBN 0-8371-0342-8, CAJE). Greenwood.
--Makers of Christianity: From Jesus to Charlemagne. LC 79-118460. (Essay & General Literature Index Reprint Ser.). 1971. Repr. of 1934 ed. 12.50 o.p. (ISBN 0-8046-1402-4). Kennikat.
Casebere, James. In the Second Half of the Twentieth Century. (Illus.). 16p. (Orig.). 1982. pap. 4.00 (ISBN 0-939784-01-7). CEPA Gall.
Casebere, Jim, jt. auth. see Beckman, Ericka.
Casebier, Allen & Casebier, Janet J., eds. Social Responsibilities of the Mass Media. LC 78-58603. 1978. pap. text ed. 11.50 (ISBN 0-8191-0539-2). U Pr of Amer.
Casebier, Janet J., jt. ed. see Casebier, Allen.
Caserio, M. C., jt. auth. see Roberts, John D.
Casese, Antonio. The New Humanitarian Law of Armed Conflict, 2 vols. 1979. Set. lib. bdg. 88.00; lib. bdg. 44.00 ea. Vol. 1 (ISBN 0-379-20458-4). Vol. 2 (ISBN 0-379-20468-1). Oceana.
Casewit, Curtis. Quit Smoking. 1983. pap. 8.95 (ISBN 0-914918-44-3). Para Res.
Casewit, Curtis W. Freelance Writing: Advice from the Pros. 192p. 1974. pap. 4.95 (ISBN 0-02-079290-5, Collier). Macmillan.
--Making a Living in the Fine Arts: Advice from the Pros. 160p. 1981. 10.95 (ISBN 0-02-522420-4). Macmillan.
--Skiing Colorado: A Complete Guide to America's Number 1 Ski State. LC 75-21060. 160p. 1975. pap. 4.95 (ISBN 0-85699-123-6). Chatham Pr.
Casey, jt. auth. see Kraft.
Casey, Brigid, jt. auth. see Lavine, Sigmund A.

Casey, Clifford B. Mirages, Mysteries & Reality: Brewster County, Texas, the Big Bend of the Rio Grande. (Illus.). 496p. 1974. 12.50 o.p. (ISBN 0-933512-14-7). Pioneer Bk TX.

Casey, Daniel J. & Rhodes, Robert E., eds. Friends & Relations: Irish American Short Stories. 1983. 16.95 (ISBN 0-686-83941-2). Devin.

Casey, Dayle A. Liberty & Law: The Nature of Individual Rights. Brown, Richard H. & Halsey, Van R., eds. (Amherst Ser). (gr. 9-12). 1972. pap. text ed. 4.92 cancelled o.p. (ISBN 0-201-00906-4, Sch Div). A-W.

Casey, Douglas. The International Man. 14.95 o.p. (ISBN 0-932496-01-6). Green Hill.

Casey, Douglas R. Crisis Investing. 2nd ed. LC 79-64112. 1980. 12.50 (ISBN 0-936906-00-6). Stratford Pr.

--The Expatriate Investor. LC 78-74579. 1979. pap. 9.95 o.p. (ISBN 0-89696-049-8, An Everest House Book). Dodd.

--International Investing. 150p. 1981. pap. 9.95 (ISBN 0-89696-130-3, An Everest House Book). Dodd.

Casey, J. The Kingdom of Valencia in the Seventeenth Century. LC 77-88669. (Cambridge Studies in Early Modern History). (Illus.). 1979. 42.50 (ISBN 0-521-21939-6). Cambridge U Pr.

Casey, James F. Fire Service Hydraulics. 2nd ed. (Illus.). 1970. 16.00 (ISBN 0-686-12258-5). Fire Eng.

Casey, James F., ed. The Fire Chief's Handbook. 4th ed. (Illus.). 1978. 22.95 (ISBN 0-686-12257-7). Fire Eng.

Casey, James P. Pulp & Paper: Chemistry & Technology, Vol. 4. 3rd ed. 600p. 1983. price not set (ISBN 0-471-03178-X, Pub. by Wiley-Interscience). Wiley.

Casey, James P., ed. Pulp & Paper: Chemistry & Chemical Technology, 2 vols. 3rd ed. LC 79-13435. 1980. Vol. 1. 78.00 (ISBN 0-471-03175-5, Pub. by Wiley-Interscience); Vol. 2. 73.00 (ISBN 0-471-03176-3). Wiley.

Casey, Joseph H., ed. see Grisez, Germain & Shaw, Russell.

Casey, Lydian. Outdoor Gardening. LC 74-11890. (Early Craft Bks.). (Illus.). 32p. (gr. 1-4). 1975. PLB 3.95g (ISBN 0-8225-0864-8). Lerner Pubns.

Casey, Marion. Charles McCarthy. 260p. 1982. text ed. 6.00. ALA.

Casey, Mary, jt. auth. see Bate, Marjorie.

Casey, Mary C., jt. auth. see Bate, Marjorie D.

Casey, R. & Rawson, P. F. The Boreal Lower Cretaceous Geological Journal Special Issue, No. 5. (Liverpool Geological Society & the Manchester Geological Association). 448p. 1973. 64.95 o.s.i. (ISBN 0-471-27752-5, Pub. by Wiley-Interscience). Wiley.

Casey, R., jt. auth. see Thompson, R.

Casey, Ralph D., ed. Press in Perspective. LC 63-16657. xviii, 218p. 1963. 17.50x o.p. (ISBN 0-8071-0339-X). La State U Pr.

Casey, Rita, jt. auth. see Sowell, Evelyn.

Casey, Robert L. Journey to the High Southwest: A Traveler's Guide. (Illus.). 368p. (Orig.). 1983. pap. 14.95 (ISBN 0-914718-78-9). Pacific Search.

Casey, Stephen, jt. auth. see Listokin, David.

Casey, W. W. How to Meet Men (For Ladies Only) 16p. pap. 3.00x (ISBN 0-943462-01-0). CaseCo.

--You, Too can Beat Police Radar & Avoid Speeding Tickets. 220p. pap. 19.95x (ISBN 0-943462-02-9). CaseCo.

Casey, W. Wilson. TV Trivia Quiz. 32p. pap. 1.95x (ISBN 0-686-36931-9). CaseCo.

Casgrove, D. J. Inositol Phosphates: Their Chemistry, Biochemistry & Physiology. (Studies in Organic Chemistry: Vol. 4). 1980. 40.50 (ISBN 0-444-41874-1). Elsevier.

Cash, Arthur H. Laurence Sterne: The Early & Middle Years. LC 75-18378. (Illus.). 1975. 60.00x (ISBN 0-416-82210-X). Methuen Inc.

Cash, Donna, jt. auth. see Carr, Jo.

Cash, Earl. John A. Williams: The Evolution of a Black Writer. LC 73-92796. 1974. cancelled 0.00 o.p. (ISBN 0-89388-142-2). Okpaku Communications.

Cash, Johnny. Man in Black: His Own Story in His Own Words. (Large Print Ser.). 1976. kivar 4.95 o.p. (ISBN 0-310-22327-X); pap. 3.50 o.p. (ISBN 0-310-22322-9). Zondervan.

Cash, Joseph H. Working the Homestake. (Illus.). 150p. 1973. 6.95 (ISBN 0-8138-0755-7). Iowa St U Pr.

Cash, Kathy. Designing & Using Simulations. (Technical Note Ser.: No. 20). 30p. (Orig.). pap. 1.00 (ISBN 0-932288-66-9). Ctr Intl Ed U of MA.

Cash, Philip, et al, eds. Medicine in Colonial Massachusetts, 1620-1820. LC 80-68589. (Illus.). xxiv, 425p. 1980. 25.00x (ISBN 0-8139-0908-2, Colonial Soc MA). U Pr of Va.

Cash, Phyllis. How to Write a Research Paper. (How to Ser.). 128p. 1975. pap. 4.95 (ISBN 0-671-47093-0). Monarch Pr.

Cashatt, Everett D., jt. auth. see Schuberth, Christopher J.

Cashdan, A. & Grugeon, E., eds. Language in Education: A Source Book. 1972. 18.95x (ISBN 0-7100-7430-1); pap. 8.95 (ISBN 0-7100-7431-X). Routledge & Kegan.

Cashdan, Sheldon. Abnormal Psychology. LC 70-39029. (Foundations of Modern Psychology). (Illus.). 160p. 1972. 9.95 (ISBN 0-13-000802-8). P-H.

Cashel Diocesan Library. County Tipperary, Republic of Ireland. Catalogue of the Cashel Diocesan Library. 1973. 95.00 (ISBN 0-8161-1065-4, Hall Library). G K Hall.

Cashel, Sue, jt. auth. see Boreta, Anne.

Cashen, William R. Farthest North College President: Charles E. Bunnel & the Early History of the University of Alaska. (Illus.). 387p. 1972. 7.95 o.p. (ISBN 0-912006-10-2). U of Alaska Pr.

Cashin, J. A., jt. auth. see Wiseman, J. A.

Cashin, James & Polimeni, Ralph S. Cost Accounting. 1981. 26.95 (ISBN 0-07-010213-9, C); instrs.' manual 30.00 (ISBN 0-07-010214-7); study guide 9.00 (ISBN 0-07-010257-0); overhead transparencies 350.00 (ISBN 0-07-075018-1); job order costing practice set 8.95 (ISBN 0-07-010258-9); process costing practice set 8.95 (ISBN 0-07-010259-7); exam questions 19.95 (ISBN 0-07-010215-5). McGraw.

Cashin, James A. Handbook for Auditors. 1971. 69.95 (ISBN 0-07-010200-7, P&RB). McGraw.

Cashin, James A. & Lerner, Joel J. Schaum's Outline of Accounting II. 2nd ed. (Schaum's Outline Ser.). 288p. 1980. pap. 6.95 (ISBN 0-07-010252-X, SP). McGraw.

Cashin, James A., jt. auth. see Moss, Morris H.

Cashin, James A., et al. Schaum's Outline of Cost Accounting Two. (Schaum's Outline Ser.). Orig. Title: Schaum's Outline of Advanced Cost Accounting. 240p. 1982. pap. 7.95 (ISBN 0-07-010207-4). McGraw.

Cashinella, Brian, jt. auth. see Borrell, Clive.

Cashion, Catherine, jt. ed. see DiNoto, Andrea.

Cashman, Richard I. The Myth of the Lokamanya: Tilak & Mass Politics in Maharashtra. LC 72-97734. 1975. 30.00x (ISBN 0-520-02407-9). U of Cal Pr.

Cashman, Seamus, jt. ed. see Gaffney, Sean.

Cashman, T. & Keys, W. Data Processing: A Text & Project Manual. 2nd ed. 1974. 18.60 (ISBN 0-07-010206-6, G); instructor's key 5.60 (ISBN 0-07-010220-1). McGraw.

Cashman, Thomas J., jt. auth. see Shelly, Gary B.

Cashmore, Ernest. Black Sportsmen. 224p. (Orig.). 1982. pap. 12.95 (ISBN 0-7100-9054-4). Routledge & Kegan.

Cashmore, Ernest & Troyna, Barry. Black Youth in Crisis. 180p. 1982. text ed. 27.50x (ISBN 0-04-362052-3); pap. 10.95 (ISBN 0-04-362053-1). Allen Unwin.

Casida, John E., ed. Pyrethrum: The Natural Insecticide. 1973. 46.00 o.s.i. (ISBN 0-12-162950-3). Acad Pr.

Casida, L. E. Industrial Microbiology. LC 68-22302. 460p. 1968. 42.95 (ISBN 0-471-14060-0). Wiley.

Casier, Edgar. Faune Ichthyologique Du London Clay: Text & Atlas. (Illus.). xiv, 496p. 1966. 100.00x (ISBN 0-565-00654-1, Pub. by British Mus Nat Hist England). Sabbot-Natural Hist Bks.

Casimir, Hendrik B. Haphazard Reality: Half a Century of Science. LC 82-48112. (Sloan Foundation Books). 356p. 1983. 15.00 (ISBN 0-06-015028-9, HarpT). Har-Row.

Casimir, M. & Bament, R. C. An Outbreak of the Australian Plague Locust, (Hortoicetes Terminiferal Walk.), During 1966-67 & the Influence of Weather on Swarm Flight. 1974. 35.00x (ISBN 0-85135-062-3, Pub. by Centre Overseas Research). State Mutual Bk.

Casini, G. Plasma Physics for Thermonuclear Fusion Reactors. (Ispra Courses on Nuclear Engineering & Technology Ser.). 496p. 1982. 74.50 (ISBN 3-7186-0091-9). Harwood Academic.

Casini, G., ed. Engineering Aspects of Thermonuclear Fusion Reactors. (Ispra Courses on Nuclear Engineering & Technology Ser.). 642p. 1982. 97.00 (ISBN 0-686-83016-4). Harwood Academic.

Caskey, Jefferson D. & Stapp, Melinda M., eds. Samuel Taylor Coleridge: A Selective Bibliography of Criticism, 1935-1977. LC 78-57765. 1978. lib. bdg. 29.95 (ISBN 0-313-20564-7, CCO/). Greenwood.

Caskey, Willie M. Secession & Restoration of Louisiana. LC 78-75302. (American Scene Ser). (Illus.). 1970. Repr. of 1938 ed. lib. bdg. 39.50 (ISBN 0-306-71263-6). Da Capo.

Casler, Darwin J. & Crockett, James R. Operational Auditing: An Introduction. Holman, Richard, ed. (Illus.). 80p. pap. text ed. 27.00 (ISBN 0-89413-097-8). Inst Inter Aud.

Casler, Robin E., ed. see American Pharmaceutical Association.

Casley, D. J. & Lury, D. A. Data Collection in Developing Countries. 1981. pap. 12.50x (ISBN 0-19-877124-X). Oxford U Pr.

Casmir, Fred L. Interaction: An Introduction to Speech Communication. LC 73-87529. 1974. text ed. 12.95x (ISBN 0-675-08874-7). Merrill.

Casmir, Fred L., ed. Intercultural & International Communication. LC 78-61912. 1978. pap. text ed. 21.25 o.p. (ISBN 0-8191-0625-9). U Pr of Amer.

Casner, A. James. American Law of Property: 1977 Supplement. 1977. pap. 70.00 (ISBN 0-316-13138-5). Little.

--Black Family Estate Plan. 2nd ed. (Student Edition Supplement to Casner's Estate Planning Ser.). 1981. pap. text ed. 14.00 o.p. (ISBN 0-316-13142-3). Little.

--Cases & Text on Property, 1982 Supplement. 1982. pap. 9.95 (ISBN 0-316-13122-9). Little.

--An Estate Family Plan for Mr. & Mrs. Harry S. Black. 3rd ed. 1982. pap. 15.00 (ISBN 0-316-13155-5). Little.

--Estate Planning, Vols. 1-6. 1980. text ed. 250.00 (ISBN 0-316-13148-2). Vol. 1. Vol. 2 (ISBN 0-316-13149-0). Vol. 3 (ISBN 0-316-13150-4). Vol. 4 (ISBN 0-316-13151-2). Vol. 5 (ISBN 0-316-13152-0). Vol. 6 (ISBN 0-316-13153-9). 1982 supplement 60.00 (ISBN 0-316-13170-9). Little.

--Estate Planning: Student Edition. 4th ed. 1150p. 1979. 28.50 (ISBN 0-316-13173-3). Little.

--Estate Planning: 1982 Supplement. 4th ed. 1982. pap. 9.95 (ISBN 0-316-13171-7). Little.

--Estate Planning: 1982 Supplement, Student Edition. LC 79-88615. 283p. 1982. 9.95 (ISBN 0-316-13171-7). Little.

Casner, A. James & Leach, W. Barton. Cases & Texts on Property. 2nd ed. 1383p. 1969. 27.50 (ISBN 0-316-13089-3). Little.

Casner, A. James, ed. American Law of Property, 8 vols. LC 52-10235. 1952. Set. 395.00 (ISBN 0-316-13145-8). Little.

Casner, A. James, ed. see American Law Institute.

Caso, Adolph. Bilingual Two Language Battery of Tests. 1983. pap. 15.00 (ISBN 0-8283-1857-3). Branden.

--Mass Media vs. the Italian Americans. 1983. pap. 4.95 (ISBN 0-8283-1830-1). Branden.

Caso, Jacques De see Pratt, James N. & De Caso, Jacques.

Caso, Ralph G. Especially Now That Boss Daley Was Gone... LC 76-66824. 1980. 5.95 o.p. (ISBN 0-533-04414-6). Vantage.

Cason, James & Rapoport, Henry. Laboratory Text in Organic Chemistry. 3rd ed. (Chemistry Ser). 1970. pap. 22.95 ref. ed. (ISBN 0-13-521435-1). P-H.

Cason, Mabel E. Song of the Trail. LC 53-10772. (Destiny Ser.). 1979. pap. 4.95 o.p. (ISBN 0-8163-0245-6). Pacific Pr Pub Assn.

Casona, Alejandro. Corona De Amor Y Muerte. Balseiro, Jose & Owre, J. Riis, eds. (Orig., Span). 1960. pap. 7.95x (ISBN 0-19-500844-8). Oxford U Pr.

Casoni, Jennifer. Sincerely, Lyndon: The Handwriting of Lyndon Baines Johnson. 100p. (Orig.). 1983. pap. 14.95 (ISBN 0-9608816-1-1). Univ Autograph.

Caspari, jt. auth. see Schauer.

Caspari, E. W. see Demerec, M.

Caspari, Fritz. Humanism & Social Order in Tudor England. LC 68-29071. 1968. 9.40 o.p. (ISBN 0-8077-1149-7); pap. text ed. 7.50x (ISBN 0-8077-1146-2). Tchrs Coll.

Caspari, Irene E. Troublesome Children in Class. (Students Library of Education). 130p. 1975. 16.95x (ISBN 0-7100-8261-4); pap. 7.50 (ISBN 0-7100-8262-2). Routledge & Kegan.

Caspary, Gerard E. Politics & Exegesis: Origen & the Two Swords. LC 77-71058. 1979. 34.50x (ISBN 0-520-03445-7). U of Cal Pr.

Caspary, Vera. Laura. 1977. Repr. of 1943 ed. lib. bdg. 16.95x (ISBN 0-89244-066-X). Queens Hse.

Caspary, Wolfgang F., ed. Sucralfate: A New Therapeutic Concept. (Illus.). 133p. 1981. pap. text ed. 26.50 cancelled o.p. (ISBN 0-8067-0341-5). Urban & S.

Casper, Barry M. & Wellstone, Paul D. Powerline: The First Battle of America's Energy War. LC 80-25903. (Illus.). 328p. 1981. lib. bdg. 18.50x (ISBN 0-87023-320-3); pap. 8.95 (ISBN 0-87023-321-1). U of Mass Pr.

Casper, Billy. Two-Hundred Ninety-Five Golf Lessons. 1973. pap. 2.95 o.s.i. (ISBN 0-695-80403-0). Follett.

Casper, Gerhard, jt. ed. see Kurland, Philip B.

Casperz, D. A. The Scottish Terrier. Foyle, Christina, ed. (Foyles Handbks). 1972. 3.95 (ISBN 0-685-55806-1). Palmetto Pub.

Cass, Angelica W. Basic Education for Adults: A Handbook for Teachers, Teacher Trainers & Leaders. LC 70-152889. 1971. 5.95 o.s.i. (ISBN 0-8096-1825-7). Follett.

Cass, David B. In the Studio: The Making of Art in Nineteenth Century France. (Illus.). 48p. pap. 6.95 (ISBN 0-931102-06-5). S & F Clark Art.

Cass, David B. & Wetenhall, John. Italian Paintings, 1859-1910: From Collections in the Northeastern Unites States. (Illus.). 82p. 1982. pap. 6.95 (ISBN 0-686-38389-3). S & F Clark.

Cass, Joan E. Helping Children Grow Through Play. LC 72-95659. 190p. 1973. 9.00x o.p. (ISBN 0-8052-3496-9). Schocken.

Cass, Loretta K. & Thomas, Carolyn B. Childhood Pathology & Later Adjustment: The Question of Prediction. LC 78-31857. (Personality Processes Ser.). 1979. 26.95 (ISBN 0-471-04553-5, Pub. by Wiley-Interscience). Wiley.

Cassady, Howard Hop-a-Long. Conditioning for Baseball: The New York Yankee's Way. LC 82-83935. (Illus.). 176p. (Orig.). 1983. pap. 7.95 (ISBN 0-88011-103-8). Leisure Pr.

Cassagnac, Granier De see De Cassagnac, Granier.

Cassanea de Mondonville, Jos. Masters of the Violin, Vol 5. Banat, Gabriel, ed. 75.00 (ISBN 0-384-03185-4). Johnson Repr.

Cassara, Ernest. The Enlightenment in America. LC 74-20962. (World Leaders Ser: No. 50). 1975. lib. bdg. 12.95 o.p. (ISBN 0-8057-3675-1, Twayne). G K Hall.

--Hosea Ballou: The Challenge to Orthodoxy. LC 81-40859. 236p. 1982. lib. bdg. 22.00 (ISBN 0-8191-2271-8); pap. text ed. 10.75 (ISBN 0-8191-2272-6). U Pr of Amer.

Cassara, Ernest, ed. History of the United States of America: A Guide to Information Sources. LC 73-17551. (American Studies Information Guide Series: Vol. 3). 1977. 42.00x (ISBN 0-8103-1266-2). Gale.

Cassard, Daniel W. & Juergenson, Elwood M. Approved Practices in Feeds & Feeding. 5th ed. LC 76-62743. (Illus.). (gr. 9-12). 1977. 16.50 (ISBN 0-8134-1901-8, 1901); text ed. 12.50x. Interstate.

Cassata, Mary & Skill, Thomas. Life on Daytime Television. Voigt, Melvin J., ed. (Communication & Information Science Ser.). 272p. 1983. text ed. 27.50 (ISBN 0-89391-138-0); pap. text ed. 14.95 (ISBN 0-89391-180-1). Ablex Pub.

Cassata, Mary B. & Totten, Herman L., eds. The Administrative Aspects of Education for Librarianship: A Symposium. LC 75-15726. 425p. 1975. 19.00 (ISBN 0-8108-0829-3). Scarecrow.

Cassavant, Sharron G. John Middleton Murry: The Critic As Moralist. (Illus.). 173p. 1982. text ed. 18.75 (ISBN 0-8173-0107-0). U of Ala Pr.

Cass-Beggs, Barbara. Your Baby Needs Music. (Illus.). 144p. 1980. 10.95 o.p. (ISBN 0-312-89767-7); pap. 5.95 o.p. (ISBN 0-312-89768-5). St Martin.

Cassedy & Nussbaum. Nine to Five Survival Guide. 1983. pap. 5.95 (ISBN 0-14-006751-5). Penguin.

Cassedy, David & Shrott, Gail. William Sidney Mount: Annotated Bibliography & Listings of Archival Holdings of the Museums at Stony Brook. (Illus., Orig.). 1983. pap. write for info. (ISBN 0-943924-05-7). Mus Stony.

Cassedy, Sylvia. In Your Own Words: A Beginner's Guide to Writing. LC 78-1237. 1979. 8.95a o.p. (ISBN 0-385-14036-3); PLB 8.95a (ISBN 0-385-14037-1). Doubleday.

Cassel & Swanson. Basic Made Easy: A Guide to Programming Microcomputers & Minicomputers. (Illus.). 272p. 1980. text ed. 18.95 (ISBN 0-8359-0399-0); pap. text ed. 14.95 (ISBN 0-8359-0398-2). Reston.

--FORTRAN Made Easy. text ed. 19.95 (ISBN 0-8359-2090-9). Reston.

Cassel, Claes-Magnus, et al. Foundations of Inference in Survey Sampling. LC 77-5114. (Probability & Mathematical Statistics Ser., Probability & Statistics Section). 1977. 38.95 (ISBN 0-471-02563-1, Pub. by Wiley-Interscience). Wiley.

Cassel, Dana K., ed. Directory of Florida Markets For Writers, 1983. 1983. 12.95. Cassell Commun Inc.

Cassel, Don. Programming Language One: A Structural Approach with PLC. 1978. pap. 18.95 (ISBN 0-87909-650-0). Reston.

--The Structured Alternative: Programming Style, Debugging & Verification. 1982. text ed. 24.95 (ISBN 0-8359-7084-1); Solutions Manual avail. (ISBN 0-8359-7085-X). Reston.

Cassel, Don & Jackson, Martin. Introduction to Computers & Information Processing: Language Edition. 1981. pap. text ed. 21.95 (ISBN 0-8359-3150-1). Reston.

--Introduction to Computers & Information Processing: Language Free Editon. 1981. text ed. 17.95 (ISBN 0-8359-3155-2); study guide o.p. 7.95 (ISBN 0-8359-3157-9); instrs'. manual o.p. avail. (ISBN 0-8359-3156-0). Reston.

Cassell, Abayomi. Liberia: History of the First African Republic, Vol. 2. 1983. 28.50x (ISBN 0-8290-1308-3). Irvington.

Cassell, Dana K., ed. Directory of Florida Markets for Writers. LC 82-70899. 92p. (Orig.). 1982. pap. 12.95 o.p. (ISBN 0-942980-00-X). Cassell Commun Inc.

Cassell, Joan, jt. ed. see Wax, Murray L.

Cassell Ltd., ed. The Patchwork Pattern Book. 1982. 26.00x (ISBN 0-289-70978-4, Pub. by Cassell England). State Mutual Bk.

Cassell, Richard A. Ford Madox Ford: A Study of His Novels. LC 76-57731. 1977. Repr. of 1962 ed. lib. bdg. 20.00x (ISBN 0-8371-9465-2, CAFF). Greenwood.

Cassells. French-English Dictionary. 1977. standard 17.95 (ISBN 0-02-052261-4); index 19.95 (ISBN 0-02-052262-2). Macmillan.

--German-English Dictionary. 1978. standard 17.95 (ISBN 0-02-052292-4); index 19.95 (ISBN 0-02-052293-2). Macmillan.

--Italian-English Dictionary. 1977. standard 19.95 (ISBN 0-02-052254-1); indexed 17.95 (ISBN 0-02-052253-3). Macmillan.

--Latin-English Dictionary. 1977. standard 16.95 (ISBN 0-686-63973-1); index 19.95 (ISBN 0-02-052258-4). Macmillan.

--Spanish-English Dictionary. 1978. standard 17.95 (ISBN 0-02-052290-8); index 19.95 (ISBN 0-02-052291-6). Macmillan.

Casselman, Barry. Language, a Magical Enterprise, the Body. (Paperplay Ser. Mini-Bks.: Vol. 7). (Illus.). 16p. 1978. saddle-stitched 2.50 (ISBN 0-939044-13-7). Lingua Pr.

Casselman, Robert C. Continuum: How Science, Psychology & Mysticism Point to a Life Beyond...& to an Extraordinary Kind of God. LC 78-7670. 1978. 9.95 o.p. (ISBN 0-399-90017-9, Marek). Putnam Pub Group.

Cassels, Alan. Fascist Italy. LC 68-9740. (Europe Since 1500Ser.). (Illus.). 1968. pap. 9.95x (ISBN 0-88295-719-8). Harlan Davidson.

Cassels, Bruce K., tr. see Breitmaier, Eberhard & Bauer, Gerhard.

Cassels, J. M. Basic Quantum Mechanics. 2nd ed. (Illus.). 206p. Date not set. pap. text ed. 13.50 (ISBN 0-333-31768-8). Scholium Intl.

Cassels, Louis. Forbid Them Not. LC 73-75885. 1973. 2.00 o.p. (ISBN 0-8309-0097-7). Ind Pr MO.

Cassem, Ned H., jt. auth. see Hackett, Thomas P.

Cassen, Robert & Jolly, Richard, eds. Rich Country Interests & Third World Development. LC 82-42561. 1982. 32.50x (ISBN 0-312-68101-1). St Martin.

Casserly, jt. auth. see Johnston.

Casserly, John J. The Ford Whitehouse: The Diary of a Speechwriter. LC 77-82185. (Illus.). 1977. 15.00 (ISBN 0-87081-106-1). Colo Assoc.

Casserly, Michael D., et al. School Vandalism: Strategies for Prevention. LC 80-8118. 1980. 19.95x (ISBN 0-669-03956-X). Lexington Bks.

Cassetty, Judith. Child Support & Public Policy. LC 77-4541. (Illus.). 1978. 19.95x (ISBN 0-669-01486-9). Lexington Bks.

Cassetty, Judith, ed. The Parental Child-Support Obligation: Research, Practice, & Social Policy. LC 81-48464. 320p. 1982. 28.95x (ISBN 0-669-05376-7). Lexington Bks.

Cassiday, Bruce. The Carpenter's Bible: A Home Owner's Bible. LC 77-82933. 1981. pap. 4.95 (ISBN 0-385-11210-6). Doubleday.

Cassiday, Bruce, ed. Roots of Detection: The Art of Deduction before Sherlock Holmes. (Recognitions). 225p. 1983. 12.95 (ISBN 0-8044-2113-7); pap. 6.95 (ISBN 0-8044-6065-5). Ungar.

Cassidy, jt. auth. see Robertson.

Cassidy, Frederick G. & Le Page, R. B., eds. Dictionary of Jamaican English. 2nd ed. LC 78-17799. 1980. 82.50 (ISBN 0-521-22165-X). Cambridge U Pr.

Cassidy, G. E. & Linnegar, S. Growing Irises. (Illus.). 160p. 1982. text ed. 15.50x o.p. (ISBN 0-7099-0706-0, Pub. by Croom Helm Ltd England). Biblio Dist.

--Growing Irises. (Illus.). 160p. 1982. 16.50 (ISBN 0-7099-0706-0). Timber.

Cassidy, Harold G. Knowledge, Experience, & Action: An Essay on Education. LC 70-81590. 1969. pap. 7.50x (ISBN 0-8077-1150-0). Tchrs Coll.

Cassidy, J. J., jt. auth. see Hjelmfelt, A. T., Jr.

Cassidy, James T. Textbook of Pediatric Rheumatology. LC 82-4951. 684p. 1982. 47.50 (ISBN 0-471-09925-2, Pub. by Wiley Med). Wiley.

Cassidy, Joan H., jt. auth. see Hotchkiss, John F.

Cassidy, John. The Hacky Sack Book. 80p. 1982. pap. 8.95 (ISBN 0-932592-05-8). Klutz Pr.

Cassidy, John A. Algernon C. Swinburne. (English Authors Ser.: No. 10). lib. bdg. 10.95 o.p. (ISBN 0-8057-1524-X, Twayne). G K Hall.

Cassidy, Laurence L. Existence & Presence: The Dialectics of Divinity. LC 80-5881. 246p. 1981. lib. bdg. 19.00 (ISBN 0-8191-1486-3); pap. text ed. 10.25 (ISBN 0-8191-1487-1). U Pr of Amer.

Cassidy, Michael. Bursting the Wineskins. 1983. 9.95; pap. 5.95 (ISBN 0-87788-094-8). Shaw Pubs.

Cassidy, Pat & Close, Jim. Basic Computer Programming for Kids. (Illus.). 192p. 1983. 17.95 (ISBN 0-13-057927-0); pap. 11.95 (ISBN 0-13-057919-X). P-H.

--Computer Graphics & Games for Kids: Apple II. (Illus.). 200p. 1983. 17.95 (ISBN 0-13-164533-1); pap. 11.95 (ISBN 0-13-164517-X). P-H.

Cassidy, Richard J. & Scharper, Philip J., eds. Political Issues in Luke-Acts. LC 82-19060. 192p. (Orig.). 1983. 16.95 (ISBN 0-88344-390-2); pap. 9.95 (ISBN 0-88344-385-6). Orbis Bks.

Cassidy, Robert. Margaret Mead: A Voice for the Century. LC 81-43435. 176p. 1982. 12.50 (ISBN 0-87663-376-9). Universe.

Cassidy, William. Knife Digest. 2nd ed. (Illus.). 1976. pap. 12.95 (ISBN 0-87364-059-4). Paladin Pr.

--Political Kidnapping. 1978. pap. 6.00 (ISBN 0-87364-141-8). Paladin Pr.

Cassie, W. F., jt. auth. see Capper, P. L.

Cassileth, Barrie R. & Cassileth, Peter A., eds. Clinical Care of the Terminal Cancer Patient. LC 82-15222. 274p. 1982. text ed. 24.00 (ISBN 0-8121-0854-X). Lea & Febiger.

Cassileth, Peter A., jt. ed. see Cassileth, Barrie R.

Cassill, R. V. Writing Fiction. 2nd ed. 192p. 1975. pap. 4.95 (ISBN 0-13-970103-6, Spec). P-H.

Cassill, R. V., ed. The Norton Anthology of Short Fiction. 2nd. ed. 1981. text ed. 11.95x (ISBN 0-393-95178-2); pap. text ed. 10.95x (ISBN 0-393-95182-0); instrs. handbook 3.95x (ISBN 0-393-95186-3). Norton.

--The Norton Anthology of Short Fiction. 1472p. 1977. pap. text ed. 10.95x complete edition (ISBN 0-393-09072-8); pap. text ed. 8.95x shorter edition (ISBN 0-393-09075-2); instr.'s handbook 2.50x (ISBN 0-393-09050-7). Norton.

Cassin, Barbara & Solomon, Sheila. Dictionary of Eye Terminology. (Illus., Orig.). 1983. 12.50x (ISBN 0-937404-07-1). Triad Pub FL.

Cassin, Maxine, ed. see Black, Charles.

Cassin, Maxine, ed. see McFerren, Martha.

Cassin, Maxine, ed. see Maddox, Everette.

Cassinelli, C. W. Total Revolution: A Comparative Study of Germany under Hitler, the Soviet Union Under Stalin, & China Under Mao. Merkl, Peter H., ed. LC 76-10302. (Studies in International & Comparative Politics: No. 10). 252p. 1976. pap. 11.75 o.p. (ISBN 0-87436-228-8); pap. 11.75 o.p. (ISBN 0-87436-228-8). ABC-Clio.

Cassinelli, G., jt. auth. see Beltrametti, E. G.

Cassini, Igor & Molli, Jeanne. I'd Do It All Over Again. (Illus.). 1977. 8.95 o.p. (ISBN 0-399-11553-6). Putnam Pub Group.

Cassin-Scott, Jack. Costumes & Settings for Staging Historical Plays. Incl. Vol. 1. The Classical Period. 1979 (ISBN 0-8238-0231-0); Vol. 2. The Medieval Period. 1979 (ISBN 0-8238-0232-9); Vol. 3. The Elizabethan & Restoration Period. 1979 (ISBN 0-8238-0236-1); Vol. 4. The Georgian Period. 1979 (ISBN 0-8238-0237-X). (Illus.). 10.95 ea. Plays.

Cassirer, Ernst. Kant's Life & Thought. Haden, James, tr. LC 81-3354. 429p. 1983. pap. text ed. 11.95x (ISBN 0-300-02982-9). Yale U Pr.

--Kant's Life & Thought. Haden, James, tr. pap. 11.95 (ISBN 0-686-42819-6, Y-451). Yale U Pr.

--The Myth of State. LC 82-18392. xii, 303p. 1983. Repr. of 1946 ed. lib. bdg. 29.75x (ISBN 0-313-23790-5, CAMO). Greenwood.

--Philosophy of Symbolic Forms, Vol. 1, Language. Manheim, Ralph, tr. 1965. pap. 6.95x (ISBN 0-300-00037-5, Y146). Yale U Pr.

--Philosophy of Symbolic Forms, Vol. 2, Mythical Thought. Manheim, Ralph, tr. 1955. 25.00x (ISBN 0-300-00354-4); pap. 6.95x (ISBN 0-300-00038-3, Y147). Yale U Pr.

--The Philosophy of Symbolic Forms, Vol. 3, The Phenomenology Of Knowledge. Manheim, Ralph, tr. 1965. pap. 8.95x (ISBN 0-300-00039-1, Y148). Yale U Pr.

--Substance & Function & Einstein's Theory of Relativity. 9.50 (ISBN 0-8446-1822-5). Peter Smith.

Cassirer, Ernst, et al, eds. Renaissance Philosophy of Man. LC 48-9358. 1956. pap. 6.50 (ISBN 0-226-09604-1, P1, Phoen). U of Chicago Pr.

Cassity, Turner. Steeplejacks in Babel. LC 73-76686. 72p. 1973. pap. 5.95 (ISBN 0-87923-070-3); 12.95. Godine.

Cassola, Carlo. Fausto & Anna. Quigley, Isabel, tr. from It. LC 75-3795. 318p. 1975. Repr. of 1960 ed. lib. bdg. 18.25x (ISBN 0-8371-8074-0, CAFAA). Greenwood.

--La Ragazza Di Bube. (Easy Readers, C). (Illus.). 1976. pap. text ed. 3.95 (ISBN 0-88436-284-1). EMC.

Casson, Hugh, illus. Wales: Prince of the Old Man of Lochnagar. (Illus.). (gr. k up). 1980. 11.95 (ISBN 0-374-35613-0). FS&G.

Casson, Lionel. Ancient Egypt. LC 65-28872. (Great Ages of Man Ser.). (Illus.). (gr. 6 up). 1965. PLB 11.97 o.p. (ISBN 0-8094-0367-6, Pub. by Time-Life). Silver.

Casson, Lionel, jt. auth. see Burriss, Eli E.

Casson, Mark. The Entrepreneur: An Economic Theory. LC 82-13802. (Illus.). 432p. 1982. text ed. 29.95x (ISBN 0-389-20328-9). B&N Imports.

--Youth Unemployment. LC 79-11242. 1979. text ed. 27.75x (ISBN 0-8419-5050-4). Holmes & Meier.

Casson, Mark, ed. The Growth of International Business. 288p. 1983. text ed. 28.50x (ISBN 0-04-330333-1). Allen Unwin.

Casson, Michael. The Craft of the Potter. LC 78-15013. (Illus.). (gr. 10-12). 1979. pap. 9.95 (ISBN 0-8120-2028-6). Barron.

Casson, Ronald W. Language, Culture & Cognition: Readings in Cognitive Anthropology. 1981. 28.95x (ISBN 0-02-320050-2). Macmillan.

Casson, Stanly. The Discovery of Man: The Story of the Inquiry into Human Origins. (Historiography: Interdisciplinary Studies: No. 2). Repr. of 1939 ed. lib. bdg. 22.50x (ISBN 0-87991-105-0). Porcupine Pr.

Cassone, Diane, jt. auth. see Cassone, Philip.

Cassone, Philip & Cassone, Diane. Hand Jobs. (Illus.). 56p. (Orig.). Date not set. pap. 6.95 (ISBN 0-9610082-0-2). Cassone Pr.

Cassou, Jean, jt. auth. see Read, Herbert.

Casstevens, Thomas B., jt. ed. see Shrivastava, B. K.

Cassuto, Alexander E., jt. auth. see Baird, Charles W.

Castagna, Edwin. Caught in the Act: The Decisive Reading of Some Notable Men & Women & Its Influence on Their Actions & Attitudes. LC 82-10276. 228p. 1982. 14.50 (ISBN 0-8108-1566-4). Scarecrow.

Castagnola, Lawrence. Parables for Little People. (Illus.). 101p. (Orig.). (gr. 4 up). 1982. pap. 5.56 (ISBN 0-89390-034-6); pap. text ed. 6.95. Resource Pubns.

Castagnoli, Ferdinando. Orthogonal Town Planning in Antiquity. 1971. 15.00 (ISBN 0-262-03042-X). MIT Pr.

Castagnoli, N., Jr., jt. ed. see Frigerio, A.

Castaing, D., et al. Hepatic & Portal Surgery in the Rat. (Illus.). 184p. 1980. 39.50x (ISBN 0-89352-101-9). Masson Pub.

Castaldi, Alfred J. & Kender, Joseph P., eds. Laureate Edition of Lehigh Reading Conference Proceedings. viii, 81p. 1972. pap. text ed. 2.50x (ISBN 0-8134-1460-1). Interstate.

Castaldi, C. R. & Brass, George A. Dentistry for the Adolescent Patient. new ed. LC 77-88308. (Illus.). 1980. text ed. 49.00 (ISBN 0-7216-2445-6). Saunders.

Castandea, Alfredo, jt. auth. see Ramirez, Manuel, 3rd.

Castaneda. Transluminal Angioplasty. (Illus.). 350p. 1983. write for info. (ISBN 0-86577-057-3). Thieme-Stratton.

Castaneda, Carlos. The Eagle's Gift. 1981. 14.95 o.s.i. (ISBN 0-671-23087-5). S&S.

--Journey to Ixtlan. 1973. pap. 4.95 (ISBN 0-671-21639-2, Touchstone Bks). S&S.

--Separate Reality. LC 79-139617. 1971. 11.95 o.p. (ISBN 0-671-20897-7). S&S.

--Separate Reality. LC 79-139617. 1971. pap. 4.95 o.p. (ISBN 0-671-21074-2, Touchstone Bks). S&S.

--The Teachings of Don Juan: A Yaqui Way of Knowledge. 1973. 11.95 o.p. (ISBN 0-671-21555-8). S&S.

--The Teachings of Don Juan: A Yaqui Way of Knowledge. LC 68-17303. 1968. 13.95 (ISBN 0-520-00217-2); pap. 3.95 (ISBN 0-520-02258-0, CAL253). U of Cal Pr.

Castaneda, James A. Agustin Moreto. (World Authors Ser.). 1974. lib. bdg. 15.95 (ISBN 0-8057-2633-0, Twayne). G K Hall.

--Mira De Amescua. LC 77-1956. (World Authors Ser.). 1977. lib. bdg. 15.95 (ISBN 0-8057-6285-X, Twayne). G K Hall.

Castaneda, Jorge. Mexico & the United Nations. LC 74-6705. (National Studies on International Organization Ser.). 244p. 1975. Repr. of 1958 ed. lib. bdg. 17.00x (ISBN 0-8371-7548-8, CAME). Greenwood.

Castaneda-Zuniga, Wilfrido, ed. Precutaneous Translamuinal Angioplasty. (Illus.). 250p. 1982. text ed. 35.00 o.p. (ISBN 0-686-81690-0). Thieme-Stratton.

Castanien, Donald G. El Inca Carcilaso De la Vega. (World Authors Ser.). lib. bdg. 15.95 (ISBN 0-8057-2928-3, Twayne). G K Hall.

Casteele, Dennis. Oldsmobile 4-4-2: A Source Book. (Illus.). 144p. 1982. pap. 12.95 (ISBN 0-934780-12-9). Bookman Dan.

Casteleyn, Mary. Planning Library Training Programmes. 176p. 1972. 20.00 (ISBN 0-233-97338-9, 05774-6, Pub. by Gower Pub Co England). Lexington Bks.

Castell, Alburey. An Introduction to Modern Philosophy. 3rd ed. 672p. 1976. 22.95 (ISBN 0-02-320070-7, 32007). Macmillan.

--An Introduction to Modern Philosophy: Examining the Human Condition. 4th ed. 656p. 1983. text ed. 21.95 (ISBN 0-02-320080-4). Macmillan.

Castell, C. P., et al. British Caenozoic Fossils: Tertiary & Quaternary. 5th ed. (Illus.). vi, 132p. 1975. pap. 4.50x (ISBN 0-686-27501-2, Pub. by Brit Mus Nat Hist). Sabbot-Natural Hist Bks.

--British Mesozoic Fossils. 5th ed. (Illus.). vi, 207p. 1975. pap. 5.50x (ISBN 0-686-27502-0, Pub. by Brit Mus Nat Hist). Sabbot-Natural Hist Bks.

Castella, P. & Baillon, D. Notes de Synthese sur l'Economie de la Ville de Bouake. (Black Africa Ser.). 94p. (Fr.). 1974. Repr. of 1970 ed. lib. bdg. 34.00x o.p. (ISBN 0-8287-0166-0, 71-2048). Clearwater Pub.

Castellan, Gilbert W. Physical Chemistry. 2nd ed. LC 75-133375. (Chemistry Ser). (Illus.). 1971. text ed. 28.95 (ISBN 0-201-00912-9). A-W.

--Physical Chemistry. 3rd ed. (Chemistry Ser.). (Illus.). 960p. 1983. text ed. 28.95 (ISBN 0-201-10386-9); Solutions Manual avail. (ISBN 0-201-10387-7). A-W.

Castelli, Louis & Cleeland, Caryn L. David Lean: A Guide to References & Resources. 1980. lib. bdg. 20.00 (ISBN 0-8161-7933-6, Hall Reference). G K Hall.

Castelliz, K., tr. see Lauer, Hans E.

Castellon, Guillermo, tr. see Garbee, Ed & Van Dyke, Henry.

Castellon, Ninoska Perez. Dulcamara. LC 82-82596. (Espejo de Paciencia Ser.). 77p. (Orig., Span. & Eng.). 1982. pap. 5.00 (ISBN 0-89729-317-7). Ediciones.

Castells, Manuel. The City & the Grassroots: A Cross-Cultural Theory of Urban Social Movements. LC 82-40099. (California Ser. in Urban Development: Vol. 2). (Illus.). 600p. 1983. 38.50x (ISBN 0-520-04756-7). U of Cal Pr.

--City, Class & Power. Lebas, Elizabeth, tr. from Fr. 1979. 25.00 (ISBN 0-312-13989-6). St Martin.

--City, Class & Power. LC 78-2978. 198p. 1982. 8.95 (ISBN 0-312-13991-8). St Martin.

--The Urban Question: A Marxist Approach. 1977. pap. 12.00x (ISBN 0-262-53035-X). MIT Pr.

Castells, Matilde O. Mundo Hispano: Lengua y Cultura. LC 80-23698. 402p. 1981. 20.55x (ISBN 0-471-03396-0); wkbk. 9.95x (ISBN 0-471-03397-9). Wiley.

Castellucis, Richard, jt. auth. see Prensky, Sol.

Castellucis, Richard L. Digital Circuits & Systems. 356p. 1981. text ed. 22.95 (ISBN 0-8359-1297-3); instrs. manual avail. (ISBN 0-8359-1298-1). Reston.

Castelvecchio, tr. see Barzini, Luigi S.

Castenada Shular, A., et al. Literatura Chicana: Texto & Contexto. 1972. ref. ed. o.p. 12.95 (ISBN 0-13-537563-0); pap. text ed. 13.95 (ISBN 0-13-537555-X). P-H.

Casteneda, Carlos. Eagle's Gift. 1983. pap. text ed. price not set (ISBN 0-671-47070-1, Touchstone Bks). S&S.

Caster, Paul. Don Juan Dialogues. (Illus.). 48p. 1982. pap. 25.00 (ISBN 0-937486-02-7). Perimeter Pr.

Castetter, William B. Personnel Function in Educational Administration. 3rd ed. 1981. text ed. 25.95 (ISBN 0-02-320140-1). Macmillan.

Casti, John. Connectivity, Complexity, & Catastrophe in Large-Scale Systems. LC 79-40818. (Wiley IIASA International Ser. on Applied Systems Analysis). 203p. 1979. 44.95 (ISBN 0-471-27661-8, Pub. by Wiley-Interscience). Wiley.

Casti, John, tr. see Salukvadze, M.

Castiglione, Baldassare. The Book of the Courtier. 1975. 10.95x (ISBN 0-460-10807-7, Evman); pap. 4.95x (ISBN 0-460-11807-2 Evman). Biblio Dist.

Castiglione, Pierina B. Italian Phonetics, Diction & Intonation. 103p. pap. 9.50x (ISBN 0-913298-48-4); Castiglione tape set 22.00 (ISBN 0-686-77593-7). S F Vanni.

Castile, George. North American Indians: An Introduction to the Chichimeca. (Illus.). 1978. text ed. 23.50 (ISBN 0-07-010233-3, C). McGraw.

Castile, George P. & Kushner, Gilbert, eds. Persistent Peoples: Cultural Enclaves in Perspective. 1981. 24.00x o.s.i. (ISBN 0-8165-0744-9); pap. text ed. 10.50x o.s.i. (ISBN 0-8165-0750-3). U of Ariz Pr.

Castile, Rand. Shiko Munakata, 1903-1975: Works on Paper (Exhibition Catalogue) (Illus.). 48p. 1982. soft-bdg. 7.50 (ISBN 0-686-37057-0). Japan Soc.

Castilhon, Jean-Louis. Essai sur les Erreurs et les Superstitions. (Holbach & His Friends Ser). 485p. (Fr.). 1974. Repr. of 1765 ed. lib. bdg. 121.00 o.p. (ISBN 0-8287-0168-7, 1520). Clearwater Pub.

Castilhon, L. Zingha, Reine d'Angola,Histoire Africaine en Deux Parties. (Bibliotheque Africaine Ser.). 295p. (Fr.). 1974. Repr. of 1769 ed. lib. bdg. 78.50x o.p. (ISBN 0-8287-0169-5, 72-2130). Clearwater Pub.

Castille, Philip & Osborne, William, eds. Southern Literature in Transition: Heritage & Promise. 176p. 1983. 19.95 (ISBN 0-87870-208-3). Memphis St Univ.

Castille, Vernon De see De Castille, Vernon.

Castillejo, Irene Claremont De see Claremont De Castillejo, Irene.

Castillo, Carlos & Bond, Otto F. University of Chicago Spanish Dictionary. 3rd rev. enl. ed. 1977. pap. 4.95 (ISBN 0-226-09674-2, Phoen). U of Chicago Pr.

Castillo, G. T. Beyond Manila: Philippine Rural Problems in Perspective. 420p. 1979. pap. 20.00 (ISBN 0-88936-191-6, IDRC116, IDRC). Unipub.

Castillo, Ronald Del see Del Castillo, Ronald.

Castle, et al. The Business Insurance Handbook. LC 80-70437. 600p. 1981. 45.00 (ISBN 0-87094-237-9). Dow Jones-Irwin.

Castle, Barbara. Castle Diaries Nineteen Seventy-Four to Seventy-Six. 788p. 1982. text ed. 49.50 (ISBN 0-8419-0689-0). Holmes & Meier.

Castle, Charles. La Belle Otero: The Last Great Courtesan. (Illus.). 192p. 1983. 14.95 (ISBN 0-7181-1935-5, Pub by Michael Joseph). Merrimack Bk Serv.

Castle, Coralie. Soup: A Cookbook. LC 73-174182. (Illus., Orig.). 1971. pap. write for info. o.p. One Hund One Prods.

Castle, Coralie & Killeen, Jacqueline. Country Inns Cookery: The Best of American Regional Cooking. LC 82-61102. (Illus.). 160p. 1982. pap. 6.95 (ISBN 0-89286-202-5). One Hund One Prods.

Castle, Coralie, jt. auth. see Baylis, Maggie.

Castle, Coralie, jt. auth. see Bryan, John.

Castle, E. B., jt. auth. see Walters, Elsa H.

Castle, Emery N. & Hemmi, Kenzo, eds. United States-Japanese Agriculture Trade Relations. LC 81-48245. 416p. 1982. 35.00x (ISBN 0-8018-2815-5); pap. 14.95x (ISBN 0-8018-2814-7). Johns Hopkins.

Castle, Emory N. & Becker, Manning H. Farm Business Management: The Decision-Making Process. 2nd ed. (Illus.). 320p. 1972. text ed. 25.95 (ISBN 0-02-320250-5, 32025). Macmillan.

Castle, H. G. Fire over England. (Illus.). 254p. 1982. 22.50 (ISBN 0-436-08900-9, Pub. by Secker & Warburg). David & Charles.

Castle, Jayne. Conflict of Interest. (Candlelight Ecstasy Ser.: No. 130). (Orig.). 1983. pap. 1.95 (ISBN 0-440-10927-2). Dell.

Castle, Kathryn. Infant & Toddler Handbook: Invitations for Optimum Early Development. 107p. 1982. pap. 12.95 (ISBN 0-89334-038-3). Humanics Ltd.

Castle, Mary. Hospital Infection Control. LC 80-13424. 251p. 1980. 25.00x (ISBN 0-471-05395-3, Pub. by Wiley Med). Wiley.

Castle, Philip. Airflow. (Paper Tiger Ser.). (Illus.). 96p. 1980. pap. 6.98 (ISBN 0-399-50495-8, Perige). Putnam Pub Group.

Castle, Raymond N., ed. Condensed Pyridazines Including Cinnolines & Phthaiazines, Vol. 27. LC 72-6304. (Heterocyclic Compounds Ser.). 1124p. 1973. 124.00 (ISBN 0-471-38211-6, Pub. by Wiley). Krieger.

Castle, Sue. The Complete New Guide to Preparing Baby Foods. rev. ed. LC 79-6099. (Illus.). 360p. 1981. 14.95 (ISBN 0-385-15884-X). Doubleday.

--Face Talk, Hand Talk, Body Talk. (gr. k-3). 1977. 9.95a o.p. (ISBN 0-385-11018-9); PLB 9.95a (ISBN 0-385-11019-7). Doubleday.

Castle, Sue, jt. auth. see Bocchicchio, Lucille.

Castle, Terry. Clarissa's Ciphers: Meaning & Disruption in Richarson's Clarissa. LC 82-2460. (Illus.). 1982. 17.50x (ISBN 0-8014-1495-4). Cornell U Pr.

Castle, Tony, ed. The New Book of Christian Quotations. 272p. 1983. pap. 9.95 (ISBN 0-8245-0551-4). Crossroad NY.

Castlehaven, James T. The Earl of Castlehaven's Memoirs of the Irish Wars with the Earl of Anglesey's: A Letter from a Person of Honour in the Country. LC 74-3345. 332p. 1974. Repr. of 1684 ed. lib. bdg. 39.00x (ISBN 0-8201-1128-7). Schol Facsimiles.

Castleman, Harry & Podrazik, Walter. The Beatles Again. LC 77-92320. (Rock & Roll Reference Ser.: No. 2). 280p. 1977. individuals 11.95 (ISBN 0-87650-086-6); institutions 15.95. Pierian.

Castleman, Harry & Podrazik, Walter J. All Together Now: First Complete Beatles Discography, 1961-75. LC 75-29523. (Rock & Roll Reference Ser.: No. 1). 410p. 1976. individual 14.95 (ISBN 0-87650-075-0); institutions 20.00. Pierian.

--Five Hundred Five Television Questions Your Friends Can't Answer. (Five Hundred Five Quiz Ser.). (Orig.). 1983. 10.95 (ISBN 0-8027-0731-9); pap. 6.95 (ISBN 0-8027-7210-2). Walker & Co.

Castleman, Kenneth R. Digital Image Processing. LC 78-27578. (Illus.). 1979. text ed. 37.95 (ISBN 0-13-212365-7). P-H.

Castleman, Michael. Sexual Solutions: An Informative Guide. 256p. 1981. 12.95 o.s.i. (ISBN 0-671-24688-7). S&S.

Castleman, Riva. Prints from Blocks: Gaugin to Now. (Illus.). 84p. 1983. pap. 8.95 (ISBN 0-87070-561-X). Museum Mod Art.

Castles, Alex C. Australia: A Chronology & Fact Book, 1606-1976. LC 77-21516. (World Chronology Ser.). 151p. 1978. 8.50 (ISBN 0-379-16313-6). Oceana.

Castlewitz, David M. VisiCalc Made Easy. 160p. (Orig.). 1983. pap. 12.95 (ISBN 0-931988-89-6). Osborne-McGraw.

Castner, Herbert, ed. see Handel, Judith.

Castoire, Marie & Posner, Richard. Gold Shield. 288p. 1982. 14.95 (ISBN 0-399-12766-6). Putnam Pub Group.

Castracane Degli Antelminelli, F. Report on the Diatoms Collected During the Voyage of H.M.S. Challenger. (Illus.). 1966. Repr. of 1886 ed. 38.40 (ISBN 3-7682-0293-3). Lubrecht & Cramer.

Castro, Angel. Cubano..., Go Home! 1972. pap. 3.00 (ISBN 0-685-48631-1). E Torres & Sons.

--Refugiados. 1971. pap. text ed. 4.00 (ISBN 0-685-48630-3). E Torres & Sons.

Castro, Fidel. Fidel Castro Speeches: Building Socialism in Cuba, Vol. 2. Taber, Michael, ed. 400p. 1983. lib. bdg. 30.00X (ISBN 0-87348-624-2); pap. 7.95X (ISBN 0-87348-650-1). Monad Pr.

--Revolutionary Struggle: Volume One (1947-1958) of the Selected Works of Fidel Castro. Bonachea, Rolando & Valdes, Nelson P., eds. 1972. 22.50x (ISBN 0-262-02065-3); pap. 4.95x (ISBN 0-262-52027-3). MIT Pr.

Castro, Jose I. The Sharks of North American Waters. LC 82-45892. (W. L. Moody, Jr., Natural History Ser.: No. 5). (Illus.). 208p. (Orig.). 1983. 19.50 (ISBN 0-89096-140-9); pap. 9.95 (ISBN 0-89096-143-3). Tex A&M Univ Pr.

Castro, Karen G., tr. see Ferreiro, Emilia & Teberosky, Ana.

Castro, Oscar & Kimbrough, Victoria. In Touch: A Beginning American English Series. Incl. students bk. 1, 1979 (ISBN 0-582-79742-X); tchr's manual 1 (ISBN 0-582-79743-8); workbook 1 (ISBN 0-582-79744-6); cassette 1; students bk. 2 (ISBN 0-582-79746-2); tchr's manual 2 (ISBN 0-582-79747-0); workbook 2 (ISBN 0-582-79748-9); cassette 2 (ISBN 0-582-79749-7); students bk. 3 (ISBN 0-582-79750-0); tchr's manual 3 (ISBN 0-582-79753-5); workbook 3 (ISBN 0-582-79752-7); cassette 3 (ISBN 0-582-79751-9). (English As a Second Language Bk.). (Illus.). 1980. pap. text ed. 4.45x ea. student bk.; tchr's manual 5.25x ea.; wkbk. 2.50x ea.; cassette 22.95 ea. Longman.

Castro, R. & De Cadenet, J. J. Welding Metallurgy of Stainless & Heat-Resisting Steels. Jain, R. C., tr. from Fr. LC 74-76582. (Illus.). 200p. 1975. 34.50 (ISBN 0-521-20431-3). Cambridge U Pr.

Castroleal, jt. auth. see Suarez.

Castroleal, Alicia. Aprende en Espanol y en Ingles: Level One-Reader A. (Aprende en Espanol y en Ingles Ser.). (Illus., Span.). (gr. 1-2). 1979. text ed. cancelled o.p. (ISBN 0-88345-409-2). Regents Pub.

--Aprende en Espanol y en Ingles: Level One-Reader B. (Aprende en Espanol y en Ingles Ser.). (Illus., Span.). 1979. text ed. write for info. o.p. (ISBN 0-88345-410-6). Regents Pub.

Castroleal, Alicia & Suarez, Diamantina V. Aprende en Espanol y en Ingles: Level 1-Reader A. 1979. pap. text ed. write for info. o.p. (ISBN 0-88345-388-6); write for info. tchr's guide o.p. (ISBN 0-88345-390-8). Regents Pub.

Castro-Magana, Mariano, jt. auth. see Collipp, Platon J.

Casty, Alan. Act of Writing & Reading: A Combined Text. (Orig.). 1966. pap. text ed. 11.95x (ISBN 0-13-003780-X). P-H.

--Improving Writing: A Positive Approach. (Illus.). 400p. 1982. pap. 10.95 (ISBN 0-13-453399-2). P-H.

--Mass Media & Mass Man. 2nd ed. LC 81-40917. 318p. 1982. pap. text ed. 12.75 (ISBN 0-8191-2261-0). U Pr of Amer.

--A Mixed Bag: A New Collection for Understanding & Response. 2nd ed. (Illus.). 256p. 1975. pap. text ed. 11.95 (ISBN 0-13-586016-4). P-H.

Casty, Alan & Tighe, Donald J. Staircase to Writing & Reading. 3rd ed. (Illus.). 1979. pap. 13.95 (ISBN 0-13-840579-4). P-H.

Casty, Alan H. The Shape of Fiction. 2nd ed. 448p. 1975. pap. text ed. 11.95x (ISBN 0-669-91066-X); instr's manual 1.95 (ISBN 0-669-91074-0). Heath.

Casualty Surgeons Association of Great Britain. Care of the Acutely Ill & Injured: Proceedings, International Congress of Emergency Surgery, Brighton, 5th, 1981. Wilson, David H. & Marsden, Andrew K., eds. LC 82-1836. 300p. 1982. 55.95 (ISBN 0-471-10238-5, Pub. by Wiley Med). Wiley.

Caswell, et al, eds. Pesticide Handbook-Entoma. 29th ed. (Incl. the out of print Consolidated List of Approved Common Names of Insecticides & Certain Other Pesticides). 1981-82. 9.00 (ISBN 0-686-23164-3); pap. 17.00 (ISBN 0-938522-09-4). Entomol Soc.

Caswell, Donald. Watching the Sun Go Down. pap. 3.00 (ISBN 0-686-81806-7). Anhinga Pr.

Catalan, Jose, jt. auth. see Hawton, Keith.

Cataldo, Bernard F., et al. Introduction to Law & the Legal Process. 3rd ed. LC 79-13193. 866p. 1980. 34.95x (ISBN 0-471-14082-1); tchr's manual 7.50 (ISBN 0-471-02267-5). Wiley.

Cataldo, Christine Z. Infant & Toddler Programs: A Guide to Very Early Childhood Education. LC 82-11418. (Illus.). 240p. Date not set. pap. text ed. 9.95 (ISBN 0-201-11020-2). A-W.

Cataldo, Corrine, jt. auth. see Whitney, Eleanor N.

Cataldo, Everett F., et al. School Desegregation Policy. LC 77-6080. (Politics of Education Ser.). (Illus.). 1978. 15.95 o.p. (ISBN 0-669-01536-9). Lexington Bks.

Cataldo, Mary A. & Benvenuti, Judi, eds. Morristown: The War Years, 1775-1783. (Illus.). 96p. (Orig.). 1979. 15.95 (ISBN 0-89062-100-4). Eastern Acorn.

Cataldo, Susan. Brooklyn-Queens Day. Owen, Maureen, ed. (Summer Ser.). 48p. (Orig.). 1982. pap. 3.00 (ISBN 0-916382-30-3). Telephone Bks.

Catalogues of the Library of the Marine Biological Association of the United Kingdom. Marine Biological Association of the United Kingdom, Library. 1978. lib. bdg. 1440.00 (ISBN 0-8161-0076-4, Hall Library). G K Hall.

Catalyst Editors. Marketing Yourself: The Catalyst Women's Guide to Successful Resumes & Interviews. LC 79-25235. 1980. 9.95 (ISBN 0-399-12452-7). Putnam Pub Group.

--What to Do with the Rest of Your Life. 1980. 16.95 o.p. (ISBN 0-671-25070-1). S&S.

Catalyst Staff. Making the Most of Your First Job. 288p. 1981. 11.95 (ISBN 0-399-12609-0). Putnam Pub Group.

Catan, John R., ed. see Owens, Joseph.

Catan, John R., tr. see Reale, Giovanni.

Catanach, I. J. Rural Credit in Western India, 1875-1930: Rural Credit & the Co-Operative Movement in the Bombay Presidency. LC 72-94986. 1970. 33.00x (ISBN 0-520-01595-9). U of Cal Pr.

Catanese, Anthony J. & Snyder, James C. Introduction to Urban Planning. (Illus.). 1979. text ed. 29.95 (ISBN 0-07-010228-7, C) (ISBN 0-07-010229-5). McGraw.

Catanese, Anthony J., et al. Urban Planning: A Guide to Information Sources. LC 78-13462. (Urban Studies Information Guide Ser.: Vol. 2). 165p. 1979. 42.00x (ISBN 0-8103-1399-5). Gale.

Catania, A. Charles. Learning. (Century Psychology Ser.). (Illus.). 1979. text ed. 23.95 (ISBN 0-13-527432-X). P-H.

Catania, Charles A. Contemporary Research in Operant Behavior. 1968. pap. 14.50x (ISBN 0-673-05496-9). Scott F.

Catanzariti, John, jt. ed. see Ferguson, E. James.

Catanzaro, Ronald J., ed. Alcoholism: The Total Treatment Approach. (Illus.). 528p. 1977. 34.50x (ISBN 0-398-00295-9). C C Thomas.

Catcheside, D. G. The Genetics of Recombination. LC 77-16201. (Genetics - Principles & Perspectives). 184p. 1978. pap. 19.95 (ISBN 0-8391-1196-7). Univ Park.

Catchpole, Clive. Owls. LC 77-8371. (New Biology Ser.). (Illus.). (gr. 4-9). 1978. 7.95 (ISBN 0-07-010232-5, GB). McGraw.

Catchside, D. G. Genetics of Recombination. (Genetics Principles & Perspectives Ser.). 182p. 1977. pap. text ed. 19.95 (ISBN 0-7131-2613-2). E Arnold.

Cate, Curtis, tr. see Saint-Exupery, Antoine De.

Cate, Phillip D. & Gill, Susan. Theophile Alexandre Steinlen. (Illus.). 166p. 1982. pap. 15.00 (ISBN 0-87905-129-9). Peregrine Smith.

Cate, Robert. How to Interpret the Bible. LC 81-86638. (Orig.). 1983. pap. 6.95 (ISBN 0-8054-1142-9). Broadman.

Cate, Ten A. Richard see Ten Cate, A. Richard.

Cateora, Philip R., jt. ed. see Andersen, Clifton R.

Cater, Douglass & Strickland, Stephen P. TV Violence & the Child: The Evolution & Fate of the Surgeon General's Report. LC 74-83207. 168p. 1975. 7.95x (ISBN 0-87154-203-X). Russell Sage.

Cates, Clifford. Air Force Collecting. LC 82-60731. (Illus.). 1982. 14.95 (ISBN 0-912958-18-9); pap. 7.95 (ISBN 0-686-96787-9). MCN Pr.

Cates, G. E., et al. Principles of Organometallic Chemistry. 1968. 16.50 (ISBN 0-412-15350-5, Pub. by Chapman & Hall). Methuen Inc.

Cates, Jerry R. Insuring Inequality: Administrative Leadership in Social Security, 1935-1954. 216p. 1982. text ed. 18.50x (ISBN 0-472-10026-2). U of Mich Pr.

Cates, Judith N. & Sussman, Marvin B., eds. Family Systems & Inheritance Patterns. LC 82-15790. (Marriage & Family Review Ser.: Vol. 5, No. 3). 128p. 1983. text ed. 19.95 (ISBN 0-86656-158-7, B158). Haworth Pr.

Cates, Paul E., ed. The Open Bible: The Christian Educators Edition. 1978. 30.00 o.p. (ISBN 0-686-08742-9). Freedom U Pr.

Cates, Rosalie. Branded. LC 79-19211. 1981. 12.95 (ISBN 0-87949-147-7). Ashley Bks.

Catesby, Mark. Natural History of Carolina, Florida & the Bahama Islands, Catalogue Volume. (Illus.). 50.00 (ISBN 0-384-07865-6). Johnson Repr.

--Natural History of Carolina, Florida & the Bahama Islands. (Illus.). Repr. 575.00 (ISBN 0-384-07315-8). Johnson Repr.

Cathcart, Helen. Anne & the Princesses Royal. 2nd ed. 205p. 1975. 8.95 o.p. (ISBN 0-491-01321-3). Transatlantic.

Cathcart, Jacqueline. Love's Fine Edge. 1983. pap. 6.95 (ISBN 0-686-84732-6, Avalon). Bouregy.

Cathcart, Kathryn. Foreseeable Future: Reading, Writing, Vocabulary with Exercises. LC 68-57468. 64p. (Orig.). 1969. text ed. 6.95x o.p. (ISBN 0-02-473940-5, 47394). Glencoe.

Cathcart, Robert, jt. ed. see Gumpert, Gary.

Cathcart, Ruth & Strong, Michael. Beyond the Classroom. (Gateway to English Program). (Illus.). 208p. (Orig.). 1981. pap. 6.95 (ISBN 0-88377-170-5). Newbury Hse.

Cather, Thomas. Voyage to America: The Journals of Thomas Cather. Yoseloff, Thomas, ed. & intro. by. LC 72-11303. (Illus.). 176p. 1973. Repr. of 1961 ed. lib. bdg. 15.00x o.p. (ISBN 0-8371-6650-0, CAVA). Greenwood.

Cather, Willa. Death Comes for the Archbishop. (YA) 1927. 15.50 (ISBN 0-394-42154-X). Knopf.

--A Lost Lady. 192p. 1972. 10.00 (ISBN 0-394-48558-0, V705, Vin); pap. 7.95 (ISBN 0-394-71705-8). Random.

--My Mortal Enemy. 1961. pap. 2.95 (ISBN 0-394-70200-X, V200, Vin). Random.

--O Pioneers. 10.95 (ISBN 0-395-07516-5); pap. 5.95 (ISBN 0-395-08365-6). HM.

--Sapphira & the Slave Girl. LC 74-20797. 1975. pap. 4.95 (ISBN 0-394-71434-2, Vin). Random.

--The Song of the Lark. 1915 ed. LC 77-15596. xvi, 490p. 1978. pap. 6.95 o.p. (ISBN 0-8032-6300-7, BB 670, Bison). U of Nebr Pr.

Catherall, Ed. Water Power. LC 81-86272. (Fun with Science Ser.). 12.68 (ISBN 0-382-06630-8). Silver.

Catherall, Ed, jt. auth. see Bird, John.

Cathers, David M. Furniture of the American Arts & Crafts Movement: Stickley & Roycroft Mission Oak. (Illus.). 1981. 19.95 (ISBN 0-452-25374-8, H397). NAL.

Catherwood, Fred. On the Job: The Christian 9 to 5. 192p. 1983. pap. 5.95 (ISBN 0-310-37261-5). Zondervan.

Cathey, James F., jt. auth. see Valfells, Sigrid.

Cathey, W. Thomas. Optical Information Processing & Holography. LC 73-14604. (Pure & Applied Optics Ser). 398p. 1974. 35.50 (ISBN 0-471-14078-3, Pub. by Wiley-Interscience). Wiley.

Cathie, John. The Political Economy of Food Aid. LC 81-9151. 200p. 1982. 25.00x (ISBN 0-312-62259-7). St Martin.

Catholic Heritage Press, jt. auth. see Tiso, Francis.

Catholic Hymnal & Service Book Editorial Committee & Doherty, John T. Catholic Hymnal. (Orig.). 1966. pap. 1.50 o.p. (ISBN 0-02-640300-5, 64030). Glencoe.

Catholic Library Association. C L A: Handbook & Membership Directory. 20.00 ea. Cath Lib Assn.

Catholic University of America, Washington, D. C. Catalog of the Oliveira Lima Library, 2 vols. 1970. Set. 190.00 (ISBN 0-8161-0873-0, Hall Library). G K Hall.

Cathon, Laura E., et al, eds. Stories to Tell to Children: A Selected List. LC 73-13317. (Illus.). 168p. 1974. pap. 4.95 (ISBN 0-8229-5246-7). U of Pittsburgh Pr.

Cativiela, A., tr. Epistolas de Pablo: Tomo III. (Comentario del Nuevo Testamento). Repr. of 1975 ed. 12.95 (ISBN 0-311-03052-1). Casa Bautista.

Cativiela, A., tr. see Schroeder, A. & Bonnet, L.

Cativiela, A., tr. see Schroeder, L. Bonnety A.

Catledge, Turner, jt. auth. see Alsop, Joseph.

Catlett, Cloe. Fifty More Hikes in Maine: Day Hikes & Backpacking Trips from the Rocky Coast to the North Maine Woods. LC 79-92571. (Fifty Hikes Ser.). (Illus., Orig.). 1980. pap. 8.95 (ISBN 0-89725-017-6). Backcountry Pubns.

Catlett, Joyce, jt. auth. see Firestone, Robert.

Catlin, Alan. Animal Acts. 92p. (Orig.). 1983. pap. 3.95 (ISBN 0-934040-10-9). Quality Ohio.

Catlin, Alberta P. & Bachand, Shirley. Practical Nursing: PreTest Self-Assessment & Review. 2nd. ed. (Nursing: Pretest Self-Assessment & Review Ser.). (Illus.). 450p. 1982. cancelled (ISBN 0-07-050994-8); pap. cancelled (ISBN 0-686-36899-1). McGraw-Pretest.

Catlin, Daniel, Jr. Liberal Education at Yale: The Yale College Course of Study 1945-1978. LC 82-17576. 264p. (Orig.). 1983. lib. bdg. 24.00 (ISBN 0-8191-2796-5); pap. text ed. 11.75 (ISBN 0-8191-2797-3). U Pr of Amer.

Catlin, George. Catlin's North American Indian Portfolio: A Reproduction. 1844 ed. 1970. Repr. of 1844 ed. 250.00 (ISBN 0-8040-0029-8, SB). Swallow.

Catlin, Robin J., ed. see PreTest Service Inc.

Catlin, Stanton L., frwd. by. Latin American Paintings & Drawings. (Illus.). 1971. pap. 3.00 (ISBN 0-88397-057-0, Pub. by Intl Exhibit Foun). C E Tuttle.

Catling, Patrick S. The Chocolate Touch. LC 78-31100. (Illus.). (gr. 4-6). 1979. Repr. of 1952 ed. PLB 7.92 (ISBN 0-688-32187-9). Morrow.

Catlow, C. R. & Mackrodt, W. C., eds. Computer Simulation of Solids. (Lecture Notes in Physics Ser.: Vol. 166). 320p. 1983. pap. 17.00 (ISBN 0-387-11588-9). Springer-Verlag.

Cato, Ingemar, jt. auth. see Olausson, Eric.

Cato, Nancy. All the Rivers Run. 1979. pap. 3.50 (ISBN 0-451-11345-4, AE1345, Sig). NAL.

--Forefathers. 704p. 1983. 15.95 (ISBN 0-312-29831-5). St Martin.

Catoe, Lynn E., ed. UFOs & Related Subjects: An Annotated Bibliography. LC 78-26124. 1979. Repr. of 1969 ed. 50.00x (ISBN 0-8103-2021-5). Gale.

Catoir, John T. The Way People Pray: An Introduction to the History of Religions. LC 73-91369. (Orig.). 1974. pap. 1.95 o.p. (ISBN 0-8091-1805-X). Paulist Pr.

Caton, Hilda, et al. Specifications for Selecting a Vocabulary & Teaching Method for Beginning Braille Readers. 76p. 1979. pap. 3.50 o.p. (ISBN 0-89128-971-2, PER971). Am Foun Blind.

Catone, Marc A. An American Generation Remembers the Beatles, No. 1. (Rock & Roll Remembrances Ser.). 256p. write for info. Pierian.

--As I Write This Letter: An American Generation Remembers the Beatles. LC 81-86107. (Rock & Roll Remberances Ser.: No. 1). 1982. individuals 17.50 (ISBN 0-87650-137-4); institutions 24.95. Pierian.

Catrambone, Gene. The Golden Touch: Frankie Carle. LC 80-80901. 1982. 8.95 (ISBN 0-87212-124-0). Libra.

Catrina, Christian, jt. auth. see Frei, Daniel.

Catron, Donald G. The Anesthesiologists Handbook. 2nd ed. (Illus.). 224p. 1976. pap. text ed. 13.95 (ISBN 0-8391-0956-3). Univ Park.

Catrou, Paul G., jt. auth. see Beeler, Myrton F.

Catsambas, Thanos. Regional Impacts of Federal Fiscal Policy. LC 77-12282. 1978. 17.95x o.p. (ISBN 0-669-01953-4). Lexington Bks.

Cattabeni, F., et al, eds. Advances in Biochemical Psychopharmacology, Vol. 24. 680p. 1980. text ed. 69.00 (ISBN 0-89004-375-2). Raven.

Cattafi, Bartolo. Cattafi Selected Poems. Swann, Brian & Feldman, Ruth, trs. from Ital. 228p. 1982. 17.50 (ISBN 0-931556-04-X); pap. 7.50 (ISBN 0-931556-05-8). Translation Pr.

Cattan, H. The Law of Oil Concessions in the Middle East & North Africa. LC 67-14400. 200p. 1967. 15.00 (ISBN 0-379-00319-8). Oceana.

Cattaneo, Frank. Shop Made Easy. (Illus.). 1971. pap. text ed. 3.50x (ISBN 0-88323-064-X, 188). Richards Pub.

Cattell, N. R. New English Grammar. 1969. pap. 5.95x (ISBN 0-262-53010-4). MIT Pr.

Cattell, R. G. Formalization & Automatic Derivation of Code Generators. Stone, Harold S., ed. LC 82-4802. (Computer Science: Systems Programming Ser.: No. 3). 158p. 1982. 34.95 (ISBN 0-8357-1316-4, Pub. by UMI Res Pr). Univ Microfilms.

Cattell, Raymond B. A New Morality from Science: Beyondism. 1973. 38.00 (ISBN 0-08-016956-2). Pergamon.

--Personality & Learning Theory: A Systems Theory of Maturation & Structured Learning, 2 vols, Vol. 2. LC 79-594. 1980. text ed. 49.00 (ISBN 0-8261-2124-1); text ed. 75.00 set. Springer Pub.

--Personality & Learning Theory: The Structure of Personality in Its Environment, 2 vols, Vol. 1. LC 79-593. 1979. text ed. 34.50 (ISBN 0-8261-2120-9); text ed. 75.00 set. Springer Pub.

Cattermole, Peter. World of Geology. (Illus.). 1971. 6.95 o.p. (ISBN 0-584-10328-X). Transatlantic.

Catterson, Joy S., ed. see Gibson, Karon W., et al.

Catto, Max. The Empty Tiger. LC 77-291. 1977. 7.95 o.p. (ISBN 0-312-24512-2). St Martin.

Catton, Bruce. The Army of the Potomac: A Trilogy, 3 vols. 1962. Set. 14.95 (ISBN 0-385-00544-X). Doubleday.

--Civil War. 1971. 8.95 o.p. (ISBN 0-07-010266-X, GB); pap. 6.95 o.p. (ISBN 0-07-010265-1). McGraw.
--Coming Fury. LC 61-12502. (Centennial History of the Civil War: Vol. 1). 17.95 (ISBN 0-385-09813-8). Doubleday.
--Gettysburg: The Final Fury. LC 73-11896. (Illus.). 128p. 1974. slipcased 17.95 (ISBN 0-385-02060-0). Doubleday.
--Glory Road: The Bloody Route from Fredericksburg to Gettysburg. LC 62-1070. 1962. 12.95 (ISBN 0-385-04167-5). Doubleday.
--Mister Lincoln's Army. LC 62-1068. 1960. 12.95 (ISBN 0-385-04310-4). Doubleday.
--Never Call Retreat, Vol. III. LC 61-12502. (Centennial History of the Civil War). 1965. 17.95 (ISBN 0-385-02615-3). Doubleday.
--Terrible Swift Sword, Vol. II. LC 62-15937. 17.95 (ISBN 0-385-02614-5). Doubleday.
--Terrible Swift Sword, Vol. 2. (The Centennial History of the Civil War Ser.). 592p. 1967. pap. 4.95 (ISBN 0-671-44925-7). WSP.
--U. S. Grant & the American Military Tradition. (The Library of American Biography Ser.). (Orig.). 1972. pap. text ed. 5.95 (ISBN 0-316-13206-3). Little.
--Waiting for the Morning Train: An American Boyhood. LC 72-76134. (Illus.). 256p. 1972. 12.95 (ISBN 0-385-07460-3). Doubleday.
Catton, William B., jt. auth. see Link, Arthur S.
Cattonar, Nell, tr. see Vidali, Vittorio.
Catudal, Jr. & Honore, M. The Diplomacy of the Quadripartite Agreement on Berlin: A New Era in East-West Politics. LC 78-345065. (Political Studies: No. 12). (Illus.). 1978. pap. 20.00x (ISBN 3-87061-138-3). Intl Pubns Serv.
Catullus. Catullus: Selected Poems. 1969. 9.95 o.p. (ISBN 0-312-12530-5). St Martin.
--The Poems of Catullus. Raphael, Frederic & McLeish, Kenneth, trs. from Lat. LC 78-66091. 1978. 8.95x (ISBN 0-87923-262-5). Godine.
--The Poems of Catullus. bilingual ed. Whigham, Peter, tr. & intro. by. LC 69-19556. 1969. 17.95x o.s.i. (ISBN 0-520-01513-4). U of Cal Pr.
--Select Poems. expurgated ed. Simpson, F. P., ed. 1879. 4.95 o.p. (ISBN 0-685-20375-1). St Martin.
--Selections from Catullus. Lyne, R. O., ed. (Latin Texts Ser.). 48p. 1973. 3.50 (ISBN 0-521-20267-1). Cambridge U Pr.
Cauchois, Y., et al, eds. Wavelengths of X-Ray Emission Lines & Absorption Edges. LC 78-40419. 1978. 160.00 (ISBN 0-08-022448-2); pap. text ed. 80.00 o.p. (ISBN 0-08-023392-9). Pergamon.
Caudano, R. & Verbist, J., eds. Electron Spectroscopy. 1136p. 1975. 127.75 (ISBN 0-444-41291-3). Elsevier.
Caudill, et al. Take Ten. LC 80-80654. (Illus.). 160p. (gr. k-2). 1980. pap. text ed. 8.95 o.p. (ISBN 0-913916-68-4, IP684). Incentive Pubns.
Caudill, Paul R. First Corinthians: A Translation with Notes. 1983. 4.95 (ISBN 0-8054-1391-X). Broadman.
--Seven Steps to Peace. LC 81-71254. 1982. pap. 3.95 (ISBN 0-8054-1527-0). Broadman.
Caudill, R. Paul. Ephesians: A Translation with Notes. LC 78-67291. 1979. pap. 3.75 o.p. (ISBN 0-8054-1375-8). Broadman.
Caudill, William. Effects of Social & Cultural Systems in Reactions to Stress. LC 58-10875. 1958. pap. 5.00 (ISBN 0-527-03302-2). Kraus Repr.
Caufield, Don. The Great Computer. 1978. 5.95 o.p. (ISBN 0-533-03618-6). Vantage.
Caughey. Decisions for Independent Living. (gr. 9-12). 1983. text ed. 5.84 (ISBN 0-87002-378-0). Bennett IL.
Caughey, John. To Kill a Child's Spirit: The Tragedy of School Segregation in Los Angeles. LC 72-89724. (Illus.). 255p. 1973. pap. text ed. 7.95 (ISBN 0-87581-146-9). Peacock Pubs.
Caughey, John & Caughey, LaRee. Los Angeles: Biography of a City. LC 75-17300. 1976. 18.95 (ISBN 0-520-03079-6); pap. 6.95 (ISBN 0-520-03410-4). U of Cal Pr.
Caughey, John W. California: The Life History of a Remarkable State's Life History. 4th ed. (Illus.). 512p. 1982. 22.95 (ISBN 0-13-112482-X). P-H.
Caughey, LaRee, jt. auth. see Caughey, John.
Caughley, Graeme. Analysis of Vertebrate Populations. LC 76-913. 1977. 44.95 (ISBN 0-471-01705-1, Pub. by Wiley-Interscience). Wiley.
Cauhape, Elizabeth. Fresh Starts: Men & Women after Divorce. 227p. 1983. 16.50 (ISBN 0-465-02553-6). Basic.
Cauhe, Joana Raspall De see Raspall de Cauhe, Joana, et al.
Caulaincourt, Armand. No Peace with Napoleon. Hanoteau, Jean, ed. Libaire, George, tr. LC 74-29631. 286p. 1975. Repr. of 1936 ed. lib. bdg. 17.75x (ISBN 0-8371-7984-X, CANP). Greenwood.
Caulcott, Evelyn. Significance Tests. (Applied Statistics Ser). 1973. 16.00x o.p. (ISBN 0-7100-7406-9); pap. 8.00 o.p. (ISBN 0-7100-8385-8). Routledge & Kegan.
Cauley, Lorinda, jt. auth. see Hancock, Sibyl.
Cauley, Lorinda B. The Animal Kids. LC 78-23632. (Illus.). (gr. k-4). 1979. 8.95 o.p. (ISBN 0-399-20677-9). Putnam Pub Group.
--The Bake-Off. LC 77-24877. (See & Read Storybooks). (gr. 1-4). 1978. PLB 6.99 (ISBN 0-399-61086-3). Putnam Pub Group.
--The Cock, the Mouse & the Little Red Hen. (Illus.). 32p. 1982. 9.95 (ISBN 0-399-20740-6); pap. 4.95 (ISBN 0-399-20930-1). Putnam Pub Group.
--Goldilocks & the Three Bears. (Illus.). 32p. (ps-2). 1981. 9.95 (ISBN 0-399-20794-5); pap. 4.95 (ISBN 0-399-20795-3). Putnam Pub Group.
--Pease Porridge Hot: A Mother Goose Cookbook. LC 77-3212. (Illus.). (gr. k-4). 1977. 6.95 (ISBN 0-399-20591-8). Putnam Pub Group.
--The Three Little Kittens. (Illus.). 32p. 1982. 7.95 (ISBN 0-399-20855-0); pap. 3.95 (ISBN 0-399-20856-9). Putnam Pub Group.
--The Ugly Duckling. LC 79-12340. (Illus.). 48p. (gr. k-3). 1979. pap. 5.95 (ISBN 0-15-692528-1, VoyB). HarBraceJ.
Cauley, Lorinda B., tr. see Pollock, Penny.
Caulfeild, S. F. & Saward, Blanche C. Encyclopedia of Victorian Needlework, 2 vols. 1972. pap. 6.00 ea. Vol. 1 o.p (ISBN 0-486-22800-2). Vol. 2 (ISBN 0-486-22801-0). Dover.
Caulfield, Betty, jt. auth. see Sakoian, Frances.
Caulfield, Don & Caulfield, Joan. The Incredible Detectives. (Illus.). (gr. 4-6). 1972. pap. 1.50 o.p. (ISBN 0-380-01282-0, 50443, Camelot). Avon.
Caulfield, Ernest. The Infant Welfare Movement in the Eighteenth Century. (Historia Medicinae Ser.). (Illus.). Repr. of 1931 ed. lib. bdg. 19.50x (ISBN 0-87991-704-0). Porcupine Pr.
Caulfield, Joan, jt. auth. see Caulfield, Don.
Caulfield, Peggy. Leaves. (Illus.). (gr. 3-7). 1962. PLB 4.29 o.p. (ISBN 0-698-30213-3, Coward). Putnam Pub Group.
Caulfield, Sean. Under the Broom Tree. LC 82-60593. 80p. 1983. pap. 3.95 (ISBN 0-8091-2493-9). Paulist Pr.
Caulfield, Sophia F. House Mottoes & Inscriptions. LC 68-21758. 1968. Repr. of 1908 ed. 30.00x (ISBN 0-8103-3322-8). Gale.
Caulfield, Sophia F. & Saward, Blanche C. Dictionary of Needlework. LC 75-172439. (Illus.). 1971. Repr. of 1882 ed. 85.00x (ISBN 0-8103-3404-6). Gale.
Caulkins, Frances M. History of Norwich Connecticut. 2nd ed. LC 76-23023. (Illus.). 728p. 1977. casebound 25.00 (ISBN 0-686-82909-3). Globe Pequot.
Causby, Ralph E., jt. auth. see Baucom, Marta E.
Causey, Denzil Y. Duties & Liabilities of Public Accountants. rev ed. LC 82-70156. (Illus.). 1982. 29.95 (ISBN 0-87094-325-1). Dow Jones-Irwin.
Causey, Don. Killer Insects. (Illus.). (gr. 4-6). 1979. PLB 7.90 s&l (ISBN 0-531-02924-7). Watts.
Causley, Charles. The Batsford Book of Stories in Verse for Children. 1979. 17.95 (ISBN 0-7134-1529-0, Pub by Batsford, England). David & Charles.
--Collected Poems 1951-1975. LC 74-30906. 294p. 1975. 17.95x (ISBN 0-87923-139-4); pap. 7.95 (ISBN 0-87923-168-8). Godine.
--Figgie Hobbin. 1974. 4.95 o.s.i. (ISBN 0-8027-6131-3); PLB 4.85 o.s.i. (ISBN 0-8027-6132-1). Walker & Co.
Causley, Charles, ed. Modern Folk Ballads. (Pocket Poet Ser.). 1966. pap. 1.25 (ISBN 0-8023-9043-9). Dufour.
Caussinus, H. & Ettinger, P. Compstat 1982: Proceedings in Computational Statistics. 500p. 1982. text ed. 32.95x (ISBN 3-7908-0280-8). Birkhauser.
Caussinus, H. & Ettinger, P., eds. Compstat 1982, Pt. 2. 383p. 1982. text ed. 18.95 (ISBN 3-7908-0283-2). Birkhauser.
Causton. Biometry of Plant Growth. 320p. 1982. text ed. 49.50 (ISBN 0-7131-2812-7). Univ Park.
Causton, David & Venus, Jill. Biometry of Plant Growth. 320p. 1981. text ed. 49.50 (ISBN 0-7131-2812-7). E Arnold.
Causton, David R. A Biologist's Mathematics. (Contemporary Biology Ser.). (Illus.). 224p. 1983. pap. text ed. price not set (ISBN 0-7131-2604-3). E Arnold.
Causton, David R. & Venus, Jill C. The Biometry of Plant Growth. 1982. 60.00x o.p. (ISBN 0-7131-2812-7). Methuen Inc.
Caute, David. The Great Fear. 1978. 16.95 o.p. (ISBN 0-671-22682-7, Touchstone Bks); pap. 6.95 o.p. (ISBN 0-671-24848-0). S&S.
Cautela, Joseph R. Behavior Analysis Forms for Clinical Intervention. LC 76-52358. 1977. spiral bdg. 24.95 (ISBN 0-87822-135-2). Res Press.
--Behavior Analysis Forms for Clinical Intervention, Vol. 2. LC 76-52358. 270p. 1981. spiral bdg. 26.95 (ISBN 0-87822-259-6, 2596). Res Press.
Cautela, Joseph R. & Cautela, Julie. Forms for Behavior Analysis with Children. 230p. (Orig.). 1983. pap. write for info. (ISBN 0-87822-267-7, 2677). Res Press.
Cautela, Julie, jt. auth. see Cautela, Joseph R.
Cauthen, Joseph C. Lumbar Spine Surgery: Indications, Techniques, Failures & Alternatives. (Illus.). 234p. 1983. lib. bdg. 45.00 (ISBN 0-683-01500-1). Williams & Wilkins.
Cauthen, Kenneth. The Ethics of Enjoyment: The Christian's Pursuit of Happiness. LC 75-13466. 128p. 1975. pap. 1.99 (ISBN 0-8042-0815-8). John Knox.
--The Impact of American Religious Liberalism. 2nd ed. LC 82-23902. 308p. 1983. pap. text ed. 12.75 (ISBN 0-8191-2762-0). U Pr of Amer.
Cauvin, Jean-Pierre, ed. see Breton, Andre.
Cauvin, Jean-Pierre, tr. see Breton, Andre.
Cauvin, Patrick. Two of a Kind. 1980. 8.95 o.s.i. (ISBN 0-440-08670-1). Delacorte.
Cauwels, Janice M. Bulimia: The Binge-Purge Compulsion. LC 82-45538. 288p. 1983. 14.95 (ISBN 0-385-18377-1). Doubleday.
Cava, Ester, et al, eds. A Pediatrician's Guide to Child Behavior Problems. LC 79-88727. 223p. 1979. text ed. 25.00x (ISBN 0-89352-075-6). Masson Pub.
Cava, Michael P. & Mitchell, Michael J. Selected Experiments in Organic Chemistry. rev. ed. 1969. pap. 15.95 (ISBN 0-8053-1871-2); 3.25 o.p. tchr's. guide (ISBN 0-8053-1873-9). Benjamin-Cummings.
Cavaco-Silva, Anibal A. Economic Effects of Public Debt. LC 77-74813. 1977. 22.50x (ISBN 0-312-23222-5). St Martin.
Cavagnaro, David. Feathers. (Illus.). 96p. 1982. pap. 12.95 (ISBN 0-912856-79-3). Graphic Arts Ctr.
Cavagnaro, David, jt. auth. see Braun, Ernest.
Cavaiani, Mabel. The High Fiber Cookbook. 1980. pap. 6.95 o.p. (ISBN 0-8092-7008-0). Contemp Bks.
Cavaille-Coll, A. Complete Theoretical Works. Huybens, G., ed. (Bibliotheca Organologica Ser.: Vol. 45). (Illus.). xiii, 218p. (Fr.). 1980. 50.00 o.s.i. (ISBN 90-6027-192-0, Pub. by Frits Knuf Netherlands). Pendragon NY.
--Devis d'un grand orgue a trois claviers et un pedalier complets projete pour la vieille Eglise Lutherienne Evangelique a Amsterdam. (Bibliotheca Organologica Ser.: Vol. 45). 52p. 1980. Repr. of 1881 ed. wrappers 17.50 o.s.i. (ISBN 90-6027-193-9, Pub. by Frits Knuf Netherlands). Pendragon NY.
Cavaioli, Frank J. & Lagumina, Salvatore J. The Peripheral Americans. LC 82-14019. 250p. 1983. lib. bdg. 9.50 (ISBN 0-89874-542-X). Krieger.
Cavaletto, M., et al. Dizionario Italiano-Bulgaro. 967p. (Ital. & Bulgarian.). 1979. leatherette 35.00 (ISBN 0-686-97340-2, M-9835). French & Eur.
Cavalier, Richard. Sales Meetings That Work: Planning & Managing Meetings to Achieve Your Goals. LC 82-72764. 250p. 1983. 21.95 (ISBN 0-87094-364-2). Dow Jones-Irwin.
Cavalier, Robert J. Ludwig Wittgenstein's Tractatus Logico-Philosophicus: A Transcendental Critique of Ethics. LC 79-3724. 1980. text ed. 18.00 (ISBN 0-8191-0915-0); pap. text ed. 10.50 (ISBN 0-8191-0916-9). U Pr of Amer.
Cavalieri, Grace, jt. auth. see Watkins, William J.
Cavaliero, Glen. Charles Williams: Poet of Theology. 224p. 1983. 8.95 (ISBN 0-8028-3579-1). Eerdmans.
Cavallaro, A., jt. ed. see Stipa, S.
Cavallaro, Ann. Careers in Food Services. 160p. (YA) 1981. 10.25 (ISBN 0-525-66698-2, 0995-300). Lodestar Bks.
Cavallero, Anthony. How to Become a Pro-Hitting .300 or Better. 1979. 5.95 o.p. (ISBN 0-533-03921-5). Vantage.
Cavalletti, Sofia. The Religious Potential of the Child. 224p. 1982. pap. 10.95 (ISBN 0-8091-2389-4). Paulist Pr.
Cavalli, F. & McGuire, W. L., eds. Proceedings of the International Symposium on Medroxyprogesterone Acetate: Geneva, Switzerland, February 24-26, 1982. (International Congress Ser.: No. 611). 632p. 1982. 95.75 (ISBN 0-444-90297-X, Excerpta Medica). Elsevier.
Cavallo, Adolph S. Tapestries of Europe & Colonial Peru in the MFA. 256p. 1968. boxed set 17.50 (ISBN 0-87846-015-2). Mus Fine Arts Boston.
Cavallo, Robert M. & Kahan, Stuart. Photography: What's the Law. 1976. 10.00 (ISBN 0-517-52534-8). Crown.
Cavan, Ruth S. & Ferdinand, Theodore N. Juvenile Delinquency. 4th ed. 448p. 1981. pap. text ed. 19.50 scp (ISBN 0-06-041206-2, HarpC). Har-Row.
Cavan, Ruth S., ed. Readings in Juvenile Delinquency. 3rd ed. LC 74-26560. 1975. pap. text ed. 16.50 scp o.p. (ISBN 0-397-47318-4, HarpC). Har-Row.
Cavan, Sherri. Twentieth Century Gothic: America's Nixon. LC 79-65722. (Illus.). 1979. 17.50 (ISBN 0-934594-00-7). Wigan Pier.
Cavanagh, Denis & Woods, Ralph F., eds. Obstetric Emergencies. 3rd ed. (Illus.). 480p. 1982. pap. text ed. 24.50 (ISBN 0-06-140627-9, Harper Medical). Lippincott.
Cavanagh, Gerald. The Businessperson in Search of Values. 1976. pap. 3.50 o.p. (65200). Glencoe.
Cavanagh, J. Digital Computer Arithmetic. 352p. 1983. 31.95 (ISBN 0-686-84225-1, C). McGraw.
Cavanagh, Michael E. The Counseling Experience: Understanding & Living It. LC 81-17050. (Psychology - Counseling Ser.). 552p. 1982. text ed. 19.95 (ISBN 0-8185-0509-5). Brooks-Cole.
Cavanagh, P. R., jt. auth. see Faria, I. E.
Cavanah, Frances. Secret of Madame Doll. LC 65-26160. (Illus.). (gr. 4-7). 1965. 6.95 o.s.i. (ISBN 0-8149-0288-X). Vanguard.
--We Came to America. (gr. 7-11). 1954. PLB 6.47 (ISBN 0-8255-2125-4). Macrae.
--We Wanted to Be Free: The Stories of Refugees & Exiles in America. LC 70-150680. (gr. 7 up). 1971. 6.25 (ISBN 0-8255-2127-0). Macrae.
Cavanah, Frances & Pannell, Lucille. Holiday Roundup. rev. ed. LC 68-18811. (Illus.). (gr. 4-6). 1968. PLB 6.97 (ISBN 0-8255-7041-7). Macrae.
Cavanah, Frances, ed. Favorite Christmas Stories. (gr. 3 up). 1948. 5.95 (ISBN 0-448-02376-8, G&D). Putnam Pub Group.
Cavanaugh, Arthur, jt. ed. see Horn, Geoffrey.
Cavanaugh, Gerald F. American Business Values in Transition. 224p. 1976. 12.95 (ISBN 0-13-024141-5); pap. text ed. 10.95x (ISBN 0-13-024133-4). P-H.
Cavanaugh, Joseph. Digital Computer Arithmetic. (Computer Science Ser.). (Illus.). 352p. 1983. 31.95 (ISBN 0-07-010282-1). McGraw.
Cavanaugh, Marjory. Withering into Truth. pap. 3.00 (ISBN 0-686-84329-0, JB42). Juniper Pr WI.
Cavanilles, A. J. Icones & Descriptiones Plantarum Quae Aut Sponte in Hispania Crescunt Aut in Hortis Hospitantur 1791-1801, 6pts. in 2 vols. 1965. 320.00 (ISBN 3-7682-0292-5). Lubrecht & Cramer.
Cavanna, Betty. Almost Like Sisters. (gr. 7 up). 1963. 10.50 (ISBN 0-688-21014-7). Morrow.
--Ballet Fever. LC 78-3684. 1978. 8.95 (ISBN 0-664-32631-5). Westminster.
--The Boy Next Door. (gr. 7 up). 1956. PLB 10.08 (ISBN 0-688-31116-4). Morrow.
Cavanna, Betty, pseud. The Diane Stories. Incl. A Date for Diane; Diane's New Love; Tourjours Diane. (gr. 4-7). 1964. 6.50 (ISBN 0-8255-2130-0). Macrae.
Cavanna, Betty. Joyride. LC 74-5930. 224p. (gr. 7 up). 1974. 9.95 (ISBN 0-688-20125-3); PLB 9.55 (ISBN 0-688-30125-8). Morrow.
--Mystery of the Emerald Buddha. LC 76-21826. (gr. 7 up). 1976. 9.95 (ISBN 0-688-22086-X); PLB 9.55 (ISBN 0-688-32086-4). Morrow.
--Paintbox Summer. 212p. 1981. Repr. PLB 15.95 (ISBN 0-89966-357-5). Buccaneer Bks.
--Ruffles & Drums. LC 75-9630. (Illus.). (gr. 7-9). 1975. 9.50 (ISBN 0-688-22035-5); PLB 9.12 (ISBN 0-688-32035-X). Morrow.
--Runaway Voyage. (gr. 7-9). 1978. PLB 9.36 (ISBN 0-688-32152-6). Morrow.
--Spice Island Mystery. LC 72-83531. (gr. 7 up). 1969. 9.95 (ISBN 0-688-21706-0). Morrow.
--Stamp Twice for Murder. LC 81-8291. 224p. (gr. 7-9). 1981. pap. 9.95 (ISBN 0-688-00700-7); PLB 9.55 (ISBN 0-688-00701-5). Morrow.
--Storm in Her Heart. LC 82-20237. (A Hiway Book: A High Interest - Low Reading Level Book). 96p. (gr. 7-10). 1983. price not set (ISBN 0-664-32700-1). Westminster.
--Two's Company. (Illus.). (gr. 5-9). 1951. 6.95 (ISBN 0-664-32080-5). Westminster.
--You Can't Take Twenty Dogs on a Date. LC 77-432. (gr. 5-9). 1977. 8.95 (ISBN 0-664-32613-7). Westminster.
Cavanna, Betty A. Touch of Magic. (Illus.). (gr. 6-9). 1961. 5.75 o.s.i. (ISBN 0-664-32253-0). Westminster.
Cavanough, Elizabeth. Sydney Holiday. 12.50 o.p. (ISBN 0-392-08667-0, ABC). Sportshelf.
Cave, Emma. Blood Bond. LC 78-20200. 1979. 12.45i (ISBN 0-06-010627-1, HarpT). Har-Row.
--Little Angie. (Fic). 1977. 7.95 o.p. (ISBN 0-698-10806-X, Coward). Putnam Pub Group.
Cave, Frank & Terrell, David. Digital & Microprocessor Technology. 448p. 1981. text ed. 22.95 (ISBN 0-8359-1326-0); instrs. manual avail. (ISBN 0-8359-1327-9). Reston.
Cave, Hugh see Eyre, A. G.
Cave, Joyce, jt. auth. see Cave, Ron.
Cave, Kathryn, ed. see Farington, Joseph.
Cave, Martin. Computers & Economic Planning. LC 79-7659. (Soviet & East European Studies). 1980. 32.50 (ISBN 0-521-22617-1). Cambridge U Pr.
Cave, Martin & Hare, Paul. Alternating Approaches to Economic Planning. 1980. 30.00 (ISBN 0-312-02147-X). St Martin.
Cave, Peter L., compiled by. Five Hundred Games. (Illus.). 160p. Date not set. pap. price not set (ISBN 0-448-02159-5, G&D). Putnam Pub Group.
Cave, Ron & Cave, Joyce. What About... Fighters. (What About Ser.). (Illus.). 32p. (gr. k-3). 1983. PLB 7.90 (ISBN 0-531-03468-2). Watts.
--What About... Missiles. (What About Ser.). (Illus.). 32p. (gr. k-3). 1983. PLB 7.90 (ISBN 0-531-03469-0). Watts.
--What About-Racing Cars? LC 82-81166. (What About Ser.). (Illus.). 32p. (gr. k-3). 1982. PLB 7.90 (ISBN 0-531-03464-X). Watts.
--What About-Space Shuttle? LC 82-81167. (What About Ser.). (Illus.). 32p. (gr. k-3). 1982. PLB 7.90 (ISBN 0-531-03465-8). Watts.
--What About Submarines? LC 82-81168. (What About Ser.). (Illus.). 32p. (gr. k-3). 1982. PLB 7.90 (ISBN 0-531-03466-6). Watts.
--What About... Tanks. (What About Ser.). (Illus.). 32p. (gr. k-3). 1983. PLB 7.90 (ISBN 0-531-03470-4). Watts.
--What About-Trains? LC 82-81169. (What About Ser.). 32p. (gr. k-3). 1982. lib. bdg. 7.90 (ISBN 0-531-03467-4). Watts.
--What About... War Ships. (What About Ser.). 32p. (gr. k-3). 1983. PLB 7.90 (ISBN 0-531-03471-2). Watts.

Cave, William, jt. auth. see Chesler, Mark A.
Cave Brown, Anthony. Bodyguard of Lies. LC 72-9749. (Illus.). 962p. (YA) 1975. 19.95i (ISBN 0-06-010551-8, HarpT). Har-Row.
Cavell, S. Must We Mean What We Say? LC 75-32911. 365p. 1976. 39.50 (ISBN 0-521-21116-6); pap. 12.95 (ISBN 0-521-29048-1). Cambridge U Pr.
Caven, Brian. The Punic Wars. LC 80-7467. (Illus.). 320p. 1980. 26.00 (ISBN 0-312-65580-0). St Martin.
Cavenagh, F. A., ed. see Mill, James & Mill, John S.
Cavenar, Jesse O. & Brodie, Keith H., eds. Critical Problems in Psychiatry. (Illus.). 512p. 1982. text ed. 29.50 (ISBN 0-397-50490-X, Lippincott Medical). Lippincott.
Cavenar, Jesse O., Jr. & Brodie, Keith H., eds. Signs & Symptoms in Psychiatry. (Illus.). 608p. 1983. text ed. 29.50 (ISBN 0-397-50489-6, Lippincott Medical). Lippincott.
Cavender, Nancy M. & Weiss, Leonard A. Thinking in Sentences: A Guide to Clear Writing. LC 81-82572. 1982. pap. 9.95 (ISBN 0-395-31690-1); instr's manual 1.00 (ISBN 0-395-31691-X). HM.
Cavendish, Arthur M. The Guidebook to British Nobility: The History of the Great English Families. (The Memoirs Collections of Significant Historical Personalities Ser.). (Illus.). 99p. 1983. 79.85 (ISBN 0-89901-086-5). Found Class Reprints.
Cavendish Laboratory, Electron Microscopy Section, jt. auth. see Saxton, W. O.
Cavendish, Richard. The Powers of Evil. LC 75-7933. 1975. 7.95 o.p. (ISBN 0-399-11484-X). Putnam Pub Group.
Cavendish, Richard, ed. Man, Myth & Magic: The Illustrated Encyclopedia of Mythology, Religion & the Unknown. 2nd ed. (Illus.). 3268p. 1983. lib. bdg. 399.95 (ISBN 0-86307-041-8). M Cavendish Corp.
Caverly, D. J., jt. auth. see Eagle, D. J.
Cavert, C. Edward. An Approach to the Design of Mediated Instruction. LC 73-87973. 1974. pap. 12.95 o.p. (ISBN 0-89240-008-0, 209). Assn Ed Comm Tech.
--Procedural Guidelines for the Design of Mediated Instruction. 1974. pap. 6.95 o.p. (ISBN 0-89240-021-8, 207). Assn Ed Comm Tech.
Cavert, C. Edward & Metcalf, Richard M. Accounting. 467p. 1982. text ed. 17.95x student guide (ISBN 0-931920-43-4). Dame Pubns.
Cavert, C. Edward, et al. Keep It Running: A Study Guide. (Illus.). 1978. pap. text ed. 12.95 (ISBN 0-07-009880-8, C); print pkg. 25.95 (ISBN 0-07-079269-0). McGraw.
Cavert, Samuel M. On the Road to Christian Unity: An Appraisal of the Ecumenical Movement. LC 78-12452. 1979. Repr. of 1961 ed. lib. bdg. 17.00x (ISBN 0-313-21184-1, CAOR). Greenwood.
Caves, D. W., jt. auth. see University of British Columbia, August 1981.
Caves, Richard E. American Industry-Structure, Conduct, Performance. 4th ed. LC 77-1075. 1977. pap. 10.95 o.p. (ISBN 0-13-027581-6). P-H.
--Multinational Enterprise & Economic Growth. LC 82-4543. (Cambridge Surveys of Economic Literature Ser.). 352p. 1983. 34.50 (ISBN 0-521-24990-2); pap. 9.95 (ISBN 0-521-27115-0). Cambridge U Pr.
Caves, Richard E. & Uekusa, Masu. Industrial Organization in Japan. 1976. 16.95 (ISBN 0-8157-1324-X); pap. 6.95 (ISBN 0-8157-1323-1). Brookings.
Caves, Richard E. & Krause, Lawrence B., eds. Britain's Economic Performance. 1980. 24.95 (ISBN 0-8157-1320-7); pap. 10.95 (ISBN 0-8157-1319-3). Brookings.
Caves, Richard E. & Roberts, Marc J., eds. Regulating the Product: Quality & Variety. LC 74-18123. 256p. 1975. prof ref 25.00x (ISBN 0-88410-272-6). Ballinger Pub.
Caves, Richard E., et al. Britain's Economic Prospects. 1968. 19.95 (ISBN 0-8157-1322-3). Brookings.
Cavett, Dick & Porterfield, Christopher. Eye on Cavett. (Illus.). 1983. 15.95 (ISBN 0-87795-463-1). Arbor Hse.
Caviedes, Cesar. The Politics of Chile: A Socio-Geographical Assessment. (Special Studies on Latin America). 1979. lib. bdg. 32.50 (ISBN 0-89158-311-4). Westview.
Cavill, I., et al. Computers in Hematology. (Computers in Medicine Ser.). 1975. 7.95 o.p. (ISBN 0-407-00037-2). Butterworth.
Cavin, Ruth. Famous Brands Cookbook. (Illus.). 384p. 1982. 14.95 (ISBN 0-8437-3393-4); pap. 9.95 (ISBN 0-8437-3394-2). Hammond Inc.
Caviness, Madeline H. Great Britain, Vol. 1: The Windows of Christ Church, Canterbury. (Illus.). 574p. 1981. text ed. 395.00x (ISBN 0-19-725995-2). Oxford U Pr.
--Stained Glass before 1540: An Annotated Bibliography. 1983. lib. bdg. 45.00 (ISBN 0-8161-8332-5, Hall Reference). G K Hall.
Cavnar, Rebecca. Winning at Losing: A Complete Program for Losing Weight & Keeping it off. (Illus.). 150p. 1983. pap. 4.95 (ISBN 0-686-82582-9). Servant.
Cavoto, Nino, tr. see Grillo, Salvatore.
Cawker, Ruth, jt. auth. see Bernstein, William.
Cawl, Farrax M. Ignorance Is the Enemy of Love: A Novel. Andrzejewski, tr. from Somali. 128p. 1982. pap. 9.95 (ISBN 0-905762-86-X, Pub. by Zed Pr England, Pub. by Zed Pr England). Lawrence Hill.
Cawley, A. C., ed. Everyman & Medieval Miracle Plays. 9.95x (ISBN 0-460-10381-4, Evman). Biblio Dist.
--The Wakefield Pageants in the Towneley Cycle. (Old & Middle English Texts). 1958. Repr. of 1975 ed. pap. 9.50x (ISBN 0-06-491013-X). B&N Imports.
Cawley, A. C. & Anderson, J. J., eds. Pearl Cleanness, Patience, & Sir Gawain & the Green Knight. 1970. 12.95x (ISBN 0-460-00346-1, Evman); pap. 2.95x (ISBN 0-460-11346-1, Evman). Biblio Dist.
Cawley, Elizabeth H., ed. see Cobden, Richard.
Cawley, Frederick D., jt. ed. see Waite, Diana S.
Cawley, J. C. & Hayhoe, F. G. Ultrastructures of Haemic Cells. LC 73-80975. (Illus.). 285p. 1973. text ed. 12.00 (ISBN 0-7216-2470-7). Saunders.
Cawley, Robert R. Henry Peacham: His Contribution to English Poetry. LC 71-127387. 185p. 1971. 16.00x (ISBN 0-271-01130-0). Pa St U Pr.
Cawood, Diana. Assertiveness for Managers. 200p. (Orig.). 1983. pap. price not set (ISBN 0-88908-562-5). Self Counsel Pr.
Caws, Mary A. Andre Breton. (World Authors Ser.: No. 117). 15.95 o.p. (ISBN 0-8057-2180-0, Twayne). G K Hall.
--A Metapoetics of the Passage: Architextures in Surrealism & After. LC 80-54468. 218p. 1981. text ed. 17.50x (ISBN 0-87451-194-1). U Pr of New Eng.
Caws, Mary A. & Riffaterre, Hermine, eds. The Prose Poem in France: Theory & Practice. 256p. 1983. 25.00x (ISBN 0-231-05434-3); pap. 12.50x (ISBN 0-231-05435-1). Columbia U Pr.
Caws, Mary A., ed. see Perse, Saint-John.
Caws, Mary A., tr. see Breton, Andre.
Caws, Mary Ann. Rene Char. (World Authors Ser.). 1977. lib. bdg. 15.95 (ISBN 0-8057-6268-X, Twayne). G K Hall.
Caws, Mary Ann & Terry, Patricia, eds. Roof Slates & Other Poems of Pierre Reverdy. LC 80-26806. (Illus.). 340p. 1981. 18.95x (ISBN 0-930350-09-X). NE U Pr.
Caws, Mary Ann, ed. see Perse, Saint-John.
Cawson, Broderick A., jt. auth. see McCracken, Alexander W.
Cawson, R. A., jt. auth. see Scully, C.
Cawson, Roderick A. & McCracken, Alexander W. Pathologic Mechanisms & Human Disease. LC 81-16832. (Illus.). 594p. 1982. pap. text ed. 24.95 (ISBN 0-8016-0939-9). Mosby.
Cawte, John. Cruel, Poor & Brutal Nations: The Assessment of Mental Health in an Australian Aboriginal Community by Short-Stay Psychiatric Field Team Methods. LC 72-188979. (Illus.). 200p. 1972. 14.00x (ISBN 0-8248-0207-1). UH Pr.
--Medicine Is the Law: Studies in Psychiatric Anthropology of Australian Tribal Societies. LC 73-77011. 320p. 1974. text ed. 16.00x (ISBN 0-8248-0251-9). UH Pr.
Cawthra, Bruce I. Industrial Property Rights in the European Economic Community. 1973 ed. 250p. 27.00 (ISBN 0-686-37377-4). Beekman Pubs.
Cayce, Edgar. Revelation: A Commentary on the Book, Based on the Study of Twenty Four Psychic Discourses of Edgar Cayce. (Twenty-Six Interpretive Readings). 1969. pap. 8.95 (ISBN 0-87604-003-2). ARE Pr.
--What I Believe. 1946. pap. 1.95 o.p. (ISBN 0-87604-021-0). ARE Pr.
Cayce, Edgar & Cayce, Hugh L. God's Other Door & the Continuity of Life. 1976. pap. 2.95 (ISBN 0-87604-007-5). ARE Pr.
Cayce, Edgar E. Atlantis, Fact or Fiction: From the Edgar Cayce Readings. 1962. pap. 1.25 o.p. (ISBN 0-87604-018-0). ARE Pr.
--Edgar Cayce on Atlantis. Cayce, Hugh L., ed. 176p. 1968. pap. 2.95 (ISBN 0-446-30760-2). Warner Bks.
Cayce, Hugh L., jt. auth. see Cayce, Edgar.
Cayce, Hugh L., ed. The Edgar Cayce Reader. 192p. 1969. pap. 2.95 (ISBN 0-446-30164-7). Warner Bks.
Cayce, Hugh L., ed. see Cayce, Edgar E.
Cayce, J. Gail. Osteopathy: Comparative Concepts - A. T. Still & Edgar Cayce. 61p. (Orig.). 1973. pap. 4.95 o.p. (ISBN 0-87604-080-6). ARE Pr.
Cayer, N. Joseph. Public Personnel Administration in the United States. LC 74-23046. 200p. (Orig.). 1975. 17.95 o.p. (ISBN 0-312-65485-5); pap. text ed. 8.95 (ISBN 0-312-65520-7). St Martin.
Cayford, John E. Fort Knox-Fortress of Maine. 120p. 1983. write for info. Cay Bel.
--Maine's Hall of Fame, Vol. 1. 300p. 1983. write for info. Cay Bel.
--The Penobscot Expedition. LC 76-21153. (Illus., Orig.). 1976. 7.95 (ISBN 0-918768-00-4); pap. 5.95 (ISBN 0-918768-01-2). Cay-Bel.
Cayley, Michael, ed. see Crashaw, Richard.
Cayre, Henri. Agricultural Plenty: A Monograph. 176p. 1982. 40.00x (ISBN 0-85614-070-8, Pub. by Gentry England). State Mutual Bk.
Cayton, Horace R., jt. auth. see Drake, St. Clair.
Cazalas, Mary W. Nursing & the Law. 3rd ed. LC 78-24253. 294p. 1979. text ed. 22.95 (ISBN 0-89443-075-0). Aspen Systems.
Cazao, Alayde, tr. see Ferguson, Charles W., et al.
Cazden, Courtney B., ed. Language in Early Childhood Education. rev. ed. (Illus.). 144p. 1980. pap. text ed. 5.00 (ISBN 0-912674-74-1). Natl Assn Child Ed.
Cazden, Elizabeth. Antoinette Brown Blackwell: A Biography. (Illus.). 288p. 1983. 14.95 (ISBN 0-935312-00-5); pap. 7.95 (ISBN 0-935312-04-8). Feminist Pr.
Cazden, Norman, et al. Folk Songs of the Catskills. LC 81-14610. 600p. 1982. lib. bdg. 69.50x (ISBN 0-87395-580-3); pap. 19.95 (ISBN 0-87395-581-1). State U NY Pr.
Cazden, Robert E. A History of the German Book Trade in America to the Civil War, 2 pts. LC 81-70545. (Studies in German Literature, Linguistics, & Culture: Vol. 1). (Illus.). 950p. 1983. 75.00 (ISBN 0-938100-09-2). Camden Hse.
Cazeau, Charles. Earthquakes. LC 73-93549. (Beginning Science Ser.). (Illus.). 32p. (gr. 2-4). 1974. lib. bdg. 4.39 (ISBN 0-695-40474-1). Follett.
Cazeau, Charles J. & Siemankowski, Francis T. Physical Geology Laboratory Manual. 3rd ed. 1982. wire coil bdg. 12.95 (ISBN 0-8403-2791-9, 40279101). Kendall-Hunt.
Cazenave, Pierre-Andre, jt. auth. see Bona, Constantin.
Cazet, Denys. The Duck with Squeaky Feet. LC 80-18018. (Illus.). 32p. (ps-2). 1980. 8.95 (ISBN 0-02-717850-1). Bradbury Pr.
--Lucky Me. LC 81-7711. (Illus.). 32p. (ps-2). Date not set. 10.95 (ISBN 0-02-717870-6). Bradbury Pr.
--Mud Baths for Everyone. LC 80-39830. (Illus.). 32p. (ps-2). 1981. 9.95 (ISBN 0-02-717860-9). Bradbury Pr.
--You Make the Angels Cry. (Illus.). 32p. (ps-k). Date not set. 10.95 (ISBN 0-87888-203-0). Bradbury Pr.
Cazimero, Momi, ed. see Belknap, Jodi P.
Cazort, Jean & Hobson, Constance T. Born to Play: The Life & Career of Hazel Harrison. LC 82-12169. (Contributions to the Study of Music & Dance Ser.: No. 3). (Illus.). 200p. 1983. lib. bdg. 27.95 (ISBN 0-313-23643-7, CBO/). Greenwood.
Cazziol, Roger J. Gloire D'Afrique. (Illus.). 1971. text ed. 2.50 (ISBN 0-521-08181-5). Cambridge U Pr.
--Kone. (Illus.). 1971. text ed. 2.50 (ISBN 0-521-07955-1). Cambridge U Pr.
--Paul et Remi. (Illus.). 40p. (Fr.). 1974. pap. text ed. 2.50 (ISBN 0-521-20433-X). Cambridge U Pr.
--Safari En Cote d'Ivoire. (Illus.). 40p. 1974. pap. 2.50 (ISBN 0-521-20434-8). Cambridge U Pr.
--Vacances Au Senegal. (Illus.). 1971. text ed. 2.50x (ISBN 0-521-08180-7). Cambridge U Pr.
CBS News & New York Times. CBS News-The New York Times Election Surveys 1980, 2 vols. LC 82-81160. 1982. Set. write for info. (ISBN 0-89138-931-8, ICPSR 7812); Vol. I. write for info. (ISBN 0-89138-933-4); Vol. II. write for info. (ISBN 0-89138-932-6). ICPSR.
CCOP-IOC SEATAR Working Group Meeting, July 1979, Bandung, Indonesia. The Geology & Tectonics of Eastern Indonesia: Proceedings. Barber, A. J. & Wiryosujono, S., eds. 356p. 1982. 60.00 (ISBN 0-08-028732-8). Pergamon.
Cea, J., jt. auth. see Haug, E. J.
Ceaser, James W. Reforming the Reforms: A Critical Analysis of the Presidential Selection Process. 216p. 1982. 18.50 (ISBN 0-88410-884-8). Ballinger Pub.
Ceausescu, E. Sterospecific Polymerization of Isoprene. (Illus.). 300p. 1982. 60.00 (ISBN 0-08-029987-3). Pergamon.
CEB & FIP Members & Staffs, compiled by. CEB-FIP Model Code for Concrete Structures, Vol. 1 & 2 (Combined) 1978. text ed. 45.00x o.p. (ISBN 0-685-65860-0). Scholium Intl.
Cebeci, T. & Bradshaw, P. Momentum Transfer in Boundary Layers. LC 76-57750. (Thermal & Fluids Engineering Ser.). (Illus.). 1977. text ed. 29.00 o.p. (ISBN 0-07-010300-3, C); 4.95 o.p. solutions manual (ISBN 0-07-010301-1). McGraw.
Cebeci, T., ed. Numerical & Physical Aspects of Aerodynamic Flows, California State University 1981: Proceedings. (Illus.). 636p. 1983. 78.00 (ISBN 0-387-11044-5). Springer-Verlag.
Cebeci, Tuncer & Smith, A. M. Analysis of Turbulent Boundary Layers. 1974. 67.00 (ISBN 0-12-164650-5); lib. ed. 82.50 (ISBN 0-12-164651-3); microfiche 48.50 (ISBN 0-12-164652-1). Acad Pr.
Cebik, L. B. Concepts, Events, & History. LC 78-64825. 1978. pap. text ed. 10.50 (ISBN 0-8191-0639-9). U Pr of Amer.
--Setting Up & Using Your Own Ham Shack. LC 81-9136. (Illus.). 308p. 1981. pap. 10.95 (ISBN 0-8306-1223-8, 1223). TAB Bks.
Cebik, L. B., ed. Reflections: An Old Man's Notes. LC 81-40384. 256p. (Orig.). 1982. lib. bdg. 23.00 (ISBN 0-8191-1974-1); pap. text ed. 11.50 (ISBN 0-8191-1975-X). U Pr of Amer.
Cebula, Richard J. Geographic Living-Cost Differentials. LC 82-48096. 208p. 1983. 27.95x (ISBN 0-669-05968-4). Lexington Bks.
Cebulash. Primary Reading Series. (gr. 1-3). complete set of 6 kits 389.85 (ISBN 0-8372-3871-4) (ISBN 0-686-43195-2). Bowmar-Noble.
Cebulash, Mel. I'm an Expert. 1982. pap. text ed. 6.95 (ISBN 0-673-16570-1). Scott F.
--Ruth Marini: Dodger Ace. LC 82-20383. (Ruth Marini on the Mound Ser.). 160p. (gr. 4up). 1983. PLB 8.95g (ISBN 0-8225-0726-9). Lerner Pubns.
--Ruth Marini of the Dodgers. LC 82-20403. (Ruth Marini on the Mound Ser.). 160p. (gr. 4up). 1983. PLB 8.95g (ISBN 0-8225-0725-0). Lerner Pubns.
Cecala, Agnes. Word Processing Skills & Applications Using the Wang System. 1983. pap. text ed. 16.95 (ISBN 0-8359-8789-2). Reston.
Ceccarelli, B., ed. see International Symposium on Cell Biology & Cytopharmacology, First.
Ceccarelli, B., et al, eds. see Nato Advanced Study Institution, et al.
Ceccerini, P. V., jt. auth. see Barlotti, A.
Cecchetti, Giovanni. Giovanni Verga. (World Authors Ser.: No. 489 Italy). 1978. 15.95 (ISBN 0-8057-6330-9, Twayne). G K Hall.
Cecchetti, Giovanni, tr. & intro. by see Verga, Giovanni.
Cecchetti, Giovanni del, tr. see Leopardi, Giacomo.
Cecchettini, P. A. CLEP Resource Manual: Introduction to Sociology. 1979. pap. 9.95 (ISBN 0-07-010306-2). McGraw.
Cecchettini, Philip A. CLEP: Introduction to Business Management. (Illus.). 1979. pap. 9.95 (ISBN 0-07-010308-9, C). McGraw.
--CLEP: Introduction to General Psychology. 1979. pap. 9.95 (ISBN 0-07-010305-4, C). McGraw.
--CLEP: Introduction to Natural Science. 1979. pap. text ed. 9.95 (ISBN 0-07-010309-7, C). McGraw.
Ceccio, Cathy M., jt. auth. see Ceccio, Joseph F.
Ceccio, Joseph F. & Ceccio, Cathy M. Effective Communication in Nursing: Theory & Practice. LC 81-15999. 315p. 1982. pap. 13.95 (ISBN 0-471-07911-1, Pub. by Wiley Med). Wiley.
Cech, Joseph J., jt. auth. see Moyle, Peter B.
Cecil, Algernon. Life of Robert Cecil. LC 71-109717. (Illus.). 1971. Repr. of 1915 ed. lib. bdg. 19.75x (ISBN 0-8371-4207-5, CERC). Greenwood.
Cecil, Andrew R. The Third Way: Enlightened Capitalism & the Search for a New Social Order. (The Andrew R. Cecil Lectures on Moral Values in a Free Society Ser.: Vol. I). 175p. 1980. 9.95x (ISBN 0-292-78041-9). U of Tex Pr.
Cecil, David, ed. see Tennyson, Alfred L.
Cecil, Joe S., jt. ed. see Boruch, Robert F.
Cecil, Martin. Meditations on the Lord's Prayer. 2nd ed. 1982. 10.95 (ISBN 0-686-27652-3). Cole-Outreach.
--On Eagle's Wings. 1977. 2.95 (ISBN 0-7051-0258-0). Cole-Outreach.
Cecil, Paula B. Management of Word Processing Operations. 1980. 26.95 (ISBN 0-8053-1759-7); instr's guide 4.95 (ISBN 0-8053-1762-7). Benjamin-Cummings.
--Word Processing in the Modern Office: Instructor's Guide. 2nd ed. 1979. 5.95 (ISBN 0-8053-1760-0); student wkbk. 6.95 (ISBN 0-8053-1761-9). Benjamin-Cummings.
Ceckler, William H., jt. auth. see Thompson, Edward V.
Ceconi, Marianne, tr. see Pavese, Cesare.
Cedar. Becoming a Lover. 1978. 1.25 (ISBN 0-8423-0120-8). Tyndale.
Cedar, Paul A. The Communicator's Commentary-James 1, 2, Peter, Jude, Vol. 2. Ogilvie, Lloyd J., ed. (The Communicator's Commentaries Ser.). 1983. 14.95. Word Pub.
Cedarbaum, Sophia. Passover: Festival of Freedom. (Illus.). (gr. k-2). 1960. 3.50 o.p. (ISBN 0-8074-0147-1, 301592). UAHC.
Cedarbaum, Sophia N. Purim: A Joyous Holiday. (Illus.). (gr. k-2). 1960. 3.50 o.p. (ISBN 0-8074-0148-X, 301562). UAHC.
Cedeno & Lazar. The Exercise Plus Pregnancy Program: Exercises for Before, During & After Pregnancy. (Illus.). 192p. 1980. pap. 4.95 (ISBN 0-688-08697-7). Quill NY.
CEDEP-INSEAD Conference, Jun. 1976. New Developments in the Applications of Bayesian Methods: Proceedings. Aykac, A. & Brumat, eds. (Contributions to Economic Analysis: Vol. 119). 1977. 70.25 (ISBN 0-444-85059-7, North-Holland). Elsevier.
Cederblom, J. B. & Blizek, William L., eds. Justice & Punishment. LC 77-3378. 1977. prof ref 22.00x (ISBN 0-88410-752-3). Ballinger Pub.
Cederblom, Jerry & Paulsen, David. Critical Reasoning. 232p. 1981. pap. text ed. 12.95x (ISBN 0-534-00965-4). Wadsworth Pub.
Cedergren, Harry R. Drainage of Highway & Airfield Pavements. LC 74-13400. (Illus.). 288p. 1974. 41.50 (ISBN 0-471-14181-X, Pub. by Wiley-Interscience). Wiley.
--Seepage, Drainage & Flow Nets. 2nd ed. LC 77-3664. 1977. 50.95 (ISBN 0-471-14179-8, Pub. by Wiley-Interscience). Wiley.
Cedering-Fox, Siv. The Blue Horse & Other Night Poems. LC 78-12793. (Illus.). 32p. (ps-3). 1979. 8.95 (ISBN 0-395-28952-1, Clarion). HM.
Cedrins, Inara, tr. see Bels, Albert.
Cegelka, Patricia T. & Prehm, Herbert J. Mental Retardation: From Categories to People. 448p. 1982. 22.95 (ISBN 0-675-09831-9). Additional Supplements May Be Obtained From Publisher. Merrill.
Cegelka, Patricia T., jt. auth. see Berdine, William H.
Cehelsky, Marta. Land Reform in Brazil: The Management of Social Change. (Westview Replica Edition Ser.). 1979. lib. bdg. 24.50 o.p. (ISBN 0-89158-075-1). Westview.
Ceidigh, P. O., jt. ed. see Keegan, B. F.

Cela, Camilo J. The Family of Pascual Duarte. 144p. 1972. pap. 2.95 (ISBN 0-380-01175-1, 60749, Bard). Avon.
--The Hive. LC 81-11540. (Neglected Books of the 20th Century Ser.). 257p. 1983. pap. 6.95 (ISBN 0-686-82496-2). Ecco Pr.
--The Hive: Neglected Books of the Twentieth Century. LC 82-11540. 1983. pap. 6.95 (ISBN 0-88001-004-5). Ecco Pr.
Celant, Germano. Bernd & Hilla Becher. LC 74-76639. (Illus.). 38p. 1974. pap. 8.00 o.p. (ISBN 0-934418-06-3). La Jolla Mus Contemp Art.
--Marcia Hafif. (Illus.). 14p. 1975. 2.00x (ISBN 0-686-99816-2). La Jolla Mus Contemp Art.
--Stephan Rosenthal. (Illus.). 14p. 1975. 3.50x (ISBN 0-686-99814-6). La Jolla Mus Contemp Art.
Celce-Murcia, Marianne, ed. Teaching English As a Second or Foreign Language. 1979. pap. text ed. 15.95 (ISBN 0-88377-125-X). Newbury Hse.
Celender, Donald. Musical Instruments in Art. LC 65-29037. (Fine Art Books). (Illus.). (gr. 5-11). 1966. PLB 4.95g (ISBN 0-8225-0160-0). Lerner Pubns.
Celenko, Theodore. A Treasury of African Art From the Harrison Eiteljorg Collection. LC 82-47954. (Illus.). 240p. 1983. 57.50x (ISBN 0-253-11057-2). Ind U Pr.
Celine, Louis-Ferdinand. Death on the Installment Plan. Manheim, Ralph, tr. LC 48-6410. 1971. pap. 8.95 (ISBN 0-8112-0017-5, NDP330). New Directions.
--Journey to the End of Night. Manheim, Ralph, tr. LC 82-7970. 1983. 19.95 (ISBN 0-8112-0846-X); pap. 7.95 (ISBN 0-8112-0847-8, NDP 542). New Directions.
--Rigadoon. Manheim, Ralph, tr. from Fr. 304p. 1975. pap. 3.95 (ISBN 0-14-004083-8). Penguin.
Cell, Derek. Doctor Bey's Book of Brats. 1978. pap. 4.95 o.p. (ISBN 0-380-46425-X, 46425). Avon.
Cell, John W. The Highest Stage of White Supremacy: The Origins of Segregation in South Africa & the American South. LC 82-4312. 320p. 1982. 34.50 (ISBN 0-521-24096-4); pap. 8.95 (ISBN 0-521-27061-8). Cambridge U Pr.
Cella, C. Ronald. Mary Johnston. (United States Authors Ser.). 1981. lib. bdg. 12.95 (ISBN 0-8057-7340-1, Twayne). G K Hall.
Cellar, jt. auth. see Appleton.
Cellier, F. E., ed. Progress in Modelling & Simulation. 1982. 55.50 (ISBN 0-12-164780-3). Acad Pr.
Cember, Herman. Introduction to Health Physics. 2nd ed. (Illus.). 475p. 1983. 35.00 (ISBN 0-08-030129-0). Pergamon.
Cembureau (European Cement Association) World Cement Directory 1980, 2 vols. 6th ed. LC 75-15776. (Illus.). 341p. (Orig.). 1980. Set. pap. 147.50x (ISBN 0-8002-2776-X). Intl Pubns Serv.
Cena, K. & Clark, J. A., eds. Bioengineering, Thermal Physiology & Comfort. (Studies in Environmental Science: Vol. 10). 1981. 64.00 (ISBN 0-444-99761-X). Elsevier.
Cence, R. J., et al, eds. Proceedings of the Seventh Hawaii Topical Conference in Particle Physics, 1977. LC 77-27006. (Particle Physics Conference Proceedings Ser). 1978. pap. text ed. 17.50x (ISBN 0-8248-0619-0). UH Pr.
Cendrars, Blaise. The Astonished Man. Rootes, Nina, tr. from Fr. 1979. 18.00 o.p. (ISBN 0-8464-0044-8). Beekman Pubs.
--Complete Postcards from the Americas: Poems of Road & Sea. LC 73-94445. 1976. 24.50x (ISBN 0-520-02716-7). U of Cal Pr.
Cenker, William. The Hindu Personality in Education: Tagore, Gandhi, & Aurobindo. LC 76-52211. 1976. 12.50x o.p. (ISBN 0-88386-759-1). South Asia Bks.
Cennini, C. D'Andrea. The Craftsman's Handbook. Thompson, D. V., Jr., tr. 8.50 (ISBN 0-8446-0542-5). Peter Smith.
Centeno, Augusto, jt. auth. see Tarr, F. C.
Centeno, Jesse. The Growing Terror & Igodsol. 1979. 4.00 o.p. (ISBN 0-8062-1390-6). Carlton.
Center for Applied Linguistics, Washington D.C. Dictionary Catalog of the Library of the Center for Applied Linguistics, Washington, D. C, 4 vols. 1974. Set. lib. bdg. 355.00 (ISBN 0-8161-1114-6, Hall Library). G K Hall.
Center for Attitudinal Healing. Another Look at the Rainbow. 1983. pap. 7.95 (ISBN 0-89087-341-0). Celestial Arts.
Center for Business & Economic Research. Economic Abstract of Alabama, 1982. Sawyer, Carolyn, ed. (Illus.). 405p. 1982. 10.00 (ISBN 0-943394-01-5). U of Ala Ctr Bus.
Center for Curriculum Design, ed. Somewhere Else: A Living-Learning Catalog. LC 82-73302. 214p. 1972. pap. 6.95 (ISBN 0-8040-0610-5). Swallow.
Center for Korean Studies. Korean Studies, Vol. I. (Korean Studies). 1977. pap. text ed. 13.50x (ISBN 0-8248-0560-7). UH Pr.
--Korean Studies, Vol. 4. 176p. 1982. 13.50 (ISBN 0-8248-0816-9). UH Pr.
Center for Migration Studies. Images: A Pictorial History of Italian Americans. Tomasi, Silvano M., ed. LC 81-67218. (Illus.). 348p. 1981. 29.95x (ISBN 0-913256-38-2, Dist. by Ozer). Ctr Migration.
Center for Research in Ambulatory Health Care Administration, ed. see Schafer, Eldon L., et al.
Center for Research in Ambulatory Health Care Administration. Medical Group Practice Management. LC 77-3330. 1977. prof ref 35.00x (ISBN 0-88410-511-3). Ballinger Pub.
--Organization & Development of a Medical Group Practice. LC 76-26953. 1976. prof ref 75.00x (ISBN 0-88410-143-6). Ballinger Pub.
--Practice Management: A Primer for Doctors & Administrators. 288p. 1983. text ed. 25.00 (ISBN 0-89946-091-7). Oelgeschlager.
Center for Research Libraries. The Center for Research Libraries Catalog, Newspaper, 1 vol. 2nd ed. 1978. Set. 136.50 set (ISBN 0-932486-20-7). Ctr Research Lib.
--The Center for Research Libraries Catalog, Serials, First Supplement, 1 vol. 1978. 136.50 set (ISBN 0-932486-21-5). Ctr Research Lib.
--The Cooperative Africana Microform Project: Cumulative Supplement. 203p. (Orig.). 1981. pap. text ed. 3.50 o.p. (ISBN 0-932486-25-8). Ctr Research Lib.
--The Cooperative Africana Microform Project: Cumulative Supplement. 246p. 1978. pap. text ed. 3.50 (ISBN 0-932486-18-5). Ctr Research Lib.
--Research Materials Available. 18p. (Orig.). 1980. pap. text ed. write for info. (ISBN 0-932486-22-3). Ctr Research Lib.
--Scientific & Technical Journals Listing, 1981. 142p. (Orig.). 1981. pap. text ed. 5.00 (ISBN 0-932486-24-X). Ctr Research Lib.
Center for Research Libraries, ed. The Center for Research Libraries Catalog Serials, 2 vols. 1972. Set. 332.00 (ISBN 0-932486-16-9). Ctr Research Lib.
--Monograph Catalog: The Center for Research Libraries Catalog, 5 vols. 1979. 332.00 set (ISBN 0-932486-13-4). Ctr Research Lib.
--Rarely Held Scientific Serials in the Midwest Inter-Library Center: Supplement I. 44p. (Orig.). 1964. pap. text ed. write for info o.p. (ISBN 0-932486-02-9). Ctr Research Lib.
--The Report of a Survey with an Outline of Programs & Policies. 24p. (Orig.). 1965. pap. text ed. write for info. (ISBN 0-932486-00-2). Ctr Research Lib.
Center for Research on Agression, Syracuse University. Prevention & Control of Agression. (General Psychology Ser.). 450p. 1983. 45.00 (ISBN 0-08-029375-1). Pergamon.
Center for Science in the Public Interest Staff, jt. auth. see Lipske, Michael.
Center for Science in the Public Interest. Ways to a Simple Lifestyle. 3.50 (ISBN 0-686-95876-4). Alternatives.
Center for Self Sufficiency Research Division Staff. The A to Z Small Business Bibliography Encyclopedia. 2000p. 1983. Set. text ed. 650.00 (ISBN 0-910811-17-2). Center Self.
Center for Self-Sufficiency Research Division. The Alternative Cooking Facilities Cookbook. 50p. 1983. pap. text ed. 12.95 (ISBN 0-910811-08-3). Center Self.
Center for Self-Sufficiency Research Division, ed. The Barter Index. 60p. Date not set. pap. text ed. 9.95 (ISBN 0-910811-09-1). Center Self.
Center for Self Sufficiency Research Division Staff. Creativity Productivity & Positivity. 50p. 1983. pap. text ed. 15.95 (ISBN 0-910811-15-6). Center Self.
Center for Self-Sufficiency Research Division, compiled by. The Food Preservation Index. 50p. 1982. pap. text ed. 12.95 (ISBN 0-910811-10-5). Center Self.
Center for Self Sufficiency Research Division Staff. Guide to Craft, Quilt, Drapery, Etc. Pattern Sources. 35p. 1983. pap. text ed. 15.95 (ISBN 0-910811-31-8). Center Self.
--Health Care Alternatives. 60p. 1983. pap. 15.95 (ISBN 0-910811-37-7). Center Self.
--Index to Self-Sufficiency Related Institutes, Associations, Organizations, Schools, & Others. 200p. 1983. pap. text ed. 19.95 (ISBN 0-910811-19-9). Center Self.
--Index to Solar Education, Home Plan Kits & Solar Related Companies. 100p. 1983. pap. text ed. 19.95 (ISBN 0-910811-35-0). Center Self.
--International Directory of Herb, Health, Vitamin & Natural Food Catalogs. 200p. 1983. pap. text ed. 15.95 (ISBN 0-910811-36-9). Center Self.
Center for Self-Sufficiency Research Division. Made from Scratch: A Reference on Cooking, Crafts, etc. 50p. Date not set. pap. text ed. 14.95 (ISBN 0-910811-07-5). Center Self.
--Making the Switch from City Living to Country Living: A Bibliography. 55p. Date not set. pap. text ed. 8.95 (ISBN 0-910811-05-9). Center Self.
--Making the Switch from City Living to Small Town Living: A Reference. 55p. Date not set. pap. text ed. 8.95 (ISBN 0-910811-06-7). Center Self.
Center For Self Sufficiency Research Division Staff. One Thousand & More Places to Find Free & Almost Free Recipes. 200p. 1983. pap. text ed. 12.95 (ISBN 0-910811-13-X). Center Self.
--Self Employment, Self Starter, & Start Your Own: A How to Bibliography. 200p. 1983. text ed. 49.95 (ISBN 0-910811-12-1). Center Self.
Center for Self-Sufficiency Research Division. Self-Sufficiency: A Bibliography. 75p. 1983. pap. text ed. 9.95 (ISBN 0-910811-00-8). Center Self.
Center for Self Sufficiency Research Division Staff. Self Sufficiency Sewing Index to Newsletters, Pattern Companies, Fabric Outlets, etc. 60p. 1983. pap. text ed. 10.95 (ISBN 0-910811-30-X). Center Self.
Center for Self Sufficiency Research Division. Self-Sufficiency Topic Index with Bibliographic Information. 500p. Date not set. text ed. 49.95 (ISBN 0-910811-01-6); pap. text ed. 39.95 (ISBN 0-910811-02-4). Center Self.
Center for Self Sufficiency Staff. Center for Self Sufficiency Directory of Recycled Cookbooks, Home Remedy Almanacs, How to Books, & Inspirational Books for Library Loan. 100p. 1983. pap. 2.00 (ISBN 0-910811-33-4). Center Self.
Center for Self-Sufficiency Staff, compiled by. Herbs: A Bibliography Index. 35p. Date not set. pap. text ed. 8.95 (ISBN 0-910811-04-0). Center Self.
Center for Self-Sufficiency Staff, ed. Plant Your Own Fruits & Vegetables & More. 50p. 1983. pap. text ed. cancelled (ISBN 0-686-82426-1). Center Self.
Center for Southern Folklore. American Folklore Films & Videotapes, Vol. 2. LC 82-9673. 424p. 1982. pap. 39.95 (ISBN 0-8352-1536-9). Bowker.
Center for Strategic & International Studies, jt. auth. see Ebinger, Charles.
Center for Study of the American Experience. The Yankee Mariner & Sea Power: America's Challenge of Ocean Space. 300p. 1982. 20.00 (ISBN 0-88474-105-2). Transaction Bks.
Centore, F. F. Persons: A Comparative Account of the Six Possible Theories. LC 78-74653. (Contributions in Philosophy: No. 13). 1979. lib. bdg. 35.00 (ISBN 0-313-20817-4, CPE/). Greenwood.
Central Commission for the Investigation of German Crimes in Poland. German Crimes in Poland, 2 vols. in one. 1982. Repr. of 1947 ed. 40.00x (ISBN 0-86527-336-7). Fertig.
Central Conference of American Rabbis. A Passover Haggadah. Rev. ed. Bronstein, Herbert, ed. 20.00 (ISBN 0-670-54187-7, Grossman). Viking Pr.
Central Electric Railfans' Association. Chicago's Rapid Transit: Rolling Stock, 1892-1947, Vol. 1, Bulletin No. 113. LC 72-96588. (Illus.). 1973. 15.00 (ISBN 0-915348-13-6). Central Electric.
Central Intelligence Agency. CIA Ammunition & Explosives Supply Catalog. (Illus.). 88p. 1975. pap. 9.95 o.p. (ISBN 0-87364-037-3). Paladin Ent.
--CIA Energy Information Reprint Series, 5 vols. Bereny, J. A., ed. Incl. Vol. I. The International Energy Situation: Outlook to 1985; Vol. 2. Prospects for Soviet Oil Production; Vol. 3. Prospects for Soviet Oil Production: A Supplemental Analysis; Vol. 4. China: Oil Production Prospects; Vol. 5. World Petroleum Outlook. 189p. 1979. pap. 54.00x (ISBN 0-89934-000-8). Solar Energy Info.
--CIA Explosives for Sabotage Manual. (Illus.). 70p. 1975. pap. 7.95 o.p. (ISBN 0-87364-036-5). Paladin Ent.
Central State University Ohio. Index to Periodical Articles by & About Blacks, Annual, 1978. 1979. lib. bdg. 65.00 (ISBN 0-8161-0323-2, Hall Library). G K Hall.
--Index to Periodical Articles by & About Negroes, Annuals, 1960-1969. 1971. lib. bdg. 15.00 ea. (Hall Library). G K Hall.
--Index to Periodical Articles by & About Negroes, Annual, 1972. 826p. 1974. lib. bdg. 49.00 (ISBN 0-8161-1106-5, Hall Library). G K Hall.
--Index to Periodical Articles by & About Negroes, Decennial Cumulation, 1950-1959. 1962. 45.00 (ISBN 0-8161-0503-0, Hall Library). G K Hall.
--Index to Periodical Articles by & About Negroes, 1960-1970, Cumulation. 1971. 65.00 (ISBN 0-8161-0847-1, Hall Library). G K Hall.
--Index to Periodicals Articles by & About Negroes, 1971. lib. bdg. 65.00 (ISBN 0-8161-0869-2, Hall Library). G K Hall.
Central State University, Wilberforce, Ohio. Hallie Q. Brown Memorial Library, Index to Periodical Articles by & About Blacks, Nineteen Seventy-Seven. 1979. lib. bdg. 62.00 (ISBN 0-8161-0256-2, Hall Library). G K Hall.
Central Statistical Office of Finland. Statistical Yearbook of Finland-Suomen Tilastollimen Vuosikirja-Statistisk Arsbok for Finland. 76th ed. Laakso, Elia, ed. LC 59-42150. (Illus.). 577p. (Eng., Finnish & Swedish.). 1981. vinyl 38.00x (ISBN 0-8002-2997-5). Intl Pubns Serv.
--Statistical Yearbook of Finland-Suomen Tilastollimen Vuosikirja-Statistisk Arsbok for Finland. 77th ed. Laakso, Elia, ed. LC 59-42150. (Illus.). 517p. (Eng., Finnish & Swedish.). 1982. vinyl 38.00x (ISBN 0-8002-3068-X). Intl Pubns Serv.
Central United Methodist Cooperative Preschool. Recipes for Happy Days. LC 77-89537. 1977. pap. 3.95 o.p. (ISBN 0-930380-00-2). Quail Run.
Centre National de la Recherce Scientifique, ed. Annuaire Francais de Droit International, Vol. XXVII (1981) LC 57-28515. 1206p. (Fr.). 1982. 125.00x (ISBN 2-222-03121-4). Intl Pubns Serv.
Centre National De la Recherche Scientifique, Paris, ed. International Directory of Medievalists, 2 vols. 5th ed. 1979. 140.00x (ISBN 0-89664-046-9, Pub. by K G Saur). Gale.
Centro Studi e Laboratori Telecomumicazioni. Optical Fiber Communication. (Illus.). 928p. 1981. 43.75 (ISBN 0-07-014882-1, P&RB). McGraw.
Cepeda, Orlando & Kelly, Mary P. Cepeda! A Career & a Comeback in the Big Leagues. (Illus.). 1982. cancelled (ISBN 0-89651-102-2). Icarus.
--Orlando! The Orlando Cepeda Story. (Illus.). 1982. cancelled (ISBN 0-89651-551-6). Icarus.
Ceppede, Jean de La see De la Ceppede, Jean.
Cera, Mary J. & Bisignano, Judith. Creating Your Future: Level 1. (Illus.). 72p. 1982. 6.95 (ISBN 0-910141-00-2, KP107). Kino Pubns.
Cerami, Charles A. More Profits, Less Risk: Your New Financial Strategy. LC 82-7775. 240p. 1982. 14.95 (ISBN 0-07-010324-0). McGraw.
Cercignani. Theory & Application of the Boltzman Equation. 1976. 38.95 (ISBN 0-444-19450-9). Elsevier.
Cerda, Gilberto, et al. Vocabulario espanol de Texas. 355p. (Span.). 1970. Repr. of 1953 ed. 19.50x o.p. (ISBN 0-292-70079-2). U of Tex Pr.
Cere, Paul. Les Population Dangereuses et les Miseres Sociales. (Conditions of the 19th Century French Working Class Ser.). 378p. (Fr.). 1974. Repr. of 1872 ed. lib. bdg. 104.75x o.p. (ISBN 0-8287-0173-3, 1093). Clearwater Pub.
Cerepak, John R. Accounting for Business. 2nd ed. LC 73-85889. 832p. 1974. text ed. 22.95 (ISBN 0-675-08881-X); Vols. 1-14 Ea. o. p. 6.50 ea. (ISBN 0-675-08823-2). Additional supplements may be obtained from publisher. Merrill.
Ceres. Herbs for Healthy Hair. LC 80-50747. (Everybody's Home Herbal Ser.). (Illus.). 62p. (Orig.). 1980. pap. 1.95 o.p. (ISBN 0-394-73947-7). Shambhala Pubns.
--Herbs to Help You Sleep. LC 80-50749. (Everybody's Home Herbal Ser.). (Illus.). 62p. (Orig.). 1980. pap. 1.95 o.p. (ISBN 0-394-73946-9). Shambhala Pubns.
Cerf, ed. see Henry, O.
Cerf, Bennett, ed. An Anthology of Famous American Stories. 1953. 5.95 o.s.i. (ISBN 0-394-60777-5). Modern Lib.
--Thirty Famous One-Act Plays. 1949. 6.95 (ISBN 0-394-60473-3). Modern Lib.
Cerf, Bennett A. Bennett Cerf's Book of Laughs. LC 59-13387. (Illus.). (gr. 1-2). 1959. 4.95 o.p. (ISBN 0-394-80011-7); PLB 5.99 (ISBN 0-394-90011-1). Beginner.
--Bennett Cerf's Book of Riddles. LC 60-13492. (Illus.). (gr. 1-2). 1960. 3.95 (ISBN 0-394-80015-X); PLB 5.99 (ISBN 0-394-90015-4). Beginner.
Cerf, Christopher, ed. Vintage Anthology of Science Fantasy. 1966. pap. 2.95 o.p. (ISBN 0-394-70326-X, V326, Vin). Random.
Cerf, Martin, jt. auth. see Atkinson, Terry.
Cerfbeer, Auguste-Edouard. Des Societes De Bienfaisance Mutuelle. (Conditions of the 19th Century French Working Class Ser.). 113p. (Fr.). 1974. Repr. of 1836 ed. lib. bdg. 38.00x o.p. (ISBN 0-8287-0174-1, 1059). Clearwater Pub.
Cermak, J. E., ed. Wind Engineering: Proceedings of the 5th International Conference, Colorado State University, USA, July 8-14, 1979, 2 vols. LC 80-40753. (Illus.). 1400p. 1980. Set. 215.00 (ISBN 0-08-024745-8). Pergamon.
Cermak, Laird S. Improving Your Memory. LC 76-26011. (McGraw-Hill Paperbacks). 1976. pap. 3.95 (ISBN 0-07-010325-9, SP). McGraw.
Cermanovic-Kuzmanovic, A. Monumenta intra fines Iugoslaviae Reperta. (Etudes Preliminaires sux Religions Orientales dan l'Empire Romain: Vol. 74). (Illus.). xi, 76p. 1982. pap. write for info. (ISBN 90-04-06533-4). E J Brill.
Ceminara, Gina. Many Lives, Many Loves. 3rd ed. LC 63-13710. 245p. 1981. pap. 6.50 (ISBN 0-87516-429-3). De Vorss.
--The Mark Twain Proposition. LC 77-13456. 1977. pap. 4.95 o.p. (ISBN 0-915442-41-8, Unilaw). Donning Co.
Cern, J. M., ed. Perturbative Quantum Chromodynamics. (Physics Reports Reprint Book Ser.: Vol. 5). 836p. 1982. 76.75 (ISBN 0-444-86420-2, North Holland). Elsevier.
Cernada, George P. Knowledge into Action. (Community Health Education Monographs: Vol. 1). 168p. 1982. pap. text ed. 9.95 (ISBN 0-89503-031-4). Baywood Pub.
Cerna-Heyrovska, J., jt. auth. see Krobloch, E.
Cernea, Michael M. Measuring Project Impact: Monitoring & Evaluation in the PIDER Rural Development Project - Mexico. (Working Paper: No. 332). vi, 131p. 1979. 5.00 (ISBN 0-686-36071-0, WP-0332). World Bank.
Cernea, Michael M. & Tepping, Benjamin J. A System of Monitoring & Evaluating Agricultural Extension Projects. (Working Paper: No. 272). vi, 115p. 1977. 5.00 (ISBN 0-686-36079-6, WP-0272). World Bank.
Cerney, J. V. Handbook of Unusual & Unorthodox Healing Methods. 1976. 14.95 o.p. (ISBN 0-13-382721-6, Parker). P-H.
Cernuda, Luis. Selected Poems of Luis Cernuda. Gibbons, Reginald, tr. from Span. LC 75-3767. 1976. 21.50x (ISBN 0-520-02984-4). U of Cal Pr.
Cernuda, Ralph & Lawson, Greg, photos by. California. (Illus.). 72p. (Orig., Eng., Span., Fr., Ger., Jap.). 1983. pap. 8.95 (ISBN 0-9606704-6-7). First Choice.
Cernuschi, Alberto. The Constructive Manifesto. LC 82-18903. 1983. 8.50 (ISBN 0-8022-2411-3). Philos Lib.

Cerny, Jaroslav. Ancient Egyptian Religion. LC 78-9931. 1979. Repr. of 1957 ed. lib. bdg. 20.00x (ISBN 0-313-21104-3, CEAE). Greenwood.

--Coptic Etymological Dictionary. LC 69-10192. 350p. 1976. 175.00 (ISBN 0-521-07228-X). Cambridge U Pr.

--Egyptian Stelae in the Bankes Collection. (Bankes Collection Bks.). 33p. 1958. pap. text ed. 10.50x (ISBN 0-900416-07-6, Pub. by Aris & Philips England). Humanities.

Cerny, Jaroslav & Gardiner, Alan. Hieratic Ostraca, Vol. I. 35p. 1957. text ed. 80.00x (ISBN 0-900416-36-X, Pub. by Aris & Philips England). Humanities.

Cerny, L. Elementary Statics & Strength of Materials. 1981. 27.50x (ISBN 0-07-010339-9). McGraw.

Cerny, Lothar. Erinnerung Bei Dickens. (Bochum Studies in English: No. 3). (Illus.). 284p. (Ger.). 1975. pap. 16.00 (ISBN 90-6032-063-8). Benjamins North Am.

Cerny, Philip & Schain, Martin, eds. French Politics & Public Policy. 1980. 26.00 (ISBN 0-312-30509-5). St Martin.

Cerny, Philip G., ed. Social Movements & Protest in France. 270p. 1982. pap. 12.00 (ISBN 0-86187-214-2). F Pinter Pubs.

Cerny, Phillip G. The Politics of Grandeur. LC 79-50232. 1980. 39.50 (ISBN 0-521-22863-8). Cambridge U Pr.

Cerny, S., jt. auth. see Smisek, M.

Ceron, J. D., Jr. Children of the Devil. 1983. 11.95 (ISBN 0-533-05656-X). Vantage.

Cerra, Frank J., ed. see Wiatrowski, Claude A. & House, Charles H.

Cerretilli & Whipp. Exercise Bioenergetics & Gas Exchange. (Grovanni Lorenzini Foundation Symposium Ser.: Vol. 9). 1981. 65.00 (ISBN 0-444-80295-9). Elsevier.

Cerreto, Frank. The Mathematics Test. (Illus.). 1979. pap. 5.95 (ISBN 0-07-010337-2, SP). McGraw.

Certo, Samuel & Brenenstuhl, Daniel L. Fundamental Readings in Modern Management: Functions & Systems. 368p. 1980. pap. write for info. o.p. (ISBN 0-697-08035-8). Wm C Brown.

Certo, Samuel C. Principles of Modern Management: Functions & Systems. 600p. 1980. text ed. write for info. o.p. (ISBN 0-697-08033-1); instr. manual avail. o.p. (ISBN 0-697-08043-9); printed tests avail. o.p. (ISBN 0-697-08045-5); experiential wkbk. avail. o.p. (ISBN 0-697-08041-2); reader avail. o.p. (ISBN 0-697-08035-8). Wm C Brown.

--Principles of Modern Management: Functions & Systems. 2nd ed. 630p. 1982. text ed. write for info (ISBN 0-697-08084-6); write for info instrs. manual (ISBN 0-697-08179-6); Experimental Wkbk avail. (ISBN 0-697-08092-7); Bk of Readings avail. (ISBN 0-697-08090-0); Lecture Enrichment Kit avail. (ISBN 0-697-08099-4); instr's. manual - Readings avail. (ISBN 0-697-08091-9); transparencies avail. Wm C Brown.

Certo, Samuel C. & Applebaum, Steven H. Principles of Modern Management: A Canadian Perspective. 630p. 1983. text ed. write for info. (ISBN 0-697-08168-0); avail. instrs.' manual (ISBN 0-697-08174-5). Wm C Brown.

Certo, Samuel C. & Brenenstuhl, Daniel C. Fundamental Readings in Modern Management. 2nd ed. 350p. 1983. pap. text ed. write for info (ISBN 0-697-08090-0); write for info instrs.' manual (ISBN 0-697-08091-9). Wm C Brown.

Cerullo, John J. The Secularization of the Soul: Psychical Research in Modern Britain. LC 81-13322. 200p. 1982. text ed. 18.50x (ISBN 0-89727-028-2). Inst Study Human.

Cerutti, Edwina. Mystic with the Healing Hands: The Life of Olga Worrall. LC 75-9317. 1977. pap. 6.95i (ISBN 0-06-061357-2, RD 244, HarpR). Har-Row.

Cerutti, Peter A., jt. ed. see Harris, Curtis C.

Cerutti, Toni. Guide to Composition in Italian. 1966. text ed. 7.95 (ISBN 0-521-04593-2). Cambridge U Pr.

Ceruzzi, Paul E. Reckoners: The Prehistory of the Digital Computer, From Relays to the Stored Program Concept, 1935-1945. LC 82-20980. (Contributions to the Study of Computer Science Ser.: No. 1). (Illus.). 240p. 1983. lib. bdg. 29.95 (ISBN 0-313-23382-9, CED/). Greenwood.

Cervantes. Don Quijote De la Mancha: Primery Parte. (Easy Reader, D). pap. 3.95 (ISBN 0-88436-056-3, 70275). EMC.

Cervantes see Allen, W. S.

Cervantes, Alex, jt. auth. see Cervantes, Esther De Michael.

Cervantes, Esther De Michael & Cervantes, Alex. Senora Pepino & Her Bad Luck Cats: Senora Pepino y Sus Gatos de Mala Suerte. LC 76-4818. (Illus., Eng. & Span.). 1976. 5.95 o.p. (ISBN 0-87917-052-2). Ethridge.

Cervantes, Irma H. Sparks, Flames & Cinders. (Illus.). 96p. 1982. 12.95 (ISBN 0-9609600-0-7). Five Windmills.

Cervantes, Miguel. Don Quixote. Putnam, Samuel, tr. & intro. by. 10.95 (ISBN 0-394-60438-5). Modern Lib.

Cervantes, Miguel De. Don Quixote. (Oxford Progressive English Readers Ser.). (Illus.). 1973. pap. text ed. 3.50x (ISBN 0-19-638224-6). Oxford U Pr.

Cervantes, Miguel De see De Cervantes, Miguel.

Cervenka, Exene, jt. auth. see Lunch, Lydia.

Cervera, Alejo De see DE Cervera, Alejo.

Cervical Spine Research Editorial Subcommittee, et al, eds. The Cervical Spine. (Illus.). 642p. 1983. text ed. 57.50 (ISBN 0-397-50510-8, Lippincott Medical). Lippincott.

Cervin, Russell A. Mission in Ferment. 1977. pap. 3.50 o.p. (ISBN 0-910452-33-4). Covenant.

Cervon, Jacqueline. The Day the Earth Shook. (gr. 6-8). 1969. 4.95 o.p. (ISBN 0-698-20029-2, Coward). Putnam Pub Group.

Cervos-Navarro, H., et al, eds. The Cerebral Vessel Wall. LC 75-25110. 288p. 1976. 34.50 (ISBN 0-89004-071-0). Raven.

Cervos-Navarro, J., ed. Brain Edema. Ferszt, R. (Advances in Neurology: Vol. 28). (Illus.). 539p. 1980. text ed. 65.50 (ISBN 0-89004-482-1). Raven.

Cervos-Navarro, J. & Fritschka, E., eds. Cerebral Microcirculation & Metabolism. 496p. 1981. text ed. 60.50 (ISBN 0-89004-590-9). Raven.

Cervos-Navarro, J., et al, eds. Pathology of Cerebrospinal Microcirculation. LC 77-84125. (Advances in Neurology Ser.: Vol. 20). 632p. 1978. 61.50 (ISBN 0-89004-237-3). Raven.

Cerwinske, Laura, jt. auth. see Rachlin, Norman S.

CES Industries, Inc. Advanced Digital Systems. (Ed-Lab Experiment Manual Ser.). (Illus.). (gr. 9-12). 1981. lab manual 12.50 (ISBN 0-86711-008-2). CES Industries.

--Advanced Digital Systems. (Ed-Lab Experiment Manual Ser.). (Illus.). 312p. (gr. 9-12). 1981. lab manual 12.50 o.p. (ISBN 0-86711-000-7). CES Industries.

CES Industries Inc. Electricity-Electronics, Bk. 1. (Ed-Lab Experiment Manual Ser.). (Illus.). 288p. (gr. 9-12). 1980. lab manual 12.50 o.p. (ISBN 0-86711-003-1). CES Industries.

CES Industries, Inc. Electronics, Bk. III. (Ed-Lab Experiment Manual Ser.). (Illus.). 232p. (gr. 9-12). 1978. lab manual 11.50 o.p. (ISBN 0-686-32842-6). CES Industries.

--Telecommunications, Bk. IV. (Ed-Lab Experiment Manual Ser.). (Illus.). 192p. (gr. 9-12). 1980. lab manual 11.50 o.p. (ISBN 0-86711-006-6). CES Industries.

CES Industries, Inc. Staff. Basic Electronics Trainer. (Ed-Lab Experiment Manual Ser.). (Illus.). (gr. 9-12). 1982. write for info. lab manual. CES Industries.

--Basic Language. (Ed-Lab Experiment Manual Ser.). (Illus.). (gr. 9-12). 1982. write for info. lab manual (ISBN 0-86711-061-9). CES Industries.

--Contactor Sensor Operation. (Ed-Lab Experiment Manual Ser.). (Illus.). (gr. 9-12). 1982. write for info. lab manual (ISBN 0-86711-063-5). CES Industries.

--Counter-Timer Module: Troubleshooting System. (Ed-Lab Experiment Manual Ser.). (Illus.). (gr. 9-12). 1982. write for info. lab manual (ISBN 0-86711-031-7). CES Industries.

--DC-AC Electronics Program. (Ed-Lab Experiment Manual Ser.). (Illus.). (gr. 9-12). 1982. write for info. lab manual (ISBN 0-86711-062-7). CES Industries.

--Fault Location & System. (Ed-Lab Experiment Manual Ser.). (Illus.). (gr. 9-12). 1982. write for info. lab manual (ISBN 0-86711-060-0). CES Industries.

--Interfaces: E-L 80, Unit 2. (Ed-Lab Experiment Manual Ser.). (Illus.). (gr. 9-12). 1982. write for info. lab manual (ISBN 0-86711-057-0). CES Industries.

--Microcomputer Technology, Unit 2. (Ed-Lab Experiment Manual Ser.). (Illus.). (gr. 9-12). 1981. lab manual 11.50 (ISBN 0-86711-023-6). CES Industries.

--Microprocessor: Student Guide. (Ed-Lab Experiment Manual Ser.). (Illus.). (gr. 9-12). 1981. write for info. lab manual (ISBN 0-86711-018-X). CES Industries.

--Microprocessors. (ED-Lab Experiment Manual Ser.). (Illus.). (gr. 9-12). write for info. lab manual (ISBN 0-86711-022-8). CES Industries.

--Microprocessors Concepts, Unit 1. (Ed-Lab Experiment Manual Ser.). (Illus.). (gr. 9-12). 1981. lab manual 9.50 (ISBN 0-86711-021-X). CES Industries.

--Programming for Ohms Law, Unit 1. (Ed-Lab Experiment Manual Ser.). (Illus.). (gr. 9-12). 1982. write for info. lab manual (ISBN 0-86711-029-5). CES Industries.

--Projects & Interfacing. (Ed-Lab Experiment Manual Ser.). (Illus.). (gr. 9-12). 1982. lab manual 9.50 (ISBN 0-86711-025-2). CES Industries.

--Pulses & Waveshaping, Bk.IV. (Ed-Lab Experiment Manual). (Illus.). (gr. 9-12). 1982. lab manual 11.50 (ISBN 0-86711-052-X). CES Industries.

--Relay Module. (Ed-Lab Experiment Manual Ser.). (Illus.). (gr. 9-12). 1981. write for info. lab manual. CES Industries.

--Robot Operation & Programming. (Ed-Lab Experiment Manual Ser.). (Illus.). (gr. 9-12). 1982. write for info. lab manual (ISBN 0-86711-032-5). CES Industries.

--Transducers. (Ed-Lab Experiment Manual). (Illus.). (gr. 9-12). 1982. write for info. lab manual (ISBN 0-86711-050-3). CES Industries.

Cesaire, Aime. Cadastre. new ed. Davis, Gregson, tr. from French. LC 75-169155. 96p. 1972. 4.95 o.p. (ISBN 0-89388-028-0); pap. 1.95 o.p. (ISBN 0-89388-029-9). Okpaku Communications.

--Discourse on Colonialism. Pinkham, Joan, tr. LC 72-178714. 96p. 1972. 4.95 o.p. (ISBN 0-686-86362-3, CL-2059); pap. 2.95 (ISBN 0-686-91524-0, PB-2266). Monthly Rev.

--The Tempest. LC 74-82723. 1974. 5.95 o.s.i. (ISBN 0-89388-174-0); pap. 2.95 o.s.i. (ISBN 0-89388-175-9). Okpaku Communications.

Cesaire, Aime see Harrison, Paul C.

Cesara, Manda. No Hiding Place: Reflections of a Woman Anthropologists. (Studies in Anthropology Ser.). 1982. 20.00 (ISBN 0-12-164880-X). Acad Pr.

Cesar Acleto O., et al, eds. Phycologia Latino-Americana, Vol. 1. (Illus.). 186p. (Span.). 1981. text ed. 24.00x (ISBN 3-7682-1297-1). Lubrecht & Cramer.

Cesarea, Eusebio de see De Cesarea, Eusebio.

Cesari, L. Surface Area. (Annuals of Mathematics Studies: No. 35). 1956. pap. 40.00 (ISBN 0-527-02752-9). Kraus Repr.

Cesari, L., jt. ed. see Bednarek, A. R.

Cesari, Lamberto, et al. Dynamical Systems: An International Symposium, Vol. I. 1976. 68.50 (ISBN 0-12-164901-6). Acad Pr.

Ceserani, Gian P. Marco Polo. (Illus.). 40p. 1982. 9.95 (ISBN 0-399-20843-7). Putnam Pub Group.

Cespedes, Guillermo. Latin America: History. 1974. 9.00 (ISBN 0-394-31810-2). Knopf.

Cess, R. D., jt. auth. see Sparrow, E. M.

Cessna Aircraft Co. Cessna, 1977 Model, 150 "Commuter" Pilot's Operating Handbook. (Illus.). 1977. pap. 7.50x (ISBN 0-911720-50-2, Cessna). Aviation.

--Cessna 1977 Model, 172 "Skyhawk" Pilot's Operating Handbook. pap. 7.50x (ISBN 0-911720-44-8, Cessna). Aviation.

Cetin, Frank. Here Is Your Hobby: Stamp Collecting. (Here Is Your Hobby Ser.). (Illus.). (gr. 5 up). 1962. PLB 5.29 o.p. (ISBN 0-399-60255-0). Putnam Pub Group.

Cetron, Marvin J. & Ralph, Christine A. Industrial Applications of Technological Forecasting. LC 80-20243. 582p. 1983. Repr. of 1971 ed. text ed. write for info. (ISBN 0-89874-238-2). Krieger.

Cetron, Marvin J., et al. Technical Resource Management: Quantitative Methods. 1970. 20.00x (ISBN 0-262-03034-9). MIT Pr.

Cevasco, G. A. J. K. Huysman: A Reference Guide to English Translations of his Works & Studies of his Life & Literature Published in England & America, 1880-1978. 1980. lib. bdg. 24.50 (ISBN 0-8161-8235-3, Hall Reference). G K Hall.

--John Gray. (English Authors Ser.). 1982. lib. bdg. 17.95 (ISBN 0-8057-6839-4, Twayne). G K Hall.

--Oscar Wilde, British Author, Poet & Wit. Rahmas, D. Steve, ed. LC 72-89209. (Outstanding Personalities Ser.: No. 45). 32p. 1972. lib. bdg. 2.95 incl. catalog cards (ISBN 0-87157-541-8); pap. 1.95 vinyl laminated covers (ISBN 0-87157-041-6). SamHar Pr.

--The Population Problem. (Topics of Our Times Ser.: No. 8). 32p. lib. bdg. 2.95 incl. catalog cards (ISBN 0-87157-809-3); pap. 1.95 vinyl laminated covers (ISBN 0-87157-309-1). SamHar Pr.

Cey, Ron, jt. auth. see Auker, Jim.

Cha, Theresa H. Dictee. 96p. 1982. 13.95 (ISBN 0-934378-10-X); pap. 6.95 (ISBN 0-934378-09-6). Tanam Pr.

Chabal, Patrick. Amilcar Cabral; Revolutionary Leadership & People's War. LC 82-14632. (African Studies: No. 37). (Illus.). 280p. Date not set. price not set (ISBN 0-521-24944-9); pap. price not set (ISBN 0-521-27113-4). Cambridge U Pr.

Chaballe, L. Y. & Masuy, L. Elsevier's Oil & Gas Field Dictionary. (in 6 languages plus Arabic suppl.). 1980. 127.75 (ISBN 0-444-41833-4). Elsevier.

Chaballe, L. Y. & Vandenberghe, J. P. Elsevier's Dictionary of Building Tools & Materials. (Eng. & Fr. & Span. & Ger. & Dutch.). 1982. 138.50 (ISBN 0-444-42047-9). Elsevier.

Chabner, Bruce A., jt. ed. see Fox, C. Fred.

Chabner, Davi-Ellen. The Language of Medicine: A Write-in Text Explaining Medical Terms. 2nd ed. (Illus.). 600p. 1981. text ed. 19.95 (ISBN 0-7216-2479-0). Saunders.

Chace, Fenner A., Jr., jt. ed. see Pequegnat, Willis E.

Chace, William M., ed. Joyce: A Collection of Critical Essays. LC 73-18496. (Illus.). 192p. 1973. 12.95 (ISBN 0-13-511303-2, Spec); pap. 4.95 (ISBN 0-13-511295-8, Spec). P-H.

Chacey, C., jt. auth. see Chambers, H.

Chachiliades, Miltiades. International Trade Theory & Policy. 2nd ed. (Economic Handbk Ser). (Illus.). 1977. text ed. 29.95 (ISBN 0-07-010344-5, C). McGraw.

Chacholiades, Miltiades. International Monetary Theory & Policy. (Illus.). 1977. 29.95 (ISBN 0-07-010340-2, C). McGraw.

--Principles of International Economics. (Illus.). 656p. 1981. text ed. 23.95 (ISBN 0-07-010345-3, C). McGraw.

Chacko, David. Brick Alley. 1981. 11.95 o.s.i. (ISBN 0-440-00862-X). Delacorte.

Chacko, G. K. Applied Operations Research: Systems Analysis in Hierarchical Decision-Making, 2 vol. set. Incl. Vol. 1. Systems Approach to Public & Private Sector Problems; Vol. 2. Operations Research to Problem Formulation & Solution. (Studies in Management Science & Solution: Vol. 3). 1976. Set. 127.75 (ISBN 0-444-10768-1, North-Holland). Elsevier.

Chacko, G. K., ed. Health Handbook: An International Reference on Care & Cure. 1979. 170.25 (ISBN 0-444-85254-9, North Holland). Elsevier.

Chacks, G. Applied Statistics in Decision Making. 1971. 27.50 (ISBN 0-444-00109-3). Elsevier.

Chacksfield, K. M., et al. Music & Language with Young Children. 190p. 1975. pap. 6.50x o.p. (ISBN 0-631-12842-5, Pub. by Basil Blackwell England). Biblio Dist.

--Music & Language with Young Children. (Illus.). 190p. 1975. 18.50x o.p. (ISBN 0-631-15330-6, Pub. by Basil Blackwell). Biblio Dist.

Chacon, Joaquin-Armando. Las Amarras Terrestres. 149p. (Span.). 1982. pap. 7.00 (ISBN 0-910061-08-4). Ediciones Norte.

Chadbourne, Ava H. Maine Place Names & the Peopling of its Towns: Cumberland County. 1982. pap. 4.95 (ISBN 0-87027-131-8). Cumberland Pr.

--Maine Place Names & the Peopling of its Towns: Franklin & Androscoggin Counties. LC 55-11060. 1957. pap. 1.00 o.p. (ISBN 0-87027-046-X). Cumberland Pr.

--Maine Place Names & the Peopling of Its Towns: Hancock County. Wheelwright, Thea, ed. LC 77-115159. (Illus.). 1970. pap. 1.95 (ISBN 0-87027-112-1). Cumberland Pr.

--Maine Place Names & the Peopling of Its Towns: Kennebec & Somerset Counties. LC 55-11060. 1957. pap. 1.00 o.s.i. (ISBN 0-87027-044-3). Cumberland Pr.

--Maine Place Names & the Peopling of Its Towns: Lincoln County. Wheelwright, Thea, ed. LC 77-115159. 1970. pap. 1.95 (ISBN 0-87027-113-X). Cumberland Pr.

--Maine Place Names & the Peopling of Its Towns: Penobscot County. LC 55-11060. 1957. pap. 1.00 o.s.i. (ISBN 0-87027-043-5). Cumberland Pr.

--Maine Place Names & the Peopling of Its Towns: Washington County. LC 77-115159. (Illus.). 1971. pap. 1.95 (ISBN 0-87027-114-8). Cumberland Pr.

--Maine Place Names & the Peopling of Its Towns: York County. LC 77-115159. (Illus., Orig.). 1971. pap. 1.95 (ISBN 0-87027-118-0). Cumberland Pr.

Chadbourne, Mary. Reflection & Recollections. 24p. (Orig.). 1982. pap. 3.50 (ISBN 0-9607370-1-4). Morel Bks.

Chadbourne, Richard & Dahlie, Hallvard, eds. The New Land: Studies in Literary Theme. 160p. 1978. pap. text ed. 6.75 (ISBN 0-88920-065-3, Pub. by Laurier U Pr Canada). Humanities.

Chadbourne, Richard M. Charles-Augustin Sainte Beuve. (World Authors Ser.). 1978. lib. bdg. 15.95 (ISBN 0-8057-6290-6, Twayne). G K Hall.

Chadda, R. S. Inventory Management in India. 2nd ed. 126p. 1971. 5.50x o.p. (ISBN 0-8188-0135-2). Paragon.

Chadderton, L. T. & Torrens, I. M. Fission Damage to Crystals. 265p. 1969. 15.95x (ISBN 0-416-12420-8). Methuen Inc.

Chaddha, K. L. & Randhawa, G. S. International Symposium on Tropical & Sub-Tropical Horticulutural, 3rd: Vol. 1, Improvement of Horticultural Plantation & Medicinal Crops. (Illus.). 325p. 1975. 25.00 (ISBN 0-88065-237-3, Pub. by Messers Today & Tomorrow Printers & Publishers). Scholarly Pubns.

Chaddick, Ron. Love's Labor Lost. LC 80-82093. (Understand Ye Shakespeare Ser.). 1980. pap. 8.95 deluxe ed. o.p. (ISBN 0-933350-35-X). Morse Pr.

Chaddock, Ron. As You Like It. LC 80-82091. (Understand Ye Shakespeare Ser.). 1980. pap. 8.95 deluxe ed. o.p. (ISBN 0-933350-34-1). Morse Pr.

--Tragedy of Macbeth. LC 80-82092. (Understand Ye Shaskespeare Ser.). 1980. pap. 8.95 deluxe ed. o.p. (ISBN 0-933350-33-3). Morse Pr.

Chadeev, V. M., jt. auth. see Rajbman, N. S.

Chader, G. J., jt. ed. see Osborne, N. O.

Chadha, K. L. & Randhawa, G. S., eds. International Symposium on Tropical & Sub-Tropical Horticulture, 3rd: Vol. 2, Nutrition of Horticultural, Plantation & Medicinal Crops. (Illus.). 266p. 1978. 20.00 (ISBN 0-88065-238-1, Pub. by Messers Today & Tomorrow Printers & Publishers). Scholarly Pubns.

Chadsey, Charles P. & Wentworth, Harold, eds. The Grosset Webster Large-Type Dictionary. (Illus.). 1978. pap. 5.95 (ISBN 0-448-14636-3, G&D). Putnam Pub Group.

Chadwick, jt. auth. see Simon, James.

Chadwick, Charles. Symbolism. (Critical Idiom Ser.). 1971. pap. 4.95x (ISBN 0-416-60910-4). Methuen Inc.

Chadwick, Edward M. Ontarian Families: Genealogies of United Empire Loyalist & other Pioneer Families of Upper Canada, 2 vols. in 1. 1983. Repr. of 1898 ed. lib. bdg. 21.00 (ISBN 0-912606-10-X). Hunterdon Hse.

Chadwick, George. Harmony: A Course of Study, 2 vols. in 1. Incl. A Key to Chadwick's Harmony. vii, 103p. LC 74-36316. (Music Reprint Ser.). xiv, 211p. 1975. Repr. of 1897 ed. lib. bdg. 35.00 (ISBN 0-306-70663-6). Da Capo.

Chadwick, George W. Judith: Lyric Drama for Solo, Chorus, & Orchestra. LC 70-169727. (Earlier American Music Ser.: Vol. 4). 176p. 1972. Repr. of 1901 ed. lib. bdg. 25.00 (ISBN 0-306-77303-1). Da Capo.

--Symphony No. Two: In B Flat, Opus 21. facsimile ed. LC 71-170930. (Earlier American Music Ser.: No. 3). 216p. 1972. Repr. of 1888 ed. 25.00 (ISBN 0-306-77304-X). Da Capo.

Chadwick, H., ed. Origen: Contra Celsum. LC 78-73132. 1980. 74.50 (ISBN 0-521-05866-X); pap. 24.50 (ISBN 0-521-29576-9). Cambridge U Pr.

Chadwick, Henry, ed. Boethius: The Consolations of Music, Logic, Theology, & Philosophy. 330p. 1981. text ed. 39.00 (ISBN 0-19-826447-X). Oxford U Pr.

Chadwick, J. The Mycenaean World. (Illus.). 224p. 1976. 42.50 (ISBN 0-521-21077-1); pap. 10.95 (ISBN 0-521-29037-6). Cambridge U Pr.

Chadwick, J., jt. auth. see Ventris, M.

Chadwick, Janet. How to Live on Almost Nothing & Have Plenty. LC 79-2246. (Illus.). 1979. 12.95 (ISBN 0-394-42811-0); pap. 7.95 (ISBN 0-394-73753-9). Knopf.

Chadwick, Jerah. The Dream Horse. 12p. (Orig.). 1980. 5.00 (ISBN 0-931188-11-3). Seal Pr WA.

Chadwick, John. Decipherment of Linear B. (Illus.). 1970. 29.95 (ISBN 0-521-04599-1); pap. 8.95x (ISBN 0-521-09596-4, 596). Cambridge U Pr.

--Mycenae Tablets Three. (Transactions Ser.: Vol. 52, Pt. 7). (Illus.). 1963. pap. 3.00 (ISBN 0-87169-527-8). Am Philos.

Chadwick, John & Chadwick, Suzanne. The Chadwick System: Discovering the Perfect Hairstyle for You. LC 82-10461. (Illus.). 250p. 1982. 17.95 (ISBN 0-671-44016-0). S&S.

Chadwick, John, et al. Knossos Tables: A Transliteration. 4th ed. (Illus.). 1971. 57.00 (ISBN 0-521-08085-1). Cambridge U Pr.

Chadwick, M. J. & Lindman, N., eds. Environmental Implications of Expanded Coal Utilization. LC 81-23560. (Illus.). 304p. 1982. 55.00 (ISBN 0-08-028734-4). Pergamon.

Chadwick, Maureen V. Mycobacteria. (Institute of Medical Laboratory Sciences Monographs). 128p. 1982. pap. text ed. write for info. (ISBN 0-7236-0595-5). Wright-PSG.

Chadwick, Owen. Catholicism & History. LC 77-77740. 1978. 22.95 (ISBN 0-521-21708-3). Cambridge U Pr.

--John Cassian. 2nd ed. 1968. 29.50 (ISBN 0-521-04607-6). Cambridge U Pr.

--The Secularization of the European Mind in the Nineteenth Century. LC 77-88670. (The Gifford Lectures in the University of Edinburgh Ser.: 1973-1974). 278p. 1976. 37.50 (ISBN 0-521-20892-0); pap. 11.95 (ISBN 0-521-29317-0). Cambridge U Pr.

Chadwick, P. Continuum Mechanics. (Illus.). 1978. pap. text ed. 9.95x o.p. (ISBN 0-04-510057-8). Allen Unwin.

Chadwick, Roxane. Don't Shoot. LC 78-6101. (Real Life Bks). (Illus.). (gr. 2-9). 1978. PLB 5.95g (ISBN 0-8225-0706-4). Lerner Pubns.

Chadwick, Suzanne, jt. auth. see Chadwick, John.

Chadwick, Whitney. Myth in Surrealist Painting, 1929-1939. Foster, Stephen, ed. LC 79-26713. (Studies in Fine Arts: The Avant-Garde, No. 1). 262p. 1980. 39.95 (ISBN 0-8357-1057-2, Pub. by UMI Res Pr). Univ Microfilms.

Chafe, Wallace, ed. The Pear Stories: Cognitive, Cultural & Linguistic Aspects of Narrative Production, Vol. 3. (Advances in Discourse Processes Ser.). (Illus.). 1980. text ed. 32.50x (ISBN 0-89391-032-5). Ablex Pub.

Chafe, William H. American Woman: Her Changing Social, Economic & Political Roles, 1920-1970. 1974. pap. 7.95 (ISBN 0-19-501785-4, GB406). Oxford U Pr.

--Civilities & Civil Rights: Greensboro, North Carolina, & the Black Struggle for Freedom. (Illus.). 1980. 19.95 (ISBN 0-19-502625-X). Oxford U Pr.

--Women & Equality: Changing Patterns in American Culture. LC 76-42639. 1977. 16.95 (ISBN 0-19-502158-4). Oxford U Pr.

Chafe, William H. & Sitkoff, Harvard, eds. A History of Our Time: Readings on Postwar America. 1982. pap. 8.95x (ISBN 0-19-503174-1). Oxford U Pr.

Chafee, Zechariah. The Blessings of Liberty. LC 72-8237. 350p. 1973. Repr. of 1956 ed. lib. bdg. 17.50x (ISBN 0-8371-6536-9, CHBL). Greenwood.

--The Inquiring Mind. LC 74-699. (American Constitutional & Legal History Ser.). 276p. 1974. Repr. of 1928 ed. lib. bdg. 32.50 (ISBN 0-306-70641-5). Da Capo.

Chafetz, Janet S. Masculine-Feminine or Human. 2nd ed. LC 77-83425. 1978. pap. text ed. 9.95 (ISBN 0-87581-231-7). Peacock Pubs.

--A Primer on the Construction & Testing of Theories in Sociology. LC 77-83430. 1978. pap. text ed. 6.95 (ISBN 0-87581-232-5). Peacock Pubs.

Chafetz, Morris E. The Alcoholic Patient: Diagnosis & Management. 300p. 1983. 22.50 (ISBN 0-87489-276-7). Med Economics.

Chaffee, Allen, ed. see Baum, L. Frank.

Chaffee, John. Designing & Making Fine Furniture. (Illus.). 192p. 1978. 14.95 o.s.i. (ISBN 0-89104-096-X, A & W Visual Library); pap. 7.95 o.s.i. (ISBN 0-89104-095-1, A & W Visual Library). A & W Pubs.

Chaffee, Margaret, jt. auth. see Bunker, Andrew F.

Chaffee, S. & Petrick, M. Using the Mass Media: Communication Problems in American Society. 1975. 18.95 (ISBN 0-07-010375-5, C). McGraw.

Chaffee, Suzy & Adler, Bill. The I Love New York Fitness Book. (Illus.). 224p. 1983. 17.95 (ISBN 0-688-02040-2). Morrow.

Chaffin, Charles, jt. auth. see Neufeld, Herm.

Chaffin, Lillie, jt. auth. see Butwin, Miriam.

Chaffin, Roger J. Microwave Semiconductor Devices: Fundamentals & Radiation Effects. LC 73-7581. 416p. 1973. 41.50 o.p. (ISBN 0-471-14311-1, Pub. by Wiley-Interscience). Wiley.

Chafin, Kenneth L. & Ogilvie, Lloyd J. The Communicator's Commentary: Corinthians 1, 2, Vol. 7. 1983. 14.95 (ISBN 0-8499-0347-5). Word Bks.

Chagall, David. The Spieler for the Holy Spirit. Young, Billie, ed. LC 72-79505. 1973. 7.95 o.p. (ISBN 0-87949-003-9). Ashley Bks.

Chahine, Robert A., ed. Coronary Artery Spasm. (Illus.). 300p. 1983. monograph 34.50 (ISBN 0-87993-192-2). Futura Pub.

Chai, Chu & Chai, Winberg. The Story of Chinese Philosophy. LC 75-17196. (Illus.). 252p. 1975. Repr. of 1961 ed. lib. bdg. 18.25x (ISBN 0-8371-8289-1, CHSC). Greenwood.

Chai, Henry, jt. auth. see Chai, Winchung.

Chai, Winberg, jt. auth. see Chai, Chu.

Chai, Winberg, ed. Essential Works of Chinese Communism. LC 75-99755. 1970. Repr. of 1969 ed. 8.50x o.p. (ISBN 0-87663-703-9, Pica Pr). Universe.

--The Search for a New China: A Capsule History, Ideology, Leadership of the Chinese Communist Party, 1921-1974. LC 74-79642. 316p. 1975. 8.95 o.p. (ISBN 0-399-11305-3). Putnam Pub Group.

Chai, Winchung & Chai, Henry. Progamming Standard COBOL. 1976. 13.75 (ISBN 0-12-166550-X). Acad Pr.

Chaika, Elaine. Language: The Social Mirror. 276p. 1982. pap. 12.95 (ISBN 0-88377-203-5). Newbury Hse.

Chaikin, Alan L. & Derlega, Valerian J. Sharing Intimacy: What We Reveal to Others & Why. 1975. 10.95 o.p. (ISBN 0-13-807867-X, Spec); pap. 3.45 o.p. (ISBN 0-13-807859-9). P-H.

Chaikin, Milton. Right Words in Right Places: A Workbook in Diction & Sentence Style. 1979. pap. text ed. 8.95 (ISBN 0-8403-2080-9). Kendall-Hunt.

Chaikin, Miriam. How Yossi Beat the Evil Urge. LC 82-47705. (A Charlotte Zolotow Bk.). (Illus.). 64p. (gr. 3-5). 1983. 8.61i (ISBN 0-06-021184-9, HarpJ); PLB 8.89g (ISBN 0-06-021185-7). Har-Row.

--I Should Worry, I Should Care. LC 78-19480. (Illus.). (gr. 3-6). 1979. 9.57i o.p. (ISBN 0-06-021174-1, HarpJ); PLB 9.89 (ISBN 0-06-021175-X). Har-Row.

--Light Another Candle: The Story & Meaning of Hanukkah. LC 80-28137. (Illus.). 80p. (gr. 3-6). 1981. 9.95 (ISBN 0-395-31026-1, Clarion); pap. 3.95 (ISBN 0-89919-057-X). HM.

--Make Noise, Make Merry: The Story & Meaning of Purim. (Illus.). 96p. (gr. 3-6). 1983. 11.50 (ISBN 0-89919-140-1, Clarion). HM.

--The Seventh Day: The Story of the Jewish Sabbath. LC 78-22789. (Illus.). (gr. 4-6). 1980. 6.95a o.p. (ISBN 0-385-14919-0); PLB (ISBN 0-385-14920-4). Doubleday.

Chaikin, Miriam & Frampton, David. The Seventh Day: The Story of the Jewish Sabbath. LC 82-16987. (Illus.). 48p. (Orig.). 1983. pap. 4.95 (ISBN 0-8052-0743-0). Schocken.

Chaiklin, J. B. & Ventry, I. M. Hearing Measurement: A Book of Readings. 2nd ed. 1982. text ed. 24.95 (ISBN 0-201-01240-5). A-W.

Chailley, Jacques. Forty Thousand Years of Music: Man in Search of Music. Myers, Rollo, tr. from Fr. LC 74-31227. (Music Reprint Ser). (Illus.). xiv, 229p. 1975. Repr. of 1964 ed. lib. bdg. 27.50 (ISBN 0-306-70661-X). Da Capo.

Chaillu, Paul B. Du see Du Chaillu, Paul.

Chaillu, Paul Du see Du Chaillu, Paul.

Chain, Steve, jt. auth. see Boas, Max.

Chaitanya, Krishna. A History of Indian Painting - Vol 2: Manuscript, Moghul & Deccani Traditions. (Illus.). 92p. 1979. text ed. 36.00x (ISBN 0-391-02591-0, Pub. by Abhinav India). Humanities.

--A History of Indian Painting: The Rajasthani Traditions, Vol. 3. 134p. 1982. text ed. 50.00x (ISBN 0-391-02413-2, Pub. by Abhinav India). Humanities.

Chaitkin, William, jt. auth. see Jencks, Charles.

Chaitow, Leon. An End to Cancer. 1978. 5.95x (ISBN 0-7225-0473-X). Cancer Control Soc.

Chajes, Alexander. Principles of Structural Stability Theory. (Civil Engineering & Engineering Mechanics Ser.). (Illus.). 288p. 1974. 34.95 (ISBN 0-13-709964-9). P-H.

Chakela, Q. K. Soil Erosion & Reservoir Sedimentation in Lesotho. 1981. text ed. 29.50x (ISBN 0-686-92528-9, Africana). Holmes & Meier.

Chaki-Sircar, Manjusri. Women of the Manipur Valley: Lai Harouba Ritual. 1982. text ed. write for info. (Pub. By Vikas India). Advent NY.

Chakrabart, C. L., ed. Progress in Analytical Atomic Spectroscopy, Vol. 1, Pt. 1. 1978. 36.00 (ISBN 0-08-022924-7). Pergamon.

Chakrabarti, Kisor K. The Logic of Gotama. LC 77-13853. (Society for Asian & Comparative Philosophy Monograph: No. 5). 1978. pap. text ed. 5.00x (ISBN 0-8248-0601-8). UH Pr.

Chakrabarty, A. M., ed. Biodegradation & Detoxification of Environmental Pollutants. 176p. 1982. 48.50 (ISBN 0-8493-5524-9). CRC Pr.

Chakraborty, R., jt. ed. see Schull, W. J.

Chakrapani, Chuck. Financial Freedom on Five Dollars a Day. (Orig.). 1983. pap. write for info. (ISBN 0-88908-564-1). Self Counsel Pr.

--The Money Spinner: A Super Easy System for Making Money. 2nd ed. (Illus.). 113p. 1981. pap. 14.95 (ISBN 0-88908-081-X). Self Counsel Pr.

Chakravarthy, Balaji S. Managing Coal: A Challenge in Adaption. LC 80-24891. 220p. 1981. 44.50x (ISBN 0-87395-467-X); pap. 19.95x (ISBN 0-87395-468-8). State U NY Pr.

Chakravarti, D., jt. ed. see Agrawal, D.

Chakravarti, M. C. Mathematics of Design & Analysis of Experiments. 1971. pap. 4.95x (ISBN 0-210-33899-7). Asia.

Chakravarty, A. S. Introduction to the Magnetic Properties of Solids. LC 80-12793. 696p. 1980. 79.95 (ISBN 0-471-07737-2, Pub. by Wiley-Interscience). Wiley.

Chakravarty, Amiya, ed. see Tagore, Rabindranath.

Chakravarty, Sukhamoy. Alternative Approaches to a Theory of Economic Growth: Marx, Marshall & Schumpeter. (R. C, Dutt Lectures on Political Economy Ser.: 1980). 1982. pap. text ed. 4.95x (ISBN 0-86131-355-0, Pub. by Orient Longman Ltd India). Apt Bks.

--Capital & Development Planning. 1969. 20.00x (ISBN 0-262-03027-6). MIT Pr.

Chakravorty, Basuda. Jyotindra Nath Mukherjee: The Humanist Revolutionary. 1982. 8.00 (ISBN 0-8364-0919-1, Pub. by Minerva India). South Asia Bks.

Chalazonitis, N. & Boisson, M., eds. Abnormal Neuronal Discharges. LC 76-58750. 447p. 1978. 42.00 (ISBN 0-89004-238-1). Raven.

Chalfant, H. Paul, compiled by. Social & Behavioral Aspects of Female Alcoholism: An Annotated Bibliography. LC 80-1021. xvi, 145p. 1980. lib. bdg. 27.50 (ISBN 0-313-20947-2, CAL/). Greenwood.

Chalfant, James M., ed. see Stanton, Robert B.

Chalfant, Paul. God in Seven Persons: Blessed Multiplicity. 1979. 12.50 o.p. (ISBN 0-533-03847-2). Vantage.

Chalfant, Stuart A. The Spokane Indians in Washington: Ethnohistorical Report on Land Use & Occupancy. 41.00 (ISBN 0-8287-1266-2). Clearwater Pub.

Chalfant, W. A. Gold, Guns & Ghost Towns. 12.95 (ISBN 0-912494-33-6); pap. 7.95. Chalfant Pr.

Chalfont, Alun. Montgomery of Alamein. LC 76-12519. 1976. 12.95 o.p. (ISBN 0-689-10744-7). Atheneum.

Chaliand, Gerard. Guerrilla Strategies: An Historical Anthology from the Long March to Afghanistan. LC 81-16347. 808p. 1982. 28.50 (ISBN 0-520-04444-4); pap. 7.95 (ISBN 0-520-04443-6). U of Cal Pr.

--Revolution in the Third World. 1978. pap. 4.95 (ISBN 0-14-004796-4). Penguin.

--The Struggle for Africa: Politics of the Great Powers. LC 82-5967. 1982. 18.50 (ISBN 0-312-76868-0). St Martin.

Chaliand, Gerard, ed. & intro. by. People Without a Country: The Kurds & Kurdistan. 292p. (Orig.). 1980. 33.00 (ISBN 0-905762-69-X, Pub. by Zed Pr England); pap. 8.50 (ISBN 0-905762-74-6, Pub. by Zed Pr England). Lawrence Hill.

Chalif, Don & Bender, Roger J. Military Pilot & Aircrew Badges of the World: 1870 to Present, Vol. 1. (Illus.). 224p. 1982. 24.95 (ISBN 0-912138-26-2). Bender Pub CA.

Chalk, John A., et al. The Devil, You Say? LC 74-6758. 160p. 1974. pap. 1.50 cancelled (ISBN 0-8344-0083-9). Sweet.

Chalk, L., jt. ed. see Metcalfe, C. R.

Chalk, William, jt. auth. see Levens, Alexander.

Chalker, Jack L. The Devil's Voyage. LC 79-7841. 336p. 1981. 11.95 o.p. (ISBN 0-385-15284-1). Doubleday.

--Medusa: A Tiger by the Tail. (The Four Lords of the Diamond Ser.: Bk. 4). 304p. (Orig.). 1983. pap. 2.95 (ISBN 0-345-29372-X, Del Rey). Ballantine.

Chall, J. S. Learning to Read: The Great Debate. updated ed. 448p. 1983. 18.95 (ISBN 0-07-010382-8, P&RB). McGraw.

--Stages of Reading Development. 293p. 1983. 18.95 (ISBN 0-07-010380-1, P&RB). McGraw.

Chall, Jeanne, jt. ed. see Carroll, John B.

Chall, Jeanne S. Learning to Read: The Great Debate. 1967. 19.95 (ISBN 0-07-010390-9, C); pap. 4.95 (ISBN 0-07-010391-7). McGraw.

Challand, Helen. Activities in the Earth Sciences. LC 82-9444. (Science Activities Ser.). (Illus.). (gr. 5 up). 1982. PLB 10.60g (ISBN 0-516-00506-5). Childrens.

--Activities in the Life Sciences. LC 82-9442. (Science Activities Ser.). (Illus.). (gr. 5 up). 1982. PLB 10.60g (ISBN 0-516-00507-3). Childrens.

--Earthquakes. LC 82-9699. (New True Bks.). (Illus.). (gr. k-4). 1982. PLB 9.25g (ISBN 0-516-01636-9). Childrens.

Challem, Jack J. Vitamin C Updated. Passwater, Richard A. & Mindell, Earl, eds. (Good Health Guide Ser.). 36p. 1983. pap. text ed. 1.45 (ISBN 0-87983-285-1). Keats.

Challener, Richard D., ed. The Legislative Origins of American Foreign Policy, 5 vols. Incl. Vol. 1. Proceedings, April 7, 1913 to March 7, 1923. 415p. lib. bdg. 40.00 (ISBN 0-8240-3030-3); Vol. 2. Proceedings, December 3, 1923 to March 3, 1933. 279p. lib. bdg. 28.00 (ISBN 0-8240-3031-1); Vol. 3. Legislative Origins of the Truman Doctrine, March to April, 1947. 235p. O.s.i. (ISBN 0-8240-3032-X); Vol. 4. Foreign Relief Aid, 1947. 401p. lib. bdg. 36.00 (ISBN 0-8240-3033-8); Vol. 5. Foreign Relief Assistance Act of 1948. 809p. lib. bdg. 65.00 (ISBN 0-8240-3034-6). (The Senate Foreign Relations Committee's Historical Ser.). 1979. Garland Pub.

Challenor, Bernard, et al. Physician's Assistant Examination Review Book. 1975. pap. 15.50 (ISBN 0-87488-422-5). Med Exam.

Challenor, J. Jeremiah. 1969. pap. 0.75 o.p. (ISBN 0-685-07646-6, 80126). Glencoe.

Challis, James & Elliman, David. Child Workers Today. 170p. 1981. 25.00x (ISBN 0-905898-06-0, Pub. by Quartermaine England). State Mutual Bk.

Challis, Mary. The Ghost of an Idea. (Raven House Mysteries Ser.). 224p. 1983. pap. cancelled (ISBN 0-373-63055-7, Pub. by Worldwide). Harlequin Bks.

Challoner, H. K. Wheel of Rebirth. 10.95 o.p. (ISBN 0-8356-5097-9). Theos Pub Hse.

Chalmers, A., ed. General Biographical Dictionary, 32 vols. rev ed. 1812-1817. Set. 1160.00 (ISBN 0-527-15900-X). Kraus Repr.

Chalmers, Amanda J., jt. auth. see McCormack, James E.

Chalmers, Bruce. Principles of Solidification. LC 76-18772. 336p. 1977. Repr. of 1964 ed. 20.50 (ISBN 0-88275-446-7). Krieger.

--The Structure & Properties of Solids: An Introduction to Materials Science. 155p. 1982. 21.95x (ISBN 0-471-26214-5, Pub. by Wiley Heyden). Wiley.

Chalmers, David M. The Muckrake Years. LC 79-22780. 176p. 1980. pap. 5.95 (ISBN 0-89874-066-5). Krieger.

Chalmers, Eric B. International Interest Rate War. LC 74-185905. 1972. 24.00 (ISBN 0-312-42280-6). St Martin.

Chalmers, George. An Introduction to the History of the Revolt of the American Colonies, 2 vols. LC 75-119049. (Era of the American Revolution Ser.). 1971. Repr. of 1845 ed. Set. lib. bdg. 85.00 (ISBN 0-306-71948-7). Da Capo.

Chalmers, Helena. Clothes, on & off the Stage: A History of Dress from the Earliest Times to the Present Day. LC 73-180965. (Illus.). xx, 292p. 1976. Repr. of 1928 ed. 40.00x (ISBN 0-8103-4033-X). Gale.

Chalmers, James A. & Leonard, Fred H. Economic Principles: Macroeconomic Theory & Policy. 1971. pap. text ed. 13.95x (ISBN 0-02-320670-5, 32067). Macmillan.

Chalmers, Mary. Merry Christmas, Harry. LC 76-58715. (Illus.). (ps-2). 7.64i o.p. (ISBN 0-06-021182-2, HarpJ); PLB 7.89 o.p. (ISBN 0-06-021183-0). Har-Row.

Chalmers, R. A. Microprocessors in Analytical Chemistry, Vol. 27, No. 7b. 64p. 1982. pap. 23.00 (ISBN 0-08-026284-8). Pergamon.

Chalmers, R. A. & Cresser, M. S. Quantative Chemical Analysis: A Laboratory Manual. 4th ed. (Analytical Chemistry Ser.). 420p. 1982. 79.95x (ISBN 0-470-27228-7). Halsted Pr.

Chalmers, R. A., ed. Gains & Losses: Errors in Trace Analysis. 90p. 1982. pap. 27.50 (ISBN 0-08-030239-4). Pergamon.

Chalmers, Robert K., jt. ed. see Banker, Gilbert S.

Chalofshy, N. & Lincoln, C. I. Up the HRD Ladder: A Guide to Professional Growth. 1983. text ed. 16.95 (ISBN 0-201-01240-5). A-W.

Chalon, Jack, jt. auth. see Turndorf, Herman.

Chaloner, W. H., jt. ed. see Redford, A.

Chalpin, Lila. William Sansom. (English Authors Ser.). 1980. lib. bdg. 12.95 (ISBN 0-8057-6781-9, Twayne). G K Hall.

Chamber, John. Small Boat & Dinghy Sailing. 11.50 (ISBN 0-392-09964-0, SpS). Sportshelf.

Chamberlain, Betty. The Artist's Guide to His Market. rev. & enl. ed. 1979. 16.95 o.p. (ISBN 0-8230-0327-2). Watson-Guptill.

--The Artist's Guide to the Art Market. 4th ed. 263p. 1983. 12.95 (ISBN 0-8230-0328-0). Watson-Guptill.

Chamberlain, Chriss & Chamberlain, Margaret. The Buttercup Buskers' Rainy Day. (Illus.). 24p. (ps-1). 1983. 8.95 (ISBN 0-434-93115-2, Pub. by Heinemann England). David & Charles.

Chamberlain, E. R. Florence in the Time of the Medici. Reeves, Marjorie, ed. (Then & There Ser.). (Illus.). 96p. (Orig.). (gr. 7-12). 1982. pap. 3.10 (ISBN 0-582-20489-5). Longman.

Chamberlain, G. V., jt. auth. see Hytten, F. E.

Chamberlain, J. Principles of Interferometric Spectroscopy. LC 78-13206. 340p. 1979. 81.95 (ISBN 0-471-99719-6). Wiley.

Chamberlain, John. The Enterprising Americans: A Business History of the United States. enl. ed. LC 73-4069. (Illus.). 304p. (YA) 1974. 16.30i (ISBN 0-06-010702-2, HarpT). Har-Row.

--Ibsen: The Open Vision. 208p. 1982. text ed. 31.50x (ISBN 0-485-11227-2, Athlone Pr). Humanities.

--A Life with the Printed Word. LC 81-85567. 204p. 1982. 14.95 (ISBN 0-89526-656-3). Regnery-Gateway.

Chamberlain, Joseph, ed. Chemistry & Physics of the Stratosphere. 1976. pap. 3.00 (ISBN 0-87590-221-9). Am Geophysical.

--Reviews of Lunar Sciences. 1977. pap. 5.00 (ISBN 0-87590-220-0). Am Geophysical.

Chamberlain, Joshua L. Passing of the Armies. 1974. 25.00 (ISBN 0-89029-021-0). Pr of Morningside.

Chamberlain, Joy. Michelle Mustn't Know. 272p. 1983. pap. 2.95 (ISBN 0-515-05699-5). Jove Pubns.

Chamberlain, Lesley. The Food & Cooking of Russia. 250p. 1982. 39.00x o.p. (ISBN 0-7139-1468-8, Pub. by Penguin Bks). State Mutual Bk.

Chamberlain, M. E. The Scramble for Africa. LC 74-177119. (Seminar Studies in History). 1974. pap. text ed. 5.95x (ISBN 0-582-35204-5). Longman.

Chamberlain, Margaret, jt. auth. see Chamberlain, Chriss.

Chamberlain, Mary. Old Wives Tales: Their History, Remedies, & Spells. 236p. 1983. pap. 7.95 (ISBN 0-86068-016-9, Virago Pr). Merrimack Bk Serv.

Chamberlain, Neil, et al. The Labor Sector. 3rd rev. ed. (Illus.). 1979. text ed. 23.95 (ISBN 0-07-010435-2). McGraw.

Chamberlain, Neil W. & Cullen, D. E. The Labor Sector. 2nd ed. Orig. Title: The Firm: Microeconomic Planning & Action. 1972. 23.95 (ISBN 0-07-010428-X, C). McGraw.

Chamberlain, Neil W. & Kuhn, J. W. Collective Bargaining. 2nd ed. 1965. 26.95 (ISBN 0-07-010437-9, C). McGraw.

Chamberlain, Neil W. & Schilling, Jane M. Impact of Strikes: Their Social & Economic Costs. LC 73-11841. 257p. 1973. Repr. of 1954 ed. lib. bdg. 20.50x (ISBN 0-8371-7066-4, CHIS). Greenwood.

Chamberlain, Peter & Ellis, Chris. Pictorial History of Tanks of the World, 1915-1945. (Illus.). 1981. 24.95 (ISBN 0-686-96628-7, Arms & Armour Pr). Stackpole.

Chamberlain, Peter & Gander, Terry. Anti-Aircraft Guns. LC 75-10159. (World War II Fact Files Ser.). (Illus.). 1975. pap. 3.95 o.p. (ISBN 0-668-03818-7). Arco.

--Self-Propelled Anti-Tank & Anti-Aircraft Guns. LC 75-10162. (World War 2 Fact Files Ser.). (Illus.). 64p. 1975. pap. 3.95 o.p. (ISBN 0-668-03897-7). Arco.

Chamberlain, Robert L. George Crabbe. (English Authors Ser.: No. 18). 12.95 o.p. (ISBN 0-8057-1132-5, Twayne). G K Hall.

Chamberlain, Russell. Rome. (The Great Cities Ser.). (Illus.). (gr. 6 up). 1976. PLB 12.00 (ISBN 0-8094-2259-X, Pub by Time-Life). Silver.

Chamberlain, V. Teen Guide to Homemaking. 5th ed. 1982. 19.92 (ISBN 0-07-007843-2). McGraw.

Chamberlain, Valerie & Kelly, Joan. Creative Home Economics Instruction. 2nd ed. O'Neill, Martha, ed. (Illus.). 256p. 1980. pap. text ed. 14.16 (ISBN 0-07-010424-7, W). McGraw.

Chamberlain, Valerie, jt. auth. see Kelly, Joan.

Chamberlain, Valerie M. & Kelly, Joan. Creative Home Economics Instruction. (Illus.). 272p. 1974. pap. text ed. 14.56 (ISBN 0-07-010423-9, W). McGraw.

Chamberlain, Von Del see Von Del Chamberlain.

Chamberlain, William H. The Russian Revolution, 2 vols. Incl. Vol. 1. 1917-1918 (ISBN 0-448-00188-8); Vol. 2. 1918-1921 (ISBN 0-448-00189-6). 1965. 4.95 ea. o.p. (ISBN 0-685-23233-6, G&D). Putnam Pub Group.

Chamberlin, Brewster, jt. ed. see Foner, Philip S.

Chamberlin, D. G., jt. auth. see Chamberlin, G. J.

Chamberlin, E. R. Preserving the Past. (Illus.). 205p. 1979. 17.50x o.p. (ISBN 0-460-04364-1, Pub. by J. M. Dent England). Biblio Dist.

Chamberlin, G. J. & Chamberlin, D. G. Color: Its Measurement, Computation, & Application. 144p. 1980. 28.95 (ISBN 0-471-25625-0, Pub. by Wiley Heyden). Wiley.

Chamberlin, G. J., jt. auth. see Thomas, L. C.

Chamberlin, J. Gordon. The Educating Act: A Phenomenological View. LC 80-6076. 202p. 1981. lib. bdg. 20.00 (ISBN 0-8191-1449-9); pap. text ed. 9.50 (ISBN 0-8191-1450-2). U Pr of Amer.

Chamberlin, Jane, illus. Saloons of San Francisco: Great & Notorious. (Illus.). 128p. (Orig.). 1982. pap. 8.95 (ISBN 0-88496-186-9). Capra Pr.

Chamberlin, Michael J., ed. see Rodriguez, Raymond L.

Chamberlin, Ralph V. Ethno-Botany of the Gosiute Indians of Utah. LC 14-11549. 1911. pap. 12.00 (ISBN 0-527-00510-X). Kraus Repr.

Chamberlin, Robert, jt. auth. see Hymovich, Debra P.

Chamberlin, Susan. Hedges, Screens & Espaliers: How to Select, Grow & Enjoy. 176p. 1982. pap. 9.95 (ISBN 0-89586-190-9). H P Bks.

Chamberlin, Susan & Pollock, Susan. Fences, Gates & Walls. 1983. pap. 9.95 (ISBN 0-89586-189-5). H P Bks.

Chamberlin, T. L. Selling & Today's Consumer: Buying? Selling? Then Do It Right! 1978. 10.00 (ISBN 0-682-49127-6, Dist. by Exposition). Life Pubns IL.

Chamberlin, Vernon A. & Schulman, Ivan A. La Rivista Ilustrada de Nueva York: History, Anthology, & Index of Literary Selections. LC 75-35891. 212p. 1976. 18.00x (ISBN 0-8262-0189-X). U of Mo Pr.

Chamberlin, Waldo, jt. auth. see Hovet, Thomas.

Chamberlin, Willard J. Entomological Nomenclature & Literature. 3rd rev. & enl. ed. LC 79-108387. vii, 141p. Repr. of 1952 ed. lib. bdg. 18.50x (ISBN 0-8371-3810-8, CHNO). Greenwood.

Chambers, A. B., et al see Dryden, John.

Chambers, Aidan. Breaktime. LC 78-19472. (gr. 7 up). 1979. 8.61i (ISBN 0-06-021256-X, HarpJ); PLB 8.89 o.p. (ISBN 0-06-021257-8). Har-Row.

--Dance on My Grave. LC 82-48258. (Charlotte Zolotow Bk.). 256p. (YA) (gr. 7 up). 1983. 12.45i (ISBN 0-06-021253-5, HarpJ); PLB 12.89g (ISBN 0-06-021254-3). Har-Row.

--Introducing Books to Children. 1973. pap. 7.50 o.p. (ISBN 0-435-80261-5). Horn Bk.

--Introducing Books to Children. 2nd ed. 224p. 1983. 22.00 (ISBN 0-87675-284-9); pap. 14.00 (ISBN 0-87675-285-7). Horn Bk.

Chambers, C. & Holliday, A. K. Intermediate Chemistry: Inorganic Chemistry. new ed. 420p. 1982. text ed. 12.95 (ISBN 0-408-10822-3). Butterworth.

--Modern Inorganic Chemistry: An Intermediate Text. 455p. 1975. 13.95 o.p. (ISBN 0-408-70663-5). Butterworth.

Chambers, Catherine, ed. see Coleman, Kenneth.

Chambers, E. J. Light & Photography for Young Experimenters. (Illus.). (gr. 9 up). 1970. pap. 10.75x (ISBN 0-7135-1531-7, LTB). Sportshelf.

Chambers, Edmund K., ed. Oxford Book of Sixteenth Century Verse. 1932. 39.95x (ISBN 0-19-812126-1). Oxford U Pr.

Chambers, Edward J., et al. National Income Analysis & Forecasting. 1975. text ed. 18.95x (ISBN 0-673-05134-X). Scott F.

Chambers, Frank. Prosateurs Francais XVIE Siecle. 1976. pap. 15.95 (ISBN 0-669-00016-7). Heath.

Chambers, Frederick, compiled by. Black Higher Education in the United States: A Selected Bibliography on Negro Higher Education & Historically Black Colleges & Universities. LC 77-91100. 1978. lib. bdg. 29.95 (ISBN 0-313-20037-8, CBH/). Greenwood.

Chambers, George. Chambersburg. (Chapbk. Ser). 1979. pap. 3.00 (ISBN 0-686-61865-3). Juniper Pr WI.

Chambers, H. & Chacey, C. Drafting & Manual Programming for Numerical Control. 1980. 31.95 (ISBN 0-13-219113-X). P-H.

Chambers, Henry A., ed. Treasury of Negro Spirituals. LC 63-14218. (Illus.). 126p. (gr. 7 up). 1983. 12.95 o.s.i. (ISBN 0-87523-145-4). Emerson.

Chambers, J. D. & Mingay, G. E. The Agricultural Revolution. 1975. pap. 14.95 (ISBN 0-7134-1358-1, Pub. by Batsford England). David & Charles.

Chambers, J. K. & Trudgill, P. Dialectology. LC 79-41604. (Cambridge Textbooks in Linguistics). (Illus.). 210p. 1980. 37.50 (ISBN 0-521-22401-2); pap. 12.95 (ISBN 0-521-29473-8). Cambridge U Pr.

Chambers, James. The Devil's Horsemen. LC 78-22055. 1979. 11.95 o.p. (ISBN 0-689-10942-3). Atheneum.

--The Norman Kings. (Kings & Queens of England Ser.). (Illus.). 224p. 1981. text ed. 17.50x (ISBN 0-297-77964-8, Pub. by Weidenfeld & Nicolson England). Biblio Dist.

Chambers, Janice E. & Yarbrough, James D., eds. Effects of Chronic Exposures to Pesticides on Animal Systems. 205p. 1982. text ed. 55.00 (ISBN 0-89004-756-1). Raven.

Chambers, Jay G. & Hartman, William T., eds. Special Education Policies: Their History, Implementation & Finance. LC 82-10515. 301p. 1982. text ed. 29.95 (ISBN 0-87722-280-0). Temple U Pr.

Chambers, John C., et al. An Executive's Guide to Forecasting. LC 74-2433. (Managers Guide Ser.). 320p. 1974. 36.95 (ISBN 0-471-14335-9, Pub. by Wiley-Interscience). Wiley.

--An Executive's Guide to Forecasting. 320p. 1983. Repr. of 1974 ed. text ed. price not set (ISBN 0-89874-585-3). Krieger.

Chambers, John H. The Achievement of Education: An Examination of Key Concepts in Educational Practice. 192p. 1983. pap. text ed. 11.50 scp (ISBN 0-06-041237-2, HarpC). Har-Row.

Chambers, John M. Computational Methods for Data Analysis. LC 77-9493. (Wiley Ser. in Probability & Mathematical Statistics: Applied Section). 1977. 32.95 (ISBN 0-471-02772-3, Pub. by Wiley-Interscience). Wiley.

Chambers, Lisa. Real Women Never Pump Iron. (Illus.). 96p. 1982. pap. 3.95 (ISBN 0-943392-10-1). Tribeca Comm.

Chambers, Mary D., jt. auth. see Esenwein, J. Berg.

Chambers, Oswald. Daily Thought for Disciples. 256p. 1983. pap. 5.95 (ISBN 0-310-22401-2). Zondervan.

--Still Higher for His Highest. LC 75-120048. 1970. Repr. of 1970 ed. 7.95 (ISBN 0-310-22410-1); large print kivar 5.95 (ISBN 0-310-22417-9). Zondervan.

Chambers, R. J. Accounting is Disarray: A Case for the Reform of Company Accounts. LC 82-48354. (Accountancy in Transition Ser.). 258p. 1982. lib. bdg. 25.00 (ISBN 0-8240-5307-9). Garland pub.

Chambers, R. W., jt. ed. see Wyatt, Alfred J.

Chambers, Raymond J. Accounting, Evaluation & Economic Behavior. LC 66-13944. 1975. Repr. of 1966 ed. text ed. 15.00 (ISBN 0-914348-15-9). Scholars Bk.

Chambers, Raymond W. England Before the Norman Conquest. LC 75-109718. Repr. of 1926 ed. lib. bdg. 17.00x (ISBN 0-8371-4208-3, CHNC). Greenwood.

Chambers, Raymond W., ed. Beowulf: An Introduction. 1959. 59.95 (ISBN 0-521-04615-7). Cambridge U Pr.

Chambers, Richard D. Fluorine in Organic Chemistry. LC 73-7824. (Interscience Monographs on Organic Chemistry Ser). 416p. 1973. 34.50 o.p. (ISBN 0-471-14330-8, Pub. by Wiley-Interscience). Wiley.

Chambers, Richard L. & Kut, Gunay, eds. Contemporary Turkish Short Stories: An Intermediate Reader. LC 76-21045. (Middle Eastern Languages & Linguistics, 3). 1977. 12.50x (ISBN 0-88297-013-5). Bibliotheca.

Chambers, Robert. Cyclopedia of English Literature: A History, Critical & Biographical, of British Authors, from the Earliest to the Present Times, 3 vols. (Illus.). 1979. Repr. of 1938 ed. Set. 191.00x (ISBN 0-8103-4213-8). Gale.

--Popular Rhymes of Scotland. LC 68-58902. 1969. Repr. of 1870 ed. 27.00x (ISBN 0-8103-3828-9). Gale.

--Rural Poverty Unperceived: Problems & Remedies. (Working Paper: No. 400). 51p. 1980. 3.00 (ISBN 0-686-36076-1, WP-0400). World Bank.

Chambers, Robert, ed. Book of Days: A Miscellany of Popular Antiquities in Connection with the Calendar, Including Anecdote, Biography & History, Curiosities of Literature, & Oddities of Human Life & Character, 2 Vols. LC 67-13009. (Illus.). 1967. Repr. of 1862 ed. 99.00x (ISBN 0-8103-3002-4). Gale.

Chambers, Ross, ed. see Felman, Shoshana, et al.

Chambers, S. Allen, ed. Discovering Historic America: Vol. I, New England. (Illus.). 320p. 1982. pap. 8.95 (ISBN 0-525-93244-5, 0869-260). Dutton.

--Discovering Historic America: Vol. II, California & the West. (Illus.). 320p. 1982. pap. 8.95 (ISBN 0-525-93246-1, 0869-290). Dutton.

--Discovering Historic America: Vol. III: The Mid-Atlantic States. (Illus.). 288p. 1983. pap. 8.95 (ISBN 0-525-93261-5, 0869-260). Dutton.

--Discovering Historic America: Vol. IV: The Southeast. (Illus.). 288p. 1983. pap. 8.95 (ISBN 0-525-93260-7, 0869-260). Dutton.

Chambers, W. N. & Burnham, Walter D., eds. The American Party Systems. rev. 2nd ed. (Illus.). 1975. pap. 8.95x (ISBN 0-19-501917-2). Oxford U Pr.

Chambers, Wicke, jt. auth. see Asher, Spring.

Chambers, Wicke & Asher, Spring, eds. The Celebration Book of Great American Traditions. LC 82-48113. (Illus.). 192p. 1983. 15.50 (ISBN 0-06-015095-5, HarpT). Har-Row.

Chamblain De Marivaux, Pierre C. De see De Chamblain De Marivaux, Pierre C.

Chamblee, Ronald F. & Evans, Marchsll C. Transax: The NCHS System for Producing Multiple Cause-of-Death Statistics, 1968-78. Madison, Eddie, ed. 55p. 1982. pap. text ed. 1.75 (ISBN 0-8406-0269-3). Natl Ctr Health Stats.

Chambless, Dianne L. & Goldstein, Alan J. Agoraphobia: Multiple Perspectives on Theory & Treatment. LC 82-7087. (Personality Processes Ser.). 227p. 1982. 26.95 (ISBN 0-471-07947-2, Pub. by Wiley-Interscience). Wiley.

Chambliss, William & Seidman, Robert. Law, Order & Power. 2nd ed. (Sociology Ser.). (Illus.). 384p. 1982. text ed. 19.95 (ISBN 0-201-10126-2). A-W.

Chambliss, William J. Crime & the Legal Process. (Sociology Ser.). 1968. text ed. 11.50 o.p. (ISBN 0-07-010460-3, C); pap. text ed. 20.95 (ISBN 0-07-010461-1). McGraw.

--Criminal Law in Action. LC 74-32149. 477p. 1975. text ed. 22.95 (ISBN 0-471-14474-6). Wiley.

--On the Take: From Petty Crooks to Presidents. LC 77-15213. (Midland Bks.: Bk. 298). 288p. 1982. pap. 7.95x (ISBN 0-253-20298-1); 22.50x (ISBN 0-253-34244-9). Ind U Pr.

Chambliss, William J. & Mankoff, Milton. Whose Law? What Order? A Conflict Approach to Criminology. LC 75-23220. 256p. 1976. pap. text ed. 16.95 (ISBN 0-471-14476-2). Wiley.

Chambliss, William J. & Ryther, Thomas E. Sociology: The Discipline & Its Direction. (Illus.). 480p. 1975. text ed. 22.95 (ISBN 0-07-010465-4, C); pap. text ed. 18.50 (ISBN 0-07-010466-2); instructor's manual 15.00 (ISBN 0-07-054368-2). McGraw.

Chamborant, C. G. De. Du Pauperisme, Ce Qu'Il Etait dans L'antiquite et Ce Qu'Il Est de Nos Jours. (Conditions of the 19th Century French Working Class Ser.). 496p. (Fr.). 1974. Repr. of 1842 ed. lib. bdg. 127.00 o.p. (ISBN 0-8287-0177-6, 1097). Clearwater Pub.

Chamelin, Neil C. & Truzzi, Marcello, eds. Criminal Law for Police Officers. 3rd ed. (Criminal Justice Ser.). 352p. 1981. text ed. 20.95 (ISBN 0-13-193821-5). P-H.

Chamelin, Neil C., et al. Introduction to Criminal Justice. 2nd ed. (Criminal Justice Ser.). (Illus.). 1979. ref. 22.95 (ISBN 0-13-480145-8). P-H.

Chamie, Joseph. Religion & Fertility: Arab Christian-Muslim Differentials. LC 80-19787. (ASA Rose Monograph Ser.). (Illus.). 176p. 1981. 24.95 (ISBN 0-521-23677-0); pap. 7.95 (ISBN 0-521-28147-4). Cambridge U Pr.

Chaminade, Cecile. Three Piano Works. Incl. Sonata in C Minor, Opus 21; Etude Symphonique, Opus 28; Six Concert Etudes, Opus 35. (Women Composers Ser.: No. 2). 1979. Repr. of 1895 ed. 19.95 (ISBN 0-306-79551-5). Da Capo.

Chamling, Dhiraj R. India & the United Nations. 1979. text ed. 17.50x (ISBN 0-210-40617-8). Asia.

Chammari, Abderraouf, jt. auth. see Beenhakker, Henri L.

Chamness, Danford. The Hollywood Guide to Film Budgeting & Script Breakdown. 2nd ed. Brooks, Susan, ed. 224p. 1981. Repr. of 1977 ed. 20.00x (ISBN 0-941806-02-2). S J Brooks.

Chamot, E. M. & Mason, C. W. Handbook of Chemical Microscopy: Chemical Methods & Inorganic Qualitative Analysis, Vol. 2. 2nd ed. 438p. 1940. 54.50 (ISBN 0-471-04122-X). Wiley.

Chamot, Emile M. & Mason, C. W. Handbook of Chemical Microscopy: Principles & Use of Microscopes & Accessories; Physical Methods for the Study of Chemical Problems, Vol. 1. 3rd ed. LC 58-12706. 52.50 (ISBN 0-471-14355-3, Pub. by Wiley-Interscience). Wiley.

Champ, Michael A. & Park, P. K. Global Marine Pollution Bibliography: For Ocean Dumping of Municipal & Industrial Wastes. 424p. 1982. 69.50x (ISBN 0-306-65205-6, Plenum Pr). Plenum Pub.

Champagne, Anthony & Dawes, Rosemary N. Courts & Modern Medicine. 320p. 1983. text ed. price not set (ISBN 0-398-04834-7). C C Thomas.

Champagne, Audrey B. & Klopfer, Leo E. Cumulative Index to Science Education, Vols. 1-60: 1916-1976. LC 20-5630. 202p. 1978. Set. pap. 21.95 (ISBN 0-471-04837-2, Pub. by Wiley-Interscience). Wiley.

Champagne, Lenora, ed. CCLM Catalog of Literary Magazines: 1983. Rev. ed. 64p. 1983. pap. 5.00x (ISBN 0-942332-02-4). Coord Coun Lit Mags.

Champagne, Roland A. Literary History in the Wake of Roland Barthes: Re-Defining the Myths of Reading. 15.00 (ISBN 0-917786-36-X). French Lit.

Champakalakshmi, A. Vaisnava Iconography in the Tamil Country. 135p. 1981. text ed. 50.00 (ISBN 0-86131-216-3, Pub. by Orient Longman Ltd India). Apt Bks.

Champie, Channing K. Worlds on Fire. 1979. 7.95 o.p. (ISBN 0-533-04082-5). Vantage.

Champigny, Robert. Sartre & Drama. 17.00 (ISBN 0-917786-31-9). French Lit.

Champine, G. Distributed Computer Systems: Impact on Management Design & Analysis. 1980. 44.75 (ISBN 0-444-86109-2). Elsevier.

Champion, Bob & Powell, Jonathan. Champion's Story: A Great Human Triumph. (Illus.). 240p. 1982. 13.95 (ISBN 0-698-11162-1, Coward). Putnam Pub Group.

Champion, Dean. Basic Statistics for Social Research. 2nd ed. 1981. text ed. 24.95x (ISBN 0-02-320600-4). Macmillan.

Champion, Dean J. The Sociology of Organizations. LC 74-12245. (Illus.). 450p. 1975. 28.00 (ISBN 0-07-010492-1, C). McGraw.

Champion, Dean J., jt. auth. see Black, James A.

Champion, Larry S. Evolution of Shakespeare's Comedy: A Study in Dramatic Perspective. LC 73-105370. 1970. 10.00x o.p. (ISBN 0-674-27140-8); pap. 4.95x o.p. (ISBN 0-674-27141-6). Harvard U Pr.

--Tragic Patterns in Jacobean & Caroline Drama. LC 77-8159. 1977. 17.00x (ISBN 0-87049-217-9). U of Tenn Pr.

Champion, Nigel, jt. auth. see Elliott, Bruce.

Champion, R. A. Learning & Activiation. LC 70-75658. (Basic Topics in Psychology Ser). 1969. pap. 8.50x o.p. (ISBN 0-471-14395-2, Pub. by Wiley-Interscience). Wiley.

Champion, Robert H., jt. auth. see Warin, Robert P.

Champion, Sara. Dictionary of Terms & Techniques in Archaeology. (Illus.). 144p. 1982. pap. 7.95 (ISBN 0-89696-162-1, An Everest House Book). Dodd.

Champion, Vici. Yet Forty Days. 1982. 6.95 (ISBN 0-533-05443-5). Vantage.

Champlin, Charles. The Movies Grow Up, Nineteen Forty to Nineteen Eighty. rev. ed. LC 82-75117. Orig. Title: The Flicks; or Whatever Became of Andy Hardy? (Illus.). xii, 284p. 1981. 25.95 (ISBN 0-8040-0363-7); pap. 12.95 (ISBN 0-8040-0364-5). Swallow.

Champlin, Connie. Puppetry & Creative Dramatics in Storytelling. Schwalb, Ann W., ed. (Illus.). 130p. (Orig.). 1980. pap. 9.95 (ISBN 0-931044-03-0). Renfro Studios.

Champlin, Joseph M. Messengers of God's Word: A Handbook for Lectors. 1983. pap. 3.95 (ISBN 0-8091-2484-X). Paulist Pr.

--Sharing Treasure, Time, & Talent: A Parish Manual for Sacrificial Giving or Tithing. LC 82-16178. 88p. (Orig.). 1982. pap. 4.95 (ISBN 0-8146-1277-6). Liturgical Pr.

--Together by Your Side: A Book for Comforting the Sick & Dying. LC 79-51016. 80p. 1979. pap. 1.95 (ISBN 0-87793-180-1). Ave Maria.

Champlin, Joseph M. & Haggerty, Brian A. Together in Peace for Children. LC 76-26348. (Illus.). 72p. (gr. 2-7). 1976. 1.50 (ISBN 0-87793-119-4). Ave Maria.

Champlin, Richard L. Trees of Newport: On the Estates of the Preservation Society of Newport County. (Illus.). 94p. 1976. pap. 4.00 (ISBN 0-917012-24-0). Preserv Soc Newport.

Champoux, Joseph E., jt. auth. see Caplan, Edwin H.

Champsaur, Paul & Milleron, Jean-Claude. Advanced Exercises in Microeconomics. Bonin, John P. & Bonin, Helene, trs. from Fr. (Illus.). 272p. 1983. text ed. 27.50x (ISBN 0-674-00525-2). Harvard U Pr.

Chan, E. C. S., jt. auth. see Pelczar, Michael, Jr.

Chan, F. Gilbert, ed. China at the Crossroads: The Communists & the Nationalists, 1927 to 1949. (Westview Replica Edition Ser.). 268p. 1980. lib. bdg. 23.00 (ISBN 0-89158-913-9). Westview.

Chan, Hok-lam. Theories of Legitimacy in Imperial China: Discussions on "Legitimate Succession" under the Jurchen-Chin Dynasty (1115-1234) 1983. price not set. U of Wash Pr.

Chan, James L., jt. auth. see Drebin, Allan R.

Chan, Jeffery, et al, eds. Aiiieeeee! an Anthology of Asian-American Writers. LC 73-88968. 256p. 1974. 7.95 (ISBN 0-88258-008-6); pap. 8.95 (ISBN 0-88258-051-5). Howard U Pr.

Chan, Jeffery P., jt. ed. see Chin, Frank.

Chan, Jerome. A Journey with the Old Man. 1982. 5.95 (ISBN 0-533-05400-1). Vantage.

Chan, Lois M. Cataloging & Classification: An Introduction. (Library Education Ser.). (Illus.). 416p. 1980. text ed. 23.50 (ISBN 0-07-010498-0, C). McGraw.

--Immroth's Guide to the Library of Congress Classification. 3rd ed. LC 80-16981. (Library Science Text Ser.). 1980. lib. bdg. 33.00x (ISBN 0-87287-224-6); pap. text ed. 21.00x (ISBN 0-87287-235-1). Libs Unl.

--Library of Congress Subject Headings: Principles & Application. LC 78-9497. (Research Studies in Library Science: No. 15). 347p. 1978. lib. bdg. 30.00 (ISBN 0-87287-187-8). Libs Unl.

Chan, Marie. Kao Shih. (World Authors Ser.). 1978. lib. bdg. 15.95 (ISBN 0-8057-6317-1, Twayne). G K Hall.

Ch'an, Master Hua, commentary by see Liang, Ch'ing.

Chan, Wing T. & Alfaruqi, Ismael R. Great Asian Religions. 1969. pap. 14.95 (ISBN 0-02-320640-3, 32064). Macmillan.

Chan Wing-Tsit. Chinese Philosophy, Nineteen Forty-Nine to Nineteen Sixty-Three: An Annotated Bibliography of Mainland China Publications. 1966. pap. 9.00x (ISBN 0-8248-0057-5, Eastwest Ctr). UH Pr.

Chanan, G., jt. auth. see Ross, J. M.

Chanana, D. R., tr. see Bloch, J.

Chance, B., Jr., jt. auth. see McDonald, Eugene T.

Chance, Britton, ed. Energy-Linked Functions of Mitochondria. 1963. 37.50 (ISBN 0-12-167862-8). Acad Pr.

Chance, Britton, et al, eds. Electronic Time Measurements. (Illus.). 1966. pap. 4.50 o.p. (ISBN 0-486-61560-X). Dover.

--Probes of Structure & Function of Macromolecules & Membranes, 2 Vols. 1971. Vol. 1. 56.50 (ISBN 0-12-167801-6); Vol. 2. 56.50 (ISBN 0-12-167802-4); Set. 81.00 (ISBN 0-685-02417-2). Acad Pr.

Chance, John K., jt. auth. see Butterworth, Douglas.

Chancellor, John & Mears, Walter R. The News Business: Getting & Writing the News as Two Top Journalists Do It. LC 82-48126. 224p. 1983. 12.95 (ISBN 0-06-015104-8, HarpT). Har-Row.

Chancellor, Philip, tr. see Wu Wei-P'Ing.

Chand, Attar. Disarmament, Detente & World Peace: A Bibliography with Selected Abstracts, 1916-1981. 167p. 1982. 22.95x (ISBN 0-940500-49-3, Pub. by Sterling India). Asia Bk Corp.

--Tibet: Past & Present 1600-1981. 257p. 1982. text ed. 24.50 (ISBN 0-391-02695-X, Pub. by Sterling India). Humanities.

Chand, Bool. Our Earth & the Universe. 3.50x o.p. (ISBN 0-210-33909-8). Asia.

Chand, Meira. The Bonsai Tree. 204p. 1983. 12.95 (ISBN 0-89919-166-5). Ticknor & Fields.

Chandaman, C. D. English Public Revenue Sixteen Sixty to Sixteen Eighty-Eight. (Illus.). 1975. 65.00x o.p. (ISBN 0-19-828268-0). Oxford U Pr.

Chandebois, Rosine & Faber, J. Automation in Animal Development. (Monographs in Developmental Biology: Vol. 16). (Illus.). iv, 150p. 1983. 69.50 (ISBN 3-8055-3666-6). S Karger.

Chander, Jagdish & Pradhan, Narindar S., eds. Studies in American Literature: Essays in Honour of William Mulder. 1977. 9.50x o.p. (ISBN 0-19-560784-8). Oxford U Pr.

Chander, Krishan. The Dreamer & Other Stories. Ratan, Jai, tr. 160p. 1970. pap. 2.50 (ISBN 0-88253-025-9, 4027). Ind-US Inc.

--Mr. Ass Comes to Town. Bouman, Helen H., tr. 167p. 1968. pap. 1.95 (ISBN 0-88253-026-7). Ind-US Inc.

Chandlee, Edward E. Six Quaker Clockmakers. (Illus.). 260p. Repr. of 1943 ed. 12.95 (ISBN 0-686-81726-5). New Eng Pub.

Chandler. Tournament Chess, Vol. 1. Miles, A. J., ed. 128p. 1981. pap. 24.00 (ISBN 0-08-026888-9). Pergamon.

Chandler, A. B. The Broken Cycle. (Science Fiction Ser.). 1979. pap. 1.75 o.p. (ISBN 0-87997-496-6, UE1496). Daw Bks.

Chandler, A. Bertram. Beyond the Galactic Rim. (Rim Worlds Ser.). 144p. 1982. 12.95 (ISBN 0-8052-8122-3, Pub. by Allison & Busby England). Schocken.

--Bring Back Yesterday. (Rim World Ser.: Vol. 3). 153p. 1982. 12.95 (ISBN 0-8052-8103-7, Pub. by Allison & Busby England). Schocken.

Chandler, A. Bertram & Hoffman, Lee. Up to the Sky in Ships: In & Out of Quandry. Hitchcock, Charles J., ed. 172p. 1982. 13.00 (ISBN 0-915368-16-1). NESFA Pr.

Chandler, Alfred D., Jr. Strategy & Structure: Chapters in the History of the American Industrial Enterprise. 1962. pap. 6.95x (ISBN 0-262-53009-0). MIT Pr.

--The Visible Hand: The Managerial Revolution in American Business. 1977. 27.50x (ISBN 0-674-94051-2, Belknap Pr); pap. 9.95 (ISBN 0-674-94052-0). Harvard U Pr.

Chandler, B. & Magnus, W. History of Combinatorial Group Theory: A Case Study of the History of Ideas. (Studies in the History of Mathematics & Physical Sciences: Vol. 9). (Illus.). 234p. 1983. 46.00 (ISBN 0-387-90749-1). Springer-Verlag.

Chandler, B., jt. auth. see Baumsiag, C. B.

Chandler, Bertram A. Big Black Mark. (Science Fiction Ser). pap. 1.50 o.p. (ISBN 0-87997-726-4, UW1355). DAW Bks.

Chandler, Betty. The Make-a-Pattern Coloring Book. (Orig.). 1977. pap. 1.95 o.s.i. (ISBN 0-8431-0235-7). Price Stern.

--Quilting Coloring Book. 1976. pap. 1.95 o.s.i. (ISBN 0-8431-0228-4). Price Stern.

Chandler, Bryn. The Coral Kill. (Orig.). 1978. pap. 1.75 o.p. (ISBN 0-451-08347-4, E8347, Sig). NAL.

--Making It. 1979. pap. 2.25 o.p. (ISBN 0-451-08756-9, E8756, Sig). NAL.

Chandler, D. S., jt. auth. see Burkholder, Mark A.

Chandler, Daniel R. The Rhetorical Tradition, Principles & Practice. 1978. pap. text ed. 9.25 (ISBN 0-8403-1934-7). Kendall-Hunt.

Chandler, David. The Campaigns of Napoleon: The Mind & Method of History's Greatest Soldier. 1182p. 1973. 45.00 (ISBN 0-02-523660-1). Macmillan.

Chandler, David & Kiernan, Ben, eds. Revolution & its Aftermath in Kampuchea. Date not set. pap. price not set. Yale U SE Asia.

Chandler, David P. A History of Cambodia. 225p. 1983. lib. bdg. 25.00x (ISBN 0-86531-578-7). Westview.

--The Land & People of Cambodia. LC 72-2270. (Portraits of the Nation Ser). (Illus.). 160p. (gr. 6 up). 1972. 10.53i (ISBN 0-397-31321-7, JBL-J). Har-Row.

Chandler, Edna W. Cowboy Andy. LC 59-4447. (Illus.). (gr. 1-2). 1959. 4.95 o.p. (ISBN 0-394-80008-7); PLB 5.99 (ISBN 0-394-90008-1). Beginner.

--Indian Paintbrush. LC 75-29160. 64p. (gr. 4-6). 1975. 6.50g o.p. (ISBN 0-8075-3639-3). A Whitman.

--Popcorn Patch. LC 77-79550. (Illus.). (gr. 4-6). 1969. 6.50g o.p. (ISBN 0-8075-6615-2). A Whitman.

Chandler, Evan. Dying Light. (Orig.). 1979. pap. 1.95 o.p. (ISBN 0-451-08465-9, J8465, Sig). NAL.

Chandler, George. International & National Library & Information Services: A Review of Recent Developments. (Recent Advances in Library & Information Services: Vol. 2). (Illus.). 230p. 1982. 20.00 (ISBN 0-08-025793-3). Pergamon.

Chandler, Harry E. How to Write What. 1978. 14.00 (ISBN 0-87170-001-8). ASM.

Chandler, John S., jt. auth. see Burton, Richard M.

Chandler, Keith. Kett's Rebellion & Other Poems. 64p. 1982. pap. text ed. 7.00x (ISBN 0-85635-277-2, 80112, Pub. by Carcanet New Pr England). Humanities.

Chandler, Lester. Inflation in the United States 1940-1948. (Fdr & the Era of the New Deal). 1976. Repr. of 1951 ed. lib. bdg. 39.50 (ISBN 0-306-70804-3). Da Capo.

Chandler, Linda S. Uncle Ike. LC 80-70520. (gr. 1-6). 1981. 5.95 (ISBN 0-8054-4264-2). Broadman.

Chandler, M. & Miles, A., eds. Tournament Chess. (Tournament Chess Ser.: Vol. 5). 176p. 1982. pap. 19.95 (ISBN 0-08-029720-X). Pergamon.

--Tournament Chess. 176p. 1982. pap. 19.95 (ISBN 0-08-029721-8). Pergamon.

--Tournament Chess, Vol. 4. 150p. 1982. 24.00 (ISBN 0-08-026893-5). Pergamon.

Chandler, Marsha A., jt. ed. see Atkinson, Michael M.

Chandler, R. Michael, jt. auth. see Stakes, Mary E.

Chandler, Ralph & Plano, Jack C. The Public Administration Dictionary. LC 81-12945. 406p. 1982. text ed. 21.95 (ISBN 0-471-09121-9); pap. text ed. 13.95 (ISBN 0-471-09119-7). Wiley.

Chandler, Raymond. The Big Sleep. 1976. pap. 1.95 o.p. (ISBN 0-394-72136-5, Vin). Random.

--The Lady in the Lake. LC 75-44962. (Crime Fiction Ser). 1976. Repr. of 1943 ed. lib. bdg. 17.50 o.s.i. (ISBN 0-8240-2358-7). Garland Pub.

--The Raymond Chandler Omnibus. LC 79-92498. 8.95 (ISBN 0-394-60492-X). Modern Lib.

Chandler, Robert, tr. The Magic Ring & other Russian Folktales. (Illus.). 90p. (gr. 2-6). 1983. pap. 2.95 (ISBN 0-571-13006-2). Faber & Faber.

Chandler, Robert F., Jr. Rice in the Tropics: A Guide to Development of National Programs. (IADS Development-Oriented Literature Ser.). 1979. lib. bdg. 23.25 (ISBN 0-89158-361-0). Westview.

Chandler, Robert W. War of Ideas: The U. S. Propaganda Compaign in Vietnam. (Special Studies in National Defense & Security Ser.). 301p. 1981. softcover 22.50 (ISBN 0-86531-082-3). Westview.

Chandler, T. J., ed. Selected Bibliography on Urban Climate. (Orig.). 1970. pap. 35.00 (ISBN 0-685-04924-8, W90, WMO). Unipub.

Chandler, Ted E. How to Have Good Health. LC 81-68045. 1982. 6.95 (ISBN 0-8054-5298-2). Broadman.

Chandler, Tertius & Fox, Gerald. Three Thousand Years of Urban Growth. LC 72-84378. (Studies in Population Ser). 1973. 59.50 (ISBN 0-12-785109-7). Acad Pr.

Chandona, Walter. How to Photograph Cats, Dogs, & Other Animals. (Illus.). 1973. 7.50 o.p. (ISBN 0-517-50349-2). Crown.

Chandor, Anthony. Choosing & Keeping Computer Staff. LC 76-357362. (Illus.). 203p. 1976. 17.50 (ISBN 0-04-658217-7). Intl Pubns Serv.

Chandra, Bipan. Nationalism & Colonialism in Modern India. 408p. 1981. text ed. 32.50x (ISBN 0-86131-194-9, Pub. by Orient Longman Ltd India). Apt Bks.

Chandra, Gyan, jt. auth. see O'Conner, Melvin C.

Chandra, Jagdish, compiled by. Bibliography of Indian Art, History & Archaeology: Dr. Anand K. Coomanaswamy Memorial Volume, Vol. 1. 1978. text ed. 65.50x (ISBN 0-391-01072-7). Humanities.

Chandra, R. K., ed. Critical Reviews in Tropical Medicine. (Vol.1). 412p. 1982. 49.50X (ISBN 0-306-40959-3, Plenum Pr). Plenum Pub.

Chandra, Ram. Road to Freedom: Revealing Sidelights. 362p. 1980. 24.95x (ISBN 0-940500-21-3); lib. bdg. 24.95x (ISBN 0-686-92327-8); text ed. 24.95x (ISBN 0-686-98511-7). Asia Bk Corp.

Chandra, Ramesh. Introductory Physics of Nuclear Medicine. 2nd ed. LC 81-17149. (Illus.). 237p. 1982. text ed. 17.50 (ISBN 0-8121-0826-4). Lea & Febiger.

Chandra, S. Superionic Solids: Principles & Applications. 1981. 68.00 (ISBN 0-444-86039-8). Elsevier.

Chandra, Subrato & Hay, Harold. Alternative Sources of Energy: Creative Cooling, No. 56. (Orig.). 1982. pap. 2.95 (ISBN 0-917328-46-9). ASEI.

Chandralekha. The Hindu Temple. 200p. 1982. 49.00x (ISBN 0-686-94078-4, Pub. by Garlandfold England). State Mutual Bk.

Chandrasekaran, A. R., jt. auth. see Krishna, Jai.

Chandrasekaran, B. & Radicchi, S., eds. Computer Program Testing. 1981. 42.75 (ISBN 0-444-86292-7). Elsevier.

Chandrasekhar, S. Liquid Crystals. LC 75-32913. (Cambridge Monographs in Physics). (Illus.). 1977. 77.50 (ISBN 0-521-21149-2). Cambridge U Pr.

--The Mathematical Theory of Black Holes. (International Ser. of Monographs on Physics). (Illus.). 750p. 1982. text ed. 89.00 (ISBN 0-686-84053-4). Oxford U Pr.

Chandrasekhara, C. S., ed. see Experts Group Meeting, National Institute of Urban Affairs, & Town & Country Planning, India, April, 1977.

Chandrasekharaiah, Kananur V. High School Students: East & West. LC 71-169241. 1971. 6.00 o.p. (ISBN 0-8022-2063-0). Philos Lib.

Chandrasekharan, K., jt. auth. see Bochner, S.

Chandrasenkhar, S. Liquid Crystals. (Cambridge Monographs in Physics). (Illus.). 352p. 1980. pap. 24.95 (ISBN 0-521-29841-5). Cambridge U Pr.

Chandresekhar. International Liquid Crystals Conference, Bangalore 1979: Proceedings. 1980. 99.95 (ISBN 0-471-25626-9). Wiley.

Chandurkar, P. J. Plant Anatomy. 256p. 1974. 40.00x (ISBN 0-686-84462-9, Pub. by Oxford & I B H India). State Mutual Bk.

Chandy, K. & Yeh, Raymond T., eds. Current Trends in Programming Methodology: Software Modeling, Vol. 3. (Illus.). 1978. ref. 24.95 (ISBN 0-13-195727-9). P-H.

Chandy, Mani K., jt. auth. see Sauer, Charles.

Chaneles, Sol, ed. Counseling Juvenile Offenders in Institutional Settings. (Journal of Offender Counseling Services & Rehabilitation Ser.: Vol. 6, No. 3). 91p. 1983. pap. text ed. 8.95 (ISBN 0-86656-170-6, B170). Haworth Pr.

--Strategies of Intervention with Public Offenders. (Journal of Offender Counseling, Services & Rehabilitation Ser.: Vol. 6, Nos. 1-2). 147p. 1982. pap. text ed. 11.95 (ISBN 0-86656-171-4, B171). Haworth Pr.

Chaney, Charles. Church Planting in America at the End of the Twentieth Century. 128p. 1982. pap. 6.95 (ISBN 0-8423-0279-4). Tyndale.

Chaney, Charles & Skee, Stanley. Plaster Mold & Model Making. LC 80-21932. 144p. 1981. Repr. of 1973 ed. text ed. 14.00 (ISBN 0-89874-282-X). Krieger.

Chaney, Clara M. & Miles, Nancy R. Remediating Learning Problems: A Developmental Curriculum. LC 73-92372. 244p. 1974. pap. text ed. 9.95x o.p. (ISBN 0-675-08816-X). Merrill.

Chaney, David. Fictions & Ceremonies: The Ethnography of Popular Narratives. LC 78-31437. 1979. 25.00 (ISBN 0-312-28814-X). St Martin.

Chaney, Earlyne. The Masters & Astara. 2nd ed. (Illus.). 100p. 1982. pap. 8.50 (ISBN 0-918936-13-6). Astara.

--Remembering. LC 74-81047. (Illus.). 380p. 1974. softcover 13.95 (ISBN 0-89031-018-1). Astara.

Chaney, Earlyne & Messick, William L. Kundalini & the Third Eye. Chaney, Sita, ed. LC 80-67635. (Illus.). 127p. 1982. pap. 12.95 (ISBN 0-918936-08-X). Astara.

Chaney, Earlyne C. Revelations of Things to Come. (Illus.). 156p. 1982. pap. 13.95 (ISBN 0-918936-12-8). Astara.

Chaney, Elsie N. Ivory Carver. (Orig.). pap. 2.00 (ISBN 0-685-08701-8). Creative Pr.

Chaney, J. F. & Ramdas, V., eds. Thermophysical Properties Research Literature Retrieval Guide 1900-1980, Vol. 5: Oxide Mixtures & Minerals. LC 81-15776. 430p. 1982. 69.50x (ISBN 0-306-67225-1); Set of 7 Vols. 695.00x (ISBN 0-686-97455-7). Plenum Pub.

--Thermophysical Properties Research Literature Retrieval Guide 1900-1980, Vol. 4: Alloys, Intermetallic Compounds & Ceramics. LC 81-15776. 756p. 1982. 110.00x (ISBN 0-306-67224-3); Set of 7 Vols. 695.00 (ISBN 0-686-97457-3). Plenum Pub.

--Thermophysical Properties Research Literature Retrieval Guide 1900-1980, Vol. 7: Coatings, Systems, Composites, Foods, Animal & Vegetable Products. 658p. 1982. 95.00 (ISBN 0-306-67227-8); Set of 7 Vols. 695.00 (ISBN 0-686-97458-1). Plenum Pub.

--Thermophysical Properties Research Literature Retrieval Guide 1900-1980, Vol. 6: Mixtures & Solutions. LC 81-155776. 516p. 1982. 89.50 (ISBN 0-306-67226-X); Set of 7 Vols. 695.00 (ISBN 0-686-97459-X). Plenum Pub.

--Thermophysical Properties Research Literature Retrieval Guide 1900-1980, Vol. 2: Inorganic Compounds. LC 81-15776. 1110p. 1982. 175.00x (ISBN 0-306-67222-7); Set of 7 Vols. 695.00 (ISBN 0-686-97461-1). Plenum Pub.

--Thermophysical Properties Research Literature Retrieval Guide 1900-1980, Vol. 3: Organic Compounds & Polymeric Materials. 2nd ed. LC 81-15776. 646p. 1982. 95.00 (ISBN 0-306-67223-5); Set of 7 Vols. 695.00 (ISBN 0-686-97462-X). Plenum Pub.

--Thermophysical Properties Research Literature Retrieval Guide 1900-1980, Vol. 1: Elements. LC 81-15776. 820p. 1982. 125.00x (ISBN 0-306-67221-9); Set of 7 Vols. 695.00 (ISBN 0-686-97464-6). Plenum Pub.

Chaney, James. Carolina Country Reader. LC 73-86780. 1973. 8.95 (ISBN 0-87716-045-7, Pub. by Moore Pub Co). F Apple.

Chaney, Lindsay & Ciepli, Michael. The Hearsts: Family & Empire, the Later Years. 1981. 16.95 o.p. (ISBN 0-671-24765-4). S&S.

Chaney, Margaret S., et al. Nutrition. 9th ed. LC 78-69546. (Illus.). 1979. text ed. 24.95 (ISBN 0-395-25448-5); o.p. inst. manual (ISBN 0-395-25449-3). HM.

Chaney, Norman. Theodore Roethke: The Poetics of Wonder. LC 81-40571. 130p. (Orig.). 1982. lib. bdg. 19.25 (ISBN 0-8191-2013-8); pap. text ed. 8.25 (ISBN 0-8191-2014-6). U Pr of Amer.

Chaney, Sita, ed. see Chaney, Earlyne & Messick, William L.

Chang. Tumors of the Central Nervous System. LC 81-17125. (Illus.). 352p. 1982. 54.50 (ISBN 0-89352-137-X). Masson Pub.

Chang, jt. auth. see Godfrey.

Chang, Arnold. Painting in the People's Republic of China: The Politics of Style. (Westview Replica Edition Ser.). 1980. lib. bdg. 16.00 (ISBN 0-89158-676-8). Westview.

Chang, C. M. & Kennedy, F. E. Advances in Computer-Aided Bearing Design. 156p. 1982. 30.00 (G00222). ASME.

Chang, Ching-sheng. Sex Histories: China's First Modern Treatise on Sex Education. 3rd ed. Levy, Howard S., tr. (Orig.). 1970. pap. 10.00 (ISBN 0-910878-03-X, Pub. by Langstaff-Levy). Oriental Bk Store.

Chang, Constance D. Chinese Menu Cookbook. LC 72-144257. (Illus.). 1971. 7.95 o.p. (ISBN 0-385-00658-6). Doubleday.

Chang, Dae H. Introduction to Criminal Justice: Theory & Application. (Orig.). 1979. pap. text ed. 14.95 (ISBN 0-8403-2102-3). Kendall-Hunt.

Chang, Diana & Greco, Leonard. The Horizon is Definitely Speaking. 48p. 1982. limited ed. 5.00x (ISBN 0-943018-02-1). Backstreet.

Chang, Florence C. Believe It or Not: An Anthology of Ancient Tales Retold. LC 80-68258. (Chinese Can Be Fun Bks.: Level 5). (Illus.). 80p. (gr. 10-12). 1980. pap. 5.75x (ISBN 0-936620-02-1); wkbk. avail. Ginkgo Hut.
--China Is Farther Than the Sun? A Beginning Chinese-English Reader. LC 80-68256. (Chinese Can Be Fun Bks.: Level 2). (Illus.). 51p. (gr. 3-4). 1980. pap. 5.00x (ISBN 0-936620-00-5); wkbk. avail. Ginkgo Hut.
--With Sound & Color: An Intermediate Chinese-English Reader. LC 80-68257. (Chinese Can Be Fun Bks.: Level 4). (Illus.). 71p. (Orig.). (gr. 7-9). 1980. pap. 5.50x (ISBN 0-936620-01-3); wkbk. avail. Ginkgo Hut.
Chang, Garma C., ed. A Treasury of Mahayana Sutras: Selections from the Maharatnakuta Sutra. Buddhist Association of the United States, tr. from Chinese. LC 82-42776. (Institute for Advanced Study of World Religion (IASWR) Ser.). 640p. 1983. 22.50x (ISBN 0-271-00341-3). Pa St U Pr.
Chang, H. C., ed. Chinese Literature: Popular Fiction & Drama. 466p. 1982. pap. 10.00 (ISBN 0-231-05367-3). Columbia U Pr.
Chang, Hsu, ed. Magnetic Bubble Technology: Integrated Circuit Magnetics for Digital Storage & Processing. LC 73-87653. 1975. 41.95 (ISBN 0-87942-033-2). Inst Electrical.
Chang, Huan-Yang & Over, Ira Earl. Selected Numerical Methods & Computer Programs for Chemical Engineers. 235p. (Orig.). 1980. pap. text ed. 11.95 (ISBN 0-88408-131-1). Sterling Swift.
Chang, Jolan. The Tao of Love & Sex: The Ancient Chinese Way to Ecstasy. 1977. pap. 7.50 (ISBN 0-525-47453-6, 0728-220). Dutton.
--The Tao of the Loving Couple: True Liberation Through the Tao. (Illus.). 168p. 1983. 14.95 (ISBN 0-525-24183-3, 01451-440); pap. 8.95 (ISBN 0-525-48042-0, 0869-260). Dutton.
Chang, K. C., ed. Food in Chinese Culture: Anthropological & Historical Perspectives. LC 75-43312. (Illus.). 448p. 1981. cloth o.p. 37.50 (ISBN 0-300-01938-6); pap. 9.95x (ISBN 0-300-02759-1, Y-402). Yale U Pr.
Chang, Luke T. China Boundary Treaties & Frontier Disputes. LC 82-3483. 443p. 1982. 45.00 (ISBN 0-379-20733-8). Oceana.
Chang, Margaret S., jt. auth. see Chang, Raymond.
Chang, N. P., ed. Five Decades of Weak Interactions, Vol. 294. (Annals of the New York Academy of Sciences Ser.). 102p. 1977. 12.00x (ISBN 0-89072-040-1). NY Acad Sci.
Chang, Pao-Min. Beijing, Hanoi & the Overseas Chinese. (China Research Monographs: No. 24). 1982. pap. 8.00x (ISBN 0-912966-50-5). IEAS.
Chang, Paul K. Control of Flow Separation: Energy Conservation, Operational Efficiency & Safety. new ed. (McGraw-Hill Series in Thermal & Fluids Engineering). (Illus.). 1976. text ed. 49.50x (ISBN 0-07-010513-8, C). McGraw.
Chang, Pauline, et al. Beginning Chinese Reader, 2 pts. Pt. 1. 4.95 (ISBN 0-686-38038-X); Pt. 2. 3.95 (ISBN 0-686-38039-8). Far Eastern Pubns.
Chang, Raymond. Chemistry. Incl. Losey, Eugene. wkbk. 9.00 (ISBN 0-394-32447-1); Goldwhite, Harold & Spielman, John. solutions to problem sets 9.00 (ISBN 0-394-32519-2). 815p. 1981. text ed. 27.00 (ISBN 0-394-31224-4). Random.
--Chinese Petroleum: An Annotated Bibliography. 1982. lib. bdg. 35.00 (ISBN 0-8161-8333-3, Hall Reference). G K Hall.
--Introduction to Chemistry. 1981. text ed. 27.00x (ISBN 0-394-31224-4); wkbk. 9.00 (ISBN 0-394-32447-1). Random.
--Physical Chemistry with Applications to Biological Systems. 2nd ed. (Illus.). 1981. text ed. 29.95 (ISBN 0-02-321040-0). Macmillan.
Chang, Raymond & Chang, Margaret S. Speaking of Chinese. (Illus.). 208p. 1983. pap. 4.95 (ISBN 0-393-30061-7). Norton.
Chang, Richard C., jt. auth. see Smith, Frank C.
Chang, S. H. The Spelling Bee Speller: The Final Rounds, Vol. 3. LC 81-90754. (The Spelling Bee Speller Ser.). 232p. (Orig.). (gr. 5-8). 1983. cancelled (ISBN 0-942462-13-0); pap. 5.95 (ISBN 0-942462-03-3). Hondale.
--The Spelling Bee Speller: The First Round, Vol. 1. LC 81-90754. (The Spelling Bee Speller Ser.). 232p. (Orig.). (gr. 5-8). 1982. cancelled (ISBN 0-942462-11-4); pap. 5.95 (ISBN 0-942462-01-7). Hondale.
--The Spelling Bee Speller: The Middle Rounds, Vol. 2. LC 81-90754. (The Spelling Bee Speller Ser.). 232p. (Orig.). (gr. 5-8). 1983. cancelled (ISBN 0-942462-12-2); pap. 5.95 (ISBN 0-942462-02-5). Hondale.
Chang, Sheldon S. L. Fundamentals Handbook of Electrical & Computer Engineering: Vol. 1: Circuits, Fields, & Electronics. LC 82-4872. 707p. 1982. 64.95 (ISBN 0-471-86215-0, Pub. by Wiley-Interscience). Wiley.
--Fundamentals Handbook of Electrical & Computer Engineering: Vol. 2: Communications, Control, Devices & Systems. LC 82-4872. 737p. 1983. 64.95 (ISBN 0-471-86213-4). Wiley.
--Fundamentals Handbook of Electrical & Computer Engineering: Vol. 3: Computer Hardware, Software & Applications. LC 82-4872. 507p. 1983. 61.95 (ISBN 0-471-86214-2, Pub. by Wiley-Interscience). Wiley.
Chang, Y. N. & Campo-Flores, Filemon. Business Policy & Strategy. 1980. pap. text ed. 15.50x (ISBN 0-673-16074-2). Scott F.
--Business Policy & Strategy: Text & Cases. 1980. text ed. 25.95x (ISBN 0-673-16073-4). Scott F.
Chang Chung-Yuan. Creativity & Taoism. (Illus.). 1970. pap. 5.95x (ISBN 0-06-131968-6, TB1968, Torch). Har-Row.
Change Institute. University of Maryland. Frontiers in Librarianship: Proceedings of Change Institute 1969. Wasserman, Paul, ed. LC 78-149958. (Contributions in Librarianship & Information Science: No. 2). 1972. lib. bdg. 35.00 (ISBN 0-8371-5823-0, WPC/). Greenwood.
Change Magazine Editors. Educating for the World View. LC 80-68195. 80p. 1980. pap. 6.95 (ISBN 0-915390-26-4). Change Mag.
Changing Times Education Service Editors. Consumer Law. rev. ed. LC 81-7720. (Illus.). 144p. 1982. pap. text ed. 5.95 (ISBN 0-88436-804-1, 30263). EMC.
--Housing. rev. ed. LC 81-400. (Illus.). 144p. 1982. pap. text ed. 5.95 (ISBN 0-88436-798-3, 30264). EMC.
--Insurance. rev. ed. LC 81-7857. (Illus.). 144p. 1982. pap. text ed. 5.95 (ISBN 0-88436-813-0, 30265). EMC.
--Marketplace. rev. ed. LC 81-4686. (Illus.). 56p. 1982. pap. text ed. 3.25 (ISBN 0-88436-801-7, 30262). EMC.
--Money Management. rev. ed. LC 81-7859. (Illus.). 64p. 1982. pap. text ed. 4.25 (ISBN 0-88436-810-6, 30261). EMC.
--Saving & Investing. rev. ed. LC 81-7860. (Illus.). 112p. 1982. pap. text ed. 4.95 (ISBN 0-88436-807-6, 30266). EMC.
Chang Kia-ngau, pseud. China's Struggle for Railroad Development. LC 74-34331. (China in the 20th Century Ser). (Illus.). vii, 340p. 1975. Repr. of 1943 ed. lib. bdg. 39.50 (ISBN 0-306-70689-X). Da Capo.
Chang Tien-Yi. The Magic Gourd. Yang, Gladys, tr. from Chinese. (Illus.). 198p. (gr. 6-10). 1979. pap. 2.50 o.p. (ISBN 0-8351-0606-3). China Bks.
Chang Wen-Ch'eng. The Dwelling of Playful Goddesses. Levy, Howard S., tr. 18.00 (ISBN 0-686-38451-2). Oriental Bk Store.
Chankin, Donald O. Anonymity & Death: The Fiction of B. Traven. LC 75-1376. 160p. 1975. 15.00x (ISBN 0-271-01190-4). Pa St U Pr.
Chankong & Haimes. Multiobjective Decision Making Theory & Methodology. (Systems Science & Engineering Ser.: Vol. 8). Date not set. 45.00 (ISBN 0-444-00710-5). Elsevier.
Chanlett, Emil T. Environmental Protection. (Illus.). 608p. 1973. text ed. 23.50 o.p. (ISBN 0-07-010520-0, C); solutions manual 3.00 o.p. (ISBN 0-07-010521-9). McGraw.
--Environmental Protection. (Environmental Engineering Ser.). 1979. text ed. 36.50 (ISBN 0-07-010531-6, C); solutions manual 7.95 (ISBN 0-07-010532-4). McGraw.
Ch'an Master Hua. Listen to Yourself; Think It Over. Heng Yin, Bhikshuni, tr. from Chinese. (Illus.). 153p. (Orig.). 1978. pap. 7.00 (ISBN 0-917512-24-3). Buddhist Text.
--The Ten Dharma Realms Are Not Beyond a Single Thought. Bhikshuni Heng Ch'ih, tr. from Chinese. (Illus.). 72p. (Orig., Eng.). 1976. pap. 4.00 (ISBN 0-917512-12-X). Buddhist Text.
Ch'an Master Hua, commentary by. Amitabha Sutra. Bhikshuni Heng Yin, et al, trs. from Chinese. (Illus.). 204p. (Orig., Eng.). 1974. pap. 8.00 (ISBN 0-917512-01-4). Buddhist Text.
Ch'an Master Hua, ed. Buddha Root Farm. Bhikshuni Heng Yin, et al, trs. (Illus.). 72p. (Orig.). 1976. pap. 4.00 (ISBN 0-917512-08-1). Buddhist Text.
Ch'an Master Hua, commentary by. The Dharani Sutra. Bhikshuni Heng Yin, tr. from Chinese. (Illus.). 352p. (Orig.). 1976. pap. 12.00 (ISBN 0-917512-13-8). Buddhist Text.
--Dharma Flower Sutra, Vol. IX. Bhikshuni Heng Yin, tr. from Chinese. (Illus.). 270p. (Orig.). 1982. pap. 9.00 (ISBN 0-917512-85-5). Buddhist Text.
--Dharma Flower Sutra, Vol. III. Bhikshuni Heng Yin, tr. from Chinese. (Illus.). 183p. (Orig.). 1979. pap. 7.95 (ISBN 0-917512-26-X). Buddhist Text.
--Dharma Flower Sutra, Vol. II. Bhikshuni Heng Yin, tr. (Illus.). 324p. (Orig., Chinese.). 1978. pap. 7.95 (ISBN 0-917512-22-7). Buddhist Text.
Ch'an Master Hua, ed. The Dharma Flower Sutra: Vol. I, Introduction. Bhikshuni Heng Yin, tr. from Chinese. (Illus.). 85p. (Orig.). 1977. pap. 3.95 (ISBN 0-917512-16-2). Buddhist Text.
Ch'an Master Hua, commentary by. Flower Adornment (Avatamsaka) Sutra: Chapter 15, The Ten Dwellings. Bhikshuni Heng Yin, et al, trs. from Chinese. (Illus.). 188p. (Orig.). 1981. pap. 8.00 (ISBN 0-917512-77-4). Buddhist Text.
--Flower Adornment Sutra, Chapter 16: Brahma Conduct. Bhikshuni Heng Hsien, tr. from Chinese. (Illus.). 86p. (Orig.). 1981. pap. 4.00 (ISBN 0-917512-80-4). Buddhist Text.
--Flower Adornment Sutra: Chapter 17, Merit & Virture from First Bringing Forth the Mind. Bhikshu Hen Shun, et al, trs. from Chinese. (Illus.). 196p. (Orig.). 1982. pap. 7.00 (ISBN 0-917512-83-9). Buddhist Text.
--Flower Adornment Sutra: Chapter 26, The Ten Grounds, Part Two. Bhikshuni Heng Hsien, tr. from Chinese. (Illus.). 206p. (Orig.). 1981. pap. 8.00 (ISBN 0-917512-74-X). Buddhist Text.
--Flower Adornment Sutra, Chapter 39: Entering the Dharma Realm, Part Four. Bhikshun Heng Tao, tr. from Chinese. (Illus.). 280p. (Orig.). 1981. pap. 8.00 (ISBN 0-917512-76-6). Buddhist Text.
--Flower Adornment Sutra, Chapter 39: Entering the Dharma Realm, Part III. Bhikshuni Heng Tao, et al, trs. from Chinese. (Illus.). 250p. (Orig.). 1981. pap. 8.50 (ISBN 0-917512-73-1). Buddhist Text.
--Flower Adornment Sutra: Chapter 39, Entering the Dharma Realm, Part V. Bhikshuni, Heng Tao, et al, trs. (Illus.). 310p. 1982. pap. 9.00 (ISBN 0-917512-81-2). Buddhist Text.
--Flower Adornment Sutra: Chapter 40, Universal Worthy's Conduct & Vows. Buddhist Text Translation Society, tr. from Chinese. (Illus.). 316p. (Orig.). 1982. pap. 10.00 (ISBN 0-917512-84-7). Buddhist Text.
--The Shurangama Mantra, Vol. I. Buddhist Rext Translation Society, tr. from Chinese. (Illus.). 296p. (Orig.). 1981. pap. 8.50 (ISBN 0-917512-69-3). Buddhist Text.
Ch'an Master Hua, ed. Shurangama Mantra, Vol. 2. Buddhist Text Translation Society, tr. (Illus.). 210p. 1982. pap. 7.50 (ISBN 0-917512-82-0). Buddhist Text.
Ch'an Master Hua, commentary by. The Shurangama Sutra, Vol. 1. Bhikshuni Heng Ch'ih, tr. from Chinese. (Illus.). 289p. (Orig.). 1977. pap. 8.50 (ISBN 0-917512-17-0). Buddhist Text.
--The Shurangama Sutra, Vol. 2. Bhikshuni Heng Ch'ih, tr. from Chinese. (Illus.). 212p. (Orig.). 1979. pap. 8.50 (ISBN 0-917512-25-1). Buddhist Text.
--Shurangama Sutra, Vol. 6. Bhikshuni Heng Ch'ih, tr. (Illus.). 220p. (Orig.). 1981. pap. 8.50 (ISBN 0-917512-37-5). Buddhist Text.
--The Sixth Patriarch's Sutra. Bhikshuni Heng Yin, tr. from Chinese. (Illus.). 235p. (Orig.). 1977. 15.00 (ISBN 0-917512-19-7); pap. 10.00 (ISBN 0-917512-33-2). Buddhist Text.
--The Sutra in Forty-Two Sections. Bhikshuni Heng Ch'ih, tr. from Chinese. (Illus.). 114p. (Orig., Eng.). 1977. pap. 4.00 (ISBN 0-917512-15-4). Buddhist Text.
--Sutra of the Past Vows of Earth Store Bodhisattva. Bhikshu Heng Ching, et al, trs. from Chinese. (Illus., Eng.). 1976. 16.00 (ISBN 0-915078-00-7); pap. 9.00 o.s.i (ISBN 0-917512-09-X). Buddhist Text.
--Varja Prajna Paramita Sutra. Bhikshuni Heng Ch'ih, tr. from Chinese. (Illus.). 180p. (Orig.). pap. 8.00 (ISBN 0-917512-02-2). Buddhist Text.
Ch'an Master Hua, jt. ed. see Ch'an Master Yung Chia.
Ch'an Master Hua, jt. ed. see Lien Ch'in.
Ch'an Master Hua, commentary by see Master Ch'ing Liang.
Ch'an Master Yung Chia & Ch'an Master Hua, eds. The Song of Enlightenment. Bhikshu Heng Yo, et al, trs. from Chinese. (Illus., Orig.). Date not set. pap. (ISBN 0-917512-20-0). Buddhist Text. Postponed.
Channell, Paul J., ed. see AIP Conference, 91st, Los Alamos, 1982.
Channels Magazine, jt. auth. see Brown, Les.
Channing, C. P., jt. auth. see T. Fujii.
Channing, Edward. Jeffersonian System, Eighteen One to Eighteen Eleven. LC 69-13855. Repr. of 1906 ed. lib. bdg. 16.25x (ISBN 0-8371-0995-7, CHJS). Greenwood.
Channing, Edward & Coolidge, Archibald C. The Barrington-Bernard Correspondence, & Illustrative Matter, 1760-1770. LC 75-109612. (Era of the American Revolution Ser). 1970. Repr. of 1912 ed. lib. bdg. 39.50 (ISBN 0-306-71909-6). Da Capo.
Channing, Marion L. The Textile Tools of Colonial Homes. 6th ed. LC 75-229981. (Illus.). 64p. 1971. pap. 3.00 (ISBN 0-9600496-1-4). Channing Bks.
Channing, Marion L. & Russell, Laura. Laura Russell Remembers. (Illus.). 80p. 1970. pap. 3.00 (ISBN 0-9600496-2-2). Channing Bks.
Channing, Susan, ed. see Davidson, Martha, et al.
Channing, William E. Discourses on War. LC 71-137531. (Peace Movement in America Ser). lxi, 229p. 1972. Repr. of 1903 ed. lib. bdg. 18.95x (ISBN 0-89198-059-8). Ozer.
Channon, D. F., jt. auth. see Stopford, J. M.
Channon, Derek F. The Strategy & Structure of British Enterprise. LC 72-94362. 300p. 1973. 15.00x (ISBN 0-87584-101-5). Harvard Busn.
Chan-Palay, Victoria, jt. auth. see Conference, Bethesda, Md, June, 1981.
Chansky, Norman M. Untapped Good: The Rehabilitation of School Dropouts. (Illus.). 288p. 1966. photocopy ed. spiral 24.50x (ISBN 0-398-00302-5). C C Thomas.
Chant, Barry. Straight Talk About Sex. (Illus.). (gr. 10-12). 1977. pap. 2.50 (ISBN 0-88368-078-5). Whitaker Hse.
Chant, Chris. Jetliner: From Takeoff to Touchdown. LC 82-81164. (Inside Story Ser.). (Illus.). 40p. 1982. PLB 9.90 (ISBN 0-531-03461-5). Watts.
Chant, Joy. Grey Mane of Morning. 352p. 1982. pap. 3.50 (ISBN 0-553-22666-5). Bantam.
Chantikian, Kosrof. Prophecies & Transformations. LC 75-35012. (Modern Poets Ser.). 88p. (Orig.). 1978. pap. 3.95 (ISBN 0-916426-01-7). KOSMOS.
Chantiles, V. L. The Food of Greece. (Illus.). 1979. Repr. 4.98 o.p. (ISBN 0-517-27888-X). Crown.
Chantre, Jean-Claude. Les Considerations Religieuses et Esthetiques D'un "Sturmer und Dranger". 650p. (Fr.). 1982. write for info. (ISBN 3-261-04989-8). P Lang Pubs.
Chantry, Walter. Signs of the Apostles. 1979. pap. 3.95 (ISBN 0-85151-175-9). Banner of Truth.
Chantry, Walter J. God's Righteous Kingdom. 151p. (Orig.). 1980. pap. 3.95 (ISBN 0-85151-310-7). Banner of Truth.
Chan Wai-Kai. Active Network Feedback Amplifier Theory. LC 79-16997. (Illus.). 550p. 1980. text ed. 37.50 (ISBN 0-07-010779-3, C). McGraw.
Chao. Design & Application of Tumor Prostheses. 1983. price not set (ISBN 0-86577-081-6). Thieme-Stratton.
Chao, Denise W. Le Style du Journal d'un Cure de Campagne de Georges Bernanos. LC 80-67223. 120p. (Fr.). 1981. lib. bdg. 16.75 (ISBN 0-8191-1644-0). U Pr of Amer.
Chao, Edmund Y. & Ivins, John C. Design & Application for Tumor Prostheses. (Illus.). 375p. 1983. write for info. Thieme-Stratton.
Chao, J. A. & Woyczynski, W. A., eds. Martingale Theory in Harmonic Analysis & Banach Spaces, Cleveland, Ohio 1981: Proceedings. (Lecture Notes in Mathematics: Vol. 939). 225p. 1982. pap. 12.00 (ISBN 0-387-11569-2). Springer-Verlag.
Chao, Kang. Capital Formation in Mainland China, 1952-1965. LC 72-85526. 1974. 34.50x (ISBN 0-520-02304-8). U of Cal Pr.
Chao, L. Statistics: Methods & Analyses. 2nd ed. 1974. text ed. 24.95 (ISBN 0-07-010525-1, C); solutions manual 15.95 (ISBN 0-07-010526-X). McGraw.
Chao, Lincoln L. Introduction to Statistics. LC 79-13686. 1979. text ed. 24.95 (ISBN 0-8185-0321-1); study guide 7.95 (ISBN 0-686-82873-9). Brooks-Cole.
--Statistics for Management. LC 79-22706. 1980. text ed. 23.95 o.p. (ISBN 0-8185-0367-X); study guide 6.95 o.p. (ISBN 0-8185-0409-9). Brooks-Cole.
Chao, Paul. Chinese Kinship. 220p. 1983. 30.00 (ISBN 0-7103-0020-4). Routledge & Kegan.
Chao, Yuen Ren. A Grammar of Spoken Chinese. LC 65-10576. 1968. 46.50x (ISBN 0-520-00219-9). U of Cal Pr.
Chao, Yuen-Ren. Language & Symbolic Systems. (Orig.). 1968. 34.50 (ISBN 0-521-04616-5); pap. 12.95 (ISBN 0-521-09457-7, 457). Cambridge U Pr.
Chaosium, Inc. Runequest. 1982. text ed. 14.95 (ISBN 0-8359-6870-7). Reston.
Chapel, Charles E. Gun Collector's Handbook of Values: Nineteen Eighty to Eighty-One. 13th rev. ed. (Illus.). 1979. 16.95 (ISBN 0-698-11011-0, Coward); pap. 8.95 (ISBN 0-698-11010-2). Putnam Pub Group.
--The Gun Collector's Handbook of Values: 1977-78. rev. ed. 1977. 17.95 o.p. (ISBN 0-698-10825-6, Coward). Putnam Pub Group.
Chapel, Jeannie. Victorian Taste: The Complete Catalogue of Paintings at the Royal Holloway College. (Illus.). 144p. 1983. pap. 25.00 (ISBN 0-8390-0302-1). Allanheld & Schram.
Chapelle, Howard I., jt. auth. see Adney, Edwin T.
Chapey, Roberta. Language Intervention Strategies in Adult Aphasia. (Illus.). 381p. 1981. 34.00 (ISBN 0-686-69565-8, 1511-7). Williams & Wilkins.
Chapian, Marie. Free to Be Thin. LC 79-15656. (Illus.). 192p. 1979. pap. 4.95 (ISBN 0-87123-560-9, 210560); study guide by Neva Coyle 64 pgs. 2.50 (ISBN 0-87123-163-8, 210163). Bethany Hse.
--Love & Be Loved. 192p. 1983. pap. 5.95 (ISBN 0-8007-5092-6, Power Bks). Revell.
Chapin & Hassett. Credit & Collection Principles & Practice. 7th ed. 1960. text ed. 31.95 (ISBN 0-07-010538-3, C). McGraw.
Chapin, Bradley. Criminal Justice in Colonial America, Sixteen Hundred & Six to Sixteen Sixty. LC 82-2753. 224p. 1983. text ed. 18.00x (ISBN 0-8203-0624-X). U of Ga Pr.
Chapin, F. Stuart, Jr. Human Activity Patterns in the City: Things People Do in Time & in Space. LC 74-5364. (Urban Research Ser). 272p. 1974. 21.95 o.p. (ISBN 0-471-14563-7, Pub. by Wiley-Interscience). Wiley.
Chapin, F. Stuart, Jr. & Weiss, Shirley F., eds. Urban Growth Dynamics: In a Regional Cluster of Cities. LC 76-54709. 496p. 1977. Repr. of 1962 ed. 22.00 (ISBN 0-88275-486-6). Krieger.
Chapin, Francis S. Experimental Designs in Sociological Research. LC 73-16867. (Illus.). 297p. 1974. Repr. of 1955 ed. lib. bdg. 20.00x (ISBN 0-8371-7239-X, CHSO). Greenwood.
Chapin, J. & Messick, R. California: People of a Region. 4th ed. (Our Nation, Our World Ser.). 288p. 1984. text ed. 18.48 (ISBN 0-07-010561-8); tchr's ed. 21.76 (ISBN 0-07-010562-6); blackline masters 7.20 (ISBN 0-07-010563-4). McGraw.
Chapin, June R. & Felton, Randall G. Chronicles of Time: A World History. (Illus.). 768p. (gr. 10). 1983. 19.92 (ISBN 0-07-001112-5, W); tchr's resource guide 14.56 (ISBN 0-07-001113-3). McGraw.

Chapin, Louis, intro. by. Fifty Charles M. Russel Paintings of The Old American West. 1978. 8.98 o.p. (ISBN 0-517-25421-2). Crown.

Chapin, Ned. Three-Sixty - Three-Seventy Programming in Assembly Language. 1973. text ed. 33.00 (ISBN 0-07-010552-9, C). McGraw.

Chapin, Schuyler G. Musical Chairs: A Life in the Arts. LC 77-5814. (Illus.). 1977. 12.50 o.p. (ISBN 0-399-11970-1). Putnam Pub Group.

Chapin-Park, Sue, jt. auth. see Park, William R.

Chaplain, O. S., Jr. Snookums Sneaks Through. (Third Grade Bk.). (Illus.). (gr. 3-4). PLB 5.95 o.p. (ISBN 0-513-00410-6). Denison.

Chaplan, Marie, jt. auth. see Backus, William.

Chaplin, George & Paige, Glenn D., eds. Hawaii Two Thousand: Continuing Experiment in Anticipatory Democracy. 500p. 1973. 14.95 (ISBN 0-8248-0252-7). UH Pr.

Chaplin, Gordon. Joyride. 192p. 1982. 14.95 (ISBN 0-698-11185-0, Coward). Putnam Pub Group.

Chaplin, Hamako & Martin, Samuel. Advanced Japanese Conversation. 1976. 8.95 (ISBN 0-686-15389-8); tapes avail. Far Eastern Pubns.

Chaplin, Hamako I., jt. auth. see Jorden, Eleanor H.

Chaplin, Jack W. Metal Manufacturing Technology. (gr. 10 up). 1976. text ed. 19.96 (ISBN 0-87345-132-5). McKnight.

Chaplin, James P. & Demers, Aline. Primer of Neurology & Neurophysiology. LC 78-6680. 1978. pap. text ed. 17.95 (ISBN 0-471-03027-9, Pub. by Wiley Med). Wiley.

Chaplin, L. Tarin, jt. auth. see Blom, Lynne A.

Chaplin, Ralph. Wobbly. LC 70-166089. (Civil Liberties in American History Ser). 1972. Repr. of 1948 ed. lib. bdg. 49.50 (ISBN 0-306-70212-6). Da Capo.

Chaplin, Ralph, et al. Centralia Case: Three Views of the Armistice Day Tragedy at Centralia, Washington, November 11, 1919. LC 77-160845. (Civil Liberties in American History Ser). 1971. Repr. of 1924 ed. lib. bdg. 35.00 (ISBN 0-306-70211-8). Da Capo.

Chapman. Business in Society. 1981. text ed. 26.95 (ISBN 0-408-10693-X); pap. text ed. 19.95 (ISBN 0-408-10694-8). Butterworth.

--Medical Dictionary for the Lay Person. 1983. pap. 4.95 (ISBN 0-8120-2247-5). Barron.

Chapman & Rutland. Book of Speed. (Young Engineer Bks.). (gr. 4-6). 1978. 10.95 (ISBN 0-86020-183-X, Usborne-Hayes). EDC.

Chapman, jt. ed. see Milligan.

Chapman, A. & Gale, A. Psychology & People. (Psychology for Professional Groups Ser.). 528p. 1982. text ed. 27.75x (ISBN 0-333-33145-1, Pub. by Macmillan England); pap. text ed. 13.00x (ISBN 0-333-33147-8). Humanities.

Chapman, A. H. Harry Stack Sullivan: His Life & His Work. LC 75-42926. 288p. 1976. 8.95 o.p. (ISBN 0-399-11734-2). Putnam Pub Group.

--Parents Talking, Kids Talking. LC 78-15271. 1979. 8.95 o.p. (ISBN 0-399-12259-1). Putnam Pub Group.

Chapman, A. H. & Almeida, Elza M. The Interpersonal Basis of Psychiatric Nursing. 1972. 12.50 o.p. (ISBN 0-399-40047-8). Putnam Pub Group.

Chapman, A. R. Biology of Seaweeds. 160p. 1979. pap. text ed. 13.95 (ISBN 0-8391-1340-4). Univ Park.

Chapman, Abraham, ed. Black Voices: An Anthology of Afro-American Literature. 1968. pap. 4.95 (ISBN 0-451-62205-7, ME2205, Ment). NAL.

--Jewish-American Literature: An Anthology. 727p. pap. 2.25 (ISBN 0-686-95132-8). ADL.

Chapman, Al. Coloring Book of New Mexico Santos. Smith, James C., Jr., ed. Ortega, Pedro R., tr. 48p. (Span. & Eng.). (gr. 1-8). 1982. pap. 2.50 (ISBN 0-913270-19-9). Sunstone Pr.

Chapman, Alan J. Heat Transfer. 3rd ed. (Illus.). 653p. 1974. text ed. 31.95 (ISBN 0-02-321450-3). Macmillan.

Chapman, Alexander. Turn Right at the Fountain. rev. ed. 304p. 1973. pap. 1.95 o.p. (ISBN 0-451-09153-1, J9153, Sig). NAL.

Chapman, Anne. Drama & Power in a Hunting Society: The Selk'nam of Tierra del Fuego. LC 82-4286. (Illus.). 240p. 1982. 39.50 (ISBN 0-521-23884-6). Cambridge U Pr.

Chapman, Annie B., jt. auth. see Hart, Albert B.

Chapman, Anthony J. & Foot, Hugh C., eds. Humor & Laughter: Theory, Research & Applications. LC 73-14378. 348p. 1976. 51.95x o.p. (ISBN 0-471-14612-9, Pub. by Wiley-Interscience). Wiley.

Chapman, Antony, ed. see Fransella, Fay.

Chapman, Antony, ed. see Hall, John.

Chapman, Antony, ed. see Holdsworth, Ruth.

Chapman, Antony, ed. see Purser, Harry.

Chapman, Antony J. & Foot, Hugh C. It's a Funny Thing Humour: The International Conference on Humor & Laughter. LC 76-53731. 400p. 1977. text ed. 48.00 (ISBN 0-08-021376-6). Pergamon.

Chapman, Antony J., jt. auth. see McGhee, Paul E.

Chapman, Antony J., et al. Pedestrian Accidents. 250p. 1982. 44.95 (ISBN 0-471-10057-9, Pub. by Wiley-Interscience). Wiley.

Chapman, B. & Potter, A. M., eds. Wimm: Political Questions. 294p. 1974. 24.00 (ISBN 0-7190-0594-9). Manchester.

Chapman, Benjamin. Card-Guide to New Testament Exegesis. 2.95 (ISBN 0-8010-2396-3). Baker Bk.

Chapman, C. B. Fibres. 1974. 5.95x (ISBN 0-87245-508-4). Textile Bk.

Chapman, Carl H. Osage Indians, Vol. Three: The Origin of the Osage Indian Tribe: an Ethnographical, Historical & Archaeological Study. (American Indian Ethnohistory Ser.: Plains Indians). (Illus.). lib. bdg. 42.00 o.s.i. (ISBN 0-8240-0749-2). Garland Pub.

Chapman, Carl H., ed. see Hamilton, Henry W. & Griffin, James B.

Chapman, Claire. Teaching Squash. 1977. pap. 10.75x (ISBN 0-7135-1951-7, SpS). Sportshelf.

Chapman, Clark R. Planets of Rock & Ice: From Mercury to the Moons of Saturn. (Illus.). 256p. 1982. 13.95 (ISBN 0-684-17484-7, ScribT). Scribner.

Chapman, Colin. Christianity on Trial. 1975. pap. text ed. 7.79 (ISBN 0-8423-0246-8). Tyndale.

Chapman, D. Biological Membranes, 3 vols. Vol. 1 1968. o.s. 70.00 (ISBN 0-12-168540-3); Vol. 2 1973. 51.50 (ISBN 0-12-168542-X); Vol. 3 1976. 57.50 (ISBN 0-12-168544-6). Acad Pr.

Chapman, D. J., jt. auth. see Chapman, V. J.

Chapman, D. J., jt. ed. see Round, F. E.

Chapman, Danny. Circus Buffoon. 238p. (Orig.). 1983. pap. 6.00 (ISBN 0-686-38858-5). S K Chapman.

Chapman, E., jt. auth. see Uvarov, B. P.

Chapman, E. N. Getting into Business. LC 75-20279. 319p. 1976. 19.95x o.p. (ISBN 0-471-14600-5). Wiley.

Chapman, E. N. & Martin, William. Self-Paced Guide for SSK: With Applications for the Hospitality Industry. 3rd ed. 96p. 1982. pap. text ed. 5.95 (ISBN 0-574-20638-8, 13-3638). SRA.

Chapman, E. N. & Williams, Catherine. A Self-Paced Guide to the Health Care Industry to Accompany SSK. 3rd ed. 96p. 1983. pap. text ed. write for info. (ISBN 0-574-20567-5). SRA.

Chapman, Edgar L. The Magic Labyrinth of Philip Jose Farmer. LC 81-21603. (The Milford Series-Popular Writers of Today: Vol. 38). 64p. 1983. lib. bdg. 9.95x (ISBN 0-89370-158-0); pap. text ed. 3.95x (ISBN 0-89370-258-7). Borgo Pr.

Chapman, Edward M. New England Village Life. LC 72-143643. 1971. Repr. of 1937 ed. 34.00x (ISBN 0-8103-3699-5). Gale.

Chapman, Elwood. College Survival: Find Yourself, Find a Career. 2nd ed. 230p. 1981. pap. text ed. 7.95 (ISBN 0-574-20615-9, 13-3615). SRA.

--Dynamic Retailing. 416p. 1980. pap. text ed. 17.95 (ISBN 0-574-20610-8, 13-3610); instr's. guide avail. (ISBN 0-574-20611-6, 13-3611). SRA.

Chapman, Elwood N. Career Search. LC 75-35758. (Illus.). 200p. 1976. pap. text ed. 7.95 (ISBN 0-574-20005-3, 13-3005); instr's guide avail. (ISBN 0-574-20006-1, 13-3006). SRA.

--From Campus to Career Success. LC 78-9085. 304p. 1978. pap. text ed. 8.95 (ISBN 0-574-20580-2, 13-3580); instr's guide avail. (ISBN 0-574-20581-0, 13-3581). SRA.

--Supervisor's Survival Kit. 3rd ed. 224p. 1981. pap. text ed. 9.95 (ISBN 0-574-20635-3, 13-3635); instr. guide avail. (ISBN 0-574-20636-1, 13-3636); self-paced exercise guide 3.95 (ISBN 0-574-20637-X, 13-3637). SRA.

--Your Attitude Is Changing. 1966. pap. text ed. 8.95 (ISBN 0-574-15300-4, 15-0300 TEXT). SRA.

--Your Attitude Is Showing. 3rd ed. LC 77-14526. 1977. pap. text ed. 8.95 (ISBN 0-574-20575-6, 13-3575); leader's guide 1.10 (ISBN 0-574-20576-4, 13-3576); study guide 3.95 (ISBN 0-574-20577-2, 13-3577). SRA.

--Your Attitude is Showing. 4th ed. 96p. 1982. text ed. 8.95 (ISBN 0-574-20680-9, 13-3680); write for info leader's guide (ISBN 0-574-20681-7, 13-3681); self-paced exercise guide 4.95 (ISBN 0-574-20682-5, 13-3682). SRA.

Chapman, Emalee. Fast Italian Meals. (Illus.). 168p. 1983. pap. 7.95 (ISBN 0-89286-210-6). One Hund One Prods.

Chapman, Eugenia & Major, Jill C. Clean Your House & Everything in It. (Illus.). 160p. 1982. pap. 6.95 (ISBN 0-448-12263-4, G&D). Putnam Pub Group.

Chapman, Frank. The Spell of Hungry Wolf. 47p. 1975. pap. 2.50 (ISBN 0-913270-42-3). Sunstone Pr.

--Yesterday's Town: Tonbridge. 1981. 39.50x o.p. (ISBN 0-86023-149-6, Pub. by Barracuda England). State Mutual Bk.

Chapman, G. Body Fluids & Their Functions. (Studies in Biology: No. 8). 80p. 1980. pap. text ed. 8.95 (ISBN 0-7131-2796-1). E Arnold.

Chapman, Gary. Toward a Growing Marriage. LC 79-21376. 1979. 7.95 o.p. (ISBN 0-8024-8789-0); pap. 4.95 (ISBN 0-8024-8787-4). Moody.

Chapman, Gary & Bryant, Steven, eds. Melodic Index to Haydn's Instrumental Music: A Thematic Locator for the Hoboken Thematisch-Bibliographisches Werkverzeichnis, Vols. I & II. (Thematic Catalogue Ser.: No. 8). 120p. 1981. lib. bdg. 21.00 (ISBN 0-918728-19-3). Pendragon NY.

Chapman, Gary D. Hope for the Separated. LC 81-18667. 160p. 1982. pap. 5.95 (ISBN 0-8024-3616-1). Moody.

Chapman, George. George Chapman: Selected Poems. Wain, Eirian, ed. (Fyfield). 1978. pap. 5.25x (ISBN 0-85635-242-X, Pub. by Carcanet New Pr England). Humanities.

Chapman, Glenn. These, My People. 1978. 6.95 o.p. (ISBN 0-533-03049-8). Vantage.

Chapman, Graham, et al. Monty Python's the Life of Brian. (Illus.). 1979. pap. 9.95 o.p. (ISBN 0-448-16568-6, G&D). Putnam Pub Group.

Chapman, Harold, jt. auth. see Sansom, W. M.

Chapman, Harry, jt. auth. see Chapman, Jane.

Chapman, Herman H. & Meyer, Walter H. Forest Mensuration. (The American Forestry Ser). (Illus.). 1949. 19.95 o.p. (ISBN 0-07-010647-9, C). McGraw.

Chapman, Hester W. The Challenge of Anne Boleyn. LC 74-79681. (Illus.). 320p. 1974. 7.95 o.p. (ISBN 0-698-10612-1, Coward). Putnam Pub Group.

Chapman, J. B. Dr. Schuessler's Biochemistry. 1973. 6.95x (ISBN 0-7225-0639-2, Pub. by Thorsons). Formur Intl.

Chapman, J. B. & Perry, Edward L. The Biochemic Handbook. Orig. Title: Biochemic Theory & Practice. 1976. pap. 1.50 (ISBN 0-89378-051-0). Formur Intl.

Chapman, J. W. & Drifte, R., eds. Japan's Quest for Comprehensive Security: Defense, Diplomacy & Dependence. LC 81-48263. 272p. 1982. 25.00x (ISBN 0-312-44070-7). St Martin.

Chapman, Jane & Chapman, Harry. Psychology of Health Care: A Humanistic Perspective. LC 82-21873. 250p. 1983. pap. text ed. 12.95 (ISBN 0-534-01291-4). Brooks-Cole.

Chapman, Jane R. Economic Realities & Female Crime: Program Choices & Economic Rehabilitation. LC 79-3785. 240p. 1980. 23.95x (ISBN 0-669-03515-7). Lexington Bks.

Chapman, Jean. The Sugar-Plum Christmas Book. (Teacher Resource Collections Ser.). (Illus.). 190p. 1982. lib. bdg. 17.25 (ISBN 0-516-08952-8). Childrens.

--Velvet Paws & Wiskers. (Teacher Resource Collections Ser.). (Illus.). 168p. 1982. lib. bdg. 17.25 (ISBN 0-516-08953-6). Childrens.

Chapman, Jefferson. The Icehouse Bottom Site. (Illus.). 146p. 1975. pap. 7.95x (ISBN 0-87049-179-2, Pub. by U of TN Dept of Anthropology). U of Tenn Pr.

Chapman, Jeffrey I. Proposition Thirteen & Land Use: A Case Study of Fiscal Limits in California. LC 79-3749. 1981. 24.95x (ISBN 0-669-03471-1). Lexington Bks.

Chapman, John. Adult English One. (Illus.). 1978. pap. 9.95 (ISBN 0-13-008821-8). P-H.

--Adult English Three. 1978. pap. 9.95 (ISBN 0-13-008862-5). P-H.

--Adult English Two. (Illus.). 1978. pap. 9.95 (ISBN 0-13-008839-0). P-H.

--Welcome to English: Let's Begin. (Welcome to English Ser.). (Illus.). 48p. 1980. pap. 2.75 o.p. (ISBN 0-88345-379-7); tchr's manual 2.95 o.p. (ISBN 0-88345-448-3). Regents Pub.

Chapman, John, jt. auth. see Richardson, Robin.

Chapman, John D. & Sherman, John C., eds. Oxford Regional Economic Atlases: The United States & Canada. 2nd ed. (Illus.). 1975. pap. 11.95x (ISBN 0-19-894308-3). Oxford U Pr.

Chapman, John F., jt. ed. see Bursk, Edward C.

Chapman, Keeler C. & Traister, John E. Homes for the Nineteen-Eighties: An Energy & Construction Design Aid. LC 82-5929. (Illus.). 256p. pap. 16.95 (ISBN 0-8306-1425-7). TAB Bks.

Chapman, Kim W. The Magic Hat. 2nd ed. LC 76-20842. (Illus.). 47p. (gr. k-4). 1976. pap. 3.25 (ISBN 0-914996-10-X). Lollipop Power.

Chapman, L. Disordered Thought in Schizophrenia. 1974. 27.95 (ISBN 0-13-216192-3). P-H.

Chapman, L. J. & Putnam, D. F. Physiography of Southern Ontario. 2nd ed. LC 66-6736. (Illus.). 1966. 27.50x o.p. (ISBN 0-8020-1944-7); pap. 7.50 o.p. (ISBN 0-8020-6071-4); maps 12.50x o.p. (ISBN 0-8020-2107-7). U of Toronto Pr.

Chapman, L. R. The Process of Learning Mathematics. LC 71-178683. 405p. 1972. text ed. 72.00 o.s.i. (ISBN 0-08-016623-7); pap. text ed. 21.00 (ISBN 0-08-017357-8). Pergamon.

Chapman, Laura H. Approaches to Art in Education. 444p. 1978. text ed. 21.95 (ISBN 0-15-502896-0, HC). HarBraceJ.

Chapman, Linda L., et al. Louis H. Sullivan Architectural Ornament Collection: Southern Illinois University at Edwardsville. LC 81-51083. (Illus.). 79p. (Orig.). 1981. pap. 10.00 (ISBN 0-89062-136-5, Pub by Southern Illinois Univ Edwardsville). Pub Ctr Cult Res.

Chapman, M. A. & Lewis, M. H. An Introduction to the Freshwater Crustacea of New Zealand. (Illus.). 261p. 1983. 19.95 (ISBN 0-00-216905-3, Pub. by W Collins Australia). Intl Schol Bk Serv.

Chapman, M. Winslow. Gelded Centaur. LC 68-8884. 1968. 4.00 o.p. (ISBN 0-8233-0012-9). Golden Quill.

--Seen from Space. 1972. 4.00 o.p. (ISBN 0-685-02640-X). Golden Quill.

Chapman, Margaret. Directing the Work of Others. (Illus.). 1972. pap. 0.35, 10 for 2.00 (ISBN 0-88441-023-4, 19-981-010). GS.

Chapman, Marvey. Marmac Guide to Los Angeles: 1984 Olympic Games Edition. Nicholson, Diana, ed. (Marmac Guide Ser.). (Illus.). 304p. (Orig.). 1983. pap. 6.95 (ISBN 0-939944-14-6). Marmac Pub.

Chapman, O. L., ed. Organic Photochemistry, Vol. 2. 1969. 52.25 o.p. (ISBN 0-8247-1097-5). Dekker.

Chapman, Orville L. Organic Syntheses, Vol. 60. LC 21-17747. (Organic Syntheses Ser.). 156p. 1981. 22.50 (ISBN 0-471-09359-9, Pub. by Wiley-Interscience). Wiley.

Chapman, Phil. Electricity. (Young Scientist Ser.). (gr. 5-9). 1976. 6.95 (ISBN 0-86020-077-9, Usborne-Hayes); PLB 9.95 (ISBN 0-88110-006-4); pap. 3.95 (ISBN 0-686-36305-1). EDC.

Chapman, R. E. Petroleum Geology: A Concise Study. LC 72-97426. 310p. 1976. pap. 30.00 (ISBN 0-444-41432-0). Elsevier.

Chapman, R. F. Biology of Locusts. (Studies in biology: No. 71). 72p. 1978. pap. text ed. 8.95 (ISBN 0-7131-2619-1). E Arnold.

--A Laboratory Study of Roosting Behavior in Hoppers of the African Migratory Locust (Locusta Migratoria Migratorioides R & F) 1955. 35.00x (ISBN 0-85135-007-0, Pub. by Centre Overseas Research). State Mutual Bk.

Chapman, R. W., ed. see Austen, Jane.

Chapman, Raymond. The Language of English Literature. 160p. 1982. pap. text ed. 9.95 (ISBN 0-7131-6371-2). E Arnold.

--Short Way to Better English. pap. 6.50x (ISBN 0-392-04585-0, SpS). Sportshelf.

Chapman, Raymond, jt. ed. see Gottlieb, Nora.

Chapman, Renate. House of Shadows. 1982. pap. 6.95 (ISBN 0-686-84750-4, Avalon). Bouregy.

--Milmorra House. (YA) 1978. 6.95 (ISBN 0-685-53391-3, Avalon). Bouregy.

--Waters Dark & Deep. 1982. 6.95 (ISBN 0-686-84191-3, Avalon). Bouregy.

Chapman, Robert. Pilot Fatigue: A Deadly Cover Up. (Illus.). 1982. 10.95 (ISBN 0-682-49900-5, Banner). Exposition.

Chapman, Robert, et al, eds. The Archaeology of Death. LC 80-41751. (New Directions in Archaeology Ser.). (Illus.). 200p. 1981. 29.95 (ISBN 0-521-23775-0). Cambridge U Pr.

Chapman, Robert C., jt. auth. see Brandt, John C.

Chapman, Robert D., jt. auth. see Brandt, John C.

Chapman, Roger, jt. auth. see Landon, Robbins H.

Chapman, Ronald F. Leonard Wood & Leprosy in the Philippines: The Culion Leper Colony, 1921-1927. LC 80-6301. (Illus.). 238p. (Orig.). 1982. lib. bdg. 21.75 (ISBN 0-8191-1976-8); pap. text ed. 10.75 (ISBN 0-8191-1977-6). U Pr of Amer.

Chapman, Ruth. Fingerprints. (gr. 3-6). 1981. 6.95 (ISBN 0-86653-045-2, GA 274). Good Apple.

Chapman, S. & Cowling, T. G. Mathematical Theory of Non-Uniform Gases. 3rd ed. LC 70-77285. (Illus.). 1970. 49.50 (ISBN 0-521-07577-7). Cambridge U Pr.

Chapman, Stanley, jt. ed. see Brena, Steven.

Chapman, Stephen & Nakielny, Richard. A Guide to Radiological Procedures. 1981. pap. text ed. 17.95x (ISBN 0-02-857410-9, Bailliere-Tindall). Saunders.

Chapman, Stephen, ed. see Bishop, Douglas D.

Chapman, Suzanne E., ed. Early American Design Motifs. LC 73-86040. (Illus.). 160p. 1974. 7.95 (ISBN 0-486-23084-8); pap. 4.50 (ISBN 0-486-22985-8). Dover.

Chapman, T. Time: A Philosophical Analysis. 1982. 29.50 (ISBN 90-277-1465-7, Pub. by Reidel Holland). Kluwer Boston.

Chapman, V. J. Mangrove Vegetation. 1976. 60.00 (ISBN 3-7682-0926-1). Lubrecht & Cramer.

--Salt Marshes & Salt Deserts of the World. 2nd ed. 1974. 60.00 (ISBN 3-7682-0927-X). Lubrecht & Cramer.

Chapman, V. J. & Chapman, D. J. The Algae. 2nd ed. 500p. 1975. 25.00 (ISBN 0-312-01715-4). St Martin.

--Seaweeds & Their Uses. 1980. 49.95x (ISBN 0-412-15740-3, Pub. by Chapman & Hall England). Methuen Inc.

Chapman, V. J., ed. The Marine Algae of New Zealand: Phaeophyceae, Vol.2. 1961. pap. 16.00 (ISBN 3-7682-0077-9). Lubrecht & Cramer.

Chapman, Vera. Blaedud the Birdman. 1980. pap. 1.95 o.s.i. (ISBN 0-380-45070-4, 45070). Avon.

--The King's Damsel. 1978. pap. 1.50 o.p. (ISBN 0-380-01916-7, 37606). Avon.

--Miranty & the Alchemist. 80p. 1983. pap. 2.25 (ISBN 0-380-79269-9, Camelot). Avon.

--The Wife of Bath. 1978. pap. 1.75 o.p. (ISBN 0-380-38976-2, 38976). Avon.

Chapman, Victoria L. Let's Go to a Service Station. new ed. (Let's Go Ser.). (Illus.). 48p. (gr. 2-5). 1974. PLB 4.29 o.p. (ISBN 0-399-60805-2). Putnam Pub Group.

--Let's Go to a Supermarket. (Let's Go Ser.). (Illus.). (gr. 3-5). 1972. PLB 4.29 o.p. (ISBN 0-399-60402-2). Putnam Pub Group.

Chapnick, Howard, ed. see Thoreau, Henry D.

Chapnick, Howard, ed. see Whitman, Walt.

Chappel, Allen H., tr. see Aichinger, Ilse.

Chappell, Annette J. Skiing Is for Me. LC 78-12411. (The Sports for Me Bks). (Illus.). (gr. 5 up). 1978. PLB 6.95g (ISBN 0-8225-1082-0). Lerner Pubns.

Chappell, Annette Jo, jt. auth. see Dickmeyer, Lowell A.

Chappell, Carl L. Virgil I. Grissom: Boy Astronaut. (Childhood of Famous Americans Ser). 200p. (gr. 8 up). 1971. 3.95 o.p. (ISBN 0-672-51622-5). Bobbs.

Chappell, Clovis G. Chappell's Special Day Sermons. (Pocket Pulpit Library). 204p. 1983. pap. 3.95. Baker Bk.

Chappell, David W., jt. ed. see Saso, Michael.

Chappell, Fred. Driftlake: A Lieder Cycle. 8p. (Orig.). 1981. pap. 6.00 o.s.i. (ISBN 0-931182-07-7); pap. 8.00 signed, Swedish marbled wrappers o.s.i. (ISBN 0-686-34577-0). Iron Mtn Pr.

--River: A Poem. LC 73-91773. 52p. 1975. pap. 4.95 o.p. (ISBN 0-8071-0094-3). La State U Pr.

Chappell, Helen. All Things in Their Season. (Orig.). 1983. pap. 3.95 (ISBN 0-440-10057-7). Dell.

--The Waxing Moon: A Gentle Guide to Magick. LC 73-89670. (Illus.). 1974. pap. 3.95 o.p. (ISBN 0-8256-3032-0, 030032, Quick Fox). Putnam Pub Group.

Chappell, Jeannette. Destination Uncharted. 1965. 3.00 o.p. (ISBN 0-8233-0013-7). Golden Quill.

Chappell, R. T. & Read, W. L. Business Communications. 232p. 1980. 30.00x (ISBN 0-7121-0272-8, Pub. by Macdonald & Evans). State Mutual Bk.

Chappell, Sally & Van Zanten, Ann. Barry Byrne & John Lloyd Wright: Architecture & Design. LC 82-71372. 72p. 1982. pap. 9.95 (ISBN 0-686-97827-7, 10416-8). U of Chicago Pr.

Chappell, Sally K. & Zanten, Ann V. Barry Byrne & John Lloyd Wright: Architecture & Design. LC 82-71372. (Illus.). 72p. 1982. pap. 9.95 (ISBN 0-913820-11-3). Chicago Hist.

Chappell, Warren, ed. The Nutcracker: Based on the Alexandre Dumas pere Version of the Story by E. T. A. Hoffmann. LC 80-15576. (Illus.). 40p. (gr. k-6). 1980. pap. 5.95 (ISBN 0-8052-0660-4). Schocken.

Chappelow, Allan. Shaw the Villager & Human Being. 380p. 1982. 40.00x (ISBN 0-284-39176-X, Pub. by C Skilton Scotland). State Mutual Bk.

Chapple, Eliot D. The Biological Foundations of Individuality & Culture. LC 79-23284. 388p. (Orig.). 1980. lib. bdg. 19.50 (ISBN 0-89874-041-X). Krieger.

Chapple, Eliot D. & Coon, Carlton S. Principles of Anthropology. LC 77-9616. 768p. 1978. Repr. 35.50 (ISBN 0-88275-583-8). Krieger.

Chapple, J. Elizabeth Gaskell: A Portrait in Letters. (Illus.). 192p. 1982. text ed. 26.00x (ISBN 0-7190-0799-2). Verry.

Chapple, Jonathan, jt. auth. see Porter, Jimathan.

Chapple, Richard. A Dostoevsky Dictionary. 512p. 1983. 30.00 (ISBN 0-88233-727-0). Ardis Pubs.

Chapra, Steven, jt. auth. see Reckhow, Kenneth H.

Chapuis, R. J. One Hundred Years of Telephone Switching (1878-1978) Part 1, 1878-1960's - Manual & Electromechanical Switching. (Studies in Telecommunications: Vol. 1). 464p. 1982. 106.50 (ISBN 0-444-86289-7, North Holland). Elsevier.

Chaput, Richard. All I Can Give. LC 72-83553. (Illus.). 158p. 1972. pap. 0.95 o.p. (ISBN 0-8189-1104-2, Pub. by Alba Bks). Alba.

Char, John K. Holistic Dentistry. Date not set. cancelled (ISBN 0-9601978-3-4). G A Eversaul.

Char, Rene. No Siege Is Absolute. Wright, Franz, tr. from Fr. LC 82-84378. (Lost Roads Ser.: No.22). 55p. (Orig., Fr. & Eng.). 1983. pap. 5.95 (ISBN 0-918786-25-8). Lost Roads.

Char, S. V. Readings in the Constitutional History of India. 720p. 1982. 49.00x (ISBN 0-19-561264-7). Oxford U Pr.

Char, T. Narasimha. Principles & Precedents of Estate Duty. 1971. lib. bdg. 20.00x o.p. (ISBN 0-210-31160-6). Asia.

Char, Tin-Yuke, ed. The Sandalwood Mountains: Readings & Stories of the Early Chinese in Hawaii. LC 74-76375. 400p. 1975. 14.95 (ISBN 0-8248-0305-1). UH Pr.

Charak, Sukhder S. History & Culture of Himalayan States, Vol. 1. (Himachal Pradesh Ser.: Pt. 1). (Illus.). 1979. text ed. 36.75x (ISBN 0-391-01047-6). Humanities.

--History & Culture of Himalayan States, Vol. 2. (Himachal Pradesh Ser.: Pt. 2). 1979. text ed. 36.75x (ISBN 0-391-01176-6). Humanities.

--History & Culture of Himalayan States, Vol. 3: Himachal Pradesh, Pt. 3. 385p. 1979. text ed. 36.75x (ISBN 0-391-01747-0). Humanities.

Charak, Sukhdev Singh. History & Culture of Himalayan States of the Jammu Kingdom, Vol. V, Pt. II. 421p. 1981. text ed. 36.75x (ISBN 0-391-02232-6, Pub. by UBS India). Humanities.

Charalambous, J. Mass Spectrometry of Metal Compounds. 320p. 1975. 34.95 o.p. (ISBN 0-408-70678-3). Butterworth.

Charap, Stanley H., jt. auth. see Chikazumi, Sushin.

Charatsis, E. G., ed. Proceedings of the Econometric Society European Meeting, 1979: Papers in Memory of Stefan Valavanis. (Contributions to Economic Analysis Ser.: Vol. 138). 1982. 98.00 (ISBN 0-444-86184-X). Elsevier.

Charbon, M. H. Historische en theoretische werken tot Eighteen Hundred: Catalogus van de muziekbibliotheek van het Haags Gemeentemuseum, 2 vols. (Haags Gemeente-Museum Ser.). 1973. 45.00 o.s.i. (ISBN 90-6027-073-8, Pub. by Frits Knuf Netherlands). Pendragon NY.

Charbonneau, Harvey C. & Webster, Gordon L. Industrial Quality Control. (Illus.). 1978. ref. 23.95 (ISBN 0-13-464255-4). P-H.

Charbonneau, Louis. The Brea File. LC 80-698. 312p. 1983. 15.95 (ISBN 0-385-15508-5). Doubleday.

Chard, Chester S. Northeast Asia in Prehistory. LC 73-2040. (Illus.). 232p. 1974. 18.50x (ISBN 0-299-06430-1). U of Wis Pr.

Chard, T. An Introduction to Radioimmunoassay & Related Techniques. 2nd, rev. & enl. ed. (Laboratory Techniques in Biochemistry & Molecular Biology Ser.: Vol. 6, Pt. 2). 284p. 1982. 79.00 (ISBN 0-444-80420-X); pap. 30.00 (ISBN 0-444-80424-2). Elsevier.

Chardin, Pierre Teilhard De see Teilhard De Chardin, Pierre.

Charette, Beverly R., ed. Christian Nursery Rhymes. (Illus.). (ps-3). 1982. PLB 9.25g (ISBN 0-516-09225-1). Childrens.

Chargaff, Erwin. Voices in the Labyrinth: Nature, Man & Science. 190p. 1978. 9.95 (ISBN 0-8164-9322-7). Seabury.

Chari, M. V. & Silvester, P., eds. Finite Elements in Electrical & Magnetic Field Problems. LC 79-10377. (Wiley Series in Numerical Methods in Engineering). 1980. 49.95 (ISBN 0-471-27578-6, Pub. by Wiley-Interscience). Wiley.

Charite, Raymond C. La see La Charite, Raymond C.

Charities Aid Foundation, ed. Directory of Grant-Making Trusts (Great Britain), 1981. 7th ed. LC 74-188784. 1050p. 1981. 92.50x o.p. (ISBN 0-904757-11-0). Intl Pubns Serv.

Chariton, Igumen. The Art of Prayer. Kadloubovsky, Palmer, tr. 288p. 1966. 23.50 (ISBN 0-571-06899-5). Faber & Faber.

Charke, Charlotte C. Narrative of the Life of Mrs. Charlotte Charke. LC 70-81365. (Illus.). 1969. Repr. of 1755 ed. 37.00x (ISBN 0-8201-1065-5). Schol Facsimiles.

Charkey, Edward S. Electromechanical System Components. LC 73-37364. 1972. 59.95 (ISBN 0-471-14700-1, Pub. by Wiley-Interscience). Wiley.

Charles, Amy, ed. see Herbert, George.

Charles, Bernard H. Pottery & Porcelain: A Glossary of Terms. (Illus.). 320p. 1983. pap. 8.95 (ISBN 0-88254-278-8). Hippocrene Bks.

Charles, C. M. Educational Psychology: The Instructional Enedeavor. 2nd ed. LC 75-43611. 438p. 1976. pap. text ed. 15.95 (ISBN 0-8016-0952-6). Mosby.

--Elementary Classroom Management: A Handbook for Excellence in Teaching. Akers, Lane, ed. (Illus.). 452p. (Orig.). 1983. pap. text ed. 12.50x (ISBN 0-582-28349-3). Longman.

--Individualizing Instruction. 2nd ed. LC 79-26645. (Illus.). 284p. 1980. pap. 14.95 (ISBN 0-8016-0974-7). Mosby.

Charles, C. M. & Malian, Ida. The Special Student: Practical Help for the Classroom Teacher. LC 80-13053. (Illus.). 246p. 1980. pap. text ed. 13.95 (ISBN 0-8016-1132-6). Mosby.

Charles, C. M., ed. Learning Centers That Teach. 1978. pap. 10.75 o.p. (ISBN 0-8191-0367-5). U Pr of Amer.

Charles, Carol M., et al. Schooling, Teaching & Learning: American Education. LC 77-13496. (Illus.). 466p. 1978. text ed. 22.95 (ISBN 0-8016-0966-6). Mosby.

Charles, David & Hurry, David J. Medical Examination Review: Obstetrics & Gynecology, Vol. 4. 5th ed. 1983. pap. text ed. 11.95 (ISBN 0-87488-104-8). Med Exam.

Charles, Donald. Calico Cat at School. LC 81-6096. (Calico Cat Story Bks.). (Illus.). 32p. (ps-3). 1981. 9.25 (ISBN 0-516-03445-6); pap. 2.95 (ISBN 0-516-43445-4). Childrens.

--Calico Cat's Exercise Book. LC 82-9640. (Calico Cat's Storybooks). (Illus.). (ps-3). 1982. PLB 9.25g (ISBN 0-516-03457-X); pap. 2.95 (ISBN 0-516-43457-8). Childrens.

--Count on Calico Cat. LC 74-8007. (Calico Cat Story Bks.). (Illus.). 32p. (ps-3). 1974. PLB 9.25 (ISBN 0-516-03435-9); pap. 2.95 (ISBN 0-516-43435-7). Childrens.

--Fat Fat Calico Cat. LC 77-7154. (Calico Cat Story Bks.). (Illus.). 32p. (gr. 3). 1977. PLB 9.25 (ISBN 0-516-03456-1); pap. 2.95 (ISBN 0-516-43456-X). Childrens.

--Letters from Calico Cat. LC 74-8181. (Calico Cat Story Bks.). (Illus.). 32p. (ps-3). 1974. PLB 9.25 (ISBN 0-516-03519-3); pap. 2.95 (ISBN 0-516-43519-1). Childrens.

Charles, Edgar D. & Kronenfeld, Jennie J., eds. Social & Economic Impacts of Coronary Artery Disease. LC 79-1554. 160p. 1980. 21.95x (ISBN 0-669-02912-2). Lexington Bks.

Charles, G. J., jt. auth. see Patsavos, L. J.

Charles, J. Norman & Charles, Sharon. Vida Abundante en Familia. Carrodeguas, Andy & Marosi, Esteban, eds. Romanenghi de Powell, Elsa R., tr. 192p. (Span.). 1982. pap. 2.25 (ISBN 0-8297-1317-4). Life Pubs Intl.

Charles, John, jt. auth. see Yates, Miles.

Charles, K. J. Total Development: Essays Toward an Integration of Marxian & Gandhian Perspectives. 1983. text ed. write for info. (ISBN 0-7069-2075-9, Pub. by Vikas India). Advent NY.

Charles, Marie. Smoldering Embers, No. 65. 1982. pap. 1.75 (ISBN 0-515-06676-1). Jove Pubns.

Charles, Marie. Scenes from the Heart. (Second Chance at Love Ser.: No. 107). 1.75 (ISBN 0-515-06871-3). Jove Pubns.

Charles, Milene. The Soviet Union & Africa: The History of the Involvement. LC 80-67227. 250p. 1980. lib. bdg. 19.75 (ISBN 0-8191-1255-0); pap. text ed. 10.00 (ISBN 0-8191-1256-9). U Pr of Amer.

Charle's Scribner's Sons. Concise Dictionary of American History. 860p. 1982. 60.00 (ISBN 0-686-83678-2, ScribT). Scribner.

Charles, Searle F. Minister of Relief: Harry Hopkins & the Depression. LC 74-2585. (Illus.). 286p. 1974. Repr. of 1963 ed. lib. bdg. 17.25x (ISBN 0-8371-7407-4, CHMR). Greenwood.

Charles, Sharon, jt. auth. see Charles, J. Norman.

Charles, Steven. Vitreous Microsurgery. (Illus.). 200p. 1981. lib. bdg. 32.00 (ISBN 0-683-01550-8). Williams & Wilkins.

Charles, Vera K. Introduction to Mushroom Hunting. LC 73-85355. (Illus.). 1974. Repr. of 1931 ed. 2.50 (ISBN 0-486-20667-X). Dover.

Charles-Edwards, D., ed. Physiological Determinants of Crop Growth. Date not set. 26.00 (ISBN 0-12-169360-0). Acad Pr.

Charles-Picard, Gilbert, ed. see Larousse.

Charlesworth, Andrew, ed. An Atlas of Rural Protest in Britain, 1548-1900. LC 82-8362. (Illus.). 224p. 1982. 25.00x (ISBN 0-8122-7853-4). U of Pa Pr.

Charlesworth, B. Evolution in Age-Structured Populations. LC 79-8909. (Cambridge Studies in Mathematical Biology: No. 1). 250p. 1980. 44.50 (ISBN 0-521-23045-4); pap. 14.95 (ISBN 0-521-29786-9). Cambridge U Pr.

Charlesworth, James C. America's Changing Role As a World Leader. Lambert, Richard D., ed. LC 76-85466. (Annals Ser.: 384). 1969. 15.00 (ISBN 0-87761-118-1); pap. 7.95 (ISBN 0-87761-117-3). Am Acad Pol Soc Sci.

Charlesworth, James C., ed. Changing American People: Are We Deteriorating or Improving? LC 68-27641. (Annals of the American Academy of Political & Social Science: No. 378). 1968. 15.00 (ISBN 0-87761-109-2); pap. 7.95 (ISBN 0-87761-108-4). Am Acad Pol Soc Sci.

Charlesworth, James C. & Lambert, Richard D., eds. New American Posture Toward Asia. new ed. LC 72-120283. (Annals of the American Academy of Political & Social Science: No. 390). 1970. 15.00 (ISBN 0-87761-128-9); pap. 7.95 (ISBN 0-87761-127-0). Am Acad Pol Soc Sci.

Charlesworth, James H., ed. Old Testament Pseudepigrapha, Vol. I: Apocalyptic Literature & Testaments. LC 80-2443. 1000p. 1983. 35.00 (ISBN 0-385-09630-5). Doubleday.

Charlesworth, Maria L. Ministering Children. Lurie, Alison & Schiller, Justin G., eds. LC 75-32166. (Classics of Children's Literature Ser.: 1621-1932). PLB 38.00 o.s.i. (ISBN 0-8240-2279-3). Garland Pub.

Charlesworth, Max. The Existentialists & Jean-Paul Sartre. 1976. 18.95 (ISBN 0-312-27580-3). St Martin.

Charlesworth, R. & Radeloff, D. J. Experiences in Math for Young Children. LC 77-80039. 1978. pap. text ed. 11.80 (ISBN 0-8273-1660-7); instructor's guide 3.75 (ISBN 0-8273-1661-5). Delmar.

Charlesworth, Rosalind. Understanding Child Development. LC 81-66763. (Child Care Ser.). (Illus.). 246p. (Orig.). 1983. text ed. 16.00 (ISBN 0-8273-1855-3); instructor's guide 3.00 (ISBN 0-8273-1856-1). Delmar.

Charlesworth, Sarah. In-Photography. (Illus.). 16p. (Orig.). 1982. pap. 4.00 (ISBN 0-939784-03-3). CEPA Gall.

Charley, Helen. Food Science. 2nd ed. LC 81-11366. 564p. 1982. text ed. 22.50 (ISBN 0-471-06206-5). Wiley.

--Food Science. LC 80-17047. 530p. 1970. 25.95x o.p. (ISBN 0-471-07063-7). Wiley.

--Food Study Manual. 3rd ed. LC 79-75636. (Illus.). 275p. (Orig.). 1971. 17.95 (ISBN 0-471-07064-5, 14195); 24.95 (ISBN 0-471-06160-3). Wiley.

Charlier, Roger. Harnessing Ocean Energies: Tapping Ocean Energies to Produce Inexhaustible, Pollution-Free Electricity. 1977. Repr. 8.00x (ISBN 0-686-21178-2). Maple Mont.

Charlier, Roger H. & Gordon, Bernard L. Ocean Resources: An Introduction to Economic Oceanography. LC 78-61393. (Illus.). 1978. pap. text ed. 9.75 (ISBN 0-8191-0599-6). U Pr of Amer.

Charlier, Roger H., et al. Marine Science & Technology: An Introduction to Oceanography. LC 80-5234. (Illus.). 498p. 1980. pap. text ed. 16.75 (ISBN 0-8191-1065-5). U Pr of Amer.

Charlip, Remy. It Looks Like Snow. LC 81-20106. 24p. 1982. pap. 2.70 (ISBN 0-688-01542-5). Greenwillow.

Charlot, G., et al, eds. Selected Constants: Oxidation & Reduction Potentials of Inorganic Substances in Aqueous Solutions. 78p. 1976. text ed. write for info. (ISBN 0-08-020836-3). Pergamon.

Charlot, Jean. An Artist on Art: Collected Essays of Jean Charlot, 2 Vols. LC 77-120323. (Illus.). 1972. Set. box 40.00 (ISBN 0-87022-118-3). UH Pr.

Charlsen, David, jt. auth. see Bullard, Brian.

Charlsen, David, jt. auth. see Rosenberg, Jeff.

Charlton, Andrew & DeVries, John. Jazz & Commercial Arranging, 2 vols. 1982. Vol. I, 208p. pap. 17.95 (ISBN 0-13-509869-6); Vol. II, 176p. 16.95 (ISBN 0-13-509893-9). P-H.

Charlton, Bill, jt. auth. see Bentley, John.

Charlton, D. G., jt. ed. see Potts, D. C.

Charlton, David, ed. Etienne-Nicolas Mehul, Three Symphonies (3,4,5) (The Symphony 1720-1840 Series D: Vol. 8). 1982. lib. bdg. 90.00 (ISBN 0-8240-3812-6). Garland Pub.

Charlton, Elizabeth. Jeremy & the Ghost. LC 78-72120. (Illus.). (gr. k-3). 1979. 6.75 (ISBN 0-89799-118-4); pap. 3.50 (ISBN 0-89799-019-6). Dandelion Pr.

--Terrible Tyrannosaurus. LC 80-26318. (Illus.). 32p. (ps-3). 1982. 5.95 (ISBN 0-525-66724-5). Dandelion Pr.

Charlton, H. Dark Comedies of Shakespeare. LC 74-100728. (Studies in Shakespeare, No. 24). 1970. Repr. of 1937 ed. lib. bdg. 19.95x (ISBN 0-8383-0340-4). Haskell.

Charlton, H. B. Shakespearian Comedy. 1966. pap. 13.95x (ISBN 0-416-69260-5). Methuen Inc.

Charlton, Henry. Shakespeare's Comedies: The Consummation. LC 71-100738. (Studies in Shakespeare, No. 24). 1970. Repr. of 1937 ed. lib. bdg. 18.95x (ISBN 0-8383-0339-0). Haskell.

Charlton, James. The Charades Book. LC 82-48227. (Illus.). 160p. (Orig.). 1983. pap. 6.68i (ISBN 0-06-091025-9, CN 1025, CN). Har-Row.

Charlton, Leigh & Swanberg, Annette. Glad Rags II. LC 81-18036. (Illus.). 192p. (Orig.). 1981. pap. 8.95 (ISBN 0-87701-178-8). Chronicle Bks.

Charlton, Mark. The Gateway Guide to the ZX-81 & ZX-80. 176p. 1981. pap. 9.95 (ISBN 0-916688-41-0). Creative Comp.

Charlton, Robert E. Yellowstone Fishing Guide. (Illus.). 51p. (Orig.). 1982. pap. 4.10 (ISBN 0-686-35969-0). Tri-County.

Charman, Sarah, jt. auth. see Kraus, Richard.

Charmatz, Jan P. & Daggett, Harriet S., eds. Comparative Studies in Community Property Law. LC 77-1740. 1977. Repr. of 1955 ed. lib. bdg. 17.75x (ISBN 0-8371-9523-3, CHCST). Greenwood.

Charmaz, Kathleeen C. Social Reality of Death... (Sociology Ser.). 1980. text ed. 12.95 (ISBN 0-201-01033-X). A-W.

Charmglow. The Complete Barbecue Cookbook: Recipes for the Gas Grill & Water Smoker. (Illus.). 192p. 1983. 14.95 (ISBN 0-8092-5554-5). Contemp Bks.

Charnas, Suzy. The Vampire Tapestry. 1980. 11.95 o.p. (ISBN 0-671-25415-4). S&S.

Charnas, Suzy M. Motherlines. 1979. pap. 1.95 o.p. (ISBN 0-425-04157-3). Berkley Pub.

Charnay, J. P. Islamic Culture & Socio-Economic Change. (Social, Economic & Political Studies of the Middle East: No. 4). xii, 82p. 1981. text ed. 15.25x (ISBN 0-686-97630-4, Pub. by E J Brill Holland). Humanities.

Charneco. Competencias para la Oficina Moderna. 360p. 9.50 (ISBN 0-07-010649-5). McGraw.

Charney, David. Sensei. 448p. Date not set. pap. 3.25 (ISBN 0-441-75887-8). Ace Bks.

Charney, Elliott. Molecular Basis of Optical Activity: Optical Rotary Dispersion & Circular Dichroism. LC 79-9705. 1979. 39.95x (ISBN 0-471-14900-4, Pub. by Wiley-Interscience). Wiley.

Charney, Jonathan I., ed. The New Nationalism & the Use of Common Spaces: Issues in Marine Pollution & the Exploitation of Antarctica. LC 81-65006. (Illus.). 358p. 1982. text ed. 39.50x (ISBN 0-86598-012-8). Allanheld.

Charney, Maurice. Comedy High & Low: An Introduction to the Experience of Comedy. (Illus.). 1978. text ed. 12.95x (ISBN 0-19-502430-3); pap. text ed. 6.95x o.p. (ISBN 0-19-502320-X). Oxford U Pr.

--How to Read Shakespeare. 1971. 7.95 o.p. (ISBN 0-07-010655-X, GB); pap. 4.95 o.p. (ISBN 0-07-010659-2). McGraw.

--Julius Caesar. (Parallel Text Ser.). 1975. pap. 2.95 o.p. (ISBN 0-671-18739-2). Monarch Pr.

--Sexual Fiction. 200p. 1981. 14.95x (ISBN 0-416-31930-0); pap. 6.50 (ISBN 0-416-31940-8). Methuen Inc.

Charniak, E. & Wilks, Y. Computational Semantics. (Fundamental Studies in Computer Science: Vol. 4). 1976. 36.25 (ISBN 0-7204-0469-X, North-Holland). Elsevier.

Charnock, Richard S. Ludus Patronymicus: Or, the Etymology of Curious Surnames. LC 68-23141. 1968. Repr. of 1868 ed. 30.00x (ISBN 0-8103-3122-5). Gale.

Charny, Israel W. Strategies Against Violence: Design for Nonviolent Change. LC 78-3135. 1978. lib. bdg. 32.50 o.p. (ISBN 0-89158-151-0). Westview.

Charon, J. Symbolic Interactionism: An Introduction, an Interpretation, an Integration. 1979. pap. 13.95 (ISBN 0-13-870105-9). P-H.

Charosh, Mannis. Number Ideas Through Pictures. LC 73-4370. (Young Math Ser.). (Illus.). 40p. (gr. 1-5). 1974. PLB 10.89 (ISBN 0-690-00156-8, TYC-J). Har-Row.

--Straight Lines, Parallel Lines, Perpendicular Lines. LC 76-106569. (Young Math Ser). (Illus.). (gr. 1-4). 1970. 7.95 o.p. (ISBN 0-690-77992-5, TYC-J); PLB 10.89 (ISBN 0-690-77993-3). Har-Row.

Charp, Sylvia, jt. auth. see Ball, Marion J.

Charpin, J., et al, eds. Allergology. (International Congress Ser.: No. 251). (Abstracts - 8th Congress). 1971. 80.50 (ISBN 90-219-0164-1, Excerpta Medica). Elsevier.

Charques, Richard. The Twilight of Imperial Russia. (Illus.). 1974. pap. 6.95x (ISBN 0-19-519787-9, GB). Oxford U Pr.

Charran, R. & Maharaj, B. Va De Cuento. (Illus.). 1977. pap. text ed. 2.95x (ISBN 0-582-76616-8). Longman.

Charren, Peggy & Sandler, Martin W. Changing Channels: Living (Sensibly) with Television. LC 82-16243. (Illus.). 320p. 1982. 24.95 (ISBN 0-201-07253-X); pap. 11.95 (ISBN 0-201-07254-8). A-W.

Charron, Jean D. The Wisdom of Pierre Charron: An Original & Orthodox Code of Morality. LC 78-12595. (Illus.). 1979. Repr. of 1961 ed. lib. bdg. 16.00x (ISBN 0-313-21064-0, CHWO). Greenwood.

Charroux, Robert. The Mysteries of the Andes. 1977. pap. 2.25 o.p. (ISBN 0-380-01702-4, 33779). Avon.

Charry, Lawrence B. Comprehension Crosswords, 10 bks. Incl. Bk. 1. (gr. 3) (ISBN 0-89061-175-0, 101); Bk. 2. (gr. 4) (ISBN 0-89061-176-9, 102); Bk. 3. (gr. 5) (ISBN 0-89061-177-7, 103); Bk. 4. (gr. 6) (ISBN 0-89061-178-5, 104); Bk. 5. (gr. 7) (ISBN 0-89061-179-3, 105); Bk. 6. (gr. 8) (ISBN 0-89061-180-7, 1-6); Bk. 7. (gr. 9) (ISBN 0-89061-181-5, 107); Bk. 8. (gr. 10) (ISBN 0-89061-182-3, 108); Bk. 9. (gr. 11) (ISBN 0-89061-183-1, 109); Bk. 10. (gr. 12) (ISBN 0-89061-184-X, 110). (24p ea.). (gr. 3-12). 1979. pap. 10.00x ea. spirit masters. Jamestown Pubs.

Charter, D., jt. ed. see Betty, M.

Charteris, Evan E. John Sargent... with Reproductions from His Paintings & Drawings. LC 70-164163. (Illus.). xii, 308p. 1972. Repr. of 1927 ed. 42.00x (ISBN 0-8103-3946-3). Gale.

Charteris, Leslie. The Saint Goes On. 1982. pap. 2.50 (ISBN 0-441-74882-1, Pub. by Charter Bks). Ace Bks.

--The Saint Goes West. 200p. 1982. pap. 2.50 (ISBN 0-441-74883-X, Pub. by Charter Bks). Ace Bks.

Charters, Ann. Jack Kerouac. 2nd rev. ed. LC 75-30147. (Phoenix Bibliographies Ser.). (Illus.). 1975. 10.00 (ISBN 0-916228-06-1); pap. 3.50 o.p. (ISBN 0-916228-07-X). Phoenix Bk Shop.

--Kerouac. (Illus.). 416p. 1974. pap. 2.50 o.p. (ISBN 0-446-81331-1). Warner Bks.

--Nobody: The Story of Bert Williams. (Roots of Jazz Ser.). (Illus.). 157p. 1983. Repr. of 1970 ed. lib. bdg. 19.50 (ISBN 0-306-76190-4). Da Capo.

Charters, Janet. The General. (Illus.). 1961. 12.00 (ISBN 0-7100-1173-3). Routledge & Kegan.

Charters, Samuel. The Legacy of the Blues: Art & Lives of Twelve Great Bluesmen. LC 76-51809. (Roots of Jazz Ser.). (Illus.). 1977. 22.50 (ISBN 0-306-70847-7); pap. 6.95 (ISBN 0-306-80054-3). Da Capo.

--Mr. Jabi & Mr. Smythe. 190p. 1983. 12.95 (ISBN 0-7145-2779-3, Pub. by M Boyars). Merrimack Bk Serv.

--Roots of the Blues. (Illus.). 1982. pap. 5.95 (ISBN 0-399-50598-9, Perige). Putnam Pub Group.

--Sweet As the Showers of Rain. LC 76-50484. (Illus.). 224p. 1977. pap. 5.95 (ISBN 0-8256-0178-9, Quick Fox). Putnam Pub Group.

Charters, Samuel B. The Country Blues. LC 75-14122. (The Roots of Jazz Ser.). (Illus.). 288p. 1975. lib. bdg. 25.00 (ISBN 0-306-70678-4); pap. 6.95 (ISBN 0-306-80014-4). Da Capo.

--Jazz: New Orleans 1885-1963. (Roots of Jazz Ser.). 173p. 1983. Repr. of 1963 ed. lib. bdg. 17.50 (ISBN 0-306-76189-0). Da Capo.

Charters, Samuel B. & Kunstadt, Leonard. Jazz: A History of the New York Scene. (Roots of Jazz Ser.). 1981. Repr. of 1962 ed. lib. bdg. 32.50 (ISBN 0-306-76055-X). Da Capo.

Chartham, Robert. Advice to Women. pap. 1.25 o.p. (ISBN 0-451-07304-5, Y7304, Sig). NAL.

--The Sensuous Couple. 2nd ed. 192p. 1981. pap. 2.50 (ISBN 0-345-29543-9); 12 copy counter display 30.00 (ISBN 0-686-96670-8). Ballantine.

--Sex for Beginners. pap. 1.25 o.p. (ISBN 0-451-07008-9, Y7008, Sig). NAL.

Chartier, Armand. Litterature Historique: Populaire Franco-Amercaine. 108p. (Fr.). 1981. pap. text ed. 3.00x (ISBN 0-911409-40-8). Natl Mat Dev.

Chartier, Armand B. Barbey D'Aurevilly. (World Authors Ser.). 1977. lib. bdg. 15.95 (ISBN 0-8057-6305-8, Twayne). G K Hall.

Chartier, Jean-Pierre & Culhane, Terry. L' Anglais Chez Soi: English Alone (Francophone Edition) (Illus.). 160p. pap. 45.00 (ISBN 0-08-025308-3). Pergamon.

Chartock, Roselle & Spencer, Jack. The Holocaust Years: Society on Trial. 244p. Repr. 2.50 (ISBN 0-686-95069-0). ADL.

Chartrand, Mark R. Skyguide. LC 81-70086. (A Golden Field Guide Ser.). (Illus.). 280p. 1982. 9.95 (ISBN 0-307-47010-5, Golden Pr); pap. 6.95 (ISBN 0-307-13667-1). Western Pub.

--Skyguide Gift Box. (Illus.). 280p. 1982. 12.95 (ISBN 0-307-47011-3). Western Pub.

Charudattan, R. & Walker, H. Lynn. Biological Control of Weeds with Plant Pathogens. LC 82-1879. 304p. 1982. 42.50x (ISBN 0-471-08598-7, Pub. by Wiley-Interscience). Wiley.

Charvat, William. Emerson's American Lecture Engagements: A Chronological List. 1961. pap. 4.00 o.p. (ISBN 0-87104-069-7). NY Pub Lib.

Charvat, William, et al, eds. see Hawthorne, Nathaniel.

Charvet, John. A Critique of Freedom & Equality. (Cambridge Studies in the History & Theory of Politics). 224p. 1982. 39.50 (ISBN 0-521-23727-0). Cambridge U Pr.

--Feminism. (Modern Ideologies Ser.). 168p. 1982. text ed. 15.00x (ISBN 0-460-10255-9, Pub. by J. M. Dent England); pap. text ed. 7.95x (ISBN 0-460-11255-4, Pub. by J. M. Dent England). Biblio Dist.

--The Social Problem in the Philosophy of Rousseau. LC 73-88311. 136p. 1974. 24.95 (ISBN 0-521-20189-6). Cambridge U Pr.

Charwat, Andrew F., et al see Heat Transfer & Fluid Mechanics Institute.

Chasan, Daniel J. Up for Grabs: Inquiries into Who Wants What. LC 77-23881. 134p. 1977. 9.95 (ISBN 0-914842-18-8); pap. 5.95 (ISBN 0-914842-17-X). Madrona Pubs.

Chasco, Edmond De see De Chasca, Edmund.

Chase & Ducat. Chase & Ducat Constitutional Interpretation, Cases-Essays-Materials. 2nd ed. LC 79-14772. 1490p. 1979. text ed. 25.95 (ISBN 0-8299-2052-8); supplement avail. (ISBN 0-314-69638-5). West Pub.

Chase, Agnes, ed. see Smithsonian Institution, Washington, D. C.

Chase, Allan. Magic Shots: A Human & Scientific Account of the Long & Continuing Struggle to Eradicate Infectious Diseases by Vaccination. LC 82-12505. 600p. 1982. 19.95 (ISBN 0-688-00787-2). Morrow.

--The Truth About STD: The Old Ones - Herpes & Other New Ones - the Primary Causes - the Available Cures. 188p. 1983. 10.95 (ISBN 0-688-01896-3). Morrow.

--The Truth About STD: The Old Ones--Herpes & Other New Ones--the Primary Causes--the Available Cures. 188p. 1983. pap. 5.95 (ISBN 0-688-01835-1). Quill NY.

Chase, Alston H. & Phillips, Henry, Jr., eds. New Greek Reader. LC 54-12234. (Illus.). (gr. 10 up). 1954. pap. text ed. 12.00x o.p. (ISBN 0-674-61550-6). Harvard U Pr.

Chase, C. I. Elementary Statistical Procedures. 2nd ed. 1976. text ed. 21.50 (ISBN 0-07-010681-9, C). McGraw.

Chase, Catherine. An Alphabet Book. LC 78-72095. (Illus.). (gr. k). 1979. 6.75 (ISBN 0-89799-087-0); pap. 3.50 (ISBN 0-89799-000-5). Dandelion Pr.

--Baby Mouse Goes Searching. LC 81-2243. (Illus.). 32p. (ps-3). 1982. 6.75 (ISBN 0-525-66742-3). Dandelion Pr.

--Baby Mouse Goes Shopping. (Illus.). 32p. (ps-2). 1981. 6.75 o.p. (ISBN 0-525-66742-3, 0655-200). Lodestar Bks.

--Hot & Cold. LC 78-72101. (First Reader Ser.). (Illus.). (gr. k-3). 1979. 6.75 (ISBN 0-89799-110-9); pap. 3.50 (ISBN 0-89799-021-8). Dandelion Pr.

--Pete, the Wet Pet. LC 81-2203. (Illus.). 32p. (ps-3). 1982. 6.75 (ISBN 0-525-66746-6). Dandelion Pr.

--See the Fly Fly. LC 78-72104. (First Reader Ser.). (Illus.). (gr. k-3). 1979. 6.75 (ISBN 0-89799-133-8); pap. 3.50 (ISBN 0-89799-023-4). Dandelion Pr.

Chase, Charlotte, jt. auth. see Harrell, Pauline C.

Chase, Chris. The Great American Waistline: Putting It on & Taking It off. 1981. 14.95 (ISBN 0-698-11069-2, Coward). Putnam Pub Group.

Chase, Chris, jt. auth. see Ford, Betty.

Chase, Colin, ed. The Dating of Beowulf. (Toronto Old English Ser.: No. 7). 275p. 1981. 27.50x (ISBN 0-8020-5576-1). U of Toronto Pr.

Chase, Deborah. The Medically-Based No-Nonsense Beauty Book. LC 74-7728. 352p. 1974. 15.50 (ISBN 0-394-48049-X). Knopf.

Chase, Edward L. Big Book of Horses. (Illus.). (gr. 4-6). 1970. 1.95 (ISBN 0-448-02241-9, G&D). Putnam Pub Group.

Chase, Elaine R. Best Laid Plans. (Finding Mr. Right Ser.). 224p. 1983. pap. 2.75 (ISBN 0-380-82743-3, 82743-3). Avon.

Chase, Elliot. Goodbye Goliath. 192p. 1983. 11.95 (ISBN 0-684-17844-3, ScribT). Scribner.

Chase, Ernest D. Romance of Greeting Cards: An Historical Account of the Origin, Evolution, & Development. LC 76-159914. (Tower Bks). (Illus.). 1971. Repr. of 1926 ed. 45.00x (ISBN 0-8103-3903-X). Gale.

Chase, Francine. A Visit to the Hospital. (Elephant Bks.). (Illus.). (gr. k-3). 1977. pap. 2.95 o.s.i. (ISBN 0-448-14011-X, G&D). Putnam Pub Group.

Chase, Francis S. Education Faces New Demands. LC 56-12940. (Horace Mann Lecture Ser.). 1956. 4.95x o.p. (ISBN 0-8229-1012-8). U of Pittsburgh Pr.

Chase, Gordon & Reveal, Betsy. How to Manage in the Public Sector. 192p. 1983. pap. text ed. 9.95 (ISBN 0-201-10127-0). A-W.

Chase, Harold, et al, eds. Biographical Dictionary of the Federal Judiciary. LC 76-18787. (Illus.). 256p. 1976. 78.00x (ISBN 0-8103-1125-9). Gale.

Chase, Harold W., jt. auth. see Ducat, Craig R.

Chase, Harry E. Eden in Winter. LC 78-71941. 1978. write for info. (ISBN 0-9601662-2-X). C Schneider.

Chase, Helen M., jt. auth. see Chase, William D.

Chase, Ilka. New York Twenty Two. LC 73-112322. 308p. Repr. of 1951 ed. lib. bdg. 16.25x (ISBN 0-8371-4710-7, CHNY). Greenwood.

Chase, Joan. During the Reign of the Queen of Persia. LC 82-48680. 288p. 1983. 14.37i (ISBN 0-06-015136-6, HarpT). Har-Row.

Chase, Joan A., jt. auth. see Ames, Louise B.

Chase, John. Exterior Decoration: Hollywood's Inside-Out Houses. Gebhard, David, ed. LC 82-9268. (California Architecture & Architects Ser.: No. 2). (Illus.). 128p. 1982. pap. 19.95 (ISBN 0-912158-88-3). Hennessey.

--Frenchmen, Desire, Good Children & Other Streets of New Orleans. (Illus.). 1949. 12.95 (ISBN 0-88289-384-X). Pelican.

--Frenchmen, Desire, Good Children & Other Streets of New Orleans. LC 49-48566. 1982. 12.95 (ISBN 0-88289-384-X). Pelican.

Chase, Leslie. Proven Techniques for Increasing Database Use. 1983. 49.95 (ISBN 0-942774-09-4). Info Indus.

Chase, Leslie, jt. ed. see Rosenau, Fred. S.

Chase Manhattan Bank. The Cashier. (Illus.). 96p. (gr. 10-12). 1975. pap. 8.92 wktext (ISBN 0-07-010690-8, G); cassettes 250.00 (ISBN 0-07-087715-7). McGraw.

Chase, Merrill W., jt. ed. see Williams, Curtis A.

Chase, Michael & Weitzman, Elliott, eds. Sleep Disorders: Basic & Clinical Research. (Advances in Sleep Research: Vol. 8). (Illus.). 604p. 1983. text ed. 85.00 (ISBN 0-89335-166-0). SP Med & Sci Bks.

Chase, Naomi F. A Child Is Being Beaten: Violence Against Children, an American Tragedy. LC 76-25577. (McGraw-Hill Paperbacks). 1976. pap. 4.95 (ISBN 0-07-010685-1, SP). McGraw.

Chase, Richard, ed. Old Songs & Singing Games. LC 72-85499. (Illus.). 64p. 1973. pap. 2.00 (ISBN 0-486-22879-7). Dover.

Chase, Robert A. Atlas of Hand Surgery. LC 72-97907. (Illus.). 438p. 1973. text ed. 60.00 (ISBN 0-7216-2495-2). Saunders.

Chase, Salmon P. Diary & Correspondence of Salmon P. Chase. LC 74-75301. (Law, Politics, & History Ser). 1971. Repr. of 1903 ed. lib. bdg. 59.50 (ISBN 0-306-71264-4). Da Capo.

--Inside Lincoln's Cabinet. Donald, David, ed. Repr. of 1954 ed. 17.00 o.p. (ISBN 0-527-16200-0). Kraus Repr.

Chase, Samuel. Trial of Samuel Chase, an Associate Justice of the Supreme Court Impeached by the House of Representatives, 2 vols. LC 69-11324. (Law, Politics, & History Ser). 1970. Repr. of 1805 ed. Set. lib. bdg. 79.50 (ISBN 0-306-71181-8). Da Capo.

Chase, Sara. Moving to Win: The Physics of Sports. LC 77-638. (Illus.). 128p. (gr. 7 up). 1977. PLB 6.64 o.p. (ISBN 0-671-32834-4). Messner.

Chase, Stuart. Government in Business. LC 71-136849. 296p. 1971. Repr. of 1935 ed. lib. bdg. 15.50x (ISBN 0-8371-5283-6, CHGB). Greenwood.

Chase, Thomas N., jt. ed. see Friedhoff, Arnold H.

Chase, U. & Sweedler, M. E. Hopf Algebras & Galois Theory Two. LC 75-84143. (Lecture Notes in Mathematics: Vol. 97). (Orig.). 1969. pap. 10.70 o.p. (ISBN 0-387-04616-X). Springer-Verlag.

Chase, Virginia. Speaking of Maine: A Selection from the Writings of Virginia Chase. Shea, Margaret, ed. (Illus.). 128p. (Orig.). 1983. pap. price not set (ISBN 0-89272-164-2). Down East.

Chase, W. P. Management of System Engineering. 228p. Repr. of 1974 ed. text ed. 26.50 (ISBN 0-471-14915-2). Krieger.

Chase, William C. The American Law School & the Rise of Administrative Government. 192p. 1982. text ed. 18.50 (ISBN 0-299-09100-7). U of Wis Pr.

Chase, William D. & Chase, Helen M. Chases' Calendar of Annual Events: Special Days, Weeks & Months in 1983. rev. ed. (Illus.). 180p. (Orig.). 1982. pap. 12.95 (ISBN-0-913082-30-9). Apple Tree.

Chase, Wilton P. Management of Systems Engineering. LC 73-18445. (Systems Engineering & Analysis Ser.). (Illus.). 176p. 1974. 29.95 o.p. (ISBN 0-471-14915-2, Pub. by Wiley-Interscience). Wiley.

Chase-Dunn, Christopher K. Socialist States in the World-System. (Sage Focus Editions). 320p. 1982. 25.00 (ISBN 0-8039-1878-X); pap. 12.50 (ISBN 0-8039-1879-8). Sage.

Chasen, Nancy H. Policy Wise: The Practical Guide to Insurance Decisions for Older Consumers. (American Association of Retired Persons Publications). 148p. 1983. pap. 5.95 (ISBN 0-673-24806-2). Scott F.

Chasen, Sylvan H. Geometric Principles & Procedures for Computer Graphic Applications. LC 78-7998. (Illus.). 1978. 27.00 (ISBN 0-13-352559-7). P-H.

Chase-Riboud, Barbara. Sally Hemings. 416p. 1980. pap. 3.50 (ISBN 0-380-48686-5, 59386-6). Avon.

Chasis, David A. Plastic Piping Systems. LC 75-45420. 216p. 1976. 25.00. Indus Pr.

Chaska. The Nursing Profession. (Illus.). 1977. pap. text ed. 21.00 (ISBN 0-07-010695-9, HP). McGraw.

Chasman, Herbert. Who Gets the Business? 200p. 1983. 14.95 (ISBN 0-910580-73-1). Farnswth Pub.

Chasse, Paul. Les Arts et La Litterature Ches la Franco-Americains de la nouvelle-angleterre. (Fr.). (gr. 9-10). 1975. pap. text ed. 1.25 (ISBN 0-911409-10-6). Natl Mat Dev.

Chasseaud, L. F., jt. auth. see Bridges, J. W.

Chasseaud, L. F., jt. ed. see Bridges, J. W.

Chast, Roz. Unscientific Americans. LC 82-4959. (Illus.). 1982. pap. 7.95 (ISBN 0-686-83029-6). Dial.

Chastain, James G., tr. see Stadelmann, Rudolph.

Chastain, Joel W., Jr., ed. U. S. Research Reactors. (AEC Technical Information Center Ser.). 78p. 1957. pap. 11.50 (ISBN 0-87079-380-2, TID-7013); microfiche 4.50 (ISBN 0-87079-483-3, TID-7013). DOE.

Chastain, Josephine K. Word Pictures. 112p. 1983. 7.00 (ISBN 0-682-49950-1). Exposition.

Chastain, Kenneth. Developing Second Language Skills: Theory to Practice. 2nd ed. 1976. 18.95 (ISBN 0-395-31008-3). HM.

--Spanish Grammar in Review: Patterns for Communication. pap. 14.50 (ISBN 0-395-30966-2). HM.

Chastain, Thomas. The Diamond Exchange. LC 80-1118. 240p. 1981. 10.95 o.p. (ISBN 0-385-14438-5). Doubleday.

--High Voltage. 1981. pap. 2.50 o.p. (ISBN 0-425-04831-4). Berkley Pub.

Chastek, Winifred K. Keyboard Skills: Sight Reading, Transposition, Harmonization, Improvisation. 1967. 14.95x (ISBN 0-534-00666-3). Wadsworth Pub.

Chaston, Gloria, jt. auth. see Jaussi, Laureen.

Chaston, I. R., intro. by. Asian Mining '81. 311p. (Orig.). pap. text ed. 100.00x (ISBN 0-900488-61-1). IMM North Am.

Chateaubriand, Francois R. De see De Chateaubriand, Francois R.

Chateaubriand, Francois-Rene de. Atala & Rene. Putter, Irving, tr. 1952. pap. 5.95x (ISBN 0-520-00223-7, CAMPUS8). U of Cal Pr.

Chateau-Lyon, P. L. La Henriade. Repr. of 1780 ed. 138.00 o.p. (ISBN 0-8287-0182-2). Clearwater Pub.

Chatelain, Agnes, jt. ed. see Cimino, Louis.

Chatelain, Alfred V. Ancient Europe in the Vision of the Rarest Available Steel Engravings. (Illus.). 99p. Repr. of 1887 ed. 227.75 (ISBN 0-89901-112-8). Found Class Reprints.

Chatelaine, Kenneth L. Harry Stack Sullivan: The Formative Years. LC 80-6251. 577p. (Orig.). 1981. lib. bdg. 30.00 (ISBN 0-8191-1552-5); pap. text ed. 19.00 (ISBN 0-8191-1553-3). U Pr of Amer.

Chatelin, Francoise. Special Approximation of Linear Operators. (Computer Science & Applied Mathematics Ser.). Date not set. price not set (ISBN 0-12-170620-6). Acad Pr.

Chater, Hara H. & Williams, A. O. An Enumeration of the Flowering Plants of Nepal: Vol. 3, Dicotyledons. (Illus.). 226p. 1982. pap. text ed. 81.50 (ISBN 0-565-00854-4). Sabbot-Natural Hist Bks.

Chater, Shirley. Operation Update: The Search for Rhyme & Reason. 32p. 1976. 3.50 (ISBN 0-686-38326-5, 14-1608). Natl League Nurse.

Chatfield, C. Analysis of Time Series: An Introduction. 2nd ed. 1980. pap. 16.95x (ISBN 0-412-22460-7, Pub. by Chapman & Hall). Methuen Inc.

Chatfield, C. & Collins, A. J. Introduction to Multivariate Analysis. 1980. 29.95x (ISBN 0-412-16030-7, Chapman & Hall England); pap. 18.95x (ISBN 0-412-16040-4). Methuen Inc.

Chatfield, Charles, ed. Peace Movements in America. LC 72-94294. 1973. 7.50x o.p. (ISBN 0-8052-3495-0); pap. 3.95 (ISBN 0-8052-0386-9). Schocken.

Chatfield, Christopher. Statistics for Technology: A Course in Applied Statistics. 2nd ed. 1978. pap. 12.50x (ISBN 0-412-15750-0, Pub. by Chapman & Hall). Methuen Inc.

Chatfield-Taylor, Joan. Backstage at the Opera. LC 82-12877. (Illus.). 132p. (Orig.). 1982. pap. 12.95 (ISBN 0-87701-271-7). Chronicle Bks.

--Picnics. LC 79-64872. (Illus.). 1980. pap. 5.95 (ISBN 0-394-73760-1). Taylor & NG.

Chatham, Doug. Shepherd's Church. Date not set. 1.75 (ISBN 0-89989-026-1). Cross Roads.

--The Shepherd's Touch. 1.95 (ISBN 0-89989-025-3). Cross Roads.

Chatham, James R. & Ruiz-Fornells, Enrique. Dissertations in Hispanic Languages & Literatures: An Index of Dissertations Completed in the United States & Canada, Vol. 1, 1876-1966. LC 70-80093. 136p. 1970. 15.50x (ISBN 0-8131-1183-8). U Pr of Ky.

Chatham, Margaret & Knapp, Barbara. Patient Education Handbook. (Illus.). 192p. 1981. pap. text ed. 12.95 (ISBN 0-89303-055-4). R J Brady.

Chatham, Robert. Advice to Men. pap. 1.25 o.p. (ISBN 0-451-07303-7, Y7303, Sig). NAL.

Chattapadhyaya. Muhammad, the Prophet of Islam. 1981. 1.25 (ISBN 0-686-97878-1). Kazi Pubns.

Chatten, Elizabeth N. Samuel Foote. (English Authors Ser.). 1980. lib. bdg. 13.95 (ISBN 0-8057-6779-7, Twayne). G K Hall.

Chattergy, Rahul & Pooch, Udo W. Top-Down, Modular Programming in FORTRAN with WATFIV. (Orig.). 1980. pap. 14.95 (ISBN 0-316-13826-6). Little.

Chattergy, Rahul, jt. auth. see Pooch, Udo W.

Chatterjee, P. K. & Wetherall, P. J. Winding Engine Calculations for the Mining. 1982. 33.00 (ISBN 0-419-12650-3, Pub. by E & FN Spon). Methuen Inc.

Chatterjee, Samprit & Price, Bertram. Regression Analysis by Example. LC 77-24510. (Probability & Mathematical Statistics Ser.: Applied Probability Section). 1977. 28.50 (ISBN 0-471-01521-0, Pub. by Wiley-Interscience). Wiley.

Chatterjee, Satya N., ed. Organ Transplantation. LC 81-21862. (Illus.). 640p. 1982. text ed. 52.50 (ISBN 0-7236-7008-0). Wright-PSG.

--Renal Transplantation. 295p. 1980. 29.00 (ISBN 0-89004-308-6). Raven.

Chatterji, M., ed. Space Location & Regional Development. 240p. 1976. pap. 17.50x (ISBN 0-85086-054-7, Pub. by Pion England). Methuen Inc.

Chatterji, Manas. Energy & Environment in the Developing Countries. LC 80-42143. 357p. 1982. 47.95x (ISBN 0-471-27993-5, Pub. by Wiley-Interscience). Wiley.

--Management & Regional Science for Economic Development. 1982. lib. bdg. 30.00 (ISBN 0-89838-108-8). Kluwer-Nijhoff.

Chatters, A. W. & Hajarnavis, C. R. Rings with Chain Conditions. LC 80-19315. (Research in Mathematics Ser.: No. 44). 198p. (Orig.). 1980. pap. text ed. 21.95 (ISBN 0-273-08446-1). Pitman Pub MA.

Chatterton, E. Keble. Battles by Sea. (Illus.). 271p. 1975. Repr. of 1925 ed. 13.50x o.p. (ISBN 0-87471-619-5). Rowman.

--Whalers & Whaling: The Story of the Whaling Ships up to the Present Day. LC 79-178626. (Illus.). 248p. 1975. Repr. of 1925 ed. 34.00x (ISBN 0-8103-4028-3). Gale.

Chatterton, Pauline. Coordinated Crafts for the Home. (Illus.). 1980. 19.95 (ISBN 0-399-90060-8, Marek). Putnam Pub Group.

Chatterton, Robert T., jt. auth. see Zaneveld, L. J.

Chatterton, Thomas. Thomas Chatterton: Selected Poems. Lindop, Greves, ed. (Fyfield Ser.). 1979. 7.95 o.p. (ISBN 0-902145-54-1, Pub. by Carcanet New Pr England) (ISBN 0-902145-55-X). Humanities.

Chatterton, Wayne. Alexander Woollcott. (United States Authors Ser.). 1978. lib. bdg. 12.95 (ISBN 0-8057-7210-3, Twayne). G K Hall.

Chatterton, Wayne, jt. auth. see Heasley Cox, Martha.

Chatterton, William A. Consumer & Small Business Bankruptcy: A Complete Working Guide. LC 82-12040. 256p. 1982. text ed. 89.50 (ISBN 0-87624-101-1). Inst Busn Plan.

Chatto, Beth. The Damp Garden. 224p. 1982. 40.00x (ISBN 0-460-04551-2, Pub. by J M Dent). State Mutual Bk.

--The Dry Garden. (Illus.). 176p. 1979. 13.95x o.p. (ISBN 0-460-04317-X, Pub. by J. M. Dent England). Biblio Dist.

Chatto, William A. Treatise on Wood Engraving, Historical & Practical. LC 69-16477. (Illus.). 1969. Repr. of 1861 ed. 56.00x (ISBN 0-8103-3531-X). Gale.

Chatton, E. Les Peridiniens Parasites. 1975. Repr. lib. bdg. 72.00x (ISBN 3-87429-100-6). Lubrecht & Cramer.

Chatton, Milton J., jt. ed. see Krupp, Marcus A.

Chattopadhyay, Kamaladevi. Tribalism in India. (Illus.). 1978. text ed. 17.75x (ISBN 0-7069-0652-7). Humanities.

Chattopadhyay, S. B. Principles & Procedures of Plant Protection. 480p. 1980. 69.00x (ISBN 0-686-84466-1, Oxford & I B H India). State Mutual Bk.

Chattopadhyaya, Alaka, tr. see Taranatha, Lama.

Chattopadhyaya, D. P., ed. Studies in the History of Indian Philosophy, 3 vols. 1981. text ed. 39.25x (ISBN 0-391-01805-1). Humanities.

Chatwin, Bruce. On the Black Hill. 256p. 1983. 14.95 (ISBN 0-670-52492-1). Viking Pr.

--The Viceroy of Ouidah. pap. 5.15 (ISBN 0-686-36917-3). Summit Bks.

Chatwin, Bruce, jt. auth. see Mapplethorpe, Robert.

Chaubey, N. P., jt. ed. see Rangarao, B. V.

Chaucer, Geoffrey. The Canterbury Tales. Hieatt, A. Kent & Hieatt, Constance, eds. Hieatt, A. Kent & Hieatt, Constance, trs. from Eng. (Bantam Classics Ser.). 421p. (gr. 9-12). 1981. pap. 2.95 (ISBN 0-553-21013-0). Bantam.

--Canterbury Tales. Skeat, Walter W., ed. (World's Classics Ser.). 15.95 o.p. (ISBN 0-19-250076-7). Oxford U Pr.

--Canterbury Tales. Coghill, Nevill, tr. (Classics Ser.). (Orig.). (YA) (gr. 9 up). 1951. pap. 2.95 (ISBN 0-14-044022-4). Penguin.

--Canterbury Tales (Selected) An Interlinear Translation. Hopper, Vincent F., ed. LC 70-99791. 1970. 6.00 o.p. (ISBN 0-8120-5015-0); pap. text ed. 5.95 (ISBN 0-8120-0039-0). Barron.

--Chaucer: The Prioress Prologue & Tale. Winny, J., ed. LC 74-19531. (Selected Tales from Chaucer Ser.). 64p. 1974. pap. text ed. 4.50 (ISBN 0-521-20744-4). Cambridge U Pr.

--Chaucer's World: A Pictorial Companion. Hussey, M., ed. (Selected Tales from Chaucer). (Orig.). 1967. 24.95 (ISBN 0-521-05354-4); pap. 9.50 (ISBN 0-521-09430-5). Cambridge U Pr.

--General Prologue to the Canterbury Tales. Winny, J., ed. (Selected Tales from Chaucer). 1965. text ed. 5.95x (ISBN 0-521-04629-7). Cambridge U Pr.

--Introduction to Chaucer. Hussey, Maurice, et al, eds. (Selected Tales from Chaucer). (Orig.). 1965. 24.95 (ISBN 0-521-05353-6); pap. 8.95x (ISBN 0-521-09286-8). Cambridge U Pr.

--The Miller's Tale. (Illus.). 1973. pap. 3.95 (ISBN 0-88388-022-9). Bellerophon Bks.

--The Miller's Tale. Ross, Thomas W., ed. LC 81-40286. (A Variorum Edition of the Works of Geoffrey Chaucer: Vol. II). 288p. 1983. 38.50 (ISBN 0-8061-1785-0). U of Okla Pr.

--The Portable Chaucer. rev. ed. Morrison, Theodore, ed. LC 75-2224. (Viking Portable Library: P 81). 1977. pap. 6.95 (ISBN 0-14-015081-1). Penguin.

--The Tales of Canterbury: Complete. Pratt, Robert A., ed. LC 72-9380. (Illus.). 587p. 1974. text ed. 23.95 (ISBN 0-395-14052-8). HM.

--Wife of Bath's Prologue & Tale. Winny, J., ed. (Selected Tales from Chaucer). 1966. text ed. 5.95x (ISBN 0-521-04630-0). Cambridge U Pr.

--The Wife of Bath's Prologue & Tale & the Clerk's Prologue & Tale. Cigman, Gloria, ed. LC 75-17976. (London Medieval & Renaissance Ser.). 94p. 1976. text ed. 16.50x (ISBN 0-8419-0225-9); pap. 9.50x (ISBN 0-8419-0226-7). Holmes & Meier.

Chaucer, Geoffrey see Swan, D. K.

Chaudhari, R. V., jt. auth. see Ramachandran, P. A.

Chaudhry, M. L. & Templeton, J. G. A First Course in Bulk Queues. 550p. 1983. write for info. (ISBN 0-471-86260-6, Pub. by Wiley-Interscience). Wiley.

Chaudhry, Shadid A. People's Democratic Republic of Yemen: A Review of Economic & Social Development. vi, 169p. 1979. pap. 15.00 (ISBN 0-686-36126-1, RC-7903). World Bank.

Chaudhuri, Buddhadeb. The Barkreshwar Temple. 117p. 1981. text ed. 13.75x (ISBN 0-391-02380-2, Pub. by Concept India). Humanities.

Chaudhuri, K. N. Economic Development of India Under the East India Company 1814-58. LC 78-129932. (European Understanding of India Ser). 1971. 44.50 (ISBN 0-521-07933-0). Cambridge U Pr.

Chaudhuri, N. P. Abstract Algebra. 288p. 12.95x (ISBN 0-07-451563-2). McGraw.

Chaudhuri, Nirad C. Hinduism. 1979. 24.95x (ISBN 0-19-520112-4). Oxford U Pr.

--Hinduism: A Religion to Live by. 1979. pap. 6.95 (ISBN 0-19-520221-X, GB 612). Oxford U Pr.

Chaudhuri, Pramit. The Indian Economy: Poverty & Development. LC 77-88457. 1979. 25.00x (ISBN 0-312-41378-5). St Martin.

Chaudhuri, R. H. Social Aspects of Fertility in India. 200p. 1982. 40.00x (ISBN 0-686-94060-1, Pub. by Garlandfold England). State Mutual Bk.

Chaudhuri, Tapan & Chaudhuri, Tukin, eds. Differential Diagnosis in Nuclear Medicine. (Illus.). 400p. 1983. text ed. write for info (ISBN 0-397-50502-7, Lippincott Medical). Lippincott.

Chaudhuri, Tukin, jt. ed. see Chaudhuri, Tapan.

Chaudier, Louann. Leading Consultants in Computer Software & Programming 1983-1984. 300p. (Orig.). 1983. pap. 39.50 (ISBN 0-943692-06-7). J Dick.

Chaudier, Louann, ed. Leading Consultants in Technology 1983. 160p. 1983. 28.00. J Dick.

Chauhan, Ela, jt. auth. see Harris, Helen.

Chauliaguet, Charles, et al. Solar Energy in Buildings. LC 8-27031. 1979. 36.95 (ISBN 0-471-27570-0, Pub. by Wiley-Interscience). Wiley.

Chaung, Y. H. & Hill, J. M. The Bangladesh Fertilizer Sector. McCune, D. L., intro. by. (Technical Bulletin Ser.: No. T-11). (Illus.). 61p. (Orig.). 1978. pap. 4.00 (ISBN 0-88090-010-5). Intl Fertilizer.

Chau Phan Thien. Vietnamese Communism: A Research Bibliography. LC 75-16961. 359p. 1975. lib. bdg. 39.95 (ISBN 0-8371-7950-5, CVC/). Greenwood.

Chaussy, C., et al. Extracorporeal Shock Wave Lithotripsy. (Illus.). viii, 112p. 1982. pap. 36.00 (ISBN 3-8055-3620-8). S Karger.

Chave, Edith H., jt. auth. see Hobson, Edmund.

Chavel, Charles. Holidays & Festivals. (Illus.). 1956. 4.00 o.p. (ISBN 0-914080-44-X). Shulsinger Sales.

Chavez, Carlos. Toward a New Music: Music & Electricity. Weinstock, Herbert, tr. from Span. LC 74-28308. (Illus.). 180p. 1975. Repr. of 1937 ed. lib. bdg. 22.50 (ISBN 0-306-70719-5). Da Capo.

Chavez, Fray A. But Time & Chance: The Biography of Padre Martinez of Taos. Hausman, Gerald, ed. LC 81-27. 196p. 1981. 15.95 (ISBN 0-913270-96-2); pap. 8.95 (ISBN 0-913270-95-4). Sunstone Pr.

--La Conquistadora: The Autobiography of an Ancient Statue. (Illus.). 1975. pap. 5.95 (ISBN 0-913270-43-1). Sunstone Pr.

Chavez, Moises. Hebreo Biblico Juego de Dos Tomos, 2 vols. (Span., Vol. I - 568 pgs., Vol. II - 240 pgs.). 1981. Set. pap. 28.95 (ISBN 0-311-42070-2, Edit Mundo). Casa Bautista.

Chavignerie, Emile B. De La see De La Chavignerie, Emile B. & Auvray, Louis.

Chavkin, Samuel. Murder in Chile. (Illus.). 288p. 1982. 13.95 (ISBN 0-89696-137-0, An Everest House Book). Dodd.

Chay, John. The Problems & Prospects of American East Asian Relations. LC 76-27694. (Special Studies on China & East Asia). 1977. lib. bdg. 27.50 o.p. (ISBN 0-89158-113-8). Westview.

Chay, John, jt. ed. see Kwak, Tai-Hwan.

Chaya, Ruth K., jt. auth. see Miller, Joan M.

Chayefsky. Television Plays. 1971. pap. 9.50 (ISBN 0-671-21133-1, Touchstone Bks). S&S.

Chayefsky, Paddy. Altered States. LC 77-11542. 1978. 12.45i (ISBN 0-06-010727-8, HarpT). Har-Row.

Chayen, Joseph, et al. Practical Histochemistry. LC 72-8596. 280p. 1973. 36.95 (ISBN 0-471-14950-0, Pub. by Wiley-Interscience). Wiley.

Chayes, Abraham & Lewis, W. Bennett, eds. International Arrangements for Nuclear Fuel Reprocessing. LC 76-52961. 280p. 1977. prof ref 25.00x (ISBN 0-88410-052-9). Ballinger Pub.

Chayes, Abram. The Cuban Missile Crisis. (International Crisis & the Role of Law Ser.). 1974. 11.95x (ISBN 0-19-519758-5); pap. text ed. 5.95x (ISBN 0-19-825320-6). Oxford U Pr.

Chaykin, Sterling. Biochemistry Laboratory Techniques. LC 76-52458. (Illus.). 178p. 1977. Repr. of 1966 ed. lib. bdg. 9.95 (ISBN 0-88275-517-X). Krieger.

Chazan, Barry I. & Soltis, Jonas F., eds. Moral Education. LC 72-89127. 1972. pap. 7.25x o.p. (ISBN 0-8077-1156-X). Tchrs Coll.

Chazan, Naomi H. An Anatomy of Ghanaian Politics: Managing Political Recession, 1969-1982. (Special Study on Africa). 350p. 1982. lib. bdg. 25.00 (ISBN 0-86531-439-X). Westview.

Chazarain, J. & Piriou, A. Introduction to the Theory of Linear Partial Differential Equations. (Studies in Mathematics & Its Applications: Vol. 14). 560p. 1982. 74.50 (ISBN 0-444-86452-0, North Holland). Elsevier.

Chazdeau, Melvin G. De see De Chazeau, Melvin G. & Kahn, Alfred E.

Chazov, E. I. & Smirnov, V. N., eds. Vessel Wall in Athero & Thrombogenesis: Studies in the U. S. S. R. (Illus.). 224p. 1982. pap. 56.90 (ISBN 0-387-11384-3). Springer-Verlag.

Cheatham, Carole B. Cost Management for Profit Centers. LC 81-6944. 247p. 1981. 59.50 (ISBN 0-87624-106-2). Inst Busn Plan.

Cheatham, Frank & Cheatham, Jane. Design Concepts & Application. (Illus.). 256p. 1983. pap. cancelled (ISBN 0-13-201897-7). Univ Park.

Cheatham, Jane, jt. auth. see Cheatham, Frank.

Cheatham, K. Follis. The Best Way Out. LC 81-47528. 168p. (YA) (gr. 12 up). 1982. 9.95 (ISBN 0-15-206741-8, HJ). HarBraceJ.

Cheatham, Margaret. Peter Tuttle & the Great Mr. Paddy. 1983. 7.95 (ISBN 0-533-05505-9). Vantage.

Cheatham, T. Richard. Communication & Law Enforcement. (Procom Ser.). 1983. pap. text ed. 7.95 (ISBN 0-673-15556-0). Scott F.

Cheatum, E. P. Common Pests of the Garden, Yard, Home, & Their Control. (Illus.). 1973. pap. 1.75x o.p. (ISBN 0-934786-29-1). G Davis.

Chebotarev, E. I., et al, eds. see International Astronomical Union Symposium, 45th, Leningrad, 1970.

Chebotarev, G. Analytical & Numerical Methods of Celestial Mechanics. 1967. 22.50 (ISBN 0-444-00023-2). Elsevier.

Chebyshev, Pafnuti L. Oeuvres: Collected Papers, 2 Vols. LC 61-17956. (Fr). 99.50 set (ISBN 0-8284-0157-8). Chelsea Pub.

--Theorie der Congruenzen. 2nd ed. LC 71-113123. xvii, 366p. (Ger.). 1972. text ed. 16.50 (ISBN 0-8284-0254-X). Chelsea Pub.

Checinski, Michael. Poland: Communism, Nationalism, Anti-Semitism. 320p. 1982. text ed. 22.95x (ISBN 0-918294-18-5). Karz-Cohl Pub.

Checkland, P. B. Systems Thinking, Systems Practice. LC 80-41381. 352p. 1981. 37.95 (ISBN 0-471-27911-0, Pub. by Wiley-Interscience). Wiley.

Checkland, Sydney. British Public Policy Seventeen Seventy Six To Nineteen Thirty-Nine: An Economic & Social Perspective. LC 82-9552. 432p. price not set (ISBN 0-521-24596-6); pap. price not set (ISBN 0-521-27086-3). Cambridge U Pr.

Checkover, V., jt. auth. see Averbakh, Y.

Checroun, Natalie. Pull Up a Chair. LC 67-15704. (People & Their Useful Things Ser.). (Illus.). (gr. 5-10). 1967. PLB 3.95g (ISBN 0-8225-0265-8). Lerner Pubns.

Chedd, Graham. The New Biology. LC 74-174816. (Science & Discovery Books). (Illus.). (gr. 12). 11.50 o.s.i. (ISBN 0-465-04998-2). Basic.

Chedid, Andree. From Sleep Unbound. Spencer, Sharon, tr. from Fr. LC 82-75430. 170p. 1983. 18.95 (ISBN 0-8040-0399-8); pap. 8.95 (ISBN 0-8040-0837-X). Swallow.

Cheeger, J. & Ebin, D. G. Comparison Theorems in Riemannian Geometry. LC 74-83725. (Mathematical Library: Vol. 9). 174p. 1975. 42.75 (ISBN 0-444-10764-9, North-Holland). Elsevier.

Cheek. Drawing Hands. (Grosset Art Instruction Ser.: Vol. 15). pap. 2.95 (ISBN 0-448-00524-7, G&D). Putnam Pub Group.

--Quick Sketching. (Grosset Art Instruction Ser.: Vol. 34). pap. 1.95 o.p. (ISBN 0-448-00543-3, G&D). Putnam Pub Group.

Cheek, Earl H., Jr. & Cheek, Martha C. Reading Instruction Through Content Teaching. 1983. text ed. 17.95 (ISBN 0-675-20026-1). Additional supplements may be obtained from publisher. Merrill.

Cheek, Martha C., jt. auth. see Cheek, Earl H., Jr.

Cheek, William F. Black Resistance Before the Civil War. 1970. pap. text ed. 7.95 (ISBN 0-02-473550-7, 47355). Macmillan.

Cheeks, James. How Proper Planning Can Reduce Your Income Taxes. rev. ed. LC 73-16036. cancelled o.s.i. (ISBN 0-87576-034-1). Pilot Bks.

Cheeks, James E. How to Compensate Executives. 3rd ed. LC 82-71349. 312p. 1982. 19.95 (ISBN 0-87094-341-3). Dow Jones-Irwin.

Cheeks, James E. & Wolf, Gordon D. How to Compensate Executives. rev. ed. LC 78-74885. 1979. 19.95 o.p. (ISBN 0-87094-172-0). Dow Jones-Irwin.

Cheesman, John, et al. The Grace of God in the Gospel. 1976. pap. 3.45 (ISBN 0-85151-153-8). Banner of Truth.

Chee Soo. The Tao of Long Life: The Chinese Art of Ch'ang Ming. 176p. 1983. pap. 7.95 (ISBN 0-85030-320-6). Newcastle Pub.

Cheetham, Erika, ed. & tr. The Prophecies of Nostradamus. 1975. pap. 5.95 (ISBN 0-399-50345-5, Perige). Putnam Pub Group.

--The Prophecies of Nostradamus: The Man Who Saw Tomorrow. 448p. 1982. pap. 3.95 (ISBN 0-425-05772-0). Berkley Pub.

Cheetham, Juliet. Social Work with Immigrants. (Library of Social Work). 242p. 1972. 12.95x o.p. (ISBN 0-7100-7365-8); pap. 8.95 (ISBN 0-7100-7366-6). Routledge & Kegan.

Cheetham, Juliet, ed. Social Work & Ethnicity. (National Institute & Social Services Library: No. 43). 256p. 1982. text ed. 28.50x (ISBN 0-04-362050-7); pap. text ed. 12.95x (ISBN 0-04-362051-5). Allen Unwin.

Cheetham, Nicolas. Keepers of the Keys: A History of the Popes from St. Peter to John Paul II. LC 82-16950. (Illus.). 352p. 1983. 17.95 (ISBN 0-684-17863-X, ScribT). Scribner.

Cheever, John. Oh What a Paradise It Seems. 112p. 1983. pap. 2.50 (ISBN 0-345-30883-2). Ballantine.

--The Wapshot Chronicle, 2 vols. in 1. Bd. with The Wapshot Scandal. LC 79-1806. 1979. 15.00i o.p. (ISBN 0-06-010741-3, HarpT). Har-Row.

--The Wapshot Scandal. 1973. pap. 2.25i o.p. (ISBN 0-06-080296-0, P296, PL). Har-Row.

Cheever, Susan. A Handsome Man. 224p. 1982. pap. 2.50 (ISBN 0-449-24570-5, Crest). Fawcett.

--Looking for Work. 1980. 8.95 o.p. (ISBN 0-671-25054-X). S&S.

Chefdor, Monique. Blaise Cendrars. (World Authors Ser.). 1980. 13.95 (ISBN 0-8057-6413-5, Twayne). G K Hall.

Cheffers, John T. & Evual, Thomas. Introduction to Physical Education: Concepts of Human Movement. (Illus.). 1978. text ed. 20.95 (ISBN 0-13-493031-2). P-H.

Cheifetz & Avenoso. Logic & Set Theory. LC 76-126359. 1973. 7.95x (ISBN 0-916060-01-2). Math Alternatives.

Cheifetz, Philip, ed. see DeSanto, et al.

Cheigh, Jhoong S., et al, eds. Manual of Clinical Nephrology of the Rogosin Kidney Center. (Developments in Nephrology: No. 1). (Illus.). 470p. 1981. PLB 65.00 o.p. (ISBN 90-247-2397-3, Pub. by Martinus Nijhoff Netherlands). Kluwer Boston.

Chejne, A. Ibn-al-Hazm. 19.95 (ISBN 0-686-97869-2). Kazi Pubns.

Chejne, A. G. Ibn Hazm. 19.95 (ISBN 0-686-83558-1); pap. 14.95 (ISBN 0-686-83558-1). Kazi Pubns.

Chejne, Anver. Ibn Hazm al Undulasi. 320p. (Orig.). 1982. 19.95x (ISBN 0-935782-03-6); pap. 14.95x (ISBN 0-935782-04-4). Kazi Pubns.

Chejne, Anwar G. Islam & the West: The Moriscos. LC 82-703. 368p. 1983. 44.50x (ISBN 0-87395-603-6); pap. 16.95x (ISBN 0-87395-606-0). State U NY Pr.

Chek-Chart. Automotive Preview, 1983. 16p. 1982. pap. text ed. 2.00x (ISBN 0-88098-019-2). H M Gousha.

--Car & Light Truck Diesel Engine Service Manual. (Automotive Service Ser.). 128p. (gr. 12). 1983. pap. text ed. 9.95x (ISBN 0-88098-016-8); 3.50x (ISBN 0-686-84028-3). H M Gousha.

--Car Care Guide, 1983. 320p. (gr. 12). 1983. pap. text ed. 39.75 (ISBN 0-88098-022-2, 0162-3443). H M Gousha.

--Complete Automotive Service Library. (Automotive Service Ser.). (Illus.). 665p. (gr. 12). 1983. pap. text ed. 50.85 (ISBN 0-88098-044-3). H M Gousha.

--Lubrications Recommendations Wall Chart, 1983. 12p. (gr. 12). 1983. pap. 4.10 (ISBN 0-88098-018-4). H M Gousha.

--Master Lubrication Handbook, 1983. 792p. 1983. 80.60x (ISBN 0-88098-020-6); Supplement 64.25 (ISBN 0-88098-021-4). H M Gousha.

--Nineteen-Eighty Three Lubrication Recommendations & Capacities Booklet. 36p. (gr. 12). 1983. pap. text ed. 4.75 (ISBN 0-88098-017-6). H M Gousha.

--Tractor & Farm Implement Lubrication Guide, 1983. 384p. 1983. pap. 34.00x (ISBN 0-88098-023-0). H. M. Gousha.

--Tractor Digest, 1983. (Illus.). 16p. (gr. 12). 1983. pap. text ed. 4.20 (ISBN 0-88098-047-8, 0731-4698). H M Gousha.

--Truck Lubrication Guide, 1983. 80p. 1983. pap. text ed. 31.80x (ISBN 0-88098-024-9). H M Gousha.

Chek-Chart, ed. Service Bulletin, 1983. (Automotive Service Ser.). (Illus.). 96p. 1983. pap. 12.80x (ISBN 0-88098-048-6, 0731-471X). H M Gousha.

Chekhov, A. P. Chekhov's Poetics. Cruise, Edwina & Dragt, Donald, trs. from Rus. 1983. 27.50 (ISBN 0-88233-780-7); pap. 7.50 (ISBN 0-88233-781-5). Ardis Pubs.

Chekhov, Anton. Anton Chekhov's Short Stories. Matlaw, Ralph E., ed. Garnett, Constance, et al, trs. (Critical Edition). 1979. text ed. 24.95 o.p. (ISBN 0-393-04528-5); pap. text ed. 6.95x o.s.i. (ISBN 0-393-09002-7). Norton.
--Anton Chekov's Plays. Bristow, Eugene K., ed. (Norton Critical Edition Ser.). 1978 12.95 o.s.i. (ISBN 0-393-04432-7); pap. 7.95x, 1977 o.s.i. (ISBN 0-393-09163-5). Norton.
--Best Plays. Young & Stark, trs. LC 56-8837. 6.95 (ISBN 0-394-60459-8). Modern Lib.
--Best Plays. Young, Stark, tr. 1966. pap. 3.95 (ISBN 0-686-38906-9, Mod LibC). Modern Lib.
--Chekhov: The Early Stories 1883-88. Miles, Patrick & Pitcher, Harvey, trs. (Illus.). 224p. 1983. 13.95 (ISBN 0-02-524620-8). Macmillan.
--Chekhov, the Major Plays: Ivanov, Sea Gull, Uncle Vanya, Three Sisters, Cherry Orchard. Dunnigan, Ann, tr. 1964. pap. 2.95 (ISBN 0-451-51767-9, CL1767, Sig Classics). NAL.
--A Father. Goldberg, Isaac, ed. Long, R. E., tr. (International Pocket Library). pap. 3.00 (ISBN 0-686-77250-4). Branden.
--Five Major Plays. Hingley, Ronald, tr. Incl. The Cherry Orchard; Ivanov; The Seagull; Three Sisters; Uncle Vanya. 330p. 1977. pap. 4.95 (ISBN 0-19-502250-5, GB 466). Oxford U Pr.
--Letters on the Short Story, the Drama & Other Literary Topics. Friedland, Louis S., ed. 346p. 1982. Repr. of 1924 ed. lib. bdg. 35.00 (ISBN 0-686-81845-8). Darby Bks.
--The Oxford Chekhov. Hingley, Ronald, ed. & tr. Incl. Vol. 1. Short Plays. 1968. 32.50x (ISBN 0-19-211349-6); Vol. 2. Platonov, Ivanov, the Seagull. 1967. 32.50x (ISBN 0-19-211347-X); Vol. 5. Stories, 1889-1891. 1970. 27.50x (ISBN 0-19-211353-4); Vol. 6. Stories, 1892-1893. 1971. 32.50x (ISBN 0-19-211363-1); Vol. 8. Stories, 1895-1897. 300p. 1965. 32.50x (ISBN 0-19-211340-2). Oxford U Pr.
--The Oxford Chekhov, Vol. 3: Uncle Vanya, Three Sisters, The Cherry Orchard. Hingley, Ronald, tr. 364p. 1964. 32.50x (ISBN 0-19-211339-9). Oxford U Pr.
--The Oxford Chekhov, Vol. 4: Stories, 1888-1889. Hingley, Ronald, tr. 302p. 1980. 39.50x (ISBN 0-19-211389-5). Oxford U Pr.
--The Portable Chekhov. Yarmolinsky, Avrahm, ed. (Viking Portable Library: P 35). 1977. pap. 6.95 (ISBN 0-14-015035-8). Penguin.
--Sea Gull. Eisemann, Fred & Murphy, Oliver F., trs. Bd. with Tragedian in Spite of Himself. (Orig.). pap. 2.50 (ISBN 0-8283-1454-3). Branden.
--Seven Short Novels. Makanowitzky, Barbara, tr. from Rus. 1971. pap. 7.95 (ISBN 0-393-00552-6, Norton Lib). Norton.
--Ward Six & Other Short Novels. Dunnigan, Ann, tr. (Orig.). 1965. pap. 3.50 (ISBN 0-451-51690-7, CE1690, Sig Classics). NAL.
Chekhov, Anton see Goldberg, Isaac.
Chekhov, Anton see Laurel Editions Editors.
Chekki, Dan A., ed. Community Development: Theory & Method of Planned Change. LC 79-907884. xiv, 258p. 1980. text ed. 27.50x (ISBN 0-7069-0819-8, Pub. by Vikas India). Advent NY.
--Participatory Democracy in Action: International Profiles of Community Development. xvi, 306p. 1980. text ed. 27.50x (ISBN 0-7069-0923-2, Pub. by Vikas India). Advent NY.
Cheldelin, Larry. Your Baby's Secret World: Four Clinics for New Parents. 1983. pap. 9.50 (ISBN 0-686-96559-0). Branden.
Cheldelin, Larry V. Your Baby's Secret World: Four Phases for Effective Parenting (A Professional & Practical Guide) Brown, J., ed. (Illus., Orig.). 1983. pap. 9.50 (ISBN 0-8283-1850-6). Branden.
Chelf, Carl P. Public Policymaking in America: Difficult Choices, Limited Solutions. 1981. text ed. 19.95x (ISBN 0-673-16276-1). Scott F.
Cheli, R. & Aste, H. Duodenitis. LC 75-16096. (Illus.). 106p. 1976. 15.00 o.p. (ISBN 0-88416-125-0). Wright-PSG.
Chelkowski, A. Dielectric Physics. (Studies in Physical & Theoretical Chemistry: Vol. 9). 1980. 74.50 (ISBN 0-444-99766-0). Elsevier.
Chell, G. G., ed. Developments in Fracture Mechanics, Vols. 1 & 2. Vol. 1, 1979. 53.50 (ISBN 0-85334-858-8, Pub. by Applied Sci England); Vol. 2, 1981. 59.50 (ISBN 0-85334-973-8). Elsevier.
Chellis, Robert D. Pile Foundations. 2nd ed. (Soil Mechanic Foundations Library). (Illus.). 1961. 47.50 (ISBN 0-07-010751-3, P&RB). McGraw.
Chellis, Robert D., et al, eds. Congregate Housing for Older People: A Solution for the 1980's. LC 81-47983. 240p. 1982. 24.95x (ISBN 0-669-05210-8). Lexington Bks.
Chelminsk, Rudy. Paris. (The Great Cities Ser.). (Illus.). (gr. 6 up). 1977. PLB 12.00 (ISBN 0-8094-2279-4, Pub. by Time-Life). Silver.
Chelminski, Rudolph, jt. auth. see Ruo-Wang, Bao.
Chelvam, Reginald T. Why Einstein Was Wrong: Or The Scroll Theory of Cosmology & of Matter. LC 82-71689. (Illus.). 268p. (Orig.). 1982. pap. 19.95 (ISBN 0-943796-00-8). Penso Pubns.
Chem Systems, Inc. Parametric Analysis Support for Alcohol Fuels Process Development. (Progress in Solar Energy Ser.: Suppl.). 150p. 1983. pap. text ed. 13.50 (ISBN 0-89553-136-4). Am Solar Energy.
--Process Design & Economic for Ethanol from Corn Stover Via Dilute Acid. (Progress in Solar Energy Ser.: Suppl.). 150p. 1983. pap. text ed. 13.50 (ISBN 0-89553-137-2). Am Solar Energy.
Chemers, Martin M., jt. auth. see Altman, Irwin.
Chemey, David R., ed. see Cheney, David R. & Hunt, Leigh.
Chemi, James M. Stanley Stearns: U. S. Duck Stamp Designer. 1966. pap. 1.00 plasti-sheen bdg. o.p. (ISBN 0-686-09669-X). Am Philatelic.
Chemical Engineering, compiled By. Industrial Waste Water & Solid Waste Engineering. LC 80-12608. 376p. 1980. pap. 35.75 (ISBN 0-07-010694-0, Chem Eng). McGraw.
Chemical Engineering Magazine. Fluid Movers: Pumps, Compressors, Fans & Blowers. (Chemical Engineering Bks.). (Illus.). 384p. 1980. 35.75 (ISBN 0-07-010769-6, P&RB). McGraw.
--Industrial Air Pollution Engineering. 1980. 30.25 (ISBN 0-07-010693-2). McGraw.
--Modern Cost Engineering Methods & Data. 1979. 42.50 (ISBN 0-07-010733-5, P&RB). McGraw.
--Physical Properties. 1979. 49.90 (ISBN 0-07-010715-7). McGraw.
--Pneumatic Conveying of Bulk Materials. Kraus, Milton N., ed. (Chemical Engineering Bks.). 352p. 1980. 31.50 (ISBN 0-07-010724-6, P&RB). McGraw.
--Process Heat Exchange. (Chemical Engineering Book Ser.). (Illus.). 624p. 1980. 34.50 (ISBN 0-07-010742-4, P&RB). McGraw.
--Process Technology & Flowsheets. LC 79-12117. (Chemical Engineering Bks). 384p. 1980. 30.75 (ISBN 0-07-010741-6, P&RB). McGraw.
--Safe & Efficient Plant Operation & Maintenance. LC 80-14762. (Chemical Engineering Ser.). 400p. 1980. 35.75 (ISBN 0-07-010707-6). McGraw.
--Selecting Materials for Process Equipment. (Chemical Engineering Ser.). 280p. 1980. 30.25 (ISBN 0-07-010692-4). McGraw.
--Separation Techniques I: Liquid-Liquid Systems. (Chemical Engineering Book Ser.). 384p. 1980. 35.75 (ISBN 0-07-010711-4). McGraw.
--Separation Techniques II: Gas-Liquid-Solid Systems. (Chemical Engineering Book Ser.). 400p. 1980. 32.50 (ISBN 0-07-010717-3). McGraw.
--Skills Vital to Successful Managers. 1979. 31.50 (ISBN 0-07-010737-8, P&RB). McGraw.
Chemical Engineering Magazine, jt. auth. see Matley, Jay.
Chemical Engineering Magazine, jt. ed. see Deutsch, David J.
Chemitz, Martin. Ministry, Word, & Sacraments: An Enchiridion. Poellot, Luther, tr. 1981. pap. 15.95 (ISBN 0-570-03295-4, 15-2730). Concordia.
Chemnitz, Martin. Examination of the Council of Trent. Kramer, Fred, tr. from Lat. LC 79-143693. 1971. 21.95 (ISBN 0-570-03213-X, 15-2113). Concordia.
--Examination of the Council of Trent: Part II. 1979. 22.95 (ISBN 0-570-03272-5, 15-2717). Concordia.
Chemsak, John A. & Linsky, E. G. Checklist of Cerambycidae: The Longhormed Beetles. (Checklist of the Beetle of Canada United States, Mexico, Central America & the West Indies Ser.). 138p. (Orig.). 1982. pap. text ed. 18.00x (ISBN 0-937548-04-9). Plexus Pub.
Chen, et al. The Cuisine of China. 1983. 18.95 (ISBN 0-8120-5361-3). Barron.
Chen, C. H. Nonlinear Maxium Entropy Spectral Analysis Methods for Signal Recognition. (Pattern Recognition & Image Processing Research Studies). 190p. 1982. 29.95 (ISBN 0-471-10497-3, Pub by Res Stud Pr). Wiley.
Chen, C. H., ed. Computer-Aided Seismic Analysis & Discrimination. (Methods in Geochemistry & Geophysics Ser: Vol. 13). 1978. 35.50 o.p. (ISBN 0-444-41681-1). Elsevier.
Chen, C. T. Analysis & Synthesis of Linear Control Systems. 1978. 21.50x (ISBN 0-9604338-0-5). Pond Woods.
Chen, C. V. Commercial, Business & Trade Laws of Taiwan. Date not set. loose-leaf 100.00 (ISBN 0-379-22004-0). Oceana.
Chen, Ching-Chih. Applications of Operations Research Models to Libraries: A Case Study in the Use of Monographs in the Francis A. Countway Library of Medicine, Harvard University. LC 75-28210. 192p. 1976. 22.50x (ISBN 0-262-03056-X). MIT Pr.
--Library Management Without Bias. Stueart, Robert D., ed. LC 80-82482. (Foundations in Library & Information Sciences Ser.: Vol. 13). 300p. (Orig.). 1981. 37.50 (ISBN 0-89232-163-6). Jai Pr.
Chen, Ching-chih & Bressler, Stacey E. Microcomputers in Libraries. (Applications in Information Management & Technology Ser.). (Illus.). 259p. (Orig.). 1982. pap. text ed. 22.95 (ISBN 0-918212-61-8). Neal-Schuman.
Chen, Ching-Chih, ed. Scientific & Technical Information Sources. 1977. 35.00x (ISBN 0-262-03062-4). MIT Pr.
Chen, Daniel, jt. auth. see Weber, Jeffrey R.
Chen, F. H. Foundations on Expansive Soils. (Developments in Geotechnical Engineering Ser.: Vol. 12). 1976. 53.25 (ISBN 0-444-41393-6). Elsevier.
Chen, G., ed. General Theory of Systems Applied to Management & Organization: Application. (System Inquiry Ser.). 323p. 1980. pap. text ed. 12.95 (ISBN 0-686-36598-4). Intersystems Pubns.
Chen, Hollis C. Theory of Electromagnetic Waves: A Co-Ordinate Free Approach. (McGraw-Hill Ser. in Electrical Engineering). (Illus.). 464p. 1983. text ed. 35.00x (ISBN 0-07-010688-6, C). McGraw.
Chen, James. Meet Brother Nee. Leung, G. K., tr. from Chinese. 1976. pap. 1.95 o.p. (ISBN 0-940232-06-5). Christian Bks.
Chen, James C., jt. auth. see Meade, George P.
Chen, James K., jt. auth. see Tsien, Tsuen-Hsuin.
Ch'En, Jerome & Tarling, Nicholas, eds. Studies in the Social History of China & South-East Asia. LC 69-13791. (Illus.). 1970. 54.50 (ISBN 0-521-07452-5). Cambridge U Pr.
Chen, Joyce. Joyce Chen Cook Book. LC 82-49008. (Illus.). 224p. 1983. pap. 7.12i (ISBN 0-06-464060-4, BN 4060). B&N NY.
Chen, Kan, ed. Technology & Social Institutions. LC 74-77658. 1974. 17.95 (ISBN 0-87942-035-9). Inst Electrical.
Ch'en, Kenneth K. Buddhism: The Light of Asia. LC 67-30496. 1968. 7.95 o.p. (ISBN 0-8120-6012-1); pap. text ed. 4.25 (ISBN 0-8120-0272-5). Barron.
Chen, King C., ed. China & the Three Worlds: A Foreign Policy Reader. LC 78-51973. 1979. 22.50 (ISBN 0-87332-134-0); pap. 12.95 (ISBN 0-87332-118-9). M E Sharpe.
Chen, Lincoln C. & Scrimshaw, Nevin S., eds. Diarrhea & Malnutrition: Interactions, Mechanisms & Interventions. 310p. 1983. 39.50x (ISBN 0-306-41046-X, Plenum Pr). Plenum Pub.
Chen, Lung-Chu & Lasswell, Harold D. Formosa, China, & the United Nations: Formosa in the World Community. 1967. 8.95 o.p. (ISBN 0-312-29960-5, F42800). St Martin.
Ch'en, Paul H. The Formation of the Early Meiji Legal Order: The Japanese Code of 1871 & Its Chinese Foundation. (London Oriental Ser.: Vol. 35). 1982. 29.95x (ISBN 0-19-713601-X). Oxford U Pr.
Chen, Peter. Entity-Relationship Approach to Sysyems Analysis & Design. 1980. 85.00 (ISBN 0-444-85487-8). Elsevier.
Chen, Philip S. & Chen, Samuel M. A New Pocket Handbook of Chemistry. rev. ed. LC 82-10023. 1983. lib. bdg. write for info. (ISBN 0-89874-532-2). Krieger.
Chen, S. H., et al, trs. see K'ung, Shang-Jen.
Chen, S. S. & Paidoussis, M. P., eds. Flow-Induced Vibration of Circular Cylindrical Structures-1982. (PVP Ser.: Vol. 63). 223p. 1982. 44.00 (H00220). ASME.
Chen, Samuel M., jt. auth. see Chen, Philip S.
Chen, Shu-Jen, jt. auth. see Sawatzky, Jasper J.
Chen, Stephen. Missouri in the Federal System. LC 80-54752. (Illus.). 234p. (Orig.). 1981. lib. bdg. 22.50 (ISBN 0-8191-1720-X); pap. text ed. 11.50 (ISBN 0-8191-1721-8). U Pr of Amer.
Chen, T. P. Aquaculture Practices in Taiwan. 1978. 30.00x (ISBN 0-685-63392-6). State Mutual Bk.
Chen, T. Y., jt. auth. see Large, George E.
Chen, Tony, illus. Wild Animals. LC 80-53105. (Board Bks.). (Illus.). 14p. (ps). 1981. boards 3.50 (ISBN 0-394-84748-2). Random.
Chen, Virginia, compiled by. The Economic Conditions of East & Southeast Asia: A Bibliography of English-Language Material, 1965 to 1977. LC 78-57762. 840p. 1978. lib. bdg. 75.00 (ISBN 0-313-20565-5, CEC/). Greenwood.
Chen, W. F. Plasticity in Reinforced Concrete. (Illus.). 576p. Date not set. text ed. 42.95 (ISBN 0-07-010687-8). McGraw. Postponed.
Chen, W. F. & Saleeb, S. F. Constitutive Equations for Engineering Materials: Elasticity & Modeling, Vol. 1. LC 81-16433. 580p. 1982. 68.50x (ISBN 0-471-09149-9, Pub. by Wiley-Interscience). Wiley.
Chen, W. K. Applied Graph Theory: Graphs & Electrical Networks. 2nd rev. ed. (North-Holland Ser. in Applied Mathematics & Mechanics: Vol. 13). 1976. text ed. 47.00 (ISBN 0-444-10870-X, North-Holland); pap. text ed. 42.75 (ISBN 0-444-10871-8). Elsevier.
Chen, Wai-Fah. Limit Analysis & Soil Plasticity. LC 74-84058. (Developments in Geotechnical Engineering: Vol. 7). 638p. 1975. 127.75 (ISBN 0-444-41249-2). Elsevier.
Chen, Wai-Kai. Linear Networks & Systems. 608p. 1983. text ed. 34.95 (ISBN 0-534-01343-0). Brooks-Cole.
Chen, Wayne H. Linear Network Design & Synthesis. (Electrical & Electronic Eng. Ser). 1964. 42.50 o.p. (ISBN 0-07-010756-4, P&RB). McGraw.
Chenault, Joann & Burnford, J. F. Human Services Professional Development: Future Directions. 1978. text ed. 18.95 (ISBN 0-07-010732-7, C). McGraw.
Chenery, Hollis & Keesing, Donald B. The Changing Composition of Developing Country Exports. (Working Paper: No. 314). 51p. 1979. 3.00 (ISBN 0-686-36205-5, WP-0314). World Bank.
Chenery, Janet. Wolfie. LC 78-77950. (Science I Can Read Books). (Illus.). (gr. k-3). 1969. 6.95 o.p. (ISBN 0-06-021261-6, HarpJ); PLB 8.89 o.p. (ISBN 0-06-021264-0). Har-Row.
Chenevert, C. Skip, Jr., jt. auth. see Mitchell, Walter.
Chenevert, Melodie. STAT: Special Techiques in Assertiveness Training for Women in the Health Professions. (Illus.). 144p. 1983. text ed. 10.95 (ISBN 0-8016-1135-0). Mosby.
Cheney, C. R. From Becket to Langton. 1956. 19.00 (ISBN 0-7190-0064-5). Manchester.
Cheney, Christopher R. Episcopal Visitation of Monasteries in the Twelfth Century. rev. ed. 224p. 1983. lib. bdg. 17.50x (ISBN 0-87991-638-9). Porcupine Pr.
Cheney, Cora. Vermont: The State with the Storybook Past. LC 76-13804. (gr. 5-9). 1976. 10.95 o.p. (ISBN 0-8289-0440-5). Greene.
Cheney, Daniel P. & Mumford, Thomas M., Jr. Shellfish & Seaweed Harvests of Puget Sound. (A Puget Sound Bk.). (Illus.). 144p. (Orig.). 1983. pap. 8.95 (ISBN 0-686-43218-5, Pub. by Wash Sea Grant). U of Wash Pr.
Cheney, David M. Son of Minos. LC 64-25838. (gr. 7). 8.00x (ISBN 0-8196-0142-X). Biblo.
Cheney, David R. & Hunt, Leigh. Musical Evenings: Or Selections, Vocal & Instrumental. Chemey, David R., ed. LC 64-12876. 68p. 1964. 6.00x (ISBN 0-8262-0033-8). U of Mo Pr.
Cheney, Frances N. & Williams, Wiley J. Fundamental Reference Sources. 2nd ed. 300p. 1980. 15.00 (ISBN 0-8389-0308-8). ALA.
Cheney, Frances N., ed. see Tate, Allen.
Cheney, Glenn A. El Salvador: Country in Crisis. (Impact Bks). (Illus.). 96p. (gr. 7 up). Date not set. PLB 8.90 (ISBN 0-531-04423-8). Watts.
--Mohandas Gandhi. (Impact Biography Ser.). (Illus.). 128p. (gr. 7 up). 1983. PLB 8.90 (ISBN 0-531-04600-1). Watts.
Cheney, Lois A. God Is No Fool. (Orig.). pap. 1.50 o.s.i. (ISBN 0-89129-251-9). Jove Pubns.
Cheney, Lynne. Sisters. (Orig.). 1981. pap. 2.50 o.p. (ISBN 0-451-11204-0, AE 1204, Sig). NAL.
Cheney, Lynne V., jt. auth. see Cheney, Richard B.
Cheney, Richard B. & Cheney, Lynne V. Kings of the Hill: Power & Personality in the House of Representatives. (Illus.). 224p. 1983. 14.95 (ISBN 0-8264-0230-5). Crossroad NY.
Cheney, Roberta C. Names on the Face of Montana. 320p. (Orig.). 1983. pap. 9.95 (ISBN 0-87842-150-5). Mountain Pr.
Cheney, Sheldon. Men Who Have Walked with God. 1974. pap. 3.45 o.s.i. (ISBN 0-440-55596-5, Delta). Dell.
Cheney, Ward & Kincaid, David. Numerical Math & Computing. LC 79-17230. 1980. text ed. 24.95 (ISBN 0-8185-0357-2). Brooks-Cole.
Cheng & Smith. Tai Chi. 16.50x (ISBN 0-685-22124-5). Wehman.
Cheng, jt. auth. see Bulla.
Cheng, Chu-Yuan. China's Economic Development: Growth & Structural Change. (Illus.). 500p. (Orig.). 1981. lib. bdg. 35.00 (ISBN 0-89158-788-8); pap. 15.95 (ISBN 0-89158-892-2). Westview.
Cheng, Chung-Ying. Tai Chen's Inquiry into Goodness. LC 70-113573. 1971. 10.00x (ISBN 0-8248-0093-1, Eastwest Ctr). UH Pr.
Cheng, Chung-ying, ed. Philosophical Aspects of the Mind-Body Problem. 240p. 1975. text ed. 14.00x (ISBN 0-8248-0342-6). UH Pr.
Cheng, D. C. A Comparison of Fourteen Commercial Viscometers & Home-Made Instruments, 1978. 1981. 85.00x (ISBN 0-686-97047-0, Pub. by W Spring England). State Mutual Bk.
--A Study Into the Possiblity of Scale-Up in Thixotropic Pipe-Flow, 1979. 1981. 45.00x (ISBN 0-686-97142-6, Pub. by W Spring England). State Mutual Bk.
Cheng, D. K. Field & Wave Electromagnetics. 640p. 1983. text ed. 29.95 (ISBN 0-201-01239-1). A-W.
Cheng, Francois. Chinese Poetic Writing: With an Anthology of Tang Poetry. Riggs, Donald A. & Seaton, Jerome P., trs. from Chinese. LC 81-48382. (Studies in Chinese Literature & Society Midland Books: No.284). 288p. 1983. 25.00x (ISBN 0-253-31358-9); pap. 12.95x (ISBN 0-253-20284-1). Ind U Pr.
Cheng, K. L. & Ueno, Keihei. CRC Handbook of Organic Analytical Reagents. 544p. 1982. 74.00 (ISBN 0-8493-0771-6). CRC Pr.
Cheng, L., ed. Marine Insects. 1976. 156.25 (ISBN 0-444-11213-8, North-Holland). Elsevier.
Cheng, Lorraine, ed. see New York Academy of Sciences, Feb 20-22, 1980.
Cheng, Peter P. C. Truce Negotiations Over Korea & Quemoy. 1977. pap. text ed. 8.75 o.p. (ISBN 0-8191-0290-3). U Pr of Amer.
Cheng, R. M., jt. auth. see Bozie, S. M.
Cheng, T-K. Archaeological Studies in Szechwan. 1957. 52.50 (ISBN 0-521-04635-1). Cambridge U Pr.
Chenier, L. S. de. Recherches Historiques sur les Maures et Histoire de l'Empire de Maroc, 3 vols. (Bibliotheque Africaine Ser.). (Fr.). 1974. Repr. of 1787 ed. lib. bdg. 371.00x o.p. (ISBN 0-8287-0184-9). Clearwater Pub.
Chenieux-Gendron, Jacqueline, jt. auth. see Bonnet, Marquerite.
Chenoff, Larry & Chernoff, Neil, eds. Short-Term Bioassays in the Analysis of Complex Environmental Mixtures: Part III. (Environmental Science Reseach: Vol. 27). 511p. 1983. 69.50x (ISBN 0-306-41191-1, Plenum Pr). Plenum Pub.
Chenoweth, H., jt. auth. see Jensen, A. C.
Chenoweth, H., jt. auth. see Jensen, Alfred E.

Chenoweth, H. H., jt. auth. see Jensen, A.

Chenoweth, Harry H., jt. auth. see Jensen, Alfred.

Chenoweth, Harry H., jt. auth. see Jensen, Alfred E.

Chenoweth, Linda. God's People: Nursery Leader's Guide. 64p. 1981. 2.95 o.p. (ISBN 0-686-74751-8). Westminster.

--God's People Share. Duckert, Mary, ed. 64p. 1981. nursery ldrs. guide 2.95 (ISBN 0-664-24337-1); pap. 1.10 (ISBN 0-664-24336-3); resource Packet 7.95 (ISBN 0-664-24338-X). Westminster.

Chenoweth, Patricia & Chenoweth, Thomas. How to Raise & Train a Lhasa Apso. (Orig.). pap. 2.95 (ISBN 0-87666-334-X, DS1097). TFH Pubns.

Chenoweth, Thomas, jt. auth. see Chenoweth, Patricia.

Chenoweth, Vida. Melodic Perception & Analysis: A Manual on Ethnic Melody. 132p. 1972. pap. 6.00x (ISBN 0-7263-0239-2); microfiche 2.25x (ISBN 0-88312-356-8). Summer Inst Ling.

--The Usarufas & Their Music. (Museum of Anthropology Publications: No. 5). 258p. 1979. 14.95x (ISBN 0-88312-154-9); microfiche 3.00x (ISBN 0-88312-242-1). Summer Inst Ling.

Chenowith, H., jt. auth. see Jensen, A. C.

Chenu, M. D. Nature, Man, & Society in the Twelfth Century: Essays on New Theological Perspectives in the Latin West. Taylor, Jeromr & Little, Lester K., eds. Taylor, Jerome & Little, Lester K., trs. LC 68-15574. (Midway Reprint Ser.). xxii, 362p. 1968. pap. write for info. (ISBN 0-226-10256-4). U of Chicago Pr.

Chenuz, Frida J. Sealyham Terriers. Foyle, W. G., ed. (Foyle Handbks). (Illus.). 1973. 3.95 (ISBN 0-685-55795-2). Palmetto Pub.

Chen Wai-Fah & Atsuta, T. Theory of Beam Columns Vol 2: Space Behavior & Design. 1977. text ed. 67.50x (ISBN 0-07-010759-9, C). McGraw.

Chen Wai-Fah & Atsuta, Toshio. Theory of Beam Columns, Vol. 1: In-Plane Behavior & Design. LC 76-49647. 1977. text ed. 59.00 (ISBN 0-07-010754-8, C). McGraw.

Cheny, David, jt. auth. see Sanders, Steven.

Cheok, Cheong Kee & Lean, Lim Lin. Demographic Impact on Socio-Economic Development. LC 81-71612. (Development Studies Centre Monograph: No. 29). 129p. (Orig.). 1982. pap. text ed. 14.95 (ISBN 0-909150-69-9, 1224). Bks Australia.

Chepesiuk, Ronald & Shankman, Arnold, eds. American Indian Archival Material: A Guide to Holdings in the Southeast. LC 82-15447. xiii, 323p. 1982. lib. bdg. 39.95 (ISBN 0-313-23731-X, CAI/). Greenwood.

Cheraksin & Ringsdorf. Predictive Medicine. 1972. 5.95x o.p. (ISBN 0-87983-150-2). Cancer Control Soc.

Cheraskin, E. & Ringsdorf, W. New Hope for Incurable Diseases. 1.65x (ISBN 0-668-02671-5). Cancer Control Soc.

Cherbuliez, A. E. Etudes sur les Causes de la Misere. (Conditions of the 19th Century French Working Class Ser). 352p. (Fr.). 1974. Repr. of 1853 ed. lib. bdg. 91.00x o.p. (ISBN 0-8287-0185-7, 1082). Clearwater Pub.

--Richesse ou Pauvrete. Exposition des Causes et des Effets de la Distribution Actuelle des Richesses Sociales. (Conditions of the 19th Century French Working Class Ser.). 184p. (Fr.). 1974. Repr. of 1841 ed. lib. bdg. 56.00x o.p. (ISBN 0-8287-0186-5, 1056). Clearwater Pub.

Cherches, Peter, jt. auth. see Acker, Kathy.

Cheremisinoff, Nicholas P. Wood for Energy Production. LC 79-56114. (Illus.). 1980. 24.95 (ISBN 0-250-40336-6). Ann Arbor Science.

Cheremisinoff, Nicholas P. & Azbel, David S. Fluid Mechanics & Unit Operations. LC 82-48638. (Illus.). 1100p. 1983. 49.95 (ISBN 0-250-40541-5). Ann Arbor Science.

Cheremisinoff, Nicholas P. & Cheremisinoff, Paul N. Cooling Towers: Selection, Design, Practice. LC 81-65711. 1981. text ed. 49.95 (ISBN 0-250-40407-9). Ann Arbor Science.

--Industrial & Hazardous Wastes Impoundment. LC 78-71428. 1979. 49.95 (ISBN 0-250-40280-7). Ann Arbor Science.

Cheremisinoff, Nicholas P. & Azbel, David S., eds. Liquid Filtration. LC 82-46063. (Illus.). 400p. 1983. 49.95 (ISBN 0-250-40600-4). Ann Arbor Science.

Cheremisinoff, Nicholas P. & Cheremisinoff, Paul N., eds. Unit Conversions & Formulas Manual. LC 79-55140. (Illus.). 1980. pap. 8.95 (ISBN 0-250-40331-5). Ann Arbor Science.

Cheremisinoff, Nicholas P. & Gupta, Ramesh, eds. Handbook of Fluids In Motion. LC 82-70706. (Illus.). 1200p. 1983. 79.95 (ISBN 0-250-40458-3). Ann Arbor Science.

Cheremisinoff, Nicholas P., et al. Chemical & Nonchemical Disinfection. LC 80-68827. (Illus.). 170p. 1981. 29.50 (ISBN 0-250-40390-0). Ann Arbor Science.

Cheremisinoff, P. N. Gasohol Sourcebook: (Abstracts) LC 81-66258. 1981. text ed. 29.95 (ISBN 0-250-40425-7). Ann Arbor Science.

Cheremisinoff, Paul N. Air Particulate Instrumentation & Analysis. LC 81-66260. 350p. 1981. text ed. 39.95 (ISBN 0-250-40465-6). Ann Arbor Science.

--Bioconversion Sourcebook. 1982. text ed. cancelled (ISBN 0-250-40424-9). Ann Arbor Science.

Cheremisinoff, Paul N. & Cheremisinoff, Peter P. Industrial Noise Control Handbook. LC 76-46023. 1977. 45.00 (ISBN 0-250-40144-4). Ann Arbor Science.

Cheremisinoff, Paul N. & Ellerbusch, Fred. Sourcebook of Environmental Regulation. LC 79-54872. 1980. cancelled (ISBN 0-250-40326-9). Ann Arbor Science.

Cheremisinoff, Paul N. & Morresi, Angelo C. Environmental Assessment & Impact Statement Handbook. LC 76-50989. 1977. 49.95 (ISBN 0-250-40158-4). Ann Arbor Science.

Cheremisinoff, Paul N. & Regino, Thomas. Principles & Applications of Solar Energy. LC 78-50308. 1978. 19.95 (ISBN 0-250-40247-5). Ann Arbor Science.

Cheremisinoff, Paul N., jt. auth. see Cheremisinoff, Nicholas P.

Cheremisinoff, Paul N., jt. auth. see Teresinski, Michael F.

Cheremisinoff, Paul N. & Ellerbusch, Fred, eds. Carbon Adsorption Handbook. LC 77-93382. (Illus.). 1978. 59.95 (ISBN 0-250-40236-X). Ann Arbor Science.

Cheremisinoff, Paul N. & Perlis, Harlan J., eds. Automatic Process Control. LC 80-70757. 192p. 1981. text ed. 39.95 (ISBN 0-250-40400-1). Ann Arbor Science.

Cheremisinoff, Paul N., jt. ed. see Cheremisinoff, Nicholas P.

Cheremisinoff, Paul N., jt. auth. see Cheremisinoff, Nicholas P.

Cheremisinoff, Peter P., jt. auth. see Cheremisinoff, Paul N.

Cherepanov, A. I. As Military Advisor In China. 333p. 1982. 8.70 (ISBN 0-8285-2290-1, Pub. by Progress Pubs USSR). Imported Pubns.

Cherescavich, Gertrude D. A Textbook for Nursing Assistants. 3rd ed. LC 72-12852. (Illus.). 442p. 1973. 16.95 o.p. (ISBN 0-8016-0957-7). Mosby.

Cherfas, Jeremy. Man Made Life: An Overview of the Science, Technology & Commerce of Genetic Engineering. 279p. 1983. 15.95 (ISBN 0-394-52926-X). Pantheon.

Cherian, Thyparambil C., jt. auth. see Ribner, Richard.

Cherin, Allen H. An Introduction to Optical Fibers. (McGraw-Hill Series in Electrical Engineering). (Illus.). 336p. 1982. text ed. 34.95x (ISBN 0-07-010703-3, C); write for info. Solutions manual (ISBN 0-07-010704-1). McGraw.

Cherkasky, Paul. The Rochester Diet. 288p. 1983. 14.95 (ISBN 0-8119-0488-1). Fell.

Cherkin, Arthur, et al, eds. Physiology & Cell Biology of Aging. LC 77-94148. (Aging Ser.: Vol. 8). 245p. 1979. text ed. 28.50 (ISBN 0-89004-283-7). Raven.

Chermisinoff, Nicholas P. Fluid Flow: Pumps, Pipes & Channels. LC 81-68034. (Illus.). 702p. 1981. 39.95 (ISBN 0-250-40432-X). Ann Arbor Science.

Chern, S. S., ed. Studies in Global Geometry & Analysis. LC 67-16033. (MAA Studies: No. 4). 197p. 1967. 16.50 o.s.i. (ISBN 0-88385-104-0). Math Assn.

Chernaik, Warren L. The Poet's Time: Politics & Religion in the Work of Andrew Marvell. LC 82-4395. 250p. Date not set. 37.50 (ISBN 0-521-24773-X). Cambridge U Pr.

Cherne, J. The Learning Disabled Child in Your Church School. (09). 1983. pap. 3.50 (ISBN 0-570-03883-9). Concordia.

Chernenko, Konstantin U. Human Rights in Soviet Society. LC 81-6948. 144p. (Orig.). 1982. pap. 2.50 (ISBN 0-7178-0588-3). Intl Pub Co.

Chernev, Irving. Most Instructive Games of Chess Ever Played. 1973. pap. 3.95 o.p. (ISBN 0-671-21536-1, Fireside). S&S.

Chernev, Irving & Harkness, Kenneth. Invitation to Chess. 7.95 o.p. (ISBN 0-671-38000-1); pap. 3.95 (ISBN 0-671-21270-2, Fireside). S&S.

Cherney, Paul, jt. auth. see Rebikoff, Dimitri.

Chernichovsky, Dov & Meesook, Oey Astra. Regional Aspects of Family Planning & Fertility Behavior in Indonesia. (Working Paper: No. 462). 62p. 1981. 3.00 (ISBN 0-686-36192-X, WP-0462). World Bank.

Chernin, Dennis, et al. Ancient & Modern Medicine: A Preventive & Therapeutic Synthesis. LC 80-82149. 200p. (Orig.). Date not set. pap. cancelled o.s.i. (ISBN 0-89389-068-5). Himalayan Intl.

Chernin, Kim. In My Mother's House. LC 82-19514. 320p. 1983. 14.95 (ISBN 0-89919-167-3). Ticknor & Fields.

--The Obsession. LC 81-47224. 224p. 1982. pap. 4.76i (ISBN 0-06-090967-6, CN 967, CN). Har-Row.

Chernoff, George & Sarbin, Hershel. Photography & the Law. 5th ed. (Illus.). 1977. 13.95 o.p. (ISBN 0-8174-2437-7, Amphoto); pap. 8.95 (ISBN 0-8174-2422-9). Watson-Guptill.

Chernoff, Herman. Sequential Analysis & Optimal Design: Proceedings. (CBMS Regional Conference Ser.: Vol. 8). (Illus.). v, 119p. (Orig.). 1972. pap. text ed. 11.00 (ISBN 0-89871-006-5). Soc Indus-Appl Math.

Chernoff, Herman & Moses, L. E. Elementary Decision Theory. LC 59-9337. (Illus.). 364p. 1959. 30.50x o.p. (ISBN 0-471-15213-7). Wiley.

Chernoff, John M. African Rhythm & African Sensibility: Aesthetics & Social Action in African Musical Idioms. LC 79-189. xviii, 262p. 1981. 9.95 (ISBN 0-226-10345-5, Phoen); cassette tape 15.00 (ISBN 0-686-86803-X, 10346-3). U of Chicago Pr.

Chernoff, Neil, jt. ed. see Chenoff, Larry.

Chernow, Burt. Gabor Peterdi: Paitings. LC 82-50989. (Illus.). 120p. 1983. 29.95 (ISBN 0-8008-3121-7). Taplinger.

--Lester Johnson: The Kaleidoscopic Crowd. LC 74-34550. (Illus.). 72p. 1975. 12.00 (ISBN 0-685-56529-7, Dist. by David Anderson Gallery). D Anderson.

Cherns, A. B. Social Science Organization & Policy: First Ser.: Belgium, Chile, Egypt, Hungary, Nigeria, Sri Lanka. (Illus.). 352p. (Orig.). 1974. pap. 21.00 (ISBN 92-3-101084-0, U614, UNESCO). Unipub.

Cherns, Albert B., jt. ed. see Davis, Louis E.

Cherny, Robert W. & Issel, William. San Francisco. Hundley, Norris, Jr. & Schutz, John A., eds. LC 81-67253. (Golden State Ser.). (Illus.). 120p. 1981. pap. text ed. 5.95x (ISBN 0-87835-120-5). Boyd & Fraser.

Chernyshevsky, Nikolai G. What Is to Be Done. abr. ed. Turkerich, I. B., ed. (Russian Library Ser). (Orig.). 1961. pap. 2.95 o.p. (ISBN 0-394-70723-0, V723, Vin). Random.

Cheronis, Nicholas D. & Entrikin, John B. Identification of Organic Compounds: A Students Text Using Semimicro Techniques. 1963. 47.00 (ISBN 0-470-15279-6, Pub. by Wiley-Interscience). Wiley.

Cheronis, Nicholas D., et al. Semimicro Qualitative Organic Analysis: The Systematic Identification of Organic Compounds. 3rd ed. LC 80-461. 1072p. 1983. Repr. of 1965 ed. lib. bdg. write for info. (ISBN 0-89874-124-6). Krieger.

Cherrett, J. M. & Sager, G. R., eds. Origins of Pest, Parasite, Disease & Weed Problems. (British Ecological Society Symposia Ser.). 413p. 1977. 55.95 o.s.i. (ISBN 0-470-99121-6). Halsted Pr.

Cherrett, J. M., et al. The Control of Injurious Animals. (Biological Science Texts Ser.). 1972. 15.95 o.p. (ISBN 0-312-16905-1). St Martin.

Cherrier, Francois. Fascinating Experiments in Physics. Egan, E. W., tr. LC 78-57789. (Illus.). (gr. 5 up). 1978. 14.95 (ISBN 0-8069-3104-3); PLB 17.79 (ISBN 0-8069-3105-1). Sterling.

Cherrington, David J. Personnel Management: Human Resource Management. 670p. 1983. text ed. write for info. (ISBN 0-697-08085-4); instrs' manual avail. (ISBN 0-697-08192-3); study guide avail. (ISBN 0-697-08094-3). Wm C Brown.

Cherrington, Ernest H. Evolution of Prohibition in the United States of America: A Chronological History of the Liquor Problem & the Temperance Reform in the United States from the Earliest Settlements to the Consummation of National Prohibition. LC 69-14916. (Criminology, Law Enforcement, & Social Problems Ser.: No. 40). 1969. Repr. of 1920 ed. 13.50x (ISBN 0-87585-040-5). Patterson Smith.

--Exploring the Moon Through Binoculars & Small Telescopes. (Illus.). 224p. 1983. pap. 10.00 (ISBN 0-486-24491-1). Dover.

Cherrington, J. Owen. Accounting Basics. (Business Ser.). 431p. 1981. text ed. 16.95x (ISBN 0-534-00902-6); wkbk. 7.95 (ISBN 0-534-00903-4). Kent Pub Co.

Cherry. Plating Waste Treatment. LC 81-68033. 324p. 1982. 39.95 (ISBN 0-250-40417-6). Ann Arbor Science.

Cherry, Annie, ed. see Brown, Shiron L.

Cherry, B. W. Polymer Surfaces. LC 80-40013. (Cambridge Solid State Science Ser.). (Illus.). 150p. 1981. 37.50 (ISBN 0-521-23082-9); pap. 15.95 (ISBN 0-521-29792-3). Cambridge U Pr.

Cherry, C. God's New Israel: Religious Interpretations of American Destiny. 1971. pap. 16.95 (ISBN 0-13-357335-4). P-H.

Cherry, Colin. On Human Communication: A Review, a Survey & a Criticism. 3rd ed. 1978. text ed. 25.00x (ISBN 0-262-03065-9); pap. 7.95x (ISBN 0-262-53038-4). MIT Pr.

Cherry, Conrad, ed. see Wyllie, Robert W.

Cherry, E. M. & Hooper, D. E. Amplifying Devices & Low-Pass Amplifier Design. LC 67-29933. 1968. 77.00 o.p. (ISBN 0-471-15345-1, Pub. by Wiley-Interscience). Wiley.

Cherry, G. E. The Evolution of British Town Planning. LC 74-470. (Illus.). 275p. 1974. 31.95x o.p. (ISBN 0-470-15350-4). Halsted Pr.

Cherry, George. ADA Programming Structures: With an Introduction to Structured Concurrent Programming. 400p. 1981. text ed. 16.95 (ISBN 0-8359-0151-3). Reston.

Cherry, George W. PASCAL Programming Structures: An Introduction to Systematic Programming. (Illus.). 336p. 1980. text ed. 19.95 (ISBN 0-8359-5463-3); pap. text ed. 16.95 (ISBN 0-8359-5462-5). Reston.

Cherry, Gordon. The Politics of Town Planning. LC 81-20772. 192p. 1982. pap. 7.95 cancelled (ISBN 0-582-29540-8). Longman.

Cherry, Gordon E., ed. Shaping an Urban World: Planning in the Twentieth Century. LC 80-17276. 1980. 30.00 (ISBN 0-312-71618-4). St Martin.

Cherry, Joetta & Tomlin, Gwynne. Disco Dancing. LC 79-51213. (Illus.). (gr. 2 up). 1979. lib. bdg. 8.45 (ISBN 0-448-13613-9, G&D); pap. 3.95 (ISBN 0-448-16562-7). Putnam Pub Group.

Cherry, John A., jt. auth. see Freeze, R. Allan.

Cherry, John F. see Davis, Jack L.

Cherry, Kelly. In the Wink of an Eye. 320p. 15.95 (ISBN 0-15-144656-3). HarBraceJ.

Cherry, Laurence B., jt. auth. see Cherry, Rona B.

Cherry, Marlin O. Zoology Laboratory Workbook. 4th ed. 152p. 1982. pap. text ed. 6.95x (ISBN 0-89641-108-7). American Pr.

Cherry, Raymond. General Plastics: Projects & Procedures. rev. ed. (Illus.). (gr. 10-12). 1967. text ed. 16.64 (ISBN 0-87345-162-7). McKnight.

--Leathercrafting: Procedures & Projects. LC 79-83885. (Illus.). 1979. pap. 7.28 (ISBN 0-87345-153-8, B81925). McKnight.

Cherry, Richard L., et al. The Essay: Structure & Purpose. 1975. pap. text ed. 12.95 (ISBN 0-395-18610-2). HM.

Cherry, Richard L., et al, eds. A Return to Vision. 2nd ed. Conley, Robert J. & Hirsch, Bernard A. 432p. 1975. pap. text ed. 12.95 (ISBN 0-395-17836-3); instr's manual 1.10 (ISBN 0-395-17869-X). HM.

Cherry, Robert D. Macroeconomics. LC 79-3130. (Economics Ser.). 1980. text ed. 22.95 (ISBN 0-201-00911-0). A-W.

Cherry, Rona B. & Cherry, Laurence B. The World of American Business: An Introduction. (Illus.). 1977. text ed. 23.50 scp o.p. (ISBN 0-06-041268-2, HarpC); study guide scp 8.50 o.p. (ISBN 0-06-041264-X). Har-Row.

Cherry, Sheldon. For Women of All Ages: A Gynecologist's Guide to Modern Female Health Care. (YA) 1980. pap. 2.95 o.p. (ISBN 0-451-09253-8, E9253, Sig). NAL.

--Understanding Pregnancy. rev. ed. 224p. 1983. 11.95 (ISBN 0-672-52758-8). Bobbs.

Cherry, Sheldon H. For Women of All Ages: A Gynecologist's Guide to Modern Female Health Care. (Illus.). 1979. 13.95 o.p. (ISBN 0-02-524730-1). Macmillan.

Cherry, William. Whom the Gods Would Destroy. 1980. 5.95 o.p. (ISBN 0-533-04378-6). Vantage.

Cherryh, C. J. Brothers of Earth. (Science Fiction Ser). 1976. pap. 1.95 o.p. (ISBN 0-87997-470-2, UJ1470). DAW Bks.

--Downbelow Station. (Science Fiction Ser.). 1981. pap. 2.75 (ISBN 0-87997-828-7, UE1828). Daw Bks.

--The Dreamstone. 1983. pap. 2.75 (ISBN 0-686-43164-2). DAW Bks.

--The Faded Sun: Kesrith. (Science Fiction Ser). (Orig.). 1978. pap. 2.95 (ISBN 0-87997-813-9, UE1813). DAW Bks.

--The Faded Sun: Kutath. (Science Fiction Ser.). (Orig.). 1980. pap. 2.50 (ISBN 0-87997-743-4, UE1743). DAW Bks.

--The Faded Sun: Shon'jir. (Science Fiction Ser.). 1979. pap. 2.50 (ISBN 0-87997-753-1, UE1753). DAW Bks.

--Port Eternity. 192p. 1982. pap. 2.50 (ISBN 0-686-95153-0). DAW Bks.

Cherryh, C. J., jt. auth. see Henneberg, N. C.

Cherryholmes, C. Understanding the United States: Grade 5. (McGraw-Hill Social Studies). (Illus.). 1979. text ed. 16.24 (ISBN 0-07-011985-6); Actionbk 4.16 (ISBN 0-07-012005-6); posters 28.52 (ISBN 0-07-012035-8); tchr's ed. 23.24 (ISBN 0-07-011995-3). McGraw.

Cherryholmes, C. & Manson, G. Investigating Societies. (Illus.). (gr. 6). 1979. 15.20 (ISBN 0-07-011986-4); Actionbk. 4.16 (ISBN 0-07-012006-4); posters 28.52 (ISBN 0-07-012036-6); tests 69.00 (ISBN 0-07-012056-0); tchr's ed. 25.08 (ISBN 0-07-011996-1). McGraw.

--Our Communities. (Illus.). (gr. 3). text ed. 13.00 (ISBN 0-07-011983-X, W); Actionbk. 3.00 (ISBN 0-07-012003-X); tchr's ed. action bk. 4.00 (ISBN 0-07-011973-2); tests 57.04 (ISBN 0-07-012043-9); tchr's ed. 21.40 (ISBN 0-07-011993-7). McGraw.

--Studying Cultures. (Illus.). (gr. 4). 1979. text ed. 14.92 (ISBN 0-07-011984-8); tchr's ed. 22.76 (ISBN 0-07-011994-5); Actionbk. 4.16 (ISBN 0-07-012004-8); posters 28.52 (ISBN 0-07-012034-X). McGraw.

Cherryholmes, C., et al. Discovering Others. (McGraw-Hill Social Studies). (Illus., For use with gr. 1). 1979. tchr's. bk. 20.48 (ISBN 0-07-011911-2, W). McGraw.

Cherryholmes, Lynn. Learning About People. (Illus.). (gr. 2). 1979. tchr's. ed. 11.08 (ISBN 0-07-011982-1, W); tchr's. ed. of wkbk. 2.16 (ISBN 0-07-011992-9); actionbk. 2.08 (ISBN 0-07-012002-1). McGraw.

Chertoff, Mordecai S., jt. ed. see Curtis, Michael.

Chertok, L., ed. see International Brain Research Organization.

Cherulnik, Paul D. Behavioral Research: Assessing the Validity of Research Findings in Psychology. 336p. 1983. text ed. 15.50 scp (ISBN 0-06-041258-5, HarpC). Har-Row.

Chesbro, George. City of Whispering Stone. 1979. pap. 1.95 o.p. (ISBN 0-451-08812-3, J8812, Sig). NAL.

Chesebro & Hamsher. Orientations to Public Communication. Applbaum, Ronald & Hart, Roderick, eds. (MODCOM Modules in Speech Communication Ser.). 1976. pap. text ed. 2.75 (ISBN 0-574-22513-7, 13-5513). SRA.
Cheshire, Jenny. Variation in an English Dialect: A Sociolinguistic Study. LC 82-4189. (Cambridge Studies in Linguistics: No. 37). (Illus.). 150p. 1982. 29.50 (ISBN 0-521-23802-1). Cambridge U Pr.
Cheshire, N. M. The Nature of Psychodynamic Interpretation. LC 75-1391. 1975. 30.25 o.p. (ISBN 0-471-15365-6, Pub. by Wiley-Interscience). Wiley.
Chesler, Bernice. In & Out of Boston With (or Without) Children. 4th ed. LC 81-86605. (Illus.). 352p. 1982. pap. 9.95 (ISBN 0-87106-968-7). Globe Pequot.
Chesler, Evan R. The Russian Jewry Reader. 147p. pap. 2.45 (ISBN 0-686-95145-X). ADL.
Chesler, Mark A. & Cave, William. A Sociology of Education. (Illus.). 1981. text ed. 21.95x (ISBN 0-02-322150-X). Macmillan.
Chesler, Phyllis. With Child: A Diary of Motherhood. LC 79-7081. 1979. 12.45 (ISBN 0-690-01835-5). T Y Crowell.
Chesman, Andrea. Pickles & Relishes: One Hundred Thirty Recipes, Apple to Zucchini. (Illus.). 160p. (Orig.). 1983. pap. 5.95 (ISBN 0-88266-321-6). Garden Way Pub.
Chesman, Andrea, ed. see Ballantyne, Janet.
Chesneau Du Marsais, C. Logique et Principes de Grammaire: Nouvelle Edition Plus Traite d'Inversion, 2 vols. (Linguistics 13th-18th Centuries Ser.). (Fr.). 1974. Repr. of 1792 ed. Set. lib. bdg. 204.00x o.p. (ISBN 0-8287-0187-3). Clearwater Pub.
--Veritables Principes de la Grammaire. (Linguistics 13th-18th Centuries Ser.). 56p. (Fr.). 1974. Repr. of 1729 ed. 18.00x o.p. (ISBN 0-8287-0188-1, 71-5042). Clearwater Pub.
Chesneaux, Jean. Pasts & Futures: Or What Is History for? 1978. 10.95 o.p. (ISBN 0-500-25062-6). Thames Hudson.
Chesner, Richard. Living Corals. (Illus.). 1979. 45.00 o.p. (ISBN 0-517-53854-7, C N Potter Bks). Crown.
Chesney, Allen, ed. Chattanooga Album: Thirty-Two Historic Postcards. LC 82-17330. (Illus.). 16p. 1983. pap. 3.95 (ISBN 0-87049-381-7). U of Tenn Pr.
Chesney, Kellow. Anti-Society: An Account of the Victorian Underworld. LC 70-113999. (Illus.). 1970. 14.95 (ISBN 0-87645-022-2). Gambit.
Chesney, Marion. Duke's Diamonds. 160p. (Orig.). 1983. pap. 2.25 (ISBN 0-449-20085-X, Crest). Fawcett.
Chesnut, D. B. Finite Groups & Quantum Theory. LC 81-19351. 270p. 1982. Repr. of 1974 ed. lib. bdg. 26.50 (ISBN 0-89874-468-7). Krieger.
--Finite Groups & Quantum Theory. LC 74-9840. 254p. 1974. 25.00 o.p. (ISBN 0-471-15445-8, Pub. by Wiley-Interscience). Wiley.
Chesnutt, C. House Behind the Cedars. 1969. pap. 1.95 o.p. (ISBN 0-02-049380-0, Collier). Macmillan.
Chesnutt, Margaret. Studies in Short Stories of William Carleton. (Gothenborg Studies in English: No. 34). 1976. pap. text ed. 18.50x (ISBN 91-7346-027-3). Humanities.
Chess, Stella & Thomas, Alexander, eds. Annual Progress in Child Psychiatry & Child Development, 12 vols. Incl. Vol. 1. 1968. o.p.; Vol. 2. 1969. (ISBN 0-87630-002-6); Vol. 3. 1970. (ISBN 0-87630-003-4); Vol. 4. 1971. (ISBN 0-87630-004-2); Vol. 5. 1972. o.p.; Vol. 6. 1973 (ISBN 0-87630-062-X); Vol. 7. 1974 (ISBN 0-87630-101-4); Vol. 8. 1975 (ISBN 0-87630-107-3); Vol. 9. 1976; Vol. 10. 1977; Vol. 11. 1978 (ISBN 0-87630-180-4); Vol. 12. 1979 (ISBN 0-87630-216-9). LC 68-23452. (Illus.). Vols. 2-4 & 6-12. 25.00 ea. Brunner-Mazel.
--Annual Progress in Child Psychiatry & Child Development 1980. LC 66-4030. 600p. 1980. 30.00 (ISBN 0-87630-247-9). Brunner-Mazel.
--Annual Progress in Child Psychiatry & Child Development, 1982. LC 68-23452. 600p. 1982. 35.00 (ISBN 0-87630-317-3). Brunner-Mazel.
Chess, Stella, et al. Your Child Is a Person: A Psychological Approach to Parenthood Without Guilt. 224p. 1977. pap. 3.95 (ISBN 0-14-004439-6). Penguin.
Chess, Victoria. Catcards. (Illus.). 24p. (gr. 1-5). 1982. pap. 4.95 spiral (ISBN 0-02-042300-4). Macmillan.
--Catcards for Christmas: A Purrfectly Wonderful Collection of Christmas Cards. (Illus.). 24p. 1982. pap. 4.95 spiral (ISBN 0-02-042240-7). Macmillan.
--Poor Esme. LC 82-2924. (Illus.). 32p. (ps-3). 1982. Reinforced bdg. 12.95 (ISBN 0-8234-0455-2). Holiday.
Chess Visions, Inc. Staff, compiled by. Minor Piece Endgames: Yuri Averbakh Endgames Cassettes. (Illus.). 60p. 1982. 21.90 (ISBN 0-939786-03-6). Chess Visions.
Chess Visions, Inc. Staff, ed. Rook & Minor Pieces: Yuri Averbakh Endgame Cassettes. (Illus.). 56p. 1982. 21.90 (ISBN 0-939786-04-4). Chess Visions.
Chesseman, G. W. & Cookson, R. F. Condensed Pyrannes, Vol. 35. 835p. 1979. 194.95 (ISBN 0-471-38204-3, Pub. by Wiley-Interscience). Wiley.
Chessman, G. Wallace. Theodore Roosevelt & the Politics of Power. LC 68-20501. (Library of American Biography Ser.). 1969. 5.00 o.p. (ISBN 0-316-13871-1); pap. 5.95 o.p. (ISBN 0-316-13870-3). Little.
Chessmore, Roy A. Profitable Pasture Management. LC 78-70056. 1979. 14.50 (ISBN 0-8134-2056-3, 2056). Interstate.
Chesswas, J. D., jt. auth. see Vaizey, J.
Chestang, Leon W., jt. ed. see Cafferty, Pastora S.
Chester, Andrew, tr. see Schweizer, Edward.
Chester, Carole. California & the Golden West. LC 82-61197. (Pocket Guide Ser.). (Illus.). 1983. pap. 4.95 (ISBN 0-528-84894-1). Rand.
--Travel for Lovers. (Illus.). 154p. 1976. 11.50 o.p. (ISBN 0-7134-3095-8). Hippocrene Bks.
Chester, Daniel N., ed. Lessons of the British War Economy. LC 70-157956. 260p. 1972. Repr. of 1951 ed. lib. bdg. 18.00x (ISBN 0-8371-6175-4, CHWE). Greenwood.
Chester, Deborah. French Slippers. 1981. 11.95 (ISBN 0-698-11071-4, Coward). Putnam Pub Group.
--A Love So Wild. LC 79-11874. 1980. 9.95 o.s.i. (ISBN 0-698-11007-2, Coward). Putnam Pub Group.
Chester, Edward W. United States Oil Policy & Diplomacy: A Twentieth Century Overview. LC 82-8379. (Contributions in Economics & Economic History Ser.: No. 52). (Illus.). 384p. 1983. lib. bdg. 35.00 (ISBN 0-313-23174-5, CUO/). Greenwood.
Chester, Giraud, et al. Television & Radio. 5th ed. (Illus.). 1978. ref. ed. 23.95 (ISBN 0-13-902981-8). P-H.
Chester, Helen. Cocktails. (Illus.). 80p. 1983. pap. 4.95 (ISBN 0-312-14634-5). St Martin.
Chester, Joyce & Avis, Peter. Make it Count: Puzzles. 72p. 1978. 15.00x o.p. (ISBN 0-7121-2102-1, Pub. by Macdonald & Evans). St Martin.
Chester, Margaret. Linsang. 1983. 4.95 (ISBN 0-533-05594-6). Vantage.
Chester, Michael. Let's Go on a Space Shuttle. new ed. LC 76-9652. (Let's Go Ser). (Illus.). 48p. (gr. 3-5). 1976. PLB 4.29 o.p. (ISBN 0-399-60960-1). Putnam Pub Group.
--Let's Go to a Recycling Center. new ed. (Let's Go Ser.). (Illus.). (gr. 3-5). 1977. PLB 3.86 o.p. (ISBN 0-399-61062-6). Putnam Pub Group.
--Let's Go to Fight a Forest Fire. (Let's Go Ser.). (Illus.). (gr. 4-6). 1978. PLB 4.29 o.p. (ISBN 0-399-61108-8). Putnam Pub Group.
--Let's Go to Stop Air Pollution. (Let's Go Ser.). (Illus.). (gr. 2-4). 1968. PLB 4.29 o.p. (ISBN 0-399-60400-6). Putnam Pub Group.
--Robots in Space. (Science Survey Ser.). (Illus.). (gr. 5-7). 1965. PLB 4.89 o.p. (ISBN 0-399-60541-X). Putnam Pub Group.
--Water Monster. LC 72-92925. (Illus.). (gr. 4-7). 1978. pap. 3.95 (ISBN 0-448-14674-6, G&D). Putnam Pub Group.
Chester, R., jt. ed. see Riley, J. P.
Chester, W. Mechanics. (Illus.). 1980. text ed. 50.00x (ISBN 0-04-510058-6); pap. text ed. 24.95x (ISBN 0-04-510059-4). Allen Unwin.
Chesterfield, Ray, jt. auth. see Ruddle, Kenneth.
Chesterman, Charles W. The Audubon Society Field Guide to North American Rocks & Minerals. LC 78-54893. (Illus.). 1979. 12.50 (ISBN 0-394-50269-8). Knopf.
Chesterman, James. Classical Terracotta Figures. LC 75-10550. (Illus.). 104p. 1975. 12.95 o.p. (ISBN 0-87951-037-4). Overlook Pr.
Chesterman, Robert, ed. Conversations with Conductors. 128p. 1976. 11.50x o.p. (ISBN 0-87471-860-0). Rowman.
Chesters, G., jt. auth. see Broome, P.
Chesters, G., jt. ed. see Broome, P.
Chesterton, G. K. The Father Brown Omnibus. 1983. 13.95 (ISBN 0-396-08159-2). Dodd.
--The Father Brown Stories. 718p. 1982. Repr. of 1929 ed. lib. bdg. 45.00 (ISBN 0-8495-0867-3). Arden Lib.
--The Innocence of the Father Brown. LC 75-44963. (Crime Fiction Ser). 1976. Repr. of 1911 ed. lib. bdg. 17.50 o.s.i. (ISBN 0-8240-2359-5). Garland Pub.
--Robert Browning. 1903. 4.95 o.p. (ISBN 0-312-10675-0). St Martin.
--Saint Francis of Assisi. LC 57-1230. 1957. pap. 2.95 (ISBN 0-385-02900-4, Im). Doubleday.
--What I Saw in America. 2nd ed. LC 68-16226. (American Scene Ser). 1968. Repr. of 1922 ed. 37.50 (ISBN 0-306-71009-9). Da Capo.
Chesterton, Gilbert K. Orthodoxy. LC 74-2837. 299p. 1974. Repr. of 1909 ed. lib. bdg. 17.25x (ISBN 0-8371-7438-4, CHOR). Greenwood.
Chesterton, Z. Ridley. British Tugs. pap. 4.00x (ISBN 0-392-14470-0, SpS). Sportshelf.
Chestnut, Lauraline G., jt. ed. see Rowe, Robert D.
Chestnut, Mary B., jt. ed. see Woodward, C. V.
Chetin, Helen. Angel Island Prisoner. Harvey, Catherine, tr. LC 82-51170. (Illus., Chinese-English.). (gr. 3 up). 1982. 7.00. New Seed.
--Frances Ann Speaks Out: My Father Raped Me. 2nd ed. (Illus.). 20p. (gr. 6 up). 1981. pap. 2.50 o.p. (ISBN 0-938678-05-1). New Seed.
Chettur, S. K. Steel Frame & I: Life in the Indian Civil Service. 1963. 4.50x o.p. (ISBN 0-210-34087-8). Asia.
Chetwood, William R. The Voyages, & Adventures of Captain Robert Boyle. LC 79-170565. (Foundations of the Novel Ser.: Vol. 46). lib. bdg. 50.00- o.s.i. (ISBN 0-8240-0558-9). Garland Pub.
Cheung, Dominic. Feng Chih. (World Authors Ser.). 1979. lib. bdg. 15.95 (ISBN 0-8057-6356-2, Twayne). G K Hall.
Cheung, Wai Yiu. Calcium & Cell Function, Vol. 3. (Molecular Biology Ser.). 432p. 1983. 64.00 (ISBN 0-12-171403-9); subscription 54.50. Acad Pr.
Cheung, Y. K. Finite Strip Method in Structural Analysis. Neal, B. G., ed. 130p. 1976. text ed. 34.00 (ISBN 0-08-018308-5). Pergamon.
Chevalier, C. Ulysse. Repertoire Des Sources Historiques Du Moyen Age: Bio-Bibliographie, 2 vols. 2nd ed. 1905-07. Set. 172.00 (ISBN 0-527-16700-2). Kraus Repr.
Chevalier, Christa. Little Green Pumpkins. Tucker, Cathy, ed. LC 81-12999. (Illus.). 32p. (ps-1). 1982. 8.25 (ISBN 0-8075-4593-7). A Whitman.
Chevalier, Denys. Maillol. (QLP Art Ser). (Illus.). 1970. 7.95 (ISBN 0-517-02688-0). Crown.
--Paul Klee. (Quality-Low-Price Art Ser.). Date not set. 7.95 (ISBN 0-517-50302-6). Crown.
--Picasso: Blue & Rose Periods. (Q L P Art Ser.). (Illus.). 1969. 7.95 (ISBN 0-517-00904-8). Crown.
Chevalier, Francois. Land & Society in Colonial Mexico: The Great Hacienda. Eustis, Alvin, tr. Simpson, Lesley B., ed. & frwd. by. 1963. 27.50x (ISBN 0-520-00229-6); pap. 8.95 (ISBN 0-520-04653-6). U of Cal Pr.
Chevalier, Georges. The Sacred Magician. 1976. pap. 5.95x o.p. (ISBN 0-8464-0807-4). Beekman Pubs.
Chevalier, Haakon M., tr. see Malraux, Andre.
Chevalier, Jacques. Civilization & the Stolen Gift: Capital, Kin, & Cult in Eastern Peru. 484p. 1982. 49.50x (ISBN 0-8020-5520-6). U of Toronto Pr.
Chevalier, Michel. Questions des Travailleurs: L'Amelioration du Sort des Ouvriers. Les Salaires, l'Organisation du Travail. (Conditions of the 19th Century French Working Class Ser.). 32p. (Fr.). 1974. Repr. of 1848 ed. lib. bdg. 23.00x o.p. (ISBN 0-8287-0189-X, 1001). Clearwater Pub.
Chevalier, Ulysse. Repertoire Des Sources Historiques Du Moyen Age: Topo-Bibliographie, 2 Vols. 2nd ed. 1894-1903. Set. 90.00 o.s.i. (ISBN 0-527-16710-X). Kraus Repr.
Chevallier, Emile. Les Salaires au Dix-Neuvieme Siecle. (Conditions of the 19th Century French Working Class Ser.). 299p. (Fr.). 1974. Repr. of 1887 ed. lib. bdg. 79.50x o.p. (ISBN 0-8287-0190-3, 1094). Clearwater Pub.
Chevallier, Raymond. Roman Roads. LC 74-82845. 1976. 50.00x (ISBN 0-520-02834-1). U of Cal Pr.
Chevassu, J. Beoumi: Etude Economique d'un Centre Semi-Urbain. (Black Africa Ser.). 154p. (Fr.). 1974. Repr. of 1968 ed. lib. bdg. 47.00 o.p. (ISBN 0-8287-0191-1, 71-2060). Clearwater Pub.
--Essai de Definition de Quelques Indicateurs de Structure et de Fonctionnement de l'Economie des Centres semi-Urbains. (Black Africa Ser.). 48p. (Fr.). 1974. Repr. of 1970 ed. 29.00x o.p. (ISBN 0-8287-0192-X, 71-2058). Clearwater Pub.
--Etude de Quelques Centres Semiurbains. (Black Africa Ser.). (Illus.). 254p. (Fr.). 1974. Repr. of 1968 ed. lib. bdg. 74.00 o.p. (ISBN 0-8287-0193-8, 71-2057). Clearwater Pub.
--Rapport Preliminaire d'Tude des Centres Semi-Urbains. (Black Africa Ser.). 54p. (Fr.). 1974. Repr. of 1967 ed. 24.00x o.p. (ISBN 0-8287-0194-6, 71-2055). Clearwater Pub.
Chevassu, J. & Michotte, J. Les Zones Rurales et les Centres Secondaires de la Region de Bouake. (Black Africa Ser.). 96p. (Fr.). 1974. Repr. of 1969 ed. lib. bdg. 34.00x o.p. (ISBN 0-8287-0196-2, 71-2049). Clearwater Pub.
Chevigny, Hector & Braverman, Sydell. Adjustment of the Blind. 1950. 42.50x (ISBN 0-685-89731-1). Elliots Bks.
Cheville, Norman F. Cell Pathology. 2nd ed. (Illus.). 516p. 1983. text ed. 44.95x (ISBN 0-8138-0310-1). Iowa St U Pr.
Cheviot, Andrew, ed. Proverbs, Proverbial Expressions, & Popular Rhymes of Scotland. LC 68-23144. 1969. Repr. of 1896 ed. 34.00x (ISBN 0-8103-3198-5). Gale.
Chevli & Farmer. Tits & Clits, No. 1. (Women's Humor Ser.). (Illus.). 1972. 1.25 (ISBN 0-918440-00-9). Nanny Goat.
Chevy Chase Manuscripts, ed. see Johnson, Hubert R.
Chew, Al H., et al. Technical Mathematics. LC 75-25011. (Illus.). 576p. 1976. text ed. 23.00 (ISBN 0-395-24009-3); instr's. manual 2.95 (ISBN 0-395-24010-7). HM.
Chew, Alexander L. The Lollipop Test: A Diagnostic Screening Test for School Readiness. 14p. pap. 19.95 (ISBN 0-89334-028-6). Humanics Ltd.
Chew, Allen F. An Atlas of Russian History: Eleven Centuries of Changing Borders. 1967. pap. text ed. 9.95x (ISBN 0-300-01445-7). Yale U Pr.
Chew, Charles & Schlawin, Sheila. To Teach Writing Right. St. Clair, Robert N., ed. (Language & Literacy Ser.). (Orig.). 1983. pap. 14.95 (ISBN 0-88499-604-2). Inst Mod Lang.
Chew, Doris N. Ada Nield Chew: The Life & Writings of a Working Woman. 256p. 1983. pap. 8.95 (ISBN 0-86068-294-3, Virago Pr). Merrimack Bk Serv.
Chew, Helena & Weinbaum, Martin. The London Eyre of Twelve Forty-Four. 1970. 50.00x (ISBN 0-686-96614-7, Pub by London Rec Soc England). State Mutual Bk.
Chew, Helena M. London Possessory Assizes: A Calendar. 1965. 50.00x (ISBN 0-686-96618-X, Pub by London Rec Soc England). State Mutual Bk.
Chew, Helena M. & Kellaway, William, eds. London Assize of Nuisance,1301-1431: A Calendar. 1973. 50.00x (ISBN 0-686-36878-9, Pub by London Rec Soc England). State Mutual Bk.
Chew, Paul A., ed. Southwestern Pennsylvania Painters, 1800-1945. LC 81-52933. (Illus.). 178p. (Orig.). 1983. pap. 12.95 (ISBN 0-686-38092-4). Westmoreland.
--Southwestern Pennsylvania Painters, 1800-1945. LC 81-52933. (Illus.). xii, 166p. 1983. pap. 12.95 (ISBN 0-686-43201-0). U of Pittsburgh Pr.
Chew, Ruth. Wednesday Witch. LC 72-75598. (Illus.). (gr. 4-6). 1972. 8.95 (ISBN 0-8234-0210-X). Holiday.
--The Wishing Tree. new ed. 144p. (gr. 7-12). 1980. 8.95 (ISBN 0-8038-8099-5). Hastings.
Chewning, Betty. Staff Manual for Teaching Patients about Hypertension. LC 78-27337. (Illus.). 340p. 1979. pap. 37.75 o.p. (ISBN 0-87258-251-5, 070119). Am Hospital.
--Staff Manual for Teaching Patients about Hypertension. LC 82-8745. (Illus.). 372p. 1982. 47.50 (ISBN 0-87258-400-3, AHA-070122). Am Hospital.
Chewning, Emily, jt. auth. see Chwast, Seymour.
Chey, William Y., ed. Functional Disorders of the Digestive Tract. 335p. 1982. text ed. write for info. (ISBN 0-89004-859-2). Raven.
Cheyette, Frederic, ed. Lordship & Community in Medieval Europe. LC 75-12657. 448p. 1975. Repr. of 1968 ed. 16.50 (ISBN 0-88275-283-9). Krieger.
Cheyette, H., jt. auth. see Cheyette, I.
Cheyette, I. & Cheyette, H. Teaching Music Creatively in the Elementary School. 1969. text ed. 26.95 (ISBN 0-07-010745-9, C). McGraw.
Cheyne, George. The English Malady. LC 76-49853. (History of Psychology Ser.). 1976. Repr. of 1733 ed. 38.00x (ISBN 0-8201-1281-X). Schol Facsimiles.
--An Essay of Health & Long Life. 1977. 40.00 o.p. (ISBN 0-85362-166-7, Oriel). Routledge & Kegan.
Cheyney, Arnold & Capone, Donald. The Map Corner. 1983. pap. text ed. 12.95 (ISBN 0-673-16615-5). Scott F.
Cheyney, Arnold B. Teaching Children of Different Cultures in the Classroom: A Language Approach. (Elementary Education Ser.). 1976. pap. text ed. 11.95 (ISBN 0-675-08622-1). Merrill.
Chi, M. T., ed. Trends in Memory Development. (Contributions to Human Development: Vol. 9). (Illus.). xiv, 160p. 1983. pap. 76.75 (ISBN 3-8055-3661-5). S Karger.
Chi, Pang-Yuan, et al, eds. An Anthology of Contemporary Chinese Literature: Taiwan: 1949-1974, Poems & Essays, Vol. 1. LC 75-42791. 340p. 1976. 17.50 (ISBN 0-295-95502-3, Pub. by Natl Inst Comp Taiwan); pap. 9.50 (ISBN 0-295-95628-3); 2 Vol. Set 35.00. U of Wash Pr.
--An Anthology of Contemporary Chinese Literature: Taiwan: 1949-1974, Short Stories, Vol. 2. LC 75-42791. 484p. 1976. 17.50 (ISBN 0-295-95503-1, Pub. by Natl Inst Comp Taiwan); pap. 9.50 (ISBN 0-295-95629-1); 2 Vol. Set 35.00. U of Wash Pr.
Chi, S. W. Heat Pipe Theory & Practice: A Sourcebook. LC 76-9761. (McGraw-Hill-Hemisphere Ser. Thermal & Fluids Engineering). (Illus.). 1976. text ed. 39.50 (ISBN 0-07-010718-1, C). McGraw.
Chia, L. S. & MacAndrews, C. Southeast Asian Seas: Frontiers for Development. 1982. 36.50x (ISBN 0-07-099247-9). McGraw.
Chia, L. S., jt. auth. see C.
Chia-Ao, see Chang Kia-ngau, pseud.
Chia Lan-Po. Cave Home of Peking Man. (Illus.). 1975. pap. 2.95 o.p. (ISBN 0-8351-0024-3). China Bks.
Chiang, A. Fundamental Methods of Mathematical Economics. 2nd ed. 1974. text ed. 29.00 (ISBN 0-07-010780-7, C); instructor's manual 20.00 (ISBN 0-07-010786-6). McGraw.
--Fundamental Methods of Mathematical Economics. 3rd ed. 736p. 1983. 23.95 (ISBN 0-07-010813-7). McGraw.
Chiang, Chin L. Life Table & Its Applications. LC 82-20331. 1983. lib. bdg. 29.50 (ISBN 0-89874-570-5). Krieger.
Chiang, Chin Long. Stochastic Processes: Some Problems & Solutions. 1983. write for info. (ISBN 0-89874-214-5). Krieger.
Chiang, Gregory K., jt. ed. see Seybolt, Peter J.
Chiang, Hai H. Electronics for Nuclear Instrumentation, Theory & Applications. 1983. lib. bdg. price not set (ISBN 0-89874-483-0). Krieger.
Chiang, Monlin. Tides From the West: A Chinese Autobiography. 1947. text ed. 23.50x (ISBN 0-686-83825-4). Elliots Bks.
Chiang Kai-Shek. China's Destiny. LC 76-24849. 260p. 1976. Repr. of 1947 ed. lib. bdg. 32.50 (ISBN 0-306-70821-3). Da Capo.
Chiang Yee. China Revisited. (Illus.). 1977. 9.95 (ISBN 0-393-08791-3). Norton.

Chiappelli, Fredi, ed. First Images of America: The Impact of the New World. LC 75-7191. 1976. 165.00x (ISBN 0-520-03010-9). U of Cal Pr.
Chiappetta, Vincent J., jt. auth. see Greulach, Victor A.
Chiara, jt. auth. see Piero.
Chiara, G. Di see Di Chiara, G. & Gessa, G. L.
Chiara, Joseph De see De Chiara, Joseph.
Chiara, Joseph De see De Chiara, Joseph & Callender, John.
Chiarelli, Luigi see Dent, Anthony.
Chiarenza, Carl. Aaron Siskind: Pleasures & Terrors. 1982. 55.00 o.p. (ISBN 0-8212-1522-1). NYGS.
Chiarenza, G. A. & Pakakostopoulos, D., eds. Clinical Application of Cerebral Evoked Potentials in Pediatric Medicine: Proceedings of the International Conference, Milan, Italy, January 14-16, 1982. (International Congress Ser.: No. 595). 416p. 1982. 69.25 (ISBN 0-444-90278-3, Excerpta Medica). Elsevier.
Chiaro, Mario A. Del see Del Chiaro, Mario A.
Chia-Shun Yih. Stratified Flows. LC 79-24817. 1980. 31.00 (ISBN 0-12-771050-7). Acad Pr.
Chia-Shun Yih, ed. Advances in Applied Mechanics, Vol. 19. LC 48-8503. 1979. 50.00 (ISBN 0-12-002019-X); lib ed. 59.50 (ISBN 0-12-002049-1); microfiche 32.00 (ISBN 0-12-002050-5). Acad Pr.
Chiasson, Robert B. Laboratory Anatomy of Necturus. 3rd ed. (Laboratory Anatomy Ser). 72p. 1976. wire coil write for info. o.p. (ISBN 0-697-04623-0). Wm C Brown.
Chia-Sun Yih see Von Mises, Richard & Von Karman, Theodore.
Chiazze, Leonard, Jr. & Lundin, Frank E., eds. Methods & Issues in Occupational & Environmental Epidemiology. LC 82-72346. (Illus.). 225p. 1982. 39.95 (ISBN 0-250-40576-8). Ann Arbor Science.
Chiba, H., et al, eds. Food Science & Technology: Proceedings of the 5th International Congress. LC 79-20898. (Developments in Food Science Ser.: Vol. 2). 448p. 1980. 85.00 (ISBN 0-444-99770-9). Elsevier.
Chibata, Ichiro & Fukui, Saburo, eds. Enzyme Engineering, Vol. 6. 560p. 1982. 59.50x (ISBN 0-306-41121-0, Plenum Pr). Plenum Pub.
Chibnall, Albert C. Protein Metabolism in the Plant. 1939. 39.50x (ISBN 0-685-69795-9); pap. 14.50x (ISBN 0-685-69796-7). Elliots Bks.
Chibnall, Marjorie, ed. Charters & Custumals of the Abbey of Holy Trinity, Caen. (Records of Social & Economic History Ser.). (Illus.). 194p. 1983. 37.50 (ISBN 0-19-726009-8). Oxford U Pr.
Chibucos, Thomas R., ed. Toward Broader Conceptualization of Child Mistreatment. LC 80-82468. (Special Issue of Infant Mental Health Journal: Vol. 1, No. 4). 73p. 1980. pap. 8.95 (ISBN 0-89885-052-5). Human Sci Pr.
Chibwe, E. C. Afro-Arab Relations in the New World Order. LC 77-90935. 1978. 25.00 (ISBN 0-312-01063-X). St Martin.
Chicago Area Transportation Center. Year Two-Thousand Alternative Transportation Futures Conference: Proceedings. 145p. 1976. pap. 1.50 (ISBN 0-686-94050-4, Trans). Northwestern U Pr.
Chicago Association of Commerce & Industry, Committee of Investigation on Smoke Abatement. Chicago Report on Smoke Abatement: A Landmark Survey of the Technology & History of Air Pollution Control. Linsky, Benjamin & Linsky, B., eds. 1971. 35.75 o.p. (ISBN 0-08-022303-6). Pergamon.
--Smoke Papers of the Chicago Association of Commerce Collected 1911-1915 for Preparation of Report Entitled Smoke Abatement & Electrification of Railway Terminals. Linsky, Benjamin, ed. 1915. 218.00 o.p. (ISBN 0-08-022302-8). Pergamon.
Chicago, Judy. Through the Flower: My Struggle As a Woman Artist. LC 76-52900. 1977. pap. 7.95 o.p. (ISBN 0-385-12696-4, Anch). Doubleday.
--Through the Flower: My Struggle As a Woman Artist. rev. and updated ed. LC 81-43748. (Illus.). 216p. 1982. pap. 8.95 (ISBN 0-385-18084-5, Anch). Doubleday.
Chichester, C. O., ed. Advances in Food Research, Vol. 28. 403p. 1982. 49.50 (ISBN 0-12-016428-0); lib ed 64.50 (ISBN 0-12-016498-1); microfiche 35.00 (ISBN 0-12-016499-X). Acad Pr.
Chichester, C. O., et al see Mrak, E. M., et al.
Chichester, Francis. Solo to Sydney. 224p. 1982. 30.00x (ISBN 0-85177-254-4, Pub. by Conway Maritime England). State Mutual Bk.
Chichester, Sir Francis. Solo to Sydney. LC 81-48449. (Illus.). 208p. 1982. 13.95 (ISBN 0-8128-2865-8). Stein & Day.
Chichester, Michael & Wilkinson, John. The Uncertain Ally. 264p. 1982. text ed. 38.00x (ISBN 0-566-00534-4). Gower Pub Ltd.
Chichvarin, V. A. International Nature Conservation Law: Environment Law. Date not set. cancelled (ISBN 0-379-00585-9). Oceana.
Chick, Edson. Dances of Death: Wedekind, Brecht, Durrenmatt, & the Satiric Tradition. (Studies in German Literature, Linguistics, & Culture: Vol. 19). (Illus.). 190p. 1983. 16.95x (ISBN 0-938100-04-1). Camden Hse.
Chick, Joyce M. Innovations in the Use of Career Information. (Guidance Monograph). 1970. pap. 2.40 o.p. (ISBN 0-685-03739-8, 9-78841). HM.
Chicken, J. C. Nuclear Power Hazard Control Policy. LC 80-40992. (Illus.). 300p. 1981. 40.00 (ISBN 0-08-023254-X); pap. 15.00 (ISBN 0-08-023255-8). Pergamon.
Chickering, Howell D., Jr., ed. Beowulf: A Dual Language Edition. LC 75-21250. (Anchor Literary Library). 1982. pap. 8.95 (ISBN 0-385-06213-3, Anch). Doubleday.
Chickering, Jesse. Immigration into the United States. LC 70-145473. (The American Immigration Library). 94p. 1971. Repr. of 1848 ed. lib. bdg. 8.95x (ISBN 0-89198-006-7). Ozer.
Chicksberg, Abraham A. Come Back, Jewish Youth Come Back Home. LC 83-60003. 1983. pap. 3.95 (ISBN 0-88400-094-X). Shengold.
Chicorel, Marietta, ed. Chicorel Abstracts to Reading & Learning Disabilities, Vol. 19, 1980: Annual Edition. (Illus.). 380p. 1982. 95.00 (ISBN 0-934598-80-0). Am Lib Pub Co.
--Chicorel Abstracts to Reading & Learning Disabilities, 1981, Vol. 19. (Chicorel Index Ser.). 380p. 1983. 95.00x (ISBN 0-934598-83-5). Am Lib Pub Co.
Chidgey, Graham. Monarch Guide to the Wines of Burgandy. (Illus.). 1978. pap. 2.95 o.p. (ISBN 0-672-28361-1). Monarch Pr.
Chiefari, Janet. Introducing the Drum & Bugle Corps. LC 82-45379. (Illus.). 128p. (gr. 5 up). 1982. PLB 10.95 (ISBN 0-396-08088-X). Dodd.
Chieffo, Clifford. Contemporary Oil Painter's Handbook. LC 75-40302. (Illus.). 160p. 1976. 18.95 (ISBN 0-13-170167-3). P-H.
Chieger, Bob. Voices of Baseball: Quotations of the Summer Game. LC 82-73027. 288p. (Orig.). 1983. pap. 7.95 (ISBN 0-689-70646-4). Atheneum.
Chielens, Edward E. The Literary Journal in America, 1900-1950: A Guide to Information Sources. LC 74-11534. (American Literature, English Literature, & World Literature in English Information Guide Ser.: Vol. 16). 1977. 42.00x (ISBN 0-8103-1240-9). Gale.
Chielens, Edward E., ed. The Literary Journal in America to 1900: A Guide to Information Sources. LC 74-11533. (American Literature, English Literature & World Literatures in English Information Guide Ser.: Vol. 3). 228p. 1975. 42.00x (ISBN 0-8103-1239-5). Gale.
Chien. Novel Drug Delivery Systems. (Drugs & the Pharmaceutical Sciences Ser.). 584p. 1982. 65.00 (ISBN 0-8247-1831-3). Dekker.
Chien, Robert I., ed. Issues in Pharmaceutical Economics. LC 78-19726. 1979. 21.95x (ISBN 0-669-02729-4). Lexington Bks.
Chien, Szuma. Selections from Records of the Historian. 1979. 12.95 (ISBN 0-8351-0617-9); pap. 7.95 (ISBN 0-8351-0618-7). China Bks.
Chien, Yi-Tzuu, jt. auth. see Booth, Taylor L.
Ch'ien Chung-shu. Fortress Besieged. Kelly, Jeanne & Mao, Nathan K., trs. LC 78-24846. (Chinese Literature in Translation Ser.). 416p. 1980. 17.50x (ISBN 0-253-16518-0). Ind U Pr.
Chien-Tung, Shui, jt. auth. see Martin, Bernard.
Chiera, E. Lists of Personal Names from the Temple School of Nippur: A Syllabary of Personal Names. (Publications of the Babylonian Section: Vol. 11-1). (Illus.). 88p. 1916. x soft bound 7.00 (ISBN 0-686-11923-1). Univ Mus of U PA.
--Lists of Personal Names from the Temple School of Nippur: Lists of Akkadian Personal Names. (Publications of the Babylonian Section: Vol. 11-2). (Illus.). 85p. 1916. soft bound 7.00x (ISBN 0-686-11924-X). Univ Mus of U PA.
--Old Babylonian Contracts. (Publications of the Babylonian Section: Vol. 8-2). (Illus.). 115p. 1922. bound 7.00xsoft (ISBN 0-686-11922-3). Univ Mus of U PA.
Chigier, N. A., jt. auth. see Beer, J. M.
Chigier, N. A., ed. Progress in Energy & Combustion Science, Vol. 7. (Illus.). 316p. 1982. 130.00 (ISBN 0-08-029124-4). Pergamon.
Chih, Yu-Ju. Advanced Newspaper Readings. 5.95 (ISBN 0-686-09970-2); tapes avail. (ISBN 0-686-09971-0). Far Eastern Pubns.
--A Primer of Newspaper Chinese. rev. ed. 8.95 (ISBN 0-686-09972-9); tapes avail. (ISBN 0-686-09973-7). Far Eastern Pubns.
Chihara, jt. auth. see ICTA Conference, Kyoto 1977, 5th.
Chih-Liang, Na. Chinese Jades: Archaic & Modern. (Illus.). 1977. 25.00 (ISBN 0-685-67980-2). Minneapolis Inst Arts.
Chijioke, F. A. Ancient Africa. LC 75-80850. (Illus.). (gr. 5-8). 1969. pap. 3.95x (ISBN 0-8419-0013-2, Africana). Holmes & Meier.
Chikan, A. Economics & Management of Inventories, 2 pts. (Studies in Production & Engineering Economics: Vol. 2). 1982. Set. 159.75 (ISBN 0-444-99718-0); Pt. A. 55.50 (ISBN 0-444-99720-2); Pt. B. 110.75 (ISBN 0-444-99719-9). Elsevier.
Chikazumi, Sushin & Charap, Stanley H. Physics of Magnetism. LC 78-2315. 566p. 1978. Repr. of 1964 ed. lib. bdg. 33.50 (ISBN 0-88275-662-1). Krieger.
Chiland, Colette, jt. auth. see Anthony, E. James.
Chilcote, R. & Edelstein, J., eds. Latin America: The Struggle with Dependency & Beyond. LC 74-8393. (States & Societies of the Third World Ser.). 781p. 1974. text ed. 26.50 o.p. (ISBN 0-470-15555-8); pap. text ed. 12.95x o.p. (ISBN 0-470-15556-6). Halsted Pr.
Chilcote, Ronald H. Theories of Comparative Politics: The Search for a Paradigm. 492p. (Orig.). 1981. lib. bdg. 35.00 (ISBN 0-89158-970-8); pap. 15.00 (ISBN 0-89158-971-6). Westview.
Chilcote, Ronald H., ed. Dependency & Marxism: Toward a Resolution of the Debate. (Latin American Perpsective Ser.: No. 1). 179p. 1982. lib. bdg. 18.95 (ISBN 0-86531-457-8); pap. text ed. 9.95 (ISBN 0-86531-458-6). Westview.
Chilcote, Ronald H. & Edelstein, Joel C., eds. Latin America: The Struggle with Dependency & Beyond. 800p. 1974. 24.50 o.p. (ISBN 0-87073-068-1); pap. 11.50 (ISBN 0-87073-069-X). Schenkman.
Chilcote, Ronald H. & Johnson, Dale L., eds. Theories of Development: Mode of Production or Dependency? (Class, State & Development Ser.: Vol. 2). (Illus.). 272p. 1983. 25.00 (ISBN 0-8039-1925-5); pap. 12.50 (ISBN 0-8039-1926-3). Sage.
Child. Organization. 2nd ed. 1983. text ed. 21.00 (ISBN 0-06-318221-1, Pub. by Har-Row Ltd England); pap. text ed. 10.50 (ISBN 0-06-318222-X, Pub. by Har-Row Ltd England). Har-Row.
Child, Francis J. English & Scottish Popular Ballads, 5 vols. 1965. Vols. 1-5. pap. 7.50 ea.; Vol. 1. pap. (ISBN 0-486-21409-5); Vol. 2. pap. o.p. (ISBN 0-486-21410-9); Vol. 3 o.p. pap. (ISBN 0-486-21411-7); Vol. 4. pap. (ISBN 0-486-21412-5); Vol. 5. pap. (ISBN 0-486-21413-3). Dover.
Child, Frank S. Colonial Parson of New England. LC 74-19532. 1974. Repr. of 1896 ed. 30.00x (ISBN 0-8103-3667-7). Gale.
Child, H. Thomas Hardy. LC 72-3631. (Studies in Thomas Hardy, No. 14). 1972. Repr. of 1916 ed. lib. bdg. 29.95x (ISBN 0-8383-1584-4). Haskell.
Child, John. Trees of the Sydney Region. pap. 7.50x o.p. (ISBN 0-392-06871-0, ABC). Sportshelf.
--Unequal Alliance: The Inter-American Military System, Nineteen Thirty-Eight to Nineteen Seventy-Nine. (A Westview Replica Edition Ser.). 254p. 1980. 27.00 (ISBN 0-89158-677-6). Westview.
Child, John & Partridge, Bruce. Lost Managers: Supervisors in Industry & Society. LC 81-17979. (Management & Industrial Relations Ser.: No. 1). (Illus.). 1982. 29.95 (ISBN 0-521-23356-9); pap. 9.95 (ISBN 0-521-29931-4). Cambridge U Pr.
Child, John, jt. ed. see Finan, John J.
Child, Julia. French Chef Cookbook. (Illus.). 1968. 15.50 (ISBN 0-394-40135-2). Knopf.
Child, L. Maria, ed. see Brent, Linda.
Child, Lydia M. Lydia Maria Child: Selected Letters, 1817-1880. Meltzer, Milton & Holland, Patricia G., eds. LC 82-8464. (New England Writer's Ser.). 610p. 1982. lib. bdg. 35.00x (ISBN 0-87023-332-7). U of Mass Pr.
--Over the River & Through the Wood. LC 74-79700. (Illus.). 32p. (ps-3). 1974. 7.95 (ISBN 0-698-20301-1, Coward). Putnam Pub Group.
Child, M. S. Molecular Collision Theory. 1974. 49.50 o.p. (ISBN 0-12-172650-9). Acad Pr.
Child Study Association. Brothers & Sisters Are Like That: Stories to Read Yourself. LC 78-158703. (Illus.). (gr. 1-4). 1971. 8.95 o.p. (ISBN 0-690-16041-0, TYC-J); PLB 10.89 o.p. (ISBN 0-690-16042-9). Har-Row.
Child Study Association of America. Pets & More Pets. LC 69-11825. (Illus.). (gr. 1-5). 1969. 8.95i o.p. (ISBN 0-690-61661-9, TYC-J). Har-Row.
--What to Tell Your Child About Sex. LC 74-6972. 150p. 1975. Repr. 17.50x (ISBN 0-87668-169-0). Aronson.
Child Study Association Of America - Children's Book Committee. Children's Books of the Year 1969. LC 67-14889. (Children's Books of the Year Ser). (Orig.). 1970. pap. 0.75 (ISBN 0-87183-171-6). Child Study.
Child Study Children's Association, ed. Friends Are Like That! Stories to Read Yourself. LC 78-22513. (Illus.). (gr. 3-6). 1979. 10.53i (ISBN 0-690-03979-4, TYC-J); PLB 10.89 (ISBN 0-690-03980-8). Har-Row.
Child, Susan. Charlie's Daughter. 1982. pap. 2.50 (ISBN 0-451-11409-4, AE1409, Sig). NAL.
Child Welfare League of America, Committee on Standards. CWLA, Committee on Standards: Child Welfare League of America Standards for Unmarried Parents. LC 52-4649. 1971. pap. 7.50 (ISBN 0-87868-093-4, UM-13). Child Welfare.
Child Welfare League of America Staff. The New Tax Law: A Guide for Child Welfare Organizations. 1981. 3.00 (ISBN 0-87868-211-2, AM-33). Child Welfare.
Childbirth Education Association of Jacksonville, Fla., Inc & Brinkley, Ginny. Your Child's First Journey: A Guide to Prepared Birth from Pregnancy to Parenthood. (Avery's Childbirth Education Ser.). (Illus.). 256p. (Orig.). 1982. pap. 9.95 (ISBN 0-89529-150-9). Avery Pub.
Childe, V. Gordon. Man Makes Himself. 1952. pap. 1.50 o.p. (ISBN 0-451-61508-5, MW1508, Ment). NAL.
Childe, Vere G. Bronze Age. LC 63-18050. 1930. 12.00x (ISBN 0-8196-0123-3). Biblo.
--Prehistoric Communities of the British Isles. 2nd ed. LC 76-114498. (Illus.). 1971. Repr. of 1947 ed. lib. bdg. 17.50x (ISBN 0-8371-4732-8, CHPC). Greenwood.
Childers, D. G., ed. Modern Spectrum Analysis. LC 78-55097. 1978. 35.95 (ISBN 0-87942-107-X). Inst Electrical.
Childers, Donald G. & Durling, Allen E. Digital Filtering & Signal Processing. LC 75-8776. (Illus.). 539p. 1975. text ed. 37.50 (ISBN 0-8299-0056-X). West Pub.
Childers, Milton, jt. auth. see Bailey, Robert.
Childers, Thomas. Information & Referral: Libraries & Information Science. Davis, Charles H., ed. (Libraries & Information Science Ser.). 384p. (Orig.). 1983. text ed. 37.50. Ablex Pub.
Children's Television Workshop. The Best of the Electric Company. (Electric Company Book Ser.). (Illus.). (gr. k-6). 1977. pap. text ed. 1.95 o.s.i. (ISBN 0-448-14487-5, G&D). Putnam Pub Group.
--The Electric Company Crazy Cut-Ups. (Electric Company Books Ser.). (gr. k-6). 1977. pap. text ed. 1.95 o.s.i. (ISBN 0-448-14486-7, G&D). Putnam Pub Group.
--The Electric Company Easy Reader's Activity Book. Incl. No. 1 (ISBN 0-448-14009-8); No. 2 (ISBN 0-448-14010-1). (Illus.). (gr. k-5). 1977. pap. 1.25 ea. o.s.i. (G&D). Putnam Pub Group.
Children's TV Workshop & Stein, Sara. Sesame Street Begins at Home. 1979. 13.95 o.p. (ISBN 0-671-22482-4). S&S.
Children's TV Workshop, ed. Sesame Street Book of Letters. (Illus.). (gr. k-2). 1971. pap. 0.75 o.p. (ISBN 0-451-04499-1, Q4499, Sig). NAL.
Childress, Alice. A Hero Ain't Nothin' but a Sandwich. 100p. (gr. 5-9). 1973. 7.95 (ISBN 0-698-20278-3, Coward). Putnam Pub Group.
--Let's Hear It for the Queen. LC 76-16075. (Illus.). (gr. 3-5). 1976. 6.95 o.p. (ISBN 0-698-20388-7, Coward). Putnam Pub Group.
--Rainbow Jordan. (Illus.). (gr. 7 up). 1981. 9.95 (ISBN 0-698-20531-6, Coward). Putnam Pub Group.
--A Short Walk. LC 79-14262. 1979. 9.95 o.p. (ISBN 0-698-10844-2, Coward). Putnam Pub Group.
--When the Rattlesnake Sounds: A Play About Harriet Tubmen. LC 75-10456. (Illus.). 32p. (gr. 7-11). 1975. 6.95 (ISBN 0-698-20342-9, Coward). Putnam Pub Group.
Childress, Harvey. Expanding Outlines of the New Testament Books. 5.95 (ISBN 0-89137-536-8). Quality Pubns.
Childress, Harvey A. The Lord's Own Church. 1980. pap. 1.50 (ISBN 0-88027-086-1). Firm Foun Pub.
Childress, James F. Who Should Decide? Paternalism in Health Care. 225p. 1982. text ed. 21.95x (ISBN 0-19-503127-X); pap. text ed. 11.95x o.p. (ISBN 0-19-503128-8). Oxford U Pr.
Childress, R. L. Fundamentals of Finite Mathematics. (Illus.). 1976. ref. ed. 25.95 (ISBN 0-13-339325-9). P-H.
Childress, Robert L. Calculus for Business & Economics. 2nd ed. LC 77-2855. (Illus.). 1978. text ed. 23.95 (ISBN 0-13-111534-0). P-H.
--Mathematics for Managerial Decisions. LC 73-17352. (Illus.). 656p. 1974. ref. ed. 23.95 (ISBN 0-13-562231-X). P-H.
Childress, Stephen. Mechanics of Swimming & Flying. LC 80-23364. (Cambridge Studies in Mathematical Biology: No. 2). (Illus.). 170p. 1981. 37.50 (ISBN 0-521-23613-4); pap. 14.95 (ISBN 0-521-28071-0). Cambridge U Pr.
Childs, Alan W. & Melton, Gary B., eds. Rural Psychology. 455p. 1982. 39.50x (ISBN 0-306-41045-1, Plenum Pr). Plenum Pub.
Childs, Barton see Steinberg, Arthur G., et al.
Childs, David. Britain Since Nineteen Forty-Five: A Political History. LC 79-8507. 1979. 25.00 (ISBN 0-312-09880-4). St Martin.
--The GDR: Moscow's German Ally. 192p. 1983. text ed. 30.00x (ISBN 0-04-335046-1); pap. text ed. 14.50 (ISBN 0-04-335047-X). Allen Unwin.
--Germany since Nineteen Eighteen. LC 80-5321. 1980. 25.00 (ISBN 0-312-32628-9). St Martin.
Childs, David & Johnson, Jeffrey. West Germany: Politics & Society. 1981. 26.00 (ISBN 0-312-86300-4). St Martin.
Childs, David, ed. The Changing Face of Western Communism. 1980. 27.50 o.p. (ISBN 0-312-12951-3). St Martin.
Childs, Edmund. William Caxton: A Portrait in a Background. LC 77-25770. 1979. 8.95 o.p. (ISBN 0-312-88068-5). St Martin.
Childs, Harwood L. Reference Guide to the Study of Public Opinion. LC 73-12777. Repr. of 1934 ed. 34.00x (ISBN 0-8103-3704-5). Gale.
Childs, J. Encyclopedia of Long Term Financing & Capital Management. 1976. 34.95 o.p. (ISBN 0-13-276113-0). P-H.
Childs, John. Armies & Warfare in Europe, 1648-1789. 208p. 1982. text ed. 22.50x (ISBN 0-8419-0820-6). Holmes & Meier.
--The Army, James II & the Glorious Revolution. 27.50 (ISBN 0-312-04949-8). St Martin.
Childs, Marquis. The Farmer Takes a Hand: The Electric Power Revolution in Rural America. LC 73-19736. (Fdr & the Era of the New Deal Ser.). (Illus.). 256p. 1974. Repr. of 1952 ed. lib. bdg. 35.00 (ISBN 0-306-70478-1). Da Capo.
Childs, Marquis & Engel, Paul. This Is Iowa. Andrews, Clarence A., ed. (Illus.). 320p. 1982. board 14.95 (ISBN 0-934582-05-X). Midwest Heritage.

Childs, Marquis W. This Is Democracy: Collective Bargaining in Scandinavia. 1938. 34.50x (ISBN 0-685-89790-7). Elliots Bks.

Childs, Michael. An Introduction to Mastery. (Orig.). 1982. pap. 10.00 (ISBN 0-910247-00-5). Source Unlimited.

Childs, W. H. Physical Constants. 9th ed. 1972. pap. 7.95x (ISBN 0-412-21050-9, Pub. by Chapman & Hall). Methuen Inc.

Chilimidos, R. S. Auto Theft Investigation. LC 79-155290. 1971. 14.00x (ISBN 0-910874-18-2). Legal Bk Co.

Chilingar, G. Carbonate Rocks, 2 pts. 1967. Pt. A: Occurrence & Classification. 36.90 (ISBN 0-444-40106-7); Pt. B: Physical & Chemical Aspects. 36.90 (ISBN 0-444-40107-5). Elsevier.

Chilingar, G. V., jt. ed. see Larsen, G.

Chilingarian, G. V. & Wolf, K. Compaction of Coarse-Grained Sediments, 2 pts. LC 73-85220. (Developments in Sedimentology Ser.: Vol. 18 A & B). 550p. 1975-77. Pt. 1. 93.75 (ISBN 0-444-41152-6); Pt. 2. 106.50 (ISBN 0-444-41361-8). Elsevier.

Chilingarian, G. V., jt. auth. see Rieke, H. H.

Chilingarian, G. V., jt. auth. see Yen, T. F.

Chilingarian, G. V. & Yen, T. F., eds. Bitumens, Asphalts & Tar Sands. 1978. 83.00 (ISBN 0-444-41619-6). Elsevier.

Chillingarian, G. V. Drilling & Drilling Fluids. (Development in Petroleum Science Ser.: Vol. 11). 1981. 119.25 (ISBN 0-444-41867-9). Elsevier.

Chillingsworth, D. R. Differential Topology with a View to Applications. (Research Notes in Mathematics Ser.: No. 9). 302p. (Orig.). 1976. pap. text ed. 26.50 (ISBN 0-273-00283-X). Pitman Pub MA.

Chilman, Catherine S. Adolescent Sexuality in a Changing American Society: Social & Psychological Perspectives for the Human Service Professions. (Personality Processes Ser.). 320p. 1983. price not set (ISBN 0-471-09162-6, Pub. by Wiley-Interscience). Wiley.

Chilson, Richard. Faith of Catholics: An Introduction. rev. ed. LC 72-81229. 320p. 1975. pap. 3.95 (ISBN 0-8091-1873-4, Deus). Paulist Pr.

Chilton, C. H., jt. auth. see Perry, Robert H.

Chilton, Carl S., Jr. The Successful Professional Client Accounting Practice. LC 82-15143. 217p. 1983. 39.95 (ISBN 0-13-868208-9, Busn). P-H.

Chilton, M. What Goes on in Shipbuilding? 1977. soft cover 15.00 o.p. (ISBN 0-85941-027-7); cased 10.00 o.p. (ISBN 0-85941-041-2). State Mutual Bk.

Chilton, P. A. The Poetry of Jean de la Ceppede: A Study in Text & Content. (Oxford Modern Languages & Literature Monographs). 1977. 34.95x (ISBN 0-19-815529-8). Oxford U Pr.

Chilton Staff. Design & Analysis of Dental-Oral Research. 2nd ed. 460p. 1982. 44.50 (ISBN 0-03-056157-4). Praeger.

Chilton Staff, ed. McCall's Big Book of Christmas Knit & Crochet. LC 82-70537. 304p. (Orig.). 1982. pap. 12.95 (ISBN 0-8019-7252-3). Chilton.

--McCall's Big Book of Knit Crochet. LC 82-70538. (Illus.). 304p. (Orig.). pap. 12.95 (ISBN 0-8019-7253-1). Chilton.

Chilton, Thomas. Strong Water: Nitric Acid, Its Sources, Methods of Manufacture, & Uses. 1968. 16.00 (ISBN 0-262-03023-3). MIT Pr.

Chilton's Automotive Editorial Department. Chilton's Repair & Tune-up Guide for Inboard-Outdrives: 1968-1972. LC 73-1268. (Illus.). 251p. 1973. 7.95 o.p. (ISBN 0-8019-5781-8). Chilton.

Chilton's Automotive Editorial Department Staff. Datsun Two Ten & Twelve Hundred, Nineteen Seventy-Three to Nineteen Eighty-Two. 1982. pap. 9.95 (ISBN 0-686-94085-7). Chilton.

Chilton's Automotive Editorial Dept. Chilton's Mechanics' Handbook: Engine Rebuilding, Engine Repair, Engine Theory, Vol. II. (Illus.). 1980. 16.95 (ISBN 0-8019-7006-7); pap. 14.95 (ISBN 0-686-82877-1). Chilton.

Chilton's Editorial Department, ed. Chilton's Import Car Repair Manual, 1975-81. LC 78-20243. (Illus.). 1536p. 1981. 19.95 (ISBN 0-8019-7029-6). Chilton.

--Chilton's Mechanics' Handbook: Automobile Sheet Metal Repair, Vol. III. (Illus.). 300p. 1981. pap. 14.95 (ISBN 0-8019-7034-2). Chilton.

--Chilton's Mechanics' Handbook: Engine Rebuilding, Engine Repair, Engine Theory, Vol. II. (Illus.). 300p. (Orig.). 1981. pap. text ed. 14.95 (ISBN 0-8019-7007-5). Chilton.

Chilton,s Editorial Department Staff. Family Book of Tests. 1982. 7.95 (ISBN 0-8019-7278-7). Chilton.

Chilver, P. & Gould, G. Learning & Language in the Classroom: Discusive Talking & Writing Across the Curriculum. 110p. 1982. 19.90 (ISBN 0-08-026777-7). Pergamon.

Chimienti, Teresa, ed. see Schmitt, Conrad J.

Chin, David & Staples, Michael. Hop Gar Kung Fu. LC 80-107762. (Illus.). 94p. 1976. pap. 4.50 (ISBN 0-86568-005-1). Unique Pubns.

Chin, Edwin, Jr. & Shrewsbury, Marvin M. Coloring Atlas of Human Anatomy. 208p. 1982. pap. text ed. 8.95 (ISBN 0-15-511800-5, HC). HarBraceJ.

Chin, Felix. Cable Television: A Selected Bibliography. 63p. 1978. pap. 3.00 o.p. (ISBN 0-686-37396-0). Vance Biblios.

Chin, Frank & Chan, Jeffery P., eds. The Big AIIIEEEEE. 1983. 15.95 (ISBN 0-88258-108-2). Howard U Pr.

Chin, Kenneth S. Understanding & Winning Casino Blackjack. LC 78-68949. 113p. 1979. 7.95 o.p. (ISBN 0-533-04204-6). Vantage.

Chin, Kin Wah. The Defence of Malaysia & Singapore: The Transformation of a Security System 1957-1971. LC 82-4330. (International Studies). 200p. 1983. 39.50 (ISBN 0-521-24325-4). Cambridge U Pr.

China Institute of International Affairs. China & the United Nations. LC 74-6706. (National Studies on International Organization Ser). 285p. 1975. Repr. of 1959 ed. lib. bdg. 17.75x (ISBN 0-8371-7542-9, CIUN). Greenwood.

China Ministry of Information & Tong, Hollington K., eds. China Handbook, Nineteen Thirty-Seven to Nineteen Forty-Five: A Comprehensive Survey of Major Developments in China. rev. enl. ed. (China in the 20th Century Ser). (Illus.). xvi, 862p. 1975. Repr. of 1947 ed. lib. bdg. 95.00 (ISBN 0-306-70701-2). Da Capo.

China National Stamp Corp. Staff. Postage Stamp Catalog of PRC (1949-1980) (Illus.). 132p. (Orig.). 1982. pap. 15.00 (ISBN 0-8351-1033-8). China Bks.

Chinaglia, Giorgio & Kane, Basil. Chinaglia. 1980. 11.95 o.p. (ISBN 0-671-25049-3). S&S.

Chinard, Francis P., jt. auth. see Bauman, John W.

Chinard, Gilbert, ed. & tr. George Washington As the French Knew Him. LC 69-13858. Repr. of 1940 ed. lib. bdg. 15.00x o.p. (ISBN 0-8371-1058-0, CHGW). Greenwood.

Chinen, Jon J. Great Mahele: Hawaii's Land Division of 1848. LC 57-14473. (Orig.). 1958. pap. 2.50x (ISBN 0-87022-125-6). UH Pr.

Chinery. A Field Guide to the Insects of Britain & Northern Europe. 29.95 (ISBN 0-686-42784-X, Collins Pub England). Greene.

Chinery, Michael. Enjoying Nature with Your Family: Learn, Look & Conserve. (Illus.). 1977. 12.95 o.p. (ISBN 0-517-53007-4). Crown.

Chinese Association of Automation, ed. Trends & Progress in Control Systems Theory & Its Application: Proceedings of the Symposium on Control Systems. 800p. 1982. write for info. (ISBN 0-677-31040-4). Gordon.

Chinese-English Translation Assistance Group. Chinese Dictionaries: An Extensive Bibliography of Dictionaries in Chinese & Other Languages. LC 82-923. 49.95 (ISBN 0-313-23505-8). Greenwood.

Chinese Experts & Staff of the Peoples. The Chinese Way to A Long & Healthy Life. Medical Publishing House, Beijin, China, ed. (Illus.). 224p. 1983. 14.95 (ISBN 0-88254-792-5). Hippocrene Bks.

Chinese Mechanical Engineering Society & Chinese Society of Theoretical & Applied Mechanics, eds. Finite Element Methods: Proceedings of the 1981 Symposium, Hefei, People's Republic of China. 400p. 1982. write for info. (ISBN 0-677-31020-X). Gordon.

Chinese Society of Theoretical & Applied Mechanics, jt. ed. see Chinese Mechanical Engineering Society.

Chinese, U. S. Symposium on Systems Analysis & Gray, Paul. Proceedings. (Systems Engineering & Analysis Ser.). 600p. 1982. 45.00 (ISBN 0-471-89585-7, Pub. by Wiley-Interscience). Wiley.

Ching, Julia, ed. & tr. see Wang, Yang-ming.

Ching-Chih Chen. Health Sciences Information Sources. 808p. 1981. 55.00x (ISBN 0-262-03074-8). MIT Pr.

Ching-hih Chen & Hernon, Peter. Information Seeking: Assessing & Anticipating User Needs. 222p. 1982. 22.95 (ISBN 0-918212-50-2). Neal-Schuman.

Ching-hih Chen & Schweizer, Susanna. Online Bibliographic Searching: Learning Manual. 1981. 21.95 (ISBN 0-918212-59-6). Neal-Schuman.

Ching Ping, jt. auth. see Bloodworth, Dennis.

Ching-Yao Hsieh, jt. auth. see Aschheim, Joseph.

Ching Yee, Janice. The Fast Gourmet from Hawaii. (Illus.). (gr. 10 up). 1977. 14.95 (ISBN 0-931420-06-7); text ed. 9.00 o.p. (ISBN 0-685-88633-6). Pi Pr.

--God's Busiest Angels. (Illus.). (gr. k-6). 1975. 1.75 (ISBN 0-931420-10-5); pap. 1.05 o.p. (ISBN 0-685-88634-4). Pi Pr.

--God's Meekest Angels. (Illus.). (gr. k-6). 1981. pap. 1.75. Pi Pr.

--God's Naughtiest Angels. (Illus.). (gr. k-6). 1974. 1.75 (ISBN 0-931420-08-3); pap. 1.05 o.p. (ISBN 0-685-88635-2). Pi Pr.

--God's Purest Angels. (Illus.). (gr. k-6). 1976. 1.75 (ISBN 0-931420-08-3); pap. 1.05 o.p. (ISBN 0-685-88636-0). Pi Pr.

--Success Is a Good Word. (gr. 9 up). 1979. 5.00 (ISBN 0-931420-22-9); pap. 3.00 o.p. (ISBN 0-685-99723-5). Pi Pr.

--This Gift I Present of Poetry from Hawaii. 3rd ed. (Poetry Gift Ser.). (Illus.). 54p. (gr. 8 up). 1980. pap. 5.00. Pi Pr.

Chinitz, Benjamin, ed. City & Suburb. LC 76-1850. 181p. 1976. Repr. of 1965 ed. lib. bdg. 15.50x (ISBN 0-8371-8679-X, CHCS). Greenwood.

Chinmoy, Sri. Commentaries on the Bhagavad Gita. LC 78-189999. (Illus.). 192p. pap. 2.50 o.s.i. (ISBN 0-89345-214-9, Steinerbks). Garber Comm.

--The Garden of Love-Light, Vols 1 & 2. Chinmoy, Sri, tr. from Bengali. (Illus., Orig.). 1973. pap. 2.00 ea.; pap. write for info. (ISBN 0-88497-031-0); pap. write for info. (ISBN 0-88497-032-9); Vol. 1 & 2. pap. write for info. (ISBN 0-88497-030-2). Aum Pubns.

--Mother India's Lighthouse: India's Spiritual Leaders. LC 74-189998. 288p. 1973. pap. 3.95 (ISBN 0-89345-219-X, Steinerbks). Garber Comm.

Chinn, Gary. The Garrett Wade Book of Woodworking Tools. LC 79-7082. (Illus.). 1980. 19.18i (ISBN 0-690-01840-1). T Y Crowell.

Chinn, Peggy L. & Jacobs, Maeona K. Theory & Nursing: A Systematic Approach. LC 82-7912. (Illus.). 222p. 1983. pap. text ed. 13.95 (ISBN 0-8016-0961-5). Mosby.

Chinn, Peggy L., ed. Advances in Nursing Theory Development. LC 82-13945. 299p. 1982. 27.50 (ISBN 0-89443-842-5). Aspen Systems.

Chinn, Peggy L., jt. ed. see Brown, Barbara J.

Chinn, Philip C., et al. Mental Retardation: A Life Cycle Approach. 2nd ed. LC 78-31835. 492p. 1979. text ed. 20.95 (ISBN 0-8016-0968-2). Mosby.

--Two-Way Talking with Parents of Special Children: A Process of Positive Communication. LC 77-26980. (Illus.). 196p. 1978. pap. text ed. 12.95 o.p. (ISBN 0-8016-0973-9). Mosby.

Chinn, W. G. & Steenrod, N. E. First Concepts of Topology. LC 66-20367. (New Mathematical Library: No. 18). 1975. pap. 8.75 (ISBN 0-88385-618-2). Math Assn.

Chinn, William G., jt. auth. see Blakeslee, David W.

Chinoy, Ely & Hewitt, John. Sociological Perspectives: Basic Concepts & Their Applications. 3rd ed. 1974. pap. text ed. 7.50x (ISBN 0-394-31869-2). Random.

Chin-Sheng, Chou. An Economic History of China. Kaplan, Edward H., tr. from Chinese. LC 74-620032. (Program in East Asian Studies Occasional Papers Ser: No. 7). Orig. Title: Chung-Kuo Ching-Chi Shih. (Illus.). 250p. 1974. pap. 6.60 (ISBN 0-914584-07-3). West Wash Univ.

Chinweizu, Onwuchekwa J. & Madubuike, Ihechukwu. Toward the Decolonization of African Literature, Vol. I. 320p. 1983. 12.95 (ISBN 0-88258-122-8); Vol. I. pap. 6.95 (ISBN 0-88258-123-6). Howard U Pr.

Chiodini, P. G. & Liuzzi, A. The Regulation of Growth Hormone Secretion, Vol. 1. Horrobin, D. F., ed. (Annual Research Reviews Ser.). 1979. 24.00 (ISBN 0-88831-050-1). Eden Pr.

Chipeta, Chinyamata. Economics of Indigenous Labor. 1982. 9.95 (ISBN 0-533-04995-4). Vantage.

Chiplin, Brian & Sloane, Peter. Tackling Discrimination in the Workplace: An Analysis of Sex Discrimination in Britain. LC 82-4384. (Management & Industrial Relations Ser.: No. 2). (Illus.). 190p. Date not set. price not set (ISBN 0-521-24565-6); pap. price not set (ISBN 0-521-28788-X). Cambridge U Pr.

Chiplin, Brian, et al. Can Workers Manage? (Hobart Papers Ser.: No. 77). 1978. pap. 5.75 o.p. (ISBN 0-255-36103-3). Transatlantic.

Chipman, Clark, ed. Emergency Department Orthopaedics. LC 82-8768. 200p. 1982. 26.50 (ISBN 0-89443-803-4). Aspen Systems.

Chipman, Donald, jt. ed. see Peden, Creighton.

Chipman, J. S. & Kindleberger, C. P., eds. Flexible Exchange Rates & the Balance of Payments: Essays in Memory of Egon Sohmen. (Studies in International Economics: Vol. 7). 1981. 57.50 (ISBN 0-444-86045-2). Elsevier.

Chipman, Nathaniel. Principles of Government: A Treatise on Free Institutions. LC 76-99478. (American Constitutional & Legal History Ser.). 1970. Repr. of 1833 ed. 39.50 (ISBN 0-306-71851-0). Da Capo.

Chipman, R. A. Transmission Lines. (Schaum Outline Ser.). 1968. pap. 8.95 (ISBN 0-07-010747-5, SP). McGraw.

Chipp, Herschel B. Georges Braque: The Late Paintings 1940-1963. 1982. pap. text ed. 18.50 (ISBN 0-943044-00-6). Phillips Collect.

Chipp, Sylvia A. & Green, Justin J., eds. Asian Women in Transition. LC 79-20517. (Illus.). 256p. 1980. text ed. 18.95x (ISBN 0-271-00251-4); pap. text ed. 9.95x (ISBN 0-271-00257-3). Pa St U Pr.

Chippendale, G. M. Eucalypts of the Western Australian Goldfields. 1982. 30.00x (ISBN 0-686-97915-X, Pub. by CSIRO Australia). State Mutual Bk.

Chipperfield, Jimmy. My Wild Life. LC 75-23487. (Illus.). 224p. 1976. 8.95 o.p. (ISBN 0-399-11616-8). Putnam Pub Group.

Chirban, John T. Human Growth & Faith: Intrinsic & Extrinsic Motivation in Human Development. LC 81-40175. (Illus.). 221p. (Orig.). 1981. lib. bdg. 21.75 (ISBN 0-8191-1784-6); pap. text ed. 10.75 (ISBN 0-8191-1785-4). U Pr of Amer.

Chirelstein, Marvin A., jt. auth. see Brudney, Victor.

Chirgwin, B. & Plumpton, C. A. Course of Mathematics for Engineers & Scientists. 2nd ed. 1983. Vol. 1, 1970. text ed. 37.00 o.p. (ISBN 0-08-006388-8); pap. text ed. 18.00 (ISBN 0-08-021678-1); Vol. 2, 1972. pap. text ed. 16.50 (ISBN 0-08-015970-2); Vol. 3, 1978. pap. text ed. 15.00 (ISBN 0-08-023042-3); Vol. 4. text ed. 11.21 (ISBN 0-08-021634-X). Pergamon.

Chirgwin, F. J. & Oldfield, P. The Library Assistant's Manual. 118p. 1978. 12.00 o.p. (ISBN 0-208-01666-X, Linnet). Shoe String.

Chirgwin, John F. & Oldfield, Phyllis. The Library Assistant's Manual. 2nd, rev. ed. 144p. 1983. 14.00 (ISBN 0-85157-350-9, Pub. by Bingley England). Shoe String.

Chirichigno, F. Norma. Clave Para Identificar los Peces Del Peru. (Institut del Mar del Peru Ser.: Informe 44). (Illus.). 388p. (Span.). 1978. pap. text ed. 56.00x (ISBN 3-87429-131-6). Lubrecht & Cramer.

Chirife, Jorge, jt. ed. see Iglesias, Hector A.

Chirigos, Michael A., ed. Control of Neoplasia by Modulation of the Immune System. LC 76-5665. (Progress in Cancer Research & Therapy Ser.: Vol. 2). 619p. 1977. 48.00 (ISBN 0-89004-125-3). Raven.

--Immune Modulation & Control of Neoplasia by Adjuvant Therapy. LC 76-5665. (Progress in Cancer Research & Therapy: Vol. 7). 519p. 1978. 53.50 (ISBN 0-89004-220-9). Raven.

Chirigos, Michael A., jt. ed. see Goldstein, Allan L.

Chirigos, Michael A., et al, eds. Mediation of Cellular Immunity in Cancer by Immune Modifiers. (Progress in Cancer Research & Therapy Ser.: Vol. 19). 288p. 1981. text ed. 34.50 (ISBN 0-89004-628-X). Raven.

Chirikjian, J. C. & Papas, T. S., eds. Structural Analysis of Nucleic Acids. (Gene Amplification & Analysis Ser.: Vol. 2). 1981. 92.00 (ISBN 0-444-00636-2). Elsevier.

Chirlian, Paul M. Basic Network Theory. LC 68-25648. (Electrical & Electronic Eng. Ser). (Illus.). 1968. 38.50 o.p. (ISBN 0-07-010788-2, C); ans. bk. 7.95 o.p. (ISBN 0-07-010789-0). McGraw.

--Introduction to Fourth. 350p. (Orig.). 1982. pap. write for info. (ISBN 0-916460-36-3). Matrix Pub.

Chironis, Nicholas P. Mechanisms, Linkages, & Mechanical Controls. 1965. 47.00 (ISBN 0-07-010775-0, P&RB). McGraw.

Chironis, Nicholas P., ed. Management Guide for Engineers & Technical Administrators. LC 68-8661. 1969. 29.50 o.p. (ISBN 0-07-010794-7, P&RB). McGraw.

Chirot, D., tr. see Stahl, Henri.

Chirot, H. C., tr. see Stahl, Henri.

Chirovsky, Nicholas L. A History of the Russian Empire, Vol. 1. LC 72-78164. (Illus.). 440p. 1973. 15.00 (ISBN 0-8022-2091-6). Philos Lib.

--An Introduction to Ukranian History, Vol. II: The Lithuanian-Rus' Commonwealth, the Polish Domination & the Cossack-Hetman State. (Illus.). 359p. 1983. 25.00 (ISBN 0-8022-2407-5). Philos Lib.

Chisam, Scott C. & Wennerstrom, Steve. Inside Track for Women. (Illus.). 1980. pap. 6.95 (ISBN 0-8092-7102-8). Contemp Bks.

Chisholm. Castle Times. 1983. 5.95 (ISBN 0-86020-622-X, 310031); pap. 2.95 (ISBN 0-86020-621-1, 310032). EDC.

--First Guide to History. 1983. 10.95 (ISBN 0-86020-625-4, 21151). EDC.

--Our Earth: Let's Find Out About. (gr. 2-5). 1982. 5.95 (ISBN 0-86020-583-5, Usborne-Hayes); lib. bdg. 8.95 (ISBN 0-88110-016-1); pap. 2.95 (ISBN 0-86020-582-7). EDC.

--Prehistoric Times. 1983. 5.95 (ISBN 0-86020-624-6, 310011); 2.95 (ISBN 0-86020-623-8, 310012). EDC.

--Roman Times. 1982. 5.95 (ISBN 0-86020-620-3, 310021); pap. 2.95 (ISBN 0-86020-619-X, 310022). EDC.

Chisholm, jt. auth. see Hawsby.

Chisholm, Anthony H. & Tyers, Rodney, eds. Food Security in Asia & the Pacific Rim: Perspectives & Policy Issues. LC 81-48396. (Illus.). 384p. 1982. 29.95x (ISBN 0-669-05356-2). Lexington Bks.

Chisholm, D., ed. Developments in Heat Exchanger Technology, Vol. 1. 1980. 65.75 (ISBN 0-85334-913-4, Pub. by Applied Sci England). Elsevier.

Chisholm, Derrick M., et al. Introduction to Oral Medicine. (Illus.). 1979. text ed. 10.00 (ISBN 0-7216-2593-2). Saunders.

Chisholm, E. Operas of Leos Janacek. 1971. 25.00 (ISBN 0-08-012854-8); pap. 10.75 (ISBN 0-08-012853-X). Pergamon.

Chisholm, Emily, tr. see Thurian, Max.

Chisholm, J. S. Vectors in Three-Dimensional Space. LC 77-82492. (Illus.). 1978. 63.50 (ISBN 0-521-21832-2); pap. 17.95 (ISBN 0-521-29289-1). Cambridge U Pr.

Chisholm, James. South Pass, 1868: James Chisholm's Journal of the Wyoming Gold Rush. Homsher, Lola M., ed. LC 60-12692. (Pioneer Heritage Ser: Vol. 3). (Illus.). vi, 350p. 1960. pap. 6.50 (ISBN 0-8032-5824-0, BB 606, Bison). U of Nebr Pr.

Chisholm, L. J. Units of Weight & Measure: International (Metric) & U. S. Customary. LC 74-20726. (Illus.). 256p. 1975. Repr. of 1967 ed. 34.00x (ISBN 0-8103-4163-8). Gale.

Chisholm, Roderick. Theory of Knowledge. 2nd ed. (Foundations of Philosophy Ser.). 1977. text ed. 15.95 (ISBN 0-13-914168-5); pap. text ed. 9.95 (ISBN 0-13-914150-2). P-H.

Chisholm, Roderick, tr. see Brentano, Franz.

Chisholm, Roderick M. Person & Object: A Metaphysical Study. LC 75-29952. (The Paul Carus Lecture Ser.). 230p. 1976. 16.00x (ISBN 0-87548-341-0). Open Court.

--The Problem of the Criterion (Nineteen Seventy-Three Aquinas Lecture) gold stamped titles 7.95 (ISBN 0-87462-138-0). Marquette.

Chisholm, Roderick M., ed. Realism & the Background of Phenomenology. vii, 308p. 1981. lib. bdg. 24.00 (ISBN 0-917930-34-7); pap. text ed. 8.50x (ISBN 0-917930-14-2). Ridgeview.

Chisholm, Roger & McCarty, Marilu. Principles of Economics. 1981. text ed. 24.50x (ISBN 0-673-15492-0). Scott F.

--Principles of Macroeconomics. 2nd ed. 1981. pap. text ed. 16.50x (ISBN 0-673-15493-9). Scott F.

--Principles of Microeconomics. 2nd ed. 1981. pap. text ed. 16.50x (ISBN 0-673-15402-5). Scott F.

Chisholm, William, et al, eds. Colloquium on Interrogativity, Cleveland, Ohio, October 5th 1981-May 3rd 1982: Proceedings. (Typological Studies in Language: 4). 250p. 1983. 30.00 (ISBN 9-0272-2868-X); pap. 20.00 (ISBN 9-0272-2864-7). Benjamins North Am.

Chisholm, William L., et al, eds. Proceedings of a Colloquium on Interrogativity. 250p. 1983. 30.00 (ISBN 90-272-2868-X); pap. 20.00 (ISBN 90-272-2864-7). Benjamins North Am.

Chisman, Forrest P. Attitude Psychology & the Study of Public Opinion. LC 76-10345. (Illus.). 1977. 17.95x (ISBN 0-271-01227-7). Pa St U Pr.

Chisnell, R. F. Vibrating Systems. (Library of Mathematics). 1966. Repr. of 1960 ed. pap. 5.00 o.p. (ISBN 0-7100-4350-3). Routledge & Kegan.

Chisolm, D. M., jt. auth. see Mason, D. K.

Chisolm, Evelyn. Pride of Baltimore & Renaissance of the Baltimore Clipper. (Illus.). 48p. 1977. pap. 2.95 (ISBN 0-686-36636-0). Md Hist.

Chisolm, Kitty & Ferguson, John. Rome: The Augustan Age: A Source Book. (Illus.). 734p. 1981. text ed. 54.00x (ISBN 0-19-872108-0); pap. text ed. 29.95x (ISBN 0-19-872109-9). Oxford U Pr.

Chissell, Joan. Schumann. Rev. ed. (The Master Musicians Ser.). (Illus.). 268p. 1977. text ed. 12.95 (ISBN 0-460-03170-8, Pub. by J. M. Dent England). Biblio Dist.

Chissick, S. S. & Derricott, R. Occupational Health & Safety Management. LC 79-41218. 720p. 1981. 94.95 (ISBN 0-471-27646-4, Pub. by Wiley-Interscience). Wiley.

Chissick, S. S., jt. auth. see Michaels, L.

Chissick, S. S., jt. auth. see Price, W. C.

Chissick, Seymour, jt. auth. see Derricott, Robert.

Chiswick, Barry, ed. Gateway: U. S. Immigration Issues & Policies. 1982. 22.95 (ISBN 0-8447-2221-9); pap. 12.95 (ISBN 0-8447-2220-0). Am Enterprise.

Chiswick, Barry, jt. auth. see San Juan, P.

Chiswick, Barry R. & Chiswick, Stephen J. Statistics & Econometrics. (Illus.). 1975. pap. 17.50 o.p. (ISBN 0-8391-0694-7). Univ Park.

Chiswick, Stephen J., jt. auth. see Chiswick, Barry R.

Chiteji, Frank M. The Development & Socio-Economic Impact of Transportation in Tanzania Eighteen Eighty-Four - Present. LC 80-5092. 151p. 1980. pap. text ed. 8.75 (ISBN 0-8191-1041-8). U Pr of Amer.

Chitnis, Suma. A Long Way to Go: Report on a Survey of Scheduled Caste High School & College Students in Fifteen States in India. 350p. 1981. 39.95x (ISBN 0-940500-67-1, Pub by Allied Pubs India). Asia Bk Corp.

Chittenden, Hiram Martin. H. M. Chittenden: A Western Epic. Le Roy, Bruce, ed. LC 61-64226. (Illus.). 136p. (Ed. limited to 1000 copies). 1961. 10.00 (ISBN 0-917048-17-2); deluxe ed. 25.00 (ISBN 0-686-96919-7). Wash St Hist Soc.

Chittenden, L. E. Report of the Debates & Proceedings of the Peace Convention Held in Washington, D.C., Feb. 1861. LC 70-158578. 626p. 1971. Repr. of 1864 ed. lib. bdg. 79.50 (ISBN 0-306-70190-1). Da Capo.

Chittenden, Margaret. The Face in the Mirror. 288p. (Orig.). 1980. pap. 2.25 o.p. (ISBN 0-523-40362-3). Pinnacle Bks.

--Merrymaking in Great Britain. LC 73-12822. (Around the World Holidays Ser). (Illus.). 96p. (gr. 4-7). 1974. PLB 7.12 (ISBN 0-8116-4952-0). Garrard.

--The Mystery of the Missing Pony. LC 79-19084. (Mystery Ser.). (Illus.). (gr. 3). 1980. PLB 6.89 (ISBN 0-8116-6411-2). Garrard.

--The Other Child. (Orig.). 1979. pap. 1.75 o.p. (ISBN 0-523-40361-5). Pinnacle Bks.

Chittick, Donald E. Philosophies in Conflict: The Creation-Evolution Controversy. 1983. price not set (ISBN 0-88070-019-X). Multnomah.

Chittick, H. Neville & Rotberg, Robert I., eds. East Africa & the Orient: Cultural Syntheses in Pre-Colonial Times. LC 73-89568. 350p. 1975. text ed. 45.00x (ISBN 0-8419-0142-2, Africana). Holmes & Meier.

Chittick, William C., tr. see Muhammad.

Chittister, Joan. Climb Along the Cutting Edge: An Analysis of Change in Religious Life. pap. 7.95 o.p. (ISBN 0-8091-2038-0). Paulist Pr.

--Women, Ministry & the Church. LC 82-62418. 1983. pap. 7.95 (ISBN 0-8091-2528-5). Paulist Pr.

Chittum, Ida. The Ghost Boy of el Toro. LC 78-1079. 1978. 8.00 (ISBN 0-8309-0201-5). Ind Pr MO.

--A Nutty Business. (Illus.). 32p. (gr. 1-4). 1973. PLB 4.29 o.p. (ISBN 0-399-60842-7). Putnam Pub Group.

--The Secrets of Madam Renee. (Illus.). 200p. (gr. 4-6). 1975. 6.50 o.p. (ISBN 0-8309-0127-2). Ind Pr MO.

Chittum, Joseph. Excitement in Problem Solving. LC 81-80161. 1983. 10.95 (ISBN 0-86666-025-9). GWP.

Chitwood, Deb. The Magic Ring. LC 82-62432. (Illus.). 32p. (ps-3). 1983. 9.95 (ISBN 0-942044-01-0). Polestar.

Chiu, Arthur, jt. ed. see Ishizaki, Hatsuo.

Chiu, Hong-Yee & Muriel, Amador, eds. Stellar Evolution. 827p. 1972. 42.50x (ISBN 0-262-12058-5). MIT Pr.

Chiu, Hungdah. China & the Taiwan Issue. LC 79-14270. (Praeger Special Studies Ser.). 1979. 34.95 (ISBN 0-03-048911-3). Praeger.

Chiu, Hungdah & Downen, Robert. Multi-System Nations & International Law, the International Status of Germany, Korea & China. LC 81-85785. (Occasional Papers Reprints Series in Contemporary Asian Studies, No. 8-1981). 203p. (Orig.). 1982. pap. text ed. 5.00 (ISBN 0-686-96991-X). Occasion Papers.

Chiu, Hungdah, ed. Chinese Yearbook of International Law & Affairs, 1981, Vol. I. (Chinese Yearbook of International Law & Affairs Ser.). 392p. 1982. pap. text ed. 7.00 (ISBN 0-942182-93-6). Occasion Papers.

--Socialist Legalism: Reform & Continuity in Post-Mao People's Republic of China. (Occasional Papers-Reprints Series in Contemporary Asian Studies: No. 1). 35p. (Orig.). 1982. pap. text ed. 2.00 (ISBN 0-686-91988-2). Occasion Papers.

Chiu, Kwong Ki see Kwong Ki Chaou.

Chiu, Lee C., jt. auth. see Yiu-Chiu, Victoria S.

Chiu, Ray C. Myocardial Protection in Regional & Global Ischemia, Vol. 1. (Annual Research Reviews). 177p. 1981. 26.00 (ISBN 0-88831-097-8). Eden Pr.

Chiu, Tony. Onyx. 352p. 1981. pap. 2.75 o.p. (ISBN 0-425-05004-1). Berkley Pub.

Chiu, Y. & Mullish, H. Crunchers: Twenty-One Games for the Timex Sinclair 1000 (2K) (McGraw-Hill VTX Ser.). 128p. 1982. 8.95 (ISBN 0-07-010831-5, GB). McGraw.

Chiu Hone-Yee, et al. Stellar Astronomy, 2 Vols. 1969. Vol. 1,388. 103.00 (ISBN 0-677-13790-7); Vol. 2,368. 81.00x (ISBN 0-677-13800-8); Set. 159.00x (ISBN 0-677-12980-7). Gordon.

Chiu Hone-Yeel & Muriel, Amador. Galactic Astronomy, Vols. 1 & 2. 1970. Vol. 1,344. 81.00x (ISBN 0-677-13750-8); Vol. 2,310. 70.00x (ISBN 0-677-13760-5); Set. 136.00 (ISBN 0-677-13770-2). Gordon.

Chivers. Chemistry Three Checkbook. 1982. 22.50 (ISBN 0-408-00662-5); pap. text ed. 9.95 (ISBN 0-408-00658-7). Butterworth.

--Chemistry Two Checkbook. 1981. text ed. 19.95 (ISBN 0-408-00637-4); pap. 9.95 (ISBN 0-408-00622-6). Butterworth.

Chivers, Thomas H. Nacoochee. LC 77-24233. 1977. Repr. of 1837 ed. 25.00x (ISBN 0-8201-1295-X). Schol Facsimiles.

--Path of Sorrow (1832), Eonchs of Ruby (1851), Memoralia (1849), Virginalia (1853), Sons of Usna (1858, 5 vols. in 1. LC 79-22103. 1979. 63.00x (ISBN 0-8201-1340-9). Schol Facsimiles.

--Unpublished Plays of Thomas Holley Chivers. LC 79-29747. 57.00x (ISBN 0-8201-1350-6). Schol Facsimiles.

Chivian, Eric, et al, eds. see International Physicians for the Prevention of Nuclear War.

Chi Wen-Shun, ed. Readings in Chinese Communist Ideology. LC 67-11201. 1968. 34.50x (ISBN 0-520-00232-6). U of Cal Pr.

Chi-Yun, Chen. Hsun Yweh: The Life & Reflections of an Early Confucian. LC 74-79135. (Studies in Chinese History, Literature & Institutions). 300p. 1975. 49.50 (ISBN 0-521-20394-5). Cambridge U Pr.

Chlad, Dorothy. Matches & Fireworks are not Toys. LC 81-18125. (Safety Town Bks.). (Illus.). (gr. k-3). 1982. PLB 9.25g (ISBN 0-516-01982-1); pap. 2.95 (ISBN 0-516-41982-X). Childrens.

--Strangers. LC 81-18109. (Safety Town Bks.). (Illus.). (gr. k-3). 1982. PLB 9.25g (ISBN 0-516-01984-8); pap. 2.95 (ISBN 0-516-41984-6). Childrens.

--When I Cross the Street-By Myself. LC 81-18108. (Safety Town Bks.). (Illus.). (gr. k-3). 1982. PLB 9.25g (ISBN 0-516-01985-6); pap. 2.95 (ISBN 0-516-41985-4). Childrens.

Chlamtac, Imrich, jt. auth. see Franta, W. R.

Chlapowski, F. Biochemistry: PreTest Self-Assessment & Review. 3rd ed. (PreTest Basic Science Review Bk.). 184p. 1982. 11.95 (ISBN 0-07-051932-3). McGraw.

Chleboun, William, jt. auth. see DeNevi, Donald.

Chmielarz, Sharon. Different Arrangements. LC 82-61650. (Minnesota Voices Project Ser.: No. 10). (Illus.). 103p. 1982. pap. 3.00 (ISBN 0-89823-042-X). New Rivers Pr.

Chmielewski, Edward. The Polish Question in the Russian State Duma. LC 77-100411. 1970. 13.50x (ISBN 0-87049-110-5). U of Tenn Pr.

Chmura, G. L. & Ross, N. W. The Environmental Impacts of Marinas & Their Boats: A Literature Review with Management Considerations. (Marine Memo Ser.: No. 45). 32p. 1978. 1.00 (ISBN 0-938412-29-9, P675). URI Mas.

Cho, Cheng & Dudding, Burton. Pediatric Infectious Diseases. (Medical Outline Ser.). 1978. pap. 28.50 (ISBN 0-87488-659-7). Med Exam.

Cho, Chin-Kuei. An Introduction to Software Quality Control. LC 80-15244. (Business Data Processing Ser.). 445p. 1980. 37.95 (ISBN 0-471-04704-X, Pub. by Wiley-Interscience). Wiley.

Cho, Chun H. Measurement & Control of Liquid Level: An Independent Learning Module of the Instrument Society of America. LC 82-48156. 288p. 1982. text ed. 39.95x (ISBN 0-87664-625-9). Instru Soc.

Cho, Emily & Grover, Linda. Looking Terrific: Express Yourself Through the Language of Clothing. LC 78-2910. (Illus.). 1978. 10.95 o.p. (ISBN 0-399-12039-4). Putnam Pub Group.

Cho, Emily & Lueders, Hermine. Looking, Working, Living Terrific 24 Hours a Day. (Illus.). 160p. 1982. 13.95 (ISBN 0-399-12745-3). Putnam Pub Group.

Cho, Lee-Jay, ed. Introduction to Cencuses of Asia & the Pacific, 1970-1974. LC 76-7232. 1976. pap. text ed. 6.00x (ISBN 0-8248-0468-6, Eastwest Ctr). UH Pr.

Cho, Lee-Jay & Kobayashi, Kazumasa, eds. Fertility Transition of East Asian Populations. (Monographs of the Center for Southeast Asian Studies, Kyoto University). 1979. text ed. 20.00x (ISBN 0-8248-0648-4); pap. text ed. 13.00x (ISBN 0-8248-0649-2). UH Pr.

Cho, Lee-Jay, et al. Population Growth of Indonesia: An Analysis of Fertility & Mortality Based on the 1971 Population Census. 1980. text ed. 14.00x (ISBN 0-8248-0691-3, Pub. by Ctr Southeast Asian Studies Kyoto Univ Japan); pap. text ed. 8.00x (ISBN 0-8248-0696-4). UH Pr.

Cho, Paul Y. Guupos Familiares y el Crecimiento de la I Glesia. Carrodeguas, Andy, ed. Lacy, Susana B., tr. 204p. (Span.). 1982. pap. 2.25 (ISBN 0-8297-1347-6). Life Pubs Intl.

Choate, Joyce S., jt. auth. see Rakes, Thomas A.

Choate, Judith. Awful Alexander. LC 74-28281. 32p. (ps-k). 1976. 6.95 o.p. (ISBN 0-385-01819-3). Doubleday.

Choate, Judith & Green, Jane. Scrapcraft: 50 Easy-to-Make Handicrafts Projects. LC 72-89814. 64p. (gr. 4-7). 1973. 7.95 o.p. (ISBN 0-385-09419-1). Doubleday.

Choate, Pat & Walter, Susan. America in Ruins: The Decaying Infrastructure. (Duke Press Policy Studies). 100p. 1983. pap. 9.75 (ISBN 0-8223-0554-2). Duke.

Choate, Pat, jt. auth. see Schwartz, Gail G.

Choate, R., ed. A Guide to Sources of Information on the Arts in Australia. (Guides to Australian Information Sources Ser.). 120p. 1983. pap. 10.50 (ISBN 0-08-029835-4). Pergamon.

Choate, Robert A., ed. Documentary Report of the Tanglewood Symposium. LC 68-57058. 160p. (Orig.). 1968. pap. 10.00x (ISBN 0-940796-02-3, 1011). Music Ed.

Choate, Sharr. Creative Casting. (Arts & Crafts Ser). (Illus.). 1966. 14.95 (ISBN 0-517-02445-4). Crown.

Choate, Sharr & De May, Bonnie C. Creative Gold & Silversmithing: Jewelry, Decorative Metalcraft. (Arts & Crafts Ser). (Illus.). 1970. 11.95 o.p. (ISBN 0-517-54309-5); pap. 8.95 (ISBN 0-517-52413-9). Crown.

Choate, Stuart A., jt. auth. see Shulte, Albert P.

Choca, James. Manual for Clinical Psychology Practicums. LC 80-18731. 172p. 1980. pap. 10.95 (ISBN 0-87630-240-1). Brunner-Mazel.

Chock, Judy & Miner, Margaret. Birth. LC 77-2603. (Illus.). 1978. 15.34i (ISBN 0-690-01434-1). T Y Crowell.

Choco, John & Choco, Ronalyn. Britain & Ireland: On Your Own. LC 81-71884. (Illus.). 225p. 7.95 (ISBN 0-939596-01-6). Country Rd.

Choco, Ronalyn, jt. auth. see Choco, John.

Chodat, R. & Fischer, W. La Vegetation du Paraguay: Resultats Scientifiques d'une Mission Botanique au Paraguay. Repr. of 1977 ed. 48.00 (ISBN 3-7682-1106-1). Lubrecht & Cramer.

Chodoff, Paul, jt. ed. see Bloch, Sidney.

Chodoff, Richard. Doctor for the Prosecution: A Fighting Surgeon Takes the Stand. LC 82-20410. 320p. 1983. 15.95 (ISBN 0-399-12767-4). Putnam.

Chodorov, Edward see Freedley, George.

Chodorow, Stanley. Christian Political Theory & Church Politics in the Mid-Twelfth Century: The Ecclesiology of Gratian's Decretum. LC 71-138512. (UCLA Center for Medieval & Renaissance Studies). 1972. 38.50x (ISBN 0-520-01850-8). U of Cal Pr.

--The Other Side of Western Civilization - Readings in Everyday Life: The Ancient World to the Reformation, Vol. 1. 2nd ed. 363p. 1979. pap. text ed. 11.95 (ISBN 0-15-567648-2, HC). HarBraceJ.

Chodorow, Stanley, jt. auth. see Hoyt, Robert S.

Choe, Boum Jone & Lambertini, Adrain. Global Energy Prospects. (Working Paper: No. 489). 50p. 1981. 5.00 (ISBN 0-686-36153-9, WP-0489). World Bank.

Choffray, Jean-Marie & Lilien, Gary L. Market Planning for New Industrial Products. LC 80-11347. (Ronald Ser. on Marketing Management). 264p. 1980. 29.95 (ISBN 0-471-04918-2, Ronald). Ronald Pr.

Choh Hao Li, ed. Hormonal Proteins & Peptides, Vol. 1. LC 82-22770. Date not set. price not set (ISBN 0-12-447211-7). Acad Pr.

--Hormonal Proteins & Peptides: Prolactin, Vol. 8. LC 80-11061. 1980. 34.50 (ISBN 0-12-447208-7). Acad Pr.

Choi, Frederick D., jt. auth. see Mueller, Gerhard G.

Choi, H., jt. auth. see Rohsenow, Warren M.

Choi, Sung C. Introductory Applied Statistics in Science. (Illus.). 1978. ref. ed. 24.95 (ISBN 0-13-501619-3). P-H.

Choi, Thomas & Greenberg, Jay N., eds. Social Science Approaches to Health Services Research. 350p. 1983. text ed. write for info (ISBN 0-914904-83-3). Health Admin Pr.

Choi, Yearn H. Introduction to Public Administration. LC 79-20383. (Orig.). 1979. pap. 5.95 o.p. (ISBN 0-915442-90-6). Donning Co.

Choi Hong Hi. Tae Kwon-Do. (Illus.). 1980. deluxe ed. 49.00x large vol. (ISBN 0-686-66273-3). Wehman.

Choksi, Armeane M. State Intervention in the Industrialization of Developing Countries: Selected Issues. (Working Paper: No. 341). xx, 193p. 1979. 5.00 (ISBN 0-686-36188-1, WP-0341). World Bank.

Choksy, Lois. Kodaly Context. 1981. 18.95 (ISBN 0-13-516674-8); pap. 13.95 (ISBN 0-13-516666-7). P-H.

--The Kodaly Method: Comprehensive Music Education from Infant to Adult. LC 73-18316. (Illus.). 224p. 1974. 18.95 (ISBN 0-13-516765-5); pap. 14.95 (ISBN 0-13-516757-4). P-H.

Cholakian, Patricia F. & Cholakian, Rouben C., eds. The Early French Novella: An Anthology of Fifteenth & Sixteenth Century Tales. LC 79-171179. 1972. 27.00x o.p. (ISBN 0-87395-090-9); pap. 7.95 o.p. (ISBN 0-87395-220-0). State U NY Pr.

Cholakian, Rouben C., jt. ed. see Cholakian, Patricia F.

Choldin, Marianna T., ed. Access to Resources in the Eighties: Proceedings of the First International Conference of Slavic Librarians & Information Specialists. (Russica Bibliography Ser.). (Orig.). 1982. pap. 7.50 (ISBN 0-686-97604-5). Russica Pubs.

Cholerton, John. The World of Mime. pap. 4.00x (ISBN 0-392-09737-0, SpS). Sportshelf.

Cholerton, Judy. Auditions & First Rehearsal. pap. 3.00x (ISBN 0-392-09740-0, SpS). Sportshelf.

--Hints on Tap Dancing. pap. 3.00x (ISBN 0-392-09690-0, SpS). Sportshelf.

--Modern Musical Enchainments. pap. 3.00x (ISBN 0-392-09723-0, SpS). Sportshelf.

--Posture & Care of Arms in Dancing. pap. 3.00x (ISBN 0-392-09706-0, SpS). Sportshelf.

Cholnoky, B. J. Die Oekologie der Diatomeen in Binnengewaessern. (Illus.). 1968. 60.00 (ISBN 3-7682-5421-6). Lubrecht & Cramer.

Cholnoky, B. J., ed. Diatomaceae I. 1966. 48.00 (ISBN 3-7682-5421-6). Lubrecht & Cramer.

Cholnoky, B. J., jt. ed. see Gerloff, J.

Cholst, Sheldon. The Psychology of the Artist. LC 91-7319. 1978. pap. 9.95 (ISBN 0-931174-00-7). Beau Rivage.

Chommie, J. G. El Derecho De los Estados Unidos: 3 Vols. (Orig., Span.). 1963. Set. pap. 24.00 (ISBN 0-379-00396-1); pap. 8.00 ea. Oceana.

Chomsky, Noam. Aspects of the Theory of Syntax. 1965. 22.00x (ISBN 0-262-03011-X); pap. 5.95 (ISBN 0-262-53007-4). MIT Pr.

--Lectures on Government & Binding. 384p. 1981. 45.00x (ISBN 90-70176-28-9); pap. 25.00x (ISBN 90-70176-13-0). Foris Pubns.

--Modular Approaches to the Study of the Mind. (SDSU Distinguished Research Lecture Ser.). 120p. 1983. 12.00 (ISBN 0-916304-56-6); pap. 6.00 (ISBN 0-916304-55-8). Campanile.

--Problems of Knowledge & Freedom: The Russell Lectures. 1972. pap. 2.95 (ISBN 0-394-71815-1, V815, Vin). Random.

Chong & Marin. Cheech & Chong's Next Movie. 1980. pap. 2.50 o.s.i. (ISBN 0-515-05709-6). Jove Pubns.

Chong, Jun. Kicking Strategy: The Art of Korean Sparring. LC 82-83443. (Illus.). 99p. (Orig.). 1983. pap. 5.95 (ISBN 0-86568-037-X, 351). Unique Pubns.

Chong-Bun Yap, jt. auth. see Brumlik, Joel.

Chong Sun Kim. Reverand Sun Myung Moon. LC 78-52115. 1978. pap. text ed. 8.25 (ISBN 0-8191-0494-9). U Pr of Amer.

Chopey, Nicholas & Hicks, Tyler G. Handbook of Chemical Engineering Calculations. (Illus.). 608p. 1983. 49.50 (ISBN 0-07-010805-6, P&RB). McGraw.

Chopin, Frederic. Waltzes & Scherzos, Vols. IX, XII, V. (Music Scores Ser.). (Illus.). 208p. 1983. pap. 6.95 (ISBN 0-486-24316-8). Dover.

Chopin, Fryderyk. Selected Correspondence of Fryderyk Chopin. Hedley, Arthur, ed. (Music Reprint Ser.). 1980. Repr. of 1963 ed. 35.00 (ISBN 0-306-79579-5). Da Capo.

Chopin, Kate. The Awakening & Selected Short Stories. (Bantam Classics Ser.). 224p. (Orig.). (gr. 9-12). 1981. pap. 1.95 (ISBN 0-553-21057-2). Bantam.

--The Awakening & Selected Stories. Baym, Nina, ed. 1981. pap. 3.95 (ISBN 0-686-38907-7, Mod LibC). Modern Lib.

Chopra, H. S., jt. ed. see Lall, K. B.

Chopra, Kasturi L. Thin Film Phenomena. LC 78-12782. 864p. 1979. Repr. of 1969 ed. 44.50 (ISBN 0-88275-746-6). Krieger.

Chopra, P. N. Sikkim. 114p. 1979. 14.95x (ISBN 0-940500-65-5). Asia Bk Corp.

Chopra, P. N., jt. auth. see Majumdar, R. C.

Chopra, P. N., ed. Religions & Communities of India. 316p. 1982. text ed. 32.25x (ISBN 0-391-02748-4). Humanities.

--Religions & Communities of India. 324p. 1982. 65.00x (ISBN 0-85692-081-9, Pub. by J M Dent). State Mutual Bk.

Chopra, Pran. India's Second Liberation. 1974. 17.50x (ISBN 0-262-03048-9). MIT Pr.

--On an Indian Border. 1966. 7.00x o.p. (ISBN 0-210-26931-6). Asia.

--Uncertain India: A Political Profile of Two Decades of Freedom. 1969. 25.00x (ISBN 0-262-03030-6). MIT Pr.

Chopra, V. P. India's Industrialisation & Mineral Exports 1951-52 to 1960-61 & Projections to 1970-71. 6.50x o.p. (ISBN 0-210-22727-3). Asia.

Chopyak, Josephine. A Turtle's Pond. 1983. 4.95 (ISBN 0-533-05471-0). Vantage.

Chorafas. Warehousing. 1975. 29.50 (ISBN 0-444-19526-2). Elsevier.

Chorafas, Dimitri N. Databases Management Systems for Distributed Computer & Networks. (Illus.). 240p. 1983. 24.95 (ISBN 0-89433-184-1). Petrocelli.

Chorafas, Dimitris N. Office Automation: The Productivity Challenge. (Illus.). 304p. 1982. text ed. 26.95 (ISBN 0-13-631028-1). P-H.

Chorao, Kay. Oink & Pearl. LC 80-8439. (An I Can Read Bk.). (Illus.). 64p. (gr. k-3). 1981. 7.64i (ISBN 0-06-021272-1, HarpJ); PLB 8.89g (ISBN 0-06-021273-X). Har-Row.

Chorba, Ronald W., jt. auth. see Bommer, Michael R. W.

Chorley, Henry F. Modern German Music: Recollections & Criticisms, 2 vols. LC 79-110994. (Music Reprint Ser.). 1973. Repr. of 1854 ed. 65.00 (ISBN 0-306-71911-8). Da Capo.

--Music & Manners in France & Germany, 3 Vols. 1983. Repr. of 1844 ed. Set. lib. bdg. 89.50 (ISBN 0-306-76217-X). Da Capo.

--Thirty Years' Musical Recollections. Newman, Ernest, ed. LC 77-183330. 411p. Date not set. Repr. of 1926 ed. price not set. Vienna Hse.

--Thirty Years of Musical Recollections, 2 Vols. 1983. Repr. of 1862 ed. Set. lib. bdg. 59.50 (ISBN 0-306-76216-1). Da Capo.

Chorley, R. J. & Haggett, P. Socio-Economic Models in Geography. 468p. 1968. pap. 12.95x (ISBN 0-416-29630-0). Methuen Inc.

Chorley, R. J., jt. auth. see Barry, Roger G.

Chorley, R. J., et al. History of the Study of Landforms; or, the Development of Geomorphology, Vol. 2: The Life & Work of William Morris Davis. 874p. 1973. 75.00x (ISBN 0-416-26890-0). Methuen Inc.

Chorley, Richard J., ed. Integrated Models in Geography. Haggett, Peter. 1969. pap. 12.50x (ISBN 0-416-29840-0). Methuen Inc.

--Introduction to Fluvial Processes. (Illus.). 1971. pap. 14.95x (ISBN 0-416-68820-9). Methuen Inc.

--Introduction to Geographical Hydrology. (Illus.). 1971. pap. 11.95x (ISBN 0-416-68830-6). Methuen Inc.

--Water, Earth & Man. 1969. 53.00x (ISBN 0-416-12030-X). Methuen Inc.

Chorley, Richard J. & Haggett, Peter, eds. Models in Geography. 1967. 82.00x (ISBN 0-416-29020-5). Methuen Inc.

Chorley, Richard J., jt. ed. see Board, Christopher.

Chorlton, Frank. Textbook of Dynamics. (Mathematics & Its Applications Ser.). 263p. 1981. pap. 18.95x o.s.i. (ISBN 0-470-27165-5). Halsted Pr.

--Vector & Tensor Methods. LC 75-16460. (Mathematics & Its Applications Ser.). 332p. 1976. 49.95x o.p. (ISBN 0-470-15604-X). Halsted Pr.

Chorlton, Frank, ed. Textbook of Dynamics. LC 77-85395. (Mathematics & Its Applications Ser.). 1978. Repr. of 1963 ed. 34.95x o.s.i. (ISBN 0-470-99325-1). Halsted Pr.

Chorlton, W. Cloud Dwellers of the Himalayas: The Bhotia. (Peoples of the Wild Ser.). 1982. 15.96 (ISBN 0-7054-0705-5, Pub. by Time-Life). Silver.

Chorlton, Windsor. Ice Ages. (Planet Earth Ser.). 1983. lib. bdg. 19.92 (ISBN 0-8094-4329-5, Pub. by Time-Life). Silver.

Chormack, D. & Dowsett, B. O. Troilboom: An Assessment of Design Concept & General Reliability, 1977. 1981. 35.00x (ISBN 0-686-97155-8, Pub. by W Spring England). State Mutual Bk.

Choron, Sandra & Hughes, John. National Lampoon's Class Reunion. (Orig.). 1982. pap. 2.95 (ISBN 0-440-16717-5). Dell.

Chorover, Stephan. From Genesis to Genocide: The Meaning of Human Nature & the Power of Behavior Control. 256p. 1979. pap. 5.95 (ISBN 0-262-53039-2). MIT Pr.

Chose, T. K., et al, eds. Downstream Processing. (Advances in Biochemical Engineering-Biotechnology: Vol. 26). (Illus.). 225p. 1983. 33.50 (ISBN 0-387-12096-3). Springer-Verlag.

Chotas, James, jt. auth. see Sturm, James L.

Chothia, J. Forging a Language. LC 78-73239. (Illus.). 1980. 29.95 (ISBN 0-521-22569-8). Cambridge U Pr.

Chotzinoff, Samuel. Toscanini: An Intimate Portrait. LC 76-7576. (Music Reprint Ser.). 1976. Repr. of 1956 ed. lib. bdg. 21.50 (ISBN 0-306-70777-2). Da Capo.

Chou, Cynthia L. My Life in the United States. 1970. 9.75 o.p. (ISBN 0-8158-0244-7). Chris Mass.

Chou, Hung-hsiang. Oracle Bone Collections in the United States. LC 74-34551. (Publications, Occasional Papers, Archaeology: Vol. 10). 1976. pap. 21.00x (ISBN 0-520-09534-0). U of Cal Pr.

Chou, Prudence. Lao She: An Intellectual's Role & Dilemma in Modern China. (China Research Monographs: No. 20). 150p. (Orig.). 1982. pap. cancelled o.p. (ISBN 0-912966-38-6). IEAS.

Chou, Prudence S. Lao She: The Dilemma of an Intellectual in Modern China. Date not set. price not set. Quintessence.

Chou, Shelley N. & Seljeskog, Edward L., eds. Spinal Deformities & Neurological Dysfunction. LC 76-5665. (Seminars in Neurological Surgery). 300p. 1978. 37.00 (ISBN 0-89004-183-0). Raven.

Chou, Tsu-Wei, jt. auth. see Vinson, Jack R.

Chou Ching-Wen. Ten Years of Storm: The True Story of the Communist Regime in China. Ming Lai, tr. LC 72-12632. 323p. 1973. Repr. of 1960 ed. lib. bdg. 17.50x (ISBN 0-8371-6685-3, CHTY). Greenwood.

Choucri, Nazli. Energy & Development in Latin America: Perspectives for Public Policy. LC 81-47741. 240p. 1982. 24.95x (ISBN 0-669-04799-6). Lexington Bks.

--International Energy Futures: Petroleum Prices, Power & Payments. (Illus.). 250p. 1981. 30.00x (ISBN 0-262-03075-6). MIT Pr.

Choudhuri, A. D. The Face of Illusion in American Drama. 1980. text ed. 13.00x (ISBN 0-391-01728-4). Humanities.

Choudhury, Golam. Chinese Perception of the New World. 1978. pap. text ed. 8.50 (ISBN 0-8191-0527-9). U Pr of Amer.

Choudhury, Golam W. China in World Affairs: The Foreign Policy of the PRC since 1970. (Special Studies on China & East Asia). (Orig.). 1982. lib. bdg. 27.50 (ISBN 0-89158-937-6); pap. 12.95 (ISBN 0-86531-329-6). Westview.

Choudhury, Masudul A. An Islamic Social Welfare Function. Quinlan, Hamid, ed. LC 82-74125. (Illus.). 60p. 1983. pap. 2.00 (ISBN 0-89259-041-6). Am Trust Pubns.

Choudhury, P. Roy see Heat Transfer & Fluid Mechanics Institute.

Choudhury, Sadananda. Economic History of Colonialism. 1979. text ed. 14.25x (ISBN 0-391-01852-3). Humanities.

Chouinard, A., jt. ed. see Losos, G.

Choukri, Mohamed. Tennessee Williams in Tangier. Bowles, Paul, tr. from Arabic. LC 78-60367. 85p. 1979. pap. 6.00 o.s.i. (ISBN 0-932274-00-5); signed limited o.p. (ISBN 0-932274-01-3). Cadmus Eds.

Chourou, Bechir, jt. auth. see Carpenter, Allan.

Choux, M., ed. Shunts & Problems in Shunts. (Monographs in Neural Sciences: Vol. 8). (Illus.). x, 230p. 1982. pap. 69.00 (ISBN 3-8055-2465-X). S Karger.

Chow, Brian G., rev. by see Walker, Westbrook A.

Chow, Chuen-Yen. An Introduction to Computational Fluid Mechanics. LC 78-27555. 396p. 1979. text ed. 35.95 (ISBN 0-471-15608-6). Wiley.

Chow, Chuen-Yen, jt. auth. see Kuethe, Arnold M.

Chow, Gregory C. Analysis & Control of Dynamic Economic Systems. LC 74-22433. (Probability & Mathematical Statistics Ser). 316p. 1975. 40.95x (ISBN 0-471-15616-7, Pub. by Wiley-Interscience). Wiley.

--Econometric Analysis by Control Methods. LC 81-571. (Wiley Series in Probability & Mathematical Statistics). 320p. 1981. 41.50 (ISBN 0-471-08706-8, Pub. by Wiley-Interscience). Wiley.

--Econometrics. 416p. 1983. text ed. 31.95 (ISBN 0-07-010847-1, C). McGraw.

Chow, J. H., ed. Time-Scale Modeling of Dynamic Networks with Applications to Power Systems. (Lecture Notes in Control & Information Sciences Ser.: Vol. 46). 218p. 1983. pap. 12.00 (ISBN 0-387-12106-4). Springer-Verlag.

Chow, Marilyn P., et al. Handbook of Pediatric Primary Care. LC 78-19731. 1979. 35.00x (ISBN 0-471-01771-X, Pub. by Wiley Med). Wiley.

Chow, P. L., et al, eds. Multiple Scattering & Waves in Random Media. 1981. 42.75 (ISBN 0-444-86280-3). Elsevier.

Chow, Ven Te, ed. Advances in Hydroscience, Vol. 13. 393p. 1982. 53.00 (ISBN 0-12-021813-5); lib. ed. 69.00 (ISBN 0-12-021880-1); microfiche 37.50 (ISBN 0-12-021881-X). Acad Pr.

Chow, Woo F. Principles of Tunnel Diode Circuits. LC 64-20080. 387p. 1964. text ed. 20.50 (ISBN 0-471-15615-9, Pub. by Wiley). Krieger.

Chow Chen-Ho. Customs of Su-Chow. Bd. with Legends from Northern Chiang-Su. Hsiao Han. (Folklore Series of National Sun Yat-Sen University: No. 14). (Chinese.). 15.00x (ISBN 0-89986-066-4). Oriental Bk Store.

Chowder, Ken. Blackbird Days. LC 79-1704. 256p. 1980. 11.49i (ISBN 0-06-011496-7, HarpT). Har-Row.

--Delicate Geometry. LC 81-48052. 352p. 1982. 12.45i (ISBN 0-06-014973-6, HarpT). Har-Row.

Chowdhury, Anwarullah. Agrarian Social Relations & Rural Development in Bangladesh. LC 81-19062. 260p. 1983. text ed. 24.50x (ISBN 0-86598-077-2). Allanheld.

Chowdhury, Nira P. Researches on Living Pteridophytes in India, Burma & Ceylon. (Illus.). 1971. text ed. 6.95x o.p. (ISBN 0-210-22349-9). Asia.

Chowdhury, R. H. Social Aspects of Fertility. 200p. 1982. text ed. 27.50x (ISBN 0-7069-1211-X, Pub by Vikas India). Advent NY.

Chowning, Larry S. Barcat Skipper: Tales of a Tangier Waterman. LC 82-74135. 160p. 1983. 11.95 (ISBN 0-87033-300-3). Cornell Maritime.

Chow Ven-Te. Handbook of Applied Hydrology: A Compendium of Water Resources Technology. 1964. 75.00 (ISBN 0-07-010774-2, P&RB). McGraw.

--Open-Channel Hydraulics. (Civil Engineering Ser). 1959. 39.50 (ISBN 0-07-010776-9, C). McGraw.

Chow Ven Te, ed. Advances in Hydroscience, 12 vols. Incl. Vol. 1. 1964. 63.00 (ISBN 0-12-021801-1); Vol. 2. 1966. 63.00 (ISBN 0-12-021802-X); Vol. 3. 1967. 63.00 (ISBN 0-12-021803-8); Vol. 4. 1968. 63.00 (ISBN 0-12-021804-6); Vol. 5. 1969. 63.00 (ISBN 0-12-021805-4); Vol. 6. 1970. 63.00 (ISBN 0-12-021806-2); Vol. 7. 1971. 63.00 (ISBN 0-12-021807-0); Vol. 8. 1972. 63.00 (ISBN 0-12-021808-9); Vol. 9. 1973. 57.00 (ISBN 0-12-021809-7); Vol. 10. 1975. 72.00 (ISBN 0-12-021810-0); lib. ed. 92.50 (ISBN 0-12-021874-7); microfiche 52.00 (ISBN 0-12-021875-5); Vol. 11. 1978. 63.00 (ISBN 0-12-021811-9); lib ed. 80.50 (ISBN 0-12-021876-3); microfiche 45.50 (ISBN 0-12-021877-1); Vol. 12. 1978. 58.50 (ISBN 0-12-021812-7); 76.00 (ISBN 0-12-021878-X); 46.50 (ISBN 0-12-021879-8). Acad Pr.

Chretien, J. & Hirsch, A., eds. Diseases of the Pleura. (Illus.). 360p. 1983. write for info (ISBN 0-89352-181-7). Masson Pub.

Chretien, J. & Marsac, J., eds. Sarcoidosis & Other Granulomatous Disorders: 9th International Conference, Paris, 31 August - 4 September 1981. (Illus.). 950p. 1982. 120.00 (ISBN 0-08-027088-3). Pergamon.

Chrimes, K. M., ed. see Xenophon.

Chrimes, S. B. Henry VII. LC 72-78947. (English Monarch Ser.). (Illus.). 400p. 1973. 40.00x (ISBN 0-520-02266-1); pap. 8.95 o.p. (ISBN 0-520-04414-2). U of Cal Pr.

--An Introduction to the Administrative History of Mediaeval England. 3rd ed. (Studies in Mediaeval History: Vol. 7). 285p. 1966. 36.00x o.p. (ISBN 0-631-09170-X, Pub. by Basil Blackwell); pap. 8.95x (ISBN 0-631-12141-2, Pub. by Basil Blackwell). Biblio Dist.

Chrisman, Cheryl L. Problems in Small Animal Neurology. LC 81-6065. (Illus.). 461p. 1982. text ed. 37.50 (ISBN 0-8121-0811-6). Lea & Febiger.

Chrisman, Harry. The Ladder of Rivers: The Story of I. P. Olive. LC 62-22284. (Illus.). 426p. 1983. 18.95 (ISBN 0-8040-0179-0, 82-71157); pap. 9.95 (ISBN 0-8040-0845-0, 82-76164). Ohio U Pr.

Chrisman, Harry E. The Ladders of Rivers: The Story of I. P. (Print) Olive. LC 82-711574. 426p. 1983. 18.95 (ISBN 0-8040-0179-0); pap. 9.95 (ISBN 0-8040-0845-0). Swallow.

--Lost Trails of the Cimarron. LC 82-73344. (Illus.). 313p. 1964. pap. 7.95 (ISBN 0-8040-0615-6, SB). Swallow.

--The One Thousand & One Most Asked Questions about the American West. LC 82-75281. (Illus.). 300p. 1982. 25.95 (ISBN 0-8040-0382-3); pap. 9.95 (ISBN 0-8040-0383-1). Swallow.

Chrisman, Harry E. & Herron, Jim. Fifty Years on the Owl Hoot Trail: Jim Herron, the First Sheriff of No Man's Land, Oklahoma Territory. LC 82-70704. (Illus.). xxvi, 356p. 1969. 12.00 o.p. (ISBN 0-8040-0114-6); pap. 8.95 (ISBN 0-8040-0614-8, Sb). Swallow.

Chrisman, N. J., jt. auth. see Friedl, J.

Chrisman, P. Oswin, ed. see State Bar of Texas Professional Efficiency & Economic Research Committee.

Christ, Carol. Diving Deep & Surfacing: Women Writers on Spiritual Quest. LC 79-51153. 176p. 1980. 10.10 o.p. (ISBN 0-8070-6362-2); pap. 5.95 (ISBN 0-8070-6363-0). Beacon Pr.

Christ, Carol P. & Plaskow, Judith. Womanspirit Rising: A Feminist Reader in Religion. LC 78-3363. (Orig.). 1979. pap. 7.95i (ISBN 0-06-061385-8, RD 275, HarpR). Har-Row.

Christ, Charles L., jt. auth. see Garrels, Robert M.

Christ Episcopal Church. Pass the Plate. Underhill, Alice & Stewart, Bobbie, eds. 384p. 1981. pap. write for info. (ISBN 0-939114-13-5). Christ Episcopal.

Christ, F. & Adams, R. You Can Learn to Learn. 750.00 (ISBN 0-13-976704-5). P-H.

Christ Foundation Staff. A Spiritual Sex Manual. LC 82-72079. (Illus.). 176p. 1982. pap. 6.95 (ISBN 0-910315-01-9). Christ Found.

Christ, Frank L. Study - Reading College Textbooks. 1966. pap. text ed. 6.95 (ISBN 0-574-17180-0, 13-0180). SRA.

Christ, Ronald, tr. see Vargas Llosa, Mario.

Christ, William & Delone, Richard P. Introduction to Materials & Structure of Music. (Illus.). 390p. 1975. pap. text ed. 18.95 (ISBN 0-13-485532-9). P-H.

Christ, William, et al. Materials & Structure of Music, Vol. 2. 2nd ed. (Illus.). 512p. 1973. ref. ed. 20.95 o.p. (ISBN 0-13-560367-6); wkbk. 11.95 o.p. (ISBN 0-13-560383-8). P-H.

--Materials & Structures of Music, Vol. 1. 3rd ed. 1980. text ed. 20.95 (ISBN 0-13-540417-7); wkbk. 11.95 (ISBN 0-13-560425-7). P-H.

Christakes, George. Albion W. Small. (World Leaders Ser.). 1978. lib. bdg. 13.95 (ISBN 0-8057-7718-0, Twayne). G K Hall.

Christanand, M. P. The Philosophy of Indian Monotheism. 132p. 1980. text ed. 12.50x (ISBN 0-333-90313-7). Humanities.

Christelow, Eileen. Mr. Murphy's Marvelous Invention. (Illus.). 40p. (gr. 4). 1983. 10.50 (ISBN 0-89919-141-X, Clarion). HM.

Christen, Carol A. Career Education & Home Economics. LC 74-11977. (Guidance Monograph). 1975. pap. 2.40 o.p. (ISBN 0-395-20050-4). HM.

Christenberry, William. William Christenberry: Photographs 1961-1981. (Illus.). 96p. 1983. 30.00 (ISBN 0-89381-110-6). Aperture.

Christenbury, Leila, ed. Developing Lifelong Readers. 55p. 3.00 (ISBN 0-686-95295-2); members 2.50 (ISBN 0-686-99488-4). NCTE.

Christensen, jt. auth. see Levin.

Christensen, C. Explorando: Affective Learning Activities for Intermediate Practice in Spanish. 1977. pap. text ed. 12.95 (ISBN 0-13-295980-1). P-H.

Christensen, Carl. Index Filicum. 1973. 106.00 (ISBN 3-87429-048-4). Lubrecht & Cramer.

--Index Filicum: Supplementum, Vols. 1, 2 & 3. 1973. 68.00 (ISBN 3-87429-049-2). Lubrecht & Cramer.

Christensen, Carl C. Art & the Reformation in Germany. (Studies in the Reformation Ser.: Vol.2). (Illus.). 269p. 1981. 18.95x (ISBN 0-8214-0388-5, 82-82816, Co-Pub by Wayne State U Pr). Ohio U Pr.

Christensen, Chuck & Christensen, Winnie. Acts 1-12: God Moves in the Early Church. rev. ed. (Fisherman Bible Studyguides). 1979. saddle stitch 2.50 (ISBN 0-87788-007-7). Shaw Pubs.

--Acts 13-28: God Moves in a Pagan World. rev. ed. (Fisherman Bible Studyguides). 1979. saddle stitch 2.50 (ISBN 0-87788-008-5). Shaw Pubs.

--James: Faith in Action. LC 75-33442. (Fisherman Bible Studyguides Ser.). 1975. saddle-stitched 2.50 (ISBN 0-87788-421-8). Shaw Pubs.

--Mark: God in Action. LC 72-88935. (Fisherman Bible Studyguides Ser.). 96p. 1972. saddle-stitched 2.50 (ISBN 0-87788-309-2). Shaw Pubs.

Christensen, Clay B. & Wolfe, David E. Vistas Hispanicas: Introduccion a la Lengua y la Cultura. 2nd ed. 18.95 (ISBN 0-395-30972-7); Instr's. manual 3.00 (ISBN 0-395-30974-3); Student wkbk. & lab manual 8.95 (ISBN 0-395-30973-5); Tapes (cassette) 150.00 (ISBN 0-395-30975-1). HM.

Christensen, Daphne, jt. auth. see Pikarsky, Milton.

Christensen, Darrel E., et al, eds. Contemporary German Philosophy, Vol. 1. 320p. 1982. 17.50x (ISBN 0-271-00336-7). Pa St U Pr.

Christensen, Deborah. My Baha'i Book. (Sunflower Bks. for Young Children: Bk. 1). (Illus., Orig.). (ps-2). 1980. pap. 2.00 (ISBN 0-87743-141-8, 353-001-10). Baha'i.

--My Favorite Prayers & Passages. (Sunflower Bks. for Young Children: Bk. 2). (Illus., Orig.). (ps-2). 1980. pap. 2.00 (ISBN 0-87743-142-6, 353-002-10). Baha'i.

--Our Baha'i Holy Places. (Sunflower Bks. for Young Children: Bk. 4). (Illus., Orig.). (ps-2). 1980. pap. 2.00 (ISBN 0-87743-144-2, 353-004-10). Baha'i.

Christensen, Don R. How-to-Draw Tips From the Top Cartoonists. LC 82-70285. (Illus.). 80p. 1982. pap. 8.49 (ISBN 0-9608068-0-6). Donnar Pubns.

Christensen, Doris, jt. auth. see Feeney, Stephanie.

Christensen, Dorothea H. George the Alligator. 1979. 4.50 o.p. (ISBN 0-533-04149-X). Vantage.

Christensen, Edith A., ed. Approved Methods of the American Association of Cereal Chemists. 8th ed. LC 82-46081. 1200p. 1983. text ed. 140.00 member (ISBN 0-686-43049-2); text ed. 190.00 non-member (ISBN 0-913250-31-7). Am Assn Cereal Chem.

Christensen, Edward, jt. ed. see MacKenzie, Ossian.

Christensen, Edwin R., jt. auth. see Lambert, Michael J.

Christensen, Erwin O. Index of American Design. (Illus.). 229p. 1950. 22.95 o.p. (ISBN 0-02-525240-2). Macmillan.

Christensen, Gardell D. Colonial New York. LC 69-15223. (Colonial History Ser). (Illus.). (gr. 5 up). 1969. 7.95 o.p. (ISBN 0-525-67102-1). Lodestar Bks.

Christensen, Howard B. Statistics: Step-by-Step. LC 76-10903. (Illus.). 1977. text ed. 24.50 (ISBN 0-395-24527-3); instr's. manual with solutions 3.50 (ISBN 0-395-24528-1). HM.

Christensen, J. Ippolito & Ashner, S. Shapiro. Needlepoint & Bargello Stitchery. LC 80-51926. (Illus.). 96p. 1980. pap. 5.95 (ISBN 0-8069-8932-7). Sterling.

Christensen, J. P. Topology & Borel Structure, Vol. 10. (Mathematical Studies). 1974. pap. 36.25 (ISBN 0-444-10608-1, North-Holland). Elsevier.

Christensen, James E. & Fisher, Jamer E. Analytic Philosophy of Education As a Sub-Discipline of Educology: An Introduction to Its Techniques & Application. LC 79-66235. 1979. pap. text ed. 9.50 (ISBN 0-8191-0802-2). U Pr of Amer.

Christensen, James E., ed. Perspectives on Education As Educology. LC 80-6078. 396p. 1981. lib. bdg. 27.50 (ISBN 0-686-77672-0); pap. text ed. 16.00 (ISBN 0-8191-1394-8). U Pr of Amer.

Christensen, James J., jt. auth. see Izatt, Reed M.

Christensen, James J., et al. Handbook of Metal-Ligand Heats & Related Thermodynamic Quantities. rev., 2nd ed. 1975. 75.50 (ISBN 0-8247-6317-3). Dekker.

Christensen, James M., ed. Gastrointestinal Motility. 543p. 1980. 52.50 (ISBN 0-89004-503-8, 566). Raven.

Christensen, James R. & Larrison, Earl J. Mammals of the Pacific Northwest. LC 82-60054. (Illus.). 1982. 17.95 (ISBN 0-89301-085-5). U Pr of Idaho.

Christensen, John B. & Telford, Ira. Synopsis of Gross Anatomy With Clinical Correlations. 4th ed. (Illus.). 400p. 1982. pap. text ed. 20.00 (ISBN 0-06-140632-5, Harper Medical). Lippincott.

Christensen, Karen, jt. auth. see Christensen, Roger.

Christensen, Leon. Christensen's Collection. 4.00 o.s.i. (ISBN 0-8283-1268-0). Branden.

Christensen, M. N., jt. auth. see Gilbert, C. M.

Christensen, Mary L. Basic Laboratory Procedures in Diagnostic Virology. (Illus.). 128p. 1977. spiral 12.50x (ISBN 0-398-03617-9). C C Thomas.

Christensen, Paula J., jt. auth. see Griffith, Janet W.

Christensen, R. Belief & Behavior. Date not set. price not set (ISBN 0-938876-16-3). Entropy ltd.

--Entropy Minimax Sourcebook, Vol. VII: Data Distributions. Date not set. price not set (ISBN 0-938876-17-1). Entropy Ltd.

Christensen, R. M. Mechanics of Composite Materials. LC 79-14093. 1979. 44.95x (ISBN 0-471-05167-5, Pub. by Wiley-Interscience). Wiley.

--Theory of Viscoelasticity: An Introduction. 2nd ed. 357p. 1982. 45.00 (ISBN 0-12-174252-0). Acad Pr.

Christensen, Roger & Christensen, Karen. The Ultimate Movie, TV & Rock Directory. 372p. (Orig.). Date not set. price not set (ISBN 0-9608038-0-7). Cardiff. Postponed.

Christensen, Val J., jt. auth. see Heasley, Victor L.

Christensen, Winnie. Women Who Believed God. (Fisherman Bible Studyguides). 80p. 1983. saddle-stiched 2.50 (ISBN 0-87788-936-8). Shaw Pubs.

Christensen, Winnie, jt. auth. see Christensen, Chuck.

Christenson, Boyd & Hanson, Nancy E. Boyd Christenson Interviews. (Illus.). 212p. 1983. 15.95 (ISBN 0-911007-00-8). Prairie Hse.

Christenson, Christina & Johnson, Thomas W. Supervising. 336p. Date not set. price not set Instrs' Resource Manual. A-W.

Christenson, Christina, et al. Supervising. (Management Ser.). (Illus.). 500p. 1982. text ed. 21.95 (ISBN 0-201-03431-X). A-W.

Christenson, Evelyn. Cambiame, Senor! 224p. Date not set. 2.75 (ISBN 0-88113-035-4). Edit Betania.

--Gaining Through Losing. 1980. 9.95 (ISBN 0-88207-795-3); pap. 4.95 (ISBN 0-88207-344-3). Victor Bks.

--Lord, Change Me. 1977. pap. 4.50 (ISBN 0-88207-756-2). Victor Bks.

--Perder Para Ganar. 1983. 2.95 (ISBN 0-88113-243-8). Edit Betania.

--Two by Evelyn. 1979. 9.95 (ISBN 0-88207-791-0). Victor Bks.

Christenson, Evelyn & Blake, Viola. What Happens When Women Pray. 144p. 1975. pap. 4.50 (ISBN 0-88207-715-5). Victor Bks.

Christenson, Larry. The Christian Family: Tenth Anniversary Edition. LC 75-324692. 224p. (Avail. 1978 paper ed. 3.50 ISBN 0-87123-088-7, order no. 200088). 1970 8.95, (ISBN 0-87123-062-3); pap. 4.95, 1980 (ISBN 0-87123-114-X, 210114); study guide 1.50 (ISBN 0-87123-046-1). Bethany Hse.

--La Familia Cristiana. 238p. Date not set. price not set (ISBN 0-88113-080-X); guia 3.25 (ISBN 0-88113-081-8). Edit Betania.

--Hacia Donde Va la Familia? 32p. Date not set. 1.25 (ISBN 0-88113-110-5). Edit Betania.

--La Mente Renovada. 128p. Date not set. 1.95 (ISBN 0-88113-199-7). Edit Betania.

--La Pareja Cristiana. Date not set. 2.95 (ISBN 0-88113-314-0). Edit Betania.

--Speaking in Tongues. LC 97-5595. 1968. pap. 2.95 (ISBN 0-87123-518-8, 200518). Bethany Hse.

--Which Way the Family? 24p. 1973. pap. 0.75 o.p. (ISBN 0-87123-643-5, 260643). Bethany Hse.

--The Wonderful Way That Babies Are Made. 48p. (Orig.). (ps up). 1982. 6.95 (ISBN 0-87123-627-3, 230627). Bethany Hse.

Christenson, R. M. & McWilliams, R. O. Voice of the People. 2nd ed. 1967. pap. text ed. 18.95 o.p. (ISBN 0-07-010782-3, C). McGraw.

Christenson, Reo M. American Politics: Understanding What Counts. (Illus.). 341p. 1980. pap. text ed. 14.50 scp (ISBN 0-06-041259-3, HarpC). Har-Row.

Christenson, Toni & Feia, Marian R. The Tree Book: Teaching Responsible Enviromental Education, Vol. 1. (Illus.). 78p. (Orig.). 1981. tchr's ed. 6.95 (ISBN 0-686-36286-1). Creative Curriculum.

Christesen, Barbara. The First Olympic Games. LC 78-15976. (Famous Firsts Ser.). (Illus.). 1978. PLB 10.76 (ISBN 0-89547-043-8). Silver.

Christian, jt. auth. see Desai.

Christian, Barbara. Black Women Novelists: The Development of a Tradition, 1892-1976. LC 79-8953. (Contributions in Afro-American & African Studies: No. 52). xiv, 275p. 1980. lib. bdg. 29.95 (ISBN 0-313-20750-X, CBW/). Greenwood.

Christian, Diane, jt. auth. see Jackson, Bruce.

Christian, Donna, jt. ed. see Wolfram, Walt.

Christian, Erich. LC-Filters: Design, Testing, & Manufacturing. (Ser. on Filters: Design, Manufacturing & Applications). 256p. 1983. 25.00 (ISBN 0-471-09053-0, Pub. by Wiley Interscience). Wiley.

Christian, Ernest S., Jr. State Taxation of Foreign Source Income. LC 81-70922. 1982. 3.50 (ISBN 0-910586-44-6). Finan Exec.

Christian, Esther. Family Enrichment: A Manual for Promoting Family Togetherness. Sorenson, Don L., ed. LC 82-70356. 160p. 1982. pap. text ed. 5.95x (ISBN 0-932796-12-5). Ed Media Corp.

Christian, Frederick H. Frank Angel Federal Marshal: Massacre in Madison. 160p. 1980. pap. 1.50 o.p. (ISBN 0-523-40589-8). Pinnacle Bks.

--Manhunt in Quemado. (Frank Angel, Federal Marshal Ser.: No. 3). 160p. 1981. pap. 1.75 o.p. (ISBN 0-523-41545-1). Pinnacle Bks.

--Ride Out to Vengeance. (Frank Angel, Federal Marshal Ser.: No. 4). 160p. 1981. pap. 1.75 o.p. (ISBN 0-523-41546-X). Pinnacle Bks.

--Shootout at Silver King. (Justice Ser.: No. 6). pap. 1.50 o.p. (ISBN 0-523-40588-X). Pinnacle Bks.

Christian, Gary D. Analytical Chemistry. 3rd ed. LC 79-19692. 643p. 1980. text ed. 29.95x (ISBN 0-471-05181-0); solutions manual 6.95 (ISBN 0-471-06377-0). Wiley.

Christian, Gary D. & Feldman, Fredric J. Atomic Absorption Spectroscopy: Applications in Agriculture, Biology & Medicine. LC 78-23204. 512p. 1979. Repr. of 1970 ed. lib. bdg. 30.50 (ISBN 0-88275-797-0). Krieger.

Christian, Glynn. A Fragile Paradise: Fletcher Christian of H.M.S. Bounty. 1982. 22.50 (ISBN 0-316-14063-5, Pub. by Atlantic Monthly Pr). Little.

Christian, Jeffrey M. & Reibsamen, Gary G. World Guide to Battery Powered Road Transportation. (Illus.). 352p. 1980. 55.00 (ISBN 0-07-010790-4, P&RB). McGraw.

Christian, John. Management, Machines & Methods in Civil Engineering. LC 81-2434. (Construction Management & Engineering Ser.). 360p. 1981. 39.95x (ISBN 0-471-06334-7, Pub. by Wiley-Interscience). Wiley.

Christian, John, intro. by. Symbolists & Decadents. LC 77-9152. (Art for All Ser). (Illus.). 1978. pap. 5.95 o.p. (ISBN 0-312-78193-8). St Martin.

Christian, K. R., et al. Simulation of Grazing Systems. 121p. 1978. pap. 14.50 (ISBN 0-686-93181-5, PDC106, Pudoc). Unipub.

Christian, M. B. The Goosehill Gang, 4 bks. Incl. The Goosehill Gang & the Chocolate Cake Caper: Illustrating 1 John 3: 18 (ISBN 0-570-03606-2, 39DD1031); The Goosehill Gang & the Disappearing Dues: Illustrating Matthew 22: 39 (ISBN 0-570-03607-0, 39DD1032); The Goosehill Gang & the Test Paper Thief: Illustrating Matthew 5: 39 (ISBN 0-570-03608-9, 39DD1033); The Goosehill Gang & the Vanishing Sandwich: Illustrating Luke 10: 37 (ISBN 0-570-03609-7, 39DD1034). (Illus.). (gr. 1-4). 1977. pap. 3.55 set o.p. (ISBN 0-686-67954-7); pap. 1.10 ea. o.p. Concordia.

Christian, Mary B. Sebastian, Super Sleuth. LC 73-2257. (Illus.). 64p. (gr. 3-6). 1974. 4.50 (ISBN 0-87955-208-5); PLB 3.48 (ISBN 0-87955-808-3). O'Hara.

--Sebastian (Super Sleuth) & the Crummy Yummies Caper. LC 82-20861. (Sebastian (Super Sleuth) Mystery Ser.). (Illus.). 64p. (gr. 2-5). 1983. 6.95 (ISBN 0-02-718430-7). Macmillan.

--Sebastian (Super Sleuth) & the Hair of the Dog Mystery. LC 82-10066. (Sebastian Super Sleuth Mystery Ser.). (Illus.). 64p. (gr. 1-4). 6.95 (ISBN 0-02-718260-6). Macmillan.

--Swamp Monsters. LC 82-1574. (Illus.). 56p. (ps-3). 1983. lib. bdg. 8.89 (ISBN 0-8037-7616-0, 0383-120); pap. 3.95 (ISBN 0-8037-7614-4). Dial Bks Young.

--The Test Paper Thief. (Goosehill Gang Ser.). (Illus.). 32p. (gr. 1-4). 1976. pap. 1.10 o.p. (ISBN 0-570-03608-9, 39-1033). Concordia.

--The Ventriloquist. (Break-of-day Ser.). (Illus.). 48p. 1982. lib. bdg. 6.99 (ISBN 0-698-30735-6, Coward). Putnam Pub Group.

Christian, Nick. Homicide Zone Four. (Orig.). 1978. pap. 1.95 o.p. (ISBN 0-451-08285-0, J8285, Sig). NAL.

--Intensive Fear. 256p. (Orig.). 1980. pap. 2.25 o.p. (ISBN 0-451-09341-0, E9341, Sig). NAL.

Christian, Paul. Listing & Selling Techniques: For Revolutionary Income in the 80's. 1982. 100.00 o.p. (ISBN 0-686-30528-0). Exec Reports.

Christian, Paula. The Cruise. LC 82-60183. 224p. (Orig.). 1982. pap. 8.95 (ISBN 0-931328-09-8). Timely Bks.

Christian, Portia, ed. Agricultural Enterprises Management in an Urban-Industrial Society: A Guide to Information Sources. LC 76-27856. (Management Information Guide: No. 34). 1978. 42.00x (ISBN 0-8103-0834-7). Gale.

Christian, Portia & Hicks, Richard, eds. Ethics in Business Conduct: A Guide to Information Sources. LC 77-127411. (Management Information Guides Ser.: No. 21). 1970. 42.00x (ISBN 0-8103-0821-5). Gale.

Christian Publications, Inc., ed. Fifty-Two Visual Ideas for Opening Assemblies, 3 vols. 2.50 ea. Vol. 1 (ISBN 0-87509-271-3). Vol. 2 (ISBN 0-87509-272-1). Vol. 3 (ISBN 0-87509-273-X). Chr Pubns.

Christian, R., jt. auth. see Wiener, R.

Christian, Ralph J., jt. auth. see Adams, G. Rollie.

Christian, Reginald F. Tolstoy: A Critical Introduction. LC 69-19373. 1970. 49.50 (ISBN 0-521-07493-2); pap. 12.95 (ISBN 0-521-09585-9, 585). Cambridge U Pr.

Christian, Roy. Factories, Forges & Foundries: Industrial Buildings of Britain. (Local Search Ser.). (Illus.). 1974. 8.75 o.p. (ISBN 0-7100-7901-X). Routledge & Kegan.

Christian, W. P., et al. Schedule-Induced Behavior, Vol. 1. 1977. 14.40 (ISBN 0-904406-52-0). Eden Pr.

Christian, William, ed. The Idea File of Harold Adam Innis. 1980. 25.00x o.p. (ISBN 0-8020-2350-9); pap. 8.50 (ISBN 0-8020-6382-9). U of Toronto Pr.

Christian, William A. An Interpretation of Whitehead's Metaphysics. LC 77-5619. 1977. Repr. of 1959 ed. lib. bdg. 35.00x (ISBN 0-8371-9638-8, CHIW). Greenwood.

Christian Writers Inst. The Successful Writers & Editors Guidebook Market Guide, 1983-1984. 1982. 5.95 (ISBN 0-88419-186-9). Creation Hse.

Christiani, Adolph. The Principles of Expression in Pianoforte Playing. LC 74-1348. (Music Reprint Ser.). 303p. 1974. Repr. of 1886 ed. lib. bdg. 27.50 (ISBN 0-306-70623-7). Da Capo.

Christiani, Dounia B., ed. see Ibsen, Henrik.

Christiano, David & Young, Lisa, eds. Human Rights Organizations & Periodicals Directory. 1982 ed. 1982. lib. bdg. 22.00 (ISBN 0-686-95282-0). Meiklejohn Civ.

Christians, Clifford G., ed. see Ellul, Jacques, et al.

Christiansen, Harley D. Casebook of Test Interpretation in Counseling. (Illus.). 96p. (Orig.). 1983. pap. text ed. 7.95 (ISBN 0-915456-05-2). P Juul Pr.

--Key Readings in Testing. 96p. (Orig.). 1983. pap. text ed. 7.95 (ISBN 0-915456-06-0). P Juul Pr.

Christiansen, K. O., jt. ed. see Mednick, Sarnoff A.

Christiansen, Larry K. & Strate, James W. Attitude Development for Retail Management. (Gregg-McGraw-Hill Marketing Ser.). (Illus.). 256p. 1981. wkbk. 7.05 (ISBN 0-07-010820-X). McGraw.

Christiansen, M. N. Breeding Plants for Less Favorable Environments. Lewis, Charles F., ed. LC 81-10346. 459p. 1982. 53.50 (ISBN 0-471-04483-0, Pub. by Wiley-Interscience). Wiley.

Christiansen, Monty L. Park Planning Handbook: Fundamentals of Physical Planning for Parks & Recreation Areas. LC 77-51844. 413p. 1977. text ed. 32.95x (ISBN 0-471-15619-1). Wiley.

Christiansen, Pauline G. From Inside Out: Writing from Subjective to Objective. (Orig.). 1978. pap. text ed. 10.95 (ISBN 0-316-14068-6); tchrs' manual unavail. (ISBN 0-316-14069-4). Little.

Christiansen, Rex. A Regional History of the Railways of Great Britain: Vol. 7: The West Midlands. 2nd ed. (Illus.). 305p. 1983. 24.95 (ISBN 0-7153-8468-6). David & Charles.

Christiansen, Sigurd. Chaff Before the Wind. Anderson, Isaac, tr. LC 73-22750. 319p. 1974. Repr. of 1934 ed. lib. bdg. 17.50x (ISBN 0-8371-7349-3, CHCB). Greenwood.

--Two Living & One Dead. Bjorkman, Edwin, tr. from Norwegian. LC 73-22751. 288p. 1975. Repr. of 1932 ed. lib. bdg. 17.25x (ISBN 0-8371-7348-5, CHTL). Greenwood.

Christianson, Arne. The Future Is Now. 1983. 8.95 (ISBN 0-533-05552-0). Vantage.

Christianson, Birgitta, tr. see Koustrup, Soren.

Christianson, Birgitta, tr. see Krustrup, Erik V.

Christianson, Elin B., ed. New Special Libraries: A Summary of Research. LC 80-11507. 1980. 7.25 o.p. (ISBN 0-87111-271-X). SLA.

Christianson, John, tr. see Koustrup, Soren.

Christianson, John, tr. see Krustrup, Erik V.

Christie, Agatha. Appointment with Death. 1981. pap. 2.50 (ISBN 0-440-10246-4). Dell.

--Cards on the Table. 1980. pap. 2.50 (ISBN 0-440-11052-1). Dell.

--A Caribbean Mystery. 1982. pap. 2.50 (ISBN 0-671-42250-2). PB.

--Death Comes as the End. LC 82-73252. (Greenway Edition). 1982. 9.95 (ISBN 0-396-08109-6). Dodd.

--Double Sin. 1983. pap. 2.95 o.s.i. (ISBN 0-440-12144-2). Dell.

--Elephants Can Remember. 1976. pap. 2.50 (ISBN 0-440-12329-1). Dell.

--Endless Night. 1982. pap. 2.75 (ISBN 0-671-44727-0). PB.

--The Four-Fifty from Paddington. LC 82-73250. (Greenway Edition). 1982. 9.95 (ISBN 0-396-08110-X). Dodd.

--Golden Ball & Other Stories. pap. 2.50 (ISBN 0-440-13272-X). Dell.

--The Labours of Hercules. (Greenway Edition). 1967. 8.95 (ISBN 0-396-05578-8). Dodd.

--The Man in the Brown Suit. 1981. pap. 2.50 (ISBN 0-440-15230-5). Dell.

--Mister Parker Pyne, Detective. 224p. 1981. pap. 2.50 (ISBN 0-440-15888-5). Dell.

--Murder in Retrospect. 192p. 1981. pap. 2.50 (ISBN 0-440-16030-8). Dell.

--The Mysterious Affair at Styles. 1980. pap. 8.95 o.p. (ISBN 0-8161-3105-8, Large Print Bks). G K Hall.

--N or M? 1981. pap. 2.50 (ISBN 0-440-16254-8). Dell.

--Partners in Crime. 1981. pap. 2.50 (ISBN 0-440-16848-1). Dell.

--Peril at End House. LC 82-73253. (Greenway Edition). 1982. 9.95 (ISBN 0-396-08111-8). Dodd.

--Poirot Investigates. 208p. 1982. pap. 2.50 (ISBN 0-553-14851-6). Bantam.

--The Postern of Fate. LC 73-14390. 244p. 1973. 6.95 o.p. (ISBN 0-396-06881-2). Dodd.

--The Regatta Mystery. 1983. pap. 2.95 (ISBN 0-440-17336-1). Dell.

--Sad Cypress. LC 82-73251. (Greenwood Edition). 1982. 9.95 (ISBN 0-396-08112-6). Dodd.

--Surprise Surprise. 1979. pap. 2.50 (ISBN 0-440-18389-8). Dell.

--There Is a Tide. 1977. pap. 2.50 (ISBN 0-440-18692-7). Dell.

--Thirteen Clues for Miss Marple. 1983. pap. 2.95 (ISBN 0-440-18755-9). Dell.

--The Underdog & Other Stories. 1978. pap. 2.50 (ISBN 0-440-19228-5). Dell.

--Witness for the Prosecution. 1983. pap. 2.95 (ISBN 0-440-19619-1). Dell.

Christie, Archibald. Samplers & Stitches. LC 73-151461. (Illus.). 1971. 6.95 (ISBN 0-8208-0339-1). Hearthside.

Christie, Bruce. Face to File Communication: A Psychological Approach to Information Systems. LC 80-41686. (Wiley Ser. in Information Processing). 320p. 1981. 35.75x (ISBN 0-471-27939-0, Pub. by Wiley Series in Information Processing). Wiley.

Christie, F. M. Graded German Comprehension. 1968. pap. text ed. 3.00x o.p. (ISBN 0-435-38160-1). Heinemann Ed.

Christie, George A., jt. auth. see Fisher, Richard B.

Christie, Ian R. Wars & Revolutions: Britain, 1760-1815. (New History of England Ser.). (Illus.). 384p. 1982. text ed. 22.50x (ISBN 0-674-94760-6). Harvard U Pr.

Christie, Ian R., jt. auth. see Brown, Lucy M.

Christie, Les. Dating & Mating: From a Christian View. Underwood, Jon, ed. (Illus.). 80p. (Orig.). 1983. pap. 2.95 (ISBN 0-87239-643-6, 39972). Standard Pub.

Christie, Linda & Curry, Jess, Jr. The ABC's of Microcomputers: A Computer Literacy Primer. (Illus.). 228p. 1983. 15.95 (ISBN 0-13-000620-3); pap. 7.95 (ISBN 0-13-000612-2). P-H.

Christie, M. J., jt. ed. see Venables, P. H.

Christie, Margaret J. & Mellett, Peter. Foundations of Psychosomatics. LC 80-42011. 432p. 1982. 35.95x (ISBN 0-471-27855-6, Pub. by Wiley-Interscience). Wiley.

Christie, Robert H., ed. Twenty-Two Authentic Banquets from India. 192p. 1975. pap. 2.50 o.p. (ISBN 0-486-23200-X). Dover.

Christie, W. W. Lipid Analysis: Isolation, Separation, Identification & Structural Analysis of Lipids. 2nd ed. LC 82-491. (Illus.). 220p. 1982. 50.00 (ISBN 0-08-023791-6); 18.00 (ISBN 0-08-023792-4). Pergamon.

Christie, Yves, et al. Art of the Christian World A.D. 200-1500: A Handbook of Styles & Forms. LC 81-85851. (Illus.). 500p. 1982. 35.00 (ISBN 0-8478-0426-7). Rizzoli Intl.

Christie-Murray, David. The Illustrated Children's Bible. LC 77-73187. (Illus.). 256p. 1982. 7.95 (ISBN 0-448-14293-7, G&D). Putnam Pub Group.

Christine, Lois. The Secret Life of Numbers. 208p. (Orig.). 1983. pap. 8.00 (ISBN 0-936878-06-1). Lorian Pr.

Christ-Janer, Albert. George Caleb Bingham. LC 74-2303. (Illus.). 134p. 1975. 40.00 o.p. (ISBN 0-8109-0220-6). Abrams.

Christman, Donald A. Successful Negotiating Strategies for School Boards & Administrators. 1978. Complete Kit. loose-leaf binding 85.00 o.p. (ISBN 0-07-079264-X, P&RB). McGraw.

Christman, Donald A., ed. see Holtje, Herbert F.

Christman, Elizabeth. Flesh & Spirit. 1980. pap. 2.25 o.p. (ISBN 0-380-52142-3, 52142). Avon.

Christman, Ernst H. Primer on Refraction. (Illus.). 128p. 1972. pap. 11.75x spiral (ISBN 0-398-02258-5). C C Thomas.

Christman, H. K., jt. auth. see Gish, Ira M.

Christman, Henry M., ed. see Warren, Earl.

Christman, L. C. Jerboa: Mysterious Visits by Uncle Odis. 1979. 6.95 o.p. (ISBN 0-533-04014-0). Vantage.

Christman, Ronald & Schibilla, Linda. Lessons on Doctrine: For Youth (Workbook) (Illus.). 64p. (Orig.). (gr. 6 up). 1982. pap. 3.50 (ISBN 0-87239-603-7, 3377). Standard Pub.

Christman, Russell F. & Gjessing, Egil, eds. Aquatic & Terrestrial Humic Materials. LC 82-71526. (Illus.). 525p. 1982. 39.95 (ISBN 0-250-40550-4). Ann Arbor Science.

Christner, Barbara, jt. auth. see Hershberger, Mary.

Christofalo, Vincent J., jt. ed. see Rothblat, George H.

Christoffel, Tom. Health & the Law: A Handbook for Health Professionals. 464p. 1982. text ed. 29.95 (ISBN 0-02-905370-6). Free Pr.

Christoffel von Grimmelshausen, Hans J. The Singular Life Story of Heedless Hopalong. Hiller, Robert L. & Osborne, John C., trs. 148p. 1981. 12.95 (ISBN 0-8143-1688-3). Wayne St U Pr.

Christofides, Nicos, et al, eds. Combinatorial Optimization. LC 78-11131. 1979. 74.95 (ISBN 0-471-99749-8, Pub. by Wiley-Interscience). Wiley.

Christol, Carl Q. The Modern International Law of Outer Space. (Pergamon Policy Studies on International Politics). (Illus.). 945p. 1982. 85.00 (ISBN 0-08-029367-0, K130). Pergamon.

Christopeit, N., jt. ed. see Kohlmann, M.

Christoph, James B. & Brown, Bernard E., eds. Cases in Comparative Politics. 3rd ed. 350p. 1976. pap. 10.95 (ISBN 0-316-13997-1). Little.

Christophe, Henri. Henry Christophe & Thomas Clarkson, a Correspondence. Griggs, Earl L. & Praton, Clifford H., eds. LC 68-23281. (Illus.). 1968. Repr. of 1952 ed. lib. bdg. 16.25x (ISBN 0-8371-0091-7). Greenwood.

Christopher, A. J. South Africa. (The World's Landscapes Ser.). (Illus.). 256p. (Orig.). 1982. pap. text ed. 15.95x (ISBN 0-582-49001-4). Longman.

Christopher, Barbara. Fruit & Vegetable Iron-On Transfer Patterns. (Dover Needlework Ser.). (Illus.). 1977. pap. 1.95 (ISBN 0-486-23556-4). Dover.

Christopher, Beth. Love for the Taking. (Finding Mr. Right Ser.). 208p. 1983. pap. 2.75 (ISBN 0-380-83311-5). Avon.

Christopher, Catherine. Complete Book of Doll Making & Collecting. 2nd rev. ed. LC 76-102176. 1970. pap. 4.95 (ISBN 0-486-22066-4). Dover.

--The Complete Book of Doll Making & Collecting. 2nd & rev. ed. (Illus.). 9.00 (ISBN 0-8446-0058-X). Peter Smith.

Christopher D. Smithers Foundation. A Company Program on Alcoholism. 1.00 o.p. (ISBN 0-686-92159-3, 9080). Hazelden.

--The Key Role of Labor in Employee Alcoholism Programs. 1.00 o.p. (ISBN 0-686-92161-5, 9120). Hazelden.

Christopher, Dean A. Manual Communication. 544p. 1976. pap. text ed. 24.95 (ISBN 0-8391-0811-7). Univ Park.

Christopher, Edward E. Behavioral Theory for Managers. 1977. pap. text ed. 10.75 (ISBN 0-8191-0352-7). U Pr of Amer.

Christopher, Edward E., jt. auth. see Christopher, Rachelle G.

Christopher, Frederick J. Basketry. (Illus.). 1952. pap. 2.25 (ISBN 0-486-20677-7). Dover.

Christopher, John. City of Gold & Lead. (gr. 5 up). 1970. pap. 2.75 (ISBN 0-02-042700-X, Collier). Macmillan.

--Introductory Technical Mathematics. (Illus.). 448p. 1982. 21.95 (ISBN 0-13-501635-5). P-H.

--Lotus Caves. LC 74-78074. (gr. 5-7). 1971. pap. 3.95 (ISBN 0-02-042690-9, Collier). Macmillan.

--New Found Land. LC 82-18354. 160p. (gr. 5-9). 1983. 9.95 (ISBN 0-525-44049-6, 0966-290). Dutton.

--The Sword of the Spirits. LC 74-20762. (gr. 5-9). 1976. pap. 2.75 (ISBN 0-02-042640-2, 04264, Collier). Macmillan.

--White Mountains. (gr. 5 up). 1970. pap. 3.95 (ISBN 0-02-042710-7, Collier). Macmillan.

--The World in Winter. (Alpha Bks.). 96p. (Orig.). 1979. pap. text ed. 2.95x (ISBN 0-19-424238-2). Oxford U Pr.

Christopher, John see Allen, W. S.

Christopher, Kenneth. Ten Catholics: Lives to Remember. (Nazareth Bks). 120p. 1983. pap. 3.95 (ISBN 0-86683-715-9). Winston Pr.

Christopher, Martin, jt. ed. see Wentworth, Felix.

Christopher, Martin, et al. Effective Marketing Management. 208p. 1981. text ed. 37.25x (ISBN 0-566-02237-0). Gower Pub Ltd.

Christopher, Matt. Catch That Pass! LC 77-77442. (Illus.). (gr. 4-6). 1969. 7.95 (ISBN 0-316-13932-7). Little.

--The Diamond Champs. (gr. 4-6). 1977. 6.95 (ISBN 0-316-13972-6). Little.

--Drag Strip Racer. 180p. (gr. 4-6). 1982. 8.95g (ISBN 0-316-13904-1). Little.

--Football Fugitive. (Illus.). 128p. (gr. 4-6). 1976. 6.95 (ISBN 0-316-13971-8). Little.

--Front Court Hex. (Illus.). 144p. (gr. 4-6). 1974. 6.95 (ISBN 0-316-13920-3). Little.

--Glue Fingers. (Illus.). 48p. (gr. 1-3). 1975. 6.95 (ISBN 0-316-13939-4). Little.

--Ice Magic. (Illus.). (gr. 4-6). 1973. 7.95 (ISBN 0-316-13958-0). Little.

--Jackrabbit Goalie. LC 78-5438. (Illus.). (gr. 1-3). 1978. 6.95 (ISBN 0-316-13975-0). Little.

--Jinx Glove. (Illus.). 48p. (gr. 1-3). 1974. 7.95 (ISBN 0-316-13965-3). Little.

--Johnny Long Legs. LC 78-113437. (Illus.). (gr. 4-6). 1970. 5.95 o.p. (ISBN 0-316-13948-3). Little.

--Kid Who Only Hit Homers. (gr. 4-6). 1972. 7.95 (ISBN 0-316-13918-1). Little.

--Look Who's Playing First Base. LC 74-129907. (Illus.). (gr. 4-6). 1971. 7.95 (ISBN 0-316-13933-5). Little.

--No Arm in Left Field. (Illus.). 160p. (gr. 4-6). 1974. 7.95 (ISBN 0-316-13964-5). Little.

--Power Play. (Illus.). (gr. 1-3). 1976. 6.95 (ISBN 0-316-14015-5). Little.

--Soccer Halfback. (Illus.). (gr. 4-6). 1978. 7.95 (ISBN 0-316-13946-7). Little.

--Stranded. (Illus.). 176p. (gr. 4-6). 1974. 6.95 (ISBN 0-316-13935-1). Little.

--The Submarine Pitch. (Illus.). (gr. 4-6). 1976. 6.95 o.p. (ISBN 0-316-13969-6). Little.

--The Team That Stopped Moving. (Illus.). 128p. (gr. 4-6). 1975. 5.95 o.p. (ISBN 0-316-13940-8). Little.

--Tight End. 128p. (gr. 3 up). 1981. 7.95 (ISBN 0-316-32672-0). Little.

--The Year Mom Won the Pennant. LC 68-11110. (Illus.). (gr. 4-6). 1968. 6.95 (ISBN 0-316-13954-8). Little.

Christopher, Maurine. Black Americans in Congress. rev. ed. LC 76-8943. (Illus.). 1976. 12.95i o.p. (ISBN 0-690-01102-4). T Y Crowell.

Christopher, Milbourne. ESP, Seers & Physics. LC 78-127607. (Illus.). 1970. 10.95i (ISBN 0-690-26815-7, TYC-T); pap. 5.95i o.p. (ISBN 0-690-01674-3, TYC-T). T Y Crowell.

--Houdini: A Pictorial Life. (Illus.). 1976. 16.30i (ISBN 0-690-01152-0). T Y Crowell.

--Milbourne Christopher's Magic Book. 1979. pap. 2.25 o.p. (ISBN 0-451-08823-9, E8823, Sig). NAL.

--Search for the Soul. LC 78-3298. 1979. 12.45 (ISBN 0-690-01760-X). T Y Crowell.

Christopher, Nicholas. On Tour with Rita. LC 81-17209. 1982. 11.95 (ISBN 0-394-51921-3); pap. 6.95 (ISBN 0-394-74998-7). Knopf.

Christopher, Rachelle G. & Christopher, Edward E. Job Enrichment: How Far Have We Come? LC 79-8992. 1979. pap. text ed. 8.50 (ISBN 0-8191-0857-X). U Pr of Amer.

Christopher, Robert. Japan Explained: The Mind of the New Goliath. 1983. price not set (ISBN 0-671-44947-8, Linden). S&S.

Christopher Street. Aphrodisiac. 320p. 1980. 12.95 o.s.i. (ISBN 0-698-11035-8, Coward). Putnam Pub Group.

Christopher Street Editors, ed. Aphrodisiac: Fiction from Christopher Street. 324p. 1982. pap. 6.95 (ISBN 0-399-50603-9, Perige). Putnam Pub Group.

Christophersen, Edward R. Little People. rev. ed. LC 79-112461. 1977. 10.50 (ISBN 0-89079-031-0); pap. 8.50 (ISBN 0-89079-032-9). H & H Ent.

Christopherson, Ragnar, tr. see Madsen, Stephan T.

Christopherson, Victor A., et al. Rehabilitation Nursing: Perspectives & Applications. (Illus.). 512p. (Orig.). 1973. 21.50 (ISBN 0-07-010815-3, HP). McGraw.

Christopherson, W. M., jt. auth. see Riotton, G.

Christopherson, William, jt. auth. see Riotton, C.

Christophorou, L. G. Atomic & Molecular Radiation Physics. LC 72-129159. (Wiley Monographs in Chemical Physics). 627p. 1971. 128.95x o.p. (ISBN 0-471-15629-9, Pub. by Wiley-Interscience). Wiley.

Christophorou, L. G., ed. Gaseous Dielectrics III: Proceedings of the Third International Symposium on Gaseous Dielectrics, Knoxville, Tennessee, USA, March 7-11, 1982. LC 82-9825. (Illus.). 600p. 1982. 95.00 (ISBN 0-08-029381-6, A110). Pergamon.

Christopoulos, George A. Prehistory & Protohistory to Eleven Hundred B.C. Bastias, John C., ed. Sherrard, Philip, tr. LC 75-18610. (History of the Hellenic World Ser.: Vol. 1). (Illus.). 420p. 1975. 43.50 (ISBN 0-271-01199-8). Pa St U Pr.

Christopoulos, George A. & Bastias, John C., eds. The Archaic Period, 1100-479 BC. Sherrard, Philip, tr. LC 75-27171. (History of the Hellenic World Ser.: Vol. 2). (Illus.). 620p. 1975. 47.50 (ISBN 0-271-01214-5). Pa St U Pr.

Christovich, et al. New Orleans Architecture, Vol. 5: Esplanade Ridge. LC 72-172272. (New Orleans Architecture Ser.). (Illus.). 1977. 22.50 (ISBN 0-88289-151-0). Pelican.

Christovich, Mary L., ed. see Wilson, Samuel, Jr. & Lemann, Bernard.

Christy, Albert. Numeral Philosophy. 82p. 4.00 (ISBN 0-686-38232-3). Sun Bks.

Christy, Arthur, ed. Asian Legacy & American Life, Essays. LC 68-9541. (Illus.). 1968. Repr. of 1945 ed. lib. bdg. 19.00x (ISBN 0-8371-0046-1, CHAL). Greenwood.

Christy, Craig. Uniformitarianism in Linguistics. (Studies in the History of Linguistics: 31). 200p. 1983. 20.00 (ISBN 90-272-4513-4). Benjamins North Am.

Christy, Dennis T. Essentials of Precalculus Mathematics. 2nd ed. 598p. 1981. text ed. 21.95 (ISBN 0-06-041303-4, HarpC); answers to even-numbered exercises avail. (ISBN 0-06-361192-9). Har-Row.

Christy, Francis T., Jr., et al, eds. Law of the Sea: Caracas & Beyond. LC 75-12540. (Law of the Sea Institute Ser). 448p. 1975. prof ref 25.00x (ISBN 0-88410-029-4). Ballinger Pub.

Christy, G. A. & Clendenin, J. C. Introduction to Investments. 8th ed. (Finance Ser.). 784p. 1982. 24.95x (ISBN 0-07-010833-1). McGraw.

--Introduction to Investments. 5th ed. (Illus.). 704p. 1973. text ed. 24.95 (ISBN 0-07-010825-0, C); instructors' manual 5.50 (ISBN 0-07-010826-9). McGraw.

Christy, G. A., et al. Introduction to Investments. 7th ed. (Finance Ser.). (Illus.). 1977. text ed. 24.95 (ISBN 0-07-010827-7, C); instructor's manual 15.95 (ISBN 0-07-010828-5). McGraw.

Christy, Howard C. The American Girl. LC 76-4778. 1976. lib. bdg. 39.50 (ISBN 0-306-70854-X); pap. 8.95 (ISBN 0-306-80042-X). Da Capo.

Christy, James. The Puppet Ministry. 1978. 2.50 (ISBN 0-8341-0532-2). Beacon Hill.

Christy, Joe. How to Buy a Used Airplane. 2nd ed. (Illus.). 1979. 6.95 (ISBN 0-8306-9799-3); pap. 3.95 o.p. (ISBN 0-8306-2272-1, 2272). TAB Bks.

--The Private Pilot's Handy Reference Guide. (Illus.). 224p. 1980. 14.95 (ISBN 0-8306-9663-6, 2325); pap. 9.95 (ISBN 0-8306-2325-6, 2325). TAB Bks.

Christy, Joe & Johnson, Clay. Your Pilot's License. rev. ed. (Illus.). 1978. 7.95 (ISBN 0-8306-9917-1); pap. 3.95 o.p. (ISBN 0-8306-2237-3, 2237). TAB Bks.

Christy, Joe & Ludvigsen, Karl. New MG Guide. 1958. pap. 3.95 (ISBN 0-8306-2020-6, 2020). TAB Bks.

Christy, Joe & Shamburger, Page. Curtiss Hawk Fighters. 1971. pap. 3.95 (ISBN 0-8306-2210-1, 2210). TAB Bks.

Christy, John & Friedman, David. Racing Cobras: A Definitive Illustrated History. (Illus.). 208p. 1982. 24.95 (ISBN 0-85045-457-3, Pub. by Osprey England). Motorbooks Intl.

Christy, Ron & Jones, Billy M. The Complete Information Bank for Entrepreneurs & Small Business Managers. LC 81-70750. (Illus.). 300p. 19.50 (ISBN 0-941958-00-0, Wichita Ctr Entrep SBM). WSU Hist Resources.

Christy, Van A. Expressive Singing: Song Anthology: Vol. II - High Voice, Medium Voice, Low Voice. 2nd ed. 240p. 1982. Vol. II high voice. write for info. wire coil (ISBN 0-697-03532-8); Vol. II medium voice. write for info. wire coil (ISBN 0-697-03531-X); Vol. II low voice. write for info. wire coil (ISBN 0-697-03530-1). Wm C Brown.

--Expressive Singing, Song Anthology Vols. 1 & 2, 3 Pts. Ea. 1966. plastic comb write for info. o.p. Vol.1, High Voice Ed. 194p (ISBN 0-697-03646-4). Vol.1, Med. Voice Ed. 194p (ISBN 0-697-03647-2). Vol. 1, Low Voice Ed. 194p (ISBN 0-697-03648-0). Vol.2, High Voice Ed. 202p (ISBN 0-697-03656-1). Vol.2, Med. Voice Ed. 202p (ISBN 0-697-03657-X). Vol.2, Low Voice Ed. 202p (ISBN 0-697-03658-8). Wm C Brown.

Chronic, Halka. Pages of Stone - The Geologic Origins of Our National Parks & Monuments Vol. I: The Rocky Mountains & the Northwest. (Illus.). 225p. (Orig.). 1983. write for info o.p. (ISBN 0-87108-636-0); pap. 14.95 o.p. (ISBN 0-87108-608-5). Pruett.

--Roadside Geology of Arizona. 320p. 1983. pap. 9.95 (ISBN 0-87842-147-5). Mountain Pr.

--Roadside Geology of Colorado: Roadside Geology Ser. LC 79-11148. (Illus.). 322p. 1980. pap. 9.95 (ISBN 0-87842-105-X). Mountain Pr.

Chronicle Guidance Publications. Chronicle Guide for Transfers. rev. ed. 170p. 1982. pap. 10.25 (ISBN 0-912578-50-5). Chron Guide.

--Chronicle Student Aid Annual, 1982. rev. ed. 395p. 1982. pap. 14.50 (ISBN 0-912578-04-1). Chron Guide.

Chronicle Guidance Publications, Inc. Chronicle Four-Year College Databook, 1982. LC 79-644820. 1982. pap. 14.50 (ISBN 0-912578-42-4). Chron Guide.

--Chronicle Two-Year College Databook, 1982. LC 79-644821. 1982. pap. 12.75 (ISBN 0-912578-43-2). Chron Guide.

--Chronicle Vocational School Manual. Downes, Paul, ed. (Orig.). 1982. pap. 12.25 (ISBN 0-912578-51-3). Chron Guide.

Chronicle Guidance Research Staff. Chronicle Career Index. rev. ed. 150p. 1982. pap. 11.25 (ISBN 0-912578-52-1). Chron Guide.

Chronis, Valerie. Valerie. pap. 3.00 (ISBN 0-686-81814-8). Anhinga Pr.

Chroust & Muhlbacher, eds. Firmware Microprogramming & Restructurable Hardware. 1980. 38.50 (ISBN 0-444-86056-8). Elsevier.

Chroust, Anton-Hermann. Aristotle, New Light on His Life & Some of His Lost Works, 2 vols. Incl. Vol. 1. Some Novel Interpretations of the Man & His Life. 448p (ISBN 0-268-00517-6); Vol. 2. Observations on Some of Aristotle's Lost Works. 495p (ISBN 0-268-00518-4). LC 73-8892. 1973. Set. text ed. 60.00 (ISBN 0-268-00522-2); text ed. 30.00 ea. U of Notre Dame Pr.

Chrysander, F. Melius, ed. see Handel, George.

Chrysler Learning, Inc. Weldtech Series in Welding: Basic Gas Metal-Arc Welding. (Illus.). 128p. 1983. pap. text ed. 9.95 (ISBN 0-13-948075-7). P-H.

--Weldtech Series in Welding: Basic Shielded Metal-Arc Welding. 128p. 1983. pap. 9.95 (ISBN 0-13-948083-8). P-H.

--Weldtech Series in Welding: Oxyacetylene Welding, Cutting, & Brazing. (Illus.). 80p. 1983. pap. 9.95 (ISBN 0-13-948091-9). P-H.

Chrysostom, John. The Divine Liturgy of Our Father Among the Saints, John Chrysostom, Archbishop of Constantinople. Holy Transfiguration Monastery, tr. from Greek. 94p. 1982. plastic covers, comb. binding 10.00x (ISBN 0-913026-54-9). St Nectarios.

Chrysostomos, Archimandrite. Orthodoxy & Papism. Williams, Theodore M., ed. 70p. 1982. pap. 4.00 (ISBN 0-911165-00-2). Ctr Trad Orthodox.

Chrysovitsiotis, I. Greek-English, English Greek Commercial, Economics & Related Fields Technical Dictionary. 2nd rev ed. 45.00 (ISBN 0-685-79112-2). Heinman.

Chryssostomidis, Chryssostomos & Connor, Jerome J., eds. Behaviour of Off-Shore Structures: Proceedings of the Third International Conference, 2 Vols. LC 82-11749. 1622p. 1982. Set. text ed. 149.00 (ISBN 0-89116-343-3). Hemisphere Pub.

Chrystal, George. Textbook of Algebra, 2 Vols. 7th ed. LC 64-21987. (gr. 9-12). text ed. 15.95 ea. (ISBN 0-8284-0084-9); pap. text ed. 4.95 ea. o.p. (ISBN 0-8284-0181-0). Chelsea Pub.

Chrystie, Thomas L. & Fabozzi, Frank J., eds. Left Hand Financing: An Emerging Field of Techniques in Corporate Finance. LC 82-72366. 1982. 27.50 (ISBN 0-87094-342-1). Dow Jones-Irwin.

Chrzanowski, Gerald. Interpersonal Approach to Psychoanalysis: Contemporary View of Harry Stack Sullivan. LC 77-1951. 242p. 1977. 18.95x o.s.i. (ISBN 0-470-99071-6). Halsted Pr.

Chrzanowski, Gerard, jt. ed. see Arietti, Silvano.

Chu, Alfred E., jt. auth. see Triebel, Walter A.

Chu, Charles. Ch'i Pai-Shih: His Life & Works. 4.75 (ISBN 0-686-09948-6); tapes avail. (ISBN 0-686-09949-4). Far Eastern Pubns.

Chu, Don-chean. Chairman Mao: Education of the Proletariat. LC 78-61107. 478p. 1980. 15.00 (ISBN 0-8022-2236-6). Inst Sino-Amer.

--Patterns of Education for the Developing Nations: Tao's Work in China 1917-1946. LC 66-5481. xi, 177p. 1966. 2.00; pap. 1.00. Inst Sino-Amer.

--Philosophic Foundations of American Education. LC 70-150045. 392p. 1971. pap. 7.00 (ISBN 0-686-35889-9). Inst Sino-Amer.

Chu, Donald. Dimensions of Sport Studies. LC 81-16425. 299p. 1982. text ed. 18.95 (ISBN 0-471-08576-6). Wiley.

Chu, Franklin D. & Trotter, Sharland. The Madness Establishment: Ralph Nader's Study Group Report on the National Institute of Mental Health. LC 73-83701. 232p. 1974. 12.95 (ISBN 0-670-44734-X, Grossman). Viking Pr.

Chu, Godwin. Radical Change Through Communication in Mao's China. LC 77-3874. 1977. text ed. 17.50x (ISBN 0-8248-0515-1, Eastwest Ctr). UH Pr.

Chu, Godwin, et al. Communication & Development in China. (Communication Monographs: No. 1). 1977. pap. text ed. 2.00x o.p. (ISBN 0-8248-0548-8). UH Pr.

Chu, Godwin, et al, eds. Communication for Group Transformation in Development. (Communications Monographs: No. 2). 1977. pap. text ed. 5.00x o.p. (ISBN 0-8248-0549-6). UH Pr.

Chu, Godwin C., ed. Popular Media in China: Shaping New Cultural Patterns. LC 78-13282. 1978. text ed. 14.00x (ISBN 0-8248-0622-0, Eastwest Ctr). UH Pr.

Chu, Godwin C. & Hsu, Francis L., eds. Moving a Mountain: Cultural Change in China. LC 79-22037. (Illus.). 1979. text ed. 20.00x (ISBN 0-8248-0667-0, Eastwest Ctr). UH Pr.

Chu, Godwin C., et al, eds. Institutional Exploration in Communication Technology. (Communications Monographs: No. 4). 1978. pap. text ed. 4.00x (ISBN 0-8248-0664-6, Eastwest Ctr). UH Pr.

Chu, Grace, ed. see Namba, Ayako.

Chu, Grace Z. Pleasures of Chinese Cooking. 1962. 9.95 o.p. (ISBN 0-671-58010-8); pap. 3.95 (ISBN 0-671-22181-7). S&S.

Chu, H. F. How to Know the Immature Insects. (Pictured Key Nature Ser.). 240p. 1949. wire coil write for info. (ISBN 0-697-04806-3); Wm C Brown.

Chu, John W. Selections from the New Testament in Chinese. 4.25 (ISBN 0-686-09969-9). Far Eastern Pubns.

Chu, Michael, ed. The New China: A Catholic Response. LC 76-56958. 180p. 1977. pap. 4.95 o.p. (ISBN 0-8091-2004-6). Paulist Pr.

Chu, Show-Chih R. Chinese Grammar & English Grammar: A Comparative Study. 417p. 1982. 12.95 (ISBN 0-686-37976-4); pap. 10.95 (ISBN 0-686-37977-2). Inst Sino-Amer.

Chu, Show-chih Rai. Chinese for the English-Speaking Student: An Approach Through English Grammar, Vol. 1. LC 72-87136. 330p. 1973. 11.95 (ISBN 0-686-37783-4); pap. 9.95 (ISBN 0-686-37784-2); tapes 14.95 (ISBN 0-686-37785-0). Inst Sino-Amer.

--Chinese for the English-Speaking Student: An Approach Through English Gammar, Vol. 2. 424p. 1976. 12.95; pap. 10.95; tapes 19.95. Inst Sino-Amer.

Chu, Yaohan. Digital Computer Design Fundamentals. 1962. 34.50 (ISBN 0-07-010800-5, C). McGraw.

--Software Blueprint & Examples. LC 81-48268. (Computer Science Ser.). (Illus.). 544p. 1982. 39.95x (ISBN 0-669-05329-5). Lexington Bks.

Chua, J. E. & Ling, S. C. The Management of Business. 2nd ed. 1982. 10.00x (ISBN 0-07-099026-3). McGraw.

Chua, L. & Lin, P. Computer-Aided Analysis of Electronic Circuits: Algorithms & Computational Techniques. 1975. 36.95 (ISBN 0-13-165415-2). P-H.

Chua, Leon O. Introduction to Nonlinear Network Theory, 3 vols. LC 78-9734. 1978. Repr. of 1969 ed. Vol. 1, Foundations Of Nonlinear Network Theory, 315 P. lib. bdg. 19.50 (ISBN 0-88275-588-9); Vol. 2, Resistive Nonlinear Networks, 480 P. lib. bdg. 22.50 (ISBN 0-88275-865-9); Vol. 3, Dynamic Nonlinear Networks, 438 P. lib. bdg. 24.00 (ISBN 0-88275-866-7); Set. lib. bdg. 55.00 (ISBN 0-686-86256-2). Krieger.

Chuang Hsin-Cheng. Evening Chats at Yenshan; or, the Case of Teng T'o. (Current Chinese Language Project: No. 14). 46p. 1970. pap. 2.00x (ISBN 0-912966-01-7). IEAS.

Chuang, Wei. The Song-Poetry of Wei Chuang (836-910 A.D.) Wixted, John T., tr. from Chinese. & intro. by. (Occasional Paper; Arizona State Univ., Center for Asian Studies: No. 12). (Illus.). iii, 144p. 1979. pap. text ed. 4.00 (ISBN 0-939252-08-2). ASU Ctr Asian.

Chuang, Yao H. Fuentes de Informacion sobre el Mercado Internacional de Fertilizantes. Ralph McElroy Company, tr. (Reference Manual Ser.: RS-2). 47p. (Orig., Span.). 1980. pap. text ed. 4.00 (ISBN 0-88090-031-8). Intl Fertilizer.

Ch'Uan-K'Ai Leung, Kenneth, jt. auth. see Klein, Jeffery A.

Chuaqui, R. B. Axiomatic Set Theory of Classes: Impredicative Theories of Classes. (North-Holland Mathematics Studies Ser.: Vol. 51). 1981. 59.75 (ISBN 0-686-81236-0). Elsevier.

Chubak, Sadeq. Sadeq Chubak: An Anthology. Bagley, F. R., ed. LC 81-17970. (Modern Persian Literature Ser.). 1983. 35.00x (ISBN 0-88206-048-1). Caravan Bks.

Chubb, Hilkka. Learning Today for Tomorrow: Education in the Environment. 1979. tchrs' materials 5.25 (ISBN 0-686-74264-8). U Pr of Amer.

Chubb, J. Faith Possesses Understanding: A Suggestion for a New Direction in Rational Theology. 200p. 1982. text ed. 14.00x (ISBN 0-391-02756-5, Pub. by Concept India). Humanities.

Chubb, John E. Interest Groups & the Bureaucracy: The Politics of Energy. LC 82-60106. (Illus.). 336p. 1983. 29.50x (ISBN 0-8047-1158-5). Stanford U Pr.

Chubb, Judith. Patronage, Power & Poverty in Southern Italy: A Tale of Two Cities. LC 82-1325. (Cambridge Studies in Modern Political Economies). (Illus.). 320p. 1983. 39.50 (ISBN 0-521-23637-1). Cambridge U Pr.

Chubb, Michael. One Third of Our Time? An Introduction to Recreation, Behavior & Resources. LC 80-25131. 742p. 1981. text ed. 29.95x (ISBN 0-471-15637-X). Wiley.

Chubin, Shahram, ed. Domestic Political Factors. LC 81-572. (Security in the Persian Gulf Ser.: Vol. 1). 104p. 1981. pap. text ed. 10.00x (ISBN 0-86598-044-6). Allanheld.

Chu-Chi, W. English-Chinese Dictionary of Physical Terms. 218p. 1973. Leatherette 25.00 (ISBN 0-686-92350-2, M-9258). French & Eur.

Chudacoff, Edward, jt. auth. see Berry, Wallace.

Chudacoff, Howard P. The Evolution of American Urban Society. 2nd ed. (Illus.). 256p. 1981. pap. text ed. 14.95 (ISBN 0-13-293605-4). P-H.

Chudley. Construction Technology 2 Checkbook. Date not set. pap. text ed. 8.95. Butterworth.

--Construction Technology 3 Checkbook. 1982. text ed. write for info. (ISBN 0-408-00686-2); pap. text ed. 9.95 (ISBN 0-408-00604-8). Butterworth.

--Construction Technology 4 Checkbook. 1983. text ed. write for info.; pap. text ed. write for info. (ISBN 0-408-00605-6). Butterworth.

Chudy, Harry T. The Complete Guide to Automotive Refinishing. (Illus.). 464p. 1982. reference 19.95 (ISBN 0-13-160440-6). P-H.

Chue, S. H. Thermodynamics: A Rigorous Postulatory Approach. LC 76-44878. 1978. 50.95 o.p. (ISBN 0-471-99455-3, Pub. by Wiley-Interscience); pap. 17.50 o.p. (ISBN 0-471-99461-8). Wiley.

Chugh, Y. P., intro. by. State-of-the-Art of Ground Control in Longwall Mining & Mining Subsidence. LC 82-71991. (Illus.). 271p. (Orig.). 1982. pap. text ed. 38.00x (ISBN 0-89520-400-2, 400-2). Soc Mining Eng.

Chui, Charles K., jt. auth. see Allen, G. D.

Chuinard, Eldon G. Only One Man Died: The Medical Aspects of the Lewis & Clark Expedition. 2nd ed. LC 78-73417. (Western Frontiermen Ser.: No. 19). (Illus.). 444p. 1980. 29.00 o.p. (ISBN 0-87062-128-9). A H Clark.

Chujoy, Anatole & Manchester, P. W. Dance Encyclopedia. 1967. 24.95 o.p. (ISBN 0-671-22586-3). S&S.

--The Dance Encyclopedia. (Illus.). 1978. pap. 8.95 o.p. (ISBN 0-671-24027-7, Touchstone Bks). S&S.

Chukayne, Edward C., jt. auth. see Bush, Lee O.

Chu-Kia, Wang. Introductory Structural Analysis with Matrix Methods. LC 72-667. 240p. 1973. ref. ed. 33.95 (ISBN 0-13-501650-9). P-H.

Chu-Kia Wang & Salmon, Charles G. Introductory Structural Analysis. (Illus.). 656p. 1983. 29.95 (ISBN 0-13-501569-3). P-H.

Chukovsky, K. Cock-the-Roach. 22p. 1981. pap. 1.60 (ISBN 0-8285-2217-0, Pub. by Progress Pubs USSR). Imported Pubns.

Chukovsky, Kornei. Alexander Blok as Man & Poet. Burgin, Diana, ed. O'Connor, Katherine, tr. LC 82-1809. 1982. 17.50 (ISBN 0-88233-485-9). Ardis Pubs.

--The Telephone. Smith, William J., tr. from Russian. LC 75-32921. (Illus.). 48p. (gr. 4-6). 1977. 7.95 o.s.i. (ISBN 0-440-08532-2, Sey Lawr); PLB 7.45 o.s.i. (ISBN 0-440-06040-0). Delacorte.

Chukumba, Stephen U. The Big Powers Against Ethiopia. 1977. pap. text ed. 18.50 (ISBN 0-8191-0230-X). U Pr of Amer.

Chumbley, Lee C. Ophthalmology in Internal Medicine. (Illus.). 288p. 1981. 32.50 (ISBN 0-7216-2578-9). Saunders.

Chun, Bong D., et al. Traditional Korean Legal Attitudes. (Korean Research Monographs: No. 2). 101p. 1980. pap. 8.00x (ISBN 0-912966-30-0). IEAS.

Chun, Ki-Taek, et al. Measures for Psychological Assessment: A Guide to 3,000 Original Sources & Their Applications. LC 74-620127. 688p. 1975. 30.00x (ISBN 0-87944-168-2). Inst Soc Res.

Chun, Patrick. Cardiopulmonary Technology Examination Review Book, Vol. 1. 2nd ed. 1980. pap. 15.50 (ISBN 0-87488-473-X). Med Exam.

Chun, Richard. Advancing in Tae Kwon Do. LC 82-47519. (Illus.). 352p. 1983. 34.62i (ISBN 0-06-015029-7, HarpT). Har-Row.

--Moo Duk Kwan, Vol. II. LC 81-186107. (Illus.). 220p. (Orig.). 1983. pap. 8.95 (ISBN 0-89750-085-7, 422). Ohara Pubns.

--Tae Kwon-Do. 39.95 (ISBN 0-685-70709-1). Wehman.

Chung, Chong-Wha, ed. Meetings & Farewells: Modern Korean Studies. LC 80-506. 1981. 25.00 (ISBN 0-312-52855-8). St Martin.

Chung, David. Anesthesia in Patients with Ischemic Heart Disease. (Current Topics in Anesthesia Ser.: No. 6). 192p. 1982. text ed. 32.50 (ISBN 0-7131-4407-6). E Arnold.

Chung, Edward K. Cardiac Arrhythmias: Self-Assessment, Vol. II. (Illus.). 462p. 1982. pap. 35.00 (ISBN 0-683-01574-5). Williams & Wilkins.

--Cardiac Arrhythmias: Self-Assessment. (Illus.). 465p. 1977. pap. text ed. 27.00 o.p. (ISBN 0-683-01573-7). Williams & Wilkins.

--Principles of Cardiac Arrhythmias. 3rd ed. 824p. 1982. lib. bdg. 75.00 (ISBN 0-683-01567-2). Williams & Wilkins.

--Principles of Cardiac Arrythmias. 2nd ed. 1977. 54.00 o.p. (ISBN 0-683-01568-0). Williams & Wilkins.

--Quick Reference to Cardiovascular Diseases. 2nd ed. (Illus.). 672p. 1982. text ed. 35.00 (ISBN 0-397-50482-9, Lippincott Medical). Lippincott.

Chung, Edward K. & Chung, Lisa S. Introduction to Clinical Cardiology. (Karger Continuing Education Ser.: Vol. 4). (Illus.). 502p. 1983. 59.00 (ISBN 3-8055-2997-X). S Karger.

Chung, J. S. Offshore Mechanics-Artic Engineering-Deepsea Systems Symposium, First: Proceedings, 2 Vols, Vol. 1. 1982. 45.00 (I00148). ASME.

Chung, J. S., ed. Offshore Mechanics-Artic Engineering-Deepsea Systems Symposium, First: Proceedings, 2 Vols, Vol. 2. 289p. 1982. 45.00 (I00148). ASME.

Chung, Kae H., ed. Academy of Management 1982: Proceedings. 12.00 (ISBN 0-686-97952-4). Acad of Mgmt.

Chung, Kai L. A Course in Probability Theory. 2nd ed. (Probability & Mathematical Statistics: A Series of Monographs & Textbooks). 1974. 20.00 (ISBN 0-12-174650-X). Acad Pr.

Chung, Lisa S., jt. auth. see Chung, Edward K.

Chung, T. J. Finite Element Analysis in Fluid Dynamics. 1978. text ed. 48.00 o.p. (ISBN 0-07-010830-7, C). McGraw.

Chung, William K., jt. auth. see Denison, Edward F.

Chung-Yuan, Chang. Original Teachings of Cha'an Buddhism. pap. 9.95 (ISBN 0-394-62417-3, V-333, Vin). Random.

Chunn, Jay, II & Dunston, Patricia, eds. Mental Health & People of Color: Curriculum Development & Change. (Illus.). 688p. 1983. 24.95 (ISBN 0-88258-097-3). Howard U Pr.

Chupack, Henry. Roger Williams. (United States Authors Ser.). 13.95 (ISBN 0-8057-0808-1, Twayne). G K Hall.

Chupco, Lee & Coachman, Ward. Creek (Muscogee) New Testament Concordance. 167p. 1982. pap. 15.00 spiral bdg. (ISBN 0-940392-10-0). Indian U Pr.

Chupp, C. & Sherf, A. F. Vegetable Diseases & Their Control. (Illus.). 1960. 32.50x (ISBN 0-471-06807-1, Pub. by Wiley-Interscience). Wiley.

Church Administration Department. Illustrating the Gospel of Matthew. LC 81-68044. 1982. pap. 4.95 (ISBN 0-686-82872-0). Broadman.

Church, Albert. Taxation of Nonrenewable Resources. LC 80-8784. (Illus.). 352p. 1981. 32.95x (ISBN 0-669-04367-2). Lexington Bks.

Church, Albert M. Conflicts Over Resource Ownership: The Use of Public Policy by Private Interests. LC 82-47942. (Lincoln Institute of Land Policy Bk.). 256p. 1982. 24.95x (ISBN 0-669-05712-6). Lexington Bks.

Church, Alfred J. Lucius, Adventures of a Roman Boy. LC 60-16706. (gr. 7-11). 8.00x (ISBN 0-8196-0108-X). Biblo.

--Roman Life in the Days of Cicero. LC 61-24994. (gr. 7-11). 12.00x (ISBN 0-8196-0105-5). Biblo.

Church, Alonzo. Calculi of Lambda Conversion. 1941. pap. 8.00 o.s.i. (ISBN 0-527-02722-7). Kraus Repr.

--Introduction to Mathematical Logic, Pt. 1. 1944. pap. 13.00 (ISBN 0-527-02729-4). Kraus Repr.

Church, Carol B. Billie Jean King: Queen of the Courts. Bender, David L. & Mc Cuen, Gary E., eds. (Focus on Famous Women Ser). (Illus.). (gr. 3-9). 1976. 8.95 (ISBN 0-912616-41-5); read-along cassette 9.95 (ISBN 0-89908-240-8). Greenhaven.

--Carol Burnett: Star of Comedy. Bender, David L. & Mc Cuen, Gary E., eds. (Focus on Famous Women Ser). (Illus.). (gr. 3-9). 1976. 8.95 (ISBN 0-912616-42-3); read-along cassette 9.95 (ISBN 0-89908-241-6). Greenhaven.

--Dorothy Day: Friend of the Poor. Bender, David L. & Mc Cuen, Gary E., eds. (Focus on Famous Women Ser). (Illus.). (gr. 3-9). 1976. 8.95 (ISBN 0-912616-45-8); read-along cassette 9.95 (ISBN 0-89908-244-0). Greenhaven.

--Indira Gandhi: Rose of India. Bender, David L. & McCuen, Gary E., eds. (Focus on Famous Women Ser). (gr. 3-9). 1976. 8.95 (ISBN 0-912616-43-1); read-along cassette 9.95 (ISBN 0-89908-242-4). Greenhaven.

--Margaret Mead: Student of the Global Village. Bender, David L. & McCuen, Gary E., eds. (Focus on Famous Women Ser). (Illus.). (gr. 3-9). 1976. 8.95 (ISBN 0-912616-46-6); read-along cassette 9.95 (ISBN 0-89908-245-9). Greenhaven.

--Rose Kennedy: No Time for Tears. Bender, David L. & Mc Cuen, Gary E., eds. (Focus on Famous Women Ser.). (Illus.). (gr. 3-9). 1976. 8.95 (ISBN 0-912616-44-X); read-along cassette 9.95 (ISBN 0-89908-243-2). Greenhaven.

Church, David B. & Pond, Wilson G. Basic Animal Nutrition & Feeding. 2nd ed. 300p. 1982. text ed. 21.95x o.p. (ISBN 0-471-86169-3). Wiley.

Church, F. J., tr. see Plato.

Church, Frederic C., Jr. Avoiding Surprises: Eight Steps to an Efficient, Low-Cost Corporate Risk Management & Insurance Program. LC 81-71318. (Illus.). 286p. 1982. 17.95 (ISBN 0-9607398-0-7). Boston Risk Magmt.

Church, Gene. No Man's Blood. LC 82-83577. 379p. 1983. pap. 7.95 (ISBN 0-86666-155-7). GWP.

Church, Gene & Carnes, Conrad D. Brainwash. LC 82-82415. (Illus.). 164p. 1983. pap. 5.95 (ISBN 0-86666-129-8). GWP.

Church, Helen N., jt. auth. see Pennington, Jean.

Church, Horace K. Excavation Handbook. 1981. 55.00 (ISBN 0-07-010840-4). McGraw.

Church, J. M., jt. auth. see Shumbs, H. R.

Church, James C. Practical Plumbing Design Guide. LC 78-18823. (Illus.). 1979. 30.95 (ISBN 0-07-010832-3, P&RB). McGraw.

Church, Joseph. America the Possible: Why & How the Constitution Should Be Re-Written. 280p. 1982. 14.95 (ISBN 0-02-525580-0). Macmillan.

Church, Joseph, jt. auth. see Stone, L. Joseph.

Church, Margaret. Structure & Theme: Don Quixote to James Joyce. 300p. 1983. 16.00 (ISBN 0-8142-0348-5). Ohio St U Pr.

Church of England. Certaine Sermons or Homilies Appointed to Be Read in the Churches in the Time of Elizabeth 1st, 1547-1571, 2 vols. in 1. LC 68-17016. 1968. Repr. of 1623 ed. 42.00x (ISBN 0-8201-1008-6). Schol Facsimiles.

Church of Scotland - General Assembly - Committee On Public Worship And Aids To Devotion. Prayers for the Christian Year. 2nd ed. 1952. 8.50x (ISBN 0-19-145602-0). Oxford U Pr.

Church, Olive. Shadow Mountain Lodge, Typing Practice Set. (Illus.). (gr. 9-12). 1977. pap. 7.96 (ISBN 0-07-010835-8, G); tchr's manual & key 4.95 (ISBN 0-07-010836-6). McGraw.

Church, Peggy P. House at Otowi Bridge: The Story of Edith Warner & Los Alamos. LC 60-13408. (Zia Bks.). (Illus.). 149p. 1973. pap. 4.95 (ISBN 0-8263-0281-5). U of NM Pr.

--Peggy Pond Church, New & Selected Poems. 2nd ed. Trusky, Tom, ed. LC 75-29917. (Modern & Contemporary Western Poets). 80p. (Orig.). 1976. pap. 3.00 (ISBN 0-916272-02-8). Ahsahta Pr.

Church, R. J. Some Geographical Aspects of Western African Development. LC 72-634680. (Papers in International Studies: Africa: No. 10). (Illus.). 1971. pap. 3.50x (ISBN 0-89680-043-1, Ohio U Ctr Intl). Ohio U Pr.

Church, R. J., et al. Africa & the Islands. 4th ed. LC 77-3459. 542p. 1977. pap. text ed. 18.95x o.s.i. (ISBN 0-470-99085-6). Halsted Pr.

Church, Randolph W. Appellate Litigation: A Virginia Law Practice System. 250p. 1982. looseleaf with forms 75.00 (ISBN 0-87215-510-2). Michie-Bobbs.

Church, Richard W. Spencer. LC 67-23879. 1968. Repr. of 1906 ed. 37.00x (ISBN 0-8103-3057-1). Gale.

Church, Robert. Turtles. (Illus., Orig.). pap. 2.50 o.p. (ISBN 0-87666-226-2, M515). TFH Pubns.

Church, Ruth E. Entertaining with Wine. LC 76-3625. (Illus.). 1979. 16.95 (ISBN 0-528-81019-7); pap. 7.95 o.p. (ISBN 0-528-88014-4). Rand.

--Wines of the Midwest. LC 82-75828. (Illus.). vii, 248p. 1982. cloth 21.95 (ISBN 0-8040-0779-9); pap. 9.95 (ISBN 0-8040-0426-9). Swallow.

Church, Thomas, et al. Gardens Are for People. 2nd ed. (Illus.). 256p. 1983. 34.95 (ISBN 0-07-010844-7, P&RB). McGraw.

Church, Vivian. Colors Around Me. LC 75-154209. (Illus.). 28p. (gr. k-3). 1971. 7.95 (ISBN 0-910030-15-4). Afro Am.

Church, William F., ed. Greatness of Louis Fourteenth. 2nd ed. (Problems in European Civilization Ser.). 1972. pap. text ed. 5.95 (ISBN 0-669-82016-4). Heath.

--Influence of the Enlightenment on the French Revolution. 2nd ed. (Problems in European Civilization Ser). 1974. pap. text ed. 5.95 (ISBN 0-669-82024-5). Heath.

Churches Alive Inc. Esteeming. LC 79-52130. (Love One Another Bible Study). (Illus.). 1979. wkbk. 2.00 (ISBN 0-934396-03-5). Churches Alive.

Churches Alive Staff. God's Family Bible Study. LC 82-72563. 70p. 1983. pap. text ed. write for info. (ISBN 0-934396-34-5). Churches Alive.

--God's Family Leader's Guide. LC 82-72564. 50p. 1983. pap. text ed. write for info. (ISBN 0-934396-35-3). Churches Alive.

--Helping People to Solo. 66p. 1977. pap. text ed. 2.25 o.p. (ISBN 0-934396-27-2). Churches Alive.

Churchill, Allen. Eyewitness: Hitler. 1979. 15.00 o.s.i. (ISBN 0-8027-0625-8). Walker & Co.

--Park Row. LC 73-14193. 344p. 1973. Repr. of 1958 ed. lib. bdg. 18.75x (ISBN 0-8371-7146-6, CHPR). Greenwood.

Churchill, Caryl. Traps, Traps. 52p. (Orig.). 1981. pap. 4.95 (ISBN 0-686-91741-3). Pluto Pr.

Churchill, Charles. Poetical Works. Grant, Douglas, ed. 1956. 54.00x (ISBN 0-19-811316-1). Oxford U Pr.

Churchill College, Cambridge England. Human Factors in Telecommunications, International Symposium, 8th. 1977. 75.00 (ISBN 0-686-37980-2). Info Gatekeepers.

Churchill, David. It, Us & the Others. LC 78-19827. (gr. 5 up). 1979. 5.95 o.p. (ISBN 0-06-021268-3, HarpJ); PLB 6.89 o.p. (ISBN 0-06-021269-1). Har-Row.

Churchill, E. L., jt. auth. see Byrne, L. S.

Churchill, Gilbert A. Marketing Research. 3rd ed. 704p. 1983. text ed. 26.95 (ISBN 0-03-060608-X). Dryden Pr.

Churchill, Lindsey. Questioning Strategies in Sociolinguistics. LC 78-11032. 1978. pap. text ed. 8.95 o.p. (ISBN 0-88377-117-9). Newbury Hse.

Churchill, Neil C., et al. Computer-Based Information Systems for Management. 166p. 14.95 (ISBN 0-86641-048-1, 6947). Natl Assn Accts.

Churchill, Peter. Horse Racing. (Illus.). 168p. 1981. 12.95 o.p. (ISBN 0-7137-1016-0); pap. 6.95 o.p. (ISBN 0-7137-1115-9). Sterling.

Churchill, Richard. I Bet I Can-I Bet You Can't. LC 82-50551. (Illus.). 128p. (gr. 3 up). 1982. 7.95 (ISBN 0-8069-4664-4); lib. bdg. 9.99 (ISBN 0-8069-4665-2). Sterling.

Churchill, Robin & Nordquist, Myron, eds. New Directions in the Law of the Sea: Documents, 11 vols. LC 72-12713. 1975. Vol. 3. lib. bdg. 35.00 (ISBN 0-379-00496-8); Vols. 1, 2, & 4-11. lib. bdg. 45.00 ea. (ISBN 0-379-00029-6). Oceana.

Churchill, Ruel V. Operational Mathematics. 3rd ed. 1971. text ed. 32.00 (ISBN 0-07-010870-6, C). McGraw.

Churchill, Ruel V. & Brown, James W. Complex Variables & Applications. 3rd ed. (Illus.). 352p. 1974. text ed. 31.00 (ISBN 0-07-010855-2, C). McGraw.

--Fourier Series & Boundary Value Problems. 3rd ed. 1978. text ed. 32.00 (ISBN 0-07-010843-9, C). McGraw.

Churchill, Sarah. Keep on Dancing. (Illus.). 1981. 14.95 (ISBN 0-698-11022-6, Coward). Putnam Pub Group.

Churchill, Stacy. The Peruvian Model of Innovation: The Reform of Basic Education. (Experiments & Innovations in Education Ser: No. 22). 54p. 1977. pap. 2.75 o.p. (ISBN 92-3-101385-8, U447, UNESCO). Unipub.

Churchill, T., tr. see Herder, Johann G.

Churchill, Ward, ed. Marxism & Native Americans. 250p. Date not set. 20.00 (ISBN 0-89608-178-8); pap. 7.50 (ISBN 0-89608-177-X). South End Pr.

Churchill, William. Weather Words of Polynesia. LC 8-11468. (AAA. M.: No. 7). 1907. pap. 12.00 (ISBN 0-527-00506-1). Kraus Repr.

Churchill, Winston S. Defending the West. 1981. 40.00x (ISBN 0-85117-210-5, Pub. by M Temple Smith). State Mutual Bk.

Churchland, P. M. Scientific Realism & the Plasticity of Mind. LC 78-73240. (Cambridge Studies in Philosophy). (Illus.). 1979. 24.95 (ISBN 0-521-22632-5). Cambridge U Pr.

Churchman, C. West. The Systems Approach. rev. & updated ed. (YA) (gr. 7-12). 1983. pap. 3.95 (ISBN 0-440-38407-9, LE). Dell.

--Thought & Wisdom. (Systems Inquiry Ser.). 150p. 1982. pap. text ed. 9.95 (ISBN 0-686-37578-5). Intersystems Pubns.

Churchman, C. West, et al. Thinking for Decisions: Deductive Quantitative Methods. LC 74-34494. (Illus.). 500p. 1975. text ed. 22.95 (ISBN 0-574-18225-X, 13-2225); solutions manual 1.95 (ISBN 0-574-18226-8, 13-2226). SRA.

Churchouse, Jack. Glamour Ships of the Union Steam Ship Company. (Illus.). 104p. 26.95 (ISBN 0-908582-41-2, Pub. by Salem Hse Ltd). Merrimack Bk Serv.

Churchward, L. G. Contemporary Soviet Government. 2nd ed. 385p. 1975. text ed. 24.95 (ISBN 0-444-19518-1). Elsevier.

--The Soviet Intelligentsia: An Essay on the Social Structure & Roles of the Soviet Intellectuals During the 1960's. (Illus.). 218p. 1973. 22.50 (ISBN 0-7100-7475-1). Routledge & Kegan.

Churchwell, Jan W. Who's Who in Technology Today Nineteen Eighty-Two to Nineteen Eighty-Three, 4 vols. 3rd ed. 3300p. 1982. Vol. 1 Electronic & Physics Technologies. 80.00 (ISBN 0-686-98437-4); Vol 2 Mechanical, Civil & Earth Science Technologies. 80.00 (ISBN 0-686-98438-2); Vol. 3 Chemical & Bioscience Technologies. 80.00 (ISBN 0-686-98439-0); Index. 145.00 (ISBN 0-686-98440-4); Set. 385.00 (ISBN 0-943692-00-8). J Dick.

Churg, Jacob, et al. Kidney Disease: Present Status. (International Academy of Pathology Monograph Ser.: No. 20). 1979. 43.00 o.p. (ISBN 0-683-01671-7). Williams & Wilkins.

Chuse, R. Pressure Vessels: The ASME Code Simplified. 1977. 24.50 (ISBN 0-07-010872-2). McGraw.

Chusid, E. Leslie, ed. The Selective & Comprehensive Testing of Adult Pulmonary Function. LC 82-84736. 400p. 1983. price not set monograph (ISBN 0-87993-195-7). Futura Pub.

Chusid, Joseph G. Correlative Neuroanatomy & Functional Neurology. 18th ed. LC 82-82712. (Illus.). 476p. 1982. lexotone cover 15.00 (ISBN 0-87041-012-1). Lange.

Chusid, Martin. A Catalogue of Verdi's Operas. (Music Indexes & Bibliographies: No. 5). 1974. pap. 17.00 (ISBN 0-913574-05-8). Eur-Am Music.

Chusid, Martin, ed. Rigoletto: Melodrama in Three Acts, 2 Vol. set. LC 82-15985. (The Works of Giuseppe Verdi: No. 1, Vol. 17). 1983. Score 406 p. 200.00x (ISBN 0-226-85306-3). Commentary viii, 92. U of Chicago Pr.

Chuta, E., jt. auth. see Allal, M.

Chute, G. M. & Chute, R. D. Electronics in Industry. 4th ed. 1971. 24.10 o.p. (ISBN 0-07-010932-X, G). McGraw.

Chute, George M. & Chute, Robert D. Electronics in Industry. 5th ed. (Illus.). 1979. text ed. 26.95 (ISBN 0-07-010934-6). McGraw.

Chute, Marchette. Introduction to Shakespeare. (gr. 7 up). 1951. 9.95 (ISBN 0-525-32587-5, 0966-290). Dutton.

--Shakespeare of London. 1950. pap. 7.95 (ISBN 0-525-47001-8, 0772-230). Dutton.

--Stories from Shakespeare. 1971. pap. 3.50 (ISBN 0-451-62183-2, ME2183, Ment). NAL.

--Stories from Shakespeare. (gr. 7 up). 1979. 10.95 (ISBN 0-529-05533-3, Philomel). Putnam Pub Group.

Chute, R. D., jt. auth. see Chute, G. M.

Chute, Robert D., jt. auth. see Chute, George M.

Chute, Robert M. Uncle George. 52p. 1977. pap. 1.00 (ISBN 0-686-74424-1). Cider Pr.

--Voices Great & Small. 24p. 1977. pap. 1.00 (ISBN 0-686-74423-3). Cider Pr.

Chvany, Catherine V. & Brecht, Richard D., eds. Morphosyntax in Slavic. (Illus.). v, 316p. (Orig.). 1981. pap. 14.95 (ISBN 0-89357-070-2). Slavica.

Chwast, Seymour. Tall City, Wide Country: A Book to Read Forward & Backward. (Illus.). 32p. (ps-k). 1983. 8.50 (ISBN 0-670-69236-0). Viking Pr.

Chwast, Seymour & Chewning, Emily. The Illustrated Flower. (Illus.). 1977. 10.95 o.p. (ISBN 0-517-52876-2, Harmony); pap. 5.95 o.p. (ISBN 0-517-52913-0). Crown.

Chwast, Seymour, jt. auth. see Suares, J. C.

Chwast, Seymour, jt. auth. see Suares, Jean-Claude.

Chyatte, Samuel, ed. Rehabilitation in Chronic Renal Failure. (Rehabilitation Medicine Library Ser.). 1979. 19.00 o.p. (ISBN 0-683-01578-8). Williams & Wilkins.

Chynn, K. Y. & Finby, N. Manual of Cranial Computerized Tomography. (Illus.). vi, 106p. 1982. 118.75 (ISBN 3-8055-3432-9). S Karger.

Chyssostomidis, C., jt. ed. see Dyer, Irra.

Chyzowych, Walt. The World Cup. (Illus.). 176p. 1982. 15.95 (ISBN 0-89651-900-7). Icarus.

Ciabotti, Patricia. Gaming It up with Shakespeare. Smith, Linda H., ed. 1980. pap. 4.95 (ISBN 0-936386-09-6). Creative Learning.

Ciampi, C. Artificial Intelligence & Legal Information Systems. 1982. 57.50 (ISBN 0-444-86414-8). Elsevier.

Ciancio, June. Scat Cat Finds a Friend. (Make-a-Bk). (Illus.). 32p. (Orig.). (ps-6). 1975. pap. 1.95 o.p. (ISBN 0-8467-0047-6, Pub. by Two Continents). Hippocrene Bks.

Ciancio, Sebastian & Bourgault, Priscilla. Pharmacology for Dental Professionals. (Illus.). 1979. text ed. 24.00 (ISBN 0-07-010953-2, HP). McGraw.

Cianciolo, Patricia. Picture Books for Children. 2nd ed. LC 80-39958. 254p. 1981. pap. 15.00 (ISBN 0-8389-0315-0). ALA.

Ciaramitaro, Barbara. Help for Depressed Mothers. Meyer, Linda, ed. LC 81-70362. 155p. 1982. 12.95 (ISBN 0-9603516-4-7); pap. 7.95 (ISBN 0-686-80938-6). C Franklin Pr.

Ciarcia, Steve. Build Your Own Z-80 Computer. 473p. 1980. 21.95 o.p. (ISBN 0-07-010961-3, BYTE Bks); pap. 15.95 (ISBN 0-07-010962-1). McGraw.

Ciardelli, F. & Salvadori, P., eds. Fundamental Aspects & Recent Developments in Optical Rotatory Dispersion & Circular Dichroism. 1973. 99.95 (ISBN 0-471-25629-3, Pub. by Wiley Heyden). Wiley.

Ciardi, John. A Browser's Dictionary. LC 79-1658. 464p. 1980. 17.26i (ISBN 0-06-010766-9, HarpT). Har-Row.

--For Instance. 1979. 12.95 o.p. (ISBN 0-393-01255-7); pap. 4.95 (ISBN 0-393-00939-4). Norton.

--A Second Browser's Dictionary: Native's Guide to the Unknown American Language. LC 82-48658. 420p. 1983. 16.30i (ISBN 0-06-015125-0, HarpT). Har-Row.

Ciardi, John & Williams, Miller. How Does a Poem Mean. 2nd ed. LC 74-11592. 432p. 1975. 14.95 (ISBN 0-395-18605-9). HM.

Ciardi, John, jt. auth. see Roberts, Joseph B., Jr.

Ciardi, John, ed. Mid-Century American Poets. lib. bdg. 7.00 o.p. (ISBN 0-8057-5818-6, Twayne). G K Hall.

Ciardi, John, tr. Purgatorio by Dante. 1971. pap. 3.50 (ISBN 0-451-62206-5, ME2206, Ment). NAL.

Ciardi, John, tr. see Alighiere, Dante.

Ciavolella, M., tr. see Caro, Annibal.

Ciba. Cerebral Vascular Smooth Muscle & Its Control. (Ciba Symposium Ser.: No. 56). 1978. 45.75 (ISBN 0-444-90026-8). Elsevier.

--Metabolic Activities of the Lung. (Ciba Symposia Ser.: No. 78). 1981. 71.50 (ISBN 0-444-90159-0). Elsevier.

Ciba Foundation. Aromatic Amino Acids in the Brain: Proceedings. (Ciba Foundation Symposium: No. 22). 1974. 34.00 (ISBN 90-219-4023-X, Excerpta Medica). Elsevier.

--Atherogenesis; Initiating Factors: Proceedings. (Ciba Foundation Symposium: No. 12). 1973. 24.75 (ISBN 0-444-15008-0, Excerpta Medica). Elsevier.

--Blood Cells & Vessel Walls: Functional Interractions. (Ciba Symposium Ser.: No. 71). 1980. 47.00 (ISBN 0-444-90112-4). Elsevier.

--Development of Mammalian Absorptive Processes. (Ciba Symposium Ser.: Vol. 70). 1980. 47.50 (ISBN 0-444-90101-9). Elsevier.

--Drug Concentrations in Neuropsychiatry. (Ciba Symposium Ser.: No. 74). 1980. 50.00 (ISBN 0-444-90137-X). Elsevier.

--Environmental Chemicals, Enzyme Function & Human Disease. (Ciba Symposium Ser.: No. 76). 1980. 69.00 (ISBN 0-444-90157-4). Elsevier.

--Health & Disease in Tribal Societies. (Ciba Symposium Ser.: No. 49). 1977. 39.75 (ISBN 0-444-15271-7). Elsevier.

--Perinatal Infections. (Ciba Symposia Ser.: No. 77). 1980. 56.25 (ISBN 0-444-90158-2). Elsevier.

--Protein Degradation in Health & Disease. (Ciba Symposium Ser.: No. 75). 1980. 76.75 (ISBN 0-444-90148-5). Elsevier.

--Sex, Hormones & Behaviour. (CIBA Foundation Symposium: No. 62). 1979. 47.00 (ISBN 0-444-90045-4). Elsevier.

--Sulphur in Biology. (Ciba Symposium Ser.: Vol. 72). 1980. 55.75 (ISBN 0-444-90108-6). Elsevier.

--Trends in Enzyme Histochemistry & Cytochemistry. (Ciba Symposium Ser.: No. 73). 1980. 58.50 (ISBN 0-444-90135-3). Elsevier.

Ciba Foundation, ed. Acute Diarrhea in Childhood. (Ciba Foundation Symposium: No. 42). 1976. 42.75 (ISBN 90-219-4047-7, Excerpta Medica). Elsevier.

--Embryogenesis in Mammals. (Ciba Foundation Symposium: No. 40). 1976. 35.00 (ISBN 0-444-15206-7). Elsevier.

--Monoamine Oxidase & Its Inhibition. (CIBA Foundation Symposium: No. 39). 1976. 48.00 (ISBN 0-444-15205-9, North-Holland). Elsevier.

CIBA Foundation Symposium. Biological Roles of Copper. (Ciba Symposium Ser.: No. 79). 1981. 61.50 (ISBN 0-444-90177-9). Elsevier.

Cibber, Colley. Colley Cibber: Three Sentimental Comedies. Sullivan, Maureen, ed. LC 73-77168. (Studies in English: No. 184). (Illus.). 352p. 1974. 32.50x o.p. (ISBN 0-300-01532-1). Yale U Pr.

Cibis, Gerhard W., tr. see Pau, Hans.

Cibula, Adam B. Biological Science Laboratory Guide, Vol. 1. 1976. pap. text ed. 7.95 (ISBN 0-8403-1049-8). Kendall-Hunt.

--Biological Science Laboratory Guide: Preliminary Edition, Vol. 2. 1977. pap. text ed. 7.95 (ISBN 0-8403-1844-8). Kendall-Hunt.

--Biological Sciences Laboratory Guide, Volume 3. 1977. pap. text ed. 4.95 (ISBN 0-8403-1732-8). Kendall-Hunt.

Cibulka, James G. & O'Brien, Timothy J. Inner City Private Elementary Schools: A Study. 225p. 1982. pap. 11.95 (ISBN 0-87462-463-0). Marquette.

Cibulskis, Margaret M. Essentials of Pharmacology. 240p. 1982. pap. text ed. 9.75 (ISBN 0-397-54334-4, Lippincott Medical). Lippincott.

Cicchetti, Charles J & Gillen, William J. The Marginal Cost & Pricing of Electricity: An Applied Approach. LC 77-2312. 1977. prof ref 30.00x (ISBN 0-88410-612-8). Ballinger Pub.

Cicchetti, Charles J. & Smith, V. Kerry. The Costs of Congestion: An Econometric Analysis of Wilderness Recreation. LC 75-29261. 1976. prof ref 20.00x (ISBN 0-88410-452-4). Ballinger Pub.

Cicciarella, Charles. The Sport of Skin Diving. (Illus.). 68p. (Orig.). 1982. pap. text ed. 3.95x (ISBN 0-89641-100-1). American Pr.

Cicciarello, Charles. Water Polo. 108p. 1981. pap. text ed. 3.95x (ISBN 0-89641-066-8). American Pr.

Cicco, Philip Di see Krutza, William J. & Dicicco, Philip P.

Cicero. Cicero: Epistulae Ad Quintum Fratrem et M. Brutum. Bailey, D. R., ed. (Cambridge Classical Texts & Commentaries Ser.: No. 22). 300p. 1981. 49.50 (ISBN 0-521-23053-5). Cambridge U Pr.

--Cicero on Oratory & Orators. Watson, J. S., tr. LC 73-103108. (Landmarks in Rhetoric & Public Address Ser.). 431p. 1970. 12.50x o.p. (ISBN 0-8093-0438-4). S Ill U Pr.

--Cicero, Select Letters. Bailey, D. R., ed. LC 78-67430. (Cambridge Greek & Latin Classics). 250p. 1980. 39.50 (ISBN 0-521-22492-6); pap. 13.95x (ISBN 0-521-29524-6). Cambridge U Pr.

--Epistulae Ad Familiares: 47-43 B.C, Vol. 2. Bailey, D. R., ed. LC 76-11079. (Classical Texts & Commentaries Ser.: No. 17). 1977. 82.00 (ISBN 0-521-21152-2). Cambridge U Pr.

--Epistulae Ad Familiares: 62-47 B.C, Vol. 1. Bailey, D. R., ed. LC 76-11079. (Classical Texts & Commentaries Ser.: No. 16). 1977. 82.00 (ISBN 0-521-21151-4). Cambridge U Pr.

--Verres in Sicily. Grose-Hodge, Humfrey & Davies, E. W., eds. (Latin). text ed. 6.95 (ISBN 0-521-04653-X). Cambridge U Pr.

Cicero, Marcus T. The Basic Works. Hadas, Moses, ed. 1964. pap. 3.75 (ISBN 0-686-38908-5, Mod LibC). Modern Lib.

Cichetti, Barbara, jt. auth. see Willson, Peggy.

Cichy, F. C. & Schenck, H. V. Corrosion of Steel & Aluminum Scuba Tanks. (Technical Report Ser.: No. 62). 20p. 1978. 2.00 (ISBN 0-938412-05-1, P769). URI Mas.

Ciechanowski, J. M. The Warsaw Rising of Nineteen Forty Four. LC 73-79315. (Soviet & East European Studies). 348p. 1974. 42.50 (ISBN 0-521-20203-5). Cambridge U Pr.

Ciekot, Jerald & Miriam-Therese. Hunger on Spaceship Earth Simulation Game. pap. 1.50 (ISBN 0-686-95393-2). Am Fr Serv Comm.

Ciepli, Michael, jt. auth. see Chaney, Lindsay.

Cierjacks, S., ed. Neutron Sources: For Applied & Pure Nuclear Research. (Neutron Physics & Nuclear Data in Science & Technology Ser.: Vol. 2). 370p. 1982. 65.00 (ISBN 0-08-029351-4). Pergamon.

Ciesielski, Stephen D. & Edison, Nancy, eds. Baltimore Renaissance: Poetry. (New Poets Ser.: Vol. 8). 50p. 1980. pap. 4.00 o.s.i. (ISBN 0-932616-06-2). New Poets.

Ciesielski, Z. Approximation & Function Spaces: Proceedings of the International Conference in Gdansk, Aug. 1979. 1982. 117.00 (ISBN 0-444-86143-2). Elsevier.

Ciesielski, Zbigniew, ed. Probability Theory. LC 80-469088. (Banach Center Publications: Vol. V). 289p. 1979. 47.50x (ISBN 0-8002-2270-9). Intl Pubns Serv.

Cieslewicz, W. J., tr. see Makogon, Yuri F.

Cifelli, Edward M. David Humphreys. (United States Authors Ser.). 1982. lib. bdg. 14.95 (ISBN 0-8057-7363-0, Twayne). G K Hall.

Ciferri, A. & Krigbaum, W. R., eds. Polymer Liquid Crystals. 394p. 1982. 59.00 (ISBN 0-12-174680-1). Acad Pr.

Ciferri, A. & Ward, I. M., eds. Ultra-High Modulus Polymers. (Illus.). 1979. 63.75x (ISBN 0-85334-800-6, Pub. by Applied Sci England). Elsevier.

Cifton, Merrit. Live Free or Die. 16p. 1982. pap. 1.00 (ISBN 0-686-37938-1). Samisdat.

Cigler, Allan & Loomis, Burdett. Interest Group Politics. 325p. 1983. pap. 9.25 (ISBN 0-87187-247-1). Congr Quarterly.

Cigman, Gloria, ed. see Chaucer, Geoffrey.

Cigno, A., jt. auth. see Day, R. H.

Ciklamini, Marlene. Snorri Sturluson. (World Authors Ser.). 1978. 15.95 (ISBN 0-8057-6334-1, Twayne). G K Hall.

Cikovsky, Nicolai, Jr., intro. by. & Lectures on the Affinity of Painting with the Other Fine Arts by Samuel F. B. Morse. LC 82-13551. (Illus.). 144p. 1983. text ed. 20.00x (ISBN 0-8262-0389-2). U of Mo Pr.

Cilento, G., jt. ed. see Adam, Waldemar.

Cilento, Raphael, jt. auth. see Crabbe, Buster.

Ciliotta, Claire, jt. auth. see Livingston, Carole.

Cimasoni, G. Crevicular Fluid Updated. (Monographs in Oral Science: Vol. 12). (Illus.). viii, 142p. 1983. 60.00 (ISBN 3-8055-3705-0). S Karger.

Ciminero, Anthony R., jt. auth. see Lahey, Benjamin B.

Ciminero, Anthony R., et al, eds. Handbook of Behavioral Assessment. LC 76-54170. (Personality Processes Ser). 1977. 49.95 (ISBN 0-471-15797-X, Pub. by Wiley-Interscience). Wiley.

Cimino, Louis & Chatelain, Agnes, eds. Directory of Practicing Anthropologists. 1981. pap. 6.00 (ISBN 0-686-36594-1). Am Anthro Assn.

Cimorell-Strong, Jacqueline M. Language Facilitation: A Cognitive Approach. 1983. pap. text ed. price not set (ISBN 0-8391-1799-X, 18449). Univ Park.

Cindro, N., ed. Nuclear Molecular Phenomena. 1978. 66.00 (ISBN 0-444-85116-X, North-Holland). Elsevier.

Cindro, N. & Ricci, R. A., eds. Dynamics of Heavy-Ion Collisions: Proceedings of Adriatic Europhysics Conference on the Dynamics of Heavy-Ion Collisions, 3rd, Hvar Croatia, Yugoslavia, May 25-30, 1981. 382p. 1982. 64.00 (ISBN 0-444-86332-X). Elsevier.

Cinel, Dino. From Italy to San Francisco: The Immigrant Experience. LC 80-53224. (Illus.). 360p. 1982. 25.00x (ISBN 0-8047-1117-8). Stanford U Pr.

Cini, Zelda, et al. Hollywood: Land & Legend. (Illus.). 192p. 1980. 19.95 o.p. (ISBN 0-87000-486-7, Arlington Hse). Crown.

Cinlar, E. Introduction to Stochastic Processes. (Illus.). 448p. 1975. ref. ed. 28.95 (ISBN 0-13-498089-1). P-H.

Cinlar, E., et al, eds. Seminar on Stochastic Processes, 1981. (Progress in Probability & Statistics: Vol. 1). 248p. 1982. text ed. 17.50 (ISBN 3-7643-3072-4). Birkhauser.

Cinnamon, Pamela A. & Swanson, Marilyn A. Everything About Exchange Values for Foods. LC 81-53064. 1981. 3.50 (ISBN 0-89301-083-9). U Pr of Idaho.

Cinningham, Lavern L., jt. ed. see Arnold, L. E.

Cintron, Ralph. Maria, Maria, Look! Mills, Ralph J., Jr., ed. 1982. 1.50 (ISBN 0-942582-04-7). Erie St Pr.

Cioffari, Bernard & Edmonds, Dean. Experiments in College Physics. 7th ed. 1983. pap. text ed. 16.95x (ISBN 0-669-00489-8). Heath.

Cioffari, Vincenzo. Beginning Italian. 3rd ed. 1979. text ed. 18.95x (ISBN 0-669-00580-0); wkbk. & lab manual 8.95x (ISBN 0-669-00581-9); tapes-reels 70.00 (ISBN 0-669-00582-7); cassettes 45.00 (ISBN 0-669-00583-5). Heath.

Cioffari, Vincenzo & Gonzalez, Emilio. Repaso Pratico y Cultural. 4th ed. 1977. text ed. 18.95x (ISBN 0-669-96461-1); wkbk. 7.95x (ISBN 0-669-96479-4); 6 cassette set 40.00 (ISBN 0-669-00333-6); 6 reel set 25.00 (ISBN 0-669-97782-9). Heath.

Cioffari, Vincenzo, ed. & tr. see Da Pisa, Guido.

Cioffi, F., jt. ed. see Borger, R.

Cioffi, Frank. Formula Fiction? An Anatomy of American Science Fiction, 1930-1940. LC 82-6112. (Contributions to the Study of Science Fiction & Fantasy Ser.: No. 3). 192p. 1982. lib. bdg. 25.00 (ISBN 0-313-23326-8, CIF/). Greenwood.

Cioffi, Luigi A., et al, eds. Body Weight Regulatory System: Normal & Disturbed Mechanisms. 388p. 1981. text ed. 43.00 (ISBN 0-89004-659-X). Raven.

Cioffredi, Peg & Cioffredi, Terry. These Guys Can Cook! 96p. (Orig.). 1982. pap. 4.95 (ISBN 0-686-82510-1). Elijah Pr.

Cioffredi, Terry, jt. auth. see Cioffredi, Peg.

Cioni, Ray & Cioni, Sally. The Babe & the Lamb: A Droodles Christmas Adventure. (The Droodles Books). 8.95 (ISBN 0-89191-635-0, 56358). Cook.

Cioni, Sally, jt. auth. see Cioni, Ray.

Cioran, E. M. Drawn & Quartered. Howard, Richard, tr. from Fr. LC 81-2872. 192p. 1982. 15.95 (ISBN 0-394-51811-X); pap. 7.95 (ISBN 0-394-17841-6). Seaver Bks.

--The Trouble with Being Born. Howard, Richard, tr. from Fr. LC 81-51526. Orig. Title: L'Inconvenient d'etre Ne. 208p. 1982. pap. 5.95 o.p. (ISBN 0-394-17847-5). Seaver Bks.

Cioran, Sam, tr. see Sologub, Fyodor.

Cioran, Samuel D. Vladmir Soloviev & the Knighthood of the Divine Sophia. 280p. 1977. text ed. 11.00 (ISBN 0-88920-043-2, Pub. by Wilfred Laurier U Pr Canada); pap. text ed. 7.00x (ISBN 0-88920-042-4). Humanities.

Cioranescu, Alexandre. Ion Barbu. (World Authors Ser.). 1981. lib. bdg. 15.95 (ISBN 0-8057-6432-1, Twayne). G K Hall.

CIOS. Management & the World of Tomorrow: Key Issues for Management in Economic Growth Technological Change & Human Welfare. 472p. 1981. text ed. 40.25x (ISBN 0-566-02239-7). Gower Pub Ltd.

Ciosek, Karen, jt. auth. see Donnelly, Thomas R.

Cipolla, C. M. Public Health & the Medical Profession in Renaissance Italy. LC 25-22984. (Illus.). 1976. 27.50 (ISBN 0-521-20959-5). Cambridge U Pr.

Cipolla, Carlo M. Faith, Reason & the Plague in Seventeenth-Century Tuscany. Kittel, Muriel, tr. from Ital. LC 79-2479. (Illus.). 1980. 12.95x (ISBN 0-8014-1230-7). Cornell U Pr.

--Fighting the Plague in Seventeenth-Century Italy. (Curti Lecture Ser.). 162p. 1980. 15.00 (ISBN 0-299-08340-3); pap. 6.95 (ISBN 0-299-08344-6). U of Wis Pr.

--The Monetary Policy of Fourteenth Century Florence. 100p. 1982. 14.95x (ISBN 0-520-04606-4). U of Cal Pr.

Cipra, Barry. Mistakes---& How to Avoid Them. 70p. Date not set. pap. text ed. price not set (ISBN 3-7643-3083-X). Birkhauser.

Cipriano, Robert, ed. Special Olympics. (Special Education Ser.). (Illus., Orig.). 1980. pap. 15.00 (ISBN 0-89568-111-0). Spec Learn Corp.

Cipriano, Robert E., jt. auth. see Ball, Edith L.

Ciria, Alberto. Parties & Power in Modern Argentina, 1930-1946. Astiz, Carlos A. & McCarthy, Mary F., trs. LC 70-129642. 1974. 44.50x (ISBN 0-87395-079-8). State U NY Pr.

Ciriani, Tito A., ed. Mathematical Models for Surface Water Hydrology: Proceedings of the Workshop Held at the IBM Scientific Center, Pisa Italy. LC 76-13457. 1977. 88.00x (ISBN 0-471-99400-6, Pub. by Wiley-Interscience). Wiley.

Cirilius, Marcus. Prehistoric Epic! 1978. 6.95 o.p. (ISBN 0-533-03456-6). Vantage.

Cirino, Antonio. U. S. Soccer vs the World. 300p. (Orig.). 1983. pap. 9.95 (ISBN 0-910641-00-5). Damon Pr.

Cirino, Linda, jt. auth. see Arbeiter, Jean.

Cirker, Blanche. The Book of Kells: Selected Plates in Full Color. (Fine Art, History of Art Ser.). (Illus.). 32p. 1982. pap. 4.50 (ISBN 0-486-24345-1). Dover.

Cirker, Blanche, jt. auth. see Cirker, Hayward.

Cirker, Blanche, ed. Needlework Alphabets & Designs. pap. 2.95 (ISBN 0-486-23159-3). Dover.

Cirker, Blanche, ed. see Bewick, Thomas.

Cirker, Blanche, jt. ed. see Cirker, Hayward.

Cirker, Hayward & Cirker, Blanche. Dictionary of American Portraits. Dover Editorial Staff, ed. 1967. 65.00 (ISBN 0-486-21823-6). Dover.

--Golden Age of the Poster. 1971. pap. 6.95 (ISBN 0-486-22753-7). Dover.

Cirker, Hayward & Cirker, Blanche, eds. Twenty-Four Art Nouveau Postcards in Full Colors: From Classic Posters. (Illus.). 12p. (Orig.). Date not set. pap. 2.95 (ISBN 0-486-24389-3). Dover.

Cirker, Haywood, ed. Italian Master Drawings from the Uffizi. (Fine Art Ser.). (Illus.). 96p. (Orig.). 1983. pap. 5.00 (ISBN 0-486-24467-9). Dover.

Cirovic, Michael M. Basic Electronics. 2nd ed. (Illus.). 1979. text ed. 22.95 (ISBN 0-8359-0370-2); solutions manual avail. (ISBN 0-8359-0371-0). Reston.

Cisin, Fred & Parvin, Jack. How to Keep Your Honda Car Alive: A Manual of Step by Step Procedures for the Compleat Idiot. (Illus.). 272p. (Orig.). 1983. pap. 14.00 (ISBN 0-912528-25-7). John Muir.

Cisin, Ira H., jt. auth. see Cahalan, Don.

Ciske, Karen L. & Mayer, Gloria G., eds. Primary Nursing. LC 79-90370. 103p. 1980. pap. text ed. 12.95 (ISBN 0-913654-60-4). Aspen Systems.

Cismaru, Alfred. Boris Vian. (World Authors Ser.: France: No. 293). 1974. lib. bdg. 15.95 (ISBN 0-8057-2951-8, Twayne). G K Hall.

--Marguerite Duras. (World Authors Ser.: France: No. 147). lib. bdg. 10.95 o.p. (ISBN 0-8057-2280-7, Twayne). G K Hall.

Cisneros, Jose, tr. see Simmons, Marc.

Cissell, Helen, et al. Mathematics of Finance. 6th ed. 1982. 23.95 (ISBN 0-395-31692-8); instr's manual 2.50 (ISBN 0-395-31693-6). HM.

Cissley, Charles H. Management Science in Life Companies. LC 75-32898. (FLMI Insurance Education Program Ser.). 1975. pap. text ed. 6.00 (ISBN 0-915322-15-3). LOMA.

--Systems & Data Processing in Insurance Companies. LC 77-70940. (FLMI Insurance Education Program Ser.). (Illus.). 1977. pap. text ed. 9.50 o.p. (ISBN 0-915322-26-9); 4.00 o.p. wkbk. (ISBN 0-915322-27-7). LOMA.

--Systems & Data Processing in Insurance Companies. rev. ed. LC 82-80670. (FLMI Insurance Education Program Ser.). 287p. 1982. text ed. 12.00 (ISBN 0-915322-55-2). LOMA.

--Systems & Data Processing in Insurance Companies: Student Guide. (FLMI Insurance Education Program). 208p. 1982. pap. 5.00 workbook (ISBN 0-915322-56-0). LOMA.

Ciszek, Walter J. & Flaherty, Daniel. He Leadeth Me. LC 73-79654. 240p. 1975. pap. 3.95 (ISBN 0-385-02805-9, Im). Doubleday.

Ciszek, Walter J. & Flaherty, Daniel L. He Leadeth Me. LC 73-79654. 216p. 1973. 6.95 o.p. (ISBN 0-385-04051-2). Doubleday.

--With God in Russia. pap. 4.50 (ISBN 0-385-03954-9, D200, Im). Doubleday.

Cita, M. B., jt. ed. see Schlanger, S. O.

Citino, David. The Appassionata Poems. 72p. (Orig.). 1983. pap. 4.50 (ISBN 0-914946-35-8). Cleveland St Univ Poetry Ctr.

Citizens Planning & Housing Association. Beyond the White Marble Steps. (Illus.). 103p. 1979. pap. 3.50 (ISBN 0-686-36491-0). Md Hist.

Citizens' Police Committee. Chicago Police Problems. LC 69-16230. (Criminology, Law Enforcement, & Social Problems Ser.: No. 89). 1969. Repr. of 1931 ed. 12.00x (ISBN 0-87585-089-8). Patterson Smith.

Citizens' Research Foundation. Model State Statute: Politics, Elections & Public Office. 3.00 (ISBN 0-686-20523-5). CRF.

--Money & Politics: A Report of the Citizens' Research Foundation Conference. 3.00 (ISBN 0-686-20522-7). CRF.

Citizens' Research Foundtion. Political Contributors & Lenders of 10,000 Dollars or More in 1972. 25.00 (ISBN 0-686-20525-1). CRF.

Citizen's Scholarship Foundation of America, ed. see Johnson, Marlys C. & Thompson, Linda J.

Citizens's Research Foundation. Political Contributors of 500 Dollars or More in 1972 to Candidates & Committees in Twelve States. 25.00 (ISBN 0-686-20524-3). CRF.

Citroen. Valse Zilvermerken in Nederland. Date not set. 21.50 (ISBN 0-686-94103-9). Elsevier.

Citroen, K. A. Amsterdam Silversmiths & Their Marks. (Studies in Silver Ser.: Vol. 1). 352p. 1975. 153.25 (ISBN 0-444-10730-4, North-Holland). Elsevier.

City of Los Angeles, City Attorney's Office. Los Angeles Municipal Code, 5 vols. 4th rev. ed. 3300p. 1979. Set. looseleaf 325.00 (ISBN 0-911110-33-X); with current 1983 changes avail. (ISBN 0-685-26720-2). Parker & Son.

Ciucci, Giorgio, et al. The American City: From the Civil War to the New Deal. Luigia La Penta, Barbara, tr. from Ital. 1979. 60.00x (ISBN 0-262-03069-1). MIT Pr.

Ciuffreda, A. R., ed. Fracture Toughness of Heavy-Wall Welded Tankage Steel, Series MPC-5, 1977. 1977. pap. text ed. 15.00 o.p. (ISBN 0-685-86867-2, G00125). ASME.

Ciupik, Larry A. The Universe. LC 77-27567. (Read About Science Ser.). (Illus.). (gr. k-3). 1978. PLB 13.30 (ISBN 0-8393-0089-1). Raintree Pubs.

Civan, Mortimer M. Epithelial Ions & Transport: Application of Biophysical Techniques. (Life Sciences Ser.). 216p. 1983. 59.95 (ISBN 0-471-04869-0, Pub. by Wiley-Interscience). Wiley.

Civica Biblioteca Berio (Berio Civic Library). Genoa. Catalogo Della Raccolta Colombiana (Catalog of the Columbus Collection) 1963. lib. bdg. 75.00 (ISBN 0-8161-0637-1, Hall Library). G K Hall.

Civitello, Andrew M., Jr. Construction Operations Manual of Policies & Procedures. LC 82-16156. 300p. 1983. looseleaf bdg. 149.50 (ISBN 0-13-168773-5, Busn). P-H.

Civrieux, Marc de see De Civrieux, Marc.

Cizankas, Victor I. & Hanna, Donald G. Modern Police Management & Organization. (Illus.). 256p. 1977. text ed. 19.95 (ISBN 0-13-597104-7). P-H.

Cizevskij, Dmitrij. History of Nineteenth-Century Russian Literature, 2 vols. Zenkovsky, Serge A., ed. Porter, Richard N., tr. from Ger. Incl. Vol. 2. The Realistic Period. 218p. 1974. o.p. 15.00x ea.; Vol. 1. o.p.; Vol. 2. o.p.; pap. 7.95x ea.; Vol. 1. pap. (ISBN 0-8265-1188-0); Vol. 2. pap. (ISBN 0-8265-1190-2). Vanderbilt U Pr.

Claassen, ed. see Dauphine Conference on Money & International Money Problems, 3rd, Paris.

Claassen, E. M., ed. see Paris-Dauphine Conference on Money & International Monetary Problems, 5th, 1981.

Clack, Alice & Leitch, Carol. Amusements Developing Algebra Skills, Vol. 1 & 2. 1975. pap. 6.95ea. (ISBN 0-686-57841-4). Vol. 1 (ISBN 0-910974-76-4). Vol. 2 (ISBN 0-910974-77-2). dittomasters for ea. vol o.p. 12.95 (ISBN 0-686-57842-2). Midwest Pubns.

Clack, Jerry. An Anthology of Alexandrian Poetry. (The Classical World Special Ser.). 570p. 1982. pap. 15.00 (ISBN 0-942012-00-3). Classical Assoc.

Claes, Frans M., compiled by. A Bibliography of Netherlandic Dictionaries: Dutch-Flemish. (Orig.). 1980. lib. bdg. 50.00 (ISBN 0-686-83480-1). Kraus Intl.

Claessens, Bob & Rousseau, Jeanne. Our Bruegel (Pieter Bruegel the Elder) (Illus.). 75.00 o.s.i. (ISBN 0-912728-11-6). Newbury Bks.

Clagett, Marshall, ed. Critical Problems in the History of Science. 1957. 25.00x o.p. (ISBN 0-299-01870-9); pap. 9.95x o.p. (ISBN 0-299-01874-1). U of Wis Pr.

Clagett, Marshall, tr. Nicole Oresme & the Medieval Geometry of Qualities & Motions. (Medieval Science Pubns., No. 12). (Illus.). 728p. 1968. 50.00x (ISBN 0-299-04880-2). U of Wis Pr.

Claghorn, Charles E. Biographical Dictionary of Jazz. 377p. 1983. 25.00 (ISBN 0-13-077966-0, Busn). P-H.

Claghorn, K. H; see Bernard, William S.

Clague, Christopher, jt. auth. see Betancourt, Roger.

Clague, Maryhelen. Beyond the Shining River. 372p. 1980. 13.95 o.s.i. (ISBN 0-698-11021-8, Coward). Putnam Pub Group.

--Moment of the Rose. 448p. 1983. pap. 2.95 (ISBN 0-449-12444-4, GM). Fawcett.

--So Wondrous Free. 1979. pap. 2.25 o.p. (ISBN 0-451-09047-0, E9047, Sig). NAL.

Clahsen, Harald. Spacherwerb in der Kindeit. 180p. (Ger.). 1982. pap. 17.00 o.p. (ISBN 3-87808-548-6). Benjamins North Am.

--Spracherwerb in der Kindheit. (Language Development Ser.: No. 4). 180p. (Orig., German.). 1982. pap. 17.00 (ISBN 3-87808-548-6). Benjamins North Am.

Clahsen, Harold, et al. Deutsch als Zweitsprache Der Spracherwerb Auslandischer Arbeiter. (Language Development (LD) Ser.: No. 3). 320p. (Ger.). 1982. 42.00 (ISBN 3-87808-253-3); pap. 22.00 (ISBN 3-87808-544-3). Benjamins North Am.

Claiborn, Charles D., jt. auth. see Strong, Stanley R.

Claiborn, William, jt. ed. see Specter, Gerald.

Claiborn, William L., et al. Working with Police Agencies: The Inter-relations Between Law Enforcers & the Behavioral Scientist. Sprafkin, Robert, ed. LC 75-17450. (Continuing Series in Community-Clinical Psychology: Vol. III). 200p. 1976. text ed. 24.95 (ISBN 0-87705-224-7). Human Sci Pr.

Claiborn, William L., jt. ed. see Cohen, Lawrence.

Claiborne, Craig. Cooking with Herbs & Spices. new, rev., enl. ed. LC 71-123921. Orig. Title: Herb & Spice Cookbook. (Illus.). 1970. 14.37i (ISBN 0-06-010784-7, HarpT). Har-Row.

--Craig Claiborne's Favorites From the New York Times, Vol. 3. 1981. pap. 2.95 (ISBN 0-446-93808-4). Warner Bks.

Claiborne, Craig & Frabey, Pierre. The Master Cooking Course: A Step-by-Step Visual Guide to the Preparation & Techniques of Four Gourmet Meals. (Illus.). 1982. 15.95 (ISBN 0-698-11167-2, Coward). Putnam Pub Group.

Claiborne, Craig & Franey, Pierre. Classic French Cooking. LC 79-124640. (Foods of the World Ser.). (Illus.). (gr. 6 up). 1970. PLB 17.28 (ISBN 0-8094-0074-X, Pub. by Time-Life). Silver.

--The Master Cooking Course: A Step-By-Step Visual Guide to the Preparation & Techniques of Four Gourmet Meals. (Illus.). 128p. 1982. pap. 9.95 (ISBN 0-399-50586-5, Perige). Putnam Pub Group.

--The Spiral Cooking Course. (Illus.). 128p. 1982. 15.95 (ISBN 0-686-82376-1, Perige); spiral bdg. 9.95 (ISBN 0-399-50586-5). Putnam Pub Group.

--Veal Cookery. LC 78-2123. (Illus.). 1978. 14.37i (ISBN 0-06-010773-1, HarpT). Har-Row.

Claiborne, Craig & Lee, Virginia. The Chinese Cookbook. 1976. pap. 9.95i (ISBN 0-397-01173-3, LP-103). Har-Row.

--The Chinese Cookbook. LC 82-48827. (Illus.). 476p. (Orig.). 1983. pap. 9.56i (ISBN 0-06-464063-9, BN 4063). B&N NY.

Claiborne, Robert & Goudsmit, Samuel. Time. Rev. ed. LC 80-52115. (Life Science Library). (Illus.). (gr. 5 up). 1966. PLB 13.40 (ISBN 0-8094-4051-2, Pub. by Time-Life). Silver.

Clain. Self Assessment Questions & Answers on Clinical Surgery. 240p. 1980. pap. 10.00 (ISBN 0-7236-0546-7). Wright-PSG.

Clain-Stefanelli, E. E. Russian Gold Coins. 1962. 5.00 (ISBN 0-685-51560-5, Pub by Spink & Son England). S J Durst.

Clair, Daphne. Depuis Toujours. (Harlequin Romantique). 192p. 1983. pap. 1.95 (ISBN 0-373-41192-8). Harlequin Bks.

Clair, Earl E. La see La Clair, Earl E.

Clair, Joy St. see St. Clair, Joy.

Clair, Robert St. see St. Clair, Robert.

Clairaut, Alexis-Claude. Recherches Sur les Courbes a Double Courbure. Repr. of 1731 ed. 43.00 o.p. (ISBN 0-8287-0198-9). Clearwater Pub.

--Theorie De la Figure De la Terre, Tiree Des Principes De L'hydrostatique. Repr. of 1743 ed. 90.00 o.p. (ISBN 0-8287-0199-7). Clearwater Pub.

Clairborne, Craig. Cooking with Herbs & Spices. LC 82-48224. (Illus.). 376p. 1983. pap. 7.64i (ISBN 0-06-090998-6, CN 998, CN). Har-Row.

Claire, Anne. Andro, Star of Bethlehem. Mahany, Patricia, ed. (Happy Day Bks.). (Illus.). 24p. (ps-2). 1983. pap. 1.29 (ISBN 0-87239-631-2, 3551). Standard Pub.

Claire, Elizabeth. A Foreign Student's Guide to Dangerous English. (Illus.). 92p. (Orig.). 1980. pap. 5.95 (ISBN 0-937630-00-4). Eardley Pubns.

Claire, Rosine. The New French Gourmet Vegetarian Cookbook. LC 75-9086. 1979. pap. 5.95 o.p. (ISBN 0-89087-058-6). Celestial Arts.

Claire, Vivian. David Bowie. LC 76-56571. (Illus., Orig.). 1977. pap. 3.95 (ISBN 0-8256-3911-5, Quick Fox). Putnam Pub Group.

--Judy Collins. LC 77-78538. (Illus.). 1977. pap. 3.95 (ISBN 0-8256-3914-X, Quick Fox). Putnam Pub Group.

--Linda Ronstadt. LC 77-88753. 1978. pap. 3.95 (ISBN 0-8256-3918-2, Quick Fox). Putnam Pub Group.

--Linda Ronstadt: A Photo-Bio. 1979. pap. 2.25 o.s.i. (ISBN 0-515-05159-4). Jove Pubns.

Claire, William, ed. see Van Doren, Mark.

Clakson, Margaret. Destined for Glory: The Meaning of Suffering. 144p. 1983. pap. 4.95 (ISBN 0-8028-1953-2). Eerdmans.

Claman, Henry N., ed. see New York Academy of Sciences Annals of, October 19-21, 1981.

Clammer, David. Zulu War. (Illus.). 192p. 1971. 14.95 o.p. (ISBN 0-7153-5672-0). David & Charles.

Clammer, John, ed. The New Economic Anthropology. LC 75-37254. 250p. 1979. 22.50x (ISBN 0-312-56630-1). St Martin.

Clampitt, Amy. The Kingfisher. (Poetry Ser.: No. 9). 150p. 1983. 11.95 (ISBN 0-394-52840-9); pap. 6.95 (ISBN 0-394-71251-X). Knopf.

Clancey, Peter L. Nineteen Improving Schools & Why Their "Formula for Success". (Illus.). 206p. (Orig.). 1982. pap. text ed. 7.95 (ISBN 0-911467-00-9). Educ Leadership.

Clancy, John. John Clancy's Christmas Cookbook. (Illus.). 1982. 17.50 (ISBN 0-87851-207-1). Hearst Bks.

--Site Surveying & Leveling. 256p. 1981. pap. text ed. 9.95 (ISBN 0-7131-3439-9). E Arnold.

Clancy, John & Field, Frances. Clancy's Oven Cookery. 1976. 8.95 o.s.i. (ISBN 0-440-01372-0, E Friede). Delacorte.

Clancy, Joseph P., tr. see Horace.

Clancy, Judith & Fisher, M. F. Not a Station but a Place. LC 79-20885. (Illus.). 72p. 1979. bds. 9.95 (ISBN 0-912184-03-5); pap. 5.95 (ISBN 0-686-82983-2). Synergistic Pr.

Clancy, Laurie. A Collapsible Man. (Illus.). 1977. 7.95 o.p. (ISBN 0-685-80820-3); lib. bdg. 6.95 o.p. (ISBN 0-685-80821-1); pap. 3.95 o.p. (ISBN 0-685-80822-X). St Martin.

--Xavier Herbert. (World Authors Ser.). 1981. lib. bdg. 15.95 (ISBN 0-8057-6394-5, Twayne). G K Hall.

Clancy, Michael, jt. auth. see Cooper, Doug.

Clapham, Arthur R., ed. The IBP Survey of Conservation Sites: An Experimental Study. LC 79-50233. (International Biological Programme Ser.: No. 24). (Illus.). 500p. 1980. 60.00 (ISBN 0-521-22697-X). Cambridge U Pr.

Clapham, Arthur R., et al. Flora of the British Isles. 2nd ed. 1962. 75.00 (ISBN 0-521-04657-2); illustrations, 4 pts. 37.50 ea. Cambridge U Pr.

Clapham, C. Liberia and Sierra Leone. LC 75-32447. (African Studies: No.20). (Illus.). 160p. 1976. 24.95 (ISBN 0-521-21095-X). Cambridge U Pr.

Clapham, C. R. Introduction to Abstract Algebra. (Library of Mathematics). 1969. pap. 5.00 o.p. (ISBN 0-7100-6626-0). Routledge & Kegan.

Clapham, W. B., Jr. Human Ecosystems. 1981. pap. 15.95x (ISBN 0-02-322510-6). Macmillan.

--Natural Ecosystems. 1973. pap. 12.95x (ISBN 0-02-322500-9, 32250). Macmillan.

--Natural Ecosystems. 2nd ed. 256p. 1983. pap. 11.95 (ISBN 0-686-38033-9). Macmillan.

Clapin, Sylvia. New Dictionary of Americanisms. LC 68-17985. 1968. Repr. of 1902 ed. 42.00x (ISBN 0-8103-3244-2). Gale.

Clapp, Andrew D. Merger Yearbook Nineteen Eighty. 1981. 68.00 (ISBN 0-939008-03-3). Cambridge Corp.

Clapp, B. W. The University of Exeter: A History. 208p. 1982. 40.00x (ISBN 0-85989-133-X, Pub. by Exeter Univ England). State Mutual Bk.

Clapp, Jeremy, jt. ed. see Langan, John.

Clapp, John M., jt. auth. see Case, Frederick E.

Clapp, Margaret A. Forgotten First Citizen: John Bigelow. LC 68-10075. 1968. Repr. of 1947 ed. lib. bdg. 17.00x o.p. (ISBN 0-8371-0047-X, CLJB). Greenwood.

Clapp, Patricia. Witch's Children. (gr. 7 up). 1982. 9.00 (ISBN 0-688-00890-9). Lothrop.

Clapp, William W. Record of the Boston Stage. LC 69-13861. Repr. of 1853 ed. lib. bdg. 18.00x (ISBN 0-8371-0350-9, CLBS). Greenwood.

Clapper, Raymond. Watching the World. (FDR & the Era of the New Deal Ser.). 1975. Repr. of 1944 ed. 45.00 (ISBN 0-306-70730-6). Da Capo.

Clapperton, Chalmers, ed. Scotland: A New Study. (Illus.). 344p. 1983. 37.50 (ISBN 0-7153-8084-2). David & Charles.

Clar, Eric. The Aromatic Sextet. LC 72-616. 128p. 1973. pap. 11.50 o.p. (ISBN 0-471-15840-2, Pub. by Wiley-Interscience). Wiley.

Clar, Lawrence & Hart, James. Calculus with Analytic Geometry for the Technologies. (Ser. in Technological Mathematics). (Illus.). 1980. text ed. 20.95 (ISBN 0-13-111856-0). P-H.

--Mathematics for the Technologies with Calculus. (P-H Series in Technical Mathematics). (Illus.). 1978. ref. ed. 27.95 (ISBN 0-13-562553-X). P-H.

Clar, Lawrence M. & Hart, James A. Mathematics for Business & Consumers. (Illus.). 1980. text ed. 22.95x (ISBN 0-02-322540-8). Macmillan.

--Mathematics for the Technologies. (Illus.). 1978. text ed. 23.95 (ISBN 0-13-565200-6). P-H.

Clardy, Betty S., jt. auth. see Clardy, Jesse V.

Clardy, Jesse V. & Clardy, Betty S. The Superfluous Man in Russian Letters. LC 80-5080. 189p. 1980. text ed. 19.25 (ISBN 0-8191-1039-6); pap. text ed. 9.50 (ISBN 0-8191-1040-X). U Pr of Amer.

Clare, A. W. & Corney, R. H., eds. Social Work & Primary Health Care. Date not set. 35.00 (ISBN 0-12-174740-9). Acad Pr.

Clare, A. W. & Lader, M., eds. Psychiatry & General Practice. 1982. 23.50 (ISBN 0-12-174720-4). Acad Pr.

Clare, Christopher R. Designing Logic Systems Using State Machines. (Illus.). 250p. 1973. text ed. 19.95 o.p. (ISBN 0-07-011120-0, C). McGraw.

Clare, E. N., jt. auth. see Bibby, W.

Clare, Francis. Your, Move God. 128p. 1982. pap. 4.50 (ISBN 0-89221-102-4). New Leaf.

Clare, J. N. & Sinclair, M. A., eds. Search & the Human Observer. (Illus.). 198p. 1979. pap. 21.50x (ISBN 0-85066-193-5). Intl Pubns Serv.

Clare, James S. Winchester College. 1982. 50.00x (ISBN 0-686-98443-9, Pub. by Cave Pubns England). State Mutual Bk.

Clare, John. Clare's Countryside. (Illus.). 1981. 19.95 (ISBN 0-434-98013-7, Pub. by W Heinemann). David & Charles.

--The Journals, Essays, & the Journey from Essex. Tibble, Anne, ed. 139p. 1980. text ed. 18.95x (ISBN 0-85635-344-2, Pub. by Carcanet New Pr England). Humanities.

--The Midsummer Cushion. Tibble, Anne & Thornton, Kelsey, eds. 519p. 1980. 22.50 o.p. (ISBN 0-85635-250-0, Pub. by Carcanet New Pr England). Humanities.

--The Rural Muse. 184p. 1982. text ed. 12.50x (ISBN 0-85635-397-3, 80449, Pub. by Carcanet New Pr England). Humanities.

Clare, M. V., Sr., tr. see Eugene, P. M.

Clare, Tom. Archaeological Sites of Devon & Cornwall. 160p. 1982. 50.00x (ISBN 0-86190-057-X, Pub. by Moorland). State Mutual Bk.

Claremon, Neil. East by Southwest. 1970. pap. 1.95 o.p. (ISBN 0-671-20602-8, Touchstone Bks). S&S.

Claremont, Chris & Simonson, Walter. Marvel & DC Present: The Uncanny X-Men & the New Teen Titans. 160p. (Orig.). 1983. pap. 2.95 cancelled o.p. (ISBN 0-446-30529-4). Warner Bks.

Claremont, Lewis De see De Claremont, Lewis.

Claremont De Castillejo, Irene. Knowing Woman: Feminine Psychology. 192p. 1974. pap. 4.76i (ISBN 0-06-090349-X, CN349, CN). Har-Row.

Clarendon Press, Cartographic Dept. Oxford Regional Economic Atlas: Western Europe. Clayton, K. M. & Kormoss, I. B., eds. 1971. 17.50x (ISBN 0-19-894306-7); pap. 6.95x (ISBN 0-19-894307-5). Oxford U Pr.

Clareson, Thomas D. Reader's Guide to Robert Silverberg. Schlobin, Roger C., ed. (Reader's Guides to Contemporary Science Fiction & Fantasy Authors Ser.: Vol. 18). (Illus., Orig.). 1983. 11.95x (ISBN 0-916732-48-7); pap. text ed. 5.95x (ISBN 0-916732-47-9). Starmont Hse.

Clareson, Thomas D., ed. Extrapolation: A Science Fiction Newsletter, Volumes 1-10, 1959-1969. (Science Fiction Ser.). 1978. lib. bdg. 35.00 o.p. (ISBN 0-8398-2441-6, Gregg). G K Hall.

Clarey, Elizabeth M. & Dixson, Robert J. Pronunciation Exercises in English. (gr. 9 up). 1963. pap. text ed. 3.50 (ISBN 0-88345-135-2, 17418); 18.00 p. with 3 records (ISBN 0-685-02029-0); cassettes 25.00 (ISBN 0-686-86692-4). Regents Pub.

Clarfield, Gerard H. United States Diplomatic History, Vol. 1. LC 72-5519. 256p. 1973. pap. text ed. 11.50 (ISBN 0-395-14026-9). HM.

Clarida, Glen, jt. auth. see Stringer, James.

Clarizio, Harvey F. & McCoy, George F. Behavioral Disorders in Children. 2nd ed. 1976. text ed. 22.95 scp o.p. (ISBN 0-690-00853-8, HarpC). Har-Row.

Clarizo, Harvey F. & McCoy, George F. Behavior Disorders in Children. 3rd ed. 672p. 1983. text ed. 18.50 scp (ISBN 0-06-041304-2, HarpC); instr's. manual avail. (ISBN 0-06-361270-4). Har-Row.

Clark. Advances in Infared & Raman Spectroscopy, Vol. 9. 1982. 112.00 (ISBN 0-471-26215-3). Wiley.

--Advances in Infrared & Raman Spectroscopy, Vol. 8. 114.00 (ISBN 0-471-25640-4, Pub. by Wiley Heyden). Wiley.

--Community Care. 2nd ed. 7.95 (ISBN 0-471-25641-2, Pub. by Wiley Heyden). Wiley.

Clark & Matko. Soviet Economic Facts: 1917-1981. LC 81-23299. 200p. 1983. 25.00x (ISBN 0-312-74758-6). St Martin.

Clark, jt. auth. see MacLeod.

Clark, A. P. Principles of Digital Data Transmission. LC 76-23217. 1976. 27.95x o.s.i. (ISBN 0-470-98913-0). Halsted Pr.

Clark, Ailsa M. Starfishes. new ed. Orig. Title: Starfishes & Their Relations. (Illus.). 1977. pap. 9.95 (ISBN 0-87666-466-4, PS-750). TFH Pubns.

Clark, Al. The Film Yearbook 1983. (Illus.). 192p. (Orig.). 1983. pap. 12.95 (ISBN 0-394-62465-3, Ever). Grove.

Clark, Alan. Aces High: The War in the Air Over the Western Front 1914-1918. (Illus.). 320p. 1973. 10.00 o.p. (ISBN 0-399-11103-4). Putnam Pub Group.

Clark, Alice. Working Life of Women in the Seventeenth Century. 368p. 1982. pap. 8.95 (ISBN 0-7100-9045-5). Routledge & Kegan.

Clark, Alice S., jt. ed. see Hoadley, Irene B.

Clark, Andrew H. Invasion of New Zealand by People, Plants & Animals: The South Island. LC 71-100249. Repr. of 1949 ed. lib. bdg. 20.50x (ISBN 0-8371-2982-6, CLIN). Greenwood.

Clark, Ann L. Leadership Technique in Expectant Parent Education. 2nd ed. LC 73-77722. (Illus.). 144p. 1973. pap. text ed. 5.00 o.p. (ISBN 0-8261-0562-9). Springer Pub.

Clark, Ann L., et al. Childbearing: A Nursing Perspective. 2nd ed. LC 78-24575. (Illus.). 1052p. 1979. text ed. 23.00x (ISBN 0-8036-1831-X). Davis Co.

Clark, Ann N. Along Sandy Trails. (37 Color Photos, 32p). (gr. 4-6). 1969. PLB 5.95 o.p. (ISBN 0-670-11485-5). Viking Pr.

--Hoofprint on the Wind. (Illus.). 160p. (gr. 4-6). 1972. PLB 8.95 o.p. (ISBN 0-670-37874-7). Viking Pr.

Clark, Anne & Rivin, Zelma. Homesteading in Urban U. S. A. LC 77-2939. 198p. 1977. text ed. 24.95 (ISBN 0-275-24060-6). Praeger.

Clark, Barbara. Growing up Gifted. 1979. text ed. 22.95 (ISBN 0-675-08276-5). Merrill.

--Growing up Gifted. 544p. 1983. pap. text ed. 21.95 (ISBN 0-675-20060-1). Merrill.

Clark, Barbara R. Reflections. Davis, Ruby & Gerstung, Estella, eds. Clark, Carl R. & Williams, Cecil J. 72p. (Orig.). (gr. 4-12). 1982. pap. 4.95 (ISBN 0-686-37922-5). Williams Com.

Clark, Barrett H. Great Short Biographies of Modern Times, the Sevententh, Eighteenth, & Nineteenth Centuries. 1406p. 1982. Repr. of 1928 ed. lib. bdg. 65.00 (ISBN 0-89987-136-4). Darby Bks.

Clark, Ben T. Russian for Americans. 3rd ed. 672p. 1983. text ed. 24.50 scp (ISBN 0-06-041296-8, HarpC); instr. manual avail. (ISBN 0-06-361250-X); scp tapes 229.00 (ISBN 0-06-047441-6). Har-Row.

Clark, Bernadine, ed. The Writer's Resource Guide. 2nd ed. 504p. 1983. 16.95 (ISBN 0-89879-102-2). Writers Digest.

Clark, Bill. A Paper Ark. LC 78-65531. (Illus.). 1979. 14.95 o.p. (ISBN 0-89696-033-1, An Everest House Book). Dodd.

Clark Boardman Company, compiled by. Federal Rules of Civil Procedure. LC 81-18095. (Federal Practice Ser.). 1982. 45.00 (ISBN 0-87632-114-7). Boardman.

Clark, Braddie. You Let Me Cry Again. LC 76-12220. 1976. 7.95 (ISBN 0-87716-064-3, Pub. by Moore Pub Co). F Apple.

Clark, Brian. Whose Life is it Anyway? 160p. 1980. pap. 2.50 (ISBN 0-380-52407-4, 52407). Avon.

Clark, Brian F. Genetic Code. (Studies in Biology: No. 83). 80p. 1978. pap. text ed. 8.95 (ISBN 0-7131-2647-7). E Arnold.

Clark, Burton R. The Higher Education System: Academic Organization in Cross-National Perspective. LC 82-13521. 1983. text ed. 24.95x (ISBN 0-520-04841-5). U of Cal Pr.

Clark, C. Shakespeare & Psychology. (Studies in Shakespeare Ser.: No. 24). 1981. lib. bdg. 48.95x (ISBN 0-8383-2143-7). Haskell.

Clark, C. E., jt. ed. see Bruccoli, Matthew J.

Clark, C. E. Frazer, Jr., ed. Hawthorne at Auction 1894-1971. LC 70-38939. (A Bruccoli Clark Book, Authors at Auction Ser.). 400p. 1972. 42.00x (ISBN 0-8103-0919-X). Gale.

--Nathaniel Hawthorne Journal. Incl. 1973. 25.00 (ISBN 0-910972-50-8); 1974. 1973. 25.00 (ISBN 0-910972-39-7); 1975. 23.00 o.p. (ISBN 0-685-83822-6). Bruccoli.

Clark, C. E., Jr. & Bruccoli, Matthew J., eds. Pages: The World of Books, Writers & Writing, Vol. 1. LC 76-20369. (Illus.). 1976. 30.00x (ISBN 0-8103-0925-4). Gale.

Clark, C. E., Jr., jt. ed. see Bruccoli, Matthew J.

Clark, C. Frazer, Jr., ed. Nathaniel Hawthorne Journal Nineteen Seventy-Eight. (Bruccoli Clark Bk.). (Illus.). 400p. Date not set. 40.00 (ISBN 0-8103-0929-7). Gale. Postponed.

Clark, C. Wells, ed. see Bigl, Joseph H., et al.

Clark, Carl R. see Clark, Barbara R.

Clark, Carol R., jt. auth. see Schallert, William F.

Clark, Carolyn & Shea, Carole A. Management in Nursing. (Illus.). 1979. text ed. 21.50 (ISBN 0-07-011135-9, HP). McGraw.

Clark, Carolyn C. Mental Health Aspects of Community Health Nursing. (Illus.). 1978. pap. text ed. 14.95 (ISBN 0-07-011150-2, HP). McGraw.

Clark, Champ. The Badlands. LC 74-18063. (American Wilderness). (Illus.). (gr. 6 up). 1974. PLB 15.96 (ISBN 0-8094-1209-8, Pub. by Time-Life). Silver.

--Flood. LC 81-18545. (Planet Earth Ser.). lib. bdg. 19.92 (ISBN 0-8094-4309-0, Pub. by Time-Life). Silver.

Clark, Charles A. Directory of Scholarships. 172p. pap. 15.00x (ISBN 0-686-31596-0). Adv Acceptance.

Clark, Charles B. When Hot Springs Was a Pup. (Illus.). 1976. pap. 2.50 o.p. (ISBN 0-917624-01-7). Lame Johnny.

Clark, Charles E. The Eastern Frontier: The Settlement of Northern New England, 1610-1763. LC 82-40477. 460p. 1983. pap. 16.50 (ISBN 0-87451-252-2). U Pr of New Eng.

--Maine During the Colonial Period: A Bibliographical Guide. (Maine History Bibliographical Guide Ser.). 1974. pap. 4.00 o.p. (ISBN 0-915592-14-2). Maine Hist.

Clark, Charles L., ed. A Guide to Theories of Economic Development: Cross-National Tests. LC 82-82662. (Theoretical Information Control Guides Ser.). 321p. (Orig.). 1982. 60.00 (ISBN 0-87536-734-8). HRAFP.

Clark, Charlie, III. Sexual Geometry. Sanfilippo, Rose E., ed. LC 82-91125. 112p. 1983. 19.95 (ISBN 0-9609808-0-6). New Pen Pub Co.

Clark, Chris & Rush, Sheila. How to Get Along with Black People: A Handbook for White Folks & Some Black Folks Too. LC 73-162960. 156p. 1973. pap. 5.95 (ISBN 0-89388-018-3). Okpaku Communications.

Clark, Christine L. The Make-It-Yourself Shoe Book. 1977. 11.95 o.p. (ISBN 0-394-41057-2); pap. 5.95 (ISBN 0-394-73303-7). Knopf.

Clark, Colin. National Income Nineteen Twenty-Four to Nineteen Thirty-One. LC 67-33571. Repr. of 1932 ed. 22.50x (ISBN 0-678-05161-5). Kelley.

--Population Growth & Land Use. 2nd ed. LC 77-78978. (Illus.). 1977. 26.00 (ISBN 0-312-63141-3). St Martin.

--Regional & Urban Location. LC 81-21510. 1982. 32.50x (ISBN 0-312-66903-8). St Martin.

--Taxmanship. (Hobart Paperbk: No. 26). 1977. pap. 2.50 o.s.i. (ISBN 0-255-36000-2). Transatlantic.

--The Theoretical Side of Calculus. LC 78-6731. 256p. 1978. Repr. of 1972 ed. lib. bdg. 11.50 o.p. (ISBN 0-88275-680-X). Krieger.

Clark, Colin W. Mathematical Bioeconomics: The Optimal Management of Renewable Resources. LC 76-16473. (Pure & Applied Mathematics Ser.). 1976. 36.00x (ISBN 0-471-15856-9, Pub. by Wiley-Interscience). Wiley.

Clark, Connie, jt. auth. see Hayward, Mary.

Clark, D. Cecil. Using Instructional Objectives in Teaching. 168p. 1972. pap. 7.95x (ISBN 0-673-07620-2). Scott F.

Clark, D. J. & Mundhenk, N. Translator's Handbook on the Books of Obadiah & Micah. (Helps for Translators Ser.). 1982. pap. 3.00 (ISBN 0-8267-0129-9, 08567). Am Bible.

Clark, D. P. & Ashall, C. Field Studies on the Australian Plague in the Channel Country of Queensland. 1969. 35.00x (ISBN 0-85135-047-X, Pub. by Centre Overseas Research). State Mutual Bk.

Clark, D. T. & Feast, W. J. Polymer Surfaces. LC 77-17426. 1978. 89.95 (ISBN 0-471-99614-9, Pub by Wiley-Interscience). Wiley.

Clark, David Allen. Jokes, Puns, & Riddles. LC 67-19070. (gr. 3-7). 1968. 5.95a o.p. (ISBN 0-385-09018-8); PLB 5.95a (ISBN 0-385-09019-6). Doubleday.

Clark, David G., et al, eds. Mass Media & the Law. 478p. 1970. 24.50 (ISBN 0-471-15851-8, Pub. by Wiley). Krieger.

Clark, David L. L. A. on Foot. (Illus.). 1983. 4.95 (ISBN 0-913290-03-3). Camaro Pub.

Clark, David R. Critical Essays on Hart Crane. (Critical Essays on American Literature). 1982. lib. bdg. 28.50 (ISBN 0-8161-8380-5, Twayne). G K Hall.

--Yeats at Songs & Choruses. LC 81-16096. (Illus.). 368p. 1983. lib. bdg. 30.00x (ISBN 0-87023-358-0). U of Mass Pr.

Clark, David S., compiled by. Index to Maps of the American Revolution in Books & Periodicals. LC 74-7543. (Illus., Orig.). 1974. lib. bdg. 29.95 (ISBN 0-8371-7582-8, DAR/). Greenwood.

Clark, David W. & Kaiser, Robert L., eds. Guide to the Administration of Charitable Remainder Trusts. 3rd ed. 1978. looseleaf binder 38.50 o.p. (ISBN 0-89964-018-4). CASE.

Clark, Dennis. The Irish in Philadelphia: Ten Generations of Urban Experience. LC 72-95884. 264p. 1974. 29.95 (ISBN 0-87722-057-3). Temple U Pr.

Clark, Dennis R., jt. auth. see Kalman, Sumner M.

Clark, Diane, jt. auth. see Stein, Joe.

Clark, Dick. Looking Great, Staying Young. LC 80-684. 256p. 1980. 11.95 o.p. (ISBN 0-672-52657-3). Bobbs.

Clark, Don. Loving Someone Gay. 1978. pap. 3.50 (ISBN 0-451-11677-1, AE1677, Sig). NAL.

Clark, Donald B. Alexander Pope. (English Authors Ser.). 1966. lib. bdg. 11.95 (ISBN 0-8057-1452-9, Twayne). G K Hall.

--Way to LVEI. 1978. pap. 7.95 (ISBN 0-8403-1915-0). Kendall Hunt.

Clark, Donald B. & Dickinson, Leon T. English Literature: A College Anthology. (Illus.). 1960. text ed. 24.95 (ISBN 0-02-322590-4). Macmillan.

Clark, Donald S. & Varney, Wilbur R. Physical Metallurgy for Engineers. 2nd ed. (Illus.). 1962. text ed. 20.95 (ISBN 0-442-01570-4). Van Nos Reinhold.

Clark, Dorothy. Shepherd's Pie. (Julia MacRae Blackbird Bks.). (Illus.). 48p. (gr. k-3). 1983. 5.95 (ISBN 0-531-04577-3, MacRae). Watts.

Clark, Douglas L. Starting a Successul Business on the West Coast. 194p. (Orig.). 1982. pap. 12.95 (ISBN 0-88908-910-8). Self Counsel Pr.

Clark, Edna M. Ohio Art & Artists. LC 74-13860. xvi, 509p. 1975. Repr. of 1932 ed. 56.00x (ISBN 0-8103-4058-5). Gale.

Clark, Eleanor. Eyes, Etc. 1978. lib. bdg. 10.95 o.p. (ISBN 0-8161-6554-8, Large Print Bks). G K Hall.

--Rome & a Villa. enl. ed. LC 74-5979. 384p. 1982. pap. 8.95 (ISBN 0-689-70630-8, 1). Atheneum.

Clark, Electa. Robert Peary: Boy of the North Pole. (Childhood of Famous Americans Ser). (Illus.). (gr. 3-7). 3.95 o.p. (ISBN 0-672-50160-0). Bobbs.

Clark, Eliot. Theodore Robinson: His Life & His Art. LC 79-91552. (Illus.). 78p. (Orig.). 1979. 25.00 (ISBN 0-940114-11-9); pap. 16.00 o.s.i. (ISBN 0-940114-10-0). R H Love Gall.

Clark, Elizabeth & Richardson, Herbert W., eds. Women & Religion: Readings in the Western Tradition from Aeschylus to Mary Daly. LC 76-9975. 1976. pap. 6.95xi (ISBN 0-06-061398-X, RD-178, HarpR). Har-Row.

Clark, Elizabeth A. Clement's Use of Aristotle: The Aristotelian Contribution of Clement of Alexandria's Refutation of Gnosticism. LC 77-93913. (Texts & Studies in Religion: Vol. 1). vii, 182p. 1981. Repr. of 1977 ed. text ed. 29.95 (ISBN 0-88946-984-9). E Mellen.

--Jerome, Chrysostom, & Friends: Essays & Translations. LC 79-66374. (Studies in Women & Religion: Vol. 1). xi, 254p. 1979. soft cover 34.95x o.p. (ISBN 0-88946-548-7). E Mellen.

--Jerome, Chrysostom, & Friends: Essays & Translations. (Studies in Women & Religion: Vol. 2). xi, 254p. 1983. Repr. of 1979 ed. 39.95x (ISBN 0-88946-541-X). E Mellen.

Clark, Elizabeth F. & De Winter, Francis, eds. Use of Solar Energy for the Cooling of Buildings. (International Solar Energy Society, American Section, Workshop Ser.). 1978. pap. text ed. 36.00x (ISBN 0-89553-012-0). Am Solar Energy.

Clark, Ella E. Indian Legends of the Pacific Northwest. (Illus.). (YA) (gr. 9-12). 1953. pap. 5.95 (ISBN 0-520-00243-1, CAL18). U of Cal Pr.

Clark, Erskine. Wrestlin Jacob: A Portrait of Religion in the Old South. LC 78-52453. 1979. pap. 3.99 (ISBN 0-8042-1089-6). John Knox.

Clark, Eve V., jt. auth. see Clark, Herbert H.

Clark, Ewen M. & Forbes, J. A. Evaluating Primary Care: Some Experiments in Quality Measurement in an Academic Unit of Primary Medical Care. (Illus.). 236p. 1979. 25.00x (ISBN 0-85664-856-6, Pub. by Croom Helm Ltd England). Biblio Dist.

Clark, F. D. & Lorenzoni, A. B. Applied Cost Engineering. (Cost Engineering Ser.: Vol. 1). 1978. 26.50 (ISBN 0-8247-6654-7). Dekker.

Clark, Fiona. Hats. (Illus.). 1982. text ed. 13.95x (ISBN 0-7134-3774-X). Drama Bk.

Clark, Floyd B. The Constitutional Doctrines of Justice Harlan. LC 74-87560. (Law, Politics & History Ser). 1969. Repr. of 1915 ed. lib. bdg. 29.50 (ISBN 0-306-71391-8). Da Capo.

Clark, Frances. ABC Papers. 32p. (gr. k-6). 1947. pap. text ed. 5.20 (ISBN 0-87487-198-0). Summy.

Clark, Frances & Goss, Louise. Keyboard Musician for the Adult Beginner. 208p. (Orig.). 1980. pap. text ed. 19.85 (ISBN 0-87487-103-4). Summy.

--The Music Tree, 3 parts. Incl. Part A. 7.05 (ISBN 0-87487-121-2); Part B. 7.15 (ISBN 0-87487-122-0); Part C. 7.20 (ISBN 0-87487-123-9). (Frances Clark Library for Piano Students). 1973. Summy.

--The Music Tree: Time to Begin. (Frances Clark Library for Piano Students). 1973. pap. text ed. 7.60 (ISBN 0-87487-120-4). Summy.

--Playtime: Supplementary Music, 3 parts. Incl. Part A. 4.05 (ISBN 0-87487-137-9); Part B. 3.95 (ISBN 0-87487-138-7); Part C. 3.95 (ISBN 0-87487-139-5). (Frances Clark Library for Piano Students). 1976. Summy.

--Supplementary Solos: Levels 3 & 4. (Frances Clark Library for Piano Students). 1974. pap. 6.65 (ISBN 0-87487-140-9). Summy.

--Teaching the Music Tree: A Handbook for Teachers. (Frances Clark Library for Piano Students). 1973. pap. text ed. 4.25 (ISBN 0-87487-124-7). Summy.

Clark, Frances & Goss, Louise, eds. Contemporary Piano Literature. Incl. Book 1. 1961. pap. text ed. 4.25 (ISBN 0-87487-107-7); Book 2. 1955. pap. text ed. 4.50 (ISBN 0-87487-108-5); Books 3 & 4. 1957. pap. text ed. 7.50 (ISBN 0-87487-109-3); Books 5 & 6. pap. text ed. 7.50 (ISBN 0-87487-110-7). (Frances Clark Library for Piano Students Ser.). (Illus.). Summy.

--Piano Literature of the 17th, 18th, & 19th Centuries. Incl. Bk. 1. 1964. pap. text ed. 4.80 (ISBN 0-87487-125-5); Bk. 2. (Illus.). 1954. pap. text ed. 4.75 (ISBN 0-87487-126-3); Bks. 3, 4a & 4b. (Illus.). 1957. pap. text ed. 7.70 (ISBN 0-87487-127-1); Bks. 5a & 6a. (Illus.). 1974. pap. text ed. 6.50 (ISBN 0-87487-128-X); Bk. 5b. (Illus.). 1957. pap. text ed. 6.00 (ISBN 0-87487-129-8); Bk. 6b. (Illus.). 1956. pap. text ed. 7.95 (ISBN 0-87487-130-1). (Frances Clark Library for Piano Students). Summy.

--Piano Technic, 6 bks. Incl. Bk. 1. 1954. pap. text ed. 6.70 (ISBN 0-87487-131-X); Bk. 2. 1955. pap. text ed. 5.95 (ISBN 0-87487-132-8); Bk. 3. 1955. pap. text ed. 6.30 (ISBN 0-87487-133-6); Bk. 4. 1960. pap. text ed. 6.70 (ISBN 0-87487-134-4); Bk. 5. 1960. pap. text ed. 6.70 (ISBN 0-87487-135-2); Bk. 6. 1960. pap. text ed. 6.70 (ISBN 0-87487-136-0). (Frances Clark Library for Piano Students). Summy.

Clark, Frances, ed. see George, Jon.

Clark, Frances, ed. see Kraehenbuehl, David.

Clark, Frank. Mathematics For Data Processing. 2nd ed. 1982. text ed. 21.95 (ISBN 0-8359-4263-5); instr's. manual avail. (ISBN 0-8359-4264-3). Reston.

Clark, Frank J. Mathematics for Data Processing. LC 73-8868. (Illus.). 432p. 1974. 19.95 (ISBN 0-87909-470-2). Reston.

Clark, Frank P. Special Effects in Motion Pictures. (Illus.). 238p. 1982. pap. text ed. 20.00 (ISBN 0-940690-00-4). Soc Motion Pic & TV Engrs.

Clark, G. Britain's Naval Heritage. 1982. 40.00x (ISBN 0-11-290365-7, Pub. by HMSO). State Mutual Bk.

Clark, G. C., jt. auth. see Punt, W.

Clark, G. M. Structure of Non-Molecular Solids: A Co-Ordinated Polyhedron Approach. (Illus.). xii, 365p. 1972. 51.25 (ISBN 0-85334-544-9, Pub. by Applied Sci England). Elsevier.

Clark, Gail. The Baroness of Bow Street. LC 78-22609. 1979. 9.95 o.p. (ISBN 0-399-12334-2). Putnam Pub Group.

--Dulcie Bligh. LC 77-21672. 1978. 8.95 o.p. (ISBN 0-399-12053-X). Putnam Pub Group.

Clark, Geoffrey A. The Asturian of Cantabria: Early Holocene Hunter-Gatherers in Northern Spain. (Anthropological Papers Ser.: No. 41). 160p. 1983. pap. 18.95x monograph (ISBN 0-8165-0800-3). U of Ariz Pr.

Clark, George & Kasten, Frederick H. History of Staining. (Illus.). 144p. 1983. lib. bdg. price not set (ISBN 0-683-01705-5). Williams & Wilkins.

Clark, George B. Industrial High Explosives: Composition & Calculations for Engineers. Raese, Jon W., ed. LC 80-18063. (CSM Quarterly Ser.: Vol. 75, No. 1). (Illus.). 100p. (Orig.). 1980. pap. 10.00 (ISBN 0-686-63161-7). Colo Sch Mines.

Clark, George N. English History: A Survey. 1971. 29.50x (ISBN 0-19-822339-0). Oxford U Pr.

Clark, Gordon, jt. ed. see Layne, Ken.

Clark, Grahame. Aspects of Prehistory. LC 73-94989. 1970. 27.50x (ISBN 0-520-01584-3); pap. 4.50x o.p. (ISBN 0-520-02630-6). U of Cal Pr.

Clark, Grover. Economic Rivalries in China. 1932. 42.50x (ISBN 0-685-69799-1). Elliots Bks.

Clark, Halsey. Depths of Danger. (Periscope Ser.: No. 3). (Orig.). 1983. pap. 3.25 (ISBN 0-440-01888-9). Dell.

Clark, Harry. A Venture in History: The Production, Publication, & Sale of the Works of Hubert Howe Bancroft. LC 72-173900. 1973. pap. 30.00x (ISBN 0-520-09417-4). U of Cal Pr.

Clark, Harry H., jt. auth. see Rathbun, John W.

Clark, Harry H., jt. ed. see Allen, Gay W.

Clark, Henry B., ed. see Linnell, Robert.

Clark, Henry B., II. Freedom of Religion in America: Historical Roots, Philosophical Concepts, Contemporary Problems. 143p. 1982. pap. 6.95 (ISBN 0-87855-925-6). Transaction Bks.

Clark, Herbert H. & Clark, Eve V. Psychology & Language: An Introduction to Psycholinguistics. (Illus.). 608p. 1977. text ed. 26.95 (ISBN 0-15-572815-6, HC). HarBraceJ.

Clark, Howard, ed. Twentieth Century Interpretations of the Odyssey. 132p. 1983. 9.95 (ISBN 0-13-934851-4); pap. 4.95 (ISBN 0-13-934844-1). P-H.

Clark, Hyla. The Tin Can Book. (Art Bks). (Illus., Orig.). 1977. pap. 6.95 (ISBN 0-451-79965-8, G9965, Sig). NAL.

Clark, Ian, jt. ed. see Bowman, Larry W.

Clark, Ira. Christ Revealed: The History of the Neotypological Lyric in the English Renaissance. LC 82-2696. (University of Florida Humanities Monographs: No. 51). xiv, 218p. 1982. pap. 15.00x (ISBN 0-8130-0712-7). U Presses Fla.

Clark, Isobel. Practical Geostatistics. (Illus.). 1979. 28.75x (ISBN 0-85334-843-X, Pub. by Applied Sci England). Elsevier.

--Practical Geostatistics. 1979. 28.75 (ISBN 0-85334-843-X). Elsevier.

Clark, J. Formicidae of Australia, Vol. 1. 1982. 40.00x (ISBN 0-686-97912-5, Pub. by CSIRO Australia). State Mutual Bk.

--Handbook for Office Workers. 3rd ed. 1982. 13.95 (ISBN 0-442-21494-4). Van Nos Reinhold.

Clark, J., et al. Thin Seam Coal Mining Technology. LC 82-7968. (Energy Tech. Rev. 80). (Illus.). 385p. 1983. 36.00 (ISBN 0-8155-0909-X). Noyes.

--Global Simulation Models: A Comparative Study. LC 74-32231. 135p. 1975. 29.00 o.p. (ISBN 0-471-15899-2, Pub. by Wiley-Interscience). Wiley.

Clark, J. A., jt. ed. see Cena, K.

Clark, J. A., jt. ed. see Cooper, C. A.

Clark, J. B., jt. ed. see Comins, N. R.

Clark, J. C. & Buckingham, P. D. Short-Lived Radioactive Gases for Clinical Use. 1975. 34.95 o.p. (ISBN 0-407-39770-1). Butterworth.

Clark, J. M., et al. Putnam's Contemporary German Dictionary. (Putnam's Contemporary Foreign Language Dictionaries). 1973. 3.50 o.p. (ISBN 0-399-11145-X). Putnam Pub Group.

Clark, J. R., ed. Chemistry & Physics of Minerals. pap. 7.50 (ISBN 0-686-60385-0). Polycrystal Bk Serv.

Clark, J. W. The Language & Style of Anthony Trollope. (Andre Deutsch Language Library). 1977. lib. bdg. 21.00 o.p. (ISBN 0-233-96641-2). Westview.

Clark, James. Cars. LC 80-17876. (A Look Inside Ser.). (Illus.). 48p. (gr. 4-12). 1981. PLB 14.25 (ISBN 0-8172-1405-4). Raintree Pubs.

Clark, James D. & Orgel, Stephen, eds. The Bugbears. LC 78-66768. (Renaissance Drama Ser.). 1979. lib. bdg. 28.50 o.s.i. (ISBN 0-8240-9749-1). Garland Pub.

Clark, James E., tr. Ojibway Indians Coloring Book. 32p. (Ojibway.). 1978. pap. 2.00 bilingual ed. (ISBN 0-87351-146-8); pap. 1.50 Eng. only o.p. (ISBN 0-87351-135-2). Minn Hist.

Clark, James L. & Clark, Lyn R. How Three: A Handbook for Office Workers. 3rd ed. 297p. 1982. 9.95x (ISBN 0-534-01116-0). Kent Pub Co.

--How Two: Handbook for Office Workers. 2nd ed. (Business Ser.). 280p. 1979. pap. text ed. 8.95x o.p. (ISBN 0-534-00635-3). Kent Pub Co.

Clark, Jane E., jt. auth. see Scott, J. A.

Clark, Jean. The Marriage Bed. LC 82-13134. 320p. 1983. 15.95 (ISBN 0-399-12746-1). Putnam Pub Group.

Clark, Jewell T., compiled by. A Guide to Church Records in the Archives Branch, Virginia State Library. x, 271p. (Orig.). 1981. pap. 5.00 o.s.i. (ISBN 0-88490-105-X). VA State Lib.

Clark, Joe. Tennessee Hill Folk. LC 72-2880. (Illus.). 96p. 1972. 10.95 (ISBN 0-8265-1183-X). Vanderbilt U Pr.

Clark, John B. Philosophy of Wealth. 2nd ed. LC 67-25955. Repr. of 1887 ed. 19.50x (ISBN 0-678-00275-4). Kelley.

Clark, John G. Mesolithic Settlement of Northern Europe. LC 75-95090. Repr. of 1936 ed. lib. bdg. 18.50 (ISBN 0-8371-2579-0, CLMS). Greenwood.

Clark, John G. & Piggott, Stuart. Prehistoric Societies. (Illus.). 1965. text ed. 7.90x (ISBN 0-685-01991-8). Phila Bk Co.

Clark, John G., ed. Frontier Challenge: Responses to the Trans-Mississippi West. LC 79-121649. 1971. 10.00x o.p. (ISBN 0-7006-0070-1). Univ Pr KS.

Clark, John H. A Map of Mental States. (Illus.). 224p. 1983. pap. price not set (ISBN 0-7100-9235-0). Routledge & Kegan.

Clark, John J. & Clark, Margaret T. A Statistics Primer for Managers. (Illus.). 272p. 1982. write for info. (ISBN 0-02-905800-7). Free Pr.

Clark, John M. Studies in the Economics of Overhead Costs. 1981. pap. 23.00x (ISBN 0-226-10851-1). U of Chicago Pr.

Clark, John P. Casualties, Poems Nineteen Sixty-Six to Nineteen Sixty-Eight. LC 73-113090. 1970. 9.50x (ISBN 0-8419-0096-5, Africana); pap. 6.00x (ISBN 0-8419-0041-8, Africana). Holmes & Meier.

--Max Stirner's Egoism. 111p. (Orig.). pap. 3.00 (ISBN 0-900384-14-X). Left Bank.

--Ozidi: A Play. (Orig.). 1966. 3.95x o.p. (ISBN 0-19-211375-5). Oxford U Pr.

Clark, John P., jt. auth. see Hollinger, Richard C.

Clark, John R. The Beaches of Maui County. LC 80-13857. (Illus.). 1980. pap. 7.95 (ISBN 0-8248-0694-8). UH Pr.

--The Beaches of O'ahu. LC 77-8244. (Illus., Orig.). 1977. pap. 4.95 (ISBN 0-8248-0510-0). UH Pr.

--Coastal Ecosystem Management: A Technical Manual for the Conservation of Coastal Zone Resources. LC 76-40125. 1977. 70.50 o.p. (ISBN 0-471-15854-2, Pub by Wiley-Interscience). Wiley.

Clark, John W., jt. auth. see Partridge, Eric.

Clark, John W., et al. Water Supply & Pollution Control. 3rd ed. 661p. 1977. text ed. 33.95 scp (ISBN 0-7002-2495-5, HarpC); solution manual avail. (ISBN 0-7002-2496-3). Har-Row.

Clark, Joseph A. & Moudy, James M. A Hope of Wisdom: Essays on Education. LC 73-75007. (Centennial Publications Ser). 86p. 1973. text ed. 5.00 (ISBN 0-912646-44-6). Tex Christian.

Clark, Joseph S. Congress, the Sapless Branch. LC 74-1778. 268p. 1976. Repr. of 1964 ed. lib. bdg. 18.50x (ISBN 0-8371-7398-1, CLCO). Greenwood.

Clark, Joshua V. Onondaga, or, Reminiscences of Earlier & Later Times, Being a Series of Historical Sketches Relative to Onondaga.., 2 vols. LC 73-12561. (Illus.). 796p. 1973. Repr. of 1849 ed. Set. 36.00 o.s.i. (ISBN 0-527-17665-6). Kraus Repr.

Clark, Julia B., et al. Pharmacological Basis of Nursing Practice. LC 81-14192. (Illus.). 702p. 1982. pap. text ed. 26.95 (ISBN 0-8016-4061-X). Mosby.

Clark, Kenneth. An Introduction to Rembrandt. LC 77-3745. (Illus.). 160p. 1979. 12.95i (ISBN 0-06-430860-X, Icon Edns); pap. 8.95i (ISBN 0-06-430092-7, I*N 92). Har-Row.

--Landscape into Art. rev. & enl. ed. (Icon Editions). (Illus.). 1978. pap. 8.95i (ISBN 0-06-430088-9, IN-88, HarpT); 19.95 (ISBN 0-06-010781-2). Har-Row.

--Nude: A Study of Ideal Form. (Illus.). pap. 5.95 o.p. (ISBN 0-385-09388-8, A168, Anch). Doubleday.

Clark, Kenneth, ed. Ruskin Today. 350p. 1983. pap. 5.95 (ISBN 0-14-006326-9). Penguin.

Clark, Kim B., jt. auth. see Abernathey, William J.

Clark, L. R., et al. The Ecology of Insect Populations in Theory & Practice. 1974. pap. 10.95x (ISBN 0-412-21170-X, Pub. by Chapman & Hall). Methuen Inc.

Clark, Lawrence. Sayula Popoluca Texts. (Publications in Linguistics & Related Fields Ser.: No. 6). 216p. 1961. pap. 2.00 (ISBN 0-88312-006-2); microfiche 3.00x (ISBN 0-88312-406-8). Summer Inst Ling.

Clark, Lawrence & Clark, Nancy. Vocabulario Popoluca de Sayula. (Vocabularios Indigenas Ser.: No. 4). 165p. 1960. pap. 3.00x (ISBN 0-88312-663-X); microfiche 2.25 (ISBN 0-88312-365-7). Summer Inst Ling.

Clark, Lawrence P. Designs for Evaluating Social Programs. (Learning Packages in the Policy Sciences Ser.: No. 11). 44p. 1979. pap. text ed. 2.50x (ISBN 0-936826-00-2). Pol Stud Assocs.

--Introduction to Surveys & Interviews. (Learning Packages in the Policy Sciences Ser.: No. 12). (Illus.). 56p. 1978. pap. text ed. 2.50x (ISBN 0-936826-01-0). Pol Stud Assocs.

Clark, Leon E. Through African Eyes: Coming of Age in Africa, Vol. 1. 120p. 1982. pap. 5.95 (ISBN 0-938960-07-5). CITE.

--Through African Eyes: From Tribe to Town - Problems of Adjustment, Vol. 2. (Illus.). 125p. 1981. pap. 5.95 (ISBN 0-938960-08-3). CITE.

--Through African Eyes: Nation-Building - Tanzania & the World. (Vol. 6). (Illus.). 160p. 1981. pap. 5.95 (ISBN 0-938960-12-1). CITE.

--Through African Eyes: The African Past & the Coming of the European. (Vol. 3). (Illus.). 144p. 1981. pap. 5.95 (ISBN 0-938960-09-1). CITE.

--Through African Eyes: The Colonial Experience An Inside View, Vol. 4. 135p. 1981. pap. 5.95 (ISBN 0-938960-10-5). CITE.

--Through African Eyes: The Rise of Nationalism - Freedom Regained, Vol. 5. 141p. 1981. pap. 5.95 (ISBN 0-938960-11-3). CITE.

Clark, Leonard H. & Klein, Raymond L. The American Secondary School Curriculum. 2nd ed. (Illus.). 544p. 1972. text ed. 23.95x (ISBN 0-02-322580-7, 32258). Macmillan.

Clark, Leonard H. & Starr, Irving S. Secondary School Teaching Methods. 4th ed. (Illus.). 512p. 1981. text ed. 22.95 (ISBN 0-02-322650-1, 322650). Macmillan.

Clark, Leonard H., jt. auth. see Callahan, Joseph F.

Clark, Leslie L., ed. see International Congress on Technology & Blindness, 1st, 1962.

Clark, Linda. The Best of Linda Clark, Vol. 2. LC 77-352686. (Illus.). 1983. pap. 6.95 (ISBN 0-87983-249-5). Keats.

--Color Therapy. LC 74-75389. 1975. 7.95 (ISBN 0-8159-5206-6). Devin.

--Get Well Naturally. 1974. Repr. of 1965 ed. 7.95 (ISBN 0-8159-5605-3). Devin.

--Handbook of Natural Remedies. pap. 2.95x (ISBN 0-671-42382-7). Cancer Control Soc.

--Help Yourself to Health. 1972. 1.50x (ISBN 0-515-03395-2). Cancer Control Soc.

--How to Improve Your Health. LC 78-61329. 1979. pap. 4.95 (ISBN 0-87983-180-4). Keats.

--Light on Your Health Problems. LC 72-83522. (Pivot Original Health Book). 240p. 1972. pap. 1.50 o.p. (ISBN 0-87983-026-3). Keats.

--Rejuvenation. 1978. 12.95 (ISBN 0-8159-6718-7). Devin.

--Stay Young Longer. (Orig.). pap. 1.95 o.s.i. (ISBN 0-515-05076-8). Jove Pubns.

Clark, Linda & Lee, Kay. Beauty Questions & Answers. 1977. pap. 2.25 o.s.i. (ISBN 0-515-05647-2). Jove Pubns.

Clark, Linda, et al. Your Natural Health Sampler. LC 73-80031. (Pivot Health Bk.). 128p. 1973. pap. 1.25 o.p. (ISBN 0-87983-058-1). Keats.

Clark, Louis H. The Complete Guide for the Manufacturer's Rep: How to Get & Hold Key Accounts. 264p. 1975. 4.25 (ISBN 0-07-011160-X, P&RB). McGraw.

Clark, Lyn R., jt. auth. see Clark, James L.

Clark, M. Gardner. The Development of China's Steel Industry & Soviet Technical Aid. LC 72-619194. 168p. 1973. pap. 7.00 (ISBN 0-87546-292-8); pap. 10.00 special hard bdg. (ISBN 0-87546-293-6). ILR Pr.

Clark, Malcolm. The Need to Question: An Introduction to Philosophy. LC 72-5579. 304p. 1973. text ed. 17.95 (ISBN 0-13-610857-1). P-H.

Clark, Malcolm, Jr., intro. by see Deady, Matthew P.

Clark, Margaret. Health in the Mexican-American Culture: A Community Study. 2nd ed. 1970. 21.00x (ISBN 0-520-01666-1); pap. 3.85 o.p. (ISBN 0-520-01668-8, CAL192). U of Cal Pr.

Clark, Margaret G. Benjamin Banneker: Astronomer & Scientist. LC 74-131055. (Americans All Ser). (Illus.). (gr. 3-6). 1971. PLB 7.12 (ISBN 0-8116-4564-9). Garrard.

--Their Eyes on the Stars: Four Black Writers. LC 73-3499. (Toward Freedom Ser.). (Illus.). (gr. 5-9). 1973. PLB 3.98 (ISBN 0-8116-4804-4). Garrard.

Clark, Margaret S. & Fiske, Susan T. Affect & Cognition: The Seventeenth Annual Carnegie Symposium on Cognition. (Ongoing Ser.). 368p. 1982. text ed. 36.00x (ISBN 0-89859-212-7). L Erlbaum Assocs.

Clark, Margaret T., jt. auth. see Clark, John J.

Clark, Margery. Poppy Seed Cakes. (ps-1). 9.95 (ISBN 0-385-07457-3); PLB o.p. (ISBN 0-385-03834-8). Doubleday.

Clark, Marlyn E. Optimal Design in Cardiovascular Fluid Mechanics: Our Amazing Circulatory System. LC 76-24995. (ICR Technical Monograph No. 5). (Illus.). 1976. pap. 5.95 (ISBN 0-89051-028-8). CLP Pubs.

Clark, Martin, jt. auth. see Morris, Henry M.

Clark, Martin E. Choosing Your Career: The Christian's Decision Manual. 120p. (Orig.). 1983. pap. 3.95 (ISBN 0-8010-2483-8). Baker Bk.

Clark, Mary H. The Cradle Will Fall. (General Ser.). 1980. lib. bdg. 13.95 (ISBN 0-8161-3121-X, Large Print Bks). G K Hall.

--The Cradle Will Fall. 1980. 10.95 o.p. (ISBN 0-671-25268-2, 25268). S&S.

--A Cry in the Night. (General Ser.). 1983. lib. bdg. 15.95 (ISBN 0-8161-3486-3, Large Print Bks). G K Hall.

--Where Are the Children. 256p. 1976. pap. 3.95 (ISBN 0-440-19593-4). Dell.

Clark, Mary L. Dinosaurs. LC 81-7750. (The New True Books). (Illus.). 48p. (gr. k-4). 1981. PLB 9.25 (ISBN 0-516-01612-1). Childrens.

Clark, Mason A., ed. The Healing Wisdom of Doctor P. P. Quimby. (Illus.). 128p. (Orig.). 1982. pap. text ed. 8.95 (ISBN 0-931400-02-3). Frontal Lobe.

Clark, Mavis T. If the Earth Falls In. LC 75-4781. 176p. (gr. 6 up). 1975. 6.95 o.p. (ISBN 0-395-28900-9, Clarion). HM.

Clark, Melanie B. A Treasury of Poetry. 1981. 4.50 (ISBN 0-8062-1687-5). Carlton.

Clark, Merrian E. Ford's Deck Plan Guide. rev. ed. LC 74-27649. 1982. 50.00 (ISBN 0-916486-58-3). M Clark.

--Ford's International Cruise Guide. 35th ed. LC 75-27925. (Winter 1982-83 Ser.). 160p. 1982. pap. 7.95. M Clark.

--Ford's International Cruise Guide. 37th ed. LC 75-27925. (Illus.). 160p. 1983. pap. 7.95 (ISBN 0-916486-71-0). M Clark.

--Ford's International Cruise Guide: Spring 1983. 36th ed. LC 75-27925. (Illus.). 160p. 1983. pap. 7.95 (ISBN 0-916486-69-9). M Clark.

Clark, Merrian E., ed. Ford's Freighter Travel Guide: Summer 1983. 61st ed. LC 54-3845. (Illus.). 144p. 1983. pap. 6.95 (ISBN 0-916486-70-2). M Clark.

Clark, Michael, jt. auth. see Small, John.

Clark, Michael D. Coherent Variety: The Idea of Diversity in British & American Conservative Thought. LC 82-9228. (Contributions in Political Science Ser.: No. 86). 248p. 1983. lib. bdg. 35.00 (ISBN 0-313-23284-9, CCV/). Greenwood.

--Worldly Theologians: The Persistence of Religion in Nineteenth Century American Thought. LC 80-5840. 328p. (Orig.). 1982. lib. bdg. 23.25 (ISBN 0-8191-1778-1); pap. text ed. 12.75 (ISBN 0-8191-1779-X). U Pr of Amer.

Clark, Michael P. Michel Foucault: An Annotated Bibliography Took Kit for A New Age. Cain, William, ed. LC 82-48474. (Modern Critics & Critical Schools Ser.). 600p. 1982. lib. bdg. 60.00 (ISBN 0-8240-9253-8). Garland Pub.

Clark, N. & Peters, M. Scorable Self-Care Evaluation (SSCE) LC 82-61594. 64p. 1983. pap. 16.00 (ISBN 0-913590-95-9). Slack Inc.

Clark, Nancy. Littleton: A Pictorial History. Friedman, Donna R., ed. LC 80-39601. (Illus.). 208p. 1981. pap. 12.95 o.p. (ISBN 0-89865-112-3). Donning Co.

Clark, Nancy, jt. auth. see Clark, Lawrence.

Clark, Nancy, ed. see Lodo, Venerable L.

Clark, Olivene. Heirloom of Memories. 1983. 8.50 (ISBN 0-8062-2137-2). Carlton.

Clark, Paul F. The Miners' Fight for Democracy: Arnold Miller & the Reform of the United Mine Workers. LC 81-2011. (Cornell Studies in Industrial & Labor Relations: No. 21). (Illus.). 194p. 1981. 16.95 (ISBN 0-87546-086-0); pap. 9.95 (ISBN 0-87546-087-9). ILR Pr.

Clark, Peter. Henry Hallam. (English Authors Ser.). 1982. lib. bdg. 15.95 (ISBN 0-8057-6818-1, Twayne). G K Hall.

Clark, Philip. Tyrants of the Twentieth Century. LC 81-86279. (In Profile Ser.). PLB 12.68 (ISBN 0-382-06633-2). Silver.

Clark, R. see Kalven, H., Jr.

Clark, R. A., jt. auth. see Klebanoff, S.

Clark, R. B. & Panchen, A. L. Synopsis of Animal Classification. 126p. 1971. 8.95x (ISBN 0-412-21250-1, Pub. by Chapman & Hall England). Methuen Inc.

Clark, R. B., intro. by. The Long-Term Effects of Oil Pollution on Marine Populations, Communities & Ecosystems: Proceedings. (RSL Philosophies. Transactions Series B, Vol. 297: No. 1087). (Illus.). 260p. 1982. text ed. 80.00x (ISBN 0-85403-188-X). Scholium Intl.

Clark, R. B., jt. ed. see Heywood, V. H.

Clark, R. J. & Hester, R. E., eds. Advances in Infrared & Raman Spectroscopy, 5 vols. Vol. 1. 1975 ed. 83.95 (ISBN 0-471-25631-5, Pub. by Wiley Heyden); Vol. 2. 1976 ed. 83.95 (ISBN 0-471-25632-3); Vol. 3. 1977 ed. 83.95 (ISBN 0-471-25633-1); Vol. 4. 1978 ed. 114.00 (ISBN 0-471-25634-X). Wiley.

--Advances in Infrared & Raman Spectroscopy, Vol. 5. 1978. casebound 114.00 (ISBN 0-471-25636-6, Pub. by Wiley Heyden). Wiley.

--Advances in Infrared & Raman Spectroscopy, Vol. 6. (Advances in Infrared & Raman Spectroscopy Ser.). 372p. 1980. 114.00 (ISBN 0-471-25637-4, Pub. by Wiley Heyden). Wiley.

--Advances in Infrared & Raman Spectroscopy, Vol. 7. (Advances in Infrared & Raman Spectroscopy Ser.). 1980. 114.00 (ISBN 0-471-25639-0, Pub. by Wiley Heyden). Wiley.

Clark, R. L. & Rushforth, S. R. Diatom Studies of the Headwaters of Henrys Fork of the Snake River, Island Park, Idaho, USA. (Bibliotheca Phycologica Ser.: No. 33). 1977. pap. text ed. 20.00x (ISBN 3-7682-1149-5). Lubrecht & Cramer.

Clark, Ralph D. Case Studies in Echocardiography: A Diagnostic Workbook. LC 76-1212. (Illus.). 1977. pap. 25.00 (ISBN 0-7216-2594-0). Saunders.

Clark, Randolph L., ed. Year Book of Cancer 1983. 1983. 40.00 (ISBN 0-8151-1791-4). Year Bk Med.

Clark, Randolph L., et al, eds. Year Book of Cancer, 1982. (Illus.). 575p. 1982. 39.95 (ISBN 0-8151-1790-6). Year Bk Med.

Clark, Randy & Koehler, Stephen. The UCSD PASCAL Handbook. (Software Ser.). (Illus.). 384p. 1982. text ed. 21.95 (ISBN 0-13-935544-8); pap. text ed. 15.95 (ISBN 0-13-935536-7). P-H.

Clark, Raymond C. Language Teaching Techniques. LC 80-84109. (Pro Lingua Language Resource Handbook Ser.: No. 1). (Illus.). 128p. (Orig.). 1980. pap. 6.50x (ISBN 0-86647-000-X). Pro Lingua.

Clark, Robert, jt. auth. see Duk Song Son.

Clark, Robert, jt. auth. see Minium, Edward W.

Clark, Robert, jt. auth. see Zuck, Roy B.

Clark, Robert C., et al. The Shaping of Art & Architecture in Nineteenth Century America. LC 78-145766. (Illus.). 1972. pap. 12.50 o.s.i. (ISBN 0-87099-024-1). Metro Mus Art.

Clark, Robert E., jt. auth. see Brubaker, J. Omar.

Clark, Robert M. Analysis of Urban Solid Waste Services: A Systems Approach. LC 77-85088. 1978. 24.00 o.p. (ISBN 0-250-40199-1). Ann Arbor Science.

Clark, Robert M. & Gillean, James I. Resource Recovery Planning & Management. LC 80-70320. 1981. text ed. 29.95 (ISBN 0-250-40298-X). Ann Arbor Science.

Clark, Robert P. Power & Policy in the Third World. 2nd ed. LC 81-19705. 168p. 1982. pap. text ed. 11.95x (ISBN 0-471-09008-5). Wiley.

Clark, Robert P., jt. auth. see White, Louise G.

Clark, Rodney. The Japanese Company. 1979. 30.00x (ISBN 0-300-02310-3); pap. 8.95x (ISBN 0-300-02646-3). Yale U Pr.

Clark, Roger E. Executive Visicalc: Application for the Apple. LC 82-11663. (Microcomputer Bks.-Executive). 192p. 1982. pap. 14.95 (ISBN 0-201-10242-0). A-W.

Clark, Ronald G. Manter & Gatz's Essentials of Clinical Neuroanatomy & Neurophysiology. 5th ed. LC 74-10887. (Illus.). 181p. 1975. pap. text ed. 7.95x o.p. (ISBN 0-8036-1850-6). Davis Co.

Clark, Ronald W. Benjamin Franklin: A Biography. LC 82-40115. (Illus.). 480p. 1983. 22.95 (ISBN 0-394-50222-1). Random.

--Edison: The Man Who Made the Future. LC 76-56653. (Illus.). 1977. 12.95 o.p. (ISBN 0-399-11952-3). Putnam Pub Group.

--Einstein: The Life & Times. (Illus.). 1972. pap. 4.95 (ISBN 0-380-01159-X, 596423, Discus). Avon.

Clark, Roy. The Longshoremen. 1974. 5.95 o.p. (ISBN 0-7153-6484-7). David & Charles.

Clark, Sam. Designing & Building Your Own House Your Own Way. 1978. 16.95 o.s.i. (ISBN 0-395-25486-8); pap. 8.95 (ISBN 0-395-26685-8). HM.

Clark, Sandra. Elizabethan Pamphleteers: Popular Moralistic Pamphlets, 1580-1640. LC 81-72064. (Illus.). 320p. 1982. 30.00 (ISBN 0-8386-3173-8). Fairleigh Dickinson.

--Moonlight Enough. (Harlequin Romances Ser.). 192p. 1983. pap. 1.75 (ISBN 0-373-02533-5). Harlequin Bks.

Clark, Sara, jt. auth. see Wittliff, William.

Clark, Stephen B. Building Christian Communities: Strategy for Renewing the Church. LC 75-189990. 192p. 1972. pap. 2.95 o.p. (ISBN 0-87793-043-0). Ave Maria.

Clark, Stephen R. Aristotle's Man: Speculations Upon Aristotelian Anthropology. 256p. 1975. 44.00x o.p. (ISBN 0-19-824516-5). Oxford U Pr.

--The Moral Status of Animals. 1977. 22.50x o.p. (ISBN 0-19-824578-5). Oxford U Pr.

--The Nature of the Beast: Are Animals Moral? 136p. 1982. text ed. 14.95 (ISBN 0-19-219130-6). Oxford U Pr.

Clark, Steve. The Complete Book of Baseball Cards. LC 76-4255. (Illus.). 128p. 1976. pap. 6.95 o.p. (ISBN 0-448-12508-0, G&D). Putnam Pub Group.

--The Complete Book of Baseball Cards. (Illus.). 128p. (gr. 3-9). 1982. pap. 6.95 (ISBN 0-448-12323-1, G&D). Putnam Pub Group.

Clark, Steven B. Unordained Elders & Renewal Communities. LC 75-35329. 1976. pap. 3.50 o.p. (ISBN 0-8091-1916-1). Paulist Pr.

Clark, Susan L. & Wasserman, Julian N. The Poetics of Conversion: Number Symbolism & Alchemy in Gottfried's "Tristan". (Utah Studies in Literature & Linguistics: Vol. 7). 168p. 1977. pap. write for info. (ISBN 3-261-02085-7). P Lang Pubs.

Clark, Sydney P. Structure of the Earth. (Foundations of Earth Science Ser). 1971. pap. text ed. 11.95 (ISBN 0-13-854646-0). P-H.

Clark, T. & Penycate, J. Psychopath: The Case of Patrick Mackay. (Illus.). 1976. 12.00 (ISBN 0-7100-8402-1). Routledge & Kegan.

Clark, T. J. & Godfrey, S., eds. Asthma. LC 76-57835. (Illus.). 1977. text ed. 14.00 (ISBN 0-7216-2596-7). Saunders.

Clark, T. W., ed. The Novel in India: Its Birth & Development. LC 70-119719. 1970. 29.50x (ISBN 0-520-01725-0). U of Cal Pr.

Clark, Terry N., ed. Comparative Community Politics. LC 72-98030. 415p. 1974. 19.95x o.s.i. (ISBN 0-470-15858-1). Halsted Pr.

Clark, Thom B., jt. auth. see Reeves, Charles A.

Clark, Thomas A. Blacks in Suburbs. LC 79-12171. 1979. pap. text ed. 17.50 (ISBN 0-88285-061-X). Ctr Urban Pol Res.

--Some Particulars. 1971. pap. 5.00 (ISBN 0-912330-12-0, Dist. by Inland Bk). Jargon Soc.

--A Still Life. LC 77-71653. (Illus.). 1977. signed limited ed 17.50 o.p. (ISBN 0-912330-29-5). Jargon Soc.

--Ways Through Bracken. 1980. signed ltd. ed. 20.00x (ISBN 0-912330-44-9); pap. 7.50 (ISBN 0-686-96760-7). Jargon Soc.

Clark, Thomas B. Omai: First Polynesian Ambassador to England. 1969. Repr. of 1940 ed. 9.00 (ISBN 0-87022-140-X). UH Pr.

Clark, Tom. The Great Naropa Poetry Wars. LC 79-55794. 92p. 1980. 20.00 o.p. (ISBN 0-932274-07-2); pap. 5.00 o.p. (ISBN 0-932274-06-4). Cadmus Eds.

--Under the Fortune Palms. 72p. 1982. 40.00x (ISBN 0-918824-38-9). Turkey Pr.

Clark, Trinkett, jt. auth. see Carmean, E. A., Jr.

Clark, V. A. & Tarter. Preparation for Basic Statistics. 1968. pap. text ed. 12.95 (ISBN 0-07-011131-6, C). McGraw.

Clark, Virginia. Wedding Flowers, Decorations, & Etiquette. 1970. 8.95 (ISBN 0-8208-0054-6). Hearthside.

Clark, Virginia A., jt. auth. see Dunn, Olive J.

Clark, Vivian V., ed. Outpatient Services: Journal Articles. 2nd ed. 348p. 1973. 10.00 o.s.i. (ISBN 0-686-68575-X, 1498). Healthcare Fin Man Assn.

Clark, W. A., jt. auth. see Nelson, Howard J.

Clark, W. E. The Tissues of the Body. 6th ed. (Illus.). 1977. pap. text ed. 29.50x o.p. (ISBN 0-19-857163-1). Oxford U Pr.

Clark, W. Mansfield. Oxidation Reduction Potentials of Organic Systems. LC 60-5143. 600p. 1971. Repr. of 1960 ed. 22.50 (ISBN 0-88275-009-7). Krieger.

Clark, Walter. The Papers of Walter Clark, 2 vols. Brooks, Aubrey J. & Lefler, Hugh T., eds. Incl. Vol. 1. xv, 607p. 1948 (ISBN 0-8078-0526-2); Vol. 2. vii, 608p. 1950 (ISBN 0-8078-0591-2). 25.00x ea. U of NC Pr.

Clark, Walter V. Ox Bow Incident. (RL 10). 1943. pap. 2.50 (ISBN 0-451-51497-1, CE1497, Sig Classics). NAL.

Clark, Warren E. Traffic Management & Collision Investigation. (Illus.). 320p. 1982. 20.95 (ISBN 0-13-926162-1). P-H.

Clark, William. Sing Peace to Cedar River. Brunelle, Jim, ed. (Illus.). 240p. 1983. pap. 10.95 (ISBN 0-930096-41-X). G Gannett.

Clark, William, jt. auth. see Lewis, Meriwether.

Clark, William, ed. Modeling Housing Market Search. LC 82-872. 256p. 1982. 30.00x (ISBN 0-312-53536-8). St Martin.

Clark, William B. Critical Essays on Robert Penn Warren. (Critical Essays on American Literature). 1981. 25.00 (ISBN 0-8161-8424-0, Twayne). G K Hall.

--Lambert Wickes: Sea Raider & Diplomat-the Story of a Naval Captain of the Revolution. 1932. 49.50x (ISBN 0-685-69800-9). Elliots Bks.

Clark, William D. Conducting Technique. LC 78-66123. 1979. pap. text ed. 10.00 (ISBN 0-8191-0684-4). U Pr of Amer.

--Rotary Power Lawn Mower Noise. (Illus.). 1978. pap. text ed. 45.00x o.p. (ISBN 0-89671-015-7). Southeast Acoustics.

Clark, William D., ed. see Given, H. Kyle, III.

Clark, William E. Fire Fighting Principles & Practices. (Illus.). 1974. 17.50 (ISBN 0-686-12259-3). Fire Eng.

Clark, Wilson. Energy for Survival: The Alternative to Extinction. LC 72-89297. (Illus.). 672p. 1975. pap. 9.95 (ISBN 0-385-03564-0, Anch). Doubleday.

Clarke. Biology of the Arthropoda. 1975. 22.50 (ISBN 0-444-19559-9). Elsevier.

Clarke & Wilson. Foam Floation: Theory & Application. 480p. 1983. price not set (ISBN 0-8247-1775-9). Dekker.

Clarke, A. B. & Disney, R. L. Probability & Random Processes for Engineers & Scientists. 1970. 36.95 (ISBN 0-471-15980-8). Wiley.

Clarke, A. D. & Lewis, M. M., eds. Learning, Speech & Thought in the Mentally Retarded. (Illus.). 92p. 1972. 6.95 o.p. (ISBN 0-407-24950-8). Butterworth.

Clarke, Adam. Clarke's Commentary: One Vol. Ed. 22.95 (ISBN 0-8010-2321-1). Baker Bk.

Clarke, Alfred C., jt. auth. see Curry, Timothy J.

Clarke, Allan. Soccer: How to Become a Champ. (Illus.). 1976. pap. 5.95 o.s.i. (ISBN 0-86002-131-9). Transatlantic.

Clarke, Amanda. Growing up in Elizabethan Times. LC 79-56439. (Growing up Ser.). (Illus.). 72p. (gr. 7 up). 1980. text ed. 14.95 o.p. (ISBN 0-7134-3364-7, Pub. by Batsford England). David & Charles.

Clarke, Anna. One of Us Must Die. LC 80-1669. (Crime Club Ser.). 192p. 1980. 10.95 o.p. (ISBN 0-385-17295-8). Doubleday.

--The Poisoned Web. 182p. 1982. 10.95 (ISBN 0-312-61992-8). St Martin.

--We the Bereaved. LC 82-45539. (Crime Club Ser.). 192p. 1982. 11.95 (ISBN 0-385-18359-3). Doubleday.

Clarke, Arthur. Song of Songs. 6.50 (ISBN 0-937396-40-0); pap. 4.00 (ISBN 0-937396-39-7). Walterick Pubs.

Clarke, Arthur C. Arthur C. Clarke Trilogy, 3 bks. (Reader's Request Ser.). 1980. Set. lib. bdg. 45.00 (ISBN 0-8161-3139-2, Large Print Bks). G K Hall.

--Childhood's End. LC 53-10419. 1980. pap. 2.50 (ISBN 0-345-29730-X, Del Rey). Ballantine.

--The City & the Stars. 192p. (RL 7). 1973. pap. 2.50 (ISBN 0-451-12034-5, AE2034, Sig). NAL.

--The Deep Range. (RL 7). 1974. pap. 2.50 (ISBN 0-451-12361-1, AE2361, Sig). NAL.

--Expedition to Earth. LC 78-95868. 181p. 6.95 o.p. (ISBN 0-15-129461-5). HarBraceJ.

--Fall of Moondust. 224p. (RL 7). 1974. pap. 1.95 (ISBN 0-451-09795-5, E9795, Sig). NAL.

--The Fountains of Paradise. (Reader's Request Ser.). 1980. lib. bdg. 15.95 (ISBN 0-8161-3039-6, Large Print Bks). G K Hall.

--Glidepath. 208p. 1973. pap. 2.25 (ISBN 0-451-11529-5, AE1529, Sig). NAL.

--Imperial Earth. (Reader's Request Ser.). 1980. lib. bdg. 16.95 (ISBN 0-8161-3037-X, Large Print Bks). G K Hall.

--Imperial Earth. LC 75-30595. 303p. 1976. 7.95 o.p. (ISBN 0-15-144233-9). HarBraceJ.

--Islands in the Sky. 1979. lib. bdg. 9.50 (ISBN 0-8398-2516-1, Gregg). G K Hall.

--The Lost Worlds of 2001. 1979. lib. bdg. 12.50 (ISBN 0-8398-2509-9, Gregg). G K Hall.

--The Nine Billion Names of God. 204p. (RL 7). Date not set. pap. 1.75 o.p. (ISBN 0-451-08381-4, E8381, Sig). NAL.

--The Nine Billion Names of God. 1974. pap. 2.50 (ISBN 0-451-11715-8, AE1715, Sig). NAL.

--Prelude to Mars. LC 65-16953. 1965. 8.50x o.p. (ISBN 0-15-173922-6). HarBraceJ.

--Reach for Tomorrow. LC 71-95869. 5.75x o.p. (ISBN 0-15-175960-X). HarBraceJ.

--Rendezvous with Rama. (Reader's Request Ser.). 1980. lib. bdg. 15.95 (ISBN 0-8161-3038-8, Large Print Bks). G K Hall.

--Rendezvous with Rama. LC 73-3497. 1973. 8.95 o.p. (ISBN 0-15-176835-8). HarBraceJ.

--Report on Planet Three & Other Speculations. 1973. pap. 2.50 (ISBN 0-451-11573-2, AE1573, Sig). NAL.

--The Sands of Mars. (RL 7). pap. 2.50 (ISBN 0-451-12312-3, AE2312, Sig). NAL.

--Tales of Ten Worlds. LC 62-16730. (gr. 10 up). 1962. 6.95 o.p. (ISBN 0-15-187980-X). HarBraceJ.

--Tales of Ten Worlds. (RL 7). 1973. pap. 2.50 (ISBN 0-451-11093-5, AE1093, Sig). NAL.

--Two Thousand & One: A Space Odyssey. 1972. pap. 2.95 (ISBN 0-451-11864-2, AE1864, Sig). NAL.

--Two Thousand & Ten: Odyssey Two. 320p. 1982. 14.95 (ISBN 0-345-30305-9, Del Rey). Ballantine.

--The Wind from the Sun: Stories of the Space Age. 176p. (RL 7). 1973. pap. 1.95 (ISBN 0-451-11475-2, AJ1475, Sig). NAL.

Clarke, B. M., jt. auth. see Crocetti, Gino.

Clarke, Basil F. Church Builders of the Nineteenth Century. LC 69-10849. (Illus.). Repr. of 1938 ed. 19.50x (ISBN 0-678-05513-0). Kelley.

--Parish Churches of London. (Illus.). 30.00 o.p. (ISBN 0-8038-0205-6). Architectural.

Clarke, Bob, jt. auth. see De Bartolo, Dick.

Clarke, Boden. Lords Temporal & Lords Spiritual. LC 80-10979. (Stokvis Studies in Historical Chronology & Thought: No. 1). 128p. 1983. lib. bdg. 11.95x (ISBN 0-89370-800-3); pap. 5.95x (ISBN 0-89370-900-X). Borgo Pr.

Clarke, Boden & Burgess, Mary A. Eastern Churches Review: An Index to Volumes One Through Ten, 1966-1978. LC 80-2550. (Borgo Reference Library: Vol. 6). 64p. 1983. lib. bdg. 9.95x (ISBN 0-89370-812-7); pap. text ed. 3.95x (ISBN 0-89370-912-3). Borgo Pr.

Clarke, Brenna K. The Emergence of the Irish Peasant Play at the Abbey Theatre. Beckerman, Bernard, ed. LC 82-4757. (Theater & Dramatic Studies: No. 12). 236p. 1982. 39.95 (ISBN 0-8357-1293-1, Pub. by UMI Res Pr). Univ Microfilms.

Clarke, Brian. Architectural Stained Glass. LC 79-211. (Illus.). 1979. 36.50 (ISBN 0-07-011264-9, Architectural Rec Bks). McGraw.

Clarke, C. A. Human Genetics & Medicine. (Studies in Biology Ser). 1971. 13.95 o.p. (ISBN 0-312-39935-9). St Martin.

Clarke, Charlotte. A Narrative on the Life of Mrs. Charlotte Clarke, Daughter of Colley Cibber. 223p. 1982. Repr. of 1755 ed. lib. bdg. 30.00 (ISBN 0-8495-0879-7). Arden Lib.

Clarke, Claudia, tr. see Moog, Helmut.

Clarke, Colin G. & Hodgkiss, Alan G. Jamaica in Maps. LC 74-84659. (Graphic Perspectives of Developing Countries Ser.). (Illus.). 125p. 1975. text ed. 35.00x (ISBN 0-8419-0175-9, Africana). Holmes & Meier.

Clarke, Cyril A. Human Genetics & Medicines. 2nd ed. (Studies in Biology: No. 20). 80p. 1978. pap. text ed. 8.95 (ISBN 0-7131-2667-1). E Arnold.

Clarke, D. Computer Aided Structural Design. LC 78-1511. 1978. 44.95 (ISBN 0-471-99641-6, Pub. by Wiley-Interscience). Wiley.

Clarke, D. H. The Blue Water Dream. 1981. 12.95 o.s.i. (ISBN 0-679-51004-4). McKay.

Clarke, D. S., Jr. Deductive Logic: An Introduction to Evaluation Technique & Logical Theory. LC 73-10459. 255p. 1973. pap. 7.95x (ISBN 0-8093-0657-3). S Ill U Pr.

Clarke, David H. Exercise Physiology. LC 75-9735. 1975. 20.95 (ISBN 0-13-294967-9). P-H.

Clarke, David H. & Clarke, H. Harrison. Research Processes in Physical Education, Recreation & Health. (Physical Education Ser). 1970. text ed. 22.95 (ISBN 0-13-774463-3). P-H.

Clarke, David H., jt. auth. see Clarke, H. Harrison.

Clarke, Donald. The Encyclopedia of How It's Made. LC 78-58391. (Illus.). 200p. 1978. 16.95 o.s.i. (ISBN 0-89479-035-8). A & W Pubs.

Clarke, Donald, ed. The Encyclopedia of How It Works. LC 76-56962. (Illus.). 248p. 1977. 16.95 o.s.i. (ISBN 0-89479-002-1). A & W Pubs.

--Encyclopedia of How It's Built. LC 79-51588. (Illus.). 184p. 1979. 16.95 o.s.i. (ISBN 0-89479-047-1). A & W Pubs.

Clarke, Duncan L., jt. ed. see Brauch, Hans G.

Clarke, E. G. & Clarke, Myra L. Veterinary Toxicology. 2nd ed. 328p. 1981. text ed. write for info. o.p. (ISBN 0-8121-0824-8). Lea & Febiger.

Clarke, E. G., ed. Isolation & Identification of Drugs, Vol. 1. 896p. 1969. 52.00 (ISBN 0-85369-061-8, Pub. by Pharmaceutical). Rittenhouse.

--Isolation & Identification of Drugs, Vol. 2. 400p. 1975. 38.00 (ISBN 0-85369-095-2, Pub. by Pharmaceutical). Rittenhouse.

Clarke, Edward H. Demand Revelation & the Provision of Public Goods. 264p. 1980. prof ref 30.00x (ISBN 0-88410-686-1). Ballinger Pub.

Clarke, Edwin, ed. Modern Methods in the History of Medicine. 1971. text ed. 50.50x (ISBN 0-485-11121-7, Athlone Pr). Humanities.

Clarke, F. L. The Tangled Web of Price Variation Accounting: The Development of Ideas Underlying Professional Prescriptions in Six Counties. LC 82-82485. (Accountancy in Transition Ser.). 466p. 1982. lib. bdg. 55.00 (ISBN 0-8240-5300-1). Garland Pub.

Clarke, F. R. Healey William: Life & Music. 480p. 1983. 37.50x (ISBN 0-8020-5549-4). U of Toronto Pr.

Clarke, Frank, tr. see Van Oyen, Hendrik.

Clarke, Frank H., ed. How Modern Medicines Are Developed. new ed. LC 76-41063. (Illus.). 151p. 1977. 10.00 (ISBN 0-87993-073-X). Futura Pub.

Clarke, G. M. Statistics & Experimental Design. 2nd ed. (Contemporary Biology Ser). 2000p. 1980. pap. text ed. 24.95 o.p. (ISBN 0-7131-2797-X). Univ Park.

Clarke, G. M. & Cooke, D. A Basic Course in Statistics. LC 78-10749. 368p. 1979. pap. text ed. 24.95x o.s.i. (ISBN 0-470-26527-2). Halsted Pr.

Clarke, G. W., ed. see Lawler, Thomas C.

Clarke, Garry E. Essays on American Music. LC 76-52606. (Contributions in American History: No. 62). (Illus.). 1977. lib. bdg. 25.00 (ISBN 0-8371-9484-9, CAM/). Greenwood.

Clarke, Geoffrey M. Statistics & Experimental Design. 200p. 1980. pap. text ed. 19.50 (ISBN 0-7131-2797-X). E Arnold.

Clarke, Gillian. Letter from a Far Country. 80p. 1982. pap. text ed. 7.00x (ISBN 0-85635-427-9, 80150, Pub. by Carcanet New Pr England). Humanities.

Clarke, H., et al. Political Choice in Canada. 1979. text ed. 24.95 o.p. (ISBN 0-07-082783-4). McGraw.

Clarke, H. C. Menu Terminology. 1969. pap. 7.95 (ISBN 0-08-006525-2). Pergamon.

Clarke, H. Harrison. Application of Measurement to Health & Physical Education. 5th ed. (Illus.). 464p. 1976. 21.95x (ISBN 0-13-039024-0). P-H.

Clarke, H. Harrison & Clarke, David H. Developmental & Adapted Physical Education. 2nd ed. (Illus.). 1978. ref. ed. 20.95 (ISBN 0-13-208421-X). P-H.

Clarke, H. Harrison, jt. auth. see Clarke, David H.

Clarke, Harold. The Splendour of Ireland. (Illus.). 64p. 1982. 15.95 (ISBN 0-900346-36-1, Pub. by Salem Hse Ltd.). Merrimack Bk Serv.

Clarke, Harold D., jt. ed. see Kornberg, Allan.

Clarke, Heather F., jt. auth. see Robinson, Geoffrey C.

Clarke, Herman F. John Coney, Silversmith: 1655-1722. LC 71-87562. (Architecture & Decorative Art Ser.: Vol. 38). (Illus.). lx, 104p. 1971. Repr. of 1932 ed. lib. bdg. 32.50 (ISBN 0-306-71393-4). Da Capo.

Clarke, Herman F. & Foote, Henry W. Jeremiah Dummer: Colonial Craftsman & Merchant 1645-1718. LC 75-87563. (Architecture & Decorative Art Ser). (Illus.). 1970. Repr. of 1935 ed. 29.50 (ISBN 0-306-71394-2). Da Capo.

Clarke, Ida C. American Women & the World War. LC 74-75233. (The United States in World War 1 Ser.). xix, 545p. 1974. Repr. of 1918 ed. lib. bdg. 25.95x (ISBN 0-89198-096-2). Ozer.

Clarke, J., et al, eds. Working Class Culture: Studies in History & Theories. 1980. 25.00x (ISBN 0-312-88978-X). St Martin.

Clarke, J. Christopher & Jackson, Arthur. Hypnosis & Behavior Therapy: The Treatment of Anxiety & Phobias. 1983. text ed. price not set (ISBN 0-8261-3450-5). Springer Pub.

Clarke, J. H. & Benforado, J., eds. Wetlands of Bottomland Hardwood Forests. (Developments in Agricultural & Managed-Forest Ecology Ser.: Vol. 11). 1981. 81.00 (ISBN 0-444-42020-7). Elsevier.

Clarke, J. Harold. Growing Berries & Grapes at Home. (Illus.). 9.00 (ISBN 0-8446-5474-4). Peter Smith.

Clarke, J. I. Population Geography & Developing Countries. 1972. 19.00 (ISBN 0-08-016445-5); pap. 9.50 (ISBN 0-08-016446-3). Pergamon.

Clarke, J. I. & Fisher, W. B. Populations of the Middle East & North Africa: A Geographical Approach. LC 72-80410. 432p. 1972. text ed. 44.50x (ISBN 0-8419-0125-2). Holmes & Meier.

Clarke, Jack A., ed. Research Materials in the Social Sciences. 2nd ed. 64p. 1967. pap. 5.95 (ISBN 0-299-01923-3). U of Wis Pr.

Clarke, Jack A. see Prakken, Sarah L.

Clarke, John H. A Clinical Repertory to the Dictionary of Materia Medica. 1979. 15.95x (ISBN 0-85032-061-5, Pub. by C. W. Daniels). Formur Intl.

--The Prescriber. 1972. 8.95x (ISBN 0-85032-088-7, Pub. by C. W. Daniels). Formur Intl.

Clarke, John H., ed. American Negro Short Stories. 355p. 1966. pap. 10.95 (ISBN 0-8090-2530-2, AmCen); pap. 6.95 (ISBN 0-8090-0080-6). Hill & Wang.

Clarke, John M. Organic Dependence & Disease: Their Origin & Significance. 1921. 32.50x (ISBN 0-686-51283-9). Elliots Bks.

Clarke, Katherine A., tr. see Giono, Jean.

Clarke, Kenneth K. & Hess, Donald T. Communication Circuits: Analysis & Design. LC 78-125610. (Engineering Ser). 1971. text ed. 32.95 (ISBN 0-201-01040-2). A-W.

Clarke, M. J., et al. Copper, Molybdenum, & Vanadium in Biological Systems. (Structure & Bonding: Vol. 53). (Illus.). 166p. 1983. 37.00 (ISBN 0-387-12042-4). Springer-Verlag.

Clarke, M. J., et al, eds. Structure vs. Special Properties. (Structure & Bonding Ser.: Vol. 52). (Illus.). 204p. 1982. 48.00 (ISBN 0-387-11781-4). Springer-Verlag.

Clarke, M. P. Parliamentary Privilege in the American Colonies. LC 76-166322. (American Constitutional & Legal History Ser.). 304p. 1971. Repr. of 1943 ed. lib. bdg. 35.00 (ISBN 0-306-70237-1). Da Capo.

Clarke, M. R., ed. Advances in Computer Chess 3: Proceedings of the International Conference, London, April, 1981. 170p. 1982. 25.00 (ISBN 0-08-026898-6). Pergamon.

Clarke, Mary. The Sadler's Wells Ballet: A History & an Appreciation. LC 77-563. (Series in Dance Ser.). 1977. Repr. of 1955 ed. lib. bdg. 25.00 (ISBN 0-306-70863-9). Da Capo.

Clarke, Mary & Crisp, Clement. Ballet Art. (Illus.). 1978. pap. 6.95 o.p. (ISBN 0-517-53455-X, C N Potter Bks). Crown.

Clarke, Mary & Vaughn, David, eds. The Encyclopedia of Dance & Ballet. LC 76-52325. (Illus.). 1977. 25.00 o.p. (ISBN 0-399-11955-8). Putnam Pub Group.

Clarke, Michael & Penny, Nicholas, eds. The Arrogant Connoisseur: Richard Payne Knight 1751-1824. 208p. 1982. 45.00 (ISBN 0-7190-0871-9). Manchester.

Clarke, Myra L., jt. auth. see Clarke, E. G.

Clarke, Nina H. Establishment of Nineteenth-Century Black Churches in Maryland & the District of Columbia. 1983. 12.95 (ISBN 0-533-05366-8). Vantage.

Clarke, Norman, jt. ed. see Brown, Sanborn C.

Clarke, P. B., jt. auth. see Hunsinger, Marjorie.

Clarke, P. F. Lancashire & the New Liberalism. (Illus.). 1971. 54.50 (ISBN 0-521-08075-4). Cambridge U Pr.

Clarke, P. H. & Richmond, M. H., eds. Genetics & Biochemistry of Pseudomonas. LC 73-18926. 366p. 1975. 70.25 o.p. (ISBN 0-471-15896-8, Pub. by Wiley-Interscience). Wiley.

Clarke, Paul D. The Science of Child-Adolescent Behavior. LC 78-57578. 1978. pap. text ed. 11.50 (ISBN 0-8191-0529-5). U Pr of Amer.

Clarke, Pauline. Return of the Twelves. (Illus.). (gr. 4-6). 1963. 7.95 o.p. (ISBN 0-698-20117-5, Coward). Putnam Pub Group.

--The Return of the Twelves. 1981. PLB 9.95 (ISBN 0-8398-2718-0, Gregg). G K Hall.

--The Two Faces of Silenus. 169p. (gr. 5 up). 1972. 5.95 o.p. (ISBN 0-698-20186-8, Coward). Putnam Pub Group.

Clarke, Peter. Liberals & Social Democrats. LC 78-6970. 1978. 39.50 (ISBN 0-521-22171-4); Dec. 1981. pap. 14.95 (ISBN 0-521-28651-4). Cambridge U Pr.

--West Africa & Islam. 280p. 1982. pap. text ed. 19.95 (ISBN 0-7131-8029-3). E Arnold.

Clarke, Peter & Evans, Susan H. Covering Campaigns: Journalism in Congressional Elections. LC 82-60738. 168p. 1983. 17.95x (ISBN 0-8047-1159-3). Stanford U Pr.

Clarke, Peter J. Plastics for Schools: Applied Polymer Science. 191p. (gr. 9 up). 1973. pap. 9.95 o.p. (ISBN 0-263-05380-6). Transatlantic.

Clarke, Prescott & Gregory, J. S., eds. Western Reports on the Taiping: A Selection of Documents. LC 81-68942. 484p. 1982. text ed. 25.00x (ISBN 0-8248-0807-X); pap. text ed. 15.95x (ISBN 0-8248-0809-6). UH Pr.

Clarke, R. M. Alfa Romeo Spider 1966-1981. (Illus.). 100p. 1982. pap. 11.95 (ISBN 0-907073-56-5, Pub. by Brooklands Bks England). Motorbooks Intl.

--American Motors Muscle Cars 1966-1970. (Illus.). 100p. 1982. pap. 11.95 (ISBN 0-907073-58-1, Pub. by Brooklands Bks England). Motorbooks Intl.

--Camaro Muscle Cars 1966-1972. (Illus.). 100p. 1982. pap. 11.95 (ISBN 0-907073-65-4, Pub. by Brooklands Bks England). Motorbooks Intl.

--Chevrolet Muscle Cars 1966-1971. (Illus.). 100p. 1982. pap. 11.95 (ISBN 0-907073-61-1, Pub. by Brooklands Bks England). Motorbooks Intl.

--Jaguar XJS 1975-1980. (Brooklands Bks.). (Illus.). 100p. (Orig.). 1981. pap. 11.95 (ISBN 0-907073-07-7, Pub. by Brooklands Bks England). Motorbooks Intl.

--Lamborghini Countach Collection, No. 1. (Illus.). 70p. 1982. pap. 8.95 (ISBN 0-907073-64-6, Pub. by Brooklands Bks England). Motorbooks Intl.

--Opel GT 1968-1973. (Illus.). 100p. 1982. pap. 11.95 (ISBN 0-907073-63-8, Pub. by Brooklands Bks England). Motorbooks Intl.

Clarke, Rebecca. Trio for Piano, Violin & Cello. LC 80-20960. (Women Composer Ser.: No. 5). (Illus.). 64p. 1980. Repr. of 1928 ed. 19.95 (ISBN 0-306-76053-3). Da Capo.

Clarke, Richard. The Copperdust Hills. 1983. 11.95 (ISBN 0-8027-4018-9). Walker & Co.

Clarke, Richard H., ed. Triplet State ODMR Spectroscopy: Techniques & Applications to Biophysical Systems. LC 81-10486. 566p. 1982. 59.00x (ISBN 0-471-07988-X, Pub. by Wiley-Interscience). Wiley.

Clarke, Robert L., ed. Afro-American History: Sources for Research. LC 80-19197. 1981. 17.50 (ISBN 0-88258-018-3). Howard U Pr.

Clarke, Ronald O. & Liste, Peter C. Environmental Spectrum: Social & Economic Views on the Quality of Life. 175p. 1974. pap. text ed. 3.95x (ISBN 0-442-21611-4). Van Nos Reinhold.

Clarke, Rosy. Antique Japanese Furniture: A Guide to Evaluating & Restoring. LC 82-21916. (Illus.). 168p. (Orig.). 1983. pap. 17.50 (ISBN 0-8348-0178-7). Weatherhill.

Clarke, Samuel. Precious Bible Promises. 1959. 3.50 o.s.i. (ISBN 0-448-01654-0). Putnam Pub Group.

--The Works, 4 vols. LC 75-11207. (British Philosophers & Theologians of the 17th & 18th Centuries: Vol. 12). 1976. Repr. of 1742 ed. Set. lib. bdg. write for info. o.s.i. (ISBN 0-8240-1762-5); lib. bdg. 42.00 ea. o.s.i. Garland Pub.

Clarke, Simon. Marx, Marginalism & Modern Sociology. (Contemporary Social Theory Ser.). 272p. 1982. text ed. 29.95x (ISBN 0-333-29252-9, Pub. by Macmillan England); pap. text ed. 11.95x (ISBN 0-333-29253-7). Humanities.

Clarke, Steve, compiled by. The Who in Their Own Words. (Illus.). 1980. pap. 5.95 (ISBN 0-8256-3949-2, Quick Fox). Putnam Pub Group.

Clarke, Thomas E., ed. Above Every Name: The Lordship of Christ & Social Systems. LC 80-82082. (Woodstock Studies). 312p. (Orig.). 1980. pap. 7.95 (ISBN 0-8091-2338-X). Paulist Pr.

Clarke, Thurston. By Blood & Fire. 288p. 1981. 12.95 (ISBN 0-399-12605-8). Putnam Pub Group.

--The Last Caravan. LC 77-9533. (Illus.). 1978. 10.95 o.p. (ISBN 0-399-11900-0). Putnam Pub Group.

Clarke, Tom. New Pentecost or New Passion? The Direction of Religious Life Today. LC 73-84049. 192p. 1974. pap. 3.95 o.p. (ISBN 0-8091-1792-4). Paulist Pr.

Clarke, W. H. An Outline of the Structure of the Pipe Organ. (Bibliotheca Organologica: Vol. 59). 130p. 1978. wrappers 20.00 o.s.i. (ISBN 90-6027-374-5, Pub. by Frits Knuf Netherlands). Pendragon NY.

Clarke, W. J., et al, eds. Myeloproliferative Disorders of Animals & Man: Proceedings. LC 70-605836. (AEC Symposium Ser.). 765p. 1970. pap. 27.25 (ISBN 0-87079-280-6, CONF-680529); microfiche 4.50 (ISBN 0-87079-281-4, CONF-680529). DOE.

Clarke, William C. Place & People: An Ecology of a New Guinean Community. LC 78-126764. (Illus.). 1971. 36.00x (ISBN 0-520-01791-9). U of Cal Pr.

Clarke, William N. Immortality. 1920. text ed. 24.50x (ISBN 0-686-83578-6). Elliots Bks.

Clarke-Stewart, Alison & Koch, Joanne. Children: Development Through Adolescence. 625p. 1983. text ed. 23.95 (ISBN 0-471-03069-4); tchrs. manual avail. (ISBN 0-471-87302-0); solutions avail. (ISBN 0-471-87197-4). Wiley.

Clarke-Stewart, K. Alison, jt. auth. see Fein, Greta G.

Clarkson, Grosvenor B. Industrial America in the World War: The Strategy Behind the Line, 1917-1918. LC 74-75234. (The United States in World War 1 Ser). (Illus.). xiii, 573p. 1974. Repr. of 1923 ed. lib. bdg. 28.95x (ISBN 0-89198-097-0). Ozer.

Clarkson, Kenneth, et al. West's Business Law: Text & Cases. (Illus.). 1980. text ed. 24.95 (ISBN 0-8299-0295-3); study guide 5.95 (ISBN 0-8299-0305-4); instrs.' manual avail. (ISBN 0-8299-0466-2). West Pub.

Clarkson, Kenneth, et al, eds. Federal Trade Commission Since 1970: Economic Regulation & Bureaucratic Behavior. (Illus.). 448p. 1981. 42.50 (ISBN 0-521-23378-X). Cambridge U Pr.

Clarkson, Kenneth W. & Miller, Roger L. Industrial Organization. (Illus.). 576p. 1981. 23.95x (ISBN 0-07-042036-X). McGraw.

Clarkson, Kenneth W., et al. West's Business Law: Alternate UCC Comprehensive Edition. 880p. 1981. text ed. 24.95 (ISBN 0-8299-0366-6). West Pub.

--Alternate Test Items to Accompany West's Business Law: Alternate UCC Comprehensive Edition. 1980. write for info. (ISBN 0-8299-0526-X). West Pub.

Clarkson, Rosetta E. Herbs, Their Culture & Uses. (Illus.). 1949. 12.95 (ISBN 0-02-526020-0). Macmillan.

Clarkson, Stephen. Canada & the Reagan Challenge. (Illus.). 383p. 1983. 19.95 (ISBN 0-89490-091-9). Enslow Pubs.

Clark-Stewart, Alison. Day-Care. (The Developing Child Ser.). (Illus.). 160p. 1982. text ed. 9.95x (ISBN 0-674-19403-9); pap. 3.95 (ISBN 0-674-19404-7). Harvard U Pr.

Clary, Chanda, jt. auth. see Brown, Donald D.

Clary, Jack. The Gamemakers: Winning Philosophies of Eight NFL Coaches. (Illus.). 256p. 1976. 10.95 o.s.i. (ISBN 0-695-80630-0). Follett.

Clary, Wayne. OS Debugging for the COBOL Programmer. Eckols, Steve & Taylor, Judy, eds. LC 80-84122. (Illus.). 312p. (Orig.). 1981. pap. text ed. 20.00 (ISBN 0-911625-10-0). M Murach & Assoc.

--OS JCL. Taylor, Judy, ed. LC 80-82867. (Illus.). 330p. 1980. pap. text ed. 22.50 (ISBN 0-911625-08-9). M Murach & Assoc.

Clarys, J. Swimming II. (Intl. Series on Sport Sciences: Vol. 2). 352p. 1975. text ed. 24.95 o.p. (ISBN 0-8391-0817-6). Univ Park.

Clasing, Henry K., Jr., jt. auth. see Rudd, Andrew.

Clason, ed. Elsevier's Dictionary of Tools & Ironware. (Eng., Fr., Span., Ital., Dutch & Ger.). 1982. 74.50 (ISBN 0-444-42085-1). Elsevier.

Clason, Carla, tr. see Evans, David & Hoxeng, James.

Clason, George S. Richest Man in Babylon. 1955. 10.25 (ISBN 0-8015-6360-7, 0995-300, Hawthorn); pap. 4.95 (ISBN 0-8015-6366-6, 0481-140, Hawthorn). Dutton.

Clason, W. Elsevier's Dictionary of Chemical Engineering, 2 Vols. (Eng., Fr., Span., Ital., Dutch, & Ger.). 1969. Set. 170.25 (ISBN 0-444-40736-7); Vol. 1. 85.00 (ISBN 0-444-40714-6); Vol. 2. 85.00 (ISBN 0-444-40715-4). Elsevier.

--Elsevier's Dictionary of Television, & Video Recording. LC 74-77577. 608p. (Eng. & Ger. & Fr. & Span. & Ital. & Dutch.). 1975. 113.00 (ISBN 0-444-41224-7). Elsevier.

Clason, W. E. Elsevier's Dictionary of Cinema, Sound & Music. (Eng., Fr., Span., Ital., Dutch, & Ger., Polyglot). 1956. 117.00 (ISBN 0-444-40117-2). Elsevier.

--Elsevier's Dictionary of Computers, Automatic Control & Data Processing. 2nd ed. (Eng., Fr., Span., & Ital., Polyglot). 1971. 85.00 (ISBN 0-444-40928-9). Elsevier.

--Elsevier's Dictionary of Electronics & Waveguides. 2nd ed. (Eng., Fr., Span., Ital., Dutch & Ger., Polyglot). 1965. 106.50 (ISBN 0-444-40119-9). Elsevier.

--Elsevier's Dictionary of General Physics. (Eng., Fr., Span., Ital., Dutch & Ger., Polyglot). 1962. 110.75 (ISBN 0-444-40122-9). Elsevier.

--Elsevier's Dictionary of Metallurgy & Metal Working. (Eng., Fr., Span., Ital., Dutch & Ger.). 1978. 136.25 (ISBN 0-444-41695-1). Elsevier.

--Elsevier's Dictionary of Nuclear Science & Technology. 2nd rev. ed. (Eng. & Fr. & Span. & Ital. & Dutch & Ger., Polyglot). 1970. 121.50 (ISBN 0-444-40810-X). Elsevier.

--Elsevier's Electrotechnical Dictionary. (Eng. & Fr. & Span. & Ital. & Dutch & Ger., Polyglot). 1965. 113.00 (ISBN 0-444-40118-0). Elsevier.

--Elsevier's Telecommunication Dictionary. 2nd rev. ed. (Eng. & Fr. & Ital. & Span. & Dutch & Ger.). 1976. 113.75 (ISBN 0-444-41394-4). Elsevier.

Clasper, Paul. Theological Ferment: Personal Reflections. 226p. (Orig.). 1982. pap. 6.75x (ISBN 0-686-37687-0, Pub. by New Day Philippines). Cellar.

Clasper, Paul D. The Yogi, the Commissar & the Third World Church. 92p. (Orig.). 1982. pap. 5.75 (ISBN 0-686-37580-7, Pub. by New Day Philippines). Cellar.

Class, Robert A. & Koehler, Robert E., eds. Current Techniques in Architectural Practice. (Illus.). 275p. 1976. 35.00X o.p. (ISBN 0-07-002324-7, Architectural Res Bks). McGraw.

Classen, E., tr. see Bjerre, Andreas.

Clastres, Pierre. Chronicle of the Guayaki Indians. 320p. 1982. cancelled 19.50 (ISBN 0-8264-0198-8). Continuum.

Claude, Inis L., Jr. Power & International Relations. 1962. text ed. 17.00 (ISBN 0-394-30133-1). Random.

Claudel, Paul. The Book of Christopher Columbus: A Lyrical Drama in Two Parts. 1930. 47.50x (ISBN 0-686-51348-7). Elliots Bks.

--Break of Noon. 1960. pap. 1.95 o.p. (ISBN 0-89526-933-3). Regnery-Gateway.

--The Satin Slipper or the Worst Is Not the Surest. 1931. 42.50x o.p. (ISBN 0-686-51305-3). Elliots Bks.

Claudin, Fernando. The Communist Movement: From Comintern to Cominform. Pearce, Brian, tr. from Fr. LC 74-25015. 739p. 1976. Set. 27.00 set. (ISBN 0-85345-366-7, CL3667). Monthly Rev.

--Communist Movement: From Comintern to Cominform, 2 vols. Pearce, Brian, tr. from Fr. LC 74-25015. (Eng.). 1977. pap. 11.90 set (ISBN 0-686-86361-5, PB4072). Monthly Rev.

Claus, Audrey, jt. auth. see Kottmeyer, William.

Claus, Audrey, jt. auth. see Kottmeyer, William A.

Claus, Karen E. & Bailey, June T. Living with Stress & Promoting Well Being: A Handbook for Nurses. LC 80-14605. (Illus.). 1980. pap. text ed. 13.95 (ISBN 0-8016-1148-2). Mosby.

--Power & Influence in Health Care: A New Approach to Leadership. LC 76-57769. (Illus.). 192p. 1977. pap. 12.95 o.p. (ISBN 0-8016-0417-6). Mosby.

Claus, Karen E., jt. auth. see James, R.

Clausen, Andy. Extreme Unction. 1974. saddle stich bdg 5.00 (ISBN 0-915214-05-9). Litmus.

Clausen, Chris A., III & Mattson, Guy C. Principles of Industrial Chemistry. LC 78-9450. 1978. 33.95x (ISBN 0-471-02774-X, Pub. by Wiley-Interscience). Wiley.

Clausen, Edwin & Bermingham, Jack. Pluralism, Racism & Public Policy: The Search for Equality. (University Bks.). 1981. lib. bdg. 19.95 (ISBN 0-8161-9041-0, Univ Bks). G K Hall.

Clausen, J. Immunochemical Techniques for the Identification & Estimation of Macromolecules. Rev. ed. (Laboratory Techniques in Biochemistry & Molecular Biology Ser.: Vol. 1, Pt. 3). 1981. pap. 26.00 (ISBN 0-444-80244-4, North-Holland). Elsevier.

Clausen, Jan. Mother, Daughter, Sister, Lover: A Collection of Short Stories Dealing with Woman's Relations to Woman. LC 80-16386. (The Crossing Press Feminist Ser.). (Orig.). 1980. 13.95 (ISBN 0-89594-034-5); pap. 4.95 (ISBN 0-89594-033-7). Crossing Pr.

--A Movement of Poets: Thoughts on Poetry & Feminism. 56p. 1982. pap. 3.95 (ISBN 0-9602284-1-1). Crossing Pr.

Clausen, Joy, et al. Maternity Nursing Today. 2nd ed. (Illus.). 1976. text ed. 28.95 (ISBN 0-07-011284-3, HP). McGraw.

Clausen, W. V., et al, eds. see Virgil.

Clauser, H., jt. auth. see Brady, G. S.

Clauser, Henry. Industrial & Manufacturing Materials. (Illus.). 416p. 1975. text ed. 26.95 (ISBN 0-07-011285-1, G). McGraw.

Clausewitz, Carl Von see Von Clausewitz, Carl.

Clausewitz, Karl Von see Von Clausewitz, Karl.

Clausner, Marlin D. Rural Santo Domingo: Settled, Unsettled, & Resettled. LC 72-95881. 323p. 1973. 24.95 o.p. (ISBN 0-87722-012-3). Temple U Pr.

Claussen, Evelyn B., jt. auth. see Claussen, Martin P.

Claussen, Martin P. & Claussen, Evelyn B. The Voice of Christian & Jewish Dissenters in America: U. S. Internal Revenue Service Hearings, December 1978. xv, 591p. 1982. pap. 25.00. Piedmont.

Claussen, Paulette M. Speech-Langauge-Hearing Update: The Standard Reference Guide, Vol. 5, No. 1. 100p. 1982. pap. 40.00 (ISBN 0-943002-00-1). Update Pubns AZ.

--Speech-Language-Hearing Update: The Standard Reference Guide, Vol. 5, No. 2. 790p. 1982. 40.00 (ISBN 0-686-84041-0). Update Pubns AZ.

--Speech-Language-Hearing Update: The Standard Reference Guide, Vol. 6, No. 1. 80p. 1982. 40.00 (ISBN 0-943002-02-8). Update Pubns AZ.

Claus-Walker, Jacqueline, jt. auth. see Halstead, Lauro S.

Clavel, Pierre. Opposition Planning in Wales & Appalachia. LC 82-10322. 251p. 1982. text ed. 27.95 (ISBN 0-87722-276-2). Temple U Pr.

Clavell, James. King Rat. 1982. pap. 3.95 (ISBN 0-440-14546-5). Dell.

--King Rat. 1982. 17.95 (ISBN 0-440-04392-1). Delacorte.

--Shogun. 1982. pap. 3.50 (ISBN 0-440-17800-2). Dell.

--Shogun. 1983. 21.95 (ISBN 0-440-08721-X). Delacorte.

--Tai-Pan. 1983. 19.95 (ISBN 0-440-08724-4). Delacorte.

Clavell, James, ed. see Sun Tzu.

Clawson, Dan. Bureaucracy & the Labor Process: A Study of U. S. Industry 1860-1920. LC 79-3885. 352p. 1980. 16.50 o.p. (ISBN 0-85345-542-2). Monthly Rev.

Clawson, Elmer. Our Economy: How It Works. 1980. 13.20 (ISBN 0-201-01057-7, Sch Div); tchr's. ed. 8.64 (ISBN 0-201-01058-5). A-W.

Clawson, Marion. Uncle Sam's Acres. LC 74-106685. Repr. of 1951 ed. lib. bdg. 19.00x (ISBN 0-8371-3356-4, CLSA). Greenwood.

Clawson, Robert W., jt. auth. see Kaplan, Lawrence S.

Claxton, John D. & Anderson, Dennis C. Consumers & Energy Conservation: International Perspectives on Research & Policy Options. 318p. 1981. 31.95 (ISBN 0-03-059659-9). Praeger.

Clay, A. T. Documents from the Temple Archives of Nippur Dated in the Reigns of Cassite Rulers with Incomplete Dates. (Publications of the Babylonian Section, Ser. A: Vol. 15). (Illus.). 68p. 1906. soft bound 8.00x (ISBN 0-686-11914-2). Univ Mus of U PA.

--Legal & Commercial Transactions Dated in the Assyrian, Neo-Babylonian & Persian Periods, Chiefly from Nippur. (Publications of the Babylonian Section, Ser. A: Vol 8, No. 1). (Illus.). 85p. 1908. soft bound 8.00x (ISBN 0-686-11913-4). Univ Mus of U PA.

Clay, Albert T. Neo-Babylonian Letters From Erech. 1920. text ed. 26.50x (ISBN 0-686-83634-0). Elliots Bks.

Clay, Clarence S. & Medwin, Herman. Acoustical Oceanography: Principles & Applications. LC 77-1133. (Ocean Engineering Ser.). 1977. text ed. 52.95x (ISBN 0-471-16041-5, Pub. by Wiley-Interscience). Wiley.

Clay, Grady. Close-up: How to Read the American City. LC 79-26307. (Illus.). 1980. pap. 7.95 (ISBN 0-226-10945-3, P863, Phoen). U of Chicago Pr.

Clay, Henry, II. The Papers of Henry Clay, 7 vols. Hopkins, James F. & Hargreaves, Mary W., eds. Incl. Vol. 1. The Rising Statesman, 1797-1814. 1060p. 1959 (ISBN 0-8131-0051-8); Vol. 2. The Rising Statesman, 1815-1820. 952p. 1961 (ISBN 0-8131-0052-6); Vol. 3. Presidential Candidate, 1821-1824. 944p. 1963 (ISBN 0-8131-0053-4); Vol. 4. Secretary of State, 1825. 1004p. 1972 (ISBN 0-8131-0054-2); Vol. 5. Secretary of State, 1826. 1104p. 1973 (ISBN 0-8131-0055-0); Vol. 6. Secretary of State, 1827. 1456p. 1981 (ISBN 0-8131-0056-9); Vol. 7. Secretary of State, 1828-1829. 832p. 1982 (ISBN 0-8131-0057-7). LC 59-13605. 35.00x ea. U Pr of Ky.

Clay, Horace F. & Hubbard, James C. Tropical Exotics. LC 77-7363. (Hawaii Garden Ser: No. 1). (Illus.). 1977. 40.00 (ISBN 0-8248-0465-1). UH Pr.

--Tropical Shrubs. LC 77-7363. (Hawaii Garden Ser: No. 2). (Illus.). 1977. 40.00 (ISBN 0-8248-0466-X). UH Pr.

Clay, James H. & Krempel, D. Theatrical Image. 1967. text ed. 31.50 (ISBN 0-07-011286-X, C). McGraw.

Clay, Katherine, ed. Microcomputers in Education: A Handbook of Resources. LC 82-12596. 112p. 1982. lib. bdg. 18.50 (ISBN 0-89774-064-5). Oryx Pr.

Clay, Marie, jt. auth. see Butler, Dorothy.

Clay, Marie M. Observing Young Readers: Selected Papers. LC 82-12047. 256p. 1982. text ed. 15.00x (ISBN 0-686-97787-4). Heinemann Ed.

Clay, Patrice. We Work with Horses. (Illus.). 160p. (YA) (gr. 7-12). 1980. 8.95 (ISBN 0-399-20735-X). Putnam Pub Group.

Clay, Patrice A. Your Own Horse: A Beginner's Guide to Horse Care. (Illus.). 1977. 7.95 (ISBN 0-399-20538-1). Putnam Pub Group.

Clay, Patrick. Firebolt. (Sargeant Hawk Ser.: No. 5). 240p. (Orig.). 1982. pap. 2.25 o.s.i. (ISBN 0-8439-1169-7, Leisure Bks). Nordon Pubns.

Clay, Phillip L. Neighborhood Renewal: Trends & Strategies. LC 78-14153. 1979. 17.95x (ISBN 0-669-02681-6). Lexington Bks.

Clay, Rotha M. Hermits & Anchorites of England. LC 68-21759. (Illus.). 1968. Repr. of 1914 ed. 34.00x (ISBN 0-8103-3424-0). Gale.

Clay, William C. The Dow Jones-Irwin Guide to Estate Planning. 5th ed. LC 82-72367. 150p. 1982. 12.95 (ISBN 0-87094-361-8). Dow Jones-Irwin.

Clay, William C., Jr., jt. auth. see Martin, Gerald D.

Clayat, E. de see De Clayat, E.

Claybaugh, Amos L., jt. auth. see Burron, Arnold.

Claybrook, Billy G. File Management Techniques. 300p. 1983. text ed. 15.95 (ISBN 0-471-04596-9); solutions bk. avail. (ISBN 0-471-87575-9). Wiley.

Claycombe, W. Wayne, jt. auth. see Sullivan, William F.

Claycombe, William W. & Sullivan, William G. Foundations of Mathematical Programming. (Illus.). 304p. 1975. 21.95 (ISBN 0-87909-282-3); o.p. students manual o.p. Reston.

Claydon, L. F. Renewing Urban Teaching. LC 73-77266. (Illus.). 180p. 1974. 24.95 (ISBN 0-521-20268-X); pap. 10.95 (ISBN 0-521-09844-0). Cambridge U Pr.

Clayes, Stanley A. Drama & Discussion. 2nd ed. (Illus.). 1978. pap. text ed. 14.95 (ISBN 0-13-219030-3). P-H.

Clayman, Barbara. The Dukes of Hazzard. (Movie & TV Tie-Ins Ser.). (Illus.). 32p. (gr. 5-8). 1982. lib. bdg. 6.95 cancelled (ISBN 0-87191-878-1); pap. 3.25 (ISBN 0-89812-287-2). Creative Ed.

Clayman, Henry M. & Jaffe, Norman S. Intraocular Lens Implantation: Techniques & Complications. LC 82-8267. (Illus.). 300p. 1983. text ed. 59.50 (ISBN 0-8016-1080-X). Mosby.

Claypool, Bob. Saturday Night at Gilley's. (Illus.). 1980. write for info. Delilah Bks.

Claypool, Jane. Alcohol & You. LC 80-25660. (Impact Bks.). (Illus.). 1981. 8.90 (ISBN 0-531-04259-6). Watts.

--Career Prep: Working In A Hospital. (Jem High Interest-Low Reading Level Ser.). (Illus.). 64p. (gr. 7-9). 1983. PLB 9.29 (ISBN 0-671-44889-7). Messner.

--How to Get a Good Job. (Triumph Bks.). (Illus.). 96p. (gr. 7 up). 1982. PLB 8.90 (ISBN 0-531-04493-9). Watts.

--Jasmine Finds Love. LC 82-13633. (A Hiway-Floweromance Bk.). (gr. 7-10). 1982. 8.95 (ISBN 0-664-32699-4). Westminster.

--A Love For Violet. LC 82-10980. (A Hiway-Floweromance Bk.). (gr. 7-10). 1982. 8.95 (ISBN 0-664-32697-8). Westminster.

--Unemployment. (Impact Ser.). 96p. (gr. 7 up). 1983. PLB 8.90 (ISBN 0-531-04586-2). Watts.

--Why Do Some People Get Fat? (Creative's Little Question Books). (Illus.). 32p. (gr. 3-4). 1982. lib. bdg. 5.95 (ISBN 0-87191-898-6). Creative Ed.

Claypool, John. The Light Within You: Looking At Life Through New Eyes. 1983. 9.95 (ISBN 0-8499-0273-8). Word Bks.

--Tracks of a Fellow Struggler. 1976. pap. 1.25 o.s.i. (ISBN 0-89129-208-X). Jove Pubns.

Clayre, Alasdair, ed. The Political Economy of the Third Sector: Co-Operation & Participation. 1980. 27.50x (ISBN 0-19-877137-1); 14.95x (ISBN 0-19-877138-X). Oxford U Pr.

Clays-Sky, Gino. Jonquil Rose: Just One More Cowboy. (Illus.). pap. 4.00 (ISBN 0-686-23233-X). Five Trees.

Clayton, Aileen. The Enemy is Listening. (Ballantine Espionage Intelligence Library: No. 22). 416p. 1982. pap. 3.95 (ISBN 0-345-30250-8). Ballantine.

Clayton, Anthony. Communication for New Loyalties: African Soldiers' Songs. LC 78-17653. (Papers in International Studies: Africa: No. 34). (Illus.). 1978. pap. 6.00x (ISBN 0-89680-069-5, Ohio U Ctr Intl). Ohio U Pr.

Clayton, Barbara & Whitley, Kathleen. Exploring Coastal Massachusetts. (Illus.). 1983. pap. 12.95 (ISBN 0-686-84716-4). Dodd.

Clayton, Bernard. The Breads of France. LC 77-94452. (Illus.). 1978. 15.00 (ISBN 0-672-52071-0); pap. 8.95 (ISBN 0-672-52693-X). Bobbs.

Clayton, Bob. Outstanding Black Collegians, 1982. 100p. 1982. 54.95 (ISBN 0-686-36273-X). Ebonics.

Clayton, Bruce D., jt. auth. see Ryan, Sheila A.

Clayton, Bruce D., jt. auth. see Squire, Jessie.

Clayton, C. Sing a Song of Gladness. (Arch Bk.). (Illus.). 32p. (gr. k-4). 1974. pap. 0.89 (ISBN 0-570-06087-7, 59-1302). Concordia.

Clayton, Donald D. Principles of Stellar Evolution & Nucleosynthesis. LC 68-12263. 1968. text ed. 29.95 o.p. (ISBN 0-07-011295-9, C). McGraw.

Clayton, E. S. Agrarian Development in Peasant Economies. 1964. 16.50 o.p. (ISBN 0-08-010562-9); pap. 7.75 o.p. (ISBN 0-08-010561-0). Pergamon.

Clayton, Florence E., jt. auth. see Clayton, George D.

Clayton, G. Operational Amplifiers. 2nd ed. 1979. text ed. 29.95 (ISBN 0-408-00370-7). Butterworth.

Clayton, G. B. Operational Amplifier Experimental Manual. new ed. 112p. 1983. text ed. price not set (ISBN 0-408-01106-8); pap. price not set (ISBN 0-408-01239-0). Butterworth.

Clayton, George D. & Clayton, Florence E. Patty's Industrial Hygiene & Toxicology: General Principles, Vol. 1. 3rd rev. ed. LC 77-17515. 1978. 128.95x (ISBN 0-471-16046-6, Pub. by Wiley-Interscience). Wiley.

--Patty's Industrial Hygiene & Toxicology, Vol. 2C. 3rd. rev. ed. 1296p. 1982. 100.00x (ISBN 0-471-09258-4, Pub. by Wiley-Interscience). Wiley.

Clayton, Irene, jt. auth. see Schmottlach, Neil.

Clayton, J. Irsud. (Science Fiction Ser.). (Orig.). 1981. pap. 2.50 (ISBN 0-87997-839-2, UE 1839). DAW Bks.

Clayton, J. P., jt. auth. see Sykes, S. W.

Clayton, J. P., ed. Ernst Troeltsch & the Future of Theology. LC 75-44576. 1976. 37.50 (ISBN 0-521-21074-7). Cambridge U Pr.

Clayton, Jan, jt. auth. see Marx, Samuel.

Clayton, Jo. Maeve: A Novel of the Diadem. (Science Fiction Ser.). 1979. pap. 2.25 (ISBN 0-87997-760-4, UE1760). DAW Bks.

Clayton, John, ed. Illinois Fact Book & Historical Almanac, 1673-1968. LC 68-21417. (Illus.). 576p. 1970. 15.00x o.p. (ISBN 0-8093-0380-9). S Ill U Pr.

Clayton, Joseph D. The Ruger Number One Rifle. Amber, John T., ed. (Know Your Gun Ser.: No. 2). (Illus.). 212p. 1982. 39.95 (ISBN 0-941540-06-5). Blacksmith Corp.

Clayton, Joyce A., jt. auth. see Clayton, Robert D.

Clayton, K. M., ed. see Clarendon Press, Cartographic Dept.

Clayton, Lawrence A. Caulkers & Carpenters in a New World: The Shipyards of Colonial Guayaquil. LC 80-11547. (Papers in International Studies Latin American Ser.: No. 8). (Orig.). 1980. pap. text ed. 15.00 (ISBN 0-89680-103-9, Ohio U Ctr Intl). Ohio U Pr.

Clayton, Nanalee. Young Living. rev. ed. (Illus.). (gr. 7-8). 1983. text ed. 15.00 (ISBN 0-87002-382-9); tchr's. guide 10.00 (ISBN 0-87002-387-X); price not set student ed. (ISBN 0-87002-399-3). Bennett IL.

Clayton, P. The Filtration Efficiency of a Range of Filter Media for Sub-Micrometre Aerosols, 1978. 1981. 50.00x (ISBN 0-686-97079-9, Pub. by W Spring England). State Mutual Bk.

Clayton, P. & Wallin, S. C. An Environmental Study of an Activated Carbon Plant, 1978. 1981. 40.00x (ISBN 0-686-97068-3, Pub. by W Green England). State Mutual Bk.

Clayton, P., jt. auth. see Bailey, D. L.

Clayton, P., et al. An Investigation of the Lead Emissions from a Lead Works & Their Effect on Ambient Lead Concentrations, 1977. 1982. 50.00x (ISBN 0-686-97095-0, Pub. by W Spring England). State Mutual Bk.

Clayton, Pat. The Cohabitation Guide. 224p. 1981. pap. 20.00x o.p. (ISBN 0-7045-0374-3, Pub. by Wildwood House). State Mutual Bk.

Clayton, Paula J. & Barrett, James E., eds. Treatment of Depression: Old Controversies & New Approaches. (American Psychopathological Association Ser.). 1982. text ed. write for info. (ISBN 0-89004-745-6). Raven.

Clayton, Peter & Gammond, Peter. Fourteen Miles on a Clear Night. LC 78-5685. (Illus.). 1978. Repr. of 1966 ed. lib. bdg. 18.00x (ISBN 0-313-20475-6, CLFM). Greenwood.

Clayton, Peter A. The Rediscovery of Ancient Egypt: Artists & Travellers in the 19th Century. (Illus.). 1983. 37.50 (ISBN 0-500-01284-9). Thames Hudson.

Clayton, Peter A., rev. by see Lurker, Manfred.

Clayton, Philip T., jt. auth. see Smolin, Pauline.

Clayton, R. K. Photosynthesis: Physical Mechanisms & Chemical Patterns. LC 79-27543. (IUPAB Biophysics Ser.: No. 4). 295p. 1981. 42.50 (ISBN 0-521-22300-8); pap. 14.95 (ISBN 0-521-29443-6). Cambridge U Pr.

Clayton, R. M. & Truman, D. E., eds. Stability & Switching in Cellular Differentiation. (Advances in Experimental Medicine & Biology). 484p. 1982. 62.50x (ISBN 0-306-41181-4, Plenum Pr). Plenum Pub.

Clayton, Richard R. Family Marriage & Social Change. 2nd ed. 1979. text ed. 21.95 (ISBN 0-669-01957-7); instr's manual 1.95 (ISBN 0-669-01956-9). Heath.

Clayton, Robert D. & Clayton, Joyce A. Concepts & Careers in Physical Education. 3rd ed. 174p. 1982. pap. text ed. 9.95x (ISBN 0-8087-2972-1). Burgess.

Clayton, Robert D., jt. auth. see Torney, John A., Jr.

Clayton, Roderick K. Light & Living Matter: A Guide to the Study of Photobiology, Vol. 2: The Biological Part. LC 76-55697. (Illus.). 254p. (Orig.). 1977. pap. text ed. 6.50 o.p. (ISBN 0-88275-493-9). Krieger.

Clayton, Stanley & Lewis, T. L. Gynecology by Ten Teachers. 396p. 1981. pap. text ed. 19.50 (ISBN 0-7131-4394-0). E Arnold.

--Obstetrics by Ten Teachers. 552p. 1980. text ed. 26.50 (ISBN 0-7131-4365-7). E Arnold.

Clayton, Thomas H. Close to the Land: The Way We Lived in North Carolina, 1820-1870. Nathans, Sydney, ed. LC 82-20143. (The Way We Lived in North Carolina Ser.). (Illus.). viii, 98p. 11.95 (ISBN 0-8078-1551-9); pap. 6.95 (ISBN 0-8078-4103-X). U of NC Pr.

Clayton, W. E. Review of the Fertilizer Distribution & Handling System in Bangladesh. (IFDC Miscellaneous Publication Ser.: A-2). 1981. 4.00 (ISBN 0-686-95959-0). Intl Fertilizer.

Clayton, W. W. History of Davidson County, Tennessee. (Illus.). 1971. Repr. of 1880 ed. 85.00 (ISBN 0-918450-03-9). C Elder.

Clayton-Jones, E., jt. ed. see Finckh, E.

Cleaf, David W. van see Brooks, Douglas M. & Van Cleaf, David W.

Clean Air Society. International Clean Air Conference, 7th, Australia. International Clean Air Conference, 1981: Proceedings. LC 81-66259. 1981. text ed. 49.95 (ISBN 0-250-40415-X). Ann Arbor Science.

Clean Air Society of Australia & New Zealand, ed. International Clean Air Conference. LC 78-51051. 1978. 50.00 o.p. (ISBN 0-250-40254-8). Ann Arbor Science.

Cleaning Consultant Services, Inc. The Comprehensive Custodial Training Manual. 1980. 48.00x (ISBN 0-9601054-1-7). Cleaning Consul.

Clear, Kathleen G. Dance Magazine College Guide: 1982-83. 2nd ed. 170p. 1982. pap. 10.95 (ISBN 0-930036-06-9). Dance Mag Inc.

Clear, Todd R. & O'Leary, Vincent. Controlling the Offenders in the Community: Reforming the Community Supervision Function. LC 81-47444. 208p. 1982. 29.95x (ISBN 0-669-04633-7). Lexington Bks.

Clear, Val. Making Money with Birds. (Illus.). 192p. 1981. 12.95 (ISBN 0-87666-825-2, H-1031). TFH Pubns.

Cleare, John. Mountaineering. (Illus.). 176p. 1980. 12.95 o.p. (ISBN 0-7137-0946-4, Pub. by Blandford Pr England); pap. 6.95 o.p. (ISBN 0-7137-1082-9). Sterling.

Clearinghouse for Hospital Management Engineering, compiled by. Multi-Institutional Arrangements in Urban Hospitals: A Collection of Case Studies. LC 81-19075. 136p. 1981. 15.00 (ISBN 0-87258-365-1, AHA-103140). Am Hospital.

Clearman, Brian. Transportation Markings: A Study in Communication. LC 80-6184. (Illus.). 489p. (Orig.). 1981. lib. bdg. 26.75 (ISBN 0-8191-1653-X); pap. text ed. 16.50 (ISBN 0-8191-1654-8). U Pr of Amer.

Cleary, A., et al. Educational Technology: Implications for Early & Special Education. LC 75-1239. 1976. 39.95 (ISBN 0-471-16045-8, Pub. by Wiley-Interscience). Wiley.

Cleary, Alan. Instrumentation for Psychology. LC 77-1250. 1978. 34.25 o.p. (ISBN 0-471-99483-9, Pub. by Wiley-Interscience). Wiley.

Cleary, Beverly. Beezus & Ramona. (gr. 4-6). 1979. pap. 2.50 (ISBN 0-440-40665-X, YB). Dell.

--Beezus & Ramona. (Illus.). (gr. 3-7). 1955. 8.50 (ISBN 0-688-21076-7); PLB 9.12 (ISBN 0-688-31076-1); pap. 1.50 o.p. (ISBN 0-688-25078-5). Morrow.

--Ellen Tebbits. (gr. 4-6). 1979. pap. 2.50 (ISBN 0-440-42299-X, YB). Dell.

--Ellen Tebbits. (Illus.). (gr. 3-7). 1951. 9.50 (ISBN 0-688-21264-6); PLB 9.12 (ISBN 0-688-31264-0). Morrow.

--Emily's Runaway Imagination. (gr. k-6). 1980. pap. 2.50 (ISBN 0-440-42215-9, YB). Dell.

--Emily's Runaway Imagination. (Illus.). (gr. 3-7). 1961. 10.75 (ISBN 0-688-21267-0); PLB 10.32 (ISBN 0-688-31267-5). Morrow.

--Fifteen. (Illus.). (gr. 6-9). 1956. 10.50 (ISBN 0-688-21285-9); PLB 10.08 (ISBN 0-688-31285-3). Morrow.

--Henry & Beezus. (Illus.). (gr. 3-7). 1952. 9.95 (ISBN 0-688-21383-9); PLB 9.55 (ISBN 0-688-31383-3). Morrow.

--Henry & Ribsy. (gr. 3 up). 1979. pap. 2.50 (ISBN 0-440-43296-0, YB). Dell.

--Henry & Ribsy. (Illus.). (gr. 3-7). 1954. 9.95 (ISBN 0-688-21382-0); PLB 9.55 (ISBN 0-688-31382-5); pap. 1.50 o.p. (ISBN 0-688-25382-2). Morrow.

--Henry & the Clubhouse. (Illus.). (gr. 3-7). 1962. 9.50 (ISBN 0-688-21381-2); PLB 9.12 (ISBN 0-688-31381-7). Morrow.

--Henry & the Paper Route. (gr. k-6). 1980. pap. 2.25 (ISBN 0-440-43298-7, YB). Dell.

--Henry & the Paper Route. (Illus.). (gr. 3-7). 1957. 9.95 (ISBN 0-688-21380-4); PLB 9.55 (ISBN 0-688-31380-9). Morrow.

--Henry Huggins. (gr. 4-6). 1979. pap. 2.50 (ISBN 0-440-43551-X, YB). Dell.

--Henry Huggins. (Illus.). (gr. 3-7). 1950. 9.50 (ISBN 0-688-25385-7); PLB 9.12 (ISBN 0-688-31385-X). Morrow.

--Jean & Johnny. (Illus.). (gr. 6-9). 1959. 10.50 (ISBN 0-688-21740-0); PLB 10.08 (ISBN 0-688-31740-5). Morrow.

--The Luckiest Girl. (gr. 7 up). 1958. PLB 11.28 (ISBN 0-688-31741-3). Morrow.

--Mitch & Amy. (gr. k-6). 1980. pap. 2.50 (ISBN 0-440-45411-5, YB). Dell.

--Mitch & Amy. (Illus.). (gr. 3-7). 1967. 9.95 (ISBN 0-688-21688-9); PLB 9.55 (ISBN 0-688-31688-3). Morrow.

--The Mouse & the Motorcycle. (gr. k-6). 1980. pap. 2.50 (ISBN 0-440-46060-3, YB). Dell.

--The Mouse & the Motorcycle. (Illus.). (gr. 2-6). 1965. 9.50 (ISBN 0-688-21698-6); PLB 9.12 (ISBN 0-688-31698-0). Morrow.

--Otis Spofford. (Illus.). (gr. 3-7). 1953. 9.50 (ISBN 0-688-21720-6); PLB 9.12 (ISBN 0-688-31720-0); pap. 1.50 o.p. (ISBN 0-688-26720-3). Morrow.

--Ramona & Her Father. LC 77-1614. (gr. 3-7). 1977. 9.50 (ISBN 0-688-22114-9); PLB 9.12 (ISBN 0-688-32114-3). Morrow.

--Ramona & Her Friends. pap. 9.00 (ISBN 0-440-47222-9). Dell.

--Ramona & Her Mother. (gr. k-6). 1980. pap. 2.50 (ISBN 0-440-47243-1, YB). Dell.

--Ramona & Her Mother. LC 79-10323. (Illus.). 192p. (gr. 4-6). 1979. 9.75 (ISBN 0-688-22195-5); PLB 9.36 (ISBN 0-688-32195-X). Morrow.

--Ramona the Brave. LC 74-164968. (Illus.). 192p. (gr. 3-7). 1975. 9.50 (ISBN 0-688-22015-0); PLB 9.12 (ISBN 0-688-32015-5). Morrow.

--Ramona the Pest. (gr. 4-7). 1982. pap. 2.50 (ISBN 0-440-47209-1, YB). Dell.

--Ramona the Pest. (Illus.). (gr. 3-7). 1968. 9.50 (ISBN 0-688-21721-4); PLB 9.12 (ISBN 0-688-31721-9). Morrow.

--The Real Hole. (Illus.). (ps-1). 1960. PLB 8.59 (ISBN 0-688-31655-7). Morrow.

--Ribsy. (Illus.). (gr. 3-7). 1964. 9.50 (ISBN 0-688-21662-5); PLB 9.12 (ISBN 0-688-31662-X). Morrow.

--Runaway Ralph. (gr. k-6). 1981. pap. 2.25 (ISBN 0-440-47519-8, YB). Dell.

--Runaway Ralph. (Illus.). (gr. 3-7). 1970. 9.75 (ISBN 0-688-21701-X); PLB 9.36 (ISBN 0-688-31701-4). Morrow.

--Sister of the Bride. (Illus.). (gr. 7 up). 1963. PLB 11.04 (ISBN 0-688-31742-1). Morrow.

--Socks. (gr. k-6). 1980. pap. 2.50 (ISBN 0-440-48256-9, YB). Dell.

--Socks. LC 72-10298. (Illus.). 192p. (gr. 3-7). 1973. 9.50 (ISBN 0-688-20067-2); PLB 9.12 (ISBN 0-688-30067-7). Morrow.

Cleary, Edward & Graham, Michael. Handbook of Illinois Evidence: 1982 Supplement. LC 79-89121. 175p. 1982. write for info. o.p. (ISBN 0-316-14723-0). Little.

Cleary, Edward W. & Graham, Michael H. Handbook of Illinois Evidence. 1979. text ed. 55.00 (ISBN 0-316-14720-6); 1983 supplement avail. Little.

--Handbook of Illinois Evidence: 1981 Supplement. LC 79-89121. 96p. 1982. pap. 12.50 (ISBN 0-316-14723-0). Little.

Cleary, Florence D. Blueprints for Better Reading. 2nd ed. 1972. 17.00 (ISBN 0-8242-0406-9). Wilson.

Cleary, J. B. & Lacombe, J. English Style Skill-Builders: A Self-Improvement Program for Transcribers & Typists. 2nd ed. 1974. 9.32 (ISBN 0-07-011303-3, G); tchr's manual & key 8.40 (ISBN 0-07-011304-1). McGraw.

Cleary, J. B. & Lacombe, J. M. English Style Skill Builders: A Self-Improvement Program for Transcribers & Typists. 1980. text ed. 9.96 (ISBN 0-07-011305-X); tchr's manual & key 7.55 (ISBN 0-07-011306-8). McGraw.

Cleary, J. C., jt. auth. see Cleary, Thomas.

Cleary, James P. & Levenbach, Hans. The Professional Forecaster: The Forecasting Process Through Data Analysis. (Quantitative Methods for Managers Ser.). (Illus.). 400p. 1981. text ed. 31.50 (ISBN 0-534-97960-2). Lifetime Learn.

Cleary, James P., jt. auth. see Levenbach, Hans.

Cleary, Jon. The Beaufort Sisters. LC 78-71416. 1979. 10.95 o.p. (ISBN 0-688-03444-6). Morrow.

--High Road to China. 320p. 1983. pap. 2.95 (ISBN 0-446-31178-2). Warner Bks.

--Spearfield's Daughter. LC 82-14542. 567p. 1983. Repr. 15.95 (ISBN 0-688-01736-3). Morrow.

Cleary, Thomas. The Flower Ornament Scripture: A Translation of the Avatamsaka Sutra Vol. I. Orig. Title: Avatamsaka Sutra (Sanskrit) Hua-yen (Chinese) 500p. (Chinese.). 1983. 25.00 (ISBN 0-87773-767-3). Great Eastern.

Cleary, Thomas & Cleary, J. C. The Blue Cliff Record. LC 76-14202. 1978. 25.00 o.p. (ISBN 0-87773-706-1, Prajna). Great Eastern.

Cleary, Thomas, tr. see Dogen.

Cleave, Charles Van see Van Cleave, Charles.

Cleaveland, Agnes M. No Life for a Lady. LC 77-6825. (Illus.). viii, 356p. 1977. pap. 6.95 (ISBN 0-8032-5868-2, BB 652, Bison). U of Nebr Pr.

Cleaver, Bill, jt. auth. see Cleaver, Vera.

Cleaver, Claire M. Step into Sales: A Woman's Guide to Personal & Financial Success Through Home Merchandising. LC 82-90238. (Illus.). 250p. (Orig.). 1982. 18.95 o.p. (ISBN 0-942356-01-2); pap. 14.95 (ISBN 0-942356-00-4). Concepts by Claire.

Cleaver, David S., jt. auth. see Hsiao, James C.

Cleaver, Eldridge. Soul on Ice. 224p. 1968. 11.95 (ISBN 0-07-011307-6, GB). McGraw.

Cleaver, Kevin M. Economic & Social Analysis of Projects & of Price Policy: The Morocco Fourth Agricultural Credit Project. (Working Paper: No. 369). 59p. 1980. 3.00 (ISBN 0-686-36084-2, WP-0369). World Bank.

Cleaver, Vera & Cleaver, Bill. Delpha Green & Company. (RL 5). 1976. pap. 1.25 o.p. (ISBN 0-451-06907-2, Y6907, Sig). NAL.

--Dust of the Earth. (RL 5). 1977. pap. 1.25 o.p. (ISBN 0-451-07658-3, Y7658, Sig). NAL.

--Ellen Grae & Lady Ellen Grae. (RL 4). 1978. pap. 1.95 (ISBN 0-451-09832-3, J9832, Sig). NAL.

--Grover. (RL 5). 1975. pap. 1.75 (ISBN 0-451-11313-6, AE1313, Sig). NAL.

--Hazel Rye. LC 81-48603. 160p. (gr. 5-7). 1983. 11.06i (ISBN 0-397-31951-7, JBL-J); PLB 11.89g (ISBN 0-397-31952-5). Har-Row.

--Where the Lilies Bloom. 1974. pap. 1.95 (ISBN 0-451-12292-5, AJ2292, Sig). NAL.

--The Whys & Wherefores of Littabelle Lee. 1976. pap. 1.50 o.p. (ISBN 0-451-07225-1, W7225, Sig). NAL.

Cleaves, A. B., jt. auth. see Schultz, John R.

Cleaves, Cheryl & Hobbs, Margie. Basic Mathematics for Trades & Technologies. (Illus.). 640p. 1983. text ed. 21.95 (ISBN 0-686-81986-1). P-H.

Cleaves, Peter S. Bureaucratic Politics & Administration in Chile. LC 73-76111. 1974. 37.50x (ISBN 0-520-02448-6). U of Cal Pr.

Clebsch, William. Christianity in European History. 1979. 21.95x (ISBN 0-19-502471-0); pap. text ed. 6.95x (ISBN 0-19-502472-9). Oxford U Pr.

Clebsch, William A. Christian Interpretations of the Civil War. Wolf, Richard C., ed. LC 76-84556. (Facet Bks.). (Orig.). 1969. pap. 1.00 o.p. (ISBN 0-8006-3054-8, 1-3054). Fortress.

Clecak, Peter. America's Quest for Self: Dissent & Fulfillment in the 60s & 70s. 368p. 1983. 22.50 (ISBN 0-19-503226-8). Oxford U Pr.

Cleckley, Hervey. The Mask of Sanity. LC 82-2124. (Medical Library). 285p. 1982. pap. 8.95 (ISBN 0-452-25341-1, 1158-X). Mosby.

Cleckley, Hervey M. Mask of Sanity. 5th ed. LC 75-31875. 472p. 1976. 23.50 o.p. (ISBN 0-8016-0985-2). Mosby.

Cleckley, Hervey M., jt. auth. see Thigpen, Corbett.

Clee, Suzanne, jt. auth. see Jensen, Tom.

Cleef, A. M. The Vegetation of the Paramos of the Colombian Cordillera Oriental. (Dissertationes Botanicae: Vol. 61). (Illus.). 320p. 1981. text ed. 24.00x (ISBN 3-7682-1302-1). Lubrecht & Cramer.

Cleeland, Caryn L., jt. auth. see Castelli, Louis.

Cleeton, Claud E. Strategies for the Options Trader. LC 78-11230. 1979. 34.95 (ISBN 0-471-04973-5, Pub. by Wiley-Interscience). Wiley.

Cleeve, Brian. Hester. LC 79-660. 1980. 10.95 (ISBN 0-698-10987-2, Coward). Putnam Pub Group.

--Judith. LC 78-5781. 1978. 8.95 o.p. (ISBN 0-698-10910-4, Coward). Putnam Pub Group.

--Kate. 352p. 1977. 8.95 o.p. (ISBN 0-698-10812-4, Coward). Putnam Pub Group.

--Sara. LC 75-38970. 384p. 1976. 8.95 o.p. (ISBN 0-698-10700-4, Coward). Putnam Pub Group.

Cleevely, R. J. World Palaeontological Collections. 450p. 1982. 80.00 (ISBN 0-7201-1655-4, Pub. by Mansell England). Wilson.

Clegg, A. B. The Changing Primary School: Teachers Speak on Adapting to New Ways. LC 72-183617. 1972. 6.95x o.p. (ISBN 0-8052-3439-X). Schocken.

Clegg, Edward. Race & Politics: Partnership in the Federation of Rhodesia & Nyasaland. LC 75-3731. 280p. 1975. Repr. of 1960 ed. lib. bdg. 18.25x (ISBN 0-8371-8061-9, CLRPO). Greenwood.

Clegg, Holly Berkowitz & Jarrett, Beverly. From a Louisiana Kitchen. (Illus.). 256p. 1983. pap. 9.95 (ISBN 0-686-82622-1). Wimmer Bks.

Clegg, Hugh A. The Changing System of Industrial Relations in Great Britain: A Completely Rewritten Version of "The System of Industrial Relations in Great Britain". 479p. 1979. 45.50x o.p. (ISBN 0-631-11091-7, Pub. by Basil Blackwell England); pap. 21.00x o.p. (ISBN 0-631-11101-8). Biblio Dist.

Clegg, Ian. Workers' Self-Management in Algeria. (Illus.). 256p. 1971. 8.95 (ISBN 0-85345-200-8, CL2008). Monthly Rev.

Clegg, J. B., jt. auth. see Weatherall, D. J.

Clegg, James S., jt. ed. see Crowe, John H.

Clegg, John. Your Book of Freshwater Life. (Illus.). (gr. 7 up). 1968. 5.95 o.p. (ISBN 0-571-08399-4). Transatlantic.

Clegg, Peter & Watkins, Derry. The Complete Greenhouse Book: Building & Using Greenhouses from Cold Frames to Solar Structures. LC 78-24572. (Illus.). 288p. 1978. 14.95 o.p. (ISBN 0-88266-142-6); pap. 10.95 (ISBN 0-88266-141-8). Garden Way Pub.

Clegg, Peter D. & Wolfe, Ralph D. Home Energy for the Eighties. LC 79-9412. (Illus.). 1979. pap. 10.95 o.p. (ISBN 0-88266-158-2). Garden Way Pub.

Cleghorn, Reese, jt. auth. see Watters, Pat.

Cleland & King. Project Management Handbook. 752p. 1983. 44.50 (ISBN 0-442-23878-9). Van Nos Reinhold.

Cleland, Charles. Mental Retardation: A Developmental Approach. (Spec. Educ. Ser.). 1978. ref. ed. 24.95x (ISBN 0-13-576504-8). P-H.

Cleland, Charles C. & Swartz, Jon D. Exceptionalities Through the Life Span: An Introduction. 1982. text ed. 22.95x (ISBN 0-02-322860-1). Macmillan.

Cleland, D. I. & King, W. R. Systems Analysis & Project Management. 3rd ed. 1983. write for info. (ISBN 0-07-011311-4). McGraw.

Cleland, David I. & King, William R. Management: A Systems Approach. (Management Ser.). (Illus.). 456p. 1972. text ed. 25.95 (ISBN 0-07-011314-9, C). McGraw.

--Systems Analysis & Project Management. 2nd ed. (Management Ser.). (Illus.). 416p. 1975. text ed. 23.95 (ISBN 0-07-011310-6, C). McGraw.

Cleland, David I. & Kocaoglu, Dundar F. Engineering Management. (Industrial Engineering & Management Science Ser.). (Illus.). 528p. 1981. text ed. 28.00 (ISBN 0-07-011316-5, C). McGraw.

Cleland, James. The Institution of a Young Noble Man. LC 47-12445. 1979. Repr. of 1607 ed. 40.00x (ISBN 0-8201-1216-X). Schol Facsimiles.

Cleland, Lucille H. Trails & Trials of the Pioneers of the Olympic Peninsula. 312p. Repr. of 1959 ed. 18.95 o.p. (ISBN 0-8466-2302-1); pap. 14.95 (ISBN 0-8466-0302-0, SJS-302). Shorey.

Cleland, Max. Strong at the Broken Places. 180p. 1980. PLB 6.95 o.p. (ISBN 0-912376-55-4). Chosen Bks Pub.

Clem, Alan. American Electoral Politics: Strategies for Renewal. 1980. pap. text ed. 9.95 (ISBN 0-442-24475-4). Van Nos Reinhold.

Cleman, Wolfgang, ed. see Shakespeare, William.

Clemeau, Carol. The Ariadne Clue. 208p. 1982. 12.95 (ISBN 0-684-17764-1). Scribner.

Clemen & Eigsti. Comprehensive Family & Community Health Nursing. (Illus.). 544p. 1981. text ed. 25.00 (ISBN 0-07-011324-6). McGraw.

Clemen, Wolfgang. English Tragedy Before Shakespeare. 1980. 38.00x (ISBN 0-416-74380-3). Methuen Inc.

Clemen, Wolfgang H. The Development of Shakespeare's Imagery. 2nd ed. 237p. 1977. 35.00x (ISBN 0-416-85740-X); pap. 14.50x (ISBN 0-416-85730-2). Methuen Inc.

Clemence, Richard, jt. auth. see Stout, Ruth.

Clemenceau, Georges. American Reconstruction, Eighteen Sixty-Five to Eighteen Seventy. 2nd ed. LC 68-16229. (American Scene Ser). 1969. Repr. of 1928 ed. 35.00 (ISBN 0-306-71010-2). Da Capo.

Clemencon, H., ed. see Symposium Lausanne, Switzerland Aug. 16 to 20 1976.

Clemens, Bryan T. The Counselor & Religious Questioning & Conflicts. LC 72-1844. (Guidance Monograph). 1973. pap. 2.40 o.p. (ISBN 0-395-14205-9). HM.

Clemens, Clara. My Husband Gabrilowitsch. (Music Reprint Ser.). 1979. Repr. of 1938 ed. 29.50 (ISBN 0-306-79563-9). Da Capo.

Clemens, Dale P. Fiberglass Rod Making. (Stoeger Bks). 1977. pap. 5.95 o.s.i. (ISBN 0-695-80861-3). Follett.

--Fiberglass Rod Making. (Illus.). 212p. pap. 8.95 (ISBN 0-88317-042-6). Stoeger Pub Co.

Clemens, David A. The Cutting Edge, Vol. 2. LC 79-52420. (Steps to Maturity Ser.). 1975. student's manual 13.95x (ISBN 0-86508-003-8); tchr's. manual 15.95x (ISBN 0-86508-004-6). BCM Inc.

Clemens, Diane S. Yalta. 368p. 1972. pap. 7.95 (ISBN 0-19-501618-1, GB). Oxford U Pr.

Clemens, Paul, ed. see Gawain, Elizabeth.

Clemens, S., jt. auth. see O'Daffer, P.

Clemenson, Heather. English Country Houses & Landed Estates. LC 82-3298. (Illus.). 256p. 1982. 30.00x (ISBN 0-312-25414-8). St Martin.

Clement & Hutton. Artists of the 19th Century. 1969. 50.00 (ISBN 0-686-43125-1). Apollo.

Clement, Ambroise. Recherches sur les Causes de l'Indigence. (Conditions of the 19th Century French Working Class Ser.). 368p. (Fr.). 1974. Repr. of 1846 ed. lib. bdg. 95.00x o.p. (ISBN 0-8287-0204-7, 1002). Clearwater Pub.

Clement, Charles B. Limited Bid. cancelled. Green Hill.

Clement, Clara E. Handbook of Christian Symbols & Stories of the Saints, As Illustrated in Art. LC 70-159863. 1971. Repr. of 1886 ed. 39.00 o.p. (ISBN 0-8103-3288-4). Gale.

--Handbook of Legendary & Mythological Art. LC 68-26616. (Illus.). 1969. Repr. of 1881 ed. 45.00x (ISBN 0-8103-3175-6). Gale.

--Saints in Art. LC 77-89303. 1976. Repr. of 1899 ed. 40.00x (ISBN 0-8103-3030-X). Gale.

Clement, Evelyn, jt. ed. see Grove, Pierce.

Clement, Felix & Larousse, Pierre. Dictionnaire Des Operas, 2 Vols. LC 69-15617. (Music Reprint Ser). 1969. Repr. of 1905 ed. Set. 110.00 (ISBN 0-306-71197-4). Da Capo.

Clement, Hal. Mission of Gravity. (Science Fiction Ser.). 1978. lib. bdg. 12.00 o.p. (ISBN 0-8398-2426-2, Gregg). G K Hall.

Clement, John A., jt. auth. see Stryker, John A.

Clement, Nemours H. Romanticism in France. (MLA Rev. Fund Ser.). 1938. pap. 45.00 (ISBN 0-527-17800-4). Kraus Repr.

Clement, Paul A., jt. auth. see Packard, Pamela M.

Clement, Preston & Johnson, W. Electrical Engineering Science. (Electrical & Electronic Eng. Ser). 1960. text ed. 35.50 o.p. (ISBN 0-07-011320-3, C) (ISBN 0-07-011319-X). McGraw.

Clement, Preston R. & Johnson, Walter C. Electrical Engineering Science. LC 82-14796. 602p. 1983. lib. bdg. write for info (ISBN 0-89874-442-3). Krieger.

Clemente, Elizabeth M. de see Van Ness, Bethann & De Clemente, Elizabeth M.

Clemente, F. F. Di see Di Clemente, F. F.

Clemente, Frank & Lambert, Richard D., eds. The New Rural America. LC 76-27028. (Annals Ser.: No. 429). 1977. 15.00 (ISBN 0-87761-208-0); pap. 7.95 (ISBN 0-87761-209-9). Am Acad Pol Soc Sci.

Clemente, Vince, jt. auth. see Carney, Jo.

Clementes, Julia. The Flower Arranger's Bedside Book. (Illus.). 80p. 1982. 12.50 (Pub. by Batsford England). David & Charles.

Clementi, Enrico & Sarma, Ramaswamy, eds. Structure & Dynamics of Nucleic Acids & Proteins. (Illus.). 600p. 1983. text ed. 49.00 (ISBN 0-940030-04-7). Adenine Pr.

Clementi, F., ed. see International Symposium on Cell Biology & Cytopharmacology, First.

Clementi, Muzio. Collected Works, 13 vols in 5. LC 70-75299. (Music Reprint Ser). 1973. 69.50 ea.; Set. 325.00 (ISBN 0-306-77260-4); fascicle of flute & violin pts. 18.50 (ISBN 0-306-77267-1); fascicle of cello pts. 18.50 (ISBN 0-306-77268-X). Da Capo.

--Gradus ad Parnassum: Twenty-Nine Selected Studies for Piano. (Carl Fischer Music Library: No. 388). 76p. Date not set. pap. 6.00 (ISBN 0-8258-0119-2, L 388). Fischer Inc NY.

--Introduction to the Art of Playing on the Pianoforte. LC 70-125067. 1974. Repr. of 1801 ed. lib. bdg. 22.50 (ISBN 0-306-70004-2). Da Capo.

Clements. Dog & Puppies. 1983. 5.95 (ISBN 0-86020-647-5, 15111); pap. 2.95 (ISBN 0-86020-646-7, 15112). EDC.

Clements, Colleen D. Medical Genetics Casebook: A Clinical Introduction to Medical Ethics Systems Theory. LC 81-8220. (Contemporary Issues in Biomedicine, Ethics, & Society Ser.). 256p. 1982. 24.50 (ISBN 0-686-97802-1). Humana.

Clements, Colleen D., jt. auth. see Teichler-Zallen, Doris.

Clements, David. Soccer Tips. LC 77-25009. (Illus.). 64p. (gr. 4-6). 1978. PLB 6.97 o.p. (ISBN 0-671-32956-1). Messner.

Clements, David L. Boundary Value Problems Governed by Second Order Elliptic Systems. LC 80-20820. (Monographs & Studies: No. 12). 176p. 1981. text ed. 53.95 (ISBN 0-273-08502-6). Pitman Pub MA.

Clements, Harry F. Sugarcane Crop Logging & Crop Control: Principles & Practices. LC 79-9894. (Illus.). 1980. text ed. 40.00x (ISBN 0-8248-0508-9). UH Pr.

Clements, Imelda W. & Buchanan, Diane E. Family Therapy: A Nursing Perspective. LC 81-13129. 356p. 1982. 16.95 (ISBN 0-471-08146-9, Pub. by Wiley Med). Wiley.

Clements, Imelda W. & Roberts, Florence B. Family Health: A Theoretical Approach to Nursing Care. LC 81-13129. 416p. 1983. 15.95 (ISBN 0-471-08536-7, Pub. by Wiley Med). Wiley.

Clements, John. Chronology of the United States. LC 70-175181. (Illus.). 320p. 1975. 31.95 (ISBN 0-07-011328-9, P&RB). McGraw.

Clements, Julia. Treasury of Rose Arrangements & Recipes. LC 59-7987. 1959. 3.50 (ISBN 0-8208-0012-0). Hearthside.

Clements, Kendrick A. William Jennings Bryan: Missionary Isolationist. LC 82-8342. (Illus.). 232p. 1983. text ed. 19.95x (ISBN 0-87049-364-7). U of Tenn Pr.

Clements, R. E. Prophecy & Tradition. LC 74-3713. 96p. 1975. pap. 2.75 (ISBN 0-8042-0110-2). John Knox.

Clements, Robert W., jt. auth. see Tetreault, Wilfred F.

Clements, Ronald E. Old Testament Theology. LC 79-16704. (New Foundations Theological Library). (Peter Toon & Ralph Martin series editors). 1980. 12.95 (ISBN 0-8042-3701-8). John Knox.

Clements, Zacharie J. & Burrell, Leon F. I Want to Make It: A Primer for Minority Students & Others Who Want to be Successful in College. LC 82-50564. 125p. (Orig.). (gr. 7-12). 1983. pap. 5.95 (ISBN 0-88247-686-6). R & E Res Assoc.

Clemes, Harris & Bean, Reynold. Self Esteem: The Key to Your Child's Well-Being. 350p. 1981. 12.95 (ISBN 0-399-12529-9). Putnam Pub Group.

--Self-Esteem: The Key to Your Child's Well-Being. 1982. pap. 3.50 (ISBN 0-8217-1096-6). Zebra.

Cleminshaw, Clarence H. Beginner's Guide to the Skies. LC 76-28317. 1977. 12.45 (ISBN 0-690-01214-4). T Y Crowell.

Clemmer, Richard B., jt. auth. see Schreiber, Arthur F.

Clemmow, P. C. An Introduction to Electromagnetic Theory. LC 73-77174. (Illus.). 320p. 1973. 46.50 (ISBN 0-521-20239-6); pap. 17.95 (ISBN 0-521-09815-7). Cambridge U Pr.

Clemmow, P. C. & Dougherty, J. P. Electrodynamics of Particles & Plasmas. 1969. text ed. 19.50 o.p. (ISBN 0-201-01143-3, Adv Bk Prog). A-W.

Clemoes, Peter, ed. Anglo Saxon England II. LC 78-190423. (Illus.). 350p. Date not set. price not set (ISBN 0-521-24918-X). Cambridge U Pr.

Clemoes, Peter & Hughes, Kathleen, eds. England Before the Conquest. LC 76-154508. (Illus.). 1971. 59.50 (ISBN 0-521-08191-2). Cambridge U Pr.

Clemoes, Peter A., ed. Anglo-Saxon England. Incl. Vol. 1. 320p. 1972. 54.50 (ISBN 0-521-08557-8); Vol. 2. 300p. 1973. 54.50 (ISBN 0-521-20218-3); Vol. 3. 320p. 1974. 54.50 (ISBN 0-521-20574-3); Vol. 4. 270p. 1975. 54.50 (ISBN 0-521-20868-8); Vol. 5. 1976. 54.50 (ISBN 0-521-21270-7); Vol. 6. 1977. 54.50 (ISBN 0-521-21701-6); Vol. 7. 1979. 54.50 (ISBN 0-521-22164-1); Vol. 8. 1980. 57.50 (ISBN 0-521-22788-7); vol. 9, 1981 56.00 (ISBN 0-521-23449-2). LC 78-190423. (Illus.). Cambridge U Pr.

Clendenin, J. C., jt. auth. see Christy, G. A.

Clendenin, William R. History of Music. (Quality Paperback Ser.: No. 272). (Illus.). 464p. 1974. pap. 6.95 (ISBN 0-8226-0272-5). Littlefield.

Clendening, Corinne P. & Davies, Ruth A. Challenging the Gifted Child. (Serving Special Populations Ser.). 1983. 32.50 (ISBN 0-8352-1682-9). Bowker.

Clene, Inc., compiled by. Who's Who in Continuing Education. 304p. 1979. 40.00x (ISBN 0-89664-024-8, Pub. by K G Saur). Gale.

Cleobury, F. H. Liberal Christian Orthodoxy. 164p. 1963. 15.95 (ISBN 0-227-67668-8). Attic Pr.

--Return to Natural Theology. 246p. 1967. 15.95 (ISBN 0-227-67722-6). Attic Pr.

Clepper, H. Origins of American Conservation. 493p. Repr. of 1966 ed. text ed. 25.95 (ISBN 0-471-06850-0). Krieger.

Clepper, Henry. Careers in Conservation: Opportunities in Natural Resource Management. 2nd ed. LC 78-21917. 1979. 29.95x (ISBN 0-471-05163-2). Ronald Pr.

Clepper, Henry, ed. Leaders of American Conservation. LC 75-155206. 354p. 1971. 17.95 o.p. (ISBN 0-8260-2045-3, 16263, Pub. by Wiley-Interscience). Wiley.

Clerc, Charles & Leiter, Louis. Seven Contemporary Short Novels. 3rd ed. 1982. pap. text ed. 13.50x (ISBN 0-673-15569-2). Scott F.

Clerc, Charles & Leiter, Louis H. Seven Contemporary Short Novels. 1969. pap. 13.50x (ISBN 0-673-05676-7). Scott F.

--Seven Contemporary Short Novels. 2nd ed. 1975. pap. 13.50x (ISBN 0-673-07971-6). Scott F.

Clerc, Charles, ed. Approaches to "Gravity's Rainbow". 315p. 1983. 25.00 (ISBN 0-8142-0337-X). Ohio St U Pr.

Clerc, J. T. & Pretsch, E. Structural Analysis of Organic Compounds by Combined Application of Spectroscopic Methods. (Studies in Analytical Chemistry: Vol. 1). 1982. 57.50 (ISBN 0-444-99748-2). Elsevier.

Clerc, Michel. Contribution a l'Etude des Relations Vitaminiques A et C. (Black Africa Ser.). 182p. (Fr.). 1974. Repr. of 1963 ed. lib. bdg. 53.50x o.p. (ISBN 0-8287-0205-5, 71-2013). Clearwater Pub.

--Deadly Payoff. 1979. pap. 1.95 o.p. (ISBN 0-451-08553-1, J8553, Sig). NAL.

Clergue. Practical Nude Photography. (Practical Ser.). (Illus.). 1983. 22.95x (ISBN 0-240-51202-2). Focal Pr.

Clergue, Lucien. Nude Workshop. LC 82-70177. (Illus.). 112p. 1982. 40.00 (ISBN 0-670-51824-7, Studio). Viking Pr.

Clerman, Robert J. & Joglekar, Rajani. Biotechnology & Energy Use. LC 77-85093. (Electrotechnology Ser.: Vol. 8). (Illus.). 189p. 1981. 39.95 (ISBN 0-250-40485-0). Ann Arbor Science.

Clerman, Robert J., jt. auth. see Joglekar, Rajani.

Clermont, Kevin M. Civil Procedure. LC 82-2742. (Black Letter Ser.). 308p. 1982. pap. text ed. 10.95 (ISBN 0-314-65090-3). West Pub.

Clermont, Kevin M., ed. Federal Rules of Civil Procedure. 1982 ed. 416p. 1982. pap. text ed. write for info. (ISBN 0-88277-089-6). Foundation Pr.

Cleron, Jean P. Saudi Arabi Two Thousand: A Strategy for Growth. LC 77-9238. 1978. 26.00x (ISBN 0-312-69978-6). St Martin.

Cleton, F., et al. Advances in Acute Leukaemia. 1975. 83.25 (ISBN 0-444-10765-7). Elsevier.

Cleugh, James. The Marquis & the Chevalier: A Study in the Psychology of Sex As Illustrated by the Lives & Personalities of the Marquis De Sade, 1740-1814 & the Chevalier Von Sacher-Masoch, 1836-1905. LC 70-142317. (Illus.). 295p. 1972. Repr. of 1952 ed. lib. bdg. 19.25x (ISBN 0-8371-5920-2, CLMC). Greenwood.

Cleugh, James, tr. see Flaceliere, Robert.

Cleugh, James, tr. see Wendt, Herbert.

Cleve, John. The Crusader: Books 3 & 4, The Accursed Tower & The Passionate Princess. LC 80-1000. 384p. (Orig.). 1981. pap. 4.95 (ISBN 0-394-17736-3, B-441, BC). Grove.

--Spaceways, No. 10: The Yoke of Shen. (Orig.). 1983. pap. 2.50 (ISBN 0-425-06063-2). Berkley Pub.

--Spaceways, No. 11: The Iceworld Connection. 224p. (Orig.). 1983. pap. 2.50 (ISBN 0-425-06067-5). Berkley Pub.

Cleve, P. T. & Grunow, A. Beitraege zur Kenntnis der arctischen Diatomeen. 1976. pap. text ed. 19.60 (ISBN 3-87429-101-4). Lubrecht & Cramer.

Cleve, Spike Van see Van Cleve, Spike.

Cleve, Thomas C. Van see Van Cleve, Thomas C.

Cleve-Euler, A. Die Diatomeen Von Schweden und Finnland, 5 pts. (Kungl. Sv. Vetenskapsak Handl Ser.). (Illus.). 1968. pap. 140.00 (ISBN 3-7682-0550-9). Lubrecht & Cramer.

Cleveland, Ana D., jt. auth. see Cleveland, Donald B.

Cleveland, David. The April Rabbits. LC 78-2044. (Illus.). (gr. k-4). 1978. 6.95 (ISBN 0-698-20463-8, Coward). Putnam Pub Group.

--The Frog on Robert's Head. (Illus.). (gr. 1-4). 1981. 8.95 (ISBN 0-698-20512-X, Coward). Putnam Pub Group.

Cleveland, Donald B. & Cleveland, Ana D. Introduction to Indexing & Abstracting. 250p. 1982. lib. bdg. 19.50 (ISBN 0-87287-346-3). Libs Unl.

Cleveland Foundation. Criminal Justice in Cleveland. Pound, Roscoe & Frankfurter, Felix, eds. LC 68-55769. (Criminology, Law Enforcement, & Social Problems Ser.: No. 8). (Illus.). 1968. Repr. of 1922 ed. 30.00x (ISBN 0-87585-008-1). Patterson Smith.

Cleveland, Harlan. The Future Executive: A Guide for Tomorrow's Managers. LC 79-138715. 128p. 1972. 14.37i (ISBN 0-06-010817-7, HarpT). Har-Row.

Cleveland, Harlan, jt. auth. see Wolf, Joseph J.

Cleveland, Harold Van B. & Brittain, W. Bruce. The Great Inflation: A Monetarist View. LC 76-41068. 72p. 1976. 3.50 (ISBN 0-89068-003-5). Natl Planning.

Cleveland, L. David. Harvard Square Restaurants & a Guidebook of History. (Illus.). 150p. (Orig.). 1983. pap. text ed. 4.95 (ISBN 0-938534-00-9). Soup to Nuts.

Cleveland Public Library - John G. White Department. Catalog of the Chess Collection, Including Checkers, 2 Vols. (Ser. Seventy). 1964. Set. 125.00 (ISBN 0-8161-0681-9, Hall Library). G K Hall.

Cleveland Symposium on Macromolecules, 1st, Case Western Reserve Univ., Oct. 1976. Proceedings. Walton, A. G., ed. 1977. 64.00 (ISBN 0-444-41561-0). Elsevier.

Cleveland, William A. Britannica Atlas. (YA) (gr. 9 up). 1982. 65.00 ea. (ISBN 0-85229-403-4). Ency Brit Ed.

Clevenger, A. W., jt. auth. see Belting, Paul E.

Clevenger, Theodore, Jr. & Matthews, Jack. The Speech Communication Process. 1971. pap. 8.95x (ISBN 0-673-05734-8). Scott F.

Cleverdon, Ardelle, ed. see Cabibi, John F.

Cleverdon, Ardelle, ed. see Purington, Robert C.

Cleverdon, Dorothy, et al. Play in a Hospital: Why & How. (Illus.). 54p. (Orig.). 1971. pap. 2.00x (ISBN 0-686-01102-3); pap. text ed. 1.50x (ISBN 0-936426-08-X). Play Schs.

Cleverley, William O. Financial Management of Health Care Facilities. 394p. 1976. 18.75 (ISBN 0-686-68581-4, 14915). Healthcare Fin Man Assn.

--Handbook of Health Care Accounting & Finance, 2 vols. LC 82-6784. 1385p. 1982. text ed. 120.00 set (ISBN 0-89443-364-4). Aspen Systems.

Clevin, Jorgen. Pete & Johnny to the Rescue. LC 74-4926. (Illus.). 64p. (ps-k). 1974. 3.50 (ISBN 0-394-82995-6); PLB 4.69 (ISBN 0-394-92995-0). Random.

Clewes, Dorothy. The End of Summer. (gr. 7-11). 1971. 5.95 o.p. (ISBN 0-698-20041-1, Coward). Putnam Pub Group.

Clewlow, C. William, Jr. & Wells, Helen F., eds. The Archaeology of Oak Park, Ventura County, California, Vol. 2. (Monograph Ser.: No. V). (Illus.). 222p. 1978. pap. 8.00 (ISBN 0-917956-27-3). UCLA Arch.

Clewlow, C. William, Jr. & Whitley, David S., eds. The Archaeology of Oak Park, Ventura County, California: Vol. III. (Institute of Archaeology Monograph: No. XI). (Illus.). 186p. (Orig.). 1979. pap. 8.00 (ISBN 0-917956-08-7). UCLA Arch.

Clewlow, C. William, Jr., et al, eds. History & Prehistory at Grass Valley, Nevada. (Monographs: No. VII). (Illus.). 173p. 1978. pap. 6.50 o.p. (ISBN 0-917956-29-X). UCLA Arch.

--Archaeological Investigations at the Ring Brothers Site Complex, Thousand Oaks, California. (Institute of Archaeology Monographs: No. 13). (Illus.). 156p. 1979. pap. 10.00 (ISBN 0-917956-13-3). UCLA Arch.

Clewlow, Carol. Hong Kong, Macau & Canton. (Travel Paperbacks Ser.). (Illus.). 192p. 1981. pap. 5.95 o.p. (ISBN 0-88254-611-2, Pub. by Lonely Planet Australia). Hippocrene Bks.

Clezy. Modification of the Mother-Child Interchange. 176p. 1979. pap. text ed. 16.95 (ISBN 0-8391-1319-6). Univ Park.

Click, J. W. & Baird, Russel N. Magazine Editing & Production. 2nd ed. 300p. 1978. text ed. write for info. o.p. (ISBN 0-697-04329-0). Wm C Brown.

Click, Marilyn J. & Ueberle, Jerrie K. R Reinforcement Contracts. 1981. text ed. 4.00 (ISBN 0-8134-2198-5). Interstate.

Click, Phyllis. Administration of Schools for Young Children. 2nd ed. LC 79-55285. (Early Childhood Education Ser.). 244p. 1981. pap. text ed. 12.80 (ISBN 0-8273-1575-9); instr's. guide 3.75 (ISBN 0-8273-1576-7). Delmar.

Clief, Ron Van see Van Clief, Ron.

Clief, Sylvia Van see Heide, Florence P. & Van Clief, Sylvia.

Cliff, A. D. & Ord, J. K. Spatial Autocorrelation. (Monographs in Spatial & Environmental Analysis). (Illus.). 178p. 1974. 15.50x (ISBN 0-85086-036-9, Pub. by Pion England). Methuen Inc.

Cliff, A. D., et al. Elements of Spatial Structure. LC 74-12973. (Geographical Studies: No. 6). (Illus.). 206p. 1974. 39.50 (ISBN 0-521-20689-8). Cambridge U Pr.

--Spatial Diffusion: An Historical Geography of Epidemics in an Island Community. (Cambridge Geographical Studies: No. 14). (Illus.). 244p. 1981. 42.50 (ISBN 0-521-22840-9). Cambridge U Pr.

Cliff, Michelle. Abeng. 180p. (Orig.). 1983. pap. write for info. (ISBN 0-930436-18-0). Persephone.

Cliff, W. J. Blood Vessels. LC 74-31789. (Biological Structure & Functions Ser.: No. 6). (Illus.). 224p. 1976. 60.00 (ISBN 0-521-20753-3). Cambridge U Pr.

Cliffe, A. E. Let Go & Let God. 1951. pap. 3.95 (ISBN 0-13-531509-3). P-H.

Clifford, A. A. Multivariate Error Analysis: A Handbook of Error Propagation & Calculation in Many-Parameter Systems. (Illus.). ix, 112p. 1973. 24.75 (ISBN 0-85334-566-X, Pub. by Applied Sci England). Elsevier.

Clifford, Alan. The Middle Ages. Yapp, Malcolm, et al, eds. (World History Ser.). (Illus.). (gr. 10). 1980. Repr. of 1977 ed. lib. bdg. 6.95 (ISBN 0-89908-028-6); pap. text ed. 2.25 (ISBN 0-89908-003-0). Greenhaven.

Clifford, Alec, tr. see Sweeting, George.

Clifford, Alejandro, tr. see Ten Boom, Corrie.

Clifford, Brian R., jt. auth. see Lloyd-Bostock, Sally M.

Clifford, C. R., ed. Lace Dictionary: Including Historic & Commercial Terms, Technical Terms, Native & Foreign. (Illus.). 156p. 1981. Repr. of 1913 ed. 30.00x (ISBN 0-8103-4311-8). Gale.

Clifford, Dennis. Plan Your Estate: Wills, Probate Avoidance, Trust & Taxes. 3rd ed. 1983. pap. 15.95 (ISBN 0-917316-53-3). Nolo Pr.

Clifford, Derek. Collecting English Watercolours. LC 75-34749. (Illus.). 1976. 40.00 o.p. (ISBN 0-685-63272-5). St Martin.

Clifford, E., jt. auth. see Hampton, C. W.

Clifford, Esther R. Knight of Great Renown. LC 60-14361. (Illus.). 1961. 15.00x o.s.i. (ISBN 0-226-11019-2). U of Chicago Pr.

Clifford, Eth. The Strange Reincarnations of Hendrick Verloom. (gr. 3-6). 1982. PLB 8.95 (ISBN 0-395-32433-5); 8.70. HM.

--The Year of the Three-Legged Deer. (gr. 3 up). 1973. pap. 0.95 o.s.i. (ISBN 0-440-49647-0). Dell.

Clifford, Gay. The Transformations of Allegory. 1974. 13.95x (ISBN 0-7100-7976-1). Routledge & Kegan.

Clifford, Harold. Maine & Her People, Suppl. on Aroostook County. rev ed. LC 57-14930. (Illus.). (YA) 1976. text ed. 8.50 o.s.i. (ISBN 0-87027-166-0). Cumberland Pr.

Clifford, Harold B. The Boothbay Region, 1906-1960. LC 61-14423. (Illus.). 368p. 1982. Repr. of 1961 ed. 15.95 (ISBN 0-87027-204-7). Cumberland Pr.

Clifford, Howard. Western Rail Guide. (Illus.). 168p. 1983. pap. 9.95 (ISBN 0-87564-540-2). Superior Pub.

Clifford, J. G., jt. auth. see Paterson, Thomas G.

Clifford, John & Waterhouse, Robert. Sentence Combining: Shaping Ideas for Better Style. 224p. (Orig.). 1983. pap. text ed. 6.95 (ISBN 0-672-61605-X); instr's. guide 3.33 (ISBN 0-672-61604-1). Bobbs.

Clifford, Laurie B. Evergreen Castles. 1983. pap. 2.95 (ISBN 0-8423-0779-6). Tyndale.

Clifford, Margaret M. Activities & Readings in Learning & Development. LC 80-84892. (Illus.). 256p. 1981. pap. text ed. 9.95 (ISBN 0-395-29924-1); frame: the ed. syke game 3.25 (ISBN 0-395-29926-8). HM.

--Practicing Educational Psychology. (Illus.). 752p. 1981. text ed. 29.50 (ISBN 0-395-29921-7); pap. text ed. 20.50 (ISBN 0-395-29922-5); instr's manual 1.00 (ISBN 0-395-29923-3); test bank 0.75 (ISBN 0-395-29925-X). HM.

Clifford, Martin. Basic Electricity & Beginning Electronics. LC 72-94809. (Illus.). 224p. 1973. 10.95 o.p. (ISBN 0-8306-3628-5); pap. 8.95 (ISBN 0-8306-2628-X, 628). TAB Bks.

--Master Handbook of Electronic Tables & Formulas. 3rd ed. (Illus.). 322p. 1980. 16.95 (ISBN 0-8306-9943-0); pap. 9.95 (ISBN 0-8306-1225-4, 1225). Tab Bks.

--Test Instruments for Electronics. LC 66-25708. 192p. 1966. 8.95 o.p. (ISBN 0-8306-6131-X); pap. 4.95 o.p. (ISBN 0-8306-5131-4, 131). TAB Bks.

Clifford, Mary L. Land & People of Liberia. LC 75-141446. (Portraits of the Nations Ser). (Illus.). 160p. (gr. 7-9). 1971. 9.57i o.p. (ISBN 0-397-31168-0, JBL-J). Har-Row.

Clifford, Nicholas. Retreat from China: British Policy in the Far East, 1937-1941. (China in the 20th Century Ser.). 1976. Repr. of 1967 ed. lib. bdg. 27.50 (ISBN 0-306-70757-8). Da Capo.

Clifford, Richard M., jt. auth. see Harms, Thelma.

Clifford, Sally A. Sacramento Cookery Book. Browder, Robyn S., ed. LC 82-2473. 300p. 1982. pap. 8.95 (ISBN 0-89865-132-8). Donning Co.

Clifford, Susan B., jt. auth. see Anderson, Pauline.

Clifford, Terry. The Diamond Healing: Tibetan Buddhist Medicine & Psychiatry. 196p. 1983. pap. 7.95 (ISBN 0-87728-528-4). Weiser.

Clifford, Timothy. The Stable of Don Juan of Austria. LC 78-53628. (Illus.). Date not set. 39.50 o.p. (ISBN 0-913870-75-7). Abaris Bks.

Clifford, William G. Books in Bottles: The Curious in Literature. LC 70-78125. 1971. Repr. of 1926 ed. 30.00x (ISBN 0-8103-3791-6). Gale.

Clifford, William K. Mathematical Papers. LC 67-28488. 1968. Repr. 35.00 (ISBN 0-8284-0210-8). Chelsea Pub.

Cliff's Notes Editors. Moby Dick Notes. (Orig.). 1966. pap. 2.95 (ISBN 0-8220-0852-1). Cliffs.

Clift, Dominique, jt. auth. see Arnopoulos, Sheila M.

Clift, Jeannette. Some Run with Feet of Clay. 128p. 1979. 9.95 (ISBN 0-8007-0901-2). Revell.

Clift, Virgil A., jt. auth. see Moseley, H. Jewel.

Clift, Wallace B. Jung & Christianity: The Challenge of Reconciliation. 192p. 1983. pap. 6.95 (ISBN 0-8245-0552-2). Crossroad NY.

Clifton, D. Business Data Systems. 1979. pap. 21.00 (ISBN 0-13-093963-3). P-H.

Clifton, David S., Jr. & Fyffe, David E. Project Feasibility Analysis: A Guide to Profitable New Ventures. LC 76-51321. 1977. text ed. 44.95 (ISBN 0-471-01611-X, Pub. by Wiley-Interscience). Wiley.

Clifton, James M., ed. Life & Labor on Argyle Island: Letter & Documents of a Savannah River Rice Plantation, 1833-1867. LC 77-85735. 365p. 1978. 20.00x (ISBN 0-8139-0951-1). U Pr of Va.

Clifton, Lucille. The Boy Who Didn't Believe in Spring. (Illus.). (gr. 3-4). 1978. 8.25 (ISBN 0-525-27145-7, 0801-240); pap. 1.95 (ISBN 0-525-45038-6, Anytime Bks). Dutton.

--Don't You Remember? (Illus.). 32p. (ps-2). 1973. 8.50 (ISBN 0-525-28840-6). Dutton.

--Everett Anderson's Goodbye. (Illus.). 32p. (gr. k-3). 1983. 9.95 (ISBN 0-03-063518-7). HR&W.

Clifton, Lucille & Di Grazia, Thomas. My Friend Jacob. LC 79-19168. 32p. (gr. k-2). 1980. 9.95 (ISBN 0-525-35487-5, 0966-290). Dutton.

Clifton, Mark. Eight Keys to Eden. Stine, Hank, ed. LC 82-12871. (Illus.). 190p. 1982. pap. 5.95 (ISBN 0-89865-258-8, Starblaze). Donning Co.

Clifton, Merrit. Baseball Stories for Boys & Girls. 20p. 1982. pap. 1.50 (ISBN 0-686-37933-0). Samisdat.

Clifton, Merritt. Learning Disabilities: What the Publicity Doesn't Tell. 24p. 1982. pap. 3.00 (ISBN 0-686-37937-3). Samisdat.

--Twenty-Four by Twelve. LC 79-84618. 92p. 1980. pap. 4.00 (ISBN 0-930012-26-7). Bandanna Bks.

Clifton, Robert & Dahms, Alan. Grassroots Administration: A Handbook for Staff & Directors of Small Community Based Social-Service Agencies. LC 79-26640. (Orig.). 1980. pap. text ed. 11.95 (ISBN 0-8185-0345-9). Brooks-Cole.

Clifton, Thomas. Music as Heard: A Study in Applied Phenomenology. LC 82-10944. (Illus.). 336p. 1983. text ed. 32.50x (ISBN 0-300-02091-0). Yale U Pr.

Clifton-Taylor, Alec. The Pattern of English Building. 2nd ed. 466p. 1972. pap. 27.50 (ISBN 0-571-09526-7). Faber & Faber.

Clignet, Remi. The Africanization of the Labor Market: Educational & Occupational Segmentations in the Camerouns. LC 75-13145. 1976. 30.00x (ISBN 0-520-03019-2). U of Cal Pr.

--Liberty & Equality in the Educational Process. LC 74-9737. 418p. 1974. 22.50 (ISBN 0-471-16057-1, Pub. by Wiley). Krieger.

Climo, Shirley. Cobweb Christmas. LC 81-43879. (Illus.). 32p. (ps-3). 1982. 10.10i (ISBN 0-690-04215-9, TYC-J); PLB 10.89g (ISBN 0-690-04216-7). Har-Row.

Clinard, M. B. Cities with Little Crime. LC 77-88672. (ASA Rose Monograph Ser.). 1978. 24.95 (ISBN 0-521-21960-4); pap. 8.95 (ISBN 0-521-29327-8). Cambridge U Pr.

Clinard, Marshall B. Black Market: A Study of White Collar Crime. LC 69-16233. (Criminology, Law Enforcement, & Social Problems Ser.: No. 87). 1969. 17.00 (ISBN 0-87585-087-1); pap. 7.50x (ISBN 0-87585-912-7). Patterson Smith.

Clinard, Marshall B. & Abbott, Daniel J. Crime in Developing Countries: A Comparative Perspective. LC 3-4031. 319p. 1973. 35.00 (ISBN 0-471-16060-1, Pub. by Wiley-Interscience). Wiley.

Clinard, Marshall B. & Yeager, Peter C. Corporate Crime. LC 80-2156. Date not set. Repr. of 1980 ed. write for info. (ISBN 0-02-906420-1). Free Pr.

Clinch, Nicholas. A Walk in the Sky: Climbing Hidden Peak. (Illus.). 232p. 1982. 18.95 (ISBN 0-89886-042-3). Mountaineers.

Cline, C. L., ed. The Owl & the Rossettis: Letters of Charles A. Howell & Dante Gabriel, Christina, & William Michael Rossetti. LC 77-88468. 1978. 17.95x (ISBN 0-271-00530-0). Pa St U Pr.

Cline, C. Terry. Missing Persons. 288p. 1983. pap. 2.95 (ISBN 0-449-20015-9, Crest). Fawcett.

Cline, C. Terry, Jr. The Attorney Conspiracy. LC 82-72059. 375p. 1983. 15.50 (ISBN 0-87795-371-6). Arbor Hse.

--Death Knell. LC 77-6935. 1977. 8.95 o.p. (ISBN 0-399-12010-6). Putnam Pub Group.

--Mindreader. LC 80-2737. 336p. 1981. 13.95 o.p. (ISBN 0-385-17372-5). Doubleday.

--Missing Persons. 1983. pap. 2.95 (ISBN 0-686-43229-0). Ballantine.

Cline, D. B., ed. see Ben Lee Memorial International Conference on Parity Nonconservation, Weak Neutral Currents & Gauge Theories, Fermi National Accelerator Laboratory, October 20-22, 1977.

Cline, Howard F. Florida Indians I. Horr, David A., ed. (American Indian Ethnohistory Ser.). 1978. lib. bdg. 42.00 o.s.i. (ISBN 0-8240-0766-2). Garland Pub.

--Florida Indians II. Horr, David A., ed. (American Indian Ethnohistory Ser.). 1978. lib. bdg. 42.00 o.s.i. (ISBN 0-8240-0767-0). Garland Pub.

Cline, Hugh F. & Sinnott, Loraine T. Building Library Collections: Policies & Practices in Academic Libraries. LC 80-8602. (Illus.). 192p. 1981. 18.95x (ISBN 0-669-04321-4). Lexington Bks.

Cline, Ray S. World Power Trends & U.S. Foreign Policy for the 1980s. (Illus.). 228p. 1980. lib. bdg. 22.00 (ISBN 0-89158-917-1); pap. 9.50 (ISBN 0-89158-790-X). Westview.

Cline, Robert F. The Tattooed Innocent & the Raunchy Grandmother: An Adult Fairy Tale, Quite Grim. LC 81-69430. 192p. (Orig.). 1983. pap. 7.95 (ISBN 0-9607082-0-0). Argos House.

Cline, Ruth H., tr. see De Troyes, Chretien.

Cline, Ruth K. & McBride, William G. A Guide to Literature for Young Adults Backround, Selection, & Use. 1983. pap. text ed. 9.95x (ISBN 0-673-16030-0). Scott F.

Cline, William R. International Debt & the Stability of the World Economy. (Policy Analyses in International Economics Ser.: No. 5). 1983. 6.00 (ISBN 0-88132-010-2). Inst Intl Eco.

--International Monetary Reform & the Developing Countries. 1976. 14.95 (ISBN 0-8157-1476-9); pap. 5.95 (ISBN 0-8157-1475-0). Brookings.

--Reciprocity: A New Approach to World Trade Policy? (Policy Analyses in International Econimics Ser.: No. 2). 48p. 1982. 6.00 (ISBN 0-88132-001-3). Inst Intl Eco.

Cline, William R. & Weintraub, Sidney. Economic Stabilization in Developing Countries. LC 80-70079. 514p. 1981. 32.95 (ISBN 0-8157-1466-1); pap. 15.95 (ISBN 0-8157-1465-3). Brookings.

Cline, William R., jt. auth. see Bergsten, C. Fred.

Cline, William R., jt. auth. see Bergsten, Fred.

Cline, William R. & Delgado, Enrique, eds. Economic Integration in Central America. LC 78-60708. 1978. 26.95 (ISBN 0-8157-1470-X). Brookings.

Cline, William R., et al. Trade Negotiations in the Tokyo Round: A Quantitative Assessment. 1978. 16.95 (ISBN 0-8157-1472-6). Brookings.

--World Inflation & the Developing Countries. 266p. 1981. 18.95 (ISBN 0-8157-1468-8); pap. 7.95 (ISBN 0-8157-1467-X). Brookings.

Clinebell, Howard. Growth Groups. 4.95 o.p. (ISBN 0-686-92336-7, 6417). Hazelden.

Clinebell, Howard J., Jr. Understanding & Counseling the Alcoholic. 8.95 o.p. (ISBN 0-686-92220-4, 4170). Hazelden.

Clinefelter, Dennis & Clinefelter, Terry. Premarital Planning. 1982. pap. 5.00 (ISBN 0-8309-0356-9). Herald Hse.

Clinefelter, Terry, jt. auth. see Clinefelter, Dennis.

Clines, D. J. & Gunn, D. M. Art & Meaning: Rhetoric in Biblical Literature. (Journal for the Study of the Old Testament, Supplement Ser.: No. 19). viii, 266p. 1982. text ed. 25.00x (ISBN 0-905774-38-8, Pub. by JSOT Pr England); pap. text ed. 19.95x (ISBN 0-905774-39-6). Eisenbrauns.

Clines, David J. I, He, We & They: A Literary Approach to Isaiah Fifty-Three. (JSOT Supplement Ser.: No. 1). 65p. 1976. pap. text ed. 8.50x o.s.i. (ISBN 0-905774-00-0, Pub. by JSOT Pr England). Eisenbrauns.

--The Theme of the Pentateuch. (JSOT Supplement Ser.: No. 10). 152p. 1978. text ed. 29.95x o.p. (ISBN 0-905774-14-0, Pub. by JSOT Pr England); pap. text ed. 16.95x (ISBN 0-905774-15-9, Pub. by JSOT Pr England). Eisenbrauns.

Clines, Francis X. About New York. LC 80-16080. 288p. 1980. 12.95 o.p. (ISBN 0-07-011384-X). McGraw.

Clinic, Mayo. Clinical Examinations in Neurology. 4th ed. LC 75-38154. (Illus.). 480p. 1976. text ed. 25.00 o.p. (ISBN 0-7216-6228-5). Saunders.

Clinical Research Centre Symposium, Sept. 1981, 2nd & Crawfurd, M. d'A. Advances in the Treatment of Inborn Errors of Metabolism: Proceedings. 384p. 1982. 47.00x (ISBN 0-471-10123-0, Pub. by Wiley Med). Wiley.

Clinker, jt. auth. see Macdermat.

Clinkscales, C. C., III, ed. see Kubek, Anthony.

Clinkscales, C. C., III, ed. see Lucas, Warren J.

Clint, Florence. Pennsylvania Area Key. 149p. 1976. 12.00 (ISBN 0-686-38096-7). Keyline Pubs.

Clinton, Catherine. The Plantation Mistress: Woman's World in the Old South 1780-1835. LC 82-3549. 368p. 1983. 18.95 (ISBN 0-394-51686-9). Pantheon.

Clinton, Daniel J. Gomez, Tyrant of the Andes. LC 70-97833. Repr. of 1936 ed. lib. bdg. 16.25x (ISBN 0-8371-2698-3, CLG). Greenwood.

Clinton, F. G. The Tin Cop. 240p. 1983. pap. 2.50 (ISBN 0-523-41923-6). Pinnacle Bks.

Clinton, Matthew. Matt Clinton's Scrapbook. LC 79-65557. (Illus.). 1979. 12.50 o.p. (ISBN 0-916620-28-X). Portals Pr.

Clio Press Ltd. Photography. (Modern Art Bibliography Ser.: No. 2). 284p. 1982. text ed. 62.00 (ISBN 0-903450-59-3). ABC-Clio.

Clipper, Lawrence J. G. K. Chesterton. (English Authors Ser.: No. 166). 1974. lib. bdg. 10.95 o.p. (ISBN 0-8057-1090-6, Twayne). G K Hall.

Clissold, Stephen. The Wisdom of the Spanish Mystics. LC 77-7650. (New Directions Wisdon Ser.). 1977. pap. 7.50 (ISBN 0-8112-0664-5, NDP442). New Directions.

Clissold, Stephen, et al, eds. Short History of Yugoslavia. LC 66-20181. (Illus.). 1968. 32.95 o.p. (ISBN 0-521-04676-9); pap. 13.95 (ISBN 0-521-09531-X). Cambridge U Pr.

Clive, Geoffrey. The Romantic Enlightenment. LC 72-8238. 219p. 1973. Repr. of 1960 ed. lib. bdg. 16.00x (ISBN 0-8371-6544-X, CLRE). Greenwood.

Clive, H. P., tr. see Taille, Jean.

Clive, John. Barossa. 1981. 12.95 o.s.i. (ISBN 0-440-00433-0). Delacorte.

--The Last Liberator. 1980. 9.95 o.s.i. (ISBN 0-440-05650-0). Delacorte.

--Macaulay: The Shaping of the Historian. 15.00 (ISBN 0-394-47278-0, Vin). Random.

Clive, John, ed. see Macaulay, Thomas B.

Clodd, Edward. Magic in Names, & in Other Things. LC 67-23906. 1968. Repr. of 1920 ed. 30.00x (ISBN 0-8103-3024-5). Gale.

--Myths & Dreams. LC 70-159918. 1971. Repr. of 1891 ed. 34.00x (ISBN 0-8103-3776-2). Gale.

--Story of the Alphabet. LC 70-123369. (Illus.). 1970. Repr. of 1938 ed. 27.00 o.p. (ISBN 0-8103-3855-6). Gale.

--Tom Tit Tot. LC 67-23907. 1968. Repr. of 1898 ed. 30.00x (ISBN 0-8103-3459-3). Gale.

Clogan, P. M., ed. Medievalia et Humanistica, Vols. 1-7. Incl. Vol. 1. LC 75-32451. 251p. 1976. (ISBN 0-521-21032-1); Vol. 2. Medieval & Renaissance Studies in Review. LC 75-32452. 223p. (ISBN 0-521-21033-X); Vol. 3. Social Dimension in Medieval & Renaissance Studies. LC 75-32453. 328p. o.p. (ISBN 0-521-21034-8); Vol. 6. LC 75-16872. 1979 (ISBN 0-521-20999-4); Vol. 7. Studies in Medieval & Renaissance Culture: Medieval Poetics. LC 76-12914. 1977. (ISBN 0-521-21331-2); Vol. 8. Studies in Medieval & Renaissance Culture Transformation & Continuity. LC 75-32451. 1978 (ISBN 0-521-21783-0); Vol. 9. LC 75-32451. 1979 (ISBN 0-521-22446-2). 37.50 ea.; Vols. 8-9. 39.50 ea. Cambridge U Pr.

Clogan, Paul M., ed. Medievalia et Humanistica: Studies in Medieval & Renaissance Culture. (New Ser.: No. 10). 264p. 1981. 27.50x (ISBN 0-8476-6944-0). Rowman.

Clogg, Mary Jo & Clogg, Richard. Greece. (World Bibliographical Ser.: No. 17). 224p. 1980. 34.50 (ISBN 0-903450-30-5). ABC Clio.

Clogg, R. A Short History of Modern Greece. LC 78-72083. (Illus.). 1979. 37.50 (ISBN 0-521-22479-9); pap. 11.95 (ISBN 0-521-29517-3). Cambridge U Pr.

Clogg, Richard, jt. auth. see Clogg, Mary Jo.

Cloke, Marjane & Wallace, Robert. The Modern Business Letter Writer's Manual. LC 69-12209. 216p. 1969. pap. 4.95 (ISBN 0-385-06952-9, Dolp). Doubleday.

Cloke, Rene. Chickweed. 4.50 (ISBN 0-392-16655-0, SpS). Sportshelf.

Cloke, Richard. Earth Ovum. LC 82-71685. 1982. pap. 3.25 (Cerulean Pr). Kent Pubns.

--Yvar, Prince of Rus. LC 80-80543. 700p. (Orig.). 1981. pap. 8.75 (ISBN 0-917458-08-7). Cerulean Pr.

Clonts, Howard A., jt. ed. see Molnar, Joseph J.

Clontz, Ralph C., Jr. Fair Credit Reporting Manual. 2nd ed. 1977. 64.00 (ISBN 0-88262-134-3). Warren.

--Truth-in-Lending Manual, 2 vols. 5th ed. 1982. Set. 87.50 (ISBN 0-88262-757-0). Warren.

Clontz, Ralph C., Jr. & Tarlow, Eric K. Equal Credit Opportunity Manual. 3rd. ed. 1979. 64.00 (ISBN 0-88262-321-4, 79-65646). Warren.

Clooney, Rosemary & Strait, Raymond. This for Remembrance. 352p. 1982. pap. 2.95 (ISBN 0-425-05968-5). Berkley Pub.

Clopton, Robert W., tr. see Dewey, John.

Clor, Harry M. The Mass Media & Democracy. 1974. pap. 10.50 (ISBN 0-395-30789-9). HM.

Clor, Harry M., jt. ed. see Goldwin, Robert A.

Close, Angela E., jt. ed. see Wendorf, Fred.

Close, Arthur C. & Colgate, Craig, Jr., eds. Washington Representatives, 1981. 5th annual ed. LC 76-21152. 532p. 1981. pap. 35.00 o.p. (ISBN 0-910416-35-4). Columbia Bks.

Close, Charles M. & Frederick, Dean K. Modeling & Analysis of Dynamic Systems. LC 77-74421. (Illus.). 1978. text ed. 35.95 (ISBN 0-395-25040-4); solutions manual 8.50 (ISBN 0-395-25031-5). HM.

Close, J. R. Motor Function in the Lower Extremity: Analyses by Electronic Instrumentation. (Illus.). 176p. 1964. photocopy ed. spiral 18.75x (ISBN 0-398-00317-3). C C Thomas.

Close, Jim, jt. auth. see Cassidy, Pat.

Close, Paul D. Sound Control & Thermal Insulation of Buildings. LC 65-28400. 510p. 1966. 26.50 (ISBN 0-442-35058-9). Krieger.

Close, R. A. English As a Foreign Language. 3rd ed. 224p. (Orig.). 1981. pap. text ed. 8.95x (ISBN 0-04-425025-8). Allen Unwin.

Close, Reg A. A Reference Grammar for Students of English. (English As a Second Language Bk.). (Illus.). 342p. 1975. pap. text ed. 10.75 (ISBN 0-582-52277-3). Longman.

Closser, Lynne, ed. see Da Free, John.

Closson, Kay. Reaching in Silence. (Contemporary Poets Ser.: No. 2). 48p. (Orig.). 1983. pap. 3.95 (ISBN 0-916982-27-0, RL227). Realities.

Closurdo, Janette S., ed. Library Management: Papers from the Management Workshop, Vol. 1. 1980. pap. 8.50 o.p. (ISBN 0-686-77554-6). SLA.

Clotfelter, Beryl E. The Universe & Its Structure. (Illus.). 448p. (Orig.). 1976. text ed. 16.95 o.p. (ISBN 0-07-011385-8, C); instructors' manual 2.95 o.p. (ISBN 0-07-011386-6). McGraw.

Clotfelter, Cecil F. & Clotfelter, Mary L., eds. Camping & Backpacking: A Guide to Information Sources. LC 79-84659. (Sports, Games, & Pastimes Information Guide Ser.: Vol. 2). 1978. 42.00x (ISBN 0-8103-1437-1). Gale.

Clotfelter, Mary L., jt. ed. see Clotfelter, Cecil F.

Clouard, Henri & Leggewie, Robert, eds. Anthologie De la Litterature Francaise, 2 vols. 2nd ed. 860p. 1975. Vol. 1. pap. text ed. 19.95x (ISBN 0-19-501877-X); Vol. 2. pap. text ed. 19.95x (ISBN 0-19-501878-8). Oxford U Pr.

Cloud, Carey C. Cloud Nine: The Dreamer & the Realist. (Illus.). 140p. 1983. 16.95 (ISBN 0-686-38768-6). Cloudcrest.

Cloud, Henry. Barbara Cartland: Crusader in Pink. LC 79-56870. (Illus.). 1980. 8.95 (ISBN 0-89696-082-X, An Everest House Book). Dodd.

Cloud, Patricia. This Willing Passion. LC 77-18048. 1978. 9.95 o.p. (ISBN 0-399-12134-X). Putnam Pub Group.

Cloud, Peter B. Elderberry Flute Song: Contemporary Coyote Tales. LC 82-4965. (Illus.). 1982. 14.95 (ISBN 0-89594-070-1); pap. 6.95 (ISBN 0-89594-069-8). Crossing Pr.

Cloudsley-Thompson, J. L. Animal Conflict & Adaptation. LC 65-26318. (Illus.). 1965. 12.00 (ISBN 0-8023-1026-5). Dufour.

--Crocodiles & Alligators. (New Biology Series). (Illus.). (gr. 4-12). 1977. PLB 6.95 o.p. (ISBN 0-07-011390-4, GB). McGraw.

--Dietary Adaptions in Animals. 76p. 1976. 39.00x (ISBN 0-686-96990-1, Pub. by Meadowfield Pr England). State Mutual Bk.

--Spiders & Scorpions. LC 74-9546. 48p. (gr. 2-7). 1975. PLB 6.95 (ISBN 0-07-011389-0, GB). McGraw.

Cloudsley-Thompson, John. Animal Migration. LC 77-14623. (Illus.). 1978. 14.95 o.p. (ISBN 0-399-12103-X). Putnam Pub Group.

--The Desert. (Illus.). 1977. 14.95 o.p. (ISBN 0-399-11885-3). Putnam Pub Group.

Clough, B. F., ed. Mangrove Ecosystems in Australia. LC 81-68098. 302p. 1982. text ed. 24.95 (ISBN 0-7081-1170-X, 1222). Bks Australia.

Clough, Jeffory J. Azoth. LC 73-9518. 52p. 1972. 4.00 (ISBN 0-911838-18-X). Windy Row.

Clough, John. Scales, Intervals, Keys & Triads: A Self-Instruction Program. (Orig., Prog. Bk.). 1964. pap. 8.95x (ISBN 0-393-09625-4, NortonC). Norton.

Clough, John & Conley, Joyce. Scales, Intervals, Keys, Triads, Rhythm & Meter. rev. ed. 1983. 9.95x (ISBN 0-393-95189-8). Norton.

Clough, Michael. A Transatlantic Symposium: Where Is South Africa Headed? (II) (Seven Springs Reports). 48p. 1980. pap. 2.00 (ISBN 0-943006-12-0). Seven Springs.

Clough, Michael, ed. Changing Realities in Southern Africa: Implications for American Policy. LC 82-12124. (Research Ser.: No. 47). x, 320p. 1982. pap. 12.50x (ISBN 0-87725-147-9). U of Cal Intl St.

Clough, R. & Penzien, J. Dynamics of Structures. (Illus.). 672p. 1975. text ed. 38.50 (ISBN 0-07-011392-0, C). McGraw.

Clough, Ralph N. Deterrence & Defense in Korea: The Role of U. S. Forces. (Studies in Defense Policy). 1976. pap. 4.95 (ISBN 0-8157-1481-5). Brookings.

--East Asia & U. S. Security. 1975. 22.95 (ISBN 0-8157-1480-7); pap. 8.95 (ISBN 0-8157-1479-3). Brookings.

Clough, Ralph N., et al. The United States, China & Arms Control. 153p. 1975. 17.95 (ISBN 0-8157-1478-5); pap. 6.95 (ISBN 0-8157-1477-7). Brookings.

Clough, Richard. A Weather Story. 1978. 5.95 o.p. (ISBN 0-533-03278-4). Vantage.

Clough, Richard H. Construction Contracting. 4th ed. LC 81-7449. 502p. 1981. 29.95 (ISBN 0-471-08657-6, Pub. by Wiley-Interscience). Wiley.

--Construction Contracting. 3rd ed. LC 74-23135. 453p. 1975. 28.95 o.p. (ISBN 0-471-16106-3, Pub. by Wiley-Interscience). Wiley.

Clough, Richard H. & Sears, Glenn A. Construction Project Management. 2nd ed. LC 78-25855. 1979. 36.95 (ISBN 0-471-04895-X, Pub. by Wiley-Interscience). Wiley.

Clough, S. B., et al. European History in a World Perspective, 2 vols. 3rd ed. Incl. Vol. 1. 848p. 13.95 o.p. (ISBN 0-669-85522-7); study guide 7.95 (ISBN 0-669-93120-9); Vol. 2. 800p. pap. text ed. 16.95 (ISBN 0-669-85530-8); study guide 7.95x (ISBN 0-669-93153-5). 1975. Heath.

--European History in a World Perspective, 3 vols. Incl. Vol. 1. 544p. pap. text ed. 14.95x (ISBN 0-669-85548-0); Vol. 2. 544p. pap. text ed. 13.95x (ISBN 0-669-85555-3); Vol. 3. 648p. pap. text ed. 14.95x (ISBN 0-669-85563-4). 1975. pap. Heath.

Clough, Shepard B. Century of American Life Insurance: A History of the Mutual Life Insurance Company of New York, 1843-1943. LC 78-100150. Repr. of 1946 ed. lib. bdg. 19.00x (ISBN 0-8371-3713-6, CLAL). Greenwood.

--European Economic History. 3rd ed. Orig. Title: The Economic Development of Western Civilization. (Illus.). 640p. 1975. text ed. 37.50 (ISBN 0-07-011393-9, C). McGraw.

--The Life I've Lived. LC 80-5503. 297p. 1981. lib. bdg. 21.75 (ISBN 0-8191-1116-3); pap. text ed. 11.50 (ISBN 0-8191-1117-1). U Pr of Amer.

Clouse, Barbara F. Writing: From Inner World to Outer World. (Illus.). 368p. 1982. pap. text ed. 11.50x (ISBN 0-07-011407-2). McGraw.

Clouse, Melvin E., ed. Clinical Lymphography. (Golden's Diagnostic Radiology Ser.: Section 7). (Illus.). 1977. 44.00 o.p. (ISBN 0-683-01883-3). Williams & Wilkins.

Clouse, Robert. Church in an Age of Orthodoxy & Enlightenment. 1980. pap. 4.95 (ISBN 0-570-06273-X, 12-2746). Concordia.

Clouse, Robert, et al. Church in History Series, 6 bks. 1980. pap. 26.95 set (ISBN 0-570-06277-2, 12-2780). Concordia.

Clouse, Robert G. & Pierard, Richard V. Streams of Civilization, Vol. II: The Modern World to the Nuclear Age. LC 78-17811. 1979. text ed. 14.95x (ISBN 0-89051-051-2, Co-Pub by Mott Media); tchr's guide 3.95x (ISBN 0-915134-47-0). CLP Pubs.

Clouser, K. Danner. Teaching Bioethics: Strategies, Problems & Resources. LC 80-10492. (The Teaching of Ethics Ser.). 77p. 1980. pap. 4.00 o.p. (ISBN 0-916558-07-X). Hastings Ctr Inst Soc.

Clouston, William A. Book of Noodles: Stories of Simpletons. LC 67-24351. 1969. Repr. of 1888 ed. 30.00x (ISBN 0-8103-3519-0). Gale.

--Popular Tales & Fictions, Their Migrations & Transformations, 2 Vols. LC 67-23920. 1968. Repr. of 1887 ed. Set. 85.00x (ISBN 0-8103-3460-7). Gale.

Clout, H. The Regional Problem in Western Europe. LC 75-7216. (Topics in Geography Ser.). (Illus.). 64p. 1976. 15.95 (ISBN 0-521-20909-9); pap. text ed. 6.95 (ISBN 0-521-09997-8). Cambridge U Pr.

Clout, Hugh. The Land of France, 1815-1914. (London Research Series in Geography: No. 1). 176p. 1983. text ed. 24.95x (ISBN 0-04-911003-9). Allen Unwin.

Clout, Hugh, jt. ed. see Salt, John.

Clout, Hugh D. The Geography of Post-War France: A Social & Economic Approach. 180p. 1972. text ed. 20.00 o.p. (ISBN 0-08-016765-9); pap. text ed. 10.00 (ISBN 0-08-016766-7). Pergamon.

--Regional Development in Western Europe. 2nd ed. LC 80-40852. 417p. 1981. 46.95x (ISBN 0-471-27846-7, Pub. by Wiley-Interscience); pap. 21.00 (ISBN 0-471-27845-9, Pub. by Wiley-Interscience). Wiley.

Clout, Hugh D., ed. Regional Development in Western Europe. LC 75-11963. 1975. 38.50 o.p. (ISBN 0-471-16112-8, Pub. by Wiley-Interscience); pap. 18.50 o.p. (ISBN 0-471-16113-6). Wiley.

Cloutier, David. Soft Lightnings. (Illus.). 54p. 1982. pap. 4.50 (ISBN 0-914278-35-5). Copper Beech.

Cloutier, David, tr. see Esteban, Claude.

Cloutier, Roger J., et al, eds. Medical Radionuclides: Radiation Dose & Effects, Proceedings. LC 70-606556. (AEC Symposium Ser.). 528p. 1970. pap. 21.25 (ISBN 0-87079-269-5, CONF-691212); microfiche 4.50 (ISBN 0-87079-270-9, CONF-691212). DOE.

Clover, Frank M. Flavius Merobaudes: A Translation & Historical Commentary. LC 75-143266. (Transactions Ser.: Vol. 61, Pt. 1). 1971. pap. 1.50 o.p. (ISBN 0-87169-611-8). Am Philos.

Clovis, Albert I., et al, eds. Consumer Protection: A Symposium. LC 72-6757. 1972. Repr. of 1968 ed. lib. bdg. 19.50 (ISBN 0-306-70524-9). Da Capo.

Clow, C., et al. Gregg Accounting, Advanced Course. 2nd ed. 1969. text ed. 17.60 (ISBN 0-07-011430-7, G); tchr's manual & key 5.90 (ISBN 0-07-011434-X); Study & Working papers Pt. 1 6.12 (ISBN 0-07-011431-5); Study & Working papers Pt. 2 6.12 (ISBN 0-07-011432-3). McGraw.

Clow, C. A. & MacDonald, R. D. Punched-Card Data Processing System. 2nd ed. 1975. 7.72 (ISBN 0-07-011424-2, G); key 3.35 (ISBN 0-07-011425-0). McGraw.

Cloward, Richard A., jt. auth. see Piven, Frances F.

Clowers, Myles L. & Letendre, Lorin. Understanding American Politics Through Fiction. 2nd ed. 1977. pap. text ed. 14.95 (ISBN 0-07-011450-1); instr's manual 15.00 (ISBN 0-07-011451-X). McGraw.

Clowers, Myles L. & Mori, Stephen. Understanding Sociology Through Fiction. LC 76-9108. 1976. pap. text ed. 13.50 (ISBN 0-07-011452-8, C); instructor's manual 3.95 (ISBN 0-07-011453-6). McGraw.

Clowers, Myles L., jt. auth. see Beck, Warren A.

Clowes, A. & Comfort, P. Process & Landform: An Outline of Contemporary Geomorphology. (Conceptual Frameworks in Geography Ser.). (Illus.). 248p. (Orig.). 1982. pap. text ed. 9.95x (ISBN 0-686-36961-0). Longman.

Clowney, Earle D, tr. see Obey, Andre.

Clowse, Barbara B., ed. Brainpower for the Cold War: The Sputnik Crisis & National Defense Education Act of 1958. LC 81-1477. (Contributions to the Study of Education: No. 3). 256p. 1981. lib. bdg. 29.95 (ISBN 0-313-22813-2, CCW/). Greenwood.

Clowse, Converse D. Measuring Charleston's Overseas Commerce, 1717-1767: Statistics from the Port's Naval Lists. LC 81-40640. (Illus.). 170p. (Orig.). 1982. lib. bdg. 22.00 (ISBN 0-8191-2055-3); pap. text ed. 10.25 (ISBN 0-8191-2056-1). U Pr of Amer.

Clubb, Louise G., tr. see Della Porta, Giambattista.

Clubb, O. E., et al, eds. The International Position of Communist China. LC 65-17379. (Hammaskjold Forums Ser.: No. 5). 116p. 1965. 10.00 (ISBN 0-379-11805-X); pap. 1.75 o.p. Oceana.

Clube, Victor & Napier, Bill. The Cosmic Serpent: A Catastrophist View of Earth History. LC 81-19699. (Illus.). 299p. 1982. 17.95 (ISBN 0-87663-379-3). Universe.

Cluett, Robert. Prose Style & Critical Reading. LC 75-40035. (New Humanistic Ser.: No. 3). (Illus.). 1976. text ed. 17.95x (ISBN 0-8077-2491-2). Tchrs Coll.

Cluff & Johnson. Clinical Concepts of Infectious Disease. 2nd ed. (Clinical Concepts in Medicine Ser.). 1978. lib. bdg. 28.50 o.p. (ISBN 0-683-01655-5). Williams & Wilkins.

Cluff, Leighton E. & Johnson, Joseph E., III. Clinical Concepts of Infectious Diseases. 3rd ed. (Illus.). 364p. 1982. lib. bdg. 37.00 (ISBN 0-683-01656-3). Williams & Wilkins.

Cluff, Leighton E., et al. Clinical Problems with Drugs. (Major Problems in Internal Medicine Ser., Vol. 5). (Illus.). 308p. 1975. text ed. 18.00 o.p. (ISBN 0-7216-2613-0). Saunders.

Clulow, C. F. To Have & to Hold: Marriage, the First Baby, & Preparing Couples for Parenthood. 168p. 1982. 16.50 (ISBN 0-08-028470-1); pap. 9.50 (ISBN 0-08-028471-X). Pergamon.

Clum, John M. Paddy Chayefsky. (United States Authors Ser.). 1976. lib. bdg. 11.95 (ISBN 0-8057-7172-7, Twayne). G K Hall.

--Ridgely Torrence. (United States Author Ser.). lib. bdg. 13.95 (ISBN 0-8057-0740-9, Twayne). G K Hall.

Clumpner, Mick. The Half-Breed. (Orig.). 1982. pap. 1.95 (ISBN 0-451-11281-4, AJ1281, Sig). NAL.

--Massacre at the Gorge. 1982. pap. 2.25 (ISBN 0-451-11743-3, AE1743, Sig). NAL.

--Nez Perce Legend. (Orig.). 1983. pap. 2.95 (ISBN 0-440-06330-2, Banbury). Dell.

Clunie, J. G. & Hayman, W. K., eds. Symposium on Complex Analysis. LC 73-92787. (London Mathematical Society Lecture Note Ser.: No. 12). 200p. 1974. 23.95 (ISBN 0-521-20452-6). Cambridge U Pr.

Clure, Beth & Rumsey, Helen. I Can Do It: Manipulative Books, 14 Bks. Incl. Come with Me (ISBN 0-8372-2169-2); Can You Guess (ISBN 0-8372-2170-6); What's Inside (ISBN 0-8372-2171-4); A Sailor Said (ISBN 0-8372-2172-2); Matching Hands (ISBN 0-8372-2173-0); Surprise Boxes (ISBN 0-8372-2174-9); What Can It Be (ISBN 0-8372-2175-7); Mirror Magic (ISBN 0-8372-2176-5); Things I Like to Do (ISBN 0-8372-0367-8); Me (ISBN 0-8372-0363-5); Cowboy Can (ISBN 0-8372-0372-4); Where Is Home (ISBN 0-8372-0364-3); Through the Day (ISBN 0-8372-0366-X); Telling Tails (ISBN 0-8372-0365-1). (Illus.). (gr. k-2). 1976. text ed. 6.90 ea.; text ed. 93.00 set o.p. (2168); tchr's. guide & 14 bks. 6.42 (ISBN 0-8372-3721-1). Bowmar-Noble.

Clurman, David & Hebard, Edna L. Condominiums & Cooperatives. LC 73-106012. (Real Estate for Professional Practitioners Ser.). 1970. 41.95 (ISBN 0-471-16130-6, Pub. by Wiley-Interscience). Wiley.

Clurman, Harold. The Fervent Years: The Group Theatre & the Thirties. (Quality Paperbacks Ser.). (Illus.). 352p. 1983. pap. 8.95 (ISBN 0-306-80186-8). Da Capo.

--On Directing. (Illus.). 336p. 1974. pap. 8.95 (ISBN 0-02-013350-2, Collier). Macmillan.

Clute, Kenneth F. The General Practitioner: A Study of Medical Education & Practice in Ontario & Nova Scotia. LC 63-4464. 566p. 1963. 40.00x o.p. (ISBN 0-8020-7032-9). U of Toronto Pr.

Clute, P. D. The Legal Aspects of Prisons & Jails. 248p. 1980. 21.75x (ISBN 0-398-04005-2); pap. 14.95x (ISBN 0-398-04006-0). C C Thomas.

Clute, Robin & Andersen, Sigrid. Juel Andersen's Carob Primer. 50p. (Orig.). 1983. pap. 3.95 (ISBN 0-916870-60-X). Creative Arts Bk.

--Juel Andersen's Tempeh Primer. 50p. (Orig.). 1983. pap. 3.95 (ISBN 0-916870-59-6). Creative Arts Bk.

Clutter, Jerome L. & Fortson, James C. Timber Management: A Quantitative Approach. 350p. 1983. text ed. 17.95 (ISBN 0-471-02961-0). Wiley.

Clutterbuck, Richard. Guerrillas & Terrorists. LC 80-83219. 125p. 1980. 12.00x (ISBN 0-8214-0590-X, 82-83798); pap. 5.95x (ISBN 0-8214-0592-6, 82-83806). Ohio U Pr.

Clutton, Cecil & Daniels, George. Watches: A Complete History of the Technical & Decorative Development of the Watch. 3rd rev. & enlarg. ed. (Illus.). 312p. 1979. 95.00 (ISBN 0-85667-058-8, Pub by Sotheby Pubns England). Biblio Dist.

Clutton-Brock, T. H. & Guinness, F. E. Red Deer: Behavior & Ecology of Two Sexes. LC 81-22025. (Wildlife Behavior & Ecology (WBE)). (Illus.). 1982. lib. bdg. 37.50x (ISBN 0-226-11056-7); pap. 12.95 (ISBN 0-226-11057-5). U of Chicago Pr.

Cluysenaar, Anne & Hewat, Sybil. Double Helix. 180p. 1982. pap. text ed. 12.50x (ISBN 0-85635-428-7, 51083, Pub. by Carcanet New Pr England). Humanities.

Cluysenaar, Anne, ed. see Singer, Burns.

Clyde, Ahmad. Cheng Ho's Voyage. LC 81-66951. (Children's Book Ser.). (Illus.). 32p. (Orig.). (gr. 3-7). 1981. pap. 1.35 (ISBN 0-89259-021-1). Am Trust Pubns.

Clyde, James E. Construction Inspection: A Field Guide to Practice. LC 79-4417. (Practical & Construction Guides Ser.). 1979. 40.95 (ISBN 0-471-05010-5, Pub by Wiley-Interscience). Wiley.

Clyde, Mary K. Flashbacks to Dawn: Eye Openers in Preparatory School circa 1914-1922. 1983. price not set (ISBN 0-533-05543-1). Vantage.

Clyde, Paul H. & Beers, Burton F. Far East: A History of Western Impacts & Eastern Responses (1830-1975) 6th ed. (Illus.). 576p. 1976. 25.95 (ISBN 0-13-302968-9). P-H.

Clydesdale, Fergus. Food Science & Nutrition: Current Issues & Answers. (Illus.). 1979. ref. 19.95 (ISBN 0-13-323162-3). P-H.

Clydesdale, Fergus M. & Francis, Frederick J. Human Ecological Issues: A Reader. 320p. (Orig.). 1980. pap. text ed. 9.95 (ISBN 0-8403-2197-X). Kendall-Hunt.

Clydesdale, Fergus S. & Francis, F. J. Food, Nutrition & You. (Illus.). 1977. lib. bdg. 17.95 (ISBN 0-13-323048-1); pap. text ed. 13.95 (ISBN 0-13-323030-9). P-H.

Clyman, Toby, tr. see Bitsilli, Peter.

Clymer, Eleanor. My Mother is the Smartest Woman in the World. LC 82-1685. (Illus.). 96p. (gr. 4-6). 1982. 8.95 (ISBN 0-689-30916-3). Atheneum.

--A Search for Two Bad Mice. LC 80-12789. (Illus.). 80p. (gr. 2-5). 1980. 9.95 (ISBN 0-689-30771-3). Atheneum.

Clymer, Floyd. Ford Model A Album. (Illus.). pap. 5.00 o.p. (ISBN 0-89287-261-6, H521). Clymer Pubns.

Clymer Publications. Corvette V-Eight, Nineteen Fifty-Five to Nineteen Sixty-Two: Complete Owner's Handbook. (Illus.). pap. 7.95 o.p. (ISBN 0-89287-082-6, A141). Clymer Pubns.

--Ford Fairmont, 1978-1982: Shop Manual. Jorgensen, Eric, ed. (Illus.). 328p. (Orig.). 11.95 (ISBN 0-89287-307-8, A174). Clymer Pubns.

Clymer Publications, ed. see Henry, Leslie R.

Clymer Publications, ed. see Hopper, Gordon E.

Clymer Publications, ed. see Page, Victor W.

Clymer Publications Staff. Volvo Service-Repair Handbook: 122s Series & P 1800, All Years. (Illus.). 224p. pap. text ed. 11.95 o.p. (ISBN 0-89287-066-4, A220). Clymer Pubns.

Cmshevner, Ernst, jt. auth. see Haslund-Christensen, Henning.

Cnossen, S., ed. Comparative Tax Studies: Essays in Honor of Richard Goode. (Contributions to Economic Analysis Ser.: Vol. 144). 450p. 1982. 76.75 (ISBN 0-444-86421-0, North Holland). Elsevier.

CNRS. New Physical, Mechanical & Chemical Properties of Very High Purity Iron. 438p. 103.00 (ISBN 0-677-30730-6). Gordon.

Coaching Clinic Editors, ed. Best of Wrestling from the Coaching Clinic. (Illus.). 1978. 14.95 o.p. (ISBN 0-13-074898-6, Parker). P-H.

Coachman, Ward, jt. auth. see Chupco, Lee.

Coad, Oral S. American Stage. 1929. text ed. 22.50x (ISBN 0-686-37861-X). Elliots Bks.

Coady, Mary-Francis. Steve Podborski. (Picture Life Ser.). (Illus.). 48p. (gr. k-3). 1983. PLB 7.90 (ISBN 0-531-04599-4). Watts.

Coaker, T. H., ed. Advances in Applied Biology, Vol. 6. LC 76-1065. (Serial Publication). 332p. 1981. 51.50 (ISBN 0-12-040906-2). Acad Pr.

--Advances in Applied Biology, Vol. 7. (Serial Publication). write for info. (ISBN 0-12-040907-0). Acad Pr.

Coakley, Jay J. Sport in Society: Issues & Controversies. 2nd ed. LC 81-14119. (Illus.). 335p. 1982. pap. text ed. 14.95 (ISBN 0-8016-1119-9). Mosby.

Coal Age Magazine. Coal Age Operating Handbook of Coal Preparation, Vol. III. (Coal Age Library of Operating Handbooks). 1979. 25.90 (ISBN 0-07-011459-5, P&RB). McGraw.

--Coal Age Operating Handbook of Underground Mining, Vol. II. 2nd ed. (Coal Age Ser.). (Illus.). 430p. 1980. 24.75 (ISBN 0-07-011461-7, P&RB). McGraw.

--Coal Age Operating Handbook of Underground Mining. 1977. 25.90 (ISBN 0-07-011457-9). McGraw.

--Operating Handbook of Coal Surface Mining. 1978. 25.90 (ISBN 0-07-011458-7). McGraw.

Coale, Samuel. Anthony Burgess. LC 81-40459. (Literature and Life Ser.). 234p. 1981. 11.95 (ISBN 0-8044-2124-2). Ungar.

--John Cheever. LC 77-4829. (Literature and Life Ser.). 1977. 11.95 (ISBN 0-8044-2126-9). Ungar.

Coalson, Glo, tr. see Wasson, Valentina P.

Coan. Basic Apple BASIC. Date not set. 10.95 (ISBN 0-686-82001-0, 5626). Hayden.

Coan, D. R. Programming Standards, 2 vols. National Computing Centre Ltd. & National Computing Centre Ltd., eds. Incl. Vol. 1. Documentation. write for info. (ISBN 0-685-30481-7); Vol. 2. Techniques. 180p. 1972. 47.50x (ISBN 0-85012-071-3). 240p. 1973. Intl Pubns Serv.

Coan, Richard W. Psychology of Adjustment: Personal Experience & Development. 558p. 1983. text ed. 22.95x (ISBN 0-471-16133-0); write for info tchr's ed. (ISBN 0-471-87196-6). Wiley.

Coarelli, Filippo. Rome. LC 78-179261. (Monuments of Civilization Ser). (Illus.). 192p. 1972. 25.00 o.p. (ISBN 0-448-02019-X, G&D). Putnam Pub Group.

Coast Community Colleges. Study Guide for the Televised Course Humanities Through the Arts. (Illus.). 288p. 1983. 12.95x (ISBN 0-07-011474-9, C). McGraw.

Coastal Engineering International Conference, 10th, Tokyo, Aug. 1966. Coastal Engineering: Proceedings. American Society of Civil Engineers, compiled By. 1580p. 1967. pap. text ed. 36.00 o.p. (ISBN 0-87262-008-5). Am Soc Civil Eng.

Coastal Resources Center. An Environmental Study of a Nuclear Power Plant at Charlestown, R. I. (Technical Report: No. 33). 234p. 1974. 5.00 o.p. (ISBN 0-686-36963-7, P373). URI Mas.

Coate. Global Issue Regimes. 238p. 1982. 28.95 (ISBN 0-03-059276-3). Praeger.

Coate, Godfrey T. & Swain, Laurence R., Jr. High-Power Semiconductor-Magnetic Pulse Generators. (Press Research Monographs, No. 39). 1967. 22.00x (ISBN 0-262-03019-5). MIT Pr.

Coate, L. Edwin & Bonner, Patricia A. Regional Environmental Management: Selected Proceedings of the National Conference. LC 74-26947. 348p. 1975. 18.00 (ISBN 0-471-16138-1, Pub. by Wiley). Krieger.

Coates, Adrian. Prelude to History. 1952. 4.75 o.p. (ISBN 0-8022-0269-1). Philos Lib.

Coates, B. E., et al. Geography & Inequality. (Illus.). 1977. text ed. 37.50x o.p. (ISBN 0-19-874069-7); pap. text ed. 9.95x (ISBN 0-19-874070-0). Oxford U Pr.

Coates, C. A. John Cowper Powys in Search of a Landscape. LC 81-19081. 204p. 1982. 27.50x (ISBN 0-389-20191-X). B&N Imports.

Coates, D. The Labor Party & the Struggle for Socialism. LC 74-19526. 272p. 1975. 39.50 (ISBN 0-521-20740-1); pap. 14.95 (ISBN 0-521-09939-0). Cambridge U Pr.

Coates, D. F. Rock Mechanics Principles. 442p. 1981. pap. text ed. 26.40 (ISBN 0-660-10933-6, Pub. by Inst Engineering Australia). Renouf.

Coates, Donald, ed. Coastal Geomorphology. (Binghamton Symposia in Geomorphology International Ser.: No. 3). (Illus.). 416p. 1980. text ed. 25.00x (ISBN 0-04-551038-5). Allen Unwin.

Coates, Donald R. Environmental Geology. LC 80-21272. 731p. 1981. text ed. 27.95x (ISBN 0-471-06379-7). Wiley.

Coates, Donald R., ed. Environmental Geomorphology & Landscape Conservation, 3 vols. Incl. Vol. 1. Prior to 1900. 1972. o.s. 55.00 (ISBN 0-12-786241-2); Vol. 2. Urban Areas. 464p. 1974. 55.00 (ISBN 0-12-786242-0); Vol. 3. Non-Urban Regions. 496p. 1973. o.s. 55.00 (ISBN 0-12-786243-9). LC 72-77882. (Benchmark Papers in Geology Ser.). (Illus.). Acad Pr.

--Geomorphology & Engineering. (Binghamton Symposia in Geomorphology: International Ser.: No. 7). (Illus.). 384p. 1980. text ed. 45.00x (ISBN 0-04-551040-7). Allen Unwin.

--Glacial Gemorphology: Binghampton Symposia in Geomorphology. (International Ser.: No. 5). (Illus.). 304p. 1981. text ed. 35.00x (ISBN 0-04-551045-8). Allen Unwin.

Coates, Donald R. & Vitek, John D., eds. Thresholds in Geomorphology. (Binghamton Symposia in Geomorphology Ser.: Vol. 9). (Illus.). 512p. (Orig.). 1980. text ed. 50.00x (ISBN 0-04-551033-4). Allen Unwin.

Coates, Edward & Flynn, Richard B., eds. Planning Facilities for Athletics, Physical Education & Recreation. rev. ed. 1979. 16.95 (ISBN 0-87670-509-3, 240-6570). AAHPERD.

Coates, Gary & Sanker, Joyce. Ali Baba & the Thieves. 1982. pap. 3.50 (ISBN 0-686-38387-7). Eldridge Pub.

--Ali Baba & the Thieves. 1982. pap. 3.50 (ISBN 0-686-38754-6). Eldridge Pub.

Coates, Jennifer. The Semantics of the Modal Auxiliaries. (Linguistics Ser.). 260p. 1983. text ed. 33.00x (ISBN 0-7099-0735-4, Pub. by Croom Helm Ltd England). Biblio Dist.

Coates, John, jt. auth. see Austen, Jane.

Coates, Robert. Investment Strategy. (Illus.). 1978. text ed. 24.95 (ISBN 0-07-011471-4). instr's guide 20.00 (ISBN 0-07-011472-2); study guide 9.95 (ISBN 0-07-011473-0). McGraw.

Coates, Robert B., et al. Diversity in a Youth Correctional System: Handling Delinquents in Massachusetts. LC 78-7311. 264p. 1979. prof ref 19.00x (ISBN 0-88410-787-6). Ballinger Pub.

Coates, Robert M. The Outlaw Years: The History of the Land Pirates of the Natchez Trace. LC 74-1087. (Illus.). 307p. 1974. Repr. of 1930 ed. 42.00x (ISBN 0-8103-3961-7). Gale.

Coates, Robert M., ed. Organic Syntheses, Vol. 59. LC 21-17747. (Series on Organic Synthesis). 1980. 22.95x (ISBN 0-471-05963-3, Pub. by Wiley-Interscience). Wiley.

Coates, Ruth A. Great American Naturalists. LC 73-21989. (Pull Ahead Bks). Orig. Title: Famous Great American Naturalists. (Illus.). 104p. (gr. 5-10). 1974. PLB 4.95g (ISBN 0-8225-0467-7). Lerner Pubns.

Coates, Sanford E. Psychical Research & Spiritualism. (Illus.). 1980. deluxe ed. 59.75 (ISBN 0-89920-006-0). Am Classical Coll Pr.

Coates, Thomas J. Adolescent Health: Crossing the Barriers. 444p. 1982. 39.50 (ISBN 0-12-177380-9). Acad Pr.

Coates, Vary T. & Finn, Bernard, eds. Retrospective Technology Assessment of Submarine Telegraphy: The Transatlantic Cable of 1866. LC 78-65157. (Illus.). 1979. pap. 12.00 (ISBN 0-911302-39-5). San Francisco Pr.

Coates, W. H. & White, H. V. Ordeal of Liberal Humanism: An Intellectual History of Western Europe Since the French Revolution, Vol 2. 1969. pap. text ed. 10.50 o.p. (ISBN 0-07-011464-1, C). McGraw.

Coates, William P. & Coates, Zelda. Soviets in Central Asia. LC 73-88983. Repr. of 1951 ed. lib. bdg. 16.25x (ISBN 0-8371-2091-8, COSA). Greenwood.

Coates, Willson H., ed. see D'Ewes, Simonds.

Coates, Zelda, jt. auth. see Coates, William P.

Coatesville-Jefferson Conference on Addiction, 1st, October 1977. Addiction Research & Treatment Converging Trends: Proceedings. Gottheil, E. L., et al, eds. LC 78-23703. 1979. 19.50 (ISBN 0-08-023025-3). Pergamon.

Coats, Joel. Insecticide Mode of Action. 472p. 1982. 59.50 (ISBN 0-12-177120-2). Acad Pr.

Coats, R. B. & Parkin, A. Computer Models in the Social Sciences. (Orig.). 1977. pap. text ed. 15.95 (ISBN 0-316-14890-3). Little.

Coats, Warren L. & Khatkhate, Deena R., Jr., eds. Money & Monetary Policy in Less Developed Countries: A Survey of Issues & Evidence. LC 79-42703. (Illus.). 834p. 1980. 40.00 (ISBN 0-08-024041-0). Pergamon.

Coatsworth, Elizabeth. The Cat Who Went to Heaven. LC 58-10917. (gr. 3-6). 1972. pap. 3.95 (ISBN 0-02-042580-5, Collier). Macmillan.

Cobb, Carl W. Antonio Machado. (World Authors Ser.: Spain: No. 161). lib. bdg. 15.95 o.p. (ISBN 0-8057-2556-3, Twayne). G K Hall.

--Contemporary Spanish Poetry: Eighteen Ninety-Eight to Nineteen Sixty-Three. LC 75-23016. (World Authors Ser.). 1976. lib. bdg. 13.95 (ISBN 0-8057-6202-7, Twayne). G K Hall.

--Federico Garcia Lorca. (World Authors Ser.). 1968. lib. bdg. 12.95 (ISBN 0-8057-2544-X, Twayne). G K Hall.

Cobb, Carl W., tr. from Span. Lorca's Romancero Gitano: A Ballad Translation & Critical Study. LC 82-17454. 136p. 1983. text ed. 15.00x (ISBN 0-87805-177-5). U Pr of Miss.

Cobb, Charles M. Practical Communication. LC 77-28696. 1978. pap. text ed. 15.50x (ISBN 0-673-16336-9). Scott F.

Cobb, David. The Adventures of Billy & Lilly, 4 bks. Incl. Dino the Dinosaur (ISBN 0-582-53107-1); Football in Space (ISBN 0-582-53106-3); Lilly's Flying Horse (ISBN 0-582-53104-7); Tennis Star (ISBN 0-582-53105-5). (English As a Second Language Bk.). (gr. 1-5). 1981. pap. 1.35 ea. Longman.

Cobb, Douglas F. VisiCalc Models for Business. LC 82-42767. 1983. pap. 14.95 (ISBN 0-88022-017-1). Que Corp.

Cobb, H. H. Improvements that Increase the Value of Your House. 1981. pap. 6.95 (ISBN 0-07-011488-9). McGraw.

Cobb, Hazel. Around the Keys & Around the Keys Again. 64p. (gr. 3-6). 1960. pap. text ed. 8.15 (ISBN 0-87487-626-5). Summy.

Cobb, Hubbard H. Improvements That Increase the Value of Your House. (Illus.). 1976. 18.95 (ISBN 0-07-011487-0, P&RB). McGraw.

Cobb, Irvin S. Exit Laughing. LC 73-19798. 1974. Repr. of 1941 ed. 47.00x (ISBN 0-8103-3687-1). Gale.

Cobb, J. B., Jr. Is It Too Late: A Theology of Ecology. 1971. pap. 3.50 o.p. (ISBN 0-02-801280-1). Glencoe.

Cobb, J. S. The American Lobster: The Biology of Homarus Americanus. (Technical Report Ser.: No. 49). 31p. 1977. 2.00 o.p. (ISBN 0-686-36969-6, P497). URI Mas.

Cobb, James, ed. see Brant, Russell A.

Cobb, John B., Jr., jt. auth. see Tracy, David.

Cobb, John B., Jr. & Schroeder, W. Widick, eds. Process Philosophy & Social Thought. LC 80-70781. (Studies in Religion & Society). 263p. 1981. 22.95x (ISBN 0-913348-18-X); pap. 9.95x (ISBN 0-913348-19-8). Ctr Sci Study.

Cobb, John B., Jr., jt. ed. see Griffin, David R.

Cobb, John B., Jr., jt. ed. see Robinson, James M.

Cobb, Jonathan & Sennett, Richard. Hidden Injuries of Class. 1973. pap. 3.95 (ISBN 0-394-71940-9, V940, Vin). Random.

Cobb, Loren & Thrall, Robert M., eds. Mathematical Frontiers of the Social & Policy Sciences. (AAAS Selected Symposium Ser.: No. 54). 186p. 1980. lib. bdg. 24.50 (ISBN 0-89158-953-8). Westview.

Cobb, Norman B., ed. see Feldman, Nans A.

Cobb, O., et al. A Performance Data Management Program for Solar Thermal Energy Systems. (Progress in Solar Energy Supplements SERI Ser.). 120p. 1983. pap. text ed. 12.00x (ISBN 0-89553-101-1). Am Solar Energy.

Cobb, Pamela. Inside the Devil's Mouth. 1st ed. LC 75-12074. 42p. 1975. pap. 3.00 (ISBN 0-916418-03-0). Lotus.

Cobb, Richard. French & Germans, Germans & French: A Personal Interpretation of France under Two Occupations; 1914-1918, 1940-1944. LC 82-40472. (Tauber Institute Ser.: No. 2). 208p. 1983. 14.00 (ISBN 0-87451-225-5). U Pr of New Eng.

--Promenades: An Historian's Appreciation of Modern French Literature. 1980. 17.95x (ISBN 0-19-211758-0). Oxford U Pr.

Cobb, Roger W., jt. auth. see Elder, Charles D.

Cobb, Vicki. Gobs of Goo. LC 82-48457. (Illus.). 40p. (gr. 1-3). 1983. 9.57i (ISBN 0-397-32021-3, JBL-J); PLB 9.89g (ISBN 0-397-32022-1). Har-Row.

--How the Doctor Knows You're Fine. LC 73-4758. (Illus.). (gr. 2-3). 1973. 9.95i o.p. (ISBN 0-397-31240-7, JBL-J). Har-Row.

--Lots of Rot. LC 80-8726. (Illus.). 40p. (gr. 1-3). 1981. 9.95 o.p. (ISBN 0-397-31938-X, JBL-J); PLB 9.89 (ISBN 0-397-31939-8); pap. 4.95 (ISBN 0-397-31960-6). Har-Row.

--Making Sense of Money. LC 74-131256. (Finding-Out Book). (Illus.). 64p. (gr. 2-4). 1971. PLB 8.95 o.p. (ISBN 0-8193-0439-5, Pub. by Parents). Enslow Pubs.

--The Secret Life of Hardware: A Science Experiment Book. LC 81-48607. (Illus.). 96p. (gr. 5 up). 1982. 9.13i (ISBN 0-397-31999-1, JBL-J); PLB 9.89g (ISBN 0-397-32000-0). Har-Row.

--Truth on Trial: The Story of Galileo Galilei. LC 79-237. (Science Discovery Ser.). (Illus.). (gr. 3-7). 1979. PLB 5.99 (ISBN 0-698-30709-7, Coward). Putnam Pub Group.

Cobb, Vicki & Darling, Kathy. Bet You Can! Science Possibilities to Fool You. 112p. (gr. 3-7). 1983. pap. 1.95 (ISBN 0-380-82180-X, Camelot). Avon.

--Bet You Can't: Scientific Impossibilities to Fool You. (Illus.). 128p. (gr. 3-7). 1983. pap. 1.95 (ISBN 0-380-54502-0, 54502-0, Camelot). Avon.

Cobb, W. A. & Van Duyn, H. Contemporary Clinical Neurophysiology. (Electroencephalography & Clinical Neurophysiology Ser.: Vol. 34, Suppl.). 1978. 110.25 (ISBN 0-444-80056-5, Biomedical Pr). Elsevier.

Cobb, Walter J., tr. see Hugo, Victor.

Cobban, A. B. King's Hall Within the University of Cambridge in the Later Middle Ages. LC 69-10193. (Studies in Medieval Life & Thought: No. 1). (Illus.). 1969. 54.50 (ISBN 0-521-04678-5). Cambridge U Pr.

Cobban, Alfred B. Social Interpretation of the French Revolution. LC 64-21535. 1968. 32.50 (ISBN 0-521-04679-3); pap. 9.95 (ISBN 0-521-09548-4). Cambridge U Pr.

Cobban, J. M. & Colebourn, R. Civis Romanus: Reader for the First Two Years of Latin. (Illus., Lat.). (gr. 8-10). 1969. text ed. 8.95 (ISBN 0-312-14175-0); o. p. key s.p. 3.95 (ISBN 0-312-14210-2). St Martin.

Cobbett, William. Poor Man's Friend. LC 75-16290. Repr. of 1829 ed. lib. bdg. 19.50x (ISBN 0-678-01039-0). Kelley.

Cobbold, Richard S. Transducers for Biomedical Measurements: Principles & Applications. LC 74-2480. (Biomedical Engineering & Health Systems Ser). 486p. 1974. 42.00x (ISBN 0-471-16145-4, Pub. by Wiley-Interscience). Wiley.

Cobbs, C. Glenn & Griffin, Frank M., Jr. Infectious Diseases Case Studies. 3rd ed. 1981. pap. 17.00 (ISBN 0-87488-011-4). Med Exam.

Cobden, Richard. American Diaries. Cawley, Elizabeth H., ed. LC 75-90488. Repr. of 1952 ed. lib. bdg. 15.00x o.p. (ISBN 0-8371-2261-9, COAD). Greenwood.

Cobden-Sanderson, T. J. Ecce Mundus Industrial Ideals, the Book Beautiful, Repr. Of 1902. Stansky, Peter & Shewan, Rodney, eds. Incl. The Arts & Crafts Moement. Repr. of 1905 ed. LC 76-18325. (Aesthetic Movement & the Arts & Crafts Movement Ser.). 1977. lib. bdg. 44.00x o.s.i. (ISBN 0-8240-2479-6). Garland Pub.

Cobelli, E. & Bergman, R. N. Carbohydrate Metabolism: Quantitative Physiology & Mathematical Modelling. LC 80-41383. 440p. 1981. 71.95 (ISBN 0-471-27912-9, Pub. by Wiley Interscience). Wiley.

Coben, Stanley. A. Mitchell Palmer: Politician. LC 79-180787. (Civil Liberties in American History Ser). (Illus.). 352p. 1972. Repr. of 1963 ed. lib. bdg. 42.50 (ISBN 0-306-70208-8). Da Capo.

Coben, Stanley, jt. auth. see Link, Arthur S.

Cobes, Jon P., jt. auth. see Heck, Shirley.

Cobham, Rosemary. Kaleidoscope Plus. 160p. 1982. 12.95 (ISBN 0-85683-046-1, Pub. by Shepheard-Walwyn). Flatiron Book Dist.

Coblans, H., ed. The Use of Physics Literature. 320p. 1975. 37.95 (ISBN 0-408-70709-7). Butterworth.

Coblans, Herbert. Librarianship & Documentation. (Grafton Books on Library Science). 1977. lib. bdg. 12.75 o.p. (ISBN 0-233-96596-3). Westview.

--Librarianship & Documentation. 144p. 1974. 17.00 (ISBN 0-233-96596-3, 05775-4, Pub. by Gower Pub Co England). Lexington Bks.

Coble, Betty J. The Private Life of the Minister's Wife. LC 81-65385. 1981. pap. 5.95 (ISBN 0-8054-6935-4). Broadman.

Coble, Charles. Nuclear Energy. (A Look Inside Ser.). (Illus.). 48p. (gr. 4 up). 1983. PLB 14.25 (ISBN 0-8172-1416-X). Raintree Pubs.

Cobleigh, Ira W. Double Your Dollars in 600 Days. 224p. 1979. 9.95 (ISBN 0-517-53777-X, Harmony). Crown.

Coblentz, Patricia, jt. auth. see Bishop, Robert.

Coblentz, Stanton. Lord of Tranerica. (YA) 6.95 (ISBN 0-685-07444-7, Avalon). Bouregy.

Coburn, Andrew. The Babysitter. 1979. 9.95 o.p. (ISBN 0-393-01189-5). Norton.

Coburn, Doris K. A Spit Is a Piece of Land: Landforms in the U. S. A. LC 77-17605. (Illus.). 128p. (gr. 4-6). 1978. PLB 7.79 o.p. (ISBN 0-671-32844-1). Messner.

Coburn, Jack, jt. ed. see Bronner, Felix.

Coburn, John. A Life to Live - a Way to Pray. 160p. (Orig.). 1973. pap. 5.95 (ISBN 0-8164-2079-3, SP80). Seabury.

Coburn, John B. Anne & the Sand Dobbies: A Story of Death for Children & Their Parents. 120p. 1980. 6.95 (ISBN 0-8164-3003-9); pap. 3.95 (ISBN 0-8164-2041-6). Seabury.

--Christ's Life, Our Life. LC 77-17172. 1978. 4.00 (ISBN 0-8164-0384-8); pap. 3.95 (ISBN 0-8164-2616-3). Seabury.

--Deliver Us from Evil: The Prayer of Our Lord. 1976. pap. 2.00 (ISBN 0-8164-2124-2). Seabury.

Coburn, Kathleen. In Pursuit of Coleridge. (Illus.). 202p. 1978. 12.75x o.p. (ISBN 0-8476-6039-7). Rowman.

Coburn, Louis. Library Media Center Problems - Case Studies. LC 73-2857. 144p. 1973. lib. bdg. 13.00 (ISBN 0-379-00019-9). Oceana.

Coburn, Louisa V., jt. ed. see Anderson, Scarvia B.

Coburn, Marjorie F., jt. auth. see Orem, R. C.

Coburn, Thomas. Devi Mahatmya. 1983. 17.50x (ISBN 0-686-42973-7). South Asia Bks.

Coca, Arthur F. Familial NonReaginic Food Allergy. 3rd ed. 300p. 1953. photocopy ed. spiral 24.50x (ISBN 0-398-04229-2). C C Thomas.

--The Pulse Test. 192p. 1982. 12.00 (ISBN 0-686-94665-0). Lyle Stuart.

Cocannouer, Joseph. Water & the Cycle of Life. 6.95 (ISBN 0-8159-7202-4). Devin.

--Weeds: Guardians of the Soil. (Illus.). pap. 6.95 (ISBN 0-8159-7205-9). Devin.

Coccari, Ronald L. see Ben-Horim, Moshe & Levy, Haim.

Coccia, Orestes P. Immediacy: The Dialectics of Non-Rational Consciousness-Prophet, Poet and Physicist. LC 80-67237. 379p. 1980. pap. text ed. 13.50 (ISBN 0-8191-1251-8). U Pr of Amer.

Coceani, Flavio, jt. auth. see Brazier, Mary A.

Coceani, Flavio & Olley, Peter M., eds. Prostaglandins & Perinatal Medicine. LC 77-17758. (Advances in Prostaglandin & Thromboxane Research Ser.: Vol. 4). 428p. 1978. 48.00 (ISBN 0-89004-216-0). Raven.

Coch, Clifford, tr. see Lengel, Olga.

Cochin, Augustin. La Condition des Ouvriers Francais d'apres les Dernier Travaux. (Conditions of the 19th Century French Working Class Ser.). 48p. (Fr.). 1974. Repr. of 1862 ed. lib. bdg. 24.50x o.p. (ISBN 0-8287-0208-X, 1107). Clearwater Pub.

Cochran, Alan. Two Plus Two. LC 79-8964. 1980. 10.95 (ISBN 0-385-15603-0). Doubleday.

Cochran, Bob. Handbook of Help & Hope. 1981. pap. 2.50 (ISBN 0-8423-1279-X). Tyndale.

Cochran, David W. Burglary Prevention: A Home Study Course. (Home Study Ser.). 28p. 1981. pap. text ed. 19.00 Bk & cassette (ISBN 0-686-96958-8). Fruition Pubns.

Cochran, Doris M. & Goin, Coleman J. The New Field Book of Reptiles & Amphibians. LC 69-18168. (Putnam Nature Field Bks.). (Illus.). 1970. 7.95 o.p. (ISBN 0-399-10292-2). Putnam Pub Group.

--The New Field Book of Reptiles & Amphibians. LC 69-18168. (Putnam Nature Field Bks.). (Illus.). 1978. pap. 4.50 o.p. (ISBN 0-399-12156-0). Putnam Pub Group.

Cochran, J. A. Analysis of Linear Integral Equations. 1972. 24.95 o.p. (ISBN 0-07-011527-3, C). McGraw.

Cochran, James A. Applied Mathematics: Principles, Techniques, & Applications. LC 82-7055. (Mathematics Ser.). 399p. 1982. text ed. 34.95 (ISBN 0-534-98026-0). Wadsworth Pub.

Cochran, John A. Money, Banking, & the Economy. 4th ed. 1979. 22.95x (ISBN 0-02-323030-4); instrs'. manual avail. Macmillan.

--Money, Banking, & the Economy. 528p. 1983. text ed. 23.95 (ISBN 0-02-323050-9). Macmillan.

Cochran, Keith. Colts Peacemaker. (Illus.). 1982. 4.95 (ISBN 0-910156-07-7). Art & Ref.

Cochran, L., jt. auth. see Whitcomb, Helen.

Cochran, Michael. Texas vs. Davis: The Only Complete Account of the Cullen Davis Murder Trials. LC 80-674. 400p. 1980. 12.95 o.p. (ISBN 0-672-52569-0). Bobbs.

Cochran, Michael H. Germany Not Guilty in 1914. LC 72-80274. 1972. 15.50 (ISBN 0-87926-009-2); pap. 2.50 (ISBN 0-87926-010-6). R Myles.

Cochran, Molly, jt. auth. see Weber, Eric.

Cochran, Negley D. E. W. Scripps. LC 73-38128. (Illus.). 315p. 1972. Repr. of 1933 ed. lib. bdg. 19.25x (ISBN 0-8371-6326-9, COSP). Greenwood.

Cochran, Sherman & Hsieh, Andrew C. K., trs. One Day in China: May 21, 1936. LC 82-48901. 304p. 1983. text ed. 19.95x (ISBN 0-300-02834-2). Yale U Pr.

Cochran, Susan Hill. The Population of Thailand: Its Growth & Welfare. (Working Paper: No. 337). iv, 73p. 1979. 5.00 (ISBN 0-686-36201-2, WP-0337). World Bank.

Cochran, Thomas C. Business in American Life: A History. LC 78-38740. 416p. 1972. 5.95 (ISBN 0-07-011520-6, P&RB); pap. 5.95 (ISBN 0-07-011525-7). McGraw.

--New York in the Confederation. LC 72-77054. (Illus.). Repr. of 1932 ed. 19.50x (ISBN 0-678-00911-2). Kelley.

--Two Hundred Years of American Business. 1978. pap. 5.95 o.s.i. (ISBN 0-440-58779-4, Delta). Dell.

Cochran, Thomas C. & Miller, William. Age of Enterprise, a Social History of Industrial America. 1968. pap. 7.50xi o.p. (ISBN 0-06-131054-9, TB1054, Torch). Har-Row.

Cochran, W. The Dynamics of Atoms in Crystals. (Structures & Properties of Solids Ser.). 160p. 1973. pap. text ed. 16.95 (ISBN 0-7131-2439-3). E Arnold.

Cochran, W. G. & Cox, G. M. Experimental Designs. 2nd ed. LC 57-5908. (Wiley Series in Probability & Mathematics Statistics, Applied Problem & Statistics Section). 617p. 1957. 35.95 (ISBN 0-471-16203-5). Wiley.

Cochran, William C. Western Reserve & the Fugitive Slave Law: A Prelude to the Civil War. LC 71-127273. 1972. Repr. of 1920 ed. 29.50 (ISBN 0-306-71212-1). Da Capo.

Cochran, William G. Contributions to Statistics. LC 81-13077. (Wiley Series in Probability & Mathematical Statistics: Probability & Mathematical Section). 1835p. 1982. 85.00x (ISBN 0-471-09786-1, Pub. by Wiley-Interscience). Wiley.

--Sampling Techniques. 3rd ed. LC 77-728. (Probability & Mathematical Statistics Ser.). 428p. 1977. text ed. 30.95 (ISBN 0-471-16240-X). Wiley.

Cochrane, jt. auth. see Meadow, Charles T.

Cochrane, A. L. Effectiveness & Efficiency: Random Reflections on Health Services. 104p. 1972. 25.00x (ISBN 0-686-97002-0, Pub. by Nuffield England). State Mutual Bk.

Cochrane, Charles N. Christianity & Classical Culture: A Study of Thought & Action from Augustus to Augustine. 1957. pap. 9.95 (ISBN 0-19-500207-5, GB). Oxford U Pr.

Cochrane, D. Glynn. The Cultural Appraisal of Development Projects. LC 78-31130. 154p. 1979. 22.95 o.p. (ISBN 0-03-047586-4). Praeger.

Cochrane, Don B., et al. The Domain of Moral Education. LC 79-54303. 312p. 1979. pap. 9.95 o.p. (ISBN 0-8091-2175-1). Paulist Pr.

Cochrane, Eric. Florence in the Forgotten Centuries 1527-1800: A History of Florence & the Florentines in the Age of the Grand Dukes. 608p. 1973. 16.00x o.s.i. (ISBN 0-226-11150-4). U of Chicago Pr.

Cochrane, James L. Macroeconomics Before Keynes. 1970. pap. 8.95x (ISBN 0-673-05010-6). Scott F.

Cochrane, James L., et al. Macroeconomics: Analysis & Policy. 398p. 1974. text ed. 16.50x (ISBN 0-673-07639-3). Scott F.

Cochrane, Rollin. ETC.-Problemes Du Francais Ecrit. LC 72-9378. (Illus.). 304p. 1973. text ed. 14.95 (ISBN 0-13-289983-3). P-H.

Cochrane, Susan H., et al. The Effects of Education on Health. (Working Paper: No. 405). 95p. 1980. 5.00 (ISBN 0-686-36037-0, WP-0405). World Bank.

Cock, J., jt. auth. see Nestel, B.

Cock, James H. Cassava. (IADS Development-Oriented Literature Ser.). 175p. 1983. lib. bdg. 18.00x (ISBN 0-86531-356-3). Westview.

Cock, Valerie. Dressmaking Simplified. 2nd ed. (Illus.). 1976. 14.00x o.p. (ISBN 0-8464-0344-7). Beekman Pubs.

Cockburn, Aiden, jt. auth. see Cockburn, Eve.

Cockburn, Aiden & Cockburn, Eve, eds. Mummies, Disease & Ancient Cultures. (Illus.). 352p. 1980. 54.50 (ISBN 0-521-23020-9). Cambridge U Pr.

Cockburn, Alexander. The Falklands Crisis. (SOS Ser.: No. 3). 1982. pap. 2.95 (ISBN 0-86676-009-1). Riverrun NY.

--Idle Passion: Chess & the Dance of Death. 1975. pap. 2.95 o.p. (ISBN 0-452-25109-5, Z5109, Plume). NAL.

Cockburn, Eve & Cockburn, Aiden. Mummies, Diseases & Ancient Cultures. Abridged ed. LC 79-25682. (Illus.). 256p. Date not set. price not set (ISBN 0-521-27237-8). Cambridge U Pr.

Cockburn, Eve, jt. ed. see Cockburn, Aiden.

Cockburn, Forrester & Gitzelmann, Richard, eds. Inborn Errors of Metabolism in Humans. LC 82-12709. 308p. 1982. 54.00 (ISBN 0-8451-3008-0). A R Liss.

Cockburn, Henry. Memorials of His Time. Miller, Karl, ed. LC 74-5737. (Classics of British Historical Literature Ser). xxviii, 446p. 1974. text ed. 19.50x o.s.i. (ISBN 0-226-11164-4). U of Chicago Pr.

Cockburn, W., jt. auth. see Street, H. E.

Cockburn-Smith, Beth. Cooking with Yogurt. (Illus.). 128p. 1981. 7.95 o.p. (ISBN 0-600-39543-X, 8181). Larousse.

Cockcroft, A. N. & Lameijer, J. N. Guide to the Collision Avoidance Rules. 3rd ed. (Illus.). 240p. 1982. text ed. 17.50x (ISBN 0-540-07278-8). Sheridan.

Cocker, H., jt. auth. see Pizetti, I.

Cockerell, Sydney C. & Plummer, John. Old Testament Miniatures. LC 75-82000. (K). 1969. 90.00 o.s.i. (ISBN 0-8076-0513-1). Braziller.

Cockerham, William. Medical Sociology. 2nd ed. 250p. 1982. 22.95 (ISBN 0-13-573410-X). P-H.

Cockerill, A. & Silberton, A. The Steel Industry. (Department of Applied Economics, Occasional Papers Ser: No. 42). (Illus.). 128p. 1974. pap. 17.95 (ISBN 0-521-09878-5). Cambridge U Pr.

Cockerill, A. W. Sir Percy Sillitoe: The Biography of the Former Head of M-15. 223p. 1976. 8.95 o.p. (ISBN 0-491-01702-2). Transatlantic.

Cockett, Mary. Look at the Little One. LC 75-42224. (Stepping Stones Ser.). (Illus.). 24p. (gr. k-3). 1976. 7.00 (ISBN 0-516-03585-1). Childrens.

Cocking, J. M. Proust: Collected Essays on the Writer & His Art. LC 81-6105. (Cambridge Studies in French: No. 1). (Illus.). 344p. 1982. 49.50 (ISBN 0-521-23790-4); pap. 14.95 (ISBN 0-521-28799-5). Cambridge U Pr.

Cockle, G. R. Those Bicentennials...from American Rails. LC 78-50294. (Illus.). 1983. 35.00 (ISBN 0-916160-04-1). G R Cockle.

--Union Pacific's Snow Fighters. LC 81-65095. (Overland Railbook). (Illus.). 208p. 1983. pap. 23.50 (ISBN 0-916160-09-2). G R Cockle.

Cockle, George R. Frisco in Transition. (Overland Railbook Ser.). (Illus.). 208p. 1983. pap. 23.50 (ISBN 0-916160-13-0). G R Cockle.

--Union Pacific Forties...on the Move. LC 81-65096. (Overland Railbook Ser.). (Illus.). 208p. 1983. pap. 23.50 (ISBN 0-916160-10-6). G R Cockle.

Cockman, N. Live Like a King: Leader's Guide. 1979. pap. 4.95 leader's guide (ISBN 0-8024-4906-9). Moody.

Cockroft, A. N. & Lameijer, J. Guide to the Collision Avoidance Rules. 2nd ed. 224p. 1976. 13.50x o.p. (ISBN 0-540-07272-9). Sheridan.

Cockroft, James. Mexico. LC 81-84740. 1982. 24.00 (ISBN 0-85345-560-0, CL5600). Monthly Rev.

Cocks, Anna S. Courtly Jewelry. (The Victoria & Albert Museum Introduction to the Decorative Arts Ser.). (Illus.). 48p. 1982. 9.95 (ISBN 0-88045-001-0). Stemmer Hse.

Cocks, George, jt. auth. see Preis, Sandra.

Cocks, L. R., ed. The Evolving Earth. LC 80-42171. (Chance, Change & Challenge Ser.). (Illus.). 290p. 1981. 77.50 (ISBN 0-521-23810-2); pap. 24.95 (ISBN 0-521-28229-2). Cambridge U Pr.

Cocks, Leslie V. & Van Rede, C. Laboratory Handbook for Oil & Fat Analysts. 1966. 66.00 o.p. (ISBN 0-12-178550-5). Acad Pr.

Coco, Charlene D. Intravenous Therapy: A Handbook for Practice. LC 79-19930. 170p. 1980. pap. text ed. 13.95 (ISBN 0-8016-0995-X). Mosby.

Cocomas Committee & Nakanishi, Motoo. Corporate Design Systems. (Illus.). 125p. 32.50 (ISBN 0-686-61692-8). Art Dir.

Cocoran, John, ed. see Han, Bong Soo.

Cocozzoli, Gary, jt. ed. see Keresztesi, Michael.

Cocteau, Jean. Appogiatures: Bilingual. 1983. 6.00 (ISBN 0-686-38844-5). Man-Root.

--Cocteau's World. 488p. 1972. Repr. text ed. 21.25x (ISBN 0-7206-0420-6, Pub. by Owen England). Humanities.

--Les Enfants Terribles. (Easy Readers, B). (Illus.). 1975. pap. text ed. 3.95 (ISBN 0-88436-286-8). EMC.

--The Grand Ecart. Galantiere, Lewis, tr. from Fr. LC 74-22403. 153p. 1977. Repr. of 1925 ed. 18.50x (ISBN 0-86527-257-3). Fertig.

--Infernal Machine & Other Plays. LC 63-18631. (Translations by W. H. Auden, Albert Bermel, E. E. Cummings, Dudley Fitts, Mary Hoeck & John Savacool). 1967. pap. 10.25 (ISBN 0-8112-0022-1, NDP235). New Directions.

--Maalesh: A Theatrical Tour in the Middle-East. Hoeck, Mary C., tr. LC 77-26022. (Illus.). 1978. Repr. of 1956 ed. lib. bdg. 15.75x (ISBN 0-313-20054-8, COMT). Greenwood.

Cocteau, Jean & Williams, Dorothy. The Miscreant. (Illus.). 164p. 1982. 13.95 (ISBN 0-7206-5480-7, Pub. by Peter Owen). Merrimack Bk Serv.

Cocteau, Jean, jt. auth. see Aragon, Louis.

Cocteau, Jean see Dent, Anthony.

Codd, Clara M. Meditation, Its Practice & Results. 4th ed. 1968. 2.25 (ISBN 0-8356-7212-3). Theos Pub Hse.

Codd, L. W., jt. auth. see Terpstra, P.

Codding, George A., Jr. & Safran, William. Ideology & Politics: The Socialist Party of France. (Westview Special Studies in European Politics & Society). 1978. lib. bdg. 28.50 (ISBN 0-89158-182-0). Westview.

Coddington, Alan. Keynesian Economics: The Search for First Principles. 144p. 1983. text ed. 18.50x (ISBN 0-04-330334-X). Allen Unwin.

Coddington, Earl A. & Levinson, N. Theory of Ordinary Differential Equations. (International Pure & Applied Mathematics Ser). 1955. text ed. 34.00 o.p. (ISBN 0-07-011542-7, C). McGraw.

Code, Charles F, ed. see American Physiological Society.

Code, Keith. A Twist of the Wrist: The Motorcycle Road Racers Handbook. LC 82-73771. (Illus.). 120p. 1983. 14.95 (ISBN 0-918226-08-2). Acrobat.

Coder, S. Maxwell. Israel's Destiny. LC 78-9659. 1978. pap. 2.95 (ISBN 0-8024-4182-3). Moody.

--Jude: The Acts of the Apostates. (Everyman's Bible Commentary Ser). 1967. pap. 4.50 (ISBN 0-8024-2065-6). Moody.

Coder, S. Maxwell, ed. NASB Gospel of John: Horton Edition. (Acorn Ser.). 96p. (Orig.). 1976. pap. 6.00 package of 10 (ISBN 0-8024-3193-3). Moody.

Codevilla, Angelo. Modern France. LC 74-56. 272p. 1974. 17.00 (ISBN 0-87548-150-7). Open Court.

Codex Alimentarius Commission. First Supplement to the List of Additives Evaluated for Their Safety-in-Use in Food. 27p. 1975. pap. 3.00 o.p. (ISBN 0-685-62844-2, FAO). Unipub.

Codlin, Ellen M., ed. ASLIB Directory: Information Sources in Science, Techonology & Commerce, Vol. 1. 4th ed. 634p. 1981. 75.00x (ISBN 0-686-72837-8, Pub by Aslib England). Gale.

--ASLIB Directory: Information Sources in the Social Sciences, Medicine & the Humanities, Vol. 2. 4th ed. 871p. 1981. 145.00x (ISBN 0-686-72838-6, Pub. by Aslib England). Gale.

Codrescu, Andrei. In America's Shoes. 256p. 1983. 14.95 (ISBN 0-87286-149-X); pap. 7.50 (ISBN 0-87286-148-1). City Lights.

--Selected Poems 1970-1980. LC 82-19532. 137p. 1983. pap. 7.00 (ISBN 0-915342-38-3). SUN.

Codrescu, Andrei & Notley, Alice. Three Zero, Turning Thirty. Wright, Keith & Wright, Jeff, eds. (Illus.). 54p. (Orig.). 1982. pap. 5.00 (ISBN 0-938878-14-X). Hard Pr.

Cody, Al. The Black Rider. (YA) 1977. 6.95 (ISBN 0-685-81421-1, Avalon). Bouregy.

--The Cry of the Cat. (YA) 1980. 6.95 (ISBN 0-686-73934-5, Avalon). Bouregy.

--Forbidden River. (YA) 1973. 6.95 (ISBN 0-685-29160-X, Avalon). Bouregy.

--The Fort at the Dry. (YA) 1977. 6.95 (ISBN 0-685-75640-8, Avalon). Bouregy.

--Powder Burns. 256p. (YA) 1973. 6.95 (ISBN 0-685-31777-3, Avalon). Bouregy.

--Return to Fort Yavapa. (YA) 1975. 6.95 (ISBN 0-685-52990-8, Avalon). Bouregy.

--The Thundering Hills. 256p. (YA) 1973. 6.95 (ISBN 0-685-32413-3, Avalon). Bouregy.

Cody, Fred. Make-Believe Summer: A Victorian Idyll. LC 79-23067. (Illus.). 96p. 1980. 10.95 o.s.i. (ISBN 0-89479-058-7). A & W Pubs.

Cody, Liza. Bad Company. 260p. 1982. 11.95 (ISBN 0-684-17760-9, ScribT). Scribner.

--Dupe. 256p. 1983. pap. 2.50 (ISBN 0-446-30367-4). Warner Bks.

Cody, Martin L. & Diamond, Jared M., eds. Ecology & Evolution of Communities. LC 74-27749. (Illus.). 838p. 1975. text ed. 35.00x o.p. (ISBN 0-674-22444-2, Belknap Pr); pap. 15.00x (ISBN 0-674-22446-9). Harvard U Pr.

Cody, William. Life of Buffalo Bill. (Classics of the Old West). 1982. lib. bdg. 17.28 (ISBN 0-8094-4015-6). Silver.

Cody, William J., Jr. & White, William. Software Manual for the Elementary Functions. (Illus.). 288p. 1980. text ed. 19.95 (ISBN 0-13-822064-6). P-H.

Coe, Brian. The History of Movie Photography. (Illus.). 176p. 1982. 19.95 (ISBN 0-904069-38-9). NY Zoetrope.

Coe, Brian, jt. auth. see Millward, Michael.

Coe, Brian W. Cameras: From Daguerrotype to Instant Pictures. (Illus.). 1978. 15.95 o.p. (ISBN 0-517-53381-2). Crown.

Coe, Charles K. Internal Control Checklist: Optimizing the Flow & Control of Revenues & Expenditures. 25p. (Orig.). 1978. pap. 3.00 o.p. (ISBN 0-89854-003-8). U of GA Inst Govt.

Coe, Eva J., jt. auth. see Bolton, Ethel S.

Coe, Evan, et al, eds. Images of America: Selected Readings Based on Alistair Cooke's America. 1977. pap. text ed. 15.00 (ISBN 0-394-32118-9). Knopf.

Coe, Graham. Colloquial English. (Illus.). 192p. (Orig.). 1981. pap. 9.50 (ISBN 0-7100-0740-X); cassette 12.95 (ISBN 0-7100-0967-4). Routledge & Kegan.

Coe, Harold B. Incorporation & Business Guide for Washington. 2nd ed. 112p. 1981. 9.95 (ISBN 0-88908-717-2); forms 11.95 incorporation (ISBN 0-686-35986-0). Self Counsel Pr.

Coe, Jacques. Fame, Fraud & Fortune: Seventy-four Years in Wall Street. (Illus.). 320p. 1983. 9.95 (ISBN 0-682-49917-X). Exposition.

Coe, Joffre L. The Formative Cultures of the Carolina Piedmont. LC 64-21423. (Transaction Ser.: Vol. 54, Pt. 5). 1980. Repr. of 1964 ed. 10.00 (ISBN 0-87169-545-6). Am Philos.

Coe, Joyce. The Donkey Who Served the King. (Arch Bk. Ser.: No. 15). (Illus.). (gr. k-3). 1978. 0.89 (ISBN 0-570-06120-2, 59-1238). Concordia.

Coe, M. E. How to Write for Television. 160p. 1980. 9.95 (ISBN 0-517-53850-4, Michelman Bks); pap. 5.95 o.p. (ISBN 0-517-54103-3). Crown.

Coe, Marguerite. Basic Skills Parts of Speech Workbook. (Basic Skills Workbooks). 32p. (gr. 5-9). 1983. 0.99 (ISBN 0-8209-0547-X, EW-2). ESP.

--Capitalization Skills. (English Ser.). 24p. (gr. 4-7). 1979. wkbk. 5.00 (ISBN 0-8209-0183-0, E-11). ESP.

--The Eight Parts of Speech. (English Ser.). 24p. (gr. 4-7). 1979. wkbk. 5.00 (ISBN 0-8209-0181-4, E-9). ESP.

Coe, Michael D. The Maya Scribe & His World. LC 73-17731. (Illus.). 160p. 1978. Repr. of 1973 ed. 50.00x o.p. (ISBN 0-8139-0568-0, Dist. by U Pr of Va). Grolier Club.

--Old Gods & Young Heroes: The Pearlsman Collection of Maya Ceramics. LC 82-70987. (Illus.). 130p. 1982. 42.50 (ISBN 0-295-95970-3, Pub. by Israel Museum); pap. 24.95 (ISBN 0-295-95981-9). U of Wash Pr.

Coe, Michael D. & Diehl, Richard A. In the Land of the Olmec, 2 vols. (Illus.). 1980. Set. 100.00x (ISBN 0-292-77549-0); Vol. 1, The Archaeology Of San Lorenzo Techochtitan, 436pp. Vol. 2, The People of the River, 204pp. U of Tex Pr.

Coe, Richard. Form & Substance: An Advance Rhetoric. LC 81-630. 428p. 1981. text ed. 17.95x (ISBN 0-673-15660-5). Scott F.

--The Vision of Jean Genet. 344p. 1983. 17.95 (ISBN 0-7206-0080-4, Pub by Peter Owen). Merrimack Bk Serv.

Coe, Richard L. The Kenya National Youth Service: A Governmental Response to Young Political Activists. LC 73-620220. (Papers in International Studies: Africa). pap. 4.00 (ISBN 0-89680-053-9, Ohio U Ctr Intl). Ohio U Pr.

Coe, Richard N. Eugene Ionesco. 6.00 o.p. (ISBN 0-8446-5711-5). Peter Smith.

Coe, Rodney M. Sociology of Medicine. 2nd ed. (Illus.). 1978. text ed. 23.95 (ISBN 0-07-011560-5, C). McGraw.

Coe, Rodney M. & Pepper, Max. Community Medicine: Some New Perspectives. (Illus.). 1978. pap. text ed. 12.95 o.p. (ISBN 0-07-011548-6, HP). McGraw.

Coe, Ross A. Warrior of Vengeance: Trails of Peril, No. 2. 224p. (Orig.). 1982. pap. 2.25 o.p. (ISBN 0-523-41710-1). Pinnacle Bks.

Coe, Wesley R. Biology of the Nemerteans of the Atlantic Coast of North America. 1943. pap. 42.50x (ISBN 0-686-51347-9). Elliots Bks.

Coe, William R. Piedras Negras Archaeology: Artifacts, Caches & Burials. (Museum Monographs). (Illus.). 245p. 1959. bound 10.00xsoft (ISBN 0-934718-11-3). Univ Mus of U PA.

Coe, William R. & Haviland, William A. Introduction to the Archaeology of Tikal, Guatemala. LC 82-21799. (Tikal Reports Ser.: No. 12). (Illus.). xii, 100p. 1982. 20.00 (ISBN 0-934718-43-1). Univ Mus of U PA.

Coedes, G. The Indianized States of South-East Asia. Vella, Walter F., ed. Cowing, Susan B., tr. from Fr. LC 67-29224. 434p. 1975. pap. text ed. 4.95x (ISBN 0-8248-0368-X, Eastwest Ctr). UH Pr.

--Indianized States of Southeast Asia. Vella, Walter F., ed. Cowing, Susan B., tr. (Illus., Fr. & Eng.). 1968. 17.50x (ISBN 0-8248-0071-0, Eastwest Ctr). UH Pr.

--The Making of Southeast Asia. Wright, H. M., tr. LC 66-4402. (gr. 9-12). 1969. 18.50x o.p. (ISBN 0-520-00248-2); pap. 4.95x o.p. (ISBN 0-520-01420-0, CAMPUS20). U of Cal Pr.

Coen, Franklin. The Plunderers. LC 79-14289. 1980. 10.95 (ISBN 0-698-10998-8, Coward). Putnam Pub Group.

Coen, Rena N. Black Man in Art. LC 78-84405. (Fine Art Books). (Illus.). (gr. 5-11). 1970. PLB 4.95g (ISBN 0-8225-0163-5). Lerner Pubns.

--Kings & Queens in Art. LC 64-8042. (Fine Arts Bks). (Illus.). (gr. 5-11). 1965. PLB 4.95g (ISBN 0-8225-0155-4). Lerner Pubns.

--Medicine in Art. LC 79-84408. (Fine Art Books). (Illus.). (gr. 5-11). 1970. PLB 4.95g (ISBN 0-8225-0166-X). Lerner Pubns.

--Old Testament in Art. LC 77-84410. (Fine Art Books). (Illus.). (gr. 5-11). 1970. PLB 4.95g (ISBN 0-8225-0168-6). Lerner Pubns.

--Red Man in Art. LC 72-267. (Fine Art Books for Young People). (Illus.). 72p. (gr. 5-12). 1972. PLB 4.95g (ISBN 0-8225-0171-6). Lerner Pubns.

Coerr, Eleanor. The Bell Ringer & the Pirates. LC 82-47700. (An I Can Read Bk.). (Illus.). 64p. (gr. k-3). 1983. 7.64i (ISBN 0-06-021354-X, HarpJ); PLB 8.89g (ISBN 0-06-021355-8). Har-Row.

--The Big Balloon Race. LC 80-8368. (An I Can Read Bk.). (Illus.). 64p. (gr. k-3). 1981. 7.64i (ISBN 0-06-021352-3, HarpJ); PLB 8.89g (ISBN 0-06-021353-1). Har-Row.

--Mystery of the Golden Cat. LC 68-13871. (Illus.). (gr. 1-5). 1968. 3.85 o.p. (ISBN 0-8048-0413-3). C E Tuttle.

Coerr, Eleanor & Evans, William E. Gigi: A Baby Whale Borrowed for Science & Returned to the Sea. (Illus.). (gr. 6-8). 1980. 8.95 o.p. (ISBN 0-399-20558-6). Putnam Pub Group.

Coerr, Eleanor B. Biography of a Giant Panda. LC 74-83019. (Nature Biography Ser.). (Illus.). (gr. 3-5). 1975. PLB 6.59 o.p. (ISBN 0-399-60920-2). Putnam Pub Group.

--Biography of a Kangaroo. LC 75-20468. (Nature Biography Ser.). (Illus.). 64p. (gr. 2-4). 1976. PLB 6.59 o.p. (ISBN 0-399-60967-9). Putnam Pub Group.

--Jane Goodall. LC 75-32503. (Beginning Biographies Ser.). (Illus.). (gr. k-3). 1976. PLB 5.99 (ISBN 0-399-60994-6). Putnam Pub Group.

--The Mixed-up Mystery Smell. LC 75-20353. (See & Read Books). (Illus.). 48p. (gr. 2-4). 1976. PLB 6.29 o.p. (ISBN 0-399-60957-1). Putnam Pub Group.

--Sadako & the Thousand Paper Cranes. LC 76-9872. (Illus.). (gr. 3-5). 1977. 8.95 (ISBN 0-399-20520-9). Putnam Pub Group.

--Waza Wins at Windy Gulch. LC 76-21224. (See & Read Storybooks). (Illus.). (gr. k-3). 1977. PLB 6.29 o.p. (ISBN 0-399-61053-7). Putnam Pub Group.

Coetzee, J. F., ed. Recommended Methods for Purification of Solvents. (International Union of Pure & Applied Chemistry). 1982. 20.00 (ISBN 0-08-022370-2). Pergamon.

Coetzee, J. M. Dusklands. 1974. cased 8.00 o.s.i. (ISBN 0-86975-035-6, Pub by Ravan Press). Three Continents.

Coetzee, J. M., tr. see Emants, Marcellus.

Coetzer, P. W., jt. auth. see Geyser, O.

Coetzer, P. W. & Le Roux, J. H., eds. Index to Periodical Articles on South African Political & Social History Since 1902: Bibliographies on South African Political History, Vol. 3. 1982. lib. bdg. 95.00 (ISBN 0-8161-8518-2, Hall Reference). G K Hall.

Coeurderoy, Ernest. Hurrah!!! Ou, la Revolution par les Cosaques. (Nineteenth Century Russia Ser.). 437p. (Fr.). 1974. Repr. of 1854 ed. lib. bdg. 110.00 o.p. (ISBN 0-8287-0209-8, R6). Clearwater Pub.

Coeure, G. Analytic Functions & Manifolds in Infinite Dimensional Spaces. 1974. pap. 16.50 (ISBN 0-444-10621-9). Elsevier.

Cofer, Charles N. Motivation & Emotion. 1972. pap. 10.95x (ISBN 0-673-05016-5). Scott F.

Cofer, Charles N., ed. Human Motivation: A Guide to Information Sources. rev. ed. (The Psychology Information Guide Ser.: Vol. 4). 175p. 1980. 42.00x (ISBN 0-8103-1418-5). Gale.

Coffee, Frank. Everything You Need to Know About Creative Home Financing: New Affordable Ways to buy (& sell) a Home, Condo, or Co-Op. 256p. 1983. 15.50 (ISBN 0-671-44295-3); pap. write for info. S&S.

Coffeen, J. A. Seismic Exploration Fundamentals. 277p. 1978. 43.95x (ISBN 0-87814-046-8). Pennwell Pub.

Coffer, William E. Phoenix: The Decline & Rebirth of the Indian People. 272p. 1982. pap. 9.95 (ISBN 0-442-21128-7). Van Nos Reinhold.

Coffer, William E. & Hosh, Koi. Sleeping Giants. LC 79-64248. 1979. pap. text ed. 8.25 (ISBN 0-8191-0760-3). U Pr of Amer.

Coffey. Rodd's Chemistry of Carbon Compounds, Vol. 4, Pt. A: Three, Four & Five Membered Heterocyclic Compounds. 1973. 149.00 (ISBN 0-444-41093-7). Elsevier.

Coffey, ed. Rodd's Chemistry of Carbon Compounds, Vol. 4, Pt. G: Heterocyclic Compounds - 6 Membered Heterocyclic Compounds with a Single Nitrogen Atom from Group V of the Periodic Table. 1977. 127.75 (ISBN 0-444-41644-7). Elsevier.

Coffey, Alan, jt. auth. see Eldefonso, Edward.

Coffey, Alan, et al. Human Relations: Law Enforcement in a Changing Community. 2nd ed. (Criminal Justice Ser.). (Illus.). 1976. 20.95 o.p. (ISBN 0-13-445692-0). P-H.

--Human Relations: Law Enforcement in a Changing Community. 3ed. ed. (Illus.). 304p. 1982. reference 21.95 (ISBN 0-13-445700-5). P-H.

Coffey, Alan R. Correctional Administration: The Management of Institutions, Probation, & Parole. (Illus.). 320p. 1975. 20.95 (ISBN 0-13-188284-8). P-H.

--The Prevention of Crime & Delinquency. (Illus.). 400p. 1975. 17.95 o.p. (ISBN 0-13-699157-2). P-H.

Coffey, Alan R. & Eldefonso, Edward. Process & Impact of Justice. (Criminal Justice Ser.). 1975. pap. text ed. 11.95x (ISBN 0-02-471750-9, 47175). Macmillan.

Coffey, Alan R., et al. An Introduction to the Criminal Justice System & Process. (Criminal Justice Ser.). (Illus.). 384p. 1974. ref. ed. 18.95 o.p. (ISBN 0-13-481127-5). P-H.

Coffey, Ann C., ed. Changing Patterns of Power in the Persian Gulf. 1983. price not set prof ref (ISBN 0-88410-914-3). Ballinger Pub.

Coffey, Brian. The Voice of the Night. LC 79-7327. 1980. 10.95 o.p. (ISBN 0-385-15258-2). Doubleday.

Coffey, D. J. see Henderson, G. M., et al.

Coffey, David. A Veterinary Surgeon's Guide for Cat Owners. (Illus.). 216p. 1983. 14.95 (ISBN 0-437-02501-2, Pub. by World's Work). David & Charles.

--A Veterinary Surgeon's Guide to Dogs. (Illus.). 199p. 1980. 14.95 (ISBN 0-437-02500-4, Pub. by World's Work). David & Charles.

Coffey, Frank. Modern Masters of Horror. 256p. 1981. 12.95 o.p. (ISBN 0-698-11051-X, Coward). Putnam Pub Group.

Coffey, Frank & Biracree, Tom. The Pride of Portland: The Story of the Trail Blazers. LC 78-57408. (Illus.). 1980. 9.95 o.p. (ISBN 0-89696-007-2, An Everest House Book). Dodd.

Coffey, Michael. Roman Satire. LC 76-28824. 1976. 16.95x (ISBN 0-416-85120-7); pap. 16.95x (ISBN 0-416-85130-4). Methuen Inc.

Coffey, P. & Presley, J. R. European Monetary Integration. LC 70-178243. 1972. 18.95 o.p. (ISBN 0-312-26950-1). St Martin.

Coffey, Peter. The Social Economy of France. LC 73-85269. 160p. 1974. 22.50 (ISBN 0-312-73220-1). St Martin.

Coffey, Peter, ed. The Economic Policies of the Common Market. LC 78-11747. 1979. 26.00x (ISBN 0-312-23447-3). St Martin.

Coffey, S. Rodd's Chemistry of Carbon Compounds, Vol. 4, Pt. E: Heterocyclic Compounds; Six-Membered Monoeterocyclic Compounds. 1978. 127.75 (ISBN 0-444-41363-4). Elsevier.

--Rodd's Chemistry of Carbon Compounds, Vol. 4, Pt. H: Heterocyclic Compounds. 2nd ed. 1978. 127.75 (ISBN 0-444-41575-0). Elsevier.

Coffey, S., ed. Rodd's Chemistry of Carbon Compounds, Vol. 4, Pt. K: Six Membered Heterocyclic Compounds with Two or More Hetero-Atoms. 1979. 136.25 (ISBN 0-444-41647-1). Elsevier.

Coffey, Thomas. The Long Thirst. 1976. pap. 2.25 o.p. (ISBN 0-440-34967-2, LE). Dell.

Coffey, Thomas M. Hap: The Story of the U. S. Air Force & the Man Who Built It, Gen. Henry "Hap" Arnold. LC 81-69928. 390p. 1982. 19.95 (ISBN 0-670-36069-4). Viking Pr.

Coffey, William J. Geography: Towards a General Spatial Systems Approach. 320p. 1981. 29.95x (ISBN 0-416-30970-4); pap. 13.95x (ISBN 0-416-30980-1). Methuen Inc.

Coffield, Frank, et al. A Cycle of Deprivation? 1981. text ed. 24.00x (ISBN 0-435-82145-8). Heinemann Ed.

Coffin, Charles M., intro. by see Donne, John.

Coffin, George. Bridge Summary Complete. (Illus., Orig.). pap. 3.00 (ISBN 0-8283-1427-6, 40, IPL). Branden.

Coffin, George, jt. auth. see Andrews, Joseph.

Coffin, Glenyce. Intervention-Intercession. 32p. (Orig.). 1982. pap. 0.75 (ISBN 0-930756-71-1). Women's Aglow.

Coffin, Henry S. In a Day of Social Rebuilding: Lectures on the Ministry of the Church. 1919. 29.50x (ISBN 0-686-51402-5). Elliots Bks.

Coffin, Joseph. Complete Book of Coin Collecting. 6th, rev. ed. LC 78-10529. (Illus.). 1979. 8.95 (ISBN 0-698-10954-6, Coward); pap. 5.95 (ISBN 0-698-10967-8). Putnam Pub Group.

--The Complete Book of Coin Collecting. 5th rev. ed. (Illus.). 1976. 7.95 o.p. (ISBN 0-698-10738-1, Coward). Putnam Pub Group.

Coffin, Kenneth B., jt. auth. see Leslie, Louis A.

Coffin, Levi. Reminiscences of Levi Coffin. LC 68-55510. Repr. of 1876 ed. 35.00x (ISBN 0-678-00430-7). Kelley.

Coffin, Lyn, tr. see Akhmatova, Anna.

Coffin, Tristram P. Uncertain Glory: Folklore & the American Revolution. LC 77-147812. 1971. 32.00x (ISBN 0-8103-5040-8). Gale.

Coffin, Tristram P. & Cohen, Henning, eds. Folklore: From the Working Folk of America. LC 79-97699. (Illus.). 504p. 1970. pap. 4.95 (ISBN 0-385-03881-X, Anch). Doubleday.

Coffinberger, Richard L. & Samuels, Linda B. Business & Its Legal Environment: Study Guide & Workbook. 176p. 1983. 8.95 (ISBN 0-13-101022-0). P-H.

Coffman, Burton. Commentary on James, First & Second; Peter, First, Second & Third, John, Jude. (Firm Foundation Commentary Ser.). 1979. 10.95 (ISBN 0-88027-075-6). Firm Foun Pub.

Coffman, C. C. Spacedust One. LC 78-63089. (Illus.). 1979. 6.50 o.p. (ISBN 0-533-03958-4). Vantage.

Coffman, Carl. Unto a Perfect Man. 4th ed. 1982. pap. 7.95 (ISBN 0-943872-83-9). Andrews Univ Pr.

Coffman, Edward G., Jr. & Denning, Peter J. Operating Systems Theory. LC 73-491. 400p. 1973. ref. ed. 28.95 (ISBN 0-13-637868-4). P-H.

Coffman, Edward G., Jr., ed. Computer & Job-Shop Scheduling Theory. LC 75-19255. 299p. 1976. 39.95x (ISBN 0-471-16319-8, Pub. by Wiley-Interscience). Wiley.

Coffman, James B. Commentary on Revelation. (Firm Foundation Commentary Ser.). 1979. 10.95 (ISBN 0-88027-076-4). Firm Foun Pub.

--Commentary on the Minor Prophets, Vol. 2. (Firm Foundation Commentary Ser.). 383p. 1981. 8.95 (ISBN 0-88027-079-9). Firm Foun Pub.

--Commentary on the Minor Prophets, Vol. 3. (Firm Foundation Commentary Ser.). 322p. 1983. 10.95 (ISBN 0-88027-107-8). Firm Foun Pub.

--Commentary on the Minor Prophets, Vol. 4. (Firm Foundation Commentary Ser.). 1983. 10.95 (ISBN 0-88027-108-6). Firm Foun Pub.

--Commentary on the New Testament, 12 vols. (Firm Foundation Commentary Ser.). 125.00 (ISBN 0-88027-077-2). Firm Foun Pub.

Coffman, Mary, jt. auth. see Butturff, Diane.

Coffman, Mary E. French Grammar. (Schaum Outline Ser.). 1973. 3.95 o.p. (ISBN 0-07-011552-4, SP). McGraw.

Coffman, Ralph J. Solomon Stoddard. (United States Authors Ser.). 1978. lib. bdg. 13.95 (ISBN 0-8057-7198-0, Twayne). G K Hall.

Coffman, S. F., ed. Church Hymnal. (657 hymns). 1927. 6.95x (ISBN 0-8361-1106-0). Herald Pr.

--Life Songs No. 2. (With Responsive Readings). 1938. 6.95x (ISBN 0-8361-1116-8). Herald Pr.

Coffman, Sara J. How to Improve Your Test-Taking Skills. 3rd ed. 1982. pap. text ed. 3.95 (ISBN 0-89917-373-X). TIS Inc.

--How to Survive at College. 3rd ed. 1982. pap. text ed. 13.95 (ISBN 0-89917-363-2). TIS Inc.

--How to Survive at College. 2nd ed. 1981. pap. 10.95x o.p. (ISBN 0-89917-339-X). TIS Inc.

Coffman, Tom. Catch a Wave: A Case Study of Hawaii's New Politics. rev. 2nd ed. LC 72-98011. 1973. pap. text ed. 3.95x (ISBN 0-8248-0270-5). UH Pr.

Coffman, Virginia. The Evil at Queen's Priory. 1978. pap. 1.75 o.p. (ISBN 0-451-08403-9, E8403, Sig). NAL.

--The Gaynor Women. (Reader's Request Ser.). 1980. lib. bdg. 16.95 (ISBN 0-8161-3047-7, Large Print Bks). G K Hall.

--A Haunted Place. 1978. pap. 1.50 o.p. (ISBN 0-451-07934-5, W7934, Sig). NAL.

--Hyde Place. (General Ser.). 1981. lib. bdg. 14.95 (ISBN 0-8161-3256-9, Large Print Bks). G K Hall.

--Isle of the Undead. 1978. pap. 1.50 o.p. (ISBN 0-451-08032-7, W8032, Sig). NAL.

--Marsanne. (Reader's Request Ser.). 1980. lib. bdg. 14.95 (ISBN 0-8161-3049-3, Large Print Bks). G K Hall.

--Mist at Darkness. 1974. pap. 0.95 o.p. (ISBN 0-451-06138-1, Q6138, Sig). NAL.

--Veronique. (Reader's Request Ser.). 1980. lib. bdg. 17.50 (ISBN 0-8161-3048-5, Large Print Bks). G K Hall.

--Virginia Coffman Romances, 4 bks. (Reader's Request Ser.). 1980. Set. lib. bdg. 60.00 (ISBN 0-8161-3140-6, Large Print Bks). G K Hall.

Coffman, William E. Frontiers of Educational Measurement & Information Systems. 1973. pap. 6.56 o.p. (ISBN 0-395-18061-9). HM.

Coffman, William E., jt. ed. see Randhawa, Bikkar S.

Coffron, J. Understanding & Troubleshooting the Microprocessors. 1980. 23.95 (ISBN 0-13-936625-3). P-H.

Coffron, James. Using & Troubleshooting the Z-8000. 1982. text ed. 19.95 (ISBN 0-8359-8157-6); pap. text ed. 14.95 (ISBN 0-8359-8156-8). Reston.

Coffron, James W. Getting Started in Digital Troubleshooting. (Illus.). 1979. text ed. 19.95 (ISBN 0-8359-2507-2); instrs'. manual o.p. avail. (ISBN 0-8359-2508-0). Reston.

--Practical Hardware Details for 8080, 8085, Z80, & 6800 Microprocessor Systems. (Illus.). 352p. 1981. text ed. 24.95 (ISBN 0-13-691089-0). P-H.

--Practical Troubleshooting for Microprocessors. (Illus.). 256p. 1981. text ed. 22.95 (ISBN 0-13-694273-3). P-H.

Coffron, James W. & Long, William E. Practical Interfacing Techniques for Microprocessor Systems. (Illus.). 432p. 1983. 26.95 (ISBN 0-13-691394-6). P-H.

Cofone, Charles J., ed. Favorite Christmas Carols. (Illus.). 64p. 1975. pap. 3.00 (ISBN 0-486-20445-6). Dover.

Cogan, B. H. & Smith, K. G. Insects: Instructions for Collectors, No. 4a. 5th rev. ed. (Illus.). vi, 169p. 1974. pap. 7.00x (ISBN 0-565-05705-7, Pub. by Brit Mus Nat Hist). Sabbot-Natural Hist Bks.

Cogan, Morris L. Clinical Supervision. LC 72-85906. 250p. 1973. text ed. 26.50 (ISBN 0-395-14027-7). HM.

Cogan, Robert & Escot, Pozzi. Sonic Design: Practice & Problems. (Illus.). 160p. 1981. text ed. 15.95 (ISBN 0-13-822734-9). P-H.

--Sonic Design: The Nature of Sound & Music. (Illus.). 544p. 1976. 22.95 (ISBN 0-13-822726-8). P-H.

Cogan, Sara, compiled by. The Jews of Los Angeles, No. 3. (Western Jewish Americana Ser. Publications). 237p. 1980. 24.95 (ISBN 0-686-30816-6); pap. 14.95 (ISBN 0-686-30817-4). Magnes Mus.

Cogdell, Roy T., jt. auth. see Sitaram, K. S.

Cogell, Elizabeth C. Ursula K. Leguin: A Primary & Secondary Bibliography. 1983. lib. bdg. 39.95 (ISBN 0-8161-8155-1, Hall Reference). G K Hall.

Coger, Leslie I. & White, Melvin R. Reader's Theatre Handbook. 3rd ed. 1981. pap. text ed. 14.50x (ISBN 0-673-15270-7). Scott F.

Coggan, Donald. Name Above All Names. 48p. 1981. pap. 2.95 o.p. (ISBN 0-281-03803-1). Seabury.

Cogger, H. G. Australian Reptiles in Colour. (Illus.). 1967. 7.50 (ISBN 0-8248-0067-2, Eastwest Ctr). UH Pr.

Coggeshall, Almy & Coggeshall, Anne. Twenty-Five Ski Tours in the Adirondacks: Cross-Country Skiing Adventures in the Southern Adirondacks, the Capital District & Tug Hill. LC 79-88594. (Twenty-Five Ski Tours Ser.). (Illus.). 144p. 1979. pap. 5.95 (ISBN 0-89725-008-7). Backcountry Pubns.

Coggeshall, Anne, jt. auth. see Coggeshall, Almy.

Coggeshall, Charles P. & Coggeshall, Thellwell R. The Coggeshalls in America: Genealogy of the Descendants of John Coggeshall of Newport with a Brief Notice of Their English Antecedents. (Illus.). 424p. 1983. Repr. of 1930 ed. 35.00 (ISBN 0-87152-374-4). Reprint.

Coggeshall, Thellwell R., jt. auth. see Coggeshall, Charles P.

Coggin & Spooner. How to Build a Bus Ministry. 0.95 (ISBN 0-8054-9405-7). Broadman.

Coggin, Philip, jt. ed. see Semper, Edward.

Coggins, Frank W. Moped Maintenance Manual. LC 78-24727. (Illus.). 1979. 12.50 o.p. (ISBN 0-89196-054-6, Domus Bks); pap. 6.95 o.p. (ISBN 0-89196-053-8). Quality Bks IL.

Coggins, Jack. The Campaign for North Africa. LC 79-7585. (Illus.). 1980. 15.00 o.p. (ISBN 0-385-04351-1). Doubleday.

--Horseman's Bible. LC 66-17921. (Outdoor Bible Ser.). 1966. pap. 4.95 (ISBN 0-385-03167-X). Doubleday.

Coggins, R. J. Samaritans & Jews: The Origins of Samaritanism Reconsidered. LC 74-3712. (Growing Points in Theology Ser.). 176p. 1974. pap. 3.49 (ISBN 0-8042-0109-9). John Knox.

Coggins, Richard. Who's Who in the Bible. (Illus.). 232p. 1981. 18.50x (ISBN 0-389-20183-9). B&N Imports.

Coggins, Richard J. & Phillips, Anthony C., eds. Israel's Prophetic Tradition. LC 81-17065. (Illus.). 290p. 1982. 39.50 (ISBN 0-521-24223-1). Cambridge U Pr.

Coggins, Wade T. & Frizen, Edwin L., Jr. Reaching Our Generation. (Illus., Orig.). 1982. pap. 5.95 (ISBN 0-87808-188-7). William Carey Lib.

Coghill, Mary A. Games & Simulatons in Industrial & Labor Relations Training. (Key Issues Ser.: No. 7). 32p. 1971. pap. 2.00 (ISBN 0-87546-207-3). ILR Pr.

--Lie Detector in Employment. (Key Issues Ser.: No. 2). 40p. 1973. pap. 2.00 (ISBN 0-87546-208-1). ILR Pr.

Coghill, Mary A., jt. auth. see Miller, Frank B.

Coghill, Mary A., jt. auth. see Shafer, Richard A.

Coghill, Nevill. Shakespeare's Professional Skills. 1964. 44.50 (ISBN 0-521-04681-5). Cambridge U Pr.

Coghill, Nevill, tr. see Chaucer, Geoffrey.

Coghlan, David A. Automotive Brake System. 1980. pap. text ed. 14.95 (ISBN 0-534-00822-4, Breton Pubs). Wadsworth Pub.

Cogley, John. A Canterbury Tale: Experiences & Reflections: 1916-1976. 1976. 2.00 (ISBN 0-8164-0322-8). Seabury.

Cognard, Jacques. Alignment of Nematic Liquid Crystals & Their Mixtures. (Molecular Crystals & Liquid Crystals Supplement Ser.). 78p. 1982. 27.00 (ISBN 0-677-05905-1). Gordon.

Cogniat, Raymond. Bonnard. (Q L P Art Ser). (Illus.). 1968. 7.95 (ISBN 0-517-09889-X). Crown.

--The Century of the Impressionists. (Illus.). 1968. 12.98 o.p. (ISBN 0-517-01320-7). Crown.

--Chagall. (Q L P Art Ser). (Illus.). 1965. 7.95 (ISBN 0-517-03719-X). Crown.

--Dufy. (Q L P Art Ser). (Illus.). 7.95 (ISBN 0-517-03721-1). Crown.

--Pissarro. (Q L P Art Ser.). 1976. 7.95 (ISBN 0-517-52477-5). Crown.

--Sisley: Q.L.P. (Illus.). 1978. 7.95 (ISBN 0-517-53321-9). Crown.

--Soutine. (Q L P Art Ser.). (Illus.). 96p. 1974. 7.95 (ISBN 0-517-51136-3). Crown.

Cogniaux, Alfredus. Orchidaceae, 4 vols. (Flora Brasiliensis Ser.: Vol. 3, Pts. 4-6). (Illus.). 970p. (Lat.). 1975. Repr. Set. lib. bdg. 180.00x (ISBN 3-87429-080-8). Lubrecht & Cramer.

Cogoli, John E. Photo-Offset Fundamentals. 4th ed. (Illus.). (gr. 10-12). 1980. text ed. 19.96 (ISBN 0-87345-235-6); study guide 6.00 (ISBN 0-87345-236-4); filmstrips & ans. avail. 398.00 (ISBN 0-685-42198-8). McKnight.

Cogswell, Betty & Sussman, Marvin B., eds. Family Medicine: A New Approach to Health Care. LC 81-6980. (Marriage & Family Review Ser.: Vol. 4, Nos. 1 & 2). 197p. 1982. text ed. 28.00 (ISBN 0-917724-25-9, B25); pap. text ed. 14.95 (ISBN 0-917724-80-1, B80). Haworth Pr.

Cogswell, Elliot C. The History of Nottingham, Deerfield & Northwood, N.H. LC 72-80064. 1972. Repr. of 1878 ed. 45.00x (ISBN 0-912274-18-2). NH Pub Co.

Cogswell, James. No Place Left Called Home. (Orig.). 1983. pap. write for info. (ISBN 0-377-00128-7). Friend Pr.

Cogswell, Leander W. History of the Town of Henniker. 1973. Repr. of 1880 ed. 45.00X (ISBN 0-912274-29-8). NH Pub Co.

Cogswell, Seddie. Tenure, Nativity & Age As Factors in Iowa Agriculture,1850-1880. (Replica Ser). (Illus.). 170p. 1975. pap. text ed. 5.00x o.p. (ISBN 0-8138-1685-8). Iowa St U Pr.

Cogswell, Theodore. The Wall Around the World. 1973. pap. 1.25 o.p. (ISBN 0-515-03278-6, N3278). Jove Pubns.

Cohan, George M. Twenty Years on Broadway & the Years It Took to Get There: The True Story of a Trouper's Life from the Cradle to the Closed Shop. LC 76-138106. (Illus.). 264p. 1972. Repr. of 1925 ed. lib. bdg. 20.50x (ISBN 0-8371-5682-3, COTY). Greenwood.

Cohan, Steven & Backscheider, P. R., eds. The Plays of James Boaden. LC 78-66608. (Eighteenth Century English Drama Ser.). lib. bdg. 50.00 (ISBN 0-8240-3579-8). Garland Pub.

Cohane, John P. The Key. (Illus.). 256p. 1969. 7.95 o.p. (ISBN 0-517-50733-1). Crown.

Cohen. Biological Role of the Nucleic Acids. 1966. 5.50 (ISBN 0-444-19962-4). Elsevier.

--Protein Phosphorylation in Regulation: Recently Discovered Systems of Enzyme Regulation by Reversible Phosphorylation. (Molecular Aspects of Cell Regulation Ser.: Vol. 1). 1980. 69.00 (ISBN 0-444-80226-6). Elsevier.

--Public Construction Contracts & the Law. 1961. 45.50 (ISBN 0-07-011557-5, P&RB). McGraw.

Cohen & Holliday. Statistics For the Social Sciences. 320p. 1982. text ed. 31.50 (ISBN 0-06-318219-X, Pub. by Har-Row Ltd England); pap. text ed. 18.50 (ISBN 0-06-318220-3, Pub. by Har-Row Ltd England). Har-Row.

Cohen & Van Heyningen. Molecular Actions of Toxins & Viruses. (Molecular Aspects of Cellular Regulation Ser.: Vol. 2). 1982. 79.25 (ISBN 0-444-80400-5). Elsevier.

Cohen, jt. auth. see Hadary.

Cohen, A. Deviance & Control. 1966. pap. text ed. 10.95 (ISBN 0-13-208389-2). P-H.

Cohen, Aaron. International Encyclopedia of Women Composers, Vol. II. 240p. 1983. 50.00 (ISBN 0-8352-1524-5). Bowker.

Cohen, Aaron & Cohen, Elaine. Planning the Electronic Office. (Illus.). 288p. Date not set. 29.95 (ISBN 0-07-011583-4, P&RB). McGraw.

Cohen, Abner. Custom & Politics in Urban Africa: A Study of Hausa Migrants in Yoruba Towns. LC 68-55743. 1969. 28.00x (ISBN 0-520-01571-1); pap. 8.50x (ISBN 0-520-01836-2, CAMPUS43). U of Cal Pr.

--The Politics of Elite Culture: Explorations in the Dramaturgy of Power in a Modern African Society. LC 80-5469. 200p. 1981. 24.50x (ISBN 0-520-04120-8); pap. 8.50x (ISBN 0-520-04275-1, CAMPUS 270). U of Cal Pr.

Cohen, Abner, ed. Urban Ethnicity. (ASA Monographs: No. 12). 360p. 1974. 27.95x (ISBN 0-422-74080-2, Pub. by Tavistock England). Methuen Inc.

Cohen, Alan. The Dragon Doesn't Live Here Anymore: Loving Fully Living Freely. (Illus.). 400p. (Orig.). 1981. pap. 7.95 (ISBN 0-910367-30-2). Eden Co.

--Have You Hugged a Monster Today. (Illus.). 64p. 1982. 3.95. Eden Co.

--Rising in Love. 150p. (Orig.). 1982. pap. 5.95 (ISBN 0-910367-31-0). Eden Co.

--Setting the Seen: Creative Visualization for Deep Relaxation & Stress Management. 36p. (Orig.). 1982. pap. 2.95 (ISBN 0-910367-33-7). Eden Co.

Cohen, Alan, jt. ed. see Sherwood, William.

Cohen, Allan Y., jt. auth. see Marin, Peter.

Cohen, Allen Y., jt. auth. see Marin, Peter.

Cohen, Alvin P., ed. see Boodberg, Peter A.

Cohen, Andrew. A Sociolinguistic Approach to Bilingual Education. 1975. 13.95 (ISBN 0-912066-34-2). Newbury Hse.

Cohen, Andrew D. Describing Bilingual Education Classrooms: The Role of the Teacher in Evaluation. LC 80-80307. 64p. (Orig.). 1980. pap. 4.50 (ISBN 0-89763-050-5). Natl Clearinghse Bilingual.

--Testing Language Ability in the Classroom. 1981. pap. text ed. 11.95 (ISBN 0-88377-155-1). Newbury Hse.

Cohen, Arnold B. Bankruptcy: Secured Transactions & Other Debtor-Creditor Matters. 646p. 1981. 55.00 (ISBN 0-87215-398-3). Michie-Bobbs.

Cohen, Arthur M. Objectives for College Courses. LC 70-116583. 128p. (Orig.). 1970. pap. text ed. 4.95x o.p. (ISBN 0-02-473280-X, 47328). Glencoe.

Cohen, B. Developing Sociological Knowledge: Theory & Method. 1980. pap. 14.95 (ISBN 0-13-205153-2). P-H.

Cohen, B. Bernard. Writing About Literature. rev ed. 256p. 1973. pap. 7.95x (ISBN 0-673-07653-9). Scott F.

Cohen, Barbara. The Demon Who Would Not Die. LC 82-1739. (Illus.). 32p. (gr. k-3). 1982. 11.95 (ISBN 0-689-30917-1). Atheneum.

--Gooseberries to Oranges. (gr. 1-3). 1982. 10.50 (ISBN 0-688-00690-6); PLB 9.55 (ISBN 0-688-00691-4). Morrow.

--King of the Seventh Grade. (gr. 4 up). 1982. 9.00 (ISBN 0-688-01302-3). Lothrop.

--Queen for a Day. LC 80-28115. 160p. (gr. 3 up). 1981. 8.95 (ISBN 0-688-00437-7); lib. bdg. 8.59 (ISBN 0-688-00438-5). Lothrop.

Cohen, Barbara & Lovejoy, Bahija. Seven Daughters & Seven Sons. LC 81-8092. 216p. (gr. 5-9). 1982. 10.95 (ISBN 0-689-30875-2). Atheneum.

Cohen, Barry D., ed. see Jospe, Michael, et al.

Cohen, Ben. Bridge Quiz. 5.50x o.p. (ISBN 0-392-09849-0, SpS). Sportshelf.

Cohen, Benjamin J. The European Monetary System: An Outsider's View. LC 81-4167. (Essays in International Finance Ser.: No. 142). 1981. pap. text ed. 2.50x (ISBN 0-88165-049-8). Princeton U Int Finan Econ.

Cohen, Bernard. Deviant Street Networks: Prostitution in New York. LC 80-8039. 1980. 22.95x (ISBN 0-669-03949-7). Lexington Bks.

Cohen, Bernard, ed. Vestibuar & Oculomotor Physiology: International Meeting of the Barany Society, Vol. 374. LC 81-14230. 892p. 1981. 177.00 (ISBN 0-89766-137-0); pap. 177.00 (ISBN 0-89766-138-9). NY Acad Sci.

Cohen, Bernard L. Concepts of Nuclear Physics. LC 70-138856. (Fundamentals of Physics Ser). (Illus.). 1971. text ed. 22.95 o.p. (ISBN 0-07-011556-7, C). McGraw.

Cohen, Bernard P. & Lee, Hans. Conflict, Conformity & Social Status. LC 74-21852. (Progress in Mathematical Social Sciences Ser: Vol. 7). 240p. 1975. 19.95 (ISBN 0-444-41269-7). Elsevier.

Cohen, Brenda. Means & Ends in Education. (Introduction Studies in Philosophy of Education). 128p. 1982. text ed. 19.50x (ISBN 0-04-370122-1); pap. text ed. 7.50x (ISBN 0-04-370123-X). Allen Unwin.

Cohen, Bruce J. Introductor to Sociology. (Schaum's Outline Ser.). 1979. pap. 5.95 (ISBN 0-07-011591-5, SP). McGraw.

Cohen, Chapman. Essays in Freethinking, 4 vols. Vol. I 1980. pap. 6.00 (ISBN 0-911826-15-7); Vol. II 1981. pap. 6.00 (ISBN 0-686-85588-4); Vol. III 1981. pap. 6.00 (ISBN 0-686-91496-1); Vol. IV 1981. pap. 6.00 (ISBN 0-686-96652-X); Set. pap. 20.00 (ISBN 0-686-96653-8). Am Atheist.

Cohen, D. & Wirth, J. R., eds. Testing Linguistic Hypotheses. LC 74-14163. 227p. 1974. text ed. 12.50x o.s.i. (ISBN 0-470-16419-0). Halsted Pr.

Cohen, D. Walter, jt. auth. see Goldman, Henry M.

Cohen, Daniel. America's Very Own Monsters. LC 82-4961. (Illus.). 48p. (gr. 2-4). 1982. PLB 7.95 (ISBN 0-396-08069-3). Dodd.

--The Encyclopedia of Monsters. LC 82-4574. (Illus.). 256p. 1983. 10.95 (ISBN 0-396-08102-9). Dodd.

--ESP: The Search Beyond the Senses. LC 77-3615. (Illus.). (gr. 7 up). 1977. pap. 1.75 (ISBN 0-15-629045-6, VoyB). HarBraceJ.

--Frauds, Hoaxes, & Swindles. LC 78-12309. (Triumph Ser.). (Illus.). (gr. 4 up). 1979. PLB 8.90 s&l (ISBN 0-531-02295-1). Watts.

--Horror in the Movies. (Illus.). 96p. (gr. 3 up). 1982. 10.50 (ISBN 0-89919-074-X, Clarion). HM.

--How to Buy a Car. LC 82-6899. (Triumph Bks.). (Illus.). 96p. (gr. 9 up). 1982. PLB 8.90 (ISBN 0-531-04494-7). Watts.

--The Human Side of Computers. LC 75-10951. 128p. (gr. 7-12). 1975. PLB 7.95 o.p. (ISBN 0-07-011572-9, GB). McGraw.

--The Magic of the Little People. LC 73-19236. (Illus.). 96p. (gr. 3 up). 1974. PLB 6.64 o.p. (ISBN 0-671-32638-4). Messner.

--Monster Dinosaur. LC 82-48460. (Illus.). 128p. (gr. 3-6). 1983. 9.57i (ISBN 0-397-31953-3, JBL-J); PLB 9.89g (ISBN 0-397-31954-1). Har-Row.

--Monsters, Giants & Little Men from Mars. LC 74-4534. 256p. (gr. 4-7). 1975. 6.95a o.p. (ISBN 0-385-03267-6); PLB 6.95a (ISBN 0-385-06943-X). Doubleday.

--Real Magic. LC 82-45388. (High Interest, Low Vocabulary Ser.). (Illus.). 112p. (gr. 4). 1982. PLB 7.95 (ISBN 0-396-08095-2). Dodd.

--The Science of Spying. (gr. 7-12). 1977. PLB 7.95 (ISBN 0-07-011578-8, GB). McGraw.

--Southern Fried Rat & Other Gruesome Tales. (Illus.). 128p. 1983. 9.95 (ISBN 0-87131-400-2). M Evans.

--The Tomb Robbers. LC 79-22760. (Illus.). 96p. (gr. 5-8). 1980. 9.95 (ISBN 0-07-011566-4, GB). McGraw.

--Video Games. (Illus.). (gr. 4 up). 1982. pap. 1.95 (ISBN 0-671-45872-8). Archway.

Cohen, Daniel J. The Body Snatchers. LC 74-32115. (The Weird & Horrible Library). (gr. 6 up). 1975. 9.57i (ISBN 0-397-31560-0, JBL-J); pap. 2.95 (ISBN 0-397-31610-0). Har-Row.

Cohen, David. How to Win Criminal Cases by Establishing a Reasonable Doubt. 1970. 29.50 (ISBN 0-13-439505-0). Exec Reports.

--Sleep & Dreaming: Origin, Nature & Functions. 1979. text ed. 38.00 o.p. (ISBN 0-08-021467-3). Pergamon.

Cohen, David, ed. Explaining Linguistic Phenomena. LC 74-12463. 207p. 1974. 12.95 o.p. (ISBN 0-470-16425-5, Pub. by Wiley). Krieger.

--Multi-Ethnic Media: Selected Bibliographies in Print. 1975. pap. text ed. 3.00 (ISBN 0-8389-3170-7). ALA.

Cohen, Donna, jt. auth. see Eisdorfer, Carl.

Cohen, Doron J. & Brillinger, Peter C. Introduction to Data Structures & Non-Numeric Computation. (Illus.). 656p. 1972. ref. ed. 28.95 (ISBN 0-13-479899-6). P-H.

Cohen, Dorothy. Consumer Behavior. 504p. 1981. text ed. 24.95 (ISBN 0-394-31160-4). Random.

Cohen, E. G., ed. Fundamental Problems in Statistical Mechanics, Vol. 5: Proceedings. 1981. 68.00 (ISBN 0-444-86137-8). Elsevier.

Cohen, Edmund D. C. G. Jung & the Scientific Attitude. (Littlefield Adams Quality Paperbacks: No. 322). 167p. 1976. pap. 3.95x (ISBN 0-8226-0322-5). Littlefield.

Cohen, Edward, jt. auth. see Koll, F.

Cohen, Edwin. Oral Interpretation: The Communication of Literature. LC 77-8655. 1977. text ed. 15.95 (ISBN 0-574-22555-2, 13-5555). SRA.

Cohen, Edwin, jt. auth. see Eaton, J. Robert.

Cohen, Elaine, jt. auth. see Cohen, Aaron.

Cohen, Ellen M. Auto Calendar Disk. (Professional Software Ser.). 1983. text ed. 65.00 (ISBN 0-471-87459-0). Wiley.

Cohen, Eugene N. & Eames, Edwin. Cultural Anthropology. (Orig.). 1982. pap. text ed. 16.95 (ISBN 0-316-14991-8); tchrs'. manual avail. (ISBN 0-316-14989-6). Little.

Cohen, Fred. Standards Relating to Dispositional Procedures. LC 76-14414. (IJA-ABA Juvenile Justice Standards Project Ser.). 80p. 1980. prof ref 14.00x (ISBN 0-88410-233-5); pap. 7.00x prof ref (ISBN 0-88410-808-2). Ballinger Pub.

Cohen, Fred, jt. auth. see Rutherford, Andrew.

Cohen, Gail. U. S. College-Sponsored Programs Abroad: Academic Year. 185p. 1983. pap. 9.95 (ISBN 0-87206-113-2). Inst Intl Educ.

Cohen, Gail, ed. Vacation Study Abroad, Vol. 2. 180p. 1982. 8.00 o.p. (ISBN 0-87206-114-0). Inst Intl Educ.

Cohen, Gail A. Vacation Study Abroad. LC 80-647933. 190p. 1983. pap. 9.95 o.p. (ISBN 0-87206-114-0). Inst Intl Educ.

Cohen, Gail A., ed. The Learning Traveler: U. S. College Sponsored Programs Abroad, Academic Year, Vol. 1. rev. ed. LC 73-75994. 180p. 1982. pap. 9.95 (ISBN 0-87206-099-3). Inst Intl Educ.

--The Learning Traveler: Vacation Study Abroad, Vol. II. rev. ed. LC 73-78423. 180p. 1982. pap. 9.95 (ISBN 0-87206-100-0). Inst Intl Educ.

--The Learning Traveler Vol. 1: U. S. College-Sponsored Programs Abroad: Academic Year. rev. ed. 186p. 1981. pap. text ed. 8.00 o.p. (ISBN 0-87206-108-6). Inst Intl Educ.

--The Learning Traveler: Vol. 1-U.S. College-Sponsored Programs Abroad: Academic Year. rev. ed. Orig. Title: Summer Study Abroad. 192p. 1983. pap. text ed. 9.95 (ISBN 0-87206-119-1). Inst Intl Educ.

--The Learning Traveler: Vol. 2-Vacation Study Abroad. rev. ed. LC 80-647000933. Orig. Title: Summer Study Abroad. 185p. 1983. pap. text ed. 9.95 (ISBN 0-87206-120-5). Inst Intl Educ.

Cohen, Gary. Understanding Revelation. LC 77-18065. 1978. 7.95 (ISBN 0-8024-9022-0). Moody.

Cohen, Gary G. & Runyon, Catherine. Weep Not for Me. LC 80-10773. 192p. 1980. pap. 3.95 (ISBN 0-8024-4309-5). Moody.

Cohen, Gary G. & Vandermey, H. Ronald, eds. Hosea-Amos. (Everyman's Bible Commentary). 128p. 1981. pap. 4.50 (ISBN 0-8024-2028-1). Moody.

Cohen, Gene D., jt. ed. see Miller, Nancy.

Cohen, Gillian, ed. Psychology of Cognition. 2nd ed. Date not set. price not set (ISBN 0-12-178760-5); pap. price not set (ISBN 0-12-178762-1). Acad Pr.

Cohen, Gourevitch. France in the Troubled World Economy. 1982. text ed. 39.95 (ISBN 0-408-10787-1). Butterworth.

Cohen, Gustav, tr. see Hanslick, Eduard.

Cohen, Habiba S. Elusive Reform: The New French Universities, 1968-1978. (Westview Replica Edition). 1978. lib. bdg. 25.00 o.p. (ISBN 0-89158-195-2). Westview.

Cohen, Hennig, jt. ed. see Levernier, James.

Cohen, Hennig, ed. see Melville, Herman.

Cohen, Henning, jt. ed. see Coffin, Tristram P.

Cohen, Henry. Business & Politics in America from the Age of Jackson to the Civil War: The Career Biography of W. W. Corcoran. LC 79-98708. (Illus.). 409p. 1971. lib. bdg. 35.00 (ISBN 0-8371-3300-9, CBP/). Greenwood.

Cohen, Henry, ed. Criminal Justice History: An International Annual, 2 vols. 1981. 24.00ea. (ISBN 0-686-37101-1). Crime Justice Hist.

Cohen, Howard, jt. auth. see Buchele, Robert.

Cohen, Hyman L. & Brumlik, Joel. Manual of Electroneuromyography. 2nd ed. (Illus.). 288p. 1976. text ed. 19.50 (ISBN 0-06-140644-9, Harper-Medical). Lippincott.

Cohen, I., ed. see Balfour, A. J.

Cohen, I. B. The Newtonian Revolution. LC 79-18637. 1981. 42.50 (ISBN 0-521-22964-2). Cambridge U Pr.

Cohen, I. Bernard. The Birth of a New Physics. 1983. pap. write for info (ISBN 0-393-30045-5). Norton.

--The Newtonian Revolution: With Illustrations of the Transformation of Scientific Ideas. LC 79-18637. (Illus.). 404p. Date not set. pap. 16.95 (ISBN 0-521-27380-3). Cambridge U Pr.

Cohen, I. L. Urim & Thumim: The Secret of God. Murphy, G., ed. (Illus.). 280p. 1983. 16.95 (ISBN 0-910891-00-1). New Research.

Cohen, Irene. The Predators. LC 7-935632. (Illus.). 1978. 14.95 o.p. (ISBN 0-399-11973-6). Putnam Pub Group.

Cohen, Irun, jt. auth. see Rosenberg, Eugene.

Cohen, Irving S., jt. auth. see Logan, Rayford W.

Cohen, J. Single Server Queue. 2nd ed. (Applied Mathematics & Mechanics Ser.: Vol. 8). 1982. 89.50 (ISBN 0-444-85452-5). Elsevier.

Cohen, J., jt. auth. see Scherf, D.

Cohen, J. J., et al, eds. Nephrology Forum. (Illus.). 376p. 1983. pap. 34.50 (ISBN 0-387-90764-5). Springer-Verlag.

Cohen, J. L., et al, eds. Logic, Methodology & Philosophy of Science, No. 6. (Studies in Logic & the Foundation of Mathematics: Vol. 104). Date not set. 125.75 (ISBN 0-444-85423-1). Elsevier.

Cohen, J. M. Journeys Down the Amazon. 216p. 1976. 11.50 o.p. (ISBN 0-85314-193-2). Transatlantic.

Cohen, Jack. Reproduction. 1977. 19.95 (ISBN 0-408-70798-4). Butterworth.

Cohen, Jack S. Magnetic Resonance in Biology, Vol. 2. (Magnetic Resonance in Biology Ser.). 280p. 1983. price not set (ISBN 0-471-05175-6, Pub. by Wiley-Interscience). Wiley.

Cohen, Jack S., jt. auth. see Portugal, Franklin H.

Cohen, Jack S., ed. Noninvasive Problems of Tissue Metabolism. LC 81-10436. 270p. 1982. 49.50x (ISBN 0-471-08893-5, Pub. by Wiley-Interscience). Wiley.

Cohen, Jacob & Cohen, Patricia. Applied Multiple Regression: Correlation Analysis for the Behavioral Sciences. 2nd ed. 512p. 1983. text ed. write for info. (ISBN 0-89859-268-2). L Erlbaum Assocs.

Cohen, James S. & Stieglitz, Maria N. Career Education For Physically Disabled Students: Classroom Business Ventures. LC 79-91614. (Illus.). 50p. 1980. 5.00 (ISBN 0-686-38798-8). Human Res Ctr.

Cohen, James S., jt. auth. see Stieglitz, Maria.

Cohen, James S., jt. auth. see Stieglitz, Maria N.

Cohen, Jamey. Dmitri. 1981. pap. 2.75 o.p. (ISBN 0-451-09663-0, E9663, Sig). NAL.

Cohen, Jane, jt. auth. see Miller, Elizabeth.

Cohen, Jean L. Class & Civil Society: The Limits of Marxian Critical Theory. LC 82-11104. 256p. 1983. lib. bdg. 20.00x (ISBN 0-87023-380-7). U of Mass Pr.

Cohen, Jean L. & Goirand, Roger. Your Baby. (Illus.). 216p. 1982. 17.95 (ISBN 0-13-978130-7); pap. 8.95 (ISBN 0-13-978122-6). P-H.

Cohen, Jean P. & Goirand, Roger. Your Baby: Pregnancy, Delivery, & Infant Care. (Illus.). 304p. 1982. 17.95 (ISBN 0-13-978130-7, Spec); pap. 8.95 (ISBN 0-13-978122-6). P-H.

Cohen, Jean-Pierre. Childhood: The First Six Years. (Illus.). 256p. 1983. 17.95 (ISBN 0-13-131300-2); pap. 8.95 (ISBN 0-13-131292-8). P-H.

Cohen, Jerome, et al, eds. Psychosocial Aspects of Cancer. Orig. Title: Research Issues in Psychological Dimensions of Cancer. 336p. 1982. text ed. 36.50 (ISBN 0-89004-494-5). Raven.

Cohen, Jerome B., et al. Guide to Intelligent Investing. LC 77-83590. 1978. 13.95 (ISBN 0-87094-152-6). Dow Jones-Irwin.

Cohen, Jerry S. & Mintz, Morton. America, Inc. 1973. pap. 3.95 o.s.i. (ISBN 0-440-50432-5, Delta). Dell.

Cohen, Joan, et al. Hitting Our Stride: Good News About Women in Their Middle Years. 1980. 10.95 o.s.i. (ISBN 0-440-03656-9). Delacorte.

Cohen, Joel, jt. auth. see Seixas, Vic, Jr.

Cohen, Joel, ed. see Torre, Joe & Ryan, Nolan.

Cohen, Joel H. Jim Palmer: Great Comeback Competitor. (Putnam Sports Shelf). (Illus.). (gr. 5 up). 1978. PLB 6.29 o.p. (ISBN 0-399-61114-2). Putnam Pub Group.

--Joe Morgan: Great Little Big Man. LC 78-7493. (Sports Shelf Ser.). (Illus.). (gr. 6-8). 1978. PLB 6.29 o.p. (ISBN 0-399-61125-8). Putnam Pub Group.

--Manny Sanguillen: Jolly Pirate. LC 75-4426. (Putnam Sports Shelf). 128p. (gr. 5 up). 1975. PLB 5.29 o.p. (ISBN 0-399-60952-0). Putnam Pub Group.

--Steve Garvey: Storybook Star. LC 77-2648. (Putnam Sports Shelf). (Illus.). 1977. PLB 6.29 o.p. (ISBN 0-399-61099-5). Putnam Pub Group.

Cohen, Joel H., jt. auth. see Schollander, Don.

Cohen, John, ed. Psychology: An Outline for the Intending Student. (Outlines Ser). 1968. pap. 7.95 o.p. (ISBN 0-7100-2998-5). Routledge & Kegan.

Cohen, Jonathan. Poems from the Island. 16p. 1979. pap. 3.00 (ISBN 0-935252-10-X); signed ltd. ed. 8.00 (ISBN 0-686-82977-8). Street Pr.

Cohen, Joyce T., compiled by. Insights: Self-Portraits by Women. LC 78-58501. (Illus.). 1978. 20.50x (ISBN 0-87923-246-3); pap. 7.95 (ISBN 0-87923-247-1). Godine.

Cohen, Kalman J. & Cyert, Richard M. Theory of the Firm: Resource Allocation in a Market Economy. 2nd ed. (Illus.). 640p. 1975. 24.95 (ISBN 0-13-913798-X). P-H.

Cohen, Kalman J. & Gibson, Stephen E. Management Science in Banking. LC 78-60934. 549p. 1982. text ed. 19.95 (ISBN 0-471-87748-4). Wiley.

Cohen, Kalman J. & Gibson, Stephen G. Management Science in Banking. 1978. text ed. 16.95 o.p. (ISBN 0-88262-245-5, 78-060934). Warren.

Cohen, Karen C., ed. see Dyer, D., et al.

Cohen, Karen C., ed. see Stephanopoulos, G.

Cohen, Kathleen & Croix, Horst de la. Study Guide to Art through the Ages. 7th. ed. 309p. study guide 7.95 (ISBN 0-15-503761-7). HarBraceJ.

Cohen, Kathleen R. Metamorphosis of a Death Symbol: The Transi Tomb in the Late Middle Ages & the Renaissance. LC 78-138511. (California Studies in the History of Art: Vol. 15). 1974. 70.00x (ISBN 0-520-01844-3). U of Cal Pr.

Cohen, Ken. A Child's Guide to Yoga. (Illus.). 1983. 9.95 (ISBN 0-915520-55-9). Ross Erikson.

Cohen, L. & Manion, L. Multicultural Classrooms: Perspectives for Teachers. 256p. 1983. text ed. 27.25x (ISBN 0-7099-0719-2, Pub. by Croom Helm Ltd England). Biblio Dist.

Cohen, L. & Thomas, J., eds. Educational Research in Britain Nineteen Seventy to Nineteen Eighty. (NFER Research Publications Ser.). 567p. 1982. text ed. 105.00x (ISBN 0-85633-243-7, NFER). Humanities.

Cohen, L. Jonathan. The Probable & the Provable. (Clarendon Library of Logic & Philosophy). 1977. 39.95x (ISBN 0-19-824412-6). Oxford U Pr.

Cohen, Lawrence & Claiborn, William L., eds. Crisis Intervention. 2nd ed. (Community-Clinical Psychology Ser.: Vol. IV). (Illus.). 208p. 1982. 24.95x (ISBN 0-89885-107-6); pap. 12.95x (ISBN 0-89885-108-4). Human Sci Pr.

Cohen, Lawrence H. Neighborhood Stories, 4 bks. Incl. Bk. 1: Vocabulary (ISBN 0-89061-200-5, 351). Jamestown Pubs; Bk. 2: Detail (ISBN 0-89061-201-3, 352). Jamestown Pubs; Bk. 3: Inference & Conclusion (ISBN 0-89061-202-1, 353). Jamestown Pubs; Bk. 4: Subject Matter & Main Idea (ISBN 0-89061-203-X, 354). Jamestown Pubs. (Illus., Orig., 53p ea.). (gr. 3-4). 1981. tchrs.' ed 25.00 (ISBN 0-89061-204-8); wkbk 4.50 ea.; of four 18.00 set. Jamestown Pubs.

Cohen, Lawrence S., et al. Physical Conditioning & Cardiovascular Rehabilitation. LC 80-23058. 324p. 1981. 30.00 (ISBN 0-471-08713-0, Pub. by Wiley-Med). Wiley.

Cohen, Leah, jt. auth. see Backhouse, Constance.

Cohen, Leon J. Listen & Learn French. 3.50 (ISBN 0-486-20875-3); with records 15.95 (ISBN 0-486-98875-9). Dover.

Cohen, Leon J. & Rogers, A. C. Digalo En Ingles, (Say It in English for Spanish-Speaking People) (Orig.). pap. 1.50 (ISBN 0-486-20802-8). Dover.

--Say It in Spanish. (Orig.). 1951. pap. 1.75 (ISBN 0-486-20811-7). Dover.

Cohen, Leslie. Nourishing a Happy Affair: Nutrition Alternatives for Individual & Family Needs. (Illus.). 150p. (Orig.). 1983. pap. 5.95 (ISBN 0-943914-02-7). Larson Pubns Inc.

Cohen, Leslie, jt. auth. see Bissell, Christa.

Cohen, M., ed. The Poems & Letters of Digby Mackworth Dolben, 1848-1867. 1981. 50.00x o.p. (ISBN 0-86127-219-6, Pub. by Avebury Pub England). State Mutual Bk.

Cohen, M. & Lucofsky, G., eds. Amorphous & Liquid Semiconductors. 1972. 122.00 (ISBN 0-7204-0249-2, North Holland). Elsevier.

Cohen, M. Bruce, jt. auth. see Jones, Seymour.

Cohen, M. Michael, Jr. The Child with Multiple Birth Defects. 200p. 1982. text ed. 32.00 (ISBN 0-89004-496-1, 453). Raven.

Cohen, M. Michael, Sr. Minor Tooth Movement in the Growing Child. LC 76-8570. (Illus.). 1977. text ed. 22.00 o.p. (ISBN 0-7216-2632-7). Saunders.

Cohen, Margo P. & Foa, Piero P., eds. Special Topics in Endocrinology & Metabolism, Vol. 4. (Special Topics in Endocrinology & Metabolism). 251p. 1982. 38.00 (ISBN 0-8451-0703-8). A R Liss.

Cohen, Marjorie A. The Shopper's Guide to New York for International & U. S. Visitors. Soule, Sandra, ed. (Illus.). 288p. (Orig.). 1981. 10.95 o.p. (ISBN 0-9606054-0-1). Two Zees.

Cohen, Marjorie A., ed. see Sherman, Margaret E.

Cohen, Marshall, jt. auth. see Copeland, Roger.

Cohen, Marshall, jt. ed. see Mast, Gerald.

Cohen, Martin. In Quest of Telescopes. 131p. 1982. 13.95 (ISBN 0-521-24989-9). Cambridge U Pr.

Cohen, Martin, jt. auth. see Anderson, James L.

Cohen, Martin A & Croner, Helga, eds. Christian Mission-Jewish Mission. LC 82-60856. 1982. pap. 7.95 (ISBN 0-8091-2475-0). Paulist Pr.

--Christian Mission-Jewish Mission. 224p. pap. 7.95 (ISBN 0-8091-2475-0). Paulist Pr.

Cohen, Marvin. Aesthetics in Life & Art: Existence in Function & Essence & Whatever Else Is Important, Too. 120p. (Orig.). 1983. pap. 8.95 (ISBN 0-940584-02-6). Gull Bks.

--The Monday Rhetoric of the Love Club & Other Parables. LC 72-93979. 128p. 1973. 8.25 o.p. (ISBN 0-8112-0474-X); pap. 3.75 (ISBN 0-8112-0475-8, NDP352). New Directions.

Cohen, Matt. Colors of War. 10.00 o.p. (ISBN 0-7710-2175-5). Methuen Inc.

Cohen, Maury, jt. auth. see Bourne, Geoffrey H.

Cohen, Maynard M., ed. Biochemistry of Neural Disease. (Illus.). 1975. text ed. 27.50 (ISBN 0-06-140646-5, Harper Medical). Lippincott.

Cohen, Melvin R. Laparoscopy, Culdoscopy & Gynecography: Technique & Atlas. LC 72-126452. (Major Problems in Obstetrics & Gynecology: Vol. 1). (Illus.). 1970. 15.00 o.p. (ISBN 0-7216-2650-5). Saunders.

Cohen, Michael. Urban Growth & Economic Development in the Sahel. (Working Paper: No. 315). 120p. 1979. 5.00 (ISBN 0-686-36230-6, WP-0315). World Bank.

Cohen, Miriam. No Good in Art. LC 79-16566. (Illus.). 32p. (gr. k-3). 1980. 9.75 (ISBN 0-688-80234-6); PLB 9.36 (ISBN 0-688-84234-8). Greenwillow.

--See You Tomorrow, Charles. LC 82-11834. (Illus.). 32p. (gr. k-3). 1983. 9.00 (ISBN 0-688-01804-1); PLB 8.59 (ISBN 0-688-01805-X). Greenwillow.

--So What? (Illus.). (ps-3). 1982. 9.00 (ISBN 0-688-01202-7); PLB 8.59 (ISBN 0-688-00909-3). Greenwillow.

Cohen, Mitch, ed. Berlin: Contemporary Writing from Berlin. LC 77-642342. (Rockbottom Specials Ser.). (Illus., Eng. & Ger.). 1983. 18.00 (ISBN 0-930012-23-2); pap. 8.50 (ISBN 0-930012-22-4). Bandanna Bks.

Cohen, Mitchell, ed. see Borochov, Ber.

Cohen, Morris L., et al, eds. Law & Science: A Selected Bibliography. rev. ed. 155p. 1980. 20.00x (ISBN 0-262-03073-X). MIT Pr.

Cohen, Morris R. The Meaning of Human History. 2nd ed. LC 61-10174. (The Paul Carus Lectures Ser.). (Illus.). ix, 320p. 1961. 21.00 (ISBN 0-87548-100-0); pap. 8.50 (ISBN 0-87548-101-9). Open Court.

Cohen, Morris R. & Nagel, Ernest. An Introduction to Logic. LC 62-21468. 1962. pap. 3.95 (ISBN 0-15-645125-5, Harv). HarBraceJ.

Cohen, Morton H., ed. see Carroll, Lewis.

Cohen, Nancy Wainer & Estner, Lois J. Silent Knife: Cesarean Prevention & Vaginal Birth after Cesarean (VBAC) (Illus.). 480p. 1983. 29.95x (ISBN 0-89789-026-4); pap. 14.95x. J F Bergin.

Cohen, Neal P., jt. auth. see Kugel, Yerachmiel.

Cohen, Nicholas & Sigel, Michael, eds. The Reticuloendothelial System: Phylogeny & Ontogeny of the RES. (Vol. 3). 750p. 1982. 89.50x (ISBN 0-306-40928-3, Plenum Pr). Plenum Pub.

Cohen, Norm, ed. see Randolph, Vance.

Cohen, Patricia. A Calculating People: The Spread of Numeracy in Early America. LC 82-7089. (Illus.). 272p. 1983. lib. bdg. 22.50x (ISBN 0-226-11283-7). U of Chicago Pr.

Cohen, Patricia, jt. auth. see Cohen, Jacob.

Cohen, Peter J. Metabolic Aspects of Anesthesia. LC 74-12356. (Illus.). 116p. 1975. text ed. 11.00x o.p. (ISBN 0-8036-1970-7). Davis Co.

Cohen, Peter Z. Calm Horse, Wild Night. LC 82-1746. 168p. (gr. 4-8). 1982. 10.95 (ISBN 0-689-30918-X). Atheneum.

Cohen, Philip. Control of Enzyme Activity. (Outline Studies in Biology). 1976. pap. 6.50x (ISBN 0-412-13060-2, Pub. by Chapman & Hall). Methuen Inc.

Cohen, R. Dominance & Defiance: A Study of Martial Instability in an Islamic African Society. 1971. pap. 4.00 (ISBN 0-686-36563-1). Am Anthro Assn.

Cohen, R. B., et al, eds. see Hymer, S.

Cohen, R. J. Binge! It's Not a State of Hunger...It's a State of Mind. 1979. cancelled (ISBN 0-02-526950-X). Macmillan.

Cohen, R. S., ed. see Colloquim for the Philosophy of Science, Boston, 1969-1972.

Cohen, Raymond. Threat Perception in International Crisis. LC 79-3964. 214p. 1979. 22.50 (ISBN 0-299-08000-5). U of Wis Pr.

Cohen, Richard. Don't Mention the Moon. 1983. 15.95 (ISBN 0-399-31009-6). Seaview Bks.

Cohen, Richard M., et al. The Scrapbook History of Pro Football. expanded & updated ed. LC 79-7463. (Illus.). 1979. pap. 10.00 o.p. (ISBN 0-672-52614-X). Bobbs.

Cohen, Robert. Acting Power. LC 77-89918. 266p. 1978. text ed. 15.95 (ISBN 0-87484-408-8). Mayfield Pub.

--The Theatre. LC 80-84012. (Illus.). 433p. 1981. pap. text ed. 16.95 (ISBN 0-87484-459-2). Mayfield Pub.

Cohen, Robert & Harrop, John. Creative Play Direction. (Theater & Drama Ser). (Illus.). 304p. 1974. ref. ed. 18.95 (ISBN 0-13-190918-5). P-H.

Cohen, Robert & Wartofsky, Marx. Language, Logic, & Method. 1983. 69.50 (ISBN 90-277-0725-1, Pub. by Reidel Holland). Kluwer Boston.

Cohen, Robert, ed. Children's Conceptions of Spatial Relationships. LC 81-48564. 1982. 7.95x (ISBN 0-87589-875-0). Jossey-Bass.

Cohen, Robert D. & Jody, Ruth. Freshman Seminar: A New Orientation. LC 77-1682. (Westview Special Studies in Higher Education Ser.). 1978. PLB 20.00 o.p. (ISBN 0-89158-098-0); pap. text ed. 10.50 o.p. (ISBN 0-89158-099-9). Westview.

Cohen, Robert S. & Wartofsky, Marx. Epistemology, Methodology, & the Social Sciences. 1983. lib. bdg. 48.00 (ISBN 90-277-1454-1, Pub. by Reidel Holland). Kluwer Boston.

Cohen, Robert S., ed. see Neurath, Otto.

Cohen, Roberta G. & Lipkin, Gladys B. Therapeutic Group Work for Health Professionals. LC 79-12388. 1979. text ed. 19.95 o.p. (ISBN 0-8261-2310-4); pap. text ed. 12.50 (ISBN 0-8261-2311-2). Springer Pub.

Cohen, Robin, ed. see Nzula, A., et al.

Cohen, Roger, jt. auth. see Copeland, Roger.

Cohen, Rona, jt. auth. see Bagley, Vicky.

Cohen, Ronald & Mohl, Raymond. The Paradox of Progressive Education: The Gary Plan & Urban Schooling. (National University Publications,Interdisciplinary Urban Ser). 1979. 20.00 (ISBN 0-8046-9237-8). Kennikat.

Cohen, Ronald J. & Maiano, William E. Legal Guidebook in Mental Health. (Illus.). 624p. 1982. text ed. 39.95 (ISBN 0-02-905740-X). Free Pr.

Cohen, Rose. Out of the Shadow. LC 77-145475. (The American Immigration Library). 352p. 1971. Repr. of 1918 ed. lib. bdg. 17.95x (ISBN 0-89198-007-5). Ozer.

Cohen, Rosetta M. Domestic Scenes. 1982. pap. 4.00 (ISBN 0-936600-02-0). Riverstone Foothills.

Cohen, Rudolf. Patterns of Personality Judgement. Schaeffer, Dirk L., tr. 1973. 52.50 (ISBN 0-12-178950-0). Acad Pr.

Cohen, S., jt. auth. see Wood, M.

Cohen, S., et al. Mechanisms of Immunopathology. LC 78-18290. (Basic & Clinical Immunologies Ser.). 1979. 50.95 (ISBN 0-471-16429-1, Pub. by Wiley Medical). Wiley.

Cohen, S. I. & Ross, R. N. Handbook of Clinical Psychobiology & Pathology, 2 Vols. Date not set. Vol. 1. 25.00 (ISBN 0-07-011621-0); Vol. 2. 35.00 (ISBN 0-07-011622-9). McGraw.

Cohen, Sam. The Truth About the Neutron Bomb: The Inventor of the Bomb Speaks Out. LC 82-14239. 260p. 1983. 12.50 (ISBN 0-688-01646-4). Morrow.

Cohen, Sandee. All We Know of Heaven. (Orig.). 1981. pap. 2.75 o.p. (ISBN 0-451-09891-9, E9891, Sig). NAL.

Cohen, Sandra B. Resource Teaching: A Mainstreaming Simulation. 1978. pap. text ed. 5.95 o.p. (ISBN 0-675-08351-6); 140.00, 4 cassettes 4 filmstrips o.p. (ISBN 0-686-86342-9); avail. additional suppl. mat. o.p. Merrill.

Cohen, Sandra B. & Plaskon, Stephen P. Language Arts for the Mildly Handicapped. (Special Education Ser.). 544p. 1980. text ed. 19.95 (ISBN 0-675-08131-9). Merrill.

Cohen, Sanford. Issues in Labor Policy. new ed. (Economics). 1977. pap. text ed. 12.95 (ISBN 0-675-08517-9). Merrill.

--Labor in the United States. 5th ed. (Economics Ser.). 1979. text ed. 24.95 (ISBN 0-675-08299-4). Merrill.

Cohen, Sara K. Whoever Said Life Is Fair? Growing Through Life's Injustices. 1982. pap. 4.95 o.p. (ISBN 0-425-05318-0). Berkley Pub.

Cohen, Sarah B., ed. From Hester Street to Hollywood: The Jewish-American Stage & Screen. LC 82-47924. (Jewish Literature & Culture Ser.). 288p. 1983. 22.50x (ISBN 0-253-32500-5). Ind U Pr.

Cohen, Selma J. Stravinsky & the Dance: A Survey of Ballet Productions 1910-1962. LC 62-15840. (Illus., Orig.). 1962. pap. 5.00 o.p. (ISBN 0-87104-169-3). NY Pub Lib.

Cohen, Sharleen C. The Ladies of Beverly Hills. 470p. 1983. 14.95 (ISBN 0-440-04621-1). Delacorte.

Cohen, Sheldon S; see Weaver, Glenn.

Cohen, Shlomo. Bahamas Diver's Guide. (Illus.). 1979. 15.95 o.p. (ISBN 0-932200-03-6, Amphoto). Watson-Guptill.

--Red Sea Diver's Guide. (Illus.). 1979. 15.95 o.p. (ISBN 0-932200-00-1, Amphoto). Watson-Guptill.

--Sea I Love. (Illus.). 1979. 8.95 o.p. (ISBN 0-932200-04-4, Amphoto). Watson-Guptill.

Cohen, Sidney. The Alcoholism Problem: Selected Issues. 192p. 1983. text ed. 19.95 (ISBN 0-86656-209-5, B209); pap. text ed. 10.95 (ISBN 0-86656-179-X). Haworth Pr.

--Clinical Gastroenterology: A Problem Oriented Approach. (Biomedical Engineering & Health Systems Ser.). 440p. 1982. 25.00 (ISBN 0-471-08071-3, Pub. by Wiley Med). Wiley.

--The Drug Dilemma. 2nd ed. (Health Education Paperback Ser.). 144p. 1975. 16.95 (ISBN 0-07-011587-7, C); pap. text ed. 9.50 (ISBN 0-07-011588-5). McGraw.

--The Substance Abuse Problems. 408p. 1981. text ed. 29.95 (ISBN 0-917724-18-6, B18); pap. text ed. 19.95 (ISBN 0-917724-22-4, B22). Haworth Pr.

Cohen, Sidney, jt. auth. see Alpert, Richard.

Cohen, Sidney, ed. Drug Abuse & Alcoholism: Current Critical Issues. LC 79-25648. (Collected Essay Ser.). 1981. pap. text ed. 6.95 (ISBN 0-917724-10-0, B10). Haworth Pr.

Cohen, Sol, compiled by. Education in the United States: A Documentary History, 5 vols. LC 73-3099. 1974. Set. lib. bdg. 225.00 (ISBN 0-313-20141-2). Greenwood.

Cohen, Stan. The Civil War in West Virginia: A Pictorial History. rev. ed. LC 82-80964. (Illus.). 160p. (Orig.). 1982. pap. text ed. 8.95 (ISBN 0-933126-17-4). Pictorial Hist.

--The Eisenhowers: Gettysburg's First Family. (Illus.). 48p. 1983. 4.95 (ISBN 0-933126-25-5). Pictorial Hist.

--Yukon River Steamboats: A Pictorial History. LC 82-81717. (Illus.). 128p. (Orig.). 1982. pap. text ed. 8.95 (ISBN 0-933126-19-0). Pictorial Hist.

Cohen, Stan B. The Civil War in West Virginia: A Pictorial History. 3rd ed. LC 76-2880. (Illus.). 206p. 1976. pap. 5.95 o.p. (ISBN 0-933126-02-6). Pictorial Hist.

--Missoula County Images. (Illus.). 264p. 1982. 19.95 (ISBN 0-933126-24-7). Pictorial Hist.

Cohen, Stanley. Folk Devils & Moral Panics. 1980. 26.00 (ISBN 0-312-29699-1). St Martin.

--Law Enforcement Guide to United States Supreme Court Decisions. (Illus.). 232p. 1972. 19.75x (ISBN 0-398-02261-5). C C Thomas.

--Three Thirty Park. 1977. 8.95 o.p. (ISBN 0-399-11901-9). Putnam Pub Group.

Cohen, Stanley, ed. see American Consulting Engineers Council.

Cohen, Stanley, et al, eds. Biology of the Lymphokines. LC 78-825. 1979. 48.50 (ISBN 0-12-178250-6). Acad Pr.

Cohen, Stanley N. & Armstrong, Marsha F. Drug Interactions: A Handbook for Clinical Use. LC 74-11082. 385p. 1974. 24.00 (ISBN 0-683-01942-2). Krieger.

Cohen, Stephan, jt. auth. see Sussman, Alan.

Cohen, Stephen & Burns, Richard C. Pathways of the Pulp. 2nd ed. LC 79-15286. 780p. 1979. pap. 49.95 (ISBN 0-8016-1009-5). Mosby.

Cohen, Stephen D. The Making of United States International Economic Policy: Principles, Problems, & Proposals for Reform. LC 77-7469. 1977. text ed. 29.95 o.p. (ISBN 0-03-021926-4); pap. 12.95 o.p. (ISBN 0-03-021921-3). Praeger.

Cohen, Stephen D. & Meltzer, Ronald L. U. S. International Economic Policy in Action. 224p. 1982. 28.95 (ISBN 0-03-061906-8); pap. 12.95 (ISBN 0-03-063308-7). Praeger.

Cohen, Stephen P. The Indian Army: Its Contribution to the Development of a Nation. LC 77-111421. 1971. 36.00x (ISBN 0-520-01697-1). U of Cal Pr.

Cohen, Stephen S. Modern Capitalist Planning: The French Model. new ed. 1977. 36.00x (ISBN 0-520-02793-0); pap. 9.50x (ISBN 0-520-02892-9, CAMPUS 141). U of Cal Pr.

Cohen, Steven M. & Hyman, Paula, eds. The Evolving Jewish Family. 256p. 1983. text ed. 30.00x (ISBN 0-8419-0860-5). Holmes & Meier.

Cohen, Stewart. Social & Personality Development in Childhood. 1976. pap. 9.95x (ISBN 0-02-323140-8, 32314). Macmillan.

Cohen, Stuart, ed. Proceedings of Towing Tank Conference, 2 vols. LC 81-65041. 1329p. 1981. Set. text ed. 98.00 (ISBN 0-250-40444-3). Ann Arbor Science.

Cohen, Stuart J., ed. New Directions in Patient Compliance. (Illus.). 1979. 18.95x (ISBN 0-669-02721-9). Lexington Bks.

Cohen, Theodore J. & Bray, Jacqueline H. The Magic Machine. (Illus.). (ps-3). 1979. 2.00 (ISBN 0-07-011579-6, BYTE Bks). McGraw.

Cohen, Tirza, jt. ed. see Bonne-Tamir, Batsheva.

Cohen, U., jt. auth. see Moore, Gary T.

Cohen, Warren I. America's Response to China: An Interpretive History of Sino-American Relations. 2nd ed. LC 80-13383. (America & the World Ser.). 271p. 1980. pap. text ed. 12.95 (ISBN 0-471-06089-5). Wiley.

Cohen, Warren I., ed. New Frontiers in American-East Asian Relations. (Studies of the East Asian Institute). 344p. 1983. text ed. 30.00x (ISBN 0-231-05630-3); pap. 15.00 (ISBN 0-231-05631-1). Columbia U Pr.

Cohen, Wayne R. & Friedman, Emanuel A., eds. Management of Labor. 1983. price not set (ISBN 0-8391-1816-3, 17884). Univ Park.

Cohen, William A. Building a Mail Order Business: A Complete Manual for Success. LC 81-16071. 442p. 1982. 17.95 (ISBN 0-471-08803-X, Pub. by Wiley-Interscience). Wiley.

--The Entrepeneur & Small Business Problem Solver: A Complete Guide to Owning & Operating Your Own Business. 445p. 1983. 31.95x o.p. (ISBN 0-471-86740-3). Ronald Pr.

Cohen, William S. & Lasson, Kenneth. How to Get the Most Out of Washington: Using Congress to Move the Federal Bureaucracy. 256p. 1982. 14.95x (ISBN 0-87196-537-2). Facts on File.

Cohen, Yaveff & Converse, Phillip E. Representation & Development in Brazil, Nineteen Seventy-Two to Nineteen Seventy-Three. 2nd ed. write for info (ISBN 0-89138-950-4). ICPSR.

Cohen-Stratyner, Barbara. Biographical Dictionary of Dance. 1982. lib. bdg. 75.00x (ISBN 0-02-870260-3). Schirmer Bks.

Cohen-Tannoudji, Claude, et al. Quantum Mechanics, 2 vols. LC 76-5874. 1978. Vol. 1. 48.95 o.p. (ISBN 0-471-16432-1, Pub. by Wiley-Interscience); 43.95 o.p. (ISBN 0-471-16434-8); Vol. 1. pap. 28.50 o.p. (ISBN 0-471-16433-X); Vol. 2. pap. 26.95 o.p. (ISBN 0-471-16435-6). Wiley.

Cohler, David. Gamemaker. 1981. pap. 2.50 o.p. (ISBN 0-451-09766-1, E9766, Sig). NAL.

Cohler, David K. The Gamemaker. LC 79-6035. 1980. 10.00 o.p. (ISBN 0-385-15650-2). Doubleday.

Cohn. Pancreatic Cancer: New Directions in Therapeutic Management. LC 81-4945. (Masson Cancer Management Ser.). 128p. 1981. 33.00x (ISBN 0-89352-133-7). Masson Pub.

Cohn, Adrian, jt. auth. see Bell, James K.

Cohn, Adrian A., jt. auth. see Bell, James K.

Cohn, Alvin W. Crime & Justice Administration. LC 76-798. 1976. text ed. 18.50 scp o.p. (ISBN 0-397-47344-3, HarpC). Har-Row.

Cohn, Arthur. The Collector's Twentieth-Century Music in the Western Hemisphere. LC 74-167848. (Music Ser.). 1972. Repr. of 1961 ed. 27.50 (ISBN 0-306-70404-8). Da Capo.

--Recorded Classical Music: A Critical Guide to Compositions & Performances. 2164p. 1981. 75.00 (ISBN 0-686-97300-3). Macmillan.

--Twentieth-Century Music in Western Europe: The Compositions & Recordings. LC 70-39297. 510p. 1972. Repr. of 1965 ed. lib. bdg. 42.50 (ISBN 0-306-70460-9). Da Capo.

Cohn, D. V., et al, eds. Hormonal Control of Calcium Metabolism. (International Congress Ser.: No. 511). 1981. 98.75 (ISBN 0-444-90193-0). Elsevier.

Cohn, David L. Life & Times of King Cotton. LC 73-11996. 286p. 1974. Repr. of 1956 ed. lib. bdg. 15.75x (ISBN 0-8371-7115-6, COKC). Greenwood.

Cohn, Davis L., jt. auth. see Melsa, James L.

Cohn, Don J., tr. see Lao She.

Cohn, E. J. Manual of German Law, 2 Vols. LC 67-28195. 1968-71. Set. 58.00 (ISBN 0-686-96820-4); Vol. 1. 35.00 (ISBN 0-379-00296-5); Vol. 2. 23.00 (ISBN 0-379-00297-3). Oceana.

Cohn, E. J., et al, eds. Handbook of Institutional Arbitration in International Trade: Rules, Facts & Figures. 1977. 64.00 (ISBN 0-7204-0567-X, North-Holland). Elsevier.

Cohn, Elchanan. The Economics of Education. 2nd ed. LC 78-13277. 480p. 1978. text ed. 22.50x (ISBN 0-88410-185-1). Ballinger Pub.

Cohn, Elchanan, et al. Input-Output Analysis in Public Education. LC 75-19249. 160p. 1975. prof ref 22.00x (ISBN 0-88410-155-X). Ballinger Pub.

Cohn, Ellen R. & McWilliams, Betty J. Clinical Orofacial Assessment. 200p. 1983. text ed. 20.00 (ISBN 0-941158-13-6, D1078-8). Mosby.

Cohn, Florence, et al. Real Estate Ad Guide. 1982. cancelled (ISBN 0-8359-6510-4). Reston.

Cohn, Georg. Existentialism & Legal Science. LC 67-14397. 148p. 1967. 12.00 (ISBN 0-379-00302-3). Oceana.

Cohn, Laurence S. Effective Use of ANS COBOL Computer Programming Language: A Supplemental Text for Programmers Working with IBM's OS & DOS Systems. LC 75-5584. (Business Data Processing Ser). 178p. 1975. 31.95x o.p. (ISBN 0-471-16436-4, Pub. by Wiley-Interscience). Wiley.

Cohn, Lawrence H. & Gallucci, Vincenzo, eds. Cardiac Bioprosthesis: Proceedings of the Second International Symposium. (Illus.). 596p. 1982. text ed. 65.00 (ISBN 0-914316-34-6). Yorke Med.

Cohn, Louis F. & McVoy, Gary R. Environmental Analysis of Transportation Systems. LC 81-14637. 374p. 1982. 44.95x (ISBN 0-471-08098-5, Pub. by Wiley-Interscience). Wiley.

Cohn, Marian R., jt. auth. see Bristow, Camille.

Cohn, Marvin. Helping Your Teen-Age Student: What Parents Can Do to Improve Reading & Study Skills. 1980. pap. 2.50 o.p. (ISBN 0-451-09502-2, E9502, Sig). NAL.

Cohn, Nik, jt. auth. see Peelaert, Guy.

Cohn, Norman. Europe's Inner Demons: An Enquiry Inspired by the Great Witch-Hunt. 1977. pap. 5.95 (ISBN 0-452-00584-1, F584, Mer). NAL.

--Pursuit of the Millennium. rev ed. 1970. pap. 9.95 (ISBN 0-19-500456-6, 321, GB). Oxford U Pr.

--Warrent for Genocide. LC 80-21733. pap. 15.00 (ISBN 0-89130-423-1, 14 00 23). Scholars Pr CA.

Cohn, P. M. Algebra, 2 vols. LC 73-2780. Vol. 1, 1974, 384p. 41.50 o.p. (ISBN 0-471-16430-5, Pub. by Wiley-Interscience); Vol. 2, 1977. 34.95 (ISBN 0-471-01823-6); Vol. 1. pap. 23.95 (ISBN 0-471-16431-3, Pub. by Wiley-Interscience). Wiley.

--Algebra, Vol. 1. 2nd ed. 410p. 1982. 23.95 (ISBN 0-471-10168-0, Pub. by Wiley-Interscience); pap. 23.95x (ISBN 0-471-10169-9). Wiley.

--Linear Equations. (Library of Mathematics). 1971. pap. 4.95 (ISBN 0-7100-6181-1). Routledge & Kegan.

--Skew Field Constructions. LC 76-46854. (London Mathematical Society Lecture Note Series: No. 27). (Illus.). 1977. limp bdg. 29.95x (ISBN 0-521-21497-1). Cambridge U Pr.

Cohn, Richard M. Difference Algebra. LC 77-28532. 372p. 1980. Repr. of 1965 ed. lib. bdg. 21.50 (ISBN 0-88275-651-6). Krieger.

Cohn, Robert G. Mallarme's un Coup de Des: An Exegesis. 1949. text ed. 24.50x (ISBN 0-686-83613-8). Elliots Bks.

Cohn, Robert L. The Shape of Sacred Space: Four Biblical Studies. LC 80-11086. (Studies in Religion: No. 23). pap. 8.50 (ISBN 0-89130-384-7, 01-00-23). Scholars Pr CA.

Cohn, Rosanne. Discover Seattle with Kids. 3rd ed. LC 80-12134. (Illus.). 160p. (Orig.). 1982. pap. 5.95 (ISBN 0-916076-55-5). Writing.

Cohn, Sherman L. Constitutional Law: Part One, the Federal Judiciary. 1968. pap. 6.00x o.p. (ISBN 0-685-14176-4). Lerner Law.

--Current Materials on Civil Procedure. 1972. pap. 14.95 o.p. (ISBN 0-685-14184-5). Lerner Law.

Cohn, Sidney A. & Gottlieb, Marvin. Anatomy Review. 6th ed. LC 80-20349. (Basic Science Review Bks.). 1980. pap. 11.95 (ISBN 0-87488-201-X). Med Exam.

Cohn, Sidney A. & Gottlieb, Marvin I. Head & Neck Anatomy Review. (Basic Science Review Bks.). 1976. spiral bdg. 12.95 o.p. (ISBN 0-87488-222-2). Med Exam.

Cohn, Theodore & Lindberg, Roy. Survival & Growth: Management Strategies for the Small Firm. 1978. pap. 2.25 (ISBN 0-451-61624-3, ME1624, Ment). NAL.

Cohn, Waldo, ed. Progress in Nucleic Acid Research & Molecular Biology, Vol. 27. (Serial Publication). 320p. 1982. 37.00 (ISBN 0-12-540027-6); Lib. ed. 48.50 (ISBN 0-686-81656-0); Microfische 26.00 (ISBN 0-12-540099-3). Acad Pr.

Cohn, Waldo E., ed. Progress in Nucleic Acid Research & Molecular Biology, Vol. 24. 1980. 37.50 (ISBN 0-12-540024-1); lib. ed. 48.50 (ISBN 0-12-540092-6); microfiche ed. 26.00 (ISBN 0-12-540093-4). Acad Pr.

Cohn, Werner. The Gypsies. 1973. pap. text ed. 5.95 o.p. (ISBN 0-8461-1362-7). Benjamin-Cummings.

Cohn-Vossen, Stephan, jt. auth. see Hilbert, David.

Cohrs, Timothy. Tendencies. 240p. 1983. 12.95 (ISBN 0-312-79099-6). St Martin.

Coil, Henry W. Conversations on Freemasonry. 1980. Repr. soft cover 12.50 (ISBN 0-88053-035-9). Macoy Pub.

Coit, Margaret L. The Growing Years, 1789-1829. LC 63-8572. (Life History of the United States). (Illus.). (gr. 5 up). 1974. PLB 10.60 (ISBN 0-8094-0552-0, Pub. by Time-Life). Silver.

--John C. Calhoun. LC 50-5234. 1977. 16.95 (ISBN 0-910220-85-9). Berg.

--The Sweep Westward, 1829-1849. LC 63-8572. (Life History of the United States). (Illus.). (gr. 5 up). 1974. PLB 10.60 (ISBN 0-8094-0553-9, Pub. by Time-Life). Silver.

Coit, Stanton, tr. see Hartmann, Nicolai.

Cok, Mary V., et al. All in Order: Information Systems for the Arts. LC 81-9506. (Illus.). 191p. 1981. pap. 7.95 (ISBN 0-89062-132-2, Pub by National Assembly State Arts Agencies). Pub Ctr Cult Res.

Cokayne, G. E. The Complete Peerage - Of England, Scotland, Ireland, Great Britain & the United Kingdom, Extant, Extinct or Dormant, 6 Vols. 2850p. Repr. Set. text ed. 675.00x (ISBN 0-904387-82-8, Pub. by Alan Sutton England). Humanities.

Coke, Desmond. Art of Silhouette. LC 73-110809. (Illus.). 1970. Repr. of 1913 ed. 34.00x (ISBN 0-8103-3549-2). Gale.

Coke, Paul T. Mountain & Wilderness. 1978. pap. 1.00 (ISBN 0-8164-2177-3). Seabury.

Coke, Tom S. Life in a Fishbowl. 1978. pap. 3.95 (ISBN 0-88207-764-3). Victor Bks.

--More Than Just You. 1979. pap. 3.95 (ISBN 0-88207-578-0). Victor Bks.

Coke, Van Deren. Nordfeldt the Painter. LC 71-183866. (Illus.). 149p. 1972. 12.00 o.p. (ISBN 0-8263-0221-1). U of NM Pr.

--The Painter & the Photograph: From Delacroix to Warhol. rev ed. LC 75-129804. (Illus.). 324p. 1972. pap. 24.95x (ISBN 0-8263-0325-0). U of NM Pr.

Coke, Van Deren, ed. One Hundred Years of Photographic History: Essays in Honor of Beaumont Newhall. LC 74-83381. (Illus.). 192p. 1975. 17.50x o.p. (ISBN 0-8263-0344-7). U of NM Pr.

Coker, Elizabeth B. The Grasshopper King: A Story of Two Confederate Exiles in Mexico During the Reign of Maximillian & Carllota. 336p. 1981. 13.50 o.p. (ISBN 0-525-10716-9, 01311-390). Dutton.

Coker, Gylbert. Naptime. LC 78-50415. (Illus.). (ps-2). 1978. 5.95 o.s.i. (ISBN 0-440-06303-5); PLB 5.47 o.s.i. (ISBN 0-440-06304-3). Delacorte.

Coker, Hazel P., jt. auth. see Coker, William S.

Coker, Jerry. The Jazz Idiom. (Illus.). 96p. 1975. 7.95 o.p. (ISBN 0-13-509851-3, Spec); pap. 2.95 o.p. (ISBN 0-13-509844-0, Spec). P-H.

--Listening to Jazz. 148p. 1982. 9.95 (ISBN 0-13-537217-8); pap. 5.95 (ISBN 0-13-537225-9). P-H.

Coker, Lawrence T. & Gaddis, Robert S., eds. Protective Coatings for Structural Steel in New Construction for the Pulp & Paper Industry. (TAPPI PRESS Reports). 38p. 1980. pap. 34.95 (ISBN 0-89852-380-X, 01-01-R080). TAPPI.

Coker, Paul. The Mad Book of Pet Care, Etiquette & Advice. 192p. (Orig.). 1983. pap. 1.95 (ISBN 0-446-30065-9). Warner Bks.

Coker, Peter. Etching Techniques. 1976. 22.50 (ISBN 0-7134-3063-X, Pub. by Batsford England). David & Charles.

Coker, W. C. The Clavarias of the United States & Canada. 1932. Repr. 32.00 (ISBN 3-7682-0913-X). Lubrecht & Cramer.

--The Saprolegniaceae with Notes on Other Water Molds. (Illus.). 1969. Repr. of 1923 ed. 25.60 (ISBN 3-7682-0620-3). Lubrecht & Cramer.

Coker, W. C. & Beers, A. H. The Stipitate Hydnums of the Eastern U.S. (Illus.). 1970. Repr. of 1951 ed. 25.60 (ISBN 3-7682-0695-5). Lubrecht & Cramer.

Coker, W. C. & Couch, J. N. The Gastromycetes of the Eastern U. S. & Canada. 1969. pap. 25.60 (ISBN 3-7682-0602-5). Lubrecht & Cramer.

Coker, William S. & Coker, Hazel P. The Siege of Mobile, Seventeen Eighty in Maps: With Data on Troop Strength, Military Units, Ships, Casualties, & Prisoners of War. LC 82-675288. (Spanish Borderlands Ser.: Vol. 9). (Illus.). 131p. (Orig.). 1982. pap. text ed. 12.95x (ISBN 0-933776-11-X). Perdido Bay.

Colaianne, A. J. Piers Plowman: An Annotated Bibliography of Editions & Criticism, 1550-1977. LC 78-7631. (Garland Reference Library of the Humanities: Vol. 121). 1978. lib. bdg. 18.00 o.s.i. (ISBN 0-8240-9822-6). Garland Pub.

Colaice, William M. see Squire, Lucy F., et al.

Colander, David, jt. auth. see Lerner, Abba.

Colander, David C. Solutions to Unemployment. 229p. 1981. pap. text ed. 8.95 (ISBN 0-15-582456-2, HC). HarBraceJ.

Colander, David C., ed. Selected Economic Writings of Abba P. Lerner. (Selected Economic Writings Ser.). 752p. 1983. text ed. 65.00X (ISBN 0-8147-1385-8). NYU Pr.

--Solutions to Inflation. 220p. 1979. pap. text ed. 8.95 (ISBN 0-15-582450-3, HC). HarBraceJ.

Colangelo, Cheryl, jt. auth. see Bergen, Adrienne F.

Colangelo, Nicholas & Zaffrann, Ronald T. New Voices in Counseling the Gifted. 1979. pap. text ed. 15.95 (ISBN 0-8403-1998-3). Kendall-Hunt.

Colangelo, Nicholas, jt. auth. see Pulvino, Charles J.

Colangelo, Nicholas & Pulvino, Charles, eds. Counseling the Elderly. 1980. 3.00 (ISBN 0-686-36384-1). Am Personnel.

Colangelo, Nicholas, et al. The Human Relations Experience: Exercises in Multiculteral Nonsexist Education. LC 81-18104. (Psychology - Counseling Ser.). 274p. 1982. pap. text ed. 9.95 (ISBN 0-534-01104-7). Brooks-Cole.

--Multicultural Nonsexist Education: A Human Relations Approach. 1979. pap. text ed. 15.95 (ISBN 0-8403-2052-3). Kendall-Hunt.

Colangelo, V. & Thornton, P. A. Engineering Aspects of Product Liability. 1981. 75.00 (ISBN 0-87170-103-0). ASM.

Colangelo, Vito J. & Heiser, F. A. Analysis of Metallurgical Failures. LC 73-19773. (Science & Technology of Materials Ser). 384p. 1974. 42.50x (ISBN 0-471-16450-X, Pub. by Wiley-Interscience). Wiley.

Colbeck, John, jt. auth. see Billington, Dora.

Colbeck, Maurice. Yorkshire Moorlands. (Illus.). 160p. 1983. 22.50 (ISBN 0-7134-3803-7, Pub. by Batsford England). David & Charles.

Colbert, E. H., jt. ed. see Kay, Marshall.

Colbert, Edwin H. An Outline of Vertebrate Evolution. Head, J. J., ed. LC 81-67987. (Carolina Biology Readers Ser.). (Illus.). 32p. (gr. 10 up). 1983. pap. 2.00 (ISBN 0-89278-331-1, 45-9731). Carolina Biological.

Colbert, Evelyn S. The Left Wing in Japanese Politics. LC 73-5263. 353p. 1973. Repr. of 1952 ed. lib. bdg. 18.50x (ISBN 0-8371-6880-5, COJP). Greenwood.

Colbert, Paul. Life is a Spiritual Experience. LC 82-70932. 91p. 1982. pap. 4.95 (ISBN 0-9608164-0-2). Flower Truth.

Colbert, Roman. Brief Spanish Reference Grammar. 1975. text ed. 5.50x (ISBN 0-442-21616-5). Van Nos Reinhold.

Colbin, Annemarie. The Book of Whole Meals: A Seasonal Guide to Assembling Balanced Vegetarian Breakfasts, Lunches & Dinners. 240p. (Orig.). 1983. pap. 7.95 (ISBN 0-345-30982-0). Ballantine.

Colborn, J. G. The Thermal Structure of the Indian Ocean. (International Indian Ocean Expedition Oceanographic Monographs: No. 2). 144p. 1975. text ed. 17.50x (ISBN 0-8248-0349-3, Eastwest Ctr). UH Pr.

Colborne, Robert. Fundamentals of Merchandise Presentation. LC 82-61469. (Illus.). 208p. 1983. 18.00 (ISBN 0-911380-59-0). Signs of Times.

Colbourn, Trevor, jt. auth. see Bedford, Henry F.

Colburn, C. B., ed. Developments in Inorganic Nitrogen Chemistry, Vol. 2. 1973. 42.75 (ISBN 0-444-40962-9, Pub. by Applied Sci England). Elsevier.

Colburn, Robert E. Fire Protection & Suppression. Williams, Carlton, ed. (Illus.). 352p. 1975. text ed. 22.50 (ISBN 0-07-011680-6, 11680-6, G); instructor's manual 4.50 (ISBN 0-07-011681-4). McGraw.

Colburn, William & Weinberg, Sanford. Listening & Audience Analysis. rev. ed. Applbaum, Ronald & Hart, Roderick, eds. (MODCOM, Modules in Speech Communication Ser.). 1980. pap. text ed. 2.75 (ISBN 0-574-22568-4, 13-5568). SRA.

Colby, Averil. Patchwork. (Illus.). 1976. pap. 10.50 o.p. (ISBN 0-8231-5009-7). Branford.

--Patchwork. (Illus.). 202p. 1982. pap. 12.95 (ISBN 0-684-17605-X, ScribT). Scribner.

--Patchwork Quilts. 1965. 17.50 (ISBN 0-7134-3025-7, Pub. by Batsford England). David & Charles.

--Pincushions. 1975. 19.95 o.p. (ISBN 0-7134-3030-3, Pub. by Batsford England). David & Charles.

Colby, Benjamin N. & Van Den Berghe, Pierre L. Ixil Country: A Plural Society in Highland Guatemala. LC 68-16740. 1969. 27.50x (ISBN 0-520-01515-0). U of Cal Pr.

Colby, C. B. Air Force Academy: Cadets, Training & Equipment. (Illus.). (gr. 4-7). 1962. PLB 5.29 o.p. (ISBN 0-698-30005-X, Coward). Putnam Pub Group.

--Aircraft of World War One: Fighters, Scouts, Bombers & Observation Planes. (Illus.). (gr. 4-7). 1962. PLB 5.99 (ISBN 0-698-30003-3, Coward). Putnam Pub Group.

--America's Natural Wonders: Strange Forests, Mysterious Caverns, & Amazing Formations. (Illus.). (gr. 4-7). 1956. PLB 5.29 o.p. (ISBN 0-698-30009-2, Coward). Putnam Pub Group.
--Annapolis: Cadets, Training & Equipment. (Illus.). (gr. 4-7). 1964. PLB 5.99 (ISBN 0-698-30014-9, Coward). Putnam Pub Group.
--Arms of Our Fighting Men: Personnel Weapons, Bazookas, Big Guns. rev. ed. (Illus.). (gr. 4-7). 1972. PLB 5.99 (ISBN 0-698-30432-2, Coward). Putnam Pub Group.
--Astronauts in Training: How Our Astronauts Prepare for Space Exploration. (Illus.). (gr. 4-7). 1969. PLB 5.99 (ISBN 0-698-30018-1, Coward). Putnam Pub Group.
--Atom at Work: How Nuclear Power Can Benefit Man. (Illus.). (gr. 4-7). 1968. PLB 5.29 o.p. (ISBN 0-698-30020-3, Coward). Putnam Pub Group.
--Beyond the Moon: Future Explorations in Interplanetary Space. (Illus.). (gr. 4-7). 1971. PLB 5.29 o.p. (ISBN 0-698-30023-8, Coward). Putnam Pub Group.
--Big Game: Animals of the Americas, Africa & Asia. (Illus.). (gr. 4-7). 1967. PLB 5.29 o.p. (ISBN 0-698-30024-6, Coward). Putnam Pub Group.
--Bomber Parade: Headliners in Bomber Plane History. (Illus.). (gr. 4-7). 1960. PLB 5.29 (ISBN 0-698-30027-0, Coward). Putnam Pub Group.
--Border Patrol: How U. S. Agents Protect Our Borders from Illegal Entry. (Illus.). 48p. (gr. 4-7). 1974. PLB 5.99 (ISBN 0-698-30542-6, Coward). Putnam Pub Group.
--Chute! Air Drop for Defense & Sport. (Illus.). 48p. (gr. 4-7). 1973. PLB 5.99 o.p. (ISBN 0-698-30447-0, Coward). Putnam Pub Group.
--Civil War Weapons: Small Arms, & Artillery of the Blue & Gray. (Illus.). (gr. 4-7). 1962. PLB 5.99 (ISBN 0-698-30046-7, Coward). Putnam Pub Group.
--Cliff Dwellings: Ancient Ruins from America's Past. (Illus.). (gr. 4-7). 1965. PLB 5.19 o.p. (ISBN 0-698-30048-3, Coward). Putnam Pub Group.
--Communications: How Man Talks to Man Across Land, Sea & Space. (Illus.). (gr. 4-7). 1964. PLB 5.99 o.p. (ISBN 0-698-30051-3, Coward). Putnam Pub Group.
--Countdown: Rockets & Missiles for National Defense. rev. ed. LC 70-125328. (Illus.). (gr. 4-7). 1970. PLB 5.99 o.p. (ISBN 0-698-30056-4, Coward). Putnam Pub Group.
--Danger Fighters: Men & Ships of the U.S. Coast Guard. (Illus.). (gr. 4-7). 1953. PLB 5.29 o.p. (ISBN 0-698-30060-2, Coward). Putnam Pub Group.
--Early American Crafts: Tools, Shops & Products. (Illus.). (gr. 4-7). 1967. PLB 5.99 (ISBN 0-698-30066-1, Coward). Putnam Pub Group.
--FBI: How the G-Men Use Science As Well As Weapons to Combat Crime. rev. ed. (Illus.). (gr. 4-7). 1970. PLB 5.99 o.p. (ISBN 0-698-30073-4, Coward). Putnam Pub Group.
--Fighter Parade: Headliners in Fighter Plane History. (Illus.). (gr. 4-7). 1960. PLB 5.99 (ISBN 0-698-30076-9, Coward). Putnam Pub Group.
--Fighting Gear of World War One: Equipment & Weapons of the American Doughboy. (Illus.). (gr. 4-7). 1961. PLB 5.99 (ISBN 0-698-30077-7, Coward). Putnam Pub Group.
--Fighting Gear of World War Two: Equipment & Weapons of the American G. I. (Illus.). (gr. 4-7). 1961. PLB 5.99 (ISBN 0-698-30078-5, Coward). Putnam Pub Group.
--Firearms by Winchester: A Part of U.S. History. (Illus.). (gr. 4-7). 1957. PLB 5.99 (ISBN 0-698-30079-3, Coward). Putnam Pub Group.
--First Boat: How to Pick It & Use It for Fun Afloat. (Illus.). (gr. 4-7). 1956. PLB 4.79 o.p. (ISBN 0-698-30080-7, Coward). Putnam Pub Group.
--First Bow & Arrow: How to Use It Skillfully for Outdoor Fun. (Illus.). (gr. 4-7). 1955. PLB 4.79 o.p. (ISBN 0-698-30081-5, Coward). Putnam Pub Group.
--First Camping Trip: How to Make It Easier & More Comfortable. (Illus.). (gr. 4-7). 1955. PLB 4.79 o.p. (ISBN 0-698-30082-3, Coward). Putnam Pub Group.
--First Fish: What You Should Do to Catch Him. (Illus.). (gr. 4-7). 1953. PLB 4.79 o.p. (ISBN 0-698-30084-X, Coward). Putnam Pub Group.
--First Hunt: With Success & Safety. (Illus.). (gr. 4-7). 1957. PLB 4.79 o.p. (ISBN 0-698-30085-8, Coward). Putnam Pub Group.
--First Rifle: How to Shoot It Straight & Use It Safely. (Illus.). (gr. 4-7). 1954. 5.99 (ISBN 0-698-30086-6, Coward). Putnam Pub Group.
--Fish & Wildlife: The Story of the Work of the U. S. Fish & Wildlife Service. (Illus.). (gr. 4-7). 1955. 5.29 o.p. (ISBN 0-698-30088-2, Coward). Putnam Pub Group.
--Frogmen: Training, Equipment & Operations of Our Navy's Undersea Fighters. (Illus.). (gr. 4-7). 1954. PLB 5.29 o.p. (ISBN 0-698-30096-3, Coward). Putnam Pub Group.
--Hidden Treasure: What, Where, & How to Find It. (Illus.). 48p. (gr. 4-7). 1975. PLB 5.99 (ISBN 0-698-30572-8, Coward). Putnam Pub Group.
--Historic American Forts: From Frontier Stockade to Coastal Fortress. (Illus.). (gr. 4-7). 1963. PLB 5.19 o.p. (ISBN 0-698-30189-7, Coward). Putnam Pub Group.
--Historic American Landmarks: From the Old North Church to the Santa Fe Trail. (Illus.). (gr. 4-7). 1968. PLB 5.29 o.p. (ISBN 0-698-30190-0, Coward). Putnam Pub Group.
--Jets of the World: New Fighters, Bombers, & Transports. (Illus.). (gr. 4-7). 1966. PLB 5.99 (ISBN 0-698-30202-8, Coward). Putnam Pub Group.
--Leatherneck: The Training, Weapons, & Equipment of the U. S. Marine Corps. (Illus.). (gr. 4-7). 1957. PLB 5.99 o.p. (ISBN 0-698-30212-5, Coward). Putnam Pub Group.
--Moon Exploration: Space Stations, Moon Maps, Lunar Vehicles. LC 76-125328. (Illus.). (gr. 4-7). 1970. 5.99 (ISBN 0-698-30239-7, Coward). Putnam Pub Group.
--Musket to M-14: Pistols, Rifles & Machine Guns Through the Years. (Illus.). (gr. 4-7). 1960. PLB 5.99 (ISBN 0-698-30246-X, Coward). Putnam Pub Group.
--National Guard: Purpose, Training & Equipment. (Illus.). (gr. 4-7). 1968. PLB 5.19 o.p. (ISBN 0-698-30250-8, Coward). Putnam Pub Group.
--Night People: Workers from Dusk to Dawn. (Illus.). (gr. 4-7). 1972. PLB 5.19 o.p. (ISBN 0-698-30257-5, Coward). Putnam Pub Group.
--North American Air Defense Command: How the U.S.A. & Canada Stand Guard Together. (Illus.). (gr. 4-7). 1969. PLB 5.19 o.p. (ISBN 0-698-30261-3, Coward). Putnam Pub Group.
--Our Space Age Army: Weapons, Vehicles & Aircraft of the Modern U.S. Army. (Illus.). (gr. 4-7). 1961. PLB 5.99 o.p. (ISBN 0-698-30273-7, Coward). Putnam Pub Group.
--Our Space Age Jets: A Completely Revised Edition of Our Fighting Jets. (Illus.). (gr. 4-7). 1959. PLB 5.99 (ISBN 0-698-30274-5, Coward). Putnam Pub Group.
--Our Space Age Navy: Carriers, Aircraft, Submarines & Missles. (Illus.). (gr. 4-7). 1962. PLB 5.99 o.p. (ISBN 0-698-30275-3, Coward). Putnam Pub Group.
--Park Ranger: Equipment, Training & Work of the National Park Rangers. rev. ed. LC 71-150276. (Illus.). (gr. 4-7). 1971. PLB 5.29 o.p. (ISBN 0-698-30278-8, Coward). Putnam Pub Group.
--Police: Skill & Science Combat Crime. rev. ed. (Illus.). (gr. 4-7). 1971. PLB 5.99 (ISBN 0-698-30285-0, Coward). Putnam Pub Group.
--Railroads U. S. A. Steam Trains to Super Trains. (Illus.). (gr. 4-7). 1970. PLB 5.99 (ISBN 0-698-30288-5, Coward). Putnam Pub Group.
--Revolutionary War Weapons: Pole Arms, Hand Guns, Shoulder Arms & Artillery. (Illus.). (gr. 4-7). 1963. PLB 5.99 (ISBN 0-698-30290-7, Coward). Putnam Pub Group.
--Sailing Ships: Great Ships Before the Age of Steam. (Illus.). (gr. 4-7). 1970. PLB 5.99 (ISBN 0-698-30301-6, Coward). Putnam Pub Group.
--Secret Service: History, Duties & Equipment. (Illus.). (gr. 4-7). 1966. PLB 5.29 o.p. (ISBN 0-698-30309-1, Coward). Putnam Pub Group.
--Ships of Commerce: Liners, Tankers, Freighters, Floating Grain Elevators, Tugboats. (Illus.). (gr. 4-7). 1963. PLB 5.29 o.p. (ISBN 0-698-30312-1, Coward). Putnam Pub Group.
--Ships of Our Navy: Carriers, Battleships, Destroyers, Transports & Landing Craft. (Illus.). (gr. 4-7). 1963. PLB 5.99 (ISBN 0-698-30313-X, Coward). Putnam Pub Group.
--The Signal Corps Today: Its History & Role in Modern Warfare. (Illus.). (gr. 4-7). 1966. PLB 5.29 o.p. (ISBN 0-698-30314-8, Coward). Putnam Pub Group.
--Small Game: Animals of the Americas. (Illus.). (gr. 4-7). 1968. PLB 5.29 o.p. (ISBN 0-698-30317-2, Coward). Putnam Pub Group.
--Smoke Eaters: Trucks, Training & Tools of the Nation's Firemen. (Illus.). (gr. 4-7). 1954. PLB 5.19 o.p. (ISBN 0-698-30318-0, Coward). Putnam Pub Group.
--Space Age Fire Fighters: New Weapons in the Fireman's Arsenal. LC 73-82034. (Illus.). 48p. (gr. 4-7). 1974. PLB 5.99 (ISBN 0-698-30531-0, Coward). Putnam Pub Group.
--Space Age Spinoffs: Space Program Benefits for All Mankind. (Illus.). 48p. (gr. 4-7). 1972. PLB 5.99 (ISBN 0-698-30420-9, Coward). Putnam Pub Group.
--Special Forces: The U.S. Army's Experts in Unconventional Warfare. (Illus.). (gr. 4-7). 1964. PLB 5.99 (ISBN 0-698-30326-1, Coward). Putnam Pub Group.
--Submarine: Men & Ships of the U.S. Submarine Fleet. (Illus.). (gr. 4-7). 1953. PLB 5.99 (ISBN 0-698-30342-3, Coward). Putnam Pub Group.
--Submarine Warfare: Men, Weapons, & Ships. (Colby Bks). (Illus.). (gr. 5-9). 1967. PLB 5.99 (ISBN 0-698-30343-1, Coward). Putnam Pub Group.
--Survival: Training in Our Armed Services. (Illus.). (gr. 4-7). 1965. PLB 5.29 o.p. (ISBN 0-698-30346-6, Coward). Putnam Pub Group.
--Today's Camping: New Equipment for the Modern Camper. (Illus.). 48p. (gr. 4-7). 1973. PLB 5.19 o.p. (ISBN 0-698-30448-9, Coward). Putnam Pub Group.
--Trucks on the Highway: Pickups, Panels, Flat Beds, Big Rigs & Special Purpose Cargo Movers. (Illus.). (gr. 5-7). 1964. PLB 5.99 (ISBN 0-698-30376-8, Coward). Putnam Pub Group.
--Two Centuries of Sea Power, 1776-1976. (Illus.). (gr. 4-7). 1976. PLB 5.99 (ISBN 0-698-30628-7, Coward). Putnam Pub Group.
--Two Centuries of Weapons: 1776-1976. LC 75-10459. (Illus.). 48p. (gr. 4-7). 1976. PLB 5.99 (ISBN 0-698-30596-5, Coward). Putnam Pub Group.
--Underseas Frontiers: An Introduction to Oceanography. LC 77-7561. (Illus.). (gr. 4-7). 1977. PLB 5.99 (ISBN 0-698-30676-7, Coward). Putnam Pub Group.
--Underwater World: Adventure Under the Surface of the Sea. (Illus.). (gr. 4-7). 1966. PLB 5.19 o.p. (ISBN 0-698-30385-7, Coward). Putnam Pub Group.
--West Point: Cadets, Training & Equipment. (Illus.). (gr. 4-7). 1963. PLB 5.29 o.p. (ISBN 0-698-30392-X, Coward). Putnam Pub Group.
--Wildlife in Our National Parks: Birds, Reptiles & Mammals. (Illus.). (gr. 4-7). 1965. PLB 5.29 o.p. (ISBN 0-698-30410-1, Coward). Putnam Pub Group.
Colby, C. B., ed. Camper's & Backpacker's Bible. (Stoeger Bks). (Illus.). 1977. pap. 7.95 o.s.i. (ISBN 0-695-80725-0). Follett.
Colby, Constance T., intro. by see Taber, Gladys.
Colby, Curtis. Bill's Great Idea. LC 73-14590. (Adventures in the Glen Ser.). 1973. PLB 4.95 o.p. (ISBN 0-88436-022-9); pap. 3.95 (ISBN 0-88436-023-7). EMC.
--The Fight for the Glen. LC 73-14586. (His Adventures in the Glen Ser). 1973. 4.95 o.p. (ISBN 0-88436-027-X); pap. 3.95 (ISBN 0-88436-028-8). EMC.
--Goose Rescue. LC 73-14585. (Adventures in the Glen Ser.). 1973. 4.95 o.p. (ISBN 0-88436-018-0); pap. 3.95 (ISBN 0-88436-019-9). EMC.
--Night Watch in the Glen. LC 73-14596. (Adventures in the Glen Ser.). 1973. 4.95 o.p. (ISBN 0-88436-016-4); pap. 3.95 (ISBN 0-88436-017-2). EMC.
--Otter in Danger. LC 73-14591. (His Adventures in the Glen Ser). 1973. 4.95 o.p. (ISBN 0-88436-020-2); pap. 3.95 (ISBN 0-88436-021-0). EMC.
--Wilderness Adventure. LC 73-14603. (Adventure in the Glen Ser.). 1973. 4.95 o.p. (ISBN 0-88436-025-3); pap. 3.95 (ISBN 0-88436-026-1). EMC.
Colby, Jean P. Plimoth Plantation: Then & Now. (Famous Museum Ser). (Illus.). 1970. 7.95g o.p. (ISBN 0-8038-5757-8). Hastings.
Colby, K. M. Artificial Paranoia: A Computer Simulation of Paranoid Processes. 1975. text ed. 18.50 (ISBN 0-08-018162-7); pap. text ed. 9.75 (ISBN 0-08-018161-9). Pergamon.
Colby, Kenneth M. Primer for Psychotherapists. 1951. 19.95 (ISBN 0-471-06901-9, Pub. by Wiley-Interscience). Wiley.
Colby, Kenneth M. & Spar, James E. The Fundamental Crisis in Psychiatry: Unreliability of Diagnosis. 236p. 1983. 24.75x (ISBN 0-398-04788-X). C C Thomas.
Colby, Robert A., jt. auth. see Gelfand, Morris A.
Colby, Vineta, jt. ed. see Kunitz, Stanley J.
Colby, W. E. A Century of Transportation in Shasta County 1821-1920. (ANCRR Occasional Paper: No. 7). 105p. 1982. 7.50 (ISBN 0-686-38931-X). Assn NC Records.
Colchie, Elizabeth S., jt. auth. see Witty, Helen.
Colchie, Thomas, tr. see Rubiao, Murilo.
Colclaser, R. A. Microelectronics Process & Device Design. 333p. 1980. 32.95 (ISBN 0-471-04339-7); solutions manual 8.50 (ISBN 0-471-08709-2). Wiley.
Colcock, Bentley P. Diverticular Disease of the Colon. LC 79-158398. (Major Problems in Clinical Surgery Ser.: Vol. 11). (Illus.). 1971. 12.50 o.p. (ISBN 0-7216-2636-X). Saunders.
Coldsborough, June. Little Puppy. (Shaggies Ser.). (Illus.). 12p. (ps-2). 1982. board 3.95 (ISBN 0-671-43159-5, Little Simon). S&S.
Coldsmith, Don. Follow the Wind. LC 82-45391. (DD Western Ser.). 192p. 1983. 11.95 (ISBN 0-385-17502-7). Doubleday.
--Trail of the Spanish Bit. LC 79-8559. (Double D Western Ser.). 192p. 1980. 10.95 (ISBN 0-385-15178-0). Doubleday.
Coldstream, J. N. Geometric Greece. LC 77-78085. (Illus.). 1977. 32.50x (ISBN 0-312-32365-4). St Martin.
Cole. Geography of USSR. 3rd ed. 1983. text ed. 34.95 (ISBN 0-408-49752-1). Butterworth.
--Nungu & the Elephant. 117p. 1980. lib. bdg. 7.95 o.p. (ISBN 0-07-011696-2). McGraw.
Cole & Foxcroft. Control of Pig Reproduction. 1982. text ed. 99.95 (ISBN 0-408-10768-5). Butterworth.
Cole, A. J. Macro Processors. 2nd ed. LC 81-10068. (Cambridge Computer Science Texts Ser.: No. 4). 240p. 1982. 27.95 (ISBN 0-521-24259-2); pap. 13.95 (ISBN 0-521-28560-7). Cambridge U Pr.
Cole, A. J. & Morrison, R. An Introduction to Programming with S-Algol. LC 82-14568. 192p. 1983. 15.95 (ISBN 0-521-25001-3). Cambridge U Pr.
Cole, A. T., jt. ed. see Dawson, M.
Cole, Adrian. The Coming of the Voidal. Stine, Hank, ed. (Voidal Trilogy Ser.). (Illus.). 198p. (Orig.). 1983. pap. 5.95 (ISBN 0-89865-287-1). Donning Co.
Cole, Anne P. Yesterday's Children. LC 79-62929. 1979. 5.95 o.p. (ISBN 0-533-04220-8). Vantage.
Cole, Arthur C. The Whig Party in the South. 1959. 10.00 (ISBN 0-8446-1126-3). Peter Smith.
Cole, Arthur C., Jr. Pogonomyrmex Harvester Ants: A Study of the Genus in North America. LC 68-17144. (Illus.). 1968. 18.95x (ISBN 0-87049-085-0). U of Tenn Pr.
Cole, B. R., jt. auth. see Hume-Rothery, W.
Cole, Barry, ed. Television Today: A Close-up View. Readings from TV Guide. 1981. 22.50x (ISBN 0-19-502798-1). Oxford U Pr.
--Television Today: A Close-up View, Readings from TV Guide. (Galaxy Book Ser.: No. 618). 1981. pap. 9.95 (ISBN 0-19-502799-X, GB). Oxford U Pr.
Cole, Benjamin. It Happened up in Maine. (Illus.). 1980. pap. 7.95 o.s.i. (ISBN 0-941238-02-4). Penobscot Bay.
Cole, Bernard D. Gunboats & Marines: The United States Navy in China, Nineteen Twenty-Five to Nineteen Twenty-Eight. LC 81-72063. (Illus.). 232p. 1982. 28.50 (ISBN 0-87413-203-7). U Delaware Pr.
Cole, Bill. Miles Davis: A Musical Biography. LC 74-2405. 1974. 7.95 o.p. (ISBN 0-688-00203-X); pap. 5.95 o.p. (ISBN 0-688-05203-7). Morrow.
Cole, Brock. The King at the Door. LC 78-20064. (Illus.). (gr. 1-3). 1979. 8.95a (ISBN 0-385-14718-X); PLB (ISBN 0-385-14719-8). Doubleday.
--No More Baths. LC 78-22790. (Illus.). (gr. 1-3). 1980. 10.95a (ISBN 0-385-14714-7); PLB (ISBN 0-385-14715-5). Doubleday.
--The Winter Wren. (Illus.). 32p. (gr. 1 up). 1983. 10.95 (ISBN 0-374-38454-1). FS&G.
Cole, Bruce. I Was Needled by Uncle Sam. Ashton, Sylvia, ed. LC 78-5413. cancelled o.s.i. (ISBN 0-87949-123-X). Ashley Bks.
--The Renaissance Artist at Work: From Pisano to Titian. LC 82-48102. (Icon Editions). (Illus.). 208p. 1983. 19.23i (ISBN 0-06-430902-9, HarpT). Har-Row.
--Sienese Painting: From Its Origins to the Fifteenth Century. LC 79-3670. (Icon Editions Ser.). (Illus.). 224p. 1980. 25.00i (ISBN 0-06-430901-0, HarpT). Har-Row.
Cole, Bruce, jt. ed. see Thompson, Norma H.
Cole, C. Donald. Christian Perspectives on Controversial Issues. 128p. (Orig.). 1983. pap. 2.95 (ISBN 0-686-82149-1). Moody.
--I Believe... 160p. 1983. pap. 2.95 (ISBN 0-8024-0353-0). Moody.
Cole, C. Robert & Moody, Michael E., eds. The Dissenting Tradition: Essays for Leland H. Carlson. LC 74-27706. xxiii, 272p. 1975. 17.00x (ISBN 0-8214-0176-9, 82-81735). Ohio U Pr.
Cole, Carole O., jt. auth. see McIntosh, Carol P.
Cole, Clara. Basic Needs. (Social Studies). (gr. 2-3). 1977. wkbk. 5.00 (ISBN 0-8209-0259-4, SS-26). ESP.
--Personal Health. (Health Ser.). 24p. (gr. 4-9). 1979. wkbk. 5.00 (ISBN 0-8209-0346-9, H-7). ESP.
Cole, David. Dixon's Book of Photography. (Illus.). 150p. 1975. 15.00 o.p. (ISBN 0-241-02276-2). Transatlantic.
Cole, David, et al. The Korean Economy: Issues of Development. LC 79-620015. (Korea Research Monographs: No. 1). 1979. pap. 3.50 o.p. (ISBN 0-912966-20-3). IEAS.
Cole, David C. & Park, Yung C. Financial Development in Korea, 1945-1978. (Harvard East Asian Monographs: No. 106). 340p. 1983. text ed. 15.00x (ISBN 0-674-30147-1). Harvard U Pr.
Cole, David C., et al. Korean Development: The Interplay of Politics & Economics. LC 75-131468. (Center for International Affairs Ser). (Illus.). 1971. 18.00x o.p. (ISBN 0-674-50563-8). Harvard U Pr.
Cole, David L. The Quest for Industrial Peace. LC 77-26873. (Meyer Kestnbaum Lectures). 1978. Repr. of 1962 ed. lib. bdg. 12.00x (ISBN 0-313-20072-6, COQI). Greenwood.
Cole, Donald B. & Blum, John M. Handbook of American History. (Illus.). 337p. (Orig.). 1968. pap. text ed. 11.95 (ISBN 0-15-530830-0, HC). HarBraceJ.
Cole, Donald W. Professional Suicide. 256p. 1980. 16.50 (ISBN 0-07-011697-0, P&RB). McGraw.
Cole, Dora J. & Wichman, Juliet R. Early Kauai Hospitality: A Family Cookbook of Receipts, 1820-1920. 1977. 12.00 (ISBN 0-686-86235-X). Kauai Museum.
Cole, Dorothy B. Meaningful Moments for Effective Living. 1977. pap. 1.75 (ISBN 0-685-81999-X). Creative Pr.
Cole, Douglas. Suffering & Evil in the Plays of Christopher Marlowe. LC 70-148617. 1971. Repr. of 1962 ed. text ed. 12.50x (ISBN 0-87752-134-4). Gordian.
Cole, Duane. The Flying Coles: Famous Aerobatic Team. LC 74-20037. (Illus.). 1974. 8.50 (ISBN 0-911721-18-5); pap. 6.95x (ISBN 0-911721-18-5). Aviation.
Cole, E. R. Act & Potency. LC 80-65625. 1980. pap. 4.95 (ISBN 0-931958-00-8). Apeiron Pr.
Cole, E. R. & Edwards, James, eds. Grand Slam: 13 Great Short Stories About Bridge. LC 75-7673. 1975. 7.95 o.p. (ISBN 0-399-11520-X). Putnam Pub Group.
Cole, Ethel. American Farmer. (Social Studies). 24p. (gr. 5-9). 1976. wkbk. 5.00 (ISBN 0-8209-0245-4, SS-12). ESP.

Cole, F. C. Traditions of the Tinguian, a Study in Philippine Folk-Lore: The Tinguian Social Religious & Economic Life of a Philippine Tribe. (Chicago Field Museum of Natural History Fieldiana Anthropology Ser). Repr. of 1922 ed. pap. 56.00 (ISBN 0-527-01874-0). Kraus Repr.

Cole, Frank. Doctor's Shorthand. LC 71-132176. 1970. 12.50 o.p. (ISBN 0-7216-2643-2). Saunders.

Cole, Frank R. & Schlinger, Evert L. The Flies of Western North America. LC 68-10687. (Illus.). 1969. 82.50x (ISBN 0-520-01516-9). U of Cal Pr.

Cole, Frank W. Reservoir Engineering Manual. 2nd ed. (Illus.). 393p. 1969. 24.95x (ISBN 0-87201-779-6). Gulf Pub.

Cole, G. D. Guild Socialism Restated. (Social Science Classics Ser.). 224p. 1980. text ed. 29.95 (ISBN 0-87855-386-X); pap. text ed. 6.95 (ISBN 0-87855-817-9). Transaction Bks.

--History of Socialist Thought, 5 vols. Incl. Vol. 1. Forerunners: Seventeen Eighty-Nine to Eighteen-Fifty. 1953. 29.95 o.p. (ISBN 0-312-38430-0); Vol. 2. Marxism & Anarchism: Eighteen-Fifty to Eighteen-Ninety. 1954. 29.95 o.p. (ISBN 0-312-38465-3); Vol. 3, 2 Pts. Second International: Eighteen Eighty-Nine to Nineteen-Fourteen. 1956. 50.00 o.p. (ISBN 0-312-38500-5); Vol. 4, 2 Pts. Communism & Social Democracy: Nineteen-Fourteen to Nineteen Thirty-One. 1958. 50.00 o.p. (ISBN 0-312-38535-8); Vol. 5. Socialism & Fascism: Nineteen Thirty-One to Nineteen Thirty-Nine. 1960. 29.95 o.p. (ISBN 0-312-38570-6). St Martin.

Cole, George. Studies in Class Structure. LC 76-2503. 195p. 1976. Repr. of 1955 ed. lib. bdg. 16.00x (ISBN 0-8371-8779-6, COSS). Greenwood.

Cole, George D. Introduction to Economic Theory: Seventeen-Fifty to Nineteen-Fifty. 1952. 18.95 (ISBN 0-312-42665-8). St Martin.

--Life of William Cobbett. LC 77-114502. 1971. Repr. of 1947 ed. lib. bdg. 20.75x (ISBN 0-8371-4781-6, COLC). Greenwood.

--Persons & Periods. LC 73-75412. Repr. of 1938 ed. 25.00x (ISBN 0-678-00495-1). Kelley.

--What Marx Really Meant. LC 79-90489. Repr. of 1934 ed. lib. bdg. 19.25x (ISBN 0-8371-3082-4, COWM). Greenwood.

Cole, Gerald A. Textbook of Limnology. 3rd ed. (Illus.). 434p. 1983. text ed. 24.95 (ISBN 0-8016-1004-4). Mosby.

Cole, H. A., ed. Petroleum & the Continental Shelf of North-West Europe, Volume 2: Environmental Protection. LC 75-14329. 126p. 1975. 42.95 o.s.i. (ISBN 0-470-16483-2). Halsted Pr.

Cole, Harry E. Stage Coach & Tavern Tales of the Old Northwest. Kellogg, Louise P., ed. LC 77-137353. 1972. Repr. of 1930 ed. 40.00x (ISBN 0-8103-3073-3). Gale.

Cole, Henderson, ed. Instrumentation for Tomorrow's Crystallography. pap. 7.50 (ISBN 0-686-60382-6). Polycrystal Bk Serv.

Cole, Herbert. Heraldry & Floral Forms As Used in Decoration. LC 74-164180. (Tower Bks). (Illus.). 1971. Repr. of 1922 ed. 40.00x (ISBN 0-8103-3913-7). Gale.

Cole, Howard N. Coronation & Royal Commemorative Medals 1887-1977. 68p. 1981. 25.00x (ISBN 0-903754-11-8, Pub. by Picton England). State Mutual Bk.

Cole, J. A. View from the Peak. 1979p. 16.95 (ISBN 0-571-11414-8). Faber & Faber.

Cole, J. P. The Development Gap: Analysis of World Poverty & Inequality. LC 80-40284. 454p. 1981. 49.95x (ISBN 0-471-27796-7, Pub. by Wiley-Interscience). Wiley.

Cole, Jack & Cole, Martha. Language Lessons for the Special Education Classroom. 200p. 1983. price not set (ISBN 0-89443-932-4). Aspen Systems.

Cole, Jack T., jt. auth. see Cole, Martha L.

Cole, Jacquelyn M. & Cole, Maurice F. Advisory Councils: A Theoretical & Practical Guide for Program Planners. (Illus.). 224p. 1983. text ed. 22.95 (ISBN 0-13-018184-6). P-H.

Cole, James H. The People Versus the Taipings: Bao Lisheng's "Righteous Army of Dongan". (China Research Monographs: No. 21). 72p. 1981. pap. 6.00x (ISBN 0-912966-39-4). IEAS.

Cole, James L. & Stwalley, William C., eds. High Temperature Chemistry. (ACS Symposium Ser.: No. 179). 1982. write for info. (ISBN 0-8412-0689-9). Am Chemical.

Cole, Jean. Trimaran Against the Trades. LC 77-96854. 1970. 7.95 (ISBN 0-8286-0047-3). De Graff.

Cole, Jim. Ninety-Nine Tips & Tricks for the New Pocket Computers. 128p. (Orig.). 1982. pap. 7.95 (ISBN 0-86668-019-5). ARCsoft.

Cole, Joan. A Lenten Journey with Jesus. 48p. 1982. pap. 1.50 (ISBN 0-89243-172-5). Liguori Pubns.

Cole, Joanna. A Bird's Body. LC 82-6446. (Illus.). 48p. (gr. k-3). 1982. 8.50 (ISBN 0-686-98318-1); lib. bdg. 7.63 (ISBN 0-688-01471-2). Morrow.

--Cars & How They Go. LC 82-45575. (Illus.). 32p. (gr. 2-6). 1983. 9.57i (ISBN 0-690-04261-2, TYC-J); PLB 9.89g (ISBN 0-690-04262-0). Har-Row.

--A Chick Hatches. (Illus.). 48p. (gr. k-3). 1976. PLB 9.55 (ISBN 0-688-32087-2). Morrow.

--Dinosaur Story. LC 74-5931. (Illus.). 32p. (gr. k-3). 1974. PLB 8.16 (ISBN 0-688-31826-6). Morrow.

--Find the Hidden Insect. LC 79-18648. (Illus.). 40p. (gr. k-3). 1979. 8.75 (ISBN 0-688-22203-X); PLB 8.40 (ISBN 0-688-32203-4). Morrow.

--A Fish Hatches. (Illus.). (gr. k-3). 1978. 9.75 (ISBN 0-688-22153-X); PLB 8.40 (ISBN 0-688-32153-4). Morrow.

--A Frog's Body. LC 80-10705. (Illus.). 48p. (gr. k-3). 1980. 8.75 (ISBN 0-688-22228-5); PLB 8.40 (ISBN 0-688-32228-X). Morrow.

--Fun on Wheels. (Illus.). (ps-1). 1977. 8.95 (ISBN 0-688-22102-5); PLB 8.59 (ISBN 0-688-32102-X). Morrow.

--Get Well, Clown-Arounds! (Illus.). 48p. (ps-3). 1983. 5.50 (ISBN 0-8193-1095-6); PLB 5.95 (ISBN 0-8193-1096-4). Parents.

--A Horse's Body. LC 80-28147. (Illus.). 48p. (gr. k-3). 1981. 7.95 (ISBN 0-688-00362-1); PLB 6.67 (ISBN 0-688-00363-X). Morrow.

--My Puppy Is Born. LC 72-14201. (Illus.). 40p. (gr. k-3). 1973. PLB 8.16 (ISBN 0-688-30078-2). Morrow.

--Plants in Winter. LC 73-1771. (A Let's-Read-&-Find-Out Science Bk). (Illus.). (ps-3). 1973. 7.95 o.p. (ISBN 0-690-62885-4, TYC-J); PLB 10.89 (ISBN 0-690-62886-2). Har-Row.

--A Snake's Body. LC 81-9443. (Illus.). 48p. (gr. k-3). 1981. 8.59 (ISBN 0-688-00702-3); PLB 8.55 (ISBN 0-688-00703-1). Morrow.

Cole, Johanna. Fleas. (Illus.). 64p. (gr. 3-7). 1973. PLB 8.16 (ISBN 0-688-31844-4). Morrow.

Cole, John. The Poor of the Earth. LC 75-46616. 1976. 23.50 (ISBN 0-89158-538-9). Westview.

Cole, John N. The Amaranth: From the Past for the Future. (Illus.). 1979. 12.95 o.p. (ISBN 0-87857-240-6). Rodale Pr Inc.

Cole, Jonathan O., ed. Clinical Research in Alcoholism: PRR 24. 178p. 1968. pap. 5.00 o.p. (ISBN 0-685-24867-4, P024-0). Am Psychiatric.

Cole, Jonathan O. & Barrett, James E., eds. Psychopathology in the Aged. (American Psychopathology Association Ser.). 332p. 1980. text ed. 35.00 (ISBN 0-89004-406-6). Raven.

Cole, Jonathan R. & Cole, Stephen. Social Stratification in Science. LC 73-78166. 1973. 16.50x (ISBN 0-226-11338-8); pap. 9.00x (ISBN 0-226-11339-6). U of Chicago Pr.

Cole, Justine. The Copeland Bride. (Orig.). 1983. pap. 3.50 (ISBN 0-440-11235-4). Dell.

Cole, Kenneth S. Membranes, Ions & Impulses: A Chapter of Classical Biophysics. LC 67-24121. (Biophysics Series: No. 1). (Illus.). 1968. 44.00x (ISBN 0-520-00251-2). U of Cal Pr.

Cole, Leander J. My Canadian Ancestry in Retrospect. 1979. 6.95 o.p. (ISBN 0-533-03924-X). Vantage.

Cole, Lee, jt. auth. see Cuthbertson, Tom.

Cole, Lee S. Vehicle Identification 1983. (Illus.). 80p. (Orig.). 1983. pap. 6.50 (ISBN 0-939818-06-X). Lee Bks.

Cole, Leonard A. Politics & the Restraint of Science. 160p. 1983. 17.95 (ISBN 0-86598-125-6). Rowman.

Cole, Lisa A., jt. auth. see Harrell, Rhett D.

Cole, Lucy. Cooking for the One You Love. LC 82-71743. 228p. 1982. 16.95 (ISBN 0-8119-0448-2). Fell.

Cole, M. & Scribner, S. Culture & Thought: A Psychological Introduction. LC 73-16360. 227p. 1974. pap. 13.95 (ISBN 0-471-16477-1). Wiley.

Cole, Maija J., jt. ed. see Keeler, Mary F.

Cole, Margaret. Life of G. D. H. Cole. 1972. 10.00 o.p. (ISBN 0-312-48405-4, L48900). St Martin.

Cole, Margaret, ed. see Webb, Beatrice.

Cole, Margaret R. Never too Old for God. Tanner, Don, ed. LC 81-52132. (Illus.). 128p. 1979. pap. 2.25 (ISBN 0-88005-001-2, UPL 001-2). Uplift Bks.

Cole, Marianne. Gentle Awakening. (Second Chance at Love Ser.: No. 101). Date not set. pap. 1.75 (ISBN 0-515-06865-9). Jove Pubns.

Cole, Martha, jt. auth. see Cole, Jack.

Cole, Martha L. & Cole, Jack T. Effective Intervention with the Language Impaired Child. LC 80-28037. 291p. 1981. text ed. 28.50 (ISBN 0-89443-344-X). Aspen Systems.

Cole, Martin, jt. auth. see Birch, Alan.

Cole, Maurice F., jt. auth. see Cole, Jacquelyn M.

Cole, Michael & Frampton, Susan. Dining In--Vail. (Dining In--Ser.). (Illus.). 1983. pap. 8.95 (ISBN 0-89716-059-2). Peanut Butter.

Cole, Michael, ed. The Selected Writings of A. R. Luria. LC 78-64342. 1979. 30.00 (ISBN 0-87332-127-8). M E Sharpe.

Cole, Owne. Sikhism & its Indian Context, 1469-1708: The Attitude of Guru Nanak & Early Sikhism to Indian Religious Beliefs & Practices. 352p. 1982. 59.00x o.p. (ISBN 0-232-51508-5, Pub. by Darton-Longman-Todd England). State Mutual Bk.

Cole, P. D. Modern & Traditional Elites in the Politics of Lagos. LC 74-76578. (African Studies: No. 12). 264p. 1975. 37.50 (ISBN 0-521-20439-9). Cambridge U Pr.

Cole, Patricia. Language Disorders in PreSchool Children. 208p. 1982. 21.95 (ISBN 0-13-522862-X). P-H.

Cole, Peter, ed. Studies in Modern Hebrew Syntax & Semantics: Transformational Generative Approach. new ed. (North Holland Linguistics Ser.: Vol. 32). 1976. 38.50 (ISBN 0-7204-0543-2, North-Holland). Elsevier.

Cole, R. T. The Recollections of R. Taylor Cole: Educator, Emmissary, Development Planner. (Illus.). 275p. 1983. 20.000 (ISBN 0-686-97725-4). Duke.

Cole, R. T., jt. ed. see Canavan, Francis S.

Cole, R. Wellesley. Kossoh Town Boy. (Illus.). 1960. 5.95 (ISBN 0-521-04686-6). Cambridge U Pr.

Cole, Rex V. Perspective for Artists. LC 77-15743. (Illus.). 288p. 1976. pap. 4.50 (ISBN 0-486-22487-2). Dover.

Cole, Richard L. Introduction to Political Research. (Illus.). 1980. pap. text ed. 13.95x (ISBN 0-02-323350-8). Macmillan.

Cole, Robert. The Book of Houses: An Astrological Guide to the Harvest Cycle in Human Life. LC 80-16931. 132p. 1980. pap. 4.95 o.p. (ISBN 0-934558-04-3); pap. 4.95 (ISBN 0-934558-01-9). Entwhistle Bks.

Cole, Robert, jt. auth. see Stralen, D. Van.

Cole, Robert E. Japanese Blue Collar: The Changing Tradition. LC 77-107656. 1971. 12.75 o.p. (ISBN 0-520-01681-5); pap. 8.95x o.s.i. (ISBN 0-520-02354-4, CAMPUS86). U of Cal Pr.

--Work, Mobility, & Participation: A Comparative Study of American & Japanese Industry. LC 77-80468. 304p. 1979. 24.50x o.s.i. (ISBN 0-520-03542-9); pap. 8.95x (ISBN 0-520-04204-2, CAMPUS 263). U of Cal Pr.

Cole, Robert S. The Practical Handbook of Public Relations. (Illus.). 224p. 1981. text ed. 19.95 (ISBN 0-13-691162-5, Spec); pap. text ed. 8.95 (ISBN 0-13-691154-4). P-H.

Cole, Roland J. & Tegeler, Philip D. Government Requirements of Small Business. LC 79-3046. (Human Affairs Research Center Ser.). 192p. 1980. 21.95x (ISBN 0-669-03307-3). Lexington Bks.

Cole, Ronald A., ed. Perception & Production of Fluent Speech. LC 79-25481. (Illus.). 576p. 1980. text ed. 39.95x (ISBN 0-89859-019-1). L Erlbaum Assocs.

Cole, Rufus. Human History: The Seventeenth Century & the Stuart Family, 2 Vols. LC 59-8900. 1959. 10.00 set o.s.i. (ISBN 0-87027-042-7); Vol. 1. (ISBN 0-87027-047-8); Vol. 2. (ISBN 0-87027-048-6). Cumberland Pr.

Cole, Sam. Global Models & the International Economic Order. LC 77-30175. 1978. text ed. 14.50 o.p. (ISBN 0-08-022991-3); pap. text ed. 4.80 (ISBN 0-08-022025-8). Pergamon.

Cole, Sandy, ed. see Grayson, Don, et al.

Cole, Sandy, ed. see Ives, Ronald, et al.

Cole, Sandy, ed. see Lee, James, et al.

Cole, Sheila. Working Kids on Working. (gr. 5 up). 1980. 10.75 (ISBN 0-688-41959-3); PLB 10.32 (ISBN 0-688-51959-8). Morrow.

Cole, Sonia. Leakey's Luck: The Life of Louis Seymour Bazett Leakey. 448p. 1975. 15.95 o.p. (ISBN 0-15-149456-8). HarBraceJ.

Cole, Stanely. Amphoto Guide to Basic Photography. (Illus.). 1978. 9.95 o.p. (ISBN 0-8174-2443-1, Amphoto); pap. 7.95 (ISBN 0-8174-2115-7). Watson-Guptill.

Cole, Stephen. The Sociological Method. 3rd ed. 1980. pap. 10.95 (ISBN 0-395-30857-7). HM.

--The Sociological Orientation. 2nd ed. 1979. pap. 16.50 (ISBN 0-395-30579-9); Instr's. manual 2.50 (ISBN 0-395-30580-2). HM.

Cole, Stephen, jt. auth. see Cole, Jonathan R.

Cole, Susan, jt. auth. see Porter, Douglas R.

Cole, Tom. A Short History of San Francisco. LC 81-2588. (Illus.). 144p. (Orig.). 1981. pap. 8.95 (ISBN 0-938530-00-3, 00-3). Lexikos.

Cole, W. A., jt. auth. see Deane, Phyllis.

Cole, Wayne S. Roosevelt & the Isolationists, Nineteen Thirty-Two to Nineteen Forty-Five. LC 82-8624. xii, 685p. 1983. 26.50x (ISBN 0-8032-1410-3). U of Nebr Pr.

Cole, William. Give Up? LC 78-6842. (Illus.). (gr. 4-6). 1978. PLB 7.90 s&l (ISBN 0-531-02249-8). Watts.

Cole, William, ed. Beastly Boys & Ghastly Girls. LC 64-20962. (Illus.). (gr. 3-6). 1964. PLB 7.99 o.p. (ISBN 0-399-61173-8, Philomel). Putnam Pub Group.

--Birds & the Beasts Were There. LC 77-3586. (Illus.). (gr. k-12). 1963. PLB 7.99 o.p. (ISBN 0-529-03724-4, Philomel). Putnam Pub Group.

--Dinosaurs & Beasts of Yore. (Illus.). (gr. 3 up). 1979. 8.95 (ISBN 0-399-20763-5, Philomel). Putnam Pub Group.

--Humorous Poetry for Children. LC 55-5283. (Illus.). 1955. PLB 8.99 o.p. (ISBN 0-529-03480-8, Philomel). Putnam Pub Group.

--I Went to the Animal Fair. LC 75-23020. (Illus.). (gr. k-3). 6.95 (ISBN 0-529-03530-8, Philomel). Putnam Pub Group.

--I'm Mad at You. LC 77-25497. (Illus.). (gr. 1-4). 1978. 8.95 o.s.i. (ISBN 0-529-05363-2, Philomel). Putnam Pub Group.

--Poem Stew. LC 81-47106. (Illus.). 96p. (gr. 3-6). 1981. 10.10i o.p. (ISBN 0-397-31963-0, JBL-J); PLB 9.98g (ISBN 0-397-31964-9). Har-Row.

--Poems for Seasons & Celebrations. (Illus.). (gr. 6 up). 1961. PLB 7.99 (ISBN 0-529-03660-6, Philomel). Putnam Pub Group.

--Poems of Magic & Spells. LC 60-5802. (Illus.). (gr. 6 up). 1960. PLB 8.99 o.s.i. (ISBN 0-529-03587-1, Philomel). Putnam Pub Group.

Cole, William E., jt. auth. see Harris, Diana K.

Cole, William E., jt. auth. see Moore, Clyde B.

Coleberd, Frances. Hidden Country Villages of California. LC 77-21926. (Illus.). 180p. 1982. pap. 7.95 (ISBN 0-87701-252-0). Chronicle Bks.

Colebourn, R., jt. auth. see Cobban, J. M.

Colecchia, Francesca. Garcia Lorca: An Annotated Bibliography of Criticism. LC 78-68301. (Reference Library of Humanities Ser.). 1979. lib. bdg. 34.00 o.s.i. (ISBN 0-8240-9800-5). Garland Pub.

Colegate, Isabel. Statues in a Garden. 1964. pap. 2.95 (ISBN 0-686-82408-3). Avon.

Colella, Albert M., et al. Systems Simulation. LC 73-11645. 288p. 1974. 23.95 (ISBN 0-669-90308-6). Lexington Bks.

Coleman & Brownlee. Financial Accounting for Management. LC 81-65306. (Accounting Ser.). 441p. Date not set. 27.00 (ISBN 0-936328-03-7); text ed. 19.95 (ISBN 0-686-83172-1). Dame Inc.

Coleman & Davidson, Bill. Gary Coleman: Medical Miracle. (Illus.). 1981. 9.95 (ISBN 0-698-11093-5, Coward). Putnam Pub Group.

Coleman, A. Flaubert's Literary Development in the Light of His Memories D'un Fou Novembre, & Education Sentimentale. (Elliott Monographs: Vol. 1). 1914. pap. 15.00 (ISBN 0-527-02605-0). Kraus Repr.

Coleman, Alexander, ed. Cinco Maestros: Cuentos modernos de Hispanoamerica. 318p. (Span.). 1969. pap. text ed. 10.95 (ISBN 0-15-507551-9, HC); instr's. manual 0.50 (ISBN 0-15-507552-7, HC). HarBraceJ.

Coleman, Arthur & Tyler, Gary R. Drama Criticism, 2 vols. Incl. Vol. 1. A Checklist of Interpretation Since 1940 of English & American Plays. LC 82-70456. 457p. 1966. 18.00x (ISBN 0-8040-0069-7); Vol. 2. A Checklist of Interpretation Since 1940 of Classical & Continental Plays. LC 82-72437. 446p. 1970. 18.00x (ISBN 0-8040-0500-1). Swallow.

Coleman, B. D. Money: How to Save It, Spend It, & Make It. 1969. 24.00 (ISBN 0-08-012936-6); pap. text ed. 10.75 o.p. (ISBN 0-08-012935-8). Pergamon.

Coleman, B. I., ed. The Idea of the City in Nineteenth-Century Britain. (Birth of Modern Britain Ser). 256p. 1973. 18.95x (ISBN 0-7100-7591-X); pap. 7.95 (ISBN 0-7100-7592-8). Routledge & Kegan.

Coleman, Bill & Coleman, Patty. God's Own Child. rev. ed. 64p. 1983. Parent's Book. pap. text ed. 3.95 (ISBN 0-89622-188-1); Leader's Guide. wkbk. 1.00 (ISBN 0-89622-187-3). Twenty-Third.

Coleman, Bruce & Hileman, Josephine. Coming to America. (Newbury House Readers Ser.: Stage 3 Intermediate). 48p. (Orig.). (gr. 7-12). 1981. pap. text ed. 2.95 (ISBN 0-88377-196-9). Newbury Hse.

Coleman, Mrs. Chapman. Life of John J. Crittenden, 2 Vols. LC 72-99469. (American Public Figures Ser). 1970. Repr. of 1871 ed. Set. lib. bdg. 89.50 (ISBN 0-306-71843-X). Da Capo.

Coleman, Charles J. Personnel: An Open System Approach. 1979. text ed. 19.95 (ISBN 0-316-15124-6); Tchr's ed. avail. (ISBN 0-316-15125-4). Little.

Coleman, D. A., ed. Demography of Immigrants & Minority Groups in the United Kingdom. Date not set. pap. price not set (ISBN 0-12-179780-5). Acad Pr.

Coleman, David, jt. ed. see Sors, Andrew I.

Coleman, David S., jt. auth. see Gaines, George, Jr.

Coleman, Donald C. Sir John Banks, Baronet & Businessman. LC 74-30845. (Illus.). 215p. 1975. Repr. of 1963 ed. lib. bdg. 17.00x (ISBN 0-8371-7932-7, COJB). Greenwood.

Coleman, Dorothy. The Gallo-Roman Muse. LC 79-71. 1979. 37.50 (ISBN 0-521-22254-0). Cambridge U Pr.

--Rabelais: A Critical Study in Prose Fiction. LC 76-173822. 1971. 49.50 (ISBN 0-521-08125-4); pap. 13.95 (ISBN 0-521-29458-4). Cambridge U Pr.

Coleman, Dorothy G., jt. ed. see Bayley, Peter.

Coleman, Dorothy S., et al. Collector's Encyclopedia of Dolls. (Illus.). 1968. 35.00 (ISBN 0-517-00059-8). Crown.

--The Collector's Book of Dolls' Clothes: Costumes in Miniature, 1700-1929. (Illus.). 640p. 1975. 35.00 (ISBN 0-517-52031-1). Crown.

Coleman, Eleanor S. Captain Gustavus Conyngham, U.S.N. Pirate or Privateer, 1747-1819. LC 82-13596. (Illus.). 196p. 1983. lib. bdg. 22.25 (ISBN 0-8191-2692-6); pap. text ed. 10.00 (ISBN 0-8191-2693-4). U Pr of Amer.

Coleman, Emily & Edwards, Betty. Brief Encounters. LC 77-16908. 1979. pap. 8.95 (ISBN 0-385-15579-4, Anch). Doubleday.

Coleman, Eric. Dinghies for All Waters: Safe Family Cruising & Day Sailing. (Illus.). 176p. 1976. 12.00 o.p. (ISBN 0-370-10459-5); pap. 9.95 o.p. (ISBN 0-685-69467-4). Transatlantic.

Coleman, F. G., tr. see McDonald, Hope.

Coleman, Francis. Great Britain. LC 75-44870. (Macdonald Countries Ser.). (Illus.). (gr. 6 up). 1976. PLB 12.68 (ISBN 0-382-06102-0, Pub. by Macdonald Ed). Silver.

Coleman, Freada A., jt. ed. see McDermott, Beatrice S.

Coleman, H. W. & Pfund, P. A., eds. Engineering Applications of Laser Velocimetry. 1982. 40.00 (H00230). ASME.

Coleman, Harry. Camping Out with Your New Van or Minibus: A Survival Manual for International Campers. 352p. 1982. 19.95 (ISBN 0-87196-308-6). Facts on File.

Coleman, Henry, jt. auth. see Shaw, Martin.

Coleman, Howard W. Case Studies in Broadcast Management. rev.,enl.,2nd ed. 1978. 10.75 (ISBN 0-8038-1220-5); pap. text ed. 6.50x (ISBN 0-8038-1221-3). Hastings.

Coleman, J. Introductory Psychology. 1977. 19.95x (ISBN 0-7100-8442-0); pap. 14.00 o.p. (ISBN 0-7100-8443-9). Routledge & Kegan.

Coleman, J. R. & Kaminsky, F. C. Ambulatory Care Systems, Vol. 4: Designing Medical Services for Health Maintenance Organizations. LC 76-55865. (Illus.). 1977. 29.95x (ISBN 0-669-01327-7). Lexington Bks.

--Ambulatory Care Systems, Vol. 5: Financial Design & Administration of Health Maintenance Organizations. LC 76-55865. 1977. 28.95x (ISBN 0-669-01328-5). Lexington Bks.

Coleman, J. Winston. The Squire's Sketches of Lexington. 1972. 6.95 (ISBN 0-87642-009-9). Henry Clay.

Coleman, James. Microwave Devices. 1982. text ed. 22.95 (ISBN 0-8359-4386-0). Reston.

Coleman, James C. Contemporary Psychology & Effective Behavior. 4th ed. 1979. text ed. 23.50x (ISBN 0-673-15202-2); student's guide 7.95x (ISBN 0-673-15203-0). Scott F.

Coleman, James C., jt. auth. see Glaros.

Coleman, James C., et al. Abnormal Psychology & Modern Life. 6th ed. 1980. text ed. 29.95x (ISBN 0-673-15213-8); pap. 8.95x student's guide (ISBN 0-673-15283-9). Scott F.

Coleman, James S. Nigeria: Background to Nationalism. LC 58-10286. (California Library Reprint Series: No. 28). 1971. 44.00x (ISBN 0-520-02070-7). U of Cal Pr.

Coleman, James S., et al. Parents, Teachers & Children: Prospects for Choice in American Education. LC 77-89164. 336p. 1977. pap. text ed. 5.95 (ISBN 0-917616-18-9). ICS Pr.

--High School Achievement: Public, Catholic, & Private Schools Compared. LC 81-68411. 1982. 20.75 (ISBN 0-465-02956-6). Basic.

Coleman, Jean. Chapter Twenty-Nine. 1979. pap. 2.50 (ISBN 0-686-38054-1). Bridge Pub.

Coleman, Jerry, et al. The Scouting Report: 1983. LC 82-48225. (Illus.). 672p. (Orig.). 1983. pap. 12.45i (ISBN 0-06-091027-5, CN 1027, CN). Har-Row.

Coleman, John. Coleman's Drive. 1966. 4.95 o.p. (ISBN 0-685-52076-5). Transatlantic.

Coleman, John, jt. ed. see Baum, Gregory.

Coleman, John A. The Evolution of Dutch Catholicism, 1958-1974. LC 74-22958. 1979. 35.00x (ISBN 0-520-02885-6). U of Cal Pr.

Coleman, John C. Nature of Adolescence. 1980. 22.50x (ISBN 0-416-72620-8); pap. 10.95x (ISBN 0-416-72630-5). Methuen Inc.

--Relationships in Adolescence. 1974. 25.00x (ISBN 0-7100-7868-4). Routledge & Kegan.

Coleman, John C., ed. The School Years: Current Issues in the Socialization of Young People. (Psychology in Progress Ser.). 180p. 1979. 25.00x (ISBN 0-416-71190-1); pap. 12.95x (ISBN 0-416-71200-2). Methuen Inc.

Coleman, John E. Questions-Answers-Explanations Flight Instructor Instrument-Airplane Written Test Guide. (Illus.). 98p. 1982. pap. text ed. 13.50 (ISBN 0-941272-06-0). Astro Pubs.

Coleman, John R. Blue-Collar Journal: A College President's Sabbatical. LC 73-21902. 1974. 11.49i (ISBN 0-397-01030-3). Har-Row.

Coleman, Joseph. Word Processing Simplified & Self-Taught. (Simplified & Self-Taught Ser.). (Illus.). 128p. 1983. lib. bdg. 9.95 (ISBN 0-668-05599-5); pap. 4.95 (ISBN 0-668-05601-0). Arco.

--Your Career in Law Enforcement. LC 79-14314. (Arco's Career Guidence Ser.). 1979. lib. bdg. 7.95 (ISBN 0-668-04740-2, 4740); pap. 4.50 (ISBN 0-668-04751-8, 4751). Arco.

Coleman, Jules. Justice & the Costs of Accidents: A Philosophic Analysis. (Philosophy & Society Ser.). 250p. 1983. text ed. 25.00x (ISBN 0-8476-7183-6). Rowman.

Coleman, Ken & Valenti, Dan. Diary of a Sportscaster. LC 82-82096. 176p. (Orig.). 1982. pap. 6.95 (ISBN 0-943514-03-7). Literations.

--Ken Coleman's Red Sox Quiz Book. 96p. 1983. pap. 4.95 (ISBN 0-943514-04-5). Literations.

Coleman, Kenneth. Colonial Georgia: A History. (A History of the American Colonies Ser.). 1976. lib. bdg. 30.00 (ISBN 0-527-18712-7). Kraus Intl.

--U. S. Financial Institutions in Crisis: How Safe are Your Savings? Chambers, Catherine & Lewis, David, eds. 13p. 1982. pap. 5.95 (ISBN 0-942632-01-X). Seraphim Pr.

Coleman, Laurence V. Historic House Museums. LC 71-175318. (Illus.). xii, 187p. 1973. Repr. of 1933 ed. 37.00x (ISBN 0-8103-3118-7). Gale.

Coleman, Les & Pedemonti, Richard D. Squeal. (Illus.). 1982. 15.95 (ISBN 0-939026-03-1). Spoonwood Pr.

Coleman, Lonnie. The Legacy of Beulah Land. 1981. pap. 3.95 (ISBN 0-440-15085-X). Dell.

--Mark. 1981. 13.95 o.p. (ISBN 0-671-42785-7). S&S.

Coleman, Lucien E. The Exciting Christian Life: Bible Study on Christian Growth. 36p. 1982. pap. 3.50 (ISBN 0-939298-11-2). J M Prods.

Coleman, Lucien E., Jr. Como Ensenar la Biblia. Diaz, Jorge E., tr. Orig. Title: How to Teach the Bible. 265p. (Span.). 1982. 7.75 (ISBN 0-311-11039-8). Casa Bautista.

--How to Teach the Bible. LC 79-52001. 1980. 9.95 (ISBN 0-8054-3428-3). Broadman.

Coleman, M., ed. Autistic Syndromes. 1976. 35.50 (ISBN 0-7204-0590-4, North Holland). Elsevier.

Coleman, Mary, ed. Neonatal Neurology. 444p. 1981. text ed. 67.50 (ISBN 0-8391-1584-9). Univ Park.

Coleman, Mary A. Disappearances. pap. 3.00 (ISBN 0-686-81811-3). Anhinga Pr.

Coleman, P. Technologist As Writer: An Introduction to Technical Writing. 1971. text ed. 13.45 (ISBN 0-07-011783-7, G). McGraw.

Coleman, P. G. & Sharma, S. C., eds. Positron Annihilation: Proceedings of the Sixth International Conference on Positron Annihilation, The University of Texas at Arlington, April 3-7, 1982. 1016p. 1983. 123.50 (ISBN 0-444-86534-9, North Holland). Elsevier.

Coleman, Patty, jt. auth. see Coleman, Bill.

Coleman, Peter & Shrubb, Lee, eds. Quadrant: Twenty-Five Years. LC 82-19998. 568p. 1983. 22.50 (ISBN 0-7022-1820-0). U of Queensland Pr.

Coleman, Richard. Gospel-Telling: The Art & Theology of Children's Sermons. 128p. (Orig.). 1982. pap. 7.95 (ISBN 0-8028-1927-3). Eerdmans.

Coleman, Robert, ed. see Virgil.

Coleman, Robert E. Evangelism in Perspective. LC 75-31306. 3.95 (ISBN 0-87509-080-X); pap. 2.50 (ISBN 0-87509-081-8). Chr Pubns.

--The Songs of Heaven. 160p. 1980. pap. 4.95 (ISBN 0-8007-5097-7, Power Bks). Revell.

--The Spirit & the Word. 96p. 1975. pap. 1.50 o.p. (ISBN 0-8007-8192-9, Spire Bks). Revell.

Coleman, Ronny J. & Russell, Raymond M. Fire Truck Toys for Men & Boys. (Catalogue of Toy Fire Apparatus Ser.: Vol. II). (Illus.). 168p. 1982. pap. 10.95 (ISBN 0-910105-01-4). Phenix Pub.

--Fire Truck Toys for Men & Boys. (Catalogue of Toy Fire Apparatus Ser.: Vol. I). (Illus.). 168p. 1981. pap. 9.95 (ISBN 0-910105-00-6). Phenix Pub.

Coleman, Satis N. Bells: Their History, Legends, Making, & Uses. LC 74-159919. (Illus.). 1971. Repr. of 1928 ed. 44.00 o.p. (ISBN 0-8103-3906-4). Gale.

Coleman, Sherman S. Complex Foot Deformities in Children. LC 82-15249. (Illus.). 301p. 1983. write for info (ISBN 0-8121-0857-4). Lea & Febiger.

--Congenital Dysplasia & Dislocation of the Hip. LC 78-59669. 286p. 1978. 54.50 (ISBN 0-8016-1018-4). Mosby.

Coleman, Terry. The Liners: A History of the North Atlantic Crossing. LC 77-76. (Illus.). 1977. 14.95 o.p. (ISBN 0-399-11958-2). Putnam Pub Group.

Coleman, Thomas E. Modern Drug Store Merchandising: How to Increase Your Sales & Profits. LC 75-28348. 214p. 1975. 15.95 (ISBN 0-86730-401-4). Lebhar Friedman.

--Retail Drug Store Management & Control. LC 78-70424. 1978. 19.95 (ISBN 0-86730-402-2). Lebhar Friedman.

Coleman, Thomas G. Blood Pressure Control, Vol. 1. 248p. 1981. 32.50 (ISBN 0-88831-088-9). Eden Pr.

Coleman, Thomas G., ed. Computer Simulation of Physiological Systems. 40p. pap. 10.00 (ISBN 0-686-36684-0). Soc Computer Sim.

Coleman, Vernon. Paper Doctors: A Critical Assessment of Medical Research. 1977. 12.95 o.s.i. (ISBN 0-85117-109-5). Transatlantic.

Coleman, W. Biology in the Nineteenth Century. LC 77-83989. (Cambridge History of Science Ser.). (Illus.). 1978. 29.95 (ISBN 0-521-21861-6); pap. 10.95 (ISBN 0-521-29293-X). Cambridge U Pr.

Coleman, Wanda. Imagoes. 160p. (Orig.). 1983. 14.00 (ISBN 0-87685-510-9); pap. 8.50 (ISBN 0-87685-509-5); deluxe ed. 25.00 (ISBN 0-87685-511-7). Black Sparrow.

Coleman, William. Courageous Christians. (Wonderful World of the Bible Ser.). (gr. 4-8). 1983. 14.95 (ISBN 0-89191-558-3). Cook.

--Death Is a Social Disease: Public Health & Political Economy in Early Industrial France. 354p. 1982. text ed. 35.00 (ISBN 0-299-08950-9). U of Wis Pr.

--Une Douzaine de Chretiens Audacieux. Cosson, Annie, ed. Martin, Marie T., tr. from Eng. 160p. (Fr.). 1983. pap. 2.00 (ISBN 0-8297-1240-2). Life Pubs Intl.

--Far Out Facts About the Bible. (gr. 4-9). 1980. pap. 2.50 o.p. (ISBN 0-89191-336-X). Cook.

--Peter. LC 85-894. 160p. (Orig.). 1982. pap. 4.95 (ISBN 0-89081-305-1, 3051). Harvest Hse.

--Understanding Suicide. (Orig.). 1979. pap. 2.50 o.p. (ISBN 0-89191-186-3). Cook.

Coleman, William, et al, eds. A Casebook of Grant Proposals in the Humanities. LC 81-18859. 248p. 1982. 29.95 (ISBN 0-918212-45-6). Neal-Schuman.

Coleman, William L. Chesapeake Charlie & the Haunted Ship. (Chesapeake Charlie Ser.). 112p. (Orig.). 1983. pap. 2.95 (ISBN 0-87123-282-0). Bethany Hse.

--Escucha a los Animales. 144p. Date not set. 2.50 (ISBN 0-88113-063-X). Edit Betania.

--Getting Ready for My First Day of School. 128p. (Orig.). (gr. k). 1983. pap. 4.95 (ISBN 0-87123-274-X). Bethany Hse.

--Mi Maquina Maravillosa. 144p. Date not set. 2.95 (ISBN 0-88113-309-4). Edit Betania.

--Un Punado de Audaces. Marosi, Esteban & Carrodeguas, Andy, eds. Sipowicz, Edwin, tr. 192p. (Span.). 1980. pap. 2.25 (ISBN 0-8297-1116-3). Life Pubs Intl.

--What Children Need to Know When Parents Get Divorced. 128p. (gr. k-5). 1983. pap. 3.95 (ISBN 0-87123-612-5). Bethany Hse.

Coleman, William V. Prayer-Talk: Casual Conversations with God. LC 82-74085. 112p. (Orig.). 1983. pap. 3.95 (ISBN 0-87793-265-4). Ave Maria.

Colenso, M., tr. see Vainshtein, Sevyan.

Coleridge, A. D., tr. see Schone, Alfred & Hiller, Ferdinand.

Coleridge, A. D., tr. see Von Hellborn, Heinrich K.

Coleridge, Christabel. Charlotte Mary Yonge, Her Life & Letters. LC 77-75961. (Library of Lives & Letters). 1969. Repr. of 1903 ed. 37.00x (ISBN 0-8103-3891-2). Gale.

Coleridge, E. H., ed. see Coleridge, Samuel T.

Coleridge, Herbert. A Dictionary of the First or Oldest Words in the English Language: From the Semi-Saxon Period of Ad 1250 to 1300, Consisting of an Alphabetical Inventory of Every Word Found in the Printed English Literature of the 13th Century. LC 74-19205. 103p. 1975. Repr. of 1863 ed. 34.00 o.p. (ISBN 0-8103-4119-0). Gale.

Coleridge, Samuel T. Coleridge: Selected Poems. Bald, R. C., ed. LC 56-6819. (Crofts Classics Ser.). 1956. pap. text ed. 3.25x (ISBN 0-88295-023-1). Harlan Davidson.

--Poems of Samuel Taylor Coleridge. Coleridge, E. H., ed. (Oxford Standard Authors Ser.). 1912. 29.95 (ISBN 0-19-254120-X). Oxford U Pr.

--Selected Poetry & Prose. Stauffer, Donald, ed. (YA) 1951. pap. 4.95 (ISBN 0-394-30952-9, T52, Mod LibC). Modern Lib.

Colerus, Egmont. Mathematics for Everyman: From Simple Numbers to the Calculus. (Illus.). 1957. 10.95 (ISBN 0-87523-104-7). Emerson.

Coles, C. L. Game Conservation in a Changing Countryside. 14.50x (ISBN 0-273-40133-5, SpS). Sportshelf.

Coles, Clarence & Young, Howard. Johnson-Evinrude Outboard Tune-up & Repair Manual, Vol. II. 1980. pap. 21.95 o.p. (ISBN 0-89330-008-X). Caroline Hse.

--Johnson-Evinrude Outboard Tune-up & Repair Manual, Vol. IV. 1980. pap. 21.95 o.p. (ISBN 0-89330-010-1). Caroline Hse.

--Johnson-Evinrude Outboard Tune-up & Repair Manual, Vol. I. 1980. pap. 21.95 o.p. (ISBN 0-89330-007-1). Caroline Hse.

--Johnson Three & Four Cylinder Outboard Tune-up & Repair Manual. 1980. pap. 21.95 o.p. (ISBN 0-89330-009-8). Caroline Hse.

--Mercruiser: Stern Drive Tune-up & Repair Manual. 1980. pap. 21.95 o.p. (ISBN 0-89330-005-5). Caroline Hse.

--Mercury Outboard Tune-up & Repair Manual. 1980. pap. 21.95 o.p. (ISBN 0-89330-006-3). Caroline Hse.

--OMC Stern Drive: Tune-up & Repair Manual. 1980. pap. 21.95 o.p. (ISBN 0-89330-004-7). Caroline Hse.

Coles, Clarence W. & Glenn, Harold T. Glenn's Complete Bicycle Manual: Selection, Maintenance, Repair. (Illus.). 352p. 1973. 9.95 (ISBN 0-517-50092-2); pap. 8.95 (ISBN 0-517-50093-0). Crown.

Coles, E. C. Guide to Medical Computing. (Computers in Medicine Ser.). (Illus.). 112p. 1973. 8.95 o.p. (ISBN 0-407-54800-9). Butterworth.

Coles, Harry L. War of Eighteen-Twelve. LC 65-17283. (Chicago History of American Civilization Ser: No. 22). (Illus.). 1965. pap. 7.50 (ISBN 0-226-11350-7, CHAC22). U of Chicago Pr.

Coles, J. M. & Harding, A. F. The Bronze Age in Europe: An Introduction to the Prehistory of Europe, 2000-700 BC. LC 79-14507. (Illus.). 1979. 40.00 (ISBN 0-312-10597-5). St Martin.

Coles, Jane H., jt. auth. see Coles, Robert.

Coles, John. Experimental Archaeology. LC 79-41520. 1980. 26.00 (ISBN 0-12-179750-3); pap. 12.00 (ISBN 0-12-179752-X). Acad Pr.

--Field Archaeology in Britain. 267p. 1972. pap. 12.95x (ISBN 0-416-76540-8). Methuen Inc.

Coles, Robert. Children of Crisis, Vol. 2: Migrants, Sharecroppers, Mountaineers. (Children of Crisis Ser.). (Illus.). 1972. 15.00 (ISBN 0-316-15171-8, Pub. by Atlantic Monthly Pr); pap. 10.95 (ISBN 0-316-15176-9). Little.

--Children of Crisis, Vol. 3: The South Goes North. LC 70-162332. (Children of Crisis Ser.). (Illus.). 704p. 1972. 15.00 (ISBN 0-316-15172-6, Pub. by Atlantic Monthly Pr); pap. 10.95 (ISBN 0-316-15177-7). Little.

--Children of Crisis, Vol. 4: Eskimos, Chicanos, Indians. (Children of Crisis Ser.). 1978. 15.00 (ISBN 0-316-15162-9, Atlantic-Little, Brown); pap. 10.95 (ISBN 0-316-15161-0). Little.

--Children of Crisis Vol. 5: Privileged Ones: the Well-off & Rich in America. LC 73-10825. (Children of Crisis Ser.). (Illus.). 1978. pap. 12.95 (ISBN 0-316-15150-5, Pub. by Atlantic-Little Brown) (ISBN 0-316-15149-1). Little.

--The Mind's Fate: Ways of Seeing Psychiatry & Psychoanalysis. 1975. 10.00 (ISBN 0-316-15179-3, Pub by Atlantic Monthly Pr.); pap. 4.95 o.p. (ISBN 0-316-15155-6). Little.

--The Old Ones of New Mexico. LC 73-82776. (Illus.). 74p. 1980. Repr. of 1973 ed. 8.95 o.p. (ISBN 0-8263-0301-3). U of NM Pr.

Coles, Robert & Coles, Jane H. Women of the Crisis Two: Lives of Work & Dreams. 1980. 10.95 o.s.i. (ISBN 0-440-09635-9, Sey Lawr). Delacorte.

Coles, Robert M., frwd. by see Sheehan, Susan.

Coles-Mogford, A. M., jt. auth. see Drummond, A. M.

Colet, John. John Colet's Commentary on First Corinthians. O'Kelly, Bernard, tr. from Lat. 1983. 22.00 (ISBN 0-86698-056-3). Medieval & Renaissance NY.

Coletta. Multiploy. 1982. lib. bdg. 19.95 (ISBN 0-8359-4742-4). Reston.

Coletta, Paolo E. Bowman Hendry McCalla: A Fighting Sailor. LC 79-66975. (Illus.). 1979. pap. text ed. 11.50 (ISBN 0-8191-0863-4). U Pr of Amer.

--French Ensor Chadwick: Scholarly Warrior. LC 80-67240. 264p. 1980. lib. bdg. 21.25 (ISBN 0-8191-1153-8); pap. text ed. 12.00 (ISBN 0-8191-1154-6). U Pr of Amer.

--William Jennings Bryan. Incl. Vol. 1. Political Evangelist, 1860-1908. (Illus.). xiv, 486p. 1964. 22.95x (ISBN 0-8032-0022-6); Vol. 3. Political Puritan, 1915-1925. (Illus.). xiv, 334p. 1969. 21.95x (ISBN 0-8032-0024-2). LC 64-11352. (Illus.). U of Nebr Pr.

Colette. Break of Day. McLeod, Enid, tr. 143p. 1974. pap. 5.25 (ISBN 0-374-51221-3). FS&G.

--Break of Day. 128p. 1983. pap. 2.50 (ISBN 0-345-30858-1). Ballantine.

--Claudine in Paris. 192p. 1982. pap. 2.50 (ISBN 0-345-30708-9). Ballantine.

--Colette at the Movies: Criticism & Screenplays. Virmaux, Alain & Virmaux, Odette, eds. Smith, Sarah W., tr. from Fr. LC 79-6148. (Ungar Film Library). (Illus.). 300p. 1980. 11.95 (ISBN 0-8044-2125-0); pap. 5.95 (ISBN 0-8044-6086-8). Ungar.

--The Complete Claudine. White, Antonia, tr. from French. Incl. Claudine at School; Claudine & Annie; Claudine in Paris; Claudine Married. 632p. 1976. 20.00 o.p. (ISBN 0-374-12691-7); pap. 10.95 (ISBN 0-374-51379-1). FS&G.

--GiGi. 1973. pap. 1.25 o.p. (ISBN 0-451-50698-7, CY698, Sig Classics). NAL.

--The Other Woman. 1975. pap. 2.50 (ISBN 0-451-51593-5, CE1593, Sig Classics). NAL.

--The Pure & the Impure. Briffault, Herma, tr. 175p. 1967. 7.95 (ISBN 0-374-23920-7); pap. 6.25 (ISBN 0-374-50692-2). FS&G.

Coletti, Mina S. & Giesea, Roberta. Family Idea, Bk. 2. LC 82-14612. 279p. 1982. pap. 5.95 (ISBN 0-87747-925-9). Deseret Bk.

Coletti-Previero, M. A., jt. ed. see Previero, A.

Coley, Christopher M., jt. auth. see Wolfe, Sidney M.

Coley, George. Reflections of the Colony of New South Wales. 14.50x (ISBN 0-392-04392-0, ABC). Sportshelf.

Colford, Paul D., jt. auth. see Egan, John P.

Colgan, Michael. Your Personal Vitamin Profile: A Medical Scientist Shows You How to Chart Your Individual Vitamin & Mineral Formala. 1982. 14.95 (ISBN 0-688-01505-0); pap. 7.45 (ISBN 0-688-01506-9). Morrow.

Colgan, Patrick. Comparative Social Recognition. 288p. 1983. 37.50 (ISBN 0-471-09350-5, Pub. by Wiley-Interscience). Wiley.

Colgan, Patrick W. Quantitative Ethology. LC 78-999. 1978. 39.95x (ISBN 0-471-02236-5, Pub. by Wiley-Interscience). Wiley.

Colgan, Susan, jt. ed. see Madigan, Mary Jean.

Colgate, Craig, Jr., ed. National Trade & Professional Associations of the United States & Canada & Labor Unions, 1981. 16th annual ed. Broida, Patricia. LC 74-647774. 416p. 1981. pap. 35.00 o.p. (ISBN 0-910416-34-6). Columbia Bks.

Colgate, Craig, Jr., jt. ed. see Close, Arthur C.

Colgate, John A. Administration of Intramural & Recreational Activities: Everyone Can Participate. LC 77-9265. 278p. 1978. text ed. 27.95x (ISBN 0-471-01728-0). Wiley.

Colglazier, E. William, jt. ed. see Lundstedt, Sven B.

Colgrave, Bertram, ed. see Bede The Venerable.

Colgren, John. The Computer Revolution. (gr. 4-8). 1982. 5.95 (ISBN 0-86653-067-3, GA 421). Good Apple.

Colie, Rosalie. The Resources of Kind: Genre-Theory in the Renaissance. LC 72-95307. 1974. 24.50x (ISBN 0-520-02397-8). U of Cal Pr.

Colin, Lawrence, jt. ed. see Hunten, Donald M.

Colin, Patrick I. Caribbean Reef Invertebrates & Plants. (Illus.). 1978. 29.95 (ISBN 0-87666-460-5, H-971). TFH Pubns.

Colinvaux, Paul. The Fates of Nations: A Biological Theory of History. 1980. 12.95 o.p. (ISBN 0-671-25204-6). S&S.

Colker, David. Running Away from Home: A Guide to Running Trails in 32 Cities Across America. (Orig.). 1979. pap. 2.50 o.s.i. (ISBN 0-515-05398-8). Jove Pubns.

Colker, Marvin L., ed. Analecta Dublinensia: Three Medieval Latin Texts in the Library of Trinity College Dublin. LC 75-1954. 1975. 22.00X (ISBN 0-910956-56-1). Medieval Acad.

Coll, Alberto R. The Western Heritage & American Values: Law, Theology, & History. Thompson, Kenneth W., ed. LC 81-43761. (American Values Projected Abroad Ser.: Vol. I). 126p. 1982. lib. bdg. 18.75 (ISBN 0-8191-2526-1); pap. text ed. 8.00 (ISBN 0-8191-2527-X). U Pr of Amer.

Collacott, R. A. Mechanical Fault Diagnosis & Condition Monitoring. 1977. 75.00x (ISBN 0-412-12930-2, Pub. by Chapman & Hall). Methuen Inc.

Collacott, Ralph A. Vibration Monitoring & Diagnosis: Techniques for Cost-Effective Plant Maintenance. LC 78-13602. 333p. 1979. 69.95 o.p. (ISBN 0-470-26524-8). Halsted Pr.

Collan, Edward. Auden: A Carnival of Intellect. 320p. 1983. 25.00 (ISBN 0-19-503168-7). Oxford U Pr.

Collar, Grant H., Jr., jt. auth. see Collar, Jerry D.

Collar, Jerry D. & Collar, Grant H., Jr. Belize (British Honduras) The Country & People, Tourism & Investment. 52p. 1972. pap. 3.00 o.p. (ISBN 0-686-05679-5). G Collar.

Collard, Elizabeth, jt. auth. see Collard, Howard.

Collard, Howard & Collard, Elizabeth. Vocabulario Mayo, Vol. 6. rev. ed. 225p. 1974. pap. 4.00x (ISBN 0-88312-657-5); microfiche 3.00 (ISBN 0-88312-318-5). Summer Inst Ling.

Collatz, L. & Mainardus, G., eds. Numerische Methoden der Approximationstheorie, 4 vols. (International Series of Numerical Mathematics: Nos. 16, 26, 30 & 42). (Illus., Ger.). 1972-78. Vol. 1, 256p. 34.65x (ISBN 3-7643-0633-5); Vol. 2, 199p. 30.80x (ISBN 3-7643-0764-1); Vol. 3, 334p. pap. 35.75x (ISBN 3-7643-0824-9); Vol. 4, 344p. pap. 44.00x (ISBN 3-7643-1025-1). Birkhauser.

Collatz, L., jt. ed. see Albrecht, J.

Collectors Club Library. New York. Philately: The Catalog of the Collectors Club Library. 1974. lib. bdg. 115.00 (ISBN 0-8161-1047-6, Hall Library). G K Hall.

Colledge, jt. auth. see Lenton.

College & Education Division. Barron's Profiles of American Colleges: Regional Editions. (gr. 10-12). 1981. Northeast. pap. text ed. 6.95 (ISBN 0-8120-2271-8); West. pap. text ed. 4.95 (ISBN 0-8120-2272-6); South. pap. text ed. 5.75 (ISBN 0-8120-2273-4); Midwest. pap. text ed. 5.75 (ISBN 0-8120-2274-2). Barron.

College Division of Barron's Educational Ser., Inc. Barron's Compact Guide to Colleges. 2nd ed. LC 80-26124. (Illus.). 352p. (gr. 11-12). 1980. pap. 2.95 o.p. (ISBN 0-8120-2288-2). Barron.

College Division of Barrons Educational Series. Barrons Profiles of American Colleges: The West. 176p. (gr. 10-12). 1983. pap. 4.95 (ISBN 0-8120-2468-0). Barron.

--Barrons Profiles of American Colleges: The South. 320p. (gr. 10-12). 1983. pap. 5.75 (ISBN 0-8120-2469-9). Barron.

--Barrons Profiles of American Colleges: The Midwest. 288p. (gr. 10-12). 1983. pap. 5.75 (ISBN 0-8120-2470-2). Barron.

College Entrance Examination Board. CLEP General & Subject Examinations: Descriptions & Sample Questions. 1981. pap. 3.00 o.p. (ISBN 0-87447-013-7, 200631). College Bd.

Collender, Stanley E. The Guide to the Federal Budget: Fiscal 1984 Edition. LC 82-643840. 150p. (Orig.). 1983. pap. text ed. 10.00 (ISBN 0-87766-321-1). Urban Inst.

Colleran, Joseph M., tr. from Latin. see Anselm of Canterbury.

Colles, Henry C., ed. see Parry, Charles H.

Collester, J. Bryan, ed. European Communities: A Guide to Information Sources. LC 73-17506. (International Relations Information Guide Ser.: Vol. 3). 1979. 42.00x (ISBN 0-8103-1322-7). Gale.

Collet, Collet D. History of Taxes on Knowledge: Their Origin & Repeal. LC 75-142565. 1971. Repr. 34.00x (ISBN 0-8103-3615-4). Gale.

Colleta, Anthony. Working Together: A Guide to Parent Involvement. Fritts, Susan R., tr. LC 76-26758. 1976. pap. text ed. 14.95 (ISBN 0-89334-002-2). Humanics Ltd.

Colleton, John. Between Cloris & Amy. 1976. pap. 2.75 (ISBN 0-451-11256-3, AE1256, Sig). NAL.

--The Delights of Anna. (Orig.). 1980. pap. 3.50 (ISBN 0-451-12188-0, AE2188, Sig). NAL.

--On or About the First Day in June. (Orig.). 1978. pap. 2.50 (ISBN 0-451-11584-8, E1584, Sig). NAL.

--Replenishing Jennifer. (Orig.). 1975. pap. 2.50 (ISBN 0-451-11585-6, AE1585, Sig). NAL.

--The Seduction of Marianna. (Orig.). 1980. pap. 2.95 (ISBN 0-451-12167-8, AE2167, Sig). NAL.

--Up in Mamie's Diary. (Orig.). 1975. pap. 2.25 (ISBN 0-451-09230-9, E9230, Sig). NAL.

Collett, Ritter. Super Stripes: Paul Brown & the Super Bowl Bengals. LC 82-83268. (Illus.). 224p. 1982. 13.95 (ISBN 0-913428-34-5). Landfall Pr.

Collett, Sidney. All About the Bible: A Popular Handbook. 324p. 1972. Repr. 11.95 (ISBN 0-8007-0004-X). Revell.

Colletta, Nat J. American Schools for the Natives of Ponape: A Study of Education & Culture Change in Micronesia. 1980. pap. text ed. 10.00x (ISBN 0-8248-0634-4, Eastwest Ctr). UH Pr.

Colletta, Nat J., jt. auth. see Knight, Peter T.

Colletti. De Rousseau a Lenine. (Publications Gramma Ser.). 318p. 1972. 33.00x (ISBN 0-677-50645-7). Gordon.

Colletti, Jack J. & Colletti, Paul J. A Freehand Approach to Technical Drawing. 336p. 1974. pap. 16.95 ref. ed. (ISBN 0-13-330548-1). P-H.

Colletti, Lucio. Marxism & Hegel. 1979. 20.00x (ISBN 0-8052-7020-5, Pub. by NLB); pap. 7.95 (ISBN 0-8052-7061-2). Schocken.

Colletti, Ned, jt. auth. see Ibach, Bob.

Colletti, Paul J., jt. auth. see Colletti, Jack J.

Colletti, Paul J., jt. auth. see Weinberg, Norman.

Colley, Ann C. Tennyson & Madness. LC 82-13689. 192p. 1983. 20.00 (ISBN 0-8203-0648-7). U of Ga Pr.

Colley, John L. Production, Operation, Planning & Control: Text & Cases. LC 77-72811. 1977. text ed. 33.50x (ISBN 0-8162-1726-2); instructor's manual 6.95 (ISBN 0-8162-1786-6). Holden-Day.

Colley, John L., Jr., et al. Operations Planning & Control. LC 77-4804. 1978. text ed. 24.00x (ISBN 0-8162-1736-X). Holden-Day.

Colliander, T. The Way of the Ascetics. 130p. 1978. 3.50 o.p. (ISBN 0-913026-19-0). St Nectarios.

Collias, Joe G. Frisco Power. LC 82-9347. (Locomotives & Trains of the St. Louis-San Francisco Railway 1903-1953 Ser.). (Illus.). 320p. Date not set. 35.00 (ISBN 0-8310-7155-9). Howell North.

Collie, C. H. Kinetic Theory & Entropy. LC 81-8332. (Illus.). 416p. 1983. pap. text ed. 22.00x (ISBN 0-582-44368-7). Longman.

Collie Club Of America. Complete Collie. LC 61-14210. (Complete Breed Book Ser.). (Illus.). 1962. 11.95 o.p. (ISBN 0-87605-105-0). Howell Bk.

--The New Collie. LC 82-19049. 304p. 1983. 14.95 (ISBN 0-87605-130-1). Howell Bk.

Collie, David, ed. see Ssu Shu.

Collie, M. J. Stirling Engine Design & Feasibility for Automotive Use. LC 79-13444. (Energy Technology Review Ser.: No. 47). (Illus.). 1979. 36.00 o.p. (ISBN 0-8155-0763-1). Noyes.

Collie, M. J., ed. Etching Compositions & Processes. LC 82-7894. (Chemical Technology Rev. 210). (Illus.). 308p. 1983. 42.00 (ISBN 0-8155-0913-8). Noyes.

Collie, Michael. George Borrow: Eccentric. LC 82-4397. (Illus.). 250p. 1983. 39.50 (ISBN 0-521-24615-6). Cambridge U Pr.

Collier & Helfrich. Mount Desert Island & Acadia National Park. (Illus.). 1978. 9.95 o.p. (ISBN 0-89272-078-6); pap. 8.95 (ISBN 0-89272-044-1). Down East.

Collier, et al. Kids' Stuff: Kindergarten - Nursery School. rev. ed. LC 78-70904. (The Kids' Stuff Set). 264p. (ps-k). 1982. pap. 10.95 (ISBN 0-913916-00-5, IP005). Incentive Pubns.

Collier, Arthur. Clavis Universalis: New Inquiry After Truth, Being a Demonstration of the Non-Existence or Impossibility of an External World, 1713. Wellek, Rene, ed. LC 75-11208. (British Philosophers & Theologians of the 17th & 18th Centuries Ser.). lib. bdg. 42.00 o.s.i. (ISBN 0-8240-1763-3). Garland Pub.

Collier, B. A. Maverick Trail. (YA) 1978. 6.95 (ISBN 0-685-05592-2, Avalon). Bouregy.

--One Foot in the Stirrup. (YA) 1978. 6.95 (ISBN 0-685-53392-1, Avalon). Bouregy.

--Trouble at Crossed Forks. (YA) 1979. 6.95 (ISBN 0-685-93880-8, Avalon). Bouregy.

Collier, Basil. Hidden Weapons. 386p. 1982. 35.00 (ISBN 0-241-10788-1, Pub. by Hamish Hamilton England). David & Charles.

Collier, Boyd, et al. Dynamic Ecology. (Biology Ser.). (Illus.). 528p. 1973. ref. ed. 23.95 (ISBN 0-13-221283-8). P-H.

Collier, C. Patrick. Geometry for Teachers. LC 75-25017. (Illus.). 352p. 1976. text ed. 20.50 o.p. (ISBN 0-395-20661-8). solutions manual 1.90 o.p. (ISBN 0-395-24219-3). HM.

Collier, Calhoun C. & Houston, Robert W. Modern Elementary Education: Teaching & Learning. (Illus.). 352p. 1976. text ed. 19.95x (ISBN 0-02-323770-8, 32377). Macmillan.

Collier, Carole. Five Hundred Five Wine Questions Your Friends Can't Answer. (Five Hundred Five Quiz Ser.). 160p. (Orig.). 1983. 11.95 (ISBN 0-8027-0730-0); pap. 6.95 (ISBN 0-8027-7209-9). Walker & Co.

Collier, Christopher, jt. auth. see Collier, James L.

Collier, Christopher see Weaver, Glenn.

Collier, David. Chinese-English Dictionary of Colloquial Terms Used in Modern Chinese Literature. 10.75 (ISBN 0-686-38037-1). Far Eastern Pubns.

Collier, Francis, et al. Quantitative Laboratory Experiments in General Chemistry. LC 75-26087. (Illus.). 288p. 1976. spiral bdg. 13.50 (ISBN 0-395-18982-9). HM.

Collier, G. Jazz. (Resources of Music Ser.). (Illus.). 200p. 1975. 22.95 (ISBN 0-521-20561-1); pap. 7.95 (ISBN 0-521-09887-4); tape o.p. 16.95 (ISBN 0-521-20854-8); record 11.95 (ISBN 0-521-20563-8). Cambridge U Pr.

Collier, George, ed. The Inca & Aztec States, Fourteen Hundred - Eighteen Hundred: Anthropology & History. (Studies in Anthropology Ser.). 438p. 1982. 47.00 (ISBN 0-12-181180-8). Acad Pr.

Collier, Gordon. Make Your Own World. 10.95 (ISBN 0-912576-04-9). R Collier.

Collier, Gordon, tr. see Grabes, Herbert.

Collier, Graham. Form, Space & Vision. 3rd ed. LC 75-167911. 1972. pap. text ed. 21.95 (ISBN 0-13-329458-7). P-H.

Collier, Gunning. Developmental Economics: Theories & Evidence. text ed. write for info (ISBN 0-408-10660-3). Butterworth.

Collier, Helen V. Counseling Women: A Guide for Therapists. (Illus.). 352p. 1982. text ed. 24.95 (ISBN 0-02-905840-6). Free Pr.

Collier, I., jt. auth. see Lewis, S.

Collier, J. G. Convective Boiling & Condensation. 2nd ed. (Illus.). 460p. 1981. text ed. 67.50 (ISBN 0-07-011798-5). McGraw.

Collier, J. W. Wood Finishing. 1967. 13.75 o.p. (ISBN 0-08-011242-0). Pergamon.

Collier, James L. CB. (Career Concise Guides Ser.). (Illus.). (gr. 7 up). 1977. PLB 8.90 s&l o.p. (ISBN 0-531-00095-8). Watts.

Collier, James L. & Collier, Christopher. Jump Ship to Freedom. LC 81-65492. 192p. (gr. 7 up). 1981. 10.95 (ISBN 0-440-04205-4). Delacorte.

Collier, Jeremy. Collier Tracts Seventeen Three to Seventeen Eight: Mr. Collier's Disuasive from the Playhouse. Bd. with A Farther Vindication of the Short View of the English Stage. Collier, Jeremy; The Person of Quality's Answer to Mr. Colliers Letters Being a Disswasive from the Playhouse. Dennis, John; A Representation of the Impiety & Immorality of the English Stage; Some Thoughts Concerning the Stage in a Letter to a Lady. Collier, Jeremy; The Stage-Beaux Toss'd in a Blanket. Gildon, Charles. LC 70-170462. (The English Stage Theory: Vol. 35). lib. bdg. 50.00 o.s.i. (ISBN 0-8240-0618-6). Garland Pub.

Collier, John. On the Gleaming Way: Navajos, Eastern Pueblos, Zunis, Hopis, Apaches & Their Land, & Their Meanings to the World. LC 82-71595. 163p. (Photos, Orig). 1962. pap. 5.95 (ISBN 0-8040-0232-0, SB). Swallow.

Collier, John G., jt. auth. see Lauterpacht, Elihu.

Collier, Joseph M., ed. Essays in American History & Culture, Vol. 1. (Illus.). 1982. pap. text ed. 3.50 (ISBN 0-942738-00-4). Amer Studies.

Collier, Kathleen W. & Ross, Mary C. Joseph Collier, Pioneer Photographer. (Illus.). 1983. price not set (ISBN 0-87108-633-6). Pruett.

Collier, Keith. Construction Contracts. (Illus.). 1979. ref. ed. 23.95 (ISBN 0-8359-0912-3); text ed. 18.95. Reston.

--Fundamentals of Construction Estimating & Cost Accounting. (Illus.). 400p. 1974. 23.95 (ISBN 0-13-335604-3). P-H.

Collier, Larry. How to Fly Helicopters. (Modern Aviation Ser.). (Illus.). 1979. 9.95 (ISBN 0-8306-9840-X); pap. 8.95 (ISBN 0-8306-2264-0, 2264). TAB Bks.

Collier, Louise W. Pilgrimage: A Tale of Old Natchez. 416p. (Orig.). 1983. pap. 9.95 (ISBN 0-918518-26-1). St Luke TN.

Collier, Paul & Lal, Deepak. Poverty & Growth in Kenya. (Working Paper: No. 389). 76p. 1980. 5.00 (ISBN 0-686-36149-0, WP-0389). World Bank.

Collier, Peter & Horowitz, David. The Rockefellers: An American Dynasty. (Illus.). 1977. pap. 4.95 (ISBN 0-451-11370-5, AE1370, Sig). NAL.

Collier, Peter, ed. Dilemmas of Democracy: Readings in American Government. 385p. (Orig.). 1976. pap. text ed. 10.95 o.p. (ISBN 0-15-517650-1, HC). HarBraceJ.

Collier, Philip E. It Seems to Me. 1982. 3.95 (ISBN 0-86544-019-0). Salvation Army.

Collier, Phyllis. How to Marry a Winner. 203p. 1982. 11.95 (ISBN 0-13-423624-6); pap. 5.95 (ISBN 0-13-423616-5). P-H.

Collier, Raymond O., Jr. & Hummel, Thomas J., eds. Experimental Design & Interpretation. LC 76-18039. (Readings in Educational Research Ser.). 1977. 30.75 (ISBN 0-8211-0225-7); text ed. 28.00 10 or more copies (ISBN 0-685-71415-2). McCutchan.

Collier, Richard. Bridge Across the Sky: The Berlin Blockade & Airlift. LC 77-17384. 1978. 12.95 o.p. (ISBN 0-07-011796-9, GB). McGraw.

--War in the Desert. LC 77-81945. (World War II Ser.). (gr. 6 up). 1977. PLB 19.92 (ISBN 0-8094-2475-4). Silver.

Collier, Robert. The Amazing Secrets of the Masters of the Far East. 10.95 (ISBN 0-912576-02-2). R Collier.

--Be Rich. 1970. pap. 2.00 (ISBN 0-910140-24-3). Anthony.

--Prayer Works. 1950. pap. 3.75 (ISBN 0-910140-04-9). Anthony.

Collier, S. Ideas & Politics of Chilean Independence, 1808-1833. (Cambridge Latin American Studies). 1968. 47.50 (ISBN 0-521-04690-4). Cambridge U Pr.

Collier, Sophia. Soul Rush: The Odyssey of a Young Woman of the '70s. LC 77-13901. 1978. 8.95 o.p. (ISBN 0-688-03276-1). Morrow.

Collier, William L., et al. Income, Employment & Food Systems in Javanese Coastal Villages. LC 77-620017. (Papers in International Studies: Southeast Asia: No. 44). (Illus.). pap. 10.00x (ISBN 0-89680-031-8, Ohio U Ctr Intl). Ohio U Pr.

Collier, Zena. Seven for the People: Public Interest Groups at Work. LC 79-136. 192p. (gr. 7 up). 1979. PLB 8.29 o.p. (ISBN 0-671-32926-X). Messner.

Colligan, Doug, jt. auth. see Teresi, Dick.

Colligan, Michael J., et al, eds. Mass Psychogenic Illness: A Social Psychological Analysis. 272p. 1982. 29.95 (ISBN 0-89859-160-0). L Erlbaum Assocs.

Colligan, Owen A., ed. Saint John Damascene: Dialectica, Version of Robert Grosseteste. (Text Ser.). 1953. 3.00 o.p. (ISBN 0-686-11552-X). Franciscan Inst.

Collignon, Jean, ed. see Mauriac, Francois.

Collin, H. B., jt. auth. see Augusteyn, R. C.

Collin, Laure. Histoire Abregee De la Musique et Des Musiciens. (Music Reprint Ser.). (Fr.). 1977. Repr. of 1897 ed. lib. bdg. 35.00 (ISBN 0-306-70875-2). Da Capo.

Collin, Richard, jt. auth. see Collin, Rima.

Collin, Rima & Collin, Richard. The New Orleans Cookbook. LC 74-7729. 320p. 1975. 16.50 (ISBN 0-394-48898-9). Knopf.

Collin, Robert E. Field Theory of Guided Waves. (International Pure & Applied Physics Ser.). 1960. text ed. 41.50 o.p. (ISBN 0-07-011802-7, C). McGraw.

--Foundations for Microwave Engineering. 1966. 45.00 (ISBN 0-07-011801-9, C). McGraw.

Collin, Robert E. & Zucker, F. J. Antenna Theory, Pts. 1-2. (Inter-University Electronics Ser.). 1969. Pt. 1. text ed. 55.00 (ISBN 0-07-011799-3, C); Pt. 2. text ed. 59.50 (ISBN 0-07-011800-0). McGraw.

Collin, Wilkie. The Moonstone. (Bantam Classics Ser.). 464p. (YA) (gr. 9-12). 1982. pap. 2.95 (ISBN 0-553-21084-X). Bantam.

Colling, Gene. Bicyclist's Guide to Yellowstone National Park. (Illus.). 64p. 1983. pap. 4.95 (ISBN 0-934318-15-8). Falcon Pr MT.

Colling, Russell L. Hospital Security. 2nd ed. 1982. text ed. 29.95 (ISBN 0-409-95048-3). Butterworth.

--Hospital Security. LC 75-46098. (Illus.). 384p. 1976. 19.95 o.p. (ISBN 0-913708-22-4). Butterworth.

Collingridge, David. Critical Decision Making: A New Theory of Social Choice. LC 82-6017. 1982. 25.00x (ISBN 0-312-17418-7). St Martin.

--The Social Control of Technology. 1981. 26.00 (ISBN 0-312-73168-X). St Martin.

Collings, jt. auth. see McBurney, D.

Collings, A. J. & Luxon, S. G. Safe Use of Solvents. 37.00 (ISBN 0-12-181250-2). Acad Pr.

Collings, Michael R. Reader's Guide to Piers Anthony. Schlobin, Roger C., ed. (Reader's Guides to Contemporary Science Fiction & Fantasy Authors Ser.: Vol. 20). (Illus., Orig.). 1983. 10.95x (ISBN 0-916732-53-3); pap. text ed. 4.95x (ISBN 0-916732-52-5). Starmont Hse.

Collingswood, Hermann. A Collection of Fifty-Five Dramatic Illustrations in Full Colours of the Cathedral Cities of Italy. (The Masterpieces of World Architectual Library). (Illus.). 107p. 1983. Repr. of 1911 ed. 287.75 (ISBN 0-89901-081-4). Found Class Reprints.

Collingwood, Guillermo. Las Dos Naturalezas del Creyente. 2nd ed. Bennett, Gordon H., ed. Bautista, Sara, tr. from Eng. (La Serie Diamante). (Illus.). 52p. (Span.). 1982. pap. 0.85 (ISBN 0-942504-03-8). Overcomer Pr.

Collingwood, Lucy. Reaching Up Reproducibles. (Perspectives II Ser.). 129p. (gr. 7-12). 1982. pap. 10.00 (ISBN 0-87879-322-4). Acad Therapy.

Collingwood, Peter. Peter Collingwood: His Weaves & Weaving. Tidball, Harriet, ed. LC 63-2332. (Shuttle Craft Guild Monograph: No. 8). (Illus.). 46p. 1963. pap. 8.45 (ISBN 0-916658-08-2). HTH Pubs.

Collingwood, R. G. & Richmond, Ian. The Archaeology of Roman Britain. 2nd ed. 1969. 55.00x (ISBN 0-416-27580-X). Methuen Inc.

Collingwood, R. J. Essay on Metaphysics. LC 71-183823. 354p. 1972. pap. 5.95 (ISBN 0-89526-996-1). Regnery-Gateway.

Collingwood, Robin G. Autobiography. 1939. 9.95x (ISBN 0-19-824694-3). Oxford U Pr.

--Idea of History. Knox, T. M., ed. 1956. pap. 9.95 (ISBN 0-19-500205-9, 1, GB). Oxford U Pr.

--Idea of Nature. 1960. pap. 5.95 (ISBN 0-19-500217-2, GB). Oxford U Pr.

--Principles of Art. 1958. pap. 8.95 (ISBN 0-19-500209-1, GB). Oxford U Pr.

--Speculum Mentis: The Map of Knowledge. LC 82-15552. 327p. 1982. Repr. of 1924 ed. lib. bdg. 39.75x (ISBN 0-313-23701-8, COSM). Greenwood.

Collingwood, Stuart D. Life & Letters of Lewis Carroll. LC 67-23871. 1967. Repr. of 1899 ed. 34.00x (ISBN 0-8103-3061-X). Gale.

Collini, Alexandre. Mon Sejour Aupres De Voltaire, et Lettres Inedites Que M'ecrivit Cet Homme Celebre Jusqu'a la Derniere Annee De Sa Vie. Repr. of 1807 ed. 109.00 o.p. (ISBN 0-8287-0210-1). Clearwater Pub.

Collini, Stefan. Liberalism & Sociology: Lt. Hobhouse & Political Argument in English, 1880-1914. LC 78-23779. 1979. 34.50 (ISBN 0-521-22304-0). Cambridge U Pr.

Collins. Geochemistry of Oilfield Waters. (Developments in Petroleum Science Ser: Vol. 1). 430p. 1975. 81.00 (ISBN 0-444-41183-6). Elsevier.

--Synopsis of Chest Diseases. 224p. 1979. pap. 16.00 (ISBN 0-7236-0526-2). Wright-PSG.

Collins, jt. auth. see Lappe.

Collins, et al. Aleutian Islands: Their People & Natural History. facsimile ed. (Illus.). 157p. Date not set. pap. 15.00 (ISBN 0-8466-0186-9, SJS186). Shorey.

Collins, A. Frederick. The Radio Amateur's Handbook. 14th ed. LC 78-3303. (Illus.). 1979. 11.49 (ISBN 0-690-01772-3). T Y Crowell.
Collins, A. Frederick & Hertzberg, Robert. The Radio Amateur's Handbook. 15th, rev. ed. LC 82-48666. (Illus.). 416p. 1983. 10.53i (ISBN 0-06-181366-4, HarpT). Har-Row.
Collins, A. J., jt. auth. see Chatfield, C.
Collins, Ace, jt. auth. see Mandrell, Louise.
Collins, Adrian, tr. see Nietzsche, Friedrich.
Collins, Adrian A. Federal Income Taxation of Employee Benefits. LC 76-163722. 770p. 1971. looseleaf with 1978 rev. pages & suppl. 47.50 o.p. (ISBN 0-87632-077-9). Boardman.
Collins, Al J. & Frazier, Gregory. Tales from the Purple Grotto: Great Jazz & Good Times in Broadcasting. (Illus.). 200p. (Orig.). 1983. pap. 7.95 (ISBN 0-89844-084-X). Troubador Pr.
Collins, Alberta C. & Dawson, Mildred A. Alphabet Soup. rev. ed. (Cornerstone Ser.). (gr. 2-3). 1978. pap. text ed. 5.32 (ISBN 0-201-41022-2, Sch Div); tchr's. ed. 6.76 (ISBN 0-201-41023-0). A-W.
Collins, Anthony. Essai sur la Nature et la Destination de l'Ame. (Holbach & His Friends Ser). 302p. (Fr.). 1974. Repr. of 1769 ed. lib. bdg. 80.00x o.p. (ISBN 0-8287-0211-X, 1553). Clearwater Pub.
--Examen des Propheties qui Servent de Fondement a la Religion Chretienne. (Holbach & His Friends Ser). 181p. (Fr.). 1974. Repr. of 1768 ed. lib. bdg. 60.00x o.p. (ISBN 0-8287-0212-8, 1577). Clearwater Pub.
Collins, Beverly & Mees, Inger. Working with the Sounds of English & Dutch. vii, 72p. 1982. pap. write for info. (ISBN 90-04-06836-8). E J Brill.
Collins, Billy. Pokerface. 1977. pap. text ed. 4.00 (ISBN 0-918298-04-0). Kenmore.
Collins, Bob, jt. auth. see Andretti, Mario.
Collins, Bobby & White, Fred. Elementary Forestry. 1981. text ed. 18.95 (ISBN 0-8359-1647-2); instr's. manual free (ISBN 0-8359-1646-4). Reston.
Collins, Bruce. Origins of America's Civil War. LC 81-81340. 165p. 1981. text ed. 24.50x (ISBN 0-8419-0714-5); pap. text ed. 13.50x (ISBN 0-8419-0715-3). Holmes & Meier.
Collins, Bud & Hollander, Zander, eds. Bud Collins Modern Encyclopedia of Tennis. LC 79-8919. (Illus.). 416p. 1980. 24.95 o.p. (ISBN 0-385-13093-7). Doubleday.
Collins, C. H. Microbiological Hazards. Date not set. text ed. price not set (ISBN 0-408-10650-6). Butterworth.
Collins, C. H. & Lyne, P. Microbiological Methods. 4th ed. 1976. 29.95 (ISBN 0-408-70716-X). Butterworth.
Collins, Carroll L., jt. auth. see Horn, Carin E.
Collins, Charlotte. Not Healed? LC 82-73707. 1983. pap. text ed. 2.50 (ISBN 0-932050-15-8). New Puritan.
Collins, Christopher. The Act of Poetry. 1970. pap. text ed. 3.95 (ISBN 0-394-30119-6, 30119). Phila Bk Co.
Collins, D. Aspects of British Politics, 1904-1919. 1966. 27.00 o.p. (ISBN 0-08-010987-X); pap. 12.75 o.p. (ISBN 0-08-010986-1). Pergamon.
Collins, D., et al. Background to Archaeology: Britain in Its European Setting. (Illus.). 128p. (Orig.). 1973. 17.95 o.p. (ISBN 0-521-20155-1); pap. 6.95x (ISBN 0-521-09808-4). Cambridge U Pr.
Collins, D. G. An English-Laos Dictionary. 238p. 1982. Repr. of 1906 ed. 90.00x (ISBN 0-576-03128-3, Gregg Intl). State Mutual Bk.
Collins, D. H., ed. Power Sources Two: Proceedings, International Symposium on Batteries, 6th. LC 62-22327. 1970. inquire for price o.p. (ISBN 0-08-013435-1). Pergamon.
Collins, Dan S. Andrew Marvell: A Reference Guide. 1981. lib. bdg. 32.00 (ISBN 0-8161-8017-2, Hall Reference). G K Hall.
Collins, David R. Charles Lindbergh: Hero Pilot. LC 77-13956. (Discovery Ser.). (Illus.). (gr. 2-5). 1978. PLB 6.69 (ISBN 0-8116-6322-1). Garrard.
--Football Running Backs: Three Ground Gainers. LC 75-23346. (Sports Library). (Illus.). 96p. (gr. 3-6). 1976. PLB 7.12 (ISBN 0-8116-6677-8). Garrard.
--Harry S. Truman: People's President. LC 74-20965. (Discovery Ser). (Illus.). 80p. (gr. 2-5). 1975. PLB 6.69 (ISBN 0-8116-6318-3). Garrard.
--If I Could, I Would. LC 78-27430. (Imagination Books). (Illus.). (gr. 1-5). 1979. PLB 6.69 (ISBN 0-8116-4417-0). Garrard.
--Linda Richards: First American Trained Nurse. LC 73-5889. (Discovery Ser). (Illus.). 80p. (gr. 2-5). 1973. PLB 6.69 (ISBN 0-8116-6313-2). Garrard.
Collins, Dennis & Boor, Jacklyn. Real Estate Options: How to Score in a Tight Market. 192p. 1983. 13.95 (ISBN 0-13-765123-6); pap. 6.95 (ISBN 0-13-765115-5). P-H.
Collins, Donald, jt. auth. see Poynter, Margaret.
Collins, Doris L., jt. auth. see Joel, Lucille A.
Collins, Dwane R., jt. auth. see Collins, Myrtle T.
Collins, E. W., jt. auth. see Kreutker, C. W.
Collins, Ed. Make Your Kid an Athlete. 1982. write for info. o.p. Green Hill.
Collins, Edward A., et al. Experiments in Polymer Science. LC 73-650. 530p. 1973. pap. text ed. 24.95 (ISBN 0-471-16585-9, Pub. by Wiley-Interscience). Wiley.
Collins, Edward, Jr. International Law in a Changing World. 1970. text ed. 23.00 (ISBN 0-394-30098-X, RanC). Random.
Collins, Edward M., tr. see Von Clausewitz, Karl.
Collins, Edward W. Geological Circular 82-3: Surficial Evidence of Tectonic Activity & Erosion Rates, Palestine, Keechi, & Oakwood Salt Domes, East Texas. (Illus.). 39p. 1982. 1.75 (ISBN 0-686-37547-5). U of Tex Econ Geology.
Collins, Edward W., et al. Oakwood Salt Dome, East Texas: Surface Geology & Drainage Analysis. (Geological Circular Ser.: No. 81-6). (Illus.). 23p. 1982. 1.25 (ISBN 0-686-36994-7). U of Tex Econ Geology.
Collins, Eric J., jt. auth. see Collins, Ian D.
Collins, F. S. The Green Algae of North America & Supplements 1-2. 1970. 60.00 (ISBN 3-7682-0680-7). Lubrecht & Cramer.
Collins, Fletcher, Jr. A Medieval Songbook: Troubadour & Trouvers. 1982. 14.95x (ISBN 0-8139-0970-8). U Pr of Va.
--Production of Medieval Church Music-Drama. LC 78-168610. (Illus.). xiii, 356p. 1972. 20.00 (ISBN 0-8139-0373-4). U Pr of Va.
Collins, Frank, jt. auth. see Seiler, Robert E.
Collins, Gary. The Rebuilding of Psychology. 1977. 6.95 (ISBN 0-8423-5314-3); pap. 6.95 (ISBN 0-8423-5315-1). Tyndale.
Collins, Gary R. Beyond Easy Believism. 1982. 8.95 (ISBN 0-8499-0332-7). Word Pub.
--Calm Down. 2nd ed. 160p. 1983. pap. 4.95 (ISBN 0-88449-096-3, A424631). Vision Hse.
Collins, George R., ed. see Miliutin, Nikolai A.
Collins, Gerarda M., jt. auth. see Parker, Robert P.
Collins, Glenn. How to Be a Guilty Parent. (Illus.). 1983. 8.95 (ISBN 0-8129-1034-6). Times Bks.
Collins, Harold R. Amos Tutuola. (World Authors Ser.). 13.95 (ISBN 0-8057-2902-X, Twayne). G K Hall.
--The New English of the Onitsha Chapbooks. LC 78-630645. (Papers in International Studies: Africa: No. 1). 1968. pap. 3.00 (ISBN 0-89680-035-0, Ohio U Ctr Intl). Ohio U Pr.
Collins, Harry M. Law of International Oil & Gas. 1982. bdr. loose-leaf 85.00 (ISBN 0-379-20728-1). Oceana.
Collins, Henry B., et al. The Far North: 2000 Years of American Eskimo & Indian Art. LC 77-3132. (Illus.). 320p. 1977. 22.50x (ISBN 0-253-32120-4); pap. 17.50x o.p. (ISBN 0-253-28105-9). Ind U Pr.
Collins, Henry H., Jr. & Ransom, Jay E., eds. Harper & Row's Complete Field Guide to North American Wildlife: Eastern Edition. LC 80-8198. (Illus.). 810p. 1981. 17.50i (ISBN 0-690-01977-7, HarpT); flexible vinyl cover 12.95i (ISBN 0-690-01971-8); western edition 17.50i (ISBN 0-690-01979-3). Har-Row.
Collins, Hugh. Marxism & Law. (Marxist Introductions Ser.). (Illus.). 200p. 1982. 22.00 (ISBN 0-19-876093-0). Oxford U Pr.
Collins, Ian D. & Collins, Eric J. Window Selection: A Guide for Architects & Designers. (Illus.). 1977. text ed. 21.95 (ISBN 0-408-00285-9). Butterworth.
Collins, Irene. Napoleon & His Parliaments, Eighteen Hundred to Eighteen Fifteen. 1979. 26.00x (ISBN 0-312-55892-9). St Martin.
Collins, Irene, ed. Government & Society in France: Eighteen Fourteen to Eighteen Forty-Eight. LC 78-143997. (Documents of Modern History Ser). 1971. 22.50 (ISBN 0-312-34160-1). St Martin.
Collins, J. A. Failure of Materials in Mechanical Design: Analysis, Prediction, Prevention. LC 80-20674. 629p. 1981. 44.95x (ISBN 0-471-05024-5, Pub. by Wiley-Interscience). Wiley.
Collins, J. H. The Mineralogy of Cornwall & Devon. 1981. 50.00x (ISBN 0-686-97167-1, Pub. by D B Barton England). State Mutual Bk.
Collins, J. H. & Masotti, L. Computer-Aided Design of Surface Acoustic Wave Devices. 1976. 64.00 (ISBN 0-444-41476-2). Elsevier.
Collins, Jackie. Chances. (Orig.). 1982. 14.95 (ISBN 0-446-51237-0); pap. 3.95 (ISBN 0-446-30268-6). Warner Bks.
--The Hollywood Zoo. 320p. 1980. pap. 2.50 o.p. (ISBN 0-523-40969-9). Pinnacle Bks.
--The Love Killers. Orig. Title: Love Head. 192p. 1975. pap. 2.95 (ISBN 0-446-30816-1). Warner Bks.
--Lovers & Gamblers. 1979. 12.95 o.p. (ISBN 0-448-15179-0, G&D). Putnam Pub Group.
--Lovers & Gamblers. 592p. 1980. pap. 3.95 (ISBN 0-446-30782-3). Warner Bks.
--The Stud. 1982. pap. 2.50 (ISBN 0-451-12221-6, AE2221, Sig). NAL.
--The World Is Full of Divorced Women. 416p. (Orig.). 1981. pap. 3.95 (ISBN 0-446-30783-1). Warner Bks.
Collins, Jacquelin, jt. auth. see Blakeley, Brian L.
Collins, James. British Empiricists: Locke, Berkeley, Hume. (Orig.). 1967. pap. 3.50 o.p. (ISBN 0-02-813460-5). Glencoe.
--CCD Methods in Modern Catechetics. (Orig.). 1966. pap. 2.95 o.p. (ISBN 0-685-07615-6, 80130). Glencoe.
--Continental Rationalists: Descartes, Spinoza, Leibniz. (Orig.). 1967. pap. 3.50 o.p. (ISBN 0-02-813480-X). Glencoe.
Collins, James C. Accident Reconstruction. (Illus.). 308p. 1979. 23.75x (ISBN 0-398-03907-0). C C Thomas.
Collins, James D. Lure of Wisdom. 1962. 7.95 (ISBN 0-87462-127-5). Marquette.
Collins, James F., ed. Handbook of Clinical Ophthalmology. LC 82-12657. 600p. 1982. 69.50 (ISBN 0-89352-190-6). Masson Pub.
Collins, James L., jt. auth. see Craig, William N.
Collins, James R., et al, eds. Hine's Insurance Counsel: 1982-83 Edition. 74th ed. 611p. 1982. 10.00x (ISBN 0-910911-00-2). Hines Legal Direct.
Collins, Jean. She Was There: Stories of Pioneering Women Journalists. LC 80-36769. (Illus.). 192p. (gr. 7 up). 1980. PLB 8.79 o.p. (ISBN 0-671-33082-9). Messner.
Collins, Jean E., jt. auth. see Ozer, Mark N.
Collins, Jim. First to the Moon. LC 78-13611. (Famous Firsts Ser.). (Illus.). 1978. PLB 10.76 (ISBN 0-89547-051-9). Silver.
Collins, John. Daniel, One-Two Maccabees, with Excursus on Apocalyptic Genre, Vol. 15. 1982. 12.95 (ISBN 0-89453-250-2); pap. 9.95 (ISBN 0-686-32769-1). M Glazier.
--U. S. Defense Planning: A Critique. 325p. 1982. lib. bdg. 30.00 (ISBN 0-86531-549-3); pap. text ed. 11.95 (ISBN 0-86531-554-X). Westview.
Collins, John, jt. auth. see Lovett, William.
Collins, John A. & Murawski, Kris, eds. Massive Transfusion in Surgery & Trauma. LC 82-18657. (Progress in Clinical & Biological Research Ser.: Vol. 108). 319p. 1982. 32.00 (ISBN 0-8451-0108-0). A R Liss.
Collins, John J. Between Athens & Jerusalem: Jewish Indentity in the Hellenistic Diaspora. 272p. Date not set. 14.95 (ISBN 0-8245-0491-7). Crossroad NY.
--Primitive Religion. (Littlefield Adams Quality Paperbacks Ser.: No. 342). 256p. 1978. pap. 4.95 (ISBN 0-8226-0342-X). Littlefield.
Collins, John N. Foreign Conflict Behavior & Domestic Disorder in Africa. (Foreign & Comparative Studies, Eastern African: No. 4). 128p. (Orig.). 1971. pap. text ed. 5.50x o.p. (ISBN 0-915984-02-4). Syracuse U Foreign Comp.
Collins, Joseph, jt. auth. see Lappe, Frances M.
Collins, Joseph, jt. auth. see Lappe, Francis M.
Collins, Joseph, et al. What Difference Could a Revolution Make? Food & Farming in the New Nicaragua. 200p. 1982. pap. 4.95 (ISBN 0-935028-10-2). Inst Food & Develop.
Collins, Judy. Judy Collins Song Book. (Illus.). 1969. pap. 8.95 (ISBN 0-448-01918-3, G&D). Putnam Pub Group.
Collins, K. J. & Weiner, J. S. Human Adaptability: A History & Compendium of Research in the International Biological Program. LC 76-39634. 1977. text ed. 32.50x o.p. (ISBN 0-312-39637-6). St Martin.
Collins, L. W., jt. ed. see Wendlandt, W. W.
Collins, Larry & La Pierre, Dominique. The Fifth Horseman. 496p. 1981. pap. 3.50 (ISBN 0-380-54734-1, 60889-8). Avon.
Collins, Larry & Lapierre, Dominique. The Fifth Horseman. 1980. 14.95 o.s.i. (ISBN 0-671-24316-0). S&S.
--Freedom at Midnight. 608p. 1976. pap. 4.95 (ISBN 0-380-00693-6, 617471). Avon.
--Mountbatten & the Partition of India. viii, 191p. 1982. text ed. 20.00x (ISBN 0-7069-1787-1, Pub. by Vikas India). Advent NY.
Collins, Lyndhurst, ed. The Use of Models in the Social Sciences. LC 75-22018. 227p. 1975. 19.75 o.p. (ISBN 0-89158-507-9). Westview.
Collins, Lyndhurst & Walker, David F., eds. Locational Dynamics of Manufacturing Activity. LC 73-21939. 412p. 1975. 64.95x (ISBN 0-471-16582-4, Pub. by Wiley-Interscience). Wiley.
Collins, M. B., jt. auth. see Banner, F. T.
Collins, M. E. Ireland, Eighteen Hundred to Nineteen Seventy. (Illus.). 1976. pap. text ed. 7.95x (ISBN 0-582-22140-4). Longman.
Collins, Mabel. Light on the Path. Incl. Through the Gates of Gold. verbatim ed. LC 68-21157. 1976. 6.00 o.p. (ISBN 0-911500-37-5); pap. 3.50 o.p. (ISBN 0-911500-38-3). Theos U Pr.
Collins, Mallary M. & Fontenelle, Don, 2nd. Changing Student Behaviors: A Positive Approach. 192p. 1981. text ed. 11.25x (ISBN 0-87073-657-4); pap. text ed. 6.95. Schenkman.
Collins, Margaret S., et al, eds. Science & the Question of Human Equality. (AAAS Selected Symposium: No. 58). 180p. 1981. softcover 17.50 (ISBN 0-89158-952-X). Westview.
Collins, Marjorie A. Dedication: What It's All About. LC 76-18069. 1976. pap. 3.50 (ISBN 0-87123-103-4, 210103). Bethany Hse.
Collins, Marva & Tamarkin, Civia. Marva Collins Way. 227p. 1982. 12.95 (ISBN 0-87477-235-4). J P Tarcher.
Collins, Mary & Power, David, eds. A Creative Tradition. (Concilium 1983: Vol. 162). 128p. (Orig.). 1983. pap. 6.95 (ISBN 0-8164-2442-X). Seabury.
Collins, Mattie. Communication in Health Care: The Human Connection in the Life Cycle. 2nd ed. LC 82-3482. (Illus.). 276p. 1982. pap. text ed. 11.95 (ISBN 0-8016-1081-8). Mosby.
Collins, Max. Hard Cash. (Nolan Ser.: No. 5). 192p. (Orig.). 1982. pap. 1.95 o.p. (ISBN 0-523-41163-4). Pinnacle Bks.
--No Cure for Death. 192p. 1983. 12.95 (ISBN 0-8027-5488-0). Walker & Co.
--Nolan: Bait Money, No. 1. 192p. pap. 1.95 o.p. (ISBN 0-523-41159-6). Pinnacle Bks.
Collins, Michael. Freak. 216p. 1983. 9.95 (ISBN 0-396-08104-5). Dodd.
Collins, Michael, jt. auth. see Capie, Forrest.
Collins, Michael, ed. see Scarlatti.
Collins, Myrtle T. & Collins, Dwane R. Survival Kit for Teachers (& Parents) LC 74-10230. 1975. pap. text ed. 10.95x (ISBN 0-673-16443-8). Scott F.
Collins, Nancy W. Professional Women & Their Mentors: A Practical Guide to Mentoring for the Woman Who Wants to Get Ahead. 192p. 1982. 12.95 (ISBN 0-13-725994-8); pap. 6.95 (ISBN 0-13-725986-7). P-H.
Collins, Nell & Moster, Mary Beth. The Valley is Bright. 102p. 1983. pap. 4.95 (ISBN 0-8407-5835-9). Nelson.
Collins, Nigel, jt. auth. see Cotterell, Arthur.
Collins, Norman. The Husband's Story. LC 78-3594. 1978. 10.95 o.p. (ISBN 0-689-10898-2). Atheneum.
Collins, P. D. An Introduction to Regge Theory & High-Energy Physics. LC 76-2233. (Cambridge Monographs on Mathematical Physics). (Illus.). 1977. 110.00 (ISBN 0-521-21245-6). Cambridge U Pr.
Collins, Pat. How to Be a Really Nice Person: Doing the Right Things - Your Way. 256p. 1983. 11.95 (ISBN 0-87131-406-1). M Evans.
Collins, Pat L. Tumble, Tumble, Tumbleweed. (gr. 1-4). 8.25 (ISBN 0-686-36220-9). Whitman Pub.
Collins, Patricia. Mary. 208p. 1981. 18.00x o.p. (ISBN 0-86188-115-X, Pub. By Judy Piatkus). State Mutual Bk.
--Your Daughter Is Brain Damaged: A Mother's Story. (Illus.). 256p. 1981. 11.95 o.p. (ISBN 0-525-93152-X). Dutton.
Collins, Paul, ed. Administration for Development in Nigeria: Introduction & Readings. 337p. (Orig.). 1980. pap. text ed. 11.95x (ISBN 0-686-82988-3). Transaction Bks.
Collins, Philip. Thackeray: Interviews & Recollections, 2 vols. LC 81-21327. 20.00 ea. (ISBN 0-312-79488-6). St Martin.
Collins, Philip, ed. Dickens: Interviews & Recollections, 2 vols. (Illus.). 1981. 28.50x ea. Vol. 1, 210 1 Pgs (ISBN 0-389-20042-5). Vol. 2, 200 Pgs (ISBN 0-389-20043-3). B&N Imports.
Collins, Philip, ed. see Dickens, Charles.
Collins, R. E. Flow of Fluids Through Porous Materials. 270p. 1961. 37.95x (ISBN 0-87814-072-7). Pennwell Pub.
Collins, R. M. Chapters from the Unwritten History of the War Between the States. 335p. 1982. 30.00 (ISBN 0-89029-066-0). Pr of Morningside.
Collins, R. S. Gold. LC 82-80279. (Illus.). 192p. 1982. cancelled (ISBN 0-528-81550-4). Rand.
Collins, Randall, ed. Sociological Theory 1983. (Social & Behavioral Science Ser.). 1983. text ed. 19.95x (ISBN 0-87589-557-3). Jossey-Bass.
Collins, Raymond A., ed. The Giant Handbook of Electronic Circuits. (Illus.). 882p. 1980. 24.95 o.p. (ISBN 0-8306-9673-3, 1300); pap. 18.95 (ISBN -08306-9662-8, 1300). TAB Bks.
Collins, Raymond F. Introduction to the New Testament. (Illus.). 480p. 1983. 24.95 (ISBN 0-385-18126-4). Doubleday.
Collins, Robert G. Critical Essays on John Cheever. (Critical Essays on American Literature Ser.). 1982. lib. bdg. 32.00 (ISBN 0-8161-8623-5). G K Hall.
Collins, Robert O. African History: Text & Readings. 1971. text ed. 10.50 (ISBN 0-394-30135-8, 30135). Phila Bk Co.
--Europeans in Africa. 1970. pap. text ed. 3.50x (ISBN 0-394-31004-7). Phila Bk Co.
Collins, Robert O. & Tignor, Robert L. Egypt & the Sudan. (Orig.). (YA) (gr. 9-12). 1967. pap. 1.95 o.p. (ISBN 0-13-246603-1, Spec, Spec). P-H.
Collins, Rowland L., ed. Beowulf. Pearson, Lucien D., tr. LC 64-10837. (Midland Bks.: No. 73). 128p. 1965. pap. 1.75x (ISBN 0-253-20073-3). Ind U Pr.
Collins, S. H. Emigrant's Guide to the United States of America, Containing All Things Necessary to Be Known by Every Class of Persons Emigrating to That Continent. LC 70-145476. (The American Immigration Library). vi, 144p. 1971. Repr. of 1830 ed. lib. bdg. 9.95x (ISBN 0-89198-008-3). Ozer.
Collins, Sarah. Beauty: Making It Happen. LC 78-75105. (Illus.). 1979. pap. 5.95 (ISBN 0-89169-549-4). Reed Bks.
Collins, Shelia, jt. auth. see Golden, Renny.
Collins, Susanna. Breathless Dawn. (Second Chance at Love Ser.: No. 94). 192p. 1983. pap. 1.75 (ISBN 0-515-06858-6). Jove Pubns.
--Hard to Handle. (Second Chance at Love Ser.: No. 14). 192p. (Orig.). 1981. pap. 1.75 o.s.i. (ISBN 0-515-05704-5). Jove Pubns.
--On Wings of Magic. 192p. 1982. pap. 1.75 (ISBN 0-515-06650-8). Jove Pubns.
Collins, Trish. Grinkles: A Keen Halloween Story. (Easy-Read Story Bks.). (Illus.). 32p. (gr. k-3). 1981. 8.60 (ISBN 0-531-02471-7); 7.90 (ISBN 0-531-04190-5). Watts.
Collins, Vincent P. Me, Myself & You. 2.95 o.p. (ISBN 0-686-92381-2, 6540). Hazelden.
Collins, W. Andrews, jt. auth. see Sprinthall, Norman A.
Collins, W. Lucas. Montagne. 192p. 1982. Repr. of 1879 ed. lib. bdg. 25.00 (ISBN 0-89760-166-1). Telegraph Bks.

Collins, W. P., ed. Perspectives on State & Local Politics. LC 74-5202. (Illus.). 288p. 1974. pap. text ed. 12.95 o.p. (ISBN 0-13-660548-6). P-H.

Collins, Wilkie. Man & Wife. (Illus.). 239p. 1983. pap. 5.00 (ISBN 0-486-24451-2). Dover.

--Woman in White. 1982. pap. 4.95x (ISBN 0-460-01464-1, Evman). Biblio Dist.

--The Woman in White: T. V. edition. Symons, Julian, ed. 1982. pap. 3.95 (ISBN 0-14-005980-6). Penguin.

Collins, Wilkie see Bleiler, E. F.

Collins, William. Introduction to Computer Programming with PASCAL. 350p. Date not set. pap. text ed. 15.95 (ISBN 0-02-323780-5). Macmillan.

--The Works of William Collins. Wendorf, Richard & Ryskamp, Charles, eds. (English Texts Ser.). (Illus.). 1979. text ed. 52.00x (ISBN 0-19-812749-9). Oxford U Pr.

Collins, William F., jt. ed. see Tindall, George T.

Collinson, A. S. Introduction to World Vegetation. 1977. text ed. 17.95x o. p. (ISBN 0-04-581012-5); pap. text ed. 10.95x (ISBN 0-04-581013-3). Allen Unwin.

Collinson, Francis, jt. ed. see Campbell, John L.

Collinson, John. The History & Antiquities of the County of Somerset. 2001p. 1982. text ed. 168.00x (ISBN 0-86299-003-3, Pub. by Alan Sutton England). Humanities.

Collinson, M. P. Farm Management in Peasant Agriculture. (Encore Edition Ser.). 470p. 1983. write for info. softcover (ISBN 0-86531-558-2). Westview.

Collinson, Patrick. Archbishop Grindal, 1519-1589: The Struggle for a Reformed Church in England. LC 78-65474. 1979. 42.50x (ISBN 0-520-03831-2). U of Cal Pr.

Collipp, Platon J. & Castro-Magana, Mariano. Pediatric & Adolescent Endocrinology Case Studies. (Case Studies Ser.). 1982. pap. text ed. write for info. (ISBN 0-87488-054-8). Med Exam.

Collis, Clive, jt. auth. see Turner, R. Kerry.

Collis, J., ed. & tr. see Linden, Wilhelm Zur.

Collis, J., tr. from Ger. Cinderella. (Illus.). 23p. (gr. 2-3). 1978. 10.25 (ISBN 0-85440-332-9, Pub. by Steinerbooks). Anthroposophic.

Collis, John S., Jr. Lumbar Discography. (Illus.). 192p. 1963. photocopy ed. spiral 21.75x (ISBN 0-398-00336-X). C C Thomas.

Collis, L., jt. auth. see Fookes, P. J.

Collis, Louise. Memoirs of a Medieval Woman. LC 82-48226. (Illus.). 288p. 1983. pap. 6.68i (ISBN 0-06-090992-7, CN 992, CN). Har-Row.

Collis, Margaret. Early Explorations. LC 77-83012. (Using the Environment Ser.). (Illus.). 1977. pap. text ed. 12.85 (ISBN 0-356-04353-3). Raintree Pubs.

--Investigations, Pts. 1 & 2. LC 77-83013. (Using the Environment). (Illus.). 1977. Pt. 1. pap. text ed. 12.85 (ISBN 0-356-04354-1); Pt. 2. pap. text ed. 12.85 (ISBN 0-356-04355-X). Raintree Pubs.

--Tackling Problems, Pt. 1. LC 77-83014. (Using the Environment Ser.). (Illus.). 1977. pap. text ed. 12.85 (ISBN 0-356-04356-8). Raintree Pubs.

--Tackling Problems, Pt. 2. LC 77-83014. (Using the Environment Ser.). (Illus.). 1977. pap. text ed. 12.85 (ISBN 0-356-05000-9). Raintree Pubs.

--Ways & Means. LC 77-83015. (Using the Environment Ser.). (Illus.). 1977. pap. text ed. 12.85 (ISBN 0-356-05001-7). Raintree Pubs.

Collis, Maurice. First Holy One. LC 70-110819. Repr. of 1948 ed. lib. bdg. 15.75x (ISBN 0-8371-3222-3, COFH). Greenwood.

--The Journey up. (Illus.). 9.95 o.p. (ISBN 0-571-09000-1). Faber & Faber.

--Raffles. Date not set. cancelled o.s.i. (ISBN 0-571-09227-6). Faber & Faber.

Collison, Beth, jt. ed. see Harris, Diana.

Collison, David. Stage Sound. LC 75-6799. (Illus.). 154p. 1976. text ed. 15.00x o.p. (ISBN 0-910482-65-9). Drama Bk.

--Stage Sound. 2nd, rev. ed. (Illus.). 1982. 20.00x (ISBN 0-304-30987-7). Drama Bk.

Collison, Kathleen, jt. auth. see Brockmeyer, Lloyd.

Collison, Mary, jt. auth. see Collison, Robert.

Collison, Robert & Collison, Mary. Dictionary of Foreign Quotations. LC 81-22090. 416p. 1982. pap. 11.95 (ISBN 0-89696-158-3, An Everest House Book). Dodd.

Collison, Robert & Roe, John. Scolma Directory of Libraries & Special Collections on Africa. 3rd ed. 120p. 1973. 17.50 o.p. (ISBN 0-208-01332-6, Archon). Shoe String.

Collison, Robert L. Uganda. (World Bibliographical Ser.: No. 11). 159p. 1981. text ed. 25.20 (ISBN 0-903450-17-8). ABC-Clio.

Collister, Edward A., jt. auth. see Harrison, Alice W.

Collman, Charles A. Our Mysterious Panics, 1830-1930: A Story of Events & the Men Involved. LC 68-28621. 1968. Repr. of 1931 ed. lib. bdg. 20.75x (ISBN 0-8371-0050-X, COMP). Greenwood.

Collman, James P. & Hegedus, Louis S. Principles & Applications or Organotransition Metal Chemistry. LC 79-57228. 715p. 1980. 27.00x (ISBN 0-935702-03-2). Univ Sci Bks.

Collodi. Pinocchio. (Easy Reader, B). pap. 3.95 (ISBN 0-88436-050-4, 55254). EMC.

Collodi, Carlo. Adventures of Pinocchio. (Illus.). (gr. 4-6). 1946. Illus. Jr. Lib 5.95 (ISBN 0-448-05801-4, G&D); Companion Lib. Ed. 2.95 (ISBN 0-448-05471-X); deluxe ed. 8.95 (ISBN 0-448-06001-9). Putnam Pub Group.

--Adventures of Pinocchio. (Illus.). 96p. (gr. 3-6). 1982. 9.95 (ISBN 0-528-82071-0). Rand.

--Pinocchio. (Illus.). 1982. pap. 3.95 (ISBN 0-399-20892-5, Philomel). Putnam Pub Group.

Collon, Dominique. Catalogue of the Western Asiatic Seals in the British Museum: Cylinder Seals II. (Akkadian-Post Akkadian-Ur III Periods). 240p. 1982. 110.00x (ISBN 0-7141-1104-X, Pub. by Brit Mus Pubns England). State Mutual Bk.

Colloni, Carlo. The Adventures of Pinocchio. (The Illustrated Junior Library). (Illus.). 272p. 1982. pap. 5.95 (ISBN 0-448-11001-6, G&D). Putnam Pub Group.

Colloque Sur la Programmation, Paris, 9-11 April, 1974. Programming Symposium: Proceedings. Robinet, B., ed. LC 74-19256. (Lecture Notes in Computer Science Ser.: Vol. 19). v, 425p. 1975. pap. 22.00 o.p. (ISBN 0-387-06859-7). Springer-Verlag.

Colloquim for the Philosophy of Science, Boston, 1969-1972. Boston Studies in the Philosophy of Science, Vol.13: Logical & Epistemological Studies in Contemporary Physics, Proceedings. Cohen, R. S. & Wartofsky, M. W., eds. LC 73-83557. (Synthese Library: No.59). 462p. 1974. 53.00 (ISBN 90-277-0391-4); pap. 28.95 (ISBN 90-277-0377-9). Kluwer Boston.

Colloquium, June 27-28, 1980. An Information Agenda for the Nineteen Eighties: Proceedings. Rochell, Carlton, ed. LC 80-28685. 154p. 1981. pap. 8.00 (ISBN 0-8389-0336-3). ALA.

Collu, R., et al, eds. Brain Neurotransmitters & Hormones. 425p. 1982. text ed. 50.50 (ISBN 0-89004-763-4). Raven.

Collu, Robert, et al, eds. Central Nervous System Effects of Hypothalamic Hormones. LC 77-94310. 453p. 1978. text ed. 45.00 (ISBN 0-89004-347-7). Raven.

--Pediatric Endocrinology. (Comprehensive Endocrinology Ser.). 660p. 1981. text ed. 65.50 (ISBN 0-89004-543-7). Raven.

Collum, Charles R. Dallas Nude. (Illus.). 1979. 28.50 o.p. (ISBN 0-8174-2950-6, Amphoto). Watson-Guptill.

--Dallas Nude: A Photographic Essay. (Illus.). 96p. 1980. pap. 14.95 o.p. (ISBN 0-8174-3756-8, Amphoto). Watson-Guptill.

Collymore, Peter. The Architecture of Ralph Erskine. 180p. 1982. 90.00x (ISBN 0-246-11250-6, Pub. by Granada England). State Mutual Bk.

Colman, A. Game Theory & Experimental Games: The Study of Strategic Interaction. (International Ser. in Experimental Social Psychology: Vol. 4). 300p. 1982. 38.00 (ISBN 0-08-026070-5); pap. 17.95 (ISBN 0-08-026069-1). Pergamon.

Colman, Carol. Love & Money: What Your Finances Say About Your Personal Relationships. 300p. 1983. 15.95 (ISBN 0-698-11189-3, Coward). Putnam Pub Group.

Colman, Hila. Accident. (gr. 7-9). 1981. pap. 1.95 (ISBN 0-671-46123-0). Archway.

--Accident. LC 80-20509. 160p. (gr. 7-9). 1980. 9.75 (ISBN 0-688-22238-2); PLB 9.36 (ISBN 0-688-32238-7). Morrow.

--After the Wedding. LC 75-11587. 192p. (gr. 7 up). 1975. PLB 8.16 (ISBN 0-688-32043-0). Morrow.

--Bride at Eighteen. (gr. 7 up). 1966. PLB 8.59 (ISBN 0-688-31122-9). Morrow.

--The Case of the Stolen Bagels. LC 77-10029. (Illus.). (gr. 2-4). 1977. reinforced lib. bdg. 5.95 o.p. (ISBN 0-517-53064-3). Crown.

--Diary of a Frantic Kid Sister. (gr. 4-6). 1975. pap. 1.95 (ISBN 0-671-46376-4). Archway.

--Ellie's Inheritance. LC 79-19009. (gr. 7-9). 1979. 6.95 o.s.i. (ISBN 0-688-22204-8); PLB 8.40 (ISBN 0-688-32204-2). Morrow.

--The Family Trap. 192p. 1982. 9.50 (ISBN 0-688-01472-0). Morrow.

--Family Trap. 1982. write for info. Macmillan.

--The Girl from Puerto Rico. (gr. 7 up). 1961. 8.95 (ISBN 0-688-21343-X). Morrow.

--The Happenings at North End School. LC 77-117224. (gr. 7 up). 1970. 8.95 (ISBN 0-688-21374-X). Morrow.

--Nobody Has to Be a Kid Forever. (gr. 5-7). 1977. pap. 1.95 (ISBN 0-671-46122-2). Archway.

--Nobody Has to Be a Kid Forever. LC 75-25810. 128p. (gr. 3-6). 1976. 5.95 o.p. (ISBN 0-517-52521-6). Crown.

--Rachel's Legacy. (gr. 7 up). 1978. 9.75 (ISBN 0-688-22154-8); PLB 9.36 (ISBN 0-688-32154-2). Morrow.

--Sometimes I Don't Love My Mother. (gr. 7 up). 1977. 9.95 (ISBN 0-688-22121-1); PLB 9.55 (ISBN 0-688-32121-6). Morrow.

--Tell Me No Lies. LC 77-15862. (Illus.). (gr. 6 up). 1978. 6.95 o.p. (ISBN 0-517-53229-8). Crown.

--What's the Matter with the Dobsons. 1982. pap. 1.95 (ISBN 0-671-43143-9). Archway.

Colman, J. Barry, ed. Readings in Church History: The Reformation & the Absolute States, 1517-1789, Vol. 2. pap. 7.95 o.p. (ISBN 0-8091-1963-3). Paulist Pr.

Colman, John. John Locke's Moral Philosophy. 280p. 1982. text ed. 27.50 (ISBN 0-686-82135-1, Pub. by Edinburgh U Pr Scotland). Columbia U Pr.

Colman, Libby, jt. auth. see Bing, Elizabeth.

Colman, Robert W. & Hirsh, Jack, eds. Hemostasis & Thrombosis. (Illus.). 1248p. 1982. text ed. 115.00x (ISBN 0-397-50435-7, Lippincott Medical). Lippincott.

Colman, Stuart. They Kept on Rockin' The Giants of Rock 'n' Roll. (Illus.). 160p. (Orig.). 1982. pap. 9.95 (ISBN 0-686-97925-7, Pub. by Blandford Pr England). Sterling.

Colman, Willaim P. & Colon, G. A. Surgery of the Skin. (Advanced Textbook Ser.). 1983. text ed. price not set (ISBN 0-87488-185-4). Med Exam.

Colmer, John. Coleridge to Catch 22: Images of Society. LC 77-25948. 1978. 22.50 (ISBN 0-312-14720-1). St Martin.

--E. M. Forster: The Personal Voice. 256p. 1975. 21.00x (ISBN 0-7100-8209-6). Routledge & Kegan.

Colnett, James. Colnett's Journal Aboard the Argonaut from April 26, 1789 to November 3, 1791. Howay, F. W., ed. LC 68-28614. 1968. Repr. of 1940 ed. lib. bdg. 30.75x o.p. (ISBN 0-8371-5063-9, COJC). Greenwood.

Colnett, Vincent, jt. auth. see Wethern, George.

Colodny, Robert G., ed. Logic, Laws, & Life: Some Philosophical Complications. LC 76-50886. (Philosophy of Science Ser.). 1977. 17.95x (ISBN 0-8229-3346-2). U of Pittsburgh Pr.

Colombeau, J. F. Differential Calculus & Holomorphy. (Mathematical Studies: Vol. 64). 1982. 59.75 (ISBN 0-444-86397-4). Elsevier.

Colombo, F., et al, eds. Epidemiological Evaluation of Drugs. LC 77-24938. (Illus.). 334p. 1977. 27.50 o.p. (ISBN 0-88416-217-6). Wright-PSG.

Colombo, J. P., ed. see Richterich, R.

Colombo, John R. Colombo's Canadian References. 1977. 29.95x (ISBN 0-19-540253-7). Oxford U Pr.

Colon, A. R. Pediatric Hepatology. (Medical Outline Ser.). 1982. pap. text ed. 25.00 (ISBN 0-87488-407-1). Med Exam.

Colon, G. A., jt. auth. see Colman, Willaim P.

Colon, Jesus. A Puerto Rican in New York & Other Sketches. LC 82-6100. (Illus.). 204p. (Orig.). 1982. pap. 3.75 (ISBN 0-7178-0589-1). Intl Pub Co.

Colonial Penn Group, Inc. Perspectives on Aging: Exploding the Myths. (Colonial Penn Lecture Ser.). 336p. 1981. prof ref 25.00x (ISBN 0-88410-734-5). Ballinger Pub.

Colonial Williamsburg Foundation Staff. Favorite Meals from Williamsburg: A Menu Cookbook. Sheppard, Donna C., ed. (Illus.). 1982. 9.75 (ISBN 0-03-062433-9). HR&W.

Colonna, Francesco. Hypnerotomachia Poliphili. LC 75-27842. (Renaissance & the Gods Ser.: Vol. 1). 1976. Repr. of 1499 ed. lib. bdg. 73.00 o.s.i. (ISBN 0-8240-2050-2). Garland Pub.

--Hypnerotomachia: The Strife of Love in a Dreame (1592). Dallington, Robert, tr. from Latin. LC 73-16223. 208p. 1973. Repr. lib. bdg. 35.00x (ISBN 0-8201-1124-4). Schol Facsimiles.

Colony, Horatio. The Amazon's Hero. 4.75 o.s.i. (ISBN 0-8283-1340-7). Branden.

--Demon in Love. 3.00 o.s.i. (ISBN 0-8283-1214-1). Branden.

--Early Land. 1967. 3.00 o.s.i. (ISBN 0-8283-1216-8). Branden.

--The Emperor & the Bee Boy. 1000p. 1976. 4.75 o.s.i. (ISBN 0-8283-1638-4). Branden.

--Flying Ones. 1967. 3.00 o.s.i. (ISBN 0-8283-1218-4). Branden.

--Magic Child. 3.00 o.s.i. (ISBN 0-8283-1215-X). Branden.

--Some Phoenix Blood. LC 69-11622. 1969. 3.75 o.s.i. (ISBN 0-8283-1008-4). Branden.

--Three Loves the Same. 1967. 3.00 o.s.i. (ISBN 0-8283-1217-6). Branden.

Colony, Horatio, ed. Flower Myth. 3.75 o.s.i. (ISBN 0-8283-1278-8). Branden.

Colorado, Antonio J. The First Book of Puerto Rico. rev. ed. LC 77-17520. (First Bks.). (Illus.). (gr. 3-5). 1978. PLB 7.90 s&l (ISBN 0-531-01292-1). Watts.

Colorado Dietectic Association Conference - 1969. Dimensions of Nutrition: Proceedings. Dupont, Jacqueline, ed. LC 71-134852. (Illus.). 1974. pap. 8.95x o.p. (ISBN 0-87081-006-5). Colo Assoc.

Colorado Energy Research Institute, Colorado School of Mines. Water & Energy in Colorado's Future. 330p. 1981. lib. bdg. 28.75 (ISBN 0-86531-118-8). Westview.

Colorado School of Mines. Subject Catalog of the Arthur Lakes Library of the Colorado School of Mines. 1977. lib. bdg. 570.00 (ISBN 0-8161-0072-1, Hall Library). G K Hall.

Colorado Springs Fine Arts Center. Woodworking in the Rockies. LC 82-71534. (Illus.). 1982. 6.00 (ISBN 0-686-37084-8). Taylor Museum.

Colourmaster. Day Outings. (Travel in England Ser.). (Illus.). 96p. 1975. 8.95 o.p. (ISBN 0-85936-004-0). Transatlantic.

--Historic Buildings. (Travel in England Ser.). (Illus.). 64p. 1975. 7.95 o.p. (ISBN 0-85933-129-6). Transatlantic.

--Lake District (Cumberland, Lancashire, Westmoreland) (Travel in England Ser.). (Illus.). 96p. 1975. Repr. 7.95 o.p. (ISBN 0-85933-006-0). Transatlantic.

--London's Pageantry. (Travel in England Ser.). (Illus.). 64p. 1975. 7.95 o.p. (ISBN 0-85933-110-5). Transatlantic.

--Pubs & Pub Signs. (Travel in England Ser.). (Illus.). 64p. 1975. 7.95 o.p. (ISBN 0-85933-105-9). Transatlantic.

--Southern England (Kent, Sussex, Hampshire, Isle of Wight) (Travel in England Ser.). (Illus.). 96p. 1975. 7.95 o.p. (ISBN 0-85933-007-9). Transatlantic.

--West Country (Cornwall, Devon, Dorset, Somerset) (Travel in England Ser.). (Illus.). 96p. 1975. 7.95 o.p. (ISBN 0-685-51761-6). Transatlantic.

Colowich, Sidney P. & Kaplan, Nathan O., eds. Methods in Enzymology: Vol. 93, Pt. F: Immunochemical Techniques, Conventional Antibodies, FC Receptors & Cytotoxicity. 393p. 1983. price not set (ISBN 0-12-181993-0). Acad Pr.

Colowick, S. & Langone, John, eds. Methods in Enzymology: Immunological Techniques, Vol. 84, Pt. D. LC 82-1678. 736p. 1982. 65.00 (ISBN 0-12-181984-1). Acad Pr.

Colowick, S. P. & Lands, William, eds. Methods in Enzymology: Vol. 86, Prostaglandins & Arachidonate Metabolites. LC 82-6791. 1982. 67.50 (ISBN 0-12-181986-8). Acad Pr.

Colowick, Sidney & Dennis, Martha, eds. Methods in Enzymology, Vol. 75: Cumulative Subject Index, Vols. 31, 32 & 34. (Serial Publication). 1982. 85.00 (ISBN 0-12-181975-2). Acad Pr.

Colowick, Sidney & Packer, Lester, eds. Methods in Enzymology: Biomembranes - Visual Pigments & Purple Membranes, Vol. 88. 750p. 1982. 78.00 (ISBN 0-12-181988-4). Acad Pr.

Colowick, Sidney & Wood, Willis, eds. Methods in Enzymology: Vol. 89, Carbohydrate Metabolism, Part D. 656p. 1982. 59.00 (ISBN 0-12-181989-2). Acad Pr.

--Methods in Enzymology: Vol. 90, Part E, Carbohydrate Metabolism. 559p. 1982. 58.00 (ISBN 0-12-181990-6). Acad Pr.

Colowick, Sidney P. & Frederiksen, D. W., eds. Methods in Enzymology: Vol. 85 Structural & Contractile Proteins - The Contractile Apparatus & the Cytoskeleton. 774p. 1982. 69.50 (ISBN 0-12-181985-X). Acad Pr.

Colowick, Sidney P. & Kaplan, Nathan O., eds. Methods in Enzymology, Vol. 87. 752p. 1982. 74.50 (ISBN 0-12-181987-6). Acad Pr.

--Methods in Enzymology: Vol. 91, Pt. 1: Enzyme Structure. Date not set. 69.00 (ISBN 0-12-181991-4). Acad Pr.

--Methods in Enzymology: Vol. 92, Pt. E: Immunochemical Techniques. Date not set. 65.00 (ISBN 0-12-181992-2). Acad Pr.

Colowick, Sidney P. & Kaplan, Sidney O., eds. Methods in Enzymology: Polyamines, Vol. 94. Date not set. price not set (ISBN 0-12-181994-9). Acad Pr.

Colquhoun, Archibald, tr. see Calvino, Italo.

Colquhoun, Norman. Painting: A Creative Approach. LC 68-21280. Orig. Title: Paint Your Own Pictures. 1969. pap. 3.50 (ISBN 0-486-22000-1). Dover.

Colquhoun, P. A New & Appropriate New System of Education for the Labouring People. 98p. 1971. Repr. of 1806 ed. 15.00x (ISBN 0-7165-1773-6, Pub. by Irish Academic Pr Ireland). Biblio Dist.

Colquhoun, Patrick. Treatise on the Commerce & Police of the River Thames. LC 69-14917. (Criminology, Law Enforcement & Social Problems Ser.: No. 41). (Map). 1969. Repr. of 1800 ed. 30.00x (ISBN 0-87585-041-3). Patterson Smith.

--Treatise on the Police of the Metropolis. 7th ed. LC 69-14918. (Criminology, Law Enforcement & Social Problems Ser.: No. 42). 1969. Repr. of 1806 ed. 30.00x (ISBN 0-87585-042-1). Patterson Smith.

Colquhoun, Robert. Life Begins at Midnight. 13.50 (ISBN 0-392-08555-0, SpS). Sportshelf.

Colquhoun, W. P. & Rutenfranz, J., eds. Studies of Shiftwork. 468p. 1981. write for info. (ISBN 0-85066-210-9, Pub. by Taylor & Francis). Intl Pubns Serv.

Colquitt, Betsy F., ed. Studies in Medieval, Renaissance, American Literature: A Festschrift. LC 78-165852. 200p. 1971. pap. 6.95x (ISBN 0-912646-19-5). Tex Christian.

Colson, Charles W. Life Sentence. (Illus.). 320p. 1981. pap. 6.95 (ISBN 0-8007-5059-4, Power Bks). Revell.

Colson, Elizabeth. The Makah Indians. LC 73-15051. (Illus.). 308p. 1974. Repr. of 1953 ed. lib. bdg. 21.00x (ISBN 0-8371-7153-9, COMI). Greenwood.

Colson, Greta, jt. auth. see Colson, John.

Colson, John & Colson, Greta. English. (Illus.). 212p. tape included 17.50x (ISBN 0-686-09303-8, Dist. by Hippocrene Books Inc.). Leviathan Hse.

Colson, John H. & Armour, William J. Sports Injuries & Their Treatment. rev. ed. (Illus.). 234p. 1983. text ed. 32.50x (ISBN 0-09-124180-4, SpS). Sportshelf.

Colt, Zandra. Splendid Savage. (Second Chance at Love Ser.: No. 92). 1982. pap. 1.75 (ISBN 0-686-81796-6). Jove Pubns.

Colter, Cyrus. Beach Umbrella. LC 82-72916. 225p. 1971. pap. 4.95 (ISBN 0-8040-0555-9). Swallow.

--The Hippodrome: A Novel. LC 82-73385. 213p. 1973. 10.95 (ISBN 0-8040-0625-3). Swallow.

Commager, Henry S. & Muessig, Raymond H. The Study & Teaching of History. 2nd ed. (Social Science Seminar, Secondary Education Ser.: No. C28). 136p. 1980. pap. text ed. 7.95 (ISBN 0-675-08317-6). Merrill.
Commager, Henry S. & Nevins, Allan. Pocket History of the United States. enl. ed. (YA) (gr. 9-12). 1982. pap. 3.95 (ISBN 0-671-42697-4). WSP.
Commager, Henry S., jt. auth. see Morison, Samuel E.
Commager, Henry S., ed. see Hamilton, Madison.
Commager, Henry S., ed. see Savage, Henry, Jr.
Commager, Henry S., ed. see Smelser, Marshal L.
Commager, Henry S., ed. see Smelser, Marshall.
Commager, Henry S., ed. see Thomas, Emory M.
Commager, Henry S., et al. Education in a Free Society, Vol. 2. LC 58-13595. 1960. 5.95 o.p. (ISBN 0-8229-1014-4). U of Pittsburgh Pr.
Commager, Steele, ed. see Crump, Mary M.
Commager, Steele, ed. see Lilja, Saara.
Commanger, Henry S. The Defeat of America: Presidential Power & the National Character. LC 74-19472. 1975. 8.95 o.s.i. (ISBN 0-671-21776-3); pap. 2.95 o.p. (ISBN 0-671-21777-1). S&S.
--The Ending of an Era: What Lies Ahead? (Vital Issues, Vol. XXIX 1979-80: No. 9). 0.50 (ISBN 0-686-81614-5). Ctr Info Am.
Commins, Dorothy, ed. Favorite Songs for Children. (Illus.). (ps). 1965. 1.95 (ISBN 0-448-04210-X, G&D). Putnam Pub Group.
Commins, Dorothy B., ed. Favorite Christmas Songs & Stories. (Illus.). (gr. 2-5). 1962. 1.95 (ISBN 0-448-00321-X, G&D). Putnam Pub Group.
Commins, E. Weak Interactions. 1973. text ed. 41.00 (ISBN 0-07-012372-1, C). McGraw.
Commire, Anne, ed. Something about the Author, Vol. 28. 250p. 1982. 50.00x (ISBN 0-8103-0082-6). Gale.
--Something about the Author, Vol. 29. 250p. 1982. 50.00x (ISBN 0-8103-0081-8). Gale.
--Something About the Author: Facts & Pictures About Contemporary Authors & Illustrators of Books for Young People. Incl. Vol. 1. 1971 (ISBN 0-8103-0050-8); Vol. 2. 1972 (ISBN 0-8103-0052-4); Vol. 3. 1972 (ISBN 0-8103-0054-0); Vol. 4. 1973 (ISBN 0-8103-0056-7); Vol. 5. 1973 (ISBN 0-8103-0058-3); Vol. 6. 1974 (ISBN 0-8103-0060-5); Vol. 7. 1975 (ISBN 0-8103-0062-1); Vol. 8. 1975. (ISBN 0-8103-0064-8); Vol. 9. 1976. (ISBN 0-8103-0066-4); Vol. 10. 1976. (ISBN 0-8103-0068-0); Vol. 11. 1977. (ISBN 0-8103-0070-2); Vol. 12. 1977. (ISBN 0-8103-0072-9); Vol. 13. 1978. (ISBN 0-685-43929-1); Vol. 14. 1978 (ISBN 0-8103-0095-8); Vol. 15. 1979 (ISBN 0-8103-0096-6); Vol. 16. 1979 (ISBN 0-8103-0097-4); Vol. 17. 1979 (ISBN 0-8103-0098-2); Vol. 18. 1980 (ISBN 0-8103-0099-0); Vol. 19. 1979 (ISBN 0-8103-0051-6); Vol. 20. 1980 (ISBN 0-8103-0053-2); Vol. 21. 1980 (ISBN 0-8103-0093-1); Vol. 22. 1980 (ISBN 0-8103-0085-0); Vol. 23. 1981 (ISBN 0-8103-0086-9); Vol. 24. 1981 (ISBN 0-8103-0087-7); Vol. 25. 1981 (ISBN 0-8103-0084-2); Vol. 26. 1982 (ISBN 0-8103-0089-3); Vol. 27. 1982 (ISBN 0-8103-0083-4). LC 72-27107. (Illus.). (gr. 7-12). 50.00x ea. Gale.
--Yesterday's Authors of Books for Children: Facts & Pictures About Authors & Illustrators of Books for Young People, 2 vols. LC 76-17501. (Yesterday's Authors of Books for Children Ser.). (Illus.). (gr. 7-12). 50.00x ea.; Vol. 1, 1977. (ISBN 0-8103-0073-7); Vol. 2 1978. (ISBN 0-8103-0090-7). Gale.
Commission d'enquete de Saint-Petersbourg. Conspiration de Russie. (Nineteenth Century Russia Ser.). 144p. (Fr.). 1974. Repr. of 1826 ed. lib. bdg. 45.00x o.p. (ISBN 0-8287-1352-9, R1). Clearwater Pub.
Commission for Aeronautical Meteorology, Extraordinary Session, 1969. Report. pap. 20.00 (ISBN 0-686-93915-8, W113, WMO). Unipub.
Commission for Aeronautical Meteorology, 5th Session, 1971. Report. pap. 20.00 (ISBN 0-686-93916-6, W119, WMO). Unipub.
Commission for Atmospheric Sciences, 6th Session. Abridged Final Report of the Sixth Session. abr. ed. 97p. (Orig.). 1974. pap. 25.00 (ISBN 92-63-10371-2, W144, WMO). Unipub.
Commission for Atmospheric Sciences, 6th Session, 1973. Report. (Publications Ser.: No. 371). pap. 25.00 (ISBN 0-686-93917-4, W144, WMO). Unipub.
Commission for Basic Systems, 6th Session, 1974. Report. pap. 25.00 (ISBN 0-686-93919-0, W151, WMO). Unipub.
Commission for (Hydrometeorology) Hydrology, 4th Session, 1972. Report. pap. 20.00 (ISBN 0-686-93920-4, W124, WMO). Unipub.
Commission for Inland Fisheries of Latin America, 1st Session. Report. (FAO Fisheries Reports: No. 222). 22p. 1979. pap. 6.00 (ISBN 0-686-94012-1, F1855, FAO). Unipub.
Commission for Instruments & Methods of Observation, 6th Session, 1973. Report. pap. 20.00 (ISBN 0-686-93924-7, W1, WMO). Unipub.
Commission for Marine Meteorology, 6th Session. Abridged Final Report of the Sixth Session. 117p. 1973. pap. 20.00 (ISBN 0-685-39010-1, W129, WMO). Unipub.
Commission for (Maritime) Marine Meteorology, 6th Session, 1972. Report. pap. 20.00 (ISBN 0-686-93922-0, W129, WMO). Unipub.
Commission for Special Applications of Meteorology & Climatology, 6th Session, 1973. Report. pap. 25.00 (ISBN 0-686-93925-5, W142, WMO). Unipub.
Commission for the European Communities, Directorate-General for Research, Science & Education, ed. Inventory of Major Research Facilities in the European Community, 2 vols. 1561p. 1977. text ed. 120.00x (ISBN 3-7940-3019-2, Pub. by K G Saur). Gale.
Commission of European Communities, ed. Plutonium Recycling Scenario in Light Water Reactors: Assessment of the Environmental Impact of the European Community. 240p. 1982. write for info. (ISBN 3-7186-0118-4). Harwood Academic.
--Research & Development on Radioactive Waste Management & Storage: First Annual Progress Report of the European Community Programme 1980-84. (Radioactive Waste Management: A Series of Monographs & Tracts Ser.: Vol. 4). 129p. 1982. write for info. (ISBN 3-7186-0115-X). Harwood Academic.
Commission of European Communities, Directorate-Center for Research-Science & Education, ed. Food: Multilingual Thesaurus. 1979. 4 vols. & index 240.00x (ISBN 0-89664-036-1, Pub. by K G Saur). Gale.
Commission of the European Communities. Coke Oven Techniques. 350p. 1983. pap. 40.00x (ISBN 0-8448-1422-9). Crane-Russak Co.
--European Community Oil & Gas Research & Development Projects. 250p. 1983. 55.00x (ISBN 0-8448-1437-7). Crane-Russak Co.
--Law & Practice Relating to Pollution Control in the Member States of the European Communities: France. 1983. 40.00x (ISBN 0-8448-1442-3). Crane-Russak.
--Law & Practice Relating to Pollution Control in the Member States of the European Communities: Greece. 1983. 40.00x (ISBN 0-8448-1445-8). Crane-Russak.
--Law & Practice Relating to Pollution Control in the Member States of the European Communities: Federal Republic of Germany. 1983. 40.00x (ISBN 0-8448-1443-1). Crane-Russak.
--Law & Practice Relating to Pollution Control in the Member States of the European Communities: Denmark. 1983. 40.00x (ISBN 0-8448-1441-5). Crane-Russak.
--Law & Practice Relating to Pollution Control in the Member States of the European Communities: Italy. 1983. 40.00x (ISBN 0-8448-1447-4). Crane-Russak.
--Law & Practice Relating to Pollution Control in the Member States of the European Communities: Belgium & Luxembourg. 1983. 40.00x (ISBN 0-8448-1435-0). Crane-Russak.
--Law & Practice Relating to Pollution Control in the Member States of the European Communities: Netherlands. 1983. 40.00x (ISBN 0-8448-1448-2). Crane-Russak.
--Law & Practice Relating to Pollution Control in the Member States of the European Communities: Ireland. 1983. 40.00x (ISBN 0-8448-1446-6). Crane-Russak.
--Law & Practice Relating to Pollution Control in the Member States of the European Communities: Comparative Volume. 1983. 40.00x (ISBN 0-8448-1450-4). Crane-Russak.
--Law & Practice Relating to Pollution Control in the Member States of the European Communities: United Kingdom. 1983. 40.00x (ISBN 0-8448-1449-0). Crane-Russak.
Commission of the European Communities, ed. Veterinary Multilingual Thesaurus, 4 vols. 1122p. 1979. 4 vols. & index 400.00x (ISBN 3-598-07082-9, Pub. by K G Saur). Gale.
Commission on Critcal Choices, et al. Power & Security. LC 75-44722. (Critical Choices for Americans Ser.: Vol. 4). 1976. 18.95x (ISBN 0-669-00416-2). Lexington Bks.
Commission on Critical Choice. How Others See Us. LC 75-44720. (Critical Choices for Americans Ser.: Vol. 3). 1976. 16.95x (ISBN 0-669-00420-0). Lexington Bks.
Commission on Critical Choices. The Americans: Nineteen Seventy-Six. Kristol, Irving, ed. Weaver, Paul H. LC 75-44719. (Critical Choices for Americans Ser.: Vol. 2). 1976. 21.95x (ISBN 0-669-00415-4). Lexington Bks.
--The Middle East: Oil, Conflict & Hope, Vol. 10. LC 75-44728. (Critical Choices for Americans Ser.). 1976. 27.95x (ISBN 0-669-00424-3). Lexington Bks.
--The Soviet Empire: Expansion & Detente. Griffith, William E., ed. LC 75-44727. (Critical Choices for Americans Ser.: Vol. IX). 1976. 24.95x (ISBN 0-669-00421-9). Lexington Bks.
--Trade, Inflation & Ethics. LC 75-44723. (Critical Choices for Americans Ser.: Vol. 5). 1976. 21.95 (ISBN 0-669-00419-7). Lexington Bks.
--Values of Growth. LC 75-44724. (Critical Choices for Americans Ser.: Vol. VI). 1976. 16.95x (ISBN 0-669-00418-9). Lexington Bks.
--Vital Resources, Vol. I. LC 75-44718. (Critical Choices for Americans Ser.). 1976. 19.95x (ISBN 0-669-00413-8). Lexington Bks.
--Western Europe: The Trials of Partnership. Landes, David S., ed. LC 75-44726. (Critical Choices of Americans Ser.: Vol. 8). 1976. 24.95x (ISBN 0-669-00423-5). Lexington Bks.
Commission on Critical Choices & Hellman, Donald C. China & Japan: A New Balance of Power. LC 75-44730. (Critical Choices for Americans Ser.: Vol. XII). 1976. 23.95 (ISBN 0-669-00426-X). Lexington Bks.
--Southern Asia: The Politics of Poverty & Peace. LC 75-44731. (Critical Choices for Americans Ser.: Vol. XIII). 1976. 23.95 (ISBN 0-669-00427-8). Lexington Bks.
Commission on Critical Choices & Kitchen, Helen. Africa: From Mystery to Maze, Vol. XI. LC 75-44729. (Critical Choices for Americans Ser.). 1976. 24.95 (ISBN 0-669-00425-1). Lexington Bks.
Commission on Freedom of the Press, ed. see Leigh, Robert D.
Commission to Study the Organization of Peace. Organizing Peace in the Nuclear Age. Holcombe, Arthur N., ed. LC 75-31831. 245p. 1975. Repr. of 1959 ed. lib. bdg. 17.00x (ISBN 0-8371-8441-X, HOOP). Greenwood.
Commission to Study the Organization of Peace & Holcombe, Arthur N. Strengthening the United Nations. LC 74-7536. 276p. 1976. Repr. of 1957 ed. lib. bdg. 18.50x (ISBN 0-8371-7579-8, HOUN). Greenwood.
Commissioner of Education. Strengthening Bilingual Education. LC 80-116022. 102p. 1979. pap. 3.50 o.p. (ISBN 0-89763-017-3). Natl Clearinghse Bilingual Ed.
Commitee for Reporting Tribunal Jurisprudence. Matrimonial Jurisprudence United States, 1973: Summaries of Selected Cases. 86p. 1975. pap. 3.00x (ISBN 0-943616-10-7). Canon Law Soc.
Committe, Thomas C., et al. Managerial Finance for the Seventies. (Finance Ser.). 1972. text ed. 26.95 (ISBN 0-07-012371-3, C); instructor's manual 7.95 (ISBN 0-07-012374-8). McGraw.
Committee for Economic Development Staff. Productivity Policy: Key to the Nation's Economic Future. (CED Statement on National Policy Ser.). 122p. (Orig.). 1983. 10.50x (ISBN 0-87186-776-1); pap. 8.50x (ISBN 0-87186-076-7). Comm Econ Dev.
Committee for Reporting Tribunal Jurisprudence. Matrimonial Jurisprudence United States, 1975-1976: Summaries of Selected Cases. 158p. (Orig.). 1977. pap. 4.00x (ISBN 0-943616-11-5). Canon Law Soc.
Committee for the Development of Subject Access to Chicano Literature. A Cumulative Index to Selected Chicano Periodicals Published Between 1967 and 1978. 1981. lib. bdg. 80.00 (ISBN 0-8161-0363-1, Hall Library). G K Hall.
Committee For The Survey Of Chemistry. Basic Chemical Research in Government Laboratories. 1966. pap. 4.75 (ISBN 0-685-17304-6). Natl Acad Pr.
Committee for Truth in History & Grimstad, William. Six Million Reconsidered: An Examination of Jewish Genocide. 1982. lib. bdg. 69.95 (ISBN 0-87700-445-5). Revisionist Pr.
Committee of the Children's Services Division. I Read, You Read, We Read, I See, You See, We See, I Hear, You Hear, We Hear, I Learn, You Learn, We Learn. LC 76-152684. (gr. k-6). 1971. pap. 4.00 (ISBN 0-8389-3124-3). ALA.
Committee on Boarding Schools. International Students in the Independent School: A Handbook. 1981. pap. 7.00 (ISBN 0-686-83733-9). NAIS.
Committee on Classroom Practices, jt. ed. see Carter, Candy.
Committee on Drinking Water, National Research Council. Drinking Water & Health. Incl. Vol. I. 1977. 26.50 (ISBN 0-309-02619-9); Vol. II. 1980. 15.50 (ISBN 0-309-02931-7); Vol. III. 1980. 17.00 (ISBN 0-309-02932-5). Natl Acad Pr.
Committee on Economics Teaching Material for Asian Universities. Economic Theory & Practice in the Asian Setting, 4 vols. Incl. Vol. 1. Macroeconomics. LC 75-20408. o.p. (ISBN 0-470-14272-3); Vol. 2. Microeconomics. LC 75-20409 (ISBN 0-470-14273-1); Vol. 3. The Economics of Agriculture. LC 75-20412. o.p. (ISBN 0-470-14270-7); Vol. 4. The Economics of Development. LC 75-20411 (ISBN 0-470-14271-5). (Economic Theory & Practice in the Asian Setting Ser.). 1975. pap. 12.95x ea. o.p. Halsted Pr.
Committee on Filler Metals. Specification for Nickel & Nickel Alloy Bare Welding Rods & Electrodes: AWS A5.14-76. LC 76-29850. 1976. pap. 8.00 (ISBN 0-685-71367-9). Am Welding.
Committee on Fisheries, 10th Session, Rome, 1975. Report. (FAO Fisheries Reports: No. 162). 45p. 1975. pap. 7.50 (ISBN 0-686-93983-2, F805, FAO). Unipub.
Committee on Fisheries, 2nd Session, Rome, 1967. Report. (FAO Fisheries Report: No. 46). 44p. 1967. pap. 7.50 (ISBN 0-686-93005-3, F1666, FAO). Unipub.
Committee on Fisheries, 2nd, Session, Rome, 1967. Report, Appendix G: The State of Ocean Use Management. (FAO Fisheries Reports). 17p. 1967. pap. 7.50 (ISBN 0-686-93093-2, F1667, FAO). Unipub.
Committee on Fisheries, 4th Session, Rome, 1969. Report. (FAO Fisheries Reports: No. 72). 44p. 1969. pap. 7.50 (ISBN 0-686-93025-8, F1679, FAO). Unipub.
Committee on Fisheries, 5th Session, Rome, 1970. Report. (FAO Fisheries Reports: No. 86). 44p. 1970. pap. 7.50 (ISBN 0-686-93050-9, F1687, FAO). Unipub.
Committee on Fisheries, 6th Session, Rome, 1971. Report. (FAO Fisheries Reports: No. 103). 50p. 1971. pap. 7.50 (ISBN 0-686-93054-1, F1694, FAO). Unipub.
Committee on Fisheries, 8th Session, Rome, 1973. Report. (FAO Fisheries Reports: No. 135). 47p. 1973. pap. 6.00 (ISBN 0-686-93094-0, F1711, FAO). Unipub.
Committee on Interior Lighting for Public Conveyances of the IES. Public Conveyances: Road-Rail Interior Lighting. new ed. (Illus.). 20p. 1974. tech. manual 6.50 (ISBN 0-87995-004-8, IES CP-12); member 3.25. Illum Eng.
Committee on Jury Standards & American Bar Association. Standards Relating to Juror Use & Management. 196p. 1982. 10.00 (ISBN 0-89656-063-5). Natl Ctr St Courts.
Committee on Natural Resources, 1st Session. Proceedings. (Water Resources Development Ser.: No. 46). pap. 12.00 (ISBN 0-686-93059-2, UN76/2F2, UN). Unipub.
Committee on Natural Resources, 2nd Session. Proceedings. (Energy Resources Development Ser.: No. 15). pap. 9.50 (ISBN 0-686-92986-1, UN76/2F11, UN). Unipub.
Committee on Natural Resources, 3rd Session. Proceedings. (Mineral Resources Development Ser.: No. 43). pap. 7.00 (ISBN 0-686-92981-0, UN77/2F13, UN). Unipub.
Committee on Natural resources, 4th Session. Proceedings. (Water Resources Development Ser.: No. 48). pap. 11.00 (ISBN 0-686-92904-7, UN78/2F12, UN). Unipub.
Committee on Pattern Jury Charges of the State Bar of Texas. Texas Pattern Jury Charges, Vol. 3. LC 78-13954. 380p. 1982. 65.00 (ISBN 0-938160-28-1, 6315). State Bar TX.
Committee on Population. Growth of U. S. Population. 1965. pap. 2.50 (ISBN 0-309-01279-1). Natl Acad Pr.
Committee on Pre & Postoperative Care American College of Surgeons. Manual of Surgical Intensive Care. Kinney, John M., ed. LC 76-51009. (Illus.). 1977. text ed. 18.00 (ISBN 0-7216-1164-8). Saunders.
Committee on Scholarly Communications with the Peoples Republic of China National Research Council. Pure & Applied Mathematics in the Peoples Republic of China. 1977. pap. 14.50 (ISBN 0-686-25566-6, PB279 509); microfiche 4.50 (ISBN 0-686-25567-4). Natl Tech Info.
Committee on Taxation, Resources, & Economic Development. Property Taxation, Land Use & Public Policy. Lynn, Arthur D., Jr., ed. 268p. 1976. 25.00 (ISBN 0-299-06920-6). U of Wis Pr.
Committee on the Safety of Nuclear Installations Specialist Meeting. Transient Two-Phase Flow: Proceedings. Plesset, Milton, et al, eds. LC 82-23422. (Illus.). 800p. 1983. text ed. 75.00 (ISBN 0-89116-258-5). Hemisphere Pub.
Committee on the Undergraduate Program in Mathematics. A Basic Library Test for Four Year Colleges. 1977. pap. 9.00 (ISBN 0-88385-423-6). Math Assn.
Committee On Underwater Telecommunications Division Of Physical Sciences. Present & Future Civil Uses of Underwater Sound. LC 76-606666. (Illus., Orig.). 1970. pap. 5.25 o.p. (ISBN 0-309-01771-8). Natl Acad Pr.
Committee On Urban Technology - Division Of Engineering. Long-Range Planning for Urban Research & Development: Technological Considerations. (Illus., Orig.). 1969. pap. 5.75 (ISBN 0-309-01729-7). Natl Acad Pr.
Committee to Defend Czech Socialists, ed. Voices of Czechoslovak Socialists. 1977. pap. 4.95 o.p. (ISBN 0-686-23504-5, Merlin Pr). Carrier Pigeon.
Commodore Computer Staff. User's Guide. Date not set. pap. 12.95 (ISBN 0-672-22010-5). Sams.
Common Council for American Unity. The Alien & the Immigration Law. LC 72-6923. Repr. of 1958 ed. lib. bdg. 20.75x (ISBN 0-8371-6503-2, ALIL). Greenwood.
Common, Thomas, tr. see Nietzsche, Friedrich.
Common Women Collective Staff. Women in U. S. History: An Annotated Bibliography. LC 77-350179. (Illus.). 2.60 (ISBN 0-9601122-1-9). Common Women.
Commons, John R. Myself: The Autobiography of John R. Commons. (Illus.). 222p. 1963. pap. 5.95x (ISBN 0-299-02924-7). U of Wis Pr.
Commons, John R. & Andrews, John B. Principles of Labor Legislation. 4th ed. LC 66-22620. Repr. of 1936 ed. 35.00x (ISBN 0-678-00207-X). Kelley.
Commons, Michael & Nevin, John A., eds. Discriminative Properties of Reinforcement Schedules. (The Quantitative Analysis of Behavior Ser.: Vol. I). 480p. 1981. prof ref 42.50x (ISBN 0-88410-377-3). Ballinger Pub.

Commons, Michael L. & Nevin, John A., eds. Quantitative Analyses of Behavior: Discriminative Properties of Reinforcement Schedules, Vol. I. 480p. 1981. prof ref 42.50x (ISBN 0-88410-377-3). Ballinger Pub.
--Quantitative Analyses of Behavior, Vol. V: Reinforcement Value The Effect of Delay in Intervening Variables. (Quantitative Analyses of Behavior: Vol. V). 500p. 1983. price not set prof. ref. (ISBN 0-88410-893-7). Ballinger Pub.
Commons, Michael L., et al, eds. Quantitative Analyses of Behavior: Acquisition, Vol. III. 560p. 1983. prof ref 37.50x (ISBN 0-88410-740-X). Ballinger Pub.
--Quantitative Analyses of Behavior Vol. II: Matching & Maximizing Accounts. 624p. 1982. prof ref 55.00x (ISBN 0-88410-739-6). Ballinger Pub.
--Quantitative Analyses of Behavior, Vol. IV: Discrimination Processes. LC 81-2654. 550p. 1983. price not set prof. ref. (ISBN 0-88410-741-8). Ballinger Pub.
Commonwealth Institute Seminar, Nov. 26, 1980, London. The Commonwealth & World Peace: A Report by the English-Speaking Union of the Commonwealth & the International Peace Academy. (IPA Report Ser.: No. 11). 1980. 6.00x (ISBN 0-686-36948-3). Intl Peace.
Commonwealth Relations Office, Great Britain. Catalogue of European Printed Books, India Office Library, 10 Vols. 1964. Set. 800.00 (ISBN 0-8161-0671-1, Hall Library). G K Hall.
--Index of Post-Nineteen Thirty Seven European Manuscript Accessions. India Office Library. 1964. 95.00 (ISBN 0-8161-0687-8, Hall Library). G K Hall.
Commonwealth Scientific & Industrial Research Institute (CSIRO) A Curious & Diverse Flora. Commonwealth Scientific & Industrial Research Institute (CSIRO) & Australian Academy of Science, eds. 1982. of slides 35.00 set (ISBN 0-686-43170-7, Pub. by CSIRO). Intl Schol Bk Serv.
Communication Skill Builders & VORT Corporation Editors. A Guide to Instructional Materials. 176p. 1981. pap. text ed. 5.00 (ISBN 0-88450-745-9, 3139-B). Communication Skill.
Communications Company. The Great Computer Calendar. 1982. pap. 7.95 (ISBN 0-8359-2574-9); 10-pack 79.50 (ISBN 0-8359-2573-0). Reston.
Communications Research Machines, Inc. Educational Psychology: A Contemporary View. 2nd ed. (CRM Bks.). pap. text ed. 12.95x o.s.i. (ISBN 0-394-32101-4). Random.
--Life & Health. 3rd ed. 589p. 1980. text ed. 23.00 (ISBN 0-394-32207-X). Random.
--Physical Science Today. (CRM Bks.). 1973. text ed. 14.95x o.p. (ISBN 0-394-30281-8). Random.
--Social Psychology: Explorations in Understanding. (CRM Bks.). 1980. text ed. 21.00x (ISBN 0-394-32550-8). Random.
--Understanding Psychology. 3rd ed. 498p. 1980. text ed. 20.00 (ISBN 0-394-32289-4); wkbk. 6.95 (ISBN 0-394-32413-7). Random.
Communicative Disorders Faculty California State University. A Style Guide for Writers in Communicative Disorders. 120p. 1980. pap. text ed. 7.95 (ISBN 0-88450-749-1, 7780-B). Communication Skill.
Como, Jay. Surviving on the Job. 1982. 6.36 (ISBN 0-686-36298-5); instr's. guide 5.28 (ISBN 0-686-37287-5). McKnight.
Comoss & Burke. Cardiac Rehabilitation: A Comprehensive Nursing Approach. text ed. 23.50 (ISBN 0-686-97966-4, Lippincott Nursing). Lippincott.
Compagnon, A. Les Classes Laborieuses, Leur Condition Actuelle, Leur Avenir par la Reorginisation du Travail. (Conditions of the 19th Century French Working Class Ser.). 354p. (Fr.). 1974. Repr. of 1858 ed. lib. bdg. 91.50x o.p. (ISBN 0-8287-0215-2, 1076). Clearwater Pub.
Compaine, Benjamin. The Newspaper Industry in the Nineteen Eighties: An Assessment of Economics & Technology. LC 80-10121. (Communications Library). 1980. text ed. 29.95x (ISBN 0-914236-37-7). Knowledge Indus.
Compaine, Benjamin M. The Book Industry in Transition: An Economic Analysis of Book Distribution & Marketing. LC 78-7527. (Communications Library Ser). (Illus.). 235p. 1978. text ed. 29.95 (ISBN 0-914236-16-4). Knowledge Indus.
--The Business of Consumer Magazines. LC 82-180. (Communications Library). 198p. 1982. text ed. 32.95 (ISBN 0-86729-020-X). Knowledge Indus.
Compaine, Benjamin M., ed. Who Owns the Media? Concentration of Ownership in the Mass Communications Industry. 2nd ed. (Communications Library Ser.). 550p. 1982. text ed. 45.00 (ISBN 0-86729-007-2). Knowledge Indus.
--Who Owns the Media? Concentration of Ownership in the Mass Communications Industry. LC 79-15891. (Communications Library). 1979. text ed. 24.95x (ISBN 0-914236-36-9). Knowledge Indus.
Companion, Audrey. Chemical Bonding. 1964. text ed. 7.95 o.p. (ISBN 0-07-012369-1, C). McGraw.
Companion, Audrey L. Chemical Bonding. 2nd ed. (Illus.). 1979. text ed. 10.00 o.p. (ISBN 0-07-012383-7, C); pap. text ed. 10.50 (ISBN 0-07-012379-9). McGraw.
Compayre, Gabriel. Abelard & the Origin & Early History of the Universities. LC 75-90094. (BCL Ser.: II). 1969. Repr. of 1893 ed. 11.50 (ISBN 0-404-01639-1). AMS Pr.
--Abelard & the Origin & Early History of the Universities. LC 69-13863. Repr. of 1893 ed. lib. bdg. 17.00x (ISBN 0-8371-0357-6, COAB). Greenwood.
Comper, W. D. Heparin (& Related Polysaccharides) Structural & Functional Properties. 280p. 1981. 56.00 (ISBN 0-677-05040-2). Gordon.
Comprone, Joseph J. Form & Substance: The Modern Essay. 496p. 1976. pap. text ed. write for info. (ISBN 0-697-03714-2); tchr's guide avail. (ISBN 0-697-03715-0). Wm C Brown.
--From Experience to Expression: A College Rhetoric. 2nd ed. LC 80-82348. (Illus.). 528p. 1981. text ed. 15.50 (ISBN 0-395-29310-3); instr's manual 0.50 (ISBN 0-395-29311-1). HM.
Compte-Rendu au Roi. Compte-Rendu au Roi sur l'Emploi des Fonds Alloues Depuis 1839 pour l'Enseignement Religieux et Elementaire des Noirs et de l'Execution des Lois des 18 et 19 Juillet 1845 Relatives au Regime des Esclaves, a l'Introduction des Travailleurs Libres aux Colonies, etc... (Slave Trade in France Ser., 1744-1848). 119p. (Fr.). 1974. Repr. of 1846 ed. lib. bdg. 39.50x o.p. (ISBN 0-8287-0216-0, TN164). Clearwater Pub.
Comptex Associates Staff. Getting the Job you Want with the Audiovisual Portfolio: A Practical Guide for Job Hunters & Career Changers. 1981. 12.95 (ISBN 0-686-37449-5). Competent Assocs.
Compton, Agnes, tr. see Supka, Magdolna B.
Compton, Al. Armonia Familiar. 1981. pap. 1.10 (ISBN 0-311-46078-X). Casa Bautista.
Compton, Alan. Comunicacion Cristiana. 1982. Repr. of 1979 ed. 3.95 (ISBN 0-311-13833-0). Casa Bautista.
Compton, Bill, jt. auth. see Johns, J. Murray.
Compton, Charles. Inside Chemistry. (Illus.). 1979. text ed. 23.00 (ISBN 0-07-012350-0, C); instructor's manual 11.00 (ISBN 0-07-012351-9). McGraw.
Compton, Charles H. Memories of a Librarian. 1954. 5.00 (ISBN 0-937322-06-7). St Louis Public Library.
Compton, D. G. Ascendancies. 12.95 o.p. (ISBN 0-399-12484-5). Putnam Pub Group.
--The Continuous Katherine Mortenhoe. 15.00 (ISBN 0-8398-2567-6, Gregg). G K Hall.
--The Steel Crocodile. 240p. 1976. Repr. of 1970 ed. lib. bdg. 11.50 (ISBN 0-8398-2327-4, Gregg). G K Hall.
--Synthajoy. 1977. Repr. of 1968 ed. lib. bdg. 12.50 (ISBN 0-8398-2373-8, Gregg). G K Hall.
Compton, D. M. & Schoen, A. H. The Mossbauer Effect. LC 62-16305. 332p. 1962. 25.00 o.p. (ISBN 0-686-86260-0). Krieger.
Compton, Eric N. Inside Commercial Banking. LC 80-13269. 191p. 1980. 24.95 (ISBN 0-471-07974-X, Pub. by Wiley-Interscience). Wiley.
Compton, Joy B. A Decade of Glory. (Illus.). 64p. 1983. 10.50 (ISBN 0-89962-322-0). Todd & Honeywell.
Compton, Merlin D. Ricardo Palma. (World Authors Ser.). 1982. lib. bdg. 15.95 (ISBN 0-8057-6435-6, Twayne). G K Hall.
Compton, Norma & Hall, Olive. Foundations of Home Economics Research: A Human Ecology Approach. LC 72-81810. 1972. pap. text ed. 13.95x (ISBN 0-8087-0338-2). Burgess.
Compton, Norma, jt. auth. see Touliatos, John.
Compton, R. R. Manual of Field Geology. LC 61-17357. 378p. 1962. 24.95 (ISBN 0-471-16698-7). Wiley.
Compton, Rae. Complete Book of Traditional Knitting. (Illus.). 240p. 1983. 19.95 (ISBN 0-686-83844-0, ScribT). Scribner.
Compton, W. V., jt. auth. see Quinlan, P. M.
Compton-Burnett, I. Daughters & Sons. 1937. 12.50 (ISBN 0-575-01796-1, Pub by Gollancz, England). David & Charles.
--A Father & His Fate. 1957. 11.95 o.p. (ISBN 0-575-01580-2, Pub. by Gollancz England). David & Charles.
--A God & his Gifts. 1963. 14.95 (ISBN 0-575-02578-6, Pub by Gollancz, England). David & Charles.
--A Heritage & its History. 1959. 14.95 (ISBN 0-575-02723-1, Pub by Gollancz, England). David & Charles.
--The Present & the Past. 1953. 14.95 (ISBN 0-575-01416-4, Pub by Gollancz, England). David & Charles.
--Two Worlds & Their Ways. 1949. 13.95 (ISBN 0-575-02610-3, Pub by Gollancz, England). David & Charles.
Compton-Burnett, Ivy. Darkness & Day. 254p. 1974. 10.00x o.p. (ISBN 0-575-01795-3). Intl Pubns Serv.
--Father & His Fate. 1969. 12.50x o.p. (ISBN 0-575-01580-2). Intl Pubns Serv.
Compton-Burnett, J., tr. see Steiner, Rudolf.
Compton-Burnett, Judith, tr. see Steiner, Rudolf.
Compton-Burnett, Juliet, tr. see Savitch, Marie.
Compton-Burnett, V., tr. see Steiner, Rudolf.
Computer Assisted Learning Symposium, 1981. Computer Assisted Learning: Selected Proceedings. Smith, P. R., ed. (Journal of Computers & Education Ser.: No. 6). 150p. 1982. 33.00 (ISBN 0-08-028111-7). Pergamon.
Computer Consultants Ltd. European Computer Survey Nineteen Sixty-Nine to Seventy. 6th ed. LC 74-102635. 1969. inquire for price o.p. (ISBN 0-08-016026-3). Pergamon.
--European Computer Users Handbook, 1969-70. LC 63-25287. 1971. inquire for price (ISBN 0-08-016027-1); inquire for price. Pergamon.
Computer Engineering Div., ASME. Computer in Engineering Nineteen Eighty-Two: Vol. 3-Mesh Generation; Finite Elements; Computers in Structural Optimization; Computers in the Engineering Workplace; Computers in Energy Systems; Personal Computing, 4 Vol. Set. 1982. 60.00 ea. (G00217); 200.00 set (G00219). ASME.
--Computers In Engineering, 1982: Vol. 1-Computer-Aided Design, Manugacturing, & Simulation, 4 Vol. Set. 1982. 60.00 (G00215); 200.00 set (G00215). ASME.
--Computers In Engineering 1982: Vol. 1-Robots & Robotics, 4 Vols. 1982. 60.00 (G00216); 200.00 set (G00219). ASME.
Computer Information Services, Chicago Hospital Council. Shared Hospital Computer Services Evaluation. 165p. 1975. 15.00 (ISBN 0-686-68578-4, 14912). Healthcare Fin Man Assn.
Computer Innovations Staff, jt. auth. see Pakin, Sandra.
Computer Usage Co., Inc. Computer Usage-Fundamentals. 2nd ed. Weiss, Eric, ed. (Illus.). 416p. 1975. text ed. 27.95 (ISBN 0-07-012402-7, C); instructor's manual 9.95 (ISBN 0-07-012410-8). McGraw.
Computer Usage Co., Inc. & Weiss, E. A. Computer Usage-Applications. 1970. pap. text ed. 19.95 (ISBN 0-07-012384-5, C). McGraw.
Computer Usage Company Inc. & Weiss, E. A. Computer Usage-Three Sixty Fortran Programming. 1969. pap. text ed. 22.95 o.p. (ISBN 0-07-012381-0, C). McGraw.
Comrie, B. The Languages of the Soviet Union. (Cambridge Language Surveys Ser.: No. 2). (Illus.). 320p. 1981. 59.50 (ISBN 0-521-23230-9); pap. 17.95 (ISBN 0-521-29877-6). Cambridge U Pr.
Comstock, Anthony. Frauds Exposed; or, How People Are Deceived & Robbed, & Youth Corrupted. LC 69-16234. (Criminology, Law Enforcement, & Social Problems Ser.: No. 79). (Illus.). 1969. Repr. of 1880 ed. 25.00x (ISBN 0-87585-079-0). Patterson Smith.
Comstock, Betsy, et al, eds. Phenomonology & Treatment of Psychiatric Emergencies. 288p. 1983. text ed. 30.00 (ISBN 0-89335-182-2). SP Med & Sci Bks.
Comstock, Philip, jt. auth. see Stern, Robert N.
Comte, August. Social Statics & Social Dynamics: The Theory of Order & the Theory of Progress. (The Most Meaningful Classics in World Culture Ser.). (Illus.). 101p. 1983. Repr. of 1899 ed. 67.85 (ISBN 0-89901-103-9). Found Class Reprints.
Comtre Corp. Multiprocessors & Parallel Processing. Enslow, D. H., ed. LC 73-18147. 352p. 1974. 34.95x (ISBN 0-471-16735-5, Pub. by Wiley-Interscience). Wiley.
Comyn, J. & Johnson, R. Wills & Intestacies. LC 78-92109. 1970. 14.75 o.p. (ISBN 0-08-006691-7); pap. 6.25 (ISBN 0-08-006690-9). Pergamon.
Comyn, James. Irish at Law. 1981. 21.50 (ISBN 0-436-10580-2, Pub. by Secker & Warburg). David & Charles.
Conaghan, John, ed. Dryden: A Selection. 1978. 33.50x (ISBN 0-416-80160-9); pap. 19.50x (ISBN 0-416-80170-6). Methuen Inc.
Conan Doyle, Arthur. Adventures & Memoirs of Sherlock Holmes. 1946. 3.95 o.s.i. (ISBN 0-394-60206-4, M206). Modern Lib.
--The Case of the Five Orange Pips. Pauk, Walter & Harris, Raymond, eds. (Jamestown Classics Ser.). (Illus.). 41p. (gr. 5). 1976. pap. text ed. 2.00x (ISBN 0-89061-062-2, 545); tchrs. ed. 3.00 (ISBN 0-89061-063-0, 547). Jamestown Pubs.
--The Case of the Six Napoleons. Pauk, Walter & Harris, Raymond, eds. (Jamestown Classics Ser.). (Illus.). 45p. (gr. 5). 1976. pap. text ed. 2.00x (ISBN 0-89061-058-4, 537); tchrs. ed. 3.00 (ISBN 0-89061-059-2, 539). Jamestown Pubs.
--The Complete Adventures & Memoirs of Sherlock Holmes. (Illus.). 336p. 1976. pap. 3.95 o.p. (ISBN 0-517-52512-7, C N Potter Bks). Crown.
--Complete Professor Challenger Stories. 1952. 20.00 (ISBN 0-7195-0360-4). Transatlantic.
--The Musgrave Ritual. Pauk, Walter & Harris, Raymond, eds. (Jamestown Classics Ser.). (Illus.). 39p. (gr. 6-12). 1976. pap. text ed. 2.00x (ISBN 0-89061-056-8, 533); tchrs. ed. 3.00 (ISBN 0-89061-057-6, 535). Jamestown Pubs.
--The Red-Headed League. Pauk, Walter & Harris, Raymond, eds. (Jamestown Classics Ser.). (Illus.). 47p. (gr. 6-12). 1976. pap. text ed. 2.00x (ISBN 0-89061-060-6, 541); tchrs. ed. 3.00 (ISBN 0-89061-061-4, 543). Jamestown Pubs.
--Sherlock Holmes: Selected Stories. (World's Classics Ser.). 1980. pap. 3.95 (ISBN 0-19-281530-X). Oxford U Pr.
--Sir Nigel. 16.95 (ISBN 0-7195-3228-0). Transatlantic.
--White Company. 15.95 o.p. (ISBN 0-7195-3225-6). Transatlantic.
Conan Doyle, Arthur see Allen, W. S.
Conan Doyle, Arthur see Doyle, Arthur Conan.
Conan Doyle, Arthur see Eyre, A. G.
Conan Doyle, Arthur see Swan, D. K.
Conant. Two Modes of Thought. 1970. pap. 1.95 o.p. (ISBN 0-671-20468-8, Touchstone Bks). S&S.
Conant, James B., ed. Overthrow of the Phlogiston Theory: The Chemical Revolution of 1775-1789. LC 50-8087. (Case Histories in Experimental Science Ser: No. 2). (Illus.). 1950. pap. 3.00x o.p. (ISBN 0-674-64950-8). Harvard U Pr.
--Pasteur's & Tyndall's Study of Spontaneous Generation. LC 53-9042. (Case Histories in Experimental Science Ser: No. 7). (Illus.). 1953. pap. 3.00x o.p. (ISBN 0-674-65700-4). Harvard U Pr.
Conant, Jonathan B. Cochran's German Review Grammar. 3rd ed. LC 73-21535. 384p. 1974. text ed. 18.95 (ISBN 0-13-139501-7). P-H.
Conant, K. J. Cluny, les Eglises et la Maison Du Chef D'Ordre. LC 65-25374. 1968. pap. 35.00x (ISBN 0-910956-51-0). Medieval Acad.
Conant, Melvin A. The Oil Factor in U.S. Foreign Policy, 1980-1990. LC 81-47714. (A Council on Foreign Relations Book Ser.). (Illus.). 144p. 1981. 14.95x (ISBN 0-669-04728-7); pap. 8.95x (ISBN 0-669-05206-X). Lexington Bks.
Conant, Melvin A. & Gold, Fern R. The Geopolitics of Energy. LC 77-20668. (Special Studies in Natural Resources & Energy Management Ser.). (Illus.). 1978. lib. bdg. 28.50 o.p. (ISBN 0-89158-404-8). Westview.
Conant, Michael. Railroad Mergers & Abandonments. LC 82-15834. (Publications of the Institute of Business & Economic Research, University of California). xiii, 212p. 1982. Repr. of 1964 ed. lib. bdg. 29.75x (ISBN 0-313-23694-1, CORAM). Greenwood.
Conant, Norman F., et al. Manual of Clinical Mycology. 3rd ed. LC 76-135321. (Illus.). 1971. 17.50 o.p. (ISBN 0-7216-2646-7). Saunders.
Conant, Ralph W. The Conant Report: A Study of the Education of Librarians. 1980. 22.50x (ISBN 0-262-03072-1). MIT Pr.
Conant, Ralph W. & Molz, R. Kathleen, eds. The Metropolitan Library. 256p. 1973. 20.00x (ISBN 0-262-03041-1). MIT Pr.
Conant, Robert, jt. auth. see Bedford, Frances.
Conant, Roger. The Political Poetry & Ideology of F. I. Tiutchev. (Ardis Essay Ser.: No. 6). 1983. 10.00 (ISBN 0-88233-624-X). Ardis Pubs.
Conant, Roger C. Electrical Circuits Problems & Laboratory Manual. (Illus.). 1980. 4.50x o.p. (ISBN 0-917974-33-6). Waveland Pr.
Conard, Alfred F. & Knauss, Robert L. Editor's Notes to Enterprise Organization. (University Casebook Ser.). 154p. 1982. pap. text ed. write for info. (ISBN 0-88277-108-6). Foundation Pr.
Conard, Alfred F., et al. Corporations-Cases, Statutes & Analysis. 2nd ed. LC 82-15888. (University Casebook Ser.). 805p. 1982. text ed. write for info. Foundation Pr.
--Editor's Notes to Corporations. 2nd ed. (University Casebook Ser.). 99p. 1982. pap. write for info. (ISBN 0-88277-117-5). Foundation Pr.
Conard, Howard. Uncle Dick Wootton. LC 80-22533. (Classics of the Old West Ser.). lib. bdg. 17.28 (ISBN 0-8094-3951-4). Silver.
Conard, Robert C. Heinrich Boll. (World Authors Ser.). 14.95 (ISBN 0-8057-6464-X, Twayne). G K Hall.
Conarroe, Richard R., ed. Executive Search: A Guide for Recruiting Outstanding Executives. LC 78-24605. 124p. 1979. Repr. of 1976 ed. lib. bdg. 12.50 o.p. (ISBN 0-88275-814-4). Krieger.
Conason, Emil & Metz, Ella. The Salt-Free Diet Cook Book. pap. 3.95 (ISBN 0-448-01827-6, G&D). Putnam Pub Group.
Conaway, Judith. City Crafts from Secret Cities. LC 77-88640. (Illus.). (gr. 3-7). 1978. lib. bdg. 8.97 o.s.i. (ISBN 0-695-40874-7). Follett.
Conaway, Judith, adapted by. King Kong. LC 82-15078. (Step-Up Adventures Ser.). (Illus.). 96p. (gr. 2-5). 1983. 2.50 (ISBN 0-394-85617-1); PLB 4.99 (ISBN 0-394-95617-6). Random.
--Twenty-Thousand Leagues under the Sea. (Step-Up Adventures Ser.: No. 6). (Illus.). 96p. (gr. 2-5). 1983. 1.95 (ISBN 0-394-85333-4); PLB 4.99 (ISBN 0-394-95333-9). Random.
Concannon, Joe, jt. auth. see Rodgers, Bill.
Concept-Research & Reference Division, ed. Who's Who of Indian Geographers. 139p. 1982. text ed. 15.25x (ISBN 0-391-02808-1, Pub. by Concept India). Humanities.
Concha, Joseph. Chokecherry Hunters & Other Poems. 31p. 1976. pap. 2.25 (ISBN 0-913270-57-1). Sunstone Pr.
Conconi, Charles & House, Toni. The Washington Sting. LC 78-13519. 1979. 10.95 o.p. (ISBN 0-698-10889-2, Coward). Putnam Pub Group.
Condax, Kate D. Riding: An Illustrated Guide. LC 82-16460. (Illus.). 208p. 1983. 14.95 (ISBN 0-668-05424-7, 5424). Arco.
Conde, D. F. & Harris, N. Modern Air Conditioning Practice. 3rd ed. 464p. 1983. 26.50x (ISBN 0-07-026833-9, G); write for info. solutions manual (ISBN 0-07-026834-7). McGraw.
Conde, D. F., jt. auth. see Harris, Norman C.

Conde, John A. The Cars That Hudson Built. LC 80-53376. (Illus.). 224p. 1980. 19.95 (ISBN 0-9605048-0-X). Arnold-Porter Pub.
--Cars with Personalities. LC 82-73487. (Illus.). 256p. 1982. 21.95 (ISBN 0-9605048-1-8). Arnold Porter Pub.
Conde Nast, ed. see Bride's Magazine Editors.
Conde Nast Publications Inc. Glamour's Health & Beauty Book. (Illus.). 1978. 14.95 o.s.i. (ISBN 0-671-23089-1). S&S.
Conde Nast Pubns., Inc. Glamour's Success Book. 1979. 10.95 o.s.i. (ISBN 0-671-24682-8). S&S.
Conde, Nicholas. The Religion. 384p. 1982. 13.95 (ISBN 0-453-00412-1, H412). NAL.
--The Religion. 1983. pap. 3.50 (ISBN 0-686-43068-9, Sig). NAL.
Condemi, John J. & Schwartz, Robert. Allergy & Clinical Immunology. 2nd ed. (Medical Examination Review Book Ser.: No. 26). 1983. write for info (ISBN 0-87488-132-3). Med Exam.
Conder, Alan D. Training the Driving Pony. LC 76-770. (Illus.). 1977. 6.95 (ISBN 0-686-85659-7); pap. 3.95 (ISBN 0-668-03951-5). Arco.
Conder, John R. & Young, Colin L. Physiochemical Measurements by Gas Chromatography. LC 78-9899. 1979. 119.95 (ISBN 0-471-99674-2, Pub. by Wiley-Interscience). Wiley.
Conder, Joseph M. & Hopkins, Gilbert N. The Self-Insurance Decision. 119p. pap. 12.95 (ISBN 0-86641-002-3, 81124). Natl Assn Accts.
Condie, K. C. Archean Greenstone Belts. (Developments in Pre-Cambrain Geology Ser.: Vol. 3). 1981. 106.50 (ISBN 0-444-41854-7). Elsevier.
Condillac, E. B. De. Principes Generaux de Grammaire pour Toutes les Langues. (Linguistics 13th-18th Centuries Ser.). 368p. (Fr.). 1974. Repr. of 1798 ed. lib. bdg. 95.00x o.p. (ISBN 0-8287-0217-9, 71-5038). Clearwater Pub.
Condillac, Etienne Bonnot de. Essay on the Origin of Human Knowledge. Nugent, Thomas, tr. from Fr. LC 76-161929. (Hist. of Psych. Ser.). 1971. Repr. of 1756 ed. 45.00x (ISBN 0-8201-1090-6). Schol Facsimiles.
Condillac, Etienne Bonnot De see De Condillac, Etienne Bonnot.
Condit, Carl. American Building: Materials & Techniques from the Beginning of the Colonial Settlements to the Present. 2nd ed. (Illus.). xiv, 330p. 1982. lib. bdg. 20.00x (ISBN 0-226-11448-1); pap. 9.95 (ISBN 0-226-11450-3, CHAC25). U of Chicago Pr.
Condit, Carl W. American Building: Materials & Techniques from the Beginning of the Colonial Settlements to the Present. LC 67-30127. (Chicago History of American Civilization Ser). (Illus.). 1969. 7.00x o.s.i. (ISBN 0-226-11451-1); pap. 4.95 o.s.i. (ISBN 0-226-11453-8, CHAC25). U of Chicago Pr.
--Chicago. Incl. Nineteen Ten to Nineteen Twenty-Nine - Building, Planning, & Urban Technology. LC 72-94791 (ISBN 0-226-11458-9, P693); Nineteen Thirty to Nineteen Seventy - Building, Planning & Urban Technology. LC 73-19996 (ISBN 0-226-11459-7, P694). (Illus.). 1976. pap. 5.45 ea. o.s.i. (Phoen). U of Chicago Pr.
--Chicago Nineteen Thirty-Nineteen Seventy: Building, Planning, & Urban Technology, Vol. 2. 1974. 12.50x (ISBN 0-226-11457-0). U of Chicago Pr.
--The Port of New York: A History of the Rail & Terminal System from the Grand Central Electrification to the Present, Vol. 2. LC 79-16850. 384p. 40.00x (ISBN 0-226-11461-9). U of Chicago Pr.
Condit, Ira J. Ficus: The Exotic Species. 1969. pap. 8.00x (ISBN 0-931876-10-9, 4025). Ag Sci Pubns.
Condon, Arnold & Lloyd, A. C. Transcribing Speed Studies. 1974. 8.96 (ISBN 0-07-012398-5, G). McGraw.
Condon, Arnold, et al. Transcription Thirty-Six. new ed. (Illus.). (gr. 11-12). 1976. pap. text ed. 6.96 (ISBN 0-07-012400-0, G); instructor's manual 7.50 (ISBN 0-07-012401-9); prep bk. 3.96 (ISBN 0-07-012404-3); transparencies 175.00 (ISBN 0-07-086175-7); tapes 315.00 (ISBN 0-07-087585-5). McGraw.
Condon, Camy & Nagasawa, Kimiko. Kites, Crackers & Craftsmen. Narita, Kikue, ed. (Illus.). 144p. (Orig.). 1974. pap. 7.50 (ISBN 0-8048-1402-3, Pub. by Shufunotomo Co Ltd Japan). C E Tuttle.
Condon, Camy, jt. auth. see Nagasawa, Kimiko.
Condon, E. U. & Odabasi, H. Atomic Structure. LC 77-88673. (Illus.). 1980. 83.50 (ISBN 0-521-21859-4); pap. 27.95 (ISBN 0-521-29893-8). Cambridge U Pr.
Condon, E. W. & Odishaw, Hugh, eds. Handbook of Physics. 2nd ed. 1967. 89.90 (ISBN 0-07-012403-5, P&RB). McGraw.
Condon, Edward U. & Shortley, George H. Theory of Atomic Spectra. (Orig.). 1935. pap. 32.50 (ISBN 0-521-09209-4). Cambridge U Pr.
Condon, J. J., jt. ed. see Fox, P. F.
Condon, John C. InterAct: Japanese & North Americans. LC 81-85730. 90p. (Orig.). Date not set. pap. text ed. 10.00 (ISBN 0-933662-49-1). Intercult Pr.
Condon, John C. & Yousef, Fathi S. An Introduction to Intercultural Communication. LC 74-14633. (No. 19). 326p. 1975. pap. 8.95 (ISBN 0-672-61328-X, SC19). Bobbs.
Condon, John C., Jr. Interpersonal Communication. 1977. text ed. 12.95x (ISBN 0-02-324210-8, 324210). Macmillan.
--Semantics & Communication. 2nd ed. (Illus.). 128p. 1975. pap. text ed. 11.95x (ISBN 0-02-324220-5, 32422). Macmillan.
Condon, M. A. Office Printers: A Practical Evaluation Guide. (Office Technology in the Eighties Ser.: No. 5). 57p. 1982. pap. 17.50x (ISBN 0-85012-371-2). Intl Pubns Serv.
Condon, Margaret. Topographics. (Outlaws Ser.: Vol. 1). 1977. signed, numbered 4.95; pap. 3.00 (ISBN 0-917624-06-8). Lame Johnny.
Condon, R. J. Our Pagan Christmas. 12p. 1981. pap. 2.00 (ISBN 0-686-83178-0). Am Atheist.
Condon, Richard. Death of a Politician. LC 78-16015. 1978. 9.95 o.s.i. (ISBN 0-399-90018-7, Marek). Putnam Pub Group.
--The Entwining. 429p. 1980. 12.95 (ISBN 0-399-90089-6, Marek). Putnam Pub Group.
--Prizzi's Honor. 320p. 1982. 13.95 (ISBN 0-698-11143-5, Coward). Putnam Pub Group.
--Prizzi's Honor. 320p. 1983. pap. 3.50 (ISBN 0-425-05778-X). Berkley Pub.
Condon, Robert. Data Processing with Applications. 2nd ed. (Illus.). 432p. 1980. text ed. 18.95 (ISBN 0-8359-1254-X); wkbk. 8.95 (ISBN 0-8359-1256-6); instrs.' manual avail. (ISBN 0-8359-1255-8). Reston.
--Data Processing with Applications. abr. ed. 1981. pap. text ed. 15.95 (ISBN 0-8359-1259-0). Reston.
Condorcet. Un Ami De Voltaire a M. D'epremesnil. Repr. of 1780 ed. 27.00 o.p. (ISBN 0-8287-0218-7). Clearwater Pub.
Condorcet, Marie J. Essai sur l'Application de l'Analyse aux Probabilites des Decisions Rendues a la Pluralite des Voix. LC 75-113124. 495p. (Fr.). 1973. Repr. of 1785 ed. 29.50 (ISBN 0-8284-0252-3). Chelsea Pub.
Condorelli, L., ed. Internal Medicine, 2 pts. (International Congress Ser.: Vol. 502). 1981. Set. 195.75 (ISBN 0-444-90136-1). Elsevier.
Condry, Dorothea. Firebird of Unlimited Happiness. (Illus.). 116p. 1981. pap. 7.50 (ISBN 0-942316-01-0). Pueblo Pub Pr.
--The Sign. 16p. 1981. pap. 1.00 o.p. (ISBN 0-686-30661-9). Samisdat.
Condry, Steve, ed. see Long, Harold & Wheeler, Allen.
Cone, Carl B. Hounds in the Morning: Sundry Sports of Merry England; Excerpts from the Sporting Magazine, 1792-1836. LC 81-51017. (Illus.). 224p. 1981. 16.00x (ISBN 0-8131-1411-X). U Pr of Ky.
Cone, Carroll. Energy Management for Industrial Furnaces. LC 80-10435. 1980. 39.95x (ISBN 0-471-06037-2, Pub. by Wiley-Interscience). Wiley.
Cone, Cynthia A. & Pelto, Pertti J. Guide to Cultural Anthropology. rev ed. 1969. pap. 7.95x o.p. (ISBN 0-673-05985-5). Scott F.
Cone, Edward T. The Composer's Voice. LC 73-80830. (Illus.). 1974. 24.50x (ISBN 0-520-02508-3). U of Cal Pr.
--The Composer's Voice. (Ernest Bloch Lecture Ser.). 194p. 1982. pap. 6.95 (ISBN 0-520-04647-1). U of Cal Pr.
Cone, Edward T., jt. ed. see Boretz, Benjamin.
Cone, Ferne G. Knutty Knitting for Kids. LC 76-50323. (Illus.). (gr. 4 up). 1977. 3.49 (ISBN 0-695-80739-0, Dist. by Caroline Hse); PLB 6.99 (ISBN 0-695-40739-2). Follett.
Cone, James. God of the Oppressed. 1978. pap. 6.95 (ISBN 0-8164-2607-4). Seabury.
Cone, James H. Black Theology & Black Power. LC 70-76462. (Orig.). 1969. pap. 5.95 (ISBN 0-8164-2003-3, SP59). Seabury.
--Black Theology of Liberation. LC 74-120333. 1970. pap. 6.95 (ISBN 0-397-10098-1, LP-053). Har-Row.
--The Spirituals & the Blues. pap. 4.95 (ISBN 0-8164-2073-4, SP74). Seabury.
--The Spirituals & the Blues: An Interpretation. LC 80-19382. viii, 152p. 1980. Repr. of 1972 ed. lib. bdg. 19.25x (ISBN 0-313-22667-9, COSB). Greenwood.
Cone, Joan. Easy Game Cooking. (Illus.). 139p. 1974. pap. 4.95 (ISBN 0-686-36726-X). Md Hist.
--Easy Game Cooking: One Hundred & Twenty-Four Savory, Home-Tested, Money-Saving Recipes & Menus for Game Birds & Animals. LC 74-75347. 1974. spiral bdg 5.95 o.p. (ISBN 0-914440-01-2); pap. 2.50 o.p. (ISBN 0-914440-29-2). EPM Pubns.
Cone, John D. & Hayes, Steven C. Environmental Problems-Behavioral Solutions. LC 80-12471. (Environment & Behavior Ser.). 280p. (Orig.). 1980. pap. text ed. 11.95 o.p. (ISBN 0-8185-0392-0). Brooks-Cole.
Cone, Margaret & Gombrich, Richard, eds. The Perfect Generosity of Price Vessantara: A Buddhist Epic. (Illus.). 1977. 39.00x (ISBN 0-19-826530-1). Oxford U Pr.
Cone, Molly. Mishmash & The Robot. (gr. 2-5). 1981. 7.95 (ISBN 0-395-30345-1). HM.
--Mishmash & The Venus Flytrap. (Illus.). (gr. 3-5). 1979. pap. 1.75 (ISBN 0-671-45069-7). Archway.
--Other Side of the Fence. (gr. 5-8). 1967. 6.95 o.p. (ISBN 0-395-06713-8). HM.
--Paul David Silverman Is a Father. LC 82-18205. (Illus.). 64p. (gr. 2 up). 1983. 9.95 (ISBN 0-525-44050-X, 0966-290). Dutton.
--Ringling Brothers. LC 70-132295. (Biography Ser). (Illus.). (gr. 2-5). 1971. 10.53i (ISBN 0-690-70287-6, TYC-J); PLB 10.89 (ISBN 0-690-70288-4). Har-Row.
Cone, Polly, ed. see Wechsberg, Joseph & Witzmann, Reingard.
Cone, Poly, et al, eds. see Ettesvold, Paul M.
Cone, Richard A. & Dowling, John E., eds. Membrane Transduction Mechanisms. LC 78-65280. (Society of General Physiologists Ser.). 248p. 1979. text ed. 32.00 (ISBN 0-89004-236-5). Raven.
Conesa, Salvador H. & Argote, M. L. A Visual Aid to the Examination of Nerve Roots. (Illus.). 1976. text ed. 10.95 o.p. (ISBN 0-02-858080-X, Pub. by Bailliere-Tindall). Saunders.
Confederate States Of America - Congress. Journal of the Congress of the Confederate States of America, 1861-1865, 7 Vols. Repr. of 1905 ed. Set. 450.00 (ISBN 0-527-18930-8). Kraus Repr.
Confederate States Of America - War Department. Southern History of the War. Repr. of 1863 ed. 29.00 o.s.i. (ISBN 0-527-18950-2). Kraus Repr.
Confer, Grayce. Faith & Fried Potatoes. 184p. 1982. pap. 4.95 (ISBN 0-8341-0732-5). Beacon Hill.
Confer, Grayce B. Faith & Fried Potatoes. 1978. pap. 4.95 (ISBN 0-685-87960-7). Creative Pr.
Confer, William N. & Ables, Billie S. Multiple Personality: Etiology, Diagnosis & Treatment. LC 82-2969. 1983. 29.95 (ISBN 0-89885-081-9). Human Sci Pr.
Conference, Bethesda, Md, June, 1981 & Chan-Palay, Victoria. Cytochemical Methods in Neuroanatomy: Proceedings. LC 82-7826. (Neurology & Neurobiology Ser.: Vol. 1). 580p. 1982. 96.00 (ISBN 0-8451-2700-4). A R Liss.
Conference for Revision of the Universal Copyright Convention, Paris, 1971. Records: Proceedings. 295p. (Orig.). 1974. pap. 18.25 o.p. (ISBN 92-3-101047-6, UNESCO). Unipub.
Conference in Honor of Anna Goldfeder, Feb 17-19, 1982. Cell Proliferation, Cancer, & Cancer Therapy: Proceedings, Vol. 397. Baserga, Renato, ed. 328p. 1982. 65.00 (ISBN 0-89766-184-2); pap. write for info. (ISBN 0-89766-185-0). NY Acad Sci.
Conference of European Statisticians. Correspondence Table Between the Standard International Trade Classification of the United Nations (SITC) & the Standard Foreign Trade Classification of the Council for Mutual Economic Assistance (SFTC). 22.00 (ISBN 0-686-43224-X, E/R.82.II.E.10). UN.
Conference on Aging, 2nd, University of Michigan. Planning the Older Years. Donohue, Wilma & Tibbitts, Clark, eds. Repr. of 1950 ed. lib. bdg. 20.50x (ISBN 0-8371-0386-X, MIUA). Greenwood.
Conference on Aging, 5th, University of Michigan, 1952. Housing the Aging. LC 76-26114. (Conference on Aging). 1976. Repr. of 1954 ed. lib. bdg. 20.50x (ISBN 0-8371-9043-6, DOHA). Greenwood.
Conference on Blood Viscosity in Heart Disease, Thromboembo-Lism & Cancer, Sydney Australia, May, 1978. Health Needs & Health Services in Rural Ghana. De Kadt, E., et al, eds. 140p. 1981. pap. 14.80 (ISBN 0-08-028136-2). Pergamon.
Conference on Cellular Dynamics, Fifth Interdisciplinary. Proceedings. Peachey, L. D., ed. 1969. 101.00 (ISBN 0-677-13300-6). Gordon.
Conference on Communication, Language & Sex, 1st Annual. Communication, Language, & Sex: Proceedings. Berryman, Cynthia & Eman, Virginia, eds. 1980. pap. text ed. 15.95 (ISBN 0-88377-136-5). Newbury Hse.
Conference on Computer Technology in Education for 1985 at Arlie House, Warrenton, Va., Sept. 15-18, 1975. Communications & Computers: Implications for Education, Proceedings. Seidel, Robert J. & Rubin, Martin L., eds. 1977. 29.50 (ISBN 0-12-635050-7). Acad Pr.
Conference on Confidentiality of Health Records, Key Biscayne, Fla., Nov. 6-9, 1974. Confidentiality: Report of the Conference on Confidentiality of Health Records. Springarn, Natalie D., ed. 58p. 1975. pap. 2.00 o.p. (ISBN 0-685-63944-4, P175-0). Am Psychiatric.
Conference on Fish Behaviour in Relation to Fishing Techniques & Tactics, Bergen, Norway, 1968-69. Proceedings, Vols. 1 & 3. (FAO Fisheries Reports: No. 62). Vol. 1, 51p. pap. 7.50 (ISBN 0-686-92921-7, F1674, FAO); Vol. 3, 427p. pap. 25.50 (ISBN 0-686-98784-5). Unipub.
Conference on Fishery Administration & Services, Rome, 1966. Report, 3 Vols. (FAO Fisheries Reports: No. 43, Vols. 1-3). 1967. Vol. 1, 169p. pap. 11.50 (ISBN 0-686-92992-6, F1661, FAO); Vol. 2, 310p. pap. 20.25 (ISBN 0-686-98836-1, F1662); Vol. 3, 286p. pap. 18.75 (ISBN 0-686-98837-X, F1663). Unipub.
Conference on High-Temperature Systems, 3rd. Proceedings: The Performance of High-Temperature Systems, 2 vols. Bahn, Gilbert S., ed. Incl. Vol. 1. 280p. 1968. 70.00x (ISBN 0-677-10600-9); Vol. 2. 360p. 1969. 89.00x (ISBN 0-677-12960-2). Gordon.
Conference on Income Support Policies for the Aging-University of Chicago. Income Support Policies for the Aged. Tolley, George S. & Burkhauser, Richard V., eds. LC 77-4155. 1977. prof ref 19.50x (ISBN 0-88410-359-5). Ballinger Pub.
Conference on Instruments & Measurements. Proceedings, 2 vols. Von Koch, H. & Ljungberg, G., eds. Incl. Vol. 1. Chemical Analysis, Electric Quantities, Nucleonics & Process Control. 57.00 o.p. (ISBN 0-12-725701-2); Vol. 2. Nuclear Instrumentation, Measurement of Electric & Magnetic Quantities, Reactor Control. 68.00 o.p. (ISBN 0-12-725702-0). 1961. Acad Pr.
Conference on Intellectual Trends in Latin America, University of Texas, 1945. Papers. LC 69-19001. Repr. of 1945 ed. lib. bdg. 16.25x (ISBN 0-8371-1037-8, TLIT). Greenwood.
Conference on Learning, Remembering & Forgetting, 3rd. Proceedings: Readiness to Remember, 2 pts. Kimble, D. P., ed. Incl. Vol. 1. 354p. 70.00x (ISBN 0-677-14420-2); Vol. 2. 310p. 70.00x (ISBN 0-677-14430-X). 762p. 1969. Set. 123.00x (ISBN 0-677-13420-7). Gordon.
Conference on Mathematical Programming, 3rd, Matrafured, Hungary, 1975. Studies on Mathematical Programming: Proceedings. Prekopa, A., ed. LC 80-496383. (Mathematical Methods of Operations Research). 200p. 1980. 22.50x (ISBN 963-05-1854-6). Intl Pubns Serv.
Conference on Non-Fossil Fuel & Non-Nuclear Fuel Energy Strategies, Honolulu, USS, January 1979. Renewable Energy Prospects: Proceedings. Bach, W., et al, eds. 340p. 1980. 24.00 (ISBN 0-08-024252-9). Pergamon.
Conference on Phenomenology Pure & Applied, 5th, Lexington, 1972. Language & Language Disturbances: Proceedings. Straus, Erwin, ed. 1973. text ed. 12.50x (ISBN 0-391-00333-X). Duquesne.
Conference on Plant Growth Substances, 9th. Plant Growth Regulation: Proceedings. (Proceedings in Life Sciences). 1977. 39.00 o.p. (ISBN 0-387-08113-5). Springer-Verlag.
Conference on Proposed Legislation in The United States & on the British National Health Care Experience. National Health Insurance Schemes: Proceedings. 75p. 1972. 3.00 (ISBN 0-89215-038-6). U Cal LA Indus Rel.
Conference on Qualitative Theory of Nonlinear Differential & Integral Equations, Wisconsin. Advances in Differential & Integral Equations: Studies in Applied Mathematics Five. Nohel, John S., ed. (Illus.). xvi, 207p. 1969. text ed. 16.50 (ISBN 0-89871-037-5). Soc Indus-Appl Math.
Conference on Research Designs in General Semantics, 1st, Pennsylvania State University. Proceedings. new ed. Johnson, Kenneth G., ed. 298p. 1974. 58.00x (ISBN 0-677-14370-2). Gordon.
Conference on Surface Properties of Materials, Held at the University of Missouri, Rolla, June 24-27, 1974. Surface Properties of Materials: Proceedings. Levenson, L. L., ed. (Journal of Surface Science: Vol. 48). 294p. 1975. Repr. of 1975 ed. 38.50 (ISBN 0-444-10846-7, North-Holland). Elsevier.
Conference On Value Inquiry - 1st & 2nd. Value Theory in Philosophy & Social Science: Proceedings. Laszlo, Ervin & Wilbur, James B., eds. LC 73-84239. (Current Topics of Contemporary Thought Ser.). 1973. 27.00x (ISBN 0-677-14160-2). Gordon.
Conference On Value Inquiry - 3rd. Human Values & Natural Science: Proceedings. Laszlo, Ervin & Wilbur, James B., eds. (Current Topics of Contemporary Thought Ser.: Vol. 4). 310p. 1970. 46.00x (ISBN 0-677-13960-8). Gordon.
Confino, Michael. Natalie Herzen: Daughter of a Revolutionary. LC 73-86555. 416p. 1974. 24.50x (ISBN 0-912050-15-2, Library Pr). Open Court.
Conford, Ellen. And This Is Laura. (gr. 5-7). 1978. pap. 2.25 (ISBN 0-671-44379-8). Archway.
--Eugene the Brave. LC 77-24241. (gr. 1-3). 1978. pap. 8.95 (ISBN 0-316-15292-7). Little.
--Lenny Kandell, Smart Aleck: . 128p. (gr. 4-6). 1983. 9.25i (ISBN 0-316-15313-3). Little.
--The Luck of Pokey Bloom. (Illus.). 144p. (gr. 4-6). 1975. 8.95 (ISBN 0-316-15305-2). Little.
--Me & the Terrible Two. (Illus.). 128p. (gr. 4-6). 1974. 8.95 (ISBN 0-316-15303-6). Little.
--Seven Days to a Brand-New Me. 96p. (gr. 5 up). 1981. 8.25i (ISBN 0-316-15311-7). Little.
--To All My Fans, with Love from Sylvie. 192p. (gr. 7 up). 1982. 9.95 (ISBN 0-316-15312-5). Little.
Confucius. The Analects. Lau, D. C., tr. 1979. pap. 3.95 (ISBN 0-14-044348-7). Penguin.
--Analects. Waley, Arthur, tr. 1966. pap. 4.95 (ISBN 0-394-70173-9, V173, Vin). Random.
--Analects of Confucius. Soothill, William E., ed. LC 68-8580. (Illus.). 1968. Repr. of 1910 ed. 17.50 o.p. (ISBN 0-8188-0082-8). Paragon.
--The Most Compelling Sayings by Confucius. Lynall, Leonard D., tr. (Most Meaningful Classics in World Culture Ser.). (Illus.). 166p. 1983. 83.45 (ISBN 0-89266-387-1). Am Classical Coll Pr.
--Sayings of Confucius. Ware, James R., tr. (Orig.). pap. 2.95 (ISBN 0-451-62168-9, ME2168, Ment). NAL.
--The Wisdom of Confucius. Yutang, Lin, ed. 5.95 (ISBN 0-394-60426-1). Modern Lib.

Congar, Samuel H., ed. Records of the Town of Newark, New Jersey, from its Settlement in 1666 to its Incorporation as a City in 1836, Vol. 6. 308p. 1966. pap. 8.50 (ISBN 0-686-81799-0). NJ Hist Soc.

Congar, Yves. Challenge to the Church: The Case of Archbishop Lefebvre. LC 76-53715. 1977. pap. 1.95 o.p. (ISBN 0-87973-689-5). Our Sunday Visitor.

--I Believe in the Holy Spirit, 3 Vols. Incl. The Experience of the Spirit. 300p. Vol. 1 (ISBN 0-8164-0518-2); Vol. 2. Lord & Giver of Life. 300p (ISBN 0-8164-0535-2); Vol. 3. The River of Life Flows in the East & in the West. 300p (ISBN 0-8164-0537-9). 300p. 1983. 24.95 ea.; Set. 70.00 (ISBN 0-8164-0540-9). Seabury.

Congdon, Don, ed. Combat-World War II, 2 vols. Incl. European Theater of Operations. 19.95 (ISBN 0-87795-457-7); Pacific Theater of Operations. 19.95 (ISBN 0-87795-458-5). (Illus.). Date not set. Arbor Hse.

Congdon, Herbert W. Early American Homes for Today: A Treasury of Decorative Details & Restoration Procedures. 1982. pap. 9.95 (ISBN 0-87233-065-6). Bauhan.

Congdon, Lee. The Young Lukacs. LC 82-11162. xiii, 235p. 1983. 21.00x (ISBN 0-8078-1538-1). U of NC Pr.

Congdon, Tim. Monetary Control in Britain. 150p. 1982. 50.00x (ISBN 0-333-26831-8, Pub. by Macmillan England). State Mutual Bk.

Conger. Friction Skin. (Comparison & Identification). Date not set. price not set (ISBN 0-444-41323-5). Elsevier.

Conger, Flora S. & Rose, Irene B. Child Care Aide Skills. (Careers in Home Economics Ser.). (Illus.). 1979. pap. text ed. 15.96 (ISBN 0-07-012420-5, G); tchr's manual & key 4.00 (ISBN 0-07-012429-9); wkbk. 5.96 (ISBN 0-07-012421-3). McGraw.

Conger, John J. Adolescence & Youth: Psychological Development in a Changing World. 2nd ed. (Illus.). 1977. text ed. 24.50 scp o.p. (ISBN 0-06-041362-X, HarpC). Har-Row.

--Contemporary Issues in Adolescent Development. 522p. 1975. pap. text ed. 13.50 scp o.p. (ISBN 0-06-041363-8, HarpC). Har-Row.

Conger, John J. & Peterson, Anne C. Adolescence & Youth: Psychological Development in a Changing World. 3rd ed. 670p. 1983. text ed. 22.50 (ISBN 0-06-041357-3); write for info instr's manual (ISBN 0-06-361342-5). Har-Row.

Conger, Yves M. After Nine Hundred Years: The Background of the Schism Between the Eastern & Western Churches. LC 78-6154. 1978. Repr. of 1959 ed. lib. bdg. 18.75x (ISBN 0-313-20493-4, COAN). Greenwood.

Congressional Quarterly, ed. see Schroeder, Richard.

Congress of Neurological Surgeons. Clinical Neurosurgery, Vol. 26. Carmel, Peter W., ed. 1979. 47.50 (ISBN 0-683-02021-8). Williams & Wilkins.

Congress of the International Economic Association, 4th, Budapest, Hungary. Economic Integration: Worldwide, Regional, Sectoral: Proceedings. Machlup, Fritz, ed. LC 76-10281. 1977. 49.95x o.p. (ISBN 0-470-01381-8). Halsted Pr.

Congress of the International Institute of Public Finance Tokyo, 37th, 1981. Public Finance & Growth: Proceedings. Stolper, Wolfgang, ed. 320p. 1983. 30.00 (ISBN 0-8143-1751-0). Wayne St U Pr.

Congress of the U. S., Office of Technology Assessment. Nuclear Proliferation & Safeguards. LC 77-60024. (Praeger Special Studies). 1977. 27.95 o.p. (ISBN 0-03-041601-9). Praeger.

Congress Senate Committee on Foreign Relations. Decade of American Foreign Policy: Basic Documents, 1941-1949. LC 68-55112. (Illus.). 1968. Repr. of 1950 ed. lib. bdg. 72.00 (ISBN 0-8371-0698-2, DEAF). Greenwood.

Congressional Information Service, Inc., ed. ASI Annual. 2262p. 1981. lib. bdg. 590.00 (ISBN 0-686-75380-1). Cong Info.

Congressional Information Service, Inc. Staff. ASI Annual, 1974, 2 Vols. LC 73-82599. 400.00 (ISBN 0-912380-23-3). Cong Info.

--ASI Annual, 1981, 2 Vols. LC 73-82599. 715.00 (ISBN 0-912380-95-0). Cong Info.

--CIS-Index 1975 Annual, 2 Vols. 220.00 (ISBN 0-912380-32-2). Cong Info.

--CIS-Index 1976 Annual, 2 Vols. 220.00 (ISBN 0-912380-41-1). Cong Info.

--CIS-Index 1978 Annual, 2 Vols. 260.00 (ISBN 0-912380-60-8). Cong Info.

--CIS-Index 1981 Annual, 2 Vols. LC 79-158879. 370.00 (ISBN 0-686-84194-8). Cong Info.

Congressional Information Service, Inc. Staff, ed. CIS Online User Guide & Thesaurus. 400p. 1982. loose-leaf 75.00 (ISBN 0-686-43131-6). Cong Info.

Congressional Information Service, Inc. Staff. CIS U. S. Congressional Committee Hearings Index: Part VI, 1953-1958. 3600p. 1982. 1625.00 (ISBN 0-686-43134-0). Cong Info.

--CIS US Congressional Committee Hearings Index: Pt. VIII, 1965-1969, 2 Vols. 1625.00 (ISBN 0-686-84196-4). Cong Info.

--CIS US Congressional Committee Hearings Index: Pt. VII, 1959-1964, 2 Vols. 1625.00 (ISBN 0-686-84197-2). Cong Info.

Congressional Information Service, Inc., ed. CIS Index 1980 Annual. 2214p. 1981. lib. bdg. 320.00 (ISBN 0-686-75115-9). Cong Info.

--Statistical Reference Index Annual, 1980, 2 Vols. 1659p. 1981. lib. bdg. 365.00 (ISBN 0-686-75116-7). Cong Info.

Congressional Information Service, Inc. Staff. Statistical Reference Index Annual, 1981, 2 Vols. 380.00 (ISBN 0-912380-89-6). Cong Info.

Congressional Office of Technology Assessment. The Direct Use of Coal: Prospects & Problems of Production & Combustion. 432p. 1981. prof ref. 35.00x (ISBN 0-88410-648-9). Ballinger Pub.

--Energy from Biological Processes: Technical & Environmental Analyses. 248p. 1981. prof ref 35.00x (ISBN 0-88410-647-0). Ballinger Pub.

Congressional Quarterley Staff. Congressional Ethics. 2nd ed. LC 80-16173. 224p. (Orig.). 1980. pap. 8.25 (ISBN 0-87187-154-8). Congr Quarterly.

Congressional Quarterly. Guide to the U. S. Supreme Court. LC 79-20210. 1022p. 1979. 90.00 (ISBN 0-87187-184-X). Congr Quarterly.

--Health Policy: The Legislative Agenda. Congressional Quarterly, ed. LC 80-18847. 236p. 1980. pap. 8.75 (ISBN 0-87187-199-8). Congr Quarterly.

--Inside Congress. 2nd ed. LC 79-20000. 200p. 1979. pap. 8.25 (ISBN 0-87187-177-7). Congr Quarterly.

Congressional Quarterly, ed. National Party Conventions: Eighteen Thirty-One to Nineteen Seventy-Six. 2nd ed. LC 79-20005. 1979. pap. 8.25 (ISBN 0-87187-189-0). Congr Quarterly.

Congressional Quarterly, ed. see Crabb, Cecil V. & Holt, Pat M.

Congressional Quarterly Inc. Advances in Science. LC 78-25601. (Editorial Research Reports). 196p. 1979. pap. 7.50 (ISBN 0-87187-142-4). Congr Quarterly.

Congressional Quarterly, Inc. America in the 1980's. LC 79-25320. (Editorial Research Reports Ser.). 192p. 1980. pap. 7.50 (ISBN 0-87187-194-7). Congr Quarterly.

Congressional Quarterly Inc. American Regionalism: Our Economic, Cultural & Political Makeup. LC 80-18934. (Editorial Research Reports). 208p. 1980. pap. 7.50 (ISBN 0-87187-194-7). Congr Quarterly.

--Changing American Family. LC 79-12753. (Editorial Research Reports). 216p. 1979. pap. 7.50 (ISBN 0-87187-149-1). Congr Quarterly.

--Dollar Politics. 3rd ed. LC 81-19572. 176p. 1981. pap. 9.25 (ISBN 0-87187-220-X). Congr Quarterly.

Congressional Quarterly, Inc. Elections, 1982. LC 82-2347. 112p. (Orig.). 1982. pap. 9.25 (ISBN 0-87187-228-5). Congr Quarterly.

Congressional Quarterly Inc. Energy Policy. 2nd ed. LC 81-1225. 280p. 1981. pap. 9.25 (ISBN 0-87187-167-X). Congr Quarterly.

--Environment & Health. LC 81-15155. 236p. 1981. pap. 9.25 (ISBN 0-87187-224-2). Congr Quarterly.

--Federal Regulatory Directory: 1980-1981. Congressional Quarterly Inc., ed. 931p. 1980. pap. text ed. 25.00 (ISBN 0-87187-153-X). Congr Quarterly.

--Federal Regulatory Directory: 1981-1982. LC 79-644368. 875p. 1981. 29.95 (ISBN 0-87187-201-3). Congr Quarterly.

--Members of Congress Since Seventeen Eighty-Nine. 2nd ed. LC 81-660. 184p. 1981. pap. 8.25 (ISBN 0-87187-165-3). Congr Quarterly.

--Middle East. 5th ed. LC 81-15206. 288p. (Orig.). 1981. pap. 9.25 (ISBN 0-87187-211-0). Congr Quarterly.

Congressional Quarterly, Inc. Origins & Development of Congress. LC 82-7372. 352p. (Orig.). 1982. pap. 8.25 (ISBN 0-87187-235-8). Congr Quarterly.

Congressional Quarterly Inc. Politics in America. Ehrenhardt, Alan, ed. LC 81-9848. 1382p. 1981. 29.50 (ISBN 0-87187-208-0). Congr Quarterly.

--President Carter, Nineteen Eighty. LC 81-3255. 196p. (Orig.). 1981. pap. 7.95 (ISBN 0-87187-206-4). Congr Quarterly.

--President Reagan. LC 81-2283. (Presidency Ser.). 129p. (Orig.). 1981. pap. 7.95 (ISBN 0-87187-172-6). Congr Quarterly.

Congressional Quarterly, Inc. Soviet Union. LC 82-2408. 292p. (Orig.). 1982. pap. 9.25 (ISBN 0-87187-232-3). Congr Quarterly.

--State Politics & Redistricting, 2 Pts. 444p. (Orig.). 1982. Set. pap. 16.00 (ISBN 0-87187-233-1). Congr Quarterly.

--Washington Information Directory: 1982-1983. LC 75-646321. 168p. (Orig.). 1982. pap. text ed. 27.50 (ISBN 0-87187-230-7). Congr Quarterly.

Congressional Quarterly Inc. Washington Information Directory: 1983-1984. LC 75-646321. 1983. 29.95 (ISBN 0-87187-255-2). Congr Quarterly.

Congressional Quarterly Inc., ed. America Votes, Vol. 14. LC 56-10132. 427p. 1981. 65.00 (ISBN 0-87187-218-8). Congr Quarterly.

--Budgeting for America. LC 81-17376. 236p. (Orig.). 1981. pap. 9.25 (ISBN 0-87187-214-5). Congr Quarterly.

--China: U. S. Policy since 1945. LC 79-27840. 369p. (Orig.). 1980. pap. 11.95 (ISBN 0-87187-188-2). Congr Quarterly.

--Congress & the Nation: 1977-1980, Vol. 5. 1240p. 1981. 90.00 (ISBN 0-87187-216-1). Congr Quarterly.

--Supreme Court & Its Work. LC 81-12622. 288p. (Orig.). 1981. pap. 8.75 (ISBN 0-87187-210-2). Congr Quarterly.

Congressional Quarterly Inc. Staff. Congressional Quarterly Almanac: 1981. LC 47-41081. 1043p. 1982. 105.00 (ISBN 0-87187-231-5). Congr Quarterly.

--Congressional Quarterly Almanac: 1982. LC 47-41081. 1200p. 1983. 115.00 (ISBN 0-686-42802-1). Congr Quarterly.

--Defense Policy. 3rd ed. 200p. 1983. pap. 8.95 (ISBN 0-87187-258-7). Congr Quarterly.

--Earth, Energy & Environment. LC 81-12621. (Editorial Research Reports Ser.). 212p. 1977. pap. 7.50 (ISBN 0-87187-107-6). Congr Quarterly.

--Editorial Research Reports, 2 Vols. 1982. Vol. I: 1981, 768p. 65.00 (ISBN 0-87187-241-2). Vol. I I: 1982, 800p. Congr Quarterly.

--Education in America: Quality vs. Cost. LC 81-12621. (Editorial Research Reports Ser.). 208p. 1981. pap. 7.95 (ISBN 0-87187-212-9). Congr Quarterly.

--Energy Issues: New Directions & Goals. LC 82-2523. (Editorial Research Reports Ser.). 216p. 1982. pap. 7.95 (ISBN 0-87187-234-X). Congr Quarterly.

--Environmental Issues: Prospects & Problems. LC 82-4975. (Editorial Research Reports Ser.). 168p. 1982. pap. 7.95 (ISBN 0-87187-238-2). Congr Quarterly.

--Federal Regulatory Directory: 1983-1984. LC 79-644368. 900p. 1983. 29.95 (ISBN 0-87187-257-9). Congr Quarterly.

--Guide to Congress. 3rd ed. 1208p. 1982. 90.00 (ISBN 0-87187-239-0). Congr Quarterly.

--Guide to Current American Government: Fall 1982. LC 61-16893. 160p. 1982. pap. 7.25 (ISBN 0-87187-236-6). Congr Quarterly.

--Guide to Current American Government: Fall 1983. LC 61-16893. 164p. 1983. pap. 7.95 (ISBN 0-87187-261-7). Congr Quarterly.

--Guide to Current American Government: Spring 1983. LC 61-16893. 156p. 1982. pap. 7.95 (ISBN 0-87187-245-5). Congr Quarterly.

--Guide to Current American Government: Spring 1984. LC 61-16893. 164p. 1983. pap. 8.50 (ISBN 0-87187-267-6). Congr Quarterly.

Congressional Quarterly, Inc. Staff. Historic Documents, Vols. 1-5. 1973-77. 54.00 ea. Vol. 1: 1972, 987p (ISBN 0-87187-043-6). Vol. 2: 1973, 1020p (ISBN 0-87187-054-1). Vol. 4: 1975, 982p (ISBN 0-87187-069-X). Vol. 4: 1975, 982p (ISBN 0-87187-090-8). Vol. 5: 1976, 1003p (ISBN 0-87187-103-3). Congr Quarterly.

Congressional Quarterly Inc. Staff. Historic Documents: 1982, Vol. XI. LC 72-97888. 1000p. 1983. 57.00 (ISBN 0-87187-257-9). Congr Quarterly.

--How Congress Works. LC 61-16893. 240p. 1983. pap. 9.25 (ISBN 0-87187-254-4). Congr Quarterly.

--Jobs for Americans. LC 77-18994. (Editorial Research Reports). 189p. 1978. pap. 7.50 (ISBN 0-87187-120-3). Congr Quarterly.

--National Health Issues. LC 77-12770. (Editorial Research Reports). 207p. 1977. pap. 7.50 (ISBN 0-87187-118-1). Congr Quarterly.

--Politics in America. LC 81-9848. Date not set. 26.95 (ISBN 0-686-42806-4). Congr Quarterly.

--Powers of Congress. 2nd ed. LC 82-14331. 388p. 1982. pap. 8.25 (ISBN 0-87187-242-0). Congr Quarterly.

--Presidential Elections since Seventeen Eigthty-Nine. 3rd ed. 200p. 1983. pap. 8.95 (ISBN 0-87187-268-4). Congr Quarterly.

--The Public's Right to Know. LC 80-20610. (Editorial Research Reports). 194p. 1980. pap. 7.50 (ISBN 0-87187-157-2). Congr Quarterly.

--Reagan's First Year. LC 82-1386. 184p. 1982. pap. 8.95 (ISBN 0-87187-225-0). Congr Quarterly.

--Regulations: Process & Politics. LC 82-14292. 192p. 1982. pap. 9.25 (ISBN 0-87187-243-9). Congr Quarterly.

--The Rights Revolution. LC 78-31931. (Editorial Research Reports). 224p. 1979. pap. 7.50 (ISBN 0-87187-144-0). Congr Quarterly.

--Roll Call: 1982. 1983. pap. 12.95 (ISBN 0-87187-252-8). Congr Quarterly.

--Supreme Court, Justice & the Law. 1983. pap. 9.25 (ISBN 0-87187-253-6). Congr Quarterly.

--U. S. Foreign Policy: Future Directions. LC 79-15637. (Editorial Research Reports). 224p. 1979. pap. 7.50 (ISBN 0-87187-187-4). Congr Quarterly.

--The Washington Lobby. 4th ed. LC 82-12525. 192p. 1982. pap. 9.25 (ISBN 0-87187-240-4). Congr Quarterly.

--The Women's Movement: Agenda for the Eighties. LC 81-17277. (Editorial Research Reports Ser.). 208p. 1981. pap. 7.95 (ISBN 0-87187-223-4). Congr Quarterly.

--Work Life in the Nineteen Eighties. LC 81-3171. (Editorial Research Reports Ser.). 200p. 1981. pap. 7.95 (ISBN 0-87187-207-2). Congr Quarterly.

--Youth Problems. LC 82-18222. (Editorial Research Reports. Ser.). 184p. 1982. pap. 7.95 (ISBN 0-87187-244-7). Congr Quarterly.

Congressional Quarterly Service. Congress & the Nation, 4 vols. Incl. Vol. 1: 1945-1964. 2015p. 1965. 90.00 (ISBN 0-685-28880-3); Vol. 2: 1965-1968. 1120p. 1969. 90.00 (ISBN 0-87187-004-5); Vol. 3, 1969-1972. 1178p. 1973. 90.00 (ISBN 0-87187-055-X); Vol. 4, 1972-1976. 1217p. 1977. 90.00 (ISBN 0-87187-112-2). LC 65-22351. Congr Quarterly.

Congressional Quarterly Staff. Guide to U. S. Elections. LC 75-659. 1103p. 1975. 60.00 (ISBN 0-87187-072-X). Congr Quarterly.

--Presidential Election since Seventeen Eighty-Nine. 2nd ed. LC 78-31928. 200p. 1979. pap. 8.25 (ISBN 0-87187-145-9). Congr Quarterly.

--Supreme Court & Individual Rights. Congressional Quarterly Staff, ed. LC 79-26967. 312p. (Orig.). 1980. pap. 8.95 (ISBN 0-87187-195-5). Congr Quarterly.

--Taxes, Jobs, & Inflation. LC 78-13735. 168p. 1978. pap. 7.50 (ISBN 0-87187-139-4). Congr Quarterly.

--Urban America: Policies & Problems. LC 78-13734. 1978. pap. 7.50 (ISBN 0-87187-138-6). Congr Quarterly.

Congressional Quarterly Staff, ed. Consumer Protection: Gains & Setbacks. LC 78-2927. 216p. 1978. pap. 7.50 (ISBN 0-87187-130-0). Congr Quarterly.

Congressional Research Service & Education & Public Welfare Division, eds. Millions for the Arts: Federal & State Cultural Programs. LC 72-78232. 64p. 20.00 (ISBN 0-686-95368-1). Wash Intl Arts.

Congreve, William. The Comedies of William Congreve: The Old Batchelor, the Double Dealer, Love for Love, the Way of the World. Henderson, Anthony, ed. LC 82-1182. (Plays by Renaissance & Restoration Dramatists Ser.). 407p. 1982. 39.50 (ISBN 0-521-24747-0); pap. 14.95 (ISBN 0-521-28932-7). Cambridge U Pr.

Congreve, William see Morrell, Janet M.

Congwen, Shen. Recollections of West Hunan. Yang, Gladys, tr. from Chinese. 196p. (Orig.). 1982. pap. 4.95 (ISBN 0-295-96016-7, Pub. by Chinese Lit Beijing). U of Wash Pr.

Coni, N., et al. Aids to Prescribing. 112p. 1982. pap. text ed. 12.00 (ISBN 0-632-00599-8, B1041-9). Mosby.

Coniaris, A. Dynamic Preaching Skills for the Orthodox Pulpit. 1982. cancelled o.p. (ISBN 0-937032-26-3). Light&Life Pub Co MN.

--Gems from the Sunday Gospel Lessons in the Orthodox Church, Vol. II. pap. 5.95 (ISBN 0-937032-13-1). Light&Life Pub Co MN.

--Gems from the Sunday Gospel Lessons in the Orthodox Church, Vol. 1. 1975. pap. 4.95 (ISBN 0-937032-12-3). Light&Life Pub Co MN.

--Getting Ready for Marriage in the Orthodox Church. 1972. pap. 1.25 (ISBN 0-937032-11-5). Light&Life Pub Co MN.

Coniaris, A. M. Introducing the Orthodox Church. 1982. pap. 6.95. Light&Life Pub Co MN.

--The Message of the Sunday Gospel Readings, Vol. 1. 1982. pap. 6.95 (ISBN 0-937032-26-3). Light&Life Pub Co MN.

--The Message of the Sunday Gospels, Vol. 2. 1983. pap. 6.95 (ISBN 0-937032-29-8). Light&Life Pub Co MN.

--The Stewardship Challange for the Orthodox Christian. 1883. pap. 6.95 (ISBN 0-937032-30-1). Light&Life Pub Co MN.

--These Are the Sacraments. 1981. pap. 5.95 (ISBN 0-937032-22-0). Light&Life Pub Co MN.

Coniglio, Jamie W. Introduction to Library Research in Education. (Westview Guides to Library Research Ser.). 130p. 1982. lib. bdg. 16.50 (ISBN 0-86531-234-6). Westview.

Coniker, Jerome F. Devotions & Prayers in Honor of St. Joseph. (Living Meditation & Prayer Bklt. Library). (Illus.). 34p. (Orig.). 1978. pap. text ed. 2.50 (ISBN 0-932406-04-1). AFC.

--Peaceful Seed Living, Vols. 1 & 2. 2nd ed. LC 78-66369. (Living Meditation & Prayerbook Ser.). (Illus.). 156p. 1981. pap. text ed. 3.00 ea. (ISBN 0-932406-00-9). AFC.

--Prayers & Recommended Practices. 2nd ed. LC 78-66374. (Living Meditation & Prayerbook Ser.). (Illus.). 91p. pap. text ed. 4.00 (ISBN 0-932406-01-7). AFC.

Coniker, Jerome F., ed. see Seeley, Burns K.

Coninx, Raymond G. Foreign Exchange Dealer's Handbook. LC 82-81900. 1982. 20.00x (ISBN 0-87551-350-6). Pick Pub.

--Foreign Exchange Dealer's Manual. 168p. 1983. 30.00x (ISBN 0-85941-152-4, Pub. by Woodhead-Faulkner England). State Mutual Bk.

--Foreign Exchange Today. rev. ed. 171p. 1980. 22.95x o.p. (ISBN 0-470-27025-X). Halsted Pr.

Conisbee, L. R. A List of Names Proposed for Genera & Subgenera of Recent Mammals from the Publication of T. S. Palmer's Index Generum Mammalium 1904 to the End of 1951. 110p. 1953. 11.00 (ISBN 0-565-00210-4). Sabbot-Natural Hist Bks.

Conk, Margo A. The United States Census & Labor Force Change: A History of Occupation Statistics, 1870-1940. Berkhofer, Robert, ed. LC 79-28085. (Studies in American History & Culture: No. 11). 240p. 1980. 39.95 (ISBN 0-8357-1078-5, Pub. by UMI Res Pr). Univ Microfilms.

Conkin, Paul K. New Deal. 2nd ed. LC 75-1148. (American History Ser.). (Illus.). 1975. pap. 5.95x (ISBN 0-88295-722-8). Harlan Davidson.

Conkin, Paul K. & Stromberg, Roland N. The Heritage & Challenge of History. 1971. pap. text ed. 11.95 scp o.p. (ISBN 0-06-041342-5, HarpC). Har-Row.

Conkis, William T. The Complete Collection of the Original Herbal Manuscript. 169p. 1982. pap. 7.95 (ISBN 0-943638-00-3). Herbal Perception.

Conklin, Barbara. The Summer Jenny Fell in Love. (Sweet Dreams Ser.). 1982. pap. 1.95 (ISBN 0-553-20789-X). Bantam.

Conklin, Drue K., ed. The Official Scrabble Players Handbook. 1976. 10.00 o.p. (ISBN 0-517-52546-1, Harmony); pap. 5.95 o.p. (ISBN 0-517-52547-X). Crown.

Conklin, Gladys. The Bug Club Book: A Handbook for Young Bug Collectors. (Illus.). 96p. (gr. 4-7). 1966. 7.95 o.p. (ISBN 0-8234-0017-4). Holiday.

--Elephants of Africa. LC 72-179099. (Illus.). 40p. (gr. k-3). 1972. PLB 8.95 o.p. (ISBN 0-8234-0201-0). Holiday.

--I Caught a Lizard. (Illus.). 40p. (gr. k-3). 1967. PLB 6.95 (ISBN 0-8234-0054-9). Holiday.

--Lucky Ladybugs. (Illus.). 32p. (gr. k-3). 1968. PLB 9.95 (ISBN 0-8234-0072-7). Holiday.

--The Octopus & Other Cephalopods. LC 77-3818. (Illus.). 64p. (gr. 4-6). 1977. pap. 8.95 o.p. (ISBN 0-8234-0306-8). Holiday.

--Tarantula, the Giant Spider. LC 72-75596. (Illus.). 32p. (gr. k-3). 1972. PLB 6.95 (ISBN 0-8234-0208-8). Holiday.

Conklin, Harold C. Hanunoo Agriculture: A Report on an Integral System of Shifting Cultivation in the Phillipines FAO Forestry Development Paper No. 12. LC 75-28745. (Illus.). 209p. 1975. text ed. 19.50x scholars (ISBN 0-911830-22-7); pap. 29.50x institutions (ISBN 0-685-69785-1). Elliots Bks.

--Ifugao Bibliography. LC 68-29881. (Bibliography Ser.: No. 11). vi, 75p. 1968. 5.50x (ISBN 0-686-30907-3). Yale U SE Asia.

Conklin, Marilyn. Poochie: Many Mottos. (Shaped Color Bk.). (Illus.). 32p. (ps up). 1983. pap. 0.99 (ISBN 0-307-21223-8). Western Pub.

--Poochie: My Favorite Things. (Shaped Color Bks.: No. 1222). (Illus.). 32p. (ps up). 1983. pap. 0.99 (ISBN 0-307-21222-X). Western Pub.

--Poochie Press-Out Pretties. (Press-Out Bk.: No. 2860). (Illus.). 8p. (ps up). 1983. 1.29 (ISBN 0-307-21186-X). Western Pub.

--Poochie Sticker Fun. (Sticker Fun Bk.: No. 2192-47). (Illus.). 16p. (gr. 1-5). 1983. 0.99 (ISBN 0-307-21192-4). Western Pub.

--Poochie: The Buddy Bk. (Shaped Color Bk.). (Illus.). 32p. (ps up). 1983. pap. 0.99 (ISBN 0-307-21221-1). Western Pub.

--Poochie: Ways to Make Wishes. (Shaped Color Bks.: No. 1220). (Illus.). 32p. (ps up). 1983. pap. 0.99 (ISBN 0-307-21220-3). Western Pub.

Conklin, Marilyn & Conklin, Marilyn. Poochie. (Color Bk.: No. 1148-20). (Illus.). 72p. (ps-4). 1983. pap. 0.99 (ISBN 0-307-21148-7). Western Pub.

Conklin, Mike. Inside Football. 1978. 9.95 o.p. (ISBN 0-685-25150-0); pap. 7.95 (ISBN 0-8092-7585-6). Contemp Bks.

Conklin, Mike, jt. auth. see Zolna, Ed.

Conklin, Nancy, jt. auth. see Lourie, Margaret.

Conklin, Paul. Tomorrow a New World. (FDR & the Era of the New Deal Ser.). 1976. Repr. of 1959 ed. lib. bdg. 39.50 (ISBN 0-306-70805-1). Da Capo.

Conkling, Edgar C. & Yeates, Maurice H. Man's Economic Environment. (Geography Ser.). 1976. text ed. 32.50 (ISBN 0-07-012408-6, C). McGraw.

Conkling, Edgar C., jt. auth. see Berry, Brian J. L.

Conlan, Jim & Deliman, Tracy. Atari Pilot for Beginners. 1982. text ed. 19.95 (ISBN 0-8359-0302-8); pap. 14.95 (ISBN 0-8359-0301-X). Reston.

Conlee, Jaelyn. Satin & Steele, No. 71. 1982. pap. 1.75 (ISBN 0-515-06682-6). Jove Pubns.

Conley, Diane, ed. Peterson's Annual Guides to Graduate Study: Graduate & Professional Programs: An Overview, 1983. 700p. 1982. pap. 13.95 (ISBN 0-87866-185-9). Petersons Guides.

--Peterson's Guides to Graduate Study: Humanities & Social Sciences, 1983. 1200p. 1982. pap. 18.95 (ISBN 0-87866-186-7). Petersons Guides.

Conley, Ellen A. Soho Madonna. 1980. pap. 2.25 o.p. (ISBN 0-380-75614-5, 75614). Avon.

Conley, John. Complications of Head & Neck Surgery. LC 79-416. (Illus.). 1979. text ed. 49.50 (ISBN 0-7216-2649-1). Saunders.

--Regional Flaps of the Head & Neck. LC 76-11603. (Illus.). 1976. text ed. 40.00 (ISBN 0-7216-2647-5). Saunders.

Conley, Joyce, jt. auth. see Clough, John.

Conley, Lucy. Gone to the Zoo. 1979. 5.90 (ISBN 0-686-25258-6). Rod & Staff.

--The Priceless Privilege. 1981. 6.00 (ISBN 0-686-30773-9). Rod & Staff.

Conley, Patrick T. The Blackstone Valley: A Sketch of Its River, Its Canal & Its People. 24p. 1983. pap. 2.75 (ISBN 0-917012-41-0). RI Pubns Soc.

--The Constitutional Significance of Trevett vs. Weeden (1786) (Illus.). 10p. 1976. pap. 1.25 (ISBN 0-917012-43-7). RI Pubns Soc.

--Providence: A Pictorial History. Friedman, Donna R., ed. LC 80-27671. (Illus.). 205p. 1981. pap. 12.95 o.p. (ISBN 0-89865-128-X). Donning Co.

--Rhode Island Constitutional Development, 1636-1775: A Survey. 35p. 1968. pap. 2.75 (ISBN 0-917012-42-9). RI Pubns Soc.

--Rhode Island Profile. (Illus.). 60p. (Orig.). 1983. pap. 2.95 (ISBN 0-917012-40-2). RI Pubns Soc.

Conley, Robert J. see Cherry, Richard L., et al.

Conley, Robert J., ed. see Tahlequah Indian Writer's Group.

Conley, Virginia & Freisner, Arlyne. Evaluation of Students in Baccalaureate Nursing Programs. 98p. 1977. 5.95 (ISBN 0-686-38296-X, 15-1684). Natl League Nurse.

Conley, Virginia, jt. auth. see Epstein, Rhoda.

Conlin, Joseph R. The American Radical Press: 1880-1960, 2 vols. LC 72-9825. 1974. Set. lib. bdg. 50.00 (ISBN 0-8371-6625-X, AMR). Greenwood.

--Big Bill Haywood & the Radical Union Movement. LC 79-80015. (Men & Movements Ser). (Illus.). 1969. 12.95x (ISBN 0-8156-2140-X). Syracuse U Pr.

--Bread & Roses Too. LC 79-95505. (Contributions in American History Ser.: No. 1). 1970. lib. bdg. 25.00 (ISBN 0-8371-2344-5, COB/). Greenwood.

--Quotations in American History. LC 82-13790. 256p. 1983. text ed. cancelled (ISBN 0-389-20315-7). B&N Imports.

Conlin, Marion. Marion Conlin's Home Cooking School. rev. ed. 224p. 1981. Repr. of 1972 ed. 12.95 (ISBN 0-87518-216-X). Dillon.

Conlin, Mary Lou. Concepts of Communication: Reading, Ideas Module, Inferences Module. LC 77-78895. (Illus.). 1978. pap. text ed. 13.50 (ISBN 0-395-25492-2); instr's. guide 1.00 (ISBN 0-395-25493-0). HM.

--Concepts of Communication: Writing: Summary, Paragraph, Essay-Test, Theme Module. 2nd ed. LC 79-49830. 1980. pap. text ed. 12.95 (ISBN 0-395-28735-9); instr's. manual 1.10 (ISBN 0-395-28485-6). HM.

--Concepts of Communication: Writing: Writing Skills Module. 2nd ed. LC 79-49830. 1980. pap. text ed. 13.50 (ISBN 0-395-28484-8); instrs.' manual 1.10. HM.

--Patterns: A Short Prose Reader. 400p. 1983. pap. text ed. 10.95 (ISBN 0-686-42947-8); write for info. instr's. manual (ISBN 0-395-32599-4). HM.

Conlon, Denis J., ed. Richard Sans Peur. (Studies in the Romance Languages & Literatures: No.192). 120p. (Orig.). 1978. pap. 9.00x (ISBN 0-8078-9192-4). U of NC Pr.

Conlon, Frank F. A Caste in a Changing World: The Chitrapur Saraswat Brahmans, 1700-1935. LC 75-7192. 1977. 31.50x (ISBN 0-520-02998-4). U of Cal Pr.

Conlon, Frank S., ed. see Blee, Ben W.

Conlon, John J. Walter Pater & the French Tradition. LC 81-65458. 180p. 1982. 21.50 (ISBN 0-8387-5016-8). Bucknell U Pr.

Conlon, V. M. Camera Techniques in Archaeology. LC 73-82631. (Illus.). 112p. 1973. 19.95 o.p. (ISBN 0-312-11445-1). St Martin.

Conn, Charles P. Making It Happen. 128p. 1981. 8.95 (ISBN 0-8007-1252-8). Revell.

--An Uncommon Freedom: The Amway Experience & Why It Grows. 208p. 1983. pap. 2.95 (ISBN 0-425-05870-0). Berkley Pub.

--The Winner's Circle. 1980. pap. 2.75 (ISBN 0-425-05639-2). Berkley Pub.

Conn, Charles P. & Miller, Barbara. Kathy. 1981. pap. 2.75 (ISBN 0-425-05766-6). Berkley Pub.

Conn, Charles P., jt. auth. see DeVos, Richard M.

Conn, Charles P., jt. auth. see Miller, Barbara.

Conn, Charles W. The Acts of the Apostles. 1966. 4.95 (ISBN 0-87148-009-3); pap. 3.95 (ISBN 0-87148-010-7). Pathway Pr.

--The Anatomy of Evil. LC 80-21103. 160p. 1981. 8.95 (ISBN 0-8007-1177-7). Revell.

--Rudder & the Rock. 1976. pap. 3.95 (ISBN 0-87148-733-0). Pathway Pr.

Conn, E. E., jt. ed. see Stumpf, P. K.

Conn, Floyd & Conn, Sadie. They Followed The Rivers. (Illus.). 241p. 1981. 14.50x (ISBN 0-9607602-0-2). Kiowa Pr.

Conn, Frances G. & Fromer, Margot J. How to Quit Smoking in Thirty Days Without Cracking Up. (Illus.). 84p. (Orig.). 1982. pap. 5.95 (ISBN 0-910107-00-9). Phillips Neuman.

Conn, George H. Horse Selection & Care for Beginners. pap. 5.00 (ISBN 0-87980-193-X). Wilshire.

--How to Get a Horse & Live with It. LC 69-15783. (Illus.). 1969. 10.00 o.p. (ISBN 0-668-02782-7). Arco.

Conn, Harold & Lieberthal, Moilton M. The Hepatic Coma Syndromes & Lactulose. (Illus.). 1979. 49.00 o.p. (ISBN 0-683-02100-1). Williams & Wilkins.

Conn, Harvie. Evangelism: Doing Justice & Preaching Grace. 112p. (Orig.). 1982. pap. 3.95 (ISBN 0-310-45311-9). Zondervan.

Conn, Howard, ed. Current Therapy 1981. (Illus.). 1100p. 1981. pap. 34.00 o.p. (ISBN 0-7216-2709-9). Saunders.

Conn, Howard F., ed. Current Therapy Nineteen Eighty. LC 49-8328. (Illus.). 988p. 1980. text ed. 29.50 o.p. (ISBN 0-7216-2708-0). Saunders.

Conn, Howard F. & Conn, Rex B., eds. Current Diagnosis - 5. LC 66-15617. (Illus.). 1977. text ed. 35.00 o.p. (ISBN 0-7216-2674-2). Saunders.

Conn, Michael P., ed. Cellular Regulation of Secretion & Release. (Cell Biology Ser.). 514p. 1982. 65.00 (ISBN 0-12-185058-7). Acad Pr.

Conn, Paul. The Possible Dream. 1978. pap. 2.75 (ISBN 0-425-05491-8). Berkley Pub.

Conn, Rex B., jt. ed. see Conn, Howard F.

Conn, Robert L., jt. auth. see Bolten, Steven E.

Conn, Sadie, jt. auth. see Conn, Floyd.

Conn, W. David, ed. Energy & Material Resources: Attitudes, Values, & Public Policy. (AAAS Selected Symposium 75). 200p. 1982. lib. bdg. 22.00 (ISBN 0-86531-521-3). Westview.

Conn, Walter E. Conscience: Development & Self-Transcendence. LC 80-24043. 280p. (Orig.). 1981. pap. 12.95 (ISBN 0-89135-025-X). Religious Educ.

Connah, Graham. Three Thousand Years in Africa: Man & His Environment in the Lake Chad Region of Nigeria. LC 79-41508. (New Studies in Archaeology). (Illus.). 268p. 1981. 65.00 (ISBN 0-521-22848-4). Cambridge U Pr.

Connally, Eugenia M. Welcome to Washington. (Illus.). 36p. 1981. pap. 3.95 (ISBN 0-936478-03-9). Interpretive Pubns.

Conneau, Theophilus. A Slaver's Log Book: Or, 20 Years' Residence in Africa. 1972. pap. 2.75 o.p. (ISBN 0-380-01773-3, 35063, Discus). Avon.

Connell, Charles. They Gave Us Shakespeare: John Heminge & Henry Condell. (Illus.). 110p. 1982. 14.95 (ISBN 0-85362-193-4, Oriel). Routledge & Kegan.

Connell, Dorothy. Sir Phillip Sidney: The Maker's Mind. (Illus.). 1978. 28.50x (ISBN 0-19-812081-8). Oxford U Pr.

Connell, Evan S. Mr. Bridge. LC 81-81513. 384p. 1981. pap. 10.50 (ISBN 0-86547-054-5); boxed, set hardcover trade with Evan Connell's Mrs. Bridge 35.00 (ISBN 0-86547-057-X). N Point Pr.

--Mrs. Bridge. LC 81-81514. 256p. 1981. pap. 8.50 (ISBN 0-86547-056-1); boxed set hardcover trade with Evan Connell's Mr. Bridge 35.00 (ISBN 0-86547-057-X). N Point Pr.

--Saint Augustine's Pigeon: The Selected Stories. Blaisdell, Gus, ed. LC 80-18186. 304p. 1980. 15.00 (ISBN 0-86547-013-8); pap. 10.00 (ISBN 0-86547-014-6). N Point Pr.

Connell, Evan S., Jr. Double Honeymoon. LC 75-34386. 1976. 7.95 o.p. (ISBN 0-399-11663-X). Putnam Pub Group.

Connell, John. The End of Tradition: Country Life in Central Surrey. (Illus.). 1978. 21.95x (ISBN 0-7100-8844-2). Routledge & Kegan.

Connell, John, jt. ed. see Moore, Mick.

Connell, Kenneth H. The Population of Ireland, 1750-1845. LC 74-9165. 293p. 1975. Repr. of 1950 ed. lib. bdg. 27.50x (ISBN 0-8371-7620-4, COPI). Greenwood.

Connell, Maureen. Mary Lacey. LC 80-7893. 288p. 1981. 13.41i (ISBN 0-690-01950-5, HarpT). Har-Row.

Connell, R. W. Ruling Class, Ruling Culture. LC 76-22981. (Illus.). 1977. 34.50 (ISBN 0-521-21392-4); pap. 10.95 (ISBN 0-521-29133-X). Cambridge U Pr.

Connell, Stephen & Galbraith, Ian A. Electronic Mail: A Revolution in Business Communications. LC 82-44. (Information & Communications Management Guides Ser.). 141p. 1982. text ed. 32.95 (ISBN 0-86729-015-3); pap. text ed. 22.95 (ISBN 0-86729-016-1). Knowledge Indus.

Connell, W. F., et al. Studying the Local Community: Education in Action. LC 78-55229. 1978. text ed. 19.95x (ISBN 0-86861-256-1); pap. text ed. 8.95x (ISBN 0-86861-264-2). Allen Unwin.

Connell, William F. Educational Thought & Influence of Matthew Arnold. LC 74-109305. 1971. Repr. of 1950 ed. lib. bdg. 18.25x (ISBN 0-8371-3580-X, COMA). Greenwood.

Connelly, J. A. Analog Integrated Circuits: Devices, Circuits, Systems & Applications. LC 74-20947. 401p. 1975. 42.95x (ISBN 0-471-16854-8, Pub. by Wiley-Interscience). Wiley.

Connelly, James F. & Fratangelo, Robert A. Elementary Technical Mathematics. (Illus.). 1978. text ed. 26.95x (ISBN 0-02-324430-5). Macmillan.

--Elementary Technical Mathematics with Calculus. 1979. 29.95x (ISBN 0-02-324440-2). Macmillan.

--Precalculus Mathematics: A Functional Approach. 2nd ed. (Illus.). 1979. text ed. 23.95x (ISBN 0-02-324400-3). Macmillan.

--Precalculus Mathematics: A Functional Approach, Study Guide. 2nd ed. (Illus.). 1980. pap. text ed. 10.95x (ISBN 0-02-324420-8). Macmillan.

Connelly, Michael, jt. auth. see Sims, Jean.

Connelly, Naomi, jt. ed. see Goldberg, Mitilda E.

Connelly, Peter. Hannibal & the Enemies of Rome. LC 79-65844. (Armies of the Past Ser.). PLB 12.68 (ISBN 0-382-06307-4). Silver.

Connelly, R. J. Whitehead vs. Hartshorne: Basic Metaphysical Issues. LC 80-69053. 172p. (Orig.). 1981. lib. bdg. 20.00 (ISBN 0-8191-1420-0); pap. text ed. 9.50 (ISBN 0-8191-1421-9). U Pr of Amer.

Connelly, Robert J. Last Rights: Death & Dying in Texas Law & Experience. 196p. 1983. pap. 8.95 (ISBN 0-931722-21-7). Corona Pub.

Connelly, Shirley, jt. auth. see Peterson, Carol W.

Connelly, Stephen E. Allan Seager. (United States Authors Ser.). 144p. 1983. lib. bdg. 16.95 (ISBN 0-8057-7386-X, Twayne). G K Hall.

Connelly, Thomas G., et al, eds. Morphogenesis & Pattern Formation. 312p. 1981. 38.00 (ISBN 0-89004-635-2). Raven.

Connely, Willard. Laurence Sterne As Yorick. LC 79-17312. (Illus.). 1979. Repr. of 1958 ed. lib. bdg. 21.00x (ISBN 0-313-22000-X, COLS). Greenwood.

Conner, Bettina, jt. auth. see Ridgeway, James.

Conner, Daniel E. Confederate in the Colorado Gold Fields. Berthrong, Donald J. & Davenport, Odessa, eds. LC 70-88149. (Illus.). 1970. 12.95 o.p. (ISBN 0-8061-0891-6). U of Okla Pr.

Conner, David A., jt. auth. see Vogt, Lawrence J.

Conner, Floyd & Snyder, John. Day-by-Day in Cincinnati Reds History. LC 82-83938. (Illus.). 300p. (Orig.). 1983. pap. 9.95 (ISBN 0-88011-106-2). Leisure Pr.

Conner, Mac, et al, illus. Cities & Suburbs. (Bowmar-Noble Social Studies Program). Orig. Title: Man & His World. (Illus.). (gr. 3). text ed. 8.43 o.p. (ISBN 0-8372-3684-3); tchrs. ed. 12.09 o.p. (ISBN 0-8372-3685-1); tests 9.96 o.p. (ISBN 0-8372-3727-0). Bowmar-Noble.

--Groups & Communities. rev. ed. (Bowmar-Noble Social Studies Program). (Illus.). 184p. (gr. 2). 1979. text ed. 7.47 o.p. (ISBN 0-8372-3682-7); tchrs. ed. 9.96 o.p. (ISBN 0-8372-3683-5); test 9.96 o.p. (ISBN 0-8372-3726-2). Bowmar-Noble.

--People & Culture. rev. ed. (Bowmar-Noble Social Studies Program). Orig. Title: Man & His World. (Illus.). 477p. (gr. 6). 1979. text ed. 11.37 o.p. (ISBN 0-8372-3690-8); tchrs. ed. 14.49 o.p. (ISBN 0-8372-3691-6); test 9.96 o.p. (ISBN 0-8372-3730-0). Bowmar-Noble.

--People & the Land. rev. ed. (Bowmar-Noble Social Studies Program). Orig. Title: Man & His World. (Illus.). 349p. (gr. 4). 1979. text ed. 9.15 o.p. (ISBN 0-8372-3686-X); tchrs. ed. 12.39 o.p. (ISBN 0-8372-3687-8); test 9.96 o.p. (ISBN 0-8372-3728-9). Bowmar-Noble.

Conner, Macet Al & Contreras, Gerry, illus. You & Your Family. rev. ed. (Bowmar-Noble Social Studies Program). Orig. Title: Man & His World. (Illus.). 152p. (gr. 1). 1979. text ed. 6.69 o.p. (ISBN 0-8372-3680-0); tchrs. ed. 9.63 o.p. (ISBN 0-8372-3681-9). Bowmar-Noble.

Conner, Michael. I Am Not the Other Houdini. LC 77-11794. 1979. pap. 1.95i o.p. (ISBN 0-06-080470-X, P 470, PL). Har-Row.

Conner, Patrick. People at Home. LC 82-1832. (Looking At Art Ser.). (Illus.). 48p. 1982. 11.95 (ISBN 0-689-50252-4, McElderry Bk). Atheneum.

--People at Work. LC 82-1812. (Looking at Art Ser.). (Illus.). 48p. 1982. 11.95 (ISBN 0-689-50253-2, McElderry Bk). Atheneum.

Conner, Paul. Celibate Love. LC 78-71330. 1979. 9.95 o.p. (ISBN 0-87973-827-8). Our Sunday Visitor.

Conner, Roger. Breaking Down the Barriers: The Changing Relationship Between Illegal Immigration & Welfare. 1982. pap. text ed. 2.50 (ISBN 0-935776-03-6). F A I R.

Conner, T. Doctrina Cristiana. Robleto, Adolfo, tr. Orig. Title: Christian Doctrine. 408p. (Span.). 1981. pap. 7.50 (ISBN 0-311-09012-5). Casa Bautista.

Conner, Terri & Sanderson, Joyce. Live Love Laugh. Dowdney, Donna & Sanderson, Conner, eds. (Illus.). 52p. (Orig.). 1981. pap. 6.95 (ISBN 0-9606904-0-9). Conner & Sanderson.

Conner, Valerie J. The National War Labor Board: Stability, Social Justice, & the Voluntary State in World War I. LC 82-13362. (Supplementary Volumes to The Papers of Woodrow Wilson). vii, 232p. 1983. 23.50x (ISBN 0-8078-1539-X). U of NC Pr.

Conner, William B. Math's & Music's Metasonics, 2 vols. Incl. Vol. 1-Creativity through Calculator Harmonic Braiding. LC 82-51200 (ISBN 0-9603536-5-8); Vol. 2-Creativity through Keyboard Harmonic Braiding. LC 82-74235 (ISBN 0-9603536-6-6). Set. pap. 36.50 GBC punched (ISBN 0-9603536-7-4). Tesla Bk Co.

Conners, Bernard F. Dancehall. new ed. 288p. 1983. 14.95 (ISBN 0-672-52757-X). Bobbs.

Connerton, P. The Tragedy of Enlightenment. LC 79-16102. (Cambridge Studies in the History & Theory of Politics). 1980. 32.50 (ISBN 0-521-22842-5); pap. 8.95 (ISBN 0-521-29675-7). Cambridge U Pr.

Connery, Donald. Guilty Until Proven Innocent. (Illus.). 1977. 9.95 o.p. (ISBN 0-399-11823-3). Putnam Pub Group.

Connery, Donald S. The Scandinavians. 1972. 9.95 o.p. (ISBN 0-671-21336-9). S&S.

Connery, Robert Howe. The Navy & the Industrial Mobilization in World War II. LC 73-166951. (FDR & the Era of the New Deal Ser). 526p. 1972. Repr. of 1951 ed. lib. bdg. 59.50 (ISBN 0-306-70322-X). Da Capo.

Connes, G. Dictionary of the Characters & Scenes in the Novels, Romances & Short Stories of H. G. Wells. LC 73-174698. (Reference Ser., No. 44). 1971. Repr. of 1926 ed. lib. bdg. 46.95x (ISBN 0-8383-1353-1). Haskell.

Connick, C. Milo. Jesus: The Man, the Mission, & the Message. 2nd ed. (Illus.). 512p. 1974. 22.95 (ISBN 0-13-509521-2). P-H.

--The New Testament: An Introduction to Its History, Literature, & Thought. 2nd ed. LC 76-180754. (Illus.). 512p. 1978. text ed. 21.95x (ISBN 0-8221-0205-6). Dickenson.

Conniff, Richard, ed. The Devil's Book of Verse. (Illus.). 1983. 14.95 (ISBN 0-89696-186-9). Dodd.

Connis, Richard T., et al, eds. Training the Mentally Handicapped for Employment: A Comprehensive Manual. LC 81-1979. (Illus.). 192p. (Orig.). 1981. pap. text ed. 19.95 o.p. (ISBN 0-89885-001-0). Human Sci Pr.

Connolly. The International Monetary System. 352p. 1982. 33.95 (ISBN 0-03-061794-4). Praeger.

Connolly, Arlene F. & Kelley, Jean. Curriculum in Graduate Education in Nursing: Part III-Development & Improvement of Graduate Education in Nursing. 46p. 1977. 4.50 (ISBN 0-686-38256-0, 15-1679). Natl League Nurse.

Connolly, Cyril. Enemies of Promise. 268p. 1983. cancelled 13.95 (ISBN 0-89255-077-5); pap. 6.95 (ISBN 0-89255-078-3). Persea Bks.

--The Rock Pool. 190p. 1982. cancelled 12.95 (ISBN 0-89255-073-2); pap. 5.95 (ISBN 0-89255-059-7). Persea Bks.

--Selected Essays. Quennell, Peter, ed. 336p. 1983. 15.95 (ISBN 0-89255-072-4). Persea Bks.

--The Unquiet Grave. 156p. 1982. cancelled 12.95 (ISBN 0-89255-074-0); pap. 5.95 (ISBN 0-89255-058-9). Persea Bks.

Connolly, Cyril, jt. auth. see Zerbe, Jerome.

Connolly, Cyril, tr. see Jarry, Alfred.

Connolly, Francis X., jt. ed. see Blehl, Vincent.

Connolly, James E. Public Speaking As Communication. LC 73-90806. 1974. pap. text ed. 7.95x (ISBN 0-8087-0344-7). Burgess.

Connolly, John F., ed. DePalma's the Management of Fractures & Dislocations: An Atlas, 2 vols. 3rd ed. (Illus.). 2000p. 1981. Set. text ed. 110.00 (ISBN 0-7216-2666-1); Vol. 1. 55.00 (ISBN 0-7216-2702-1); Vol. 2. 55.00 (ISBN 0-7216-2703-X). Saunders.

Connolly, John R. Dimensions of Belief & Unbelief. LC 80-67241. 373p. 1981. lib. bdg. 24.25 (ISBN 0-8191-1389-1); pap. text ed. 14.00 (ISBN 0-8191-1390-5). U Pr of Amer.

Connolly, John S., jt. ed. see Bolton, James R.

Connolly, Julian W. Ivan Bunin. (World Authors Ser.). 1982. lib. bdg. 18.95 (ISBN 0-8057-6513-1, Twayne). G K Hall.

Connolly, Paul H. Building Family: An Act of Faith. LC 82-74073. 96p. 1982. pap. 4.95 (ISBN 0-87029-186-6, 20277-0). Abbey.

Connolly, Peter. The Greek Armies. LC 79-65846. (Armies of the Past Ser.). PLB 12.68 (ISBN 0-382-06308-2). Silver.

--Pompeii. LC 79-65847. (Armies of the Past Ser.). PLB 12.68 (ISBN 0-382-06309-0). Silver.

--The Roman Army. LC 79-65845. (Armies of the Past Ser.). PLB 12.68 (ISBN 0-382-06306-6). Silver.

Connolly, Robert D. Paper Collectibles, Identification & Value Guide. (Illus.). pap. 9.95 (ISBN 0-89689-022-8). Wallace-Homestead.

Connolly, Terence. Engineers & Organizations. LC 82-22703. (Industrial Engineering Ser.). 384p. 1983. pap. text ed. 18.95 (ISBN 0-534-01409-7). Brooks-Cole.

Connolly, Terence L., ed. see Thompson, Francis.

Connolly, Thomas, jt. auth. see Veazie, Walter.

Connolly, Thomas E., ed. see Hawthorne, Nathaniel.

Connolly, Thomas J. Foundations of Nuclear Engineering. LC 77-26916. 344p. 1978. text ed. 38.50x (ISBN 0-471-16858-0). Wiley.

Connolly, Vivian. Love in Exile. (Superromance Ser.). 295p. 1983. pap. 2.95 (ISBN 0-373-70063-6, Pub. by Worldwide). Harlequin Bks.

Connolly, W. E. Appearance & Reality in Politics. 224p. 1981. 29.95 (ISBN 0-521-23026-8). Cambridge U Pr.

Connolly, William E., jt. auth. see Best, Michael H.

Connolly, William H. & Gordon, Glen. Social Structure & Political Theory. 1974. pap. text ed. 5.95x o.p. (ISBN 0-669-83923-X). Heath.

Connor, Anthony J. Baseball for the Love of It: Hall of Famers Tell It Like It Was. (Illus.). 288p. 1982. 16.95 (ISBN 0-02-527500-3). Macmillan.

Connor, D. Russell & Hicks, Warren W. B G on the Record: A Bio-Discography of Benny Goodman. rev. ed. LC 79-79599. (Illus.). 1969. 22.95 o.p. (ISBN 0-87000-059-4, Arlington Hse). Crown.

Connor, F. R. Modulation. (Introductory Topics in Electronics & Telecommunication). 144p. 1982. pap. text ed. 9.95 (ISBN 0-7131-3457-7). E Arnold.

--Noise. (Introductory Topics in Electronics & Telecommunications). 144p. 1982. pap. text ed. 9.95 (ISBN 0-7131-3459-3). E Arnold.

--Signals. (Introductory Topics in Electronics & Telecommunication). 144p. 1982. pap. text ed. 9.95 (ISBN 0-7131-3458-5). E Arnold.

Connor, Jerome J., jt. ed. see Chryssostomidis, Chryssostomos.

Connor, John J. On-the-Job-Training. (Illus.). 112p. 1983. pap. text ed. 14.95 (ISBN 0-934634-56-4). Intl Human Res.

Connor, John M. Market Power of Multinationals: A Quantitative Analysis of U. S. Corporations in Brazil & Mexico. LC 77-14302. (Praeger Special Studies). 1977. 31.95 o.p. (ISBN 0-03-023036-5). Praeger.

Connor, John W., jt. auth. see Gillespie, Margaret C.

Connor, Joseph E. & Devos, Burnell H., Jr., eds. Guide to Accounting Controls: Establishing, Evaluating, & Monitoring Control Systems. LC 79-64169. 1979. 96.00 (ISBN 0-88262-333-8). Warren.

Connor, Leo E. Administration of Special Education Programs. LC 61-11500. 1961. pap. text ed. 4.75x (ISBN 0-8077-1182-9). Tchrs Coll.

Connor, Patrick E. Dimensions in Modern Management. 3rd ed. LC 81-84072. 1982. pap. 14.95 (ISBN 0-395-31723-1). HM.

--Organizations: Theory & Design. 1979. text ed. 25.95 (ISBN 0-574-19380-4, 13-2380); instr's guide avail. (ISBN 0-574-19381-2, 13-2381). SRA.

Connor, Seymour V. Texas: A History. LC 71-136037. (Illus., Orig.). 1971. text ed. 22.95x (ISBN 0-88295-724-4). Harlan Davidson.

Connor, Ursula. How to select & Buy a Personal computer: For Small Business, for Department Heads, for the Home, for Self-Employed Professionals. 1983. pap. 9.95 (ISBN 0-686-81787-7). Devin.

Connors, Joseph J. Borromini & the Roman Oratory: Style & Society. (Illus.). 528p. 1980. 50.00x (ISBN 0-262-03071-3). MIT Pr.

Connors, Kenneth A. A Textbook of Pharmaceutical Analysis. 3rd ed. LC 81-19742. 664p. 1982. 55.00x (ISBN 0-471-09034-4, Pub. by Wiley-Interscience). Wiley.

--A Textbook of Pharmaceutical Analysis. 2nd ed. LC 74-34134. 611p. 1975. 42.95x o.p. (ISBN 0-471-16853-X, Pub. by Wiley-Interscience). Wiley.

Connors, Kenneth A., et al. Chemical Stability of Pharmaceuticals: A Handbook for Pharmacists. LC 78-1759. 1979. 36.50x (ISBN 0-471-02653-0, Pub. by Wiley-Interscience). Wiley.

Connors, Tracy D. The Nonprofit Organization Handbook. LC 78-26691. (Illus.). 1979. 44.95 (ISBN 0-07-012422-1, P&RB). McGraw.

Connors, Tracy D. & Callaghan, Christopher T., eds. Financial Management for Nonprofit Organizations. 400p. 1982. 29.95 (ISBN 0-8144-5732-0). Am Mgmt.

Connotillo, Barbara C., ed. Agriculture Study in the U. S. LC 79-90889. 1980. pap. text ed. 4.50 (ISBN 0-87206-097-7). Inst Intl Educ.

--Practical Guide for Foreign Visitors. 1979. pap. text ed. 3.50 (ISBN 0-87206-096-9). Inst Intl Educ.

--Summer Learning Options U. S. A. 100p. (Orig.). pap. text ed. 8.95 (ISBN 0-87206-122-1). Inst Intl Educ.

Conoley, Collie W., jt. auth. see Conoley, Jane C.

Conoley, Jane C. & Conoley, Collie W. School Consultation: A Guide to Practice & Training. (Pergamon General Psychology Ser.: No. 111). (Illus.). 260p. 1982. 25.00 (ISBN 0-08-027566-4); pap. 12.95 (ISBN 0-08-027565-6). Pergamon.

Conolly, Leonard W. & Wearing, J. P., eds. English Drama & Theatre, 1800-1900: A Guide to Information Sources. LC 73-16975. (American Literature, English Literature, & World Literatures in English Information Guide Ser.: Vol. 12). 1978. 42.00x (ISBN 0-8103-1225-5). Gale.

Conomos, T. J., ed. San Francisco Bay: The Urbanized Estuary. 469p. (Orig.). 1979. 16.95 (ISBN 0-934394-00-8). AAASPD.

Conot, Robert E. Justice at Nuremberg: The First Comprehensive, Dramatic Account of the Trial of the Leaders. LC 82-48395. (Illus.). 640p. 1983. 19.18i (ISBN 0-06-015117-X, HarpT). Har-Row.

Conover, David. Finding Marilyn. LC 81-47699. (Illus.). 256p. 1981. 14.95 (ISBN 0-448-12020-8, G&D). Putnam Pub Group.

Conover, Donald W., jt. auth. see Woodson, Wesley E.

Conover, Helen F., jt. auth. see Mugridge, Donald H.

Conover, Herbert S. Grounds Maintenance Handbook. 3rd ed. (Illus.). 512p. 1976. 37.50 (ISBN 0-07-012412-4, P&RB). McGraw.

Conover, Hobart & Berlye, Milton. Business Dynamics. 481p. 1982. text ed. 15.50 (ISBN 0-672-97973-X); tchr's ed. 6.67 (ISBN 0-672-97978-0); wkbk. 5.95 (ISBN 0-672-97977-2). Bobbs.

Conover, Mary B., jt. auth. see Tilkian, Sarko M.

Conover, Mary H. Cardiac Arrhythmias: Exercises in Pattern Interpretation. 2nd ed. LC 77-24509. (Illus.). 1978. pap. text ed. 14.95 (ISBN 0-8016-1024-9). Mosby.

Conover, Mary H., jt. auth. see Marriott, Henry J.

Conover, W. J. Practical Nonparametric Statistics. 2nd ed. LC 80-301. (Probability & Mathematical Statistics Ser.). 493p. 1980. 35.95 (ISBN 0-471-02867-3). Wiley.

Conquest, Robert. The Politics of Ideas in the U. S. S. R. LC 76-27307. 1976. Repr. of 1967 ed. lib. bdg. 19.00x (ISBN 0-8371-9049-5, COPO). Greenwood.

Conrad, Agnes C., jt. auth. see Gast, Ross H.

Conrad, Alfred F., et al. Enterprise Organization: Cases, Statutes & Analysis on Licensing, Employment, Agency, Partnerships, Associations, & Corporations. 3rd ed. LC 82-10902. (University Casebook Ser.). 1423p. 1982. text ed. write for info. (ISBN 0-88277-058-6). Foundation Pr.

Conrad, Andree, ed. Information & Knowledge: How They Get Around - What Happens to Them in the Process. 160p. 1983. 8.95 (ISBN 0-8180-2301-5). Horizon.

Conrad, Andree, tr. see Donoso, Jose.

Conrad, Barnaby. Fire Below Zero. (Orig.). 1981. pap. 2.75 o.s.i. (ISBN 0-440-12524-3). Dell.

Conrad, Barnaby & Mastorakis, Nico. Keepers of the Secret. 256p. pap. 2.95 (ISBN 0-515-05544-1). Jove Pubns.

Conrad, Barnaby & Mortensen, Neils. Endangered. LC 77-13920. 1978. 8.95 o.p. (ISBN 0-399-12171-4). Putnam Pub Group.

Conrad, Beverly. Doggytales. (Orig.). 1980. pap. 2.95 o.s.i. (ISBN 0-440-52132-7, Delta). Dell.

--Kitty Tales. (Orig.). 1980. pap. 2.95 o.s.i. (ISBN 0-440-51458-4, Delta). Dell.

Conrad, Clifton. The Undergraduate Curriculum: A Guide to Innovation & Reform. (Westview Special Studies in Higher Education). 1979. lib. bdg. 21.00 (ISBN 0-89158-196-0). Westview.

Conrad, Clifton F., jt. auth. see Bullock, G. William, Jr.

Conrad, Dan & Hedin, Diane, eds. Youth Participation & Experiential Education. LC 81-20114. (Child & Youth Services Ser.: Vol. 4, Nos. 3 & 4). 163p. 1982. text ed. 20.00 (ISBN 0-917724-99-2, B99). Haworth Pr.

Conrad, Daniel L. The Quick Proposal Workbook. 119p. 13.95 (ISBN 0-686-82294-3, 37A). Public Management.

Conrad, Daniel L. & Public Management Institute Staff. The New Grants' Planner. rev. ed. 400p. 47.50 (ISBN 0-686-82257-9, 30B). Public Management.

Conrad, Eleanor. The Teddy-Bear Circus. (Kindergarten Read-to Bks.). (Illus.). (gr. k-2). PLB 5.95 o.p. (ISBN 0-513-00477-7). Denison.

Conrad, Eva & Maul, Terry. Introduction to Experimental Psychology. LC 81-1647. 542p. 1981. text ed. 22.95 (ISBN 0-471-06005-4). Wiley.

Conrad, Glenn R. & Brasseaux, Carl A. A Selected Bibliography of Scholarly Literature on Colonial Louisiana & New France. 150p. 10.00 (ISBN 0-940984-06-7). U of SW LA Ctr LA Studies.

Conrad, Glenn R., ed. see De Villiers du Terrage, Marc.

Conrad, J. TV Commercial: How Is It Made. 1983. 10.25 (ISBN 0-442-21866-4); pap. price not set (ISBN 0-442-21867-2). Van Nos Reinhold.

Conrad, Jack R. The Horn & the Sword. LC 72-9822. (Illus.). 222p. 1973. Repr. of 1957 ed. lib. bdg. 15.50x (ISBN 0-8371-6604-7, COHO). Greenwood.

Conrad, John J., jt. auth. see Cox, Steven M.

Conrad, John P. Future of Corrections. Sellin, Thorsten, ed. LC 69-16927. (Annals: No. 381). 1969. pap. 7.95 (ISBN 0-87761-112-2). Am Acad Pol Soc Sci.

--Justice & Consequences. LC 78-348. 192p. 1981. 19.95x (ISBN 0-669-02190-3). Lexington Bks.

Conrad, John P. & Dinitz, Simon. In Fear of Each Other: Studies of Dangerousness in America. LC 77-286. (The Dangerous Offender Project). 1977. 17.95 (ISBN 0-669-01478-8). Lexington Bks.

Conrad, John W. Ceramic Formulas: A Guide to Clay, Glaze, Enamel, Glass & Their Colours. 309p. 1973. 17.95 (ISBN 0-02-527610-7). Macmillan.

--Contemporary Ceramic Techniques. 1979. 20.95 (ISBN 0-13-169540-1). P-H.

Conrad, Joseph. Great Short Works of Joseph Conrad. Allen, Jerry, ed. pap. 3.50i (ISBN 0-06-083039-5, P3039, PL). Har-Row.

--Heart of Darkness. Walker, Franklin, ed. Bd. with The Secret Sharer. (Bantam Classics Ser.). 204p. (Critical suppl. includes biography, reviews, essays). (gr. 10-12,RL 10). 1981. pap. 1.75 (ISBN 0-553-21026-2). Bantam.

--Heart of Darkness. LC 81-38511. 128p. 1982. Repr. of 1926 ed. 10.00x (ISBN 0-8376-0458-3). Bentley.

--Heart of Darkness & the Secret Sharer. 1971. pap. 1.50 (ISBN 0-451-51668-0, CW1668, Sig Classics). NAL.

--Lord Jim. (Bantam Classics Ser.). 271p. (gr. 9-12). 1981. pap. 1.95 (ISBN 0-553-21027-0). Bantam.

--Lord Jim. lib. bdg. 16.95 (ISBN 0-89966-057-6). Buccaneer Bks.

--Lord Jim. LC 44-22843. 1927. 14.95 (ISBN 0-385-04265-5). Doubleday.

--Lord Jim. Moser, Thomas, ed. (Critical Editions Ser). (Annotated). 1968. pap. text ed. 7.95x (ISBN 0-393-09656-4). Norton.

--Nigger of "Narcissus", Typhoon, Falk, & Other Stories. Sherry, Norman, ed. 1978. Repr. of 1974 ed. 12.95x (ISBN 0-460-00980-X, Evman); pap. 3.50x (ISBN 0-460-01980-5, Evman). Biblio Dist.

--Nostromo. pap. 2.95 (ISBN 0-451-51455-6, CE1455, Sig Classics). NAL.

--Nostromo. LC 82-42865. 8.95 (ISBN 0-394-60431-8). Modern Lib.

--An Outcast of the Islands. 296p. 1976. pap. 3.50 (ISBN 0-14-004054-4). Penguin.

--A Personal Record. LC 82-73728. xvii, 220p. 1982. pap. 6.95 (ISBN 0-910395-05-5). Marlboro Pr.

--Secret Agent. 1953. pap. 4.95 (ISBN 0-385-09352-7, Anch). Doubleday.

--A Set of Six. 356p. 1977. Repr. of 1908 ed. lib. bdg. 16.95x (ISBN 0-89966-264-1). Buccaneer Bks.

--Tales of Unrest. 1977. pap. 2.95 (ISBN 0-14-003885-X). Penguin.

--Three Great Tales. Incl. Nigger of the Narcissus; Heart of Darkness; Typhoon. 1958. pap. 3.95 (ISBN 0-394-70155-0, V-155, Vin). Random.

--Typhoon & Other Tales. pap. 3.95 (ISBN 0-451-51779-2, CE1779, Sig Classics). NAL.

--Victory. LC 32-26954. 1957. pap. 4.95 (ISBN 0-385-09314-4, Anch). Doubleday.

--Youth & The End of the Tether. 176p. 1976. pap. 2.95 (ISBN 0-14-004055-2). Penguin.

Conrad, Joseph & Ford, Madox F. Romance. LC 82-73434. 541p. Repr. of 1928 ed. lib. bdg. 37.50x (ISBN 0-88116-002-4). Brenner Bks.

Conrad, Joseph & Hueffer, Ford M. The Inheritors. (Science Fiction Ser.). 352p. 1976. Repr. of 1901 ed. lib. bdg. 15.00 o.p. (ISBN 0-8398-2350-9, Gregg). G K Hall.

Conrad, Joseph see Swan, D. K.

Conrad, Kenneth & Bressler, Rubin. Drug Therapy for the Elderly. LC 81-38398. (Illus.). 371p. 1982. pap. text ed. 21.95 (ISBN 0-8016-0782-5). Mosby.

Conrad, Leo, jt. auth. see Zimmerman, Steven.

Conrad, Nancy L. Return of Yesterday. 1978. 6.95 o.p. (ISBN 0-533-03155-9). Vantage.

Conrad, Peter. Imagining America. (Illus.). 1980. 16.95x (ISBN 0-19-502651-9). Oxford U Pr.

--Romantic Opera & Literary Form. (Quantum Bk.). (Illus.). 185p. 1981. 18.50x (ISBN 0-520-03258-6, CAL 527); pap. 6.95 (ISBN 0-520-04508-4, CAL527). U of Cal Pr.

Conrad, Peter & Kern, Rochelle, eds. Sociology of Health & Illness: Critical Perspectives. 500p. 1981. text ed. 18.95x (ISBN 0-312-74065-4); pap. text ed. 12.95x (ISBN 0-312-74066-2). St Martin.

Conrad, Peter F. Identifying Hyperactive Children: A Study in the Medicalization of Deviant Behavior. LC 75-44559. (Illus.). 1976. 16.95x o.p. (ISBN 0-669-00499-5). Lexington Bks.

Conrad, Phil. Trial & Terror. 1978. 7.95 o.p. (ISBN 0-533-03620-8). Vantage.

Conrad, Randy. Your Community Recreation Planning: A Guide for Local Involvement in Comprehensive Recreation Planning. 160p. 1977. pap. 5.00 (ISBN 0-686-84029-1). U OR Ctr Leisure.

Conrad, Robert, ed. Brazilian Slavery: An Annotated Research Bibliography. 1977. lib. bdg. 19.00 (ISBN 0-8161-7855-0, Hall Reference). G K Hall.

Conrad, Robert & Hool, Bryce, eds. Taxation of Mineral Resources. LC 80-8392. (Lincoln Institute of Land Policy Book). 1980. 17.95x (ISBN 0-669-04104-1). Lexington Bks.

Conrad, Susan P. Perish the Thought: Intellectual Women in Romantic America, 1830-1860. LC 75-25463. (Illus.). 1976. 19.95x (ISBN 0-19-501995-4). Oxford U Pr.

Conrad, William R., Jr. & Glenn, William E. The Effective Voluntary Board of Directors: What it is & How it Works. rev. ed. (Illus.). 225p. 1983. pap. text ed. 8.95x (ISBN 0-8040-0836-1, 82-76081). Ohio U Pr.

Conrader, Constance, jt. auth. see Conrader, Jay.

Conrader, Jay & Conrader, Constance. The Northwoods Wildlife Region. (American Wildlife Region Ser.: No. 9). (Illus.). 192p. (Orig.). 1982. lib. bdg. 12.95 (ISBN 0-87961-126-X); pap. 7.95 (ISBN 0-87961-127-8). Naturegraph.

Conradi, Peter J. John Fowles. (Contemporary Writers Ser.). 1982. pap. 4.25 (ISBN 0-416-32250-6). Methuen Inc.

Conrads, Ulrich, ed. Programs & Manifestoes on 20th-Century Architecture. 1971. 14.50x o.p. (ISBN 0-262-03039-X); pap. 5.95 (ISBN 0-262-53030-9). MIT Pr.

Conrow, Robert & Hecksel, Arlene. Herbal Pathfinders: A Sourcebook for the Herbal Renaissance. (Illus.). 320p. 1983. pap. 9.95 (ISBN 0-88007-128-1). Woodbridge Pr.

Conroy, Barbara. Learning Packaged to Go: A Directory & Guide to Staff Development & Training Packages. 1983. price not set (ISBN 0-89774-065-3). Oryx Pr.

--Library Staff Development & Continuing Education: Principles & Practices. LC 78-18887. 296p. 1978. 27.50 (ISBN 0-87287-177-0). Libs Unl.

Conroy, F. F., jt. auth. see Hellerman, Herbert.

Conroy, Hilary & Miyakawa, T. Scott, eds. East Across the Pacific. LC 72-77825. 322p. 1972. pap. 19.75 o.p. (ISBN 0-87436-087-0). ABC-Clio.

Conroy, Hilary, jt. ed. see Coox, Alvin D.

Conroy, Hilary, jt. ed. see Wray, Harry.

Conroy, Jack. The Disinherited. xii, 310p. 1982. pap. 6.95 (ISBN 0-88208-150-0). Lawrence Hill.

--Disinherited. Date not set. pap. 5.95 o.p. (ISBN 0-686-95777-6). Jefferson Natl.

Conroy, John, jt. auth. see Kraft, Eve.

Conroy, Joseph F. Aventure En Normandie: Reader 2. LC 81-7784. (A L'aventure! Ser). (Illus.). 40p. (Orig., Fr.). (gr. 7-12). 1982. pap. 1.95 (ISBN 0-88436-855-6, 40260). EMC.

--Danger sur la Cote d'azur: Reador 4. LC 81-7820. (A L'aventure! Ser.). (Illus.). 40p. (Orig., Fr.). (gr. 7-12). 1982. pap. 1.95 (ISBN 0-88436-857-2, 40263). EMC.

--Destination: France! Reader 1. LC 81-7816. (A L'aventure! Ser.). (Illus.). 40p. (Orig., Fr.). (gr. 7-12). 1982. pap. 1.95 (ISBN 0-88436-854-8, 40259). EMC.

--Guide Terrestre, ou La Terre et Ses Singes. (Orig.). (gr. 7-12). 1975. pap. text ed. 5.50 (ISBN 0-87720-461-6). AMSCO Sch.

--Sur la Route de la Contrebande. LC 81-7817. (A L'aventure! Ser.: Reader 3). (Illus.). 40p. (Orig., French.). (gr. 7-12). pap. 1.95 (ISBN 0-88436-856-4, 40261). EMC.

Conroy, Larry & O'Connell, Paul. The Consumer Cost Guide to Car Repair. (Illus.). 144p. 1983. text ed. 12.95 (ISBN 0-13-168872-3); pap. 5.95 (ISBN 0-13-168864-2). P-H.

Conroy, Lawrence E., et al. General Chemistry Laboratory Operation. 3rd ed. 1977. pap. 13.95x (ISBN 0-02-324330-9, 32433). Macmillan.

Conroy, Mary. The Rational Woman's Guide to Self-Defense. new ed. LC 74-18873. (Illus.). 128p. (Orig.). 1975. pap. 2.50 (ISBN 0-448-11943-9, G&D). Putnam Pub Group.

Conroy, Mary & Ritvo, Edward. Every Woman Can: A Common-Sense Guide to Safety, Security & Self-Defense. LC 82-82355. 224p. (Orig.). 1982. pap. 6.95 (ISBN 0-448-16062-5, G&D). Putnam Pub Group.

Conroy, Pat. The Water Is Wide. 1979. pap. 3.50 (ISBN 0-380-46037-8, 63586-0). Avon.

Conroy, William T., Jr. Villiers de L'Isle-Adam. (World Author Ser.). 1978. 15.95 (ISBN 0-8057-6332-5, Twayne). G K Hall.

Conry, Tom, jt. auth. see Science Action Coalition.

Conseil Colonial de Bourbon. Avis du Conseil Colonial de Bourbon sur Diverses Propositions Concernant l'Esclavage. (Slave Trade in France Ser., 1744-1848). 28p. (Fr.). 1974. Repr. of 1839 ed. lib. bdg. 17.00 o.p. (ISBN 0-8287-1332-4, TN 147). Clearwater Pub.

Conseil International De la Langue Francaise. Glossary of the Environment. LC 76-19547. 138p. 1977. 23.95 o.p. (ISBN 0-275-23760-5). Praeger.

Conseiller. Curare & Curarisation. 1980. 73.75 (ISBN 90-219-0443-8). Elsevier.

--Liver-Anaesthesia & Critical Care. 1980. 58.50 (ISBN 90-219-0445-4). Elsevier.

Conseiller, C., et al, eds. Anaesthesia & Postoperative Care in Uncommon Diseases: Post Graduate Course. Proceedings of International Meeting of Anaesthesiology & Resuscitation, XIIth, C. H. U. PetieSalpetriere, Paris 1980. 442p. 1982. 73.75 (ISBN 90-2-190473-X). Elsevier.

--Volatile Halogenated Anaesthetics: Post-Graduate Course. Proceedings of International Meeting of Anaesthesiology & Resuscitation, C. H. U. PetieSalpetriere, Paris, 1980. 242p. 1981. 55.50 (ISBN 90-219-0474-8). Elsevier.

Consentino, John. Computer Graphics Marketplace. 2nd ed. 64p. 1983. pap. 25.00 (ISBN 0-89774-086-6). Oryx Pr.

Conservation Foundation Staff. State of the Environment 1982. LC 82-8257. (Illus.). 439p. (Orig.). 1982. pap. 15.00 (ISBN 0-89164-070-3). Conservation Foun.

Considine, Douglas M. Chemical & Process Technology Encyclopedia. 1184p. 1974. 69.50 (ISBN 0-07-012423-X, P&RB). McGraw.

--Encyclopedia of Instrumentation & Control. LC 80-24422. 814p. 1981. Repr. of 1971 ed. text ed. 49.50 (ISBN 0-89874-281-1). Krieger.

--Energy Technology Handbook. 1977. 74.95 (ISBN 0-07-012430-2, P&RB). McGraw.

Considine, Douglas M. & Ross, S. D. Process Instruments & Controls Handbook. 2nd ed. 1344p. 1974. 49.50 o.p. (ISBN 0-07-012428-0, P&RB). McGraw.

Considine, Tim. The Language of Sport. Doering, Henry & Fisher, Patricia, eds. 352p. 1982. pap. 8.95 (ISBN 0-911818-24-3). World Almanac.

--The Language of Sport. 352p. 1982. 15.95x (ISBN 0-87196-653-0). Facts on File.

--The Photographic Dictionary of Soccer. (Illus., Orig.). 1979. pap. 6.95 o.p. (ISBN 0-446-87953-3). Warner Bks.

Constable, A. T. A Collection of Some of the Greatest Paintings by Raphael in the Form of Full Colours Reproduction. (Illus.). 91p. 1983. 98.85 (ISBN 0-86650-061-8). Gloucester Art.

Constable, Anthony. Early Wireless. (Illus.). 160p. 1981. 19.95 o.p. (ISBN 0-8069-3116-7). Sterling.

Constable, Giles. Attitudes Toward Self-Inflicted Suffering in the Middle Ages. (Stephen J. Brademas Lectures Ser.). 28p. (Orig.). Date not set. pap. text ed. 2.50 (ISBN 0-916586-87-1). Hellenic Coll Pr.

Constable, Giles, jt. ed. see Benson, Robert L.

Constable, Ian J., jt. auth. see Lim, Arthur.

Constable, Robert. Prerogativa Regis: Tertia Lectura Roberti Constable De Lyncolnis Inne. Thorne, Samuel E., ed. 1949. 47.50x (ISBN 0-685-69876-9). Elliots Bks.

Constable, Trevor J. The Cosmic Pulse of Life: The Revolutionary Biological Power Behind UFO's. LC 77-72046. (Illus.). 446p. 1977. pap. 10.00 (ISBN 0-89345-049-9, Steinerbks). Garber Comm.

Constable, W. G. Canaletto: Giovanni Antonio Canal(1697-1768, 2 vols. 2nd ed. Links, J. G., ed. 1977. Set. 139.00x o.p. (ISBN 0-19-817324-5). Oxford U Pr.

--The Painter's Workshop. (Illus.). 1980. pap. 3.50 (ISBN 0-486-23836-9). Dover.

Constabulary Force Commissioners, Great Briain. First Report of the Constabulary Force Commissioners Appointed to Inquire As to the Best Means of Establishing an Efficient Constabulary Force in the Countries of England & Wales. LC 76-172561. (Criminology, Law Enforcement, & Social Problems Ser.: No. 165). (Intro. added). Date not set. cancelled 15.00 (ISBN 0-87585-165-7). Patterson Smith.

Constance, Garnett, tr. see Tolstoy, Leo.

Constance, J. D. Electrical Engineering for Professional Engineers Examinations. 3rd ed. 1981. 18.95 (ISBN 0-07-012455-8). McGraw.

--Mechanical Engineering for Professional Engineers' Examination. 3rd ed. 1981. 18.95 (ISBN 0-07-012457-4). McGraw.

Constance, John D. Electrical Engineering for Professional Engineers' Examinations. 3rd ed. (Illus.). 544p. 1975. 32.50 (ISBN 0-07-012448-5, P&RB). McGraw.

--How to Become a Professional Engineer. 3rd ed. LC 77-17941. (Illus.). 1978. 32.50 (ISBN 0-07-012449-3, P&RB); pap. 14.95 (ISBN 0-07-012456-6). McGraw.

--Mechanical Engineering for Professional Engineers' Examinations. 2nd ed. 1969. 24.50 o.p. (ISBN 0-07-012443-4, P&RB). McGraw.

Constandse, A. K. & Hofstee, E. W. Rural Sociology in Action. (FAO Economic & Social Development Ser.: No. 10). 64p. 1964. pap. 5.25 (ISBN 0-686-92693-5, F1459, FAO). Unipub.

Constans, H. Philip, Jr. Fit for Freedom. LC 79-6405. 141p. 1980. pap. text ed. 8.25 (ISBN 0-8191-0945-2). U Pr of Amer.

Constant, Benjamin. Adolphe. 2nd ed. Rudler, G., ed. (Modern French Texts Ser.). 1941. pap. write for info. (ISBN 0-7190-0142-0). Manchester.

--Discours a la Chambre sur la Traite des Noirs. (Slave Trade in France Ser., 1744-1848). 48p. (Fr.). 1974. Repr. of 1827 ed. lib. bdg. 27.00x o.p. (ISBN 0-8287-0221-7, TN148). Clearwater Pub.

Constant, Benjamin, tr. see Godwin, William.

Constantine. Rockburg Railroad Murder. 1982. pap. 6.95 (ISBN 0-686-84624-9, Nonpareil Bks). Godine.

Constantine & Hobbs. Know Your Woods. 1975. text ed. 17.95 (ISBN 0-87002-903-7). Bennett IL.

Constantine, John & Wallis, Julia. The Thames & Hudson Maunual of Professional Photography. (Thames & Hudson Manual Ser.). (Illus.). 1983. pap. 10.95 (ISBN 0-500-68025-6). Thames Hudson.

Constantine, K. C. The Man Who Liked Slow Tomatoes. LC 81-47321. 256p. 1982. 12.95 (ISBN 0-87923-407-5). Godine.

--The Man Who Liked Slow Tomatoes. 1983. pap. 2.95 (ISBN 0-14-006621-7). Penguin.

Constantine, Larry L., jt. auth. see Yourdon, Edward.

Constantine, Mildred. Tina Modotti: A Fragile Life. (Illus.). 224p. 1983. 30.00. Rizzoli Intl.

Constantine, Stephen. The Making of British Colonial Development Policy 1914-1940. 200p. 1983. text ed. 32.50 (ISBN 0-7146-3204-X, F Cass Co). Biblio Dist.

Constantinescu, F. & Magyari, E. Problems in Quantum Mechanics. 1971. pap. text ed. 45.00 o.p. (ISBN 0-08-006826-X); text ed. 25.00 (ISBN 0-08-019008-1). Pergamon.

Constantinides, A., et al, eds. see Biochemical Engineering Conference, 2nd, Henniker, New Hampshire, July 13-18, 1980.

Constantinides, A. G., jt. ed. see Bogner, R. E.

Constantinides, Paris. Functional Electronic Histology. 1974. 111.75 (ISBN 0-444-40998-X). Elsevier.

Constantino, Ernesto. Ilokano Dictionary. McKaughan, Howard P., ed. (PALI Language Texts: Philippines). (Orig.). 1971. pap. text ed. 10.00x (ISBN 0-87022-152-3). UH Pr.

--Ilokano Reference Grammar. McKaughan, Howard P., ed. LC 71-152463. (PALI Language Texts: Philippines). (Orig.). 1971. pap. text ed. 2.50x o.p. (ISBN 0-87022-153-1). UH Pr.

Constantino, Renato. A History of the Philippines: From the Spanish Colonization to the Second World War. LC 76-28979. 459p. 1976. 21.50 (ISBN 0-85345-394-2, CL-3942). Monthly Rev.

Constellation International Editors, ed. Your Personal Forecast. Incl. Aries (ISBN 0-448-14168-X); Taurus (ISBN 0-448-14169-8); Gemini (ISBN 0-448-14170-1); Cancer (ISBN 0-448-14171-X); Leo (ISBN 0-448-14172-8); Virgo (ISBN 0-448-14173-6); Libra (ISBN 0-448-14174-4); Scorpio (ISBN 0-448-14175-2); Sagittarius (ISBN 0-448-14176-0); Capricorn (ISBN 0-448-14177-9); Aquarius (ISBN 0-448-14178-7); Pisces (ISBN 0-448-14179-5). (Illus.). 1979. pap. 1.50 ea. o.p. (G&D). Putnam Pub Group.

Consumer Electronics Group. New World of Audio: A Music Lover's Guide. Date not set. pap. 8.95 (ISBN 0-672-21946-8). Sams.

Consumer Group, Inc., jt. auth. see Darack, Arthur.

Consumer Guide. The Complete Guide to Stereo Equipment. 1979. 12.95 o.p. (ISBN 0-671-24767-0); pap. 7.95 o.p. (ISBN 0-671-24837-5). S&S.

--Complete Medicine Book. 1981. cancelled o.p. (ISBN 0-671-25501-0). S&S.

--The Fastest, Cheapest, Best Way to Clean Everything. 1981. 10.95 o.p. (ISBN 0-671-25500-2, 25500). S&S.

Consumer Guide, ed. Consumer Guide: Nineteen Eighty-One Buying Guide. 1981. pap. 3.50 o.p. (ISBN 0-451-09623-1, E9623, Sig). NAL.

--Consumer Guide: Nineteen Eighty-One Cars. 1981. pap. 3.50 o.p. (ISBN 0-451-09625-8, 9625, Sig). NAL.

--The Tool Catalog. LC 78-4729. (Illus.). pap. 8.95i o.p. (ISBN 0-06-090731-2, CN-731, CN). Har-Row.

Consumer Guide & Dickinson, Peter, eds. Your Retirement: A Complete Planning Guide. 128p. 1981. 12.95 (ISBN 0-89104-271-7, A & W Visual Library); pap. 4.95 (ISBN 0-89104-270-9, A & W Visual Library). A & W Pubs.

Consumer Guide Editorial Staff, ed. Consumer Guide Fix-It. (Illus.). 1976. 8.95 o.p. (ISBN 0-671-22249-X); pap. 3.95 o.p. (ISBN 0-671-22226-0). S&S.

Consumer Guide Editors. Blue Ribbon Canning & Preserving. (Joy of Living Ser.). 1976. pap. 1.95 o.p. (ISBN 0-671-22410-7). S&S.

--Computer Careers: Where the Jobs Are & How to Get Them. 256p. 1981. 6.95 (ISBN 0-449-90064-9, Columbine). Fawcett.

--The Cook's Store. (Illus.). 1978. 14.95 o.p. (ISBN 0-671-24589-9); pap. 7.95 o.p. (ISBN 0-671-24590-2). S&S.

--Decorating Your Office for Success. LC 78-20157. (Illus.). 1979. 13.41i (ISBN 0-06-010854-1, HarpT). Har-Row.

--The Easy-to-Understand Guide to Word Processing. (Illus., Orig.). 1982. pap. cancelled (ISBN 0-671-46172-9). Doubleday.

--The Energy Savers Catalog. (Illus.). 1977. pap. 6.95 o.p. (ISBN 0-399-12038-6). Putnam Pub Group.

--Food Preserver. 1979. 12.95 o.p. (ISBN 0-671-24591-0, 22227-9); pap. 6.95 (ISBN 0-671-24592-9). S&S.

--Health Careers: Where the Jobs Are & How to Get Them. Date not set. pap. 6.95 (ISBN 0-449-90075-4, Columbine). Fawcett.

--How to Win at E.T. the Video Game. 32p. 1983. pap. 2.50 (ISBN 0-440-13767-5). Dell.

--The Ultimate Householder's Book: Over 4000 Invaluable Tips to Save You Time & Money. (Illus.). 732p. 1982. 17.95 (ISBN 0-89479-113-3). A & W Pubs.

Consumer Guide Editors, jt. auth. see Beatty, Virginia.

Consumer Guide Editors, jt. auth. see Beatty, Virginia L.

Consumer Guide Editors, jt. auth. see Dickinson, Peter A.

Consumer Guide Editors, ed. see Berland, Theodore.

Consumer Guide Magazine Editors. Consumer Guide-Complete Buying Guide to Stereo & Tape Recorders. 384p. (Orig.). 1974. pap. 1.95 o.p. (ISBN 0-451-05814-3, J5814, Sig). NAL.

--Consumer Guide: Photographic Equipment Test Reports. (Orig.). 1974. pap. 1.95 o.p. (ISBN 0-451-06082-2, J6082, Sig). NAL.

--Model Cars. (Orig.). 1978. pap. 2.95i o.p. (ISBN 0-06-090639-1, CN 639, CN). Har-Row.

--Model Military Toys. (Orig.). 1978. pap. 2.95i o.p. (ISBN 0-06-090641-3, CN 641, CN). Har-Row.

--Model Trains. (Orig.). 1978. pap. 2.95i o.p. (ISBN 0-06-090640-5, CN 640, CN). Har-Row.

Consumer Guide Magazine Editors, ed. Consumer Guide---Complete Guide to Fishing Equipment. (Orig.). 1975. pap. 1.95 o.p. (ISBN 0-451-06667-7, J6667, Sig). NAL.

--Consumer Guide---Complete Guide to Golfing Equipment. (Orig.). 1975. pap. 1.95 o.p. (ISBN 0-451-06668-5, J6668, Sig). NAL.

Consumer Guide Publications International Editors. Favorite Brands Name Recipes, Soups & Sandwiches. 144p. (Orig.). 1982. pap. 2.50 (ISBN 0-449-24571-3, Crest). Fawcett.

Consumer Guides Editors. An Easy-to-Understand Guide to Home Computers. 1982. pap. 3.95 (ISBN 0-686-84861-6, AE2031, Sig). NAL.

Consumers Guide Editors. Rating the Exercises. Kuntzlemann, Charles T., ed. LC 77-18438. 1978. 10.95 (ISBN 0-688-03293-1). Morrow.

Consumers Union. Consumer Reports Buying Guide 1983. 400p. 1982. pap. 3.50 (ISBN 0-385-18349-6). Doubleday.

--Top Tips from Consumer Reports: How to Do Things Better, Faster, Cheaper. 320p. (Orig.). 1983. pap. 6.70 (ISBN 0-316-15344-3). Little.

Contant, H. & Duthie, H. C. The Phytoplankton of Lac St-Jean, Quebec. (Bibliotheca Phycologica Ser.: No. 40). (Illus.). 1978. pap. text ed. 16.00x (ISBN 3-7682-1198-3). Lubrecht & Cramer.

Contant d'Orville, Andre-Guillaume. Histoire des Differents Peuple du Monde, Vol. 4. (Bibliotheque Africaine Ser.). 530p. (Fr.). 1974. Repr. of 1770 ed. lib. bdg. 130.50x o.p. (ISBN 0-8287-0222-5, 72-2150). Clearwater Pub.

Conte, A., ed. Algebraic Threefolds, Varenna, Italy 1981, Second Session: Proceedings. (Lecture Notes in Mathematics: Vol. 947). 315p. 1982. pap. 16.50 (ISBN 0-387-11587-0). Springer-Verlag.

Conte, Jon R. & Shore, David A., eds. Social Work & Child Sexual Abuse. LC 82-11952. (Journal of Social Work & Human Sexuality Ser.: Vol. 1, Nos. 1 & 2). 200p. 1982. text ed. 20.00 (ISBN 0-917724-50-X, B50). Haworth Pr.

Conte, Michael, et al. Employee Ownership. 70p. 1981. pap. 8.00x (ISBN 0-87944-255-7). Inst Soc Res.

Conte, S. D. & De Boor, C. Elementary Numerical Analysis: An Algorithmic Approach. 3rd ed. 1980. 26.95 (ISBN 0-07-012447-7). McGraw.

Conte, Sylvester B. & Kemme, Douglas H. Positioning Technique Handbook for Radiologic Technologists. LC 78-5245. 289p. 1978. pap. text ed. 15.50 (ISBN 0-8016-1031-1). Mosby.

Contemporary Folk Poetry Staff. Quechua Peoples Poetry. 70p. 1982. pap. 6.00 o.p. (ISBN 0-686-97207-4). Curbstone.

Contemporary Perspectives, Inc. Problem Solving Mathematics: Level E. (Problem Solving in Mathematics Ser.). 96p. (gr. 5). 1982. text ed. write for info. (ISBN 0-87895-548-8); tchrs. guide avail. (ISBN 0-87895-549-6). Modern Curr.

Contempre, Yvette. The Grand Island of Jatte. LC 79-65866. (Children's Art Ser.). PLB 11.96 (ISBN 0-382-06332-5). Silver.

--The Tower of Babel. LC 79-65866. (Children's Art Ser.). PLB 11.96 (ISBN 0-382-06327-9). Silver.

Contenau, G. Everyday Life in Babylon & Assyria. (Illus.). 1954. 19.95 o.p. (ISBN 0-312-27160-3). St Martin.

Content, Robin, jt. auth. see Smelser, Neil J.

Conti, Natale & Tritonio, Antonio M. Mythologiae & Mythologia. Orgel, Stephen, ed. LC 78-68194. (Philosophy of Images Ser.: Vol. 13). (Illus.). 1980. lib. bdg. 66.00 o.s.i. (ISBN 0-8240-3687-5). Garland Pub.

Conti, R. Institutiones Mathematicae: Linear Differential Equations & Control, Vol. 1. 1977. 27.50 (ISBN 0-12-363601-9). Acad Pr.

Continuing Working Party on Fishery Statistics in the North Atlantic Area, 5th Session, 1967. Report. (FAO Fisheries Report: No. 45). 33p. 1967. pap. 7.50 (ISBN 0-686-93002-9, F1665, FAO). Unipub.

Contosta, David R. Henry Adams & the American Experiment. (Library of American Biography). 176p. (Orig.). 1980. 10.95 (ISBN 0-316-15401-6); pap. 5.95 (ISBN 0-316-15400-8). Little.

Contractor, Farok J. International Technology Licensing: Compensation, Costs, & Negotiation. LC 80-8768. 208p. 1981. 26.95x (ISBN 0-669-04359-1). Lexington Bks.

Contreras, Gloria, jt. ed. see Simms, Richard L.

Contreras, H. A Theory of Word Order with Special Reference to Spanish. (Linguistics Ser.: Vol. 29). 1976. pap. 23.25 (ISBN 0-7204-6210-X, North-Holland). Elsevier.

Contreras, Moyra, tr. see Rodieck, Jorma.

Controversies in Nephrology Conference Sponsored by the American Kidney Fund. Controversies in Nephrology, Vol. 2: Proceedings. Schreiner, George E., ed. (Controversies in Nephrology, 2nd). 390p. 1981. text ed. 57.25x (ISBN 0-89352-144-2). Masson Pub.

Convention on International Trade in Endangered Species of Wild Fauna & Flora. Guidelines for the Transport & Preparation of Shipment of Live Wild Animals & Plants. 109p. 1981. pap. 13.00 (ISBN 0-686-93565-9, 0105-UPB100, UNEP); pap. 13.00 Fr. ed. (ISBN 0-686-99140-0, 0105-UPB102); pap. 13.00 Span. ed. (ISBN 0-686-99141-9, 0105-UPB101). Unipub.

Convention on International Trade in Endangered Species of Wild Fauna & Flora, Conference of the Parties, 1st Meeting, Berne, 1976. Proceedings. 554p. 1981. pap. 44.00 (ISBN 0-686-93127-0, IUCN). Unipub.

Converse, Gordon, et al. Fishers of Men: The Way of the Apostles. LC 80-23760. 1980. 14.95 o.p. (ISBN 0-13-319673-9). P-H.

Converse, Jean M. & Schuman, Howard. Conversations at Random: Survey Research As Interviewers See It. LC 73-15840. (Illus.). 121p. 1974. pap. 8.00x (ISBN 0-87944-248-4). Inst Soc Res.

Converse, John M., et al. Symposium on Diagnosis & Treatment of Craniofacial Anomalies, Vol. 20. LC 79-27063. 534p. 1979. text ed. 89.50 (ISBN 0-8016-1030-3). Mosby.

Converse, Philip E., jt. ed. see Campbell, Angus.

Converse, Phillip E., jt. auth. see Campbell, Angus.

Converse, Phillip E., jt. auth. see Cohen, Yaveff.

Conway, Anne. The Conway Letters: Being the Correspondence of Anne, Viscountess Conway, Henry More & Their Friends. Nicolson, M. H., ed. 1930. 65.00x (ISBN 0-685-89745-1). Elliots Bks.

Conway, B. E. Electrochemical Data. LC 69-10078. (Illus.). 1969. Repr. of 1952 ed. lib. bdg. 19.75x (ISBN 0-8371-1630-9, COED). Greenwood.

--Ionic Hydration in Chemistry & Biophysics. (Studies in Physical & Theoretical Chemistry: Vol. 12). Date not set. 125.75 (ISBN 0-444-41947-0). Elsevier.

Conway, Brian E., jt. ed. see Bockris, J. O'M.

Conway, J. B. Functions of One Complex Variable. Halmos, P. R., ed. LC 72-96938. (Lecture Notes in Mathematics: Vol. 11). (Illus.). xiv, 314p. 1973. text ed. 10.70 (ISBN 0-387-07028-1). Springer-Verlag.

Conway, Jill K. Society & the Sexes in Early Industrial America: Part One of a Bibliographical Guide to the Study of the History of American Women. LC 82-48041. 350p. 1982. lib. bdg. 40.00 (ISBN 0-8240-9936-2). Garland Pub.

Conway, Jim. Los Hombres En Su Crisis De Media Vida. Orig. Title: Men in Mid-Life Crisis. 256p. 1982. pap. 4.95 (ISBN 0-311-46088-7). Casa Bautista.

Conway, John, tr. see Baumer, Franz.

Conway, John, tr. see Tank, Kurt L.

Conway, John B. Subnormal Operators. (Research Notes in Mathematics: No. 51). 400p. 1981. pap. text ed. 28.50 (ISBN 0-273-08520-4). Pitman Pub MA.

Conway, Judith. Manos: South American Crafts for Children. LC 78-3228. (Illus.). 1978. lib. bdg. 4.47 (ISBN 0-695-41189-6). Follett.

Conway, Laura. The Undying Past. 1980. 8.95 o.p. (ISBN 0-525-22595-1). Dutton.

Conway, Lorraine. Marine Biology. (gr. 5-8). 1982. 5.95 (ISBN 0-86653-056-8, GA 400). Good Apple.

--Oceanography. (gr. 5-8). 1982. 5.95 (ISBN 0-86653-066-5, GA401). Good Apple.

--Science Graphs & Word Games. (Superific Science Ser.: Bk. V). 48p. (gr. 5-8). 1981. 4.95 (ISBN 0-86653-029-0, GA 257). Good Apple.

Conway, Lynn, jt. auth. see Mead, Carver.

Conway, M. D. Omitted Chapters of History Disclosed in the Life & Papers of Edmund Randolph. LC 73-124041. (American Public Figures Ser). 1971. Repr. of 1888 ed. lib. bdg. 52.50 (ISBN 0-306-70995-3). Da Capo.

Conway, Madeleine & Kirk, Nancy. The Museum of Modern Art Artists' Cookbook. LC 77-82029. (Illus.). 1977. pap. 8.95 o.p. (ISBN 0-87070-219-X). Museum Mod Art.

Conway, Madeleine, jt. auth. see Moss, Lydia.

Conway Maritime Press Ltd., ed. Conway's All the World's Fighting Ships 1947-1982. 480p. 125.00x (ISBN 0-85177-225-0, Pub. by Conway Maritime England). State Mutual Bk.

Conway, Martin R. Outer Banks Guide. Knott, Susan, ed. LC 82-72996. (Illus.). 64p. (Orig.). 1983. pap. 4.50 (ISBN 0-938634-02-X). Carabelle.

Conway, Moncure. Autobiography: Memoirs, & Experiences of Moncure Daniel Conway, 2 Vols. LC 76-87495. (American Public Figures Ser). (Illus.). 1970. Repr. of 1904 ed. lib. bdg. 115.00 (ISBN 0-306-71402-7). Da Capo.

Conway, Patricia, jt. auth. see Jensen, Robert.

Conway, R. S. The Making of Latin: An Introduction to Latin, Greek & English Etymology. 1983. 20.00 (ISBN 0-89241-335-2); pap. 12.50 (ISBN 0-89241-341-7). Caratzas Bros.

Conway, Richard W., et al. Theory of Scheduling. 1967. 26.95 (ISBN 0-201-01189-1). A-W.

Conway, Robert S. Harvard Lectures on the Vergilian Age. LC 67-13861. 1928. 9.00x (ISBN 0-8196-0182-9). Biblo.

Conway, Sally. You & Your Husband's Mid-Life Crisis. 1982. pap. 2.50 (ISBN 0-451-11560-0, AE1560, Sig). NAL.

Conway, Steve. Logging Practices. rev. ed. LC 82-80487. (A Forest Industries Bk.). (Illus.). 432p. 1982. 42.50 (ISBN 0-87930-143-0); pap. 35.00 (ISBN 0-87930-144-9). Miller Freeman.

Conway-Rutkowski, Barbara L. Carini & Owens Neurological & Neurosurgical Nursing. 8th ed. LC 81-14161. (Illus.). 803p. 1982. pap. text ed. 24.95 (ISBN 0-8016-1035-4). Mosby.

Conwell. Acres of Diamonds. (Inspirational Classics Ser.). 64p. 1975. 4.95 (ISBN 0-8007-1141-6); pap. 2.25 (ISBN 0-8007-8091-4, Spire Bks). Revell.

Conwell, E. M., jt. ed. see Epstein, A. J.

Conwell, Russell H. Acres of Diamonds. 1972. pap. 2.25 (V2762). Jove Pubns.

Conybeare, William J. Perversion; or, the Causes & Consequences of Infidelity, 1856. Wolff, Robert L., ed. LC 75-497. (Victorian Fiction Ser.). 1975. lib. bdg. 66.00 o.s.i. (ISBN 0-8240-1572-X). Garland Pub.

Conyers, Diana. An Introduction to Social Planning in the Third World. LC 80-14714. 224p. 1982. 35.95x (ISBN 0-471-10043-9, Pub. by Wiley-Interscience); pap. 14.50 (ISBN 0-471-10044-7). Wiley.

Conyers, James E. & Wallace, Walter L. Black Elected Officials: A Study of Black Americans Holding Governmental Office. LC 74-30881. 208p. 1976. 9.95x (ISBN 0-87154-206-4). Russell Sage.

Conyngham, William J. The Modernization of Soviet Industrial Management: Socio-Economic Development & the Search for Viability. LC 81-21630. (Soviet & East European Studies). (Illus.). 256p. 1982. 34.50 (ISBN 0-521-24381-5). Cambridge U Pr.

Conyngton, Thomas. A Manual of Partnership Relations. LC 6-693. 221p. 1982. Repr. of 1905 ed. lib. bdg. 27.50 (ISBN 0-89941-178-9). W S Hein.

Conze, Edward. Buddhism: Its Essence & Development. pap. 3.95xi o.p. (ISBN 0-06-130058-6, TB 58, Torch). Har-Row.

--Buddhist Meditation. 190p. 1972. pap. 6.95 o.p. (ISBN 0-04-294073-7). Allen Unwin.

--A Short History of Buddhism. 1982. text ed. 10.95x (ISBN 0-04-294109-1); pap. 5.95 (ISBN 0-04-294123-7). Allen Unwin.

Conze, Edward, ed. & tr. The Large Sutra on Perfect Wisdom, with the Divisions of the Abhisamayalankara. LC 71-189224. 1975. 49.00x (ISBN 0-520-02240-8). U of Cal Pr.

Conze, Edward & Lancaster, Lewis, eds. Buddhist Scriptures: A Bibliography. LC 77-83380. (Reference Library of the Humanities: Vol. 113). 161p. 1982. lib. bdg. 21.00 (ISBN 0-8240-9848-X). Garland Pub.

Conze, Edward, tr. from Sanskrit. & pref. by. The Perfection of Wisdom in Eight Thousand Lines & Its Verse Summary. LC 72-76540. (Wheel Ser.: No. 1). 348p. 1973. 12.00 (ISBN 0-87704-048-6); pap. 6.00 (ISBN 0-87704-049-4). Four Seasons Foun.

Conze, Werner. The Shaping of the German Nation: A Historical Analysis. Mellon, Neville, tr. LC 79-5140. 1979. 20.00 (ISBN 0-312-71623-0). St Martin.

Coody, Betty. Using Literature with Young Children. 3rd ed. 220p. 1983. pap. write for info. (ISBN 0-697-06068-3). Wm C Brown.

Coody, Betty F. Using Literature with Young Children. 2nd ed. 200p. 1979. pap. text ed. write for info. o.p. (ISBN 0-697-06211-2); instr. manual avail. o.p. Wm C Brown.

Coogan, Michael D., ed. Stories from Ancient Canaan. LC 77-20022. 1978. softcover 5.95 (ISBN 0-664-24184-0). Westminster.

Coogan, William H. & Woshinsky, Oliver H. The Science of Politics: An Introduction to Hypothesis Formation & Testing. 242p. (Orig.). 1982. lib. bdg. 22.25 (ISBN 0-8191-2652-7); pap. text ed. 10.50 (ISBN 0-8191-2653-5). U Pr of Amer.

Coogler, O. J. Structured Mediation in Divorce Settlements: A Handbook for Marital Mediators. LC 77-15814. 1978. 18.95x (ISBN 0-669-02343-4). Lexington Bks.

Cook. Drawing Cats. (The Grosset Art Instruction Ser.: No. 8). (Illus.). 48p. Date not set. pap. 2.95 (ISBN 0-448-00517-4, G&D). Putnam Pub Group.

--Drawing Dogs. (The Grosset Art Instruction Ser.: No. 10). (Illus.). 48p. Date not set. pap. 2.95 (ISBN 0-448-00519-0, G&D). Putnam Pub Group.

--A Programmed Introduction to In Spectroscopy. 38.00 (ISBN 0-471-25644-7); pap. 29.95 (ISBN 0-471-25643-9). Wiley.

Cook, jt. auth. see Blance.

Cook, jt. auth. see Perard.

Cook, A. H. Celestial Masers. LC 76-14028. (Cambridge Monographs on Physics). (Illus.). 1977. 32.50 (ISBN 0-521-21344-4). Cambridge U Pr.

--Interiors of the Planets. (Cambridge Planetary Science Ser.: No. 1). (Illus.). 360p. 1981. 64.50 (ISBN 0-521-23214-7). Cambridge U Pr.

Cook, A. J. English for Life, Book 1-People & Places: International Edition. 32p. 1981. teachers' guide & cassettes 24.00 (ISBN 0-08-024565-X); pap. 1.95 (ISBN 0-686-77941-X). Pergamon.

Cook, Albert. Adapt the Living. LC 82-75018. viii, 83p. 1980. 12.95x (ISBN 0-8040-0350-5); pap. 6.95 (ISBN 0-8040-0359-9). Swallow.

--Charges. LC 82-70241. 154p. 1970. 10.95 (ISBN 0-8040-0036-0); pap. 5.95 (ISBN 0-8040-0037-9). Swallow.

--Enactment: Greek Tragedy. LC 82-72742. 175p. 1971. 13.95x (ISBN 0-8040-0539-7). Swallow.

--French Tragedy: The Power of Enchantment. LC 82-75737. xvi, 124p. 1981. 14.95x (ISBN 0-8040-0548-6). Swallow.

--Oedipus Rex: A Mirror for Greek Drama. LC 81-71992. 178p. 1982. pap. text ed. 5.50x (ISBN 0-917974-84-0). Waveland Pr.

--Shakespeare's Enactment: The Dynamics of Renaissance Theatre. LC 82-73849. 257p. 1975. 15.00x (ISBN 0-8040-0695-4). Swallow.

Cook, Albert, ed. see Aeschylus & Sophocles.

Cook, Albert, ed. & tr. see Homer.

Cook, Albert M. & Webster, John G., eds. Clinical Engineering: Principles & Practices. (Illus.). 1979. text ed. 35.00 (ISBN 0-13-137737-X). P-H.

--Therapeutic Medical Devices: Application & Design. (Illus.). 656p. 1981. 39.95 (ISBN 0-13-914796-9). P-H.

Cook, Albert S. Biblical Quotations in Old English Prose Writers: Second Series. LC 74-7275. 1903. lib. bdg. 40.00 (ISBN 0-686-96720-8). Folcroft.

--Concordance to Beowulf. LC 68-23146. 1968. Repr. of 1911 ed. 34.00x (ISBN 0-8103-3169-1). Gale.

Cook, Albert S., ed. see Eglamour.

Cook, Alice H. Introduction to Japanese Trade Unionism. LC 66-63380. 228p. 1966. pap. 5.00 (ISBN 0-87546-014-3); pap. 8.00 special hard bdg. (ISBN 0-87546-266-9). ILR Pr.

--The Working Mother: A Survey of Problems & Programs in Nine Countries. 2nd rev. ed. LC 78-620004. 84p. 1978. pap. 4.75 (ISBN 0-87546-067-4). ILR Pr.

Cook, Alice H. & Douty, Agnes M. Labor Education Outside the Unions: A Review of Postwar Programs in Western Europe & the United States. 148p. 1958. pap. 2.00 (ISBN 0-87546-015-1); pap. 5.00 special hard bdg. (ISBN 0-87546-267-7). ILR Pr.

Cook, Alice H. & Hayashi, Hiroko. Working Women in Japan: Discrimination, Resistance, & Reform. LC 80-17706. (Cornell International Industrial & Labor Relations Reports: No. 10). 128p. 1980. 12.50 o.s.i. (ISBN 0-87546-078-X); pap. 7.95 (ISBN 0-87546-079-8). ILR Pr.

Cook, Alicia S. Contemporary Perspectives on Adulthood & Aging. 384p. 1983. text ed. 19.95 (ISBN 0-02-324600-6). Macmillan.

Cook, Alta L., tr. see Tougas, Gerard.

Cook, Andrea, jt. auth. see Cook, Frank.

Cook, B. W. & Jones, K. A Programmed Introduction to Infrared Spectroscopy. 1972. 38.00 (ISBN 0-471-25644-7, Wiley Heyden); pap. 29.95 (ISBN 0-471-25643-9). Wiley.

Cook, Barbara. How to Raise Good Kids. LC 78-7844. 192p. 1978. pap. 3.95 (ISBN 0-87123-233-2, 210233). Bethany Hse.

Cook, Barbara I. Counseling Women. LC 72-1838. (Guidance Monograph). 1973. pap. 2.60 o.p. (ISBN 0-395-14199-0). HM.

Cook, Ben. Legend in Crimson: A Photo History of Alabama Football. Wells, Lawrence, ed. (Illus.). 192p. 1982. 29.95 (ISBN 0-916242-20-X, Pub. by Sports Yearbook Company). Yoknapatawpha.

Cook, Blanche W., ed. Crystal Eastman on Women & Revolution. (Illus.). 1978. 22.50x (ISBN 0-19-502445-1). Oxford U Pr.

--Crystal Eastman on Women & Revolution. 1978. pap. 8.95 (ISBN 0-19-502446-X, GB 556, GB). Oxford U Pr.

Cook, Blanche W., et al. Past Imperfect: Alternative Essays in American History from Colonial Times to the Cold War. 1973. Vols.1 & 2. pap. text ed. 6.95x ea. Phila Bk Co.

Cook, Bob. Speaking in Tongues: Is That All There Is? (Discovery Bks.). 48p. (YA) (gr. 9-12). 1982. pap. text ed. 1.35 (ISBN 0-88243-932-4, 02-0932). Gospel Pub.

Cook, Bridget, jt. auth. see Stott, Geraldine.

Cook, Bruce. The Beat Generation. LC 82-20918. 248p. 1983. Repr. of 1971 ed. lib. bdg. 35.00x (ISBN 0-313-23073-0, COBG). Greenwood.

--Brecht in Exile. LC 82-2926. 240p. 1983. 16.00 (ISBN 0-03-060278-5). HR&W.

Cook, C. Donald, ed. see International Symposium on the Future of Union Catalogue, University of Toronto, May 21-22 1981.

Cook, Catherine E., ed. see Carus, Paul.

Cook, Charles T., ed. see Spurgeon, Charles H. C. H.

Cook, Chris. Sources in British Political History, 1900-1951, Vols. 3 & 4. Incl. Vol. 3. A Guide to the Private Papers of Members of Parliament, A-K. LC 77-71207 (ISBN 0-312-74656-3); Vol. 4. A Guide to the Private Papers of Members of Parliament, L-Z. LC 77-71188 (ISBN 0-312-74657-1). 1977. 25.00x ea. St Martin.

--Sources in British Political History, 1900-1951: A Guide to the Papers of Selected Public Servants. LC 75-15220. 320p. 1975. Vol. 1. 25.00 (ISBN 0-312-74620-2); Vol. 2. 25.00 (ISBN 0-312-74655-5). St Martin.

Cook, Chris & Keith, Brendan. British Historical Facts: 1830-1900. LC 74-76689. 400p. 1975. text ed. 29.95 o.p. (ISBN 0-312-10290-9). St Martin.

Cook, Chris & Killingray, David. African Political Facts Since Nineteen Forty-Five. 256p. 1983. 19.95x (ISBN 0-87196-381-7). Facts on File.

Cook, Chris & Stevenson, John. The Atlas of Modern Warfare. LC 78-50013. (Illus.). 1978. 22.50 o.p. (ISBN 0-399-12173-0). Putnam Pub Group.

Cook, Chris & Weeks, Jeffery. Sources in British Political History 1900-1951: A Guide to the Private Papers of Selected Writers, Intellectuals & Publicists, Vol. 5. LC 75-4012. 1978. 25.00 (ISBN 0-312-74658-X). St Martin.

Cook, Chris, jt. auth. see Powell, Ken.

Cook, Chris & Ramsden, John, eds. Trends in British Politics Since 1945. LC 77-17789. 1978. 22.50x (ISBN 0-312-81754-1). St Martin.

Cook, Chris, jt. ed. see Peele, Gillian.

Cook, Chris, jt. ed. see Pimlott, Ben.

Cook, Chris, jt. ed. see Sked, Alan.

Cook, Christopher. A Short History of the Liberal Party, 1900-1975. 192p. 1976. 19.95x o.p. (ISBN 0-312-72065-3). St Martin.

Cook, Christopher, jt. auth. see McKie, David.

Cook, Clarence. The House Beautiful: Essays on Beds & Tables, Stools & Candlesticks. LC 78-14326. (Illus.). 336p. 1980. Repr. of 1878 ed. 35.00 (ISBN 0-88427-029-7). North River.

Cook, Constance E. Nuclear Power & Legal Advocacy: The Environmentalists & the Courts. LC 79-3277. 176p. 1980. 19.95x (ISBN 0-669-03441-X). Lexington Bks.

Cook, Curtis W., jt. auth. see Basil, Douglas.

Cook, D. B. Ab Initio Valence Calculations in Chemistry. LC 73-15144. 271p. 1974. 46.95x o.s.i. (ISBN 0-470-17000-X). Halsted Pr.

--Structures & Approximations for Electrons in Molecules. LC 77-15665. 295p. 1978. 54.95x o.s.i. (ISBN 0-470-99348-0). Halsted Pr.

Cook, Daniel J., tr. see Leibniz, Gottfried W.

Cook, Daniel W., jt. auth. see Bolton, Brian.

Cook, David. Small World of Ants. LC 80-85049. (Gloucester Press Ser.). (gr. k-3). 1981. PLB 7.90 (ISBN 0-531-03452-6). Watts.

--Small World of Bees & Wasps. LC 80-85050. (Gloucester Press Ser.). (gr. k-3). 1981. PLB 7.90 (ISBN 0-531-03453-4). Watts.

--Small World of Reptiles. LC 80-85052. (Gloucester Press Ser.). (gr. k-3). 1981. PLB 7.90 (ISBN 0-531-03455-0). Watts.

Cook, David, jt. auth. see Pitt, Valerie.

Cook, David M. The Theory of the Electromagnetic Field. (Illus.). 560p. 1975. ref. ed. 30.95 (ISBN 0-13-913293-7). P-H.

Cook, Desmond L. Program Evaluation & Review Technique: Applications in Education. LC 78-57981. 1978. pap. text ed. 6.25 (ISBN 0-8191-0657-7). U Pr of Amer.

Cook, Don. Ten Men & History. LC 80-1062. 528p. 1981. 14.95 o.p. (ISBN 0-385-14908-5). Doubleday.

Cook, Donald. AACR2 Decisions & Rule Interpretations. 480p. 1982. text ed. 50.00 (ISBN 0-8389-3281-9). ALA.

Cook, Donald, jt. ed. see Schimmelpfeng, Richard H.

Cook, Donald J. Elements of Chemistry. 384p. 1974. pap. text ed. 11.95x o.p. (ISBN 0-442-21631-9). Van Nos Reinhold.

Cook, Dorian, tr. see Djilas, Milovan.

Cook, Dorothy E. & Monro, Isabel S., eds. Short Story Index: Basic Volume, 1900-1949. Incl. Supplement 1950-1954. Cook, Dorothy E. & Fidell, Estelle A., eds. 394p. 1956. 15.00 (ISBN 0-686-66648-8); Supplement 1955-1958. Fidell, Estelle A. & Flory, Esther V., eds. 341p. 1960. 15.00 (ISBN 0-686-66649-6); Supplement 1959-1963. Fidell, Estelle A., ed. 487p. 1965. 19.00 (ISBN 0-686-66650-X); Supplement 1964-1968. Fidell, Estelle A., ed. 599p. 1969. 24.00 (ISBN 0-686-66651-8); Supplement 1969-1973. Fidell, Estelle A., ed. 1974. 35.00 (ISBN 0-686-66652-6); Supplement 1974. Bogart, Gary L. & Fidell, Estelle A., eds. 1975. 20.00 o.p. (ISBN 0-686-66653-4); 1976. 20.00 o.p. (ISBN 0-686-66654-2); 1977. 20.00 o.p. (ISBN 0-686-66655-0); Supplement, 1974-1978. Bogart, Gary L., ed. 50.00 (ISBN 0-686-66656-9). 1553p. 1953. 27.00 (ISBN 0-8242-0384-4). Wilson.

Cook, Earl F., ed. Tufflavas & Ignimbrites. 1966. 23.95 (ISBN 0-444-00008-9, North Holland). Elsevier.

Cook, Earleen H. The Insane or Mentally Impaired Defendant: A Selected Bibliography. (Public Administration Ser.). 57p. 1983. pap. 8.25 (ISBN 0-88066-355-3). Vance Biblios.

Cook, Eleanor & Hosek, Chaviva, eds. Centre & Labyrinth: Essays in Honour of Northrop Frye. 328p. 1982. 35.00x (ISBN 0-8020-2496-3). U of Toronto Pr.

Cook, Elizabeth. The Ordinary & the Fabulous. 2nd ed. LC 75-7213. 204p. 1976. 27.95 (ISBN 0-521-20825-4); pap. 9.95 (ISBN 0-521-09961-7). Cambridge U Pr.

Cook, Eugene A., ed. see Texas Attorneys or Professors of Law.

Cook, F., et al. Language Arts Typing. 3rd ed. 1979. text ed. 12.96 (ISBN 0-07-012477-9); tchr's manual & key 7.40 (ISBN 0-07-012479-5). McGraw.

Cook, Francis H. Hua-Yen Buddhism: The Jewel Net of Indra. LC 76-43288. (Institute for Advanced Study of World Religions Ser.). 1977. 16.75x (ISBN 0-271-01245-5). Pa St U Pr.

Cook, Frank & Cook, Andrea. The Casualty Roll For the Crimes 1854-1855. 269p. 1981. 90.00 (ISBN 0-686-98448-X, Pub. by Picton England). State Mutual Bk.

Cook, Fred J. The Crimes of Watergate. LC 81-10497. (Illus.). 192p. (gr. 9 up). 1981. lib. bdg. 9.90 (ISBN 0-686-76378-5). Watts.

--Franklin D. Roosevelt: Valiant Leader. (American Hero Biographies). (Illus.). (gr. 3-5). 1969. PLB 4.49 o.p. (ISBN 0-399-60183-X). Putnam Pub Group.

--The Great Energy Scam: Private Billions vs. Public Good. 256p. 1983. 15.95 (ISBN 0-02-527800-2). Macmillan.

Cook, G. C. & Phipps, Lloyd J. Six Hundred More Things to Make for the Farm & Home. (Illus.). (gr. 9-12). 1952. 19.35 (ISBN 0-8134-0198-4); text ed. 14.50x. Interstate.

Cook, Gary D., ed. see Hardenbrook, Harry.

Cook, Gladys E. Big Book of Cats. (Illus.). (gr. k-3). 1965. 1.50 o.s.i. (ISBN 0-448-00339-2, G&D). Putnam Pub Group.

--Drawing Horses, Dogs & Cats. Duenewald, Doris, ed. LC 78-52824. (Elephant Books Ser.). (Illus.). 1971. pap. 4.95 (ISBN 0-448-16156-7, G&D). Putnam Pub Group.

Cook, Glen. Stars' End. 352p. (Orig.). 1982. pap. 2.95 (ISBN 0-446-30156-6). Warner Bks.

Cook, Glenn C. Five Hundred More Things to Make for Farm & Home. (Illus.). (gr. 9-12). 1944. 19.35 (ISBN 0-8134-0038-4); text ed. 14.50x. Interstate.

Cook, H. C. Manual of Histological Demonstration Techniques. 1974. 19.95 o.p. (ISBN 0-407-74700-1). Butterworth.

Cook, Harriet N. Bible Alphabet of Animals. rev. ed. (Illus.). pap. 4.25 (ISBN 0-686-15488-6). Rod & Staff.

Cook, J. E. & Earlley, Elsie C. Remediating Reading Disabilities: Simple Things That Work. LC 79-20412. 266p. 1979. text ed. 27.00 (ISBN 0-89443-154-4). Aspen Systems.

Cook, James. Explorations of Captain James Cook in the Pacific, as Told by Selections of His Own Journals, 1768-1779. Price, A. Grenfell, ed. (Illus.). pap. 6.00 (ISBN 0-486-22766-9). Dover.

--The Explorations of Captain James Cook in the Pacific as Told by Selections of His Own Journals 1768-1779. Price, A. Grenfell, ed. (Illus.). 10.00 (ISBN 0-8446-4531-1). Peter Smith.

Cook, James, jt. auth. see Wigley, Richard.

Cook, James F. Governors of Georgia. (Illus.). 320p. 1979. 12.95 (ISBN 0-686-83449-6). Strode.

Cook, Jeffrey. The Architecture of Bruce Goff. LC 78-2135. (Icon Editions). (Illus.). 1978. 22.50i o.p. (ISBN 0-06-430950-9, HarpT). Har-Row.

--Award-Winning Passive Solar House Designs. Stetson, Fred, ed. (Illus.). 176p. 1983. pap. 10.95 (ISBN 0-88266-313-5). Garden Way Pub.

Cook, Jeffrey & Prowler, Donald, eds. Passive Systems Seventy-Eight: A Selection of the Leading Passive Solar Papers of the Year Presented at National Solar Conferences in Philadelphia & Denver. 1978. pap. text ed. 27.00x (ISBN 0-89553-016-3). Am Solar Energy.

Cook, Jerry. Amor, Aceptacion y Perdon. Carrodeguas, Andy, et al, eds. Silva, Jose, tr. from Eng. Orig. Title: Love, Acceptance & Forgiveness. 201p. (Span.). 1982. pap. 2.00 (ISBN 0-8297-1121-X). Life Pubs Intl.

Cook, John, ed. School Librarianship. (Illus.). 272p. 1981. 25.00 (ISBN 0-08-024814-4); pap. 16.00 (ISBN 0-08-024813-6). Pergamon.

Cook, John A. & Wool, Robert. All You Need to Know About Banks. 202p. 1983. 13.95 (ISBN 0-553-05025-7). Bantam.

Cook, John P. Composite Construction Methods. LC 76-26020. (Practical Construction Guides Ser.). 1977. 47.95 (ISBN 0-471-16905-6, Pub by Wiley-Interscience). Wiley.

--Construction Sealants & Adhesives. LC 70-121905. (Practical Construction Guides Ser). 1970. 39.50 (ISBN 0-471-16900-5, Pub. by Wiley-Interscience). Wiley.

Cook, John S., ed. Biogenesis & Turnover of Membrane Macromolecules. LC 75-25111. (Society of General Physiologists Ser: Vol. 31). 304p. 1976. 30.00 (ISBN 0-89004-092-3). Raven.

Cook, John W. & Winkle, Gary M. Auditing: Philosophy & Technique. 2nd ed. LC 79-88718. (Illus.). 1980. text ed. 26.95 (ISBN 0-395-28660-3); instr's. manual 3.50; suppl. test bank 1.25 (ISBN 0-395-32067-4). HM.

Cook, Joseph J. Famous Firsts in Basketball. new ed. LC 75-25766. (Famous Firsts Ser.). (Illus.). 64p. (gr. 5-8). 1976. PLB 4.97 o.p. (ISBN 0-399-60976-8). Putnam Pub Group.

--Famous Firsts in Tennis. LC 77-21855. (Famous Firsts Ser.). (Illus.). (gr. 5 up). 1978. PLB 4.49 o.p. (ISBN 0-399-61111-8). Putnam Pub Group.

Cook, Joseph J. & Wisner, William L. Coastal Fishing for Beginners. LC 77-6488. (Illus.). (gr. 5 up). 1977. PLB 5.95 o.p. (ISBN 0-396-07487-1). Dodd.

Cook, Joyce L., jt. auth. see Bull, T. R.

Cook, K. M., tr. see Anikin, A. V.

Cook, Kathleen, et al, trs. see Laurina, Vera & Pushkariov, Vasily.

Cook, Kenneth. Play Little Victims. 1978. text ed. 8.25 (ISBN 0-08-023123-3). Pergamon.

Cook, L., jt. ed. see Gordy, W.

Cook, L. B., jt. auth. see Rhodes, R. S.

Cook, L. M. Coefficients of Natural Selection. 1971. text ed. 7.50x o.p. (ISBN 0-09-104190-2, Hutchinson U Lib); pap. text ed. 7.75x o.p. Humanities.

--Population Genetics: Outline Studies in Biology. 1976. pap. 6.50x (ISBN 0-412-13930-8, Pub. by Chapman & Hall). Methuen Inc.

Cook, Leah, ed. Devotion for Every Day, 183-84. 384p. 1983. pap. 3.95 (ISBN 0-87239-618-5). Standard Pub.

--Devotion for Every Day, 1983-84. large type ed. 384p. 1983. pap. 5.95 (ISBN 0-87239-619-3). Standard Pub.

Cook, Leland. St. Patrick's Cathedral. (Illus.). 160p. 1981. 24.95 (ISBN 0-8256-3169-6, Quick Fox); pap. 9.95 (ISBN 0-8256-3158-0, Quick Fox). Putnam Pub Group.

Cook, Lennox. The Manipulator. LC 78-9353. 1978. 8.95 o.p. (ISBN 0-698-10927-9, Coward). Putnam Pub Group.

Cook, Lloyd A. Intergroup Education. LC 71-100151. Repr. of 1954 ed. lib. bdg. 20.50x (ISBN 0-8371-3397-1, COIE). Greenwood.

Cook, Lyndon W. & Cannon, Donald W. Exodus & Beyond. (Essays in Mormon History Ser.). 264p. Date not set. pap. 7.95 (ISBN 0-89036-151-7). Hawkes Pub Inc.

Cook, Lyndon W., jt. ed. see Cannon, Donald Q.

Cook, M., jt. auth. see Argyle, M.

Cook, M., jt. auth. see Crone, Patricia.

Cook, M. A., ed. The History of the Ottoman Empire Seventeen Thirty. LC 75-38188. (Illus.). 232p. 1976. 39.50 (ISBN 0-521-20891-2); pap. 12.95 (ISBN 0-521-09991-9). Cambridge U Pr.

Cook, Malcolm. Soccer Coaching & Team Management. (Illus.). 160p. (Orig.). 1983. pap. 7.95 (ISBN 0-7158-0795-1, Pub. by EP Publishing England). Sterling.

Cook, Marcy. Codecracker I. (gr. 3-6). 1982. 8.50 (ISBN 0-88488-235-7). Creative Pubns.

--Codecracker II. (gr. 4-8). 1982. 8.50 (ISBN 0-88488-236-5). Creative Pubns.

--Codecracker Two. (gr. 4-8). 1982. 8.50 (ISBN 0-88488-236-5). Creative Pubns.

--Think About It: Language Arts Problems of the Day. (gr. 4-8). 1981. 8.50 (ISBN 0-88488-234-9). Creative Pubns.

--Think About It: Mathematics Problems of the Day. (gr. 4-8). 1981. 8.50 (ISBN 0-88488-233-0). Creative Pubns.

Cook, Margaret G. New Library Key. 3rd ed. 264p. 1975. pap. 7.00 (ISBN 0-8242-0541-3). Wilson.

Cook, Marjorie. To Walk on Two Feet. LC 77-17369. 1978. 8.95 (ISBN 0-664-32628-5). Westminster.

Cook, Melva, jt. auth. see Brown, Richard.

Cook, Melva, jt. auth. see Hinkle, Joseph.

Cook, Mercer & Henderson, Stephen E. Militant Black Writer in Africa & the United States. LC 69-17324. 150p. 1969. pap. 6.95 (ISBN 0-299-05394-6). U of Wis Pr.

Cook, Mercer, ed. & tr. see Diop, Cheikh A.

Cook, Myra, jt. auth. see Piechowiak, Ann.

Cook, P. A., jt. ed. see Bell, D. J.

Cook, Patsy A., ed. Directory of Oral History Programs in the United States. 138p. 59.95 (ISBN 0-667-00680-X). Microfilming Corp.

Cook, Paul H. Tintagel. 224p. (Orig.). 1981. pap. 2.25 o.p. (ISBN 0-425-05055-6). Berkley Pub.

Cook, Paul J. Estimating for the General Contractor. 225p. 1982. text ed. 32.00 (ISBN 0-911950-48-6); pap. 27.50 (ISBN 0-911950-49-4). Means.

Cook, Peter & Webb, Barbara, eds. The Complete Book of Sailing. LC 76-19620. (Illus.). 1977. 19.00 (ISBN 0-385-11531-8). Doubleday.

Cook, Peter D. Start & Run Your Own Succussful Business: An Entrepreneur's Guide. LC 82-4336. 256p. 1982. 14.95 (ISBN 0-8253-0107-6). Beaufort Bks NY.

Cook, Philip J. & Lambert, Richard D., eds. Gun Control. (The Annals of the American Academy of Political & Social Science Ser.: No. 455). 250p. 1981. 7.50x o.p. (ISBN 0-87761-262-5); pap. 7.95x (ISBN 0-87761-263-3). Am Acad Pol Soc Sci.

Cook, R. D. & Weisberg, S. Residuals & Influence in Regression. (Monographs on Statistics & Applied Probability). 1982. 25.00x (ISBN 0-412-24280-X, Pub. by Chapman & Hall). Methuen Inc.

Cook, R. J., jt. auth. see Baker, K. F.

Cook, R. M. Greek Art. (Illus.). 222p. 1973. 12.95 o.p. (ISBN 0-374-16670-6). FS&G.

Cook, Ramona G. Aeolus Drives. LC 71-75354. 1969. 4.00 o.p. (ISBN 0-8233-0129-X). Golden Quill.

Cook, Ramsay & Mitchinson, Wendy, eds. The Proper Sphere: Woman's Place in Canadian Society. 1976. pap. 8.95x o.p. (ISBN 0-19-540272-3). Oxford U Pr.

Cook, Ray L. Soil Management for Conservation & Production. LC 62-8770. (Illus.). 527p. 1962. 30.95 (ISBN 0-471-16995-1). Wiley.

Cook, Reginald L. Robert Frost: A Living Voice. LC 74-78982. (New England Writers Ser.). 360p. 1974. 15.00x (ISBN 0-87023-165-0). U of Mass Pr.

Cook, Richard I. Bernard Mandeville. (English Authors Ser.). 1974. lib. bdg. 13.95 (ISBN 0-8057-1371-9, Twayne). G K Hall.

--Sir Samuel Garth. (English Authors Ser.). 1980. lib. bdg. 14.95 (ISBN 0-8057-6775-4, Twayne). G K Hall.

Cook, Richard J. Rails Across the Midlands. 2nd ed. LC 64-16409. (Illus.). 1968. 16.95 o.p. (ISBN 0-87095-018-5). Golden West.

Cook, Richard J. & Gardi, Gavin L. How to Design & Build Thermosiphoning Air Panels. iv, 36p. (Orig.). pap. 2.00 (ISBN 0-939294-13-3). Beach Leaf.

Cook, Richard M. Carson McCullers. LC 75-2789. (Modern Literature Ser.). 160p. 1975. 11.95 (ISBN 0-8044-2128-5). Ungar.

Cook, Robert A. Ahora Que Creo: Now That I Believe. (Bk, Span). 1957. pap. 2.95 (ISBN 0-8024-0120-1); pap. 4.95 package of 10. Moody.

--Now That I Believe. 1956. pap. 2.95 (ISBN 0-8024-5982-X). Moody.

Cook, Robert A., jt. auth. see Georgopoulos, Basil S.

Cook, Robert C. Human Fertility: The Modern Dilemma. LC 72-156185. 1971. Repr. of 1951 ed. lib. bdg. 18.75x (ISBN 0-8371-6128-2, COHU). Greenwood.

Cook, Robert D. Concepts & Applications of Finite Element Analysis. 2nd ed. LC 80-26255. 537p. 1981. text ed. 42.95 (ISBN 0-471-03050-3); 30.00 (ISBN 0-471-08200-7). Wiley.

--Concepts & Applications of Finite Element Analysis. A Textbook for Beginning Courses in the Finite Method As Used for the Analysis of Displacement, Strain & Stress. LC 74-7053. 402p. 1974. text ed. 34.95x o.p. (ISBN 0-471-16915-3). Wiley.

Cook, Robert S., Jr. Zoning for Downtown Urban Design: How Cities Control Development. LC 79-48033. 1980. 21.95x (ISBN 0-669-03642-0). Lexington Bks.

Cook, Robin. Brain. 320p. 1980. 11.95 (ISBN 0-399-12563-9). Putnam Pub Group.

--Coma. (RL 7). 1977. pap. 3.50 (ISBN 0-451-11852-9, AE1852, Sig). NAL.

--Fever. 288p. 1982. 13.95 (ISBN 0-399-12637-6). Putnam Pub Group.

--Fever. 1983. pap. 3.95 (ISBN 0-686-84405-X, Sig). NAL.

--Sphinx. (General Ser.). 1979. lib. bdg. 14.95 (ISBN 0-8161-3014-0, Large Print Bks). G K Hall.

--Sphinx. 1980. pap. 3.50 (ISBN 0-451-12219-4, AE2219, Sig). NAL.

--Sphinx. LC 79-1071. 1979. 10.95 (ISBN 0-399-12328-8). Putnam Pub Group.

--Sphinx: Movie Edition. 1981. pap. 2.95 o.p. (ISBN 0-451-09745-9, E9745, Sig). NAL.

Cook, Samuel F. Drummond Island: The Story of the British Occupation 1815-1828. LC 73-90803. (Illus.). 124p. (YA) 1974. pap. 4.50 o.p. (ISBN 0-912382-14-7). Black Letter.

Cook, Scott. Zapotec Stoneworkers: The Dynamics of Rural Simple Commodity Production in Modern Mexican Capitalism. LC 81-40584. (Illus.). 454p. (Orig.). 1982. lib. bdg. 28.50 (ISBN 0-8191-2419-2); pap. text ed. 16.25 (ISBN 0-8191-2420-6). U Pr of Amer.

Cook, Sherburne F. The Conflict Between the California Indian & White Civilization. LC 75-23860. 1976. 46.50x (ISBN 0-520-03142-3); pap. 6.95 (ISBN 0-520-03143-1, CAL332). U of Cal Pr.

--The Population of the California Indians 1769-1970. LC 74-27287. 1976. 28.50x (ISBN 0-520-02923-2). U of Cal Pr.

Cook, Sherburne F. & Borah, Woodrow. Essays in Population History, 3 vols. Incl. Vols. 1 & 2. Mexico & the Caribbean. 1971. 39.00x ea. Vol. 1 (ISBN 0-520-01764-1). Vol. 2 (ISBN 0-520-02272-6); Vol. 3. Mexico & California. 1979. 36.50x (ISBN 0-520-03560-7). U of Cal Pr.

Cook, Stanley, jt. auth. see Whaley, Stephen.

Cook, Stanley J. & Suter, Richard W. The Scope of Grammar: A Study of Modern English. Talkington, William A., ed. (Illus.). 1980. text ed. 19.50x (ISBN 0-07-012460-4). McGraw.

Cook, Stephani & Lumiere, Richard. Healthy Sex...& Keeping it That Way. (Orig.). 1983. 13.50 (ISBN 0-671-45493-5); pap. 6.25 (ISBN 0-671-45899-X). S&S.

Cook, Sterling & Southard, Edna C. Anette Covington: Paintings & Drawings. LC 82-82113. 50p. (Orig.). 1982. pap. 5.00 o.p. (ISBN 0-686-97736-X). Miami Univ Art.

--Annette Covington: Paintings & Drawings. LC 82-82113. (Illus.). 50p. (Orig.). 1982. pap. 5.00 (ISBN 0-940784-02-5). Miami Univ Art.

Cook, Susannah. A Closer Look at Bears & Pandas. LC 76-27970. (Closer Look at Ser.). (Illus.). (gr. 8 up). 1979. pap. 1.95 (ISBN 0-531-03448-8). Watts.

Cook, Thomas & Campbell, Donald T. Quasi-Experimentation. 1979. pap. 18.95 (ISBN 0-395-30790-2). HM.

Cook, Thomas, jt. ed. see Scioli, Frank.

Cook, Thomas D., et al. Sesame Street Revisited. LC 74-25853. 420p. 1975. 15.00x (ISBN 0-87154-207-2). Russell Sage.

Cook, Thomas J., jt. auth. see Scioli, Frank P.

Cook, Thomas M. & Russell, Robert A. Introduction to Management Science. 2nd ed. (Illus.). 640p. 1981. text ed. 26.95 (ISBN 0-13-486092-6); study guide 10.95 (ISBN 0-13-486118-3). P-H.

Cook, Tim. Vagrant Alcoholics. 1975. 20.00x (ISBN 0-7100-8118-9). Routledge & Kegan.

Cook, V. J. English for Life: Meeting People, Bk. 2. (Illus.). 160p. 1982. pap. 4.95 (ISBN 0-08-024608-7); pap. 2.95 Student's Bk. (ISBN 0-08-025306-7, S100). Pergamon.

--English for Life, Vol. I: People & Places. (Illus.). 144p. 1980. pap. 4.50 (ISBN 0-08-024564-1, S110); wkbk. 2.95 (ISBN 0-08-027231-2). Pergamon.

Cook, V. J. & Esnol, A. English for Life Book I Francophone: Livre de l'eleve. (Pergamon Institute of English Courses Ser.). (Illus.). 151p. 1983. pap. 5.95 (ISBN 0-08-024580-3). Pergamon.

Cook, V. J., et al. English for Life Book I Francophone Teachers' Guide: Guide du Professeur. (Pergamon Institute of English Courses Ser.). 64p. 1983. pap. 2.95 (ISBN 0-08-024582-X). Pergamon.

Cook, W. D. & Kuhn, W. D. Planning Processes in Developing Countries: Techniques & Achievements. (TIMS Studies in the Management Sciences: Vol. 17). 1982. 64.00 (ISBN 0-444-86344-3, North Holland). Elsevier.

Cook, W. Robert. The Theology of John. LC 79-10261. 1979. 11.95 (ISBN 0-8024-8629-0). Moody.

Cook, Whitfield. Taxi to Dubrovnik. 320p. 1981. 12.95 o.s.i. (ISBN 0-440-08693-0). Delacorte.

Cook, William A. Natural Childbirth: Fact & Fallacy. LC 81-19021. 216p. 1982. text ed. 16.95 (ISBN 0-88229-655-8). Nelson-Hall.

Cook, William J., Jr. Security Systems: Considerations, Layout, Performance. Date not set. pap. 9.95 (ISBN 0-672-21949-2). Sams.

Cook, William R. & Herzman, Ronald B. The Medieval World View: An Introduction. (Illus.). 320p. 1982. 14.95x (ISBN 0-19-503089-3); pap. 6.95x (ISBN 0-19-503090-7). Oxford U Pr.

Cookbook Committee of Lutheran General Hospital. Cooking in General. 350p. 1978. 10.00 (ISBN 0-686-82545-4). Serv League IL.

Cooke, Alan, ed. see Universite Laval,Centre d'Etudes Nordiques, Quebec.

Cooke, Alistair. Alistair Cooke's America. 1973. 30.50 (ISBN 0-394-48726-5). Knopf.

--A Generation on Trial: U. S. A. vs Alger Hiss. LC 82-11870. 371p. 1982. Repr. of 1968 ed. lib. bdg. 35.00x (ISBN 0-313-23373-X, COGE). Greenwood.

--Six Men. 1978. pap. 2.75 (ISBN 0-425-04689-3, Dist. by Putnam). Berkley Pub.

Cooke, Alistair, ed. see Mencken, Henry L.

Cooke, Ann. Giraffes at Home. LC 79-158686. (A Let's-Read-&-Find-Out Science Bk.). (Illus.). (gr. k-3). 1972. 10.53i (ISBN 0-690-33082-0, TYC-J); PLB 10.89 (ISBN 0-690-33083-9). Har-Row.

Cooke, Ann & Cooke, Frank. Cooking with Music. (Illus.). 150p. 1983. pap. 12.95 (ISBN 0-940076-01-2); cassette 6.95. Fiesta City.

Cooke, Arthur L., ed. see Stroup, Thomas B.

Cooke, Bernard. Sacraments & Sacramentality. 240p. 1983. pap. 7.95 (ISBN 0-89622-161-X). Twenty-Third.

Cooke, Bernard J. Beyond Trinity. 1969. 7.95 (ISBN 0-87462-134-8). Marquette.

Cooke, Brian. The Fall & Rise of Steam. (Illus.). 128p. 1982. 22.95 (ISBN 0-86720-623-3). Sci Bks IntL.

Cooke, Clarence M. Our Daily Life: An Oregon Civics. (Illus.). 1946. text ed. 7.95 (ISBN 0-8323-0166-3). Binford.

Cooke, D. & Craven, A. H. Basic Statistical Computing. 176p. 1982. pap. text ed. 13.95 (ISBN 0-7131-3441-0). E Arnold.

Cooke, D., jt. auth. see Clarke, G. M.

Cooke, David C. Bomber Planes That Made History. (Illus.). (gr. 4-6). 1959. PLB 4.49 o.p. (ISBN 0-399-60064-7). Putnam Pub Group.

--Famous U. S. Air Force Bombers. LC 72-5947. (Illus.). 64p. (gr. 5 up). 1973. 6.95 (ISBN 0-396-06695-X). Dodd.

--Fighter Planes That Made History. (Illus.). (gr. 4-8). 1958. PLB 5.49 o.p. (ISBN 0-399-60166-X). Putnam Pub Group.

--Inventions That Made History. LC 68-24508. (Illus.). (gr. 5 up). 1969. PLB 4.89 o.p. (ISBN 0-399-60302-6). Putnam Pub Group.

--Racing Cars That Made History. (Illus.). (gr. 5-9). 1960. PLB 4.49 o.p. (ISBN 0-399-60529-0). Putnam Pub Group.

--The Tribal People of Thailand. (Illus.). (gr. 5-9). 1972. PLB 4.39 o.p. (ISBN 0-399-60740-4). Putnam Pub Group.

Cooke, Deryck. Gustav Mahler: An Introduction to His Music. 1980. 22.95 (ISBN 0-521-23175-2); pap. 6.95 (ISBN 0-521-29847-4). Cambridge U Pr.

--I Saw the World End: A Study of Wagner's Ring. 1979. 22.50 (ISBN 0-19-315316-5). Oxford U Pr.

--Vindications: Essays on Romantic Music. LC 82-4295. 160p. 1982. 24.95 (ISBN 0-521-24765-9); pap. 7.95 (ISBN 0-521-28947-5). Cambridge U Pr.

Cooke, Donald E. Presidents in Uniform. LC 69-14455. (Illus.). (gr. 6-9). 1969. PLB 8.95 o.s.i. (ISBN 0-8038-5746-2). Hastings.

Cooke, E. M. Clinical Microbiology for Medical Students. Gibson, G. L., ed. 1983. 18.95 (ISBN 0-471-90017-6, Pub. by Wiley Med). Wiley.

Cooke, Edward F. & Janosik, G. Edward. Guide to Pennsylvania Politics. LC 79-14132. (Illus.). 1980. Repr. of 1957 ed. lib. bdg. 17.25x (ISBN 0-313-21994-X, COGP). Greenwood.

Cooke, F. W., et al. Materials for Reconstructive Surgery, Vol. 9, No. 4. 292p. 1975. 18.00 (ISBN 0-471-17025-9, Pub. by JW). Krieger.

Cooke, Frank, jt. auth. see Cooke, Ann.

Cooke, Frank E. Kids Can Write Songs, Too. (Illus.). 120p. 1983. pap. 7.95 (ISBN 0-940076-02-0). Fiesta City.

Cooke, Fred J. Ku Klux Klan: America's Recurring Nightmare. LC 80-19325. (Illus.). 160p. (YA) (gr. 7 up). 1981. PLB 9.29 o.p. (ISBN 0-671-34055-7). Messner.

Cooke, G. W. Fertilizing for Maximum Yield. 3rd ed. 320p. 1982. 8.95. Macmillian.

--Fertilizing for Maximum Yield. 3rd ed. 473p. 1982. 32.50 (ISBN 0-02-949310-2). Free Pr.

Cooke, Gary. Butterfish & Other Poems. (Flowering Quince Poetry Ser.: No. 2). (Illus.). 24p. (Orig.). 1978. pap. 4.00 (ISBN 0-940592-03-7). Heyeck Pr.

Cooke, George W. John Sullivan Dwight: A Biography. LC 79-90210. (Music Reprint Ser). 1969. Repr. of 1898 ed. 32.50 (ISBN 0-306-71818-9). Da Capo.

Cooke, Gillian. A Celebration of Christmas. (Illus.). 176p. 1980. 16.95 (ISBN 0-399-12525-6). Putnam Pub Group.

Cooke, Hope, jt. auth. see D'Amboise, Jaques.

Cooke, Jacqueline, jt. auth. see Travers, Robert M.

Cooke, James J., ed. see French Colonial Historical Society.

Cooke, James J., ed. see French Colonial Historical Society, 5th Meeting.

Cooke, James J., jt. ed. see Heggoy, Alf A.

Cooke, John. George Bernanos: A Study of Christian Commitment. 1981. 30.00x o.p. (ISBN 0-86127-202-1, Pub. by Avebury Pub England). State Mutual Bk.

--Georges Bernanos: A Study of Christian Commitment. 1981. 50.00x o.p. (ISBN 0-86127-202-1, Pub. by Avebury Pub England). State Mutual Bk.

Cooke, John, jt. auth. see Bernard, George.

Cooke, John, jt. auth. see Nichols, David.

Cooke, K. L., ed. see SIMS Conference on Epidemiology, Alta, UT, July 8-12, 1974.

Cooke, Marcus & Dennis, Anthony J., eds. Polynuclear Aromatic Hydrocarbons: Physical & Biological Chemistry. (International Symposium on Polynuclear Aromatic Hydrocarbons, Sixth). 1982. 65.00 (ISBN 0-935470-13-1). Battelle.

Cooke, Michael. The Ancient Curse of the Baskervilles. LC 82-83499. 96p. pap. 4.95 (ISBN 0-934468-14-1). Gaslight.

Cooke, Nelson M. & Adams, Herbert F. Arithmetic Review for Electronics. 1968. 17.95 (ISBN 0-07-012516-3, G); answers to review problems 1.00 (ISBN 0-07-012517-1). McGraw.

--Basic Mathematics for Electronics. 4th ed. (Illus.). 1976. text ed. 23.95 (ISBN 0-07-012512-0, G); study guide 11.95 (ISBN 0-07-000305-X). McGraw.

Cooke, Nelson M., et al. Basic Mathematics for Electronics. 5th ed. LC 82-226. (Illus.). 688p. 1982. 23.95x (ISBN 0-07-012514-7). McGraw.

Cooke, Peter N. Energy Saving in Distribution. 262p. 1981. text ed. 54.00x (ISBN 0-566-02155-2). Gower Pub Ltd.

--Inflation Management in Motor Transport Operations. 192p. 1978. text ed. 30.25x (ISBN 0-566-02056-4). Gower Pub Ltd.

Cooke, Robert, jt. auth. see Rosenfeld, Charles.

Cooke, Roderic. The Biology of Symbiotic Fungi. LC 76-56175. 1977. 45.95x (ISBN 0-471-99467-7, Pub. by Wiley-Interscience). Wiley.

Cooke, Ronald U. & Doornkamp, John C. Geomorphology in Environmental Management: An Introduction. (Illus.). 1974. text ed. 29.50x o.p. (ISBN 0-19-874020-4); pap. text ed. 15.95x (ISBN 0-19-874021-2). Oxford U Pr.

Cooke, Ronald U. & Warren, Andrew. Geomorphology in Deserts. 1974. 35.00x (ISBN 0-520-02280-7). U of Cal Pr.

Cooke, Thomas D., ed. The Present State of Scholarship in Fourteen Century Literature. (Illus.). 304p. 1983. 23.80 (ISBN 0-8262-0379-5). U of MO Pr.

Cooke-Macgregor, Francis. After Plastic Surgery: Adaption & Adjustment. 160p. 1979. 19.95x (ISBN 0-686-84385-1). J F Bergin.

Cook-Gumperz, Jenny. Social Control & Socialization: A Study of Class Differences in the Language of Maternal Control. (Primary Socialization, Language & Education Ser.). 300p. 1973. 24.95x (ISBN 0-7100-7409-3). Routledge & Kegan.

Cookman, jt. auth. see Teacher.

Cookridge, E. H. The Orient Express: The Life & Times of the World's Most Famous Train. LC 78-57119. (Illus.). 1980. pap. 6.95i (ISBN 0-06-090770-3, CN 770, CN). Har-Row.

Cooks, R. G., et al. Metastable Ions. LC 72-97419. 312p. 1973. 61.75 (ISBN 0-444-41119-4). Elsevier.

Cookson, Arthur. From Harrow to Hawk. 1978. 6.95 o.p. (ISBN 0-533-03213-X). Vantage.

Cookson, Catherine. Color Blind. 1977. pap. 1.75 (ISBN 0-451-07394-0, E7394, Sig). NAL.

--Dwelling Place. LC 78-142476. 1971. 6.95 o.p. (ISBN 0-672-51525-3). Bobbs.

--The Gambling Man. LC 75-12578. 288p. 1975. 7.95 o.p. (ISBN 0-688-02948-5). Morrow.

--The Garment. 1974. pap. 1.50 o.p. (ISBN 0-451-06481-X, W6481, Sig). NAL.

--Nipper. LC 73-159017. (gr. 5-9). 1971. 3.95 o.p. (ISBN 0-672-51577-6). Bobbs.

--The Tide of Life. 288p. 1976. 8.95 o.p. (ISBN 0-688-03032-7). Morrow.

--The Whip. 384p. 1983. 14.95 (ISBN 0-686-37591-2). Summit Bks.

Cookson, R. F., jt. auth. see Chesseman, G. W.

Coole, Arthur B. Coins in China's History. 4th ed. (Illus.). 1965. 25.00 (ISBN 0-912706-01-5). Akers.

--A Trouble Shooter for God in China. (Illus.). 1976. 20.00 (ISBN 0-912706-05-8). Akers.

Coole, Arthur B., et al. Encyclopedia of Chinese Coins, Vol. 1, Bibliography Of Far Eastern Numismatology & A Coin Index. (Illus.). 1967. 35.00 (ISBN 0-912706-04-X). Akers.

Coolen, jt. auth. see Roddy.

Cooley, Charles H. Human Nature & the Social Order. (Social Science Classics Ser.). (Illus.). 482p. 1983. 19.95 (ISBN 0-87855-918-3). Transaction Bks.

--Social Organization: A Study of the Larger Mind. (Social Science Classics Ser.). 457p. 1983. pap. 19.95 (ISBN 0-87855-824-1). Transaction Bks.

Cooley, Leland. The Dancer. 1979. pap. 2.75 o.p. (ISBN 0-451-08651-1, E8651, Sig). NAL.

Cooley, Marcia & Shaffer, Carol. Fundamentals of Nursing for Human Needs. 1982. text ed. 17.95 (ISBN 0-8359-2175-1); instrs'. manual avail. (ISBN 0-8359-2176-X). Reston.

--Nursing Skills for Human Needs. 1982. pap. text ed. 11.95 (ISBN 0-8359-5038-7). instructor's manual o.p. avail. (ISBN 0-8359-2176-X). Reston.

Cooley, Peter, jt. auth. see Bennett, John.

Cooley, Robert N. & Schreiber, Melvyn H. Radiology of the Heart & Great Vessels. 3rd ed. (Golden's Diagnostic Radiology Ser: Section 4). (Illus.). 676p. 1978. 78.00 (ISBN 0-683-02103-6). Williams & Wilkins.

Cooley, Stella G., jt. auth. see Jensen, Joyce D.

Cooley, Susan D. Country Walks in Connecticut: A Guide to the Nature Conservancy Preserves. (Illus.). 224p. (Orig.). 1982. pap. 6.95 (ISBN 0-910146-41-1). Appalach Mtn.

Cooley, Thomas, ed. The Norton Sampler: Short Essays for Composition. 2nd ed. (gr. 12). 1981. pap. text ed. 8.95x (ISBN 0-393-95179-0); write for info. instrs'. hdbk. (ISBN 0-393-95183-9). Norton.

Cooley, Thomas M. A Treatise on the Constitutional Limitations. LC 78-87510. (American Constitutional & Legal History Ser). 720p. 1972. Repr. of 1868 ed. lib. bdg. 75.00 (ISBN 0-306-71403-5). Da Capo.

Cooley, W. C., ed. see Smoldyrev, A. Ye.

Cooley, William W. & Lohnes, Paul R. Multivariate Data Analysis. LC 70-127661. (Illus.). 364p. 1971. 28.95 (ISBN 0-471-17060-7). Wiley.

Coolidge, Archibald C., jt. auth. see Channing, Edward.

Coolidge, Charles E. Zig-Zag. 1983. 6.95 (ISBN 0-686-84429-7). Vantage.

Coolidge, Dane. Gringo Gold. (Western Fiction Ser.). 1981. lib. bdg. cancelled o.s.i. (ISBN 0-8398-2679-6, Gregg). G K Hall.

Coolidge, Julian L. Treatise on Algebraic Plane Curves. (Illus.). 1959. pap. 5.00 o.p. (ISBN 0-486-60543-4). Dover.

--Treatise on the Circle & the Sphere. LC 78-128872. 1971. text ed. 27.50 (ISBN 0-8284-0236-1). Chelsea Pub.

Coolidge, Susan. What Katy Did. 1983. pap. 1.95 (ISBN 0-14-035011-X, Puffin). Penguin.

Cooling, B. Franklin. War, Business, & American Society: Historical Perspectives on the Military-Industrial Complex. LC 76-18163. (National University Pubns. Ser. in American Studies). 1977. 19.50 (ISBN 0-8046-9156-8). Kennikat.

Cooling, W. Colebrook. Arbitration Presentation: Box Seat at a Labor Management Dispute. 1978. manual 22.00 (ISBN 0-89806-006-0, 122); members 11.00; play package 90.00 (ISBN 0-89806-008-7, 152); members 45.00. Inst Indus Eng.

--Simplified Low-Cost Maintenance Control. rev. ed. 128p. 1983. 24.95 (ISBN 0-8144-5657-X). Am Mgmt Assns.

Coolman, Anne L., ed. see Mitchell, Susan.

Coomaraswamy, Ananda K. The Arts & Crafts of India & Ceylon. (Illus.). 259p. 1964. 7.95 o.p. (ISBN 0-374-10616-9); pap. 2.95 o.p. (ISBN 0-374-50340-0). FS&G.

--Christian & Oriental Philosophy of Art. 1957. pap. 3.00 (ISBN 0-486-20378-6). Dover.

--The History of Indian & Indonesian Art. (Illus.). pap. 6.00 o.s.i. (ISBN 0-486-21436-2). Dover.

--Spiritual Authority & Temporal Power in the Indian Theory of Government. 1942. pap. 10.00 (ISBN 0-527-02696-4). Kraus Repr.

--Transformation of Nature in Art. 1937. pap. 4.95 (ISBN 0-486-20368-9). Dover.

Coomaraswamy, Ananda K. & Nivedita, Sr. Myths of the Hindus & Buddhists. (Illus.). (gr. 4-8). pap. 5.50 (ISBN 0-486-21759-0). Dover.

Coombes, David, ed. The Power of the Purse: A Symposium on the Role of European Parliaments in Budgetary Decisions. LC 75-23959. (Illus.). 394p. 1976. text ed. 30.95 o.p. (ISBN 0-275-05790-9). Praeger.

Coombes, John. Capital Transfer Tax. 90.00 (ISBN 0-903486-25-3, Pub. by Prof Bks England). State Mutual Bk.

Coombs, A. J. & Madgic, R. F. Variable Modular Scheduling. 1972. pap. 4.00 o.p. (ISBN 0-02-640800-7, 64080). Glencoe.

Coombs, C. A. The Arena of International Finance. 243p. 1976. 28.95 o.p. (ISBN 0-471-01513-X, Pub. by Wiley-Interscience). Wiley.

Coombs, Charles. Auto Racing. LC 73-153770. (Illus.). (gr. 5-9). 1971. 9.95 (ISBN 0-688-21053-8); PLB 8.59 (ISBN 0-688-31053-2). Morrow.

--Be a Winner in Baseball. (Illus.). 128p. (gr. 5-9). 1973. PLB 9.12 (ISBN 0-688-30093-6). Morrow.

--Be a Winner in Basketball. LC 75-17778. (Illus.). 128p. (gr. 5-9). 1975. PLB 9.12 (ISBN 0-688-32039-2); pap. 2.45 (ISBN 0-688-27039-5). Morrow.

--Be a Winner in Horsemanship. LC 76-17118. (Illus.). 128p. (gr. 5-9). 1976. 8.95 (ISBN 0-688-22080-0); PLB 8.59 (ISBN 0-688-32080-5). Morrow.

--Be a Winner in Ice Hockey. LC 73-10769. (Illus.). 128p. (gr. 5-9). 1974. PLB 9.12 (ISBN 0-688-30099-5); pap. 2.45 (ISBN 0-688-25099-8). Morrow.

--Bicycling. (Illus.). (gr. 5-9). 1972. 9.50 (ISBN 0-688-20032-X); PLB 6.95 o.s.i. (ISBN 0-688-30032-4). Morrow.

--Coal in the Energy Crisis. LC 80-13701. (Illus.). 128p. (gr. 4-6). 1980. 8.75 (ISBN 0-688-22239-0); PLB 8.40 (ISBN 0-688-32239-5). Morrow.

--Drag Racing. (Illus.). (gr. 5-9). 1970. PLB 8.59 (ISBN 0-688-31243-8). Morrow.

--Hot-Air Ballooning. LC 80-26704. (Illus.). 128p. (gr. 4-6). 1981. 8.95 (ISBN 0-688-00364-8); PLB 8.59 (ISBN 0-688-00365-6). Morrow.

--Mopeding. (Illus.). (gr. 4-6). 1978. 8.75 (ISBN 0-688-22155-6); PLB 8.40 (ISBN 0-688-32155-0). Morrow.

--Motorcycling. LC 68-23911. (gr. 5-9). 1968. PLB 8.95 (ISBN 0-688-21564-5); pap. 8.59 (ISBN 0-688-31564-X). Morrow.

--Passage to Space: The Shuttle Transportation System. LC 79-1176. (Illus.). (gr. 4-6). 1979. 9.25 (ISBN 0-688-22188-2); PLB 8.88 (ISBN 0-688-32188-7). Morrow.

--Pipeline Across Alaska. LC 77-28986. (Illus.). (gr. 5-9). 1978. 8.25 (ISBN 0-688-22139-4); PLB 7.92 (ISBN 0-688-32139-9). Morrow.

--Skylab. LC 79-168471. (Illus.). (gr. 5-9). 1972. PLB 8.59 (ISBN 0-688-31812-6). Morrow.

--Tankers, Giants of the Sea. LC 79-9376. (Illus.). 128p. (gr. 4-6). 1979. 8.75 (ISBN 0-688-22205-6); PLB 8.40 (ISBN 0-688-32205-0). Morrow.

Coombs, Charles I. Be a Winner in Skiing. LC 77-2621. (gr. 5-9). 1977. 8.95 (ISBN 0-688-22131-9); PLB 8.59 (ISBN 0-688-32131-3). Morrow.

Coombs, Clyde, et al. Mathematical Psychology: An Elementary Introduction. 1969. text ed. 23.95 o.p. (ISBN 0-13-562157-7). P-H.

Coombs, Clyde F. Printed Circuits Handbook. 1979. 42.50 (ISBN 0-07-012608-9, P&RB). McGraw.

Coombs, Clyde F., Jr. Basic Electronic Instrument Handbook. LC 72-1394. (Handbook Ser.). (Illus.). 832p. 1972. 49.50 (ISBN 0-07-012615-1, P&RB). McGraw.

Coombs, Clyde H. Psychology & Mathematics: An Essay on Theory. 104p. 1983. text ed. 12.50 (ISBN 0-472-10034-3). U of Mich Pr.

Coombs, G. H., jt. auth. see Gutteridge, W. E.

Coombs, Gary B. Goleta Depot: The History of a Rural Railroad Station. LC 82-83472. (Illus.). 96p. (Orig.). 1982. 8.00 (ISBN 0-911773-00-2); pap. 5.00 (ISBN 0-911773-01-0). Inst Am Res.

Coombs, H. & Coombs, P., eds. Journal of a Somerset Rector: John Skinner, 1772-1879. 15.00 o.p. (ISBN 0-87556-253-1). Saifer.

Coombs, John, tr. see Schwendowius, Barbara & Domling, Wolfgang.

Coombs, Marie T., jt. auth. see Nemeck, Francis K.

Coombs, Michael J., jt. ed. see Sime, Max S.

Coombs, Nina. Love So Fearful. (Rapture Romance Ser.: No. 1). 1983. pap. 1.95 (ISBN 0-451-12003-5, AJ2003, Sig). NAL.

Coombs, Norman. The Black Experience in America. LC 73-186717. (The Immigrant Heritage of America Ser.). 1972. lib. bdg. 11.95 o.p. (ISBN 0-8057-3208-X, Twayne). G K Hall.

Coombs, P., jt. ed. see Coombs, H.

Coombs, Patricia. Dorrie & the Witches' Camp. LC 82-9986. (Illus.). 48p. (gr. 1-5). 1983. 8.00 (ISBN 0-688-01507-7); PLB 7.63 (ISBN 0-688-01508-5). Lothrop.

Coombs, Robert H. & St. John, Joanne. Making It in Medical School. 1979. 10.00 o.p. (ISBN 0-686-77951-7); pap. 6.95 o.p. (ISBN 0-89335-056-7). Petersons Guides.

Coombs, Rod, jt. auth. see Green, K.

Coombs, W. E. & Palmer, W. J. Construction Accounting & Financial Management. 2nd ed. (Modern Structure Ser.). 1977. 39.50 (ISBN 0-07-012610-0, P&RB). McGraw.

--A Handbook of Construction Accounting & Financial Management. 3rd ed. 576p. 1983. 37.50 (ISBN 0-07-012611-9). McGraw.

Coon, C. S. Caravan: The Story of the Middle East. rev. ed. LC 75-45344. 390p. 1976. Repr. of 1958 ed. 19.50 (ISBN 0-88275-393-2). Krieger.

Coon, Carleton S. The Races of Europe. LC 76-184840. (Illus.). 739p. 1972. Repr. of 1939 ed. lib. bdg. 47.50x (ISBN 0-8371-6328-5, CORE). Greenwood.

--Racial Adaptations. LC 82-8010. (Illus.). 1982. text ed. 24.95 (ISBN 0-8304-1012-0); pap. text ed. 12.95 (ISBN 0-88229-806-2). Nelson-Hall.

--A Reader in Cultural Anthropology. LC 76-78. 634p. 1977. Repr. of 1948 ed. lib. bdg. 24.50 (ISBN 0-88275-394-0). Krieger.

Coon, Carleton S., et al. Yengema Cave Report. (Museum Monograph). (Illus.). 77p. 1968. 3.50x (ISBN 0-934718-23-7). Univ Mus of U PA.

Coon, Carlton S., jt. auth. see Chapple, Eliot D.

Coon, Dennis. Essentials of Psychology: Exploration & Application. 2nd ed. (Illus.). 550p. 1982. pap. text ed. 18.95 (ISBN 0-314-63162-3). West Pub.

--Introduction to Psychology. 3rd ed. (Exploration & Application). (Illus.). 700p. 1983. text ed. 22.95 (ISBN 0-314-69642-3); tchrs.' manual avail. (ISBN 0-314-71085-X); study guide avail. (ISBN 0-314-71086-8). West Pub.

Coon, Dennis L. Introduction to Psychology Exploration & Application. 2nd ed. (Illus.). 1980. text ed. 21.95 (ISBN 0-8299-0303-8). study guide 8.50 (ISBN 0-8299-0304-6); instrs.' manual avail. (ISBN 0-8299-0467-0). West Pub.

Coon, Kathy. Dog Intelligence Test. 1978. pap. 2.95 o.s.i. (ISBN 0-380-01903-5, 37358). Avon.

Coon, Nelson. Gardening for Fragrance: Indoors & Out. (Illus., Orig.). 1970. 5.95 (ISBN 0-8208-0068-6). Hearthside.

--Using Plants for Healing. 5.95 (ISBN 0-8208-0053-8). Hearthside.

--Using Wayside Plants. rev. ed. (Illus.). 1969. 5.95 (ISBN 0-8208-0061-9). Hearthside.

Cooney, Barbara. Miss Rumphius. LC 82-2837. (Illus.). 32p. (gr. k-3). 1982. 12.95 (ISBN 0-670-47958-6). Viking Pr.

Cooney, Caroline B. The Paper Caper. (Illus.). 64p. (gr. 9-12). 1981. 6.95 (ISBN 0-698-20506-5, Coward). Putnam Pub Group.

--Safe As the Grave. LC 78-24412. (Illus.). (gr. 3-5). 1979. 6.95 (ISBN 0-698-20479-4, Coward). Putnam Pub Group.

--Sand Trap. 192p. pap. 2.50 (ISBN 0-380-83295-X). Avon.

Cooney, Ellen. Small Town Girl. LC 82-23379. 208p. (gr. 5 up). 1983. 9.95 (ISBN 0-395-33881-6). HM.

Cooney, Margaret, jt. auth. see Talbott, G. Douglas.

Cooney, Nancy. The Wobbly Tooth. LC 77-14943. (Illus.). 1978. 6.95 (ISBN 0-399-20615-9). Putnam Pub Group.

Cooney, Nancy E. The Blanket That Had to Go. (Illus.). 32p. (gr. 4-8). 1981. 7.95 (ISBN 0-399-20716-3). Putnam Pub Group.

--The Wobbly Tooth. (Illus.). 32p. (Orig.). (gr. k-3). 1981. pap. 2.95 (ISBN 0-399-20776-7, Peppercorn). Putnam Pub Group.

Cooney, Nancy H. Sex, Sexuality, & You: A Handbook for Growing Christians. 100p. (Orig.). 1980. pap. text ed. 3.50 (ISBN 0-697-01741-9); tchrs.' resource guide 1.00 (ISBN 0-697-01742-7). Wm C Brown.

Cooney, Rian. Icarus. LC 82-2865. (Kestrel Chap Bks.). 48p. (Orig.). 1982. pap. 4.00 (ISBN 0-914974-35-1). Holmgangers.

Cooney, Thomas J., et al. Geometry with Applications & Problems Solving. 1982. pap. text ed. 20.60 (ISBN 0-201-00974-9, Sch Div); tchr's. manual 22.56 (ISBN 0-201-00975-7). A-W.

--Dynamics of Teaching Secondary Mathematics. 1975. 21.95 o.p. (ISBN 0-395-18617-X). HM.

Cooney, William P., 3rd, jt. auth. see Brooker, Andrew F.

Coons, John E. & Sugarman, Stephen D. Education by Choice: The Case for Family Control. LC 77-20318. 1978. 16.95x (ISBN 0-520-03613-1); pap. 4.95 (ISBN 0-520-03837-1). U of Cal Pr.

Coons, Kenelm. Seafood Seasons-How to Plan Profitable Purchasing of Fish & Shellfish: A Guide to Natural Cycles & Regulatory Controls for the Seafood Buyer. Dore, Ian, ed. (Osprey Seafood Handbooks). 1983. 48.00 (ISBN 0-943738-02-4); pap. 40.00 (ISBN 0-943738-03-2). Osprey Bks.

Coons, Quentin & Krusell, Cynthia H. The Winslows of "Carewell". Before & after the Mayflower. 1975. 3.00 (ISBN 0-686-38915-8). Pilgrim Hall.

Coontz, Otto. Hornswoggle Magic. (gr. 3-7). 1981. 8.95 (ISBN 0-316-15536-5). Little.

--The Night Walkers. (gr. 5 up). 1982. PLB 9.95 (ISBN 0-395-32557-9); 9.70. HM.

--The Quiet House. LC 78-18347. (Illus.). (gr. 1-3). 1978. 6.95 o.p. (ISBN 0-316-15533-0). Little.

Coontz, Sydney. Population Theories & the Economic Interpretation. (International Library of Sociology). 202p. 1957. 14.95x (ISBN 0-7100-3361-3). Routledge & Kegan.

Coop, J. E. Sheep & Goat Production. (World Animal Science Ser.: Vol. 10). 1982. 121.50 (ISBN 0-444-41989-6). Elsevier.

Coop, Richard H. & White, Kinnard. Psychological Concepts in the Classroom. 1974. pap. text ed. 13.50 scp o.p. (ISBN 0-06-041347-6, HarpC). Har-Row.

Coope, Rosalys. Salomon de Brosse & the Development of the Classical Style in French Architecture from 1565 to 1630. LC 70-127381. (Illus.). 295p. 1972. 50.00x (ISBN 0-271-00140-2). Pa St U Pr.

Cooper. Introduction to Japanese History & Culture. 1971. pap. 3.94 (ISBN 0-08-017484-1). Pergamon.

--Software Quality Management. 1979. 25.00 (ISBN 0-89433-093-4). Petrocelli.

Cooper, jt. auth. see Day.

Cooper, A. A. An Inquiry Concerning Virtue, or Merit. Walford, D. E., ed. 152p. 1977. 15.50 (ISBN 0-7190-0657-0). Manchester.

Cooper, Alice & Gaines, Steve. Me, Alice: The Autobiography of Alice Cooper. LC 75-40488. (Illus.). 288p. 1976. 7.95 o.p. (ISBN 0-399-11535-8). Putnam Pub Group.

Cooper, Allan D. U. S. Economic Power & Political Influence in Namibia, 1700-1982. (Replica Edition). 300p. 1982. softcover 22.00 (ISBN 0-86531-920-0). Westview.

Cooper, B. S., jt. auth. see Westwood, W.

Cooper, Barry. Michel Foucault: An Introduction to the Study of his Thought. (Studies in Religion & Society: Vol. 2). 176p. 1982. 29.95x (ISBN 0-88946-867-2). E Mellen.

Cooper, Bernard R., ed. Scientific Problems of Coal Utilization: Proceedings. LC 78-9553. (DOE Symposium Ser.). 424p. 1978. pap. 18.50 (ISBN 0-87079-400-0, CONF-770509); microfiche 4.50 (ISBN 0-87079-378-0, CONF-770509). DOE.

Cooper, Bev, jt. auth. see McCullough, Bonnie.

Cooper, Bruce C., jt. auth. see Croce, Pat.

Cooper, Bruce S. Collective Bargaining, Strikes, & Financial Costs in Public Education: A Comparative Review. LC 81-71248. xix, 120p. (Orig.). 1982. pap. 7.85 (ISBN 0-86552-079-8). U of Oreg ERIC.

Cooper, C. A. & Clark, J. A., eds. Employment, Economics & Technology: The Impact of Technological Change on the Labor Market. LC 82-42543. 180p. 1982. 25.00x (ISBN 0-312-24459-2). St Martin.

Cooper, C. Everett. Up Your Asteroid! a Science Fiction Farce. LC 77-866. 1977. lib. bdg. 9.95x (ISBN 0-89370-106-8); pap. 3.95x (ISBN 0-89370-206-4). Borgo Pr.

Cooper, C. L. & Marshall, J. White Collar & Professional Stress. 257p. 1980. 44.95x (ISBN 0-471-27760-6, Pub. by Wiley-Interscience). Wiley.

Cooper, C. L. & Payne, R. Stress at Work. (Studies in Occupational Stress). 293p. 1978. 49.95 (ISBN 0-471-99547-9, Pub. by Wiley-Interscience). Wiley.

Cooper, Carl, jt. auth. see Humble, Lance.

Cooper, Cary. Psychology & Management. (Psychology for Professional Groups Ser.). 275p. 1981. text ed. 25.00x (ISBN 0-333-31856-0, Pub. by Macmillan England); pap. text ed. 10.95x (ISBN 0-333-31875-7). Humanities.

Cooper, Cary & Torrington, Derek. After Forty: The Time for Achievement. 211p. 1981. 23.95x (ISBN 0-471-28043-7, Pub. by Wiley Interscience). Wiley.

Cooper, Cary L. Learning from Others in Groups: Experimental Learning Approaches. LC 78-26987. (Illus.). 1979. lib. bdg. 29.95 (ISBN 0-313-20922-7, COL/). Greenwood.

--The Stress Check: Coping with the Stresses of Life & Work. (Illus.). 176p. 1980. 11.95 (ISBN 0-13-852640-0, Spec); pap. 5.95 (ISBN 0-13-852632-X). P-H.

--Stress Research: Issues for the Eighties. 150p. 1983. not set 29.95 (ISBN 0-471-10246-6, Pub. by Wiley-Interscience). Wiley.

--Theories of Group Processes. LC 74-28089. (Individuals, Groups & Organizations Ser.). 275p. 1975. 49.95 (ISBN 0-471-17117-4, Pub. by Wiley-Interscience); pap. text ed. 22.00 (ISBN 0-471-99452-9). Wiley.

Cooper, Cary L. & Alderfer, Clayton. Advances in Experiential Social Processes. LC 77-22060. (Advances in Experimental Social Processes Ser.: Vol. 1). 1978. 42.95 (ISBN 0-471-99546-0, Pub. by Wiley-Interscience). Wiley.

Cooper, Cary L. & Marshall, Judi. Understanding Executive Stress. LC 77-16077. 1978. text ed. 14.00 (ISBN 0-89433-059-4). Petrocelli.

Cooper, Cary L. & Payne, Roy. Current Concerns in Occupational Stress. LC 79-40641. (Wiley Ser. on Studies in Occupational Stress). 1980. 45.00x (ISBN 0-471-27624-3, Pub. by Wiley-Interscience). Wiley.

Cooper, Cary L., jt. auth. see Alderfer, Clayton P.

Cooper, Cary L., jt. auth. see Jones, Andrew N.

Cooper, Cary L., jt. ed. see Marshall, Judi.

Cooper, Cary L., jt. ed. see Payne, Roy.

Cooper, Charles. English Table in History & Literature. LC 68-21760. 1968. Repr. of 1929 ed. 30.00x (ISBN 0-8103-3520-4). Gale.

--Policy Interventions for Technological Innovation in Developing Countries. (Working Paper: No. 441). 59p. 1980. 5.00 (ISBN 0-686-36148-2, WP-0441). World Bank.

Cooper, Chester L., ed. Growth in America. LC 75-35359. (Contributions in American Studies: No. 21). (Illus.). 320p. 1976. lib. bdg. 29.95 (ISBN 0-8371-8596-3, CGA). Greenwood.

Cooper, Christine & Hildesley, Angela. Carefree Cookbook. 1976. 8.95 o.p. (ISBN 0-600-31879-6). Transatlantic.

Cooper, Dale, et al. The Outdoor Handbook. (Illus.). 1978. 13.95 o.p. (ISBN 0-600-36743-6). Transatlantic.

Cooper, Darien. How to Be Happy Though Young. 1979. 5.95 (ISBN 0-8007-5048-9, Power Bks). Revell.

Cooper, Darien & Carroll, Anne K. Darien Cooper's Happy Husband Book. 1980. text ed. 9.95 (ISBN 0-88207-785-6). Victor Bks.

Cooper, Darien B. You Can Be the Wife of a Happy Husband. LC 74-77450. 156p. 1974. pap. 4.95 (ISBN 0-88207-711-2). Victor Bks.

Cooper, Darien B. & Carroll, Anne K. We Became Wives of Happy Husbands. 168p. 1976. pap. 4.95 (ISBN 0-88207-731-7). Victor Bks.

Cooper, David D. The Lesson of the Scaffold: The Public Execution Controversy in Victorian England. LC 73-92901. (Illus.). xi, 212p. 1974. 13.95x (ISBN 0-8214-0148-3, 82-81511). Ohio U Pr.

Cooper, David G. Architectural & Engineering Salesmanship. LC 78-15367. 1978. 23.95x (ISBN 0-471-03642-0, Pub. by Wiley-Interscience). Wiley.

Cooper, David J. Brooks Range Passage. (Illus.). 208p. 1982. 14.95 (ISBN 0-89886-061-X). Mountaineers.

Cooper, David L., jt. auth. see Richards, W. Graham.

Cooper, Davis. Daily Devotions for Newlyweds. LC 81-67204. 1983. 5.95 (ISBN 0-8054-5646-5). Broadman.

Cooper, Dennis. Idols. LC 79-66660. 1979. pap. 4.95 (ISBN 0-686-28355-4). Sea Horse.

--Tenderness of the Wolves. LC 81-15104. 76p. 1981. 13.95 (ISBN 0-89594-066-3); pap. 4.95 (ISBN 0-89594-065-5). Crossing Pr.

Cooper, Derek. The Bad Food Guide. (Illus.). 1967. 13.95 o.p. (ISBN 0-7100-1229-2). Routledge & Kegan.

--The Beverage Report. (Illus.). 1970. 10.00 o.p. (ISBN 0-7100-6625-2). Routledge & Kegan.

--The Gullibility Gap. (Illus.). 1974. 12.50 o.p. (ISBN 0-7100-7972-9). Routledge & Kegan.

--Skye. (Illus.). 1970. 22.50 o.p. (ISBN 0-7100-6820-4). Routledge & Kegan.

Cooper, Diana. Animal Hotel. 224p. 1983. 12.95 (ISBN 0-312-03782-1). St Martin.

Cooper, Donald. Theatre Year, 1980. (Illus.). 1982. pap. 15.95 (ISBN 0-686-84198-0). Drama Bk.

--Theatre Year, 1981. (Illus.). 1982. pap. 15.95 (ISBN 0-686-84199-9). Drama Bk.

--Theatre Year, 1982. (Illus.). 1983. pap. 15.95 (ISBN 0-686-84200-6). Drama Bk.

Cooper, Doug. Standard Pascal Uses Reference Manual. 1983. write for info (ISBN 0-393-95332-7). Norton.

Cooper, Doug & Clancy, Michael. Oh! PASCAL! 1982. pap. 17.95x (ISBN 0-393-95205-3). Norton.

Cooper, Edward L. Comparative Immunology. (Foundations of Immunology Ser.). (Illus.). 480p. 1976. 23.95x o.p. (ISBN 0-13-153429-7). P-H.

Cooper, Elizabeth. Harim & the Purdah: Studies of Oriental Women. LC 68-23147. 1975. Repr. of 1915 ed. 37.00x (ISBN 0-8103-3167-5). Gale.

--Rosie's Hospital Story. LC 80-52525. (Starters Ser.). PLB 8.00 (ISBN 0-382-06498-4). Silver.

Cooper, Elizabeth K. Insects & Plants: The Amazing Partnership. LC 63-7893. (Illus.). (gr. 4-6). 1963. 6.95 o.p. (ISBN 0-15-238701-3, HJ). HarBraceJ.

Cooper, Ella G., jt. auth. see Goodall, Helen S.

Cooper, Emmanuel. Electric Kiln Pottery: The Complete Guide. (Illus.). 144p. 1982. 24.95 (ISBN 0-7134-4037-6, Pub. by Batsford England). David & Charles.

Cooper, Erwin. Aqueduct Empire. (Illus.). 1968. 12.50 o.p. (ISBN 0-87062-008-8). A H Clark.

Cooper, Eugene. The Woodcarvers of Hong Kong. LC 78-75255. (Cambridge Studies in Social Anthropology: No. 29). (Illus.). 1980. 27.95 (ISBN 0-521-22699-6). Cambridge U Pr.

Cooper, F. T., tr. see Donauer, Friedrich.

Cooper, Frank E. Administrative Agencies & the Courts. LC 51-62547. (Michigan Legal Studies). xxv, 470p. 1982. Repr. of 1951 ed. lib. bdg. 35.00 (ISBN 0-89941-171-1). W S Hein.

--Writing in Law Practice. 1963. text ed. 19.00 (ISBN 0-672-81021-2, Bobbs-Merrill Law). Michie-Bobbs.

Cooper, Fred C. Banking Law Anthology, 1983, Vol.1. (National Law Anthology Ser.). 1983. 59.95 (ISBN 0-914250-23-X). Intl Lib.

Cooper, Fred C., ed. Public Utilities Law Anthology, 1980-1981, Vol. VI. LC 74-77644. (National Law Anthology Ser.). 1982. text ed. 59.95 (ISBN 0-914250-24-8). Intl Lib.

Cooper, Frederic T., jt. auth. see Maurice, Arthur B.

Cooper, George. A Voluntary Tax? New Perspectives on Sophisticated Estate Tax Avoidance. LC 78-20853. (Studies of Government Finance). 1979. 11.95 (ISBN 0-8157-1552-8); pap. 4.95 (ISBN 0-8157-1551-X). Brookings.

Cooper, George H. Building Construction Estimating. 3rd ed. 1971. 22.95 (ISBN 0-07-012931-2, G). McGraw.

Cooper, Gwen & Haas, Evelyn. Wade a Little Deeper Dear. 1978. pap. 4.50 (ISBN 0-87735-044-2). Wade Bks.

Cooper, H. B. & Rossano, A. T. Source Testing for Air Pollution Control. 228p. 1974. Repr. of 1971 ed. text ed. 24.50 (ISBN 0-07-012760-3, C). McGraw.

Cooper, H. H. C., jt. ed. see Wicks, Robert J.

Cooper, H. John, jt. auth. see Davie, Peter.

Cooper, Helen. John Trumbull: The Hand & Spirit of a Painter. LC 82-50609. (University Art Gallery Publication Ser.). (Illus.). 256p. 1982. text ed. 45.00x (ISBN 0-300-02928-4); pap. 19.95x (ISBN 0-300-02932-2). Yale U Pr.

Cooper, Helen, ed. see Burnham, Patricia M. & Price, Martin.

Cooper, Henry. Boxing. (Pelham Pictorial Sports Instruction Ser.). (Illus.). 1977. 10.95 o.p. (ISBN 0-7207-0790-0). Transatlantic.

Cooper, Henry R. The Igor Tale: An Annotated Bibliography of Twentieth-Century Non-Soviet Scholarship on the Slovo O polku Igoreve. LC 77-85703. 1978. 27.50 (ISBN 0-87332-111-1). M E Sharpe.

Cooper, Henry R., Jr. France Preseren. (Twayne's World Authors Ser.). 1981. lib. bdg. 15.95 (ISBN 0-8057-6462-3, Twayne). G K Hall.

Cooper, Henry R., Jr., jt. ed. see Lencek, Rado L.

Cooper, I. S., ed. Cerebellar Stimulation in Man. LC 77-76925. 232p. 1978. 31.00 (ISBN 0-89004-206-3). Raven.

Cooper, J. Microprocessor Background for Management Personnel. 208p. 1981. 19.95 (ISBN 0-13-580829-4). P-H.

Cooper, J., jt. auth. see Curtis, A.

Cooper, J., jt. ed. see Rose, J. W.

Cooper, J. David, et al. The What & How of Reading Instruction. 1979. pap. text ed. 17.95 (ISBN 0-675-08287-0). Additional supplements may be obtained from publisher. Merrill.

Cooper, J. W. Introduction to PASCAL for Scientists. LC 80-28452. 260p. 1981. 22.50x (ISBN 0-471-08785-8, Pub. by Wiley-Interscience). Wiley.

Cooper, Jack R. & Bloom, Floyd E. The Biochemical Basis of Neuropharmacology. 4th ed. (Illus.). 1982. text ed. 21.95x (ISBN 0-19-503093-1); pap. text ed. 11.95 (ISBN 0-19-503094-X). Oxford U Pr.

Cooper, Jack R., et al. The Biochemical Basis of Neuropharmacology. 3rd ed. (Illus.). 1978. text ed. 15.95x o.p. (ISBN 0-19-502346-3); pap. text ed. 8.95x o.p. (ISBN 0-19-502347-1). Oxford U Pr.

Cooper, Jackie, ed. Mackintosh Architecture. LC 77-89987. 1978. 15.95 o.p. (ISBN 0-312-11244-0). St Martin.

Cooper, James. Correspondence of James Fenimore Cooper, 2 Vols. LC 71-160159. (American Biography Ser., No. 32). 1971. Repr. of 1922 ed. Set. lib. bdg. 79.95x (ISBN 0-8383-1295-0). Haskell.

Cooper, James F. Deerslayer. (RL 7). pap. 2.95 (ISBN 0-451-51645-1, CE1645, Sig Classics). NAL.

--The Deerslayer. 5th ed. (Bantam Classics Ser.). 528p. (YA) (gr. 9-12). 1982. pap. 2.95 (ISBN 0-553-21085-8). Bantam.

--Early Critical Essays, 1820-1822. LC 55-11038. 1977. Repr. 30.00x (ISBN 0-8201-1228-3). Schol Facsimiles.

--Gleanings in Europe: France. Philbrick, Thomas & Denne, Constance A., eds. (The Writings of James Fenimore Cooper Ser.). 380p. 1983. 30.00x (ISBN 0-87395-368-1). State U NY Pr.

--Gleanings in Europe: Italy. Denne, Constance A., ed. (The Writings of James Fenimore Cooper Ser.). 1980. 34.50x (ISBN 0-87395-365-7); pap. 10.95x (ISBN 0-87395-460-2). State U NY Pr.

--Letters & Journals of James Fenimore Cooper, 6 vols. Beard, James F., ed. Incl. 1960. Vols. 1-2.set. 40.00x o.p. (ISBN 0-674-52550-7); Vols. 3-4. 1964. Set. 40.00x (ISBN 0-674-52551-5); Vols. 5-6. 1968. Set. 40.00x (ISBN 0-674-52552-3). (Illus., Belknap Pr). Harvard U Pr.

--Pathfinder. (RL 10). 1964. pap. 3.50 (ISBN 0-451-51708-3, CE1708, Sig Classics). NAL.

--The Pathfinder. Dixson, Robert J., ed. (American Classics Ser.: Bk. 4). (gr. 9 up). 1973. pap. text ed. 3.25 (ISBN 0-88345-200-6, 18123); cassettes 40.00 (ISBN 0-685-38992-8); 40.00 o.p. tapes (ISBN 0-685-38993-6). Regents Pub.

--The Pathfinder: Or the Inland Sea. (Writings of James Fenimore Cooper Ser.). 1980. 34.50x (ISBN 0-87395-360-6); pap. 10.95x (ISBN 0-87395-477-7). State U NY Pr.

--Pioneers. (RL 10). pap. 3.50 (ISBN 0-451-51621-4, CE1621, Sig Classics). NAL.

--The Pioneers. Beard, James F., ed. LC 77-21795. (Writings of James Fenimore Cooper Ser.). 1980. 34.50x (ISBN 0-87395-359-2); pap. 10.95x (ISBN 0-87395-423-8). State U NY Pr.

--Satanstoe. LC 62-9515. xviii, 425p. 1962. pap. 4.50x (ISBN 0-8032-5036-3, BB 138, Bison). U of Nebr Pr.

--Tales for Fifteen. LC 59-6525. 1977. Repr. of 1823 ed. 35.00x (ISBN 0-8201-1247-X). Schol Facsimiles.

--Wyandotte. Philbrick, Thomas & Philbrick, Marianne, eds. (The Writings of James Fenimore Cooper Ser.). 518p. 1981. 34.50x (ISBN 0-87395-414-9); pap. 10.95x (ISBN 0-87395-469-6). State U NY Pr.

Cooper, James F see Swan, D. K.

Cooper, James F., ed. Correspondence of James Fenimore-Cooper, 2 Vols. 776p. 1983. Repr. of 1922 ed. lib. bdg. 200.00 set (ISBN 0-89760-167-X). Telegraph Bks.

Cooper, James F., et al. Gleanings in Europe: England. Ringe, Donald A. & Staggs, Kenneth W., eds. (The Writings of James Fenimore Cooper Ser.). 383p. 1981. 34.50x (ISBN 0-87395-367-3); pap. 10.95x (ISBN 0-87395-459-9). State U NY Pr.

Cooper, James Fenimore. The Last of the Mohicans. (Bantam Classics Ser.). 384p. (Orig.). (gr. 7-12). 1981. pap. 2.50 (ISBN 0-553-21054-8). Bantam.

--The Last of the Mohicans. Sappenfield, James A. & Feltskog, E. N., eds. (Definitive Edition of the Writings of James Fenimore Cooper Ser.). 500p. 1982. 30.00x (ISBN 0-87395-362-2); pap. 9.95x (ISBN 0-87395-470-X). State U NY Pr.

Cooper, James M. & DeVault, M. Vere. Competency Based Teacher Education. LC 72-83478. 123p. 1973. 20.75x (ISBN 0-8211-0010-6); text ed. 18.60 in copies of 10 (ISBN 0-686-66847-2). McCutchan.

Cooper, James M., jt. auth. see Ryan, Kevin.

Cooper, James M., et al. Classroom Teaching Skills: A Handbook. 1977. pap. text ed. 14.95x o.p. (ISBN 0-669-94722-9); instr's manual 1.95 o.p. (ISBN 0-669-97899-X); wkbk. 9.95x o.p. (ISBN 0-669-94730-X). Heath.

--Classroom Teaching Skills: A Handbook. 2nd ed. 544p. 1982. pap. text ed. 15.95 (ISBN 0-669-04369-9); instr's guide 1.95 (ISBN 0-669-04370-2). Heath.

Cooper, James R. & Guntermann, Karl L. Real Estate & Urban Land Analysis. LC 73-10397. (Special Ser. in Real Estate & Urban Land Economics). (Illus.). 544p. 1974. 33.95x o.p. (ISBN 0-669-90415-5). Lexington Bks.

Cooper, James R., jt. auth. see Pyhrr, Stephen A.

Cooper, James W. The Minicomputer in the Laboratory. 2nd ed. LC 82-8490. 381p. 1983. 29.00 (ISBN 0-471-09012-3, Pub. by Wiley-Interscience). Wiley.

--The Minicomputer in the Laboratory: With Examples Using the PDP-11. LC 76-44255. 1977. 28.50x (ISBN 0-471-01883-X, Pub. by Wiley-Interscience). Wiley.

--Spectroscopic Techniques for Organic Chemists. LC 79-23952. 1980. 26.50x (ISBN 0-471-05166-7, Pub. by Wiley-Interscience). Wiley.

Cooper, Jane, et al, eds. Extended Outlooks: The Iowa Review Collection of Contemporary Women Writers. 400p. 1982. 17.95 (ISBN 0-02-528080-5); pap. 9.95 (ISBN 0-02-049690-7). Macmillan.

Cooper, Jean, et al. Helping Language Development. LC 77-27524. 1978. 15.95 (ISBN 0-312-36757-0). St Martin.

Cooper, Jeffrey. How to Make Love to an Extraterrestrial. LC 82-62491. 96p. (Orig.). 1983. pap. 3.50 (ISBN 0-688-01888-2). Quill NY.

Cooper, Jerome. Sincerely Your Friend Letters of Mr. Justice Hugo L. Black. LC 73-1797. 16p. 1973. pap. 1.00 o.p. (ISBN 0-8173-9360-9). U of Ala Pr.

Cooper, Jerry M. The Army & Civil Disorder: Federal Military Intervention in Labor Disputes, 1877-1900. LC 79-7064. (Contributions in Military History: No. 19). 1980. lib. bdg. 29.95 (ISBN 0-313-20958-8, CAD/). Greenwood.

Cooper, Jilly. Jolly Marsupial. 1982. write for info. o.p. (ISBN 0-413-51290-8). Methuen Inc.

--Supermen & Super Women. 1982. pap. write for info. o.p. Methuen Inc.

Cooper, Jo. Handfeeding Baby Birds. (Illus.). 1979. 4.95 (ISBN 0-87666-992-5, KW-017). TFH Pubns.

Cooper, John C. Cults: A Directory. 160p. (Orig.). Date not set. pap. 6.95 o.p. (ISBN 0-8298-0458-7). Pilgrim NY. Postponed.

Cooper, John C., jt. auth. see McManus, Una.

Cooper, John L. The Police & the Ghetto. (National University Publications, Multi-Disciplinary Studies in the Law). 1980. 16.50 o.p. (ISBN 0-8046-9250-5). Kennikat.

--The Seventh Decade: A Study of the Women's Liberation Movement. (Orig.). 1980. pap. text ed. 9.95 (ISBN 0-8403-2175-9). Kendall-Hunt.

Cooper, John M., et al. Kinesiology. 5th ed. LC 81-11116. (Illus.). 452p. 1982. text ed. 21.95 (ISBN 0-8016-1040-0). Mosby.

Cooper, John M., Jr. The Vanity of Power: American Isolationism & the First World War. LC 70-95508. (Contributions in American History: No. 3). 1969. lib. bdg. 29.95 (ISBN 0-8371-2342-9, COP/). Greenwood.

Cooper, John N., jt. auth. see Smith, Alpheus.

Cooper, John O. Measuring Behavior. 2nd ed. (Special Education Ser.). (Illus.). 224p. 1981. pap. text ed. 12.95 (ISBN 0-675-08078-9). Merrill.

Cooper, John R. Mel Martin: First Base Jinx. (Mel Martin Baseball Stories Ser.: No. 4). 208p. (gr. 3-7). 1982. 8.95 (ISBN 0-671-44539-1); pap. 2.95 (ISBN 0-671-44548-0). Wanderer Bks.

--Mel Martin: The Mystery at the Ball Park. (Mel Martin Baseball Stories Ser.: No. 1). 208p. (gr. 3-7). 1982. 8.95 (ISBN 0-671-44536-7); pap. 2.95 (ISBN 0-671-44545-6). Wanderer Bks.

--Mel Martin: The Phantom Homer. (Mel Martin Baseball Stories Ser.: No. 3). 208p. (gr. 3-7). 1982. 8.95 (ISBN 0-671-44538-3); pap. 2.95 (ISBN 0-671-44547-2). Wanderer Bks.

--Mel Martin: The Southpaw's Secret. (Mel Martin Baseball Stories Ser.: No. 2). 208p. (gr. 3-7). 1982. 8.95 (ISBN 0-671-44537-5); pap. 2.95 (ISBN 0-671-44546-4). Wanderer Bks.

Cooper, Joseph. Cameras & Operating Techniques. (Nikon Handbook Ser.). (Illus.). 1979. 15.95 o.p. (ISBN 0-8174-2487-3, Amphoto); pap. 9.95 o.p. (ISBN 0-8174-2159-9). Watson-Guptill.

--Close-Up Photography & Copying. (Nikon Handbook Ser.). (Illus.). 1979. 14.95 o.p. (ISBN 0-8174-2489-X, Amphoto); pap. 8.95 o.p. (ISBN 0-8174-2161-0). Watson-Guptill.

--Exposure Control & Lighting. (Nikon Hanbook Ser.). (Illus.). 1979. 13.95 o.p. (ISBN 0-8174-2490-3, Amphoto); pap. 7.95 o.p. (ISBN 0-8174-2162-9). Watson-Guptill.

--Lenses & Lens Systems. (Nikon Handbook Ser.). 1979. 15.95 o.p. (ISBN 0-8174-2488-1, Amphoto); pap. 9.95 o.p. (ISBN 0-8174-2160-2). Watson-Guptill.

--Special Applications Motor Drives, Underwater Photography, & Auxiliary Systems. (Nikon Handbook Ser.). (Illus.). 1979. 14.95 o.p. (ISBN 0-8174-2492-X, Amphoto); pap. 8.95 o.p. (ISBN 0-8174-2164-5). Watson-Guptill.

--Special Effects, Shooting Situations, & Darkroom Techniques. (Nikon Handbook Ser.). (Illus.). 1979. 14.95 o.p. (ISBN 0-8174-2491-1, Amphoto); pap. 8.95 o.p. (ISBN 0-8174-2163-7). Watson-Guptill.

Cooper, Joseph D. Asahi Pentax Manual. (Illus.). 1975. looseleaf 27.50 o.p. (ISBN 0-8174-1439-8, Amphoto). Watson-Guptill.

--Honeywell Pentax Manual. (Illus.). 1975. looseleaf 27.50 o.p. (ISBN 0-8174-0439-2, Amphoto). Watson-Guptill.

--Polaroid Pocket Companion. 1967. pap. 2.95 o.p. (ISBN 0-8174-0165-2, Amphoto). Watson-Guptill.

Cooper, Kay. All About Goldfish As Pets. LC 76-26519. (Illus.). 64p. (gr. 3 up). 1976. PLB 6.97 o.p. (ISBN 0-671-32801-8). Messner.

--All About Rabbits As Pets. LC 74-7592. (Illus.). 64p. (gr. 3 up). 1974. PLB 6.97 o.s.i. (ISBN 0-671-32694-5). Messner.

--A Chipmunk's Inside-Outside World. LC 72-11958. (Illus.). 64p. (gr. 3 up). 1973. PLB 4.79 o.p. (ISBN 0-671-32566-3). Messner.

--C'mon Ducks! LC 77-25089. (Illus.). 64p. (gr. 3 up). 1978. PLB 6.97 o.p. (ISBN 0-671-32905-7). Messner.

Cooper, Kenneth. Aerobics. 1968. 1.00x (ISBN 0-686-32626-1). Cancer Control Soc.

--The Aerobics Program for Total Well-Being: Exercise, Diet & Emotional Balance. (Illus.). 1982. 16.95 (ISBN 0-87131-380-4). M Evans.

Cooper, Lane, tr. Rhetoric of Aristotle. (Orig.). 1960. pap. text ed. 13.95 (ISBN 0-13-780692-2). P-H.

Cooper, Laura G. & Smith, Marilyn Z. Standard FORTRAN: A Problem-Solving Approach. LC 72-4395. 288p. (Orig.). 1973. pap. text ed. 17.50 (ISBN 0-395-14028-5). HM.

Cooper, Lynn. Forgotten Love. Bd. with From Paris with Love. 1982. pap. 2.75 (ISBN 0-451-11361-6, AE1361, Sig). NAL.

Cooper, Lynna. Deep Water, Deep Love. (Adventures in Love Ser.: No. 29). 1982. pap. 1.75 (ISBN 0-451-11746-8, AE1746, Sig). NAL.

--Forgotten Love. (Orig.). 1979. pap. 1.75 o.p. (ISBN 0-451-08569-8, E8569, Sig). NAL.

--From Paris with Love. (Orig.). 1980. pap. 1.75 o.p. (ISBN 0-451-09128-0, E9128, Sig). NAL.

--Hearts in the Highlands. 1980. pap. 2.50 (ISBN 0-451-11568-6, AE1568, Sig). NAL.
--The Hired Wife. Bd. with The Moon in Eclipse. Slack, Claudia. 1981. pap. 2.75 (ISBN 0-451-11089-7, AE1089, Sig). NAL.
--Inherit My Heart. (Orig.). 1981. pap. 1.95 o.p. (ISBN 0-451-09782-3, J9782, Sig). NAL.
--My Treasure, My Love. 1978. pap. 1.50 o.p. (ISBN 0-451-07936-1, W7936, Sig). NAL.
--Offer of Marriage. pap. 1.50 o.p. (ISBN 0-451-08457-8, W8457, Sig). NAL.
--Portrait of Love. (Orig.). 1980. pap. 1.75 o.p. (ISBN 0-451-09495-6, E9495, Sig). NAL.
Cooper, M. Drapery. Date not set. price not set (ISBN 0-442-21875-3). Van Nos Reinhold.
Cooper, M. J., jt. auth. see Hanley, W. S.
Cooper, M. K. Private Lies. 1979. 9.95 o.p. (ISBN 0-671-24738-7). S&S.
Cooper, Margaret C. Code Name: Clone. (Illus.). 192p. (gr. 4-6). 1982. 8.95 (ISBN 0-8027-6474-6); PLB 9.85 (ISBN 0-8027-6475-4). Walker & Co.
Cooper, Marian & Bredow, Miriam. The Medical Assistant. 4th ed. (Illus.). 1978. text ed. 24.50 (ISBN 0-07-012751-4); wkbk. 14.95 (ISBN 0-07-012752-2); tchr's manual wkbk. 15.00 (ISBN 0-07-012753-0). McGraw.
Cooper, Mark N. The Transformation of Egypt. LC 82-15317. 288p. 1982. text ed. 22.50x (ISBN 0-8018-2836-8). Johns Hopkins.
Cooper, Martin see Abraham, Gerald, et al.
Cooper, Martin, tr. see Druskin, Mikhail S.
Cooper, Matthew. The German Air Force Nineteen Thirty-Three to Nineteen Forty-Five: An Anatomy of Failure. (Illus.). 375p. 1981. 19.95 (ISBN 0-86720-565-2). Sci Bks Intl.
Cooper, Max D. & Dayton, Delbert H., eds. Development of Host Defenses. LC 76-51866. 320p. 1977. 34.50 (ISBN 0-89004-117-2). Raven.
Cooper, Michael. Rationing Health Care. LC 74-32600. 150p. 1975. 24.95x o.p. (ISBN 0-470-17119-7). Halsted Pr.
Cooper, Michele, jt. auth. see Cahill, Susan.
Cooper, Morton. Resnick's Odyssey. LC 78-14008. 1978. 9.95 o.p. (ISBN 0-688-03379-2). Morrow.
Cooper, Nancy, jt. auth. see Bin-Nun, Judy.
Cooper, Nanthapa, jt. auth. see Cooper, Robert.
Cooper, Norman W. Finding Your Self. new ed. 96p. 1974. pap. 4.50 (ISBN 0-87516-183-9). De Vorss.
--Love That Heals. 1977. pap. 4.50 (ISBN 0-87516-228-2). De Vorss.
Cooper, Pamela J. Speech Communication for the Classroom Teacher. (Illus.). 296p. (Orig.). 1980. pap. text ed. 15.95 (ISBN 0-89787-303-3). Gorsuch Scarisbrick.
Cooper, Patricia & Buferd, Norma B. The Quilters: Women & Domestic Art. LC 76-2765. (Illus.). 1977. pap. 12.95 (ISBN 0-385-12039-7). Doubleday.
Cooper, Patricia J., ed. Better Homes & Gardens Woman's Health & Medical Guide. LC 79-55161. (Illus.). 696p. 1981. 29.95 (ISBN 0-696-00275-2). BH&G.
Cooper, Paul R. & Fleischer, Alan S. Head Injury. (Illus.). 424p. 1982. lib. bdg. 49.00 (ISBN 0-683-02106-0). Williams & Wilkins.
Cooper, Peter L. Signs & Symptoms: Thomas Pynchon & the Contemporary World. LC 82-6929. 288p. 1983. 19.95 (ISBN 0-520-04537-8). U of Cal Pr.
Cooper, Philip D. & Robinson, Larry M. Health Care Marketing Mamagement: A Case Approach. LC 82-3904. 361p. 1982. text ed. 34.50 (ISBN 0-89443-394-6). Aspen Systems.
Cooper, Phillip J. Public Law & Public Administration. 474p. 1983. text ed. 21.95 (ISBN 0-87484-526-2). Mayfield Pub.
Cooper, Phyllis. Feminine Gymnastics. 3rd ed. LC 80-65135. 1980. spiral bdg. 12.95x (ISBN 0-8087-2962-4). Burgess.
Cooper, R. A. & Weekes, A. J. Data, Models & Statistical Analysis. 400p. 1983. text ed. 30.00x (ISBN 0-389-20382-3); pap. text ed. 19.50x (ISBN 0-389-20383-1). B&N Imports.
Cooper, Raymond D. & Wood, Robert W., eds. Physical Mechanisms in Radiation Biology: Proceedings. LC 74-600124. (AEC Technical Information Center Ser.). 332p. 1974. pap. 16.25 (CONF-721001); microfiche 4.50 (ISBN 0-87079-303-9, CONF-721001). DOE.
Cooper, Robert & Cooper, Nanthapa. Culture Shock! Thailand. 256p. 1983. 8.95 (ISBN 0-686-42988-5). Hippocrene Bks.
Cooper, Robert, jt. auth. see Gordon, Lawrence A.
Cooper, Robert D. Health & Welfare Fund Operations & Expenses: Summary Report & Fact Book for Multiemployer Plans. 47p. (Orig.). 1982. pap. 12.50 (ISBN 0-89154-200-0). Intl Found Employ.
Cooper, Robert L., jt. auth. see Fishman, Joshua.
Cooper, Robert L., ed. Language Spread: Studies in Diffusion & Social Change. LC 81-47567. 368p. 1982. 17.50 (ISBN 0-253-32000-3). Ind U Pr.
Cooper, Robert L., jt. ed. see Spolsky, Bernard.
Cooper, Robert M. Lost on Both Sides. Dante Gabriel Rossetti: Critic & Poet. LC 71-91957. 268p. 1970. 15.50x (ISBN 0-8214-0069-X, 82-80752). Ohio U Pr.
Cooper, Robert W., jt. auth. see Rosenblum, Leonard A.
Cooper, Rodney H., jt. auth. see Johnson, Leroy F.
Cooper, Rosaleen & Palmer, Ann. Games from an Edwardian Childhood. (Illus.). 96p. 1982. 9.95 (ISBN 0-7153-8317-5). David & Charles.
Cooper, Rosalind. Spirits & Liqueurs. (Illus.). 112p. 1982. pap. 5.95 (ISBN 0-89586-194-1). H P Bks.
Cooper, S. A. Concise International Dictionary of Mechanical Geography. 6.00 o.p. (ISBN 0-685-28348-8). Philos Lib.
Cooper, S. K. & Fraser, D. R. The Financial Marketplace. 1982. 23.95 (ISBN 0-201-00196-9); instrs' guide 9.95 (ISBN 0-201-10196-3). A-W.
Cooper, St. G. The Natural Resources of Trinidad & Tobago. Bacon, P. R., ed. 225p. 1981. 44.50x (ISBN 0-8448-1416-4). Crane-Russak Co.
Cooper, Sandi. Soups & Salads. Lawrence, Betsy, ed. LC 81-70441. (Great American Cooking Schools Ser.). (Illus.). 84p. 1982. pap. 6.95 (ISBN 0-941034-13-5). I Chalmers.
--Soups & Salads. LC 82-48659. (Great American Cooking Schools Ser.). (Illus.). 80p. 1983. 8.61i (ISBN 0-06-015151-X, HarpT). Har-Row.
Cooper, Saul & Hodges, William F., eds. The Mental Health Construction Field, Vol. XI. 224p. 1983. text ed. 24.95x (ISBN 0-89885-130-0). Human Sci Pr.
Cooper, Shawn. The Clinical Use & Interpretation of the Wechsler Intelligence Scale for Children-Revised. (Illus.). 284p. 1983. 24.50x (ISBN 0-398-04750-2). C C Thomas.
Cooper, Signe, jt. auth. see McGriff, Erline P.
Cooper, Signe S. The Practice of Continuing Education in Nursing. LC 82-13872. 340p. 1982. 28.50 (ISBN 0-89443-664-3). Aspen Systems.
Cooper, Susan. The Dark Is Rising. LC 72-85916. 232p. (gr. 6 up). 1973. 10.95 (ISBN 0-689-30317-3, McElderry Bk). Atheneum.
--Over Sea, Under Stone. LC 79-10489. (Illus.). (gr. 4-7). 1979. pap. 5.95 (ISBN 0-15-670542-7, VoyB). HarBraceJ.
--The Silver Cow. LC 82-13928. (Illus.). 32p. (ps-4). 1983. 11.95 (ISBN 0-689-50236-2, McElderry Bk). Atheneum.
Cooper, T. B. & Gershon, S. Lithium: Controversies & Unresolved Issues. (International Congress Ser.: Vol. 478). 1980. 193.25 (ISBN 0-444-90093-4). Elsevier.
Cooper, Terrance C. The Tools of Biochemistry. LC 76-30910. 1977. 32.50x (ISBN 0-471-17116-6, Pub. by Wiley-Interscience). Wiley.
Cooper, Terry & Ratner, Marilyn. Many Friends Cookbook: An International Cookbook for Boys & Girls. LC 79-24832. (Illus.). 64p. (gr. 3-6). 1980. pap. 6.95 (ISBN 0-399-20755-4, Philomel). Putnam Pub Group.
Cooper, Thomas. Treatise on the Law of Libel & the Liberty of the Press. LC 71-107408. (Civil Liberties in American History Ser). 1970. Repr. of 1833 ed. lib. bdg. 25.00 (ISBN 0-306-71892-8). Da Capo.
--Two Essays: On the Foundation of Civil Government & On the Constitution of the United States. LC 72-99477. (American Constitutional & Legal History Ser). 1970. Repr. of 1826 ed. lib. bdg. 19.50 (ISBN 0-306-71852-9). Da Capo.
Cooper, Thomas, ed. see Elyot, Thomas.
Cooper, Tom. Starch Lover's Diet. LC 82-60495. 128p. 1982. 4.95 (ISBN 0-931948-39-8). Peachtree Pubs.
Cooper, W. Warm Air Heating for Climate Control. 1980. 23.95 (ISBN 0-13-944231-6). P-H.
Cooper, W. E. ABC of Flower Growing. (Illus.). 9.50 (ISBN 0-392-06742-0, LTB). Sportshelf.
--ABC of Garden Pests & Diseases. (Illus.). 9.50x (ISBN 0-686-63609-0, LTB). Sportshelf.
--ABC of Gardening. (Illus.). 9.50x (ISBN 0-392-06739-0, LTB). Sportshelf.
Cooper, W. F. & Fordham. Electrical Safety Engineering. 1977. 64.95 (ISBN 0-408-00289-1). Butterworth.
Cooper, W. Norman. Dance with God. LC 81-69932. 128p. (Orig.). 1982. 7.50 (ISBN 0-87516-491-9); pap. 4.50 (ISBN 0-87516-468-4). De Vorss.
--The Ultimate Destination. 95p. 1980. 7.50 (ISBN 0-87516-413-7); pap. 4.50 (ISBN 0-87516-381-5). De Vorss.
Cooper, W. W. & Ijiri, Yuji. Eric Louis Kohler: Accounting's Man of Principles. (Illus.). 1978. 19.95 (ISBN 0-8359-1773-8). Reston.
Cooper, William & Wiesbecker, Henry. Solid State Devices & Integrated Circuits. 1982. text ed. 21.95 (ISBN 0-8359-7045-0); solutions manual avail. (ISBN 0-8359-7046-9). Reston.
Cooper, William D. Electronic Instrumentation & Measurement Techniques. 2nd ed. LC 77-24528. (Illus.). 1978. ref. ed. 23.95 (ISBN 0-13-251710-8). P-H.
Cooper, William E. Speech Perception & Production. LC 79-17281. (Language & Being Ser.). 1979. 22.50 (ISBN 0-89391-027-9). Ablex Pub.
Cooper, William J. Chemistry in Water Reuse, Vol. 2. 647p. 1981. text ed. 49.95 (ISBN 0-250-40391-9). Ann Arbor Science.
Cooper, William J., ed. Chemistry in Water Reuse, Vol. 1. LC 80-70321. 557p. 1981. text ed. 49.95 (ISBN 0-250-40377-3). Ann Arbor Science.
Cooper, William J., Jr., ed. see Hundley, Daniel R.
Cooper, William R. Archaic Dictionary. LC 73-76018. 1969. Repr. of 1876 ed. 66.00x (ISBN 0-8103-3885-8). Gale.
Cooper, Wyatt. Families: A Memoir & a Celebration. LC 75-9347. (Illus.). 224p. 1975. 12.45i (ISBN 0-06-010857-6, HarpT). Har-Row.
Cooperative Group of Shandong Medical College & Shandong College of Traditional Chinese Medicine, Jinan, China. Anatomical Atlas of Chinese Acupuncture Points. 265p. 1983. 32.00 (ISBN 0-08-029784-6). Pergamon.
Cooper-Hill, James & Greenberg, Martin J. Cases & Material on Mortgages & Real Estate Finance. (Contemporary Legal Education Ser.). 632p. 1982. 27.50 (ISBN 0-87215-499-8). Michie-Bobbs.
Cooperman, Avram M. & Hoerr, Stanley O. Surgery of the Pancreas: A Text & Atlas. LC 77-23621. (Illus.). 1977. 54.50 (ISBN 0-8016-1032-X). Mosby.
Cooperman, Carolyn & Rhoades, Chuck. New Methods for Puberty Education. (Illus.). 1983. 20.00 (ISBN 0-9609366-0-2). NW Plan Parent.
Cooperman, Lee H., jt. ed. see Orkin, Frederick K.
Cooperrider, Edward A., tr. see Steinwede, Dietrich.
Coopers & Lybrand. Employer Accounting for Pension Costs & Other Post-Retirement Benefits. LC 81-68568. 1981. 7.10 (ISBN 0-686-83748-7). Finan Exec.
--International Tax Summaries 1982: A Guide for Planning & Decisions. (Wiley Ronald Series in Professional Accounting & Business). 912p. 1982. 55.00x (ISBN 0-471-87576-7). Ronald Pr.
Coopersmith, Georgia. Directions in Metal: Work Produced at the Johnson Atelier Technical Institute of Sculpture. (Illus.). 24p. (Orig.). 1982. pap. 8.00 (ISBN 0-942746-02-3). Brainerd.
--Twentieth Anniversary Exhibition of the Vogels Collection. (Illus.). 94p. Date not set. pap. 12.50. Brainerd.
Coopersmith, Harry. New Jewish Songbook. LC 65-14593. pap. 7.50x (ISBN 0-87441-060-6). Behrman.
Coopersmith, Stanley. Antecedents of Self-Esteem. 2nd ed. (Illus.). xii, 284p. 1981. pap. 13.00 (ISBN 0-89106-017-0, 7283). Consulting Psychol.
Coopland. Letter to King Richard II. 186p. 1982. 53.00x (ISBN 0-85323-283-0, Pub. by Liverpool Univ England). State Mutual Bk.
Cooray, L. J. Conventions, the Australian Constitution & the Future. xix, 235p. 1979. 24.00x (ISBN 0-9596568-1-2). Rothman.
Coordinating Working Party on Atlantic Fishery Statistics 7th Session, Rome, 1971. FAO-ICES-ICNAF-ICCAT: Report. (FAO Fisheries Reports: No. 121). 49p. 1971. pap. 7.50 (ISBN 0-686-93226-9, F1704, FAO). Unipub.
Coordinating Working Party on Atlantic Fishery Statistics, 6th Session, Copenhagen, 1969. Report. (FAO Fisheries Reports: No. 70). 29p. 1969. pap. 7.50 o.p. (ISBN 0-686-93022-3, F1677, FAO). Unipub.
Coote, Jack H. Monochrome Darkroom Practice. (Illus.). 320p. 1982. 28.95 (ISBN 0-240-51061-5). Focal Pr.
--Monochrome Darkroom Practice. rev. ed. (Illus.). 320p. 1983. pap. 13.95 (ISBN 0-240-51700-8). Butterworth.
Cootes, R. J. The Middle Ages. (Longman Secondary Histories Ser.). (Illus.). 208p. (Orig.). (gr. 6-12). 1980. pap. text ed. 8.75 (ISBN 0-582-20510-7). Longman.
Cootes, R. J. & Snellgrove, L. E. The Ancient World. (Longman Secondary Histories Ser.). (Illus.). 208p. (gr. 6-12). 1978. pap. text ed. 8.75 (ISBN 0-582-20503-4). Longman.
Cootner, Cathryn. Tent & Town: Rugs & Embroideries from Central Asia. LC 82-49068. (The H. McCoy Jones Collection). (Illus.). 16p. 1982. pap. 2.95x (ISBN 0-88401-043-0). Fine Arts Mus.
Cootner, Cathryn M., jt. ed. see Sharpe, William F.
Coover, James. Musical Instrument Collections: Catalogs & Cognate Literature. LC 81-19901. (Detroit Studies in Music Bibliography Ser.: No. 47). 1981. 25.00 (ISBN 0-89990-013-5). Info Coord.
Coover, Robert. Charlie in the House of Rue. Peich, Michael, ed. (Fiction Ser.: No. 1). (Illus.). 1980. 12.00 o.p. (ISBN 0-915778-30-0); ltd. signed ed. 50.00x (ISBN 0-915778-31-9). Penmaen Pr.
--Pricksongs & Descants. 1970. pap. 4.95 (ISBN 0-452-25321-7, Z5321, Plume). NAL.
Coover, Shriver L. Programmed Blueprint Reading. 3rd ed. 1975. text ed. 15.28 o.p. (ISBN 0-07-013063-9, W); tests 16.40 o.p. (ISBN 0-07-013064-7). McGraw.
Coox, Alvin D. The Anatomy of a Small War: The Soviet-Japanese Struggle for Changkufeng-Khasan, 1938. LC 76-51924. (Contributions in Military History: No. 13). 1977. lib. bdg. 35.00 (ISBN 0-8371-9479-2, CSJ/). Greenwood.
Coox, Alvin D. & Conroy, Hilary, eds. China & Japan: Search for Balance Since World War I. LC 77-10006. 468p. 1978. text ed. 36.50 o.p. (ISBN 0-87436-275-X). ABC-Clio.
Copass, Michael, jt. auth. see Eisenberg, Mickey S.
Cope, jt. auth. see Goldman.
Cope, Arthur C., ed. Organic Reactions, Vol. 11. LC 42-20265. 510p. 1975. Repr. of 1960 ed. 29.50 (ISBN 0-88275-881-0). Krieger.
--Organic Reactions, Vol. 12. LC 42-20265. 546p. 1975. Repr. of 1962 ed. 29.50 (ISBN 0-88275-882-9). Krieger.
--Organic Reactions, Vol. 13. LC 42-20265. 390p. 1979. Repr. of 1962 ed. 29.50 (ISBN 0-88275-836-5). Krieger.
--Organic Reactions, Vol. 14. LC 42-20265. 506p. 1978. Repr. of 1965 ed. 29.50 (ISBN 0-88275-730-X). Krieger.
--Organic Reactions, Vol. 15. LC 42-20265. 616p. 1978. Repr. of 1967 ed. 29.50 (ISBN 0-88275-731-8). Krieger.
--Organic Reactions, Vol. 16. LC 42-20265. 456p. 1975. Repr. of 1968 ed. 29.50 (ISBN 0-88275-883-7). Krieger.
Cope, C. B. & Fuller, W. H. The Scientific Management of Hazardous Wastes. LC 82-14650. (Illus.). 375p. Date not set. 69.50 (ISBN 0-521-25100-1). Cambridge U Pr.
Cope, David. New Music Composition. LC 76-21376. 1977. pap. text ed. 12.95 (ISBN 0-02-870630-7). Schirmer Bks.
--New Music Notation. LC 75-32585. 1976. perfect bdg. 7.95 (ISBN 0-8403-1315-2). Kendall-Hunt.
--Quiet Lives. (Vox Humana Ser.). 1983. 12.95 (ISBN 0-89603-048-2); pap. 4.95 (ISBN 0-89603-049-0). Humana.
Cope, David, jt. auth. see Goldman, Myer.
Cope, David E. Organisation Development & Action Research in Hospitals. 176p. 1981. text ed. 44.50x (ISBN 0-566-00387-2). Gower Pub Ltd.
Cope, David H. New Directions in Music. 3rd ed. 286p. 1981. pap. text ed. write for info. (ISBN 0-697-03448-8). Wm C Brown.
Cope, Donald M., jt. auth. see Brickner, William H.
Cope, Dwight W. & Schoude, Lee E. Plastics. LC 77-21618. (Illus.). 112p. 1982. text ed. 5.80 (ISBN 0-87006-426-6). Goodheart.
Cope, Emma E. How to Decipher & Study Old Documents: Being a Guide to the Reading of Ancient Manuscripts, the Key to the Family Deed Chest. 2nd ed. LC 73-18446. 1974. Repr. of 1903 ed. 37.00x (ISBN 0-8103-3701-0). Gale.
Cope, G. M. & Rayner, P. A. The Standard Catalogue of English Milled Coinage, 1662-1972. 1978. 22.00 o.p. (ISBN 0-685-51072-7, Pub by Spink & Son England). S J Durst.
Cope, Gabriele E. Librarianship at a Four Year University: Programs, Syllabi, Bibliography for Library Technicians. 2nd ed. LC 81-69381. 295p. (Orig.). 1981. pap. 17.95x (ISBN 0-933540-02-7). Ego Bks.
Cope, Gabriele E. & Hoffman, Kay Y. Coping with the OCLC Subsystem. 2nd ed. LC 78-108748. 1979. pap. 9.40x (ISBN 0-933540-01-9). Ego Bks.
Cope, Gilbert. Symbolism in the Bible & the Church. 1959. 10.00 (ISBN 0-8022-0300-0). Philos Lib.
Cope, Harley F. Command at Sea. 3rd ed. Bucknell, Howard, 3rd, ed. LC 66-28158. 1966. 9.50x o.p. (ISBN 0-87021-124-2). Naval Inst Pr.
Cope, Jack. The Adversary Within. 208p. 1982. text ed. 19.00x (ISBN 0-391-02697-6, 40255, Pub. by David Philip Pub Africa). Humanities.
Cope, R. & Sawko, F. Computer Methods for Civil Engineering. 336p. 1982. 19.00 (ISBN 0-07-084129-2). McGraw.
Cope, Robert E. Successful Participative Management in Smaller Companies. 125p. (Orig.). 1982. pap. text ed. 18.00 (ISBN 0-9610044-0-1). QDP Inc.
Cope, Zachary. Cope's Early Diagnosis of the Acute Abdomen. 15th ed. Silen, William, ed. (Illus.). 1979. text ed. 17.95x (ISBN 0-19-502455-9); pap. text ed. 10.95x (ISBN 0-19-502456-7). Oxford U Pr.
--History of the Acute Abdomen. 1965. 19.50x (ISBN 0-19-265104-8). Oxford U Pr.
Copeland, Adrian D. Textbook of Adolescent Psychopathology & Treatment. (Illus.). 152p. 1974. 14.75x (ISBN 0-398-03114-2); 9.75x (ISBN 0-398-03115-0). C C Thomas.
Copeland, Benny R. & Sullivan, Nelson G. Cost Accounting: Accumulation, Analysis, & Control. 1977. text ed. 23.95 (ISBN 0-8299-0122-1); check figures bklt. avail. (ISBN 0-8299-0470-0); solutions manual avail. (ISBN 0-8299-0469-7). West Pub.
Copeland, Beth. Spartan Singer. (Orig.). 1975. pap. 1.25x (ISBN 0-914994-02-6, CB-003). Cider Pr.
Copeland, Bonnie C. Lady of Moray. LC 79-51400. 1979. 13.95 o.p. (ISBN 0-689-10996-2). Atheneum.
Copeland, Carolyn. Tankas from the Koelz Collection: Museum of Anthropology, University of Michigan. (Michigan Papers on South & Southeast Asia: No. 18). (Illus.). xii, 99p. (Orig.). 1980. pap. 11.50x (ISBN 0-89148-018-8). Ctr S&SE Asian.
Copeland, Clyde X., ed. see Junior League of Jackson, Mississippi.
Copeland, E. B. Hymenophyllum. Bd. with Trichomanes; Genera Hymenophyllacearum. (Illus.). 460p. (Repr. of 1933-38 eds.). 1975. lib. bdg. 64.00x (ISBN 3-87429-079-4). Lubrecht & Cramer.
Copeland, E. L. El Cristianismo y Otras Religiones. Mora, Abdias A., tr. Orig. Title: Christianity & World Religious. (Illus.). 192p. (Span.). 1981. pap. 3.50 (ISBN 0-311-05760-8, Edit Mundo). Casa Bautista.
Copeland, Edward M. Surgical Oncology. LC 82-8608. 744p. 1983. 58.95x (ISBN 0-471-07997-9, Pub. by Wiley Med). Wiley.

Copeland, Hedary R. A Lipreading Practice Manual for Teenagers & Adults. 2nd ed. LC 71-83512. 1969. pap. text ed. 7.50 (ISBN 0-88200-082-9, B1091). Alexander Graham.
Copeland, J. E., ed. see Linguistic Association of Canada & the U.S.
Copeland, J. L. Transport Properties of Ionic Liquids. 84p. 1974. 25.00x (ISBN 0-677-02830-X). Gordon.
Copeland, John, jt. auth. see Gurland, Barry J.
Copeland, Keith. Aids for the Severely Handicapped. 152p. 1974. 59.00x (ISBN 0-686-98010-7, Pub. by Pitman Bks England). State Mutual Bk.
Copeland, Lewis, ed. High School Subjects Self Taught. 3rd rev. ed. LC 64-13835. 1967. 17.95 (ISBN 0-385-04949-8). Doubleday.
--Ten Thousand Jokes, Toasts & Stories. LC 66-737. 1965. 14.95 (ISBN 0-385-00163-0). Doubleday.
Copeland, Lori. Playing for Keeps. (Candlelight Ecstasy Ser.: No. 134). (Orig.). 1983. pap. 1.95 (ISBN 0-440-17171-7). Dell.
Copeland, Melvin T. & Rogers, Elliott C. Saga of Cape Ann. LC 60-10075. (Illus.). 1966. pap. 4.95 o.p. (ISBN 0-87027-061-3). Cumberland Pr.
Copeland, Mildred, et al. Occupational Therapy for Mentally Retarded Children: Guidelines for Occupational Therapy Aides & Certified Occupational Therapy Assistants. (Illus.). 1976. 19.95 (ISBN 0-8391-0930-X). Univ Park.
Copeland, Morris A. Fact & Theory in Economics. Morse, Chandler, ed. LC 73-8564. 347p. 1973. Repr. of 1958 ed. lib. bdg. 20.00x (ISBN 0-8371-6965-8, COFA). Greenwood.
Copeland, O. Multifluid Thermodynamic Power Cycles: An Invention Report & a Preliminary Assessment of the Potential. (Progress in Solar Energy Supplements SERI Ser.). 1983. pap. text ed. 7.50x (ISBN 0-89553-093-7). Am Solar Energy.
Copeland, Paul W. The Land & People of Jordan. rev. ed. LC 72-5362. (Portraits of the Nation Ser.). (Illus.). (gr. 6 up). 1972. 10.53i (ISBN 0-397-31403-5, JBL-J). Har-Row.
Copeland, Peter. Civil War Uniforms Coloring Book. (Illus.). 1977. pap. 2.00 (ISBN 0-486-23535-1). Dover.
--From Antietam to Gettysburg: A Civil War Coloring Book. (Illus.). 48p. (Orig.). (gr. 3 up). 1983. pap. 2.25 (ISBN 0-486-24476-8). Dover.
--Uniforms of the Napoleonic Wars Coloring Book. (Coloring Bks.). (Illus.). 48p. (Orig.). (gr. 3 up). 1982. pap. 2.50 (ISBN 0-486-24390-7). Dover.
Copeland, Peter & Martin, John. Story of Glass Coloring Book. (Illus.). pap. 2.00 (ISBN 0-486-24199-8). Dover.
Copeland, Peter F. American Military Uniforms, 1639-1968: A Coloring Book. (Coloring Book Ser.). 48p. (Orig.). 1976. pap. 2.25 (ISBN 0-486-23239-5). Dover.
--Pirates & Buccaneers Coloring Book. (Illus.). 1977. pap. 2.00 (ISBN 0-486-23393-6). Dover.
--Working Dress in Colonial & Revolutionary America. LC 76-15309. (Contributions in American History: No. 58). (Illus.). 1977. lib. bdg. 45.00 (ISBN 0-8371-9033-9, COD/). Greenwood.
--World War One Uniforms Coloring Book. (Illus.). pap. 2.00 (ISBN 0-486-23579-3). Dover.
Copeland, R. M., et al. Financial Accounting. LC 79-18276. 517p. 1980. 29.95x (ISBN 0-471-17173-5); working papers, 340 p. 3.00x (ISBN 0-471-05994-3); study guide, 205 p. 10.95x (ISBN 0-471-02289-6). Wiley.
Copeland, Richard W. How Children Learn Mathematics. 3rd ed. (Illus.). 1978. text ed. 20.95x (ISBN 0-02-324780-0). Macmillan.
--Math Activities for Children: A Diagnostic Approach. (Elementary Curriculum Ser.). 1979. pap. text ed. 11.95 (ISBN 0-675-08316-8). Merrill.
Copeland, Robert. Spode's Willow Pattern & Other Design After the Chinese. (Illus.). 280p. 1980. 50.00 (ISBN 0-8478-0264-7). Rizzoli Intl.
Copeland, Roger & Cohen, Marshall. What is Dance? Readings in Theory & Criticism. (Illus.). 512p. 1983. pap. 10.95 (ISBN 0-19-503197-0, GB 720, GB). Oxford U Pr.
Copeland, Roger & Cohen, Roger. What is Dance? Readings in Theory & Criticism. (Illus.). 512p. 1983. 29.95 (ISBN 0-19-503217-9). Oxford U Pr.
Copeland, Ronald M. & Dascher, Paul E. Managerial Accounting: An Introduction to Planning, Information Processing & Control. 2nd ed. LC 74-5147. 658p. 1978. text ed. 32.50x (ISBN 0-471-17171-9); study guide 11.50x (ISBN 0-471-02346-9). Wiley.
Copeland, Ronald M. & Ingram, Robert W. Municipal Financial Reporting & Disclosure Quality. LC 82-11580. (Illus.). 156p. Date not set. pap. text ed. 4.76 (ISBN 0-201-10197-1). A-W.
Copeland, Thomas E. & Weston, J. Fred. Financial Theory & Corporate Policy. LC 78-73366. 1979. text ed. 26.95 (ISBN 0-201-00971-4); solution manual 5.95 (ISBN 0-201-00972-2). A-W.
--Financial Theory & Corporate Policy. 2nd ed. LC 82-11662. (Illus.). 704p. 1983. text ed. 26.95 (ISBN 0-201-10291-9). A-W.
Copeland, Tom. A Consultation in Writing. 52p. 3 ring spiral 25.00 (ISBN 0-934140-05-7). Toys N Things.
Copeland, Tom, ed. Basic Guide to Record Keeping & Taxes. 5th rev. ed. (Business Ideas for Family Day Care Providers Ser.). (Illus.). 40p. (Orig.). 1982. pap. 4.50 (ISBN 0-934140-07-3). Toys N Things.
--Parents in the Workplace: A Management Resource for Employers. (Illus.). 30p. folder 16.50 (ISBN 0-934140-17-0). Toys N Things.
Copeland, William C. Audit-Proof Contracting for Federal Money for Children's Services. LC 76-47868. 1976. pap. text ed. 7.00 (ISBN 0-87868-161-2, CHI-3). Child Welfare.
--Managing Federal Money for Children's Services. LC 77-8655. 1978. pap. text ed. 7.00 (ISBN 0-87868-162-0, CHI-4). Child Welfare.
--Obtaining Federal Money for Children's Services. LC 76-28577. 1976. pap. text ed. 7.00 (ISBN 0-87868-160-4, CHI-2). Child Welfare.
Copeland, William C. & Seneca Corporation. Finding Federal Money for Childrens Services: Title XX & Other Programs. LC 76-10077. 1976. pap. 7.00 (ISBN 0-87868-159-0, CHI-1). Child Welfare.
Copeland, Willis, jt. auth. see Boyan, Norman.
Copeman, George. The Chief Executive & Business Growth. 358p. 1974. 12.00x o.p. (ISBN 0-900537-00-0). Hippocrene Bks.
--The Managing Director. 2nd ed. 283p. 1982. text ed. 36.75x (ISBN 0-09-147280-6, Pub. by Busn Bks England). Renouf.
--What Every Director Wants to Know About the Business. pap. 2.50x o.p. (ISBN 0-686-09304-6). Hippocrene Bks.
Copen, Melvyn R., jt. auth. see Richman, Barry M.
Copenhaver, jt. auth. see Braunstein.
Copenhaver, Edward H. Surgery of the Vulva & Vagina: A Practical Guide. (Illus.). 100p. 1981. text ed. 30.00 (ISBN 0-7216-2718-8). Saunders.
Copes, Jane see Herron, Dudley.
Copi, Irving M. Introduction to Logic. 6th ed. 1982. text ed. 22.95x (ISBN 0-02-324920-X). Macmillan.
--Symbolic Logic. 5th ed. 1979. text ed. 22.95x (ISBN 0-02-324980-3). Macmillan.
Copi, Irving M. & Gould, James A. Readings on Logic. 2nd ed. 1972. pap. 9.95x (ISBN 0-02-324910-2, 32491). Macmillan.
Coplan, Kate & Rosenthal, Constance. Guide to Better Bulletin Boards. LC 76-102937. 232p. 1970. 20.00 (ISBN 0-379-00369-4). Oceana.
Coplan, Michael A., jt. auth. see Moore, John H.
Copland, Aaron. Copland on Music. LC 76-13512. 1976. Repr. of 1960 ed. lib. bdg. 27.50 (ISBN 0-306-70775-6). Da Capo.
--Copland on Music. 1963. pap. 7.95 (ISBN 0-393-00198-9, Norton Lib). Norton.
--What to Listen for in Music. rev. ed. (Illus.). 1957. 14.95 (ISBN 0-07-013089-2, GB). McGraw.
--What to Listen for in Music. rev. ed. (RL 9). 1964. pap. 2.25 (ISBN 0-451-62072-0, ME2072, Ment). NAL.
Copland, Ian. The British Raj & the Indian Princes. 1982. 18.50x (ISBN 0-8364-0893-4, Pub. by Macmillan India). South Asia Bks.
Coplen, Dotty. Parenting A Path Through Childhood. 1982. pap. 7.25 (ISBN 0-903540-61-4, Pub. by Floris Books). St George Bk Serv.
Coplen, Ron, compiled by. Special Libraries: A Cumulative Index. 94p. 1982. 18.75 (ISBN 0-686-81712-5). SLA.
Copleston, Frederick. History of Philosophy: Greece & Rome, 2 pts, Vol. 1. Pt. 1. pap. 3.95 (ISBN 0-385-00210-6, Im); Pt. 2. pap. 4.50 (ISBN 0-385-00211-4). Doubleday.
--History of Philosophy: Late Mediaeval & Renaissance Philosophy, 2 Pts, Vol. 3. 1953. pap. 3.95 pt. 1 (ISBN 0-385-01632-8, Im); pap. 4.95 pt. 2 (ISBN 0-385-06532-9, Im, D136B). Doubleday.
--History of Philosophy: Mediaeval Philosophy, 2 Pts, Vol. 2. Pt. 1. pap. 5.50 (ISBN 0-385-01631-X, Im); Pt. 2. pap. 4.95 (ISBN 0-385-03235-8, Im). Doubleday.
--History of Philosophy: Modern Philosophy: Bentham to Russell, 2 pts, Vol. 8. 1966. Pt. 1. pap. 2.45 (ISBN 0-385-01637-9, Im); Pt. 2. pap. 3.95 (ISBN 0-385-06543-4). Doubleday.
--History of Philosophy: Modern Philosophy: The French Enlightenment to Kant, 2 pts, Vol. 6. Pt. 1. pap. 2.45 (ISBN 0-385-01635-2, Im); Pt. 2. pap. 4.50 (ISBN 0-385-06514-0, Im). Doubleday.
--History of Philosophy: Seventeenth & Eighteenth Century British Philosophers, 2 pts, Vol. 5. pap. 3.95 Pt. 1 (ISBN 0-385-01634-4, Im); pap. 3.95 Pt. 2 (ISBN 0-385-06540-X). Doubleday.
Copley, A., ed. Biorheology: Abstracts of the Second International Congress, No. 2. 1975. pap. text ed. 23.50 o.p. (ISBN 0-08-019962-3). Pergamon.
--Biorheology: Proceedings of the Second International Congress. 1975. pap. text ed. 47.00 o.p. (ISBN 0-08-019963-1). Pergamon.
Copley, Frank O. Exclusus Amator: A Study in Latin Love Poetry. (APA Philological Monographs). pap. 18.00 (ISBN 0-686-95232-4, 40-00-17). Scholars Pr CA.
Copley, Frank S. A Set of Alphabets in Modern Use with Examples of Each Style; Letters, Cyphers, Figures, Monograms, Borders, Compasses & Flourishes. 200p. pap. 15.00 (ISBN 0-87556-490-9). Saifer.
Copley, John S. Letters & Papers of John Singleton Copley & Henry Pelham, 1739-1776. LC 78-100615. (Library of American Art Ser.). (Illus.). 1970. Repr. of 1914 ed. lib. bdg. 42.50 (ISBN 0-306-71406-X). Da Capo.
Copley, R. Evan. Harmony: Baroque to Contemporary, Pt. I. 198p. 1978. pap. text ed. 10.60x (ISBN 0-87563-158-4). Stipes.
--Harmony: Baroque to Contemporary, Pt. II. 198p. 1979. pap. text ed. 11.60x (ISBN 0-87563-175-4). Stipes.
Coplin, William. Teaching Policy Studies. 1978. pap. 6.00 (ISBN 0-918592-26-7). Policy Studies.
Coplin, William D. Introduction to International Politics. 3rd ed. (Illus.). 1980. text ed. 22.95 (ISBN 0-13-485383-0). P-H.
Coplin, William D. & O'Leary, Michael K. Analyzing Public Policy Issues. (Learning Packages in the Policy Sciences Ser.: No. 17). (Illus.). 50p. 1980. pap. text ed. 2.50x (ISBN 0-936826-06-1). Pol Stud Assocs.
Coplin, William D. & Rochester, J. Martin. Dyadic Disputes, 1922-1968. 1976. codebk write for info. (ISBN 0-89138-021-3). ICPSR.
Coplin, William D., ed. Teaching Policy Studies: A Guide to What, How & Where. LC 77-9186. (Policy Studies Organization Ser.). 1978. 21.95x (ISBN 0-669-01829-5, Dist. by Transaction Bks). Lexington Bks.
Copp, Charles A., jt. ed. see Pacholski, Richard A.
Copp, David & Wendell, Susan, eds. Pornography & Censorship. 350p. 1982. 19.95 (ISBN 0-87975-181-9); pap. 9.95 (ISBN 0-87975-182-7). Prometheus Bks.
Copp, David H., jt. auth. see Crawford, Rudd A., Jr.
Coppa, F. J. Camillo di Cavour. (World Leaders Ser.). lib. bdg. 12.95 (ISBN 0-8057-3018-4, Twayne). G K Hall.
Coppa, Frank J. Pope Pius IX. (World Leaders Ser.). 1979. lib. bdg. 14.95 (ISBN 0-8057-7727-X, Twayne). G K Hall.
Coppa, Frank J. & Curran, Thomas J. The Immigrant Experience in America. (Immigrant Heritage of America Ser). 1977. lib. bdg. 11.95 (ISBN 0-8057-8406-3, Twayne). G K Hall.
Coppel, Alfred. The Apocalypse Brigade. 352p. pap. 3.50 (ISBN 0-441-02572-2, Pub. by Charter Bks). Ace Bks.
--The Burning Mountain: A Novel of the Invasion of Japan. LC 82-47674. 448p. 1983. 15.95 (ISBN 0-15-114978-X). HarBraceJ.
Coppen, A., jt. ed. see Paykel, E. S.
Coppenger, Mark T. A Christian View of Justice. Date not set. pap. 6.95 (ISBN 0-8054-6126-4). Broadman. Postponed.
Coppens, Peter R. De see De Coppens, Peter R.
Coppens, Peter R. de see De Coppens, Peter R.
Coppens, Philip, ed. Experimental & Theoretical Studies of Electron Densities. pap. 7.50 (ISBN 0-686-60379-6). Polycrystal Bk Serv.
Copper, Basil. The House of the Wolf. (Illus.). 350p. 1983. 14.95 (ISBN 0-87054-095-5). Arkham.
Copper, John F., jt. auth. see Kintner, William R.
Copperman, Paul. The Literacy Hoax: The Decline of Reading, Writing, & Learning in the Public Schools & What We Can Do About It. LC 78-18703. 1979. pap. 5.95 (ISBN 0-688-08353-6). Quill NY.
Copperud, Roy H. & Nelson, Roy P. Editing the News. 300p. 1983. pap. text ed. write for info. (ISBN 0-697-04353-3). Wm C Brown.
Coppi, B., ed. Theory of Magnetically Confined Plasmas: Proceedings. (Commission of the European Communities Ser.: Eur 5737). (Illus.). 1979. pap. 99.00 (ISBN 0-08-023434-8). Pergamon.
Coppin, Ezra. Too Proud to Die. LC 82-50238. 160p. (Orig.). 1982. pap. 4.95 (ISBN 0-88449-082-3, A424615). Vision Hse.
Coppins, Richard, jt. auth. see Wu, Nesa.
Coppock, J. T. & Duffield, B. S. Recreation in the Countryside: A Spatial Analysis. LC 75-9115. (Illus.). 250p. 1975. 26.00 (ISBN 0-312-66605-5). St Martin.
Coppock, J. T., jt. auth. see Sewell, W. Derrick.
Coppock, J. T. & Wilson, C. B., eds. Environmental Quality: With Emphasis on Urban Problems. 207p. 1974. 22.95x o.p. (ISBN 0-470-17205-3). Halsted Pr.
--Environmental Quality-with Emphasis on Urban Problems. LC 74-9579. 207p. 1974. 12.95 (ISBN 0-470-17205-3). Krieger.
Copps, Dale. The Savage Survivor: Three Hundred Million Years of the Shark. (gr. 7 up). 1976. 5.95 o.s.i. (ISBN 0-685-78821-0, Dist. by Westwind Pr); lib. ed. 5.97 o.s.i. (ISBN 0-695-40663-9). Follett.
--The Sherlock Holmes Puzzle Book. (Illus.). 160p. 1981. pap. 5.95 (ISBN 0-385-14839-9, Dolp). Doubleday.
Copps, E., ed. Menander: Four Plays (The Hero, Epitrepontes, Periceiromene & Samia) (College Classical Ser.). 1981. lib. bdg. 25.00x (ISBN 0-89241-366-2); pap. text ed. 12.50x (ISBN 0-686-94739-8). Caratzas Bros.
Copson, Edward T. Asymptotic Expansions. (Cambridge Tracts in Mathematics & Mathematical Physics). 1965. 24.95 (ISBN 0-521-04721-8). Cambridge U Pr.
--Partial Differential Equations. LC 74-12965. (Illus.). 316p. 1975. 49.50 (ISBN 0-521-20583-2); pap. 18.95 (ISBN 0-521-09893-9). Cambridge U Pr.
Copus, David A. & Rosenzweig, Linda E., eds. OFCCP & Federal Contract Compliance. LC 81-80406. 233p. 1981. text ed. 25.00 (ISBN 0-686-73152-2, A1-1278). PLI.
Coral, Lenore see Munby, A. N.
Corancez, Olivier De. De Jean-Jacques Rousseau. (Rousseauism, 1788-1797). 1978. Repr. lib. bdg. 29.00x o.p. (ISBN 0-8287-0224-1). Clearwater Pub.
Coray, G., jt. ed. see Nievergelt, J.
Coray, Henry. Son of Tears: St. Augustine. 1977. pap. 1.75 o.p. (ISBN 0-89310-002-1). Carillon Bks.
Corben, H. C. & Stehle, Philip. Classical Mechanics. 2nd ed. LC 74-141. 402p. 1974. Repr. of 1960 ed. 25.00 (ISBN 0-88275-162-X). Krieger.
Corbet, jt. auth. see Ovenden.
Corbet, John H. Physical Geography Manual. 1976. pap. text ed. 11.95 (ISBN 0-8403-0963-5). Kendall-Hunt.
Corbett. Roman Art. 4.98 o.p. (ISBN 0-517-30375-2). Crown.
Corbett & Ovenden. The Mammals of Britain & Europe. pap. 15.95 (ISBN 0-686-42745-9, Collins Pub England). Greene.
Corbett, Arthur. History of the Institution of Engineers: Australia 1919-1969. 288p. 1973. text ed. 19.50x (ISBN 0-207-12516-3, Pub. by Inst Engineering Australia). Renouf.
Corbett, Bayliss, ed. CENSORED: Hard-to-Locate Sources of Information on Current Affairs. 12th, rev. ed. LC 81-642893. 53p. (Orig.). 1982. pap. 10.00 (ISBN 0-933152-03-5). Bayliss Corbett.
Corbett, E. V. The Fundamentals of Library Organization & Administration: A Practical Guide. 1978. lib. bdg. 37.50x (ISBN 0-85365-540-5, Pub. by Lib Assn England); pap. text ed. 17.95x (ISBN 0-85365-840-4). Oryx Pr.
Corbett, Edith O. Mouse, Mouser & Mousest. LC 80-67054. (The Saturday Evening Post Read-to-Me Ser.). (Illus.). 96p. (Orig.). (ps up). 1983. 7.95 (ISBN 0-89387-050-1, Co-Pub by Sat Eve Post). Curtis Pub Co.
--The Playtime Shoebox. LC 78-24438. (Illus.). 128p. (gr. 3-5). 1979. PLB 7.79 o.p. (ISBN 0-671-32927-8). Messner.
Corbett, Edmund V. Illustrations Collection: Its Formation, Classification & Exploitation. LC 72-164185. (Illus.). 1971. Repr. of 1941 ed. 34.00x (ISBN 0-8103-3786-X). Gale.
Corbett, Edward P. The Little English Handbook: Choices & Conventions. 3rd ed. LC 80-23739. 259p. 1981. pap. text ed. 9.95x (ISBN 0-673-15662-1). Scott F.
--The Little Rhetoric. LC 76-45081. 1977. pap. text ed. 12.50x (ISBN 0-673-15663-X). Scott F.
--The Little Rhetoric & Handbook. 2nd ed. 550p. 1982. pap. text ed. 14.50x (ISBN 0-673-15733-4); tchrs.' ed avail. Scott F.
Corbett, Edward P., ed. The Essay: Subjects & Stances. (English Literature Ser). (277). 1974. pap. text ed. 11.95 (ISBN 0-13-283515-0). P-H.
Corbett, Edward P. J. The Little Rhetoric & Handbook with Readings. 1983. pap. text ed. 16.50x (ISBN 0-673-15830-6). Scott F.
Corbett, J. Elliott. Prophets on Main Street. rev. ed. LC 77-79597. 1977. pap. 7.25 (ISBN 0-8042-0841-7). John Knox.
Corbett, J. W., jt. ed. see Urli, N. B.
Corbett, James A. & Moore, Philip S., eds. Petri Pictaviensis Allegoriae Super Tabernaculum Moysi. (Mediaeval Studies Ser.: No. 3). 1938. 21.95 (ISBN 0-268-00207-X). U of Notre Dame Pr.
Corbett, James W. & Ianniello, Louis C., eds. Radiation-Induced Voids in Metals: Proceedings. LC 72-600048. (AEC Symposium Ser.). 884p. 1972. pap. 30.00 (ISBN 0-87079-320-9, CONF-710601); microfiche 4.50 (ISBN 0-87079-321-7, CONF-710601). DOE.
Corbett, Margaret D. How to Improve Your Sight. (Illus.). 1970. 2.98 o.p. (ISBN 0-517-06745-5). Crown.
Corbett, Percy E. Study of International Law. (Orig.). 1955. pap. text ed. 2.35 (ISBN 0-685-19772-7). Phila Bk Co.
Corbett, Philip B. Petronius. (World Authors Ser.: No. 97). 13.95 o.p. (ISBN 0-8057-2698-5, Tawyne). G K Hall.
Corbett, Scott. The Baseball Bargain. LC 74-86618. (Illus.). (gr. 4-6). 1970. 5.95 o.p. (ISBN 0-316-15683-3, Pub. by Atlantic Monthly Pr). Little.
--The Disappearing Dog Trick. (The Trick Ser). (Illus.). (gr. 4-6). 1963. 6.95 o.p. (ISBN 0-316-15706-6, Pub. by Atlantic Monthly Pr). Little.
--The Discontented Ghost. (gr. 7 up). 1978. 10.95 (ISBN 0-525-28775-2, 01064-310, Unicorn Bk). Dutton.
--Dr. Merlin's Magic Shop. (Illus.). (gr. 1-5). 1973. 4.95 o.p. (ISBN 0-316-15709-0, Pub. by Atlantic Monthly Pr). Little.
--The Foolish Dinosaur Fiasco. (Illus.). (gr. 1-3). 1978. 6.95 (ISBN 0-316-15657-4, Pub. by Atlantic Monthly Pr). Little.
--Grave Doubts. LC 82-47916. 144p. (gr. 3-7). 1982. 10.95g (ISBN 0-316-15659-0, Pub. by Atlantic Monthly Pr). Little.
--Great McGoniggle Rides Shotgun. (gr. k-6). 1980. pap. 1.25 (ISBN 0-440-43313-4, YB). Dell.

--The Hangman's Ghost Trick. (Illus.). (gr. 4-6). 1977. 6.95 (ISBN 0-316-15728-7, Atlantic-Little, Brown). Little.
--Home Computers: A Simple & Informative Guide. (Illus.). 128p. (gr. 5 up). 1980. 8.95 (ISBN 0-316-15658-2, Pub. by Atlantic Monthly Pr); pap. 5.70i (ISBN 0-316-15712-0). Little.
--Jokes to Read in the Dark. LC 79-23129. (Illus.). 80p. (gr. 5-9). 1980. 9.95 (ISBN 0-525-32796-7); pap. 2.95 (ISBN 0-525-45052-1, Unicorn Bk). Dutton.
--The Lemonade Trick. (The Trick Ser). (Illus.). (gr. 4-6). 1960. 7.95 (ISBN 0-316-15694-9, Pub. by Atlantic Monthly Pr). Little.
--The Red Room Riddle. (A Corbett Riddle Bk.). (Illus.). 128p. (gr. 4-6). 1972. 6.95 (ISBN 0-316-15719-8, Pub. by Atlantic Monthly Pr.). Little.
--Run for the Money. (Illus.). (gr. 4-6). 1973. 5.95 (ISBN 0-316-15707-4, Pub. by Atlantic Monthly Pr). Little.
--What Makes a Boat Float? LC 76-94498. (gr. 4-6). 1970. 6.95 (ISBN 0-316-15713-9, Pub. by Atlantic Monthly Pr). Little.
--What Makes TV Work. (Illus.). (gr. 3 up). 1965. 4.95 o.p. (ISBN 0-316-15696-5, Pub. by Atlantic Monthly Pr). Little.
Corbett, W. J. The Song of Pentecost. (Illus.). 224p. (gr. 5 up). 1983. 11.95 (ISBN 0-525-44051-8, 01258-370). Dutton.
Corbetta, Francesco, jt. auth. see Bianchini, Francesco.
Corbiere. The Centenary Corbiere. Warner, Val, tr. from Fr. LC 74-18607. 290p. 1975. 12.00 (ISBN 0-8023-1256-X); pap. 5.95 (ISBN 0-85635-061-3). Dufour.
Corbiere, Tristan. The Centenary Corbiere. bi-lingual ed. Warner, Val, tr. from Fr. (Translation Ser.). 1980. 12.95 o.p. (ISBN 0-85635-060-5, Pub. by Carcanet New Pr England). Humanities.
Corbiere-Gille, Gisele, jt. auth. see Waldinger, Renee.
Corbierre, Anne. Paris. LC 80-50996. (Rand McNally Pocket Guide Ser.). (Illus.). 1983. pap. 4.95 (ISBN 0-528-84273-0). Rand.
Corbin, Alan, jt. ed. see Briggs, Michael.
Corbin, Charles B. & Corbin, David E. Homemade Play Equipment. (Illus.). 115p. 1981. pap. text ed. 3.95x (ISBN 0-89641-058-7). American Pr.
Corbin, David E., jt. auth. see Corbin, Charles B.
Corbin, Frederick T., ed. World Soy Bean Research Conference II: Proceedings. 1980. lib. bdg. 45.00 (ISBN 0-89158-678-4). Westview.
Corbin, H. Dan. Recreation Leadership. 3rd ed. LC 70-76313. 1970. text ed. 20.95 (ISBN 0-13-767970-X). P-H.
Corbin, Henry. Avicenna & the Visionary Recital. Trask, Willard R., tr. from French. (Dunquin Ser.: No. 13). 278p. 1980. pap. text ed. 13.50 (ISBN 0-88214-213-5). Spring Pubns.
--The Man of Light in Iranian Sufism. Pearson, Nancy, tr. from Fr. LC 77-6013. 1978. pap. 9.95 (ISBN 0-394-73441-6). Shambhala Pubns.
Corbin, Patricia. Designers Design for Themselves. (Illus.). 96p. 1981. 11.95 (ISBN 0-525-93135-X). Dutton.
--Summer Cottages & Castles: Scenes from the Good Life. (Illus.). 144p. 1983. 29.95 (ISBN 0-525-93279-8, 02908-870). Dutton.
Corbin, Peter, jt. auth. see Thoman, Richard S.
Corbin, Richard, ed. see Henry, O.
Corbin, William. The Day Willie Wasn't. LC 76-126446. (Illus.). (gr. k-3). 1971. PLB 4.69 o.p. (ISBN 0-698-30061-0, Coward). Putnam Pub Group.
--The Everywhere Cat. (Illus.). (ps-1). 1970. PLB 4.49 o.p. (ISBN 0-698-30072-6, Coward). Putnam Pub Group.
--The Golden Mare. (Illus.). (gr. 6-7). 1955. 5.95 o.p. (ISBN 0-698-20054-3, Coward). Putnam Pub Group.
--The Pup with the Up & Down Tail. (Illus.). (gr. 2-6). 1972. 5.95 o.p. (ISBN 0-698-20169-8, Coward). Putnam Pub Group.
--Smoke. (gr. 5-9). 1967. 7.95 o.p. (ISBN 0-698-20131-0, Coward). Putnam Pub Group.
Corbitt, David L. Formation of the North Carolina Counties, 1663-1943. 1975. pap. 8.00 (ISBN 0-86526-032-X). NC Archives.
Corbitt, Helen. Helen Corbitt Cooks for Company. LC 74-599. 1974. 14.95 (ISBN 0-395-18491-6). HM.
Corbitt, Helen L. Helen Corbitt's Cookbook. (Illus.). 1976. 11.95 (ISBN 0-395-07577-7). HM.
Corbitt, Mary K., ed. Results from the Second Mathematics Assessment of the NAEP. LC 81-4322. 167p. 1981. 9.00 (ISBN 0-87353-172-8). NCTM.
Corbman, B. Textiles: Fiber to Fabric. 6th ed. 608p. 1982. text ed. 23.95x (ISBN 0-07-013137-6, C). McGraw.
Corbman, B. P., jt. auth. see Potter, Maurice D.
Corbman, Bernard P. Textiles: Fiber to Fabric. 5th ed. (Illus.). 512p. (gr. 12). 1975. text ed. 23.35 (ISBN 0-07-013125-2, G); instructor's manual & key 6.95 (ISBN 0-07-013126-0). McGraw.
Corbman, Bernard P. & Krieger, Murray. Mathematics of Retail Merchandising. 2nd ed. 450p. 1972. 29.95x (ISBN 0-471-06587-0). Ronald Pr.
Corbon, Anthime. De l'Enseignement Professionnel. 4th ed. (Conditions of the 19th Century French Working Class Ser.). 192p. (Fr.). 1974. Repr. lib. bdg. 55.50x o.p. (ISBN 0-8287-0226-8, 1144). Clearwater Pub.
--Le Secret du Peuple de Paris. (Conditions of the 19th Century French Working Class Ser.). 412p. (Fr.). 1974. Repr. of 1863 ed. lib. bdg. 95.50x o.p. (ISBN 0-8287-0227-6, 1084). Clearwater Pub.
Corbridge, D. E. Phosphorus: An Outline of Its Chemistry, Biochemistry & Technology. 2nd ed. 1980. 85.00 (ISBN 0-444-41887-3). Elsevier.
Corbridge, S. The Structural Chemistry of Phosphorus. LC 64-4605. 560p. 1974. 106.50 (ISBN 0-444-41073-2). Elsevier.
Corbus, Howard F. & Swanson, Laura L. Adopting the Problem-Oriented Medical Record in Nursing Homes: A Do-It-Yourself Manual. LC 78-53068. 98p. 1978. pap. 12.95 (ISBN 0-913654-44-2). Aspen Systems.
Corbusier. Verde to San Carlos. LC 68-24017. (Illus.). 1971. 8.95 (ISBN 0-912762-16-0); deluxe ed. 40.00 (ISBN 0-912762-17-9). King.
Corcoran, A. Wayne. Costs: Accounting, Analysis & Control. LC 77-18798. (Accounting & Information Systems Ser.). 786p. 1978. text ed. 38.95x (ISBN 0-471-17251-0). Wiley.
Corcoran, Barbara. All the Summer Voices. LC 73-76316. (Illus.). 208p. (gr. 5-9). 1973. 6.25 o.p. (ISBN 0-689-30107-3). Atheneum.
--Making It. 1982. pap. 1.95 cancelled o.p. (ISBN 0-671-44219-8). Archway.
--Sasha, My Friend. LC 69-703589. 1969. 7.95 o.p. (ISBN 0-689-20582-1). Atheneum.
--Strike! LC 82-13759. 168p. (gr. 6 up). 1983. 10.95 (ISBN 0-689-30952-X). Atheneum.
--A Watery Grave. LC 82-1726. 180p. (gr. 4-6). 1982. 9.95 (ISBN 0-689-30919-8). Atheneum.
Corcoran, Eileen. Meeting Basic Competencies in Communications. 1979. pap. 2.75x (ISBN 0-88323-152-2, 242); tchr's answer key 1.00x (ISBN 0-88323-156-5, 246). Richards Pub.
--Meeting Basic Competencies in Math. 1978. pap. text ed. 2.75x (ISBN 0-88323-138-7, 227); tchrs answer key free (ISBN 0-88323-141-7, 230). Richards Pub.
--Reading for Survival. 1978. pap. 2.75x (ISBN 0-88323-145-X, 234); tchr's. answer key free (ISBN 0-88323-151-4, 240). Richards Pub.
Corcoran, Eileen L. Finding Ourselves. 1971. pap. text ed. 2.75x (ISBN 0-88323-014-3, 114). Richards Pub.
--Know Your Signs - Be a Better Driver, Bk. 1. (Know Your Signs Ser.). 1982. pap. 3.95x (ISBN 0-88323-049-6, 258). Richards Pub.
--Know Your Signs - Be a Better Driver: Driving Interstate & Superhighways. (Know Your Signs Ser.). 1973. pap. 3.95x (ISBN 0-88323-112-3, 200). Richards Pub.
--Meeting Basic Competencies in Practical Science & Health: A Workstudy Book to Improve Daily Living Skills. (Illus.). 1979. 2.75x (ISBN 0-88323-146-8, 237); tchrs answer key free (ISBN 0-88323-154-9, 245). Richards Pub.
--Meeting Basic Competencies in Reading. 1977. pap. text ed. 2.75x (ISBN 0-88323-134-4, 221); tchrs answer key 1.00 (ISBN 0-88323-144-1, 232). Richards Pub.
--Rights & Duties of Citizens: Practice Materials for Foundations of Citizenship. Bk. 1 1964. pap. 2.50x o.p. (ISBN 0-88323-061-5, 159); Bk. 2 1965. pap. 2.50x o.p. (ISBN 0-88323-062-3, 160); Bk. 3 1970. pap. 2.50x o.p. (ISBN 0-88323-063-1, 161). Richards Pub.
--Weather & Us, Bk. 1. (Science Ser.). 1967. pap. 1.50x (ISBN 0-88323-078-X, 175). Richards Pub.
--Weather & Us, Bk. 2. (Science Ser.). 1967. pap. 1.50x (ISBN 0-88323-079-8, 176). Richards Pub.
Corcoran, Eileen L. & Pavka, John. What Is Electricity? (Science Ser.). 1966. pap. 1.50x (ISBN 0-88323-080-1, 177). Richards Pub.
Corcoran, John & Farkas, Emil. The Complete Martial Arts Catalogue. 1977. 10.95 o.p. (ISBN 0-685-76281-5); pap. 7.95 o.p. (ISBN 0-671-22668-1). S&S.
Corcoran, John, jt. auth. see Farkas, Emil.
Corcoran, John, ed. see Tarski, Alfred.
Corcoran, M. Jerome. Catholic Elementary School Principal. 1st ed. 1961. 9.95 o.p. (ISBN 0-02-829220-0). Glencoe.
Corcoran, Theresa S. Vida Dutton Scudder. (United States Authors Ser.). 1982. lib. bdg. 15.95 (ISBN 0-8057-7354-1, Twayne). G K Hall.
Cord, Robert L., et al. Political Science: An Introduction. 688p. 1974. Repr. text ed. 22.95 (ISBN 0-13-687889-X); study guide & access wkbk. 7.95 (ISBN 0-13-687913-6). P-H.
Cord, William O. An Introduction to Richard Wagner's Der Ring Des Nibelungen: A Handbook. LC 82-14417. (Illus.). 175p. 1983. text ed. 19.95x (ISBN 0-8214-0648-5, 82-84176); pap. 11.95 (ISBN 0-8214-0708-2, 82-84770). Ohio U Pr.
Corda, A. C. Icones Fungorum Hucusque Cognitorum. 1963. 152.00 (ISBN 3-7682-7050-5). Lubrecht & Cramer.
Cordasco, Francesco. American Medical Imprints, 1820-1910: A Checklist of Publications Illustrating the History & Progress of Medical Science & Education & the Healing Arts in the United States. 850p. 1983. 125.00 (ISBN 0-940198-01-0). Junius-Vaughn.
--Bilingual Schooling in the United States: A Sourcebook for Educational Personnel. 1976. 33.12x (ISBN 0-07-013127-9, W). McGraw.
--A Brief History of Education. 2nd rev. ed. (Quality Paperback Ser.: No. 67). 1976. pap. 4.95 (ISBN 0-8226-0067-6). Littlefield.
--Immigrant Children in American Schools: A Classified & Annotated Bibliography with Selected Source Documents. LC 76-45096. 1976. lib. bdg. 35.00x (ISBN 0-678-00743-8). Kelley.
--Register of Eighteenth Century Bibliographies & References: A Chronological Quarter-Century Survey Relating to English Literature, Booksellers, Newspapers, Periodicals, Printing & Publishing, Aesthetics, Art & Music, Economics, History & Science, a Preliminary Contribution. LC 76-4182. 1968. Repr. of 1950 ed. 30.00x (ISBN 0-8103-3521-2). Gale.
Cordasco, Francesco & Gatner, Elliott S. Research & Report Writing. rev. ed. (Quality Paperback: No. 277). 146p. 1974. pap. 3.95 (ISBN 0-8226-0277-6). Littlefield.
Cordasco, Francesco, ed. Bilingual Education in American Schools: A Guide to Information Sources. Bernstein, George. LC 79-15787. (Education Information Guide Ser.: Vol. 3). 1979. 42.00x (ISBN 0-8103-1447-9). Gale.
--Italian Americans: A Guide to Information Sources. LC 78-4833. (Ethnic Studies Information Guide Ser.: Vol. 2). 1978. 42.00x (ISBN 0-8103-1397-9). Gale.
--Jacob Riis Revisited. LC 72-93134. Repr. of 1970 ed. lib. bdg. 25.00x (ISBN 0-678-00706-3). Kelley.
Cordasco, Francesco & Alloway, David N., eds. Medical Education in the United States: A Guide to Information Sources. LC 79-24030. (Education Information Guide Ser.: Vol. 8). 1980. 42.00x (ISBN 0-8103-1458-4). Gale.
--Sociology of Education: A Guide to Information Sources. LC 78-10310. (Education Information Guide Ser.: Vol. 2). 1979. 42.00x (ISBN 0-8103-1436-3). Gale.
Cordasco, Francesco, ed. see Harper, Richard C.
Cordasco, Francesco, ed. see Knoche, Carl H.
Cordasco, Francesco, ed. see Mostwin, Danuta.
Cordasco, Francesco, ed. see Wilhelm, Hubert G.
Cordasco, Francesco, et al. The Puerto Rican Experience: A Sociological Sourcebook. (Quality Paperback: No. 259). (Orig.). 1975. Repr. of 1973 ed. pap. 5.95 (ISBN 0-8226-0259-8). Littlefield.
Cordasco, Francesco, et al, eds. History of American Education: A Guide to Information Sources. LC 79-23010. (Education Information Guide Ser.: Vol. 7). 1979. 42.00x (ISBN 0-8103-1382-0). Gale.
--The School in the Social Order: A Sociological Introduction to Educational Understanding. LC 81-40495. 438p. 1981. pap. text ed. 16.50 (ISBN 0-8191-1731-5). U Pr of Amer.
Corday & Swan. Clinical Strategies in Ischemic Heart Disease: New Concepts & Current Controversies. 1979. 56.00 o.p. (ISBN 0-683-02080-3). Williams & Wilkins.
Corddry, Thomas. Kibby & the Red Elephant. LC 72-13771. (Illus.). (gr. 3-6). 1973. 4.95 (ISBN 0-87955-106-2). O'Hara.
Cordeau, J., ed. see International Symposium on Neurophysiology.
Cordell, Geoffrey A. Introduction to Alkaloids: A Biogenetic Approach. LC 80-39651. 1056p. 1981. 150.00 (ISBN 0-471-03478-9, Pub. by Wiley-Interscience). Wiley.
Cordemoy, Geraud de. Philosophical Discourse Concerning Speech (1668) & a Discourse Written to a Learned Frier (1670) LC 72-6400. (History of Psychology Ser.). 224p. 1972. Repr. 29.00x (ISBN 0-8201-1106-6). Schol Facsimiles.
Corden, W. M. Inflation, Exchange Rates, & the World Economy: Lectures on Int'l Monetary Economics. rev. ed. (Studies in Business & Society Ser.). 160p. 1981. 15.00x (ISBN 0-226-11585-2). U of Chicago Pr.
--Inflation, Exchange Rates, & the World Economy: Lectures on International Monetary Economics. LC 76-58331. (Studies in Business & Society). 1977. pap. 4.00x (ISBN 0-226-11584-4). U of Chicago Pr.
--Trade Policy & Economic Welfare. (Illus.). 1974. text ed. 45.00x (ISBN 0-19-828199-4); pap. text ed. 17.95x (ISBN 0-19-828401-2). Oxford U Pr.
Corden, W. M. & Fels, Gerhard, eds. Public Assistance to Industry: Protection & Subsidies in Britain & Germany. new ed. LC 76-19791. (Illus.). 1976. lib. bdg. 36.25 o.p. (ISBN 0-89158-632-6). Westview.
Cordenoy, E. Jacob De. Flore De l'Ile De la Reunion (Mascarene Islands) 1972. Repr. of 1895 ed. 60.00 (ISBN 3-7682-0758-7). Lubrecht & Cramer.
Corder, A. S. Maintenance Management Techniques. 1976. 22.50 o.p. (ISBN 0-07-084459-3, P&RB). McGraw.
Corder, George E. Your Brain-Image Power. LC 82-90505. (How to Selfsex & Imagize Your Way to Super-Successful Living). 200p. 1983. lib. bdg. 25.00 (ISBN 0-9609246-0-4). G E Corder.
--Your Brain-Image Power: How to Selfsex & Imagize Your Way to Super-Successful Living. LC 82-90505. 200p. 1983. lib. bdg. 25.00 (ISBN 0-9609246-0-4). Brain-Image.
Corder, Jim. Shakespeare, Nineteen Sixty-Four. 1965. 8.00x (ISBN 0-912646-20-9). Tex Christian.
Corder, Jim W. Contemporary Writing: Process & Practice. 1979. text ed. 15.50x (ISBN 0-673-15100-X). Scott F.
--Contemporary Writing: Process & Practice. 2nd ed. 1983. pap. text ed. 13.95x (ISBN 0-673-15430-0). Scott F.
--Contemporary Writing with Handbook. 2nd ed. 1983. text ed. 15.95x (ISBN 0-673-15443-2). Scott F.
--Handbook of Current English. 6th ed. 1981. text ed. 13.50x (ISBN 0-673-15587-0); pap. 13.50x (ISBN 0-673-15425-4). Scott F.
--Rhetoric: A Text-Reader on Language & Its Uses. (Orig.). 1965. pap. text ed. 5.50 (ISBN 0-685-19762-X). Phila Bk Co.
Corder, Jim W. & Kendall, Lyle H., Jr. College Rhetoric. 1962. text ed. 5.50x (ISBN 0-685-19687-9). Phila Bk Co.
Corder, Jim W., et al. Starpoint: A Shining Place. LC 78-26132. (Illus., Orig.). 1978. pap. 4.95 (ISBN 0-912646-50-0). Tex Christian.
Corder, S. Pit. Error Analysis & Interlanguage. 128p. 1981. pap. text ed. 11.95x (ISBN 0-19-437073-9). Oxford U Pr.
Cordes, Alfred. The Descent of the Doves: Camus's Journey to the Spirit. LC 79-3811. 1980. text ed. 20.75 o.p. (ISBN 0-8191-0931-2); pap. text ed. 11.50 o.p. (ISBN 0-8191-0932-0). U Pr of Amer.
Cordes, Carole V., jt. auth. see Babin, Edith H.
Cordes, Eugene & Schaeffer, Riley S. Chemistry. (Rice Chemistry Ser.). (Illus.). 702p. 1973. text ed. 29.50 scp o.p. (ISBN 0-06-041359-X, HarpC); instructor's manual avail. o.p. (ISBN 0-06-361393-X). Har-Row.
Cordes, Eugene H., jt. auth. see Mahler, Henry R.
Cordes, Lianne. The Reflecting Pond. 1980. pap. 6.95 (ISBN 0-89486-121-2). Hazelden.
Cordier, J., jt. ed. see Lowenthal, F.
Cordier, Sherwood S. The Air & Sea Lanes of the North Atlantic: Their Security in the Nineteen Eighties. LC 81-40180. 90p. (Orig.). 1981. pap. text ed. 6.50 (ISBN 0-8191-1587-8). U Pr of Amer.
--Calculus of Power: The Current Soviet-American Conventional Military Balance in Central Europe. 3rd ed. LC 79-5435. 1980. pap. text ed. 8.00 (ISBN 0-8191-0883-9). U Pr of Amer.
Cording, Edward J., jt. ed. see American Society of Civil Engineers.
Cordingley, Patrick, jt. auth. see Limb, Sue.
Cordingly, David. Marine Painting in England, 1700-1900. (Illus.). 1974. 17.95 o.p. (ISBN 0-517-51229-7, C N Potter Bks). Crown.
Cordle, Thomas. Andre Gide. LC 74-80079. (Griffin Authors Ser). 183p. 1975. pap. 4.95 o.p. (ISBN 0-312-03640-X). St Martin.
--Andre Gide. (World Authors Ser.: France: No. 86). lib. bdg. 12.50 o.p. (ISBN 0-8057-2364-1, Twayne). G K Hall.
Cordner, Gary W., jt. auth. see Hudzik, John.
Cordner, Michael, ed. see Etherege, George.
Cordon, William A. Properies, Evaluation & Control of Engineering Materials. 1979. text ed. 32.50 (ISBN 0-07-013123-6, C); solution manual 7.95 (ISBN 0-07-013124-4). McGraw.
Cordova, Efren, jt. auth. see Morris, James O.
Cords, Nicholas & Gerster, Patrick. Myth & the American Experience, Vol. 1. 2nd ed. 1978. pap. text ed. 13.95x (ISBN 0-02-471880-7). Macmillan.
Cords, Nicholas, jt. auth. see Gerster, Patrick.
Corduneanu, Constantin. Principles of Differential & Integral Equations. 2nd ed. LC 77-2962. 1977. text ed. 14.95 (ISBN 0-8284-0295-7). Chelsea Pub.
Cordwell, Miriam & Rudoy, Marion. The Complete Book of Men's Hair Styles & Hair Care. LC 75-147328. (Illus.). 128p. 1974. 4.95 o.p. (ISBN 0-517-51533-4). Crown.
Cordy, Peter, ed. Creative Source - Fourth Annual. 4th ed. 442p. 1983. 45.00 (ISBN 0-920986-03-X). Wilcord Pubns.
Core, Earl L., jt. auth. see Strausbaugh, P. D.
Core, George & Sullivan, Walter. Writing from the Inside. 1983. 8.95x (ISBN 0-393-95246-0); instr.' manual avail. (ISBN 0-393-95337-8). Norton.
Core, Lucy, ed. The Louisiana Almanac, 1983-84 Edition. 512p. (Orig.). 1983. pap. 9.95 (ISBN 0-88289-297-5). Pelican.
Core, Lucy, ed. see Women of Christ Church Cathedral.
Corea, Gena. The Hidden Malpractice. 1978. pap. 1.95 o.s.i. (ISBN 0-515-04522-5). Jove Pubns.
Corelli, Marie. A Romance of Two Worlds. LC 72-81601. 328p. 1982. Repr. of 1973 ed. 12.00 (ISBN 0-89345-401-X, Spirit Fiction). Garber Comm.
Cores, Lucy. Katya. 1980. 10.95 o.p. (ISBN 0-312-45096-6). St Martin.
Corey, E. Raymond & Star, Steven H. Organization Strategy: A Marketing Approach. LC 79-132151. 1971. 25.00x (ISBN 0-87584-088-4). Harvard Busn.
Corey, E. Raymond, ed. Industrial Marketing: Cases & Concepts. 2nd ed. (Illus.). 432p. 1976. 24.95 (ISBN 0-13-464248-1). P-H.

Corey, Gerald. I Never Knew I Had a Choice. 2nd. ed. LC 82-4300. (Psychology Ser.). 400p. 1982. pap. text ed. 14.95 (ISBN 0-534-01201-9). Brooks-Cole.

--Theory & Practice of Counseling & Psychotherapy. 2nd ed. LC 81-6139. 270p. 1981. text ed. 18.95 (ISBN 0-8185-0455-2). Brooks-Cole.

--Theory & Practice of Group Counseling. LC 80-18985. 500p. 1980. text ed. 19.95 (ISBN 0-8185-0400-5). Brooks-Cole.

Corey, Gerald & Corey, Marianne S. Groups: Process & Practice. LC 77-8324. (Illus.). 1977. pap. text ed. 12.95 o.p. (ISBN 0-8185-0235-5). Brooks-Cole.

Corey, Helen. Art of Syrian Cookery. LC 61-18785. 1962. 12.95 (ISBN 0-385-00295-5). Doubleday.

Corey, Joseph, jt. auth. see Bodle, Yvonne.

Corey, Marianne S., jt. auth. see Corey, Gerald.

Corey, Mary & Westermark, Victoria. Fer Shur! How to be a Valley Girl - Totally! 64p. 1982. pap. 2.50 (ISBN 0-553-23237-1). Bantam.

Corey, Stephen M. Audio-Visual Materials of Instruction, Pt. 1. LC 49-8494. (National Society for the Study of Education 48th Yearbook Ser.). 1949. lib. bdg. 6.50 o.s.i. (ISBN 0-226-60004-1). U of Chicago Pr.

Corey, Stephen M., ed. In-Service Education for Teachers, Supervisors & Administrators. LC 57-631. (National Society for the Study of Education Yearbooks Ser: No. 56 Pt. 1). 1956. 6.50x o.s.i. (ISBN 0-226-60040-8). U of Chicago Pr.

Corfield, P. J. The Impact of English Towns, Seventeen Hundred to Eighteen Hundred. 224p. 1982. 23.95 (ISBN 0-19-215830-9); pap. 9.95x (ISBN 0-19-289093-X). Oxford U Pr.

Corfield, Virginia. A Celestial Fix: Reflections in Psalm 119, 89-132. LC 82-90797. (Reflection Ser.: Bk. 3). 121p. 1983. 8.95 (ISBN 0-9603298-3-8). Provident.

Coriell, Rebekah, jt. auth. see Coriell, Ron.

Coriell, Ron & Coriell, Rebekah. A Child's Book of Character Building, Bk. Two. (ps-2). 1981. 8.95 (ISBN 0-8007-1265-X). Revell.

--Show & Tell. (Character Builders Ser.). (ps-2). 1980. 1.35 o.p. (ISBN 0-8007-7007-2, Christian School Curriculum). Revell.

Corillion, Robert. Les Charophycees de France et de l'Europe Occidentale. 1972. 70.40 (ISBN 3-87429-014-X). Lubrecht & Cramer.

Corinne, Tee. Labiaflowers. 48p. (Orig.). 1981. pap. 3.95 (ISBN 0-930044-20-7). Naiad Pr.

--Yantras of Womanlove. 100p. (Orig.). 1982. pap. 6.95 (ISBN 0-930044-30-4). Naiad Pr.

Corinth, K. Fashion Showmanship: Everything You Need to Know to Give a Fashion Show. 24.95x (ISBN 0-87245-061-9). Textile Bk.

Corinth, Kay. Fashion Showmanship: Everything You Need to Know to Give a Fashion Show. LC 76-109430. (Illus.). 280p. 1970. 24.95 (ISBN 0-471-17480-7). Wiley.

Cork, jt. auth. see Cox.

Cork, R. Margaret. The Forgotten Children. 1.95 o.p. (ISBN 0-686-92094-5). Hazelden.

Cork, Seamus. Irish Erotic Art. 96p. 1981. 5.95 (ISBN 0-312-43601-7); prepack 79.50 (ISBN 0-312-43602-5). St Martin.

Corke, jt. ed. see Bruck.

Corke, Helen. In Our Infancy: An Autobiography, Pt. 1, 1882-1912. LC 74-31799. (Illus.). 250p. 1975. 34.50 (ISBN 0-521-20797-5). Cambridge U Pr.

Corkin, Suzanne, et al, eds. Alzheimer's Disease: A Report of Progress in Research. (Aging Ser.: Vol. 19). 550p. 1982. text ed. 49.00 (ISBN 0-89004-685-9). Raven.

Corkum, Collin J. & Corkum, Jerria G. Spelling & Meaning Systems. 205p. (Orig.). 1982. pap. 9.95 (ISBN 0-686-37778-8). Brainstorm Bks.

--Word Power Systems. 220p. 1983. pap. 9.95. BrainStorm Bks.

Corkum, Collin J. & Girard-Corkum, Jerria. Spelling Systems for All Ages & Levels of Achievement. 130p. 1981. write for info. o.s.i. BrainStorm Bks.

Corkum, Jerria G., jt. auth. see Corkum, Collin J.

Corl, Carolyn K., jt. auth. see Straatveit, Tyyne.

Corlett, E. N. & Richardson, J. Stress, Work Design & Productivity. (Wiley Ser. on Studies in Occupational Stress). 271p. 1981. 37.95x (ISBN 0-471-28044-5, Pub. by Wiley-Interscience). Wiley.

Corlett, E. N., jt. ed. see Gudnason, C. H.

Corlett, P. N. Practical Programming. 2nd ed. LC 75-161295. (School Mathematics Project Handbooks). (Illus.). 1971. 27.95 (ISBN 0-521-08198-X); pap. 11.95x (ISBN 0-521-09740-1). Cambridge U Pr.

Corlett, William & Moore, John. Questions of Human Existence As Answered by Major World Religions: The Buddha Way. LC 79-15685. 160p. (YA) 1980. 8.95 o.p. (ISBN 0-87888-153-0). Bradbury Pr.

--Questions of Human Existence As Answered by Major World Religions: The Hindu Sound. LC 79-15815. 160p. (YA) 1980. 8.95 o.p. (ISBN 0-87888-151-4). Bradbury Pr.

--Questions of Human Existence As Answered by Major World Religions: The Islamic Space. LC 79-15204. 160p. (YA) 1980. 8.95 o.p. (ISBN 0-87888-154-9). Bradbury Pr.

--Questions of Human Existence As Answered by Major World Religions: The Judaic Law. LC 79-16432. 160p. (YA) 1980. 8.95 o.p. (ISBN 0-87888-152-2). Bradbury Pr.

--Questions of Human Existence As Answered by Major World Religions: The Question of Religion. LC 79-15140. 112p. (YA) 1980. 8.95 o.p. (ISBN 0-87888-149-2). Bradbury Pr.

--Questions of Human Existence As Answered by Major World Religions: The Christ Story. LC 79-15687. 160p. (YA) 1980. 8.95 o.p. (ISBN 0-87888-150-6). Bradbury Pr.

Corlett, William T. Medicine Man of the Early American Indian & His Cultural Background. (Illus.). 369p. 1935. photocopy ed. spiral 34.50x (ISBN 0-398-04233-0). C C Thomas.

Corlew, Robert E., jt. auth. see Burns, G. Frank.

Corlew, Robert E., jt. auth. see Nicholson, James L.

Corley, Edwin. The Genesis Rock. LC 79-7045. 1980. 12.95 o.p. (ISBN 0-385-15018-0). Doubleday.

--Long Shots. LC 80-1089. 408p. 1981. 13.95 o.p. (ISBN 0-385-15922-6). Doubleday.

Corley, Nora T., ed. Travel in Canada: A Guide to Information Sources. (Geography & Travel Information Guide Ser.: Vol. 4). 350p. 1982. 42.00x (ISBN 0-8103-1493-2). Gale.

Corley, R. H., et al. Oil Palm Research. (Developments in Crop Science Ser.: Vol. 1). 1976. 117.00 (ISBN 0-444-41471-1). Elsevier.

Corley, Robert, jt. auth. see Windal, Floyd.

Corley, Robert N. & Holmes, Eric M. Principles of Business Law. 12th ed. (Illus.). 960p. 1983. 25.95 (ISBN 0-13-701250-0); student gd. & wkbk. 8.95 (ISBN 0-13-701276-4). P-H.

Corley, Robert N. & Robert, William J. Principles of Business Law. 11th ed. 1979. 25.95 (ISBN 0-13-701318-3); pap. 8.95 student guide & wkbk., 3rd ed. (ISBN 0-13-701326-4). P-H.

Corley, Robert N., et al. The Legal Environment of Business. 5th ed. (Illus.). 608p. 1981. 24.95 (ISBN 0-07-013186-4, C); instructor's manual 15.95 (ISBN 0-07-013187-2); test file 15.95 (ISBN 0-07-013189-9). McGraw.

--Fundamentals of Business Law. 3rd ed. (Illus.). 800p. 1982. text ed. 22.95 (ISBN 0-13-332189-4); study guide 8.95 (ISBN 0-13-332247-5). P-H.

--Real Estate & the Law. 453p. 1982. text ed. 28.95 (ISBN 0-394-32546-X). Random.

Corliss, Augustus, compiled by. Old Times of North Yarmouth, Maine. LC 76-52883. (Illus.). 1977. 55.00x (ISBN 0-912274-72-7). NH Pub Co.

Corliss, Clark E. Patten's Elements of Embryology. (Illus.). 1976. text ed. 27.00 (ISBN 0-07-013150-3, HP). McGraw.

Corliss, Richard. Talking Pictures: Screenwriters in the American Cinema. rev. ed. LC 72-94413. 416p. Date not set. pap. 8.95 (ISBN 0-87951-159-1). Overlook Pr.

Corliss, William R. Lightning, Auroras, Nocturnal Lights & Related Luminous Phenomena. LC 82-99902. (A Catalog of Geophysical Anomalies Ser.). (Illus.). 248p. 1982. 11.95 (ISBN 0-915554-09-7). Sourcebook.

--Tornadoes, Dark Days, Anomalous Precipitation, & Related Weather Phenomena. (Catalog of Geophysical Anomalies Ser.). (Illus.). 250p. 1983. 11.95 (ISBN 0-915554-10-0). Sourcebook.

Corliss, William R., compiled by. Handbook of Unusual Natural Phenomena. LC 78-22625. (Illus.). 432p. 1983. pap. 12.95 (ISBN 0-385-14754-6, Anch). Doubleday.

Cormack, D. Criteria for the Selection of Oil Spill Containment & Recovery Equipment for Use at Sea, 1979. 1981. 40.00x (ISBN 0-686-97051-9, Pub. by W Spring England). State Mutual Bk.

Cormack, D. & Nichols, J. A. Feasability Study of Aerial Application of Oil Dispersant Concentrates for Oil Spill Clearance, 1977. 1981. 40.00x (ISBN 0-686-97078-0, Pub. by W Spring England). State Mutual Bk.

Cormack, D., jt. auth. see Martinelli, F. N.

Cormack, D., jt. auth. see Parker, H. D.

Cormack, D., et al. Oil Mop Device for Oil Recovery on the Open Sea, 1979. 1982. 39.00x (ISBN 0-686-97137-X, Pub. by W Spring England). State Mutual Bk.

Cormack, M. Catalogue of Drawings & Watercolour in the Fitzwilliam Museum, Cambridge. M. W. Turner, R. A., 1775-1851. LC 75-12158. (Illus.). 132p. 1975. 34.50 (ISBN 0-521-20955-2). Cambridge U Pr.

Cormack, Margaret L. The Hindu Woman. LC 74-6750. 207p. 1974. Repr. of 1953 ed. lib. bdg. 15.50x (ISBN 0-8371-7557-7, COHW). Greenwood.

Cormack, Mary P., jt. auth. see Barrett, M. Edgar.

Cormack, R. M. Ecological Sampling. 1981. pap. 5.95x o.p. (ISBN 0-412-15390-4, Pub. by Chapman & Hall England). Methuen Inc.

Cormack, Sandy. Small Arms: A Concise History of Their Development. (Illus.). 154p. 1983. 16.95 (ISBN 0-686-43006-9, Profile Pr England). Hippocrene Bks.

Corman & Tunison. Zipper Art. (The Grosset Art Instruction Ser.: No. 82). (Illus.). 48p. Date not set. pap. price not set (ISBN 0-448-00593-X, G&D). Putnam Pub Group.

Corman, Avery. The Old Neighborhood. 1980. 10.95 o.p. (ISBN 0-671-41475-5, 41475, Linden). S&S.

Corman, Calvin W. Commercial Law: Cases & Materials. 1976. 27.50 (ISBN 0-316-15740-6). Little.

Corman, Cid. Aegis: Selected Poems 1970-1980. 112p. 1983. 14.95 (ISBN 0-930794-57-5); pap. 5.95 (ISBN 0-930794-58-3). Station Hill Pr.

Cormany, Christine. How to Raise & Train a Whippet. (Orig.). pap. 2.95 (ISBN 0-87666-409-5, DS1131). TFH Pubns.

Cormier, Edmond. Hope, Hopelessness, & the Alcoholic. (Orig.). 1978. pap. 1.50 o.p. (ISBN 0-89486-052-6). Hazelden.

Cormier, Louise S. & Cormier, William H. Behavioral Counseling: Operant Procedures, Self-Management Strategies, & Recent Innovations. LC 74-11956. (Guidance Monograph). 1975. pap. 2.40 o.p. (ISBN 0-395-20032-6). HM.

Cormier, Louise S., jt. auth. see Cormier, William H.

Cormier, Raymond J., ed. Voices of Conscience: Essays on Medieval & Modern French Literature in Memory of James D. Powell & Rosemary Hodgins. LC 76-15343. 282p. 1977. 29.95 (ISBN 0-87722-090-5). Temple U Pr.

Cormier, Raymond J., tr. see Frappier, Jean.

Cormier, Robert. After the First Death. 224p. 1983. pap. 2.50 (ISBN 0-380-48652-0, 48652, Flare). Avon.

--The Chocolate War. 192p. (gr. 7 up). 1975. pap. 2.25 (ISBN 0-440-94459-7, LFL). Dell.

--Eight Plus One. 192p. 1982. pap. 2.25 (ISBN 0-553-22690-8). Bantam.

--I Am the Cheese. 1978. pap. 2.25 (ISBN 0-440-94060-5, LFL). Dell.

Cormier, Sherilyn N., jt. auth. see Hackney, Harold L.

Cormier, William H. & Cormier, Louise S. Behavioral Counseling: Initial Procedures, Individual & Group Strategies. LC 74-11962. (Guidance Monograph). 1975. pap. 2.40 o.p. (ISBN 0-395-20037-7). HM.

Cormier, William H., jt. auth. see Cormier, Louise S.

Cornaby, Barney, ed. Management of Toxic Substances in Our Ecosystems: Taming the Medusa. LC 81-67257. (Illus.). 186p. 1981. 22.50 (ISBN 0-686-84680-X). Ann Arbor Science.

Cornaby, W. Arthur. A String of Chinese Peach-Stones. LC 70-175730. (Illus.). xvi, 478p. 1974. Repr. of 1895 ed. 37.00x (ISBN 0-8103-3125-X). Gale.

Cornacchia, Harold J. & Barrett, Stephen. Consumer Health: A Guide to Intelligent Decisions. 2nd ed. LC 80-11515. (Illus.). 338p. 1980. pap. text ed. 14.95 (ISBN 0-8016-1037-0). Mosby.

--Shopping for Health Care: The Essential Guide to Products & Services. 1982. pap. 9.95 (ISBN 0-452-25366-7, Plume). NAL.

--Shopping for Health Care: The Essential Guide to Products & Services. LC 82-6405. (Medical Library). 381p. 1982. pap. 9.95 (ISBN 0-686-84856-X, 1140-7). Mosby.

Cornacchia, Harold J. & Staton, Wesley M. Health in the Elementary Schools. 5th ed. LC 78-21076. (Illus.). 434p. 1979. text ed. 19.95 (ISBN 0-8016-1062-1). Mosby.

Cornacchia, Harold J., et al. Drugs in the Classroom: A Conceptual Model for School Programs. 2nd ed. LC 77-22968. (Illus.). 336p. 1978. pap. text ed. 15.95 (ISBN 0-8016-1043-5). Mosby.

Cornberg, Sol & Gebauer, Emanuel L. Stage Crew Handbook. rev. ed. LC 56-11916. (Illus.). 1957. 13.41xi (ISBN 0-06-031560-1, HarpT). Har-Row.

Corne, Chris, jt. auth. see Baker, Philip.

Corneg, Martha, jt. auth. see Neufeld, M. Lynne.

Corneille. L' Illusion Comique. 2nd ed. Marks, J., ed. (Modern French Texts Ser.). 1969. pap. write for info. (ISBN 0-7190-0323-7). Manchester.

Cornelia, Elizabeth. Australia. LC 78-56592. (Countries Ser.). (Illus.). 1978. PLB 12.68 (ISBN 0-382-06182-9). Silver.

Cornelison, Isaac J. The Relation of Religion to Civil Government in the United States. LC 75-107409. (Civil Liberties in American History Ser). 1970. Repr. of 1895 ed. lib. bdg. 45.00 (ISBN 0-306-71890-1). Da Capo.

Cornelisse, J. W., et al. Rocket Propulsion & Spaceflight Dynamics. LC 78-40059. (Aerospace Engineering Ser.). 505p. 1979. text ed. 87.95 (ISBN 0-273-01141-3). Pitman Pub MA.

Cornelius. Food Service Careers. 1979. text ed. 18.00 (ISBN 0-87002-206-7); tchr's guide free; student's guide 3.76 (ISBN 0-87002-165-6). Bennett IL.

Cornelius, Chase, jt. auth. see Cornelius, Sue.

Cornelius, Debra. Who Cares? Handbook on Sex Education & Counseling Services for Disabled People. 276p. 1982. pap. text ed. 16.95 (ISBN 0-8391-1727-2). Univ Park.

Cornelius, E. T., Jr., jt. auth. see Alexander, L. G.

Cornelius, Edwin T., jt. auth. see Byrne, Donn.

Cornelius, Edwin T., Jr. Interview: Listening Comprehension for High Intermediate & Advanced Students. (English As a Second Language Bk.). (Illus.). 128p. 1981. pap. text ed. 5.25x (ISBN 0-582-79700-4); cassette 13.95x (ISBN 0-582-79702-0); bk. & cassette in tote 16.50x (ISBN 0-582-79782-9). Longman.

--New English Course, 6 bks. Incl. Book 1. student text 4.75 (ISBN 0-89285-125-2); tchr's. annotated ed. 6.95 (ISBN 0-89285-137-6); wkbk. 2.00 (ISBN 0-89285-131-7); cassette 120.00 (ISBN 0-89285-119-8); cassette tape 18.00 (ISBN 0-89285-113-9); Book 2. student text 4.75 (ISBN 0-89285-126-0); tchr's annotated ed. 6.95 (ISBN 0-89285-138-4); wkbk. 2.00 (ISBN 0-89285-132-5); cassette 120.00 (ISBN 0-89285-120-1); cassette tape 18.00 (ISBN 0-89285-114-7); Book 3. student text 4.75 (ISBN 0-89285-127-9); tchr's annotated ed. 6.95 (ISBN 0-89285-139-2); wkbk. 2.00 (ISBN 0-89285-133-3); cassette 120.00 (ISBN 0-89285-121-X); cassette tape 18.00 (ISBN 0-89285-115-5); Book 4. student text 4.75 (ISBN 0-89285-128-7); tchr's annotated ed. 6.95 (ISBN 0-89285-140-6); wkbk. 2.00 (ISBN 0-89285-134-1); cassette 120.00 (ISBN 0-89285-122-8); cassette tape 18.00 (ISBN 0-89285-116-3); Book 5. student text 4.75 (ISBN 0-89285-129-5); tchr's annotated ed. 6.95 (ISBN 0-89285-141-4); wkbk. 2.00 (ISBN 0-89285-135-X); cassette 120.00 (ISBN 0-89285-123-6); cassette tape 18.00 (ISBN 0-89285-117-1); Book 6. student text 4.75 (ISBN 0-89285-130-9); tchr's annotated ed. 6.95 (ISBN 0-89285-142-2); wkbk. 2.00 (ISBN 0-89285-136-8); cassette 120.00 (ISBN 0-89285-124-4); cassette tape 18.00 (ISBN 0-89285-118-X); Bks. 1-6. progress quizzes & placement tests avail.. (Illus.). 1979. pap. text ed. 4.75 ea. English Lang.

Cornelius, Hal & Lewis, William. Career Guide for Sales & Marketing. Levy, Valerie, ed. (Career Blazers Guides). 1983. pap. 7.95 (ISBN 0-671-47169-4). Monarch Pr.

--Word Processing. (Career Blazers Guides Ser.). 192p. pap. 7.95 (ISBN 0-671-45869-8). Monarch Pr.

Cornelius, L. A. Grammar & Composition for Schools. 390p. 1981. pap. text ed. 5.95x (ISBN 0-86131-291-0, Pub. by Orient Longman Ltd India). Apt Bks.

Cornelius, Richard. Concentrated Chemical Concepts. 12p. 1982. text ed. 15.00 (ISBN 0-471-87486-8). Wiley.

Cornelius, Sue & Cornelius, Chase. City in Art. LC 65-29036. (Fine Art Books). (Illus.). (gr. 5-11). 1966. PLB 4.95g (ISBN 0-8225-0159-7). Lerner Pubns.

Cornelius, Temple H. & Marshall, John B. Golden Treasures of the San Juan. LC 82-73450. 235p. 1961. pap. 5.95 (ISBN 0-8040-0636-9, SB). Swallow.

Cornelius, Wayne A. Building the Cactus Curtain: Mexico & U. S. Responses, from Wilson to Carter. 1980. 8.95 o.p. (ISBN 0-520-03888-6). U of Cal Pr.

Cornell, C. A., jt. auth. see Benjamin, J.

Cornell, Claire P., jt. auth. see Gelles, Richard J.

Cornell, Dale D. & Erickson, Frances G. Marriage: The Phoenix Contract. 1983. 20.00 (ISBN 0-87527-264-9). Green.

Cornell, James C., Jr. Lost Lands & Forgotten People. LC 78-57795. (Illus.). (gr. 5 up). 1978. 8.95 o.p. (ISBN 0-8069-3926-5); PLB 8.29 o.p. (ISBN 0-8069-3927-3). Sterling.

--Nature at Its Strangest: True Stories from the Files of the Smithsonian Institution's Center for Short-Lived Phenomena. LC 74-82336. (Illus.). 128p. (gr. 3 up). 1974. 7.95 (ISBN 0-8069-3924-9); PLB 9.99 (ISBN 0-8069-3925-7). Sterling.

Cornell, Jean G. Louis Armstrong: Ambassador Satchmo. LC 75-188567. (Americans All Ser.). (Illus.). 96p. (gr. 3-6). 1972. PLB 6.48 o.p. (ISBN 0-8116-4576-2). Garrard.

--Mahalia Jackson: Queen of Gospel Song. LC 73-14713. (Americans All Ser). (Illus.). 96p. (gr. 3-6). 1974. PLB 7.12 (ISBN 0-8116-4581-9). Garrard.

--Ralph Bunche: Champion of Peace. LC 75-20368. (Americans All Ser). 96p. (gr. 3-6). 1976. PLB 7.12 (ISBN 0-8116-4583-5). Garrard.

Cornell, Jimmy. Modern Ocean Cruising: Boats, Gear & Crews Surveyed. (Illus.). 250p. 1983. 19.95 (ISBN 0-229-11687-6, Pub. by Adlard Coles). Sheridan.

Cornell, John B. & Smith, Robert J. Two Japanese Villages: Matsunagi, a Japanese Mountain Community, Kurusu, a Japanese Agricultural Community. LC 77-90491. Repr. of 1956 ed. lib. bdg. 20.25 (ISBN 0-8371-2130-2, COJV). Greenwood.

Cornell, Joseph A. Computers in Hospital Pharmacy Management: Fundamentals & Applications. 225p. 1983. write for info. (ISBN 0-89443-673-2). Aspen Systems.

Cornell, Joseph B. Sharing Nature with Children. LC 78-74650. (Illus.). 143p. 1979. pap. 5.95 (ISBN 0-916124-14-2). Ananda.

Cornell, Julien D. The Conscientious Objector & the Law. Bd. with Conscience & the State: Legal & Administrative Problems of Conscientious Objectors, 1943-1944. LC 75-137532. (Peace Movement in America Ser). 264p. 1972. Repr. of 1943 ed. lib. bdg. 16.95x (ISBN 0-89198-060-1). Ozer.

Cornell, Luis L. Kipling in India. 224p. 1982. Repr. of 1966 ed. lib. bdg. 35.00 (ISBN 0-89760-165-3). Telegraph Bks.

Cornell, R., jt. auth. see Dudick, T. S.

Cornell, Richard. Your Career in Music. LC 77-13361. (Arco Career Guidance Ser.). 1979. lib. bdg. 7.95 (ISBN 0-668-04459-4); pap. 4.50 (ISBN 0-668-04461-6). Arco.

Cornell, Sara. Art: A History of Changing Style. 456p. 1983. 29.95 (ISBN 0-686-84550-1); pap. text ed. 19.95 (ISBN 0-686-84551-X). P-H.

Cornell, Tim & Matthews, John. Atlas of the Roman World. (Illus.). 240p. 1982. 35.00 (ISBN 0-87196-652-2). Facts on File.

Cornell University. Third Supplement to the Cumulation of the Library Catalog Supplements of the New York State School of Industrial & Labor Relations. 1979. lib. bdg. 180.00 (ISBN 0-8161-0260-0, Hall Library). G K Hall.

Cornell University Agricultural Waste Management Conference, 10th, 1978. Best Management Practices for Agriculture & Silviculture: Proceedings. Loehr, Raymond C. & Haith, Douglas A., eds. LC 78-67494. 1979. 35.00 o.p. (ISBN 0-250-40271-8). Ann Arbor Science.

Cornell University. Libraries. Catalogue of the Witchcraft Collection in the Cornell University Library. LC 76-41552. 1977. lib. bdg. 110.00 (ISBN 0-527-19705-X). Kraus Intl.

Cornell University Libraries. Petrarch: Catalogue of the Petrarch Collection in Cornell University Library. LC 74-3398. 1974. 90.00 (ISBN 0-527-19700-9). Kraus Intl.

Cornell University, Martin P. Catherwood Library. Cumulation of the Library Catalog Supplements of the New York State School of Industrial and Labor Relations, First Supplement. 1977. lib. bdg. 120.00 (ISBN 0-8161-0055-1, Hall Library). G K Hall.

Cornell University New York State School of Industrial & Labor Relations. Cumulation of the Library Catalog Supplements of Martin P. Catherwood Library of the New York State School of Industrial & Labor Relations, 9 vols. 1976. Set. lib. bdg. 1235.00 (ISBN 0-8161-0022-5, Hall Library). G K Hall.

Cornell University, New York State School of Industrial & Labor Ralations Staff. Library Catalog of the Martin P. Catherwood Library of the New York State School of Industrial & Labor Relations, 12 vols. 1967. Set. lib. bdg. 1140.00 (ISBN 0-8161-0757-2, PHall Library). G K Hall.

Cornell University, New York State School of Industrial & Labor Relations. Library Catalog of the Martin P. Catherwood Library of the New York State School of Industrial & Labor Relations, First Supplement. 873p. 1967. lib. bdg. 110.00 (ISBN 0-8161-0772-6, Hall Library). G K Hall.

Cornell University, New York State School of Industrial & Labor Relations Staff. Library Catalog of the Martin P. Catherwood Library of the New York State School of Industrial & Labor Relations, Second Supplement. 1968. lib. bdg. 120.00 (ISBN 0-8161-0844-7, Hall Library). G K Hall.

--Library Catalog of the Martin P. Catherwood Library of the New York State School of Industrial & Labor Relations, Third Supplement. 1969. lib. bdg. 120.00 (ISBN 0-8161-0878-1, Hall Library). G K Hall.

--Library Catalog of the Martin P. Catherwood Library of the New York State School of Industrial & Labor Relations, Fourth Supplement. 1970. lib. bdg. 120.00 (ISBN 0-8161-0911-7, Hall Library). G K Hall.

--Library Catalog of the Martin P. Catherwood Library of the New York State School of Industrial & Labor Relations, Fifth Supplement. 1972. 120.00 (ISBN 0-8161-0986-9, Pub. by HHall Library). G K Hall.

--Library Catalog of the Martin P. Catherwood Library of the New York State School of Industrial & Labor Relations, Sixth Supplement. 1973. lib. bdg. 120.00 (ISBN 0-8161-1072-7, Hall Library). G K Hall.

--Library Catalog of the Martin P. Catherwood Library of the New York State School of Industrial & Labor Relations, Seventh Supplement. 1974. lib. bdg. 120.00 (ISBN 0-8161-1079-4, Hall Library). G K Hall.

Cornell University Staff. Libraries, Cornell University: Southeast Asia Catalog, 7 vols. 1976. Set. lib. bdg. 665.00 (Hall Library). G K Hall.

Cornell Waste Management Conference, 9th. Food, Fertilizer & Agricultural Residues: Proceedings. Loehr, Raymond C., ed. LC 77-85092. 1977. 40.00 o.p. (ISBN 0-250-40190-8). Ann Arbor Science.

Cornell Waste Management Conference, 8th. Land As a Waste Management Alternative. Loehr, Raymond C., ed. LC 76-46019. 1977. 49.95 o.p. (ISBN 0-250-40140-1). Ann Arbor Science.

Corner, D. C. & Stafford, D. C. Open-End Investment Funds in the European Economic Community & Switzerland. LC 76-17101. 1977. lib. bdg. 47.75 o.p. (ISBN 0-89158-620-2). Westview.

Corner, Desmond C. & Mayes, David G., eds. Modern Portfolio Theory & Financial Institutions. 1982. text ed. 36.00x (ISBN 0-8419-5093-8). Holmes & Meier.

Corner, E. A Monograph of Thelephora. (Illus.). 1968. 16.00 (ISBN 3-7682-5427-5). Lubrecht & Cramer.

--Supplement to "A Monograph of Clavaria & Allied Genera". (Illus.). 1970. pap. 48.00 (ISBN 3-7682-5433-X). Lubrecht & Cramer.

Corner, E. J. The Life of Plants. LC 81-11436. 1981. 9.95 (ISBN 0-226-11586-0, Phoen). U of Chicago Pr.

--Phylloporus Quel & Paxillus Fr. in Malaya & Borneo. (Illus.). 1971. pap. 12.00 (ISBN 3-7682-0741-2). Lubrecht & Cramer.

Corner, E. J. H. The Seeds of Dicotyledons, 2 vols. LC 74-14434. (Illus.). 860p. 1976. Vol. 1. 85.00 (ISBN 0-521-20688-X); Vol. 2. 125.00 (ISBN 0-521-20687-1). Cambridge U Pr.

Corner, George W. Dr. Kane of the Arctic Seas. LC 72-88531. 319p. 1972. 24.95 (ISBN 0-87722-022-0). Temple U Pr.

Corner, George W., ed. see Rush, Benjamin.

Corner, J. & Hawthorn, J. Communication Studies: An Introductory Reader. 256p. 1980. pap. text ed. 13.95 (ISBN 0-7131-6278-3). E Arnold.

Corner, M. A., ed. see Ninth International Summer School of Brain Research.

Corner, Philip. Popular Entertainments. 16p. 1981. pap. 3.00 (ISBN 0-914162-56-X). Knowles.

Cornet, Joseph, jt. auth. see Thompson, Robert.

Cornett, Jim. Wildlife of the Southwest Deserts. (Illus.). 80p. (Orig.). 1975. pap. 4.95 (ISBN 0-686-10617-2). Nature Trails.

Cornett, Joe D. & Beckner, Weldon. Introductory Statistics for the Behavioral Sciences. (Educational Psychology Ser). 280p. 1975. text ed. 17.95 (ISBN 0-675-08757-0). Additional supplements may be obtained from publisher. Merrill.

Corney, Alan. Atomic & Laser Spectroscopy. (Illus.). 1977. text ed. 29.95x (ISBN 0-19-851138-8); pap. 24.95x o.p. (ISBN 0-19-851148-5). Oxford U Pr.

Corney, R. H., jt. ed. see Clare, A. W.

Cornfeld, Gaalyah. The Historical Jesus: A Scholarly View of the Man & His World. LC 82-14860. (Illus.). 224p. 1983. 16.95 (ISBN 0-02-528200-X). Macmillan.

Cornfeld, Gaalyah & Maier, Paul L., eds. Josephus: The Jewish War. 560p. 1982. 39.95 (ISBN 0-310-39210-1). Zondervan.

Cornfield, Robert, jt. auth. see Martins, Peter.

Cornford, A. J. The Market for Owned Houses in England & Wales Since Nineteen Forty-Five. 1979. text ed. 33.25x (ISBN 0-566-00195-0). Gower Pub Ltd.

Cornford, Francis. Plato's Cosmology: The Timaeus of Plato. 4th ed. (International Library of Psychology, Philosophy & Scientific Method). 1971. text ed. 23.75x o.p. (ISBN 0-7100-3126-2); pap. text ed. 24.75x o.p. Humanities.

Cornford, Francis M. Before & After Socrates. 23.95 (ISBN 0-521-04726-9); pap. 6.95 (ISBN 0-521-09113-6). Cambridge U Pr.

--Thucydides Mythistoricus. LC 69-13866. Repr. of 1907 ed. lib. bdg. 16.25x (ISBN 0-8371-1055-6, COTH). Greenwood.

--Unwritten Philosophy & Other Essays. Guthrie, William K., ed. 1967. 24.95 (ISBN 0-521-04727-7); pap. 7.95x o.p. (ISBN 0-521-09444-5). Cambridge U Pr.

Corngold, Stanley. The Commentators' Despair: The Interpretation of Kafka's Metamorphosis. LC 72-189558. 1973. 15.00 o.p. (ISBN 0-8046-9017-0, Natl U); pap. 9.95 o.p. (ISBN 0-8046-9051-0). Kennikat.

Cornick, Delroy L. & Elkin, Robert. Analyzing Costs in a Residential Group Care Facility: A Step-by-Step Manual. LC 78-89708. 1969. pap. 7.95 (ISBN 0-87868-062-4, 1-33). Child Welfare.

Cornil, C. Urethral Obstruction in Boys. 1975. 32.75 (ISBN 0-444-16706-4). Elsevier.

Corning Museum of Glass. American & European Pressed Glass in the Corning Museum of Glass. (Illus.). 500p. (Orig.). pap. 25.00 (ISBN 0-486-24330-3). Dover.

Corning, P. A. The Synergism Hypothesis: A Theory of Progressive Evolution. 1983. pap. price not set (ISBN 0-07-013172-4). McGraw.

Cornish, et al. Sampling Systems for Process Analyzers. 1981. 99.95 (ISBN 0-408-00261-1). Butterworth.

Cornish, Clive G. Basic Accounting for the Small Business: Simple, Foolproof Techniques for Keeping Your Books Straight & Staying Out of Trouble. 2nd ed. (Illus.). 161p. 1980. pap. 4.50 (ISBN 0-88908-906-X). Self Counsel Pr.

Cornish, Sam. Grandmother's Pictures. (Illus.). 1978. pap. 0.95 o.p. (ISBN 0-380-01912-4, 37416, Camelot). Avon.

Cornish-Bowden, A. Basic Mathematics for Biochemists. 1981. 18.95x (ISBN 0-412-23000-3, Pub. by Chapman & Hall); pap. 8.95x (ISBN 0-412-23010-0). Methuen Inc.

Cornish-Bowden, Athel. Fundamentals of Enzyme Kinetics. LC 79-40116. (Illus.). 1979. text ed. 24.95 (ISBN 0-408-10617-4). Butterworth.

Cornog, Martha, jt. auth. see Neufeld, M. Lynne.

Corns, Albert R. Bibliography of Unfinished Books in the English Language. Sparke, Archibald, ed. LC 67-28093. 1968. Repr. of 1915 ed. 34.00x (ISBN 0-8103-3208-6). Gale.

Corns, Thomas N. The Development of Milton's Prose Style. (English Monographs). 132p. 1982. 19.95x (ISBN 0-19-811717-5). Oxford U Pr.

Cornu, A. Compilation of Mass Spectral Data, 2 vols. Massot, R., ed. 1975. Vol. 1. 95.00 (ISBN 0-471-25646-3, Pub. by Wiley Heyden); Vol. 2. 171.00 (ISBN 0-471-25647-1); Set. 226.00 (ISBN 0-471-25648-X). Wiley.

Cornu, A. & Massot, R. List of Conversion Factors for Atomic Impurities to PPM by Weight. 1968. 59.95 (ISBN 0-471-25645-5, Wiley Heyden). Wiley.

Cornu, A., jt. auth. see Leclerc, J. C.

Cornwall, I. W. Bones for the Archaeologist. 2nd rev. ed. (Illus.). 264p. 1974. 15.00x o.p. (ISBN 0-460-04229-7, Pub. by J. M. Dent England). Biblio Dist.

Cornwall, John. Modern Capitalism: Its Growth & Transformation. LC 77-81846. (Illus.). 1978. 22.50 (ISBN 0-312-53784-0). St Martin.

Cornwall, Judson. La Alabanza Que Liberta. 160p. Date not set. 2.25 (ISBN 0-88113-002-8). Edit Betania.

--La Fe No Fingida. Carrodeguas, Andy & Marosi, Esteban, eds. Oyola, Eliezar, tr. from Eng. Orig. Title: Unfeigned Faith. 201p. (Span.). 1982. pap. 2.25 (ISBN 0-8297-1174-0). Life Pubs Intl.

--Freeway under Construction. 1978. bklt. .95 (ISBN 0-88270-304-8, Pub. by Logos). Bridge Pub.

--Give Me-Make Me. 1979. 1.25 (ISBN 0-88270-387-0). Bridge Pub.

--Heaven. 1978. pap. 3.95 (ISBN 0-89728-008-3). Omega Pubns Or.

Cornwell, Ada, ed. see Junaluska Historical Society.

Cornwell, Bernard. Sharpe's Gold. 352p. Date not set. pap. 3.25 (ISBN 0-441-76089-9). Ace Bks.

--Sharpe's Sword. (Sharpe Saga Ser.). 352p. 1983. 15.75 (ISBN 0-670-63941-9). Viking Pr.

Cornwell, Clifton, jt. auth. see Gibson, James W.

Cornwell, Debbra, jt. auth. see Cornwell, Stephen.

Cornwell, Keith. The Flow of Heat. 1977. 21.00 o.p. (ISBN 0-442-30177-4); pap. 11.50x (ISBN 0-442-30168-5). Van Nos Reinhold.

Cornwell, Malcolm. Formed by His Word: Patterns of Scriptural Prayer. (Orig.). 1978. pap. 2.50 (ISBN 0-914544-20-9). Living Flame Pr.

Cornwell, Mary, ed. see Junaluska Historical Society.

Cornwell, N. The Life, Times & Milieu of V. F. Odoyevsky, 1804-1869. 1981. 80.00x o.p. (ISBN 0-86127-207-2, Pub. by Avebury Pub England). State Mutual Bk.

Cornwell, Richard E. The Miniwarehouse: A Guide for Investors & Managers. 92p. 1975. pap. 14.95 (ISBN 0-912104-19-8). Inst Real Estate.

Cornwell, Richard E. & Victor, Buzz. Self-Service Storage: The Handbook for Investors & Managers. rev. ed. Moore, Betty T., ed. LC 81-86050. (Institute of Real Estate Management Monographs: Series on Specific Property Types). Orig. Title: The Miniwarehouse. (Illus.). 200p. 1983. pap. text ed. 19.95 (ISBN 0-912104-54-6). Inst Real Estate.

Cornwell, Robert C., jt. auth. see Manship, Darwin.

Cornwell, Stephen & Cornwell, Debbra. Cooking in the Nude: For Playful Gourmets. (Illus.). 64p. 1982. pap. 3.95 (ISBN 0-943678-00-5). Wellton Bks.

Coroles, Yvonne, jt. auth. see Curtis, Lindsay R.

Corona, Simon, tr. see Yates, K. M.

Coronado, Rosa. Cooking the Mexican Way. LC 82-254. (Easy Menu Ethnic Cookbooks Ser.). (Illus.). 48p. (gr. 5 up). 1982. PLB 7.95g (ISBN 0-8225-0907-5). Lerner Pubns.

Corpi, Lucha. Palabras de Mediodia (Noon Words) Rodriquez-Nieto, Catherine, tr. (Illus.). 1980. 11.50 (ISBN 0-936470-00-3); pap. 5.95 (ISBN 0-936470-01-1). El Fuego Aztlan.

Corporate Monitor, Inc. Educational Software Directory. 1982. pap. text ed. 22.50 (ISBN 0-87287-352-8). Libs Unl.

Corr, C. A., jt. auth. see Wass, H.

Corr, Charles A. & Corr, Donna M. The Hospice Care: Principles & Practice. (Death & Suicide Ser.: Vol. 5). 1983. text ed. 26.95 (ISBN 0-8261-3540-4); text ed. 22.95 Quantities of 10 or more (ISBN 0-686-83090-3). Springer Pub.

Corr, Charles A., jt. ed. see Pacholski, Richard A.

Corr, Charles A., jt. ed. see Wass, Hannelore.

Corr, Donna M., jt. auth. see Corr, Charles A.

Corrace, Douglas & Bond, Edward. Glasgow. (Illus.). 128p. 1983. 22.95 (ISBN 0-00-435667-5, Collins Pub England). Greene.

Corradini, Claudia. Lab & Excerise Book for Elementary Italian. 2nd ed. 1977. pap. text ed. 9.25 (ISBN 0-8191-0245-8). U Pr of Amer.

Corradini, V., tr. see Carducci, Joshua.

Corran, H. S. Isle of Man. (Islands Ser.). 1977. 13.50 o.p. (ISBN 0-7153-7417-6). David & Charles.

Corras, James & Zerowin, Jeffrey. Improving College Admission Test Scores: Verbal Workbook. 184p. (Orig.). (gr. 11-12). 1982. pap. write for info. (ISBN 0-88210-135-8). Natl Assn Principals.

Correa, F. G., tr. see Canright, D. M.

Correa, Hector & El Torky, Mohamed A. The Biological & Social Determinants of the Demographic Transition. LC 82-16042. (Illus.). 298p. (Orig.). 1983. lib. bdg. 24.25 (ISBN 0-8191-2754-X); pap. text ed. 12.75 (ISBN 0-8191-2755-8). U Pr of Amer.

Correale, William H. A Building Code Primer. (Illus.). 1978. pap. text ed. 14.95x (ISBN 0-07-013171-6, C). McGraw.

Corredor-Matheos, J., jt. auth. see Artigas, J. Llorens.

Correll, Donovan S. Flora of the Bahamian Archipelago. (Illus.). 1692p. 1982. lib. bdg. 120.00x (ISBN 3-7682-1289-0). Lubrecht & Cramer.

Corren, Grace. The Attic Child. 1979. pap. 1.95 o.p. (ISBN 0-523-40322-4). Pinnacle Bks.

--The House of Counted Hatreds. 160p. 1980. pap. 1.75 o.p. (ISBN 0-523-40649-5). Pinnacle Bks.

Correnti, Samuel, jt. auth. see Block, Stanley.

Corrette, M. Methode pour apprende aisement a jouir de la Flute Traversiere. (The Flute Library: Vol. 6). 1978. Repr. of 1740 ed. wrappers 22.50 o.s.i. (ISBN 90-6027-195-5, Pub. by Frits Knuf Netherlands). Pendragon NY.

Correu, Larry M. Beyond the Broken Marriage. LC 82-13661. 144p. 1982. pap. 7.95 (ISBN 0-664-24446-7). Westminster.

Correu, Larry M., ed. The Best of These Days. LC 82-13415. 132p. 1983. 8.95 (ISBN 0-664-21391-X). Westminster.

Corrick, James A. The Human Brain: Minds & Matter. LC 82-18461. (Arco How-It-Works Ser.). (Illus.). 192p. 1983. 12.95 (ISBN 0-668-05519-7). Arco.

Corrie, Jane. Man with Two Faces. (Harlequin Romances Ser.). 192p. 1983. pap. 1.75 (ISBN 0-373-02551-3). Harlequin Bks.

--Miss Catastrophe. (Collection Harlequin Ser.). 192p. 1983. pap. 1.95 (ISBN 0-373-49336-3). Harlequin Bks.

Corrie, Sandra & Stine, Laura, eds. Journal for the Protection of All Beings, No. 3. (Illus.). 1969. pap. 1.50 o.p. (ISBN 0-87286-024-8). City Lights.

Corrigan, B. C. Tailgating-The Lincoln-Douglas Debates: A Tour of the Seven Original Debate Sites on the Eve of Their 125th Anniversary. LC 82-73684. 60p. 1982. pap. write for info. ADS Pr.

Corrigan, Barbara. How to Make Pants & Jeans That Really Fit. LC 77-74295. (gr. 9 up). 1978. pap. 6.95 o.p. (ISBN 0-385-12786-3). Doubleday.

Corrigan, Beatrice, ed. Curious Annals: New Documents Relating to Browning's Roman Murder Story. LC 56-3780. 142p. 1971. 15.00x o.p. (ISBN 0-8020-7007-8). U of Toronto Pr.

Corrigan, Beatrice, ed. see Erasmus, Desiderius.

Corrigan, Eileen M. Alcoholic Women in Treatment. 1979. text ed. 19.95x (ISBN 0-19-502653-5). Oxford U Pr.

Corrigan, John D., jt. auth. see Bennett, Millard.

Corrigan, John T., ed. Anglo-American Cataloging Rules: One Year Later. (CLA Studies in Librarianship: No. 6). (Illus.). 61p. pap. 8.00 (ISBN 0-87507-023-X). Cath Lib Assn.

Corrigan, Paul & Leonard, Peter. Social Work Practice Under Capitalism: A Marxist Approach. (Critical Texts in Social Work & the Welfare State Ser.). 1978. text ed. 14.00x o.p. (ISBN 0-333-21601-6, MacMillian); pap. text ed. 6.00x o.p. (ISBN 0-333-21602-4); pap. text ed. 10.50x o.p. (ISBN 0-333-21601-6). Humanities.

Corrigan, Philip, et al. Socialist Construction & Marxist Theory: Bolshevism & Its Critique. LC 78-7591. 1978. 15.00 (ISBN 0-85345-469-8, CL-4698); pap. 7.50 (ISBN 0-85345-580-5). Monthly Rev.

Corrigan, Robert W. The Making of Theatre: From Drama to Performance. 1981. pap. text ed. 9.95x (ISBN 0-673-15403-3). Scott F.

--The World of the Theatre. 1979. text ed. 18.95x (ISBN 0-673-15107-7). Scott F.

Corrigan, Robert W. & Loney, Glenn M., eds. Comedy: A Critical Anthology. LC 78-150137. (Orig.). 1971. pap. text ed. 12.95 (ISBN 0-395-04325-5). HM.

--Forms of Drama. LC 74-150136. 906p. (Orig.). 1972. pap. text ed. 12.95 (ISBN 0-395-04327-1). HM.

Corrigan, Thomas F. The Teddy Bear Wore Expensive Shoes. 1978. 4.95 o.p. (ISBN 0-533-03073-0). Vantage.

Corrin, Jay P. G. K. Chesterton & Hilaire Belloc: The Battle Against Modernity. LC 81-4756. xvi, 262p. 1981. text ed. 20.95x (ISBN 0-8214-0604-3, 82-83897). Ohio U Pr.

Corrin, Sara. A Time to Laugh: Thirty Stories for Young Children. Corrin, Stephen, ed. LC 81-670036. (Faber Fanfares Ser.). (Illus.). 204p. (Orig.). (ps-5). 1980. pap. 3.25 (ISBN 0-571-11487-3). Faber & Faber.

Corrin, Sara & Corrin, Stephen, eds. More Stories for Seven-Year-Olds. LC 79-670248. 184p. (gr. 1-3). 1979. 11.95 (ISBN 0-571-11196-3). Faber & Faber.

--Once upon a Rhyme: 101 Poems for Young Children. (Illus.). 160p. (gr. 1-4). 1982. 9.95 (ISBN 0-571-11913-1). Faber & Faber.

Corrin, Sara, et al. Stories for Five Year-Olds & Other Young Readers. Corrin, Stephen, ed. (Illus.). 168p. (ps-5). 1973. 8.95 (ISBN 0-571-10162-3). Faber & Faber.

Corrin, Stephen, jt. ed. see Corrin, Sara.

Corrin, Stephen, jt. ed. see Corrin, Sara.

Corrin, Stephen, ed. see Corrin, Sara, et al.

Corrin, Stephen, jt. ed. see Corrin, Sara.

Corrin, Stephen, tr. see Eliade, Mircea.

Corrin, Stephen, tr. see Gernyet, N. & Jagdfeld, G.

Corringham, Mary. I, Jane Austen. 1971. 8.75 o.p. (ISBN 0-7100-7102-7). Routledge & Kegan.

Corris, Peter, ed. & intro. by see Wawn, William T.

Corry, Bernard, jt. ed. see Peston, Maurice.

Corry, J. E., et al, eds. Isolation & Identification Methods for Food Poisoning Organisms. LC 81-71577. (Society for Applied Bacteriology Technical Ser.: No. 17). 1982. 55.50 (ISBN 0-12-189950-0). Acad Pr.

Corsaro, Maria & Korzenlowsky, Carole. A Woman's Guide to a Safe Abortion. LC 82-15652. (Illus.). 120p. 1983. 12.95 (ISBN 0-03-060603-9); pap. 9.95 (ISBN 0-03-060602-0). HR&W.

Corsaut, Maurine J. Hematology Laboratory Manual. (Illus.). 162p. 1982. spiral 21.75x (ISBN 0-398-04524-0). C C Thomas.

Corse, Larry B. & Corse, Sandra B. Articles on American & British Literature: An Index to Selected Periodicals, 1950-1977. LC 82-75521. xii, 413p. 1981. 30.00x (ISBN 0-8040-0408-0). Swallow.

Corse, Sandra B., jt. auth. see Corse, Larry B.

Corsellis, Jane. Painting Figures in Light. (Illus.). 144p. 1982. 22.50 (ISBN 0-8230-3631-6). Watson-Guptill.

Corser, Frank & Corser, Rose. Tahiti Traveler's Guide. 3rd, rev. ed. (Illus.). 52p. 1981. pap. 3.50 (ISBN 0-686-38091-6). F & R Corser.

Corser, Rose, jt. auth. see Corser, Frank.

Corsini, G. U., jt. ed. see Gessa, G. L.

Corsini, Raymond. Handbook of Innovative Psychotherapies. LC 80-29062. (Personality Processes Ser.). 1016p. 1981. 44.95x (ISBN 0-471-06229-4, Pub. by Wiley-Interscience). Wiley.

Corsini, Raymond J. Current Psychotherapies. 2nd ed. LC 78-61880. 1979. pap. text ed. 15.50 (ISBN 0-87581-240-6). Peacock Pubs.

Corsini, Raymond J. & Marsella, Anthony J. Personality Theories, Research & Assessment. LC 82-61261. 620p. 1983. text ed. 21.50 (ISBN 0-87581-288-0). Peacock Pubs.

Corsini, Raymond J. & Painter, Genevieve. The Practical Parent: The ABC's of Child Discipline. LC 74-1801. 262p. 1975. 13.41i (ISBN 0-06-010873-8, HarpT). Har-Row.

Corsini, Raymond J., jt. auth. see Gazda, George M.

Corsini, Raymond J., jt. auth. see Ignas, Edward.

Corsini, Raymond J., jt. auth. see Manaster, Guy J.

Corsini, Raymond J., jt. auth. see Wedding, Dan.

Corsini, Raymond J., ed. Current Personality Theories. 1977. text ed. 17.95 o.p. (ISBN 0-87581-204-X, 204). Peacock Pubs.

Corsini, Raymond J., jt. ed. see Ignas, Edward.

Corso, Gregory. Earth Egg. (Illus.). 1974. pap. 10.00 (ISBN 0-934450-01-3); pap. 20.00 signed ed. (ISBN 0-934450-00-5). Unmuzzled Ox.

--The Japanese Notebook Ox. 1974. pap. 4.95x (ISBN 0-934450-05-6). Unmuzzled Ox.

Corso, Steve Del see Del Corso, Steven, et al.

Corson, Christopher. Maya Anthropomorphic Figurines from Jaina Island, Campeche. (No. 1). (Illus.). 218p. 1976. pap. 8.95 (ISBN 0-87919-053-1). Ballena Pr.

Corson, Helen B. Does Your Diet Work? LC 80-8427. (Illus.). 105p. (Orig.). 1980. pap. 7.95 (ISBN 0-9605358-0-2). MIND.

Corson, James C., ed. Notes & Index to Sir Herbert Grierson's Edition of the Letters of Sir Walter Scott. 1979. 105.00x (ISBN 0-19-812718-9). Oxford U Pr.

Corson, John J. The Governance of Colleges & Universities: Modernizing Structure & Processes. rev. ed. 1975. 17.95 (ISBN 0-07-013205-4, P&RB). McGraw.

Corson, John J. & Harris, Joseph P. Public Administration in Modern Society. LC 81-7262. (Foundations of American Government & Political Science Ser.). 155p. 1981. Repr. of 1963 ed. lib. bdg. 20.75x (ISBN 0-313-22668-7, COPU/). Greenwood.

--Public Administration in Modern Society. 1963. pap. text ed. 6.95 o.p. (ISBN 0-07-013188-0, C). McGraw.

Corson, Richard. Champions at Speed. LC 78-25853. (Illus.). (gr. 6 up). 1979. 5.95 o.p. (ISBN 0-396-07656-4). Dodd.

--Fashions in Eyeglasses. (Illus.). 1967. 50.00 (ISBN 0-8023-1111-3). Dufour.

--Stage Makeup. 6th ed. (Illus.). 464p. 1981. text ed. 28.95 (ISBN 0-13-840512-3). P-H.

Cort, Ned. Boxer Unit-OSS, No. 2: Alpine Gambit. (Men of Action Ser.). 160p. (Orig.). 1981. pap. 1.95 o.s.i. (ISBN 0-446-30019-5). Warner Bks.

Cortada, James W. EDP Cost & Charges: Finance, Budgets & Cost Control in Data Processing. (Data Processing Management Ser.). (Illus.). 1980. text ed. 29.95 (ISBN 0-13-235655-4). P-H.

--Two Nations Over Time: Spain & the United States, 1776-1977. LC 77-94752. (Contributions in American History: No. 74). 1978. lib. bdg. 29.95 (ISBN 0-313-20319-9, CTN/). Greenwood.

Cortada, James W., compiled by. Bibliographic Guide to Spanish Diplomatic History: Fourteen Sixty to Nineteen Seventy-Seven. LC 77-4565. 1977. lib. bdg. 35.00 (ISBN 0-8371-9685-X, CBG/). Greenwood.

Cortada, James W., ed. Spain in the Twentieth-Century World: Essays on Spanish Diplomacy, 1898-1978. LC 78-75257. (Contributions in Political Science: No. 30). 1980. lib. bdg. 29.95 (ISBN 0-313-21326-7, CST/). Greenwood.

Cortazar, Julio. End of the Game: And Other Stories. 1978. pap. 6.25i (ISBN 0-06-090637-5, CN 637, CN). Har-Row.

--We Love Glenda So Much & Other Tales. Rabassa, Gregory, tr. from Span. LC 82-48732. 1983. 11.95 (ISBN 0-394-53024-1). Knopf.

Cortazar, Mercedes. Astrogifts. LC 80-7665. (Illus.). 192p. (Orig.). 1980. pap. 5.95i o.p. (ISBN 0-06-090798-3, CN 798, CN). Har-Row.

Cortazzo, Carmen. Nowhere to Go but Home. 176p. (Orig.). 1982. pap. cancelled (ISBN 0-523-41626-1). Pinnacle Bks.

Cortelazzo, Manlio. I Dialetti E la Dialettologia in Italia (Fini Al 1800) (ARS Linguistica Ser.: No. 4). 146p. (Orig., Ital.). 1980. pap. 22.00 (ISBN 3-87808-354-8). Benjamins North Am.

Cortes, Carlos E., et al. Understanding You & Them: Tips for Teaching About Ethnicity. 66p. pap. 3.95 (ISBN 0-686-95026-7). ADL.

Cortes, F., et al. Systems Analysis for Social Scientists. LC 73-23061. 1974. 32.95 o.p. (ISBN 0-471-17509-9, Pub. by Wiley-Interscience). Wiley.

Cortes, Funes H. & Rozencweig, M., eds. New Approaches in Cancer Therapy. (European Organization for Research on Treatment of Cancer (EORTC) Monograph: Vol. 11). 225p. 1982. text ed. 45.00 (ISBN 0-89004-781-2). Raven.

Cortes-Conde, Roberto & Hunt, Shane J., eds. Latin American Economies: Growth & the Export Sector, 1880-1930. 260p. 1983. write for info. (ISBN 0-8419-0771-4). Holmes & Meier.

Cortes Conde, Roberto & Stein, Stanley J., eds. Latin America: A Guide to Economic History 1830-1930. LC 74-30534. 1977. 62.50x (ISBN 0-520-02956-9). U of Cal Pr.

Cortesi, David. A Programmer's Notebook: Utilities for the CP-M80. 1983. text ed. 21.95 (ISBN 0-8359-5642-3); pap. text ed. 16.95 (ISBN 0-8359-5641-5). Reston.

Cortesi, Lawrence. The Deadly Skies. 1983. pap. 3.25 (ISBN 0-8217-1132-6). Zebra.

--Rogue Sergeant. 224p. 1982. pap. 2.50 o.p. (ISBN 0-505-51854-6). Tower Bks.

Cortey, Noel. Modern Elementary Linear Algebra. LC 78-57573. 1978. pap. text ed. 8.00 (ISBN 0-8191-0524-4). U Pr of Amer.

Corti, Egon C. The Rise of the House of Rothschild. 430p. 1972. pap. 4.95 (ISBN 0-88279-112-5). Western Islands.

Corti, V., tr. see Artaud, Antonin.

Cortina Company. Conversational Brazilian-Portuguese in 20 Lessons. 192p. 1980. pap. 3.95 (ISBN 0-06-463607-0, EH 607, EH). B&N NY.

Cortis, Gerald. Social Context of Teaching. (Psychology & Education Ser.). 1977. text ed. 8.00x o.p. (ISBN 0-7291-0018-9); pap. text ed. 5.25x o.p. (ISBN 0-7291-0013-8). Humanities.

Cortissoz, Royal. John Lafarge, A Memoir & A Study. LC 70-87508. (Library of American Art Ser). (Illus.). 1971. Repr. of 1911 ed. lib. bdg. 27.50 (ISBN 0-306-71405-1). Da Capo.

Cortner, Richard C. The Supreme Court & Civil Liberties Policy. LC 75-21071. 225p. 1976. text ed. 14.95 o.p. (ISBN 0-87484-337-5); pap. 8.95 (ISBN 0-87484-336-7). Mayfield Pub.

Cortot, Alfred. French Piano Music. Andrews, Hilda, tr. from Fr. LC 77-4108. (Music Reprint, 1977 Ser.). 1977. Repr. of 1932 ed. 22.50 (ISBN 0-306-70896-5). Da Capo.

Cortright, Barbara. The Reach of Solitude: The Paintings of Taylor. (Illus.). 1983. 25.00 (ISBN 0-8397-7073-1). Eriksson.

Cortright, David. International Soldiers' Movement. 23p. 1975. 0.50 (ISBN 0-686-43098-0). Recon Pubns.

Corts, Paul, jt. auth. see Kell, Carl.

Corts, Paul R., jt. auth. see Kell, Carl L.

Corum, Claudia W. An Introduction to the Swazi (Siswati) Language. (African Language Texts Ser.). (Orig.). pap. text ed. 5.00 (ISBN 0-941934-01-2). Ind U Afro-Amer Arts.

Corwen, Leonard. There's a Job for You In: Advertising, Commercial Art, Fashion, Films, Public Relations & Publicity, Publishing, Television & Radio, Travel & Tourism. (Illus.). 192p. (Orig.). 1983. pap. 8.95 (ISBN 0-8329-0273-X). New Century.

--Your Future in Publishing. LC 72-91800. 144p. 1975. pap. 4.50 (ISBN 0-668-03428-9). Arco.

Corwin, Arthur F., ed. Immigrants & Immigrants: Perspectives on Mexican Labor Migration to the United States. LC 77-84756. (Contributions in Economics & Economic History: No. 17). (Illus.). 1978. lib. bdg. 29.95 (ISBN 0-8371-9848-8, CII/). Greenwood.

Corwin, Edward S. John Marshall & the Constitution. 1919. text ed. 8.50x (ISBN 0-686-83597-2). Elliots Bks.

--Liberty Against Government: The Rise, Flowering, & Decline of a Famous Judicial Concept. LC 77-4090. 1978. Repr. of 1948 ed. lib. bdg. 26.00x (ISBN 0-8371-9589-6, COLAG). Greenwood.

Corwin, Harry O. & Jenkins, John B. Conceptual Foundation of Genetics: Selected Readings. LC 75-26092. (Illus.). 448p. 1976. pap. text ed. 15.50 (ISBN 0-395-24064-6). HM.

Corwin, Ronald G. Reform & Organizational Survival. LC 72-10367. 496p. 1973. 22.50 (ISBN 0-471-17519-6, Pub. by Wiley). Krieger.

Corwin, Ronald G., ed. Research in the Sociology of Education & Socialization, Vol. 2. 316p. 1980. 42.50 (ISBN 0-89232-158-X). Jai Pr.

--Research in the Sociology of Education & Socialization, Vol. 3. 325p. 1981. 42.50 (ISBN 0-89232-187-3). Jai Pr.

Corwin, Sheila. Marriage & the Family & Child-Rearing Practices. Zak, Therese A., ed. (Lifeworks Ser.). (Illus.). 160p. 1981. text ed. 5.00 (ISBN 0-07-013198-8). McGraw.

Corwin, Thomas M. Twentieth-Century Physics: Remodeling the Universe. (Illus.). 350p. 1982. text ed. write for info. (ISBN 0-8162-1870-6); write for info. instr's. manual (ISBN 0-8162-1871-4). Holden Day.

Corwith, Bonnie. Transitions of a Purple Rabbit. 1983. 7.95 (ISBN 0-533-05463-X). Vantage.

Cory, Beverly. Grammar & Usage. (Learning Workbooks Language Arts). (gr. 4-6). pap. 1.50 (ISBN 0-8224-4179-9). Pitman.

--Phonics & Spelling. (Learning Workbooks Language Arts). (gr. 4-6). pap. 1.50 (ISBN 0-8224-4176-4). Pitman.

--Word Meaning. (Learning Workbooks Language Arts). (gr. 4-6). pap. 1.50 (ISBN 0-8224-4178-0). Pitman.

--Word Structure. (Learning Workbooks Language Arts). (gr. 4-6). pap. 1.50 (ISBN 0-8224-4177-2). Pitman.

Cory, Carol & Lintner, Jay. Peace Futuring. (Orig.). 1983. pap. 1.95 Leader's Bk. (ISBN 0-686-84608-7); pap. 1.95 Student's Bk. (ISBN 0-686-84609-5). Pilgrim NY.

Cory, Desmond. The Night Hawk. 188p. 1983. pap. 2.95 (ISBN 0-8027-3024-8). Walker & Co.

Cory, Herbert E. The Intellectuals & the Wage Works: A Study in Educational Psychoanalysis. 273p. 1982. Repr. of 1919 ed. lib. bdg. 50.00 (ISBN 0-686-81846-6). Darby Bks.

Coryell, Julie & Friedman, Laura. Jazz Rock Fusion, the People, the Music. 1978. pap. 9.95 o.s.i. (ISBN 0-440-54409-2, Delta). Dell.

Coscarelli, Diego, ed. Barron's Regents Exams & Answers: Italian. rev. ed. LC 75-39381. 250p. (gr. 10-12). 1982. pap. text ed. 3.95 (ISBN 0-8120-3149-0). Barron.

Coscia, Louis W., pseud. The Promised One. 192p. Date not set. price not set. Todd & Honeywell.

Cosentino, Christine, jt. ed. see Gerber, Margy.

Cosentino, Donald J. Defiant Maids & Stubborn Farmers: Tradition & Invention in Mende Story Performance. LC 81-15517. (Studies in Oral & Literate Culture: No. 4). (Illus.). 260p. 1982. 34.50 (ISBN 0-521-24197-9). Cambridge U Pr.

Cosentino, Rodolfo. Atlas of Anatomy & Surgical Approaches in Orthopaedic Surgery, Vol. 2: Lower Extremity. (Illus.). 276p. 1973. pap. 24.50x spiral (ISBN 0-398-00350-5). C C Thomas.

Cosenza, Mario E., compiled by. Biographical & Bibliographical Dictionary of the Italian Humanists & of the World of Classical Scholarship in Italy, 1300-1800, 5 Vols. 1962. Set. 475.00 (ISBN 0-8161-0626-6, Hall Library); Vol. 6. suppl. (1967) 105.00 (ISBN 0-8161-0765-3). G K Hall.

Cosenza, Mario E., ed. Biographical & Bibliographical Dictionary of the Italian Printers & of Foreign Printers in Italy from the Introduction of the Art of Printing into Italy to 1800. 1968. lib. bdg. 95.00 (ISBN 0-8161-0766-1, Hall Library). G K Hall.

Cosenza, Mario E., compiled by. Checklist of the Non-Italian Humanists, 1300-1800. 1969. lib. bdg. 75.00 (ISBN 0-8161-0839-0, Hall Library). G K Hall.

Coser, Lewis. Masters of Sociological Thought: Ideas in Historical & Social Context. 2nd ed. (Illus.). 611p. 1977. text ed. 22.95 (ISBN 0-15-555130-2, HC). HarBraceJ.

Coser, Lewis & Howe, Irving. The New Conservatives. rev. ed. 1977. pap. 5.95 o.p. (ISBN 0-452-00463-2, F463, Mer). NAL.

Coser, Lewis, jt. auth. see Howe, Irving.

Coser, Lewis A. Functions of Social Conflict. LC 56-6874. 1964. pap. text ed. 7.95 (ISBN 0-02-906810-X). Free Pr.

--Sociology Through Literature. 2nd ed. 544p. 1972. pap. text ed. 16.95 (ISBN 0-13-821538-3). P-H.

Coser, Lewis A., et al. Books: The Culture & Commerce of Publishing. LC 81-66100. 350p. 1982. 19.00 (ISBN 0-465-00759-7). Basic.

Cosgrave, Gerald P. Choices for Tomorrow. 1978. pap. text ed. 4.95x (ISBN 0-8077-8065-0, Guidance Center). Tchrs Coll.

Cosgrove, Carol A. & Twitchett, Kenneth J. New International Actors: The United Nations & the European Economic Community. LC 73-111412. 1970. 18.95 (ISBN 0-312-56805-3); pap. text ed. 6.95 o.p. (ISBN 0-312-56770-7). St Martin.

Cosgrove, David O. & McCready, V. Ralph. Ultrasound Imaging: Liver Spleen Pancreas. 367p. 1982. 75.00x (ISBN 0-471-10068-4, Pub. by Wiley Med). Wiley.

Cosgrove, John J. Upon This Rock: A Tale of Peter. LC 77-94404. 1978. pap. 4.95 o.p. (ISBN 0-87973-775-1). Our Sunday Visitor.

Cosgrove, Mark P. B. F. Skinner's Behaviorism: An Analysis. 128p. (Orig.). 1982. pap. 5.95 (ISBN 0-310-44491-8). Zondervan.

Cosgrove, Stephen. Jake O'Shawnasey. (gr. 1-6). 1975. pap. 1.50 o.s.i. (ISBN 0-8431-0558-5). Price Stern.

--Morgan Mine. (Serendipity Bks.). (Illus.). 32p. (gr. 1-6). 1982. pap. 1.50 (ISBN 0-686-97768-8). Price Stern.

Cosgrove, Steve. In Search of Saveopotomas. (Serendipity Bks). (Illus.). (gr. k-4). 1978. PLB 7.95 (ISBN 0-87191-661-4). Creative Ed.

--Jake O'Shawnasey. (Serendipity Bks.). (Illus.). (gr. k-4). 1978. PLB 7.95 (ISBN 0-87191-654-1). Creative Ed.

Cosgrove-Twitchett, Carol. Europe & Africa. 212p. 1978. text ed. 30.50x (ISBN 0-566-00182-9). Gower Pub Ltd.

Coshof, Karen, et al. The Haunted Dollhouse. LC 82-50640. (Illus.). 96p. 1982. 5.95 (ISBN 0-89480-206-2). Workman Pub.

Coslow, Samson. Make Money on the Interest Rate Roller Coaster. 288p. 1982. 14.95 (ISBN 0-698-11155-9, Coward). Putnam Pub Group.

Cosman, Anna. How to Read & Write Poetry. (First Bks.). (Illus.). (gr. 5-8). 1979. PLB 8.90 s&l (ISBN 0-531-02261-7). Watts.

Cosmi, Ermelando, jt. ed. see Scarpelli, Emilie.

Cosmi, Ermelando V., jt. ed. see Scarpelli, Emile M.

C.O.S.P.A.R International Space Science Symposium, 7th, Vienna, 1966. Life Sciences & Space Research: Proceedings, Vol. 5. Brown, A. H. & Favorite, F. G., eds. 1969. text ed. 19.75x o.p. (ISBN 0-7204-1364-8). Humanities.

C.O.S.P.A.R International Space Science Symposium - London - Jul 26-27 1967. Moon & Planets: A Session of the Joint Open Meeting of Working Groups One, Two & Five of the Tenth Plenary Meeting of COSPAR, Vol. 2. Dollfus, A., ed. (Illus., Part Fr). 1968. 14.25x o.p. (ISBN 0-7204-0129-1). Humanities.

C.O.S.P.A.R International Space Science Symposium - 7th - Vienna. Moon & Planets: Proceedings, Vol. 1. Dollfus, A., ed. 1967. text ed. 15.00x o.p. (ISBN 0-7204-0116-X, Pub. by North Holland). Humanities.

C.O.S.P.A.R., 11th Plenary Meeting, Tokyo, 1968. Life Sciences & Space Research: Proceedings, Vol. 7. Vishniac, W. & Favorite, F. G., eds. LC 63-6132. (Illus.). 1969. text ed. 20.00x o.p. (ISBN 0-7204-1367-2, Pub. by North Holland). Humanities.

C.O.S.P.A.R., 12th Meeting, Prague, 1969. Life Sciences & Space Research: Proceedings, Vol. 8. Vishniac, W. & Favorite, F. G., eds. LC 63-6132. (Illus., Orig.). 1970. pap. text ed. 25.25x o.p. (ISBN 0-7204-1365-6). Humanities.

Cossi, Olga. Fire Mate. LC 77-1334. (Illus.). 1977. 5.50 o.p. (ISBN 0-8309-0163-9). Ind Pr MO.

Cosslett, Tess. The Scientific Movement & Victorian Literature. LC 82-10284. 1982. 22.50x (ISBN 0-312-70298-1). St Martin.

Cosslett, V. E. & Barer, R., eds. Advances in Optical & Electron Microscopy. Vol. 1. 1966. 44.50 (ISBN 0-12-029901-1); Vol. 2. 1968. 66.00 (ISBN 0-12-029902-X); Vol. 3. 1969. 45.50 (ISBN 0-12-029903-8); Vol. 4. 1971. 67.00 (ISBN 0-12-029904-6); Vol. 5. 1973. 61.00 (ISBN 0-12-029905-4); Vol. 6, 1976. 52.50 (ISBN 0-12-029906-2); Vol. 7, 1979. 57.50 (ISBN 0-12-029907-0). Acad Pr.

--Advances in Optical & Electron Microscopy, Vol. 8. (Serial Publication). 281p. 1982. 58.00 (ISBN 0-12-029908-9). Acad Pr.

Cossman, E. Joseph. How I Made One Million Dollars in Mail Order. (Illus.). 1963. 14.95 (ISBN 0-13-397406-5). P-H.

Cosson, Annie, ed. Comment Reussir Votre Mariage. Orig. Title: I Want My Marriage to be Better. 176p. 1982. pap. 1.60 (ISBN 0-8297-0845-6). Life Pubs Intl.

Cosson, Annie, ed. see Carlson, G. R.

Cosson, Annie, ed. see Coleman, William.

Cosson, Annie, ed. see Getz, Gene A.

Cosson, Annie, ed. see Grams, Betty J.

Cosson, Annie, ed. see Halley.

Cosson, Annie, ed. see Kennedy, D. J.

Cosson, Annie, ed. see Lindsey, Hal.

Cosson, Annie, ed. see McDowell, Josh.

Cosson, Annie, ed. see Mears, Henrietta C.

Cosson, Annie, ed. see Rexroat, Stephen.

Cosson, Annie, ed. see Rodriguez, Cookie.

Cosson, Annie, ed. see Taylor, Thomas.

Cosson, Annie, tr. see Harris, Ralph.

Cosson, Annie, et al, eds. see Harris, Ralph.

Costa, Betty & Costa, Marie. A Practical Guide to Microcomputers in Small Libraries & Media Centers. 175p. 1983. lib. bdg. 19.50 (ISBN 0-87287-354-4). Libs Unl.

Costa, C. D., ed. Horace. (Greek & Latin Studies). 176p. 1973. 18.50x (ISBN 0-7100-7597-9). Routledge & Kegan.

--Seneca. (Greek & Latin Studies Ser.). 252p. 1974. 22.00x (ISBN 0-7100-7900-1). Routledge & Kegan.

Costa, E. & Gessa, G. L., eds. Nonstriatal Dopaminergic Neurons. LC 76-5661. (Advances in Biochemical Psychopharmacology Ser.: Vol. 16). 728p. 1977. 65.50 (ISBN 0-89004-127-X). Raven.

Costa, E. & Giacobini, S., eds. Biochemistry of Simple Neuronal Models. (Advances in Biochemical Psychopharmacology Ser.: Vol. 2). 382p. 1970. text ed. 24.00 (ISBN 0-911216-10-3). Raven.

Costa, E. & Greengard, P., eds. Mechanism of Action of Benzodiazepines. LC 75-10978. (Advances in Biochemical Psychopharmacology Ser.: Vol. 14). 190p. 1975. 25.50 (ISBN 0-89004-039-7). Raven.

Costa, E. & Greengard, Paul, eds. Advances in Biochemical Psychopharmacology, Vol. 1. LC 73-84113. (Illus.). 1969. 20.00 (ISBN 0-911216-06-5). Raven.

Costa, E. & Holmstedt, B., eds. Gas Chromatography-Mass Spectrometry in Neurobiology. LC 73-84113. (Advances in Biochemical Psychopharmacology Ser.: Vol. 7). (Illus.). 183p. 1973. 27.00 (ISBN 0-911216-48-0). Raven.

Costa, E. & Racagni, G., eds. Typical & Atypical Antidepressants: Molecular Mechanisms. (Advances in Biochemical Psychopharmacology Ser.: Vol. 31). 405p. 1982. text ed. 49.50 (ISBN 0-89004-686-7). Raven.

Costa, E. & Sandler, M., eds. Monoamine Oxidases - New Vistas. LC 73-84113. (Advances in Biochemical Psychopharmacology Ser.: Vol. 5). (Illus.). 466p. 1972. 38.00 (ISBN 0-911216-19-7). Raven.

Costa, E. & Trabucci, M., eds. Regulatory Peptides: From Molecular Biology to Function. (Advances in Biochemical Psychopharmacology Ser.: Vol. 33). 1982. text ed. 65.00 (ISBN 0-89004-797-9). Raven.

Costa, E., jt. ed. see Ebadi, M.

Costa, E., jt. ed. see Greengard, P.

Costa, E., et al, eds. Gaba & Benzodiazepine Receptors. (Advances in Biochemical Psychopharmacology Ser.: Vol. 26). 321p. 1981. text ed. 39.50 (ISBN 0-89004-530-5). Raven.

--Serotonin, New Vistas: Biochemistry & Behavioral & Clinical Studies. LC 73-91166. (Advances in Biochemical Psychopharmacology Ser.: Vol. 11). 446p. 1974. 34.50 (ISBN 0-911216-69-3). Raven.

--Serotonin, New Vistas: Histochemistry & Pharmacology. LC 73-91165. (Advances in Biochemical Psychopharmacology Ser.: Vol. 10). 345p. 1974. 34.50 (ISBN 0-911216-68-5). Raven.

--First & Second Messengers: New Vistas. LC 75-14583. (Advances in Biochemical Psychopharmacology Ser: Vol. 15). 514p. 1976. 45.50 (ISBN 0-89004-084-2). Raven.

Costa, Erminio & Trabucchi, Marco, eds. Neural Peptides & Neural Communication. (Advances in Biochemical Psychopharmacology Ser.: Vol. 22). 670p. 1980. text ed. 67.50 (ISBN 0-89004-375-2). Raven.

Costa, Francisco Da see Mickle, M. M. & Da Costa, Francisco.

Costa, G. & Gatto, R. R., eds. Theory of Fundamental Interactions: Proceedings of the International School of Physics, Enrico Fermi Course LXXXI, Varenna, Italy, July 21 - August 2, 1980. (Enrico Fermi International Summer School of Physics Ser.: Vol. 81). 300p. 1982. 61.75 (ISBN 0-444-86156-4, North Holland). Elsevier.

Costa, John E. & Baker, Victor R. Surficial Geology Building with the Earth. 608p. 1981. text ed. 28.95x (ISBN 0-471-03229-8). Wiley.

Costa, Joseph H. & Nelson, Gordon K. Child Abuse & Neglect: Legislation, Reporting & Prevention. LC 77-3836. 1978. 28.95x (ISBN 0-669-01670-5). Lexington Bks.

Costa, Joseph J. Abuse of Women: Legislation, Reporting, & Prevention. LC 81-48512. 1982. write for info. (ISBN 0-669-05374-0). Lexington Bks.

Costa, Margaret. Four Seasons Cookery Book. 1979. 28.00x o.p. (ISBN 0-8464-0423-0). Beekman Pubs.

Costa, Marie, jt. auth. see Costa, Betty.

Costa, Ray. How to Be a Male Exotic Dancer. (Illus.). 114p. (Orig.). pap. text ed. 9.95 (ISBN 0-686-38733-3). Costa.

Costa, Rebecca, et al. A Parent's Guide to Children: The Challenge. LC 77-90090. (Illus., Orig.). 1978. pap. 4.25 (ISBN 0-8015-5734-8, 0413-120, Hawthorn). Dutton.

Costa, Richard H. H. G. Wells. (English Authors Ser.). 1966. lib. bdg. 11.95 (ISBN 0-8057-1568-1, Twayne). G K Hall.

--Malcolm Lowry. LC 75-185451. (World Authors Ser.: Canada: No. 217). lib. bdg. 10.95 o.p. (ISBN 0-8057-2548-2, Twayne). G K Hall.

Costabel, Eva D. A New England Village. LC 82-13738. (Illus.). 64p. (gr. 4 up). 1983. 11.95 (ISBN 0-689-30972-4). Atheneum.

Costain, David W., jt. auth. see Green, A. Richard.

Costain, Thomas B. The Conquering Family. LC 62-20488. 1964. 6.95 (ISBN 0-385-04088-1). Doubleday.

--The Last Plantagenets. LC 62-52105. 1962. 6.95 (ISBN 0-385-00142-8). Doubleday.

--White & the Gold. LC 53-7236. 5.95 (ISBN 0-385-04526-3); limited ed. 35.00. Doubleday.

Costales, Claire & Berry, Jo. Staying Dry: A Practical Solution to Alcohol Abuse. rev. ed. 1983. pap. 4.95 (ISBN 0-8307-0885-5). Regal.

Costantini, Humberto, tr. see Slote, Alfred.

Costanza, Mary S. The Living Witness: Art in the Concentration Camps & Ghettos. 1982. 19.95 (ISBN 0-02-906660-3). Free Pr.

Costanzo, Christie. Mommy & Me Exercises the Kidnastics Program. (Illus.). 72p. (Orig.). 1983. pap. 5.95 (ISBN 0-917982-28-2). Cougar Bks.

Costanzo, P. R., jt. auth. see Shaw, M.

Costanzo, P. R., jt. auth. see Shaw, M. E.

Costas, Orlando E. The Integrity of Mission: The Inner Life & Outreach of the Church. LC 79-1759. 1979. pap. 5.72i (ISBN 0-06-061586-9, RD 235, HarpR). Har-Row.

Coste, Adolphe. Hygiene Sociale contre le Pauperisme. (Conditions of the 19th Century French Working Class Ser.). 543p. (Fr.). 1974. Repr. of 1882 ed. lib. bdg. 134.00x o.p. (ISBN 0-8287-0228-4, 1085). Clearwater Pub.

Coste, Brigitte, jt. auth. see Braude, Beatrice.

Coste D'Arnobat, Pierre-Nicolas. Voyages au Pays de Bambouc. (Bibliotheque Africaine Ser.). 64p. (Fr.). 1974. Repr. of 1789 ed. lib. bdg. 27.50x o.p. (ISBN 0-8287-0229-2, 72-2138). Clearwater Pub.

Costello, Augustine. Our Police Protectors: History of the New York Police. 3rd ed. LC 79-129324. (Criminology, Law Enforcement, & Social Problems Ser.: No. 127). (Illus.). 653p. (With intro. added). 1972. Repr. of 1885 ed. lib. bdg. 25.00x (ISBN 0-87585-127-4). Patterson Smith.

Costello, C. G. Symptoms of Psychopathology: A Handbook. LC 78-88309. 679p. 1970. 45.95x o.p. (ISBN 0-471-17520-X). Wiley.

Costello, Chris & Strait, Raymond. Lou's on First: The Biography of Lou Costello. (Illus.). 384p. 1983. pap. 6.95 (ISBN 0-312-49914-0). St Martin.

Costello, David F. The Desert World. LC 77-184973. (Illus.). 256p. 1972. 9.95i o.p. (ISBN 0-690-23513-5). T Y Crowell.

--The Seashore World. LC 79-7641. (Illus.). 256p. 1980. 14.37i (ISBN 0-690-01235-7). Har-Row.

Costello, Donald P. Fellini's Road. LC 82-50286. 224p. 1983. text ed. 16.95 (ISBN 0-268-00958-9); pap. text ed. 9.95 (ISBN 0-268-00961-9). U of Notre Dame Pr.

Costello, Elaine. Signing: How to Speak with Your Hands. 1983. pap. 9.95 (ISBN 0-686-43070-0). Bantam.

Costello, Jeanne & Witty, Doreen. Lighten-Up. Neumayer, Lisa, ed. (Illus.). 288p. (Orig.). 1983. pap. write for info. (ISBN 0-9609894-1-2). Costello & Witty.

Costello, John J. & Gowdy, Spenser O. Mathematics for the Management, Life & Social Sciences. 703p. 1982. text ed. 24.95 (ISBN 0-15-555240-6, HC); answers 2.95 (ISBN 0-15-555241-4). HarBraceJ.

Costello, John J., et al. Finite Mathematics with Applications. 524p. 1981. text ed. 22.95 (ISBN 0-15-527400-7, HC); solutions 1.95 (ISBN 0-15-527401-5). HarBraceJ.

Costello, Mary C. Between Fixity & Flux. 1966. pap. 5.95x (ISBN 0-8132-0255-8). Cath U Pr.

Costello, Maurice J. & Gibbs, Richard C. Palms & Soles in Medicine. (Illus.). 720p. 1967. photocopy ed. spiral 60.25x (ISBN 0-398-00351-3). C C Thomas.

Costello, Nancy A. Katu Vocabulary. 124p. 1971. pap. 2.00x o.s.i. (ISBN 0-88312-778-4); microfiche 2.25. Summer Inst Ling.

Costello, V. F. Urbanization in the Middle East. LC 76-11075. (Urbanization in Developing Countries Ser.). (Illus.). 1977. 22.95 (ISBN 0-521-21324-X); pap. 8.95 (ISBN 0-521-29110-0). Cambridge U Pr.

Costeloe, M. P. Church Wealth in Mexico. (Cambridge Latin American Studies: No. 2). 1968. 22.95 (ISBN 0-521-04729-3). Cambridge U Pr.

Costeloe, Michael see Steele, Colin.

Coster, J., jt. ed. see Lewis, S. M.

Coster, Jean. Dictionary for Automotive Engineering. 298p. 1983. 38.00 (ISBN 3-598-10430-8, Pub. by K G Saur). Shoe String.

Costich, Julia F. Antonin Artaud. (World Authors Ser.). 1978. lib. bdg. 15.95 (ISBN 0-8057-6333-3, Twayne). G K Hall.

Costigan, Daniel M. Electronic Delivery of Documents & Graphics. 344p. 1978. 24.25 (ISBN 0-686-98117-0). Telecom Lib.

Costikyan, Barbara H. Be Kind to Your Dog At Christmas, & Other Ways to Have Happy Holidays & a Lucky New Year. LC 81-22343. (Illus.). 56p. (gr. 8-11). 1982. 9.95 (ISBN 0-394-84963-9); PLB 9.99 (ISBN 0-394-94963-3). Pantheon.

Costin. Plaid for Abnormal Psychology. 1976. pap. 6.95 o.p. (ISBN 0-256-01480-9, 11-1032-00). Dow Jones-Irwin.

Costin, Lela B. Child Welfare: Policies & Practices. new ed. (Illus.). 432p. 1972. text ed. 15.95 o.p. (ISBN 0-07-013202-X, C). McGraw.

--Child Welfare: Policies & Practices. 2nd ed. (Illus.). text ed. 23.50 (ISBN 0-07-013206-2, C); instructor's manual 15.00 (ISBN 0-07-013207-0). McGraw.

Costley, Dan L. & Todd, Ralph. Human Relations in Organizations. (Management Ser.). (Illus.). 1978. pap. text ed. 16.95 (ISBN 0-8299-0211-2); instrs. manual avail. (ISBN 0-8299-0471-9). West Pub.

--Human Relations in Organizations. 2d ed. (Illus.). 570p. 1983. text ed. 17.95 (ISBN 0-314-69643-1); write for info. instr's. manual (ISBN 0-314-71087-6). West Pub.

Costlow, John D., ed. Fertility of the Sea, 2 vols. LC 74-132383. (Illus.). 646p. 1971. Set. 105.00x (ISBN 0-677-14730-9). Gordon.

Costopoulos, William C. The Price of Aquittal. 1982. 12.50 (ISBN 0-8062-1944-0). Carlton.

Cotchett, Joseph W. & Elkind, Arnold B. Federal Courtroom Evidence. LC 75-26155. 249p. 1980. incl. 1983 suppl. 38.50 (ISBN 0-911110-20-8). Parker & Son.

Cotchett, Joseph W., jt. auth. see Haight, Fulton.

Cote, Wilfred A., ed. Cellular Ultrastructure of Woody Plants. LC 65-15851. (Illus.). 1965. 29.95x (ISBN 0-8156-5015-9). Syracuse U Pr.

Cotera, Martha P., tr. see Hazen, Nancy.

Cotes, Peter. Trial of Elvira Barney. LC 76-45510. (Celebrated Trials Ser.). (Illus.). 1977. 5.95 o.p. (ISBN 0-7153-7294-7). David & Charles.

Cotgreave, Alfred. Contents-Subject Index to General & Periodical Literature. LC 74-31272. 1971. Repr. of 1900 ed. 64.00 o.p. (ISBN 0-8103-3778-9). Gale.

Cotgrove, Stephen. Catastrophe or Cornucopia: The Environment, Politics & the Future. LC 81-148827. 1982. 35.95x (ISBN 0-471-10079-X, Pub. by Wiley-Interscience); pap. 19.95x (ISBN 0-471-10166-4). Wiley.

Cothen, Joe H. The Preacher's Notebook on Isaiah. 1983. pap. 6.95 (ISBN 0-88289-365-3). Pelican.

Cothren, Paige. Let None Deal Treacherously. 256p. (Orig.). 1981. pap. 5.00 (ISBN 0-937778-03-6). Fulness Hse.

Cotliar, William, jt. auth. see Riordan, John J.

Cotlier, Edward & Maumenee, Irene H., eds. Genetic Eye Diseases: Retinitis Pigmentosa & Other Inherited Eye Disorders. LC 82-13049. (Birth Defects; Original Article Ser.: Vol. 18, No. 6). 746p. 1982. 76.00 (ISBN 0-8451-1050-0). A R Liss.

Cotman & Poste. Cell Surface & Neuron & Neuronal Function. (Cell Surface Reviews Ser.: Vol. 6). 1981. 121.75 (ISBN 0-444-80202-9). Elsevier.

Cotman, Carl W., jt. auth. see Angevine, Jay B., Jr.

Cotman, Carl W., ed. Neuronal Plasticity. LC 77-72807. 349p. 1978. 34.50 (ISBN 0-89004-210-1). Raven.

Cotner, Robert C. Readings in American History, 2 vols. 4th ed. LC 75-37038. (Illus.). 1976. Vol. 1. pap. text ed. 12.50 o.p. (ISBN 0-395-17810-X); Vol. 2. pap. text ed. 13.50 (ISBN 0-395-17811-8). HM.

Cotran, Ramzi, jt. auth. see Leaf, Alexander.

Cotran, Ramzi, jt. auth. see Majno, Guido.

Cott, Christine H. Dangerous Delight. (Superromances Ser.). 384p. 1983. pap. 2.50 (ISBN 0-373-70050-4). Harlequin Bks.

--Toute la Tendresse du Monde. (Harlequin Seduction Ser.). 332p. 1983. pap. 3.25 (ISBN 0-373-45015-X). Harlequin Bks.

Cott, Jonathan. Stockhausen. 1973. 10.95 o.p. (ISBN 0-671-21495-0). S&S.

Cott, Nancy, ed. The Root of Bitterness: Documents of the Social History of American Women. 1972. pap. 9.75 (ISBN 0-525-47328-9, 0947-280). Dutton.

Cotter, C. Astronomical & Mathematical Foundations of Geography. 1966. 9.00 (ISBN 0-444-19960-8). Elsevier.

Cotter, Cornelius P., ed. Political Science Annual, Vol. 4. LC 66-29710. 1973. 16.25 (ISBN 0-672-51808-2). Bobbs.

Cotter, Michael, ed. Vietnam. 1977. lib. bdg. 54.00 (ISBN 0-8161-8050-4, Hall Reference). G K Hall.

Cotter, Patrick & Bowdler, George A. Voter Participation in Central America, 1954-1981: An Exploration. LC 81-43714. (Illus.). 276p. (Orig.). 1982. lib. bdg. 23.25 (ISBN 0-8191-2214-9); pap. text ed. 11.50 (ISBN 0-8191-2215-7). U Pr of Amer.

Cotter, R. Business Policy Game: A Player's Manual. 1973. 14.95 (ISBN 0-13-107433-4). P-H.

Cotterell, Arthur. A Dictionary of World Mythology. LC 79-65889. (Illus.). 1980. 12.95 o.s.i. (ISBN 0-399-12464-0). Putnam Pub Group.

--A Dictionary of World Mythology. (Illus.). 256p. 1982. pap. 5.95 (ISBN 0-399-50619-5, Perige). Putnam Pub Group.

Cotterell, Arthur & Collins, Nigel. Futureprobe. 1974. pap. text ed. 6.00x o.p. (ISBN 0-435-10175-7); tchr's ed. 3.00x o.p. (ISBN 0-435-10176-5). Heinemann Ed.

Cotterell, Laurence, jt. auth. see Reilly, Catherine W.

Cotterell, M., tr. see Steiner, Rudolf.

Cotterill, H. R., tr. see Barrili, Anton G.

Cotterill, J. A., jt. auth. see Cunliffe, W. J.

Cottingham, Clement, jt. auth. see Gomez, Rudolph.

Cottingham, Clement, ed. Race, Poverty & the Urban Underclass. LC 81-47712. (Illus.). 224p. 1982. 24.95x (ISBN 0-669-04730-9). Lexington Bks.

Cottingham, John, ed. & tr. Descartes' Conversation with Burman. 1974. pap. 9.95x (ISBN 0-19-824671-4). Oxford U Pr.

Cottino-Jones, Marga. Order from Chaos: Social & Aesthetic Harmonies in Boccaccio's Decameron. LC 82-17418. 210p. (Orig.). 1983. lib. bdg. 21.75 (ISBN 0-8191-2840-6); pap. text ed. 10.75 (ISBN 0-8191-2841-4). U Pr of Amer.

Cottle, Basil. The Plight of English. 1976. 7.95 o.p. (ISBN 0-87000-307-0, Arlington Hse). Crown.

Cottle, Joseph. The Fall of Cambria, a Poem, 2 vols. in 1. LC 75-31186. (Romantic Context Ser.: Poetry 1789-1830: Vol. 38). 1978. Repr. of 1808 ed. lib. bdg. 47.00 o.s.i. (ISBN 0-8240-2137-1). Garland Pub.

--Messiah; a Poem. LC 75-31187. (Romantic Context Ser.: Poetry 1789-1830: Vol. 39). 1978. Repr. of 1815 ed. lib. bdg. 47.00 o.s.i. (ISBN 0-8240-2138-X). Garland Pub.

Cottle, R. W., jt. ed. see Balinski, M. L.

Cottle, R. W., et al, eds. Variational Inequalities & Complementarity Problems: Theory & Applications. Giannessi, F. & Lions, J. L. LC 79-40108. 408p. 1980. 55.95 (ISBN 0-471-27610-3, Pub. by Wiley-Interscience). Wiley.

Cottle, Rex L., et al. Labor & Property Rights in California Agriculture: An Economic Analysis of the CALRA. LC 82-40318. (Texas A&M University Economics Ser.: No. 6). 136p. 1982. 18.50x (ISBN 0-89096-132-8). Tex A&M Univ Pr.

Cottle, Thomas J. Barred from School: Two Million Children. LC 76-20607. 1976. 7.95 (ISBN 0-915220-12-1); pap. 3.95 (ISBN 0-915220-40-7, 24165). New Republic.

--Black Testimony: Voices of Britain's West Indians. 184p. 1980. 22.95 (ISBN 0-87722-186-3). Temple U Pr.

--Busing. LC 76-7740. 1976. pap. 3.95 (ISBN 0-8070-0495-2, BP561). Beacon Pr.

--Children in Jail. LC 75-77440. 1977. 10.10x (ISBN 0-8070-0492-8); pap. 4.95x (ISBN 0-8070-0493-6, BP589). Beacon Pr.

--Golden Girl: The Story of an Adolescent Suicide. 304p. 14.95 (ISBN 0-399-12639-2). Putnam Pub Group.

--Hidden Survivors: Portraits of Poor Jews in America. LC 79-26718. 1980. 9.95 o.p. (ISBN 0-13-387357-9). P-H.

--Like Fathers, Like Sons: Portraits of Intimacy & Strain. (Modern Sociology Ser.). 300p. 1981. 15.95 (ISBN 0-89391-054-6); pap. 9.95 (ISBN 0-89391-087-2). Ablex Pub.

Cottle, Thomas J., jt. auth. see Greenblat, Cathy.

Cottle, William C. Interest & Personality Inventories. (Guidance Monograph). 1968. pap. 2.60 o.p. (ISBN 0-395-09929-3). HM

Cottle, William C. & Downie, N. M. Preparation for Counseling. 2nd ed. 1970. text ed. 22.95 o.p. (ISBN 0-13-697227-6). P-H.

Cottman & Blassingame. Out Island Doctor. (Illus.). 288p. 8.95 (ISBN 0-913428-18-3); pap. 4.95 (ISBN 0-686-83953-6). Landfall Pr.

Cottman, Gwen. Traveling in Africa. 36p. 1982. 3.00 (ISBN 0-912444-24-X). Gaus.

Cotton, Albert F. Progress in Inorganic Chemistry, Vol. 7. LC 59-13035. 1966. 29.50 (ISBN 0-470-17675-X, Pub. by JW). Krieger.

Cotton, Albert F. & Wilkinson, Geoffrey. Basic Inorganic Chemistry. LC 75-26832. 579p. (Arabic Translation available). 1976. 30.50 (ISBN 0-471-17557-9). Wiley.

Cotton, Albert F., ed. Progress in Inorganic Chemistry, Vol. 3. 552p. 1983. Repr. of 1962 ed. write for info (ISBN 0-89874-014-2). Krieger.

--Progress in Inorganic Chemistry, Vol. 8. 1983. Repr. of 1967 ed. write for info. Krieger.

Cotton, Charles. Selected Poems. Robinson, Ken, ed. 128p. 1982. pap. text ed. 6.25x (ISBN 0-85635-413-9, 51122, Pub. by Carcanet New Pr England). Humanities.

Cotton, Charles, jt. auth. see Walton, Izaak.

Cotton, F. Albert. Chemical Applications of Group Theory. 2nd ed. LC 76-129657. 1971. 35.95x (ISBN 0-471-17570-6, Pub. by Wiley-Interscience). Wiley.

Cotton, F. Albert & Walton, Richard A. Multiple Bonds Between Metal Atoms. LC 81-11371. 466p. 1982. 47.50x (ISBN 0-471-04686-8, Pub. by Wiley-Interscience). Wiley.

Cotton, F. Albert & Wilkinson, Geoffrey. Advanced Inorganic Chemistry: A Comprehensive Text. 4th ed. LC 79-22506. 1980. 34.95x (ISBN 0-471-02775-8, Pub. by Wiley-Interscience). Wiley.

Cotton, Henry. The Typographical Gazetteer. LC 76-159922. 1975. Repr. of 1825 ed. 34.00x (ISBN 0-8103-4121-2). Gale.

Cotton, Ira W., ed. Office Automation Conference Digest Nineteen-Eighty. LC 80-80155. (Illus.). ix, 373p. 1980. pap. 16.00 (ISBN 0-88283-002-3). AFIPS Pr.

Cotton, Ira W., jt. ed. see Blanc, Robert P.

Cotton, James H. Royce on the Human Self. LC 69-10080. (Illus.). 1968. Repr. of 1954 ed. lib. bdg. 19.25x (ISBN 0-8371-0053-4, COHS). Greenwood.

Cotton, Joseph P., ed. The Constitutional Decisions of John Marshall, 2 Vols. LC 67-25445. (Law, Politics & History Ser.). 1969. Repr. of 1905 ed. Set. lib. bdg. 75.00 ea. (ISBN 0-306-70947-3). Da Capo.

Cotton, Leo, ed. Mr. Boston Deluxe Official Bartender's Guide. 61st, rev. ed. 224p. 1983. pap. 4.95 (ISBN 0-446-37043-6, 37-043-6). Warner Bks.

Cotton, Leonard, jt. auth. see Taylor, Selwyn.

Cotton, Nathan. Quantity Baking Recipes: Combined Edition, 2 vols. Incl. Vol. I. Cakes, Icings & Cheesecakes. 292p (ISBN 0-8436-2265-2); Vol. II. Breads, Pastries, Pies & Cookies. 284p (ISBN 0-8436-2272-5). 1983. Set. text ed. 39.95 (ISBN 0-8436-2273-3); text ed. 21.95 ea. CBI Pub.

Cotton, R. E., jt. auth. see Thomson, A. D.

Cottone, James A., et al. Outline of Forensic Dentistry. (Illus.). 1982. 19.95 (ISBN 0-8151-1868-6). Year Bk Med.

Cottonwood, Joe. Famous Potatoes. 1979. 10.95 o.s.i. (ISBN 0-440-03098-6, Sey Lawr). Delacorte.

--Famous Potatoes. 1979. pap. 4.95 o.s.i. (ISBN 0-440-52334-6, Delta). Dell.

--Frank City (Goodbye) 1981. 12.95 o.s.i. (ISBN 0-440-02910-4). Delacorte.

--Frank City (Goodbye) 1981. pap. 5.95x o.s.i. (ISBN 0-440-52906-9, Delta). Dell.

Cottrall, M. B. Fundamentals of Clinical Radionuclide Imaging. 1982. 25.00x (ISBN 0-686-92013-9, Pub. by Brit Inst Radiology England). State Mutual Bk.

Cottrell, Barbara J., jt. auth. see Larsen, Lawrence H.

Cottrell, Beekman W., jt. auth. see Slack, Robert C.

Cottrell, Jack. The Bible Says. 128p. (YA) 1983. pap. 2.25 (ISBN 0-87239-480-8). Standard Pub.

Cottrell, James E. & Turndorf, Herman. Anesthesia & Neurosurgery. LC 79-24676. (Illus.). 434p. 1979. text ed. 69.50 (ISBN 0-8016-1036-2). Mosby.

Cottrell, Jane E. Alberto Moravia. LC 73-84599. (Literature and Life Ser.). 174p. 1974. 11.95 (ISBN 0-8044-2131-5). Ungar.

Cottrell, John. Mexico City. (The Great Cities Ser.). (Illus.). 1979. lib. bdg. 12.00 (ISBN 0-8094-3105-X); 10.00 (ISBN 0-8094-3106-8). Silver.

Cottrell, Leonard. Land of the Pharaohs. LC 60-11464. (Illus.). (gr. 6 up). 1960. PLB 7.99 o.p. (ISBN 0-529-03612-6, Philomel). Putnam Pub Group.

--Up in a Balloon. LC 69-17423. (Illus.). (gr. 8 up). 1970. 12.95 (ISBN 0-87599-142-4). S G Phillips.

--Warrior Pharaohs. (Illus.). (gr. 6-8). 1969. PLB 4.89 o.p. (ISBN 0-399-60656-4). Putnam Pub Group.

Cottrell, Robert D. Colette. LC 73-84598. (Literature and Life Ser.). 1974. 11.95 (ISBN 0-8044-2130-7). Ungar.

--Simone De Beauvoir. LC 74-34131. (Literature and Life Ser.). 1975. 11.95 (ISBN 0-8044-2132-3). Ungar.

Couch, Houston B. Diseases of Turfgrasses. 3rd ed. 1984. write for info. (ISBN 0-89874-211-0). Krieger.

Couch, J. N., jt. auth. see Coker, W. C.

Couch, James. Fundamentals of Statistics for the Behavioral Sciences. LC 81-51854. 423p. 1982. text ed. 18.95 (ISBN 0-312-31195-8); study guide 6.95 (ISBN 0-312-31197-4); Instr's. manual. St Martin.

Couch, John D., jt. auth. see Barrett, William A.

Couch, Larry. Dada Dog. Strahan, Bradley R., ed. (Illustrated Chapbook Ser.). (Illus.). 24p. 1983. pap. text ed. 2.50 (ISBN 0-938872-04-4). Black Buzzard.

Couch, Leon W. Digital & Analog Communication Systems. 672p. 1983. text ed. 34.95 (ISBN 0-02-325240-5). Macmillan.

Couchman, Bob & Couchman, Win. James: Hear It! Live It! (Carpenter Studyguides). 64p. 1982. saddle-stitched leader's handbook 2.95 (ISBN 0-87788-423-4); member's handbook 1.95 (ISBN 0-87788-422-6). Shaw Pubs.

--Ruth & Jonah: People in Process. (Carpenter Studyguides Ser.). 64p. 1983. saddle-stiched members' handbk. 1.95 (ISBN 0-87788-736-5); leader's handbook 2.95 (ISBN 0-87788-737-3). Shaw Pubs.

--Small Groups: Timber to Build up God's House. LC 82-798. (Carpenter Studyguide Ser.). 96p. 1982. pap. 2.95 (ISBN 0-87788-097-2). Shaw Pubs.

Couchman, Charles B. The Balance Sheet. LC 82-48355. (Accountancy in Transition Ser.). 300p. 1982. lib. bdg. 30.00 (ISBN 0-8240-5308-7). Garland Pub.

Couchman, Win, jt. auth. see Couchman, Bob.

Coudenhove-Kalergi, Heinrich J. Anti-Semitism Throughout the Ages. Coudenhove-Kalergi, Richard, ed. Rappoport, Angelo S., tr. LC 73-97274. (Illus.). 288p. 1973. Repr. of 1935 ed. lib. bdg. 17.50x (ISBN 0-8371-2595-2, COAS). Greenwood.

Coudenhove-Kalergi, Richard, ed. see Coudenhove-Kalergi, Heinrich J.

Coudert, Allison, jt. auth. see Adams, Laurie.

Coudert, Jo. Advice from a Failure. LC 65-26996. pap. 6.95 (ISBN 0-8128-6182-5). Stein & Day.

--The Alcoholic in Your Life. LC 70-185955. 264p. 1981. pap. 8.95 (ISBN 0-8128-6121-3). Stein & Day.

Coudroglou, Aliki. Work, Women & the Stuggle For Self-Sufficiency: The Win Experience. LC 82-13679. 214p. 1982. lib. bdg. 22.25 (ISBN 0-8191-2654-3); pap. text ed. 10.75 (ISBN 0-8191-2655-1). U Pr of Amer.

Coue, Emile. My Method. 97p. 4.50 (ISBN 0-686-38229-3). Sun Bks.

Couer de Jesus d' Elbee, Jean du. I Believe In Love. Teichert, Marilyn & Stebbins, Madeline, trs. LC 82-24134. (Fr.). 1983. pap. 3.95 (ISBN 0-932506-21-6). St Bedes Pubns.

Couffer, Jack & Couffer, Mike. African Summer. new ed. LC 76-7917. (Illus.). 96p. (gr. 6 up). 1976. 6.95 o.p. (ISBN 0-399-20544-6). Putnam Pub Group.

--Canyon Summer. LC 77-4323. (Illus.). (gr. 6-9). 1977. 6.95 o.p. (ISBN 0-399-20585-3). Putnam Pub Group.

--Galapagos Summer. LC 75-7530. (Illus.). 96p. (gr. 6 up). 1975. 6.95 o.p. (ISBN 0-399-20458-X). Putnam Pub Group.

--Salt Marsh Summer. LC 78-18718. (Illus.). (gr. 6-8). 1978. 6.95 o.p. (ISBN 0-399-20645-0). Putnam Pub Group.

Couffer, Mike, jt. auth. see Couffer, Jack.

Couger, Dan & McFadden, Fred. First Course in Data Processing with BASIC. LC 80-22130. 443p. 1981. pap. text ed. 23.95x (ISBN 0-471-08046-2). Wiley.

--First Course in Data Processing with BASIC, COBOL, FORTRAN, RPG II. 2nd ed. LC 80-22129. 532p. 1981. pap. text ed. 24.95x (ISBN 0-471-05581-6). Wiley.

Couger, Daniel & Zawacki, Robert A. Motivating & Managing Computer Personnel. 213p. 1980. 27.95 (ISBN 0-471-08485-9, Pub. by Wiley-Interscience). Wiley.

Couger, J. Daniel & McFadden, Fred R. Introduction to Computer-Based Information Systems. LC 74-28437. 655p. 1975. text ed. 33.95 (ISBN 0-471-17736-9). Wiley.

Coughanowr, Donald R. & Koppel, L. B. Process Systems Analysis & Control. (Chemical Engineering Ser.). (Illus.). 1965. 36.50 (ISBN 0-07-013210-0, C). McGraw.

Coughlan, Bill & Franke, Monte. Going CO-OP: The Complete Guide to Buying & Owning Your Own Apartment. LC 82-72501. 224p. 1983. 14.42 (ISBN 0-8070-0868-0); pap. 7.21 (ISBN 0-8070-0869-9). Beacon Pr.

Coughlan, Margaret N., ed. Children's Books 1981. LC 65-60014. 16p. 1982. pap. 2.50 (ISBN 0-686-97938-9). Lib Congress.

Coughlan, Robert. The Private World of William Faulkner. LC 72-78474. 1972. Repr. of 1954 ed. lib. bdg. 15.00x o.p. (ISBN 0-8154-0424-7). Cooper Sq.

--World of Michelangelo. LC 66-16540. (Library of Art Ser.). (Illus.). (gr. 6 up). 1966. 19.92 (ISBN 0-8094-0261-0, Pub. by Time-Life). Silver.

Coughlin, C. E. A Series of Lectures on Social Justice. LC 71-173652. (FDR & the Era of the New Deal). 242p. 1971. Repr. of 1935 ed. lib. bdg. 32.50 (ISBN 0-306-70373-4). Da Capo.

Coughlin, Edward V. Adelardo Lopez de Ayala. (World Authors Ser.). 1977. lib. bdg. 15.95 (ISBN 0-8057-6303-1, Twayne). G K Hall.

Coughlin, George C. Here Is Your Career: The Law. LC 78-14176. (Here Is Your Career Ser.). (Illus.). (gr. 6-12). 1979. 7.95 (ISBN 0-399-20655-8). Putnam Pub Group.

Coughlin, George G. Your Introduction to Law. 4th ed. LC 74-29435. 320p. 1982. pap. 5.72i (ISBN 0-06-463563-5, EH 563, EH). B&N NY.

Coughlin, R. & Driscoll, F. Operational Amplifiers & Linear Integrated Circuits. 312p. 1977. text ed. 23.95 (ISBN 0-13-637850-1). P-H.

Coughlin, R. E., et al. Urban Analysis for Branch Library System Planning. LC 71-133496. (Contributions in Librarianship & Information Science: No. 1). 1972. lib. bdg. 25.00 (ISBN 0-8371-5161-9, CLP/). Greenwood.

Coughlin, R. F. & Driscoll, F. F. Semiconductor Fundamentals. (Illus.). 336p. 1976. 21.95x (ISBN 0-13-806406-7). P-H.

Coughlin, Robert F. & Driscoll, Frederick F., Jr. Operational Amplifiers & Linear Integrated Circuits. 2nd ed. (Illus.). 400p. 1982. 23.95 (ISBN 0-13-637785-8). P-H.

Coughlin, William J. Day of Wrath. 1980. 9.95 o.s.i. (ISBN 0-440-02152-9). Delacorte.

Coughtrey, P. J., jt. auth. see Martin, M. H.

Coughtry, Jay. The Notorious Triangle: Rhode Island & the African Slave Trade, 1700-1807. LC 81-4324. 361p. 1981. 32.95 (ISBN 0-87722-218-5). Temple U Pr.

Couhig, Marcelle R. Asphodel Plantation Cookbook. LC 78-24263. 144p. 1980. spiral bdg. 6.95 (ISBN 0-88289-194-4). Pelican.

Coukis, Basil P., tr. see Papanoutsos, Evangelos P.

Coulacos, Spero & Carey, Robert J. How to Recover from Heart Disease. LC 82-82306. 352p. 1983. 15.95 (ISBN 0-448-07367-6, G&D). Putnam Pub Group.

Couldrey, Vivienne. Swans of Brhyadr. LC 78-11777. 1979. 8.95 o.p. (ISBN 0-698-10945-7, Coward). Putnam Pub Group.

Coulet du Gard, Rene. Dictionary of Spanish Place Names of the Northwest Coast of America: California, Vol. I. 190p. 1982. 24.00 (ISBN 0-939586-01-0). Edns Des Deux Mondes.

--Dictionary of Spanish Place Names of the Northwest Coast of America: Oregon, Washington State, British Columbia, Alaska, Vol. II. 190p. 1983. 24.00 (ISBN 0-939586-02-9). Edns Des Deux Mondes.

Coullery, Marie-Therese & Newstead, Martin S. Netsuke: Selected Pieces. (Baur Collection Catalogues Ser.: Vol. 6). (Illus.). 1978. 235.00 (ISBN 0-685-39558-8). Routledge & Kegan.

Coulon, F. de see Kunt, M. & De Coulon, F.

Couloumbis, Ted & Wolfe, James. Introduction to International Relations: Power & Justice. 2nd ed. 448p. 1982. pap. 22.95 (ISBN 0-13-485292-3). P-H.

Couloumbis, Theo. A., jt. auth. see Wolfe, James H.

Coulson, Andrew. Tanzania: A Political Economy. (Illus.). 410p. 1982. 34.95x (ISBN 0-19-828292-3); pap. 15.95 (ISBN 0-19-828293-1). Oxford U Pr.

Coulson, C. A. The Shape & Structure of Molecules. 2nd ed. McWeeny, Roy, rev. by. 112p. 1982. 18.95 (ISBN 0-19-855517-2); pap. 8.95 (ISBN 0-19-855518-0). Oxford U Pr.

Coulson, Charles A. Science, Technology, & the Christian. LC 78-16421. 1978. Repr. of 1960 ed. lib. bdg. 15.75x (ISBN 0-8371-9041-X, COSCI). Greenwood.

Coulson, J., ed. The Pocket Oxford Russian-English Dictionary. 1975. 10.95x (ISBN 0-19-864113-3). Oxford U Pr.

Coulson, J. M. Chemical Engineering: An Introduction to Design, Vol. 6. (Illus.). 720p. 1983. 75.01 (ISBN 0-08-022969-7); pap. 29.50 (ISBN 0-08-022970-0). Pergamon.

Coulson, J. R. & Peacock, D. G., eds. Chemical Engineering, Vol. 3. 2nd ed. (Chemical Engineering Ser.: Vol. 3). (Illus.). 1979. text ed. 81.00 (ISBN 0-08-023818-1); pap. text ed. 24.00 (ISBN 0-08-023819-X). Pergamon.

Coulson, Jessie. Dostoevsky: A Self Portrait. LC 75-26212. (Illus.). 279p. 1975. Repr. of 1962 ed. lib. bdg. 19.00x (ISBN 0-8371-8405-3, CODO). Greenwood.

Coulson, Jessie, tr. see Dostoevsky, Feodor.

Coulson, Margaret & Riddell, Carol. Approaching Sociology. rev. ed. 144p. 1980. 12.95x (ISBN 0-7100-0574-1); pap. 5.95x (ISBN 0-7100-0575-X). Routledge & Kegan.

Coulson, Margaret A. & Riddell, C. Approaching Sociology: A Critical Introduction. (Students Library of Sociology). 1970. 9.75 o.p. (ISBN 0-7100-6877-8); pap. 3.95 o.p. (ISBN 0-7100-6878-6). Routledge & Kegan.

Coulson, N. J. Succession in the Muslim Family. 1971. 47.50 (ISBN 0-521-07852-0). Cambridge U Pr.

Coulson, Robert. Fighting Fair. 224p. 1983. price not set. Free Pr.

Coulson, Walter F., ed. Surgical Pathology, 2 vols. LC 78-17028. (Illus.). 1978. 150.00x (ISBN 0-397-50386-5, Lippincott Medical). Lippincott.

Coulson, William D. & Leonard, Albert, Jr. Cities of the Delta-Naukratis, Preliminary Report on the 1977-1978 & 1980 Seasons Part I. LC 81-52798. (American Research Center in Egypt, Reports: Vol. 4). (Illus.). xiv, 118p. (Orig.). 1982. 20.50x (ISBN 0-89003-081-2); pap. 15.00x (ISBN 0-89003-080-4). Undena Pubns.

Coulson, William D., jt. ed. see McDonald, William A.

Coulson, William R. A Sense of Community: That Education Might Be Personal. LC 73-76604. 1973. pap. text ed. 6.95x (ISBN 0-675-08929-8). Merrill.

Coulter, Catherine. The Autumn Countess. 1979. pap. 2.25 (ISBN 0-451-11445-0, AE1445, Sig). NAL.

--Devil's Embrace. 1982. pap. 3.50 (ISBN 0-451-11853-7, AE1853, Sig). NAL.

--The Generous Earl. (Orig.). 1981. pap. 1.95 o.p. (ISBN 0-451-09899-4, J9899, Sig). NAL.

--Lord Deverill's Heir. 1980. pap. 2.25 (ISBN 0-451-11398-5, AE1398, Sig). NAL.

--Lord Harry's Folly. 1980. pap. 2.25 (ISBN 0-451-11534-1, AE1534, Sig). NAL.

--The Rebel Bride. (Orig.). 1979. pap. 2.25 (ISBN 0-451-11719-0, AE1719, Sig). NAL.

Coulter, E. Merton. Confederate States of America Eighteen Sixty-Five-Eighteen Seventy-Seven. LC 50-6319. (History of the South, Vol. 7). (Illus.). x, 644p. 1950. 25.00x (ISBN 0-8071-0007-2). La State U Pr.

--South During Reconstruction Eighteen Sixty-Five to Eighteen Seventy-Seven. LC 48-5161. (History of the South Ser.: Vol. 8). (Illus.). 1947. 25.00x (ISBN 0-8071-0008-0). La State U Pr.

Coulter, Harris L. Homoeopathic Medicine. LC 74-190020. 1972. pap. 1.65 (ISBN 0-89378-072-3). Formur Intl.

Coulter, N. Arthur, Jr. Synergetics: An Adventure in Human Development. 1976. 14.95 o.p. (ISBN 0-13-879981-4, Parker). P-H.

Coulter, Rita K. Discover the French Connection Between St. Louis & New Orleans. 1977. 16.95x (ISBN 0-932380-01-8); lib. bdg. 9.95x (ISBN 0-686-96751-8). Interhouse Pub.

Coulthard, Alfred J. & Watts, Martin. Windmills of Somerset & the Men Who Worked Them. 113p. 1982. 29.00x (ISBN 0-7050-0060-5, Pub. by C Skilton Scotland). State Mutual Bk.

Coulthard, Malcolm. Introduction to Discourse Analysis. (Applied Linguistics & Language Study Ser.). 1978. pap. text ed. 10.75 (ISBN 0-582-55087-4). Longman.

Coulthard, Malcolm, et al. Discourse Intonation & Language Teaching. (Applied Linguistics & Language Study Ser.). 1980. pap. text ed. 10.75 (ISBN 0-582-55366-0); cassette 16.00x (ISBN 0-582-55367-9). Longman.

Coulthard, R. M., jt. auth. see Sinclair, J.

Coulton, Claudia J. Social Work Quality Assurance Programs: A Comparative Analysis. LC 79-64941. 102p. 1979. pap. 6.50x (ISBN 0-87101-080-1, CBH-080-1). Natl Assn Soc Wkrs.

Council for Economic Planning & Development (Republic of China) Taiwan Statistical Data Book, 1982. LC 72-219425. (Illus.). 318p. (Orig.). 1982. pap. 12.50x (ISBN 0-8002-3027-2). Intl Pubns Serv.

Council of Europe, ed. Population Decline in Europe: Implications of a Declining or Stationary Population. LC 78-3106. (Illus.). 1978. 36.00x (ISBN 0-312-63125-1). St Martin.

Council of Europe for Cultural Cooperation. Paedogogica Europaea, Vol. 5. 1971. 14.25 (ISBN 0-444-99978-7). Elsevier.

Council of Industrialized Building Research. Building Research & Documentation. 1961. 38.50 (ISBN 0-444-40109-1). Elsevier.

Council of New York Law Associates & Volunteer Lawyers for the Arts, eds. New York Not-for-Profit Organization Manual. rev. ed. 190p. 1982. pap. 20.00 (ISBN 0-686-37424-X). Coun NY Law.

Council of State Governments. The Handbook of Interstate Crime Control. LC 77-2991. 1977. Repr. of 1966 ed. lib. bdg. 17.25x (ISBN 0-8371-9567-5, CSHI). Greenwood.

Council of State Governments Staff, ed. State & Local Government Purchasing. 2nd ed. 750p. (Orig.). 1982. pap. 21.00 (ISBN 0-87292-033-X). Coun State Govts.

Council on Economic Priorities & Boothe, Joan N. Cleaning Up: The Cost of Refinery Pollution Control. LC 75-10535. 1977. 22.95 o.p. (ISBN 0-03-040936-5). Praeger.

Council on Economic Priorities (CEP) Paper Profits: Pollution in the Pulp & Paper Industry. 480p. 1972. 20.00x o.s.i. (ISBN 0-262-03045-4). MIT Pr.

Council on Education in the Geological Sciences & Wright, F. F. Estuarine Oceanography. (Illus.). 80p. 1974. pap. text ed. 13.95 (ISBN 0-07-012336-5, C). McGraw.

Council on Foreign Relations, Inc. (New York) Catalog of the Foreign Relations Library, First Supplement. 1979. lib. bdg. 325.00 (ISBN 0-8161-0306-2, Hall Library). G K Hall.

Council on Foreign Relations Inc., New York. Catalog of the Foreign Relations Library, 9 Vols. 1969. Set. lib. bdg. 835.00 (ISBN 0-8161-0840-4, Hall Library). G K Hall.

Council on International Educational Exchange. Where to Stay U. S. A. (Illus.). 368p. 1980-81. pap. 4.95 o.p. (ISBN 0-671-25496-0). Frommer-Pasmantier.

Council on Interracial Books for Children, Inc. Chronicles of American Indian Protest. 2nd, rev. ed. 400p. (gr. 11-12). pap. 6.95 (ISBN 0-930040-30-9). CIBC.

--Guidelines for Selecting Bias-Free Textbooks & Storybooks. LC 80-165903. 105p. 1980. pap. 7.95 (ISBN 0-930040-33-3). CIBC.

--Racism & Sexism in Children's Books. (Interracial Digest Ser.: No. 2). (Illus.). 48p. (Orig.). (gr. 11-12). 1978. pap. 4.50 (ISBN 0-930040-29-5). CIBC.

--Stereotypes, Distortions & Omissions in U. S. History Textbooks: A Content Analysis Instrument for Detecting Racism & Sexism. 143p. (gr. 11-12). 1977. pap. 8.95x (ISBN 0-930040-03-1). CIBC.

Council on Learning. The Role of the Scholarly Disciplines. 43p. pap. 4.95 (ISBN 0-686-97920-6). Change Mag.

Council on Legal Education Opportunity. Allan Bakke versus Regents of the University of California, 6 vols. Slocum, Alfred A., ed. LC 78-3573. 1978. lib. bdg. 44.00 ea. (ISBN 0-379-20297-2); Set. lib. bdg. 264.00. Oceana.

Council on Population & Environment (COPE) Population, Environment & People. LC 72-169019. 225p. (Orig.). 1971. 23.95 o.p. (ISBN 0-07-012405-1, C); pap. 2.95 o.p. (ISBN 0-07-012407-8). McGraw.

Cound, John J. Civil Procedure Supplement for Use with All Pleading & Procedure Casebooks, 1982. (American Casebook). 411p. 1982. pap. text ed. 7.95 (ISBN 0-314-66385-1). West Pub.

Counsell, J. N. & Horning, D. H. Vitamin C (Ascorbic Acid) 1981. 65.75 (ISBN 0-85334-109-5, Pub. by Applied Sci England). Elsevier.

Counsilman, James. Science of Swimming. 1968. ref. ed. 22.95 (ISBN 0-13-795385-2). P-H.

Count de St. Germain. The Theory of the Mounts of the Hand & the Message They Convey to the Future of Man. (Illus.). 131p. 1983. Repr. of 1898 ed. 115.45 (ISBN 0-89901-110-1). Found Class Reprints.

Counter, Constance & Tani, Karl. Palette in the Kitchen. (Illus.). 1973. pap. 5.95 (ISBN 0-913270-28-8). Sunstone Pr.

Country Beautiful Editors, jt. auth. see Allen, Dorothy H.

Country Beautiful Editors, ed. see Gridley, Marion E.

Country Beautiful Magazine Editors, jt. auth. see Allen, Dorothy H.

Country Magazine Eds., ed. How to Save Money on the Farm. pap. 8.50x (ISBN 0-392-08166-0, ABC). Sportshelf.

Country Music Magazine, jt. ed. see Carr, Patrick.

Countryman, Jack. Atlantis & the Seven Stars. LC 77-9182. 1979. 7.95 o.p. (ISBN 0-312-05946-9). St Martin.

Countryman, Kathleen M., jt. auth. see Gekas, Alexandra B.

Countryman, Vern. Cases & Materials on Debtor & Creditor. 2nd ed. 1974. pap. 25.00 (ISBN 0-316-15803-8). Little.

Countryman, Vern & Kaufman, Andrew L. Commercial Law: Cases & Materials. 722p. 1971. 22.00 o.p. (ISBN 0-316-15810-0). Little.

Countryman, Vern, et al. The Lawyer in Modern Society. 2nd ed. 1976. 25.50 (ISBN 0-316-15800-3). Little.

Countryside Books, ed. Home Landscaping. (Illus.). 144p. cancelled (ISBN 0-88453-002-7, Pub by A B Morse). Berkshire Traveller.

Countryside Staff, ed. The Countryside A-Z Guide to Vegetables. (A-Z Ser.). (Orig.). 1983. pap. 7.95 (ISBN 0-88453-038-8). Countryside Bks.

Counts, David R. Grammar of Kaliai-Kove. LC 72-627917. (Oceanic Linguistics Special Publication: No. 6). (Orig.). 1970. pap. text ed. 6.00x (ISBN 0-87022-156-6). UH Pr.

Counts, George S. Bolshevism, Fascism & Capitalism. 1932. text ed. 12.50x (ISBN 0-686-83492-5). Elliots Bks.

--Country of the Blind: The Soviet System of Mind Control. LC 79-100153. Repr. of 1949 ed. lib. bdg. 18.50x (ISBN 0-8371-3680-6, CCOB). Greenwood.

Couper, Alstair, ed. The Times Atlas of the Oceans. (Illus.). 256p. 1983. 75.00 (ISBN 0-686-82708-2). Sci Bks Intl.

Couper, Heater & Murtagh, Terence. Heavens Above! (Illus.). 64p. (gr. 5 up). 1981. lib. bdg. 9.90 (ISBN 0-531-04287-1). Watts.

Couper, Heather & Henbest, Nigel. All About Space. (Full Color Fact Books). (Illus.). 32p. (gr. 4-12). 1982. PLB 7.95 (ISBN 0-8219-0014-5, 35545). EMC.

Couper, J. M. Looking for a Wave. 1975. 6.95 o.p. (ISBN 0-87888-085-2). Bradbury Pr.

Coupland, R. E. & Fujita, T., eds. Chromaffin, Enterochromaffin & Related Cells: A NATO Foundation Symposium. (Illus.). 1976. 115.75 (ISBN 0-444-41448-7, North Holland). Elsevier.

Coupland, R. T., ed. Grassland Ecosystems of the World. LC 77-83990. (International Biological Programme Ser.: No. 18). 1979. 80.00 (ISBN 0-521-21867-5). Cambridge U Pr.

Coupland, Reginald. American Revolution & the British Empire. LC 65-18801. 1965. Repr. of 1930 ed. 7.50x o.p. (ISBN 0-8462-0601-3). Russell.

Courant, R. Differential & Integral Calculus, 2 vols. Incl. Vol. 1. 630p. 1937. 38.00 (ISBN 0-471-17820-9); Vol. 2. 692p. 1936. 38.00x (ISBN 0-471-17853-5). Pub. by Wiley-Interscience). Wiley.

Courant, R. & Hilbert, D. Methods of Mathematical Physics, 2 Vols. Set. 92.50x (ISBN 0-471-17990-6, Pub. by Wiley-Interscience); Vol. 1, 1953. 45.95x (ISBN 0-470-17952-X); Vol. 2, 1962. 61.95x (ISBN 0-470-17985-6). Wiley.

Courant, R., jt. ed. see Behnke, H.

Courant, Richard & John, Fritz. Introduction to Calculus & Analysis, 2 vols. LC 65-16403. 912p. 1965. Vol. 1, 661 P. 49.95 (ISBN 0-470-17860-4); Vol. 2, 1974, 954 P. 47.50x (ISBN 0-471-17862-4, Pub. by Wiley-Interscience). Wiley.

Courant, Richard & Robbins, Herbert. What Is Mathematics? An Elementary Approach to Ideas & Methods. (Illus.). 1979. pap. 12.95 (ISBN 0-19-502517-2, GB576, GB). Oxford U Pr.

Courcy, G. I. C. Paganini: The Genoese, 2 vols. LC 76-5892. (Music Reprint Series). 1977. Repr. of 1957 ed. Set. lib. bdg. 65.00 (ISBN 0-306-70872-8). Da Capo.

Courjon, Jean, et al, eds. Clinical Applications of Evoked Potentials in Neurology. (Advances in Neurology Ser.: Vol. 32). 592p. 1982. text ed. 65.00 (ISBN 0-89004-619-0). Raven.

Courlander, Harold. The Crest & the Hide & Other African Stories. (Illus.). 144p. 1982. 11.95 (ISBN 0-698-20536-7, Coward). Putnam Pub Group.

--The Drum & the Hoe: Life & Lore of the Haitian People. (California Library Reprint Ser.: No. 31). (Illus.). 436p. 1981. Repr. of 1973 ed. 30.00x (ISBN 0-520-02364-1). U of Cal Pr.

--King's Drum & Other African Stories. LC 62-14242. (Illus.). (gr. 3-7). 1962. 6.50 o.p. (ISBN 0-15-242925-5, HJ). HarBraceJ.

--King's Drum: And Other African Stories. LC 62-14242. (Illus.). (gr. 3-7). 1970. pap. 3.95 (ISBN 0-15-647190-6, VoyB). HarBraceJ.

--Tales of Yoruba Gods & Heroes. LC 72-84307. 256p. 1972. 6.95 o.p. (ISBN 0-517-50063-9). Crown.

Cournos, John see Haydn, Hiram.

Cournos, John, intro. by. American Short Stories of the Nineteenth Century. 250p. 1983. pap. text ed. 4.95x (ISBN 0-460-01840-X, Pub. by Evman England). Biblio Dist.

Cournos, John, tr. see Sologub, Feodor.

Cournoyer, Norman G. & Marshall, Anthony. Hotel, Restaurant & Travel Law. 2nd ed. 1983. text ed. 26.95 (ISBN 0-534-01273-6). Breton Pubs.

Cournulier, Benoit De see De Cornulier, Benoit.

Couro, Ted. San Diego County Indians As Farmers & Wage Earners. pap. 1.00 (ISBN 0-686-69102-4). Acoma Bks.

Courriere, C. Histoire de la Litterature Contemporaine en Russie. (Nineteenth Century Russia Ser.). 442p. (Fr.). 1974. Repr. of 1875 ed. lib. bdg. 111.00 o.p. (ISBN 0-8287-0232-2, R70). Clearwater Pub.

Coursen, H. R. The Leasing out of England: Shakespeare's Second Henriad. LC 81-40354. (Illus.). 234p. (Orig.). 1982. PLB 22.25 (ISBN 0-8191-2455-9); pap. text ed. 10.75 (ISBN 0-8191-2456-7). U Pr of Amer.

--Winter Dreams. St. Cyr, Napoleon, ed. LC 82-4152. (Orig.). 1982. pap. 4.00 (ISBN 0-910380-04-X). Cider Mill.

Coursodon, J. P. & Sauvage, Pierre. American Directors, 2 Vols. 1983. Vol. I, 448p. 21.95 (ISBN 0-07-013263-1, GB); pap. 11.95 (ISBN 0-07-013261-5); Vol. II, 432p. 21.95 (ISBN 0-07-013264-X); pap. 11.95 (ISBN 0-07-013262-3). McGraw.

Coursodon, J. P., jt. auth. see Besnard, M.

Court, J., jt. auth. see Dierauf, E., Jr.

Court, John M. Myth & History in Revelation: The Book of Revelation. LC 79-16586. 1980. 6.49 (ISBN 0-8042-0346-6). John Knox.

Court, Nathan A. Modern Pure Solid Geometry. 2nd ed. LC 64-18134. 1979. text ed. 17.95 (ISBN 0-8284-0147-0). Chelsea Pub.

Court, William H. British Economic History, Eighteen Seventy to Nineteen Fourteen. 1966. 64.50 (ISBN 0-521-04731-5); pap. 19.95x (ISBN 0-521-09362-7). Cambridge U Pr.

Court de Gebelin, A. Histoire Naturelle de la Parole. (Linguistics 13th-18th Centuries Ser.). 400p. (Fr.). 1974. Repr. of 1772 ed. lib. bdg. 102.00 o.p. (ISBN 0-8287-0233-0, 71-5039). Clearwater Pub.

Courtenay, Ashley. Let's Halt Awhile in Great Britain Hotel Guide, 1982. (Orig.). 1982. pap. 14.95 (ISBN 0-8038-4339-9). Hastings.

--Let's Halt Awhile in Ireland, 1980. 1980. pap. 5.95 o.p. (ISBN 0-8038-4330-5). Hastings.

Courter, G., jt. auth. see Courter, P.

Courter, J. W. Aladdin, the Magic Name in Lamps. 17.50 (ISBN 0-87069-001-9, 99001). Wallace-Homestead.

Courter, P. & Courter, G. The Filmmaker's Craft. 1983. 29.95 (ISBN 0-442-21708-0). Van Nos Reinhold.

Courtes, J., jt. auth. see Greimas, A. J.

Courtes, Jean Marie, jt. auth. see Devisse, Jean.

Courthion, Pierre. Impressionism. LC 79-142740. (Illus.). 206p. 1971. 40.00 (ISBN 0-8109-0202-8). Abrams.

--Impressionism. concise ed. Shepley, John, tr. (Illus.). 1977. 17.50 (ISBN 0-8109-1112-4); pap. 10.95 (ISBN 0-8109-2067-0). Abrams.

Courtier, Gary. Midwife. 1982. pap. 3.95 (ISBN 0-451-11503-1, AE1503, Sig). NAL.

Courtine, Robert J., jt. auth. see Vence, Celine.

Courtine, Robert J., ed. The Master Chefs of France Recipe Book. (Illus.). 192p. 1982. 24.95 (ISBN 0-89696-140-0, An Everest House Book). Dodd.

Courtis, S. A., jt. auth. see Watters, Garnette.

Courtiss, Eugene H. Male Aesthetic Surgery. 1st ed. LC 81-14147. (Illus.). 426p. 1982. text ed. 84.50 (ISBN 0-8016-1115-6). Mosby.

Courtiss, Eugene H., ed. Aesthetic Surgery: Trouble - How to Avoid It & How to Treat It. LC 78-4958. 274p. 1978. text ed. 43.50 o.p. (ISBN 0-8016-1060-5). Mosby.

Courtivron, Isabelle De see Marks, Elaine & De Courtivron, Isabelle.

Courtney, Alice E. & Whipple, Thomas W. Sex Stereotyping in Advertising. 1983. price not set (ISBN 0-669-03955-1). Lexington Bks.

Courtney, Andrew. Muzzle Loading Today. (Illus.). 96p. (Orig.). 1981. pap. 8.50x o.p. (ISBN 0-85242-731-X). Intl Pubns Serv.

Courtney, Caroline. Abandoned for Love. 224p. (Orig.). 1981. pap. 1.75 (ISBN 0-446-94607-9). Warner Bks.

--Courier of Love. 240p. (Orig.). 1982. pap. 1.95 o.p. (ISBN 0-446-90961-0). Warner Bks.

--Dangerous Engagement. 1979. pap. 1.75 o.p. (ISBN 0-446-94052-6). Warner Bks.

--Duchess in Disguise. (General Ser.). 1979. lib. bdg. 12.50 (ISBN 0-8161-3002-7, LargePrint Bks). G K Hall.

--The Fortunes of Love. 1980. pap. 1.75 o.p. (ISBN 0-446-94055-0). Warner Bks.

--Heart of Honor. 1980. pap. 1.75 o.p. (ISBN 0-446-94294-4). Warner Bks.

--Libertine in Love. 1980. pap. 1.75 o.p. (ISBN 0-446-94295-2). Warner Bks.

--Love of My Life. 208p. (Orig.). 1981. pap. 1.75 o.p. (ISBN 0-446-94609-5). Warner Bks.

--Love Triumphant. 1980. pap. 1.75 o.p. (ISBN 0-446-94293-6). Warner Bks.

--Love Unmasked. (General Ser.). 1980. lib. bdg. 11.95 (ISBN 0-8161-3096-5, Large Print Bks). G K Hall.

--A Lover's Victory. 192p. (Orig.). 1981. pap. 1.75 o.p. (ISBN 0-446-90611-5). Warner Bks.

--Love's Masquerade. 1980. pap. 1.75 o.p. (ISBN 0-446-94292-8). Warner Bks.

--The Masquerading Heart. (Regency Romance Ser.: No. 18). 208p. (Orig.). 1982. pap. 1.95 (ISBN 0-446-90612-3). Warner Bks.

--Tempestuous Affair. (Orig.). 1981. pap. 1.75 o.p. (ISBN 0-446-94608-7). Warner Bks.

--A Wager for Love. 1980. lib. bdg. 13.95 o.p. (ISBN 0-8161-3020-5, Large Print Bks). G K Hall.

Courtney, Damien A., tr. see Pressat, Roland.

Courtney, Dayle. The House That Ate People. Korth, Bob, ed. (Thorne Twins Adventure Ser.). (Illus.). 192p. (Orig.). (gr. 7-12). 1983. pap. 2.79 (ISBN 0-87239-683-5, 2903). Standard Pub.

--Shadow of Fear. Korth, Bob, ed. (Thorne Twins Adventure Ser.). (Illus.). 192p. (gr. 7-12). 1983. pap. 2.79 (ISBN 0-87239-682-7, 2902). Standard Pub.

--The Sinister Circle. Korth, Bob, ed. (Thorne Twins Adventure Ser.). (Illus.). 192p. (Orig.). (gr. 7-12). 1983. pap. 2.79 (ISBN 0-87239-684-3, 2904). Standard Pub.

--The Trail of Bigfoot. Korth, Bob, ed. (Thorne Twins Adventure Ser.). (Illus.). 192p. (Orig.). (gr. 7-12). 1983. pap. 2.79 (ISBN 0-87239-681-9, 2901). Standard Pub.

Courtney, E. A Commentary on the Satires of Juvenal. 650p. 1981. text ed. 84.00x (ISBN 0-485-11190-X, Athlone Pr). Humanities.

Courtney, G. J. Je Vous Presente. (Illus.). 1970. pap. text ed. 2.95x (ISBN 0-582-36008-0). Longman.

Courtney, P. P. Plantation Agriculture. (Advanced Economic Geographies Ser.). 296p. 1982. 35.00x (ISBN 0-7135-1256-3, Pub. by Bell & Hyman England). State Mutual Bk.

Courtney, Ragan. Meditations for the Suddenly Single. pap. 5.95 (ISBN 0-310-70301-8). Zondervan.

Courtney, Richard. The Dramatic Curriculum. 144p. 1980. text ed. 10.00x (ISBN 0-89676-061-8); pap. text ed. 7.95x (ISBN 0-89676-063-4). Drama Bk.

--Outline History of British Drama. LC 82-6595. (Quality Paperback Ser.: No. 373). 346p. (Orig.). 1982. pap. text ed. 8.95 (ISBN 0-8226-0373-X). Littlefield.

Courtney, Richard, jt. ed. see Schattner, Gertrud.

Courtney, William P. Secrets of Our National Literature: Chapters in the History of the Anonymous & Pseudonymous Writings of Our Countrymen. LC 68-21761. 1968. Repr. of 1908 ed. 37.00x (ISBN 0-8103-3140-3). Gale.

Courtney, Winifred F. Young Charles Lamb, 1775-1802. (Gotham Library). 244p. 1982. 30.00 (ISBN 0-8147-1382-3). NYU Pr.

Courtright, Gordon. Trees & Shrubs for Western Gardens. LC 79-65785. (Illus.). 1979. 43.00 (ISBN 0-917304-13-6). Timber.

Courville, Jacques, et al, eds. The Inferior Olivary Nucleus: Anatomy & Physiology. (Illus.). 407p. 1980. text ed. 54.00 (ISBN 0-89004-414-7). Raven.

Coury, Elaine. Terence's Bembine Phormio: A Palaeographic Examination. (Illus.). 150p. 59.00 (ISBN 0-86516-011-2). Bolchazy-Carducci.

Coury, Elaine, ed. Phormio: A Comedy by Terence. (Illus.). 224p. 1982. pap. text ed. 8.95x (ISBN 0-686-84392-4). Bolchazy-Carducci.

Coury, Fred F., ed. A Practical Guide to Minicomputer Applications. LC 70-182820. 1972. 17.95 o.p. (ISBN 0-87942-005-7). Inst Electrical.

Coury, Victor M., et al. Preparation for the Dental Admission Test. (Illus.). 1980. pap. text ed. 8.95 o.p. (ISBN 0-07-013238-0, C). McGraw.

Cousin, Elvire, tr. see Getz, Gene A.

Cousin D'Avallon, C. Y. Voltairiana, Ou Recueil Des Bons Mots. Repr. of 1801 ed. 51.00 o.p. (ISBN 0-8287-0234-9). Clearwater Pub.

Cousineau, Robert H. Humanism & Ethics: An Introduction to the Letter on Humanism by Heidegger. 137p. 1972. text ed. 15.00x (ISBN 0-391-00407-7). Humanities.

Cousins, Albert N. & Nagpaul, Hans. Urban Life: The Sociology of Cities & Urban Society. LC 78-14427. 1979. text ed. 25.95x (ISBN 0-471-03026-0). Wiley.

Cousins, Geoffrey. Golf in Britain. 1975. 17.95 (ISBN 0-7100-8028-X). Routledge & Kegan.

Cousins, Geoffrey & Scott, Tom. A Century of Opens. 1972. 10.00 o.p. (ISBN 0-584-10037-X). Transatlantic.

Cousins, K. Residential Conservation Service Inspector-Installer Examination Guide. (Progress in Solar Energy Supplements SERI Ser.). 60p. 1983. pap. text ed. 9.00x (ISBN 0-89553-087-2). Am Solar Energy.

Cousins, M. F. Engineering Drawing from the Beginning. 1964. Vol. 1. 1964. 30.00 o.p. (ISBN 0-08-010839-3); pap. 12.00 o.p. (ISBN 0-08-010840-7). Pergamon.

Cousins, Michael J. & Bridenbaugh, Phillip O. Neural Blockade in Clinical Anesthesia & Management of Pain. (Illus.). 1188p. 1980. text ed. 115.00x (ISBN 0-397-50439-X, Lippincott Medical). Lippincott.

Cousins, Norman. Anatomy of an Illness. 9.95x (ISBN 0-393-01252-2); pap. 4.95x (ISBN 0-553-01293-2). Cancer Control Soc.

--Dr. Schweitzer of Lambarene. LC 73-7075. (Illus.). 254p. 1973. Repr. of 1960 ed. lib. bdg. 17.75x o.p. (ISBN 0-8371-6902-X, CODS). Greenwood.

--Healing & Belief. LC 82-81098. 64p. 1982. 65.00 (ISBN 0-88014-041-0). Mosaic Pr OH.

--Human Options. 224p. 1983. pap. 5.95 (ISBN 0-425-05875-1). Berkley Pub.

--The Physician in Literature. 500p. 1982. text ed. 16.95 (ISBN 0-7216-2739-0). Saunders.

Cousteau, Jacques. Jacques Cousteau: The Ocean World. (Illus.). 1979. 60.00 (ISBN 0-8109-0777-1). Abrams.

Cousteau, Jacques-Yves & Cousteau, Philippe. The Shark: Splendid Savage of the Sea. (Undersea Discoveries Ser.). (Illus.). 228p. 1832. pap. 10.95 (ISBN 0-89104-112-5, A & W Visual Library). A & W Pubs.

Cousteau, Jacques-Yves & Diola, Philippe. Dolphins. (Undersea Discoveries Ser.). (Illus.). 304p. 1983. pap. 10.95 (ISBN 0-89104-076-5, A & W Visual Library). A & W Pubs.

Cousteau, Jacques-Yves & Diole, Philippe. Dolphins: Playful Mammals of the Sea. LC 74-9481. (Undersea Discoveries Ser.). (Illus.). 304p. 1983. pap. 10.95 (ISBN 0-89104-076-5, A & W Visual Library). A & W Pubs.

--The Whale: Mighty Monarch of the Sea. (Undersea Discoveries Ser.). (Illus.). 304p. 1983. pap. 10.95 (ISBN 0-89104-077-3, A & W Visual Library). A & W Pubs.

Cousteau, Philippe, jt. auth. see Cousteau, Jacques-Yves.

Coustillas, Pierre, ed. Politics in Literature in the Nineteenth Century. 1974. pap. text ed. 10.00x o.p. (ISBN 0-685-41700-X). Humanities.

Coustillas, Pierre, ed. see Gissing, George.

Coutant, Helen. The Gift. LC 82-7810. (Illus.). 48p. (gr. 2-5). 1983. 9.95 (ISBN 0-394-85499-3); lib. bdg. 9.99 (ISBN 0-394-95499-8). Knopf.

Coute, A. & Tell, G. Ultrastructure de la Paroi Cellulaire des Desmidiacees au Microscope Electronique a Balayage. (Nova Hedwigia Beiheft: No. 68). (Illus.). 228p. (Fr.). 1982. lib. bdg. 60.00x (ISBN 3-7682-5468-2). Lubrecht & Cramer.

Coutinho, A. Pereira. Flora de Portugal. 2A ed. dirigido pel Ruy Telles Plahinha. (Historia Naturalis Classica 98). 1973. Repr. lib. bdg. 80.00x (ISBN 3-7682-0931-8). Lubrecht & Cramer.

Coutinho, John De S. Advanced Systems Development Management. LC 76-30531. (Systems Engineering & Analysis Ser.). 433p. 1977. 42.50x o.s.i. (ISBN 0-471-01487-7, Pub. by Wiley-Interscience). Wiley.

Coutinho, Mauricio, jt. auth. see Possas, Mario L.

Couto, Richard A. Streams of Idealism & Health Care Innovation: An Assessment of Service Learning & Community Mobilization. (Illus.). 1982. text ed. 18.95x (ISBN 0-8077-2724-5). Tchrs Coll.

Coutsouradis, D., et al, eds. High Temperature Alloys for Gas Turbines. (Illus.). 1978. text ed. 98.50x (ISBN 0-85334-815-4, Pub. by Applied Sci England). Elsevier.

Coutts, T. J. Electrical Conduction in Thin Metal Films. 244p. 1974. 55.50 (ISBN 0-444-41184-4). Elsevier.

Couture, G. L. & Gladden, L. The Aging Game. 1983. 14.95x (ISBN 0-686-29897-7). Cancer Control Soc.

Couturier, Jean J., jt. auth. see Schick, Richard P.

Couzens, Reginald C. Stories of the Months & Days. LC 70-124662. (Illus.). 1971. Repr. of 1923 ed. 47.00x (ISBN 0-8103-3013-X). Gale.

Cove, D. J. Genetics. LC 75-160089. (Illus.). 1972. 39.50 (ISBN 0-521-08255-2); pap. text ed. 10.95x (ISBN 0-521-09663-4). Cambridge U Pr.

Cove, Mary & Regan, Jane. Teaching Religion Effectively Program. 96p. 1982. pap. 3.50 (ISBN 0-697-01825-3); program manual 24.95 (ISBN 0-697-01826-1). Wm C Brown.

Covelli, Pasquale. Borrowing Time: Growing up with Juvenile Diabetes. LC 79-7083. 1979. 11.49 (ISBN 0-690-01841-X). T Y Crowell.

Covello, Charles J. Real Estate Buying - Selling Guide for Washington. 2nd ed. (Illus.). 83p. 1983. pap. price not set (ISBN 0-88908-723-7). Self Counsel Pr.

Covello, Leonard & D'Agnostino, Guido. Teacher in the Urban Community. (Quality Paperback: No. 242). 1970. pap. 4.95 (ISBN 0-8226-0242-3). Littlefield.

Coven, Brenda. American Women Dramatists of the Twentieth Century: A Bibliography. LC 82-5942. 244p. 1982. 15.00 (ISBN 0-8108-1562-1). Scarecrow.

Coveney, D., jt. auth. see Medlicott, W. N.

Coveney, James. Glossary of English & German Management Terms. (English for Special Purposes Bk.). 1977. pap. text ed. 6.95x (ISBN 0-582-55525-6). Longman.

Coveney, James & Amey, J. Glossary of Spanish & English Management Terms. (English for Special Purposes Bk.). 1978. pap. text ed. 6.95x (ISBN 0-582-55541-8). Longman.

Coveney, James & Moore, Shelia J., eds. Glossary of French & English Management Terms. (English for Special Purposes Bk.). 158p. 1972. pap. text ed. 6.95x (ISBN 0-582-55502-7). Longman.

Coventry, Camilla, tr. see Shestov, Lev.

Coventry, Mark B., ed. Year Book of Orthopedics, 1982. (Illus.). 1982. 37.00 (ISBN 0-8151-1883-X). Year Bk Med.

--Year Book of Orthopedics, 1983. 1983. 40.00 (ISBN 0-8151-1884-8). Year Bk Med.

Covert, Alice L. The Distant Drum. 256p. (YA) 1974. 6.95 (ISBN 0-685-49584-1, Avalon). Bouregy.

--The Glass House. (YA) 1972. 6.95 (ISBN 0-685-25147-0, Avalon). Bouregy.

Covert, Alice L. & O'More, Peggy. The Alien Heart. Bd. with Make Way for Spring. 1982. pap. 2.50 (ISBN 0-451-11893-6, AE1893, Sig). NAL.

Covert, Paul. Cages. (New Writers Ser.). 1971. 3.95 (ISBN 0-686-86288-0). Liveright.

Covert, Richard P. & McNulty, Elizabeth G. Management Engineering for Hospitals. 32p. 1981. pap. 8.75 (ISBN 0-87258-341-4, AHA-133175). Am Hospital.

Covey, Joan. Pony Express '76' 14.00 (ISBN 0-686-37636-6). Snohomish Pub.

Covey, Liz, jt. auth. see Ingham, Rosemary.

Coville, Rollin E. Wasps of the Genus Trypoxylon Subgenus Trypargilum in North America: Hymenoptera: Sphecidae. (Publications in Entomology: Vol. 97). 1982. pap. 14.00x (ISBN 0-520-09651-7). U of Cal Pr.

Covina, Gina. The City of Hermits. LC 82-74335. 232p. (Orig.). 1983. 11.95 (ISBN 0-9609626-2-X); pap. 6.95 (ISBN 0-9609626-1-1). Barn Owl Bks.

Covina, Gina & Galana, Laurel, eds. Lesbian Reader. 1975. pap. 5.95 (ISBN 0-9609626-0-3). Amazon Pr.

Covington, A. K. & Jones, P., eds. Hydrogen-Bonded Solvent Systems. 366p. 1968. write for info. (ISBN 0-85066-025-4, Pub. by Taylor & Francis). Intl Pubns Serv.

Covington, Faison, jt. auth. see Owensby, Lou R.

Covington, Robert N. & Goldman, Alvin L. Legislation Protecting the Individual Employee: Unit Two, Labor Relations & Social Problems. 750p. 1982. text ed. 17.50 o.p. (ISBN 0-87179-377-6). BNA.

Covington, Robert N. see Labor Law Group.

Covino, Frank. The Digest Book of Downhill Skiing. (The Sports & Leisure Library). (Illus.). 96p. 1979. pap. 2.95 o.s.i. (ISBN 0-695-81320-X). Follett.

--Skier's Digest. 2nd ed. (DBI Bks). (Illus.). 288p. (Orig.). 1976. pap. 7.95 o.s.i. (ISBN 0-695-80596-7). Follett.

Covino, Frank, ed. see Killy, Jean-Claude.

Covino, Marge & Jordan, Pat. Woman's Guide to Shaping Your Body with Weights. (Illus.). 1978. 12.45i (ISBN 0-397-01301-9). Har-Row.

Covino, William A., jt. auth. see Bobrow, Jerry.

Cowan, Anita P., jt. auth. see Stettner, Allison G.

Cowan, Charles. Are You Speaking the Word? 1.00 o.s.i. (ISBN 0-89274-119-8, HH-119). Harrison Hse.

--Reward of Confidence. 40p. 1978. pap. 1.00 o.s.i. (ISBN 0-89274-110-4). Harrison Hse.

Cowan, D. R. Sales Analysis from the Management Standpoint. LC 67-24325. 210p. 1967. 15.00 (ISBN 0-379-00072-5). Oceana.

Cowan, Dale. Deadly Sleep. (Twilight Ser.). (gr. 5 up). 1982. pap. 1.95 (ISBN 0-440-91961-4, LFL). Dell.

Cowan, David. Introduction to Modern Literary Arabic. 1958. pap. 13.95 (ISBN 0-521-09240-X). Cambridge U Pr.

Cowan, Elizabeth. Readings for Writing. 1983. pap. text ed. 9.95x (ISBN 0-673-15845-4). Scott F.

--Writing: Brief Edition. 1983. pap. text ed. 13.95x (ISBN 0-673-15735-0). Scott F.

Cowan, Elizabeth, jt. auth. see Cowan, Gregory.

Cowan, Geoffrey. Fun with Magic. LC 74-17714. (Illus.). 48p. (gr. 3-6). 1975. 3.95 (ISBN 0-448-11909-9, G&D). Putnam Pub Group.

Cowan, George M. Some Aspects of the Lexical Structure of a Mazatec Historical Text. (Publications in Linguistics & Related Fields Ser.: No. 11). 146p. 1965. pap. 1.50 (ISBN 0-88312-011-9); microfiche 2.25 (ISBN 0-88312-411-4). Summer Inst Ling.

Cowan, Glen. Table Tennis-How to Play the Game. (Illus.). 96p. 1972. pap. 2.95 o.p. (ISBN 0-448-01517-X, G&D). Putnam Pub Group.

Cowan, Gregory & Cowan, Elizabeth. Writing. 1980. text ed. 21.95x (ISBN 0-673-15665-6). Scott F.

Cowan, Gregory & McPherson, Elizabeth. Plain English Please: A Rhetoric. 4th ed. 477p. 1980. pap. text ed. 12.50 (ISBN 0-394-32367-X). Random.

Cowan, H. J. An Historical Outline of Architectural Science. 2nd, enl. ed. 1978. 20.50 (ISBN 0-444-00250-2). Elsevier.

--Predictive Methods for the Energy Conserving Design of Buildings. (Illus.). 128p. 1983. pap. 33.50 (ISBN 0-08-029838-9). Pergamon.

--Solar Energy Applications in the Design of Buildings. 1980. 49.25 (ISBN 0-85334-883-9, Pub. by Applied Sci England). Elsevier.

Cowan, Henry J. Design of Reinforced Concrete Structures. (Illus.). 304p. 1982. 26.95 (ISBN 0-13-201376-2). P-H.

--The Master Builders: A History of Structural & Environmental Design from Ancient Egypt to the Nineteenth Century. LC 77-5125. 1977. 37.50 (ISBN 0-471-02740-5, Pub. by Wiley-Interscience). Wiley.

--Science & Building: Structural & Environmental Design in the Nineteenth & Twentieth Centuries. LC 77-7297. 1978. 42.95 (ISBN 0-471-02738-3, Pub. by Wiley-Interscience). Wiley.

Cowan, Henry J. & Dixon, John. Building Science Laboratory Manual. (Illus.). 1978. text ed. 24.75x (ISBN 0-85334-747-6, Pub. by Applied Sci England). Elsevier.

Cowan, Ian B. The Scottish Reformation. LC 82-5834. 256p. 1982. 25.00x (ISBN 0-312-70519-0). St Martin.

Cowan, J. L. Pleasure & Pain. LC 68-13019. 1968. 22.50 (ISBN 0-312-61705-4). St Martin.

Cowan, Jack C. & Weintritt, Donald J. WaterFormed Scale Deposits. 606p. 1976. 69.95x (ISBN 0-87201-896-2). Gulf Pub.

Cowan, Kenneth. Implant & Transplant Surgery. 1972. pap. 6.95 o.p. (ISBN 0-7195-2249-8). Transatlantic.

Cowan, Lyn. Masochism: A Jungian View. LC 82-16957. 137p. (Orig.). 1982. pap. 8.50 (ISBN 0-88214-320-4). Spring Pubns.

Cowan, Marian M. Tzotzil Grammar. (Publications in Linguistics & Related Fields Ser.: No. 18). 119p. 1969. pap. 2.25x (ISBN 0-88312-020-8); microfiche 2.25x (ISBN 0-88312-420-3). Summer Inst Ling.

Cowan, Marianne, tr. see Nietzsche, Friedrich.

Cowan, Martin B., jt. ed. see Tucker, Stefan F.

Cowan, Marvin W. Los Mormones: Sus Doctrinas Refutadas a la Luz De la Biblia. De La Fuente, Tomas, tr. from Eng. 160p. 1981. pap. 3.50 (ISBN 0-311-05763-2). Casa Bautista.

Cowan, Michael A., jt. auth. see Egan, Gerard.

Cowan, Paul. An Orphan in History: Retrieving a Jewish Legacy. LC 80-1803. 264p. 1982. 15.95 (ISBN 0-385-15055-5). Doubleday.

Cowan, Philip. Behind the Beatles Songs. LC 79-50646. (Illus.). pap. 2.95 (ISBN 0-448-16546-5, G&D). Putnam Pub Group.

Cowan, R. S., jt. auth. see Stafleu.

Cowan, Robert J., jt. ed. see Weintraub, Sam.

Cowan, S. T. Cowan & Steel's Manual for the Identification of Medical Bacteria. (Illus.). 240p. 1974. 39.50 (ISBN 0-521-20399-6). Cambridge U Pr.

--A Dictionary of Microbial Taxonomy. Hill, L. R., ed. LC 77-85705. (Illus.). 1978. 45.00 (ISBN 0-521-21890-X). Cambridge U Pr.

Cowan, Sam. Handbook of Modern Electronics Math. LC 82-11260. 254p. 1983. 21.95 (ISBN 0-13-380485-2). P-H.

Cowan, Thomas A., ed. American Jurisprudence Reader. LC 56-12585. (Docket Ser.: Vol. 8). 256p. (Orig.). 1956. 15.00 (ISBN 0-379-11308-2); pap. 2.50 (ISBN 0-379-11308-2). Oceana.

Cowan, W. & Cuenod, M., eds. Use of Axonal Transport for Studies of Neuronal Connectivity. 1975. 118.50 (ISBN 0-444-41347-2). Elsevier.

Cowan, W. M., et al, eds. Annual Review of Neuroscience, Vol. 6. (Illus.). 1983. text ed. 27.00 (ISBN 0-8243-2406-4). Annual Reviews.

Cowan, W. Maxwell, ed. Studies in Developmental Neurobiology: Essays in Honor of Viktor Hamburger. (Illus.). 1981. text ed. 49.50x (ISBN 0-19-502927-5). Oxford U Pr.

Cowan, Z. Individual Liberty & the Law. 1977. 10.00 o.p. (ISBN 0-379-00597-2). Oceana.

Coward, Harold & Kawamura, Leslie, eds. Religion & Ethnicity. 181p. 1978. pap. text ed. 5.75 (ISBN 0-88920-064-5, Pub. by Wilfred Laurier U Pr Canada). Humanities.

Coward, Harold & Penelhum, Terence, eds. Mystics & Scholars: The Calgary Conference on Mysticism 1976. 121p. 1977. pap. text ed. 5.75x (ISBN 0-919812-04-X, Pub. by Wilfred Laurier U Pr Canada). Humanities.

Coward, Harold G. Bhartrhari. (World Authors Ser.). 1976. lib. bdg. 15.95 (ISBN 0-8057-6243-4, Twayne). G K Hall.

Coward, Harold G., ed. Language in Indian Philosophy & Religion. 98p. 1978. pap. text ed. 5.25x (ISBN 0-919812-07-4, Pub. by Wilfred Laurier U Pr Canada). Humanities.

Coward, Noel. The Lyrics of Noel Coward. LC 73-77884. 432p. 1973. 12.95 (ISBN 0-87951-011-0); pap. 8.95 (ISBN 0-87951-061-7). Overlook Pr.

--Plays: Five. 432p. 1983. pap. 7.50 (ISBN 0-394-62456-4, B486, BC). Grove.

--Plays: Four. 512p. (Orig.). 1981. pap. 9.95 (ISBN 0-394-17943-9, B-462, BC). Grove.

--Plays: One. 384p. (Orig.). 1981. pap. 9.95 (ISBN 0-394-17940-4, B-459, BC). Grove.

--Plays: Three. 432p. (Orig.). 1981. pap. 9.95 (ISBN 0-394-17942-0, B-461, BC). Grove.

--Plays: Two. 384p. (Orig.). 1981. pap. 9.95 (ISBN 0-394-17941-2, B-460, BC). Grove.

Coward, Noel P. Star Quality: Six Stories. LC 75-109288. Repr. of 1951 ed. lib. bdg. 15.50x (ISBN 0-8371-3831-0, COSQ). Greenwood.

Coward, Rosalind. Patriarchal Precedents: Sexuality & Social Relations. 280p. (Orig.). 1983. pap. 9.95 (ISBN 0-7100-9324-1). Routledge & Kegan.

Cowart, David. Thomas Pynchon: The Art of Allusion. LC 79-20157. (Crosscurrents-Modern Critiques-New Ser.). 168p. 1980. 12.95 (ISBN 0-8093-0944-0). S Ill U Pr.

Cowart, David, ed. Twentieth-Century American Science Fiction Writers, 2 vols. (Dictionary of Literary Biography Ser.: Vol. 8). 1981. 148.00x set (ISBN 0-8103-0918-1, Bruccoli Clark). Gale.

Cowart, J. B., jt. auth. see Osmond, J. K.

Cowart, Jack, et al. Henri Matisse Paper Cut-Outs. (Illus.). 1978. 25.00 o.p. (ISBN 0-8109-1301-1). Abrams.

Cowasjee, Saros. So Many Freedoms: A Study of the Major Fiction of Mulk Raj Anand. 1978. 14.95x o.p. (ISBN 0-19-560887-9). Oxford U Pr.

Cowden, Ronald R., jt. ed. see Harrison, Frederick W.

Cowdrey, Albert E. This Land, This South: An Environmental History. Roland, Charles P., ed. LC 82-20154. (New Perspectives on the South Ser.). 256p. 1983. 23.00 (ISBN 0-8131-0302-9). U Pr of Ky.

Cowdry, E. V. Aging Better. (Illus.). 500p. 1972. spiral, photocopy ed. 49.50x (ISBN 0-398-02263-1). C C Thomas.

Cowdry, E. V., jt. auth. see Emmel, Victor E.

Cowel, Lucinda, jt. auth. see Gilliam, Terry.

Cowell, Barbara, jt. auth. see Wilson, John.

Cowell, Cyril. Your Book of Animal Drawing. (gr. 7 up). pap. 7.50 o.p. (ISBN 0-571-05139-1). Transatlantic.

Cowell, E. B. The Jataka; or Stories of the Buddha's Former Births, 3 vols. Repr. of 1895 ed. 21.00x ea o.p. Vol. 1, 1973 (ISBN 0-8002-1612-1). Vol. 2, 1973 (ISBN 0-8002-1613-X). Vol. 3, 1979, Repr. Of 1901 Ed (ISBN 0-8002-1614-8). Intl Pubns Serv.

Cowell, E. B., jt. ed. see Beynon, L. R.

Cowell, F. A. Measuring Inequality: Techniques for the Social Sciences. LC 77-20851. 193p. 1978. 14.95x o.s.i. (ISBN 0-470-99349-9). Halsted Pr.

Cowell, Frank R. History, Civilization & Culture: An Introduction to the Historical & Social Philosophy of Pitirum A. Sorokin. LC 78-14112. (Illus.). 1979. Repr. of 1950 ed. 22.50 (ISBN 0-88355-784-3). Hyperion Conn.

Cowell, Henry & Cowell, Sidney. Charles Ives & His Music. (Music Reprint Ser.). x, 253p. 1981. Repr. of 1969 ed. 25.00 (ISBN 0-306-76125-4). Da Capo.

Cowell, Sidney, jt. auth. see Cowell, Henry.

Cowen, David. The Cells of Neural Tissue & Their Pathologic Reactions. LC 76-720307. (Neuropathology, an Illustrated Course Ser.). 29p. 1977. 100.00x o.p. (ISBN 0-8036-2911-7). Davis Co.

Cowen, John E., ed. Teaching Reading through the Arts. 118p. 1983. pap. 7.00 (ISBN 0-87207-733-0). Intl Reading.

Cowen, R. History of Life. 1975. 14.50 (ISBN 0-07-013260-7, C). McGraw.

Cowen, Richard & Lipps, Jere H. Controversies in the Earth Sciences: A Reader. LC 75-1395. (Illus.). 439p. 1975. pap. text ed. 14.95 (ISBN 0-8299-0044-6). West Pub.

Cowen, Roy C. Christian Dietrich Grabbe. (World Authors Ser.). lib. bdg. 15.95 (ISBN 0-8057-2396-X, Twayne). G K Hall.

Cowen, Zelman. American-Australian Private International Law. LC 57-13050. 1957. 9.00 o.p. (ISBN 0-379-11408-9). Oceana.

Cowen, Zelman & Carter, P. B. Essays on the Law of Evidence. LC 72-11327. 278p. 1973. Repr. of 1956 ed. lib. bdg. 18.25x (ISBN 0-8371-6665-9, COEL). Greenwood.

Cowen, Zelman & Zines, Leslie. Federal Jurisdiction in Australia. 1979. text ed. 39.95x (ISBN 0-19-550556-5). Oxford U Pr.

Cowgill, George R. The Vitamin B: Requirements of Man. 1934. 47.50x (ISBN 0-686-50034-2). Elliots Bks.

Cowgill, Joy. Wagon Train Nineteen Fifty-Eight. (Illus.). 78p. 1980. pap. 5.00 (ISBN 0-916552-21-7). Acoma Bks.

Cowherd, Raymond G. Political Economists & the English Poor Laws: A Historical Study of the Influence of Classical Economics on the Formation of Social Welfare Policy. LC 76-8301. xvii, 300p. 1977. 18.00x (ISBN 0-8214-0233-1, 82-82352). Ohio U Pr.

Cowhey, Peter F. see Aronson, Jonathan D.

Cowhig, Jerry. The World Under the Microscope. (The World of Nature Ser.). (Illus.). 128p. 1973. 1.98 o.p. (ISBN 0-517-12044-5, Bounty Books). Crown.

Cowie, A. P. & Mackin, Ronald. Oxford Dictionary of Current Idiomatic English: Verbs with Prepositions & Particles, Vol. 1. 1975. 13.95x (ISBN 0-19-431145-7). Oxford U Pr.

Cowie, Alfred T., jt. ed. see Kon, S. K.

Cowie, L. W. The Pilgrim Fathers. (Putnam Documentary History Ser.). (Illus.). 1972. 6.95 o.p. (ISBN 0-399-10633-2). Putnam Pub Group.

--The Railway Age. LC 79-64162. (Adventures in History Ser.). PLB 12.68 (ISBN 0-382-06296-5). Silver.

Cowie, Leonard W. Sixteenth-Century Europe. (Illus.). 1977. pap. text ed. 10.95x o.p. (ISBN 0-05-002828-6). Longman.

Cowie, Peter. Ingmar Bergman: A Critical Biography. (Illus.). 352p. 1982. 19.95 (ISBN 0-684-17771-4, ScribT). Scribner.

Cowie, Peter, ed. International Film Guide 1983. (International Film Guide Ser.). (Illus.). 496p. 1982. pap. 10.95 (ISBN 0-900730-00-5). NY Zoetrope.

Cowie, V. A Study of the Early Development of Mongols. LC 75-99554. 1970. write for info. (ISBN 0-08-006828-6). Pergamon.

Cowing, Susan B., tr. see Coedes, G.

Cowle, Jerry. Discover the Trees. LC 76-51174. (Illus.). (gr. 5 up). 1977. 7.95 o.p. (ISBN 0-8069-3734-3); PLB 7.49 o.p. (ISBN 0-8069-3735-1). Sterling.

Cowles, C. S. Family Journey Into Joy. 168p. 1982. pap. 3.95 (ISBN 0-8341-0803-8). Beacon Hill.

Cowles, H. Robert. Opening the Old Testament. LC 80-65149. (Illus.). 158p. (Orig.). 1980. pap. 5.50 (ISBN 0-87509-279-9); Leader's Guide. 3.50 (ISBN 0-87509-283-7). Chr Pubns.

Cowles, Jane. Informed Consent. 256p. 1976. 8.95 o.p. (ISBN 0-698-10682-2, Coward). Putnam Pub Group.

Cowles, Julia. The Diaries of Julia Cowles. Mosely, ed. 1931. 32.50x (ISBN 0-685-89746-X). Elliots Bks.

Cowles, Laurence G. Analysis & Design of Transistor Circuits. 328p. 1966. 16.50 (ISBN 0-442-01710-3, Pub. by Van Nos Reinhold). Krieger.

Cowles, Milly, jt. auth. see Walsh, Kevin.

Cowles, Virginia. The Astors. LC 79-2219. (Illus.). 1979. 17.95 o.p. (ISBN 0-394-41478-0). Knopf.

--The Last Tsar. LC 77-147. (Illus.). 1977. 14.95 o.p. (ISBN 0-399-11974-4). Putnam Pub Group.

Cowles, Willard B. Treaties & Constitutional Law. LC 75-18356. 315p. 1975. Repr. of 1941 ed. lib. bdg. 18.25x (ISBN 0-8371-8316-2, COTC). Greenwood.

Cowley, Alan H., ed. Compounds Containing Phosphorous-Phosphorus Bonds. LC 72-90631. (Benchmark Papers in Inorganic Chemistry Ser). 400p. 1973. text ed. 52.50 o.s.i. (ISBN 0-12-786262-5). Acad Pr.

Cowley, Fraser. Critique of British Empiricism. LC 68-10754. 1968. 17.95 o.p. (ISBN 0-312-17640-6). St Martin.

Cowley, J. M. Diffraction Physics. 2nd ed. 1981. 64.00 (ISBN 0-444-86121-1). Elsevier.

Cowley, J. M., jt. auth. see Weisselberg, R. C.

Cowley, John. Personnel Management in Libraries. 112p. 1982. 13.00 (ISBN 0-85157-324-X, Pub. by Bingley England). Shoe String.

Cowley, Joseph. The Chrysanthemum Garden. 1981. 11.95 o.p. (ISBN 0-671-41632-4). S&S.

Cowley, Malcolm. A Second Flowering: Works & Days of the Lost Generation. (Illus.). 320p. 1973. 10.95 (ISBN 0-670-62826-3). Viking Pr.

Cowley, Malcolm, ed. see Emerson, Ralph W.

Cowley, Malcolm, ed. see Faulkner, William.

Cowley, Malcolm, ed. see Hawthorne, Nathaniel.

Cowley, Malcolm, ed. see Whitman, Walt.

Cowley, R. A., jt. auth. see Bruce, A. D.

Cowley, R. Adams & Trump, Benjamin F. Pathophysiology of Shock, Anoxia & Ischemia. 722p. 1981. 75.00 (ISBN 0-683-02149-4, 2149-4). Williams & Wilkins.

Cowling, E. R., jt. ed. see Horsfall, J. G.

Cowling, Elizabeth. The Cello: New Edition. (Illus.). 240p. 1983. 17.95 (ISBN 0-686-83826-2, ScribT). Scribner.

Cowling, Ellis B., jt. ed. see Horsfall, James G.

Cowling, Maurice. Eighteen Sixty-Seven: Disraeli, Gladstone & Revolution. (Cambridge Studies in the History & Theory of Politics). 1967. 54.50 (ISBN 0-521-04740-4). Cambridge U Pr.

--The Impact of Hitler: British Politics & British Policy 1933-1940. LC 74-12968. (Cambridge Studies in the History & Theory of Politics). 448p. 1975. 64.50 (ISBN 0-521-20582-4). Cambridge U Pr.

--Religion & Public Doctrine in Modern England. (Cambridge Studies in the History & Theory of Politics). 498p. 1981. 54.50 (ISBN 0-521-23289-9). Cambridge U Pr.

Cowling, T. G. Magnetohydrodynamics. LC 76-38002. (Monographs on Astronomical Subjects). 135p. 1977. 39.50x o.s.i. (ISBN 0-8448-1060-6). Crane-Russak Co.

Cowling, T. G., jt. auth. see Chapman, S.

Cowman, Charles E. & Serrano, Antonio. Manantiales En el Desierto. Orig. Title: Stream in the Desert. 1980. pap. 4.95 (ISBN 0-311-40028-0, Edit Mundo). Casa Bautista.

Cowman, Mrs. Charles E. Cumbres De Inspiracion. Robleto, Adolfo, tr. 1982. Repr. of 1979 ed. pap. 4.25 (ISBN 0-311-40026-4). Casa Bautista.

--Streams in the Desert, Vol. 2. large print ed. 384p. 1976. 7.95 (ISBN 0-310-22537-X). Zondervan.

Cowper, W. Correspondence of William Cowper, 4 Vols. LC 68-24904. (English Biography Ser., No. 31). 1969. Repr. of 1904 ed. lib. bdg. 99.95x (ISBN 0-8383-0156-8). Haskell.

Cowper, William. The Letters & Prose Writings of William Cowper, Vol. III: Letters, 1787-1791. King, James & Ryskamp, Charles, eds. (Illus.). 1982. 79.00x (ISBN 0-19-812608-5). Oxford U Pr.

--The Letters & Prose Writings of William Cowper, Vol. I, 1750-1781 & Vol. II, 1782-1786. King, James & Ryskamp, Charles, eds. (Illus.). 1979. 69.00x (ISBN 0-19-811863-5); Vol. II, 1981 98.00, (ISBN 0-19-812607-7). Oxford U Pr.

--Verse & Letters. Spiller, Brian, ed. (The Reynard Library). 1968. 20.00x o.p. (ISBN 0-674-93470-9). Harvard U Pr.

Cowperthwait, John H. Money, Silver & Finance. LC 69-19666. Repr. of 1892 ed. lib. bdg. 15.50x (ISBN 0-8371-0363-0, COMS). Greenwood.

Cowser, K. E. & Richmond, C. R., eds. Synthetic Fossil Fuel Technology: Potential Health & Environmental Effects. LC 80-68338. 288p. 1980. 39.95 (ISBN 0-250-40358-7). Ann Arbor Science.

Cox & Cork. Butterflies & Moths. (First Nature Bks.). (gr. 2-5). 1980. 5.95 (ISBN 0-86020-478-2, Usborne-Hayes); PLB 8.95 (ISBN 0-88110-073-0); pap. 2.95 (ISBN 0-86020-477-4). EDC.

Cox & Johnston. Conflict, Politics & the Urban Scene. LC 81-16620. 288p. 1983. 25.00x (ISBN 0-312-16233-2). St Martin.

Cox, jt. auth. see Thompson.

Cox, A. & Kemp, T. J. Introductory Photochemistry. 1972. text ed. 22.50 (ISBN 0-07-094176-9, C). McGraw.

Cox, Albert W. Sonar & Underwater Sound. LC 74-15547. (Illus.). 1975. 20.95 o.p. (ISBN 0-669-95935-9). Lexington Bks.

Cox, Allan. The Cox Report on the American Corporation. 448p. 1982. 21.95 (ISBN 0-440-01548-0). Delacorte.

Cox, Alwyn see Allen, W. S.

Cox, Andrew, jt. auth. see Mason, Joseph.

Cox, Annette. Art-as-Politics: The Abstract Expressionist Avant-Garde & Society. Foster, Stephen, ed. LC 82-4760. (Studies in Fine Arts: The Avant-Garde: No. 26). 216p. 1982. 39.95 (ISBN 0-8357-1318-0, Pub. by UMI Res Pr). Univ Microfilms.

Cox, Archibald. Law & the National Labor Policy. LC 82-20930. 111p. 1983. Repr. of 1960 ed. lib. bdg. 27.50x (ISBN 0-313-23794-8, COLN). Greenwood.
--The Role of the Supreme Court in American Government. 128p. 1976. 14.95x (ISBN 0-19-827411-4). Oxford U Pr.
--The Role of the Supreme Court in American Government. x1976 ed. LC 75-29958. 1977. pap. 4.95 (ISBN 0-19-519909-X, 482, GB). Oxford U Pr.

Cox, Arthur M. The Dynamics of Detente. 1976. 8.95 o.p. (ISBN 0-393-05592-2). Norton.

Cox, B., jt. auth. see Vale, J.

Cox, Barbara G. & Macaulay, Janet. Nuevas Fronteras-New Frontiers: Un Programa de Aprendizaje Bilingue para Ninos-A Bilingual Early Learning Program. LC 81-81331. 1982. 636.00 (ISBN 0-08-028280-6). Pergamon.

Cox, Barbara G., ed. Hispanic American Periodicals Index, 1975. LC 75-642408. 1978. lib. bdg. 125.00x (ISBN 0-87903-400-9). UCLA Lat Am Ctr.
--Hispanic American Periodicals Index, 1976. LC 75-642408. 1979. lib. bdg. 125.00x (ISBN 0-87903-401-7). UCLA Lat Am Ctr.

Cox, Barry, jt. auth. see Foster, R. W.

Cox, Bernard. Pleasure Steamers. (Illus.). 64p. (Orig.). 1983. 12.50 (ISBN 0-7153-8333-7). David & Charles.

Cox, Brian. Five Hundred Things to Do in Washington for Free. (Illus.). 192p. 1983. pap. 5.95 (ISBN 0-8329-0262-4). New Century.

Cox, C. B. The Free Spirit: A Study of Liberal Humanism in the Novels of George Eliot, Henry James, E. M. Forster, Virginia Woolf, Angus Wilson. LC 80-13281. 195p. 1980. Repr. of 1963 ed. lib. bdg. 20.00x (ISBN 0-313-22449-8, COFS). Greenwood.

Cox, C. B. & Boyson, Rhodes, eds. Black Paper 1977. 1978. pap. 4.75 o.p. (ISBN 0-85117-117-6). Transatlantic.

Cox, C. Benjamin. The Censorship Game & How to Play It. LC 77-82256. (Bulletin Ser.: No. 50). 1977. pap. 4.20 (ISBN 0-87986-011-1, 498-15258). Coun Soc Studies.

Cox, Carole F. Hesse, Goethe, Jung, You, & Me: A Story. pap. 2.95 o.p. (ISBN 0-686-09886-2). Star Pub Fla.

Cox, Charles, jt. auth. see Beck, John.

Cox, Christopher. A Key West Companion. (Illus.). 208p. 1983. 19.95 (ISBN 0-312-45182-2). St Martin.

Cox, D. H. A Third Century Hoard of Tetradrachms from Gordion. (Museum Monograph). (Illus.). v, 20p. 1953. 1.50x (ISBN 0-934718-01-6). Univ Mus of U PA.

Cox, D. R. Analysis of Binary Data. 1970. 17.50x (ISBN 0-412-15340-8, Pub. by Chapman & Hall). Methuen Inc.
--Applied Statistics: Principles & Examples. 1981. 32.00x (ISBN 0-412-16560-0, Pub. by Chapman & Hall); pap. 15.95x (ISBN 0-412-16570-8). Methuen Inc.
--Renewal Theory. (Monographs on Statistic & Applied Probability). 1967. pap. 7.95x (ISBN 0-412-20570-X, Pub. by Chapman & Hall). Methuen Inc.

Cox, D. R. & Hinkley, D. V. Theoretical Physics. 1979. 17.95x o.p. (ISBN 0-412-16160-5, Pub. by Chapman & Hall). Methuen Inc.

Cox, D. R. & Isham, V. Point Processes. 17.95x (ISBN 0-412-21910-7, Pub. by Chapman & Hall England). Methuen Inc.

Cox, D. R. & Lewis, P. A. The Statistical Analysis of Series of Events. (Monographs on Statistics & Applied Probability). 1966. 17.50x (ISBN 0-412-21800-3, Pub. by Chapman & Hall). Methuen Inc.

Cox, D. R. & Smith, W. L. Queues: Receptors & Recognition Series B. Incl. Vol. 13. Receptor Regulation; Vol. 12. Purinergic Receptors; Vol. 11. Membrane Receptors; Vol. 10. Neurotransmitter Receptors, Part 2: Biogenic Amines; Vol. 9. Neurotransmitter Receptors, Part 1: Amino Acids, Peptides & Benzodiazepines; Vol. 8. Virus Receptors, Part 2: Animal Viruses; Vol. 7. Virus Receptors, Part 1: Bacterial Viruses; Vol. 6. Bacterial Adherence; Vol. 5. Taxis & Behavior; Vol. 4. Specificity of Embryological Interactions; Vol. 3. Microbial Interactions; Vol. 2. Intercellular Junctions & Synapses; Vol. 1. The Specificity & Action of Animal, Bacterial & Plant Toxins. 1971. pap. 11.50x (ISBN 0-412-10930-1, Pub. by Chapman & Hall England). Methuen Inc.

Cox, David. Modern Psychology: The Teachings of Carl Gustav Jung. 1968. pap. 3.95 (ISBN 0-06-463231-8, EH 231, EH). B&N NY.

Cox, David R. Planning of Experiments. LC 58-13457. (Probability & Statistics Ser.). (Illus.). 308p. 1958. 39.95x (ISBN 0-471-18183-8). Wiley.

Cox, Deborah & Davis, Juliet. Thirty Days to a Beautiful Bottom. 1982. pap. 2.95 (ISBN 0-553-01472-2). Bantam.

Cox, Dermot. Proverbs, with Introduction to Sapiential Books, Vol. 17. 1982. 10.95 (ISBN 0-89453-251-0); pap. 6.95 (ISBN 0-686-32770-5). M Glazier.

Cox, Diane & Peck, Cynthia V. Reading Games in the Classroom. (Illus.). 82p. 1977. pap. text ed. 6.00x (ISBN 0-89061-280-3, 427). Jamestown Pubs.

Cox, Dorothy. Modern Upholstery. (Illus.). 152p. 1980. pap. 12.50x (ISBN 0-7135-1599-6, LTB). Sportshelf.

Cox, E. Aubrey. Bottoms Up with a Rear Admiral. LC 79-79091. 1969. 7.95 (ISBN 0-87716-004-X, Pub. by Moore Pub Co). F Apple.

Cox, E. R. & Bold, H. C. Taxonomic Investigations of Stigeoclonium. (Phycological Studies: No. 7). (Illus.). 1979. pap. text ed. 22.40 (ISBN 3-87429-130-8). Lubrecht & Cramer.

Cox, Edward F. Twelve for Twelve. 64p. 1982. pap. 3.50 (ISBN 0-8341-0787-2). Beacon Hill.

Cox, Edwin, jt. auth. see Boot, John C.

Cox, Eunice W., jt. auth. see Winters, Stanley A.

Cox, Frances M. Aging in a Changing Village Society: A Kenyan Experience. (Orig.). 1977. pap. text ed. 3.00 (ISBN 0-910473-03-X). Intl Fed Ageing.

Cox, Frank D. Human Intimacy: Marriage, the Family & Its Meaning. 2nd ed. (Illus.). 560p. 1981. 21.95 (ISBN 0-8299-0367-4). West Pub.
--Human Intimacy: Marriage, the Family & Its Meaning. (Illus.). 1978. text ed. 16.95 o.s.i. (ISBN 0-8299-0152-3); instrs.' manual avail. o.s.i. (ISBN 0-8299-0473-5). West Pub.

Cox, Fred M., et al, eds. Strategies of Community Organizations: A Book of Readings. 3rd ed. LC 77-83396. 1979. pap. text ed. 14.95 (ISBN 0-87581-230-9). Peacock Pubs.
--Tactics & Techniques of Community Practice. LC 76-41998. 1977. pap. text ed. 14.95 (ISBN 0-87581-221-X, 221). Peacock Pubs.

Cox, G. E. The Gospel According to St. Matthew. (Student Christian Movement Press - Torch Bible Ser.). (Orig.). 1952. pap. 6.95 o.p. (ISBN 0-19-520294-5). Oxford U Pr.

Cox, G. M., jt. auth. see Cochran, W. G.

Cox, Gary, jt. auth. see Austin, Michael J.

Cox, Geoffrey J., jt. auth. see Ayling, Tony.

Cox, George. Lindbergh: An American Epic. 1975. 5.00 o.p. (ISBN 0-8233-0228-8). Golden Quill.

Cox, George D., tr. see Zola, Emile.

Cox, George W. Introduction to the Science of Comparative Mythology & Folklore. LC 68-20124. 1968. Repr. of 1883 ed. 34.00x (ISBN 0-8103-3425-9). Gale.

Cox, H. & Morgan, D. City Politics & the Press. LC 72-96678. (Illus.). 200p. 1973. 27.95 (ISBN 0-521-20162-4). Cambridge U Pr.

Cox, Halley J. & Stasack, Edward. Hawaiian Petroglyphs. LC 78-111491. (Special Publication Ser.: No. 60). (Illus.). 108p. 1977. pap. 9.00 (ISBN 0-910240-09-4). Bishop Mus.

Cox, Harold E., jt. auth. see Bowman, Stanley F.

Cox, Harvey. Just as I Am. LC 82-11631. 160p. 1983. 10.95 (ISBN 0-687-20687-1). Abingdon.
--The Seduction of the Spirit. 1974. pap. 5.95 o.p. (ISBN 0-671-21728-3, Touchstone Bks). S&S.

Cox, Harvey & Fletcher, Joseph, eds. Situation Ethics Debate. LC 68-11991. 1968. pap. 2.65 (ISBN 0-664-24814-4). Westminster.

Cox, Helen. Midwifery Manual: A Guide for Auxiliary Midwives. (McGraw-Hill International Health Services Ser.). (Illus.). 1976. pap. text ed. 6.95 o.p. (ISBN 0-07-099250-9, C). McGraw.

Cox, Homer T. Henry Seton Merriman. (English Authors Ser.). 14.95 (ISBN 0-8057-1384-0, Twayne). G K Hall.

Cox, J., jt. auth. see Mize, Joe H.

Cox, J. Halley & Davenport, William. Hawaiian Sculpture. LC 73-151453. 1974. 20.00 (ISBN 0-8248-0281-0). UH Pr.

Cox, James. Financial Information, Accounting & the Law: Cases & Materials. 1980. text ed. 25.00 (ISBN 0-316-15861-5). Little.

Cox, James W. A Guide to Biblical Preaching. LC 76-13491. 144p. 1976. pap. 6.95 (ISBN 0-687-16230-0). Abingdon.

Cox, Jim, jt. auth. see Robison, James.

Cox, Jimmie, jt. auth. see Robinson, James.

Cox, John. Overkill: Weapons of the Nuclear Age. LC 77-27663. (Illus.). (gr. 7 up). 1978. 7.95i o.p. (ISBN 0-690-03856-9, TYC-J); PLB 9.89 (ISBN 0-690-03857-7). Har-Row.

Cox, John E. Surgery of the Reproductive Tract in Large Animals. 210p. 1982. pap. 40.00x (ISBN 0-686-92031-7, Pub. by Liverpool Univ England). State Mutual Bk.

Cox, John J., jt. auth. see Rubinstein, Mark.

Cox, John L., jt. auth. see Vogt, Judith F.

Cox, K. G., et al. Introduction to the Practical Study of Crystals, Minerals & Rocks. 1969. 8.75 o.p. (ISBN 0-07-094053-3, P&RB). McGraw.
--Interpretation of Igneous Rocks. 1979. text ed. 50.00x (ISBN 0-04-552015-1); pap. text ed. 24.95x (ISBN 0-04-552016-X). Allen Unwin.
--An Introduction to the Practical Study of Crystals, Minerals, & Rocks. rev. ed. LC 74-13833. 235p. 1975. text ed. 16.95x o.s.i. (ISBN 0-470-18139-7). Halsted Pr.

Cox, K. R., et al, eds. Locational Approaches to Power & Conflict. LC 76-127983. 345p. 1974. 19.95x o.s.i. (ISBN 0-470-18122-2). Halsted Pr.

Cox, Keith, jt. auth. see Kotler, Philip.

Cox, Kevin R. Location & Public Problems. 352p. 1979. 16.95x (ISBN 0-416-60091-3). Methuen Inc.
--Location & Public Problems: A Political Geography of the Contemporary World. LC 78-71125. (Illus.). 1979. text ed. 14.95x (ISBN 0-88425-015-6). Maaroufa Pr.

Cox, Kevin R., ed. Urbanization & Conflict in Market Societies. LC 77-76158. (Illus.). 1978. text ed. 12.95x (ISBN 0-88425-007-5). Maaroufa Pr.

Cox, Kevin R. & Golledge, Reginald G., eds. Behaviour Problems in Geography Revisited. 1982. 26.95x (ISBN 0-416-72430-2); pap. 12.95x (ISBN 0-416-72440-X). Methuen Inc.

Cox, Klaudia, ed. see Cypress, Beulah K.

Cox, Klaudia, ed. see Ganley, James P. & Roberts, Jean.

Cox, Klaudia, ed. see Gardocki, Gloria J.

Cox, Klaudia, ed. see Landis, J. Richard & Eklund, Stephen A.

Cox, Klaudia, tr. see Fulwood, Robinson & Johnson, Clifford L.

Cox, M. History of Sir John Deane's Grammar School, Northwich. 1976. 25.00 (ISBN 0-7190-1282-1). Manchester.

Cox, M. V., ed. Are Young Children Egocentric? 1980. 25.00 (ISBN 0-312-04839-4). St Martin.

Cox, Martha H. see Heasley Cox, Martha & Chatterton, Wayne.

Cox, Michael A. Oxycal vs. Arthritis. 171p. (Orig.). 1982. pap. 5.95 (ISBN 0-686-43305-X). R Tanner Assocs Inc.

Cox, N. S., jt. ed. see Balmforth, C. K.

Cox, Nicole & Federici, Silvia. Counter-Planning from the Kitchen: Wages for Housework - a Perspective on Capital & the Left. 2nd ed. 24p. 1976. pap. 1.75 (ISBN 0-905046-03-X). Falling Wall.

Cox, Norman W., ed. Encyclopedia of Southern Baptists, Vols. I & II. LC 58-5417. (Illus.). 1958. 39.95 (ISBN 0-8054-6501-4). Broadman.

Cox, P. H. Progress in Radiopharmacology 3. 1983. pap. text ed. 44.00 (ISBN 90-247-2768-5, Pub. by Martinus Nijhoff Netherlands). Kluwer Boston.

Cox, P. H., ed. Progress in Radiopharmacology, Vol. 1. 1979. 55.50 (ISBN 0-444-80178-2, North Holland). Elsevier.
--Progress in Radiopharmacology, Vol. 2: Selected Topics. 1981. 64.75 (ISBN 0-444-80323-8). Elsevier.

Cox, Palmer. Another Brownie Book. (Illus.). (gr. k-3). 1890. pap. 2.00 o.p. (ISBN 0-486-21625-X). Dover.
--The Brownies: Their Book. (Illus.). (gr. 2-6). 1887. pap. 3.95 (ISBN 0-486-21265-3). Dover.

Cox, Peter. Dwarf Rhododendrons. (Illus.). 296p. 1973. 17.95 (ISBN 0-02-528560-2). Macmillan.

Cox, Peter R., ed. Demography. 5th ed. LC 70-92245. (Illus.). 1976. 54.50 (ISBN 0-521-21003-8); pap. 19.95 (ISBN 0-521-29020-1). Cambridge U Pr.

Cox, R. The Botticelli Madonna. 1979. 9.95 (ISBN 0-07-013291-7). McGraw.

Cox, R., jt. auth. see Johnson, R.

Cox, R. A., ed. Offshore Medicine: Medical Care of Employees in the Offshore Oil Industry. (Illus.). 208p. 1982. 35.60 (ISBN 0-387-11111-5). Springer-Verlag.

Cox, R. H., jt. auth. see Leyden, D. E.

Cox, R. Merritt. Eighteenth Century Spanish Literature. (World Authors Ser.). 1979. lib. bdg. 13.95 (ISBN 0-8057-6367-8, Twayne). G K Hall.
--Juan Melendez Valdes. (World Authors Ser.). 1974. lib. bdg. 15.95 (ISBN 0-8057-2918-6, Twayne). G K Hall.
--Tomas de Iriarte. (World Authors Ser.). lib. bdg. 15.95 (ISBN 0-8057-2456-7, Twayne). G K Hall.

Cox, Richard. Teaching Volleyball. LC 80-65110. 1980. pap. text ed. 6.95x (ISBN 0-8087-2929-2). Burgess.

Cox, Richard, jt. auth. see Durieux, Caroline.

Cox, Richard H. Locke on War & Peace. LC 82-42514. 240p. 1983. pap. text ed. 10.75 (ISBN 0-8191-2662-4). U Pr of Amer.

Cox, Richard H., ed. John Locke: Second Treatise of Government. (Crofts Classics Ser.). 200p. 1982. text ed. 10.95x (ISBN 0-88295-124-6); pap. text ed. 3.75x (ISBN 0-88295-125-4). Harlan Davidson.
--Religious Systems & Psychotherapy. 520p. 1973. 29.75x (ISBN 0-398-02753-6). C C Thomas.

Cox, Robert V. Deadly Pursuit. LC 77-76773. 192p. 1977. 8.95 (ISBN 0-8117-0481-5). Stackpole.

Cox, Ronald J. The Gospel Jesus. LC 75-43431. 1976. pap. 2.95 o.p. (ISBN 0-87973-774-3). Our Sunday Visitor.

Cox, Rosann M., jt. auth. see Vick, Marie.

Cox, S. W. & Filby, D. E. Instrumentation in Agriculture. (Illus.). 160p. 1972. text ed. 14.95x o.p. (ISBN 0-8464-0519-9). Beekman Pubs.

Cox, Stafford G., et al. Wellness R.S.V.P. 1981. pap. 6.95 (ISBN 0-8053-2304-X). Benjamin Cummings.

Cox, Steven M. & Conrad, John J. Juvenile Justice: A Guide to Practice & Theory. 300p. 1978. text ed. write for info. (ISBN 0-697-08206-7); instructor's resource manual avail. Wm C Brown.

Cox, Steven M. & Fitzgerald, Jack D. Police & Community Relations: Critical Issues. 320p. 1983. text ed. write for info. (ISBN 0-697-08219-9); instrs.' manual avail. (ISBN 0-697-08222-9). Wm C Brown.

Cox, T. Disadvantaged Eleven Year Olds. 140p. 1983. 18.90 (ISBN 0-08-028911-8). Pergamon.
--Stress. 208p. 1978. pap. text ed. 18.95 (ISBN 0-8391-1219-X). Univ Park.

Cox, Thornton. Southern France. (Thornton Cox's Travellers' Guide Ser.). 1979. pap. 4.95 o.p. (ISBN 0-8038-7156-2). Hastings.
--Thornton Cox's Traveller's Guide to East Africa. new ed. (Illus.). 200p. 1980. pap. 5.95 o.s.i. (ISBN 0-8038-7215-1). Hastings.

Cox, Thorton. The Caribbean. (Thorton Cox's Travellers' Guides Ser.). 1979. pap. 4.95 o.p. (ISBN 0-8038-7156-2). Hastings.
--Thorton Cox Travel Guide to Egypt. (Thorton Cox Travel Guides). (Illus.). 120p. 1983. pap. 6.95 (ISBN 0-88254-809-3, Pub. by Geographia England). Hippocrene Bks.

Cox, Victoria, jt. auth. see Applebaum, Stan.

Cox, Virginia D. & Weathers, Willie T. Old Houses of King & Queen County, Virginia. LC 73-89225. (Illus.). 450p. 1973. 17.50x (ISBN 0-8139-0848-5). U Pr of Va.

Cox, Wesley. How to Install Your Own Telephones, Extensions & Accessories & Kiss Ma Bell Goodbye. (Illus.). 1983. pap. 4.95 (ISBN 0-517-54936-0). Crown.

Cox, William E. Industrial Marketing Research. LC 78-11480. (Marketing Management Ser.). 1979. 34.95x (ISBN 0-471-03467-3, Pub. by Wiley-Interscience). Wiley.

Cox, William R. Home Court Is Where You Find It. LC 79-6641. (gr. 6 up). 1980. 7.95 (ISBN 0-396-07798-6). Dodd.

Coxe, Brinton. An Essay on Judicial Power & Unconstitutional Legislation. LC 79-99476. 1970. Repr. of 1893 ed. 47.50 (ISBN 0-306-71853-7). Da Capo.

Coxe, Tench. View of the United States of America Between the Years 1787 & 1794. LC 64-24342. Repr. of 1794 ed. 35.00x (ISBN 0-678-00070-0). Kelley.

Coxe, Weld. Marketing Architectural & Engineering Services. 2nd ed. 1982. text ed. 24.95 (ISBN 0-442-22011-1). Van Nos Reinhold.

Coxeter, H. S. Introduction to Geometry. 2nd ed. LC 72-93909. 469p. 1969. 33.95 (ISBN 0-471-18283-4). Wiley.
--Unverganglich Geometrie. 2nd, Rev. ed. (Wissenschaft und Kultur Ser.: 17). 552p. 1982. text ed. 44.00x (ISBN 3-7643-1195-9). Birkhauser.

Coxeter, H. S. & Moser, W. O. Generators & Relations for Discrete Groups. 3rd rev. ed. LC 72-79063. (Ergebnisse der Mathematik und Ihrer Grenzgebiete: Vol. 14). (Illus.). 174p. 1972. 39.00 (ISBN 0-387-09212-9). Springer-Verlag.

Coxeter, H. S., et al. The Fifty-Nine Icosahedra. (Illus.). 30p. 1982. pap. 12.00 (ISBN 0-387-90770-X). Springer-Verlag.

Coxeter, Harold S. Regular Complex Polytopes. LC 73-75855. (Illus.). 208p. 1975. 54.50 (ISBN 0-521-20125-X). Cambridge U Pr.

Coxford, Lola M. Resume Writing Made Easy. 124p. 1982. pap. 4.95 (ISBN 0-686-84489-0). Gorsuch Scarisbrick.

Coxhead, David & Hiller, Susan. Dreams: Visions of the Night. (Illus.). 1977. pap. 8.95 o.p. (ISBN 0-500-81012-5). Thames Hudson.

Coxhead, Nona. Mindpower. LC 77-3845. 1977. 8.95 o.p. (ISBN 0-312-53350-0). St Martin.

Coxhead, Nona, jt. auth. see Cade, C. Maxwell.

Coxon, A. P. & Jones, C. L. Measurement & Meanings: Techniques & Methods of Studying Occupational Cognition. LC 78-26705. 1979. 27.50x (ISBN 0-312-52418-8). St Martin.

Coxon, A. P., jt. ed. see Davies, P. M.

Coxon, A. P. M. The User's Guide to Multidimensional Scaling. 320p. 1982. text ed. 28.00 (ISBN 0-435-82251-9). Heinemann Ed.

Coxon, Anthony P. & Jones, Charles L. Class & Hierarchy: The Social Meaning of Occupations. (Illus.). 1979. 27.50 (ISBN 0-312-14256-0). St Martin.
--The Images of Occupational Prestige: A Study in Social Cognition. LC 77-90093. 1978. 27.50x (ISBN 0-312-40928-1). St Martin.

Coxon, DeWayne. Energy Bootstrapping in Israel. 90p. 1983. 11.95 (ISBN 0-910213-03-8); pap. 6.95 (ISBN 0-910213-02-X). Jordan Pub.
--Practical Solar Heating Manual with Blueprints for Air & Water Systems. LC 81-65327. 96p. 1981. text ed. 19.95 softcover (ISBN 0-250-40446-X). Ann Arbor Science.

Coxon, J. M. & Halton, B. Organic Photochemistry. LC 73-82447. (Chemistry Texts Ser). (Illus.). 270p. 1974. 35.50 (ISBN 0-521-20322-8); pap. 16.95 (ISBN 0-521-09824-6). Cambridge U Pr.

Coy, Harold. Congress. LC 80-24914. (First Books about Washington Ser.). (gr. 4 up). 1981. PLB 8.90 (ISBN 0-531-04250-2). Watts.
--First Book of the Supreme Court. LC 80-25701. (First Bks). (Illus.). (gr. 7 up). 1958. PLB 4.90 o.p. (ISBN 0-531-00648-4). Watts.
--Presidents. (First Bks.). (Illus.). (gr. 4-6). 1977. PLB 8.90 s&l (ISBN 0-531-02906-9). Watts.
--Supreme Court. LC 80-25701. (First Books About Washington Ser.). (gr. 4 up). 1981. PLB 8.90 (ISBN 0-531-04252-9). Watts.

Coy, Kendrick. Multi-Sensory Educational Aids from Scrap. (Illus.). 232p. 1980. spiral 19.50x (ISBN 0-398-03934-8). C C Thomas.

Coy, Peter M. Love Song. (Contemporary Poets Ser.). 62p. (Orig.). 1982. pap. 3.95 (ISBN 0-911027-00-9). Fevertree Pr.

Coyaud, Maurice. Introduction a l'Etude Des Langages Documentaires. LC 66-26623. (Alabama Linguistic & Philological Ser: Vol. 12). 148p. 1966. 12.00 o.p. (ISBN 0-8173-0105-4). U of Ala Pr.

Coyer, Gabriel-Francois. Chinki. (Utopias in the Enlightenment Ser.). 96p. (Fr.). 1974. Repr. of 1768 ed. lib. bdg. 34.50 o.p. (ISBN 0-8287-0235-7, 026). Clearwater Pub.

--Decouverte de l'Isle Frivole. (Utopias in the Enlightenment Ser.). 55p. (Fr.). 1974. Repr. of 1751 ed. 24.00x o.p. (ISBN 0-8287-0236-5, 050). Clearwater Pub.

Coyle, David C. Breakthrough to the Great Society. LC 65-11941. 225p. 1965. 7.50 (ISBN 0-379-00240-X). Oceana.

Coyle, Dominick J. Minorities in Revolt. LC 81-65866. (Illus.). 256p. 1982. 28.50 (ISBN 0-8386-3120-7). Fairleigh Dickinson.

Coyle, J. D., jt. auth. see Barltrop, J. A.

Coyle, John J. & Bardi, Edward. The Management of Business Logistics. LC 75-37998. (Illus.). 450p. 1976. text ed. 17.95 o.s.i. (ISBN 0-8299-0074-8). West Pub.

--The Management of Business Logistics. 2nd ed. 500p. 1980. text ed. 22.95 (ISBN 0-8299-0325-9); instrs.' manual avail. (ISBN 0-8299-0472-7). West Pub.

Coyle, John J. & Bardi, Edward J. Transportation. (Illus.). 542p. 1982. text ed. 24.50 (ISBN 0-314-63158-5). West Pub.

Coyle, Joseph T. & Enna, Salvatore J., eds. Neuroleptics: Neurochemical, Behavioral, & Clinical Perspectives. (Central Nervous System Pharmacology Ser.: Vol. 3). 1982. text ed. write for info. (ISBN 0-89004-735-9). Raven.

Coyle, L. Patrick. The World Encyclopedia of Food. (Illus.). 800p. 1982. 40.00x (ISBN 0-87196-417-1). Facts on File.

Coyle, Neva. Free to Be Thin Daily Planner. 128p. (Orig.). 1983. pap. 5.95 (ISBN 0-87123-284-7). Bethany Hse.

Coyle, R. G. Management System Dynamics. LC 76-40144. 463p. 1977. 71.95x (ISBN 0-471-99444-8, Pub. by Wiley-Interscience); pap. 32.95 (ISBN 0-471-99451-0). Wiley.

Coyle, Terence, jt. auth. see Hale, Robert B.

Coyle, Wallace. Roger Williams: A Reference Guide. (Reference Publications Ser.). 1977. lib. bdg. 16.00 o.p. (ISBN 0-8161-7986-7, Hall Reference). G K Hall.

--Stanley Kubrick: A Guide to Reference & Resources. 1980. lib. bdg. 26.00 (ISBN 0-8161-8058-X, Hall Reference). G K Hall.

Coyle, Wallace, jt. ed. see Fowler, William M.

Coyle, William. Research Papers. 5th ed. LC 79-14110. 1980. pap. 6.95 o.p. (ISBN 0-672-61500-2). Odyssey Pr.

Coyle, William, ed. Young Man in American Literature: The Initiation Theme. LC 68-31707. (Perspectives on American Lit. Ser). (Orig.). 1969. pap. 9.50 (ISBN 0-672-63147-4). Odyssey Pr.

Coyne, John. Hobgoblin. 228p. 1981. 12.95 (ISBN 0-399-12643-0). Putnam Pub Group.

--The Legacy. 1979. pap. 2.95 (ISBN 0-425-05612-0). Berkley Pub.

--The Piercing. 1980. pap. 2.95 (ISBN 0-425-05476-4). Berkley Pub.

--The Piercing. LC 78-7337. 1979. 8.95 o.p. (ISBN 0-399-12172-2). Putnam Pub Group.

--The Searing. 1980. 9.95 (ISBN 0-399-12547-7). Putnam Pub Group.

Coyne, Marla & Smith, Nancy. For Crying Out Cloud: A Study of Acid Rain. Johnson, Harriett S., ed. LC 81-50050. (Illus.). 64p. (Orig.). (gr. 4-7). 1981. pap. text ed. 3.95 (ISBN 0-935698-02-7). Tasa Pub Co.

Coyner, Athleen B., jt. auth. see Zelle, Raeone.

Coynik, David. Film: Real to Reel. rev. ed. (Illus., Orig.). 1976. pap. text ed. 13.50 scp o.p. (ISBN 0-06-382530-9, HarpC). Har-Row.

Coysh, A. W. The Dictionary of Blue & White Pottery. (Illus.). 1981. 44.50 (ISBN 0-907462-06-5). Antique Collect.

Coysh, A. W. & Stefano, Frank, Jr. Collecting Ceramic Landscapes-British & American Landscapes on Printed Pottery. (Illus.). 80p. 1981. 15.00 (ISBN 0-8048-1407-4, Pub by Lund Humphries England). C E Tuttle.

Cozad, Dale. Water Supply for Fire Protection. (Illus.). 304p. 1981. text ed. 22.95 (ISBN 0-13-945964-2). P-H.

Cozart, Leon. Life: The Pursuit of Happiness & Death. LC 81-90517. 1982. 6.95 (ISBN 0-533-05227-0). Vantage.

Cozen, Michalel P. & Lewis, Geroge K. Boston: A Geographical Portrait. LC 76-4791. (Contemporary Metropolitan Analysis Ser.). 104p. 1976. pap. 8.95x (ISBN 0-88410-432-X). Ballinger Pub.

Cozens, W. H. Lessons in Chess Strategy. (Routledge Chess Handbooks). 124p. 1968. pap. 4.95 (ISBN 0-7100-5223-5). Routledge & Kegan.

Cozzens, J. & Faith, C. Simple Noetherian Rings. LC 75-10037. (Cambridge Tracts in Mathematics Ser.). 140p. 1975. 26.95x (ISBN 0-521-20734-7). Cambridge U Pr.

Cozzens, James G. Ask Me Tomorrow. LC 40-11104. (Modern Classic Ser.). 1969. 11.95 (ISBN 0-15-109041-6). HarBraceJ.

--The Just & the Unjust. LC 42-17992. (Modern Classic Ser.). 1950. 11.95 (ISBN 0-15-146577-0). HarBraceJ.

--The Just & the Unjust. LC 42-17992. 1965. pap. 6.95 (ISBN 0-15-646578-7, Harv). HarBraceJ.

Cozzi, Angelo, photos by. Innocence in the Mirror. LC 78-52475. (Illus.). 1978. 12.95 o.p. (ISBN 0-688-03376-8). Morrow.

Crabb, Cecil V. & Holt, Pat M. Invitation to Struggle: Congress, the President & Foreign Policy. Congressional Quarterly, ed. LC 79-27912. (Politics & Public Policy Ser.). 248p. (Orig.). 1980. pap. 8.75 (ISBN 0-87187-196-3). Congr Quarterly.

Crabb, Cecil V., jt. ed. see Sandoz, Ellis.

Crabb, Cecil V., Jr. American Foreign Policy in the Nuclear Age. 3rd ed. 1972. pap. text ed. 23.50 scp o.p. (ISBN 0-06-041382-4, HarpC). Har-Row.

--American Foreign Policy in the Nuclear Age. 4th ed. 608p. 1983. pap. text ed. 18.50 scp (ISBN 0-06-041391-3, HarpC). Har-Row.

Crabb, John H., tr. from Fr. Constitution of Belgium & the Belgian Civil Code as Amended to September 1, 1982 in the Moniteur Belge. LC 82-18059. ix, 428p. 1982. text ed. 65.00x (ISBN 0-8377-0425-1). Rothman.

Crabb, Lawrence J., Jr. The Marriage Builder: A Blueprint for Couples & Counselors. 176p. 1982. 8.95 (ISBN 0-310-22580-9). Zondervan.

Crabb, Lawrence J., Jr. & Crabb, Lawrence J., Sr. Adventures of Captain Al Scabbard, No. 1. LC 80-27223. 128p. (Orig.). (gr. 6-8). 1981. pap. 3.95 (ISBN 0-8024-0280-1). Moody.

--The Adventures of Captain Al Scabbard, No. 2. LC 80-27358. 128p. (Orig.). (gr. 6-8). 1981. pap. 3.95 (ISBN 0-8024-0281-X). Moody.

Crabb, M. C. ZZ-Two-Homotopy Theory. (London Mathematical Lecture Note Ser.: No. 44). 100p. (Orig.). 1980. pap. 16.95 (ISBN 0-521-28051-6). Cambridge U Pr.

Crabbe, Buster & Cilento, Raphael. Buster Crabbe's Arthritis Exercise Book. 1980. 9.95 o.p. (ISBN 0-671-24019-6, 24019). S&S.

Crabbe, David & McBride, Richard, eds. The World Energy Book: An A-Z, Atlas, & Statistical Sourcebook. (Illus.). 1979. pap. 12.50x (ISBN 0-262-53036-8). MIT Pr.

Crabbe, J. A., jt. ed. see Jermy, A. C.

Crabbe, J. C., jt. auth. see Rigter, H.

Crabbe, John. Hi-Fi in the Home. (Illus.). 1971. 9.95 o.p. (ISBN 0-7137-0589-2). Transatlantic.

Crabbe, Katharyn F. J. R. R. Tolkien. LC 81-4793. (Literature and Life Ser.). 200p. 1981. 11.95 (ISBN 0-8044-2134-X); pap. 4.95 (ISBN 0-8044-6091-4). Ungar.

Crabill, Calvin, jt. auth. see Stein, Sherman.

Crable, Richard E. Argumentation As Communication: Reasoning with Receivers. 312p. 1976. text ed. 14.95 (ISBN 0-675-08609-4). Merrill.

Crabtree, Catherine G. A'la Aspen: Restaurant Recipes. rev. ed. 1983. pap. 9.95 (ISBN 0-937070-05-X). Crabtree.

--Ala Texas: Restaurant Recipes. 1983. pap. 9.95 (ISBN 0-937070-04-1). Crabtree.

--A'la Vail: Restaurant Recipes. LC 80-67564. pap. 9.95 cancelled (ISBN 0-937070-03-3). Crabtree.

Crabtree, Harold. Spinning Tops & Gyroscopic Motion. LC 66-23755. (Illus.). 1977. text ed. 12.95 (ISBN 0-8284-0204-3). Chelsea Pub.

Crabtree, Helen K. Saddle Seat Equitation. LC 79-97656. 1970. 12.95 o.p. (ISBN 0-385-03170-X). Doubleday.

--Saddle Seat Equitation. rev. ed. LC 81-43770. (Illus.). 384p. 1982. 19.95 (ISBN 0-385-17217-6). Doubleday.

Crace, Max D. & McJunkin, James N. Visions of Vietnam: Drawings & Photographs of the Vietnam War. (Illus.). 248p. 1983. 25.00 (ISBN 0-89141-175-5). Presidio Pr.

Craddock, C. H., ed. see Virgil.

Craddock, Fred B. John. Hayes, John H., ed. LC 82-48095. (Knox Preaching Guides Ser.). 149p. 1982. pap. 4.95 (ISBN 0-8042-3241-5). John Knox.

Cradock, S. & Hinchcliffe, A. J. Matrix Isolation. LC 74-31786. (Illus.). 140p. 1975. 32.50 (ISBN 0-521-20759-2). Cambridge U Pr.

Craemer, Willy De see De Craemer, Willy.

Craeybeckx, A. S. Elsevier's Dictionary of Photography. (Eng., Fr., & Ger., Polyglot). 1965. 113.00 (ISBN 0-444-40146-6). Elsevier.

Crafford, F. S. Jan Smuts: A Biography. LC 69-10081. (Illus.). 1968. Repr. of 1943 ed. lib. bdg. 19.25x (ISBN 0-8371-0054-2, CRJS). Greenwood.

Craft, Ann & Craft, Michael. Sex & The Mentally Handicapped. Rev. ed. 1982. pap. 7.95 (ISBN 0-7100-9293-8). Routledge & Kegan.

Craft, Ann & Craft, Michael, eds. Sex Education & Counselling for Mentally Handicapped People. 336p. 1983. pap. text ed. 19.95 (ISBN 0-8391-1773-6, 19496). Univ Park.

Craft, Benjamin C. & Hawkins, M. F. Applied Petroleum Reservoir Engineering. 1959. 36.95 (ISBN 0-13-041285-6). P-H.

Craft, J. L., jt. ed. see Craig, R. G.

Craft, J. L., jt. ed. see Whelan, A.

Craft, M. & Miles, L. Patterns of Care for the Mentally Subnormal. 1967. 24.00 o.s.i. (ISBN 0-08-012265-5); pap. 10.75 (ISBN 0-08-012264-7). Pergamon.

Craft, M., ed. Psychopathic Disorders. 1966. inquire for price o.p. (ISBN 0-08-011618-3); pap. 6.05 o.p. (ISBN 0-08-011617-5). Pergamon.

Craft, Michael, jt. auth. see Craft, Ann.

Craft, Michael, jt. ed. see Craft, Ann.

Craft, Robert. Present Perspectives. LC 82-48886. 1983. 18.95 (ISBN 0-394-53073-X). Knopf.

Craft, Robert, jt. auth. see Stravinsky, Igor.

Craft, Robert, ed. Stravinsky: Selected Correspondence, Vol. 1. LC 81-47495. (Illus.). 416p. 1981. 27.50 (ISBN 0-394-51870-5). Knopf.

Craft, Ruth. Pieter Brueghel's The Fair. LC 76-10256. (gr. 2-4). 1976. 10.53i (ISBN 0-397-31698-4, JBL-J). Har-Row.

Crafts, Alden S. Modern Weed Control. LC 74-76383. (Illus.). 1975. 24.50x (ISBN 0-520-02733-7). U of Cal Pr.

Crafts, Alden S., jt. auth. see Ashton, Floyd M.

Crafts, Glenna C. How to Raise & Train a Norwegian Elkhound. (Orig.). pap. 2.95 (ISBN 0-87666-342-0, DS1101). TFH Pubns.

Crafts, Roger C. A Textbook of Human Anatomy. 2nd ed. LC 78-11424. 1979. 39.50x (ISBN 0-471-04454-7, Pub. by Wiley Med). Wiley.

Cragan, John F. & Wright, David W. Communications Small Group Discussions: A Case Study Approach. (Illus.). 400p. 1980. text ed. 16.95 (ISBN 0-8299-0338-0); instrs.' manual avail. (ISBN 0-8299-0474-3). West Pub.

--Introduction to Speech Communication. LC 80-52302. 400p. 1980. pap. text ed. 11.95x (ISBN 0-917974-45-X). Waveland Pr.

Cragg, Dan, jt. auth. see Elting, John R.

Cragg, J. B. Advances in Ecological Research, Vol. 13. (Serial Publication). write for info. (ISBN 0-12-013913-8). Acad Pr.

Cragg, J. B., ed. Advances in Ecological Research. Vol. 1 1963. 33.50 (ISBN 0-12-013901-4); Vol. 2 1965. 41.00 (ISBN 0-12-013902-2); Vol. 3 1966. 51.50 (ISBN 0-12-013903-0); Vol. 4 1967. o.s. 49.50 (ISBN 0-12-013904-9); Vol. 6 1969. 45.50 (ISBN 0-12-013906-5); Vol. 7 1971. 47.00 (ISBN 0-12-013907-3); Vol. 8 1974. 66.00 (ISBN 0-12-013908-1); Vol. 9 1975. 63.00 (ISBN 0-12-013909-X); Vol. 10, 1978. 28.50 (ISBN 0-12-013910-3). Acad Pr.

--Advances in Ecological Research, Vol. 12. (Serial Publication). 1982. 35.50 (ISBN 0-12-013912-X). Acad Pr.

Cragg, John G. & Malkiel, Burton G. Expectations & the Structure of Share Prices. (National Bureau of Economic Research-Monograph). 192p. 1982. lib. bdg. 24.00x (ISBN 0-226-11668-9). U of Chicago Pr.

Cragg, Shelia. A Whirldwind Named Tim. 2nd, Rev. ed. 192p. 1982. pap. text ed. 3.50 (ISBN 0-88449-099-8, A324572). Vision Hse.

Craggs, J. D., jt. auth. see Meek, J. M.

Craggs, Stewart R. William Walton: A Thematic Catalogue. 1977. 39.00x (ISBN 0-19-315433-1). Oxford U Pr.

Craghan, John. Esther, Judith, Tobit, Jonah, Ruth, Vol. 16. 1982. 10.95 (ISBN 0-89453-249-9); pap. 7.95 (ISBN 0-686-32768-3). M Glazier.

Craghan, John F. Love & Thunder: A Sprituality of the Old Testament. 248p. 1983. pap. text ed. 10.95 (ISBN 0-8146-1279-2). Liturgical Pr.

--Yesterday's Word Today. LC 82-12648. 496p. 1982. pap. 14.95 (ISBN 0-8146-1273-3). Liturgical Pr.

Crago, Hugh, jt. auth. see Crago, Maureen.

Crago, Maureen & Crago, Hugh. Prelude to Literacy: A Young Child's Encounter with Pictures & Story. (Illus.). 320p. 1983. price not set (ISBN 0-8093-1077-5). S Ill U Pr.

Cragoe, Edward J. Diuretics: Chemistry, Pharmacology & Medicine. (Chemistry & Pharmacology of Drugs Ser.). 688p. 1983. 80.00 (ISBN 0-471-08366-6, Pub. by Wiley-Interscience). Wiley.

Craig, et al. Hearing Aids & You. 121p. (gr. 4 up). 3.95 o.p. (ISBN 0-86575-028-9). Dormac.

--Your Child's Hearing Aid. 46p. 1976. 3.00 (ISBN 0-86575-029-7). Dormac.

Craig, Albert M. Choshu in the Meiji Restoration. 2nd ed. (Harvard Historical Monographs: No. 47). 424p. 1973. text ed. 18.50x (ISBN 0-674-12850-8). Harvard U Pr.

Craig, Albert M., jt. auth. see Reischauer, Edwin O.

Craig, Alec. The Banned Books of England & Other Countries: A Study of the Conception of Literary Obscenity. LC 77-9968. 1977. Repr. of 1962 ed. lib. bdg. 19.25x (ISBN 0-8371-9709-0, CRBB). Greenwood.

Craig, Alisa. Murder Goes Mumming. large print ed. LC 82-3276. 289p. 1982. Repr. of 1981 ed. 9.95x (ISBN 0-89621-354-4). Thorndike Pr.

--Murder Goes Mumming. 192p. 1982. pap. 2.50 (ISBN 0-553-22702-5). Bantam.

--Terrible Tide. LC 82-45867. (Crime Club Ser.). 192p. 1983. 11.95 (ISBN 0-385-18700-9). Doubleday.

Craig, Allen T., jt. auth. see Hogg, Robert V.

Craig, Barbara. The Evolution of a Mystery Play: Le Sacrifice d'Abraham. 20.00 (ISBN 0-917786-30-0). French Lit.

Craig, Byron. Learner Workbook for Fundamentals of Mathematics. (Orig.). (gr. 10 up). 1983. pap. text ed. 129.95 o.p. (ISBN 0-88408-153-2). Sterling Swift.

Craig, C. Samuel, jt. auth. see Douglas, Susan P.

Craig, C. Samuel, jt. auth. see Sternthal, Brian.

Craig, Christine. Quadrille for Tigers. Date not set. pap. price not set (ISBN 0-942610-02-4). Mina Pr. Postponed.

Craig, David, ed. see Dickens, Charles.

Craig, Dennis. Horse Racing. 250p. 30.00 (ISBN 0-87556-059-8). Saifer.

Craig, Eleanor. One, Two, Three: The Story of Matt, a Feral Child. 1978. 10.95 o.p. (ISBN 0-07-013342-5, GB). McGraw.

--P. S. Your Not Listening. 224p. 1973. pap. 2.95 (ISBN 0-451-12194-5, AE2194, Sig). NAL.

Craig, Frances, jt. auth. see Craig, John.

Craig, G. Child Development. 1979. 23.95 (ISBN 0-13-131250-2); study guide & wkbk. 8.95 (ISBN 0-13-131268-5). P-H.

Craig, G. A. Europe Since Eighteen Fifteen. LC 77-140148. 884p. 1971. 22.50 (ISBN 0-03-084699-4, Pub. by HR&W). Krieger.

Craig, Gordon A. The Battle of Koniggratz: Prussia's Victory Over Austria, 1866. LC 75-35334. (Illus.). 211p. 1976. Repr. of 1964 ed. lib. bdg. 25.00x (ISBN 0-8371-8563-7, CRBK). Greenwood.

--From Bismarck to Alexander: Aspects of German Statecraft. LC 78-1080. (The Albert Shaw Lectures on Diplomatic History, 1958). 1979. Repr. of 1958 ed. lib. bdg. 18.50x (ISBN 0-313-21233-3, CRFB). Greenwood.

--The Germans. 348p. 1982. 15.95 (ISBN 0-399-12436-5). Putnam Pub Group.

--Germany, Eighteen Sixty-Six to Nineteen Forty-Five. (History of Modern Europe Ser.). 1978. 25.00 (ISBN 0-19-822113-4); pap. 14.95x (ISBN 0-19-502724-8). Oxford U Pr.

--Politics of the Prussian Army Sixteen Forty Nineteen Forty-Five. 1964. pap. 9.95 (ISBN 0-19-500257-1, GB). Oxford U Pr.

Craig, Gordon A., ed. see Kehr, Eckart.

Craig, Grace, jt. auth. see Specht, Riva.

Craig, Grace J. Human Development. 2nd ed. (Illus.). 1980. text ed. 23.95 (ISBN 0-13-444984-3); study guide 7.95 (ISBN 0-13-445015-9). P-H.

Craig, Hardin. The Enchanted Glass: The Elizabethan Mind in Literature. LC 75-11492. 293p. 1975. Repr. of 1952 ed. lib. bdg. 18.50x (ISBN 0-8371-8200-X, CREG). Greenwood.

Craig, Hardin & Bevington, David. An Introduction to Shakespeare. rev. ed. 1975. pap. 12.50x (ISBN 0-673-07972-4). Scott F.

Craig, Hazel T. Thresholds to Adult Living. 1976. text ed. 19.80 o.p. (ISBN 0-87002-175-3); tchr's. guide 8.40 (ISBN 0-87002-283-0). Bennett IL.

Craig, Helen. Mouse House Days of the Week. LC 82-60211. (Illus.). 30p. (ps-1). 1983. 2.95 (ISBN 0-394-85286-9). Random.

Craig, J. C., et al. Labour Market Structure, Industrial Organisation & Low Pay. LC 82-4265. (University of Cambridge Dept. of Applied Economics Occasional Papers: No. 54). 200p. 1982. 24.50 (ISBN 0-521-24579-6). Cambridge U Pr.

Craig, J. W. Design of Lossy Filters. 1970. 22.00x (ISBN 0-262-03038-1). MIT Pr.

Craig, James. Graphic Design Career Guide: How to Get a Job & Establish a Career in Design. (Illus.) 176p. (Orig.). 1983. pap. 14.95 (ISBN 0-8230-2151-3). Watson-Guptill.

Craig, James R. Intimacy Training. 200p. (Orig.). 1983. pap. 12.95 (ISBN 0-686-38457-1). J R Craig.

Craig, James R. & Vaughan, David J. Ore Microscopy & Ore Petiography. LC 80-39786. 406p. 1981. 31.95 (ISBN 0-471-08596-0, Pub. by Wiley-Interscience). Wiley.

Craig, James R., jt. auth. see Vaughan, David J.

Craig, James V. Domestic Animal Behavior: Causes & Implications for Animal Care & Management. (Illus.). 400p. 1981. text ed. 24.95 (ISBN 0-13-218339-0). P-H.

Craig, Jasmine. Imprisoned Heart. (Second Chance at Love Ser.: No. 118). 1983. pap. 1.75 (ISBN 0-515-07206-0). Jove Pubns.

--Stormy Reunion, No. 80. 1982. pap. 1.75 (ISBN 0-515-06691-5). Jove Pubns.

Craig, Jean. Heart of the Orchestra: The Story of the Violin & Other Strings. LC 62-20802. (Musical Books for Young People Ser). (Illus.). (gr. 5-11). 1962. PLB 3.95g (ISBN 0-8225-0053-1). Lerner Pubns.

--Spring Is Like the Morning. (Illus.). (gr. 2-4). 1965. PLB 4.97 o.p. (ISBN 0-399-60603-3). Putnam Pub Group.

--Woodwinds. LC 62-20806. (Musical Books for Young People Ser). (Illus.). (gr. 5-11). 1963. PLB 3.95g (ISBN 0-8225-0062-0). Lerner Pubns.

Craig, John. Chappie & Me. LC 79-664. 1979. 8.95 o.p. (ISBN 0-396-07660-2). Dodd.

--Zach. 256p. (gr. 7 up). 1972. 6.95 o.p. (ISBN 0-698-20187-6, Coward). Putnam Pub Group.

Craig, John & Craig, Frances. Track & Field. (First Bks.). (Illus.). (gr. 4 up). 1979. PLB 8.90 s&l (ISBN 0-531-02264-1). Watts.

Craig, John C. Programs for the Casio Handheld Computer. (Illus., Orig.). 1982. pap. 19.95 (ISBN 0-88006-054-9). Green Pub Inc.

Craig, Julia F., jt. auth. see McVicar, Marjorie.

Craig, Lois A., jt. auth. see Federal Architecture Project Staff.

Craig, M. J. The Man Whose Name Was Not Thomas. LC 78-22626. (Illus.). 32p. (gr. k-3). 1981. 9.95a (ISBN 0-385-15064-4); PLB (ISBN 0-385-15065-2). Doubleday.

Craig, M. Jean. The Donkey Prince. LC 75-45477. (gr. k-3). 1977. 7.95a (ISBN 0-385-11294-7); PLB o.p. (ISBN 0-385-11295-5). Doubleday.

Craig, M. S. To Play the Fox. LC 82-7442. 1982. 10.95 (ISBN 0-396-08099-5). Dodd.

Craig, Marjorie. Miss Craig's Twenty-One Day Shape up Program for Men & Women. (Illus.). 1968. 13.95 (ISBN 0-394-40993-0). Random.

Craig, Mary. Mother Teresa. (Profiles Ser.). (Illus.). 64p. (gr. 4-6). 1983. 7.95 (ISBN 0-241-10933-7, Pub. by Hamish Hamilton England). David & Charles.

Craig, Mary S. Lyon's Pride. 352p. 1983. pap. 3.50 (ISBN 0-515-05295-7). Jove Pubns.

Craig, Maurice. Architecture in Ireland. (Aspects of Ireland Ser.). (Illus.). 57p. (Orig.). 1978. pap. 5.95 (ISBN 0-906404-01-0, Pub. by Dept Foreign Ireland). Irish Bks Media.

Craig Norback & Co. The Gerber Baby Encyclopedia. (Orig.). 1983. pap. price not set (ISBN 0-440-53292-2). Dell.

Craig, Oman. Childhood Diabetes: The Facts. (The Facts Ser.). (Illus.). 126p. 1982. 12.95 (ISBN 0-19-261330-8). Oxford U Pr.

Craig, Oman & Apley, John. Childhood Diabetes. 2nd ed. (Postgraduate Pediatric Ser.). 1981. text ed. 47.00 (ISBN 0-407-00209-X). Butterworth.

Craig, Patricia, jt. auth. see Cadogan, Mary.

Craig, Paul. My Look at Life Itself. 1978. 6.95 o.p. (ISBN 0-533-03444-2). Vantage.

Craig, Paul P., ed. Energy Decentralization. Levine, Mark D. (AAAS Selected Symposium 72). 175p. 1982. lib. bdg. 18.50 (ISBN 0-86531-407-1). Westview.

Craig, Paula M. Mr. Wiggle's Book. (Early Childhood Bk.). (Illus.). (ps-2). PLB 4.95 o.p. (ISBN 0-513-01177-3). Denison.

Craig, R., jt. auth. see Jarvis, R. C.

Craig, R. G. & Craft, J. L., eds. Applied Geomorphology. (Binghamton Symposia in Geomorphology, Internatonal Ser.: No. 11). (Illus.). 350p. 1982. text ed. 35.00x (ISBN 0-04-551050-4). Allen Unwin.

Craig, R. G. & Labovitz, M. L., eds. Future Trends in Geomathematics. 1982. 28.00x (ISBN 0-85086-080-6, Pub by Pion England). Methuen Inc.

Craig, Richard A. Upper Atmosphere: Meteorology & Physics. (International Geophysics Ser.: Vol. 8). 1965. 45.50 (ISBN 0-12-194850-1). Acad Pr.

Craig, Robert. Creepers. 1982. pap. 2.95 (ISBN 0-451-11823-5, AE1823, Sig). NAL.

--Storm & Sorrow in the High Pamirs. 1980. 10.95 o.p. (ISBN 0-671-25154-6). S&S.

Craig, Robert C. & Dupuis, Adrian M. American Education: Its Origins & Issues. 1963. text ed. 6.95 o.p. (ISBN 0-02-813650-0); teachers' manual 1.25 o.p. (ISBN 0-685-07607-5). Glencoe.

Craig, Robert G. Restorative Dental Materials. 6th ed. LC 80-12105. (Illus.). 478p. 1980. pap. text ed. 27.95 (ISBN 0-8016-3866-6). Mosby.

Craig, Robert G. & O'Brien, William J. Dental Materials: Properties & Manipulation. 3rd ed. Powers, John M., ed. (Illus.). 327p. 1983. pap. text ed. 15.95 (ISBN 0-8016-1084-2). Mosby.

Craig, Robert G., et al. Dental Materials: Properties & Manipulation. 2nd ed. LC 78-16677. (Illus.). 1979. pap. text ed. 14.95 (ISBN 0-8016-1072-9); wkbk. o.p. 6.95 (ISBN 0-8016-1073-7). Mosby.

Craig, Robert G., et al, eds. Dental Materials: A Problem Oriented Approach. LC 77-18734. (Illus.). 276p. 1978. text ed. 15.95 o.p. (ISBN 0-8016-1064-8). Mosby.

Craig, Robert J. & Yeatts, Harry W. The Complete Guide for Writing Technical Articles. 1976. pap. text ed. 10.00 o.p. (ISBN 0-89806-020-6, 25). Inst Indus Eng.

Craig, Roy R. Structural Dynamics: An Introduction to Computer Methods. LC 80-39798. 527p. 1981. text ed. 39.95 (ISBN 0-471-04499-7). Wiley.

Craig, Sidney D. Raising Your Child: Not by Force But by Love. LC 72-10436. 1982. pap. 6.95 (ISBN 0-664-24413-0). Westminster.

Craig, Stephanie, tr. see Reboul, Antoine.

Craig, Thomas, ed. Commonwealth Universities Yearbook 1981, 4 vols. 57th ed. LC 59-24175. (Illus.). 2700p. (Orig.). 1981. Set. pap. 155.00x o.p. (ISBN 0-85143-066-X). Intl Pubns Serv.

Craig, Tracey L., ed. see American Association for State & Local History.

Craig, Victor. Smart Choices. (Illus.). 112p. 1982. pap. 19.95 (ISBN 0-941156-00-1). Clear View Pubns.

Craig, W. J., ed. see Shakespeare, William.

Craig, William D. Germanic Coinages. 2nd ed. 1983. lib. bdg. 50.00 (ISBN 0-915262-74-6). S J Durst.

Craig, William L. The Son Rises. LC 11-267. 260p. 1981. 7.95 (ISBN 0-8024-7948-0). Moody.

Craig, William N. & Collins, James L. New Vistas for Competitive Employment of Deaf. (Monograph: No. 2). 110p. 1970. pap. text ed. 3.00 (ISBN 0-914494-04-X). Am Deaf & Rehab.

Craige, Betty J., ed. Relativism in the Arts. LC 82-4726. 216p. text ed. 19.00x (ISBN 0-8203-0625-8). U of Ga Pr.

Craige, Betty Jean. Lorca's "Poet in New York". The Fall into Consciousness. LC 76-24339. (Studies in Romance Languages: No. 15). 112p. 1977. 10.50x (ISBN 0-8131-1349-0). U Pr of Ky.

Craighead, Frank C., Jr. Track of the Grizzly. LC 78-8563. (Sierra Club Paperback Library). (Illus.). 272p. 1982. pap. 9.95 (ISBN 0-87156-322-3). Sierra.

Craighead, J. J. & Sumner, J. S. A Definitive System for Analysis of Grizzly Bear Habitat & Other Wilderness Resources Utilizing LANDSAT Multispectral Imagery & Computer Technology. Mitchell, J. A. & Lyons, L. J., eds. (Illus.). 304p. (Orig.). 1982. pap. text ed. 27.50 (ISBN 0-910439-01-X). Wildlife-Wildlands.

Craighead, W. Edward, et al. Behavior Modification. 2nd ed. LC 80-83115. 576p. 1981. text ed. 24.50 (ISBN 0-395-29721-4); instr's. manual 1.00 (ISBN 0-395-30090-8). HM.

Craigie, E. Horne & Gibson, William C. The World of Ramon y Cajal: With Selections from His Nonscientific Writings. (Illus.). 308p. 1968. photocopy ed. spiral 27.50x (ISBN 0-398-00354-8). C C Thomas.

Craigie, J. S., jt. auth. see Hellebust, J. A.

Craigie, Pearl M. The School for Saints, Repr. Of 1897 Ed. Wolff, Robert L., ed. Bd. with Robert Orange. Repr. of 1900 ed. LC 75-463. (Victorian Fiction Ser.). 1975. lib. bdg. 66.00 o.s.i. (ISBN 0-8240-1541-X). Garland Pub.

Craigie, Peter. Ugarit & the Old Testament. 128p. (Orig.). 1983. pap. 5.95 (ISBN 0-8028-1928-1). Eerdmans.

Craigie, William A. & Hulbert, James R., eds. Dictionary of American English on Historical Principles, 4 Vols. LC 36-21500. 1938-1944. Set. 250.00x (ISBN 0-226-11741-3); 40.00 o.s.i. (ISBN 0-686-76907-4); Vol. 1. o.s.i. (ISBN 0-226-11737-5); Vol. 2. o.s.i. (ISBN 0-226-11738-3); Vol. 3. o.s.i. (ISBN 0-226-11739-1); Vol. 4. o.s.i. (ISBN 0-226-11740-5). U of Chicago Pr.

Craigie, Sir William. Dictionary of the Older Scottish Tongue, 4 vols. 29 pts. 1967. Vol. I A-C. 70.00x o.p. (ISBN 0-226-11674-3); Vol. II D-G. 60.00x o.p. (ISBN 0-226-11675-1); Vol. III H-L. 80.00x o.p. (ISBN 0-226-11677-8); Vol. IV M-N. 50.00x o.p. (ISBN 0-226-11678-6); Pts. 5-8, 26, 27-29. vols. I-IV 260.00 o.p. (ISBN 0-226-11679-4); Pts. 8-29. o.s.i. 16.00 ea. o.p. U of Chicago Pr.

Craik, D. J., ed. Magnetic Oxides, 2 vols. LC 73-14378. 1280p. 1975. Set. 260.00x (ISBN 0-471-18356-3, Pub. by Wiley-Interscience). Wiley.

Craik, Dinah M. Little Lame Prince. (Illus.). (gr. 4-6). companion lib. ed. o.s.i. 7.95 (ISBN 0-448-06017-5, G&D); Illus. Jr. Ed. 5.95 (ISBN 0-686-66436-1); deluxe ed. 8.95 (ISBN 0-686-66437-X). Putnam Pub Group.

Craik, Kenneth J. Nature of Explanation. 1943. 27.50 (ISBN 0-521-04755-2); pap. 9.95 (ISBN 0-521-09445-3, 445). Cambridge U Pr.

Craik, Rebecca L., jt. auth. see Bishop, Beverly.

Craik, T. W. Tudor Interlude. 1958. text ed. 15.00x (ISBN 0-7185-1014-3, Leicester). Humanities.

Craik, T. W., ed. see Shakespeare, William.

Craik, Thomas, et al. Revels History of Drama in English, Vol. 2: 1500-1576. 1980. 53.00x (ISBN 0-416-13030-5). Methuen Inc.

Craik, W. A. Elizabeth Gaskell & the English Provincial Novel. 1975. pap. 5.95x o.p. (ISBN 0-416-82640-7). Methuen Inc.

Crail, Ted. Apetalk & Whalespeak: The Quest for Interspecies Communication. 320p. 1983. pap. 7.95 (ISBN 0-8092-5527-8). Contemp Bks.

Crain, Ernest, jt. auth. see Maxwell, William E.

Crain, Ernest, et al. The Challenge of Texas Politics: Text with Readings. (Illus.). 1980. pap. 14.50 (ISBN 0-8299-0339-9). West Pub.

Crain, Robert L., et al. Making Desegregation Work: How Schools Create Social Climate. (Rand Educational Policy Study Ser.). 304p. 1982. prof ref 25.00x (ISBN 0-88410-199-1). Ballinger Pub.

Crain, Sharie & Drotning, Phillip T. Taking Stock. 1979. pap. 4.95 o.p. (ISBN 0-8092-7374-8). Contemp Bks.

Crain, Stanley M. Neurophysiologic Studies in Tissue Culture. LC 75-14567. 292p. 1976. 32.50 (ISBN 0-89004-048-6). Raven.

Crain, William C. Theories of Development: Concepts & Applications. (Illus.). 1980. text ed. 21.95 (ISBN 0-13-913566-9). P-H.

Crain, William L., tr. from Fr. Racine's Phedre & Iphigenia. LC 82-81873. (Illus.). 150p. (Orig.). 1982. pap. 16.00 (ISBN 0-88127-002-4). Oracle Pr LA.

Craine, James F. & Gudeman, Howard E. The Rehabilitation of Brain Functions: Principles, Procedures, & Techniques of Neurotraining. 358p. 1981. pap. 29.75x spiral (ISBN 0-398-04605-0). C C Thomas.

Cralley, Lester & Cralley, Lewis. Patty's Industrial Hygiene & Toxicology: Theory & Rationale of Industrial Hygiene Practice, Vol. 3. LC 78-27102. 1979. 67.50x (ISBN 0-471-02698-0, Pub by Wiley-Interscience). Wiley.

Cralley, Lester V. & Cralley, Lewis J., eds. Industrial Hygiene Aspects of Plant Operations, Vol. 1. 774p. 1982. 47.50 (ISBN 0-02-949350-1). Free Pr.

Cralley, Lewis, jt. auth. see Cralley, Lester.

Cralley, Lewis J., jt. ed. see Cralley, Lester V.

Cram, Mildred. Forever. 1935. 8.95 (ISBN 0-394-42540-5). Knopf.

--Sir. 1973. 4.95 (ISBN 0-913270-11-3). Sunstone Pr.

Cram, Penny Hauser see Hauser-Cram, Penny & Carrozza-Martin, Fay.

Cram, R. A. My Life in Architecture. Repr. of 1936 ed. 18.00 o.s.i. (ISBN 0-527-20310-6). Kraus Repr.

Crambach, A., jt. ed. see Deyl, Z.

Cramblit, Joella & Loebel, JoAnn. Flowers Are for Keeping: How to Dry Flowers & Make Gifts & Decorations. LC 79-12892. (Illus.). 128p. (gr. 5 up). 1979. PLB 8.29 o.p. (ISBN 0-671-33007-1). Messner.

Cramer, Carl, ed. The Down East Guide to Maine Antique Shops. 3rd ed. 176p. (Orig.). 1981. pap. 6.95 (ISBN 0-89272-121-9, PIC174). Down East.

Cramer, Gwendoline. Thoughts & Feelings. 1978. 4.95 o.p. (ISBN 0-533-03473-6). Vantage.

Cramer, H. & Schultz, J., eds. Cyclic Nucleotides: Mechanisms of Action. LC 76-45361. 1977. 79.95 (ISBN 0-471-99456-1, Pub. by Wiley-Interscience). Wiley.

Cramer, Harold. Random Variables & Probability Distribution. 3rd ed. (Cambridge Tracts in Mathematics & Mathematical Physics). 1970. 24.95 (ISBN 0-521-07685-4). Cambridge U Pr.

Cramer, J. Grant, tr. see Grundtvig, Svendt.

Cramer, J. S., ed. Relevance & Precision. 1976. 36.75 (ISBN 0-7204-0534-3, North-Holland). Elsevier.

Cramer, James A., jt. ed. see McDonald, William F.

Cramer, Kenneth R. & Pai, Shi I. Magnetofluid Dynamics for Engineer & Applied Physicists. (Illus.). 360p. 1973. text ed. 28.50 (ISBN 0-07-013425-1, C). McGraw.

Cramer, Malinda E. Divine Science & Healing. 1974. 6.95 (ISBN 0-686-24349-8); pap. 4.50 (ISBN 0-686-24350-1). Divine Sci Fed.

Cramer, Stanley, jt. ed. see Hansen, James.

Cramers, C. A., ed. see International Symposium, 3rd, Amsterdam, Sept. 1976.

Cramlet, Ross C. Woodturning Visualized. rev ed. 1973. pap. 7.50 (ISBN 0-02-813770-1). Glencoe.

--Woodwork Visualized. rev. ed. (Illus., Orig.). 1967. pap. text ed. 7.50 (ISBN 0-02-813790-6). Glencoe.

Cramp, D. G. Quantitative Approaches to Metabolism: The Role of Tracers & Models in Clinical Medicine. LC 81-21992. 390p. 1982. 54.95 (ISBN 0-471-10172-9, Pub. by Wiley-Interscience). Wiley.

Cramp, Stanley, ed. Handbook of the Birds of Europe, the Middle East, & North Africa: The Birds of the Western Paleartic, Vol. III: Waders to Gulls. (Illus.). 920p. 1983. 89.00 (ISBN 0-19-857506-8). Oxford U Pr.

Crampin, M., jt. auth. see Pirani, F. A.

Crampon, L. J. The Characteristics of the Tourist or Travel Market of a Give Destination Area. 74p. 1964. 3.50 o.p. (ISBN 0-686-64172-8). U CO Busn Res Div.

Crampton Associates, ed. Airport Transit Guide. (Illus.). 64p. (Orig.). 1982. pap. write for info. (ISBN 0-9610142-0-2). Crampton Assoc.

Crampton, Beecher. Grasses in California. (California Natural History Guides Ser.). (Illus., Orig.). 1974. 14.95x (ISBN 0-520-02739-6); pap. 5.95 (ISBN 0-520-02507-5). U of Cal Pr.

Crampton, Esme. A Handbook of the Theatre. 264p. (Orig.). 1982. pap. text ed. 12.00x (ISBN 0-435-18185-8). Heinemann Ed.

Crampton, Patricia, tr. see Broger, Achim.

Crampton, Patricia, tr. see Gyllenskold, Karin.

Crampton, Patricia, tr. see Koerner, Wolfgang.

Crampton, Patricia, tr. see Valencak, Hannelore.

Cranach, M. Von see Von Cranach, M.

Cranach, Mario Von see Von Cranach, Mario.

Cranberry, Nola, tr. see Shely, Patricia.

Cranberry, Nola, tr. see Woggon, Guillermo.

Cranch, Christopher P. Collected Poems, 1835-1892. DeFalco, Joseph, ed. LC 70-161930. 1971. 75.00x (ISBN 0-8201-1091-4). Schol Facsimiles.

Crandall, B. J. Morphology & Development of Branches in the Leafy Hepaticae. (Illus.). 1970. 32.00 (ISBN 3-7682-5430-5). Lubrecht & Cramer.

Crandall, D. R. & Mullineaux, D. R. Pleistocene Sequence in Southeastern Part of the Puget Sound Lowland, Washington. (Reprint Ser.: No. 2). (Illus.). 14p. 1958. 0.25 (ISBN 0-686-36910-6). Geologic Pubns.

Crandall, Dorothy & Ambuter, Jeanne. Mrs. Filbert's His & Her's Cookbook. 7.95 o.p. (ISBN 0-916752-13-5). Green Hill.

Crandall, G. Douglas. Experiments in Biochemistry. (Illus.). 128p. 1982. pap. 9.95 (ISBN 0-19-503185-7). Oxford U Pr.

Crandall, K. C. & Seabloom, R. W. Engineering Fundamentals in Measurements, Probability, Statistics & Dimensions. 1970. pap. 18.50 (ISBN 0-07-013439-1, C). McGraw.

Crandall, Lee S. Management of Wild Mammals in Captivity. LC 64-10498. (Illus.). 1964. 37.00x (ISBN 0-226-11758-8). U of Chicago Pr.

Crandall, Richard E. PASCAL for the Sciences. (Self-Teaching Guides). 224p. 1983. pap. text ed. 12.95 (ISBN 0-471-87242-3). Wiley.

Crandall, Robert W. Controlling Industrial Pollution: The Economics & Politics of Clean Air. LC 82-45982. 220p. 1983. 24.95 (ISBN 0-8157-1604-4); pap. 9.95 (ISBN 0-8157-1603-6). Brookings.

--The U. S. Steel Industry in Recurrent Crisis: Policy Options in a Competitive World. LC 81-4642. 200p. 1981. 22.95 (ISBN 0-8157-1602-8); pap. 8.95 (ISBN 0-8157-1601-X). Brookings.

Crandall, Ruth. Buzzy Bee Story Book. Sparks, Judith, ed. (A Happy Day Bk.). (Illus.). 24p. (gr. 1-3). 1980. 1.29 (ISBN 0-87239-409-3, 3641). Standard Pub.

Crandall, Stephen H. Engineering Analysis. LC 82-20335. 428p. 1983. Repr. of 1956 ed. lib. bdg. write for info. (ISBN 0-89874-577-2). Krieger.

--Engineering Analysis: A Survey of Numerical Procedures. (Engineering Societies Monographs Ser). 1956. text ed. 34.50 (ISBN 0-07-013430-8, C). McGraw.

Crandall, Stephen H. & Karnopp, Dean C. Dynamics of Mechanical & Electromechanical Systems. LC 82-9890. 466p. 1982. Repr. of 1968 ed. lib. bdg. 36.00 (ISBN 0-89874-529-2). Krieger.

Crandall, Stephen H., et al. Introduction to the Mechanics of Solids. 2nd ed. (Illus.). 640p. 1972. text ed. 33.95 (ISBN 0-07-013436-7, C). McGraw.

--An Introduction to the Mechanics of Solids. 3rd ed. (Illus.). 1978. text ed. 34.95 (ISBN 0-07-013441-3, C); solution manual 20.50 (ISBN 0-07-013442-1). McGraw.

--Dynamics of Mechanical & Electromechanical Systems. 1968. text ed. 36.00 o.p. (ISBN 0-07-013433-2, C). McGraw.

Crandall-Stotler, Barbara & Jacobson, Katherine. Bios: Process & Diversity. 2nd ed. 1978. wire coil 12.95 (ISBN 0-8403-1409-4). Kendall-Hunt.

Crane, A. & Lemoine, J. An Introduction to the Regenerative Method for Simulation Analysis. (Lecture Notes in Control & Information Sciences: Vol. 4). 1977. pap. text ed. 9.70 o.p. (ISBN 0-387-08408-8). Springer-Verlag.

Crane, Barbara J. GS 1 Skill Booklet. (Crane Reading System - English Ser.). (Illus.). (gr. k-2). 1977. pap. text ed. 13.20 per 10 (ISBN 0-89075-041-6). Crane Pub Co.

Crane, Bonnie L. Blanche Ames: Artist & Activist. (Illus.). 40p. (Orig.). 1982. pap. 4.95 (ISBN 0-934358-10-9). Brockton Art.

Crane, Caroline. Coast of Fear. 1982. pap. 2.50 (ISBN 0-451-11456-6, AE1456, Sig). NAL.

--The Foretelling. LC 82-1409. 224p. 1982. 10.95 (ISBN 0-396-08056-1). Dodd.

--Summer Girl. LC 79-15811. 1979. 8.95 o.p. (ISBN 0-396-07735-8). Dodd.

--Summer Girl. 1981. pap. 2.50 o.p. (ISBN 0-451-09806-4, E9806, Sig). NAL.

--Wife Found Slain. 1982. pap. 2.50 (ISBN 0-451-11614-3, AE1614, Sig). NAL.

Crane, Caroling. The Third Passenger. LC 82-19923. 1983. 10.95 (ISBN 0-396-08132-0). Dodd.

Crane, Debra J. & Berson, Misha, eds. Young Stages: A Guide to Theatre & Dance for Youth in the San Francisco Bay Area. LC 82-51320. (Illus.). 72p. (Orig.). 1982. pap. 5.00 (ISBN 0-9605896-1-9). Theatre Ctr Bay.

Crane, Diana. The Sanctity of Social Life: Physicians Treatment of Critically Ill Patients. LC 74-15510. 186p. 1975. 14.95x (ISBN 0-87154-209-9). Russell Sage.

Crane, Donald P. Personnel: The Management of Human Resources. 3rd ed. 752p. 1982. text ed. 23.95x (ISBN 0-534-01070-9). Kent Pub Co.

Crane, Dwight B., jt. auth. see Bradley, Stephen P.

Crane, Dwight D. & Riley, Michael J. NOW Accounts. LC 77-6580. 1978. 19.95x o.p. (ISBN 0-669-01612-8). Lexington Bks.

Crane, Edgar G., Jr. Legislative Review of Government Programs: Tools for Accountability. LC 76-12846. (Special Studies). 1977. text ed. 34.95 o.p. (ISBN 0-275-23720-6). Praeger.

Crane, Frederick G. Insurance Principles & Practices. LC 79-19510. 525p. 1980. text ed. 28.95x (ISBN 0-471-01763-9). Wiley.

Crane, Hart. Complete Poems & Selected Letters & Prose of Hart Crane. 1966. pap. 5.95 (ISBN 0-385-01531-3, A537, Anch). Doubleday.

Crane, Hewitt D. The New Social Marketplace: Notes on Effecting Social Change in America's Third Century. LC 80-11674. (Communication & Information Science Ser.). (Illus.). 112p. 1980. text ed. 17.50 (ISBN 0-89391-063-5). Ablex Pub.

Crane, J. D. El Espiritu Santo en la Experiencia del Cristiano. De Lerin, Olivia, tr. Orig. Title: The Christian's Esperience of the Holy Spirit. 128p. 1982. Repr. of 1979 ed. 5.95 (ISBN 0-311-09093-1). Casa Bautista.

--Manual Para Predicadores Laicos. 122p. 1982. pap. 2.10 (ISBN 0-311-42039-7). Casa Bautista.

Crane, J. R. Fighting Yankees & Other Yarns. LC 67-16828. (Illus.). 1973. pap. 3.95 (ISBN 0-87027-137-7). Cumberland Pr.

Crane, James. Guia de Estudios Sobre Manual Para Predicadores Laicos. 88p. 1982. pap. 3.50. Casa Bautista.

Crane, James D. El Sermon Eficaz. 308p. Date not set. pap. 4.50. Casa Bautista.

Crane, James D. & Diaz, Jorge E. Lecciones Para Nuevos Creyentes. 64p. 1981. pap. 1.65 (ISBN 0-311-13835-7); write for info. (ISBN 0-311-13838-1). Casa Bautista.

Crane, John. Laboratory Experiments for Microprocessor Systems. (Illus.). 192p. 1980. pap. text ed. 13.95 (ISBN 0-13-519694-9). P-H.

Crane, John K. T. H. White. (English Authors Ser.). 1974. lib. bdg. 12.95 (ISBN 0-8057-1573-8, Twayne). G K Hall.

Crane, John R., ed. see Zucconi, Paul J.

Crane, Jules M. Introduction to Marine Biology (a Laboratory Text) LC 73-76466. 1973. pap. text ed. 11.95 (ISBN 0-675-08954-9). Additional supplements may be obtained from publisher. Merrill.

Crane, Keith, tr. see Pecsi, Kalman.

Crane, Keith, tr. see Varnusz, Egon.

Crane, Lawrence, jt. auth. see McCormack, P. D.

Crane, Leah. Dark Ecstasy. (Superromances Ser.). 384p. 1983. pap. 2.95 (ISBN 0-373-70066-0, Pub. by Worldwide). Harlequin Bks.

Crane, Mary. Rape: Avoidance & Resistance, A Nonviolent Approach. (Orig.). 1982. pap. 3.50 (ISBN 0-940460-04-1). Peace & Gladness.

Crane, P. W. Worked Examples in Basic Electronics. 1967. inquire for price o.p. (ISBN 0-08-012217-5); pap. 7.00 o.p. (ISBN 0-08-012216-7). Pergamon.

Crane, Ray De see De Crane, Ray.

Crane, Rhonda J. The Politics of International Standards: France & the Color TV War. LC 79-4231. (Communication & Information Science Ser.). 1979. 17.50x (ISBN 0-89391-019-8). Ablex Pub.

Crane, Richard, jt. auth. see Weisz, Michael.

Crane, Ronald S. Languages of Criticism & the Structure of Poetry. LC 54-4048. (Alexander Lectures Ser.). 1953. 20.00x (ISBN 0-8020-5017-4); pap. 6.50 (ISBN 0-8020-6024-2). U of Toronto Pr.

Crane, Santiago D., tr. see Blackwood, A. W.

Crane, Stephan. The Red Badge of Courage. 1983. pap. 2.95 (ISBN 0-14-039021-9). Penguin.

Crane, Stephen. The Blue Hotel & Other Stories. Orig. Title: Maggie & Other Stories. 1982. pap. 3.95 (ISBN 0-671-46036-6). WSP.

--Bride Comes To Yellow Sky. (Creative's Classics Ser.). (Illus.). 40p. (gr. 6-12). 1982. lib. bdg. 7.95 (ISBN 0-87191-827-7). Creative Ed.

--Great Short Works of Stephen Crane: Red Badge of Courage, Monster, Maggie, Open Boat, Blue Hotel, Bride Comes to Yellow Sky & Other Works. rev ed. Colvert, J., ed. pap. 3.50i (ISBN 0-06-083032-8, P3032, PL). Har-Row.

--Maggie: A Girl of the Streets (Eighteen Ninety-Three) Gullason, Thomas A., ed. (Norton Critical Edition). 1980. 20.95x (ISBN 0-393-01222-0); pap. 5.95x (ISBN 0-393-95024-7). Norton.

--The Open Boat. (Creative's Classic Ser.). (Illus.). 64p. (gr. 6-12). 1982. lib. bdg. 7.95 (ISBN 0-87191-826-9). Creative Ed.

--The Red Badge of Courage. (Bantam Classics Ser.). 149p. (Orig.). (gr. 7-12). 1981. pap. 1.50 (ISBN 0-553-21011-4). Bantam.

--Red Badge of Courage. 1951. pap. 3.75 (ISBN 0-394-30945-6, T45, Mod LibC). Modern Lib.

--The Red Badge of Courage. rev. ed. Dixson, Robert J., ed. (American Classics Ser.: Bk. 10). (gr. 9 up). 1974. pap. text ed. 3.25 (ISBN 0-88345-206-5, 18129); cassettes 40.00 (ISBN 0-685-38931-6, 18129); 35.00 o.p. tapes (ISBN 0-685-38932-4). Regents Pub.

--Red Badge of Courage & Selected Stories. (RL 7). 1952. pap. 1.50 (ISBN 0-451-51592-7, CW1592, Sig Classics). NAL.

--The Works of Stephen Crane: Vol. 10: Poems & Literary Remains. Bowers, Fredson, ed. LC 68-8536. 1975. 20.00x (ISBN 0-8139-0610-5). U Pr of Va.

--The Works of Stephen Crane, Vol. 3. Bowers, Fredson, ed. Bd. with The Third Violet; Active Service. LC 68-8536. 492p. 1976. 20.00 (ISBN 0-8139-0666-0). U Pr of Va.

--Works of Stephen Crane: Vol. 4, The O'Ruddy. Bowers, Fredson, ed. LC 68-8536. (Illus.). 362p. 1971. 17.50x (ISBN 0-8139-0341-6). U Pr of Va.

--Works of Stephen Crane: Vol. 5, Tales of Adventure. Bowers, Fredson, ed. LC 68-8536. (Illus.). 242p. 1970. 17.50x (ISBN 0-8139-0302-5). U Pr of Va.

--Works of Stephen Crane: Vol. 7, Tales of Whilomville. Bowers, Fredson, ed. Incl. The Monster; His New Mittens. LC 68-8536. (Illus.). 277p. 1969. 17.50x (ISBN 0-8139-0259-2). U Pr of Va.

--Works of Stephen Crane, Vol. 8: Tales, Sketches, & Reports. Bowers, Fredson, ed. LC 68-8536. (Illus.). 1183p. 1973. 37.50x (ISBN 0-8139-0405-6). U Pr of Va.

--Works of Stephen Crane, Vol. 9, Reports of War. Bowers, Fredson, ed. LC 68-8536. (Illus.). 678p. 1971. 27.50x (ISBN 0-8139-0342-4). U Pr of Va.

Crane, Teresa. Molly. 537p. 1982. 13.95 (ISBN 0-698-11072-2, Coward). Putnam Pub Group.

Crane, Theodore. Architectural Construction: The Choice of Structural Design. 2nd ed. LC 56-7153. 1956. 38.95 (ISBN 0-471-18447-0, Pub. by Wiley-Interscience). Wiley.

Crane, Theodore R., ed. Colleges & the Public Seventeen Eighty-Seven to Eighteen Sixty-Two. LC 63-9583. (Orig.). 1963. text ed. 10.00 (ISBN 0-8077-1200-0); pap. text ed. 5.00x (ISBN 0-8077-1197-7). Tchrs Coll.

Crane, Thomas F. Italian Popular Tales. LC 68-21762. 1968. Repr. of 1885 ed. 37.00x (ISBN 0-8103-3462-3). Gale.

Crane, Verner W. Benjamin Franklin & A Rising People. (Library of American Biography). 219p. 1962. pap. text ed. 5.95 (ISBN 0-316-16012-1). Little.

--The Southern Frontier, 1670-1732. 384p. 1982. pap. text ed. 7.95x (ISBN 0-393-00948-3). Norton.

Crane, Walter. Artist's Reminiscences. LC 68-21763. (Illus.). 1968. Repr. of 1907 ed. 34.00x (ISBN 0-8103-3522-0). Gale.

--The Bases of Design. Stansky, Peter & Shewan, Rodney, eds. LC 76-17756. (Aesthetic Movement & the Arts & Crafts Movement Ser.: Vol. 10). 1977. Repr. of 1898 ed. lib. bdg. 44.00 o.s.i. (ISBN 0-8240-2459-1). Garland Pub.

--Of the Decorative Illustration of Books Old & New. LC 68-30611. 1968. Repr. of 1905 ed. 42.00x (ISBN 0-8103-3299-X). Gale.

Cranefield, Paul F., jt. auth. see Hoffman, Brian F.

Cranefield, Paul F., ed. Two Great Scientists of the Nineteenth Century: Correspondence of Emil Du Bois-Reymond & Carl Ludwig. Ayed, Sabine L., tr. from Ger. LC 79-24140. 204p. 1982. text ed. 15.00x (ISBN 0-8018-2351-X). Johns Hopkins.

Cranefield, Paul F. & Hoffman, Brian F., eds. Paired Pulse Stimulation of the Heart. 1968. 7.50 (ISBN 0-87470-009-4). Rockefeller.

Cranford, Carolyn E., ed. see American Automobile Association.

Crangle, D. J. The Magnetic Properties of Solids. (Structures & Properties of Solids Ser.). 192p. 1977. pap. text ed. 16.95 (ISBN 0-7131-2574-8). E Arnold.

Crank, D. H., et al. Methods of Teaching Shorthand & Transcription. 1982. 17.85 (ISBN 0-07-013465-0). McGraw.

Crankshaw, Edward. The Fall of the House of Habsburg. 1983. pap. 7.95 (ISBN 0-14-006459-1). Penguin.

Cranley, Mecca, jt. auth. see Ziegel, Erna.

Cranmer, John L. Basic Drilling Engineering Manual. 168p. 1982. 49.95x (ISBN 0-87814-199-5). Pennwell Books Division.

Cranmer, John L., Jr. BASIC Reservoir Engineering Manual. 240p. 1982. 49.95x (ISBN 0-87814-196-0). Pennwell Books Division.

Cranmer-Byng, J. L., ed. see Murray, Margaret A.

Crano, William D. & Brewer, Marilyn B. Principles of Research in Social Psychology. (Illus.). 336p. 1972. text ed. 29.50 (ISBN 0-07-013455-3, C). McGraw.

Cranor, Rosalind. Elvis Collectibles. 368p. Date not set. 12.95 (ISBN 0-89145-205-2). Collector Bks.

Cranston, Edwin A., tr. see Okada, Barbara T.

Crant, Phillip, tr. see Bazin, Herve.

Cranton, Elmer M., jt. auth. see Passwater, Richard A.

Cranwell, John P. Gourmet's Gamut. 1979. 7.50 o.p. (ISBN 0-533-03824-3). Vantage.

Cranz, Galen. The Politics of Park Design: A History of Urban Parks in America. (Illus.). 352p. 1982. 25.00x (ISBN 0-262-03086-1). MIT Pr.

Crapanzano, V. & Garrison, V. Case Studies in Spirit Possession. LC 76-26653. 457p. 1977. 43.95 (ISBN 0-471-18460-8). Wiley.

Crapanzano, Vincent. The Hamadsha: A Study in Moroccan Ethnopsychiatry. LC 72-75529. 1973. 33.00x (ISBN 0-520-02241-6); pap. 8.95x (ISBN 0-520-04510-6). U of Cal Pr.

Crapo, Henry H. & Rota, Gian-Carlo. On the Foundations of Combinatorial Theory: Combinatorial Geometries. 1970. pap. 10.00x (ISBN 0-262-53016-3). MIT Pr.

Crapol, Edward P. America for Americans: Economic Nationalism & Anglophobia in the Late Nineteenth Century. LC 71-176287. (Contributions in American History Ser.: No. 28). 248p. 1973. lib. bdg. 27.50 (ISBN 0-8371-6273-4, CRA/). Greenwood.

Crapps, Robert W., et al. Introduction to the New Testament. LC 72-75637. (Illus.). 566p. 1969. 27.50 (ISBN 0-471-07010-6, Pub. by Wiley Med). Wiley.

Crapsey, Edward. Nether Side of New York. LC 69-14919. (Criminology, Law Enforcement, & Social Problems Ser.: No. 46). 1969. Repr. of 1872 ed. 12.00x (ISBN 0-87585-046-4). Patterson Smith.

Crary, jt. auth. see Petrone, Louis.

Crary, A. P., ed. Antarctic Snow & Ice Studies Two. LC 64-60078. (Antarctic Research Ser.: Vol. 16). (Illus.). 1971. 32.00 (ISBN 0-87590-116-6). Am Geophysical.

Crary, David T., et al. Personal Finance. 7th ed. LC 79-27578. 1980. text ed. 29.95x, 718 p. (ISBN 0-471-05639-1). study guide, 208 p. 12.95x (ISBN 0-471-07802-6). Wiley.

Crary, Elizabeth. I Want It. LC 82-2129. (Children's Problem Solving Bks.). (Illus.). 32p. (Orig.). (ps-2). 1982. PLB 8.95 (ISBN 0-9602862-5-X); pap. 3.95 (ISBN 0-9602862-2-5). Parenting Pr.

--I Want to Play. LC 82-3610. (Children's Problem Solving Bks.). (Illus.). 32p. (Orig.). (ps-2). 1982. PLB 8.95 (ISBN 0-9602862-7-6); pap. 3.95 (ISBN 0-9602862-4-1). Parenting Pr.

--My Name Is Not Dummy. (Children's Problem Solving Bks.). (Illus.). 32p. (Orig.). (ps-2). 1983. PLB 8.95 (ISBN 0-9602862-9-2); pap. 3.95 (ISBN 0-9602862-8-4). Parenting Pr.

Crary, Jonathan & Levin, Kim. Eleanor Antin: The Angel of Mercy. (Illus.). 1977. pap. 3.00x (ISBN 0-934418-02-0). La Jolla Mus Contemp Art.

Crasemann, Bernd, ed. Xray & Atomic Inner-Shell Physics, 1982. LC 82-74075. (AIP Conf. Proc. Ser.: No. 94). 802p. 1982. lib. bdg. 44.50 (ISBN 0-88318-193-2). Am Inst Physics.

Crashaw, Richard. Selected Poems. Cayley, Michael, ed. (Fyfield). 1979. 7.95 o.p. (ISBN 0-902145-56-8, Pub. by Carcanet New Pr England); pap. 4.95 o.p. (ISBN 0-902145-57-6). Humanities.

Crass, Richard A. New Trends in Trauma. LC 82-42831. 175p. (Orig.). 1983. pap. price not set (ISBN 0-940122-07-3). Multi Media CO.

Crater, Don R. Cone Crafting. (Illus.). 52p. (Orig.). 1980. pap. 6.95 (ISBN 0-940654-00-8). Tribune Pub.

Craton, Michael. Testing the Chains: Resistance to Slavery in the British West Indies. LC 82-71600. (Illus.). 336p. 1982. 25.00x (ISBN 0-8014-1252-8). Cornell U Pr.

Cratty, B. Teaching Motor Skills. (Man in Action Ser.). (Illus.). 1973. pap. text ed. 10.95 (ISBN 0-13-893958-6). P-H.

Cratty, Bryant J. Active Learning: Games to Enhance Academic Abilities. (Physical Education Ser). (Illus.). 1971. pap. text ed. 11.95 (ISBN 0-13-003491-6). P-H.

--Career Potentials in Physical Activity. LC 79-136631. (Physical Education Ser). 1971. ref. ed. 19.95 (ISBN 0-13-114710-2). P-H.

--Perceptual-Motor Behavior & Educational Processes. (Illus.). 284p. 1971. photocopy ed. spiral 24.50x (ISBN 0-398-00359-9). C C Thomas.

--Psychology in Contemporary Sport: Guidelines for Coaches & Athletes. (Illus.). 336p. 1973. ref. ed. 20.95 (ISBN 0-13-734079-6). P-H.

--Social Psychology in Athletics. (Illus.). 320p. 1981. text ed. 20.95 (ISBN 0-13-817650-7). P-H.

Cratty, Bryant J., jt. auth. see Vanek, Miroslav.

Cratty, Bryant S. Perceptual & Motor Development in Infants & Young Children. 2nd ed. 1979. 19.95 (ISBN 0-13-657023-2). P-H.

Craven, A. H., jt. auth. see Cooke, D.

Craven, B. D. Functions of Several Variables. 144p. 1981. 23.00x (ISBN 0-412-23330-4, Pub by Chapman & Hall England); pap. 9.95x (ISBN 0-412-23340-1). Methuen Inc.

--Mathematical Programming & Control Theory. (Mathematics Ser.). 1978. pap. 14.95x (ISBN 0-412-15500-1, Pub. by Chapman & Hall). Methuen Inc.

Craven, George M. Object & Image: An Introduction to Photography. (Illus.). 256p. 1975. ref. ed. 19.95 o.p. (ISBN 0-13-628925-8). P-H.

Craven, John. Ocean Engineering Systems. 1971. pap. 16.00x o.p. (ISBN 0-262-03040-3). MIT Pr.

Craven, John P. The Management of Pacific Marine Resources: Present Problems & Future Trends. (Illus.). 96p. 1982. lib. bdg. 12.00 o.p. (ISBN 0-86531-424-1). Westview.

Craven, John V. Industrial Organization, Anti-Trust & Public Policy. (Middlebury College Conference Series in Economic Issues). 1982. lib. bdg. 25.00 (ISBN 0-89838-103-7). Kluwer-Nijhoff.

Craven, Margaret. Again Calls the Owl. 1981. pap. 2.50 (ISBN 0-440-10074-7). Dell.

--Again Calls the Owl. (General Ser.). 1980. lib. bdg. 9.50 (ISBN 0-8161-3115-5, Large Print Bks). G K Hall.

--Again Calls the Owl. LC 79-22388. (Illus.). 1980. 7.95 o.p. (ISBN 0-399-12453-5). Putnam Pub Group.

--The Home Front. 252p. 1981. 11.95 (ISBN 0-399-12568-X). Putnam Pub Group.

--Walk Gently This Good Earth. LC 77-22492. 1977. 6.95 o.p. (ISBN 0-399-12040-8). Putnam Pub Group.

Craven, Paul J., Jr., jt. auth. see Baker, Robert A.

Craven, Robert R. Guide to Fishing: Westchester & Putnam Counties. 96p. 1982. pap. 4.95 (ISBN 0-686-35793-0). Outdoor Pubns.

Craven, Robert R., compiled by. Billiards, Bowling, Table Tennis, Pinball & Video Games: A Bibliographic Guide. LC 82-21077. 162p. 1983. lib. bdg. 29.95 (ISBN 0-313-23462-0, CBB/). Greenwood.

Craven, Sara. La Pierre Des Voeux. (Harlequin Collection Ser.). 192p. 1983. pap. 1.95 (ISBN 0-373-49337-1). Harlequin Bks.

--Sup with the Devil. (Harlequin Presents Ser.). 192p. 1983. pap. 1.95 (ISBN 0-373-10599-1). Harlequin Bks.

Craven, Thomas, ed. Treasury of Art Masterpieces. rev. ed. (Illus.). 1958. 19.95 o.p. (ISBN 0-671-74320-1). S&S.

--A Treasury of Art Masterpieces. 1977. pap. 9.95 o.p. (ISBN 0-671-22776-9). S&S.

Craven, Wesley F. The Colonies in Transition, 1660-1713. (New American Nation Ser). 1968. 22.07xi (ISBN 0-06-010913-0, HarpT). Har-Row.

--The Legend of the Founding Fathers. LC 82-25241. (New York University, Stokes Foundation, Anson G. Phelps Lectureship on Early American History Ser.). vii, 222p. 1983. Repr. of 1956 ed. lib. bdg. 27.50x (ISBN 0-313-23840-5, CRLE). Greenwood.

Cravens, Dorras. Reading Colors. (ps-1). 1981. 5.95 (ISBN 0-86653-018-5, GA247). Good Apple.

Cravens, Gwyneth. Love & Work. 368p. 1983. pap. 2.95 (ISBN 0-449-20047-7, Crest). Fawcett.

--Speed of Light. LC 78-21585. 1979. 9.95 o.p. (ISBN 0-671-25127-9). S&S.

Cravens, Richard, jt. auth. see Crockett, James U.

Cravens, Sydney P., jt. ed. see Aycock, Wendell M.

Craver, Charles B., jt. auth. see Smith, Arthur B., Jr.

Craver, Samuel, jt. auth. see Ozmon, Howard.

Cravis, Howard. Communications Network Analysis. LC 75-39314. 1981. 23.95x (ISBN 0-669-00443-X). Lexington Bks.

Crawford. Pathology of Ischaemic Heart Disease. (Postgraduate Pathology Ser.). 1978. 49.95 (ISBN 0-407-00091-7). Butterworth.

Crawford & Wild. Obstetric Clinical Care. 1980. 73.75 (ISBN 0-444-80211-8). Elsevier.

Crawford, Albert B. Incentives to Study: A Survey of Student Opinions. 1929. 47.50x (ISBN 0-685-69804-1). Elliots Bks.

Crawford, Albert B. & Burnham, Paul S. Forecasting College Achievement: A Survey of Aptitude Tests for Higher Education, Part I., General Considerations in the Measurement of Academic Progress. 1946. 39.50x (ISBN 0-686-51387-8). Elliots Bks.

Crawford, Arthur W. Monetary Management Under the New Deal. LC 70-173988. (FDR & the Era of the New Deal Ser.). 380p. 1972. Repr. of 1940 ed. lib. bdg. 49.50 (ISBN 0-306-70374-2). Da Capo.

Crawford, C. C. Genesis, Vol. I. LC 77-1140. (The Bible Study Textbook Ser.). 1966. 14.30 o.s.i. (ISBN 0-89900-002-9). College Pr Pub.

--Survey Course in Christian Doctrine, Vol. 1 & 2. (Bible Study Textbook Ser.). 221p. (Orig.). 1970. 13.80 (ISBN 0-89900-053-3). College Pr Pub.

--What the Bible Says about Faith. LC 82-72621. (What the Bible Says Ser.). 380p. 1982. 13.50 (ISBN 0-89900-089-4). College Pr Pub.

Crawford, Charles. Bad Fall. LC 72-82889. 144p. (gr. 7 up). 1972. PLB 9.89 o.p. (ISBN 0-06-021369-8, HarpJ). Har-Row.

--Three-Legged Race. LC 74-2622. 160p. (gr. 7-12). 1974. PLB 9.89 o.p. (ISBN 0-06-021367-1, HarpJ). Har-Row.

Crawford, Charles, ed. see Vaughan, Virginia C.

Crawford, Charles W., ed. Memphis Memories: Thirty-Two Historic Postcards. (Illus.). 16p. 1983. pap. 3.95 (ISBN 0-87049-382-5). U of Tenn Pr.

Crawford, Clan, Jr. Strategy & Tactics in Municipal Zoning. (Illus.). 1979. 27.95 o.p. (ISBN 0-13-850990-5, Busn). P-H.

Crawford, Diane. Savage Eden, No. 79. 1982. pap. 1.75 (ISBN 0-515-06690-7). Jove Pubns.

Crawford, Donald W. Kant's Aesthetic Theory. LC 73-15259. 200p. 1974. 25.00 o.p. (ISBN 0-299-06510-3, 651). U of Wis Pr.

Crawford, Dorothy J. Kerkeosiris: An Egyptian Village in the Ptolemaic Period. LC 70-96083. (Classical Studies). (Illus.). 1971. 39.50 (ISBN 0-521-07607-2). Cambridge U Pr.

Crawford, E. David, ed. Genitourinary Cancer Surgery. Borden, Thomas A. LC 81-23624. (Illus.). 575p. 1982. text ed. 98.50 (ISBN 0-8121-0812-4). Lea & Febiger.

Crawford, Elizabeth D., jt. ed. see De Montreville, Doris.

Crawford, Elizabeth D., tr. from Ger. The Seven Ravens: The Brothers Grimm. LC 80-25365. Orig. Title: Die Sieben Raven. (Illus.). 24p. (gr. k-3). 1981. 9.95 (ISBN 0-688-00371-0); PLB 9.55 (ISBN 0-688-00372-9). Morrow.

Crawford, Elizabeth D., tr. see Broger, Achim.

Crawford, Elizabeth D., tr. see Fuchshuber, Annegert.

Crawford, Elizabeth D., tr. see Grimm Brothers.

Crawford, Elizabeth D., tr. see Koci, Marta.

Crawford, Elizabeth D., tr. see Rettich, Margaret.

Crawford, Elizabeth D., tr. see Rettich, Margret.

Crawford, Fred D. H. M. Tomlinson. (English Authors Ser.). 1981. lib. bdg. 14.95 (ISBN 0-8057-6800-9, Twayne). G K Hall.

--Mixing Memory & Desire: The Waste Land & Modern British Novels. LC 82-477. 170p. 1982. 17.95x (ISBN 0-271-00308-1). Pa St U Pr.

Crawford, Harold B., ed. see McPartlnd, Joseph F.

Crawford, Harold B., ed. see Transamerica Delaval Inc.

Crawford, Harriet, ed. Subterranean Britain. LC 79-16858. 1979. 20.00x (ISBN 0-312-77477-X). St Martin.

Crawford, J. R. Lovely Peggy: A Play in Three Acts Based on the Love Romance of Margaret Woffington & David Garrick. 1911. 19.50x (ISBN 0-686-51412-2). Elliots Bks.

Crawford, James. Australian Courts of Law. 1982. 42.50x (ISBN 0-19-554344-0). Oxford U Pr.

--The Creation of States in International Law. 1979. 58.00x (ISBN 0-19-825347-8). Oxford U Pr.

Crawford, Jeffrey L., et al. Computer Application in Mental Health: A Source Book. 1983. price not set prof ref (ISBN 0-88410-712-4). Ballinger Pub.

Crawford, Jerry L. Acting: In Person & In Style. 3rd ed. 480p. 1983. pap. text ed. write for info. (ISBN 0-697-04234-0). Wm C Brown.

Crawford, John, jt. auth. see Le Sueur, Meridel.

Crawford, John & Morin, J. Donald, eds. The Eye in Childhood. Date not set. price not set (ISBN 0-8089-1503-7). Grune.

Crawford, John C. Totontepec Mixe Phonotagmemics. (Publications in Linguistics & Related Fields Ser.: No. 8). 197p. 1963. pap. 3.00x o.p. (ISBN 0-88312-008-9); pap. 3.00 (ISBN 0-88312-408-4); microfiche 3.00 (ISBN 0-88312-313-4). Summer Inst Ling.

Crawford, John S. Wolves, Bears & Bighorns: Wilderness Observations & Experiences of a Professional Outdoorsman. LC 80-22007. (Illus.). 192p. 1980. 25.00 (ISBN 0-88240-146-7); pap. 19.00 (ISBN 0-88240-144-0). Alaska Northwest.

Crawford, John T., III & Hustrulid, William A., eds. Open Pit Planning & Design. LC 79-52269. (Illus.). 367p. 1979. text ed. 30.00x (ISBN 0-89520-253-0). Soc Mining Eng.
Crawford, John W. Discourse: Essay on English & American Literature. (Costerus New Ser.: No. XIV). 1978. pap. text ed. 25.00x o.p. (ISBN 90-6203-672-4). Humanities.
Crawford, Joyce. Stranger in Our Darkness. LC 68-57163. 1968. 8.95 (ISBN 0-87716-000-7, Pub. by Moore Pub Co). F Apple.
Crawford, Kenneth, jt. auth. see Simmons, Paul D.
Crawford, Linda. Vanishing Acts. LC 81-84523. 320p. 1982. 15.95 (ISBN 0-399-31000-2). Seaview Bks.
Crawford, Lucy. Supervisory Skills in Marketing. Dorr, Eugene, ed. (Occupational Manuals & Projects in Marketing Ser.). (Illus.). (gr. 9-10). 1977. pap. text ed. 7.32 (ISBN 0-07-013471-5, G); teacher's manual & key 4.50 (ISBN 0-07-013472-3). McGraw.
Crawford, Lucy & Lynch, Richard. Finance & Credit. (Career Competencies in Marketing). (Illus.). (gr. 11-12). 1978. pap. text ed. 7.32 (ISBN 0-07-013481-2, G); teacher's manual & key 4.50 (ISBN 0-07-013482-0). McGraw.
Crawford, Lucy C. & Meyer, Warren G. Organization & Administration of Distributive Education. LC 70-187803. 336p. 1972. text ed. 20.95 (ISBN 0-675-09112-8). Merrill.
Crawford, Marion A., tr. see Balzac, Honore De.
Crawford, Marjorie F. Kinder Art Drawing. (Illus.). 57p. 1982. 7.00 (ISBN 0-9610102-0-7). Edutech.
Crawford, Mark H., jt. ed. see Jablonski, Donna M.
Crawford, Marshall A., jt. auth. see Grauer, Robert G.
Crawford, Martin. Air Pollution Control Theory. 1976. text ed. 39.95 (ISBN 0-07-013490-1, C); solutions manual 27.95 (ISBN 0-07-013491-X). McGraw.
Crawford, Mary C. In the Days of the Pilgrim Fathers. LC 74-129572. 1970. Repr. of 1921 ed. 37.00x (ISBN 0-8103-3470-4). Gale.
--Little Pilgrimages Among Old New England Inns: Being an Account of Little Journeys to Various Quaint Inns & Hostelries of Colonial New England. LC 76-107629. (Illus.). 1970. Repr. of 1907 ed. 34.00x (ISBN 0-8103-3536-0). Gale.
--Social Life in Old New England. LC 71-102645. (Tower Bks). (Illus.). 1971. Repr. of 1914 ed. 47.00 o.p. (ISBN 0-8103-3924-2). Gale.
Crawford, Michael. The Roman Republic. (Fontana History of the Ancient World Ser.). 1978. text ed. 24.75x o.p. (ISBN 0-391-00832-3). Humanities.
Crawford, Michael, jt. auth. see Kays, William M.
Crawford, Michael & Whitehead, David, eds. Archaic & Classical Greece: A Selection of Ancient Sources in Translation. LC 82-4355. 700p. Date not set. price not set (ISBN 0-521-22775-5); pap. price not set (ISBN 0-521-29638-2). Cambridge U Pr.
Crawford, R. J. Plastics Engineering. (Illus.). 360p. 1981. 75.00 (ISBN 0-08-026262-7); pap. 25.00 (ISBN 0-08-026263-5). Pergamon.
Crawford, R. M. M., jt. ed. see Hook, Donal D.
Crawford, Richard. Andrew Law, American Psalmodist. (Music Ser.). (Illus.). xix, 424p. 1981. Repr. of 1968 ed. lib. bdg. 35.00 (ISBN 0-306-76090-8). Da Capo.
--Men, Women & Bridge: Startling Tales of the Bridge Table. LC 77-93316. (Illus.). 1978. 8.95 o.p. (ISBN 0-8069-4934-1); lib. bdg. 8.29 o.p. (ISBN 0-8069-4935-X). Sterling.
Crawford, Richard, ed. The Civil War Songbook: Complete Original Sheet Music for 37 Songs. (Illus.). 157p. 1977. pap. 6.00 (ISBN 0-486-23422-3). Dover.
Crawford, Robert. In Art We Trust: Boards of Trustees in the Performing Arts. 88p. 1982. pap. text ed. 12.50x (ISBN 0-9602942-3-6). Drama Bk.
Crawford, Robert, jt. auth. see Barnard, David.
Crawford, Robert H. Mosfet in Circuit Design. (Texas Instruments Electronics Ser). (Illus.). 1967. 38.50 (ISBN 0-07-013475-8, P&RB). McGraw.
Crawford, Robert P. The Techniques of Creative Thinking. 1964. Repr. of 1954 ed. flexible cover 7.00 (ISBN 0-87034-010-7). Fraser Pub Co.
Crawford, Ronald L. Lignin Biodegradation & Transformation. LC 80-39557. 154p. 1981. 33.95x (ISBN 0-471-05743-6, Pub. by Wiley-Interscience). Wiley.
Crawford, Rudd A., Jr. & Copp, David H. Introduction to Computer Programming. 1969. pap. 7.32 (ISBN 0-395-02252-5). HM.
Crawford, S. Cromwell. The Evolution of Hindu Ethical Ideals. (Asian Studies at Hawaii: No. 28). 197p. 1982. pap. text ed. 14.00x (ISBN 0-8248-0782-0). UH Pr.
Crawford, T., ed. see McKinney, B.
Crawford, Tad. Legal Guide for the Visual Artist. 1977. pap. 6.95 (ISBN 0-8015-4472-6, Hawthorn). Dutton.
Crawford, Teri. The First Wild West Rodeo. LC 78-14549. (Famous Firsts Ser.). (Illus.). 1978. PLB 10.76 (ISBN 0-89547-058-6). Silver.
--Protectors of the Wilderness: The First Forest Rangers. LC 78-14492. (Famous Firsts Ser.). (Illus.). 1978. PLB 10.76 (ISBN 0-89547-049-7). Silver.
Crawford, W. Rex, tr. see Vasconcelos, Jose.
Crawford, William. Report on the Penitentiaries of the United States. LC 69-16235. (Criminology, Law Enforcement, & Social Problems Ser.: No. 97). 1969. Repr. of 1835 ed. 45.00x (ISBN 0-87585-097-9). Patterson Smith.
Crawford, Williame & Kerstrat, Francoise. New Code of Civil Procedure in France, Bk. 1. De Grivart, tr. from Fr. LC 77-25936. 214p. 1978. 32.50 (ISBN 0-379-20266-2). Oceana.
Crawford-Currie, Ronald. Cross-Country Skiing. LC 82-8620. 160p. 1982. 19.95 (ISBN 0-442-21512-6). Van Nos Reinhold.
Crawfurd, M. d'A, jt. auth. see Clinical Research Centre Symposium, Sept. 1981, 2nd.
Crawhall, Joseph. Old Aunt Elspa's ABC. (Illus.). pap. 3.95 (ISBN 0-85967-503-3). Green Tiger Pr.
--Quaint Cuts in the Chap Book Style. 88p. 1974. Repr. of 1889 ed. 4.50 (ISBN 0-486-23020-1). Dover.
Crawley, Aileen. The Shadow of God. 320p. 1983. 12.95 (ISBN 0-312-71406-8). St Martin.
Crawley, C. W. The Question of Greek Independence: A Study of British Policy in the Near East, 1821-1833. LC 74-144130. 272p. 1973. Repr. of 1930 ed. 23.50x (ISBN 0-86527-161-5). Fertig.
Crawley, Eduardo. Dictators Never Die: Nicaragua & the Somoza Dynasty. LC 78-31151. 1979. 18.95 (ISBN 0-312-20007-2). St Martin.
Crawley, Ernest. Mystic Rose: A Study of Primitive Marriage & of Primitive Thought in Its Bearing on Marriage, 2 Vols. rev. & enl. ed. Besterman, Theodore, ed. LC 72-164193. 1971. Repr. of 1927 ed. 47.00x (ISBN 0-8103-3781-9). Gale.
Crawley, Frank, jt. auth. see Bartholomew, Rolland.
Crawley, Geoffrey, ed. British Journal of Photography Annual 1983. 123rd ed. (Illus.). 222p. 1983. 24.95 (ISBN 0-900414-28-6, Pub. by Henry Greenwood & Co Ltd England). Writers Digest.
Crawley, Gerald M. Energy. (Illus.). 320p. 1975. text ed. 21.95x (ISBN 0-02-325580-3, 32558). Macmillan.
Crawley, Lawrence, et al. Reproduction, Sex, & Preparation for Marriage. 2nd ed. (Illus.). 256p. 1973. pap. 14.95 (ISBN 0-13-773937-0). P-H.
Crawley, Richard, tr. see Thucydides.
Crawley, Stanley M. & Dillion, Robert W. Steel Buildings: Analysis & Design. 2nd ed. LC 76-39934. 591p. 1977. text ed. 35.95x (ISBN 0-471-18552-3). Wiley.
Crawley, Tony. Screen Dreams: The Hollywood Pinup. (Illus.). 160p. (Orig.). 1982. pap. 9.95 (ISBN 0-933328-40-0). Delilah Bks.
Crawley, William B., Jr. Bill Tuck: A Political Life in Harry Byrd's Virginia. LC 78-16751. (Illus.). 281p. 1978. 14.95x (ISBN 0-8139-0766-7). U Pr of Va.
Crawley, Winston & Miller, Charles. A Structured Approach to FORTRAN. 1982. text ed. 24.95 (ISBN 0-8359-7092-2); pap. text ed. 16.95 (ISBN 0-8359-7091-4); instrs'. manual avail. (ISBN 0-8359-7093-0). Reston.
Crawshaw, Alwyn. How To Paint with Acrylics. 64p. 1982. pap. 5.95 (ISBN 0-89586-158-5). H P Bks.
--How To Paint with Watercolors. 64p. 1982. pap. 5.95 (ISBN 0-89586-157-7). H P Bks.
C. Raymond Van Dusen. Self-Publishing: How to Cash in on Your Writing Ability Now. (Royal Court Reports Ser.: No. 3). (Illus.). 67p. (Orig.). 1982. pap. 3.95 (ISBN 0-941354-02-4). Royal Court.
Crayton, Spurgeon E. Screams of Protest. (Illus.). 1982. 10.00 (ISBN 0-8315-0188-X). Speller.
Craz, Albert G. Getting to Know the Mississippi River. (Getting to Know Ser.). (Illus.). (gr. 3-5). 1965. PLB 3.97 o.p. (ISBN 0-698-30136-6, Coward). Putnam Pub Group.
Craz, Albert G. & Mavragis, Edward P. Writing: The Business Letter. (Writing Ser.). 68p. 1981. wkbk. 3.95 (ISBN 0-9602800-1-4). Comp Pr.
--Writing: The Composition. (Writing Ser.). 66p. 1981. wkbk. 3.95 (ISBN 0-9602800-3-0). Comp Pr.
--Writing: The Report. (Writing Ser.). 66p. 1981. wkbk. 3.95 (ISBN 0-9602800-2-2). Comp Pr.
CRDI, Ottawa. Les Priorities de la Recherca sur la Politique Scientifique et Technique en Africque: Compte Rendu du Colloque tenu a l'Universite d'Ife (Nigeria) du 3-6 Decembre 1979. 32p. 1981. pap. 5.00 (ISBN 0-88936-280-7, IDRC-162F, IDRC). Unipub.
--Le Role des Arbres au Sahel: Compte Rendu du Colloque tenu a Dakar (Senegal) du 5 au 10 Novembre 1979. 92p. 1980. pap. 7.00 o.p. (ISBN 0-88936-262-9, IDRC-158F, IDRC). Unipub.
Creagh, Patrick. The Lament of the Border-Guard. 63p. 1980. pap. text ed. 7.95x (ISBN 0-85635-314-0, Pub. by Carcanet New Pr England). Humanities.
Creal, Margaret. The Man Who Sold Prayers. (Bessie Bks.). 192p. 1983. 12.45i (ISBN 0-06-039017-4, HarpT). Har-Row.
Crealock, Henry H. Deer Stalking in the Highlands of Scotland. 1982. 500.00x (ISBN 0-686-94026-1, Pub. by A Atha Pub). State Mutual Bk.
Creamer, Robert H. Machine Design. 2nd ed. LC 75-12093. (Engineering Technology Ser.). (Illus.). 544p. 1976. text ed. 26.95 (ISBN 0-201-01178-6); instr's guide 1.50 (ISBN 0-201-01179-4). A-W.
Creamer, T. & Hixson, S., eds. Chinese Dictionaries: An Extensive Bibliography of Dictionaries in Chinese & Other Languages. LC 82-923. 432p. 1982. lib. bdg. 49.95 (ISBN 0-686-97183-3, MDC). Greenwood.
Crean, John E., jt. auth. see Briggs, Jeanine.
Crean, John E., et al. Deutsche Sprach und Landeskunde. Incl. Ratyck, Joanna. wkbk. 8.00 (ISBN 0-394-32649-0); Crean, John E. lab manual 8.00 (ISBN 0-394-32650-4). 608p. 1981. text ed. 22.00 (ISBN 0-394-32648-2). Random.
Creasey, John. The Baron & the Unfinished Portrait. 190p. 1983. pap. 2.95 (ISBN 0-8027-3002-7). Walker & Co.
--The Baron in France. 190p. 1983. pap. 2.95 (ISBN 0-8027-3001-9). Walker & Co.
--Help from the Baron. 188p. 1983. pap. 2.95 (ISBN 0-8027-3000-0). Walker & Co.
--The Toff & the Fallen Angels. 192p. 1983. pap. 2.95 (ISBN 0-8027-3004-3). Walker & Co.
Creasey, William A. Cancer: An Introduction. (Illus.). 1981. text ed. 21.95x (ISBN 0-19-502951-8); pap. text ed. 14.95x (ISBN 0-19-502952-6). Oxford U Pr.
--Drug Disposition in Humans: The Basis of Clinical Pharmacology. (Illus.). 1979. text ed. 21.95x (ISBN 0-19-502460-5); pap. text ed. 13.95x (ISBN 0-19-502461-3). Oxford U Pr.
Creasey, William A., ed. Clinical Pharmacology. Symposium Proceedings. 248p. 1975. text ed. 32.00 (ISBN 0-08-018949-0). Pergamon.
Creasman, William T., jt. auth. see DiSaia, Philip J.
Creason, Nancy S. Effects of External Funding: On Instructional Components of Baccalaureate & Higher Degree Nursing Programs. (League Exchange Ser.: No. 119). 74p. 1978. 5.95 (ISBN 0-686-38147-5, 15-1732). Natl League Nurse.
Creasy, Robert K., jt. auth. see Hales, Dianne.
Creasy, Rosalind. The Complete Book of Edible Landscaping. LC 81-14465. (Illus.). 400p. (Orig.). 1982. 25.00 (ISBN 0-87156-249-9); pap. 14.95 (ISBN 0-87156-278-2). Sierra.
Creative Concepts. Bluegrass Complete: Complete Words, Music & Guitar Chords for Eighty-Nine Songs. (Illus.). 192p. (Orig.). pap. 9.95 (ISBN 0-486-24503-9). Dover.
Creative Services Division. The Official NFL Encyclopedia of Pro Football. 1982. 27.95 (ISBN 0-453-00431-8, H431). NAL.
Creaton, David. The Beasts of My Fields. 1978. pap. 1.95 o.s.i. (ISBN 0-380-38497-3, 38497). Avon.
Crebillon, Claude P. Letters from the Marchioness De M to the Count De R, Vol. 60. LC 72-170590. (Novel in England, 1700-1775). lib. bdg. 50.00 o.s.i. (ISBN 0-8240-0572-4). Garland Pub.
--The Wayward Head & Heart. Bray, Barbara, tr. LC 78-16439. 1978. Repr. of 1963 ed. lib. bdg. 20.00x (ISBN 0-313-20578-7, CRWH). Greenwood.
Crecine, John P., ed. The New Educational Programs in Public Policy, the First Decade. (Public Policy & Government Organizations: Supplement No. 1). 275p. 1981. 42.50 (ISBN 0-686-73775-X). Jai Pr.
--Public Policy & Government Organization, Vol. 1. 350p. 1981. 42.50 (ISBN 0-89232-044-3). Jai Pr.
--Public Policy & Government Organization, Vol. 2. 350p. 1981. 42.50 (ISBN 0-89232-210-1). Jai Pr.
Crecy, Jeanne. Night Hunters: Winter Keeper. 1982. pap. 2.50 (ISBN 0-451-11581-3, AE1581, Sig). NAL.
Crede, Charles E., jt. auth. see Harris, Cyril M.
Creech, Kenneth, jt. auth. see Easley, Wayne.
Creed, R. S., et al. Reflex Activity of the Spinal Cord. (Illus.). 1972. 32.50x (ISBN 0-19-857355-3). Oxford U Pr.
Creed, Virginia. France. rev. ed. LC 77-83911. (World Culture Ser.). (Illus.). 168p. (gr. 6 up). 1978. text ed. 11.20 ea. 1-4 copies o.s.i. (ISBN 0-88296-188-8); text ed. 8.96 ea. 5 or more copies o.s.i.; tchrs' guide 8.94 o.s.i. (ISBN 0-686-85956-1). Fideler.
Creed, Virginia & Douglas Jackson, W. A. France & Soviet Union. rev. ed. LC 77-83892. (World Cultures Ser.). (Illus.). 298p. (gr. 6 up). 1978. text ed. 12.43 ea. 1-4 copies (ISBN 0-88296-154-3); text ed. 9.94 ea. 5 or more copies; tchrs'. guide 8.96 (ISBN 0-88296-369-4). Fideler.
Creedy, Judith & Wall, Norbert. Real Estate Investment by Objective. LC 79-14085. (Illus.). 416p. 1979. 24.95 (ISBN 0-07-013495-2, P&RB). McGraw.
Creedy, Thomas. Economics of Labor. 1982. text ed. 19.95 (ISBN 0-408-10826-6). Butterworth.
Creekmore, Anna M. & Pokornowski, Ila M., eds. Textile History: Readings. LC 81-40873. (Illus.). 342p. (Orig.). 1982. lib. bdg. 34.75 (ISBN 0-8191-2197-5); pap. text ed. 14.75 (ISBN 0-8191-2198-3). U Pr of Amer.
Creekmore, Betsey B. Making Gifts from Oddments & Outdoor Materials. (Illus.). 1970. 8.95 (ISBN 0-8208-0069-4). Hearthside.
--Traditional American Crafts: A Practical Guide to 300 Years of Methods & Materials. LC 68-8517. (Illus.). 1968. 10.00 (ISBN 0-8208-0327-8). Hearthside.
Creekmore, Hubert, ed. Lyrics of the Middle Ages. LC 69-13869. Repr. of 1959 ed. lib. bdg. 15.75x (ISBN 0-8371-0365-7, CRLM). Greenwood.
Creel, Herlee G., et al. Literary Chinese by the Inductive Method, 3 Vols. Incl. Vol. 1. Hsiao Ching. rev ed. LC 48-8466. 1948. Repr. 8.50x (ISBN 0-226-12034-1); Vol. 2. Selections from the Lun Yu. LC 38-1458. 1939. 14.00x (ISBN 0-226-12032-5); Vol 3. The Mencius. LC 38-1458. 1952. 14.00x (ISBN 0-226-12033-3). U of Chicago Pr.
Creel, Herrlee G. Origins of Statecraft in China: The Western Chou Empire, Vol. 1. LC 73-110072. 1970. 25.00x (ISBN 0-226-12043-0); pap. 8.95, 1983 (ISBN 0-226-12044-9). U of Chicago Pr.
--What Is Taoism? And Other Studies in Chinese Cultural History. LC 77-102905. 1977. pap. 3.95 o.s.i. (ISBN 0-226-12042-2, P724, Phoen). U of Chicago Pr.
--What Is Taoism? And Other Studies in Chinese Cultural History. LC 77-102905. (Midway Reprint Ser.). viii, 192p. 1982. pap. text ed. 8.00x (ISBN 0-226-12047-3). U of Chicago Pr.
Creeley, Robert. The Collected Poems of Robert Creeley. LC 81-19668. 576p. 1983. 27.50 (ISBN 0-520-04243-3). U of Cal Pr.
Creeley, Robert, jt. auth. see Olson, Charles.
Creer, K. M., ed. see Royal Society Discussion Meeting, January 27-28, 1982, Proceedings.
Crees, J. Meredith Revisited & Other Essays. LC 67-30813. (Studies in Fiction, No. 34). 1969. Repr. of 1921 ed. lib. bdg. 28.95x (ISBN 0-8383-0713-2). Haskell.
Creese, Raymond, ed. see Unwin, Raymond.
Creese, Thomas M. & Haralick, Robert M. Differential Equations for Engineers. 1978. text ed. 27.50 (ISBN 0-07-013510-X, C); instructor's manual 15.00 (ISBN 0-07-013511-8). McGraw.
Creff, Albert & Wernick, Robert. Dr. Creff's 1-2-3 Sports Diet. 1979. 8.95 o.p. (ISBN 0-698-10890-6, Coward). Putnam Pub Group.
Crefield, Donna. From This Land. 384p. (Orig.). 1980. pap. 2.50 o.p. (ISBN 0-523-40522-7). Pinnacle Bks.
Creger, W. P., et al, eds. Annual Review of Medicine: Selected Topics in the Clinical Sciences, Vol. 34. LC 51-1659. (Illus.). 1983. text ed. 27.00 (ISBN 0-8243-0534-5). Annual Reviews.
Creger, William P., et al, eds. Annual Review of Medicine: Selected Topics in the Clinical Sciences, Vol. 27. LC 51-1659. (Illus.). 1976. text ed. 17.00 (ISBN 0-8243-0527-2). Annual Reviews.
Cregier, Don M. Bounder from Wales: Lloyd George's Career Before the First World War. LC 76-4894. 328p. 1976. 22.00x (ISBN 0-8262-0203-9). U of Mo Pr.
--Chiefs Without Indians: Asquith, Lloyd George, & the Liberal Remnant, 1916-1935. LC 82-17546. (Illus.). 330p. (Orig.). 1983. lib. bdg. 23.50 (ISBN 0-8191-2806-6); pap. text ed. 12.50 (ISBN 0-8191-2807-4). U Pr of Amer.
Creigh, Dorothy W. A Primer for Local Historical Societies. LC 76-231. 1976. pap. 7.95 (ISBN 0-910050-20-1). AASLH.
--Tales from the Prairie, 4 vols. Incl. Vol. 1. 1977. pap. 2.95 (ISBN 0-934858-03-9); Vol. 2. 1973. pap. 3.95 (ISBN 0-934858-04-7); Vol. 3. 1976. pap. 5.95 (ISBN 0-934858-05-5); Vol. 4. 1979. pap. 9.95 (ISBN 0-934858-06-3). LC 74-157038. (Illus.). Set. pap. write for info. Adams County.
Creighton, B., tr. see Junger, Ernst.
Creighton, Douglas G. Jacques-Francois Deluc of Geneva & His Friendship with Jean-Jacques Rousseau. LC 82-5332. (Romance Monographs: No. 42). 128p. 1983. write for info. Romance.
Creighton, Helen. Law Every Nurse Should Know. 3rd ed. LC 74-31835. 385p. 1975. text ed. 13.00 o.p. (ISBN 0-7216-2752-8). Saunders.
Creighton, Joanne V. Joyce Carol Oates. (United States Authors Ser.). 1979. lib. bdg. 10.95 (ISBN 0-8057-7212-X, Twayne). G K Hall.
Creighton, John. British Buses Since 1945. (Illus.). 144p. 1983. 16.95 (ISBN 0-7137-1258-9, Pub. by Blandford Pr England). Sterling.
Creighton, Mandell. Cardinal Wolsey. 226p. 1982. Repr. of 1888 ed. lib. bdg. 35.00 (ISBN 0-8495-0878-9). Arden Lib.
Creighton, Margaret S. Dogwatch & Liberty Days: Seafaring Life in the Nineteenth Century. LC 73-1982. (Illus.). 85p. 1982. pap. 12.50 (ISBN 0-87577-070-3). Peabody Mus Salem.
Creighton, Thomas H. The Lands of Hawaii: Their Use & Misuse. LC 77-16124. 1978. text ed. 17.50x (ISBN 0-8248-0482-1). UH Pr.
Creighton, Thomas R. Southern Rhodesia & the Central African Federation. LC 75-32456. (Illus.). 1976. Repr. of 1961 ed. lib. bdg. 18.50x (ISBN 0-8371-8543-2, CRSR). Greenwood.
Creighton, Warren S. The Contributions of Mussolini to the Civilization of Mankind. (Illus.). 137p. 1981. 61.55 (ISBN 0-89266-282-4). Am Classical Coll Pr.
--The Contributions of Mussolini to the Civilization of Mankind. (Illus.). 115p. 1983. 75.45 (ISBN 0-86722-038-4). Inst Econ Pol.
Crelinsten, Ronald D. & Szabo, Denis. Hostage-Taking: Theory & Practice. (Illus.). 1979. 18.95x (ISBN 0-669-02841-X). Lexington Bks.
Crelinsten, Ronald D., et al, eds. Terrorism & Criminal Justice. LC 77-887185. (Illus.). 1978. 19.95x (ISBN 0-669-01983-6). Lexington Bks.
Crellin, John K. Medical Care in Pioneer Illinois. LC 82-81512. (Southern Illinois University Medical Humanities Ser.). (Illus.). 128p. 1982. 15.95 (ISBN 0-686-35864-3). Pearson Museum.

Cremer, L. & Muller, H. Principles & Applications of Room Acoustics, Vols. 1 & 2. Shultz, T. J., tr. (Illus.). 1982. Geometrical, Statistical & Psychological Room Acoustics. 94.50 (ISBN 0-85334-114-1, Pub. by Applied Sci England); Wave Theoretical Room Acoustics. 69.75 (ISBN 0-85334-113-3). Elsevier.

Cremers, A. B. & Kriegel, H. P., eds. Theoretical Computer Science: Proceedings, Dortmund, FRG, 1983. (Lecture Notes in Computer Science Ser.: Vol. 145). 367p. 1983. pap. 16.50 (ISBN 0-387-11973-6). Springer-Verlag.

Cremers van der Does, Eline. The Agony of Fashion. (Illus.). 128p. 1980. 17.50 o.p. (ISBN 0-7137-1058-6, Pub. by Blandford Pr England). Sterling.

Cremin, B. J., et al. Radiological Diagnosis of Digestive Tract Disorders in the Newborn: A Guide to Radiologists, Surgeons, & Paediatricians. (Illus.). 1973. 21.95 o.p. (ISBN 0-407-38375-1). Butterworth.

Cremin, Lawrence A. The Wonderful World of Ellwood Patterson Cubberley: An Essay on the Historiography of American Education. LC 65-20759. (Orig.). 1965. text ed. 6.50x (ISBN 0-8077-1215-9); pap. text ed. 3.25x (ISBN 0-8077-1212-4). Tchrs Coll.

Cremin, Lawrence A., ed. Republic & the School: Horace Mann on the Education of Free Men. 7th ed. LC 57-9102. (Orig.). 1957. pap. text ed. 4.50x (ISBN 0-8077-1206-X). Tchrs Coll.

Cremlyn, R. Pesticides: Preparation & Mode of Action. LC 77-28590. 1978. 46.00x (ISBN 0-471-99631-9, Pub. by Wiley-Interscience); pap. 24.95 (ISBN 0-471-27669-3). Wiley.

Cremona, Joseph. Buogiorno Italia! (Illus.). 304p. (Ital.). 1982. pap. text ed. 8.95 (ISBN 0-563-16479-4, 55261, Pub. by British Broadcasting Corp England). EMC.

Cremony, John C. Life Among the Apaches. LC 80-25871. (Classics of the Old West Ser.). PLB 17.28 (ISBN 0-8094-3955-7). Silver.

--Life among the Apaches. LC 82-16106. 322p. 1983. pap. 6.50e not set (ISBN 0-8032-6312-0, BB 828, Bison). U of Nebr Pr.

Crener, Maxime A., jt. auth. see Overgaard, Herman O.

Crenner, James. Aging Ghost. 1964. 3.00 o.p. (ISBN 0-8233-0015-3). Golden Quill.

Crenshaw. Bedside Manners. 1983. 14.95 (ISBN 0-07-013581-9). McGraw.

Crenshaw, A. H., jt. auth. see Edmonson, A. S.

Crenshaw, George. Belvedere. 256p. (Orig.). 1982. pap. 2.50 (ISBN 0-523-49004-6). Pinnacle Bks.

--Belvedere III. 256p. 1983. pap. 2.50 (ISBN 0-523-49027-5). Pinnacle Bks.

Crenshaw, Martha, ed. see Horowitz, Irving L. & Dror, Yehezkel.

Crenshaw, Mary A. Prescription Junkie: One Woman's Triumph over Pill Addiction. 288p. 1980. 10.95 o.p. (ISBN 0-517-53746-X, C N Potter Bks). Crown.

--The Super-Foods Diet Book. 256p. 1983. 12.95 (ISBN 0-02-528820-2). Macmillan.

Crepeau, Georges. Belanger: Ou L'Histoire D'un Crime. (Novels by Franco-Americans in New England 1850-1940 Ser.). 49p. (Orig., Fr.). (gr. 10 up). 1979. pap. 4.50 (ISBN 0-911409-14-9). Natl Mat Dev.

Crepin, F. Primitiae Monographiae Rosarum: Meteriaux Pour Servir a L'Histoire Des Roses, 6 pts. in 1 vol. 1972. Repr. of 1882 ed. 40.00 (ISBN 3-7682-0759-5). Lubrecht & Cramer.

Crescent. I Hate My Brother Harry. LC 82-47706. (Illus.). 32p. (ps-3). 1983. 9.57i (ISBN 0-06-021757-X, HarpJ); PLB 9.89g (ISBN 0-06-021758-8). Har-Row.

Cresci, Martha W. Complete Book of Model Business Letters. 1976. 16.95 (ISBN 0-13-157438-8). P-H.

Crescimanno, Russell. Culture, Consciousness, & Beyond: An Introduction. LC 82-17425. 102p. (Orig.). lib. bdg. 18.75 (ISBN 0-8191-2811-2); pap. text ed. 8.00 (ISBN 0-8191-2812-0). U Pr of Amer.

Crespi, R. S. Patenting in the Biological Sciences: A Practical Guide for Research Scientists in Biotechnology & the Pharmaceutical & Agrochemical Industries. LC 81-19771. 1982. 38.00 (ISBN 0-471-10151-6, Pub. by Wiley-Interscience). Wiley.

Crespigny, R. de see De Crespigny, R. R.

Crespin, Vick S., et al. Walker's Manual for Construction Cost Estimating. Frank R. Walker Company, ed. (Illus.). 128p. 1981. pap. 12.95 (ISBN 0-911592-85-7). F R Walker.

Crespy, Mary A., ed. Pipeline Rates on Crude Petroleum Oil. 800p. Date not set. 150.00 (ISBN 0-686-29443-2). CSG Pr.

Cress, Donald A., tr. see Descartes, Rene.

Cress, Donald A., tr. see Rousseau, Jean-Jacques.

Cress, Mary. Automation. (Science Ser.). 24p. (gr. 6 up). 1977. wkbk. 5.00 (ISBN 0-8209-0153-9, S-15). ESP.

Cress, P., et al. Fortran IV with Watfor & Watfiv. 1970. ref. ed. 18.95 (ISBN 0-13-329433-1). P-H.

--Structured FORTRAN with Watfiv-S. 1980. pap. 18.95 (ISBN 0-13-854752-1). P-H.

Cresser, M. S., jt. auth. see Chalmers, R. A.

Cresser, Malcolm S. Solvent Extraction in Flame Spectroscopic Analysis. 1978. 52.95 o.p. (ISBN 0-408-71307-0). Butterworth.

Cressey, Donald R. Other People's Money: A Study in the Social Psychology of Embezzlement. LC 73-7907. (Criminology, Law Enforcement, & Social Problems Ser.: No. 202). 204p. 1973. Repr. of 1953 ed. lib. bdg. 15.00x (ISBN 0-87585-202-5). Patterson Smith.

Cressey, Donald R. & Ward, David A., eds. Delinquency, Crime & Social Process. 1969. text ed. 29.50 scp o.p. (ISBN 0-06-041414-6, HarpC). Har-Row.

Cressey, George B. Asia's Land & People. 3rd ed. (Geography Ser). (Illus.). 1963. text ed. 21.50 o.p. (ISBN 0-07-013640-8, C). McGraw.

Cressey, Paul G. Taxi-Dance Hall: A Sociological Study in Commercialized Recreation & City Life. LC 68-57596. (Illus.). 1968. Repr. of 1932 ed. lib. bdg. 19.00x (ISBN 0-8371-0366-5, CRTD). Greenwood.

--Taxi-Dance Hall: A Sociological Study in Commercialized Recreation & City Life. LC 69-16236. (Criminology, Law Enforcement, & Social Problems Ser.: No. 76). (Illus., With intro. essay added). 1969. Repr. of 1932 ed. 12.50x (ISBN 0-87585-076-6). Patterson Smith.

Cresson, B. C., jt. auth. see Flanders, H. J.

Cresswell, Anthony M. & Murphy, Michael J., eds. Education & Collective Bargaining: Readings in Policy & Research. LC 76-46121. 1977. 23.00 (ISBN 0-8211-0227-3); text ed. 20.75x 10 or more copies (ISBN 0-686-82935-2). McCutchan.

Cresswell, Anthony M., et al. Teachers, Unions, & Collective Bargaining in Public Education. LC 79-91436. 350p. 1980. text ed. 24.25 (ISBN 0-8211-0229-X); text ed. 22.00 10 or more copies (ISBN 0-686-86307-0). McCutchan.

Cresswell, Helen. Dear Shrink. LC 82-7728. 204p. (gr. 7 up). 1982. 9.95 (ISBN 0-02-725560-3). Macmillan.

Cresswell, Maxwell J., jt. auth. see Hughes, George E.

Cresswell, R. W., jt. auth. see Young, A. P.

Cresswell, Rachel L., jt. auth. see Fry, Elizabeth.

Cresswell, Roy. Quality in Urban Planning & Design. 1979. pap. 43.95 (ISBN 0-408-00363-4). Butterworth.

Cressy, David. Education in Tudor & Stuart England. LC 75-32933. 160p. 1976. 22.50 (ISBN 0-312-23730-8). St Martin.

--Literacy & the Social Order. (Illus.). 250p. 1980. 32.50 (ISBN 0-521-22514-0). Cambridge U Pr.

Cressy, Earl H. Daughters of Changing Japan. LC 75-390. 305p. 1975. Repr. of 1955 ed. lib. bdg. 19.75x (ISBN 0-8371-8023-6, CRDJ). Greenwood.

Crestol, Jack & Schneider, Herman M. Tax Planning for Investors: The Nineteen Eighty-Two Guide to Securities, Investments, & Tax Shelters. LC 82-71350. 175p. 1982. 14.95 (ISBN 0-87094-298-0). Dow Jones-Irwin.

Creswell, jt. auth. see Grove.

Creswell, John. Generals & Admirals: The Story of Amphibious Command. LC 75-8486. (Illus.). 1976. Repr. of 1952 ed. lib. bdg. 16.00x (ISBN 0-8371-8151-8, CRGAD). Greenwood.

Creswell, K. A. A Bibliography of the Architecture, Arts & Crafts of Islam. 2nd. ed. 100.00 o.s.i. (ISBN 0-89410-306-7). Three Continents.

Creswell, Thomas J., jt. auth. see McDavid, Virginia.

Creswell, William H., Jr., jt. auth. see Anderson, Carl L.

Creswick, Alice. The Red Book of Fruit Jars, No. 3. pap. 11.95 (ISBN 0-89145-076-9). Wallace-Homestead.

Cretser, Gary A. & Leon, Joseph J., eds. Intermarriage in the United States. LC 82-6213. (Marriage & Family Review Ser.: Vol. 5, No. 1). 119p. 1982. text ed. 20.00 (ISBN 0-917724-60-7, B60); pap. text ed. 9.95 (ISBN 0-917724-83-6, B83). Haworth Pr.

Creutzfeldt, W., ed. Acarbose: Proceedings of the International Symposium on Acarbose Effects on Carbohydrate & Fat Metabolism, First, Montreux, October 8-10, 1981. (International Congress Ser.: No. 594). 588p. 1982. 81.00 (ISBN 0-444-90283-X, Excerpta Medica). Elsevier.

Creveld, Marijke. Epilithic Lichen Communities in the Alpine Zone of Southern Norway. (Bibliotheca Lichenologica: Vol. 17). (Illus.). 288p. 1981. text ed. 40.00x (ISBN 3-7682-1313-7). Lubrecht & Cramer.

Creveld, Martin L. Van see Van Creveld, Martin L.

Crew, Henry, tr. from Latin. The Photismi De Lumine of Maurolycus: A Chapter in Late Medieval Optics. 1940. 12.50x (ISBN 0-686-30225-7). R S Barnes.

Crew, Michael A. & Kleindorfer, Paul R. Public Utility Economics. LC 78-24611. 1979. 24.00x (ISBN 0-312-65569-X). St Martin.

Crew, Michael A., ed. Issues in Public-Utility Pricing & Regulation. LC 79-6033. 1980. 24.95x (ISBN 0-669-03606-4). Lexington Bks.

--Problems in Public-Utility Economics & Regulation. 192p. 1979. 19.95x (ISBN 0-669-02775-8). Lexington Bks.

--Regulatory Reform & Public Utilities. LC 81-47749. 288p. 1982. 28.95x (ISBN 0-669-04834-8). Lexington Bks.

Crew, P. Mack. Calvinist Preaching & Iconoclasm in the Netherlands, 1544-1569. LC 77-77013. (Studies in Early Modern History). 1978. 34.95 (ISBN 0-521-21739-3). Cambridge U Pr.

Crewe, Jonathan. Unredeemed Rhetoric: Thomas Nashe & the Scandal of Authorship. LC 82-6554. 144p. 1982. text ed. 15.00x (ISBN 0-8018-2848-1). Johns Hopkins.

Crewe, Nancy M. & Zola, Irving K. Independent Living for Physically Disabled People: Developing, Implementing & Evaluating Self-Help Rehabilitation Programs. LC 82-48067. (Social & Behavioral Science Ser.). 1983. text ed. 19.95x (ISBN 0-87589-556-5). Jossey-Bass.

Crews, Donald. Harbor. (Illus.). (ps-1). 1982. 9.50 (ISBN 0-688-00861-5); PLB 8.59 (ISBN 0-688-00862-3). Morrow.

--Parade. LC 82-20927. (Illus.). 32p. (gr. k-3). 1983. 10.00 (ISBN 0-688-01995-1); PLB 9.55 (ISBN 0-688-01996-X). Greenwillow.

Crews, Frederick. Out of My System: Psychoanalysis, Ideology, & Critical Method. 1975. 17.95x (ISBN 0-19-501947-4). Oxford U Pr.

--The Random House Handbook. 3rd ed. 512p. 1980. text ed. 14.00 (ISBN 0-394-32378-5). Random.

Crews, Frederick & Schell, Orville. Starting Over: A College Reader. 1969. pap. text ed. 4.95 (ISBN 0-685-55618-2). Phila Bk Co.

Crews, Frederick C., ed. see Hawthorne, Nathaniel.

Crews, Harry. Blood & Grits. LC 78-54605. 1979. 11.49i (ISBN 0-06-010933-5, HarpT). Har-Row.

--Childhood, the Biography of a Place. (General Ser.). 1979. lib. bdg. 12.95 (ISBN 0-8161-6752-4, Large Print Bks). G K Hall.

--A Childhood: The Biography of a Place. LC 78-54677. 1978. 11.49i (ISBN 0-06-010932-7, HarpT). Har-Row.

Crews, Judson. The Clock of Moss. Berge, Carol & Boyer, Dale, eds. LC 82-73828. (Ahsahta Press Modern & Contemporary Poetry of the West Ser.). 60p. (Orig.). 1983. pap. 3.00 (ISBN 0-916272-21-4). Ahsahta Pr.

Crews, Judson, ed. see Greasybear, Charley J.

Creyke, W. E. & Sainsbury, I. E. Design with Non-Ductile Materials. (Illus.). xix, 290p. 1982. 57.50 (ISBN 0-85334-149-4, Pub. by Applied Sci England). Elsevier.

Cribb, A. B., jt. auth. see Cribb, J. W.

Cribb, J. W. & Cribb, A. B. Wild Medicine in Australia. (Illus.). 228p. 1982. 19.95 (ISBN 0-00-216446-9, Pub. by W Collins Australia); pap. text ed. 19.95 (ISBN 0-686-95223-5). Intl Schol Bk Serv.

Crichton, George H. Nicola Pisano & the Revival of Sculpture in Italy. LC 78-59011. (Illus.). 1981. Repr. of 1938 ed. cancelled o.p. (ISBN 0-88355-686-3). Hyperion Conn.

Crichton, Ian. The Art of Dying. 166p. 1983. 15.95 (Pub. by Peter Owen). Merrimack Bk Serv.

Crichton, J. D. Once & Future Liturgy. pap. 4.95 o.p. (ISBN 0-8091-2131-X). Paulist Pr.

Crichton, Michael. Jasper Johns. LC 77-78150. (Illus.). 1977. 45.00 o.p. (ISBN 0-8109-1161-2). Abrams.

--The Terminal Man. (YA) 1972. 13.50 (ISBN 0-394-44768-9). Knopf.

Crichton, Ronald. Falla. LC 81-71303. (BBC Music Guides Ser.). 104p. (Orig.). 1983. pap. 5.95 (ISBN 0-295-95926-6). U of Wash Pr.

Crick, jt. auth. see Dupuy.

Crick, B. & Heater, D. New Directions in Curriculum Studies. 180p. 1979. write for info. (ISBN 0-905273-07-9, Pub. by Taylor & Francis). Intl Pubns Serv.

Crick, Bernard. The American Science of Politics: Its Origin & Conditions. LC 82-15829. xv, 252p. 1982. lib. bdg. 35.00x (ISBN 0-313-23696-8, CRAS). Greenwood.

Crick, Francis. Life Itself. 1982. pap. 4.80 (ISBN 0-671-25563-0, Touchstone Bks). S&S.

Crick, Malcolm. Explorations in Language & Meaning: Towards a Semantic Anthropology. LC 76-17290. 1977. text ed. 39.95x o.p. (ISBN 0-470-15144-7). Halsted Pr.

Cricket Magazine Editors, jt. auth. see Leverich, Kathleen.

Crickmay, Anthony. Dancers. LC 81-48551. (Illus.). 128p. 1982. 50.00 (ISBN 0-688-01239-6). Morrow.

Crickmay, Marie C. Help the Stroke Patient to Talk. (Illus.). 132p. 1977. pap. 11.75x (ISBN 0-398-03593-8). C C Thomas.

Crickmer, D. F. & Zegeer, D. A., eds. Elements of Practical Coal Mining. 2nd ed. LC 79-57346. (Illus.). 847p. 1981. 44.00x (ISBN 0-89520-270-0, 270-0). Soc Mining Eng.

Criddle, W. J. & Ellis, G. P. Spectral & Chemical Characterization of Organic Compounds: A Laboratory Handbook. 2nd ed. LC 80-40497. 115p. 1980. 39.00x (ISBN 0-471-27813-0, Pub. by Wiley-Interscience); pap. 15.95x (ISBN 0-471-27812-2). Wiley.

Crider, Allen B., ed. Mass Market Publishing in America. 1982. lib. bdg. 35.00 (ISBN 0-8161-8590-5, Hall Reference). G K Hall.

Crider, Andrew B., et al. Psychology. 1983. text ed. 23.95x (ISBN 0-673-15316-9). Scott F.

Crider, Charles C. & Kistler, Robert C. The Seventh-Day Adventist Family: An Empirical Study. 296p. 1979. pap. 3.95 (ISBN 0-943872-77-4). Andrews Univ Pr.

Crider, Virginia. The Lost God. 1968. pap. 1.10 (ISBN 0-686-05590-X). Rod & Staff.

Criel, Geert, jt. auth. see Lutsenburg Maas, Jacob van.

Crighton, D. B., et al, eds. Control of Ovulation. new ed. LC 78-40043. 1978. 74.95 o.p. (ISBN 0-408-70924-3). Butterworth.

Crighton, Richard. The Million Dollar Lift. 288p. 1981. pap. 2.50 o.p. (ISBN 0-380-76604-3, 76604). Avon.

Crile, George, Jr. Surgery: Your Choices, Your Alternatives. (General Ser.). 1980. lib. bdg. 13.95 (ISBN 0-8161-6764-8, Large Print Bks). G K Hall.

Crile, George W. Bipolar Theory of Living Processes. 2nd ed. 1981. Repr. of 1955 ed. 18.95x (ISBN 0-686-76728-4). Regent House.

Criley, J. Michael, jt. auth. see French, William J.

Crim, Keith R., jt. ed. see Buttrick, George A.

Crim, Keith R., et al, eds. The Interpreter's Dictionary of the Bible, Supplementary Volume. LC 62-9387. (Illus.). 1976. 20.00 (ISBN 0-687-19269-2). Abingdon.

Crim, Lottie R. Come Care with Me. LC 82-73369. (Illus.). 1983. pap. 4.50 (ISBN 0-8054-5431-4). Broadman.

Crime & Justice History Group, ed. Criminal Justice History: An International Annual, Vol. 2. (Illus.). 210p. 1981. 24.00 (ISBN 0-686-98515-X). John Jay Pr.

Crimes, T. P. & Harper, J. C. Trace Fossils Two: Geological Journal Special Issue, No. 9. (Liverpool Geological Society & the Manchester Geological Association). 360p. 1980. 81.95 (ISBN 0-471-27756-8, Pub. by Wiley-Interscience). Wiley.

Crimmins, John J., jt. auth. see Hugard, Jean.

Crimmins, Timothy, jt. ed. see Shumsky, Neil L.

Crimp, Susan, jt. auth. see Millard, Clive.

Crinklaw, Frances & Frizzi, Richard J. Teaching Consonant Blends & Digraphs in Context. (Word Analysis Library Ser.). (Illus.). 1980. spiral bdg. 17.50x (ISBN 0-87628-958-8, C-9588-9); dup masters 17.50x (ISBN 0-87628-959-6, C-9596-2). Ctr Appl Res.

--Teaching Consonants in Context. (Word Analysis Library). (Illus.). 1980. spiral bdg. 17.50x (ISBN 0-87628-956-1, C-9561-6); dup masters 17.50x (ISBN 0-87628-965-0, C-9650-7). Ctr Appl Res.

--Teaching Vowels & Vowel Digraphs in Context. (Word Analysis Library Ser.). (Illus.). 1980. spiral bdg. 17.50x (ISBN 0-87628-966-9, C-9669-7); dup. masters 17.50x (ISBN 0-87628-963-4, C-9634-1). Ctr Appl Res.

Crippen, G. M. Distance Geometry & Conformational Calculations. LC 80-42044. (Chemometrics Research Studies). 1981. 29.95 (ISBN 0-471-27991-9, Pub. by Research Studies Pr). Wiley.

Crippen, Lee F. Simon Cameron: Ante Bellum Years. LC 76-168674. (American Scene Ser). 1972. Repr. of 1942 ed. lib. bdg. 39.50 (ISBN 0-306-70362-9). Da Capo.

Crippen, Thomas G. Christmas & Christmas Lore. LC 69-16067. (Illus.). x, 223p. 1972. Repr. of 1923 ed. 47.00x (ISBN 0-8103-3029-6). Gale.

Cripps, E. L., ed. Space-Time Concepts in Urban & Regional Models. (London Papers in Regional Science). 238p. 1974. pap. 15.50x (ISBN 0-85086-044-X, Pub. by Pion England). Methuen Inc.

Cripps, Louise. Puerto Rico: The Case for Independence. 192p. 4.50 o.p. (ISBN 0-87073-334-6). Schenkman.

Cripps, Louise L. The Spanish Caribbean: From Columbus to Castro. 1979. lib. bdg. 20.00 (ISBN 0-8161-9003-8, Univ Bks). G K Hall.

Cripps, Martin. An Introduction to Computer Hardware. 1978. text ed. 22.95 (ISBN 0-316-16114-4). Little.

Cripps, Richard S. Amos. 1981. lib. bdg. 13.50 (ISBN 0-86524-081-7, 3001). Klock & Klock.

Cripps, Thomas. Slow Fade to Black: The Negro in American Film, 1900-1942. (Illus.). 1977. pap. 9.95 (ISBN 0-19-502130-4, 484, GB). Oxford U Pr.

Cripwell, Kenneth. Language. Yapp, Malcolm, et al, eds. (World History Ser.). (Illus.). (gr. 10). 1980. Repr. of 1977 ed. lib. bdg. 6.95 (ISBN 0-89908-146-0); pap. text ed. 2.25 (ISBN 0-89908-121-5). Greenhaven.

Crisi, J. Bruce. What to Do When the Family Hurts. 1982. pap. 5.95 (ISBN 0-8423-7996-7). Tyndale.

Crisler, Jesse E. & McElrath, Joseph R., Jr. Frank Norris: A Reference Guide. (No. 3). 145p. 1974. 18.00 (ISBN 0-8161-1097-2, Hall Reference). G K Hall.

Crisler, Lois. Arctic Wild. LC 73-4073. (Illus.). 320p. (Memorial ed.). (YA) 1973. 12.45i (ISBN 0-06-010917-3, HarpT). Har-Row.

--Arctic Wild. LC 57-8168. 1979. pap. 2.25i o.p. (ISBN 0-06-080012-7, P12, PL). Har-Row.

Crisp, Arthur H. & Stonehill, Edward. Sleep, Nutrition & Mood. LC 75-16121. 1976. 37.95 (ISBN 0-471-18688-0, Pub. by Wiley-Interscience). Wiley.

Crisp, Clement, jt. auth. see Clarke, Mary.

Crisp, Quentin. How to Become a Virgin. 192p. 1983. pap. 6.95 (ISBN 0-312-39543-4). St Martin.

--The Naked Civil Servant. 1978. pap. 2.25 o.p. (ISBN 0-451-08292-3, E8292, Sig). NAL.

Crisp, S., jt. auth. see Wilson, A. D.

Crisp, Tony. Do You Dream: How to Gain Insight into Your Dreams. 1972. pap. 9.50 (ISBN 0-525-47326-2, 0922-280). Dutton.

Crisp, William. Spytrap. 200p. 1983. 12.95 (ISBN 0-686-38837-2). Pantheon.

Crispens, Charles G., Jr. Essentials of Medical Genetics. (Illus.). 1971. text ed. 13.50 (ISBN 0-06-140669-4, Harper Medical). Lippincott.

Crispin, Edmund. Buried for Pleasure. LC 75-44967. (Crime Fiction Ser). 1976. Repr. of 1949 ed. lib. bdg. 17.50 o.s.i. (ISBN 0-8240-2362-5). Garland Pub.

--Buried for Pleasure. LC 49-8208. 1980. pap. 2.84i (ISBN 0-06-080506-4, P 506, PL). Har-Row.

--The Case of the Gilded Fly. 1980. pap. 2.50 (ISBN 0-380-50187-2, 63552-6). Avon.

--The Case of the Gilded Fly. (General Ser.). 1980. lib. bdg. 13.95 (ISBN 0-8161-3018-3, Large Print Bks). G K Hall.

--Holy Disorders. (General Ser.). 1980. lib. bdg. 13.95 (ISBN 0-8161-3111-2, Large Print Bks). G K Hall.

Crispin, John. Pedro Salinas. (World Authors Ser.). 1974. lib. bdg. 15.95 (ISBN 0-8057-2784-1, Twayne). G K Hall.

Crispin, John, jt. auth. see Crispin, Ruth K.

Crispin, Ruth K. & Crispin, John. Progress in Spanish: Grammar & Practice for the Second Year. 2nd ed. 1978. text ed. 16.95x o.p. (ISBN 0-673-15147-6). Scott F.

--Workbook & Laboratory Manual for Progress in Spanish. 2nd ed. 1978. pap. 6.95x o.p. (ISBN 0-673-15148-4). Scott F.

Crispino, James A. The Assimilation of Ethnic Groups: The Italian Case. 175p. 1980. text ed. 14.95x (ISBN 0-913256-39-0, Dist by Ozer). Ctr Migration.

Criss, Wayne E., jt. ed. see Sharma, Rameshwar K.

Criss, Wayne E., et al, eds. Control Mechanisms in Cancer. LC 75-30234. (Progress in Cancer Research & Therapy Ser: Vol.1). 488p. 1976. 50.00 (ISBN 0-89004-083-4). Raven.

Crissy, W. J., et al. Selling: The Personal Force in Marketing. LC 76-45848. (Marketing Ser.). 1977. text ed. 30.50 (ISBN 0-471-18757-7). Wiley.

Crist, Larry, et al, trs. see Greimas, A. J. & Courtes, J.

Crist, Lyle M. Man Expressed: The Realm of Writing. 1971. pap. text ed. 6.95x o.p. (ISBN 0-02-474600-2, 47460). Glencoe.

Crist, Steven. Offtrack: Bets & Pieces. LC 79-6662. 168p. 1981. 9.95 o.p. (ISBN 0-385-15215-9). Doubleday.

Cristiani, Therese S., jt. auth. see George, Rickey L.

Cristofer, Michael. The Shadow Box. 1977. pap. 2.25 o.p. (ISBN 0-380-01865-9, 46839, Bard). Avon.

--The Shadow Box. LC 77-21670. 1977. 8.95 (ISBN 0-910482-90-X). Drama Bk.

Cristol, Steven M., et al. Essentials of Media Planning: A Marketing Viewpoint. LC 75-21743. (Illus.). 96p. (Orig.). 1976. pap. text ed. 9.95x (ISBN 0-87251-019-0). Crain Bks.

Cristoplos, F., jt. ed. see Valletutti.

Cristy, Ann. Enthralled. (Second Chance at Love Ser.: No. 103). Date not set. pap. 1.75 (ISBN 0-515-06867-5). Jove Pubns.

--Torn Asunder. 192p. 1982. pap. 1.75 (ISBN 0-515-06660-5). Jove Pubns.

Criswell, John W. Planned Maintenance for Productivity & Energy Conservation. (Illus.). 250p. 1983. text ed. 36.00 (ISBN 0-915586-71-1). Fairmont Pr.

Criswell, W. A. Acts: An Exposition. 948p. 1983. Repr. 19.95 (ISBN 0-310-44150-1). Zondervan.

--Criswell's Guidebook for Pastors. LC 79-7735. 1980. 11.95 (ISBN 0-8054-2536-5). Broadman.

--Did Man Just Happen? (Orig.). 1980. pap. text ed. 2.50 o.p. (ISBN 0-8024-2212-8). Moody.

--Great Doctrines of the Bible, Vol. 1 & 2. 192p. 1982. Repr. 16.90 (ISBN 0-310-43868-3). Zondervan.

--Great Doctrines of the Bible, Vol. 2. 192p. 1982. 9.95 (ISBN 0-310-43860-8). Zondervan.

Critchfield, Howard J. General Climatology. 3rd ed. (Illus.). 416p. 1974. ref. ed. 26.95 (ISBN 0-13-350264-3). P-H.

Critchfield, Margot, jt. auth. see Dwyer, Thomas.

Critchfield, Margot, jt. auth. see Dwyer, Thomas A.

Critchfield, Richard. Villages. 412p. 1983. pap. 10.95 (ISBN 0-385-18375-5, Anch). Doubleday.

Critchley, Julian. The North Atlantic & the Soviet Union in the 1980's. 170p. 1982. 49.00x (ISBN 0-333-29469-6, Pub. by Macmillan England). State Mutual Bk.

Critchley, Macdonald. The Divine Banquet of the Brain. LC 78-24621. 279p. 1979. text ed. 21.50 (ISBN 0-89004-348-5). Raven.

Critchley, Macdonald, ed. Butterworths Medical Dictionary. 2nd ed. LC 77-30154. 1978. 59.95 (ISBN 0-407-00061-5). Butterworth.

Critchley, Macdonald, et al, eds. Headache: Physiopathological & Clinical Concepts. (Advances In Neurology Ser.: Vol. 33). 438p. 1982. 50.50 (ISBN 0-89004-636-0). Raven.

Critchlow, Keith. Islamic Patterns. LC 76-8694. (Illus.). 1976. 24.95x o.p. (ISBN 0-8052-3627-9); pap. 9.95 (ISBN 0-8052-0537-3). Schocken.

Crites, J. O. Vocational Psychology. 1969. text ed. 32.50 (ISBN 0-07-013780-3, C). McGraw.

Crites, John O. Career Counseling: Models, Methods & Materials. (Illus.). 240p. 1981. text ed. 17.50x (ISBN 0-07-013781-1, C). McGraw.

Crites, Laura, ed. The Female Offender: A Total Look at Women in the Criminal Justice System. 1977. 23.95x (ISBN 0-669-00635-1). Lexington Bks.

Critser, James R. Radiological Equipment. 115p. 1982. 80.00 (ISBN 0-914428-97-7, 10R-81). Lexington Data.

Critser, James R., Jr. Biotechnical Engineering: Equipment & Processes. (Ser.14-82). 1983. 210.00 (ISBN 0-88178-011-1). Lexington Data.

--Blood Technology. (Ser.10BT-82). 1983. 100.00 (ISBN 0-88178-004-9). Lexington Data.

--Cardiac Technology. (Ser. 10CT-81). 123p. 1982. 100.00 (ISBN 0-914428-95-0). Lexington Data.

--Clinical Assays. (Ser.10CA-82). 1983. 100.00 (ISBN 0-88178-003-0). Lexington Data.

--Energy Systems: Solar, Wind, Water, Geothermal, Ser. 11-82. 1983. 150.00 (ISBN 0-88178-001-4). Lexington Data.

--Energy Systems: Solar, Wind, Water Geothermal, Ser. 11-81. (Ser.11-81). 204p. 1983. 150.00 (ISBN 0-88178-000-6). Lexington Data.

--Laser Manufacture & Technology 1973. Incl. 150.00 o.p. (ISBN 0-914428-18-7). (Ser. 6-73). 1974. Lexington Data.

--Medical Diagnostic Apparatus: Systems. (Ser.10DAS-82). 1983. 100.00 (ISBN 0-88178-006-5). Lexington Data.

--Medical Therapeutic Apparatus Systems. 131p. 1982. 80.00 (ISBN 0-914428-98-5, 10TAS-81). Lexington Data.

--Membrane Separation Processes. (Ser.5-82). 1983. 135.00 (ISBN 0-88178-002-2). Lexington Data.

--Prosthetics & Contact Lens. 126p. 1982. 80.00 (ISBN 0-914428-96-9, 10PC-81). Lexington Data.

Critser, James R. Jr., Jr. Cancer: Diagnosis & Therapy. (Ser.10CDT-82). 1983. 80.00 (ISBN 0-88178-005-7). Lexington Data.

Crittenden, Faith J. Discharge Planning for Health Care Facilities. 224p. 1983. pap. text ed. 17.95 (ISBN 0-89303-210-7). R J Brady.

Crittenden, John A. Parties & Elections in the United States. (Illus.). 464p. 1982. 22.95 (ISBN 0-13-650903-7). P-H.

Crittenden, Roger. The Thames & Hudson Manual of Film Editing. (Illus.). 1982. 17.95 (ISBN 0-500-67023-4); pap. 9.95 (ISBN 0-500-68023-X). Thames Hudson.

Croasdale, Hannah & Bicudo, Carlos E. A Synopsis of North American Desmids, Part II; Desmidiaceae: Placodermae Section 5, The Filamentous Genera. LC 70-183418. (Illus.). vi, 122p. 1983. 26.50x (ISBN 0-8032-3661-1). U of Nebr Pr.

Croce, Arlene. Afterimages. LC 78-4592. 1979. 12.95 (ISBN 0-394-41093-9, Vin). Random.

Croce, Benedetto. Aesthetic. Ainslie, Douglas, tr. LC 78-58500. 544p. 1978. pap. 9.95 (ISBN 0-87923-255-2, Nonpareil Bk.). Godine.

--Essays on Marx & Russia. DeGennaro, Angelo A., tr. LC 66-17538. (Milestones of Thought Ser.). 1966. pap. 2.95 (ISBN 0-8044-6098-1). Ungar.

--Historical Materialism & the Economics of Karl Marx. LC 78-66239. (Social Science Classics). 225p. 1981. 29.95 (ISBN 0-87855-313-4); pap. text ed. 6.95 (ISBN 0-87855-695-8). Transaction Bks.

--History As the Story of Liberty. Sprigge, Sylvia, tr. LC 71-105123. 1970. pap. 5.95 (ISBN 0-89526-980-5). Regnery-Gateway.

Croce, Camille, compiled by. Directory of Member Agencies, 1980. rev. ed. LC 21-3975. 87p. 1980. pap. 10.00 o.p. (ISBN 0-87304-177-1). Family Serv.

Croce, Pat & Cooper, Bruce C. Conditioning for Ice Hockey Year-Round. LC 82-83917. (Illus.). 176p. (Orig.). 1983. pap. 7.95 (ISBN 0-88011-090-2). Leisure Pr.

Crocetti, Gino. Graduate Record Examination Aptitude Test (GRE) LC 82-184750. 528p. (Orig.). 1983. pap. 6.95 (ISBN 0-668-05479-4, 5479). Arco.

Crocetti, Gino & Clarke, B. M. Law School Admission Test: Preparation for the New Test. 416p. (Orig.). 1982. pap. 7.95 (ISBN 0-668-05427-1, 5427). Arco.

Crocetti, Guido M., et al. Contemporary Attitudes Toward Mental Illness. LC 73-80071. (Contemporary Community Health Ser.). 1974. 10.95x o.p. (ISBN 0-8229-3273-3). U of Pittsburgh Pr.

Crocker, Betty. Betty Crocker's Breads. (Illus.). 1974. PLB 7.62 o.p. (ISBN 0-307-69574-3, Golden Pr); pap. 3.95 (ISBN 0-307-09919-9). Western Pub.

--Betty Crocker's Cookbook. 1969. text ed. 13.32 ringbound o.p. (ISBN 0-07-013816-8, W). McGraw.

--Betty Crocker's Cooking with Wine. 1979. pap. 3.95 (ISBN 0-307-09923-7, Golden Pr). Western Pub.

--Betty Crocker's Deluxe Wedding Plan Book. 1979. 6.95 (ISBN 0-307-09553-3, Golden Pr). Western Pub.

--Betty Crocker's Salads. (Illus.). 1977. PLB 9.15 o.p. (ISBN 0-307-69900-5, Golden Pr); pap. 3.95 (ISBN 0-307-09900-8). Western Pub.

Crocker, Chester A., jt. ed. see Bissel, Richard E.

Crocker, George N. Roosevelt's Road to Russia. LC 74-26540. (FDR & the Era of the New Deal Ser.). (Illus.). xvii, 312p. 1975. Repr. of 1959 ed. lib. bdg. 39.50 (ISBN 0-306-70714-4). Da Capo.

Crocker, John. Bermuda, Bahamas, Hispanola, Puerto Rico & the Virgin Islands. 17.50x (ISBN 0-87556-062-8). Saifer.

Crocker, John R., ed. The Student Guide to Catholic Colleges & Universities 1982-1983. 1982. 46.00x (ISBN 0-8434-0769-7). McGrath.

Crocker, Lionel. Harry Emerson Fosdick's Art of Preaching: An Anthology. (Illus.). 296p. 1971. 19.75x o.p. (ISBN 0-398-00368-8). C C Thomas.

Crocker, Richard L. The Early Medieval Sequence. LC 74-84143. 1977. 55.00x (ISBN 0-520-02847-3). U of Cal Pr.

--History of Musical Style. (Music Ser). 1966. text ed. 19.95 o.p. (ISBN 0-07-013850-8, C). McGraw.

Crocker, Sabin. Piping Handbook. 5th ed. King, R. C., ed. 1967. 62.50 (ISBN 0-07-013841-9, P&RB). McGraw.

Crockett, Arthur. Three Secret Prophecies of Fatima Revealed. (Illus.). 72p. 1982. pap. 8.95 (ISBN 0-938294-13-X). Global Comm.

Crockett, H. Dale. Focus on Watergate: An Examination of the Moral Dilemma of Watergate in the Light of Civil Religion. LC 81-16952. 130p. 1981. 10.95x (ISBN 0-86554-017-9). Mercer Univ Pr.

Crockett, James R., jt. auth. see Casler, Darwin J.

Crockett, James U. Annuals. LC 78-140420. (Time-Life Encyclopedia of Gardening). (Illus.). (gr. 6 up). 1971. lib. bdg. 17.28 (ISBN 0-8094-1082-6, Pub. by Time-Life). Silver.

--Bulbs. LC 78-140420. (Time-Life Encyclopedia of Gardening). (Illus.). (gr. 6 up). 1971. lib. bdg. 17.28 (ISBN 0-8094-1102-4, Pub. by Time-Life). Silver.

--Evergreens. LC 78-140420. (Time-Life Encyclopedia of Gardening). (Illus.). (gr. 6 up). 1971. lib. bdg. 17.28 (ISBN 0-8094-1106-7, Pub. by Time-Life). Silver.

--Flowering House Plants. LC 78-140420. (Time-Life Encyclopedia of Gardening). (Illus.). 1971. lib. bdg. 17.28 (ISBN 0-8094-1098-2, Pub. by Time-Life). Silver.

--Flowering Shrubs. LC 78-140420. (Time-Life Encyclopedia of Gardening). (Illus.). (gr. 6 up). 1972. lib. bdg. 17.28 (ISBN 0-8094-1114-8, Pub. by Time-Life). Silver.

--Landscape Gardening. LC 78-140420. (Time-Life Encyclopedia of Gardening). (Illus.). (gr. 6 up). 1971. lib. bdg. 17.28 (ISBN 0-8094-1090-7, Pub. by Time-Life). Silver.

--Perennials. LC 78-140420. (Time-Life Encyclopedia of Gardening). (Illus.). (gr. 6 up). 1972. lib. bdg. 17.28 (ISBN 0-8094-2328-6, Pub. by Time-Life). Silver.

--Roses. LC 78-140420. (Time-Life Encyclopedia of Gardening). (Illus.). (gr. 6 up). 1971. lib. bdg. 17.28 (ISBN 0-8094-1086-9, Pub. by Time-Life). Silver.

--Trees. LC 78-140420. (The Time-Life Encyclopedia of Gardening Ser.). (Illus.). 1972. lib. bdg. 17.28 (ISBN 0-8094-1119-9). Silver.

--Vegetables & Fruits. LC 78-140420. (Time-Life Encyclopedia of Gardening). (Illus.). 1972. lib. bdg. 17.28 (ISBN 0-8094-1071-0, Pub. by Time-Life). Silver.

Crockett, James U. & Allen, Oliver E. Decorating with Plants. LC 77-95146. (The Time-Life Encyclopedia of Gardening Ser.). (Illus.). 1978. lib. bdg. 17.28 (ISBN 0-8094-2580-7). Silver.

--Pruning & Grafting. LC 78-15795. (The Time-Life Encyclopedia of Gardening Ser.). (Illus.). 1978. lib. bdg. 17.28 (ISBN 0-8094-2634-X). Silver.

--Shade Gardens. (The Time-Life Encyclopedia of Gardening Ser.). (Illus.). 1979. lib. bdg. 17.28 (ISBN 0-8094-2646-3); 14.64 (ISBN 0-8094-2647-1). Silver.

--Winter Gardens. LC 79-18814. (Time-Life Encyclopedia of Gardening). lib. bdg. 17.28 (ISBN 0-8094-2614-5). Silver.

Crockett, James U. & Cravens, Richard. Pests & Diseases. LC 77-89155. (The Time-Life Encyclopedia of Gardening Ser.). (Illus.). 1977. lib. bdg. 17.28 (ISBN 0-8094-2567-X). Silver.

--Vines. LC 78-31771. (The Time-Life Encyclopedia of Gardening Ser.). (Illus.). 1979. lib. bdg. 17.28 (ISBN 0-8094-2596-3). Silver.

Crockett, James U. & Murphy, Wendy B. Gardening under Lights. LC 77-92113. (The Time-Life Encyclopedia of Gardening Ser.). (Illus.). 1978. lib. bdg. 17.28 (ISBN 0-8094-2571-8). Silver.

--Japanese Gardens. LC 79-15137. (The Time-Life Encyclopedia of Gardening Ser.). (Illus.). 1979. lib. bdg. 17.28 (ISBN 0-8094-2630-7); 14.64 (ISBN 0-686-66221-0). Silver.

Crockett, James U. & Perl, Philip. Cacti & Succulents. LC 78-58300. (The Time-Life Encyclopedia of Gardening Ser.). (Illus.). 1978. lib. bdg. 17.28 (ISBN 0-8094-2588-2). Silver.

--Miniatures & Bonsai. LC 78-20889. (The Time-Life Encyclopedia of Gardening Ser.). (Illus.). 1979. lib. bdg. 17.28 (ISBN 0-8094-2642-0). Silver.

Crockett, James U. & Prendergast, C. Easy Gardens. (The Time-Life Encyclopedia of Gardening Ser.). (Illus.). 1979. lib. bdg. 17.28 (ISBN 0-8094-2638-2). Silver.

Crockett, James U. & Skelsy, Alice F. Orchids. LC 78-18249. (The Time-Life Encyclopedia of Gardening Ser.). (Illus.). 1978. lib. bdg. 17.28 (ISBN 0-8094-2592-0). Silver.

Crockett, James U. & Tanner, Ogden. Garden Construction. LC 78-1383. (The Time-Life Encyclopedia of Gardening Ser.). (Illus.). 1978. lib. bdg. 17.28 (ISBN 0-8094-2584-X). Silver.

--Rock & Water Gardens. LC 79-13072. (The Time-Life Encyclopedia of Gardening Ser.). (Illus.). 1979. lib. bdg. 17.28 (ISBN 0-8094-2626-9); 14.64 (ISBN 0-8094-2627-7). Silver.

Crockett, James V. Foliage House Plants. LC 78-140420. (Time-Life Encyclopedia of Gardening). (Illus.). (gr. 6 up). 1972. lib. bdg. 17.28 (ISBN 0-8094-1098-2, Pub. by Time-Life). Silver.

--Lawns & Ground Covers. LC 78-140420. (Time-Life Encyclopedia of Gardening). (Illus.). (gr. 6 up). 1971. lib. bdg. 17.28 (ISBN 0-8094-1094-X, Pub. by Time-Life). Silver.

Crockett, James V., et al. Greenhouse Gardening. LC 76-51513. (Time-Life Encyclopedia of Gardening). (Illus.). (gr. 6 up). 1977. PLB 17.28 (ISBN 0-8094-2563-7, Pub by Time-Life). Silver.

Crockford, H. D., et al. Laboratory Manual of Physical Chemistry. 2nd ed. 352p. 1975. text ed. 20.50 (ISBN 0-471-18884-1). Wiley.

Crocombe, Ron, ed. see Ta'unga.

Croft, B. A. & Hoyt, S. C. Integrated Management of Insect Pests of Pome & Stone Fruit. (Environemental Science & Technology Texts & Monographs). 464p. 1983. 52.50 (ISBN 0-471-05334-1, Pub. by Wiley-Interscience). Wiley.

Croft, Barbara L. The Checklist Kit for Resume Writing & Job Application Letters. 16p. 1982. 3.50 (ISBN 0-9609580-0-2). Different Drum.

Croft, Barbara Y., jt. ed. see Price, Ronald R.

Croft, David R. & Lilley, David G. Heat Transfer Calculations Using Finite Difference Equations. (Illus.). 1977. 57.50x (ISBN 0-85334-720-4, Pub. by Applied Sci England). Elsevier.

Croft, Doreen. Be Honest with Yourself. 1976. pap. text ed. 9.95x o.p. (ISBN 0-534-00452-0). Wadsworth Pub.

Croft, Doreen & Hess, Robert D. Activities Handbook for Teachers of Young Children. 3rd ed. LC 79-90365. 1980. pap. text ed. 13.95 (ISBN 0-395-28698-0). HM.

Croft, Doreen J., jt. auth. see Hess, Robert.

Croft, J. R. & Kanis, A. Handbooks of the Flora of Papua New Guinea, Vol. II. (Illus.). 276p. 1982. text ed. 37.50 (ISBN 0-522-84204-6, Pub. by Melbourne U Pr Australia). Intl Schol Bk Serv.

Croft, Kenneth. A Practice Book on English Stress & Intonation. 81p. 1961. pap. 5.50 (ISBN 0-87789-013-7); cassette tapes 90.00 (ISBN 0-87789-125-7). Eng Language.

--Reading & Word Study: For Students of English As a Second Language. (Illus.). 1969. pap. text ed. 11.95 (ISBN 0-13-756742-1). P-H.

--Reading on English As a Second Language: For Teachers & Teacher Trainees. 1980. 16.95 (ISBN 0-316-16137-3). Little.

Croft, L. R. Handbook of Protein Sequences: A Compilation of Amino Acid Sequences of Proteins. LC 79-41487. 644p. 1980. 119.95 (ISBN 0-471-27703-7). Wiley.

--Protein Sequence Determination. LC 79-41488. 157p. 1980. pap. 16.95 (ISBN 0-471-27710-X). Wiley.

Croft, Mary K., jt. auth. see Steward, Joyce S.

Croft, Pauline. The Spanish Company. 1973. 50.00x (ISBN 0-686-96611-2, Pub by London Rec Soc England). State Mutual Bk.

Croft, T., et al. American Electricians' Handbook. 9th ed. 1970. 38.50 (ISBN 0-07-013929-6, P&RB). McGraw.

Croft, Terrell, et al. American Electrician's Handbook. 10th ed. 1664p. 1980. 46.75 (ISBN 0-07-013931-8, P&RB). McGraw.

Crofton, H. T., jt. auth. see Smart, Bath C.

Crofton, John & Douglas, Andrew. Respiratory Diseases. 3rd ed. (Illus.). 836p. 1981. 72.50 (ISBN 0-8016-1142-3, Blackwell). Mosby.

Crofts, Freeman W. The Cheyne Mystery. (Crime Ser). 1978. pap. 2.95 (ISBN 0-14-000917-5). Penguin.

--Inspector French's Greatest Case. (Crime Ser). 1978. pap. 2.95 o.p. (ISBN 0-14-000918-3). Penguin.

--The Pit-Prop Syndicate. (Crime Ser.). 1978. pap. 2.95 (ISBN 0-14-000512-9). Penguin.

Croghan, Martin J. & Croghan, Penelope P. Idealogical Training in Communist Education. LC 79-47986. 209p. 1980. text ed. 20.00 (ISBN 0-8191-0992-4); pap. text ed. 10.50 (ISBN 0-8191-0993-2). U Pr of Amer.

--Role Models & Readers: A Sociological Analysis. LC 79-5430. 1980. pap. 9.50 (ISBN 0-8191-0879-0). U Pr of Amer.

Croghan, Penelope P., jt. auth. see Croghan, Martin J.

Croghan, Tonita, jt. auth. see Brace, Betty L.

Crohn, Burrill B. Understand Your Ulcer. rev. ed. (Illus.). 1950. 8.50x (ISBN 0-911378-26-X). Sheridan.

Croinin, D. O., jt. auth. see Dillon, Myles.

Croisdale, D. W., et al, eds. Computerised Braille Production: Today & Tomorrow. 422p. 1983. pap. 17.20 (ISBN 0-387-12057-2). Springer-Verlag.

Croissant, Kay & Dees, Catherine. Continuum: The Immortality Principle. LC 79-109190. 1978. pap. 4.75 o.p. (ISBN 0-934704-00-7, Pub. by Palm Publications Pr.). Theos U Pr.

Croix, Don La see Kaufman, Peter B. & La Croix, Don.

Croix, Grethe La see La Croix, Grethe.

Croix, Horst de la, jt. auth. see Cohen, Kathleen.

Croix, Horst de la see De la Croix, Horst & Tansey, Richard G.

Croke, B. F. & Harris, J. D. Religious Conflict in Fourth Century Rome. (Sources in Ancient History Ser.). 139p. (Orig.). 1982. pap. 21.00x (ISBN 0-424-00091-1, Pub. by Sydney U Pr Australia). Intl Schol Bk Serv.

Croker, Thomas. Researches in the South of Ireland: A Source Book of Irish Folk Tradition. 1969. Repr. of 1824 ed. 27.00x (ISBN 0-7165-0077-9, Pub. by Irish Academic Pr Ireland). Biblio Dist.

Croker, Thomas C. Fairy Legends & Tradition of the South Ireland. LC 82-5885. 1983. 50.00 (ISBN 0-8201-1380-8). Schol Facsimiles.

Crokett, Christina. To Touch a Dream. (Super Romances Ser.). 384p. 1983. pap. 2.95 (ISBN 0-373-70055-5, Pub. by Worldwide). Harlequin Bks.

Croll, Carolyn. Too Many Babas. LC 78-22474. (I Can Read Bks.). (Illus.). 64p. (gr. k-3). 1979. 7.64i o.p. (ISBN 0-06-021383-3, HarpJ); PLB 8.89 (ISBN 0-06-021384-1). Har-Row.

Croll, Elisabeth. The Politics of Marriage in Contemporary China. LC 80-40586. (Contemporary China Institute Publications Ser.). (Illus.). 224p. 1981. 39.50 (ISBN 0-521-23345-3). Cambridge U Pr.

Croll, Neil A. Behaviour of Nematodes: Their Activity, Senses & Responses. LC 75-124954. 1971. 17.95 o.p. (ISBN 0-312-07245-7). St Martin.

Croll, R. D. & Doery, A. C. Successful Conferences. 38p. 1983. pap. 2.50 (ISBN 0-643-00371-1, Pub. by CSIRO Australia). Intl Schol Bk Serv.

Cromartie, Bill. Braggin' Rights: A Game by Game History of the Alabama-Auburn Football Rivalry 1893 to 1981. LC 82-82118. (Great Rivalry Ser.). (Illus.). 400p. 1982. 9.95 (ISBN 0-88011-070-8). Leisure Pr.

--Georgia-Georgia Tech Football. (College Sports Ser.: Football). 1981. 10.95 o.p. (ISBN 0-87397-124-8). Strode.

Cromartie, Bill, jt. auth. see Peterson, James A.

Crombie, A. C. Augustine to Galileo. (Illus.). 1979. text ed. 20.00x (ISBN 0-674-05273-0). Harvard U Pr.

Cromer, A. Physics in Science & Industry. 1980. text ed. 27.50 (ISBN 0-07-014437-0); supplementary materials avail. McGraw.

Cromer, Alan. Physics for the Life Sciences. 2nd ed. (Illus.). 1976. text ed. 27.50 (ISBN 0-07-014434-6); instructor's manual 15.00 (ISBN 0-07-014436-2); study guide 12.95 (ISBN 0-07-014435-4). McGraw.

Cromer, Alan & Boughton, Robert. Laboratory Physics for the Life Sciences. (Illus.). 256p. 1974. text ed. 6.95 o.p. (ISBN 0-07-014432-X, C). McGraw.

Cromie, Alice. Tour Guide to the Old West. 1982. pap. 9.95 (ISBN 0-8129-6323-7). Times Bks.

Cromie, Robert. Chicago. LC 80-17624. (Illus.). 128p. 1980. 35.00 (ISBN 0-528-81102-9); pap. 8.95 o.p. (ISBN 0-528-88061-6). Rand.

Cromie, Robert & Roth, Hy. The Little People. LC 79-51195. (Illus.). 1980. 15.95 (ISBN 0-89696-024-2, An Everest House Book). Dodd.

Cromie, William. Skylab: The Story of Man's First Station in Space. LC 74-25983. (Illus.). 192p. (gr. 7 up). 1976. 10.95 (ISBN 0-679-20300-1). McKay.

Commelinck, M., jt. auth. see Roucoux, A.

Crompton, Anne. The Untamed. 256p. (Orig.). 1981. pap. 2.75 o.p. (ISBN 0-523-41151-0). Pinnacle Bks.

Crompton, Anne E. The Ice Trail. 128p. (gr. 3-7). 1980. 9.50 (ISBN 0-416-30691-8). Methuen Inc.

--The Sorcerer. LC 82-61042. 176p. 1982. Repr. of 1971 ed. 16.95 (ISBN 0-933256-36-1). Second Chance.

--The Sorcerer. LC 82-61042. (Illus.). 176p. pap. 8.95 (ISBN 0-933256-37-X). Second Chance.

Crompton, D. W. & Newton, B. A., eds. Trends & Perspectives in Parasitology, Vol. 1. LC 80-42159. (Illus.). 150p. 1981. 24.95 (ISBN 0-521-23821-8); pap. 10.95 (ISBN 0-521-28242-X). Cambridge U Pr.

Crompton, John. Snake. (Illus.). 1969. 7.50 o.p. (ISBN 0-571-05524-9). Transatlantic.

Crompton, Margaret. Adolescents & Social Workers. Davies, Martin, ed. (Community Care & Practice Handbooks). vi, 91p. (Orig.). 1983. pap. text ed. 7.95x (ISBN 0-435-82189-X). Heinemann Ed.

--Passionate Search: A Life of Charlotte Bronte. 252p. 1982. Repr. of 1955 ed. lib. bdg. 40.00 (ISBN 0-686-94645-6). Century Bookbindery.

Crompton, Rosemary, jt. auth. see Wedderburn, Dorothy.

Crompton, T. R. Chemical Analysis of Additives in Plastics. 2nd ed. 1977. Pergamon.

--Small Batteries: Primary Cells, Vol. 2. LC 81-11495. 224p. 1983. 64.95x (ISBN 0-470-27356-9). Halsted Pr.

Cromwell, Leslie & Arditti, M. Medical Instrumentation for Health Care. (Illus.). 1976. Ref. Ed. 24.95 (ISBN 0-13-572602-6). P-H.

Cromwell, Leslie, et al. Biomedical Instrumentation & Measurements. 2nd ed. (Illus.). 1980. text ed. 26.95 (ISBN 0-13-076448-5). P-H.

Cromwell, Liz & Hibner, Dixie. Finger Frolics: Fingerplays for Young Children. 2nd ed. 1976. pap. 7.95 o.p. (ISBN 0-933212-09-7, Dist. by Gryphon House). Partner Pr.

Cromwell, Paul F., Jr. & Keefer, George. Readings on Police-Community Relations. 2nd ed. (Criminal Justice Ser.). 1978. pap. 15.95 (ISBN 0-8299-0156-6). West Pub.

Cromwell, Paul F., Jr., jt. auth. see Killinger, George G.

Cromwell, Ronald, et al. The Kvebaek Family Sculpture Technique: A Diagnostic & Research Tool in Family Therapy. 39p. 1980. pap. 3.95 (ISBN 0-932930-30-1). Pilgrimage Inc.

Cronan, Marion & Atwood, June. First Foods. rev. ed. (gr. 7-9). 1976. text ed. 15.40 (ISBN 0-87002-168-0); tchr's guide free. Bennett IL.

Cronan, Marion L. & Atwood, June. Foods in Homemaking. rev. ed. (Illus.). (gr. 9-12): 1972. text ed. 21.20 (ISBN 0-87002-121-4); tchr's guide free. Bennett IL.

Cronbach, Abraham. The Quest for Peace. LC 79-137533. (Peace Movement in America Ser). ix, 223p. 1972. Repr. of 1937 ed. lib. bdg. 16.95x (ISBN 0-89198-061-X). Ozer.

Crone, Alla. Winds over Manchuria. (Orig.). 1983. pap. 3.50 (ISBN 0-440-18853-9). Dell.

Crone, G. R. The Discovery of the East. LC 72-173296. 1971. 17.95 o.p. (ISBN 0-312-21245-3). St Martin.

--Maps & Their Makers: An Introduction to the History of Cartography. (Illus.). 1978. 22.50 o.p. (ISBN 0-208-01724-0, Archon). Shoe String.

Crone, Marie-Luise. Untersuchungen Zur Reichskirchenpolitik Lothars III, 1125-1137: Zwischen Reichskirchlicher Tradition Und Reformkurie. 398p. 1982. write for info (ISBN 3-8204-7019-0). P Lang Pubs.

Crone, Moira. The Winnebago Mysteries. 144p. 1982. 10.95 (ISBN 0-914590-68-5); pap. 4.95 (ISBN 0-914590-69-3). Fiction Coll.

Crone, Patricia. Slaves on Horses. LC 79-50234. 1980. 44.50 (ISBN 0-521-22961-8). Cambridge U Pr.

Crone, Patricia & Cook, M. Hagarism. LC 75-41714. 1980. pap. 12.95 (ISBN 0-521-29754-0). Cambridge U Pr.

--Hagarism: The Making of the Islamic World. LC 75-41714. 268p. 1977. 32.50 (ISBN 0-521-21133-6). Cambridge U Pr.

Crone, Rainer F. Numerals, Nineteen Twenty-Four to Nineteen Seventy-Seven. (Illus.). 84p. 1978. pap. 10.00 o.p. (ISBN 0-87451-983-7). U Pr of New Eng.

Croner, Helga. Stepping Stones to Further Jewish-Christian Relations: An Unabridged Collection of Christian Documents. 157p. pap. 10.00 (ISBN 0-686-95183-2). ADL.

Croner, Helga & Klenicki, Leon, eds. Issues in the Jewish-Christian Dialogue: Jewish Perspectives on Covenant Mission & Witness. 190p. 7.95 (ISBN 0-686-95172-7). ADL.

Croner, Helga, jt. ed. see Cohen, Martin A.

Croner, Helga, jt. ed. see Boadt, Lawrence.

Croner, John A. The Basque & the Boy. LC 80-15675. 1982. 14.95 (ISBN 0-87949-176-0). Ashley Bks.

Croney, John. Anthropometry for Designers. rev. ed. 144p. 1981. pap. 12.00 o.p. (ISBN 0-442-22013-8). Van Nos Reinhold.

Cronin, Anthony. Heritage Now: Irish Literature in the English Language. 215p. 1983. 17.95x (ISBN 0-312-36993-X). St Martin.

--New & Selected Poems. 128p. 1982. pap. text ed. 8.50x (ISBN 0-85635-367-1, 40680, Pub. by Carcanet New Pr England). Humanities.

Cronin, Gaynell & Cronin, Jim. Saints for Today. 1978. pap. 7.55 o.p. (ISBN 0-88479-014-2). Arena Lettres.

Cronin, Isaac. The International Squid Cookbook. (Illus.). 96p. 1981. pap. 6.95 (ISBN 0-915572-61-3). Aris Bks.

Cronin, Isaac & Harlow, Jay. The California Seafood Cookbook. (Illus.). 300p. 1983. 16.95 (ISBN 0-943186-04-8); pap. 10.95 (ISBN 0-943186-03-X). Aris Bks.

Cronin, James E. & Sirianni, Carmen, eds. Work, Community & Power: The Experience of Labor in Europe & America, 1900-1925. 1983. write for info. (ISBN 0-87722-308-4); pap. write for info. (ISBN 0-87722-309-2). Temple U Pr.

Cronin, Jim, jt. auth. see Cronin, Gaynell.

Cronin, John F. Social Principles & Economic Life. 1966. 6.95 o.p. (ISBN 0-02-813980-1). Glencoe.

Cronin, L. Eugene, ed. Estuarine Research, 2 vols. Incl. Vol 1. Chemistry & Biology. 58.50 (ISBN 0-12-197501-0); Vol 2. Geology & Engineering. 59.00 (ISBN 0-12-197502-9). 1975. 96.50 set (ISBN 0-685-72436-0). Acad Pr.

Cronin, Lawrence J. Resources for Religious Education of Retarded People. 1977. pap. 2.00 o.p. (ISBN 0-88479-009-6). Arena Lettres.

Cronin, Morton J. Vocabulary One Thousand: With Words in Context. 2nd ed. 180p. 1981. pap. text ed. 9.95 (ISBN 0-15-594987-X, HC); instr's. manual 1.50 (ISBN 0-15-594988-8). HarBraceJ.

Cronin, Richard. Shelley's Poetic Thoughts. 1981. 25.00 (ISBN 0-312-71664-8). St Martin.

Cronin, Thomas E., et al. U. S. V. Crime in the Streets. LC 80-8842. (Illus.). 224p. 1981. 17.50x (ISBN 0-253-19017-7). Ind U Pr.

Cronin, Vincent. The View from Planet Earth: Man Looks at the Cosmos. LC 82-16654. (Illus.). 384p. 1983. pap. 6.95 (ISBN 0-688-01479-8). Quill NY.

Cronk, George. The Message of the Bible: An Orthodox Christian Perspective. LC 82-7355. 293p. (Orig.). 1982. pap. 8.95 (ISBN 0-913836-94-X). St Vladimirs.

Cronk, Louise H., jt. auth. see Handy, Ralph S.

Cronk, Walter. Golden Light. 3rd ed. LC 64-15645. (Illus.). 1973. Repr. of 1964 ed. 7.95 (ISBN 0-87516-018-2). De Vorss.

Cronkhite, C. L. Automation & Law Enforcement. (Illus.). 160p. 1974. 13.50x (ISBN 0-398-03200-9); pap. 8.75x (ISBN 0-398-03201-7). C C Thomas.

Cronon, E. David. Josephus Daniels in Mexico. (Illus.). 384p. 1960. 17.50 (ISBN 0-299-02061-4); pap. 6.95 (ISBN 0-299-02064-9). U of Wis Pr.

Cronon, William. Changes in the Land. (Illus.). 1982. 14.50 (ISBN 0-8090-3405-0); pap. 6.75 (ISBN 0-8090-0158-6). Hill & Wang.

Cronquist, jt. auth. see Gleason.

Cronquist, Arthur. Vascular Flora of the Southeastern United States: Vol. 1-Asteraceae. Radford, Albert E., ed. LC 79-769. xv, 261p. 1980. 25.00x (ISBN 0-8078-1362-1). U of NC Pr.

Cronstedt, Val. Engineering Management & Administration. 1961. 27.50 o.p. (ISBN 0-07-014480-X, P&RB). McGraw.

Croog, Sydney H. & Levine, Sol. Life After a Heart Attack: Social & Psychological Factors Eight Years Later. LC 81-6702. 328p. 1982. 26.95 (ISBN 0-89885-071-1). Human Sci Pr.

Crook, Bette & Crook, Charles L. Famous Firsts in Medicine. new ed. (Famous Firsts Ser.). (Illus.). 96p. (gr. 5 up). 1974. PLB 4.97 o.p. (ISBN 0-399-60861-3). Putnam Pub Group.

Crook, Charles L., jt. auth. see Crook, Bette.

Crook, D. P. Diplomacy During the American Civil War. LC 75-25678. (America in Crisis Ser). 209p. 1975. pap. text ed. 14.50 (ISBN 0-471-18856-5). Wiley.

Crook, David & Crook, Isabel. The First Years of Yangyi Commune. (International Library of Sociology). 288p. 1979. 22.50 (ISBN 0-7100-3463-6). Routledge & Kegan.

--Revolution in a Chinese Village: Ten Mile Inn. (International Library of Sociology). 190p. 1979. 20.00 (ISBN 0-7100-3393-1). Routledge & Kegan.

Crook, Howard. The Brownstone Cavalry. 400p. 1983. pap. 3.50 (ISBN 0-425-05935-9). Berkley Pub.

Crook, Isabel, jt. auth. see Crook, David.

Crook, J. Mordaunt. William Burges & the High Victorian Dream. LC 81-1592. (Illus.). 632p. 1981. 55.00 (ISBN 0-226-12117-8). U of Chicago Pr.

Crook, M. A. & Johnson, P., eds. Liquid Scintillation Counting, Vol. 3. 1974. 66.95 (ISBN 0-471-25656-0, Wiley Heyden). Wiley.

--Liquid Scintillation Counting, Vol. 5. 1978. casebound 83.95 (ISBN 0-471-25653-6, Wiley Heyden). Wiley.

Crook, Roger H. An Open Book to the Christian Divorcee. LC 73-87064. pap. 4.95 (ISBN 0-8054-5217-6). Broadman.

Crook, William G. Are You Allergic? rev. ed. 1978. pap. 5.95 (ISBN 0-933478-02-X). Prof Bks.

--Can Your Child Read? Is He Hyperactive? rev. ed. 1977. pap. 5.95 (ISBN 0-933478-01-1). Prof Bks.

--Your Allergic Child. LC 73-1682. 171p. 1973. 9.50 o.p. (ISBN 0-686-65359-9). Krieger.

Crookall, R. Interpretation of Cosmic & Mystical Experiences. 187p. 1969. 11.95 (ISBN 0-227-67729-3). Attic Pr.

Crooke, John. Better Tennis. (Better Ser.). (Illus.). (gr. 7 up). 1976. 16.95x (ISBN 0-7182-0486-7, SpS). Sportshelf.

Crooks, J. Drugs & the Elderly. 320p. 1979. text ed. 49.95 o.p. (ISBN 0-8391-1438-9). Univ Park.

Crooks, James B. Politics & Progress: The Rise of Urban Progressivism in Baltimore, 1895-1911. LC 68-21805. (Illus.). x, 260p. 1968. 20.00x o.p. (ISBN 0-8071-0417-5). La State U Pr.

Crooks, Robert & Baur, Karla. Our Sexuality. 1983. 21.95 (ISBN 0-8053-1914-X). Benjamin-Cummings.

Crooks, Thomas C. & Hancock, Harry L. Basic Technical Mathematics. 1969. text ed. 21.95x (ISBN 0-02-325640-0, 32564). Macmillan.

Crookshank, Anne O. Irish Art from Sixteen Hundred. (Aspects of Ireland Ser.: Vol. 4). (Illus.). 80p. Date not set. pap. 5.95 (ISBN 0-906404-04-5, Pub. by Dept Foreign Ireland). Irish Bks Media.

Crookston, Peter, ed. Village England. (Illus.). 256p. 1980. 16.95 o.p. (ISBN 0-09-142320-1, Pub. by Hutchinson England). Methuen Inc.

Croom, Emily A. Unpuzzling Your Past: A Basic Guide to Genealogy. LC 82-24514. (Illus.). 128p. 1983. pap. 7.95 (ISBN 0-932620-21-3). Betterway Pubns.

Croome, D. J. & Roberts, B. M. Air Conditioning & Ventilation of Buildings, Vol. 1. 2nd ed. LC 79-40965. (International Ser. in Heating, Ventilation & Refrigeration: Vol. 14). (Illus.). 1981. text ed. 60.00 (ISBN 0-08-024779-2). Pergamon.

Croome, D. J. & Sherratt, A. F., eds. Condensation in Buildings. (Illus.). 1972. text ed. 39.00x (ISBN 0-85334-548-1, Pub. by Applied Sci England). Elsevier.

Croome, Derek J. Noise & Design of Buildings & Services. LC 81-12631. (Illus.). 160p. (Orig.). 1982. pap. text ed. 39.95x (ISBN 0-86095-877-9). Longman.

Croonenburg, Englebert J. Van see Van Croonenburg, Englebert J.

Cropley, A. J. Towards a System of Lifelong Education: Some Practical Considerations. LC 80-40417. (Advances in Lifelong Education Ser.: Vol. 7). (Illus.). 234p. 1980. 25.00 o.p. (ISBN 0-08-026068-3); pap. 12.25 (ISBN 0-08-026067-5). Pergamon.

Cropper, William H. Quantum Physicists & an Introduction to Their Physics. 1970. pap. 9.95x (ISBN 0-19-500861-8). Oxford U Pr.

Crosbie, Ray, et al, eds. Towards Real-Time Simulation... Languages, Models & systems. (SCS Simulation Ser.: Vol. 6, Nos. 1 & 2). 30.00 (ISBN 0-686-36671-9). Soc Computer Sim.

Crosby, et al. Building College Spelling Skills. 192p. (Orig.). 1981. pap. text ed. 8.95 (ISBN 0-316-16186-1); tchr's manual avail. (ISBN 0-316-16188-8). Little.

Crosby, Alexander L. Pond Life. LC 64-12627. (Junior Science Books Ser). (Illus.). (gr. 2-5). 1964. PLB 6.69 (ISBN 0-8116-6169-5). Garrard.

--The Rimac: River of Peru. LC 67-10021. (Illus.). (gr. 5). 1965. PLB 3.98 (ISBN 0-8116-6366-3). Garrard.

Crosby, Alfred W., Jr. The Columbian Exchange: Biological and Cultural Consequences of 1492. LC 73-140916. (Contributions in American Studies: No. 2). 268p. 1972. lib. bdg. 27.50 (ISBN 0-8371-5821-4, CCE/); pap. 3.95 (ISBN 0-8371-7228-4). Greenwood.

--Epidemic & Peace, 1918. LC 75-23861. (Illus.). 337p. 1976. lib. bdg. 29.95 (ISBN 0-8371-8376-6, CPD/). Greenwood.

Crosby, Benjamin, jt. auth. see Lindenberg, Marc.

Crosby County Historical Commission. A History of Crosby County, 1876-1977. 1978. 75.00x (ISBN 0-686-31815-3). Crosby County.

Crosby, Ernest. Garrison the Non-Resistant. LC 72-137534. (Peace Movement in America Ser.). 141p. 1972. Repr. of 1905 ed. lib. bdg. 11.95x (ISBN 0-89198-062-8). Ozer.

Crosby, Gary & Firestone, Ross. Going My Own Way. LC 82-45196. (Illus.). 312p. 1983. 15.95 (ISBN 0-385-17055-6). Doubleday.

Crosby, John. Men In Arms. LC 82-40168. 256p. 1983. 14.95 (ISBN 0-8128-2885-2). Stein & Day.

Crosby, John F., jt. auth. see Williams, Carl E.

Crosby, Kathryn. My Life With Bing. LC 82-74361. (Illus.). 358p. 1983. 29.95 (ISBN 0-938728-01-6). Collage Inc.

Crosby, N. T. Food Packaging Materials: Aspects of Analysis & Migration of Contaminants. (Illus.). 190p. 1981. 33.00 (ISBN 0-85334-926-6, Pub. by Applied Sci England). Elsevier.

Crosby, Nina & Marten, Elizabeth. The Zoo. (gr. 3-6). 1980. 6.95 (ISBN 0-916456-73-0, GA187). Good Apple.

Crosby, Nina, jt. auth. see Marten, Elizabeth.

Crosby, Philip. Quality Is Free: The Art of Making Quality Free. 1979. 19.95 (ISBN 0-07-014512-1, P&RB). McGraw.

Crosby, Philip B. The Art of Getting Your Own Sweet Way. 2nd ed. (Illus.). 240p. 1981. 16.50 (ISBN 0-07-014515-6). McGraw.

--Quality Is Free: The Art of Making Quality Certain. 1980. pap. 3.50 (ISBN 0-451-62129-8, ME2129, Ment). NAL.

Crosby, Phoebe. Stars. LC 60-9233. (Junior Science Ser.). (Illus.). (gr. 2-5). 1960. PLB 6.69 (ISBN 0-8116-6153-9). Garrard.

Crosby, R. M. & Liston, R. A. The Waysiders: Reading & the Dyslexic Child. LC 76-12222. (John Day Bk.). 1976. 11.49 (ISBN 0-381-98290-4). T Y Crowell.

Crosby, Robert W., ed. Cities & Regions As Nonlinear Decision Systems. (AAAS Selected Symposium: No. 77). 200p. 1983. lib. bdg. 25.00 (ISBN 0-86531-530-2). Westview.

Crosby, Sumner M., et al. The Royal Abbey of Saint-Denis in the Time of Abbot Suger (1122-1151) Shultz, Ellen, ed. LC 80-28849. (Illus.). 128p. 1981. pap. 12.95 (ISBN 0-87099-261-9). Metro Mus Art.

Crosby, Travis L. English Farmers & the Politics of Protection. 228p. 1977. text ed. 20.75x o.p. (ISBN 0-85527-116-7). Humanities.

Crosher, Judith & Strongman, Harry. The Greeks. LC 77-86190. (Peoples of the Past Ser.). (Illus.). 1977. PLB 12.68 (ISBN 0-382-06119-5). Silver.

Crosher, Judith, et al. The Aztecs. LC 77-86189. (Peoples of the Past Ser.). (Illus.). 1977. PLB 12.68 (ISBN 0-382-06123-3). Silver.

Crosignani, P. G. & Rubin, B. L., eds. Genetic Control of Gamete Production & Function. LC 82-71233. (Serono Clinical Colloquia on Reproduction Ser.: No. 3). 1982. write for info. o.s.i. (ISBN 0-8089-1505-3, 790947). Grune.

Croskery, Sidney E. While I Remember. 1982. 27.00x (ISBN 0-85640-260-5, Pub. by Blackstaff Pr). State Mutual Bk.

Crosland, Andrew, compiled by. Concordance to F. Scott Fitzgerald's the Great Gatsby. LC 74-11607. (A Bruccoli Clark Book). 425p. 1975. 68.00x (ISBN 0-8103-1005-8). Gale.

--Concordance to the Complete Poetry of Stephen Crane. LC 74-30426. (A Bruccoli Clark Book). 1975. 76.00x (ISBN 0-8103-1006-6). Gale.

Crosland, Jessie, tr. Medieval French Literature. LC 76-17313. 1976. Repr. of 1956 ed. lib. bdg. 19.25x (ISBN 0-8371-8971-3, CRMF). Greenwood.

Crosland, M. P. Gay-Lussac: Scientist & Bourgeois. LC 77-91084. (Illus.). 1978. 45.00 (ISBN 0-521-21979-5). Cambridge U Pr.

Crosland, Margaret. Raymond Radiquet: A Biographical Study with Selections from His Work. 153p. 1982. 12.95 (ISBN 0-7206-0413-3, Pub. by Peter Owen). Merrimack Bk Serv.

Crosland, Margaret, tr. see Linhart, Robert.

Crosland, Margaret, tr. see Pavese, Cesare.

Crosland, Susan. Tony Crosland. (Illus.). 422p. 1983. 19.95 (ISBN 0-224-01787-X, Pub by Jonathan Cape). Merrimack Bk Serv.

Cross, Aleene. Home Economics Evaluation. LC 73-75679. 1973. text ed. 21.95 (ISBN 0-675-08933-6). Merrill.

Cross, Amanda. The James Joyce Murder. large type ed. LC 82-6027. 275p. 1982. Repr. of 1982 ed. 9.95 (ISBN 0-89621-373-0). Thorndike Pr.

--Poetic Justice. (YA) (gr. 7 up). 1979. pap. 2.95 (ISBN 0-380-44222-1, 82388-8). Avon.

--The Question of Max. 1977. pap. 2.50 (ISBN 0-380-01770-9, 58818-8). Avon.

--The Question of Max. 1977. lib. bdg. 10.95 o.p. (ISBN 0-8161-6451-7, Large Print Bks). G K Hall.

--The Theban Mysteries. large print ed. LC 82-5469. 275p. 1982. Repr. of 1979 ed. 9.95x (ISBN 0-89621-362-5). Thorndike Pr.

Cross, Arthur L. Anglican Episcopate & the American Colonies. ix, 368p. 1964. Repr. of 1902 ed. 19.50 o.p. (ISBN 0-208-00420-3, Archon). Shoe String.

Cross, Barbara M., ed. Educated Woman in America: Selected Writings of Catharine Beecher, Margaret Fuller & M. Carey Thomas. LC 65-23578. (Illus.). 1965. text ed. 10.00 (ISBN 0-8077-1221-3); pap. text ed. 5.00x (ISBN 0-8077-1218-3). Tchrs Coll.

Cross, Charles A., jt. auth. see Moore, Patrick.

Cross, Colin. The Liberals in Power: 1905-1914. LC 75-40998. 1976. Repr. of 1963 ed. lib. bdg. 20.25x (ISBN 0-8371-8706-0, CRLP). Greenwood.

Cross, Donna W. Mediaspeak: How Television Makes Up Your Mind. 288p. 1983. 16.95 (ISBN 0-698-11131-1, Coward). Putnam Pub Group.

--Word Abuse: How the Words We Use, Use Us. LC 78-11025. 1979. 9.95 (ISBN 0-698-10906-6, Coward); pap. 5.95 (ISBN 0-698-10968-6). Putnam Pub Group.

Cross, Donna W., jt. auth. see Woolfolk, William.

Cross, Doris. Columns. 68p. 1982. pap. 12.00 (ISBN 0-917588-07-X). Trike.

Cross, Dorothy. Movable Property in the Nuzi Documents. 1937. pap. 10.00 (ISBN 0-527-02684-0). Kraus Repr.

Cross, Eric. The Late Operas of Antonio Vivaldi, 1727-1738, 2 vols. Fortune, Nigel, ed. LC 81-77. (British Studies in Musicology: No. 1). 616p. 1981. Set. 84.95 (ISBN 0-8357-1158-7, Pub. by UMI Res Pr). Vol. 1 (ISBN 0-8357-1255-9). Vol. 2 (ISBN 0-8357-1256-7). Univ Microfilms.

Cross, F. L. & Livingstone, Elizabeth A. The Oxford Dictionary of the Christian Church. 1974. 60.95x (ISBN 0-19-211545-6). Oxford U Pr.

Cross, Frank L., jt. ed. see Young, Richard A.

Cross, Frank L., Jr., jt. auth. see Hesketh, Howard E.

Cross, Frank M., ed. Symposia Celebrating the Seventy-Fifth Anniversary of the Founding of the American Schools of Oriental Research: 1900-1975. LC 79-10226. (Zion Research Foundation, Occasional Publications: Vol. 1 & 2). 183p. 1979. pap. text ed. 8.00x (ISBN 0-89757-503-2, Am Sch Orient Res). Eisenbrauns.

Cross, Frank R. Elementary School Career Education: A Humanistic Model. LC 73-92002. (Occupational Education Ser.). 160p. 1974. pap. text ed. 8.95 o.p. (ISBN 0-675-08824-0). Merrill.

Cross, Gary P., et al. Conflict & Human Interaction. 1979. pap. text ed. 11.95 (ISBN 0-8403-1990-8). Kendall-Hunt.

Cross, Gary S. Immigrant Workers in Industrial France: The Making of a New Laboring Class. 1983. write for info. (ISBN 0-87722-300-9). Temple U Pr.

Cross, George L. Blacks in White Colleges: Oklahoma's Landmark Cases. 1975. pap. 5.95 (ISBN 0-8061-1267-0). U of Okla Pr.

Cross, Gilbert, jt. auth. see Wallace, Forrest.

Cross, Gillian. The Demon Headmaster. (Illus.). 174p. (gr. 3-7). 1983. bds. 6.95 (ISBN 0-19-271460-0, Pub. by Oxford U Pr Childrens). Merrimack Bk Serv.

Cross, Gordon R. The Psychology of Learning: An Introduction for Students of Education. 1974. text ed. 31.00 o.s.i. (ISBN 0-08-018136-8); pap. text ed. 17.00 (ISBN 0-08-018135-X). Pergamon.

Cross, Hansell F. All About Sex & Reproduction in a Nutshell: A Short Reference of Biological Facts. 1983. 10.00 (ISBN 0-533-05302-1). Vantage.

Cross, Helen R. A Curiosity for the Curious. LC 77-3400. (Illus.). (gr. 3-6). 1978. 7.95 o.p. (ISBN 0-698-20423-9, Coward). Putnam Pub Group.

--Isabella Mine. (Illus.). (gr. 3-7). 1982. 9.00 (ISBN 0-688-00885-2). Lothrop.

Cross, Henry, Jr., jt. auth. see Avery, David D.

Cross, Ira B. A History of the Labor Movement in California. (California Library Reprint Ser.). 1974. Repr. 33.00x (ISBN 0-520-02646-2). U of Cal Pr.

Cross, J. A. Lord Swinton. 320p. 1983. 45.00 (ISBN 0-19-822602-0). Oxford U Pr.

Cross, James E., jt. auth. see Bazire, Joyce.

Cross, James E. & Hill, Thomas D., eds. The Prose Solomon & Saturn; & Adrian & Ritheus. (McMaster Old English & Texts Ser.). 1982. 35.00x (ISBN 0-8020-5472-2); pap. 12.50 (ISBN 0-8020-6509-0). U of Toronto Pr.

Cross, Jeanne. Simple Printing Methods. LC 72-39812. (Illus.). 48p. (gr. 6 up). 1972. 10.95 (ISBN 0-87599-192-0). S G Phillips.

Cross, John, jt. auth. see Galliher, John.

Cross, K. W., et al, eds. Foetal & Neonatal Physiology: Proceedings. LC 72-93673. (Illus.). 600p. 1973. 99.00 (ISBN 0-521-20178-0). Cambridge U Pr.

Cross, L. S. Paul's Letters Made Easy for Devotions. 120p. (Orig.). 1982. pap. 4.95 (ISBN 0-89221-090-7, Pub by SonLife). New Leaf.

Cross, M. Urbanization & Urban Growth in the Caribbean. LC 78-67307. (Urbanization in Developing Countries Ser.). 1979. 29.95 (ISBN 0-521-22426-8); pap. 8.95 (ISBN 0-521-29491-6). Cambridge U Pr.

Cross, Michael. U. S. Corporate Personnel Reduction Policies. 134p. 1982. text ed. 35.50x (ISBN 0-566-00501-8). Gower Pub Ltd.

Cross, N. J., jt. auth. see Allen, G. R.

Cross, P. C., jt. auth. see Allen, H. C., Jr.

Cross, R. C., ed. see Symposium On Relaxation Methods In Relation To Molecular Structure Aberystwyth - 1965.

Cross, Richard K. Malcolm Lowry: A Preface to His Fiction. LC 79-16091. 1980. 12.50x (ISBN 0-226-12125-9). U of Chicago Pr.

Cross, Rupert. Precedent in English Law. 3rd. ed. 252p. 1977. pap. text ed. 13.95x (ISBN 0-19-876073-6). Oxford U Pr.

Cross, Samuel H., ed. Russian Primary Chronicle: Laurentian Text. Sherbowitz-Wetzor, O. P., tr. LC 53-10264. 1968. Repr. of 1953 ed. 10.00x (ISBN 0-910956-34-0). Medieval Acad.

Cross, T. P. Motif-Index of Early Irish Literature. 1952. 30.00 o.s.i. (ISBN 0-527-20700-4). Kraus Repr.

Cross, W. & Florio, C. You Are Never Too Old to Learn. 1978. pap. 8.95 (ISBN 0-07-014514-8, C). McGraw.

Cross, Wilbur. Egypt. LC 82-9465. (Enchantment of the World). (Illus.). (gr. 5-9). 1982. PLB 13.25g (ISBN 0-516-02762-X). Childrens.

--Kids & Booze: What You Must Know to Help Them. 1979. 10.95 o.p. (ISBN 0-87690-355-3); pap. 5.95 (ISBN 0-87690-314-6, 0578-170). Dutton.

--Kids & Booze: What You Must Know to Help Them. 5.95 o.p. (ISBN 0-686-92227-1, 5017). Hazelden.

--Naval Battles & Heroes. LC 60-13854. (American Heritage Junior Library). 154p. (YA) (gr. 7 up). 1960. 12.95 (ISBN 0-06-021375-2, HarpJ); PLB 14.89 o.p. (ISBN 0-06-021376-0). Har-Row.

Cross, Wilbur L. The Modern English Novel. 1928. 24.50x (ISBN 0-686-51417-3). Elliots Bks.

Crossan, John D. Cliffs of Fall: Paradox & Polyvalence in the Parables of Jesus. 128p. 1980. 9.95 (ISBN 0-8164-0113-6). Seabury.

Crossan, John D., ed. Semeia Nineteen: The Book of Job & Ricocur's Hermeneutics. (Semeia Ser.). 9.95 (ISBN 0-686-96266-4, 06 20 19). Scholars Pr CA.

--Semeia Seventeen: Gnomie Wisdom. (Semeia Ser.). 9.95 (ISBN 0-686-96253-2, 06 20 17). Scholars Pr CA.

--Semeia Ten: Narrative Syntax: Traditions & Reviews. (Semeia Ser.). 9.95 (ISBN 0-686-96237-0, 06 20 10). Scholars Pr CA.

Crossan, R. M. & Nance, H. Master Standard Data: The Economic Approach to Work Measurement. 2nd ed. 1972. 21.50 o.p. (ISBN 0-07-014516-4, P&RB). McGraw.

Crossan, Richard M. & Nance, Harold W. Master Standard Data: The Economic Approach to Work,Measurement. rev. ed. LC 80-11165. 268p. 1980. Repr. of 1972 ed. lib. bdg. 16.00 (ISBN 0-89874-133-5). Krieger.

Crosse, Howard & Hempel, Goerge. Management Policies for Commercial Banks. 3rd ed. (Illus.). 1980. text ed. 22.95 (ISBN 0-13-549030-8). P-H.

Crossette, Barbara. America's Wonderful Little Hotels & Inns: 1981-82. (Illus.). 400p. 1981. 14.95 o.p. (ISBN 0-312-92016-4); pap. 8.95 o.p. (ISBN 0-312-92017-2). St Martin.

Crossette, Barbara, ed. America's Wonderful Little Hotels & Inns: 1982-83. 3rd ed. LC 82-2325. (Illus.). 496p. (Orig.). 1982. write for info. (ISBN 0-312-92019-9); pap. 12.95. Congdon & Weed.

Crossick, Geoffrey, ed. The Lower-Middle Class in Britain, 1870-1914. LC 76-25410. 1977. 22.50x (ISBN 0-312-49980-9). St Martin.

Crosskey, William W. Politics & the Constitution in the History of the United States, 4 bks, Vols I & II. LC 77-90070. (Midway Reprint Ser.). 1978. Set. pap. text ed. 48.00x o.s.i. (ISBN 0-226-12132-1). U of Chicago Pr.

Crossland, Bernard. Explosive Welding of Metals & Its Applications. (Series on Advanced Manufacturing). (Illus.). 1982. 48.00x (ISBN 0-19-859119-5). Oxford U Pr.

Crossley, Ceri. Edgar Quinet (1803-1875) A Study in Romantic Thought. LC 82-82432. (French Forum Monographs: No. 43). 149p. (Orig.). 1983. pap. 10.00x (ISBN 0-917058-42-9). French Forum.

Crossley, Frederick H. The English Abbey: Its Life & Work in the Middle Ages. LC 82-25127. (Illus.). xiv, 114p. 1983. Repr. of 1935 ed. lib. bdg. 45.00x (ISBN 0-313-23849-9, CRFE). Greenwood.

Crossley, Robert. Reader's Guide to H. G. Wells. Schlobin, Roger C., ed. (Reader's Guides to Contemporary Science Fiction & Fantasy Authors Ser.: Vol. 19). (Illus., Orig.). 1982. 10.95x (ISBN 0-916732-51-7); pap. text ed. 4.95x (ISBN 0-916732-50-9). Starmont Hse.

Crossley-Holland, Kevin & Mitchell, Bruce. The Battle of Maldon & Other Old English Poems. LC 65-13048. 138p. 1975. pap. 3.95 o.p. (ISBN 0-312-07000-4). St Martin.

Crossley-Holland, Kevin, jt. auth. see Paton Walsh, Jill.

Crossley-Holland, Kevin, ed. The Anglo-Saxon World. LC 82-24331. 200p. 1983. text ed. 22.50x (ISBN 0-389-20367-X). B&N Imports.

Crossman, Eileen. Mountain Rain. 1982. pap. 5.95 (ISBN 0-85363-146-8). OMF Bks.

Crossman, Morton. Together at Last. 1983. 7.95 (ISBN 0-533-05365-X). Vantage.

Crosson, R. S., et al. Compilation of Earthquake Hypo-Centers in Western Washington: 1977. (Information Circular Ser.: No. 66). (Illus.). 1979. 0.50 (ISBN 0-686-38467-9). Geologic Pubns.

Crosson, Robert S. & Noson, Linda. Compilation of Earthquake Hypo-Centers in Western Washington: 1975. (Information Circular Ser.: No.64). (Illus.). 12p. 1978. 0.50 (ISBN 0-686-34738-2). Geologic Pubns.

Crosson, Robert S., jt. auth. see Noson, Linda L.

Crosswait, C. Bruce, jt. auth. see Wilkes, Mary.

Crosswell, C. Legal & Financial Aspects of International Business. LC 80-14900. 350p. 1980. 40.00 (ISBN 0-379-20683-8). Oceana.

Crosten, William L. French Grand Opera: An Art & a Business. LC 73-171381. 132p. 1972. Repr. of 1948 ed. lib. bdg. 25.00 (ISBN 0-306-70405-6). Da Capo.

Crothers, Donald M., jt. auth. see Eisenberg, David.

Crottel, L. & Mendez, M. Lapland. (Illus.). 1968. 17.50x o.p. (ISBN 0-686-66879-0, N503). Vanous.

Crotty, Norma M., jt. auth. see Jacobs, James B.

Crotty, Robert & Manley, Gregory. Commentaries on the Readings of the Lectionary: Cycles A, B, C. 1975. pap. 12.95 (ISBN 0-916134-20-2). Pueblo Pub Co.

Crotty, William. Party Reform. 1983. pap. text ed. 10.95x (ISBN 0-582-28177-6). Longman.

Crotty, William J. & Jacobson, Gary C. American Parties in Decline. 267p. 1980. pap. text ed. 8.95 (ISBN 0-316-16222-1). Little.

Crotty, William J., ed. Paths to Political Reform. (Policy Studies Organization Bk.). 400p. 1980. 28.95 o.s.i. (ISBN 0-669-02395-7). Lexington Bks.

Crouch, Colin. The Politics of Industrial Relations. (Political Issues of Modern Britain Ser.). 1979. text ed. 25.25x (ISBN 0-391-01163-4). Humanities.

Crouch, Colin, ed. State & Economy in Contemporary Capitalism. LC 78-26539. 1979. 26.00x (ISBN 0-312-75601-1). St Martin.

Crouch, Edmond & Wilson, Richard. Risk-Benefit Analysis. 240p. 1982. prof ref 25.00x (ISBN 0-88410-667-5). Ballinger Pub.

Crouch, James & Carr, Micheline. Anatomy & Physiology: A Laboratory Manual. LC 76-56507. (Illus.). 369p. 1977. spiral 14.95 (ISBN 0-87484-356-1). Mayfield Pub.

Crouch, James E. Introduction to Human Anatomy. 5th ed. (Illus.). 256p. 1973. pap. 12.95 (ISBN 0-87484-206-9). Mayfield Pub.

--Introduction to Human Anatomy: A Laboratory Manual. 6th ed. (Illus.). 236p. 1983. spiral bdg. 11.95 (ISBN 0-87484-540-8). Mayfield Pub.

Crouch, James E. & McClintic, Robert J. Human Anatomy & Physiology. 2nd ed. LC 76-868. 809p. 1976. text ed. 33.95 (ISBN 0-471-18918-9). lab manual 13.95 (ISBN 0-471-58170-4); students manual 8.50 (ISBN 0-471-01715-9). Wiley.

Crouch, Marcus. The Whole World Storybook. (Illus.). 160p. (gr. k-4). 1983. text ed. 12.95 (ISBN 0-19-278103-0, Pub. by Oxford U Pr Childrens). Merrimack Bk Serv.

Crouch, Milton & Raum, Hans, eds. Directory of State & Local History Periodicals. LC 77-4396. 1977. pap. 7.00 (ISBN 0-8389-0246-4). ALA.

Crouch, Owen. What the Bible Says about the Bible. LC 81-65515. (What the Bible Says Ser.). 400p. 1981. 13.50 (ISBN 0-89900-082-7). College Pr Pub.

Crouch, R., et al. Preparatory Mathematics for Elementary Teachers. 595p. 1965. text ed. 13.50x o.p. (ISBN 0-471-18913-8, Pub. by Wiley). Krieger.

Crouch, Ralph B. Finite Mathematics with Statistics for Business. 1968. solutions manual 15.95 (ISBN 0-07-014519-9, C). McGraw.

Crouch, Richard E. Interstate Custody Litigation: A Guide to Use & Court Interpretation of the Uniform Child Custody Jurisdiction Act. LC 81-6082. 148p. 1981. pap. text ed. 12.50 (ISBN 0-87179-357-1). BNA.

Crouch., S. L. & Starfield, A. M. Boundary Element Methods in Solid Mechanics. (Illus.). 1982. text ed. 35.00x (ISBN 0-04-620010-X). Allen Unwin.

Crouch, Steve. Steinbeck Country. LC 72-95690. (Images of America Ser.). (Illus.). 192p. 1975. 18.50 o.p. (ISBN 0-517-52715-4); pap. 9.95 (ISBN 0-517-52716-2). Crown.

Crouch, Thomas W. A Yankee Guerrillero: Frederick Funston & the Cuban Insurrection, 1896-1897. LC 75-20193. (Illus.). 176p. 1975. 9.95x o.p. (ISBN 0-87870-027-7). Memphis St Univ.

Crouch, W. G., jt. auth. see Zetler, Robert L.

Crouch, Winston W. Organized Civil Servants: Public Employer-Employee Relations in California. LC 77-91767. 1978. 29.50x (ISBN 0-520-03626-3). U of Cal Pr.

Crouch, Winston W., et al. California Government & Politics. 7th ed. (Illus.). 288p. 1981. pap. 12.95 (ISBN 0-13-112433-1). P-H.

Croucher, John S. Operations Research: A First Course. (Illus.). 320p. 1980. 29.00 (ISBN 0-08-024798-9); pap. 16.50 (ISBN 0-08-024797-0). Pergamon.

Croucher, Michael & Reid, Howard. The Fighting Arts. (Illus.). 1983. price not set (ISBN 0-671-47158-9). S&S.

Croucher, N. Outdoor Pursuits for Disabled People. 180p. 1981. pap. text ed. 13.00x (ISBN 0-85941-186-9). Verry.

Croucher, Ronald & Woolley, Alan R. Fossils, Minerals & Rocks: Collection & Preservation. LC 82-1282. (Illus.). 64p. 1982. 6.50 (ISBN 0-521-24736-5, Copublished with the British Museum). Cambridge U Pr.

Crouchett, Lorraine J. Filipinos in California: From the Days of the Galleon to the Present. LC 82-73374. (Illus.). 168p. 1983. 10.95x (ISBN 0-910823-00-6). Downey Place.

Crough, Colin. Student Revolt. 1971. 6.95 o.p. (ISBN 0-370-01320-4). Transatlantic.

Crouse, Anna & Crouse, Russel. Peter Stuyvesant of Old New York. (Landmark Ser.: No. 3). (gr. 4-6). 1954. PLB 4.27 (ISBN 0-394-90343-9); pap. 2.95 (ISBN 0-394-80343-4). Random.

Crouse, Anna & Crouse, Russell. Alexander Hamilton & Aaron Burr. (Landmark Ser.: No. 85). 1963. 2.95 (ISBN 0-394-80385-X, BYR); PLB 5.99 (ISBN 0-394-90385-4). Random.

Crouse, Russel, jt. auth. see Crouse, Anna.

Crouse, Russell, jt. auth. see Crouse, Anna.

Crouse, W. H. & Anglin, D. L. Automotive Air Conditioning. 2nd ed. 304p. 1982. text ed. 17.95x (ISBN 0-07-014857-0, C); wkbk. 8.95x (ISBN 0-07-014858-9). McGraw.

--Automotive Brakes, Suspension & Steering. 6th ed. 1983. 19.95 (ISBN 0-07-014828-7). McGraw.

--Automotive Emission Control. 3rd ed. 1983. text ed. write for info. (ISBN 0-07-014816-3); write for info. instr's planning guide; write for info wkbk. (ISBN 0-07-014817-1). McGraw.

--Automotive Tune-Up. 1983. text ed. 17.95 (ISBN 0-07-014836-8); wkbk. 8.95 (ISBN 0-07-014837-6). McGraw.

Crouse, William H. Automotive Electrical Equipment. 8th ed. (Automotive Technology Ser.). 1975. text ed. 17.95 (ISBN 0-07-014666-7, G); wkbk. 8.95 (ISBN 0-07-014688-8); instructor's planning guide 4.50 (ISBN 0-07-014667-5). McGraw.

--Automotive Electronics & Electrical Equipment. 9th ed. (Illus.). 1980. pap. text ed. 17.95 (ISBN 0-07-014831-7); instructor's planning guide 3.00 (ISBN 0-07-014833-3); wkbk. 8.95 (ISBN 0-07-014832-5). McGraw.

--Automotive Mechanics. 6th ed. (gr. 10 up). 1970. text ed. 19.05 o.p. (ISBN 0-07-014668-3, G); instructor's planning guide 4.50 o.p. (ISBN 0-07-014681-0) (ISBN 0-07-014682-9). McGraw.

--Automotive Service Business: Operation & Management. 1972. pap. text ed. 16.50 (ISBN 0-07-014605-5, G). McGraw.

--Small Engines: Operation & Maintenance. (Automotive Technology Ser). (Illus.). 448p. 1973. pap. text ed. 17.95 (ISBN 0-07-014691-8, G); wkbk. 7.95 (ISBN 0-07-014692-6). McGraw.

Crouse, William H. & Anglin, D. L. Automotive Fuel, Lubricating & Cooling Systems. 5th ed. 1976. 17.95 (ISBN 0-07-014648-9, G); wkbk. 8.95 (ISBN 0-07-014649-7); instructor's planning guide 4.50 (ISBN 0-07-014656-X). McGraw.

--Automotive Mechanics. 7th ed. (Illus.). 640p. (gr. 11-12). 1975. text ed. 21.50 (ISBN 0-07-014535-0, G); instructor's manual 7.95 (ISBN 0-07-014536-9); study guide 8.95 (ISBN 0-07-014539-3); testbk. 6.95 (ISBN 0-07-014537-7); wkbk 9.95 (ISBN 0-07-014538-5). McGraw.

Crouse, William H. & Anglin, Donald L. The Auto Book. 2nd ed. (Illus.). 1978. text ed. 21.50 (ISBN 0-07-014560-1, G); instructor's manual 6.00 (ISBN 0-07-014564-4); study guide 8.95 (ISBN 0-07-014561-X); wkbk. 8.95 (ISBN 0-07-014562-8); auto text bk. 7.95 (ISBN 0-07-014563-6). McGraw.

--Automotive Air Conditioning: A Complete Program. (Automotive Technology Ser.). (Illus.). 1977. soft bdg. 17.95 (ISBN 0-07-014591-1, G); wkbk 8.95 (ISBN 0-07-014593-8); transparencies 145.00 (ISBN 0-07-014594-6); instructor's planning guide 4.50 (ISBN 0-07-014592-X). McGraw.

--Automotive Automatic Transmissions. 6th ed. LC 81-14262. (Illus.). 304p. 1983. pap. 16.05 (ISBN 0-07-014771-X, G); instr's planning guide 3.00 (ISBN 0-07-014773-6); wkbk. 8.00 (ISBN 0-07-014772-8). McGraw.

--Automotive Body Repair & Refinishing. (Illus.). 1980. text ed. 25.00 (ISBN 0-07-014791-4); instructor's planning guide 3.50 (ISBN 0-07-014793-0); wkbk. 9.95. McGraw.
--Automotive Chassis & Body. 5th ed. (Automotive Technology Ser.). (Illus.). 416p. 1975. soft cover 17.95 (ISBN 0-07-014653-5, G); wkbk. 8.95 (ISBN 0-07-014654-3); instructor's planning guide 4.50 (ISBN 0-07-014655-1). McGraw.
--Automotive Emission Control. 2nd ed. (Automotive Technology Ser.). (Illus.). 1977. pap. text ed. 17.95 (ISBN 0-07-014640-3, G); wkbk. 8.95 (ISBN 0-07-014641-1); instrs planning guide 4.50 (ISBN 0-07-014642-X). McGraw.
--Automotive Engines. 5th ed. (Automotive Technology Ser.). 1975. 17.95 (ISBN 0-07-014602-0, G); wkbk. 8.95 (ISBN 0-07-014603-9); instr's. planning guide 4.50 (ISBN 0-07-014604-7). McGraw.
--Automotive Engines. 6th ed. (Illus.). 96p. 1980. 17.95 (ISBN 0-07-014825-2, G); instructor's planning guide 3.00 (ISBN 0-07-014827-9); wkbk. 8.95 (ISBN 0-07-014826-0). McGraw.
--Automotive Fuel, Lubricating & Cooling Systems. 6th ed. Gilmore, D. E., ed. (Illus.). 352p. 1980. pap. text ed. 17.95 (ISBN 0-07-014862-7, G); wkbk. 8.95 (ISBN 0-07-014863-5). McGraw.
--Automotive Manual Transmissions & Power Trains. 6th ed. LC 81-17206. (Illus.). 352p. 1983. pap. text ed. 16.05 (ISBN 0-07-014776-0, G); wkbk. 8.00 (ISBN 0-07-014777-9); instr's planning guide 3.00 (ISBN 0-07-014778-7). McGraw.
--Automotive Technician's Handbook. (Illus.). 1979. 32.95 (ISBN 0-07-014751-5). McGraw.
--Automotive Tools, Fasteners, & Measurements: A Text-Workbook. (Automotive Technology Series). (Illus.). (gr. 9-12). 1977. pap. text ed. 10.95 (ISBN 0-07-014630-6, G). McGraw.
--Automotive Transmissions & Power Trains. 5th ed. 1976. 17.95 (ISBN 0-07-014637-3, G); wkbk. 8.95 (ISBN 0-07-014638-1); instructor's planning guide 4.50 (ISBN 0-07-014646-2). McGraw.
--Automotive Tune-up. (Automotive Technology Series). (Illus.). (gr. 12). 1977. soft-cover 17.95 (ISBN 0-07-014810-4, G); instructors guide 4.50 (ISBN 0-07-014812-0); wkbk 8.95 (ISBN 0-07-014811-2). McGraw.
--Motor Vehicle Inspection. (Illus.). 1978. 25.95 (ISBN 0-07-014813-9, G); instructor's planning guide 3.50 (ISBN 0-07-014814-7); wkbk 9.95 (ISBN 0-07-014815-5). McGraw.
--Motorcycle Mechanics. LC 81-217. (Illus.). 384p. 1982. pap. text ed. 17.95 (ISBN 0-07-014781-7); wkbk. 128p. 6.95 (ISBN 0-07-014782-5). McGraw.
--Pocket Automotive Dictionary, with Metric Conversion Table. new ed. (Automotive Technology Ser). 1976. pap. text ed. 4.95 (ISBN 0-07-014752-3, G). McGraw.
--Small Engine Mechanics. 2nd ed. LC 79-4658. (Illus.). 1979. pap. text ed. 18.95 (ISBN 0-07-014795-7, G); instructor's planning guide 3.50 (ISBN 0-07-014797-3); wkbk. 7.95 (ISBN 0-07-014796-5). McGraw.
--Workbook for Motorcycle Mechanics. (Illus.). 128p. 1982. 6.95 (ISBN 0-07-014782-5). McGraw.
Crouser, R. L. It's Unlucky to be Behind at the End of the Game: And Other Great Sports Retorts. (Illus.). 160p. 1983. 10.95 (ISBN 0-688-01968-4). Morrow.
--It's Unlucky to be Behind at the End of the Game and Other Great Sports Retorts. (Illus.). 160p. (Orig.). 1983. pap. 3.95 (ISBN 0-688-01970-6). Quill NY.
Crout, D. H. Chemistry of Natural Products. 1984. price not set (ISBN 0-87735-213-5). Freeman C.
Crout, D. H., jt. auth. see Geissman, T. A.
Crout, George. Lucky Cloverleaf. (Upper Grade Bk.). (Illus.). (gr. 4-6). PLB 2.00 o.p. (ISBN 0-513-00494-7). Denison.
Crouzet, Francois. The Victorian Economy. Forster, A. S., tr. 400p. 1982. text ed. 32.50x (ISBN 0-231-05542-0); pap. 16.00x (ISBN 0-231-05543-9). Columbia U Pr.
Crow, A., jt. auth. see Crow, Lester D.
Crow, Alice, jt. auth. see Crow, Lester D.
Crow, Carl. He Opened the Door of Japan. LC 74-5552. (Illus.). 275p. 1974. Repr. of 1939 ed. lib. bdg. 17.75x (ISBN 0-8371-7512-7, CROD). Greenwood.
Crow, Charles L., jt. ed. see Kerr, Howard.
Crow, D. R. Principles & Applications of Electrochemistry. 2nd ed. LC 79-75. (Chemistry Textbook Ser.). 238p. 1979. pap. 14.95x (ISBN 0-412-16020-X, Pub. by Chapman & Hall England). Methuen Inc.
Crow, David. Polarography of Metal Complexes. 1969. 29.50 (ISBN 0-12-198050-2). Acad Pr.
Crow, Donna F. The Frantic Mother Cookbook. LC 82-81918. (Orig.). 1982. pap. 4.95 (ISBN 0-89081-356-6). Harvest Hse.
--Professor Q's Mysterious Machine. (Making Choices Ser.: No. 3). (gr. 3-8). 1983. pap. 2.50 (ISBN 0-89191-562-1). Cook.
Crow, Gary A. Children at Risk: A Handbook of the Signs & Symptoms of Early Childhood Difficulties. LC 77-87859. 1978. 12.95 (ISBN 0-8052-3675-9). Schocken.
--Crisis Intervention: A Social Interaction Approach. 1978. 11.95 o.s.i. (ISBN 0-695-81163-0). Follett.
Crow, James F. Genetics Notes: An Introduction to Genetics. 8th ed. 352p. 1982. pap. text ed. write for info. (ISBN 0-8087-4805-X). Burgess.
--How Well Can We Assess Genetic Risk? Not Very. 9.00 (ISBN 0-913392-56-1). NCRP Pubns.
Crow, Jeffrey J. & Tise, Larry E., eds. The Southern Experience in the American Revolution. LC 77-21519. xvii, 310p. 1979. 21.00x (ISBN 0-8078-1313-3); pap. 8.00x (ISBN 0-8078-4059-9). U of NC Pr.
Crow, John A. The Epic of Latin America. LC 78-62860. 1000p. 1980. 38.00x (ISBN 0-520-04107-0); pap. 14.95 (ISBN 0-520-03776-6, CAL. NO. 458). U of Cal Pr.
Crow, Judson O. McDowell County, North Carolina, Land Entry Abstracts 1843-1869, Vol. 1. LC 82-20499. 504p. 1983. pap. 25.00 (ISBN 0-87152-365-5). Reprint.
Crow, Lester C. Introduction to Guidance: Basic Principles & Practices. 2nd ed. 464p. 1960. 16.50 (ISBN 0-442-21291-7, Pub. by Van Nos Reinhold). Krieger.
Crow, Lester D. Principles of Guidance. 251p. 1982. pap. write for info. (ISBN 0-932970-33-8). L D Crow.
--Psychology of Childhood for Students of Child Psychology. 211p. 1981. pap. write for info. o.s.i. (ISBN 0-932970-24-9). Prinit Pr.
Crow, Lester D. & Crow, A. Adolescent Development & Adjustment. 2nd ed. 1965. 16.95 o.p. (ISBN 0-07-014694-2, C). McGraw.
Crow, Lester D. & Crow, Alice. How to Study. 1963. pap. 3.95 (ISBN 0-02-013500-9, Collier). Macmillan.
--Human Development & Learning. 2nd ed. LC 74-26685. 590p. 1975. Repr. of 1965 ed. 23.50 (ISBN 0-88275-252-9). Krieger.
Crow, Michael M., ed. High Sulfur Coal Exports: An International Analysis. 1983. write for info. (ISBN 0-8093-1122-4). S Ill U Pr.
Crow, Ruth & McCarthy, Ginny, eds. Teenage Women in the Juvenile Justice Sustem: Changing Values. 169p. (Orig.). 1979. pap. 6.00 (ISBN 0-9608696-1-1). New Dir Young Women.
Crow, W. B. Occult Properties of Herbs. (Paths to Inner Power Ser). 1980. pap. 2.50 (ISBN 0-87728-097-5). Weiser.
Crowder, C. M., ed. English Society & Government in the Fifteenth Century. LC 68-79460. (Selections from History Today Ser.,No. 2). (Illus.). 1967. 7.95 (ISBN 0-05-000809-9); pap. 4.95 (ISBN 0-685-09164-3). Dufour.
--Unity, Heresy & Reform 1378-1460: The Conciliar Response to the Great Schism. LC 76-56693. (Documents of Medieval History Ser). 224p. 1977. 21.50x o.p. (ISBN 0-312-83318-0). St Martin.
Crowder, David L. Tales of Eastern Idaho. (Illus.). 150p. (Orig.). 1981. pap. text ed. 8.95 (ISBN 0-9607304-1-9). KID Broadcasting.
Crowder, Michael. The Story of Nigeria. 4th ed. 432p. 1978. pap. 9.95 (ISBN 0-571-04947-8). Faber & Faber.
--West Africa: An Introduction to Its History. (Illus.). 1977. pap. text ed. 8.95x (ISBN 0-582-60003-0). Longman.
Crowder, Richard. Carl Sandburg. (United States Authors Ser.). 1963. lib. bdg. 10.95 (ISBN 0-8057-0648-8, Twayne). G K Hall.
Crowder, Vernon & Jolly, Sonny. Concepts of Physical Education. (Illus., Orig.). pap. text ed. 8.95 (ISBN 0-88136-002-3). Jostens.
Crowdis, David G. & Wheeler, Brandon W. Introduction to Mathematical Ideas. LC 68-27505. (Illus.). 1969. text ed. 21.95 (ISBN 0-07-014705-1, C). McGraw.
--Trigonometry: A Functional Approach. 1971. text ed. 13.50 o.p. (ISBN 0-07-014710-8, C); instructor's manual 1.95 o.p. (ISBN 0-07-014711-6). McGraw.
Crowdis, David G. & Wheeler,. W. Elementary Algebra. 1970. text ed. 20.00 o.p. (ISBN 0-07-014707-8, C). McGraw.
Crowdis, David G., et al. Concepts of Calculus with Applications to Business & Economics. 1975. text ed. 22.95 (ISBN 0-02-473010-6); tchrs' manual free (ISBN 0-02-473020-3). Macmillan.
Crowe, Alf. A Guide to Autogyros. 2nd ed. (Illus.). 64p. 1982. pap. 8.00 (ISBN 0-933078-08-0). M Arman.
Crowe, Andrew. A Field Guide to the Native Edible Plants of New Zealand. (Illus.). 196p. 1983. 19.95 (ISBN 0-00-216983-5, Pub. by W Collins Australia). Intl Schol Bk Serv.
Crowe, Cameron. Fast Times at Ridgemont High: A True Story. 1981. 14.95 o.p. (ISBN 0-671-25290-9); pap. 5.95 (ISBN 0-671-25291-7). S&S.
Crowe, Cecily. Abbeygate. 1977. 8.95 o.p. (ISBN 0-698-10819-1, Coward). Putnam Pub Group.
Crowe, Clayton T., jt. auth. see Roberson, John A.
Crowe, Clayton T. see Heat Transfer & Fluid Mechanics Institute.
Crowe, Frederick E. Method in Theology: An Organon for Our Time. LC 80-81015. (Pere Marquette Ser.). 68p. 1980. 7.95 (ISBN 0-87462-519-X). Marquette.
--Time of Change. 1968. 4.50 o.p. (ISBN 0-685-07668-7, 80162). Glencoe.
Crowe, James W., jt. auth. see Brennan, William T.
Crowe, John H. & Clegg, James S., eds. Anhydrobiosis. LC 73-12354. (Benchmark Papers in Biological Concepts Ser.). 496p. 1973. text ed. 55.00 o.s.i. (ISBN 0-12-786277-3). Acad Pr.
Crowe, Keith J. A History of the Original Peoples of Northern Canada. (Illus.). 172p. 1974. 7.95 o.p. (ISBN 0-7735-0233-5); pap. 6.95 (ISBN 0-7735-0220-3). McGill-Queens U Pr.
Crowe, P. R. Concepts in Climatology. LC 77-174727. 355p. 1972. 32.50 (ISBN 0-312-16065-8). St Martin.
Crowe, Patrick H. Teacher Survival Handbook. LC 82-60573. 125p. (Orig.). 1983. pap. 8.95 (ISBN 0-88247-680-7). R & E Res Assoc.
Crowe, Robert L. Clyde Monster. (Illus.). (ps-3). 1976. 10.75 (ISBN 0-525-28025-1, 01044-310). Dutton.
Crowe, Rosalie & Brinkernoff, Sidney, eds. Early Yuma. LC 75-27825. (Illus.). 144p. 1976. 17.95 o.p. (ISBN 0-87358-144-X). Northland.
Crowe, Steve. Satellite Television & Your Backyard Dish. Krieger, Robin, ed. LC 81-90593. (Illus.). 200p. (Orig.). 1982. 20.00 (ISBN 0-910419-00-0); pap. 15.00 (ISBN 0-910419-01-9); trade special 15.00 (ISBN 0-910419-02-7). Satellite.
Crowe, Sylvia. Garden Design. 1959. 8.95 (ISBN 0-8208-0043-0). Hearthside.
Crowe, Walter C., et al. Laboratory Manual in Adapted Physical Education & Recreation: Experiments, Activities, & Assignments. (Illus.). 1977. pap. text ed. 9.50 o.p. (ISBN 0-8016-1099-0). Mosby.
--Priciples & Methods of Adapted Physical Education & Recreation. 4th ed. LC 81-1004. (Illus.). 524p. 1981. text ed. 23.95 (ISBN 0-8016-0327-7). Mosby.
Crowell, Benedict & Wilson, Robert F. The Armies of Industry: Our Nation's Manufacture of Munitions for a World in Arms, 1917-1918, 2 vols. in one. LC 74-75235. (The United States in World War 1 Ser). (Illus.). xxviii, 738p. 1974. Repr. lib. bdg. 49.95x (ISBN 0-89198-101-2). Ozer.
--Demobilization: Our Industrial & Military Demobilization After the Armistice, 1918-1920. LC 74-75236. (The United States in World War 1 Ser). (Illus.). xvi, 333p. 1974. Repr. of 1921 ed. lib. bdg. 22.95x (ISBN 0-89198-102-0). Ozer.
--The Giant Hand: Our Mobilization & Control of Industry & Natural Resources, 1917-1918. LC 74-75237. (The United States in World War 1 Ser). (Illus.). xxx, 191p. 1974. Repr. of 1921 ed. lib. bdg. 18.95x (ISBN 0-89198-099-7). Ozer.
--The Road to France: The Transportation of Troops & Military Supplies, 1917-1918, 2 vols. in one. LC 74-75238. (The United States in World War 1 Ser). (Illus.). xv, 675p. 1974. Repr. of 1921 ed. lib. bdg. 42.95x (ISBN 0-89198-100-4). Ozer.
Crowell, John, ed. see Miller, Perry.
Crowell, Laura E., jt. auth. see Scheidel, Thomas M.
Crowell, Lynda & Mariotti, Maryanne. The Parent's Guide to Austin, 1982-83. (Illus.). 208p. 1982. pap. 5.95 (ISBN 0-938934-02-3). C&M Pubns.
Crowell, Pattie & Stanford, Ann. Critical Essays on Anne Bradstreet. (Critical Essays on American Literature Ser.). 330p. 1983. lib. bdg. 42.50 (ISBN 0-8161-8643-X). G K Hall.
Crowell, Richard A. Stock Market Strategy. (Illus.). 1977. 32.50 (ISBN 0-07-014720-5, P&RB). McGraw.
Crowell, Richard H. & Slesnick, William E. Calculus with Analytic Geometry. (Illus.). 1968. 24.95x (ISBN 0-393-09782-X). Norton.
Crowell, Robert M., jt. auth. see Ojemann, Robert G.
Crowell, Thomas, Jr., ed. see Bender, James F.
Crowest, Frederick J. Musicians' Wit, Humour, & Anecdote. LC 72-78131. (Illus.). 1971. Repr. of 1902 ed. 43.00 o.p. (ISBN 0-8103-3729-0). Gale.
--The Story of British Music From the Earliest Times to the Tudor Period. 404p. 1983. pap. 6.95 (ISBN 0-88072-002-6). Tanager Bks.
Crowfoot. Weep with Me. Date not set. 1.95 (ISBN 0-89989-028-8). Cross Roads.
Crowfoot, James & Bryant, Bunyan. Action for Educational Equity: A Guide for Parents & Members of Community Groups. 184p. (Orig.). 1982. pap. text ed. 9.00 (ISBN 0-917754-19-0). Inst Responsive.
Crowhurst, Norman. Electronic Musical Instruments. LC 70-133801. (Illus.). 1971. 8.95 o.p. (ISBN 0-8306-1546-6); pap. 5.95 o.p. (ISBN 0-8306-0546-0, 546). TAB Bks.
Crowl, Philip A. The Intelligent Traveller's Guide to Historic Britain. LC 81-19469. (Illus.). 832p. 1983. 39.95 (ISBN 0-312-92337-6); pap. 19.95 (ISBN 0-312-92338-4). Congdon & Weed.
Crowl, Phillip. The Intelligent Traveller's Guide to Historic Britain. (Illus.). 600p. 1982. 39.95 (ISBN 0-312-92337-6); pap. 19.95 (ISBN 0-312-92338-4). St Martin.
Crowley, Aleister. Astrology. Skinner, Stephen, ed. 224p. 25.00x o.p. (ISBN 0-85978-001-5, Pub. by Spearman England). State Mutual Bk.
--The Book of Thoth. LC 79-16399. (Illus.). 287p. 1977. pap. 8.95 (ISBN 0-913866-12-1). US Games Syst.
--Eight Lectures on Yoga. pap. 2.95 (ISBN 0-87728-122-X). Weiser.
--Holy Books. pap. 2.95 o.p. (ISBN 0-685-01086-4). Weiser.
--The Law Is for All. 2nd ed. Regardie, Israel, ed. 368p. 1983. pap. 10.95 (ISBN 0-941404-25-0). Falcon Pr AZ.
--The Magical Record of the Beast 666. Symonds, John & Grant, Kenneth, eds. 326p. 1979. 40.50 (ISBN 0-7156-0636-0, Pub. by Duckworth England); pap. 17.00 o.p. (ISBN 0-7156-1208-5, 386, Pub. by Duckworth England); limited ed. slipcase 95.00 (ISBN 0-686-37758-3). Biblio Dist.
--The Magical Record of the Beast 666. Symonds, John & Grant, Kenneth, eds. 326p. 1972. 16.95 (ISBN 0-7156-0636-0). US Games Syst.
Crowley, Aleister & Motta, Marcelo. Ofiflamme: The Law, Vol. 6. (No. 4). 1983. 11.00 (ISBN 0-933454-08-2, Pub by OTO). SOTOA.
--Oriflamme: Mapick & Mysticism, Vol. 6. (No. 2). 1982. 15.00 (ISBN 0-933454-06-6, Pub by OTO). SOTOA.
--Oriflamme: Mapick in Theory & Practice, Vol. 6. (No. 3). 1983. 22.00 (ISBN 0-933454-07-4, Pub. by OTO). SOTOA.
--Oriflamme: Yoga & Mapick, Vol. 6. (No. 1). 8.00 (ISBN 0-933454-05-8, Pub by OTO). SOTOA.
Crowley, Aleister & Regardie, Israel. Magick Without Tears. 3rd ed. 560p. 1982. 49.94 (ISBN 0-941404-16-1); pap. 13.95 (ISBN 0-941404-17-X). Falcon Pr Az.
--The World's Tragedy. 200p. 1982. pap. 11.95 (ISBN 0-941404-18-8). Falcon Pr Az.
Crowley, Aleister see Kerval, Alastor de, pseud.
Crowley, Aleister see Yuen, Ko, pseud.
Crowley, Carleen. All About Clothes. (Gregg-McGraw-Hill Ser. for Independent Living). 1978. pap. text ed. 7.96 (ISBN 0-07-014765-5); wkbk. 4.96 (ISBN 0-07-014766-3); tchrs' manual 4.00 (ISBN 0-07-014767-1). McGraw.
Crowley, Charles B. Universal Mathematics in Aristotelian-Thomistic Philosophy: The Hermeneutics of Aristotelian Texts Relative to Universal Mathematics. LC 79-48093. 239p. 1980. text ed. 20.75 (ISBN 0-8191-1009-4); pap. text ed. 10.00 (ISBN 0-8191-1010-8). U Pr of Amer.
Crowley, Ellen, ed. Reverse Acronyms, Initialisms, & Abbreviations Dictionary. 8th ed. (The Acronyms, Initialisms, & Abbreviations Dictionary Ser.: Vol. 3). 1600p. 1982. 120.00x (ISBN 0-8103-0507-0). Gale.
Crowley, Ellen T., ed. Acronyms, Initialisms, & Abbreviations Dictionary, Vol. 1. 7th ed. 1500p. 1980. 92.00 o.p. (ISBN 0-8103-0504-6). Gale.
--New Acronyms, Initialisms, & Abbreviations. 7th ed. (Acronyms, Initialisms & Abbreviation Dictionay: Vol. 2). 200p. 1981. pap. 85.00 set o.p. (ISBN 0-8103-0501-1). Gale.
Crowley, Frances G. Domingo Faustino Sarmiento. (World Authors Ser.). lib. bdg. 15.95 (ISBN 0-8057-2798-1, Twayne). G K Hall.
Crowley, Frank, ed. A New History of Australia. LC 78-14279. 639p. 1975. text ed. 42.50x (ISBN 0-8419-6100-X). Holmes & Meier.
Crowley, J. S. & Zimmerman, L. Z. Residential Passive Solar Design. 256p. 1983. 34.95 (ISBN 0-07-014769-8, P&RB). McGraw.
Crowley, James B., tr. see Toshihiko, Shimada, et al.
Crowley, John W. George Cabot Lodge. LC 75-44429. (United States Authors Ser.). 1976. lib. bdg. 13.95 (ISBN 0-8057-7165-4, Twayne). G K Hall.
Crowley, Kitty A. First Women of the Skies. LC 78-21907. (Famous Firsts Ser.). (Illus.). 1978. PLB 10.76 (ISBN 0-89547-063-2). Silver.
Crowley, Leonard V. Introduction to Human Disease. 700p. 1983. text ed. 23.95 (ISBN 0-534-01264-7). Brooks-Cole.
Crowley, M., jt. ed. see Nixon, D. W.
Crowley, Mary C. Think Mink! 128p. 1976. 7.95 o.p. (ISBN 0-8007-0810-5). Revell.
Crowley, Maude. Azor & the Blue-Eyed Cow. (Children's Literature Ser.). 1980. PLB 7.95 (ISBN 0-8398-2605-2, Gregg). G K Hall.
Crowley, Thomas H. Understanding Computers. (Orig.). (YA) (gr. 9-12). 1967. pap. 4.95 o.p. (ISBN 0-07-014761-2, SP). McGraw.
Crowley, william, ed. Rushton's Rowboats & Canoes, 1903. LC 82-48169. (Illus.). 128p. 1983. pap. 15.00 (ISBN 0-87742-164-1). Intl Marine.
Crown, Francis, Jr. Confederate Postmaster Provisionals. Date not set. lib. bdg. 100.00x (ISBN 0-88000-124-0). Quarterman. Postponed.
Crown, J. C., jt. auth. see Bittinger, M. L.
Crown, J. Conrad & Bittinger, Marvin L. Finite Mathematics: A Modeling Approach. 2nd ed. LC 80-19472. (Mathematics Ser.). (Illus.). 480p. 1981. text ed. 23.95 (ISBN 0-201-03145-0); instrs' manual 3.50 (ISBN 0-686-85479-9). A-W.
Crown, J. Conrad, jt. auth. see Bittinger, Marvin L.
Crown, June, jt. ed. see Paton, W. D.
Crown, Patricia. Drawings by E. F. Burney. LC 82-21300. (Illus.). 80p. 1982. pap. 7.50 (ISBN 0-87328-124-1). Huntington Lib.
Crown, Paul. What You Should Know About Building Your Mailing Lists. LC 72-13927. (Business Almanac Ser.: No. 20). 121p. 1973. 5.95 (ISBN 0-379-11220-5). Oceana.
Crown, S. Essential Principles of Psychiatry. LC 72-128608. 307p. 1970. text ed. 15.00 (ISBN 0-911216-16-2). Raven.
Crowner, David L. & Marschall, Laurence A., eds. Computers & Human Communication: Problems & Prospects. LC 79-52964. 1979. pap. text ed. 9.75 o.p. (ISBN 0-8191-0787-5). U Pr of Amer.

Crownhart-Vaughan, E. A., jt. ed. see Golovin, Pavel N.

Crownhart-Vaughan, E. A., jt. tr. see Dmytryshyn, Basil.

Crownhart-Vaughan, E. A., tr. see Golovin, Pavel N.

Crownhart-Vaughan, E. A., jt. auth. see Vaughan, Thomas.

Crownhart-Vaughn, E. A., ed. see Golovin, Pavel N.

Crowningshield, Gerald & Gorman, Kenneth A. Cost Accounting: Principles & Managerial Applications. 4th ed. LC 78-69551. (Illus.). 1979. text ed. 27.50 (ISBN 0-395-26797-8); instr's. manual 4.75 (ISBN 0-395-26798-6). HM.

Crownover, Arthur, Jr. Gibson's Suits in Chancery. 6th ed. 950p. 1982. text ed. 65.00 (ISBN 0-87215-440-8). Michie-Bobbs.

Crowson, P. S. Tudor Foreign Policy. LC 73-81733. 288p. 1973. 22.50 (ISBN 0-312-82285-5). St Martin.

Crowther, Bosley. Reruns: Fifty Memorable Films. LC 78-6271. (Illus.). 1978. 17.50 o.p. (ISBN 0-399-12112-9); pap. 7.95 o.p. (ISBN 0-399-12230-3). Putnam Pub Group.

--Vintage Films. LC 76-19038. (Illus.). 1977. 15.00 o.p. (ISBN 0-399-11637-0). Putnam Pub Group.

Crowther, Geoff. Korea-A Travel Survival Kit. (Lonely Planet Travel Ser.). (Illus.). 160p. (Orig.). 1983. pap. 6.95 (ISBN 0-88254-673-2, Pub. by Lonely Planet Australia). Hippocrene Bks.

--South America on a Shoestring. (Illus.). 1980. pap. 10.95 o.p. (ISBN 0-908086-08-3). Hippocrene Bks.

Crowther, J. R., jt. auth. see Wardley, R. C.

Crowther, Jonathan. Intermediate Crosswords, for Learners of English as a Foreign Language. 46p. 1980. pap. 3.25x (ISBN 0-19-581751-6). Oxford U Pr.

Crowther, Patricia & Arnold. The Witches Speak. 1976. pap. 3.50 o.p. (ISBN 0-87728-285-4). Weiser.

Crowther, Richard L. Affordable Passive Solar Homes. 160p. 1983. 15.00 (ISBN 0-89553-129-1). Am Solar Energy.

Crowther, Robert. Jungle Jumble. (Illus.). 32p. (ps-1). 1983. 6.25 (ISBN 0-670-41076-4). Viking Pr.

--The Most Amazing Hide-&-Seek Alphabet Book. LC 77-79334. (Illus.). (ps-1). 1978. 10.95x (ISBN 0-670-48996-4, Co-Pub by Kestrel Bks). Viking Pr.

--The Most Amazing Hide & Seek Counting Book. (Illus.). 14p. 1981. 10.95 (ISBN 0-670-48997-2). Viking Pr.

Crowther-Hunt, Norman. Two Early Political Associations: The Quakers & the Dissenting Deputies in the Age of Sir Robert Walpole. LC 78-23805. 1979. Repr. of 1961 ed. lib. bdg. 20.75x (ISBN 0-313-21036-5, HUTW). Greenwood.

Croxton, Anthony H. Railways of Zimbabwe. (Illus.). 316p. 1982. 22.50 (ISBN 0-7153-8130-X). David & Charles.

Croxton, C. Introduction to Liquid State Physics. LC 74-13153. 283p. 1975. 46.00x o.p. (ISBN 0-471-18933-2, Pub. by Wiley-Interscience); pap. 23.00x o.p. (ISBN 0-471-18934-0). Wiley.

Croxton, Clive A. Statistical Mechanics of the Liquid Surface. LC 79-40819. 287p. 1980. 79.95 (ISBN 0-471-27663-4, Pub. by Wiley-Interscience). Wiley.

Croxton, P. C., jt. auth. see Bray, K. M.

Croy, O. R. Croy's Camera Trickery. 13.50 o.p. (ISBN 0-8038-1216-7). Hastings.

--Design by Photography. 1972. 12.95 o.p. (ISBN 0-8174-0624-7, Amphoto). Watson-Guptill.

--The Photographic Portrait. 2nd ed. (Illus.). 204p. 1975. 19.95 (ISBN 0-240-50912-9). Focal Pr.

Croy, Otto R. Croy's Camera Trickery. (Illus.). 1977. 19.95 o.s.i. (ISBN 0-240-50958-7). Focal Pr.

Croydon, Michael. Ivan Albright. LC 78-5369. (Illus.). 308p. 1978. 85.00 o.p. (ISBN 0-89659-002-X); limited ed. 1950.00 o.p. (ISBN 0-89659-015-1). Abbeville Pr.

Croydon, Michael, compiled by see Jeong, Tung Hon.

Croydon, W. F. & Parker, E. H. Dielectric Film on Gallium Arsenide. (Electrocomponent Science Monograph: Vol. 2). 160p. 1981. 23.00 (ISBN 0-677-05710-5). Gordon.

Crozier, Alice. Novels of Harriet Beecher Stowe. LC 73-83010. 1969. Repr. of 1896 ed. 17.95 (ISBN 0-19-500521-X). Oxford U Pr.

Crozier, Brian. Strategy of Survival. (Illus.). 1978. 8.95 o.p. (ISBN 0-87000-421-2, Arlington Hse). Crown.

Crozier, Michel. The World of the Office Worker. LC 76-141150. 240p. 1973. pap. 3.75 o.p. (ISBN 0-8052-0407-5). Schocken.

Crozier, Patrick. Introduction to Electronics. 1983. 24.95 (ISBN 0-686-92674-9, Breton Pubs). Wadsworth Pub.

Cruce, Emeric. Le Nouveau Cynee. Repr. of 1623 ed. 60.00 o.p. (ISBN 0-8287-0241-1). Clearwater Pub.

Cruchon, Steve & Smith, Harry. Instant Bowling. pap. 3.95 (ISBN 0-448-01515-3, G&D). Putnam Pub Group.

Cruden, Alexander. Cruden's Concordance. 1982. pap. 3.95 (ISBN 0-515-06741-5). Jove Pubns.

--Cruden's Concordance: Handy Reference Edition. (Baker's Paperback Reference Library). 344p. 1982. pap. 6.95 (ISBN 0-8010-2478-1). Baker Bk.

--Cruden's Concordance to the Old & New Testaments. unabridged ed. 14.95 (ISBN 0-8007-0058-9); pap. 3.95 (ISBN 0-8007-8055-8, Spire Bks). Revell.

--Cruden's Unabridged Concordance. LC 54-11084. 17.95 (ISBN 0-8054-1123-2). Broadman.

Cruden, Robert. Many & One: A Social History of the United States. (Illus.). 1980. text ed. 18.95 (ISBN 0-13-555714-3). P-H.

Cruickshank, Allan D. Cruickshank's Photographs of Birds of America. LC 77-70078. (Illus.). 1977. pap. 7.95 (ISBN 0-486-23497-5). Dover.

Cruickshank, Charles. Deception in World War II. (Illus.). 1980. 17.95 (ISBN 0-19-215849-X). Oxford U Pr.

Cruickshank, Don, ed. see Wilson, Edward M.

Cruickshank, Helen G., ed. John & William Bartram's America. (American Naturalists Ser.). (Illus.). 12.00 (ISBN 0-8159-5101-9). Devin.

Cruickshank, James. Soil Geography. (Illus.). 265p. 16.95 o.p. (ISBN 0-686-74073-4); pap. 8.95 (ISBN 0-7153-5847-2). David & Charles.

Cruickshank, John. Benjamin Constant. (World Authors Ser.). 1974. lib. bdg. 12.95 (ISBN 0-8057-2242-4, Twayne). G K Hall.

--Variations on Catastrophe: Some French Responses to the Great War. 1982. 34.95x (ISBN 0-19-212599-0). Oxford U Pr.

Cruickshank, Marjorie. Children & Industry. 189p. 1981. text ed. 15.00x (ISBN 0-7190-0809-3, Pub. by Manchester England). Humanities.

Cruickshank, William M. & Johnson, G. Orville. Education of Exceptional Children & Youth. 3rd ed. (Illus.). 736p. 1975. 27.95 (ISBN 0-13-240382-X). P-H.

Cruickshank, William M. & Tash, Eli, eds. Academics & Beyond: The Best of ACLD, Vol. 4. (The Best of ACLD Ser.). 256p. pap. text ed. 13.95 (ISBN 0-8156-2272-4). Syracuse U Pr.

Cruickshanks, Eveline, ed. Ideology & Conspiracy: Aspects of Jacobitism 1689-1759. 231p. 1982. text ed. 31.50x (ISBN 0-85976-084-7, 40740, Pub. by John Donald Scotland). Humanities.

--Parliamentary History, 1982, Vol. 1. 256p. 1983. text ed. 28.25x (ISBN 0-86299-013-0, Pub. by Sutton England); pap. text ed. 17.00x (ISBN 0-86299-014-9). Humanities.

Cruickshrank, John, ed. French Literature & Its Background, 6 vols. Incl. Vol. 1. Sixteenth Century. (No. 138). 1968. o.p. (ISBN 0-19-285020-2); Vol. 2. Seventeenth Century. (No. 171). 1969. 7.95x o.p. (ISBN 0-19-285028-8); Vol. 3. Eighteenth Century. (No. 139). 1968. 7.95x o.p. (ISBN 0-19-285021-0); Vol. 4. Early Nineteenth Century. (No. 172). 1969. 7.95x o.p. (ISBN 0-19-285029-6); Vol. 5. Late Nineteenth Century. (No. 173). 1969. 7.95x o.p. (ISBN 0-19-285033-4); Vol. 6. Twentieth Century. (No. 184). 1970. 7.95x o.p. (ISBN 0-19-285043-1). (Oxford Paperbacks Ser.). Oxford U Pr.

Cruikshank, Donald R., ed. Teaching Is Tough. (Applied Education Ser.). (Illus.). 368p. 1980. text ed. 14.95 (ISBN 0-13-893495-9, Spec); pap. 6.95 (ISBN 0-13-893487-8). P-H.

Cruikshank, George. Cruikshank Prints for Hand Coloring. pap. 5.00 (ISBN 0-486-23684-6). Dover.

Cruikshank, George see Lear, Edward.

Cruikshank, Margaret L. Thomas Babington Macaulay. (English Author Ser.). 1978. lib. bdg. 14.95 (ISBN 0-8057-6686-3, Twayne). G K Hall.

Cruikshank, W. Psychology of Exceptional Children & Youth. 4th ed. 1980. 27.95 (ISBN 0-13-733808-2). P-H.

Cruikshank, Warren L., jt. auth. see Burke, John D.

Cruise, Ben. The Musicians of Bremen. (Little Golden Bks.). (Illus.). 24p. (ps-2). 1983. 0.89 (ISBN 0-307-02074-6, Golden Pr). Western Pub.

Cruise, Boyd & Harton, Merle. Signor Faranta's Iron Theatre. LC 82-83592. (Illus.). 150p. 1982. 15.95x (ISBN 0-917860-13-6). Historic New Orleans.

Cruise, Edwina, tr. see Bitsilli, Peter.

Cruise, Edwina, tr. see Chekhov, A. P.

Cruise, Robert J., jt. auth. see Blitchington, Peter.

Cruit, Ronald L. Intruder in Your Home: How to Defend Yourself Legally With A Firearm. LC 82-42727. 288p. 1983. 17.95 (ISBN 0-686-83443-7). Stein & Day.

Crum, J. K. Art of Inner Listning. 1975. pap. write for info (ISBN 0-515-09484-6, PV092). Jove Pubns.

Crumb, R. Carload O' Comics. LC 76-29200. (Illus.). 1977. pap. 6.95 o.s.i. (ISBN 0-914646-10-9). Belier Pr.

--The Complete Fritz the Cat. LC 78-60512. (Illus.). pap. 6.00 o.s.i. (ISBN 0-914646-16-8). Belier Pr.

Crumbaker, Marge & Tucker, Gabe. Up & Down with Elvis Presley. (Illus.). 320p. 1981. 12.95 (ISBN 0-399-12571-X). Putnam Pub Group.

Crumbley, D. L. & Milam, Edward E. Estate Planning in the '80s. 224p. 1983. 15.95 (ISBN 0-8144-5758-4). Am Mgmt.

Crumbley, D. Larry. Readings in Selected Tax Problems of the Oil Industry. 280p. 1982. 35.00x (ISBN 0-87814-201-0). Pennwell Books Division.

Crumbley, D. Larry & Grossman, Steven D. Readings in Oil Industry Accounting. 238p. 1980. 35.00x (ISBN 0-87814-123-5). Pennwell Pub.

Crumbley, D. Larry & Reese, Craig E. Readings in the Crude Oil Windfall Profit Tax. 280p. 1982. 35.00x (ISBN 0-87814-185-5). Pennwell Books Division.

--Readings in the Windfall Profit Tax. 375p. 1982. 35.00x o.p. (ISBN 0-87814-185-5). Pennwell Books Division.

Crumeyrolle, A. & Grifone, J., eds. Symplectic Geometry. (Research Notes in Mathematics Ser.: No. 80). 280p. 1983. pap. text ed. 22.95 (ISBN 0-273-08575-1). Pitman Pub MA.

Crumley, James. Dancing Bear. 256p. 1983. 12.95 (ISBN 0-686-43169-3). Random.

Crummy, Philip. Aspects of Anglo-Saxon & Norman Colchester. (CBA Research Reports Ser.: No. 39). 100p. 1981. pap. text ed. 32.95x (ISBN 0-906780-06-3, Pub. by Coun Brit Archaeology). Humanities.

Crump, Donald J., ed. Giants from the Past. LC 81-47893. (Books for World Explorers: No. IV). 104p. (gr. 3-8). 1983. 6.95 (ISBN 0-87044-424-7); PLB 8.50 (ISBN 0-87044-429-8). Natl Geog.

--Preserving America's Past. LC 81-48076. (Special Publications: No. 17). 200p. 1983. 6.95 (ISBN 0-87044-415-8); lib. bdg. 8.50 (ISBN 0-87044-420-4). Natl Geog.

Crump, G. B. Petroanalysis 81: Proceedings of the Institute of Petroleum London 1982. 416p. 1982. 83.95 (ISBN 0-471-26217-X, Pub. by Wiley Interscience). Wiley.

Crump, Irving. Our Merchant Marine Academy, Kings Point. LC 74-5553. (Illus.). 236p. 1975. Repr. of 1958 ed. lib. bdg. 17.75x (ISBN 0-8371-7511-9, CRMA). Greenwood.

--Our United States Coast Guard Academy. LC 74-5554. (Illus.). 241p. 1975. Repr. of 1961 ed. lib. bdg. 17.75x (ISBN 0-8371-7510-0, CRCG). Greenwood.

Crump, J. I., Jr., ed. Selections from the Shui-Hu Chuan. 3.25 (ISBN 0-686-09967-2). Far Eastern Pubns.

Crump, Mary M. The Epyllion from Theocritus to Ovid. Commager, Steele, ed. LC 77-70761. (Latin Poetry Ser.). 1978. lib. bdg. 32.00 o.s.i. (ISBN 0-8240-2966-6). Garland Pub.

Crump, R. W. Charlotte & Emily Bronte, 1846-1915: A Reference Guide. 1982. lib. bdg. 27.50 (ISBN 0-8161-7953-0, Hall Reference). G K Hall.

Crump, R. W., ed. The Complete Poems of Christina Rosetti. LC 78-5571. 1979. 25.00x (ISBN 0-8071-0358-6). La State U Pr.

Crump, Rebecca W. Christina Rossetti: A Reference Guide. (General Ser.). 1976. lib. bdg. 21.00 (ISBN 0-8161-7847-X, Hall Reference). G K Hall.

Crump, Spencer. Fundamentals of Journalism. (Illus.). 224p. 1974. text ed. 17.95 (ISBN 0-07-014835-X, G). McGraw.

--Rail Car, Locomotive & Trolley Builders: An All-Time Directory. 1980. write for info. (ISBN 0-87046-032-3, Pub. by Trans-Anglo). Interurban.

Crump, Spencer, ed. see Martin, Cy & Martin, Jeannie.

Crumrine, Lynne S. Phonology of Arizona Yaqui with Texts. LC 61-64124. (Anthropological Papers: No. 5). 1961. pap. 2.00x o.p. (ISBN 0-8165-0132-7). U of Ariz Pr.

Crunkilton, John, jt. auth. see Hillison, John.

Crunkilton, John R. & Krebs, Al H. Teaching Agriculture Through Problem Solving. 3rd ed. 1981. text ed. 12.95x (ISBN 0-8134-2199-3). Interstate.

Cruseturner, Wayne. Forever & Ever. 240p. (Orig.). 1981. pap. 2.50 o.s.i. (ISBN 0-515-05529-8). Jove Pubns.

Cruson, Charlene S., ed. see Steindler, Gerry.

Crutcher, Chris. Running Loose. LC 82-20935. 160p. (gr. 1 up). 1983. 9.00 (ISBN 0-688-02002-X). Greenwillow.

Crutchfield, James, jt. ed. see Brown, Gardner M., Jr.

Crutchfield, Marjorie A. Elementary Social Studies: An Inter-Disciplinary Approach. (Elementary Education Ser.). 1978. text ed. 16.95 (ISBN 0-675-08365-6). Additional supplements may be obtained from publisher. Merrill.

Crutchley, Brooke. To Be a Printer. 200p. 1980. 22.50 (ISBN 0-521-23663-0). Cambridge U Pr.

Cruttenden, Alan. Language in Infancy & Childhood: A Linguistic Introduction to Language Acquisition. LC 78-22106. 1979. 25.00 (ISBN 0-312-46606-4). St Martin.

Cruttwell, Patrick, ed. see Johnson, Samuel.

Cruz, Felix de la, jt. ed. see Lubs, Herbert.

Cruz, Felix F. De La see Davidson, Richard L. & De La Cruz, Felix F.

Cruz, Felix F. de la see De la Cruz, Felix F.

Cruz, J. B., Jr., ed. System Sensitivity Analysis. LC 72-93263. (Benchmark Papers in Electrical Engineering & Computer Science Ser). 450p. 1973. text ed. 52.50 o.s.i. (ISBN 0-12-786285-4). Acad Pr.

Cruz, Joan C. Desires of Thy Heart. (Orig.). 1977. pap. 1.95 o.p. (ISBN 0-451-07738-5, J7738, Sig). NAL.

Cruz, Jose B. & Van Valkenburg, M. E. Signals in Linear Circuits. 480p. 1974. text ed. 32.50 (ISBN 0-395-16971-2); instr's. manual 8.50 (ISBN 0-395-17838-X). HM.

Cruz, Manny & Symington, Nikki. Alice Barnes-American Activist. Kern, Ann T., ed. (Illus.). 52p. (Orig.). 1982. pap. 7.50 (ISBN 0-686-38731-7). Connections CA.

Cruz, Mercedes Santa see Santa Cruz, Mercedes.

Cruz, Nicky & Buckingham, Jamie. Run Baby Run. (gr. 9-12). 1982. pap. 2.50 (ISBN 0-515-06737-7). Jove Pubns.

Cruz, Vera Da see Da Cruz, Vera.

Cryer, Colin W. Numerical Functional Analysis. (Monographs on Numerical Analysis). 592p. 1982. 39.00 (ISBN 0-19-853410-8). Oxford U Pr.

Cryer, Gene, ed. see Bleich, Arthur H. & McCullough, Jerry.

Cryer, Philip E. Diagnostic Endocrinology. 2nd ed. (Illus.). 1979. text ed. 19.95x (ISBN 0-19-502525-3); pap. text ed. 9.95x (ISBN 0-19-502526-1). Oxford U Pr.

Crymes, Ruth, et al. Developing Fluency in English: With Sentence-Combining Practice in Nominalization. (Illus.). 256p. 1974. pap. text ed. 11.50 (ISBN 0-13-204826-4). P-H.

Crystal. Linguistic Controversies. 288p. 1982. text ed. 44.95 (ISBN 0-7131-6349-6). Univ Park.

Crystal, D. Prosodic Systems & Intonation in English. LC 69-13792. (Cambridge Studies in Linguistics: No. 1). (Illus.). 1969. 54.50 (ISBN 0-521-07387-1); pap. 18.95 (ISBN 0-521-29058-9). Cambridge U Pr.

--Working with LARSP. (Studies in Language Disability & Remediation: Vol 1A). 359p. 1979. pap. 25.50 (ISBN 0-444-19469-X). Elsevier.

Crystal, D. J., jt. auth. see Bolton, W. F.

Crystal, David. Child Language, Learning & Linguistics. 114p. 1976. pap. text ed. 9.95 (ISBN 0-7131-5891-3). E Arnold.

--The English Tone of Voice: Essays in Intonation, Prosody & Paralanguage. LC 76-5970. (Illus.). 200p. 1976. 25.00x (ISBN 0-312-25550-0). St Martin.

--A First Dictionary of Linguistics & Phonetics. (Language Library Ser.). 404p. 1980. lib. bdg. 34.00 (ISBN 0-86531-051-3, Pub. by Andre Deutsch); pap. text ed. 12.00 o.p. (ISBN 0-86531-050-5). Westview.

--Profiling Linguistic Disability. 224p. 1982. pap. text ed. 19.95 (ISBN 0-7131-6354-2). E Arnold.

--What is Linguistics? 96p. 1974. pap. text ed. 9.95 (ISBN 0-7131-5741-0). E Arnold.

Crystal, David, ed. Linguistic Controversies. 256p. 1982. text ed. 44.95 (ISBN 0-7131-6349-6). E Arnold.

Crystal, Stephen. America's Old Age Crisis: Public Policy & the Two Worlds of Aging. 1982. 16.50 (ISBN 0-465-00124-6). Basic.

Csaba, L., et al, eds. Networks from the User's Point of View. 1981. 81.00 (ISBN 0-444-86291-9). Elsevier.

Csakany, et al. Universal Algebra. 1982. 138.50 (ISBN 0-444-85405-3). Elsevier.

Csakany, B. & Schmidt, J. Contributions to Universal Algebra. (Colloquia Mathematica Ser.: Vol. 17). 1978. 106.50 (ISBN 0-7204-0725-7, North-Holland). Elsevier.

Csakany, B. & Rosenberg, I., eds. Finite Algebra & Multiple-Valued Logic. (Colloquia Mathematica: Vol. 28). 880p. 1982. 127.75 (ISBN 0-444-85439-8). Elsevier.

Csanady, G. T. Circulation in the Coastal Ocean. 1982. 52.50 (ISBN 90-277-1400-2, Pub. by Reidel Holland). Kluwer Boston.

Csapodi, Csaba. Bibliotheca Corviniana: The Library of King Matthias Corvinus of Hungary. 2nd, Rev. ed. Horn, Z., tr. LC 82-187248. (Illus.). 334p. (Hungarian.). 1981. 50.00x (ISBN 963-207-617-6). Intl Pubns Serv.

Csaszar, A. Topology, 2 vols. (Colloquia Mathematica Ser.: Vol. 23). 1980. Set. 149.00 (ISBN 0-444-85406-1). Elsevier.

Csath, Geza. Opium & Other Stories. 1983. pap. 4.95 (ISBN 0-14-006689-6). Penguin.

Cserr, Helen F., et al, eds. see Symposium Held at the Mount Desert Island Biological Laboratory, Salisbury Cove, Maine, Sept. 1974.

Csida, Joseph. The Music-Record Career Handbook. rev. ed. 360p. 1980. 16.95 (ISBN 0-8230-7581-8, Billboard Bks). Watson-Guptill.

Csida, Joseph & Csida, June B. American Entertainment. (Illus.). 1978. 30.00 o.p. (ISBN 0-8230-7506-0, Billboard Bks). Watson-Guptill.

Csida, June B., jt. auth. see Csida, Joseph.

Csikos-Nagy, Bela. Socialist Economic Policy. LC 72-90020. 1979. 25.00 (ISBN 0-312-73745-9). St Martin.

Csikszentmihalyi, Mihaly, jt. auth. see Getzels, Jacob W.

Csillery, Klara K. Hungarian Village Furniture. 1972. 4.25x o.p. (ISBN 0-8002-0828-5). Intl Pubns Serv.

Csiro, R. W. & Tavast, R. R., eds. Distributed Computer Control Systems 1982: Proceedings of the 4th IFAC Workshop, DCCS-82, Tallinn, USSR, 24-26 May 1982. (IFAC Proceedings Ser.). 175p. 1983. 43.00 (ISBN 0-08-028675-5). Pergamon.

Csizmadia, I. G. Molecular Structure & Conformation: Recent Advances. (Progress in Theoretical Organic Chemistry Ser.: Vol. 3). 1982. 93.75 (ISBN 0-444-42089-4). Elsevier.

Csizmadia, I. G., ed. Applications of Mo Theory in Organic Chemistry. (Progress in Theoretical Organic Chemistry Ser.: Vol. 2). 1977. 106.50 (ISBN 0-444-41565-3). Elsevier.

Csokits, Janos, tr. see Pilinszky, Janos.

Csomos, G. Clinical Hepatology: History-Present State-Outlook. (Illus.). 430p. 1982. 42.00 (ISBN 0-387-11838-1). Springer-Verlag.

Csorgo, M., et al, eds. Statistics & Related Topics. 1981. 53.25 (ISBN 0-444-86293-5). Elsevier.

Csuti, Blair. Type Specimens of Recent Mammals in the Museum of Vertebrate Zoology, University of California, Berkeley. (U. C. Publications in Zoology Ser.: Vol. 114). 80p. 1981. 10.50x (ISBN 0-520-09622-3). U of Cal Pr.

Cua, A. S. Dimensions of Moral Creativity: Paradigms, Principles, & Ideals. LC 77-16169. 1978. 16.75x (ISBN 0-271-00540-8). Pa St U Pr.

--The Unity of Knowledge & Action: A Study in Wang Yang-Ming's Moral Psychology. LC 81-23060. 152p. 1982. text ed. 12.95x (ISBN 0-8248-0786-3). UH Pr.

Cua, Antonio S. Reason & Virtue: A Study in the Ethics of Richard Price. LC 66-10868. xv, 196p. 1966. 12.00x (ISBN 0-8214-0014-2, 82-80158). Ohio U Pr.

Cuadra, Carlos & Luke, Ann W., eds. The Annual Review of Information Science & Technology, Vol. 5, 1970. LC 66-25096. 1970. text ed. 35.00 (ISBN 0-85229-156-6). Knowledge Indus.

Cuadra, Carlos, et al, eds. Annual Review of Information Science & Technology, Vol. 10. LC 66-25096. 1975. 27.50 (ISBN 0-87715-210-1). Am Soc Info Sci.

Cuadra, Carlos A. The Annual Review of Information Science & Technology, Vol 10, 1975. Luke, Ann W., ed. LC 66-25096. 1975. text ed. 35.00 (ISBN 0-686-67625-4). Knowledge Indus.

Cuadra, Carlos A., ed. The Annual Review of Information Science & Technology, Vol. 3, 1968. LC 66-25096. (Illus.). 1968. text ed. 35.00 (ISBN 0-685-94669-X). Knowledge Indus.

Cuadra, Carlos A. & Luke, Ann W., eds. The Annual Review of Information Science & Technology, Vol. 4, 1969. LC 66-25096. 1969. text ed. 35.00 (ISBN 0-85229-147-7). Knowledge Indus.

--The Annual Review of Information Science & Technology, Vol. 7, 1972. LC 66-25096. (Illus.). 1972. text ed. 35.00 (ISBN 0-87715-206-3). Knowledge Indus.

--The Annual Review of Information Science & Technology, Vol. 8, 1973. LC 66-25096. 1973. text ed. 35.00 (ISBN 0-87715-208-X). Knowledge Indus.

--The Annual Review of Information Science & Technology, Vol. 9, 1974. LC 66-25096. (Illus.). 1974. text ed. 35.00 (ISBN 0-87715-209-8). Knowledge Indus.

Cuatrecasas, P., ed. The Specificity & Action of Animal, Bacterial & Plant Toxins. (Recptors & Recognition Series B.: Vol. 1). 1976. 63.00 (ISBN 0-412-09730-3, Pub. by Chapman & Hall). Methuen Inc.

Cuatrecasas, P. & Greaves, M. F., eds. Receptors & Recognition, Series A, 6 vols. Incl. Vol. 1. 175p. 1976 (ISBN 0-412-13800-X); Vol. 2. 229p. 1976 (ISBN 0-412-13810-7); Vol. 3. 166p. 1977 (ISBN 0-412-14310-0); Vol. 4. 258p. 1977 (ISBN 0-412-14330-5); Vol. 5. 212p. 1978 (ISBN 0-412-15270-3); Vol. 6. 199p. 1978 (ISBN 0-412-15290-8). 100.00 set (ISBN 0-412-15950-3, Pub. by Chapman & Hall England). Methuen Inc.

Cuban Economic Research Project, University of Miami. Labor Conditions in Communist Cuba. LC 63-21349. 1963. pap. 2.95x o.p. (ISBN 0-87024-303-9). U of Miami Pr.

Cubbedge, Robert, jt. auth. see Lansdorp, Robert.

Cubberley, William. The Commodity Market Today. 62p. (Orig.). 1979. pap. 11.00 (ISBN 0-686-37422-3). Future Pub TN.

Cube, Hans L. von see Von Cube, Hans L. & Staimle, Fritz.

Cubieres-Palmezeaux, M. De. La Vengeance de Pluton, ou Suite des Muses Rivales. Repr. of 1778 ed. 28.00 o.p. (ISBN 0-8287-0242-X). Clearwater Pub.

Cubit, Harry. Electrical Construction Cost Estimating. (Illus.). 320p. 1981. 31.50 (ISBN 0-07-014885-6). McGraw.

Cubitt, Heather. Russia under the Last Tsar. Reeves, Marjorie, ed. (Then & There Ser.). (Illus.). 96p. (Orig.). (gr. 7-12). 1980. pap. text ed. 3.10 (ISBN 0-582-22141-2). Longman.

--Spain & Her Empire Under Philip II. Reeves, Marjorie, ed. (Then & There Ser.). (Illus.). 96p. (Orig.). (gr. 7-12). 1976. pap. text ed. 3.10 (ISBN 0-582-20434-8). Longman.

Cubitt, J. M. & Reyment, R. A. Quantitative Stratigraphic Correlation. LC 81-21926. (International Geological Correlation Programme Ser.). 320p. 1983. 49.50x (ISBN 0-471-10171-0, Pub. by Wiley-Interscience). Wiley.

Cubitt, J. M. & Henley, S., eds. Statistical Analysis in Geology. LC 78-17368. (Benchmark Papers in Geology Ser.: Vol. 37). 340p. 1978. 48.50 (ISBN 0-87933-335-9). Hutchinson Ross.

Cuca, Roberto. Family Planning Programs: An Evaluation of Experience. (Working Paper: No. 345). xii, 134p. 1979. 5.00 (ISBN 0-686-36195-4, WP-0345). World Bank.

Cucuel, G. La Poupliniere et la Musique De Chambre Au XVIII Siecle. LC 70-158961. (Music Ser). (Fr.). 1971. Repr. of 1913 ed. lib. bdg. 49.50 (ISBN 0-306-70186-3). Da Capo.

Cucumber Group. Why Cucumbers Are Better Than Men. (Illus.). 32p. 1983. pap. 2.95 (ISBN 0-87131-399-5). M Evans.

Cuddihy, John M. No Offense: Civil Religion & Protestant Taste. 1978. 5.00 (ISBN 0-8164-0385-6). Seabury.

Cuddihy, William. Agricultural Price Management in Egypt. (Working Paper: No. 388). x, 164p. 1980. 5.00 (ISBN 0-686-36062-1, WP-0388). World Bank.

Cuddy, Dennis L. Contemporary American Immigration: Interpretive Essays (European & Non-European, 2 vols. (Immigrant Heritage of America Ser.). 1982. Non-european. 17.50 (ISBN 0-8057-8420-9, Twayne); European. 17.50 (ISBN 0-8057-8421-7); lib. bdg. 29.95 (ISBN 0-8057-8422-5). G K Hall.

Cuddy, J. D. International Price Indexation. (Illus.). 1977. 19.95 o.p. (ISBN 0-347-01140-3, 00684-X, Pub. by Saxon Hse England). Lexington Bks.

Cude, Wilfred. A Due Sense of Differences: An Evaluative Approach to Canadian Literature. LC 80-67244. 237p. lib. bdg. 20.00 (ISBN 0-8191-1206-2); pap. text ed. 10.50 (ISBN 0-8191-1207-0). U Pr of Amer.

Cudihy, John M. The Ordeal of Civility. 1976. pap. 3.45 o.s.i. (ISBN 0-440-56555-3, Delta). Dell.

Cudjoe, Selwyn R. Resistance & Caribbean Literature. LC 76-25616. xii, 319p. 1981. 20.00x (ISBN 0-8214-0353-2, 82-82451); pap. 8.95x (ISBN 0-8214-0573-X, 82-82469). Ohio U Pr.

Cudlipp, Edythe. Vitamins. (Good Health Books Ser.). 1978. pap. 2.95 (ISBN 0-448-14824-2, G&D). Putnam Pub Group.

Cudworth, Marsha & Michaels, Howard. Victorian Holidays: A Guide to Guesthouses, Bed & Breakfast Inns & Restaurants of Cape May, N. J. 2nd rev. & enlarged ed. LC 82-83816. 125p. (Orig.). pap. 6.95 (ISBN 0-9608554-1-6). Lady Raspberry.

Cuello, A., ed. Co-Transmission. 224p. 1982. 85.00x (ISBN 0-333-32592-3, Pub. by Macmillan England). State Mutual Bk.

Cuello, A. C. Brain Microdissection Techniques. 160p. 1983. write for info. (ISBN 0-471-10523-6, Pub. by Wiley-Interscience); pap. write for info. (ISBN 0-471-90019-2, Pub. by Wiley-Interscience). Wiley.

--Immunohistochemistry. (IBRO Handbook Ser.: Methods in the Neurosciences). 500p. 1982. write for info. (ISBN 0-471-10245-8, Pub. by Wiley-Interscience); pap. write for info. (ISBN 0-471-90052-4). Wiley.

Cuenca, Alfredo O., Jr. Second Selected Poems. 84p. (Orig.). 1982. pap. 7.50x (ISBN 0-686-37567-X, Pub. by New Day Philippines). Cellar.

Cuenod, M., jt. ed. see Cowan, W.

Cuenod, M., et al, eds. see International Symposium, Switzerland, Sept. 1978.

Cuesta, Benedicto. El Paisano: Nuevo Mexico: Vida y Dilema. 1976. pap. 4.95 (ISBN 0-913270-59-8). Sunstone Pr.

Cueva, Agustin. The Process of Political Domination in Ecuador. Salti, Danielle, tr. LC 79-809. 109p. 1981. 19.95 (ISBN 0-87855-338-X). Transaction Bks.

Cuff, David J. & Mattson, Mark T. Thematic Maps. 1982. 14.95x (ISBN 0-416-60221-5). Methuen Inc.

Cuff, P. J., tr. see Gabba, Emilio.

Cuff, Robert, jt. ed. see Porter, Glenn.

Cugiani, M., jt. auth. see Archetti, F.

Cuisin, Michel. Animals of African Plains. LC 80-53904. (Nature's Hidden World Ser.). 11.96 (ISBN 0-382-06454-2). Silver.

--Birds of Prey. LC 80-53901. (Nature's Hidden World Ser.). 11.96 (ISBN 0-382-06455-0). Silver.

--Lakes & Rivers. LC 80-53905. (Nature's Hidden World Ser.). 11.96 (ISBN 0-382-06452-6). Silver.

--Mountain Animals. LC 80-53905. (Nature's Hidden World Ser.). PLB 11.96 (ISBN 0-382-06452-6). Silver.

--Woods & Forests. LC 80-53902. (Nature's Hidden World Ser.). 11.96 (ISBN 0-382-06369-4). Silver.

Cukor, Gyorgy. Strategies of Industrialisation in the Developing Countries. LC 73-89996. 288p. 1974. 26.00 (ISBN 0-312-76440-5). St Martin.

Culberson, Chicita F. Chemical & Botanical Guide to Lichen Products. 1979. pap. text ed. 36.00 (ISBN 3-87429-165-0). Lubrecht & Cramer.

Culberson, W. L., ed. see Tuckerman, E.

Culbert, David H. News for Everyman: Radio & Foreign Affairs in Thirties America. LC 75-23862. 238p. 1976. lib. bdg. 27.50 (ISBN 0-8371-8260-3, CRC/). Greenwood.

Culbert, M. L. Vitamin B-17: Forbidden Weapon Against Cancer. 1974. 8.95 o.p. (ISBN 0-87000-279-1, Arlington Hse). Crown.

Culbert, Michael L. Freedom from Cancer. new ed. LC 76-43206. (Illus.). 1976. pap. 4.95 (ISBN 0-89245-007-X). Seventy-Six.

--What the Medical Establishment Won't Tell You That Could SAVE YOUR LIFE! Friedman, Robert S., ed. LC 82-9607. 280p. (Orig.). 1983. pap. 7.95 (ISBN 0-89865-256-1). Donning Co.

Culbert, Michael L., jt. auth. see Harper, Harold W.

Culbert, Samuel A. & McDonough, John J. The Invisible War: Pursuing Self-Interests at Work. LC 79-18682. 1980. 18.95 (ISBN 0-471-05855-6, Pub. by Wiley-Interscience). Wiley.

Culbert, T. Patrick, jt. auth. see Schusky, Ernest.

Culbert, T. Patrick, ed. The Classic Maya Collapse. LC 72-94657. (School of American Research: Advanced Seminar Ser). (Illus.). 549p. 1977. pap. 12.50x o.p. (ISBN 0-8263-0463-X). U of NM Pr.

Culbertson, Jack A. & Henson, Curtis. Performance Objectives for School Principals. LC 74-75367. 1974. 19.95x (ISBN 0-8211-0223-0); text ed. 17.95x (ISBN 0-685-42628-9). McCutchan.

Culbertson, James T. Consciousness: Natural & Artifical. LC 81-81617. 1983. 9.95 (ISBN 0-87212-152-6). Libra.

Culbertson, John M. Money & Banking. 2nd ed. 1976. text ed. 24.95 (ISBN 0-07-014886-4, C); instructor's manual 15.95 (ISBN 0-07-014887-2). McGraw.

Culbertson, Robert G. & Tezak, Mark R. Order Under Law-Readings in Criminal Justice. 272p. 1981. pap. text ed. 7.95x (ISBN 0-917974-52-2). Waveland Pr.

Culbertson, William S. Alexander Hamilton: An Essay. 1916. 24.50x (ISBN 0-686-50039-3). Elliots Bks.

Culbreth, M., jt. auth. see Gold, Frances J.

Culey, Alma G. Australian Bibliography on the Biology of the Sheep Industry. 1982. 30.00x (ISBN 0-686-97922-2, Pub. by CSIRO Australia). State Mutual Bk.

Culhane, P. T., jt. auth. see O'Toole, L. M.

Culhane, Terry, jt. auth. see Chartier, Jean-Pierre.

Culick, F. E., ed. Guggenheim Aeronautical Laboratory at the California Institute of Technology: The First Fifty Years. LC 82-50314. (Illus.). 1983. pap. 7.50 (ISBN 0-911302-46-8). San Francisco Pr.

Culicover, Peter W. Syntax. 2nd ed. 356p. 1982. 24.50 (ISBN 0-12-199256-X). Acad Pr.

Culicover, Peter W., jt. auth. see Wexler, Kenneth.

Culin, Charlotte. Cages of Glass, Flowers of Time. LC 79-14460. (gr. 7 up). 1979. 10.95 (ISBN 0-02-725450-X). Bradbury Pr.

Culinary Arts Institute, tr. see Goock, Roland.

Culinary Arts Institute Staff, jt. auth. see Carter, Linda.

Culinary Arts Institute Staff, ed. Bread & Soup Cookbook. LC 76-26728. (Adventures in Cooking Ser.). (Illus.). 1976. 3.95 o.s.i. (ISBN 0-8326-0553-0, 1510); pap. 3.95 (ISBN 0-686-96700-3, 2510). Delair.

--Italian Cookbook. LC 77-72330. (Adventures in Cooking Ser.). (Illus.). 1977. pap. 3.95 (ISBN 0-8326-0570-0, 2509). Delair.

--The New World Encyclopedia of Cooking. rev. ed. LC 72-5575. (Illus.). 1980. 17.95 (ISBN 0-8326-0540-9, 1403-N). Delair.

Culinary Arts Institute Staff, jt. ed. see De Proft, Melanie.

Cullen, Bernard. Hegel's Social & Political Thought. LC 79-10730. 1979. 25.00x (ISBN 0-312-36674-4). St Martin.

Cullen, Catherine, tr. see Favret-Saada, Jeanne.

Cullen, D. E., jt. auth. see Chamberlain, Neil W.

Cullen, Donald E. National Emergency Strikes. LC 68-66472. (ILR Paperback Ser.: No. 7). 144p. 1968. pap. 3.00 (ISBN 0-87546-032-1). ILR Pr.

Cullen, Francis T., Jr. Theories of Crime & Deviance: Accounting for Form & Content. 224p. Date not set. text ed. 27.50x (ISBN 0-86598-073-X). Allanheld.

Cullen, Frank, jt. auth. see Cullen, Mary Anne.

Cullen, I. G., ed. Analysis & Decision in Regional Policy. (London Papers in Regional Science). 232p. 1979. 19.50x (ISBN 0-85086-070-9, Pub. by Pion England). Methuen Inc.

Cullen, J., jt. auth. see Davis, P. H.

Cullen, Mary Anne & Cullen, Frank. The Eighty Proof Cookbook: An Introduction to Cooking with High Sprits. 192p. 1982. pap. 6.95 (ISBN 0-312-24053-8); pap. 69.50 prepack (ISBN 0-312-24054-6). St Martin.

Cullen, Matthew & Woolrey, Sharon. World Congress on Land Policy: Nineteen Eighty Proceedings. LC 81-47762. 544p. 1982. 34.95x (ISBN 0-686-98362-9). Lexington Bks.

Cullen, Patrick. Spenser, Marvell, & Renaissance Pastoral. LC 76-123566. 1970. 10.00x o.p. (ISBN 0-674-83195-0). Harvard U Pr.

Cullen, Patrick & Roche, Thomas P., Jr., eds. Spenser Studies: A Renaissance Poetry Annual, Vol. III. (Spenser Studies). 209p. 1982. 21.50x (ISBN 0-8229-3457-4). U of Pittsburgh Pr.

--Spenser Studies: A Renaissance Poetry Annual, Vol. IV. 160p. 1983. 14.95x (ISBN 0-8229-3476-0). U of Pittsburgh Pr.

Cullen, Susan E., jt. ed. see Pierce, Carl W.

Cullen, Timothy, tr. see Frantzeskakis, Ion F.

Cullen, W. R., jt. auth. see Addison, A. W.

Culler, A. D., ed. see Arnold, Matthew.

Culler, Arthur D. The Imperial Intellect. LC 55-8700. Repr. of 1955 ed. lib. bdg. 17.25x (ISBN 0-8371-7683-2, CUII). Greenwood.

Culler, Jonathan. On Deconstruction: Theory & Criticism After Structuralism. LC 82-7414. 320p. 1982. 22.50x (ISBN 0-8014-1322-2). Cornell U Pr.

--Roland Barthes. 128p. 1983. 19.95 (ISBN 0-19-520420-4). Oxford U Pr.

--Roland Barthes. 128p. 1983. pap. 4.95 (ISBN 0-19-520421-2, GB738, GB). Oxford U Pr.

Culler, R. D. Skiffs & Schooners. LC 74-17905. (Illus.). 406p. 1975. 25.00 (ISBN 0-87742-047-5). Intl Marine.

Cullertson, Alan N. & Kenney, D. E. Contract Administration Manual for the Design Professional: How to Establish, Systematize, & Monitor Construction Contract Controls. (Illus.). 320p. 1983. 34.95 (ISBN 0-07-014894-5, P&RB). McGraw.

Culley, jt. auth. see Lazer.

Culley, James, jt. auth. see Lazer, William.

Culley, M. B. The Pilchard. 1971. 59.00 (ISBN 0-08-016523-0). Pergamon.

Culley, Robert C. Studies in the Structure of Hebrew Narrative. LC 75-37159. (Semeia Studies). 128p. 1976. pap. 3.95 o.p. (ISBN 0-8006-1504-2, 1-1504). Fortress.

Culley, Robert C., ed. Semeia Fifteen: Perspectives on Old Testament Narrative. (Semeia Ser.). 9.95 (ISBN 0-686-96241-9, 06 20 15). Scholars Pr CA.

Culley, Robert C. & Overholt, Thomas W., eds. Semeia Twenty-One: Anthropological Perspectives on Old Testament Prophecy. 9.95 (ISBN 0-686-96279-6, 06 20 21). Scholars Pr CA.

Culliford, Peyo see Peyo.

Culliford, Pierre see Peyo, pseud.

Culligan, Matthew J. & Sedlacek, Keith. How to Avoid Stress Before It Kills You. 2.98 o.p. (ISBN 0-517-30556-9). Crown.

Culligan-Hogan, Matthew J. Quest for the Galloping Hogan. 1979. 7.95 o.p. (ISBN 0-517-53665-X). Crown.

Cullin, William H. How to Conduct Foreign Military Sales: The United States Guide 1980 (with FY82 update) LC 82-1228. 456p. loose-leaf 115.00 (ISBN 0-87179-379-2). BNA.

Cullinan, Bernice, ed. Black Dialects & Reading. LC 73-88933. 1974. pap. 7.00 o.p. (ISBN 0-8141-0322-7); pap. 5.00 members o.p. (ISBN 0-686-86382-8). NCTE.

Cullinan, Bernice E., et al. Literature & the Child. 594p. 1981. text ed. 22.95 (ISBN 0-15-551110-6, HC). HarBraceJ.

Cullinan, Douglas & Epstein, Michael. Special Education for Adolescents: Issues & Perspectives. (Special Education Ser.). 1979. text ed. 24.95 o.p. (ISBN 0-675-08407-5). Merrill.

Cullinan, Justine, jt. ed. see Boland, Bill M.

Cullinan, Thomas. The Bedeviled. LC 77-25418. 1978. 10.00 o.p. (ISBN 0-399-12153-6). Putnam Pub Group.

--The Eighth Sacrament. LC 77-4189. 1977. 7.95 o.p. (ISBN 0-399-12011-4). Putnam Pub Group.

Culling, C. F. Handbook of Histopathological & Histochemical Techniques. 3rd ed. 1974. 67.50 (ISBN 0-407-72901-1). Butterworth.

--Modern Microscopy: Elementary Theory & Practice. 1974. 8.95 o.p. (ISBN 0-407-75400-8). Butterworth.

Cullingan, Matthew J. Getting Back to the Basics of Selling. (Ace Business Library). 128p. 1982. pap. 2.95 (ISBN 0-441-28256-3). Ace Bks.

Cullingford, R. A., et al. Timescales in Geomorphology. LC 79-40517. 1980. 89.95 (ISBN 0-471-27600-6, Pub. by Wiley-Interscience). Wiley.

Cullinhan, Douglas & Epstein, Michael. Behavior Disorders of Children & Adolescents. (Illus.). 384p. 1983. 23.95 (ISBN 0-13-072041-0). P-H.

Cullins, Laura, jt. auth. see Cullins, Warren.

Cullins, Warren & Cullins, Laura. Zeballos, Its Gold Its People Yesterday & Today: An Historical Documentation. (Orig.). 1982. pap. 9.75 (ISBN 0-9608386-0-0). Cullins.

Cullis, A. G. & Joy, D. C., eds. Microscopy of Semiconducting Materials, 1981. 464p. 1981. 75.00x o.p. (ISBN 0-85498-151-9, Pub. by A Hilger). State Mutual Bk.

Cullis, J. G., et al. The Economics of Outpatient Clinic Location. 207p. 1981. text ed. 42.75x (ISBN 0-566-00303-1). Gower Pub Ltd.

Culliton, Joseph. Non-Violence-Central to Christian Spirituality: Perspectives from Scriptures to the Present. LC 82-7964. (Toronto Studies in Theology: Vol. 8). 312p. 1982. 39.95x (ISBN 0-88946-964-4). E Mellen.

Cullity, B. D. Elements of X-Ray Diffraction. 2nd ed. LC 77-73950. (Illus.). 1978. text ed. 31.95 (ISBN 0-201-01174-3). A-W.

Cullity, Berrard D. Introduction to Magnetic Materials. LC 71-159665. 1972. text ed. 32.95 (ISBN 0-201-01218-9). A-W.

Cullmann, Oscar. Christ & Time: The Primitive Christian Conception of Time & History. rev. ed. 1964. 11.95 (ISBN 0-664-20488-0). Westminster.

--New Testament: An Introduction for the General Reader. LC 68-12796. 1968. pap. 3.65 (ISBN 0-664-24817-9). Westminster.

Cullmann, Oscar & Leenhardt, Franz J. Essays on the Lord's Supper. LC 58-8979. 1958. pap. 4.25 (ISBN 0-8042-3748-4). John Knox.

Cullom, Shelby. Fifty Years of Public Service: Personal Recollections of Shelby M. Cullom. LC 75-87504. (American Public Figures Ser.). 1969. Repr. of 1911 ed. lib. bdg. 55.00 (ISBN 0-306-71410-8). Da Capo.

Cullop, Floyd G. Constitution of the United States: An Introduction. (Education Ser). (Orig.). 1969. pap. 1.95 (ISBN 0-451-11541-4, AJ1541, Sig). NAL.

Cullum. Handbook of Engineering Design. text ed. write for info (ISBN 0-408-00558-0). Butterworth.

Cullum, J. K. & Willoughby, R. A. Lanczos Algorithms for Large, Symmetric Eigenvalue Computations. (Progress in Scientific Computing Ser.). Date not set. text ed. price not set (ISBN 3-7643-3058-9). Birkhauser.

Cullup, Michael. Reading Geographies. 96p. 1982. pap. text ed. 7.00x (ISBN 0-85635-429-5, 51124, Pub. by Carcanet Pr England). Humanities.

Cullup, Michael & Pavlik, Cheryl. Write About: Writing Activities for Intermediate Students. 96p. (gr. 10-12). 1982. pap. text ed. write for info. (ISBN 0-88018-050-1). Atlantis Pub.

Cully, Iris & Cully, Kendig B. From Aaron to Zerubabbel: Profiles of Bible People. 168p. (Orig.). 1976. pap. 1.00 (ISBN 0-8164-1232-4). Seabury.

Cully, Kendig B., jt. auth. see Cully, Iris.

Culp. Keys to Good Language, Levels 2-6. (gr. 2-6). Level 2. pap. 1.83 (ISBN 0-8372-4300-9); Levels 3-6. pap. 2.67 ea.; tchr's ed. 2.19 (ISBN 0-8372-4301-7); Levels 3-6. tchr's eds. 3.39 ea.; dupl. masters avail. Bowmar-Noble.

Culp, Archie W. Principles of Energy Conversion. (Illus.). 1979. text ed. 34.95 (ISBN 0-07-014892-9, C). McGraw.

Culp, Mary B. & Spann, Sylvia. Me? Teach Reading? LC 79-4309. 1979. pap. text ed. 11.95x (ISBN 0-673-16397-0). Scott F.

Culp, Robert D. & Bauman, Edward J., eds. Guidance & Control 1982. LC 57-43769. (Advances in the Astronautical Sciences Ser.: Vol. 48). (Illus.). 558p. (Orig.). 1982. lib. bdg. 65.00x (ISBN 0-87703-170-3); pap. text ed. 50.00x (ISBN 0-87703-171-1). Am Astronaut.

Culp, Wesner, Clup, Inc., jt. auth. see Owen, William F.

Culpan, Norman, jt. auth. see Reeves, James.

Culpeper, Nicholas. Complete Herbal. (Illus.). 1960. 14.95 (ISBN 0-685-21926-7). Wehman.

--Culpeper's Color Herbal. (Illus.). 224p. (Orig.). 1983. pap. 12.95 (ISBN 0-8069-7690-X). Sterling.

--Culpeper's Complete Herbal. (Illus.). 1959. 14.95 (ISBN 0-8069-3900-1); lib. bdg. 11.69 o.p. (ISBN 0-8069-3901-X). Sterling.

Culpepper, Fred, jt. auth. see Miller, Rex.

Culpepper, R. Alan. Anatomy of the Fourth Gospel: A Study in Literary Design. LC 82-16302. 256p. 1983. 19.95 (ISBN 0-8006-0693-0, 1-693). Fortress.

Culton, Martha. This is That. (Illus.). 1983. 6.95 (ISBN 0-533-05647-0). Vantage.

Cultural Assistance Center. Public & Private Support for the Arts in New York City: A Review with Recommendations for Improvement in the 80's. LC 80-65497. 160p. (Orig.). 1980. pap. 6.00x (ISBN 0-89062-098-9, Pub. by Cultural Assist). Pub Ctr Cult Res.

Cultural Assistance Center Staff. A Guide to New York City Museums. 2nd ed. (Illus.). 64p. Date not set. pap. 1.50 (ISBN 0-486-24454-7). Dover.

Culver, Carmen M. & Hoban, Gary J. Power to Change: Issues for the Innovative Educator. Goodlad, John I., ed. (IDEA Reports on Schooling). (Illus.). 380p. 1973. text ed. 14.95 (ISBN 0-07-014890-2, P&RB). McGraw.

Culver, Charles A. Musical Acoustics. 4th ed. 1956. text ed. 29.50 (ISBN 0-07-014904-6). McGraw.

Culver, David C. Cave Life: Evolution & Ecology. (Illus.). 208p. 1982. text ed. 25.00x (ISBN 0-674-10435-8). Harvard U Pr.

Culver, Dorothy C. Bibliography of Crime & Criminal Justice: Nineteen Twenty-Seven to Nineteen Thirty-One. LC 69-16228. (Criminology, Law Enforcement, & Social Problems Ser.: No. 99). 1969. Repr. of 1934 ed. 24.00x (ISBN 0-87585-099-5). Patterson Smith.

Culver, Dorothy C., ed. Bibliography of Crime & Criminal Justice: Nineteen Thirty-Two to Nineteen Thirty-Seven. LC 69-16227. (Criminology, Law Enforcement, & Social Problems Ser.: No. 100). 1969. Repr. of 1939 ed. 24.00x (ISBN 0-87585-100-2). Patterson Smith.

Culver, John H. & Syer, John C. Power & Politics in California. LC 79-18497. 236p. 1980. pap. text ed. 11.50 (ISBN 0-471-04866-6). Wiley.

Culver, Sylvia A. Keep the River Flowing. 92p. 1979. pap. 2.50 (ISBN 0-8341-0592-6). Beacon Hill.

Culverwel, Nathanael. An Elegant & Learned Discourse on the Light of Nature, 1652: Nathanael Colverwel (1618-1651) Wellek, Rene, ed. LC 75-11215. (British Philosophers & Theologians of the 17th & 18th Centuries Ser.). 1978. lib. bdg. 42.00 o.s.i. (ISBN 0-8240-1769-2). Garland Pub.

Culyer, A. J. The Political Economy of Social Policy. 1980. 29.00 (ISBN 0-312-62242-2). St Martin.

Culyer, A. J., ed. Economic Policies & Social Goals: Aspects of Public Choice. LC 74-23031. 308p. 1975. 32.50 (ISBN 0-312-23450-3). St Martin.

Culyer, A. J., et al, eds. An Annotated Bibliography of Health Economics. LC 77-79018. 1977. 40.00x (ISBN 0-312-03873-9). St Martin.

Cumberland, Charles C. Mexico: The Struggle for Modernity. LC 68-15891. (Latin American Histories Ser). (Orig.). 1968. pap. 6.95x (ISBN 0-19-500766-2). Oxford U Pr.

Cumberlege, Vera. Shipwreck. LC 73-93553. (Picture Bk). 32p. (gr. k-3). 1974. 4.95 o.s.i. (ISBN 0-695-80478-2); lib. bdg. 4.98 o.s.i. (ISBN 0-695-40478-4). Follett.

Cumbler, John T. A Moral Response to Industrialism: The Lectures of Reverend Cook in Lynn, Massachusetts. LC 81-9338. (American Social History Ser.). 180p. 1982. 30.50x (ISBN 0-87395-558-7); pap. 9.95x (ISBN 0-87395-559-5). State U NY Pr.

--Working-Class Community in Industrial America: Work, Leisure, & Struggle in Two Industrial Cities, 1880-1930. LC 78-57768. (Contributions in Labor History: No. 8). 1979. lib. bdg. 29.95 (ISBN 0-313-20615-5, CWC/). Greenwood.

Cumes, J. W. The Indigent Rich: A Theory of General Equilibrium in a Keynesian System. 224p. 1972. 20.00 (ISBN 0-08-017534-1). Pergamon.

--Inflation: A Study in Stability. 202p. 1975. text ed. 20.00 (ISBN 0-08-018167-8). Pergamon.

Cuming, G. J., ed. Mission of the Church & the Propagation of the Faith. LC 77-108105. (Cambridge Studies in Church History: No. 6). 1970. 39.50 (ISBN 0-521-07752-4). Cambridge U Pr.

Cuming, G. J. & Baker, Derek, eds. Councils & Assemblies. LC 70-132384. (Cambridge Studies in Church History: No. 7). 1971. 52.50 (ISBN 0-521-08038-X). Cambridge U Pr.

Cuming, G. J., jt. ed. see Jasper, R. C.

Cuming, Geoffrey. A History of Anglican Liturgy. 450p. 1982. 50.00x (ISBN 0-333-30661-9, Pub. by Macmillan England). State Mutual Bk.

Cuming, Maurice W. Personnel Management in the National Health Service. 320p. 1978. 35.00x (ISBN 0-686-92035-X, Pub. by Heinemann England). State Mutual Bk.

Cumings, Bruce. Child of Conflict: The Korean-American Relationship 1943-1953. LC 82-48871. (Publications on Asia of the School of International Studies: No. 37). 350p. 1983. 22.50 (ISBN 0-295-95995-9). U of Wash Pr.

Cumings, J. N., ed. see Migraine Symposium, 4th, London, 1971.

Cumings, J. N., ed. see Migraine Symposium, 5th, London, 1972.

Cumings, Pamela. Widow's Walk. 320p. 1981. 11.95 o.p. (ISBN 0-517-54332-X). Crown.

Cumming & Funder. Endocrinology, 1980. 1980. 59.75 (ISBN 0-444-80267-3). Elsevier.

Cumming, A. P., jt. auth. see Wright, P.

Cumming, Elaine & Cumming, John H. Closed Ranks: An Experiment in Mental Health Education. LC 57-9073. (Commonwealth Fund Publications Ser). 1957. 12.50x o.p. (ISBN 0-674-13600-4). Harvard U Pr.

Cumming, Gordon, jt. auth. see Scadding, J G.

Cumming, John. Contribution Towards a Bibliography Dealing with Crime & Cognate Subjects. 3rd ed. LC 71-108220. (Criminology, Law Enforcement, & Social Problems Ser.: No. 103). 1970. Repr. of 1935 ed. 12.00x (ISBN 0-87585-103-7). Patterson Smith.

--Runners & Walkers. LC 80-54683. (Illus.). 192p. 1981. 16.95 (ISBN 0-89526-664-4); pap. 9.95 (ISBN 0-89526-889-2). Regnery-Gateway.

Cumming, John & Burns, Paul, eds. Prayers for Our Times. 144p. 1983. 10.95 (ISBN 0-8245-0071-7); pap. 4.95 (ISBN 0-8245-0107-1). Crossroad NY.

Cumming, John H., jt. auth. see Cumming, Elaine.

Cumming, Marsue & Epton, Arli, eds. Theatre Profiles Three. (Illus.). 350p. (Orig.). 1977. pap. 9.95 (ISBN 0-930452-02-X). Theatre Comm.

Cumming, Robert. Just Imagine. (Illus.). 64p. (gr. 4 up). 1982. 12.95 (ISBN 0-684-17762-5, ScribT). Scribner.

Cumming, Robert G. Case Studies of Psychiatric Emergencies. 1983. 16.95 (ISBN 0-8391-1811-2, 19283). Univ Park.

Cumming, Valerie. Gloves. (Illus.). 1982. 13.95x (ISBN 0-7134-1008-6). Drama Bk.

Cumming, William ME. Follow ME. LC 76-47721. 6.95 (ISBN 0-917920-01-5); pap. 1.95 (ISBN 0-917920-00-7). Mustardseed.

Cummings, Abbott L. The Framed Houses of Massachusetts Bay, 1625-1725. LC 78-8390. (Illus.). 1979. 40.00x (ISBN 0-674-31680-0, Belknap Pr); pap. 12.95 (ISBN 0-674-31681-9, Belknap Pr). Harvard U Pr.

Cummings, David, jt. auth. see Pipkin, Bernard.

Cummings, Donald W. & Herum, John, eds. Tempo: Life, Work & Leisure. (Illus.). 336p. 1974. pap. text ed. 12.95 (ISBN 0-395-17839-8, 3-12925); instructors' guide 2.50 (ISBN 0-395-17867-3, 3-12926). HM.

Cummings, E. E. Collected Poems. LC 63-37949. 12.95 (ISBN 0-15-118563-8). HarBraceJ.

--Enormous Room. new ed. LC 77-114387. 1950. 5.95 o.s.i. (ISBN 0-87140-956-9); pap. 3.25 o.s.i. (ISBN 0-686-86289-9, L-001). Liveright.

--The Enormous Room. 5.95 (ISBN 0-394-60427-X). Modern Lib.

--Fairy Tales. LC 75-8515. (Illus.). 39p. (gr. 2-3). 1975. pap. 2.95 (ISBN 0-15-629895-3, VoyB). HarBraceJ.

--I: Six Non Lectures. LC 53-10472. (Charles Eliot Norton Lectures Ser: 1952-1953). 1953. 4.50x o.p. (ISBN 0-686-82914-X); pap. 3.95 o.p. (ISBN 0-674-44000-5). Harvard U Pr.

--Ninety-Five Poems. LC 58-10909. 1958. 8.50 o.p. (ISBN 0-15-166450-1). HarBraceJ.

--Ninety-Five Poems. LC 58-10909. 1971. pap. 1.95 (ISBN 0-15-665950-6, Harv). HarBraceJ.

--One Times One. LC 54-10935. 55p. 1972. pap. 2.95 (ISBN 0-15-668800-X, Harv). HarBraceJ.

--Seventy Three Poems. LC 63-20271. 92p. 6.95 o.p. (ISBN 0-15-181360-4). HarBraceJ.

--Seventy Three Poems. LC 63-20271. 1971. pap. 4.95 (ISBN 0-15-680676-2, Harv). HarBraceJ.

Cummings, Gordon, et al. Soft Tissue Changes in Contractures, Vol. 1. (Orthopedic Physical Therapy Ser.). (Illus.). 1983. pap. 12.75x (ISBN 0-936030-02-X). Stokesville Pub.

Cummings, H. Wayland & Long, Larry W. Managing Communication in Organizations: An Introduction. 361p. 1982. pap. text ed. 15.95x (ISBN 0-89787-314-9). Gorsuch Scarisbrick.

Cummings, Harold J. Prescription for Tomorrow. LC 80-25723. 112p. 1980. 6.95 (ISBN 0-87863-034-1). Farnswth Pub.

Cummings, Homer & McFarland, Carl. Federal Justice. LC 76-109552. (American Constitutional & Legal History Ser). 1970. Repr. of 1937 ed. lib. bdg. 59.50 (ISBN 0-306-71906-1). Da Capo.

Cummings, Hubertis. Indebtedness of Chaucer's Works to the Italian Works of Boccaccio. LC 65-21098. (Studies in Comparative Literature, No. 35). 1969. Repr. of 1916 ed. lib. bdg. 27.95x (ISBN 0-8383-0534-2). Haskell.

Cummings, Ian. Marx, Engels & National Movements. LC 80-10283. 224p. 1980. 27.50 (ISBN 0-312-51792-0). St Martin.

Cummings, J. T. & Moll, H. Prayers for College Students. LC 12-2962. 1982. pap. 4.95 (ISBN 0-570-03869-3). Concordia.

Cummings, Jean. Alias the Buffalo Doctor. LC 82-79770. (Illus.). 266p. 1981. 11.95 (ISBN 0-8040-0815-9). Swallow.

--Why They Call Him The Buffalo Doctor. LC 82-79789. 309p. 1971. 10.95 (ISBN 0-8187-0035-1). Swallow.

Cummings, Joe. Thailand: A Travel Survival Kit. (Lonely Planet Travel Ser.). (Illus.). 144p. (Orig.). 1982. 30.00 (ISBN 0-88254-672-4, Pub. by Lonely Planet Australia). State Mutual Bk.

Cummings, John. Deuteronomy. 1982. lib. bdg. 16.00 (ISBN 0-86524-085-X, 0501). Klock & Klock.

Cummings, Kathleen R. Architectural Records in Chicago. (Illus.). 92p. 1981. pap. 12.95 (ISBN 0-86559-052-4). Art Inst Chi.

Cummings, Keith. The Technique of Glass Forming. (Illus.). 168p. 1980. 24.95 (ISBN 0-7134-1612-2, Pub. by Batsford England). David & Charles.

Cummings, L. L. & Schwab, Donald P. Performance in Organizations: Determinants & Appraisal. 200p. 1973. pap. 10.95x (ISBN 0-673-07627-X). Scott F.

Cummings, L. L., jt. auth. see Harnett, D. L.

Cummings, L. L. & Staw, Barry, eds. Research in Organizational Behavior, Vol. 3. 356p. 1981. 42.50 (ISBN 0-89232-151-2). Jai Pr.

Cummings, L. L., jt. ed. see Staw, Barry.

Cummings, Larry L., jt. ed. see Staw, Barry M.

Cummings, Michael R., jt. auth. see Klug, William S.

Cummings, Milton C., Jr. & Wise, David. Democracy under Pressure: An Introduction to the American Political System. 4th ed. 689p. 1981. text ed. 22.95 (ISBN 0-15-517343-X, HC); study guide 7.95 (ISBN 0-15-517344-8). HarBraceJ.

Cummings, Nancy B. & Michael, Alfred F., eds. Immune Mechanisms in Renal Disease. 550p. 1982. 65.00x (ISBN 0-306-40948-8, Plenum Pr). Plenum Pub.

Cummings, O. R. Street Cars of Boston, Vol. 6: Birneys, Type 5, Semiconvertibles, Parlor, Private, & Mail Cars. (Illus.). 84p. (Orig.). 1980. pap. 9.00 o.p. (ISBN 0-911940-34-0). Cox.

Cummings, Paul. Artists in Their Own Words. LC 79-16474. 1979. 12.95 o.p. (ISBN 0-312-05512-9). St Martin.

Cummings, Paul, ed. Dictionary of Contemporary American Artists. 3rd ed. LC 76-10548. 1977. 35.00 o.p. (ISBN 0-312-20090-0). St Martin.

Cummings, R. D., tr. see Plato.

Cummings, Ray. Girl in the Golden Atom. LC 73-13251. (Classics of Science Fiction Ser.). (Illus.). 357p. 1973. 12.50 (ISBN 0-88355-107-1); pap. 3.95 (ISBN 0-88355-136-5). Hyperion Conn.

--Tarrano the Conqueror. Del Ray, Lester, ed. LC 75-400. (Library of Science Fiction). 1975. lib. bdg. 17.50 o.s.i. (ISBN 0-8240-1406-5). Garland Pub.

Cummings, Richard. Contemporary Selling. 1979. 20.95 (ISBN 0-395-30584-5); Instr's. manual 1.10 (ISBN 0-395-30585-3). HM.

--Make Your Own Comics for Fun & Profit. (gr. 7 up). 1975. 9.95 o.p. (ISBN 0-8098-3929-6). McKay.

Cummings, Thomas G., ed. Systems Theory for Organization Development. LC 79-42906. (Individuals, Groups & Organizations Ser.). 362p. 1980. 53.95 (ISBN 0-471-27691-X, Pub. by Wiley-Interscience). Wiley.

Cummings, Thomas S. Historic Annals of the National Academy of Design. LC 71-87503. (Library of American Art). 1969. Repr. of 1865 ed. lib. bdg. 42.50 (ISBN 0-306-71411-6). Da Capo.

Cummings, Violet. Has Anybody Really Seen Noah's Ark? 416p. 1982. pap. 8.95 (ISBN 0-89051-086-5). CLP Pubs.

Cummings, William W. & Koslow, Irving, eds. Scott Specialized Catalogue of United States Stamps, 1982. 60th ed. (Illus.). 790p. 1981. softcover 18.00 o.p. (ISBN 0-89487-042-4). Scott Pub Co.

Cummings, William W. & Weinfield, Barbara A., eds. Scott Standard Postage Stamp Catalogue, 1982, Vol. 1. (Illus.). 992p. 1981. softcover 18.00 o.p. (ISBN 0-89487-038-6). Scott Pub Co.

--Scott Standard Postage Stamp Catalogue, 1982, Vol. 2. (Illus.). 1056p. 1981. softcover 18.00 o.p. (ISBN 0-89487-039-4). Scott Pub Co.

--Scott Standard Postage Stamp Catalogue, 1982, Vol. 3. (Illus.). 1056p. 1981. softcover 18.00 o.p. (ISBN 0-89487-040-8). Scott Pub Co.

--Scott Standard Postage Stamp Catalogue, 1982, Vol. 4. (Illus.). 960p. 1981. softcover 18.00 o.p. (ISBN 0-89487-041-6). Scott Pub Co.

Cummins, D. Duane & White, William G. The American Frontier. rev. ed. (Inquiries into American History Ser.). (gr. 11-12). 1972. pap. text ed. 4.50 (ISBN 0-02-641220-9, 64122); tchr's. ed. o.p. 5.28 (ISBN 0-02-641250-0, 64125). Glencoe.

--The American Revolution. rev. ed. (Inquiries into American History Ser.). (gr. 11-12). 1973. pap. text ed. 4.50 (ISBN 0-02-641280-2, 64128); tchr's ed. o.p. 5.28 (ISBN 0-02-641330-2, 64133). Glencoe.

--Consensus & Turmoil: The 1950's & 1960's. (Inquiries into American History Ser). (gr. 11-12). 1973. pap. 4.50 (ISBN 0-02-641380-9, 64138); tchrs' ed. o.p. 5.28 (ISBN 0-02-641390-6, 64139). Glencoe.

--Contrasting Decades: The Nineteen Twenties & Nineteen Thirties. (Inquiries into American History Ser.). (gr. 11-12). 1973. pap. 4.50 (ISBN 0-02-641350-7, 64135); tchrs' ed. o.p. 5.28 (ISBN 0-02-641360-4, 64136). Glencoe.

--The Federal Period. (Inquiries into American History Ser). (gr. 11-12). 1973. pap. 4.50 (ISBN 0-685-03316-3, 64142); tchrs' manual o.p. 2.68 (ISBN 0-685-03317-1, 64143). Glencoe.

--Industrialism: The American Experience. (Inquiries into American History Ser.). (gr. 11-12). 1972. pap. text ed. 4.50 (ISBN 0-02-641460-0, 64146); tchr's ed. o.p. 5.28 (ISBN 0-02-641470-8, 64147). Glencoe.

--Our Colonial History: Plymouth & Jamestown. (Inquiries into American History Ser). (gr. 11-12). 1973. pap. 4.50 (ISBN 0-02-641540-2, 64154); tchrs' ed. o.p. 5.28 (ISBN 0-02-641550-X, 64155). Glencoe.

Cummins, Duane D. & White, William G. Origins of the Civil War. (Inquiries into American History Ser.). (gr. 11-12). 1973. pap. 4.50 (ISBN 0-02-641500-3, 64150); tchrs' ed. o.p. 5.28 (ISBN 0-02-641510-0, 64151). Glencoe.

Cummins, J. David & Smith, Barry D. Risk Classification in Life Insurance. 1982. lib. bdg. 45.00 (ISBN 0-89838-114-2). Kluwer-Nijhoff.

Cummins, J. David, et al. Risk Classification in Life Insurance. LC 81-47873. (Illus.). 1982. cancelled (ISBN 0-669-05112-8). Lexington Bks.

Cummins, Kenneth, jt. auth. see Fawcett, Harold.

Cummins, Kenneth W., jt. auth. see Merritt, Ricard W.

Cummins, Martha H. & Slade, Carole. Writing the Research Paper: A Guide & Sourcebook. LC 78-69613. (Illus.). 1979. pap. text ed. 10.95 (ISBN 0-395-27259-9); instr's manual 0.50 (ISBN 0-395-27260-2). HM.

Cummins, Patricia W. Literary & Historical Perspectives of the Middle Ages. 232p. 1982. 8.00 (ISBN 0-937058-15-7). West Va U Pr.

Cummins, Walter, jt. auth. see Gordon, George G.

Cummins, William H. The Great Italian Villas of the Renaissance. (The Masters of World Architecture Library). (Illus.). 148p. 1982. Repr. of 1908 ed. 137.85 (ISBN 0-686-83080-6). Found Class Reprints.

Cumper, G. E., ed. The Economy of the West Indies. LC 73-19112. 273p. 1975. Repr. of 1960 ed. lib. bdg. 18.25x (ISBN 0-8371-7300-0, CUEW). Greenwood.

Cumpston, I. M., ed. The Growth of the British Commonwealth: 1880-1932. (Documents of Modern History Ser.). 192p. 1973. 20.00 (ISBN 0-312-35140-2). St Martin.

Cunanan, Augustina S., jt. auth. see Cabrera, Neonetta C.

Cundiff, Edward W. & Still, Richard R. Basic Marketing: Concepts, Decisions & Strategies. 2nd ed. LC 79-138478. 1971. ref. ed. 24.95 (ISBN 0-13-062638-4); study guide 4.95 (ISBN 0-13-062620-1). P-H.

Cundiff, Edward W., jt. auth. see Still, Richard R.

Cundiff, Edward W., et al. Fundamentals of Modern Marketing. 3rd ed. 1980. text ed. 24.95 (ISBN 0-13-341388-8). P-H.

Cundy, et al. Infection Control in Health Care Facilities. (Illus.). 232p. 1977. 24.95 (ISBN 0-8391-1158-4). Univ Park.

Cundy, Henry M. & Rollett, A. P. Mathematical Models. 2nd ed. (Illus.). 1961. 15.95 (ISBN 0-19-832504-5). Oxford U Pr.

Cundy, Percival, tr. see Franko, Ivan.

Cundy, Percival, tr. see Ukrainka, Lesia.

Cuneo, Mary L. Inside a Sand Castle & Other Secrets. (Illus.). (gr. k-3). 1979. reinforced bdg. 6.95 o.p. (ISBN 0-395-27805-8). HM.

Cuney-Hare, Maud. Negro Musicians & Their Music. LC 74-4108. (Music Reprint Ser.). 1974. Repr. of 1936 ed. 39.50 (ISBN 0-306-70652-0). Da Capo.

Cunff, Madeleine Le. Sur le Vif. (Illus., Fr.). 1977. pap. text ed. 6.95 (ISBN 0-88436-454-2). EMC.

Cunge, J. A. & Holley, F. M. Practical Aspects of Computational River Hydraulics. LC 79-25810. (Water Resources Engineering Ser.). 420p. 1981. text ed. 76.95 (ISBN 0-273-08442-9). Pitman Pub MA.

Cunge, J. A., jt. auth. see Abbott, M. B.

Cunha, Dorothy G., jt. auth. see Cunha, George M.

Cunha, George M. & Cunha, Dorothy G. Library & Archives Conservation: 1980's & Beyond, 2 Vols. LC 82-10806. 1983. Vol. I. write for info. (ISBN 0-8108-1587-7); Vol. II Bibliography. write for info. (ISBN 0-8108-1604-0). Scarecrow.

Cuni, Antonio, tr. see Emanuel, W. D.

Cunitz, Jonathan A. Computer Cases in Accounting. (Illus.). 96p. 1972. pap. 11.95 ref. ed. (ISBN 0-13-166140-X). P-H.

Cunliffe, B. Rome & Her Empire. 1978. 50.00 (ISBN 0-07-014915-1). McGraw.

Cunliffe, B. W. & Fulford, M. G., eds. Corpus Signorum Imperii Romani, Great Britain: Vol. 1, Fascicle 2, Bath & the Rest of Wesswex. (British Academy). (Illus.). 1982. 98.00x (ISBN 0-19-726004-7). Oxford U Pr.

Cunliffe, Barry. The Celtic World. LC 79-13213. (Illus.). 1979. 39.95 o.p. (ISBN 0-07-014918-6). McGraw.

--The Regni. (People of Roman Britain Ser.). 1973. text ed. 17.50x o.p. (ISBN 0-7156-0669-7). Humanities.

--Roman Bath Discovered. (Illus.). 1971. 27.50 (ISBN 0-7100-6826-3). Routledge & Kegan.

Cunliffe, Barry, ed. Coinage & Society in Britain & Gaul: Some Current Problems. (CBA Research Reports Ser.: No. 38). 100p. 1981. pap. text ed. 25.95x (ISBN 0-906780-04-7, Pub. by Coun Brit Archaeology). Humanities.

Cunliffe, Frederick & Piazza, Peter B. Criminalistics & Scientific Investigation. (Ser. in Criminal Justice). (Illus.). 1980. text ed. 22.95 (ISBN 0-13-193284-5). P-H.

Cunliffe, John. Mr. Gosling & the Runaway Chair. LC 80-2696. (Illus.). 32p. (ps-3). 1981. 8.95 o.p. (ISBN 0-233-96956-X). Andre Deutsch.

Cunliffe, Lesley, jt. auth. see Brown, Craig.

Cunliffe, Marcus. American Presidents & the Presidency. 2nd rev. ed. LC 76-19101. 1976. 15.00 o.p. (ISBN 0-07-014936-4, GB). McGraw.

--George Washington: Man & Monument. (RL 9). pap. 1.75 o.p. (ISBN 0-451-61814-9, ME1814, Ment). NAL.

--Nation Takes Shape: Seventeen Eighty-Nine - Eighteen Thirty-Seven. LC 59-5770. (Chicago History of American Civilization Ser). 1960. o.s. 10.00x (ISBN 0-226-12666-8); pap. 6.95 (ISBN 0-226-12667-6, CHAC3). U of Chicago Pr.

Cunliffe, W. Gordon. Gunter Grass. (World Authors Ser.: Germany: No. 65). 1969. lib. bdg. 10.95 o.p. (ISBN 0-8057-2400-1, Twayne). G K Hall.

Cunliffe, W. J. & Cotterill, J. A. The Acnes: Clinical Features, Pathogenesis & Treatment. LC 75-21145. (Major Problems in Dermatology Ser.: Vol. 6). (Illus.). 306p. 1975. 15.00 (ISBN 0-7216-2785-4). Saunders.

Cunniff, Patrick F. Environmental Noise Pollution. LC 76-48146. 210p. 1977. 36.50x (ISBN 0-471-18943-X). Wiley.

Cunningham. Cunningham's Manual of Practical Anatomy: Head & Neck & Brain, Vol. 3. 14th ed. Romanes, G. J., ed. (Illus.). 1979. 12.95x (ISBN 0-19-263205-1). Oxford U Pr.

--Cunningham's Manual of Practical Anatomy: Thorax and Abdomen, Vol. 2. 14th ed. Romanes, G. J., ed. (Illus.). 1977. pap. text ed. 12.95x (ISBN 0-19-263135-7). Oxford U Pr.

--Cunningham's Manual of Practical Anatomy: Upper & Lower Limbs, 3 vols. 14th ed. Romanes, G. J., ed. (Illus.). 270p. 1976. Vol. 1. pap. text ed. 12.95x (ISBN 0-19-263129-2); Vol. 2 o.p. pap. text ed. 11.95 (ISBN 0-19-263135-7); Vol. 3 o.p. pap. text ed. 11.95 (ISBN 0-19-263205-1). Oxford U Pr.

Cunningham, Alastair J., jt. ed. see Sercarz, Eli E.

Cunningham, Ann Marie & Fitzpatrick, Mariana. Future Fire: Weapons for the Apocalypse. 256p. 1983. pap. 8.95 (ISBN 0-446-37031-2). Warner Bks.

Cunningham, Beryl M. & Holtrop, Wm. Woodshop Tool Maintenance. rev. ed. (Illus.). 296p. 1974. text ed. 21.96 (ISBN 0-87002-145-1). Bennett IL.

Cunningham, Bob. Ten-Five, Alaska Skip. LC 76-51138. (Neil Hawkins CB Adventure Ser.). (Illus.). (gr. 4-5). 1977. PLB 6.95 (ISBN 0-913940-58-5). Crestwood Hse.

--Ten-Seven, for Good Sam. LC 76-51143. (Neil Hawkins CB Adventure Ser.). (Illus.). (gr. 4-5). 1977. PLB 6.95 (ISBN 0-913940-59-3). Crestwood Hse.

--Ten-Seventy, Range Fire. LC 76-51141. (Neil Hawkins CB Adventure Ser.). (Illus.). (gr. 4-5). 1977. PLB 6.95 (ISBN 0-913940-56-9). Crestwood Hse.

--Ten Thirty-Three Emergency. LC 76-51139. (CB Adventure Ser.). (Illus.). (gr. 4). 1977. PLB 6.95 (ISBN 0-913940-57-7). Crestwood Hse.

--Ten-Two Hundred, Come on Smokey! LC 76-51142. (Neil Hawkins CB Adventure Ser.). (Illus.). (gr. 4-5). 1977. PLB 6.95 (ISBN 0-913940-55-0). Crestwood Hse.

Cunningham, Bronnie. Best Book of Riddles, Puns & Jokes. LC 78-1238. 1979. 7.95a o.p. (ISBN 0-385-12981-5); PLB 7.95a (ISBN 0-385-12982-3). Doubleday.

Cunningham, Bronnie, compiled by. Funny Business. (Illus.). (gr. 3-8). 1979. pap. 2.50 o.p. (ISBN 0-14-031071-1, Puffin). Penguin.

Cunningham, Bruce L., jt. auth. see McKinney, Peter.

Cunningham, Carolyn, compiled by. Montana Weather. (Illus.). 156p. 1982. pap. 6.95 (ISBN 0-938314-03-3). MT Mag.

Cunningham, Cathy. Curse of Valkyrie House. 176p. 1981. pap. 1.95 (ISBN 0-8439-0970-6, Leisure Bks). Nordon Pubns.

Cunningham, Chet. Your Bike: How to Keep Your Motorcycle Running. LC 74-16626. (Illus.). (gr. 6 up). 1975. 6.95 o.p. (ISBN 0-399-20435-0). Putnam Pub Group.

--Your Wheels: How to Keep Your Car Running. new ed. (Illus.). 128p. (gr. 6 up). 1973. PLB 5.29 o.p. (ISBN 0-399-60830-3). Putnam Pub Group.

Cunningham, Donald H., jt. auth. see Sparrow, W. Keats.

Cunningham, Donald H. & Estrin, Herman A., eds. The Teaching of Technical Writing. LC 75-37652. 221p. (Orig.). 1975. pap. 7.70 o.p. (ISBN 0-8141-5175-2); pap. 5.50 members o.p. (ISBN 0-686-86472-7). NCTE.

Cunningham, Donna. Being a Lunar Type in a Solar World. 334p. 1982. pap. 9.95 (ISBN 0-87728-522-5). Weiser.

Cunningham, E. V. The Case of the Kidnapped Angel. (Nightingale Series Paperbacks). 1983. pap. 7.95 (ISBN 0-8161-3471-5, Large Print Bks). G K Hall.

--The Case of the Poisoned Eclairs. (Nightingale Ser.). 1982. pap. 7.95 (ISBN 0-8161-3333-6, Large Print Bks). G K Hall.

--The Case of the Sliding Pool. 1981. 10.95 o.s.i. (ISBN 0-440-01114-0). Delacorte.

--The Case of the Sliding Pool. 1983. pap. 2.95 (ISBN 0-440-12092-6). Dell.

Cunningham, Earlene B. Mechanisms of Metabolism. (Illus.). 1977. text ed. 32.50 (ISBN 0-07-014927-5, C). McGraw.

Cunningham, Edward G., jt. auth. see Bux, William E.

Cunningham, Frank. James David Forbes: Pioneer Scottish Glaciologist. 475p. 1983. 60.00x (ISBN 0-7073-0320-6, Pub. by Scottish Academic Pr Scotland). Columbia U Pr.

Cunningham, G. H. The Gasteromycetes of Australia & New Zealand. (Bibliotheca Mycologica 67). 1979. Repr. of 1942 ed. lib. bdg. 32.00 (ISBN 3-7682-1231-9). Lubrecht & Cramer.

Cunningham, Gustavus W. Idealistic Argument in Recent British & American Philosophy. LC 76-98750. Repr. of 1933 ed. lib. bdg. 21.00x (ISBN 0-8371-2833-1, CUBA). Greenwood.

Cunningham, Hugh. Leisure in the Industrial Revolution Seventeen Eighty to Eighteen Eighty. LC 80-13354. 1980. 26.00 (ISBN 0-312-47894-1). St Martin.

Cunningham, J., jt. auth. see Williams, D. F.

Cunningham, J. V. Collected Essays of J. V. Cunningham. LC 75-21800. xii, 463p. 1977. o.p 20.00 (ISBN 0-8040-0670-9); pap. 9.95 (ISBN 0-8040-0671-7). Swallow.

--Collected Poems & Epigrams. LC 82-72551. 142p. 1971. pap. 9.95 (ISBN 0-8040-0517-6). Swallow.

--Exclusions of a Rhyme: Poems & Epigrams. LC 82-74227. 120p. (Orig.). 1960. 10.00x (ISBN 0-8040-0763-2); pap. 6.95 (ISBN 0-8040-0102-2). Swallow.

--Journal of John Cardan. LC 82-71108. 56p. 1964. 2.95x (ISBN 0-8040-0173-1). Swallow.

--Woe or Wonder: The Emotional Effect of Shakespearean Tragedy. LC 82-72296. 134p. 1964. pap. 4.50x (ISBN 0-8040-0323-8). Swallow.

Cunningham, J. V., ed. The Problem of Style. 300p. 1983. pap. 8.95 (ISBN 0-941324-03-6). Van Vactor & Goodheart.

Cunningham, James. Sources of Finance for Higher Education in America. LC 79-6081. 165p. 1980. pap. text ed. 9.50 (ISBN 0-8191-0980-0). U Pr of Amer.

Cunningham, James & Cunningham, Partricia. Reading in Elementary Classrooms: Strategies & Observations. LC 82-7814. 512p. 1982. text ed. 17.95x (ISBN 0-582-28390-6). Longman.

Cunningham, James V. & Kotler, Milton. Building Neighborhood Organizations. 224p. 1983. text ed. 15.95x (ISBN 0-268-00668-7); pap. text ed. 7.95x (ISBN 0-268-00669-5). U of Notre Dame Pr.

Cunningham, Jo. The Autumn Leaf Story. (Illus.). pap. 6.50 (ISBN 0-686-51517-X, 99073); price guide 3.00 (ISBN 0-686-51518-8). Wallace-Homestead.

Cunningham, John. The Poetics of Byron's Comedy in Don Juan. (Salzburg - Romantic Reassessment Ser.: No. 106). 242p. 1982. pap. text ed. 25.00x (ISBN 0-391-02778-6, Pub. by Salzburg Austria). Humanities.

Cunningham, John D. Human Biology. 544p. 1983. text ed. 26.95 scp (ISBN 0-06-041451-0, HarpC); instr's. manual avail.; test bank avail. (ISBN 0-06-361454-5). Har-Row.

Cunningham, John J. Introduction to Nutritional Physiology. (Illus.). 400p. 19.95 (ISBN 0-89313-031-1); text ed. 19.95 (ISBN 0-686-38084-3). G F Stickley.

Cunningham, John R., jt. auth. see Johns, Harold E.

Cunningham, Julia. The Silent Voice. (gr. k-6). 1983. pap. 2.50 (ISBN 0-440-48404-9, YB). Dell.

--Wolf Roland. LC 82-19068. 96p. (gr. 5 up). 1983. 9.95 (ISBN 0-394-85892-1); PLB 9.99 (ISBN 0-394-95892-6). Pantheon.

Cunningham, Kitty. Conversations with a Dancer. (Illus.). 192p. 1980. 12.95 o.p. (ISBN 0-312-16942-6). St Martin.

Cunningham, Laura. Third Parties. 288p. 1980. 11.95 (ISBN 0-698-11040-4, Coward). Putnam Pub Group.

Cunningham, Lawrence, ed. Mother of God. LC 82-47741. 132p. 1982. 21.63i (ISBN 0-686-97232-5, HarpR). Har-Row.

Cunningham, Lawrence S. Saint Francis of Assisi. (World Authors Ser.). 1976. lib. bdg. 13.95 (ISBN 0-8057-6249-3, Twayne). G K Hall.

Cunningham, Lee N., tr. see Edington, D. W.

Cunningham, Louis & Peters, Herman J. Counseling Theories: A Selective Examination for School Counselors. LC 72-83704. 1973. text ed. 17.95 (ISBN 0-675-09066-0). Merrill.

Cunningham, Luvern L. Governing Schools: New Approaches to Old Issues. LC 70-137520. 1971. pap. text ed. 9.95 (ISBN 0-675-09256-6). Merrill.

Cunningham, Luvern L. & Gephart, William J., eds. Leadership: The Science & the Art Today. LC 60-2874. 1973. text ed. 12.95 (ISBN 0-87581-155-8). Peacock Pubs.

Cunningham, Luverne, et al, eds. Educational Administration: The Developing Decades. LC 76-27956. 1977. 24.75x (ISBN 0-8211-0226-5); text ed. 22.25x (ISBN 0-685-71408-X). McCutchan.

Cunningham, Madelyn. Monique. (Historical Romance Ser.). (Orig.). 1979. pap. 2.50 o.s.i. (ISBN 0-515-05113-6). Jove Pubns.

Cunningham, Michael R., jt. auth. see Lee, Sherman E.

Cunningham, Partricia, jt. auth. see Cunningham, James.

Cunningham, Patricia M., et al. Classroom Reading Instruction, K-5: Alternative Approaches. 1977. pap. text ed. 11.95 (ISBN 0-669-00324-7). Heath.

Cunningham, Richard, tr. see Bombal, Maria L.

Cunningham, Richard G. Annotated Bibliography of the Work of the Canon Law Society of America 1965-1980. 121p. (Orig.). 1982. pap. 4.50x (ISBN 0-943616-06-9). Canon Law Soc.

Cunningham, Robert, jt. auth. see Patchin, Robert I.

Cunningham, Robert, jt. ed. see Carlson, Rick J.

Cunningham, Robert, tr. see Boros, Ladislaus.

Cunningham, Robert J., tr. see Ratzinger, Joseph C.

Cunningham, Robert, Jr. Governing Hospitals: Trustees & the New Accountabilities. LC 75-44127. 188p. 1976. pap. 17.50 (ISBN 0-87258-182-9, AHA-196111). Am Hospital.

Cunningham, Robert M., Jr. Asking & Giving: A Report on Hospital Philanthropy. LC 79-28315. 148p. (Orig.). 1980. pap. 17.50 (ISBN 0-87258-300-7, AHA-064130). Am Hospital.

--The Healing Mission & the Business Ethic. 305p. 1982. 23.95 (ISBN 0-931028-21-3). Pluribus Pr.

--Wellness at Work. LC 81-15500. 137p. 1982. pap. text ed. 7.95 (ISBN 0-914818-08-2, Inquiry Bk). Blue Cross Shield.

Cunningham, Robert S. Halos & Pitchforks: Philosophical Ramblings of a Wandering Physician. 1983. 8.95 (ISBN 0-533-05614-4). Vantage.

Cunningham, Scott. Magical Herbalism: The Secret Craft of the Wise. Weschcke, Carl L., et al, eds. (Llewellyn's Practical Magick Ser.). (Illus.). xvi, 241p. (Orig.). 1982. pap. 7.95 (ISBN 0-87542-120-2). Llewellyn Pubns.

Cunningham, Susan, jt. auth. see Swenson, Gwen.

Cunningham, William. Systematic Planning for Educational Change. LC 81-84692. 339p. 1982. text ed. 19.95 (ISBN 0-87484-551-3). Mayfield Pub.

Cunningham, William & Mahanand, Marilyn. Blacks in the Performing Arts. Date not set. cancelled (ISBN 0-208-01849-2, Lib. Prof Pubns). Shoe String.

Cunningham, William G. The Aircraft Industry: A Study in Industrial Location. (Illus.). 1951. 6.00 o.p. (ISBN 0-685-53317-4, Pub. by Lorrin Morrison). Aviation.

Cunningham, William H. & Lopreato, Sally C. Energy Use & Conservation Incentives: A Study of the Southwestern United States. LC 77-7485. (Praeger Special Studies). 1977. text ed. 26.95 o.p. (ISBN 0-03-022276-1). Praeger.

Cunnington, C. Willett & Cunnington, Phillis. Handbook of English Costume in the Eighteenth Century. rev. ed. (Illus.). 1972. 15.00 (ISBN 0-8238-0128-4). Plays.

--Handbook of English Costume in the Nineteenth Century. 1970. 15.95 (ISBN 0-8238-0080-6). Plays.

Cunnington, Phillis. Medieval & Tudor Costume. (Illus.). 1968. 7.95 o.p. (ISBN 0-8238-0137-3). Plays.

Cunnington, Phillis, jt. auth. see Cunnington, C. Willett.

Cunnison, J., jt. auth. see Scott, William R.

Cunnyngham, Phyllis. Vita Breathing. LC 78-67971. 144p. (Orig.). 1981. pap. cancelled (ISBN 0-448-15469-2, G&D). Putnam Pub Group.

CUNY Linguistics Conference on Vowel Harmony, May 14, 1977. Issues in Vowel Harmony: Proceedings. Vago, Robert, ed. (Studies in Language Companion Ser.: No. 6). 1979. text ed. 35.75x o.p. (ISBN 0-686-58502-X). Humanities.

Cunynghame, Henry H. Time & Clocks: A Description of Ancient & Modern Methods of Measuring Time. LC 77-78127. (Illus.). 1970. Repr. of 1906 ed. 30.00x (ISBN 0-8103-3576-X). Gale.

Cuomo, George. Family Honor. LC 82-45459. 696p. 1983. 17.95 (ISBN 0-385-11077-4). Doubleday.

Cuplan. Classified Directory of Artists's Signatures, Symbols, & Monograms. Date not set. 185.00. Apollo.

Cuplan, Robert D., et al. Job Demands & Worker Health. 358p. 1980. pap. 17.00x (ISBN 0-87944-265-4). Inst Soc Res.

Cupp, Easter E. Marine Plankton Diatoms of the West Coast of North America. 1977. pap. text ed. 38.40x (ISBN 3-87429-125-1). Lubrecht & Cramer.

Cupper, Jack & Cupper, Lindsay. Hawks in Focus: A Study of Australia's Birds of Prey. (Illus.). 208p. 1982. 30.00 (ISBN 0-686-97177-9). Buteo.

Cupper, Lindsay, jt. auth. see Cupper, Jack.

Cuppleditch, David. Phil May: The Artist & His Wit. 128p. 1982. 50.00x (ISBN 0-284-98592-9, Pub. by C Skilton Scotland). State Mutual Bk.

Cupps, Thomas R. & Fauci, Anthony S. The Vasculitides. 1981. pap. 32.50. Saunders.

Cuppy, Will. How to Attract the Wombat. LC 82-20072. (Illus.). 192p. 1949. pap. 5.95 (ISBN 0-226-12828-8). U of Chicago Pr.

--How to Become Extinct. LC 82-17649. (Illus.). 114p. 1941. pap. 4.95 (ISBN 0-226-12826-1). U of Chicago Pr.

Curatorial Staff, Metropolitan Museum of Art. Metropolitan Museum of Art: Notable Acquisitions, 1965-1975. LC 75-31761. (Illus.). 304p. 1975. pap. 12.50 (ISBN 0-87099-141-8). Metro Mus Art.

Curators at the Musei Vaticani & the Metropolitan Museum of Art. The Vatican Collections: The Papacy & Art. Shultz, Ellen & Horbar, Amy, eds. (Illus.). 256p. 1982. 24.50 (ISBN 0-87099-321-6); pap. 14.95 (ISBN 0-87099-320-8). Metro Mus Art.

Curchak, Norma, et al. Legal Typewriting. 2nd ed. (Illus.). 1980. pap. text ed. 9.95 (ISBN 0-07-014940-2); instructor's manual 5.45 (ISBN 0-07-014941-0). McGraw.

Curcic, Slobodan. Gracanica: King Milutin's Church & Its Place in Late Byzantine Architecture. LC 79-11984. (Illus.). 1980. 29.50x (ISBN 0-271-00218-2). Pa St U Pr.

Curcio, Louis L. & Galanti, Marie E. Nouveau Visage Du Monde Francais. 2nd ed. 203p. 1981. 14.50 (ISBN 0-395-30978-6). HM.

Curds, C. R., et al. British & Other Freshwater Ciliated Protozoa: Part 2. LC 81-15541. (Synopses of the British Fauna Ser.: No. 23). 400p. Date not set. price not set (ISBN 0-521-25033-1). Cambridge U Pr.

Cure, Karen. MiniVacations, U.S.A. (Illus.). 256p. (Orig.). 1976. pap. 6.95 o.s.i. (ISBN 0-695-80529-0). Follett.

Curelaru, M., jt. auth. see Eisenstadt, S. N.

Cureton, E. E. & D'Agostino, R. B. Factor Analysis: An Applied Approach. (Illus.). 480p. 1982. text ed. 39.95 (ISBN 0-89859-048-5). L Erlbaum Assocs.

Cureton, Thomas K. Physiological Effects of Exercise Programs on Adults. (Illus.). 228p. 1971. photocopy ed. spiral 23.00x (ISBN 0-398-00377-7). C C Thomas.

Curhan, Joan P., et al. Tracing the Multinationals: A Sourcebook on U. S. - Based Enterprise. LC 77-9979. 456p. 1977. prof ref 40.00x (ISBN 0-88410-655-1). Ballinger Pub.

Curie, Barbara. Buzzy Bee Goes to School. Mahany, Patricia, ed. (Happy Day Bks.). (Illus.). 24p. (ps-2). 1983. 1.29 (ISBN 0-87239-633-9, 3553). Standard Pub.

--Buzzy Bee Says "Bee Happy". (A Happy Day Bk.). (Illus.). 24p. (gr. k-3). 1979. 1.29 (ISBN 0-87239-355-0, 3625). Standard Pub.

Curl, James C. Developmental Arithmetic: An Individualized Approach. (Illus.). 272p. 1973. text ed. 13.95 (ISBN 0-07-014945-3, W); instructor's manual 13.95 (ISBN 0-07-014946-1). McGraw.

Curl, James S. The Victorian Celebration of Death: The Architecture & Planning of the 19th-Century Necropolis. LC 70-184048. 1972. 31.00x (ISBN 0-8103-2000-2). Gale.

Curle, Adam. Education for Liberation. LC 73-13309. 144p. 1973. 7.95 o.p. (ISBN 0-470-18950-9). Krieger.

Curlee-Salisbury, Joan. When the Woman You Love is an Alcoholic. 2.45 o.p. (ISBN 0-686-92104-6). Hazelden.

Curley, Daniel. Ann's Spring. LC 76-30652. (Illus.). (gr. 3-7). 1977. 6.50i o.p. (ISBN 0-690-01266-7, TYC-J). Har-Row.

--Billy Beg & the Bull. LC 77-11551. (Illus.). (gr. 4-6). 1978. 6.95i (ISBN 0-690-03808-9, TYC-J); PLB 6.79 o.p. (ISBN 0-690-03831-3). Har-Row.

Curley, E. M. Spinoza's Metaphysics: An Essay in Interpretation. LC 70-85073. 1969. 14.00x o.p. (ISBN 0-674-83210-8). Harvard U Pr.

Curley, Lois, jt. ed. see Hestenes, Roberta.

Curley, Richard T. Elders, Shades, & Women: Ceremonial Change in Lango, Uganda. LC 70-634788. 1973. 24.50x (ISBN 0-520-02149-5). U of Cal Pr.

Curme, George O. English Grammar. (Orig.). 1947. pap. 4.76i (ISBN 0-06-460061-0, CO 61, COS). B&N NY.

C.U.R.N. Project, Michigan Nurses Association. Clean Intermittent Catherization. Horsley, Joanne, ed. (Using Research to Improve Nursing Practice Ser.). 112p. 1982. 14.00 (ISBN 0-8089-1463-4, 792061). Grune.

Curnow, D. H., jt. auth. see Worth, H. G.

Curnow, Wystan, jt. auth. see Allen, Jim.

Curnow, Wystan, ed. Essays on New Zealand Literature. 1973. pap. text ed. 15.00x o.p. (ISBN 0-435-18195-5). Heinemann Ed.

Curran. Gross Pathology, a Colored Atlas. 30.00 o.p. (ISBN 0-85602-030-3). Wiley.

Curran, Charles E. American Catholic Social Ethics: Twentieth Century Approaches. LC 82-4829. 336p. 1982. 21.95 (ISBN 0-268-00603-2). U of Notre Dame Pr.

--Moral Theology: A Continuing Journey. LC 81-23160. xiv, 238p. 1983. pap. text ed. 6.95 (ISBN 0-268-01351-9, 85-13517). U of Notre Dame Pr.

--Politics, Medicine & Christian Ethics: A Dialogue with Paul Ramsey. LC 72-91521. 240p. (Orig.). 1973. 1.50 o.p. (ISBN 0-8006-0500-4, 1-500). Fortress.

Curran, Charles E. & McCormick, Richard. Readings in Moral Theology: No. 1, Moral Norms & Catholic Tradition. LC 79-84237. 1979. pap. 7.95 (ISBN 0-8091-2203-0). Paulist Pr.

Curran, Connie L. & Lengacher, Cecile A. Preparation for Practice: Self-Study Modules in Medical-Surgical Nursing. 413p. 1981. pap. text ed. 16.50 (ISBN 0-397-54373-5, Lippincott Nursing). Lippincott.

--Preperation for Practice: Self-Study in Medical-Surgical Nursing. 413p. pap. text ed. 16.50 o.p. (ISBN 0-397-54373-5, Lippincott Nursing). Lippincott.

Curran, Dolores. I'm Telling: Confessions of a Middle-Age, Middle Class Parent. LC 77-14822. (Emmaus Book). 128p. 1978. pap. 1.95 (ISBN 0-8091-2073-9). Paulist Pr.

--Traits of a Healthy Family: Fifteen Traits Commonly Found in Healthy Families by Those Who Work With Them. LC 82-70489. 300p. 1983. 14.95 (ISBN 0-86683-643-8). Winston Pr.

Curran, Donald J., ed. see Groves, Harold M.

Curran, J. T. Fetal Heart Monitoring. 1975. 21.95 o.p. (ISBN 0-407-00014-3). Butterworth.

Curran, James P. & Monti, Peter, eds. Social Skills Training: A Practical Handbook for Assessment & Treatment. LC 81-6374. 447p. 1982. 29.50 (ISBN 0-89862-610-2). Guilford Pr.

Curran, Joseph. Introductory Sociology. LC 76-30856. 1977. 14.95 (ISBN 0-07-014947-X, C); instructor's manual 2.95 (ISBN 0-07-014948-8). McGraw.

Curran, June. Drawing Home Plans: A Simplified Drafting System for Planning & Design. Giumarra, Nancy & Weine, Ruth, eds. LC 78-72188. (Illus.). 1979. 24.95 (ISBN 0-932370-01-2); pap. 14.95 (ISBN 0-932370-02-0). Brooks Pub Co.

--Drawing Home Plans: A Simplified Drafting System for Planning & Design. LC 78-72188. (Illus.). 241p. 24.95x (ISBN 0-932370-01-2); pap. 14.95 (ISBN 0-932370-02-0). W Kaufmann.

--Profile Your Lifestyle: Questions to Ask Yourself Before Building, Buying, or Remodeling. LC 78-72187. 159p. 1979. pap. 7.95 (ISBN 0-932370-00-4). W Kaufmann.

Curran, R. C. Color Atlas of Histopathology. 2nd ed. (Illus.). 1972. text ed. 39.50x (ISBN 0-19-519151-X). Oxford U Pr.

Curran, R. C. & Jones, E. L. Gross Pathology: A Color Atlas. (Illus.). 1974. text ed. 37.50x (ISBN 0-19-519797-6). Oxford U Pr.

Curran, Stuart, ed. Le Bossu & Voltaire on the Epic: Rene le Bossu, Treatise of the Epic Poem, 1695 & Voltaire, Essay on Epic Poetry, 1727. LC 73-133363. 1970. 42.00x (ISBN 0-8201-1086-8). Schol Facsimiles.

Curran, Susan. New Technology & Insurance. 1981. 50.00x (ISBN 0-686-97106-X, Pub. by Fourmat England). State Mutual Bk.

Curran, Susan & Mitchell, Horace. Office Automation: An Essential Management Strategy. 210p. 1982. 18.00x (ISBN 0-8448-1420-2). Crane-Russak Co.

Curran, Susan, jt. auth. see Pask, Gordon.

Curran, Thomas J. Xenophobia & Immigration, 1820-1930. LC 74-10865. (The Immigrant Heritage of American Ser). 1975. lib. bdg. 10.95 o.p. (ISBN 0-8057-3294-2, Twayne). G K Hall.

Curran, Thomas J., jt. auth. see Coppa, Frank J.

Curran, William & Shapiro, E. Donald. Law, Medicine & Foresnic Science. 3rd ed. LC 81-81207. 1181p. 1982. text ed. 28.00 (ISBN 0-316-16510-7). Little.

Curran, William J. & Shapiro, E. Donald. Law, Medicine & Forensic Science. 2nd ed. 1046p. 1970. 25.50 o.p. (ISBN 0-316-16512-3). Little.

Curren, Anna M. Clinical Nursing Skills. (Illus.). 370p. 1983. pap. text ed. 21.95 (ISBN 0-918082-02-1). Wallcur Inc.

Curren, Art. Kitbashing Model Railroad Structures. (Illus., Orig.). 1985. pap. price not set (ISBN 0-89024-059-0). Kalmbach.

Curren, Polly. I Know a Plumber. (Community Helper Bks.). (Illus.). (gr. k-3). 1976. PLB 4.29 o.p. (ISBN 0-399-61032-4). Putnam Pub Group.

--I Know an Electrician. (Community Helper Bks.). (Illus.). (gr. k-3). 1977. PLB 4.29 o.p. (ISBN 0-399-61061-8). Putnam Pub Group.

Current Biography staff, jt. auth. see Moritz, Charles.

Current, R. N. John C. Calhoun. (World Leaders Ser.). 12.95 (ISBN 0-8057-3659-X, Twayne). G K Hall.

Current, Richard N. Daniel Webster & the Rise of National Conservatism. (The Library of American Biography). 215p. 1962. pap. text ed. 5.95 (ISBN 0-316-16515-8). Little.

Current-Garcia, Eugene. O. Henry. (United States Authors Ser.). 1972. lib. bdg. 10.95 (ISBN 0-8057-0368-3, Twayne). G K Hall.

Current-Garcia, Eugene & Patrick, Walton R. American Short Stories. 4th ed. 1981. pap. text ed. 13.50x (ISBN 0-673-15570-6). Scott F.

--What Is the Short Story? Studies in the Development of a Literary Form. rev. ed. 1974. pap. 10.95x (ISBN 0-673-07886-8). Scott F.

Currey, Cecil B. Follow Me & Die. LC 82-48509. 304p. 1983. 17.95 (ISBN 0-8128-2892-5). Stein & Day.

Currey, L. W. & Reginald, R. Science Fiction & Fantasy Reference Guide: An Annotated History of Critical & Biographical Works. LC 80-22715. (Borgo Reference Library: Vol. 4). 64p. (Orig.). 1983. lib. bdg. 9.95x (ISBN 0-89370-145-9); pap. text ed. 3.95x (ISBN 0-89370-245-5). Borgo Pr.

Currey, L. W., jt. auth. see Reginald, R.

Currey, L. W., jt. ed. see Hartwell, David G.

Curriculum Committee of St. Paul Technical Vocational Institute. Mathematics for Careers. LC 78-52661. (Mathematics Ser.). 1980. pap. text ed. 15.00 o.p. (ISBN 0-8273-1676-3); instructor's guide 1.75 o.p. (ISBN 0-8273-1677-1). Delmar.

Curriculum Design & Development Course Team. Curriculum Design. LC 75-20255. 529p. 1975. pap. 24.95x o.p. (ISBN 0-470-99202-6). Halsted Pr.

Currie, Angela, jt. auth. see Currie, Graham.

Currie, B. & Sharpe, R. A. Structural Detailing Level II. (Illus.). 160p. pap. text ed. 14.95x (ISBN 0-7121-1985-X). Intl Ideas.

Currie, Barbara. Pioneers in the American West, 1780-1840. Reeves, Marjorie, ed. (Then & There Ser.). (Illus.). 92p. (Orig.). (gr. 7-12). 1969. pap. text ed. 3.10 (ISBN 0-582-20454-2). Longman.

--Railroads & Cowboys in the American West. Reeves, Marjorie, ed. (Then & There Ser.). (Illus.). 112p. (Orig.). (gr. 7-12). 1974. pap. text ed. 3.10 (ISBN 0-582-20533-6). Longman.

Currie, D. & Nobay, R., eds. Macroeconomic Analysis: Essays in Macroeconomics & Econometrics. (Illus.). 506p. 1981. 44.00x (ISBN 0-7099-0311-1, Pub. by Croom Helm Ltd England). Biblio Dist.

Currie, D., et al, eds. Microeconomic Analysis: Essays in Microeconomics & Economic Development. (Illus.). 510p. 1981. 44.00x (ISBN 0-7069-0709-4, Pub. by Croom Helm Ltd England). Biblio Dist.

Currie, Donald J. Abdominal Pain. (Illus.). 1979. text ed. 21.95 (ISBN 0-07-014942-9, HP). McGraw.

Currie, Donald J. & Smialowski, Arthur. Photographic Illustration for Medical Writing. (Illus.). 132p. 1962. photocopy ed. spiral 14.75x (ISBN 0-398-00379-3). C C Thomas.

Currie, Elliott, jt. auth. see Skolnick, Jerome.

Currie, Elliott, jt. ed. see Skolnick, Jerome H.

Currie, G., ed. see Lakatos, Imre.

Currie, Graham & Currie, Angela. Cancer: The Biology of Malignant Disease. 128p. 1983. pap. text ed. 16.50 (ISBN 0-7131-4400-9). E Arnold.

Currie, Harold W. Eugene V. Debs. LC 76-3780. (United States Authors Ser.). 1976. lib. bdg. 12.95 (ISBN 0-8057-7167-0, Twayne). G K Hall.

Currie, Ian. You Cannot Die. LC 79-16697. (Illus.). 1978. 9.95x o.p. (ISBN 0-416-00191-2). Methuen Inc.

Currie, J. M. The Economic Theory of Agricultural Land Tenure. LC 80-41114. (Illus.). 1981. 34.50 (ISBN 0-521-23634-7). Cambridge U Pr.

Currie, Janice K., jt. auth. see Heyneman, Stephen P.

Currie, Lloyd A., ed. Nuclear & Chemical Dating Techniques. (ACS Symposium Ser.: No. 176). 1982. write for info. (ISBN 0-8412-0669-4). Am Chemical.

Currie, Russel M. Work Study. 1978. pap. 23.50x (ISBN 0-273-00959-1, LTB). Sportshelf.

Currie, S., jt. auth. see Behan, P. O.

Currier, Richard L., ed. see Meshorer, Ya'akov.

Currin, Beverly M. The Hope That Never Disappoints. 128p. (Orig.). 1983. pap. 6.95 (ISBN 0-687-17415-5). Abingdon.

Currry, Susan & Rich, Susan, eds. Kline Guide to the Chemical Industry. 4th ed. (Illus.). 590p. 1980. pap. 147.00 (ISBN 0-917148-13-4). Kline.

Curry. Press Control Around the World. 304p. 1982. 29.95 (ISBN 0-03-059869-9). Praeger.

--The World of Mexican Cooking. pap. 4.95 (ISBN 0-686-81679-X). Corona Pub.

Curry, Barbara. Model Aircraft. (First Bks.). (Illus.). (gr. 4 up). 1979. PLB 8.90 s&l (ISBN 0-531-02260-9). Watts.

--Model Historical Aircraft. LC 82-4779. (First Bks.). (Illus.). 72p. (gr. 4 up). 1982. PLB 8.90 (ISBN 0-531-04465-3). Watts.

Curry, Dudley & Frame, Robert. Accounting Principles: A Multimedia Program. LC 72-95544. 1973. Modules 1-15. pap. text ed. 19.95 (ISBN 0-675-08992-1). Merrill.

Curry, Estell H., jt. auth. see Silvius, George H.

Curry, Jane. The River's in My Blood: Riverboat Pilots Tell Their Stories. LC 82-11068. xx, 279p. 1983. 17.50 (ISBN 0-8032-1416-2). U of Nebr Pr.

Curry, Jane, ed. see Holley, Marietta.

Curry, Jess, Jr., jt. auth. see Christie, Linda.

Curry, John. Animal Skeletons. (Studies in Biology: No. 21). 56p. 1978. pap. text ed. 8.95 (ISBN 0-7131-2284-6). E Arnold.

Curry, Kenneth. Sir Walter Scott's Edinburgh Annual Register. LC 77-8136. 1977. 17.95x (ISBN 0-87049-208-X). U of Tenn Pr.

--Southey. (Author Guides). 1975. 18.00 o.p. (ISBN 0-7100-8112-X). Routledge & Kegan.

Curry, Leonard P. The Free Black in Urban America, 1800-1850: The Shadow of the Dream. LC 80-27811. (Illus.). 416p. 1981. lib. bdg. 27.50x (ISBN 0-226-13124-6). U of Chicago Pr.

Curry, Lerond. Protestant-Catholic Relations in America: World War I Through Vatican II. LC 79-183352. 136p. 1972. 12.00x o.p. (ISBN 0-8131-1265-6). U Pr of Ky.

Curry, Lloyd W. Science Fiction & Fantasy Authors: A Bibliography of First Printings of Their Fiction & Selected Nonfiction. Hartwell, David G., ed. 1979. lib. bdg. 48.00 o.p. (ISBN 0-686-61018-0, Hall Reference). G K Hall.

Curry, Nancy L. Fencing. LC 82-83919. (Illus.). 144p. (Orig.). 1983. pap. 6.95 (ISBN 0-918438-99-3). Leisure Pr.

Curry, R. N. Fundamentals of Natural Gas Conditioning. 128p. 1981. 32.95x (ISBN 0-87814-162-6). Pennwell Pub.

Curry, Richard A. Ramon de Mesonero Romanos. (World Authors Ser.). 1976. lib. bdg. 15.95 (ISBN 0-8057-6226-4, Twayne). G K Hall.

Curry, Robert L., Jr., jt. auth. see Rothchild, Donald.

Curry, Stephen H. & Whelpton, Robin. Manual of Laboratory Pharmcokinetics: Experiments in Biopharmaceutics, Biochemical Pharmacology & Pharmacokinetics with a Consideration of Relevant Instrumental & Chromatographic Techniques. 250p. 1983. write for info. (ISBN 0-471-10247-4, Pub. by Wiley-Interscience). Wiley.

Curry, Timothy J. & Clarke, Alfred C. Introducing Visual Sociology. (Illus.). 1978. pap. text ed. 6.95 (ISBN 0-8403-2267-4, 40226701). Kendall-Hunt.

Curry, W. H. Sun Rising on the West: The Saga of Henry Clay & Elizabeth Smith. 1979. 21.00x (ISBN 0-686-31817-X). Crosby County.

Curry, W. Lawrence, ed. Anthems for the Junior Choir, 5 bks. 1.50 ea. Westminster.

--Service Music for the Adult Choir. 2.50 ea. (ISBN 0-664-10059-7). Westminster.

Curtain, Mary. Armond & the First Christmas. (Arch Bk.: No. 16). (Illus.). 1979. 0.89 (ISBN 0-570-06129-6, 59-1247). Concordia.

Curth, Helen O., tr. see Korting, Gunter W. & Denk, R.

Curth, William, tr. see Korting, Gunter W. & Denk, R.

Curth, William, et al, trs. see Korting, Gunter W.

Curthoys, J. S., jt. ed. see Atrens, D. M.

Curti, Merle. American Philanthropy Abroad: A History. 1963. 42.50 (ISBN 0-8135-0422-8). Rutgers U Pr.

Curti, Merle, et al, eds. American Issues: The Social Record, 2 Vols. 4th rev. ed. LC 75-132875. 1971. Vol. 1. pap. 6.50x o.p. (ISBN 0-397-47230-7, HarpC); Vol. 2. pap. 6.95x o.p. (ISBN 0-397-47231-5, HarpC). Har-Row.

Curti, Merle E. The Learned Blacksmith: The Letters & Journals of Elihu Burritt. LC 70-137536. (Peace Movement in America Ser). ix, 241p. 1972. Repr. of 1937 ed. lib. bdg. 16.95x (ISBN 0-89198-063-6). Ozer.

--Peace or War: The American Struggle, 1636-1936. LC 70-143428. (Peace Movement in America Ser.). 374p. 1972. Repr. of 1936 ed. lib. bdg. 20.95x (ISBN 0-89198-064-4). Ozer.

Curtin, Bernadette M., jt. auth. see Hecklinger, Fred J.

Curtin, Leah & Flaherty, M. Josephine. Nursing Ethics: Theories & Pragmatics. (Illus.). 378p. 1981. text ed. 17.95 (ISBN 0-89303-051-1); pap. text ed. 15.95 (ISBN 0-89303-053-8). R J Brady.

Curtin, Philip D. Economic Change in Precolonial Africa: Senegambia in the Era of the Slave Trade, 2 vols. LC 74-5899. (Illus.). 1975. Vol. 1, 394p. 35.00 (ISBN 0-299-06640-1); Supplementary Evidence, 164p. 35.00 (ISBN 0-299-06650-9). U of Wis Pr.

--Image of Africa: British Ideas & Action, 1780-1850, 2 vols. in 1. (Illus.). 1964. 37.50x (ISBN 0-299-03020-2); Vol. 1, 302p. pap. 9.95 (ISBN 0-299-83025-X); Vol. 2, 248p. pap. 9.95 (ISBN 0-299-83026-8). U of Wis Pr.

Curtin, Philip D., ed. Africa & the West: Intellectual Responses to European Culture. LC 77-176409. 272p. 1972. 30.00 (ISBN 0-299-06121-3); pap. 12.50 (ISBN 0-299-06124-8). U of Wis Pr.

Curtin, Richard T. Income Equity Among U. S. Workers: The Bases & Consequences of Deprivation. LC 76-24349. (Praeger Special Studies). 1977. 25.95 o.p. (ISBN 0-275-23780-X). Praeger.

Curtin, Richard T., ed. Surveys of Consumers, 1974-75: Contributions to Behavioral Economics. LC 72-619718. 336p. 1976. 16.00x (ISBN 0-87944-209-3). Inst Soc Res.

Curtin, Rosalie, et al. R.C.I.A. A Practical Approach to Christian Initiation. 136p. (Orig.). 1981. pap. 10.95 (ISBN 0-697-01759-1). Wm C Brown.

Curtin, W. G., et al. Structural Masonry Designer's Manual. (Illus.). 448p. 1982. text ed. 85.00x (ISBN 0-246-11208-5). Sheridan.

Curtis. Practical Math for Business: 3-e. 1983. pap. text ed. 16.95 (ISBN 0-686-84525-0); Instr's. annotated ed. 17.95 (ISBN 0-686-84526-9). HM.

Curtis, et al. Educational Resources Management System. 3.75 (ISBN 0-685-57172-6). Assn Sch Busn.

Curtis, A. & Cooper, J. Mathematics of Accounting. 4th ed. 1961. 24.95 (ISBN 0-13-563908-5); text ed. 29.95 (ISBN 0-686-66514-7). P-H.

Curtis, A. S. Cell Surface: Its Molecular Role in Morphogenesis. 1967. 63.50 (ISBN 0-12-199650-6). Acad Pr.

Curtis, Alan. Practical Math for Business. 2nd ed. LC 77-73944. (Illus.). 1978. pap. text ed. 17.50 (ISBN 0-395-25431-0); instr's. ed. 14.95 (ISBN 0-395-25432-9). HM.

Curtis, Alan R. Practical Math for Business. 3d ed. LC 82-84521. 368p. 1983. pap. text ed. 16.95 (ISBN 0-395-32698-2); instr's. annotated ed. 17.95 (ISBN 0-395-32699-0). HM.

Curtis, Anthony. The Lyle Antiques Identification Guide. (Illus.). 174p. 1981. pap. 4.95 (ISBN 0-698-11114-1, Coward). Putnam Pub Group.

--The Lyle Offical Arms & Armour Review. 416p. 1981. 24.95 (ISBN 0-698-11116-8, Coward). Putnam Pub Group.

--The Lyle Offical Arts Review. 516p. 1981. 24.95 (ISBN 0-698-11117-6, Coward). Putnam Pub Group.

--The Lyle Offical Books Review. 348p. 1981. 24.95 (ISBN 0-698-11115-X, Coward). Putnam Pub Group.

--The Lyle Official Antiques Review 1983. 1982. 24.95 (ISBN 0-698-11190-7, Coward); pap. 14.95 (ISBN 0-698-11204-0). Putnam Pub Group.

Curtis, Anthony, compiled by. Antiques & Their Values. Incl. China (ISBN 0-698-11121-4); Furniture (ISBN 0-698-11159-1); Glass (ISBN 0-698-11158-3); Silver (ISBN 0-698-11160-5). 1982. pap. 5.95 ea. (Coward). Putnam Pub Group.

Curtis, Anthony, ed. The Lyle Official Antiques Review, 1982. (Illus.). 1981. 24.95 (ISBN 0-698-11119-2, Coward); flexible bdg. with jacket 14.95 (ISBN 0-698-11120-6). Putnam Pub Group.

Curtis, Benjamin R. A Memoir of Benjamin Robbins Curtis, 2 Vols. LC 77-75298. (The American Scene Ser.). 1970. Repr. of 1879 ed. 115.00 (ISBN 0-306-71267-9). Da Capo.

Curtis, Bob. Food Service Security: Internal Control. LC 75-33513. 256p. 1975. 21.95 (ISBN 0-86730-214-3). Lebhar Friedman.

--Security Control: External Theft. LC 76-163714. (Security Control Ser.). 1971. 21.95 (ISBN 0-86730-504-5). Lebhar Friedman.

--Security Control: Internal Theft. LC 72-90623. (Security Control Ser.). 1973. 21.95 (ISBN 0-86730-503-7). Lebhar Friedman.

Curtis, Brian A., et al. An Introduction to the Neurosciences. LC 74-145556. (Illus.). 830p. 1972. 27.50 (ISBN 0-7216-2810-9); 15.00, filmstrip (ISBN 0-7216-9818-2). Saunders.

Curtis, Bruce. William Graham Sumner. (United States Authors Ser.). 1981. lib. bdg. 12.95 (ISBN 0-8057-7324-X, Twayne). G K Hall.

Curtis, Charles, et al. Perspectives on God: Sociological, Theological & Philosophical. LC 78-62943. 1978. pap. text ed. 10.00 (ISBN 0-8191-0605-4). U Pr of Amer.

Curtis, Charles J. Contemporary Protestant Thought. Devine, J. Frank & Rousseau, Richard W., eds. (Contemporary Theology Ser). 1970. pap. text ed. 4.95 o.p. (ISBN 0-02-814040-0). Glencoe.

Curtis, Charles W. & Reiner, Irving. Methods of Representation Theory: With Applications to Finite Groups & Orders, Vol. I. LC 81-7416. (Pure & Applied Mathematics: Wiley-Interscience Series of Tests, Monographs & Tracts). 819p. 1981. 59.95x (ISBN 0-471-18994-4, Pub. by Wiley-Interscience). Wiley.

--Representation Theory of Finite Groups & Associative Algebras. LC 62-16994. (Pure & Applied Mathematics Ser). 1962. 59.95 (ISBN 0-470-18975-4, Pub. by Wiley-Interscience). Wiley.

Curtis, Dan B. & Brewer, Robert S. Speaking As a Farmer: Winning FFA Speeches, Principles of Speech Preparation & Presentation. 256p. 1980. pap. text ed. 9.95 (ISBN 0-8403-2248-8). Kendall-Hunt.

Curtis, David A. Strategic Planning for Smaller Business: Improving Corporate Performance & Personal Reward. LC 82-48171. 224p. 1983. 21.95x (ISBN 0-669-06011-9). Lexington Bks.

Curtis, Donald. Science of Mind in Daily Living. 1975. pap. 5.00 (ISBN 0-87980-299-5). Wilshire.

--Your Thoughts Can Change Your Life. pap. 5.00 (ISBN 0-87980-179-4). Wilshire.

Curtis, Donald R., ed. Indianapolis Dining Guide, 1983. (Illus.). 272p. (Orig.). 1982. pap. 6.95 (ISBN 0-9607968-1-9). Indytype.

Curtis, Doris M., et al. How to (Try to) Find on Oil Field. 96p. 1981. 23.95x (ISBN 0-87814-166-9). Pennwell Pub.

Curtis, Dunn see Bellairs, Ruth, et al.

Curtis, Edward S. Indian Days of the Long Ago. (Illus.). 1978. 8.95 (ISBN 0-913668-46-X); pap. 4.95 (ISBN 0-913668-45-1). Ten Speed Pr.

--Portraits from North American Indian Life. 192p. 1981. pap. 10.95 o.s.i. (ISBN 0-89104-003-X, A & W Visual Library). A & W Pubs.

Curtis, Eileen & Renier, Judith. Girl on a Mountain-New Leaves. 1973. pap. 4.00 o.p. (ISBN 0-912950-15-3). Blue Oak.

Curtis, Francis D. Digest of Investigations in the Teaching of Sciences in the Elementary & Secondary Schools. LC 74-153694. 1971. Repr. of 1926 ed. text ed. 12.95x (ISBN 0-8077-1223-X). Tchrs Coll.

--Digest of Investigations in the Teaching of Science, Third. LC 74-153694. 1971. Repr. of 1939 ed. text ed. 13.50x (ISBN 0-8077-1226-4). Tchrs Coll.

--Reviews of Research in Science Education Series, 6 vols. 1971. Set. 62.50x (ISBN 0-8077-2433-5). Tchrs Coll.

--Second Digest of Investigations in the Teaching of Science. LC 74-153694. 1971. Repr. of 1931 ed. text ed. 13.50x (ISBN 0-8077-1225-6). Tchrs Coll.

Curtis, G. H., jt. auth. see Williams, Howell.

Curtis, George T. Constitutional History of the United States: From Their Declaration of Independence to the Close of Their Civil War, 2 vols. (American Constitution & Legal History Ser.). 1100p. 1974. Repr. of 1896 ed. Set. lib. bdg. 145.00 (ISBN 0-306-70611-3). Da Capo.

Curtis, George W., ed. see Downing, Andrew J.

Curtis, Helena. Biology. 3rd ed. LC 78-68582. (Illus.). 1979. text ed. 27.95x (ISBN 0-87901-100-9); study guide 7.95x (ISBN 0-87901-101-7); lab topics in biolology 11.95x (ISBN 0-87901-103-3). Worth.

Curtis, Helena & Barnes, N. Sue. Invitation to Biology. 3rd ed. 1981. text ed. 25.95x (ISBN 0-87901-131-9); study guide 7.95 (ISBN 0-87901-139-4). Worth.

Curtis, Helene & Dudley, Cliff. All That I Have. LC 77-81394. 1979. pap. 2.95 (ISBN 0-89221-044-3). New Leaf.

Curtis, J. & Scott, W. Social Stratification: Canada. 2nd ed. 1979. pap. 13.25 (ISBN 0-13-818633-2). P-H.

Curtis, Jack. The Man in Place. (Illus.). 36p. 1982. 35.00x (ISBN 0-918824-33-8). Turkey Pr.

Curtis, Jack D. & Detert, Richard A. How to Relax: A Holistic Approach to Stress Management. LC 80-84021. 222p. 1981. pap. 9.95 (ISBN 0-87484-527-0). Mayfield Pub.

Curtis, Jack H., et al. Sociology: An Introduction. (Illus.). 1967. text ed. 5.60 o.p. (ISBN 0-02-814050-8); instructor's manual 3.52 o.p. (ISBN 0-02-814070-2). Glencoe.

Curtis, James. Between Flops: A Biography of Preston Sturges. LC 81-48009. (Illus.). 352p. 1982. 15.95 (ISBN 0-15-111932-5). HarBraceJ.

--James Whale. LC 82-5965. (Filmmakers Ser.: No. 1). 267p. 1982. 16.50 (ISBN 0-8108-1561-3). Scarecrow.

Curtis, James C. Andrew Jackson & the Search for Vindication. (Library of American Biography). 1976. 7.50 (ISBN 0-316-16554-9); pap. text ed. 5.95 (ISBN 0-316-16553-0). Little.

Curtis, James R., jt. auth. see Boswell, Thomas D.

Curtis, Jane & Curtis, Will. Welcome the Birds to Your Home. LC 79-20819. (Illus.). 1980. 9.95 o.s.i. (ISBN 0-8289-0353-0); pap. 5.95 (ISBN 0-8289-0354-9). Greene.

Curtis, Jim, ed. see Walther, Mina.

Curtis, John. Current Resources in Family Therapy. 40p. 1981. pap. 3.95 (ISBN 0-686-33182-6). Pilgrimage Inc.

Curtis, John & Greene, John. Counseling Resources: An Annotated Bibliography. 52p. 1980. softcover 4.85 o.p. (ISBN 0-932930-17-4). Pilgrimage Inc.

--Human Sexuality: An Annotated Bibliography. 70p. 1980. softcover 5.95 (ISBN 0-932930-16-6). Pilgrimage Inc.

--Premarital, Marital, & Family Therapy: An Annotated Bibliography. 72p. 1979. pap. 5.95 o.p. (ISBN 0-932930-15-8). Pilgrimage Inc.

Curtis, John, et al. Building Research Skills. Rev. ed. 145p. 1982. softcover 11.95 (ISBN 0-932930-14-X). Pilgrimage Inc.

Curtis, John D. & Papenfuss, Richard L. Health Instruction: A Task Approach. LC 79-56570. 1980. pap. text ed. 10.95x (ISBN 0-8087-2914-4). Burgess.

Curtis, John P., jt. auth. see De Talavera, Frances.

Curtis, John T. Vegetation of Wisconsin: An Ordination of Plant Communities. (Illus.). 672p. 1959. 25.00 (ISBN 0-299-01940-3). U of Wis Pr.

Curtis, Joseph E. Recreation: Theory & Practice. LC 78-31266. (Illus.). 1979. pap. text ed. 16.50 (ISBN 0-8016-1183-0). Mosby.

Curtis, Joseph E., jt. auth. see Kraus, Richard G.

Curtis, Joy, jt. auth. see Benjamin, Martin.

Curtis, Laura. The Elusive Daniel Defoe. 200p. 1983. 19.50x (ISBN 0-389-20063-8). B&N Imports.

Curtis, Lindsay R. Cigarrillo: Contaminante, No. 1. Repr. of 1978 ed. pap. 1.10 (ISBN 0-311-46073-9). Casa Bautista.

Curtis, Lindsay R. & Coroles, Yvonne. Pregnant & Lovin' It. LC 77-82012. (Illus.). 1977. pap. 5.95 (ISBN 0-912656-82-4). H P Bks.

Curtis, Lynn A. Violence, Race, & Culture. 1977. pap. text ed. 8.95x (ISBN 0-669-01066-9). Heath.

Curtis, Michael, ed. People & Politics in the Middle East. LC 72-140617. 325p. 1971. pap. 4.95 (ISBN 0-87855-500-5). Transaction Bks.

--Religion & Politics in the Middle East. 300p. 1982. lib. bdg. 25.25 (ISBN 0-86531-065-3); pap. 11.95 (ISBN 0-86531-388-1). Westview.

Curtis, Michael & Chertoff, Mordecai S., eds. Israel: Social Structure & Change. 443p. pap. 4.95 (ISBN 0-686-95160-3). ADL.

Curtis, Nancy. Cockatiels. (Orig.). pap. 3.95 (ISBN 0-87666-420-6, M517). TFH Pubns.

Curtis, Norman E. The Centurion. 1980. 5.70 o.p. (ISBN 0-310-22941-3). Zondervan.

Curtis, Patricia. Animal Partners: Training Animals to Help People. (Illus.). 144p. (gr. 7 up). 1982. 10.95 (ISBN 0-525-66791-1, 01063-320). Lodestar Bks.

--The Indoor Cat: How to Understand, Enjoy & Care for House Cats. LC 79-6578. (Illus.). 192p. 1981. 10.95 (ISBN 0-385-15368-6). Doubleday.

--The Indoor Cat: How to Understand, Enjoy & Care for House Cats. (Illus.). 192p. 1982. pap. 4.95 (ISBN 0-399-50596-2, Perige). Putnam Pub Group.

Curtis, Philip. Invasion of the Comet People: A Capers Book. LC 82-9923. (Illus.). 128p. (gr. 3-5). 1983. 1.95 (ISBN 0-394-85490-X); lib. bdg. 4.99 (ISBN 0-394-95490-4). Knopf.

Curtis, R. K. Evolution or Extinction: The Choice Before Us-A Systems Approach to the Study of the Future. 420p. 1982. 50.00 (ISBN 0-08-027933-3); pap. 25.00 (ISBN 0-08-027932-5). Pergamon.

Curtis, Richard. How to Be Your Own Literary Agent. 1983. 12.95 (ISBN 0-395-33123-4). HM.

--Life of Malcolm X. (Illus.). (gr. 7up). 1971. 6.25 (ISBN 0-8255-2786-4). Macrae.

Curtis, Richard F., jt. auth. see Borhek, James T.

Curtis, Richard H. The Aviatrix. (Skymasters Ser.: No. 7). 320p. (Orig.). 1983. pap. 3.25 (ISBN 0-440-00333-4, Emerald). Dell.

--Cry of the Condor. (The Skymasters Ser.: No. 10). (Orig.). 1983. pap. 3.25 (ISBN 0-440-01510-3). Dell.

--Every Man an Eagle. (Skymasters Ser.: No. 8). (Orig.). 1983. pap. 3.25 (ISBN 0-440-02276-2, Emerald). Dell.

--Through Clouds of Flame. (Skymasters Ser.: No. 9). 1983. pap. 3.25 (ISBN 0-440-08765-1). Dell.

Curtis, Robert H. Pacific Hospital. (Orig.). 1980. pap. 1.95 o.p. (ISBN 0-451-09018-7, J9018, Sig). NAL.

Curtis, Stanley J. Education in Britain Since 1900. LC 71-104264. Repr. of 1952 ed. lib. bdg. 15.75x (ISBN 0-8371-3913-9, CUEB). Greenwood.

Curtis, Tony. Kid Andrew Cody & Julie Sparrow. 1978. pap. 2.25 o.p. (ISBN 0-451-08010-6, E8010, Sig). NAL.

Curtis, Tony, ed. The Antiques Collector's Pocketbook. (Illus.). 1978. 6.95 (ISBN 0-902921-03-7). Apollo.

--Art Nouveau-Deco. (Illus.). 1978. 2.00 (ISBN 0-902921-87-8). Apollo.

--Bronze. (Illus.). 1978. 2.00 (ISBN 0-902921-40-1). Apollo.

--China. (Illus.). 1978. 2.00 (ISBN 0-902921-43-6). Apollo.

--Furniture. (Illus.). 1978. 2.00 (ISBN 0-902921-46-0). Apollo.

--Instruments. (Illus.). 1978. 2.00 (ISBN 0-902921-39-8). Apollo.

--Ivory. (Illus.). 1978. 2.00 (ISBN 0-902921-85-1). Apollo.

--Kitchen Equipment. (Illus.). 1978. 2.00 (ISBN 0-902921-41-X). Apollo.

--Lyle Official Antiques Review, 1983. (Illus.). 1983. 24.95. Apollo.

--Militaria. (Illus.). 1978. 2.00 (ISBN 0-902921-49-5). Apollo.

--Musical Instruments. (Illus.). 1978. 2.00 (ISBN 0-902921-50-9). Apollo.

--Oriental Art. (Illus.). 1978. 2.00 (ISBN 0-902921-88-6). Apollo.

--Oriental Rugs. (Illus.). 1978. 2.00 (ISBN 0-902921-51-7). Apollo.

--Pewter. (Illus.). 1978. 2.00 (ISBN 0-902921-54-1). Apollo.

--Tables. (Illus.). 1978. 2.00 (ISBN 0-902921-86-X). Apollo.

--Veteran & Vintage Cars. (Illus.). 1978. 2.00 (ISBN 0-902921-53-3). Apollo.

Curtis, W. Robert. What Follows Service Integration? Simulated Decentralized State Organizations Delivering Comprehensive Human Services. (Organizational Development of State Human Services Ser.). (Orig.). 1979. pap. 2.95 o.p. (ISBN 0-89995-005-1). Social Matrix.

Curtis, Will, jt. auth. see Curtis, Jane.

Curtis, William. Modern Architecture Since Nineteen Hundred. 400p. 1983. text ed. 39.95 (ISBN 0-13-586667-7); pap. text ed. 21.95 (ISBN 0-13-586666-9). P-H.

Curtiss, Eleanor. For Young Souls. 1941. pap. 1.95 (ISBN 0-87516-303-3). De Vorss.

Curtiss, Ellen T. & Untersee, Philip A. Corporate Responsibilities & Opportunities to 1990. (Arthur D. Little Books). (Illus.). 1979. 28.95x (ISBN 0-669-02848-7). Lexington Bks.

Curtiss, F. H., jt. auth. see Curtiss, H. A.

Curtiss, H. A. & Curtiss, F. H. Gems of Mysticism. 83p. 3.50 (ISBN 0-686-38219-6). Sun Bks.

--The Key to the Universe. 391p. 1981. pap. 13.50 o.p. (ISBN 0-89540-069-3, SB-069). Sun Pub.

--The Voice of Isis. 472p. 17.50 (ISBN 0-686-38238-2). Sun Bks.

Curtiss, Richard D. Thomas E. Williams & the Fine Arts Press. (Illus.). 120p. 1973. 30.00 (ISBN 0-87093-091-5). Dawsons.

Curtiss, Richard D., et al, eds. A Guide for Oral History Programs. 1973. 10.00 (ISBN 0-930046-03-X). CSUF Oral Hist.

Curtiss, Ursula. Death of a Crow. LC 82-19951. 1983. 9.95 (ISBN 0-396-08130-4). Dodd.

--Widow's Web. LC 56-5742. 1983. pap. 2.95 (ISBN 0-396-08164-9). Dodd.

Curtius, H. C., jt. ed. see Wachter, H.

Curtler, Hugh M. A Prologue to Philosophy. rev. ed. LC 79-51465. 1979. pap. text ed. 6.75 (ISBN 0-8191-0750-6). U Pr of Amer.

Curto, Josephine. Biography of an Alligator. new ed. LC 75-10452. (Nature Biography Ser.). 64p. (gr. 2-4). 1976. PLB 5.49 o.p. (ISBN 0-399-60968-7). Putnam Pub Group.

--How to Become a Single Parent: A Guide for Single People Considering Adoption or Natural Parenthood Alone. 252p. 1983. 14.95 (ISBN 0-13-396192-3); pap. 6.95 (ISBN 0-13-396184-2). P-H.

Curto, Peter. Realities. 1983. 5.95 (ISBN 0-533-05454-0). Vantage.

Curtola, Giovanni. The Simon & Schuster Book of Oriental Carpets. LC 82-10268. (Illus.). 216p. 1982. 26.95 (ISBN 0-671-45696-2). S&S.

Curts, Paul. Luther's Variations in Sentence Arrangement From the Modern Literary Usage With Primary Reference to the Position of the Verb. 1910. pap. text ed. 29.50x (ISBN 0-686-83611-1). Elliots Bks.

Curtsinger, William R. & Brower, Kenneth. Wake of the Whale. (Illus.). 1979. 35.00 o.p. (ISBN 0-525-22950-7). Dutton.

Curvin, Robert & Porter, Bruce. Blackout Looting: New York City, July 13, 1977. LC 78-20817. 1979. 13.95x o.p. (ISBN 0-470-26669-4); pap. text ed. 6.95 o.p. (ISBN 0-470-26627-9). Halsted Pr.

Curwen, C. A. Taiping Rebel: The Deposition of Li Hsiu-Ch' eng. LC 76-8292. (Cambridge Studies in Chinese History, Literature & Institutions). (Illus.). 1977. 49.50 (ISBN 0-521-21082-8). Cambridge U Pr.

Curwen, Henry. History of Booksellers, the Old & the New. LC 68-19656. (Illus.). 1968. Repr. of 1873 ed. 37.00x (ISBN 0-8103-3300-7). Gale.

Curwen, Samuel. Journal & Letters of Samuel Curwen, an American in England, from 1775-1783. Ward, George A., ed. LC 70-14720. (Era of the American Revolution Ser). 1970. Repr. of 1864 ed. lib. bdg. 85.00 (ISBN 0-306-71923-1). Da Capo.

Curwin, Richard & Fuhrmann, Barbara. Discovering Your Teaching Self: Humanistic Approaches to Effective Teaching. LC 74-11371. (Curriculum & Teaching Ser.). (Illus.). 256p. 1975. pap. text ed. 16.95 (ISBN 0-13-216077-3). P-H.

Curwin, Richard & Mendler, Allen. The Discipline Book: A Complete Guide to School & Classroom Management. (Illus.). 1979. pap. 9.95 (ISBN 0-8359-1336-8). Reston.

Curzon & Cutress. Trace Elements & Dental Diseases. (Illus.). 432p. 1983. text ed. 35.00 (ISBN 0-7236-7035-8). Wright PSG.

Curzon, Daniel. From Violent Men: A Novel. (Orig.). 1983. pap. write for info. (ISBN 0-930650-04-2). D Brown Bks.

Curzon, G., ed. The Biochemistry of Psychiatric Disturbances. LC 80-40498. 144p. 1980. 39.00x (ISBN 0-471-27814-9, Pub. by Wiley-Interscience). Wiley.

Curzon, L. B. Law of Evidence. 288p. 1978. 39.00x (ISBN 0-7121-1244-8, Pub. by Macdonald & Evans). State Mutual Bk.

Curzon, Lucia. The Dashing Guardian. (Second Chance at Love Ser.: No. 123). 1983. pap. 1.75 (ISBN 0-515-07211-7). Jove Pubns.

--Queen of Hearts, No. 87. 1982. pap. 1.75 (ISBN 0-515-06698-2). Jove Pubns.

Curzon, Victoria. The Essentials of Economic Integration. LC 73-88026. 300p. 1974. 27.50 (ISBN 0-312-26425-9). St Martin.

Cusack & James. Four Winds & a Family. 10.50x (ISBN 0-392-16669-0, ABC). Sportshelf.

Cusack, Anne, jt. auth. see Cusack, Michael.

Cusack, David F., ed. Agroclimate Information for Development: Reviving the Green Revolution. 300p. 1982. lib. bdg. 20.00 (ISBN 0-86531-429-2). Westview.

Cusack, Isabel L. Ivan the Great. LC 77-26593. (Illus.). (gr. 1-4). 1978. 5.95i o.p. (ISBN 0-690-03860-7, TYC-J); PLB 5.79 o.p. (ISBN 0-690-03861-5). Har-Row.

Cusack, Michael & Cusack, Anne. Plant Mysteries: A Scientific Inquiry. LC 78-12665. (Illus.). 160p. (gr. 7 up). 1978. PLB 7.29 o.p. (ISBN 0-671-32897-2). Messner.

Cusack, Michael J. Is There a Bermuda Triangle? Science & Sea Mysteries. LC 76-2717. (Illus.). 128p. (gr. 7 up). 1976. PLB 8.29 o.p. (ISBN 0-671-32783-6). Messner.

Cusatelli, G. Dizionario Garzanti della Lingua Italiana. 1008p. (Ital.). 1979. 19.95 (ISBN 0-686-97335-6, M-9189). French & Eur.

--Dizionario Garzanti della Lingua Italiana. 2008p. (Ital.). 1980. 49.95 (ISBN 0-686-97336-4, M-9190). French & Eur.

Cusens, A. R. & Pama, R. P. Bridge Deck Analysis. LC 74-3726. 278p. 1975. 56.95 (ISBN 0-471-18998-7, Pub. by Wiley-Interscience). Wiley.

Cusens, Anthony R., jt. auth. see Loo, Yew C.

Cushieri, A. & Moossa, A. R. Essential Surgical Practice. (Illus.). 1152p. 1982. text ed. 65.00 (ISBN 0-7236-0622-6). Wright-PSG.

Cushing. Quantifier Meanings. (Linguistics Ser.: Vol. 48). 1982. pap. 44.75 (ISBN 0-444-86445-8, North Holland). Elsevier.

Cushing, Anthony, jt. auth. see Lange, Joseph.

Cushing, Barry E. Accounting Information Systems & Business Organizations. 2nd ed. LC 77-83024. (Illus.). 1978. text ed. 26.95 (ISBN 0-201-01016-X). A-W.

--Accounting Information Systems & Business Organizations. 3rd ed. LC 81-2411. (Accounting Ser.). (Illus.). 808p. 1981. text ed. 26.95 (ISBN 0-201-10111-4). A-W.

Cushing, D. H. Fisheries Biology: A Study in Population Dynamics. 2nd ed. LC 79-5405. (Illus.). 320p. 1981. 18.50 (ISBN 0-299-08110-9). U of Wis Pr.

--Marine Ecology & Fisheries. LC 74-82218. (Illus.). 228p. 1975. 55.00 (ISBN 0-521-20501-8); pap. 21.95 (ISBN 0-521-09911-0). Cambridge U Pr.

--Science & the Fisheries. (Studies in Biology: No. 85). 64p. 1978. pap. text ed. 9.85 (ISBN 0-686-43113-8). E Arnold.

Cushing, G. F., ed. Hungarian Prose & Verse. (London East European Ser.). 1956. text ed. 15.50x o.p. (ISBN 0-485-17501-0, Athlone Pr). Humanities.

Cushing, Harvey, jt. auth. see Bailey, Percival.

Cushing, William. Initials & Pseudonyms: A Dictionary of Literary Disguises, 2 Vols. 936p. 1982. Repr. of 1888 ed. Set. 79.00x (ISBN 0-8103-3962-5). Gale.

Cushman, Doug. Once upon a Pig. LC 82-80873. (Platt & Munk Storybooks). (Illus.). 48p. (gr. k-3). 1982. 5.95 (ISBN 0-448-47492-1, G&D). Putnam Pub Group.

Cushman, Doug, compiled by. & illus. Trolls. LC 80-84446. (Illus.). 48p. (ps-3). 1981. 6.95 (ISBN 0-448-47490-5, G&D). Putnam Pub Group.

Cushman, George M. Movie-Making in Eighteen Lessons. (Illus.). 1971. pap. 4.95 o.p. (ISBN 0-8174-0537-2, Amphoto). Watson-Guptill.

Cushman, Kathleen & Miller, Edward, eds. How to Produce a Small Newspaper: A Guide for Independent Journalists. 2nd, Rev. ed. (Illus.). 192p. (Orig.). 1983. pap. 8.95 (ISBN 0-916782-39-5). Harvard Common Pr.

Cushman, Keith. D. H. Lawrence at Work: The Emergence of the Prussian Officer Stories. LC 77-22149. 1978. 14.95x (ISBN 0-8139-0728-4). U Pr of Va.

Cushman, M. L. Governance of Teacher Education. LC 76-52063. 1977. 21.75x (ISBN 0-8211-0228-1); text ed. 19.50 (ISBN 0-686-82936-0). McCutchan.

Cushman, R. F. & Stover, A. The McGraw-Hill Construction Form Book. 448p. 1983. 34.50 (ISBN 0-07-014995-X, P&RB). McGraw.

Cushman, R. M., et al. Sourcebook of Hydrologic & Ecological Features: Water Resource Regions of the Conterminous United States. LC 79-56108. (Illus.). 1980. 29.95 (ISBN 0-250-40355-2). Ann Arbor Science.

Cushman, Robert F. Avoiding Liability in Architectural Design & Construction: An Authoritative & Practical Guide for Design Professionals. 448p. 1983. 45.00 (ISBN 0-471-09579-6, Pub. by Wiley-Interscience). Wiley.

--Cases in Constitutional Law. 5th ed. 1979. ref. 27.95 (ISBN 0-13-118299-4). P-H.

--Leading Constitutional Decisions. 16th ed. 480p. 1982. pap. text ed. 16.95 (ISBN 0-13-527374-9). P-H.

--Leading Constitutional Decisions. 15th ed. 1977. pap. text ed. 13.95 o.p. (ISBN 0-13-527358-7). P-H.

Cushman, Robert F. & Palmer, William J. Businessman's Guide to Construction: The Dow Jones Guide to Planning, Designing, Financing, Contracting & Insuring of Industrial; Institutional Commercial & Other Buildings. LC 79-20894. 1980. 37.50 o.p. (ISBN 0-87128-580-0, Pub. by Dow Jones). Dow Jones-Irwin.

Cushman, Robert F. & Perry, Sherryl R. Planning, Financing & Constructing Health Care Facilities. LC 82-16343. 386p. 1982. 34.00 (ISBN 0-89443-839-5). Aspen Systems.

Cushner, Nicholas P. Farm & Factory: The Jesuits & the Development of Agrarian Capitalism in Colonial Quito. LC 81-13537. 274p. 1982. 42.50x (ISBN 0-87395-570-6); pap. 13.95x (ISBN 0-87395-571-4). State U NY Pr.

--Landed Estates in the Colonial Philippines. LC 75-27615. (Monograph Ser.: No. 20). (Illus.). 146p. 1976. 11.50x (ISBN 0-686-30899-9). Yale U SE Asia.

--Landed Estates in the Colonial Philippines. (Illus.). x, 146p. 1976. pap. 11.50 (ISBN 0-686-38047-9). Yale U SE Asia.

Cusine, Douglas J. & Grant, John P., eds. The Impact of Marine Pollution. LC 80-670. 324p. 1980. text ed. 32.50x (ISBN 0-916672-54-9). Allanheld.

Cuskey, Walter R. & Wathey, Richard B. Female Addiction: A Longitudinal Study. LC 80-8338. (Illus.). 192p. 1981. 22.95x (ISBN 0-669-04029-0). Lexington Bks.

Cusmano, Anthony J. How to Better Understand Photochemistry for Better Photography. LC 82-61711. 1982. pap. 9.95 (ISBN 0-943214-03-3). Media Pubns.

--How to Turn Your Camera into a Money Machine. LC 82-73115. 1982. pap. 9.95 (ISBN 0-943214-02-5). Media Pubns.

--How to Use the Microcomputer in Your Small Business. LC 82-60723. (Orig.). 1982. pap. 12.95 (ISBN 0-943214-01-7). Media Pubns.

Cussans, John E. Handbook of Heraldry. LC 76-132520. 1971. Repr. of 1893 ed. 42.00x (ISBN 0-8103-3012-1). Gale.

Cussen, Joseph A., jt. auth. see Dominicis, Maria C.

Cussler, Clive. Pacific Vortex. 346p. 1983. pap. 3.50 (ISBN 0-553-22866-8). Bantam.

Cussler, E. L. Multicomponent Diffusion. (Chemical Engineering Monographs: Vol. 3). 1976. 44.75 (ISBN 0-444-41326-X). Elsevier.

Cust, M. M. Needlework As Art. Stansky, Peter & Shewan, Rodney, eds. LC 76-17770. (Aesthetic Movement & the Arts & Crafts Movement Ser.). 1978. Repr. of 1886 ed. lib. bdg. 44.00x o.s.i. (ISBN 0-8240-2474-5). Garland Pub.

Custance, Roger. Winchester College: Sixth-Centenary Essays. (Illus.). 1982. 48.00x (ISBN 0-19-920103-X). Oxford U Pr.

Custer, Elizabeth B. Boots & Saddles: Or Life in Dakota with General Custer. (Western Frontier Library: No. 17). (Illus.). 11.95 (ISBN 0-8061-0487-2); pap. 6.95 (ISBN 0-8061-1192-5). U of Okla Pr.

--Following the Guidon. (Western Frontier Library: Vol. 33). (Illus.). 341p. pap. 5.95 o.p. (ISBN 0-8061-1354-5). U of Okla Pr.

--Tenting on the Plains. LC 72-145498. (Western Frontier Library: Vols. 46, 47, 48). (Illus.). 1971. boxed set 18.95 (ISBN 0-8061-0943-2). U of Okla Pr.

Custodio, Sidney & Dudley, Cliff. Love Hungry Priest. 144p. (Orig.). 1983. pap. 2.95 (ISBN 0-89221-099-0). New Leaf.

Cusumano, Michele. Just As the Boy Dreams of White Thighs Under Flowered Skirts. 28p. (Orig.). 1980. pap. 2.50 (ISBN 0-935252-24-X); op 5.00 (ISBN 0-686-63441-1). Street Pr.

Cutbirth, Nancy, jt. ed. see Cutts, John P.

Cutcliffe, Stephen H., et al, eds. Technology & Values in American Civilization: A Guide to Information Sources. (American Information Guide Ser.: Vol. 9). 680p. 1980. 42.00x (ISBN 0-8103-1475-4). Gale.

Cutforth, A. E. Methods of Amalgamation. LC 82-48358. (Accountancy in Transition Ser.). 354p. 1982. lib. bdg. 35.00 (ISBN 0-8240-5310-9). Garland Pub.

Cutforth, Arthur E. Audits. LC 82-48357. (Accountancy in Transition Ser.). 164p. 1982. lib. bdg. 20.00 (ISBN 0-8240-5309-5). Garland Pub.

Cuthbert, John A. West Virginia Folk Music. 185p. 1982. 10.00 (ISBN 0-937058-12-2). West Virginia U Pr.

Cuthbert, Mabel J. How to Know the Fall Flowers. (Pictured Key Nature Ser.). 206p. 1948. wire coil write for info. 0.00 (ISBN 0-697-04810-1). Wm C Brown.

Cuthbert, Thomas R. Circuit Design Using Personal Computers. 512p. 1983. 39.95 (ISBN 0-471-87700-X, Pub. by Wiley-Interscience). Wiley.

Cuthbertson, A., jt. ed. see Kempster, A. J.

Cuthbertson, Lulu L., jt. auth. see Cuthbertson, Stuart.

Cuthbertson, Stuart. Italian Verb Wheel. 1937. 3.95x (ISBN 0-669-30221-X). Heath.

Cuthbertson, Stuart & Cuthbertson, Lulu L. French Verb Wheel. 1935. 3.95 (ISBN 0-669-26674-4). Heath.

--German Verb Wheel. 1935. 3.95x (ISBN 0-669-28753-9). Heath.

--Spanish Verb Wheel. 1935. 3.95 o.p. (ISBN 0-669-31427-7). Heath.

Cuthbertson, Tom. Anybody's Roller Skating Book. LC 81-50301. (Illus.). (YA) 1981. not cancelled 8.95 (ISBN 0-89815-042-6); pap. 4.95 (ISBN 0-89815-040-X). Ten Speed Pr.

--The Bike Bag Book. LC 81-50252. (Illus.). 144p. (Orig.). 1981. pap. 2.95 plastic cover (ISBN 0-89815-039-6). Ten Speed Pr.

Cuthbertson, Tom & Cole, Lee. I Can Swim, You Can Swim. (Illus., Orig.). (gr. 4-8). 1979. pap. 4.00 (ISBN 0-913668-79-6). Ten Speed Pr.

Cutie, Anthony J., jt. auth. see Plakogiannis, Fotios M.

Cutillo, Brian, jt. tr. see Rimpoche, Kunga.

Cutino, Peter & Bledsoe, Dennis, eds. Polo: The Manual for Coach & Player. new ed. (Illus.). 225p. 1975. pap. 7.95 (ISBN 0-685-56491-6). Swimming.

Cutland, N. J. Computability: An Introduction to Recursive Function Theory. LC 79-51823. 1980. 54.50 (ISBN 0-521-22384-9); pap. 17.95 (ISBN 0-521-29465-7). Cambridge U Pr.

Cutler, et al, eds. Correspondence of James Polk, 1842-1843, Vol.6. LC 75-84005. (Polk Project Ser.). 1982. 30.00x (ISBN 0-8265-1211-9). Vanderbilt U Pr.

Cutler, Anthony. Transfigurations: Studies in the Dynamics of Byzantine Iconography. LC 75-1482. (Illus.). 226p. 1975. 27.50x (ISBN 0-271-01194-7). Pa St U Pr.

Cutler, Carol. Haute Cuisine for Your Hearts Delight. 192p. 1973. 6.95 (ISBN 0-517-50048-5, C N Potter Bks). Crown.

--Six Minute Souffle. 1983. pap. 8.95 o.p. (ISBN 0-517-54901-8, C N Potter). Crown.

--The Six-Minute Souffle & Other Culinary Delights: Carol Cutler's Complete Guide to Time-Saving Elegant Meals. (Illus.). 1976. 12.95 o.p. (ISBN 0-517-52381-7, C N Potter Bks). Crown.

Cutler, Charles L; see Weaver, Glenn.

Cutler, E. F. & Alvin, K. L. The Plant Cuticle. (Linn Soc Symposium Ser.: No. 10). 1982. for info. 90.00rite (ISBN 0-12-199920-3). Acad Pr.

Cutler, Ivor. The Animal House. (Illus.). (gr. k-3). 1977. 7.95 (ISBN 0-688-22110-6); PLB 7.63 (ISBN 0-688-32110-0). Morrow.

Cutler, James E. Lynch-Law: An Investigation into the History of Lynching in the United States. LC 69-14920. (Criminology, Law Enforcement, & Social Problems Ser.: No. 70). (Illus.). 1969. Repr. of 1905 ed. 11.00x (ISBN 0-87585-070-7). Patterson Smith.

Cutler, John. Understanding Aircraft Structures. 176p. 1981. 14.95x o.p. (ISBN 0-8464-1242-X). Beekman Pubs.

Cutler, Julian S. Seasons of Friendship. 1983. 3.95 (ISBN 0-8378-2032-4). Gibson.

Cutler, Kathy. Festive Bread Book. 288p. 1982. 14.95 (ISBN 0-8120-5453-9). Barron.

Cutler, Laurence S., jt. ed. see Dietz, Albert G.

Cutler, Phillip. AC Circuit Analysis: With Illustrative Problems. (Illus.). 304p. 1974. pap. 11.95 o.p. (ISBN 0-07-014996-8, G); solutions 1.50 o.p. (ISBN 0-07-014997-6). McGraw.

--D C Circuit Analysis with Illustrative Problems. rev. ed. Orig. Title: Outline for DC Circuit Analysis with Illustrative Problems. (Illus.). 208p. 1974. pap. text ed. 10.95 o.p. (ISBN 0-07-015008-7, G); solutions 1.95 o.p. (ISBN 0-07-015009-5). McGraw.

--Linear Electronic Circuits with Illustrative Problems. 1972. text ed. 11.95 o.p. (ISBN 0-07-015004-4, G). McGraw.

--Solid State Device Theory, with Illustrative Problems. 1972. text ed. 11.95 o.p. (ISBN 0-07-015002-8, G). McGraw.

Cutler, R., tr. from Rus. see Bakunin, Mikhail.

Cutler, Roland. The Gates of Sagittarius. 304p. 1981. pap. 2.75 o.p. (ISBN 0-380-56085-2, 56085). Avon.

Cutler, Ron. The Medusa Syndrom. 1983. pap. 2.95 (ISBN 0-686-43060-3, Sig). NAL.

Cutler, Wade E. Triple Your Reading Speed. LC 70-93505. (Prog. Bk.). 1970. lib. bdg. 7.50 o. p. (ISBN 0-668-02084-9); pap. 5.00 (ISBN 0-668-02083-0). Arco.

Cutler, Wayne & Harris, Michael H., eds. Justin Winsor: Scholar-Librarian. LC 80-19310. (Heritage of Librarianship Ser.: No. 5). 196p. 1980. lib. bdg. 25.00 (ISBN 0-87287-200-9). Libs Unl.

Cutler, Wayne, et al, eds. Correspondence of James K. Polk 1839-1841. LC 75-84005. (Polk Project Ser.: Vol. 5). 1980. 25.00x (ISBN 0-8265-1208-9). Vanderbilt U Pr.

Cutler, William W., 3rd & Gillette, Howard, Jr., eds. The Divided Metropolis: Social & Spatial Dimensions of Philadelphia, 1800-1975. LC 79-7729. (Contributions in American History: No. 85). (Illus.). 1980. lib. bdg. 29.95 (ISBN 0-313-21351-8, GDM/). Greenwood.

Cutler, Winnifred, et al. Menopause: A Guide for Women & the Men who Love Them. (Illus.). 1983. 15.00 (ISBN 0-393-01709-5). Norton.

Cutress, jt. auth. see Curzon.

Cutress, Bryan. Tennis. LC 80-50935. (Intersport Ser.). 13.00 (ISBN 0-382-06435-6). Silver.

Cutright, Phillips & Jaffe, Fredericks S. Impact of Family Planning Programs on Fertility: The U. S. Experience. LC 76-12847. 1976. text ed. 26.95 o.p. (ISBN 0-275-23350-2). Praeger.

Cutt, W. Towrie. Seven for the Sea. LC 73-93556. 96p. (gr. 3-6). 1974. 4.95 o.s.i. (ISBN 0-695-80480-4); lib. bdg. 4.98 o.s.i. (ISBN 0-695-40480-6). Follett.

Cutten, George B. Mind: Its Origin & Goal. 1925. 24.50x (ISBN 0-685-89766-4). Elliots Bks.

--Speaking with Tongues: Historically & Psychologically Considered. 1927. 32.50x (ISBN 0-685-69805-X). Elliots Bks.

Cutter, C. A. Cutter's Rules for a Printed Dictionary Catalog: A Special Report of the U. S. Commissioner of Education, Pt. 2. 262p. 1971. Repr. of 1876 ed. 20.00x o.p. (ISBN 0-87471-313-7). Rowman.

Cutter, Charles & Oppenheim, Micha F. Jewish Reference Sources: A Select, Annotated Bibliographic Guide. 180p. 1983. lib. bdg. 19.95 (ISBN 0-8240-9347-X). Garland Pub.

Cutter, Fred. Art & the Wish to Die. 302p. 1983. text ed. 24.95x (ISBN 0-88229-370-2). Nelson-Hall.

Cutting, G. W. Process Audits on Mineral Dressing Processes: Their Generation & Practical Use, 1978. 1981. 69.00x (ISBN 0-686-97143-4, Pub. by W Spring England). State Mutual Bk.

Cutting, James E., jt. ed. see Kavanagh, James F.

Cutting, Jorge. La Salvacion: Su Seguridad, Creteza y Gozo. 2nd ed. Daniel, Roger P., ed. Bautista, Sara, tr. from Eng. (La Serie Diamante). 48p. (Span.). 1982. pap. 0.85 (ISBN 0-942504-05-4). Overcomer Pr.

--La Venida del Senor. 2nd ed. Bennett, Gordon H., ed. Bautista, Sara, tr. from Eng. (La Serie Diamante). 48p. (Span.). 1982. pap. 0.85 (ISBN 0-942504-10-0). Overcomer Pr.

Cutting, Rose M. John & William Bartram, William Byrd II & St. John De Crevcoeur: A Reference Guide. 1976. lib. bdg. 24.00 (ISBN 0-8161-1176-6, Hall Reference). G K Hall.

Cuttino, G. P., ed. Gascon Register A, Vol. 3. (British Academy Ser.). 1976. 22.50x o.p. (ISBN 0-19-725966-9). Oxford U Pr.

Cutts, A. M. Dios y Sus Ayudantes. (Illus.). 48p. (Span.). 1981. pap. 1.10 (ISBN 0-311-38548-6). Casa Bautista.

Cutts, Edward L. Scenes & Characters of the Middle Ages. LC 67-27866. (Social History Reference Ser.). (Illus.). 1968. Repr. of 1872 ed. 40.00x (ISBN 0-8103-3257-4). Gale.

Cutts, J. Harry, jt. auth. see Krause, William J.

Cutts, John P. & Cutbirth, Nancy, eds. Love's Changelinges Change. LC 74-84570. (North American Mentor Texts & Studies Ser.: No. 2). (Based on Sir Philip Sidney's Arcadia, 1590). 1974. pap. 10.00 (ISBN 0-87423-009-8). Westburg.

Cutul, Ann-Marie, ed. Twentieth-Century European Painting: A Guide to Information Sources. LC 79-24249. (Art & Architecture Information Guide Ser.: Vol. 9). 1980. 42.00x (ISBN 0-8103-1438-X). Gale.

Cuyler, Margery. The All-Around Christmas Book. (Illus.). 96p. (gr. 2-5). 1982. 11.50 (ISBN 0-03-060387-0); pap. 4.95 (ISBN 0-03-062183-6). HR&W.

Cuzin, Jean-Pierre, jt. auth. see Laclotte, Michel.

Cvetlovic, Dragos, et al, eds. Spectra of Graphs: Theory & Applications. LC 79-50490. (Pure & Applied Mathematics Ser.). 1980. 59.00 o.s.i. (ISBN 0-12-195150-2). Acad Pr.

Cwiklo, William E. Computers in Litigation Support. 1979. 25.00 o.p. (ISBN 0-07-091038-3, Petrocelli Bks). McGraw.

Cyert, Richard M. The American Economy, Nineteen Sixty to Two Thousand. LC 82-48600. (Charles C. Moskowitz Memorial Lecture Ser.: Vol. XXLII). 1983. 12.95 (ISBN 0-02-923100-0). Free Pr.

Cyert, Richard M. & March, J. G. Behavioral Theory of the Firm. 1963. ref. ed. 24.95 (ISBN 0-13-073304-0). P-H.

Cyert, Richard M., jt. auth. see Cohen, Kalman J.

Cykler, Edmund, jt. auth. see Wold, Milo.

Cykler, Edmund, jt. auth. see Wold, Milo A.

Cylke, Kurt, jt. ed. see Massis, Bruce E.

Cypert, Samuel A. Writing Effective Business Letters, Memos, Proposals, & Reports. 192p. 1983. 12.95 (ISBN 0-8092-5605-3). Contemp Bks.

Cyphers, Emma. New Book of Foliage Arrangements. rev. ed. LC 64-21085. (Illus.). 1965. 4.95 (ISBN 0-8208-0018-X). Hearthside.

Cyphers, Emma H. Fruit & Vegetable Arrangements. rev. ed. 4.50 (ISBN 0-8208-0014-7). Hearthside.

Cypress, Beulah K. Medication Therapy in Office Visits for Selected Diagnoses: National Ambulatory Medical Care Survey, United States, 1980. Cox, Klaudia, ed. (Ser. 13: No. 71). 65p. 1982. pap. text ed. 1.85 (ISBN 0-8406-0266-9). Natl Ctr Health Stats.

Cypser, R. J. Communications Architecture for Distributed Systems. LC 76-52673. (Illus.). 1978. text ed. 29.95 (ISBN 0-201-14458-1). A-W.

--Communications Architecture for Distributed Systems. 711p. 1978. 21.95 (ISBN 0-686-98122-7). Telecom Lib.

Cyr, Don. Teaching Your Children Photography: A Step-by-Step Guide. (Illus.). 1977. pap. 6.95 o.p. (ISBN 0-8174-2416-4, Amphoto); Spanish Ed. pap. 9.95 o.p. (ISBN 0-8174-0335-3). Watson-Guptill.

Cyriax, James & Russell, Gillean. Textbook of Orthopaedic Medicine: Treatment by Manipulation, Massage & Injection, Vol. II. 10th ed. (Illus.). 1980. text ed. 52.00 (ISBN 0-02-857490-7, Pub. by Balliere-Tindall). Saunders.

Cyrs, Thomas E., Jr., ed. Handbook for the Design of Instruction in Pharmacy Education. 200p. Date not set. 6.50 (ISBN 0-686-83878-5). Am Assn Coll Pharm.

Cyzyk, Janet. Entering the Reader's World, 3 bks. Mendyk, Dennis, ed. (Adult Literacy Training Ser.). (Illus.). 160p. 1983. pap. 4.33 ea. Bk. 1 (ISBN 0-8428-9503-5). Bk. 2 (ISBN 0-8428-9504-3). Bk. 3 (ISBN 0-8428-9505-1). Cambridge Bk.

Cyzyk, Janet L. Baltimore County Design: Administrator's Manual. Maryland State Dept. of Education, ed. (Correlates Test to Adult Literacy Ser.). (Illus.). 128p. 1982. pap. text ed. 13.26 (ISBN 0-8428-9501-9); student test bklt. 3.00 (ISBN 0-8428-9500-0). Cambridge Bk.

Czaja, Paul C. Writing with Light: A Simple Workshop in Basic Photography. LC 72-93261. 96p. (gr. 6 up). 1973. 6.95 (ISBN 0-85699-068-X). Chatham Pr.

Czajka, Peter A. & Duffy, James P. Poisoning Emergencies: A Guide for Emergency Medical Personnel. LC 79-20542. 1980. pap. text ed. 12.95 (ISBN 0-8016-1205-5). Mosby.

Czaky, Mick, ed. How Does It Feel? Exploring the World of the Senses. 1980. pap. 15.95 o.p. (ISBN 0-517-53829-6, Harmony); pap. 9.95 o.p. (ISBN 0-686-85836-0). Crown.

--How Does It Feel? Exploring the World of Your Senses: Exploring the Five Senses. (Illus.). 1979. 15.95 o.p. (ISBN 0-517-53829-6); pap. 9.95 o.p. (ISBN 0-517-53983-7). Crown.

Czarnecki, D. B. & Blinn, D. W. Diatoms of Southwestern USA: Diatoms of Lower Lake Powell & Vicinity, Vol. 1. (Bibliotheca Phycologica: No. 28). 1977. pap. text ed. 16.00 (ISBN 3-7682-1102-9). Lubrecht & Cramer.

--Diatoms of Southwestern USA: Diatoms of the Colorado River in Grand Canyon National Park and Vicinity, Vol. 2. (Illus.). 1978. pap. text ed. 20.00 (ISBN 3-7682-1182-7). Lubrecht & Cramer.

Czarnowski, M. S. Productive Capacity of Locality As a Function of Soil & Climate with Particular Reference to Forest Land. LC 64-16087. (University Studies, Biological Science Ser: Vol. 5). (Illus.). xviii, 174p. 1964. 17.50x o.p. (ISBN 0-8071-0422-1). La State U Pr.

Czech, Hella, tr. see Portmann, Adolf.

Czege, A. Wass De see De Czege, A. Wass.

Czeisler, Charles A. & Guilleminault, Christian, eds. REM Sleep: Its Temporal Distribution. (Sleep Reprint Ser.: Vol. 2, Nos. 3-4, 1980). 126p. 1980. pap. text ed. 14.00 (ISBN 0-89004-527-5). Raven.

Czeizing, Panorama. Budapest. 3rd ed. (Illus.). 1970. 5.00x (ISBN 0-89918-372-7, H-372). Vanous.

Czempiel, Ernst-Otto & Rustow, Dankwart A., eds. The Euro-American System: Economic & Political Relations Between North America & Western Europe. LC 76-4557. 1976. 32.25 o.p. (ISBN 0-89158-601-6). Westview.

Czerkas, Sylvia M. & Glut, Donald F. Dinosaurs, Mammoths, & Cavemen: The Art of Charles R. Knight. LC 80-65359. (Illus.). 120p. 1982. 24.95 (ISBN 0-525-93242-9, 02422-730); pap. 14.95 (ISBN 0-525-47709-8, 01451-440). Dutton.

Czermak, Herberth. The Trial Notes. (Orig.). 1976. pap. text ed. 2.75 (ISBN 0-8220-1304-5). Cliffs.

Czerniak, Eli. Reinforced Concrete Columns, 2 vols. Incl. Vol. 1. Working Stress Design for Concrete Columns. (Illus.). 424p. 18.00 (ISBN 0-8044-4166-9); Vol. 2. Working Stress Design Charts for Spiral Columns. (Illus.). 320p. 15.00 (ISBN 0-8044-4167-7). Set. 33.00 (ISBN 0-8044-4165-0). Ungar.

Czerniewska, Pam, jt. auth. see Gannon, Peter.

Czerny, Carl. On the Proper Performance of All Beethoven's Works for the Piano. Badura-Skoda, Paul, ed. 1970. pap. 19.00 (ISBN 3-7024-0111-3, 47-13340ENJ). Eur-Am Music.

--School of Practical Composition, 3 vols. (Music Reprint Ser.). 1979. Repr. of 1848 ed. Set. lib. bdg. 95.00 (ISBN 0-306-79595-7). Da Capo.

Czerwinski, Frank L., jt. auth. see Samaras, Thomas T.

Czestochowski, Joseph. The American Landscape Tradition: A Study & Gallery of Paintings. (Illus.). 160p. 1983. 35.75 (ISBN 0-525-93206-2, 03471-1040); pap. 20.75 (ISBN 0-525-47674-1, 02015-650). Dutton.

Czichos. Tribology: A Systems Approach to the Science of Friction, Lubrication & Wear. (Tribology Ser.: Vol. 1). 1978. 68.00 (ISBN 0-444-41676-5). Elsevier.

Czitrom, Daniel J. Media & the American Mind: From Morse to McLuhan. LC 81-14810. xiv, 254p. 1982. 19.95x (ISBN 0-8078-1500-4); pap. 7.95x (ISBN 0-8078-4107-2). U of NC Pr.

Czoboly, E., jt. auth. see Sih, G.

Czudnowski, M. M., jt. ed. see Eulau, H.

Czudnowski, Moshe M., ed. Does Who Governs Matter? (International Yearbook for Studies of Leaders & Leadership Ser.). 300p. 1982. 25.00x (ISBN 0-87580-085-8); pap. 12.50 (ISBN 0-87580-529-9). N Ill U Pr.

--Political Elites & Social Change: Studies in Elite Roles & Attitudes. (International Yearbook for Studies of Leaders & Leadership). 300p. 1983. price not set (ISBN 0-87580-093-9); pap. price not set (ISBN 0-87580-530-2). N Ill U Pr.

D

D. Bradford Barton Ltd., ed. American Flying Boats: A Pictorial Survey. 1981. 25.00x (ISBN 0-686-97136-1, Pub. by D B Barton England). State Mutual Bk.

Daalder, Hans & Shils, Edward, eds. Universities, Politicians & Bureaucrats: Europe & the United States. LC 81-9936. (Illus.). 700p. 1982. 79.50 (ISBN 0-521-23673-8). Cambridge U Pr.

Daball, Raymond F. Graphic Design with Calligraphy Now. cancelled o.s.i. (ISBN 0-87027-187-3). Cumberland Pr.

D'Abate, Richard. To Keep the House from Falling in. 39p. 1973. 2.95 (ISBN 0-87886-028-2). Ithaca Hse.
Dabey, John, ed. see Achebe, Chinua.
Dabney, Joseph. Herk: Hero of the Skies. pap. 8.95 (ISBN 0-932298-16-8). Copple Hse.
Dabney, Joseph E. Herk, Hero of the Skies. 12.95 o.p. (ISBN 0-932298-07-9). Green Hill.
--Mountain Spirits II. 1981. pap. 6.95 (ISBN 0-932298-05-2). Copple Hse.
Dabney, Lewis, ed. The Portable Edmund Wilson. (Portable Library Ser.: No. 98). 1983. 18.75 (ISBN 0-670-77078-7). Viking Pr.
Dabney, Lewis M., ed. see Wilson, Edmund.
Dabney, Virginius. Dry Messiah: The Life of Bishop Cannon. LC 73-110825. (Illus.). vii, 353p. Repr. of 1949 ed. lib. bdg. 17.75x (ISBN 0-8371-3225-8, DADM). Greenwood.
--Virginia: The New Dominion. LC 78-157580. (Illus.). 1971. pap. 9.95 o.p. (ISBN 0-385-00391-9). Doubleday.
--Virginia: The New Dominion, a History from 1607 to the Present. LC 78-157580. (Illus.). 629p. 14.95 o.p. (ISBN 0-385-07150-7). U Pr of Va.
DaBoll, Irene B., jt. auth. see DaBoll, Raymond F.
DaBoll, Raymond F. & DaBoll, Irene B. Recollections of the Lyceum & Chautauqua Circuits Plus Notes on Calligraphy & Scribal Writing. LC 66-19773. (Illus.). 188p. 1974. 16.95 (ISBN 0-87027-107-5); pap. 10.95 o.s.i. (ISBN 0-87027-133-4). Cumberland Pr.
Dabrowski, Richard A. Designs for the Woodcarver. LC 76-1141. (Illus.). 1982. Repr. of 1976 ed. spiral bdg. 9.50 (ISBN 0-918036-02-X). Woodcraft Supply.
D'Accone, Frank. Allesandro Scarlatti's Gli equivoci nel sembiante: The History of a Baroque Opera. 2nd ed. (Pendragon Press Monographs in Musicology Ser.). 150p. 1983. lib. bdg. 27.00 (ISBN 0-918728-21-5). Pendragon NY.
Dacey, John S. Adolescents Today. 2nd ed. 1982. text ed. 21.95x (ISBN 0-673-16023-8). Scott F.
--Adult Development. 1982. text ed. 21.95x (ISBN 0-673-16021-1). Scott F.
Dacey, Philip. Gerard Manley Hopkins Meets Walt Whitman in Heaven & Other Poems. (Illus.). 100p. 1982. 22.50 (ISBN 0-915778-43-2); signed 75.00 (ISBN 0-915778-44-0); pap. 8.50 (ISBN 0-915778-45-9). Penmaen Pr.
Dachslager, Howard & Yayashi, Masato. Learning BASIC Programming: A Systematic Approach. 280p. 1983. pap. text ed. 18.95 (ISBN 0-534-01422-4). Brooks-Cole.
Dacie, J. V. Haemolytic Anaemias-Congenital & Acquired. 2nd rev. & enl. ed. Incl. Pt. 1. The Congenital Anaemias. (Illus.). 339p. 1960. 39.50 o.p. (ISBN 0-8089-0581-3); Pt. 2. The Auto-Immune Anaemias. (Illus.). 371p. 1962. 39.50 o.p. (ISBN 0-8089-0582-1); Pt. 3. Secondary or Symptomatic Haemolytic Anaemias. (Illus.). 274p. 1967. o.p. (ISBN 0-8089-0583-X); Pt. 4. Drug-Induced Haemolytic Anaemias. (Illus.). 368p. 1967. 30.75 o.p. (ISBN 0-8089-0584-8). Grune.
Dacons, J. C., jt. auth. see Philips, J. P.
Da Costa, Francisco, jt. auth. see Mickle, M. M.
Da Costa, Michael. Finance & Development: The Role of International Commercial Banks in the Third World. (Replica Edition). 120p. 1982. lib. bdg. 17.00x (ISBN 0-86531-917-0). Westview.
Dacre, Charlotte. Hours of Solitude: A Collection of Original Poems by Charlotte Dacre, Better Known by the Name Rosa Matilda, 2 vols. in 1. Reiman, Donald, ed. LC 75-31190. (Romantic Context Ser.: Poetry 1789-1830: Vol. 42). 1979. Repr. of 1805 ed. lib. bdg. 47.00 o.s.i. (ISBN 0-8240-2141-X). Garland Pub.
Da Cruz, Vera. C. M. B. Questions & How to Answer Them. 5th ed. (Illus.). 1977. pap. 5.95 o.p. (ISBN 0-571-04919-2). Faber & Faber.
Dacso, Michael M. Restorative Medicine in Geriatrics. (Illus.). 340p. 1963. photocopy ed. spiral 27.50x (ISBN 0-398-00385-8). C C Thomas.
Dacy, Joe, II. Hypnosphere. 1983. 9.95 (ISBN 0-533-05282-3). Vantage.
Dada, Victor B. Choose the Sex of Your Baby: A Psychological Approach. 1983. 7.95 (ISBN 0-533-05256-4). Vantage.
D'Adamo, James. One Man's Food: Is Someone Else's Poison. 320p. 1980. 10.95 (ISBN 0-399-90092-6, Marek). Putnam Pub Group.
Dadayan, V. S. Macroeconomic Models. 208p. 1981. 7.00 (ISBN 0-8285-2271-5, Pub. by Progress Pubs USSR). Imported Pubns.
Dadd, R. H., jt. ed. see Mittler, T. E.
Daddad, Wadi D. Educational & Economic Effects of Promotion & Repetition Practices. (Working Paper: No. 319). 52p. 1979. 3.00 (ISBN 0-686-36054-0, WP-0319). World Bank.
Dadoo, Y. M., et al. South African Communist Speak, 1915-1980. 474p. 1981. pap. 25.00x (ISBN 0-686-83901-3, Pub. by Inkuleko). Imported Pubns.
Dadourian, H. M. Introduction to Analytic Geometry & the Calculus. LC 80-39791. 256p. 1983. Repr. of 1949 ed. lib. bdg. price not set (ISBN 0-89874-267-6). Krieger.
Dadson, Theresa. Index to the Legion Observer: Volumes Two Through Nine, 1967-1974. 1979. lib. bdg. 35.00 (ISBN 0-8161-8294-9, Hall Reference). G K Hall.
D.A.E. Project University of Washington. D.A.E Project: Instructional Materials for Dental Health Professions, 25 Bks. Incl. Bk. 1. Establish Patient Relationships. 9.95x (ISBN 0-8077-6041-2); Bk. 2. Self-Care One. 7.95x (ISBN 0-8077-6042-0); Vol. 3. Self-Care Two. 7.95x (ISBN 0-8077-6043-9); Vol. 4. Coronal Polish. 9.95x (ISBN 0-8077-6044-7); Vol. 5. Topical Fluoride. 6.95x (ISBN 0-8077-6045-5); Vol. 6. Normal Radiographic Landmarks. 8.95x (ISBN 0-8077-6046-3); Vol. 7. Oral Inspection. 5.95x (ISBN 0-8077-6047-1); Vol. 8. Oral Inspection. 4.95x (ISBN 0-8077-6048-X); Margination: Overhang Removal. 8.95x (ISBN 0-8077-6049-8); Vol. 10. Root Planning. 5.95x (ISBN 0-8077-6050-1); Vol. 11. Take Study Model Impressions. 7.95x (ISBN 0-8077-6051-X); Vol. 12. Pour & Separate Models. 5.95x (ISBN 0-8077-6052-8); Vol. 13. Trim & Finish Models. 4.95x (ISBN 0-8077-6053-6); Vol. 14. Instrument Transfer One. 6.95x (ISBN 0-8077-6054-4); Vol. 15. Instrument Transfer: Restorative. 6.95x (ISBN 0-8077-6055-2); Vol. 16. Instrument Transfer: **Endodontics. 4.95x (ISBN 0-8077-6056-0); Vol. 17. Instrument Transfer: Oral Surgery. 6.95x (ISBN 0-8077-6057-9); Vol. 18. Instrument Transfer: Periodontics. 6.95x (ISBN 0-8077-6058-7); Vol. 19. Maintain Operating Field. 6.95x (ISBN 0-8077-6059-5); Vol. 20. Rubber Dam. 8.50x (ISBN 0-8077-6060-9); Vol. 21. Microbiology. 5.95x (ISBN 0-8077-6061-7); Vol. 22. Sterilization & Disinfection. 8.50x (ISBN 0-8077-6062-5); Vol. 23. Dental Handpieces. 4.95x (ISBN 0-8077-6063-3); Vol. 24. Maintain Equipment & Operatory. 9.95x (ISBN 0-8077-6064-1); Vol. 25. Maintain Sterilization & Laboratory Equipment. 6.95x (ISBN 0-8077-6065-X); Faculty Guide & Test Items 9.95x (ISBN 0-8077-6066-8). 1982. Tchrs Coll.**
Daemmrich, Horst S. Wilhelm Raabe. (World Authors Ser.). 1981. lib. bdg. 13.95 (ISBN 0-8057-6436-4, Twayne). G K Hall.
Daeschner, Charles. Pediatrics: An Approach to Independent Learning. LC 82-8438. 646p. 1983. pap. 24.95x (ISBN 0-471-05992-7, Pub. by Wiley Med). Wiley.
Dafalla, Hassan. The Nubian Exodus. LC 75-4496. (Illus.). 360p. 1975. 18.00x o.p. (ISBN 0-87663-715-2, Pica Pr). Universe.
Dafflon, Bernard. Federal Finance in Theory & Practice with Special Reference to Switzerland. 176p. 1977. 90.00x (ISBN 0-7121-5624-0, Pub. by Macdonald & Evans). State Mutual Bk.
Da Free, John. Crazy DA Must Sing Inclined to His Weaker Side: Confessional Poems of Liberation & Love. 1982. pap. 6.95 (ISBN 0-686-82091-6). Dawn Horse Pr.
--Forehead, Breath & Smile: An Anthology of Devotional Readings from the Spiritual Teaching of Master. 1982. 20.95 (ISBN 0-913922-70-6). Dawn Horse Pr.
--The Hymn of the Master. (Illus.). 106p. (Orig.). 1982. pap. 8.95 (ISBN 0-913922-71-4). Dawn Horse Pr.
--I Am Happiness: A Rendering for Children of the Spiritual Adventure. Bodha, Daji & Closser, Lynne, eds. (Illus., Orig.). (gr. 2 up). 1982. pap. 9.95 (ISBN 0-913922-68-4). Dawn Horse Pr.
--The Liberator, Eleutherios. (Illus.). 114p. 1982. 12.95 (ISBN 0-913922-66-8); pap. 6.95 (ISBN 0-913922-67-6). Dawn Horse Pr.
--Nirvananasara. (Orig.). 1982. pap. 9.95 (ISBN 0-913922-65-X). Dawn Horse Pr.
--The Yoga of Consideration & the Way I Teach. (Orig.). 1982. pap. 3.95 (ISBN 0-913922-63-3). Dawn Horse Pr.
Da Free John. Easy Death: On the Sacred Ordeal of Keeping Attention in the Sacrifice. 500p. Date not set. Vol. 1. pap. price not set. Vol. 2: Lion Sutia (ISBN 0-913922-58-7). Dawn Horse Pr.
Daft, Richard L. Organization Theory & Design. (Management Ser.). (Illus.). 570p. 1982. text ed. 19.95 (ISBN 0-314-69645-8). West Pub.
Daft, Richard L., jt. auth. see Campbell, John P.
Daftuar, C. Job Attitudes in Indian Management: A Study in Need Deficiencies & Need Importance. 80p. 1982. text ed. 10.75x (ISBN 0-391-02718-2, Pub. by Concept). Humanities.
Da Gama, Bosco, jt. ed. see Phantom, D. S.
Da Gama, Jose B. The Uruguay: A Historical Romance of South America. Garcia, Frederick & Stanton, Edward, eds. Burton, Richard F., tr. LC 81-15920. 270p. (Port.). 1982. 27.50x (ISBN 0-520-04524-6). U of Cal Pr.
D'Agapeyeff, Alexander. Codes & Ciphers. LC 73-19772. (Illus.). 1974. Repr. of 1939 ed. 30.00 o.p. (ISBN 0-8103-3716-9). Gale.
Dagel, John F. Diesel Engine Repair. LC 81-615. 586p. 1982. text ed. 25.95x (ISBN 0-471-03542-4); tchrs' manual (ISBN 0-471-86373-4). Wiley.
Dager, Deborah. Heartaches. 224p. 1983. pap. 1.95 (ISBN 0-449-70042-9, Juniper). Fawcett.
Dagg, Anne I., jt. auth. see Gauthier-Pilters, Hilde.
Daggett, Harriet S., jt. ed. see Charmatz, Jan P.
Daggett, Windsor P. A Down-East Yankee from the District of Maine. LC 20-21414. (Illus.). 1920. pap. 4.00 o.p. (ISBN 0-915592-07-X). Maine Hist.
Dagher, Joseph P. Technical Communication: A Practical Guide. (Illus.). 1978. pap. text ed. 14.95 (ISBN 0-13-898247-3). P-H.
--Writing a Practical Guide. LC 74-11784. (Illus.). 1976. pap. text ed. 12.95 (ISBN 0-395-18621-8); instr's. manual 1.35 (ISBN 0-395-18803-2). HM.
Dagher, Yusuf. Arabic Dictionary of Pseudonyms. (Arabic.). 1982. 16.00x (ISBN 0-86685-300-6). Intl Bk Ctr.
Daglio, S. Daniel, tr. see Yates, Kyle M. & Owens, J. J.
Daglish, E. Fitch. The Basset Hound. (Foyle's Handbks). 1973. 3.95 (ISBN 0-685-55818-5). Palmetto Pub.
--Beagles. Foyle, Christina, ed. (Foyle's Handbks). 1973. 3.95 (ISBN 0-685-55802-9). Palmetto Pub.
--Dog Breeding. Foyle, Christina, ed. 1973. 3.95 (ISBN 0-685-55810-X). Palmetto Pub.
--Training Your Dog. LC 76-10739. (Illus.). 1976. bds. 2.25 o.p. (ISBN 0-668-03978-7). Arco.
Dagmar, et al, trs. see Tichy, M. & Rakosnik, J.
Dagnal, Cynthia. Starting Your Own Rock Band. (Illus.). 96p. (Orig.). 1983. pap. 5.95 (ISBN 0-8092-5606-1). Contemp Bks.
Dagnino, Alfonso G. see Alegria, Fernando, et al.
D'Agnostino, Guido, jt. auth. see Covello, Leonard.
D'Agostino, Bruno. Greece. (Monuments of Civilization Ser.: No. 6). (Illus.). 192p. 1975. 25.00 o.p. (ISBN 0-448-02023-8, G&D). Putnam Pub Group.
Dagostino, Frank. Materials of Construction. 1981. text ed. 21.95 (ISBN 0-8359-4286-4). Reston.
--Mechanical & Electrical Systems in Building. 1982. text ed. 25.95 (ISBN 0-8359-4312-7). Reston.
--Mechanical & Electrical Systems in Construction & Architecture. (Illus.). 1978. ref. ed. 27.95 (ISBN 0-87909-511-3); solutions manual avail. (ISBN 0-87909-510-5). Reston.
Dagostino, Frank R. Contemporary Architectural Drawing: Residential & Commercial. 1977. 20.95 (ISBN 0-87909-132-0). Reston.
--Estimating in Building Construction. 2nd ed. (Illus.). 1978. text ed. 23.95 (ISBN 0-87909-275-0). solutions manual free (ISBN 0-8359-2749-0). Reston.
D'Agostino, Peter. Coming & Going. LC 82-61856. 88p. 1982. pap. 9.95 (ISBN 0-917986-18-0). NFS Pr.
D'Agostino, Peter, ed. Transmission. 350p. (Orig.). 1983. 22.95 (ISBN 0-934378-25-8); pap. 10.95 (ISBN 0-934378-26-6). Tanam Pr.
D'Agostino, Peter & Muntadas, Antonio, eds. The Un-Necessary Image. LC 82-51275. (Illus.). 104p. (Orig.). 1982. pap. 8.95 (ISBN 0-934378-30-4). Tanam Pr.
D'Agostino, R. B., jt. auth. see Cureton, E. E.
D'Agostino, Robert A., et al. Mastering Reading Comprehension Skills. LC 81-20494. (Illus.). 224p. (Orig.). 1982. pap. 6.95 (ISBN 0-668-05125-6). Arco.
Daguerre, Louis J. Historical & Descriptive Account of the Various Processes of the Daguerreotype & the Diorama. LC 36-3404. 1969. Repr. of 1839 ed. 9.00 o.s.i. (ISBN 0-527-21100-1). Kraus Repr.
Dahdah. Dictionary of Arabic Grammar, in Charts & Tables. (Illus., Arabic-Arabic.). 1982. 30.00x (ISBN 0-86685-292-1). Intl Bk Ctr.
Dahendorf, Ralf. On Britain. LC 82-60102. 198p. 1982. pap. 6.95 (ISBN 0-226-13410-5). U of Chicago Pr.
Dahl, A. M. & Knick, Allison, eds. Directory of Directors in the City of New York & Suburbs. rev. ed. 725p. 1981. 125.00 o.s.i. (ISBN 0-936612-02-9). DODC.
Dahl, Arlene. Beyond Beauty. 1980. pap. 11.95 o.p. (ISBN 0-671-24555-4). S&S.
Dahl, Curtis. Robert Montgomery Bird. (United States Authors Ser.). 13.95 (ISBN 0-8057-0060-9, Twayne). G K Hall.
Dahl, Dale C. & Hammond, Jerome W. Market & Price Analysis: The Agricultural Industries. (Illus.). 1976. text ed. 22.95 o.p. (ISBN 0-07-015060-5, C). McGraw.
Dahl, Dolores. Make Ready. LC 82-99847. (Illus.). 91p. (Orig.). 1982. pap. 4.95 (ISBN 0-9608960-0-7). Single Vision.
Dahl, Fred, jt. auth. see Sippl, Charles J.
Dahl, Hartvig. Word Frequencies of Spoken American English. 300p. 1980. 85.00x (ISBN 0-930454-07-3, Pub. by Verbatim). Gale.
Dahl, Mark V. Common Office Dermatology. Date not set. price not set (ISBN 0-8089-1497-9). Grune.
Dahl, Mikkel. Scripture Defogged for the Millions. 1979. 6.95 o.p. (ISBN 0-533-03351-9). Vantage.
Dahl, Norman C. & Wiesner, Jerome B., eds. World Change & World Security. (MIT Bicentennial Studies Ser.). 1978. 16.50 (ISBN 0-262-04058-1). MIT Pr.
Dahl, Otto C. Early Phonetic & Phonemic Changes in Austronesia. 176p. 1982. 18.00 (ISBN 82-00-09530-4). Universitet.
--Proto-Austronesian. 2nd ed. (Scandinavian Institute of Asian Studies Monograph: No. 15). 146p. (Orig.). 1977. pap. text ed. 11.00x o.p. (ISBN 0-7007-0064-1). Humanities.
Dahl, Roald. The BFG. (Illus.). (gr. k up). 1982. 10.95 (ISBN 0-374-30469-6); slipcased limited ed. 30.00 (ISBN 0-374-30471-8). FS&G.
--Charlie & the Great Glass Elevator: The Further Adventures of Charlie Bucket & Willie Wonka, the Chocolate-Maker Extraordinaire. (Illus.). (gr. k-7). 1972. 8.95 (ISBN 0-394-82472-5); PLB 8.99 (ISBN 0-394-92472-X). Knopf.
--Danny: The Champion of the World. (Illus.). 208p. (gr. 3 up). 1975. PLB 7.99 (ISBN 0-394-93103-3). Knopf.
--Dirty Beasts. (Illus.). 32p. (gr. 1 up). 1983. 10.95 (ISBN 0-374-31790-9). FS&G.
--Fantastic Mister Fox. LC 74-118704. (Illus.). (gr. k-3). 1970. PLB 6.99 (ISBN 0-394-90497-4). Knopf.
--James & the Giant Peach. (Illus.). (gr. 3 up). 1961. 11.95 (ISBN 0-394-81282-4); PLB 11.99 (ISBN 0-394-91282-9). Knopf.
--Roald Dahl's Revolting Rhymes. LC 82-15263. (Illus.). 48p. 1983. 9.95 (ISBN 0-394-85422-5); lib. bdg. 9.99 (ISBN 0-394-95422-X). Knopf.
--Selected Stories. 1968. 3.95 o.s.i. (ISBN 0-394-60242-0, 242). Modern Lib.
--The Twits. 96p. 1982. pap. 1.95 (ISBN 0-553-15167-3). Bantam.
Dahl, Robert A. Congress & Foreign Policy. LC 82-25123. x, 305p. 1983. Repr. of 1950 ed. lib. bdg. 35.00x (ISBN 0-313-23788-3, DACF). Greenwood.
--Democracy in the United States. 4th ed. 1981. 16.95 (ISBN 0-395-30793-7); Instr's. manual 1.25 (ISBN 0-395-30794-5). HM.
--Modern Political Analysis. 3rd ed. (Foundations of Modern Political Science Ser). (Illus.). 176p. 1976. ref. ed. o.p. 8.95x (ISBN 0-13-596999-9); pap. text ed. 9.95 (ISBN 0-13-596981-6). P-H.
--Polyarchy: Participation & Opposition. LC 70-140534. 1971. 20.00 o.p. (ISBN 0-686-86919-2); pap. 7.95x (ISBN 0-300-01565-8, Y254). Yale U Pr.
Dahlberg, Arthur O. How to Lower Interest Rates. 1983. 14.95 (ISBN 0-8159-5718-1). Devin.
Dahlberg, Charles C. & Jaffe, Joseph. Stroke: A Doctor's Personal Story of His Recovery. (Illus.). 1977. 12.95 o.p. (ISBN 0-393-08720-4). Norton.
Dahlhaus, Carl. Analysis & Value Judgement. 2nd ed. Levarie, Siegmund, tr. from Ger. (Pendragon Press Monographs in Musicology Ser.). Orig. Title: Analyse und Werturteil. 150p. 1983. lib. bdg. 32.00 (ISBN 0-918728-20-7). Pendragon NY.
--Richard Wagner's Music Dramas. Whittall, Mary, tr. LC 78-68359. 1979. 22.95 (ISBN 0-521-22397-0). Cambridge U Pr.
Dahlhaus, Carl & Eggebrecht, Hans H. Brockhaus Riemann Musiklexikon, Vol. 1, A-K. (Ger.). 1978. 99.50 o.s.i. (ISBN 3-7653-0303-8). Eur-Am Music.
Dahlie, Hallvard. Brian Moore. (World Authors Ser.). 1981. lib. bdg. 15.95 (ISBN 0-8057-6475-5, Twayne). G K Hall.
Dahlie, Hallvard, jt. ed. see Chadbourne, Richard.
Dahlin, Therrin C. & Gillum, Gary P. The Catholic Left in Latin America: A Comprehensive Bibliography. 1981. lib. bdg. 35.00 (ISBN 0-8161-8396-1, Hall Reference). G K Hall.
Dahlinger, John D. & Leighton, Frances S. The Secret Life of Henry Ford. LC 77-15422. (Illus.). 1978. 10.95 o.p. (ISBN 0-672-52377-9). Bobbs.
Dahlstedt, Marden. Shadow of the Lighthouse. LC 73-88537. (Illus.). 160p. (gr. 3-7). 1974. 6.50 o.p. (ISBN 0-698-20291-0, Coward). Putnam Pub Group.
--The Stopping Place. new ed. LC 75-43616. (Illus.). 160p. (gr. 5 up). 1976. 6.95 o.p. (ISBN 0-399-20496-2). Putnam Pub Group.
--The Terrible Wave. (Illus.). 128p. (gr. 4-7). 1972. 5.95 o.p. (ISBN 0-698-20188-4, Coward). Putnam Pub Group.
Dahlstrom, jt. auth. see Bang.
Dahlstrom, jt. auth. see Muus.
Dahlstrom, jt. auth. see Schoitz.
Dahlstrom, J. & Ryel, D. Promises to Keep: Reading & Writing About Values. 1977. pap. text ed. 13.95 (ISBN 0-13-731059-5). P-H.
Dahmke, Mark. Microcomputer Operating Systems. 240p. 1981. pap. 16.95 (ISBN 0-07-015071-0). McGraw.
Dahms, Alan, jt. auth. see Clifton, Robert.
Dahms, Alan M. Thriving: Beyond Adjustment. LC 79-17954. 1980. pap. text ed. 19.95 (ISBN 0-8185-0358-0). Brooks-Cole.
Dahneke, Barton E. Measurement of Suspended Particles By Quasi-Elastic Light Scattering. 400p. 1982. 39.95 (ISBN 0-471-87289-X, Pub. by Wiley-Interscience). Wiley.
Dahnert, Ulrich. Die Orgeln Gottfried Silbermanns in Mitteldeutschland. (Bibliotheca Organologica Ser.: Vol. 34). 1971. Repr. of 1953 ed. 50.00 o.s.i. (ISBN 0-686-30876-X, Pub. by Frits Knuf Netherlands); wrappers 37.50 o.s.i. (ISBN 0-686-30877-8, Pub. by Frits Knuf Netherlands). Pendragon NY.
Dahnsen, Alan. Aircraft. LC 77-15092. (Easy-Read Fact Bks). (Illus.). (gr. 2-4). 1978. 8.60 (ISBN 0-531-01351-0). Watts.
--Bicycles. LC 78-7346. (Easy-Read Fact Bks.). (Illus.). (gr. 2-4). 1978. PLB 8.60 s&l (ISBN 0-531-01372-3). Watts.
Dahood, Roger G., jt. ed. see Ackerman, Robert W.
Dahrendorf, ed. Europe's Economy in Crisis. 1982. text ed. 24.95x (ISBN 0-8419-0806-0). Holmes & Meier.

Dai, Bingham. Opium Addiction in Chicago. LC 72-124503. (Criminology, Law Enforcement, & Social Problems Ser.: No. 126). (Intro. index added). 1970. 17.00x (ISBN 0-87585-126-6). Patterson Smith.

Daiches, David. Glasgow. 256p. 1982. pap. 7.95 (ISBN 0-686-95233-2, Pub. by Granada England). Academy Chi Ltd.

--The Last Stuart: The Life & Times of Bonnie Prince Charlie. (Illus.). 320p. 1973. 10.00 o.p. (ISBN 0-399-11109-3). Putnam Pub Group.

--Literature & Gentility in Scotland. 120p. 1982. 12.50x (ISBN 0-85224-438-X, Pub. by Edinburgh U Pr Scotland). Columbia U Pr.

--Virginia Woolf. LC 78-12655. 1979. Repr. of 1963 ed. lib. bdg. 19.75x (ISBN 0-313-21187-6, DAVW). Greenwood.

--Willa Cather: A Critical Introduction. LC 71-136061. 1971. Repr. of 1951 ed. lib. bdg. 25.00 (ISBN 0-8371-5211-9, DAWC). Greenwood.

Daiches, David, ed. A Companion to Scottish Culture. (Illus.). 441p. 1982. 42.50 (ISBN 0-8419-0792-7). Holmes & Meier.

--Idea of a New University: An Experiment in Sussex. 1971. pap. 4.95x o.p. (ISBN 0-262-54011-8). MIT Pr.

Daiches, Sol. People in Distress: A Geographical Perspective on Psychological Wellbeing. LC 81-4308. (University of Chicago, Department of Geography Research Paper Ser.: No. 197). (Illus.). 199p. 1981. pap. 8.00 (ISBN 0-89065-104-3). U Chicago Dept Geog.

Daigle, Pierre V. The Seeker. 126p. 1973. pap. 3.95 o.p. (ISBN 0-914216-08-2). Acadian Pub.

Daigneault, Aubert, ed. Studies in Algebraic Logic. LC 74-84580. (Studies in Mathematics: No. 9). 1975. 16.50 (ISBN 0-88385-109-1). Math Assn.

Daigneault, Ernest A., jt. auth. see Brown, R. Don.

Daigon, Arthur & Dempsey, Richard A. School: Pass at Your Own Risk. (Illus.). 228p. 1973. pap. text ed. 16.95 (ISBN 0-13-793877-2). P-H.

Daiker, Donald A., et al. The Writer's Options: Combining to Composing. 2nd ed. 388p. 1982. pap. text ed. 12.50 scp (ISBN 0-06-041476-6, HarpC); instructors manual avail. (ISBN 0-06-361493-6). Har-Row.

Dail, Shirley M. Jesus Said "Leave Her Alone". (Illus.). 1979. pap. 2.95x (ISBN 0-9602440-0-X). Jesus-First.

Dailey, Charles A. & Madsen, Ann M. Good Judgement About People. new ed. LC 78-31339. (Illus.). 1979. 18.95 (ISBN 0-07-015086-9, P&RB). McGraw.

--How to Evaluate People in Business: The Track-Record Method of Making Correct Judgments. LC 82-16233. 240p. 1983. pap. 9.95 (ISBN 0-07-015087-7, P&RB). McGraw.

Dailey, Dwight M. Concert Pieces for the Tenor Saxophone. 1950. write for info (ISBN 0-685-21777-9). Wahr.

Dailey, Janet. Foxfire Light. (Nightingale Series Paperbacks). 1983. pap. 8.95 (ISBN 0-8161-3494-4, Large Print Bks). G K Hall.

--L'Epouse De Juin. (Harlequin Romantique). 192p. 1983. pap. 1.95 (ISBN 0-373-41194-4). Harlequin Bks.

--The Second Time. (Nightingale Series Paperbacks). 1983. pap. 7.95 (ISBN 0-8161-3517-7, Large Print Bks). G K Hall.

--Stands a Calder Man. (Orig.). 1983. pap. 6.95 (ISBN 0-671-83609-9). PB.

--Wildcatter's Woman. (Nightingale Ser.). 1982. pap. 6.95 (ISBN 0-8161-3440-5, Large Print Bks). G K Hall.

Dailey, Timothy E., jt. auth. see Wickman, Peter M.

Daily, Charles A. Using the Track Record Approach: The Key to Successful Personnel Selection. 176p. 1982. 16.95 (ISBN 0-8144-5695-2). Am Mgmt.

Daily, Elaine K. & Schroeder, John S. Hemodynamic Waveforms: Exercises in Identification & Analysis. 1st ed. (Illus.). 308p. 1983. pap. text ed. 15.95 (ISBN 0-8016-1212-8). Mosby.

Daily, Elaine K., jt. auth. see Schroeder, John S.

Daily, James M. Interpersonal Skills for the Manager. LC 82-73405. 275p. 1982. ringed binder 29.95 (ISBN 0-87094-350-2). Dow Jones-Irwin.

Daimler, Harriet, pseud. Darling. 176p. (Orig.). 1983. pap. 3.95 (ISBN 0-394-62458-0, B489, BC). Grove.

Dainow, Joseph. The Role of Judicial Decisions & Doctrine in Civil Law & in Mixed Jurisdictions. LC 73-90871. xviii, 350p. 1974. 27.50x (ISBN 0-8071-0080-3). La State U Pr.

Dainow, Joseph, ed. Essays on the Civil Law of Obligations. LC 75-96256. xii, 314p. 1969. 25.00x (ISBN 0-8071-0912-6). La State U Pr.

Daintith, John, ed. Dictionary of Chemistry. Orig. Title: Facts on File Dictionary of Chemistry. (Illus.). 240p. 1982. pap. 5.72i (ISBN 0-06-463559-7). B&N NY.

Dair, Carl. Design with Type. LC 66-23932. 1967. 20.00 o.p. (ISBN 0-8020-1426-7); pap. 12.95. U of Toronto Pr.

Dais, Eugene E. Law & the Ecological Challenge: Amintaphil, Vol. 2. LC 78-61842. 1979. lib. bdg. 32.50 (ISBN 0-930342-66-6). W S Hein.

Daitz, Stephen G. Euripides' "Hekabe". (Sound Seminars Ser.). 50p. Date not set. with 2 cassettes 29.95x (ISBN 0-88432-084-7, S23650). J Norton Pubs.

--Pronunciation of Ancient Greek: A Practical Guide. 10p. Date not set. with 2 cassettes 19.95x (ISBN 0-88432-083-9, S23660). J Norton Pubs.

Daitzman, Reid J. Mental Jogging. LC 79-16602. 1980. 9.95 o.s.i. (ISBN 0-399-90053-5, Marek). Putnam Pub Group.

Daitzman, Reid J., ed. Diagnosis & Intervention in Behavior Therapy & Behavioral Medicine, Vol. 1. 320p. 1983. text ed. 34.95x (ISBN 0-8261-4040-8). Springer Pub.

Daix, Pierre. Cubists & Cubism. LC 82-60070. (Skira Great Art Movement Ser.). (Illus.). 176p. 1982. 65.00 (ISBN 0-8478-0457-7). Rizzoli Intl.

Dajani, Burhan. The Palestine Yearbook 1973. (Arabic.). 1977. 30.00 (ISBN 0-686-18944-2). Inst Palestine.

Dajani, Burhan, ed. The Palestine Yearbook, 1972. (Arabic.). 1977. 30.00 (ISBN 0-686-18943-4). Inst Palestine.

Dake, Charles R. A Strange Discovery. (Science Fiction Ser). 336p. 1975. Repr. of 1899 ed. lib. bdg. 14.00 o.p. (ISBN 0-8398-2302-9, Gregg). G K Hall.

Dake, L. P. Fundamentals of Reservoir Engineering. (Developments in Petroleum Science: Vol. 8). 1979. pap. text ed. 30.00 (ISBN 0-444-41830-X). Elsevier.

Dakers, Elaine K. Titus Oates. LC 71-114506. (Illus.). 1971. Repr. of 1949 ed. lib. bdg. 18.50x (ISBN 0-8371-4783-2, DATO). Greenwood.

Dakhil, Fahd, et al. Housing Problems in Developing Countries: Proceedings of IAHS International Conference 1978, 2 vols. LC 78-65357. 1979. Set. 95.95x (ISBN 0-471-27561-1); 95.95x ea. Vol. 1 (ISBN 0-471-27558-1). Vol. 2 (ISBN 0-471-27559-X, Pub. by Wiley-Interscience). Wiley.

Dakin, Douglas. The Greek Struggle for Independence, 1821-1833. LC 72-89798. 1973. 34.50x (ISBN 0-520-02342-0). U of Cal Pr.

--The Unification of Greece: Seventeen-Seventy to Nineteen Twenty-Three. LC 76-187329. 1972. 25.00 (ISBN 0-312-83300-8). St Martin.

Dakin, John. Feedback from Tomorrow. (Research in Planning & Design Ser.). 492p. 1980. 33.50x (ISBN 0-85086-071-7, Pub. by Pion England). Methuen Inc.

Dakin, Julian. The Language Laboratory & Language Learning. (Longman Handbooks for Language Teachers). 1973. pap. text ed. 6.95x (ISBN 0-582-55228-1). Longman.

Dakyns, Jannie R. The Middle Ages in French Literature 1851-1900. new ed. (Oxford Modern Languages & Literature Monographs). 1973. 29.95x o.p. (ISBN 0-19-815522-0). Oxford U Pr.

Dalal-Clayton, D. B., ed. Black's Agricultural Dictionary. (Illus.). 512p. 1981. 28.50x (ISBN 0-389-20261-4). B&N Imports.

Daland, Robert T. Exploring Brazilian Bureaucracy: Performance & Pathology. LC 80-67246. 455p. 1981. lib. bdg. 27.00 (ISBN 0-8191-1468-5); pap. text ed. 17.00 (ISBN 0-8191-1469-3). U Pr of Amer.

Dalbey, Alice F. The Visitor's Guide to Point Reyes National Seashore. LC 73-89770. (Orig.). 1974. pap. 4.95 (ISBN 0-85699-098-1). Chatham Pr.

Dalbor, John B. & Sturcken, H. Tracy. Spanish in Review. LC 78-27055. 337p. 1979. pap. text ed. 18.95x (ISBN 0-471-03991-8). wkbk., 1840 p. 9.50 (ISBN 0-471-03992-6). Wiley.

Dalby, David. Black Through White: Patterns of Communication. (Hans Wolff Memorial Lecture Ser.). (Orig.). 1970. pap. text ed. 2.00 (ISBN 0-941934-02-0). Ind U Afro-Amer Arts.

Dalby, Stuart. Make Your Own Musical Instruments. 1978. 19.95 o.p. (ISBN 0-7134-0545-7, Pub. by Batsford England). David & Charles.

Dalcq, A., et al, eds. Anatomy. (International Congress Ser.: No. 70). (Abstracts). 1963. pap. 14.75 (ISBN 90-219-1107-8, Excerpta Medica). Elsevier.

Dale, Alexander. Healthy Hair & Common Sense. 9.95x (ISBN 0-911638-02-4). Cancer Control Soc.

Dale, Alzina S. The Outline of Sanity: A Life of G. K. Chesterton. 350p. 1982. 18.95 (ISBN 0-8028-3550-3). Eerdmans.

Dale, Anthony. Fashionable Brighton Eighteen Twenty to Eighteen Sixty. 2nd ed. (Illus.). 1967. 12.50 o.p. (ISBN 0-85362-028-8, Oriel). Routledge & Kegan.

Dale, Barbara & Roeber, Johanna. The Pregnancy Exercise Book. 1982. cancelled (ISBN 0-394-52730-5); pap. 6.95 (ISBN 0-394-71119-X). Pantheon.

Dale, Charles W., jt. auth. see Oliva, Ralph A.

Dale, E. Management: Theory & Practice. (Management Ser.). (Illus.). 1978. text ed. 23.95 (ISBN 0-07-015188-1, C); instructors manual 21.00 (ISBN 0-07-015189-X). McGraw.

Dale, Edgar & O'Rourke, Joseph. The Living Word Vocabulary. LC 81-50682. 704p. 1981. lib. bdg. 49.95 (ISBN 0-7166-3115-6). World Bk.

Dale, Ernest. Management: Theory & Practice. 3rd ed. (Management Ser.). (Illus.). 816p. 1973. text ed. 14.95 o.p. (ISBN 0-07-015165-2, C); pap. text ed. 15.95 (ISBN 0-07-015162-8); instructors manual 15.95 (ISBN 0-07-015166-0). McGraw.

Dale, J. R. & Applebe, G. E. Pharmacy, Law & Ethics. 2nd ed. 629p. 1979. 21.00 (ISBN 0-85369-128-2, Pub. by Pharmaceutical). Rittenhouse.

Dale, Jean N. The Monkey's Paw. rev. ed. (Reading & Exercise Ser.: No. 5). 1975. pap. 3.25 (ISBN 0-89285-054-X); cassette tapes 29.50 (ISBN 0-89285-072-8). ELS Intl.

--Tale from Tangier. rev. ed. (Reading & Exercise Ser.: No. 6). 1975. pap. 3.25 (ISBN 0-89285-055-8); cassette tapes 29.50 (ISBN 0-89285-073-6). ELS Intl.

Dale, Jean N. & Sheeler, Willard D. The Angry Sea. rev. ed. (Reading & Exercise Ser.: No. 2). 1975. pap. 3.25 (ISBN 0-89285-051-5); cassette tapes 29.50 (ISBN 0-89285-069-8). ELS Intl.

--The Quiet Man. rev. ed. (Reading & Exercise Ser.: No. 4). 1975. pap. 3.25 (ISBN 0-89285-053-1); cassette tapes 29.50 (ISBN 0-89285-071-X). ELS Intl.

--Winds of Virtue. rev. ed. (Reading & Exercise Ser.: No. 3). 1975. pap. 3.25 (ISBN 0-89285-052-3); cassette tapes 29.50 (ISBN 0-89285-070-1). ELS Intl.

Dale, Jean N. & Sheeler, Williard D. The Whistler. rev. ed. (Reading & Exercise Ser.: No. 1). 1975. pap. 3.25 (ISBN 0-89285-050-7); cassette tapes 29.50 (ISBN 0-89285-068-X). ELS Intl.

Dale, John E. The Growth of Leaves. (No. 137). 64p. 1982. pap. text ed. 8.95 (ISBN 0-7131-2836-4). E Arnold.

Dale, John E. & Milthorpe, Frederick L. The Growth & Functioning of Leaves. LC 82-4377. (Illus.). 550p. Date not set. price not set (ISBN 0-521-23761-0). Cambridge U Pr.

Dale, Kathleen. Brahms: A Biography, with a Survey of Books, Editions & Recordings. (Concertgoer's Companion Ser.). 118p. 1970. 11.50 o.p. (ISBN 0-208-01056-4, Archon). Shoe String.

--Nineteenth Century Piano Music: A Handbook for Pianists. LC 70-87500. (Music Ser.). 1974. Repr. of 1954 ed. 29.50 (ISBN 0-306-71414-0). Da Capo.

Dale, Laura A., jt. auth. see Murphy, Gardner.

Dale, Nell B. & Orshalick, David W. Introduction to Pascal & Structured Design. 448p. Date not set. pap. 17.95 (ISBN 0-669-04797-X). Heath.

Dale, Norman, tr. see Guillot, Rene.

Dale, Peter. Mortal Fire. LC 74-29409. x, 181p. 1976. 12.00 (ISBN 0-8214-0185-8, 82-81859); pap. 7.00 (ISBN 0-8214-0187-4, 82-81867). Ohio U Pr.

--One Another: A Sonnet Sequence. (Poetry Ser.). 1979. 7.95 o.p. (ISBN 0-902400-21-5, Pub. by Carcanet New Pr England); pap. 4.95 o.p. (ISBN 0-902400-22-3). Humanities.

Dale, Philip S. & Ingram, David. Child Language: An International Perspective. 416p. 1981. pap. 19.95 (ISBN 0-8391-1608-X). Univ Park.

Dale, R., et al. Education & the State, Vol. I. (Schooling & the National Interest). 395p. 1981. write for info. (ISBN 0-905273-16-8, Pub. by Taylor & Francis); pap. write for info. (ISBN 0-905273-15-X, Pub. by Taylor & Francis). Intl Pubns Serv.

Dale, Robert D., jt. auth. see Bruster, Bill G.

Dale, Rodney, ed. see Sassoon, George.

Dale, Roger, et al, eds. Schooling & Capitalism: A Sociological Reader. (Open University Set Texts). 1976. 16.95x (ISBN 0-7100-8493-5); pap. 8.50 (ISBN 0-7100-8494-3). Routledge & Kegan.

Dale, Stan & Beauchamp, Val. Fantasies Can Set You Free. LC 80-66195. 124p. (Orig.). 1980. pap. 6.95 o.p. (ISBN 0-686-78690-4). Celestial Arts.

Dale, W. Andrew. Management of Arterial Occlusive Disease. (Illus.). 1971. 37.50 o.p. (ISBN 0-8151-2213-6). Year Bk Med.

Dale-Green, Patricia. The Archetypal Cat. 2nd ed. Orig. Title: Cult of the Cat. (Illus.). 189p. 1983. pap. 13.50 (ISBN 0-88214-700-5). Spring Pubns.

D'Alembert, jt. ed. see Diderot.

D'Alembert, Family. Strangler's Moon. (E.E. Doc Smith Ser: No. 2). 1976. pap. 1.75 o.s.i. (ISBN 0-515-04731-7). Jove Pubns.

D'Alembert, Jean L. Preliminary Discourse to the Encyclopedia of Diderot. Schwab, Richard & Rex, Walter, trs. LC 63-21831. (Orig.). 1963. 7.50 (ISBN 0-672-51037-5); pap. 6.95 (ISBN 0-672-60276-8, LLA88). Bobbs.

Dalen, J. T. Van see Lessell, S. & Van Dalen, J. T.

Dales, D. N., jt. auth. see Thiessen, Frank.

Dales, Dave, jt. auth. see Theissen, Frank.

Dales, Davis, jt. auth. see Thiessen, Frank J.

Dales, Richard C. The Intellectual Life of Western Europe in the Middle Ages. LC 79-5515. 1980. pap. text ed. 10.25 (ISBN 0-8191-0900-2). U Pr of Amer.

--Marius on the Elements. 200p. 1977. 19.95x (ISBN 0-520-02856-2). U of Cal Pr.

D'Alessandro, Arthur D., jt. auth. see Dolan, Frances M.

D'Alessio, Barbara, jt. ed. see Goldstein, Sherry.

Dalessio, Donald J., jt. auth. see Diamond, Seymour.

Dalessio, Donald J., ed. see Wolff, Harold G.

D'Alessio, Gregory J., jt. auth. see Schiffman, Yale M.

D-Alessio, Gregory J., jt. auth. see Schiffman, Yale M.

Dalet, Roger. How to Give Yourself Relief from Pain: By the Simple Pressure of a Finger. LC 79-3825. (Illus.). 176p. 1982. pap. 8.95 (ISBN 0-8128-6153-1). Stein & Day.

--Safeguard Your Health & Beauty with Finger Massage. 156p. 1980. 22.00x (ISBN 0-686-97048-9, Pub. by Rider England). State Mutual Bk.

Daley, Arthur. All the Home Run Kings. (Putnam Sports Shelf). (Illus.). (gr. 4-9). 1972. 6.95 o.p. (ISBN 0-399-20249-8). Putnam Pub Group.

Daley, Brian. A Tapestry of Magics. 304p. 1983. pap. 2.95 (ISBN 0-686-82483-0, Del Rey). Ballantine.

Daley, D. J., jt. auth. see Stoyan, D.

Daley, John, ed. The Vatican: Spirit & Art of Christian Rome. (Illus.). 1983. 39.50 (ISBN 0-686-43091-3). Metro Mus Art.

Daley, Ken. Basic Film Technique. (Media Manual Series). (Illus.). 160p. 1980. pap. 10.95 (ISBN 0-240-51016-X). Focal Pr.

Daley, Martin & Wilson, Margo. Sex, Evolution & Behavior. 2nd ed. 400p. 1983. pap. text ed. write for info. (ISBN 0-87150-767-6, 4511). Grant Pr.

Daley, Nelda K. & Shannon, Thomas R. The American Social Structure, Preliminary Edition. 1978. pap. text ed. 10.95 (ISBN 0-8403-1933-9). Kendall-Hunt.

Daley, Robert. Year of the Dragon. 1982. pap. 3.95 (ISBN 0-451-11817-0, AE1817, Sig). NAL.

Daley, William J., et al. Ethylene Oxide Control in Hospitals. LC 79-22184. 48p. (Orig.). 1979. pap. 10.00 (ISBN 0-87258-291-4, AHA-031400). Am Hospital.

Dal Fabbro, Mario. How to Build Modern Furniture. 3rd ed. 1976. 11.95 o.p. (ISBN 0-07-015185-7, P&RB). McGraw.

--How to Make Children's Furniture & Play Equipment. 2nd ed. (Illus.). 192p. 1974. 19.95 (ISBN 0-07-015186-5, P&RB). McGraw.

--Upholstered Furniture: Design & Construction. LC 69-13602. (Illus.). 1969. 7.20 (ISBN 0-07-015180-6, P&RB). McGraw.

Dalgish, Gerard M. A Dictionary of Africanisms: Contributions of Sub-Saharan Africa to the English Language. LC 82-9366. (Illus.). 244p. 1982. lib. bdg. 35.00 (ISBN 0-313-23585-6, DDA/). Greenwood.

Dalgliesh, Alice. Bears on Hemlock Mountain. LC 52-11023. 1981. pap. 2.95 (ISBN 0-686-84870-5, A-133, Pub. by Aladdin). Atheneum.

Dalglish, Edward H. Layman's Bible Book Commentary: Jeremiah, Lamentations, Vol. 11. 1983. 4.75 (ISBN 0-8054-1181-X). Broadman.

Dali, Salvador. The Unspeakable Confessions of Salvador Dali. Parinaud, Andre, as told to. Salemson, Harold J., tr. from Fr. LC 81-11232. Orig. Title: Comment on Devient Dali. (Illus.). 302p. 1981. pap. 6.95 (ISBN 0-688-00010-X). Quill NY.

Da Liu. The Taoist Health Exercise Book. LC 74-78308. (Illus.). 1974. pap. 3.95 o.p. (ISBN 0-8256-3029-0, 030029, Quick Fox). Putnam Pub Group.

Dalke, J. David, jt. auth. see Hart, Lois B.

DallaCosta, Mariarosa & James, Selma. The Power of Women & the Subversion of the Community. 80p. 1981. pap. 3.50 (ISBN 0-9502702-4-5). Falling Wall.

Dallas, D. B., ed. see Society of Manufacturing Engineers.

Dallas, Eneas S. Poetics: An Essay on Poetry. (Classics in Art & Literary Criticism, House Ser). Repr. of 1852 ed. 27.00 (ISBN 0-384-11435-0). Johnson Repr.

Dallas, Gregor. The Imperfect Peasant Economy: The Loire Country, 1800-1914. LC 81-21558. (Illus.). 352p. 1982. 34.50 (ISBN 0-521-24060-3). Cambridge U Pr.

Dallas Museum of Fine Arts. Gallery Buffet Soup Cookbook. (Illus.). 126p. 1977. 7.50 (ISBN 0-686-36728-6). Md Hist.

Dallas, Patricia. Dallas in Wonderland. LC 78-50949. (Illus.). 1979. 9.95 (ISBN 0-89169-511-7). Reed Bks.

Dallas, Philip. Italian Wines. 2nd ed. LC 82-24195. (Books on Wine). 336p. 1983. 24.95 (ISBN 0-571-18071-X); pap. 11.95 (ISBN 0-571-11994-8). Faber & Faber.

Dallas, Richard J. & Thompson, James M. Clerical & Secretarial Systems for the Office. (Office Occupations Ser.). (Illus.). 448p. 1975. ref. ed. 20.95 (ISBN 0-13-136390-5). P-H.

Dallas-Damis, Athena. Windswept. (Orig.). 1981. pap. 2.50 o.p. (ISBN 0-451-09666-5, E9666, Sig). NAL.

Dallas-Damis, Athena, tr. see Kazantzakis, Nikos.

Dallek, Robert. The American Style of Foreign Policy: Cultural Politics & Foreign Affairs. LC 82-48877. 336p. 1983. 16.95 (ISBN 0-394-51360-6). Knopf.

--Franklin D. Roosevelt & American Foreign Policy, 1932-1945. (A Galaxy Book: No. 628). 1979. 29.95 (ISBN 0-19-502457-5); pap. 10.95 (ISBN 0-19-502894-5, GB628). Oxford U Pr.

Dalley, Terence, ed. The Complete Guide to Illustration & Design: Techniques & Materials. LC 79-13326. (Illus.). Date not set. cancelled (ISBN 0-8317-1612-6, Mayflower Bks). Smith Pubs. Postponed.

Dallier, Aline, intro. by. Combative Acts, Profiles & Voices: An Exhibition of Women Artists from Paris. (Illus.). 14p. 1976. pap. 3.00 (ISBN 0-89062-127-6, Pub by A.I.R. Gallery). Pub Ctr Cult Res.

Dallimore, Arnold. Forerunner of the Charismatic Movement. (Orig.). 1983. pap. 7.95 (ISBN 0-8024-0286-0). Moody.

Dallin, Alexander. The Soviet Union at the United Nations: An Inquiry into Soviet Motives & Objectives. LC 75-27679. (Illus.). 244p. 1976. Repr. of 1962 ed. lib. bdg. 19.25x (ISBN 0-8371-8454-1, DASU). Greenwood.

Dallin, Alexander, compiled by. Soviet Conduct in World Affairs. LC 75-31359. 318p. 1976. Repr. of 1960 ed. lib. bdg. 19.25x (ISBN 0-8371-8511-4, DASCW). Greenwood.

Dallin, David J. New Soviet Empire. 1951. 37.50x (ISBN 0-685-69806-8). Elliots Bks.

--Real Soviet Russia. 1947. 27.50x (ISBN 0-685-69807-6). Elliots Bks.

--Russia & Postwar Europe. 1943. 27.50x (ISBN 0-685-69808-4). Elliots Bks.

--Soviet Russia's Foreign Policy, 1939-42. 1942. 49.50x (ISBN 0-685-88556-9). Elliots Bks.

Dallin, Leon, jt. auth. see Winslow, Robert W.

Dallin, Lynn. Cancer Causes & Natural Controls. LC 82-13765. 1983. 19.95 (ISBN 0-87949-224-4). Ashley Bks.

Dallinger, Jane. Grasshoppers. LC 80-27806. (Lerner Natural Science Bks.). (Illus.). (gr. 4-10). 1981. PLB 8.95g (ISBN 0-8225-1455-9). Lerner Pubns.

--Spiders. LC 80-27548. (Lerner Natural Science Bks.). (Illus.). (gr. 4-10). 1981. PLB 8.95g (ISBN 0-8225-1456-7). Lerner Pubns.

Dallinger, Jane & Johnson, Sylvia A. Frogs & Toads. LC 80-27667. (Lerner Natural Science Bks.). (Illus.). (gr. 4-10). 1982. PLB 8.95g (ISBN 0-8225-1454-0). Lerner Pubns.

Dallinger, Jane & Overbeck, Cynthia. Swallowtail Butterflies. LC 82-15294. (Lerner Natural Science Bks.). (Illus.). 48p. (gr. 4-10). 1982. PLB 8.95g (ISBN 0-8225-1465-6). Lerner Pubns.

Dallinger, Nat. Unforgettable Hollywood. LC 82-3479. (Illus.). 1982. 17.50 (ISBN 0-688-01323-6). Morrow.

Dallington, Robert, tr. see Colonna, Francesco.

Dallison, Dennis. Reflections of My Life: The Apology of John the Baptist. Norman, Ruth, ed. 77p. (Orig.). 1982. pap. text ed. 2.50 (ISBN 0-932642-75-6). Unarius.

Dallman, Elaine, et al, eds. Woman Poet: The Midwest. (Woman Poet Ser.). 1983. casebound 12.95 (ISBN 0-935634-05-3); pap. text ed. 6.00 (ISBN 0-935634-04-5). Women-in-Lit.

--Woman Poet: The South. (Woman Poet Ser.). 1984. casebound 12.95 (ISBN 0-935634-07-X); pap. text ed. 6.00 (ISBN 0-935634-06-1). Women-in-Lit.

Dallmeyer, R. David. Physical Geology Laboratory Text & Manual: A Guide for the Study of Earth. 2nd ed. 1978. wire coil bdg. 11.50 (ISBN 0-8403-1231-8). Kendall-Hunt.

Dally, Ann. Inventing Motherhood: The Consequences of an Ideal. LC 82-10517. 360p. 1983. 19.95 (ISBN 0-8052-3830-1). Schocken.

--Understanding. LC 78-66254. 192p. 1983. pap. 6.95 (ISBN 0-8128-6104-3). Stein & Day.

Dally, James W. & Riley, William F. Experimental Stress Analysis. 2d ed. LC 77-393. (Illus.). 1977. text ed. 36.50x (ISBN 0-07-015204-7, C). McGraw.

Dally, Peter & Gomez, Joan. Anorexia Nervosa. (Illus.). 220p. 1980. 27.50 o.p. (ISBN 0-8151-2261-6). Year Bk Med.

--Obesity & Anorexia Nervosa: A Question of Shape. 128p. 1980. pap. 6.95 (ISBN 0-571-11472-5). Faber & Faber.

Dalman, Gustaf H. Words of Christ. 1981. lib. bdg. 13.50 (ISBN 0-86524-080-9, 9509). Klock & Klock.

Dal Masetto, Antonio. El ojo de la perdiz. 214p. (Span.). 1980. pap. 8.00 (ISBN 0-910061-01-7). Ediciones Norte.

Dal Maso, Leonardo B. Rome of the Popes. (Italia Artistica Ser.). (Illus.). 128p. 1975. pap. 16.50x (ISBN 0-8002-1937-6). Intl Pubns Serv.

D'Alonzo, Bruno J. Educating Adolescents with Learning & Behavior Problems. 600p. 31.00 (ISBN 0-89443-847-6). Aspen Systems.

Dalrymple, Bryon. How to Call Wildlife. LC 74-33568. (Funk & W Bk.). (Illus.). 192p. 1975. 10.53i (ISBN 0-308-10208-8); pap. 4.50 o.p. (ISBN 0-308-10209-6, TYC-T). T Y Crowell.

Dalrymple, Byron. The Complete Book of Deer Hunting. (Stoeger Bks). 1975. pap. 5.95 o.s.i. (ISBN 0-695-80561-4). Follett.

--Modern Book of the Black Bass. (Stoeger Bks). (Illus.). 232p. 1976. pap. 5.95 o.s.i. (ISBN 0-695-80656-4). Follett.

Dalrymple, Byron W. The Complete Book of Deer Hunting. 256p. pap. 8.95 (ISBN 0-88317-050-7). Stoeger Pub Co.

--How to Rig & Fish Natural Baits. (Funk & W Bk.). (Illus.). 1976. 7.95 o.p. (ISBN 0-308-10289-4); pap. 4.50i (ISBN 0-308-10291-6, TYC-T). T Y Crowell.

Dalrymple, Dana & Dalrymple, Helen. Appalachian Trail Guide Southern Pennsylvania to Northern Virginia (Susquehanna River to Shenandoah National Park) 10th rev. ed. (Orig.). 1979. pap. 6.00 (ISBN 0-915746-12-3). Potomac Appalach.

Dalrymple, Douglas J. Sales Management: Concepts & Cases. (Wiley Series in Marketing). 485p. 1982. text ed. 26.95x (ISBN 0-471-07867-0); tchrs. manual 16.00 (ISBN 0-471-09963-5). Wiley.

Dalrymple, Douglas J. & Parsons, Leonard J. Marketing Mangement: Text & Cases. 2nd ed. LC 79-24833. (Wiley Ser. in Marketing). 723p. 1980. text ed. 30.95x (ISBN 0-471-03606-4). Wiley.

Dalrymple, Helen, jt. auth. see Dalrymple, Dana.

Dalrymple, Helen W., jt. auth. see Goodrum, Charles A.

Dalrymple, Martha, jt. auth. see Goldstone, Harmon H.

Dalrymple, Paul, et al. A Year of Snow Accumulation at Plateau Station; Thermal Properties & Heat Transfer Processes of Low-Temperature Snow; Radiative Heat Transfer; Process in Snow & Ice; Papers 1, 2, 3 & 4: Meteorological Studies at Plateau Station, Antarctica. Businger, Joost A., ed. (Antarctic Research Ser.: Vol. 25). 1977. pap. 13.50 (ISBN 0-87590-125-5). Am Geophysical.

Dalrymple, Willard, jt. auth. see Diehl, Harold S.

Dalrymple, Willard & Purcell, Elizabeth F., eds. Campus Health Programs. LC 76-29247. (Illus.). 1976. 7.50 o.p. (ISBN 0-914362-15-1). J Macy Foun.

Dalsass, Diana. The Good Cake Book. (Illus.). 272p. 1982. 12.95 (ISBN 0-453-00432-6, H432). NAL.

Dalton. Microbial Growth on C1 Compounds. 1981. 66.95 (ISBN 0-471-26098-3, Wiley Heyden). Wiley.

--The Miracle of Flight. 1977. 16.95 (ISBN 0-07-015207-1). McGraw.

Dalton & Stanley. South Pacific Handbook. (Illus.). 578p. 1982. 12.95 (ISBN 0-686-43406-4). Bradt Ent.

Dalton, Bill. Indonesia Handbook. (Illus.). 492p. Date not set. write for info. Moon Pubns CA.

--Indonesian Handbook. (Illus.). 1978. 9.50 o.p. (ISBN 0-9603322-0-0, Pub. by Moon Pubns). C E Tuttle.

Dalton, Bill, ed. see Stanley, David.

Dalton, Dan R., jt. auth. see Schuler, Randall S.

Dalton, David. Rolling Stone. 1979. pap. 4.95 (ISBN 0-8256-3929-8, Quick Fox). Putnam Pub Group.

--The Rolling Stones in Their Own Words. (Illus.). 128p. 1981. pap. 5.95 (ISBN 0-8256-3926-3, Quick Fox). Putnam Pub Group.

Dalton, David & Farren, Mick. Rolling Stones: In Their Own Words. (Illus.). 128p. (Orig.). 1983. pap. 6.95 (ISBN 0-399-41007-4). Delilah Bks.

Dalton, Dennis, jt. ed. see Wilson, Jeyaratnam.

Dalton, Elyse. Mirrors of the Heart. (Adventures in Love Ser.: No. 35). 1982. pap. 1.95 (ISBN 0-451-11875-8, AJ1875, Sig). NAL.

Dalton, G. E. Managing Agricultural Systems. xii, 163p. Date not set. 24.75 (ISBN 0-85334-165-6, Pub. by Applied Sci England). Elsevier.

Dalton, Gene W., et al. The Distribution of Authority in Formal Organizations. (Paperback Ser). 240p. 1973. pap. 3.95 o.p. (ISBN 0-262-54021-5). MIT Pr.

Dalton, Gene W., et al, eds. Organizational Structure & Design. 1970. pap. 13.50x (ISBN 0-256-00607-5). Irwin.

Dalton, George. Economic Systems & Society. (Education Ser). 1974. pap. 4.95 (ISBN 0-14-080912-0). Penguin.

Dalton, George, ed. Research in Economic Anthropology, Vol. 1. (Orig.). 1978. lib. bdg. 42.50 (ISBN 0-89232-040-0). Jai Pr.

--Research in Economic Anthropology, Vol. 2. 390p. 1979. 42.50 (ISBN 0-89232-085-0). Jai Pr.

--Research in Economic Anthropology, Vol. 4. 375p. 1981. 42.50 (ISBN 0-89232-189-X). Jai Pr.

--Research in Economic Anthropology: Annual, Vol. 3. 400p. (Orig.). 1980. lib. bdg. 42.50 (ISBN 0-89232-114-8). Jai Pr.

Dalton, George, ed. see Murra, John V.

Dalton, John. The Professional Cosmetologist. 2nd ed. (Illus.). 1979. text ed. 18.95 (ISBN 0-8299-0186-8); pap. text ed. 12.50 (ISBN 0-8299-0231-7); study guide 8.95 (ISBN 0-8299-0280-5). state board review questions 4.95 (ISBN 0-8299-0290-2); answer key 1.00 (ISBN 0-8299-0264-3). West Pub.

Dalton, John R. Basic Clinical Urology. 288p. 1982. text ed. 17.50 (ISBN 0-06-140664-3, Lippincott Medical). Lippincott.

Dalton, Katharina. Depression After Childbirth: How to Recognize & Treat Postnatal Illness. (Illus.). 192p. 1981. 16.95x (ISBN 0-19-217701-X); pap. 7.95x (ISBN 0-19-286008-9). Oxford U Pr.

--Once a Month. 2nd ed. 1983. pap. 6.95 (ISBN 0-89793-030-4). Hunter Hse.

Dalton, Lawrence. Those Elegant Rolls-Royce. 350p. 1981. 75.00x (ISBN 0-686-97075-6, Pub. by D Watson England). State Mutual Bk.

Dalton, Marie, jt. auth. see Wheeler, Carol A.

Dalton, Stephen. Caught in Motion: High Speed Nature Photography. 1982. 18.95 (ISBN 0-442-21951-2). Van Nos Reinhold.

Dalven, Rae. Anna Comnena. LC 78-169634. (World Authors Ser.: Greece: No. 213). lib. bdg. 15.95 o.p. (ISBN 0-8057-2240-8, Twayne). G K Hall.

Dalven, Rae, tr. see Ritsos, Yannis.

Dalvi, Quasia, jt. auth. see Hensher, David.

Dalwood, C., jt. auth. see Biggs, P.

Daly, Barbara J. Intensive Care Nursing. LC 78-78019. (Current Clinical Nursing Ser.). 1979. pap. 19.00 (ISBN 0-87488-575-2). Med Exam.

Daly, Carroll J. The Snarl of the Beast. 1981. 13.95 (ISBN 0-8398-2658-3, Gregg). G K Hall.

Daly, David D., jt. ed. see Klass, Donald W.

Daly, Donald F. Aim for a Job in Air Conditioning & Refrigeration. LC 70-114141. (Career Guidance Ser). 1971. pap. 4.50 (ISBN 0-668-02224-8). Arco.

--Your Career in Air Conditioning, Refrigeration & Related Engineering Careers. LC 78-701. 1979. lib. bdg. 7.95 (ISBN 0-668-04562-0); pap. 4.50 (ISBN 0-668-04573-6). Arco.

Daly, Gabriel. Asking the Father: A Study of the Prayer of Petition. 1982. 8.95 (ISBN 0-89453-277-4); pap. 5.95 (ISBN 0-686-32776-4). M Glazier.

Daly, Howell V., et al. An Introduction to Insect Biology & Diversity. (Illus.). 1978. text ed. 31.50 (ISBN 0-07-015208-X, C). McGraw.

Daly, J. M. Recognition & Specificity in Plant Host-Parasite Interactions. 370p. 1979. text ed. 49.50 o.p. (ISBN 0-8391-1440-0). Univ Park.

Daly, James & Bergman, Lee. A Hero's Welcome: The Conscience of Sergeant James Daly VS. the United States Army. LC 74-17652. (Illus.). 288p. 1975. 8.50 o.p. (ISBN 0-672-52030-3). Bobbs.

Daly, John P. A Generative Syntax of Penoles Mixtec. (Publications in Linguistics Ser.: No. 42). 90p. 1973. pap. 4.00x (ISBN 0-88312-052-6); microfiche 1.50x (ISBN 0-88312-452-1). Summer Inst Ling.

Daly, John W., et al, eds. Physiology & Pharmacology of Adenosine Derivatives. 350p. 1982. text ed. write for info. (ISBN 0-89004-833-9). Raven.

Daly, Kathleen. Dinosaurs. (Look-Look Ser.). (Illus.). 1977. PLB 5.38 o.p. (ISBN 0-307-61835-8, 11835, Golden Pr); pap. 1.25 o.p. (ISBN 0-307-11835-5). Western Pub.

--Raggedy Ann & Andy. 1977. pap. 2.95 o.s.i. (ISBN 0-440-57269-X, Delta). Dell.

Daly, Kathleen N. Body Words: A Dictionary of the Human Body, How It Works, & Some of the Things That Affect It. LC 79-7598. (Illus.). 176p. (gr. 4-6). 1980. 10.95 (ISBN 0-385-11485-0); PLB o.p. (ISBN 0-385-11486-9). Doubleday.

--A Child's Book of Animals. LC 74-16145. 48p. (gr. k-3). 1975. 7.95a o.p. (ISBN 0-686-85889-1); PLB (ISBN 0-385-09751-4). Doubleday.

--A Child's Book of Insects. LC 74-14994. (gr. k-4). 1977. 7.95a o.p. (ISBN 0-686-85891-3); PLB (ISBN 0-385-09744-1). Doubleday.

--The Macmillan Picture Wordbook. LC 82-6619. (Illus.). 80p. (ps-1). 1982. 7.95 (ISBN 0-02-725600-6). Macmillan.

--The Simon & Schuster Question & Answer Book. Barish, Wendy, ed. (Illus.). 320p. (gr. 3 up). 1982. 8.95 (ISBN 0-671-44427-1). Wanderer Bks.

Daly, Lloyd W. Iohannis Philoponi: De Vocabulis Quae Diversum Signification Exhibent Secundum Differentiam Accentus. LC 81-72156. (Memoirs Ser.: Vol. 151). 1983. 20.00 (ISBN 0-87169-151-5). Am Philos.

Daly, Marsha. Steve Martin--A Wild & Crazy Guy: An Unauthorized Biography-Well, Excuuuse Us! (Orig.). 1980. pap. 2.25 o.p. (ISBN 0-451-09206-6, E9206, Sig). NAL.

Daly, Maureen. Seventeenth Summer. 293p. 1981. Repr. PLB 16.95x (ISBN 0-89966-355-9). Buccaneer Bks.

--Seventeenth Summer. (Illus.). (gr. 9 up). 1942. 7.95 o.p. (ISBN 0-396-02322-3). Dodd.

--What's Your P. Q. - Personality Quotient? rev. ed. (Illus.). (gr. 9 up). 1966. 5.95 o.p. (ISBN 0-396-03365-2). Dodd.

Daly, N. R., ed. Advances in Mass Spectrometry, Vol. 7 In 2 Parts. 1977. 380.00 (ISBN 0-471-25657-9, Pub. by Wiley Heyden). Wiley.

Daly, Peter M. Index Emblematicus: The Emblems of Andreas Alciatus, Vol. 1. 800p. 1983. 95.00x (ISBN 0-8020-2425-4). U of Toronto Pr.

--Literature in the Light of the Emblem: Structural Parallels Between the Emblem & Literature in the Sixteenth & Seventeenth Centuries. LC 79-11863. (Illus.). 1979. 25.00x o.p. (ISBN 0-8020-5390-4). U of Toronto Pr.

Daly, Peter M., ed. The European Emblem: Towards an Index Emblematicus. 152p. pap. text ed. 9.75 (ISBN 0-88920-090-4, Pub. by Wilfred Laurier U Pr Canada). Humanities.

Daly, Reginald D. Changing World of the Ice Age. 1934. text ed. 19.50 (ISBN 0-686-83502-6). Elliots Bks.

Daly, Richard R. After Day One. 32p. (Orig.). Date not set. pap. text ed. 4.00 (ISBN 0-686-83760-6). ALA.

Daly, Robert. God's Altar: The World & the Flesh in Puritan Poetry. LC 77-76182. 1978. 18.95x (ISBN 0-520-03480-5). U of Cal Pr.

Daly, Saralyn R. Katherine Mansfield. (English Authors Ser.: No. 23). 1965. lib. bdg. 12.95 o.p. (ISBN 0-8057-1372-7, Twayne). G K Hall.

Daly, Saralyn R., tr. from Span. see Ruiz, Juan.

Daly, Treve, jt. auth. see Thompson, Raymond.

Dalzell, George W., jt. auth. see Canfield, George L.

Dalzell, J. Ralph. Plan Reading for Home Builders. 2nd ed. LC 72-7068. Orig. Title: Home Blueprint Reading for Builders. (Illus.). 160p. 4.25 (ISBN 0-07-015221-7, P&RB). McGraw.

--Repairing & Remodeling Guide for Home Interiors: Planning, Materials, Methods. 2nd ed. Merritt, Fred, ed. Orig. Title: Remodeling Guide for Home Interiors. (Illus.). 448p. 1973. 16.50 o.p. (ISBN 0-07-015222-5, P&RB). McGraw.

Dalzell, Ralph J. Repairing & Remodeling Guide for Home Interiors: Planning, Materials, Methods. 2nd ed. LC 72-13413. 432p. 1956. Repr. of 1973 ed. 21.50 o.p. (ISBN 0-07-015222-5). Krieger.

Dalzell, Ralph J. & Merritt, Frederick. Plan Reading for Home Builders. 2nd ed. LC 82-14057. 186p. 1983. Repr. of 1972 ed. write for info. (ISBN 0-89874-393-1). Krieger.

Dalzell, W. R. The Shell Guide to the History of London. (Illus.). 1982. 29.95 (ISBN 0-393-01593-9). Norton.

Dam, Kenneth W., jt. auth. see Shultz, George P.

Dam, Mogens, ed. see Epilepsy International Symposium, 12th. Copenhagen, Denmark, et al.

Damachi, U. G., et al, eds. Industrial Relations in Africa. LC 79-12765. 35.00x (ISBN 0-312-41457-9). St Martin.

Damachi, Ukandi G, et al. Development Paths in Africa & China. LC 75-45447. 1976. 27.50 o.p. (ISBN 0-89158-541-9). Westview.

Damask, A. C. & Swenberg, C. E., eds. Medical Physics, Vol. 3. Date not set. price not set (ISBN 0-12-201203-8). Acad Pr.

D'Amato, Alex, jt. auth. see D'Amato, Jane.

D'Amato, Alex, jt. auth. see D'Amato, Janet.

D'Amato, Francesco. Nuclear Cytology in Relation to Development. LC 76-46045. (Developmental & Cell Biology Ser.: No. 6). 1977. 60.00 (ISBN 0-521-21508-0). Cambridge U Pr.

D'Amato, Jane & D'Amato, Alex. Algonquian & Iroquois Crafts for You to Make. LC 79-15487. (Illus.). 96p. (gr. 3 up). 1979. PLB 8.29 o.p. (ISBN 0-671-32979-0). Messner.

D'Amato, Janet & D'Amato, Alex. African Crafts for You to Make. LC 70-75690. (Illus.). 64p. (gr. 4 up). 1969. PLB 7.79 o.p. (ISBN 0-671-32130-7). Messner.

--Colonial Crafts for You to Make. LC 74-19005. (Illus.). 64p. (gr. 4-6). 1975. 8.29 o.p. (ISBN 0-671-32706-2). Messner.

D'Amato, M. R. Experimental Psychology: Methodology, Psychophysics & Learning. 1970. text ed. 30.00 (ISBN 0-07-015230-6, C). McGraw.

Da Matta, Roberto. A Divided World: Apinaye Social Structure. (Studies in Cultural Anthropology: No. 6). (Illus.). 216p. 1982. text ed. 40.00x (ISBN 0-674-21288-6). Harvard U Pr.

Damberger. Voyage dans l'Interieur de l'Afrique, 2 vols. (Bibliotheque Africaine Ser.). 676p. (Fr.). 1974. Repr. of 1801 ed. lib. bdg. 175.50x o.p. (ISBN 0-8287-0246-2). Clearwater Pub.

D'Amboise, Christopher. Leap Year: A Year in the Life of a Dancer. LC 82-45352. (Illus.). 206p. 1982. 17.95 (ISBN 0-385-17449-7). Doubleday.

D'Amboise, Jaques & Cooke, Hope. Teaching the Magic of Dance. (Illus.). 1983. price not set (ISBN 0-671-47026-4). S&S.

D'Ambrosie, Charles A., jt. auth. see Archer, Stephen H.

D'Ambrosio, Charles A. Principles of Modern Investments. LC 75-34094. (Illus.). 512p. 1976. text ed. 23.95 (ISBN 0-574-19210-7, 13-2210); instr's guide avail. (ISBN 0-574-19211-5, 13-2211). SRA.

D'Ambrosio, Charles A., jt. auth. see Archer, Stephen N.

D'Ambrosio, Richard. Leonora. 1978. 9.95 o.p. (ISBN 0-07-015226-8, GB). McGraw.

Dame, F. J., et al. Exploratory Business: Distributive, Clerical, Accounting-Data Processing, Stenographic Occupations. 5th ed. 1971. text ed. 7.44 (ISBN 0-07-015227-6, G); tchr's. manual & key 7.40 (ISBN 0-07-015228-4). McGraw.

D'Amelio, Dan. Silvabamba. LC 77-74837. (Pacesetters Ser.). (Illus.). 64p. (gr. 4 up). 1978. PLB 8.65 (ISBN 0-516-02158-3). Childrens.

Damian, Peter. Book of Gomorrah: An Eleventh-Century Treaties Against Clerical Homosexual Practices. Payer, Pierre J., tr. 120p. 1982. pap. text ed. 7.50x (ISBN 0-88920-123-4, 40794, Pub. by Wilfred Laurier U Pr Canada). Humanities.

Damiani, Bruno M. Francisco Lopez De Ubeda. (World Authors Ser.). 1977. lib. bdg. 15.95 (ISBN 0-8057-6271-X, Twayne). G K Hall.

--Montemayor's Diana, Music, & the Visual Arts. 1982. 11.00x (ISBN 0-942260-28-7). Hispanic Seminary.

Damiani, Bryno M. Francisco Deligado. (World Authors Ser.: No. 335). 12.50 o.p. (ISBN 0-8057-2265-3, Twayne). G K Hall.

Damis, John. Conflict in Northwest Africa: The Western Sahara Dispute. (Publication Ser.: 278). (Illus.). 196p. 1983. 19.95 (ISBN 0-8179-7781-3). Hoover Inst Pr.

Damjan, Mischa. The False Flamingoes. LC 70-105399. (Illus.). 32p. (ps-3). 5.95 (ISBN 0-87592-016-0). Scroll Pr.

--Goodbye Little Bird. Bell, Anthea, tr. from Ger. LC 82-20954. (Illus.). 20p. (gr. 2-4). 1983. PLB 11.95 (ISBN 0-571-12520-4). Faber & Faber.

--The Little Seahorse. LC 82-20953. (Illus.). (gr. 2-6). 1983. PLB 11.95 (ISBN 0-571-12519-0). Faber & Faber.

Damjanov, Ivan. General Pathology. 2nd ed. (Medical Outline Ser.). 1982. pap. 23.50 (ISBN 0-87488-628-7). Med Exam.

--Ultrastructural Pathology of Human Tumors, Vol. 1. Horrobin, D. F., ed. LC 79-319782. (Annual Research Reviews Ser.). 1979. 24.00 (ISBN 0-88831-045-5). Eden Pr.

--Ultrastructural Pathology of Human Tumors, Vol. 2. Horrobin, D. F., ed. (Annual Research Reviews). 144p. 1980. 24.00 (ISBN 0-88831-082-X). Eden Pr.

Damjanov, Ivan & Knowles, Barbara, eds. The Human Teratomas. (Contemporary Biomedicine Ser.). 416p. 1983. 49.50 (ISBN 0-89603-040-7). Humana.

Damlouji, Namir F. & Feighner, John. Psychiatry Specialty Board Review. 1983. pap. text ed. price not set. Med Exam.

Damm, Helene Von see Von Damm, Helene.

Dammann, Nancy. A Social History of the Frontier Nursing Service. (Illus.). 179p. (Orig.). 1982. pap. 5.95 (ISBN 0-9609376-0-9). Soc Change Pr.

Dammers, Richard H. Richard Steele. (English Authors Ser.). 1982. lib. bdg. 13.95 (ISBN 0-8057-6837-8, Twayne). G K Hall.

Damon, Lee. Laugh with Me, Love with Me. (Second Chance at Love Ser.: No. 120). 1983. pap. 1.75 (ISBN 0-515-07208-7). Jove Pubns.

Damon, Lorraine, jt. auth. see Naidech, Howard J.

Damon, Phillip. Modes of Analogy in Ancient & Medieval Verse. (California Library Reprint Series: No. 33). 1973. 19.95x (ISBN 0-520-02366-8). U of Cal Pr.

Damon, S. Foster. A Blake Dictionary: The Ideas & Symbols of William Blake. LC 65-18187. (Illus.). 472p. 1965. text ed. 35.00x (ISBN 0-87057-088-9, Pub. by Brown U Pr). U Pr of New Eng.

--A Blake Dictionary: The Ideas & Symbols of William Blake, with a New Index by Morris Eaves. LC 78-65433. (Illus.). 1979. pap. 15.00 (ISBN 0-394-73688-5). Shambhala Pubns.

Damon, S. Foster, ed. see Blake, William.

Damon, William. Social & Personality Development: Essays on the Growth of the Child. 504p. 1983. pap. text ed. 19.95x (ISBN 0-393-95307-6). Norton.

--Social & Personality Development: From Infancy Through Adolescence. (Illus.). 1983. 25.00 (ISBN 0-393-01742-7); pap. text ed. 12.95x04381580x (ISBN 0-393-95248-7). Norton.

Damore, Leo. In His Garden. 656p. 1982. pap. 3.95 o.p. (ISBN 0-425-05707-0). Berkley Pub.

Da Mota, A. Teixeira. Some Aspects of Portugese Colonisation & Sea Trade in West Africa in the 15th & 16th Centuries. (Hans Wolff Memorial Lecture Ser.). 29p. (Orig.). 1978. pap. text ed. 2.50 (ISBN 0-941934-22-5). Ind U Afro-Amer Arts.

D'Amoto, Richard F., jt. auth. see McGinnis, Michael R.

Damp, Margaret M. Finding Fulfillment in the Manse. 115p. 1978. pap. 2.95 o.p. (ISBN 0-8341-0544-6). Beacon Hill.

Damp, Philip. Growing Dahlias. (Illus.). 140p. 1981. 12.50x o.p. (ISBN 0-7099-0800-8, Pub. by Croom Helm Ltd England). Biblio Dist.

Damp, Phillip. Growing Dahlias. (Illus.). 139p. 1982. 12.95 (ISBN 0-7099-0800-8). Timber.

Dampier, Robert. To the Sandwich Islands on H.M.S. Blonde. Joerger, Pauline K., ed. LC 73-147156. 1971. 14.00 (ISBN 0-87022-176-0). UH Pr.

Dampier, William. Voyage to New Holland. 256p. 1982. text ed. 22.50x (ISBN 0-904387-75-5, Pub. by Alan Sutton England); pap. text ed. 10.50x (ISBN 0-86299-006-8). Humanities.

Damron, O. Rex & O'Neill, Daniel J. An Introduction to Interpersonal & Public Communication. 139p. 1981. pap. text ed. 5.95x (ISBN 0-89641-021-8). American Pr.

Damrosch, Barbara. Theme Gardens. LC 82-60062. (Illus.). 224p. 1982. 19.95 (ISBN 0-89480-218-6); pap. 10.95 (ISBN 0-89480-217-8). Workman Pub.

Damrosch, Walter J. My Musical Life. LC 71-109725. (Illus.). 376p. 1972. Repr. of 1923 ed. lib. bdg. 18.75x (ISBN 0-8371-4215-6, DAML). Greenwood.

Dams, T., et al, eds. Food & Population: Priorities in Decision Making. 208p. 1979. text ed. 26.00x (ISBN 0-566-00250-7). Gower Pub Ltd.

Dan, Alice, et al. The Menstrual Cycle: A Synthesis of Interdisciplinary Research, Vol. 1. LC 80-18837. (Illus.). 1980. text ed. 28.00 (ISBN 0-8261-2630-8); text ed. 48.00 vol. 1-2 set. Springer Pub.

Dan, B. Van see Van Dan, B.

Dan, Joseph, ed. The Teachings of Hasidism. (Orig.). 1983. pap. text ed. 9.95x (ISBN 0-87441-346-X). Behrman.

Dana, Barbara. Crazy Eights. LC 77-25645. (gr. 7 up). 1978. 7.95o.p. (ISBN 0-06-021388-4, HarpJ); PLB 9.89 (ISBN 0-06-021389-2). Har-Row.

--Zucchini. LC 80-8448. (A Charlotte Zolotow Bk.). (Illus.). 128p. (gr. 3-5). 1982. 10.10i (ISBN 0-06-021394-9, HarpJ); PLB 10.89g (ISBN 0-06-021395-7). Har-Row.

Dana, Bill, jt. auth. see Peter, Laurence J.

Dana, E. S. & Hurlbut, C. S. Minerals & How to Study Them. 3rd ed. 323p. 1949. pap. 16.50 (ISBN 0-471-19195-7). Wiley.

Dana, H. E. El Mundo Del Nuevo Testamento. Villarello, Ildefonso, tr. 288p. 1977. pap. 4.95 (ISBN 0-311-04342-9). Casa Bautista.

Dana, H. E. & Mantey, J. R. Gramatica Griega Del Nuevo Testamento. Robleto, Adolfo & De Clark, Catalina, trs. 1979. pap. 10.50 (ISBN 0-311-42010-9). Casa Bautista.

Dana, H. E. & Mantey, R. Manual Grammar of the Greek New Testament: With Index. 1957. text ed. 19.95x (ISBN 0-02-327070-5, 32707). Macmillan.

Dana, J. D., et al. Systems of Minerology, 3 vols. 7th ed. Incl. Vol. 1. Elements, Sulfides, Sulfosalts, Oxides. 1944. 66.50 (ISBN 0-471-19239-2); Vol. 2. Halides, Nitrates, Borates, Carbonates, Sulfates, Phosphates, Arsenates, Tungstates, Molybdates. 1951. 66.95 (ISBN 0-471-19272-4); Vol. 3. Silica Minerals. 1962. 49.95 (ISBN 0-471-19287-2). Pub. by Wiley-Interscience). Wiley.

Dana, Julian. The Sacramento: River of Gold. (Illus.). 306p. Date not set. pap. 7.95 (ISBN 0-934136-22-X). Western Tanager.

Dana, Richard H., Jr. Two Years Before the Mast. Date not set. pap. 3.50 (ISBN 0-451-51764-4, CE1764, Sig Classics). NAL.

Dana, Robert. In a Fugitive Season. LC 82-75943. 80p. 1979. 10.95 (ISBN 0-8040-0804-3); pap. 5.95 (ISBN 0-8040-0805-1). Swallow.

--Power of the Visible. LC 82-72833. 71p. 1971. 8.95 (ISBN 0-8040-0551-6); pap. 4.95 (ISBN 0-8040-0646-6). Swallow.

Dana, Samuel T. & Fairfax, Sally K. Forest & Range Policy. 2nd ed. (Illus.). 496p. 1980. text ed. 29.50 (ISBN 0-07-015288-8, P&RB). McGraw.

Dana, William S. How to Know the Wild Flowers. rev. ed. Hylander, Clarence J., ed. (Illus.). 1963. pap. 6.00 (ISBN 0-486-20332-8). Dover.

Dance, Bill, jt. auth. see Sosin, Mark.

Dance, J. B. Cold Cathode Tubes. (Illus.). 1969. 10.00x o.p. (ISBN 0-685-20566-5). Transatlantic.

Dance, Peter, jt. auth. see Abbott, Tucker.

Dance, S. P. The Collector's Encyclopedia of Shells. 2nd ed. 1982. 24.95 (ISBN 0-07-015292-6). McGraw.

Dance, Stanley. The World of Earl Hines. (Da Capo Quality Paperbacks). (Illus.). 334p. 1983. pap. 10.95 (ISBN 0-306-80182-5). Da Capo.

Dance, Stanley, ed. Jazz Era: The Forties. (Roots of Jazz Ser.). 253p. 1983. Repr. of 1961 ed. lib. bdg. 27.50 (ISBN 0-306-76191-2). Da Capo.

Dancis, J. & Hwang, J. C., eds. Perinatal Pharmacology: Problems & Priorities. LC 73-91163. 240p. 1974. 30.00 (ISBN 0-911216-70-7). Raven.

Danco, Katharine L. From the Other Side of the Bed: A Woman Looks at Life in the Family Business. LC 81-13032. 1981. 19.95 (ISBN 0-9603614-2-1). Univ Pr OH.

Danco, Leon A. Inside the Family Business. LC 80-23512. (N A). 1980. 19.95 (ISBN 0-9603614-1-3). Univ Pr OH.

Danco, Leon A. & Jonovic, Donald J. Outside Directors in the Family Owned Business: Why, When, Who & How. LC 81-12931. 1981. 29.95 (ISBN 0-9603614-3-X). Univ Pr OH.

Dancu, Dumitru, jt. auth. see Dancu, Juliana.

Dancu, Juliana & Dancu, Dumitru. Romanian Icons on Glass. (Illus.). 179p. 1983. 13.50 (ISBN 0-8143-1711-1). Wayne St U Pr.

Dandamayev, M. A., ed. Societies & Languages of the Ancient Near East: Studies in Honour of I. M. Diakonoff. 380p. 1982. pap. 48.00x (ISBN 0-686-82295-1, 51309, Pub. by Aris & Phillips England) (ISBN 0-85668-205-5). Humanities.

Dandekar, Hemalata C. The Planner's Use of Information: Techniques for Collection, Organization & Communication. (Environmental Design Ser.: Vol. 2). 272p. 1982. text ed. 29.75 (ISBN 0-87933-429-0). Hutchinson Ross.

Dandekar, M. M. & Sharma, N. K. Water Power Engineering. 1980. pap. text ed. 15.00x o.p. (ISBN 0-7069-0700-0, Pub. by Vikas India). Advent NY.

Dandekar, R. N. The Age of Guptas & Other Essays. 1982. 30.00 (ISBN 0-8364-0916-7, Pub. by Ajanta). South Asia Bks.

Dandekar, V. M. Peasant Worker Alliance. (R. C. Dutt Lectures on Political Economy: 1979). 104p. 1981. pap. text ed. 8.95 (ISBN 0-86131-274-0, Pub. by Orient Longman Ltd India). Apt Bks.

--Peasant-Worker Alliance: Its Basis in the Indian Economy, R. C. Dutt Lectures on Political Economy, 1979. 104p. 1981. cloth 20.00x (ISBN 0-686-94093-8, Pub. by Sangam Bks England). State Mutual Bk.

Dandekar, Varsha. Salads of India. 90p. 1983. 13.95 (ISBN 0-89594-075-2); pap. 4.95 (ISBN 0-89594-074-4). Crossing Pr.

Dandelot, jt. auth. see Dorst.

Dando, William A. The Geography of Famine. LC 80-11145. (Scripta Series in Geography). 209p. 1980. 32.95x o.p. (ISBN 0-470-26956-1). Halsted Pr.

D'Andrea, Jeanne, ed. see Barron, Stephanie, et al.

Dandy, J. E., ed. List of British Vascular Plants: Prepared by J. E. Dandy for the British Museum (Natural History) & the Botanical Society of the British Isles. xvi, 176p. 1982. Repr. of 1958 ed. 12.50x (ISBN 0-565-00449-2, Pub. by Brit Mus Nat Hist England). Sabbot-Natural Hist Bks.

Daneke, Gregory A. & Lagassa, George K. Energy Policy & Public Administration. LC 79-3182. 336p. 1980. 31.95x (ISBN 0-669-03395-2). Lexington Bks.

Daneke, Gregory A., jt. auth. see Steiss, Alan W.

Daneke, Gregory A., ed. Energy, Economics & the Environment: Toward a Comprehensive Perspective. LC 81-47690. 304p. 1981. 29.95x (ISBN 0-669-04717-1). Lexington Bks.

Daneker, Gail, jt. auth. see Grossman, Richard.

Daneliuk, F. A. Un Systeme Interactif sur Mini-Ordinateur pour la Recherche Documentaire et la Gestion de Bibliotheques. 19p. 1979. pap. 2.00 o.p. (ISBN 0-88936-192-4, IDRC-TS14F, IDRC). Unipub.

Danella, Utta. Those Von Tallien Women. 352p. 1980. pap. 2.75 o.p. (ISBN 0-380-47506-5, 47506). Avon.

Daneman, Meredith. A Chance to Sit Down. 176p. 1981. pap. 2.25 o.s.i. (ISBN 0-380-54163-7, 54163). Avon.

Daner, Selma, et al. The Passover Feast Two. 1978. 9.75 (ISBN 0-686-27071-1). Am Mizrachi Women.

Danforth, Amy. Birch Hollow Jubilee. (Illus.). 24p. (gr. 4-8). 1982. pap. 2.00 (ISBN 0-940072-01-7). Dragonfly Pr.

--Patchwork of Poems. (Illus.). 20p. (Orig.). (gr. 1-6). 1981. pap. 3.00 (ISBN 0-940072-00-9). Dragonfly Pr.

Danforth, David N., ed. Obstetrics & Gynecology. 4th ed. (Illus.). 1200p. 1982. text ed. 59.00 (ISBN 0-06-140696-1, Harper Medical). Lippincott.

Dang, Nghiem. Viet-Nam: Politics & Public Administration. (Illus.). 1966. 15.00x o.p. (ISBN 0-8248-0049-4, Eastwest Ctr). UH Pr.

D'Angelo, A., jt. ed. see Mannucci, P. M.

D'Angelo, Edward, et al. Contemporary East European Marxism, Vol. II. (Praxis: Vol. 7). 275p. 1982. pap. text ed. 27.75x (ISBN 0-391-02788-3). Humanities.

D'Angelo, Frank J. Process & Thought in Composition. 2nd ed. 1980. text ed. 12.95 (ISBN 0-316-16981-1); tchr's ed. avail. (ISBN 0-316-16986-2). Little.

D'Angelo, Gary, jt. auth. see Stewart, John.

D'Angelo, Henry. Microcomputer Structures. 1981. 18.95 (ISBN 0-07-015294-2, BYTE Bks); instr's manual 8.95 (ISBN 0-07-015298-5). McGraw.

D'Angelo, Louise. Too Busy for God? Think Again! 120p. 1975. pap. 2.50 (ISBN 0-686-81631-5). TAN Bks Pubs.

D'Angelo, Mary R. Moses in the Letter to the Hebrews. LC 78-12917. (Society of Biblical Literature, Dissertation Ser.: No. 42). 1979. 12.00 o.p. (ISBN 0-89130-265-4, 060142); pap. 9.95 (ISBN 0-89130-333-2). Scholars Pr Ca.

Dangerfield, George. Awakening of American Nationalism, 1815-1828. (New American Nation Ser.). pap. 7.95xi (ISBN 0-06-133061-2, TB3061, Torch). Har-Row.

--The Damnable Question: A Study in Anglo-Irish Relations. pap. 5.95 o.p. (ISBN 0-316-17201-4, Atlantic-Little, Brown). Little.

--The Damnable Question: A Study of Anglo-Irish Relations. 1976. 14.95 o.p. (ISBN 0-316-17200-6, Pub. by Atlantic Monthly Pr); pap. 5.95 o.p. (ISBN 0-316-17201-4). Little.

--Defiance to the Old World: The Story Behind the Monroe Doctrine. (Crossroads of America Ser.). (gr. 4-8). 1970. PLB 4.49 o.p. (ISBN 0-399-60124-4). Putnam Pub Group.

--The Era of Good Feelings. LC 51-14815. 1963. pap. 5.50 (ISBN 0-15-629000-6, Harv). HarBraceJ.

--Strange Death of Liberal England, 1910-1914. (Illus.). 1961. pap. 3.95 (ISBN 0-399-50227-0, 50, Perigee). Putnam Pub Group.

Dangerfield, Royden, ed. see Gordon, David R.

D'Angerville, Count, ed. Living Descendants of Blood Royal in America: World Nobility & Peerage, Vol. 4. (Illus.). 1142p. 1970. 45.00x (ISBN 0-902516-00-0). Intl Pubns Serv.

Dangoor, Daniella, tr. see Hocquenghem, Guy.

Danhof, Kenneth & Smith, Carol. Computing System Fundamentals: An Approach Based on Microcomputers. LC 79-14933. 1981. text ed. 26.95 (ISBN 0-201-01298-7); instrs' manual 2.00 (ISBN 0-201-01245-6). A-W.

Daniel & Terrell. Business Statistics: Basic Concepts & Methodology. 1982. text ed. 28.95 (ISBN 0-686-84527-7); write for info. supplementary material. HM.

Daniel, A. R. Baker's Dictionary. 2nd ed. 1971. 18.50 (ISBN 0-444-20121-1). Elsevier.

--Bakery Materials & Methods. 4th ed. 1978. Repr. 20.50 (Pub. by Applied Sci England). Elsevier.

--Bakery Questions Answered. 1972. 18.50 (ISBN 0-85334-540-6, Pub. by Applied Sci England). Elsevier.

--Up-to-Date Confectionery. 4th ed. (Illus.). 1978. pap. text ed. 28.75x (ISBN 0-85334-791-3, Pub. by Applied Sci England). Elsevier.

Daniel, Anita. Story of Albert Schweitzer. (World Landmark Ser.: No. 33). (Illus.). (gr. 7-9). 1957. 2.95 (ISBN 0-394-80533-X, BYR); PLB 5.99 (ISBN 0-394-90533-4). Random.

Daniel, Becky. I Can Draw a Circus. (ps-3). 1982. 5.95 (ISBN 0-86653-082-7, GA 428). Good Apple.

Daniel, Becky & Daniel, Charlie. Good Apple & Teacher Helpers. 1981. 9.95 (ISBN 0-86653-047-9, GA 282). Good Apple.

--Rainbow Factory. (ps-2). 1982. 5.95 (ISBN 0-86653-063-0, GA 427). Good Apple.

--Ready, Set...Read! (ps-3). 1979. 5.95 (ISBN 0-916456-45-5, GA114). Good Apple.

Daniel, Charles, jt. auth. see Smith, Page.

Daniel, Charlie, jt. auth. see Daniel, Becky.

Daniel, Cletus E. The ACLU & the Wagner Act: An Inquiry into the Depression-Era Crisis of American Liberalism. LC 80-22450. (Cornell Studies in Industrial & Labor Relations: No. 20). 146p. 1981. 13.50 o.s.i. (ISBN 0-87546-082-8); pap. 7.95 (ISBN 0-87546-083-6). ILR Pr.

Daniel, Colin. Demon Tree. (Twilight Ser.: No. 9). (YA) (gr. 7-12). 1983. pap. 1.95 (ISBN 0-440-92097-3, LFL). Dell.

Daniel, Cuthbert. Applications of Statistics to Industrial Experimentation. LC 76-2012. (Applied Probability & Statistics Ser.). 294p. 1976. 39.95x (ISBN 0-471-19469-7, Pub. by Wiley-Interscience). Wiley.

Daniel, Cuthbert & Wood, Fred S. Fitting Equations to Data: Computer Analysis of Multifactor Data. 2nd ed. LC 79-11110. (Probability & Mathematical Statistics Ser.: Applied Section). 1980. 36.95 (ISBN 0-471-05370-8, Pub. by Wiley-Interscience). Wiley.

Daniel, E. J. Any Other Song: A Plea for Holistic Communication. LC 79-24892. 185p. 1980. pap. text ed. 10.95 o.p. (ISBN 0-87619-460-9). R J Brady.

Daniel, E. Valentine, jt. auth. see Keyes, Charles F.

Daniel, Eleanor, rev. by see Leavitt, Guy P.

Daniel, George, ed. see Camus, Albert.

Daniel, George B., ed. see Sartre, Jean-Paul.

Daniel, Glenda. Dune Country: A Guide for Hikers & Naturalists. LC 82-74193. (Illus.). 167p. 1977. pap. 6.95 (ISBN 0-8040-0757-8). Swallow.

Daniel, James W., jt. auth. see Noble, Ben.

Daniel, Joe & Britton, Phil. Texas on the Halfshell: Tex-Mex, Barbecue, Chili & Lone Star Delights. LC 81-43408. (Illus.). 240p. 1982. pap. 12.95 (ISBN 0-385-17904-9, Dolp). Doubleday.

Daniel, John. Ava Gardner. (Illus.). 224p. 1983. 10.95 (ISBN 0-312-06240-0). St Martin.

--In the Quiet of the Land. 24p. 1982. pap. write for info. (ISBN 0-9605512-1-2). Clearwater OR.

Daniel, Katinka S. Kodaly Approach, Method Book One. 2nd ed. LC 79-53162. 204p. 1979. wire 21.00 (ISBN 0-916656-13-6); materials for transparencies 21.00 (ISBN 0-916656-14-4). Mark Foster Mus.

--Kodaly in Kindergarten: Fifty Lesson Plans, Curriculum, Song Collection. LC 81-68473. (Illus.). 190p. (Orig.). 1981. wire bdg. 18.50 (ISBN 0-916656-15-2, MF-15). Mark Foster Mus.

Daniel, Katinka S., jt. auth. see Zemke, Lorna.

Daniel, Keith W. Francis Poulenc: His Artistic Development & Musical Style. Buelow, George, ed. LC 81-19767. (Studies in Musicology: No. 52). 400p. 1982. 49.95 (ISBN 0-8357-1284-2, Pub. by UMI Res Pr). Univ Microfilms.

Daniel, Lusk. O, Rosie. LC 78-23579. (Illus., Orig.). 1979. pap. 5.95x (ISBN 0-914140-04-3). Carpenter Pr.

Daniel, Megan. The Sensible Courtship. 1982. pap. 2.25 (ISBN 0-451-11739-5, H420). NAL.

Daniel, Norman A. Heroes & Saracens: A Reinterpretation of the Chansons de Geste. 196p. 1983. 27.50 (ISBN 0-85224-430-4, Pub. by Edinburgh U Pr). Columbia U Pr.

Daniel, Oliver. Stokowski: A Counterpoint of View. LC 82-2443. (Illus.). 1982. 24.95 (ISBN 0-396-07936-9). Dodd.

Daniel, P. Africanisation, Nationalisation & Inequality. LC 78-31563. (DAE-Industrial Relations & Labour Ser.). 1979. 37.50 (ISBN 0-521-22179-4); pap. 17.95x (ISBN 0-521-29623-4). Cambridge U Pr.

Daniel, Pete, jt. auth. see Smock, Raymond.

Daniel, R. P. Gospel & the Path of Separation. pap. 2.50 (ISBN 0-88172-016-X). Believers Bkshelf.

--Let's Play Bible Detective. 36p. pap. 2.00 (ISBN 0-88172-017-8). Believers Bkshelf.

--Outline of Booth's Chart of the Ages. pap. 2.00 (ISBN 0-88172-018-6). Believers Bkshelf.

--Outlines for Christian Youth. pap. 4.50 (ISBN 0-88172-019-4). Believers Bkshelf.

--The Tabernacle Talks Today. pap. 3.95 (ISBN 0-88172-020-8). Believers Bkshelf.

Daniel, R. P., ed. see Dennett, E.

Daniel, R. P., ed. see Hole, F. B.

Daniel, Ralph T. The Anthem in New England Before Eighteen Hundred. (Music Reprint Ser.). 1979. Repr. of 1966 ed. 32.50 (ISBN 0-306-79511-6). Da Capo.

Daniel, Ralph T., jt. auth. see Apel, Willi.

Daniel, Robert L. American Philanthropy in the Near East, 1820-1960. LC 74-81451. xii, 322p. 1970. 15.00x (ISBN 0-8214-0063-0, 82-80695). Ohio U Pr.

Daniel, Roger P., ed. see Cutting, Jorge.

Daniel, Roger P., ed. see Mackintosh, Carlos H.

Daniel, Samuel, tr. see Giovio, Paolo.

Daniel, Sol, jt. ed. see Gilbert, Leopold.

Daniel, Theodore W. & Helms, John. Baker's Principles of Silviculture. 2nd ed. (Illus.). 1979. text ed. 32.00 (ISBN 0-07-015297-7, C). McGraw.

Daniel, Walter C. Black Journals of the United States. LC 81-13440. (Historical Guides to the World's Periodicals & Newspapers). 400p. 1982. lib. bdg. 45.00 (ISBN 0-313-20704-6, DBJ). Greenwood.

--Images of the Preacher in Afro-American Literature. LC 80-67247. 250p. (Orig.). 1981. lib. bdg. 20.00 (ISBN 0-8191-1662-9); pap. 10.25 (ISBN 0-8191-1663-7). U Pr of Amer.

Daniel, Wayne W. Applied Nonparametric Statistics. LC 77-74515. (Illus.). 1978. text ed. 27.50 (ISBN 0-395-25795-6); solutions manual 1.25 (ISBN 0-395-25796-4). HM.
--Biostatistics: A Foundation for Analysis in the Health Sciences. 2nd ed. LC 77-28253. (Probability & Mathematical Statistics Ser.). 504p. 1978. text ed. 28.95 (ISBN 0-471-02591-7). Wiley.
--Introductory Statistics with Applications. LC 76-10897. (Illus.). 1977. text ed. 24.95 (ISBN 0-395-24430-7); instr's. guide with solutions 3.50 (ISBN 0-395-24431-5); study guide 10.50 (ISBN 0-395-24843-4). HM.
Daniel, Wayne W. & Terrell, James C. Business Statistics: Basic Concepts & Methodology. 2nd ed. LC 78-69607. (Illus.). 1979. text ed. 25.95 (ISBN 0-395-26762-5); instr's. manual 2.25 (ISBN 0-395-26763-3); study guide 10.50 (ISBN 0-395-26764-1). HM.
--Business Statistics: Basic Concepts & Methodology. LC 82-83254. 832p. 1982. text ed. 26.95 (ISBN 0-395-32601-X); write for info. instr's. resource manual (ISBN 0-395-32602-8); study guide 10.95 (ISBN 0-395-32603-6). HM.
Daniel, William & Fleiszar, Kathleen. Genetics & Variation. (Illus.). 471p. text ed. 21.80 (ISBN 0-87563-220-3). Stipes.
Daniel, William A., Jr. Adolescents in Health & Disease. LC 77-5074. (Illus.). 392p. 1977. pap. text ed. 15.95 o.p. (ISBN 0-8016-1201-2). Mosby.
Daniel, Yuli. Prison Poems. Burg, David & Boyars, Arthur, trs. LC 76-186888. 80p. (Rus. - Eng.). 1972. 6.50 (ISBN 0-87955-501-7); pap. 2.95 (ISBN 0-87955-503-3). O'Hara.
Daniele, Joseph W. Early American Metal Projects. LC 75-130495. 16.64 (ISBN 0-87345-142-2). McKnight.
--How to Build a Clock-With Thirty Five Plans & Complete Instructions. (Illus.). 224p. 1982. pap. 12.95 (ISBN 0-940166-01-1). Old Main Bks.
Danielian, Ronald L., jt. auth. see Stanley, Timothy W.
Daniell, David. Coriolanus in Europe. 192p. 1981. text ed. 29.50x (ISBN 0-485-11192-6). Humanities.
Daniell, Jere R. Colonial New Hampshire - A History. LC 81-6046. (A History of the American Colonies Ser.). 1982. lib. bdg. 30.00 (ISBN 0-527-18715-1). Kraus Intl.
Daniell, Jo, illus. Thorn Bird Country. (Illus.). 128p. 1983. pap. 12.95 (ISBN 0-446-37573-X). Warner Bks.
Danielle, Timothy T. The Lawyers: The Inns of Court. LC 76-25744. 353p. 1976. 17.50 (ISBN 0-379-00593-X). Oceana.
Danielli, J. F., jt. auth. see Bourne, G. H.
Danielli, J. F., jt. ed. see Bourne, G. H.
Danielli, J. F., ed. see Symposium on Molecular Pharmacology, 3rd, Buffalo 1968, et al.
Danielli, J. F., et al, eds. Recent Progress in Surface Science, 3 vols. Incl. Vol. 1. 1964. 61.00 (ISBN 0-12-571801-2); Vol. 2. 1964. 69.00 (ISBN 0-12-571802-0); Vol. 3. 1970. 67.00 (ISBN 0-12-571803-9). Acad Pr.
Danielli, James, jt. ed. see Bourne, Geoffrey.
Danielli, James F., ed. International Review of Cytology Supplement: Vol. 15: Aspects of Cell Regulation. Date not set. price not set (ISBN 0-12-364376-7). Acad Pr.
Danielli, James F., jt. ed. see Bourne, Geoffrey H.
Danielou, Jean. The Dead Sea Scrolls & Primitive Christianity. Attanasio, Salvator, tr. from Fr. LC 78-21516. 1979. Repr. of 1958 ed. lib. bdg. 17.75x (ISBN 0-313-21144-2, DADE). Greenwood.
--A History of Early Christian Doctrine Before the Council of Nicaea. Baker, John A., tr. Incl. Vol. 1. The Theology of Jewish Christianity. 1977. 25.00 o.p. (ISBN 0-664-21061-9); Vol. 2. Gospel Message & Hellenistic Culture. LC 72-7090. 17.50 (ISBN 0-664-20961-0); Vol. 3. The Origins of Latin Christianity. LC 76-44380. 1977. 27.50 (ISBN 0-664-21064-3). Westminster.
Daniels, Alan & Yeates, Don. Design & Analysis of Software Systems. 257p. 1983. pap. 15.00 (ISBN 0-89433-212-0). Petrocelli.
Daniels, Alan & Yeates, Donald, eds. Systems Analysis. (Illus.). 1971. text ed. 17.95 (ISBN 0-574-17885-6, 13-0885); instr's guide avail. (ISBN 0-574-17886-4, 13-0886). SRA.
Daniels, Anders, jt. auth. see Bach, Wilfred.
Daniels, Arthur M. A Journal of Sibley's Indian Expedition During the Summer of 1863 & Record of the Troops Employed. (Illus.). 154p. 1980. Repr. 30.00 (ISBN 0-911506-13-6). Thueson.
Daniels, Aubrey C., jt. auth. see Rosen, Theodore A.
Daniels, Bennet, jt. auth. see Daniels, Else.
Daniels, Bruce C. Dissent & Conformity: The Rhode Island Town. (Illus.). Date not set. price not set (ISBN 0-8195-5083-3). Wesleyan U Pr.
Daniels, Bruce C; see Weaver, Glenn.
Daniels, Camilla-Chapin, et al, trs. see Figner, Vera N.
Daniels, Cora L. & Stevans, C. M., eds. Encyclopedia of Superstitions, Folklore & the Occult Sciences of the World, 3 vols. LC 70-141151. 1971. Repr. of 1903 ed. 107.00x (ISBN 0-8103-3286-8). Gale.
Daniels, D. J., ed. New Movements in the Study & Teaching of Chemistry. 1977. 14.00 o.s.i. (ISBN 0-85117-077-3). Transatlantic.
Daniels, D. J., ed. see Buttle, J. W.
Daniels, David. The Golden Age of Contract Bridge. LC 78-25629. (Illus.). 224p. 1982. 15.95 (ISBN 0-8128-2576-4); pap. 7.95 (ISBN 0-8128-6166-3). Stein & Day.
Daniels, Dorothy. Bridal Black. (Orig.). 1980. pap. 1.75 o.p. (ISBN 0-451-09211-2, Sig). NAL.
--The Cormac Legend. 1979. pap. 2.25 (ISBN 0-451-11555-4, AE1555, Sig). NAL.
--For Love & Valcour. 480p. 1983. pap. 3.50 (ISBN 0-446-30256-2). Warner Bks.
--House of Silence. (Orig.). 1980. pap. 1.75 o.p. (ISBN 0-451-09423-9, E9423, Sig). NAL.
--The Lanier Riddle. 224p. (Orig.). 1972. pap. 1.75 o.p. (ISBN 0-446-84806-9). Warner Bks.
--Night Shadow. (Orig.). 1979. pap. 1.75 o.p. (ISBN 0-451-08763-1, E8763, Sig). NAL.
--The Purple & the Gold. (Orig.). 1980. pap. 1.95 o.p. (ISBN 0-451-09118-3, J9118, Sig). NAL.
Daniels, Douglas H. Pioneer Urbanites: A Social & Cultural History of Black San Francisco. 260p. 1980. 29.95 (ISBN 0-87722-169-3). Temple U Pr.
Daniels, Elam J. Como Ser Feliz En el Matrimonio. Orig. Title: How to Be Happily Married. 96p. 1981. pap. 2.10 (ISBN 0-311-46066-6). Casa Bautista.
Daniels, Elizabeth A. Jessie White Mario: Risorgimento Revolutionary. LC 78-158178. (Illus.). vii, 199p. 1972. 13.95 (ISBN 0-8214-0103-3, 82-81081). Ohio U Pr.
Daniels, Ellen S., ed. How to Raise Money: Special Events for Arts Organizations. 32p. 1981. pap. 3.00 o.p. (ISBN 0-915400-30-8). Am Council Arts.
Daniels, Else & Daniels, Bennet. Vacation at Sea: A Travel Guide for Cruises. (Illus.). 1979. pap. 5.95 (ISBN 0-346-12423-9). Cornerstone.
--Vacation at Sea: A Travel Guide for Cruises. (Illus.). 1979. 8.95 o.p. (ISBN 0-671-18438-5). Sovereign Bks.
Daniels, Farrington. Direct Use of the Sun's Energy. (Illus., Orig.). 1964. 27.50x o.p. (ISBN 0-300-00399-4). Yale U Pr.
--Direct Use of the Sun's Energy. LC 64-20913. 391p. 1983. pap. text ed. 7.95x (ISBN 0-300-02986-1). Yale U Pr.
--Direct Use of the Sun's Energy. pap. 7.95 (ISBN 0-686-42820-X, Y-457). Yale U Pr.
Daniels, Farrington, jt. auth. see Alberty, Robert A.
Daniels, Farrington, et al. Experimental Physical Chemistry. 7th ed. 1970. text ed. 32.50 (ISBN 0-07-015339-6, C). McGraw.
Daniels, G. Divorce Guide for Washington. 2nd ed. 74p. 1980. 7.95 (ISBN 0-88908-716-4); divorce forms 9.95 (ISBN 0-686-35988-7). Self Counsel Pr.
Daniels, George & Markarian, Ohannes. Watches & Clocks in the Sir David Salomons Collection. (Illus.). 320p. 1983. 65.00x (ISBN 0-85667-074-X, Pub. by Sotheby Pubns England). Biblio Dist.
Daniels, George, jt. auth. see Clutton, Cecil.
Daniels, George H. & Rose, Mark H., eds. Energy & Transport: Historical Perspectives on Policy Issues. (Sage Focus Editions: Vol. 52). (Illus.). 288p. 1982. 25.00 (ISBN 0-8039-0786-9); pap. 12.50 (ISBN 0-8039-0787-7). Sage.
Daniels, Gilbert, ed. see Bonar, Ann.
Daniels, Gilbert, ed. see Hine, Jacqui.
Daniels, Guy, tr. see Casals, Felipe G.
Daniels, Harvey A. Famous Last Words: The American Language Crisis Reconsidered. 1983. 19.95 (ISBN 0-8093-1055-4); pap. 10.95x (ISBN 0-8093-1093-7). S Ill U Pr.
Daniels, J; see Bernard, William S.
Daniels, J. R. Firegold. LC 75-10476. 192p. 1975. 7.95 o.p. (ISBN 0-698-10679-2, Coward). Putnam Pub Group.
Daniels, Jack, et al. Conditioning for Distance Running: The Scientific Aspects. LC 77-22538. (American College of Sports Medicine Ser.). 106p. 1978. text ed. 17.95 (ISBN 0-471-19483-2). Wiley.
Daniels, James W. Elementary Linear Algebra & Its Applications. (Illus.). 368p. 1981. text ed. 23.95 (ISBN 0-13-258293-7). P-H.
Daniels, Jerry C., jt. ed. see Ritzmann, Stephan E.
Daniels, John D. & Ogram, Ernest W., Jr. International Business: Environments & Operations. 3rd ed. (Illus.). 252p. Date not set. pap. price not set Instrs' Manual (ISBN 0-201-10224-2). A-W.
Daniels, John D., et al. International Business: Environments & Operations. 2nd ed. LC 78-67456. 1979. text ed. 25.95 (ISBN 0-201-01395-9); instr's manual avail. (ISBN 0-201-01396-7). A-W.
--International Business Environments & Operations. 3rd ed. LC 81-170636. (Illus.). 531p. 1982. text ed. 25.95 (ISBN 0-201-10223-4). A-W.
Daniels, John S. Smoke of the Gun. Bd. with Wild Riders. Hoffman, Lee. 1979. pap. 1.95 o.p. (ISBN 0-451-08667-8, J8667, Sig). NAL.
Daniels, John S., jt. auth. see Hickok, Will.
Daniels, Jonathan. The End of Innocence. LC 73-37285. (FDR & the Era of the New Deal Ser.). 351p. 1972. Repr. of 1954 ed. 39.50 (ISBN 0-306-70423-4). Da Capo.
--Frontier on the Potomac. LC 70-37284. (FDR & the Era of the New Deal Ser). 262p. 1972. Repr. of 1946 ed. lib. bdg. 35.00 (ISBN 0-306-70425-0). Da Capo.
--Prince of Carpetbaggers. LC 74-3742. (Illus.). 319p. 1974. Repr. of 1958 ed. lib. bdg. 17.75x (ISBN 0-8371-7466-X, DAPO). Greenwood.
--A Southerner Discovers the South. LC 68-16228. (The American Scene Ser.). 1970. Repr. of 1938 ed. lib. bdg. 42.50 (ISBN 0-306-71011-0). Da Capo.
Daniels, Les. Living in Fear: A History of Horror in the Mass Media. (Quality Paperbacks Ser.). (Illus.). 256p. 1983. pap. 12.95 (ISBN 0-306-80193-0). Da Capo.
Daniels, Lynda M., jt. auth. see Kochar, Mahendra S.
Daniels, M. E. Fireplaces & Wood Stoves. LC 76-26948. (Illus.). 1977. 13.95 o.p. (ISBN 0-672-52175-X). Bobbs.
Daniels, Megan. The Unlikely Rivals. 1981. pap. 2.25 (ISBN 0-451-11076-5, AE1076, Sig). NAL.
Daniels, Norman. Reading Rawls. LC 74-25908. 1975. 15.00x o.s.i. (ISBN 0-465-06854-5); pap. 8.95x o.s.i. (ISBN 0-465-06855-3). Basic.
Daniels, P. W. Office Location & the Journey to Work: A Comparative Study of Five Urban Centers. 175p. 1980. text ed. 30.00x (ISBN 0-566-00352-X). Gower Pub Ltd.
--Service Industries: Growth & Location. 2nd ed. LC 82-4260. (Cambridge Topics in Geography Ser.). (Illus.). 96p. 1982. 12.95 (ISBN 0-521-23730-0). Cambridge U Pr.
--Spatial Patterns of Office Growth & Location. LC 78-8386. 414p. 1979. 54.95 (ISBN 0-471-99675-0). Wiley.
Daniels, Patricia. Aladdin & the Magic Lamp. LC 79-27304. (Raintree Fairy Tales). (Illus.). 24p. (gr. k-3). 1980. PLB 12.50 (ISBN 0-8393-0257-6). Raintree Pubs.
--Ali Baba & the Forty Thieves. LC 79-27042. (Raintree Fairy Tales). (Illus.). 24p. (gr. k-3). 1980. PLB 12.50 (ISBN 0-8393-0255-X). Raintree Pubs.
--Beauty & the Beast. LC 79-28433. (Raintree Fairy Tales). (Illus.). 24p. (gr. k-3). 1980. PLB 12.50 (ISBN 0-8393-0258-4). Raintree Pubs.
--Cinderella. LC 79-28526. (Raintree Fairy Tales). (Illus.). 24p. (gr. k-3). 1980. PLB 12.50 (ISBN 0-8393-0253-3). Raintree Pubs.
--Rumpelstiltskin. LC 79-27140. (Raintree Fairy Tales). (Illus.). 24p. (gr. k-3). 1980. PLB 12.50 (ISBN 0-8393-0252-5). Raintree Pubs.
--Sinbad the Sailor. LC 79-28588. (Raintree Fairy Tales). (Illus.). 24p. (gr. k-3). 1980. PLB 12.50 (ISBN 0-8393-0256-8). Raintree Pubs.
--Sleeping Beauty. LC 79-26974. (Raintree Fairy Tales). (Illus.). 24p. (gr. k-3). 1980. PLB 12.50 (ISBN 0-8393-0254-1). Raintree Pubs.
--Snow White & the Dwarfs. LC 79-28431. (Raintree Fairy Tales Ser.). (Illus.). 24p. (gr. k-3). 1980. lib. bdg. 12.50 (ISBN 0-8393-0251-7). Raintree Pubs.
Daniels, Patrick. Early Photography. LC 78-60790. (Illus.). 1978. pap. 4.95 o.p. (ISBN 0-312-22465-6). St Martin.
Daniels, Paul R. Teaching the Gifted Learning Disabled Child. 400p. 1983. 26.50 (ISBN 0-89443-928-6). Aspen Systems.
Daniels, Pearl G. Portrait of Fred D. Gray. 4.50 o.p. (ISBN 0-533-01472-7). Vantage.
Daniels, Richard W. Approximation Methods for Electronic Filter Design: With Applications to Passive, Active & Digital Networks. (Illus.). 448p. 1974. 33.50 o.p. (ISBN 0-07-015308-6, P&RB). McGraw.
Daniels, Robert V. Studying History: How & Why. 3rd ed. 128p. 1981. pap. text ed. 8.95 (ISBN 0-13-858738-8). P-H.
Daniels, Robert V., ed. Stalin Revolution: Foundations of Soviet Totalitarianism. 2nd ed. (Problems in European Civilization Ser.). 1973. pap. 5.95 (ISBN 0-669-82495-X). Heath.
Daniels, Roger. The Bonus March: An Episode of the Great Depression. LC 75-133497. (Illus.). 352p. 1971. lib. bdg. 29.95 (ISBN 0-8371-5174-0, DBM/). Greenwood.
--Concentration Camps North America: Japanese in the United States & Canada During World War II. LC 80-19813. 260p. 1981. Repr. of 1971 ed. text ed. 9.50 (ISBN 0-89874-025-8). Krieger.
--The Politics of Prejudice: The Anti-Japanese Movement in California & The Struggle for Japanese Exclusion. (California Library Reprint Ser.). 1978. 24.00x (ISBN 0-520-03412-0); pap. 3.45 (ISBN 0-520-03411-2). U of Cal Pr.
Daniels, Roger & Kitano, Harry H. American Racism: Exploration of the Nature of Prejudice. 1969. pap. text ed. 10.95 (ISBN 0-13-028993-0). P-H.
Daniels, Shirley. All You Need to Know About Microcomputers: The Small Business Manager's Advisory. LC 79-64577. (Illus.). 144p. 1979. pap. text ed. 7.95 (ISBN 0-89914-003-3). Third Party Pub.
Daniels, Steven. How Two Gerbils, Twenty Goldfish, Two Hundred Games, Two Thousand Books & I Taught Them How to Read. LC 78-141992. (Illus.). 1971. pap. 4.95 (ISBN 0-664-24913-2). Westminster.
Daniels, Stuart R. Inelastic Steel Structures. LC 65-25460. (Illus.). 1966. 14.50x (ISBN 0-87049-064-8). U of Tenn Pr.
Daniels, V. G., jt. ed. see Huang, C. L.
Daniels, Velma. Kat: The Tale of a Calico Cat. LC 77-13788. (Illus.), (gr. k-7). 1977. 8.95 (ISBN 0-88289-180-4). Pelican.
Daniels, Velma S. Celebrate Joy! 1982. pap. 2.50 (ISBN 0-451-11945-2, AE1945, Sig). NAL.
Daniels, Winthrop M. Recollections of Woodrow Wilson. 1944. 19.50x (ISBN 0-685-89776-1). Elliots Bks.
Danielsen, Albert L. The Evolution of OPEC. LC 81-85395. 305p. 1982. pap. text ed. 19.95 (ISBN 0-15-129394-5). HarBraceJ.
Danielsen, Niels. Papers in Theoretical Linguistics. 250p. 1983. 25.00 (ISBN 90-272-3509-0). Benjamins North Am.
Danielson, Albert. The Evolution of OPEC. 304p. (Orig.). 1982. pap. text ed. 8.95 (ISBN 0-15-518795-3). HarBraceJ.
Danielson, Albert L. & Kamerschen, David R., eds. Current Issues in Public-Utility Economics: Essays in Honor of James C. Bonbright. LC 81-48612. 352p. 1983. 34.95x (ISBN 0-669-05440-2). Lexington Bks.
Danielson, Dorothy & Hayden, Rebecca. Using English: Your Second Language. (Illus.). 228p. 1973. pap. text ed. 11.95x (ISBN 0-13-939678-0). P-H.
Danielson, Dorothy, et al. Reading in English: For Students of ESL. 2nd ed. (Illus.). 1980. pap. text ed. 11.95 (ISBN 0-13-753442-6). P-H.
Danielson, Elena, jt. auth. see Palm, Charles.
Danielson, Henry. Arthur Machen: A Bibliography. LC 79-149784. 1971. Repr. of 1923 ed. 30.00x (ISBN 0-8103-3682-0). Gale.
Danielson, Michael N. & Murphy, Walter F. American Democracy. 10th ed. (Illus.). 608p. 1983. text ed. price not set (ISBN 0-8419-0839-7). Holmes & Meier.
Danielson, Wayne, jt. auth. see Prejean, Blanche.
Danielsson, Bror, ed. Middle English Falconry Treatises, Pt. 1. (Mediaeval English Hunt, Cynegetica Anglica: Vol. 2). 1980. pap. text ed. price not set (ISBN 0-391-01141-3). Humanities.
--Middle English Falconry Treatises, Pt. 2. (Mediaeval English Hunt Ser.: Vol. 3). 1980. text ed. cancelled (ISBN 0-640-96753-0); pap. text ed. price not set (ISBN 0-391-01177-4). Humanities.
Daniken, Eric von see Von Daniken, Eric.
Daniken, Erich Von see Von Daniken, Erich.
Daniken, Erich von see Von Daniken, Erich.
Daniken, Erich Von see Von Daniken, Erich.
Danikin, Y., jt. auth. see Pshenichny, B.
Danilevskii, J. A. Lappo see Lappo-Danilevskii, J. A.
Daniloff, Raymond G. & Schuckers, Gordon H. Physiology of Speech & Hearing: An Introduction. 1980. text ed. 27.95 (ISBN 0-13-674747-7). P-H.
Daninos, Pierre. Carnets Du Major W. Marmaduke Thompson. (Illus.). 1963. pap. text ed. 6.95x (ISBN 0-521-04767-6). Cambridge U Pr.
Danion, Boots. Handcapping in the Winner's Circle: How to Win at the Track. Pollack, Martin, ed. LC 82-73261. 192p. (Orig.). 1982. pap. 9.95 (ISBN 0-936836-05-9). Alliance Pubs.
Danish Association of Advertising Agencies, ed. Media Scandinavia, 1982. 31st ed. LC 72-623099. 618p. (Eng. & Danish.). 1982. 75.00x (ISBN 87-87827-13-1). Intl Pubns Serv.
Danish, Steve, et al. Helping Skills: A Basic Training Program. 2nd ed. 1980. wkbk softcover 119 p. 9.95 (ISBN 0-87705-484-3); leaders manual 68 5.95x (ISBN 0-87705-483-5); Set. 12.95x. Human Sci Pr.
Danishefsky, Isidore. Biochemistry for Medical Sciences. 1980. text ed. 26.95 (ISBN 0-316-17198-0). Little.
Dank, Milton. Albert Einstein. (Impact Biography Ser.). (Illus.). 128p. (gr. 7up). 1983. PLB 8.90 (ISBN 0-531-04587-0). Watts.
Danker, Frederick W. Multipurpose Tools for Bible Study. rev. ed. 1970. pap. 10.95 (ISBN 0-570-03734-4, 12-2638). Concordia.
Danker, Frederick W., jt. auth. see Gingrich, Wilbur F.
Danker, Harold, jt. auth. see Steinberg, Richard M.
Dankert, Clyde E., et al, eds. Hours of Work. LC 78-27581. (Industrial Relations Research Association Publication: No. 32). 1979. Repr. of 1965 ed. lib. bdg. 19.75x (ISBN 0-313-20903-0, DAHW). Greenwood.
Danko, Xena, tr. see Poliakova, Liudmila V.
Dankoff, Robert, tr. Wisdom of Royal Glory-Kutadgu Bilig: A Turko-Islamic Mirror for Princes. LC 82-20159. (Publications of The Center for Middle Eastern Studies: No. 16). 320p. 1983. 25.00 (ISBN 0-226-97179-1). U of Chicago Pr.
Danks, Lawrence J. Real Estate Advertising. 260p. 1982. 24.95 (ISBN 0-88462-420-X). Real Estate Ed Co.
Danks, Maureen C. & Mitchell, Lawrence J. Study Guide to Accompany Biology, the Study of Life, by Bernstein & Bernstein. 258p. 1982. 8.95 (ISBN 0-15-505442-2, HC). HarBraceJ.
Danky, James P. & Hady, Maureen B. Native American Press in Wisconsin & the Nation: Proceedings of the Conference on the Native American Press in Wisconsin & the Nation, April 22-23, 1982. LC 82-17634. 197p. 1982. pap. 6.50. U Wis Lib Sch.
Danky, James P., ed. Genealogical Research: An Introduction to the Resources of the State Historical Society of Wisconsin. LC 79-15148. 1979. pap. 3.00 (ISBN 0-87020-180-8). State Hist Soc Wis.
Danky, James P., jt. ed. see Hedy, Maureen E.
Danley, Jerry J. Useful Science. (Illus.). 1977. pap. 2.95x (ISBN 0-88323-127-1, 216); tchr's key free (ISBN 0-88323-132-8, 222). Richards Pub.

Danly, Robert L. In the Shade of Spring Leaves: The Life & Writings of Higuchi Ichiyo, a Woman of Letters in Meiji Japan. LC 81-50434. (Illus.). 355p. 1983. pap. text ed. 10.95 (ISBN 0-300-02981-0). Yale U Pr.

--In the Shade of Spring Leaves: The Life & Writings of Higuchi Ichiyo, a Woman of Letters in Meiji Japan. pap. 10.95 (ISBN 0-686-42821-8, Y-456). Yale U Pr.

Dann, F. Know Your Newspaper. (Orig.). 1977. pap. 2.95 (ISBN 0-671-18772-4). Monarch Pr.

Dann, Jack & Zebrowski, George. Faster Than Light. 352p. 1982. pap. 2.95 (ISBN 0-441-22825-9, Pub. by Ace Science Fiction). Ace Bks.

Dann, Jack, ed. Wandering Stars: Anthology of Jewish Fantasy & Science Fiction. LC 73-4146. 252p. 1974. 8.95 o.p. (ISBN 0-06-010944-0, HarpT). Har-Row.

Danna, Jo. Why Retire? New Jobs, New Workstyles & How to Find Them, Vol. 1. (Illus.). 325p. 1983. 16.95 (ISBN 0-9610036-0-X); pap. 12.95 (ISBN 0-9610036-1-8). Palomino Pr.

Danna, Mark, jt. auth. see Poynter, Dan.

Danne, A. H., jt. ed. see Spedding, E. H.

Dannebring, David D. & Starr, Martin K. Management Science: An Introduction. (Quantitative Methods in Management Ser.). 1981. 28.95 (ISBN 0-07-015352-3, C); study guide (by Chen & Dannenbring) 11.95 (ISBN 0-07-015353-1); instr's. manual 15.00 (ISBN 0-07-015354-X). McGraw.

Dannen, Donna, jt. auth. see Dannen, Kent.

Dannen, Kent & Dannen, Donna. Rocky Mountain National Park Hiking Trails-Including Indian Peaks. LC 77-25701. (Illus.). 288p. 1978. pap. 6.95 o.p. (ISBN 0-914788-06-X). East Woods.

Dannenbaum, Julie. More Fast & Fresh. LC 82-48114. (Illus.). 256p. 1983. 14.37i (ISBN 0-06-015084-X, HarpT). Har-Row.

Dannenberg, Linda. The Paris Way of Beauty. 1979. 10.95 o.p. (ISBN 0-671-24723-9). S&S.

Dannenfeldt, Karl H. Church of the Renaissance & Reformation. LC 77-98300. (Church in History Ser). 1978. pap. 4.95 (ISBN 0-570-06271-3, 12-2726). Concordia.

Dannenfeldt, Karl H., ed. The Renaissance. 2nd ed. (Problems in European Civilization Ser). 1973. pap. text ed. 5.95 (ISBN 0-669-90530-5). Heath.

Danner, Douglas. Pattern Discovery: Antitrust. LC 81-82088. 1981. 65.00 (ISBN 0-686-35942-9). Lawyers Co-Op.

--Pattern Discovery: Employment Discrimination. LC 81-82088. 1981. 65.00 (ISBN 0-686-35943-7). Lawyers Co-Op.

--Pattern Discovery: Securities. LC 81-82088. 1982. 65.00 (ISBN 0-686-37165-8). Lawyers Co-Op.

Danner, Peter L. An Ethics for the Affluent. LC 80-5528. 424p. 1980. lib. bdg. 25.00 (ISBN 0-8191-1163-5); pap. text ed. 15.25 (ISBN 0-8191-1164-3). U Pr of Amer.

Dannhaeuser, Norbert. Contemporary Trade Strategies in the Philippines. 288p. Date not set. 30.00 (ISBN 0-8135-0950-5). Rutgers U Pr.

Dannies, P. & Kozarich, J. W. Pharmacology: Pretest Self-Assessment & Review. 192p. Date not set. 11.95 (ISBN 0-07-051935-8). McGraw.

D'Annunzio, Gabriele. Daughter of Jorio: A Pastoral Tragedy. Porter, Charlotte, et al, trs. LC 69-10064. Repr. of 1907 ed. lib. bdg. 15.50x (ISBN 0-8371-0005-4, DADJ). Greenwood.

--Tales of My Native Town. Mantellini, Rafael, tr. LC 69-10065. Repr. of 1920 ed. lib. bdg. 17.75x (ISBN 0-8371-0056-9, DANT). Greenwood.

Danoff, Judith, et al. Open for Children: For Those Interested in Early Childhood Education. (Illus.). 1977. text ed. 19.95 (ISBN 0-07-015343-4, C); pap. text ed. 16.50 (ISBN 0-07-015342-6). McGraw.

Danon, D., ed. Aging: A Challenge to Science & Society--Vol. 1, Biology. (Illus.). 1981. 65.00x (ISBN 0-19-261254-9). Oxford U Pr.

Danon, J. Lectures on the Mossbauer Effect. LC 68-19092. (Documents on Modern Physics Ser). 150p. (Orig.). 1968. 39.00x (ISBN 0-677-01530-5). Gordon.

Danon, Samuel & Rosenburg, Samuel N., trs. from Fr. Ami & Amile. 10.00 (ISBN 0-917786-20-3). French Lit.

Danos, Paul & Imhoff, Eugene A., Jr. Intermediate Accounting. (Illus.). 1088p. 1983. 32.00 (ISBN 0-13-469338-8); practice set 6.95 (ISBN 0-13-469619-0). P-H.

Danowski, F. Fishermen's Wives: Coping with an Extraordinary Occupation. (Marine Bulletin Ser.: No. 37). 78p. 1980. 2.00 o.p. (ISBN 0-686-36986-6, P862). URI Mas.

Danowski, T. S. Diabetes As a Way of Life. 3rd ed. (Illus.). 224p. 1974. 6.95 o.p. (ISBN 0-698-10581-8, Coward). Putnam Pub Group.

--Diabetes As a Way of Life. 4th, rev. ed. LC 78-10197. (Illus.). 1979. 8.95 o.s.i. (ISBN 0-698-10947-3, Coward). Putnam Pub Group.

--Sustained Weight Control: The Individual Approach. 2nd ed. 194p. 1973. pap. text ed. 3.75x o.p. (ISBN 0-8036-2331-3). Davis Co.

Dansereau, P. Biogeography: An Ecological Perspective. (Illus.). 1957. 32.50 o.s.i. (ISBN 0-471-06808-X, Pub. by Wiley-Interscience). Wiley.

Danson, Lawrence. Max Beerbohm & The Mirror of the Past. (Illus.). 96p. 1982. 15.00 (ISBN 0-686-97665-7). Princeton Lib.

Dante. Literature in the Vernacular. Purcell, Sally, tr. from Ital. 96p. (Orig.). 1981. pap. 6.95 o.p. (ISBN 0-85635-274-8, 40134, Pub. by Carcanet New Pr England); pap. text ed. 6.95x o.p. (ISBN 0-85635-274-8). Humanities.

--Purgatorio: The Divine Comedy of Dante Alighieri. Mandelbaum, Allen, tr. (The California Dante Ser.: Vol. II). (Illus.). 1982. 22.50 (ISBN 0-520-04516-5). U of Cal Pr.

Dante Society of America, Inc. Dante Studies: With the Annual Report of the Dante Society. Pellegrini, Anthony L., ed. Incl. Vol. 85. Artinian, Robert, et alcontrib. by. vi, 144p. 1967; Vol. 86. Fergusson, Francis, et alcontrib. by. viii, 196p. 1968; Vol. 87. Contini, Gianfranco, et alcontrib. by. viii, 205p. 1969; Vol. 88. Bernardo, Aldo S., et alcontrib. by. viii, 227p. 1970; Vol. 89. Brown, Emerson, Jr., et alcontrib. by. viii, 148p. 1971; Vol. 90. Berk, Philip R., et alcontrib. by. viii, 216p. 1972; Vol. 91. Bergin, Thomas G., et alcontrib. by. 1973; Vol. 92. Barkens, David, et alcontrib. by. 1974; Vol. 93. Mills, Marguerite, et alcontrib. by. 1975; Vol. 94; Vol. 95; Vol. 96; Vol. 97; Vol. 98. LC 15-2183. pap. 15.00x ea. State U NY Pr.

Dante University of America Press, ed. Dante in the Twentieth Century. (Dante Studies). 1981. 15.00 (ISBN 0-937832-16-2); leather 25.00. Branden.

Dante Alighieri. Dante's Inferno. Tiller, Terence, ed. LC 67-25235. (Bilingual). 1967. 5.95x o.p. (ISBN 0-8052-3048-3). Schocken.

--De Vulgari Eloquentia. Howell, A. G. Ferrers, tr. 79p. 1981. pap. 7.95 (ISBN 0-900615-25-7, Pub. by Element Bks England). Hydra Bk.

--The Divine Comedy, 3 vols. rev. ed. Sinclair, John D, tr. Incl. Vol. 1. Inferno. 1961. pap. 7.95 (ISBN 0-19-500412-4, GB65); Vol 2. Purgatorio. 1961. pap. 7.95 (ISBN 0-19-500413-2, GB66); Vol. 3. Paradiso. 1961. pap. 7.95 (ISBN 0-19-500414-0, GB67). pap. (GB). Oxford U Pr.

--The Divine Comedy: The Inferno, Vol. 1. Singleton, Charles S., tr. from Italian. LC 68-57090. (Bollingen Ser: Lxxx). (Illus.). 1088p. (Bilingual ed.). 1980. pap. 12.50x (ISBN 0-691-01832-4). Princeton U Pr.

--De Monarchia & Four Political Letters. Hardie, Colin & Nicholl, Donald, trs. from Ital. LC 81-52139. Date not set. pap. 8.95 (ISBN 0-89526-880-9). Regnery Gateway.

--Translation of the Latin Works of Dante Alighieri. LC 69-13874. Repr. of 1904 ed. lib. bdg. 15.50x (ISBN 0-8371-1799-2, DAAT). Greenwood.

Danto, Arthur C. Jean-Paul Sartre. LC 75-19019. (Modern Masters Ser.). 175p. 1975. 8.95 o.p. (ISBN 0-670-40630-9). Viking Pr.

--The Transfiguration of the Commonplace: A Philosophy of Art. 288p. 1983. pap. text ed. 6.95x (ISBN 0-674-90346-3). Harvard U Pr.

Danto, Bruce L., et al, eds. The Human Side of Homicide. 336p. 1982. 24.00 (ISBN 0-231-04964-1). Columbia U Pr.

Danton, J. Periam. Between M.L.S. & Ph.D. LC 74-133380. 1970. pap. 5.00 (ISBN 0-8389-0089-5). ALA.

D'Antonio, William V., ed. see Drucker, Peter F., et al.

Dany, M. & Laloy, J. R. Le Francais de L'Hotellerie et du Tourisme. 186p. (Fr.). 1980. pap. 14.95 (ISBN 0-686-97381-X, M-9311). French & Eur.

Danzer, Hal C., jt. auth. see Kass-Annese, Barbara.

Danziger, Christopher. South African History, 1910-1970: Cartoons. (Illus.). 1978. 10.50x o.p. (ISBN 0-19-570117-8). Oxford U Pr.

Danziger, James N. & Dutton, William H. Computers & Politics. 320p. 1983. pap. 15.00 (ISBN 0-231-04889-0). Columbia U Pr.

Danziger, Jeff. The Complete Reagan Diet. LC 82-61449. (Illus.). 96p. (Orig.). 1982. pap. 3.20 (ISBN 0-688-01908-0). Quill NY.

Danziger, Marlies K. Oliver Goldsmith & Richard Brinsley Sheridan. LC 77-6946. (Literature and Life Ser.). 1978. 11.95 (ISBN 0-8044-2129-3). Ungar.

Danziger, Marlies K. & Johnson, Wendell S. The Critical Reader: Analyzing & Judging Literature. LC 78-4302. 1978. 11.95 (ISBN 0-8044-2135-8); pap. 4.95 (ISBN 0-8044-6096-5). Ungar.

Danziger, Marlies K. & Johnson, Wendell S., eds. Poetry Anthology. (Orig.). 1967. pap. text ed. 14.00 (ISBN 0-394-30187-0). Random.

Danziger, Paula. Can You Sue Your Parents for Malpractice? pap. 1.95 (ISBN 0-686-74495-0, LE). Dell.

--Can You Sue Your Parents for Malpractice. (YA) 1980. pap. 1.95 (ISBN 0-440-91066-8, LFL). Dell.

--The Cat Ate My Gymsuit. (gr. k-6). 1980. pap. 2.25 (ISBN 0-440-41612-4, YB). Dell.

Danzin, A. Science & the Second Renaissance of Europe. 1979. pap. text ed. 27.00 (ISBN 0-08-022442-3). Pergamon.

Dao, Wong Ming. Stone Made Smooth. 1982. pap. 6.95 (ISBN 0-907821-00-6). OMF Bks.

Dao, Wong Ming see Dao, Wong Ming.

Daoudi, M. S. The Meaning of Kahlil Gibran. 160p. 1982. 9.95 (ISBN 0-8065-0804-3). Citadel Pr.

Daoust, H., jt. auth. see Stepek, J.

Da Parigi, Tomaso, jt. auth. see De Sommevoire, Alexis.

Daperr, H. H., ed. Advances in Nutritional Research, Vol. 5. 270p. 1983. 39.50x (ISBN 0-306-41095-8, Plenum Pr). Plenum Pub.

Daphne & Nelson. Beauty Unknown: Twenty-Seven Psychic Drawings of Spirit Beings with Their Messages for Our Planet. LC 74-20173. (New Age Ser.: No. 503). (Illus.). 1976. 7.00 (ISBN 0-89007-007-5). C Stark.

Daphne & Nelson, eds. Beauty Unknown Color Lithographs. (New Age Ser.: No. 502). 1976. 12.00 (ISBN 0-89007-502-6). C Stark.

Da Pisa, Guido. Guido Da Pisa's Commentary on Dante's Inferno. Cioffari, Vincenzo, ed. & tr. LC 74-11248. xxv, 750p. 1974. 44.50x (ISBN 0-87395-259-6). State U NY Pr.

Dapkus, Dave, jt. auth. see Mosby, Jack.

Dapogny, James. Ferdinand "Jelly Roll" Morton: The Collected Piano Music. (Illus.). 576p. (Orig.). 1982. pap. 23.95 (ISBN 0-87474-351-6). Smithsonian.

Dapples, Edward C. Basic Geology for Science & Engineering. LC 59-5880. 620p. 1973. Repr. of 1959 ed. 23.50 (ISBN 0-88275-106-9). Krieger.

D'Appolonia, Elio, jt. ed. see Pattison, Harry C.

D'Aprix, Roger. Communicating for Productivity. (Continuing Management Education Ser.). 112p. 1982. text ed. 14.95 (ISBN 0-06-041547-9, HarpC). Har-Row.

Dapunt, Otto, jt. auth. see Wittliff, James L.

Dapunt, Otto, jt. ed. see Wittliff, James L.

Daquine, Sonia. Si Nos Chemins Se Croisent. (Collection Colombine Ser.). 192p. 1983. pap. 1.95 (ISBN 0-373-48068-7). Harlequin Bks.

Dar, B. A. Quranic Ethics. pap. 3.50 (ISBN 0-686-18602-8). Kazi Pubns.

Darack, Arthur. The Consumers Digest Automobile Repair Book. (Illus.). 1978. pap. 12.50 (ISBN 0-07-015344-2, SP); pap. 7.95 (ISBN 0-07-015345-0). McGraw.

--The Guide to Home Appliance Repair. (Illus., Orig.). 1979. pap. 8.95 (ISBN 0-07-015360-4). McGraw.

Darack, Arthur & Consumer Group, Inc. Used Cars: How to Avoid Highway Robbery. (Illus.). 256p. 1983. 18.95 (ISBN 0-13-940056-7); pap. 7.95 (ISBN 0-13-940049-4). P-H.

Darbar, Gyanvati, ed. see Prasad, Rajendra.

Darbishire, Helen. The Poet Wordsworth. LC 79-14336. 182p. 1980. Repr. of 1965 ed. lib. bdg. 20.75x (ISBN 0-313-21483-2, DAWO). Greenwood.

Darbishire, Helen, ed. see Wordsworth, William.

Darboux, Gaston. Theorie Generale Des Surfaces, 4 Vols. 2nd ed. LC 67-16997. (Fr). 1968. Set. 85.00 (ISBN 0-8284-0216-7). Chelsea Pub.

Darby, David, jt. auth. see Ojakangas, Richard.

Darby, H. C., ed. A New Historical Geography of England After 1600. LC 76-26029. 1978. 64.50 (ISBN 0-521-22123-4); pap. 19.50 o.p. (ISBN 0-521-29145-3). Cambridge U Pr.

--A New Historical Geography of England Before 1600. LC 76-26141. 1978. 54.50 (ISBN 0-521-22122-6); pap. 21.95 (ISBN 0-521-29144-5). Cambridge U Pr.

Darby, J. N. The Collected Writings, 35 vols. Set. 105.00 (ISBN 0-88172-055-0); 3.50 ea. Believers Bkshelf.

--Letters of J. N. Darby, 3 vols. Set. 12.95 (ISBN 0-88172-061-5); 4.50 ea. Believers Bkshelf.

--Notes & Comments on Scripture, 7 vols. Set. 20.00 (ISBN 0-88172-068-2); 3.25 ea. Believers Bkshelf.

--Notes & Jottings on Scripture. 3.95 (ISBN 0-88172-069-0). Believers Bkshelf.

--Synopsis of the Books of the Bible, 5 vols. Set. 27.50 (ISBN 0-88172-070-4). Believers Bkshelf.

Darby, John & Williamson, Arthur. Violence & the Social Services in Northern Ireland. (Studies in Social Policy & Welfare). 1978. text ed. 24.00x (ISBN 0-435-82261-6). Heinemann Ed.

Darby, Joseph R., jt. auth. see Sears, J. Kern.

Darby, Ken. The Brownstone House of Nero Wolfe. 192p. 1983. 13.45i (ISBN 0-316-17280-4). Little.

Darby, McIhael. Intermediate Macroeconomics. (Illus.). 1979. text ed. 24.95 (ISBN 0-07-015348-5, C); instructor's manual 7.95 (ISBN 0-07-015349-3). McGraw.

Darby, Tom. The Feast: Meditations on Politics & Time. 256p. 1982. 30.00x (ISBN 0-8020-5578-8). U of Toronto Pr.

Darby, W. J., et al, eds. Annual Review of Nutrition, Vol. 2. (Illus.). 1982. text ed. 22.00 (ISBN 0-8243-2802-7). Annual Reviews.

--Annual Review of Nutrition, Vol. 3. 330p. 1983. 27.00 (ISBN 0-8243-2803-5). Annual Reviews.

Darbyshire, A. E. A Grammer of Style. (Andre Deutsch Language Library). 1977. lib. bdg. 12.75 o.p. (ISBN 0-233-96009-0). Westview.

D'Arcais, G. B., jt. auth. see Levelt, W. J.

D'Arcais, G. B. Flores see Flores D'Arcais, G. B. & Levelt, W. J.

D'Arcangelo, B. F., et al. Mathematics for Plumbers & Pipe Fitters. 3rd rev. ed. (Applied Mathematics Ser.). (Illus.). 244p. 1982. pap. text ed. 7.80 (ISBN 0-8273-1291-1); instr's. guide 3.75 (ISBN 0-8273-1292-X). Delmar.

D'Arcangelo, Bartholomew, et al. Blueprint Reading for Plumbers: Residential & Commercial. rev. ed. LC 78-24844. (Blueprint Reading Ser.). (gr. 7). 1980. pap. text ed. 13.80 (ISBN 0-8273-1367-5); instr's. guide 4.25 (ISBN 0-8273-1368-3). Delmar.

Darch, Colin, ed. Africa Index to Continental Periodical Literature. 1982. cancelled (ISBN 3-598-21822-2, Pub. by K G Saur). Shoe String.

D'Arcy, jt. auth. see Griffin.

Darcy, C. P. The Encouragement of the Fine Arts in Lancashire, 1760-1860. 1977. 22.00 (ISBN 0-7190-1330-5). Manchester.

Darcy, Clare. Allegra. 1976. pap. 1.95 (ISBN 0-451-09611-8, J9611, Sig). NAL.

--Caroline & Julia. LC 81-51969. 192p. 1982. 10.95 (ISBN 0-8027-0694-0). Walker & Co.

--Elyza. (YA) (RL 9). 1977. pap. 2.25 (ISBN 0-451-11023-4, AE1023, Sig). NAL.

--Eugenia. (RL 9). 1978. pap. 2.50 (ISBN 0-451-11274-1, AE1274, Sig). NAL.

--Gwendolen. 1979. lib. bdg. 11.95 o.p. (ISBN 0-8161-6745-1, Large Print Bks). G K Hall.

--Gwendolen. 1979. pap. 1.95 o.p. (ISBN 0-451-08847-6, J8847, Sig). NAL.

--Letty. (General Ser.). 1980. lib. bdg. 12.95 (ISBN 0-8161-3127-9, Large Print Bks). G K Hall.

--Regina. 1978. pap. 2.50 (ISBN 0-451-11113-3, AE1113, Sig). NAL.

--Rolande. 1979. lib. bdg. 10.95 o.p. (ISBN 0-8161-6670-6, Large Print Bks). G K Hall.

D'Arcy, Martin C. The Meeting of Love & Knowledge: Perennial Wisdom. LC 78-23621. 1979. Repr. of 1957 ed. lib. bdg. 16.00x (ISBN 0-313-21145-0, DAME). Greenwood.

--The Sense of History. LC 73-16797. 309p. 1974. Repr. of 1959 ed. lib. bdg. 16.25x (ISBN 0-8371-7230-6, DASE). Greenwood.

D'Arcy, Martin S. The Nature of Belief. LC 72-10693. 236p. 1976. Repr. of 1958 ed. lib. bdg. 18.50x (ISBN 0-8371-6616-0, DANB). Greenwood.

D'Arcy, P. F. & Griffin, J. P. Iatrogenic Diseases: Annual Updates. 2nd ed. Incl. Update 1981. (Illus.). 1981. text ed. 67.50 (ISBN 0-19-261263-8); Update 1982. 288p. 1983. 49.50 (ISBN 0-19-261356-1). Oxford U Pr.

D'Arcy, Pamela. Angel in the House. (Orig.). 1980. pap. 1.75 o.s.i. (ISBN 0-515-05199-3). Jove Pubns.

--Magic Moment. 192p. (Orig.). 1980. pap. 1.75 o.s.i. (ISBN 0-515-05200-0). Jove Pubns.

Darden, Ellington. The Athlete's Guide to Sports Medicine. (Illus.). 1981. pap. 7.95 (ISBN 0-8092-7159-1). Contemp Bks.

--Especially for Women. 2nd ed. LC 82-83949. (Illus.). 224p. 1983. pap. 7.95 (ISBN 0-88011-118-6). Leisure Pr.

--The Nautilus Nutrition Book. (Illus.). 352p. 1981. 14.95 (ISBN 0-8092-5891-9); pap. 8.95 (ISBN 0-8092-5890-0). Contemp Bks.

Darden, Ellington, ed. see Allman, Fred L., Jr.

Darden, W. R. & Lusch, R. F., eds. Patronage Behavior & Retail Management. 512p. 1983. 39.00 (ISBN 0-444-00704-0). Elsevier.

D'Ardenne, S. R. & Doboson, E. J., eds. Siente Katerine: Re-Edited from Ms Bodley 34 & Other Manuscripts. (Early English Text Soc. Ser. Supplementary Texts). 1981. text ed. 44.00x (ISBN 0-19-722407-5). Oxford U Pr.

Dardess, John W. Confucianism & Autocracy: Professional Elites in the Founding of the Ming Dynasty. LC 82-4822. 400p. 1983. text ed. 35.00x (ISBN 0-520-04659-5). U of Cal Pr.

Dardess, Margaret B., jt. ed. see Aoki, Michiko Y.

Dardis, Tom. Harold Lloyd. 1983. write for info. (ISBN 0-670-45227-0). Viking Pr.

Dardjowidjojo, Soenjono. Sentence Patterns of Indonesian. LC 78-6687. (Pali Language Texts: Indonesia). 1978. pap. text ed. 15.00x (ISBN 0-8248-0418-X). UH Pr.

Dare, Christopher, jt. auth. see Pincus, Lily.

Dare, Dan. Rogue Planet. (Illus.). 112p. 1981. pap. 9.95 (ISBN 0-8256-9553-8, Quick Fox). Putnam Pub Group.

Darell-Brown, Susan. The Mississippi. LC 78-62982. (Rivers of the World Ser.). (Illus.). 1978. PLB 12.68 (ISBN 0-382-06204-3). Silver.

Darey-Bembe, Francoise & Bembe, John P. Day by Day with God. 1982. 4.95 (ISBN 0-8215-9908-9). Sadlier.

Darga, Norbert. The Survival Bible. LC 82-4261. 1982. 16.95 (ISBN 0-672-52760-X); pap. 12.95 (ISBN 0-672-52707-3). Bobbs.

Dargassies, S. S. Neurological Development in the Full-Term & Premature Neonate. 1977. 94.00 (ISBN 90-219-2109-X, North Holland). Elsevier.

Darian, Mujana. Thoughts to Take Home for Advent. 1976. pap. 1.95 o.p. (ISBN 0-8199-0446-5). Franciscan Herald.

Darian, Steven G. The Ganges in Myth & History. LC 77-21374. 1978. text ed. 10.95x (ISBN 0-8248-0509-7). UH Pr.

D'Arienzo, Raymond V. & Moracco, John C. Stress in Teaching: A Comparison of Perceived Occupational Stress Factors Between Special Education & Regular Classroom Teachers. 158p. (Orig.). 1982. lib. bdg. 21.25 (ISBN 0-8191-1874-5); pap. text ed. 9.75 (ISBN 0-8191-1875-3). U Pr of Amer.

Darilek, Richard E. A Loyal Opposition in Time of War: The Republican Party & the Politics of Foreign Policy from Pearl Harbor to Yalta. LC 75-44655. (Contributions in American History: No.49). 288p. (Orig.). 1976. lib. bdg. 27.50 (ISBN 0-8371-8773-7, DLO/). Greenwood.

DaRin, Doris. Sean O'Casey. LC 75-10107. (Literature and Life Ser.). 1977. 11.95 (ISBN 0-8044-2136-6). Ungar.
Darin-Drabkin, H., jt. auth. see Tuma, Elias H.
Daringer, Helen F. Adopted Jane. LC 47-30260. (Illus.). 225p. (gr. 3-7). 1973. pap. 1.25 (ISBN 0-15-602950-2, VoyB). HarBraceJ.
--Stepsister Sally. LC 52-7083. (Illus.). (gr. 3-7). 1966. pap. 1.45 (ISBN 0-15-684951-8, VoyB). HarBraceJ.
Dario, Ruben. Selected Poems of Ruben Dario. Kemp, Lysander, tr. from Sp. (Texas Pan American Ser.). (Illus.). 149p. 1965. 6.95x o.p. (ISBN 0-292-73370-4). U of Tex Pr.
Darisse, Alan, jt. auth. see Archibald, John.
Dark, Philip J. An Illustrated Catalogue of Benin Art. 1982. lib. bdg. 65.00 (ISBN 0-8161-0382-8, Hall Library). G K Hall.
Dark, Sidney & Grey, Rowland. W. S. Gilbert, His Life & Letters. LC 71-164210. 1971. Repr. of 1923 ed. 34.00x (ISBN 0-8103-3789-4). Gale.
Darke, Hubert, tr. see Siyar al-Muluk.
Darke, Jo. Cornish Landscapes. (Illus.). 64p. 1983. 12.50 (ISBN 0-7134-4187-9, Pub. by Batsford England). David & Charles.
--Lake District Landscapes. (Illus.). 64p. 1983. 12.50 (ISBN 0-7134-4185-2, Pub. by Batsford England). David & Charles.
--South Coast Landscapes. (Illus.). 64p. 1983. 12.50 (ISBN 0-7134-4189-5, Pub. by Batsford England). David & Charles.
--Yorkshire Landscapes. (Illus.). 64p. 1983. 12.50 (ISBN 0-7134-4183-6, Pub. by Batsford England). David & Charles.
Darken, Lawrence S. & Gurry, R. W. Physical Chemistry of Metals. (Metallurgy & Metallurgical Engineering Ser.). 1953. text ed. 25.95 o.p. (ISBN 0-07-015355-8, C). McGraw.
Darkes, Anna S. How to Make & Use Overhead Transparancies. LC 77-7888. (Illus.). 1977. pap. 3.95 (ISBN 0-8024-3652-8). Moody.
Darley, H. C., jt. auth. see Gray, George.
Darley, J. Psychology. 1981. 23.95 (ISBN 0-13-733154-1); pap. 8.95 (ISBN 0-13-733188-6). P-H.
Darling. With Love from Darling's Kitchen. 1982. pap. 9.95 (ISBN 0-930440-17-X). Royal Pub Co.
Darling, Frank C. The Westernization of Asia: A Comparative Political Analysis. 1979. lib. bdg. 21.95 (ISBN 0-8161-9005-4, Univ Bks). G K Hall.
Darling, John. Sea Anglers' Guide to Britian & Ireland. 160p. 1982. 60.00x (ISBN 0-7188-2509-8, Pub. by Lutterworth Pr England); pap. 40.00x (ISBN 0-7188-2510-1). State Mutual Bk.
Darling, John, jt. auth. see Rhodius, Hans.
Darling, John R., jt. auth. see Lipson, Harry A.
Darling, Kathy. Ants Have Pets. LC 77-9079. (For Real Ser.). (Illus.). (gr. 1-6). 1977. PLB 6.69 (ISBN 0-8116-4305-0). Garrard.
--Bug Circus. LC 76-17021. (For Real Books). (Illus.). (gr. 2-5). PLB 6.69 (ISBN 0-8116-4301-8). Garrard.
--Jack Frost & the Magic Paint Brush. LC 76-14465. (Imagination Ser.). (Illus.). (gr. k-5). 1977. lib. bdg. 6.69 (ISBN 0-8116-4402-2). Garrard.
--The Jelly Bean Contest. LC 72-3450. (Venture Ser). (Illus.). 64p. (gr. 2). 1972. PLB 6.89 (ISBN 0-8116-6970-X). Garrard.
--Little Bat's Secret. LC 74-8175. (Venture Ser). (Illus.). 64p. (gr. 2). 1974. PLB 6.89 (ISBN 0-8116-6975-0). Garrard.
--The Mystery in Santa's Toyshop. LC 77-19090. (Mystery Ser.). (Illus.). (gr. k-3). 1978. PLB 6.79 (ISBN 0-8116-6402-3). Garrard.
--Paul & His Little-Big Dog. LC 77-22267. (For Real Ser.). (Illus.). (gr. k-4). 1977. PLB 6.69 (ISBN 0-8116-4307-7). Garrard.
--Pecos Bill Finds a Horse. LC 79-12079. (American Folktales Ser.). (Illus.). (gr. 2-5). 1979. PLB 6.69 (ISBN 0-8116-4047-7). Garrard.
Darling, Kathy & Freed, Debbie. Games Gorillas Play. LC 76-17324. (For Real Bks). (Illus.). 40p. (gr. k-3). 1976. PLB 6.69 (ISBN 0-8116-4302-6). Garrard.
Darling, Kathy, jt. auth. see Cobb, Vicki.
Darling, Lois & Darling, Louis. Before & After Dinosaurs. (Illus.). (gr. 5-9). 1959. PLB 8.16 (ISBN 0-688-31077-X). Morrow.
--Sixty Million Years of Horses. (Illus.). (gr. 3-7). 1960. PLB 8.16 (ISBN 0-688-31000-1). Morrow.
--Turtles. (Illus.). (gr. 3-7). 1962. PLB 8.16 (ISBN 0-688-31547-X). Morrow.
--Worms. LC 77-102408. (Illus.). 48p. (gr. 2-5). 1972. pap. 8.16 (ISBN 0-688-31773-1). Morrow.
Darling, Louis, jt. auth. see Darling, Lois.
Darling, Louise, ed. Handbook of Medical Library Practice, Vol. 1. 4th ed. 344p. 1982. 22.50 (ISBN 0-686-97361-5). Med Lib Assn.
Darling, Lowell. One Hand Shaking: A California Campaign Diary. LC 79-3345. 224p. 1980. 5.95 (ISBN 0-15-668747-X, Harv); pap. 5.95o.p. (ISBN 0-15-668747-X, Harv). HarBraceJ.
Darling, Renny. Cordon Red, White, & Blue: The Great New American Cuisine. (Illus.). 1981. pap. 9.95 (ISBN 0-930440-15-3). Recipes-of-the-Month.
--Great Beginnings & Happy Endings: Hors D'Oeuvres & Desserts for Standing Ovations. (Illus., Orig.). 1979. pap. 9.95 (ISBN 0-930440-11-0). Recipes-of-the-Month.
--The Joy of Eating: A Simply Delicious Cookbook. LC 76-27499. 1978. 15.95 (ISBN 0-930440-06-4). Recipes-of-the-Month.
--The Joy of Eating: A Simply Delicious Cookbook. LC 76-27499. (Illus.). 1976. pap. 9.95 (ISBN 0-930440-00-5). Recipes-of-the-Month.
--The Joy of Eating French Food: Great French Dishes Made Easy. LC 77-85742. (Illus.). 1977. pap. 9.95 (ISBN 0-930440-05-6). Recipes-of-the-Month.
--The Joy of Entertaining: Renny Darling's Party Planner. LC 78-53363. 1978. 15.95 (ISBN 0-930440-10-2); pap. 9.95 (ISBN 0-930440-08-0). Recipes-of-the-Month.
--The Love of Eating: 2-Minute Breads & Other Culinary Magic. LC 77-85732. (Illus.). 1977. pap. 9.95 (ISBN 0-930440-01-3). Recipes-of-the-Month.
--The Momma Cookbook: Gourmet Recipes for Family & Friends. LC 77-85737. (Illus.). 1977. pap. 9.95 (ISBN 0-930440-04-8). Recipes-of-the-Month.
--Renny Darling's Diet Gourmet: The Yes, Yes, Yes Cookbook. (Illus.). 1982. pap. 9.95 (ISBN 0-930440-16-1). Recipes-of-the-Month.
--Renny Darling's Party Planner. (Illus.). 1978. 15.95 (ISBN 0-930440-02-1); pap. 9.95 (ISBN 0-930440-03-X). Recipes-of-the-Month.
--Selections from "the Joy of Eating". 1978. pap. 9.95 (ISBN 0-930440-07-2). Recipes-of-the-Month.
--Sugar & Spice & Everything Nice. (Illus.). 1981. pap. 9.95 (ISBN 0-930440-14-5). Recipes-of-the-Month.
--Sweet Dreams: My Greatest Desserts. (Illus.). 1980. pap. 9.95 (ISBN 0-930440-13-7). Recipes-of-the-Month.
--With Love from Mama & Me: Gourmet Recipes for Family & Friends. (Illus.). 1980. pap. 9.95 (ISBN 0-930440-12-9). Recipes-of-the-Month.
Darlington, C. D. Evolution of Man & Society. 1970. 12.95 o.p. (ISBN 0-671-20171-9). S&S.
Darlington, C. D. & LaCour, L. F. The Handling of Chromosomes. 6th ed. LC 75-20130. 201p. 1976. 22.95x o.p. (ISBN 0-470-19527-4). Halsted Pr.
Darlington, C. LeRoy & Eigenfeld, Neil. The Chemical World: Activities & Explorations. LC 76-4597. (Illus.). 1977. text ed. 16.96 (ISBN 0-395-24070-0). HM.
Darlington, Joy. Fast Friends. LC 78-22732. 1979. 8.95 o.p. (ISBN 0-385-15158-6). Doubleday.
--Those Van der Meer Women. LC 78-14839. 1979. 10.00 o.p. (ISBN 0-399-12174-9). Putnam Pub Group.
Darlington, Katya. The Labrador Retriever. 1977. pap. 3.50 (ISBN 0-7028-1094-0). Palmetto Pub.
Darlington, P. J. Evolution for Naturalists: The Simple Principles & Complex Reality. LC 79-22897. 1980. 26.50x (ISBN 0-471-04783-X, Pub. by Wiley-Interscience). Wiley.
Darlington, Sandy, ed. see DeVegh, Elizabeth.
Darlington, Sandy, ed. see Dranow, Ralph.
Darmstaedter, Ludwig, et al. Handbuch Zur Geschichte der Naturwissenschaften und der Technik. 2nd rev. enl. ed. LC 9-606. 1908. 46.00 o.s.i. (ISBN 0-527-21500-7). Kraus Repr.
Darnall, Jean. Heaven, Here I Come. LC 77-91521. 1978. pap. 2.95 o.p. (ISBN 0-88419-148-6). Creation Hse.
Darnbrough, A. & Kinrade, F. Directory for the Disabled: A Handbook of Information & Opportunities for Disabled & Handicapped People. X ed. 242p. 1981. pap. text ed. 15.00 (ISBN 0-85941-184-2). Verry.
Darnell, A. C., jt. auth. see O'Brien, D. P.
Darnell, D. K. & Brockriede, W. Persons Communicating. (Speech Communication Ser.). (Illus.). 256p. 1976. pap. text ed. 17.95 (ISBN 0-13-657387-8). P-H.
Darnell, Donald G. William Hickling Prescott. (United States Authors Ser.). 1975. lib. bdg. 13.95 (ISBN 0-8057-0598-8, Twayne). G K Hall.
Darnell, Frank & Simpson, Patricia. Rural Education: In Pursuit of Excellence. 244p. 1982. pap. 29.95 (ISBN 0-686-84840-3, Pub. by CSIRO Australia). Intl Schol Bk Serv.
Darnton, Maida C., tr. see Lucas-Dubreton, J.
Darnton, Robert. Mesmerism: The End of the Enlightenment in France. LC 68-25607. (Illus.). 1971. pap. 5.95 o.p. (ISBN 0-8052-0269-2). Schocken.
Da Rosa, A. M., jt. auth. see Ibarra, F.
Daroy, Esther V. The Drumbeater & Other Stories. 144p. (Orig.). 1982. pap. 5.75 (ISBN 0-686-37579-3, Pub. by New Day Philippines). Cellar.
D'Aroy, Pat, jt. ed. see Barr, Mary.
Darr, Ann. Cleared for Landing. LC 78-6640. 1978. 10.95 o.p. (ISBN 0-931848-00-8); pap. 4.50 (ISBN 0-931848-01-6). Dryad Pr.
Darr, Jack. How to Test Almost Everything Electronic. LC 66-30560. 1967. 10.95 (ISBN 0-685-24819-4); pap. 4.95 (ISBN 0-8306-6132-8, 132). TAB Bks.
Darr, K., jt. ed. see Rakich, J.
Darracott, J., ed. see Fitzwilliam Museum.
Darracott, Joseph. The World of Charles Ricketts. (Illus.). 200p. 1980. 29.95 o.p. (ISBN 0-416-00711-2). Methuen Inc.
Darracott, Joseph C., ed. The First World War in Posters. (Illus., Orig.). 1974. 9.95 o.p. (ISBN 0-486-23027-9); pap. 6.00 (ISBN 0-486-22979-3). Dover.
Darragh, Colleen. The Pregnancy Day-By-Day Book. (Illus.). 192p. 1983. 9.57i (ISBN 0-06-015152-8, HarpT). Har-Row.
Darrah, L. B. Food Marketing. rev. ed. 387p. 1971. 33.95 (ISBN 0-471-06588-9). Wiley.
Darrell, Elizabeth. The Gathering Wolves. 388p. 1980. 13.95 o.p. (ISBN 0-698-11061-7, Coward). Putnam Pub Group.
--The Jade Alliance. LC 79-14342. 1979. 11.95 o.p. (ISBN 0-399-12342-3). Putnam Pub Group.
Darrell, Jesse, tr. see Steiner, Rudolf.
Darroch, Nadina. Cooking with Coffee. (Illus.). 112p. (Orig.). 1979. pap. 3.95 o.s.i. (ISBN 0-89104-229-6, A & W Visual Library). A & W Pubs.
Darroch, Vivian & Silvers, Ronald J. Interpretive Human Studies: An Introduction to Phenomenological Research. LC 82-13636. 276p. 1983. lib. bdg. 23.50 (ISBN 0-8191-2698-5); pap. text ed. 11.50 (ISBN 0-8191-2699-3). U Pr of Amer.
Darrough, Masako N. & Blank, Robert H., eds. Biological Differences & Social Equality: Implications for Social Policy. (Illus.). 272p. 1983. lib. bdg. 29.95 (ISBN 0-313-23022-6, DAS/). Greenwood.
Darrow, Clarence. Crime, Its Cause & Treatment. LC 70-172562. (Criminology, Law Enforcement, & Social Problems Ser.: No. 148). 320p. (Intro. added). 1972. Repr. of 1922 ed. 14.00x (ISBN 0-87585-143-6). Patterson Smith.
--An Eye for an Eye. LC 76-79093. 1969. 9.95 (ISBN 0-87716-011-2, Pub. by Moore Pub Co). F Apple.
--Resist Not Evil. LC 78-172567. (Criminology, Law Enforcement & Social Problems Ser.: No. 148). 200p. (With intro. & index added). 1972. lib. bdg. 10.00 cancelled (ISBN 0-87585-148-7); pap. 4.00 (ISBN 0-87585-903-8). Patterson Smith.
--The Skeleton in the Closet. 1936. pap. 3.00 (ISBN 0-686-77085-4). Branden.
Darrow, Clarence & Lewis, Arthur. Darrow-Lewis Debate on the Theory of Non-resistance Evil. pap. 3.00 (ISBN 0-686-96400-4). Am Atheist.
Darrow, Clarence see Drummond, Henry.
Darrow, Clarence S. Resist Not Evil. LC 77-137538. (Peace Movement in America Ser). 179p. 1972. Repr. of 1903 ed. lib. bdg. 12.95x (ISBN 0-89198-065-2). Ozer.
Darrow, Clarence S. & Lewis, Arthur M. Marx Versus Tolstoy: A Debate. LC 73-137537. (Peace Movement in America Ser). 124p. 1972. Repr. of 1911 ed. lib. bdg. 10.95x (ISBN 0-89198-066-0). Ozer.
Darrow, Frank M. Cybernetics versus Homeostasis. (Illus.). 1977. pap. 4.00 (ISBN 0-686-82893-3). Darrow.
--Girls, & Boys, & Women. (Illus.). 1977. pap. 3.50 o.p. (ISBN 0-685-86446-4). Darrow.
--Life Styles & Sex. 68p. (Orig.). 1971. pap. text ed. 3.00 (ISBN 0-912636-02-5). Darrow.
--Middle Childhood & Future Lifestyles. new ed. 175p. (Orig.). 1972. 3.00 o.p. (ISBN 0-685-25551-4). Darrow.
--Sex Ethics for Survival. (Illus.). 1968. pap. text ed. 2.00 (ISBN 0-685-08747-6). Darrow.
--Wifestyles & Lifestyles. new ed. 34p. 1974. 2.50 o.p. (ISBN 0-912630-02-7). Darrow.
Darrow, Frank M., et al. An Experiment. (Orig.). 1977. pap. 2.50 o.p. (ISBN 0-685-80844-0). Darrow.
Darrow, Helen F. Social Studies for Understanding. LC 64-18225. (Orig.). 1964. pap. text ed. 4.50 (ISBN 0-8077-1230-2). Tchrs Coll.
Darrow, Ken, ed. see Thorburn, Craig.
Darst, David H. Juan Boscan. (World Authors Ser.). 1978. lib. bdg. 15.95 (ISBN 0-8057-6316-3, Twayne). G K Hall.
Darst, David M. The Complete Bond Book: A Guide to All Types of Fixed-Income Securities. (Illus.). 352p. (Orig.). 1975. 33.95 (ISBN 0-07-017390-7, P&RB). McGraw.
--The Handbook of the Bond & Money Markets. LC 80-36816. (Illus.). 461p. 1981. 34.95 (ISBN 0-07-015401-5, P&RB). McGraw.
Dart, Alan, jt. auth. see Cardy, Lynn.
Dart, Allan K. E S L Grammar Quiz Book for Intermediate to Advanced Students of English As a Second Language. 256p. 1982. pap. 10.95 (ISBN 0-13-283812-5). P-H.
Dart, Allen K. ESL Grammar Workbook 1: For Intermediate Speakers & Writers of English As a Second Language. 1978. pap. text ed. 10.95 (ISBN 0-13-283663-7). P-H.
--ESL Grammar Workbook 2: For Intermediate Speakers & Writers of English As a Second Language. 1978. pap. text ed. 10.95 (ISBN 0-13-283671-8). P-H.
Dart, P. J., jt. ed. see Ayanaba, A.
Dart, R. K. & Stretton, R. J. Microbiological Aspects of Pollution Control. (Fundamentals of Pollution Control & Environmental Sciences Ser.: Vol. 6). 1980. 53.25 (ISBN 0-444-41918-7). Elsevier.
Dart, Thurston. Interpretation of Music. pap. 4.95xi (ISBN 0-06-131978-3, TB1978, TB). Har-Row.
Dartington, T., et al. Life Together. 148p. 1981. 17.95x (ISBN 0-422-77900-8, Pub. by Tavistock England); pap. 8.95x (ISBN 0-422-77910-5). Methuen Inc.
Dartmouth College Library, Hanover, N. H. Dictionary Catalog of the Stefansson Collection on the Polar Regions, 8 Vols. 1967. Set. lib. bdg. 690.00 (ISBN 0-8161-0676-2, Hall Library). G K Hall.
Dartnell, A. Trees & Shrubs of the British Isles. 11.50x (ISBN 0-392-06756-0, LTB). Sportshelf.
Darton, Harvey F. Arnold Bennett. 127p. 1982. lib. bdg. 17.50 (ISBN 0-8495-1139-9). Arden Lib.
Darton, Michael, ed. A Modern Concordance to the New Testament. LC 75-34831. 1977. 12.95 (ISBN 0-385-07901-X). Doubleday.
Darvall, Frank O. Popular Disturbances & Public Order in Regency England. LC 68-58973. Repr. of 1934 ed. lib. bdg. 25.00x (ISBN 0-678-00458-7). Kelley.
Darvall, Lixi. How to Get What You Want in Nine Languages (incl. Hebrew) 160p. 1982. pap. 4.95 (ISBN 0-686-43007-7, Carta Maps & Guides Pub Isreal). Hippocrene Bks.
Darvas, Robert & Lukacs, Paul. Spotlight on Card Play: A New Approach to the Practical Analysis of Bridge Hands. (Master Bridge Ser.). (Illus.). 160p. 1982. pap. 9.50 (ISBN 0-575-03078-X, Pub. by Gollancz England). David & Charles.
Darvick, Herman M. Collecting Autographs. LC 81-1847. (Illus.). 96p. (gr. 4-7). 1981. PLB 8.29 o.p. (ISBN 0-671-34025-5). Messner.
Darvill, Fred T., Jr. Hiking the North Cascades. LC 81-14451. (Sierra Club Totebook Ser.). (Illus.). 384p. (Orig.). 1982. pap. 9.95 (ISBN 0-87156-297-9). Sierra.
--Mountaineering Medicine: A Wilderness Medical Guide. 10th ed. Winnett, Thomas, ed. (Illus.). 60p. 1983. pap. 1.95 (ISBN 0-89997-021-4). Wilderness Pr.
--North Cascades Highway Guide. 1973. pap. 1.00 o.p. (ISBN 0-915740-03-6). Darvill Outdoor.
--Stehekin: The Enchanted Valley. LC 80-16628. (Illus.). 128p. (Orig.). 1981. pap. 6.95 (ISBN 0-913140-42-2). Signpost Bk Pub.
Darwell, Stephen, ed. see Butler, Joseph.
Darwin, B. Dickens. LC 73-8958. (Studies in Dickens, No. 52). 1973. Repr. of 1933 ed. lib. bdg. 31.95x (ISBN 0-8383-1710-3). Haskell.
Darwin, C. A Monograph of the Sub-Class Cirripedia: 1851-54, 2 vols. in 1. (Illus.). 1964. 48.00 (ISBN 3-7682-0114-7). Lubrecht & Cramer.
Darwin, Charles. Darwin on Earthworms: The Formation of Vegetable Mould Through the Action of Worms. (Illus.). 160p. 1976. 7.95 (ISBN 0-916302-10-5); pap. 5.95 (ISBN 0-916302-06-7). Bookworm NY.
--Darwin on Humus & the Earthworm: The Formation of Vegetable Mould. 4th ed. 1966. text ed. 5.00x p.p. (ISBN 0-571-06778-6). Humanities.
--The Descent of Man & Selection in Relation to Sex. LC 73-20158. (Illus.). 672p. 1974. Repr. of 1874 ed. 52.00 o.p. (ISBN 0-8103-3963-3). Gale.
--The Expression of Emotion in Man & Animals. Rachman, S. J., ed. (Classics in Psychology & Psychiatry Ser.). 432p. 1983. Repr. of 1872 ed. write for info. (ISBN 0-904014-39-8). F Pinter Pubs.
--Expression of the Emotions in Man & Animals. LC 65-17286. (Illus.). 1965. pap. 7.00x (ISBN 0-226-13656-6, P526, Phoen). U of Chicago Pr.
--Origin of Species. pap. 3.50 (ISBN 0-451-62102-6, ME2102, Ment). NAL.
--The Origin of Species. abr. ed. Appleman, Philip, ed. 1975. pap. text ed. 3.95x (ISBN 0-393-09219-4). Norton.
--The Origin of Species & the Descent of Man. 8.95 (ISBN 0-394-60398-2). Modern Lib.
--The Origin of the Species. (Rowman & Littlefield University Library). 488p. 1972. 15.00x (ISBN 0-87471-662-4); pap. 8.00x (ISBN 0-87471-663-2). Rowman.
--Origin of the Species. 1982. pap. 3.95 (ISBN 0-14-043205-1). Penguin.
--The Structure & Distribution of Coral Reefs. (Library Reprint Ser.). 1976. 30.00x (ISBN 0-520-03282-9). U of Cal Pr.
Darwin, Charles R. The Descent of Man & His Selection in Relation to Sex. LC 72-3894. (Illus.). xvi, 688p. 1972. write for info. (ISBN 0-404-08409-5). AMS Pr.
--Diary of the Voyage of H. M. S. Beagle. Barlow, Nora, ed. LC 34-6168. 1969. Repr. of 1933 ed. 25.00 o.s.i. (ISBN 0-527-21600-3). Kraus Repr.
--The Different Forms of Flowers on Plants of the Same Species. LC 72-3900. (Illus.). viii, 352p. 1972. write for info. (ISBN 0-404-08414-1). AMS Pr.
--The Effects of Cross & Self Fertilisation in the Vegetable Kingdom, Vol. 13. LC 72-3898. viii, 482p. 1972. write for info. AMS Pr.
--Expression of the Emotions in Man & Animals. LC 73-90703. Repr. of 1955 ed. lib. bdg. 18.50x (ISBN 0-8371-2291-0, DAEM). Greenwood.
--The Formation of Vegetable Mould, Through the Action of Worms, with Observations on Their Habits. LC 72-3903. (Illus.). vii, 326p. 1972. write for info. (ISBN 0-404-08416-8). AMS Pr.
--Foundations of the Origin of Species. Darwin, Francis, ed. LC 10-1422. 1909. 13.00 o.s.i. (ISBN 0-527-21610-0). Kraus Repr.

--Geological Obsevations on the Volcanic Islands & Parts of South America Visited during the Voyage of H.M.S. Beagle. LC 72-3889. (Illus.). xiii, 648p. 1972. write for info. (ISBN 0-404-08403-6). AMS Pr.
--Insectivorous Plants, Vol. 12. LC 72-3897. (Illus.). x, 462p. 1972. write for info. AMS Pr.
--Journal of Researches into the Natural History & Geology of the Countries Visited during the Voyage of the H.M.S. Beagle Round the World, Under the Command of Capt. Fitz Roy R.N, 2 Vols. LC 72-3887. (Illus.). x, 519p. 1972. write for info. (ISBN 0-404-08401-X). AMS Pr.
--The Life & Letters of Charles Darwin, 2 Vols. Darwin, Francis, ed. LC 72-3904. (Illus.). 1972. write for info. (ISBN 0-404-08417-6). AMS Pr.
--The Movement & Habits of Climbing Plants. LC 72-3896. (Illus.). viii, 208p. write for info. (ISBN 0-404-08411-7). AMS Pr.
--The Origin of Species by Means of Natural Selection. LC 72-3891. (Illus.). write for info. (ISBN 0-404-08404-4). AMS Pr.
--The Power of Movement in Plants. 2nd ed. LC 65-23402. 1966. Repr. of 1881 ed. lib. bdg. 55.00 (ISBN 0-306-70921-X). Da Capo.
--The Power of Movement in Plants. 3rd ed. LC 72-3901. (Illus.). x, 592p. 1972. write for info. (ISBN 0-404-08415-X). AMS Pr.
--The Structure & Distribution of Coral Reefs. 3rd ed. LC 73-147085. (Illus.). xx, 344p. 1972. write for info. (ISBN 0-404-08402-8). AMS Pr.
--The Variation of Animals & Plants Under Domestication, 2 Vols. LC 72-3893. (Illus.). 1972. write for info. (ISBN 0-404-08407-9). AMS Pr.
--The Various Contrivances by Which Orchids are Fertilised by Insects. 2nd ed. LC 72-3892. (Illus.). xvi, 300p. 1972. write for info. (ISBN 0-404-08406-0). AMS Pr.
--Voyage of the "Beagle". 1979. 10.95x (ISBN 0-460-00104-3, Evman); pap. 5.95x (ISBN 0-460-01104-9, Evman). Biblio Dist.

Darwin, Erasmus. The Botanic Garden; a Poem in Two Parts. Reiman, Donald H., ed. Bd. with Pt. 1. Containing the Economy of Vegetation; Pt. 2. The Loves of the Plants. with Philosopical Notes. LC 75-31194. (Romantic Context Ser.: Poetry 1789-1830). 1979. Repr. of 1791 ed. lib. bdg. 47.00 o.s.i. (ISBN 0-8240-2145-2). Garland Pub.
--The Golden Age, a Poetical Epistle from Erasmus D-N M.D., to Thomas Beddoes, Repr. Of 1794 Ed. Reiman, Donald H., ed. Bd. with The Temple of Nature; or the Origin of Society: A Poem, with Philosophical Notes. Repr. of 1803 ed. LC 75-31195. (Romantic Context Ser.: Poetry 1789-1830: Vol. 47). 1979. lib. bdg. 47.00 o.s.i. (ISBN 0-8240-2146-0). Garland Pub.

Darwin, Francis, ed. see Darwin, Charles R.

Darwin, Gary. Darwin's Thumb Tip Miracles. Fenton, Robert & Fenton, Irene, eds. (Illus.). 129p. (Orig.). (gr. 8 up). 1981. 20.00 (ISBN 0-939024-00-4); text ed. 20.00 (ISBN 0-686-98459-5); pap. 13.95 (ISBN 0-939024-01-2). Rare Pub.

Darwin, George. Scientific Papers: 1907-16, 5 vols. LC 8-16429. 1976. Set. 300.00 (ISBN 0-527-21620-8). Kraus Repr.

Darwin, John. Britain, Egypt & the Middle East. LC 80-14718. 1980. 26.00 (ISBN 0-312-09736-0). St Martin.

Dary, David. Cowboy Culture: A Saga of Five Centuries. LC 80-2699. (Illus.). 416p. 1981. 18.50 (ISBN 0-394-42605-3). Knopf.
--How to Write News for Broadcast & Print Media. LC 72-94811. 192p. 1973. 9.95 o.p. (ISBN 0-8306-3643-9, 643). TAB Bks.

Dary, David A. The Buffalo Book. 448p. 1983. pap. 3.95 (ISBN 0-380-00475-5, 62786, Discus). Avon.
--The Buffalo Book: The Full Saga of the American Animal. LC 82-73575. (Illus.). 374p. 1973. 18.00 (ISBN 0-8040-0653-9, SB); limited ed. o.p. 100.00 (ISBN 0-8040-0717-9). Swallow.

Dary, Davis. Cowboy Culture. 1982. pap. 7.95 (ISBN 0-380-60632-1). Avon.

Daryabadi, A. M. Holy Quaran Arabic-English. 19.95 (ISBN 0-686-83591-3). Kazi Pubns.

Daryanani, Gobind. Principles of Active Network Synthesis & Design. LC 76-20659. 495p. 1976. text ed. 36.95 (ISBN 0-471-19545-6). Wiley.

Daryanani, Sital. Building Systems Design with Programmable Calculators. 1980. 39.50 (ISBN 0-07-015415-5, P&RB). McGraw.

Das. Fundamentals of Soil Dynamics. Date not set. 39.50 (ISBN 0-444-00705-9). Elsevier.

Das, Arvind N. Agrarian Movements in India: Studies on 20th Century Bihar. (Illus.). 200p. 1982. text ed. 29.50x (ISBN 0-7146-3216-3, F Cass Co). Biblio Dist.

Das, B. S. The Sikkim Saga. (Illus.). 1982. text ed. write for info. (ISBN 0-7069-1971-8, Pub. by Vikas India). Advent NY.

Das, Bhagavan. Essential Unity of All Religions. LC 66-6517. 1966. pap. 2.75 o.p. (ISBN 0-8356-0007-6, Quest). Theos Pub Hse.

Das, Braja. Advanced Soil Mechanics. (Illus.). 528p. 1982. text ed. 34.95 (ISBN 0-07-015416-3, C). McGraw.

Das, D. K., jt. auth. see Prabhudesai, R. K.

Das, H. C. Tantricism: A Study of the Yogini Cult. (Illus.). 88p. 1981. text ed. 21.50x (ISBN 0-391-02791-3, 41007, Pub. by Sterling India). Humanities.

Das, J. P. & Mulcaby, R., eds. Theory & Research in Learning Disabilities. LC 82-112219. 300p. 1982. 37.50x (ISBN 0-306-41112-1, Plenum Pr). Plenum Pub.

Das, K. G. Controlled-Release Technology: Bioengineering Analysis. 240p. 1983. 50.00 (ISBN 0-471-08680-0, Pub. by Wiley-Interscience). Wiley.

Das, Kamala. The Descendants. (Writers Workshop Redbird Ser.). 35p. 1975. o.s.i. 8.00 (ISBN 0-88253-526-9); pap. text ed. 4.00 (ISBN 0-88253-525-0). Ind-US Inc.

Das, Manas M. The Rooted Alien: A Study of Hardy's Poetic Sensibility. 160p. 1982. text ed. 13.75x (ISBN 0-391-02805-7). Humanities.

Das, P. C., jt. auth. see Sibinga, C. Th.

Das, R. J. Joseph Conrad: A Study in Existential Vision. 132p. 1980. text ed. 10.00x (ISBN 0-391-01915-5). Humanities.

Das, R. R., jt. auth. see Misra, R.

Das, Swami Harihar & Ito, Dee. The Healthy Body Handbook: A Basic Guide to Diet & Nutrition, Yoga for Health, & Natural Cures for a Healthy Body. LC 79-2802. (Illus.). 1980. pap. 5.95i o.p. (ISBN 0-06-090730-4, CN 730, CN). Har-Row.

Dasa, Mandalesuaraba, et al, eds. see Goswami, Satsuarupa D.

Dasa, Mandalesvara, ed. see Das Goswami, Satsvarupa.

Dascal, Marcelo. Pragmatics & the Philosophy of Mind. (Pragmatics & Beyond Ser.). 120p. 1983. pap. 16.00 (ISBN 90-272-2503-6). Benjamins North Am.

Dascenzo, Frank, jt. auth. see Groat, Dick.

Dascher, Paul E. & Janell, Paul A. Accounting: A Book of Readings. LC 80-70470. 539p. 1983. pap. text ed. 11.95x (ISBN 0-931920-30-2). Dame Pubns.

Dascher, Paul E., jt. auth. see Copeland, Ronald M.

Dasent, G. W., tr. see De Paola, Tomie.

Dasent, George W. East O' the Sun & West O' the Moon. LC 70-97214. (gr. 1 up). 1970. pap. 6.00 (ISBN 0-486-22521-6). Dover.
--East O' the Sun & West O' the Moon. (Norwegian Folk Tales). (Illus.). 8.25 (ISBN 0-8446-0573-5). Peter Smith.
--Popular Tales from the Norse: With an Introductory Essay on the Origin & Diffusion of Popular Tales. 3rd ed. LC 74-136733. clii, 443p. 1971. Repr. of 1888 ed. 37.00x (ISBN 0-8103-3796-7). Gale.

Das Goswami, Satsvarupa. Japa Reform Notebook. Bimala dasi & Mandalesvara dasa, eds. 145p. (Orig.). 1982. pap. text ed. 2.95 (ISBN 0-911233-07-5). Gita Nagari.
--Letters from Srila Prabhupada, Vol. 1. Mandalesvara dasa & Gaura Purnima dasa, eds. 274p. (Orig.). 1982. pap. text ed. 3.95 (ISBN 0-911233-03-2). Gita Nagari.
--One Hundred & Eight Rosebushes: Preaching in Germany. Mandalesvara dasa & Bimala dasi, eds. (Prahupada-lila Ser.). 44p. (Orig.). 1982. pap. text ed. 2.00 (ISBN 0-911233-04-0). Gita-Nagari.
--Srila Prbhupada in Latin America. Dasa, Mandalesvara & Dasi, Bimala, eds. (Prabhupada-lila). (Orig.). Vol. 7. pap. text ed. 2.00 (ISBN 0-911233-05-9). Gita-Nagari.

Dasgupta, A. K. Economic Theory & the Developing Countries. LC 74-83520. 250p. 1975. 22.50 (ISBN 0-312-23590-9). St Martin.

Das Gupta, A. K. A Theory of Wage Policy. (Illus.). 1976. pap. 3.95x o.p. (ISBN 0-19-560699-X). Oxford U Pr.

Das Gupta, Ashin. Malabar in Asian Trade, 1740-1800. (Cambridge South Asian Studies: No. 3). 1967. 27.95 (ISBN 0-521-04784-6). Cambridge U Pr.

Dasgupta, Gautam, ed. see Breuer, Lee.

Das Gupta, Jyotirindra. Authority, Priority, & Human Development. (Illus.). 126p. 9.95x (ISBN 0-19-561391-0). Oxford U Pr.
--Language Conflict & National Development: Group Politics & National Language Policy in India. LC 75-94992. (Center for South & Southeast Asia Studies, UC Berkeley). 1970. 27.50x (ISBN 0-520-01590-8). U of Cal Pr.

Dasgupta, P. S. & Heal, G. M. Economic Theory & Exhaustible Resources. LC 79-51749. (Cambridge Economic Handbooks Ser.). 1980. 47.50 (ISBN 0-521-22991-X); pap. 18.95x (ISBN 0-521-29761-3). Cambridge U Pr.

Dasgupta, Partha. The Control of Resources. (Illus.). 240p. 1983. text ed. 22.50x (ISBN 0-674-16980-8). Harvard U Pr.

Dasgupta, Surendranath. A History of Indian Philosophy, 5 vols. 1975. o.p. (ISBN 0-685-81609-5); Vol. 1. pap. text ed. 8.75x (ISBN 0-8426-0963-6); Vol. 2. pap. text ed. 11.50x (ISBN 0-8426-0975-X); Vol. 3. pap. text ed. 11.50x (ISBN 0-8426-0976-8); Vol. 4. pap. text ed. 8.75x (ISBN 0-8426-0977-6); Vol. 5. pap. text ed. 4.75x (ISBN 0-8426-0964-4). Humanities.
--Indian Idealism. 1962. 27.95 (ISBN 0-521-04783-8); pap. 8.95x (ISBN 0-521-09194-2). Cambridge U Pr.
--Indian Philosophy, 5 vols. 1922-55. Set. 230.00 (ISBN 0-521-08865-8); Vol. 1. 57.50 (ISBN 0-521-04778-1); Vol. 2. 65.50 (ISBN 0-521-04779-X); Vol. 3. 65.50 (ISBN 0-521-04780-3); Vol. 4. 55.00 (ISBN 0-521-04781-1); Vol. 5. 29.95 (ISBN 0-521-04782-X). Cambridge U Pr.

Dash, Bhagan & Kashyap, Lalitesh. Basic Principles of Ayurveda. 655p. 1980. 38.75x (ISBN 0-391-02208-3). Humanities.

Dash, Bhagwan & Kashyap, L. Diagnosis & Treatment of Diseases in Ayurveda. (Todarananda Ayurveda Saukhyam: Vol. 2). 640p. 1981. text ed. 38.75x (ISBN 0-391-02472-8, Pub. by Concept India). Humanities.

Dash, Samuel, et al. Eavesdroppers. LC 71-136498. (Civil Liberties in American History Ser). (Illus.). 1971. Repr. of 1959 ed. lib. bdg. 35.00 (ISBN 0-306-70074-3). Da Capo.

Dash, V. & Kashyap, L., eds. Materia Medica of Ayurveda. 1980. text ed. 40.00x (ISBN 0-391-01813-2). Humanities.

Dasheff, Bill & Dearborn, L. Good Garb. (Orig.). 1980. pap. 9.95 o.s.i. (ISBN 0-440-52588-8, Delta). Dell.

Dashefsky, Arnold. Ethnic Identity in Society. 1976. pap. 12.95 (ISBN 0-395-30587-X). HM.

Dashew, Linda, jt. auth. see Dashew, Steve.

Dashew, Steve & Dashew, Linda. The Circumnavigators' Handbook. (Illus.). 1983. 34.50x (ISBN 0-393-03275-2). Norton.

Dashiell, Segar C. Smithfield: A Pictorial History. LC 77-18259. (Illus.). 1977. 15.95 o.p. (ISBN 0-915442-44-2). Donning Co.

Dasi, Bimala, ed. see Das Goswami, Satsvarupa.

Da Silva, jt. ed. see Wilson, Barbara.

Da Silva, Raul, et al. Evidence of Terror in Chile. MacBeth, Brian, tr. from Swedish. 1974. pap. text ed. 2.45 o.p. (ISBN 0-85036-199-0, Merlin Pr). Carrier Pigeon.

Da Silva, Zenia S. Beginning Spanish: A Concept Approach. 4th ed. (Illus.). 1978. text ed. 23.95 scp o.p. (ISBN 0-06-041506-1, HarpC); scp tape manual 9.50 o.p. (ISBN 0-06-041507-X); scp tapes 315.00 o.p. (ISBN 0-06-047488-2). Har-Row.
--On with Spanish: A Concept Approach. 3rd ed. 438p. 1982. text ed. 21.50 scp (ISBN 0-06-041525-8, HarpC); instr's manaul avail. (ISBN 0-06-361511-8); tapes 295.00 (ISBN 0-06-047443-2); scp 8.95 (ISBN 0-06-041526-6). Har-Row.
--Spanish: A Short Course. 2nd ed. (Illus.). 1980. text ed. 22.50 scp (ISBN 0-06-041524-X, HarpC); instructor's manual avail. (ISBN 0-06-361507-X); scp wkbk. & tape man 8.50 (ISBN 0-06-041518-5); scp tapes 295.00 (ISBN 0-06-047492-0). Har-Row.

Dasilva, Zenia Sacks. Beginning Spanish: A Concept Approach. 5th ed. 608p. 1983. text ed. 24.50 scp (ISBN 0-06-041508-8, HarpC); scp wkbk. 8.50 (ISBN 0-06-041509-6); instr's. manual avail. (ISBN 0-06-361538-X); scp reel to reel tapes 295.00 (ISBN 0-686-83089-X); scp cassettes 295.00 (ISBN 0-06-047446-7). Har-Row.

Dasmann, R. F. Environmental Conservation. 4th ed. 436p. 1976. 18.95 (ISBN 0-471-19602-9). Wiley.
--Planet in Peril? Man & the Biosphere Today. 135p. (Ger., Hungarian, Persian & Span. eds. also avail.). 1972. pap. 4.50 o.p. (ISBN 92-3-100947-8, UNESCO). Unipub.

Dasmann, Raymond F. California's Changing Environment. Hundley, Norris & Schutz, John A., eds. LC 81-66064. (Golden State Ser.). (Illus.). 110p. 1981. pap. text ed. 5.95x (ISBN 0-87835-116-7). Boyd & Fraser.
--Wildlife Biology. 2nd ed. LC 80-19006. 212p. 1981. text ed. 20.95x (ISBN 0-471-08042-X). Wiley.

Dasmann, Raymond F., et al. Ecological Principles for Economic Development. LC 72-8597. 252p. 1973. pap. 24.95 (ISBN 0-471-19606-1, Pub. by Wiley-Interscience). Wiley.

Dasoyan, K. A. & Aguf, I. A. Lead Accumulator. 1968. 5.95x o.p. (ISBN 0-210-27168-X). Asia.

Dass, Baba Hari. Sweeper to Saint: Stories of Holy India. Renu, Ma, ed. LC 80-52021. (Illus.). 208p. (Orig.). 1981. pap. 6.95 (ISBN 0-918100-03-8). Sri Rama.

Dass, Baba Hari, et al. Silence Speaks--from the Chalkboard of Baba Hari Dass. LC 76-53902. (Illus.). 224p. (Orig.). 1982. pap. 5.95 (ISBN 0-918100-01-1). SRI Rama.

Dass, Ram. Miracle of Love: Stories About Neem Karoli Baba. (Illus.). 1979. pap. 12.95 (ISBN 0-525-47611-3, 01257-380). Dutton.

D'Assaily, Gisele & Falconnet, Paulette. Tak-Tak the Dachshund. LC 63-17652. (gr. 1-3). 1963. 3.50 o.s.i. (ISBN 0-8076-0237-X). Braziller.

Dasso, C. H. Nuclear Physics. (Proceedings). 1982. 95.75 (ISBN 0-444-86401-6). Elsevier.

Dasso, Jerome & Kuhn, Gerald W. Real Estate Finance. (Illus.). 464p. 1983. 24.95 (ISBN 0-13-762757-2). P-H.

Dasso, Jerome, jt. auth. see Ring, Alfred A.

Dasso, Jerome, et al. Fundamentals of Real Estate. (Illus.). 1977. ref. ed. 23.95 (ISBN 0-13-343426-5); student guide 9.95 (ISBN 0-13-343442-7). P-H.

Data Notes Publishing Staff. Aluminum Recycling: Data Notes. 30p. 1983. pap. text ed. 9.95 (ISBN 0-911569-40-5). Data Notes Pub.
--Automobile Recycling: Data Notes. 30p. pap. text ed. 9.95 (ISBN 0-911569-50-2). Data Notes Pub.
--Clothing Recycling: Data Notes. 1983. pap. text ed. 9.95 (ISBN 0-911569-49-9). Data Notes Pub.
--Directory of Colleges that Offer Credit for Life Experience. 300p. 1983. text ed. 49.95 (ISBN 0-911569-07-3). Data Notes Pub.
--Directory of Flea Market Directories, Books, References. 200p. 1983. pap. text ed. 14.95 (ISBN 0-911569-57-X). Data Notes Pub.
--Directory of Refunding Periodicals, Books, Clubs, Associations. 200p. 1983. text ed. 29.95 (ISBN 0-911569-06-5). Data Notes Pub.
--Directory of Women's Associations & Organizations Based in Arizona. 1983. pap. text ed. 9.95 (ISBN 0-911569-32-4). Data Notes Pub.
--Directory of Women's Associations & Organizations Based in Colorado. 1983. pap. text ed. 9.95 (ISBN 0-911569-33-2). Data Notes Pub.
--Directory of Women's Associations & Organizations Based in California. 1983. pap. text ed. 9.95 (ISBN 0-911569-27-8). Data Notes Pub.
--Directory of Women's Associations & Organizations Based in District of Columbia. 1983. pap. text ed. 9.95 (ISBN 0-911569-28-6). Data Notes Pub.
--Directory of Women's Associations & Organizations Based in England. 1983. pap. text ed. 9.95 (ISBN 0-911569-39-1). Data Notes Pub.
--Directory of Women's Associations & Organizations Based in Florida. 1983. pap. text ed. 9.95 (ISBN 0-911569-37-5). Data Notes Pub.
--Directory of Women's Associations & Organizations Based in Georgia. 1983. pap. text ed. 9.95 (ISBN 0-911569-31-6). Data Notes Pub.
--Directory of Women's Associations & Organizations Based in Iowa. 1983. pap. text ed. 9.95 (ISBN 0-911569-34-0). Data Notes Pub.
--Directory of Women's Associations & Organizations Based in Jersey. 1983. pap. text ed. 9.95 (ISBN 0-911569-35-9). Data Notes Pub.
--Directory of Women's Associations & Organizations Based in Massachusetts. 1983. pap. text ed. 9.95 (ISBN 0-911569-30-8). Data Notes Pub.
--Directory of Women's Associations & Organizations Based in Maryland. 1983. pap. text ed. 9.95 (ISBN 0-911569-36-7). Data Notes Pub.
--Directory of Women's Associations & Organizations Based in Minnesota. 1983. pap. text ed. 9.95 (ISBN 0-911569-38-3). Data Notes Pub.
--Directory of Women's Associations & Organizations Based in New York. 1983. pap. text ed. 9.95 (ISBN 0-911569-26-X). Data Notes Pub.
--Directory of Women's Associations & Organizations Based in Texas. 1983. pap. text ed. 9.95 (ISBN 0-911569-29-4). Data Notes Pub.
--Equipment Recycling: Data Notes. 30p. 1983. pap. text ed. 9.95 (ISBN 0-911569-48-0). Data Notes Pub.
--Furniture Recycling: Data Notes. 30p. 1983. pap. 9.95 (ISBN 0-911569-45-6). Data Notes Pub.
--Glass Recycling: Data Notes. 30p. 1983. pap. text ed. 9.95 (ISBN 0-911569-42-1). Data Notes Pub.
--Kitchen Recycling: Data Notes. 35p. 1983. pap. text ed. 9.95 (ISBN 0-911569-51-0). Data Notes Pub.
--Metal Recycling: Data Notes. 30p. 1983. pap. text ed. 9.95 (ISBN 0-911569-44-8). Data Notes Pub.
--One Thousand & More Places to Look for Continuing Education. 200p. 1983. text ed. 49.95 (ISBN 0-911569-05-7). Data Notes Pub.
--Paper Recycling: Data Notes. 30p. 1983. pap. text ed. 9.95 (ISBN 0-911569-41-3). Data Notes Pub.
--Rubber Recycling: Data Notes. 30p. 1983. pap. text ed. 9.95 (ISBN 0-911569-43-X). Data Notes Pub.
--Shelter Recycling: Data Notes. 30p. 1983. pap. text ed. 9.95 (ISBN 0-911569-46-4). Data Notes Pub.
--U. S. Directory of Business Start Up Fees. 1983. text ed. 59.95 50 pg. (ISBN 0-911569-13-8); pap. text ed. 29.95 160 pg. (ISBN 0-911569-08-1). Data Notes Pub.
--U. S. Directory of Places to Locate Recyclable Scrap. 60p. 1983. text ed. 19.95 (ISBN 0-911569-14-6). Data Notes Pub.
--Wood Recycling: Data Notes. 30p. 1983. pap. text ed. 9.95 (ISBN 0-911569-47-2). Data Notes Pub.

Data Notes Publishing Staff, compiled by. Creative Financing Data Notes. 65p. Date not set. 15.95 (ISBN 0-686-37650-1). Data Notes Pub.
--Data Notes Bibliographical Reference Handbook. 250p. Date not set. pap. text ed. 22.95 (ISBN 0-686-37654-4). Data Notes Pub.
--The Foreign Trade Index. 55p. Date not set. pap. cancelled (ISBN 0-686-37652-8). Data Notes Pub.
--Generics Data Notes. 75p. Date not set. 10.95 (ISBN 0-686-37653-6). Data Notes Pub.

Data Notes Publishing Staff, ed. Telemarketing, Telephone Sales & Telephone Soliciting; Data Notes. 70p. 1983. 12.95 (ISBN 0-686-37647-1). Data Notes Pub.

Data Processing Management Association, jt. auth. see Awad, Elias M.

Date, C. J. Introduction to Database Systems. 3rd ed. LC 80-17603. (IBM Systems Programming Ser.). (Illus.). 704p. 1981. text ed. 26.95 (ISBN 0-201-14471-9). A-W.
--Introduction to Database Systems. LC 82-3900. 480p. Date not set. text ed. 25.95 (ISBN 0-201-14474-3). A-W.

Dathorne, O. R. Dark Ancestor: The Literature of the Black Man in the Caribbean. LC 80-22581. xii, 292p. 1981. 20.00x (ISBN 0-8071-0757-3). La State U Pr.

Dati, Gregorio, jt. auth. see Pitti, Buonaccorso.

Datnow, Claire-Louise, et al. Downtown-An Outdoor Classroom. (Illus.). 54p. 1981. 10.00 (ISBN 0-686-36929-7). Birmingham Hist Soc.

Dator, James & Bezold, Clement. Judging the Future. LC 81-51228. 151p. 1981. pap. text ed. 10.00x (ISBN 0-8248-0770-7, Soc Sci Res Inst). UH Pr.

Datta, Gouri. Of Amaranths & Else. 1983. 5.95 (ISBN 0-533-05691-8). Vantage.

Datta, S. K., ed. Earthquake Ground Motion & Its Effects On Structures. (AMD Ser.: Vol. 53). 197p. 1982. 40.00 (H00241). ASME.

Datta, S. P. & Ottaway, J. H. Biochemistry: (Concise Medical Textbook) 3rd ed. (Illus.). 1976. pap. text ed. 17.50 o.p. (ISBN 0-02-857530-X, Pub. by Bailliere-Tindall). Saunders.

Datta, Surajit K. De see De Datta, Surajit K.

D'Attilio, Anthony. Seashore Life Coloring Book. 48p. 1973. pap. 1.95 (ISBN 0-486-22930-0). Dover.

Datz, S., ed. Physics of Electronic & Atomic Collisions: Abstracts of Contributed Papers. 1981. 127.75 (ISBN 0-444-86322-2). Elsevier.

--Physics of Electronic & Atomic Collisions: Invited Papers of the International Conference on the Physics of Electronic & Atomic Collisions, XIIth, Gatlinburg, TN, July 15-21, 1981. 872p. 1982. 132.00 (ISBN 0-444-86323-0). Elsevier.

Dau, Frederick W. Florida Old & New. LC 74-13957. 1975. Repr. of 1934 ed. 32.00 o.p. (ISBN 0-8103-4060-7). Gale.

Dau, P. C. Plasmapheresis & the Immunobiology of Myasthenia Gravis. 371p. 1979. 60.00 (ISBN 0-471-09477-3, Pub. by Wiley Med). Wiley.

Dau, W. H., tr. see Walther, Carl F.

Daub, Edward E. Fire. LC 77-26664. (Read About Science Ser.). (Illus.). (gr. k-3). 1978. PLB 13.30 (ISBN 0-8393-0080-8). Raintree Pubs.

Daub, Edward E., et al. Comprehending Technical Japanese. LC 74-5900. 440p. 1975. 32.50 (ISBN 0-299-06680-0). U of Wis Pr.

Daub, Guido H., jt. auth. see Seese, William S.

Daube, David. Forms of Roman Legislation. LC 78-12308. 1979. Repr. of 1956 ed. lib. bdg. 17.25x (ISBN 0-313-21146-9, DAFR). Greenwood.

Dauben, Joseph W. Georg Cantor: His Mathematics & Philosophy of the Infinite. 1979. 27.50x o.p. (ISBN 0-674-34871-0). Harvard U Pr.

Dauben, William G. Organic Reactions, Vol. 29. 500p. 1983. 40.00 (ISBN 0-471-87490-6, Pub. by Wiley-Interscience). Wiley.

Dauben, William G., ed. Organic Reactions, Vol. 17. LC 42-20265. 346p. 1975. Repr. of 1969 ed. 29.50 (ISBN 0-88275-884-5). Krieger.

--Organic Reactions, Vol. 18. LC 42-20265. 476p. 1978. Repr. of 1970 ed. 29.50 (ISBN 0-88275-732-6). Krieger.

--Organic Reactions, Vol. 19. LC 42-20265. 446p. 1975. Repr. of 1972 ed. 29.50 (ISBN 0-88275-885-3). Krieger.

--Organic Reactions, Vol. 20. LC 42-20265. 506p. 1981. Repr. of 1973 ed. 39.50 (ISBN 0-89874-390-7). Krieger.

--Organic Reactions, Vols. 21-28. LC 42-20265. (Organic Reaction Ser.). Vol. 21, 1974, 417p. 34.95 (ISBN 0-471-19622-3, Pub by Wiley-Interscience); Vol. 22, 1975, 474p. 36.95 (ISBN 0-471-19623-1); Vol. 23, 1976, 520p. 39.50 (ISBN 0-471-19624-X); Vol. 24, 1976, 431p. 44.95x (ISBN 0-471-19625-8); Vol. 25, 1977, 490p. 43.50 (ISBN 0-471-01741-8); Vol. 26, 1979, 488p. 35.95 (ISBN 0-471-05209-4); Vol. 27, 1982, 405p. 45.00 (ISBN 0-471-09657-1); Vol. 28, 1982, 347p. 39.50 (ISBN 0-471-86141-3). Wiley.

Daubenmire, Rexford. Plants & Environment: A Textbook of Plant Autecology. 3rd ed. LC 73-13826. 422p. 1974. text ed. 28.95 (ISBN 0-471-19636-3). Wiley.

Daubenmire, Rexford F. Plant Communities: A Textbook of Plant Synecology. 1968. text ed. 29.50 scp (ISBN 0-06-041548-7, HarpC). Har-Row.

Dauber, Roslyn & Cain, Melinda, eds. Women & Technological Change in Developing Countries. (AAAS Selected Symposium: No. 53). 250p. 1980. lib. bdg. 25.00 (ISBN 0-89158-791-8); text ed. 12.00. Westview.

Daubie, Julie. La Femme Pauvre Au Dix-Neuvieme Siecle. Condition Economique. Condition Professionnelle, 3 vols. (Conditions of the 19th Century French Working Class Ser.). (Fr.). 1974. Repr. of 1869 ed. Set. lib. bdg. 205.00x o.p. (ISBN 0-8287-0249-7). Vol. 1 (1139). Vol. 2 (1140). Vol. 3 (1141). Clearwater Pub.

D'Aubigne, J. H. Life & Times of Martin Luther. pap. 10.95 o.p. (ISBN 0-8024-4899-2). Moody.

Daubitz, Paul & Ross, Robert. The Public Manager's Phone Book. 142p. 1979. 35.00 (ISBN 0-686-98039-5). Telecom Lib.

Daudel, R. The Fundamentals of Theoretical Chemistry. 1968. 28.00 (ISBN 0-08-012300-7). Pergamon.

Daudel, R. & Pullman, A., eds. Quantum Theory of Chemical Reactions. 1982. lib. bdg. 32.50 (ISBN 90-277-1467-3, Pub. by Reidel Holland). Kluwer Boston.

Daudel, Raymond, et al. Quantum Chemistry: Methods & Applications. LC 59-15340. (Illus.). 586p. 1960. 28.00 (ISBN 0-470-19668-8, Pub. by Wiley). Krieger.

Daudet, A. Bi-Linguals French-English Lettres De Mon Moulin. A. Daudet. Mansion, J. E., tr. from Fr. (Harrap's Bilingual Ser.). 62p. 1955. 5.00 (ISBN 0-911268-42-1). Rogers Bk.

Daudet, Alphonse. Lettres De Mon Moulin. (Easy Readers, Ser. A). 48p. (Fr.). 1976. pap. text ed. 2.95 (ISBN 0-88436-225-6, 40266). EMC.

--Suffering: Eighteen Eighty-Seven to Eighteen Ninety-Five. 1934. 22.50x (ISBN 0-686-51319-3). Elliots Bks.

Daudon, Rene. French in Review. 2nd ed. 433p. 1962. text ed. 16.95 (ISBN 0-15-528850-4, HC); tapes, 10 reels 125.00 (ISBN 0-15-528851-2, HC). HarBraceJ.

Dauer, Rosamond. The Three Hundred Pound Cat. (Illus.). pap. 2.25 (ISBN 0-380-62745-0, Camelot). Avon.

D'Augelli, Anthony, et al. Helping Others. LC 80-17819. 170p. 1980. pap. text ed. 9.95 (ISBN 0-8185-0401-3). Brooks-Cole.

Daugert, Stanley M. The Philosophy of Thorstein Veblen. vii, 134p. Repr. of 1950 ed. lib. bdg. 15.00x (ISBN 0-87991-651-6). Porcupine Pr.

Daugherty, Billy J. This New Life. 40p. Date not set. pap. text ed. cancelled o.s.i. (ISBN 0-89274-080-9). Harrison Hse.

Daugherty, Billy Joe. More Faith Power to You. 1978. pap. 2.50 o.s.i. (ISBN 0-89274-100-7). Harrison Hse.

Daugherty, D. H., et al. A Bibliography of Periodical Literature in Musicology & Allied Fields, No. 1 & 2. LC 71-177974. 148p. 1971. Repr. of 1940 ed. lib. bdg. 32.50 (ISBN 0-306-70413-7). Da Capo.

Daugherty, Harry M. Inside Story of the Harding Tragedy. LC 75-27054. 348p. 1975. pap. 4.95 (ISBN 0-88279-118-4). Western Islands.

Daugherty, J. S. & Powell, R. E. Sheet-Metal Pattern Drafting & Shop Problems. rev. ed. 196p. 1975. pap. text ed. 15.00 (ISBN 0-87002-155-9). Bennett IL.

Daugherty, James. Andy & the Lion. (Illus.). (gr. 1-4). 1938. PLB 12.95 (ISBN 0-670-12433-8). Viking Pr.

Daugherty, James, ed. & illus. see Emerson, Ralph W.

Daugherty, Richard D., jt. auth. see Kirk, Ruth.

Daugherty, Robert L. & Franzini, Joseph B. Fluid Mechanics: With Engineering Applications. 7th ed. (Illus.). 1977. text ed. 35.00 (ISBN 0-07-015427-9, C); solutions manual 25.00 (ISBN 0-07-015428-7). McGraw.

Daugherty, Sarah B. The Literary Criticism of Henry James. LC 80-36753. xiv, 232p. 1981. 16.95x (ISBN 0-8214-0440-7, 82-83277). Ohio U Pr.

--The Literary Criticism of Henry James. LC 80-36753. xiv, 232p. 1982. pap. text ed. 8.95x (ISBN 0-8214-0697-3, 82-84663). Ohio U Pr.

Daugherty, Wayne, jt. auth. see Houck, John.

Daughters of St. Paul. More Than a Knight. (Encounter Ser.). (Illus.). 100p. 1982. 3.00 (ISBN 0-8198-4714-3, EN0204); pap. 2.00 (ISBN 0-8198-4715-1). Dghtrs St Paul.

--Preparing to Receive Jesus Christ. (Way, Truth & Life Ser.). 1978. 1.00 (ISBN 0-8198-0548-3); tchr's manual 3.00 (ISBN 0-8198-0549-1); activity book 0.75 (ISBN 0-8198-0550-5). Dghtrs St Paul.

Daughters of St. Paul, tr. see Ricciardi, Antonio.

Daujat, Jean. The Faith Applied. 1963. 5.95 o.p. (ISBN 0-933932-22-7). Scepter Pubs.

D'Aulaire, Edgar P., jt. auth. see D'Aulaire, Ingri.

D'Aulaire, Ingri & D'Aulaire, Edgar P. Abraham Lincoln. rev. ed. (gr. k-4). 1957. 12.95a (ISBN 0-385-07669-X); PLB (ISBN 0-385-07674-6). Doubleday.

--Animals Everywhere. (ps-1). 1954. 7.95a o.p. (ISBN 0-686-85885-9); PLB (ISBN 0-385-07703-3). Doubleday.

--Benjamin Franklin. (gr. 1-4). 1950. 9.95 (ISBN 0-385-07219-8); PLB o.p. (ISBN 0-385-07603-7). Doubleday.

--Columbus. LC 55-9011. (gr. k-4). 9.95 o.p. (ISBN 0-385-07606-1). Doubleday.

--D'Aulaire Book of Greek Myths. 1982. pap. 6.95 (ISBN 0-385-15787-8). Doubleday.

--D'Aulaires' Book of Greek Myths. LC 62-15877. 1962. 14.95a (ISBN 0-385-01583-6); PLB (ISBN 0-385-07108-6). Doubleday.

--D'Aulaires' Trolls. LC 76-158897. 64p. (gr. 1-3). 1972. 8.95a (ISBN 0-385-08255-X); 50.00 o.p. limited ed. (ISBN 0-385-04343-0); PLB (ISBN 0-385-01275-6). Doubleday.

--D'Aularies' Trolls. (Illus.). 1978. pap. 2.95 (ISBN 0-385-13339-1, Zephyr). Doubleday.

--Don't Count Your Chicks. 40p. (ps-1). 1973. PLB 10.95 (ISBN 0-385-07609-6). Doubleday.

--Don't Count Your Chicks. (ps-1). 1973. pap. 2.95 o.p. (ISBN 0-385-05233-2, Zephyr). Doubleday.

--George Washington. (gr. 1-4). 12.95 (ISBN 0-385-07306-2); PLB (ISBN 0-385-07611-8). Doubleday.

--Norse Gods & Giants. LC 67-19109. (gr. 3-7). 1967. 12.95 o.p. (ISBN 0-385-04908-0); PLB 12.95 (ISBN 0-385-07235-X). Doubleday.

--Ola. (gr. k-4). 1939. 6.95 o.p. (ISBN 0-385-07670-3). Doubleday.

--Pocahontas. (gr. 1-4). 1949. 7.95a (ISBN 0-385-07454-9); PLB (ISBN 0-385-07650-9). Doubleday.

--The Terrible Troll-Bird. LC 75-6762. 48p. (gr. k-3). 1976. 8.95a o.p. (ISBN 0-686-85898-0); PLB 8.95a (ISBN 0-385-03475-X). Doubleday.

D'Aulnoy, Marie C. Tales of the Fairies in Three Parts, Compleat: As Extracted from the Second Edition in English of Her "Diverting Works". Lurie, Alison & Schiller, Justin G., eds. LC 75-32137. (Classics of Children's Literature Ser.: 1621-1932). PLB 38.00 o.s.i. (ISBN 0-8240-2254-8). Garland Pub.

Daum, Susan M. & Stellman, Jeanne M. Work Is Dangerous to Your Health: A Handbook of Health Hazards in the Workplace & What You Can Do About Them. pap. 5.95 (ISBN 0-394-71918-2, V-918, Vin). Random.

Daumal, Rene. Mount Analogue: A Novel of Symbolically Authentic Non-Euclidean Adventures in Mountain Climbing. Shattuck, Roger, tr. from Fr. 120p. 1974. pap. 3.50 (ISBN 0-14-003947-3). Penguin.

Daumas, Maurice, ed. History of Technology & Invention: Progress Through the Ages, 2 vols. Incl. Vol. 1. The Origins of Technological Civilization (ISBN 0-517-50727-7); Vol. 2. The First Stages of Mechanization (ISBN 0-517-50728-5). (Illus.). 1969. 30.00 ea. Crown.

Daumier, Honore. Doctors & Medicine. 136p. 1981. 29.95 (ISBN 0-86710-001-X). Edns Vilo.

Dauncey, Helen. Is It Poisonous, 1980. 1980. pap. text ed. 2.95 (ISBN 0-933916-04-3). IMS Pr.

Dauncey, Richard, ed. Lab Index 1980. (Annual Ser.). 1980. pap. text ed. 45.00 o.p. (ISBN 0-933916-03-5). IMS Pr.

Daunton, Martin. House & Home in the Victorian City. 400p. 1983. text ed. 55.00x (ISBN 0-8419-0836-2). Holmes & Meier.

Dauphin, Sue. Houston by Stages: A History of the Theatre in Houston. 1981. 14.95 (ISBN 0-89015-303-5). Eakin Pubns.

Dauphine Conference on Money & International Money Problems, 3rd, Paris. Stabilization Policies in Interdependent Economies: Proceedings. Salin & Claassen, eds. 1972. 37.25 (ISBN 0-444-10368-6, North-Holland). Elsevier.

D'Auri, Laura, ed. see Sanadi, Lalita.

D'Auria, Michael & Ryan, Herbert F. Legal Terms & Concepts in Criminal Justice. 2nd. ed. 168p. 1982. pap. 7.95 (ISBN 0-89529-153-3). Avery Pub.

Dause, Charles A., jt. auth. see Ziegelmueller, George W.

Daussant, J. Seed Portions. LC 82-71240. write fro info. (ISBN 0-12-204380-4). Acad Pr.

Dausset, J., jt. ed. see Fougereau, M.

Dauster, Frank. Xavier Villaurrutia. (World Authors Ser.). 1971. lib. bdg. 14.95x (ISBN 0-686-82929-8). Irvington.

Dauster, Frank & Lyday, Leon F. En un Acto. 1974. pap. text ed. 5.95 (ISBN 0-442-21991-1). Van Nos Reinhold.

Dauster, Frank, ed. Xavier Villaurrutia. (World Authors Ser.). 15.95 (ISBN 0-8057-2964-X, Twayne). G K Hall.

Dauw, Dean C. Creativity & Innovation in Organizations. 380p. 1980. pap. text ed. 14.95x (ISBN 0-917974-42-5). Waveland Pr.

--Up Your Career. 3rd ed. LC 79-57133. (Illus.). 256p. 1980. pap. text ed. 9.95 (ISBN 0-917974-40-9). Waveland Pr.

Dauzat, Joann, jt. auth. see Dauzat, Sam V.

Dauzat, Sam V. & Dauzat, Joann. Reading: The Teacher & the Learner. LC 80-19435. 447p. 1981. text ed. 19.95 (ISBN 0-471-02668-9). Wiley.

Daval, Jean-Luc. Photography: History of an Art. Dexter, R. F., tr. from Fr. LC 82-60033. (Illus.). 272p. 1982. 60.00 (ISBN 0-8478-0460-7). Rizzoli Intl.

DaVall, G. M., jt. auth. see Ernest, John W.

Davar, Ashok. The Wheel of King Asoka. (Picture Bk). (gr. 1 up). 1977. 6.95 o.s.i. (ISBN 0-695-80709-9); lib. ed. 6.99 o.s.i. (ISBN 0-695-40709-0). Follett.

Dave, Smita. Christopher Marlowe. 118p. 1974. text ed. 6.00x (ISBN 0-391-00367-4). Humanities.

Davenant, William. The Shorter Poems & Songs from the Plays & Masques. Gibbs, A. M., ed. 1972. 39.00x o.p. (ISBN 0-19-812434-1). Oxford U Pr.

Davenport, Cyril. The Book: Its History & Development. LC 79-164212. (Tower Bks). (Illus.). viii, 258p. 1971. Repr. of 1930 ed. 37.00x (ISBN 0-8103-3944-7). Gale.

Davenport, Donald H. Index to Business Indices. LC 70-153015. 1971. Repr. of 1937 ed. 31.00 o.p. (ISBN 0-8103-3706-1). Gale.

Davenport, Guy. Eclogues: Eight Stories by Guy Davenport. LC 80-29027. (Illus.). 256p. 1981. 20.00 (ISBN 0-86547-029-4); pap. 11.00 (ISBN 0-86547-030-8). N Point Pr.

--The Geography of the Imagination. LC 80-23870. 400p. 1981. 20.00 o.p. (ISBN 0-86547-000-6); pap. 15.00 (ISBN 0-86547-001-4). N Point Pr.

Davenport, Guy, tr. & intro. by. Archilochos, Sappho, Alkman: Three Lyric Poets of the Late Greek Bronze Age. LC 78-65467. 1980. 18.50x (ISBN 0-520-03823-1). U of Cal Pr.

Davenport, H. The Higher Arithmetic. 5th ed. LC 81-21786. 180p. 1982. 22.95 (ISBN 0-521-24422-6); pap. 9.95 (ISBN 0-521-28678-6). Cambridge U Pr.

--The Higher Arithmetic: An Introduction to the Theory of Numbers. 172p. 1983. pap. 4.00 (ISBN 0-486-24452-0). Dover.

Davenport, Howard, jt. auth. see Andrews, Bart.

Davenport, J. S. European Crowns & Talers Since 1800. 1964. 35.00 (ISBN 0-685-51551-6, Pub by Spink & Son England). S J Durst.

Davenport, John. Letters of John Davenport, Puritan Divine. Calder, Isabel M., ed. 1937. 57.50x (ISBN 0-685-69794-0). Elliots Bks.

Davenport, John S. Large Sized Coins of the World. (Illus.). 1983. lib. bdg. 50.00 (ISBN 0-686-79429-X). S J Durst.

Davenport, Marge. Northwest Glory Days. (Illus.). 208p. (Orig.). 1983. pap. 6.95 (ISBN 0-938274-02-3). Paddlewheel.

Davenport, Michael G. The Fully Illustrated Book of the Most Notorious French Females at the Beginning of the Century. (A Memoir Collection of Significant Historical Personalities Ser.). (Illus.). 113p. 1983. 98.75 (ISBN 0-86650-048-0). Gloucester Art.

Davenport, Millia. Book of Costume. 33.00x (ISBN 0-87245-073-2). Textile Bk.

Davenport, Odessa, ed. see Conner, Daniel E.

Davenport, Peter, jt. ed. see Thompson, Philip.

Davenport, R. L., jt. auth. see Kutscher, Charles F.

Davenport, Rita. Making Time, Making Money: A Step-By-Step Program to Set Your Goals & Achieve Success. 256p. 1982. 14.95 (ISBN 0-312-50801-8); pap. 6.95 (ISBN 0-312-50802-6). St Martin.

--Sourdough Cookery. LC 77-71168. (Illus.). 1977. 5.95 o.p. (ISBN 0-89586-155-0); pap. 4.95 o.p. (ISBN 0-912656-63-8). H P Bks.

Davenport, W. Athens. (The Great Cities Ser.). (Illus.). 1978. 12.00 (ISBN 0-8094-2299-9). Silver.

--Probability & Random Processes: An Introduction for Applied Scientists & Engineers. 1970. 39.50 (ISBN 0-07-015440-6, C). McGraw.

Davenport, W. A. Fifteenth Century English Drama: The Early Moral Plays & their Literary Relations. LC 82-3665. 160p. 1982. text ed. 37.50x (ISBN 0-8476-7120-8). Rowman.

Davenport, W. H. The One Culture. LC 70-106054. 1971. 13.75 (ISBN 0-08-016322-X). Pergamon.

Davenport, William, jt. auth. see Cox, J. Halley.

Davern, Jeanne, ed. see Architectural Record Magazine.

Daveson, Mons. My Lord Kasseem. (Harlequin Romances Ser.). 192p. 1983. pap. 1.75 (ISBN 0-686-37699-4). Harlequin Bks.

Davey, Graham. Animal Learning & Conditioning. 512p. 1981. pap. text ed. 19.95 (ISBN 0-8391-4149-1). Univ Park.

Davey, Graham, ed. Applications of Conditioning Theory. (Psychology in Progress Ser.). 1981. 27.00x (ISBN 0-416-73560-6); pap. 10.95x (ISBN 0-416-73570-3). Methuen Inc.

Davey, H. & Mercer, H. Real Estate Principles in California. 4th ed. 1981. 23.95 (ISBN 0-686-70163-1). P-H.

Davey, Harold W. Contemporary Collective Bargaining. 3rd ed. LC 74-152315. 1972. ref. ed. 21.95 o.p. (ISBN 0-13-169607-6). P-H.

Davey, Henry. History of English Music. 3rd ed. LC 69-15620. (Music Ser). 1969. Repr. of 1921 ed. lib. bdg. 39.50 (ISBN 0-306-71133-8). Da Capo.

Davey, Herbert. The Law Relating to the Mentally Defective. (Historical Foundations of Forensic Psychiatry & Psychology Ser.). 568p. 1980. Repr. of 1914 ed. lib. bdg. 55.00 (ISBN 0-306-76070-3). Da Capo.

Davey, Homer C., jt. auth. see Driscoll, Donald C.

Davey, J. R., jt. auth. see Bennett, William R.

Davey, J. T. & Johnston, H. B. The African Migratory Locust (Locusta Migratoria Migratorioides) R & FO in Nigeria. 91p. 1956. 35.00x (ISBN 0-85135-009-7, Pub. by Centre Overseas Research). State Mutual Bk.

Davey, John, jt. auth. see Case, Doug.

Davey, Kenneth. Financing Regional Government: International Practices & Their Relevance to the Third World. (Public Administration in Developing Countries Ser.). 220p. 1983. 24.95 (ISBN 0-471-10356-X, Pub. by Wiley-Interscience). Wiley.

Davey, Nelson J. These Are the Times. 1983. 8.95 (ISBN 0-533-05555-5). Vantage.

Davey, Norman & Ling, Roger. Wall-Painting in Roman Britain. (Illus.). 232p. 1982. pap. text ed. 25.25x (ISBN 0-904387-96-8, Pub. by Alan Sutton England). Humanities.

Davey, Patrick J. Financial Management of Company Pension Plans. (Report Ser: No. 611). 117p. (Orig.). 1973. pap. 17.50 (ISBN 0-8237-0022-4). Conference Bd.

Davia, N. C. & Thomas, D. An Assessment of the Model Six-V Oil Skimm ER Supplied by Engineering & General Equipment Ltd., 1980. 1981. 30.00x (ISBN 0-686-97036-5, Pub. by W Spring England). State Mutual Bk.

Davia, N. C., jt. auth. see Thomas, D. H.

Daviau, Donald, tr. see Urbach, Reinhard.

Daviau, Donald G. & Buelow, George J. The "Ariadne Auf Naxos" of Hugo von Hofmannsthal & Richard Strauss. (Studies in the Germanic Languages & Literatures: No. 80). ix, 269p. 1975. 18.00x (ISBN 0-8078-8080-9). U of NC Pr.

Daviau, Donald G. & Fischer, Ludwig, eds. Das Exilerlebnis: Verhandlungen Des Vierten Symposium Uber Deutsche und Oesterreichische Exilliteratur. LC 81-70544. (Illus.). 530p. (Ger.). 1982. 37.00x (ISBN 0-938100-17-3). Camden Hse.

David, A. R. A Guide to Religious Ritual at Abydos. 182p. 1981. pap. text ed. 40.00x (ISBN 0-85668-060-5, Pub. by Aris & Phillips England). Humanities.

David, A. R., ed. The Manchester Museum Mummy Project. 1979. 25.50 (ISBN 0-7190-1293-7). Manchester.

David, Andrew. Country Music Stars: People at the Top of the Charts. LC 79-55241. (Illus.). 96p. 1980. 5.98 o.p. (ISBN 0-89196-063-5, Domus Bks). Quality Bks IL.

--River Thrill Sports. LC 82-24966. (Superwheels & Thrill Sports Bks.). (Illus.). 48p. (gr. 4up). 1983. PLB 7.95g (ISBN 0-8225-0506-1). Lerner Pubns.

David, Bruce E. How to Get Everything you Want from Life: The Secret of Power. 62p. (Orig.). 1982. pap. write for info. (ISBN 0-9609734-0-0). Worth Print.

David, Carl. Collecting & Care of Fine Art. (Illus.). 160p. 1981. 10.00 (ISBN 0-517-54287-0). Crown.

David, Chella S., jt. auth. see Ferrone, Soldano.

David, D. J. PET-CBM Basics. 140p. 1983. pap. 7.95 (ISBN 0-918398-47-9). Dilithium Pr.

David, D. J. & Staley, H. B. Analytical Chemistry of Polyurethanes. LC 78-12430. (High Polymer Ser.: Vol. 16, Pt. 3). 1979. Repr. of 1969 ed. lib. bdg. 36.50 (ISBN 0-88275-753-9). Krieger.

David, David S. Calcium Metabolism in Renal Failure & Nephrolithiasis. LC 76-30308. (Perspectives in Nephrology & Hypertension Ser.). 1977. 54.50 o.p. (ISBN 0-471-19673-8, Pub. by Wiley Medical). Wiley.

David, Ed. The Intelligent Idiot's Guide to Getting the Most Out of Your Home Video. LC 82-13292. (Illus.). 224p. (Orig.). 1982. lib. bdg. 19.50 (ISBN 0-89471-178-4); pap. 8.95 (ISBN 0-89471-177-6). Running Pr.

David, Edward, ed. Inside Asquith's Cabinet: From the Diaries of Charles Hobhouse. LC 77-84941. (Illus.). 1978. 26.00x (ISBN 0-312-41868-X). St Martin.

David, Elizabeth. English Bread & Yeast Cookery: American Edition. Hess, Karen, notes by. 1982. pap. 10.95 (ISBN 0-14-046539-1). Penguin.

--French Country Cooking. (Handbook Ser.). 1959. pap. 4.95 (ISBN 0-14-046043-8). Penguin.

--French Provincial Cooking. rev. ed. LC 80-8369. (Illus.). 520p. 1982. write for info (ISBN 0-06-014827-6, HarpT). Har-Row.

David, Eric. Sangres. (Orig.). 1983. pap. 5.95 (ISBN 0-686-43102-2). Avant Bks.

David, Felicien. Melodies Orientales & other Piano Works. (Music Reprint Ser.). 100p. 1983. Repr. lib. bdg. write for info (ISBN 0-306-76214-5). Da Capo.

David, H. The Statistical Package STATCAT: Source Programs & User Manual. 800p. 1982. 102.25 (ISBN 0-444-86453-9, North Holland). Elsevier.

David, Heather M. Admiral Rickover & the Nuclear Navy. (Lives to Remember Ser.). (gr. 4-9). 1970. PLB 4.97 o.p. (ISBN 0-399-60004-3). Putnam Pub Group.

David, Irene, jt. auth. see David, Lester.

David, Irwin T. & Sturgeon, C. Eugene. How to Evaluate & Improve Internal Controls in Government Units. LC 81-83910. (Illus.). 111p. 1981. pap. 18.00 Nonmember (ISBN 0-686-84336-3); pap. 16.00 Member (ISBN 0-686-84337-1). Municipal.

David, J., ed. see Reiter, Russel J.

David, J. H., et al. Guidelines for Discharge Planning. 59p. 1973. 9.00 o.p. (ISBN 0-913590-15-0). Slack Inc.

David, Jack, jt. auth. see Lecker, Robert.

David, Jack, jt. ed. see Lecker, Robert.

David, Janina, tr. see Ziemian, Joseph.

David, Jay. Autocize. LC 78-23751. (Illus.). 1980. pap. 4.95 (ISBN 0-688-08399-4). Quill NY.

David, Katalin. Treasures in Hungarian Ecclesiastical Collections. Hoch, Elizabeth, tr. from Hungarian. (Illus.). 150p. 1982. 27.50x (ISBN 963-13-1460-X). Intl Pubns Serv.

David, Leonard, jt. auth. see Borg, Nicholas.

David, Lester. The Lonely Lady of San Clemente. 1979. pap. 2.50 o.p. (ISBN 0-425-04253-7). Berkley Pub.

David, Lester & David, Irene. Ike & Mamie: The Story of the General & His Lady. (Illus.). 272p. 1981. 12.95 (ISBN 0-399-12644-9). Putnam Pub Group.

David, M. Geostatistical Ore Reserve Estimation. (Developments in Geomathematics: Vol. 2). 1977. 51.00 (ISBN 0-444-41532-7). Elsevier.

David, Marcel. Adult Education in Yugoslavia. 1962. pap. 4.00 o.p. (ISBN 92-3-100495-6, UB3, UB). Unipub.

David, Marjorie, ed. see Sterne, Laurence.

David, Martin A. The Dancer's Audition Book. LC 82-50546. (Illus.). 160p. 1982. 15.95 (ISBN 0-8069-7046-4); lib. bdg. 18.79 (ISBN 0-8069-7047-2); pap. 8.95 (ISBN 0-8069-7638-1). Sterling.

David, Michael, jt. ed. see Saunders, Peter E.

David, P. A. Technical Choice, Innovation & Economic Growth. (Illus.). 320p. 1975. 42.50 (ISBN 0-521-20518-2); pap. 13.95x (ISBN 0-521-09875-0). Cambridge U Pr.

David, Paul T. Party Strength in the United States 1872-1970. LC 77-183897. xii, 310p. 1972. 13.95x (ISBN 0-8139-0396-3). U Pr of Va.

David, Paul T. & Pollock, Ross. Executives for Government: Central Issues of Federal Personnel Administration. LC 76-48706. 1977. Repr. of 1958 ed. lib. bdg. 17.00x (ISBN 0-8371-9335-4, DAEG). Greenwood.

David, Paul T. & Everson, David H., eds. The Presidential Election & Transition, 1980-1981. 304p. 1983. price not set (ISBN 0-8093-1109-7). S Ill U Pr.

David, Pedro R., ed. The World of the Burglar: Five Criminal Lives. LC 73-82774. 298p. 1974. 10.00x (ISBN 0-8263-0304-8); pap. 5.95 (ISBN 0-8263-0332-3). U of NM Pr.

David, R. W. Shakespeare in the Theatre. LC 77-82494. (Illus.). 278p. 1981. pap. 16.95 (ISBN 0-521-28490-2). Cambridge U Pr.

--Shakespeare in the Theatre. LC 77-82494. (Illus.). 1978. 29.95 (ISBN 0-521-21833-0). Cambridge U Pr.

David, Rene & Brierly, John E. Major Legal Systems in the World Today: An Introduction to the Comparative Study of Law. 2nd ed. LC 78-67751. 1978. 30.00 (ISBN 0-02-907590-4); pap. text ed. 15.95 (ISBN 0-02-907610-2). Free Pr.

David, William & Gibson, Margaret. Reincarnation & the Soul in the Parables of Jesus. 80p. 1980. pap. 4.50 o.p. (ISBN 0-87516-412-9). De Vorss.

David, Zdenek V., jt. auth. see Kann, Robert A.

Davidge, R. W. Mechanical Behaviour of Ceramics. LC 77-90206. (Cambridge Solid State Science Ser.). (Illus.). 1980. pap. 10.95 (ISBN 0-521-29309-X). Cambridge U Pr.

Davidian, H. H. Rhododendron Species, Vol. I. (Illus.). 1982. cloth 59.95 (ISBN 0-917304-71-3). Timber.

David-Juba, Robert. Flights...into Time. 2nd ed. LC 82-81680. (Illus.). 66p. 1982. pap. 7.95 (ISBN 0-686-82317-6, JNP-03). Joyful Noise.

Davidman, Joy. Smoke on the Mountain: An Interpretation of the Ten Commandments. LC 54-6099. 1970. pap. 4.50 (ISBN 0-664-24919-1). Westminster.

David-Neel, Alexandra. The Power of Nothingness. large type ed. LC 82-10387. 217p. 1982. Repr. of 1982 ed. 9.95 (ISBN 0-89621-382-X). Thorndike Pr.

Davidoff. Handbook of the Spinal Cord, Vol. 1. 592p. 1982. write for info. (ISBN 0-8247-1708-2). Dekker.

Davidoff, Frank & Rossi, John, eds. Digital Video. (Illus.). 114p. 1982. pap. text ed. 25.00 (ISBN 0-940690-02-0). Soc Motion Pic & TV Engrs.

Davidoff, Linda L. Introduction to Psychology. 2nd ed. (Illus.). 1980. text ed. 24.00 (ISBN 0-07-015504-6, C); instructor's manual 18.00 (ISBN 0-07-015505-4); active learning resources 14.50 (ISBN 0-07-015507-0); test file 30.00 (ISBN 0-07-015506-2). McGraw.

Davidov, H. Botanical Dictionary: Russian-English-German-French-Latin. 335p. 1981. Repr. of 1960 ed. lib. bdg. 32.00x (ISBN 3-87429-197-9). Lubrecht & Cramer.

Davidovici, Sorin, ed. see Sydenham, Peter H.

Davidow-Goodman, Ann. Let's Draw Animals. (Illus.). (gr. 1-5). 1960. 1.95 (ISBN 0-448-02917-0, G&D). Putnam Pub Group.

--Let's Draw Dinosaurs. LC 77-94034. (Step-by-Step Books Ser.). (Illus.). (gr. 1-6). 1978. pap. 1.95 (ISBN 0-448-14990-7, G&D). Putnam Pub Group.

Davidowitz, Steve. Betting Thoroughbreds: A Professional's Guide for the Horseplayer. Rev. ed. (Illus.). 232p. 1983. pap. 7.25 (ISBN 0-525-48046-3, 0772-230). Dutton.

Davidowitz, Steven. Betting Thoroughbreds: Professional's Guide for the Horseplayer. (Illus.). 1977. 8.95 o.p. (ISBN 0-525-06632-2); pap. 5.25 (ISBN 0-525-47620-2, 0510-150). Dutton.

Davids, Anthony. Children in Conflict: A Casebook. LC 73-20108. 227p. 1974. pap. text ed. 13.95 (ISBN 0-471-19699-1). Wiley.

Davids, Jules. America & the World of Our Time. text ed. 11.95 (ISBN 0-685-77200-4). Phila Bk Co.

Davids, Jules, ed. American Diplomatic & Public Papers: The United States & China, 14 vols. LC 81-9058. (Ser. 3: The Sino-Japanese War to the Russo-Japanese War, 1894-1905). 4500p. 1982. Set. lib. bdg. 795.00 (ISBN 0-8420-2185-X). Scholarly Res Inc.

--American Diplomatic & Public Papers, The United States & China: The Treaty System & the Taiping Rebellion, 1842-1860, 21 vols. LC 73-77510. (Ser. 1). 1974. Set. 1095.00 (ISBN 0-8420-1703-8). Scholarly Res Inc.

Davids, Kenneth. Coffee: A Guide to Buying, Brewing & Enjoying. LC 76-13003. (Illus.). 192p. 1976. 8.95 o.p. (ISBN 0-89286-103-7); pap. 5.95 o.p. (ISBN 0-89286-102-9). One Hund One Prods.

Davids, L. Robert. Baseball Research Journal 1982. (Illus.). 183p. (Orig.). 1982. pap. 5.00 (ISBN 0-910137-01-3). Soc Am Baseball Res.

--This Date in Baseball History. rev. ed. (Illus.). 56p. (Orig.). 1982. pap. 2.50 (ISBN 0-910137-00-5). Soc Am Baseball Res.

Davids, L. Robert, ed. Baseball Research Journal. (Illus.). 160p. (Orig.). 1983. pap. 5.00 (ISBN 0-910137-06-4). Soc Am Baseball Res.

Davids, Richard C. Lords of the Arctic: A Journey Among the Polar Bears. (Illus.). 224p. 1982. 29.95 (ISBN 0-02-529630-2). Macmillan.

Davids, Robert L, ed. Insider's Baseball. (Illus.). 288p. 1983. 13.95 (ISBN 0-686-83657-X, ScribT). Scribner.

Davidsohn, Israel & Stern, Kurt. Problem Solving in Immunohematology. 2nd ed. LC 77-93058. 117p. 1978. pap. text ed. 20.00 o.p. (ISBN 0-89189-035-1, 45-6-012-00). Am Soc Clinical.

Davidson. Short History of Chess. 1981. pap. 5.95 o.p. (ISBN 0-679-14550-8). McKay.

Davidson & Taylor. Revision Notes on Building Services. 1978. Repr. of 1975 ed. 4.95 o.p. (ISBN 0-408-00186-0). Butterworth.

Davidson, et al. Financial Accounting. 3rd ed. 764p. 1982. 26.95 (ISBN 0-03-059871-0). Dryden Pr.

Davidson, A. Handbook of Precision Engineering, Vol. 5: Joining Techniques. (Illus.). 297p. 1972. 37.50 (ISBN 0-07-015472-4, P&RB). McGraw.

Davidson, Abraham. Early American Modernist Painting: 1910-1935. LC 80-8223. (Icon Editions). (Illus.). 320p. 1981. 25.00i (ISBN 0-06-430975-4, HarpT); pap. 14.37i (ISBN 0-06-430120-6, IN-120). Har-Row.

Davidson, Alan. North Atlantic Seafood. (Handbook Ser.). 1983. pap. cancelled (ISBN 0-14-046493-X). Penguin.

Davidson, Alan, tr. see Dumas, Alexandre.

Davidson, Alan J. Radiologic Diagnosis of Renal Parenchymal Disease. LC 76-20086. (Monografhs in Clinical Radiology: No. 11). (Illus.). 1977. text ed. 33.00 o.p. (ISBN 0-7216-2925-3). Saunders.

Davidson, Amanda. Teddy's First Christmas. LC 82-82092. (Illus.). 24p. (ps-2). 1982. 7.70 (ISBN 0-03-062616-1). HR&W.

Davidson, Angus, tr. see Berto, Giuseppe.

Davidson, Angus, tr. see Moravia, Alberto.

Davidson, Arnold E. Mordecai Richler. LC 82-40282. (Literature & Life Ser.). 190p. 1983. 11.95 (ISBN 0-8044-2140-4). Ungar.

Davidson, Avram. Collected Fantasies. 1982. pap. 2.50 (ISBN 0-686-97651-7). Berkley Pub.

Davidson, B. R. European Farming in Australia: An Economic History of Australian Farming. 1981. 57.50 (ISBN 0-444-41993-4). Elsevier.

Davidson, Basil. African Kingdoms. LC 66-25647. (Great Ages of Man Ser.). (Illus.). (gr. 6 up). 1966. lib. bdg. 19.96 (ISBN 0-8094-0371-4, Pub. by Time-Life). Silver.

--No Fist Is Big Enough to Hide the Sky: The Liberation of Guinea Bissau & Cape Verde. 208p. 1982. 9.95 (ISBN 0-905762-93-2, Pub. by Zed Pr England). Lawrence Hill.

Davidson, Ben. The Skateboard Book. rev. ed. (Illus.). 1979. pap. 4.95 o.p. (ISBN 0-448-12484-X, G&D). Putnam Pub Group.

Davidson, Bill, jt. auth. see Caesar, Sid.

Davidson, Bill, jt. auth. see Coleman.

Davidson, Bruce. Subway. LC 82-47812. Date not set. 100.00 (ISBN 0-394-52293-1). Knopf. Postponed.

Davidson, C. W. Transmission Lines for Communications & Digital Systems. 1978. 39.95x o.p. (ISBN 0-470-99160-7). Halsted Pr.

--Transmission Lines For Communications. LC 78-4546. 218p. 1982. 19.95x (ISBN 0-470-27358-5). Halsted Pr.

Davidson, Caroline. A Woman's Work Is Never Done: A History of Housework in the British Isles 1650-1950. (Illus.). 256p. 1983. 19.95 (ISBN 0-7011-3901-3, Pub. by Chatto & Windus). Merrimack Bk Serv.

Davidson, Cathy N. Critical Essays on Ambrose Bierce. (Critical Essays on American Literature Ser.). 1982. 28.50 (ISBN 0-8161-8393-7, Twayne). G K Hall.

Davidson, Clifford, ed. A Middle English Treatise on the Playing of Miracles. LC 81-40028. 93p. 1981. lib. bdg. 15.75 (ISBN 0-8191-1514-2); pap. text ed. 7.00 (ISBN 0-8191-1515-0). U Pr of Amer.

Davidson, David, jt. auth. see Blot, David.

Davidson, Diane, ed. see Shakespeare, William.

Davidson, Donald & Suppes, Patrick. Decision Making: An Experimental Approach. LC 77-13439. 1977. Repr. of 1957 ed. lib. bdg. 16.00x (ISBN 0-8371-9854-2, DAVD). Greenwood.

Davidson, Donald J., ed. see Field, Frederick Vanderbilt.

Davidson, E. H., ed. see Poe, Edgar Allan.

Davidson, Ellen, jt. auth. see Schniedewind, Nancy.

Davidson, Florence E., jt. auth. see Blackman, Margaret B.

Davidson, Frank P. & Meador, C. Lawrence, eds. How Big & Still Beautiful? Macro-Engineering Revisited. (AAAS Selected Symposium: No. 30). 383p. 1980. lib. bdg. 32.50 (ISBN 0-89158-792-6). Westview.

Davidson, Frank P., et al. Macroengineering & the Infra-Structure of Tomorrow. 1979. lib. bdg. 26.00x o.p. (ISBN 0-89158-294-0). Westview.

Davidson, Georgie. Origami. LC 75-44992. (Larousse Craft Ser.). (Illus.). 1978. pap. 8.95 (ISBN 0-88332-027-4, 8036). Larousse.

Davidson, Glen W. Living with Dying. LC 74-14186. 112p. (Orig.). 1975. pap. 4.50 (ISBN 0-8066-1468-4, 10-3980); study guide 00.30 (10-3981). Augsburg.

Davidson, Gregory, jt. auth. see Poole, Lon.

Davidson, Harold G. The Lost Works of Edward Borein. LC 78-68394. (Illus.). 1978. 25.00 (ISBN 0-686-14435-X); ltd. ed. of 200 signed & numbered copies 100.00 (ISBN 0-686-14436-8). H G Davidson.

Davidson, Helen H., jt. auth. see Klopfer, Bruno.

Davidson, Homer. Small-Screen TV Servicing Manual. LC 75-13009. (Illus.). 240p. 1975. vinyl 9.95 (ISBN 0-8306-5778-9); pap. 6.95 o.p. (ISBN 0-8306-4778-3, 778). TAB Bks.

Davidson, Isobel. Real Stories from Baltimore County History. LC 70-9245. (Illus.). x, 296p. Repr. of 1917 ed. 30.00x (ISBN 0-8103-5033-5). Gale.

Davidson, J. A., intro. by. Resource Developments in the Eighties. (Chemeca Ser.). 338p. (Orig.). 1982. pap. text ed. 54.00x (ISBN 0-85825-169-8, Pub. by Inst Engineering Australia). Renouf.

Davidson, J. F., ed. Fluidization. Keairns, D. L. LC 77-82495. (Illus.). 1978. 62.50 (ISBN 0-521-21943-4). Cambridge U Pr.

Davidson, J. F., jt. ed. see Von Kaulla, K. N.

Davidson, J. R. Strachan see Strachan-Davidson, J. R.

Davidson, J. W. Samoa Mo Samoa: The Emergence of the Independent State of Western Samoa. 1967. 37.50x (ISBN 0-19-550060-1). Oxford U Pr.

Davidson, James D. The Squeeze. 1980. 11.95 o.p. (ISBN 0-671-40084-3). S&S.

Davidson, James J. The Artistic Work of James L. Davidson: A Pictorial Look at an Artist. 1983. 6.95 (ISBN 0-533-05356-0). Vantage.

Davidson, James M., jt. ed. see Overcash, Michael R.

Davidson, James W. & Rugge, John. The Complete Wilderness Paddler. LC 82-40021. 288p. Date not set. pap. 5.95 (ISBN 0-394-71153-X, Vin). Random.

Davidson, Jane, tr. see Dumas, Alexandre.

Davidson, Jeffrey, jt. auth. see Watson, Thomas.

Davidson, Jesse. Famous Firsts in Aviation. (Famous Firsts Ser.). 72p. (gr. 6-8). 1974. PLB 4.97 o.p. (ISBN 0-399-60902-4). Putnam Pub Group.

Davidson, Jessica. How to Improve Your Spelling & Vocabulary. (gr. 7 up). 1980. PLB 8.90 (ISBN 0-531-04133-6). Watts.

Davidson, Joan & Lloyd, Richard, eds. Conservation & Agriculture. LC 77-697. 1978. 51.00x (ISBN 0-471-99502-9, Pub. by Wiley-Interscience). Wiley.

Davidson, Joan W., ed. see Wilson, Woodrow.

Davidson, Joel & Komp, R. J. The Solar Electric Home: A Photovoltaics How-To Handbook. (Illus.). 150p. 1983. pap. 10.00 (ISBN 0-937948-04-7). AATEC Pubns.

Davidson, John. Diabolus Amans. Fletcher, Ian, ed. Bd. with The North Wall. LC 76-20055. (Decadent Consciousness Ser.: Vol. 6). 1978. Repr. of 1885 ed. lib. bdg. 38.00 o.s.i. (ISBN 0-8240-2755-8). Garland Pub.

Davidson, Joseph B. Inside Horseracing. (Illus.). 282p. (Orig.). 1974. pap. 6.00 o.p. (ISBN 0-668-03332-0). Arco.

Davidson, Josephine, jt. auth. see Reggio, Kathryn.

Davidson, Judith. Japan: Where East Meets West. Hopkins, Terry, ed. (Discovering Our Heritage Ser.). (Illus.). 112p. (gr. 5 up). 1982. PLB 9.95 (ISBN 0-87518-230-5). Dillon.

Davidson, Laurie & Gordon, Laura K. The Sociology of Gender. 1979. pap. 13.95 (ISBN 0-395-30588-8). HM.

Davidson, Lionel. Murder Games. LC 77-26790. 1978. 8.95 o.p. (ISBN 0-698-10908-2, Coward). Putnam Pub Group.

--The Night of Wenceslas. LC 82-47557. 224p. 1982. pap. 2.84i (ISBN 0-06-080595-1, P595, PL). Har-Row.

Davidson, Margaret. Louis Braille: The Boy Who Invented Books for the Blind. (Illus.). 96p. (gr. 2-5). 1972. 7.95g o.p. (ISBN 0-8038-4281-3). Hastings.

--Seven True Dog Stories. (gr. 2-4). 1977. 6.95 o.s.i. (ISBN 0-8038-6738-7). Hastings.

--Seven True Horse Stories. (Illus.). (gr. 2-5). 1979. 6.95g o.s.i. (ISBN 0-8038-6760-3). Hastings.

Davidson, Mark. Uncommon Sense: The Life & Thought of Ludwig von Bertalanffy (1901-1972), Father of General Systems Theory. LC 82-16900. 256p. 1983. 16.95 (ISBN 0-87477-165-X). HM.

Davidson, Marshall. Life in America, 2 vols. LC 74-10940. 1104p. 1974. Set. 25.00 o.p. (ISBN 0-395-17214-4). HM.

Davidson, Martha, et al. The Leather District & the Fort Point Channel: The Boston Photo-Documentary Project. Channing, Susan, ed. 72p. (Orig.). 1982. 5.00 (ISBN 0-932246-02-8). Artists Found.

Davidson, Mary S. A Superstar Called Sweetpea. (YA) (gr. 6-9). 1982. pap. 1.95 (ISBN 0-440-97877-7, LFL). Dell.

Davidson, Mayer B. Diabetes Mellitus: Diagnosis & Treatment. LC 81-84. 480p. 1981. Combined Ed. 22.00 (ISBN 0-471-09543-5, Pub. by Wiley Med). Wiley.

Davidson, Melvin G. PL-One Programming with PL-C. LC 72-7635. 224p. (Orig.). 1973. pap. text ed. 15.50 (ISBN 0-395-14518-X). HM.

Davidson, Muriel. Hot Spot. LC 79-23690. 1980. 10.95 (ISBN 0-399-90072-1, Marek). Putnam Pub Group.

--Til Death You Do Pay. 372p. 1981. 13.95 (ISBN 0-399-90131-0, Marek). Putnam Pub Group.

Davidson, Norman R. Statistical Mechanics. (Advanced Chemistry Ser.). (Illus.). 1962. text ed. 35.00 (ISBN 0-07-015454-6, C). McGraw.

Davidson, Owen & Jones, C. M. Lawn Tennis: The Great Ones. 7.50 o.p. (ISBN 0-7207-0380-8). Transatlantic.

Davidson, P. Moonlighting: A Complete Guide to Over 200 Exciting Part-Time Jobs. 288p. 1983. 7.95 (ISBN 0-07-049607-2, GB). McGraw.

Davidson, Paul C., ed. see Barbour, Pamela G. & Spivey, Morma G.

Davidson, R. J. Methods in Nonlinear Plasma Theory. (Pure & Applied Physics Ser.). 1972. 63.00 (ISBN 0-12-205450-4). Acad Pr.

Davidson, R. L. Handbook of Water-Soluble Gums & Resins. 1980. 47.75 (ISBN 0-07-015471-6). McGraw.

Davidson, R. L., jt. auth. see Bland, William F.

Davidson, Ralph & Lyon, William F. Insect Pests of Farm, Garden, & Orchard. 7th ed. LC 78-31366. 596p. 1979. text ed. 29.95x o.p. (ISBN 0-471-03538-6). Wiley.

Davidson, Ralph H. & Lyon, William F. Insect Pests of Farm, Garden & Orchard. 7th ed. LC 78-31366. 596p. 1981. pap. text ed. 16.95 (ISBN 0-471-86314-9). Wiley.

Davidson, Ralph K. Price Discrimination in Selling Gas & Electricity. LC 75-35023. (The Johns Hopkins Univ Ser. in Hist. & Pol. Sci., Ser.: No. 72, No. 1). 1976. Repr. of 1955 ed. lib. bdg. 18.25x (ISBN 0-8371-8575-0, DAPRD). Greenwood.

Davidson, Richard J. & Schwartz, Gary E., eds. Consciousness & Self-Regulation: Advances in Research & Theory, Vol. 3. 225p. 1982. 25.00x (ISBN 0-306-41214-4, Plenum Pr). Plenum Pub.

Davidson, Richard L. & De La Cruz, Felix F. Somatic Cell Hybridization. LC 74-75725. 312p. 1974. 34.50 (ISBN 0-911216-75-8). Raven.

Davidson, Richard M. Typology in Scripture: A Study of Hermeneutical Structures. (Andrews University Seminary Doctoral Dissertation Ser.: Vol. 2). (Orig.). 1981. pap. 8.95 (ISBN 0-943872-34-0). Andrews Univ Pr.

Davidson, Robert, ed. Creative Ideas for Advent. 114p. (Orig.). 1980. pap. 9.95 (ISBN 0-940754-06-1). Ed Ministries.

Davidson, Robert L. & Sittig, Marshall, eds. Water-Soluble Resins. 2nd ed. LC 68-9136. 240p. 1968. 15.95 (ISBN 0-686-86267-8). Krieger.

Davidson, Roger & Oleszek, Walter. Congress & Its Members. Way, Jean, ed. LC 81-5446. 488p. (Orig.). 1981. pap. 10.95 (ISBN 0-87187-202-1). Congr Quarterly.

Davidson, S. & Weil, R. Handbook of Cost Accounting. 1978. 38.50 (ISBN 0-07-015452-X). McGraw.

Davidson, Sara. Loose Change: Three Women of the Sixties. LC 76-2766. 1977. 11.95 o.p. (ISBN 0-385-03630-2). Doubleday.

--Real Property. LC 79-55371. 1980. 10.95 o.p. (ISBN 0-385-15573-5). Doubleday.

Davidson, Sharon V., et al. Nursing Care Evaluation: Concurrent & Retrospective Review Criteria. LC 77-5069. 420p. 1977. 24.95 o.p. (ISBN 0-8016-1210-1). Mosby.

Davidson, Sidney & Weil, Roman. Handbook of Modern Accounting. 2nd ed. (Illus.). 1977. 54.95 (ISBN 0-07-015451-1, P&RB). McGraw.

Davidson, Sidney, et al. Inflation Accounting: A Guide for the Accountant & the Financial Analyst. 1976. 31.00 (ISBN 0-07-015478-3, P&RB). McGraw.

Davidson, Stephen M. Medicaid Decisions: Systematic Analysis of the Cost Problem. LC 80-10998. 1980. prof ref 25.00x (ISBN 0-88410-142-8). Ballinger Pub.

Davidson, Stephen M., et al. The Cost of Living Longer: National Health Insurance & the Elderly. LC 79-2756. 160p. 1980. 22.95x (ISBN 0-669-03242-5). Lexington Bks.

Davidson, Tom & Steely, Judy. Using Learning Centers with Not Yet Readers: An Aid for ABC Darians. LC 77-20781. (Illus.). 1978. text ed. 12.95 o.p. (ISBN 0-87620-937-1); pap. text ed. 11.95x o.p. (ISBN 0-673-16455-1). Scott F.

Davidson, Tom, et al. The Learning Center Book: An Integrated Approach. LC 74-33858. (Illus.). 176p. 1976. case ed. 11.95x (ISBN 0-673-16382-2); pap. text ed. 11.95x o.p. (ISBN 0-673-16381-4). Scott F.

Davidson, W. R., et al. Retailing Management. 4th ed. 883p. 1975. 32.95 (ISBN 0-471-06591-9); instrs'. manual o.p. (ISBN 0-471-07457-8). Wiley.

Davidson, William H. Global Strategic Management. (Marketing Management Ser.). 348p. 1982. 27.95x (ISBN 0-471-09314-9). Ronald Pr.

Davidson, William V. Historical Geography of the Bay Islands, Honduras: Anglo-Hispanic Conflict in the Western Caribbean. (Illus.). 1974. 16.95x (ISBN 0-87651-207-4); pap. 9.50x (ISBN 0-686-96890-5). Southern U Pr.

Davie, D. Heydey of Sir Walter Scott. Repr. of 1961 ed. 9.00 o.s.i. (ISBN 0-527-21900-2). Kraus Repr.

Davie, Donald. Collected Poems, Nineteen Fifty to Nineteen Seventy. LC 72-82671. 1972. 25.00 (ISBN 0-19-519712-7). Oxford U Pr.

--Collected Poems Nineteen Seventy to Nineteen Eighty-Three. 192p. 1983. pap. text ed. 12.50x (ISBN 0-85635-462-7, Pub. by Carcanet New Pr England). Humanities.

--In the Stopping Train: And Other Poems. 1980. text ed. 9.95x (ISBN 0-19-520175-2). Oxford U Pr.

--The Poet in the Imaginary Museum. Alpert, Barry, ed. LC 77-85356. 1978. 17.50 o.p. (ISBN 0-89255-029-5). Persea Bks.

--These the Companions: Recollections by Donald Davie. 1982. 22.50 (ISBN 0-521-24511-7). Cambridge U Pr.

--Thomas Hardy & British Poetry. LC 70-188291. 1972. 14.95x (ISBN 0-19-501572-X). Oxford U Pr.

--Three for Water Music. 64p. (Orig.). 1981. pap. text ed. 6.50x (ISBN 0-85635-363-9, Pub. by Carcanet New Pr England). Humanities.

Davie, Donald, ed. & tr. see Pasternak, Boris.

Davie, J. T. & Morrison, R. Recursive Descent Compiling. LC 81-6778. (Computers & Their Applications). 195p. 1982. pap. 29.95x (ISBN 0-470-27361-5). Halsted Pr.

Davie, Maurice, ed. see Sumner, William G.

Davie, Maurice R. Constructive Immigration Policy. 1923. pap. 19.50x (ISBN 0-685-69809-2). Elliots Bks.

Davie, Peter & Cooper, H. John. First Bull Run (1861) (Knight's Battles for Wargamers Ser.). (Illus.). 100p. 1973. 3.95 o.p. (ISBN 0-88254-210-9). Hippocrene Bks.

Davier, jt. auth. see Burrows.

Davies. Cavitation in Real Liquids. 1964. 12.50 (ISBN 0-444-40153-9). Elsevier.

--Conduction System of the Heart. 1982. text ed. 99.95 (ISBN 0-407-00133-6). Butterworth.

--Construction Site: Production 4 Checkbook. 1982. text ed. 22.50 (ISBN 0-408-00675-7); pap. 12.50 (ISBN 0-408-00656-0). Butterworth.

Davies & Beatty. Literature of the Romantic Period, 1750-1850. 228p. 1982. 40.00x (ISBN 0-85323-353-5, Pub. by Liverpool Univ England). State Mutual Bk.

Davies, A. Meaning of the Dead Sea Scrolls. pap. 1.95 (ISBN 0-451-61745-2, ME2097, Ment). NAL.

Davies, A. F. Skills, Outlooks, Passions: A Psychoanalytic Contribution to the Study of Politics. 2nd ed. LC 78-54575. (Illus.). 456p. 1981. 59.00 (ISBN 0-521-22081-5); pap. 16.95 (ISBN 0-521-29349-9). Cambridge U Pr.

Davies, A. G., jt. ed. see Seyferth, D.

Davies, Alastair. An Annotated Critical Bibliography of Modernism, No. 1. LC 82-13864. (Harvester-Barnes & Noble Annotated Critical Bibliographies Ser.). 276p. 1982. text ed. 35.00x (ISBN 0-389-20303-3). B&N Imports.

Davies, Andrew. The Fantastic Feats of Doctor Boox. LC 72-93651. (Illus.). 64p. (gr. 1-3). 1973. 4.95 (ISBN 0-02-726240-5). Bradbury Pr.

--Marmalade & Rufus. 1983. 8.95 (ISBN 0-517-54632-9). Crown.

Davies, Arthur C. The Science & Practice of Welding. 7th ed. LC 77-71408. (Illus.). 1977. 27.95x (ISBN 0-521-21557-9). Cambridge U Pr.

Davies, Barbara S. & Davies, J. Clarence, 3rd. The Politics of Pollution. 2nd ed. LC 74-20996. (Studies in Contemporary America Ser.). 256p. 1975. 7.50 o.p. (ISBN 0-672-53720-6); pap. 6.95 (ISBN 0-672-63720-0). Pegasus.

Davies, Barrie. At the Mermaid Inn: Wilfred Campbell, Archibald Lampman, Duncan Campbell Scott in the Globe 1892-93. (Literature of Canada; Poetry & Prose in Reprint). 1979. 35.00x o.p. (ISBN 0-8020-2299-5); pap. 9.50 (ISBN 0-8020-6333-0). U of Toronto Pr.

Davies, Benjamin. Baker's Harmony of the Gospels. (Baker's Paperback Reference Library). 192p. 1983. pap. 6.95 (ISBN 0-8010-2928-7). Baker Bk.

Davies, Bernard. Use of Groups in Social Work Practice. 1975. 16.95x (ISBN 0-7100-8085-9); pap. 6.50 o.p. (ISBN 0-7100-8086-7). Routledge & Kegan.

Davies, Bettilu D. Tall Trouble. LC 81-11326. 160p. 1981. pap. 2.95 (ISBN 0-8024-8112-4). Moody.

Davies, Bleddyn. Universality, Selectivity & Effectiveness in Social Policy. LC 80-457434. (Studies in Social Policy & Welfare). 1978. text ed. 27.00x (ISBN 0-435-82266-7). Heinemann Ed.

Davies, Brian. Seal Song. (Large Format Ser). (Illus.). 1979. pap. 7.95 (ISBN 0-14-004740-9). Penguin.

--Social Control & Education. 1976. pap. 7.50x (ISBN 0-416-55810-0). Methuen Inc.

Davies, Brian E., ed. Applied Soil Trace Elements. LC 79-40640. 482p. 1980. 71.95 (ISBN 0-471-27625-1, Pub. by Wiley-Interscience). Wiley.

Davies, Brinley. Business Finance & the City of London. 2nd ed. (Studies in the British Economy). (Orig.). 1980. pap. text ed. 6.00x o.p. (ISBN 0-435-84579-9). Heinemann Ed.

--United Kingdom & the World Monetary System: Studies in the British Economy Ser. 2nd ed. 1976. pap. text ed. 7.00x o.p. (ISBN 0-435-84350-8). Heinemann Ed.

Davies, Brinley & Foad, John. Statistics for Economics. 1977. pap. text ed. 8.50x o.p. (ISBN 0-435-84330-3). Heinemann Ed.

Davies, Bronwyn. Life in the Classroom & the Playground: The Accounts of Primary School Children. (Social Worlds of Childhood Ser.). 224p. 1983. 27.50 (ISBN 0-7100-9210-5). Routledge & Kegan.

Davies, Bruce & Thomas, Geoffrey, eds. Science & Sporting Performance: Management or Manipulation? (Illus.). 250p. 1982. 32.50 (ISBN 0-19-857594-7). Oxford U Pr.

Davies, C., et al. Organization for Program Management. LC 78-27660. 1980. 43.95 (ISBN 0-471-27571-9, Pub. by Wiley-Interscience). Wiley.

Davies, D. E. Seasonal Breeding & Migrations of the Desert Locust (Schistocerca Gregaria Forskal) in North-Eastern Africa & the Middle East. 1952. 35.00x (ISBN 0-85135-010-0, Pub. by Centre Overseas Research). State Mutual Bk.

Davies, D. H., ed. Zambia in Maps. LC 73-653626. (Graphic Perspectives in Developing Countries Ser). 128p. 1972. text ed. 34.60x (ISBN 0-8419-0081-7, Africana). Holmes & Meier.

Davies, D. M., ed. Textbook of Adverse Drug Reactions. 2nd ed. (Illus.). 1981. text ed. 75.00x (ISBN 0-19-261270-0). Oxford U Pr.

Davies, D. R. & Schackleton, V. J. Psychology & Work. (Essential Psychology Ser.). 1975. pap. 4.50x (ISBN 0-416-82290-8). Methuen Inc.

Davies, D. R. & Tune, G. S. Human Vigilance Performance. 1970. 24.95 (ISBN 0-444-19717-6). Elsevier.

Davies, D. W. & Barber, D. L. Communication Networks for Computers. LC 73-2775. (Computing Ser). 575p. 1973. 84.95x (ISBN 0-471-19874-9, Pub. by Wiley-Interscience). Wiley.

Davies, D. W., et al. Computer Networks & Their Protocols. LC 78-21973. (Wiley Series in Computing). 487p. 1979. 71.95 (ISBN 0-471-99750-1, Pub. by Wiley Interscience). Wiley.

Davies, David, jt. auth. see Bussink, Willem.

Davies, David W. & Wrigley, Elizabeth S., eds. Concordance to the Essays of Francis Bacon. LC 73-8947. 392p. 1973. 64.00x (ISBN 0-8103-1004-X). Gale.

Davies, Don, ed. Communities & Their Schools. (Study of the Schooling in the United States Ser.). 352p. 1981. 19.95 (ISBN 0-07-015503-8, P&RB). McGraw.

Davies, E. J. & Simpson, P. G. Induction Heating Handbook. 460p. 1979. 39.95 (ISBN 0-07-084515-8). McGraw.

Davies, E. W., ed. see Cicero.

Davies, Evan. The Book of Dulwich. 1977. 20.00x o.p. (ISBN 0-86023-003-1). State Mutual Bk.

Davies, Frederick. Death of a Hit-Man. 224p. 1982. 10.95 (ISBN 0-312-18640-1). St Martin.

Davies, G. Henton. Exodus. (Student Christian Movement Press Ser. - Torch Bible Ser.). (Orig.). 1967. pap. 7.95 (ISBN 0-19-520295-3). Oxford U Pr.

Davies, G. I. The Way of the Wilderness. LC 77-95442. (Society for Old Testament Monographs). (Illus.). 1979. 27.95 (ISBN 0-521-22057-2). Cambridge U Pr.

Davies, Glyn A. Virtual Work in Structural Analysis. LC 81-15926. 325p. 1982. 38.00x (ISBN 0-471-10112-5, Pub. by Wiley-Interscience). Wiley.

Davies, Hugh. International Electronic Music Catalog. 1968. 25.00x (ISBN 0-262-04012-3). MIT Pr.

Davies, Hunter. The Beatles. rev. ed. LC 77-25031. 1978. 14.95 (ISBN 0-07-015463-5, GB). McGraw.

--William Wordsworth: A Biography. LC 80-66004. (Illus.). 1980. 17.95 o.p. (ISBN 0-689-11087-1). Atheneum.

Davies, Hunter & Herrmann, Frank. Great Britain. (Illus.). 288p. 1983. 31.50 (ISBN 0-241-10755-5, Pub. by Hamish Hamilton England). David & Charles.

Davies, I. Aging in Animals. (Studies in Biology: No. 151). 64p. 1983. pap. text ed. 8.95 (ISBN 0-7131-2863-1). E Arnold.

Davies, I. K. Objectives in Curriculum Design. new ed. (Illus.). 1976. text ed. 13.95 o.p. (ISBN 0-07-084065-2, C). McGraw.

Davies, Ian, jt. auth. see Raistrick, Duncan.

Davies, Ivor K. Competency Based Learning: Management, Technology, & Design. Orig. Title: The Management of Learning. 254p. 1973. text ed. 32.50 (ISBN 0-07-084420-8, C). McGraw.

Davies, J. & Hughes, S. Pricing in Practice. (Studies in the British Economy Ser.). 1975. pap. text ed. 6.50x o.p. (ISBN 0-435-84563-2). Heinemann Ed.

Davies, J., ed. Esenin: A Biography in Memoirs, Letters, & Documents. 286p. 1982. 22.50 (ISBN 0-88233-491-3). Ardis Pubs.

Davies, J. C. Yesterday's Town: Victorian Harborough. 1981. 39.50x o.p. (ISBN 0-86023-118-6, Pub. by Barracuda England). State Mutual Bk.

Davies, J. Clarence, 3rd, jt. auth. see Davies, Barbara S.

Davies, J. G., ed. The Westminster Dictionary of Worship. LC 78-25582. (Illus.). 1979. 15.95 (ISBN 0-664-21373-1). Westminster.

Davies, J. W. Physiological Responses to Burning Injury. 1982. 67.00 (ISBN 0-12-206080-6). Acad Pr.

Davies, Jack. Ffolks. 320p. (Orig.). 1980. pap. 2.50 o.s.i. (ISBN 0-515-05430-5). Jove Pubns.

Davies, Jack & Lawry, Robert P. Institutions & Methods of the Law: Introductory Teaching Materials. LC 81-23956. (American Casebook Ser.). 542p. 1982. text ed. 17.95 (ISBN 0-314-64216-1). West Pub.

Davies, Jane, jt. auth. see Andrian, Gustave W.

Davies, John. Poems. Krueger, Robert, ed. (Oxford English Texts Ser). (Illus.). 1974. 54.00x (ISBN 0-19-812716-2). Oxford U Pr.

Davies, John, jt. auth. see Spenser, Edmund.

Davies, John S. Beginning to Compose. Incl. Bk. 1. Writing Melodies (ISBN 0-19-321063-0); Bk. 2. Writing in Two Parts (ISBN 0-19-321064-9). (gr. 4-6). 1976. pap. 4.25 (ISBN 0-686-86546-4); tchr's bk. 5.25 (ISBN 0-19-321062-2). Oxford U Pr.

Davies, John T. The Legend Makers. 1983. 12.95 (ISBN 0-686-34309-3). Amber Crest.

Davies, Jonathan, jt. auth. see Brenner, Vincent C.

Davies, Jonathan J. CPA Liability: A Manual for Practitioners. (Modern Accounting Perspectives & Practices Ser.). 266p. 1983. write for info (ISBN 0-471-06290-1). Ronald Pr.

Davies, Kenneth J., jt. auth. see Wronski, Wojcech.

Davies, Kirk. Earth's Final Hours. 330p. (Orig.). 1982. pap. 9.95 (ISBN 0-9609174-0-3). Pacific Inst.

Davies, Laurence. Cesar Franck & His Circle. LC 77-4231. (Music Reprint Ser.). (Illus.). 1977. Repr. of 1970 ed. lib. bdg. 35.00 (ISBN 0-306-77410-0). Da Capo.

Davies, M. Functions of Biological Membranes. (Outline Studies in Biology). 1973. pap. 6.50x (ISBN 0-412-11350-3, Pub. by Chapman & Hall). Methuen Inc.

Davies, M. S., et al. A Directory of Clothing Research. 1968. 7.00 o.s.i. (ISBN 0-87245-603-X). Textile Bk.

Davies, Margaret L., ed. Life As We Have Known It. 184p. 1975. pap. 4.95 (ISBN 0-393-00772-3, Norton Lib). Norton.

Davies, Margery. Woman's Place Is at the Typewriter: Office Work & Office Workers, 1870-1930. LC 82-13694. (Class & Culture Ser.). 264p. 1982. text ed. 22.95 (ISBN 0-87722-291-6). Temple U Pr.

Davies, Marilyn A., jt. auth. see Foley, Theresa S.

Davies, Martin. The Gold Machine. 1979. pap. 1.95 o.p. (ISBN 0-523-40396-8). Pinnacle Bks.

--Prisoners of Society: Attitudes & After-Care. (International Library of Sociology Ser.). 1974. 20.00x (ISBN 0-7100-7989-3). Routledge & Kegan.

--Support Systems in Social Work. (Library of Social Work). 1977. 18.95x (ISBN 0-7100-8616-4); pap. 8.95 (ISBN 0-7100-8617-2). Routledge & Kegan.

Davies, Martin, ed. see Crompton, Margaret.

Davies, Michael. Newman Against the Liberals. 1978. 11.00 o.p. (ISBN 0-87000-394-1, Arlington Hse). Crown.

Davies, N. de Garis. A Corpus of Inscribed Egyptian Funerary Cones, Pt. 1. (Illus.). 7p. 1957. text ed. 45.00x (ISBN 0-900416-12-2, Pub. by Aris & Philips England). Humanities.

Davies, Nigel. The Ancient Kingdoms of Mexico. 284p. 1982. 30.00x o.p. (ISBN 0-7139-1245-6, Pub. by Penguin Bks). State Mutual Bk.

Davies, Nina. Scenes from Some Theban Tombs. (Private Tombs at Thebes Ser.: Vol. IV). 22p. 1963. text ed. 26.00x (ISBN 0-686-73619-2, Pub. by Aris & Philips England). Humanities.

Davies, Nina M. Tutankhamun's Painted Box. 22p. 1962. pap. 30.00x (ISBN 0-900416-22-X, Pub. by Aris & Philips England). Humanities.

Davies, P. A., ed. see Specialist Symposium on Geophysical Fluid Dynamics, European Geophysical Society, Fourth Meeting, Munich September, 1977.

Davies, P. C. The Forces of Nature. LC 78-72084. (Illus.). 1979. 39.50 (ISBN 0-521-22523-X); pap. 12.95 (ISBN 0-521-29535-1). Cambridge U Pr.

--The Physics of Time Asymmetry. LC 74-81536. 1974. 33.00x (ISBN 0-520-02825-2); pap. 6.50x (ISBN 0-520-03247-0). U of Cal Pr.

--The Search for Gravity Waves. (Illus.). 160p. 1980. 14.95 (ISBN 0-521-23197-3). Cambridge U Pr.

--Space & Time in the Modern Universe. LC 76-27902. (Illus.). 1977. 35.50 (ISBN 0-521-21445-9); pap. 13.95 (ISBN 0-521-29151-8). Cambridge U Pr.

Davies, P. C. W. The Accidental Universe. LC 81-21592. (Illus.). 160p. 1982. 19.95 (ISBN 0-521-24212-6); pap. 9.95 (ISBN 0-521-28692-1). Cambridge U Pr.

Davies, P. M. & Coxon, A. P., eds. Key Texts on Multidimensional Scaling. xx, 352p. 1982. text ed. 20.00x (ISBN 0-435-82253-5). Heinemann Ed.

Davies, Paul. The Edge of Infinity. 1982. 12.95 (ISBN 0-671-44063-2). S&S.

--The Edge of Infinity. 1983. pap. 6.95 (ISBN 0-671-46062-5, Touchstone Bks). S&S.

Davies, Penelope & Stewart, Philippa. Tutankhamun's Egypt. LC 77-92805. (The History Makers Ser.). 1978. 7.95 o.p. (ISBN 0-312-82369-X); pap. 4.95 o.p. (ISBN 0-312-82370-3). St Martin.

Davies, Peter. Davies' Dictionary of Golfing Terms. 1980. 13.95 o.p. (ISBN 0-671-24761-1). S&S.

--Fly Away Paul. LC 73-90314. 224p. (gr. 7 up). 1974. 5.95 o.p. (ISBN 0-517-51437-0). Crown.

--Roots: Family Histories of Familiar Words. (Illus.). 224p. 1981. 21.95 (ISBN 0-07-015449-X, P&RB). McGraw.

Davies, Peter J., jt. auth. see Galston, Arthur W.

Davies, Philip. Qumran. 1982. 35.00x (ISBN 0-7188-2458-X, Pub. by Lutterworth Pr England). State Mutual Bk.

Davies, R. Developments in Food Microbiology, Vol. 1. 1982. 49.25 (ISBN 0-85334-999-1, Pub. by Applied Sci England). Elsevier.

Davies, R. & Grant, M. D. London & Its Railways. (Illus.). 224p. (Orig.). 1983. 23.95 (ISBN 0-7153-8107-5). David & Charles.

Davies, R., et al. Intermediate Moisture Foods. (Illus.). 1976. 49.25 (ISBN 0-85334-702-6, Pub. by Applied Sci England). Elsevier.

Davies, R. E. Airlines of the United States Since 1914. (Illus.). 746p. 1983. Repr. of 1972 ed. text ed. 35.00x (ISBN 0-87474-356-7). Smithsonian.

--A History of the World's Airlines. (Airlines History Project Ser.). (Illus.). Date not set. 39.50 (ISBN 0-404-19325-0). AMS Pr.

Davies, R. G., jt. auth. see Richards, O. W.

Davies, R. L., jt. auth. see Diamond.

Davies, R. T., ed. Medieval English Lyrics. 384p. 1966. 17.95 (ISBN 0-571-05522-2); pap. 9.95 (ISBN 0-571-06571-6). Faber & Faber.

Davies, R. Trevor, tr. from Lat. & Fr. Documents Illustrating the History of Civilization in Medieval England: 1066-1500. 413p. 1982. Repr. of 1926 ed. lib. bdg. 50.00 (ISBN 0-8495-1140-2). Arden Lib.

Davies, R. W., ed. The Soviet Union. (Illus.). 1978. text ed. 22.50x (ISBN 0-04-947022-1); pap. text ed. 8.95x (ISBN 0-04-947023-X). Allen Unwin.

Davies, Rhiannon. Advanced Needlework Notebook. 1970. pap. text ed. 6.50x o.p. (ISBN 0-435-42831-4). Heinemann Ed.

--Needlework Notebook. 1968. pap. text ed. 5.50x o.p. (ISBN 0-435-42830-6). Heinemann Ed.

Davies, Richard O. Housing Reform During the Truman Administration. LC 65-25641. 1966. 12.00x o.p. (ISBN 0-8262-0046-X). U of Mo Pr.

Davies, Robert, ed. York Records of the Fifteenth Century. 304p. 1976. Repr. of 1843 ed. text ed. 21.00x (ISBN 0-904586-02-2, Pub. by Alan Sutton England). Humanities.

Davies, Robertson. A Mixture of Frailties. LC 78-74578. 1979. 12.50 (ISBN 0-89696-051-X, An Everest House Book). Dodd.

--The Rebel Angels. 1983. pap. 3.95 (ISBN 0-14-006271-8). Penguin.

Davies, Ross. Retail Planning in the European Community. 1979. text ed. 37.25x (ISBN 0-566-00308-2). Gower Pub Ltd.

Davies, Rupert E. The Problems of Authority in the Continental Reformers: A Study of Luther, Zwingli, & Calvin. LC 78-5871. 1978. Repr. of 1946 ed. lib. bdg. 20.00x (ISBN 0-313-20487-X, DAPA). Greenwood.

Davies, Rupert E., jt. ed. see Flew, Robert N.

Davies, Ruth A., jt. auth. see Clendening, Corinne P.

Davies, S. The Diffusion of Process Innovations. LC 78-15143. 1979. 37.50 (ISBN 0-521-22193-5). Cambridge U Pr.

Davies, S. G., ed. Organotransition Metal Chemistry: Applications to Organic Synthesis. (Organic Chemistry Ser.: Vol. 2). (Illus.). 428p. 1982. 85.00 (ISBN 0-08-026202-3). Pergamon.

Davies, S. J. In Spite of Dungeons. 160p. 1978. pap. text ed. 7.50x (ISBN 0-904387-11-9, Pub. by Alan Sutton England). Humanities.

Davies, Samuel. Collected Poems. Davis, Richard B., ed. LC 68-17019. 1968. 34.00x (ISBN 0-8201-1011-6). Schol Facsimiles.

Davies, Saunders, tr. see Lauer, Hans E.

Davies, Stella & Levitt, John. What's in a Name. 1970. 12.95 o.p. (ISBN 0-7100-6753-4). Transatlantic.

Davies, Stevan. The Gospel of Thomas & Christian Wisdom. 160p. 1983. pap. 9.95 (ISBN 0-8164-2456-X). Seabury.

Davies, Stevan L. The Revolt of the Widows: The Social World of the Apocryphal Acts. LC 80-11331. 150p. 1980. 12.95x (ISBN 0-8093-0958-0). S Ill U Pr.

Davies, Stevie. Images of Kinship in "Pardise Lost". Milton's Politics & Christian Liberty. LC 82-17485. 256p. 1983. text ed. 21.00x. U of Mo Pr.

Davies, Sue, tr. see Schnitzler, Arthur.

Davies, Terry F. Autoimmune Endocrine Disease. 500p. 1983. write for info. (ISBN 0-471-09778-0, Pub. by Wiley-Interscience). Wiley.

Davies, Thomas D. Star Sight Reduction Tables for Forty-Two Stars: Assumed Altitude Method of Celestial Navigation. LC 79-7464. 1980. 28.50x o.p. (ISBN 0-87033-250-3). Cornell Maritime.

Davies, Thomas L. Shoots: A Guide to Your Family's Photographic Heritage. LC 77-84356. (Illus.). 1978. 7.95 o.p. (ISBN 0-89169-033-6). Addison Hse.

--Shoots: A Guide to Your Family's Photographic Heritage. LC 77-84356. (Illus.). 1977. pap. 4.95 o.p. (ISBN 0-89169-012-3). Addison Hse.

--Supplementary English Glossary. LC 68-23468. 1968. Repr. of 1881 ed. 47.00x (ISBN 0-8103-3245-0). Gale.

Davies, Valentine. Miracle on Thirty-Fourth Street. LC 47-4221. (YA) (gr. 7-12). 1967. pap. 2.50 (ISBN 0-15-660453-1, Harv). HarBraceJ.

Davies, W. D. The Gospel & the Land: Early Christianity & Jewish Territorial Doctrine. LC 72-82228. 1974. 29.50x (ISBN 0-520-02278-5). U of Cal Pr.

--Jewish & Pauline Studies. LC 82-48620. 432p. 1983. text ed. 29.95 (ISBN 0-8006-0694-9). Fortress.

--System Identification for Self Adaptive Control. LC 70-128756. 1970. 37.75 o.p. (ISBN 0-471-19885-4, Pub. by Wiley-Interscience). Wiley.

Davies, Walford, ed. see Thomas, Dylan.

Davies, Wendy. Wales in the Early Middle Ages. (Studies in the Early History of Britain: Vol. 2). 300p. 1982. text ed. 46.25x (ISBN 0-7185-1163-8, Leicester). Humanities.

Davies, William D. Sermon on the Mount. (Orig.). 1966. pap. 7.95 (ISBN 0-521-09384-8, 384). Cambridge U Pr.

--Setting of the Sermon on the Mount. 1964. 69.50 (ISBN 0-521-04797-8); pap. 19.95 (ISBN 0-521-29124-0). Cambridge U Pr.

Davies, William H. Captive Lion & Other Poems. 1921. 19.50x (ISBN 0-685-89738-9). Elliots Bks.

Davies-Rodgers, Ellen. The Great Book: Calvary Protestant Episcopal Church. Memphis, Tennessee 1832-1972. 1973. 30.00 (ISBN 0-685-84989-9). Plantation.

Davin, D. M. Closing Times. 1975. 15.00x (ISBN 0-19-212197-9). Oxford U Pr.

Davin, Dan. Roads from Home. (New Zealand Fiction Ser.). 1977. 12.50x o.p. (ISBN 0-19-647948-7). Oxford U Pr.

Da Vinci, Leonardo. Codex Atlanticus. 12000.00 (ISBN 0-384-32302-2). Johnson Repr.

--The Corpus of the Anatomical Studies in the Collection of Her Majesty Queen Elizabeth II at the Royal Library, Windsor Castle. facsimile ed. 1978. 8000.00. Johnson Repr.

--Leonardo da Vinci Drawings. (Illus.). Date not set. pap. 2.50 (ISBN 0-486-23951-9). Dover.

--Leonardo on the Human Body. O'Malley, Charles D. & Saunders, J. B., trs. (Fine Art Ser.). (Illus.). 506p. 1983. pap. 10.00 (ISBN 0-486-24483-0). Dover.

--Transcriptions of the Codex Atlanticus, 12 vols. Set. 900.00 (ISBN 0-384-32303-0). Johnson Repr.

Davin-Power, Maurice. Shadows in the Sun. (Irish Play Ser.). pap. 2.95x (ISBN 0-912262-64-8). Proscenium.

Davinson, D. E. The Periodicals Collection. 244p. 1978. 26.50 (ISBN 0-233-96918-7, 05776-2, Pub. by Gower Pub Co England). Lexington Bks.

Davinson, Donald. The Periodicals Collection. 2nd ed. (A Grafton Book). 1978. lib. bdg. 27.50 (ISBN 0-89158-883-3). Westview.

Davio, Marc, et al. Discrete & Switching Functions. 1978. text ed. 97.50x (ISBN 0-07-015509-7, C). McGraw.

Davis. A Career in Advertising. 13.50x o.p. (ISBN 0-392-07440-0, LTB). Sportshelf.

--Cheese, Vols. 2 & 3. Vol. 2, 1965. 16.00 (ISBN 0-686-43056-5); Vol. 3, 1977. 45.00. Elsevier.

--Davis Dictionary of the Bible. 21.95 (ISBN 0-8054-1124-0). Broadman.

--Human Cancer: Its Characterization & Treatment. (International Congress Series.: Vol. 484 & Advances in Tumor Prevention & Detective: Vol. 5). 1980. 98.00 (ISBN 0-444-90175-2). Elsevier.

Davis & Spillman. Cardiac Rehabilitation for the Patient & Family. 1982. pap. text ed. 9.07 (ISBN 0-8359-0676-0). Reston.

Davis, jt. auth. see Osmond, Marie.

Davis, A., tr. see Graeff, H. & Kuhn, W.

Davis, A. E. & Bolin, T. D. Symptom Analysis & Physical Diagnosis in Medicine. 1977. text ed. 20.00 (ISBN 0-08-021245-X); pap. text ed. 13.50 (ISBN 0-08-021244-1). Pergamon.

Davis, A. Jann. Please See My Need. (Illus.). pap. 5.95x (ISBN 0-9609184-0-X). Satellite Cont.

Davis, Adelle. Let's Cook It Right. LC 62-9440. 1970. pap. 3.95x (ISBN 0-451-11161-3, Pub. by NAL). Formur Intl.

--Let's Cook It Right. 1970. 6.95x (ISBN 0-15-150166-1); pap. 1.75x (ISBN 0-686-36360-4). Cancer Control Soc.

--Let's Eat Right to Keep Fit. 1970. pap. 2.50x (ISBN 0-451-07951-5). Cancer Control Soc.

--Let's Eat Right to Keep Fit. LC 71-128463. 1970. pap. 2.95 (ISBN 0-451-09644-4, Pub. by NAL). Formur Intl.

--Let's Eat Right to Keep Fit. 1970. pap. 2.95 (ISBN 0-451-11608-9, AE1608, Sig). NAL.

--Let's Get Well. pap. 3.50x (ISBN 0-451-09147-7). Cancer Control Soc.

--Let's Get Well. LC 65-19054. 1972. pap. 3.50 (ISBN 0-451-09852-8, Pub. by NAL). Formur Intl.

--Let's Get Well. pap. 3.50 (ISBN 0-451-09852-8, E9852, Sig). NAL.

--Let's Stay Healthy. 1981. 12.95x (ISBN 0-15-150443-1). Cancer Control Soc.

--You Can Get Well. 1975. pap. 2.95 (ISBN 0-87904-033-5). Lust.

Davis, Alan, ed. Maps: The Eighties. 100p. 1983. 5.00 (ISBN 0-686-38061-4). Moons Quilt Pr.

Davis, Alan & Horobin, Gordon, eds. Medical Encounters: The Experience of Illness & Treatment. LC 76-44646. 1977. text ed. 18.95x o.p. (ISBN 0-312-52605-9). St Martin.

Davis, Albert R., jt. auth. see Rawls, Walter, Jr.

Davis, Alexander J. Rural Residences. (Architecture & Decorative Art Ser.). 1980. Repr. of 1838 ed. 95.00 (ISBN 0-306-71165-6). Da Capo.

Davis, Alexandra & Davis, O. B. Exercises in Reading & Writing. LC 82-17719. (gr. 8-12). 1982. pap. 5.75 (ISBN 0-86709-031-6). Boynton Cook Pubs.

Davis, Alice V. Timothy Turtle. LC 40-32634. (Illus.). (gr. k-3). 1940. 5.95 o.p. (ISBN 0-15-288368-1, HJ). HarBraceJ.

--Timothy Turtle. LC 40-32634. (Illus.). (gr. 1-4). 1972. pap. 3.95 (ISBN 0-15-690450-0, VoyB). HarBraceJ.

Davis, Allen F. & Woodman, Harold D. Conflict & Consensus in Early American History. 5th ed. 1980. pap. text ed. 11.95 (ISBN 0-669-02489-9). Heath.

--Conflict & Consensus in Modern American History. 5th ed. 1980. pap. text ed. 11.95 (ISBN 0-669-02490-2). Heath.

Davis, Allen F. & Haller, Mark H., eds. The Peoples of Philadelphia: A History of Ethnic Groups & Lower Class Life, 1790-1940. LC 72-95879. 311p. 1973. 24.95 (ISBN 0-87722-053-0); pap. 8.95 (ISBN 0-87722-035-2). Temple U Pr.

Davis, Allen F., ed. see Bannister, Robert C.

Davis, Allen F., ed. see Bordin, Ruth.

Davis, Allen F., ed. see Farrell, James J.

Davis, Allen F., ed. see Hill, Mary A.

Davis, Allen F., ed. see Marsh, Margaret.

Davis, Allen F., ed. see Meikle, Jeffrey.

Davis, Allen F., ed. see Sizer, Sandra S.

Davis, Allison. Leadership, Love & Aggression. 256p. 15.95 (ISBN 0-15-149348-0). HarBraceJ.

--Psychology of the Child in the Middle Class. LC 60-15158. (Horace Mann Lecture Ser.). 1960. 4.95x o.p. (ISBN 0-8229-1066-7). U of Pittsburgh Pr.

Davis, Angela Y. Women, Race & Class. Date not set. 13.50 (ISBN 0-394-51039-9). Random.

--Women, Race & Class. LC 82-40414. 288p. 1983. pap. 5.95 (ISBN 0-394-71351-6, Vin). Random.

Davis, Ann. The Residential Solution: State Alternatives to Family Care. (Tavistock Library of Social Work Practice). 158p. 1981. 19.95x (ISBN 0-422-77320-4, Pub. by Tavistock England); pap. 9.50x (ISBN 0-422-77330-1, Pub. by Taavistock England). Methuen Inc.

Davis, Ann N. & Richardson, Robert A. The Helicopter: Its Importance to Commerce & to the Public. 138p. 1978. 10.00 o.p. (ISBN 0-911721-70-3, Pub. by Helicopter Assn). Aviation.

Davis, Anne B., jt. auth. see Kalkman, Markian E.

Davis, Anthony. Tackle Motorcycle Sport This Way. (Tackle Ser.). (Illus.). 1976. pap. 6.95x o.p. (ISBN 0-09-103521-X, SpS). Sportshelf.

Davis, Arthur P. From the Dark Tower: Afro-American Writers, 1900 to 1960. LC 73-88969. 352p. 1974. 10.95x (ISBN 0-88258-004-3). Howard U Pr.

Davis, Arthur P. & Redding, Saunders, eds. Cavalcade: Negro American Writing from 1760 to the Present. LC 70-20257. 1971. text ed. 24.50 (ISBN 0-395-04345-X). HM.

Davis, Audrey, ed. see Hammond, Bernice.

Davis, B. D. Electrical & Electronic Technologies: A Chronology of Events & Inventors from 1900 to 1940. LC 82-16739. 220p. 1983. 16.00 (ISBN 0-8108-1590-7). Scarecrow.

Davis, B. P. The Economics of Automatic Testing: Electronics Components & Sub-Assemblies. 320p. 1982. 42.50 (ISBN 0-07-084584-0, P&RB). McGraw.

Davis, Barry. Understanding DC Power Supplies. (Illus.). 240p. 1983. 18.95 (ISBN 0-13-936831-0); pap. 12.95 (ISBN 0-13-936823-X). P-H.

Davis, Bernard. Food Commodities--Catering, Processing, Storing. 1978. pap. 16.50 (ISBN 0-434-90297-7, Pub. by Heinemann). David & Charles.

Davis, Bernard & Davis, Elizabeth, eds. Poets of the Early Seventeenth Century. (Boutledge English Texts). 1967. pap. 4.95 (ISBN 0-7100-4512-3). Routledge & Kegan.

Davis, Bernard D. & Flaherty, Patricia, eds. Human Diversity: Its Causes & Social Significance. LC 76-7002. (American Academy of Arts and Sciences Ser.). 192p. 1976. prof ref 16.50x (ISBN 0-88410-047-2). Ballinger Pub.

Davis, Bernard E. Edmund Spenser: A Critical Study. LC 62-10228. 1962. Repr. of 1933 ed. 8.50x o.p. (ISBN 0-8462-0164-X). Russell.

Davis, Bertha & Whitfield, Susan. The Coal Question. LC 82-4716. (Impact Ser.). (Illus.). 96p. (gr. 7 up). 1982. PLB 8.90 (ISBN 0-531-04484-X). Watts.

--How to Improve Your Comprehension. (gr. 7 up). 1980. PLB 8.90 (ISBN 0-531-04132-8). Watts.

Davis, Bertram H. Thomas Percy. (English Authors Ser.). 12.95 (ISBN 0-8057-6804-1, Twayne). G K Hall.

Davis, Bette. Mother Goddam. rev. ed. 1979. pap. 2.75 o.p. (ISBN 0-425-04119-0). Berkley Pub.

Davis, Bette, jt. auth. see Stine, Whitney.

Davis, Betty, jt. auth. see Stine, Whitney.

Davis, Bob J., ed. Information Sources in Transportation, Material Management, & Physical Distribution: An Annotated Bibliography & Guide. LC 75-23864. (Orig.). 1976. lib. bdg. 65.00 (ISBN 0-8371-8379-0, DBT/). Greenwood.

Davis, Brian L. Badges & Insignia of the Third Reich 1933-1945. (Illus.). 160p. 1983. 16.95 (ISBN 0-7137-1130-2, Pub. by Blandford Pr England). Sterling.

Davis, Bruce & Davis, Genny W. The Magical Child Within You. LC 82-84601. (Illus.). 112p. 1983. pap. 5.95 (ISBN 0-911717-00-5). Inner Light Pub.

Davis, Bruce & Wright, Genny. Hugs & Kisses. LC 77-5283. (Illus.). 96p. 1978. 4.95 (ISBN 0-89480-008-6); pap. 3.50 (ISBN 0-89480-106-6). Workman Pub.

Davis, Bruce L., compiled by. Criminological Bibliographies: Uniform Citations to Bibliographies, Indexes, & Review Articles of the Literature of Crime Study in the United States. LC 78-59442. 1978. lib. bdg. 29.95 (ISBN 0-313-20545-0, DCR/). Greenwood.

Davis, Burke. Amelia Earhart. (Lives to Remember Ser.). 192p. (gr. 6 up). 1972. PLB 5.49 o.p. (ISBN 0-399-60723-4). Putnam Pub Group.

--Biography of a Fish Hawk. LC 76-49987. (Nature Biography Ser.). (Illus.). (gr. 3-6). 1977. PLB 6.59 o.p. (ISBN 0-399-61084-7). Putnam Pub Group.

--Biography of a King Snake. LC 74-16625. (Nature Biography Ser.). (Illus.). (gr. 3-5). 1975. PLB 6.59 o.p. (ISBN 0-399-60919-8). Putnam Pub Group.

--Biography of a Leaf. new ed. LC 75-42028. (Nature Biography Ser.). (Illus.). 64p. (gr. 2-5). 1972. PLB 5.49 o.p. (ISBN 0-399-60746-3). Putnam Pub Group.

--Getting to Know Jamestown. (Getting to Know Ser.). (Illus.). (gr. 3-5). 1971. PLB 3.97 o.p. (ISBN 0-698-30130-7, Coward). Putnam Pub Group.

--Getting to Know Thomas Jefferson's Virginia. (Getting to Know Ser.). (Illus.). (gr. 3-5). 1971. PLB 3.97 o.p. (ISBN 0-698-30161-7, Coward). Putnam Pub Group.

--Mr. Lincoln's Whiskers. LC 77-29208. (Illus.). (gr. 3-5). 1979. 6.95 (ISBN 0-698-20455-7, Coward). Putnam Pub Group.

--Newer & Better Organic Gardening. LC 75-42028. (Illus.). 96p. (gr. 5 up). 1976. 5.95 o.p. (ISBN 0-399-20510-1). Putnam Pub Group.

--Runaway Balloon: The Last Flight of Confederate Airforce One. (Illus.). 48p. (gr. 5 up). 1976. 5.95 o.p. (ISBN 0-698-20372-0, Coward). Putnam Pub Group.

--Sherman's March. LC 79-5550. (Illus.). 1980. 16.50 (ISBN 0-394-50739-8). Random.

Davis, Burnie. How to Activate Miracles in Your Life & Ministry. 125p. 1982. pap. 3.95 (ISBN 0-89274-230-5, HH-230). Harrison Hse.

Davis, C., et al, eds. The Geometric Vein: The Coxeter Festschrift. (Illus.). 512p. 1982. 48.00 (ISBN 0-387-90587-1). Springer-Verlag.

Davis, Calvin V. & Sorensen, K. E. Handbook of Applied Hydraulics. 3rd ed. (Illus.). 1968. 75.00 (ISBN 0-07-015538-0, P&RB). McGraw.

Davis, Cecil T. Monumental Brasses of Gloucestershire. (Illus.). 1970. 12.50x o.p. (ISBN 0-87556-068-7). Saifer.

Davis, Charles. Body As Spirit: The Nature of Religious Feeling. 160p. 1976. 2.00 (ISBN 0-8164-0288-4). Seabury.

--Industrial Electronics: Design & Application. LC 72-92570. 1973. text ed. 26.95x (ISBN 0-675-09010-5). Additional supplements may be obtained from publisher. Merrill.

Davis, Charles G. Shipping & Craft in Silhouette. LC 70-162509. (Tower Bks). (Illus.). 221p. 1972. Repr. of 1929 ed. 34.00x (ISBN 0-8103-3945-5). Gale.

Davis, Charles H. & Lundeen, Gerald W. Illustrative Computer Programming for Libraries: Selected Examples for Information Specialists. 2nd ed. LC 81-1128. (Contributions in Librarianship & Information Science Ser.: No. 39). (Illus.). 120p. 1981. lib. bdg. 17.50 (ISBN 0-313-22151-0, DAD/). Greenwood.

Davis, Charles H. & Rush, James E. Guide to Information Science. LC 78-75240. (Illus.). 1979. lib. bdg. 29.95 (ISBN 0-313-20982-0, DGI/). Greenwood.

--Guide to Information Science. LC 78-75240. xvii, 305p. 1980. pap. text ed. 9.95 (ISBN 0-313-22603-2, DGI:). Greenwood.

--Information Retrieval & Documentation in Chemistry. LC 72-791. (Contributions in Librarianship & Information Science: No. 8). 1974. lib. bdg. 25.00 (ISBN 0-8371-6364-1, DAI/). Greenwood.

Davis, Charles H., ed. see Childers, Thomas.

Davis, Charles T., jt. auth. see Fabre, Michel.

Davis, Cheri. W. S. Merwin. (United States Authors Ser.). 1981. lib. bdg. 11.95 (ISBN 0-8057-7301-0, Twayne). G K Hall.

Davis, Christopher. Plains Indians. (Illus.). (gr. 5-8). 1978. PLB 9.40 s&l (ISBN 0-531-01429-0, Gloucester Press). Watts.

Davis, Christopher M., jt. ed. see Stern, Robert M.

Davis, Cos H., Jr. Ministering to Mobile Families. LC 80-71222. 1982. pap. 3.95 (ISBN 0-8054-3232-9). Broadman.

Davis, Creath. How to Win in a Crisis. 2nd ed. 224p. 1980. pap. 4.95 o.p. (ISBN 0-310-23181-7). Zondervan.

Davis, D. Dwight, jt. auth. see Schmidt, Karl P.

Davis, David B. Antebellum American Culture: An Interpretive Anthology. 1979. pap. text ed. 11.95 (ISBN 0-669-01476-1). Heath.

Davis, David C., et al, eds. Service Parts Management Reprints. LC 82-72118. 123p. 1982. pap. 10.50 (ISBN 0-935406-19-0). Am Prod & Inventory.

Davis, Deane C. Nothin' But the Truth: More Yankee Yarns. LC 82-80343. (Illus.). 224p. 1982. 10.95 (ISBN 0-933050-10-0); pap. 6.95 (ISBN 0-933050-14-3). New Eng Pr VT.

Davis, Dennis, jt. auth. see Kraus, Sidney.

Davis, Dick, ed. see Traherne, Thomas.

Davis, Dorothy S. A Gentle Murderer. 1980. lib. bdg. 11.95 (ISBN 0-8398-2650-8, Gregg). G K Hall.

--A Gentle Murderer. 224p. 1982. pap. 2.50 o.p. (ISBN 0-380-60715-8, 60715). Avon.

Davis, Douglas, intro. by. Photography As Fine Art. (Illus.). 224p. 1983. 50.00 (ISBN 0-525-24184-1, 038-83). Dutton.

Davis, Douglas & Simmons, Allison, eds. The New Television: A Public - Private Art. 1976. 22.50x (ISBN 0-262-04050-6); pap. 7.95 (ISBN 0-262-54031-2). MIT Pr.

Davis, E. Challenging Colonialism: Bank Misr & Egyptian Industrialization, 1920-1941. 1982. 23.50 (ISBN 0-691-07640-5). Princeton U Pr.

Davis, E. H., jt. auth. see Poulos, H. G.

Davis, E. W. & Yeomans, K. A. Company Finance & the Capital Market. LC 74-16990. (Department of Applied Economics, Occasional Papers: No. 39). (Illus.). 200p. 1975. 29.95 (ISBN 0-521-20144-6); pap. 15.95 (ISBN 0-521-09792-4). Cambridge U Pr.

Davis, Earl C. Somebody Cares. LC 81-71255. 1983. 6.95 (ISBN 0-8054-5211-7). Broadman.

Davis, Earle. The Flint & the Flame: The Artistry of Charles Dickens. 333p. 1982. Repr. of 1964 ed. lib. bdg. 35.00 (ISBN 0-89760-142-4). Telegraph Bks.

Davis, Ed. Teachers As Curriculum Evaluators. (Classroom & Curriculum in Australia Ser.: No. 4). 180p. 1981. text ed. 22.50x (ISBN 0-86861-090-9); pap. text ed. 9.95x (ISBN 0-86861-098-4). Allen Unwin.

Davis, Edith M. & Millman, Michael L. Health Care for the Urban Poor: Directions for Policy. (Conservation of Human Resources Ser.: No. 21). 220p. 1983. text ed. 30.00x (ISBN 0-86598-088-8). Allanheld.

Davis, Edward D. A Half Century of Struggle for Freedom in Florida. LC 82-50932. 1982. write for info. (ISBN 0-9610068-0-3). Drake's Ptg & Pub.

Davis, Edward M. Staff One: Perspectives on Effective Police Management. (Illus.). 1978. ref. ed. 21.95 (ISBN 0-13-840256-6); pap. text ed. 15.95 (ISBN 0-13-840249-3). P-H.

Davis, Edward W., ed. Project Management: Techniques, Applications & Managerial Issues. 1976. pap. text ed. 18.00 (ISBN 0-89806-024-9, 220); pap. text ed. 9.00 members. Inst Indus Eng.

Davis, Edward Z. Translations of German Poetry in American Magazines, 1741-1810. LC 66-27663. 1966. Repr. of 1905 ed. 30.00x (ISBN 0-8103-3209-4). Gale.

Davis, Eleanor H. Abraham Fornander: A Biography. LC 78-31368. 1979. 13.95 (ISBN 0-8248-0459-7). UH Pr.

Davis, Elizabeth, jt. ed. see Davis, Bernard.

Davis, Ellen N. The Vapheio Cups & Aegean Gold & Silver Ware. LC 76-23609. (Outstanding Dissertations in the Fine Arts). (Illus.). 1977. Repr. of 1973 ed. lib. bdg. 63.00 o.s.i. (ISBN 0-8240-2681-0). Garland Pub.

Davis, Elwood C., jt. auth. see Nance, Virginia L.

Davis, Elwyn. Introductory Modern Algebra. LC 73-87837. 1974. text ed. 17.95 (ISBN 0-675-08872-0). Merrill.

Davis, Emily C. Ancient Americans: The Archaeological Story of Two Continents. LC 74-12555. (Illus.). 311p. 1975. Repr. of 1931 ed. lib. bdg. 22.50x o.p. (ISBN 0-8154-0497-2). Cooper Sq.

Davis, Eurmett. Only in Dreams. (Illus.). 32p. (Orig.). (ps-3). 1983. pap. 4.75 (ISBN 0-940742-10-1). Carnival Pr.

Davis, F. James. Understanding Minority Dominant Relations: Sociological Contributions. LC 77-90671. 1979. 17.95x (ISBN 0-88295-210-2). Harlan Davidson.

Davis, F. T. Business Acquisitions Desk Book. 2nd ed. LC 81-6464. 415p. 1981. 65.00 (ISBN 0-87624-049-X). Inst Busn Plan.

Davis, Fanny. Getting to Know Turkey. (Getting to Know Ser.). (Illus.). (gr. 3-5). 1972. PLB 3.97 o.p. (ISBN 0-698-30163-3, Coward). Putnam Pub Group.

Davis, Fei-Ling. Primitive Revolutionaries of China: A Study of Secret Societies in the Late Nineteenth Century. LC 76-45585. 1977. 14.00x (ISBN 0-8248-0522-4). UH Pr.

Davis, Flora. Eloquent Animals. LC 77-18021. 1978. 8.95 o.p. (ISBN 0-698-10892-2, Coward). Putnam Pub Group.

--Inside Intuition: What We Know About Nonverbal Communication. 240p. 1975. pap. 2.50 (ISBN 0-451-11117-6, AE1117, Sig). NAL.

--Living Alive. LC 79-7490. 456p. 1980. 12.95 o.p. (ISBN 0-385-14506-3). Doubleday.

Davis, Forrest. The Atlantic System: The Story of Ango-American Control of the Seas. LC 73-3012. 363p. 1973. Repr. of 1941 ed. lib. bdg. 17.00x o.p. (ISBN 0-8371-6833-3, DAAS). Greenwood.

Davis, Frances R. & Parker, Robert P., Jr., eds. Teaching for Literacy: Reflections on the Bullock Report. LC 78-16898. 1978. text ed. 12.95x (ISBN 0-87586-060-5); pap. text ed. 7.95x (ISBN 0-87586-061-3). Agathon.

Davis, Frank. Early Eighteenth Century English Glass. (Country Life Collectors Guides Ser). 1972. 4.95 o.p. (ISBN 0-600-43601-2). Transatlantic.

--The Fisherman's Guide to Lake Pontchartrain. rev. ed. LC 81-23561. (Illus.). 125p. (Orig.). 1983. pap. 6.95 (ISBN 0-88289-333-5). Pelican.

--The Frank Davis Seafood Notebook. (Illus.). 256p. 1983. 14.95 (ISBN 0-88289-309-2). Pelican.

--The Plain Man's Guide to Second-Hand Furniture. 1972. 8.95 o.p. (ISBN 0-7181-0936-8). Transatlantic.

Davis, Frank G. The Economics of Black Community Development: An Analysis & Program for Autonomous Growth & Development. 1976. pap. text ed. 10.50 (ISBN 0-8191-0008-0). U Pr of Amer.

Davis, Franklin M. Across the Rhine. (World War II Ser.). PLB 19.92 (ISBN 0-8094-2543-2). Silver.

Davis, G. see Allen, W. S.

Davis, G. B. & Olsen, M. H. Management Information Systems: Conceptual Foundations, Structure & Development. 2nd ed. 1983. write for info. (ISBN 0-07-015828-2); write for info. instr's manual (ISBN 0-07-015830-4). McGraw.

Davis, G. B. & Olson, M. H. Elementary Structured COBOL: A Step by Step Approach. 3rd ed. 416p. 1983. 14.95 (ISBN 0-07-015788-X); write for info. inst's manual (ISBN 0-07-015789-8). McGraw.

Davis, Gary & Scott, Joseph. Training Creative Thinking. LC 78-8376. 316p. 1978. Repr. of 1971 ed. lib. bdg. 15.00 (ISBN 0-88275-688-5). Krieger.

Davis, Gary A. & Warren, Thomas F. Psychology of Education: New Looks. 1974. pap. text ed. 14.95x (ISBN 0-669-84574-4). Heath.

Davis, Gene. Agriculture & Automotive Diesel Mechanics. (Illus.). 256p. 1983. 17.95 (ISBN 0-13-018838-7). P-H.

Davis, Gene, jt. auth. see Baldwin, Deirdra.

Davis, Genevieve. The Children of Passion. 1980. pap. 2.50 o.p. (ISBN 0-523-40393-3). Pinnacle Bks.

Davis, Genny W., jt. auth. see Davis, Bruce.

Davis, George. Coming Home. (Howard University Press Library of Contemporary Literature). 208p. 1983. pap. 6.95 (ISBN 0-88258-118-X). Howard U Pr.

--The Posthumous Papers of the Pickwick Club. LC 72-3167. (Studies in Dickens, No. 52). 1972. Repr. of 1928 ed. lib. bdg. 22.95x (ISBN 0-8383-1533-X). Haskell.

--Your Career in Energy-Related Occupations. LC 79-17471. (Arco's Career Guidance Ser.). (Illus.). 1980. lib. bdg. 7.95 (ISBN 0-668-04798-4, 4798-4); pap. 4.50 (ISBN 0-668-04803-4, 4803-4). Arco.

Davis, George & Watson, Glegg. Black Life in Corporate America: Swimming in the Mainstream. LC 81-43064. 216p. 1982. 14.95 (ISBN 0-385-14701-5, Anchor Pr). Doubleday.

Davis, George B., et al. The Official Military Atlas of the Civil War. (Illus.). 1978. 60.00 o.p. (ISBN 0-517-53407-X). Crown.

Davis, George R. The Local Network Handbook. (Illus.). 1982. pap. text ed. 26.95 (ISBN 0-07-015823-1, P&RB). McGraw.

Davis, Gevevieve, jt. auth. see Wilde, Mary P.

Davis, Gibbs. Fishman & Charly. LC 82-23350. 160p. (gr. 5 up). 1983. 8.95 (ISBN 0-395-33882-4). HM.

--Maud Flies Solo. LC 80-27084. 192p. (gr. 5-7). 1981. 8.95 (ISBN 0-02-726280-4). Bradbury Pr.

--Swann Song. LC 81-18066. 192p. (gr. 7 up). 1982. 9.95 (ISBN 0-02-726280-4). Bradbury Pr.

Davis, Glenn & Helfand, Gary. The Uncertain Balance: Federal Regulators in a Changing Political Economy. 224p. (Orig.). 1983. pap. text ed. 8.95x (ISBN 0-89529-184-3). Avery Pub.

Davis, Gloria, ed. What Is Modern Indonesian Culture? Papers in International Studies. LC 79-18979. (Southeast Asia Ser.: No. 52). 1979. pap. 18.00 (ISBN 0-89680-075-X, Ohio U Ctr Intl). Ohio U Pr.

Davis, Gordon. The Goering Treasure. 288p. (Orig.). 1980. pap. 2.25 (ISBN 0-89083-692-2). Zebra.

Davis, Gordon B. Computer Data Processing. 2nd ed. (Illus.). 672p. 1973. text ed. 31.95 (ISBN 0-07-015785-5, C); instructor's manual 11.00 (ISBN 0-07-015787-1); study guide 12.95 (ISBN 0-07-015786-3). McGraw.

--Computers & Information Processing. (Illus.). 1977. text ed. 27.95 (ISBN 0-07-015564-X, C); instructors manual 7.95 (ISBN 0-07-015565-8). McGraw.

--Introduction to Electronic Computers. 3rd ed. (Illus.). 1977. text ed. 28.95 (ISBN 0-07-015825-8); instructor's manual 16.50 (ISBN 0-07-015826-6). McGraw.

--Management Information Systems: Conceptual Foundations, Structure & Development. (Illus.). 480p. 1974. text ed. 29.50 (ISBN 0-07-015827-4, C); instructor's manual 8.50 (ISBN 0-07-015831-2). McGraw.

Davis, Gordon B. & Everest, Gordon. Readings in Management Information Systems. 1976. pap. 17.95 (ISBN 0-07-015835-5, C). McGraw.

Davis, Gordon B. & Hoffman, Thomas R. FORTRAN Seventy-Seven: A Structured Disciplined Style. 2nd ed. 416p. 1983. pap. text ed. 16.95x (ISBN 0-07-015903-3, C); instr's manual 15.00. McGraw.

Davis, Gordon B. & Hoffmann, Thomas R. Fortran: A Structured, Disciplined Approach. (Illus.). 1978. text ed. 18.95 (ISBN 0-07-015901-7, C); instructor's manual 17.00 (ISBN 0-07-015902-5). McGraw.

Davis, Gordon B., et al. Elementary Structured COBOL: A Step by Step Approach. LC 76-57721. 1977. pap. text ed. 18.95 (ISBN 0-07-015782-0, C); instructor's manual 13.00 (ISBN 0-07-015783-9). McGraw.

Davis, Grania. The King & the Mangoes. (Jataka Tales for Children). (Illus.). 24p. (gr. 1-6). 1975. 5.95 o.p. (ISBN 0-913546-27-5); pap. 4.95 o.p. (ISBN 0-913546-69-0). Dharma Pub.

--The Proud Peacock & the Mallard. (Jataka Tales for Children). (Illus.). 24p. (gr. 1-6). 1975. 5.95 o.p. (ISBN 0-913546-26-7); pap. 4.95 o.p. (ISBN 0-913546-70-4). Dharma Pub.

Davis, Grant, jt. ed. see Hutnik, Russell.

Davis, Grant M. & Dillard, John E., Jr. Increasing Motor Carrier Productivity: An Empirical Analysis. LC 77-7821. (Praeger Special Studies). 1977. text ed. 22.95 o.p. (ISBN 0-03-022641-4). Praeger.

Davis, Grant M. & Sherwood, Charles S. Rate Bureaus & Antitrust Conflicts in Transportation Public Policy Issues. (Special Studies). (Illus.). 138p. 1975. text ed. 20.95 o.p. (ISBN 0-275-09880-X). Praeger.

Davis, Grant M., ed. Motor Carrier Economics, Regulation, & Operation. LC 81-40650. 452p. 1981. lib. bdg. 28.50 (ISBN 0-8191-1927-X); pap. text ed. 15.50 (ISBN 0-8191-1928-8). U Pr of Amer.

Davis, Gregory H. Technology: Humanism or Nihilism: A Critical Analysis of the Philosophical Basis & Practice of Modern Technology. LC 81-40178. 304p. (Orig.). 1981. lib. bdg. 21.25 (ISBN 0-8191-1776-5); pap. text ed. 11.25 (ISBN 0-8191-1777-3). U Pr of Amer.

Davis, Gregson, tr. see Cesaire, Aime.

Davis, Guillermo H. Gramatica Elemental del Griego del Nuevo Testamento. McKibben, Jorge F., tr. 240p. 1980. Repr. of 1978 ed. 4.75 (ISBN 0-311-42008-7). Casa Bautista.

Davis, Gwen. Marriage. 1983. pap. 3.50 (ISBN 0-8217-1122-9). Zebra.

--Pretenders. pap. 1.95 o.p. (ISBN 0-451-07541-2, J7541, Sig). NAL.

--Romance. 1983. 14.50 (ISBN 0-87795-497-6). Arbor Hse.

Davis, Gwendolyn T., ed. How to Get Help for Kids: A Guide to Agencies. Services & Facilities for Abused, Emotionally Disturbed & Physically Handicapped Children. 1980. pap. 29.95 o.p. (ISBN 0-915794-18-7, 9320/78). Gaylord Prof Pubns.

Davis, H., jt. ed. see McGimsey, C. R.

Davis, H., et al. The Testing of Engineering Materials. 4th ed. 480p. 1982. 34.95x (ISBN 0-07-015656-5). McGraw.

Davis, H. L. Honey in the Horn. LC 35-16787. 380p. 1975. 14.95 (ISBN 0-910220-76-X). Berg.

Davis, H. S. Culture & Diseases of Game Fishes. (Illus.). 1953. 30.00x (ISBN 0-520-00293-8). U of Cal Pr.

Davis, H. Ted, jt. ed. see Aris, Rutherford.

Davis, Harmer E., et al. Testing & Inspection of Engineering Materials. 3rd ed. (Civil Engineering Ser.). 1964. text ed. 34.50 (ISBN 0-07-015655-7, C). McGraw.

Davis, Harold E. The Fledgling Province: Social & Cultural Life in Colonial Georgia 1733-1776. LC 76-2570. (Institute of Early American History & Culture Ser.). (Illus.). xi, 306p. 1976. 22.50x (ISBN 0-8078-1267-6). U. of NC Pr.

Davis, Harold L. Beulah Land. LC 75-136062. 1971. Repr. of 1949 ed. lib. bdg. 16.00x (ISBN 0-8371-5212-7, DABL). Greenwood.

--Team Bells Woke Me, & Other Stories. LC 73-13321. 300p. 1974. Repr. of 1953 ed. lib. bdg. 17.25x (ISBN 0-8371-7125-3, DATB). Greenwood.

--Winds of Morning. LC 77-138586. 344p. 1972. Repr. of 1952 ed. lib. bdg. 17.25x (ISBN 0-8371-5785-4, DAWM). Greenwood.

Davis, Harry L. & Silk, Alvin J. Behavioral & Management Science in Marketing. LC 77-18878. 1978. 44.95x (ISBN 0-471-07179-X). Ronald Pr.

Davis, Harwell G. The Legend of Landsee. LC 76-40829. 1976. 6.95 (ISBN 0-87397-106-X). Strode.

Davis, Hazel R., jt. auth. see Davis, James E.

Davis, Henry. Compiler Writing in PASCAL. (Pascal Notebook Ser.: Vol. 3). 150p. Date not set. pap. cancelled (ISBN 0-918398-45-2). Dilithium Pr.

--Introduction to PASCAL. (Pascal Notebook Ser.: Vol. 1). 150p. Date not set. pap. cancelled (ISBN 0-918398-43-6). Dilithium Pr.

Davis, Henry P. Training Your Own Bird Dog. rev. ed. (Illus.). 1970. 8.95 (ISBN 0-399-10810-6). Putnam Pub Group.

Davis, Henry W. The Political Thought of Heinrich Von Treitschke. LC 72-9084. 295p. 1973. Repr. of 1915 ed. lib. bdg. 16.25x (ISBN 0-8371-6568-7, DAPT). Greenwood.

Davis, Herbert, ed. see Swift, Jonathan.

Davis, Herbert J., et al, eds. Nineteenth Century Studies. LC 69-10083. 1969. Repr. of 1940 ed. lib. bdg. 17.50x (ISBN 0-8371-0057-7, DANC). Greenwood.

Davis, Hilarie. Super Think: A Guide for Asking Thought-Provoking Questions. Bachelis, Faren, ed. 88p. 1982. tchrs. ed. 8.50 (ISBN 0-931724-21-X). Dandy Lion.

Davis, Hiram S. Productivity Accounting. 3rd ed. LC 78-72037. 194p. 1980. pap. 15.00 (ISBN 0-89546-009-2). Indus Res Unit-Wharton.

Davis, Horace A. The Judicial Veto. LC 78-146152. (American Constitutional & Legal History Ser). 1971. Repr. of 1914 ed. lib. bdg. 22.50 (ISBN 0-306-70093-X). Da Capo.

Davis, Horace B. Toward a Marxist Theory of Nationalism. LC 77-91740. 1980. pap. 7.50 (ISBN 0-85345-516-3, PB5163). Monthly Rev.

Davis, Horace B., ed. & tr. see Luxemburg, Rosa.

Davis, Irene, jt. auth. see Davis, Lester.

Davis, Irvine, ed. see Walrod, Michael R.

Davis, J. C. Utopia & the Ideal Society: A Study of English Utopian Writing, 1516-1700. 410p. 1981. 54.50 (ISBN 0-521-23396-8). Cambridge U Pr.

Davis, J. C., jt. auth. see Sheehan, H. L.

Davis, J. C. & McCullagh, M. J., eds. Display & Analysis of Spatial Data. LC 74-2823. 378p. 1974. 49.25 o.p. (ISBN 0-471-19915-X, Pub. by Wiley-Interscience). Wiley.

Davis, J. G. Cheese: Annotated Bibliography with Subject Index. (Davis Cheese Ser.: Vol. 4). 1976. 40.00 (ISBN 0-444-19528-9). Elsevier.

Davis, J. H., jt. ed. see Stephenson, G. M.

Davis, J. Morton. How to Make the Economy Succeed. LC 82-15776. 336p. 1983. 14.95 (ISBN 0-87663-402-1). Universe.

Davis, J. Ronnie & Meyer, Charles W. Principles of Public Finance. (Illus.). 448p. 1983. 23.95 (ISBN 0-13-709881-2). P-H.

Davis, J. W., Jr. National Executive Branch. LC 72-96834. 1970. pap. 4.50. Free Pr.

Davis, J. William & Wright, Ruth. Texas: Political Practice & Public Policy. 3rd ed. (Government Ser.). 1982. pap. 12.95 (ISBN 0-8403-2792-7). Kendall Hunt.

Davis, Jack & Loveless, E. E. The Administrator & Educational Facilities. LC 80-1445. 272p. 1981. lib. bdg. 21.50 (ISBN 0-8191-1391-3); pap. text ed. 11.25 (ISBN 0-8191-1392-1). U Pr of Amer.

Davis, Jack, jt. auth. see Jacobs, Frank.

Davis, Jack E., tr. see Leon-Portilla, Miguel.

Davis, Jack L., ed. Papers in Cycladic Prehistory. Cherry, John F. (Institute of Archaeology Monograph: No. 14). (Illus.). 203p. 1979. pap. 12.50 (ISBN 0-917956-14-1). UCLA Arch.

Davis, James. Going to College. 1977. softcover 12.95 o.p. (ISBN 0-89158-081-6). Westview.

--Teaching Strategies for the College Classroom. LC 76-1905. (Special Studies in Higher Education Ser). 1976. 13.75x o.p. (ISBN 0-89158-033-6); softcover 10.00 o.p. (ISBN 0-89158-104-9). Westview.

Davis, James A. Elementary Survey Analysis. (Methods of Social Science Ser). (Illus.). 1971. pap. text ed. 14.95 (ISBN 0-13-260547-3). P-H.

--General Social Survey Cumulative File, 1972-1982. LC 81-82220. 1982. write for info. codebk. (ISBN 0-932132-27-8). ICPSR.

--General Social Survey, 1972. 1973. codebk. write for info. o.p. (ISBN 0-89138-060-4). ICPSR.

--General Social Survey, 1973. 1974. codebk. write for info. o.p. (ISBN 0-89138-073-6). ICPSR.

--General Social Survey, 1974. new ed. LC 75-36289. 1975. codebk. write for info. o.p. (ISBN 0-89138-119-8). ICPSR.

Davis, James A. & Gebhard, Ruth. Great Books & Small Groups. LC 77-24390. 1977. Repr. of 1961 ed. lib. bdg. 20.50x (ISBN 0-8371-9742-2, DAGB). Greenwood.

Davis, James B. La Quete de Paul Gadenne: Une Morale pour Notre Epoque. (Fr.). 12.00 (ISBN 0-917786-18-1). French Lit.

Davis, James E. Frontier America, Eighteen Hundred to Eighteen Forty: A Comparative Demographic Analysis of the Settlement Process. LC 77-77031. (Illus.). 1977. 15.50 o.p. (ISBN 0-87062-120-3). A H Clark.

Davis, James E. & Davis, Hazel R. Women's Studies. 114p. 4.50 (ISBN 0-686-95301-0); members 4.00 (ISBN 0-686-99489-2). NCTE.

Davis, James E., ed. Planning a Social Studies Program: Activities, Guidelines, & Resources. 2nd ed. 1982. pap. write for info. (ISBN 0-89994-266-0). Soc Sci Ed.

Davis, James H., Jr. Fenelon. (World Authors Ser.). 1979. lib. bdg. 14.95 (ISBN 0-8057-6384-8, Twayne). G K Hall.

Davis, James P. How to Make it through Law School: A Guide for Minority & Disadvantaged Students. 150p. 1982. 15.00x (ISBN 0-914970-23-2); pap. 7.50 (ISBN 0-914970-24-0). Conch Mag.

Davis, James R. Help Me, I'm Hurt: The Child-Victim Handbook. 168p. 1982. 9.95 (ISBN 0-686-84428-9); pap. text ed. 9.95 (ISBN 0-8403-2747-1). Kendall-Hunt.

--The Sentencing Dispositions of New York City Lower Court Criminal Judges. LC 82-45016. (Illus.). 230p. (Orig.). 1982. lib. bdg. 22.00 (ISBN 0-8191-2566-0); pap. text ed. 10.75 (ISBN 0-8191-2567-9). U Pr of Amer.

Davis, James W. National Conventions in an Age of Party Reform. LC 82-9382. (Contributions in Political Science Ser.: No. 91). 384p. 1983. lib. bdg. 35.00 (ISBN 0-313-23048-X, DNC/). Greenwood.

--Presidential Primaries: Road to the White House. LC 79-54062. (Contributions in Political Science: No. 41). 1980. lib. bdg. 29.95 (ISBN 0-313-22057-3, DPP/). Greenwood.

Davis, Jeff C., Jr. Advanced Physical Chemistry: Molecules, Structure, & Spectra. (Illus.). 1965. 35.50x (ISBN 0-471-06719-9, Pub. by Wiley-Interscience). Wiley.

Davis, Jennie. In God's Great Way. LC 82-7446. (Illus.). 32p. (gr. 1-2). 1982. lib. bdg. 4.95 (ISBN 0-686-83152-7). Dandelion Hse.

--Praise Him! Praise Him! LC 82-7238. (Illus.). 32p. (ps-k). 1982. lib. bdg. 4.95 (ISBN 0-686-83151-9). Dandelion Hse.

Davis, Jerome D. High-Cost Oil & Gas Resources. (Illus.). 266p. 1981. 40.00x (ISBN 0-85664-588-5, Pub. by Croom Helm LTD England). Biblio Dist.

Davis, Jerry C. Rehabbing for Profit. (Illus.). 224p. 1981. 34.00 (ISBN 0-07-015695-6, P&RB). McGraw.

Davis, Jesse. Classics of the Royal Ballet. LC 79-10866. (Illus.). (gr. 4 up). 1980. 7.95 o.p. (ISBN 0-698-20502-2). Putnam Pub Group.

Davis, Jim. Garfield Eats His Heart Out. (Illus.). 128p. (Orig.). 1983. pap. 4.95 (ISBN 0-345-30912-X). Ballantine.

--Garfield Goes to a Picnic. LC 82-60879. (Sniffy Bks.). (Illus.). 24p. (ps-1). 1983. pap. 3.95 (ISBN 0-394-85634-1). Random.

--The Garfield Treasury. (Orig.). 1982. pap. 7.95 (ISBN 0-345-30713-5). Ballantine.

--Here Comes Garfield. 1982. pap. 4.95 (ISBN 0-686-82437-7). Ballantine.

Davis, Joe. Hawaiian Song Album. 2.95x o.s.i. Wehman.

Davis, Joe T. Legendary Texans. 1982. 9.95 (ISBN 0-89015-336-1). Eakin Pubns.

Davis, John. The Evasive Peace. 1970. pap. 6.00 (ISBN 0-911026-01-0). New World Press NY.

Davis, John, jt. auth. see Hall, Robert.

Davis, John A., jt. ed. see Kitzinger, Sheila.

Davis, John C. Statistics & Data Analysis in Geology. LC 72-6792. (Illus.). 550p. 1973. 37.95 (ISBN 0-471-19895-1). Wiley.

Davis, John D. English Silver at Williamsburg. LC 75-4814. (Williamsburg Decorative Arts Ser.). (Illus.). viii, 254p. 1976. 15.00x o.p. (ISBN 0-87935-028-8). U Pr of Va.

--English Silver at Williamsburg. LC 75-4814. (Illus.). 254p. (Orig.). 1976. pap. 11.00x (ISBN 0-87935-028-8). U Pr of Va.

Davis, John F. An Audience with Jesus. 134p. 1982. 4.00 (ISBN 0-8198-0721-4, SP0008); pap. 3.00 (ISBN 0-8198-0722-2). Dghtrs St Paul.

--Chinese Novels. LC 76-43332. 1976. Repr. of 1822 ed. 35.00x (ISBN 0-8201-1278-X). Schol Facsimiles.

Davis, John H. Guggenheims: An American Epic. LC 77-20069. (Illus.). 1979. pap. 6.95 (ISBN 0-688-08273-4). Quill NY.

Davis, John J. Biblical Numerology. (Orig.). 1968. pap. 4.50 (ISBN 0-8010-2813-2). Baker Bk.

--Conquest & Crisis: Studies in Joshua, Judges & Ruth. (Illus.). pap. 5.95 (ISBN 0-88469-052-0). BMH Bks.

--Perfect Shepherd. pap. 5.50 (ISBN 0-88469-110-1). BMH Bks.

Davis, John M., jt. auth. see Klein, Donald F.

Davis, John M. & Maas, James W., eds. The Affective Disorders: Anthology. (Illus.). 320p. 1983. text ed. 25.00 (ISBN 0-88048-002-5). Am Psychiatric.

Davis, John M., jt. ed. see Blasewitz, A. G.

Davis, John W. Advanced Level Practical Chemistry. (gr. 9 up). text ed. 4.50 o.p. (ISBN 0-7195-0286-1). Transatlantic.

Davis, Joseph K., et al. Literature. 1977. text ed. 16.50x (ISBN 0-673-15009-7). Scott F.

Davis, Joseph S. Wheat & the AAA. LC 76-172868. (FDR & the Era of the New Deal Ser.). 468p. 1973. Repr. of 1935 ed. 59.50 (ISBN 0-306-70375-0). Da Capo.

Davis, Joyce E. Chrysalis. 6.95 (ISBN 0-686-84352-5). Olympus Pub Co.

Davis, Judy & Spellman, Shirley. Cardiac Rehabilitation for the Patient & Family. (Illus.). 176p. 1980. pap. text ed. 14.95 (ISBN 0-8359-0678-7). Reston.

Davis, Julian C. Rorschach Location Charts. 1958. spiral bdg. 14.00 (ISBN 0-8089-0594-5). Grune.

Davis, Julie & Weiss, Herman. How to Get Married: A Proven Plan for Finding the Right Mate. 64p. (Orig.). 1983. pap. 2.95 (ISBN 0-345-31102-7). Ballantine.

Davis, Julie, jt. auth. see Larkin, Regina.

Davis, Julie, jt. auth. see Shorell, Irma.

Davis, Juliet, jt. auth. see Cox, Deborah.

Davis, K. Roscoe & McKeown, Patrick G. Quantitative Models for Management. (Business Ser.). 735p. 1981. text ed. 24.95x (ISBN 0-534-00935-2). Kent Pub Co.

Davis, K. Roscoe, jt. auth. see Leitch, Robert A.

Davis, Karen. National Health Insurance: Benefits, Costs, & Consequences. (Studies in Social Economics). 182p. 1975. 18.95 (ISBN 0-8157-1760-1); pap. 7.95 (ISBN 0-8157-1759-8). Brookings.

Davis, Karen & Schoen, Cathy. Health & the War on Poverty: A Ten-Year Appraisal. (Studies in Social Economics). 1978. 18.95 (ISBN 0-8157-1758-X); pap. 7.95 (ISBN 0-8157-1757-1). Brookings.

Davis, Karl D., et al. Emergency & Disaster Nursing Continuing Education Review. 1976. pap. 12.00 (ISBN 0-87488-371-7). Med Exam.

Davis, Kathryn. At the Wind's Edge. (The Dakotas Ser.). 384p. (Orig.). 1983. pap. 3.25 (ISBN 0-523-41459-5). Pinnacle Bks.

Davis, Keith. The Challenge of Business. Kothman, Thomas H., ed. (Illus.). 544p. 1975. text ed. 29.95 (ISBN 0-07-015527-5, C); instructor's guide 7.95 (ISBN 0-07-063125-5); transparency masters 15.00 (ISBN 0-07-015529-1); student guide 8.00 (ISBN 0-07-015528-3). McGraw.

--Human Behavior at Work. 6th ed. (Management Ser.). (Illus.). 576p. 1981. text ed. 23.95x (ISBN 0-07-015516-X, C); instr's. manual & test file 18.95 (ISBN 0-07-015517-8); study guide 8.95 (ISBN 0-07-015535-6). McGraw.

Davis, Keith & Newstrom, John. Organizational Behavior: Readings & Exercises. 6th ed. (Management Ser.). (Illus.). 468p. 1981. text ed. 13.50 (ISBN 0-07-015500-3, C). McGraw.

Davis, Keith, jt. auth. see Werther, William.

Davis, Keith, ed. Advances in Descriptive Psychology, Vol. 1. 400p. 1981. 45.50 (ISBN 0-89232-179-2). Jai Pr.

Davis, Keith, ed. see Koontz, Harold & O'Donnell, Cyril.

Davis, Keith, ed. see Miles, Raymond E.

Davis, Keith, ed. see Mills, D. Quinn.

Davis, Keith, et al. Business & Society: Concepts & Policy Issues. 4th ed. (Management Ser.). (Illus.). 672p. 1980. text ed. 23.95x (ISBN 0-07-015532-1, C); instr's manual 20.00 (ISBN 0-07-015533-X). McGraw.

Davis, Ken. Better Business Writing: A Process Approach. 320p. 1983. 10.95 (ISBN 0-675-20015-6). Additional supplements may be obtained from publisher. Merrill.

Davis, Kenn. The Forza Trap. 1979. pap. 1.95 o.p. (ISBN 0-380-44552-2, 44552). Avon.

Davis, Kenneth P. Forest Management. 2nd ed. 1966. text ed. 33.50 (ISBN 0-07-015531-3, C). McGraw.

Davis, Kenneth P., jt. auth. see Brown, A. A.

Davis, Kenneth R. Marketing Management. 4th ed. LC 80-19924. (Marketing Ser.). 778p. 1981. text ed. 30.95x (ISBN 0-471-05948-X). Wiley.

Davis, Kenneth R. & Webster, Frederick E., Jr. Sales Force Management. LC 68-12886. (Illus.). 764p. 1968. 31.95x o.p. (ISBN 0-471-06593-5, 22271). Wiley.

Davis, Kenneth S. & Leopold, Luna. Water. Rev. ed. LC 80-521127. (Life Science Library). (Illus.). (gr. 5 up). 1970. PLB 13.40 (ISBN 0-8094-4075-X, Pub. by Time-Life). Silver.

Davis, L. J. Bad Money. 224p. 1982. 12.95 (ISBN 0-312-06524-8). St Martin.

Davis, L. M., jt. auth. see Winn, Charles S.

Davis, Lance & North, Douglass. Institutional Change & American Economic Growth. 1971. 34.50 (ISBN 0-521-08111-4). Cambridge U Pr.

Davis, Lance E., et al. American Economic Growth: An Economist's History of the United States. (Illus.). 1972. text ed. 33.95 scp o.p. (ISBN 0-06-041557-6, HarpC). Har-Row.

Davis, Larry. P-Fifty-One Mustang in Color. (Fighting Colors Ser.). (Illus.). 32p. 1982. softcover 5.95 (ISBN 0-89747-135-0, 6505). Squad Sig Pubns.

Davis, Larry & Greer, Don. Air War over Korea. (Aircraft Special Ser.). (Illus.). 96p. 1982. 8.95 (ISBN 0-89747-137-7, 6035). Squad Sig Pubns.

Davis, Lawrence. Theory of Action. (Foundations of Philosophy Ser.). 1979. ref. 15.95 (ISBN 0-13-913152-3); pap. text ed. 12.95 (ISBN 0-13-913145-0). P-H.

Davis Lecture Committee. Essays in the History of Medicine, in Honor of David J. Davis. LC 66-12463. 193p. 1966. 12.50 (ISBN 0-252-00048-X). U of Ill Pr.

Davis, Lennard J. Factual Fictions: The Origins of the English Novel. LC 82-12815. 272p. 1983. 24.00x (ISBN 0-231-05420-3); pap. 12.50x (ISBN 0-231-05421-1). Columbia U Pr.

Davis, Lenwood G. The Black Aged in the United States: An Annotated Bibliography. LC 80-1193. xviii, 200p. 1980. lib. bdg. 29.95 (ISBN 0-313-22560-5, DAB/). Greenwood.

--The Black Family in the United States: A Selected Bibliography of Annotated Books, Articles, & Dissertations on Black Families in America. LC 77-89109. 1978. lib. bdg. 27.50 (ISBN 0-8371-9851-8, DBF/). Greenwood.

Davis, Lenwood G. & Sims, Janet L. Black Artists in the United States: An Annotated Bibliography of Books, Articles, & Dissertations on Black Artists, Seventeen Seventy-Nine to Nineteen Seventy-Nine. LC 79-8576. 160p. 1980. lib. bdg. 27.50 (ISBN 0-313-22082-4, DBA/). Greenwood.

Davis, Lenwood G. & Sims, Janet L., eds. Marcus Garvey: An Annotated Bibliography. LC 80-653. xvi, 200p. 1980. lib. bdg. 27.50 (ISBN 0-313-22131-6, DMG/). Greenwood.

Davis, Lester & Davis, Irene. Ike & Mamie. large type ed. LC 82-5869. (Illus.). 410p. 1982. Repr. of 1981 ed. 12.95 (ISBN 0-686-82639-6). Thorndike Pr.

Davis, Lisa E. & Taran, Isabel C., eds. The Analysis of Hispanic Texts: Current Trends in Methodology. LC 76-45294. (Second York College Colloquium). 1976. lib. bdg. 16.95x (ISBN 0-916950-03-4); pap. 10.95x (ISBN 0-916950-17-4). Bilingual Pr.

Davis, Lorin R. see Heat Transfer & Fluid Mechanics Institute.

Davis, Lou Ellen. Clouds of Destiny. LC 77-15567. 1978. 9.95 o.p. (ISBN 0-399-12055-6). Putnam Pub Group.

Davis, Louis E. & Cherns, Albert B., eds. The Quality of Working Life: Problems, Prospects & the State of the Art, Vol.1. LC 74-24369. 1975. 22.95 (ISBN 0-02-907390-1); pap. text ed. 10.95 (ISBN 0-02-907380-4). Free Pr.

Davis, Louis E. & Taylor, James C., eds. Design of Jobs. 2nd ed. LC 78-23397. 1979. text ed. 21.95x (ISBN 0-673-16080-7). Scott F.

Davis, Lydia, tr. see Blanchot, Maurice.

Davis, M. Visual Design in Dress. 1980. 21.95 (ISBN 0-13-942409-1). P-H.

Davis, M., ed. The Undecidable: Basic Papers on Undecidable Propositions, Unsolvable Problems & Computable Functions. LC 65-3996. 1965. 16.50 (ISBN 0-911216-01-4). Raven.

Davis, M. H. Linear Estimation & Stochastic Control. 1977. 24.00x o.p. (ISBN 0-412-15130-8, Pub. by Chapman & Hall); pap. 16.95x (ISBN 0-412-15140-5). Methuen Inc.

Davis, M. M; see Bernard, William S.

Davis, Mac. Giant Book of Sports. (Illus.). (gr. 5-9). 1967. 4.95 o.s.i. (ISBN 0-448-04445-5, G&D). Putnam Pub Group.

--Great Sports Humor. LC 73-823. (Elephant Books). (Illus.). 128p. (gr. 3-9). 1976. pap. 3.95 o.p. (ISBN 0-448-12576-5, G&D). Putnam Pub Group.

--Great Sports Humor. (Illus.). 128p. (gr. 3-7). 1982. pap. 4.95 (ISBN 0-448-12327-4, G&D). Putnam Pub Group.

--Strange & Incredible Sports Happenings. LC 74-27940. (Elephant Bks.). (Illus.). (gr. 3-7). 1978. pap. 3.95 o.s.i. (ISBN 0-448-14617-7, G&D). Putnam Pub Group.

--Strange & Incredible Sports Happenings. Powers, Richard, ed. (Illus.). 128p. (gr. 3-7). 1982. pap. 3.95 (ISBN 0-448-12326-6, G&D). Putnam Pub Group.

Davis, Madeleine & Wallbridge, David. Boundary & Space: An Introduction to the Work of D. W. Winnicott. LC 81-10034. 212p. 1981. 19.50 (ISBN 0-87630-251-7). Brunner-Mazel.

Davis, Maggie S. The Best Way to Ripton. LC 82-2940. (Illus.). 32p. (ps-3). 1982. Reinforced bdg. 8.95 (ISBN 0-8234-0459-5). Holiday.

Davis, Malcolm, jt. auth. see Plath, Carl.

Davis, Margaret B. French. (Blue Book Ser). pap. 1.25 o.p. (ISBN 0-671-18121-1). Monarch Pr.

Davis, Martha & Skupien, Janet. Body Movement & Nonverbal Communication: An Annotated Bibliography, 1971-1981. LC 81-7881. 320p. 1982. 29.50x (ISBN 0-253-34101-9). Ind U Pr.

Davis, Martha, ed. Interaction Rhythms: Periodicity in Communicative Behavior. LC 81-2936. 336p. 1982. 34.95 (ISBN 0-89885-003-7). Human Sci Pr.

Davis, Martin. Applied Nonstandard Analysis. LC 76-28484. (Pure & Applied Mathematics Ser.). 1977. text ed. 33.95x (ISBN 0-471-19897-8, Pub. by Wiley-Interscience). Wiley.

--Computability & Unsolvability. (Mathematics Ser.). 288p. 1983. pap. 6.50 (ISBN 0-486-61471-9). Dover.

Davis, Mary. Careers in a Bank. LC 72-7645. (Early Career Bks.). (Illus.). 36p. (gr. 3-5). 1973. PLB 5.95g (ISBN 0-8225-0308-5). Lerner Pubns.

--Careers in a Medical Center. LC 72-7657. (Early Career Bks). (Illus.). 36p. (gr. 2-5). 1973. 5.95g (ISBN 0-8225-0310-7). Lerner Pubns.

--Careers in Baseball. LC 72-7646. (Early Career Bks.). (Illus.). 36p. (gr. 2-5). 1973. PLB 5.95g (ISBN 0-8225-0313-1). Lerner Pubns.

--Careers in Printing. LC 72-5416. (Early Career Bks.). (Illus.). 36p. (gr. 2-5). 1973. PLB 5.95g (ISBN 0-8225-0306-9). Lerner Pubns.

--Careers with a Telephone Company. LC 72-5412. (Early Career Bks.). (Illus.). 36p. (gr. 2-5). 1973. PLB 5.95g (ISBN 0-8225-0302-6). Lerner Pubns.

Davis, Mary Kay. The Needlework Doctor: How to Solve Every Kind of Needlework Problem. (Illus.). 320p. 1983. 24.95 (ISBN 0-13-611087-8); pap. 13.95 (ISBN 0-13-611079-7). P-H.

Davis, Mary L. Polly & the President. LC 67-15697. (General Juvenile Bks). (Illus.). (gr. k-5). 1967. PLB 3.95g (ISBN 0-8225-0264-X). Lerner Pubns.

--Women Who Changed History: Five Famous Queens of Europe. LC 74-11899. (Real World Ser.). (Illus.). 104p. (gr. 5 up). 1975. PLB 6.95g (ISBN 0-8225-0638-6). Lerner Pubns.

Davis, Matthew L., ed. Memoirs of Aaron Burr, 2 Vols. LC 73-152836. (Era of the American Revolution Ser). 1971. Repr. of 1836 ed. Set. lib. bdg. 85.00 (ISBN 0-306-70139-1). Da Capo.

Davis, Michael. William Blake: A New Kind of Man. LC 77-71059. (Illus.). 1977. 22.50x (ISBN 0-520-03443-0); pap. 6.95 (ISBN 0-520-03456-2). U of Cal Pr.

Davis, Michael, ed. In A Wiltshire Village: Scenes from Rural Victorian Life, Selected from the Writings of Alfred Williams. 192p. 1981. pap. text ed. 9.00x (ISBN 0-904387-62-3, 61185, Pub. by Alan Sutton England). Humanities.

Davis, Mikol & Lane, Earle. Rainbows of Life. (Illus., Orig.). 1978. pap. 6.95i o.p. (ISBN 0-06-090624-3, CN 624, CN). Har-Row.

Davis, Mildred J. The Art of Crewel Embroidery. (Illus.). 224p. 1962. pap. 4.95 o.p. (ISBN 0-517-50077-9). Crown.

Davis, Monte, jt. auth. see Woodcock, Alexander.

Davis, Murray S. Smut: Erotic Reality-Obscene Ideology. LC 82-16061. 328p. 1983. 20.00 (ISBN 0-226-13791-0). U of Chicago Pr.

Davis, Myrna. Bouquet: Twelve Flower Fables. (Illus.). 65p. 1982. 10.00 (ISBN 0-517-54604-3, C N Potter Bks). Crown.

--The Potato Book. LC 73-7890. (Illus.). 1978. pap. 2.95 (ISBN 0-688-05186-3). Quill NY.

Davis, Nancy. Vocabulary Improvement. 3rd ed. 1978. pap. text ed. 14.50x (ISBN 0-07-015543-7, C). McGraw.

Davis, Natalie Z. Society & Culture in Early Modern France: Eight Essays by Natalie Zemon Davis. LC 74-82777. (Illus.). 1975. 22.50x (ISBN 0-8047-0868-1); pap. 7.95 (ISBN 0-8047-0972-6, SP-142). Stanford U Pr.

Davis, Nina, jt. ed. see Kertis, Joan.

Davis, Norah D. & Lindsey, Linda. At Home in the Sun: An Open-House Tour of Solar Homes in the United States. LC 79-12867. (Illus.). 1979. 14.95 o.p. (ISBN 0-88266-152-3); pap. 12.95 o.p. (ISBN 0-88266-151-5). Garden Way Pub.

Davis, Norma A. Trade Winds Cookery. 1956. spiral bdg. 5.00 (ISBN 0-685-09015-9). Dietz.

Davis, Norman. Journeys to the Past. 1980. 9.95 (ISBN 0-910286-83-3); pap. 6.95 (ISBN 0-910286-78-7). Boxwood.

Davis, Norman, ed. The Paston Letters. (The World's Classics Ser.). (Illus.). 320p. 1983. pap. 6.95 (ISBN 0-19-281615-2, GB). Oxford U Pr.

Davis, Norman, ed. see Sweet, Henry.

Davis, O. B., jt. auth. see Davis, Alexandra.

Davis, Oscar, Jr Save Your Marriage. 1982. 4.95 (ISBN 0-686-84101-8). Carlton.

Davis, P. Medical Dictation & Transcription. 2nd ed. LC 80-27720. 468p. 1981. pap. 16.50x (ISBN 0-471-06023-2, Pub. by Wiley Med). Wiley.

Davis, P. E., jt. auth. see Smith, G. L.

Davis, P. H. & Cullen, J. The Identification of Flowering Plant Families. LC 78-8125. (Illus.). 1979. 24.95 (ISBN 0-521-22111-0); pap. 6.95x (ISBN 0-521-29359-6). Cambridge U Pr.

Davis, P. J. The Mathematics of Matrices: A First Book of Matrix Theory & Linear Algebra. 2nd ed. 348p. 1973. text ed. 24.95x o.p. (ISBN 0-471-00928-8). Wiley.

Davis, P. R., ed. Performance Under Sub-Optimal Conditions. 104p. 1971. pap. 18.50x (ISBN 0-85066-044-0, Pub. by Taylor & Francis). Intl Pubns Serv.

Davis, P. W. & Solomon, E. P. The World of Biology. 2nd ed. 1979. text ed. 24.95 (ISBN 0-07-015552-6); supplementary materials avail. McGraw.

Davis, P. W., ed. see Linguistic Association of Canada & the U.S.

Davis, P. William, jt. auth. see Soloman, Eldra P.

Davis, Pat. The Badminton Coach: A Manual for Coaches, Teachers & Players. 3rd, rev. ed. (Illus.). 160p. (gr. 9 up). 1980. text ed. 23.50x (ISBN 0-7182-1243-6, SpS). Sportshelf.

--Better Badminton. 16.95x (ISBN 0-686-83100-4, SpS). Sportshelf.

Davis, Patricia A. Two Hundred & One Russian Verbs Fully Conjugated in All the Tenses. LC 67-26140. 1970. text ed. 8.95 (ISBN 0-8120-6050-4); pap. text ed. 4.95 (ISBN 0-8120-0271-7). Barron.

Davis, Patricia M. see Larson, Mildred L.

Davis, Percival, jt. auth. see Friar, Wayne.

Davis, Peter. Hometown. 1982. 14.50 (ISBN 0-671-24556-2). S&S.

--Hometown. 1983. pap. price not set (ISBN 0-671-47059-0, Touchstone Bks). S&S.

--The Social Context of Dentistry. 189p. 1980. 27.50x (ISBN 0-7099-0152-6, Pub. by Croom Helm Ltd England). Biblio Dist.

Davis, Philip. Introduction to Moral Philosophy. LC 72-92572. 1973. text ed. 15.95x (ISBN 0-675-09003-2). Merrill.

Davis, Philip J. Circulant Matrices. LC 79-10551. (Pure & Applied Mathematics: Texts, Monographs, & Tracts). 1979. 34.95 (ISBN 0-471-05771-1, Pub. by Wiley-Interscience). Wiley.

--Interpolation & Approximation. LC 75-2568. (Illus.). 416p. 1975. pap. text ed. 7.00 (ISBN 0-486-62495-1). Dover.

Davis, Phyllis & Hershelman, N. L. Medical Shorthand. 2nd ed. LC 80-29003. 323p. 1981. pap. 16.50x (ISBN 0-471-06024-0). Wiley.

Davis, Phyllis E., jt. auth. see Smith, Genevieve.

Davis, Phyllis E., jt. auth. see Smith, Genevieve L.

Davis, Polly. English Structure in Focus. 1977. pap. text ed. 12.95 (ISBN 0-88377-077-6); answer key 3.95 (ISBN 0-88377-100-4); tchrs. manual 3.95 (ISBN 0-88377-095-4). Newbury Hse.

Davis, R., et al, eds. Advanced Bacterial Genetics. LC 80-25695. 254p. (Orig.). 1980. lab manual 30.00x (ISBN 0-87969-130-1). Cold Spring Harbor.

Davis, R. Hunt, Jr. Bantu Education & the Education of Africans in South Africa, No. 14. LC 72-85206. (Papers in International Studies: Africa). (Illus.). 1972. pap. 4.50x (ISBN 0-89680-047-4, Ohio U Ctr Intl). Ohio U Pr.

Davis, Ray J. Ecology & Conservation of Natural Resources. 1978. lib. bdg. 7.31 (ISBN 0-931054-02-8). Clark Pub.

--Ecology & Conservation of Natural Resources. rev. ed. (Illus.). 187p. 1978. pap. text ed. 7.25 o.p. (ISBN 0-931054-10-9). Clark Pub.

Davis, Ray J. & Grant, Lewis, eds. Weather Modification: Technology & Law. LC 78-55519. (AAAS Selected Symposia Ser.). 1978. lib. bdg. 17.50 (ISBN 0-89158-153-7). Westview.

Davis, Raymond E. & Kelly, J. W. Elementary Plane Surveying. 4th ed. (Illus.). 1967. text ed. 34.00 (ISBN 0-07-015771-5, C). McGraw.

--Short Course in Surveying. 1942. text ed. 18.50 o.p. (ISBN 0-07-015900-9, C). McGraw.

Davis, Raymond E., et al. Surveying Theory & Practice. 6th ed. (Illus.). 1120p. 1981. text ed. 32.50 (ISBN 0-07-015790-1); solutions manual 15.00 (ISBN 0-07-015791-X). McGraw.
Davis, Rebecca M., ed. see Niwano, Nikkyo.
Davis, Richard. Space One. 155p. (gr. 7-12). 1975. 7.95 o.p. (ISBN 0-200-71967-X). Transatlantic.
--Space Two: A New Collection of Science Fiction Stories. 140p. 1975. 8.95 o.p. (ISBN 0-200-72275-1). Transatlantic.
Davis, Richard, ed. Space Four. 1978. 10.75 o.p. (ISBN 0-200-72512-2). Transatlantic.
--Space Three. (Illus.). 1977. 7.75 o.p. (ISBN 0-200-72447-9). Transatlantic.
Davis, Richard A., compiled by. Neurosurgical Contributions of Loyal Davis: Selected Papers & Retrospective Commentaries. LC 72-93113. (Illus.). 1973. text ed. 12.00 o.p. (ISBN 0-7216-2990-3). Saunders.
Davis, Richard B., ed. see Davies, Samuel.
Davis, Richard C. & Miller, Linda A., eds. Guide to the Cataloged Collections in the Manuscript Department of the William R. Perkins Library, Duke University. LC 79-28688. 1005p. 1980. lib. bdg. 30.50 (ISBN 0-87436-299-7). ABC-Clio.
Davis, Richard C., ed. see Forest History Society.
Davis, Richard F. Modern Dairy Cattle Management. 1962. ref. ed. 18.95 o.p. (ISBN 0-13-590794-2). P-H.
Davis, Richard H. Dealing with Death. (Andrus Gerontology Ser.). Date not set. 4.95 (ISBN 0-686-94884-X). Hollander Co.
Davis, Robert. Control Tower. 1980. 10.95 o.p. (ISBN 0-399-12175-7). Putnam Pub Group.
--Gerald Griffin. (English Authors Ser.). 1980. lib. bdg. 14.95 (ISBN 0-8057-6799-1, Twayne). G K Hall.
Davis, Robert B. George Russell. (English Authors Ser.). 1977. lib. bdg. 14.95 (ISBN 0-8057-6677-4, Twayne). G K Hall.
Davis, Robert D., jt. auth. see Moon, Robert A.
Davis, Robert D., jt. auth. see Moon, Robert G.
Davis, Robert H., ed. Historical Dictionary of Colombia. LC 76-54245. (Latin American Historical Dictionaries Ser.: No. 14). (Illus.). 1977. 13.50 o.p. (ISBN 0-8108-0999-0). Scarecrow.
Davis, Robert H., et al. Learning System Design. (Illus.). 320p. 1974. text ed. 28.50 (ISBN 0-07-074334-7, C). McGraw.
Davis, Robert S., Jr. Research in Georgia: With a Special Emphasis Upon the Georgia Department of Archives & History. (Illus.). 268p. 1981. 25.00 (ISBN 0-89308-199-X); pap. 20.00 (ISBN 0-686-96889-1). Southern Hist Pr.
Davis, Rodney. Real Estate. LC 79-155. (Career Competencies in Marketing). (Illus.). (gr. 11-12). 1979. pap. text ed. 7.32 (ISBN 0-07-015672-7, G); tchrs. manual 4.50 (ISBN 0-07-015673-5). McGraw.
Davis, Roger & Northcutt, Glenn, eds. Fish Neurobiology, Vol. II: Higher Brain Areas & Functions. (Illus.). 328p. 1983. text ed. 45.00x (ISBN 0-472-10019-X). U of Mich Pr.
Davis, Roger, jt. ed. see Northcutt, Glenn.
Davis, Ronald L. A History of Music in American Life, Vol. 1: The Formative Years, 1620-1865. LC 79-25359. 320p. 1982. lib. bdg. 22.00 (ISBN 0-89874-002-9). Krieger.
--A History of Music in American Life, Vol. 2: The Gilded Years, 1865-1920. LC 79-25359. 286p. 1980. lib. bdg. 18.00 (ISBN 0-89874-003-7). Krieger.
--A History of Music in American Life, Vol. 3: The Modern Era, 1920 to the Present. LC 79-25359. 462p. 1981. lib. bdg. 29.50 (ISBN 0-89874-004-5). Krieger.
--Twentieth Century Cultural Life in Texas. Rosenbaum, Robert J., ed. (Texas History Ser.). (Illus.). 50p. 1981. pap. text ed. 1.95x (ISBN 0-89641-072-2). American Pr.
Davis, Ronald L., ed. A History of Music in American Life. LC 79-25359. Set. 59.50 (ISBN 0-89874-080-0). Krieger.
Davis, Ruby, ed. see Clark, Barbara R.
Davis, Rupert Hart see Sassoon, Seigfried.
Davis, Rupert Hart see Sassoon, Siegfried.
Davis, Russell G., jt. auth. see McGinn, Noel F.
Davis, S. H. Victims of the Miracle. (Illus.). 1977. 32.50 (ISBN 0-521-21738-5); pap. 7.95 (ISBN 0-521-29246-8). Cambridge U Pr.
Davis, S. Rufus. The Federal Principle: A Journey Through Time in Quest of Meaning. LC 75-32673. 1978. 27.50x (ISBN 0-520-03146-6). U of Cal Pr.
Davis, Sally A., ed. Artist's Market, 1983. 528p. 1982. 14.95 (ISBN 0-89879-084-0). Writers Digest.
Davis, Samuel M. Rights of Juvenile: The Juvenile Justice System. 2nd ed. LC 80-124651. 1980. 47.50 (ISBN 0-87632-104-X). Boardman.
Davis, Samuel P. History of Nevada, 2 Vols. (Illus.). 1983. 75.00 (ISBN 0-686-42715-7). Nevada Pubns.
Davis, Shirley M., jt. auth. see Swain, Philip H.
Davis, Stanley, et al. Geology: Our Physical Environment. 1975. text ed. 29.95 (ISBN 0-07-015680-8, C); instructor's manual 7.95 (ISBN 0-07-015681-6). McGraw.
Davis, Stanley M., ed. Managing & Organizing Multinational Corporations. LC 77-1760. 1979. text ed. 59.00 (ISBN 0-08-021267-0); pap. text ed. 14.00 (ISBN 0-08-021266-2). Pergamon.
--Managing & Organizing Multinational Corporations. 516p. 59.00 (ISBN 0-686-84794-6). Work in Amer.
Davis, Stanley N. & De Wiest, Roger J. M. Hydrogeology. 463p. 1966. 31.95 (ISBN 0-471-19900-1). Wiley.
Davis, Stephen. Logic & the Nature of God. LC 81-18464. 200p. 1983. 22.50x (ISBN 0-312-49448-3). St Martin.
Davis, Stephen & Simon, Peter. Reggae International. LC 82-61223. 1983. pap. 14.95 (ISBN 0-394-71313-3). Knopf.
Davis, Stephen T. Logic & the Nature of God. 200p. 1983. 9.95 (ISBN 0-8028-3321-7). Eerdmans.
Davis, Steve. Programs for the T.I. Home Computer. LC 82-90783. 150p. (Orig.). (gr. 5 up). 1983. pap. 14.95 (ISBN 0-911061-00-2). S Davis Pub.
Davis, Steven A. How to Stay Healthy in an Unhealthy World. LC 82-12581. 288p. 1983. 12.50 (ISBN 0-688-01574-3). Morrow.
Davis, Susan. Will the Real Me Please Stand Up. (Redwood Ser.). 79p. Date not set. pap. 3.95 (ISBN 0-8163-0479-3). Pacific Pr Pub Assn.
Davis, Susan S. Patience & Power: The Lives of Morrocan Village Women. 200p. 1983. 15.25 (ISBN 0-87073-503-9); pap. 8.95 (ISBN 0-87073-504-7). Schenkman.
Davis, Tenny L. Chemistry of Powder & Explosives. 500p. 1972. Repr. of 1943 ed. 14.00 (ISBN 0-913022-00-4). Angriff Pr.
Davis, Thadious M. Faulkner's "Negro". Art & the Southern Context. 304p. 1983. 25.00x (ISBN 0-8071-1047-7); pap. 10.95x (ISBN 0-8071-1064-7). La State U Pr.
Davis, Thomas. Experimentation with Microprocessor Applications. (Orig.). 1980. pap. text ed. 12.95 (ISBN 0-8359-1812-2). Reston.
Davis, Thomas B. Carlos de Alvear, Man of Revolution: The Diplomatic Career of Argentina's First Minister to the United States. LC 69-13878. Repr. of 1955 ed. lib. bdg. 17.50x (ISBN 0-8371-0373-8, DACA). Greenwood.
Davis, Thomas D. Philosophy: An Introduction Through Original Fiction & Discussion. LC 78-12329. 1978. pap. text ed. 7.95x (ISBN 0-394-32048-4). Random.
Davis, Thomas J. A Perilous Season. LC 82-48427. 480p. 1983. 15.95 (ISBN 0-02-907740-0). Free Pr.
Davis, Thomas M., jt. auth. see Johnson, Willoughby.
Davis, Thomas M. & Davis, Virginia L., eds. Edward Taylor vs. Solomon Stoddard: The Nature of the Lord's Supper. (American Literary Manuscripts Ser.). 1981. lib. bdg. 30.00 (ISBN 0-8057-9653-3, Twayne). G K Hall.
--Edward Taylor's "Church Records" & Related Sermons. (American Literary Manuscripts Ser.). 1981. lib. bdg. 35.00 (ISBN 0-8057-9650-9, Twayne). G K Hall.
--Edward Taylor's Minor Poetry. (American Literary Manuscripts Ser.). 1981. lib. bdg. 35.00 (ISBN 0-8057-9654-1, Twayne). G K Hall.
--The Unpublished Writings of Edward Taylor, 3 vols. (American Literary Manuscripts Ser.). 1981. Set. lib. bdg. 90.00 (ISBN 0-8057-9655-X, Twayne). G K Hall.
Davis, Thomas W., ed. Committees for Repeal of the Test & Corporation Acts: Minutes, Seventeen Eighty Six-Ninety & Eighteen Twenty Seven-Eight. 1978. 50.00x (ISBN 0-686-96607-4, Pub by London Rec Soc England). State Mutual Bk.
Davis, Tom, ed. see Goldsmith, Oliver.
Davis, Uri. Israel: Utopia Incorporated. 182p. 1977. 10.00 (ISBN 0-905762-12-6, Pub. by Zed Pr England); pap. 6.00 o.s.i. (ISBN 0-905762-13-4). Lawrence Hill.
Davis, Vincent, ed. see Bucknell, Howard, III.
Davis, Vincent, ed. see Sorley, Lewis.
Davis, Virginia L., jt. ed. see Davis, Thomas M.
Davis, W. Brother Against Brother. (Civil War Ser.). 1983. lib. bdg. price not set (Pub. by Time-Life). Silver.
--First Blood. (Civil War Ser.). 1983. lib. bdg. price not set (Pub. by Time-Life). Silver.
Davis, W. & Harrap, K. R., eds. Characterization & Treatment of Human Tumours. (Proceedings). 1978. 69.00 (ISBN 0-444-90014-4). Elsevier.
Davis, W. Grayburn, jt. auth. see McCormick, John.
Davis, W. Hersey, jt. auth. see Robertson, A. T.
Davis, W. S. Information Processing Systems: An Introduction to Modern Computer-Based Information Systems. 2nd ed. 1981. 19.95 (ISBN 0-201-03183-3); student wkbk. 6.95 (ISBN 0-201-03185-X); transparencies 15.00 (ISBN 0-201-03577-4); tests 3.95 (ISBN 0-201-03627-4). A-W.
Davis, W. W. El Gringo: New Mexico & Her People. LC 82-2735. (Illus.). 432p. 1982. 24.95x (ISBN 0-8032-1665-3); pap. 7.95 (ISBN 0-8032-6558-1, BB800, Bison). U of Nebr Pr.
Davis, Wade. Ted & Dottie in a Day of Fun. (Illus.). (gr. 1-2). 1967. text ed. 6.84 (ISBN 0-87443-032-1). Benson.
Davis, Wayne T., jt. ed. see Noll, Kenneth E.
Davis, William. Bench & Bar of the Commonwealth of Massachusetts, 2 vols. (American Constitutional & Legal History Ser). 1299p. 1974. Repr. of 1895 ed. Set. lib. bdg. 145.00 (ISBN 0-306-70612-1). Da Capo.
--The Best of Everything. 224p. 1981. 9.95 o.p. (ISBN 0-312-07713-0). St Martin.
--History of the Judiciary of Massachusetts. LC 74-8535. (American Constitutional & Legal History Ser). xxiv, 446p. 1974. Repr. of 1900 ed. lib. bdg. 55.00 (ISBN 0-306-70613-X). Da Capo.
Davis, William, jt. auth. see Schultes, Richard.
Davis, William, ed. The Punch Book of Inflation. LC 74-31967. 1975. 4.50 o.p. (ISBN 0-7153-7014-6). David & Charles.
Davis, William A. Maydays & Mermaids. 240p. 1983. 12.00 (ISBN 0-89540-133-9). Sun Pub.
Davis, William C. The Battle of New Market. LC 82-18705. (Illus.). 280p. 1983. pap. 7.95 (ISBN 0-8071-1078-7). La State U Pr.
--The Orphan Brigade: The Kentucky Confederates Who Couldn't Go Home. LC 79-7491. (Illus.). 336p. 1980. 12.95 o.p. (ISBN 0-385-14893-3). Doubleday.
--The Orphan: The Kentucky Confederates Who Couldn't Go Home. 352p. 1983. pap. 8.95 (ISBN 0-8071-1077-9). La State U Pr.
--Stand in the Day of Battle: The Imperiled Union 1861-1865, Vol. 2. LC 82-45521. (Illus.). 336p. 1983. 19.95 (ISBN 0-385-14895-X). Doubleday.
Davis, William C., ed. The Guns of '62: The Image of War, 1861-1865, Vol. 2. LC 81-43151. (Illus.). 460p. 1982. 35.00 (ISBN 0-385-15467-4). Doubleday.
Davis, William C., ed. see National Historical Society.
Davis, William G. Social Relations in a Philippine Market: Self-Interest & Subjectivity. LC 71-145783. 1973. 31.50x (ISBN 0-520-01904-0). U of Cal Pr.
Davis, William H. Beginner's Grammar of the Greek New Testament. 1923. 10.95xi (ISBN 0-06-061710-1, HarpR). Har-Row.
--Seventy-Five Years in California. rev. & enl. ed. Small, Harold A., ed. LC 66-11279. (Illus.). 1967. 27.50 (ISBN 0-910760-08-X). J Howell.
Davis, William H. & Golf Digest Editors. One Hundred Greatest Golf Courses & Then Some. LC 82-81714. 280p. 1982. 29.95 (ISBN 0-914178-57-1). Golf Digest.
Davis, William K., et al. Laboratory Exercises for General Botany. 4th ed. (Illus.). 94p. pap. text ed. 4.95x (ISBN 0-89641-067-6). American Pr.
Davis, William S. Computer & Business Information Processing. 2nd ed. LC 82-6864. (Illus.). 448p. 1983. pap. text ed. 17.95 (ISBN 0-201-11118-7). A-W.
--Operating Systems. 2nd ed. LC 82-3926. (Illus.). 448p. 1983. text ed. 19.95 (ISBN 0-201-11116-0). A-W.
Davis, William S. & Fisher, Richard H. Cobol: An Introduction to Structured Logic & Modular Program Design. 1979. pap. 18.95 (ISBN 0-201-01431-9); instrs'. manual 2.95 (ISBN 0-686-67461-8). A-W.
Davis, William S. & McCormack, Allison. Information Age. LC 78-55817. 1979. text ed. 19.95 (ISBN 0-201-01101-8); manual 2.95 (ISBN 0-201-01102-6). A-W.
Davis Fishman, Katherine. The Computer Establishment. 468p. 1981. 20.95 (ISBN 0-686-98079-4). Telecom Lib.
Davis-Gardner, Angela. Felice. LC 81-40234. 430p. 1982. 13.50 (ISBN 0-394-52009-2). Random.
Davis-Goff, Annabel. Night Tennis. LC 78-7334. 1978. 8.95 o.p. (ISBN 0-698-10924-4, Coward). Putnam Pub Group.
--Tailspin. 1981. 12.95 (ISBN 0-698-11023-4, Coward). Putnam Pub Group.
Davison, A., ed. Physical & Inorganic Chemistry. (Topics in Current Chemistry Ser.: Vol. III). (Illus.). 194p. 1983. 37.50 (ISBN 0-387-12065-3). Springer-Verlag.
Davison, Alex M. A Synopsis of Renal Diseases. (Illus.). 192p. 1981. pap. text ed. 16.00 (ISBN 0-7236-0569-6). Wright-PSG.
Davison, Brian. Explore a Castle. (Illus.). 128p. (gr. 4-6). 1982. 12.50 (ISBN 0-241-10763-6, Pub. by Hamish Hamilton England). David & Charles.
Davison, D. J. The Environmental Factor: An Approach for Managers. LC 77-20123. 1978. 39.95x o.s.i. (ISBN 0-470-99351-0). Halsted Pr.
Davison, J. F. Programming for Digital Computers. (Illus.). 1962. 37.00x (ISBN 0-677-00210-6). Gordon.
Davison, Kenneth E. The Presidency of Rutherford B. Hayes. LC 79-176289. (Contributions in American Studies: No. 3). 1972. lib. bdg. 29.95 (ISBN 0-8371-6275-0, DPH/); pap. 4.95 o.p. (ISBN 0-8371-7564-X, DPH). Greenwood.
Davison, Kenneth E., ed. American Presidency: A Guide to Information Sources. LC 73-17552. (The American Studies Information Guide Series, Gale Information Guide Library: Vol. 11). 200p. 1983. 42.00x (ISBN 0-8103-1261-1). Gale.
Davison, Marguerite P. A Handweavers Pattern Book. rev ed. (Illus.). 1951. 18.00 (ISBN 0-9603172-0-1). M P Davison.
--A Handweavers Source Book. (Illus.). 1953. pap. text ed. 10.95 (ISBN 0-9603172-1-X). M P Davison.
Davison, Mark L. Multidimensional Scaling. (Probability & Mathematical Statistics: Applied Probability & Statistic Section Ser.). 300p. 1983. 25.25 (ISBN 0-471-86417-X, Pub. by Wiley-Interscience). Wiley.
Davison, Michael. Ancient Rome. LC 79-57555. (Abbeville Library of Art Ser.: No. 1). (Illus.). 112p. (Orig.). 1980. pap. 4.95 o.p. (ISBN 0-89659-124-7). Abbeville Pr.
--The Glory of Greece & World of Alexander. LC 79-92450. (Illus.). 172p. 1980. pap. 14.95 o.p. (ISBN 0-89659-104-2). Abbeville Pr.
Davison, Peter. Contemporary Drama & the Popular Dramatic Tradition in England. LC 79-55526. 206p. 1983. text ed. 26.00x (ISBN 0-389-20232-0). B&N Imports.
Davison, W. Phillips, et al. News from Abroad & the Foreign Policy Public. LC 80-68024. (Headline Ser.: No. 250). (Illus.). 64p. (Orig.). 1980. pap. 3.00 (ISBN 0-87124-063-7). Foreign Policy.
Davison, Will, jt. ed. see Etzold, Thomas H.
Daviss, Diana V., ed. Bibliography of Human Rights. Date not set. looseleaf 85.00 (ISBN 0-379-20816-4). Oceana.
Davisson, Bud. The World of Sport Aviation. LC 82-1054. (Illus.). 242p. 1982. 24.00 (ISBN 0-87851-151-2). Hearst Bks.
Davitt, Thomas E. The Basic Values in Law: A Study of the Ethics -Legal Implications of Psychology & Anthropology. LC 68-24357. 1968. pap. 12.95 (ISBN 0-87462-451-7). Marquette.
--The Elements of Law. LC 59-10419. 1959. pap. 12.95 (ISBN 0-87462-475-4). Marquette.
Davitz, Joel & Davitz, Lois. Love & Understanding. LC 77-14817. (Emmaus Book). 144p. 1978. pap. 1.95 o.p. (ISBN 0-8091-2072-0). Paulist Pr.
Davitz, Joel R. & Davitz, Lois L. Evaluating Research Plans in the Behavioral Sciences: A Guide. LC 77-20296. 1977. pap. 4.50x (ISBN 0-8077-2544-7). Tchrs Coll.
Davitz, Joel R., et al. The Communication of Emotional Meaning. LC 75-31360. 1976. Repr. of 1964 ed. lib. bdg. 20.00x (ISBN 0-8371-8527-0, DACE). Greenwood.
Davitz, Lois, jt. auth. see Davitz, Joel.
Davitz, Lois L., jt. auth. see Davitz, Joel R.
Davodow-Goodman, Ann. Let's Draw Shapes. (Step-by-Step Guides). (Illus.). 80p. (gr. k-3). 1976. pap. 1.95 (ISBN 0-448-12137-9, G&D). Putnam Pub Group.
Davrout, L., tr. see Wieger, L.
Davson. The Eye. 1974. Vol. 5. by subscription 56.50 70.00 (ISBN 0-12-206755-X); Vol. 6. by subscription 65.50 53.00 (ISBN 0-12-206756-8). Acad Pr.
Davson, Hugh, ed. Eye. 2nd ed. Vol. 1. 1969. by subscription 53.00 74.50 (ISBN 0-12-206751-7); Vol. 2A 1976. by subscription 62.00 75.00 (ISBN 0-12-206752-5); Vol. 2B 1977. by subscription 62.00 75.00 (ISBN 0-12-206762-2); Vol. 3. 1970. by subscription 43.50 53.50 (ISBN 0-12-206753-3). Acad Pr.
Davy, B. & Graham, M., eds. Disease of Fish Cultured for Food in Southeast Asia: Report of a Workshop Held in Cisarua, Bogor, Indonesia, 28 November-1 December, 1978. 32p. 1979. pap. 5.00 (ISBN 0-88936-226-2, IDRC139, IDRC). Unipub.
Davy, C. see Steiner, Rudolf.
Davy, C., tr. see Steiner, Rudolf.
Davy, Charles, tr. see Steiner, Rudolf.
Davy, H. Nitrous Oxide. (Illus.). 606p. 1972. 38.50 o.p. (ISBN 0-407-33150-6). Butterworth.
Davy, Yvonne. Frau Luther. LC 78-57355. (Destiny Ser.). 1979. pap. 4.95 o.p. (ISBN 0-8163-0235-9). Pacific Pr Pub Assn.
Davye, Arnold, et al. Lagonga: A History of the Marque. 1979. 21.00 o.p. (ISBN 0-7153-7695-0). David & Charles.
Daw, George. Gun Patents 1864. 1982. 15.00x (ISBN 0-87556-251-5). Saifer.
Dawan, Elizabeth, jt. auth. see Veroff, Joseph.
Dawber, J. & Moore, A. Chemistry for the Life Science. 1973. 13.95 o.p. (ISBN 0-07-094286-2, C). McGraw.
Dawber, P. G., jt. auth. see Elliott, James P.
Dawdy, Doris O. Artists of the American West: A Biographical Dictionary, Vol. II. LC 82-75059. xiv, 345p. 1981. 22.95x (ISBN 0-8040-0352-1, SB). Swallow.
--Artists of the American West: A Biographical Dictionary, Vol. I. LC 82-73294. 275p. 1974. 20.00x (ISBN 0-8040-0607-5, SB). Swallow.
Dawe & Dornan. One-to-One: Resources for Conference-Centered Writing. (Orig.). 1981. pap. text ed. 10.95 (ISBN 0-316-17724-5); tchr's manual avail. (ISBN 0-316-17723-7). Little.
Dawe, Clyde J., et al, eds. Phyletic Approaches to Cancer. 410p. 49.50 (ISBN 0-686-86932-X, Pub. by Japan Sci Soc Japan). Intl Schol Bk Serv.
Dawe, Jessamon. Writing Business & Economic Papers, Theses & Dissertations. (Quality Paperback: No. 96). (Orig.). 1975. pap. 4.95 (ISBN 0-8226-0096-X). Littlefield.
Dawe, Jessamon & Lord, William J., Jr. Functional Business Communication. 2nd ed. (Illus.). 544p. 1974. ref. ed. 21.95 (ISBN 0-13-332007-3). P-H.
Dawe, R. D., ed. see Sophocles.
Dawes, Benjamin. Trematoda. 1946. 85.00 (ISBN 0-521-07219-0). Cambridge U Pr.
Dawes, Charles G. Journal As Ambassador to Great Britain. LC 72-109728. Repr. of 1939 ed. lib. bdg. 28.00x o.p. (ISBN 0-8371-4218-0, DAJO). Greenwood.

Dawes, Clinton J. Marine Botany. LC 1-7527. 628p. 1981. 49.95 (ISBN 0-471-07844-1, Pub. by Wiley-Interscience). Wiley.

Dawes, Geoffrey S. Foetal & Neonatal Physiology. 1968. 27.50 o.p. (ISBN 0-8151-2341-8). Year Bk Med.

Dawes, Hugh N. Public Finance & Economic Development: Spotlight on Jamaica. LC 81-40176. (Illus.). 162p. (Orig.). 1982. lib. bdg. 21.25 (ISBN 0-8191-2091-X); pap. text ed. 10.00 (ISBN 0-8191-2092-8). U Pr of Amer.

Dawes, John. Rugby Union. (Pelham Pictorial Sports Instruction Ser). (Illus.). 1977. 10.95 o.p. (ISBN 0-7207-0792-7). Transatlantic.

Dawes, Kathleen A., ed. see Dawes, Walter A.

Dawes, Rosemary N., jt. auth. see Champagne, Anthony.

Dawes, Walter A. Christianity Four Thousand Years Before Jesus. Dawes, Kathleen A., ed. (Illus.). 63p. (Orig.). 1982. pap. 4.95 (ISBN 0-938792-17-2). New Capernaum.

Dawidoff, Robert. The Education of John Randolph. 352p. Date not set. pap. text ed. 6.95 (ISBN 0-393-95287-8). Norton. Postponed.

Dawisha, Adeed & Dawisha, Karen, eds. The Soviet Union in the Middle East: Perspectives & Policies. 168p. 1982. text ed. 17.50x (ISBN 0-8419-0796-X); pap. text ed. 9.50x (ISBN 0-8419-0797-8). Holmes & Meier.

Dawisha, Adeed I. Syria & the Lebanese Crisis. LC 80-85. 200p. 1980. 26.00 (ISBN 0-312-78203-9). St Martin.

Dawisha, Karen. Soviet Foreign Policy Towards Egypt. 1979. 26.00x (ISBN 0-312-74837-X). St Martin.

Dawisha, Karen, jt. ed. see Dawisha, Adeed.

Dawkins, J. V. Developments in Polymer Characterisation, Vols. 1 & 2. Vol. 1. 45.00 (ISBN 0-85334-789-1, Pub. by Applied Sci England); Vol. 2. 55.50 (ISBN 0-85334-909-6). Elsevier.

Dawkins, J. V., ed. Developments in Polymer Characterisation, Vol. 3. 1982. 61.50 (Pub. by Applied Sci England). Elsevier.

--Developments in Polymer Characterisation, Vol. 4. Date not set. 61.50 (ISBN 0-85334-180-X, Pub. by Applied Sci England). Elsevier.

Dawkins, Marian. Animal Suffering. 1980. 20.00x (ISBN 0-412-22580-8, Pub. by Chapman & Hall England); pap. 9.95x (ISBN 0-412-22590-5). Methuen Inc.

Dawkins, Peter J., jt. auth. see Bosworth, Derek L.

Dawkins, Richard. The Selfish Gene. LC 76-29168. 1978. pap. 5.95 (ISBN 0-19-520000-4, GB500, GB). Oxford U Pr.

Dawkins, Webster L. Whatever Happened to America? 112p. 1983. 7.00 (ISBN 0-682-49965-X). Exposition.

Dawley, Gloria & Sorger, James. What to Do until the Doctor Calls Back. Guindon, Kathleen M., ed. (Illus.). 96p. (Orig.). 1982. 10.95 (ISBN 0-942696-01-8); pap. 5.95 (ISBN 0-942696-00-X). Transmediacom.

Dawood, M. Yusoff. Dysmenorrhea. (Illus.). 304p. 1981. lib. bdg. 35.00 (ISBN 0-683-02364-0). Williams & Wilkins.

Daws, Gavan. Shoal of Time: A History of the Hawaiian Islands. LC 73-92053. 507p. 1974. pap. 7.95 (ISBN 0-8248-0324-8). UH Pr.

Dawson & Drover. Early English Clocks. 99.00 (ISBN 0-686-95479-3). Antique Collect.

Dawson, et al. Modern Russian, Vol. 1. 480p. 1980. plus 24 audio-cassettes 195.00x (ISBN 0-88432-044-8, B101). J Norton Pubs.

--Modern Russian II. 482p. 1980. 24 audio cassettes incl. 195.00x (ISBN 0-88432-056-1). J Norton Pubs.

Dawson, A. J. Finn the Wolfhound. LC 63-7894. (gr. 7-9). 1966. pap. 0.75 (ISBN 0-15-630998-X, VoyB). HarBraceJ.

Dawson, Adele. Health, Happiness & the Pursuit of Herbs. LC 79-21182. (Illus.). 1980. 12.95 (ISBN 0-8289-0362-X); pap. 9.95 (ISBN 0-8289-0363-8). Greene.

Dawson, Albert C. & Dawson, Laila M. Dicho y Hecho: Beginning Spanish: A Simplified Approach. LC 80-19506. 456p. 1981. text ed. 20.95x (ISBN 0-471-06476-9). wkbk. 9.95x (ISBN 0-471-06103-4); tapes 1.00 (ISBN 0-471-06475-0). Wiley.

Dawson, Barbara. Metal Thread Embroidery. (Illus.). 216p. 1982. pap. 9.75 (ISBN 0-686-98030-1). Branford.

Dawson, Christopher H. The Historic Reality of Christian Culture: A Way to the Renewal of Human Life. LC 76-21783. (Religious Perspectives Ser: Vol. 1). 124p. 1976. Repr. of 1960 ed. lib. bdg. 15.00x o.p. (ISBN 0-8371-9001-0, DAHR). Greenwood.

Dawson, Clayton L., et al. Modern Russian, 2 pts. Incl. Part 1 (ISBN 0-87840-169-5). with 24 cassettes in an album 105.00 set (ISBN 0-686-67899-0). LC 77-5837. 1977. Repr. of 1964 ed. 13.25 ea. (ISBN 0-87840-170-9). Georgetown U Pr.

Dawson, David. No Fear in His Presence. LC 80-50261. 192p. 1980. text ed. 9.95 o.p. (ISBN 0-8307-0753-0, 5108918). Regal.

Dawson, David, jt. ed. see Tyler, H. Richard.

Dawson, David, et al. Schizophrenia in Focus: Guidelines for Treatment & Rehabilitation. 176p. 1983. 24.95 (ISBN 0-89885-096-7). Human Sci Pr.

Dawson, David M. see Tyler, Richard H.

Dawson, E. R., tr. see Akheizer, N. I.

Dawson, E. R., tr. see Akheizer, N. I. & Glazman, I. M.

Dawson, E. Y. Marine Red Algae of Pacific Mexico: Ceramiales, Dasyaceae, Rhodomelaceae, Part 8. (Illus.). 1963. pap. 8.00 (ISBN 3-7682-0209-7). Lubrecht & Cramer.

Dawson, E. Yale & Foster, Michael S. Seashore Plants of California. LC 81-19690. (California Natural History Guides Ser.: No. 47). (Illus.). 226p. 1983. 15.95 (ISBN 0-520-04138-0); pap. 7.95 (ISBN 0-520-04139-9). U of Cal Pr.

Dawson, Fielding. Krazy Kat & Seventy-Six More, Collected Stories: 1950-1976. 378p. 1982. 14.00 (ISBN 0-87685-564-8); signed ed. 25.00 (ISBN 0-87685-565-6); pap. 10.00 (ISBN 0-87685-563-X). Black Sparrow.

Dawson, George G., jt. auth. see Gordon, Sanford D.

Dawson, J. B. & Sharp, B. L., eds. Annual Reports on Analytical Atomic Spectroscopy, Vol. 10. 342p. 1982. 165.00x (ISBN 0-85186-717-0, Pub. by Royal Soc Chem England). State Mutual Bk.

Dawson, J. Frank. Place Names in Colorado. 1976. pap. 1.75x (ISBN 0-87315-067-8). Golden Bell.

Dawson, James. Australia Aborigines. (AIAS New Ser.: No. 26). 103p. 1981. text ed. 23.50x (ISBN 0-391-02220-2, Pub. by Australian Inst Australia). Humanities.

--Superspill. (Illus.). 128p. 1981. 18.95 (ISBN 0-86720-588-1). Sci Bks Intl.

Dawson, John. Seventeenth Virginia Cavalry: Or Wildcat Cavalry. 1982. 15.00 (ISBN 0-686-83061-X). Pr of Morningside.

Dawson, John & Palmer, George. Cases on Restitution. 2nd ed. 1969. 22.00 o.p. (ISBN 0-672-81193-6, Bobbs-Merrill Law). Michie-Bobbs.

Dawson, John, jt. auth. see Kirby, David.

Dawson, John A. Commercial Distribution in Europe. LC 81-2123. 1982. 27.50 (ISBN 0-312-15264-7). St Martin.

Dawson, John A., ed. The Marketing Environment. LC 78-31680. 1979. 35.00x (ISBN 0-312-51530-8). St Martin.

Dawson, John P. The Oracles of the Law. xix, 520p. 1978. Repr. of 1968 ed. lib. bdg. 49.50x (ISBN 0-313-20260-5, DAOL). Greenwood.

Dawson, Joseph C. Seeking Shelter: How to Find & Finance an Energy-Efficient Home. (Illus.). 256p. 1983. 17.95 (ISBN 0-688-00902-6). Morrow.

--Seeking Shelter: How to Find & Finance an Energy-Efficient Home. (Illus.). 256p. 1983. pap. 9.95 (ISBN 0-688-00903-4). Quill NY.

Dawson, Joseph M. America's Way in Church, State & Society. LC 79-15522. 1980. Repr. of 1953 ed. lib. bdg. 19.00x (ISBN 0-313-22006-9, DAAW). Greenwood.

Dawson, Laila M., jt. auth. see Dawson, Albert C.

Dawson, Lawrence H. Nicknames & Pseudonyms. LC 73-164216. viii, 312p. 1974. Repr. of 1908 ed. 39.00 o.p. (ISBN 0-8103-3177-2). Gale.

Dawson, M. & Cole, A. T., eds. Studies in Latin Poetry. (Yale Classical Studies: Vol. 21). 1969. 37.50 (ISBN 0-521-07395-2). Cambridge U Pr.

Dawson, Mary M. A Complete Guide to Crochet Stitches. (Illus.). 128p. 1973. pap. 4.50 (ISBN 0-517-50019-1). Crown.

Dawson, Mildred A., jt. auth. see Collins, Alberta C.

Dawson, Mildred A., jt. auth. see Newman, Georgiana C.

Dawson, Mildred A., et al. Five Words Long. 3rd ed. Bamman, Henry A., ed. (Kaleidoscope Ser.). 1978. pap. text ed. 7.48 (ISBN 0-201-40875-9, Sch Div); tchr's. ed. 8.04 (ISBN 0-201-40876-7). A-W.

Dawson, Miles M., ed. Wisdom of Confucius. pap. 2.50 (ISBN 0-8283-1462-4, 18, IPL). Branden.

Dawson, Oliver. Herbaceous Border. (Illus.). 144p. 1973. 4.95 o.p. (ISBN 0-7153-6211-9). David & Charles.

Dawson, P. R. & Wilkinson, A. The Effectiveness of Fluxes in Secondary Brass Remelting, 1977. 1981. 40.00x (ISBN 0-686-97074-8, Pub. by W Spring England). State Mutual Bk.

Dawson, P. R., jt. auth. see Rao, S.

Dawson, P. R., jt. auth. see Wilkinson, A.

Dawson, Pam. Monarch Illustrated Guide to Embroidery. pap. 6.95 o.p. (ISBN 0-671-18770-8). Monarch Pr.

Dawson, Pat. Knitting. (Monarch Illustrated Guide Ser.). 1977. pap. 6.95 o.p. (ISBN 0-671-18769-4). Monarch Pr.

Dawson, Peter. The Blizzard. 144p. 1982. pap. 1.95 (ISBN 0-553-22911-7). Bantam.

--Making a Comprehensive Work: The Road from Bomb Alley. 190p. 1981. 25.00x o.p. (ISBN 0-631-12534-5, Pub. by Basil Blackwell England); pap. 12.50x o.p. (ISBN 0-631-12619-8). Biblio Dist.

Dawson, Peter E. Evaluation, Diagnosis, & Treatment of Occlusal Problems. LC 74-12409. 407p. 1974. 62.50 (ISBN 0-8016-1216-0). Mosby.

Dawson, Peter P. & Gallegos, Frederick. Case Study II: MEDCO, Inc. (Illus.). 89p. 1973. pap. text ed. 7.95 (ISBN 0-574-17920-8, 13-0920); instr's guide avail. (ISBN 0-574-17921-6, 13-0921). SRA.

Dawson, Peter S. & King, Charles E. Population Biology: Retrospect & Prospect. 240p. 1983. text ed. 22.00 (ISBN 0-231-05252-9). Columbia U Pr.

Dawson, R., jt. ed. see Duursma, E. K.

Dawson, R. M., et al. Data for Biochemical Research. 2nd ed. 1969. 49.50x (ISBN 0-19-855334-X). Oxford U Pr.

Dawson, Ralph E., III & Dawson, Shirley. Cherokee-English Interliner, First Epistle of John of the New Testament. 25p. 1982. pap. 2.50 spiral bdg. (ISBN 0-940392-11-9). Indian U Pr.

Dawson, Raymond. Confucius. Thomas, Keith, ed. (Past Masters Ser.). 1982. 8.95 (ISBN 0-8090-3596-0); pap. 3.25 (ISBN 0-8090-1423-8). Hill & Wang.

Dawson, Raymond H. The Decision to Aid Russia, 1941. LC 73-16798. 315p. 1974. Repr. of 1959 ed. lib. bdg. 18.50x (ISBN 0-8371-7231-4, DAAR). Greenwood.

Dawson, Richard E., et al. Political Socialization. 2nd ed. (Ser. in Comparative Politics). 226p. 1977. pap. text ed. 10.95 (ISBN 0-316-17741-5). Little.

Dawson, Robert M. Government of Canada. 5th ed. Ward, Norman, rev. by. LC 63-5198. (Canadian Government Ser.). 1970. lib. bdg. 25.00x o.p. (ISBN 0-8020-1720-7); text ed. 17.50 o.p. (ISBN 0-8020-2046-1). U of Toronto Pr.

Dawson, Robert O. Sentencing: The Decision As to Type, Length, & Conditions of Sentence. 428p. 1969. pap. 7.95 o.p. (ISBN 0-316-17739-3). Little.

--Standards Relating to Adjudication. LC 77-1755. (IJA-ABA Juvenile Justice Standards Project Ser.). 112p. 1980. prof ref 20.00x (ISBN 0-88410-236-X); pap. 10.00x (ISBN 0-88410-809-0). Ballinger Pub.

Dawson, S. W. Drama & the Dramatic. (Critical Idiom Ser.). 1970. pap. 4.95x (ISBN 0-416-17280-6). Methuen Inc.

Dawson, Shirley, jt. auth. see Dawson, Ralph E., III.

Dawson, T. J. Marsupials & Monotremes. (Studies in Biology: No. 150). 80p. 1983. pap. text ed. 8.95 (ISBN 0-7131-2853-4). E Arnold.

Dawson, T. L. Chapter Four - Carpet & Yarn Printing. 75.00x (ISBN 0-686-98203-7, Pub. by Soc Dyers & Colour); pap. 50.00x (ISBN 0-686-98204-5). State Mutual Bk.

Dawson, Thomas H. Offshore Structural Engineering. (Illus.). 352p. 1982. text ed. 34.95 (ISBN 0-13-633206-4). P-H.

Dawson, Townes L. & Mounce, Earl W. Business Law: Text & Cases. 4th ed. 1979. text ed. 26.95x (ISBN 0-669-01690-X); instructor's manual free (ISBN 0-669-01691-8). Heath.

Dawson, W. A. Introductory Guide to Central Labour Legislation. 10.00x o.p. (ISBN 0-210-27188-4). Asia.

Dawson, Warren R., ed. The Banks Letters: A Calendar of the Manuscript Correspondence of Sir Joseph Banks Preserved in the British Museum, the British Museum (Natural History) & Other Collections in Great Britain. 965p. 1958. 100.00x (ISBN 0-565-00085-3, Pub. by Brit Mus Nat Hist England). Sabbot-Natural Hist Bks.

Dawson, William F. Christmas, Its Origin & Associations, Together with Its Historical Events & Festive Celebrations During Nineteen Centuries. LC 68-54857. 1968. Repr. of 1902 ed. 45.00x (ISBN 0-8103-3351-1). Gale.

Dawson, William L. Instrumentation in the Speech Clinic. LC 73-86410. 1973. pap. 1.50x (ISBN 0-8134-6549-4, 6549). Interstate.

Dax, Peter, tr. see Berrondo, Marie.

Day & Cooper. Railway Signalling Systems. 12.75x (ISBN 0-392-08779-0, SpS). Sportshelf.

Day, A. C. Compatible Fortran. LC 77-95444. (Illus.). 1979. 19.95 (ISBN 0-521-22027-0). Cambridge U Pr.

--Fortran Techniques. LC 72-78891. (Illus.). 104p. 1972. 19.95 (ISBN 0-521-08549-7); pap. 8.95 (ISBN 0-521-09719-3). Cambridge U Pr.

Day, A. Grove. Books about Hawaii: Fifty Basic Authors. LC 77-7997. 1977. text ed. 9.95x (ISBN 0-8248-0561-5). UH Pr.

--Eleanor Dark. (World Authors Ser.). 1976. lib. bdg. 15.95 (ISBN 0-8057-6224-8, Twayne). G K Hall.

--James A. Michener. 2nd ed. (United States Authors Ser.). 1977. lib. bdg. 10.95 (ISBN 0-8057-7184-0, Twayne). G K Hall.

--James Michener. 2nd ed. (United States Authors Ser.). 1977. lib. bdg. 11.95 (ISBN 0-8057-7184-0, Twayne). G K Hall.

--Modern Australian Prose, Nineteen One to Nineteen Seventy-Five: A Guide to Information Sources, Vol. 32. Day, A. Grove, ed. LC 74-11536. (American Literature, English Literature & World Literatures in English Information Guide Ser.). 425p. 1980. 42.00x (ISBN 0-8103-1243-3). Gale.

--Pacific Islands Literature: One Hundred Basic Books. LC 70-151452. 1971. 12.95x o.p. (ISBN 0-87022-180-9). UH Pr.

--Robert D. FitzGerald. (World Authors Ser.). 1974. lib. bdg. 13.95 (ISBN 0-8057-2311-0, Twayne). G K Hall.

--Sky Clears. 1951. pap. 2.45 (ISBN 0-686-95825-X). Jefferson Natl.

Day, A. Grove & Knowlton, Edgar, Jr. V. Blasco Ibanez. (World Authors Ser.). 15.95 (ISBN 0-8057-2448-6, Twayne). G K Hall.

Day, A. Grove, jt. auth. see Leib, Amos P.

Day, A. Grove, ed. see Becke, Louis.

Day, A. Grove, ed. & intro. by see Stevenson, Robert L.

Day, A. Grove, ed. see Twain, Mark.

Day, Alan J., ed. Border & Territorial Disputes. (Illus.). 450p. 1982. 75.00x (ISBN 0-582-90251-7, Longman). Gale.

Day, Alan J. & Degenhardt, Henry W., eds. Political Parties of the World. LC 80-83467. 432p. 1980. 90.00x (ISBN 0-582-90300-9). Gale.

Day, Angell. English Secretary. LC 67-10122. 1967. Repr. of 1599 ed. 38.00 (ISBN 0-8201-1012-4). Schol Facsimiles.

Day, B. F. Building Acoustics. 1969. 12.50 (ISBN 0-444-20047-9). Elsevier.

Day, Barbara. Open Learning in Early Childhood. 2nd ed. (Illus.). 224p. 1975. pap. text ed. 12.95 (ISBN 0-02-327950-8, 32795). Macmillan.

Day, Candra, jt. auth. see Hess, Patricia.

Day, Christopher. Pattern Design. 1979. 22.50 o.p. (ISBN 0-7134-3299-3, Pub. by Batsford England). David & Charles.

Day, Clarence. In the Green Mountain Country. 1934. 24.50x (ISBN 0-686-50044-X). Elliots Bks.

--Scenes from the Mesozoic & Other Drawings. 1935. 27.50x (ISBN 0-686-51306-1). Elliots Bks.

Day, D. E. Relaxation Processes in Glass: Special Journal Issue. (Journal of Non-Crystalline Solids: Vol. 14). 1974. 57.50 (ISBN 0-444-10613-8, North-Holland). Elsevier.

Day, David, jt. auth. see Jackson, Albert.

Day, David A. Construction Equipment Guide. LC 72-10163. (Practical Construction Guides Ser.). 563p. 1973. 61.95x o.p. (ISBN 0-471-19985-0, Pub. by Wiley-Interscience). Wiley.

Day, David E. Early Childhood Education: A Human Ecological Approach. 1983. text ed. 15.95x (ISBN 0-673-16029-7). Scott F.

Day, Dawn. The Adoption of Black Children. LC 77-18585. (Illus.). 1979. 19.95 (ISBN 0-669-02107-5). Lexington Bks.

Day, Dawn, jt. auth. see Newman, Dorothy K.

Day, Dee. Getting to Know Panama. (Getting to Know Ser.). (Illus.). (gr. 3-5). 1958. PLB 3.97 o.p. (ISBN 0-698-30142-0, Coward). Putnam Pub Group.

--Getting to Know Spain. (Getting to Know Ser.). (Illus.). (gr. 3-5). 1957. PLB 3.97 o.p. (ISBN 0-698-30156-0, Coward). Putnam Pub Group.

Day, Donald B. Index to the Science Fiction Magazines, 1926-1950. Rev. ed. 1982. lib. bdg. 48.00 (ISBN 0-8161-8591-3, Hall Reference). G K Hall.

Day, Dorothy. Loaves & Fishes: The Story of the Catholic Worker Movement. LC 82-48433. (Illus.). 240p. 1983. pap. 6.68i (ISBN 0-06-061771-3, HarpR). Har-Row.

--The Long Loneliness: An Autobiography. LC 81-4727. (Illus.). 1981. pap. 6.68i (ISBN 0-06-061751-9, RD363, HarpR). Har-Row.

Day, Douglas. Malcolm Lowry: A Biography. (Illus.). 1973. 19.95 (ISBN 0-19-501711-0). Oxford U Pr.

Day, Douglas, ed. see Faulkner, William.

Day, Frank P. Rockbound: A Novel. LC 73-81763. (Literature of Canada Ser.). 1973. pap. 7.95 o.p. (ISBN 0-8020-6200-8). U of Toronto Pr.

Day, G., et al. Computer Models in Marketing: Planning. 128p. 1977. pap. 13.75x (ISBN 0-89426-004-9). Scientific Pr.

Day, Gene G. Is Any Among You Sick? The Dynamics of a Healing Ministry. 1979. pap. 3.95 o.p. (ISBN 0-682-49494-1). Exposition.

Day, George S., jt. auth. see Aaker, David A.

Day, George S., jt. ed. see Aaker, David A.

Day, Glenn R., jt. auth. see Likes, Robert C.

Day, Graham & Caldwell, Lisley, eds. Diversity & Decomposition in the Labour Market. 211p. 1982. text ed. 36.50x (ISBN 0-566-00556-5). Gower Pub Ltd.

Day, Haliday T., et al. Shape of Space: Sculpture of George Sugarman. (Illus.). 114p. 1982. cancelled o.p. (ISBN 0-8390-0294-7). Allanheld & Schram.

Day, Holliday D. The Shape of Space, George Sugarman. Allen, Jane A., ed. (Illus.). 144p. (Orig.). 1981. 34.50 (ISBN 0-936364-07-6); pap. 17.95 (ISBN 0-936364-06-8). Joslyn Art.

Day, Howard D. A Guide for Adult School Crossing Guards. (Illus.). 34p. 1971. Set Of 10. photocopy ed. spiral 24.50x (ISBN 0-398-02171-6). C C Thomas.

Day, Hughes W. Beside Still Waters. 418p. 1979. 9.95 (ISBN 0-8341-0599-3). Beacon Hill.

Day, Ingeborg. Ghost Waltz: A Memoir. LC 80-16411. 240p. 1980. 11.95 o.p. (ISBN 0-670-29485-3). Viking Pr.

Day, Irene F. The Moroccan Cookbook. LC 77-88752. (Illus.). 160p. 1978. pap. 4.95 (ISBN 0-8256-3095-9, Quick Fox). Putnam Pub Group.

Day, Isobel, jt. auth. see Bewley, Beulah R.

Day, Ivan. Perfumery with Herbs. 1980. 30.00x o.p. (ISBN 0-232-51414-3, Pub. by. Darton-Longman-Todd England). State Mutual Bk.

Day, J. S. Subcontracting Policy in the Airframe Industry. 1956. write for info. (ISBN 0-08-018745-5). Pergamon.

Day, James M, jt. ed. see Laufer, William S.

Day, Janis K. A Working Approach to Human Relations in Organizations. LC 79-24589. 1980. pap. text ed. 18.95 (ISBN 0-8185-0347-5). Brooks-Cole.

Day, Jo Anne C. Art Nouveau Cut & Use Stencils. (Illus.). 64p. 1977. pap. 3.75 (ISBN 0-486-23443-6). Dover.

Day, Jocelyn. Tarnished Rainbow, No. 64. Date not set. pap. 1.75 o.p. (ISBN 0-515-06675-3). Jove Pubns.

--Tarnished Rainbow, No. 82. 1982. pap. 1.75 (ISBN 0-515-06693-1). Jove Pubns.

Day, John. Engines: The Search for Power. (Illus.). 256p. 1980. 27.50 o.p. (ISBN 0-312-25216-1). St Martin.

Day, John W., Jr., jt. ed. see Hall, Charles A.

Day, Kenneth, intro. by. William Caxton & Charles Knight. (Illus.). 240p. pap. 8.95 (ISBN 0-913720-06-2, Sandstone). Beil F C.

Day, Lewis F. Alphabets Old & New for the Use of Craftsmen. 3rd ed. LC 68-23148. 1968. Repr. of 1910 ed. 30.00x (ISBN 0-8103-3301-5). Gale.

--Nature & Ornament: Nature the Raw Material of Design. LC 74-137355. (Illus.). 1971. Repr. of 1930 ed. 34.00x (ISBN 0-8103-3328-7). Gale.

--Nature in Ornament. LC 70-159852. (Illus.). 1971. Repr. of 1898 ed. 34.00x (ISBN 0-8103-3207-8). Gale.

--Ornament & Its Application. LC 71-136735. (Illus.). 1971. Repr. of 1904 ed. 34.00x (ISBN 0-8103-3324-4). Gale.

Day, Lewis F. & Buckle, Mary. Art in Needlework: A Book About Embroidery. LC 74-159927. Repr. of 1900 ed. 34.00x (ISBN 0-8103-3062-8). Gale.

Day, M. H., ed. Human Evolution, Vol. 11. 162p. 1973. write for info. (ISBN 0-686-81310-3, Pub. by Taylor & Francis). Intl Pubns Serv.

--Vertebrate Locomotion. (Symposia of the Zoological Society of London Ser.: No. 48). 1981. 89.50 (ISBN 0-12-613348-4). Acad Pr.

Day, M. J. Plasmids. (Studies in Biology: No. 142). 56p. 1982. pap. text ed. 8.95 (ISBN 0-7131-2846-1). E Arnold.

Day, Malcolm M. Thomas Traherne. (English Author Ser.). 1982. lib. bdg. 15.95 (ISBN 0-8057-6742-8, Twayne). G K Hall.

Day, Marie F. Kingdom Come: Fact or Fantasy. 1983. 7.95 (ISBN 0-533-05309-9). Vantage.

Day, Millard F. Basic Bible Doctrine. 1953. pap. 2.95 (ISBN 0-8024-0239-9). Moody.

Day, N. R. David's Faithfulness. 85p. (Orig.). 1979. pap. 6.95 (ISBN 0-940754-02-9). Ed Ministries.

--Your Faith Is Growing! 51p. (Orig.). 1981. pap. 5.45 (ISBN 0-940754-10-X). Ed Ministries.

Day, N. Raymond. From Palm Sunday to Easter. 45p. (Orig.). 1979. pap. 5.45 (ISBN 0-940754-01-0). Ed Ministries.

Day, Peter R. Communication in Social Work. LC 72-8466. 128p. 1973. text ed. 20.00 o.p. (ISBN 0-08-017064-1); pap. text ed. 9.25 (ISBN 0-08-017065-X). Pergamon.

--Social Work & Social Control. 1981. 20.00x (ISBN 0-422-77520-7, Pub. by Tavistock); pap. 10.95x (ISBN 0-422-77530-4). Methuen Inc.

Day, Peter R., ed. The Genetic Basis of Epidemics in Agriculture, Vol. 287. (Annals of the New York Academy of Sciences). 400p. 1977. 37.00x (ISBN 0-89072-033-9). NY Acad Sci.

Day, Phyllis. Sold Twice. 1968. pap. 1.15 o.p. (ISBN 85363-078-X). OMF Bks.

Day, R. A., Jr. & Johnson, Ronald C. General Chemistry. (Illus.). 592p. 1974. text ed. 27.95 o.p. (ISBN 0-13-349340-7). P-H.

Day, R. A., Jr. & Underwood, Arthur L. Quantitative Analysis. 4th ed. (Illus.). 1980. text ed. 31.95 (ISBN 0-13-746545-9); pap. 7.95 solutions manual (ISBN 0-13-746560-2); lab manual 12.95 (ISBN 0-13-746552-1). P-H.

Day, R. H. & Cigno, A. Modelling Economic Change: The Recursive Programming Approach. (Contributions to Economic Analysis Ser.: Vol. 117). 1978. 64.00 (ISBN 0-444-85056-2, North Holland). Elsevier.

Day, Richard. Automotive Engine Tuning. 1981. pap. text ed. 15.95 (ISBN 0-8359-0270-6). Reston.

--Automotive Mechanics. (Illus.). 1980. text ed. 20.95 (ISBN 0-8359-0272-2). Reston.

--How to Service & Repair Your Own Car. rev. ed. LC 72-97173. (Popular Science Ser.). (Illus.). 1980. 14.95i o.p. (ISBN 0-06-010985-8, HarpT). Har-Row.

Day, Richard H., ed. Economic Analysis & Agricultural Policy. 340p. 1982. text ed. 35.00x (ISBN 0-8138-0532-5). Iowa St U Pr.

Day, Richard H. & Robinson, Stephan M., eds. Mathematical Topics in Economic Theory & Computation. LC 72-96283. 149p. 1972. text ed. 12.50 (ISBN 0-89871-045-6). Soc Indus-Appl Math.

Day, Robert. The Last Cattle Drive. 1977. pap. 1.95 o.p. (ISBN 0-380-01832-2, 36228). Avon.

--The Last Cattle Drive. LC 76-28173. 1977. 7.95 o.p. (ISBN 0-399-11883-7). Putnam Pub Group.

Day, Robert A. How to Write & Publish a Scientific Paper. 2nd ed. (Professional Writing Ser.). (Illus.). 180p. 1983. 17.95 (ISBN 0-686-84415-7); pap. text ed. 11.95 (ISBN 0-89495-022-3). ISI Pr.

Day, Satis B. & Day, Stacey B. A Hindu Interpretation of the Hand & Its Portents As Practiced by the Palmists of India. LC 73-85296. 5.50 (ISBN 0-912922-25-7); pap. 2.50 (ISBN 0-686-96906-5). U of Minn Bell.

Day, Stacey. Tuluak & Amaulik. LC 73-93517. (Illus.). 176p. 1973. 6.50 (ISBN 0-912922-07-9); pap. 3.75 (ISBN 0-686-96907-3). U of Minn Bell Mus.

Day, Stacey B., jt. auth. see Day, Satis B.

Day, Stacey B., et al, eds. Cancer Invasion & Metastasis: Biologic Mechanisms & Therapy. LC 77-83695. (Progress in Cancer Research & Therapy Ser: Vol. 5). 540p. 1977. 48.00 (ISBN 0-89004-184-9). Raven.

Day, Susan & McMahan, Elizabeth. The Writer's Resource: Readings for Composition. 416p. 1983. pap. text ed. 10.95 (ISBN 0-07-016152-6, C). McGraw.

Day, Susan, jt. auth. see McMahan, Elizabeth.

Day, Thomas. The History of Little Jack. Bd. with Original Stories from Real Life. Wollstonecraft, Mary. LC 75-32149. (Classics of Children's Literature, 1621-1932: Vol. 15). 1976. Repr. of 1788 ed. PLB 38.00 o.s.i. (ISBN 0-8240-2263-7). Garland Pub.

--The History of Sandford & Merton, 3 vols. in 1. LC 75-32143. (Classics of Children's Literature, 1621-1932: Vol. 11). 1977. Repr. of 1789 ed. PLB 38.00 ea. o.s.i. (ISBN 0-8240-2260-2). Garland Pub.

--Monarch College Outline on Music. pap. 4.95 o.p. (ISBN 0-671-08048-2). Monarch Pr.

Day, Wilbur V. Through Hell to Heaven. 1978. 5.95 o.p. (ISBN 0-533-03543-0). Vantage.

Day, William D. Introduction to Vector Analysis for Radio & Electronic Engineers. 14.00x o.p. (ISBN 0-685-20598-3). Transatlantic.

--Tables of La Place Transforms. 2.50 o.p. (ISBN 0-685-20639-4). Transatlantic.

Day, William H. Maximizing Small Business Profits: With Precision Management. LC 78-9407. 1979. 13.95 (ISBN 0-13-566257-5, Spec); pap. 6.95 (ISBN 0-13-566240-0, Spec). P-H.

Dayal, R. An Integrated System of World Models, Vol. 2. (North-Holland Systems & Control Ser.: Vol. 2). 1981. 59.75 (ISBN 0-444-86272-2). Elsevier.

Dayal, Raghubir, jt. auth. see Khanna, K. C.

Dayan, Moshe. Diary of the Sinai Campaign. LC 67-15231. (Illus.). 1967. pap. 1.95 o.p. (ISBN 0-8052-0140-8). Schocken.

Dayan, Yael. Three Weeks in October. 1979. 8.95 o.s.i. (ISBN 0-440-07992-6, E Friede). Delacorte.

Dayananda, James Y. Manohar Malgonkar. (World Authors Ser.). 1975. lib. bdg. 15.95 (ISBN 0-8057-2566-0, Twayne). G K Hall.

Daydi-Tolson, Santiago. The Post-Civil War Spanish Social Poets. (World Authors Ser.). 192p. 1983. lib. bdg. 19.95 (ISBN 0-8057-6533-6, Twayne). G K Hall.

Daydi-Tolson, Santiago, ed. Vicente Aleixandre: A Critical Appraisal. LC 81-65036. (Studies in Literary Analysis). 336p. 1981. lib. bdg. 16.95x (ISBN 0-916950-21-2); pap. text ed. 9.95x (ISBN 0-916950-20-4). Bilingual Pr.

Daykin, Vernon. Technical Arabic. 132p. 1980. 15.00x (ISBN 0-686-94054-7, Pub. by Lund Humphries England). State Mutual Bk.

Daynes, Byron W. & Tatalovich, Raymond. Contemporary Readings in American Government. (Orig.). 1980. pap. text ed. 10.95 (ISBN 0-669-01163-0). Heath.

Days, G. D., ed. Threshold of the McCarthy Era & the McCarthy Era, Beginning of the End. 60p. 1980. pap. 19.95 includes cassettes-cancelled (ISBN 0-918628-54-7, 54/7). Congeros Pubns.

Daytner. Surfactants in Textile Processing. (Surfactant Science Ser.). 208p. 1983. price not set (ISBN 0-8247-1812-7). Dekker.

Dayton, C. M. Design of Educational Experiments. 1970. text ed. 32.50 (ISBN 0-07-016174-7, C). McGraw.

Dayton, D. H., jt. ed. see Bellanti, J. A.

Dayton, David, ed. A Roseliep Retrospective: Poems & Other Words by & About Raymond Roseliep. LC 80-17304. (Illus.). 112p. 1980. pap. 10.00 o.p. (ISBN 0-934184-04-6). Alembic Pr.

Dayton, Delbert H., jt. ed. see Cooper, Max D.

Dayton, Delbert H., jt. ed. see Ogra, P. L.

Dayton, Donald, jt. ed. see Bryant, M. Darrol.

Dayton, Edward R. God's Purpose & Man's Plans. 1976. pap. 3.00 (ISBN 0-912552-11-5). MARC.

Dayton, Edward R. & Engstrom, Ted W. Strategy for Leadership. 240p. 1979. 12.95 (ISBN 0-8007-0994-2). Revell.

--Strategy for Living: How to Make the Best Use of Your Time & Abilities. LC 76-3935. (Orig.). 1976. 5.95 o.p. (ISBN 0-8307-0422-1, 51-070-08); pap. 5.95 (ISBN 0-8307-0424-8, 5403405); wkbk. 3.95 (ISBN 0-8307-0476-0, 5202000). Regal.

Dayton, Edward R., ed. Mission Handbook: North American Protestant Ministries Overseas. 1977. 6.00 o.p. (ISBN 0-912552-06-9). MARC.

Dayton, Eldorous L. Chantefable: The Story of the Roman Poet Catullus & His Love for Lesbia in Prose & English Verse. 120p. 1982. 16.95 (ISBN 0-943602-00-9). Gardnor Hse.

Dayton, Irene. In Oxbow of Time's River. LC 78-64440. 1978. 5.50 (ISBN 0-911838-52-X). Windy Row.

--The Panther's Eye. 80p. 1974. 4.95 (ISBN 0-911838-42-2). Windy Row.

--Seven Times the Wind. LC 76-45244. 1977. 4.95 (ISBN 0-911838-50-3). Windy Row.

--Sixth Sense Quivers. LC 76-138847. 1970. 4.00 (ISBN 0-911838-08-2). Windy Row.

Dayton, Laura. LeRoy's Birthday Circus. LC 81-2205. (Illus.). 32p. (ps-3). 1982. 6.75 (ISBN 0-525-66744-X). Dandelion Pr.

Dayus, Kathleen. Her People. (Illus.). 194p. 1983. pap. 7.95 (ISBN 0-86068-275-7, Virago Pr). Merrimack Bk Serv.

Daze, Ann M. & Scanlon, John W. Code Pink: A Practical System for Neonatal-Perinatal Resuscitation. 168p. 1981. pap. text ed. 17.95 (ISBN 0-8391-1670-5). Univ Park.

Dazeley, G. H. Organic Chemistry. LC 69-10061. 1969. text ed. 19.95x (ISBN 0-521-07171-2). Cambridge U Pr.

D'Azzo, John & Houpis, Constantine. Linear Control System Analysis & Design. 2nd ed. (Electrical Engineering Ser.). (Illus.). 864p. 1981. text ed. 35.00 (ISBN 0-07-016183-6, C); solutions manual 18.50 (ISBN 0-07-016184-4). McGraw.

D'Azzo, John J. & Houpis, Constantine. Feedback Control System Analysis & Synthesis. 2nd ed. (Electronic & Electrical Engineering Ser.). 1966. text ed. 34.50 (ISBN 0-07-016175-5, C). McGraw.

D-Din-Ahmed, Shemsu see Ahmed, Shemsu-D-Din.

De, Honore Balzac see Balzac, Honore De.

De, Monique P. Ladebat see De Ladebat, Monique P.

Dea, Kay & Sixth NASW Professional Symposium, 1979, eds. Perspectives for the Future: Social Work Practice in the 80's. LC 80-83988. 192p. (Orig.). 1980. pap. text ed. 12.95x (ISBN 0-87101-089-5, CBO-089-C). Natl Assn Soc Wkrs.

De Acha, Eduardo. Una Nota de Derecho Penal. LC 82-71757. 184p. (Orig., Span.). 1982. pap. 10.00 (ISBN 0-89729-314-2). Ediciones.

Deacon, Eileen. Making Jewelry. LC 77-7942. (Beginning Crafts Ser.). (Illus.). (gr. k-3). 1977. PLB 9.30 o.p. (ISBN 0-8393-0116-2). Raintree Pubs.

Deacon, G. E. & Deacon, Margaret B., eds. Modern Concepts of Oceanography. LC 81-6239. (Benchmark Papers in Geology Ser.: Vol. 61). 386p. 1982. 46.00 (ISBN 0-87933-390-1). Hutchinson Ross.

Deacon, Margaret B., jt. ed. see Deacon, G. E.

Deacon, Richard. A History of the British Secret Service: Covers the Development of the Intelligence System from the Days of Henry VII to the Present. 6.95 (ISBN 0-586-05116-3). Academy Chi Ltd.

--A History of the Japanese Secret Service. 320p. 1982. 40.00x (ISBN 0-584-10383-2, Pub. by Muller Ltd). State Mutual Bk.

--Kempei Tai: A History of the Japanese Secret Service. LC 82-20564. (Illus.). 306p. 14.95 (ISBN 0-8253-0131-9). Beaufort Bks NY.

--Madoc & the Discovery of America. LC 67-23398. (Illus.). 1967. 5.00 o.s.i. (ISBN 0-8076-0421-6). Braziller.

--Microwave Cookery. 5.95 (ISBN 0-912656-73-5). H P Bks.

Deaderick, Barron. Campaigns & Battles of America, Seventeen Fifty-Five to Eighteen Sixty-Five. 1959. 4.95 o.p. (ISBN 0-8158-0085-1). Chris Mass.

Deady, Matthew P. Pharisee Among Philistines: The Diary of Judge Matthew P. Deady, 1871-1892, 2 vols. Clark, Malcolm, Jr., intro. by. LC 74-75363. (Illus.). 702p. 1975. 27.95 (ISBN 0-87595-046-9); deluxe ed. 30.00 (ISBN 0-686-96825-5); pap. 21.95 (ISBN 0-686-96826-3). Oreg Hist Soc.

Deag, John. Social Behavior of Animals. (Studies in Biology: No. 118). 96p. 1980. pap. text ed. 8.95 (ISBN 0-686-43116-2). E Arnold.

Deagan, Kathleen, ed. Spanish St. Augustine: The Archaeology of a Colonial Creole Community (Monographs) (Studies in Historical Archaeology). Date not set. price not set (ISBN 0-12-207880-2). Acad Pr.

De Ajuriaguerra, J. Handbook of Child Psychiatry & Psychology. Lorion, Raymond P., tr. LC 80-80094. 678p. 1980. text ed. 34.50x (ISBN 0-89352-031-4). Masson Pub.

Deak, Edit. Rope Drawings by Patrick Ireland: An Exhibition. (Illus.). 32p. 1977. pap. 3.00x (ISBN 0-934418-04-7). La Jolla Mus Contemp Art.

Deak, Etienne & Deak, Simone. Dictionary of Colorful French Slanguage & Colloquialisms. (Illus.). 1961. pap. 4.75 o.p. (ISBN 0-525-47087-5). Dutton.

Deak, Francis & Jessup, Philip C., eds. A Collection of Neutrality Laws, Regulations & Treaties of Various Countries, 2 vols. LC 39-34164. 1976. Repr. of 1939 ed. Set. 60.00 o.s.i. (ISBN 0-527-22050-7). Kraus Repr.

Deak, Gloria-Gilda. American Views: Prospects & Vistas. LC 76-40041. (Illus.). 1976. 25.00 (ISBN 0-87104-263-0). NY Pub Lib.

Deak, Istan, jt. auth. see Mitchell, Allan.

Deak, Istvan. Weimar Germany's Left-Wing Intellectuals: A Political History of the Weltbuhne & Its Circle. LC 68-9271. (Illus.). 1968. 32.50x o.p. (ISBN 0-520-00309-8). U of Cal Pr.

Deak, Simone, jt. auth. see Deak, Etienne.

De'ak, Stephen. David Popper: Violoncello Virtuoso & Composer. (Illus.). 320p. 1980. 17.95 (ISBN 0-87666-621-7, Z-32). Paganiniana Pubns.

Deakin, Michael. Children on the Hill. LC 73-1731. 128p. 1973. 5.95 o.p. (ISBN 0-672-51843-0). Bobbs.

Deakin, Michael, jt. auth. see Frost, David.

Deakin, Motley F. Rebecca West. (English Authors Ser.). 1980. 11.95 (ISBN 0-8057-6788-6, Twayne). G K Hall.

Deal, jt. auth. see Barth.

Deal, Jacquelyn see Meltzer, Lawrence.

Deal, William S. Happiness & Harmony in Marriage. pap. 2.95 (ISBN 0-686-13723-X). Crusade Pubs.

--Living Christian in Today's World. 1973. pap. 1.25 o.p. (ISBN 0-8341-0208-0). Beacon Hill.

--The March of Holiness Through the Centuries. 1978. pap. 2.50 (ISBN 0-686-05528-4). Crusade Pubs.

--New Light on the Shepherd Psalm. 1982. write for info. Crusade Pubs.

--The Other Shepherd. 1982. 2.95 (ISBN 0-686-38053-3). Crusade Pubs.

--Pictorial Introduction to the Bible. large print 12.95 (ISBN 0-686-13725-6); pap. 3.95. Crusade Pubs.

--A Pictorial Introduction to the Bible. LC 67-20517. 438p. 1982. pap. 12.95 (ISBN 0-89081-363-9). Harvest Hse.

--Problems of the Spirit-Filled Life. 2.95 (ISBN 0-686-13724-8). Crusade Pubs.

--What Every Young Christian Should Know. 1982. write for info. Crusade Pubs.

De Alessi, Louis. Some Economic Aspects of Government Ownership & Regulation: Essays From Economia Pubblica. (LEC Occasional Paper). 50p. 1982. pap. 3.00 (ISBN 0-916770-12-5). Law & Econ U Miami.

Dealey, J. Q. Growth of American State Constitutions. LC 75-124891. (American Constitutional & Legal History Ser). 308p. 1972. Repr. of 1915 ed. lib. bdg. 39.50 (ISBN 0-306-71985-1). Da Capo.

De Alvarez, Russell R., ed. The Kidney in Pregnancy. LC 76-13184. (Clinical Obstetrics & Gynecology Ser.). 1976. 33.95 o.p. (ISBN 0-471-20030-1, Pub. by Wiley Medical). Wiley.

Deam, C. C. Flora of Indiana. 1970. Repr. of 1940 ed. 40.00 (ISBN 3-7682-0696-3). Lubrecht & Cramer.

Dean, Alan H., jt. auth. see McDonald, Jack R.

Dean, Amber. Be Home by Eleven. 192p. 1973. 4.95 o.p. (ISBN 0-399-11142-5). Putnam Pub Group.

Dean, Anabel. Bats the Night Fliers. LC 73-11975. (General Juvenile Bks). (Illus.). 32p. (gr. 7 up). 1974. PLB 5.95g (ISBN 0-8225-0291-7). Lerner Pubns.

--Fire! How Do They Fight It? LC 77-17635. (Illus.). 1978. text ed. 9.95 (ISBN 0-664-32626-9). Westminster.

--How Animals Communicate. LC 77-23281. (Illus.). 64p. (gr. 3 up). 1977. PLB 6.97 o.p. (ISBN 0-671-32818-2). Messner.

--Willie Can Fly. (Early Childhood Bk.). (Illus.). (ps-2). PLB 4.95 o.p. (ISBN 0-513-00493-9). Denison.

--Wind Sports. LC 82-13460. (Illus.). (gr. 5-9). 12.95 (ISBN 0-664-32696-X). Westminster.

Dean, Bashford. A Bibliography of Fishes, 3 vols. 1973. 128.00 (ISBN 3-87429-036-0). Lubrecht & Cramer.

Dean, Carol. One Last Kiss. 1982. pap. 2.95 (ISBN 0-8217-1112-1). Zebra.

Dean, Charles W. & De Bruyn Kops, Mary. The Crime & the Consequences of Rape. 152p. 1982. 17.50x (ISBN 0-398-04552-6); pap. 12.75x (ISBN 0-398-04627-1). C C Thomas.

Dean, Chris & Whitlock, Quentin. The Handbook of Computer-Based Training. 250p. 1983. 25.00 (ISBN 0-89397-132-4). Nichols Pub.

Dean, Dave & Hefley, Marti. Now Is Your Time to Win. 1983. 6.95 (ISBN 0-8423-4724-0). Tyndale.

Dean, David. Architecture of the 1930's. (Illus.). 160p. 1983. 25.00 (ISBN 0-8478-0485-2); pap. 15.00 (ISBN 0-8478-0484-4). Rizzoli Intl.

--English Shopfronts from Contemporary Source Books, 1792-1840. (Illus.). 1970. 20.00 (ISBN 0-85458-270-3). Transatlantic.

Dean, Dwight G., ed. Dynamics in Social Psychology. 1966. pap. text ed. 10.95x (ISBN 0-394-30137-4). Phila Bk Co.

Dean, Edith, jt. auth. see Andersen, Georg.

Dean, Frank. The Complete Book of Trick & Fancy Riding. LC 60-13312. (Illus.). 1975. boxed 14.95 (ISBN 0-87004-240-8). Caxton.

--Cowboy Fun. LC 79-91384. (Illus.). 160p. 1980. 10.95 (ISBN 0-8069-4608-3); PLB 13.29 (ISBN 0-8069-4609-1). Sterling.

Dean, G. D., jt. auth. see Read, B. E.

Dean, G. W. & Wells, M. C., eds. Forerunners of Realizable Values Accounting in Financial Reporting. LC 82-82486. (Accountancy in Transition Ser.). 342p. 1982. lib. bdg. 45.00 (ISBN 0-8240-5334-6). Garland Pub.

Dean, Howard E. Judicial Review & Democracy. (Orig.). 1966. pap. text ed. 3.25 (ISBN 0-685-19740-9). Phila Bk Co.

Dean, J. Planning Library Education Programmes. 144p. 1972. 17.00 (ISBN 0-233-95760-X, 05778-9, Pub. by Gower Pub Co England). Lexington Bks.

Dean, J. A., ed. Lange's Handbook of Chemistry. 12th ed. 1978. 41.50 (ISBN 0-07-016191-7). McGraw.

Dean, Jeff. Architectural Photography: Techniques for Architects, Preservationists, Historians, Photographers, & Urban Planners. LC 81-12830. (Illus.). 1982. 19.95 (ISBN 0-910050-54-6). AASLH.

Dean, Jennifer B. Careers in a Department Store. LC 72-5411. (Early Career Bks.). (Illus.). 36p. (gr. 2-5). 1973. PLB 5.95g (ISBN 0-8225-0301-8). Lerner Pubns.

--Careers with an Airline. LC 72-5413. (Early Career Bks.). (Illus.). 36p. (gr. 2-5). 1973. PLB 5.95g (ISBN 0-8225-0303-4). Lerner Pubns.

Dean, John. Blind Ambition: The White House Years. 1976. 13.95 o.p. (ISBN 0-671-22438-7). S&S.

Dean, John W., III. Lost Honor. LC 82-61776. 1982. 15.95 (ISBN 0-936906-15-4). Stratford Pr.

Dean, K. J. Physics & Chemistry of Baking. 3rd ed. 1980. 22.75 (ISBN 0-85334-867-7, Pub. by Applied Sci England). Elsevier.

Dean, L., jt. auth. see Blau, Judith H.

Dean, Leonard F., et al, eds. Play of Language. 3rd ed. 1971. pap. text ed. 9.95x (ISBN 0-19-501304-2). Oxford U Pr.

Dean, Lois R. Five Towns: A Comparative Community Study. (Orig.). 1968. pap. text ed. 3.50x (ISBN 0-685-19727-1). Phila Bk Co.

Dean, Malcolm, ed. Ephemeris of Chiron. rev. 2nd ed. 1982. 6.95 (ISBN 0-686-82682-5). Weiser.

Dean, Nancy & Stark, Myra, eds. In the Looking Glass: Twenty-One Modern Short Stories by Women. LC 76-48851. (YA) 1977. 8.95 o.p. (ISBN 0-399-11837-3). Putnam Pub Group.

Dean, Norman L. Energy Efficiency in Industry. 472p. 1980. prof ref 35.00x (ISBN 0-88410-056-1). Ballinger Pub.

Dean, Peter G. Teaching & Learning Mathematics. (The Woburn Education Ser.). 1982. 22.50x (ISBN 0-7130-0168-2, Pub by Woburn Pr England); pap. text ed. 12.50x (ISBN 0-7130-4007-6). Biblio Dist.

Dean, R. T. Cellular Degradative Processes. 1978. pap. 6.50x (ISBN 0-412-15190-1, Pub. by Chapman Hall). Methuen Inc.

Dean, Richard. Home Video. (Illus.). 176p. 1982. pap. 8.95 (ISBN 0-408-01166-1). Focal Pr.

Dean, Richard H. & O'Neill, James A., Jr. Vascular Disorders of Childhood. LC 82-191. (Illus.). 204p. 1983. write for info (ISBN 0-8121-0832-9). Lea & Febiger.

Dean, Robert J. Layman's Bible Book Commentary: Luke, Vol. 17. 1983. 4.75 (ISBN 0-8054-1187-9). Broadman.

Dean, Roger, ed. The Album Cover Album. LC 77-71713. (Illus.). 160p. 1977. 25.00 o.s.i. (ISBN 0-89104-085-4); pap. 10.95 o.s.i. (ISBN 0-89104-074-9). A & W Pubs.

Dean, Roger, jt. ed. see Thorgerson, Storm.

Dean, Roger T. Lysosomes. (Studies in Biology: No. 84). 64p. 1978. pap. text ed. 8.95 (ISBN 0-7131-2663-9). E Arnold.

Dean, Thomas. Post-Theistic Thinking: The Marxist-Christian Dialogue in Radical Perspective. LC 74-83202. 300p. 1975. 29.95 (ISBN 0-87722-037-9). Temple U Pr.

Dean, Thomas, jt. ed. see Raines, John C.

Dean, Vera. The United States & Russia. rev ed. LC 72-97342. (Illus.). xvi, 336p. Repr. of 1948 ed. lib. bdg. 21.75x o.p. (ISBN 0-8371-3740-3, DEUS). Greenwood.

Dean, Vera M. Nature of the Non-Western World. (Orig.). pap. 1.50 o.p. (ISBN 0-451-61224-8, MW1224, Ment). NAL.

Dean, W. B. & Farrar, G. E., Jr. Basic Concepts of Anatomy & Physiology. 2nd ed. (Illus.). 400p. 1982. pap. text ed. 14.50 (ISBN 0-397-54378-6, Lippincott Medical). Lippincott.

Dean, Warren, pref. by see Fernandes, Florestan.

Dean, William F. General Dean's Story. LC 72-12310. (Illus.). 305p. 1973. Repr. of 1954 ed. lib. bdg. 20.00x (ISBN 0-8371-6690-X, DEDS). Greenwood.

Dean, Winton. Handel & The Opera Seria. LC 79-78567. (Ernest Bloch Lectures). 1969. 38.50x (ISBN 0-520-01438-3). U of Cal Pr.

Dean, Winton & Hicks, Anthony. The New Grove Handel. (The New Grove Composer Biography Ser.). (Illus.). 1983. 16.50 (ISBN 0-393-01682-X); pap. 7.95 (ISBN 0-393-30086-2). Norton.

Dean, Winton, ed. see Dent, Edward.

Dean, Winton, ed. see Dent, Edward J.

DeAndrea, William. Five O'Clock Lightning. (Fingerprint Mysteries Ser.). 266p. 1983. pap. 5.95 (ISBN 0-312-29499-9). St Martin.

DeAndrea, William L. Killed with a Passion. LC 82-45353. (Crime Club Ser.). 192p. 1983. 11.95 (ISBN 0-385-18275-9). Doubleday.

Deane, Basil. Albert Roussel. LC 80-16642. (Illus.). vii, 188p. 1980. Repr. of 1961 ed. lib. bdg. 20.75x (ISBN 0-313-22612-1, DEAR). Greenwood.

Deane, Dee S. Black South Africans - A Who's Who: Profiles of Natal's Leading Blacks. (Illus.). 1978. text ed. 17.50x o.p. (ISBN 0-19-570148-8). Oxford U Pr.

Deane, Hazel. Powerful Is the Light. 1965. 5.95 o.p. (ISBN 0-686-24351-X). Divine Sci Fed.

Deane, Leslie. The Girl with the Golden Hair. (Orig.). 1978. pap. 2.25 o.s.i. (ISBN 0-515-04807-0). Jove Pubns.

--Star Power. 1980. pap. 2.75 o.s.i. (ISBN 0-515-05282-5). Jove Pubns.

Deane, Norma, tr. see Perrot, Jean.

Deane, P., jt. auth. see Mitchell, Brian R.

Deane, Philip. Caribbean Vacations. (Illus.). 1966. 1.95 o.p. (ISBN 0-448-01180-8, G&D). Putnam Pub Group.

Deane, Phyllis. The Evolution of Economic Ideas. LC 77-88674. (Modern Cambridge Economics Ser.). 1978. 34.50 (ISBN 0-521-21928-0); pap. 13.95 (ISBN 0-521-29315-4). Cambridge U Pr.

--The First Industrial Revolution. 2nd ed. LC 78-26388. 1980. 44.50 (ISBN 0-521-22667-8); pap. 11.95 (ISBN 0-521-29609-9). Cambridge U Pr.

Deane, Phyllis & Cole, W. A. British Economic Growth, Sixteen Eighty-Eight to Nineteen Fifty-Nine: Trends & Structure. 2nd ed. LC 67-21956. (Cambridge Department of Applied Economics Monographs). (Illus.). 1969. 49.50 (ISBN 0-521-04801-X); pap. 16.95x (ISBN 0-521-09569-7). Cambridge U Pr.

Deane, Seamus. Gradual Wars. 64p. 1975. Repr. of 1972 ed. 8.00x (ISBN 0-7165-2153-9, Pub. by Irish Academic Pr Ireland). Biblio Dist.

Deane, Seamus & Munby, A. N., eds. Sales Catalogues of Libraries of Eminent Persons: Politicians Burke, Hastings, Hollis, O'Connell & Wilkes. (Vol. 8). 396p. 1974. 20.00 o.p. (ISBN 0-7201-0367-3, Pub. by Mansell England). Wilson.

Deane, Sidney N., tr. see Anselm, St.

Deane, Sonia. Doctors in Love. (Aston Hall Romances Ser.: No. 107). 192p. (Orig.). 1980. pap. 1.50 o.p. (ISBN 0-523-41119-7). Pinnacle Bks.

De Angeli, Marguerite. The Door in the Wall: Story of Medieval London. LC 64-7025. (gr. 3-6). 10.95a (ISBN 0-385-07283-X); PLB (ISBN 0-385-05743-1); pap. 1.95 o.p. (ISBN 0-385-07909-5). Doubleday.

--Fiddlestrings. LC 73-82243. 128p. (gr. 4-7). 1974. PLB 4.95 (ISBN 0-385-08437-4). Doubleday.

--Thee Hannah. (gr. 2-5). 8.95 o.p. (ISBN 0-385-07525-1); PLB 8.95 (ISBN 0-385-06130-7). Doubleday.

--Whistle for the Crossing. LC 76-42323. (gr. 2-5). 1977. 5.95a o.p. (ISBN 0-385-11552-0); PLB 5.95a (ISBN 0-385-11553-9). Doubleday.

De Angelis, George & Francis, Edward P. The Ford Model "A"-As Henry Built It. 3rd ed. (Illus.). 234p. 1983. 16.95 (ISBN 0-911383-02-6). Motor Cities.

Deans, Alexander S. The Bee Keepers Encyclopedia. LC 75-23248. (Illus.). 1979. Repr. of 1949 ed. 58.00x (ISBN 0-8103-4176-X). Gale.

Deans, Stanley R. The Radon Transform & Some of Its Applications. 350p. 1983. 36.00 (ISBN 0-471-89804-X, Pub. by Wiley-Interscience). Wiley.

Dean-Smith, Margaret, ed. see Playford, John.

De Anton, Haberkamp G., ed. see Haensch, G.

Dear, M. J. & Taylor, S. M. Not on Our Street. 1982. 19.95x (ISBN 0-85086-096-2, Pub. by Pion England). Methuen Inc.

Dear, Michael J. & Scott, Allen J. Urbanization & Urban Planning in Capitalist Societies. 1981. 27.95x (ISBN 0-416-74640-3); pap. 15.95x (ISBN 0-416-74650-0). Methuen Inc.

De Aragon, Ray J. City of Candy & Streets of Ice Cream. LC 79-52960. (Miss Miffit Story Time Bks.). (Illus., Orig.). (gr. 1-6). 1979. text ed. 5.95 (ISBN 0-932906-05-2); pap. 2.50 (ISBN 0-932906-04-4). Pan-Am Publishing Co.

--The Great Lovers. (Non-Fiction Ser.). (Illus.). 104p. (Orig.). 1983. pap. 5.95 (ISBN 0-932906-10-9). Pan-Am Publishing Co.

De Araujo, Virginia, ed. see Andrade, Carlos D.

Dearborn, David C., frwd. by see Wyman, Thomas B.

Dearborn, Elwyn. The Down East Printmaker: Carroll Thayer Berry. (Illus.). Date not set. write for info. (ISBN 0-89272-170-7); write for info. ltd. ed. (ISBN 0-89272-169-3). Down East.

Dearborn, L., jt. auth. see Dasheff, Bill.

Dearden, C. W. The Stage of Aristophanes. (University of London Classical Ser: No. 7). 224p. 1976. text ed. 29.25x o.p. (ISBN 0-485-13707-0, Athlone Pr). Humanities.

Dearden, Garry, jt. ed. see Parlett, Malcolm.

Dearden, James S. George Allen & John Ruskin "A Romantic Addition to the History of Publishing". 96p. 1982. 50.00x (ISBN 0-284-98623-2, Pub. by C Skilton Scotland). State Mutual Bk.

Dearden, John. Cost Accounting & Financial Control Systems. LC 73-184160. 1973. text ed. 27.95 (ISBN 0-201-01507-2). A-W.

Dearden, John & Shank, John. Financial Accounting & Reporting: A Contemporary Emphasis. (Illus.). 544p. 1975. ref. ed. 27.95 (ISBN 0-13-314757-6). P-H.

Dearden, M. & Dearden, R. A Modern Course in Biology. 307p. 1969. text ed. 6.64 o.p. (ISBN 0-08-013457-2). Pergamon.

Dearden, R., jt. auth. see Dearden, M.

Dearden, R. F., et al. Educational & the Development of Reason, 3 pts. Incl. Pt. 1. Critique of Current Educational Aims. pap. 7.95 (ISBN 0-7100-8084-0); Pt. 2. Reason. pap. 8.95 (ISBN 0-7100-8101-4); Pt. 3. Education & Reason. pap. 6.95 (ISBN 0-7100-8102-2). 1975. Routledge & Kegan.

Dearholt, Donald & McSpadden, William. Electromagnetic Wave Propagation. (Illus.). 480p. 1973. text ed. 46.50 (ISBN 0-07-016205-0, C). McGraw.

Dearing, James. Making Money Making Music. 320p. 1982. 18.95 (ISBN 0-89879-089-1); pap. 12.95 (ISBN 0-89879-101-4). Writers Digest.

Dearing, John, ed. Calculator Tips & Routines: Especially for the HP-41c-41CV. LC 81-90355. 136p. 1981. pap. 15.00 (ISBN 0-942358-00-7). Corvallis Software.

Dearing, Trevor. Supernatural Healing Today. 1979. pap. 4.95 (ISBN 0-88270-340-4, Pub. by Logos). Bridge Pub.

Dearing, Vinton A. A Manual of Textual Analysis. LC 82-20947. ix, 108p. 1983. Repr. of 1959 ed. lib. bdg. 27.50x (ISBN 0-313-23734-4, DEMA). Greenwood.

--Principles & Practice of Textual Analysis. LC 73-76122. 1975. 33.00x (ISBN 0-520-02430-3). U of Cal Pr.

Dearing, Vinton A. see Dryden, John.

Dearle, Norman B. Economic Chronicle of the Great War For Great Britain & Ireland: 1914-1919. (Economic & Social History of the World War Ser.). 1929. text ed. 65.00x (ISBN 0-686-83531-X). Elliots Bks.

Dearlove, J. The Politics of Policy in Local Government. LC 73-77179. (Illus.). 300p. 1973. 32.50 (ISBN 0-521-20244-2). Cambridge U Pr.

Dearlove, John. The Reorganization of British Local Government. LC 78-18092. 1979. 44.50 (ISBN 0-521-22341-5); pap. 12.95 (ISBN 0-521-29456-8). Cambridge U Pr.

De Armand, David W., jt. auth. see Epstein, Samuel.

DeArment, Robert K. Knights of the Green Cloth: The Saga of the Frontier Gamblers. LC 81-16196. (Illus.). 432p. 1982. 19.50 (ISBN 0-8061-1726-5). U of Okla Pr.

Dearmer, Percy. Songs of Praise. Vaughan Williams, Ralph & Shaw, Martin, eds. Incl. Music Ed. rev. & enl. ed. 1932. 19.95x (ISBN 0-19-231207-3); enl. ed. 1931. 3.50x o.p. (ISBN 0-19-231205-7). Oxford U Pr.

DeArmond, Stephen J., et al. Structure of the Human Brain: A Photographic Atlas. 2nd ed. (Illus.). 1976. pap. text ed. 16.95x (ISBN 0-19-502073-1); slide set o.p. 39.50x (ISBN 0-19-501948-2). Oxford U Pr.

Dearnley, Christopher. English Church Music, 1650-1750: In Royal Chapel, Cathedral & Parish Church. (Studies in Church Music). (Illus.). 1970. 15.00x (ISBN 0-19-519136-6). Oxford U Pr.

DeArteaga, William. Past Life Visions: A Christian Exploration. 240p. 1983. pap. 11.95 (ISBN 0-8164-2414-4). Seabury.

Deary, Terry. Calamity Kate. LC 82-1326. (The Good Time Library). (Illus.). 112p. (gr. 2-6). 1982. lib. bdg. 7.95g (ISBN 0-87614-195-5). Carolrhoda Bks.

--The Lambton Worm. LC 82-1327. (The Good Time Library). (Illus.). 88p. (gr. 3-7). lib. bdg. 7.95g (ISBN 0-87614-196-3). Carolrhoda Bks.

Deasey, Denison. Education Under Six. LC 77-21081. 1978. 26.00x (ISBN 0-312-23748-0). St Martin.

Deasington, R. J. Practical Guide to Computer Communications & Networking. (Ellis Horwood Series in Computers & Their Applications). 132p. 1982. 39.95x (ISBN 0-470-27545-6). Halsted Pr.

De Assis, Joaquim M. Machado see Machado de Assis, Joaquim M.

Deasy, P. B. & Timoney, R. F. The Quality Control of Medicines: Proceedings. 1976. 85.00 (ISBN 0-444-41454-1, North Holland). Elsevier.

Deasy, P. B. & Timoney, R. F., eds. Progress in the Quality Control of Medicines. 298p. 1982. 78.75 (ISBN 0-444-80344-0). Elsevier.

Deasy, Richard M., ed. see Staples, William R.

Deatherage, George E. Construction Office Administration. 1964. 33.95 o.p. (ISBN 0-07-016211-5, P&RB). McGraw.

Deaton, David, jt. auth. see Bowers, John.

Deaton, John. Love & Sex in Marriage: Doctor's Guide to the Sensual Union. 1978. 14.95 o.p. (ISBN 0-13-540856-3, Parker). P-H.

--A Medical Doctors Guide to Youth, Health, & Longevity. 14.95 (ISBN 0-13-572503-8). P-H.

Deats, Paul, Jr., ed. Toward a Discipline of Social Ethics: Essays in Honor of Walter George Muelder. LC 70-189020. 1972. 5.00 (ISBN 0-87270-018-6). Boston U Sch of Theology.

Deaux, Kay, jt. auth. see Wrightsman, Lawrence.

De Ayala, Ramon P. Belarmino & Apolonio, Baumgarten, Murray & Berns, Gabriel, trs. from Span. 1983. pap. 5.95 (ISBN 0-520-04958-6, CAL 626). U of Cal Pr.

De Azevedo, Carlos see Azevedo, Carlos de.

DeBach, P. Biological Control by Natural Enemies. LC 73-90812. (Illus.). 325p. 1974. 42.50 (ISBN 0-521-20380-5); pap. 12.95x (ISBN 0-521-09835-1). Cambridge U Pr.

De Back, P. Paul Delvaux: Catalog Raisonne. (Illus.). 55.00 o.s.i. (ISBN 0-912729-10-4). Newbury Bks.

De Bairacli-Levy, Juliette. Common Herbs for Natural Health. LC 73-91335. (Illus.). 198p. 1974. pap. 3.95 (ISBN 0-8052-0436-9). Schocken.

--Nature's Children: A Guide to Organic Foods & Herbal Remedies for Children. LC 78-163326. (Illus.). 1978. pap. 3.95 (ISBN 0-8052-0580-2). Schocken.

De Baker. Toxicity & Side Effects of Psychotropic Drugs. (International Congress Ser.: Vol. 145). Date not set. 66.00 (ISBN 0-686-95305-3). Elsevier.

DeBakey & Gotlo. Living Heart. (Health, Nutrition & Well Being Bks). pap. 6.95 o.p. (ISBN 0-448-14685-1, G&D). Putnam Pub Group.

De Bakker, H. Major Soils & Soil Regions in the Netherlands. 192p. 105.00X (CAB Bks). State Mutual Bk.

De Bakker, J. W. & Van Vliet, J., eds. Algorithmic Languages. 1982. 47.00 (ISBN 0-444-86285-4). Elsevier.

De Balzac, Honore. Pere Goriot. Reed, Henry, tr. (Orig.). 1962. pap. 1.95 (ISBN 0-451-51603-6, CJ1603, Sig Classics). NAL.

De Balzac, Honore see Balzac, Honore De.

De Bandt, Jacques, et al. European Studies in Development. LC 79-26811. 1980. 35.00x (ISBN 0-312-27086-0). St Martin.

De Barancourt, Petit. De l'Emancipation des Noirs Du Lettres a M. le Duc de Broglie sur les Dangers De Cette Mesure. (Slave Trade in France, 1744-1848, Ser.). 330p. (Fr.). 1974. Repr. of 1845 ed. lib. bdg. 86.00x o.p. (ISBN 0-8287-0685-9, TN134). Clearwater Pub.

Debarbat, S. & Guinot, B. La Methode Des Hauteurs Egales En Astronomie. (Cours et Documents De Mathematiques et De Physique Ser.). 150p. 1970. 39.00 (ISBN 0-677-50250-8). Gordon.

DeBarthe, Frank. Life & Adventures of Frank Grouard. (Classics of the Old West Ser.). 1982. lib. bdg. 17.28 (ISBN 0-8094-4007-5). Silver.

De Bartolo, Dick & Clarke, Bob. Mad Vertising. (Orig.). 1972. pap. 1.25 o.p. (ISBN 0-451-06739-8, Y6739, Sig). NAL.

Debartolo, Dick & North, Harry. The Mad Book of Sex & Violence & Home Cooking. 192p. (Orig.). 1983. pap. 1.95 (ISBN 0-446-30033-0). Warner Bks.

DeBartolo, Dick & Woodbridge, George. A Mad Guide to Leisure Time. (Illus.). 192p. (Orig.). 1983. pap. 1.95 (ISBN 0-446-30466-2). Warner Bks.

De Bary, William T., ed. Buddhist Tradition: In India, China & Japan. 1969. 3.95 o.s.i. (ISBN 0-394-60205-6, M205). Modern Lib.

De Beaugrande, Robert. Text, Discourse, & Process: Toward a Multidisciplinary Science of Texts. (Advances in Discourse Processes Ser.: Vol. 4). 1980. text ed. 32.50x (ISBN 0-89391-033-3). Ablex Pub.

De Beaugrande, Robert see Beaugrande, Robert de.

De Beaumont, Madame. Beauty & the Beast. LC 76-57884. (Illus.). (gr. k-3). 1978. 9.95 (ISBN 0-02-726400-9). Bradbury Pr.

De Beauvoir, Simone. The Mandarins. LC 79-65852. 610p. 1979. pap. 8.95 (ISBN 0-89526-898-1). Regnery-Gateway.

--Memoirs of a Dutiful Daughter. 1974. pap. 7.21i (ISBN 0-06-090351-1, CN351, CN). Har-Row.

De Becker, Raymond. The Other Face of Love. 256p. 20.00x o.p. (ISBN 0-85435-353-4, Pub. by Spearman England). State Mutual Bk.

DeBeer, E. S. The Correspondence of John Locke, Vol. 7, Letters 2665-3286. (The Clarendon Edition of the Works of John Locke Ser.). 1982. 110.00x (ISBN 0-19-824564-5). Oxford U Pr.

De Beer, E. S., ed. see Locke, John.

DeBeer, E. S., ed. see Locke, John.

De Beer, Gavin. Archaeopteryx Lithographica: A Study Based on the British Museum Specimen. (Illus.). 68p. 1966. Repr. of 1954 ed. 23.75x (ISBN 0-565-00224-4, Pub. by Brit Mus Nat Hist England). Sabbot-Natural Hist Bks.

De Beer, Gavin R., ed. see Locke, John.

De Beer, Peter H., jt. auth. see Leonard, Robert J.

De Bekker, Leander J., jt. auth. see Vizetelly, Frank H.

Debelak, Marianne, et al. Creating Innovative Classroom Materials for Teaching Young Children. 321p. 1981. pap. text ed. 16.95 spiral bdg. (ISBN 0-15-515786-8, HC). HarBraceJ.

DeBell, Garrett. The New Environmental Handbook. LC 79-56911. 320p. (Orig.). 1980. pap. 5.95 (ISBN 0-913890-36-7). Brick Hse Pub.

De Bellecombe, L. Greyfie, jt. auth. see Roberts, Benjamin C.

DeBelleroche, J. Presynaptic Receptors: Mechanisms & Functions. 223p. 1982. 64.95X (ISBN 0-470-27345-3). Halsted Pr.

De Bellis, Jack, ed. Sidney Lanier, Henry Timrod & Paul Hamilton Hayne: A Reference Guide. 1978. lib. bdg. 25.00 (ISBN 0-8161-7967-0, Hall Reference). G K Hall.

DeBenedetti, Charles. The Origins of the Modern American Peace Movement, 1915-1929. LC 78-4994. (KTO Studies in American History). 1978. 25.00 (ISBN 0-527-22070-1). Kraus Intl.

De Benedetti, Edoardo. Visualizations in the Realm of Historical Predictions in the Light of the Kondratieff Theory. (Illus.). 131p. 1983. 87.45 (ISBN 0-86722-041-4). Inst Econ Pol.

DeBenedetti, Sergio. Nuclear Interactions. LC 73-92136. 660p. 1974. Repr. of 1964 ed. 36.50 o.p. (ISBN 0-88275-143-3). Krieger.

De Benedictis, Daniel J. The Complete Real Estate Adviser. Rev. ed. 1983. pap. 6.95 (ISBN 0-346-12578-2). Cornerstone.

De Benitez, Ana M. Prehispanic Cookbook (Cocina Prehispanica) 1960. pap. 12.50 (ISBN 0-911268-24-3). Rogers Bk.

Debenjak, D. Modern Dictionary Slovene-German-Slovene. 608p. (Slovene & Ger.). 1981. leatherette 14.95 (ISBN 0-686-97402-6, M-9702). French & Eur.

De Bertier de Sauvigny, G. & Pinkney, David H. History of France. rev. & enl. ed. Friguglietti, James, tr. LC 82-20978. (Illus.). 350p. 1983. text ed. 28.50 (ISBN 0-88273-426-1); pap. 17.95 (ISBN 0-88273-425-3). Forum Pr Il.

Debes, John L., jt. auth. see Fransecky, Roger B.

Debevoise, Neilson C. Political History of Parthia. LC 38-10721. (Illus.). 1968. Repr. of 1938 ed. lib. bdg. 19.00x (ISBN 0-8371-0374-6, DEPA). Greenwood.

Debicki, Andrew & Pupo-Walker, Enrique. Estudios Hispanoamericanos in honor of J. J. Arrom. (Studies in the Romance Languages & Literatures: No. 158). 291p. 1974. pap. 16.00x (ISBN 0-8078-9158-4). U of NC Pr.

Debicki, Andrew P. Poetry of Discovery: The Spanish Generation of 1956-1971. LC 82-40171. 240p. 1982. 19.50x (ISBN 0-8131-1461-6). U Pr of Ky.

De Bilio, Beth. Vendetta Con Brio. LC 72-9881. (Black Bat Mystery Ser). 1973. 5.95 o.p. (ISBN 0-672-51791-4). Bobbs.

Debiski, Andrew P. Damaso Alonso. (World Authors Ser.). 14.95 (ISBN 0-8057-2036-7, Twayne). G K Hall.

DeBlanc, H. J. & Sorenson, J. A. Noninvasive Brain Imaging: Computed Tomography & Radionuclides. LC 74-27242. (Illus.). 232p. 1975. 23.00 o.p. (ISBN 0-88416-137-4). Wright-PSG.

Deblander, Gabriel. The Fall of Icarus. LC 79-65865. (Children's Art Ser.). PLB 11.96 (ISBN 0-382-06329-5). Silver.

De Blasis, Celeste. The Proud Breed. LC 77-20282. 1978. 12.50 o.p. (ISBN 0-698-10870-1, Coward). Putnam Pub Group.

--The Tiger's Woman. 1981. 14.95 o.s.i. (ISBN 0-440-08819-4). Delacorte.

De Bles, Arthur. How to Distinguish the Saints in Art by Their Costumes, Symbols & Attributes. LC 68-18018. 1975. Repr. of 1925 ed. 63.00x (ISBN 0-8103-4125-5). Gale.

De Bles, Arthur see De Bles, Arthur.

DeBlij, Harm J. Wine: A Geographic Appreciation. LC 82-20648. (Illus.). 320p. 1983. text ed. 18.95 (ISBN 0-86598-091-8). Allanheld.

Deblij, Harm J., jt. auth. see Glassner, Martin I.

Deblij, Harm J., jt. auth. see Greenland, David E.

Deblock, N. J. Elsevier's Dictionary of Public Health. (Eng. & Fr. & Span. & Ital. & Dutch & Ger.). 1976. 47.00 (ISBN 0-444-41395-2). Elsevier.

De Blois, Pierre. Hystore Job: Adaptation en Vers Francaise du Compenonm in Job de Pierre de Blois. Bates, Robert C., ed. 1937. text ed. 14.50x (ISBN 0-686-83574-3). Elliots Bks.

Debnam, Betty. Alpha Betty's ABC Fun Book. (The Mini Page Fun Books). (Illus.). 24p. (gr. k-3). 1982. pap. 1.95 (ISBN 0-02-042810-3). Macmillan.

--Casey Count's Number Fun Book. (The Mini Page Fun Bks.). (Illus.). 24p. (gr. k-3). 1982. pap. 1.95 (ISBN 0-02-042830-8). Macmillan.

--The Mini Page Mighty Funny Party Book. LC 79-18687. (Alligator Original Paperback). (Illus.). 1979. pap. 5.95 (ISBN 0-8362-4208-4). Andrews & McMeel.

--The Mini Spy Mystery Fun Book. (The Mini Page Fun Books). (Illus.). 24p. (gr. k-3). 1982. pap. 1.95 (ISBN 0-02-042820-0). Macmillan.

--Peter Penquin's Puzzle-Le-Do Fun Book. (The Mini Page Fun Books). (Illus.). 24p. (gr. k-3). 1982. pap. 1.95 (ISBN 0-02-042850-2). Macmillan.

Debney, L. M., jt. ed. see Singleton, W. T.

Debo, Angie. History of the Indians of the United States. LC 73-108802. (Civilization of the American Indian Ser.: Vol. 106). (Orig.). 1970. 16.95 (ISBN 0-8061-0911-4). U of Okla Pr.

--Rise & Fall of the Choctaw Republic. 2nd ed. LC 69-7973. (Civilization of the American Indian Ser.: No. 6). (Illus.). 1934. pap. 8.95 (ISBN 0-8061-1247-6). U of Okla Pr.

Debo, Harvey V. & Diamant, Leo. Construction Superintendent's Job Guide. LC 79-17979. (Ser. on Practical Construction Guides). 1980. 29.95 (ISBN 0-471-20457-9, Pub. by Wiley-Interscience). Wiley.

De Board, Robert. The Psychoanalysis of Organizations: A Psychoanalytic Approach to Behaviour in Groups & Organizations. 158p. 1978. 18.00x (ISBN 0-422-76520-1, Pub. by Tavistock England); pap. 9.50x (ISBN 0-422-76530-9). Methuen Inc.

Deboeck, Guido & Kinsey, Bill. Managing Inofrmation for Rural Development: Lessons from Eastern Africa. (Working Paper: No. 379). vii, 70p. 1980. 5.00 (ISBN 0-686-36070-2, WP-0379). World Bank.

Deboeck, Guido & Ng, Ronald. Monitoring Rural Development in East Asia. (Working Paper: No. 439). 91p. 1980. 5.00 (ISBN 0-686-36072-9, WP-0439). World Bank.

De Boer, John J. Teaching Secondary English. LC 76-100155. Repr. of 1951 ed. lib. bdg. 18.00x (ISBN 0-8371-3426-9, DETS). Greenwood.

DeBoer, Marjorie. Crown of Desire. 704p. (Orig.). 1983. pap. 3.95 (ISBN 0-8439-1166-2, Leisure Bks). Dorchester Pub Co.

De Boer, P. A. H. Religieuze Aspecten van het Palestijnse Vraagstuk. x, 39p. 1982. pap. write for info. (ISBN 90-04-06727-2). E J Brill.

De Boer, S. P. & Driessen, E. J. Biographical Dictionary of Soviet Dissidents. 1982. lib. bdg. 165.00 (ISBN 90-247-2538-0, Pub. by Martinus Nijhoff Netherlands). Kluwer Boston.

De Boer, Theo. Foundations of Critical Psychology. Plantinga, Theodore, tr. 196p. 1982. text ed. 16.50x (ISBN 0-8207-0158-0). Duquesne.

DeBoer, Warren R. Archaeological Explorations in Northern Arizona, NA10754: A Sinagua Settlement of the Rio De Flag Phase. (Publications in Anthropology Ser.: No. 1). (Illus.). 1976. pap. 5.00 (ISBN 0-930146-08-5). Queens Coll Pr.

DeBold, Richard C., ed. see Barron, Frank.

DeBolt, Margaret W. Georgia Sampler Cookbook. Browder, Robyn, ed. LC 82-19841. (Regional Cookbook Ser.). (Illus.). 300p. (Orig.). 1983. pap. 8.95 (ISBN 0-89865-283-9). Donning Co.

--Savannah Sampler Cookbook. (Illus.). 298p. 1978. pap. 5.95 (ISBN 0-686-36729-4). Md Hist.

--Savannah Spectres. Freidman, Robert, ed. LC 82-23455. (Illus., Orig.). 1983. pap. 6.95 (ISBN 0-89865-201-4). Donning Co.

DeBolt, Margaret W. & Law, Emma. Savannah Sampler Cookbook. LC 78-1078. (Illus.). 1978. pap. 6.95 (ISBN 0-915442-49-3). Donning Co.

De Bonafous, Louis-Abel. Esprit des Livres Defendus, ou Antilogies Philosophiques, 4 vols. (Holbach & His Friends Ser). 2399p. (Fr.). 1974. Repr. of 1777 ed. lib. bdg. 587.50x o.p. (ISBN 0-8287-0104-0, 1501-4). Clearwater Pub.

Deboni, Franco, ed. Authentic Art Deco Jewelry Designs: 700 Illustrations. (Antiques Ser.). (Illus.). 96p. (Orig.). 1983. pap. 5.00 (ISBN 0-486-24346-X). Dover.

De Bono, E. Lateral Thinking. pap. 5.95i (ISBN 0-06-090325-2, CN325, CN). Har-Row.

De Bono, Edward. The Dog Exercising Machine. 1971. pap. 3.95 o.p. (ISBN 0-671-21092-0, Touchstone Bks). S&S.

--The Greatest Thinkers. LC 76-6034. (Illus.). 1976. 15.95 o.p. (ISBN 0-399-11762-8). Putnam Pub Group.

De Bono, Edward & De Saint-Arnand, Michael. The Learn to Think Coursebook. 2nd ed. 206p. 1982. 19.95 (ISBN 0-942580-01-X). E De Bono.

DeBono, Peter, jt. auth. see Bradbeer, Robin.

Deboo, Gordon J. & Burrous, Clifford N. Integrated Circuits & Semiconductor Devices: Theory & Application. 2nd ed. (Illus.). 1977. text ed. 26.95 (ISBN 0-07-016246-8, G); instructor's manual 3.00 (ISBN 0-07-016247-6). McGraw.

DeBoodt, M. & Gabriels, D. Assessment of Erosion. LC 80-41170. 563p. 1981. 81.00x (ISBN 0-471-27899-8, Pub. by Wiley-Interscience). Wiley.

De Boodt, M., ed. Assessment of Erosion. Gabriels, D. 400p. 1981. 79.00 o.p. (ISBN 0-8260-7790-0, Pub. by Wiley-Interscience). Wiley.

De Boor, C., jt. auth. see Conte, S. D.

De Borchgrave, Arnaud, jt. auth. see Moss, Robert.

Debord, G. Society of the Spectacle. 1977. 1.50 o.p. (ISBN 0-934868-07-7). Black & Red.

Debord, Pierre. Aspects Sociaux et economiques de la vie Religieuse dans l'Anatolie Greco-romaine. (Etudes Preliminaires aux Religions Orientale dans l'Empire Romain Ser.: Vol. 88). (Illus.). ix, 476p. 1982. write for info. E J Brill.

De Bourgoing, Jean, ed. see Franz Joseph, I.

De Brabander, M. see International Symposium on Microtubule Inhibitors, Belgium, 1975.

De Brabander, M. & De Mey, J., eds. Microtubules & Microtubule Inhibitors. (Janssen Research Foundation Ser.: Vol. 3). 1981. 92.00 (ISBN 0-444-80305-X). Elsevier.

De Braganca, Aquino. African Liberation Reader: Documents of the National Liberation Movements: Vol III The Strategy of Liberation. Wallerstein, Immanuel, ed. 244p. 1982. 26.95 (ISBN 0-86232-069-0, Pub. by Zed Pr England); pap. 10.50 (ISBN 0-86232-120-4, Pub. by Zed Pr England). Lawrence Hill.

--African Liberation Reader: Documents of the National Liberation Movements: Vol. II The National Liberation Movements. Wallerstein, Immanuel, ed. 244p. 1982. 26.95 (ISBN 0-86232-068-2, Pub. by Zed Pr England); pap. 10.50 (ISBN 0-86232-119-0, Pub. by Zed Pr England). Lawrence Hill.

De Brand, Roy E. Children's Sermons for Special Occasions. LC 82-72228. (Orig.). 1983. pap. 3.95 (ISBN 0-8054-4927-2). Broadman.

De Branganca, Aquino. African Liberation Reader: Documents of the National Liberation Movements: Vol. I The Anatomy of Colonialism. Wallerstein, Immanuel, ed. 244p. 1982. 26.95 (ISBN 0-86232-067-4, Pub. by Zed Pr England); pap. 10.50 (ISBN 0-86232-118-2, Pub. by Zed Pr England). Lawrence Hill.

Debray, Regis. Revolution in the Revolution? Armed Struggle & Political Struggle in Latin America. Ortiz, Bobbye, tr. from Fr., Span. LC 80-19409. 126p. 1980. Repr. of 1967 ed. lib. bdg. 19.25x (ISBN 0-313-22669-5, DERE). Greenwood.

Debreczeny, Paul. Nikolay Gogol & His Contemporary Critics. LC 66-18702. (Transactions Ser.: Vol. 56, Pt. 3). 1966. pap. 1.00 o.p. (ISBN 0-87169-563-4). Am Philos.

--The Other Pushkin: A Study of Alexander Pushkin's Prose Fiction. LC 81-85449. 392p. 1983. 32.50x (ISBN 0-8047-1143-7). Stanford U Pr.

--Temptations of the Past. 110p. 1982. pap. 6.50 (ISBN 0-938920-17-0). Hermitage MI.

Debreczeny, Paul, tr. see Pushkin, Alexander.

De Breffny, Brian. Irish Family Names: Arms, Origins & Locations. (Illus.). 190p. 1982. 19.95 (ISBN 0-393-01612-9). Norton.

--Irish Family Names: Arms, Origins, & Locations. 50.00x (ISBN 0-7171-1225-X). State Mutual Bk.

--The Synagogue. LC 78-7583. (Illus.). 1978. 24.95 o.p. (ISBN 0-02-530310-4). Macmillan.

De Bres, Pieter H. Religion in Atene: Religious Associations & the Urban Maori. 1971. text ed. 8.20x (ISBN 0-8248-0583-6). UH Pr.

Debreu, Gerard. Mathematical Economics: Twenty Papers of Gerard Debreu. LC 82-12875. (Econometric Society Monographs in Pure Theory). 320p. Date not set. price not set (ISBN 0-521-23736-X). Cambridge U Pr.

De Brie, G. A., ed. Bibliographia Philosophica, 1934-45, 2 vols. LC 51-5942. 1569p. 1954. Set. 100.00x (ISBN 0-8002-1231-2). Intl Pubns Serv.

De Brincat, Matthew see Brincat, Matthew De.

DeBrito, Ibrantino X. The American Civilization. LC 81-65252. 286p. 1982. 11.95 (ISBN 0-533-04963-6). Vantage.

DeBrizzi, John A. Ideology & the Rise of Labor Theory in America. LC 82-12024. (Contributions in Labor History Ser.: No. 14). 224p. 1983. lib. bdg. 29.95 (ISBN 0-313-23614-3, DID/). Greenwood.

De Brossard, Sebastien. Dictionaire de Musique, contenant une explication des Termes Grecs, Latins, Italiens, & Francois, les plus usitez dans la Musique. 2nd ed. (Dictionarium Musicum: Vol. 1). 1965. Repr. of 1705 ed. 62.50 o.s.i. (ISBN 90-6027-377-X, Pub. by Frits Knuf Netherlands); wrappers 47.50 o.s.i. (ISBN 90-6027-015-0, Pub. by Frits Knuf Netherlands). Pendragon NY.

De Bruin, A., ed. Biochemical Toxicology of Environmental Agents. 1976. 253.25 (ISBN 0-444-41455-X, North Holland). Elsevier.

DeBruin, Jerry. Young Scientists Explore Animals, Bk. 2. (gr. 4-7). 1982. 3.95 (ISBN 0-86653-073-8, GA 406). Good Apple.

--Young Scientists Explore the Moon, Bk. 3. (gr. 4-7). 1982. 3.95 (ISBN 0-86653-074-6, GA 407). Good Apple.

--Young Scientists Explore the World Around Them, Bk. 1. (gr. 4-7). 1982. 3.95 (ISBN 0-86653-072-X, GA 405). Good Apple.

De Brunhoff, Jean. Babar & Zephir. Haas, Merle, tr. (Illus.). (ps). 1942. 5.95 (ISBN 0-394-80579-8, BYR); PLB 5.99 (ISBN 0-394-90579-2). Random.

--Meet Babar & His Family. (Illus.). (ps-1). 1973. pap. 1.50 (ISBN 0-394-82682-5, BYR). Random.

--Travels of Babar. (Illus.). (ps). 1937. 5.95 (ISBN 0-394-80576-3, BYR); PLB 5.99 (ISBN 0-394-90576-8). Random.

De Brunhoff, Jean & De Brunhoff, Laurent. Babar's Anniversary Album. LC 81-5182. (Illus.). 144p. (ps-3). 1981. 12.95 (ISBN 0-394-84813-6); PLB 13.99 o.p. (ISBN 0-394-94813-0). Random.

De Brunhoff, Laurent. Babar & the Professor. new ed. (Illus.). (gr. k-2). 1966. 4.95 o.p. (ISBN 0-394-80590-9, BYR); PLB 5.99 (ISBN 0-394-90590-3). Random.

--Babar & the Wully-Wully. LC 75-8069. (Illus.). 36p. (gr. k-3). 1975. 4.95 o.p. (ISBN 0-394-83077-6, BYR); PLB 5.99 (ISBN 0-394-93077-0). Random.

--Babar Learns to Cook. LC 78-11769. (Picturebacks Ser.). (Illus.). (ps-1). 1979. PLB 4.99 (ISBN 0-394-94108-X, BYR); pap. 1.50 (ISBN 0-394-84108-5). Random.

--Babar Loses His Crown. LC 67-21918. (gr. k-3). 1967. 3.95 o.p. (ISBN 0-394-80045-1); PLB 5.99 (ISBN 0-394-90045-6). Beginner.

--Babar's Bookmobile. LC 73-22775. (Illus.). 24p. (ps-2). 1974. 5.95 (ISBN 0-394-82660-4, BYR). Random.

--Babar's Games. (Pop-Up Bks.: No. 13). (Illus.). (ps up). 1968. 3.95 o.p. (ISBN 0-394-81527-0). Random.

De Brunhoff, Laurent, jt. auth. see De Brunhoff, Jean.

De Brunoff, Laurent. Babar Saves the Day. LC 76-11684. (Picturebacks Ser.). (Illus.). (gr. 3-6). 1976. pap. 1.50 (ISBN 0-394-83341-4, BYR). Random.

DeBruyen, Robert L. Causing Others to Want Your Leadership. 184p. 1979. Repr. of 1976 ed. 12.95 (ISBN 0-686-36319-1). R L DeBruyen.

De Bruyn, Monica G. The Beaver Who Wouldn't Die. LC 75-2968. (Picture Bk). (Illus.). 32p. (gr. 2-4). 1975. 5.95 o.s.i. (ISBN 0-695-80586-X); lib. ed. 5.97 o.s.i. (ISBN 0-695-40586-1). Follett.

De Bruyn Kops, Mary, jt. auth. see Dean, Charles W.

De Bry, Theodore. Les Grands Voyages, 6 vols. (Ger.). 1982. Repr. of 1634 ed. lib. bdg. cancelled o.p. (ISBN 0-88354-215-3). Clearwater Pub.

Debs, Eugene V. Walls & Bars. LC 74-172574. (Criminology, Law Enforcement, & Social Problems Ser.: No. 161). (With intro & index added). 1973. Repr. of 1927 ed. 8.00x (ISBN 0-87585-161-4). Patterson Smith.

Debuer, Eddy & Debuer, Henriette. Seeing the Real Amsterdam. 1983. pap. cancelled (ISBN 0-8120-2243-2). Barron.

Debuer, Henriette, jt. auth. see Debuer, Eddy.

De Burger, James E., ed. Marriage Today: Problems, Issues & Alternatives. 750p. 1981. pap. 9.95 o.p. (ISBN 0-87073-169-6). Schenkman.

DeBurgh, W. G. Legacy of the Ancient World. 576p. 1971. Repr. 30.00x (ISBN 0-7121-1210-3, Pub. by Macdonald & Evans). State Mutual Bk.

De Burigny, Jean-Levesque. Examen Critique des Apologistes de la Religion Chretienne. (Holbach & His Friends Ser). 290p. (Fr.). 1974. Repr. lib. bdg. 77.50x o.p. (ISBN 0-8287-0153-9, 1533). Clearwater Pub.

Debus, A. G. Man & Nature in the Renaissance. LC 77-91085. (Cambridge History of Science Ser.). (Illus.). 1978. 24.95 (ISBN 0-521-21972-8); pap. 8.95 (ISBN 0-521-29328-6). Cambridge U Pr.

Debus, Allen G., jt. auth. see Rust, Brian A.

Debus, Michael. The Search for Identity, Conscience & Rebirth. 1982. pap. 2.50 (ISBN 0-903540-59-2). St George Bk Serv.

Debuskey, Matthew. The Chronically Ill Child & His Family. 224p. 1970. photocopy ed. spiral 16.75x (ISBN 0-398-00410-2). C C Thomas.

D'Eca, Raul & Greenfield, Eric V. Portuguese Grammar. 1979. pap. 4.76i (ISBN 0-06-460185-4, CO 185, COS). B&N NY.

De Cadenet, J. J., jt. auth. see Castro, R.

De Cadiz, Luis M., tr. see De Cesarea, Eusebio.

De Calan, Pierre. Cosmas or the Love of God. LC 80-508. 192p. 1980. 9.95 o.p. (ISBN 0-385-17059-9). Doubleday.

De Callieres. On the Manner of Negotiating with Princes. Whyte, A. F., tr. from Fr. LC 82-21800. 160p. 1983. pap. text ed. 8.75 (ISBN 0-8191-2923-2). U Pr of Amer.

DeCamp, L. S. Rogue Queen. pap. 1.50 o.p. (ISBN 0-451-08097-1, W8097, Sig). NAL.

De Camp, L. Sprague. The Bronze God of Rhodes. Stine, Hank, ed. (Illus.). 338p. (Orig.). 1983. lib. bdg. 12.95 (ISBN 0-89865-285-5); pap. 5.95 (ISBN 0-89865-284-7); limited ed. 35.00 (ISBN 0-89865-286-3). Donning Co.

--The Dragon of Ishtar Gate. Stine, Hank, ed. LC 82-5024. (Illus.). 218p. 1982. pap. 5.95 (ISBN 0-89865-196-4); 12.95 (ISBN 0-89865-227-8); ltd. ed. 35.00 (ISBN 0-89865-228-6). Donning Co.

--The Fringe of the Unknown. 205p. 1983. 16.95 (ISBN 0-87975-204-1). Prometheus Bks.

--The Great Fetish. LC 78-1239. (Science Fiction Ser.). 1978. 10.95 o.p. (ISBN 0-385-13139-9). Doubleday.

--The Hostage of Zir. 224p. 1982. pap. 2.50 (ISBN 0-441-34296-5, Pub. by Ace Science Fiction). Ace Bks.

--Lost Continents: The Atlantis Theme in History, Science, & Literature. 10.00 (ISBN 0-8446-0535-2). Peter Smith.

--The Prisoner of Zhamanak. 2.50 (ISBN 0-441-67937-4, Pub. by Ace Science Fiction). Ace Bks.

--The Unbeheaded King. 1983. 9.95 (ISBN 0-345-30773-9, Del Rey). Ballantine.

DeCamp, L. Sprague & Carter, Lin. Conan the Barbarian. 1982. pap. 2.50 (ISBN 0-686-97681-9). Bantam.

De Camp, L. Sprague & Howard, Robert E. Conan, the Ursurper. (Conan Ser.: No. 8). 192p. 1983. pap. 2.50 (ISBN 0-441-11602-7, Pub. by Ace Science Fiction). Ace Bks.

De Camp, L. Sprague, ed. see Howard, Robert E.

DeCampoli, Giuseppe. The Statics of Structural Components: Understanding the Basics of Structural Design. 256p. 1983. price not set (ISBN 0-471-87169-9, Pub. by Wiley-Interscience). Wiley.

De Campos, Deoclecio Redig. Michelangelo: The Last Judgment. 1979. 100.00 (ISBN 0-385-12299-3). Doubleday.

De Candolle, A. P. Collection de Memoires pour servir a l'Histoire du Regne Vegetal et plus specialement pour servir de complement a quelques parties du Prodromus Regni Vegetabilis. (Illus.). 1972. 100.00 (ISBN 3-7682-0728-5). Lubrecht & Cramer.

Decanio, Stephen J. Agriculture in the Postbellum South: The Economics of Production & Supply. 1975. 25.00x (ISBN 0-262-04047-6). MIT Pr.

DeCarava, Roy. Roy DeCarava: Photographs. Alinder, James, ed. LC 81-68286. (Illus.). 192p. 1982. 40.00 (ISBN 0-933286-26-0); Deluxe ed. 750.00 (ISBN 0-933286-29-5). Friends Photography.

Decareau, Robert V., jt. auth. see Goldblith, Samuel A.

DeCarle, Don. Practical Clock Repairing. 18.95x (ISBN 0-685-22074-5). Wehman.

De Carli, Franco. The World of Fish. Richardson, Jean, tr. LC 79-1436. (Abbeville Press Encyclopedia of Natural Science). (Illus.). 1979. 13.95 (ISBN 0-89659-035-6); pap. 7.95 o. p. (ISBN 0-89659-029-1). Abbeville Pr.

DeCarlo, Thomas. Executive's Handbook of Balanced Physical Fitness: A Guide to a Personalized Exercise Program. (Illus.). 1975. pap. 4.95 o.s.i. (ISBN 0-8096-1900-8, Assn Pr). Follett.

De Carvalho, Maria C. Karl R. Poppers Philosophie der Wissenschaftlichen und der Vorwissenschaft-Lichen Erfahrung. 203p. (Ger.). 1982. write for info. (ISBN 3-8204-7206-1). P Lang Pubs.

De Casas, Celso A. Pelon Drops Out. LC 79-13385. (Illus.). 1979. pap. 6.00 (ISBN 0-89229-006-4). Tonatiuh-Quinto Sol Intl.

De Caso, Jacques, jt. auth. see Pratt, James N.

De Cassagnac, Granier. De l'Emancipation des Esclaves, Lettres a M. De Lamartine. (Slave Trade in France, 1744-1848, Ser.). 94p. (Fr.). 1974. Repr. of 1840 ed. lib. bdg. 34.00x o.p. (ISBN 0-8287-0393-0, TN131). Clearwater Pub.

De Castille, Vernon. Health & Physical Well Being: The Essential Knowledge of the Basic Rules on Being Healthy, Staying Healthy & Live a Long & Happy Life Which Everyone, but Absolutely Everyone Ought to Possess for the Benefit & Success of His Existence. (The Essential Knowledge Series Books). (Illus.). 1978. plastic spiral bdg. 27.35 o.p. (ISBN 0-89266-121-6). Am Classical Coll Pr.

--How to Gain Tranquillity & the Pleasures of Internal Contentment & Emotional Balance Without the Taking of Pills. (Illus.). 1977. 36.00 (ISBN 0-89266-048-1). Am Classical Coll Pr.

De Castillejo, Irene Claremont see Claremont De Castillejo, Irene.

Decatur, Stephen. The Private Affairs of George Washington. LC 77-86596. (American Scene Ser). 1969. Repr. of 1933 ed. 45.00 (ISBN 0-306-71416-7). Da Capo.

De Cauhe, Joana Raspall see Raspall de Cauhe, Joana, et al.

Decaux, M., jt. auth. see Dostert, L.

De Caux, Salomon. Les Raisons des forces mouvantes, avec diverses machines tant utiles que plaisantes. (Bibliotheca Organologica Ser.: Vol. 21). 1973. Repr. of 1615 ed. 75.00 o.s.i. (ISBN 90-6027-197-1, Pub. by Frits Knuf Netherlands). Pendragon NY.

Decazes, Daisy & Banowsky, William S. Western Oklahoma: A Photographic Essay. (Illus.). 160p. (YA) 1982. 30.00 (ISBN 0-8061-1821-0). U of Okla Pr.

De Cellier, Florent. Histoire des Classes Ouvrieres en France depuis la Conquete de la Gaule jusqu'a Nos Jours. (Conditions of the 19th Century French Working Class Ser.). 486p. (Fr.). 1974. Repr. of 1859 ed. lib. bdg. 121.00 o.p. (ISBN 0-8287-0252-7, 1004). Clearwater Pub.

De Cervantes, Miguel. Don Quixote. unabr. ed. Starkie, Walter, tr. (Orig.). 1957. pap. 4.50 (ISBN 0-451-51682-6, CE1682, Sig Classics). NAL.

De Cervantes, Miguel see Cervantes, Miguel De.

DE Cervera, Alejo. Statutes of Limitations in American Conflicts of Law. LC 65-23494. 189p. 1966. 12.50 (ISBN 0-379-00259-0). Oceana.

De Cesarea, Eusebio. Historia Eclesiastica De Eusebio. De Cadiz, Luis M., tr. (Biblioteca Mundo Hispano de Obras Clasicas Ser.). (Span.). Date not set. pap. price not set (ISBN 0-311-15042-X, Edit Mundo). Casa Bautista.

De Chamblain De Marivaux, Pierre C. Le Paysan Parvenu: Or, the Fortunate Peasant. LC 78-60836. (Novel 1720-1805 Ser.: Vol. 2). 1979. lib. bdg. 45.00 o.s.i. (ISBN 0-8240-3651-4); lib. bdg. 31.00 ea. o.s.i. Garland Pub.

Dechant, Emarld V. Psychology in Teaching Reading. 2nd ed. 1977. text ed. 25.95 (ISBN 0-13-736686-8). P-H.

Dechant, Emerald. Diagnosis & Remediation of Reading Disability. (Illus.). 512p. 1981. text ed. 23.95 (ISBN 0-13-208454-6). P-H.

--How to Be Happily Married. LC 74-38983. 120p. 1972. pap. 1.65 o.p. (ISBN 0-8189-0236-1). Alba.

Dechant, Emerald V. Improving the Teaching of Reading. 3rd ed. (Illus.). 512p. 1982. reference 23.95 (ISBN 0-13-453423-9). P-H.

De Chardin, Pierre Teilhard see Teilhard De Chardin, Pierre.

DeCharms, R., et al. Enhancing Motivation: A Change Project in the Classrooms. LC 75-38701. (Social Relations Ser.). 279p. 1976. 15.95x o.p. (ISBN 0-470-01392-3). Halsted Pr.

De Chasca, Edmund. The Poem of The Cid. LC 75-30597. (World Authors Ser.,: Spain: No.378). 1976. lib. bdg. 12.50 o.p. (ISBN 0-8057-6194-2, Twayne). G K Hall.

De Chateaubriand, Francois R. The Martyrs. Wight, O. W., ed. & tr. from Fr. LC 76-15294. 451p. 1976. Repr. of 1859 ed. 35.00x (ISBN 0-86527-275-1). Fertig.

De Chateaubriand, Francois-Rene see Chateaubriand, Francois-Rene de.

De Chazeau, Melvin G. & Kahn, Alfred E. Integration & Competition in the Petroleum Industry. (Petroleum Monograph: Vol. 3). xviii, 598p. Repr. of 1959 ed. lib. bdg. 47.50x (ISBN 0-87991-149-2). Porcupine Pr.

Dechert, Charles R., ed. Social Impact of Cybernetics. 1967. pap. 1.95 o.p. (ISBN 0-671-20146-8, Touchstone Bks). S&S.

Dechesne, B. H. & Pons, C. Sexuality & Handicap: Problems of the Motor Handicapped. (Illus.). 264p. 1983. pap. 29.75x (ISBN 0-398-04746-4). C C Thomas.

De Chiara, Joseph. Handbook of Architectural Details for Commercial Buildings. 512p. 1980. 39.50 (ISBN 0-07-016215-8, P&RB). McGraw.

--Site Planning Standards. (Illus.). 1977. 36.50 (ISBN 0-07-016216-6, P&RB). McGraw.

De Chiara, Joseph & Callender, John. Time-Saver Standards for Building Types. 2nd ed. 1088p. 1980. 59.50 (ISBN 0-07-016265-4, P&RB). McGraw.

DeChow, Georgeen H. & Rines, Alice R. Preparing the Associate Degree Graduate. 71p. 1977. 5.50 (ISBN 0-686-38275-7, 23-1661). Natl League Nurse.

DeChristoforo, R. J. Woodworking Techniques: Joints & Their Applications. (Illus.). 1979. ref.ed. 18.95 (ISBN 0-8359-8785-X). Reston.

Deci, Edward L. The Psychology of Self-Determination. LC 80-8373. 1980. 22.95 (ISBN 0-669-04045-2). Lexington Bks.

Deci, Edward L., jt. auth. see Gilmer, B. V.

Deci, Edward L., et al. Readings in Industrial & Organizational Psychology. 3rd ed. Orig. Title: Readings in Industrial & Business Psychology. (Illus.). 544p. 1971. pap. text ed. 13.95 o.p. (ISBN 0-07-016206-9, C). McGraw.

DeCicco, Paul R. Life Safety Considerations in Atrium Buildings. Date not set. 4.35 (ISBN 0-686-37667-6, TR 82-3). Society Fire Protect.

Decius, J. C. & Hexter, R. M. Molecular Vibrations in Crystals. 1977. 47.50 (ISBN 0-07-016227-1). McGraw.

De Civrieux, Marc. Watunna: An Orinoco Creation Cycle. Guss, David, ed. LC 80-82440. (Illus.). 216p. 1980. 20.00 (ISBN 0-86547-002-2); pap. 12.50 (ISBN 0-86547-003-0). N Point Pr.

Deck, E., jt. auth. see Folta, J.

Deckard, Barbara S. The Women's Movement: Political, Socioeconomic, & Psychological Issues. 2nd ed. 1979. pap. text ed. 16.95 scp o.p. (ISBN 0-06-041612-2, HarpC). Har-Row.

--The Women's Movement: Political, Socioeconomic, & Psychological Issues. 3rd ed. 528p. 1983. pap. text ed. 18.50 scp (ISBN 0-06-041615-7, HarpC). Har-Row.

Decker & Backmund. Pediatric Neuroradiology. 1975. 75.95 o.p. (ISBN 0-407-00102-6). Butterworth.

Decker, Anne, et al. A Handbook on Open Admissions. LC 76-7463. (Special Studies Higher Education Ser). 1976. lib. bdg. 17.75 o.p. (ISBN 0-89158-044-1). Westview.

Decker, Cecil A. & Decker, John R. Planning & Administering Early Childhood Programs. 2nd ed. (Elementary Education Ser.: No. C22). 480p. 1980. pap. text ed. 18.95 (ISBN 0-675-08160-2). Merrill.

Decker, Clarence R. The Victorian Conscience. LC 77-8021. 1977. Repr. of 1952 ed. lib. bdg. 19.00x (ISBN 0-8371-9684-1, DEVC). Greenwood.

Decker, David L. & Shichor, David. Urban Structure & Victimization. LC 79-1865. 128p. 1982. 16.95x (ISBN 0-669-02951-3). Lexington Bks.

Decker, David R. & Duran, Ignacio. The Political, Economic & Labor Climate in Colombia. (Multinational Industrial Relations Ser.: No. 4 Latin American Studies (4C-Columbia)). 1982. pap. 18.00 (ISBN 0-89546-025-4). Indus Res Unit-Wharton.

Decker, Douglas, jt. auth. see Mackie, Dustin.

Decker, Fred W. Science Travel Guide: The Guide to Technological Expositions, Museums, Landmarks, & Science Originals. 1971. pap. 1.95X (ISBN 0-88246-017-X). Oreg St U Bkstrs.

Decker, Harold A. & Herford, Julius, eds. Choral Conducting: A Symposium. LC 72-94347. (Illus.). 320p. 1973. 23.95 (ISBN 0-13-133355-0). P-H.

Decker, John R., jt. auth. see Decker, Cecil A.

Decker, Larry, ed. Volunteer Coordinator Guide. 61p. 1961. pap. 3.00 (ISBN 0-686-84033-X). U OR Ctr Leisure.

Decker, Larry E., jt. ed. see Schoeny, Donna H.

Decker, Marjorie A. The Christian Mother Goose Baby Album in Rhyme. (Illus.). 30p. 1982. lib. bdg. 11.95 (ISBN 0-933724-12-8). Decker Pr Inc.

--Christian Mother Goose: Benjamin Bumblebee's Little Color-Grams. (Little Color-Grams Ser.). (Illus.). 96p. (gr. k-4). 1981. pap. 2.50 (ISBN 0-933724-09-8). Decker Pr Inc.

--The Christian Mother Goose Book. (Illus.). 112p. 1980. 10.95 o.p. (ISBN 0-8007-1195-5). Revell.

--Christian Mother Goose: Brother Rabbit's Little Color-Grams. (Illus.). 96p. (gr. k-4). 1981. pap. 2.50 (ISBN 0-933724-07-1). Decker Pr Inc.

--Christian Mother Goose: Charlie Cricket's Little Color-Grams. (Little Color-Grams Ser.). (Illus.). 96p. (gr. k-4). 1981. pap. 2.50 (ISBN 0-933724-08-X). Decker Pr Inc.

--Christian Mother Goose: Color-Me Keepsakes. (Color-Me Ser.). (Illus.). 64p. (gr. k-4). 1981. pap. 1.75 (ISBN 0-933724-05-5). Decker Pr Inc.

--Christian Mother Goose: Color-Me Praises. (Color-Me Ser). (Illus.). 64p. 1981. pap. 1.75 (ISBN 0-933724-03-9). Decker Pr Inc.

--Christian Mother Goose: Color-Me Rhymes No. 1. (Color-Me Ser.). (Illus.). 64p. (gr. k-4). 1981. pap. 1.75 (ISBN 0-933724-02-0). Decker Pr Inc.

--Christian Mother Goose: Grandpa Mole's Little Color-Grams. (Little Color-Grams Ser.). (Illus.). 96p. (gr. k-4). 1981. pap. 2.50 (ISBN 0-933724-06-3). Decker Pr Inc.

--The Christian Mother Goose Treasury. LC 80-69167. (Christian Mother Goose Ser.: Vol. II). (Illus.). 112p. (gr. k-4). 1980. PLB 10.95 (ISBN 0-933724-01-2). Decker Pr Inc.

--The Christian Mother Goose Treasury. (Illus.). 112p. 1980. 10.95 o.p. (ISBN 0-8007-1196-3). Revell.

Decker, Randall E. Patterns of Exposition Eight. 8th ed. 1982. pap. text ed. 9.95 (ISBN 0-316-17924-8); tchrs' manual avail. (ISBN 0-316-17925-6). Little.

--Patterns of Exposition Seven. 388p. 1980. pap. text ed. 9.95 (ISBN 0-316-17921-3); instructor's manual free (ISBN 0-316-17922-1). Little.

Decker, Raymond F., ed. Source Book on Maraging Steels. 1979. 42.00 o.p. (ISBN 0-87170-079-4). ASM.

Decker, Robert. Agenda of Psychotherapy. 48p. 1980. softcover 4.75 o.p. (ISBN 0-932930-20-4). Pilgrimage Inc.

Decker, Robert J. Effective Psychotherapy: The Silent Dialog. 76p. 1982. softcover 5.95 (ISBN 0-932930-51-4). Pilgrimage Inc.

Deckert, Frank. Big Bend: Three Steps to the Sky. Pearson, John R., ed. (Illus.). 40p. (Orig.). 1981. pap. 3.95 (ISBN 0-686-38923-9). Big Bend.

De Claremont, Lewis. Ancient Book of Formulas. 3.95. Wehman.

--Ancients Book of Magic. 3.95 o.p. Wehman.

--Seven Keys to Power. 3.95 (ISBN 0-685-22105-9). Wehman.

Declareuil, Joseph. Rome, the Law-Giver. Parker, Edward A., tr. LC 73-98752. Repr. of 1927 ed. lib. bdg. 20.75x (ISBN 0-8371-2796-3, DERL). Greenwood.

De Clark, Catalina, tr. see Dana, H. E. & Mantey, J. R.

De Clayat, E. Steinlen: The Graphic Work. (Illus.). 248p. (Fr.). 1983. Repr. of 1913 ed. 95.00 (ISBN 0-915346-71-0). A Wofsy Fine Arts.

De Clemente, Elizabeth M., jt. auth. see Van Ness, Bethann.

DeClerck, Fred & Vanhoutte, Paul M., eds. Five-Hydroxytryptamine in Peripheral Reactions. 224p. 1982. text ed. 37.00 (ISBN 0-89004-772-3). Raven.

De C. L. Huffman, Claire. Montale & the Occasions of Poetry. LC 82-61368. 356p. 1983. 25.00x (ISBN 0-691-06562-4). Princeton U Pr.

DeCombray, Richard. Goodbye Europe. LC 82-45122. 216p. 1983. 13.95 (ISBN 0-385-18097-7). Doubleday.

De Condillac, Etienne Bonnot. The Major Philosophical Works of Etienne Bonnot de Condillac. Philip, Franklin & Lane, Harlan, trs. from Fr. 448p. 1982. text ed. 36.00x (ISBN 0-89859-181-3). L Erlbaum Assocs.

Deconninck, G. Introduction to Radioanalytical Physics. (Nuclear Methods Monograph: Vol. 1). 1978. 53.25 (ISBN 0-444-99796-2). Elsevier.

De Coppens, Peter R. Ideal Man in Classical Sociology: The Views of Comte, Durkheim, Pareto, & Weber. LC 75-27174. 272p. 1976. 16.95x (ISBN 0-271-01206-4). Pa St U Pr.

--The Nature & Use of Ritual. 1977. pap. text ed. 8.50 (ISBN 0-8191-0341-1). U Pr of Amer.

--Spiritual Perspective II: The Spiritual Dimension & Implications of Love, Sex, & Marriage. LC 80-6302. 175p. (Orig.). 1981. pap. text ed. 9.50 (ISBN 0-8191-1512-6). U Pr of Amer.

De Coppens Peter, Roche see Roche De Coppens, Peter.

De Cordemoy, Geraud see Cordemoy, Geraud de.

De Cornulier, Benoit. Meaning Detatchment. (Pragmatics & Beyond Ser.). vi, 124p. 1980. pap. 14.00 (ISBN 90-272-2502-8, 7). Benjamins North Am.

DeCoster, Cyrus. Juan Valera. (World Authors Ser.). 192p. 1974. lib. bdg. 15.95 (ISBN 0-8057-2919-4, Twayne). G K Hall.

DeCoster, Cyrus C. Pedro Antonio de Alarcon. (World Authors Ser.). 1979. lib. bdg. 15.95 (ISBN 0-8057-6391-0, Twayne). G K Hall.

Decoster, D. T., et al. Accounting for Managerial Decision Making. 2nd ed. LC 77-15785. (Accounting & Information Systems Ser.). 438p. 1978. pap. text ed. 22.95 (ISBN 0-471-02204-7). Wiley.

DeCoster, David A., jt. ed. see Brown, Robert D.

Decoteau, A. E. The Handbook of Amazon Parrots. (Illus.). 221p. 1980. 14.95 (ISBN 0-87666-892-9, H-1025). TFH Pubns.

--Handbook of Cockatoos. (Illus.). 159p. 1981. 19.95 (ISBN 0-87666-826-0, H-1030). TFH Pubns.

--The Handbook of Macaws. (Illus.). 128p. 1982. 19.95 (ISBN 0-87666-844-9, H-1044). TFH Pubns.

De Coulon, F., jt. ed. see Kunt, M.

De Coursey, R. The Human Organism. 5th ed. 1980. text ed. 24.95 (ISBN 0-07-016275-1); tchr's manual avail. (ISBN 0-07-016277-8). McGraw.

DeCoursey, Russell M. The Human Organism. 4th ed. (Illus.). 672p. 1974. text ed. 24.95 (ISBN 0-07-016234-4, C). McGraw.

--Laboratory Manual of Human Anatomy & Physiology. 2nd ed. (Illus.). 256p. 1974. pap. text ed. 12.95 (ISBN 0-07-016239-5, C). McGraw.

De Courtivron, Isabelle, jt. ed. see Marks, Elaine.

De Coussemaker, C. E. Catalogue des Livres, Manuscripts et Instruments de Musique. (Auction Catalogues of Music Ser.: Vol. 4). 1976. Repr. of 1877 ed. wrappers 45.00 o.s.i. (ISBN 90-6027-198-X, Pub. by Frits Knuf Netherlands). Pendragon NY.

De Craemer, Willy. The Jamaa & the Church: A Bantu Catholic Movement in Zaire. (Oxford Studies in African Affairs). 1977. 49.50x (ISBN 0-19-822708-6). Oxford U Pr.

De Crane, Ray. Cut Your Own Taxes & Save Nineteen Eighty-One. 80p. 1980. pap. 1.50 o.p. (ISBN 0-915106-18-3). World Almanac.

Decrespigny, R. C. China: The Land & Its People. 1973. pap. 8.95 (ISBN 0-312-13265-4). St Martin.

De Crespigny, R. R. China This Century. LC 75-10977. 300p. 1975. text ed. 19.95 o.p. (ISBN 0-312-13335-9). St Martin.

DeCristoforo, R. J. Concrete & Masonry: Techniques & Design. (Illus.). 384p. 1975. 18.95 (ISBN 0-87909-149-5). Reston.

De Cristoforo, R. J. How to Build Your Own Furniture. (Illus.). 176p. pap. 3.50 o.p. (ISBN 0-06-463352-7, EH 352, EH). B&N NY.

Decroly, J. C., et al. Parametric Amplifiers. 442p. 1973. 59.95x o.s.i. (ISBN 0-470-20065-0). Halsted Pr.

Decroux, Etienne. Words on Mime. 208p. Date not set. text ed. 15.95x (ISBN 0-89676-045-6); pap. 12.95x (ISBN 0-89676-046-4). Drama Bk. Postponed.

DeCrow, Karen, jt. auth. see Seidenberg, Robert.

Decter, Midge. Liberal Parents, Radical Children. LC 75-7529. 1975. 7.95 o.p. (ISBN 0-698-10675-X, Coward). Putnam Pub Group.

De Czege, A. Wass. Eliza & the House that Jack Built. LC 82-71386. 1982. 15.00 (ISBN 0-87934-027-4). Danubian.

De Datta, Surajit K. Principles & Practices of Rice Production. LC 80-28941. 618p. 1981. 44.95x (ISBN 0-471-08074-8, Pub. by Wiley-Interscience). Wiley.

Dede, Vivian. Mr. Dumb Jokes. 1982. pap. 1.95 (ISBN 0-570-08407-5, 39-1082). Concordia.

--The Stranger at Jacob's Well. (Arch Bk: No. 20). 1983. pap. 0.89 (ISBN 0-570-06164-4). Concordia.

De Deckker, P. T., ed. see Pritchard, George.

De Deiros, Norma H. C. Dramatizaciones Infantiles Para Dias Especiales. 1981. pap. 2.50 (ISBN 0-311-07606-8). Casa Bautista.

Dedekind, R., jt. auth. see Lejeune-Dirichlet, P. G.

De Diego, Fernando. La Ingenia Hidalgo Don Quijote De la Mancha, De Cervantes. (Illus.). 1977. 35.00x (ISBN 84-400-3582-9). Esperanto League North Am.

De Dietrich, Suzanne. God's Unfolding Purpose: A Guide to the Study of the Bible. Brown, Robert M., tr. LC 60-6169. 1960. 6.95 (ISBN 0-664-20296-9). Westminster.

--The Witnessing Community: The Biblical Record of God's Purpose. LC 58-5020. 1978. pap. 3.95 (ISBN 0-664-24199-9). Westminster.

Dedijer, V., et al. History of Yugoslavia. 1974. 8.95 (ISBN 0-07-016235-2, P&RB). McGraw.

De Dillmont, Therese. The Complete DMC Encyclopedia of Needlework. (Illus.). 700p. Date not set. pap. 9.95 (ISBN 0-685-20554-1). Toggitt.

Dedmond, Emmett. Fabulous Chicago. rev. ed. LC 81-66024. (Illus.). 480p. 1983. pap. 9.95 (ISBN 0-689-70639-1, 288). Atheneum.

Dedmond, Francis B. Sylvester Judd. (United States Authors Ser.). 1980. lib. bdg. 13.95 (ISBN 0-8057-7305-3, Twayne). G K Hall.

Dedner, Burghard. Carl Sternheim. (Twayne's World Authors Ser.). 1982. lib. bdg. 18.95 (ISBN 0-8057-6518-2, Twayne). G K Hall.

De Dombal, E. T., ed. see IFIP TC Four Working Conference.

Deduck, Patricia A. Realism, Reality & the Fictional Theory of Alain Robbe-Grillet & Anais Nin. LC 82-13549. 118p. 1982. lib. bdg. 19.00 (ISBN 0-8191-2719-1); pap. text ed. 8.25 (ISBN 0-8191-2720-5). U Pr of Amer.

Dee, Elaine E., jt. auth. see Zocchi, Giusseppe.

Dee, John. The Hieroglyphic Monad. 1975. 9.95 (ISBN 0-87728-276-5). Weiser.

Dee, Nerys. Fortune-Telling by Playing Cards: A New Guide to the Ancient Art of Cartomancy. 160p. 1982. pap. 7.95 (ISBN 0-686-83073-3). Newcastle Pub.

Deecke, L., jt. ed. see Kornhuber, H. H.

Deedat, A. Is Bible God's Word? 1981. 2.75 (ISBN 0-686-97857-9). Kazi Pubns.

Deedy, John. The New Nuns. LC 82-11895. 160p. (Orig.). 1982. pap. 7.95 (ISBN 0-8190-0649-1, FC143). Fides Claretian.

Deegan, James, Jr. Priest as Manager. 1969. 7.50 o.p. (ISBN 0-685-07660-1, 80166). Glencoe.

Deegan, Paul. Catfish Hunter. (Sports Superstars Ser.). (Illus.). (gr. 3-9). 1979. PLB 6.95 o.p. (ISBN 0-87191-720-3); pap. 3.25 (ISBN 0-89812-159-0). Creative Ed.

Deegan, Paul J. Almost a Champion. LC 74-14517. (Dan Murphy Sports Ser). 40p. (gr. 3-6). 1975. PLB 6.95 (ISBN 0-87191-402-6); pap. 3.25 (ISBN 0-89812-151-5). Creative Ed.

--Close but Not Quite. LC 74-16334. (Dan Murphy Sports Ser.). 40p. (gr. 3-6). 1975. PLB 6.95 (ISBN 0-87191-405-0); pap. 3.25 (ISBN 0-89812-152-3). Creative Ed.

--Dan Moves up. LC 74-17069. (Dan Murphy Sports Ser.). 40p. (gr. 3-6). 1975. PLB 6.95 (ISBN 0-87191-406-9); pap. 3.25 (ISBN 0-89812-153-1). Creative Ed.

--Important Decision. LC 74-14514. (Dan Murphy Sports Ser.). (Illus.). 40p. (gr. 3-6). 1975. PLB 6.95 (ISBN 0-87191-401-8); pap. 3.25 (ISBN 0-89812-154-X). Creative Ed.

--Team Manager. LC 74-14515. (Dan Murphy Sports Ser.). (Illus.). 40p. (gr. 3-6). 1974. PLB 6.95 (ISBN 0-87191-403-4); pap. 3.25 (ISBN 0-89812-155-8). Creative Ed.

--Tournaments. LC 74-149436. (Dan Murphy Sports Ser.). 40p. (gr. 3-6). 1975. PLB 6.95 (ISBN 0-87191-404-2); pap. 3.25 (ISBN 0-89812-156-6). Creative Ed.

Deeken, Alfons. La Vejez: Growing Old & How to Cope with It. (Span.). pap. 1.25 o.p. (ISBN 0-686-79563-6). Paulist Pr.

Deeley, Lilla. Favorite Hungarian Recipes. 88p. 1972. pap. 2.75 (ISBN 0-486-22846-0). Dover.

Deeley, T. J. Computers in Radiotherapy: Clinical Aspects. (Computers in Medicine Ser.). (Illus.). 120p. 1972. 14.95 o.p. (ISBN 0-407-51600-X). Butterworth.

--Needle Biopsy. 1974. 13.50 o.p. (ISBN 0-407-32670-7). Butterworth.

Deeley, T. J., ed. Modern Radiotherapy & Oncology Series. Incl. Carcinoma of the Bronchus. (Illus.). 370p. 1971. 26.95 o.p. (ISBN 0-407-27540-1); Central Nervous System Tumors. 1974. 26.95 o.p. (ISBN 0-407-27590-8); Gynaecological Cancer. (Illus.). 336p. 1971. 19.95 o.p. (ISBN 0-407-27740-4); Malignant Diseases in Children. 1974. 37.75 o.p. (ISBN 0-407-27870-2). Butterworth.

--Topical Reviews in Radiotherapy & Oncology, Vol. 1. (Topical Reviews Ser.). (Illus.). 288p. 1980. text ed. 32.50 (ISBN 0-7236-0538-6). Wright-PSG.

Deeley, Thomas J. Principles of Radiation Therapy. 160p. 1976. 17.95 o.p. (ISBN 0-407-00030-5). Butterworth.

Deeley, Thomas J., ed. Modern Trends in Radiotherapy-Two. (Illus.). 1972. 29.95 o.p. (ISBN 0-407-31501-2). Butterworth.

--Topical Reviews in Radiotherapy & Oncology, Vol. 2. (Illus.). 264p. 1982. text ed. 37.50 (ISBN 0-7236-0616-1). Wright-PSG.

Deely, John. Introducing Semiotic: Its History & Doctrine. LC 82-47782. (Advances in Semiotics Ser.; Midland Bks.: Bk. 287). 264p. (Orig.). 1982. 22.50x (ISBN 0-253-33080-7); pap. 7.95 (ISBN 0-253-20287-6). Ind U Pr.

Deely, John N. & Nogar, Raymond J. The Problem of Evolution: A Study of the Philosophical Repercussions of Evolutionary Science. LC 78-163701. 1973. text ed. 9.50 (ISBN 0-390-25998-5). Hackett Pub.

Deem, Bill, jt. auth. see Muchow, Kenneth.

Deem, Bill, et al. Digital Computer Circuits & Concepts. 3rd ed. (Illus.). 1980. text ed. 22.95 (ISBN 0-8359-1299-X); free instrs'. manual (ISBN 0-8359-1300-7). Reston.

Deem, William R. Electronics Math. (Illus.). 576p. 1981. text ed. 21.95 (ISBN 0-13-252304-3). P-H.

Deeming, Bill, jt. auth. see Deeming, Sue.

Deeming, Sue & Deeming, Bill. Canning. (Illus.). 192p. 1983. pap. 7.95 (ISBN 0-89586-185-2). H P Bks.

Deems, Edward M., ed. Holy-Days & Holidays: A Treasury of Historical Material, Sermons in Full & in Brief, Suggestive Thoughts & Poetry, Relating to Holy Days & Holidays. LC 68-17940. 1968. Repr. of 1902 ed. 57.00x (ISBN 0-8103-3352-X). Gale.

Deems, Eugene F., Jr. & Pursley, Duane. North American Furbearers: A Contemporary Reference. (Illus.). 217p. 1983. text ed. 14.00 (ISBN 0-932108-08-3). Intl Assn Fish & Wildlife.

Deen. International Conference on Databases Nineteen-Eighty. 1980. 48.00 o.p. (ISBN 0-85501-495-4). Wiley.

Deen, Edith. Bible's Legacy for Womanhood. 1976. pap. write for info (ISBN 0-515-09586-9). Jove Pubns.

Deen, Leonard W. Conversing in Paradise: Poetic Genius & Identity-as-Community in Blake's Los. LC 82-20307. 288p. 1983. text ed. 23.00 (ISBN 0-8262-0396-5). U of Mo Pr.

Deen, Rosemary, jt. auth. see Ponsot, Marie.

Deen, S. M. & Hammersley, P., eds. Proceedings: International Conference on Data Bases, University of Aberdeen, July 1980. (British Computer Society Workshop Ser.). 288p. 1980. 66.95 (ISBN 0-471-25658-7, Wiley Heyden). Wiley.

Deeny, Kevin J., jt. auth. see Junkins, David R.

Deep, Samuel D. & Brincklow, William D. Introduction to Business: A Systems Approach. (Illus.). 576p. 1974. ref. ed. 24.95 o.p. (ISBN 0-13-478529-0); study guide 4.95 o.p. (ISBN 0-13-478552-5). P-H.

Deepak, A., jt. auth. see Ruhnke, L. H.

Deepak, Adarsh & Rao, K. R. Remote Sensing Applications for Rice Production. (Illus.). Date not set. price not set (ISBN 0-937194-03-4). Spectrum Pr.

Deepak, Adarsh, ed. Atmospheric Aerosols: Their Formation, Optical Properties, & Effects. LC 81-51934. (Illus.). 1982. 47.50 (ISBN 0-937194-01-8). Spectrum Pr.

Deepak, Adarsh, jt. ed. see Singh, Jag J.

Deer, W. A., et al. Rock Forming Minerals: Vol. 1A, Orthosilicates. 2nd ed. 900p. 1981. 149.95 (ISBN 0-470-26633-3). Halsted Pr.

Deere & Company. Electrical Systems: Compact Equipment. (Fundamentals of Service Compact Equipment Ser.). (Illus.). 1982. pap. text ed. 8.00 (ISBN 0-86691-028-X); wkbk. 4.40 (ISBN 0-86691-031-X). Deere & Co.

--Engines (Consumer Products) (Illus.). 100p. (Orig.). 1982. pap. text ed. 10.00 (ISBN 0-86691-004-2); wkbk. 4.40 (ISBN 0-686-85859-X). Deere & Co.

--Hydraulics: Compact Equipment. (Fundamentals of Service Compact Equipment Ser.). (Illus.). 124p. 1983. pap. text ed. 8.00 (ISBN 0-86691-029-8); wkbk. 3.60 (ISBN 0-86691-032-8). Deere & Co.

--Power Trains: Compact Equipment. (Funadamentals of Service Compact Equipment Ser.). (Illus.). 104p. 1983. pap. text ed. 8.00 (ISBN 0-86691-030-1); wkbk. 3.60 (ISBN 0-86691-033-6). Deere & Co.

Deere, Carmen & Leal, Magdalena Leon de. Women in Andean Agriculture: Peasant Production & Rural Wage Employment in Colombia & Peru. Internatiojnal Labour Office, ed. (Women, Work & Development Ser.: No. 4). xii, 172p. (Orig.). 1982. pap. 11.40 (ISBN 92-2-103106-3). Intl Labour Office.

Deerforth, Daniel. Knock Wood! Superstition Through the Ages. LC 79-164220. 200p. 1974. Repr. of 1928 ed. 37.00x (ISBN 0-8103-3964-1). Gale.

Dees, Benjamin. E. A. Baratynsky. (World Authors Ser.). 1972. lib. bdg. 15.95 (ISBN 0-8057-2092-8, Twayne). G K Hall.

Dees, Catherine, jt. auth. see Croissant, Kay.

Dees, Jerome S. Sir Thomas Elyot & Roger Ascham: A Reference Guide. 1981. 27.00 (ISBN 0-8161-8353-8, Hall Reference). G K Hall.

Deese, David & Nye, Joseph, eds. Energy & Security. 512p. 1980. prof ref 17.50x (ISBN 0-88410-640-3). Ballinger Pub.

Deese, David A. Nuclear Power & Radioactive Waste. LC 77-18496. (Illus.). 1978. 21.95 (ISBN 0-669-02114-8). Lexington Bks.

Deese, Helen, jt. auth. see Axelrod, Steven G.

Deeson, A. F. An Illustrated History of Steamships. 1977. 9.75 o.s.i. (ISBN 0-904978-05-2). Transatlantic.

Deeson, A. F. L. The Collector's Encyclopedia of Rocks & Minerals. (Illus.). 288p. 1973. 15.00 (ISBN 0-517-50550-9, C N Potter Bks). Crown.

Deetz, James. In Small Things Forgotten: The Archaeology of Early American Life. LC 76-50760. (Illus.). 1977. pap. 4.95 (ISBN 0-385-08031-X, Anch). Doubleday.

Deetz, Stanley, ed. Phenomenology in Rhetoric & Communication. LC 81-43514. (Current Continental Research Ser.: No. 3). (Illus.). 246p. (Orig.). 1982. lib. bdg. 23.00 (ISBN 0-8191-2087-1); pap. text ed. 11.25 (ISBN 0-8191-2088-X). U Pr of Amer.

De Eudaly, Maria S. Capacitando a Maestros De Ninos. pap. (ISBN 0-311-11035-5). Casa Bautista.

De Faire, Ulf & Theorell, Tores. Life Stress & Coronary Heart Disease. 250p. 1983. 18.50 (ISBN 0-87527-201-0). Green.

DeFalco, Joseph, ed. see Cranch, Christopher P.

Defaux, Gerard. Le Curieux, le glorieux et la sagesse du monde dans la premiere moitie du XVIe siecle: L'exemple de Panurge. LC 81-71430. (French Forum Monographs: No. 34). 196p. (Orig.). 1982. pap. 15.00 (ISBN 0-917058-33-X). French Forum.

--Moliere, ou les Metamorphoses du Comique: De la Comedie Morale Au Triomphe De la Folie. LC 79-53401. (French Forum Monographs: No. 18). 372p. (Fr.). 1980. pap. 17.50x (ISBN 0-917058-17-8). French Forum.

Defaux, Gerard, ed. see Yale French Studies.

De Feldy, L. Elizabeth. Common Sense Etiquette: For Business Women, Wives, Mistresses. (Illus.). 119p. lib. bdg. 15.00x (ISBN 0-935402-15-2); pap. 14.00 (ISBN 0-935402-16-0). Intl Comm Serv.

De Felice, Renzo. Fascism: An Informal Introduction to Its Theory & Practice. LC 76-13006. 128p. 1977. 1976 5.95x (ISBN 0-87855-190-5); pap. 8.95x 1977 (ISBN 0-87855-619-2). Transaction Bks.

DeFelice, S. Drug Discovery: The Pending Crisis. 94p. 1972. 10.50 o.p. (ISBN 0-683-02421-3, Pub. by W & W). Krieger.

DeFelitta, Frank. Audrey Rose. LC 75-24875. 384p. 1975. 8.95 o.p. (ISBN 0-399-11606-0). Putnam Pub Group.

De Felitta, Frank. The Entity. LC 78-9811. 1978. 10.95 o.p. (ISBN 0-399-12231-1). Putnam Pub Group.

--The Entity. 480p. 1983. pap. 3.95 o.p. (ISBN 0-446-30136-1). Warner Bks.

--Sea Trial. 1982. pap. 2.95 (ISBN 0-380-81414-5, 81414). Avon.

Deferrari, Roy. First Year Latin. 1st ed. 1958. 3.96 o.p. (ISBN 0-02-814220-9). Glencoe.

DeFeudis, F. V. see Delgado, J. M.

DeFeudis, Francis V. & Mandel, Paul, eds. Amino Acid Neurotransmitters, Vol. 29. (Advances in Biochemical Psychopharmacology). 600p. 1981. 59.00 o.p. (ISBN 0-89004-595-X). Raven.

Deffand, Madame du. Letters to & from Madame Du Deffand & Julie De Lespinasse. limited ed. Smith, W. H., ed. 1938. 32.50x (ISBN 0-685-69810-6). Elliots Bks.

Deffner, Don. The Real Word for the Real World. (Preacher's Workshop Ser.). 48p. 1977. pap. 2.50 (ISBN 0-570-07402-9, 12-2674). Concordia.

Deffner, Donald. I Hear Two Voices, God! 1983. pap. 4.95 (ISBN 0-570-03882-0). Concordia.

Deffner, Donald, jt. auth. see Andersen, Richard.

De Figueiredo, D. G., ed. Differential Equations, Sao Paulo, Brazil, 1981: Proceedings. (Lecture Notes in Mathematics: Vol. 957). 301p. 1983. pap. 16.00 (ISBN 0-387-11951-5). Springer-Verlag.

De Filippo, Eduardo. Saturday, Sunday, Monday. Waterhouse, Keith & Hall, Willis, trs. 1974. pap. text ed. 5.00x (ISBN 0-435-23201-0). Heinemann Ed.

De Finetti, Bruno. Theory of Probability: A Critical Introductory Treatment. LC 73-10744. (Probability & Mathematical Statistics Ser.: Vol. 1). 300p. 1974. 59.95 (ISBN 0-471-20141-3, Pub. by Wiley-Interscience). Wiley.

--Theory of Probability: A Critical Introductory Treatment. Machi, Antonio & Smith, Adrian, trs. LC 73-10744. (Probability & Mathematical Statistics Ser.: Vol. 2). 375p. 1975. 69.95 (ISBN 0-471-20142-1, Pub. by Wiley-Interscience). Wiley.

DeFleur. Social Problems in American Society. 1982. 16.95 (ISBN 0-686-84654-0); supplementary materials avail. HM.

DeFleur, Melvin & Lowery, Shearon. Milestones in Mass Communication Research. (Illus.). 448p. 1983. text ed. 22.50x (ISBN 0-582-28352-3); pap. text ed. 10.95x (ISBN 0-582-28353-1). Longman.

DeFleur, Melvin L. Social Problems in American Society. LC 82-81108. 640p. 1982. text ed. 16.95 (ISBN 0-395-32567-6); instr's. manual avail. (ISBN 0-395-32568-4). HM.

DeFleur, Melvin L. & Dennis, Everette E. Understanding Mass Communication. LC 80-82762. (Illus.). 528p. 1981. pap. text ed. 15.50 (ISBN 0-395-29722-2); instr's manual 1.00 (ISBN 0-395-29723-0). HM.

DeFleur, Melvin L., et al. Sociology: Human Society. 2nd brief ed. 1977. pap. 15.95x o.p. (ISBN 0-673-07928-7). Scott F.

--Sociology: Human Society. 3rd ed. 1981. text ed. 20.95x o.p. (ISBN 0-673-15211-1). Scott F.

Defliese, P. L., et al. Montgomery's Auditing. 9th ed. 1975. 55.95x (ISBN 0-471-06527-7). Ronald Pr.

--Montgomery's Auditing. 9th ed. 869p. 1975. 55.95 (ISBN 0-471-06527-7). Wiley.

Defoe. Robinson Crusoe. (Children's Classic Ser.). (gr. 3-6). 1981. 5.95 (ISBN 0-86020-554-1, Usborne-Hayes); PLB 8.95 (ISBN 0-88110-062-5); pap. 2.95 (ISBN 0-686-36310-8). EDC.

Defoe, Daniel. Captain Singleton. 1969. Repr. of 1906 ed. 8.95x (ISBN 0-460-00074-8, 74, Evman). Biblio Dist.

--Conjugal Lewdness, or Matrimonial Whoredom. LC 67-10178. 1967. Repr. of 1727 ed. 45.00x (ISBN 0-8201-1013-2). Schol Facsimiles.

--The Manufacturer, Vols. 1-86. Bd. with The British Merchant; The Weaver. LC 78-11810. 1979. Repr. of 1720 ed. 55.00x (ISBN 0-8201-1324-7). Schol Facsimiles.

--Moll Flanders. 1977. pap. 2.95x (ISBN 0-460-01837-X, Evman); 9.95x (ISBN 0-460-00837-4). Biblio Dist.

--Moll Flanders. Kelly, Edward, ed. (Critical Editions Ser.). 500p. 1973. pap. text ed. 8.95x (ISBN 0-393-09412-X). Norton.

--Robinson Crusoe. (Bantam Classics Ser.). 288p. (gr. 7-12). 1981. pap. text ed. 1.95 (ISBN 0-553-21062-9). Bantam.

--Robinson Crusoe. (Span.). 9.95 (ISBN 84-241-5636-6). E Torres & Sons.

--Robinson Crusoe. (Illus.). (gr. 4-6). 1952-63. il. jr. lib. 5.95 (ISBN 0-448-05821-9, G&D); Companion Lib. Ed. 2.95 (ISBN 0-448-05467-1); deluxe ed. 8.95 (ISBN 0-448-06021-3). Putnam Pub Group.

--Robinson Crusoe. (RL 6). pap. 1.95 (ISBN 0-451-51606-0, CJ1606, Sig Classics). NAL.

--Robinson Crusoe. LC 78-3384. (Raintree's Illustrated Classics). (Illus.). (gr. 5-8). 1978. PLB 13.30 (ISBN 0-8172-1137-3). Raintree Pubs.

--Roxana: The Fortunate Mistress. Jack, Jane, ed. (Oxford English Novels Ser.). 1964. pap. 6.95x o.p. (ISBN 0-19-281046-4). Oxford U Pr.

Defoe, Daniel see Swan, D. K.

DeFoe, Mark. Bringing Home Breakfast, No. 4. new ed. Fleming, Harold, ed. (Black Willow Chapbook Ser.). (Illus.). 20p. (Orig.). 1982. pap. 3.00 (ISBN 0-910047-02-2). Black Willow.

Defoggi, Ernest. An Engineer's Analysis (& Solution) of the Human Mind. (Illus.). 1978. 8.95x o.s.i. (ISBN 0-9602372-0-8). E Defoggi.

Defontenay, C. I. Star (Psi Cassiopeia) (Science Fiction Ser.). 208p. 1976. Repr. of 1854 ed. lib. bdg. 10.95 o.p. (ISBN 0-8398-2324-X, Gregg). G K Hall.

De Fontenay, Elisabeth. Diderot: Reason & Resonance. Mehlman, Jeffrey, tr. from Fr. LC 82-9649. 274p. 1982. 14.95 (ISBN 0-8076-1035-6). Braziller.

Deford, Frank. Everybody's All-American. 1982. pap. 3.50 (ISBN 0-451-11730-1, AE1730, Sig). NAL.

Deford, Frank, jt. auth. see Kramer, Jack.

De Ford, Miriam A. & Jackson, Joan S., eds. Who Was When? 3rd ed. 184p. 1976. 35.00 (ISBN 0-8242-0532-4). Wilson.

De Ford, Tamara. How to Survive While Raising Teenagers. Sanchez, Ray A., ed. 60p. 1983. pap. 3.95 (ISBN 0-931908-07-8). Sag Scriptory.

DeForest, John W. The Downing Legends-Stories in Rhyme. Incl. The Witch of Shiloh; The Last of the Wampanoags; The Gentle Earl; The Enchanted Voyage. 1901. 24.50x (ISBN 0-685-91097-0). Elliots Bks.

De Forest, John W. Honest John Vane. Rubin, Joseph J., ed. (Monument Edition Ser.). 15.00x (ISBN 0-271-00318-9). Pa St U Pr.

DeForest, John W. Poems: Medley & Palestina. 1902. 24.50x (ISBN 0-685-89770-2). Elliots Bks.

DeForest, P. R. & Gaenssien, R. E. Forensic Science: An Introduction to Criminalistics. 544p. 1983. 23.95 (ISBN 0-07-016267-0). McGraw.

DeForest, W. S. Photoresist: Materials & Processes. 1975. 41.50 (ISBN 0-07-016230-1, P&RB). McGraw.

De Forges, Maria T. Impressionist Painters: From Cezanne to Toulouse-Lautrec. Graig, Marjorie G., tr. (World in Color Ser.). (Illus.). 50p. 1976. 3.95 o.p. (ISBN 0-88254-389-X). Hippocrene Bks.

DeForrest, Roland. The Quest of Dirk & Honey. 256p. 1983. pap. 2.75 (ISBN 0-446-30297-X). Warner Bks.

--The Wildon Affair. (Erotica Ser.). 256p. 1983. pap. 2.75 (ISBN 0-446-30207-4). Warner Bks.

De Fossard, Esta see Rinsky, Lee A. & Fossard, Esta de.

De France, J. J. Electrical Fundamentals, 2 pts. Incl. Pt. 1. Direct Current; Pt. 2. Indirect Current. 1969. Set. text ed. 24.95 (ISBN 0-13-247197-3). P-H.

DeFrance, Joseph J. Electrical Fundamentals. 2nd ed. (Illus.). 672p. 1983. text ed. 25.95 (ISBN 0-13-247262-7). P-H.

De Francesco, Henry. Quantitative Analysis Methods for Substantive Analysts. LC 74-20886. 431p. 1975. 26.95 o.p. (ISBN 0-471-20529-X, Pub. by Wiley-Interscience). Wiley.

DeFrancis, John. Beginning Chinese Reader, 2 pts. 2nd ed. LC 76-5103. 1977. Pt. I. text ed. 40.00x (ISBN 0-300-02056-2); Pt. II. 40.00x (ISBN 0-300-02057-0); Pts. I & II. pap. 11.95x vol. I (ISBN 0-300-02060-0); pap. 13.95x vol. 2 (ISBN 0-300-02061-9). Yale U Pr.

--Character Text for Beginning Chinese. 2nd ed. LC 76-5105. 1976. text ed. 40.00x (ISBN 0-300-02055-4); pap. 12.95x (ISBN 0-300-02059-7). Yale U Pr.

--Intermediate Chinese. 1964. text ed. 40.00x o.p. (ISBN 0-300-00412-5); pap. text ed. 16.95x (ISBN 0-300-00064-2). Yale U Pr.

--Things Japanese in Hawaii. (Illus.). 224p. 1973. pap. 9.50 (ISBN 0-8248-0233-0). UH Pr.

DeFrancis, John, ed. see Lindell, Kristina.

DeFrancis, John, ed. see Yee, Dennis K.

DeFrancis, John, ed. see Yung, Teng C.

DeFrancis, John, et al. Intermediate Chinese Reader, 2 Pts. text ed. 45.00x ea. o.p.; Pt. 1 1967 o.p. 7.95x o.p. (ISBN 0-300-00413-3); Pt. 2 1968 o.p. pap. 8.50x o.p. (ISBN 0-300-00414-1); Pt. 1. pap. 19.95x (ISBN 0-300-00065-0); Pt. 2. pap. text ed. 19.95x (ISBN 0-300-00066-9). Yale U Pr.

DeFrancis, John, jt. auth. see Liang, James C.

DeFriese, Gordon. Strategies for the Promotion of Health. 1983. prof ref 25.00x (ISBN 0-88410-719-1). Ballinger Pub.

DeFriese, Gordon H. & Barker, Ben D., eds. Assessing Dental Manpower Requirements: Alternative Approaches for State & Local Planning. LC 82-11383. 184p. 1982. prof ref 20.00x (ISBN 0-88410-746-9). Ballinger Pub.

Deftos, L. J. Medullary Thyroid Carcinoma. (Beitraege zur Onkologie. Contributions to Oncology Ser.: Vol. 17). (Illus.). viii, 144p. 1983. pap. 60.00 (ISBN 3-8055-3703-4). S Karger.

De Gaetano, Giovanni & Garattini, Silvio, eds. Platelets: A Multidisciplinary Approach. LC 78-66352. (Monographs of the Mario Negri Institute for Pharmacological Research). 501p. 1978. 47.50 (ISBN 0-89004-252-7). Raven.

DeGaetano, Jean. Speech Improvement Duplicating Masters, 3 vols. 1973. Set 1. text ed. 9.95x (ISBN 0-8134-1124-6); Set 2. text ed. 9.95x (ISBN 0-8134-1442-3); Set 3. text ed. 9.95x (ISBN 0-8134-1537-3). Interstate.

Degaleesan, T. E., jt. auth. see Laddha, G. S.

De Galiana Mingot, Tomas see Mingot, Tomas De Galiana.

Degani, Meir H. Astronomy Made Simple. rev. ed. LC 76-2836. 224p. 1976. pap. 4.95 (ISBN 0-385-08854-X, Made). Doubleday.

DeGaris, Roger, tr. see Badinter, Elisabeth.

DeGaris, Roger, tr. see Bulychev, Kirill.

Degarmo, E. Paul. Engineering Economy. 6th ed. 1979. text ed. 29.95 (ISBN 0-02-328160-X). Macmillan.

--Materials & Processes in Manufacturing. 5th ed. (Illus.). 1979. text ed. 31.95x (ISBN 0-02-328120-0); instrs'. manual avail. Macmillan.

De Gasparin, A. De l'Affranchissement des Esclaves et de ses Rapports avec la Politique Actuelle. (Slave Trade in France, 1744-1848, Ser.). 76p. (Fr.). 1974. Repr. of 1839 ed. lib. bdg. 22.50x o.p. (ISBN 0-8287-0363-9, TN130). Clearwater Pub.

De Gasparin, Agenor. Esclavage et Traite. (Slave Trade in France, 1744-1848, Ser.). 276p. (Fr.). 1974. lib. bdg. 74.50x o.p. (ISBN 0-8287-0364-7, TN129). Clearwater Pub.

De Gasparis, Priscilla, jt. auth. see Bower, Robert T.

Degasperis, A., jt. auth. see Calogers, F.

DeGast, Robert. The Lighthouses of the Chesapeake. 173p. 1976. 15.00 (ISBN 0-686-36638-7). Md Hist.

--Western Wind Eastern Shore. (Illus.). 173p. 1975. 14.95 (ISBN 0-686-36750-2). Md Hist.

De Gasztold, Carmen B. Prayers from the Ark & The Creatures' Choir. Godden, Rumer, tr. (Poets Ser.). 1976. pap. 5.95 (ISBN 0-14-042200-5). Penguin.

De Gaulle, Charles. Charles De Gaulle Memoirs of Hope: Renewal & Endeavor. 1972. 10.00 o.p. (ISBN 0-671-21118-8). S&S.

--The Edge of the Sword. LC 75-26731. 128p. 1975. Repr. of 1960 ed. lib. bdg. 16.50x (ISBN 0-8371-8366-9, GAES). Greenwood.

De Gaury, Gerald. Rulers of Mecca. LC 78-63458. (Pilgrimages Ser.). (Illus.). 1982. Repr. of 1954 ed. 34.50 (ISBN 0-404-16517-6). AMS Pr.

De Gaviria, Maria C., ed. see National Library of Peru.

De Gelder, Beatrice, ed. Knowledge & Representation. (International Library of Psychology). 190p. 1982. 30.00 (ISBN 0-7100-0922-4). Routledge & Kegan.

Degen, Bruce. Jamberry. LC 82-47708. (Illus.). 32p. (ps-1). 1983. 7.64i (ISBN 0-06-021416-3, HarpJ); PLB 8.89g (ISBN 0-06-021417-1). Har-Row.

Degen, Clara, jt. ed. see Stearns, Betty.

Degenhardt, Henry W. Treaties & Alliances of the World. 3rd ed. LC 81-83479. (Keesing's Reference Publications Ser.). 409p. 1981. 75.00x (ISBN 0-8103-1602-1). Gale.

Degenhardt, Henry W., jt. ed. see Day, Alan J.

DeGennaro, Angelo A., tr. see Croce, Benedetto.

Degens, T. Transport Seven-Forty-One-R. (gr. 4-7). 1977. pap. 1.50 o.p. (ISBN 0-440-99003-3, LFL). Dell.

Degenshein, Joan & Stern, Naomi M. Successful Cosmetic Selling. rev. ed. LC 71-144088. (Chain Store Age Bks.). (Illus.). 1978. pap. 14.95 (ISBN 0-86730-403-0). Lebhar Friedman.

De George, Richard T. Business Ethics. 1982. text ed. 14.95x (ISBN 0-02-328000-X). Macmillan.

DeGeorge, Richard T. & Pichler, Joseph A., eds. Ethics, Free Enterprise, & Public Policy: Original Essays on Moral Issues in Business. 1978. text ed. 12.95x (ISBN 0-19-502467-2); pap. text ed. 9.95x (ISBN 0-19-502425-7). Oxford U Pr.

Deghan, Bijan & Webster, Grady L. Morphology & Infrageneric Relationships of the Genus "Jatropha" (Euphorbiaceae) LC 77-83116. (Publications in Botany Ser.: Vol. 74). 1979. 15.50x (ISBN 0-520-09585-5). U of Cal Pr.

Degler, C. N. Neither Black nor White: Slavery & Race Relations in Brazil & the U. S. 1971. 9.95 o.p. (ISBN 0-02-328190-1, 32819); pap. 11.95 (ISBN 0-02-328200-2, 32820). Macmillan.

Degler, Carl. The Other South. LC 82-14429. 371p. 1982. text ed. 24.95X (ISBN 0-930350-33-2); pap. text ed. 9.95x (ISBN 0-930350-34-0). NE U Pr.

Degler, Carl N. Affluence & Anxiety: America Since Nineteen Forty-Five. 2nd ed. 210p. 1975. pap. 9.95x (ISBN 0-673-07956-2). Scott F.

--The Age of the Economic Revolution: 1876-1900. 2nd ed. 1977. pap. 9.95x (ISBN 0-673-07967-8). Scott F.

--At Odds: Women & the Family in America, from the Revolution to the Present. 1980. 27.50x (ISBN 0-19-502657-8). Oxford U Pr.

--At Odds: Women & the Family in America from the Revolution to the Present. 544p. 1981. pap. 9.95 (ISBN 0-19-502934-8, GB 645, GB). Oxford U Pr.

--Out of Our Past: The Forces That Shaped Modern America. rev. ed. LC 77-88637. 1970. pap. 6.95xi (ISBN 0-06-131967-8, TB1967, Torch). Har-Row.

--Place Over Time: The Continuity of Southern Distinctiveness. LC 77-586. (Walter Lynwood Fleming Lectures in Southern History Ser.). 1982. 10.95x (ISBN 0-8071-0299-7); pap. 5.95x. La State U Pr.

Degler, Carl N., et al. The Democratic Experience, 2 vols. 5th ed. 1981. pap. text ed. 17.95x (ISBN 0-673-15450-5); Vol. 1. pap. text ed. 12.50x (ISBN 0-673-15451-3); Vol. 2. pap. text ed. 12.50x (ISBN 0-673-15452-1). Scott F.

Degli Antelminelli, F. Castracane see Castracane Degli Antelminelli, F.

Degnan, James P., jt. auth. see Hefferman, William A.

De Gobineau, Arthur. The Renaissance: Savonarola, Cesare Borgia, Julius II, Leo X, Michaelangelo. 1979. Repr. of 1913 ed. cancelled 17.50 (ISBN 0-685-33294-2). Fertig.

De Golberry, Silvain-Meinrad-Xavier see Golberry, Silvain-Meinrad-Xavier de.

De Gongora y Argote, Luis. Fourteen Sonnets & Polyphemus. 1975. 3.50 (ISBN 0-942260-07-4). Hispanic Seminary.

De Gouy, Louis P. The Bread Tray: 600 Recipes for Homemade Breads, Rolls, Muffins, & Biscuits. 9.00 (ISBN 0-8446-5024-2). Peter Smith.

--Creative Hamburger Cookery. LC 73-88330. 128p. 1974. pap. 3.00 (ISBN 0-486-23001-5). Dover.

--The Soup Book: 770 Recipes. 9.00 (ISBN 0-8446-5028-5). Peter Smith.

DeGowin, Elmer L. & DeGowin, Richard L. Bedside Diagnostic Examination. 4th ed. (Illus.). 952p. 1981. flexible bdg. 22.95x (ISBN 0-02-328030-1). Macmillan.

DeGowin, Richard L., jt. auth. see DeGowin, Elmer L.

De Graaf, Frank. Marine Tropical Aquarium Guide. (Illus.). 282p. (YA) 1982. 14.95 (ISBN 0-87666-805-8, PL-2017). TFH Pubns.

De Graaf, G. A. see Graaf, G. A. de.

DeGraaf, Richard M. & Witman, Gretchin M. Trees, Shrubs, & Vines for Attracting Birds: A Manual for the Northeast. LC 78-19698. (Illus.). 1979. 14.00x o.p. (ISBN 0-87023-266-5). U of Mass Pr.

De Gramont, Sanche. The Strong Brown God: The Story of the Niger River. LC 75-33298. 356p. 1976. 12.50 o.p. (ISBN 0-395-19782-1). HM.

De Grand, Alexander. Italian Fascism: Its Origins & Development. LC 81-23132. (Illus.). xiv, 174p. 1982. 16.50x (ISBN 0-8032-1652-1); pap. 7.95 (ISBN 0-8032-6553-0, BB 727). U of Nebr Pr.

De Grange, McQuilkin. Nature & Elements of Sociology. 1953. text ed. 59.50x (ISBN 0-686-83631-6). Elliots Bks.

DeGravelles, William D. & Kelley, John H. Injuries Following Rear-End Automobile Collisions. (Illus.). 256p. 1969. photocopy ed. spiral 22.75x (ISBN 0-398-00414-5). C C Thomas.

DeGreene, K. B. The Adaptive Organization: Anticipation & Management of Crisis. LC 81-13112. 394p. 1982. 35.95 (ISBN 0-471-08296-1, Pub. by Wiley-Interscience). Wiley.

De Greene, Kenyon. Sociotechnical Systems: Factors in Analysis, Design & Management. (Illus.). 416p. 1973. ref. ed. 25.00 (ISBN 0-13-821553-7). P-H.

De Gregoire, Abbe Henri. Oeuvres, 14 Vols. 1977. Set. lib. bdg. write for info.; lib. bdg. 630.00 (ISBN 3-262-00007-8); per vol. 45.00. Kraus Intl.

DeGregorio, George. Joe DiMaggio: An Informal Biography. LC 80-6159. 272p. 1981. 14.95 (ISBN 0-8128-2777-5); pap. 8.95 (ISBN 0-8128-6178-7). Stein & Day.

Degremont Company Editors. Water Treatment Handbook. LC 72-96505. (Illus.). 1116p. 1973. 40.00 (ISBN 0-686-02503-2). Taylor-Carlisle.

De Grivart, tr. see Crawford, Williame & Kerstrat, Francoise.

DeGrood, David. Haeckel's Theory of the Unity of Nature. (Praxis: Vol.8). 100p. 1982. pap. text ed. 11.50x (ISBN 90-6032-216-9). Humanities.

DeGrood, David H. Radical Currents in Contemporary Philosophy, Vol. II. 1983. 22.50 (ISBN 0-686-77703-4). Fireside Bks.

--Radical Currents in Contemporary Philosophy, Vol. II. 1983. 22.50 (ISBN 0-87527-029-8). Green.

DeGroot, Henry. Comstock Papers. Basso, Dave, ed. (Great Basin Abstracts Ser.). (Illus.). 100p. 1982. pap. 11.50 (ISBN 0-936332-10-7). Falcon Hill Pr.

--Comstock Papers. Basso, Dave, ed. (Great Basin Abstracts Ser.). (Illus.). 50p. 1983. pap. 19.95 (ISBN 0-936332-21-2). Falcon Hill Pr.

De Groot, Irene, jt. auth. see Niemeijer, J. W.

DeGroot, Leslie J. & Stanbury, John B. The Thyroid Diseases. 4th ed. LC 75-17916. 823p. 1975. 51.95 o.p. (ISBN 0-471-20530-3, Pub. by Wiley-Medimedia Publications). Wiley.

DeGroot, Leslie J., ed. Endocrinology, 3 vols. LC 78-24043. 1979. Vol. 1, 592pps. 57.00 (ISBN 0-8089-1114-7); Vol.2, 800pps. 77.50 (ISBN 0-8089-1168-6); Vol. 3, 880pps. 85.50 (ISBN 0-8089-1169-4). Grune.

DeGroot, M. H. Optimal Statistical Decisions. 1970. text ed. 38.95 (ISBN 0-07-016242-5, C). McGraw.

De Groot, Roy A. Cooking with the Cuisinart Food Processor. LC 76-46586. 1977. 14.95 (ISBN 0-07-016273-5, GB). McGraw.

--Revolutionizing French Cooking. LC 76-10947. 1976. 15.95 o.p. (ISBN 0-07-016240-9, GB). McGraw.

--The Wines of California, the Pacific Northwest & New York: First Classification of the Wineries & Vineyards. 448p. 1982. 19.95 (ISBN 0-671-40049-5). Summit Bks.

De Groot, S. R. & Vanleeuwen, W. A. Relativistic Kinetic Theory: Principles & Applications. 1980. 74.50 (ISBN 0-444-85453-3). Elsevier.

DeGroot, W., ed. Stormwater Detention Facilities. LC 82-73613. 448p. 1982. pap. text ed. 31.00 (ISBN 0-87262-348-3). Am Soc Civil Eng.

De Grouchy, Jean & Turleau, Catherine. Clinical Atlas of Human Chromosomes. LC 77-2282. 1977. 65.00 (ISBN 0-471-01704-3, Pub. by Wiley Medical). Wiley.

De Gruijter, Dato N. & Van Der Kamp, Leo. J., eds. Advances in Psychological & Educational Measurement. LC 76-4492. 1976. 69.95 (ISBN 0-471-01817-1, Pub. by Wiley Interscience). Wiley.

De Gruijter, J. J. Numerical Classification of Soils & Its Application in Survey. (Agricultural Research Reports Ser.: No. 855). (Illus.). 1978. pap. 22.00 (ISBN 90-220-0608-5, PDC59, Pub. by PUDOC). Unipub.

DeGrummond, Jane L. Renato Beluche: Smuggler, Privateer, & Patriot, 1780 to 1860. (Illus.). 328p. 1983. text ed. 27.50x (ISBN 0-8071-1054-X). La State U Pr.

De Gubernatis, Angelo see Gubernatis, Angelo De.

De Guibert, Joseph. The Jesuits: Their Spiritual Doctrine & Practice. Young, W. J., tr. LC 64-21430. 717p. 1964. pap. 8.00 (ISBN 0-912422-09-2). Inst Jesuit.

DeGuilmo, Joseph M. Electricity-Electronics: Principles & Applications. LC 79-54909. (Electronics Technology Ser.). (Illus.). 706p. (Orig.). 1982. pap. 21.00 (ISBN 0-8273-1686-0); instr's. guide 4.75 (ISBN 0-8273-1687-9). Delmar.

De Gutierrez, Frances A., tr. see Olson, Joan & Olson, Gene.

De Guzman & Miguel. Real Variable Methods in Fourier Analysis. (Mathematical Studies Ser.: Vol. 46). 1981. 57.50 (ISBN 0-444-86124-6). Elsevier.

De Guzman, Videa, jt. auth. see Ramos, Teresita V.

DeGuzman, Videa P. Syntactic Derivation of Tagalog Verbs. LC 78-11029. (Oceanic Linguistic Special Publication: No. 16). 1978. pap. text ed. 14.00x (ISBN 0-8248-0627-1). UH Pr.

DeHaan, Daniel F. The God You Can Know. LC 81-16948. 180p. 1982. pap. 5.95 (ISBN 0-8024-3008-2). Moody.

De Haan, Ger. Conditions on Rules. 248p. 1981. 34.25x (ISBN 90-70176-35-1); pap. 18.70x (ISBN 90-70176-08-4). Foris Pubns.

DeHaan, M. R. The Chemistry of the Blood. 160p. 1983. pap. 4.95 (ISBN 0-310-23291-0). Zondervan.

DeHaan, Martin R. The Jew & Palestine in Prophecy. 1978. pap. 5.95 (ISBN 0-310-23381-X). Zondervan.

De Haan, Martin R. Signs of the Times. 1951. 5.95 (ISBN 0-310-23471-9). Zondervan.

DeHaan, Warren V. The Optometrist's & Ophthalmologist's Guide to Pilot's Vision. LC 81-69431. 200p. 1982. 33.00 (ISBN 0-941388-00-X). Am Trend Pub.

De Halacsy, E. Conspectus Florae Graecae & Supplementum Prim, 4 vols. in 3. 1969. Set. 240.00 (ISBN 3-7682-7192-7). Lubrecht & Cramer.

De'Ham, Claude, illus. Playtime. (Moments Ser.). 20p. (Orig.). 1975. pap. 2.00 (ISBN 0-85953-038-8, Pub. by Child's Play England). Playspaces.

DeHart, Florence E. The Librarian's Psychological Commitments: Human Relations in Librarianship. LC 79-7059. (Contributions in Librarianship & Information Science: No. 27). 1979. lib. bdg. 25.00 (ISBN 0-313-21329-1, DLC/). Greenwood.

De Hartog, Jan. The Lamb's War. LC 78-20201. 500p. 1980. 13.41i (ISBN 0-06-010995-5, HarpT). Har-Row.

--The Lamb's War. 512p. 1983. pap. 3.95 (ISBN 0-449-20019-1, Crest). Fawcett.

--The Trail of the Serpent. LC 80-8228. (Cornelia & Michael Bessie Bks.). 256p. 1983. 14.37i (ISBN 0-06-039018-2, HarpT). Har-Row.

De Harven, Emile. Caminos Peligrosos. LC 75-38833. (Illus.). 140p. 1976. pap. 5.95 (ISBN 0-88436-259-0). EMC.

--Chemins Dangereux. LC 75-38836. (Illus.). 140p. 1976. pap. 5.95 (ISBN 0-88436-260-4). EMC.

--Gefahrliche Wege. LC 75-29089. (Illus.). 140p. 1976. pap. 5.45 (ISBN 0-88436-256-6). EMC.

--Suivez la Piste. LC 77-10091. 1972. pap. 4.75 (ISBN 0-912022-30-2). EMC.

DeHaven, Charlotte, jt. auth. see DeHaven, Kent C.

DeHaven, Edna P. Teaching & Learning the Language Arts. 1979. text ed. 18.95 (ISBN 0-316-17933-7); tchr's manual avail. (ISBN 0-316-17934-5). Little.

DeHaven, Kent C. & DeHaven, Charlotte. What's on Tap. (Illus., Orig.). 1982. pap. write for info. Trends & Custom.

DeHaven, Martha L., jt. auth. see Walker, Jacilyn G.

De Havenon, Andre, ed. A Touch of Paris: A Selective Guide to Paris in Plain English. (Illus.). 255p. (Orig.). 1980. pap. 8.95 (ISBN 0-933982-14-3). Bradt Ent.

De Heer, F. J., jt. auth. see Govers, T. R.

De Hegermann-Lindencrone, L. In the Courts of Memory: Eighteen Fifty-Eight to Eighteen Seventy-Five. (Music Reprint Ser.). viii, 450p. 1980. Repr. of 1911 ed. lib. bdg. 37.50 (ISBN 0-306-76012-6). Da Capo.

Dehesa, J. S., et al, eds. Interacting Bosons in Nuclei, Granada, Spain 1981: Proceedings. (Lecture Notes in Physics: Vol. 161). 209p. 1982. pap. 12.50 (ISBN 0-387-11572-2). Springer-Verlag.

De Heusch, Luc. Why Marry Her? Society & Symbolic Structures. Lloyd, Janet, tr. (Cambridge Studies in Social Anthropology: No. 33). (Illus.). 240p. 1981. 42.50 (ISBN 0-521-22460-8). Cambridge U Pr.

Dehmlow, Eckhard & Dehmlow, Sigrid. Phase Transfer Catalysis. 2nd ed. Ebel, Hans F., ed. (Monographs in Modern Chemistry: Vol. 11). 1983. price not set (ISBN 3-527-25897-3). Verlag Chemie.

Dehmlow, Sigrid, jt. auth. see Dehmlow, Eckhard.

De Honnecourt, Villard. The Sketchbook of Villard de Honnecourt. Bowie, Theodore, ed. LC 82-15540. (Illus.). 144p. 1982. lib. bdg. 35.00x (ISBN 0-313-23747-6, VISK). Greenwood.

DeHoyos, Genieve. Stewardship, the Divine Order. LC 81-82055. 200p. 1982. 6.95 (ISBN 0-88290-191-5, 1065). Horizon Utah.

DeHuszar, William I. Mortgage Loan Administration. (Illus.). 480p. 1972. text ed. 29.95 (ISBN 0-07-016257-3, C). McGraw.

Deibel, Robert H. & Lindquist, John A. General Food Microbiology: Laboratory Manual. 1982. pap. 10.95x (ISBN 0-8087-4405-4). Burgess.

Deibert, Alvin N. B. J. & the Language of the Woodland. (Illus.). 48p. (Orig.). (gr. 2-6). 1983. pap. 5.50 (ISBN 0-87743-701-7). Baha'i.

Deibler, Ellis. Semantic Relationships of Gahuku Verbs. (SIL Linguistic & Related Fields Ser.: No. 48). 159p. 1974. pap. 8.00x (ISBN 0-88312-058-5); microfiche 2.25x (ISBN 0-88312-458-0). Summer Inst Ling.

Deichman, Elizabeth S. & Evans, Patricia L. A Teaching Guide for Working with the Elderly. 27p. 1980. pap. text ed. 4.95 (ISBN 0-932910-24-6, 124). Potentials Development.

Deichman, Elizabeth S. & O'Kane, C. P. Working with the Elderly: A Training Manual. Rev. ed. 119p. (Orig.). 1980. pap. text ed. 8.95 (ISBN 0-932910-32-7). Potentials Development.

Deigan, Paul T., jt. auth. see McCarthy, Martha M.

Deigh, Khigh, ed. The Golden Oracle: The Ancient Chinese Way to Prosperity. LC 82-18471. (Illus.). 176p. 1983. 11.95 (ISBN 0-668-05661-4). Arco.

Deighan, Maurice. County Court Practice & Procedure. 1980. 40.00x (ISBN 0-686-97089-6, Pub. by Fourmat England). State Mutual Bk.

Deighton, Ken. SS-GB. (General Ser.). 1979. lib. bdg. 18.95 (ISBN 0-8161-6748-6, Large Print Bks). G K Hall.

Deighton, Lee C. Vocabulary Development in the Classroom. LC 59-8372. 1959. pap. text ed. 3.75x o.p. (ISBN 0-8077-1236-1). Tchrs Coll.

Deighton, Len. Battle of Britain. (Illus.). 224p. 1980. 19.95 (ISBN 0-698-11033-1, Coward). Putnam Pub Group.

--The Billion Dollar Brain. 1980. pap. 2.50 (ISBN 0-425-05355-5). Berkley Pub.

--Bomber. 1982. pap. 3.95 (ISBN 0-451-12029-9, AE2029, Sig). NAL.

--Funeral in Berlin. 1980. pap. 2.75 (ISBN 0-425-06123-X). Berkley Pub.

--Goodbye, Mickey Mouse. LC 82-47813. 355p. 1982. 14.95 (ISBN 0-394-51259-6). Knopf.

--Horse Under Water. 1980. pap. 2.50 (ISBN 0-425-05475-6). Berkley Pub.

--Yesterday's Spy. 1976. pap. 2.50 o.p. (ISBN 0-446-31014-X). Warner Bks.

Deikman, Arthur J. The Observing Self: Mysticism & Psychotherapy. LC 81-70486. 208p. 1983. pap. 6.97 (ISBN 0-686-82696-5). Beacon Pr.

De Imaz, Jose L. Los Que Mandan (Those Who Rule) Astiz, Carlos A., tr. from Span. LC 69-12100. 1970. 34.50x (ISBN 0-87395-044-5); pap. 10.95x (ISBN 0-87395-073-9). State U NY Pr.

Deinhardt, Carol L. Personality Assessment & Psychological Interpretation. (Illus.). 256p. 1983. 19.75x (ISBN 0-398-04752-9). C C Thomas.

Deininger, Rolf A., ed. Models for Environmental Pollution Control. LC 73-80818. (Illus.). 440p. 1973. 49.95 o.p. (ISBN 0-250-40032-4). Ann Arbor Science.

Deiros, P. A. Que Paso Con Estos Pecados? 1979. pap. 2.50 (ISBN 0-311-42063-X). Casa Bautista.

Deiros, Pablo. El Cristiano y los Problemas Eticos. 112p. 1977. pap. 2.50 (ISBN 0-311-46064-X). Casa Bautista.

Deiros, Pablo, compiled by. Figuras De Plata. 200p. 1978. pap. 3.95 (ISBN 0-311-42053-2, Edit Mundo). Casa Bautista.

Deiros, Pablo A., tr. see Duval, Evelyn M.

Deis, Paul. Inventory & Production Management in the Nineteen Eighties. (Illus.). 384p. 1983. 25.95 (ISBN 0-13-502559-1). P-H.

Deitchman, Seymour J. New Technology & Military Power: General Purpose Military Forces for the Nineteen Eighties & Beyond. (Special Studies in Military Affairs). 315p. 1981. lib. bdg. 30.75 o.p. (ISBN 0-89158-358-0); pap. 13.50 o.p. (ISBN 0-86531-307-5). Westview.

Deitel, Harvey, jt. auth. see Lorin, Harold.

Deitel, Harvey M. Introduction to Computer Programming with the BASIC Language. LC 77-2960. (Illus.). 1977. pap. 18.95 ref. ed. (ISBN 0-13-480137-7). P-H.

Deitrich, Jeff. Reluctant Resister. (Illus.). 1983. 17.00 (ISBN 0-87775-156-0); pap. 6.00 (ISBN 0-87775-157-9). Unicorn Pr.

Deitsch, Clarence R., jt. auth. see Dilts, David A.

Deitsch, Maian & Rauch, James, eds. Kline Guide to Energy. LC 81-81264. (Illus.). 525p. 1981. pap. 175.00 (ISBN 0-917148-20-7). Kline.

Deitsch, Marian, ed. Directory of U.S. & Canadian Marketing Surveys & Services. 4th ed. 1981. loose-leaf 145.00 (ISBN 0-917148-75-4). Kline.

--Kline Guide to Packaging. Rich, Susan. (Illus.). 324p. 1980. pap. 100.00. Kline.

--Kline Guide to the Plastics Industry. 2nd ed. LC 82-83394. (Illus.). 340p. 1982. pap. 147.00 (ISBN 0-917148-16-9). Kline.

DeJaeger, Robert, jt. ed. see Mathe, Georges.

De Jager, E. M., jt. ed. see Eckhaus, W.

Dejean, Philippe. Carlo-Rembrandt-Ettore-Jean Buggatti. LC 82-40344. (Illus.). 360p. 1983. 50.00 (ISBN 0-8478-0446-1). Rizzoli Intl.

Dejene, Alemneh. Non-Formal Education As a Strategy in Development: Comparative Analysis of Rural Development Projects. LC 80-5882. 131p. 1980. lib. bdg. 18.50 (ISBN 0-8191-1346-8); pap. text ed. 8.50 (ISBN 0-8191-1347-6). U Pr of Amer.

De Jesus, Ed. C., jt. ed. see McCoy, Alfred W.

DeJoia, Alex & Stenton, Adrian. Terms in Systemic Linguistics. LC 80-5089. 1980. 20.00 (ISBN 0-312-79180-1). St Martin.

Dejon, William L. Policy Formulation. LC 79-10329. 643p. 1980. text ed. 22.95x (ISBN 0-8436-0781-5); keys to the cases 8.95x (ISBN 0-8436-0787-4). Kent Pub Co.

--Principles of Management: Text & Cases. LC 77-75123. 1978. 23.95 o.p. (ISBN 0-8053-2336-8); instr's man. 8.95 o.p. (ISBN 0-8053-2337-6). Benjamin-Cummings.

DeJong. The Dutch Reformed Church in the American Colonies. LC 78-17216. 1978. pap. 8.95 (ISBN 0-8028-1741-6). Eerdmans.

DeJong, Alexander D. Help & Hope for the Alcoholic. 128p. 1982. pap. 3.95 (ISBN 0-8423-1408-3). Tyndale.

DeJong, Benjamin R. Uncle Ben's Quotebook. 1976. pap. 8.95 (ISBN 0-89081-023-0, 0230). Harvest Hse.

DeJong, Constance. The Lucy Amarillo Stories. 1978. pap. 5.00 (ISBN 0-918746-03-5). Standard Edns.

--Modern Love. 1977. pap. 5.00 (ISBN 0-918746-01-9). Standard Edns.

DeJong, Dola. The Field. Perkins, Maxwell, ed. Van Duyn, A. V., tr. from Dutch. LC 79-84437. 1979. 16.95 (ISBN 0-933256-02-7); pap. 8.95 (ISBN 0-933256-05-1). Second Chance.

--The Field. Van Duym, A. V., tr. LC 79-84437. 215p. 1983. pap. 4.95 (ISBN 0-933256-39-6). Second Chance.

De Jong, E. J. & Jancic, S. J., eds. Industrial Crystallization, '78. 588p. 1979. 100.00 (ISBN 0-686-63101-3, North Holland). Elsevier.

Dejong, Gerald F. The Dutch in America, 1609-1974. (The Immigrant Heritage of America Ser). 1975. lib. bdg. 12.50 o.p. (ISBN 0-8057-3214-4, Twayne). G K Hall.

De Jong, Kees A. & Scholten, Robert, eds. Gravity & Tectonics. LC 73-1580. (Illus.). 502p. 1973. 67.50 (ISBN 0-471-20305-X, Pub. by Wiley-Interscience). Wiley.

DeJong, Peter, ed. Pest Management in Transition. LC 79-53138. (A Westview Replica Edition Ser.). 1979. lib. bdg. 20.00 (ISBN 0-89158-679-2). Westview.

Dejong, Russell N. A History of American Neurology. 170p. 1982. text ed. 19.50 (ISBN 0-89004-680-8). Raven.

--Year Book of Neurology & Neurosurgery, 1983. 1983. 35.00 (ISBN 0-8151-2424-4). Year Bk Med.

De Jong, W., et al, eds. Hypertension & Brain Mechanisms. (Progress in Brain Research Ser.: Vol. 47). 1977. 78.50 (ISBN 0-444-41534-3, North Holland). Elsevier.

De Jonge, Alex. Dostoevsky & the Age of Intensity. LC 74-30067. 256p. 1975. text ed. 18.95 o.p. (ISBN 0-312-21805-2). St Martin.

--Fire & Water: A Life of Peter the Great. LC 79-23113. (Illus.). 1980. 12.95 o.s.i. (ISBN 0-698-11018-8, Coward). Putnam Pub Group.

--The Life & Times of Grigorii Rasputin. (Illus.). 368p. 1982. 16.95 (ISBN 0-698-11136-2, Coward). Putnam Pub Group.

DeJonge, Alex. Nightmare Culture: Lautreamont & les Chants De Maldoror. LC 73-79380. 200p. 1974. 17.95 o.p. (ISBN 0-312-57330-8). St Martin.

DeJonge, Eric. Victorian Period Furniture--1840-1860. (Illus.). 72p. (Orig.). 1982. pap. 4.95 (ISBN 0-940166-02-X). Old Main Bks.

De Jongh, Brian. Companion Guide to Mainland Greece. (Illus.). 480p. 1983. 16.95 (ISBN 0-13-154567-1); pap. 8.95 (ISBN 0-13-154559-0). P-H.

DeJonj, Marie-Christine, tr. see Rexroat, Stephen.

De Jonnes, Alexandre M. Recherches Statistiques sur l'Esclavage Colonial et sur les Moyens de le Supprimer. (Slave Trade in France, 1744-1848, Ser.). 277p. (Fr.). 1974. Repr. of 1842 ed. lib. bdg. 93.00x o.p. (ISBN 0-8287-0254-3). Clearwater Pub.

De Joode, Ton & Stolk, Anthonie. The Backyard Bestiary. (Illus.). 1982. 25.00 (ISBN 0-394-52824-7). Knopf.

De Jourlet, Marie. Legacy of Windhaven. (The Windhaven Saga). 1978. pap. 3.50 (ISBN 0-523-41784-5). Pinnacle Bks.

--Return to Windhaven. (Windhaven). 1978. pap. 3.50 (ISBN 0-523-41858-2). Pinnacle Bks.

--Storm Over Windhaven. 1977. pap. 3.50 (ISBN 0-523-41967-8). Pinnacle Bks.

--Trials of Windhaven. (Orig.). 1980. pap. 3.50 (ISBN 0-523-42013-7). Pinnacle Bks.

--Windhaven Plantation. (Orig.). 1977. pap. 3.50 (ISBN 0-523-42006-4). Pinnacle Bks.

--Windhaven's Crisis. 448p. (Orig.). 1981. pap. 3.50 (ISBN 0-523-41748-9). Pinnacle Bks.

--Windhaven's Peril. (Windhaven Ser.). 1979. pap. 3.50 (ISBN 0-523-41968-6). Pinnacle Bks.

Dejours, Pierre, ed. Principles of Comparative Respiratory Physiology. 2nd ed. LC 74-25821. 251p. 1981. 32.50 (ISBN 0-444-80279-7, North-Holland); pap. 24.50 o.p. (ISBN 0-444-10852-1). Elsevier.

De Jouvancy, Joseph. De la Maniere d'Apprendre et d'Enseigner. xiv, 138p. (Fr.). 1981. Repr. of 1892 ed. lib. bdg. 65.00 (ISBN 0-8287-1538-6). Clearwater Pub.

De Julio, Mary A. Quilts from Montgomery County, New York. (Illus.). 24p. (Orig.). 1981. pap. 3.00 (ISBN 0-9608694-0-9). Montgomery Hist.

De Juvigny, F. Leonard, jt. auth. see Fair, D. E.

De Kadt, E., et al, eds. see Conference on Blood Viscosity in Heart Disease, Thromboembo-Lism & Cancer, Sydney Australia, May, 1978.

De Kadt, Ellen, tr. see Medvedev, Roy A.

De Kait, Ellen see Medvedev, Roy A.

Dekan, Jan. Moravia Magna. Trebaticka, Heather, tr. (Illus.). 192p. 1981. 42.50 (ISBN 0-89893-084-7). CDP.

Dekar, Paul R. & Ban, Joseph D., eds. In the Great Tradition. 240p. 1982. 25.00 (ISBN 0-8170-0972-8). Judson.

De Kay, James T. Meet Christopher Columbus. LC 68-23104. (Step-up Books Ser.). (Illus.). (gr. 2-6). 1968. 3.95 o.p. (ISBN 0-394-80071-0, BYR); PLB 4.99 (ISBN 0-394-90071-5). Random.

--Meet Martin Luther King Jr. LC 78-79789. (Step-up Books Ser.). (gr. 3-6). 1969. 4.95 (ISBN 0-394-80055-9, BYR); PLB 4.99 (ISBN 0-394-90055-3). Random.

De Kay, Ormonde, Jr. N'Heures Souris Rames: The Coucy Castle Manuscript. 1980. 7.95 (ISBN 0-517-54081-9, C N Potter Bks). Crown.

Dekeijzer, Arne J., jt. auth. see Kaplan, Fredric M.

Deken, Joseph. The Electronic Cottage: Everyday Living with Your Personal Computer in the 1980's. LC 81-14016. (Illus.). 320p. 1981. 15.95 (ISBN 0-688-00664-7). Morrow.

De Kernion, Jean B., jt. auth. see Skinner, Donald G.

De Kerpely, Theresa. Arabesque. 1977. pap. 1.95 o.p. (ISBN 0-451-07424-6, J7424, Sig). NAL.

De Kerval, Alastor see Kerval, Alastor de.

De Keyser, Ignace see Haine, Malou & Keyser, Ignace de.

De Kimpe, C. R., tr. see Duchaufour, Philippe.

Dekker, George. Coleridge & the Literature of Sensibility. (Critical Studies). 270p. 1978. text ed. 20.00x (ISBN 0-686-83548-4). B&N Imports.

Dekker, H. C., et al. Planning in a Dutch & a Yugoslav Steelworks: A Comparative Study. (Illus.). 1976. pap. text ed. 23.00x o.p. (ISBN 90-6032-078-6). Humanities.

Dekker, John, jt. auth. see Briggs, Asa.

Dekker, L. & Savastano, G., eds. Simulation of Systems, 1979. 1980. 138.50 (ISBN 0-444-86123-8). Elsevier.

DeKock, M. H. Central Banking. 4th ed. LC 74-78896. 318p. 1974. 27.50 (ISBN 0-312-12740-5). St Martin.

DeKock, Roger L. & Gray, Harry B. Chemical Structure & Bonding. 1980. 25.95 (ISBN 0-8053-2310-4). Benjamin-Cummings.

De Koninck & Ivic. Topics in Arithmetical Functions. (Mathematics Studies Ser.: Vol. 43). 1980. 42.75 (ISBN 0-444-86049-5, North Holland). Elsevier.

De Koning, A. J. & Jenner, F. A., eds. Phenomenology & Psychiatry. 1982. 36.00 (ISBN 0-8089-1432-4). Grune.

DeKornfeld, Thomas J. & Finch, Jay S. Respiratory Care Case Studies, Vol. 1. 3rd ed. (Illus.). 1982. pap. 20.00 (ISBN 0-87488-019-X). Med Exam.

DeKornfeld, Thomas J., jt. auth. see Slack, Steven J.

DeKornfeld, Thomas J. & Detmar, Michael W., eds. Anesthesiology. 5th ed. LC 61-66847. (Medical Examination Review Bk.: No. 12). 1980. pap. 21.50 (ISBN 0-87488-112-9). Med Exam.

Dekornfeld, Thomas J., et al. Respiratory Therapy Examination Review Book, Vol. 2. 2nd ed. Orig. Title: Inhalation Therapy Examination Review Book, Vol. 2. 1974. spiral bdg. 12.75 (ISBN 0-87488-344-X). Med Exam.

De Korosy. Approach to Chemistry. 1969. 18.50 (ISBN 0-444-19770-2). Elsevier.

DeKosky, Robert K. Knowledge & Cosmos: Development & Decline of the Medieval Perspective. LC 79-66226. 1979. text ed. 20.75 (ISBN 0-8191-0814-6); pap. text ed. 13.50 (ISBN 0-8191-0815-4). U Pr of Amer.

DeKoven, Marianne. A Different Language: Gertrude Stein's Experimental Writing. LC 82-70558. 288p. 1983. 22.50 (ISBN 0-299-09210-0). U of Wis Pr.

Dekovic, Gene, ed. see Emerson, Ralph Waldo.

De Kreter, D. M., et al, eds. The Pituitary & Testis: Clinical & Experimental Studies. (Monographs on Endocrinology: Vol. 25). (Illus.). 200p. 1983. 50.00 (ISBN 0-387-11874-8). Springer-Verlag.

Dekretser, David, jt. ed. see Burger, Henry.

De Kruif, Paul. Hunger Fighters. LC 67-32084. (YA) (gr. 7-12). 1967. pap. 0.95 (ISBN 0-15-642430-4, Harv). HarBraceJ.

--Microbe Hunters. LC 67-34588. 1966. pap. 4.95 (ISBN 0-15-659413-7, Harv). HarBraceJ.

De Kun, N. The Mineral Resources of Africa. 1965. 139.75 (ISBN 0-444-40163-6). Elsevier.

De la Barca, Pedro C. Celos Aun Del Aire Matan. Stroud, Matthew D., tr. LC 80-54543. (Illus.). 219p. (Sp. & Eng.). 1981. 12.00 (ISBN 0-911536-90-6); pap. 8.00 (ISBN 0-686-96901-4). Trinity U Pr.

De La Billardiere, J. J. Sertum Austro-Caledonicum. (Illus.). 1968. Repr. of 1825 ed. 64.00 (ISBN 3-7682-0541-X). Lubrecht & Cramer.

De la Ceppede, Jean. Theorems. Bosley, Keith, tr. from Fr. 132p. 1983. text ed. 19.00x (ISBN 0-85635-450-3, Pub. by Carcanet Pr England). Humanities.

De La Chavignerie, Emile B. & Auvray, Louis. Dictionnaire General, 5 vols. Rosenblum, Robert, ed. LC 78-68412. 1979. Repr. of 1885 ed. lib. bdg. 275.00 o.s.i. (ISBN 0-8240-3539-9). Garland Pub.

Delacorta. Diva. 1983. price not set. Summit Bks.

Delacorte, Peter. Games of Chance. 1982. pap. 2.95 (ISBN 0-451-11510-4, AE1510, Sig). NAL.

Delacote, G., ed. Physics Teaching in Schools. 404p. 1978. pap. write for info. (ISBN 0-85066-136-6, Pub. by Taylor & Francis). Intl Pubns Serv.

Delacour, Jean. Pheasant Breeding & Care. (Illus.). 1978. 14.95 (ISBN 0-87666-434-6, AP-6450). TFH Pubns.

--The Pheasants of the World. 1982. 125.00x (ISBN 0-904558-37-1, Pub. by Saiga Pub). State Mutual Bk.

--Wild Pigeons & Doves. rev. ed. (Illus.). 189p. 1980. 14.95 (ISBN 0-87666-968-2, AP-6810). TFH Pubns.

Delacroix, Eugene. Delacroix. Marchiore, Giuseppe, ed. (Art Library Ser: Vol. 28). 1969. pap. 3.50 (ISBN 0-448-00477-1, G&D). Putnam Pub Group.

De la Croix, Horst & Tansey, Richard G. Art Through the Ages. 7th ed. 922p. 1980. text ed. 24.95 o.p. (ISBN 0-15-503758-7, HC). HarBraceJ.

--Art Through the Ages, 2 vol. ed. 7th ed. Incl. Vol. 1. Ancient, Medieval & Non-European Art. 481p. pap. text ed. 16.95 o.p. (ISBN 0-15-503759-5); pap. 16.95 o.p. (ISBN 0-15-503760-9); Vol. 2. Renaissance & Modern Art. 489p. pap. text ed. 16.95 o.p. (ISBN 0-15-503760-9). 1980. study guide 6.95 o.p. (ISBN 0-15-503761-7, HC). HarBraceJ.

De La Croix, Horst see Cohen, Kathleen & Croix, Horst de la.

De la Cruz, Felix see Lubs, Herbert & Cruz, Felix de la.

De La Cruz, Felix F., jt. auth. see Davidson, Richard L.

De la Cruz, Felix F., ed. Trisomy Twenty-One (Down Syndrome) (NICHD-Mental Retardation Research Center Ser.). 318p. 1980. text ed. 34.95 (ISBN 0-8391-1588-1). Univ Park.

De Lacy, E. A., ed. see Philodemus.

De Lacy, Ph. H., ed. see Philodemus.

De Ladebat, Monique P. The Village That Slept. 1980. PLB 8.95 (ISBN 0-8398-2610-9, Gregg). G K Hall.

De La Fage, Adrien. Essais de Diptherographie musicale ou notices, descriptions, analyses, extraits et reproductions de manuscrits relatifs a la pratique, a la theorie et a l'histoire de la musique. 1964. Repr. of 1864 ed. 62.50 o.s.i. (ISBN 90-6027-006-1, Pub. by Frits Knuf Netherlands). Pendragon NY.

De La Farelle, F. F. Du Progres Social au Profit des Classes Populaires ou Indigentes. (Conditions of the 19th Century French Working Class Ser.). 514p. (Fr.). 1974. Repr. of 1847 ed. lib. bdg. 127.50x o.p. (ISBN 0-8287-0482-1, 1095). Clearwater Pub.

De Lafayette, Marie see Lafayette, Marie.

De Lafontaine, Henry C. The King's Musick: A Transcript of Records Relative to Music & Musicians. LC 70-169648. 522p. 1973. Repr. of 1909 ed. lib. bdg. 45.00 (ISBN 0-306-70269-X). Da Capo.

De La Fuente, Julio, ed. see Malinowski, Bronislaw.

Delafuente, Lucien, jt. auth. see Metz, Elizabeth.

De La Fuente, Patricia, ed. Chicano. Date not set. 3.00 (ISBN 0-938884-02-6). RiverSedge Pr.

De La Fuente, R., ed. see World Congress of Psychiatry 5th, Mexico, D. F. Nov. 25 - Dec. 4, 1971.

De La Fuente, Tomas, tr. see Cowan, Marvin W.

De La Fuente, Tomas R. Jesus Nos Habla Por Medio De Sus Parabolas. 1978. 2.95 (ISBN 0-311-04344-5). Casa Bautista.

DeLage, Ida. ABC Christmas. LC 77-14604. (Once Upon an ABC). (Illus.). (gr. k-4). 1978. PLB 6.69 (ISBN 0-8116-4355-7). Garrard.

--ABC Easter Bunny. LC 78-14829. (Once Upon an ABC Ser.). (Illus.). (gr. k-4). 1979. PLB 6.69 (ISBN 0-8116-4356-5). Garrard.

--ABC Fire Dogs. LC 77-591. (Once Upon an ABC). (Illus.). (gr. k-4). 1977. PLB 6.69 (ISBN 0-8116-4351-4). Garrard.

--ABC Halloween Witch. LC 77-5469. (Once Upon an ABC). (Illus.). (gr. k-4). 1977. lib. bdg. 6.69 (ISBN 0-8116-4353-0). Garrard.

--ABC Pigs Go to Market. LC 77-23317. (Once Upon an ABC). (Illus.). (gr. k-4). 1977. lib. bdg. 6.69 (ISBN 0-8116-4350-6). Garrard.

--ABC Pirate Adventure. LC 77-3171. (Once Upon an ABC). (Illus.). (gr. k-4). 1977. PLB 6.69 (ISBN 0-8116-4352-2). Garrard.

--ABC Santa Claus. LC 77-5629. (Once Upon an ABC). (Illus.). (gr. k-4). 1978. PLB 6.69 (ISBN 0-8116-4354-9). Garrard.

--ABC Triplets at the Zoo. LC 79-13265. (Once Upon an ABC Ser.). (Illus.). 32p. (gr. k-4). 1980. PLB 6.69 (ISBN 0-8116-4357-3). Garrard.

--Am I a Bunny? LC 77-11639. (Ida De Lage Bks.). (Illus.). (gr. k-2). 1978. lib. bdg. 6.69 (ISBN 0-8116-6072-9). Garrard.

--Beware! Beware! a Witch Won't Share. LC 72-76326. (Old Witch Books). (Illus.). 48p. (gr. k-4). 1972. PLB 6.69 (ISBN 0-8116-4059-0). Garrard.

--A Bunny Ride. LC 74-14818. (Ida DeLage Bks.). (Illus.). 32p. (gr. k-2). 1975. PLB 6.69 (ISBN 0-8116-6065-6). Garrard.

--Bunny School. LC 76-17625. (Ida DeLage Bks.). (Illus.). 32p. (gr. k-2). 1976. PLB 6.69 (ISBN 0-8116-6071-0). Garrard.

--Farmer & the Witch. LC 66-12674. (Old Witch Books). (Illus.). (gr. k-4). 1966. PLB 6.69 (ISBN 0-8116-4050-7). Garrard.

--Frannie's Flower. LC 79-11724. (Ida DeLage Bks.). (Illus.). (gr. k-2). 1979. PLB 6.69 (ISBN 0-8116-6076-1). Garrard.

--Good Morning, Lady. LC 73-22084. (Ida DeLage Bks.). (Illus.). 32p. (gr. k-2). 1974. PLB 6.69 (ISBN 0-8116-6051-6). Garrard.

--Hello, Come in. LC 71-156079. (Venture Ser.). (Illus.). 40p. (gr. 1). 1971. PLB 6.69 (ISBN 0-8116-6708-1). Garrard.

--Old Witch & Her Magic Basket. LC 78-58520. (Old Witch Ser.). (Illus.). (gr. k-4). 1978. PLB 6.69 (ISBN 0-8116-4063-9) Garrard.

--The Old Witch & the Crows. LC 81-13227. (Old Witch Bks.). (Illus.). 48p. (gr. k-4). 1983. PLB write for info. (ISBN 0-8116-4067-1). Garrard.

--The Old Witch & the Dragon. LC 78-11283. (Old Witch Ser.). (Illus.). (gr. k-4). 1979. lib. bdg. 6.69 (ISBN 0-8116-4064-7). Garrard.

--The Old Witch & the Ghost Parade. LC 77-18185. (Old Witch Ser). (Illus.). (gr. k-4). 1978. PLB 6.69 (ISBN 0-8116-4062-0). Garrard.

--Old Witch & the Snores. LC 75-95748. (Old Witch Books). (Illus.). (gr. k-4). 1970. PLB 6.69 (ISBN 0-8116-4056-6). Garrard.

--Old Witch & the Wizard. LC 73-16039. (Old Witch Books). (Illus.). 48p. (gr. k-4). 1974. PLB 6.69 (ISBN 0-8116-4060-4). Garrard.

--The Old Witch Finds a New House. LC 79-11732. (Old Witch Ser.). (Illus.). (gr. k-4). 1979. PLB 6.69 (ISBN 0-8116-4065-5). Garrard.

--Old Witch Goes to the Ball. LC 69-15830. (Old Witch Books). (Illus.). (gr. k-4). 1969. PLB 6.69 (ISBN 0-8116-4055-8). Garrard.

--The Old Witch's Party. LC 75-45232. (Old Witch Books). (Illus.). 48p. (gr. k-4). 1976. PLB 6.69 (ISBN 0-8116-4061-2). Garrard.

--Pilgrim Children Come to Plymouth. LC 80-29180. (Illus.). 48p. (gr. 1-5). 1981. lib. bdg. 6.69 (ISBN 0-8116-6084-2). Garrard.

--The Pilgrim Children on the Mayflower. LC 79-21812. (Ida DeLage Bks.). (Illus.). 48p. (gr. 1-5). 1980. PLB 6.69 (ISBN 0-8116-4315-8). Garrard.

--Pink Pink. LC 72-11015. (Venture Ser). (Illus.). 40p. (gr. 1). 1973. PLB 6.69 (ISBN 0-8116-6725-1). Garrard.

--Weeny Witch. LC 68-10173. (Old Witch Books). (Illus.). (gr. k-4). 1968. PLB 6.69 (ISBN 0-8116-4052-3). Garrard.

--What Does a Witch Need? LC 76-143305. (Old Witch Books). (Illus.). (gr. k-4). 1971. PLB 6.69 (ISBN 0-8116-4058-2). Garrard.

--Witchy Broom. LC 69-10373. (Old Witch Books). (Illus.). (gr. k-4). 1969. PLB 6.69 (ISBN 0-8116-4054-X). Garrard.

Delagi, Edward F. & Perotto, Aldo. Anatomic Guide for Electromyographer: The Limbs. 2nd ed. (Illus.). 224p. 1982. 18.75x (ISBN 0-398-03951-8). C C Thomas.

Delagran, Louise, ed. see Masters, M.

Delagran, Louise, ed. see Meadowbrook Reference Group.

De La Harpe, J. F. Eloge De Voltaire. Repr. of 1780 ed. 41.00 o.p. (ISBN 0-8287-0489-9). Clearwater Pub.

De la Iglesia, Maria E. The International Catalogue of Catalogues: The Complete Guide to World-Wide Shopping by Mail. rev. ed. LC 81-48041. (Illus.). 224p. (Orig.). 1982. 21.11 (ISBN 0-06-014985-X, HarpT); pap. 10.53i (ISBN 0-06-090942-0, CN 942, HarpT). Har-Row.

Delaigue, Joelle, jt. auth. see Schneider, Jost.

Delaisse, L. M. A Century of Dutch Manuscript Illumination. (California Studies in the History of Art: No. VI). (Illus.). 1968. 74.50x (ISBN 0-520-00315-2). U of Cal Pr.

De La Laurencie, Lionel. Lully. LC 77-3976. (Music Reprint Ser.). (Illus., Fr.). 1977. Repr. of 1911 ed. lib. bdg. 27.50 (ISBN 0-306-70894-9). Da Capo.

Delamar, Gloria. Children's Counting-Out Rhymes, Fingerplays, Jump Rope & Ball Bounce Chants & Other Rhythms: A Comprehensive English-Language Reference. LC 82-24904. 200p. 1983. lib. bdg. 19.95x (ISBN 0-89950-064-1). McFarland & Co.

De La Mare, P. B. Electrophilic Halogenation. LC 75-13451. (Chemistry Texts Ser.). (Illus.). 280p. 1976. 45.00 (ISBN 0-521-20968-4); pap. 17.95 (ISBN 0-521-29014-7). Cambridge U Pr.

De la Mare, P. D. & Bolton, R. Electrophilic Additions to Unsaturated Systems. 2nd ed. (Studies in Organic Chemistry: Vol. 9). 1982. 91.50 (ISBN 0-444-42030-4). Elsevier.

De la Mare, Walter. Best Stories of Walter de la Mare. 400p. (Orig.). Date not set. pap. 7.95 (ISBN 0-571-13076-3). Faber & Faber.

--Molly Whuppie. (Illus.). 32p. (gr. 1 up). 1983. 10.95 (ISBN 0-374-35000-0). FS&G.

De Lamartine. Poemes Choisis. Barbier, J. L., ed. (Modern French Text Ser.). 1921. pap. write for info. (ISBN 0-7190-0147-1). Manchester.

De Lamartine, Alphonse see Lamartine, Alphonse de.

DeLamater, John & MacCorqvodale, Patricia. Premarital Sexuality: Attitudes, Relationships, Behavior. LC 78-65019. 314p. 1979. 27.50 (ISBN 0-299-07840-X). U of Wis Pr.

Delamere, C., jt. auth. see Calhoun, G. M.

Delamont, Sara. Sex Roles & the School. 1980. 17.50x (ISBN 0-416-71310-6); pap. 7.50x (ISBN 0-416-71320-3). Methuen Inc.

--Sociology of Women: An Introduction. 256p. (Orig.). 1980. text ed. 22.50x (ISBN 0-04-301119-5); pap. text ed. 8.95x (ISBN 0-04-301120-9). Allen Unwin.

Delamont, Sara, jt. ed. see Stubbs, Michael.

Delamont, Victor L. The Ministry of Music in the Church. LC 79-25918. 1980. pap. 5.95 (ISBN 0-8024-5673-1). Moody.

Delamore, I. W., jt. auth. see Israels, M. G.

DeLamotte, Roy C. The Alien Christ. LC 80-5902. 276p. 1980. lib. bdg. 21.25 (ISBN 0-8191-1304-2); pap. text ed. 11.00 (ISBN 0-8191-1305-0). U Pr of Amer.

--Jalaluddin Rumi: Songbird of Sufism. LC 80-5884. 187p. 1980. lib. bdg. 19.00 (ISBN 0-8191-1286-0); pap. text ed. 9.25 (ISBN 0-8191-1287-9). U Pr of Amer.

Delancey, Mark & Delancey, Virginia. A Bibliography of Cameroon. LC 75-1165. (African Bibliography Ser.: Vol. 4). 675p. 1975. text ed. 45.00x (ISBN 0-8419-0167-8, Africana). Holmes & Meier.

DeLancey, Mark W. African International Relations: An Annotated Bibliography. 366p. 1980. 27.50 (ISBN 0-89158-680-6). Westview.

DeLancey, Mark W., ed. Aspects of International Relations in Africa. (African Humanities Ser.). 253p. (Orig.). 1980. pap. 9.00 (ISBN 0-941934-28-4). Ind U Afro-Amer Arts.

Delancey, Virginia, jt. auth. see Delancey, Mark.
Delancy, Samuel R. Fall of the Towers. 224p. 1982. pap. 2.50 (ISBN 0-553-20309-6). Bantam.
DeLand, Antoinette. Fielding's Worldwide Guide to Cruises. rev. ed. (Illus.). 320p. 1982. pap. 12.95 (ISBN 0-688-01648-0). Morrow.
--Fielding's Worldwide Guide to Cruises. rev. ed. LC 82-62320. (Illus.). 384p. 1982. pap. 12.45 (ISBN 0-686-38814-3). Fielding.
Deland, Frank H. Cerebral Radionuclide Angiography. LC 75-292. (Illus.). 1976. text ed. 42.00 o.p. (ISBN 0-7216-3018-9). Saunders.
DeLand, Frank H. & Wagner, Henry W. Atlas of Nuclear Medicine: Reticuloendothelial System, Liver, Spleen & Thyroid, Vol. 3. LC 74-81820. (Illus.). 1972. 40.00 o.p. (ISBN 0-7216-3017-0). Saunders.
De Landa, Diego. The Maya: Diego De Landa's Account of the Affairs of Yucatan. Pagden, A. R., ed. & tr. from Span. LC 70-190752. (Illus.). 1975. cancelled 15.00 o.p. (ISBN 0-87955-303-0). O'Hara.
Delaney, Anita J., jt. ed. see Mizio, Emelicia.
Delaney, C. F., et al, eds. The Problems of Philosophy. LC 76-643. 384p. 1976. text ed. 12.95x o.p. (ISBN 0-268-01521-X). U of Notre Dame Pr.
Delaney, Daniel J., jt. auth. see Eisenberg, Sheldon.
Delaney, Edmund. The Conneticut River: New England's Historic Waterway. (Illus.). 224p. 1983. pap. 9.95 (ISBN 0-87106-980-6). Globe Pequot.
Delaney, Gayle. Living Your Dreams. LC 78-20590. 240p. 1981. pap. 6.68i (ISBN 0-06-250201-8, CN 4018, HarpR). Har-Row.
Delaney, J. W. & Garratty, G. Handbook of Hematological & Blood Transfusion Technique. 2nd ed. (Illus.). 1969. pap. text ed. 11.95x o.p. (ISBN 0-407-72852-X). Butterworth.
Delaney, John J. Pocket Dictionary of Saints. LC 82-45479. 528p. 1983. pap. 5.95 (ISBN 0-385-18274-0, Im). Doubleday.
--Saints Are Now: Eight Portraits of Modern Sanctity. LC 82-45866. 224p. 1983. pap. 4.50 (ISBN 0-385-17356-3, Im). Doubleday.
Delaney, John J., ed. Saints for All Seasons. LC 77-81438. 1978. 7.95 o.p. (ISBN 0-385-12908-4); pap. 3.95 (ISBN 0-385-12909-2, Im). Doubleday.
--Why Catholic. LC 78-14653. 1980. pap. 3.50 o.p. (ISBN 0-385-14185-8, Im). Doubleday.
Delaney, M. C. The Marigold Monster. LC 82-14739. (Illus.). 32p. (ps-3). 1983. 9.95 (ISBN 0-525-44023-2, 0966-290). Dutton.
Delaney, Mary M. Of Irish Ways. (BN 4000 Ser.). pap. 5.95 (ISBN 0-06-464035-3, BN). B&N NY.
Delaney, Ned. Terrible Things Could Happen. LC 82-10051. (Illus.). 32p. (gr. k-3). 1983. 10.00 (ISBN 0-688-01282-5); PLB 9.55 (ISBN 0-688-01284-1). Lothrop.
Delaney, Patrick R. & Adler, James R. GAAP: Transaction Approach. 528p. 1983. text ed. write for info (ISBN 0-471-86144-8). Wiley.
Delaney, Patrick R., jt. auth. see Gleim, Irvin M.
Delaney, Patrick R., jt. auth. see Gleim, Irvin N.
Delaney, Patrick R., jt. auth. see Gleim, Irwin N.
Delaney, Samuel R. The Einstein Intersection. Del Rey, Lester, ed. LC 75-402. (Library of Science Fiction). 1975. lib. bdg. 17.50 o.s.i. (ISBN 0-8240-1407-3). Garland Pub.
Delaney, Sue. The Lord, the Lion & Mutn. pap. 0.95 (ISBN 0-89985-995-X). Christ Nations.
--Mutu Finds the Way to Heaven. pap. 0.95 (ISBN 0-89985-996-8). Christ Nations.
Delanghe, R., jt. auth. see Brackt, F.
Delanglez, Jean. El Rio Del Espiritu Santo: An Essay on the Cartography of the Gulf Coast & the Adjacent Territory During the 16th & 17th Centuries. LC 48-2640. (Monograph Ser.: No. 21). (Illus.). 1945. 6.50x o.p. (ISBN 0-930060-03-2). US Cath Hist.
Delank, Claudia. Die Struktur des Zylklus "Four Quartets" Von T. S. Eliot. 327p. (Ger.). 1982. write for info. (ISBN 3-8204-5810-7). P Lang Pubs.
Delano, A. Life on the Plains & at the Diggings. LC 81-16565. (Classics of the Old West). lib. bdg. 17.28 (ISBN 0-8094-3987-5). Silver.
Delano, Anne. Field Hockey. (Physical Education Activities Ser.). 80p. 1968. pap. text ed. write for info. (ISBN 0-697-07010-7); tchrs.' manual avail. (ISBN 0-697-07217-7). Wm C Brown.
--Lacrosse for Girls & Women. (Physical Education Activities Ser.). 80p. 1970. pap. text ed. write for info. (ISBN 0-697-07018-2); tchrs.' manual avail. (ISBN 0-697-07221-5). Wm C Brown.
Delano, Poli see Alegria, Fernando, et al.
De La Nuez, Manual. Eduardo Marquina. LC 76-5796. (World Authors Ser.). 1976. lib. bdg. 15.95 (ISBN 0-8057-6238-8, Twayne). G K Hall.
Delany, M. J. Ecology of Mammals. (Tertiary Level Biology Ser.). 1982. 36.00x (ISBN 0-412-00081-4, Pub. by Chapman & Hall England); pap. 16.95x (ISBN 0-412-00091-1). Methuen Inc.
Delany, M. R. & Campbell, Robert. Search for a Place: Black Separatism & Africa, 1860. Bell, Howard, ed. 1971. pap. 2.25 o.p. (ISBN 0-472-06179-8, AA). U of Mich Pr.
Delany, Samuel. Dhalgren. 1983. pap. 3.95 (ISBN 0-553-14861-3). Bantam.
Delany, Samuel R. Babel-Seventeen. (The Science Fiction of Samuel R. Delany Ser.). 176p. 1976. Repr. of 1969 ed. lib. bdg. 9.95 o.p. (ISBN 0-8398-2328-2, Gregg). G K Hall.
--The Ballad of Beta Two. 144p. 1982. 2.50 (ISBN 0-553-20312-6). Bantam.
--The Ballad of Beta-2. (The Science Fiction of Samuel R. Delany). 1977. lib. bdg. 9.95 o.p. (ISBN 0-8398-2393-2, Gregg). G K Hall.
--Dhalgren. 1977. lib. bdg. 35.00 (ISBN 0-8398-2396-7, Gregg). G K Hall.
--Driftglass. (The Science Fiction of Samuel R. Delany). 1977. lib. bdg. 13.00 o.p. (ISBN 0-8398-2395-9, Gregg). G K Hall.
--Empire Star. (Science Fiction Ser.). 1977. lib. bdg. 9.95 o.p. (ISBN 0-8398-2394-0, Gregg). G K Hall.
--The Fall of the Towers. 1977. Repr. of 1970 ed. lib. bdg. 16.00 o.p. (ISBN 0-8398-2372-X, Gregg). G K Hall.
--The Jewels of Aptor. (Science Fiction Ser.). 176p. 1976. Repr. of 1971 ed. lib. bdg. 9.95 o.p. (ISBN 0-8398-2329-0, Gregg). G K Hall.
--Nova. 1977. lib. bdg. 12.00 (ISBN 0-8398-2397-5, Gregg). G K Hall.
--The Science Fiction of Samuel R. Delany. 1977. 110.00 o.p. (ISBN 0-686-74232-X, Gregg). G K Hall.
--Triton. 1977. Repr. of 1976 ed. lib. bdg. 15.00 o.p. (ISBN 0-8398-2371-1, Gregg). G K Hall.
Delany, Sheila, ed. Counter-Tradition: A Reader in the Literature of Dissent & Alternatives. LC 73-147018. 1971. text ed. 10.00x o.p. (ISBN 0-465-01429-1); pap. 7.50x o.p. (ISBN 0-465-01430-5). Basic.
Delany, Veronica, ed. see Cary, Patrick.
Delany, Vincent T., ed. Frederic William Maitland Reader. LC 57-10624. (Docket Ser.: Vol. 10). 256p. 1957. 15.00 (ISBN 0-379-11310-4); pap. 2.50 (ISBN 0-379-11310-4). Oceana.
De laPena, Augustin. The Psychobiology of Cancer: Automatization & Boredom in Health & Disease. 256p. 1983. 25.95x (ISBN 0-89789-002-7). J F Bergin.
De La Perriere, Guillaume see La Perriere, Guillaume de.
De La Plain, S., jt. auth. see Kiley-Worthington, M.
Delaporte. The Devil: Does He Exist & What Does He Do? 212p. pap. 4.00 (ISBN 0-686-81625-0). TAN Bks Pubs.
De La Portilla & Varela. Mejora Tu Espanol. 300p. (gr. 9-12). 1979. pap. text ed. 7.95 (ISBN 0-88345-366-5, 18427); tchr's manual, 73 pp. 5.95 (ISBN 0-88345-414-9, 18429); cassettes 25.00. Regents Pub.
De La Ramee, Louise. Dog of Flanders & Other Stories. (Companion Library). (Illus.). (gr. 7 up). 1965. 2.95 o.s.i. (ISBN 0-448-05480-9, G&D). Putnam Pub Group.
De la Ramee, Louise see Ouida, pseud.
De Laredo, E. Abecassis see Latin School of Physics, 14th Caracas, Venezuela July 10-28, 1972.
De La Rosa, Denise M., jt. auth. see Kolin, Michael J.
De la Suaree, Octavio. La Obra Literaria De Regino E. Boti. LC 77-75376. (Senda de Estudios y Ensayos). (Orig., Span.). 1977. pap. 9.95 (ISBN 0-918454-02-6). Senda Nueva.
De la Torre Bueno, Laura, jt. ed. see Graham, Munir.
Delattre, Andre, ed. see Olivier, Juste.
Delattre, Pierre. Advanced Training in French Pronunciation. 1949. pap. 3.50x (ISBN 0-910408-03-3); record 7.95 (ISBN 0-910408-04-1). Coll Store.
--Les Difficultes Phonetiques Du Francais. (Fr.). 1948. pap. 3.50x (ISBN 0-910408-02-5). Coll Store.
--Principes De Phonetique Francaise a l' Usage Des Etudiants Anglo-Americains. (Fr.). 1951. pap. 3.50x (ISBN 0-910408-01-7). Coll Store.
DeLauer, Marjel Jean. The Mystery of the Phantom Billionaire. Young, Billie, ed. LC 72-83301. 1972. 9.95 (ISBN 0-87949-005-5). Ashley Bks.
De Lauer, R. D., jt. auth. see Bussard, R. W.
Delaume, Georges. Transnational Contracts: Applicable Law & Settlement of Disputes, 5 bndrs, Vol. 1. LC 74-30028. 1975. Set. looseleaf suppl. to 1979 500.00 (ISBN 0-379-10200-5). Oceana.
Delaume, Georges R. American-French Private International Law. 2nd ed. LC 61-13055. (Bilateral Studies in Private International Law: No. 2). 221p. 1961. 15.00 (ISBN 0-379-11402-X). Oceana.
Delaunay, Charles. Django Reinhardt. James, Michael, tr. from Fr. (Quality Paperbacks Ser.). (Illus.). 247p. 1982. pap. 7.95 (ISBN 0-306-80171-X). Da Capo.
Delauney, Charles. New Hot Discography. 1948. 16.00 (ISBN 0-910468-04-4). Criterion Mus.
DeLaura, David, ed. see Newman, John H.
DeLaurence, Lauron W. Master Key. 3.95x o.p. (ISBN 0-685-22037-0). Wehman.
De Laurentis, Anthony C. You are Never too Old to Live: For People from 35 to 100 Who are Eager for New Challenges in Life. (Illus.). 117p. 1983. 19.75 (ISBN 0-89266-394-4). Am Classical Coll Pr.
DeLaurentis, Teresa & Heath, Stephen, eds. The Cinematic Apparatus. 1980. 25.00 (ISBN 0-312-13907-1). St Martin.
De La Vallieres, William. The Theory, Application & Practice of the Point & Figure Method of Stock Market Chart Analysis. (The New Stock Market Library). (Illus.). 1978. 77.75 (ISBN 0-89266-126-7). Am Classical Coll Pr.
De la Vega, Garcilaso see Garcilaso de la Vega.
De La Vega, Sara L. & Parr, Carmen S. Avanzando: Gramatica espanola y leetura. LC 77-18537. 287p. 1978. text ed. 17.95 (ISBN 0-471-02731-6); wkbk. A 10.50 (ISBN 0-471-02732-4); wkbk. B 9.95 (ISBN 0-471-02733-2). Wiley.
Delavnay, Charles. Dejango Reinhardt (Jazz) (Roots of Jazz Ser.). 247p. 1981. 25.00 (ISBN 0-306-76057-6). Da Capo.
Delaware Technical & Community College, English Department. Writing Skills for Technical Students. 400p. 1982. pap. text ed. 10.95 (ISBN 0-13-970665-8). P-H.
Delay, Jean. Youth of Andre Gide. Guicharnaud, June, tr. LC 63-13060. 1963. 12.00x o.s.i. (ISBN 0-226-14207-8). U of Chicago Pr.
Delbanco, Nicholas. Small Rain. LC 74-17481. 1975. 7.95 o.p. (ISBN 0-688-02885-3). Morrow.
--Stillness. (The Sherbrookes Trilogy). 1982. pap. 7.50 (ISBN 0-688-00978-6). Quill NY.
Del Barco, Miguel & Tiscareno, Froylan, trs. The Natural History of Baja California. (Baja California Travel Ser.: No. 43). (Illus.). 300p. 50.00 (ISBN 0-87093-243-8). Dawson's.
Delbecq, Andre, et al. Group Techniques for Program Planning: A Guide to Nominal Group & Delphi Processes. 1975. pap. 10.95x (ISBN 0-673-07591-5). Scott F.
D'Elbee. Journal du Voyage du Sieur Delbee, aux Isles, dans la Coste de Guynee. (Bibliotheque Africaine Ser.). 216p. (Fr.). 1974. Repr. of 1671 ed. lib. bdg. 61.00x o.p. (ISBN 0-8287-1066-X, 72-2152). Clearwater Pub.
Delbruck, Hans. History of the Art of War Within the Framework of Political History, Vol. II: The Germans. Renfroe, Walter J., Jr., tr. from Ger. LC 72-792. (Contributions in Military History: No. 20). (Illus.). 552p. 1980. lib. bdg. 45.00 (ISBN 0-8371-8163-1, DEC/). Greenwood.
--History of the Art of War Within the Framework of Political History, Vol. I: Antiquity. Renfroe, Walter J., Jr., tr. from Ger. LC 72-792. (Contributions in Military History: No. 9). (Illus.). 604p. 1975. lib. bdg. 45.00 (ISBN 0-8371-6365-X, DEB/). Greenwood.
Del Bueno, Dorothy. A Financial Guide for Nurses: Investing in Yourself & Others. (Illus.). 240p. 1982. text ed. 19.95 (ISBN 0-86542-007-6). Blackwell Sci.
Del Carmen, Rolando. Criminal Procedure & Evidence. (HBJ Criminal Justice Ser.). 190p. 1979. pap. text ed. 10.95 o.p. (ISBN 0-15-550490-8, HC); instructor's manual avail. o.p. (ISBN 0-15-516100-8). HarBraceJ.
Del Carmen, Vicente. Rizal: An Encyclopedic Collection, Vol. 1. (Illus.). 217p. (Orig.). 1982. 15.75 (ISBN 971-10-0058-X, Pub. by New Day Philippines); pap. 10.75 (ISBN 971-10-0059-8). Cellar.
Del Carril, Bonifacio, tr. see Saint-Exupery, Antione De.
Del Castillo, Richard G. The Los Angeles Barrio: 1850-1890-A Social History. (Illus.). 232p. 1982. 22.50x (ISBN 0-520-03816-9); pap. 6.95 (ISBN 0-520-04773-7). U of Cal Pr.
Del Castillo, Ronald. Commodity Futures Trading: The Essential Knowledge Which Everybody, but Absolutely Everybody Ought to Possess About Speculating in Commodity Futures. (Essential Knowledge Ser.). (Illus.). 1978. plastic spiral bdg. 44.95 (ISBN 0-89266-117-8). Am Classical Coll Pr.
--Commodity Futures Trading: The Essential Knowledge You Must Possess to Master the Commodity Market. (Illus.). 149p. 1981. 44.85 (ISBN 0-89266-330-8). Am Classical Coll Pr.
Del Cecchetti, Giovanni see Leopardi, Giacomo.
Del Chiaro, Mario A. Etruscan Red-Figured Vase-Painting at Caere. LC 73-85785. 1975. 52.50x (ISBN 0-520-02578-4). U of Cal Pr.
Del Corso, Steven, et al. Blue Domino. LC 78-55617. 1978. 9.95 o.p. (ISBN 0-399-11902-7). Putnam Pub Group.
Delden, E. Standard Fabrication Practices for Cane Sugar Mills. (Sugar Ser.: Vol. 1). 1981. 53.25 (ISBN 0-444-41958-6). Elsevier.
D'Elden, Karl H. Van see Van D'Elden, Karl H. & Kirchow, Evelyn.
Delderfield, Eric. Stories of Inns & their Signs in Britain. (Illus.). 1982. 12.50 o.p. (ISBN 0-7153-6249-6). David & Charles.
Delderfield, R. F. All Over the Town. 1977. 8.95 o.p. (ISBN 0-671-22920-6). S&S.
--Charlie, Come Home. 1977. Repr. lib. bdg. 16.95 o.p. (ISBN 0-8161-6448-7, Large Print Bks). G K Hall.
--Napoleon's Marshals. LC 66-16287. (Illus.). 1980. pap. 7.95 (ISBN 0-8128-6055-1). Stein & Day.
--Stop at a Winner. 1978. 9.95 o.p. (ISBN 0-671-24229-6). S&S.
Delderfield, Ronald F. Horseman Riding By. 1967. 10.95 o.p. (ISBN 0-671-31893-4). S&S.
Del Duca, Anthony see Duca, Anthony Del.
Del Duca, Louis. Commercial, Business & Trade Laws: Italy. Date not set. loose-leaf 125.00 (ISBN 0-379-22002-4). Oceana.
de Leal, Magdalena Leon see Deere, Carmen & Leal, Magdalena Leon de.
Deledda, Grazia. L'edera. (Easy Reader, C. Ser.). 96p. (Ital.). 1981. pap. text ed. 3.95 (ISBN 0-88436-884-X, 55257). EMC.
--The Mother. LC 23-16660. 1974. 12.95 (ISBN 0-910220-57-3). Berg.
De Leener, M. F., jt. auth. see Resibois, P.
DeLeenheer, A. P., ed. see International Symposium on Quantitative Mass Spectrometry in Life Sciences, 1st, State University of Ghent Belgium June 16-18 1976.
DeLeeuw, Adele. John Henry, Steel-Drivin' Man. LC 66-20136. (American Folktales Ser.). (Illus.). (gr. 2-5). 1966. PLB 6.69 (ISBN 0-8116-4004-3). Garrard.
--Paul Bunyan & His Blue Ox. LC 68-10710. (American Folktales Ser.). (Illus.). (gr. 2-5). 1968. PLB 6.69 (ISBN 0-8116-4007-8). Garrard.
--Who Can Kill the Lion. LC 66-20137. (Fantasy Ser.). (Illus.). 48p. (gr. k-4). 1966. PLB 6.69 (ISBN 0-8116-4051-5). Garrard.
De Leeuw, Cateau. Benedict Arnold: Hero & Traitor. (Spies of the World Ser.). (Illus.). 1970. PLB 4.79 o.p. (ISBN 0-399-60050-7). Putnam Pub Group.
De Leeuw, J. H. see Von Mises, Richard & Von Karman, Theodore.
De Leeuw, P. W., jt. ed. see Birkenhager, W. H.
De Leeuw, S., jt. auth. see Southworth, R.
Delehanty, Suzanne & Ashton, Dave. Eight Abstract Painters. (Illus.). 1978. pap. 4.00 o.p. (ISBN 0-88454-024-3). U of Pa Contemp Art.
De Leiris, Alain. The Drawings of Edouard Manet. LC 68-13017. (Studies in the History of Art: No. 10). 1969. 86.50x (ISBN 0-520-01547-9). U of Cal Pr.
De Leiris, Lucia. Shells of the World Coloring Book. (Coloring Bks.). (Illus.). 45p. (Orig.). (gr. 2 up). 1982. pap. 2.25 (ISBN 0-486-24368-0). Dover.
Delellis. Diagnostic Immunohistochemistry. LC 81-4949. (Masson Monographs in Diagnostic Pathology: Vol. 2). (Illus.). 360p. 1981. 68.75x (ISBN 0-89352-126-4). Masson Pub.
De Leon, Arnoldo. They Called Them Greasers: Anglo Attitudes Toward Mexicans in Texas 1821-1900. 184p. 1983. 19.95 (ISBN 0-292-70363-5); pap. 8.85 (ISBN 0-292-78054-0). U of Tex Pr.
De Leon, Daniel, tr. see Bebel, August.
De Leon, Fray L. The Unknown Light: The Poems of Fray Luis de Leon. Barnstone, Willis, tr. LC 79-15030. 1979. 33.50x (ISBN 0-87395-394-0); pap. 11.95x (ISBN 0-87395-444-0). State U NY Pr.
DeLeon, Peter. Development & Diffusion of the Nuclear Power Reactor: A Comparative Analysis. LC 79-12988. 352p. 1979. prof ref 27.50x (ISBN 0-88410-682-9). Ballinger Pub.
De Lerin, O. S. D., tr. see Hudson, R. Lofton.
De Lerin, Olivia, tr. see Crane, J. D.
De Lerin, Olivia S. Enviame a Mi: Aventuras de los esposos Davis, fundadores de la C. B. P. 64p. 1980. pap. 1.75 (ISBN 0-311-01062-8). Casa Bautista.
De Lerin, Olivia S. D., tr. see Bisagno, Juan.
Delesalle, Paul. Les Conditions de Travail Chez les Ouvriers en Instruments de Precision de Paris. (Conditions of the 19th Century French Working Class Ser.). 35p. (Fr.). 1974. Repr. of 1899 ed. lib. bdg. 21.00 o.p. (ISBN 0-8287-0255-1, 1122). Clearwater Pub.
Delesie, Luk, jt. auth. see Blanpain, Jan.
DeLespinasse, Paul. Thinking About Politics: American Government in Associational Perspective. (Orig.). 1980. pap. 14.95 (ISBN 0-442-25409-1). Van Nos Reinhold.
Delessert, Etienne. The Endless Party. Tabberner, Jeffrey, tr. from Fr. Orig. Title: San Fin la Fete. (Illus.). 32p. (ps-3). 1981. 11.95 (ISBN 0-19-279753-0). Oxford U Pr.
Deleuze, Gilles & Tomlinson, Hugh. Nietzsche & Philosophy. (European Perspectives Ser.). 275p. 1983. text ed. 25.00. Columbia U Pr.
Delf, George. Jomo Kenyatta: Towards Truth About "the Light of Kenya". LC 75-17469. 215p. 1975. Repr. of 1961 ed. lib. bdg. 16.00x (ISBN 0-8371-8307-3, DEJK). Greenwood.
Delffs, Sofie, tr. see Scheffel, Josef V.
Delfinado, Mercedes D. & Hardy, D. Elmo. A Catalog of the Diptera of the Oriental Region, Vol. 3. LC 74-174544. 1977. text ed. 40.00s (ISBN 0-8248-0346-9). UH Pr.
--Catalog of the Diptera of the Oriental Region, Vol. 1: Suborder Nematocera. LC 74-174544. 350p. 1973. text ed. 30.00x (ISBN 0-8248-0205-5). UH Pr.
--A Catalog of the Diptera of the Oriental Region, Vol. 2: Suborder Brachycera, Suborder Cyclorrhapha Through Division Aschiza. LC 74-174544. 480p. 1975. text ed. 25.00x (ISBN 0-8248-0274-8). UH Pr.
Delfinado, Mercedes D., jt. auth. see Hardy, D. Elmo.
Delfosse, Edita. How to Raise & Train an Akita. (Orig.). pap. 2.95 (ISBN 0-87666-234-3, DS1041). TFH Pubns.
Delgado, Abelardo. Letters to Louise. LC 82-50707. 1982. pap. 5.00 (ISBN 0-89229-008-0). Tonatiuh-Quinto Sol Intl.

Delgado, Enrique, jt. ed. see Cline, William R.
Delgado, Gregorio & Smith, Julian P. Management of Complications in Gynecologic Oncology. LC 81-16135. 287p. 1982. 38.00 (ISBN 0-471-05993-5, Pub. by Wiley Med). Wiley.
Delgado, J. M., ed. Behavioral Neurochemistry. DeFeudis, F. V. LC 76-22627. 270p. 1977. 20.00x o.s.i. (ISBN 0-470-15179-X). Halsted Pr.
Delgaty, Alfa & Sanchez, Augustin R. Diccionario Tzotzil De San Andres Con Variaciones Dialectales. (Vocabularios Indigenas: No. 22). (Illus.). 481p. (Orig., Tzotzil & Span.). 1978. pap. 10.00x (ISBN 0-88312-674-5); microfiche 4.50x (ISBN 0-88312-372-X). Summer Inst Ling.
Delgaty, Colin C. Vocabulario Tzotzil De San Andres. (Vocabularios Indigenas Ser.: No. 10). 81p. 1964. pap. 3.25 o.p. (ISBN 0-88312-668-0); 2.25 o.p. Summer Inst Ling.
Del Grande, J. J. & Duff, G. F. Introduccion Al Calculo Elemental. 1976. text ed. 10.30x o.p. (ISBN 0-06-310070-3, IntlDept). Har-Row.
Delhaye, J. M., et al. Thermohydraulics of Two-Phase Systems for Industrial Design & Nuclear Engineering. LC 80-14312. (Hemisphere Ser. in Thermal & Fluids Engineering). (Illus.). 544p. 1980. text ed. 46.50 (ISBN 0-07-016268-9, C). McGraw.
Delhom, L. A. Design & Application of Transistor Switching Circuits. (Texas Instruments Electronics Ser). 1968. 39.50 o.p. (ISBN 0-07-016253-0, P&RB). McGraw.
Delieb, Eric. Investing in Silver. 1967. 7.95 o.p. (ISBN 0-517-09240-9, C N Potter Bks). Crown.
DeLillo, Don. The Names. LC 82-48012. 1982. 13.95 (ISBN 0-394-52814-X). Knopf.
Deliman, Tracy, jt. auth. see Conlan, Jim.
De Limce, Alison, jt. auth. see Silk, Gerald.
De Lippe, Aschwin. Indian Medieval Sculpture: About 550-1250 A.D. (Illus.). 1978. 93.75 (ISBN 0-444-85086-4, North-Holland). Elsevier.
Delitzsch, Franz. Commentary on the Epistle to the Hebrews, 2 vols. 1978. Set. 31.50 (ISBN 0-86524-110-4, 5801). Klock & Klock.
--A New Commentary on Genesis, 2 vols. 1978. 30.50 (ISBN 0-86524-131-7, 0101). Klock & Klock.
--Old Testament History of Redemption. 1981. pap. 6.95 o.p. (ISBN 0-88469-141-1). BMH Bks.
Dell, Catherine, jt. auth. see Paton, John.
Dell, David J., et al. Guide to Hindu Religion. 1981. lib. bdg. 45.00 (ISBN 0-8161-7903-4, Hall Reference). G K Hall.
Dell, F. Generative Phonology. LC 79-14139. (Illus.). 1980. 44.50 (ISBN 0-521-22484-5); pap. 10.95x (ISBN 0-521-29519-X). Cambridge U Pr.
Dell, Helen Davis. Individualizing Instruction. LC 72-80760. (Illus.). 192p. 1972. pap. text ed. 8.95 (ISBN 0-574-18490-2, 13-1490). SRA.
Dell, Sidney. On Being Grandmotherly: The Evolution of IMF Conditionality. LC 81-6888. (Essays in International Finance Ser.: No. 144). 1981. pap. text ed. 2.50x (ISBN 0-88165-051-X). Princeton U Int Finan Econ.
Dellacherie, C. & Meyer, P. A. Probabilities & Potential. 1978. 36.25 (ISBN 0-7204-0701-X, North-Holland). Elsevier.
Della Fazia, Alba see Amoia, Alba Della Fazia.
Della Mirandola, Giovanni Pico see Pico Della Mirandola, Giovanni.
Della Porta, Giambattista. Gli Duoi Fratelli Rivali: The Two Rival Brothers. Clubb, Louise G., tr. from Italian. LC 78-64458. 350p. 1980. 27.50x (ISBN 0-520-03786-3). U of Cal Pr.
Della Torre, K. W. Von see Von Dalla Torre, K. W. & Harms, H.
Della Torree, Edward, et al. The Electromagnetic Field. LC 79-23788. 1980. Repr. of 1969 ed. text ed. 36.50 (ISBN 0-89874-100-9). Krieger.
Della Volpe, Galvano. Critique of Taste. 1978. 18.50 (ISBN 0-8052-7001-9, Pub by NLB). Schocken.
Dellenbaugh, Frederick. The Romance of the Colorado River. LC 82-3339. (Classics of the Old West Ser.). lib. bdg. 17.28 (ISBN 0-8094-4003-2). Silver.
Dellheim, Charles. The Face of the Past: The Preservation of the Medieval Inheritance in Victorian England. LC 82-4486. (Illus.). 225p. 1982. 29.95 (ISBN 0-521-23645-2). Cambridge U Pr.
Dellinger, Dave, jt. ed. see Albert, Michael.
Dell'Isola, Alphonse & Kirk, Stephen J. Life Cycle Costing for Design Professionals. (Illus.). 288p. 1981. 29.50 (ISBN 0-07-016280-8). McGraw.
Dell'Isola, Alphonse J. Value Engineering in the Construction Industry. 3rd ed. 376p. 1983. text ed. 34.50 (ISBN 0-442-26202-7). Van Nos Reinhold.
Dellon, A. Lee. Evaluation of Sensibility & Reeducation in the Hand. (Illus.). 388p. 1981. 42.00 (ISBN 0-686-77746-8, 2427-2). Williams & Wilkins.
Dell'Orto, L. Archeological Center of Rome Roman Forum. pap. 9.50 (ISBN 0-935748-45-8). Scalabooks.
Delman, B. & Froment, G. Catalyst Deactivation: Proceedings. (Studies in Surface Science & Catalysis: Vol. 6). 1980. 106.50 (ISBN 0-444-41920-9). Elsevier.
Del Mar, Alexander. History of Monetary Systems. LC 66-21669. Repr. of 1895 ed. 35.00x (ISBN 0-678-00289-4). Kelley.
Delmar, Rosalind, tr. see Aleramo, Sibilla.
Del Mar, W., jt. auth. see Pender, H.
Delmon, B., ed. see International Symposium on the Relations Between Heterogeneous & Homogeneous Catalytic Phenomena, Brussels, 1974.
Delmon, B., et al, eds. see International Symposium, Louvain, Sept., 1978.
Delmon, Philip. Ten Types of Table Wine. 1973. pap. 2.50 o.p. (ISBN 0-263-51788-8). Transatlantic.
Delmont, J., ed. Milk Intolerances & Rejection. (Illus.). x, 190p. 1983. pap. 72.00 (ISBN 3-8055-3546-5). S Karger.
Delmontegue, Robert. Man's Common Sense Guide to Physical Fitness. (Illus.). 156p. 1982. pap. 5.95 (ISBN 0-88254-707-0). Hippocrene Bks.
DeLoach, Carolyn P., jt. auth. see Malinowski, Janet S.
DeLoach, Charlene P. & Wilkins, Ronnie D. Independent Living: Services for the Disabled & Elderly. 1983. pap. text ed. price not set (ISBN 0-8391-1794-9, 16462). Univ Park.
DeLoach, Jane E. General Surgical Nursing. (Nursing Outline Ser.). 1979. pap. 12.75 (ISBN 0-87488-393-8). Med Exam.
DeLoach, Marva L., jt. ed. see Josey, E. J.
Delobel, C. & Litwin, W., eds. Distributed Data Bases. 1980. 68.00 (ISBN 0-444-85471-1). Elsevier.
DeLogu, Giuseppe, ed. see Tintoretto.
DeLonchamps, Joanne. Eden Under Glass. 1956. 2.50 o.p. (ISBN 0-8233-0019-6). Golden Quill.
Delone, Richard, et al. Aspects of Twentieth-Century Music. (Illus.). 541p. 1974. 24.95x (ISBN 0-13-049346-5). P-H.
Delone, Richard P., jt. auth. see Christ, William.
DeLong, George W. Waterfront Living: How to Buy Real Estate on the Water. LC 79-57321. (Illus., Orig.). 1983. pap. 10.00 (ISBN 0-9603414-0-4). DeLong & Assoc.
De Long, Patrick D. Art in the Humanities. 2nd ed. 1970. pap. text ed. 10.95 (ISBN 0-13-046979-3). P-H.
De Longchamps, Joanne. Warm Bloods, Cold Bloods. (Illus.). 44p. (Orig.). 1982. pap. text ed. 10.00 (ISBN 0-915596-25-3). West Coast.
De Loor, G. P., ed. Radar Remote Sensing. (Remote Sensing Reviews: Vol. 1, No. 1). 176p. 1982. 47.50 (ISBN 3-7186-0132-X). Harwood Academic.
Delora, Joann S., et al. Understanding Human Sexuality. LC 79-89744. (Illus.). 1980. pap. text ed. 16.50 (ISBN 0-395-28255-1); instr's. manual 1.00 (ISBN 0-395-28256-X); study guide 6.95 (ISBN 0-395-29079-1). HM.
--Understanding Sexual Interaction. 2nd ed. (Illus.). 672p. 1981. text ed. 20.95 (ISBN 0-395-29724-9); instr's manual 1.00 (ISBN 0-395-29725-7). HM.
Deloria, Vine. God Is Red. 384p. 1975. pap. 5.95 o.s.i. (ISBN 0-440-54401-7, Delta). Dell.
Deloria, Vine, Jr. Behind the Trail of Broken Treaties. 1974. pap. 5.95 o.s.i. (ISBN 0-440-51403-7, Delta). Dell.
--God Is Red. 1983. pap. 3.95 (ISBN 0-440-33044-0, LE). Dell.
--We Talk, You Listen. 1972. pap. 2.45 o.s.i. (ISBN 0-440-59587-8, Delta). Dell.
DeLorme, David, ed. The New Hampshire Atlas & Gazetteer. rev. ed. (Atlas & Gazetteer Ser.). (Illus.). 88p. 1983. pap. 8.95 (ISBN 0-89933-004-5). DeLorme Pub.
--The Vermont Atlas & Gazetteer. rev. ed. (Atlas & Gazetteer Ser.). (Illus.). 88p. (Orig.). 1983. pap. 8.95 (ISBN 0-89933-005-3). DeLorme Pub.
Delorme, Robert L. Latin America: Social Science Information Sources, 1967-1979. 288p. 1981. text ed. 32.75 (ISBN 0-87436-292-X). ABC-Clio.
De Lorre, C. & Willis, A., eds. Wolf-Rayet Stars: Observations, Physics, Evolution. 1982. 69.50 (ISBN 90-277-1469-X, Pub. by Reidel Holland); pap. 34.50 (ISBN 90-277-1470-3). Kluwer Boston.
De Lorris, Guillaume & De Meun, Jean. Romance of the Rose. Robbins, Harry W., tr. 1962. pap. 7.75 (ISBN 0-525-47090-5, 0752-230). Dutton.
De Los Rios Magrina, Emilios. Color Atlas of Anorectal Diseases. LC 80-51318. (Illus.). 207p. 1980. text ed. 35.00 (ISBN 0-7216-3034-0). Saunders.
Deloughery, Grace L. History & Trends of Professional Nursing. 8th ed. LC 77-386. (Illus.). 278p. 1977. pap. 17.95 (ISBN 0-8016-1974-2). Mosby.
De Louvois, J., ed. Selected Topics in Clinical Bacteriology. 1976. text ed. 17.50 o.p. (ISBN 0-02-857570-9, Pub. by Bailliere-Tindall). Saunders.
DeLozier, M. Wayne. The Marketing Communications Process. (Illus.). 1976. text ed. 25.95 (ISBN 0-07-016302-2, C); instructor's manual 15.00 (ISBN 0-07-016303-0). McGraw.
DeLozier, M. Wayne & Woodside, Arch G. Marketing Management: Strategies & Cases. (Marketing & Management Ser.). 1978. text ed. 25.95 (ISBN 0-675-08417-2). Additional supplements may be obtained from publisher. Merrill.
DeLozier, M. Wayne, jt. auth. see Lewison, Dale.
Delozier, M. Wayne, et al. Experiential Learning Exercises in Marketing. 1977. pap. text ed. 14.50x (ISBN 0-673-16085-8). Scott F.
DeLozier, Wayne. Consumer Behavior Dynamics: A Casebook. (Business Ser.). 1977. text ed. 12.95 (ISBN 0-675-08504-7). Additional supplements may be obtained from publisher. Merrill.
Delp, Mahlon H. & Manning, Robert T. Major's Physical Diagnosis: An Introduction to the Clinical Process. 9th ed. (Illus.). 650p. 1981. text ed. 22.50 (ISBN 0-7216-3002-2). Saunders.
Delp, Mahlon H. & Manning, Robert T., eds. Major's Physical Diagnosis. 8th ed. LC 74-9430. (Illus.). 690p. 1975. text ed. 19.50 o.p. (ISBN 0-7216-3012-X). Saunders.
Delpar, Helen. Borzoi Reader in Latin American History. 1972. pap. text ed. 4.25x (ISBN 0-394-31151-5). Phila Bk Co.
--The Discoverers: An Encyclopedia of Explorers & Exploration. LC 79-9259. (Illus.). 1979. 39.95 (ISBN 0-07-016264-6). McGraw.
--Encyclopedia of Latin America. LC 72-11311. (Illus.). 672p. 1974. 49.50 (ISBN 0-07-016263-8, P&RB). McGraw.
Del Portillo, Alvaro see Portillo, Alvaro del.
Del Pozo, Cal. Bunnetics: How to Shape Your Buns. LC 81-43580. (Illus.). 144p. 1982. pap. 4.95 (ISBN 0-385-17974-X, Dolp). Doubleday.
Del Ray, Lester, ed. see Cummings, Ray.
Del Ray, Lester, ed. see Le Guin, Ursula K.
Del Ray, Lester, ed. see Williamson, Jack.
Del Rey, Lester. Moon of Mutiny. 1979. lib. bdg. 9.50 (ISBN 0-8398-2518-8, Gregg). G K Hall.
Del Rey, Lester, ed. see Beresford, J. D.
Del Rey, Lester, ed. see Delaney, Samuel R.
Del Rey, Lester, ed. see Hubbard, L. Ron.
Del Rey, Lester, ed. see Smith, Edward E.
Del Rey, Lester, ed. see Van Vogt, A. E.
Del Rey, Lester, ed. see Williamson, Jack.
Del Rio, Amelia A., jt. auth. see Del Rio, Angel.
Del Rio, Angel & Del Rio, Amelia A. Antologia General de La Literatura Espanola. (Span.). 1982. pap. 15.00 (ISBN 0-86515-001-X). Edit Mensaje.
Delrio, Giovanni, ed. Steroids & Their Mechanisms of Action in Non Mammalian Vertebrates. (Progress in Cancer Research & Theory Ser.). 239p. 1980. text ed. 27.00 (ISBN 0-89004-487-2). Raven.
De L. Ryals, Clyde see Ryals, Clyde de L.
Del Sesto, Steven L. Science, Politics, & Controversy: Civilian Nuclear Power in the United States 1946-1974. (Special Studies in Sci., Tech., & Pub. Policy). 260p. 1981. lib. bdg. 26.50 o.p. (ISBN 0-89158-566-4); pap. text ed. 12.00 o.p. (ISBN 0-86531-255-9). Westview.
Delsol, Paula. Chinese Astrology. 1976. pap. 3.50 (ISBN 0-446-30831-5). Warner Bks.
Del Solar, Edmundo. Orlando Letelier: Biographical Notes & Comments. 1979. 5.95 o.p. (ISBN 0-533-03808-1). Vantage.
Delson, Donn & Hurst, Walter E. Delson's Dictionary of Radio & Records Industry Terms. Posner, Neil, ed. LC 80-24486. (Entertainment Communication Ser.: Vol. 2). 112p. (Orig.). 1981. pap. 9.95 (ISBN 0-9603574-2-4). Bradson.
Delson, Donn, jt. auth. see Michalove, Ed.
Delson, Donn, ed. see Paulson, Terry & Delson, Joyce.
Delson, Joyce, jt. auth. see Paulson, Terry.
Delson, Paula. Chinese Astrology. (Illus.). 248p. 1982. Repr. 11.95 (ISBN 0-88254-700-3). Hippocrene Bks.
Delson, Roberta M. Readings in Caribbean History & Economics: An Introduction to the Region. 360p. 1981. 60.00 (ISBN 0-677-05280-4). Gordon.
Del Tedesco, Mary M. A Rhapsody of Lines. 4.50 o.p. (ISBN 0-533-01903-6). Vantage.
Delton, Jina. Two Blocks Down. 1982. pap. 1.50 (ISBN 0-451-11477-9, AW1477, Vista). NAL.
Delton, Judy. Back Yard Angel. (Illus.). 112p. (gr. 2-5). 1983. 8.95 (ISBN 0-395-33883-2). HM.
--Brimhall Turns Detective. LC 82-9582. (Carolrhoda On My Own Bks). (Illus.). 48p. (gr. k-3). 1983. PLB 6.95g (ISBN 0-87614-203-X). Carolrhoda Bks.
--The Goose Who Wrote a Book. LC 81-15475. (Carolrhoda on My Own Bks.). (Illus.). 40p. (gr. k-3). 1982. PLB 6.95g (ISBN 0-87614-179-3). Carolrhoda Bks.
--I Never Win! LC 80-27618. (A Carolrhoda on My Own Bk). (Illus.). 32p. (gr. k-3). 1981. PLB 6.95g (ISBN 0-87614-139-4). Carolrhoda Bks.
--I'm Telling You Now. LC 82-17714. (Illus.). 32p. (ps-k). 1983. 9.95 (ISBN 0-525-44037-2, 0966-290). Dutton.
--It Happened on Thursday. Pacini, Kathy, ed. LC 77-19086. (Concept Bks.). (Illus.). (gr. 1-3). 1978. 7.50 (ISBN 0-8075-3669-5). A Whitman.
--Kitty in the Summer. (Illus.). (gr. 2-5). 1980. 8.95 (ISBN 0-395-29456-8). HM.
--On a Picnic. LC 78-1240. (gr. k-3). 1979. 6.95a o.p. (ISBN 0-686-85896-4); PLB 6.95a (ISBN 0-385-12945-9). Doubleday.
--Two Good Friends. LC 73-88181. (Illus.). 32p. (gr. k-3). 1974. reinforced lib. bdg. 5.50 o.p. (ISBN 0-517-51401-X). Crown.
--Two Is Company. LC 75-45180. (Illus.). (gr. k-3). 1976. 4.95 o.p. (ISBN 0-517-52601-8). Crown.
--Walk on a Snowy Night. LC 81-48660. (Illus.). 32p. (gr. k-3). 1982. 8.61i (ISBN 0-06-021592-5, HarpJ); PLB 8.89g (ISBN 0-06-021593-3). Har-Row.
Delton, Julie. My Uncle Nikos. LC 81-43317. (Illus.). 32p. (gr. 1-4). 1983. 10.53i (ISBN 0-690-04164-0, TYC-J); PLB 10.89g (ISBN 0-690-04165-9). Har-Row.
Del Toro, V. Control Engineering Continuous & Discrete-Time Control Systems: A Computer Orientation. Date not set. price not set o.p. (ISBN 0-07-016295-6). McGraw.
--Electromechanical Devices for Energy Conversion & Control Systems. 1968. ref. ed. 31.95 (ISBN 0-13-250068-X). P-H.
Del Toro, Vincent. Electrical Engineering Fundamentals. (Illus.). 832p. 1972. ref. ed. 29.95 (ISBN 0-13-247056-X). P-H.
--Principles of Electrical Engineering. 2nd ed. (Illus.). 800p. 1972. 29.95 (ISBN 0-13-709139-7). P-H.
De Lubac, Henri. Teilhard Explained. (Orig.). 1968. pap. 1.45 o.p. (ISBN 0-8091-1694-4, Deus). Paulist Pr.
De Lubicz, Isha Schwaller see Schwaller de Lubicz, Isha.
De Lubicz, R. A. Schwaller see Schwaller de Lubicz, R. A.
Deluc, Yves & Ruck, Heribert. Prisunic. LC 82-12756. (Illus.). 48p. (Fr.). (gr. 7-12). 1982. pap. text ed. 2.35 (ISBN 0-88436-905-6, 40287); pap. text ed. 12.00 cassettes. EMC.
De Luca, Hector F. & Frost, H. M., eds. Osteoporosis. (Recent Advances in Pathogenesis & Treatment Ser.). 528p. 1981. text ed. 49.50 (ISBN 0-8391-1630-6). Univ Park.
De Luca, Luigi M., ed. see New York Academy of Sciences, March 10-12, 1980.
DeLuca, Michael & Michaelides, Stephen. Dining In--Cleveland. (Dining In--Ser.). (Illus.). 190p. 1982. pap. 8.95 (ISBN 0-89716-034-7). Peanut Butter.
Deluca, Stuart M., jt. auth. see Stone, Alfred R.
De Lucchi, Lorna see Lucchi, Lorna De.
Delucchi, V. L., ed. Studies in Biological Control. LC 75-16867. (International Biological Programme Ser.: No. 9). (Illus.). 380p. 1975. 75.00 (ISBN 0-521-20910-2). Cambridge U Pr.
Delucia, Alan A. Compact Atlas of Idaho. (Illus.). 110p. (Orig.). Date not set. pap. 20.95x (ISBN 0-940982-02-1). Ctr Bus Devel & Res.
Delumeau, Jean. Catholicism Between Luther & Voltaire: A New View of the Counter-Reformation. Moiser, Jeremy, tr. 1977. 21.50 (ISBN 0-664-21341-3). Westminster.
Delupis, Ingrid. Finance & Protection of Investments in Developing Countries. LC 73-12149. 183p. 1973. 34.95x o.p. (ISBN 0-470-20637-3). Halsted Pr.
Delury, George E., ed. The World Almanac & Book of Facts 1975. LC 4-3781. 1974. pap. 2.75 o.p. (ISBN 0-911818-03-0). World Almanac.
--The World Almanac & Book of Facts 1977. LC 4-3781. 1976. 5.95 o.p. (ISBN 0-911818-06-5). World Almanac.
--The World Almanac & Book of Facts 1979. LC 78-437810. 1978. 6.95 o.p. (ISBN 0-911818-10-3); pap. 3.95 o.p. (ISBN 0-911818-09-X). World Almanac.
Delusse, Charles. L Art de la Flute Traversiere. (The Flute Library: Vol. 10). 1980. Repr. of 1760 ed. wrappers 35.00 o.s.i. (ISBN 90-6027-207-2, Pub. by Frits Knuf Netherlands). Pendragon NY.
Del Vasto, Lanza. Return to the Source. Sidgwick, Jean, tr. from Fr. LC 70-169817. 319p. 1972. 6.95x o.p. (ISBN 0-8052-3441-1). Schocken.
Del Vasto, Lanzo. Return to the Source. 1973. pap. 2.95 o.p. (ISBN 0-671-21684-8, Touchstone Bks). S&S.
Delves, L. M. & Walsh, J., eds. Numerical Solution of Integral Equations. (Illus.). 1974. 35.00x (ISBN 0-19-853342-X). Oxford U Pr.
Delvin, Jack. Magic of the Masters. (Illus.). (gr. 7-11). 1977. 8.95 o.p. (ISBN 0-668-04128-5); pap. 4.95 o.p. (ISBN 0-668-04132-3). Arco.
Delwiche, C. C. Denitrification, Nitrification, & Atmospheric Nitrous Oxide. LC 80-22698. 286p. 1981. 44.95x (ISBN 0-471-04896-8, Pub. by Wiley-Interscience). Wiley.
DeLynn, Jane. In Thrall. LC 81-23471. 256p. 1982. 13.95 (ISBN 0-517-54100-9, C N Potter Bks). Crown.
DeLyre, Wolf F. Essentials of Dental Radiography for Dental Assistants & Hygienists. 2nd ed. (Illus.). 1980. text ed. 22.95 (ISBN 0-13-285676-X). P-H.
De Lys, Claudia, jt. auth. see Batchelor, Julie F.
DeLyser, Femmy. Jane Fonda's Workout Book for Pregnancy, Birth & Recovery. 1982. 16.95 (ISBN 0-671-43219-2). S&S.
De Madariaga, Salvador see Madariaga, Salvador De.
De Madre, Ad. Des Ouvriers et Des Moyens D'ameliorer Leur Condition Dans les Villes. (Conditions of the 19th Century French Working Class Ser.). 140p. (Fr.). 1974. Repr. of 1863 ed. lib. bdg. 44.00x o.p. (ISBN 0-8287-0257-8, 1087). Clearwater Pub.
De Maio, Gerald, jt. auth. see Kushner, Harvey W.
De Maistre, Joseph. On God & Society: Essay on the Generative Principle of Political Constitution & Other Human Institutions. Greifer, Elisha, ed. Porter, Laurence, tr. Date not set. pap. 3.95 o.p. (ISBN 0-89526-928-7). Regnery-Gateway.
--The Works of Joseph de Maistre. Lively, Jack, ed. LC 77-148418. 1971. pap. 3.95 o.p. (ISBN 0-8052-0304-4). Schocken.
De Man, Paul. Blindness & Insight: Essays in the Rhetoric of Contemporary Criticism. 2nd, rev. ed. (Theory & History of Literature Ser.: Vol. 7). 288p. 1983. 29.50x (ISBN 0-8166-1134-3); pap. 12.95 (ISBN 0-8166-1135-1). U of Minn Pr.

Demand, Carlo. Airplanes of the Second World War Coloring Book. 48p. 1981. pap. 2.00 (ISBN 0-486-24107-6). Dover.

--Airplanes of World War I Coloring Book. 48p. 1979. pap. 1.75 (ISBN 0-486-23807-5). Dover.

Demand, Nancy H. Thebes in the Fifth Century. (States & Cities of Ancient Greece Ser.). 208p. 1983. 19.95 (ISBN 0-7100-9288-1). Routledge & Kegan.

Demanet, Abbe. Nouvelle Histoire de l'Afrique Francaise. (Bibliotheque Africaine Ser.). 664p. (Fr.). 1974. Repr. of 1767 ed. lib. bdg. 160.00x o.p. (ISBN 0-8287-0258-6, 72-2120). Clearwater Pub.

Demant, J. C. see Demantius, J. C.

Demantius, J. C. Isagoge Artis Musicae. (Dictionarium Musicum Ser.: Vol. 3). 1975. Repr. of 1607 ed. wrappers 35.00 o.s.i. (ISBN 90-6027-209-9, Pub. by Frits Knuf Netherlands). Pendragon NY.

Demaray, Donald E. Basic Beliefs. 1958. pap. 3.95 (ISBN 0-8010-2827-2). Baker Bk.

--Bible Study Sourcebook. (Illus.). 10.95 (ISBN 0-310-23621-5). Zondervan.

--Watch Out For Burnout: Its Signs, Prevention, & Cure. 112p. (Orig.). 1983. pap. 4.95. Baker Bk.

Demaray, Kathleen. Instruye al Nino. Orig. Title: Train up a Child. (Illus.). 24p. (Span.). 1982. Spiral Wire Bound 4.95 (ISBN 0-89367-085-5). Light & Life.

DeMarco, Donald. Abortion in Perspective. 1974. 7.00 (ISBN 0-910728-16-X); pap. 5.95 (ISBN 0-910728-07-0). Hayes

--The Anesthetic Society. 182p. (Orig.). 1982. pap. 5.95 (ISBN 0-931888-09-3). Christendom Pubns.

DeMarco, Gordon. October Heat. 250p. 1979. 8.95 o.p. (ISBN 0-918064-04-X); pap. 2.50 o.p. (ISBN 0-918064-05-8). Germinal Pr.

DeMarco, Tom. Controlling Software Projects: Management Measurement & Estimation. (Illus.). 296p. 1982. pap. 28.50 (ISBN 0-917072-32-4). Yourdon.

--Structured Analysis & System Specification. LC 78-51285. (Illus.). 368p. (Orig.). 1979. pap. 25.00 (ISBN 0-917072-07-3). Yourdon.

DeMare, George, jt. auth. see Steil, Lyman K.

DeMaree & McKinnon Fegan. Idaho Supplement to "Fundamentals of Real Estate" & "Real Estate Principles & Practice". 8th ed. 1981. pap. 5.95 (ISBN 0-13-765917-2). P-H.

Demaree, Kristyna P., ed. Continuity & Change in Latin America. (Proceedings of the Pacific Coast Council on Latin American Studies: Vol. 9). (Illus.). 130p. (Orig.). 1982. pap. 12.00 (ISBN 0-916304-54-X). Campanile.

Demarest, Bruce A. Who Is Jesus? 132p. 1983. pap. 4.50 (ISBN 0-88207-103-3). SP Pubns.

Demarest, Chris L. Benedict Finds a Home. (Illus.). (ps-1). 1982. 9.00 (ISBN 0-688-00154-8); PLB 8.59 (ISBN 0-688-00586-1). Lothrop.

--Clemens' Kingdom. LC 82-12731. (Illus.). 32p. (gr. k-3). 1983. 10.50 (ISBN 0-688-01655-3); PLB 10.08 (ISBN 0-688-01657-X). Lothrop.

Demarest, David P. The Ghetto Reader. Lamdin, Louis S., ed. 1970. pap. text ed. 5.50x (ISBN 0-685-77206-3). Phila Bk Co.

Demarest, David P., Jr., ed. From These Hills, from These Valleys: Selected Fiction about Western Pennsylvania. LC 75-15088. 1976. 10.95 (ISBN 0-8229-1123-X). U of Pittsburgh Pr.

Demarest, Don, et al. Marriage Encounter. LC 77-88195. 1978. 8.95 (ISBN 0-89310-051-X); pap. 3.95 o.p. (ISBN 0-89310-052-8). Carillon Bks.

Demarest, Robert, jt. auth. see Noback, Charles.

Demarest, Robert J. & Sciarra, John J. Conception, Birth & Contraception: A Visual Presentation. 2nd ed. LC 75-30954. (Illus.). 1976. 12.00 o.p. (ISBN 0-07-016259-X, GB). McGraw.

Demarest, Rosemary. Accounting Information Sources. LC 70-120908. (Management Information Guide Ser.: No. 18). 1970. 42.00x (ISBN 0-8103-0818-5). Gale.

De Margerie, Bertrand. The Christian Trinity in History. Fortman, E. J., tr. from Fr. LC 81-8735. 1982. 29.95 (ISBN 0-932506-14-3). St Bedes Pubns.

De Maria, Richard. Communal Love at Oneida: A Perfectionist Vision of Authority, Property & Sexual Order. LC 78-60958. (Texts & Studies in Religion: Vol. 2). xiii, 233p. 1978. soft cover 19.95x o.s.i. (ISBN 0-88946-986-5). E Mellen.

DeMaria, Robert. The Language of Grammar. LC 63-15677. 1973. 10.00 (ISBN 0-88427-008-4); pap. text ed. 5.95 (ISBN 0-88427-009-2). North River.

De Marillac, Charles see Marillac, Charles de.

Demaris, Ovid. The Vegas Legacy. 528p. 1983. 15.95 (ISBN 0-440-09172-1). Delacorte.

De Marivaux, Pierre C. De Chamblain see De Chamblain De Marivaux, Pierre C.

De Marly, Diana. Costume on the Stage: 1600-1940. LC 82-8799. (Illus.). 168p. 1982. text ed. 26.50x (ISBN 0-389-20317-3). B&N Imports.

--The History of Haute Couture 1850-1950. LC 79-22987. (Illus.). 216p. 1980. 38.00x (ISBN 0-8419-0586-X). Holmes & Meier.

Demarquez, Suzanne. Manuel de Falla. (Music Reprint Ser.). viii, 253p. 1983. Repr. of 1968 ed. lib. bdg. 25.00 (ISBN 0-306-76204-8). Da Capo.

De Martini, Francesco, jt. ed. see Burstein, Elias.

Demas, J. N., ed. Excited State Lifetime Measurements: Monograph. LC 82-16253. 288p. 1983. price not set (ISBN 0-12-208920-0). Acad Pr.

DeMasters, Carol. Dining In: Milwaukee. (Dining In Ser.). 210p. (Orig.). 1981. pap. 7.95 (ISBN 0-89716-099-1). Peanut Butter.

De Maubeuge, M., jt. auth. see Vokaer, Roger.

De Maupassant, Guy. Mademoiselle Fifi & Other Stories. Galsworthy, Ada, tr. Incl. Old Mother Savage; Piece of String; Sale; Two Friends; Duel; Umbrella; At Sea. (Illus.). pap. 3.00 (ISBN 0-8283-1446-2, IPL). Branden.

DeMause, Lloyd. Reagan's America. 200p. 1983. 16.95 (ISBN 0-940508-02-8). Creative Roots.

DeMause, Lloyd & Ebel, Henry, eds. Jimmy Carter & American Fantasy. 1977. 12.95 o.p. (ISBN 0-686-32129-4). Psychohistory Pr.

De May, Bonnie C., jt. auth. see Choate, Sharr.

DeMay, John A. Discovery: How to Win Your Case Without Trial. 199p. 1982. 34.95 (ISBN 0-13-215640-7, Busn). P-H.

De Mayo, Welington, jt. auth. see Palis, Jacob, Jr.

Demazure, M. & Gabriel, P. Introduction to Algebraic Geometry & Algebraic Groups. (Mathematics Studies: Vol. 39). 1980. 44.75 (ISBN 0-444-85443-6). Elsevier.

Dembeck, Adeline A. Guidebook to Man-Made Textile Fibers & Textured Yarns of the World. 3rd ed. 22.00x (ISBN 0-87245-082-1). Textile Bk.

Dember, Sol & Dember, Steven. Complete Airbush Techniques. 2nd ed. 1980. pap. write for info. (ISBN 0-672-21783-X). Sams.

Dember, Steven, jt. auth. see Dember, Sol.

Dember, William N. & Jenkins, James J. General Psychology: The Science of Behavior & Experience. 2nd ed. 700p. 1983. text ed. write for info. (ISBN 0-697-06654-1); write for info. student study guide (ISBN 0-697-06655-X); write for info. instr's manual (ISBN 0-697-06656-8). L Erlbaum Assocs.

Dembo, L. S., ed. Interviews with Contemporary Writers. LC 82-51092. 384p. 1983. 25.00 (ISBN 0-299-09330-1); pap. 8.95 (ISBN 0-299-09334-4). U of Wis Pr.

Dembo, L. S., jt. ed. see Krieger, Murray.

Dembowski. A Handbook for School District Financial Management. 1982. 11.95 (ISBN 0-910170-24-X). Assn Sch Busn.

Dembowski, P. Finite Geometries. (Ergebnisse Er Mathematik und Ihrer Grenzgebiete: Vol. 44). 1977. 35.50 (ISBN 0-387-08310-3). Springer-Verlag.

Dembowski, Peter F. Jean Froissart & His Meliador: Context, Craft & Sense. LC 82-84728. (The Edward C. Armstrong Monographs on Medieval Literature: No. 2). 224p. 1983. pap. 15.00 (ISBN 0-917058-44-5). French Forum.

Dembroski, T. M. & Schmidt, T. H., eds. Biobehavioral Bases of Coronary Heart Disease. (Karger Biobehavioral Medicine Ser.: Vol. 2). (Illus.). 530p. 1983. 95.25 (ISBN 3-8055-3629-1). S Karger.

Dembrowski, Harry E. The Union of Lublin: Polish Federalism in the Golden Age. (East European Monographs: No. 116). 384p. 1982. 27.50x (ISBN 0-88033-009-0). East Eur Quarterly.

Deme, Rona. Country Host Cookbook. (Illus.). 288p. 1980. pap. 8.95 (ISBN 0-8256-3172-6, Quick Fox). Putnam Pub Group.

De Meillon, Botha, jt. auth. see Freeman, Paul.

De Meis, jt. auth. see DeMeis, Leopoldo.

DeMeis, Leopoldo & De Meis. The Sarcoplasmic Reticulum: Transport & Energy Transduction. LC 81-2325. (Transport in the Life Sciences Ser.). 163p. 1981. 44.50 (ISBN 0-471-05025-3, Pub. by Wiley-Interscience). Wiley.

De Mello, Anthony. Sadhana: A Way to God, Christian Exercises in Eastern Form. LC 78-70521. (Study Aids on Jesuit Topics: No. 9). 146p. 1978. 6.00 (ISBN 0-912422-38-6); pap. 5.00 smyth sewn (ISBN 0-912422-37-8); pap. 4.00 (ISBN 0-912422-46-7). Inst Jesuit.

De Melo e Castro, E. M., jt. ed. see Macedo, Helder.

De Melun, Armand. De l'Intervention de la Societe pour Prevenir et Soulager la Misere. (Conditions of the 19th Century French Working Class Ser.). 71p. (Fr.). 1974. Repr. of 1849 ed. lib. bdg. 30.00 o.p. (ISBN 0-8287-0598-4, 1063). Clearwater Pub.

De Menil, Dominque, intro. by. Humble Treasures-Exhibition Catalog: Tribal Art from Negro Africa. (Illus.). 1965. pap. 1.00 o.p. (ISBN 0-913456-88-8). Interbk Inc.

De Menil, Lois P. Who Speaks for Europe: The Case of De Gaulle. LC 77-77137. 1978. 16.95x (ISBN 0-312-87025-6). St Martin.

Dement, William C., jt. auth. see Miles, Laughton E.

De Mente, Boye. Amazing Arizona. Hawkins, Mary E., ed. (Illus.). 164p. Date not set. pap. 4.95 (ISBN 0-914778-41-2). Phoenix Bks. Postponed.

--Eros' Revenge: The Brave New World of American Sex. LC 78-78307. 1979. pap. 6.95 (ISBN 0-914778-21-8). Phoenix Bks.

--Exotic Japan: The Traveler's Wonderland. LC 72-71128. (Illus.). 160p. 1976. pap. 4.95 (ISBN 0-914778-12-9). Phoenix Bks.

--How to Order Chinese Food. LC 82-80460. 64p. 1982. pap. 4.95 (ISBN 0-914778-43-9). Phoenix Bks.

--Japanese Language Guide. 164p. Date not set. pap. cancelled (ISBN 0-914778-42-0). Phoenix Bks.

Dementyev, I. U. S. A., Imperialists & Anti-Imperialists. 351p. 1979. 7.45 (ISBN 0-8285-1598-0, Pub. by Progress Pubs USSR). Imported Pubns.

DeMeo, Victoria, jt. auth. see Dutton, Beth.

Demerec, M., ed. Advances in Genetics. Incl. Vol. 1. 1947 (ISBN 0-12-017601-7); Vol. 2. 1948 (ISBN 0-12-017602-5); Vol. 3. 1950 (ISBN 0-12-017603-3); Vol. 4. 1951 (ISBN 0-12-017604-1); Vol. 5. 1953 (ISBN 0-12-017605-X); Vol. 6. 1954 (ISBN 0-12-017606-8); Vol. 7. 1955 (ISBN 0-12-017607-6); Vol. 8. 1956 (ISBN 0-12-017608-4); Vol. 9. 1958 (ISBN 0-12-017609-2); Vol. 10. Caspari, E. W. & Thoday, J. M., eds. 1961 (ISBN 0-12-017610-6); Vol. 11. 1962 (ISBN 0-12-017611-4); Vol. 12. 1964 (ISBN 0-12-017612-2); Vol. 13. 1965 (ISBN 0-12-017613-0); Vol. 14. Caspari, E. W., ed. 1968 (ISBN 0-12-017614-9); Vol. 15. Caspari, E. W., ed. 1970 (ISBN 0-12-017615-7); Vol. 16. Caspari, E. W., ed. 1971 (ISBN 0-12-017616-5); Vol. 17. The Genetics of Tribolium & Related Species. 1973. 55.50 (ISBN 0-12-017617-3); Vol. 18. 1976. 55.00 (ISBN 0-12-017618-1); Vol. 19. 1977. 59.50 (ISBN 0-12-017619-X); Suppl. 1. The Genetics of Tribolium & Related Species. Sokoloff, Alexander. 1966. 38.00 (ISBN 0-12-017661-0). Vols. 1-16. **55.00 ea. Acad Pr.**

--Advances in Genetics, Vol. 21. LC 47-30313. (Serial Publication). 384p. 1982. 36.00 (ISBN 0-12-017621-1). Acad Pr.

Demers, Aline, jt. auth. see Chaplin, James P.

De Mesquita, B. Bueno see Bueno de Mesquita, B.

Demetrakopoulos, Stephanie. Listening to Our Bodies: The Rebirth of Feminine Wisdom. LC 81-70489. 256p. 1983. 12.98 (ISBN 0-8070-6704-0). Beacon Pr.

Demetrulias, Diana & Deutsch, Alleen. New Audiences for Teacher Education. LC 82-60797. (Fastback Ser.: No. 178). 50p. 1982. pap. 0.75 (ISBN 0-87367-178-3). Phi Delta Kappa.

De Meun, Jean, jt. auth. see De Lorris, Guillaume.

De Mey, J., jt. ed. see De Brabander, M.

Demi. Cinderella on Wheels. LC 82-2996. (Illus.). 12p. (gr. 1-4). 1982. 9.95 (ISBN 0-03-059473-1). HR&W.

DeMichele, Michael D. The Italian Experience in America: A Pictorial History. LC 81-71921. (Illus.). 144p. 15.00 (ISBN 0-9607870-0-3); lib. bdg. write for info. U Scranton Ethnic.

De Michele, Vincenzo. Color Treasury of Crystals. (Bounty Bk. Ser.). (Illus.). 64p. 1974. pap. 1.98 o.p. (ISBN 0-517-51428-1). Crown.

--World of Minerals. (World of Nature Ser.). 1973. 4.98 o.p. (ISBN 0-517-12043-7, Bounty Books). Crown.

Demidoff, Lorna B. How to Raise & Train a Siberian Husky. (Orig.). pap. 2.95 (ISBN 0-87666-391-9, DS1118). TFH Pubns.

D'Emilio, John. Sexual Politics, Sexual Communities: The Making of a Homosexual Minority in the United States 1940-1970. LC 82-16000. 262p. 1983. 20.00 (ISBN 0-226-14265-5). U of Chicago Pr.

De Mille, Agnes. And Promenade Home. (Series in Dance). 1980. Repr. of 1956 ed. lib. bdg. 22.50 (ISBN 0-306-79614-7). Da Capo.

--Dance to the Piper. (Series in Dance). (Illus.). 342p. 1980. Repr. of 1951 ed. lib. bdg. 22.50 (ISBN 0-306-79613-9); Set. 35.00 (ISBN 0-306-79615-5). Da Capo.

--Reprieve. 1982. pap. 2.95 (ISBN 0-451-11914-2, AE1914, Sig). NAL.

DeMille, Agnes. Reprieve: A Memoir. LC 81-43210. 288p. 1981. 14.95 (ISBN 0-385-15721-5). Doubleday.

DeMille, Janice. Bushy's Secret Spot. (Illus.). 32p. 1981. 1.50 (ISBN 0-915630-15-X). Zion.

--From Spring to Spring. (Illus.). 32p. 1981. 1.50 (ISBN 0-915630-16-8). Zion.

--Kendra's Surprise. (Illus.). 32p. 1981. pap. 1.50 (ISBN 0-915630-17-6). Zion.

DeMille, Nelson. Cathedral. 1981. 13.95 o.s.i. (ISBN 0-440-01140-X). Delacorte.

Demille, Robert. Put Your Mother on the Ceiling. 1976. pap. 4.95 (ISBN 0-14-004379-9). Penguin.

Deming, Barbara, jt. auth. see Deming, Dick.

Deming, Dick & Deming, Barbara. Back at the Farm: Raising Livestock on a Small Scale. 288p. 1982. 17.95 (ISBN 0-442-26334-1); pap. 10.95 (ISBN 0-442-26353-8). Van Nos Reinhold.

Deming, H. G. Water: The Fountain of Opportunity. Gillam, W. S. & McCoy, W. S., eds. (Illus.). 1975. 22.50x (ISBN 0-19-501841-9). Oxford U Pr.

Deming, Mary & Haddard, Joyce. Follow the Sun: International Cookbook for Young People. LC 82-61563. (Illus.). 96p. (gr. 4-12). 1982. pap. 6.50 (ISBN 0-9609188-0-9). Sun Scope.

Deming, Richard. Metric Power: Why & How We Are Going Metric. LC 74-5039. 192p. (gr. 5 up). 1974. 8.95 (ISBN 0-525-66380-0). Lodestar Bks.

--Police Lab at Work. LC 66-29903. (Illus.). (gr. 5-7). 4.95 o.p. (ISBN 0-672-50433-2). Bobbs.

Deming, Robert H., ed. A Bibliography of James Joyce Studies. Rev., 2nd ed. (Reference Publications Ser.). 1977. lib. bdg. 39.50 (ISBN 0-8161-7969-7, Hall Reference). G K Hall.

Deming, William E. Sample Design in Business Research. LC 60-6451. (Probability & Mathematical Statistics Ser.). 1960. 54.50x (ISBN 0-471-20724-1, Pub. by Wiley-Interscience). Wiley.

De Mirabaud, Jean-Baptiste. Opinion des Anciens sur les Juifs. (Holbach & His Friends Ser). 129p. (Fr.). 1974. Repr. of 1769 ed. lib. bdg. 41.50x o.p. (ISBN 0-8287-0623-9, 1530). Clearwater Pub.

--Reflexions Impartiales sur l'Evangile. (Holbach & His Friends Ser). 111p. (Fr.). 1974. Repr. of 1769 ed. lib. bdg. 37.50x o.p. (ISBN 0-8287-0624-7, 1535). Clearwater Pub.

De Miranda, Francisco see Miranda, Francisco De.

De Moivre, Abraham. Doctrine of Chances: Including Treatise on Annuities. 3rd ed. LC 66-23756. 1967. 17.95 (ISBN 0-8284-0200-0). Chelsea Pub.

Demokan, M. S. Mode-Locking in Solid-State & Semiconductor Lasers. 227p. 1982. 39.95 (ISBN 0-471-10498-1). Res Stud Pr.

Demolen, Richard, ed. Richard Mulcaster's Positions. LC 77-168389. 1970. text ed. 11.50 (ISBN 0-8077-1238-8); pap. 5.95x (ISBN 0-8077-1235-3). Tchrs Coll.

DeMolen, Richard L., ed. Erasmus. LC 73-89992. (Documents of Modern History Ser.). 208p. 1974. 18.95 (ISBN 0-312-25795-3). St Martin.

De Molina, Sara Pais, tr. see Haas, Harold I.

De Mondonville, Jean-Joseph C. Jubilate: Motet for Five Chorus, etc. Borroff, Edith, ed. (Music Reprint Ser., 1977). (Illus.). 1977. Repr. of 1961 ed. text ed. 5.75 (ISBN 0-306-77411-9). Da Capo.

Demong, Denise, jt. auth. see Beard, Timothy F.

Demong, Denise, jt. auth. see Embery, Joan.

Demong, Phyllis. Rare & Undone Saints. 96p. 1983. pap. 3.95 (ISBN 0-380-63081-8, 63081-8). Avon.

DeMont, Billie C. & DeMont, Roger A. Accountability: An Action Model for the Public Schools. (Illus.). 1975. 9.95 (ISBN 0-88280-023-X). ETC Pubns.

DeMont, Roger A., jt. auth. see DeMont, Billie C.

De Monte, Alpha. In Return For... 240p. 1983. 11.00 (ISBN 0-682-49934-X). Exposition.

DeMonte, Claudia, jt. auth. see Bachrach, Judy.

DeMonte, John R. King James' Version of the Games of Golfe, Bk. II. (Illus.). 60p. (Orig.). 1982. pap. 7.50 (ISBN 0-9605176-1-8). Raycol Prods.

De Montfort, St. Louis Marie. True Devotion to the Blessed Virgin. 4.95 (ISBN 0-910984-49-2); pap. 3.95 (ISBN 0-910984-50-6). Montfort Pubns.

De Montreville, Doris & Crawford, Elizabeth D., eds. Fourth Book of Junior Authors & Illustrators. 370p. 1978. 20.00 (ISBN 0-8242-0568-5). Wilson.

De Moor, W. & Wijngaard, E. H., eds. Psychotherapy: Research & Training. 1980. 57.50 (ISBN 0-444-80209-6). Elsevier.

De-Moraes, Moises, tr. see Nee, Watchman.

De Moratin, Leandro F. The Maiden's Consent. De Onis, Harriet, tr. from Span. LC 62-18305. (gr. 10 up). 1963. 5.25 (ISBN 0-686-85701-1); pap. text ed. 1.95 (ISBN 0-8120-0131-1). Barron.

De Morgan, Augustus. The Encyclopedia of Eccentrics. Smith, David E., ed. 416p. 1974. pap. 10.00 (ISBN 0-87548-194-9). Open Court.

De Morgan, Augustus, jt. auth. see Smith, David E.

DeMori, Renato, jt. ed. see Suen, Ching Y.

Demoro, Harre W. Electric Railway Pioneer: Commuting on the Northwestern Pacific, 1903-1941. (Special Ser.: No. 84). (Illus.). 136p. 1983. price not set (ISBN 0-916374-55-6). Howell North. Postponed.

--Electric Railway Pioneer: Commuting on the Northwestern Pacific 1903-1941. (Special Ser.: No. 84). (Illus.). 136p. 1983. price not set (ISBN 0-916374-55-6). Interurban.

Demoro, Harre W., jt. auth. see Wurm, Ted.

De Morogues, Bigot. De la Misere des Ouvriers et de la Marche a Suivre Pour y Remedier. (Conditions of the 19th Century French Working Class Ser.). 135p. (Fr.). 1974. Repr. of 1832 ed. lib. bdg. 43.00x o.p. (ISBN 0-8287-0643-3, 1029). Clearwater Pub.

--Du Pauperisme, de la Mendicite et des Moyens d'en Prevenir les Funestes Effects. (Conditions of the 19th Century French Working Class Ser.). 683p. (Fr.). 1974. Repr. of 1834 ed. lib. bdg. 165.00x o.p. (ISBN 0-8287-0644-1, 1030). Clearwater Pub.

--Recherches des Causes de la Richesse et de la Misere des Peuples Civilises. (Conditions of the 19th Century French Working Class Ser.). 649p. (Fr.). 1974. Repr. of 1834 ed. lib. bdg. 156.00x o.p. (ISBN 0-8287-0645-X, 1031). Clearwater Pub.

Demos, John. Little Commonwealth: Family Life in Plymouth Colony. (Illus.). 1971. pap. 5.95 (ISBN 0-19-501355-7, 344, GB). Oxford U Pr.

Demos, John P. Entertaining Satan: Witchcraft & the Culture of Early New England. LC 81-22463. 560p. 1982. 25.00 (ISBN 0-19-503131-8). Oxford U Pr.

Demos, T. Radiologic Case Studies: A Study Guide for the Orthopedic Surgeon. LC 82-62398. 299p. 1983. 39.50 (ISBN 0-943432-02-2). Slack Inc.

DeMoss, Arthur & DeMoss, Nancy, eds. The Family Album: 1977 Edition. (Illus.). 1976. 7.95 o.p. (ISBN 0-87981-066-1). Holman.

DeMoss, Nancy, jt. ed. see DeMoss, Arthur.

Demosthenes. Orationes, 3 vols. Incl. Vol. 1. Nos. 1-19. Butcher, S. H., ed. 1903. 24.00x (ISBN 0-19-814518-7); Vol. 2, Pt. 1. Nos. 20-26. Butcher, S. H., ed. 1907. o.p. (ISBN 0-19-814519-5); Vol. 2, Pt. 2. Nos. 27-40. Rennie, W., ed. 1921. o.p. (ISBN 0-19-814520-9); Vol. 3. Nos. 41-60. Rennie, W., ed. 1931. 22.50x (ISBN 0-19-814521-7). (Oxford Classical Texts Ser.). Oxford U Pr.

--Public Orations. 1967. Repr. of 1954 ed. 7.95x (ISBN 0-460-00546-4, Evman). Biblio Dist.

De Mott, D. A. Corporations at the Crossroads: Governance & Reform. 1979. 47.95 (ISBN 0-07-016330-8). McGraw.

Demoulin, J. P., ed. see Teilhard De Chardin, Pierre.

De Mourgues, Odette. Racine: Or the Triumph of Relevance. (Orig.). 1967. 34.50 (ISBN 0-521-06023-0); pap. 12.95x (ISBN 0-521-09428-3). Cambridge U Pr.

--Two French Moralists. LC 77-82506. (Major European Authors Ser.). 1978. 34.50 (ISBN 0-521-21823-3). Cambridge U Pr.

Demouy, Jane K. Katherin Anne Porter's Women: The Eye of Her Fiction. 248p. 1982. text ed. 22.50x (ISBN 0-292-79018-X). U of Tex Pr.

Dempsey, Al. Miss Finney Kills Now & Then. 256p. 1982. pap. 2.50 o.p. (ISBN 0-523-48026-1). Pinnacle Bks.

Dempsey, Al & Moore, Robin. The Red Falcons. (Orig.). 1980. pap. 2.25 o.p. (ISBN 0-523-40854-4). Pinnacle Bks.

Dempsey, Al, jt. auth. see Moore, Robin.

Dempsey, Arthur, jt. auth. see Dempsey, Particia.

Dempsey, B., jt. auth. see Perrin, D. D.

Dempsey, Charles. Annibale Carracci & the Beginnings of Baroque Style. 1977. 22.00 (ISBN 0-686-92334-0). J J Augustin.

Dempsey, David & Zimbardo, Philip G. Psychology & You. 1978. text ed. 20.95x (ISBN 0-673-15086-0). Scott F.

Dempsey, Jerome A. & Reed, Charles E., eds. Muscular Exercise & the Lung. (Illus.). 416p. 1977. 45.00 (ISBN 0-299-07220-7). U of Wis Pr.

Dempsey, Michael W., ed. Illustrated Fact Book of Science. LC 82-16412. (Illus.). 236p. 1983. 9.95 (ISBN 0-668-05729-7, 5729). Arco.

Dempsey, Mike, ed. Pipe Dreams: Early Advertising Art from the Imperial Tobacco Company. (Illus.). 96p. 1983. pap. 11.95 (ISBN 0-907516-12-2, Pub by Michael Joseph). Merrimack Bk Serv.

Dempsey, Particia & Dempsey, Arthur. The Research Process in Nursing. 1980. 13.95 (ISBN 0-442-20884-7). Van Nos Reinhold.

Dempsey, Paul. The Bicycler's Bible. (Illus.). 1977. 9.95 (ISBN 0-8306-7846-8); pap. 5.95 o.p. (ISBN 0-8306-6846-2, 846). TAB Bks.

--How to Repair Diesel Engines. LC 75-20847. (Illus.). 308p. 1975. 15.95 (ISBN 0-8306-5817-3); pap. 10.95 (ISBN 0-8306-4817-8, 817). TAB Bks.

Dempsey, Paul K. Power Tuning Your Car, Truck, Van or RV. (Illus.). 1979. 9.95 (ISBN 0-8306-9784-5); pap. 5.95 o.p. (ISBN 0-8306-1157-6, 1157). TAB Bks.

Dempsey, Richard A., jt. auth. see Daigon, Arthur.

Dempsey, S. J., jt. auth. see Topping, Victor.

Dempster, Germaine. Dramatic Irony in Chaucer. 1959. text ed. 12.50x (ISBN 0-391-00492-1). Humanities.

Dempster, J. P. The Population Dynamics of the Moroccan Locust (Dociostaurus Maroccanus Thunb) in Cyprus. 1957. 35.00x (ISBN 0-85135-011-9, Pub. by Centre Overseas Research). State Mutual Bk.

Dempster, Lauramay T. The Genus Galium (Rubiaceae) in Mexico & Central America. (Publications in Botany: No. 73). 1978. pap. 11.00x (ISBN 0-520-09578-2). U of Cal Pr.

Dempster, Stuart. The Modern Trombone: A Definition of Its Idioms. LC 76-14309. (The New Instrumentation Ser.: Vol. III). 1979. 22.50x (ISBN 0-520-03252-7). U of Cal Pr.

Demsetz, H. Economic, Legal & Political Dimensions of Competition. (Lectures in Economics Ser.: Vol. 4). 1982. 27.75 (ISBN 0-444-86442-3). Elsevier.

Demtroeder, W. Laser Spectroscopy: Basic Concepts & Instrumentation. (Springer Series in Chemical Physics: Vol. 5). (Illus.). 694p. 1983. 29.00 (ISBN 0-387-10343-0). Springer-Verlag.

De Mundo Lo, Sara. Index to Spanish American Collective Biography: Mexico, Vol. 2. 1982. lib. bdg. 65.00 (ISBN 0-8161-8529-8, Hall Reference). G K Hall.

--Index to the Spanish American Collective Biography: The Andean Countries, Vol. 1. 1981. lib. bdg. 60.00 (ISBN 0-8161-8181-0, Hall Reference). G K Hall.

Demura, Fumio & Ivan, Dan. Advanced Nunchaku. Johnson, Gilbert & Adachi, Geraldine, eds. LC 76-40816. (Ser. 126). (Illus.). 1976. pap. text ed. 6.95 (ISBN 0-89750-021-0). Ohara Pubns.

Demuth, Katherine & Sekhesa, Tholoana. Basic SeSotho: An Oral Approach. (African Language Texts Ser.). (Orig.). 1978. pap. text ed. 5.00 (ISBN 0-941934-24-1). Ind U Afro-Amer Arts.

Demuth, Norman. French Opera: Its Development to the Revolution. (Music Reprint, 1978 Ser.). (Illus.). 1978. Repr. of 1963 ed. lib. bdg. 32.50 (ISBN 0-306-77576-X). Da Capo.

DeMuth, Vivienne. All Kinds of Things. (Paint by Number: No. 1482). (Illus.). 32p. (gr. 1 up). 1983. pap. 1.99 (ISBN 0-307-21482-6). Western Pub.

--Nature. (Paint by Number: No. 1480). (Illus.). 32p. (gr. 1 up). 1983. pap. 1.99 (ISBN 0-307-21480-X). Western Pub.

DeMyer, William. Technique of the Neurologic Examination. 3rd, rev. ed. (Illus.). 1980. text ed. 27.00 (ISBN 0-07-016352-9). McGraw.

DeMyer, William, ed. Psychiatry-Neurology: PreTest Self-Assessment & Review. (Illus.). 250p. (Orig.). 1982. pap. 29.95 (ISBN 0-07-051660-X). McGraw.

Den, Van Hoek see Van den Hoek, C.

Denaerde, Stefan & Stevens, Wendelle C. UFO... Contact from Planet Iarga. Lodge, Jim, tr. from Dutch. (UFO Fact Bks.). Orig. Title: Buitenaardse Beschaving. (Illus.). 368p. 1982. lib. bdg. 15.95 (ISBN 0-9608558-1-5). UFO Photo.

Denaes, Raymond. General Guide to Paris Street Atlas. 1980. pap. 12.95 (ISBN 0-933982-04-6, Pub by Editions L'indispensable). Bradt Ent.

Denaro, A. R. Elementary Electrochemistry. 2nd ed. 246p. 1971. pap. 11.95 (ISBN 0-408-70071-8). Butterworth.

Denavit, Jacques, jt. auth. see Hartenberg, Richard S.

Den Brock, A. A. van see Nieuwenhuis, Paul & Van den Brock, A. A.

Denby, David, ed. Film Seventy to Seventy-One. 1971. pap. 2.95 o.p. (ISBN 0-671-21048-3, Touchstone Bks). S&S.

Denby, Edwin. Collected Poems. LC 75-23024. 1975. 17.95 (ISBN 0-916190-00-5); pap. 8.95 (ISBN 0-916190-01-3). Full Court NY.

--Mrs. W's Last Sandwich. 1972. 6.95. Horizon.

D'Encarnacao, Patricia, jt. auth. see D'Encarnacao, Paul.

D'Encarnacao, Paul & D'Encarnacao, Patricia. How to Love Yourself Unconditionally. LC 82-99980. (Illus.). 96p. 1983. pap. larga. 12.95 with cassette (ISBN 0-9610048-0-0). Metamorphosis Pr.

D'Encausse, Helene C. Confiscated Power. LC 82-47521. (A Cornelia & Michael Bessie Bk.). 415p. 1982. 19.18i (ISBN 0-06-039009-3, HarpT). Harper Row.

Dence, Joseph B. Mathematical Techniques in Chemistry. LC 75-16337. 442p. 1975. text ed. 37.00 (ISBN 0-471-20319-X, Pub. by Wiley-Interscience). Wiley.

--Steroids & Peptides: Selected Chemical Aspects for Biology, Biochemistry & Medicine. LC 79-21236. 1980. 58.95 (ISBN 0-471-04700-7, Pub. by Wiley-Interscience). Wiley.

Denck, H., ed. see Paquet, K. J., et al.

Dendel, Esther W. The Basic Book of Fingerweaving. (Illus.). 1974. 8.95 o.p. (ISBN 0-671-21697-X). S&S.

Dendurent, H. O., ed. Thomas De Quincey: A Reference Guide. 1978. lib. bdg. 21.00 (ISBN 0-8161-7840-2, Hall Reference). G K Hall.

Dendy, William. Lost Toronto. (Illus.). 1979. 25.00 o.p. (ISBN 0-19-540294-4). Oxford U Pr.

Deneault, Henry N., jt. auth. see Govoni, Norman A.

DeNeef, A. L. Spenser & the Motives of Metaphor. LC 82-14737. 205p. 1983. 31.75 (ISBN 0-8223-0487-2). Duke.

Deneliuk, F. A. Information Retrieval & Library Management: An Interactive Minicomputer System. 16p. 1978. pap. 5.00 (ISBN 0-88936-170-3, IDRC TS14, IDRC). Unipub.

Denenberg, Herbert S., et al. Risk & Insurance. 2nd ed. 1974. 24.95 (ISBN 0-13-781294-9). P-H.

Denenberg, R. V. & Seidman, Eric. The Dog Catalog. LC 77-88433. 1978. 14.95 o.p. (ISBN 0-448-14641-X, G&D); pap. 7.95 o.p. (ISBN 0-448-14642-8). Putnam Pub Group.

De Nerval, Gerard. Les Chimeres. Rinsler, Norma, ed. 1973. text ed. 19.50x o.p. (ISBN 0-485-14702-5, Athlone Pr); pap. text ed. 10.50x o.p. (ISBN 0-485-12702-4, Athlone Pr). Humanities.

Denes, Agnes. Isometric Systems in Isotropic Space, Map Projections from the Study of Distortions, 1973-1979. LC 79-66223. (Illus.). 100p. 1979. 40.00x (ISBN 0-89822-007-6). Visual Studies.

Denes, Magda. In Necessity & Sorrow: Life & Death in an Abortion Hospital. 1977. pap. 3.95 o.p. (ISBN 0-14-004679-8). Penguin.

DeNeufville, R. & Stafford, J. Systems Analysis for Engineers & Managers. 36.50 (ISBN 0-07-016370-7, C); solutions manual 7.95 (ISBN 0-07-016371-5). McGraw.

De Neufville, Richard. Airport Systems Planning: A Critical Look at the Methods & Experience. LC 76-5994. 1976. text ed. 17.50x (ISBN 0-262-04051-4). MIT Pr.

DeNevi, Donald & Chleboun, William. The West Coast Goes to War. LC 81-6397. 200p. Date not set. 20.00 (ISBN 0-8310-7140-0). Howell-North.

Deng, Francis M. The Dinka & Their Songs. (Oxford Library of African Literature Ser.). 1973. 24.95x o.p. (ISBN 0-19-815138-1). Oxford U Pr.

--Dinka Folktales: African Stories from the Sudan. LC 73-82901. (Illus.). 200p. 1974. text ed. 32.50x (ISBN 0-8419-0138-4, Africana). Holmes & Meier.

Dengerink, Don, jt. auth. see Green, Lee.

Dengler, Dieter. Escape from Laos. 1982. pap. 2.95 (ISBN 0-8217-1113-X). Zebra.

Dengler, Sandy. Arizona Longhorn Adventure. LC 18-60. (Pioneer Family Adventure Ser.). 128p. (gr. 5-8). 1980. pap. 2.95 (ISBN 0-8024-0299-2). Moody.

--Beasts of the Field Puzzles. 1979. pap. 2.95 (ISBN 0-8024-0680-7). Moody.

--Getting into the Bible. LC 79-15064. 1979. pap. 4.95 (ISBN 0-8024-2923-8). Moody.

--The Horse Who Loved Picnics. LC 80-10691. (Pioneer Family Adventure Ser.). 128p. (gr. 4-8). 1980. pap. 2.95 (ISBN 0-8024-3589-0). Moody.

--The Melon Hound. LC 79-28218. (Pioneer Family Adventures Ser.). (Orig.). 1980. pap. 2.95 (ISBN 0-8024-5239-6). Moody.

--Mystery at McGeehan Ranch. LC 81-18694. (Pioneeer Family Adv. Ser.). 128p. 1982. pap. 2.95 (ISBN 0-8024-2972-6). Moody.

--Rescue in the Desert. LC 80-25563. (Pioneer Family Adventure Ser.). 128p. (Orig.). (gr. 4-7). 1981. pap. 2.95 (ISBN 0-8024-0874-5). Moody.

--Socorro Island Treasure. LC 82-22864. (Daniel Tremain Adventures Ser.). 128p. (gr. 5-8). 1983. pap. price not set (ISBN 0-8024-7813-1). Moody.

Denham, H. M. The Adriatic: A Sea-Guide to Venice, the Italian Shore & the Dalmatian Coast. (Illus.). 1977. 19.95 o.p. (ISBN 0-393-03204-3). Norton.

Denham, Hardy R., Jr. After You've Said I Do. 80p. (Orig.). 1983. pap. 5.95 (ISBN 0-939298-18-X). J M Prods.

Denham, John W. & Pickard, C. Glenn. Clinical Roles in Rural Health Centers. LC 78-27733. (Rural Health Center Ser.). (Illus.). 80p. 1979. prof ref 15.00x (ISBN 0-88410-537-7); pap. 9.95x (ISBN 0-88410-543-1). Ballinger Pub.

Denham, Ken. Guinea Pigs & Chinchillas. (Illus.). 93p. 1977. pap. 3.95 (ISBN 0-7028-1075-4). Avian Pubns.

Denham, Robert. Northrop Frye: A Supplementary Bibliography. 67p. (Orig.). 1979. pap. 5.00 (ISBN 0-931182-02-6). Iron Mtn Pr.

Den Hamer, H. E. Interordering: A New Method of Component Orientation. (Studies in Mechanical Engineering: Vol. 2). 1981. 51.00 (ISBN 0-444-41933-0). Elsevier.

Denhardt, Bob. The Quarter Horse. LC 82-45893. (Illus.). 280p. 1983. Repr. of 1941 ed. 14.95 (ISBN 0-89096-144-1). Tex A&M Univ Pr.

Denhardt, J. G., Jr. Complete Guide to Estate Accounting & Taxes. 3rd ed. 240p. 1978. 32.95 o.p. (ISBN 0-13-160242-X, Busn). P-H.

Denhardt, Robert M. Foundation Dams of the American Quarter Horse. 240p. 1982. 22.95 (ISBN 0-8061-1820-2). U of Okla Pr.

--The Horse of the Americas. LC 74-5955. 1975. pap. 9.95 (ISBN 0-8061-1724-9). U of Okla Pr.

Den Hartog, Jacob P. Advanced Strength of Materials. 1952. text ed. 39.50 (ISBN 0-07-016400-2, C). McGraw.

--Mechanical Vibrations. 4th ed. 1956. text ed. 39.00 (ISBN 0-07-016389-8). McGraw.

Den Hengel, John W. Van. The Home of Meaning: The Hermeneutics of the Subject of Paul Ricoeur. LC 82-40204. 356p. (Orig.). 1982. lib. bdg. 26.25 (ISBN 0-8191-2602-0); pap. text ed. 14.00 (ISBN 0-8191-2603-9). U Pr of Amer.

Denhoff, Eric & Feldman, Steven A. Management through Diet & Medication. (Pediatric Habilitation Ser.: Vol. 2). (Illus.). 280p. 1981. 26.50 (ISBN 0-8247-1565-9). Dekker.

Denhoff, Eric & Stern, Leo. Minimal Brain Dysfunction. LC 78-61473. (Illus.). 208p. 1979. 30.25x (ISBN 0-89352-038-1). Masson Pub.

Denholm, Anthony. Lord Ripon 1827-1909: A Political Biography. 302p. 1982. text ed. 28.00x (ISBN 0-7099-0805-9, Pub. by Croom Helm Ltd England). Biblio Dist.

Denholm, Richard. Basic Math with Applications. 1981. pap. text ed. 18.95x (ISBN 0-673-15233-2). Scott F.

DeNicola, Alejandro F. & Blaquier, Jorge A. Physiopathology of Hypophysical Disturbances & Diseases of Reproduction, Vol.87. LC 82-15219. (Progress in Clinical & Biological Research Ser.). 352p. 1982. 36.00 (ISBN 0-8451-0087-4). A R Liss.

Denieul-Cormier, Anne. Wise & Foolish Kings: The House of Valois. LC 77-175365. (Illus.). 1980. 11.95 o.p. (ISBN 0-385-04903-X). Doubleday.

Deniker, P., ed. Collegium Internationale Neuro-Psychopharmacologicum, 10th Congress: Proceedings, 2 vols. 1978. Set. text ed. 275.00 (ISBN 0-08-021506-8). Pergamon.

Dening, Greg. Islands & Beaches: Discourse on a Silent Land, Marquesas, 1774-1880. (Illus.). 350p. 1980. text ed. 27.50 (ISBN 0-8248-0721-9). UH Pr.

Dening, Greg, ed. see Robarts, Edward.

Denis, George, tr. see Tertz, Abram & Sinyavsky, Andrei.

Denis, Jean. Traite de L'Accord de L'Espinette. 2nd ed. LC 68-16229. (Music Ser.). 1969. Repr. of 1650 ed. 17.50 (ISBN 0-306-70950-3). Da Capo.

Denis, Jean-Jerome. Le Tresor. LC 82-10317. (Illus.). 32p. (Fr.). (gr. 7-12). 1982. pap. text ed. 1.95 (ISBN 0-88436-910-2, 40284); cassettes 12.00. EMC.

Denis, John. Alistair MacLean's Hostage Tower. 192p. 1983. pap. 2.50 (ISBN 0-449-20086-8, Crest). Fawcett.

Denis, Philippe. Notebook of Shadows: Selected Poems, 1974-1980. Irwin, Mark, tr. from Fr. LC 82-82907. (Contemporary European Poetry Ser.). Orig. Title: Cahier d'ombres. 68p. (Orig.). Date not set. lib. bdg. 10.00 (ISBN 0-910321-01-9); pap. 5.00 (ISBN 0-910321-00-0). Globe Pr.

Denis, R. G. Gambling Times Guide to Thoroughbred Racing. (Illus., Orig.). Date not set. pap. text ed. 5.95 (ISBN 0-89746-005-7). Lyle Stuart.

Denisen, Ervin L. Principles of Horticulture. 2nd ed. (Illus.). 1979. text ed. 24.95 (ISBN 0-02-328380-7); instrs'. manual avail. (ISBN 0-685-96773-5). Macmillan.

Denisoff, R. Serge. Sing a Song of Social Significance. LC 78-186631. 1972. pap. 7.50 o.p. (ISBN 0-87972-036-0). Bowling Green Univ.

--Solid Gold: The Popular Record Industry. LC 74-20194. (Cultural & Society Ser). (Illus.). 504p. 1981. pap. 5.95 o.p. (ISBN 0-87855-586-2). Transaction Bks.

Denisoff, R. Serge & Wahrman, Ralph. An Introduction to Sociology. 2nd ed. (Illus.). 1979. pap. text ed. 17.95x o.p. (ISBN 0-02-328400-5); students' guide avail. o.p.; instrs'. manual avail. o.p. Macmillan.

--An Introduction to Sociology. 3rd ed. 640p. 1983. pap. text ed. 19.95 (ISBN 0-02-328430-7). Macmillan.

Denisoff, R. Serge, et al. Theories & Paradigms in Contemporary Sociology. LC 73-90894. 450p. 1974. pap. text ed. 12.95 (ISBN 0-87581-169-8). Peacock Pubs.

Denison, Edward F. Accounting for Slower Economic Growth: The United States in the 1970s. LC 79-20341. 212p. 1979. 22.95 (ISBN 0-8157-1802-0); pap. 10.95 (ISBN 0-8157-1801-2). Brookings.

--Accounting for United States Economic Growth: 1929-1969. LC 74-278. 355p. 1974. 22.95 (ISBN 0-8157-1804-7); pap. 9.95 (ISBN 0-8157-1803-9). Brookings.

Denison, Edward F. & Chung, William K. How Japan's Economy Grew So Fast: The Sources of Postwar Expansion. 1976. 18.95 (ISBN 0-8157-1808-X); pap. 7.95 (ISBN 0-8157-1807-1). Brookings.

Denison, R. A., jt. ed. see Martin, M. J.

Denk, R., jt. auth. see Korting, Gunter W.

Denker, H. W. Implantation: The Role of Proteinases, & Blockage of Implantation Through Proteinase Inhibitors. (Advances in Anatomy, Embryology & Cell Biology: Vol. 53, Pt. 5). (Illus.). 1977. pap. 31.00 o.p. (ISBN 0-387-08479-7). Springer-Verlag.

Denker, Henry. The Healers. LC 82-20374. 352p. 1983. 13.45 (ISBN 0-688-01585-9). Morrow.

--Horowitz & Mrs. Washington. LC 79-1114. 1979. 11.95 o.p. (ISBN 0-399-12341-5). Putnam Pub Group.

--Outrage. 320p. 1983. pap. 3.50 (ISBN 0-380-62802-3). Avon.

--The Warfield Syndrome. 324p. 1981. 11.95 (ISBN 0-399-12612-0). Putnam Pub Group.

--The Warfield Syndrome. 224p. 1982. pap. 2.95 o.p. (ISBN 0-425-05631-7). Berkley Pub.

Denkinger, Marc, ed. see Olivier, Juste.

Denktash, Rauf. The Cyprus Triangle. 224p. 1982. 17.95 (ISBN 0-04-327066-2). Allen Unwin.

Denlinger, Charles & Denlinger, Elaine. Algebra Review. 116p. 1978. pap. text ed. 2.95 o.p. (ISBN 0-12-059568-0). Acad Pr.

Denlinger, Elaine, jt. auth. see Denlinger, Charles.

Denmark, F. L., jt. auth. see Sherman, J. A.

Denmark, Florence L., jt. auth. see Unger, Rhoda K.

Denmark, Florence L., ed. Psychology: The Leading Edge. new ed. (Annals of the New York Academy of Sciences: Vol. 340). 114p. 1980. 22.00x (ISBN 0-89766-068-4); pap. 22.00x (ISBN 0-89766-069-2). NY Acad Sci.

Denmark, Florence L., jt. ed. see Salzinger, Kurt.

Denmark, Florence L., et al, eds. Women: A PDI Reference Work, Vol. 1. LC 75-5161. 626p. 1977. 49.95 (ISBN 0-88437-001-1). Psych Dimensions.

Denmead, O. T., jt. auth. see Bradley, E. F.

Denn, M. Process Fluid Mechanics. 1980. 31.95 (ISBN 0-13-723163-6). P-H.

Denn, Morton M., jt. auth. see Russell, T. Fraser.

Dennard, Margaret S. You Praise the Lord Your Way, & I Will Praise Him Mine. 1979. 4.50 o.p. (ISBN 0-533-03905-3). Vantage.

Denne, Constance A., ed. see Cooper, James F.

Dennehy, Raymond. Reason & Dignity. LC 81-40364. 152p. 1982. lib. bdg. 19.75 (ISBN 0-8191-1898-2); pap. text ed. 8.75 (ISBN 0-8191-1899-0). U Pr of Amer.

Dennell, R., ed. European Economic Prehistory: A New Approach. Date not set. price not set (ISBN 0-12-209180-9). Acad Pr.

Dennemeyer, Rene. Introduction to Partial Differential Equations & Boundary Value Problems. (International Pure & Applied Mathematics Ser). 1968. text ed. 35.00 (ISBN 0-07-016396-0, C). McGraw.

Denneny, Michael, et al, eds. The Christopher Street Reader. 416p. 1983. 19.95 (ISBN 0-698-11103-6, Coward). Putnam Pub Group.

Dennerstein, Lorraine, et al. Hysterectomy: A Book to Help You Deal with the Physical & Emotional Aspects. (Illus.). 160p. 1982. 11.95x (ISBN 0-19-554371-8); pap. 6.95x (ISBN 0-19-554366-1). Oxford U Pr.

Dennett, Daniel C. Brainstorms: Philosophical Essays on Mind & Psychology. LC 78-13723. (Bradford Bks.). 384p. 1980. text ed. 24.00x (ISBN 0-262-04064-6); pap. 10.00 (ISBN 0-262-54037-1). MIT Pr.

Dennett, Daniel C., jt. auth. see Hofstadter, Douglas R.

Dennett, Daniel C., jt. ed. see Hofstadter, Douglas R.
Dennett, E. The Step I Have Taken. Daniel, R. P., ed. 53p. pap. 2.75 (ISBN 0-88172-140-9). Believers Bkshelf.
Dennett, M. W. Birth Control Laws. LC 70-119053. (Civil Liberties in American History Ser). 1970. 35.00 (ISBN 0-306-71942-8). Da Capo.
Denney. Dictionary of Spectroscopy. 2nd ed. 208p. 1982. 39.95 (ISBN 0-471-87478-7, Pub. by Wiley-Interscience). Wiley.
Denney, Myron K. Second Opinion. new ed. LC 79-50419. 1979. 8.95 (ISBN 0-448-16555-4, G&D). Putnam Pub Group.
Denney, R. C. Named Organic Reactions. 1969. text ed. 5.95 o.p. (ISBN 0-408-60250-3). Butterworth.
Denney, Richard J. & Biles, Blake A. European Environmental Laws & Regulations Notebook. 160p. 1982. Wkbk. 48.00 (ISBN 0-86587-104-3). Gov Insts.
Denney, Roland C. Dictionary of Chromatography. 2nd ed. 229p. 1982. 39.95 (ISBN 0-471-87477-9, Pub. by Wiley-Interscience). Wiley.
Denney, Ron. Chemistry. 160p. 1982. 25.00x (ISBN 0-686-81708-7, Pub. by Muller Ltd). State Mutual Bk.
Denning & Phillips. The Llewellyn Practical Guide to Group Magick. Weschcke, Carl, ed. (Orig.). Date not set. pap. 6.95 (ISBN 0-87542-182-2). Llewellyn Pubns.
--Llewellyn's Practical Guide to Astral Projection. LC 79-88141. (Illus.). 1980. pap. 6.95 (ISBN 0-87542-181-4). Llewellyn Pubns.
Denning, Charles H., Jr. First Aid for Horses. (Orig.). pap. 3.00 (ISBN 0-87980-189-1). Wilshire.
Denning, Melita & Phillips, Osborne. The Llewellyn Complete Guide to Planetary Magick. Weschcke, Carl L., ed. (Practical Magick Ser.). (Illus.). 240p. (Orig.). 1983. pap. 9.95 (ISBN 0-87542-193-8). Llewellyn Pubns.
--Llewellyn Practical Guide to the Development of Psychic Powers. 1981. 6.95 (ISBN 0-87542-191-1). Llewellyn Pubns.
--The Llewellyn Practical Guide to the Magick of the Tarot. Weschcke, Carl L., ed. LC 82-83428. (Llewellyn's Practical Magick Ser.). (Illus.). 240p. (Orig.). 1983. pap. 6.95 (ISBN 0-87542-198-9). Llewellyn Pubns.
Denning, Peter J., jt. auth. see Coffman, Edward G., Jr.
Denning, Peter J., et al. Machines, Languages & Computation. (Automatic Computation Ser.). (Illus.). 1978. ref. ed. 29.95 (ISBN 0-13-542258-2). P-H.
Dennis, A. L. Eastern Problems at the Close of the Eighteenth Century. 277p. Repr. of 1901 ed. lib. bdg. 22.50x (ISBN 0-87991-092-5). Porcupine Pr.
Dennis, Anthony J., jt. ed. see Cooke, Marcus.
Dennis, Barbara D., ed. see National Academy of Arbitrators-24th Annual Meeting.
Dennis, Barbara D., ed. see National Academy of Arbitrators-25th Annual Meeting.
Dennis, Barbara D., ed. see National Academy of Arbitrators-26th Meeting.
Dennis, Barbara D., ed. see National Academy of Arbitrators-27th Annual Meeting.
Dennis, Barbara D., ed. see National Academy of Arbitrators-28th Annual Meeting.
Dennis, Barbara D., ed. see National Academy of Arbitrators-29th Annual Meeting.
Dennis, Barbara D., ed. see National Academy of Arbitrators-30th Annual Meeting.
Dennis, Barbara D., ed. see National Academy of Arbitrators-32nd Annual Meeting.
Dennis, Barbara D., jt. ed. see Stern, James L.
Dennis, Deborah E., jt. ed. see Zikmund, Joseph.
Dennis, Ervin A. & Jenkins, John D. Comprehensive Graphic Arts. 2nd ed. (Illus.). 576p. 1983. text ed. 26.95 (ISBN 0-672-97681-1); instr's guide 6.67 (ISBN 0-672-97682-X); wkbk. 5.95 (ISBN 0-672-98447-4). Bobbs.
Dennis, Erwin A. & Jenkins, John D. Comprehensive Graphic Arts. LC 72-92620. 1974. 24.95 (ISBN 0-672-97607-2); tchrs' manual, 1975 6.67 (ISBN 0-672-97609-9); student's manual, 1976 11.50 (ISBN 0-672-97608-0). Bobbs.
Dennis, Everette, jt. auth. see Hage, George.
Dennis, Everette E., jt. auth. see DeFleur, Melvin L.
Dennis, Henry C. The American Indian, 1492-1976: A Chronology & Fact Book. 2nd ed. LC 76-46440. (Ethnic Chronology Ser.: No. 1). 177p. 1977. 8.50 (ISBN 0-379-00526-3). Oceana.
Dennis, Ivanette, ed. see Richardson Woman's Club.
Dennis, J. Richard. Fractions Are Parts of Things. LC 73-127603. (Illus.). 40p. (gr. 2-5). 1971 (ISBN 0-690-31520-1, TYC-J). PLB 10.89 (ISBN 0-690-31521-X); pap. 1.45 (ISBN 0-690-31522-8, TYC-J). Har-Row.
Dennis, Jack, ed. Socialization to Politics: A Reader. LC 72-8329. 527p. 1973. pap. text ed. 22.95x o.s.i. (ISBN 0-471-20926-0). Wiley.
Dennis, John. O, Promised Land. 160p. 1982. pap. text ed. 8.95 (ISBN 0-88377-237-X). Newbury Hse.
Dennis, John see Collier, Jeremy.
Dennis, John, jt. auth. see Griffin, Suzanne M.
Dennis, John E. & Schnabel, Robert B. Numerical Methods for Unconstrained Optimization & Nonlinear Equations. (Illus.). 272p. 1983. text ed. 27.00 (ISBN 0-13-627216-9). P-H.
Dennis, John G. Structural Geology. 532p. 1972. 32.50 (ISBN 0-471-06746-6). Wiley.
Dennis, John V. A Complete Guide to Bird Feeding. 1975. 14.95 (ISBN 0-394-47937-8). Knopf.
Dennis, Judith, jt. auth. see Adrian, Ann.
Dennis, LaRae. Know Your Poison. 1972. pap. text ed. 3.90x o.p. (ISBN 0-88246-026-9). Oreg St U Bkstrs.
Dennis, Larry, jt. auth. see Lohren, Carl.
Dennis, Lawrence J. & Eaton, William E., eds. George S. Counts: Educator for a New Age. LC 79-28182. 167p. 1980. 12.95x (ISBN 0-8093-0954-8). S Ill U Pr.
Dennis, Lisl. Travel Photography Developing a Personal Style. (Illus.). 150p. 1983. pap. 16.95 (ISBN 0-930764-42-0). Curtin & London.
Dennis, Lorraine B. Psychology of Human Behavior for Nurses. 3rd ed. LC 67-10729. (Illus.). 1967. 14.95 (ISBN 0-7216-3011-1). Saunders.
Dennis, Marshall. Mortgage Lending Fundamentals & Practices. (Illus.). 1981. text ed. 20.95 (ISBN 0-8359-4651-7); instructer's manual avail. (ISBN 0-8359-4652-5). Reston.
Dennis, Martha, jt. ed. see Colowick, Sidney.
Dennis, Nigel. An Essay on Malta. LC 73-83041. (Illus.). 64p. 1974. 6.95 (ISBN 0-8149-0732-6). Vanguard.
Dennis, Nigel F. Dramatic Essays. LC 77-28431. 1978. Repr. of 1962 ed. lib. bdg. 18.25x (ISBN 0-313-20244-3, DEDR). Greenwood.
Dennis, Norman. Public Participation & Planners. (Society Today & Tomorrow Ser.). (Illus.). Date not set. cancelled o.s.i. (ISBN 0-571-09952-1). Faber & Faber.
Dennis, P. O. Food Control in Action. 1981. 45.00 (ISBN 0-85334-894-4, Pub. by Applied Sci England). Elsevier.
Dennis, Peggy. The Autobiography of an American Communist: A Personal View of a Political Life, 1925-1975. LC 77-23607. (Illus.). 288p. 1977. 12.95 (ISBN 0-88208-081-4); pap. 5.95 o.s.i. (ISBN 0-88208-090-3). Lawrence Hill.
Dennis, Peter. The Lost Starship. LC 81-52500. (Starters Ser.). PLB 8.00 (ISBN 0-382-06509-3). Silver.
Dennis, R. Ethel. Black People of America. (gr. 9-12). 1970. 13.72 o.p. (ISBN 0-07-016397-9, W); pap. 10.60 o.p. (ISBN 0-07-016398-7). McGraw.
Dennis, R. K., ed. Algebraic K-Theory: Proceedings, Oberwolfach, FRG, 1980, Vol. II. (Lecture Notes in Mathematics Ser.: Vol. 967). 409p. 1983. pap. 20.00 (ISBN 0-387-11966-3). Springer-Verlag.
Dennis, R. W. British Ascomycetes. 3rd rev. & enl. ed. (Illus.). 1977. 80.00 (ISBN 3-7682-0552-5). Lubrecht & Cramer.
Dennis, R. W., et al. New Check List of British Agarics & Boleti. 1974. Repr. of 1960 ed. 16.00 (ISBN 3-7682-0935-0). Lubrecht & Cramer.
Dennis, Richard, ed. Handbook on Aerosols. LC 75-33965. (ERDA Technical Information Center). 148p. 1976. pap. 11.75 (ISBN 0-87079-024-2, TID-26608); microfiche 4.50 (ISBN 0-87079-237-7, TID-26608). DOE.
Dennis, Warren L. & Pottinger, J. Stanley. Federal Regulation of Banking Redlining & Community Reinvestment. LC 80-51511. 1981. 56.00 o.p. (ISBN 0-88262-476-8). Warren.
Dennis, Wayne & Skinner, B. F. Current Trends in Psychology. 225p. 1982. Repr. of 1947 ed. lib. bdg. 45.00 (ISBN 0-8495-1141-0). Arden Lib.
Dennis, Wesley. Flip & the Morning. LC 51-13521. (Illus.). (ps-1). 1977. pap. 2.95 (ISBN 0-14-050204-1, Puffin). Penguin.
Dennis, William J. Tacna & Arica: An Account of the Chile-Peru Boundary Dispute & of the Arbitration by the United States. 1931. text ed. 18.50x (ISBN 0-686-83802-5). Elliots Bks.
Dennison, Darwin. The Dine System: The Nutrition Plan for Better Health. 1982. pap. 8.95 (ISBN 0-452-25367-5, Plume). NAL.
--The Dine System: The Nutritional Plan for Better Health. LC 82-8254. (Medical Library). (Illus.). 196p. 1982. pap. 8.95 (ISBN 0-686-84854-3, 1258-6). Mosby.
Dennison, John H. Analysis of Geologic Structures. (Illus.). 1968. text ed. 14.95x (ISBN 0-393-09801-X, NortonC). Norton.
Dennison, W. F. Education in Jeopardy: Problems & Possibilities of Contraction. (Theory & Practice in Education Ser.: Vol. 3). 176p. 1981. 19.95x o.p. (ISBN 0-631-12548-5, Pub. by Basil Blackwell England); pap. 9.95x o.p. (ISBN 0-631-12889-1). Biblio Dist.
Denno, Robert F. & McClure, Mark S., eds. Variable Plants & Herbivores in Natureal & Managed Systems. Date not set. price not set (ISBN 0-12-209160-4). Acad Pr.
Dennon. CP-M Revealed. Date not set. 12.95 (ISBN 0-686-81999-3, 5204). Hayden.
Denny, James. Death of Christ. 1982. lib. bdg. 12.50 (ISBN 0-86524-090-6, 9507). Klock & Klock.
Denny, M. Ray. Comparative Psychology: An Evolutionary Analysis of Animal Behavior. LC 79-21123. 496p. 1980. text ed. 29.50x (ISBN 0-471-70930-1). Wiley.
Denny, Randal. The Habit of Happiness. 1976. 2.50 (ISBN 0-8341-0399-0). Beacon Hill.
Denny-Brown. The Cerebral Control of Movement. 222p. 1982. 50.00x (ISBN 0-85323-001-3, Pub. by Liverpool Univ England). State Mutual Bk.
Dennys, Nicholas B. The Folk-Lore of China, & Its Affinities with That of the Aryan & Semitic Races. LC 79-89262. (Illus.). iv, 163p. 1972. Repr. of 1876 ed. 37.00x (ISBN 0-8103-3932-3). Gale.
Dennys, Rodney. The Heraldic Imagination. (Illus.). 1976. 15.00 o.p. (ISBN 0-517-52629-8, C N Potter Bks). Crown.
Denoeu, Francois. Sommets Litteraires Francais. rev. ed. 1967. text ed. 20.95 o.p. (ISBN 0-669-04826-7). Heath.
Denoeu, Francois & Sices, David. Two Thousand & One French & English Idioms: Idiotismes Francais et Anglais 2001. 1982. pap. text ed. 7.95 (ISBN 0-8120-0435-3). Barron.
De Nogent, Guibert. Self & Society in Medieval France. pap. 4.95xi o.p. (ISBN 0-06-131471-4, TB1471, Torch). Har-Row.
Denomme, Robert T. Leconte de Lisle. (World Authors Ser.). 1973. lib. bdg. 15.95 (ISBN 0-8057-2518-0, Twayne). G K Hall.
Denonn, Lester E., ed. see Russell, Bertrand.
DeNorre, Rochel. A Woman of New Orleans. (Woman's Destiny Ser.: No. 2). (Orig.). 1983. pap. 2.95 (ISBN 0-440-09856-4, Banbury). Dell.
Den Ouden, Bernard see Ouden, Bernard D.
Dens, Jean-Pierre. L' Honnete Homme et la Critique du Gout: Esthetique et Societe au XVIIe Siecle. LC 81-68005. (French Forum Monographs: No. 28). 158p. (Orig.). 1981. pap. 9.50x (ISBN 0-917058-27-5). French Forum.
Denslow, Van Buren. Principles of the Economic Philosophy of Society, Government & Industry. (The Neglected American Economists Ser.). 1974. lib. bdg. 50.00 o.s.i. (ISBN 0-8240-1023-X). Garland Pub.
Densmore, Frances. Chippewa Music, 2 vols. LC 77-164513. (Illus.). 1972. Repr. of 1913 ed. Set. lib. bdg. 47.50 (ISBN 0-306-70459-5). Da Capo.
--Choctaw Music. LC 72-1883. (Music Ser.). (Illus.). 110p. 1972. Repr. of 1943 ed. lib. bdg. 15.00 (ISBN 0-306-70511-7). Da Capo.
--Handbook of the Collection of Musical Instruments in the United States National Museum. LC 79-155231. (Music Ser). 1971. Repr. of 1927 ed. lib. bdg. 27.50 (ISBN 0-306-70167-7). Da Capo.
--Mandan & Hidatsa Music. LC 72-1886. (Music Ser.). (Illus.). 236p. 1972. Repr. of 1923 ed. lib. bdg. 21.50 (ISBN 0-306-70514-1). Da Capo.
--Menominee Music. LC 72-1882. (Music Ser.). (Illus.). 286p. 1972. Repr. of 1932 ed. lib. bdg. 22.50 (ISBN 0-306-70510-9). Da Capo.
--Music of Acoma, Isleta, Cochiti, & Zuni Pueblos. LC 72-1877. (Music Ser.). (Illus.). 142p. 1972. Repr. of 1957 ed. lib. bdg. 17.50 (ISBN 0-306-70505-2). Da Capo.
--Music of the Indians of British Columbia. LC 72-1879. (Music Ser.). (Illus.). 118p. 1972. Repr. of 1943 ed. lib. bdg. 16.50 (ISBN 0-306-70507-9). Da Capo.
--The Music of the North American Indian, 14 vols. in 13. (Music Ser.). 1972. Set. 275.00 (ISBN 0-306-70517-6). Da Capo.
--Nootka & Quileute Music. LC 72-1885. (Music Ser.). (Illus.). 416p. 1972. Repr. of 1939 ed. lib. bdg. 32.50 (ISBN 0-306-70513-3). Da Capo.
--Northern Ute Music. LC 72-1887. (Music Ser.). (Illus.). 236p. 1972. Repr. of 1922 ed. lib. bdg. 22.50 (ISBN 0-306-70515-X). Da Capo.
--Papago Music. LC 72-1881. (Music Ser.). (Illus.). 276p. 1972. Repr. of 1929 ed. lib. bdg. 22.50 (ISBN 0-306-70509-5). Da Capo.
--Pawnee Music. LC 72-1880. (Music Ser.). 160p. 1972. Repr. of 1929 ed. lib. bdg. 16.50 (ISBN 0-306-70508-7). Da Capo.
--Seminole Music. LC 72-1878. (Music Ser.). (Illus.). 276p. 1972. Repr. of 1956 ed. lib. bdg. 22.50 (ISBN 0-306-70506-0). Da Capo.
--Teton Sioux Music. LC 72-1889. (Music Ser.). (Illus.). 722p. 1972. Repr. of 1918 ed. lib. bdg. 42.50 (ISBN 0-306-70516-8). Da Capo.
--Yuman & Yaqui Music. LC 72-1884. (Music Ser.). (Illus.). 272p. 1972. Repr. of 1932 ed. lib. bdg. 22.50 (ISBN 0-306-70512-5). Da Capo.
Densmore, Mary J., jt. auth. see Emanuelsen, Kathy L.
Denson, Alan. A Bibliography of the Writings of A. E. (Collected Edition of the Writings of G. W. Russell: No. IX). 1980. text ed. price not set (ISBN 0-391-01089-1). Humanities.
--Letters from A. E. (Collected Edition of the Writings of G. W. Russell VII). 1980. text ed. price not set (ISBN 0-391-01139-1). Humanities.
Denstman, Harold & Schultz, M. J. Photographic Reproduction: Methods, Techniques & Applications for Engineering & the Graphic Arts. 1963. 26.50 o.p. (ISBN 0-07-016403-7, P&RB). McGraw.
Dent, Alan. Mrs. Patrick Campbell. LC 72-9046. (Illus.). 333p. 1973. Repr. of 1961 ed. lib. bdg. 18.25x (ISBN 0-8371-6560-1, DECA). Greenwood.
Dent, Anthony, ed. International Modern Plays. Incl. Life of the Insects. Capek, Karel; Mask & the Face. Chiarelli, Luigi; Infernal Machine. Cocteau, Jean; Hannele. Hauptmann, Gerhart; Miss Julie. Strindberg, August. 1973. pap. 2.50x (ISBN 0-460-01989-9, Evman). Biblio Dist.
Dent, David, jt. auth. see Young, Anthony.
Dent, E. J., ed. see Somma, Antonio.
Dent, Edward. The Rise of Romantic Opera. Dean, Winton, ed. LC 76-14029. (Illus.). 1976. 37.50 (ISBN 0-521-21337-1). Cambridge U Pr.
Dent, Edward J. Foundations of English Opera. 2nd ed. LC 65-18501. (Music Ser). 1965. Repr. of 1928 ed. lib. bdg. 25.00 (ISBN 0-306-70905-8). Da Capo.
--The Rise of Romantic Opera. Dean, Winton, ed. LC 78-62111. 1979. pap. 10.95 (ISBN 0-521-29659-5). Cambridge U Pr.
Dent, Edward J., tr. see Bouilly, J. N.
Dent, J. B. & Blackie, M. J. Systems Simulation in Agriculture. (Illus.). 1979. 33.90x (ISBN 0-85334-827-8, Pub. by Applied Sci England). Elsevier.
Dent, J. B., jt. ed. see Blackie, M. J.
Dent, John see Allen, W. S.
Dent, Joseph B., et al. Fundamentals of Engineering Graphics. 2nd ed. (Illus.). 1979. pap. text ed. 23.95x o.p. (ISBN 0-02-328470-6). Macmillan.
Dent, Julian. Crisis in Finance: Crown, Financiers & Society in Seventeenth-Century France. LC 73-80084. 288p. 1973. 26.00 (ISBN 0-312-17360-1). St Martin.
Dent, Martin. Nigeria: The Politics of Military Rule. 200p. 1983. text ed. 30.00x (ISBN 0-7146-3138-8, F Cass Co). Biblio Dist.
Dent, Nicholas. How to Sail. LC 78-78116. 1979. 11.95 o.p. (ISBN 0-312-39613-9). St Martin.
--How to Sail: A Practical Course in Boat Handling. (Illus.). 128p. pap. 9.95 (ISBN 0-312-39625-2). St Martin.
Dent, R. W. Shakespeare's Proverbial Language: An Index. 378p. 1981. 31.00x (ISBN 0-520-03894-0). U of Cal Pr.
Dent, Roxanne. Sweetwater Saga. 1979. pap. 2.95 (ISBN 0-451-11979-7, AE1979, Sig). NAL.
Dentan, Robert C. First Reader in Biblical Theology: The Design of the Scriptures. 1965. pap. 5.95 (ISBN 0-8164-2022-X, SP20). Seabury.
--First, Second Kings & First, Second Chronicles. LC 59-10454. (Layman's Bible Commentary Ser., Vol. 7). 1964. pap. 3.95 (ISBN 0-8042-3067-6). John Knox.
--Holy Scriptures: A Survey. (Orig.). 1949. pap. 5.95 (ISBN 0-8164-2031-9, SP1). Seabury.
Dentinger, Jane. Murder on Cue. LC 82-45595. 192p. 1983. 11.95 (ISBN 0-385-18411-5). Doubleday.
Denton, Clive. Susan Hayward & the Movie. 300p. write for info. (ISBN 0-498-02316-8). A S Barnes.
Denton, D., jt. ed. see Brain, P. F.
Denton, D. A. The Hunger for Salt: An Anthropological, Physiological, & Medical Analysis. (Illus.). 665p. 1982. 149.80 (ISBN 0-387-11286-3). Springer-Verlag.
Denton, E. N., jt. auth. see Glanvill, A. B.
Denton, G. H. & Hughes, T. J. The Last Great Ice Sheets. LC 79-27808. 484p. 1980. 112.00 (ISBN 0-471-06006-2, Pub. by Wiley-Interscience). Wiley.
Denton, J. H. Robert Winchelsey & the Crown, 1294-1313. (Cambridge Studies in Medieval Life & Thought: No. 14). 1980. 47.50 (ISBN 0-521-22963-4). Cambridge U Pr.
Denton, James. Circuit Hikes in Shenandoah National Park. 11th ed. LC 80-81762. 80p. 1980. pap. 2.50 (ISBN 0-915746-15-8). Potomac Appalach.
Denton, Jeremiah, et al. Great Issues 81: A Forum on Important Questions Facing the American Public, Vol. 12. LC 75-648855. 1981. 11.95 (ISBN 0-686-97229-5). TSU Pr.
Denton, John A. Medical Sociology. LC 77-94098. (Illus.). 1978. text ed. 25.50 (ISBN 0-395-25805-7). HM.
Denton, Juanita H., jt. auth. see Denton, Wallace.
Denton, K. Safety Management. 416p. 1982. 27.50x (ISBN 0-07-016410-X). McGraw.
Denton, Molly T., ed. Guide to the Appalachian Trail & Side Trails in the Shenandoah National Park. 8th ed. LC 76-17452. 265p. 1977. pap. 6.00 o.p. (ISBN 0-915746-07-7). Potomac Appalach.
Denton, R. M. & Pogson, C. I. Metabolic Regulation. 1976. pap. 6.50x (ISBN 0-412-13150-1, Pub. by Chapman & Hall England). Methuen Inc.
Denton, R. M., jt. auth. see Randle, P. J.
Denton, Robert E., Jr. The Symbolic Dimensions of the American Presidency: Description & Analysis. LC 82-70562. 160p. 1982. pap. text ed. 7.95x (ISBN 0-917974-86-7). Waveland Pr.
Denton, Wallace & Denton, Juanita H. Creative Couples: The Growth Factor in Marriage. LC 82-17439. 156p. 1983. pap. 8.95 (ISBN 0-664-24453-X). Westminster.
D'Entreves, A. P. Natural Law: An Introduction to Legal Philosophy. 2nd rev. ed. 1964. text ed. 14.50x (ISBN 0-09-102600-8, Hutchinson U Lib); pap. text ed. 9.50x (ISBN 0-09-102601-6, Hutchinson U Lib). Humanities.
D'Entreves, Alexander P. Medieval Contribution to Political Thought: Thomas Aquinas, Marsilius of Padua, Richard Hooker. 1959. Repr. of 1939 ed. text ed. 12.50x (ISBN 0-391-00513-8). Humanities.
Denver. John Denver Songbook. 1975. 5.95 o.p. (ISBN 0-448-12176-X, G&D). Putnam Pub Group.
Denver Public Library. Catalog of the Conservation Library, 6 vols. 1974. Set. lib. bdg. 550.00 (ISBN 0-8161-1113-8, Hall Library). G K Hall.
--Catalog of the Western History Department, Denver Public Library, 7 vols. 1970. Set. lib. bdg. 665.00 (ISBN 0-8161-0864-1, Hall Library). G K Hall.

--Catalog of the Western History Department, Denver Public Library, 1st Suppl. 1975. lib. bdg. 130.00 (ISBN 0-8161-0898-6, Hall Library). G K Hall.

Denwood, P. & Piatigorsky, A., eds. Buddhist Studies: Ancient & Modern. (Collected Papers on South Asia Ser.: No. 4). 220p. 1982. text ed. 11.75x o.p. (ISBN 0-391-02479-5, Pub. by Curzon Pr England). Humanities.

Denwood, Philip & Piatigorsky, Alexander, eds. Buddhist Studies: Ancient & Modern. 220p. 1983. 22.50x (ISBN 0-389-20264-9). B&N Imports.

Denyer, Brian Lindsay. Basic Soccer Strategy: An Introduction for Young Players. LC 74-11816. 120p. (gr. 6-9). 1976. 7.95a o.p. (ISBN 0-686-85887-5); PLB (ISBN 0-385-07964-8). Doubleday.

Denyer, C. P., tr. see Halley, Henry H.

Denyer, J. C. Office Administration. 4th ed. Mugridge, A. L., rev. by. 214p. 1982. pap. 9.95 (ISBN 0-7121-1540-4). Intl Ideas.

Denyer, J. E., intro. by. International Mineral Processing Congress 1960. 5th ed. 1118p. 1960. text ed. 46.00x (ISBN 0-686-32512-5). IMM North Am.

Denyer, Ralph. The Guitar Handbook. LC 82-47805. 1982. 25.00 (ISBN 0-394-52419-5); pap. 13.95 (ISBN 0-394-71257-9). Knopf.

Denyer, Susan. African Traditional Architecture. LC 77-16428. (Illus.). 1978. text ed. 22.50x (ISBN 0-8419-0287-9, Africana); pap. 15.50x (0-8419-0336). Holmes & Meier.

Denzel, Justin. Jumbo: Giant Circus Elephant. LC 72-9349. (Famous Animal Stories Ser.). (Illus.). 48p. (gr. 2-5). 1973. PLB 6.89 (ISBN 0-8116-4850-8). Garrard.

Denzel, Justin F. Black Kettle: King of the Wild Horses. LC 73-14786. (Famous Animal Stories Ser). (Illus.). 48p. (gr. 2-5). 1974. PLB 6.89 (ISBN 0-8116-4854-0). Garrard.

--Hiboy: Young Devil Horse. LC 80-10578. (Famous Animal Stories Ser.). 48p. (gr. 3). 1980. PLB 6.89 (ISBN 0-8116-4866-4). Garrard.

--Sampson, Yankee Stallion. LC 79-22793. (Famous Animal Stories). (Illus.). 48p. (gr. 3). 1980. PLB 6.89 (ISBN 0-8116-4865-6). Garrard.

--Scat: The Movie Cat. LC 77-23300. (Famous Animal Ser.). (Illus.). (gr. 2-5). 1977. PLB 6.89 (ISBN 0-8116-4861-3). Garrard.

--Snowfoot: White Reindeer of the Arctic. LC 75-43634. (Famous Animal Stories). (Illus.). 48p. (gr. 2-5). 1976. PLB 6.89 (ISBN 0-8116-4858-3). Garrard.

--Wild Wing: Great Hunting Eagle. LC 75-6829. (Famous Animal Stories). (Illus.). 48p. (gr. 2-5). 1975. PLB 6.89 (ISBN 0-8116-4856-7). Garrard.

Denzin, N. K., jt. auth. see Spitzer, S. P.

Denzin, Norman K. The Research Act. 2nd ed. 1978. text ed. 21.95 (ISBN 0-07-016361-8, C). McGraw.

--Sociological Methods: A Sourcebook. 2nd ed. 1977. text ed. 14.95 o.p. (ISBN 0-07-016365-0, C); pap. text ed. 18.50 (ISBN 0-07-016366-9). McGraw.

--Studies in Symbolic Interaction: An Annual Compilation of Research, Vol. 1. 1978. lib. bdg. 42.50 (ISBN 0-89232-065-6). Jai Pr.

Denzin, Norman K., ed. Studies in Symbolic Interaction, Vol. 2. (Orig.). 1979. lib. bdg. 42.50 (ISBN 0-89232-105-9). Jai Pr.

--Studies in Symbolic Interaction, Vol. 3. 304p. 1980. 42.50 (ISBN 0-89232-153-9). Jai Pr.

--Studies in Symbolic Interaction, Vol. 4. 350p. 1981. 42.50 (ISBN 0-89232-232-2). Jai Pr.

--The Values of Social Science. rev. 2nd. ed. LC 72-94545. 194p. 1973. Repr. of 1970 ed. 12.95 (ISBN 0-87855-054-2). Transaction Bks.

Deo, Narsingh. Graph Theory with Applications to Engineering & Computer Science. 1974. 34.95 (ISBN 0-13-363473-6). P-H.

--System Simulation with Digital Computer. (Illus.). 224p. 1983. pap. 17.95 (ISBN 0-13-881789-8). P-H.

Deo, S. G., jt. auth. see Pandit, S. G.

De Oca, Marco A. Twenty-One Poems. Miller, Yvette E., ed. Villasenor, Laura, tr. 73p. 1982. pap. 9.00 (ISBN 0-935480-09-9). Lat Am Lit Rev Pr.

De Ockham, Guillelmi. Opera Politica, Vol. 1. 2nd ed. Offler, H. S., ed. 378p. 1974. 37.50 (ISBN 0-7190-0548-5). Manchester.

--Opera Politica, Vol. 2. Offler, H. S., ed. 504p. 1963. 44.00 (ISBN 0-7190-0081-5). Manchester.

Deogaonkar, D. Administration for Rural Development in India. 242p. 1981. text ed. 19.00x (ISBN 0-391-02275-X, Pub. by Concept India). Humanities.

Deogaonkar, S. G. Problems of Development in Tribal Areas. 192p. 1980. text ed. 14.25x (ISBN 0-391-02132-X). Humanities.

Deol, D. Charisma & Commitment: The Mind & Political Thinking of Indira Gandhi. 136p. 1981. 12.95x (ISBN 0-940500-56-6, Pub. by Sterling India). Asia Bk Corp.

De Oliveira, Joseph see Oliveira, Joseph De.

De Oliveira, Paulo. Getting In! Steps to Acceptance at a Selective College. LC 82-40503. 160p. 1982. pap. 5.95 (ISBN 0-89480-359-X). Workman Pub.

Deonanan, Carlton R., jt. auth. see Deonanan, Venus E.

Deonanan, Venus E. & Deonanan, Carlton R. Teaching Spanish in the Secondary School in Trinidad, West Indies: A Curriculum Perspective. LC 79-6199. 373p. 1980. pap. text ed. 13.00 o.p. (ISBN 0-8191-1005-1). U Pr of Amer.

De Onis, Harriet, tr. see De Moratin, Leandro F.

De Onis, Harriet, tr. see Guzman, Martin L.

De Padua, Fernando, jt. auth. see International Congress on Electro Cardiology, Lisbon, 7th, June 1980.

De Palacios, Alicia Puyana see Puyana De Palacios, Alicia.

DePalma, Anthony F. Management of Fractures & Dislocations: An Atlas, 2 vols. 2nd ed. LC 69-12877. (Illus.). 1970. Set. 75.00 o.p. (ISBN 0-686-66532-5); 37.50 ea. o.p.; Vol. 1. (ISBN 0-7216-3027-8); Vol. 2. (ISBN 0-7216-3028-6). Saunders.

--Surgery of the Shoulder. 3rd ed. (Illus.). 768p. 1983. text ed. 75.00 (ISBN 0-397-50492-6, Lippincott Medical). Lippincott.

De Paola, Thomas A. The Clown of God: An Old Story. LC 78-3845. (Illus.). 48p. (gr. k-2). 1978. 9.95 (ISBN 0-15-219175-5, HJ). HarBraceJ.

De Paola, Tomie. Big Anthony & the Magic Ring. LC 78-23631. (Illus.). (gr. k-3). 1979. pap. 3.95 (ISBN 0-15-611907-2, VoyB). HarBraceJ.

--Bill & Pete. LC 78-5330. (Illus.). (gr. k-2). 1978. 7.95 (ISBN 0-399-20646-9); pap. 4.95 (ISBN 0-399-20650-7). Putnam Pub Group.

--The Cat on the Dovrefell: A Christmas Tale. Dasent, G. W., tr. LC 78-26340. (Illus.). 32p. (gr. k-3). 1979. 8.95 (ISBN 0-399-20680-9); pap. 3.95 (ISBN 0-399-20685-X). Putnam Pub Group.

--The Clown of God. LC 78-3845. (Illus.). (ps-3). 1978. pap. 5.95 (ISBN 0-15-618192-4, VoyB). HarBraceJ.

--The Family Christmas Tree Book. LC 80-12081. (Illus.). 32p. (ps-3). 1980. PLB 9.95 (ISBN 0-8234-0416-1). Holiday.

--Francis: The Poor Man of Assisi. LC 81-6984. (Illus.). 48p. (gr. 2-5). 1982. PLB 14.95 (ISBN 0-8234-0435-8). Holiday.

--The Friendly Beasts: An Old English Christmas Carol. (Illus.). 32p. 1981. 10.95 (ISBN 0-399-20739-2); pap. 4.95 (ISBN 0-399-20777-5). Putnam Pub Group.

--Giorgio's Village. (Illus.). (gr. 1 up). Date not set. 11.95 (ISBN 0-399-20854-2). Putnam Pub Group.

--Helga's Dowry. LC 76-54953. (Illus.). 32p. (ps-3). 1977. pap. 2.95 o.p. (ISBN 0-15-233702-4, VoyB). HarBraceJ.

--The Hunter & the Animals: A Wordless Picture Book. LC 81-2875. (Illus.). 32p. (ps-3). 1981. PLB 11.95 (ISBN 0-8234-0397-1); pap. 5.95 (ISBN 0-8234-0428-5). Holiday.

--The Knight & the Dragon. (Illus.). 32p. (gr. k-2). 1980. 8.95 (ISBN 0-399-20708-2, Peppercorn); pap. 3.95 (ISBN 0-686-65654-7). Putnam Pub Group.

--Michael Bird-Boy. (Illus.). (ps-2). 1975. 5.95 o.p. (ISBN 0-13-580803-0); pap. 5.95 (ISBN 0-13-580803-0); 2.95 (ISBN 0-13-580811-1). P-H.

--Nana Upstairs & Nana Downstairs. new ed. (Illus.). 32p. (ps-3). 1973. PLB 7.99 (ISBN 0-399-60787-0). Putnam Pub Group.

--Now One Foot, Now the Other. (Illus.). 48p. (gr. 3-7). 1981. 8.95 (ISBN 0-399-20774-0); pap. 3.95 (ISBN 0-399-20775-9). Putnam Pub Group.

--Oliver Button Is a Sissy. LC 78-12624. (Illus.). 48p. (ps-3). 1979. 7.95 (ISBN 0-15-257852-8, HJ). HarBraceJ.

--Oliver Button Is a Sissy. LC 78-12624. (Illus.). (gr. k-3). 1979. pap. 2.45 (ISBN 0-15-668140-4, VoyB). HarBraceJ.

--Pancakes for Breakfast. LC 77-15523. (Illus.). (ps-2). 1978. 8.95 (ISBN 0-15-259455-8, HJ); pap. 2.50 (ISBN 0-15-670768-3, VoyB). HarBraceJ.

--The Prince of the Dolomites. LC 79-18524. (Illus.). 48p. (ps-3). 1980. pap. 4.50 (ISBN 0-15-674432-5, VoyB). HarBraceJ.

--The Quicksand Book. LC 76-28762. (Illus.). 32p. (ps-3). 1977. PLB 9.95 (ISBN 0-8234-0291-6). Holiday.

--Strega Nona's Magic Lessons. (Illus.). (gr. k up). Date not set. 11.95 (ISBN 0-15-281785-9). HarBraceJ.

--When Everyone Was Fast Asleep. LC 75-43893. (Illus.). 32p. (ps-3). 1976. PLB 6.95 (ISBN 0-8234-0278-9). Holiday.

--When Everyone Was Fast Asleep. (Picture Puffin Ser.). (Illus.). (gr. k-2). 1979. pap. 3.95 (ISBN 0-14-050310-2, Puffin). Penguin.

De Paola, Tomie see Paola, Tomie de.

De Paola, Tomie, illus. & retold by. Fin M'Coul: The Giant of Knockmany Hill. LC 80-2254. (Illus.). 32p. (ps-3). 1981. PLB 10.95 (ISBN 0-8234-0384-X); pap. 5.95 (ISBN 0-8234-0385-8). Holiday.

De Paor, Maire. Early Irish Art. (Aspects of Ireland Ser.: Vol. 3). (Illus.). 57p. 1979. pap. 5.95 (ISBN 0-906404-03-7, Pub. by Dept Foreign Ireland). Irish Bks Media.

Deparcieux, Antoine. Essai sur les Probabilitie De la Duree De la Vie Humaine. Repr. of 1760 ed. 46.00 o.p. (ISBN 0-8287-0260-8). Clearwater Pub.

Depardon, Raymond & Taback, Carol, illus. Aperture, No. 89. (Illus.). 80p. 1983. pap. 12.50 (ISBN 0-89381-112-2). Aperture.

Department of American Decorative Arts & Sculpture & Fairbanks, Jonathan L. New England Begins: The Seventeenth Century, 3 vols. Spear, Judy & Jupe, Margaret, eds. LC 82-80591. (Illus.). 604p. 1982. Set. pap. 55.00 (ISBN 0-87846-210-4). Mus Fine Arts Boston.

Department of Asiatic Art, Museum of Fine Arts. Asiatic Art in the Museum of Fine Arts, Boston. LC 82-61853. (Illus.). 216p. 1982. pap. 18.50 (ISBN 0-87846-226-0). Mus Fine Arts Boston.

Department of Energy. Photovoltaic Energy Systems: Program Summary. 220p. 1980. pap. 34.95x (ISBN 0-89934-070-9, P-040). Solar Energy Info.

Department of Foreign Affairs. Facts about Ireland. 2nd ed. (Illus.). 258p. Date not set. 14.50 (ISBN 0-906404-10-X, Pub. by Dept Foreign Ireland); pap. 9.95 (ISBN 0-906404-12-6). Irish Bks Media.

Department of Geography, University of Hawaii, compiled by. Atlas of Hawaii. LC 72-91236. (Illus.). 232p. 1973. 19.95 (ISBN 0-8248-0259-4). UH Pr.

Department of Nursing Service, University of California. Mosby's Manual of Clinical Nursing Procedures. LC 81-1379. (Illus.). 394p. 1981. pap. text ed. 21.95 (ISBN 0-8016-3592-6). Mosby.

Department of Paintings Museum of Fine Arts. Summary Catalogue of European Paintings. (Illus.). 368p. 1983. price not set (ISBN 0-87846-230-9). Mus Fine Arts Boston.

De Pasquale, Michael. Ju-Jitsu. (Monarch Illustrated Guide Ser.). (Illus.). 1977. pap. 2.95 o.p. (ISBN 0-671-18777-5). Monarch Pr.

DePasquale, Michael, Jr. Ju-Jitsu. LC 78-10717. (Illus.). 160p. (gr. 7 up). 1978. PLB 7.29 o.p. (ISBN 0-671-32963-4). Messner.

De Patterson, Paulina G. Te Damos Gracias, Dios. (Illus.). 28p. 1981. pap. 0.60 (ISBN 0-311-38508-7). Casa Bautista.

De Paul, Edith. The Viscount's Witch. (Candlelight Regency Ser.: No. 672). (Orig.). 1981. pap. 1.50 o.s.i. (ISBN 0-440-19321-4). Dell.

DePaula, H. & Mueller, C. Marketing Today's Fashion. 1980. 18.95 (ISBN 0-13-558155-9). P-H.

Depauw, Karen, jt. auth. see Seaman, Janet.

De Pauw, Linda G. Seafaring Women. (gr. 7 up). 1982. PLB 10.95 (ISBN 0-395-32434-3); 10.45. HM.

De Peters, Amalia B., jt. auth. see Lombardi, Ronald P.

Depew, Creighton A. see Heat Transfer & Fluid Mechanics Institute.

De Pizan, Christine. The Book of the City of Ladies. Richards, E. J., tr. from Fr. (Illus.). 364p. 1982. 17.95 (ISBN 0-89255-061-9). Persea Bks.

DePlatt, Lyman, ed. Genealogical Historical Guide to Latin America. LC 78-75146. (Genealogy & Local History Ser.: Vol. 4). 1978. 42.00x (ISBN 0-8103-1389-8). Gale.

De Plou, Dafne C., tr. see Drakeford, John W.

De Plou, Dafne C., tr. see Harty, Robert & Harty, Annelle.

De Poerck, R. A., jt. auth. see Krug, C. A.

De Poix, Carol. Jo, Flo & Yolanda. 35p. (ps-1). 1973. pap. 2.75 (ISBN 0-914996-04-5). Lollipop Power.

De Polnay, Peter. Garibaldi: The Legend & the Man. LC 75-22641. (Illus.). 234p. 1976. Repr. of 1960 ed. lib. bdg. 17.50x (ISBN 0-8371-8361-8, DEGA). Greenwood.

De Pons, Beatriz. Crecer Contigo. 1978. pap. 2.20 (ISBN 0-311-40037-X). Casa Bautista.

De Pont, J. J., jt. ed. see Bonting, S. L.

De Pontecoulant, Adolphe. Organographie, 2 vols. (Bibliotheca Organologica Ser.: Vol. 9). 1972. Repr. of 1861 ed. 137.50 o.s.i. (ISBN 90-6027-138-6, Pub. by Frits Knuf Netherlands). Pendragon NY.

De Pontecoulant, Louis A. see De Pontecoulant, Adolphe.

De Poor, Betty M., tr. Dios, Tu y Tu Familia. (Dios, Tu y la Vida). Orig. Title: Deus, Voce E Sua Familia. 1981. Repr. of 1978 ed. 0.95 (ISBN 0-311-46202-2). Casa Bautista.

De Powell, Elsie R., tr. see Mayhall, Jack & Mayhall, Carole.

Depp, Roberta J., jt. ed. see Wynar, Bohdan S.

Deppe, Phillip, et al. The High Risk Child: A Guide for Concerned Parents. 198p. 1981. 13.95 o.p. (ISBN 0-02-531010-0). Macmillan.

Deppe, Theodore R. Management Strategies in Financing Parks & Recreation. 250p. 1983. text ed. 17.95 (ISBN 0-471-09966-X). Wiley.

De Pree, Gladis, jt. auth. see De Pree, Gordon.

De Pree, Gordon & De Pree, Gladis. Blade of Grass. LC 65-19504. 1971. pap. 4.95 (ISBN 0-310-23641-X). Zondervan.

Depriest, Launder. Reliability in the Acquisitions Process. (Statistics Lecture Notes). 296p. 1983. write for info. (ISBN 0-8247-1792-9). Dekker.

De Proft, Melanie & Culinary Arts Institute Staff, eds. The American Family Cookbook. rev. ed. LC 71-158818. (Illus.). 1980. 14.95 (ISBN 0-8326-0536-0, 1105-N). Delair.

DeProspo, Ernest, jt. ed. see Varlejs, Jana.

Dept. of Advertising Design, Mohawk Valley Community College. Signature One, A Graphics Annual. (Illus.). 32p. 1983. pap. 7.95 (ISBN 0-86610-126-8). Meridian Pub.

Dept. of the Navy, U. S. Marine Corps. Sniping: U. S. Marine Corps Manual FMFM-1-3B. (Illus.). 270p. 1969. pap. 7.95 (ISBN 0-87364-042-X). Paladin Ent.

De Purucker, G. Clothed with the Sun: The Mystery-Tale of Jesus the Avatara. rev. ed. Small, Emmett & Todd, Helen, eds. Orig. Title: The Story of Jesus. 56p. 1972. pap. 1.00 (ISBN 0-913004-06-5). Point Loma Pub.

--Golden Precepts: A Guide to Enlightened Living. rev. 3rd ed. Todd, Helen & Small, W. Emmett, eds. 170p. 1971. 3.50 o.p. (ISBN 0-686-86619-3); pap. 2.50 (ISBN 0-913004-02-2, 913004-02). Point Loma Pub.

--Mahatmas & Genuine Occultism. rev. ed. Small, Emmett & Todd, Helen, eds. Orig. Title: The Masters & the Path of Occultism. 100p. 1972. pap. 1.50 (ISBN 0-913004-07-3). Point Loma Pub.

--Wind of the Spirit. abr. ed. Small, W. Emmett & Todd, Helen, eds. 282p. 1971. pap. 3.25 (ISBN 0-913004-00-6, 913004-00). Point Loma Pub.

--Word Wisdom in the Esoteric Tradition. (Study Ser.: No. 2). 1980. 5.95 (ISBN 0-913004-35-9, 913004-35). Point Loma Pub.

De Purucker, G. & Tingley, Katherine. H. P. Blavatsky: The Mystery. rev. ed. Small, W. Emmett & Todd, Helen, eds. (Illus.). 256p. 1974. pap. 5.25 (ISBN 0-913004-14-6). Point Loma Pub.

De Purucker, G. De see De Purucker, G.

Dequasie, Andrew. Thirsty. 1983. 11.95 (ISBN 0-8027-4017-0). Walker & Co.

De Quehen, Hugh, ed. see Butler, Samuel.

Dequeker, J. Bone Loss in Normal & Pathological Conditions. 1972. lib. bdg. 12.50 o.p. (ISBN 0-686-28545-X, Pub. by Martinus Nijhoff Netherlands). Kluwer Boston.

De Queljoe, David. Marginal Man in a Colonial Society: Abdoel Moeis' Salah Asuahan. LC 74-620028. (Papers in International Studies: Southeast Asia: No. 32). 1974. pap. 4.00x (ISBN 0-89680-019-9, Ohio U Ctr Intl). Ohio U Pr.

DeQuille, Dan. Silver Walled Palace. Basso, Dave, ed. (Great Basin Abstracts Ser.). (Illus.). 56p. 1983. pap. 19.95 (ISBN 0-936332-19-0). Falcon Hill Pr.

Dequin, Henry C. Librarians Serving Disabled Children & Young People. 306p. 1983. lib. bdg. 22.50 (ISBN 0-87287-364-1). Libs Unl.

De Quincey, Thomas. Confessions of an English Opium-Eater. 300p. 1983. pap. text ed. 4.95 o.p. (ISBN 0-460-01223-1, Evman). Biblio Dist.

De Quincy, Thomas. Confessions of an English Opium-Eater. 1978. Repr. of 1907 ed. 7.95x (ISBN 0-460-00223-6, Evman). Biblio Dist.

--Confessions of an English Opium Eater. Hayter, Alethea, ed. (English Library). 1971. pap. 3.50 (ISBN 0-14-043061-X, EL61). Penguin.

Der, Van Werff see Van Der Werff, A. & Huls, H.

Der, Veur Paul W. Van see The, Lian & Van Der Veur, Paul W.

Derato, F. C. Automotive Ignition Systems: Diagnosis & Repair. 320p. 1982. 14.95x (ISBN 0-07-016501-7). McGraw.

Derber, Milton & Young, Edwin, eds. Labor & the New Deal. LC 70-169656. (Fdr & the Era of the New Deal Ser.). 394p. 1972. Repr. of 1957 ed. lib. bdg. 39.50 (ISBN 0-306-70364-5). Da Capo.

Derby, Harry L. The Hand Cannons of Imperial Japan. Reidy, John & Welge, Albert, eds. LC 82-90099. (Illus.). 304p. 1981. 37.95 (ISBN 0-940424-00-2). Derby Pub.

Derbyshire, Desmond. Textos Hixkaryana. 206p. 1965. pap. 2.75x (ISBN 0-88312-649-4); microfiche 3.00 (ISBN 0-88312-499-8). Summer Inst Ling.

Derbyshire, E., et al. Geomorphological Processes. LC 79-5285. (Studies in Physical Geography Ser.). 312p. 1980. lib. bdg. 31.25 (ISBN 0-89158-695-4, Pub. by Dawson Pub); pap. 13.50 (ISBN 0-89158-864-7). Westview.

Derbyshire, Edward, ed. Geomorphology & Climate. LC 75-4523. 514p. 1976. 98.00 o.p. (ISBN 0-471-20954-6, Pub. by Wiley-Interscience). Wiley.

Derbyshire, Robert C. Medical Licensure & Discipline in the United States. LC 78-17712. 1978. Repr. of 1969 ed. lib. bdg. 18.50x (ISBN 0-313-20528-0, DEML). Greenwood.

D'Ercloe, A. Joseph, jt. auth. see Ontjes, David A.

D'Ercole, Joseph A., jt. auth. see Ontjes, David A.

Derden, John K., jt. auth. see Dorsey, James E.

DeReamer, Russell. Modern Safety & Health Technology. LC 79-47487. 1980. 44.95x (ISBN 0-471-05729-0, Pub. by Wiley-Interscience). Wiley.

De Reamer, Russell. Modern Safety Practices. LC 58-12708. 372p. 1958. 13.50 (ISBN 0-471-20361-0, Pub. by Wiley). Krieger.

De Recondo, A. M., ed. New Approaches in Eukaryotic DNA Replication. 375p. 1983. 47.50x (ISBN 0-306-41182-2, Plenum Pr). Plenum Pub.

De Reedy, Ginette D., tr. see Wallace, Lew.

De Regniers, Beatrice S. Little Sister & the Month Brothers. LC 75-4594. (Illus.). 48p. (ps-3). 1976. 8.95 (ISBN 0-8164-3147-7, Clarion). HM.

--May I Bring a Friend? LC 64-19562. (Illus.). (ps-2). 1964. PLB 9.95 (ISBN 0-689-20615-1). Atheneum.

--Red Riding Hood. LC 79-175561. (Illus.). (ps-3). 1972. 5.95 o.p. (ISBN 0-689-30036-0). Atheneum.

De Regniers, Beatrice S. & Haas, Irene. Little House of Your Own. LC 55-5236. (Illus.). (gr. k-3). 1955. 6.95 (ISBN 0-15-245787-9, HJ). HarBraceJ.

De Regniers, Beatrice S. & Pierce, Leona. Who Likes the Sun. LC 61-6112. (Illus.). 32p. (gr. k-3). 1961. 3.95 (ISBN 0-15-296065-1, HJ). HarBraceJ.

De Regniers, Beatrice S. see Schenk De Regniers, Beatrice.

de Regniers, Beatrice Schenk see Regniers, Beatrice Schenk de.

Derek, Sean C. Cast of Characters. (Illus.). 336p. (Orig.). 1982. pap. 3.50 (ISBN 0-8439-1126-3, Leisure Bks). Dorchester Pub Co.

De Renzo, D. J., ed. Cogeneration Technology & Economics for the Process Industries. LC 82-22279. (Energy Technology Review: No. 81). (Illus.). 395p. 1983. 42.00 (ISBN 0-8155-0932-4). Noyes.
--Wind Power: Recent Developments. LC 79-14069. (Energy Technology Review Ser.: No. 46). (Illus.). 1979. 36.00 (ISBN 0-8155-0759-3). Noyes.
De Reuterskiold, Alex, jt. auth. see Mirabaud, Paul.
Derevitzky. Fiddleheads & Mustard Blossoms. (Illus.). 1979. pap. 4.50 (ISBN 0-89272-074-3). Down East.
Derevitzky, Catherine. Tansy Cakes with Honey. (Illus.). 1980. pap. 4.95 (ISBN 0-89272-097-2, 310). Down East.
De Reyna, Rudy. Painting in Opaque Watercolor. (Illus.). 160p. 1979. pap. 9.95 o.p. (ISBN 0-8230-3776-2). Watson-Guptill.
Derfler, Frank, Jr. & Stallings, Frank. A Manager's Guide to Local Networks. (Illus.). 154p. 1983. 21.95 (ISBN 0-13-549766-3); pap. 14.95 (ISBN 0-13-549758-2). P-H.
Der Hovanessian, Diana, tr. see Manoogian, Torkom.
Deri, M. Ferroelectric Ceramics. 106p. 1969. 32.00 (ISBN 0-677-61450-0). Gordon.
Derian, Claude, jt. auth. see Bupp, Irvin C.
De Rico, Ul. The Ring of the Nibelung. (Illus.). 204p. 1980. 39.95 (ISBN 0-500-23324-1). Thames Hudson.
Derig, Betty & Sharp, Flo. The Idaho Rambler: For Gadabouts & Stay-at-Homes. rev. ed. LC 82-80104. 266p. (Orig.). 1982. pap. 7.95 (ISBN 0-686-38094-0). Rambler Pr.
DeRighi, R. The Story of the Penny Black. 8.95. StanGib Ltd.
Derijk, L. M., jt. ed. see Mansfield, J.
Dering, Edward. Parliamentary Diary of Sir Edward Dering, 1670-73. Henning, Basil D., ed. (Yale Historical Pubs. Miscellany Ser.: No. XVI). 1940. 49.50x (ISBN 0-685-69825-4). Elliots Bks.
De Rivera, Joseph. Field Theory As Human-Science: Contributions of Lewin's Berlin Group. LC 75-35530. 533p. 1976. 24.50x o.s.i. (ISBN 0-470-20368-4). Halsted Pr.
De Rivera, Joseph, ed. Conceptual Encounters: A Method for the Exploration of Human Experience. LC 80-6068. 382p. 1981. lib. bdg. 25.00 (ISBN 0-8191-1961-X); pap. text ed. 14.00 (ISBN 0-8191-1962-8). U Pr of Amer.
Der Klip, Rita Van see Van Der Klip, Rita.
Der Kulk, W. Van see Schouten, Jan A. & Van Der Kulk, W.
Derlega, Valerian & Janda, Louis H. Personal Adjustment: Selected Readings. 1979. pap. text ed. 10.95x (ISBN 0-673-15288-X). Scott F.
Derlega, Valerian J. & Janda, Louis. Personal Adjustment: The Psychology of Everyday Life. 2nd ed. 1981. text ed. 21.95x (ISBN 0-673-15470-X). Scott F.
Derlega, Valerian J., jt. auth. see Chaikin, Alan L.
Derleth, August. The Solar Pons Omnibus, 2 Vols. LC 76-17995. (Illus.). 1982. 39.95 set (ISBN 0-87054-006-8, Mycroft & Moran). Arkham.
--Wisconsin. LC 67-27861. 7.95 o.p. (ISBN 0-88361-078-7). Stanton & Lee.
Derleth, August W. Wisconsin Earth, a Sac Prairie Sampler. LC 70-113065. 1971. Repr. of 1948 ed. lib. bdg. 28.50x o.p. (ISBN 0-8371-4696-8, DEWE). Greenwood.
Derloshon, Jerry, jt. auth. see McCaffrey, Mike.
Derman, William. Serfs, Peasants, & Socialists: A Former Serf Village in the Republic of Guinea. LC 78-117148. 1973. 30.00x (ISBN 0-520-01728-5). U of Cal Pr.
Der Marel, R. Van see Van der Marel, R. & Beutelspacher, H.
Der Mehden, Fred R. Von see Von der Mehden, Fred R.
Der Meid, Louise B. Van see Van Der Meid, Louise B.
Der Meijden, R. Van see Van Der Meijden, R.
Dermenghem, Emile. Muhammad & the Islamic Tradition. Watt, Jean, tr. LC 73-15204. Repr. of 1958 ed. lib. bdg. 15.50 (ISBN 0-8371-7163-6, DEMI). Greenwood.
--Muhammad & the Islamic Tradition. Watt, Jean M., tr. from Fr. LC 81-47412. (Spiritual Masters Ser.). (Illus.). 192p. 1981. 15.00 (ISBN 0-87951-130-3). Overlook Pr.
--Muhammad & the Islamic Tradition. Watt, Jean M., tr. LC 81-47412. 192p. Date not set. 10.95 (ISBN 0-87951-073-0); pap. 6.95 (ISBN 0-87951-170-2). Overlook Pr.
Dermer, Joseph. How to Write Successful Foundation Proposals. 11.50 (ISBN 0-686-24207-6). Public Serv Materials.
--New Ways to Succeed with Foundations: A Guide for the Reagan Years. 19.50 (ISBN 0-686-37107-0). Public Serv Materials.
Dermer, Joseph, ed. America's Most Successful Fund Raising Letters. 18.95 (ISBN 0-686-24210-6). Public Serv Materials.
--Where America's Large Foundation Make Their Grants: 1977-78 Edition. 6.00 (ISBN 0-686-37132-1). Public Serv Materials.
--Where America's Large Foundations Make Their Grants: 1983-1984 Edition. 1983. 44.50 (ISBN 0-686-37909-8). Public Serv Materials.
--Where America's Large Foundations Make Their Grants: 1980-81 Edition. 7.00 (ISBN 0-686-24208-4). Public Serv Materials.
Dermer, Joseph & Wertheimer, Stephen, eds. The Complete Guide to Corporate Fund Raising. 16.75 (ISBN 0-686-37106-2). Public Serv Materials.
Dermer, O. C., et al. Biochemical Indicators of Subsurface Pollution. LC 80-67658. (Illus.). 203p. 1980. 37.50 (ISBN 0-250-40383-8). Ann Arbor Science.
Dermer, Otis C., jt. auth. see Waller, George R.
Der Merwe, Alwyn Van see Van Der Merwe, Alwyn.
Der Meulen, Jan van see Van der Meulen, Jan & Price, Nancy W.
Der Molen, H. J. Van see Van Der Molen, H. J. & Klopper, A.
Dermott, S. F. The Origin of the Solar System. LC 77-7547. 1978. 132.95 (ISBN 0-471-99529-0, Pub. by Wiley-Interscience); pap. 57.95 (ISBN 0-471-27585-9, Pub. by Wiley-Interscience). Wiley.
Dermout, Maria. The Ten Thousand Things. Beekman, E. M., ed. Koning, Hans, tr. from Dutch. (Library of the Indies). 272p. 1983. Repr. of 1958 ed. lib. bdg. 19.00x (ISBN 0-87023-384-X). U of Mass Pr.
Dern, John P. Genealogical Contribution Reprinted from the Albany Protocol: Wilhelm Christoph Berkenmeyer's Chronicle of Lutheran Affairs in New York Colony, 1731-1750. 1981. pap. 3.75 (ISBN 0-686-97286-4). Hope Farm.
--London Churchbooks & the German Emigration of 1709. (Illus.). 55p. (Ger. & Eng.). 1972. pap. 3.00 o.p. (ISBN 0-913186-01-5). Monocacy.
Dernberger, Robert F., jt. auth. see Whiting, Allen S.
Dernburg, Thomas & McDougall, Duncan. Macroeconomics. 6th ed. (Illus.). 1980. text ed. 24.95 (ISBN 0-07-016534-3). McGraw.
Dernburg, Thomas F. & McDougall, Duncan. Macroeconomics. 5th ed. 1976. text ed. 16.95 o.p. (ISBN 0-07-016526-2, C). McGraw.
Dernburg, Thomas F., et al. Studies in Household Economic Behavior. 1958. 39.50x (ISBN 0-686-51317-7). Elliots Bks.
Dernoncourt, Wayne L., jt. auth. see Robinson, James W.
De Robeck, Nesta. Music of the Italian Renaissance. LC 69-12689. (Music Ser). 1969. Repr. of 1928 ed. lib. bdg. 18.50 (ISBN 0-306-71232-6). Da Capo.
De Robertis, E. D. & Carrea, R. Biology of Neuroglia. (Progress in Brain Research: Vol. 15). 1965. 75.75 (ISBN 0-444-40165-2, North Holland). Elsevier.
DeRobertis, Eduardo & Schacht, Jochen, eds. Neurochemistry of Cholinergic Receptors. LC 73-91105. 156p. 1974. 20.00 (ISBN 0-911216-66-9). Raven.
De Robigne, Bennett M. Trial of D. M. Bennett: Upon the Charge of Depositing Prohibited Matter in the Mail. LC 72-8110. (Civil Liberties in American History Ser). 202p. 1973. Repr. of 1879 ed. lib. bdg. 27.50 (ISBN 0-306-70525-7). Da Capo.
Deroche, Andre & Huldebrand, Nicholas. The Principles of Autobody Repairing & Repainting. 3rd ed. (Illus.). 672p. 1981. text ed. 20.95 (ISBN 0-686-63447-0). P-H.
De Rochefoucauld, La Duc see Rochefoucauld, La Duc De.
DeRocher, Francoise & DeRocher, Gregory. Options: Apercus de la France. LC 79-27245. 140p. 1980. pap. text ed. 10.95x (ISBN 0-471-04260-9). Wiley.
DeRocher, Gregory, jt. auth. see DeRocher, Francoise.
De Rohan, Pierre, ed. Federal Theatre Plays: 3 Plays. LC 72-2386. (Illus.). 1973. lib. bdg. 22.50 (ISBN 0-306-70494-3). Da Capo.
De Rojas Zorrilla, Francisco, jt. ed. see MacCurdy, Raymond R.
De Rola, Stanislas Klossowski see Klossowski de Rola, Stanislas.
Deroo, Remi, jt. auth. see Roche, Douglas.
DeRoo, Sally. Exploring Our Environment: A Resource Guide-Manual-Plants. (Illus.). 168p. 1977. instr.'s manual 6.00 (ISBN 0-89039-208-0). Ann Arbor Pubs.
De Ropp, Robert. Warrior's Way. 1979. pap. 5.95 o.s.i. (ISBN 0-440-59385-9, Delta). Dell.
De Ropp, Robert S. Drugs & the Mind. 1976. pap. 3.95 o.s.i. (ISBN 0-440-54927-2, Delta). Dell.
--Eco-Tech. 336p. 1975. pap. 3.45 o.s.i. (ISBN 0-440-54537-4, Delta). Dell.
--Master Game. 1969. pap. 5.95 (ISBN 0-440-55479-9, Delta). Dell.
--Sex Energy. 1971. pap. 2.95 o.s.i. (ISBN 0-440-57851-5, Delta). Dell.
--Warrior's Way. 1979. 10.95 o.s.i. (ISBN 0-440-09438-0, Sey Lawr). Delacorte.
De Roquette-Buisson, Odile. The Canal Du Midi. (Illus.). 1983. 29.95 (ISBN 0-500-24115-5). Thames Hudson.
DeRosa, Paul & Stern, Gary H. In the Name of Money: A Professional's Guide to the Federal Reserve, Interest Rates & Money. (Illus.). 192p. 1980. 19.95 (ISBN 0-07-016521-1, P&RB). McGraw.
De Rosa, Peter. God Our Saviour. (Impact Books). 1967. 4.95 o.p. (ISBN 0-685-07640-7, 80171). Glencoe.
De Rosa, Peter & Richards, Hubert J. Christ in Our World. 1967. 3.95 o.p. (ISBN 0-685-07618-0, 80626). Glencoe.
De Rosa, Peter, ed. Introduction to Catechetics. 1968. pap. 2.75 o.p. (ISBN 0-685-07645-8, 80173). Glencoe.
DeRose, Peter & McGuire, S. W. A Concordance to the Works of Jane Austen, 3 Vols. LC 82-48281. 1647p. 1982. lib. bdg. 250.00 (ISBN 0-8240-9245-7). Garland Pub.
De Rose, Peter L. Jane Austen & Samuel Johnson. LC 78-7813. 133p. 1980. lib. bdg. 20.50 (ISBN 0-8191-1073-6); pap. text ed. 8.25 (ISBN 0-8191-1074-4). U Pr of Amer.
De Rosis, Helen. Women & Anxiety. 1979. 8.95 o.s.i. (ISBN 0-440-09398-8). Delacorte.
De Rosis, Helen A. Working with Patients: Introductory Guidelines for Psychotherapists. LC 77-896. 1977. 10.50x (ISBN 0-87586-057-5). Agathon.
De Rossi, Claude J. Learning BASIC Fast. rev. ed. LC 74-3355. (Illus.). 1979. pap. text ed. 14.95 (ISBN 0-8359-3977-4). Reston.
De Rougemont, D. The Future Is Our Concern. (Systems Science & World Order Library). 254p. 1983. 45.00 (ISBN 0-08-027395-5); pap. 16.00 (ISBN 0-08-027394-7). Pergamon.
De Rougemont, Denis. The Growl of Deeper Waters. Hazo, Samuel & Luey, Beth, trs. LC 75-33422. 1976. 10.95 o.p. (ISBN 0-8229-3315-2). U of Pittsburgh Pr.
Derow, Ellan O., jt. auth. see Carley, Michael J.
Der Pijl, L. Van see Van der Pijl, L.
Der Plas, Leendert Van see Van Der Plas, Leendert.
Der Post, Laurens Van see Van Der Post, Laurens.
Derr, Thomas S. Barriers to Ecumenism: The Holy See & the World Council on Social Questions. LC 82-18761. 128p. (Orig.). 1983. pap. 7.95 (ISBN 0-88344-031-8). Orbis Bks.
Derrett, J. Duncan. Religion, Law & the State of India. Date not set. cancelled o.s.i. (ISBN 0-571-08478-8). Faber & Faber.
Derrett, J. Duncan, tr. see Lingat, Robert.
Derrett, M., jt. auth. see Duncan, J.
Derrick, Christopher. Escape from Scepticism: Liberal Education As If Truth Mattered. 1977. pap. text ed. 2.95 (ISBN 0-89385-002-0). Sugden.
--Joy Without a Cause: Selected Essays of Christopher Derrick. 254p. 1979. pap. 4.95 (ISBN 0-89385-004-7). Sugden.
--Sex & Sacredness. LC 82-80302. 219p. (Orig.). 1982. pap. 7.95 (ISBN 0-89870-018-3). Ignatius Pr.
Derrick, Lionel. Black Massacre. (Penetrator Ser.: No. 35). (Orig.). 1980. pap. 1.50 o.p. (ISBN 0-523-40632-0). Pinnacle Bks.
--Capitol Hell. (Penetrator Ser., No. 3). 192p. (Orig.). 1974. pap. 1.50 o.p. (ISBN 0-523-40422-0). Pinnacle Bks.
--Deadly Silence. (Penetrator Ser.: No. 36). 192p. (Orig.). 1980. pap. 1.75 o.p. (ISBN 0-523-40673-8). Pinnacle Bks.
--Deepsea Shootout. (Penetrator: No. 16). (Orig.). 1976. pap. 1.50 o.p. (ISBN 0-523-40851-X). Pinnacle Bks.
--Demented Empire. (Penetrator Ser.: No. 17). 1976. pap. 1.50 o.p. (ISBN 0-523-40456-5). Pinnacle Bks.
--Divine Death: Penetrator No. 23. (Penetrator Ser.). 1977. pap. 1.50 o.p. (ISBN 0-523-40085-3). Pinnacle Bks.
--Dixie Death Squad. (Penetrator Ser.: No. 13). 192p. (Orig.). 1976. pap. 1.50 o.p. (ISBN 0-523-40426-3). Pinnacle Bks.
--Floating Death. (The Penetrator Ser.: No. 25). 1978. pap. 1.50 o.p. (ISBN 0-523-40178-7). Pinnacle Bks.
--High Disaster: Penetrator No. 22. (Penetrator Ser). (Orig.). 1977. pap. 1.50 o.p. (ISBN 0-523-40067-5). Pinnacle Bks.
--Mankill Sport. (Penetrator Ser.: No. 14). 192p. 1976. pap. 1.50 o.p. (ISBN 0-523-40427-1). Pinnacle Bks.
--The Penetrator: Blood on the Strip. (The Penetrator Ser., No. 2). 160p. (Orig.). 1973. pap. 1.25 o.p. (ISBN 0-523-40102-7). Pinnacle Bks.
--Penetrator: Hell's Hostages, No. 41. 192p. (Orig.). 1981. pap. 1.75 o.p. (ISBN 0-523-41116-2). Pinnacle Bks.
--The Penetrator No. 18: Countdown to Terror. (The Penetrator Ser.). 1977. pap. 1.50 o.p. (ISBN 0-523-40428-X). Pinnacle Bks.
--Penetrator No. 19: Panama Power Play. (The Penetrator Ser). (Orig.). 1977. pap. 1.50 o.p. (ISBN 0-523-40429-8). Pinnacle Bks.
--Penetrator No. 20: The Radiation Hit. (The Penetrator Ser.). 192p. (Orig.). 1977. pap. 1.50 o.p. (ISBN 0-523-40258-9). Pinnacle Bks.
--The Penetrator, No. 5: Mardi Gras Massacre. (Orig.). 1974. pap. 1.50 o.p. (ISBN 0-523-40424-7). Pinnacle Bks.
--The Penetrator, No. 6: Tokyo Purple. 192p. (Orig.). 1974. pap. 1.50 o.p. (ISBN 0-523-40493-X). Pinnacle Bks.
--Penetrator, No. 7: Baja Bandidos. (Orig.). 1974. pap. 1.50 o.p. (ISBN 0-523-40494-8). Pinnacle Bks.
--Penetrator, No. 8: Northwest Contract. 192p. (Orig.). 1975. pap. 1.50 o.p. (ISBN 0-523-40495-6). Pinnacle Bks.
--Penetrator, No. 9: Dodge City Bombers. 192p. (Orig.). 1975. pap. 1.50 o.p. (ISBN 0-523-40425-5). Pinnacle Bks.
--The Penetrator: The Target Is H. (The Penetrator Ser., No. 1). 192p. (Orig.). 1973. pap. 1.25 o.p. (ISBN 0-523-40101-9). Pinnacle Bks.
--Satan's Swarm. (The Penetrator Ser.: No. 49). 192p. (Orig.). 1983. pap. 2.25 (ISBN 0-523-41681-4). Pinnacle Bks.
--The Supergun Mission, No. 21. (Penetrator Ser.). (Orig.). 1977. pap. 1.25 o.p. (ISBN 0-523-40079-9). Pinnacle Bks.
Derrick, Thomas, et al, eds. Thomas Wilson's Arte Rhetorique: An Old Spelling Critical Edition. LC 81-47031. (Garland English Texts Ser.). 804p. 1982. lib. bdg. 75.00 (ISBN 0-8240-9408-5). Garland Pub.
Derrick, W. College Trigonometry. 1982. text ed. 18.95 (ISBN 0-686-94940-4); instr's guide 4.95 (ISBN 0-8053-2319-8). A-W.
Derrick, William R. & Grossman, Stanley I. Elementary Differential Equations with Applications. 2nd ed. (Mathematics Ser.). (Illus.). 576p. 1981. text ed. 24.95 (ISBN 0-201-03162-0); answer bk. 2.00 (ISBN 0-201-03166-3). A-W.
--Elementary Differential Equations with Applications: A Short Course. 2nd ed. (Mathenatics Ser.). (Illus.). 384p. 1981. text ed. 23.95 (ISBN 0-201-03164-7). A-W.
Derricott, R. Rebuild. LC 81-21942. (Properties of Materials Safety & Environmental Factors). 286p. 1982. 41.95x (ISBN 0-471-10173-7, Pub. by Wiley-Interscience). Wiley.
Derricott, R., jt. auth. see Blyth, W. A.
Derricott, R., jt. auth. see Chissick, S. S.
Derricott, Robert & Chissick, Seymour. Energy Conservation & Thermal Insulation: Properties of Materials. LC 80-41587. (Safety & Environmental Factors Ser.). 785p. 1981. 89.50x (ISBN 0-471-27930-7, Pub. by Wiley-Interscience). Wiley.
Derricotte, Toi. Natural Birth. 80p. (Orig.). 1983. 11.95 (ISBN 0-89594-102-3); pap. 4.95 (ISBN 0-89594-101-5). Crossing Pr.
Derrida, Jacques. Dissemination. Johnson, Barbara, tr. LC 81-3359. 400p. 1981. 22.50 (ISBN 0-226-14327-9); pap. 9.95 (ISBN 0-226-14334-1). U of Chicago Pr.
--Margins of Philosophy. Bass, Alan, tr. from Fr. LC 82-11137. 1983. lib. bdg. 22.50x (ISBN 0-226-14325-2). U of Chicago Pr.
--Positions. Bass, Alan, tr. from Fr. LC 80-17620. 1981. 11.95x (ISBN 0-226-14332-5); pap. 4.50 (ISBN 0-226-14331-7). U of Chicago Pr.
--Spurs: Nietzsche's Styles. Harlow, Barbara, tr. from Fr. LC 79-31. vi, 166p. 1981. pap. 5.95 (ISBN 0-226-14333-3). U of Chicago Pr.
Derry, Duncan. Concise World Atlas of Geology & Mineral Deposits: Non-Metallic Minerals, Metallic Minerals & Energy Minerals. LC 80-675233. 110p. 1980. 74.95 (ISBN 0-470-26996-0). Halsted Pr.
Derry, Evelyn F. The Christian Year. 1st ed. 1982. Repr. of 1967 ed. 9.50 (ISBN 0-903540-56-8, Pub by Floris Books). St George Bk Serv.
Derry, John. English Politics & the American Revolution. LC 76-56694. 1977. text ed. 14.95 o.p. (ISBN 0-312-25523-3). St Martin.
Derry, John & Derry, Reg. Spectral Universe. 1983. 7.95 (ISBN 0-533-05502-4). Vantage.
Derry, John W. Castlereagh. LC 75-29820. (British Political Biography Ser.). 250p. 1976. 25.00 (ISBN 0-312-12355-8). St Martin.
--Charles James Fox. 1972. 37.50 o.p. (ISBN 0-7134-1118-X, Pub. by Batsford England). David & Charles.
--Radical Tradition: Tom Paine to Lloyd George. 1967. 19.95 o.p. (ISBN 0-312-66185-1). St Martin.
Derry, Reg, jt. auth. see Derry, John.
Derry, Ruth. Scholar Dollars. (gr. 3-6). 1982. 5.95 (ISBN 0-86653-057-6, GA 415). Good Apple.
Derry, T. K. A History of Modern Norway, 1814-1972. (Illus.). 1973. 42.00x (ISBN 0-19-822503-2). Oxford U Pr.
Derry, T. K. & Blakeway, M. G. The Making of Britain, 2 vols. Incl. Vol. 1. Life & Work to the Close of the Middle Ages. pap. 6.95 o.p. (ISBN 0-7195-1816-4); Vol. 2. Life & Work from the Renaissance to the Industrial Revolution. pap. 6.95 o.p. (ISBN 0-7195-1834-2). (gr. 9-12). Set. 10.00 o.p. (ISBN 0-7195-1833-4). Transatlantic.
Derry, T. K. & Jarman, T. L. Making of Modern Britain: Life & Work from George Third to Elizabeth Second. (Illus.). 1971. pap. 3.95 o.p. (ISBN 0-7195-0304-3). Transatlantic.
Derry, Thomas K. & Williams, Trevor I. Short History of Technology from the Earliest Times to A. D. 1900. (Illus.). 1961. 29.95x (ISBN 0-19-500142-7); pap. 13.95x (ISBN 0-19-881231-0, OPB). Oxford U Pr.
Dersal, William R. Van see Van Dersal, William R.
Dershem, Larry D., ed. Library of Congress Classification Class K, Subclass KF Law of the United States Cumulative Index. (AALL Publication Ser.: No. 18). vii, 326p. 1982. looseleaf 35.00x (ISBN 0-8377-0115-5). Rothman.
Dershowitz, Alan M. The Best Defense. 1982. 16.95 (ISBN 0-394-50736-3). Random.
--The Best Defense. LC 82-40426. (Illus.). 464p. 1983. pap. 4.95 (ISBN 0-394-71380-X, Vin). Random.
Der Smissen, Betty van see Van der Smissen, Betty.
Der Starre, H. van see International Symposium on Olfaction & Taste, 7th, the Netherlands 1980.

Derthick, Martha. Between State & Nation: Regional Organizations of the United States. LC 74-727. 1974. 18.95 (ISBN 0-8157-1812-8); pap. 7.95 (ISBN 0-8157-1811-X). Brookings.

--Uncontrollable Spending for Social Services Grants. 80p. 1975. pap. 6.95 (ISBN 0-8157-1813-6). Brookings.

Dertinger, Charles J. Reflections. 1983. write for info. (ISBN 0-8062-2043-0). Carlton.

Dertouzos, Michael. Threshold Logic: A Synthesis Approach. (Press Research Monographs: No. 32). 1965. 22.50x (ISBN 0-262-04009-3). MIT Pr.

Dertouzos, Michael L. & Moses, Joel, eds. The Computer Age: A Twenty-Year View. 1979. 27.50x o.p. (ISBN 0-262-04055-7); pap. text ed. 9.95 (ISBN 0-262-54036-3). MIT Pr.

Dertouzos, Michael L., et al. Systems, Networks & Computation: Basic Concepts. LC 79-4556. 528p. 1979. Repr. of 1972 ed. lib. bdg. 25.50 (ISBN 0-88275-916-7). Krieger.

Derucher, Kenneth & Heins, Conrad. Materials for Civil & Highway Engineers. (Illus.). 416p. 1981. text ed. 31.95 (ISBN 0-13-560490-7). P-H.

Deruguine, Tania, tr. see Dyadkin, Iosif G.

DeRusso, P. M., et al. State Variables for Engineers. LC 65-21443. 608p. 1965. 50.95 (ISBN 0-471-20380-7). Wiley.

DeRuth. Portrait Painting. (Pitman Art Ser.: Vol. 48). pap. 1.95 o.p. (ISBN 0-448-00557-3, G&D). Putnam Pub Group.

Derveur, Paul W. Van see The, Lian & Van Der Veur, Paul W.

Dervin, Brenda & Voigt, Melvin J., eds. Progress in Communication Sciences, Vol. 4. 304p. 1983. text ed. 32.50 (ISBN 0-89391-102-X). Ablex Pub.

Dervin, Brenda, jt. ed. see Voigt, Melvin J.

Dervitsiotis, Kostas. Operations Management. (Industrial Engineering & Management Science). (Illus.). 784p. 1980. text ed. 27.50x (ISBN 0-07-016537-8, C); solutions manual 12.00 (ISBN 0-07-016538-6). McGraw.

Der Vlugt, Ebel Van see Van Der Vlugt, Ebed.

Der Wee, Hermann Van see Van der Wee, Hermann & Vinogradov, Vladimir A.

Derwing, Bruce L. & Priestly, Tom M. Reading Rules for Russian: A Systematic Approach to Russian Spelling & Pronunciation with Notes on Dialectal & Stylistic Variation. (Illus.). vi, 247p. (Orig.). 1980. pap. 11.95 (ISBN 0-89357-066-4). Slavica.

Derzhavina, M. Central V. I. Lenin Museum. 111p. 1979. 4.95 (ISBN 0-8285-1790-8, Pub by Progress Pubs USSR). Imported Pubns.

Der Zouwen, J. Van see Geyer, R. F. & Zouwen, J. van der.

De Sade, Marquis. Selected Letters. 14.95x (ISBN 0-8464-0833-3). Beekman Pubs.

Desade, Marquis see Sade, Marquis De.

Desai & Christian. Numerical Methods in Geotechnic Engineering. 1977. 54.50 (ISBN 0-07-016542-4). McGraw.

Desai, A. R. Urban Family & Family Planning in India. 224p. 1980. Repr. 22.95x (ISBN 0-940500-70-1). Asia Bk Corp.

Desai, Anita. Clear Light of Day. LC 80-7603. 224p. 1980. 12.45i (ISBN 0-06-010984-X, HarpT). Har-Row.

--Cry the Peacock. (Orient Paperbacks Ser.). 218p. 1980. pap. 4.50 (ISBN 0-86578-083-8). Ind-US Inc.

--Fire on the Mountain. LC 77-3788. 1977. 10.53i (ISBN 0-06-011066-X, HarpT). Har-Row.

--Fire on the Mountain. 1983. pap. 3.95 (ISBN 0-14-005347-6). Penguin.

--Games at Twilight. 1983. pap. 3.95 (ISBN 0-14-005348-4). Penguin.

Desai, C. S. Elementary Finite Element Method. (Civil Engineering & Engineering Mechanics Ser.). (Illus.). 1979. ref. ed. 33.95 (ISBN 0-13-256636-2). P-H.

Desai, C. S., jt. ed. see American Society of Civil Engineers.

Desai, Kalpana S. Iconography of Visnu. LC 73-906314. (Illus.). 159p. 1973. text ed. 17.50x o.p. (ISBN 0-8002-1525-7). Intl Pubns Serv.

Desai, Meghnad. Testing Monetarism. 250p. 1982. pap. 13.50 (ISBN 0-686-38288-9). F Pinter Pubs.

Desai, Megnad. Applied Econometrics. (Illus.). 1976. text ed. 24.95 (ISBN 0-07-016541-6, C). McGraw.

Desai, Morarji. The Story of My Life, 2 vols. LC 74-901103. (Illus.). vii, 651p. 1974. Set. 30.00x o.p. (ISBN 0-333-90016-2). South Asia Bks.

--The Story of My Life, Vol. 3. 1979. 8.50x o.p. (ISBN 0-8364-0364-9). South Asia Bks.

Desai, Narayan. Bliss to Be Young with Gandhi. (Volume I of Childhood Memoirs Ser.). (Orig.). 1983. pap. write for info. (ISBN 0-940460-01-7). Peace & Gladness.

--Childhood Memoirs, 2 Vols. (Orig.). 1983. pap. write for info. (ISBN 0-940460-03-3). Peace & Gladness.

--Reminiscences of My Father & Gandhi. (Childhood Memoirs Ser.: Vol. II). (Orig.). 1983. pap. write for info. (ISBN 0-940460-02-5). Peace & Gladness.

--Towards a Nonviolent Revolution. 176p. 4.00 o.p. (ISBN 0-686-96939-1). Greenlf Bks.

Desai, P. The Bokaro Steel Plant. 1972. pap. 15.00 (ISBN 0-444-10388-0, North-Holland). Elsevier.

Desai, R. W., ed. Johnson on Shakespeare. 1979. text ed. 13.00x (ISBN 0-86131-120-5). Humanities.

Desai, Santosh N. Hinduism in Thai Life. 163p. 1980. 34.95x (ISBN 0-940500-66-3, Pub by Popular Prakashan India). Asia Bk Corp.

Desai, Sudha V. Social Life in Maharashtra Under the Peshwas. 220p. 1980. 29.95 (ISBN 0-940500-72-8). Asia Bk Corp.

Desai, Tripta. Indo-American Relations Between 1940-1974. 1977. pap. text ed. 9.00 o.p. (ISBN 0-8191-0155-9). U Pr of Amer.

Desai, V. G., tr. see Gandhi, M. K.

De St. Jorre, John. The Brothers' War: Biafra & Nigeria. 1972. 10.00 o.p. (ISBN 0-395-13934-1). HM.

De Saint-Arnand, Michael, jt. auth. see De Bono, Edward.

De Saint-Denys, Hervey. Dreams & How to Guide Them. Schatzman, Morton, ed. 174p. 1982. text ed. 13.50x (ISBN 0-7156-1584-X, Pub. by Duckworth England). Biblio Dist.

De Saint-Exupery, Antoine. Petit Prince. (Illus., Fr.). pap. 1.95 (ISBN 0-685-20246-1). Schoenhof.

De Saint-Exupery, Antoine see Saint-Exupery, Antione De.

De Saint-Exupery, Antoine see Saint-Exupery, Antoine de.

De Saint-Exupery, Antoine see Saint-Exupery, Antoine De.

De Saint-Exupery, Antoine see Saint-Exupery, Antoine de.

De Saint-Foix, G., jt. auth. see De Wyzewa, T.

De Saint-Germaine, Comte C. see Saint-Germaine, Comte C.

De Saint-Simon, Claude-Henri. Oeuvres Completes, 7 tomes. Set. write for info. (ISBN 0-685-34971-3). French & Eur.

Desalmand, Paul, jt. auth. see Tort, Patrick.

De Salvatierra, Juan M. Selected Letters about California. Burrus, Ernest J., tr. (Baja California Travel Ser.: No. 25). 280p. 1971. 24.00 (ISBN 0-686-84003-8). Dawsons.

DeSalvo, John A., ed. see Adams, Frank O.

De Salvo, Louis J. Consumer Finance. LC 76-46450. 337p. 1977. pap. text ed. 18.95 o.p. (ISBN 0-471-04391-5). Wiley.

Desan, Wilfrid. The Planetary Man. Incl. A Noetic Prelude to a United World; An Ethical Prelude to a United World. LC 71-169233. 384p. 1972. 9.95 o.p. (ISBN 0-02-531080-1, 53108). Macmillan.

De Santa Ana, Julio. Towards a Church of the Poor, Ed. LC 80-25667. 210p. (Orig.). 1981. pap. 8.95 (ISBN 0-88344-502-6). Orbis Bks.

De Santi, Roger. Trends & Issues of Diagnostic & Remedial Readings. LC 81-43680. 202p. (Orig.). 1982. lib. bdg. 23.00 (ISBN 0-8191-2219-X); pap. text ed. 10.25 (ISBN 0-8191-2220-3). U Pr of Amer.

De Santillana, Giorgio. Reflections on Men & Ideas. 1968. 17.50x o.p. (ISBN 0-262-04016-6); pap. 5.95x (ISBN 0-262-54012-6). MIT Pr.

De Santillana, Giorgio & Von Dechend, Hertha. Hamlet's Mill. LC 69-13267. 1977. pap. 8.95 (ISBN 0-87923-215-3). Godine.

De Santis, Daniel V., jt. auth. see Levin, Edward.

DeSantis, Hugh. The Diplomacy of Silence: The American Foreign Service, the Soviet Union, & the Cold War 1933 to 1947. LC 80-16676. 1980. 23.00x (ISBN 0-226-14337-6). U of Chicago Pr.

DeSantis, Marie. Fisherwoman. 288p. 1983. 14.95 (ISBN 0-525-24149-3, 01450-450). Dutton.

DeSantis, Vincent P. The Shaping of Modern America: Eighteen Seventy-Seven to Nineteen Sixteen. 1973. pap. text ed. 10.95x (ISBN 0-88273-110-6). Forum Pr IL.

DeSanto, et al. Statistics Through Problem Solving. 2nd ed. Avenoso, Frank & Cheifetz, Philip, eds. LC 73-77244. (gr. 9-12). 1978. pap. text ed. 10.95x (ISBN 0-916060-04-7). Math Alternatives.

De Satnick, Shelly. Bridge for Everyone: A Step by Step Text & Workbook. 144p. 1982. pap. 7.95 (ISBN 0-380-81083-2, 81083). Avon.

De Sausmarez, Maurice. Basic Design. 96p. 1982. 30.00x (ISBN 0-906969-22-0, Pub. by Benn Pubns). State Mutual Bk.

Desautels, Edouard J. Advanced Uses of Visicalc R, for the IBM Personal Computer. (Microcomputer Power Ser.). 256p. 1983. pap. write for info. (ISBN 0-697-09973-3); write for info. diskette (ISBN 0-697-09974-1). Wm C Brown.

--Assembly Language Programming for PDP-11 & LSI-11 Computers: An Introduction to Computer Organization. 592p. 1982. pap. write for info. (ISBN 0-697-08164-8); solutions manual avail. (ISBN 0-697-08165-6). Wm C Brown.

--VisiCalc R for the Apple II Plus Computer. (Microcomputer Power Ser.). 160p. 1982. pap. write for info. plastic comb; Diskette avail. (ISBN 0-697-09972-5). Wm C Brown.

--VisiCalc R for the IBM Personal Computer. (Microcomputer Power Ser.). 176p. 1982. pap. write for info. plastic comb (ISBN 0-697-09967-9); Diskette avail. (ISBN 0-697-09970-9). Wm C Brown.

--VisiCalc R for the TRS-80 TM Model I & Model III Computers. 160p. 1982. pap. write for info. plastic comb (ISBN 0-697-09956-3); Diskette for Model III avail. (ISBN 0-697-09971-7). WM C Brown.

--Visicalc R for the TRS-80 TM: Model II & Model 16 Computers. 160p. 1982. pap. text ed. write for info. (ISBN 0-697-09955-5); Diskette for Model II avail. (ISBN 0-697-09969-5). Wm C Brown.

Desautels, Paul. The Gem Kingdom. 1971. 25.00 o.p. (ISBN 0-394-46533-4); pap. 8.95 (ISBN 0-394-73373-8). Random.

Desautels, Paul E. The Gem Collection. new ed. LC 79-16475. (The Treasures in the Smithsonian Ser.: No. 1). (Illus.). 77p. 1980. 12.50 (ISBN 0-87474-360-5); pap. 8.95 (ISBN 0-87474-361-3). Smithsonian.

--Rocks & Minerals. LC 73-91134. (Collector's Series: No. 1). (Illus.). 160p. 1974. 4.95 (ISBN 0-448-11540-9, G&D). Putnam Pub Group.

de Sauvigny, G. de Bertier see De Bertier de Sauvigny, G. & Pinkney, David H.

Desbarats, Peter. Gabrielle & Selena. LC 73-14661. (Illus.). 32p. (gr. k-3). 1974. pap. 0.95 (ISBN 0-15-634080-1, AVB87, VoyB). HarBraceJ.

Desborough, Vincent R. The Greek Dark Ages. LC 79-180736. 1972. 27.50 (ISBN 0-312-34720-0). St Martin.

Desbrandes, R., jt. auth. see Ketchian, S.

Descartes, Rene. Discours de la Methode. Gadoffre, G., ed. (Modern French Text Ser.). 1961. pap. write for info. (ISBN 0-7190-0144-7). Manchester.

--La Geometrie. Smith, David E. & Latham, Marcia L., trs. from Fr. & Lat. (Illus.). xiii, 259p. 1952. 17.00 (ISBN 0-87548-168-X). Open Court.

--Meditations of Descartes. Veitch, John, tr. from Fr. & Lat. xxxii, 290p. 1966. 18.00 (ISBN 0-87548-042-X). Open Court.

--Meditations on First Philosophy. Cress, Donald A., tr. from Lat. 1979. pap. text ed. 1.95 (ISBN 0-915144-57-3). Hackett Pub.

--Philosophical Works, 2 Vols. Haldane, E. S. & Ross, G. R., eds. 1967. Vol. 1. 49.50 (ISBN 0-521-06943-2); Vol. 2. 49.50 (ISBN 0-521-06944-0); Vol. 1. pap. 11.95 (ISBN 0-521-09416-X); Vol. 2. pap. 11.95 (ISBN 0-521-09417-8). Cambridge U Pr.

--Philosophical Writings. 1966. 3.95 o.s.i. (ISBN 0-394-60043-6, M43). Modern Lib.

--Principles of Philosophy. Miller, Reese P. & Miller, Valentine R., trs. 1983. lib. bdg. 59.00 (ISBN 0-686-37924-1, Pub by Reidel Holland). Kluwer Boston.

Desch, H. E. Timber: Its Structure, Properties & Utilization. 6th ed. 416p. (Orig.). 1980. pap. text ed. 24.95x (ISBN 0-917304-62-4). Timber.

Descharnes, Robert & Prevost, Clovis. Gaudi: The Visionary. LC 82-70179. (Illus.). 248p. 1982. 75.00 (ISBN 0-670-33587-8, Studio). Viking Pr.

De Schauensee, Max. The Collector's Verdi & Puccini. LC 77-28264. (Keystone Books in Music Ser.: No. KB 46). 1978. Repr. of 1962 ed. lib. bdg. 16.00x (ISBN 0-313-20241-9, SCCV). Greenwood.

Descola, Jean. Conquistadors. Barnes, Malcolm, tr. LC 72-122060. Repr. of 1957 ed. lib. bdg. 25.00x (ISBN 0-678-03151-7). Kelley.

Descombes, Vincent. Modern French Philosophy. Scott-Fox, L. & Harding, J. M., trs. 240p. 1981. 34.50 (ISBN 0-521-22837-9); pap. 11.95 (ISBN 0-521-29672-2). Cambridge U Pr.

D'Escoto, Miguel, tr. see Frei, Eduardo.

De S. Coutinho, John see Coutinho, John De S.

De Segonzac, Catherine. Jewish Yoga: A System of Visualization & Movement Rooted in Genesis. 208p. Date not set. pap. 7.95 (ISBN 0-87728-529-2). Weiser.

De Selincourt, Aubrey. World of Herodotus. LC 81-83969. 400p. 1982. pap. 12.00 (ISBN 0-86547-070-7). N Point Pr.

De Selincourt, Ernest, ed. see Wordsworth, William.

De Selincourt, Ernest, ed. see Wordsworth, William & Wordsworth, Dorothy.

De Sena, Jorge. The Poetry of Jorge de Sena. Williams, Frederick G., ed. LC 79-84616. 320p. 1980. 20.00 (ISBN 0-930012-19-4); pap. 12.50 (ISBN 0-930012-18-6). Bandanna Bks.

--Sobre Esta Praia: Eight Meditations on the Coast of the Pacific. Griffin, Jonathan, tr. LC 79-114869. (Inklings Ser.: No. 1). (Port. & Eng.). 1979. pap. 3.00 (ISBN 0-930012-31-3). Mudborn.

De Serres, F. J., et al, eds. In Vitro Metabolic Activation in Mutagenesis Testing: Proceedings of the Symposium on the Role of Metabolic Activation in Producing Mutagenic & Carcinogenic Environmental Chemicals, 1976. 1977. 75.75 (ISBN 0-7204-0612-9, North-Holland). Elsevier.

De Sevigne. Madame de Sevigne: Selected Letters. Tanrock, L. W., ed. 1982. pap. 5.95 (ISBN 0-14-044405-X). Penguin.

Desfontaines. Le Nouveau Gulliver, 2 vols. (Utopias in the Enlightenment Ser.). 499p. (Fr.). 1974. Repr. of 1730 ed. Set. lib. bdg. 137.50x o.p. (ISBN 0-8287-0266-7). Vol. 1 (046). Vol. 2 (047). Clearwater Pub.

Desharnais, A. A Review of Surgical Nursing. 1978. text ed. 11.95 (ISBN 0-07-016560-2). McGraw.

De Shazer, Steve. Patterns of Brief Family Therapy. LC 81-7239. (Guilford Family Therapy Ser.). 1982. 17.50 (ISBN 0-89862-038-4). Guilford Pr.

DeShazo, Peter. Urban Workers & Labor Unions in Chile, 1902-1927. LC 82-70557. (Illus.). 384p. 1983. 30.00 (ISBN 0-299-09220-8). U of Wis Pr.

Deshen, Schlomo, jt. auth. see Shokeid, Moshe.

Deshen, Shlomo & Zenner, Walter P. Jewish Societies in the Middle East: Community, Culture & Authority. LC 80-6285. (Illus.). 328p. (Orig.). 1982. lib. bdg. 25.50 (ISBN 0-8191-2578-4); pap. text ed. 12.75 (ISBN 0-8191-2579-2). U Pr of Amer.

Deshen, Shlomo, jt. auth. see Shokeid, Moshe.

Deshimaru, Taisen. The Zen Way to the Martial Arts: A Japanese Master Reveals the Secrets of the Samurai. Amphoux, Nancy, tr. (Illus.). 128p. 1983. pap. 5.95 (ISBN 0-525-93267-4, 0578-170). Dutton.

DeShong, Barbara L. The Special Educator: Stress & Survival. LC 81-1743. 230p. 1981. text ed. 22.95 (ISBN 0-89443-358-X). Aspen Systems.

Deshpande, C. D., et al. Impact of a Metropolitan City on the Surrounding Region. (Illus.). 167p. 1980. pap. text ed. 8.50x (ISBN 0-391-02206-7). Humanities.

Deshpande, C. K., jt. auth. see Hiranandani, L. H.

Deshpande, Madhav. Critical Studies in Indian Grammarians I, Theory of Homogeneity (Savarnya) LC 75-36896. (The Michigan Papers in South & Southeast Asian Languages & Linguistics: No. 2). xiv, 221p. (Orig.). 1975. pap. 8.00x (ISBN 0-89148-052-8). Ctr S&SE Asian.

Deshpande, Madhav M. & Hook, Peter E., eds. Aryan & Non-Aryan in India. LC 78-60016. (Michigan Papers on South & Southeast Asia: No. 14). xii, 315p. 1979. 21.00x (ISBN 0-89720-011-X); pap. 15.50x (ISBN 0-89148-014-5). Ctr S&SE Asian.

Deshpande, Vamanrao H. Indian Musical Traditions: An Aesthetic Study of the Gharanas in Hindustani Music. (Illus.). 117p. 1973. 10.00x (ISBN 0-8002-1544-3). Intl Pubns Serv.

Desikachar, T. K. Religiousness in Yoga: Lectures on Theory & Practice. Skelton, Mary L. & Carter, J. R., eds. LC 79-9643. (Illus.). 314p. 1980. text ed. 21.50 (ISBN 0-8191-0966-5); pap. text ed. 11.50 (ISBN 0-8191-0967-3). U Pr of Amer.

De Silva, Clarence W. Dynamic Testing & Seismic Qualification Practice. LC 80-8879. 416p. 1982. 47.95x (ISBN 0-669-04393-1). Lexington Bks.

De Silva, Clarence W. & Wormley, David N. Automated Guideway Transit Analysis & Design. LC 80-8927. 304p. 1983. 37.95x (ISBN 0-669-04407-5). Lexington Bks.

De Silva, K. M. A History of Sri Lanka. 550p. 1981. 38.50x (ISBN 0-520-04320-0). U of Cal Pr.

--Sri Lanka: A Survey. LC 77-73917. 1977. text ed. 25.00x (ISBN 0-8248-0568-2). UH Pr.

De Simone, Diane, jt. auth. see Durden-Smith, Jo.

Desiraju, T. Mechanisms in Transmission of Signals for Conscious Behavior. 1976. 103.50 (ISBN 0-444-41397-9, North Holland). Elsevier.

De Sismondi, Simonde see Sismondi, Simonde de.

De Sitter, Lamoraal U. Structural Geology. 2nd ed. (International Earth & Planetary Sciences Ser). 1964. text ed. 24.95 o.p. (ISBN 0-07-016573-4, C). McGraw.

Deskapagana, Kathleen, jt. auth. see Pagana, Timothy J.

Desloge, Edward A. Classical Mechanics, Vol. 1. LC 81-11402. 519p. 1982. 40.00x (ISBN 0-471-09144-8, Pub. by Wiley-Interscience). Wiley.

--Classical Mechanics, Vol. 2. LC 81-11402. 492p. 1982. 49.50x (ISBN 0-471-09145-6, Pub. by Wiley-Interscience). Wiley.

De Smedt, Evelyn. Lifearts: A Practical Guide to Total Being - Traditional Wisdom & the New Medicine. LC 76-10550. 1977. 15.00 o.p. (ISBN 0-312-48510-7); pap. 5.95 o.p. (ISBN 0-312-48545-X). St Martin.

De Smith, Josie. El Hogar Que Dios Me Dio. 1981. pap. 2.10 (ISBN 0-311-46082-8). Casa Bautista.

De Smith, Josie see Smith, Josie De.

Desmond, David P., jt. auth. see Maddux, James F.

Desmond, Glenn M. & Kelley, Richard E. Business Valuation Handbook. LC 77-365976. 1977. 42.50 o.s.i. (ISBN 0-685-83502-2). Valuation.

Desmond, Hilary. Linton Park, Number One: Charlotte. 176p. (Orig.). 1981. pap. 1.75 o.p. (ISBN 0-523-41062-X). Pinnacle Bks.

--Linton Park Number Two: Anne. 176p. (Orig.). 1981. pap. 1.75 o.p. (ISBN 0-523-41063-8). Pinnacle Bks.

Desmond, Kevin. Motorboating Facts & Feats. (Illus.). 256p. 1980. 19.95 (ISBN 0-900424-86-9, Pub by Guinness Superlatives England). Sterling.

--Richard Shuttleworth. (Illus.). 192p. 1982. 19.95 (ISBN 0-86720-629-2). Sci Bks Intl.

Desmond, Margaret G. Modifying the Work Environment for the Physically Disabled: An Accessibility Checklist for Employers. LC 80-83500. (Illus.). 128p. 1981. 8.95 (ISBN 0-686-38822-4). Human Res Ctr.

Desmond, Robert M., jt. auth. see Karlekar, Bhalchandra V.

Desmond, Robert W. Crisis & Conflict: World News Reporting Between Two Wars, 1920 to 1940, Vol. III. LC 82-8584. (World News Reporting Ser.). 544p. 1982. text ed. 30.00x (ISBN 0-87745-111-7). U of Iowa Pr.

Desmont, Mark, jt. ed. see Blaukopf, Kurt.

Desmoulins, Camille. Oeuvres, 10 Vols. 1980. lib. bdg. 540.00 (ISBN 3-601-00189-6). Kraus Intl.

Desnick, R. J., jt. ed. see Bishop, D. F.

Desnick, Robert J. & Gatt, Shimon, eds. Gaucher Disease: A Century of Delineation & Research. LC 82-4611. (Progress in Clinical & Biological Research Ser.: Vol. 95). 764p. 1982. 76.00 (ISBN 0-8451-0095-5). A R Liss.

Desnick, Robert J. & Patterson, Donald F., eds. Animal Models of Inherited Metabolic Diseases. LC 82-8961. (Progress in Clinical & Biological Research Ser.: Vol. 94). 544p. 1982. 54.00 (ISBN 0-8451-0094-7). A R Liss.

Desnick, Shirley G. Geriatric Contentment: A Guide to Its Achievement in Your Home. 76p. 1971. photocopy ed. spiral 9.75x (ISBN 0-398-00440-4). C C Thomas.

Desnoes & Edmundo. Literatures in Transition: The Many Voices of the Caribbean Area A Symposium. Minc, Rose S., ed. LC 82-84104. 180p. (Eng. & Span.). 1983. pap. 12.95 (ISBN 0-935318-10-0). Edins Hispamerica.

Desnoes, Edmundo, ed. Los Dispositivos en la flor (Cuban literatura desde la revolucion) 557p. (Span.). 1981. pap. 12.00 (ISBN 0-910061-03-3). Ediciones Norte.

De Soamo, Maitland C. Joe Call: The Lewis Giant. LC 81-3334. (Illus.). 1891. 12.50 (ISBN 0-686-83970-6). Adirondack Yes.

--Summers on the Saranacs. LC 80-81853. (Illus.). 1980. 22.50 (ISBN 0-9601158-6-2). Adirondack Yes.

Desoer, C. A. & Kuh, E. S. Basic Circuit Theory. LC 68-9551. 1969. text ed. 34.95 (ISBN 0-07-016575-0, C); instr's manual 25.00 (ISBN 0-07-016577-7). McGraw.

Desoer, C. A. & Vidyasagar, M. Feedback Systems: Input-Output Properties. (Electrical Science Ser.). 1975. 57.00 o.s.i. (ISBN 0-12-212050-7). Acad Pr.

Desoer, C. A., jt. auth. see Callier, F. M.

Desoer, C. A., jt. auth. see Zadeh, L. A.

De Sola, R. Abbreviations Dictionary. 6th ed. 1981. 38.00 (ISBN 0-444-00380-0). Elsevier.

De Sola, Ralph. Worldwide What & Where: Geographic Glossary & Traveller's Guide. LC 74-82038. 720p. 1975. text ed. 15.75 o.p. (ISBN 0-87436-147-8). ABC-Clio.

De Sola Pinto, Vivian. Peter Sterry, Platonist & Puritan, 1613-1672. Repr. of 1934 ed. lib. bdg. 16.25x (ISBN 0-8371-0193-X, PIPS). Greenwood.

De Sola Pool, Ithiel. Forecasting the Telephone. (Communications & Information Sciences Ser.). 192p. 1983. text ed. 19.50 (ISBN 0-89391-048-1). Ablex Pub.

De Sola Pool, Ithiel, ed. The Prestige Press: A Comparative Study of Political Symbols. 1970. pap. 4.95x (ISBN 0-262-66022-9). MIT Pr.

--The Social Impact of the Telephone. 512p. 1977. pap. 9.95x (ISBN 0-262-66048-2). MIT Pr.

--Talking Back: Citizen Feedback & Cable Technology. 320p. 1973. 20.00x (ISBN 0-262-16056-0). MIT Pr.

De Sole, S. Entwicklung der Drelipore von Coprinus Radiatus (Bolt.) Fr. (Bibliotheca Mycologica 88). (Illus.). 148p. 1982. pap. 20.00 (ISBN 3-7682-1343-9). Lubrecht & Cramer.

De Sommevoire, Alexis & Da Parigi, Tomaso. Tesoro Della Linqua Greca-Volgare Ed Italiana, cioe Ricchissimo dizzionario greco-volgare et italiano, 2 vols. (Gr. & Ital.). Date not set. Repr. of 1709 ed. lib. bdg. 175.00x (ISBN 0-686-72425-9). Pt. 1, Italian-Greek, Viii, 513 Pages. Pt. 2, Greek-Italian, Xxviii, 461 Pages. Caratzas Bros.

De Sormo, Maitland C. Heydays of the Adirondacks. LC 74-84746. (Illus.). 1975. 15.00 (ISBN 0-9601158-2-X); pap. 12.00 (ISBN 0-9601158-3-8). Adirondack Yes.

--Seneca Ray Stoddard, Versatile Camera Artist. LC 72-905866. (Illus.). 1972. 15.00 (ISBN 0-9601158-1-1). Adirondack Yes.

Desotelle, Joanne R., ed. Who's Who Among American Law Students, 1983. LC 81-645742. 160p. 1982. 30.00 (ISBN 0-943960-00-2). Univ Pub Bureau.

De Soto, Jose Aybar see Aybar de Soto, Jose.

DeSourdis, Ron, jt. auth. see Henry, Marilyn.

De Sousa, Maria. Lymphocyte Circulation: Experimental & Clinical Aspects. LC 80-40848. 259p. 1981. 54.95x (ISBN 0-471-27854-8, Pub. by Wiley-Interscience). Wiley.

Desoutter, D. M. Your Book of Sound. Jenkins, D. L., tr. (Illus.). (gr. 7 up). 1971. 5.95 o.p. (ISBN 0-571-09530-5). Transatlantic.

Desoutter, Denis M. Your Book of Space Travel. (gr. 7 up). 6.50 o.p. (ISBN 0-571-04720-3). Transatlantic.

Desoutter, Denny. The Boat-Owner's Practical Dictionary. (Practical Handbooks for the Yachtsman Ser.). (Illus.). 1978. 14.95 o.p. (ISBN 0-370-30041-6); pap. 10.50 o.p. (ISBN 0-370-30042-4). Transatlantic.

--The Small-Boat Skipper's Safety Book. 224p. 1972. pap. 8.50 o.s.i. (ISBN 0-370-30010-6). Transatlantic.

Desoutter, Denny, ed. see Greenfield, Pete.

De Souza, Alfred, ed. Women in Contemporary India. LC 76-900940. 1976. 18.50 (ISBN 0-88386-720-6). South Asia Bks.

DeSouza, Anthony & Foust, Brady. World Space-Economy. 1979. text ed. 24.95 (ISBN 0-675-08292-7). Merrill.

De Souza, Anthony, jt. ed. see Vogeler, Ingolf.

De Souza, Chris. Looking at Music. 48p. 1980. 8.95 o.p. (ISBN 0-442-24337-5). Van Nos Reinhold.

DeSouza, Glenn R. Energy Policy & Forecasting: Economic, Financial, & Technological Dimensions. LC 79-9671. (Arthur D. Little Bk.). 240p. 1981. 26.95x (ISBN 0-669-03614-5). Lexington Bks.

--System Methods for Socio-Economic & Environmental Impact Analysis. LC 79-7183. (Arthur D. Little Bk.). 176p. 1979. 23.95x (ISBN 0-669-02953-X). Lexington Bks.

DeSpelder, Lynne A. & Strickland, Albert L. The Last Dance: Encountering Death & Dying. 457p. 1983. text ed. 16.95 (ISBN 0-87484-535-1). Mayfield Pub.

Des Periers, Bonaventure. Bonaventure Des Periers's Novel Pastimes & Merry Tales. La Charite, Raymond C., ed. & tr. LC 70-190532. (Studies in Romance Languages: No. 6). 264p. 1972. 13.00x (ISBN 0-8131-1279-6). U Pr of Ky.

Despert, J. Louis. Children of Divorce. 1953. pap. 3.95 (ISBN 0-385-02001-5, Dolp). Doubleday.

Despert, J. Louise. The Inner Voices of Children. new ed. (Illus.). 180p. 1976. 10.95 o.p. (ISBN 0-671-22244-9); pap. 3.95 o.p. (ISBN 0-671-22245-7). S&S.

De Spinoza, Benedictus. The Principles of Descartes' Philosophy. Britan, Halbert H., tr. from Lat. LC 74-3096. 1978. pap. 6.00 (ISBN 0-87548-053-5). Open Court.

Despreau De La Condamine, S. Soirees De Ferney Ou Confidenced De Voltaire. Repr. of 1802 ed. 96.00 o.p. (ISBN 0-8287-0271-3). Clearwater Pub.

Des Pres, Terrence. The Survivor: An Anatomy of Life in the Death Camps. (Illus.). 1980. pap. 6.95 (ISBN 0-19-502703-5, GB 596, GB). Oxford U Pr.

Dessaix, Robert, tr. see Vakhtin, Boris.

Dessau, Joanna. Absolute Elizabeth. LC 78-69818. 1979. 7.95 (ISBN 0-312-00187-8). St Martin.

Dessauer, John P. Book Industry Trends, 1982. (Illus., Orig.). 1982. pap. 150.00 (ISBN 0-940016-13-3). Bk Indus Study.

Dessauer, John P., et al. Book Industry Trends, 1977. 336p. 1977. pap. 275.00 o.p. (ISBN 0-940016-04-4). Bk Indus Study.

--Book Industry Trends, 1978. (Illus.). 315p. 1978. pap. 300.00 o.p. (ISBN 0-940016-05-2). Bk Indus Study.

Dessel, N., et al. Science & Human Destiny. (Illus.). 288p. 1973. text ed. 17.50 (ISBN 0-07-016580-7, C); instructors' manual 1.00 (ISBN 0-07-016581-5). McGraw.

Dessen, Alan C. Elizabethan Drama & the Viewer's Eye. LC 76-26593. xii, 176p. 1977. 14.00x (ISBN 0-8078-1291-9). U of NC Pr.

Desser, S. S., jt. ed. see Mettrick, D. F.

Dessler, Alexander J., ed. Physics of the Jovian Magnetosphere. (Cambridge Planetary Science 3). (Illus.). 400p. 1983. 29.50 (ISBN 0-521-24558-3). Cambridge U Pr.

Dessler, G. Organization Theory: Integrating Structure & Behavior. 1980. 23.95 (ISBN 0-13-641886-4). P-H.

Dessler, Gary. Human Behavior: Improving Productivity at Work. (Illus.). 480p. 1980. text ed. 22.95 (ISBN 0-8359-2994-9); instrs' manual avail. (ISBN 0-8359-2995-7). Reston.

--Management Fundamentals: Modern Principles & Practices. 3rd ed. 1982. text ed. 21.95 (ISBN 0-8359-4215-5); student guide 9.95 (ISBN 0-8359-4217-1); instrs'. manual avail. (ISBN 0-8359-4216-3). Reston.

De Stael. Germany, 2 vols. Wight, O. W., tr. LC 82-73430. 845p. Repr. of 1864 ed. lib. bdg. 65.00x (ISBN 0-88116-010-5). Brenner Bks.

Destang, Francoise, jt. auth. see Thomas, Philippe.

DeStefano, Johanna S. Language, the Learner & the School. LC 77-13511. 221p. 1978. pap. text ed. 14.95 (ISBN 0-471-02378-7). Wiley.

Destevens, George, ed. Myocardial Infarction & Cardiac Death. LC 82-11547. Date not set. price not set (ISBN 0-12-212160-0). Acad Pr.

Destine, J., jt. ed. see Cantraine, G.

Destler, Chester M; see Weaver, Glenn.

Destler, I. M. Making Foreign Economic Policy. LC 79-5119. 256p. 1980. 18.95 (ISBN 0-8157-1822-5); pap. 7.95 (ISBN 0-8157-1821-7). Brookings.

Destler, I. M. & Sato, Hideo, eds. Coping with U.S.-Japanese Economic Conflicts. LC 81-47897. (Illus.). 320p. 1982. 25.95x (ISBN 0-669-05144-6). Lexington Bks.

Destler, I. M., et al. Managing an Alliance: The Politics of U. S.-Japanese Relations. 224p. 1976. 18.95 (ISBN 0-8157-1820-9); pap. 7.95 (ISBN 0-8157-1819-5). Brookings.

De Stoeckl, Agnes. Mistress of Versailles, the Life of Madame Du Barry. 1967. 8.95 o.p. (ISBN 0-685-20605-X). Transatlantic.

De Stroumillo, Elisabeth. Greece. (Illus.). 1974. pap. 5.95 o.p. (ISBN 0-8038-2665-6). Hastings.

De Stroumillo, Elizabeth. Traveller's Guide to Greece. 1978. pap. 5.95 (ISBN 0-8038-2665-6). Hastings.

De Summers, Jessica. Gozo Al Grecer. 48p. 1981. pap. 1.10 (ISBN 0-311-38550-8, Edit Mundo). Casa Bautista.

DesVoigne, Merritt J. Being Small Wasn't Bad at All. LC 82-90097. (Orig.). 1982. pap. 4.95x (ISBN 0-686-84843-8). Littleman.

De Syrmia, Edmond. At the Head of Nations: The Rise of the Papal & Princely House of Odescalchi. LC 76-44029. (Illus.). 116p. 1978. 10.00 (ISBN 0-914226-05-3). Cyclopedia.

Deszo, L. & Hajdu, P., eds. Theoretical Problems of Typology & the Northern Eurasian Languages. 184p. 1970. 26.00 (ISBN 90-6032-062-X). Benjamins North Am.

Detacuden, Nam U. The Simplest Explanation of God Ever Explained. 240p. 1983. 13.50 (ISBN 0-682-49951-X). Exposition.

De Talavera, Frances & Curtis, John P. San Francisco's Gaslight Era Cookbook. (Illus.). 126p. Date not set. cancelled (ISBN 0-87701-174-5); pap. cancelled (ISBN 0-87701-241-5). Chronicle Bks.

De Tella, G., jt. ed. see Kindleberger, Charles P.

De Teran, Lisa St. Aubin see St. Aubin de Teran, Lisa.

Detert, Richard A., jt. auth. see Curtis, Jack D.

De Thabrew. Popular Tropical Aquarium Plants. 1981. 30.00x (ISBN 0-686-98215-0, Pub. by Thornhill Pr England). State Mutual Bk.

Dethier, Vincent G. To Know a Fly. LC 62-21838. (Illus.). 1963. pap. 5.95x (ISBN 0-8162-2240-1). Holden-Day.

Dethier, Vincent G. & Stellar, Eliot. Animal Behavior. 3rd ed. 1970. pap. 12.95 ref ed. (ISBN 0-13-037440-7). P-H.

Dethloff, Henry C. & May, Irvin M., Jr. Southwestern Agriculture: Pre-Columbian to Modern. LC 81-48381. (Illus.). 320p. 1982. 23.75x (ISBN 0-89096-121-2). Tex A&M Univ Pr.

Dethloff, Henry C., jt. auth. see Bryant, Keith L., Jr.

Dethy, Ray C., jt. auth. see Ostrander, Raymond H.

Detloff, Virginia. Index to Spring: An Annual of Archetypal Psychology & Jungian Thought, 1941-1979. 70p. 1983. pap. write for info. (ISBN 0-88214-018-3). Spring Pubns.

Detmar, Michael W., jt. ed. see DeKornfeld, Thomas J.

Detmar, Richard C. & Smullen, Clinton W. Algebra Drill & Practice. 2nd ed. (A Software Microcomptuer Program Ser.). 1982. scp instr's manual 5.95 (ISBN 0-06-041636-X, HarpC); scp complete package 125.00 (ISBN 0-06-041635-1). Har-Row.

Detmer, Josephine & Pancoast, Patricia. Portland. Dibner, Martin, ed. LC 72-172820. (Illus.). 1973. collector's 25.00 (ISBN 0-9600612-0-7). Greater Portland.

De Tocqueville, Alexis. Democracy in America. abr. ed. Heffner, Richard D., ed. pap. 3.50 (ISBN 0-451-62218-9, ME2218, Ment). NAL.

De Tocqueville, Alexis see Tocqueville, Alexis de.

De Toledano, Ralph. Devil Take Him. LC 79-14755. 1979. 11.95 o.p. (ISBN 0-399-12113-7). Putnam Pub Group.

De Tornya, Rheba, jt. auth. see Poshek, Neila.

DeTornyay, Rheba. Strategies of Teaching Nursing. LC 73-134038. (Paperback Nursing Ser.). 1971. pap. 12.95x o.p. (ISBN 0-471-20395-5, Pub. by Wiley Medical). Wiley.

De Toro Gisbert, M. Dictionnaire Bilingue: Francais-Espagnol, Espagnol-Francais. 546p. (Fr. & Span.). 1968. pap. text ed. 7.95 (ISBN 0-686-97445-X, S-36345). French & Eur.

De Torres, Esther Z., jt. auth. see Borges, Jorge L.

De Trevino, Elizabeth B. Among the Innocent. LC 79-6858. 360p. 1981. 13.95 o.p. (ISBN 0-385-13397-9). Doubleday.

Detrick, Mia. Sushi. LC 81-12224. (Illus.). 112p. (Orig.). 1981. pap. 8.95 (ISBN 0-87701-238-5). Chronicle Bks.

Detro, Gene. When All the Wild Summer. 28p. 1983. pap. 3.00 (ISBN 0-914974-39-4). Holmgangers.

Detro, Gene, ed. see Stock, Susan.

Detroit Public Library. Automotive History Collection of the Detroit Public Library: A Simplified Guide to Its Holdings, 2 Vols. 1966. Set. 190.00 (ISBN 0-8161-0718-1, Hall Library). G K Hall.

--Catalog of the E. Azalia Hackley Memorial Collection of Negro Music, Dance & Drama. 1979. lib. bdg. 100.00 (ISBN 0-8161-0299-6, Hall Library). G K Hall.

De Troyes, Chretien. Lancelot, or The Knight of the Cart. Kibler, William W., ed. (The Garland Library of Medieval Literature). 1981. lib. bdg. 36.00 o.s.i. (ISBN 0-8240-9442-5). Garland Pub.

--Perceval: Or, the Story of the Holy Grail. 260p. 1983. 35.00 (ISBN 0-08-026296-1); pap. 17.50 (ISBN 0-08-026295-3). Pergamon.

--Perceval: The Story of the Grail. Bryant, Nigel, tr. LC 82-3696. (Arthurian Studies: No. V). 288p. 1982. text ed. 47.50x (ISBN 0-8476-7201-8). Rowman.

--Yvain; or, the Knight with the Lion. Cline, Ruth H., tr. from Fr. LC 73-85026. 222p. 1975. 6.95x (ISBN 0-8203-0327-5). U of Ga Pr.

Detshy, Mihaly. Sarosptak (Hungary) Boros, Laszlo, tr. from Hungarian. (Illus.). 118p. 1979. pap. 5.00x (ISBN 963-13-0389-6). Intl Pubns Serv.

Detsicas, Alec. Collectanea Historica. 320p. 1981. text ed. 42.00x (ISBN 0-906746-02-7, Pub. by Alan Sutton England). Humanities.

Detsky, Allan. The Economic Foundations of National Health Policy. LC 78-15292. 288p. 1978. prof ref 25.00x (ISBN 0-88410-528-8). Ballinger Pub.

Dett, P. Nathaniel. Collected Piano Works of R. Nathaniel Dett. (Illus.). 1973. pap. 16.50 (ISBN 0-87487-080-1). Summy.

Dettelbach, Cynthia G. In the Driver's Seat: The Automobile in American Literature & Popular Culture. LC 75-35342. (Contributions in American Studies: No. 25). (Illus.). 160p. 1976. lib. bdg. 25.00 (ISBN 0-8371-8593-9, DDS/). Greenwood.

Detterman, Douglas K. & Sternberg, Robert J., eds. How & How Much Can Intelligence Be Increased. 256p. 1982. 0.24.95 (ISBN 0-89391-117-8). Ablex Pub.

Detterman, Douglas K., jt. ed. see Sternberg, Robert J.

Dettman, John W. Mathematical Methods in Physics & Engineering. 2nd ed. LC 68-28412. (International Pure & Applied Mathematics Ser.). 1969. text ed. 18.95 o.p. (ISBN 0-07-016597-1, C). McGraw.

Detty, Elizabeth W., jt. auth. see Bryson, Joseph E.

De Turnebe, Odet. Satisfaction All Around: Les Contens. Beecher, Donald, tr. (Carleton Renaissance Plays Ser.). 102p. 1979. pap. text ed. 3.50x (ISBN 0-7709-0063-1, Pub. by Wilfred Laurier U Pr Canada). Humanities.

De Tussac, R. Cri des Colons Contre un Ouvrage de M. L'eveque et Senateur Gregoire. (Slave Trade in France, 1744-1848, Ser.). 314p. (Fr.). 1974. Repr. of 1810 ed. lib. bdg. 83.00x o.p. (ISBN 0-8287-0841-X). Clearwater Pub.

Detweiler, Robert. John Updike. (United States Authors Ser.). lib. bdg. 11.95 (ISBN 0-8057-0752-2, Twayne). G K Hall.

--Story, Sign, & Self: Phenomenology & Structuralism As Literary-Critical Methods. Beardslee, William A., ed. LC 76-9713. (Semeia Studies). 240p. 1978. pap. 5.95 o.p. (ISBN 0-8006-1505-0, 1-1505). Fortress.

Detweiler, Robert & Kornweibel, Theodore. Slave & Citizen: A Critical Annotated Bibliography on Slavery & Race Relations in the Americas. 300p. 1983. pap. 6.00 (ISBN 0-686-84758-X). Campanile.

Detweiler, Robert, ed. John Updike. LC 74-187611. (Twayne's United States Authors Ser.). 183p. 1972. pap. text ed. 4.95 o.p. (ISBN 0-672-61506-1). Bobbs.

--Semeia Twenty-Three: Derrida & Biblical Studies. (Semeia Ser.). 9.95 (ISBN 0-686-96296-6, 06 20 23). Scholars Pr CA.

Detweiler, Robert, et al. Environmental Decay in Its Historical Context. 1973. pap. 7.95x (ISBN 0-673-07678-4). Scott F.

Detweiler, Susan G. George Washington's Chinaware. LC 81-14993. (Illus.). 240p. 1982. 40.00 (ISBN 0-8109-1779-3). Abrams.

Detwiler, Donald S. Germany: A Short History. LC 76-4563. 288p. 1976. 14.95x o.p. (ISBN 0-8093-0491-0); pap. 9.95 (ISBN 0-8093-0768-5). S Ill U Pr.

Detwiler, Donald S. & Burdick, Charles B., eds. Introduction & Guide: Japanese & Chinese Studies & Documents, Vol. 1. (War in Asia & the Pacific Ser., 1937 to 1949). 460p. 1980. lib. bdg. 60.50 o.s.i. (ISBN 0-8240-3285-3). Garland Pub.

Deuber, Carl G. Vegetative Propagation of Conifers. 1940. pap. 29.50x (ISBN 0-686-51323-1). Elliots Bks.

Deubert, L. W. & Jenkins, C. B. Tooth-Coloured Filling Materials in Clinical Practice. 2nd ed. (Dental Practitioner Handbook Ser.: No. 16). (Illus.). 154p. 1982. pap. text ed. 17.50 (ISBN 0-7236-0628-5). Wright-PSG.

Deuchar, E. M. Cellular Interactions in Animal Development. 1975. 33.00x (ISBN 0-412-13010-6, Pub. by Chapman Hall). Methuen Inc.

Deuchar, Elizabeth M. Xenopus: The South African Clawed Frog. LC 73-18927. 246p. 1975. 45.50 o.p. (ISBN 0-471-20962-7, Pub. by Wiley-Interscience). Wiley.

Deuchler, Florens. Gothic Art. LC 72-85081. (History of Art Ser.). (Illus.). 184p. 1973. 12.50x o.p. (ISBN 0-87663-172-3). Universe.

Deudney, Daniel & Flavin, Christopher. Renewable Energy: The Power to Choose. 1983. 18.95 (ISBN 0-393-01710-9). Norton.

Deudon, Eric H. Nietzsche En France: L'antichristianisme et la Critique, 1891-1915. LC 81-43820. 176p. (Orig.). 1982. lib. bdg. 23.00 (ISBN 0-8191-2339-0); pap. text ed. 10.25 (ISBN 0-8191-2340-4). U Pr of Amer.

Deulofeu, et al. The Best from the Bottle. 1979. 12.95 (ISBN 0-8256-3157-2, Quick Fox). Putnam Pub Group.

De Unamuno, M. The Agony of Belief. Kerrigan, A. & Nozick, M., eds. 1982. 18.50 (ISBN 0-691-06498-9); pap. 6.95 (ISBN 0-691-01366-7). Princeton U Pr.

De Unamuno, Miguel. San Manuel Bueno, Martir. (Harrap's Bilingual Ser.). 55p. (Spanish.). 1957. 5.00 (ISBN 0-911268-46-4). Rogers Bk.

--Three Exemplary Novels & a Prologue. 228p. 1982. Repr. of 1930 ed. lib. bdg. 50.00 (ISBN 0-8495-5412-8). Arden Lib.

Deur, Lynne. Doers & Dreamers: Social Reformers of the 19th Century. LC 79-128808. (Pull Ahead Bks). (gr. 5-11). 1972. PLB 4.95g (ISBN 0-8225-0462-6). Lerner Pubns.

--Indian Chiefs. LC 75-128807. (Pull Ahead Bks). (Illus.). (gr. 6-11). 1972. PLB 4.95g (ISBN 0-8225-0461-8). Lerner Pubns.

--Political Cartoonists. LC 72-128809. (Pull Ahead Bks). (Illus.). (gr. 5-11). 1972. PLB 4.95g (ISBN 0-8225-0463-4). Lerner Pubns.

Deurs, George van. Anchors in the Sky: Spuds Ellyson, the First Naval Aviator. LC 78-74. (Illus.). 1978. 12.95 o.p. (ISBN 0-89141-034-1). Presidio Pr.

Deutch, B. I., et al, eds. Hyperfine Interactions. 1977. 65.25 (ISBN 0-7204-0452-5, North-Holland). Elsevier.

Deutsch, Albert, jt. auth. see Schneider, David M.

Deutsch, Alleen, jt. auth. see Demetrulias, Diana.

Deutsch, Arnold. The Human Resources Revolution: Communicate or Litigate. (Illus.). 1979. 19.95 (ISBN 0-07-016593-9, P&RB). McGraw.

Deutsch, Babette. Poetry Handbook: A Dictionary of Terms. 1962. pap. 3.95 o.p. (ISBN 0-448-00123-3, G&D). Putnam Pub Group.

--Poetry Handbook: A Dictionary of Terms. 4th ed. (Funk & W Bk.). 1974. pap. 4.95i (ISBN 0-308-10248-7, EH-548). T Y Crowell.

Deutsch, Babette, tr. see Babel, Isaac.

Deutsch, Beatrice L. Ambulatory Care Nursing Procedure & Employee Health Service Manual. 1977. spiral bdg. 12.00 o.p. (ISBN 0-87488-968-5). Med Exam.

Deutsch, Charles. Broken Bottles, Broken Dreams: Understanding & Helping the Children of Alcoholics. LC 81-5729. 232p. 1982. text ed. 17.95x O.P. (ISBN 0-8077-2664-8); pap. text ed. 13.95x (ISBN 0-8077-2663-X). Tchrs Coll.

Deutsch, David J. & Chemical Engineering Magazine, eds. Process Piping Systems. LC 80-13774. (Chemical Engineering Ser.). 484p. 1980. 43.00 (ISBN 0-07-010706-8). McGraw.

Deutsch, E., jt. ed. see Kleinberger, G.

Deutsch, Eliot. Advaita Vedanta: A Philosophical Reconstruction. LC 69-19282. 1969. pap. text ed. 3.95x (ISBN 0-8248-0271-3, Eastwest Ctr). UH Pr.

--Humanity & Divinity: An Essay in Comparative Metaphysics. LC 76-128081. 1970. 12.00x (ISBN 0-87022-190-6). UH Pr.

--On Truth: An Ontological Theory. LC 79-12754. 1979. text ed. 12.00x (ISBN 0-8248-0615-8). UH Pr.

--Personhood, Creativity & Freedom. LC 82-4891. 167p. 1982. text ed. 20.00x (ISBN 0-8248-0800-2). UH Pr.

--Studies in Comparative Aesthetics. LC 74-34028. (Society for Asian & Comparative Philosophy Monographs: No. 2). (Illus.). 112p. (Orig.). 1975. pap. text ed. 4.50x (ISBN 0-8248-0365-5). UH Pr.

Deutsch, Eliot & Van Buitenen, J. A. Source Book of Advaita Vedanta. 1971. 15.00x o.p. (ISBN 0-87022-189-2). UH Pr.

Deutsch, Francine. Child Services: On Behalf of Children. LC 82-14570. (Psychology Ser.). 350p. 1982. pap. text ed. 14.95 (ISBN 0-534-01221-3). Brooks-Cole.

Deutsch, Francine, jt. auth. see Hultsch, David F.

Deutsch, Herman B. Brennan's New Orleans Cookbook. (Illus.). 1961. 11.95 (ISBN 0-88289-382-3). Pelican.

Deutsch, Hermann B. Brennan's New Orleans Cookbook. LC 60-53567. 1982. 11.95 (ISBN 0-88289-382-3). Pelican.

Deutsch, K. Analysis of International Relations. 2nd ed. (Foundations of Modern Political Science Ser.). 1978. pap. 13.95 (ISBN 0-13-033217-8). P-H.

Deutsch, Karl W. Nationalism & Social Communication: An Inquiry into the Foundations of Nationality. (Illus.). 1953. pap. 9.95x o.p. (ISBN 0-262-54001-0). MIT Pr.

--Politics & Government: How People Decide Their Fate. 3rd ed. LC 79-90262. (Illus.). 1980. text ed. 24.95 (ISBN 0-395-28486-4); instr's. manual 1.00 (ISBN 0-395-28487-2). HM.

Deutsch, Karl W., et al. Comparative Government: Politics of Industrialized & Developing Nations. (Illus.). 494p. 1981. text ed. 20.95 (ISBN 0-395-29759-1). HM.

Deutsch, Keith. Space Travel in Fact & Fiction. (gr. 5 up). 1980. PLB 8.90 (ISBN 0-686-65170-7). Watts.

Deutsch, Lawrence J. Elementary Hearing Science. 208p. 1979. pap. text ed. 14.95 (ISBN 0-8391-1255-6). Univ Park.

Deutsch, M. & Hornstein, H. A., eds. Applying Social Psychology: Implications for Research, Practice, & Training. LC 75-15665. 287p. 1975. 14.95x o.p. (ISBN 0-470-20965-8). Halsted Pr.

Deutsch, Marilyn W., jt. ed. see Leland, Henry.

Deutsch, Michael S. Software Verification & Validation: Realistic Project Approaches. (Illus.). 288p. 1982. text ed. 23.95 (ISBN 0-13-822072-7). P-H.

Deutsch, Morton & Krauss, Robert M. Theories in Social Psychology. LC 65-25230. (Basic Topics in Psychology Ser). 1965. text ed. 11.00x (ISBN 0-465-08435-4). Basic.

Deutsch, Otto. Handel: A Documentary Biography. LC 74-3118. (Music Ser.). 942p. 1974. Repr. of 1954 ed. lib. bdg. 65.00 (ISBN 0-306-70624-5). Da Capo.

Deutsch, Ronald M., jt. auth. see Bach, George R.

Deutsch, Sid, jt. auth. see Welkowitz, Walter.

Deutsch, W., ed. The Child's Construction of Language Behavioral Development: Monographs. 408p. 1982. 39.50 (ISBN 0-12-213580-6). Acad Pr.

Deutscher, Irwin. What We Say-What We Do: Sentiments & Acts. 1973. pap. 10.95x o.p. (ISBN 0-673-07806-X). Scott F.

Deutscher, Isaac. The Prophet Armed: Trotsky, 1879-1921. 1980. pap. 9.95 (ISBN 0-19-281064-2, GB 605, GB). Oxford U Pr.

--The Prophet Outcast: Trotsky, 1929-1940. 1980. pap. 9.95 (ISBN 0-19-281066-9, GB 607, GB). Oxford U Pr.

--The Prophet Unarmed: Trotsky, 1921-1929. 1980. pap. 9.95 (ISBN 0-19-281065-0, GB 606, GB). Oxford U Pr.

--Unfinished Revolution: Russia, 1917-1967. LC 67-23012. 1969. pap. 4.95 (ISBN 0-19-500786-7, GB). Oxford U Pr.

Deutsches Archaeologisches Institute. Catalogs from the Library of the German Institute of Archaeology, 3 pts. Incl. Pt. 1. Author & Periodical Catalogs, 7 vols. Set. 665.00 (ISBN 0-8161-0824-2); Pt. 2. Classified Catalog, 3 vols. Set. 355.00 (ISBN 0-8161-0103-5); Pt. 3. Author Catalog of Periodicals, 3 vols. Set. 285.00 (ISBN 0-8161-0104-3). 1969 (Hall Library). G K Hall.

Deutschman, Aaron D., et al. Machine Design: Theory & Practice. (Illus.). 768p. 1975. text ed. 32.95x (ISBN 0-02-329000-5, 32900). Macmillan.

Deva, Govind S., ed. see Patanjali.

Devahuti. Bias in Indian Historiography. 1980. text ed. 33.50x (ISBN 0-391-02174-5). Humanities.

--Problems of Indian Historiography. 1979. text ed. 12.00x (ISBN 0-391-01862-0). Humanities.

Devahuti, ed. Problems of Indian Historiography. 1979. 13.50x o.p. (ISBN 0-8364-0352-5). South Asia Bks.

De Vall, Mark Van see Van De Vall, Mark.

Devall, William B., jt. auth. see Harry, Joseph.

Devall, William S., Jr. Junior High School Art Curriculum. LC 79-6770. 79p. 1980. pap. text ed. 7.00 (ISBN 0-8191-0951-7). U Pr of Amer.

De Valois, Ninette. Come Dance With Me: A Memoir, 1898-1956. (Illus.). xvi, 234p. (gr. 9-12). 1981. pap. 8.95 (ISBN 0-903102-02-1). Princeton Bk Co.

Devamata, Sr. Sri Ramakrishna & His Disciples. 1928. 6.50 (ISBN 0-911564-23-3). Vedanta Ctr.

DeVan, Shumway, et al. Oil Industry U. S. A. 1979-80. 1979. 65.00 (ISBN 0-686-84376-2). Oil Daily.

Devaney, Dennis M. & Kelly, Marion. Kaneohe: A History of Change. rev. ed. (Illus.). 300p. 1982. Repr. of 1976 ed. pap. 14.95 (ISBN 0-935848-14-2). Bess Pr.

Devaney, John. Bob Cousy. (Putnam Sports Shelf). (Illus.). (gr. 5 up). 1965. PLB 4.97 o.p. (ISBN 0-399-60061-2). Putnam Pub Group.

--The Bobby Orr Story. (Pro Hockey Library: No. 6). (Illus.). (gr. 5 up). 1973. 2.50 o.p. (ISBN 0-394-82612-4, BYR); PLB 3.69 (ISBN 0-394-92612-9). Random.

--Douglas MacArthur: Something of a Hero. LC 78-10820. (Illus.). (gr. 5-8). 1979. 8.95 (ISBN 0-399-20660-4). Putnam Pub Group.

--Great Upsets of Stanley Cup Hockey. LC 75-33969. (Sports Library). (Illus.). 96p. (gr. 3-6). 1976. PLB 7.12 (ISBN 0-8116-6678-6). Garrard.

--Hitler: Mad Dictator of World War II. LC 77-21057. (Illus.). (gr. 6-8). 1978. 8.95 (ISBN 0-399-20627-2). Putnam Pub Group.

--Juan Marichal: Mr. Strike. LC 74-113515. (Putnam Sports Shelf). (Illus.). (gr. 5 up). 1970. PLB 4.97 o.p. (ISBN 0-399-60330-1). Putnam Pub Group.

--The Picture Story of Terry Bradshaw. LC 77-22841. (Illus.). 64p. (gr. 3-6). 1977. PLB 6.97 o.p. (ISBN 0-671-32867-0). Messner.

--Star Pass Receivers of the NFL. (NFL Punt, Pass & Kick Library: No. 17). (Illus.). (gr. 5 up). 1972. 2.50 o.p. (ISBN 0-394-82439-3, BYR); PLB 3.69 (ISBN 0-394-92439-8). Random.

--Tiny: The Story of Nate Archibald. LC 77-3214. (Putnam Sports Shelf). (Illus.). 1977. PLB 6.29 o.p. (ISBN 0-399-61098-7). Putnam Pub Group.

Devaney, John, jt. auth. see Lorimer, Lawrence T.

Devaney, Sally, ed. see Johnson, Curtiss.

Devanney, J. W., et al. Parable Beach: A Primer in Coastal Zone Management. 1976. text ed. 12.50x (ISBN 0-262-04052-2). MIT Pr.

Devanter, Lynda Van see Van Devanter, Lynda & Morgan, Christopher.

Devarahi, pseud. The Complete Guide to Synthesizers. (Illus.). 272p. 1982. pap. 15.95 (ISBN 0-13-160630-1). P-H.

Devaraja, N. K. Hinduism & Christianity. 1970. 7.25x o.p. (ISBN 0-210-98164-4). Asia.

De Varigny, Charles. Fourteen Years in the Sandwich Islands. Korn, Alfons L., tr. LC 80-26141. (Illus.). 320p. (Fr.). 1981. 24.95 (ISBN 0-8248-0709-X). UH Pr.

De Vate, Dwight Van see Van De Vate, Dwight, Jr.

De Vaucanson, J. Le Mecanisme du Fluteur Automate: An Account of the Automation or Image Playing the German Flute. (The Flute Library: Vol. 5). 1979. Repr. of 1742 ed. 37.50 o.s.i. (ISBN 90-6027-211-0, Pub. by Frits Knuf Netherlands); wrappers 25.00 o.s.i. (ISBN 90-6027-210-2, Pub. by Frits Knuf Netherlands). Pendragon NY.

DeVault, Christine, jt. auth. see Strong, Bryan.

DeVault, M. Vere, jt. auth. see Cooper, James M.

DeVaux, Roland. Ancient Israel, 2 Vols. 1965. Vol. 1, Social Institutions. pap. 4.95 (ISBN 0-07-016599-8, SP); Vol. 2, Religious Institutions. pap. 5.95 (ISBN 0-07-016600-5). McGraw.

De Vaux, Roland. The Early History of Israel. LC 78-1883. 1978. 34.50 (ISBN 0-664-20762-6). Westminster.

DeVeaugh-Geiss, Joseph. Tardive Dyskinesia & Related Involuntary Movement Disorders. (Illus.). 222p. 1982. text ed. 35.00 (ISBN 0-7236-7006-4). Wright-PSG.

DeVeaux, Alexis. Na-ni. LC 72-9864. (Illus.). 48p. (gr. 3-5). 1973. 3.50 o.p. (ISBN 0-06-021627-1, HarpJ); PLB 5.79 o.p. (ISBN 0-06-021628-X). Har-Row.

De Veer, Florine. A Taste of the Lotus. 1979. 9.50 o.p. (ISBN 0-533-03915-0). Vantage.

De Vega, Lope. The Pilgrim: or the Stranger in His Own Country, Vol. 69. LC 71-170598. (Novel in England, 1700-1775 Ser). lib. bdg. 50.00 o.s.i. (ISBN 0-8240-0581-3). Garland Pub.

DeVegh, Elizabeth. Love: A Fearful Success. Darlington, Sandy, ed. 192p. (Orig.). 1983. pap. 3.95 (ISBN 0-9604152-7-0). Arrowhead Pr.

Deveillette, Peter, jt. auth. see Hensel, Evelyn.

De Velde, Paul Van see Steininger, G. Russell & Van de Velde, Paul.

Devellard, Jean-Paul, jt. auth. see Dolce, Donald.

De Vellis, Jean, jt. ed. see Perez-Polo, J. Regino.

Development of Petroleum & Natural Gas Resources in Asia & the Far East, 4th. Proceedings, Vols. 1 & 3. (Mineral Resources Development Ser.: No. 41). Vol. 1. pap. 19.00 (ISBN 0-686-93048-7, UN73/2F14, UN); Vol. 3. pap. 8.50 (ISBN 0-686-98882-5). Unipub.

Development Planning & Research Associates, Inc., for U. S. Dept. of Agri., Manhattan, Kansas. Wind Energy Applications in Agriculture. 204p. 1982. pap. 24.50x (ISBN 0-89934-172-1, W064). Solar Energy Info.

Devenyi, T. & Gergely, J. Amino Acid Peptides & Proteins. 1974. 56.00 (ISBN 0-444-41127-5). Elsevier.

DeVenzio, Dick. Hitting Your Targets. 96p. (Orig.). 1983. pap. 4.95 (ISBN 0-686-36862-2). Fool Court.

--Stuff! Good Players Should Know. (Illus.). 320p. 1983. 13.95 (ISBN 0-910305-00-5). Fool Court.

Dever, Alan. Community Health Analysis: A Holistic Approach. LC 79-26291. 409p. 1980. text ed. 33.50 (ISBN 0-89443-161-7). Aspen Systems.

Dever, Joseph. Cushing of Boston: A Candid Portrait. 15.00 (ISBN 0-8283-1382-2). Branden.

Dever, Richard B. Talk: Teaching the American Language to Kids. (Special Education Ser.). 1978. text ed. 23.95 (ISBN 0-675-08437-7). Merrill.

Deverall, B. J. Defence Mechanisms of Plants. LC 76-12917. (Monographs in Experimental Biology Ser.: No. 19). (Illus.). 1977. 24.95 (ISBN 0-521-21335-5). Cambridge U Pr.

Deverall, Brian. Fungal Paraitism. (Studies in Biology: No. 17). 72p. 1981. pap. text ed. 8.95 (ISBN 0-7131-2832-1). E Arnold.

Deveraux, Jude. Bronwyn. 1982. pap. write for info o.p. (ISBN 0-671-45034-4). PB.

--Velvet Song. 1983. pap. 2.95. PB.

Deverell, Dore. How I Healed My Cancer Holistically. 4.95 (ISBN 0-686-29909-4). Cancer Control Soc.

Devereux, E. J. Renaissance English Translations of Erasmus: A Bibliography to 1700. (Erasmus Ser.). 256p. 1983. 35.00x (ISBN 0-8020-2411-4). U of Toronto Pr.

Devereux, Frederick L., Jr. Famous American Horses. LC 75-13347. (Illus.). 128p. 1975. 24.95 (ISBN 0-8159-5512-X). Devin.

Devereux, George. Dreams in Greek Tragedy: An Ethno-Psycho-Analytic Study. LC 74-27288. 400p. 1976. 35.75x (ISBN 0-520-02921-6). U of Cal Pr.

--Ethnopsychoanalysis: Psychoanalysis & Anthropology As Complementary Frames of Reference. LC 74-16708. 1978. 39.75x (ISBN 0-520-02864-3). U of Cal Pr.

Devereux, Owen F. Topics in Metallurgical Thermodynamics. 416p. 1983. write for info. (ISBN 0-471-86963-5, Pub. by Wiley-Interscience). Wiley.

Devereux, William. Adult Education in Inner London 1870-1980. 352p. 1982. 50.00x (ISBN 0-85683-059-3, Pub. by Shepeard-Walwyn England). State Mutual Bk.

Deverite, Louis-Alexandre. La Vie et les Doleances D'un Pauvre-Diable. Repr. of 1789 ed. 32.50 o.p. (ISBN 0-8287-0272-1). Clearwater Pub.

De Vesme, Alexandre, jt. auth. see Massar, Phyllis D.

Devi, Indra. Forever Young, Forever Healthy. LC 53-10933. (Illus.). 1976. pap. 1.50 o.p. (ISBN 0-668-03776-8). Arco.

Devi, Maitreyi. It Does Not Die. (Translated from Bengali). 15.00 o.s.i. (ISBN 0-89253-644-6); flexible cloth 11.00 (ISBN 0-89253-645-4). Ind-US Inc.

Devi, Shakuntala. Figuring: The Joy of Numbers. LC 78-4731. 160p. 1981. pap. 3.95 (ISBN 0-06-463530-9, EH 530, EH). B&N NY.

Devi, Shyamasree & Lal, P. Tagore's Last Poems. Rev. ed. 29p. (Bengali.). 1980. 8.00 (ISBN 0-86578-120-6); pap. 4.00 (ISBN 0-86578-121-4). Ind-US Inc.

Devi, Shyamasree, tr. see Tagore, Rabindranath.

De Vido, Alfredo. Designing Your Client's House: The Architect's Guide for Meeting Design Goals & Budgets. (Illus.). 176p. 1983. 25.00 (ISBN 0-8230-7142-1, Whitney Lib). Watson-Guptill.

Devienne, F. Nouvelle Methode de Flute. new ed. (The Flute Library: Vol. 7). x, 76p. Repr. of 1800 ed. wrappers 32.50 o.s.i. (ISBN 90-6027-208-0, Pub. by Frits Knuf Netherlands). Pendragon NY.

De Vigny, Alfred. Cinq-Mars; or, a Conspiracy Under Louis XIII, 2 vols. in 1. Hazlitt, W., tr. from Fr. LC 75-1382. 1983. Repr. of 1889 ed. 27.50 (ISBN 0-86527-227-1). Fertig.

DeVille, Jard, jt. auth. see DeVille, Roberta.

Deville, Lawrrence. The Conflict Between the Foreign Policy of the United States & the Economic Interests of the Large Corporations. (Illus.). 163p. 1983. 73.85 (ISBN 0-86722-043-0). Inst Econ Pol.

DeVille, Roberta & DeVille, Jard. Lovers for Life: The Key to a Loving & Lasting Marriage. LC 80-10652. 224p. 1980. 8.95 o.p. (ISBN 0-688-03618-X). Morrow.

De Villeneuve-Bargemont, Alban. Economie Politique Chretienne, 3 vols. (Conditions of the 19th Century French Working Class Ser.). 1780p. (Fr.). 1974. Repr. of 1834 ed. lib. bdg. 437.50x o.p. (ISBN 0-8287-0865-7, 1034-6). Clearwater Pub.

De Villiers, Gerard. Embargo. (Malko Ser.: No. 15). pap. cancelled o.s.i. (ISBN 0-523-40056-X). Pinnacle Bks.

De Villiers du Terrage, Marc. The Last Years of French Louisiana. Brasseaux, Carl A. & Conrad, Glenn R., eds. Phillips, Hosea, tr. LC 82-73751. 525p. 20.00x (ISBN 0-940984-05-9). U of SW LA Ctr LA Studies.

De Vinck, Catherine. Ikon: Ode to the Virgin Mary. 30p. 1972. pap. 3.00 o.p. (ISBN 0-911726-13-6). Alleluia Pr.

De Vinck, Jose. The Words of Jesus, with Key Readings from New & Old Testaments. 320p. 1977. deluxe ed. 30.00 morocco o.p. (ISBN 0-911726-26-8); pap. 12.75x Imitation morocco O. P. o.p. (ISBN 0-911726-27-6). Alleluia Pr.

DeVinck, Jose, jt. auth. see Raya, Joseph.

De Vinck, Jose, jt. auth. see Raya, Joseph.

De Vinck, Jose M., ed. see Kucharek, Casimar.

De Vinck, Jose M., ed. see Raya, Joseph.

Devine, Bob. God in Creation. LC 82-8147. 1982. pap. 3.95 (ISBN 0-8024-3028-7). Moody.

--Mr. Baggy-Skinned Lizard. (God in Creation Ser.). (Illus.). (gr. 3-6). 1977. pap. 1.95 o.p. (ISBN 0-8024-5671-5). Moody.

--The Oyster Thief. (God in Creation Ser.). (Illus.). (gr. 3-5). 1979. pap. 1.95 o.p. (ISBN 0-8024-6267-7). Moody.

Devine, Donald F. & Kaufman, Jerome E. Mathematics for Elementary Education. LC 73-14692. 609p. 1973. 25.95 (ISBN 0-471-20969-4). Wiley.

Devine, Donald F. & Kaufmann, Jerome E. Elementary Mathematics. LC 76-24805. 525p. 1977. text ed. 26.95x (ISBN 0-471-20970-8); tchrs. manual 8.00 (ISBN 0-471-02394-9). Wiley.

Devine, George F., jt. ed. see Starr, William J.

Devine, J. Frank, ed. see Curtis, Charles J.

Devine, Laurie. Nile. 1983. 16.95 (ISBN 0-671-45170-7). S&S.

Devine, Mary. Brujeria: A Study of Mexican American Folk-Magic. Weschcke, Carl L., ed. (Orig.). 1982. pap. 7.95 (ISBN 0-87542-775-8). Llewellyn Pubns.

Devine, Michael D., et al. Energy from the West: A Technology Assessment of Western Energy Resource Development. LC 80-5936. (Illus.). 350p. 1981. 27.50 (ISBN 0-8061-1750-8); pap. 14.95 (ISBN 0-8061-1751-6). U of Okla Pr.

Devine, Michael J. John W. Foster: Politics & Diplomacy in the Imperial Era, 1873-1917. LC 80-17387. (Illus.). x, 187p. 1981. 16.50x (ISBN 0-8214-0437-7, 82-83244). Ohio U Pr.

Devine, Peter, ed. see Gafney, Leo & Beers, John C.

Devine, Thomas G. Listening Skills Schoolwide: Activities & Programs. (Orig.). 1982. pap. 6.50 (ISBN 0-8141-2956-0). NCTE.

DeVinne, Theodore L. Invention of Printing. LC 68-17971. 1969. Repr. of 1876 ed. 42.00x (ISBN 0-8103-3302-3). Gale.

Devino, Gary T. Agribusiness Finance. 1981. text ed. 11.95 (ISBN 0-8134-2191-8); pap. 8.95x (ISBN 0-686-86127-2). Interstate.

De Visscher, Michel, ed. The Thyroid Gland. (Comprehensive Endocrinology Ser.). 552p. 1980. 59.00 (ISBN 0-89004-342-6, 396). Raven.

Devisse, Jean & Courtes, Jean Marie. The Image of the Black in Western Art, Vol. II, Pt. 1: From the Demonic Threat to the Incarnation of Sainthood. Bugner, Ladislas, ed. (Illus.). 288p. 1983. 70.00 (ISBN 0-939594-02-1). Menil Found.

Devisse, Jean & Mollat, Michel. The Image of the Black in Western Art, Vol. II, Pt. 2: Africans in the Christian Ordinance of the World (Fourteenth to the Sixteenth Century) Bugner, Ladislas, ed. (Illus.). 336p. 1983. 80.00 (ISBN 0-939594-03-X). Menil Found.

DeVita, Vincent T., Jr. & Hellman, Samuel. Cancer: Principles & Practice of Oncology. (Illus.). 1504p. 1982. text ed. 125.00x (ISBN 0-397-50440-3, Lippincott Medical). Lippincott.

DeVitis, A. A. Anthony Burgess. (English Authors Ser.: No. 132). lib. bdg. 10.95 o.p. (ISBN 0-8057-1068-X, Twayne). G K Hall.

De Vitis, A. A. Graham Greene. (English Authors Ser.: No. 3). 1964. lib. bdg. 8.50 o.p. (ISBN 0-8057-1240-2, Twayne). G K Hall.

De Vitis, A. A. & Kalson, Albert E. J. B. Priestley. (English Authors Ser.). 1980. lib. bdg. 9.95 (ISBN 0-8057-6774-6, Twayne). G K Hall.

De Vito, Alfred. Teaching with Quotes. (Illus.). 130p. (Orig.). 1982. pap. 9.95 (ISBN 0-942034-01-5). Creat Ventures.

DeVito, Alfred & Krockover, Gerald H. Creative Sciencing: A Practical Approach. 2nd ed. (Illus.). 262p. 1980. text ed. 14.95 (ISBN 0-316-18159-5); tchr's manual avail. (ISBN 0-316-18162-5). Little.

DeVito, Joseph. Elements of Public Speaking. (Illus.). 480p. 1981. text ed. 17.50 scp (ISBN 0-06-041653-X, HarpC); instructor's manual avail. (ISBN 0-06-361636-X). Har-Row.

--The Psychology of Speech & Language: An Introduction to Psycholinguistics. LC 81-40762. (Illus.). 320p. 1981. pap. text ed. 11.25 (ISBN 0-8191-1820-6). U Pr of Amer.

DeVito, Joseph A. Communication: Concepts & Processes. 3rd ed. (Illus.). 320p. 1981. pap. text ed. 13.95 (ISBN 0-13-153411-4). P-H.

--The Interpersonal Communication Book. 2nd ed. (Illus.). 1980. pap. text ed. 18.95 scp (ISBN 0-06-041654-8, HarpC); instructional strategies avail. (ISBN 0-06-361635-1). Har-Row.

--The Interpersonal Communication Book. 3rd ed. 508p. 1983. pap. text ed. 14.95 scp (ISBN 0-06-041651-3, HarpC); instr's. manual avail. (ISBN 0-06-361631-9). Har-Row.

--Psycholinguistics. LC 73-183112. (Studies in Communicative Disorders Ser). 36p. 1971. pap. 1.95 o.p. (ISBN 0-672-61277-1). Bobbs.

DeVito, Michael. The Church's Faith, Bk. I. pap. 3.95 (ISBN 0-941850-06-4). Sunday Pubn.

--The Church's Worship, Bk. II. pap. 3.95 (ISBN 0-941850-07-2). Sunday Pubn.

DeVitt, Joan Q., jt. auth. see Benson, Evelyn P.

De Vlieger, M. Brain Edema. LC 80-22983. 176p. 1981. 39.95x (ISBN 0-471-04477-6, Pub. by Wiley-Med). Wiley.

Devlin. A Dictionary of Synonyms & Antonyms. 384p. 1982. pap. 2.95 (ISBN 0-446-31028-X). Warner Bks.

Devlin, Albert J., ed. Eudora Welty's Chronicle: A Story of Mississippi Life. LC 82-19996. 240p. 1983. text ed. 20.00x (ISBN 0-87805-176-7). U Pr of Miss.

Devlin, Christopher. Life of Robert Southwell, Poet & Martyr. LC 72-90498. Repr. of 1956 ed. lib. bdg. 16.25x (ISBN 0-8371-2203-1, DESO). Greenwood.

Devlin, Harry, jt. auth. see Devlin, Wende.

Devlin, John F. Syria. 135p. 1982. lib. bdg. 16.50x (ISBN 0-86531-185-4). Westview.

Devlin, K. J. Sets, Functions & Logic. 90p. 1981. 15.95x (ISBN 0-412-22660-X, Pub. by Chapman & Hall England); pap. 7.50x (ISBN 0-412-22670-7). Methuen Inc.

Devlin, Patrick. Criminal Prosecution in England. 1958. 29.50x (ISBN 0-685-69811-4). Elliots Bks.

Devlin, Polly. The Vogue Book of Fashion Photography. 1979. 35.00 o.p. (ISBN 0-671-24371-3). S&S.

Devlin, Robert & Witham, Francis. Plant Physiology. 4th ed. 500p. 1983. text ed. write for info. (ISBN 0-87150-765-X). Grant Pr.

Devlin, Thomas M. Textbook of Biochemistry: With Clinical Correlations. LC 81-13063. 1265p. 1982. 36.95x (ISBN 0-471-05039-3, Pub. by Wiley Med). Wiley.

Devlin, Wende & Devlin, Harry. Cranberry Halloween. (gr. k-3). Date not set. 9.95 (ISBN 0-590-07854-2, Four Winds). Schol Bk Serv.

De Voe, Thomas F. The Market Assistant. LC 72-174033. (Illus.). 455p. 1975. Repr. of 1867 ed. 56.00x (ISBN 0-8103-4117-4). Gale.

Devol, Kenneth S. Mass Media & the Supreme Court. 400p. (Orig.). 1982. pap. text ed. 22.50 o.p. (ISBN 0-8038-4741-6). Hastings.

Devol, Kenneth S., ed. Mass Media & the Supreme Court. rev. 3rd ed. (Communication Arts Bks.). 1982. 14.50 o.s.i. (ISBN 0-8038-4683-5); pap. text ed. 22.50x (ISBN 0-8038-4741-6). Hastings.

Devol, Terry B. & Graham, Richard B. Establishment of the First U. S. Government Post Offices in the Northwest Territory. (Illus.). 1975. 4.50 o.p. (ISBN 0-686-18057-7). Am Philatelic.

De Voltaire, Francois M. Candide, Zadig & Selected Stories. Frame, Donald, tr. pap. 2.25 (ISBN 0-451-51609-5, CE1609, Sig Classics). NAL.

Devon, Anne. Defiant Mistress. (Second Chance at Love Ser.: No. 105). Date not set. pap. 1.75 (ISBN 0-515-06869-1). Jove Pubns.

--The Rogue's Lady. 192p. 1982. pap. 1.75 (ISBN 0-686-81840-7). Jove Pubns.

Devon, T. K. & Scott, A. I. Handbook of Naturally Occurring Compounds, 2 vols. Incl. Vol. 1. Acetogenins, Shikimates & Carbohydrates. 1975. 63.50 (ISBN 0-12-213601-2); Vol. 2. Terpenes. 1972. 64.00 (ISBN 0-12-213602-0). Acad Pr.

DeVoney, Chris & Summe, Richard. CP-M Word Processor Evaluations. Noble, David, ed. (Level C Business Software Evaluations). 1982. pap. 16.50 (ISBN 0-88022-006-6). Que Corp.

--IBM's Personal Computer. Noble, David F. & Noble, Virginia D., eds. 303p. 1982. 23.95 (ISBN 0-88022-101-1); pap. 14.95 (ISBN 0-88022-100-3). Que Corp.

DeVoney, Chris, ed. see Poling, Carol.

Devonia. Honiton Lace. 1978. pap. 7.95 (ISBN 0-686-22986-X). Robin & Russ.

Devons, Ely. Essays in Economics. LC 79-17089. (Illus.). 203p. 1980. Repr. of 1961 ed. lib. bdg. 20.75x (ISBN 0-313-21296-1, DEEE). Greenwood.

De Voogl, H. J., jt. ed. see Schroeder, F. H.

De Voorde, Annouk M. Van see Van De Voorde, Annouk M.

DeVore, Irven, jt. auth. see Eimerl, Sarel.

Devore, Irven, jt. auth. see Sarel, Eimerl.

De Vore, Nicholas. Encyclopedia of Astrology. (Littlefield Adams Quality Paperbacks: No. 323). 1977. pap. 5.95 (ISBN 0-8226-0323-3). Littlefield.

DeVore, Ralph E., jt. auth. see Mallery, Mary S.

DeVore, Ronald M. The Arab-Israeli Conflict: A Historical, Political, Social, & Military Bibliography. LC 76-17575. (War-Peace Bibliography Ser.: No. 4). 273p. 1976. text ed. 32.50 o.p. (ISBN 0-87436-229-6). ABC-Clio.

DeVore, Russell B. Practical Problems in Mathematics for Heating & Cooling Technicians. LC 79-57141. (Practical Problems in Mathematics Ser.). 192p. 1981. pap. text ed. 7.80 (ISBN 0-8273-1682-8); instr's. guide 3.25 (ISBN 0-8273-1683-6). Delmar.

DeVore, Wynetta & Schlesinger, Elfriede. Ethnic-Sensitive Social Work Practice. LC 80-27538. (Illus.). 285p. 1981. pap. text ed. 13.95 (ISBN 0-8016-1268-3). Mosby.

Devos, Burnell H., Jr., jt. ed. see Connor, Joseph E.

De Vos, George & Romanucci-Ross, Lola. Ethnic Identity: Cultural Continuities & Change. xvi, 396p. 1983. pap. text ed. 12.00x (ISBN 0-226-14364-3). U of Chicago Pr.

De Vos, Raymond. History of the Monies Medals & Tokens of Monaco. 1978. 0.00 (ISBN 0-685-51123-5); lib. bdg. 80.00x (ISBN 0-685-51124-3). S J Durst.

DeVos, Richard M. & Conn, Charles P. Believe! 1975. pap. 2.95 (ISBN 0-8007-8267-4, Spire). Revell.

DeVoto, Bernard. Across the Wide Missouri. (Illus.). 608p. 1981. 8.98 (ISBN 0-517-10266-8). Crown.

--The Portable Mark Twain. (Orig.). 1983. pap. 18.75 (ISBN 0-670-73341-5). Viking Pr.

Devoto, Bernard, ed. see Twain, Mark.

De Voto, Mark, ed. see Piston, Walter.

Devreese, J. T., ed. Polarons in Ionic Crystals & Polar Semiconductors: Proceedings of the 1971 Antwerp Advanced Study Institute. 1972. 76.75 (ISBN 0-444-10409-7, North-Holland). Elsevier.

Devreese, J. T. & Van Doren, V. E., eds. Ab Initio Calculation of Phonon Spectra. 275p. 1983. 42.50x (ISBN 0-306-41119-9, Plenum Pr). Plenum Pub.

Devrient, Edward. My Recollections of Felix Mendelssohn-Bartholdy & His Letters to Me. Macfarren, Natalia, tr. LC 72-163799. 307p. Date not set. Repr. of 1869 ed. price not set. Vienna Hse.

De Vries, A. Dictionary of Symbols & Imagery. 2nd. rev. ed. 1976. 66.00 (ISBN 0-444-10607-3, North-Holland). Elsevier.

Devries, A. & Kochva, E., eds. Toxins of Animal & Plant Origin, 3 vols. LC 71-130967. (Illus.). 1084p. 1972. Set. 194.00x (ISBN 0-677-14710-4); Vol. 1-1971,512. 92.00x (ISBN 0-677-12430-9); Vol. 2-1972,338. 66.00x (ISBN 0-677-12440-6); Vol. 3-1973,292. 59.00x (ISBN 0-677-12450-3). Gordon.

DeVries, D. A. & Afgan, N. H., eds. Heat & Mass Transfer in the Biosphere: Pt. 1, Transfer Processes in the Plant Environment. LC 74-28072. (Advances in Thermal Engineering Ser.). 594p. 1975. 28.50x (ISBN 0-470-20985-2). Halsted Pr.

DeVries, David L., et al. Performance Appraisal on the Line. LC 81-10328. 160p. 1981. 24.95 (ISBN 0-471-09254-1, Pub. by Wiley-Interscience). Wiley.

De Vries, Egbert & Casanova, P. Gonzales, eds. Social Research & Rural Life in Central America, Mexico & the Caribbean Region. 1966. 7.50 o.p. (ISBN 92-3-100617-7, U612, UNESCO). Unipub.

De Vries, G. A. Contribution to the Knowledge of the Genus Cladosporium Linx Ex Fries: Thesis. (Illus.). 1967. 16.00 (ISBN 3-7682-0458-8). Lubrecht & Cramer.

De Vries, H., jt. auth. see Van Bekkum, O.

De Vries, H. P. & Rodriguez-Novas, J. The Law of the Americas. LC 65-27792. 339p. 1965. 20.00 (ISBN 0-379-00268-X). Oceana.

De Vries, Henry. Civil Law: The Anglo-American Lawyer. LC 75-11645. 544p. 1975. text ed. 27.50 (ISBN 0-379-00222-1). Oceana.

De Vries, Henry P. Civil Law & the Anglo-American Lawyer. LC 75-11645. 1976. pap. 12.50 o.p. (ISBN 0-379-00267-1). Oceana.

Devries, Herbert & Briley, Michael. Health Science. LC 78-27588. (Illus.). 1978. text ed. 18.95x (ISBN 0-673-16334-2). Scott F.

DeVries, Herbert A. & Hales, Dianne. Fitness After 50. (Illus.). 192p. 1983. pap. 5.95 (ISBN 0-686-83789-4, ScribT). Scribner.

De Vries, J. Economy of Europe in an Age of Crisis: 1600-1750. LC 75-30438. (Illus.). 240p. 1976. 37.50 (ISBN 0-521-21123-9); pap. 10.95 (ISBN 0-521-29050-3). Cambridge U Pr.

De Vries, Jan. Barges & Capitalism: Passenger Transportation in the Dutch Economy (1632-1839) 368p. 1981. pap. 16.50 (ISBN 90-6194-432-5, Pub. by Hes Pubs Netherlands). Benjamins North Am.

De Vries, Jan Vredeman see Vredeman De Vries, Jan.

DeVries, John, jt. auth. see Charlton, Andrew.

DeVries, Louis. German-English Technical & Engineering Dictionary. 2nd ed. 1966. 59.95 (ISBN 0-07-016631-5, P&RB). McGraw.

DeVries, Louis & Hochman, Stanley. French-English Science & Technology Dictionary. 4th ed. 1976. 26.95 (ISBN 0-07-016629-3, P&RB). McGraw.

DeVries, Louis & Jacolev, Leon. German-English Science Dictionary. 4th ed. 1978. 26.95 (ISBN 0-07-016602-1, P&RB). McGraw.

DeVries, Louis & Kolb, Helga. Dictionary of Chemistry & Chemical Engineering, 2 vols. 2nd ed. Incl. Vol. 1. German-English. 1978. 129.50x (ISBN 0-686-53141-8); Vol. 2. English-German. LC 77-138815. 129.50x (ISBN 0-89573-025-1). 1979. Verlag Chemie.

De Vries, Madeline & Weber, Eric. Body & Beauty Secrets of the Super Beauties. (Illus.). 1980. 11.95 o.p. (ISBN 0-399-12016-5). Putnam Pub Group.

DeVries, Martin & Berg, Robert L. The Use & Abuse of Medicine. 316p. 1982. 34.95 (ISBN 0-03-061702-2). Praeger.

DeVries, Mary A. see Prentice-Hall Editorial Staff.

DeVries, Peter. Blood of the Lamb. 1982. pap. 4.95 (ISBN 0-14-006297-1). Penguin.

De Vries, Peter. Sauce for the Goose. 1982. pap. 3.95 (ISBN 0-14-006281-5). Penguin.

--Slouching Towards Kalamazoo. 228p. 1983. 13.45i (ISBN 0-316-18172-2). Little.

DeVries, Pieter A. & Shapiro, Stephen R. Complications of Pediatric Surgery. LC 81-19678. 581p. 1982. 55.00 (ISBN 0-471-04887-9, Pub. by Wiley Med). Wiley.

DeVries, Rheta, jt. auth. see Kamii, Constance.

De Vries, Tom. On the Meaning & Future of the European Monetary System. LC 80-20510. (Essays in International Finance Ser.: No. 138). 1980. pap. text ed. 2.50x (ISBN 0-88165-045-5). Princeton U Int Finan Econ.

De Vries, W. R. & Dornfield, D. A., eds. Inspection & Quality Control in Manufacturing Systems. (PED Ser.: Vol. 6). 1982. 24.00 (H00249). ASME.

Devsis Study Team. Devsis: The Preliminary Design of an International Information System for the Development Sciences. 247p. 1976. pap. 13.00 (ISBN 0-88936-084-7, IDRC65, IDRC). Unipub.

De Vylder, Stephan. Agriculture in Chains: A Case Study in Contradictions & Constraints. 192p. 1981. 25.00 (ISBN 0-86232-041-0, Pub. by Zed Pr England). Lawrence Hill.

Dew, Desmond. Let's Try It This Way. 1983. 13.95 (ISBN 0-533-05383-8). Vantage.

Dew, Donald & Jensen, Alfred D. Phonetic Transcription. 2nd ed. 1979. text ed. 9.95 (ISBN 0-675-08309-5). Additional supplements may be obtained from publisher. Merrill.

Dew, Thomas R. Lectures on the Restrictive System. LC 68-55701. Repr. of 1829 ed. 25.00x (ISBN 0-678-00441-2). Kelley.

De Waal, Frans. Chimpanzee Politics: Power & Sex among Apes. Milnes, Janet, tr. from Dutch. LC 82-48115. (Illus.). 224p. 1983. 15.86i (ISBN 0-06-015113-7, HarpT). Har-Row.

De Waal, Hugo, tr. see Faber, Heije.

De Waal, M. Medicinal Herbs in the Bible. Meijlink, Jane, ed. 96p. Date not set. pap. write for info. (ISBN 0-87728-527-6). Weiser.

DeWaard, E. John & Klein, Aaron E. Electric Cars. LC 74-18790. (gr. 6-9). PLB 8.95 (ISBN 0-385-08143-X). Doubleday.

De Waard, J. & Nida, E. A. Translator's Handbook on the Book of Ruth. (Helps for Translators Ser.). 1976. Repr. of 1973 ed. softcover 2.60x (ISBN 0-8267-0107-8, 08518). United Bible.

De Waard, J. & Smalley, W. A. Translator's Handbook on the Book of Amos. (Helps for Translators Ser.). 1981. Repr. of 1979 ed. softcover 2.50x (ISBN 0-8267-0128-0, 08577). United Bible.

De Waard, Jan, jt. auth. see Borg, Albert J.

DeWalle. Groundwater Management & Its Public Health Aspects. 250p. 1983. 27.50 (ISBN 0-250-40530-X). Ann Arbor Science.

De Walt, B. R. Modernization in a Mexican Ejido. LC 78-3412. (Latin American Studies: No. 33). (Illus.). 1979. 37.50 (ISBN 0-521-22064-5). Cambridge U Pr.

Dewan, M. L. Agriculture & Rural Development in India: A Case Study on the Dignity of Labour. 240p. 1982. text ed. 16.25x (ISBN 0-391-02722-0, Pub. by Concept). Humanities.

Dewan, Shashi & Straughen, Alan. Power Semiconductor Circuits. LC 75-8911. 523p. 1975. 38.50 (ISBN 0-471-21180-X, Pub. by Wiley-Interscience). Wiley.

Dewan, Wilfred F. Catholic Belief & Practice in an Ecumenical Age. 1966. pap. 1.95 (ISBN 0-8091-1510-7). Paulist Pr.

Dewar, A. J., jt. auth. see Russell, W. Ritchie.

Dewar, Darrell. Fundamental Math Workbooks & Answer Key. (Illus.). (gr. 7-12). 1972. wkbk. pt. 1 7.95 (ISBN 0-88499-043-5). wkbk. pt. 2 7.95 (ISBN 0-88499-044-3). Inst Mod Lang.

Dewar, Donald L. Circulo de Calidad Manual del Miembro. (Illus.). 246p. (Orig., Span.). 1981. pap. 10.00 (ISBN 0-937670-08-1). Quality Circle.

--Control Charts No. 1: Leader Manual & Instructional Guide. (Illus.). 43p. (Orig.). 1982. pap. 12.00 (ISBN 0-937670-20-0). Quality Circle.

--Control Charts No. 1: Member Manual. (Illus.). 43p. (Orig.). 1982. pap. 12.00 (ISBN 0-937670-25-1). Quality Circle.

--Control Charts No. 2: Leader Manual & Instructional Guide. (Illus.). 43p. 1982. pap. 12.00 (ISBN 0-937670-21-9). Quality Circle.

--Control Charts No. 2: Member Manual. (Illus.). 58p. 1982. pap. 12.00 (ISBN 0-937670-26-X). Quality Circle.

--Histograms: Leader Manual & Instructional Guide. (Illus.). 50p. (Orig.). 1982. pap. 12.00 (ISBN 0-937670-19-7). Quality Circle.

--Histograms: Member Manual. (Illus.). 50p. 1982. pap. 12.00 (ISBN 0-937670-24-3). Quality Circle.

--Quality Circle Member Manual. (Quality Circle Handbook & Quality Circle Leader Manual & Instructional Guide Ser.). (Illus.). 268p. (Orig.). 1980. pap. 10.00 (ISBN 0-937670-01-4). Quality Circle.

--Quality Circle Member Manual for Financial Institutions. 3rd ed. (Illus.). 268p. 1982. pap. 10.00 (ISBN 0-937670-13-8). Quality Circle.

--Quality Circle Member Manual for Medical Facilities. 2nd ed. (Illus.). 268p. (Orig.). 1982. pap. 10.00 (ISBN 0-937670-05-7). Quality Circle.

--The Quality Circle: What You Should Know About It. (Illus.). 29p. 1980. pap. 0.75 (ISBN 0-937670-04-9). Quality Circle.

--Scatter Diagrams: Leader Manual & Instructional Guide. (Illus.). 58p. 1982. pap. 12.00 (ISBN 0-937670-22-7). Quality Circle.

--Scatter Diagrams: Member Manual. (Illus.). 58p. 1982. pap. 12.00 (ISBN 0-937670-27-8). Quality Circle.

--Stratification: Leader Manual & Instructional Guide. (Illus.). 42p. (Orig.). 1982. pap. 12.00 (ISBN 0-937670-18-9). Quality Circle.

--Stratification: Member Manual. (Illus.). 42p. (Orig.). 1982. pap. 12.00 (ISBN 0-937670-23-5). Quality Circle.

Dewar, M. J., et al, eds. Radicals in Biochemistry. (Topics in Current Chemistry Ser.: Vol. 108). (Illus.). 140p. 1983. 28.00 (ISBN 0-686-43338-6). Springer-Verlag.

--Synthetic & Structural Problems. (Topics in Current Chemistry Ser.: Vol. 106). (Illus.). 170p. 1982. 39.00 (ISBN 0-387-11766-0). Springer-Verlag.

--Wittig Chemistry: Dedicated to Professor Dr. G. Wittig. (Topics in Current Chemistry Ser.: Vol. 109). (Illus.). 220p. 1983. 43.50 (ISBN 0-387-11907-8). Springer-Verlag.

Dewar, Margaret. Industry in Trouble: The Federal Government & the New England Fisheries. LC 82-10748. 244p. 1983. text ed. 29.95 (ISBN 0-87722-283-5). Temple U Pr.

Dewar, Mary, ed. see Smith, Thomas.

Dewar, Michael J. Molecular Orbital Theory of Organic Chemistry. LC 68-21840. (Advanced Chemistry Ser). (Illus.). 1968. text ed. 24.00 o.p. (ISBN 0-07-016637-4, C). McGraw.

Dewayne, Donald F., ed. The Best Critical Studies of the Review of Philosophy & the Theory of the Soul. (Major Currents in Contemporary World History Library). (Illus.). 1981. 49.75 o.p. (ISBN 0-89266-304-9). Am Classical Coll Pr.

Dewdney, J. C., jt. auth. see Symons, Leslie.

Dewdney, John C. The U.S.S.R. LC 76-16744. (Westview Special Studies in Industrial Geography). (Illus.). 1976. lib. bdg. 30.00 o.p. (ISBN 0-89158-616-4). Westview.

DeWeerd, H. A., ed. see Marshall, George C.

Dewees, D. N., et al. Economic Analysis of Environmental Policies. LC 75-38798. (Ontario Economic Council Research Studies). 1975. pap. 8.50 (ISBN 0-8020-3335-0). U of Toronto Pr.

Dewees, Donald N. Economics & Public Policy: The Automobile Pollution Case. 208p. 1974. 25.00x (ISBN 0-262-04043-3). MIT Pr.

DeWeese, Gene. Adventures of a Two-Minute Werewolf. LC 82-45285. (Illus.). 120p. (gr. 5-8). 1983. 9.95a (ISBN 0-385-17453-5). Doubleday.

--Nightmares from Space. (Triumph Books Ser.). (Illus.). 96p. (gr. 7up). 1981. lib. bdg. 8.90 (ISBN 0-531-04338-X). Watts.

DeWeese, Jean. The Backhoe Gothic. LC 80-1670. (Romantic Suspense Ser.). 192p. 1981. 10.95 o.p. (ISBN 0-385-12099-0). Doubleday.

DeWeid. Hormones & the Brain. 352p. 1981. text ed. 39.50 (ISBN 0-8391-1645-4). Univ Park.

DeWein, Sibyl & Ashabraner, Joan. The Collector's Encyclopedia of Barbie Dolls & Collectibles. (Illus.). 1977. 17.95 o.p. (ISBN 0-517-53172-0). Crown.

DeWelt, Don. Leviticus. LC 75-328945. (The Bible Study Textbook Ser.). (Illus.). 1975. 14.30 o.s.i. (ISBN 0-89900-007-X). College Pr Pub.

--Nine Lessons on the Holy Spirit. 187p. 1978. 3.95 (ISBN 0-89900-116-5). College Pr Pub.

--The Power of the Holy Spirit, Vol. III. 1972. pap. 3.95 (ISBN 0-89900-125-4). College Pr Pub.

--Prayer Time: A Guide to Daily Worship. LC 81-82986. 736p. 1982. pap. 21.95 (ISBN 0-89900-146-7). College Pr Pub.

DeWelt, Don, jt. auth. see Johnson, B. W.

DeWelt, Don, jt. auth. see Kidwell, R. J.

D'Ewes, Simonds. Journal of Sir Simonds D'Ewes From the First Recess of the Long Parliament to the Withdrawal of King Charles From London. Coates, Willson H., ed. 1942. text ed. 24.50x (ISBN 0-686-83599-9). Elliots Bks.

DeWesse, David F. & Saunders, William H. Textbook of Otolaryngology. 6th ed. LC 81-14162. (Illus.). 495p. 1982. text ed. 33.95 (ISBN 0-8016-1273-X). Mosby.

De Wetering, Janwillen Van see Van de Wetering, Janwillen.

Dewey, Ariane, ed. & illus. Pecos Bill. LC 82-9229. (Illus.). 56p. (gr. k-3). 1983. 9.00 (ISBN 0-688-01410-0); PLB 8.59 (ISBN 0-688-01412-7). Greenwillow.

Dewey, Edward R. & Mandino, Og. Cycles: The Mysterious Forces That Trigger Events. 1976. pap. 5.95 (ISBN 0-8015-1880-6, Hawthorn). Dutton.

Dewey, Joanna. Markan Public Debate: Literary Technique, Concentric Structure & Theology in Mark 2: 1-3: 6. LC 79-17443. (Society of Biblical Literature Ser.: No. 48). 14.95 (ISBN 0-89130-337-5, 06-01-48); pap. 9.95 (ISBN 0-89130-338-3). Scholars Pr CA.

Dewey, John. The Early Works of John Dewey, 1882-1898, 5 vols. MLA-CEAA textual ed. Boydston, Jo Ann, ed. Incl. Vol. 1 (1882-1888): Collected Essays & Leibniz's New Essays Concerning the Human Understanding. Hahn, Lewis E., intro. by. 493p. 1969. 17.50x (ISBN 0-8093-0349-3); pap. 7.95 (ISBN 0-8093-0722-7); Vol. 2 (1887): Psychology. Schneider, Herbert W., intro. by. 420p. 1967. 19.95x (ISBN 0-8093-0282-9); pap. 6.95 (ISBN 0-8093-0723-5); Vol. 3 (1889-1892): Collected Essays & Outline of a Critical Theory of Ethics. Eames, S. Morris, intro. by. 495p. 1969. 17.50x (ISBN 0-8093-0402-3); pap. 7.95 (ISBN 0-8093-0724-3); Vol. 4 (1893-1894): Collected Essays & the Study of Ethics. Leys, Wayne A., intro. by. 463p. 1971. 17.50x (ISBN 0-8093-0496-1); pap. 7.95 (ISBN 0-8093-0725-1); Vol. 5 (1895-1898): Collected Essays. McKenzie, William R., intro. by. 670p. 1972. 18.95x (ISBN 0-8093-0540-2); pap. 8.95 (ISBN 0-8093-0726-X). LC 67-13938. S Ill U Pr.

--Experience & Nature. 1929. pap. 6.95 (ISBN 0-486-20471-5). Dover.

--Experience & Nature. rev. ed. (Paul Carus Lectures Ser.). 380p. 1925. 24.00 (ISBN 0-87548-096-9); pap. 10.00 (ISBN 0-87548-097-7). Open Court.

--How We Think: A Restatement of the Relation of Reflective Thinking to the Educative Process. 1933. text ed. 15.95x (ISBN 0-669-20024-7). Heath.

--Human Nature & Conduct. 5.95 (ISBN 0-394-60439-3). Modern Lib.

--John Dewey: His Contribution to the American Tradition. Edman, Irwin, ed. LC 68-21327. 1968. Repr. of 1955 ed. lib. bdg. 18.75x (ISBN 0-8371-0404-1, EDCT). Greenwood.

--Lectures in China, 1919-1920. Clopton, Robert W. & Ou, Tsuin-chen, trs. from Chinese. 300p. 1973. 16.00x (ISBN 0-8248-0212-8, Eastwest Ctr). UH Pr.

--Middle Works, Eighteen Ninety-Nine to Nineteen Twenty-Four, Vols. 13-15. Incl. Vol. 13. 30.00x (ISBN 0-8093-1083-X); Vol. 14. 22.50x (ISBN 0-8093-1084-8); Vol. 15. 25.00x (ISBN 0-8093-1085-6). LC 76-7231. 1983. S Ill U Pr.

--The Middle Works of John Dewey, Eighteen Ninety-Nine to Nineteen Twenty-Four, Vol. 12: 1920. Boydson, Jo Ann, intro. by. LC 76-7231. 320p. 1982. 22.50x (ISBN 0-8093-1004-X). S Ill U Pr.

--The Middle Works of John Dewey, Eighteen Ninety-Nine to Nineteen Twenty-Four, Vol. 11: 1918-1919. Boydston, Jo Ann, intro. by. LC 76-7231. 448p. 1982. 25.00x (ISBN 0-8093-1003-1). S Ill U Pr.

--The Middle Works of John Dewey, 1899-1924, Vols. 1-12. MLA-CEAA textual ed. Boydston, Jo Ann, ed. Incl. Vol. 1 (1899-1901): Collected Articles & "The School & Society" & "The Educational Situation". Burnett, Joe R., intro. by. 480p. 1976. 19.95x (ISBN 0-8093-0753-7); Vol. 2 (1902-1903): Collected Articles & "Studies in Logical Theory" & "The Child & the Curiculum". Hook, Sidney, intro. by. 471p. 1976. 19.95x (ISBN 0-8093-0754-5); Vol. 3 (1903-1906): Collected Articles. Baysinger, Patricia R., ed. 1977. 19.95x (ISBN 0-8093-0775-8); Vol. 5 (1908): "Ethics". Stevenson, Charles L. 1978. 24.95x (ISBN 0-8093-0834-7); Vol. 6 (1910-1911): Collected Essays & "The Problem of Truth". Thayer, H. S. 652p. 1978. 24.95x (ISBN 0-8093-0835-5); Vol. 7. Interest & Effort in Education. Ross, Ralph, intro. by. 575p. 1979. 24.95x (ISBN 0-8093-0881-9); Vol. 8. German Philosophy & Politics & Schools of Tomorrow. 582p. 24.95x (ISBN 0-8093-0882-7); Vol. 9. Democracy & Education. 426p. 1980. 19.95x (ISBN 0-8093-0933-5); Vol. 10. Collected Writings. 1980. 24.95x (ISBN 0-8093-0934-3). LC 76-7231. S Ill U Pr.

--Problems of Men. LC 68-19266. 1968. Repr. of 1946 ed. lib. bdg. 29.75x (ISBN 0-8371-0382-7, DEPM). Greenwood.

--Public & Its Problems. LC 82-71751. 236p. 1954. pap. 5.95x (ISBN 0-8040-0254-1). Swallow.

--The Thinking Mechanisms of the Human Intellect & How to Develop Them Successfully. (An Intimate Life of Man Library Book). (Illus.). 143p. 1982. 67.85 (ISBN 0-89920-047-8). Am Inst Psych.

Dewey, John & Kallen, Horace M. The Bertrand Russell Case. LC 78-37289. (Civil Liberties in American History Ser). 228p. 1972. Repr. of 1941 ed. lib. bdg. 29.00 (ISBN 0-306-70426-9). Da Capo.

Dewey, Kenneth, jt. auth. see Selsam, Millicent.

Dewey, Melvil. Dewey Decimal Classification & Relative Index. 10th & abr. ed. LC 70-164427. 1971. 18.00x (ISBN 0-910608-13-X). Forest Pr.

--Dewey Decimal Classification & Relative Index, 3 vols. 18th ed. Incl. Vol. 1. Introduction & Tables. 15.00 o.p. (ISBN 0-910608-10-5); Vol. 2. Schedules. 15.00 o.p. (ISBN 0-910608-10-5); Vol. 3. Index. 15.00 o.p. (ISBN 0-910608-11-3). LC 78-140002. (Illus.). 2692p. 1971. Set. 60.00 o.p. (ISBN 0-685-26876-4). Forest Pr.

Dewey, Robert E. & Gould, James A. Freedom: Its History, Nature & Varieties. 1970. pap. text ed. 13.95x (ISBN 0-02-329500-7, 32950). Macmillan.

Dewey, Robert E. & Hurlbutt, Robert H. Introduction to Ethics. 1977. 20.95x (ISBN 0-02-329480-9, 32948). Macmillan.

De Weydenthal, Jan B. The Communists of Poland: An Historical Outline. Staar, Richard F., ed. LC 78-59465. (Publications Ser.: No. 202). (Illus.). 236p. 1979. pap. 8.95 o.p. (ISBN 0-8179-7022-3). Hoover Inst Pr.

De Wheat, Gaye, jt. auth. see Wheat, Ed.

Dew-Hughes, D., jt. auth. see Wyatt, Oliver H.

Dewhurst, Eileen. Drink This. LC 80-2320. 192p. 1981. 10.95 o.p. (ISBN 0-385-17457-8). Doubleday.

--Whoever I Am. LC 82-45102. (Crime Club Ser.). 192p. 1983. 11.95 o.p. (ISBN 0-385-18185-X). Doubleday.

Dewhurst, Jack. Royal Confinements. 198p. 1981. 12.95 o.p. (ISBN 0-312-69466-0). St Martin.

Dewhurst, Kenneth. Dr. Thomas Sydenham (1624-1689) His Life & Original Writings. LC 66-19348. (Wellcome Institute of the History of Medicine). 1966. 29.50x (ISBN 0-520-00320-9). U of Cal Pr.

Dewhurst, Kenneth & Reeves, Nigel. Friedrich Schiller-Medicine, Psychology, & Literature: With the First English Edition of His Complete Medical & Psychological Writings. LC 76-14308. 1978. 39.95x (ISBN 0-520-03250-0). U of Cal Pr.

De Wiest, Roger J. M., jt. auth. see Davis, Stanley N.

DeWilde, Marc. Closed Graph Theorems & Webbed Spaces. (Research Notes in Mathematics Ser.: No. 19). 158p. (Orig.). 1978. pap. text ed. 19.95 (ISBN 0-273-08403-8). Pitman Pub MA.

De Wilde, P., jt. auth. see Boite, R.

De Wildemann, E. see Wildemann, E. De.

Dewine, Sue, jt. auth. see Phelps, Lynn.

DeWine, Sue, jt. auth. see Tortoriello, Thomas R.

Dewing, Rolland. Wounded Knee: The Impact & Signifigance of the Second Incident. 225p. 1983. 18.95x (ISBN 0-8290-1290-7). Irvington.

De Winter, Francis, ed. Readings in National Energy Policy: Supplement to Progress in Solar Energy, Vol. 5. (Special Publications Ser.). 1982. pap. text ed. 10.00 (ISBN 0-89553-048-1). Am Solar Energy.

De Winter, Francis, ed. see Bereny, Justin A.

De Winter, Francis, jt. ed. see Clark, Elizabeth F.

De Winton, Dorothy see Winton, Dorothy de.

Dewire, Robert, jt. auth. see Russo, Monica.

De Wispelaere, C., ed. Air Pollution Modeling & Its Application: Part 2. (NATO-Challenges of Modern Society: Vol. 3). 855p. 1983. 95.00x (ISBN 0-306-41115-6, Plenum Pr). Plenum Pub.

De Wit, Augusta. Island India. 1923. 39.50x (ISBN 0-686-51407-6). Elliots Bks.

DeWit, C. T., et al. Simulation of Assimilation, Respiration & Transpiration of Crops. LC 78-11384. 1978. pap. 22.95x o.s.i. (ISBN 0-470-26494-2). Halsted Pr.

De Wit, Dorothy. Children's Faces Looking up: Program Building for the Storyteller. LC 78-10702. 1979. 15.00 (ISBN 0-8389-0272-3). ALA.

De Wit, Toke. Epiphytic Lichens & Air Pollution in the Netherlands. 1974. 24.00 (ISBN 3-7682-1059-6). Lubrecht & Cramer.

DeWitt, C. & Peyraud, J., eds. Les Houches Lectures: 1972, Plasma Physics. new ed. 556p. 1975. 104.00x (ISBN 0-677-15740-1). Gordon.

Dewitt, David. Answering the Tough Ones. 160p. 1980. pap. 5.95 (ISBN 0-8024-8971-0). Moody.

--Beyond the Basics. 1983. pap. 5.95 (ISBN 0-8024-0178-3). Moody.

DeWitt, David P., ed. see Incropera, Frank P.

Dewitt, Edith. Bridal Path. LC 81-81944. (Illus.). 192p. 1983. 16.95 (ISBN 0-86666-039-9). GWP.

DeWitt, Howard A. Van Morrison: The Mystic's Music. (Illus.). 160p. (Orig.). 1983. pap. 12.95 (ISBN 0-686-83848-3). Horizon Bks CA.

DeWitt, Howard A. & Kirshner, Alan M. In the Course of Human Events: American Government. 296p. 1982. pap. text ed. 17.95 (ISBN 0-8403-2844-3). Kendall-Hunt.

De Witt, Johanna. The Littlest Reindeer. (Illus.). 32p. (gr. k-3). 1979. PLB 9.25 o.p. (ISBN 0-516-03534-7). Childrens.

Dewitt, Norman J., et al. College Latin. 1954. text ed. 18.95x (ISBN 0-673-05105-6). Scott F.

Dewitt, Sherri. Worker Participation & the Crisis of Liberal Democracy. (Westview Replica Edition Ser.). 150p. 1980. lib. bdg. 22.00 (ISBN 0-89158-922-8). Westview.

De Witt, Thomas E., tr. see Steinert, Marlis G.

Dewjee, Audrey, ed. see Seacole, Mary.

DeWolf, Gordon. Flora Exotica. LC 72-190443. (Illus.). 1978. pap. 7.95 (ISBN 0-87923-257-9); ltd. edition 35.00; 17.50. Godine.

DeWolf, L. Harold. Eternal Life: Why We Believe. LC 79-21670. 1980. pap. 6.95 (ISBN 0-664-24288-X). Westminster.

Dewolf, William F. A Competency-Based Instructional Module in Art Criticism: Task Analysis & Assessment Procedures. 47p. 1977. pap. text ed. 7.00 (ISBN 0-8191-0250-4). U Pr of Amer.

DeWoskin, Kenneth J. A Song for One or Two: Music & the Concept of Art in Early China. LC 81-19519. (Michigan Papers in Chinese Studies: No. 42). (Illus.). 216p. (Orig.). 1982. pap. 6.00x (ISBN 0-89264-042-1); pap. text ed. 6.00x (ISBN 0-686-96905-7). U of Mich Ctr Chinese.

Dews, Peter B., jt. ed. see Thompson, Travis.

Dews, Robert P. Early Joel. 2nd ed. 1982. 6.00x (ISBN 0-940184-03-6). R P Dews.

Dewsbury, Donald A. Comparative Animal Behavior. (Illus.). 1978. text ed. 28.95 (ISBN 0-07-016673-0, C). McGraw.

Dewsbury, Donald A., ed. Mammalian Sexual Behavior: Foundations for Contemporary Research. LC 81-6231. (Benchmark Papers in Behavior Ser.: Vol. 15). 382p. 1981. 48.00 (ISBN 0-87933-396-0). Hutchinson Ross.

De Wulf, Lucienne. Faces of Venus: Prostitution Through the Ages. LC 79-55796. 225p. Date not set. 14.95 (ISBN 0-916728-31-5). Bks in Focus.

De Wyzewa, T. & De Saint-Foix, G. Mozart W. A. Sa Vie Musicale & Son Oeuvre, 2 vols. (Music Reprint Ser.). 2274p. 1980. Repr. of 1936 ed. Set. lib. bdg. 110.00 (ISBN 0-306-79561-2). Da Capo.

Dexeus, Santiago, Jr., et al. Colposcopy. Austin, Karl L., tr. from Span. LC 74-177752. (Major Problems in Obstetrics & Gynecology: Vol. 10). (Illus.). 1977. text ed. 28.00 (ISBN 0-7216-3050-2). Saunders.

Dexter, Catherine. Gertie's Green Thumb. LC 82-21664. (Illus.). 128p. (gr. 4-7). 1983. 8.95 (ISBN 0-02-730200-8). Macmillan.

Dexter, Dave. Jazz Story: From the Nineties to the Sixties. (Illus., Orig.). (gr. 8-10). 1964. pap. 2.95 o.p. (ISBN 0-13-509463-1, Spec). P-H.

Dexter, Dave, Jr. Jazz Cavalcade. LC 77-8035. (Roots of Jazz Ser.). (Illus.). 1977. Repr. of 1946 ed. lib. bdg. 25.00 (ISBN 0-306-77431-3). Da Capo.

Dexter, Franklin B. Biographical Sketches of the Graduates of Yale College, with Annals of the College History, Seventeen Hundred One to Eighteen Fifteen, 6 vols. (Two vols. are unbound). 1912. Set. 450.00x (ISBN 0-686-51346-0). Elliots Bks.

--Sketch of the History of Yale University. 1887. 29.50x (ISBN 0-685-89783-4). Elliots Bks.

Dexter, Lincoln A., ed. Maps of Early Massachusetts. LC 79-51535. (Illus.). 1979. text ed. 11.00x o.s.i. (ISBN 0-9601210-7-2); pap. text ed. 6.50x (ISBN 0-9601210-6-4). L A Dexter.

Dexter, R. F., tr. see Daval, Jean-Luc.

Dexter, Stephen C. Handbook of Oceanographic Engineering Materials. LC 78-26196. (Ocean Engineering Ser.). 1979. 42.95 (ISBN 0-471-04950-6, Pub. by Wiley-Interscience). Wiley.

Dey, Charmaine. The Magic Candle. 64p. 1982. pap. 3.50 (ISBN 0-942272-00-5). Original Pubns.

Dey, Joseph C., Jr., ed. Golf Rules in Pictures. Rev. ed. (Illus.). 104p. 1982. pap. 4.95 (ISBN 0-448-01360-6, G&D). Putnam Pub Group.

Dey, Mukul K. Methods of Experimental Psychology. LC 79-66485. 1979. pap. text ed. 9.25 (ISBN 0-8191-0818-9). U Pr of Amer.

Dey, S. K. Destination Man: Towards a New World. 1982. 40.00x (ISBN 0-686-94084-9, Pub. by Garlandfold England). State Mutual Bk.

Deyl, Z. & Kopecky, J. Bibliography of Column Liquid Chromatography 1971-1973, & Survey of Applications, Vol. 6. (Journal of Chromatography Supplement). 1977. 110.25 (ISBN 0-444-41469-X). Elsevier.

Deyl, Z. & Crambach, A., eds. Electrophoresis: Pt. B-Applications. (Journal of Chromatography Library: Vol. 18). 462p. 1983. 95.75 (ISBN 0-444-42114-9). Elsevier.

Deyl, Z., et al. Bibliography of Column Chromatography, 1967-1970, & Survey of Applications. 1973. 88.00 (ISBN 0-444-41008-2). Elsevier.

--Bibliography of Electrophoresis, 1968-1972, & Survey of Applications, Vol. 4. (Journal of Chromatography Ser.). 1976. 85.00 (ISBN 0-444-41225-5). Elsevier.

--Electrophoresis: Pt. A. Everaerts, E. M., ed. (Journal of Chromatography Library: Vol. 18). 1980. 85.00 (ISBN 0-444-41721-4). Elsevier.

Deyl, Z., et al, eds. Liquid Column Chromatography: A Survey of Modern Techniques & Applications. (Journal of Chromatography Library: Vol. 3). 1176p. 1975. 138.50 (ISBN 0-444-41156-9). Elsevier.

Deyoung, Carol & Glittenberg, Jody. Out of Uniform & Into Trouble Again. LC 82-62400. 120p. 1983. Repr. 16.00 (ISBN 0-913590-98-3). Slack Inc.

DeYoung, Donald B., jt. auth. see Whitcomb, John C.

De Young, Garry. The Meaning of Christianity. 96p. 1982. text ed. 9.95x ten or more bks. (ISBN 0-686-81748-6); pap. 7.95x (ISBN 0-686-81749-4); tchrs' ed. 7.95 (ISBN 0-686-81750-8). De Young Pr.

De Young, Gary. Pocket Gopher & Other Poems from the Gopher State. (Illus.). 31p. Date not set. pap. 1.50 (ISBN 0-686-43167-7). De Young Pr.

De Young, Karen, compiled by. Trade & Professional Associations in California: A Directory. 2nd ed. LC 81-12274. (California Information Guides Ser.). 75p. (Orig.). 1982. pap. 20.00x (ISBN 0-912102-57-8). Cal Inst Public.

DeYoung, Lillian. Dynamics of Nursing. 4th ed. LC 80-29477. (Illus.). 235p. 1981. pap. text ed. 16.95 (ISBN 0-8016-1283-7). Mosby.

De Young, Mary. The Sexual Victimization of Children. LC 82-17197. 190p. 1982. lib. bdg. 18.95x (ISBN 0-89950-063-3). McFarland & Co.

Deyries, Bernard, et al. The Story of Music in Cartoon. LC 82-1817. (Illus.). 144p. 1982. 12.95 (ISBN 0-668-05592-8, 5592). Arco.

Deza, M. & Rosenberg, I. G., eds. Combinatorics 79, 2 Pts. (Annals of Discrete Mathematics: Vols. 8 & 9). 1981. Set. 115.00 (ISBN 0-444-86112-2); Pt. 1. 68.00 (ISBN 0-444-86110-6); Pt. 2. 68.00 (ISBN 0-444-86111-4). Elsevier.

De Zayas, Zoila. Desarrollando Destrezas en Preparacion Para el Examen Equivalencia de Escuela Superior en Espanol: Mathematicas: Developing Skills in Math for High School Equivalency Test in Spanish. (Span.). (gr. 10-12). Date not set. pap. text ed. 3.75 (ISBN 0-8120-0560-0). Barron.

Dezettel, Louis M. Home Electrical Improvements. (Audel Mini Guide Ser.). 1975. pap. 0.99 o.p. (ISBN 0-672-23823-3). Audel.

De Zirkoff, Boris. The Dream That Never Dies: Boris de Zirkoff Speaks Out on Theosophy. Small, W. Emmett, ed. (Illus.). 242p. 1983. pap. 11.50 lexitone (ISBN 0-913004-45-6). Point Loma Pub.

De Zirkoff, Boris, ed. see Blavatsky, H. P.

De Zirkoff, Boris, ed. see Blavatsky, Helena P.

De Zoete, Beryl. Dance & Magic Drama in Ceylon. (Illus.). 1957. 6.95 o.s.i. (ISBN 0-87830-032-5). Theatre Arts.

De Zoete, Beryl, tr. see Moravia, Alberto.

DeZoete, Beryl, tr. see Schmitz, Ettore.

Dezso, L. & Hajdu, P., eds. Theoretical Problems of Typology & the Northern Eurasian Languages. 184p. 1970. text ed. 34.25x o.p. (ISBN 0-685-75720-X). Humanities.

Dezso, Laszlo, ed. Contrastive Studies Hungarian-English. 122p. (Orig.). 1982. pap. 7.50x (ISBN 963-05-2719-7). Intl Pubns Serv.

D'Haen, Theo. A Communicative Approach to Fowles, Barth, Cortazar & Boon: Text to Reader. 160p. 1983. 30.00 (ISBN 90-272-2191-X); pap. 20.00 (ISBN 90-272-2201-0). Benjamins North Am.

--Text to Reader: A Communicative Approach to Fowles, Barth, Cortazar & Boon. (Utrecht Publications in Comparative Literature: 16). 160p. 1983. 30.00 (ISBN 90-272-2191-X); pap. 20.00 (ISBN 90-272-2201-0). Benjamins North Am.

D'Ham, Claude. Sport. (Moment Ser.). 20p. (Orig.). 1975. pap. 2.00 (ISBN 0-85953-035-3, Pub. by Child's Play England). Playspaces.

D'Ham, Claude, illus. On the Farm. (Moments Ser.). (Illus., Orig.). 1975. pap. 2.00 (ISBN 0-85953-036-1, Pub. by Child's Play England). Playspaces.

--The Weather. (Moments Ser.). (Illus., Orig.). 1975. pap. 2.00 (ISBN 0-85953-037-X, Pub. by Child's Play England). Playspaces.

Dhames, Dudley. On Your Feet. 8.50x (ISBN 0-392-06109-0, SpS). Sportshelf.

Dhanda, Leila. Bonsai Culture. 141p. 1980. 40.00x (ISBN 0-686-84448-3, Pub. by Oxford & I B H India). State Mutual Bk.

Dhanji, Farid. El Salvador: Demographic Issues & Prospects. ii, 69p. 1979. pap. 20.00 (ISBN 0-686-36106-7, RC-7910). World Bank.

Dhar, D. N. The Chemistry of Chalcones & Related Compounds. LC 80-39560. 285p. 1981. 43.50 (ISBN 0-471-08007-1, Pub. by Wiley-Interscience). Wiley.

Dhar, R. N. Computer Aided Power System Operation & Analysis. (Illus.). 320p. 1983. 29.95 (ISBN 0-07-451580-2, P&RB). McGraw.

D'Harnoncourt, Everard, tr. see Arrabal, Fernando.

Dhasmana, M. M. The Ramos of Arunachal. 1980. text ed. 17.25x (ISBN 0-391-01827-2). Humanities.

Dhawan, B. N., ed. see Satellite Symposium International Congress of Pharmacology, Lucknow, India 8th, July 1981.

Dhiegh, Khigh A. The Eleventh Wing. 1974. pap. 3.25 o.s.i. (ISBN 0-440-53252-3, Delta). Dell.

Dhillion, B. Reliabiltiy Engineering in Systems Design & Operation. 336p. 1982. 37.50 (ISBN 0-442-27213-8). Van Nos Reinhold.

Dhillon, Balbir S. Power System Reliability, Safety & Management. LC 82-72852. (Illus.). 350p. 1983. 39.95 (ISBN 0-250-40548-2). Ann Arbor Science.

Dhillon, Sukhraj S. Health, Happiness & Longevity Eastern & Western Approach. (Illus.). 224p. (Orig.). 1983. pap. 12.95 (ISBN 0-87040-527-6). Kodansha.

Dhir, K. K. Ferns of the Northwestern Himalayas. (Bibliotheca Pteridologica 1). (Illus.). 1979. pap. text ed. 16.00x (ISBN 3-7682-1222-X). Lubrecht & Cramer.

Dhir, K. K. & Sood, A. Fern Flora of Mussoorie Hills. (Bibliotheca Pteridologica 2). (Illus.). 1981. pap. text ed. 16.00x (ISBN 3-7682-1232-7). Lubrecht & Cramer.

Dhiravamsa. The Dynamic Way of Meditation. 160p. 1983. pap. 8.95 (ISBN 0-85500-163-1). Newcastle Pub.

--The Dynamic Way of Meditation: The Release & Cure of Pain & Suffering Through Vipassana Meditative Techniques. 160p. (Orig.). 1983. pap. 7.95 (ISBN 0-85500-163-1, Pub. by Thorsons Pubs England). Sterling.

--The Way of Non-Attachment: The Practice of Insight Meditation. LC 76-48761. 1977. 6.95 o.p. (ISBN 0-8052-3644-9). Schocken.

Dhokalia, R. P. The Codification of Public International Law. LC 66-11927. 367p. 1970. 22.50 (ISBN 0-379-00264-7). Oceana.

Dhonte, Pierre. Clockwork Debt: Trade & the External Debt of Developing Countries. LC 79-1753. 144p. 1979. 18.95x (ISBN 0-669-02925-4). Lexington Bks.

Dhrymes, P. J. Distributed Lags: Problems of Estimation & Formulation. (Advanced Textbooks in Economics: Vol. 14). 1981. 31.75 (ISBN 0-444-86013-4). Elsevier.

--Distributed Lags: Problems of Estimation & Formulation. Rev. ed. 1981. 32.00 (ISBN 0-444-86013-4). Elsevier.

D'Hulst, R. A. Jacob Jordaens. LC 82-70747. (Illus.). 1982. 95.00x (ISBN 0-8014-1519-5). Cornell U Pr.

Diabelli, Anton, et al. The Diabelli Variations: Variations on a Theme by Fifty Composers & Virtuosos. 1977. pap. write for info (ISBN 0-912028-09-2). Music Treasure.

Diagram Group. The Brain: A User's Manual. LC 81-17942. (Illus.). 191p. 1982. 14.95 (ISBN 0-686-83014-8, Coward). Putnam Pub Group.

--The Brain: A User's Manual. (Illus.). 192p. 1982. pap. 7.95 (ISBN 0-399-50622-5, Perige). Putnam Pub Group.

--Crossword Puzzles: How to Make Your Own. 160p. 1982. pap. 7.95 (ISBN 0-312-17689-9). St Martin.

--The Healthy Body: A Maintenance Manual. 1981. pap. 8.95 (ISBN 0-452-25352-7, Z5352, Plume). NAL.

--The Healthy Body: A Maintenance Manual. (Medical Library). (Illus.). 192p. 1982. pap. 8.95 (ISBN 0-452-25352-7, 1293-4). Mosby.

--Logic Puzzles. 96p. 1983. pap. 1.75 (ISBN 0-345-30478-0). Ballantine.

--Maze Puzzles. 96p. (Orig.). 1983. pap. 1.75 (ISBN 0-345-30477-2). Ballantine.

--Picture Puzzles. 96p. (Orig.). 1983. pap. 1.75 (ISBN 0-345-30476-4). Ballantine.

--The Rule Book: The Authoritative Up-To-Date Illustrated Guide to the Regulations, History,& Object of All Major Sports. (Illus.). 432p. 9.95 (ISBN 0-312-69576-4). St Martin.

--Sex: A User's Manual. (Illus.). 196p. 1981. 14.95 (ISBN 0-399-12574-4, Perige); pap. 7.95 (ISBN 0-399-50517-2). Putnam Pub Group.

--The Sports Fan's Ultimate Book of Sports Comparisons: A Visual, Statistical & Factual Reference on Comparative Abilities, Records, Rules & Equipment. (Illus.). 192p. pap. 9.95 (ISBN 0-312-75335-7). St Martin.

Dial, O. E. & Goldberg, Edward M. Privacy, Security, & Computers: Guidelines for Municipal & Other Public Information Systems. LC 74-13617. (Special Sutdies). (Illus.). 186p. 1975. 25.95 o.p. (ISBN 0-275-09890-7). Praeger.

Diamant, Leo, jt. auth. see Debo, Harvey V.

Diamant, R. M. Atomic Energy. LC 81-69254. (Illus.). 553p. 1982. text ed. 49.95 (ISBN 0-250-40491-5). Ann Arbor Science.

Diamond. Dependent Development in United Kingdom Regions with Particular Reference to Wales. (Progress in Planning Ser.: Vol. 15, Part 1). 90p. 1980. pap. 13.50 (ISBN 0-08-026809-9). Pergamon.

--Distribution, Allocation, Social Structure & Spatial Form: Elements of Planning Theory. (Progress in Planning Ser.: Vol. 14, Part 3). (Illus.). 83p. 1980. pap. 13.50 (ISBN 0-08-026808-0). Pergamon.

--The Location of Immigrant Industry Within a U. K. Assisted Area: The Scottish Experience. (Progress in Planning Ser.: Vol. 14, Part 2). (Illus.). 121p. 1980. pap. 13.50 (ISBN 0-08-026807-2). Pergamon.

--Shelter for the Poor: The Case of Poona. (Progress in Planning Ser.: Vol. 15, Pt. 3). 85p. 1981. pap. 13.50 (ISBN 0-08-026811-0). Pergamon.

Diamond & Davies, R. L. The Impact of Town Centre Shopping Schemes in Britain: Their Impact on Traditional Retail Environments. (Progress in Planning Ser.: Vol. 14, Part 1). (Illus.). 104p. 1980. pap. 13.50 (ISBN 0-08-026789-0). Pergamon.

Diamond & Wood, L. J. Adjustment in the Urban System: The Tasman Bridge Collapse & Its Effects on Metropolitan Hobart. (Progress in Planning Ser.: Vol. 15, Pt. 2). 85p. 1981. pap. 13.50 (ISBN 0-08-026810-2). Pergamon.

Diamond, Allen. The Holiest Bible. LC 79-65912. 1979. 4.95 o.p. (ISBN 0-533-04354-9). Vantage.

Diamond, Arlyn, jt. ed. see Edwards, Lee R.

Diamond, Arthur S. The Evolution of Law & Order. LC 72-9372. 342p. 1973. Repr. of 1951 ed. lib. bdg. 21.00x (ISBN 0-8371-6580-6, DIEL). Greenwood.

Diamond, Beatrice. Episode in American Journalism. LC 64-15546. 1964. 11.50 o.p. (ISBN 0-8046-0108-9). Kennikat.

Diamond, Dick. Reedy River. (Australian Theatre Workshop Ser.). 1970. 4.50x o.p. (ISBN 0-85859-003-4, 00534). Heinemann Ed.

Diamond, Donna. The Pied Piper of Hamelin. LC 80-12027. (Illus.). 32p. (ps-3). 1981. PLB 9.95 (ISBN 0-8234-0415-3). Holiday.

Diamond, Donna, adapted by. & illus. The Bremen Town Musicians: A Grimms' Fairytale. LC 80-36838. (Illus.). 32p. (gr. k-2). 1981. 8.95 o.s.i. (ISBN 0-440-00826-3); PLB 8.44 o.s.i. (ISBN 0-440-00827-1). Delacorte.

Diamond, Dorothy. Aerial Models. LC 77-82978. (Teaching Primary Science Ser.). 1978. pap. text ed. 9.85 (ISBN 0-356-05074-2). Raintree Pubs.

--Mirrors & Magnifiers. LC 77-82982. (Teaching Primary Science Ser.). (Illus.). 1977. pap. text ed. 9.85 (ISBN 0-356-05078-5). Raintree Pubs.

--Science from Wood. LC 77-82981. (Teaching Primary Science Ser.). (Illus.). 1977. pap. text ed. 9.85 (ISBN 0-356-05073-4). Raintree Pubs.

--Seeds & Seedlings. LC 77-82986. (Teaching Primary Science Ser.). (Illus.). 1977. pap. text ed. 9.85 (ISBN 0-356-05072-6). Raintree Pubs.

--Teacher's Guide to Primary Science. LC 77-82977. (Teaching Primary Science Ser.). (Illus.). 1978. 22.25 (ISBN 0-356-05082-3). Raintree Pubs.

Diamond, Dorothy & Tiffin, Robert. Musical Instruments. LC 77-82979. (Teaching Primary Science Ser.). (Illus.). 1977. pap. text ed. 9.85 (ISBN 0-356-05077-7). Raintree Pubs.

Diamond, Dorothy, jt. auth. see Bird, John.

Diamond, Dorothy, jt. auth. see Diamond, Walter.

Diamond, Dorothy B., jt. auth. see Diamond, Walter H.

Diamond, E. Nervous System: Disease, Diagnosis, Treatment. (Clinical Monographs Ser.). (Illus.). 1976. pap. 7.95 o.p. (ISBN 0-87618-065-9). R J Brady.

Diamond, E. Grey. Inside China Today: A Western View. 1983. 16.50 (ISBN 0-393-01711-7). Norton.

Diamond, Ed, jt. auth. see Mazlish, Bruce.

Diamond, Edwin. Good News, Bad News. 1978. 15.00x (ISBN 0-262-04057-3); pap. 5.95x (ISBN 0-262-54035-5). MIT Pr.

--T. V. News in Four Countries. 150p. Date not set. cancelled (ISBN 0-08-028839-1); pap. cancelled (ISBN 0-08-028838-3). Pergamon.

Diamond, Elliot, jt. auth. see Le Bendig, Michael.

Diamond, Harriet & Dutwin, Phyllis. Grammar-in Plain English. rev. ed. LC 75-2487. (gr. 9-12). 1977. pap. text ed. 6.50 (ISBN 0-8120-0545-7). Barron.

Diamond, J. & Pintel, G. Introduction to Contemporary Business. 1975. 21.95 (ISBN 0-13-487991-0); study guide 8.95 (ISBN 0-13-488015-3). P-H.

Diamond, Jacqueline. Song for a Lady. 192p. 1983. 11.95 (ISBN 0-8027-0724-6). Walker & Co.

Diamond, Jared M. Avifauna of the Eastern Highlands of New Guinea. (Illus.). 1972p. 1972. 15.00 (ISBN 0-686-35800-7). Nuttall Ornithological.

Diamond, Jared M., jt. ed. see Cody, Martin L.

Diamond, Jay & Pintel, Gerald. Mathematics of Business. 2nd ed. (Illus.). 416p. 1975. pap. text ed. 18.95 (ISBN 0-13-564013-X); wkbk. 9.95 (ISBN 0-13-564021-0). P-H.

--Principles of Marketing. (Illus.). 1980. 18.95 (ISBN 0-13-701417-1); pap. text ed. 9.95 study guide (ISBN 0-13-701425-2). P-H.

Diamond, Jay, jt. auth. see Pintel, Gerald.

Diamond, John. The Answer Within: How to Find Your Psychobiological Harmony. 288p. 1983. cancelled 13.95 (ISBN 0-89479-108-7). A & W Pubs.

--Behavioral Kinesiology & the Autonomic Nervous System. (Behavioral Kinesiology Ser.). 85p. 1983. pap. 47.50 (ISBN 0-911238-78-6). Regent House.

--The Collected Papers of John Diamond, M.D, 2 vols. 1983. pap. 19.95 ea. Vol. 1, 88p. (ISBN 0-911238-75-1). Vol. 2, 170p (ISBN 0-911238-76-X). Regent House.

--Holistic Therapy: Lectures on a Spiritual Basis of Holistic Therapy. 67p. 1983. pap. 19.95x (ISBN 0-911238-79-4). Regent House.

--Life Energy in Music: Notes on Music & Sound. 140p. 1983. pap. 19.95 (ISBN 0-915628-20-1). Zeppelin.

--Re-Mothering Experience: How to Totally Love. Orig. Title: How to Totally Love. 90p. 1983. pap. 15.95x (ISBN 0-915628-13-9). Zeppelin.

--Some Contributions of Behavioral Kineseology to Art. (Behavioral Kinesiology Ser.). 73p. 1983. pap. 29.95 (ISBN 0-915628-14-7). Zeppelin.

--Speech, Language & the Power of Breath in Behavioral Kinesiology. (Behavioral Kinesiology Ser.). 85p. 1983. pap. 47.50 (ISBN 0-911238-77-8). Regent House.

Diamond, L. H. Nephrology Reviews, Vol. 2. 320p. 1981. 32.00 (ISBN 0-471-07956-1, Pub. by Wiley Medical). Wiley.

Diamond, Louis H. & Balow, James E., eds. Nephrology Reviews 1980. 1979. 35.00x (ISBN 0-471-05472-0, Pub. by Wiley Medical). Wiley.

Diamond, Malcolm L. Contemporary Philosophy & Religious Thought: An Introduction to the Philosophy of Religion. new ed. 416p. 1974. text ed. 14.95 o.p. (ISBN 0-07-016721-4, C); pap. text ed. 18.95 (ISBN 0-07-016720-6). McGraw.

Diamond, Martin. The Founding of the Democratic Republic. LC 80-84210. 183p. 1981. pap. text ed. 7.50 (ISBN 0-87581-271-6). Peacock Pubs.

Diamond, Milton & Karlen, Arno. Sexual Decisions. (Illus.). 536p. 1980. text ed. 20.95 (ISBN 0-316-18388-1); instructor's manual free (ISBN 0-316-18390-3). Little.

Diamond, Milton, jt. auth. see Steinhoff, Patricia G.

Diamond, Neil, ed. The Neil Diamond Songbook. (Illus.). 376p. 1982. 29.95 (ISBN 0-933328-46-X). Delilah Bks.

Diamond, Norman. Ambulatory Care for the House Officer: Initial Approach to Diagnosis & Management. (House Officer Ser.). 364p. 1982. pap. 9.95 (ISBN 0-683-02504-X). Williams & Wilkins.

Diamond, R. B. & Waggoner, D. R. Etude Sur Les Engrais en Afrique de L'Ouest, Vol. Un. (Techinical Bulletins Ser.: TF-3). (Illus.). 74p. (Orig., Fr.). 1977. pap. 4.00 (ISBN 0-88090-038-5). Intl Fertilizer.

Diamond, R. B., et al. West African Fertilizer Study: Mali, Vol. III. (Technical Bulletin T-5). (Illus.). 61p. (Orig.). 1976. pap. 5.00 (ISBN 0-88090-004-0). Intl Fertilizer.

--West African Fertilizer Study: Mauritania, Vol. VII. (Technical Bulletin T-9). (Illus.). 33p. (Orig.). 1978. pap. 4.00 (ISBN 0-88090-008-3). Intl Fertilizer.

--West African Fertilizer Study: Niger, Vol. V. (Technical Bulletin - T-7). (Illus.). 46p. (Orig.). 1978. pap. 4.00 (ISBN 0-88090-006-7). Intl Fertilizer.

--West African Fertilizer Study: Senegal, Vol. II. (Technical Bulletin, T-4). (Illus.). 58p. (Orig.). pap. 4.00 (ISBN 0-88090-003-2). Intl Fertilizer.

--West African Fertilizer Study: Upper Volta, Vol. IV. (Technical Bulletin - T-6). (Illus.). 59p. (Orig.). 1977. pap. 4.00 (ISBN 0-88090-005-9). Intl Fertilizer.

--West African Fertilizer Study: Chad, Vol. VI. (Technical Bulletin - T-8). (Illus.). 55p. (Orig.). 1977. pap. 4.00 (ISBN 0-88090-007-5). Intl Fertilizer.

Diamond, R. B., jt. auth. see Zalla, T.

Diamond, R. D. & Waggoner, D. R. West African Fertilizer Study Regional Overview, Vol. I. (Technical Bulletin Ser.: T-3). 71p. (Orig.). 1977. pap. 4.00 (ISBN 0-88090-039-3). Intl Fertilizer.

Diamond, Ray B., jt. auth. see Martinez, Adolfo.

Diamond, Seymour & Dalessio, Donald J. The Practicing Physician's Approach to Headache. 3rd ed. (Illus.). 192p. 1982. lib. bdg. 29.00 (ISBN 0-683-02503-1). Williams & Wilkins.

Diamond, Seymour & Furlong, William B. More Than Two Aspirin: Help for Your Headache Problem. 372p. 1976. 8.95 o.s.i. (ISBN 0-695-80612-2). Follett.

Diamond, Solomon. Roots of Psychology: Psychology Recollected. LC 72-76919. (Illus.). 800p. 1973. text ed. 25.95x o.s.i. (ISBN 0-465-07137-6). Basic.

Diamond, Stanley. Dahomey: Transition & Conflict in State Formation. 160p. Date not set. cancelled (ISBN 0-89789-024-8). J F Bergin. Postponed.

--Totems. 96p. 1981. 20.00 o.p. signed, ltd. ed. (ISBN 0-940170-01-9); pap. 6.95 (ISBN 0-940170-03-5). Open Bk Pubns.

Diamond, Susan Z. Records Management. 192p. 1983. 21.95 (ISBN 0-8144-5729-0). Am Mgmt Assns.

Diamond, W. I. & Smith, P. Input Output Methods in Urban & Regional Planning: A Practical Guide. LC 73-66. 1977. pap. 11.00 (ISBN 0-08-021858-X). Pergamon.

Diamond, Walter & Diamond, Dorothy. International Tax Treaties of All Nations, 12 vols, Series B. LC 77-16742. 1978. lib. bdg. 50.00 ea. (ISBN 0-379-00725-8). Oceana.

Diamond, Walter H. & Diamond, Dorothy B. International Tax Treaties of All Nations, 12 vols. LC 75-33646. 1976. text ed. 50.00x ea. (ISBN 0-379-00725-8). Oceana.

Diamonstein, Barbaralee. Inside New York's Art World. LC 79-64991. (Illus.). 1980. pap. 9.95 (ISBN 0-8478-0259-0). Rizzoli Intl.

Di Amrogonas, et al. Analytical Methods in Rotor Dynamics. Date not set. price not set (ISBN 0-85334-199-0). Elsevier.

Dias, C. J. & Luckham, R., eds. Studies of Law in Social Change & Development: Lawyers in the Third World-Comparative & Developmental Perspectives. 25.00 (ISBN 0-686-35898-8); pap. 12.00 (ISBN 0-686-37202-6). Intl Ctr Law.

Diaz. Derecho Mercantil. 300p. (Span.). 1983. pap. text ed. write for info. (ISBN 0-06-310500-4, Pub. by HarLA Mexico). Har-Row.

Diaz, Andres C. & Iorillo, Nino R. Conversacion y Controversia: Topicos de Siempre. LC 72-1757. (Illus.). 272p. 1973. text ed. 15.95 (ISBN 0-13-171934-3). P-H.

Diaz, Briquets S., jt. auth. see Simmons, A.

Diaz, Carroll. Golf: A Beginner's Guide. LC 73-93342. (Illus.). 87p. 1974. pap. text ed. 12.95 o.p. (ISBN 0-87484-217-4); pap. 4.95 o.p. (ISBN 0-87484-216-6). Mayfield Pub.

Diaz, J. B., ed. Alexander Weinstein Selecta. 629p. 1978. text ed. 49.50 (ISBN 0-273-08411-9). Pitman Pub MA.

Diaz, Janet. Miguel Delibes. (World Authors Ser.). lib. bdg. 15.95 (ISBN 0-8057-2264-5, Twayne). G K Hall.

Diaz, Janet W. Ana Maria Matute. (World Authors Ser.). 12.95 (ISBN 0-8057-2600-4, Twayne). G K Hall.

Diaz, Joaquin & Viana, Luis D. Romances Tradicionales de Castilla y Leon. (Spanish Ser: No. 1). 1981. 0.12.50x (ISBN 0-942260-22-8). Hispanic Seminary.

Diaz, Jorge E. Guia De Estudios Sobre Doctrina Cristiana. (Guias De Estudio). 88p. pap. 4.50 (ISBN 0-311-43500-9). Casa Bautista.

Diaz, Jorge E., jt. auth. see Crane, James D.

Diaz, Jorge E., tr. see Coleman, Lucien E., Jr.

Diaz, May N. Tonala: Conservatism, Responsibility & Authority in a Mexican Town. LC 66-14566. 1966. 18.95x (ISBN 0-520-00321-7); pap. 2.65 o.p. (ISBN 0-520-01750-1). U of Cal Pr.

Diaz Alejandro, Carlos F., jt. auth. see Bacha, Edmar L.

Diaz-Briquets, Sergio. The Health Revolution in Cuba. (Institute of Latin American Studies Special Publication Ser.). 235p. 1983. text ed. 19.95x (ISBN 0-292-75071-4). U of Tex Pr.

--International Migration Within Latin America & the Caribbean: Some Reasearch Notes. LC 81-69418. 60p. Date not set. 7.95 (ISBN 0-686-99305-5). Ctr Migration.

Diaz-Cobo, Oscar. Bare Kills. (Illus.). 160p. 1982. pap. 10.00 (ISBN 0-87364-253-8). Paladin Ent.

Diaz-Guerrero, Rogelio, jt. ed. see Spielberger, Charles D.

Diaz Viana, Luis see Diaz, Joaquin & Viana, Luis D.

Dib, Albert. Forms & Agreements for Architects, Engineers & Contractors. LC 75-37971. 1976. with 1981 suppl. 140.00 (ISBN 0-87632-215-1). Boardman.

DiBattista, William J., jt. ed. see Kaldor, George.

Dibble, Ernest F. Young Prophet Niebuhr: Reinhold Niebuhr's Early Search for Social Justice. 1978. pap. text ed. 12.50 (ISBN 0-8191-0377-2). U Pr of Amer.

Dibelius, Martin. From Tradition to Gospel. Wolff, Bertram L., tr. 1971. 22.50 (ISBN 0-227-67752-8). Attic Pr.

Dibell, Ansen. Circle, Crescent, Star. (Science Fiction Ser.). 1981. pap. 2.25 o.p. (ISBN 0-87997-603-9, UE1603). Daw Bks.

Dibella, Geoffrey A., et al. Handbook of Partial Hospitalization. LC 81-12231. 450p. 1982. 29.95 (ISBN 0-87630-270-3). Brunner-Mazel.

Di Benedetta, C. & Balasz, R. Multidisciplinary Approach to Brain Development. (Developments in Neuroscience Ser.: Vol. 9). 1980. 94.00 (ISBN 0-444-80227-4). Elsevier.

Di Benedetto, Ubaldo, ed. New Comprehensive English-Spanish, Spanish-English Dictionary, 2 Vols. 3100p. 1977. Set. 60.00x (ISBN 84-7166-211-6). Intl Pubns Serv.

DiBernard, Barbara. Alchemy & Finnegans Wake. LC 79-22809. 1980. lib. bdg. 39.50x (ISBN 0-87395-388-6); pap. 11.95x (ISBN 0-87395-429-7). State U NY Pr.

Di'Bil b. 'Ali. Di'bil B. 'Ali: The Life and Writings of an Early 'Abbasid Poet. Zolondek, Leon, ed. & tr. LC 61-6553. 196p. 1961. 13.00x (ISBN 0-8131-1061-0). U Pr of Ky.

Dible, Donald M., ed. Build a Better You-Starting Now, Vol. 10. LC 70-63064. 256p. 1982. 12.95 (ISBN 0-88205-209-8). Showcase Fairfield.

--Build a Better You-Starting Now, Vol. 11. LC 70-63064. 256p. 1983. 12.95 (ISBN 0-88205-210-1). Showcase Fairfield.

--Build a Better You-Starting Now, Vol. 12. LC 70-863064. 256p. 1983. 12.95 (ISBN 0-88205-211-X). Showcase Fairfield.

Dibner, Bern, et al. Leonardo the Inventor. LC 80-18713. (Illus.). 192p. 1980. 9.95 o.p. (ISBN 0-07-016765-6). McGraw.

Dibner, David R. Joint Ventures for Architects & Engineers. (Illus.). 192p. 1972. 32.50 (ISBN 0-07-016760-5, P&RB). McGraw.

Dibner, Martin. The Deep Six. 228p. 1980. pap. 2.25 o.p. (ISBN 0-523-40916-8). Pinnacle Bks.

--The Devil's Paintbrush. LC 82-45460. 384p. 1983. 16.95 (ISBN 0-385-15666-9). Doubleday.

--Seacoast Maine: People & Places. (Illus.). 208p. 1982. pap. 9.95 (ISBN 0-89272-143-X, 482). Down East.

--The Trouble with Heroes. 384p. 1980. pap. 1.75 o.p. (ISBN 0-523-24914-4). Pinnacle Bks.

Dibner, Martin, ed. see Detmer, Josephine & Pancoast, Patricia.

Dibos, Pablo E. & Wagner, Henry N. Atlas of Nuclear Medicine: Bone, Vol. IV. LC 74-81820. 1978. text ed. 40.00 o.p. (ISBN 0-7216-3001-4). Saunders.

Di Brino, Nicholas. The History of the Morris Park Racecourse & the Morris Family. (Illus.). 48p. 1977. pap. 3.95 (ISBN 0-686-38455-5). Bronx County.

DiCaprio, Nicholas S. Adjustment: Fulfilling Human Potentials. (Illus.). 1980. text ed. 19.95 (ISBN 0-13-004101-7). P-H.

Dicaro, Deborah & Spigai, Frances. Patents. LC 82-72565. (Database Search Aids Ser.: Vol. 6). 150p. (Orig.). 1983. pap. 25.00 (ISBN 0-939920-08-5). Database Serv.

Di Castri, F., et al, eds. Mediterranean-Type Shrublands: Ecosystems of the World Ser. (Vol. 11). 1981. 119.25 (ISBN 0-444-41858-X). Elsevier.

Dice, Lee R. Man's Nature & Nature's Man: The Ecology of Human Communities. LC 72-9607. 329p. 1973. Repr. of 1955 ed. lib. bdg. 20.75x (ISBN 0-8371-6594-6, DIMN). Greenwood.

DiCerto, Joseph. The T. V. Team. (Illus.). 96p. (gr. 4-6). 1983. PLB 8.79 (ISBN 0-671-45948-1). Messner.

DiCesare, Mario, ed. George Herbert & the Seventeenth Century Religious Poets. (Norton Critical Editions). 401p. 1978. pap. text ed. 7.95x (ISBN 0-393-09254-2). Norton.

Dicey, Albert V. Introduction to the Study of the Law of the Constitution. LC 81-82778. 586p. 1982. 15.00X (ISBN 0-86597-002-5); pap. 7.00X (ISBN 0-86597-003-3). Liberty Fund.

--Thoughts on the Union Between England & Scotland. LC 77-114510. 1971. Repr. of 1920 ed. lib. bdg. 19.00x (ISBN 0-8371-4785-9, DIUE). Greenwood.

Dicey, E. M., tr. see Boutmy, Emile.

Dicharry, Warren F. Greek Without Grief: An Outline Guide to New Testament Greek. 3rd, rev. ed. 112p. 1982. pap. 6.95 (ISBN 0-9608630-3-6). St Thomas Seminary.

Di Chiara, G. & Gessa, G. L., eds. GABA & the Basal Gangliosides. (Advances in Biochemical Psychopharmacology Ser.: Vol. 30). 1981. text ed. 31.00 (ISBN 0-89004-752-9). Raven.

--Glutamate As a Neurotransmitter. (Advances in Biochemical Psychopharmacology Ser.: Vol. 27). 464p. 1981. text ed. 54.50 (ISBN 0-89004-420-1). Raven.

Dichter, Ernest. Handbook of Consumer Motivations: The Psychology of the World of Objects. 1964. 9.50 o.p. (ISBN 0-07-016780-X, P&RB). McGraw.

--Motivating Human Behavior. 1971. 34.95 (ISBN 0-07-016781-8, P&RB). McGraw.

--Total Self-Knowledge. LC 75-37981. 280p. 1976. 11.95 o.p. (ISBN 0-686-82973-5); pap. 4.95 (ISBN 0-8128-1919-5). Stein & Day.

Dichter, H. Handbook of American Sheet Music, 2 Pts. (Illus.). pap. 12.50 ea. (ISBN 0-87556-077-6). Saifer.

Dichter, Steve. Sinister. LC 81-86420. 192p. 1983. 10.95 (ISBN 0-86666-043-7). GWP.

Dichtl, Rudolph J., jt. auth. see Jackson, John P.

Dicicco, Philip P., jt. auth. see Krutza, William J.

Dick, Alexandra, tr. see Lagerkvist, Par.

Dick, B., jt. auth. see Dunphy, D. C.

Dick, Bernard F. Billy Wilder. (Filmmakers Ser.). 1980. lib. bdg. 11.95 (ISBN 0-8057-9274-0, Twayne). G K Hall.

--William Golding. (English Authors Ser.). 1968. lib. bdg. 11.95 (ISBN 0-8057-1224-0, Twayne). G K Hall.

Dick, Carson. Immunological Aspects of Rheumotology. 1981. 42.50 (ISBN 0-444-19474-6). Elsevier.

Dick, E., et al. GUIDE: Gathering up Information for Developmental Education for the TMR. 1979. spiral bound 18.95 (ISBN 0-87804-358-6). Mafex.

Dick, E. A., jt. auth. see Snell, W. H.

Dick, Everett. The Sod-House Frontier 1854-1890: A Social History of the Northern Plains from the Creation of Kansas & Nebraska to the Admission of the Dakotas. LC 78-24204. (Illus.). xxii, 550p. 1979. pap. 7.95 (ISBN 0-8032-6551-4, BB 700, Bison). U of Nebr Pr.

Dick, H. M. & Kissemeyer-Nielsen, F., eds. Histocompatibility Techniques. LC 79-13943. 1979. 53.00 (ISBN 0-444-80132-4, North Holland). Elsevier.

Dick, James G. Analytical Chemistry. LC 78-728. 704p. 1978. Repr. of 1973 ed. lib. bdg. 31.50 (ISBN 0-88275-580-3). Krieger.

Dick, John H., jt. auth. see Sprunt, Alexander, Jr.

Dick, Oliver L., ed. see Aubrey, John.

Dick, Philip K. Clans of the Alphane Moon. 1979. lib. bdg. 12.95 (ISBN 0-8398-2598-6, Gregg). G K Hall.

--Counter-Clock World. 1979. lib. bdg. 11.95 (ISBN 0-8398-2485-8, Gregg). G K Hall.

--Dr. Bloodmoney, or How We Got Along After the Bomb. 1977. Repr. of 1965 ed. lib. bdg. 11.00 o.p. (ISBN 0-8398-2365-7, Gregg). G K Hall.

--Eye in the Sky. 1979. lib. bdg. 14.95 (ISBN 0-8398-2481-5, Gregg). G K Hall.

--The Game-Players of Titan. 1979. lib. bdg. 13.95 (ISBN 0-8398-2482-3, Gregg). G K Hall.

--A Handful of Darkness. (Science Fiction Ser.). 1978. lib. bdg. 11.00 o.p. (ISBN 0-8398-2413-0, Gregg). G K Hall.

--The Man in the High Castle. 1979. lib. bdg. 9.95 (ISBN 0-8398-2476-9, Gregg). G K Hall.

--Solar Lottery. (Science Fiction Ser.). 208p. 1976. Repr. of 1955 ed. lib. bdg. 10.95 o.p. (ISBN 0-8398-2330-4, Gregg). G K Hall.

--The Three Stigmata of Palmer Eldritch. 1979. lib. bdg. 14.95 (ISBN 0-8398-2479-3, Gregg). G K Hall.

--Time Out of Joint. 1979. lib. bdg. 14.95 (ISBN 0-8398-2480-7, Gregg). G K Hall.

--Ubik. (Science Fiction Ser.). 1979. lib. bdg. 10.95 o.p. (ISBN 0-8398-2478-5, Gregg). G K Hall.

--Vulcan's Hammer. 1979. lib. bdg. 11.95 (ISBN 0-8398-2484-X, Gregg). G K Hall.

--The World Jones Made. 1979. PLB 12.95 (ISBN 0-8398-2483-1, Gregg). G K Hall.

--The Zap Gun. 1979. lib. bdg. 12.95 (ISBN 0-8398-2494-7, Gregg). G K Hall.

Dick, Richard J., jt. auth. see Hinkel, Daniel F.

Dick, Robert C. Black Protest: Issues & Tactics. LC 72-794. 320p. 1974. lib. bdg. 29.95 (ISBN 0-8371-6366-8, DNA/); pap. 5.95 o.p. (ISBN 0-8371-8922-5). Greenwood.

Dick, Trevor J. Economic History of Canada: A Guide to Information Sources. LC 73-17571. (Economics Information Guide Ser.: Vol. 9). 1978. 42.00x (ISBN 0-8103-1292-1). Gale.

Dick, W. & Hagerty, N. Topics in Measurement. 1970. pap. text ed. 14.95 (ISBN 0-07-016783-4, C). McGraw.

Dick, Walter & Carey, Lou. The Systematic Design of Instruction. 1978. pap. 12.50x (ISBN 0-673-15122-0). Scott F.

Dick, Walter, jt. auth. see Singer, Robert N.

Dickason, A. Sheet Metal Drawing & Pattern Development. (Illus.). 364p. 1983. pap. text ed. 28.50x (ISBN 0-273-41163-2, SpS). Sportshelf.

Dickason, Jean & Schult, Martha. Maternal & Infant Care. 2nd ed. (Illus.). 1979. text ed. 27.50 (ISBN 0-07-016796-6, HP); instructor's manual 10.00 (ISBN 0-07-016797-4). McGraw.

Dickason, Jean, et al. Maternal & Infant Drugs & Nursing Intervention. (Illus.). 1978. pap. text ed. 13.50 (ISBN 0-07-016788-5, HP). McGraw.

Dicken, Peter & Lloyd, Peter. Modern Western Society: A Geographical Perspective on Work, Home, & Well-Being. 396p. 1982. pap. text ed. 14.95 scp (ISBN 0-06-041645-9, HarpC). Harrow.

Dickens. The Courts of Europe. 1977. 24.95 (ISBN 0-07-016802-4). McGraw.

Dickens, Arthur G. English Reformation. LC 64-22987. (Fabric of British History Ser). 1968. 11.00x o.p. (ISBN 0-8052-3063-7); pap. 7.95 (ISBN 0-8052-0177-7). Schocken.

Dickens, Charles. Bleak House. 1964. pap. 4.95 (ISBN 0-451-51739-3, CE1739, Sig Classics). NAL.

--Bleak House. (Critical Edition Ser.). 1978 o.p. 24.95, (ISBN 0-393-04374-6); pap. 9.95x 1977 (ISBN 0-393-09332-8). Norton.

--Bleak House. (Bantam Classics Ser.). (YA) (gr. 10-12). 1983. pap. 3.95 (ISBN 0-553-21108-0). Bantam.

--Christmas Carol. (Illus.). 1982. 12.50 (ISBN 0-434-95857-3, Pub. by Heinemann). David & Charles.

--Christmas Carol: A Facsimile of the Manuscript & First Edition. facsimile ed. (Illus.). 1967. 18.75 o.p. (ISBN 0-685-11951-3). Heineman.

--A Christmas Carol & the Cricket on the Hearth. (Childrens Illustrated Classics Ser). (Illus.). 220p. 1973. Repr. of 1963 ed. 9.00x o.p. (ISBN 0-460-05059-1, Pub. by J. M. Dent England). Biblio Dist.

--A Christmas Carol: The Original Manuscript. 10.50 (ISBN 0-8446-0078-4). Peter Smith.

--Christmas Carol: The Public Reading Version. Collins, Philip, ed. (Illus.). 1971. 20.00 (ISBN 0-87104-228-2). NY Pub Lib.

--Christmas Stories. 1971. pap. 3.95x (ISBN 0-460-01414-5, Evman). Biblio Dist.

--David Copperfield. (Classics Ser). (gr. 9 up). pap. 2.95 (ISBN 0-8049-0065-5, CL-65). Airmont.

--David Copperfield. 864p. pap. 4.95 (ISBN 0-671-45106-5). WSP.

--Dombey & Son. pap. 3.95 (ISBN 0-451-51595-1, CE1595, Sig Classics). NAL.

--Edwin Drood & Master Humphrey's Clock. 1970. Repr. of 1915 ed. 9.95x (ISBN 0-460-00725-4, Evman). Biblio Dist.

--Great Expectations. (Bantam Classics Ser.). 454p. (gr. 9-12). 1981. pap. 2.50 (ISBN 0-553-21015-7). Bantam.

--Great Expectations. (RL 9). pap. 1.95 (ISBN 0-451-51759-8, CJ1759, Sig Classics). NAL.

--Great Expectations. McMaster, R. D., ed. (Odyssey Ser.). 512p. (Orig.). 1965. pap. text ed. 5.50 (ISBN 0-686-43042-5). Bobbs.

--Hard Times. (Bantam Classics Ser.). 301p. (gr. 9-12). 1981. pap. 1.95 (ISBN 0-553-21016-5). Bantam.

--Hard Times. Craig, David, ed. (English Library Ser.). 1969. pap. 2.25 (ISBN 0-14-043042-3). Penguin.

--The Heart of Charles Dickens: As Revealed in His Letters to Angela Burd. Johnson, Edgar, ed. LC 75-25254. 415p. 1976. Repr. of 1952 ed. lib. bdg. 24.00x o.p. (ISBN 0-8371-8397-9, DICB). Greenwood.

--Life & Adventures of Nicholas Nickleby. TV tie-in ed. Slater, Michael, ed. 1982. pap. 4.95 (ISBN 0-14-006454-0). Penguin.

--The Life & Adventures of Nicholas Nickleby. LC 82-21971. (Illus.). 1344p. 1982. 35.00x (ISBN 0-8122-7873-9); pap. 17.95x 2 vol. set (ISBN 0-8122-1135-9). U of Pa Pr.

--The Life & Adventures of Nicholas Nickleby. 1982. pap. 4.50 (ISBN 0-451-51633-8, CE1633, Sig Classics). NAL.

--Nicholas Nickleby. (Bantam Classics Ser.). 816p. (YA) (gr. 10-12). 1983. pap. 4.50 (ISBN 0-553-21086-6). Bantam.

--Our Mutual Friend. (RL 8). pap. 3.95 (ISBN 0-451-51797-0, CE1797, Sig Classics). NAL.

--Our Mutual Friend. Gill, Stephen, ed. (English Library Ser.). 1971. pap. 4.95 (ISBN 0-14-043060-1). Penguin.

--Pickwick Papers. (Picture Aids to World Geography Ser.). (gr. 10 up). 1968. pap. 2.95 (ISBN 0-8049-0191-0, CL-191). Airmont.

--Pickwick Papers. (RL 9). pap. 4.95 (ISBN 0-451-51756-3, CE1756, Sig Classics). NAL.

--The Portable Charles Dickens. Wilson, Angus, ed. 1983. pap. 6.95 (ISBN 0-14-015099-4). Penguin.

--A Tale of Two Cities. (Bantam Classics Ser.). 352p. (gr. 9-12). 1981. pap. 1.95 (ISBN 0-553-21017-3). Bantam.

--Tale of Two Cities. (Illus.). (gr. 4-6). 1948. il. jr. lib. 5.95 (ISBN 0-448-05823-5, G&D); deluxe ed. 8.95 (ISBN 0-448-06023-X). Putnam Pub Group.

--A Tale of Two Cities. (The Illustrated Junior Library). (Illus.). 432p. 1982. pap. 5.95 (ISBN 0-448-11023-7, G&D). Putnam Pub Group.

--Tale of Two Cities. (RL 7). 1960. pap. 1.95 (ISBN 0-451-51776-8, CJ1776, Sig Classics). NAL.

Dickens, Charles & Kitton, F. G. The Poems & Verses of Charles Dickens. 220p. 1983. pap. 6.95 (ISBN 0-686-38393-1). Tanager Bks.

Dickens, Charles see Allen, W. S.

Dickens, Charles see Eyre, A. G.

Dickens, Charles see Swan, D. K.

Dickens, Frank. A Curl Up & Die Day. (Illus.). 152p. 1982. 12.95 (ISBN 0-7206-0573-3, Pub. by Peter Owen). Merrimack Bk Serv.

Dickens, Frank, et al, eds. Carbohydrate Metabolism & Its Disorders, 2 Vols. 1968. Vol. 1. 84.50 o.s.i. (ISBN 0-12-214901-7); Vol. 2. 62.50 o.s.i. (ISBN 0-12-214902-5). Acad Pr.

Dickens, Milton. Speech: Cynamic Communication. 3rd. ed. 400p. (Orig.). 1974. pap. text ed. 17.95 (ISBN 0-15-583193-3); instrs'. manual avail. HarBraceJ.

Dickens, Roy S., Jr. Cherokee Prehistory: The Pisgah Phase in the Appalachian Summit Region. LC 76-1972. 1976. 17.95x (ISBN 0-87049-193-8). U of Tenn Pr.

Dickens, Susanne, jt. auth. see Knox-Thompson, Elaine.

Dickenson, Emily. For Love of Her. 1974. pap. 4.95 (ISBN 0-517-51488-5, C N Potter Bks). Crown.

Dickenson, Harry & Kleinschmidt, Robert. Technical Mechanics. (Illus.). 736p. 1974. text ed. 22.05 o.p. (ISBN 0-07-016790-7, G); instructor's manual 1.95 o.p. (ISBN 0-07-016791-5). McGraw.

Dickenson, John P. Brazil. LC 81-20827. (The World's Landscapes Ser.). text ed. 28.00x (ISBN 0-686-37903-9). Longman.

--Brazil: An Industrial Geography. (Westview Special Studies in Industrial Geography). 1978. lib. bdg. 26.00 (ISBN 0-89158-832-9, Dawson). Westview.

Dickenson, Mary. Democracy in Trade Unions: Studies in Membership Participation & Control. LC 82-2065. (Policy, Politics, & Administration Ser.). (Illus.). 249p. 1983. text ed. 32.50x (ISBN 0-7022-1666-6). U of Queensland Pr.

Dickenson, Richard B., jt. ed. see Nell, Varney R.

Dicker, jt. auth. see Greene.

Dicker, Herman. Piety & Perseverance: Jews from the Carpathian Mountains. LC 80-54595. (Illus.). 252p. 1981. 14.95 (ISBN 0-87203-094-6); pap. 8.95 (ISBN 0-87203-098-9). Hermon.

Dickerman, Marion. The Three Founders: Charles K. Stillman, Carl C. Cutler, Edward E. Bradley. (Illus.). 42p. 1965. pap. 4.00 o.p. (ISBN 0-913372-18-8). Mystic Seaport.

Dickerman, Pat. Adventure Travel, North America. LC 77-25745. (Illus.). 1978. 9.95 o.p. (ISBN 0-690-01750-2); pap. 5.95i o.p. (ISBN 0-690-01751-0). T y Crowell.

--Farm, Ranch & Country Vacations. LC 60-2113. (Adventure Guides Ser.). (Illus.). 240p. 1983. pap. 8.95 (ISBN 0-913214-04-3). Berkshire Traveller.

--Farm, Ranch, & Country Vacations. (Illus.). 1983. pap. 8.95 (ISBN 0-913214-04-3). Farm & Ranch.

Dickerman, Patricia. Adventure Travel. LC 79-57153. 256p. 1983. 8.95 (ISBN 0-913216-04-6, Pub. by Adventure Guide). Berkshire Traveller.

--Farm, Ranch, Country Vacations. LC 60-2113. 256p. 1981. 7.95 o.p. (ISBN 0-913214-03-5, Pub. by Adventure Guide). Berkshire Traveller.

Dickerman, Sherwood E., ed. see Salinger, John P.

Dickerson, F. Reed. The Fundamentals of Legal Drafting. 1965. 15.00 (ISBN 0-316-18394-6). Little.

--Legislative Drafting. LC 77-8392. 1977. Repr. of 1954 ed. lib. bdg. 15.50x (ISBN 0-8371-9688-4, DILD). Greenwood.

Dickerson, J. W., jt. auth. see Bryce-Smith, D.

Dickerson, Louise. Good Wife, Good Wife. 1977. 6.95 (ISBN 0-07-016811-3); PLB 7.95 (ISBN 0-07-016812-1). McGraw.

Dickerson, M. O., et al, eds. Problems of Change in Urban Government. 249p. 1980. pap. text ed. 9.25 (ISBN 0-88920-089-0, Pub. by Wilfred Laurier U Pr Canada). Humanities.

Dickerson, Oliver. Boston under Military Rule. LC 70-114511. 1971. Repr. of 1936 ed. lib. bdg. 15.00x o.p. (ISBN 0-8371-4734-4, DIBM). Greenwood.

Dickerson, Oliver M., ed. Boston under Military Rule 1768-1769. LC 70-118029. (Era of the American Revolution Ser). 1970. Repr. of 1936 ed. 22.50 (ISBN 0-306-71943-6). Da Capo.

Dickerson, R. E. & Geis, I. Hemoglobin: Structure, Function, Evolution & Pathology. 1983. 29.95 (ISBN 0-8053-2411-9). Benjamin-Cummings.

Dickerson, R. W. Accountants & the Law of Negligence. LC 82-48361. (Accountancy in Transition Ser.). 668p. 1982. lib. bdg. 65.00 (ISBN 0-8240-5312-5). Garland Pub.

Dickerson, Richard E. & Geis, Irving. Chemistry, Matter, & the Universe. 1976. 27.95 (ISBN 0-8053-2369-4); study guide 5.95 (ISBN 0-8053-5260-0); instr's guide 4.95 (ISBN 0-8053-2380-5). Benjamin-Cummings.

--The Structure & Action of Proteins. LC 69-11112. 1969. pap. text ed. 15.95 (ISBN 0-8053-2391-0). Benjamin-Cummings.

Dickerson, Richard E., et al. Chemical Principles. 3rd ed. LC 77-87336. 1979. pap. text ed. 28.95 (ISBN 0-8053-2398-8); instr's guide 4.95 (ISBN 0-8053-2410-0); programmed reviews 11.95 (ISBN 0-8053-6027-1); problems 13.95 (ISBN 0-8053-1587-X); study guide 8.95 (ISBN 0-8053-2399-6); transparency masters 75.00 (ISBN 0-8053-2396-1). Benjamin-Cummings.

Dickerson, Robert B., Jr. Final Placement: A Guide to the Deaths, Funerals, & Burials of Notable Americans. Irvine, Keith, ed. LC 81-52598. (Illus.). 250p. 1982. 19.95 (ISBN 0-917256-18-2). Ref Pubns.

Dickerson, Thelma M. & Dyer, Marilyn. Designing & Building a Curriculum. 98p. 1979. 5.95 (ISBN 0-686-38259-5, 16-1776). Natl League Nurse.

Dickes, E. W., tr. see Doberer, Kurt K.

Dickes, E. W., tr. see Ruppin, Arthur.

Dickes, G. J. & Nicholas, P. V. Gas Chromatrography in Food Analysis. 1976. 54.95 o.p. (ISBN 0-408-70781-X). Butterworth.

Dickey, Glenn. America Has a Better Team: The Story of Bill Walsh & San Francisco's World Champion 49ers. rev. ed. (Illus.). 192p. 1982. 14.95 (ISBN 0-936602-66-X); pap. 9.95 (ISBN 0-936602-65-1). Harbor Pub CA.

Dickey, Imogene B., jt. auth. see Bindseil, Kenneth R.

Dickey, James. Buckdancer's Choice. LC 65-21079. (Wesleyan Poetry Program: Vol. 28). (Orig.). 1965. pap. 6.95 (ISBN 0-8195-1028-9, Pub. by Wesleyan U Pr). Columbia U Pr.

--False Youth: Four Seasons. (Illus.). 1983. ltd. ed. 50.00 (ISBN 0-939722-15-1). Pressworks.

--Night Hurdling. 1982. ltd. ed. 14.95 (ISBN 0-89723-040-X). Bruccoli.

--Poems: Nineteen Fifty-Seven to Nineteen Sixty-Seven. (Poetry Series). 1968. pap. 3.95 (ISBN 0-02-069320-6, Collier). Macmillan.

--Starry Place Between the Antlers: Why I Live in South Carolina. 1981. 2.00 (ISBN 0-89723-030-2); limited signed ed. 20.00 (ISBN 0-89723-031-0). Bruccoli.

--The Zodiac. 1976. signed & slipcased manuscript ed. 400.00 (ISBN 0-89723-018-3). Bruccoli.

Dickey, John, jt. ed. see Stanton, Jeffrey.

Dickey, John W. Metropolitan Transportation Planning. 550p. 1975. text ed. 34.50 o.p. (ISBN 0-07-016795-8, C). McGraw.

Dickey, John W. & Watts, Thomas M. Analytic Techniques in Urban & Regional Planning: With Applications in Public Administration & Affairs. (Illus.). 1978. text ed. 40.00x (ISBN 0-07-016798-2, C); solutions manual 4.95 (ISBN 0-07-016799-0). McGraw.

Dickey, Lawrence D. Clinical Ecology. (Illus.). 832p. 1976. photocopy ed. spiral 95.50x (ISBN 0-398-03409-5). C C Thomas.

Dickey, Lawrence D., jt. auth. see Eagle, Robert.

Dickey, Parke A. Petroleum Development Geology. 2nd ed. 428p. 1981. 49.95x (ISBN 0-87814-174-X). Pennwell Books Division.

--Petroleum Development Geology. 398p. 1979. 49.95x o.p. (ISBN 0-87814-049-2). Pennwell Pub.

Dickey, R. I. Accountants Cost Handbook. 2nd ed. 1050p. 1960. 59.95 (ISBN 0-471-06519-6). Wiley.

Dickey, R. P. Running Lucky. LC 82-71868. (New Poetry Ser.: No. 39). 80p. 1969. 6.95 (ISBN 0-8040-0265-7). Swallow.

Dickey, R. W. Bifurcation Problems in Nonlinear Elasticity. (Research Notes in Mathematics Ser.: No. 3). 119p. 1976. pap. text ed. 18.95 (ISBN 0-273-00103-5). Pitman Pub MA.

Dickey, Richard P. Managing Contraceptive Pill Patients. 2nd rev. ed. LC 76-29294. (Illus.). 116p. 1980. vinyl 7.95 o.p. (ISBN 0-917634-08-X). Creative Infomatics.

--Managing Contraceptive Pill Patients. 3rd ed. (Illus.). 8.65 (ISBN 0-686-42717-3). Creative Infomatics.

Dickey, W., jt. auth. see Schneider, R.

Dickie, George & Sclafani, R. J. Aesthetics: A Critical Anthology. LC 76-28127. (Illus.). 1977. text ed. 18.95 (ISBN 0-312-00910-0). St Martin.

Dickins, Anthony S. & Ebert, Hilmar. One Hundred Classics of the Chessboard. (Chess Ser.). 208p. 1983. 17.00 (ISBN 0-08-026921-4); pap. 9.90 (ISBN 0-08-026920-6). Pergamon.

Dickinson, Alyce M., jt. ed. see O'Brien, Richard.

Dickinson, Anthony. Contemporary Animal Learning Theory. (Problems in the Behavioral Sciences Ser.). (Illus.). 180p. 1981. 29.95 (ISBN 0-521-23469-7); pap. 9.95 (ISBN 0-521-29962-4). Cambridge U Pr.

Dickinson, Colin & Lucas, John. The Encyclopedia of Mushrooms. LC 77-14635. (Illus.). 1979. 25.00 o.p. (ISBN 0-399-12104-8). Putnam Pub Group.

--Van Nostrand Reinhold Color Dictionary of Mushrooms. 160p. 1982. pap. 12.95 (ISBN 0-442-21998-9). Van Nos Reinhold.

Dickinson, D., ed. Practical Waste Treatment & Disposal. (Illus.). xvi, 214p. 1974. 39.00 (ISBN 0-85334-580-5, Pub. by Applied Sci England). Elsevier.

Dickinson, Darol. Photographing Livestock: The Complete Guide. LC 79-88468. (Illus.). 14.50 o.p. (ISBN 0-87358-199-7); pap. 7.95 o.p. (ISBN 0-87358-200-4). Northland.

Dickinson, E. & Stainsby, G. Colloids in Food. (Illus.). xiv, 532p. 1982. 98.50 (ISBN 0-85334-153-2, Pub. by Applied Sci England). Elsevier.

Dickinson, Edward. Music in the History of the Western Church, with an Introduction in Religious Music Among the Primitive & Ancient Peoples. LC 69-13884. Repr. of 1902 ed. lib. bdg. 19.75x (ISBN 0-8371-1062-9, DIMW). Greenwood.

--The Spirit of Music: How to Find It & How to Share It. 218p. 1982. Repr. of 1927 ed. lib. bdg. 25.00 (ISBN 0-8495-1142-9). Arden Lib.

Dickinson, Elizabeth M., jt. ed. see Harvey, John F.

Dickinson, Emily. Acts of Light: Emily Dickinson. Langton, Jane, ed. 188p. 1980. 24.95 (ISBN 0-8212-1098-X, 006505); deluxe ed. 75.00 (ISBN 0-8212-1118-8, 006513DXLE). NYGS.

--Choice of Emily Dickinson's Verse. Hughes, Ted, ed. 68p. 1968. pap. 4.95 (ISBN 0-571-08218-1). Faber & Faber.

--Selected Poems. 1948. 3.95 o.s.i. (ISBN 0-394-60025-8, M25). Modern Lib.

Dickinson, Francis & Monteith, Lesley. Handbook for Weight Reduction. (Creative Arts Communications Ser.). (Illus.). Date not set. cancelled (ISBN 0-916870-20-0). Creative Arts Bk.

Dickinson, G. Lowes. Greek View of Life. 1958. pap. 2.95x o.p. (ISBN 0-472-06022-8, 22, AA). U of Mich Pr.

Dickinson, George S. A Handbook of Style in Music. 2nd ed. LC 72-90211. (Music Reprint Ser). 1969. Repr. of 1965 ed. 19.50 (ISBN 0-306-71820-0). Da Capo.

Dickinson, Goldsworthy L. The Greek View of Life. LC 78-12661. 1979. Repr. of 1958 ed. lib. bdg. 20.50x (ISBN 0-313-21195-7, DIGV). Greenwood.

Dickinson, H. T., ed. Politics & Literature in the Eighteenth Century. (Rowman & Littlefield University Library). 234p. 1974. 9.50x (ISBN 0-87471-405-2); pap. 4.00x (ISBN 0-87471-400-1). Rowman.

Dickinson, Jane. All About Trees. LC 82-17382. (Question & Answer Bks.). (Illus.). 32p. (gr. 3-6). 1983. PLB 8.59 (ISBN 0-89375-892-2); pap. text ed. 1.95 (ISBN 0-89375-893-0). Troll Assocs.

--Wonders of Water. LC 82-17388. (Question & Answer Bks.). (Illus.). 32p. (gr. 3-6). 1983. PLB 8.59 (ISBN 0-89375-874-4); pap. text ed. 1.95 (ISBN 0-89375-875-2). Troll Assocs.

Dickinson, John. Political Writings of John Dickinson, 1764-1774. Ford, P. L., ed. LC 70-119061. (Era of the American Revolution). 1970. Repr. of 1895 ed. lib. bdg. 49.50 (ISBN 0-306-71950-9). Da Capo.

Dickinson, John C. Monastic Life in Medieval England. LC 78-25804. (Illus.). 1979. Repr. of 1961 ed. lib. bdg. 20.75x (ISBN 0-313-20774-7, DIML). Greenwood.

Dickinson, John K., tr. see Heiber, Helmut.

Dickinson, Leon T., jt. auth. see Clark, Donald B.

Dickinson, O. P., jt. auth. see Simpson, R. H.

Dickinson, Peter. The Blue Hawk. (YA) (gr. 7 up). 1976. 9.95 o.p. (ISBN 0-316-18429-2, Pub. by Atlantic Monthly Pr). Little.

--The Fires of Autumn: Sexual Activity in the Middle & Later Years. LC 73-18403. 196p. 1977. pap. 4.95 o.p. (ISBN 0-8473-1502-9). Sterling.

--King & Joker. 1977. pap. 1.50 o.p. (ISBN 0-380-01767-9, 35006). Avon.

--Travel & Retirement Edens Abroad. (Illus.). 304p. 1983. 19.95 (ISBN 0-525-93274-7, 01840-550); pap. 12.95 (01258-370). Dutton.

Dickinson, Peter, jt. ed. see Consumer Guide.

Dickinson, Peter A. The Complete Retirement Planning Book: Your Guide to Happiness, Health & Financial Security. LC 76-7608. 1976. 10.95 o.p. (ISBN 0-8415-0446-6); pap. 6.95 o.p. (ISBN 0-8415-0440-7). Dutton.

--Get More Money from Social Security, Government Benefits, Medicare, Plus... 1982 ed. Editors of Consumer Guide, ed. (Illus.). 96p. (Orig.). 1982. pap. 4.95 (ISBN 0-448-12028-3, G&D). Putnam Pub Group.

--Sunbelt Retirement: The Complete State-By-State Guide to Retiring in the South & West of the United States. 2nd ed. (Illus.). 1980. 14.95 (ISBN 0-525-93123-6); pap. 8.95 (ISBN 0-525-93107-4, 0869-290). Dutton.

Dickinson, Peter A. & Consumer Guide Editors. Get More from Social Security, Government Benefits, Medicare, Plus... (Illus.). 96p. 1981. pap. 4.50 o.p. (ISBN 0-448-14619-3, G&D). Putnam Pub Group.

Dickinson, Robert E. The Population Problem of Southern Italy: An Essay in Social Geography. LC 76-49087. (Illus.). 1977. Repr. of 1955 ed. lib. bdg. 15.50x (ISBN 0-8371-9337-0, DIPP). Greenwood.

--Regional Concept: The Anglo-American Leaders. 1976. 26.75x o.p. (ISBN 0-7100-8272-X). Routledge & Kegan.

--West European City. 2nd ed. (International Library of Society & Social Reconstruction Ser.). (Illus.). 1963. Repr. of 1951 ed. text ed. 28.75x o.p. (ISBN 0-7100-3295-1). Humanities.

Dickinson, Robert E. & Howarth, O. J. R. The Making of Geography. LC 75-38379. 1976. Repr. of 1933 ed. lib. bdg. 20.75x (ISBN 0-8371-8669-2, DIMG). Greenwood.

Dickinson, Robert L. Atlas of Human Sex Anatomy. LC 50-5564. (Illus.). 382p. 1970. Repr. of 1949 ed. 34.00 (ISBN 0-88275-014-3). Krieger.

Dickinson, W. Calvin. James Harrington's Republic. LC 82-24749. 126p. (Orig.). 1983. lib. bdg. 18.50 (ISBN 0-8191-3019-2); pap. text ed. 8.25 (ISBN 0-8191-3020-6). U Pr of Amer.

Dickison, S. K., jt. auth. see Schaub, J. H.

Dickman, Irving R. Winning the Battle for Sex Education. LC 82-61000. 64p. (Orig.). 1982. pap. 6.00 (ISBN 0-9609212-0-6). SIECUS.

Dickmeyer, Lowell A. Football Is for Me. LC 79-15445. (Sports for Me Bks.). (Illus.). (gr. 2-5). 1979. lib. bdg. 6.95g (ISBN 0-8225-1087-1). Lerner Pubns.

--Hockey Is for Me. LC 78-54362. (The Sports for Me Bks). (Illus.). (gr. 2-5). 1978. PLB 6.95g (ISBN 0-8225-1080-4). Lerner Pubns.

--Skateboarding Is for Me. LC 78-54361. (The Sports for Me Bks). (Illus.). (gr. 5 up). 1978. PLB 6.95g (ISBN 0-8225-1081-2). Lerner Pubns.

--Soccer Is for Me. LC 77-92294. (Sports for Me Books). (Illus.). (gr. k-4). 1978. PLB 6.95g (ISBN 0-8225-1076-6). Lerner Pubns.

--Track Is for Me. LC 79-1508. (Sports for Me Bks.). (Illus.). (gr. 2-5). 1979. PLB 6.95g (ISBN 0-8225-1083-9). Lerner Pubns.

Dickmeyer, Lowell A. & Chappell, Annette Jo. Tennis Is for Me. LC 77-92300. (Sports for Me Books). (Illus.). (gr. k-4). 1978. PLB 6.95g (ISBN 0-8225-1077-4). Lerner Pubns.

Dickneider, William C., Jr. & Kaplan, David. Choice & Change: An Introduction to Economics. (Illus.). 1978. pap. text ed. 14.95 (ISBN 0-8299-0165-5); test bank avail. (ISBN 0-8299-0475-1). West Pub.

Dick-Reade, Grantly. Childbirth Without Fear. rev. 4th ed. LC 77-181616. (Illus.). 1979. pap. 3.95i (ISBN 0-06-080490-4, P 490, PL). Har-Row.

Dicks, Brian. The Ancient Persians: How They Lived & Worked. 1979. 14.95 o.p. (ISBN 0-7153-7711-6). David & Charles.

--Corfu. LC 76-48823. (Islands Ser.). (Illus.). 1977. 14.95 o.p. (ISBN 0-7153-7311-0). David & Charles.

Dicks, Terrance. The Baker Street Irregulars in the Case of the Cop Catchers. 128p. (gr. 5-9). 1982. 8.95 (ISBN 0-525-66765-2, 0869-260). Lodestar Bks.

--The Baker Street Irregulars in the Case of the Missing Masterpiece. LC 79-18861. (gr. 4 up). 1979. 7.95 (ISBN 0-525-66656-7). Lodestar Bks.

--Dr. Who & the Day of the Daleks. (Dr. Who Ser.: No. 1). 1979. pap. 1.95 (ISBN 0-523-41986-4). Pinnacle Bks.

--Dr. Who & the Genesis of the Daleks. (The Dr. Who Ser.: No. 4). 1979. pap. 1.95 (ISBN 0-523-41973-2). Pinnacle Bks.

--Dr. Who & the Loch Ness Monster. (Dr. Who Ser.: No. 6). 1979. pap. 1.95 (ISBN 0-523-41791-8). Pinnacle Bks.

--Dr. Who & the Revenge of the Cybermen. (Dr. Who Ser.: No. 5). 1979. pap. 1.95 (ISBN 0-523-41620-2). Pinnacle Bks.

Dicks, Terrence. Dr. Who & the Android Invasion. (Dr. Who Ser.: No. 9). (Orig.). 1980. pap. 1.95 (ISBN 0-523-41619-9). Pinnacle Bks.

Dickson, Billy, jt. auth. see McAleer, John.

Dickson, Carter. The Department of Queer Complaints. 1981. 13.95 (ISBN 0-8398-2739-3, Gregg). G K Hall.

Dickson, D. Bruce. Prehistoric Pueblo Settlement Patterns: The Arroyo Hondo, New Mexico, Site Survey. LC 79-21542. (Arroyo Hondo Archaeological Ser.: Vol. 2). (Illus.). 1979. pap. 7.50 (ISBN 0-933452-02-0). Schol Am Res.

Dickson, David. A Commentary on the Psalms, 2 vols. 1980. 32.50 (ISBN 0-86524-017-5, 1901). Klock & Klock.

Dickson, David T. Tax Shelters for the Not-So-Rich. (Illus.). 1980. 9.95 o.p. (ISBN 0-8092-7142-7). Contemp Bks.

Dickson, Douglas N. Corporate Political Action Committees. 1983. prof ref 25.00x (ISBN 0-88410-839-2). Ballinger Pub.

Dickson, Edward M., et al. The Hydrogen Energy Economy: A Realistic Appraisal of Prospects & Impacts. LC 76-56807. (Special Studies). 1977. 33.95 o.p. (ISBN 0-275-24290-0). Praeger.

Dickson, Elizabeth & Peterson, George. Public Employee Compensation: A Twelve City Comparison. 2nd ed. LC 81-53060. 213p. 1981. pap. text ed. 12.00 (ISBN 0-87766-310-6, URI 32800). Urban Inst.

Dickson, G. W. & Wetherbe, J. Management Information Systems Management. 576p. 1982. 26.95x (ISBN 0-07-016825-3); write for info. instr's manual (ISBN 0-07-016826-1). McGraw.

--Management Information Systems Management Cases. 224p. 1982. 12.95x (ISBN 0-07-016827-X). McGraw.

Dickson, Gary L. Resident Assistant Stress Inventory: Manual & Inservice Education Guide. rev. ed. iv, 43p. 1981. pap. 3.95 (ISBN 0-943872-68-5). Andrews Univ Pr.

Dickson, George E. & Saxe, Richard W. Partners for Educational Reform & Renewal. LC 73-7241. 1973. 21.75x (ISBN 0-8211-1825-0); text ed. 19.50x (ISBN 0-685-42629-7). McCutchan.

Dickson, Gordon. Hour of the Horde. (gr. 6-8). 1970. 4.50 o.p. (ISBN 0-399-20097-5). Putnam Pub Group.

--The Outposter. 256p. (Orig.). 1982. pap. 2.95 (ISBN 0-523-48580-8). Pinnacle Bks.

--The Pritcher Mass. 256p. 1983. pap. 2.75 (ISBN 0-523-48556-5). Pinnacle Bks.

Dickson, Gordon, ed. Nebula Winners Twelve. LC 66-20974. 1978. 12.45i (ISBN 0-06-011078-3, HarpT). Har-Row.

Dickson, Gordon R. The Alien Way. 224p. 1982. pap. 2.25 (ISBN 0-441-01692-8, Pub. by Ace Science Fiction). Ace Bks.

--In Iron Years. LC 73-20509. (Doubleday Science Fiction Ser.). 256p. 1980. 11.95 o.p. (ISBN 0-385-01555-0). Doubleday.

--Spacepaw. 1983. pap. 2.50 (ISBN 0-441-77759-7, Pub. by Ace Science Fiction). Ace Bks.

--Special Delivery. pap. 1.95 (ISBN 0-686-83917-X, Pub. by Ace Science Fiction). Ace Bks.

Dickson, Gordon R. & Green, Roland. Jamie the Red. Date not set. pap. price not set (Pub. by Ace Science Fiction). Ace Bks.

Dickson, Gordon R., jt. auth. see Anderson, Poul.

Dickson, J. H. Bryophytes of the Pleistocene: The British Record & Its Chorological & Ecological Implications. 1973. 85.00 (ISBN 0-521-08576-4). Cambridge U Pr.

Dickson, James G. Diseases of Field Crops. 2nd ed. (Agricultural Sciences Ser). (Illus.). 1956. text ed. 38.50 (ISBN 0-07-016804-0, C). McGraw.

Dickson, James G., et al, eds. The Role of Insectivorous Birds in Forest Ecosystems. LC 79-12111. 1979. 34.50 (ISBN 0-12-215350-2). Acad Pr.

Dickson, Joanne, ed. Manuel Neri: Sculpture & Drawings. LC 80-71065. (Illus.). 28p. (Orig.). 1981. pap. 5.95 (ISBN 0-932216-11-0). Seattle Art.

Dickson, K. B. Historical Geography of Ghana. LC 69-19375. (Illus.). 1971. 49.50 (ISBN 0-521-07102-X); pap. 13.95x (ISBN 0-521-09657-X). Cambridge U Pr.

Dickson, Kenneth L. & Maki, Alan W., eds. Modeling the Fate of Chemicals in the Aquatic Environment. LC 82-71527. (Illus.). 413p. 1982. 27.50 (ISBN 0-250-40552-0). Ann Arbor Science.

Dickson, Leonard E. Collected Mathematical Papers, 5 vols. Albert, A. Adrian, ed. LC 69-19943. 3300p. 1975. Set. text ed. 195.00 set (ISBN 0-8284-0273-6). Chelsea Pub.

--Plane Trigonometry with Practical Applications. LC 70-114597. (Illus.). (gr. 10-12). 1970. Repr. of 1922 ed. text ed. 9.50 (ISBN 0-8284-0230-2). Chelsea Pub.

--Studies in the Theory of Numbers. LC 61-13494. 13.95 (ISBN 0-8284-0151-9). Chelsea Pub.

Dickson, Murray. Where There Is No Dentist. Blake, Michael, ed. LC 82-84067. (Illus.). 192p. (Orig.). 1983. pap. 5.00 (ISBN 0-942364-05-8). Hesperian Found.

Dickson, Naida. Biography of a Honeybee. LC 73-11976. (General Juvenile Bks). (Illus.). 48p. (gr. 1-4). 1974. PLB 5.95g (ISBN 0-8225-0292-5). Lerner Pubns.

--I'd Like... (Early Childhood Bk.). (Illus.). (ps-2). PLB 4.95 o.p. (ISBN 0-513-00509-9). Denison.

Dickson, P. Kissinger & the Meaning of History. LC 78-5633. 1978. 27.95 (ISBN 0-521-22113-7). Cambridge U Pr.

Dickson, Paul. The Official Explanations. (Illus.). 225p. 1980. 9.95 o.s.i. (ISBN 0-440-06513-5). Delacorte.

--The Official Rules. 1978. 9.95 o.s.i. (ISBN 0-440-06545-3). Delacorte.

--Out of This World. 1977. pap. text ed. 9.95 o.s.i. (ISBN 0-440-56756-4, Delta). Dell.

--Out of This World: American Space Photography. 1977. 19.95 o.s.i. (ISBN 0-440-06568-2). Delacorte.

--Toasts. (Orig.). 1982. pap. 7.95 (ISBN 0-440-58741-7, Dell Trade Pbks). Dell.

Dickson, Paul & Goulden, Joseph. There Are Alligators in Our Sewers: And Other American Credos. 396p. 1983. 15.95 (ISBN 0-440-08882-8). Delacorte.

Dickson, Robert. Robert's Dinner for Six. LC 78-64486. 1978. 6.00 (ISBN 0-937684-05-8). Tradd St Pr.

Dickson, Robert G. Divorce Guide for Alberta. 3rd ed. 91p. 1979. 7.95 (ISBN 0-88908-216-2); forms 12.95 (ISBN 0-686-35995-X). Self Counsel Pr.

Dickson, Stanley, et al. Communication Disorders: Remedial Principles & Practices. 1974. text ed. 21.95x (ISBN 0-673-07742-X). Scott F.

Dickson, T. R. Introduction to Chemistry. 3rd ed. LC 78-17406. 465p. 1979. text ed. 24.95x (ISBN 0-471-02223-3). experiments 7.95 (ISBN 0-471-04747-3); transparencies 8.00 (ISBN 0-471-04757-0); study guide 7.95 (ISBN 0-471-04748-1); tchrs. manual 10.00 (ISBN 0-471-04750-3). Wiley.

--Understanding Chemistry: From Atoms to Attitudes. LC 73-12695. 361p. 1974. text ed. 23.95x o.p. (ISBN 0-471-21285-7). Wiley.

Dickson, Tony, ed. Capital & Class in Scotland. 286p. 1982. text ed. 33.75x (ISBN 0-85976-065-0, Pub. by Donald Scotland). Humanities.

Di Clemente, F. F. Soccer Illustrated for Coach & Player. 2nd ed. 260p. 1968. 16.95x o.p. (ISBN 0-471-07138-2). Wiley.

DiClemente, Frank F. Soccer Illustrated: For Coach & Player. 2nd ed. LC 68-8624. 268p. 1968. 15.95 o.p. (ISBN 0-686-79903-8). Krieger.

--Soccer Illustrated: For Coach & Player. LC 68-8624. 268p. (Orig.). 1968. 15.95 o.p. (ISBN 0-89874-461-X). Krieger.

DiClerico, Robert. The American President. (Illus.). 1979. pap. 14.95 ref. ed. (ISBN 0-13-028555-2). P-H.

DiClerico, Roberts & Hammock, Allan S. Points of View: Readings in American Government & Politics. 2nd ed. LC 82-10358. 352p. 1983. pap. text ed. write for info. (ISBN 0-201-10350-8). A-W.

DiCosmo, F., jt. auth. see Nag Raj, T. R.

Didato, Salvatore. Psychotechniques. LC 79-50640. 1980. cancelled o.p. (ISBN 0-448-15165-0, G&D). Putnam Pub Group.

Diday, E. & Lebart, L., eds. Data Analysis & Informatics. 1980. 78.75 (ISBN 0-444-86005-3). Elsevier.

Didday, Rich. Home Computers Two Hundred Ten Questions & Answers, Vol. 1: Hardware. LC 77-9285. 265p. 1977. 11.95 (ISBN 0-918398-00-2). Dilithium Pr.

Didday, Rich L., et al. Fortran for Business People. (Illus.). 1978. pap. text ed. 17.50 (ISBN 0-8299-0101-9). West Pub.

Didday, Richard & Page, Rex. Fortran for Humans. 3rd ed. (Illus.). 450p. 1981. pap. text ed. 18.95 (ISBN 0-8299-0356-9). West Pub.

--Using BASIC. 542p. 1981. pap. text ed. 18.95 (ISBN 0-8299-0357-7). West Pub.

Didday, Richard, jt. auth. see Page, Rex.

Didday, Richard L., jt. auth. see Page, Rex L.

Diderot & D'Alembert, eds. Encyclopedie, 18 vols. (Fr., 12 vols. of plates & 6 texts). 1971-1979. Set. 3450.00 (ISBN 0-8277-3025-X). Pergamon.

--Encyclopedie; Ou, Dictionnaire Raisonne Des Sciences, Des Arts et Des Metiers, 35 Vols. 1751. Repr. 4750.00 (ISBN 0-8277-3054-3). Pergamon.

Diderot, Denis. The Letter of the Blind for the Benefit of Those Who See. (The Most Meaningful Classics in World Culture Ser.). (Illus.). 101p. 1983. 66.85 (ISBN 0-89266-383-9). Am Classical Coll Pr.

--Philosophical Thought of Diderot. (Meaningful Classics in World Culture Ser.). (Illus.). 129p. 1982. 49.75 (ISBN 0-89266-348-0). Am Classical Coll Pr.

Didier, E. L. Life & Poems of Edgar Allen Poe. LC 73-16344. (Studies in Poe, No. 23). 1974. lib. bdg. 49.95x o.p. (ISBN 0-8383-1726-X). Haskell.

Didier, J. Granites & Their Enclaves. LC 76-179999. (Developments in Petrology Ser.: Vol. 3). 412p. 1973. 85.00 (ISBN 0-444-40974-2). Elsevier.

Didier, Jean, ed. Le Bottin Gourmand. (Illus.). 1176p. (Orig., Fr.). 1982. pap. 40.00x (ISBN 2-7039-0505-X). Intl Pubns Serv.

Didion, Joan. A Book of Common Prayer. 1977. 8.95 o.p. (ISBN 0-671-22491-3). S&S.

--A Book of Common Prayer. 288p. 1983. pap. price not set (ISBN 0-671-42169-7). WSP.

--Play It As It Lays. 266p. 1983. pap. price not set (ISBN 0-671-43596-5). WSP.

--Salvador. 1983. 12.95 (ISBN 0-671-47024-8). S&S.

--Slouching Towards Bethlehem. 240p. 1983. pap. price not set (ISBN 0-671-42210-3). WSP.

DiDomenico, Joseph M. Investigative Technique for the Retail Security Investigator. LC 79-12097. 1979. 15.95 (ISBN 0-86730-530-4). Lebhar Friedman.

Di Donato, Georgia. Woman of Justice. (General Ser.). 1980. lib. bdg. 15.95 (ISBN 0-8161-3132-5, Large Print GBks). G K Hall.

Di Donato, Pietro see Donato, Pietro di.

Didriksen, Paula, tr. see Braun, Isabella.

Didsbury, Howard F., Jr., ed. Communications & the Future. 400p. 14.50 (ISBN 0-930242-16-5). World Future.

Diebel, Don. The Complete Guide to Meeting Women. 180p. 1983. pap. 8.95 (ISBN 0-937164-01-1). Gemini Pub Co.

Diebener, Wilhelm. Monograms & Decorations from the Art Nouveau Period. (Pictorial Archive Ser.). (Illus.). 144p. 1982. pap. 6.00 (ISBN 0-486-24347-8). Dover.

Diebert, Linda, jt. auth. see Tremper, Andra.

Diebold Group. Automatic Data Processing Handbook. (Illus.). 1977. 54.95 (ISBN 0-07-016807-5, P&RB). McGraw.

Diebold, John. The Role of Business in Society. 144p. 1983. 12.95 (ISBN 0-8144-5743-6). Am Mgmt.

Diebold, William, Jr. Industrial Policy As an International Issue. (Nineteen Eighty's Project (Council on Foreign Relations)). 1979. text ed. 13.95 (ISBN 0-07-016809-1); pap. 6.95 (ISBN 0-07-016810-5). McGraw.

Diebold, William, Jr., jt. auth. see Caldwell, Lawrence.

Dieckmann, Jane. Use It All: The Leftovers Cookbook. LC 81-15215. (Illus.). 368p. 1981. 18.95x (ISBN 0-89594-061-2); pap. 10.95x (ISBN 0-89594-062-0). Crossing Pr.

Dieckmann, Liselotte. Johann Wolfgang Goethe. (World Authors Ser.). 1974. lib. bdg. 12.95 (ISBN 0-8057-2378-1, Twayne). G K Hall.

Diedrich, Richard C. Guidance Personnel & Other Professionals. (Guidance Monograph). 1968. pap. 2.40 o.p. (ISBN 0-395-09908-0). HM.

Diedrich, Richard C. & Dye, H. Allan. Group Procedures: Purposes, Processes, & Outcomes. 1972. pap. text ed. 21.50 (ISBN 0-395-04364-6). HM.

Diefendorf, B. B. Paris City Councillors in the Sixteenth Century: The Politics of Patrimony. 1982. 31.50 (ISBN 0-691-05362-6). Princeton U Pr.

Diego, Fernando De see De Diego, Fernando.

Diehl, Charles. Byzantium: Greatness & Decline. Walford, Naomi, tr. (Byzantine Ser.). 1960. pap. 12.50x o.p. (ISBN 0-8135-0328-0). Rutgers U Pr.

Diehl, Charles F., jt. auth. see Stevenson, Dwight E.

Diehl, Gaston. Derain. (Q L P Art Ser.). 7.95 (ISBN 0-517-03720-3). Crown.

--Fernand Leger. (Quality-Low-Price Art Ser.). (Illus.). 96p. 1982. 7.95 (ISBN 0-517-54711-2). Crown.

--Joan Miro. (Q L P Ser.). (Illus.). 87p. 1974. 7.95 (ISBN 0-517-51671-3). Crown.

--Max Ernst. (Q L P Art Ser.). (Illus.). 96p. 1973. 7.95 (ISBN 0-517-50004-3). Crown.

--The Moderns. (Illus.). 12.50 o.p. (ISBN 0-517-01331-2). Crown.

--Pascin. (Q L P Art Series). (Illus.). 1968. 7.95 (ISBN 0-517-09890-3). Crown.

--Picasso. (Q L P Art Ser). (Illus.). 1960. 7.95 (ISBN 0-517-00501-8). Crown.

--Van Dongen. (Q L P Art Ser). (Illus.). 7.95 (ISBN 0-517-02408-X). Crown.

--Vasarely. (Q L P Art Ser.). (Illus.). 96p. 1972. 7.95 (ISBN 0-517-50800-1). Crown.

Diehl, George M. Machinery Acoustics. LC 73-12980. 204p. 1973. 29.95x (ISBN 0-471-21360-8, Pub. by Wiley-Interscience). Wiley.

Diehl, H. S., et al. Health & Safety for You. 4th ed. text ed. 17.92 (ISBN 0-07-016860-1, W); tchr's. ed. 19.72 (ISBN 0-07-016861-X); tests 2.96 (ISBN 0-07-016862-8). McGraw.

Diehl, Harold S. & Dalrymple, Willard. Healthful Living: A Textbook of Personal & Community Health. 9th ed. (Illus.). 576p. 1973. text ed. 21.00 (ISBN 0-07-016835-0, C); instructor's manual 3.95 (ISBN 0-07-016836-9). McGraw.

Diehl, Harold S., et al. Health & Safety for You. 3rd ed. (gr. 9 up). 1969. text ed. 17.48 (ISBN 0-07-016856-3, W). McGraw.

--Health & Safety for You. 5th ed. 1979. text ed. 18.64 (ISBN 0-07-016863-6); tchr's ed. 8.96 (ISBN 0-07-016864-4). McGraw.

Diehl, Helmut. Atheismus Im Religionsunterricht. 622p. (Ger.). 1982. write for info. (ISBN 3-8204-6280-5). P Lang Pubs.

Diehl, Marcy O. & Fordney, Marilyn T. Medical Transcribing: Techniques & Procedures. LC 78-52727. (Illus.). 1979. pap. text ed. 21.95 (ISBN 0-7216-3079-0). Saunders.

Diehl, P., et al. Computer Assistance in the Analysis of High-Resolution NMR Spectra. (NMR Basic Principles & Progress: Vol. 6). (Illus.). 100p. 1972. 24.00 (ISBN 0-387-05532-0). Springer-Verlag.

Diehl, Richard A., jt. auth. see Coe, Michael D.

Diehl, William. Chameleon. LC 80-40228. 1982. 14.50 (ISBN 0-394-51961-2). Random.

Diehr, George. Business Programming with BASIC. LC 76-39639. 366p. 1972. 29.95 (ISBN 0-471-21370-5). Wiley.

Diekelman, Nancy. Primary Health Care of the Well Adult. (Illus.). 1977. pap. text ed. 15.50 (ISBN 0-07-016879-2, HP). McGraw.

Diekelmann, Nancy, et al. Fundamentals of Nursing. (Illus.). 1979. text ed. 26.00 (ISBN 0-07-016885-7, HP). McGraw.

Diekman, Norman & Pile, John. Drawing Interior Architecture: A Guide to Rendering & Presentation. 176p. 1983. 32.50 (ISBN 0-8230-7159-6, Whitney Lib). Watson-Guptill.

Diekmann, Jens, jt. auth. see Schuhholz, Annaliese.

Diekmann, Miep. Slave Doctor. Mueller, Madeleine, tr. (Illus.). (gr. 7 up). 1970. 9.95 (ISBN 0-688-20123-7). Morrow.

Diekmann, O. Risk Assessment in Cost Estimating for New Technologies. (Progress in Solar Energy Supplement SERI Ser.). 75p. 1983. pap. text ed. 9.00 (ISBN 0-89553-084-8). Am Solar Energy.

Diekstra, Frans. Early & Middle English Literature. (Dutch Quarterly Review of Anglo-American Letters: Vol. 11, 1981/4). 80p. 1981. pap. text ed. 9.25x (ISBN 90-6203-933-2, Pub. by Rodopi England). Humanities.

Diel, Paul. Symbolism in Greek Mythology: Human Desire & Its Transformations. Stuart, Vincent, et al, trs. from Fr. LC 79-67696. 240p. 1980. 20.00 (ISBN 0-394-51083-6). Shambhala Pubns.

Dieleman, Dale. The Go Book. (Good Things for Youth Leaders). 64p. 1982. pap. 4.50 (ISBN 0-8010-2929-5). Baker Bk.

Dielman, Louis H., ed. see Marine, William M.

Diem, Aubrey. Western Europe: Geographical Analysis. LC 77-24617. 543p. 1979. text ed. 34.95 (ISBN 0-471-21400-0). Wiley.

Diem, Liselott. Children Learn Physical Skills, 2 vols. 1978. pap. 7.95 ea.; Vol. 1. Birth to 3 Years (ISBN 0-88314-040-3, 240-26322); Vol. 2. Ages 3-5 (ISBN 0-88314-039-X, 240-26324). AAHPERD.

--Who Can. 1977. 4.95x (ISBN 0-88314-211-2, 245-26074). AAHPERD.

Diener, Theodor O. Viroids & Viroid Diseases. LC 78-21681. 1979. 30.95x (ISBN 0-471-03504-1, Pub. by Wiley-Interscience). Wiley.

Dienes, C. Thomas, jt. auth. see Barron, Jerome A.

Dienes, G. J., ed. Studies in Radiation Effects in Solids, Vol. 4. 202p. 1975. 46.00x (ISBN 0-677-03340-0). Gordon.

Dienes, G. J., ed. see Sixth International Liquid Crystals Conference, Kyoto, Japan, June 30-July 4, 1980.

Dienes, Z. P. Science & the University. (Frank Gerstein Lecture Ser.: York Univ). 90p. 1967. 14.95 o.p. (ISBN 0-312-70280-9). St Martin.

Dienes, Zoltan P. Experimental Study of Mathematics Learning. 1963. text ed. 9.25x o.p. (ISBN 0-09-068650-0). Humanities.

Dienhart, Allan. Football Scouting Workbook. pap. 8.95x o.p. (ISBN 0-392-07843-0, SpS). Sportshelf.

Dienhart, John W. A Cognitive Approach to the Ethics of Counseling Psychology. LC 82-17393. 152p. (Orig.). 1983. lib. bdg. 18.75 (ISBN 0-8191-2817-1); pap. text ed. 8.50 (ISBN 0-8191-2818-X). U Pr of Amer.

Dienstag, Jacob I. Eschatology in Maimonidean Thought. 1982. 39.50x (ISBN 0-87068-706-9). Ktav.

Dierauf, E., Jr. & Court, J. Unified Concepts in Applied Physics. 1979. 23.95 (ISBN 0-13-938753-6). P-H.

Diercks, Char, tr. see Kutac, Edward A. & Caran, S. Christopher.

Dierker, Paul F., jt. auth. see Campbell, Howard E.

Dierks, Paul A., jt. auth. see Vargo, Richard J.

Diernisse, Villy. Retort Pouch: New Growth Industry. (Illus.). 191p. 1981. 950.00x (ISBN 0-910211-00-0). Laal Co.

Dierrsen, Gunther, jt. auth. see Frickelton, Annelise.

Dierschke, Hartmut. Internationale Vereinigung Fuer Vegetationskunde: Berichte der Internationalen Symposien: Syntaxonomie (1980) (Illus.). 614p. (Ger.). 1981. lib. bdg. 64.00x (ISBN 3-7682-1309-9, Pub. by Cramer Germany). Lubrecht & Cramer.

Dierschke, Hartmut, ed. Struktur und Dynamik von Waeldern: Rinteln, April 1981, Berichte der Internationalen Symposien der Intern'len Vereinigung fuer Vegetationskunde. (Illus.). 600p. (Orig., Ger.). 1983. lib. bdg. 64.00 (ISBN 3-7682-1334-X). Lubrecht & Cramer.

Diers Rau, Henrietta A. Healing with Herbs: Nature's Way to Better Health. LC 75-23579. 240p. 1976. pap. 2.50 (ISBN 0-668-03878-0). Arco.

Dies, Edward J. Titans of the Soil: Great Builders of Agriculture. LC 76-49613. (Illus.). 1977. Repr. of 1949 ed. lib. bdg. 21.00x (ISBN 0-8371-9329-X, DITS). Greenwood.

Diesfeld, Hans-Jochen. Health Research in Developing Countries. 238p. 1982. write for info. (ISBN 3-8204-7110-3). P Lang Pubs.

Diesing, Paul. Reason in Society: Five Types of Decisions & Their Social Conditions. LC 72-11328. 262p. 1973. Repr. of 1962 ed. lib. bdg. 29.75x (ISBN 0-8371-6660-8, DIRS); pap. 4.95 (ISBN 0-8371-8941-1, DIR). Greenwood.

Diesner, Hans-Joachim. The Great Migration. (Illus.). 255p. 1982. 35.00 o.p. (ISBN 0-88254-640-6). Hippocrene Bks.

Diessenhaus, H. I., jt. auth. see Millon, T.

Dieter, G. Engineering Design. 608p. 1983. text ed. 34.50x (ISBN 0-07-016896-2). McGraw.

Dieter, George. Mechanical Metallurgy. 2nd ed. (Illus.). 1976. text ed. 36.95 (ISBN 0-07-016891-1, C); instructor's manual 8.50 (ISBN 0-07-016892-X). McGraw.

Dieter, William. Hunter's Orange. LC 82-73280. 256p. 1983. 12.95 (ISBN 0-689-11379-X). Atheneum.

Dieterich, Daniel, ed. Teaching about Doublespeak. LC 76-4139. 200p. 1976. pap. 6.15 (ISBN 0-8141-5027-6); pap. 5.00 members (ISBN 0-686-86470-0). NCTE.

Dieterlen, F. Zur Phaenologie des aequatorialen Regenwaldes im Ost-Zaire (Kivu) nebst Planzenliste und Klimadaten. (Dissertations Botanica: No. 47). (Illus.). 1979. pap. 12.00x (ISBN 3-7682-1215-7). Lubrecht & Cramer.

Dieth, Eugen, jt. ed. see Orton, Harold.

Diethrich, Edward B., ed. Noninvasive Assessment of the Cardiovascular System. LC 82-4785. (Illus.). 432p. 1982. text ed. 39.50 (ISBN 0-7236-7019-6). Wright-PSG.

Dietiker, Simone R. En Bonne Forme. 2nd ed. 416p. 1978. pap. text ed. 15.95x (ISBN 0-669-00863-X). Heath.

--En Bonne Forme. 3rd ed. 416p. 1983. pap. 15.95 (ISBN 0-669-05255-8). Heath.

--Franc-Parler. 2nd ed. 1980. text ed. 21.95x (ISBN 0-669-02491-0); instrs.' guide 8.95 (ISBN 0-669-02494-5); wkbk. 6.95 (ISBN 0-669-02492-9); tapes-reels 60.00 (ISBN 0-669-02496-1); cassettes 30.00 (ISBN 0-669-02497-X); demo tape 1.00 (ISBN 0-669-02498-8); tapescript 1.00 (ISBN 0-669-02495-3). Heath.

Dietl, L. Kay & Neff, Marsha J. Human Needs & Social Welfare Curriculum Project. Incl. Unit I. To Promote the General Welfare? An Introduction to the United States Social Welfare System. write for info. (ISBN 0-8077-6070-6); write for info. tchrs. manual (ISBN 0-8077-6071-4); Unit II. Aging Americans-Profiles, Programs & Possibilities. write for info. (ISBN 0-8077-6072-2); write for info. tchrs. manual (ISBN 0-8077-6073-0); Youth-Search for Identity. write for info. (ISBN 0-8077-6074-9); write for info. tchrs. manual (ISBN 0-8077-6075-7); Unit IV. Single Parent Families: Choice or Chance? write for info. (ISBN 0-8077-6076-5); write for info. tchrs. manual (ISBN 0-8077-6077-3); New Directions: Alternatives to the United States Social Welfare System. write for info. (ISBN 0-8077-6078-1); write for info. tchrs. manual (ISBN 0-8077-6079-X). 1983. Tchrs Coll.

Dietrich, D., jt. ed. see Zamrik, S. Y.

Dietrich, Emerson, ed. see Elliott, Ralph N.

Dietrich, Frank H., II & Kearns, Thomas. Basic Statistics. 1983. text ed. 26.95 (ISBN 0-89517-044-2). Dellen Pub.

Dietrich, Frank H., II, jt. auth. see McClave, James T.

Dietrich, Gunter. General Oceanography. LC 63-17346. 1963. 40.50 o.p. (ISBN 0-470-21450-3, Pub. by Wiley-Interscience). Wiley.

Dietrich, John & Waggoner, Susan. The Complete Health Club Handbook. (Orig.). 1983. pap. price not set (ISBN 0-671-47027-2). S&S.

Dietrich, R. V. & Wicander, E. Reed. Rocks, Minerals & Fossils. (Self-Teaching Guides Ser.). 288p. 1983. pap. text ed. 9.95 (ISBN 0-471-89883-X). Wiley.

Dietrich, Richard, ed. The Realities of Literature. LC 70-136507. 1971. text ed. 16.50x long ed. o.p. (ISBN 0-471-00122-8); pap. text ed. 16.50x (ISBN 0-673-15675-3). Scott F.

Dietrich, Richard V. Geology & Virginia. LC 76-110752. (Illus.). xiv, 213p. 1971. 14.95x (ISBN 0-8139-0289-4). U Pr of Va.

Dietrich, Richard V. & Skinner, Brian J. Rocks & Rock Minerals. LC 79-1211. 1979. text ed. 20.95 (ISBN 0-471-02934-3). Wiley.

Dietrich, Suzanne. Matthew. LC 59-10454. (Layman's Bible Commentary Ser.: Vol. 16). 1961. pap. 3.95 (ISBN 0-8042-3076-5). John Knox.

Dietrich, Suzanne De see De Dietrich, Suzanne.

Dietrich, Wendell, ed. see Kane, John F.

Dietrich, Wendell, ed. see Orr, Robert P.

Dietrich, William G. Powee in Valentine Land. (Early Childhood Bk.). (Illus.). (ps-2). PLB 4.95 o.p. (ISBN 0-513-01192-7). Denison.

Dietz, Albert G. Dwelling House Construction. rev., 4th ed. (Illus.). 528p. 1974. 25.00x (ISBN 0-262-04044-1); pap. text ed. 9.95 (ISBN 0-262-54033-9). MIT Pr.

--Plastics for Architects & Builders. 1970. text ed. 16.50x (ISBN 0-262-54009-6). MIT Pr.

Dietz, Albert G. & Cutler, Laurence S., eds. Industrialized Building Systems for Housing. 1971. 27.50x (ISBN 0-262-04034-4). MIT Pr.

Dietz, August, Sr. Presidents of the United States: Portraits & Biographies. 2.00 (ISBN 0-685-47902-1). Dietz.

Dietz, Brian, ed. The Part & Trade of Early Elizabethan London: Documents. 1972. 50.00x (ISBN 0-686-96612-0, Pub by London Rec Soc England). State Mutual Bk.

Dietz, David. The New Outline of Science. LC 73-39220. (Illus.). 512p. 1972. 17.50 o.p. (ISBN 0-396-06526-0). Dodd.

--Stars & the Universe. (gr. 5-8). 1968. PLB 4.99 o.p. (ISBN 0-394-90906-2, BYR). Random.

Dietz, Henry A. & Moore, Richard J. Political Participation in a Non-Electoral Setting: The Urban Poor in Lima, Peru. LC 79-14218. (Papers in International Studies: Latin America: No. 6). 1979. pap. text ed. 9.00 (ISBN 0-89680-085-7, Ohio U Ctr Intl). Ohio U Pr.

Dietz, Lois, jt. auth. see Parker, William.

Dietz, Marjorie J., ed. see Free, Montague.

Dietz, Mary L. Killing for Profit: The Social Organization of Felony Homicide. (Illus.). 232p. 1983. text ed. 22.95X (ISBN 0-8304-1008-2). Nelson-Hall.

Dietz, Tim. Tales of Whales. Jack, Susan, ed. (Illus.). 160p. (Orig.). 1982. pap. 7.95 (ISBN 0-930096-33-9). G Gannett.

Dietze, Charles E. The Henderson Crusade. (Illus.). 164p. (Orig.). 1983. pap. 4.95 (ISBN 0-9610198-0-8). G G L Pub Co.

Dietze, Gunther, jt. ed. see Back, Nathan.

Dieudonne, J. History of Functional Analysis. (North Holland Mathematics Studies: Vol. 49). 1981. pap. 38.50 (ISBN 0-444-86148-3). Elsevier.

Diez, W., jt. auth. see Braun, Louis.

Di Fabio, Anthony. Rheumatoid Diseases Cured at Last. LC 82-72042. (Illus.). 96p. (Orig.). 1982. pap. 9.95 (ISBN 0-931150-12-4). Authors Co-op.

DiFederico, Frank R. Francesco Trevisani: Eighteenth Century Painter in Rome. (Illus.). 1977. 50.00 o.p. (ISBN 0-916276-02-3). Decatur Hse.

Diffor, John C., ed. Educators Guide to Free Filmstrips. 34th rev. ed. LC 50-11650. 1982. pap. 15.75 (ISBN 0-87708-122-0). Ed Prog.

Diffor, John C. & Horkheimer, Mary F., eds. Educators Guide to Free Films. 42nd rev. ed. LC 45-412. 1982. pap. 22.50 (ISBN 0-87708-121-2). Ed Prog.

Diffrient, Niels, et al. Humanscale Seven-Eight-Nine. 1981. 37.50 (ISBN 0-262-04061-1). MIT Pr.

DiFiore. Baby Strawberry Book of Toys. 121p. 1980. 2.95 o.p. (ISBN 0-07-016921-7). McGraw.

Difiore, Lawrence. Where's Goldie? LC 82-83381. (First Little Golden Bk.). (Illus.). 24p. (ps). 1983. 0.69 (ISBN 0-307-10149-5, Golden Pr); PLB price not set (ISBN 0-307-68149-1). Western Pub.

Di Francia, G. Toraldo, ed. see International School of Physics.

Di Francis. Cat Country: The Quest for the British Big Cat. (Illus.). 160p. 1983. 12.50 (ISBN 0-7153-8425-2). David & Charles.

DiFranco, Anthony. Italy: Balanced on the Edge of Time. Schneider, Tom, ed. (Discovering Our Heritage). (Illus.). 112p. (gr. 5 up). 1982. PLB 9.95 (ISBN 0-87518-229-1). Dillon.

--Pope John Paul II: Bringing Love to a Troubled World. Schneider, Thomas, ed. (Taking Part Ser.). (Illus.). 48p. (gr. 3 up). 1983. PLB 7.95 (ISBN 0-87518-241-0). Dillon Pr.

DiFranco, Ralph. A Review of Concepts & Methodologies in Scholarship on Juan De Mena. Parent, David J., ed. LC 81-4866. (ALP Medieval Studies Ser.: Vol. 7). 1981. 19.50 (ISBN 0-8357-0584-6, IS-00132, Pub. by Applied Lit Pr). Univ Microfilms.

DiGaetani, Jane B., jt. auth. see DiGaetani, John L.

DiGaetani, John L. & DiGaetani, Jane B. Writing out Loud: A Self-Help Guide to Clear Business Writing. LC 82-73623. 190p. 1983. 12.95 (ISBN 0-87094-374-X). Dow Jones-Irwin.

DiGangi, Frank E., jt. auth. see Knevel, Adelbert M.

Digby, Anne. The Quicksilver Horse. 96p. 1982. 8.95 (ISBN 0-312-66083-9). St Martin.

Digby, Sir Kenelm. Two Treatises: The Nature of Bodies; the Nature of Man's Soule, 1644. Wellek, Rene, ed. LC 75-11217. (British Philosophers & Theologians of the 17th & 18th Centuries Ser.). 1978. lib. bdg. 42.00 o.s.i. (ISBN 0-8240-1771-4). Garland Pub.

Digby, S. & Harle, J. C. Soldiers & Ceremonial in British India. 1982. 59.00x (ISBN 0-686-92032-5, Pub. by Ashmolean Mus Oxford). State Mutual Bk.

DiGennaro, Joseph. The New Physical Fitness: Exercise for Everybody. (Illus.). 1983. pap. text ed. 6.95X (ISBN 0-89582-097-8). Morton Pub.

DiGeorge, illus. Twelve Days of Christmas. (Illus.). 1967. pap. 1.00 o.p. (ISBN 0-685-11987-4). Heineman.

Digerness, David S. The Mineral Belt: Georgetown, Mining, Colorado Central Railroad, Vol. III. (Illus.). 416p. 49.00 (ISBN 0-686-84503-X). Sundance.

Digges, Thomas A. Adventures of Alonso: Containing Some Striking Anecdotes of the Present Minister of Portugal. LC 43-13609. (Monograph Ser.: No. 18). 1943. Repr. of 1775 ed. 12.00x (ISBN 0-930060-01-6). US Cath Hist.

Diggins, John P. & Kann, Mark E., eds. The Problem of Authority in America. 255p. 1981. 29.95 (ISBN 0-87722-220-7). Temple U Pr.

Diggory, Terrence. Yeats & American Poetry: The Traditional of the Self. LC 82-15070. 280p. 1983. 25.00x (ISBN 0-691-06558-6). Princeton U Pr.

Diggs, B. J. The State, Justice, & the Common Good: An Introduction to Social & Political Philosophy. 1974. pap. 7.95x (ISBN 0-673-05198-6). Scott F.

Diggs, Dorothy C. Working Manual for Altar Guilds. rev. ed. (Orig.). 1957. pap. 3.95 (ISBN 0-8192-1028-5). Morehouse.

Diggs, Ellen I. Black Chronology: From 400 B.C. to the Abolition of the Slave Trade. 1983. lib. bdg. 35.00 (ISBN 0-8161-8543-3, Hall Reference). G K Hall.

DiGiacomo, James, jt. auth. see Shannon, Thomas A.

DiGioia, L. Paul. Luke Miles. 1982. 5.95 (ISBN 0-533-05462-1). Vantage.

Di Giovanni. Jorge Luis Borges: Selected Poems 1923-1967. pap. 4.95 o.s.i. (ISBN 0-440-54307-X, Delta). Dell.

DiGiovanni, Cleto, Jr. Crisis in Central America. (Monographs in International Affairs). 1982. pap. text ed. 6.95 (ISBN 0-686-84670-2). AISI.

Di Giovanni, Norman T., tr. see Borges, Jorge L. & Bioy-Cesares, Adolfo.

Di Girolamo, Costanzo. A Critical Theory of Literature. 160p. 1981. 17.50 (ISBN 0-299-08120-6). U of Wis Pr.

Digital Research, Inc. CP-M Compatible Software Catalog. 2nd ed. Date not set. pap. 12.95 (ISBN 0-88022-018-X). Que Corp.

Digital Signal Processing Committee, ed. Programs for Digital Signal Processing. LC 79-89028. 1979. 42.95 (ISBN 0-87942-127-4); tape version 55.00 (ISBN 0-686-96748-8). Inst Electrical.

--Selected Papers in Digital Signal Processing, II. LC 75-22925. 1976. 29.95 (ISBN 0-87942-059-6). Inst Electrical.

DiGiuseppe, Raymond, jt. auth. see Wales, Susan R.

D'Ignazio, Fred. Chip Mitchell: The Case of the Stolen Computer Brains. (Illus.). 128p. (gr. 5-9). 1982. 8.95 (ISBN 0-525-66790-3, 0869-260). Lodestar Bks.

--The Creative Kid's Guide to Home Computers. LC 79-6860. (Illus.). 144p. (gr. 6). 1981. 10.95a (ISBN 0-385-15313-9); PLB (ISBN 0-385-15314-7). Doubleday.

--Messner's Introduction to the Computer. (Illus.). 288p. (gr. 9-12). 1983. PLB 9.79 (ISBN 0-671-42267-7). Messner.

--The New Astronomy: Probing the Secrets of Space. (First Bks). (Illus.). 72p. (gr. 4 up). 1982. PLB 8.90 (ISBN 0-531-04386-X). Watts.

--Small Computers. LC 80-85049. (gr. 9 up). 1981. 9.60 (ISBN 0-531-04269-3). Watts.

--The Star Wars Question & Answer Book about Computers. LC 82-19030. (Illus.). 64p. (gr. 4-8). 1983. PLB 7.99 (ISBN 0-394-95686-9); pap. 4.95 (ISBN 0-394-85686-4). Random.

D'Ignazio, Fred & Gilliam, Stan. Katie & the Computer. LC 78-74960. (Illus.). (gr. 1-4). 1979. 8.95 (ISBN 0-916688-11-9). Creative Comp.

Digrande, Joseph. The Stone & the Candle. Jones, Jean, ed. (Illus.). 60p. 1983. lib. bdg. write for info. (ISBN 0-936204-33-8); pap. write for info. (ISBN 0-936204-34-6). Jelm Mtn.

Di Grappa, Carol, ed. Landscape: Theory. LC 80-81182. (Illus.). 176p. 1982. 35.00 (ISBN 0-912810-27-0); pap. 19.95 (ISBN 0-912810-32-7). Lustrum Pr.

Di Grappa, Carol, et al, eds. Fashion: Theory. LC 80-81181. (Illus.). 176p. 1982. 35.00 (ISBN 0-912810-28-9); pap. 19.95 (ISBN 0-912810-29-7). Lustrum Pr.

Di Grassi, Giacomo see Jackson, James L.

Di Grazia, Bob, jt. ed. see Palone, Joe.

Di Grazia, Thomas, jt. auth. see Clifton, Lucille.

Dijk, T. A. Van see Van Dijk, T. A.

Dijksman, E. A. Motion Geometry of Mechanism. LC 75-3977. (Illus.). 250p. 1976. 44.50 (ISBN 0-521-20841-6). Cambridge U Pr.

Dijkstra, Edward W. A Discipline of Programming. (Illus.). 240p. 1976. 27.00x (ISBN 0-13-215871-X). P-H.

Dijkstra, J., jt. ed. see Beemster, A.

Dijkstra, W. & Van Der Zouwen, J., eds. Response Behaviour in the Survey Interview. 1982. 26.50. Acad Pr.

Dikepa, Kalio H., jt. auth. see Lieber, Michael D.

Diket, A. L. Senator John Slidell & the Community He Represented in Washington 1853-1861. LC 81-43676. 278p. (Orig.). 1982. lib. bdg. 23.00 (ISBN 0-8191-2547-4); pap. text ed. 11.50 (ISBN 0-8191-2548-2). U Pr of Amer.

--Wha' Hae Wi' (Pender) Bled. 1978. 7.50 o.p. (ISBN 0-533-03517-1). Vantage.

Dikman, M. Theory of Thin Elastic Shells. (Surveys & Reference Works in Mathematics Ser.: No. 8). 384p. 1982. text ed. 65.95 (ISBN 0-273-08431-3). Pitman Pub MA.

Dikshit, R. K. Chandellas of Jejakabhukti. 1977. 13.50x o.p. (ISBN 0-88386-934-9). South Asia Bks.

Dil, A. S., ed. see Ervin-Tripp, Susan M.

Dil, Anwar S., ed. see Polome, Edgar C.

Dilamarter, Ronald R. & Hoffman, Wayne L., eds. Field Trip Guide: Nineteen Eighty AAG Louisville Meeting. LC 80-65645. (Illus.). 96p. 1980. pap. 2.00 o.p. (ISBN 0-89291-140-9). Assn Am Geographers.

Dilampedusa, Giuseppe. The Leopard. 1975. pap. 2.50 o.p. (ISBN 0-380-00377-5, 49411). Avon.

Dilber, Edward. Meisterwerke der Deutschen Sprache. 1970. text ed. 7.50 (ISBN 0-685-55621-2, 30169). Phila Bk Co.

Dilcher, D. L. & Taylor, T. N., eds. Biostratigraphy of Fossil Plants: Sucessional & Paleoecological Analyses. LC 79-27418. 259p. 1980. 31.50. Hutchinson Ross.

Dilcher, Gerhard & Hoke, Rudolf. Grundrechte Im 19, Jahrhundert. 283p. (Ger.). 1982. write for info. (ISBN 3-8204-7100-6). P Lang Pubs.

Di Leo, Joseph. Physical Factors in Growth & Development: A Manual for Educators, Nurses, & Social Workers. LC 75-106235. 1970. pap. 3.50x (ISBN 0-8077-1244-2). Tchrs Coll.

DiLeo, Joseph H. Interpreting Children's Drawings. (Illus.). 212p. 1983. 25.00 (ISBN 0-87630-327-0); pap. 16.95 (ISBN 0-87630-331-9). Brunner-Mazel.

DiLeo, Michael & Smith, Eleanor. Two Californias: The Myths & the Realities of a State Divided Against Itself. (Illus.). 250p. (Orig.). 1983. pap. 10.95 (ISBN 0-933280-16-5). Island CA.

DiLiello, L. R. Methods in Food & Dairy Microbiology. (Illus.). 1982. lab manual 16.50 (ISBN 0-87055-411-5). AVI.

Dilisio, James E. Maryland: A Geography. (Geographies of the United States Ser.). 256p. 1983. lib. bdg. 35.00 (ISBN 0-86531-092-0); pap. text ed. 18.00 (ISBN 0-86531-474-8). Westview.

Dilker, Barbara. Stage Management Forms & Formats. LC 79-16689. (Illus.). 192p. (Orig.). 1982. pap. text ed. 13.95x (ISBN 0-910482-85-3). Drama Bk.

Dill, Marshall, Jr. Paris in Time. LC 74-30550. 1975. 10.00 o.p. (ISBN 0-399-11486-6). Putnam Pub Group.

Dill, Stephen H. Integrated Studies: Challenges to the College Curriculum. LC 82-17511. (Illus.). 158p. (Orig.). 1983. lib. bdg. 19.50 (ISBN 0-8191-2794-9); pap. text ed. 9.25 (ISBN 0-8191-2795-7). U Pr of Amer.

Dill, William R. Running the American Corporation. LC 78-16922. (American Assembly Ser.). 1978. 10.95 o.p. (ISBN 0-13-783894-8, Spec); pap. 4.95 (ISBN 0-13-783886-7). P-H.

Dill, William R. & Popov, G. Organization for Forecasting & Planning: Experience in the Soviet Union & the United States. LC 78-13620. (IIASA International Series on Applied Systems Analysis). 256p. 1979. 42.95 (ISBN 0-471-99720-X, Pub. by Wiley-Interscience). Wiley.

Dillard & Millar. Atlas of Cardiac Surgery. 1983. price not set (ISBN 0-02-329530-9). Macmillan.

Dillard, Annie. Living by Fiction. LC 81-47882. 192p. 1983. pap. 4.76i (ISBN 0-06-091044-5, CN 1044, CN). Har-Row.

--Pilgrim at Tinker Creek. LC 73-18655. 232p. 1974. 11.49i (ISBN 0-06-121980-0). Har-Row.

--Teaching a Stone to Talk: Expeditions & Encounters. LC 82-47520. 192p. 1982. 12.95 (ISBN 0-06-015030-0, HarpT). Har-Row.

Dillard, Clyde R. & Goldberg, David E. Chemistry: Reactions, Structure, & Properties. 2nd ed. (Illus.). 1978. 27.95x (ISBN 0-02-329580-5). Macmillan.

Dillard, Dudley. Economic Development of the North Atlantic Community: Historical Introduction to Modern Economics. 1967. text ed. 25.95 (ISBN 0-13-223305-3). P-H.

Dillard, Emil. Nouns & Pronouns. LC 74-75401. 80p. 1974. 5.00 (ISBN 0-911838-40-6). Windy Row.

Dillard, J. L. All-American English. 1976. pap. write for info. o.p. (ISBN 0-394-71637-X, Vin). Random.

--American Talk: Where Our Words Come from. 1977. pap. 7.95 (ISBN 0-394-40012-7, Vin). Random.

Dillard, J. L., ed. see Marckwardt, Albert H.

Dillard, Jack. Heart Stop: No Death at All. (Illus.). 42p. (Orig.). 1982. pap. write for info. (ISBN 0-940588-08-0). Hazlett Print.

Dillard, John E., Jr., jt. auth. see Davis, Grant M.

Dillard, Mabel M., jt. auth. see Benson, Brian J.

Dillard, R. H. The First Man on the Sun: A Novel. 304p. 1983. 19.95 (ISBN 0-8071-1090-6); pap. 8.95 (ISBN 0-8071-1098-1). La State U Pr.

Dillaway, Hope M. Wake up, Parents! 184p. 1974. 5.95 o.p. (ISBN 0-8158-0317-6). Chris Mass.

Dille, Robert C., ed. The Collected Works of Buck Rogers in the 25th Century. LC 76-39700. 320p. 1977. pap. 8.95 o.s.i. (ISBN 0-89104-062-5, A & W Visual Library). A & W Pubs.

Diller. Drawing for Young Artists. (The Grosset Art Instruction Ser.: No. 14). (Illus.). 48p. Date not set. pap. 2.95 (ISBN 0-448-00523-9, G&D). Putnam Pub Group.

--Young Artists Go to Europe. (Pitman Art Ser.: Vol. 27). pap. 1.95 o.p. (ISBN 0-448-00536-0, G&D). Putnam Pub Group.

Diller, jt. auth. see Haltenorth.

Diller, Aubrey. Race Mixture Among the Greeks Before Alexander. LC 70-95094. Repr. of 1937 ed. lib. bdg. 15.50x (ISBN 0-8371-3086-7, DIRM). Greenwood.

Diller, Edward. A Mythic Journey: Gunter Grass's Tin Drum. LC 73-86402. 224p. 1974. 15.00x o.p. (ISBN 0-8131-1308-3). U Pr of Ky.

Diller, Karl C. Individual Differences & Universals in Language Learning Aptitude. (Orig.). 1981. pap. text ed. 17.95 (ISBN 0-88377-164-0). Newbury Hse.

--The Language Teaching Controversy. rev ed. LC 78-7021. 1978. pap. text ed. 10.95 (ISBN 0-88377-114-4). Newbury Hse.

Diller, Phyllis & Klein, Norman. The Joys of Aging--& How to Avoid Them. LC 79-7863. (Illus.). 168p. 1981. 8.95 (ISBN 0-385-14555-1). Doubleday.

Dilley, Clyde A. & Rucker, Walter E. Math Card Games. (Illus.). 86p. (Orig.). (gr. 7-12). 1974. pap. text ed. 8.75 (ISBN 0-88488-006-0). Creative Pubns.

Dilley, Romilda. Mrrarr & Me. (Illus.). 48p. 1982. 20.00 (ISBN 0-88014-062-3). Mosaic Pr OH.

--Snared by Snarling S's. (Illus.). 48p. 1982. 18.00 (ISBN 0-88014-048-8). Mosaic Pr OH.

Dilligan, Robert J., jt. ed. see Bedford, Emmett G.

Dillingham, William B., jt. auth. see Watkins, Floyd C.

Dillingham, William P., Jr. Federal Aid to Veterans, Nineteen Seventeen to Nineteen Forty One. 1952. 5.95 o.p. (ISBN 0-8130-0061-0). U Presses Fla.

Dillion, Robert W., jt. auth. see Crawley, Stanley M.

Dillman, Don. A. Mail & Telephone Surveys: The Total Design Method. LC 78-581. 1978. 34.95x (ISBN 0-471-21555-4, Pub. by Wiley-Interscience). Wiley.

Dillmont, Therese De see De Dillmont, Therese.

Dillner, Martha H. & Olson, Joanne P. Personalizing Reading Instruction in Middle Junior & Senior High Schools. 2nd ed. 544p. 1982. pap. text ed. 17.95 (ISBN 0-02-329780-8). Macmillan.

Dillner, Martha H., jt. auth. see Olson, Joanne P.

Dillon, Anne F., et al. The Complete St. Louis Guide. (Brussels Walk Guide). (Illus.). Date not set. pap. 3.25 (ISBN 0-933508-04-2). Dillon-Donnelly. Postponed.

Dillon, Barbara. The Beast in the Bed. LC 80-15069. (Illus.). 32p. (gr. k-3). 1981. 8.95 (ISBN 0-688-22254-4); PLB 8.59 (ISBN 0-688-32254-9). Morrow.

--The Good-Guy Cake. LC 80-14514. (Illus.). 64p. (gr. k-3). 1980. 8.75 (ISBN 0-688-22240-4); PLB 8.40 (ISBN 0-688-32240-9). Morrow.

--The Good-Guy Cake. (Skylark Ser.). 64p. 1982. pap. 1.75 (ISBN 0-553-15156-8, Skylark). Bantam.

--Who Needs a Bear? LC 80-26530. (Illus.). 64p. (gr. k-3). 1981. 7.95 (ISBN 0-688-00445-8); PLB 7.63 (ISBN 0-688-00446-6). Morrow.

Dillon, Bert. A Chaucer Dictionary: Proper Names & Allusions Excluding Place Names. 1974. lib. bdg. 27.00 (ISBN 0-8161-1112-X, Hall Reference). G K Hall.

Dillon, Bert, ed. A Malory Handbook. 1978. lib. bdg. 19.00 (ISBN 0-8161-7964-6, Hall Reference). G K Hall.

Dillon, Brian D., ed. Practical Archaeology: Field & Laboratory Techniques & Archaeological Logistics. (Archaeological Research Tools Ser.: Vol. 2). 1982. pap. 8.50 (ISBN 0-917956-42-7). UCLA Arch.

--The Student's Guide to Archaeological Illustrating. rev. ed. (Archaeological Research Tools Ser.: Vol. 1). (Illus.). 154p. 1983. pap. 8.50 (ISBN 0-917956-38-9). UCLA Arch.

Dillon, Catherine. Beloved Captive. 1979. pap. 2.25 o.p. (ISBN 0-451-08921-9, E8921, Sig). NAL.

Dillon, Eilis. The Wild Geese. 1981. 13.95 o.s.i. (ISBN 0-671-22852-8). S&S.

Dillon, J. F. The Law & Jurisprudence of England & America. LC 75-99475. (American Constitutional & Legal History Ser). 1970. Repr. of 1894 ed. lib. bdg. 49.50 (ISBN 0-306-71854-5). Da Capo.

Dillon, Jacquelyn, jt. auth. see Kriechbaum, Casimer, Jr.

Dillon, Jane M. School for Young Riders. (Illus.). (YA) 8.95 o.p. (ISBN 0-668-02605-7). Arco.

Dillon, John A. Foundations of General Systems Theory. (Systems Inquiry Ser.). 300p. 1982. pap. 12.95 (ISBN 0-686-37575-0). Intersystems Pubns.

Dillon, John M., jt. auth. see O'Hehir, Brendan.

Dillon, K. V., ed. see Prange, G. W.

Dillon, Kenneth J. King & Estates in the Bohemian Lands, 1526-1564. 206p. 1976. write for info. P Lang Pubs.

Dillon, Kristine E., ed. see Linnell, Robert.

Dillon, Lawrence S. Evolution: Concepts & Consequences. 2nd ed. LC 77-9033. (Illus.). 504p. 1978. pap. text ed. 18.95 o.p. (ISBN 0-8016-1299-3). Mosby.

--The Inconstant Gene. 568p. 1982. 65.00x (ISBN 0-306-41084-2, Plenum Pr). Plenum Pub.

Dillon, Lowell I. & Lyon, Edward E. Indiana: Crossroads of America. (Regional Geography Ser.). (Illus.). 1978. pap. text ed. 10.95 (ISBN 0-8403-1893-6). Kendall-Hunt.

Dillon, Mark & Haigh, Frank. International Race Car Drivers. LC 73-22514. (Superwheels & Thrill Sports Bks.). (Illus.). 52p. (gr. 5-10). 1974. PLB 7.95g (ISBN 0-8225-0413-8). Lerner Pubns.

Dillon, Mary, ed. see Hopkins, Jack.

Dillon, Mary Earhart. Wendell Wilkie, Eighteen Ninety Two to Nineteen Fourty Four. LC 71-39040. (FDR & the Era of the New Deal Ser.). 378p. 1972. Repr. of 1952 ed. lib. bdg. 45.00 (ISBN 0-306-70456-0). Da Capo.

Dillon, Mary T. Magazine Article Writing. 1977. 9.95 o.p. (ISBN 0-87116-107-9). Writer.

Dillon, Merton L. The Abolitionists: The Growth of a Dissenting Minority. Rischin, Moses, ed. LC 73-15096. (American Minorities Ser). (Illus.). 300p. 1974. 12.50 (ISBN 0-87580-044-0); pap. 6.00 (ISBN 0-87580-513-2). N Ill U Pr.

--Benjamin Lundy & the Struggle for Negro Freedom. LC 66-15473. 1966. 17.50 o.p. (ISBN 0-252-72748-7). U of Ill Pr.

--Elijah P. Lovejoy, Abolitionist Editor. LC 80-11000. ix, 190p. 1980. Repr. of 1961 ed. lib. bdg. 20.75x (ISBN 0-313-22352-1, DIEJ). Greenwood.

Dillon, Michael. China Profiles. 1983. 29.50x (ISBN 0-7146-3152-3, F Cass Co). Biblio Dist.

--The Chinese Porcelain Industry. cancelled o.s.i. (ISBN 0-7146-3148-5, F Cass Co). Biblio Dist.

Dillon, Myles & Croinin, D. O. Teach Yourself Irish. (Teach Yourself Ser.). pap. 4.95 (ISBN 0-679-10183-7). McKay.

Dillon, Patricia. Love Alone. 304p. (Orig.). 1981. pap. 2.95 o.s.i. (ISBN 0-515-05082-2). Jove Pubns.

Dillon, Richard. California's Humbugs & Heroes. LC 70-89100. (Illus.). 375p. 1982. pap. cancelled (ISBN 0-934136-25-4). Western Tanager.

Dillon, Ronna F. & Schmeck, Ronald R., eds. Individual Differences in Cognition, Vol. 1. Date not set. 34.00 (ISBN 0-12-216401-6). Acad Pr.

Dillon, Roy. Working with Animal Supplies & Services. Lee, Jasper S., ed. (Career Preparation for Agriculture-Agribusiness Ser). (Illus.). 1980. pap. text ed. 7.96 (ISBN 0-07-016951-9, G); activity guide 4.96 (ISBN 0-07-016952-7); tchr's manual & key 3.00 (ISBN 0-07-016953-5). McGraw.

Dillon, W. R., jt. auth. see Goldstein, M.

Dillow, Jeffrey. Goldchester: More High Fantasy Adventures. 1982. text ed. 15.95 o.p. (ISBN 0-8359-2568-4); pap. text ed. 13.95 (ISBN 0-8359-2567-6). Reston.

--High Fantasy Boxed Set. 1981. pap. text ed. 21.95 (ISBN 0-8359-2830-6). Reston.

--Wizards & Warriors. 1981. text ed. 14.95 (ISBN 0-8359-8737-X); poster 5.95 (ISBN 0-8359-8738-8). Reston.

Dillow, Linda. La Esposa Virtuosa. 160p. Date not set. 2.50 (ISBN 0-88113-064-8). Edit Betania.

Dilly, Martin. This Is Model Flying. (Illus.). 188p. 1975. 9.95 o.p. (ISBN 0-241-89198-1). Transatlantic.

Dilman, Ilham & Phillips, D. Z. Sense & Delusion. (Studies in Philosophical Psychology). 1971. text ed. 6.00x o.p. (ISBN 0-391-00150-7). Humanities.

Dilmore, Gene. Quantitative Techniques in Real-Estate Counseling. LC 74-31724. (Special Ser. in Real Estate & Urban Land Economics). 272p. 1981. 25.95x (ISBN 0-669-98251-2). Lexington Bks.

DiLorenzo, Maria Kearon see DiLorenzo-Kearon, Maria.

DiLorenzo, Thomas J., jt. auth. see Bennett, James T.

DiLorenzo-Kearon, Maria. Medical Spanish. 256p. Date not set. with 12 cassettes 145.00x (ISBN 0-88432-079-0, MS20). J Norton Pubs.

DiLorenzo-Kearon, Maria A. & Kearon, Thomas P. Medical Spanish: A Conversational Approach. 256p. 1981. pap. text ed. 9.95 (ISBN 0-15-557880-4, HC). HarBraceJ.

Dilsen, N., et al, eds. Behcet's Disease. (International Congress Ser.: No. 467). 1979. 69.00 (ISBN 0-444-90068-3, Excerpta Medica). Elsevier.

Dilson, Jesse. Abacus. (Illus.). (gr. 5-8). 1969. 6.95 o.p. (ISBN 0-312-00105-3); pap. 5.95 (ISBN 0-312-00140-1). St Martin.

Dilts, David A. & Deitsch, Clarence R. Labor Relations. 512p. 1983. text ed. 24.95 (ISBN 0-02-329650-X). Macmillan.

Dilts, James D., jt. auth. see Dorsey, John.

Dilts, R., jt. auth. see Marzuki, S.

Dilts, Robert. Analytical Chemistry. 512p. 1974. text ed. 16.95x (ISBN 0-442-22158-4). Van Nos Reinhold.

Dilworth, D. A., tr. see Nishida, Kitaro.

Dilworth, David, ed. see Ogai, Mori.

Dilworth, David, tr. see Ogai, Mori.

Dilworth, J. R. Variable Plot Cruising. 1982. pap. text ed. 5.50x (ISBN 0-88246-030-7). Oreg St U Bkstrs.

Dilworth, James. Production & Operations Management: Manufacturing & Non-Manufacturing. 1979. 25.00x (ISBN 0-394-32204-5). Random.

Dima, Nicholas. Bessarabia & Bukovina: The Soviet-Romanian Territorial Dispute. (East European Monographs: No. 110). 256p. 1982. 20.00x (ISBN 0-88033-003-1). East Eur Quarterly.

DiMaggio, Paul. Hitchhiker's Field Manual. LC 74-188016. (Illus.). 288p. 1974. pap. 1.95 o.p. (ISBN 0-02-097380-2). Macmillan.

Di Majo, Ennio. Baby's First Years. (Illus.). 1977. 3.50 (ISBN 0-448-14077-2, G&D). Putnam Pub Group.

Diman, Roderic C., ed. see Alfonso X.

Dimancescu, Dan, jt. auth. see Botkin, James.

DiMarco, Anthony C. The Big Bowl Football Guide. LC 76-8361. (Illus.). 1976. pap. 3.95 o.p. (ISBN 0-399-11805-5). Putnam Pub Group.

Dimarco, Susan, jt. auth. see Fishkin, Lois.

DiMarco, Vincent. Piers Plowman: A Reference Guide. 1982. lib. bdg. 45.00 (ISBN 0-8161-8309-0, Hall Reference). G K Hall.

Dimarco, Vincent & Perelman, Leslie. The Middle English Letter of Alexander to Aristotle. (Costerus New Ser.: No. XIII). 1978. pap. text ed. 17.75x o.p. (ISBN 90-6203-662-7). Humanities.

DiMaria-Kuiper, Johannes W. Hot Under the Collar: Self-Portrait of a Gay Pastor. 1983. pap. 8.95 (ISBN 0-686-38773-2). Mercury Pr.

Dimarogonas, Andrew D. Vibration Engineering. LC 75-38518. (Illus.). 565p. 1976. text ed. 32.50 (ISBN 0-8299-0035-7). West Pub.

DiMascio, A. & Shader, R. I. Butyrophenes in Psychiatry. 128p. 1972. text ed. 14.00 (ISBN 0-911216-31-6). Raven.

DiMatteo, M. Robin & DiNicola, D. Dante. Achieving Patient Compliance: Psychology of the Medical Practitioner's Role. (Pergamon General Psychology Ser.). (Illus.). 300p. 1982. 35.00 (ISBN 0-08-027552-4); pap. 12.95 (ISBN 0-08-027551-6). Pergamon.

Dimatteo, M. Robin, jt. auth. see Kaplan, Robert.

Dimberg, Ronald G. The Sage & Society: The Life & Thought of Ho Hsin-yin. (Society for Asian & Comparative Philosophy Monographs: No. 1). 190p. (Orig.). 1974. pap. text ed. 5.75x (ISBN 0-8248-0347-7). UH Pr.

Dimbleby, Geoffrey. Ecology & Archaeology. (Studies in Biology: No. 77). 64p. 1978. pap. text ed. 8.95 (ISBN 0-7131-2632-9). E Arnold.

Dimen, Muriel & Friedl, Ernestine, eds. Regional Variation in Modern Greece & Cyprus: Toward a Perspective on the Ethnography of Greece. (Annals of the New York Academy of Sciences: Vol. 268). 465p. 1976. 32.00x (ISBN 0-89072-022-3). NY Acad Sci.

Dimendberg, David C., jt. auth. see Bowers, Warner F.

Dimen-Schein, Muriel. The Anthropological Imagination. (McGraw-Hill Paperbacks Ser.). 1977. 8.95 (ISBN 0-07-016986-1, SP). pap. 4.95 (ISBN 0-07-016985-3). McGraw.

Diment, Judith & Harvey, Anthony. Animals of Long Ago. LC 78-64663. (Fact Finders Ser.). (Illus.). 1979. PLB 8.00 (ISBN 0-382-06234-5). Silver.

Dimic, Milan V., ed. see Hutcheon, Linda.

Di Michael, Eleanor M., jt. auth. see King, Robert G.

Dimick, Kenneth & Krause, Frank. Practicum Manual for Counseling & Psychotherapy. 2nd, rev. ed. 1983. pap. text ed. 9.95x o.p. (ISBN 0-915202-23-9). Accel Devel.

Dimmitt, Cornelia, ed. Classical Hindu Mythology: A Reader in the Sanskrit Puranas. Van Buitenen, J. A. & Dimmitt, Cornelia, trs. LC 77-92643. 388p. 1978. 29.95 (ISBN 0-87722-117-0); pap. 12.95x (ISBN 0-87722-122-7). Temple U Pr.

Dimmitt, Cornelia, tr. see Dimmitt, Cornelia.

Dimmock, N. J., jt. auth. see Primrose, S. B.

Dimock, Anthony Weston & Dimock, Julian A. Florida Enchantments. LC 74-13789. (Illus.). 318p. 1975. Repr. of 1908 ed. 37.00x (ISBN 0-8103-4061-5). Gale.

Dimock, Edward C., Jr., et al. The Literatures of India: An Introduction. LC 73-87300. xiv, 265p. 1975. 12.50x o.s.i. (ISBN 0-226-15232-4). U of Chicago Pr.

Dimock, Julian A., jt. auth. see Dimock, Anthony Weston.

Dimock, Marshall E. Free Enterprise & the Administrative State. LC 76-142856. 179p. 1972. Repr. of 1951 ed. lib. bdg. 15.50x (ISBN 0-8371-5955-5, DIFE). Greenwood.

Dimock, Marshall E., jt. ed. see Haines, Charles G.

Dimond, Paul R. Dilemma of Local Government: Discrimination in the Provision of Public Services. LC 78-57187. (Illus.). 1978. 23.95x (ISBN 0-669-02372-8). Lexington Bks.

Dimond, Richard E. Study Guide for Psychology: The Exploration of Human Behavior. 1976. pap. 4.95x o.p. (ISBN 0-673-15004-6). Scott F.

Dimond, Richard E., jt. auth. see Senter, R. J.

Dimond, Stuart J. & Blizard, David, eds. Evolution & Lateralization of the Brain, Vol. 299. (Annals of the New York Academy of Sciences). 501p. 1977. 42.00x (ISBN 0-89072-045-2). NY Acad Sci.

Dimondstein, Geraldine. Children Dance in the Classroom. 1971. text ed. 19.95x (ISBN 0-02-329670-4, 32967). Macmillan.

Dimont, Max I. The Indestructible Jews. 480p. 1973. pap. 2.50 (ISBN 0-451-09371-2, E9371, Sig). NAL.

--Jews, God & History. 1972. pap. 3.95 (ISBN 0-451-12181-3, AE2181, Sig). NAL.

D'Imperio, Dan. Antique Valentines. LC 80-23002. (Illus.). 160p. write for info. (ISBN 0-498-02505-5). A S Barnes.

Dimsdale, Joel E., ed. Survivors, Victims & Perpetrators: Essays on the Nazi Holocaust. LC 79-24834. (Illus.). 474p. (Orig.). 1982. pap. text ed. 22.00 (ISBN 0-89116-351-4). Hemisphere Pub.

Dimsdale, Thomas. Vigilantes of Montana. LC 80-29395. (Classics of the Old West Ser.). lib. bdg. 17.28 (ISBN 0-8094-3959-X). Silver.

Din, M. R., jt. auth. see Malik, Imam.

Dinaburg, M. S. Photosensitive Diazo Compounds & Their Uses. (Focal Library Ser.). 1964. 46.95 (ISBN 0-240-50655-3). Focal Pr.

Dinan, John A. The Pulp Western: A Popular History of the Western Fiction Magazine in America. LC 81-21697. (I. O. Evans Studies in the Philosophy & Criticism of Literature: Vol. 2). (Illus.). 160p. 1983. lib. bdg. 11.95x (ISBN 0-89370-161-0); pap. text ed. 5.95x (ISBN 0-89370-261-7). Borgo Pr.

Dinardo, C. T., ed. Computers & Security, Vol. III. (The Information Technology Ser.). (Illus.). 247p. 1977. pap. 23.00 (ISBN 0-88283-016-3). AFIPS Pr.

Dincher, Judy, jt. auth. see Hood, Gail H.

Dinda, S. & James, K. How to Use Circle Grid Analysis for Die Tryouts. 1981. 16.00 (ISBN 0-87170-119-7). ASM.

D'Indy, Vincent. Beethoven: A Critical Biography. LC 72-125054. (Music Ser). (Illus.). 1970. Repr. of 1913 ed. lib. bdg. 16.50 (ISBN 0-306-70019-0). Da Capo.

D'Indy, Vincent, ed. see Franck, Cesar.

Dine, Jim, illus. Apocalypse: The Revelation of Saint John, the Divine. (Illus.). 64p. 1982. 1500.00 (ISBN 0-910457-00-X). Arion Pr.

Dine, S. S. Van see Van Dine, S. S.

Dineen, S. Complex Analysis in Locally Convex Spaces. (Mathematical Studies Ser.: Vol. 57). 1982. 59.75 (ISBN 0-444-86319-2, North Holland). Elsevier.

DiNenno, Philip J. Simplified Radiation Heat Transfer Calculations from Large Open Hydrocarbon Fires. Date not set. 5.35 (ISBN 0-686-37674-9, TR 82-9). Society Fire Protect.

Diner, Hasia R. In the Almost Promised Land: American Jews & Blacks, 1915-1935. LC 76-46767. (Contributions in American History: No. 59). 1977. lib. bdg. 29.95 (ISBN 0-8371-9400-8, DIA/). Greenwood.

Diner, Hasia R., ed. Women & Urban Society: A Guide to Information Sources. LC 78-13109. (Urban Studies Information Guide Ser.: Vol. 7). 1979. 42.00x (ISBN 0-8103-1425-8). Gale.

Dinerman, Miriam, ed. Social Work in a Turbulent Word: Proceedings of 7th NASW Professional Symposium. 1983. text ed. 15.95 (ISBN 0-87101-108-5, CBO-108-C). Natl Assn Soc Wkrs.

Dinerstein, Herbert S. War & the Soviet Union. LC 75-45031. 268p. 1976. Repr. of 1962 ed. lib. bdg. 18.50x (ISBN 0-8371-8658-7, DIWS). Greenwood.

Dines, David M., jt. auth. see Goldman, Amy Beth.

Dines, Glen. John Muir. (See & Read Biographies Ser.). (Illus.). 64p. (gr. 2-4). 1974. PLB 4.49 o.p. (ISBN 0-399-60880-X). Putnam Pub Group.

--Sir Cecil & the Bad Blue Beast. LC 70-125868. (Illus.). (gr. k-2). 1970. 10.95 (ISBN 0-87599-175-0). S G Phillips.

Dinesen, Betzy, ed. Rediscovery: Three Hundred Years of Stories by & about Women. 272p. 1982. pap. 3.50 (ISBN 0-380-60756-5, 60756, Bard). Avon.

Dinesen, Isak. Out of Africa. 416p. 1972. pap. 4.95 (ISBN 0-394-71740-6, V740, Vin). Random.

--Seven Gothic Tales. 1972. pap. 4.95 (ISBN 0-394-71807-0, V807, Vin). Random.

--Seven Gothic Tales. 6.95 (ISBN 0-394-60496-2). Modern Lib.

Dingle, H. & Hegmann, J. P. Evolution & Genetics of Life Histories. (Proceedings in Life Science Ser.). (Illus.). 256p. 1982. 33.80 (ISBN 0-686-97803-X). Springer-Verlag.

Dingle, H., ed. Evolution of Insect Migration & Diapause. (Proceedings in Life Sciences). 1978. 29.00 o.p. (ISBN 0-387-90294-5). Springer-Verlag.

Dingle, J. T., ed. Lysosomes: A Laboratory Handbook. 2nd ed. 1977. 85.00 (ISBN 0-7204-0627-7, North-Holland); pap. 35.75 (ISBN 0-7204-0628-5). Elsevier.

Dingle, J. T. & Gordon, J. L., eds. Cellular Interactions. (Research Monographs in Cell & Tissue Physiology: Vol. 6). 1981. 86.50 (ISBN 0-444-80330-0). Elsevier.

Dingle, J. T, et al, eds. Lysosomes in Biology & Pathology, Vols. 1-5. (Vols. 1 & 2 2nd eds). 1973-76. Vol. 1. 128.50 (ISBN 0-444-10501-8, North Holland); Vol. 2. 146.00 (ISBN 0-444-10502-6); Vol. 3. 122.75 (ISBN 0-444-10405-4); Vol. 4. 155.50 (ISBN 0-444-10810-6); Vol. 5. 113.75 (ISBN 0-444-11204-9). Elsevier.

Dingle, J. T., et al, eds. Lyposomes in Applied Biology & Therapeutics. (Lyposomes in Biology & Pathology Ser.: Vol. 6). 714p. 1979. 146.00 (ISBN 0-686-63105-6, North Holland). Elsevier.

Dingoian, George. The Tide is Turning. LC 81-86207. 64p. 1983. pap. 4.95 (ISBN 0-86666-037-2). GWP.

Dingus, Rick. The Photographic Artifacts of Timothy O'Sullivan. (Illus.). 224p. 1982. 45.00 (ISBN 0-8263-0607-1, P-52). U of NM Pr.

Dingus, S. D., jt. auth. see McCorkle, Ruth M.

Dingwall, Robert. Aspects of Illness. LC 76-39652. 1977. 20.00 (ISBN 0-312-05687-7). St Martin.

Dingwall, Robert & Lewis, Philip. The Sociology of the Professions. LC 82-3352. 244p. 1982. 25.00x (ISBN 0-312-74075-1). St Martin.

Dingwell, Joyce. Melodie du Vent. (Harlequin Romantique). 192p. 1983. pap. 1.95 (ISBN 0-373-41180-4). Harlequin Bks.

DiNicola, D. Dante, jt. auth. see DiMatteo, M. Robin.

DiNitto, Diana M. & Dye, Thomas R. Social Welfare Politics & Public Policy. (Illus.). 352p. 1983. text ed. 20.95 (ISBN 0-13-819474-2). P-H.

Dinitz, Simon, jt. auth. see Conrad, John P.

Dinitz, Simon, jt. ed. see Scott, Joseph E.

Dinitz, Simon, jt. auth. see Miller, Stuart J.

Dinkelspiel, John R. & Uchenick, Joel. Condominiums: The Effects of Conversion on a Community. LC 80-39894. 224p. 1981. 21.00 (ISBN 0-86569-059-6). Auburn Hse.

Dinkin, Robert J. Voting in Provincial America: A Study of Elections in the Thirteen Colonies, 1689-1776. LC 77-71861. (Contributions in American History: No. 64). (Illus.). 1977. lib. bdg. 29.95 (ISBN 0-8371-9543-8, DIV/). Greenwood.

--Voting in Revolutionary America: A Study of Elections in the Original Thirteen States, 1776-1789. LC 81-13266. (Contributions in American History: No. 99). (Illus.). 200p. 1982. lib. bdg. 27.50 (ISBN 0-313-23091-9, DVR). Greenwood.

Dinkler, Erich. Kunst und Geschichte Nubiens in Christlicher Zeit: Ergebnisse und Probleme Auf Grund der Jungsten Ausgrabungen. (Illus.). 379p. 1970. text ed. 92.00x o.p. (ISBN 3-7647-0216-8). Humanities.

Dinkmeyer, Don, et al. Adlerian Counseling & Psychotherapy. LC 78-17399. 1978. text ed. 19.95 (ISBN 0-8185-0264-9). Brooks-Cole.

Dinkmeyer, Don C. & Muro, James J. Group Counseling: Theory & Practice. 2nd ed. LC 77-83357. 1979. text ed. 19.50 (ISBN 0-87581-206-6). Peacock Pubs.

Dinman, Bertram D. The Nature of Occupational Cancer: A Critical Review of Present Problems. 112p. 1974. photocopy ed. spiral 14.75x (ISBN 0-398-02907-5). C C Thomas.

Dinn, Freda. Early Music for Recorders: An Introduction & Guide to Its Interpretation, & History, for Amateurs. 1974. pap. 12.00 (ISBN 0-901938-07-6, 75 A 11155). Eur-Am Music.

Dinnage, James, jt. auth. see Parry, Anthony.

Dinneen, Betty. Striped Horses: The Story of a Zebra Family. LC 82-7786. (Illus.). 96p. (gr. 4-6). 1982. 9.95 (ISBN 0-02-732200-9). Macmillan.

Dinnerstein, Leonard & Jackson, Kenneth T., eds. American Vistas: Eighteen Seventy-Seven to the Present. 4th ed. 448p. 1982. pap. 8.95 (ISBN 0-19-503166-0). Oxford U Pr.

--American Vistas: Sixteen Hundred Seven to Eighteen Seventy-Seven. 4th ed. 320p. 1982. pap. 7.95 (ISBN 0-19-503164-4). Oxford U Pr.

DiNoto, Andrea & Cashion, Catherine, eds. Trash or Treasure. 1977. 10.00 o.p. (ISBN 0-517-52915-7); pap. 6.95 (ISBN 0-517-53026-0). Crown.

Dinsdale, Tim. Loch Ness Monster. 4th ed. (Illus.). 208p. (Orig.). 1982. pap. 9.50 (ISBN 0-7100-9022-6). Routledge & Kegan.

--Project Water Horse. (Illus.). 1975. 18.95 (ISBN 0-7100-8029-8); pap. 8.95 (ISBN 0-7100-8030-1). Routledge & Kegan.

Dinsmoor, William B. Athenian Archon List in the Light of Recent Discoveries. LC 74-114512. (Illus.). 274p. 1974. Repr. of 1939 ed. lib. bdg. 20.75x (ISBN 0-8371-4735-2, DIAA). Greenwood.

Dinter, Wolfgang. Waldgesellschaften der Neiderrheinischen Sandplatten, No. 64. (Dissertationes Botanicae). (Illus.). 112p. 1982. pap. text ed. 20.00x (ISBN 3-7682-1325-0). Lubrecht & Cramer.

Dintiman, George B. How to Sprint Faster. LC 82-81448. (Illus.). 160p. (Orig.). 1983. pap. 6.95 (ISBN 0-88011-057-0). Leisure Pr.

Dintiman, George B. & Greenberg, Jerrold S. Health Through Discovery. 2nd ed. LC 82-11421. 608p. 1983. pap. text ed. 16.95 (ISBN 0-686-82162-9). A-W.

Dintiman, George B., jt. auth. see Unitas, John.

Dintiman, George B., et al. A Comprehensive Manual of Foundations & Physical Education Activities for Men & Women. (Orig.). 1979. pap. text ed. 12.95x (ISBN 0-8087-0486-9). Burgess.

Dintino, Justin J. & Martens, Frederick T. Police Intelligence Systems in Crime Control: Maintaining a Delicate Balance in a Liberal Democracy. (Illus.). 143p. 1983. text ed. price not set (ISBN 0-398-04830-4). C C Thomas.

Dinwiddie, Dottie, jt. ed. see Shurden, Kay W.

Dinwiddie, Elza, jt. auth. see Erwin, Bette J.

Diola, Philippe, jt. auth. see Cousteau, Jacques-Yves.

Diole, Philippe, jt. auth. see Cousteau, Jacques-Yves.

Diomedi, Alexander. Sketches of Indian Life in the Pacific Northwest. 1978. 10.95 (ISBN 0-87770-199-7). Ye Galleon.

Dion, Bernard A. Locally Least-Cost Error Correctors for Context-Free & Context-Sensitive Parsers. Stone, Harold, ed. LC 82-8397. (Computer Science: Systems Programming Ser.: No. 14). 102p. 1982. 34.95 (ISBN 0-8357-1358-X, Pub. by UMI Res Pr). Univ Microfilms.

Dionne, Roger, jt. auth. see Sklansky, David.

Diop, Birago. Contes Choisis. Hutchinson, Joyce, ed. 1967. text ed. 5.95x (ISBN 0-521-04836-2). Cambridge U Pr.

Diop, Cheikh A. The African Origin of Civilization: Myth or Reality. Cook, Mercer, ed. & tr. from Fr. LC 73-81746. (Illus.). 317p. 1974. 16.95 (ISBN 0-88208-021-0); pap. 8.95 (ISBN 0-88208-022-9). Lawrence Hill.

--Black Africa: Economic & Cultural Basis for a Federated State. Salemson, Harold J., tr. LC 78-62368. 132p. 1978. 7.95 (ISBN 0-88208-095-4); pap. 0.00 o.s.i. (ISBN 0-88208-096-2). Lawrence Hill.

DiOrio, Ralph A. Called to Heal. LC 82-45354. (Illus.). 264p. 1982. 14.95 (ISBN 0-385-18226-0). Doubleday.

Diosdi, Gyorgy. Ownership in Ancient & Preclassical Roman Law. 1970. 12.50x (ISBN 0-8002-1772-1). Intl Pubns Serv.

DiPalma, Guiseppe. Surviving Without Governing: The Italian Parties in Parliament. LC 75-46035. 1977. 33.00x (ISBN 0-520-03195-4). U of Cal Pr.

DiPalma, J. R. Drill's Pharmacology in Medicine. 4th ed. 1971. 47.00 (ISBN 0-07-017006-1, HP). McGraw.

DiPalma, Joseph R. Basic Pharmacology in Medicine. (Illus.). 1976. text ed. 23.95 (ISBN 0-07-017010-X, HP). McGraw.

--Basic Pharmacology in Medicine. 2nd ed. (Illus.). 640p. 1981. text ed. 27.00 (ISBN 0-07-017011-8, HP). McGraw.

DiPalma, Ray. The Gallery Goers. 21p. 1971. 1.50 (ISBN 0-87886-002-9). Ithaca Hse.

--Soli. 65p. 1973. 4.95 (ISBN 0-686-80026-5); pap. 2.95 (ISBN 0-87886-027-4). Ithaca Hse.

Di Palma, Vera. Capital Gains Tax. 224p. 1981. 35.00x (ISBN 0-7121-0460-7, Pub. by Macdonald & Evans). State Mutual Bk.

DiPaolo-Healey, Antonette, ed. The Old English Vision of St. Paul. LC 77-89928. 1978. 11.00x (ISBN 0-910956-76-6, SAM 2); pap. 5.00x (ISBN 0-910956-62-6). Medieval Acad.

Dipboye, Robert L., jt. auth. see Howell, William C.

DiPego, Gerald. With a Vengeance. LC 76-30472. 1977. 8.95 o.p. (ISBN 0-07-017012-6, GB). McGraw.

Dipersio, Michael, et al. Castles in the Sand: 10 Projects That Can Be Built in One to Six Hours. (Illus.). 128p. 1982. pap. 6.95 (ISBN 0-399-50599-7, Perige). Putnam Pub Group.

DiPiero, W. S. Solstice. (Porch Chapbook Ser.: No. 5). (Illus.). 1980. pap. 3.00 (ISBN 0-932968-15-5); signed & numbered ed. 5.00 (ISBN 0-686-96856-5). Porch Pubns.

DiPietre, Dennis D., jt. auth. see Calkins, Peter H.

DiPietro, John C. Structures in Beckett's Watt. 12.00 (ISBN 0-917786-22-X). French Lit.

Di Pietro, Phil. Short Stories of Tall Tales. 1979. 8.95 o.p. (ISBN 0-533-04164-3). Vantage.

Di Pietro, Robert, ed. Ethnic Perspectives in American Literature: Selected Essays on the European Contribution. Ifcovic, Edward, et al. LC 82-14265. 320p. 1983. 22.50x (ISBN 0-87352-126-9); pap. 12.50x (ISBN 0-87352-127-7). Modern Lang.

DiPorta, Leo. Zen Running. 1978. pap. 4.95 o.p. (ISBN 0-89696-019-6, An Everest House Book). Dodd.

DiPrima, Richard. The City & Its Problems. LC 80-70425. 89p. (Orig.). 1980. pap. text ed. 3.95 (ISBN 0-86652-004-X). Educ Indus.

--The First Amendment. LC 81-65895. (Orig.). (gr. 6-12). 1982. pap. text ed. 3.95 (ISBN 0-86652-012-0). Educ Indus.

--The Great Whales: Endangered Monarchs of the Deep. 155p. (Orig.). 1981. pap. text ed. 7.95 (ISBN 0-86652-042-2). Educ Indus.

--Headline History of the Sixties. LC 80-71081. 73p. (Orig.). (gr. 6-12). pap. text ed. 4.95 (ISBN 0-86652-011-2). Educ Indus.

--Perspective On... Inflation. LC 80-70424. 181p. (Orig.). 1980. pap. text ed. 4.95 (ISBN 0-86652-005-8). Educ Indus.

Di Prima, Richard C., jt. auth. see Boyce, William E.

DiPrima, Richard C., jt. auth. see Boyce, William E.

Dirac, P. The Development of Quantum Theory: J. Robert Oppenheimer Memorial Prize Acceptance Speech. 76p. 1971. 19.00x (ISBN 0-677-02970-5). Gordon.

Dirac, Paul A. General Theory of Relativity. LC 75-8690. 71p. 1975. 26.95 (ISBN 0-471-21575-9, Pub. by Wiley-Interscience). Wiley.

Dircks, Richard J. Richard Cumberland. (English Authors Ser.). 1976. lib. bdg. 14.95 (ISBN 0-8057-6654-5, Twayne). G K Hall.

Dirckx, John H. Dx & Rx: A Physician's Guide to Medical Writing. (Medical Publications). 1977. lib. bdg. 12.95 o.p. (ISBN 0-8161-2100-1, Pub. by Halll Medical). G K Hall.

Director, S. W. Circuit Theory: The Computational Approach. LC 75-2016. 679p. 1975. text ed. 41.95 (ISBN 0-471-21580-5); tchrs manual 10.00 (ISBN 0-471-21582-1). Wiley.

Director, S. W. & Rohrer, R. A. Introduction to System Theory. (Electronic Systems Ser). 23.00 o.p. (ISBN 0-07-017014-2, C); 1.50 o.p. solutions manual (ISBN 0-07-017015-0). McGraw.

DiRenzo, Gordon J., ed. We, the People: American Character & Social Change. LC 76-51926. (Contributions in Sociology Ser.: No. 24). (Illus.). 1977. lib. bdg. 29.95 (ISBN 0-8371-9481-4, DWP/). Greenwood.

Dirickx, Yvo M. & Jennergren, L. Peter. Systems Analysis by Multilevel Methods: With Applications to Economics & Management. LC 79-40639. (International Ser. on Applied Systems Analysis). 217p. 1979. 44.95 (ISBN 0-471-27626-X, Pub. by Wiley-Interscience). Wiley.

Dirinzer, D. History of the Alphabet. (Illus.). 1977. 16.50 (ISBN 0-912728-09-4). Newbury Bks.

Dirks, Rudolph. The Katzenjammer Kids. (Illus.). 32p. (Orig.). 1974. pap. 3.00 (ISBN 0-486-23005-8). Dover.

Dirlik, Arif. Revolution & History: Origins of Marxist Historiography in China, 1919-1937. LC 77-80469. 1978. 35.75x (ISBN 0-520-03541-0). U of Cal Pr.

Di Roma, Edward & Rosenthal, Joseph A., eds. Numerical Finding List of British Command Papers Published 1833-1962. LC 70-137702. 1971. Repr. of 1967 ed. 12.00 o.p. (ISBN 0-87104-505-2). NY Pub Lib.

Dirr, Michael. Manual of Woody Landscape Plants. 3rd ed. (Illus.). 1983. 28.80x (ISBN 0-87563-231-9); pap. text ed. 19.80 (ISBN 0-87563-226-2). Stipes.

Dirsh, V. A. Morphometrical Studies on Phases of the Desert Locust (Schistocerca Gregaria Forskal) 1953. 35.00x (ISBN 0-85135-066-6, Pub. by Centre Overseas Research). State Mutual Bk.

Dirsh, V. M. The African General of Acridoides. 1965. 60.00x (ISBN 0-521-04837-0, Pub. by Centre Overseas Research). State Mutual BK.

Diruta, G. Il Transilvano, 1593-1609. facsjmile ed. (Bibliotheca Organologica Ser.: Vol. 44). (Illus.). 154p. 1980. 75.00 o.s.i. (ISBN 90-6027-212-9, Pub. by Frits Knuf Netherlands). Pendragon NY.

Dirven, Rene, et al. The Scene of Linguistic Action & its Perspectivization by SPEAK, TALK, SAY & TELL. (Pragmatics & Beyond: III-6). 100p. (Orig.). 1983. pap. 16.00 (ISBN 90-272-2528-1). Benjamins North Am.

DiSaia, Philip J. & Creasman, William T. Clinical Gynecologic Oncology. LC 80-18687. (Illus.). 478p. 1981. text ed. 39.50 (ISBN 0-8016-1314-0). Mosby.

DiSaia, Philip J., et al. Synopsis of Gynecologic Oncology. LC 74-34307. (Clinical Monographs in Obstetrics & Gynecology Ser). 344p. 1975. 37.50 o.p. (ISBN 0-471-21590-2, Pub. by Wiley-Med). Wiley.

DiSaisa, Philip J., jt. auth. see Brown, Stephen G.

Disalvo, Vincent. Business & Public Professional Communication: Basic Skills & Principles. (Speech & Drama Ser.). 1977. text ed. 17.95 (ISBN 0-675-08486-5). Additional supplements may be obtained fom publisher. Merrill.

DiSante, Theodore. How to Select & Use Medium-Format Cameras. 192p. 1981. pap. 12.95 (ISBN 0-89586-046-5). H P Bks.

Disch, Thomas M. The Early Science Fiction Stories of Thomas M. Disch (1963-1966) 1977. lib. bdg. 13.00 (ISBN 0-8398-2370-3, Gregg). G K Hall.

--The Genocides. 1978. lib. bdg. 10.00 (ISBN 0-8398-2436-X, Gregg). G K Hall.

--Man Who Had No Idea. 1982. pap. 2.95 (ISBN 0-553-22667-3). Bantam.

--On Wings of Song. LC 78-21411. 359p. 1979. 17.50 (ISBN 0-312-58466-0). Ultramarine Pub.

--The Right Way to Figure Plumbing. 75p. (Orig.). 1972. pap. 5.95 (ISBN 0-913560-05-7). Ultramarine Pub.

--Ringtime. LC 82-19279. (Singularities Ser.). (Illus.). 48p. (Orig.). 1982. 35.00 (ISBN 0-915124-70-X); pap. 10.00 (ISBN 0-915124-71-8). Toothpaste.

--Three Hundred Thirty-Four. 1974. pap. 2.25 o.p. (ISBN 0-380-01633-8, 42630). Avon.

--Three Hundred Thirty-Four. (Science Fiction Ser.). 288p. 1976. Repr. of 1974 ed. lib. bdg. 12.50 o.p. (ISBN 0-8398-2331-2, Gregg). G K Hall.

Disch, Thomas M. & Naylor, Charles. Neighboring Lives. LC 80-19021. 351p. 1981. 15.00 (ISBN 0-684-16644-5). Ultramarine Pub.

Disch, Thomas M. & Naylor, Charles, eds. Strangeness. 1978. pap. 2.50 o.p. (ISBN 0-380-41434-1, 41434). Avon.

Disch, Thomas M., ed. see Lupoff, Richard.

Discipio, William, ed. The Behavioral Treatment of Psychotic Illness. LC 73-18292. 240p. 1974. text ed. 26.95 (ISBN 0-87705-131-3). Human Sci Pr.

Dise, Craig A., ed. Physiology: PreTest Self-Assessment & Review. 3rd ed. (Basic Science Ser.). 196p. 1982. review book 11.95 (ISBN 0-07-051936-6, HP). McGraw.

Disease Control Centers, Atlanta, Georgia. Author-Title & Subject Catalogs of the Centers for Disease Control Library. 1983. lib. bdg. 750.00 (ISBN 0-8161-0395-X, Hall Library). G K Hall.

DiSessa, Andrea, jt. auth. see Abelson, Harold.

Dishon, Daniel, ed. Middle East Record, 6 vols. Incl. Vol. 1. 1960. o.p. (ISBN 0-87855-164-6); Vol. 2. 826p. 1961 (ISBN 0-87855-165-4); Vol. 3. 668p. 1967 (ISBN 0-87855-166-2); Vol. 4. 920p. 1968 (ISBN 0-87855-167-0). vols. 2-4 69.95 ea.; Set. casebound o. p. 200.00 (ISBN 0-87855-223-5). Transaction Bks.

DiSimoni, Frank. Logbook for the Speech-Language Pathologist. rev. ed. 1981. text ed. 6.95x (ISBN 0-8134-2188-8). Interstate.

Diskin, Lahna. Reader's Guide to Theodore Sturgeon. Schlobin, Roger C., ed. LC 80-21423. (Reader's Guides to Contemporary Science Fiction & Fantasy Author Ser.: Vol. 7). (Illus., Orig.). 1981. 10.95x (ISBN 0-686-86765-3); pap. text ed. 4.95x (ISBN 0-916732-09-6). Starmont Hse.

--Theodore Sturgeon: A Primary & Secondary Bibliography. 1979. lib. bdg. 17.00 (ISBN 0-8161-8046-6, Hall Reference). G K Hall.

Disney. Mickey's Circus Adventure. 1979. 2.50 (ISBN 0-686-94469-0). Watts.

Disney, R. & Ott, T., eds. Applied Probability--Computer Science: The Interface, 2 Vols. (Progress in Computer Science). 1982. text ed. 34.00x ea. Vol. 2, 532pp (ISBN 3-7643-3067-8). Vol. 3, 514pp (ISBN 3-7643-3093-7). Birkhauser.

Disney, R. L., jt. auth. see Clarke, A. B.

Disney, Rosemary. The Splendid Art of Decorating Eggs. (Illus.). 160p. 1972. 10.00 (ISBN 0-8208-0345-6). Hearthside.

Disney, Walt. Donald Duck & the Golden Helmet. (Illus.). 36p. 1981. pap. 3.95 o.p. (ISBN 0-89659-178-6). Abbeville Pr.

--Favorite Nursery Tales. (Illus.). (ps-3). 1977. PLB 4.95 (ISBN 0-307-12068-6, Golden Pr). Western Pub.

--Goofy on Cave Man Island. (Illus.). 36p. 1981. pap. 3.95 o.p. (ISBN 0-89659-179-4). Abbeville Pr.

--The Grasshopper & the Ants. (Walt Disney Square Bks.). (Illus.). (gr. k-3). 1978. PLB 5.38 (ISBN 0-307-66090-7, Golden Pr). Western Pub.

--Lady & the Tramp. (Walt Disney Square Bks.). (Illus.). (gr. k-3). 1978. PLB 5.38 (ISBN 0-307-66091-5, Golden Pr). Western Pub.

--Mickey Mouse Joins the Foreign Legion. (Illus.). 36p. 1981. pap. 3.95 o.p. (ISBN 0-89659-175-1). Abbeville Pr.

--Mickey Mouse Meets Robin Hood. (Illus.). 36p. 1981. pap. 3.95 o.p. (ISBN 0-89659-176-X). Abbeville Pr.

--Snow White & the Seven Dwarfs. (gr. 2 up). 1979. pap. 0.95 o.s.i. (ISBN 0-448-15923-6, G&D). Putnam Pub Group.

--Snow White & the Seven Dwarfs. (Disney Movie-Go-Round Bks.). (Illus.). 10p. (ps-3). 1982. bds. 8.95 (ISBN 0-671-44897-8). Windmill Bks.

Dison, Norma. Clinical Nursing Techniques. 4th ed. LC 78-31262. (Illus.). 492p. 1979. pap. text ed. 16.95 o.p. (ISBN 0-8016-1308-6). Mosby.

--Simplified Drugs & Solutions for Nurses, Including Arithmetic. 7th ed. LC 79-28198. (Illus.). 140p. 1980. pap. text ed. 10.50 (ISBN 0-8016-1311-6). Mosby.

Dispenza, J. Reruns. 1971. pap. 2.00 o.p. (ISBN 0-02-642000-7, 64200). Glencoe.

Dispenza, Joseph. The House of Alarcon. LC 78-3598. 1978. 9.95 o.p. (ISBN 0-698-10928-7, Coward). Putnam Pub Group.

Disraeli, Benjamin. Coningsby. 1983. pap. 5.95 (ISBN 0-14-043192-6). Penguin.

--Lothair. LC 75-98810. Repr. of 1906 ed. lib. bdg. 17.25x (ISBN 0-8371-2846-3, BELO). Greenwood.

--Tancred: Or, the New Crusade. LC 79-98811. Repr. of 1877 ed. lib. bdg. 19.00x (ISBN 0-8371-3072-7, BATA). Greenwood.

Disselkoen, Laura, ed. Semana de la Pasion, Muerte y Resurreccion: Muerte y Resurreccion. 75p. 1981. pap. 2.25 (ISBN 0-311-08501-6). Casa Bautista.

Disston, Harry. Beginning the Rest of Your Life: A Guide to an Active Retirement. 160p. (Orig.). 1981. pap. 4.95 o.p. (ISBN 0-87000-518-9, Arlington Hse). Crown.

--Riding Rhymes for Young Riders. (Illus.). (gr. 1-6). 1951. pap. 1.95 (ISBN 0-87027-100-8). Cumberland Pr.

Distad, Audree. Come to the Fair. LC 77-3812. (Illus.). (gr. 3-7). 1977. 5.95 o.p. (ISBN 0-06-021686-7, HarpJ); PLB 9.89 (ISBN 0-06-021687-5). Har-Row.

Di Stasi, Lawrence. Mal Occhio: The Underside of Vision. LC 81-7. (Illus.). 160p. 1981. 17.50 (ISBN 0-86547-033-2). N Point Pr.

DiStefano, J. J., et al. Feedback & Control Systems. (Schaum's Outline Ser). (Orig.). 1967. pap. 8.95 (ISBN 0-07-017045-2, SP). McGraw.

Distel, Ann. Andre Dunoyer de Segonzac. (Quality-Low-Price Art Ser.). Date not set. 6.95 o.p. (ISBN 0-517-54004-5). Crown.

Distelberger, Rudolf, jt. auth. see Leithe-Jasper, Manfred.

Dita, P. & Georgescu, V., eds. Gauge Theories: Fundamentals Interactions & Rigorous Results. (Progress in Physics Ser.: Vol. 5). 389p. Date not set. text ed. 22.50 (ISBN 3-7643-3095-3). Birkhauser.

Ditchburn, R. W. Light, 3 vols. 3rd. ed. 1977. Vol. 1 o.p. pap. 25.00 (ISBN 0-12-218101-8); Vol. 2. pap. 23.00 (ISBN 0-12-218102-6); Vol. 3. 84.50 (ISBN 0-12-218150-6). Acad Pr.

Ditchfield, P. H. Old English Customs Extant at the Present Time. LC 68-21765. 1968. Repr. of 1896 ed. 34.00x (ISBN 0-8103-3427-5). Gale.

Ditella, Guido. Argentina under Peron, 1973-76: The Nation's Experience with a Labor-Based Government. LC 81-23281. 256p. 1982. 25.00x (ISBN 0-312-04871-8). St Martin.

Dithmar, Edward A. John Drew. 137p. 1982. Repr. of 1900 ed. lib. bdg. 35.00 (ISBN 0-89760-143-2). Telegraph Bks.

Ditlea, Steve. A Simple Guide to Home Computers. LC 78-70685. (Illus.). 192p. 1979. 10.95 o.p. (ISBN 0-89104-108-7, A & W Visual Library); pap. 4.95 o.p. (ISBN 0-89104-109-5, A & W Visual Library). A & W Pubs.

Ditlevsen, Tove. Complete Freedom & Other Stories. Brondum, Jack, tr. 96p. 1982. pap. 6.00 (ISBN 0-915306-24-7). Curbstone.

Ditmars, Raymond L. Strange Animals I Have Known. 1966. pap. 0.60 o.p. (ISBN 0-15-685632-8, HPL3, HPL). HarBraceJ.

Dito, William R., et al. Clinical Pathologic Correlations in Amniotic Fluid. (Illus.). 1975. 12.00 o.s.i. (ISBN 0-89189-010-6, 45-9-005-00). Am Soc Clinical.

Ditri, A. E., et al. Managing the EDP Function. 1971. 39.95 (ISBN 0-07-017048-7, P&RB). McGraw.

D'itri, F. M., jt. auth. see D'itri, P. A.

D'Itri, Frank M. Acid Precipitation: Effects on Ecological Systems. LC 81-69072. 1982. 39.95 (ISBN 0-250-40509-1). Ann Arbor Science.

--Land Treatment of Municipal Wastewater: Vegetation Selection & Management. LC 81-69071. 218p. 1982. 24.50 (ISBN 0-250-40508-3). Ann Arbor Science.

D'Itri, Frank M., jt. auth. see D'Itri, Patricia A.

D'itri, P. A. & D'itri, F. M. Mercury Contamination: A Human Tragedy. 311p. Repr. of 1977 ed. text ed. 28.95 (ISBN 0-471-02654-9). Krieger.

D'Itri, Patricia A. & D'Itri, Frank M. Mercury Contamination: A Human Tragedy. LC 76-58478. (Environmental Science and Technology: a Wiley-Interscience Series of Texts and Monographs). 311p. 1977. 32.50x o.p. (ISBN 0-471-02654-9, Pub. by Wiley-Interscience). Wiley.

D'Itri, Patricia W. Damon Runyon. (United States Authors Ser.). 1982. lib. bdg. 12.95 (ISBN 0-8057-7336-3, Twayne). G K Hall.

Ditter, Francis J., Jr., tr. see Halbwachs, Maurice.

Ditter, Vida Y., tr. see Halbwachs, Maurice.

Dittert, Lewis W., ed. Sprowls' American Pharmacy. 7th ed. LC 73-20013. (Illus.). 500p. 1974. 25.00 o.p. (ISBN 0-397-52058-1, Lippincott Medical). Lippincott.

Dittes, James E. Bias & the Pious: The Relationship Between Prejudice & Religion. LC 72-90263. (Study of Generations Paperbacks Ser). 104p. 1973. pap. 1.95 o.p. (ISBN 0-8066-1311-4, 10-0670). Augsburg.

Dittman, Richard & Schmieg, Glenn. Physics in Everyday Life. Rogers, Janice L. & Zappa, C. R., eds. (Schaum's Outline Seri). (Illus.). 1979. text ed. 22.50 (ISBN 0-07-017056-8, C); instructor's manual 15.00 (ISBN 0-07-017057-6). McGraw.

Dittman, Richard, jt. auth. see Zemansky, Mark.

Dittmann, Laura, ed. Curriculum Is What Happens: Planning Is the Key. rev. ed. LC 70-123390. 72p. 1977. pap. text ed. 2.00 o.p. (ISBN 0-912674-08-3, 119). Natl Assn Child Ed.

Dittmann, Laura L. & Ramseu, Marjorie, eds. Their Future Is Now: Today Is for Children. (Illus.). 1982. pap. 5.75 (ISBN 0-87173-102-9). ACEI.

Dittmann, Reidar. Eros & Psyche: Strindberg & Munch in the 1890s. Foster, Stephen, ed. LC 82-4923. (Studies in Fine Arts: The Avant-Garde: No. 27). 232p. 1982. 39.95 (ISBN 0-8357-1319-9, Pub. by UMI Res Pr). Univ Microfilms.

Dittmar, Mark. Jumbo Art Yearbook: Grade 3 & 4. (Jumbo Art Ser.). 96p. (gr. 3-4). 1981. wkbk. 14.00 (ISBN 0-8209-0046-X, JAY-34). ESP.

--Jumbo Art Yearbook: Grade 5 & 6. (Jumbo Art Ser.). 96p. (gr. 5-6). 1981. wkbk. 14.00 (ISBN 0-8209-0047-8, JAY-56). ESP.

--Jumbo Art Yearbook: Grade 7 & 8. (Jumbo Art Ser.). 96p. (gr. 7-8). 1982. wkbk. 14.00 (ISBN 0-8209-0048-6, JAY-78). ESP.

--Math Montana & Friends. (gr. 4-6). 1982. 5.95 (ISBN 0-86653-084-3, GA 430). Good Apple.

Dittmar, Norbert. A Critical Survey of Sociolinguistics: Theory & Application. LC 76-27160. (Illus.). 320p. 1977. 30.00 (ISBN 0-312-17500-0). St Martin.

Dittmer, Howard J. Phylogeny & Form in the Plant Kingdom. LC 74-264. 656p. 1974. Repr. of 1964 ed. 25.00 (ISBN 0-88275-167-0). Krieger.

Dittmer, Lowell. Liu Shao-Ch'i & the Chinese Cultural Revolution: The Politics of Mass Criticism. LC 73-85786. (Center for Chinese Studies). 1975. 30.00x (ISBN 0-520-02574-1); pap. 9.95x o.p. (ISBN 0-520-02957-7). U of Cal Pr.

Dittmer, Lowell & Ruoxi, Chen. Ethics & Rhetoric of the Chinese Cultural Revolution. LC 81-82595. (Current Chinese Language Project Ser.: No. 19). 1981. pap. 4.00x (ISBN 0-912966-47-5). IEAS.

Dittmer, Paul. Accounting Practices for Hotels, Motels, & Restaurants. LC 79-142507. 1971. text ed. 21.50 (ISBN 0-672-96062-1); tchr's manual 6.67 (ISBN 0-672-26064-6); wkbk., 1972 11.95 (ISBN 0-672-96063-X). Bobbs.

Dittmor, Ray H. Double Leverage: The Whole Truth. 1979. 5.95 (ISBN 0-533-05098-7). Vantage.

Ditzel, Paul. Railroad Yard. LC 77-12758. (Illus.). 64p. (gr. 3 up). 1977. PLB 6.97 o.p. (ISBN 0-671-32871-9). Messner.

Diulio, Eugene. Macroeconomic Theory. 256p. (Orig.). 1974. pap. text ed. 6.95 (ISBN 0-07-017049-5, SP). McGraw.

Divas, Mireille. I'm a Year Old Now. (Illus.). 176p. 1983. 15.95 (ISBN 0-13-451344-4); pap. 7.95 (ISBN 0-13-451336-3). P-H.

Divine, David. Hadrian's Wall: A Study of the North-West Frontier of Rome. LC 69-13122. (Illus.). 1969. 9.95 o.p. (ISBN 0-87645-017-6). Gambit.

Divine, J. A. & Blachford, G. Stained Glass Craft. 115p. 1972. pap. 2.50 (ISBN 0-486-22812-6). Dover.

Divine, James & Starkey, Roberta. How to Beat Test Anxiety & Score Higher on the GMAT. 160p. 1983. pap. 4.95 (ISBN 0-8120-2420-6). Barron.

Divine, Robert A. American Immigration Policy Nineteen Twenty Four to Nineteen Fifty Two. LC 70-166323. (Civil Liberties in American History Ser). 200p. 1972. Repr. of 1957 ed. lib. bdg. 27.50 (ISBN 0-306-70244-4). Da Capo.

--Eisenhower & the Cold War. 160p. 1981. pap. 4.95 (ISBN 0-19-502824-4, 621, GB). Oxford U Pr.

--Roosevelt & World War Two. 1970. pap. 4.95 (ISBN 0-14-021191-8, Pelican). Penguin.

Divine, Thomas F. Interest, an Historical & Analytical Study in Economics & Modern Ethics. 1959. 13.95 (ISBN 0-87462-405-3). Marquette.

Divinsky, Nathan J. Rings & Radicals. LC 66-1192. 1965. 17.50x o.p. (ISBN 0-8020-1368-6). U of Toronto Pr.

Divry, D. C. Divry's Greek-English Dialogues. 1947. pocket ed. 6.00 (ISBN 0-685-09028-0). Divry.

Divry, G. C. Modern English-Greek-English Desk Dictionary with Thumb Index. 768p. (Gr. & Eng.). 1979. 19.95 (ISBN 0-686-97405-0, M-9443). French & Eur.

Divry, George C. Divry's English-To-Greek Phrase & Conversation Pronouncing Manual. 1966. flexible bdg. 6.00 (ISBN 0-685-09027-2). Divry.

--Divry's New Self Taught English Method for Greeks. 1956. 6.00 (ISBN 0-685-09032-9). Divry.

--Greek Made Easy. 3rd ed. 1953. 6.00 (ISBN 0-685-09037-X). Divry.

Dix, C. H. & Aldous, W. H. Microwave Valves. 15.00x o.p. (ISBN 0-592-02728-7). Transatlantic.

Dix, Carol, jt. auth. see Scher, Jonathan.

Dix, Colin. Accomodation Operations. 176p. 1979. 20.00x (ISBN 0-7121-0174-8, Pub. by Macdonald & Evans). State Mutual Bk.

Dix, Dorothea L. Remarks on Prisons & Prison Discipline in the United States. LC 67-24731. (Criminology, Law Enforcement, & Social Problems Ser.: No. 4). 1967. Repr. of 1845 ed. 10.00x (ISBN 0-87585-004-9). Patterson Smith.

Dix, George, et al. Texas Mental Health Commitments. LC 77-91216. (Texas Law Monograph Ser.: No. 1). 195p. 1978. pap. 15.00 (ISBN 0-938160-18-4, 6311). State Bar TX.

Dix, George E. & Sharlot, M. Michael. Basic Criminal Law, Cases & Materials, Criminal Justice Ser. 2nd ed. 650p. 1980. text ed. 24.95 (ISBN 0-8299-0318-6); instrs.' manual avail. (ISBN 0-8299-0588-X). West Pub.

Dix, H. M. Environmental Pollution: Atmosphere, Land, Water & Noise. LC 80-40287. (Institution of Environmental Sciences Ser.). 286p. 1980. 45.95x (ISBN 0-471-27797-5, Pub. by Wiley-Interscience); pap. 21.95x (ISBN 0-471-27905-6). Wiley.

Dix, J. Harlan. Allergy & Clinical Immunology: Continuing Education Review. 1981. pap. text ed. 22.00 (ISBN 0-87488-435-7). Med Exam.

Dix, Owen R. & Jackson, M. P. Statistical Analysis of Lineaments & their Relation to Fracturing, Faulting & Halokinesis in the East Texas Basin. (Report of Investigations: No. 110). 30p. 1.50 (ISBN 0-686-36597-6). Bur Econ Geology.

Dixin, Xu, et al. China's Search for Economic Growth. (Illus.). 217p. (Orig.). 1982. pap. 5.95 (ISBN 0-8351-0974-7). China Bks.

Dixit, A. & Norman, V. D. Theory of International Trade. (Cambridge Economic Handbooks). 250p. 1980. 37.50 (ISBN 0-521-23481-6); pap. 15.95 (ISBN 0-521-29969-1). Cambridge U Pr.

Dixmier, J. Von Neumann Algebras. (North-Holland Mathematical Library: Vol. 27). 1981. 53.25 (ISBN 0-444-86308-7). Elsevier.

Dixon. I Can Manage. 1983. write for info. (ISBN 0-07-072902-6). McGraw.

--Surgical Application of Lasers. (Illus.). 1983. 39.50 (ISBN 0-8151-2514-3). Year Bk Med.

Dixon, A., ed. see International Congress of Rheumatology, et al.

Dixon, Adrienne, tr. see Boon, Louis P.

Dixon, Adrienne, tr. see Michiels, Ivo.

Dixon, Alan C. Network Analysis. LC 72-90475. 1973. text ed. 26.95 (ISBN 0-675-09024-5). Merrill.

Dixon, Andrew D. & Sarnat, Bernard G., eds. Factors & Mechanisms Influencing Bone Growth. LC 82-13115. (Progress in Clinical & Biological Research Ser.: Vol. 101). 657p. 1982. 96.00 (ISBN 0-8451-0101-3). A R Liss.

Dixon, Bashford. Biology of the Rhodophyta. (University Reviews of Botany: No. 4). (Illus.). 285p. 1977. pap. text ed. 20.00x (ISBN 3-87429-124-3). Lubrecht & Cramer.

Dixon, Bernard. Beyond the Magic Bullet: The Real Story of Medicine. LC 77-11811. 1978. 12.45i (ISBN 0-06-011062-7, HarpT). Har-Row.

Dixon, Charles. Advanced Calculus. LC 80-41382. 147p. 1981. 34.95 (ISBN 0-471-27913-7, Pub. by Wiley-Interscience); pap. 19.95 (ISBN 0-471-27914-5). Wiley.

Dixon, Craig L. First Aide for Pets. 24p. (Orig.). 1982. 2.95 (ISBN 0-8431-0721-9). Price Stern.

Dixon, Dorothy. Leather & Lace, No. 2: The Trembling Heart. (Orig.). 1982. pap. 2.50 (ISBN 0-686-97467-0). Zebra.

--Leather & Lace, No. 4: Flame of the West. 1982. pap. 2.50 (ISBN 0-8217-1091-5). Zebra.

--Leather & Lace, No. 5: Cimarron Rose. 1982. pap. 2.50 (ISBN 0-8217-1106-7). Zebra.

--Leather & Lace, No. 7: Diamond Queen. 1983. pap. 2.50 (ISBN 0-8217-1138-5). Zebra.

Dixon, Dougal. Geology. (Science World Ser.). (Illus.). 40p. (gr. 4 up). 1983. PLB 8.90 (ISBN 0-531-04582-X). Watts.

Dixon, Dwight R. & Dixon, Paul B. Photography: Experiments & Projects. (Illus.). 1976. pap. text ed. 13.95 (ISBN 0-02-329840-5). Macmillan.

Dixon, E. J. see Taliaferro, W. H. & Humphrey, J. H.

Dixon, Eustace A. New Jersey: Environment & Cancer. Vivian, V. Eugene, ed. (Illus.). 410p. 1982. 19.95 (ISBN 0-942848-00-4); pap. 12.95 (ISBN 0-942848-01-2). Eureka Pubns.

Dixon, F. J., Jr. see Taliaferro, W. H. & Humphrey, J. H.

Dixon, Frank, jt. ed. see Kunkel, Henry.

Dixon, Frank J. & Fisher, David W., eds. Immunopathology. (Illus.). 380p. 1983. text ed. write for info (ISBN 0-87893-148-1). Sinauer Assoc.

Dixon, Franklin W. Arctic Patrol Mystery. LC 69-12166. (Hardy Boys Ser: Vol. 48). (Illus.). (gr. 4-7). 1969. 2.95 (ISBN 0-448-08948-3, G&D). Putnam Pub Group.

--Bombay Boomerang. LC 70-100116. (Hardy Boys Ser.: Vol. 49). (Illus.). (gr. 5-9). 1970. 2.95 (ISBN 0-448-08949-1, G&D). Putnam Pub Group.

--The Clue in the Embers. LC 74-181843. (Hardy Boys Ser.: Vol. 35). (Illus.). 196p. (gr. 5-9). 1956. 2.95 (ISBN 0-448-08935-1, G&D). Putnam Pub Group.

--Clue of the Broken Blade. LC 73-119043. (Hardy Boys Ser: Vol. 21). (Illus.). (gr. 5-9). 1942. 2.95 (ISBN 0-448-08921-1, G&D). Putnam Pub Group.

--The Clue of the Hissing Serpent. new ed. (Hardy Boys Ser.: Vol. 53). (Illus.). 196p. (gr. 5-9). 1974. 2.95 (ISBN 0-448-08953-X, G&D). Putnam Pub Group.

--Clue of the Screeching Owl. (Hardy Boys Ser: Vol. 41). (Illus.). (gr. 5-9). 1962. 2.95 (ISBN 0-448-08941-6, G&D). Putnam Pub Group.

--The Crimson Flame. Barish, Wendy, ed. (Hardy Boys Ser.). 192p. (gr. 3-7). 1983. 8.95 (ISBN 0-671-42366-5); pap. 2.95 (ISBN 0-671-42367-3). Wanderer Bks.

--Crisscross Shadow. rev. ed. (Hardy Boys Ser: Vol. 32). (gr. 5-9). 1953. 2.95 (ISBN 0-448-08932-7, G&D). Putnam Pub Group.

--Danger on Vampire Trail. LC 70-130337. (Hardy Boys Ser.: Vol. 50). (Illus.). (gr. 5-9). 1971. 2.95 (ISBN 0-448-08950-5, G&D). Putnam Pub Group.
--Disappearing Floor. (Hardy Boys Ser: Vol. 19). (gr. 5-9). 1940. 2.95 (ISBN 0-448-08919-X, G&D). Putnam Pub Group.
--Figure in Hiding. (Hardy Boys Ser: Vol. 16). (gr. 5-9). 1937. 2.95 (ISBN 0-448-08916-5, G&D). Putnam Pub Group.
--The Firebird Rocket. LC 77-76131. (Hardy Boys Ser.: Vol. 57). (Illus.). (gr. 5-9). 1978. 2.95 (ISBN 0-448-08957-2, G&D); lib. bdg. 3.99 (ISBN 0-448-18957-7). Putnam Pub Group.
--Flickering Torch Mystery. (Hardy Boys Ser: Vol. 22). (gr. 5-9). 1943. 2.95 (ISBN 0-448-08922-X, G&D). Putnam Pub Group.
--Footprints under the Window. (Hardy Boys Ser: Vol. 12). (gr. 5-9). 1933. 2.95 (ISBN 0-448-08912-2, G&D). Putnam Pub Group.
--Ghost at Skeleton Rock. rev. ed. (Hardy Boys Ser: Vol. 37). (gr. 5-9). 1958. 2.95 (ISBN 0-448-08937-8, G&D). Putnam Pub Group.
--Great Airport Mystery. (Hardy Boys Ser: Vol. 9). (gr. 5-9). 1930. 2.95 (ISBN 0-448-08909-2, G&D). Putnam Pub Group.
--Hardy Boys: Billion Dollar Ransom. Barish, Wendy, ed. (Hardy Boys Ser.: 73). (Illus.). 192p. (gr. 3-7). 1982. 8.95 (ISBN 0-671-42352-5); pap. 2.75 (ISBN 0-671-42355-X). Wanderer Bks.
--Hardy Boys: Mystery of Smugglers Cove. (The Hardy Boys Ser.: No. 64). 192p. (gr. 3-7). 1980. PLB 8.95 (ISBN 0-671-41117-9); pap. 2.95 (ISBN 0-671-41112-8). Wanderer Bks.
--The Hardy Boys Number Seventy-Five: Trapped at Sea. Schneider, Meg, ed. (Illus.). 192p. (gr. 3-7). 1982. 8.95 (ISBN 0-671-42362-2); pap. 2.95 (ISBN 0-671-42363-0). Wanderer Bks.
--The Hardy Boys Number Seventy-Six: Game Plan for Disaster. Schneider, Meg, ed. (Illus.). 208p. (gr. 3-7). 1982. 8.95 (ISBN 0-671-42364-9); pap. 2.95 (ISBN 0-671-42365-7). Wanderer Bks.
--Hardy Boys: The Apeman's Secret. (Hardy Boys Ser.: No. 62). (Illus.). 192p. (Orig.). (gr. 3-7). 1980. 8.95 (ISBN 0-671-95530-6); pap. 2.95 (ISBN 0-671-95482-2). Wanderer Bks.
--Hardy Boys: The Infinity Clue. (The Hardy Boys Ser.: No. 70). (Illus.). 192p. (Orig.). (gr. 3-7). 1981. 8.95 (ISBN 0-671-42342-8); pap. 2.95 (ISBN 0-671-42343-6). Wanderer Bks.
--Hardy Boys: The Mummy Case. (The Hardy Boys Ser.: No. 63). 192p. (gr. 3-7). 1980. PLB 8.95 (ISBN 0-671-41116-0); pap. 2.95 (ISBN 0-671-41111-X). Wanderer Bks.
--Hardy Boys: The Outlaw's Silver. (The Hardy Boys Ser.: No. 67). 192p. (Orig.). (gr. 3-7). 1981. 8.95 (ISBN 0-671-42336-3); pap. 2.95 (ISBN 0-671-42337-1). Wanderer Bks.
--Hardy Boys: The Pentagon Spy. (Hardy Boys Ser.: No. 61). (Illus.). (gr. 3-7). 1980. lib. bdg. 8.95 (ISBN 0-671-95562-4); pap. 2.95 (ISBN 0-671-95570-5). Wanderer Bks.
--Hardy Boys: The Stone Idol. (Hardy Boys Ser.: No. 65). (Illus.). 192p. (gr. 3-7). 1981. 8.95 (ISBN 0-671-42289-8); pap. 2.95 (ISBN 0-671-42290-1). Wanderer Bks.
--Hardy Boys: The Submarine Caper. (Hardy Boys Ser.: No. 68). (Illus.). 192p. (Orig.). (gr. 3-7). 1981. 8.95 (ISBN 0-671-42338-X); pap. 2.95 (ISBN 0-671-42339-8). Wanderer Bks.
--Hardy Boys: The Vanishing Thieves. (Hardy Boys Ser.: No. 66). (Illus.). 176p. (Orig.). (gr. 3-7). 8.95 (ISBN 0-671-42291-X); pap. 2.95 (ISBN 0-671-42292-8). Wanderer Bks.
--Hardy Boys: Tic-Tac Terror. (The Hardy Boys Ser.: No. 74). (Illus.). 192p. (gr. 3-7). 1982. 8.95 (ISBN 0-671-42356-8); pap. 2.95 (ISBN 0-671-42357-6). Wanderer Bks.
--Hardy Boys: Track of the Zombie. (The Hardy Boys Ser.: No. 71). (Illus.). 192p. (gr. 3-7). 1982. 8.95 (ISBN 0-671-42348-7); pap. 2.95 (ISBN 0-671-42349-5). Wanderer Bks.
--Hardy Boys: Voodoo Plot. (The Hardy Boys Ser.: No. 72). (Illus.). 192p. (gr. 3-7). 1982. 8.95 (ISBN 0-671-42350-9); pap. 2.95 (ISBN 0-671-42351-7). Wanderer Bks.
--Hardy Boys Who-Dunnit Mystery Book. 64p. (gr. 3-7). Date not set. pap. 2.50 o.p. (ISBN 0-671-95721-X). Wanderer Bks. Postponed.
--Haunted Fort. (Hardy Boys Ser: Vol. 44). (gr. 5-9). 1964. 2.95 (ISBN 0-448-08944-0, G&D). Putnam Pub Group.
--Hidden Harbor Mystery. (Hardy Boy Ser: Vol. 14). (gr. 5-9). 1935. 2.95 (ISBN 0-448-08914-9, G&D). Putnam Pub Group.
--Hooded Hawk Mystery. rev. ed. (Hardy Boys Ser: Vol. 34). (Illus.). (gr. 5-9). 1955. 2.95 (ISBN 0-448-08934-3, 8934, G&D). Putnam Pub Group.
--House on the Cliff. (Hardy Boys Ser: Vol. 2). (gr. 5-9). 1927. 2.95 (ISBN 0-448-08902-5, G&D). Putnam Pub Group.
--Hunting for Hidden Gold. (Hardy Boys Ser: Vol. 5). (gr. 5-9). 1928. 2.95 (ISBN 0-448-08905-X, G&D). Putnam Pub Group.
--The Jungle Pyramid. LC 76-14297. (Hardy Boys Ser.). (Illus.). (gr. 5-9). 1977. 2.95 (ISBN 0-448-08956-4, G&D); PLB 7.25 (ISBN 0-448-18956-9). Putnam Pub Group.
--Mark on the Door. rev. ed. (Hardy Boys Ser: Vol. 13). (gr. 5-9). 1934. 2.95 (ISBN 0-448-08913-0, G&D). Putnam Pub Group.
--The Masked Monkey. (Hardy Boys Ser.: Vol. 51). (Illus.). 196p. (gr. 5-9). 1972. 2.95 (ISBN 0-448-08951-3, G&D). Putnam Pub Group.
--Melted Coins. rev. ed. LC 78-86722. (Hardy Boys Ser.: Vol. 23). (Illus.). (gr. 5-9). 1944. 2.95 (ISBN 0-448-08923-8, G&D). Putnam Pub Group.
--Missing Chums. rev. ed. (Hardy Boys Ser: Vol. 4). (gr. 5-9). 1930. 2.95 (ISBN 0-448-08904-1, G&D). Putnam Pub Group.
--The Mysterious Caravan. new ed. LC 74-10463. (Hardy Boys Ser.: Vol. 54). (Illus.). 196p. (gr. 5-9). 1975. 2.95 (ISBN 0-448-08954-8, G&D). Putnam Pub Group.
--Mystery at Devil's Paw. (Hardy Boys Ser.: Vol. 38). (Illus.). 192p. (gr. 5-9). 1959. Repr. 2.95 (ISBN 0-448-08938-6, G&D). Putnam Pub Group.
--Mystery of Cabin Island. (Hardy Boys Ser: Vol. 8). (gr. 5-9). 1929. 2.95 (ISBN 0-448-08908-4, G&D). Putnam Pub Group.
--Mystery of the Aztec Warrior. (Hardy Boys Ser: Vol. 43). (gr. 5-9). 1964. 2.95 (ISBN 0-448-08943-2, G&D). Putnam Pub Group.
--Mystery of the Chinese Junk. (Hardy Boys Ser.: Vol. 39). (gr. 5-9). 1959. 2.95 (ISBN 0-448-08939-4, G&D). Putnam Pub Group.
--Mystery of the Desert Giant. (Hardy Boys Ser.: Vol. 40). (Illus.). (gr. 5-9). 1960. 2.95 (ISBN 0-448-08940-8, G&D). Putnam Pub Group.
--Mystery of the Flying Express. LC 73-106327. (Hardy Boys Ser.: Vol. 20). (Illus.). (gr. 5-9). 1941. 2.95 (ISBN 0-448-08920-3, G&D). Putnam Pub Group.
--The Mystery of the Samurai Sword. (The Hardy Boys Ser.: No. 60). (Illus.). (gr. 3-6). 1979. 7.95 (ISBN 0-671-95506-3); pap. 2.50 (ISBN 0-671-95497-0). Wanderer Bks.
--Mystery of the Spiral Bridge. (Hardy Boys Ser: Vol. 45). (Illus.). (gr. 5-9). 1966. 2.95 (ISBN 0-448-08945-9, G&D). Putnam Pub Group.
--Mystery of the Whale Tattoo. (Hardy Boys Ser: Vol. 47). (gr. 5-9). 1967. 2.95 (ISBN 0-448-08947-5, G&D). Putnam Pub Group.
--Night of the Werewolf. (The Hardy Boys Ser.: No. 59). (Illus.). (gr. 3-6). 1979. 8.95 (ISBN 0-671-95498-9); pap. 2.95 (ISBN 0-671-95520-9). Wanderer Bks.
--Phantom Freighter. rev. ed. LC 75-115957. (Hardy Boys Ser.: Vol. 26). (Illus.). (gr. 5-9). 1947. 2.95 (ISBN 0-448-08926-2, G&D). Putnam Pub Group.
--Secret Agent on Flight 101. (Hardy Boys Ser: Vol. 46). (gr. 5-9). 1967. 2.95 (ISBN 0-448-08946-7, G&D). Putnam Pub Group.
--The Secret of Pirates' Hill. rev. ed. (Hardy Boys Ser.: Vol. 36). (Illus.). 196p. (gr. 5-9). 1957. 2.95 (ISBN 0-448-08936-X, G&D). Putnam Pub Group.
--Secret of Skull Mountain. (Hardy Boys Ser: Vol. 27). (gr. 5-9). 1948. 2.95 (ISBN 0-448-08927-0, G&D). Putnam Pub Group.
--Secret of the Caves. rev. ed. (Hardy Boys Ser: Vol. 7). (gr. 5-9). 1929. 2.95 (ISBN 0-448-08907-6, G&D). Putnam Pub Group.
--Secret of the Lost Tunnel. rev. ed. (Hardy Boys Ser: Vol. 29). (Illus.). (gr. 5-9). 1950. 2.95 (ISBN 0-448-08929-7, G&D). Putnam Pub Group.
--Secret of the Old Mill. (Hardy Boys Ser: Vol. 3). (gr. 5-9). 1927. 2.95 (ISBN 0-448-08903-3, G&D). Putnam Pub Group.
--Secret of Wildcat Swamp. (Hardy Boys Ser: Vol. 31). (gr. 5-9). 1952. 2.95 (ISBN 0-448-08931-9, G&D). Putnam Pub Group.
--Secret Panel. rev. ed. LC 74-86693. (Hardy Boys Ser.: Vol. 25). (Illus.). (gr. 5-9). 1946. 2.95 (ISBN 0-448-08925-4, G&D). Putnam Pub Group.
--Secret Warning. (Hardy Boys Ser: Vol. 17). (gr. 5-9). 1938. 2.95 (ISBN 0-448-08917-3, G&D). Putnam Pub Group.
--The Shattered Helmet. LC 72-90825. (Hardy Boys Ser.: Vol. 52). (Illus.). 196p. (gr. 5-9). 1973. 2.95 (ISBN 0-448-08952-1, G&D). Putnam Pub Group.
--Shore Road Mystery. (Hardy Boys Ser: Vol. 6). (Illus.). (gr. 5-9). 1964. 2.95 (ISBN 0-448-08906-8, G&D). Putnam Pub Group.
--Short-Wave Mystery. rev. ed. (Hardy Boys Ser: Vol. 24). (gr. 5-9). 1928. 2.95 (ISBN 0-448-08924-6, G&D). Putnam Pub Group.
--Sign of the Crooked Arrow. rev ed. LC 71-100119. (Hardy Boys Ser.: Vol. 28). (Illus.). (gr. 5-9). 1949. 2.95 (ISBN 0-448-08928-9, G&D). Putnam Pub Group.
--Sinister Sign Post. (Hardy Boys Ser: Vol. 15). (gr. 5-9). 1936. 2.95 (ISBN 0-448-08915-7, G&D). Putnam Pub Group.
--The Sting of the Scorpion. LC 78-57930. (Hardy Boys Ser.: Vol. 58). (Illus.). (gr. 3-7). 1979. 2.95 (ISBN 0-448-08958-0, G&D); PLB 7.25 (ISBN 0-448-18958-5). Putnam Pub Group.
--Tower Treasure. (Hardy Boys Ser: Vol. 1). (gr. 5-9). 1927. 2.95 (ISBN 0-448-08901-7, G&D). Putnam Pub Group.
--Twisted Claw. rev. ed. LC 77-86667. (Hardy Boys Ser.: Vol. 18). (Illus.). (gr. 5-9). 1939. 2.95 (ISBN 0-448-08918-1, G&D). Putnam Pub Group.
--Viking Symbol Mystery. (Hardy Boys Ser: Vol. 42). (gr. 5-9). 1963. 2.95 (ISBN 0-448-08942-4, G&D). Putnam Pub Group.
--Wailing Siren Mystery. rev. ed. (Hardy Boys Ser: Vol. 30). (Illus.). (gr. 5-9). 1951. 2.95 (ISBN 0-448-08930-0, G&D). Putnam Pub Group.
--What Happened at Midnight. (Hardy Boys Ser: Vol. 10). (gr. 5-9). 1931. 2.95 (ISBN 0-448-08910-6, G&D). Putnam Pub Group.
--While the Clock Ticked. (Hardy Boys Ser: Vol. 11). (gr. 5-9). 1932. 2.95 (ISBN 0-448-08911-4, G&D). Putnam Pub Group.
--The Witchmaster's Key. LC 75-17392. (Hardy Boys Ser.: Vol. 55). (Illus.). 196p. (gr. 5-9). 1976. 2.95 (ISBN 0-448-08955-6, G&D). Putnam Pub Group.
--Yellow Feather Mystery. (Hardy Boys Ser: Vol. 33). (gr. 5-9). 1954. 2.95 (ISBN 0-448-08933-5, G&D). Putnam Pub Group.

Dixon, Franklin W. & Spina, D. A. Hardy Boys Detective Handbook. rev. ed. (Hardy Boys Ser.). (Illus.). 224p. (gr. 4-7). 1972. 3.95 (ISBN 0-448-01990-6, G&D). Putnam Pub Group.
Dixon, Franklin W., jt. auth. see Keene, Carolyn.
Dixon, J. C., ed. Continuing Education in the Later Years. LC 53-12339. (Center for Gerontological Studies & Programs Ser.: No. 12). 1963. pap. 3.75 o.p. (ISBN 0-8130-0062-9). U Presses Fla.
Dixon, J. S., jt. auth. see Gosling, J. A.
Dixon, James M. English Idioms. LC 73-163172. vi, 288p. 1975. Repr. of 1927 ed. 42.00x (ISBN 0-8103-3986-2). Gale.
Dixon, Jeane. Horoscopes for Dogs. 1979. 5.95 o.p. (ISBN 0-395-27453-2). HM.
Dixon, Jesse T. Adapting Activities for Therapeutic: Recreation Service: Concepts & Applications. (Illus.). 37p. (Orig.). 1981. pap. 12.00 (ISBN 0-916304-48-5). Campanile.
Dixon, John, jt. auth. see Cowan, Henry J.
Dixon, John D. Problems in Group Theory. LC 72-76597. 1973. pap. 4.00 (ISBN 0-486-61574-X). Dover.
Dixon, John P. The Spatial Child. (Illus.). 288p. 1983. text ed. price not set (ISBN 0-398-04821-5). C C Thomas.
Dixon, John R. Design Engineering: Inventiveness, Analysis & Decision-making. LC 82-88. 1983. Repr. of 1966 ed. cancelled o.p. (ISBN 0-89874-416-4). Krieger.
--Design Engineering: Inventiveness, Analysis & Decision Making. 1966. text ed. 17.50 o.p. (ISBN 0-07-017071-1, C). McGraw.
--Thermodynamics One: An Introduction to Energy. (P-H Ser. in Mechanical Engineering). (Illus.). 512p. 1975. 31.95 (ISBN 0-13-914887-6). P-H.
Dixon, K. C. Cellular Defects in Disease. (Illus.). 504p. 1982. text ed. 35.75 (ISBN 0-632-00734-6, B 1321-3). Mosby.
Dixon, Keith. Sociological Theory: Pretence & Possibility. (Monographs in Social Theory). 142p. 1973. 18.95 (ISBN 0-7100-7601-0); pap. 7.95 (ISBN 0-7100-7698-3). Routledge & Kegan.
Dixon, L. C. Numerical Optimisation of Dynamic Systems. 1980. 53.25 (ISBN 0-444-85494-0). Elsevier.
Dixon, L. C. & Szego, G. P., eds. Towards Global Optimisation, Vols. I & II. LC 74-28195. 1975-78. Vol. I. 68.00 (ISBN 0-444-10955-2, North-Holland); Vol. II. 59.75 (ISBN 0-444-85171-2). Elsevier.
Dixon, Lawrence W. Wills, Death & Taxes: Basic Principles for Protecting Estates. LC 77-21380. (Quality Paperback: No. 228). (Orig.). 1977. pap. 3.95 (ISBN 0-8226-0228-8). Littlefield.
Dixon, Marlene. Women in Class Struggle. 3rd ed. 175p. 1983. pap. 7.95 (ISBN 0-89935-021-6). Synthesis Pubns.
Dixon, Marlene & Jonas, Susanne, eds. The New Nomads: From Immigrant Labor to Transnational Working Class. LC 82-10356. (Contemporary Marxism Ser.). (Illus.). 165p. (Orig.). 1982. pap. 6.50 (ISBN 0-89935-018-6). Synthesis Pubns.
--Revolution & Intervention in Central America. 3rd ed. LC 82-50034. (Contemporary Marxism Ser.). (Illus.). 100p. (Orig.). 1982. pap. 6.50. Synthesis Pubns.
--World Capitalist Crisis & the Rise of the Right. (Contemporary Marxism Ser.). (Illus., Orig.). 1982. pap. 6.50 (ISBN 0-89935-016-X). Synthesis Pubns.
Dixon, Marlene, et al. Quebec & the Parti Quebecois. (Orig.). 1980. pap. 3.50 o.p. (ISBN 0-89935-003-8). Synthesis Pubns.
Dixon, Mim. What Happened to Fairbanks? The Effects of the Trans-Alaska Oil Pipeline on the Community of Fairbanks, Alaska. (Social Impact Assessment Ser.: No. 1). (Illus.). 337p. 1980. lib. bdg. 23.75 (ISBN 0-89158-071-9); pap. text ed. 10.00 (ISBN 0-89158-961-9). Westview.
Dixon, N. Rex & Martin, Thomas B., eds. Automatic Speech & Speaker Recognition. LC 78-65703. 1979. 35.95 (ISBN 0-87942-117-7). Inst Electrical.
Dixon, Norman F. Preconscious Processing. LC 80-42012. 320p. 1981. 35.95x (ISBN 0-471-27982-X, Pub. by Wiley-Interscience). Wiley.
Dixon, P. The Theory of Joint Maximization. LC 74-24348. (Contributions to Economic Analysis: Vol. 91). 212p. 1975. 47.00 (ISBN 0-444-10792-4, North-Holland). Elsevier.
Dixon, P. B. & Parmenter, B. R. ORANI: A Multisectoral Model of the Australian Economy. (Contributions to Economic Analysis Ser.: Vol. 142). 356p. 1982. 68.00 (ISBN 0-444-86294-3). Elsevier.
Dixon, Pahl & Dixon, Peter. Hot Skateboarding. (Orig.). 1977. pap. 1.95 o.p. (ISBN 0-446-89653-5). Warner Bks.
Dixon, Paul B., jt. auth. see Dixon, Dwight R.
Dixon, Penelope & Ryan, Fortune. Photographers of the Farm Security Association: An Annotated Bibliography. LC 81-43333. 250p. 1983. lib. bdg. 30.00. Garland Pub.
Dixon, Peter. Creative Expression in the Primary School. (Practical Guides for Teachers Ser.). (Illus.). 136p. 1974. pap. 5.95x o.p. (ISBN 0-631-94120-7, Pub. by Basil Blackwell). Biblio Dist.
Dixon, Peter, jt. auth. see Dixon, Pahl.
Dixon, Peter, ed. Writers & Their Background: Alexander Pope. LC 72-85534. (Writers & Their Background Ser.). xx, 324p. 1972. 15.00x (ISBN 0-8214-0113-0, 82-81164); pap. 7.00x (ISBN 0-8214-0114-9, 82-81172). Ohio U Pr.
Dixon, Peter L. The True Love. 224p. (Orig.). 1981. pap. 2.50 o.p. (ISBN 0-380-78717-2, 78717). Avon.
Dixon, Peter S. & Irvine, Linda M. Seaweeds of the British Isles; Vol. 1, Rhodophyta: Pt. 1, Introduction, Nemeliales, Gigartinales. (Illus.). 1977. pap. 32.50x (ISBN 0-565-00781-5, Pub. by Brit Mus Nat Hist). Sabbot-Natural Hist Bks.
Dixon, Philip. Discoveries at Crinkley Hill. 100p. 1982. 10.00x (ISBN 0-85224-444-4, Pub. by Edinburgh U Pr Scotland). Columbia U Pr.
Dixon, R. C. Spread Spectrum Systems. LC 75-31707. 1976. text ed. 37.50 (ISBN 0-471-21629-1, Pub. by Wiley-Interscience). Wiley.
Dixon, R. G., et al. Right of Privacy: A Symposium. LC 75-147833. (Symposia on Law & Society Ser). 1971. Repr. of 1965 ed. lib. bdg. 22.50 (ISBN 0-306-70114-6). Da Capo.
Dixon, R. L. Executive's Accounting Primer. 1971. 29.95 (ISBN 0-07-017078-9, P&RB). McGraw.
Dixon, R. M. The Dyirbal Language of North Queensland: Studies in Linguistics. LC 78-190415. (No. 9). (Illus.). 448p. 1973. 59.50 (ISBN 0-521-08510-1); pap. 18.95 (ISBN 0-521-09748-7). Cambridge U Pr.
--A Grammar of Yidin. LC 76-27912. (Cambridge Studies in Linguistics: No. 19). (Illus.). 1977. 79.50 (ISBN 0-521-21462-9). Cambridge U Pr.
Dixon, R. M., ed. Grammatical Categories in Australian Languages. (AIAS Linguistic Ser.: No. 22). 768p. 1976. text ed. 57.50x (ISBN 0-391-00694-0); pap. text ed. 33.75x (ISBN 0-391-00695-9). Humanities.
Dixon, R. M. & Blake, B. J., eds. Handbook of Australian Languages, Vol. 1. xiv, 392p. 1979. 41.00 (ISBN 90-272-0512-4). Benjamins North Am.
--Handbook of Australian Languages, Vol. 2. xxiv, 427p. 1982. 41.00 (ISBN 90-272-2004-2). Benjamins North Am.
Dixon, Robert. Dynamic Astronomy. 3rd ed. (Illus.). 1980. pap. text ed. 23.95 (ISBN 0-13-221267-6). P-H.
--El Ingles en Accion-See It & Say It in English. 1978. pap. 3.50 (ISBN 0-451-12101-5, AE2101, Sig). NAL.
--The McGraw-Hill Thirty-Six Hour Accounting Course. new ed. 1976. 34.95 (ISBN 0-07-017090-8, P&RB). McGraw.
--Physical Science: A Dynamic Approach. (Illus.). 1979. pap. text ed. 23.95 (ISBN 0-13-669820-4). P-H.
Dixon, Robert, et al. Essentials of Accounting. 1966. text ed. 12.95x o.p. (ISBN 0-02-329850-2, 32985); problems & practice sets 6.95 o.p. (ISBN 0-02-329860-X, 32986). Macmillan.
Dixon, Robert C. Spread Spectrum Techniques. LC 76-18432. (IEEE Press Selected Reprint Ser). 408p. 1976. 31.00 (ISBN 0-471-02358-2); pap. 20.50 (ISBN 0-471-02359-0, Pub. by Wiley-Interscience). Wiley.
Dixon, Robert C., ed. Spread Spectrum Techniques. LC 76-18432. 1976. 15.45 (ISBN 0-87942-078-2). Inst Electrical.
Dixon, Robert G. Benchwork. LC 80-66607. (Machine Trades - Machine Shop Ser.). (Illus.). 211p. 1981. pap. text ed. 9.80 (ISBN 0-8273-1743-3); instr's. guide 2.50 (ISBN 0-8273-1744-1). Delmar.
Dixon, Roger. Going to Jerusalem: A Novel. LC 76-58023. 224p. 1977. 7.95 o.p. (ISBN 0-698-10813-2, Coward). Putnam Pub Group.
Dixon, Samuel, jt. auth. see Trojanowicz, Robert.
Dixon, Samuel L. Working with People in Crisis: Theory & Practice. LC 78-31227. (Illus.). 204p. 1979. pap. text ed. 12.95 (ISBN 0-8016-1320-5). Mosby.
Dixon, Solon. The Dixon Legend. 1982. 9.95 (ISBN 0-87397-208-2). Strode.
Dixon, Terence & Lucas, Martin. The Human Race. LC 82-14280. (New Press Ser.). 256p. 1982. 24.95 (ISBN 0-07-017080-0). McGraw.
Dixon, W. G. Special Relativity. LC 77-83991. (Illus.). 1978. 54.50 (ISBN 0-521-21871-3). Cambridge U Pr.
--Special Relativity: The Foundation of Macroscopic Physics. LC 77-83991. (Illus.). 261p. 1982. pap. 19.95 (ISBN 0-521-27241-6). Cambridge U Pr.
Dixon, W. J. & Nicholson, W. L. Exploring Data Analysis: The Computer Revolution in Statistics. LC 73-85786. 1974. 32.50x (ISBN 0-520-02470-2). U of Cal Pr.
Dixon, Wilfrid J. & Massey, F. J., Jr. Introduction to Statistical Analysis. 3rd ed. (Illus.). 1969. 29.00 (ISBN 0-07-017070-3, C). McGraw.

Dixon-Hunt, John & Holland, Faith M., eds. The Ruskin Polygon. 266p. 1982. 30.00 (ISBN 0-7190-0834-4). Manchester.
Dixson, et al. My First English-Japanese Picture Dictionary. (Illus.). (gr. 1-6). 1978. pap. text ed. 4.50 (ISBN 0-88345-260-X). Regents Pub.
Dixson, Robert J. Correct English. (Blue Bks.). pap. 1.75 o.p. (ISBN 0-671-18106-8). Monarch Pr.
--Curso Completo De Ingles, 4 bks. (gr. 9-12). 1973. Bk. 1. pap. text ed. 3.25 (ISBN 0-88345-035-6, 17998); Bk. 2. pap. text ed. 3.25 (ISBN 0-88345-036-4, 17999); Bk. 3. pap. text ed. 3.25 (ISBN 0-88345-037-2, 18118); Bk. 4. pap. text ed. 3.25 (ISBN 0-88345-038-0, 18119). cassettes 100.00 (ISBN 0-685-04772-5). Regents Pub.
--Graded Exercises in English. rev. ed. (Orig.). (gr. 8-10). 1971. pap. text ed. 3.75 (ISBN 0-88345-058-5, 18009); answer key 1.50 (ISBN 0-685-19797-2). Regents Pub.
--Ingles Practico Sin Maestro, 2 vols. (gr. 9 up). 1972. One-vol. Ed. pap. text ed. 6.50 (ISBN 0-88345-068-2, 18102); Vol. 1. pap. text ed. 3.75 (ISBN 0-88345-069-0); Vol. 2. pap. text ed. 3.75 (ISBN 0-88345-070-4). 60.00 ea.tapes o.p.; ea cassettes 60.00. Regents Pub.
--Modern Short Stories in English. rev. ed. (Illus., Orig., Sequel to Easy Reading Selections in English). (gr. 9-11). 1971. pap. text ed. 3.25 (ISBN 0-88345-117-4, 17986); 35.00 o.p. tapes (ISBN 0-685-19799-9); cassettes 40.00 (ISBN 0-685-19800-6). Regents Pub.
--Practical Guide to the Teaching of English As a Foreign Language. 1975. pap. text ed. 3.25 (ISBN 0-88345-244-8, 18132). Regents Pub.
--Tests & Drills in English Grammar, 2 bks. rev. ed. (Orig.). (gr. 7 up). 1972. Bk. 1. pap. text ed. 3.25 (ISBN 0-88345-159-X, 18007); Bk. 2. pap. text ed. 3.25 (ISBN 0-88345-160-3, 18008). Regents Pub.
Dixson, Robert J., jt. auth. see Angel, Juvenal L.
Dixson, Robert J., jt. auth. see Clarey, Elizabeth M.
Dixson, Robert J., ed. see Cooper, James F.
Dixson, Robert J., ed. see Crane, Stephen.
Dixson, Robert J., ed. see Eggleston, Edward.
Dixson, Robert J., ed. see Harte, Bret.
Dixson, Robert J., ed. see Hawthorne, Nathaniel.
Dixson, Robert J., ed. see Howells, William D.
Dixson, Robert J., ed. see James, Henry.
Dixson, Robert J., ed. see Poe, Edgar Allan.
Diyasena, W. Pre-Vocational Education in Sri Lanka. (Experiments & Innovations in Education, Asian Ser.: No. 28). 50p. 1977. pap. 2.50 (ISBN 92-3-101404-8, U743, UNESCO). Unipub.
DiZazzo, Ray, jt. auth. see Parrish, Darrell.
Dizenzo, Patricia. Phoebe. 128p. (Orig.). (gr. 8-12). 1982. pap. 1.95 (ISBN 0-553-14944-X, 13376-4). Bantam.
--Phoebe. (gr. 9 up). 1970. PLB 7.95 (ISBN 0-07-017096-7, GB). McGraw.
Dizikes, John. Britain, Roosevelt & the New Deal: British Opinion, 1932-1938. Freidel, Frank, ed. LC 78-63282. (Modern American History Ser.: Vol. 7). 200p. 1979. lib. bdg. 30.00 o.s.i. (ISBN 0-8240-3631-X). Garland Pub.
Dizon, Andrew E., jt. ed. see Sharp, Gary D.
Djenev, Kiril, jt. auth. see Katzarova-Kukudova, Raina.
Djilas, Milovan. Conversations with Stalin. Petrovich, Michael B., tr. LC 62-14470. 1963. pap. 4.95 (ISBN 0-15-622591-3, Harv). HarBraceJ.
--The New Class: An Analysis of the Communist System. LC 82-48032. 224p. 1983. Repr. of 1957 ed. write for info (ISBN 0-15-665489-X, Harv). HarBraceJ.
--The Unperfect Society: Beyond the New Class. Cook, Dorian, tr. LC 70-76568. 1970. pap. 5.95 (ISBN 0-15-693125-7, Harv). HarBraceJ.
Djokovic, D. Z. & Malzan, Jerry. Products of Reflections in U (P.Q) (Memoirs Ser.: No. 259). 5.00 (ISBN 0-8218-2259-4). Am Math.
Djoleto, Amu & Kwami, Thomas, eds. West African Prose. 1972. pap. text ed. 3.00x o.p. (ISBN 0-435-90805-7). Heinemann Ed.
Djoszegi, V. & Hoppal, M. Shamanism in Siberia. Simon, S., tr. from Rus. LC 79-300802. (Illus.). 1978. 50.00x (ISBN 963-05-1350-1). Intl Pubns Serv.
Dlouhy, Z. Disposal of Radioactive Wastes. (Studies in Environmental Science: Vol. 15). 246p. 1982. 59.75 (ISBN 0-444-99724-5). Elsevier.
Dlugatch, Irving. Dynamic Cost Reduction. LC 78-21078. (Systems & Controls for Financial Management Ser.). 1979. 39.95x (ISBN 0-471-03565-3, Pub. by Wiley-Interscience). Wiley.
Dlugolensky, Y. Clocks & Watches. 26p. 1982. pap. 2.00 (ISBN 0-8285-2292-8, Pub. by Progress Pubs USSR). Imported Pubns.
Dlugosch, Sharon. Table Setting Guide. 1980. 8.00 (ISBN 0-918420-05-9). Brighton Pubns.
--Table Setting Guide. (Orig.). 1982. pap. 3.95 (ISBN 0-918420-07-5). Brighton Pubns.
D'Mello, A. & Kruk, Z. L. Multiple Choice Questions in Pharmacology. 64p. 1982. pap. text ed. 6.95 (ISBN 0-686-43069-7). E Arnold.
Dmytryshyn, Basil. A History of Russia. (Illus.). 1977. 24.95 (ISBN 0-13-392134-4). P-H.
Dmytryshyn, Basil, ed. see Golovin, Pavel N.
Dmytryshyn, Basil & Crownhart-Vaughan, E. A., trs. Colonial Russian America: Kyrill T. Khlebnikov's Reports, 1817-1832. LC 76-43154. (North Pacific Studies Ser.: No. 2). (Illus.). 158p. 1976. 19.95 (ISBN 0-87595-053-1); pap. 12.95 (ISBN 0-87595-139-2). Oreg Hist Soc.
Dmytryshyn, Basil, tr. see Golovin, Pavel N.
Doan, Daniel. Dan Doan's Fitness Program for Hikers & Cross-Country Skiers. LC 78-58591. (Illus.). 1978. pap. 4.95 (ISBN 0-912274-98-0). Backcountry Pubns.
--Fifty Hikes in New Hampshire's White Mountains: Walks, Day Hikes, Backpacking Trips. rev. ed. LC 73-76396. (Fifty Hikes Ser.). (Illus.). 168p. 1982. pap. 7.95 o.p. (ISBN 0-942440-04-8). Backcountry Pubns.
--Fifty Hikes in New Hampshire's White Mountains: Walks, Day Hikes, & Backpacking Trips. 3rd, rev. ed. (Fifty Hikes Ser.). (Illus.). 224p. 1983. pap. 8.95 (ISBN 0-942440-12-9). Backcountry Pubns.
--Fifty More Hikes in New Hampshire: Day Hikes & Backpacking Trips from the Coast to Coos County. rev. ed. (Fifty Hikes Ser.). (Illus.). 224p. 1983. pap. 8.95 (ISBN 0-942440-06-4). Backcountry Pubns.
Doan, Rachel N., jt. auth. see Nieland, Robert G.
Doane, D. V., jt. auth. see Siebert, C. A.
Doane, Doris. Exploring Old Cape Cod. rev. ed. (Illustrated Guide Ser.). (Illus.). 1973. pap. 4.95 (ISBN 0-85699-003-5). Chatham Pr.
Doane, Doris C. & Keyes, King. How to Read Tarot Cards. (Illus.). 208p. 1979. pap. 4.33i (ISBN 0-06-463481-7, EH 481, EH). B&N NY.
Doane, George W. The Goodly Heritage of Jerseymen: The First Annual Address before the New Jersey Historical Society at Their Meeting in Trenton, on Thursday, January 15, 1846. 2nd ed. 32p. 1971. pap. 2.00 (ISBN 0-686-81822-9). NJ Hist Soc.
Doane, R. W. Common Pests. (Illus.). 398p. 1931. photocopy ed. spiral 34.75x (ISBN 0-398-04245-4). C C Thomas.
Dobb, Craig. The Performing World of the Dancer. LC 81-50298. (The Performing World Ser.). 15.20 (ISBN 0-382-06590-5). Silver.
--Young Person's Guide to the Ballet. (Masterworks of Opera Ser.). 15.96 (ISBN 0-382-06445-3). Silver.
Dobb, M. H., ed. see Ricardo, David.
Dobb, Maurice. An Essay on Economic Growth & Planning. 119p. 1977. 10.75 (ISBN 0-7100-1284-5). Routledge & Kegan.
--Political Economy & Capitalism: Some Essays in Economic Tradition. LC 76-108389. 357p. 1972. Repr. of 1945 ed. lib. bdg. 17.00x (ISBN 0-8371-3812-4, DOPE). Greenwood.
--Theories of Value & Distribution Since Adam Smith. LC 72-88619. (Illus.). 264p. 1973. 42.50 (ISBN 0-521-20100-4); pap. 15.95 (ISBN 0-521-09936-6). Cambridge U Pr.
--Welfare Economics & the Elements of Socialism. LC 69-16280. (Illus.). 1969. 47.50 (ISBN 0-521-07462-2); pap. 15.95 (ISBN 0-521-09937-4). Cambridge U Pr.
Dobbin, Muriel. A Taste for Power. 352p. 1980. 10.95 (ISBN 0-399-90095-0, Marek). Putnam Pub Group.
Dobbins, Bill. High Tech Training. 1982. 18.75 (ISBN 0-671-43860-3); pap. 9.25 (ISBN 0-671-43861-1). S&S.
Dobbins, Bill, jt. auth. see Schwarzenneger, Arnold.
Dobbins, Frank A. The Contributions of Mohammedanism to the Historical Growth of Mankind & Its Future Prospects. (Illus.). 103p. Repr. of 1883 ed. 97.75 (ISBN 0-89901-111-X). Found Class Reprints.
Dobbins, G. S. Aprenda a Ser Lider. Molina, S. P., tr. from Eng. Orig. Title: Learning to Lead. 126p. (Span.). 1980. pap. 2.50 (ISBN 0-311-17013-7). Casa Bautista.
Dobbins, Gaines S. Churchbook. 1951. 10.95 (ISBN 0-8054-2502-0). Broadman.
--Ministering Church. LC 60-9530. 1960. 8.95 (ISBN 0-8054-2505-5). Broadman.
Dobbins, Joann H. Pineapple Gold. 304p. 1983. pap. 10.95 (ISBN 0-9610540-0-X). Wimmer Bks.
Dobbins, Murrell F., jt. auth. see Touchstone, Joseph C.
Dobbins, Richard A. Atmospheric Motion & Air Pollution: An Introduction for Students of Engineering & Science. LC 79-952. (Environmental Science & Technology: Texts & Monographs). 323p. 1979. 49.95 (ISBN 0-471-21675-5, Pub. by Wiley-Interscience). Wiley.
Dobbins, Robert R. If & Only If in Analysis. 1977. pap. text ed. 10.00 (ISBN 0-8191-0344-6). U Pr of Amer.
Dobbs, B. J. The Foundations of Newton's Alchemy: Or "The Hunting of the Greene Lyon". LC 74-31795. (Cambridge Paperback Library). (Illus.). 300p. Date not set. pap. 16.95 (ISBN 0-521-27381-1). Cambridge U Pr.
Dobbs, Brian & Dobbs, Judy. Dante Gabriel Rossetti: An Alien Victorian. 1977. text ed. 20.75x (ISBN 0-686-86085-3). Humanities.
Dobbs, David & Hanks, Robert. A Modern Course on the Theory of Equations. 1980. 15.00x (ISBN 0-936428-03-1). Polygonal Pub.
Dobbs, Horace. Follow the Wild Dolphins. LC 82-5712. (Illus.). 292p. 1982. 15.95 (ISBN 0-312-29752-1). St Martin.
Dobbs, Judy, jt. auth. see Dobbs, Brian.
Dobell, Bertram. Catalogue of Books Printed for Private Circulation. LC 66-25693. 1966. Repr. of 1906 ed. 30.00x (ISBN 0-8103-3303-1). Gale.
Dobelstein, A. Politics, Economics, & the Public Welfare. 1980. 22.95 (ISBN 0-13-683979-7). P-H.
Dobereiner. Glorious World of Golf. 9.95 (ISBN 0-448-14376-3, G&D). Putnam Pub Group.
Dobereiner, Peter. Golf Rules Explained. (Illus.). 160p. 1982. Repr. of 1980 ed. 12.50 (ISBN 0-7153-8081-8). David & Charles.
Doberer, Kurt K. The Goldmakers: Ten Thousand Years of Alchemy. Dickes, E. W., tr. LC 72-597. (Illus.). 301p. 1972. Repr. of 1948 ed. lib. bdg. 16.25x (ISBN 0-8371-6355-2, DOGM). Greenwood.
Doberstein, J. W., tr. see Thielicke, Helmut.
Dobie, Ann B. & Hirt, Andrew J. Comprehension & Composition: An Introduction to the Essay. (Illus.). 1980. pap. text ed. 12.95x (ISBN 0-02-329920-7). Macmillan.
Dobie, J. Frank. Coronado's Children: Tales of Lost & Buried Treasures of the Southwest. 367p. 1982. Repr. of 1931 ed. lib. bdg. 50.00 (ISBN 0-89987-170-4). Darby Bks.
--Longhorns. 1957. pap. 3.95 o.p. (ISBN 0-448-00025-3, G&D). Putnam Pub Group.
--Some Part of Myself. 1967. 9.95 (ISBN 0-316-18790-9). Little.
--Up the Trail from Texas. (Landmark Ser, No. 60). (Illus.). (gr. 7-9). 1955. PLB 4.39 o.p. (ISBN 0-394-90360-9); 2.95 (ISBN 0-394-80360-4). Random.
Dobie, M. R., tr. see Glotz, G.
Dobie, Marryat R., tr. see Robin, Leon.
Dobin, Joel C. To Rule Both Day & Night: Astrology in the Bible, Midrash & Talmud. 256p. 1977. 11.95 (ISBN 0-89281-000-9). Inner Tradit.
Dobinson, M. A., jt. auth. see Hassal, K. A.
Dobkin, Kaye. The Queen of Hearts. 1982. pap. 3.50 (Banbury). Dell.
--The White Rabbit. (Looking Glass Ser.: No. 3). (Orig.). 1983. pap. 3.50 (ISBN 0-440-09740-1). Dell.
Dobkowski, Michael N. The Politics of Indifference: A Documentary History of Holocaust Victims in America. LC 81-40867. 486p. (Orig.). 1982. lib. bdg. 29.75 (ISBN 0-8191-2576-8); pap. text ed. 17.25 (ISBN 0-8191-2577-6). U Pr of Amer.
--The Tarnished Dream: The Basis of American Anti-Semitism. LC 78-67655. (Contributions in American History: No. 81). 1979. lib. bdg. 29.95 (ISBN 0-313-20641-4, DDR/). Greenwood.
--The Tarnished Dream: The Basis of American Anti-Semitism. 291p. Repr. 22.50 (ISBN 0-686-95113-1). ADL.
Doble, Henry F., Jr. Medical Office Design: Territory & Conflict. 320p. 1982. 42.50 (ISBN 0-87527-243-6). Green.
Dobler, Donald W., jt. auth. see Lee, Lamar, Jr.
Dobler, J., jt. auth. see Locher, Carl.
Dobler, Lavinia. Customs & Holidays Around the World. LC 62-8222. (Around the World Ser.). (Illus.). (gr. 7-12). 1962. 9.50 (ISBN 0-8303-0043-0). Fleet.
--National Holidays Around the World. LC 66-16525. (Around the World Ser.). (Illus.). (gr. 7-12). 1968. 9.50 (ISBN 0-8303-0044-9). Fleet.
Dobler, Max. Ionophores & Their Structure. LC 81-4373. 379p. 1981. 64.50 (ISBN 0-471-05270-1, Pub. by Wiley-Interscience). Wiley.
Doblin, Alfred. A People Betrayed: November 1918: A German Revolution. 1983. 19.95 (ISBN 0-88064-007-3); pap. 10.95 (ISBN 0-88064-008-1). Fromm Intl Pub.
Doboson, E. J., jt. ed. see D'Ardenne, S. R.
Dobratz, Betty A., jt. auth. see Kourvetaris, George A.
Dobree, Bonamy, et al, eds. see Henderson, Philip.
Dobree, John H. & Boulter, Eric. Blindness & Visual Handicap: The Facts. (Facts Ser.). (Illus.). 252p. 1982. 13.95x (ISBN 0-19-261328-6). Oxford U Pr.
Dobreiner, Peter. Down the Nineteenth Fairway. LC 82-73279. 256p. 1983. 12.95 (ISBN 0-689-11380-3). Atheneum.
Dobretsov, L. N. & Gomoyunova, M. V. Emission Electronics. 433p. 64.95 o.s.i. (ISBN 0-470-21680-8). Halsted Pr.
Dobrian, Walter A. & Jeffers, Coleman R., eds. Spanish Readings for Conversation. (Orig., Prog. Bk., Span). 1970. pap. text ed. 10.50 o.p. (ISBN 0-395-04367-0). HM.
Dobrin, Arnold. Ireland: The Edge of Europe. LC 70-117146. (World Neighbors Ser.). (Illus.). (gr. 6 up). 1971. 7.95 o.p. (ISBN 0-525-67030-0). Lodestar Bks.
--Little Monk & the Tiger: A Tale of Thailand. (Illus.). (gr. k-3). 1965. PLB 3.86 o.p. (ISBN 0-698-30222-2, Coward). Putnam Pub Group.
--Marshes & Marsh Life. (Illus.). (gr. 3-5). 1969. PLB 4.99 o.p. (ISBN 0-698-30229-X, Coward). Putnam Pub Group.
--Taro & the Sea Turtles. (Illus.). (gr. k-3). 1966. PLB 4.39 o.p. (ISBN 0-698-30352-0, Coward). Putnam Pub Group.
Dobrin, Arthur, jt. auth. see Bizzaro, Patrick.
Dobrin, Milton. Introduction to Geophysical Prospecting. 3rd ed. 1976. text ed. 36.50 (ISBN 0-07-017195-5). McGraw.
Dobriner, William M. Class in Suburbia. LC 81-19070. xii, 166p. 1982. Repr. of 1963 ed. lib. bdg. 19.25x (ISBN 0-313-23145-1, DOCS). Greenwood.
Dobroszycki, Lucjan & Kirshenblatt-Gimblett, Barbara. Image Before My Eyes: A Photographic History of Jewish Life in Poland, 1864-1939. LC 75-35448. (Illus.). 1979. pap. 14.95 (ISBN 0-8052-0634-5). Schocken.
Dobrota, M., jt. auth. see Hinton, R.
Dobryshman, E. M. Review of Forecast Verification Techniques. (Technical Note Ser.). 51p. 1973. pap. 10.00 (ISBN 0-685-34863-6, W106, WMO). Unipub.
Dobrzynski, L. Handbook of Surfaces & Interfaces, Vol. 3. new ed. LC 77-24776. 1979. lib. bdg. 52.50x o.s.i. (ISBN 0-8240-9855-2, Garland STPM Pr). Garland Pub.
Dobson, Austin. Samuel Richardson. LC 67-23877. 1968. Repr. of 1902 ed. 30.00x (ISBN 0-8103-3055-5). Gale.
--Thomas Bewick & His Pupils. LC 69-17340. 1968. Repr. of 1884 ed. 30.00x (ISBN 0-8103-3523-9). Gale.
Dobson, C. R. Masters & Journeyman: A Prehistory of Industrial Relations 1717 to 1800. LC 80-491631. 212p. 1980. 24.75x (ISBN 0-8476-6768-5). Rowman.
Dobson, Christopher & Payne, Ronald. The Carlos Complex: A Study in Terror. LC 76-57878. 1977. 8.95 o.p. (ISBN 0-399-11903-5). Putnam Pub Group.
Dobson, Edward D. Commodity Spreads: A Historical Chart Perspective. LC 79-112547. (Illus.). 1982. 25.00 (ISBN 0-934380-00-7). Traders Pr.
Dobson, G. E. Catalogue of the Chiroptera in the Collection of the British Museum. (Illus.). 1966. 40.00 (ISBN 3-7682-0300-X). Lubrecht & Cramer.
Dobson, Hubert E. Power to Excel. 273p. 1982. 10.95 (ISBN 0-9607256-0-1); pap. 4.95 (ISBN 0-9607256-1-X). Rich Pub Co.
Dobson, James. Dare to Discipline. 1982. pap. 2.95 (ISBN 0-553-22841-2). Bantam.
--Dare to-Discipline. pap. 4.95 (ISBN 0-8423-0631-5). Tyndale.
--Dare to Discipline. 1970. pap. 2.95 pocket ed. (ISBN 0-8423-0635-8). Tyndale.
--Dr. Dobson Answers Your Questions. 1983. 12.50 (ISBN 0-8423-0652-8). Tyndale.
--Emotions: Can You Trust Them? LC 79-91703. 144p. 1981. pap. 3.95 (ISBN 0-8307-0808-1, 5415807); pap. text ed. 2.25 (ISBN 0-8307-0866-9, 5017909). Regal.
--Preparemonos para la Adolescencia. 192p. Date not set. 2.75 (ISBN 0-88113-253-5). Edit Betania.
--The Strong-Willed Child. 1978. 9.95 (ISBN 0-8423-0664-1). Tyndale.
--What Wives Wish Their Husbands Knew About Women. 1975. 8.95 (ISBN 0-8423-7890-1). Tyndale.
--What Wives Wish Their Husbands Knew About Women. 1977. pap. 4.95 (ISBN 0-8423-7889-8). Tyndale.
Dobson, Judith, jt. auth. see Dobson, Russell.
Dobson, Margaret. Cactus Rose. (Candlelight Ecstasy Ser.: No. 145). (Orig.). 1983. pap. 1.95 (ISBN 0-440-11290-7). Dell.
Dobson, P. N. & Peterson, V. Z., eds. Proceedings of the Fifth Hawaii Topical Conference in Particle Physics (1973) LC 73-92867. 630p. (Orig.). 1974. pap. text ed. 17.50x (ISBN 0-8248-0327-2). UH Pr.
Dobson, P. N., Jr., et al, eds. Proceedings of the Sixth Hawaii Topical Conference in Particle Physics (1975) 1976. pap. text ed. 15.00x (ISBN 0-8248-0464-3). UH Pr.
Dobson, Peter N., jt. ed. see Yount, David.
Dobson, R. B. Durham Priory, Fourteen Hundred to Fourteen Fifty. LC 72-89809. (Studies in Medieval Life & Thought). 390p. 1973. 59.50 (ISBN 0-521-20140-3). Cambridge U Pr.
Dobson, R. B. & Taylor, J. Rymes of Robyn Hood: An Introduction to the English Outlaw. LC 75-31564. (Illus.). 1976. 16.95 (ISBN 0-8229-1126-4). U of Pittsburgh Pr.
Dobson, Richard L. Year Book of Dermatology, 1981. 1981. 35.50 (ISBN 0-8151-2667-0). Year Bk Med.
--Year Book of Dermatology 1983. 1983. 40.00 (ISBN 0-8151-2669-7). Year Bk Med.
Dobson, Richard L. & Thiers, Bruce H., eds. Year Book of Dermatology, 1982. (Illus.). 425p. 1982. 37.00 (ISBN 0-8151-2668-9). Year Bk Med.
Dobson, Russell & Dobson, Judith. The Language of Schooling. LC 81-40594. 86p. (Orig.). 1982. lib. bdg. 18.50 (ISBN 0-8191-1876-1); pap. text ed. 7.00 (ISBN 0-8191-1877-X). U Pr of Amer.
Dobson, Russell, et al. Staff Development: A Humanistic Approach. LC 80-67254. 175p. 1980. pap. text ed. 9.50 (ISBN 0-8191-1131-7). U Pr of Amer.
Dobson, Theodore. Inner Healing: God's Great Assurance. LC 78-65129. 216p. 1978. pap. 3.95 o.p. (ISBN 0-8091-2161-1). Paulist Pr.
Dobson, William. Child of Hell. 1982. pap. 2.95 (ISBN 0-451-11768-9, AE1768, Sig). NAL.
--The Child Player. (Orig.). 1981. pap. 1.95 o.p. (ISBN 0-451-09604-5, J9604, Sig). NAL.
--Fangs. (Orig.). 1980. pap. 1.95 o.p. (ISBN 0-451-09346-1, J9346, Sig). NAL.
--The Ripper. (Orig.). 1981. pap. 2.50 o.p. (ISBN 0-451-11205-9, AE1205, Sig). NAL.

Dobyns, Stephen. Dancer with One Leg: A Novel. 228p. 1983. 13.95 (ISBN 0-525-24169-8, 01354-410). Dutton.
--Saratoga Swimmer. 1983. pap. 2.95 (ISBN 0-14-006357-9). Penguin.
Dobyns, Zipporah. Exploring Astrology. 1983. pap. 9.95 (ISBN 0-917086-49-X, Pub. by Astro Comp Serv). Para Res.
Dobzhansky, Theodosius. Genetic Diversity & Human Equality. LC 73-76262. 1973. pap. 3.95x o.p. (ISBN 0-465-09710-3, CN-5010). Basic.
Do Carmo, Manfredo. Differential Geometry of Curves & Surfaces. 1976. 31.95 (ISBN 0-13-212589-7). P-H.
Do Carmo, Pamela B. & Patterson, Angelo T. First Aid Principles & Procedures. (Illus.). 256p. 1976. pap. text ed. 12.95 (ISBN 0-13-317933-8). P-H.
Dochterman, Delores. The Art of Taking Minutes. LC 82-42639. 208p. 1982. 12.95 (ISBN 0-9609526-0-8). Snyder Pub Co.
Dock, V. Thomas. Structured COBOL: American National Standard. (The West Series in Data & Information Systems). (Illus.). 1978. pap. text ed. 16.95 (ISBN 0-8299-0181-7). West Pub.
--Structured FORTRAN IV Programing. (Data Processing & Information System Ser.). (Illus.). 1979. pap. text ed. 17.95 (ISBN 0-8299-0249-X). West Pub.
Dock, V. Thomas & Essick, Edward. Principles of Business Data Processing. 4th ed. 512p. 1980. text ed. 18.95 (ISBN 0-574-21295-7, 13-4295); instr's guide avail. (ISBN 0-574-21296-5, 13-4296); transparency masters 30.00 (ISBN 0-574-21303-1, 13-4303); study guide 6.95 (ISBN 0-574-21297-3, 13-4297). SRA.
--Principles of Business Data Processing: (with MIS Including BASIC) 4th ed. 1980. text ed. 20.95 (ISBN 0-574-21305-8, 13-4305); instructor's guide avail. (ISBN 0-574-21301-5); study guide 7.95 (ISBN 0-574-21302-3, 13-4302). SRA.
Dock, V. Thomas, et al, eds. MIS: A Managerial Perspective. LC 77-7063. 1977. pap. text ed. 14.95 (ISBN 0-574-21050-4, 13-4050). SRA.
Dock, William. Prevention of Obstruction of Coronary & Other Vital Arteries. LC 79-50185. 316p. 1983. 42.50 (ISBN 0-87527-202-9). Green.
Dockens, William S., jt. ed. see Thompson, Travis.
Dockhorn, Jean. Essentials of Social Work Programs in Hospitals. LC 81-20613. 48p. 1982. 15.00 (ISBN 0-87258-353-8, AHA-187103). Am Hospital.
Dockrill, D. W. & Mortley, R., eds. The Via Negativa. 211p. 1983. pap. text ed. 23.25x (ISBN 0-85668-915-7, Pub. by Aris & Phillips England). Humanities.
Dockrill, M. L., jt. auth. see Lowe, C. J.
Docks, L. R. American Premium Record Guide: Identification & Values-78's, 45's & LP's. 2nd ed. 1981. pap. 14.95 o.p. (ISBN 0-517-54404-0, Americana). Crown.
Docks, Les. American Premium Record Guide: Seventy-Eight Rpms - Forty-Five Rpms - LPs, a Collectors Identification & Value Guide. (Illus.). 1979. pap. 14.95 (ISBN 0-89689-023-6). Wallace-Homestead.
Dockstader, Frederick J. The American Indian in Graduate Studies: A Bibliolgrapy of Theses & Dissertations, 2 vols, Vol. 25. (Contributions Ser.). 1973. Set. pap. 18.00 (ISBN 0-934490-06-6); Vol. 1. pap. 10.00 (ISBN 0-934490-07-4); Vol. 2. pap. 10.00 (ISBN 0-934490-08-2). Mus Am Ind.
--Weaving Arts of the North American Indian. LC 78-381. (Illus.). 1978. 25.00i o.p. (ISBN 0-690-01739-1). T Y Crowell.
Dockx, S., ed. see Symposium, Brussels.
Docter, Richard F., jt. auth. see Holmen, Milton G.
Doctor, Jan. The Mystery of Marriage: A Challenge to Forced Divorce. 1980. 8.95 o.p. (ISBN 0-682-49302-3, Testament). Exposition.
Dr. Williams' Library, London. Early Nonconformity, 1566-1800: A Catalogue of Books in Dr. Williams's Library, London, 3 pts. Incl. Pt. 1. Author Catalogue, 5 vols. Set. 380.00 (ISBN 0-8161-0797-1); Pt. 2. Subject Catalogue, 5 vols. Set. 400.00 (ISBN 0-8161-0174-4); Pt. 3. Chronological Catalogue, 2 vols. Set. 175.00 (ISBN 0-8161-0173-6). 1968 (Hall Library). G K Hall.
Doctorow, E. L. American Anthem. (Illus.). 272p. 1982. 65.00 (ISBN 0-941434-16-8, 8003); limited ed., autographed & slipcased 100.00 (ISBN 0-686-83085-7, 8011). Stewart Tabori & Chang.
--Welcome to Hard Times. 224p. 1975. 8.95 o.p. (ISBN 0-394-49833-X); pap. 3.95 (ISBN 0-394-73107-7). Random.
Doctors, Samuel I. Role of Federal Agencies in Technology Transfer. 1969. 22.50x o.p. (ISBN 0-262-04018-2). MIT Pr.
Doczi, Gyorgy. The Power of Limits: Proportional Harmonies in Nature, Art, & Architecture. LC 77-90883. (Illus.). 224p. 1981. 19.95 (ISBN 0-394-51352-5); pap. 10.95 (ISBN 0-394-73580-3). Shambhala Pubns.
Dodd, A. E. & Dodd, E. M. Peakland Roads & Trackways. 192p. 1982. 40.00x (ISBN 0-86190-066-9, Pub. by Moorland). State Mutual Bk.
Dodd, C. H. Politics & Government in Turkey. LC 78-85453. 1969. 32.50x (ISBN 0-520-01430-8). U of Cal Pr.
Dodd, Carl. Dodd's Revelations. 20p. pap. 1.00 (ISBN 0-686-83983-8). Am Atheist.
Dodd, Carley H. Dynamics of Intercultural Communication. 300p. 1982. pap. text ed. write for info. (ISBN 0-697-04191-3); instr's manual avail. (ISBN 0-697-04209-X). Wm C Brown.
Dodd, Charles H. Bible Today. 1946-1960. 19.95 (ISBN 0-521-04844-3); pap. 8.95 (ISBN 0-521-09118-7). Cambridge U Pr.
--Founder of Christianity. LC 73-90222. 306p. 1970. pap. 4.95 (ISBN 0-02-084640-1). Macmillan.
--Historical Tradition in the Fourth Gospel. 1975. 64.00 o.p. (ISBN 0-521-04847-8); pap. 15.95x (ISBN 0-521-29123-2). Cambridge U Pr.
--Interpretation of the Fourth Gospel. 64.50 (ISBN 0-521-04848-6); pap. text ed. 16.95 (ISBN 0-521-09517-4, 517). Cambridge U Pr.
--Meaning of Paul for Today. pap. 3.95 o.p. (ISBN 0-452-00311-3, F311, Mer). NAL.
Dodd, E. E. Atlas of Histology. 1979. 38.95 (ISBN 0-07-017230-7). McGraw.
Dodd, E. M., jt. auth. see Dodd, A. E.
Dodd, Edward H. The Rape of Tahiti. LC 82-21997. 1983. 18.95 (ISBN 0-396-08114-2). Dodd.
Dodd, Gerald D. & Jing, Bao-Shan. Radiology of the Nose, Paranasal Sinuses & Nasopharynx. (Golden's Diagnostic Radiology Ser.: Section 2). 264p. 1977. 46.00 o.p. (ISBN 0-683-02602-X). Williams & Wilkins.
Dodd, Henry P. Epigrammatists: A Selection from the Epigrammatic Literature of Ancient, Mediaeval & Modern Times. LC 69-16801. 1969. Repr. of 1876 ed. 45.00x (ISBN 0-8103-3524-7). Gale.
Dodd, James B. Free-Based Information Centers in Libraries. 150p. 1983. 36.50 (ISBN 0-86729-049-8); pap. 27.50 (ISBN 0-86729-048-X). Knowledge Indus.
Dodd, Lawrence D. & Oppenheimer, Bruce I. Congress Reconsidered. 2nd ed. Way, Jean, ed. LC 80-39915. 464p. 1981. pap. 10.95 (ISBN 0-87187-162-9). Congr Quarterly.
Dodd, Philip, ed. The Art of Travel: Essays on Travel Writing. 172p. 1982. text ed. 17.50x (ISBN 0-7146-3205-8, F Cass Co). Biblio Dist.
Dodd, Sue. Cataloging Machine: Readable Data Files. 268p. 1982. text ed. 35.00 (ISBN 0-8389-0365-7). ALA.
Dodd, V. R. Total Alignment of High Speed Machines: The Dodd Bar Method. 1975. 39.95x (ISBN 0-87814-074-3). Pennwell Book Division.
Dodd, W. A., jt. auth. see Cameron, J.
Dodd, W. F. Revision & Amendment of State Constitutions. LC 73-120854. (American Constitutional & Legal History Ser). 1970. Repr. of 1910 ed. lib. bdg. 42.50 (ISBN 0-306-71959-2). Da Capo.
Dodd, Walter. Evans Mound. (University of Utah Anthropological Papers: No. 106). 160p. (Orig.). 1982. pap. 10.00 (ISBN 0-87480-207-5). U of Utah Pr.
Dodd, William E. Cotton Kingdom. 1919. text ed. 8.50x (ISBN 0-686-83514-X). Elliots Bks.
Dodds, Eric R. The Greeks & the Irrational. (Sather Classical Lectures: No. 25). 1951. pap. 7.95 (ISBN 0-520-00327-6, CAL74). U of Cal Pr.
Dodds, John W. Everyday Life in Twentieth-Century America. Wright, Louis B., ed. (Everyday Life in America Ser.). (Illus.). (gr. 7-10). 1966. 6.75 o.p. (ISBN 0-399-20073-8). Putnam Pub Group.
Dodds, Lois. How Do I Look from Up There? (gr. 9-12). 1980. pap. 3.95 (ISBN 0-88207-584-5). Victor Bks.
Dodds, Robert H. Writing for Technical & Business Magazines. (Illus.). 208p. 1982. Repr. of 1969 ed. text ed. 14.95 (ISBN 0-89874-237-4). Krieger.
Dodds, W. Jean & Orlans, F. Barbara, eds. Scientific Perspectives in Animal Welfare: Symposium. LC 82-24375. Date not set. 17.50 (ISBN 0-12-219140-4). Acad Pr.
Dodes, Irving A. Mathematics: A Liberal Arts Approach with Basic. 2nd. ed. LC 79-131. 464p. 1980. lib. bdg. 21.50 (ISBN 0-88275-892-6). Krieger.
Dodge & Safonov. Eye of the Peacock. (YA) 6.95 (ISBN 0-685-07432-3, Avalon). Bouregy.
Dodge, et al. Marketing Research. 561p. 1982. text ed. 24.95 (ISBN 0-675-09847-5). Additional supplements may be obtained from publisher. Merrill.
Dodge, Alice M. Girl in Exile. (YA) 1969. 6.95 (ISBN 0-685-07435-8, Avalon). Bouregy.
Dodge, C. W. Some Lichens of Tropical Africa IV: Dermatocarpaceae to Pertusariaceae. 1964. pap. 32.00 (ISBN 3-7682-5412-7). Lubrecht & Cramer.
--Some Lichens of Tropical Africa V: Lecanoraceae to Physiaceae. 1971. pap. 40.00 (ISBN 3-7682-5438-0). Lubrecht & Cramer.
Dodge, Calvert R., ed. A World Without Prisons. LC 78-24629. 304p. 1979. 25.95x (ISBN 0-669-02706-5). Lexington Bks.
Dodge, Charlyne, ed. see Frederic, Harold.
Dodge Cost Information Systems. Dodge Construction Systems Costs, 1983. 300p. 1982. 49.95 (ISBN 0-07-017406-7, P&RB). McGraw.
--Dodge Guide to Public Works & Heavy Construction, 1983. 300p. 1982. 49.95 (ISBN 0-07-017408-3, P&RB). McGraw.
--Dodge Manual for Building, Construction, Pricing & Scheduling. 300p. 1982. 39.50 (ISBN 0-07-017407-5, P&RB). McGraw.
Dodge Cost Information Systems Division. Dodge Construction Systems Costs, 1980. 262p. 1979. pap. 39.80 o.p. (ISBN 0-07-017331-1, P&RB). McGraw.
--Dodge Manual for Building Construction Pricing & Scheduling, 1981. 292p. 1981. 29.80 o.p. (ISBN 0-07-017328-1). McGraw.
--Dodge Manual for Building Construction Pricing & Scheduling, 1980. 292p. 1979. pap. 39.80 o.p. (ISBN 0-07-017330-3, P&RB). McGraw.
Dodge, D. & Baird, D. H., eds. Continuities & Discontinuities in Political Thought. LC 74-16197. 314p. 1975. text ed. 14.95 o.p. (ISBN 0-470-21744-8); pap. text ed. 9.95x o.p. (ISBN 0-470-21745-6). Halsted Pr.
Dodge, David L. War Inconsistent with the Religion of Jesus Christ. LC 75-137540. (Peace Movement in America Ser). xxiv, 168p. 1972. Repr. of 1905 ed. lib. bdg. 13.95x (ISBN 0-89198-067-9). Ozer.
Dodge, Dorothy & Baird, Duncan H., eds. Continuities & Discontinuities in Political Thought. 350p. 1975. 15.95 o.p. (ISBN 0-87073-795-3); pap. 7.95 o.p. (ISBN 0-87073-796-1). Schenkman.
Dodge, Geraldine R. The German Shepherd Dog in America. 1956. 17.50 o.p. (ISBN 0-686-19924-3). Quest Edns.
Dodge, Guy H., ed. Jean-Jacques Rousseau: Authoritarian Libertarian? LC 77-158944. (Problems in Political Science Ser.). 1972. pap. text ed. 2.95x o.p. (ISBN 0-669-74534-0). Heath.
Dodge, Harold F. & Romig, Harry G. Sampling Inspection Tables: Single & Double Sampling. 2nd ed. LC 59-6763. (Ser. in Probability & Mathematical Statistics). (Illus.). 1959. 40.95 (ISBN 0-471-21747-6, Pub. by Wiley-Interscience). Wiley.
Dodge, Howard. Barron's How to Prepare for the College Board Achievement Tests - Mathematics Level II. LC 78-8655. 1979. pap. 7.95 (ISBN 0-8120-0325-X). Barron.
Dodge, J. Atlas of Biological Ultrastructures. 1968. 10.50 (ISBN 0-444-19949-7). Elsevier.
Dodge, Kirsten, ed. Government & Business: Prospects for Partnership. LC 80-81347. (Symposia Ser.). 238p. 1980. 8.50x (ISBN 0-89940-409-X). LBJ Sch Public Affairs.
Dodge, Louise, jt. auth. see Preston, Harriet W.
Dodge, Marshall & Bryan, Robert. Bert & I & Other Stories from Down East. Babbidge, Homer D., intro. by. (Illus.). 140p. (Orig.). 1981. 11.95 (ISBN 0-9607546-0-1); pap. 7.95. Bert & I Bks.
Dodge, Martin, jt. auth. see Dodge, Venus.
Dodge, Mary M. Hans Brinker. (Illus.). (gr. 4-6). 1945-63. il. jr. lib. 5.95 (ISBN 0-448-05811-1, G&D); Companion Lib. Ed. 2.95 (ISBN 0-448-05462-0); deluxe ed. 8.95 (ISBN 0-448-06011-6). Putnam Pub Group.
Dodge, Raymond. Conditions & Consequences of Human Variability. 1931. 39.50x (ISBN 0-685-69812-2). Elliots Bks.
Dodge, Raymond & Kahn, Eugen. The Craving for Superiority. 1931. 27.50 (ISBN 0-686-51366-5). Elliots Bks.
Dodge, Richard H. How to Read & Write in College: A Complete Course. (Second Ser.). 264p. 1982. pap. text ed. 11.50 scp (ISBN 0-06-041688-2, HarpC); master key avail. (ISBN 0-06-361689-0); Ach Test M avail. (ISBN 0-06-361688-2); Ach Test N avail. (ISBN 0-06-361687-4). Har-Row.
Dodge, Venus & Dodge, Martin. The Doll's House Do-It Yourself Book. LC 82-19486. (Illus.). 224p. 1983. 16.95 (ISBN 0-8069-5484-1); pap. 9.95 (ISBN 0-8069-7710-8). Sterling.
Dodge, Yadolah, jt. auth. see Arthanari, Subramanyam.
Dodgson, Campbell. Albrecht Durer: Engravings & Etchings. LC 67-27451. (Graphic Art Ser). 1967. Repr. of 1926 ed. 27.50 (ISBN 0-306-70976-7). Da Capo.
Dodgson, Charles L. Lewis Carroll Picture Book: A Selection from the Unpublished Writings & Drawings of Lewis Carroll, Together with Reprints from Scarce & Unacknowledged Work. LC 70-159931. (Tower Bks). (Illus.). 1971. Repr. of 1899 ed. 34.00x (ISBN 0-8103-3915-3). Gale.
Dodgson, Charles L., jt. ed. see Guiliano, Edward.
Dodgson, John, jt. auth. see Pryke, Richard.
Dodi, Andrea, jt. auth. see Giusti-Lanham, Hedy.
Dodson, C. T. Categories, Bundles & Spacetime Topology. (Shiva Mathematics Ser.: No. 1). 230p. (Orig.). 1980. pap. text ed. 21.50 (ISBN 0-906812-01-1, Pub. by Shiva Pub England). Imprint Edns.
Dodson, C. T. & Poston, T. Tensor Geometry. (Surveys & References Ser.: No. 1). 620p. (Orig.). 1979. pap. text ed. 30.95 (ISBN 0-273-01040-9). Pitman Pub MA.
--Tensor Geometry: The Geometric Viewpoint & Its Uses. new ed. (Illus.). 1979. pap. cancelled o.p. (ISBN 0-8224-1040-0). Pitman Pub MA.
--Tensor Geometry: The Geometric Viewpoint & Its Uses. (Reference Works in Mathematics Ser: No. 1). (Illus.). cancelled o.p. (ISBN 0-8224-0317-X). Pitman Pub MA.
Dodson, Carolyn, ed. see Trimble, Stephen.
Dodson, Daniel B. Looking for Zoe. LC 80-16930. 340p. 1981. 12.95 o.p. (ISBN 0-396-07878-8). Dodd.
Dodson, Edward O. & Dodson, Peter. Evolution: Process & Product. 2nd ed. 1976. 13.95x (ISBN 0-442-22164-9). Van Nos Reinhold.
Dodson, Fitzhugh. How to Discipline--with Love. 1978. pap. 3.95 (ISBN 0-451-12211-9, AE2211, Sig). NAL.
--How to Parent. 444p. 1973. pap. 3.95 (ISBN 0-451-11908-8, AE1908, Sig). NAL.
Dodson, Fitzhugh & Alexander, Ann. Your Child: Pregnancy Through Preschool. (Illus.). 416p. 1983. pap. 12.95 (ISBN 0-671-45894-9, Fireside). S&S.
Dodson, Fitzhugh & Ruben, Paula. How to Grandparent. LC 80-7849. 304p. 1981. 13.41i (ISBN 0-690-01874-6, HarpT). Har-Row.
Dodson, Peter, jt. auth. see Dodson, Edward O.
Dodson, Reynolds, jt. auth. see Rosenblatt, Seymour.
Dodson, Susan. Have You Seen This Girl. 1982. 9.95 (ISBN 0-686-36006-0). Four Winds Pr.
Dodwell, G. T. Canaries. (Illus.). 94p. 1978. 3.95 (ISBN 0-7028-1071-1). Avian Pubns.
--Encyclopedia of Canaries. (Illus.). 288p. 1976. 19.95 (ISBN 0-87666-952-6, H967). TFH Pubns.
--The Lizard Canary & Other Rare Breeds. 208p. 1982. 40.00x (ISBN 0-86230-052-5, Pub. by Saiga Pub). State Mutual Bk.
Dodwell Marketing Consultants. Industrial Groupings in Japan, 1982-83. rev. ed. LC 78-324735. (Illus.). 529p. 1982. pap. 335.00x (ISBN 0-8002-3032-9). Intl Pubns Serv.
Doe, John. Sobriety & Beyond. 7.00 o.p. (ISBN 0-686-92068-6). Hazelden.
--Sobriety Without End. 7.00 o.p. (ISBN 0-686-92069-4). Hazelden.
DOE Technical Information Center. Carbon Dioxide & Climate: A Bibliography, July 1976 through June 1981. 170p. 1981. pap. 16.00 (ISBN 0-87079-391-8, DOE/TIC-3382-RI); microfiche 4.50 (ISBN 0-87079-408-6, DOE/TIC-3382-RI). DOE.
--Cooling Towers: A Bibliography, Supplement 4. 134p. 1980. pap. 13.00 (ISBN 0-87079-173-7, DOE/TIC-3360 (SUPPL. 4)); microfiche 4.50 (ISBN 0-87079-414-0, DOE/TIC-3360 (SUPPL. 4)). DOE.
--Cooling Towers: A Bibliography, Supplement 5. 118p. 1981. pap. 11.50 (ISBN 0-87079-174-5, DOE/TIC-3360 (SUPPL. 5)); mcirofiche 4.50 (ISBN 0-87079-415-9, DOE/TIC-3360 (SUPPL. 5)). DOE.
--Energy Accounting & Management: A Bibliography. 119p. 1979. pap. 13.00 (ISBN 0-87079-190-7, TID-3375); microfiche 4.50 (ISBN 0-87079-417-5, TID-3375). DOE.
--Fuel Cells: A Bibliography, 1977 to June 1980. 239p. 1980. pap. 20.50 (ISBN 0-87079-211-3, DOE/TIC-3359 (SUPPL. 1)); microfiche 4.50 (ISBN 0-87079-421-3, DOE/TIC-3359 (SUPPL. 1)). DOE.
--Radioactive Waste Processing & Disposal: A Bibliography Covering June 1976 Through August 1978. 942p. 1980. pap. 62.50 (ISBN 0-87079-371-3, NUREG-0643 (TID-3311-S8)); microfiche 4.50 (ISBN 0-87079-441-8, NUREG-0643 (TID-3311-S8)). DOE.
--Radioactive Waste Processing & Disposal: A Bibliography Covering November 1979 Through December 1980. 900p. 1981. pap. 59.50 (ISBN 0-87079-372-1, NUREG-0644(TID-3311-S9)); microfiche 4.50 (ISBN 0-87079-442-6, NUREG-0644(TID-3311-S9)). DOE.
--Radioactive Waste Processing & Disposal: A Bibliography Covering September 1978 Through November 1979. 883p. 1980. pap. 59.50 (ISBN 0-87079-373-X, DOE/TIC-3311-S10); microfiche 4.50 (ISBN 0-87079-443-4, DOE/TIC-3311-S10). DOE.
Doebele, William A. Land Readjustment: A Different Approach to Financing Urbanization. LC 82-47967. 256p. 1982. 27.95 (ISBN 0-669-05723-1). Lexington Bks.
Doebelin, E. O. System Dynamics: Modeling & Response. LC 77-187802. 448p. 1972. 33.50 (ISBN 0-675-09120-9). Merrill.
Doebelin, Ernest O. Measurement Systems: Application & Design. 2nd ed. (Illus.). 768p. 1971. text ed. 33.50 (ISBN 0-07-017336-2, C). McGraw.
--Measurement Systems: Application & Design. 3rd ed. (Illus.). 896p. 1982. text ed. 34.50x (ISBN 0-07-017337-0). McGraw.
--System Modeling & Response: Theoretical & Experimental Approaches. LC 79-27609. 587p. 1980. text ed. 42.95 (ISBN 0-471-03211-5). Wiley.
Doebner, H. D. & Palev, T. D., eds. Twistor Geometry & Non-Linear Systems: Proceedings, Primorsko, Bulgaria, 1980. (Lecture Notes in Mathematics Ser.: Vol. 970). 216p. 1983. pap. 11.50 (ISBN 0-387-11972-8). Springer-Verlag.
Doeff, Annick M., jt. auth. see Barker, William F.
Doehaerd. Early Middle Ages in the West: Economy & Society. (Europe in the Middle Ages Ser.: Vol. 13). 1978. 59.75 (ISBN 0-444-85091-0, North-Holland). Elsevier.
Doel, Van Den H. see Van Den Doel, H.
Doelle, Leslie L. Environmental Acoustics. LC 70-159320. (Architectural Ser.). (Illus.). 300p. 1972. 47.50 (ISBN 0-07-017342-7, P&RB). McGraw.
Doelp, Alan, jt. auth. see Franklin, Jon.
Doenhoff, Albert E. Von see Abbott, Ira H. & Von Doenhoff, Albert E.
Doerffler, Alfred. Open the Meeting with Prayer. LC 55-7442. 1955. 3.50 (ISBN 0-570-03147-8, 12-2531). Concordia.

Doerge, Robert F., ed. Wilson & Gisvold's Textbook of Organic Medicinal & Pharmaceutical Chemistry. 8th ed. (Illus.). 960p. 1982. text ed. 47.50 (ISBN 0-397-52092-1, Lippincott Medical). Lippincott.

Doering, Henry, ed. The World Almanac Book of Buffs, Masters, Mavens & Uncommon Experts. LC 80-81179. 352p. (Orig.). 1980. pap. 6.95 o.p. (ISBN 0-911818-13-8). World Almanac.

Doering, Henry, ed. see Considine, Tim.

Doering, Jeanne. The Encouragers. LC 81-68641. 160p. 1982. pap. 4.95 (ISBN 0-86693-004-3). Moody.

--The Power of Encouragement. 176p. (Orig.). 1983. pap. 4.95 (ISBN 0-686-82020-7). Moody.

Doering, Mildred & Rhodes, Susan R. The Aging Worker: Research & Recommendations. 352p. 1983. 29.95 (ISBN 0-8039-1949-2). Sage.

Doeringer, Peter B. & Piore, Michael J. Internal Labor Markets & Manpower Analysis. 224p. 1971. 15.95x (ISBN 0-669-63529-4). Lexington Bks.

Doeringer, Suzannah, et al, eds. Art & Technology: A Symposium on Classical Bronzes. 1970. 16.50 o.p. (ISBN 0-262-04030-1). MIT Pr.

Doerken, Maurine. Classroom Combat: Teaching & Television. 336p. 1983. 23.95 (ISBN 0-87778-186-9). Educ Tech Pubns.

Doerksen, Harvey R., jt. auth. see Pierce, John.

Doern, G. Bruce, jt. ed. see Tupper, Allan.

Doerner, Cynthia, et al. Winning Tennis Doubles. LC 77-91151. 1978. 9.95 o.p. (ISBN 0-8092-7697-6); pap. 4.95 o.p. (ISBN 0-8092-7696-8). Contemp Bks.

Doerner, Klaus. Madmen & the Bourgeoisie: A Social History of Insanity & Psychiatry. Neugroschel, Joachim & Steinberg, Jean, trs. 368p. 1981. text ed. 25.00x (ISBN 0-631-10181-0, Pub. by Basil Blackwell England). Biblio Dist.

Doerr, Paul, jt. ed. see Lee, David.

Doerr, Wilhelm, ed. see Borchard, Franz.

Doerries, Hermann. Constantine & Religious Liberty. 1960. 32.50x (ISBN 0-686-51363-0). Elliots Bks.

Doery, A. C., jt. auth. see Croll, R. D.

Doeser, Linda & Richardson, Rosamond. The Little Garlic Book. (Illus.). 64p. 1983. 5.95 (ISBN 0-312-48864-5). St Martin.

--The Little Green Avocado Book. (Illus.). 64p. 1983. 5.95 (ISBN 0-312-48862-9). St Martin.

--The Little Pepper Book. (Illus.). 64p. 1983. 5.95 (ISBN 0-312-48864-5). St Martin.

Doetsch, G. Handbuch der Laplace Transformation, 3 vols. Incl. Vol. 1. Theorie der Laplace Transformation. 581p. 88.55x (ISBN 3-7643-0083-3); Vol. 2. Anwendungen der Laplace Transformation, 1, Abteilung. 436p. 68.75x (ISBN 3-7643-0653-X); Vol. 3. Anwendungen der Laplace Transformation, 2, Abteilung. 2nd ed. 299p. 46.75 (ISBN 3-7643-0674-2). (Mathematische Reihe Ser.: Nos. 14, 15 & 19). (Ger.). 1971-73. Birkhauser.

Doezema, Linda P., ed. Dutch Americans: A Guide to Information Sources. LC 79-13030. (Ethnic Studies Information Guide Ser.: Vol. 3). 1979. 42.00x (ISBN 0-8103-1407-X). Gale.

Dogan, Mattei & Rokkan, Stein, eds. Social Ecology. 458p. (Paperback edition of Quantitative Ecological Analysis in the Social Sciences). 1974. pap. 6.95x o.p. (ISBN 0-262-54022-3). MIT Pr.

Dogen. A Primer of Soto Zen: A Translation of Dogen's Shobogenzo Zuimonki. Masunaga, Reiho, tr. from Japanese. LC 76-126044. 1971. text ed. 7.50x (ISBN 0-8248-0094-X, Eastwest Ctr). UH Pr.

--A Primer of Soto Zen: A Translation of Dogen's Shobogenzo Zuimonki. Masunaga, Reiho, tr. from Japanese. LC 76-126044. 128p. 1975. pap. text ed. 2.95x (ISBN 0-8248-0357-4, Eastwest Ctr). UH Pr.

--Record of Things Heard from the Treasury of the Eye of the True Teaching: A Translation of the Shobogenzo Zuimonki. Cleary, Thomas, tr. from Japanese. LC 78-13112. 1980. pap. 8.00 (ISBN 0-87773-743-6, Prajna). Great Eastern.

Doggett, Edna, ed. see Reed, William.

Doggett, Joella, jt. auth. see Scheick, William J.

Dogin, Yvette. Help Yourself to a Job, 3 pts. (Illus.). (gr. 7 up). Set. text ed. 6.75 (ISBN 0-912486-00-7); Pt. 1, 1977. text ed. 2.25 (ISBN 0-912486-32-5); Pt. 2, 1980. text ed. 2.25 (ISBN 0-912486-02-3); Pt. 3, 1978. text ed. 2.25 (ISBN 0-912486-03-1). Finney Co.

--Jobs from "A" to "Z". 1982. pap. 2.75x (ISBN 0-88323-048-8, 147). Richards Pub.

--Teen-Agers at Work. rev. ed. 1983. pap. 2.95x (ISBN 0-88323-067-4, 164). Richards Pub.

Dogramaci, Ali. Developments in Econometric Analyses of Productivity. (Studies in Productivity Analysis). 1982. lib. bdg. 30.00 (ISBN 0-89838-101-0). Kluwer-Nijhoff.

Dohan, Mary H. Mr. Roosevelt's Steamboat. large print ed. LC 82-3264. 345p. 1982. Repr. of 1981 ed. 9.95x (ISBN 0-89621-357-9). Thorndike Pr.

Doheny, Margaret. The Discipline of Nursing: An Introduction. 224p. 1982. pap. text ed. 11.95 (ISBN 0-89303-058-9). R J Brady.

Doherty, Barbara. I Am What I Do: Contemplation & Human Experience. 226p. 1982. pap. 7.95 (ISBN 0-88347-129-9). Thomas More.

Doherty, Catherine D. The Gospel of a Poor Woman. 6.95 (ISBN 0-87193-151-6). Dimension Bks.

Doherty, Catherine De Hueck. Urodivoi: Fools for Good. 112p. 1983. 9.95 (ISBN 0-8245-0553-0). Crossroad NY.

Doherty, Cecelia & Ilyin, Donna. Technical Manual for ELSA: English Language Skills Assessment in a Reading Context. (ELSA Tests Ser.). 1981. pap. 3.95 (ISBN 0-88377-226-4). Newbury Hse.

Doherty, Dennis. Dimensions of Human Sexuality. LC 79-7046. 1979. 8.95 o.p. (ISBN 0-385-15040-7). Doubleday.

Doherty, Filomena, jt. auth. see T. F. H. Staff.

Doherty, John T., jt. auth. see Catholic Hymnal & Service Book Editorial Committee.

Doherty, M. Stephen. Dynamic Still Lifes in Watercolor: Sondra Freckelton's Approach to Color, Composition, & Control of the Medium. (Illus.). 144p. 1983. 22.50 (ISBN 0-8230-1583-1). Watson-Guptill.

--Paul Ortlip: His Heritage & His Art. (Illus.). 152p. 1983. 45.00 (ISBN 0-914016-91-1). Phoenix Pub.

Doherty, Michael E. & Shemberg, Kenneth M. Asking Questions About Behavior: An Introduction to What Psychologists Do. 2nd ed. 1978. pap. 8.95x (ISBN 0-673-15043-7). Scott F.

Doherty, Paul. Atlas of the Planets. LC 80-12347. (Illus.). 144p. 1980. 18.95 (ISBN 0-07-017341-9, GB). McGraw.

Doherty, R. D., jt. auth. see Martin, J. W.

Doherty, R. N. Social-Documentary Photography in the U. S. A. (Illus.). 1976. pap. 6.95 o.p. (ISBN 0-8174-0316-7, Amphoto). Watson-Guptill.

Doherty, Robert E. Industrial & Labor Relations Terms: A Glossary. 4th rev. ed. LC 79-18839. (ILR Bulletin: No. 44). 40p. 1979. pap. 2.50 (ISBN 0-87546-075-5). ILR Pr.

--Labor Relations Primer: The Story of a Union Management Agreement. (ILR Bulletin Ser.: No. 54). 1971. pap. 2.50 (ISBN 0-87546-212-X). ILR Pr.

Doherty, Robert E., jt. auth. see Aboud, Grace S.

Doherty, Robert E., ed. Public Access: Citizens & Collective Bargaining in the Public Schools. LC 79-13189. 112p. 1979. pap. 7.95 (ISBN 0-87546-073-9). ILR Pr.

Doherty, Robert E., jt. ed. see Adler, Joseph.

Doherty, Steve. How to Build Tahiti. pap. 3.00 o.s.i. (ISBN 0-685-32970-4). Seven Seas.

Doherty, W. T., jt. auth. see Zaba, Joseph.

Doherty, William J. & Baird, Macaran A. Family Therapy & Family Medicine. LC 82-3135. (Family Therapy Ser.). 285p. 1983. text ed. 22.50x (ISBN 0-89862-041-4, G35). Guilford Pr.

Dohrenwend, Barbara S. & Dohrenwend, Bruce P. Stressful Life Events: Their Nature & Effects. LC 74-6369. 340p. 1974. 36.95x (ISBN 0-471-21753-0, Pub. by Wiley-Interscience). Wiley.

Dohrenwend, Bruce P., jt. auth. see Dohrenwend, Barbara S.

Doi, A. R. Islamic Jurisprudence. 7.95 (ISBN 0-686-97870-6). Kazi Pubns.

--Non-Muslims Under Shari'ah. 1981. 4.50 (ISBN 0-686-97861-7). Kazi Pubns.

--Shari'ah & Family Law. 7.95 (ISBN 0-686-97873-0). Kazi Pubns.

Doig, Ivan. The Sea Runners. LC 82-45174. (Illus.). 288p. 1982. 13.95 (ISBN 0-689-11302-1). Atheneum.

--Winter Brothers: A Season at the Edge of America. LC 80-7933. (Illus.). 252p. 1980. 10.95 o.p. (ISBN 0-15-197186-2, Harv.). HarBraceJ.

Doig, Jameson, ed. Issues and Realities in Corrections: A Symposium. 1982. pap. 6.00 (ISBN 0-918592-58-5). Policy Studies.

Doig, Jameson W. Criminal Corrections: Ideals & Realities. LC 81-48633. (Policy Studies Organization Book). 240p. 1982. 25.95x (ISBN 0-669-05467-4). Lexington Bks.

Doiron, John, jt. auth. see Hyde, Cornelius J., III.

Doiron, Peter, jt. ed. see Barron, Neil.

Doise, W. & Douglas, G. Groups & Individuals. LC 77-84800. (Illus.). 1978. 32.50 (ISBN 0-521-21953-1); pap. 10.95 (ISBN 0-521-29320-0). Cambridge U Pr.

Doisneau, Robert. Robert Doisneau: Photographs. 144p. 1981. 70.00x o.p. (ISBN 0-86092-050-X, Pub. by Fraser Bks). State Mutual Bk.

Doke, Clement M. Bantu: Modern Grammatical, Phonetical, & Lexicographical Studies Since 1860. LC 47-5679. 119p. (Orig.). 1967. pap. 7.50x o.p. (ISBN 0-7129-0205-8). Intl Pubns Serv.

Doksum, K. A., jt. auth. see Bickel, P. J.

Doksum, Kjell, jt. ed. see Bickel, Peter J.

Dolan. The Bermuda Triangle & Other Mysteries of Nature. LC 79-22798. (Triumph Bks.). 1980. PLB 8.40 (ISBN 0-531-04113-1, A23). Watts.

Dolan, A. T., jt. ed. see Ahsen, Akhter.

Dolan, C. Terrence, ed. Systemic Mycoses-Deep Seated: Clinical Mycology II. LC 75-736235. (Atlases of Clinical Mycology: 2). (Illus.). 20p. 1975. text & slides 80.00 (ISBN 0-89189-040-8, 15-7-003-00); microfiche ed. 22.00 (ISBN 0-89189-088-2, 17-7-003-00). Am Soc Clinical.

--Systemic Mycoses-Opportunistic Pathogens: Clinical Mycology III. LC 75-736236. (Atlases of Clinical Mycology: 3). 24p. 1975. text & slides 80.00 (ISBN 0-89189-041-6, 15-7-004-00); microfiche ed. 22.00 (ISBN 0-89189-089-0, 17-7-004-00). Am Soc Clinical.

--Systemic Mycoses-Saprobic Fungi: Clinical Mycology VI. LC 80-720450. (Atlases of Clinical Mycology: 6). (Illus.). 27p. 1976. text & slides 80.00 (ISBN 0-89189-044-0, 15-7-010-00); microfiche ed. 22.00 (ISBN 0-89189-092-0, 17-7-010-00). Am Soc Clinical.

--Systemic Mycoses-Yeasts: Clinical Mycology I. LC 75-736234. (Atlases of Clinical Mycology: 1). (Illus.). 24p. 1975. text & slides 80.00 (ISBN 0-89189-039-4, 15-7-002-00); microfiche ed. 22.00 (ISBN 0-89189-087-4, 17-7-002-00). Am Soc Clinical.

Dolan, D. & Williamson, J. Teaching Problem-Solving Strategies. (Resource Bk.). 1982. 16.00 (ISBN 0-201-10231-5). A-W.

Dolan, Edward F., Jr. Adolf Hitler: A Portrait in Tyranny. (Illus.). 240p. (gr. 7 up). 1981. PLB 8.95 (ISBN 0-396-07982-2). Dodd.

--Basic Football Strategy: An Introduction for Young Players. LC 76-3438. 144p. (gr. 5-9). 1976. 7.95a o.p. (ISBN 0-385-03998-0); PLB (ISBN 0-385-04184-5). Doubleday.

--The Complete Beginner's Guide to Gymnastics. LC 78-60286. (Illus.). 1980. 9.95a (ISBN 0-385-13434-7); PLB (ISBN 0-385-13435-5). Doubleday.

--Great Moments in the Indy 500. (Triumph Bks.). (Illus.). (gr. 5 up). 1982. PLB 8.90 (ISBN 0-531-04407-6). Watts.

--Great Moments in the NBA Championships. (Triumph Bks.). (Illus.). 96p. (gr. 5 up). 1982. PLB 8.90 (ISBN 0-531-04406-8). Watts.

--Great Moments in the Superbowl. (Triumph Bks.). (Illus.). 96p. (gr. 5 up). 1982. PLB 8.90 (ISBN 0-531-04408-4). Watts.

--Great Moments in the World Series. (Triumph Bks.). (Illus.). 96p. (gr. 5 up). 1982. PLB 8.90 (ISBN 0-531-04409-2). Watts.

--Gun Control. (Impact Bks.). 96p. (gr. 7 up). 1982. PLB 8.90 o.p. (ISBN 0-531-02202-1). Watts.

--Gun Control: A Decision for Americans. LC 78-5576. (Impact Bks). (Illus.). (gr. 7 up). 1978. PLB 8.90 s&l o.p. (ISBN 0-531-02202-1). Watts.

--How to Leave Home---& Make Everybody Like It. LC 77-6500. (Illus.). (gr. 9 up). 1977. 7.95 (ISBN 0-396-07475-8). Dodd.

Dolan, Edward F., Jr. & Lyttle, Richard B. Kyle Rote, Jr. American-Born Soccer Star. LC 78-18561. 1979. 7.95 o.p. (ISBN 0-385-14098-3). Doubleday.

Dolan, Edwin G. Basic Economics. 3rd ed. 800p. 1983. text ed. 25.95 (ISBN 0-03-062381-2). Dryden Pr.

--Basic Macroeconomics: Understanding National Income, Inflation & Unemployment. 400p. 1983. pap. text ed. 16.95 (ISBN 0-03-062407-X). Dryden Pr.

--Basic Microeconomics. 3rd ed. 464p. 1983. pap. text ed. 16.95 (ISBN 0-03-062406-1). Dryden Pr.

Dolan, Edwin G., jt. auth. see Goodman, John C.

Dolan, Frances M. & D'Alessandro, Arthur D. Your Last Wish, My Love. 1979. 6.50 o.p. (ISBN 0-533-03941-X). Vantage.

Dolan, J. A. Motor Vehicle Technology & Practical Work. 1971. pap. text ed. 16.50x o.p. (ISBN 0-435-72052-X). Heinemann Ed.

Dolan, Jay P. The Immigrant Church: New York's Irish & German Catholics, 1815-1865. LC 82-23827. (Illus.). xiv, 221p. 1983. pap. text ed. 7.95x (ISBN 0-268-01151-6, 85-11511). U of Notre Dame Pr.

Dolan, John, jt. ed. see Jedin, Hubert.

Dolan, Josephine A. Nursing in Society: A Historical Perspective. 14th ed. LC 77-88313. (Illus.). 380p. 1978. 24.00 (ISBN 0-7216-3133-9). Saunders.

Dolan, Jr. Child Abuse. LC 79-26266. (gr. 7 up). 1980. PLB 8.90 (ISBN 0-531-02864-X, A29). Watts.

Dolan, Paul J., jt. ed. see Miller, Ruth.

Dolan, Thomas J. Fusion Research, 3 vols. LC 80-18383. 1000p. Set. 120.00 (ISBN 0-08-025565-5); Vol. I. pap. 25.00 (ISBN 0-08-025566-3); Vol. II. pap. 25.00 (ISBN 0-08-025567-1); Vol. III. pap. 25.00 (ISBN 0-08-028817-0). Pergamon.

Dolbeare, K. M. American Public Policy: A Citizen's Guide. 1982. 13.95x (ISBN 0-07-017405-9). McGraw.

Dolbeare, Kenneth M. Political Change in the United States: A Framework for Analysis. (Policy Impact & Political Change in America Ser.). (Illus.). 240p. 1974. text ed. 10.95 o.p. (ISBN 0-07-017403-2, C); pap. text ed. 14.95 o.p. (ISBN 0-07-017402-4). McGraw.

Dolbeare, Kenneth M. & Dolbeare, Patricia. American Ideologies. 3rd ed. 1976. pap. 12.95 (ISBN 0-395-30795-3). HM.

Dolbeare, Kenneth M. & Edelman, Murray J. American Politics: Policies, Power, & Change. 4th ed. 592p. 1981. pap. text ed. 15.95 (ISBN 0-669-03348-0); student guide 6.95 (ISBN 0-669-03957-8); instr's guide 1.95 (ISBN 0-669-03701-X). Heath.

Dolbeare, Patricia, jt. auth. see Dolbeare, Kenneth M.

Dolby, J. L. Evaluation of the Utility & Cost of Computerized Library Catalogues. 1969. 20.00x (ISBN 0-262-04023-9). MIT Pr.

Dolby, Thomas. The Shakespeare Dictionary: Forming a General Index to All the Popular Expressions, & Most Striking Passages in the Works of Shakespeare. 1982. Repr. of 1832 ed. lib. bdg. 100.00 (ISBN 0-89760-144-0). Telegraph Bks.

Dolby, William. Sima Qian War Lords: Translated with 12 Other Stories from "Historical Records". Scott, John, tr. from Chinese. 168p. 1974. 15.00x o.p. (ISBN 0-87471-597-0). Rowman.

Dolce, Donald & Devellard, Jean-Paul. The Consumer's Guide to Menswear. pap. 11.95 (ISBN 0-89696-188-5). Dodd.

Dolch, Edward W. & Dolch, M. P. Ivanhoe. (Pleasure Reading Ser). (gr. 3-12). 1961. PLB 6.69 (ISBN 0-8116-2612-1). Garrard.

Dolch, M. P., jt. auth. see Dolch, Edward W.

Dolci, Danilo. A New World in the Making. Munroe, R., tr. from It. LC 75-3990. 327p. 1976. Repr. of 1965 ed. lib. bdg. 19.25x (ISBN 0-8371-7419-8, DONW). Greenwood.

Dolciani, Mary P., et al. Intermediate Algebra for College Students. LC 71-146721. 1971. text ed. 18.00 (ISBN 0-395-12072-1); tchrs. ed. & key 6.68 (ISBN 0-395-12074-8). HM.

--Modern Introductory Analysis. 2nd ed. (gr. 11-12). 1980. text ed. 18.56 (ISBN 0-395-28697-2); tchrs.' ed. 22.93 (ISBN 0-395-28696-4); progress tests 3.24 (ISBN 0-395-19857-7); solutions 1.44 (ISBN 0-395-02369-6). HM.

Dolder, Willi, jt. auth. see Rothermund, Dietmar.

Dole, Charles E. Flight Theory & Aerodynamcs: A Practical Guide for Operational Safety. LC 81-3009. 299p. 1981. 34.95x (ISBN 0-471-09152-9, Pub. by Wiley-Interscience). Wiley.

Dole, D. J., intro. by. Agricultural Engineering, 1980: Agricultural Conferences. 290p. (Orig.). 1980. pap. text ed. 45.00x (ISBN 0-85825-138-8, Pub. by Inst Engineering Australia). Renouf.

Dolecki, Szymon, et al, eds. Mathematical Control Theory. (Banach Center Publications: Vol. I). (Illus.). 166p. 1976. 27.50x (ISBN 0-8002-2266-0). Intl Pubns Serv.

Dolejs, Ladislaw, jt. auth. see Sorm, Frantisek.

Dolenc, Danica, tr. see Mesesnel, Janez.

Dolensek, Nancy & Burn, Barbara. Mutt: The First Guide to the All-American Breed. (Illus.). 1978. 14.95 o.p. (ISBN 0-517-53185-2, C N Potter Bks); pap. 6.95 o.s.i. (ISBN 0-517-53186-0). Crown.

Dolezal, Ivan. Asian & African Studies, Vol. 18. 323p. 1982. text ed. 13.75x (ISBN 0-7007-0156-7, 41190, Pub. by Curzon Pr England). Humanities.

Dolezal, R. & Varcop, L. Process Dynamics: Automatic Control of Steam Generation Plant. (Illus.). 1970. 26.75 (ISBN 0-444-20042-8, Pub. by Applied Sci England). Elsevier.

Dolezal, V. Nonlinear Networks. 1977. 38.50 (ISBN 0-444-41571-8). Elsevier.

Dolezal, V. J. Monotone Operators & Applications in Control & Network Theory. (Studies in Automation & Control: Vol. 2). 1979. 42.75 (ISBN 0-444-41791-5). Elsevier.

Dolgin, Robert M. & Tiburzi, D. James. The Bank Income Tax Return Manual with Specimen Filled-in Returns. 1982. 55.00 (ISBN 0-88262-881-X, 80-54680). Warren.

Dolgoff, Ralph & Feldstein, Donald. Understanding Social Welfare. (Illus.). 1980. text ed. 20.50 scp o.p. (ISBN 0-06-041676-9, HarpC). Har-Row.

Dolgoff, Ralph, jt. auth. see Loewenberg, Frank.

Dolgopolva, Z., ed. Russia Dies Laughing: Jokes from Soviet Russia. (Illus.). 126p. 1983. 9.95 (ISBN 0-233-97402-4, Pub by Salem Hse Ltd). Merrimack Bk Serv.

Dolgoroukov. La Verite sur la Russie. (Nineteenth Century Russia Ser.). 404p. (Fr.). 1974. Repr. of 1860 ed. lib. bdg. 103.00 o.p. (ISBN 0-8287-0276-4, R72). Clearwater Pub.

Dolin, Anton. Friends & Memories. Wheatcroft, Andrew, compiled by. (Illus.). 192p. 1983. 29.95 (ISBN 0-7100-9199-0). Routledge & Kegan.

Dolin, Armin. Buy-Sell-Merge-Affiliate: Insurance Agency Manual & Workbook, 2 vols. LC 82-81856. 626p. 1982. Set. 75.00 (ISBN 0-87218-319-X). Vol. I, 490p. Vol. II, 136p. Natl Underwriter.

Dolin, Arnold, jt. ed. see Geiser, Elizabeth.

Dolin, Edwin, ed. see Aeschylus & Sophocles.

Doling, J. F., jt. auth. see Hobbs, F. D.

D'Olivet, Fabre. The Hebraic Tongue Restored. Redfield, Louise N., tr. 1981. 27.50 (ISBN 0-87728-332-X). Weiser.

Doll, Dixon R. Data Communications: Facilities, Networks, & System Design. LC 77-12508. 1978. 39.95x (ISBN 0-471-21768-9, Pub by Wiley-Interscience). Wiley.

--Data Communications: Facilities, Networks & System Design. 493p. 1978. 34.50 (ISBN 0-686-98099-9). Telecom Lib.

Doll, Edgar A. Measurement of Social Competence. (Illus.). 1953. 16.50 (ISBN 0-913476-09-9). Am Guidance.

Doll, Howard D. Oral Interpretation of Literature: An Annotated Bibliography with Multimedia Listings. LC 82-3344. 505p. 1982. 32.50 (ISBN 0-8108-1538-9). Scarecrow.

Doll, John P. & Orazem, Frank. Production Economics: Theory with Applications. Esposito, R., ed. LC 76-41478. (Agricultural Economics Ser.). 416p. 1978. text ed. 29.95x (ISBN 0-471-87001-3). Wiley.

Dollaghan, Helen. Helen Dollaghan's Best Main Dishes. LC 79-19385. (Illus.). 1979. 12.95 o.p. (ISBN 0-07-017380-X). McGraw.

Dollar, C. M. America Changing Time: A Brief History. LC 80-10684. 729p. 1980. 18.95x (ISBN 0-471-06087-9). Wiley.

Dollar, Charles M. America: Changing Times, Combined Edition. 2nd ed. LC 78-12242. 1088p. 1982. text ed. 22.95 (ISBN 0-471-09421-8); 22.50 (ISBN 0-471-09787-X). Wiley.

--America: Changing Times to 1865, Vol. 2. 2nd ed. LC 81-13053. 624p. 1982. text ed. 15.95x (ISBN 0-471-09417-X); study guide avail. Wiley.

--America Changing Times to 1877, Vol. 1. 2nd ed. LC 81-13053. 450p. 1981. text ed. 15.95x (ISBN 0-471-09418-8); o.p. tchrs. manual (ISBN 0-471-04906-9); avail. tchrs. manual (brief) 7.00 (ISBN 0-471-07803-4). Wiley.

Dollard, John, et al. Frustration & Aggression. LC 79-26458. 1980. Repr. of 1939 ed. lib. bdg. 21.00x (ISBN 0-313-22201-0, DOFR). Greenwood.

Dollard, John D. & Friedman, Charles N. Product Integration with Applications to Differential Equations. LC 79-20454. (Encyclopedia of Mathematics & Its Applications: Vol. 10). 1979. text ed. 29.50 (ISBN 0-201-13509-4). A-W.

Dollarhide, Kenneth, tr. Micheren's Senji-sho: An Essay on the Selection of the Proper Time. LC 82-21687. (Studies in Asian Thought & Religion: Vol. 1). 176p. 1983. 29.95x (ISBN 0-88946-051-5). Voter Ed Proj.

Dollfus, A., ed. see C.O.S.P.A.R International Space Science Symposium - London - Jul 26-27 1967.

Dollfus, A., ed. see C.O.S.P.A.R International Space Science Symposium - 7th - Vienna.

Dollfus, A., jt. ed. see Florkin, M.

Dollimore, jt. auth. see European Symposium on Thermal Analysis.

Dollimore, ed. Thermal Analysis: Proceedings, 2nd European Symposium. 1981. 62.50 o.p. (ISBN 0-85501-705-8). Wiley.

Dollimore, D. Thermal Analysis: European Symposium 2nd, Proceedings. 1981. 61.95 (ISBN 0-471-25661-7, Pub. by Wiley Heyden). Wiley.

Dollimore, D., jt. auth. see Keattch, C. J.

Dollinger, Hans. The Decline & Fall of Nazi Germany & Imperial Japan. (Illus.). 1968. 12.50 o.p. (ISBN 0-517-01313-4). Crown.

Dolloff, Francis W. & Perkinson, Roy L. How to Care for Works of Art on Paper. (Illus.). 1971. pap. 3.00 (ISBN 0-87846-136-1). Mus Fine Arts Boston.

Dolman, John, Jr. & Knaub, Richard K. The Art of Play Production. 3rd ed. (Auer Ser.). (Illus.). 1973. text ed. 25.50 scp o.p. (ISBN 0-06-041682-3, HarpC). Har-Row.

Dolmetsch, Christopher. The German Press of the Shenandoah Valley, 1789-1854. LC 81-69881. (Studies in German Literature, Linguistics, & Culture: Vol. 4). (Illus.). 157p. 1983. 19.00x (ISBN 0-938100-01-7). Camden Hse.

Dolmetsch, Mabel. Dances of England & France from 1450-1600: With Their Music & Authentic Manner of Performance. LC 74-34449. (Ser. in Dance). (Illus.). xii, 163p. 1975. lib. bdg. 21.50 (ISBN 0-306-70725-X); pap. 6.95 (ISBN 0-306-80025-X). Da Capo.

--Dances of Spain & Italy from 1400 to 1600. LC 74-28450. (Ser. in Dance). (Illus.). xii, 174p. 1975. Repr. of 1954 ed. lib. bdg. 21.50 (ISBN 0-306-70726-8). Da Capo.

Dolores, Carmen. Aunt Zeze's Tears. Goldberg, Isaac, ed. & tr. (International Pocket Library). pap. 3.00 (ISBN 0-686-77238-5). Branden.

Dolotta, T. A., et al. Data Processing in 1980-1985: A Study of Potential Limitations to Progress. LC 76-4783. 191p. 1976. 24.95 (ISBN 0-471-21783-2); pap. 12.95x o.p. (ISBN 0-471-21786-7, Pub. by Wiley-Interscience). Wiley.

Dolphin, D., jt. auth. see Dunford, H. B.

Dolphin, David. B Twelve, 2 vols, Vols. 1 & 2. LC 81-10300. 1176p. 1982. Set. 130.00x (ISBN 0-471-03655-2, Pub. by Wiley-Interscience). Wiley.

Dolphin, David & Wick, Alexander. Tabulation of Infrared Spectral Data. LC 76-48994. 1977. 24.95 o.p. (ISBN 0-471-21780-8, Pub. by Wiley-Interscience). Wiley.

Dolphin, Lambert T. Que De las Drogas, el Ocultismo y la Astrologia? Swenson, Ana Maria, tr. 1977. Repr. of 1972 ed. 1.75 (ISBN 0-311-46034-8). Casa Bautista.

Dolphin, Robert R. Collecting Beer Cans: A World Guide. 1977. pap. 4.95 o.p. (ISBN 0-517-21564-0). Crown.

Dolson, Frank. Beating the Bushes: Life in the Minor Leagues. (Illus.). 296p. 1983. 13.95 (ISBN 0-89651-055-7). Icarus.

Dolson, Hildegarde. William Penn. (Landmark Ser.: No. 98). (Illus.). (gr. 3-7). 1961. PLB 4.39 o.p. (ISBN 0-394-90398-6); pap. 2.95 (ISBN 0-394-80398-1). Random.

Dolukhanov, Paul M. Ecology & Economy in Neolithic Eastern Europe. (Illus.). 1979. 25.00x (ISBN 0-312-22613-6). St Martin.

Dolzall, Donnette & Model Railroader Staff, eds. ABC's of Model Railroading. LC 78-55680. 1978. pap. 5.75 (ISBN 0-89024-536-3). Kalmbach.

Dolzall, Gary & Dolzall, Stephen. Diesel Locomotives of Baldwin-Baldwin Lima Hamilton. Hayden, Bob, ed. (Illus., Orig.). 1983. pap. price not set (ISBN 0-89024-052-3). Kalmbach.

Dolzall, Stephen, jt. auth. see Dolzall, Gary.

Doman, Glenn. How to Teach Your Baby How to Read. 160p. 1975. pap. 4.50 (ISBN 0-385-11161-4, Dolp). Doubleday.

Domanska, Janina. The Best of the Bargain. LC 76-13010. (Illus.). 32p. (gr. k-3). 1977. 8.95 o.p. (ISBN 0-688-80062-9); PLB 10.32 (ISBN 0-688-84062-0). Greenwillow.

--Marek, the Little Fool. LC 81-6966. (Illus.). 32p. (gr. k-3). 1982. 10.00 (ISBN 0-688-00912-3); PLB 9.55 (ISBN 0-688-00913-1). Greenwillow.

--Marek, the Little Fool. (ps-3). 1982. 10.50 (ISBN 0-688-00912-3); PLB 9.55 (ISBN 0-688-00913-1). Morrow.

Domanski, Don. War in an Empty House. (House of Anansi Poetry Ser.: No. 41). 72p. (Orig.). 1982. pap. 6.95 (ISBN 0-88784-094-9, Pub. by Hse Anansi Pr Canada). U of Toronto Pr.

Domar, Rebecca A. Basic Russian. 1961. text ed. 15.95 o.p. (ISBN 0-07-017375-3, C); teachers manual & key 3.95 o.p. (ISBN 0-07-017396-6). McGraw.

Domb, C. M., ed. Phase Transitions, Vol. 7. Date not set. price not set (ISBN 0-12-220307-0). Acad Pr.

Domb, J., tr. see Lermontov, M. Y.

Domb, J., tr. see Turgenev, Ivan S.

Domb, Jessie, tr. see Tolstoi, L. N.

Dombal, E. T. De see IFIP TC Four Working Conference.

Dombrow, Bernard A. Polyurethanes. 250p. 1965. 14.25 o.p. (ISBN 0-442-15107-1, Pub. by Van Nos Reinhold). Krieger.

Dombrowski, Daniel A. Plato's Philosophy of History. LC 80-5853. 225p. 1981. lib. bdg. 20.00 (ISBN 0-8191-1356-5); pap. text ed. 10.00 (ISBN 0-8191-1357-3). U Pr of Amer.

Domencich, T. Urban Travel Demand. LC 74-30936. (Contributions to Economic Analysis Ser.: Vol. 93). 215p. 1975. 47.00 (ISBN 0-444-10830-0, North-Holland). Elsevier.

Domenico, Joseph M. Di see DiDomenico, Joseph M.

Domer, Larry R. & Bauer, Jeffrey C. Personalized Guide to Establishing Associateships & Partnerships. Snyder, Thomas L. & Felmeister, Charles J., eds. (Dental Practice Management Ser.). (Illus.). 168p. 1982. pap. text ed. 12.95 (ISBN 0-8016-4714-2). Mosby.

Domer, Larry R., jt. auth. see Snyder, Thomas L.

Domer, Larry R., et al. Dental Practice Management: Concepts & Application. LC 80-15309. (Illus.). 376p. 1980. text ed. 39.95 (ISBN 0-8016-1422-8). Mosby.

Domes, Jurgen. China After the Cultural Revolution. Goodman, David, tr. from Ger. 1977. 30.00x (ISBN 0-520-03064-8). U of Cal Pr.

Domhoff, G. William. The Powers That Be: Process of Ruling Class Domination in America. LC 78-55633. 1979. pap. 5.95 (ISBN 0-394-72649-9, Vin). Random.

--The Powers That Be: Processes of Ruling Class Domination in America. 1979. 15.00 (ISBN 0-394-49604-3); pap. 5.95. Random.

Domholdt, L. C., jt. auth. see Tuve, George L.

Domingo, Willis, tr. see Adorno, Theodor.

Domingue, G. J. Cell Wall-Deficient Bacteria: Basic Principles & Clinical Significance. 1982. text ed. 21.95 (ISBN 0-201-10162-9, Adv Bk Prog). A-W.

Dominguez. Economic Issues & Political Conflict: U. S.- Latin America Relation. 1982. text ed. 45.95. Butterworth.

Dominguez, G. S. Marketing in Regulated Environment. (Marketing Management Ser.). 341p. 1978. 38.95x o.p. (ISBN 0-471-02402-3). Wiley.

Dominguez, George S. The Business Guide to Tosca: Effects & Actions. LC 79-20054. 1979. 35.95 (ISBN 0-471-05371-6, Pub. by Wiley Interscience). Wiley.

--Government Relations: Handbook for Developing & Conducting the Company Program. LC 81-11500. 429p. 1982. 39.50 (ISBN 0-471-06421-1, Pub. by Wiley-Interscience). Wiley.

--Marketing in a Regulated Environment. LC 77-22099. (Marketing Management Ser.). 1978. 38.95x o.p. (ISBN 0-471-02402-3). Ronald Pr.

Dominguez, Jorge I. U. S. Interest & Policies in the Caribbean & Central America. 1982. pap. 4.75 (ISBN 0-8447-1097-0). Am Enterprise.

Dominguez, Richard H. Complete Book of Sports Medicine. 1983. pap. 5.95 (ISBN 0-446-37370-2). Warner Bks.

Dominguez, Richard H. & Gajda, Robert J. Total Body Training. 288p. 1983. pap. 7.95 (ISBN 0-686-84718-0). Warner Bks.

Dominguez Barbera, M. Valencia. (Spanish Guide Ser). (Illus.). 1960. 4.50x (ISBN 0-8002-2131-1). Intl Pubns Serv.

Dominiak, Geraldine F., jt. auth. see Louderback, Joseph G.

Dominiak, Geraldine F., jt. auth. see Louderback, Joseph G., 3rd.

Dominic, R. B. The Attending Physician. LC 79-1702. (A Harper Novel for Suspense Ser.). 1980. 11.49i (ISBN 0-06-011073-2, HarpT). Har-Row.

Dominic, Randolph & Barry, William. Pyrrhus Venture. 416p. 1983. 17.45i (ISBN 0-316-18934-0). Little.

Dominicis, Maria C. & Cussen, Joseph A. Casos y Cosas. 1981. pap. text ed. 9.95x o.p. (ISBN 0-673-15325-8). Scott F.

Dominick, Barbara A. A Practical, Self-Help Guide for Stutterers. 64p. 1983. 8.75x (ISBN 0-398-04794-4). C C Thomas.

Dominick, Joseph R., jt. auth. see Wimmer, Roger D.

Dominion, Jack. Marriage Faith & Love. 276p. 1981. 19.95x o.p. (ISBN 0-232-51548-4, Pub. by Darton-Longman-Todd England). State Mutual Bk.

Dominowski, R. Research Methods. 1980. 23.95 (ISBN 0-13-774315-7). P-H.

Dominy, Eric. Teach Yourself Judo. (Illus.). 1962. 8.95 (ISBN 0-87523-140-3). Emerson.

--Teach Yourself Karate. (Illus.). 1968. 8.95 (ISBN 0-87523-163-2). Emerson.

--Teach Yourself Self-Defense. (Illus.). 1963. 8.95 (ISBN 0-87523-150-0). Emerson.

Domke, Martin, ed. International Trade Arbitration. LC 73-11852. 320p. 1974. Repr. of 1958 ed. lib. bdg. 35.00x (ISBN 0-8371-7075-3, DOTA). Greenwood.

Domling, Wolfgang, jt. ed. see Schwendowius, Barbara.

Dommen, Edward, ed. Islands. (Illus.). 135p. 1981. 20.00 (ISBN 0-08-026799-8). Pergamon.

Dommergues, Y. R., tr. see Krupa, S. V.

Domning, Daryl. Sirenian Evolution in the North Pacific Ocean. (Publications in Geological Science Ser.: Vol. 118). 1978. 15.00x (ISBN 0-520-09581-2). U of Cal Pr.

Domolki, B. & Gergely, T., eds. Mathematical Logic in Computer Science. (Colloquia Mathematica Societatis Janos Bolyai Ser.: Vol. 26). 758p. 1982. 117.00 (ISBN 0-444-85440-1). Elsevier.

Domonkos, Anthony N. & Arnold, Harry L., Jr. Diseases of the Skin. 7th ed. (Illus.). 1100p. 1982. 70.00 (ISBN 0-7216-3138-X). Saunders.

Domotor, Tekla. Hungarian Folk Beliefs. LC 82-48163. (Illus.). 324p. 1983. 17.50x (ISBN 0-253-32876-4). Ind U Pr.

Domschke, Eliane, jt. auth. see Goyer, Doreen S.

Domuret, Allan J., et al. Encyclopedia for the TRS-80, Vol. 3. Putnam, Katherine & Comiskey, Kate, eds. (Illus.). 288p. 1981. text ed. 19.95 (ISBN 0-88006-031-X, EN8103); pap. text ed. 10.95 (ISBN 0-88006-032-8, EN8083). Green Pub Inc.

Don, Frank. Color Your World. 189p. 1983. pap. 4.95 (ISBN 0-89281-048-3). Destiny Bks.

--Earth Changes Ahead: The Coming of Great Catastrophes. 256p. 1983. pap. 2.75 (ISBN 0-686-33184-2). Destiny Bks.

Don, Marvin, et al, eds. Self-Assessment of Current Knowledge in Family Practice. 2nd ed. 1976. pap. 14.50 o.p. (ISBN 0-87488-261-3). Med Exam.

Donagan, Alan. Theory of Morality. LC 76-25634. 1979. pap. 5.85 (ISBN 0-226-15567-6, P838, Phoen). U of Chicago Pr.

Donaghy, Henry J. James Clarence Mangan. (English Authors Ser.). 1974. lib. bdg. 14.95 (ISBN 0-8057-1370-0, Twayne). G K Hall.

Donaghy, William, jt. auth. see Emmert, Philip.

Donaghy, William C. Our Silent Language: An Introduction to Nonverbal Communication. (Comm Comp). (Illus.). 54p. 1980. pap. text ed. 2.95x (ISBN 0-89787-304-1). Gorsuch Scarisbrick.

Donahue, Benedict. The Cultural Arts of Africa. LC 79-66646. (Illus.). 1979. pap. text ed. 10.50 (ISBN 0-8191-0845-6). U Pr of Amer.

Donahue, Bob & Donahue, Marilyn. How to Make People Like You When You Know They Don't. 1982. pap. 3.95 (ISBN 0-8423-1531-4). Tyndale.

--Things That Go Bump in the Night, & Other Fears. (YA) 1983. pap. 3.95 (ISBN 0-686-82528-4). Tyndale.

Donahue, Charles. Testament of Mary: The Gaelic Version of the Dormitio Mariae. 1942. pap. 5.00 o.p. (ISBN 0-8232-0100-7). Fordham.

Donahue, Don & Goodrick, Susan, eds. The Apex Treasury of Underground Comics. LC 74-78872. (Illus.). 192p. 1974. pap. 5.95 o.p. (ISBN 0-8256-3042-8, Quick Fox). Putnam Pub Group.

Donahue, Jack, ed. Rafts We Sail & Other Poems. LC 76-138848. 1970. 4.00 (ISBN 0-911838-09-0). Windy Row.

Donahue, John N., jt. ed. see Bastien, Joseph W.

Donahue, Kenneth, ed. see Pignatti, Terisio.

Donahue, Lois. That Taste In My Mouth Is Foot. 106p. 1982. pap. 4.95 (ISBN 0-9610104-0-1). F & L Assocs.

Donahue, Marilyn. To Catch a Golden Ring. (gr. 4-9). 1980. pap. 2.50 o.p. (ISBN 0-89191-330-0). Cook.

Donahue, Marilyn, jt. auth. see Donahue, Bob.

Donahue, Moraima. Figuras y Contrafiguras en la obra Poetica de Fernando Alegria. Miller, Yvette E., ed. 141p. 1980. pap. 7.95 (ISBN 0-935480-05-6). Lat Am Lit Rev Pr.

--La Poesia de Manuel Duran. Miller, Yvette E., ed. 242p. (Orig., Span.). 1977. 15.95 (ISBN 0-935480-01-3); pap. 8.50 (ISBN 0-935480-05-6). Lat Am Lit Rev Pr.

Donahue, Phil, et al. Donahue. 1980. 11.95 o.p. (ISBN 0-671-25207-0). S&S.

--Donahue: My Own Story. large print ed. LC 81-8779. 397p. 1981. Repr. of 1979 ed. 11.95x o.p. (ISBN 0-89621-295-5). Thorndike Pr.

Donahue, R. J., jt. auth. see Azaroff, Leonid V.

Donahue, Roy & Miller, John. Soils: An Introduction to Soils & Plant Growth. 5th ed. (Illus.). 656p. 1983. text ed. 27.95 (ISBN 0-13-822288-6). P-H.

Donahue, Roy L., et al. Our Soils & Their Management. 4th ed. LC 75-27887. 1976. Repr. of 1771 ed. 22.00 (ISBN 0-8134-1771-6); text ed. 16.50x. Interstate.

--Soils: An Introduction to Soils & Plant Growth. 4th ed. (Illus.). 1977. 26.95 (ISBN 0-13-821918-4). P-H.

Donahue, Warren. Foundations of Technical Mathematics. LC 75-96962. 478p. 1970. 27.95 (ISBN 0-471-21774-3); avail. tchrs. manual 6.00 (ISBN 0-471-21773-5). Wiley.

Donald. Practical Obstetric Problems. 5th ed. (Illus.). 1071p. 1979. text ed. 54.00 (ISBN 0-397-58247-1, Lippincott Medical). Lippincott.

Donald, Bruce H. Cutting College Costs: The Up-To-the-Minute Manual for 1983-84. 128p. 1982. pap. 7.95 (ISBN 0-525-48009-9, 0772-230). Dutton.

Donald, D. W. Compound Interest & Annuities--Certain. 1975. 21.50 (ISBN 0-434-90366-3, Pub. by Heinemann). David & Charles.

Donald, David. Lincoln Reconsidered. 1956. pap. 4.95 (ISBN 0-394-70190-9). Knopf.

--Lincoln Reconsidered: Essays on the Civil War Era. pap. 4.95 (ISBN 0-394-70190-9, V-190, Vin). Random.

Donald, David, jt. auth. see Randall, James G.

Donald, David, ed. Why the North Won the Civil War. 1962. pap. 2.95 (ISBN 0-02-031660-7, Collier). Macmillan.

Donald, David, ed. see Chase, Salmon P.

Donald, David H. Liberty & Union. 1978. pap. text ed. 11.95x (ISBN 0-669-01152-5). Heath.

--The Politics of Reconstruction, 1863-1867. LC 82-1015. (The Walter Lynnwood Fleming Lectures in Southern History). 105p. 1982. Repr. of 1967 ed. lib. bdg. 19.25x (ISBN 0-313-23481-7, DONP). Greenwood.

Donald, Elsie B. London Shopping Guide. (Penguin Handbooks Ser.). (Illus.). 1978. pap. 2.95 o.p. (ISBN 0-14-046222-8). Penguin.

Donald, Gordon. Credit for Small Farmers in Developing Countries. LC 76-7936. (Special Studies in Social, Political & Economic Development Ser.). 1976. 24.00 o.p. (ISBN 0-89158-108-1). Westview.

Donald, Kathleen & Holloway, Elizabeth. A Guide to Group Self Hypnosis for Participants & Leaders. 300p. (Orig.). 1983. pap. text ed. write for info. (ISBN 0-915202-37-9). Accel Devel.

Donald, L. & MacDonald, W. S., eds. Roll of Graduates of the University of Aberdeen, 1956-1970: With Supplement 1860-1955. 1982. 82.80 (ISBN 0-08-028469-8). Pergamon.

Donald, Leroy. Trail to Lometa. 192p. (YA) 1976. 6.95 (ISBN 0-685-62630-X, Avalon). Bouregy.

Donald, Robert & Moore, James. Writing Clear Paragraphs. 2nd ed. (Illus.). 272p. 1983. pap. text ed. 10.95 (ISBN 0-13-970004-8). P-H.

Donald, Robert B., et al. Writing Clear Paragraphs. (Illus.). 1978. pap. text ed. 11.95x (ISBN 0-13-970350-0). P-H.

Donald, Robyn. Mansion for My Love. (Harlequin Presents Ser.). 192p. 1983. pap. 1.75 (ISBN 0-373-10567-3). Harlequin Bks.

--Sous la Lune des Tropiques. (Collection Harlequin). 192p. 1983. pap. 1.95 (ISBN 0-373-49323-1). Harlequin Bks.

Donald, Vivian. Cathy's Choice. (Orig.). (YA) (RL 9). 1978. pap. 1.50 o.p. (ISBN 0-451-08033-5, W8033, Sig). NAL.

--Elizabeth in Love. (Orig.). 1979. pap. 1.75 o.p. (ISBN 0-451-08671-6, E8671, Sig). NAL.

--For Love or Money. pap. 1.25 o.p. (ISBN 0-451-07756-3, Y7756, Sig). NAL.

--The Laird & the Lady: The Royal Scot. 1978. pap. 1.75 o.p. (ISBN 0-451-08059-9, E8059, Sig). NAL.

Donaldson. Marine Painting. (Pitman Art Ser.: Vol. 44). pap. 1.95 o.p. (ISBN 0-448-00553-0, G&D). Putnam Pub Group.

--The Medium-Term Loan Market. LC 82-42619. 176p. 1982. 25.00x (ISBN 0-312-52820-5). St Martin.

Donaldson, jt. auth. see Malecki.

Donaldson, Alfred L. History of the Adirondacks, 2 vols. LC 77-12661. (Illus.). 1977. Repr. of 1921 ed. Set. 45.00 (ISBN 0-916346-26-9). Harbor Hill Bks.

Donaldson, Cyril & Le Cain, George. Tool Design. 3rd ed. (Illus.). 840p. 1973. text ed. 27.95 (ISBN 0-07-017531-4, G); answer key 4.00 (ISBN 0-07-017532-2). McGraw.

Donaldson, David D. Atlas of External Diseases of the Eye: The Cornea & Sclera, Vol. 3. 2nd ed. LC 79-20605. 514p. 1979. text ed. 90.50 (ISBN 0-8016-1434-1). Mosby.

Donaldson, E. T., ed. Chaucer's Poetry: An Anthology for the Modern Reader. 2nd ed. LC 74-22536. 1975. 24.95 o.p. (ISBN 0-8260-2781-4). Scott F.

--Chaucer's Poetry: An Anthology for the Modern Reader. 1975. text ed. 29.95x (ISBN 0-673-15667-2). Scott F.

Donaldson, Elizabeth & Donaldson, Gerald, eds. The Book of Days. LC 79-64840. (Illus.). 384p. 1979. 12.95 o.s.i. (ISBN 0-89479-055-2). A & W Pubs.

Donaldson, Elvin F., et al. Corporate Finance. 4th ed. 689p. 1975. 30.50x (ISBN 0-471-06562-5); instrs'. manual 3.00 (ISBN 0-471-07459-4). Wiley.

Donaldson, Frances & Usborne, Richard. P. G. Wodehouse 1881-1981: Addresses given by Frances Donaldson & Richard Usborne. (Wodehouse Monograph: No. 2). 44p. (Orig.). 1982. pap. 14.50 (ISBN 0-87008-101-2). Heineman.

Donaldson, Fred. Crooked Trail. 208p. (Orig.). 1982. pap. 2.25 o.s.i. (ISBN 0-8439-1134-4, Leisure Bks). Nordon Pubns.

Donaldson, G. The Scottish Reformation. 47.50 (ISBN 0-521-08675-2). Cambridge U Pr.

Donaldson, George & Swan, Malcom. Administration of Eco-Education: A Handbook for Administrators of Environmental-Conservation-Outdoor Education Programs. 136p. 7.50 (ISBN 0-88314-008-X). AAHPERD.

Donaldson, Gerald, jt. ed. see Donaldson, Elizabeth.

Donaldson, Gordon. The Scots Overseas. LC 75-36360. (Illus.). 1976. Repr. of 1966 ed. lib. bdg. 18.25x (ISBN 0-8371-8625-0, DOTSO). Greenwood.

Donaldson, Graham. Forestry. (Sector Policy Paper). 63p. 1978. pap. 5.00 (ISBN 0-686-36066-4, PP-7804). World Bank.

Donaldson, J., ed. see Ante-Nicene Fathers.

Donaldson, James A., jt. auth. see Anson, Barry.

Donaldson, James H., jt. auth. see Malecki, Donald S.

Donaldson, James O. Neurology of Pregnancy. LC 76-58600. (Major Problems in Neurology: Vol. 7). (Illus.). 1978. text ed. 30.00 (ISBN 0-7216-3139-8). Saunders.

Donaldson, Judy P. Transcultural Picture Word List: For Teaching English to Children from Any of Twenty One Language Backgrounds. LC 78-58532. 1980. pap. text ed. 21.95x (ISBN 0-918452-10-4). Learning Pubns.

--Transcultural Picture Word List: For Teaching English to Children from any of Twelve Language Backgrounds, Vol. II. LC 78-58532. 204p. (Orig.). pap. text ed. 15.95x (ISBN 0-918452-38-4). Learning Pubns.

Donaldson, L. A., jt. auth. see Troughton, J.

Donaldson, Margaret. Children's Minds. (Illus.). 1979. 10.95 o.p. (ISBN 0-393-01185-2); pap. 3.95x (ISBN 0-393-95101-4). Norton.

Donaldson, P. S., ed. A Machiavellian Treatise by Stephen Gardiner. LC 74-12963. (Studies in the History & Theory of Politics). 204p. 1976. 42.50 (ISBN 0-521-20593-X). Cambridge U Pr.

Donaldson, R. J. Parasites & Western Man. 232p. 1979. text ed. 24.50 (ISBN 0-8391-1432-X). Univ Park.

Donaldson, Robert H., ed. The Soviet Union in the Third World: Success & Failures. (Westview Special Studies in International Relations). 350p. 1980. lib. bdg. 27.50 (ISBN 0-89158-974-0); pap. text ed. 12.50 (ISBN 0-86531-158-7). Westview.

Donaldson, Scott. By Force of Will: The Life & Art of Ernest Hemingway. 1978. pap. 3.95 o.p. (ISBN 0-14-004689-5). Penguin.

Donaldson, Stephen. Chronicles of Thomas Covenant, 3 vols. 1982. pap. 7.50 boxed set (ISBN 0-345-28173-X, Del Rey). Ballantine.

Donaldson, Stephen R. Gilden-Fire. (The Illearth War ("Thomas Covenant the Unbeliever") Ser.). (Illus.). 70p. 1982. lib. bdg. 11.95 o.p. (ISBN 0-934438-54-4). Underwood-Miller.

--The One Tree. (The Second Chronicles of Thomas Covenant: Bk. 2). 496p. 1983. pap. 3.50 (ISBN 0-345-30550-7, Del Rey). Ballantine.

--White Gold Wielder. (The Second Chronicles of Thomas Covenant Ser.: Bk. 3). 1983. 14.95 (ISBN 0-345-30307-5, Del Rey). Ballantine.

Donaldson, T. Ngiyambaa: The Language of the Wangaaybuwan. LC 79-7646. (Cambridge Studies in Linguistics: No. 29). (Illus.). 320p. 1980. 64.50 (ISBN 0-521-22524-8). Cambridge U Pr.

Donaldson, T. & Werhare, P. Ethical Issues in Business: A Philosophical Approach. 1979. pap. 15.95 (ISBN 0-13-290064-5). P-H.

Donaldson, Thomas. Corporations & Morality. 288p. 1982. pap. 10.95 (ISBN 0-13-177006-3); 14.95 (ISBN 0-13-177014-4). P-H.

Donaldson, Thomas & Werhane, Patricia H. Ethical Issues in Business. 2nd ed. (Illus.). 416p. 1983. pap. 16.95 (ISBN 0-13-290148-X). P-H.

Donaldson, Thomas C. Idaho of Yesterday. LC 70-104218. Repr. of 1941 ed. lib. bdg. 25.00x o.p. (ISBN 0-8371-3335-1, DOID). Greenwood.

Donaldson, Wayne, jt. ed. see Tulving, Endel.

Donarico, Elnora. Nurse Jessica's Cruise. (YA) 1980. 6.95 (ISBN 0-686-59796-6, Avalon). Bouregy.

--Nurse Vicky's Love. (YA) 1979. 6.95 (ISBN 0-685-59935-3, Avalon). Bouregy.

Donat, Alexander. The Holocaust Kingdom: A Memoir. LC 77-89067. 1978. pap. 4.95 (ISBN 0-8052-5008-5, Pub by Holocaust Library). Schocken.

--The Holocaust Kingdom: A Memoir. 368p. pap. 5.95 (ISBN 0-686-95070-4). ADL.

Donat, Alexander, ed. The Death Camp Treblinka: A Documentary. LC 78-71296. (Illus.). 1979. 9.95 (ISBN 0-8052-5008-5, Pub. by Holocaust Library); pap. 4.95 (ISBN 0-89604-009-7). Schocken.

Donat, Lilian K., tr. see Kirschner, M. J.

Donatelli, Gary, jt. auth. see Armentani, Andy.

Donati, Maria B., et al, eds. Malignancy & the Hemostatic System. (Monographs of the Mario Negri Institute for Pharmacological Research). 148p. 1981. text ed. 19.00 (ISBN 0-89004-463-5). Raven.

Donati, Robert M., jt. auth. see Newton, William T.

Donato, Anthony. Preparing Music Manuscript. LC 77-4024. (Illus.). 1977. Repr. of 1963 ed. lib. bdg. 20.50x (ISBN 0-8371-9587-X, DOPM). Greenwood.

Donato, Georgia di see Di Donato, Georgia.

Donato, Pietro di. Christ in Concrete. LC 39-10762. 320p. 1975. 8.95 o.p. (ISBN 0-672-52161-X); pap. 5.95 o.p. (ISBN 0-672-52187-3). Bobbs.

Donatus, Cornelius. How to Anticipate the Business Future Without the Use of Computers. (Illus.). 47p. 1974. 69.50 (ISBN 0-913314-27-7). Am Classical Coll Pr.

Donauer, Friedrich. Swords Against Carthage. Cooper, F. T., tr. LC 61-12878. (Illus.). (gr. 7-11). 1932. 8.00x (ISBN 0-8196-0112-8). Biblo.

Donavan, Josephine. New England Local Color Literature: A Women's Tradition. LC 82-40252. 250p. 1982. 12.95 (ISBN 0-8044-2138-2). Ungar.

Doncaster, Islay. Traditional China. Killingray, Margaret & O'Connor, Edmund, eds. (World History Ser.). (Illus.). (gr. 10). 1980. Repr. of 1977 ed. lib. bdg. 6.95 (ISBN 0-89908-032-4); pap. text ed. 2.25 (ISBN 0-89908-007-3). Greenhaven.

Doncaster, John P. Francis Walker's Aphids. (Illus.). viii, 165p. 1961. 16.50 (ISBN 0-565-00074-8). Sabbot-Natural Hist Bks.

Donders, F. C. Accommodation & Refraction of the Eye. LC 78-27045. (Classics in Ophthalmology). 1979. Repr. of 1864 ed. lib. bdg. 32.50 (ISBN 0-88275-839-X); 00.00. Krieger.

Dondi, Beda, jt. auth. see Ray, Mary F.

Done, J. N., et al. Applications of High-Speed Liquid Chromatography. LC 74-16148. 1975. 48.00x (ISBN 0-471-21784-0, Pub. by Wiley-Interscience). Wiley.

Donea, J. M. Advanced Structural Dynamics. 1980. 74.00 (ISBN 0-85334-859-6, Pub. by Applied Sci England). Elsevier.

Donegan, Jane B. Women & Men Midwives: Medicine, Morality, & Misogyny in Early America. LC 77-87968. (Contributions in Medical History: No. 2). (Illus.). 1978. lib. bdg. 29.95 (ISBN 0-8371-9868-2, DMA/). Greenwood.

Donegan, Judith H. Cardiopulmonary Resuscitation: Physiology, Pharmacology, & Practical Application. (Illus.). 336p. 1982. 32.50x (ISBN 0-398-04625-5). C C Thomas.

Donelan, M. D. & Grieve, M. J. International Disputes: Case Histories, 1945-1970. LC 73-78089 280p. 1973. 26.00 (ISBN 0-312-42000-5). St Martin.

Donelan, M. D., jt. auth. see Northedge, F. S.

Donelson, Elaine & Gullahorn, Jeanne E., eds. Women: A Psychological Perspective. LC 76-54924. 342p. 1977. pap. text ed. 17.50 o.p. (ISBN 0-471-21781-6). Wiley.

Donelson, Kenneth, ed. Students' Right to Read. 2nd ed. (Orig.). 1972. pap. 0.25 (ISBN 0-8141-4817-4). NCTE.

Donelson, Kenneth L. & Nilsen, Alleen P. Literature for Today's Young Adults. 1980. text ed. 15.50x (ISBN 0-673-15165-4). Scott F.

Doney, Meryl. How I Am Big. (Illus.). 16p. 1983. pap. 0.99 (ISBN 0-86683-705-1). Winston Pr.

--When I Was Little. (Illus.). 16p. 1983. pap. 0.99 (ISBN 0-86683-704-3). Winston Pr.

Doney, Meryl, ed. Now We Have a New Baby. Orig. Title: Now We have a New Baby. (Illus.). 16p. 1983. pap. 0.99 (ISBN 0-686-43064-6). Winston Pr.

Doney, Willis, tr. see Malebranche, Nicolas.

Dong, Collin H. & Banks, Jane. New Hope for the Arthritic. LC 75-16388. 184p. 1975. 12.45i (ISBN 0-690-00964-X). T Y Crowell.

Dong, Eugene & Andreopoulos, Spyros. Heart Beat. LC 77-10720. (Fic). 1978. 9.95 o.p. (ISBN 0-698-10875-2, Coward). Putnam Pub Group.

Dong, Paul, jt. auth. see Stevens, Wendelle C.

Dong, Wonmo, ed. Korean-American Relations at Crossroads. xiv, 178p. 1982. 8.00 (ISBN 0-932014-07-0). AKCS.

Dong, Wonmo & Sunoo, Harold H., eds. Whither Korea? Views of Korean Christian Scholars in North America. viii, 166p. 1975. 4.00 (ISBN 0-932014-01-1). AKCS.

Dongan, Margaret, jt. auth. see Aumann, Jordan.

Dongarra, J. J., et al. Linpack User's Guide. LC 78-78206. viii, 367p. 1979. pap. text ed. 19.00 (ISBN 0-89871-172-X). Soc Indus-Appl Math.

Donges, Gregory S. Policy Making for the Mentally Handicapped. 138p. 1982. text ed. 32.00x (ISBN 0-566-00514-X). Gower Pub Ltd.

Donhoff, Marion. Foe Into Friend: The Makers of the New Germany from Konrad Adenaver to Helmut Schmidt. LC 82-10381. 214p. 1982. 18.50x (ISBN 0-312-29692-4). St Martin.

Donin, Hayim H. To Raise a Jewish Child: A Guide for Parents. LC 76-7679. 1977. 14.95 (ISBN 0-465-08626-8). Basic.

Donin, Hayyim H., ed. Sukkot. 128p. pap. 4.50 (ISBN 0-686-95148-4). ADL.

Donington, Robert. The Interpretation of Early Music. rev. ed. LC 73-81205. 1974. 39.95 o.p. (ISBN 0-312-42420-5). St Martin.

--The Interpretation of Early Music. 766p. 1982. Repr. 29.95 (ISBN 0-571-04789-0). Faber & Faber.

Donk, M. A. The Generic Names Proposed for Agaricaceae. 1962. pap. 40.00 (ISBN 3-7682-5405-4). Lubrecht & Cramer.

--The Generic Names Proposed for Hymenomycetes 1-9,12,13. 1966. pap. 20.00 (ISBN 3-7682-0347-6). Lubrecht & Cramer.

--The Generic Names Proposed for Polyporaceae. 1968. pap. 12.80 (ISBN 3-7682-0557-6). Lubrecht & Cramer.

--Revision der Niederlaendishen Heterobasidiomycetae und Homobasidiomycetae-Aphyllophoraceae, 2 parts in 1 vol. (Illus.). 1969. Repr. of 1933 ed. 32.00 (ISBN 3-7682-0621-1). Lubrecht & Cramer.

Donlan, Dan, jt. auth. see Singer, Harry.

Donlan, Walter, intro. by. Classical World Bibliography of Greek & Roman History. LC 76-52511. (Library of Humanities Reference Bks.: No. 94). lib. bdg. 30.00 o.s.i. (ISBN 0-8240-9879-X). Garland Pub.

--The Classical World Bibliography of Greek Drama & Poetry. LC 76-52510. (Library of Humanities Reference Bks.: No. 93). lib. bdg. 40.00 o.s.i. (ISBN 0-8240-9880-3). Garland Pub.

--The Classical World Bibliography of Philosophy, Religion, & Rhetoric. LC 76-52512. (Library of Humanities Reference Bks.: No. 95). lib. bdg. 42.00 o.s.i. (ISBN 0-8240-9878-1). Garland Pub.

Donleavy, J. P. Destinies of Darcy Dancer, Gentleman. 1977. 9.95 o.s.i. (ISBN 0-440-01903-6, Sey Lawr). Delacorte.

--Destinies of Darcy Dancer, Gentlemen. 1978. pap. 4.95 o.s.i. (ISBN 0-440-52029-0, Delta). Dell.

--The Plays of J. P. Donleavy. (Illus.). 464p. 1972. 10.00 o.s.i. (ISBN 0-440-07008-2, Sey Lawr). Delacorte.

--The Plays of J. P. Donleavy. 1972. pap. 3.95 o.s.i. (ISBN 0-440-57015-8, Delta). Dell.

--The Unexpurgated Code. 1976. pap. 3.95 o.s.i. (ISBN 0-440-59229-1, Delta). Dell.

Donleavy, James P. The Ginger Man. 1965. 7.95 o.s.i. (ISBN 0-440-02885-X, Sey Lawr). Delacorte.

--The Onion Eaters. 1971. 7.95 o.s.i. (ISBN 0-440-06669-7, Sey Lawr). Delacorte.

Donley, Diana, jt. ed. see Burkhalter, Pamela.

Donn. Pediatric Transillumination. 1982. 29.00 (ISBN 0-8151-2733-2). Year Bk Med.

Donn, William L. Meteorology. 3rd ed. 1965. text ed. 25.10 (ISBN 0-07-017598-5, G). McGraw.

Donnan, Elizabeth, ed. see Bayard, James A.

Donne, jt. auth. see Shakepeare.

Donne, John. Complete Poems. 1976. 9.95x (ISBN 0-460-00867-6, Evman); pap. 3.50x (ISBN 0-460-01867-1). Biblio Dist.

--The Complete Poetry & Selected Prose of John Donne. Coffin, Charles M., intro. by. LC 52-5874. 6.95 (ISBN 0-394-60440-7). Modern Lib.

--Devotions: Upon Emergent Occasions. Bd. with Death's Duel. 1959. pap. 5.95 (ISBN 0-472-06030-9, 30, AA). U of Mich Pr.

--John Donne's Sermons on the Psalms & Gospels: With a Selection of Prayers & Meditations. Simpson, Evelyn M., ed. & intro. by. LC 63-16249. 1963. 20.00x (ISBN 0-520-00338-1); pap. 2.65 (ISBN 0-520-00340-3, CAL84). U of Cal Pr.

--Letters to Several Persons of Honour. LC 77-10078. 340p. 1977. Repr. of 1651 ed. lib. bdg. 38.00x (ISBN 0-8201-1296-8). Schol Facsimiles.

--Love Poems. (Pocket Poet Ser.). 1968. pap. 1.25 (ISBN 0-289-27744-2). Dufour.

--The Love Poems of John Donne. Fowkes, Charles, ed. 128p. 1982. 8.95 (ISBN 0-312-49944-2). St Martin.

--Pseudo-Martyr. LC 74-16215. 450p. 1974. 50.00x (ISBN 0-8201-1140-6). Schol Facsimiles.

--Songs & Sonnets of John Donne. Redpath, Theodore, ed. 1967. pap. 8.95x o.p. (ISBN 0-416-69660-0). Methuen Inc.

Donne, Michael & Fowler, Cynthia. Per Ardua Ad Astra: Seventy Years of the RFC & RAF. 192p. 1982. 39.00x (ISBN 0-584-11022-7, Pub. by Muller Ltd). State Mutual Bk.

--The Wings of Britain. 192p. 1982. 50.00x (ISBN 0-584-11022-7, Pub. by Muller Ltd). State Mutual Bk.

Donne, Robert C. Determinants of Value: An Annotated Bibliography. (Bibliographic Ser.). 48p. 1976. 8.00 (ISBN 0-686-84051-8). Intl Assess.

Donne, W. B., ed. Correspondence of King George the Third with Lord North, 1768-1783. LC 76-154697. (Era of the American Revolution Ser). 1971. Repr. of 1867 ed. lib. bdg. 95.00 (ISBN 0-306-70155-3). Da Capo.

Donnell, Lloyd H. Beams, Plates & Shells. (Engineering Societies Monograph). 1976. text ed. 47.50 (ISBN 0-07-017593-4, C). McGraw.

Donnelley, Elfie. So Long Grandpa. Bell, Anthea, tr. (Illus.). 96p. (gr. 3-5). 1981. 8.95 (ISBN 0-517-54423-7). Crown.

Donnelly, G. F., et al. The Nursing System: Issues, Ethics & Politics. LC 80-12402. 224p. 1980. 13.50 (ISBN 0-471-04441-5). Wiley.

Donnelly, Gloria F. RN's Survival Sourcebook: Coping with Stress. (Illus.). 225p. 1983. softcover 10.95 (ISBN 0-87489-299-6). Med Economics.

Donnelly, Gloria F., jt. ed. see Sutterley, Doris C.

Donnelly, Honoria & Billings, Richard. Sara & Gerald. 1983. 17.95 (ISBN 0-8129-1030-3). Times Bks.

Donnelly, Jane. Call Up the Storm. (Harlequin Romances Ser.). 192p. 1983. pap. 1.75 (ISBN 0-373-02552-1). Harlequin Bks.

--Le Jardinier De Tir Glyn. (Harlequin Romantique). 192p. 1983. pap. 1.95 (ISBN 0-373-41191-X). Harlequin Bks.

Donnelly, Kerry. Doberman Pinschers. (Illus.). 1979. 4.95 (ISBN 0-87666-698-5, KW-009). TFH Pubns.

--Poodles. (Illus.). 1979. 4.95 (ISBN 0-87666-699-3, KW-010). TFH Pubns.

--Yorkshire Terriers. (Illus.). 1979. 4.95 (ISBN 0-87666-696-9, KW-007). TFH Pubns.

Donnelly, Kerry V., jt. auth. see Bruette, William A.

Donnelly, Mary L. Willett Family of Maryland, Colonial Pewters, Kentucky Pioneers. LC 82-74006. (Illus.). 712p. 1983. 40.00 (ISBN 0-939142-07-4). Private Pub.

Donnelly, Patricia J. Manual & Dissection Guide for Mammalian Anatomy. (Illus.). 116p. 1972. pap. text ed. 10.95x (ISBN 0-8036-2680-0); instructor's guide incl. (ISBN 0-8036-2681-9); & 20 slides 15.00 set (ISBN 0-686-82896-8). Davis Co.

Donnelly, Paul, jt. auth. see Williams, Kenneth.

Donnelly, R. H., et al. Active Games & Contests. 2nd ed. 672p. 1958. 21.95 (ISBN 0-471-07088-2). Wiley.

Donnelly, Richard J., et al. Active Games & Contests. 2nd ed. LC 81-19384. 686p. 1983. Repr. of 1958 ed. lib. bdg. write for info. (ISBN 0-89874-460-1). Krieger.

Donnelly, Thomas C., jt. auth. see Peel, Roy V.

Donnelly, Thomas R. & Ciosek, Karen. To Those That Have Ears. LC 82-62455. 100p. 1982. 11.95 (ISBN 0-9610268-0-4). Seventh Trumpet.

Donnenfeld, J. Etude d'un Marche Urbain Africain. (Black Africa Ser). (Illus.). 122p. (Fr.). 1974. Repr. lib. bdg. 40.00x o.p. (ISBN 0-8287-0278-0, 71-2015). Clearwater Pub.

Donner, Florinda. Shabono. 1983. pap. 3.95 (ISBN 0-440-38276-9, LE). Dell.

Donner, Martin W., jt. auth. see Ramsey, Elizabeth M.

Donner, Michael & Bramesco, Norton. Crossword Encyclopedia. LC 82-60060. (Illus.). 384p. 1982. 18.95 (ISBN 0-89480-222-4); pap. 9.95 (ISBN 0-89480-221-6). Workman Pub.

Donner, Morton, et al. The Intellectual Tradition of the West: Readings in the History of Ideas. Incl. Vol. 1. 1967. pap. 11.95x o.p. (ISBN 0-673-05578-7); Vol. 2. 1968. pap. o.p. (ISBN 0-673-05579-5). pap. Scott F.

Donner, Wolf. The Five Faces of Thailand: An Economic Geography. (Illus.). 1978. 25.00 o.p. (ISBN 0-312-29423-9). St Martin.

Donnerstein, Edward, jt. ed. see Geen, Russell.

Donnison, Polly. William the Dragon. (Illus.). 64p. (ps-3). 1973. PLB 4.64 o.p. (ISBN 0-698-30510-8, Coward). Putnam Pub Group.

Donno, Daniel, ed. see Machiavelli, Noccolo.

Donno, Daniel J., ed. see Campanella, Tommaso.

D'Onofrio, Carol & Wang, Virginia, eds. Cooperative Rural Health Education. 1976. pap. 9.00x o.p. (ISBN 0-913590-35-5). Slack Inc.

Donoghue, D. Jonathan Swift. LC 77-79053. 1969. 44.50 (ISBN 0-521-07564-5). Cambridge U Pr.

Donoghue, Denis. The Sovereign Ghost: Studies in Imagination. LC 75-27923. 1977. 19.50x (ISBN 0-520-03134-2). U of Cal Pr.

Donoghue, John D. Pariah Persistence in Changing Japan: A Case Study. 1977. pap. text ed. 8.25 (ISBN 0-8191-0170-2). U Pr of Amer.

Donoghue, William E. & Tilling, Thomas. William E. Donoghue's No-Load Mutual Fund Guide: How to Take Advantage of the Investment Opportunity of the '80s. LC 82-48116. (Illus.). 224p. 1983. write for info. (ISBN 0-06-015096-3, HarpT). Har-Row.

Donohue, Brian. How to Buy an Office Computer or Word Processor. (Illus.). 256p. 1983. 17.95 (ISBN 0-13-403113-X); pap. 8.95 (ISBN 0-13-403105-9). P-H.

Donohue, Jerry. The Structures of the Elements. LC 80-15363. 448p. 1982. Repr. of 1974 ed. lib. bdg. 29.50 (ISBN 0-89874-230-7). Krieger.

Donohue, John P. Testis Tumors. (International Perspectives in Urology: Vol. 7). (Illus.). 360p. 1983. lib. bdg. price not set (ISBN 0-683-02613-5). Williams & Wilkins.

Donohue, Joseph. Theatre in the Age of Kean. (Drama & Theatre Studies). (Illus.). 201p. 1975. 18.50x o.p. (ISBN 0-87471-698-5). Rowman.

Donohue, Joseph C. Understanding Scientific Literatures: A Bibliometric Approach. (Illus.). 101p. 1974. 17.50x (ISBN 0-262-04039-5). MIT Pr.

Donohue, Joseph C. & Kochen, Manfred, eds. Information for the Community. LC 75-40168. 1976. text ed. 12.00 o.p. (ISBN 0-8389-0208-1). ALA.

Donohue, Wilma, ed. see Conference on Aging, 2nd, University of Michigan.

Donohugh, Donald. The Middle Years. 320p. text ed. 14.95 (ISBN 0-7216-3144-4). Saunders.

Donoso, Anton. Julian Marias. (World Author Ser.). 1982. lib. bdg. 16.95 (ISBN 0-8057-6486-0, Twayne). G K Hall.

Donoso, Ephraim, jt. ed. see Friedberg, Charles K.

Donoso, Jose. Charleston & Other Stories. Conrad, Andree, tr. from Spanish. LC 76-19449. 1977. 12.95 (ISBN 0-87923-197-1); limited ed. 25.00x (ISBN 0-87923-206-4). Godine.

--The Obscene Bird of Night. St. Martin, Hardie & Mades, Leonard, trs. from Span. LC 79-88419. 1979. pap. 8.95 (ISBN 0-87923-191-2, Nonpareil Bks.). Godine.

Donovan & Green. The Wood Chair in America. LC 82-90454. (Illus.). 120p. 1982. pap. 24.95 (ISBN 0-9609844-0-2). E & S Brickel.

Donovan, Bruce E. Euripides Papyri 1: Texts from Oxyrhynelius. (American Society of Papyrology Ser.). 10.50 (ISBN 0-686-95226-X, 31-00-05). Scholars Pr CA.

Donovan, Dennis G. & Herman, Magaretha G. Sir Thomas Browne & Robert Burton: A Reference Guide. 1981. lib. bdg. 40.00 (ISBN 0-8161-8018-0, Hall Reference). G K Hall.

Donovan, J. & Madnick, S. Information Systems: Data Base, Telecommunications, Transaction Manager & Performance Education. Date not set. text ed. price not set (ISBN 0-07-039457-1); price not set instr's manual (ISBN 0-07-039458-X). McGraw.

Donovan, J. W. Tact in Court Containing Sketches of Cases Won by Skill, Wit, Art, Tact, Courage & Eloquence with Practical Illustrations in Letters of Lawyers Giving Their Best Rules for Winning Cases. 3rd rev. ed. 135p. 1983. Repr. of 1886 ed. lib. bdg. 20.00x (ISBN 0-8377-0517-7). Rothman.

Donovan, James A., ed. U. S. Military Force 1980: An Evaluation. 96p. 1980. 2.50 (ISBN 0-686-38854-2). CDI.

Donovan, Joan, et al. The Nurse Assistant. 2nd ed. (Illus.). 1977. pap. text ed. 21.00 (ISBN 0-07-017675-2, HP); instructor's manual 10.00 (ISBN 0-07-017676-0). McGraw.

Donovan, John. I'll Get There, It Better Be Worth the Trip. pap. 1.25 o.p. (ISBN 0-440-93980-1, LFL). Dell.

--I'll Get There: It Better Be Worth the Trip. LC 69-15539. (gr. 7 up). 1969. 7.95 o.p. (ISBN 0-06-021717-0, HarpJ); PLB 10.89 (ISBN 0-06-021718-9). Har-Row.

--Systems Programming. (Computer Science Ser). (Illus.). 480p. 1972. text ed. 35.95 (ISBN 0-07-017603-5, C); instr's manual 25.00 (ISBN 0-07-017604-3). McGraw.

--Wild in the World. (gr. 7 up). 1974. pap. 1.25 o.p. (ISBN 0-380-01625-7, 29264). Avon.

Donovan, John, jt. auth. see Madnick, Stuart.

Donovan, John C. The Cold Warriors: A Policy-Making Elite. 1974. 8.95x (ISBN 0-669-83931-0). Heath.

--The Nineteen Sixties: Politics & Public Policy. LC 80-5757. 142p. 1980. lib. bdg. 17.50 (ISBN 0-8191-1189-9); pap. text ed. 7.50 (ISBN 0-8191-1190-2). U Pr of Amer.

--The Politics of Poverty. 3rd ed. LC 80-5046. 201p. 1980. text ed. 18.75 (ISBN 0-8191-1025-6); pap. text ed. 8.00 (ISBN 0-8191-1026-4). U Pr of Amer.

Donovan, John C., et al. People, Power & Politics: An Introduction to Political Science. (Illus.). 384p. 1981. pap. text ed. 13.95 (ISBN 0-201-03246-5). A-W.

Donovan, John J & Mednick, Stuart E. Software Projects: Pedagogical Aids for Software Education & Research. LC 76-57693. 1977. text ed. 19.95 (ISBN 0-07-017591-8, C). McGraw.

Donovan, Josephine L. Sarah Orne Jewett. LC 80-5334. (Literature and Life Ser.). 160p. 1980. 11.95 (ISBN 0-8044-2137-4). Ungar.

Donovan, Pete. Carol Johnston: The One-Armed Gymnast. LC 82-4449. (Sports Stars Ser.). (Illus.). (gr. 2-8). 1982. PLB 7.95g (ISBN 0-516-04323-4); pap. 2.50 (ISBN 0-516-44323-2). Childrens.

Donovan, Peter. Interpreting Religious Experience. (Orig.). 1979. pap. 3.00 (ISBN 0-8164-2209-5). Seabury.

Donovan, Ronald & Orr, Marsha J. Subcontracting in the Public Sector: The New York State Experience. LC 82-6379. 1982. pap. 4.95 (ISBN 0-87546-095-X). ILR Pr.

Donsbach, Kurt. Metabolic Cancer Therapies. 1981. 1.95x (ISBN 0-686-37945-4). Cancer Control Soc.

Donsbach, Kurt & Walker, Morton. Chelation. 1981. 1.00x (ISBN 0-686-36341-8). Cancer Control Soc.

--DMSO. 1981. 1.00x (ISBN 0-686-36344-2). Cancer Control Soc.

Donsbach, Kurt & Welch, Richard. Cancer: Cause & Control. 1978. 1.00 (ISBN 0-686-36337-X). Cancer Control Soc.

Donsker, M. D., ed. see Kac, Mark.

Donsky, Joanne, jt. auth. see Bone, Barry.

Donson, Theodore B. Prints & the Print Markets: A Handbook for Buyers, Collectors, & Connoisseurs. LC 76-14487. (Illus.). 1977. 23.99i (ISBN 0-690-01160-1). T Y Crowell.

Donway, Roger, jt. auth. see Kelley, David.

Dony, John G. & Dyer, James. The Story of Luton. 160p. 1982. 35.00x (ISBN 0-900804-11-4, Pub. by White Crescent England). State Mutual Bk.

Don-Yehiya, Eliezer, jt. auth. see Liebman, Charles S.

Donze, Mary T. In My Heart Room. 64p. 1982. pap. 1.50 (ISBN 0-89243-161-X). Liguori Pubns.

Donze, Terese. In My Heart Room Coloring Book. Murphy, Mary, tr. 32p. 1982. pap. 1.50 (ISBN 0-89243-169-5). Liguori Pubns.

Doob, Joseph L. Stochastic Processes. LC 52-11857. (Wiley Series in Probability & Mathematical Statistics). 1953. 48.95x (ISBN 0-471-21813-8, Pub. by Wiley-Interscience). Wiley.

Doob, Leonard W. Becoming More Civilized, a Psychological Exploration. LC 73-6211. 333p. 1973. Repr. of 1960 ed. lib. bdg. 17.50x (ISBN 0-8371-6893-7, DOMC). Greenwood.

--Panorama of Evil: Insights from the Behavioral Sciences. LC 77-87964. (Contributions in Philosophy: No. 10). 1978. lib. bdg. 25.00 (ISBN 0-313-20030-0, DPE/). Greenwood.

--The Pursuit of Peace. LC 80-1201. x, 335p. 1981. lib. bdg. 35.00 (ISBN 0-313-22630-X, DPO/). Greenwood.

Doob, Leonard W., ed. Ezra Pound Speaking: Radio Speeches of World War II. LC 77-91288. (Contributions in American Studies: No. 37). 1978. lib. bdg. 35.00 (ISBN 0-313-20057-2, DEP/). Greenwood.

Doohan, Leonard. Luke: The Perennial Spirituality. LC 82-71449. 336p. (Orig.). 1982. pap. 10.95 (ISBN 0-939680-03-3). Bear & Co.

Dooley, Anne M. A Quest for Religious Maturity: The Obsessive-Compulsive Personality -- Implications for Pastoral Counseling. LC 80-67255. 124p. (Orig.). 1981. lib. bdg. 18.25 (ISBN 0-8191-1442-1); pap. text ed. 8.25 (ISBN 0-8191-1443-X). U Pr of Amer.

Dooley, D. J. Compton Mackenzie. (English Authors Ser.). 1974. lib. bdg. 14.95 (ISBN 0-8057-1361-1, Twayne). G K Hall.

Dooley, D. J., ed. Data Conversion Integrated Circuits. LC 80-10541. 1980. 29.95 (ISBN 0-87942-131-2). Inst Electrical.

Dooley, Dennis. Dashiell Hammett. LC 79-4824. (Recognitions Ser.). 9.95 o.p. (ISBN 0-8044-2141-2). Ungar.

Dooley, H. H. Last Rights. LC 79-6882. 1980. 10.00 o.p. (ISBN 0-385-15742-8). Doubleday.

Dooley, Kate C. The Jesus Book. LC 82-61422. 48p. (Orig.). 1983. pap. 2.95 (ISBN 0-8091-2514-5). Paulist Pr.

Dooley, Peter C. Elementary Price Theory. 2nd ed. (Illus., Orig.). 1973. pap. text ed. 10.95 (ISBN 0-13-259531-1). P-H.

--Introductory Macroeconomics. LC 81-40774. 192p. 1981. pap. text ed. 8.25 o.p. (ISBN 0-8191-1827-3). U Pr of Amer.

Dooley, Susan, jt. auth. see Hirsch, Abby.

Dooley, Thomas W. Buy Now! How Alternative Financing Can Work For You. 48p. (Orig.). 1982. pap. 2.95 (ISBN 0-88462-444-7). Real Estate Ed Co.

Doolin, James H. Residential Cooling, 2 pts. 1982. pap. 15.00 ea. Pt. 1: 50p (ISBN 0-914626-04-3). Pt. 2: 91p (ISBN 0-914626-05-1). Doolco Inc.

Doolittle. Communications & Conflict. rev. ed. Applbaum, Ronald & Hart, Roderick, eds. (MODCOM Modules in Speech Communication Ser.). 1982. pap. text ed. 2.75 (ISBN 0-574-22586-2, 13-5586). SRA.

Doolittle, Hilda. Bid Me to Live. (Imagist Ser.). (Illus.). 220p. 1982. 20.00x (ISBN 0-933806-19-1). Black Swan CT.

--The Gift. LC 82-8027. 160p. 1982. 14.95 o.p. (ISBN 0-8112-0853-2); pap. 5.95 o.p. (ISBN 0-8112-0854-0, NDP546). New Directions.

--Hedylus. rev. ed. LC 79-22495. (Imagist Ser). (Illus.). 160p. 1980. 17.50x (ISBN 0-933806-00-0). Black Swan CT.

--Notes on Thought & Vision. 44p. (Orig.). 1983. 9.95 (ISBN 0-87286-142-2); pap. 4.00 (ISBN 0-686-83068-7). City Lights.

--Tribute to Freud. 208p. 1975. pap. 2.95 o.p. (ISBN 0-07-027731-1, SP). McGraw.

Doolittle, Hilda see H. D., pseud.

Doolittle, Jerome. The Bombing Officer. LC 82-5136. 236p. 1982. 12.95 (ISBN 0-525-24105-1, 01258-370). Dutton.

--Canyons & Mesas. LC 74-77772. (American Wilderness). (Illus.). (gr. 6 up). 1974. PLB 15.96 (ISBN 0-8094-1238-1, Pub. by Time-Life). Silver.

--The Southern Appalachians. LC 75-27179. (American Wilderness). (Illus.). (gr. 6 up). 1976. PLB 15.96 (ISBN 0-8094-1347-7, Pub. by Time-Life). Silver.

Doolittle, Jesse S. & Hale, Francis J. Thermodynamics for Engineers. 608p. 1983. text ed. 29.95 (ISBN 0-471-05805-X). Wiley.

Doolittle, Rosalie & Tiedebohl, Harriet. Southwest Gardening. rev. ed. LC 52-11535. (Illus.). 222p. 1967. pap. 7.50 (ISBN 0-8263-0027-8). U of NM Pr.

Dooren, Ingrid van see Pinxten, Rik & Van Dooren, Ingrid.

Doorenbos, H., ed. Non-Surgical Treatment of Malignant Diseases. (The Jonxis Lectures Ser.: Vol. 5). 1981. 44.25 (ISBN 0-444-90179-5). Elsevier.

Doorlag, Donald H., jt. auth. see Lewis, Rena B.

Doorn, J. Van see Van Doorn, J.

Doornkamp, John C., jt. auth. see Cooke, Ronald U.

Doos, B. R. Numerical Experimentation Related to GARP. (GARP Publications Ser.: No. 6). (Illus., Orig.). 1970. pap. 10.00 (ISBN 0-685-04920-5, WE295, WMO). Unipub.

Dooyeweerd, Herman. Roots of Western Culture: Pagan, Secular & Christian Options. 1979. 12.95x (ISBN 0-88906-104-1). Radix Bks.

Dop, H. van see Nieuwstadt, F. & Van Dop, H.

Dopfer, Kurt. The New Political Economy of Development: Integrated Theory & Asian Experience. LC 79-13396. 1979. 37.50x (ISBN 0-312-56869-X). St Martin.

Dopfer, Kurt C., ed. Economics in the Future: Toward a New Paradigm. LC 76-2600. 1976. lib. bdg. 23.50 o.p. (ISBN 0-89158-548-6). Westview.

Dopp, Pearl. From the Top of a Secret Tree. (Illus., Orig.). 1979. pap. 6.95 (ISBN 0-931762-11-1). B J Phunn.

Dopp, Peggy H. & Vroman, Barbara F. Tomorrow Is a River. LC 76-52054. 1977. 12.95 (ISBN 0-931762-00-6). B J Phunn.

Dopyera, John E., jt. auth. see Lay-Dopyera, Margaret Z.

Doraiswamy, L. K. & Sharma, M. M. Heterogeneous Reactions: Analysis, Examples & Reactor Design, 2 vols. 1983. Vol. 1, Gas-solid & Solid-solid reactions, 624pgs. write for info (ISBN 0-471-05368-6, Pub. by Wiley-Interscience); Vol. 2, Fluid-Fluid-Solid Reactions, 650pgs. write for info (ISBN 0-471-86839-6, Pub. by Wiley-Interscience). Wiley.

Doran, James D. Matthew Brady: Historian with a Camera. (Illus.). 1955. 7.50 o.p. (ISBN 0-517-00104-7). Crown.

Doran, Madeleine. Something About Swans: Essays. 134p. 1973. 7.50 (ISBN 0-299-06170-1). U of Wis Pr.

Doran, Robert M. Psychic Conversion & Theological Foundations: Toward a Reorientation of the Human Sciences. LC 81-9360. (American Academy of Religion Studies in Religion Ser.). 1981. pap. 9.95 (ISBN 0-89130-522-X, 01-00-25). Scholars Pr CA.

--Subject & Psyche: Ricoeur, Jung, & the Search for Foundations. 1977. 11.75 (ISBN 0-8191-0257-1). U Pr of Amer.

Doran, Thomas J. Running Lean: How to Maximize Your People's Productivity, Boost Morale & Improve Profits. 125p. 1983. 19.95 (ISBN 0-939550-02-4); pap. 9.95 (ISBN 0-939550-03-2). DK Halcyon.

Doran, Thomas J., Jr., jt. auth. see Kubeck, James J.

Dor Bahadur Bista. People of Nepal. 4th ed. (Illus.). 210p. (gr. 9-12). 1980. 29.95x (ISBN 0-940500-20-5); lib. bdg. 29.95x (ISBN 0-686-92321-9); text ed. 29.95x (ISBN 0-686-98509-5). Asia Bk Corp.

Dordick, B. F., jt. ed. see Babb, Janice B.

Dordick, Herbert S., et al. The Emerging Network Marketplace. (Communication & Information Science Ser.). 288p. 1981. 32.50x (ISBN 0-89391-036-8). Ablex Pub.

Dore, Gustave. The Dore Illustrations for Dante's Divine Comedy. LC 75-17176. 1976. lib. bdg. 13.50x (ISBN 0-88307-605-5). Gannon.

--Dore's Illustrations for Don Quixote: A Selection of 190 Illustrations by Gustave Dore. (Illus.). 160p. 1982. pap. 6.00 (ISBN 0-486-24300-1). Dover.

--Dore's Illustrations for Rabelais: A Selection of 252 Illustrations. (Illus.). 1978. pap. 6.00 (ISBN 0-486-23656-0). Dover.

--History of Holy Russia. Weissbort, Daniel, tr. from Fr. LC 65-161410. 207p. 1972. 18.00x (ISBN 0-912050-11-X, Library Pr). Open Court.

Dore, Ian, ed. Frozen Seafood-The Buyer's Handbook: A Guide to Profitable Buying for Commercial Users. LC 82-12513. (Osprey Seafood Handbooks Ser.). 308p. 1982. text ed. 48.00 (ISBN 0-943738-00-8); pap. 40.00 (ISBN 0-943738-01-6). Osprey Bks.

Dore, Ian, ed. see Coons, Kenelm.

Dore, Ronald P. British Factory-Japanese Factory: The Origins of National Diversity in Employment Relations. LC 72-78948. 1973. 28.50x (ISBN 0-520-02268-8); pap. 9.95x (ISBN 0-520-02495-8, CAMPUS96). U of Cal Pr.

--The Diploma Disease: Education, Qualification, & Development. LC 75-22653. 1976. 30.00x (ISBN 0-520-03107-5); CAMPUS 181. pap. 7.95x o.p. (ISBN 0-520-03270-5). U of Cal Pr.

Dore, Ronald P., tr. see Fukutake, Tadashi.

Dore, Wade Van see Van Dore, Wade.

Doreen. Poetry Speaks. 1979. 4.95 o.p. (ISBN 0-533-04073-6). Vantage.

Doreian, P. & Hummon, N. P. Modeling Social Processes. new ed. (Progress in Mathematical Social Sciences: 8). 1976. 19.95 (ISBN 0-444-41465-7). Elsevier.

Dorell, J. R., tr. see Erofeev, Benedict.

Doremus, Robert H. Glass Science. LC 73-4713. (Science & Technology of Materials Ser). 349p. 1973. 42.50x (ISBN 0-471-21900-2, Pub. by Wiley-Interscience). Wiley.

Doren, Carl C. Van see Van Doren, Carl C.

Doren, Carl van see Prokosch, Frederic.

Doren, Carl Van see Van Doren, Carl.

Doren, Carlton Van see Van Doren, Carlton, et al.

Doren, Charles Van see Adler, Mortimer J. & Van Doren, Charles.

Doren, Charles Van see Roske, Ralph J. & Van Doren, Charles.

Doren, Mark Van see Bartram, William.

Doren, Mark Van see Van Doren, Mark.

Doren, V. E. Van see Devreese, J. T. & Van Doren, V. E.

Doress, Irvin & Porter, Jack N. Kids in Cults: Why they Join, Why they Stay, Why they Leave. Rev. ed. 22p. (Orig.). 1982. pap. 2.50 (ISBN 0-932270-02-6). Zalonka Pubns.

Dorf, Barbara. Beginner's Guide to Painting in Oils. (Illus.). 1972. 15.75 o.p. (ISBN 0-7207-0464-2). Transatlantic.

--Beginner's Guide to Painting the Nude. (Illus.). 171p. 1974. 14.00 o.p. (ISBN 0-7207-0636-X). Transatlantic.

--Introduction to Still Life & Flower Painting. (Illus.). 184p. 1976. 15.95 o.p. (ISBN 0-7207-0885-0). Transatlantic.

Dorf, R. C. Technology, Society & Man. LC 74-76445. (Illus.). 1974. text ed. 18.00x o.p. (ISBN 0-87835-047-0); pap. 12.95x (ISBN 0-87835-052-7). Boyd & Fraser.

Dorf, Richard. Introduction to Computers & Computer Science. 2nd ed. LC 77-81994. (Illus.). 1977. text ed. cancelled (ISBN 0-87835-061-6). Boyd & Fraser.

Dorf, Richard C. The Energy Factbook, 1980-1981. 1980. 22.95 (ISBN 0-07-017623-X). McGraw.

--Introduction to Computers & Computer Science. 3rd ed. LC 81-66059. (Illus.). 640p. 1981. text ed. 21.95x (ISBN 0-87835-113-2). Boyd & Fraser.

--Matrix Algebra: A Programmed Introduction. 260p. 1969. pap. 19.95x (ISBN 0-471-21909-6). Wiley.

--Modern Control Systems. 3rd ed. LC 79-16320. (Electrical Engineering Ser.). (Illus.). 1980. text ed. 28.95 (ISBN 0-201-01258-8). A-W.

Dorfman. Color Mixing. (Grosset Art Instruction Ser.: No. 56). pap. 2.95 (ISBN 0-448-00565-4, G&D). Putnam Pub Group.

Dorfman, Gerald A. Wage Politics in Britain, 1945-1967: Government Vs. the TUC. 160p. 1973. 7.95x o.p. (ISBN 0-8138-0300-4). Iowa St U Pr.

Dorfman, John, et al. Well-Being: An Introduction to Health. 1980. pap. text ed. 15.50x (ISBN 0-673-15088-7). Scott F.

Dorfman, John R. The Stock Market Directory. LC 81-43558. 580p. 1982. 29.95 (ISBN 0-385-17286-9). Doubleday.

Dorfman, Joseph. Economic Mind in American Civilization, 1606-1933, 5 Vols. LC 64-7764. 1946-59. Set. 100.00x (ISBN 0-678-00111-1). Vol. 1. 25.00x (ISBN 0-678-04004-4); Vol. 2. 25.00x (ISBN 0-678-04005-2); Vol. 3. 25.00x (ISBN 0-678-00539-7); Vol. 4. 25.00 (ISBN 0-678-04007-9); Vol. 5. 25.00 (ISBN 0-678-04008-7). Kelley.

Dorfman, Joseph, ed. see Veblen, Thorstein B.

Dorfman, Mark S. Introduction to Insurance. 2nd ed. (P-H Series in Security & Insurance). (Illus.). 496p. 1982. text ed. 24.95 (ISBN 0-13-485367-9). P-H.

Dorfman, R., et al. Linear Programming & Economic Analysis. 1958. text ed. 27.00 o.p. (ISBN 0-07-017621-3, P&RB). McGraw.

Dorfman, Robert, ed. Measuring Benefits of Government Investments. (Studies of Government Finance). 429p. 1965. pap. 8.95 (ISBN 0-8157-1901-9). Brookings.

Dorham, David P., ed. see Paton, George Whitecross.

Doria, Charles. The Game of Europe: A Comedy of High Gothic Romance Frankly Rendered Out of the Senseless. LC 82-755391. 107p. 1983. lib. bdg. 19.95x (ISBN 0-8040-0409-9); pap. 10.95 (ISBN 0-8040-0410-2). Swallow.

Doria, Charles, ed. The Tenth Muse: Classical Drama in Translation. LC 82-75844. vi, 587p. 1980. 25.00x (ISBN 0-8040-0781-0). Swallow.

Dorian, A. F. Dictionary of Science & Technology: German-English. 2nd ed. 1981. 121.50 (ISBN 0-444-41997-7). Elsevier.

Dorian, A. F. & Osenton, J. Elsevier's Dictionary of Aeronautics. (Eng., Fr., Span., Ital., Port., & Ger., Polyglot). 1964. 106.50 (ISBN 0-444-40177-6). Elsevier.

Dorian, A. F., compiled by. Dictionary of Science & Technology, 2 vols. 2nd, rev. ed. (Ger. & Eng.). 1982. Set. 242.75 (ISBN 0-686-85923-5). Elsevier.

Dorian, A. F., ed. Dictionary of Science & Technology, 2 Vols. 1400p. 1979. Set. 255.50 (ISBN 0-686-85924-3); Vol. I: Fr.- Eng. 127.75 (ISBN 0-444-41911-X); Vol. II: Eng. & Fr. 127.75 (ISBN 0-444-41829-6). Elsevier.

Dorian, Emil. The Quality of Witness: A Romanian Diary, 1937-1944. Dorian, Marguerite, ed. Vamos, Mara S., tr. from Romanian. 352p. 1983. 19.95 (ISBN 0-8276-0211-1). Jewish Pubn.

Dorian, Frederick. Musical Workshop. LC 77-138109. (Illus.). 1971. Repr. of 1947 ed. lib. bdg. 19.75x (ISBN 0-8371-5685-8, DOMW). Greenwood.

Dorian, Marguerite, ed. see Dorian, Emil.

Dorian, Marguerite, tr. see Caraion, Ion.

Dorin & Salisbury. Train Watcher's Log. 64p. 1981. pap. 2.95 (ISBN 0-686-98187-1). Superior Pub.

Dorin, Patrick C. The Great Northern Railway: Lines East. (Illus.). 192p. Date not set. 24.95 (ISBN 0-87564-541-0). Superior Pub.

--Yesterday's Trains. LC 81-3696. (Superwheels & Thrill Sports Bks.). (Illus.). (gr. 4 up). 1981. PLB 7.95g (ISBN 0-8225-0439-1, ASTERISKS). Lerner Pubns.

--Yesterday's Trucks. LC 81-20717. (Superwheels & Thrill Sports Bks.). (Illus.). (gr. 4 up). 1982. PLB 7.95g (ISBN 0-8225-0502-9). Lerner Pubns.

Doring, P. F. Colloquial German. (Trubners Colloquial Manuals). 1975. 9.50 o.p. (ISBN 0-7100-8031-X); pap. 4.95 o.p. (ISBN 0-7100-8032-8). Routledge & Kegan.

Doring, R., jt. auth. see Knapp, H.

Doris, Liz, ed. see Broadcast Information Bureau, Inc.

Dorje, Rinjing. Tales of Uncle Tompa: The Legendary Rascal of Tibet. LC 75-18105. (Illus.). 80p. 1975. pap. 7.95 (ISBN 0-915880-02-4). Dorje Ling.

Dorko, Dennis A. New Dreams to Dream: Here's to Life. 1978. 4.50 o.p. (ISBN 0-533-03691-7). Vantage.

Dorland, Michael. Double-Cross Circuit. LC 78-54630. 1978. 10.00 o.p. (ISBN 0-448-15162-6, G&D). Putnam Pub Group.

--The Double-Cross Circuit. 1980. pap. 1.95 o.p. (ISBN 0-451-09065-9, J9065, Sig). NAL.

Dorling. Use of Mathematical Literature. 1977. 34.95 o.p. (ISBN 0-408-70913-8). Butterworth.

Dorling, T. A. Activated Carbon Adsorption in Odour Control: The Adsorption of Styrene Vapour, 1979. 1981. 65.00x (ISBN 0-686-97008-X, Pub. by W Spring England). State Mutual Bk.

Dorling, T. A. & Sullivan, E. J. Airborne Particulate Lead Levels in Central London, 1980: Nineteen Seventy-Three to Seventy-Nine. 1981. 50.00x (ISBN 0-686-97019-5, Pub. by W Spring England). State Mutual Bk.

Dorman, C. C. North Western Album. (Illus.). 18.50x (ISBN 0-392-04067-0, SpS). Sportshelf.

Dorman, Daniel L. & Patterson, Jane R. Directory of Central Ohio Poets, 1977. 1977. pap. 1.25x (ISBN 0-914994-06-9). Cider Pr.

Dorman, James E. Recorded Dylan: A Critical Review & Discography. LC 82-60706. (Illus., Orig.). 1982. pap. 5.95 (ISBN 0-943564-00-X). Soma Pr Cal.

Dorman, John F. The Prestons of Smithfield & Greenfield in Virginia. (Filson Club Publications, Second Ser.). (Illus.). 441p. 1982. 27.50 (ISBN 0-9601072-1-5). Filson Club.

Dorman, L. I., ed. Cosmic Rays. 675p. 1974. 91.50 (ISBN 0-444-10480-1, North-Holland). Elsevier.

Dorman, Michael. The Making of a Slum. 1972. 9.95 o.s.i. (ISBN 0-440-05192-4). Delacorte.

--Witch Hunt. LC 75-32917. 192p. (gr. 7 up). 1976. 9.95 o.s.i. (ISBN 0-440-09689-8). Delacorte.

Dorman, Sonya. Planet Patrol. LC 78-1566. (gr. 6-10). 1978. 6.95 o.p. (ISBN 0-698-20435-2, Coward). Putnam Pub Group.

--Stretching Fence. LC 75-14550. 61p. 1975. 8.95 (ISBN 0-8214-0188-2, 82-81891); pap. 4.95 (ISBN 0-8214-0209-9, 82-81909). Ohio U Pr.

Dormer, K. J. Fundamental Tissue Geometry. LC 79-50235. (Illus.). 1980. 42.50 (ISBN 0-521-22326-1). Cambridge U Pr.

Dormon, James J., Jr. Theater in the Ante Bellum South, 1815-1861. xvi, 322p. 1967. 24.00x (ISBN 0-8078-1047-9). U of NC Pr.

Dorn, Al. One-Minute Photo Lessons. (Illus.). 136p. 1980. 11.95 (ISBN 0-8174-2179-3, Amphoto); pap. 7.95 (ISBN 0-686-83159-4). Watson-Guptill.

Dorn, Robert D. A Manual of the Vascular Plants of Wyoming, 2 vols. LC 76-24772. (Reference Library of Science & Technology Ser.: Vol. 4). (Illus.). 1977. Set. lib. bdg. 95.00 o.s.i. (ISBN 0-8240-9905-2). Garland Pub.

Dorn, William S. & McCracken, Daniel D. Introductory Finite Mathematics with Computing. LC 75-30647. 449p. 1976. text ed. 23.95 o.p. (ISBN 0-471-21917-7). Wiley.

Dorn, William S. & McCracken, Daniel D., eds. Numerical Methods with Fortran IV Case Studies. LC 77-37365. 477p. 1972. 34.95 (ISBN 0-471-21918-5). Wiley.

Dornan, jt. auth. see Dawe.

Dornan, James E., Jr. The U. S. War Machine. (Illus.). 1978. 22.95 o.p. (ISBN 0-517-53543-2). Crown.

--U. S. War Machine: An Encyclopedia of American Military. 272p. 1981. pap. 9.95 o.p. (ISBN 0-517-54552-7). Crown.

--The U. S. War Machine: An Illustrated Encyclopedia of American Military Equipment & Strategy. 1983. 10.95 (ISBN 0-517-54984-0). Crown.

Dornberg, John. Munich Nineteen Twenty-Three: The First Full Story of Hitler's Early Grab for Power. LC 81-48670. (Illus.). 400p. 1982. 18.22i (ISBN 0-06-038025-X, HarpT). Har-Row.

Dornbusch, Charles E. Communities of New York & the Civil War: The Recruiting Areas of the Civil War Regiments. 1962. pap. 3.00 o.p. (ISBN 0-87104-054-9). NY Pub Lib.

--G. I. Stories: A Checklist. (Gordon Lester Ford Memorial Study Ser. 3). 1950. pap. 2.00 o.p. (ISBN 0-87104-082-4). NY Pub Lib.

Dornbusch, R., jt. auth. see Fischer, S.

Dornbusch, Rudiger & Fischer, Stanley. Economics. (Illus.). 1008p. 1983. 25.95x (ISBN 0-07-017757-0); study guide 10.95 (ISBN 0-07-017759-7); instr's. manual 8.95 (ISBN 0-07-017758-9); transparency masters 8.95 (ISBN 0-07-017764-3). McGraw.

--Macroeconomics. 2nd ed. (Illus.). 736p. 1980. text ed. 24.95 (ISBN 0-07-017754-6, C); instructor's manual 18.95 (ISBN 0-07-017755-4); study guide 8.95 (ISBN 0-07-017756-2). McGraw.

--Macroeconomics. (Illus.). 1978. text ed. 17.95 (ISBN 0-07-017751-1, C). McGraw.

Dornbusch, S. M. & Schmid, C. F. Primer of Social Statistics. (Sociology Ser.). 1955. text ed. 19.50 o.p. (ISBN 0-07-017628-0, C). McGraw.

Dornbush, Rhea L., et al, eds. Chronic Cannibas Use, Vol. 282. (Annals of the New York Academy of Sciences). 430p. 1976. 32.00x (ISBN 0-89072-028-2). NY Acad Sci.

Dorner, Helene T., jt. auth. see Beeton, Douglas R.

Dorner, Jane. Cortes & the Aztecs. Reeves, Marjorie, ed. (Then & There Ser.). (Illus.). 112p. (gr. 7-12). 1972. pap. text ed. 3.10 (ISBN 0-582-20529-8). Longman.

Dorner, Peter & El-Shafie, Mahmoud A., eds. Resources & Development: Natural Resource Policies & Economic Development in an Interdependent World. (Illus.). 516p. 1980. 27.50 (ISBN 0-299-08250-4). U of Wis Pr.

Dornette, William H. Legal Aspects of Anesthesia. (Illus.). 599p. 1972. text ed. 40.00x o.p. (ISBN 0-8036-2720-3). Davis Co.

Dornfeldt, Jeanne & Knights of the Square Table. Inside Insight. 83p. (Orig.). 1982. pap. 4.95 (ISBN 0-937816-18-3). Tech Data.

Dornfield, D. A., jt. ed. see De Vries, W. R.

Dornfield, Ernst. Butterflies of Oregon. 275p. 1980. 25.00x (ISBN 0-917304-58-6). Timber.

Dornhoff, Larry L. & Hohn, Franz E. Applied Modern Algebra. (Illus.). 1978. 28.95 (ISBN 0-02-329980-0). Macmillan.

Dornier, Ann, ed. Mercian Studies. 250p. 1977. pap. text ed. 18.25x o.p. (ISBN 0-7185-1148-4, Leicester). Humanities.

Dorotheus Of Gaza. Dorotheos of Gaza: Discourses & Sayings. LC 77-4295. (Cistercian Studies Ser: No. 33). 1977. 7.00 (ISBN 0-87907-933-9). Cistercian Pubns.

Dorozynski, A. Doctors & Healers. 64p. 1975. pap. 5.00 (ISBN 0-686-93843-7, IDRC43, IDRC). Unipub.

Dorozynski, A., ed. Recherche-Operation, Application: Deroulement d'un Seminair-Atelier sur la Recherche Operationelle dans le Domaine de la Sancte Publique, tenu au Centre Universitaire des Sciences de la Sante a Yaounde, Cameroun, 6-11 Decembre 1976. 27p. 1977. pap. 2.00 o.p. (ISBN 0-88936-118-5, IDRC-081F, IDRC). Unipub.

Dorp, Rolf Von see Myrdal, Jan.

Dorr, Donal. Remove the Heart of Stone: Charismatic Renewal & the Experience of Grace. LC 78-58312. 160p. 1978. pap. 5.95 o.p. (ISBN 0-8091-2119-0). Paulist Pr.

Dorr, E., jt. auth. see Smith, G. R.

Dorr, E. L. General Methodology Manual for Occupational Manuals & Projects in Marketing Series. 1969. 6.50 o.p. (ISBN 0-07-017647-7, G); general methodology manual 7.84 o.p. (ISBN 0-07-017648-5). McGraw.

Dorr, E. L., jt. auth. see Ernest, John W.

Dorr, E. L., jt. auth. see Nye, B. C.

Dorr, E. L., jt. auth. see Walsh, L. A.

Dorr, E. L., et al. Buying & Pricing. 1971. pap. text ed. 6.56 o.p. (ISBN 0-07-017613-2, G). McGraw.

Dorr, Eugene, ed. see Bikkie, James A.

Dorr, Eugene, ed. see Crawford, Lucy.

Dorr, Eugene, ed. see Ely, Vivian & Barnes, Michael.

Dorr, Eugene, ed. see Hiserodt, Donald.

Dorr, Eugene, et al. Merchandising. 2nd ed. (Occupational Manuals & Projects in Marketing Ser.). 1977. pap. text ed. 7.32 (ISBN 0-07-017615-9, G); tchr's manual & key 4.50 (ISBN 0-07-017616-7). McGraw.

Dorr, Eugene L., ed. see Antrim, William.

Dorr, Eugene L., ed. see Ertel, Kenneth & Walsh, Lawrence.

Dorr, Eugene L., ed. see Harris, E. Edward.

Dorr, Eugene L., ed. see Klaurens, Mary.

Dorr, Eugene L., ed. see Logan, William.

Dorr, R. L. What Eight Million Women Want. LC 10-28964. Repr. of 1910 ed. 23.00 o.s.i. (ISBN 0-527-24600-X). Kraus Repr.

Dorr, Williams P. The David Curve. LC 75-7746. 1976. 7.95 (ISBN 0-87949-049-7). Ashley Bks.

Dorram, Peter. The Expert Witness. LC 82-71941. 128p. (Orig.). 1982. pap. 16.95 (ISBN 0-918286-27-1). Planners Pr.

Dorrance & Co. Editors, ed. Modern American Short Stories 1982. 1982. 9.95 (ISBN 0-8059-2850-2). Dorrance.

Dorrance, Don. Morituri. 20p. 1975. pap. 1.00 o.p. (ISBN 0-686-20752-1). Samisdat.

Dorrance, G. S. National Monetary & Financial Analysis. LC 77-82744. (Illus.). 1978. 24.00 (ISBN 0-312-55946-1). St Martin.

Dorre, Pamela. Wind over Stonehenge. LC 77-75947. (Pacesetters Ser.). (Illus.). 64p. (gr. 4 up). 1978. PLB 8.65 (ISBN 0-516-02175-3). Childrens.

Dorris, C. E see Gospel Advocate.

Dorsch, Jerry A. & Dorsch, Susan E. Understanding Anesthesia Equipment: Construction Care & Complications. 1975. 33.00 o.p. (ISBN 0-683-02614-3). Williams & Wilkins.

Dorsch, Susan E., jt. auth. see Dorsch, Jerry A.

Dorsch, T. S., ed. Essays & Studies-1972. (Essays & Studies: Vol. 25). 125p. 1972. text ed. 12.50 (ISBN 0-391-00231-7). Humanities.

Dorschner, John & Fabricio, Robert. The Winds of December. LC 79-12550. (Illus.). 1980. 15.95 (ISBN 0-698-10993-7, Coward). Putnam Pub Group.

Dorsen, Norman & Bender, Paul. Political & Civil Rights in the United States: 1982 Supplement to Volume I. 1982. pap. 9.95 (ISBN 0-316-19052-7). Little.

Dorsen, Norman, et al. Emerson, Haber & Dorsen's Political & Civil Rights in the United States, Vol. 2. 4th ed. 1979. text ed. 30.00 student ed. (ISBN 0-316-19049-7). Little.

Dorsett, Joseph L. Integrated Algebra & Trigonometry. 2nd ed. 1977. pap. text ed. 15.95 (ISBN 0-8403-1699-2). Kendall-Hunt.

Dorsey, Anne G., jt. auth. see Sciarra, Dorothy J.

Dorsey, David F., et al, eds. Design & Intent in African Literature. 137p. 1982. 22.00 (ISBN 0-89410-354-7); pap. 14.00 (ISBN 0-89410-355-5). Three Continents.

Dorsey, G. A. The Arapaho Sun Dance, the Ceremony of the Offerings Lodge. (Chicago Field Museum of Natural History Fieldiana Anthropology Ser.). 1903. 88.00 (ISBN 0-527-01864-3). Kraus Repr.

--Cheyenne. enl. ed. (Chicago Field Museum of Natural History Fieldiana Anthropology Ser). 1905. pap. 34.00 (ISBN 0-527-01869-4). Kraus Repr.

Dorsey, G. A. & Kroeber, A. L. Traditions of the Arapaho. (Chicago Field Museum of Natural History Fieldiana Anthropology Ser). 1903. pap. 48.00 (ISBN 0-527-01865-1). Kraus Repr.

Dorsey, G. A. & Voth, H. R. Oraibi Soyal Ceremony, & Oraibi Powamu Ceremony, & Mishongnovi Ceremonies of the Snake & Antelope Fraternities, & Oraibi Summer Snake Ceremony, 4 wks. in 1 vol. 1901-03. pap. 77.00 (ISBN 0-527-01863-5). Kraus Repr.

Dorsey, Gray L. American Freedoms. LC 74-20856. 1974. lib. bdg. 12.50 (ISBN 0-930342-25-9); pap. text ed. 7.50 (ISBN 0-930342-26-7). W S Hein.

Dorsey, James E. Georgia Genealogy & Local History: A Bibliography. LC 82-7594. 416p. 1983. 27.50 (ISBN 0-87152-359-0); pap. 20.00 (ISBN 0-87152-363-9). Reprint.

Dorsey, James E. & Derden, John K. Montgomery County, Georgia: A Source Book of Genealogy & History. 256p. 1983. price not set (ISBN 0-87152-377-9); pap. 20.00 (ISBN 0-87152-376-0). Reprint.

Dorsey, John & Dilts, James D. A Guide to Baltimore Architecture. (Illus.). 327p. 1981. pap. 4.95 (ISBN 0-686-36805-3). Md Hist.

Dorson, Richard M. Man & Beast in American Comic Legend. LC 81-48622. (Illus.). 192p. 1983. 20.00 (ISBN 0-253-33665-1). Ind U Pr.

--Negro Folktales in Michigan. LC 73-21099. (Illus.). 245p. 1974. Repr. of 1956 ed. lib. bdg. 17.25x (ISBN 0-8371-5989-X, DONF). Greenwood.

Dorson, Richard M., ed. Davy Crockett American Comic Legend. LC 77-2876. (Illus.). 1977. Repr. of 1939 ed. lib. bdg. 15.75x (ISBN 0-8371-9517-9, DOCR). Greenwood.

--Handbook of American Folklore. LC 82-47574. (Illus.). 608p. Date not set. 35.00x (ISBN 0-253-32706-7). Ind U Pr.

--Peasant Customs & Savage Myths Selections from the British Folklorists, 2 Vols. LC 68-16690. 1969. Set. 40.00x o.s.i. (ISBN 0-226-15867-5); Vol. 1. 13.50x o.s.i. (ISBN 0-226-15865-9); Vol. 2. 12.50x o.s.i. (ISBN 0-226-15866-7). U of Chicago Pr.

Dorson, Richard M., ed. see Stern, Stephen.

Dorst & Dandelot. A Field Guide to the Larger Mammals of Africa. 34.95 (ISBN 0-686-42779-3, Collins Pub England). Greene.

Dorsten, Jan Van see Sidney, Philip.

D'Ortigue, M. J. Dictionnaire Liturgique, Historique et Theorique de Plainchant et de Musique d'Eglise. LC 79-155353. (Music Ser). 1971. Repr. of 1854 ed. lib. bdg. 75.00 (ISBN 0-306-70165-0). Da Capo.

Dorwart, Jeffrey M. Conflict of Duty: U. S. Navy's Intelligence Dilemma 1919-1945. 228p. 1983. 22.95 (ISBN 0-87021-685-6). Naval Inst Pr.

Dorwart, Reinhold A. Administrative Reforms of Frederick William First of Prussia. LC 70-138221. 1971. Repr. of 1953 ed. lib. bdg. 16.25x (ISBN 0-8371-5578-9, DOAR). Greenwood.

Dorweiler, jt. auth. see Brown.

Dosa, Marta L., tr. Libraries in the Political Scene: Georg Leyh & German Librarianship, 1933-53. LC 72-5218. (Contributions in Librarianship & Information Science: No. 7). 256p. 1973. lib. bdg. 27.50 (ISBN 0-8371-6443-5, DGL/). Greenwood.

Dosch, Hans-Michael, jt. ed. see Gelfand, Erwin W.

Doscher, Paul, et al. Intensive Gardening Round the Year. (Illus.). 224p. 1981. pap. 10.95 (ISBN 0-8289-0399-9). Greene.

Doshay, Lewis J. Boy Sex Offender & His Later Career. LC 69-14921. (Criminology, Law Enforcement, & Social Problems Ser.: No. 59). 1969. Repr. of 1943 ed. 12.00x (ISBN 0-87585-059-6). Patterson Smith.

Doshi, Harish. Traditional Neighborhood in a Modern City. LC 74-902204. 154p. 1974. 8.50x o.p. (ISBN 0-88386-292-1). South Asia Bks.

Doskey, John S., jt. auth. see Rosenberg, Kenyon C.

Doskow, Minna. William Blake's Jerusalem. LC 81-65463. (Illus.). 388p. 1982. 37.50 (ISBN 0-8386-3090-1). Fairleigh Dickinson.

Dosmond, A. J. Here, There & Everywhere. 1982. write for info. Roush Bks.

Dosmond, J. Deerskin Map. Date not set. write for info. Roush Bks.

Dos Passos, John. Big Money. 1969. pap. 3.95 (ISBN 0-451-51791-1, CE1791, Sig Classics). NAL.

--Century's Ebb. LC 75-920. (Thirteenth Chronicle Ser.). 448p. 1975. 10.95 (ISBN 0-87645-089-3). Gambit.

--Facing the Chair: Story of the Americanization of Two Foreign-Born Workmen. LC 72-104066. (Civil Liberties in American History Ser.). 1970. Repr. of 1927 ed. 19.50 (ISBN 0-306-71871-5). Da Capo.

--Forty-Second Parallel. 1969. pap. 2.25 o.p. (ISBN 0-451-51344-4, CE1344, Sig Classics). NAL.

--The Grand Design. (District of Columbia Ser.). 1977. Repr. of 1949 ed. lib. bdg. 18.95x (ISBN 0-89244-036-8). Queens Hse.

--Ground We Stand On: Some Examples from the History of a Political Creed. LC 41-16286. Repr. of 1941 ed. 18.00 o.s.i. (ISBN 0-527-24800-2). Kraus Repr.

--Mr. Wilson's War. LC 61-12612. 1962. 7.50 (ISBN 0-385-02828-8). Doubleday.

--Number One. (District of Columbia Ser). 1977. Repr. of 1943 ed. lib. bdg. 16.95x (ISBN 0-89244-035-X). Queens Hse.

--The Prospect Before Us. LC 72-10716. (Illus.). 375p. 1973. Repr. of 1950 ed. lib. bdg. 18.75 (ISBN 0-8371-6626-8, DOPB). Greenwood.

--The Shackles of Power: Three Jeffersonian Decades. LC 66-12237. 1966. 7.95 (ISBN 0-385-02261-1). Doubleday.

--State of the Nation. LC 73-718. (Illus.). 333p. 1973. Repr. of 1944 ed. lib. bdg. 17.25x (ISBN 0-8371-6782-5, DOSN). Greenwood.

Dos Passos, John see Dos Passos, John.

Doss, Calvin L. School & Community Relations: A Book of Readings. 1976. pap. text ed. 7.00 (ISBN 0-8191-0030-7). U Pr of Amer.

Doss, Helen. Your Skin Holds You in. LC 78-2777. (Illus.). 64p. (gr. 3-6). 1978. PLB 6.97 o.p. (ISBN 0-671-32935-9). Messner.

Doss, Helen & Wells, Richard L. All the Better to Bite with. LC 76-27245. (Illus.). 64p. (gr. 3-5). 1976. PLB 7.29 o.p. (ISBN 0-671-32799-2). Messner.

Doss, Margot Patterson. A Walker's Yearbook: Fifty-Two Seasonal Walks in the San Francisco Bay Area. (Illus.). 288p. (Orig.). 1983. pap. 8.95 (ISBN 0-89141-154-2). Presidio Pr.

Doss, Martha M., ed. The Directory of Special Opportunities for Women. 290p. 1981. 18.95 (80-85274). Impact VA.

Dos Santos, Jean see Santos, Jean Dos.

Dos Santos, Joyce Audy see Audy dos Santos, Joyce.

Dos Santos, S. M., jt. auth. see Barney, G. C.

Dossat, Roy J. Principles of Refrigeration. 2nd ed. LC 78-2938. 603p. 1978. text ed. 29.95 (ISBN 0-471-03550-5); solutions manual 8.00 (ISBN 0-471-03771-0). Wiley.

Dossenbach, Hans, jt. auth. see Dossenbach, Monique.

Dossenbach, Monique & Dossenbach, Hans. Animal Babies of East Africa. new ed. LC 76-23450. (Illus.). (gr. 3-5). 1977. 5.95 o.p. (ISBN 0-399-20529-2). Putnam Pub Group.

Dostal, J. Operational Amplifiers. (Studies in Electrical & Electronic Engineering Ser.: Vol. 4). 1981. 83.00 (ISBN 0-444-99760-1). Elsevier.

Doster, et al. Barron's How to Prepare for the CLEP Subject Exams: English Composition-Freshman English. LC 78-664. (Illus.). 1978. pap. text ed. cancelled (ISBN 0-8120-0622-4). Barron.

Doster, James F. Creek Indians, 2 Vols. Horr, David A., ed. (American Indian Ethnohistory Ser.). 1978. lib. bdg. 42.00 o.s.i. (ISBN 0-8240-0788-3). Garland Pub.

Doster, Rebecca, jt. auth. see Whordley, Derek.

Doster, Rebecca J., jt. auth. see Whordley, Derek.

Doster, W., ed. Barron's How to Prepare for the CLEP Examinations - General Examination. rev. ed. LC 78-32129. 1979. pap. 7.95 (ISBN 0-8120-2011-1). Barron.

Dostert, L. & Decaux, M. Francais, Cours Avance, Styles Litteraires. 1964. text ed. 7.20 o.p. (ISBN 0-02-815560-2). Glencoe.

Dostert, L. & Lindenfeld, J. Francais, Cours Moyen, Civilisation. 1961. text ed. 6.95 o.p. (ISBN 0-02-815500-9). Glencoe.

Dostert, Pierre E., ed. see Thompson, Wayne C.

Dosti, Rose. Middle Eastern Cooking. (Illus.). 192p. 1982. pap. 9.95 (ISBN 0-89586-184-4). H P Bks.

Dosti, Rose, et al. Light Style: The New American Cuisine, The Low Calorie, Low Salt, Low Fat Way to Good Food & Good Health. LC 79-1771. (Illus.). 1982. 14.95 (ISBN 0-06-250485-1, CN-4040, HarpT); pap. 8.61i (ISBN 0-06-250487-8). Har-Row.

Dostoevsky, F. Zapiski iz Podpolia. 1982. 15.00 (ISBN 0-88233-779-3); pap. 3.50 (ISBN 0-88233-777-7). Ardis Pubs.

Dostoevsky, F. M. The Double. Harden, Evelyn, tr. from Rus. 1983. 15.00 (ISBN 0-88233-756-4); pap. 6.50 (ISBN 0-88233-757-2). Ardis Pubs.

Dostoevsky, Fedor. Notes from Underground. Matlaw, Ralph E., tr. Bd. with Grand Inquisitor. 1960. pap. 3.50 (ISBN 0-525-47050-6, 0340-110). Dutton.

Dostoevsky, Feodor. Memoirs from the House of the Dead. Hingley, Ronald, ed. Coulson, Jessie, tr. (The World's Classics Ser.). 384p. 1983. pap. 4.95 (ISBN 0-19-281613-6, GB). Oxford U Pr.

Dostoevsky, Fyodor. The Adolescent. MacAndrew, Andrew R., tr. 608p. 1981. pap. 9.95 (ISBN 0-393-00995-5). Norton.

--The Brothers Karamazov. Matlaw, Ralph, ed. Garnett, Constance, tr. (Critical Edition Ser). 1000p. 1976. 17.50x (ISBN 0-393-04426-2); pap. 9.95x (ISBN 0-393-09214-3). Norton.

--The Brothers Karamazov. Garnett, Constance, tr. 8.95 (ISBN 0-394-60415-6). Modern Lib.

--Great Short Works of Fyodor Dostoevsky. Hingley, Ronald, ed. Bird, George, et al, trs. 1968. pap. 3.50i (ISBN 0-06-083081-6, P3081, PL). Har-Row.

--The Idiot. Garnett, Constance, tr. from Russian. (Bantam Classic Ser.). 597p. (gr. 7-12). 1981. pap. 2.25 (ISBN 0-553-21039-4). Bantam.

--Notes From Underground. Durgy, Robert G., ed. Shishkoff, Serge, tr. from Russian. LC 82-45080. 288p. 1982. pap. text ed. 10.75 (ISBN 0-8191-2415-X). U Pr of Amer.

Dostoyevsky, Anna. Dostoyevsky: Reminiscences. Stillman, Beatrice, ed. & tr. (Illus.). 448p. 1975. 12.50 o.p. (ISBN 0-87140-592-X). Liveright.

Dostoyevsky, F. Karamazov Brothers, 2 vols. 1173p. 1980. Set. 15.95 (ISBN 0-8285-2244-8, Pub. by Progress Pubs USSR). Imported Pubns.

Dostoyevsky, Fedor. The Brothers Karamazov. MacAndrew, Andrew, tr. from Russian. (Classic Ser.). 936p. (gr. 9-12). 1981. pap. 2.75 (ISBN 0-553-21037-8). Bantam.

--Brothers Karamazov. Garnett, Constance, tr. (YA) 1950. pap. 5.00x (ISBN 0-394-30912-X, T12, Mod LibC). Modern Lib.

--Crime & Punishment. Garnett, Constance, tr. from Russian. (Bantam Classics Ser.). 472p. (gr. 10-12). 1981. pap. 2.50 (ISBN 0-553-21038-6). Bantam.

--Crime & Punishment. Garnett, Constance, tr. (YA) 1950. pap. 4.00 (ISBN 0-394-30911-1, T11, Mod LibC). Modern Lib.

--Crime & Punishment. Monas, Sidney, tr. pap. 2.25 (ISBN 0-451-51745-8, CE1745, Sig Classics). NAL.

Dostoyevsky, Fyodor. The Best Short Stories of Dostoyevsky. Magarshack, David, tr. 6.95 (ISBN 0-394-60477-6). Modern Lib.

--The Brothers Karamazov. 1982. pap. 5.95 o.p. (ISBN 0-14-044416-5). Penguin.

--Idiot. (Classic Ser.). 1969. pap. 2.50 (ISBN 0-451-51618-4, CE1618, Sig Classics). NAL.

--The Idiot. Garnett, Constance, tr. LC 82-42864. 10.95 (ISBN 0-394-60434-2). Modern Lib.

--Letters from the Underworld: The Gentle Maiden, & the Landlady. 1971. 9.95x (ISBN 0-460-00654-1, Evman); pap. 3.95x (ISBN 0-460-01654-7, Evman). Biblio Dist.

--Notes from Underground. Ginsburg, Mirra, tr. from Russian. (Bantam Classics Ser.). 192p. (gr. 9-12). 1981. pap. 1.95 (ISBN 0-553-21043-2). Bantam.

--Notes from Underground & Selected Stories: White Nights, Dream of a Ridiculous Man, House of the Dead. MacAndrew, Andrew R., tr. pap. 2.50 (ISBN 0-451-51442-4, CE1442, Sig Classics). NAL.

--Possessed. MacAndrew, Andrew R., tr. (Orig.). 1962. pap. 4.50 (ISBN 0-451-51747-4, CE1747, Sig Classics). NAL.

--The Possessed. Garnett, Constance, tr. Yarmolinsky, Avraham, ed. 7.95 (ISBN 0-394-60441-5). Modern Lib.

--Three Short Novels of Dostoyevsky. Yarmolinsky, Avrahm, ed. Garnett, Constance, tr. Incl. Double; Notes from the Underground; Eternal Husband. LC 60-57341. pap. 6.95 (ISBN 0-385-09435-3, A193, Anch). Doubleday.

Doswell, Andrew. Office Automation. (Information Processing). 280p. 1983. 33.95 (ISBN 0-471-10457-4, Pub. by Wiley-Interscience). Wiley.

Dotan, Aron. Ben Asher's Creed: A Study of the History of the Controversy. LC 76-27649. (Society of Biblical Literature. Masoretic Studies). 1977. pap. 9.95 (ISBN 0-89130-084-8, 06-05-03). Scholars Pr Ca.

Doten & Boulard. Costume Drawing. (Pitman Art Ser.: Vol. 2). pap. 1.95 o.p. (ISBN 0-448-00511-5, G&D). Putnam Pub Group.

Dotsenko, Paul. The Struggle for a Democracy in Siberia, 1917-1920: Eyewitness Account of a Contemporary. (Publication Ser.: No. 277). (Illus.). 145p. 1983. lib. bdg. 16.95 (ISBN 0-8179-7771-6). Hoover Inst Pr.

Dott, Robert H. & Batten, Roger L. Evolution of the Earth. 3rd ed. (Illus.). 576p. 1980. text ed. 27.50 (ISBN 0-07-017625-6, C). McGraw.

Dott, Robert H., Jr., jt. ed. see Siegfried, Robert.

Dottori, D. Mathematics for Today & Tomorrow. 2nd ed. 1975. 11.32 (ISBN 0-07-082244-1, W). McGraw.

Doty, Betty. Publish Your Own Handbound Books. LC 80-67947. (Illus.). 127p. 1980. 8.95 (ISBN 0-930822-01-3); lib. bdg. 7.95 (ISBN 0-930822-03-X). Bookery.

Doty, C. Stewart. From Cultural Rebellion to Counterrevolution: The Politics of Maurice Barres. LC 75-15337. 294p. 1976. 16.00x (ISBN 0-8214-0191-2, 82-81941). Ohio U Pr.

Doty, C. Stewart, ed. The Industrial Revolution. LC 76-14929. (European Problem Studies). 142p. 1976. pap. text ed. 5.50 o.p. (ISBN 0-88275-433-5); pap. 5.50 o.p. Krieger.

Doty, Jean & Doty, Roy. Macmillan Children's Calendar Nineteen Eighty-Two. (Illus.). 1981. pap. 5.95 (ISBN 0-02-732990-9). Macmillan.

Doty, M. R. The Empire of Summer. Brown, Steven F., ed. LC 81-50288. (Thunder City Poetry Ser.). 56p. 1981. pap. 4.50 (ISBN 0-918644-24-0). Thunder City.

Doty, Richard G. Money of the World. LC 78-66398. 1978. 14.95 o.p. (ISBN 0-448-16450-7, G&D). Putnam Pub Group.

Doty, Roy. Eye Fooled You. (Illus.). 48p. (gr. 3-7). 1983. pap. 2.95 (ISBN 0-02-042980-0, Collier). Macmillan.

--Macmillan Children's Calendar 1983. (Illus.). (gr. 3up). 1982. pap. 6.95 (ISBN 0-02-733030-3). Macmillan.

--Tinkerbell Is a Ding-a-Ling. LC 79-6973. (Illus.). (gr. 4-6). 1980. 6.95a o.p. (ISBN 0-385-13490-8); PLB 4.95 (ISBN 0-385-13491-6). Doubleday.

Doty, Roy & Maar, Len. Where Are You Going with That Energy? LC 75-36587. (gr. 2-5). 1978. 5.95a o.p. (ISBN 0-385-11519-9); PLB 5.95a (ISBN 0-385-11520-2). Doubleday.

Doty, Roy & Reuther, David. Fun to Go: A Take-Along Activity Book. (Illus.). 64p. (gr. 2-7). 1982. pap. 4.95 (ISBN 0-02-042960-6); prepack 12 59.40 (ISBN 0-686-86315-1). Macmillan.

Doty, Roy, jt. auth. see Doty, Jean.

Doty, W. D., jt. auth. see Stout, R. D.

Doty, William F. Meet Your Pastor. LC 78-56776. (Illus., Orig.). 1978. pap. 1.95 o.p. (ISBN 0-8189-1153-0, 153, Pub. by Alba Bks). Alba.

Doty, William G., ed. see Eliade, Mircea.

Doubiago, Sharon. Hard Country. 250p. (Orig.). 1982. pap. 8.00 (ISBN 0-931122-25-2). West End.

Doubleday, Neal F. A Study of Hawthorne's Early Tales. LC 76-185462. 1972. 17.25 o.p. (ISBN 0-8223-0267-5). Duke.

--Writing the Research Paper. rev. ed. 1971. pap. text ed. 6.95x (ISBN 0-669-81224-2). Heath.

Doubtfire, Stanley. Make Your Own Classical Guitar. LC 82-16860. (Illus.). 128p. 1983. Repr. of 1981 ed. 17.95 (ISBN 0-8052-3833-6). Schocken.

Doucet, Jacques. Catalogüede Fonds Speciauxde la Bibliotheque Litteraire Jacques Doucet (Paris, France) (Fonds Valery). 1972. 95.00 (ISBN 0-8161-0952-4, Hall Library). G K Hall.

--Catalogüede Fonds Speciauxde la Bibliotheque Litteraire Jacques Doucet (Paris, France) (Fonds Mauriac et Fonds Jouhandeau). 1972. 95.00 (ISBN 0-8161-0954-0, Hall Library). G K Hall.

--Catalogüede Fonds Speciauxde la Bibliotheque Litteraire Jacques Doucet (Paris, France) (Lettres a Andre Gide). 1972. 95.00 (ISBN 0-8161-0951-6, Hall Library). G K Hall.

--Catalogüede Manuscritsde la Bibliotheque Litteraire Jacques Doucet, Paris, France. 1972. 100.00 (ISBN 0-8161-0950-8, Hall Library). G K Hall.

Doudera, A. Edward & Shaw, Margery W., eds. Human Life: An Interdisciplinary Approach to the Concept of Person. 300p. (Orig.). 1983. text ed. write for info. (ISBN 0-914904-82-5). Health Admin Pr.

Doudna, Martin K. Concerned about the Planet: The Reporter Magazine & American Liberalism, 1949-1968. LC 77-10048. (Contributions in American Studies: No. 32). 1977. lib. bdg. 25.00 (ISBN 0-8371-9698-1, DCA/). Greenwood.

Dougall, Herbert E. & Gaumnitz, Jack E. Capital Markets & Institutions. 4th ed. (Foundations of Finance Ser.). (Illus.). 1980. pap. text ed. 12.95 (ISBN 0-13-113670-4). P-H.

Dougan, Clark & Weiss, Stephen. Tet, Vol. 6. Manning, Robert, ed. (The Vietnam Experience Ser.). (Illus.). 192p. 1983. 14.95 (ISBN 0-939526-06-9). Boston Pub Co.

Dougan, Michael B. Confederate Arkansas: The People & Policies of a Frontier State in Wartime. LC 76-16117. 173p. 1976. 12.50 (ISBN 0-8173-5230-9). U of Ala Pr.

Dougan, Terrell & Isbell, Lyn. We Have Been There: Families Share the Joys & Struggles of Living with Mental Retardation. 208p. (Orig.). 1983. pap. 9.95 (ISBN 0-687-44306-7). Abingdon.

Douge, Daniel. Caribbean Pilgrims: The Plight of the Haitian Refugees. 96p. 1982. 6.00 (ISBN 0-682-49890-4, University). Exposition.

Dougherty, Ching-yi, et al. Chinese Character Indexes: Vol. 1: Telegraphic Code Index. Vol. 2: Romanization Index. Vol. 3: Radical Index. Vol. 4: Total Stroke Count Index. Vol. 5: Four Corner System Index. 1963. 130.00x (ISBN 0-520-00346-2). U of Cal Pr.

Dougherty, F. C., tr. see Kazner, E., et al.

Dougherty, Flavian, ed. The Meaning of Human Suffering. LC 81-6267. 349p. 1982. 29.95 (ISBN 0-89885-011-8). Human Sci Pr.

Dougherty, Frank P. & Jopling, Samuel H. Managerial Accounting in Canada. LC 82-73436. 651p. 1983. text ed. 24.95x (ISBN 0-931920-47-7). Dame Pubns.

Dougherty, J. P., jt. auth. see Clemmow, P. C.

Dougherty, James J. The Politics of Wartime Aid: American Economic Assistance to France & French Northwest Africa, 1940-1946. LC 77-84770. (Contributions in American History: No. 71). 1978. lib. bdg. 29.95 (ISBN 0-8371-9882-8, DPW/). Greenwood.

Dougherty, James L. Union Free Management. 1972. 71.50 (ISBN 0-85013-144-8). Dartnell Corp.

Dougherty, Jim. Varmint Hunter's Digest. 1977. pap. 6.95 o.s.i. (ISBN 0-695-80838-9). Follett.

Dougherty, Kenneth see Anonym, Kenneth, pseud.

Dougherty, Patricia. American Diplomats & the Franco-Prussian War: Perceptions from Paris & Berlin. LC 80-250000089. 42p. 1980. 2.50 (ISBN 0-934742-06-5, Inst Study Diplomacy). Geo U Sch For Serv.

Dougherty, Raymond P. Archives From Erech. (Goucher College Cuneiform Inscription Ser.: Vol. 3). 1933. text ed. 27.50x (ISBN 0-686-83476-3). Elliots Bks.

Dougherty, Richard M. & Heinritz, Fred J. Scientific Management of Library Operations. 2nd ed. LC 81-18200. 286p. 1982. 15.00 (ISBN 0-8108-1485-4). Scarecrow.

Dougherty, Thomas J. Controlling the New Inflation. LC 80-8962. (Illus.). 192p. 1981. 21.95x (ISBN 0-669-04512-8). Lexington Bks.

Dougherty, Thomas J., jt. ed. see Kessel, David.

Dougherty, William F. Owl Light. 64p. pap. 4.75 (ISBN 0-939736-35-7). Wings ME.

Dougherty, William M. Introduction to Hematology. 2nd ed. LC 75-33097. (Illus.). 264p. 1976. 19.95 o.p. (ISBN 0-8016-1444-9). Mosby.

Doughty, Charles M. Travels in Arabia Deserta, 2 vols. (Illus.). 1980. Vol. 1. pap. 10.95 (ISBN 0-486-23825-3); Vol. 2. pap. 10.95 (ISBN 0-486-23826-1). Dover.

Doughty, Harold & Livesey, Herbert B. Guide to American Graduate Schools. 4th ed. LC 82-5257. 485p. 1982. pap. 14.95 (ISBN 0-14-046541-3). Penguin.

Doughty, Howard. Francis Parkman. LC 78-5521. 414p. 1978. Repr. of 1962 ed. lib. bdg. 30.00x o.p. (ISBN 0-313-20387-3, DOFP). Greenwood.

--Francis Parkman. 420p. 1983. pap. text ed. 9.95x (ISBN 0-674-31775-0). Harvard U Pr.

Doughty, J., jt. auth. see Aykroyo, W. R.

Doughty, Martin. Merchant Shipping & War. (Royal Historical Society, Studies in History: No. 31). 218p. 1982. text ed. 30.00x (ISBN 0-391-02688-7). Humanities.

Doughty, Robin W. Feather Fashions & Bird Preservation: A Study in Nature Protection. LC 72-619678. 1975. 24.50x (ISBN 0-520-02588-1). U of Cal Pr.

Doughty, Robin W., jt. ed. see Hugill, Peter J.

Doughty, Tom & George, Barbara. The Complete Book of Long-Distance & Competitive Cycling. 1983. 17.95 (ISBN 0-671-42433-5); pap. 8.95 (ISBN 0-671-42434-3). S&S.

Douglas, A. G., et al. Systematic New Product Development. LC 78-2398. 173p. 1978. 34.95x o.s.i. (ISBN 0-470-26328-8). Halsted Pr.

Douglas, Alfred. Extra-Sensory Powers: A Century of Psychical Research. LC 77-77807. (Illus.). 392p. 1982. 15.00 (ISBN 0-87951-064-1); pap. 7.95 (ISBN 0-87951-160-5). Overlook Pr.

--Oscar Wilde & Myself. 306p. 1983. Repr. of 1914 ed. lib. bdg. 45.00 (ISBN 0-686-38783-X). Century Bookbindery.

Douglas, Alfred, jt. auth. see Shaw, Bernard.

Douglas, Amanda H. Jamaica. (Inflation Fighter Ser.). 208p. 1982. pap. 1.50 o.s.i. (ISBN 0-8439-1147-6, Leisure Bks). Nordon Pubns.

Douglas, Andrew, jt. auth. see Crofton, John.

Douglas, B., et al. Concepts & Models of Inorganic Chemistry. 2nd ed. 816p. 1983. text ed. 34.95 (ISBN 0-471-21984-3). Wiley.

Douglas, Barbara. Fair Wind of Love. LC 76-18356. (Romantic Suspense Ser.). 1980. 8.95 o.p. (ISBN 0-385-08998-8). Doubleday.

--Good as New. (ps-1). 1982. 9.00 (ISBN 0-688-41983-6); PLB 8.59 (ISBN 0-688-51983-0). Morrow.

Douglas, Bodie E. & McDaniel, D. H. Concepts & Models of Inorganic Chemistry. 510p. 1965. text ed. 31.50x (ISBN 0-471-00129-5). Wiley.

Douglas, Bodie E., ed. Inorganic Syntheses, Vol. 18. LC 39-23015. (Inorganic Syntheses Ser.). 1978. 35.95x (ISBN 0-471-03393-6, Pub. by Wiley-Interscience). Wiley.

Douglas, C. E. When All Hell Breaks Loose. 1974. pap. 4.95 (ISBN 0-9601124-0-5). Tusayan Gospel.

Douglas, C. P. & Holt, K. S., eds. Mental Retardation: Prenatal Diagnosis & Infant Assessment. (Illus.). 72p. 1972. 6.95 o.p. (ISBN 0-407-26850-2). Butterworth.

Douglas, Carole N. Amberleigh. 352p. (Orig.). 1980. pap. 2.50 o.s.i. (ISBN 0-515-05715-0). Jove Pubns.

--Fair Wind, Fiery Star. 320p. (Orig.). 1981. pap. 2.75 o.s.i. (ISBN 0-515-06034-8). Jove Pubns.

--Her Own Person. (Love & Life Romance Ser.). 176p. (Orig.). 1982. pap. 1.75 (ISBN 0-345-30733-X). Ballantine.

Douglas, Casey. Le Cavalier Infidele. (Harlequin Seduction Ser.). 332p. 1983. pap. 3.25 (ISBN 0-373-45020-6, Pub. by Worldwide). Harlequin Bks.

--Proud Surrender. (Super Romances Ser.). 384p. 1983. pap. 2.95 (ISBN 0-373-70056-3, Pub. by Worldwide). Harlequin Bks.

Douglas, Charles H. Basic Music Theory. McKenzie, Wesley M., ed. 1970. pap. 3.45 (ISBN 0-910842-01-9, GE11, Pub. by GWM). Kjos.

Douglas, Colin. The Intern's Tale. LC 82-47995. 192p. 1982. pap. 7.95 (ISBN 0-394-17996-X, E831, Ever). Grove.

Douglas, D. M. Surgical Departments in Hospitals: The Surgeon's View. 1972. 8.95 o.p. (ISBN 0-407-40340-X). Butterworth.

Douglas, David. English Scholars, Sixteen Sixty to Seventeen Thirty. LC 75-3865. (Illus.). 291p. 1975. Repr. of 1951 ed. lib. bdg. 18.00x (ISBN 0-8371-8093-7, DOES). Greenwood.

Douglas, David C. The Norman Achievement: 1050-1100. LC 74-88028. 1969. 30.00x (ISBN 0-520-01383-2). U of Cal Pr.

--The Norman Fate, 1100-1154. LC 75-13155. 350p. 1976. 40.00x (ISBN 0-520-03027-3). U of Cal Pr.

--William the Conqueror: The Norman Impact upon England. (English Monarchs Ser.). 1964. 33.00x (ISBN 0-520-00348-9); pap. 5.95 (ISBN 0-520-00350-0, CAL131). U of Cal Pr.

Douglas, Donald, jt. auth. see Gaddie, Ronald E.

Douglas, Eileen. Eileen Douglas's New York Inflation Fighters' Guide. LC 82-20378. (Illus.). 256p. (Orig.). 1983. pap. 5.95 (ISBN 0-688-01851-3). Quill NY.

Douglas, Ellen. A Lifetime Burning. 224p. 1982. 13.95 (ISBN 0-394-52719-4). Random.

Douglas, Erika, ed. The Family Circle Hints Book. 1982. 12.95 (ISBN 0-8129-1016-8). Times Bks.

Douglas, Evan J. Intermediate Microeconomic Analysis: Theory & Applications. (Illus.). 576p. 1982. text ed. 24.95 (ISBN 0-13-470708-7). P-H.

--Managerial Economics: Theory, Practice & Problems. (Illus.). 1979. ref. ed. 24.95 (ISBN 0-13-550236-5). P-H.

Douglas, F. C. Land-Value Rating. 76p. 1961. pap. 1.00 (ISBN 0-911312-60-9). Schalkenbach.

Douglas, G., jt. auth. see Doise, W.

Douglas, George A. Writing for Public Relations. (Marketing & Management Ser.). 192p. 1980. pap. text ed. 11.95 (ISBN 0-675-08171-8). Merrill.

Douglas, Gilean. Silence Is My Homeland. LC 78-2324. (Illus.). 192p. 1978. 8.95 (ISBN 0-8117-1521-3). Stackpole.

Douglas, Gina. The Ganges. LC 78-62983. (Rivers of the World Ser.). (Illus.). 1978. PLB 12.68 (ISBN 0-382-06205-1). Silver.

Douglas, Harriet C. Handweaver's Instruction Manual. LC 76-24020. (Shuttle Craft Guild Monograph: No. 34). (Illus.). 41p. 1949. pap. 8.45 (ISBN 0-916658-30-9). HTH Pubs.

Douglas, I. J. Audit & Control of Mini & Microcomputers. 112p. 1982. pap. 22.50x (ISBN 0-85012-368-2). Intl Pubns Serv.

Douglas, Ian. Humid Landforms. (Illus.). 1977. text ed. 17.50x (ISBN 0-262-04054-9). Mit Pr.

Douglas, J. Construction Equipment Policy. 1975. text ed. 28.95 (ISBN 0-07-017658-2); instr's manual avail. (ISBN 0-07-017659-0). McGraw.

Douglas, J. D., ed. The New Bible Dictionary. 1344p. 1982. 24.95 (ISBN 0-8423-4667-8). Tyndale.

Douglas, J. D. & Johnson, J. M., eds. Existential Sociology. LC 76-47198. 1977. 39.50 (ISBN 0-521-21515-3); pap. 13.95 (ISBN 0-521-29225-5). Cambridge U Pr.

Douglas, Jack. Going Nuts in Brazil with Jack Douglas. 1977. 7.95 o.p. (ISBN 0-399-11838-1). Putnam Pub Group.

--Rubber Duck. LC 78-21247. 1979. 9.95 o.p. (ISBN 0-399-12176-5). Putnam Pub Group.

Douglas, Jack D. Observations of Deviance. 350p. 1981. pap. text ed. 11.75 (ISBN 0-8191-1819-2). U Pr of Amer.

Douglas, Jack D. & Johnson, John M., eds. Official Deviance: Readings in Malfeasance, Misfeasance, & Other Forms of Corruption. LC 77-5715. 1977. pap. text ed. 10.50 scp o.p. (ISBN 0-397-47361-3, HarpC). Har-Row.

Douglas, James. Construction Equipment Policy. (Construction Engineering Ser.). (Illus.). 320p. 1975. text ed. 21.00 o.p. (ISBN 0-07-017658-2, C); solutions manual avail. o.p. (ISBN 0-07-017659-0). McGraw.

--Gundog Training. (Illus.). 144p. 1983. 17.50 (ISBN 0-7153-8336-1). David & Charles.

--The Savages. (Irish Play Ser.). 6.95x (ISBN 0-912262-60-5); pap. 2.95x (ISBN 0-912262-61-3). Proscenium.

Douglas, James, et al. Modern Construction & Development Forms. 2nd ed. 1983. 56.00 (ISBN 0-88262-775-9). Warren.

Douglas, James McM. Drag Race Driver. (Putnam Sports Shelf). (gr. 5 up). 1971. PLB 6.29 o.p. (ISBN 0-399-60138-4). Putnam Pub Group.

--Hunger for Racing. (Putnam Sports Shelf). (Illus.). (gr. 7-10). 1967. PLB 4.97 o.p. (ISBN 0-399-60271-2). Putnam Pub Group.

Douglas, Jeannine G. Don't Drown in the Mainstream: Unexpurgated Edition. 66p. (Orig.). 1981. pap. text ed. 4.95 (ISBN 0-9607872-0-8). Vail Pub.

Douglas, Jim. Santa Fe Cookery: Traditional New Mexican Recipes. 1982. 8.95 (ISBN 0-385-27753-9). Dial.

Douglas, John. H. M. S. Ganges. 1980. 15.00x o.p. (ISBN 0-906418-00-3, Pub. by Roundwood). State Mutual Bk.

Douglas, John, jt. auth. see Massie, Joseph L.

Douglas, Johnson E. Successful Seed Programs: A Planning & Management Guide. (IADS Development - Oriented Literature Ser.). 353p. 1980. lib. bdg. 26.25 (ISBN 0-89158-793-4). Westview.

Douglas, Kate. Captive of the Heart. 1982. pap. 2.75 (ISBN 0-380-81125-1, 81125-1). Avon.

Douglas, Lewis W. The Liberal Tradition: A Free People & a Free Economy. LC 77-171382. (FDR & the Era of the New Deal Ser). 136p. 1972. Repr. of 1935 ed. lib. bdg. 19.50 (ISBN 0-306-70376-9). Da Capo.

Douglas, Linda. Painting & Drawing. LC 80-53611. (Whizz Kids Ser.). 8.00 (ISBN 0-382-06461-5). Silver.

Douglas, Lloyd V., et al. Teaching Business Subjects. 3rd ed. (Illus.). 1973. ref. ed. 26.95 (ISBN 0-13-891457-5). P-H.

Douglas, Martha C. Go for It: How to Get Your First Good Job. LC 79-16211. (Illus.). 1979. pap. 5.95 o.p. (ISBN 0-87701-154-0). Chronicle Bks.

--Go For It! How to Get Your First Good Job. 208p. (Orig.). (gr. 9 up). 1983. pap. 5.95 (ISBN 0-89815-090-6). Ten Speed Pr.

Douglas, Mary. Natural Symbols: Explorations in Cosmology. 1972. pap. 5.95 (ISBN 0-394-71105-X, VG42, Vin). Random.

Douglas, Mary & Tipton, Steven M., eds. Religion & America: Spirituality in a Secular Age. LC 82-72500. 256p. 1983. 13.94 (ISBN 0-8070-1106-1); pap. 8.61 (ISBN 0-8070-1107-X). Beacon Pr.

Douglas, Mary A. The Secretarial Dental Assistant. LC 75-19522. 1976. pap. 12.00 (ISBN 0-8273-0349-1); instr.'s guide 2.75 (ISBN 0-8273-0350-5). Delmar.

Douglas, Mary L., jt. auth. see Bates, Frank.

Douglas, Mary P. Pupil Assistant in the School Library. LC 57-9534. 1957. pap. 4.00 (ISBN 0-8389-0050-X). ALA.

Douglas, Mike. My Story. LC 78-2694. (Illus.). 1978. 10.00 o.p. (ISBN 0-399-11963-9). Putnam Pub Group.

Douglas, Nik. Tibetan Tantric Charms & Amulets. LC 77-70855. (Illus.). 1978. pap. 10.00 o.p. (ISBN 0-486-23589-0). Dover.

--Tibetan Tantric Charms & Amulets: 230 Examples Reproduced from Original Woodblocks. (Illus.). 17.50 (ISBN 0-8446-5749-2). Peter Smith.

Douglas, Nik, ed. see Bhattacharyya, Bhaskar.

Douglas, Norman. London Street Games. 2nd ed. LC 68-31089. 1968. Repr. of 1931 ed. 30.00x (ISBN 0-8103-3477-1). Gale.

--South Wind. 416p. 1982. pap. 5.95 (ISBN 0-486-24361-3). Dover.

Douglas, Paul H. Social Security in the United States. LC 75-136527. 384p. 1972. Repr. of 1936 ed. lib. bdg. 17.50x (ISBN 0-8371-5448-0, DOSS). Greenwood.

--Social Security in the United States: An Analysis & Appraisal of the Federal Social Security Act. 2nd ed. LC 70-167847. (FDR & the Era of the New Deal). 1971. Repr. of 1939 ed. lib. bdg. 55.00 (ISBN 0-306-70323-8). Da Capo.

Douglas, Peter. The Ideal Home Book of Interiors. 128p. 1983. pap. 9.95 (ISBN 0-7137-1327-5, Pub. by Blandford Pr England). Sterling.

Douglas, Peter, jt. auth. see Walsh, Barry.

Douglas, Ronald M. The Irish Book: A Miscellany of Facts & Fancies, Folklore & Fragments, Poems & Prose to Do with Ireland & Her People. LC 74-164227. xxvi, 393p. 1972. Repr. of 1936 ed. 34.00 o.p. (ISBN 0-8103-3166-7). Gale.

Douglas, Roy. Advent of War, Nineteen Thirty-Nine to Nineteen Forty. LC 78-12266. 1979. 22.50 (ISBN 0-312-00650-0). St Martin.

--In the Year of Munich. LC 77-82823. (Illus.). 1978. 25.00 (ISBN 0-312-41179-0). St Martin.

--Land, People & Politics. LC 75-32929. 250p. 1976. text ed. 17.95 o.p. (ISBN 0-312-46480-0). St Martin.

--Nineteen Thirty-Nine: A Retrospect Forty Years After. 101p. 1983. 19.50 (ISBN 0-208-02020-9, Archon Bks). Shoe String.

Douglas, S. W. & Williamson, H. D. Principles of Veterinary Radiography. 3rd ed. (Illus.). 296p. 1980. text ed. 37.50 o.p. (ISBN 0-8121-0757-8). Lea & Febiger.

Douglas, Stephan A. & PeDerson, Paul. Blood, Believer, & Brother: The Development of Voluntary Associations in Malaysia. LC 73-620255. (Illus.). 1973. pap. 4.50x o.s.i. (ISBN 0-89680-017-2, Ohio U Ctr Intl). Ohio U Pr.

Douglas, Stephen, jt. auth. see Lincoln, Abraham.

Douglas, Susan P. & Craig, C. Samuel. International Marketing Research. 384p. 1983. 24.95 (ISBN 0-13-473132-8). P-H.

Douglas, Tom. Group Processes in Social Work: A Theoretical Synthesis. LC 78-8401. 1979. 37.95x (ISBN 0-471-99676-9, Pub. by Wiley-Interscience). Wiley.

Douglas, William O. The Anatomy of Liberty. pap. 1.95 o.p. (ISBN 0-671-03281-X, Touchstone Bks). S&S.

--Go East, Young Man. 544p. 1975. pap. 4.25 o.s.i. (ISBN 0-440-54521-8, Delta). Dell.

--Go East, Young Man: The Early Years. LC 81-4196. (Illus.). 544p. pap. 7.95 (ISBN 0-394-71165-3, Vin). Random.

--A Living Bill of a Rights. 72p. pap. 0.75 (ISBN 0-686-95045-3). ADL.

--Points of Rebellion. LC 79-107197. 1970. pap. 7.95 (ISBN 0-394-44068-4, V603, Vin). Random.

Douglas, Winsome. Discovering Embroidery. (Illus.). 1973. 4.95 o.p. (ISBN 0-263-69981-1). Transatlantic.

Douglas-Home, William & Muggeridge, Malcolm. P. G. Wodehouse: Three Talks & a Few Words at a Festive Occasion. (Wodehouse Monograph Ser.: No. 4). 48p. (Orig.). 1983. pap. 16.50 limited ed. (ISBN 0-87008-103-9). Heineman.

Douglas Jackson, W. A., jt. auth. see Creed, Virginia.

Douglas-Morris, K. J., jt. auth. see Perkins, Roger.

Douglass, A. E. Climatic Cycle & Tree Growth, 3 vols. in one. (Vols. 1 & 2, A Study of the Annual Rings of Trees in Relation to Climate & Solar Activity; Vol. 3, A Study of Cycles). 1971. 60.00 (ISBN 3-7682-0720-X). Lubrecht & Cramer.

Douglass, Amanda H. The Heavens Blaze Forth. (Inflation Fighters Ser.). 192p. 1982. pap. cancelled o.s.i. (ISBN 0-8439-1136-0, Leisure Bks). Nordon Pubns.

Douglass, Barbara. Skateboard Scramble. LC 78-12480. (Illus.). (gr. 3-6). 1979. 8.95 (ISBN 0-664-32641-2). Westminster.

Douglass, David & Krieger, Joel. A Miner's Life. 116p. (Orig.). 1983. pap. 8.95 (ISBN 0-7100-9473-6). Routledge & Kegan.

Douglass, E. P. Rebels & Democrats. LC 77-160853. (Era of the American Revolution Ser.). 368p. 1971. Repr. of 1955 ed. 45.00 (ISBN 0-306-70402-1). Da Capo.

Douglass, Ellsworth. Pharaoh's Broker. (Science Fiction Ser.). 336p. 1976. Repr. of 1899 ed. lib. bdg. 15.00 o.p. (ISBN 0-8398-2342-8, Gregg). G K Hall.

Douglass, Frederick. Frederick Douglass: The Narrative & Selected Writings. 1981. pap. 4.95 (ISBN 0-686-38904-2, Mod LibC). Modern Lib.

--Life & Times of Frederick Douglass: The Complete Autobiography. 1962. pap. 8.95 (ISBN 0-02-002350-2, Collier). Macmillan.

--The Life & Writings of Frederick Douglass: Supplementary Volume: 1844-1860, Vol. 5. Foner, Philip S., ed. 1975. 15.00 o.p. (ISBN 0-7178-0453-4); pap. 5.95 o.p. (ISBN 0-7178-0454-2). Intl Pub Co.

--My Bondage & My Freedom. (Black Rediscovery Ser). 1969. pap. 6.50 (ISBN 0-486-22457-0). Dover.

--Narrative of the Life of Frederick Douglass, an American Slave. (RL 7). 1968. pap. 1.95 (ISBN 0-451-12191-0, AJ2191, Sig). NAL.

Douglass, Gordon K. The New Interdependence: The European Community & the United States. LC 79-5121. 160p. 1979. 19.95x (ISBN 0-669-03203-4). Lexington Bks.

Douglass, Herb, jt. auth. see Walton, Lew.

Douglass, J. H., et al. Units in Woodworking. LC 79-8737. (Industrial Arts Ser.). 320p. 1981. text ed. 17.00 (ISBN 0-8273-1332-2); pap. text ed. 13.00 (ISBN 0-8273-1333-0); comprehensive tests 1.00 (ISBN 0-8273-1335-7); instr's guide 2.50 (ISBN 0-8273-1334-9). Delmar.

Douglass, J. Harvey. Projects in Wood Furniture. rev. ed. LC 67-21721. (Illus.). (gr. 7 up). 1967. text ed. 16.64 (ISBN 0-87345-027-2). McKnight.

Douglass, Judy D. Old Maid Is a Dirty Word. LC 77-74149. (Illus.). 1977. pap. 1.95 o.p. (ISBN 0-918956-37-4). Campus Crusade.

Douglass, Leslie S. Women in Business: How to Make Yourself Marketable. (Illus.). 192p. 1980. 10.95 (ISBN 0-13-962019-2, Spec); pap. 4.95 (ISBN 0-13-962001-X). P-H.

Douglass, Malcolm P., ed. Writing & Reading in a Balanced Curriculum. (Claremont Reading Conference Yearbook Ser.). 222p. (Orig.). 1982. pap. 11.00 (ISBN 0-941742-00-8). Claremont Grad.

Douglass, Paul. Guide to Planning the Farm Estate: With Checklists & Forms. 2nd ed. (IBP Ser. in Estate Planning & Administration). 1979. text ed. 39.50 o.p. (ISBN 0-87624-172-0). Inst Busn Plan.

Douglass, Ralph. Calligraphic Lettering. 3rd ed. 1975. 12.95 (ISBN 0-8230-0551-8); spiral avail. Watson-Guptill.

Douglass, William A. & Etulain, Richard W., eds. Basque Americans: A Guide to Information Sources. (Ethnic Studies Information Guide Ser.: Vol. 6). 175p. 1981. 42.00x (ISBN 0-8103-1469-X). Gale.

Douglass, William C. & Walker, Morton. DMSO: The New Healing Power. (Illus.). 1983. 14.95 (ISBN 0-8159-5315-1). Devin.

Douglass, William S. Echalar & Murelaga: Opportunity & Rural Exodus in Two Spanish Basque Villages. LC 74-28932. 200p. 1975. 26.00 (ISBN 0-312-22540-7). St Martin.

Douglas-Wilson, J. & McLachlan, Gordon, eds. Health Service Prospects: An International Survey. 358p. 1973. 35.00x (ISBN 0-686-96986-3, Pub. by Nuffield England). State Mutual Bk.

Douglis, Philip N. Pictures for Organizations. LC 82-60042. (Communications Library). (Illus.). 233p. (Orig.). 1982. pap. 35.00 (ISBN 0-931368-10-3). Ragan Comm.

Douhait, Rudolph D. The Political Chaos of the World & the Violent Leadership Role of Communist Russia. (Illus.). 127p. 1983. 67.45 (ISBN 0-86722-033-3). Inst Econ Pol.

Douillard, Jeanne & Snow, Suzanne. Chasons de Chez-Nous. (Illus.). 61p. (Fr., Music). (gr. k-6). 1978. pap. text ed. 1.00x (ISBN 0-911409-01-7). Natl Mat Dev.

Doukhan, Jacques B. The Genesis Creation Story: Its Literary Structure. (Andrews University Seminary Doctoral Dissertation Ser.: Vol. 5). xii, 303p. 1982. pap. 8.95 (ISBN 0-943872-37-5). Andrews Univ Pr.

Doulis, Thomas. Disaster & Fiction: The Impact of the Asia Minor Disaster of 1922 on Modern Greek Fiction. LC 75-22654. 1977. 27.50x (ISBN 0-520-03112-1). U of Cal Pr.

--George Theotokas. (World Authors Ser.). 1975. lib. bdg. 15.95 (ISBN 0-8057-2881-3, Twayne). G K Hall.

Doull, John, et al, eds. Casarett & Doull's Toxicology. 2nd ed. LC 79-18632. (Illus.). 1980. text ed. 36.00x (ISBN 0-02-330040-X). Macmillan.

Doumanis, Mariella, ed. Mothering in Greece: Behavioral Development. Date not set. price not set. Acad Pr.

Doumas, Christon G. Thera: Pompeii of the Ancient Aegean. (New Aspects of Antiquity Ser.). (Illus.). 1983. 29.95 (ISBN 0-500-39016-9). Thames Hudson.

Doumato, Lamia, ed. American Drawing: A Guide to Information Sources. LC 79-63743. (Art & Architecture Information Guide Ser.: Vol. 11). 1979. 42.00x (ISBN 0-8103-1441-X). Gale.

Doumergu, Emil. Saudi Arabia & the Explosion of Terrorism in the Middle East. (The Great Currents of History Library Book). (Illus.). 137p. 1983. 77.85 (ISBN 0-86722-016-3). Inst Econ Pol.

Doupnik, Joseph, jt. auth. see Banks, Peter M.

Doursther, H. Dictionnaire Universel Des Poeds et Mesures Anciens et Modernes, Contenant Des Ables Des Monnaies De Tous les Pays. (Fr.). 1840. pap. text ed. 42.25x o.p. (ISBN 90-6041-012-2). Humanities.

Douskou, Iris. Athens: The City & It's Museums. (Athenon Illustrated Guides Ser.). (Illus.). 112p. 1983. pap. 14.00 (ISBN 0-88332-313-3, Pub. by Ekdotike Athenon Greece). Larousse.

Doust, W. A. Salvage Adventures in Turkey. 1979. 7.95 o.p. (ISBN 0-533-04085-X). Vantage.

Douthit, Nathan. The Coos Bay Region, 1890-1944: Life on a Coastal Frontier. Rev. ed. (Illus.). 190p. 1982. pap. 10.95 (ISBN 0-9607192-0-2); 16.95. River W Bks.

Douthitt, C. B. & McMillan, J. A. Trigonometry. 1977. text ed. 15.00 (ISBN 0-07-017670-1); solns. manual avail. (ISBN 0-07-017671-X). McGraw.

Douthwaite, Graham. Jury Instructions on Damages in Tort Actions. 1981. text ed. 37.50 (ISBN 0-87473-137-2). A Smith Co.

Douty, Agnes M., jt. auth. see Cook, Alice H.

Douty, Esther M. The Brave Balloonists: America's First Airmen. LC 73-19642. (How They Lived Ser.). (Illus.). 96p. (gr. 3-6). 1969. PLB 7.12 (ISBN 0-8116-6926-2). Garrard.

Douvan, Elizabeth & Gold, Martin. The Individual & Social Environment: An Integration of Social Psychology. cancelled o.s.i. (ISBN 0-88410-360-9). Ballinger Pub.

Douwes, Klaas. Grondig ondersoeck van de Toonen der Musyk. (Early Music Theory in the Low Countries Ser.: Vol. 2). 1971. Repr. of 1699 ed. wrappers 25.00 o.s.i. (ISBN 90-6027-142-4, Pub. by Frits Knuf Netherlands). Pendragon NY.

Dove, Jack. The Audio-Visual. 304p. 1975. 22.50 (ISBN 0-233-96643-9, 05779-7, Pub. by Gower Pub Co England). Lexington Bks.

--McColvin & Reeves' Music Libraries, 2 Vols. rev. ed. 1965. Vol. I, 176 p. 15.00 (ISBN 0-233-95769-3, 05782-0, Pub. by Gower Pub Co England); Vol. II, 744 p. 31.50 (ISBN 0-233-95768-5, 05781-9). Lexington Bks.

Dove, Patricia, ed. This is Salt Lake City. (Illus.). 224p. (Orig.). 1981. pap. 5.95 (ISBN 0-686-36856-8). Ram Pub Inc.

Dover Editorial Staff, ed. see Cirker, Hayward & Cirker, Blanche.

Dover, G. A. & Flavell, R. B., eds. Genome Evolution. (Systematics Association Ser.: Vol. 20). 388p. 1982. 33.50 (ISBN 0-12-221380-7); pap. 17.50 (ISBN 0-12-221382-3). Acad Pr.

Dover, K. J. Greek Popular Morality in the Time of Plato & Aristotle. LC 73-94451. 1975. 33.00x (ISBN 0-520-02721-3). U of Cal Pr.

--Lysias & the Corpus Lysiacum. LC 68-63337. (Sather Classical Lectures: No. 39). 1968. 31.50x (ISBN 0-520-00351-9). U of Cal Pr.

Dover, K. J., ed. see Plato.

Dover, K. J., ed. see Theocritus.

Dovey, D. M., et al. Heat Treatment of Metals. 1963. 7.50 o.p. (ISBN 0-201-01609-5, Adv Bk Prog). A-W.

Dow, Allen. The Official Guide to Ballroom Dancing. LC 79-55239. (Illus.). 96p. 1980. 5.98 o.p. (ISBN 0-89196-065-1, Domus Bks). Quality Bks IL.

--The Official Guide to Jazz Dancing. LC 79-55238. (Illus.). 96p. 1980. 5.98 o.p. (ISBN 0-89196-064-3, Domus Bks). Quality Bks IL.

--The Official Guide to Latin Dancing. LC 79-55240. (Illus.). 96p. 1980. 5.98 o.p. (ISBN 0-89196-067-8, Domus Bks). Quality Bks IL.

Dow, Charles H. Scientific Stock Speculation. 101p. 1971. 7.50 o.s.i. (ISBN 0-685-25835-1). Windsor.

Dow, Clista. Lunchroom Waste: A Study of "How Much & How Come". Smith, Linda H., ed. 1978. pap. 4.95 (ISBN 0-936386-04-5). Creative Learning.

Dow Education Systems. Basic Industrial Mathematics: A Text Workbook. 1972. text ed. 16.95 (ISBN 0-07-017660-4, G); ans. key 3.50 (ISBN 0-07-017661-2). McGraw.

Dow, Emily R. How to Make Doll Clothes. (Illus.). (gr. 5-8). 1953. 5.50 o.p. (ISBN 0-698-20064-0, Coward). Putnam Pub Group.

Dow, G. Steven. Your Aquarium - Your Vacation - Your Relocation. (Illus.). 64p. (Orig.). 1976. pap. 2.95 o.p. (ISBN 0-87666-456-7, M528). TFH Pubns.

Dow, George. The Great Central Eighteen Sixty Four to Eighteen Ninety Nine. 27.50x (ISBN 0-392-15442-0, SpS). Sportshelf.

Dow, George F. Arts & Crafts in New England. 1704-1775. LC 67-2035. (Architecture & Decorative Art Ser). (Illus.). 1967. Repr. of 1927 ed. lib. bdg. 35.00 (ISBN 0-306-70955-4). Da Capo.

Dow, Gwyneth, ed. Teacher Learning. (Routledge Education Bks.). 110p. 1982. pap. 12.95 (ISBN 0-7100-9020-X). Routledge & Kegan.

Dow, J. C. Management of the British Economy, 1940-56. LC 64-21542. (National Institute of Economic & Social Research Economic & Social Studies: No. 22). 1970. pap. 16.95x (ISBN 0-521-09467-4). Cambridge U Pr

Dow, James E. A Prussian Liberal: The Life of Eduard Von Simson. LC 81-40312. 226p. (Orig.). 1982. lib. bdg. 21.25 (ISBN 0-8191-1984-9); pap. text ed. 10.25 (ISBN 0-8191-1985-7). U Pr of Amer.

Dow, Paul E. Discretionary Justice: A Critical Inquiry. 304p. 1981. prof ref 30.00x (ISBN 0-88410-835-X). Ballinger Pub.

Dow, Philip, ed. Golden Gate Watershed: Nineteen American Poets. (Illus.). 400p. cloth 24.95 (ISBN 0-15-136418-4). HarBraceJ.

Dow, Phillip, ed. Golden Gate Watershed: Nineteen American Poets. 400p. pap. 10.95 (ISBN 0-15-636101-9, Harv). HarBraceJ.

Dow, Roger W. Business English. LC 78-18253. 451p. 1979. 17.95 (ISBN 0-471-36661-7); wkbk. 8.95 (ISBN 0-471-04959-X); avail. tchrs. manual (ISBN 0-471-05251-5). Wiley.

Dow, Sheila C. & Earl, Peter E. Money Matters: A Keynesian Approach to Monetary Economics. LC 82-11380. 280p. 1982. text ed. 28.50x (ISBN 0-389-20323-8). B&N Imports.

Dow, Steven. Breeding Angelfish for the Hobbyist & Professional. LC 76-1982. 1976. 5.95 (ISBN 0-915096-04-8). Palmetto Pub.

--Success with Corydoras Catfish. LC 77-2814. (Pet Reference Ser.: No. 4). (Illus.). 90p. 1977. pap. 5.95 (ISBN 0-915096-05-6). Palmetto Pub.

Dowben, Robert M. & Shay, Jerry W., eds. Cell & Muscle Motility, Vol. 3. 295p. 1983. 39.50x (ISBN 0-306-41157-1, Plenum Pr). Plenum Pub.

Dowbenko, George. Homegrown Holography. LC 76-16450. (Illus.). 1978. 13.95 o.p. (ISBN 0-8174-2113-0, Amphoto); pap. 8.95 o.p. (ISBN 0-8174-2406-7). Watson-Guptill.

Dowbenko, Uri. Marijuana Double-Take. 2nd ed. 64p. (Orig.). 1982. pap. 3.95 (ISBN 0-686-36145-8). Sirius Pubns.

Dowd, Alton. Deep River. LC 76-56711. 1977. 9.95 (ISBN 0-87716-074-0, Pub. by Moore Pub Co). F Apple.

Dowd, D. W., et al, eds. Medical, Moral & Legal Implications of Recent Medical Advances: A Symposium. LC 71-152124. (Symposia on Law & Society Ser). 1971. Repr. of 1968 ed. lib. bdg. 19.50 (ISBN 0-306-70128-6). Da Capo.

Dowd, E. Thomas. Leisure Counseling: Concepts & Applications. (Illus.). 392p. 1983. text ed. price not set (ISBN 0-398-04824-X). C C Thomas.

Dowd, J. E., jt. auth. see Glasunov, I. S.

Dowd, Merle E., jt. auth. see Call, Frances.

Dowd, Thomas, jt. auth. see Franks, Ronald.

Dowdall, Jim, jt. auth. see Bygrave, Mike.

Dowdell, D. Secrets of the ABCs. LC 65-22301. (Illus.). (gr. 2 up). 1968. PLB 6.75x (ISBN 0-87783-035-5). Oddo.

Dowdell, Dorothy. Hibiscus Lagoon. large type ed. LC 82-10336. 267p. 1982. Repr. of 1981 ed. 9.95 (ISBN 0-89621-379-X). Thorndike Pr.

--The Impossible Dream. (Candlelight Romance Ser.: No. 678). (Orig.). 1981. pap. 1.75 o.s.i. (ISBN 0-440-14177-X). Dell.

--The Impossible Dream. LC 82-16751. 286p. 1982. Repr. of 1981 ed. 9.95 (ISBN 0-89621-390-0). Thorndike Pr.

Dowden, Anne O. This Noble Harvest: A Chronicle of Herbs. LC 79-12021. (Illus.). 1979. 12.95 (ISBN 0-529-05548-1, Philomel). Putnam Pub Group.

Dowden, Wilfred S., ed. The Journal of Thomas Moore, Vol. 1. LC 79-13541. 400p. 1983. 50.00 (ISBN 0-87413-145-6). U Delaware Pr.

Dowdey, Clifford. Bugles Blow No More. LC 37-27301. 1971. Repr. of 1937 ed. 14.95 (ISBN 0-910220-07-7). Berg.

Dowdey, Landon G., ed. Journey to Freedom: A Casebook with Music. LC 82-71116. 106p. 1969. 7.95 (ISBN 0-8040-0174-X); pap. 4.50x (ISBN 0-8040-0175-8). Swallow.

Dowdney, Donna, ed. see Conner, Terri & Sanderson, Joyce.

Dowdy, Mac. The Book of Ely. 1981. 39.50x o.p. (ISBN 0-86023-117-8, Pub. by Barracuda England). State Mutual Bk.

Dowell, Arlene T. AACR 2 Headings: A Five-Year Projection of Their Impact on Catalogs. (Research Studies in Library Science: No. 17). 180p. 1982. lib. bdg. 22.50 (ISBN 0-87287-330-7). Libs Unl.
--Cataloging with Copy: A Decision-Makers Handbook. LC 76-1844. (Illus.). 295p. 1976. lib. bdg. 22.50 (ISBN 0-87287-153-3). Libs Unl.
Dowell, Arlene T., ed. see Frost, Carolyn O.
Dowell, Coleman. White on Black on White. 224p. 1983. 14.95 (ISBN 0-88150-000-3). Countryman.
Dowell, Eldridge F. History of Criminal Syndicalism Legislation in the United States. LC 73-87517. (American History, Politics & Law Ser.). 1969. Repr. of 1939 ed. lib. bdg. 25.00 (ISBN 0-306-71426-4). Da Capo.
Dowell, Linus. Didactic Strategies in Physical Education. (Illus.). 232p. (Orig.). 1980. pap. text ed. 9.95x (ISBN 0-89641-047-1). American Pr.
--Principles of Mechanical Kinesiology. 506p. 1982. pap. text ed. 20.95x (ISBN 0-89641-109-5). American Pr.
Dowell, Paul W., jt. auth. see Kirkland, James W.
Dowell, Richard W., jt. auth. see Pizer, Donald.
Dowell, Stephen. History of Taxation & Taxes in England, 4 Vols. 2nd ed. LC 67-5737. Repr. of 1884 ed. 115.00x (ISBN 0-678-05167-4). Kelley.
Dowell, Susan S., jt. auth. see Kitching, Frances.
Dowing, David & Herman, Gary. Jane Fonda. (Illus.). 1980. pap. 5.95 (ISBN 0-8256-3944-1, Quick Fox). Putnam Pub Group.
Dowland, Robert. Varietie of Lute Lessons. Hunt, Edgar, ed. 1958. 24.00 (ISBN 0-901938-45-9, 75-A10441). Eur-Am Music.
Dowler, Wayne. Dostoevsky, Grigor'ev, & Native Soil Conservatism. 240p. 1982. 27.50x (ISBN 0-8020-5604-0). U of Toronto Pr.
Dowley, Tim. Eerdmans' Handbook to the History of Christianity. LC 77-5616. 1977. 24.95 (ISBN 0-8028-3450-7). Eerdmans.
--J. S. Bach: His Life & Times. expanded ed. (Life & Times Ser.). (Illus.). 192p. 1981. 12.95 (ISBN 0-87666-584-9, Z-53). Paganiniana Pubns.
--Mick Jagger & the Stones. (Illus.). 128p. (gr. 6 up). 1983. pap. 9.95 (ISBN 0-88254-734-8). Hippocrene Bks.
Dowley, Timothy. Bach: His Life & Times. (Midas-Composer Life & Times Ser.). (Illus.). 144p. 1983. 16.95 (ISBN 0-85936-145-4, Pub. by Midas Bks England). Hippocrene Bks.
Dowlin, Kenneth E. The Electronic Library: The Promise & the Process. (Applications in Information Management & Technology Ser.). (Illus.). 225p. lib. bdg. 24.95 (ISBN 0-918212-75-8). Neal-Schuman.
Dowlin, Seward T. Schaum's Outline of Mathematics for Economists. (Illus., Orig.). 1979. pap. 8.95 (ISBN 0-07-017760-0, SP). McGraw.
Dowling, Ann & Williams, John e. Sound & Sources of Sound. LC 82-15687. 260p. 1983. 59.95 (ISBN 0-470-27370-4); pap. 29.95 (ISBN 0-470-27388-7). Halsted Pr.
Dowling, Barbara T. & McDougal, Marianne. Business Concepts for English Practice. 192p. 1982. pap. text ed. 10.95 (ISBN 0-88377-240-X); 3.50. Newbury Hse.
Dowling, Edward T., jt. auth. see Salvatore, Dominick.
Dowling, Jerry L. Criminal Investigation. (HBJ Criminal Justice Ser.). 219p. 1979. pap. text ed. 9.95 o.p. (ISBN 0-15-516090-7, HC); instructor's manual avail. o.p. HarBraceJ.
--Teaching Materials on Criminal Procedure. (Criminal Justice Ser.). 1976. text ed. 19.95 o.s.i. (ISBN 0-8299-0616-9); pap. text ed. instrs.' manual avail. o.s.i. (ISBN 0-8299-0617-7). West Pub.
Dowling, John. Diego De Saavedra Fajardo. (World Authors Ser.). 1977. lib. bdg. 15.95 (ISBN 0-8057-6200-0, Twayne). G K Hall.
--Leandro Fernandez de Moratin. (World Authors Ser.: No. 149). lib. bdg. 15.95 (ISBN 0-8057-2630-6, Twayne). G K Hall.
Dowling, John E., jt. ed. see Cone, Richard A.
Dowling, M. & Glahe, F. R., eds. Readings in Econometric Theory. LC 79-128867. 1970. pap. 12.50 (ISBN 0-87081-004-9). Colo Assoc.
Dowling, R. H. & Hofmann, A. F. The Medical Treatment of Gallstones. 400p. 1982. text ed. write for info. (ISBN 0-85200-206-8, Pub. by MTP Pr England). Kluwer Boston.
Dowling, R. H., jt. auth. see Robinson, J. W.
Dowling, William F. & Sayles, Leonard R. How Managers Motivate. 1978. text ed. 23.95 (ISBN 0-07-017668-X, C); instructors' manual 15.00 (ISBN 0-07-017669-8). McGraw.
Down, C. G. & Stocks, J. Environmental Impact of Mining. LC 77-23129. 371p. 1977. 69.95x o.p. (ISBN 0-470-99086-4). Halsted Pr.
Down, Edith. What's to Eat? 1981. text ed. 13.16 (ISBN 0-87002-333-0); tchr's. ed. 7.96 (ISBN 0-87002-364-0). Bennett IL.
Downard, William L. The Cincinnati Brewing Industry: A Social & Economic History. LC 72-96398. (Illus.). 173p. 1973. 15.00 (ISBN 0-8214-0122-X, 82-81248). Ohio U Pr.
--Dictionary of the History of the American Brewing & Distilling Industries. LC 79-6826. (Illus.). xxv, 268p. 1980. lib. bdg. 45.00 (ISBN 0-313-21330-5, DOD/). Greenwood.
Downen, Robert, jt. auth. see Chiu, Hungdah.
Downer, Alan S., ed. see Sheridan, Richard B.
Downes, David L. Indoor Photography. (Photographer's Library). 168p. 1983. pap. 12.95 (ISBN 0-240-51115-8). Focal Pr.
Downes, Kerry. Hawksmoor. 2nd. ed. 1980. 60.00x (ISBN 0-262-04060-3). MIT Pr.
--Rubens. (Art Ser.). (Illus.). 288p. 1981. 29.50 o.s.i. (ISBN 0-906379-04-0, Pub. by Jupiter Bks England). Hippocrene Bks.
Downes, Olin, jt. auth. see Siegmeister, Elie.
Downes, Paul, ed. see Chronicle Guidance Publications, Inc.
Downey, Bill. Uncle Sam Must Be... Losing the War: Black Marines of the 51st. LC 82-5879. (Illus.). 224p. (Orig.). 1982. pap. 7.95 (ISBN 0-89407-050-9). Strawberry Hill.
Downey, Douglas W., ed. see Standard Educational Corporation.
Downey, Glanville. Constantinople in the Age of Justinian. (Centers of Civilization Ser.: No. 3). 1980. pap. 6.95 (ISBN 0-8061-1708-7). U of Okla Pr.
Downey, J., jt. auth. see Fisher, J.
Downey, Joan M., jt. auth. see Irvin, Judith L.
Downey, John C. & Kelly, James L. Biological Illustrations: Techniques & Exercises. (Illus.). 178p. 1982. pap. text ed. 11.75x (ISBN 0-8138-0201-6). Iowa St U Pr.
Downey, Matthew T., ed. Teaching American History: New Directions. LC 81-86080. 115p. (Orig.). 1982. pap. 7.25 (ISBN 0-87986-043-X). Coun Soc Studies.
Downey, Murray W. Books of Books, Vols. 1-7. Incl. Vol. 1. The Books of Moses. 64p. 1976. (ISBN 0-87509-054-0); Vol. 2. Historical Books. 73p. 1976. pap. text ed. (ISBN 0-87509-055-9); Vol. 3. The Poetical Books. 81p. 1976. pap. text ed. (ISBN 0-87509-056-7); The Major Prophets. 69p. 1976. pap. text ed. (ISBN 0-87509-057-5); Vol. 5. The Minor Prophets. 81p. 1976. pap. text ed. (ISBN 0-87509-058-3); Vol. 6. The Synoptic Gospels & Acts. 78p. 1978. pap. text ed. (ISBN 0-87509-059-1); Vol. 7. Pauline Epistle I. 65p. 1979. pap. text ed. (ISBN 0-87509-060-5). (Theological Education by Extension Ser.). pap. text ed. 2.75 ea. o.p. (ISBN 0-87509-053-2). Chr Pubns.
Downey, Robert J. & Roth, Jordan T. Baton Techniques for Officer Survival. (Illus.). 288p. 1983. pap. 29.75x spiral (ISBN 0-398-04781-2). C C Thomas.
Downey, Robert J. & Roth, Jordon T. Weapon Retention Techniques for Officer Survival. (Illus.). 120p. 1981. 17.50x (ISBN 0-398-04108-3). C C Thomas.
Downey, Susan B. The Excavations at Dura-Europos: The Stone & Plaster Sculpture (Final Report III, Part I, Fascicle 2) LC 77-88106. (Monumenta Archaeologica: No. 5). (Illus.). 1978. 46.00 (ISBN 0-917956-04-4). UCLA Arch.
Downey, W. David & Trocke, John K. Agribusiness Management. (Illus.). 480p. 1980. text ed. 23.00 (ISBN 0-07-017645-0, C); study guide 9.95 (ISBN 0-07-017646-9); study guide 8.95 (ISBN 0-07-017649-3). McGraw.
Downey, W. K., ed. Food Quality & Nutrition: Research Priorities for Thermal Processing. (Illus.). 1980. text ed. 63.75x (ISBN 0-85334-803-0, Pub. by Applied Sci England). Elsevier.
Downie, Freda. Plainsong. 1981. 11.50 (ISBN 0-436-13251-6, Pub. by Secker & Warburg). David & Charles.
Downie, J. A. Robert Harley & the Press. LC 78-67810. 1979. 39.50 (ISBN 0-521-22187-0). Cambridge U Pr.
Downie, Jill. Turn of the Century. 1982. pap. 3.50 (ISBN 0-380-80861-7, 80861). Avon.
Downie, John. High Fidelity. 48p. 1981. pap. 2.50 (ISBN 0-86212-002-0). Falling Wall.
--Mary Ann; an Elegy. 126p. 1981. pap. 5.95 (ISBN 0-86212-000-4). Falling Wall.
Downie, Leonard, Jr. The New Muckrakers. 1978. pap. 2.50 o.p. (ISBN 0-451-61628-6, ME1628, Ment). NAL.
--The New Muckrakers. LC 76-4832. 288p. 1976. 10.95 (ISBN 0-915220-13-X, 23039). New Republic.
Downie, N. M. & Heath, Robert W. Basic Statistical Methods. 4th ed. 1974. text ed. 23.50 scp o.p. (ISBN 0-06-042731-0, HarpC); scp study guide 8.50 o.p. (ISBN 0-06-042734-5). Har-Row.
--Basic Statistical Methods. 5th ed. 352p. 1983. text ed. 20.50 scp (ISBN 0-06-041728-5, HarpC); scp study guide 7.50 (ISBN 0-06-041723-4). Har-Row.
Downie, N. M., jt. auth. see Cottle, William C.
Downie, Norville M. Types of Test Scores. (Guidance Monograph). 1968. pap. 2.40 o.p. (ISBN 0-395-09926-9). HM.
Downie, Patricia A., ed. Cash's Textbook of Medical Conditions for Physiotherapists. 6th ed. (Illus.). 1979. pap. text ed. 13.75 o.p. (ISBN 0-686-77776-X, Lippincott Nursing). Lippincott.
--Cash's Textbook of Neurology for Physiotherapists. 3rd ed. 464p. 1981. pap. text ed. 17.00 (ISBN 0-397-58281-1, Lippincott Nursing). Lippincott.
Downie, R. S., et al. Education & Personal Relationships: A Philosophical Study. 184p. 1974. pap. 8.95x (ISBN 0-416-76210-7). Methuen Inc.
Downing, A. B., ed. Euthanasia & the Right to Death: The Case for Voluntary Euthanasia. (Contemporary Issues Ser.: No. 2). 1970. text ed. 18.00x (ISBN 0-391-00022-5). Humanities.
Downing, A. F. & Scully, V. J., Jr. Architectural Heritage of Newport, Rhode Island: 1640-1915. 2nd ed. (Illus.). 1967. 14.98 (ISBN 0-517-09719-2, C N Potter Bks). Crown.
Downing, Alfred. The Region of the Upper Columbia River & How I Saw it. 50p. 1980. 7.50 (ISBN 0-686-98303-3); pap. 4.95 (ISBN 0-87770-234-9). Ye Galleon.
Downing, Andrew J. Architecture of Country Houses. LC 68-16230. (Architecture & Decorative Art Ser). (Illus.). 1968. Repr. of 1850 ed. 45.00 (ISBN 0-306-71034-X). Da Capo.
--Rural Essays. Curtis, George W., ed. LC 69-13713. (Architecture & Decorative Art Ser.). 640p. 1975. Repr. of 1854 ed. lib. bdg. 45.00 (ISBN 0-306-71035-8). Da Capo.
Downing, David. Atlas of Territorial & Border Disputes. (Illus.). 121p. 1980. 13.50x (ISBN 0-450-04804-7). Intl Pubns Serv.
--The Devil's Virtuosos. (War Bks.). 280p. 1983. pap. 2.25 (ISBN 0-87216-609-0). Jove Pubns.
--The Devil's Virtuosos: German Generals at War, 1940-1945. LC 76-45770. 1977. 10.95 o.p. (ISBN 0-312-19862-0). St Martin.
--Robert Redford. (Illus.). 224p. 1983. pap. 11.95 (ISBN 0-312-68747-8). St Martin.
Downing, Douglas. Computer Programming the Easy Way. (Easy Way Ser.). 288p. 1983. pap. 6.95 (ISBN 0-8120-2626-8). Barron.
Downing, George D. Basic Marketing. LC 79-142984. 448p. 1971. 17.95x (ISBN 0-675-09233-7). Additional supplements may be obtained from publisher. Merrill.
--Professional Sales Management. LC 81-4694. (Grid Series in Marketing). 620p. 1983. text ed. 26.95 (ISBN 0-88244-235-5). Grid Pub.
Downing, Jim, jt. auth. see Bendt, Ingela.
Downing, Joan. Baseball Is Our Game. LC 82-4418. (Sports Primers Ser.). (Illus.). (gr. k-3). 1982. PLB 9.25g (ISBN 0-516-03402-2); pap. 2.95 (ISBN 0-516-43402-0). Childrens.
Downing, John. The Coast of Puget Sound: Its Processes & Development. (A Puget Sound Bk.). (Illus.). 150p. (Orig.). 1983. pap. 8.95 (ISBN 0-295-95944-4, Pub. by Wash Sea Grant). U of Wash Pr.
Downing, John & Leong, Che Kan. Psychology of Reading. 1982. text ed. 25.95 (ISBN 0-02-330020-5). Macmillan.
Downing, M. E. Landscape Construction. 1977. 25.00x (ISBN 0-419-10890-4, Pub. by E & FN Spon). Methuen Inc.
Downing, Niki. A Natural Talent & Other Stories. 1982. 13.00 o.p. (ISBN 0-533-05337-4). Vantage.
--The Wings of the Morning. 1983. 10.95 (ISBN 0-533-05581-4). Vantage.
Downing, Paul, ed. Cross-National Comparisons in Environmentals Protection. (Orig.). 1982. pap. 6.00 (ISBN 0-918592-57-7). Policy Studies.
Downing, Sybil, jt. auth. see Barker, Jane V.
Downing, Thomas. Thomas Downing Paintings Nineteen Sixty-Two to Nineteen Sixty-Seven. (Illus.). 24p. 1968. 3.00x (ISBN 0-686-99834-0). La Jolla Mus Contemp Art.
Downs, Anthony. No Vacancy: Rental Housing in the 1980's. 225p. 1983. 24.95 (ISBN 0-8157-1922-1); pap. 9.95 (ISBN 0-8157-1921-3). Brookings.
--Urban Problems & Prospects. 2nd ed. 1976. pap. 15.50 (ISBN 0-395-30590-X). HM.
Downs, Anthony, jt. auth. see Bradbury, Katharine L.
Downs, Anthony, jt. ed. see Bradbury, Katharine L.
Downs, Donald, jt. auth. see Veniard, John.
Downs, Fane & Flukinger, Roy. Abilene: An American Centennial. LC 82-60427. (Illus.). 104p. 1982. 24.50 (ISBN 0-292-70364-3, Pub. by R N Richardson Pr). U of Tex Pr.
Downs, Florence S. & Newman, Margaret A. A Sourcebook of Nursing Research. 3rd ed. (Illus.). 225p. Date not set. pap. price not set (ISBN 0-8036-2792-0). Davis Co.
Downs, Gary E. & Gerlovich, Jack A. Practical Science Safety for Elementary Teachers. (Illus.). 96p. 1982. pap. text ed. 8.50 (ISBN 0-8138-1641-6). Iowa St U PR.
Downs, Hugh. Thirty Dirty Lies About Old. (General Ser.). 1979. lib. bdg. 9.95 (ISBN 0-8161-6758-3, Large Print Bks). G K Hall.
Downs, Hugh & Roll, Richard J. Hugh Downs' The Best Years Book: How to Plan for Fulfillment, Security, & Happiness in the Retirement Years. 1981. 14.95 o.s.i. (ISBN 0-440-00693-7, E Friede). Delacorte.
Downs, James F. Cultures in Crisis. 2nd ed. 1975. pap. text ed. 10.95 (ISBN 0-02-472300-2, 47230). Macmillan.
Downs, James, Jr. Principles of Real Estate Management. 12th ed. Kirk, Nancye J., ed. LC 79-92870. (Illus.). 386p. 1980. lib. bdg. 21.95 (ISBN 0-912104-43-0). Inst Real Estate.
Downs, Kathy. My ABC Zoo Book. Mahany, Patricia, ed. (Happy Day Bks.). (Illus.). 24p. (ps-2). 1983. 1.29 (ISBN 0-87239-642-8, 3562). Standard Pub.
--My Book of Friends. Rev. ed. Miller, Marjorie, ed. (Illus.). 28p. (Orig.). (ps-3). Date not set. PLB 4.95 (ISBN 0-87239-557-X, 2882). Standard Pub. Postponed.
Downs, M., jt. auth. see Northern, Jerry L.
Downs, Michael. James Harrington. (English Authors Ser.). 1977. lib. bdg. 14.95 (ISBN 0-8057-6693-6, Twayne). G K Hall.
Downs, Robert B. American Library Resources: A Bibliographical Guide Supplement 1961-1970. LC 51-11156. 1972. text ed. 30.00 (ISBN 0-8389-0116-6). ALA.
--Books That Changed the World. 2nd ed. LC 78-13371. 1978. text ed. 20.00 (ISBN 0-8389-0270-7). ALA.
--Famous American Books. LC 72-172256. 394p. 1971. 16.95 (ISBN 0-07-017665-5, P&RB). McGraw.
--Famous Books: Great Writings in the History of Civilization. (Quality Paperback: No. 297). 278p. (Orig.). 1975. pap. 3.95 (ISBN 0-8226-0297-0). Littlefield.
--Friedrich Froebel. (World Leaders Ser.). 1978. lib. bdg. 13.95 (ISBN 0-8057-7668-0, Twayne). G K Hall.
--Heinrich Pestalozzi. (World Leaders Ser.). 1975. lib. bdg. 13.95 (ISBN 0-8057-3560-7, Twayne). G K Hall.
--Henry Barnard. LC 77-1775. (World Leaders Ser.). 1977. 12.95 (ISBN 0-8057-7710-5, Twayne). G K Hall.
--Horace Mann. (World Leaders Ser: No. 29). 1974. lib. bdg. 12.95 o.p. (ISBN 0-8057-3544-5, Twayne). G K Hall.
--In Search of New Horizons. LC 78-13656. 1978. text ed. 20.00 (ISBN 0-8389-0269-3). ALA.
--Landmarks in Science: Hippocrates to Carson. LC 82-154. 305p. 1982. lib. bdg. 23.50 (ISBN 0-87287-295-5). Libs Unl.
Downs, Robert B., ed. American Library Resources: A Bibliographical Guide Supplement, 1971-1980. 224p. 1981. text ed. 30.00 (ISBN 0-8389-0342-8). ALA.
--Bear Went Over the Mountain: Tall Tales of American Animals. LC 73-148835. 1971. Repr. of 1964 ed. 34.00x (ISBN 0-8103-3279-5). Gale.
Downs, Robert B., et al. Memorable Americans. 400p. 1983. lib. bdg. 23.50 (ISBN 0-87287-360-9). Libs Unl.
Downs, Robert C. Peoples. LC 73-10704. 1974. 6.95 o.p. (ISBN 0-672-51900-3). Bobbs.
Downs, T. Nelson. The Art of Magic. Hilliard, John N., ed. 352p. 1980. pap. 5.00 (ISBN 0-486-24005-3). Dover.
Dowrick, D. J. Earthquake Resistant Design: A Manual for Engineers. LC 76-26171. 1977. 67.95 (ISBN 0-471-99433-2, Pub. by Wiley-Interscience). Wiley.
Dowrick, F. E. Human Rights. 1979. text ed. 28.00x (ISBN 0-566-00281-7). Gower Pub Ltd.
Dowrick, Stephanie & Grundberg, Sibyl, eds. Why Children? LC 80-84688. 1981. 6.95 (ISBN 0-15-696362-0, Harv); pap. 6.95o.p. (ISBN 0-15-696362-0). Harbracej.
Dowse, R. E. & Hughes, J. A. Political Sociology. LC 76-39229. 457p. 1972. pap. 16.95x (ISBN 0-471-22146-5). Wiley.
Dowsett, B. O., jt. auth. see Chormack, D.
Dowsett, David J., jt. auth. see Ennis, Joseph T.
Dowsett, Dick. God, That's Not Fair. 1982. pap. 2.95 (ISBN 0-85363-148-4). OMF Bks.
Dowson, Duncan, jt. auth. see Hamrock, Bernard J.
Dowson, Ernest & Moore, Arthur. A Comedy of Masks. Fletcher, Ian & Stokes, John, eds. LC 76-20066. (Decadent Consciousness Ser.: Vol. 8). 1977. Repr. of 1896 ed. lib. bdg. 38.00 o.s.i. (ISBN 0-8240-2757-4). Garland Pub.
Dowson, John. A Classical Dictionary of Hindu Mythology & Religion, Geography, History & Literature. 11th ed. 28.00 (ISBN 0-7100-1302-7). Routledge & Kegan.
Doyle, A. Self-Sufficiency & Back to Basics Workbook. 60p. Date not set. 9.95 (ISBN 0-939476-81-9). Biblio Pr GA.
Doyle, A., ed. The Children's Index. LC 81-71747. 200p. (Orig.). 1982. pap. text ed. 21.95 (ISBN 0-939476-44-4). Biblio Pr GA.
--The Self Sufficiency & Back to Basics Index. LC 82-70238. 55p. (Orig.). 1982. pap. text ed. 9.95 (ISBN 0-939476-46-0). Biblio Pr GA.
Doyle, A. C. Fundraiser's Workbook: Based on Guide for Fundraisers. 8.95 (ISBN 0-939476-76-2). Biblio Pr GA.
--How to Be Your Own Publisher, Advertiser, Promoter, Etc. Date not set. 59.95 (ISBN 0-939476-19-3); pap. text ed. 49.95 (ISBN 0-939476-18-5). Biblio Pr GA.
--Recycling Workbook: Based on Recycling for Living, Fun & Profit. 50p. 1983. 8.95 (ISBN 0-939476-50-9). Biblio Pr GA.
--Self-Sufficiency Workbook. 50p. 1983. 10.95 (ISBN 0-939476-77-0). Biblio Pr GA.
--A Series of Suggestions. 300p. 1983. text ed. 75.00 (ISBN 0-939476-92-4). Biblio Pr GA.
--Survival Suggestions for Libraries. 1982. pap. 4.00 (ISBN 0-939476-48-7). Biblio Pr GA.
Doyle, A. C., ed. Single Source: A Bibliography for Singles. 75p. 1982. pap. 9.95 (ISBN 0-939476-71-1). Biblio Pr GA.
Doyle, A. Conan. A Duet with an Occasional Chorus. LC 80-67707. (Conan Doyle Centennial Ser.). (Illus.). 1983. 14.95 (ISBN 0-934468-48-6). Gaslight.

--The New Revelation. 122p. Date not set. pap. 5.00 (ISBN 0-89540-103-7, SB-103). Sun Pub.
--The Parasite. LC 80-67704. (Conan Doyle Centennial Ser.). (Illus.). 100p. cancelled (ISBN 0-934468-45-1). Gaslight.
--The Sherlock Holmes Illustrated Omnibus: The Complete Texts & Original Drawings of The Adventures of Sherlock Holmes, Memoirs of Sherlock Holmes, The Hound of the Baskervilles, & The Return of Sherlock Holmes. LC 75-37293. (Illus.). 704p. 1976. pap. 9.95 o.p. (ISBN 0-8052-0507-1). Schocken.
--Strange Studies from Life & Other Narratives: The Complete True Crime Writings of Sir Arthur Conan Doyle. (Conan Doyle Centennial Ser.). 96p. 1983. 11.95 (ISBN 0-934468-49-4). Gaslight.
--The Tragedy of the Korosko. LC 80-67706. (Conan Doyle Centennial Ser.). (Illus.). 202p. 1983. 11.95 (ISBN 0-934468-47-8). Gaslight.

Doyle, Alfreda. Guide for Fundraisers. 52p. 1981. pap. text ed. 7.95 (ISBN 0-939476-30-4). Biblio Pr GA.
--How to Make Simple Potpourri to Give as Gifts. 35p. 1983. pap. 7.95 (ISBN 0-939476-61-4). Biblio Pr GA.
--I Can, I Shall, I Will. 50p. 1983. pap. text ed. 8.95 (ISBN 0-939476-54-1). Biblio Pr GA.
--Just As It Was Given to Me. 50p. 1983. pap. text ed. 5.95 (ISBN 0-939476-55-X). Biblio Pr GA.
--Posie the Positive Train. Date not set. 6.95 (ISBN 0-939476-27-4); pap. 4.95 (ISBN 0-939476-28-2). Biblio Pr GA.
--Posie the Positive Train Workbook. 60p. 1983. 4.95 (ISBN 0-939476-63-0). Biblio Pr GA.
--Starting a Self Sufficiency Library; Suggested Places to Look for Used & Inexpensive Books. 25p. 1983. pap. text ed. 4.00 (ISBN 0-910811-32-6). Center Self.
--Suggestions for Types of Recycling Businesses. 50p. 1983. pap. text ed. 22.95 (ISBN 0-910811-34-2). Center Self.
--Unusual & Different Greeting Cards & Forms to Duplicate. 45p. 1983. pap. text ed. 9.95 (ISBN 0-939476-59-2). Biblio Pr GA.

Doyle, Alfreda, compiled by. Refrences on Prosperity. 35p. 1983. pap. 6.95 (ISBN 0-939476-62-2). Biblio Pr GA.

Doyle, Alfreda C. Business Recycling Suggestions. 26p. 1983. pap. text ed. 6.95 (ISBN 0-910811-24-5). Center Self.
--Creative Suggestions on Obtaining Company Benefits for a Small Business. 26p. 1983. pap. text ed. 6.95 (ISBN 0-910811-21-0). Center Self.
--Suggestions for Becoming Self Sufficient. 90p. 1983. pap. text ed. 15.95 (ISBN 0-910811-29-6). Center Self.
--Suggestions for Hunting Aluminum Cans & Other Aluminum. 26p. 1983. pap. text ed. 6.95 (ISBN 0-910811-26-1). Center Self.
--Suggestions for Making Money Addressing & Stuffing Envelopes Or How to Run a Small Letter Shop Service. 26p. 1983. pap. text ed. 9.95 (ISBN 0-910811-20-2). Center Self.
--Suggestions for Starting a Business from Businesses That Are Going Out of Business. 26p. 1983. pap. text ed. 16.95 (ISBN 0-910811-25-3). Center Self.
--Suggestions for Telemarketing Operations. 26p. 1983. pap. text ed. 6.95 (ISBN 0-910811-27-X). Center Self.
--Suggestions for Thrifty Ways to Legally Obtain Cashoffs Or Cents Off Coupons. 26p. 1983. pap. text ed. 6.95 (ISBN 0-910811-22-9). Center Self.
--Survival Suggestions for Libraries (Continued...) 25p. 1983. pap. 9.95 (ISBN 0-939476-93-2). Biblio Pr GA.
--Survival Suggestions for the Holidays & Other Gift Giving Occassions. 26p. 1983. pap. text ed. 6.95 (ISBN 0-910811-28-8). Center Self.
--Survival Suggestions for Urban Dwellers. 26p. 1983. pap. text ed. 6.95 (ISBN 0-910811-23-7). Center Self.

Doyle, Arthur C. Adventures of Sherlock Holmes. 1930. Repr. of 1892 ed. 12.45i (ISBN 0-06-011070-8, HarpT). Har-Row.
--Annotated Sherlock Holmes, 2 Vols. Baring-Gould, William S., ed. (Illus.). 1967. Set. 39.95 (ISBN 0-517-50291-7, C N Potter Bks). Crown.
--The Hound of the Baskervilles. (Oxford Progressive English Readers Ser.). (Illus.). (gr. k-6). 1973. pap. text ed. 3.50x (ISBN 0-19-638267-X). Oxford U Pr.

Doyle, Arthur C., as told to see Saffron, Robert.

Doyle, Arthur Conan. Complete Sherlock Holmes. LC 65-6074. 18.95 (ISBN 0-385-00689-6); two-volume edition 19.95 (ISBN 0-385-04591-3). Doubleday.
--Six Notable Adventures of Sherlock Holmes. (gr. 3 up). Date not set. price not set (ISBN 0-448-41101-6, G&D). Putnam Pub Group.

Doyle, Arthur Conan see Conan Doyle, Arthur.

Doyle, Barbara. Midnight Embrace. (Orig.). 1980. pap. 1.25 o.s.i. (ISBN 0-440-15132-5). Dell.

Doyle, Brendan & Fox, Matt. Meditations with TM Julian of Norwich. LC 82-73955. (Meditations with TM). (Illus.). 128p. (Orig.). 1982. pap. 6.95 (ISBN 0-939680-11-4). Bear & Co.

Doyle, Brian B. & Scheiber, Stephen C., eds. The Impaired Physician. 200p. 1983. 24.50x (ISBN 0-306-41081-8, Plenum Pr). Plenum Pub.

Doyle, Charles. James K. Baxter. (World Authors Ser.). 1976. lib. bdg. 15.95 (ISBN 0-8057-6227-2, Twayne). G K Hall.
--William Carlos Williams & the American Poem. LC 81-8925. 224p. 1982. 20.00x (ISBN 0-312-88064-2). St Martin.

Doyle, Conan. Adventure of the Speckled Band & Other Stories of Sherlock Holmes. (RL 6). pap. 1.95 (ISBN 0-451-51642-7, CJ1642, Sig Classics). NAL.

Doyle, Darrell J., jt. ed. see Segal, Harold.

Doyle, David N. & Edwards, Owen D., eds. America & Ireland, Seventeen Seventy Six to Nineteen Seventy Six: The American Identify & the Irish Connection. LC 79-7066. 1980. lib. bdg. 29.95 (ISBN 0-313-21119-1, DOA/). Greenwood.

Doyle, Dennis M. Efficient Accounting & Record Keeping. Brownstone, David, ed. LC 78-2474. (The Small Business Profit Program Ser.). 116p. 1977. pap. text ed. 5.95 (ISBN 0-471-05044-X). Wiley.

Doyle, Edward, tr. see Scottus, Sedulius.

Doyle, Edward G. & Lipsman, Samuel L. America Takes Over, Vol. 4. Manning, Robert, ed. LC 82-61227. (Vietnam Experience Ser.). (Illus.). 192p. 1982. 14.95 (ISBN 0-939526-03-4). Boston Pub Co.

Doyle, Esther M. & Floyd, Virginia H., eds. Studies in Interpretation, No. 2. 375p. 1977. pap. text ed. 27.75x (ISBN 90-6203-070-X). Humanities.

Doyle, Harrison. How to Sustain that Electrical Lifeforce Within You. 1983. 9.95 (ISBN 0-918462-08-8). Hillside.

Doyle, J. Introduction to Electrical Wiring. 2nd ed. (Illus.). 1980. text ed. 20.95 (ISBN 0-8359-3185-4). Reston.

Doyle, J. G. Louis Moreau Gottschalk. (Bibliographies in American Music). 1983. write for info. (ISBN 0-911772-66-9). Info Coord.

Doyle, James, jt. ed. see Campbell, Jane.

Doyle, James A. Catholic Press Directory. 128p. 1983. pap. 10.00 (ISBN 0-686-30366-0). Cath Pr Assn.
--The Male Experience. 320p. 1983. pap. text ed. write for info. (ISBN 0-697-06553-7). Wm C Brown.

Doyle, John R., Jr. Arthur Shearly Cripps. (World Authors Ser.). 1975. lib. bdg. 15.95 (ISBN 0-8057-6216-7, Twayne). G K Hall.
--Francis Carey Slater. (World Authors Ser.). lib. bdg. 15.95 (ISBN 0-8057-2834-1, Twayne). G K Hall.
--Thomas Pringle. (World Authors Ser.). lib. bdg. 15.95 (ISBN 0-8057-2718-3, Twayne). G K Hall.
--William Charles Scully. (World Authors Ser.). 1978. lib. bdg. 15.95 (ISBN 0-8057-6331-7, Twayne). G K Hall.

Doyle, Kathleen E. & Hoover, Jan. Cooperative Law for California Retail Consumer Co-Ops. 316p. 1982. pap. text ed. 7.00 (ISBN 0-686-82421-0). Calif Dept Co.

Doyle, Kenneth O., Jr. Evaluating Teaching. LC 79-9673. 192p. 1983. 20.95x (ISBN 0-669-03613-7). Lexington Bks.

Doyle, L. B. Information Retrieval & Processing. LC 75-1179. (Information Science Ser.). 1975. 39.95 (ISBN 0-471-22151-1, Pub. by Wiley-Interscience). Wiley.

Doyle, M. P., jt. auth. see Neckers, D. C.

Doyle, Marvyl & Mittwer, Marie. Basic Reading Patterns: Words & Sentences. (gr. 10 up). 1969. pap. text ed. 11.95 (ISBN 0-13-068031-1). P-H.

Doyle, Michael P. & Mungall, William S. Experimental Organic Chemistry. LC 79-18392. 490p. 1980. text ed. 21.95 (ISBN 0-471-03383-9); avail. tchrs. manual (ISBN 0-471-08053-5). Wiley.

Doyle, Paul A. Liam O'Flaherty. (English Authors Ser.: No. 108). lib. bdg. 10.95 o.p. (ISBN 0-8057-1424-3, Twayne). G K Hall.
--Pearl Buck. (U. S. Authors Ser.: No. 85). 1965. lib. bdg. 8.50 o.p. (ISBN 0-8057-0112-5, Twayne). G K Hall.
--Pearl S. Buck. rev. ed. (United States Authors Ser.). 1980. lib. bdg. 10.95 (ISBN 0-8057-7325-8, Twayne). G K Hall.

Doyle, Peter & Hart, Norman. Case Studies in International Marketing. 272p. (Orig.). 1982. pap. 19.95 (ISBN 0-434-90370-1, Pub. by W Heinemann); pap. 14.95 tchr's manual (ISBN 0-434-90371-X). David & Charles.

Doyle, Phyllis B., et al. Helping the Severely Handicapped Child: A Guide for Parents & Teachers. LC 78-3300. (John Day Book in Special Education). (Illus.). 1979. 12.45i (ISBN 0-381-90063-0). T Y Crowell.

Doyle, Robert V. Careers to Preserve Our Shrinking World: Working & Living with Appropriate Technology. LC 81-1880. (Illus.). 190p. (gr. 7 up). 1981. PLB 10.79 o.p. (ISBN 0-671-34046-8). Messner.

Doyle, Thomas P., ed. Marriage Studies: Reflections in Canon Law & Theology, Vol. 1. 155p. (Orig.). 1980. pap. 4.00x (ISBN 0-943616-03-4). Canon Law Soc.
--Marriage Studies: Reflections in Canon Law & Theology, Vol. 2. 202p. (Orig.). 1982. pap. 4.50x (ISBN 0-943616-04-2). Canon Law Soc.

Doyle, Walter & Good, Thomas L., eds. Focus on Teaching: Readings from the Elementary School Journal. 290p. 1983. lib. bdg. 22.00x (ISBN 0-226-16177-3); pap. 8.95 (ISBN 0-226-16178-1). U of Chicago Pr.

Doyle, William. Old European Order Sixteen Sixty to Eighteen Hundred. (Short Oxford History of the Modern World Ser.). (Illus.). 1978. 36.00x (ISBN 0-19-913073-6); pap. 15.95x (ISBN 0-19-913131-7). Oxford U Pr.
--Origins of the French Revolution. 272p. 1981. 37.50x (ISBN 0-19-873020-9); pap. 19.95x (ISBN 0-19-873021-7). Oxford U Pr.
--The Parliament of Bordeaux & the End of the Old Regime: 1771-1790. LC 74-77768. 1974. text ed. 27.50 o.p. (ISBN 0-312-59675-8). St Martin.

Doyle, William, jt. ed. see Milburn, Josephine.

Doyno, Victor, ed. Mark Twain: American Skeptic. LC 82-60382. 350p. 1982. 18.95 (ISBN 0-87975-189-4); pap. 9.95 (ISBN 0-87975-190-8). Prometheus Bks.

Dozer, Donald M. Portrait of the Free State. 638p. 1976. 17.50 (ISBN 0-686-36828-2). Md Hist.

Dozier, Jeffrey, jt. auth. see Marsh, William.

Dozier, Zoe. Home Again, My Love. (YA) 1978. 6.95 (ISBN 0-685-86408-1, Avalon). Bouregy.
--The Warm Side of the Island. (YA) 1978. 6.95 (ISBN 0-685-53394-8, Avalon). Bouregy.

Dozois, Gardner, ed. The Best SF Stories of the Year, No. 8. (Orig.). 1980. pap. 2.25 o.s.i. (ISBN 0-440-11232-X). Dell.

Dozoretz, Eileen & Pearl, Shirley. California Personal Injury, a Guide for Law Office Paper Work & Procedure: With 1977 Supplement. LC 74-83831. 1974. 15.00x (ISBN 0-910874-33-6). Legal Bk Co.

Dr. A., pseud. The Sensuous Dirty Old Man. pap. 1.50 o.p. (ISBN 0-451-07199-9, W7199, Sig). NAL.

Drabble, Margaret. Realms of Gold. 368p. 1982. pap. 3.95 (ISBN 0-553-22603-7). Bantam.

Drabble, Phil. Country Matters. (Illus.). 216p. 1983. 15.95 (ISBN 0-7181-2177-5, Pub by Michael Joseph). Merrimack Bk Serv.
--Design for a Wilderness. (Illus.). 137p. 1974. 7.75 o.p. (ISBN 0-7207-0706-4). Transatlantic.
--My Beloved Wilderness. (Illus.). 150p. 1972. 7.50 o.s.i. (ISBN 0-7207-0519-3). Transatlantic.
--Of Pedigree Unknown: Sporting & Working Dogs. (Illus.). 1977. 8.75 o.s.i. (ISBN 0-7181-1447-7). Transatlantic.
--Pleasing Pets. (Illus.). 252p. 1976. 7.50 o.p. (ISBN 0-86002-050-9). Transatlantic.

Drabeck, Bernard A., et al. Structures for Composition. 2nd ed. LC 77-77675. (Illus.). 1978. pap. text ed. 12.95 (ISBN 0-395-25567-8); instrs.' manual 0.50 (ISBN 0-395-25568-6). HM.
--Exploring Literature. LC 81-82566. 1982. 14.95 (ISBN 0-395-31694-4); instr's manual 1.00 (ISBN 0-686-97254-6). HM.

Drabek, Thomas E. & Key, William H. Conquering Disaster: Family Recovery & Long Term Consequences. 485p. 1983. text ed. 39.50x (ISBN 0-8290-1000-9). Irvington.

Drabek, Thomas E., jt. auth. see Haas, J. Eugene.

Drabkin, I. E., ed. see Galilei, Galileo.

Drabkin, Marjorie. Word Mastery: A Guide to the Understanding of Words. Bromberg, Murray, ed. LC 75-34906. 1978. pap. 5.95 (ISBN 0-8120-0526-0). Barron.

Drach, Robert F., jt. auth. see Herzfeld, Thomas J.

Drachkovitch, Milorad, ed. East Central Europe: Yesterday, Today, Tomorrow. (Publication Ser.: No. 240). 417p. 1982. 25.95x (ISBN 0-686-86067-5). Hoover Inst Pr.

Drachkovitch, Milorad M., ed. Fifty Years of Communism in Russia. LC 68-8178. 1968. 19.95x (ISBN 0-271-00068-6). Pa St U Pr.

Drachman, Theodore S. The Deadly Dream. 224p. 1982. 9.95 (ISBN 0-8397-1900-0). Eriksson.

Drachsler, Julius. Intermarriage in New York City: A Statistical Study of the Amalgamation of European Peoples. LC 74-145477. (The American Immigration Library). 204p. 1971, Repr. of 1921 ed. lib. bdg. 12.95x (ISBN 0-89198-009-1). Ozer.

Drackett, Phil. The Book of Cromer. 1981. 39.50x o.p. (ISBN 0-86023-144-5, Pub. by Barracuda England). State Mutual Bk.
--The Book of the Veteran Car. (Illus.). 144p. 1974. 9.50 o.p. (ISBN 0-7207-0654-8). Transatlantic.
--Car Makers. LC 80-51161. (Careers Ser.). PLB 12.68 (ISBN 0-382-06414-3). Silver.
--Inns & Harbours of North Norfolk. 150p. 1980. 11.00x o.p. (ISBN 0-902628-88-7, Pub. by RAC). State Mutual Bk.

Drackett, Phil, ed. Encyclopedia of the Motor Car. (Illus.). 1979. 30.00 o.p. (ISBN 0-517-53833-4). Crown.

Dracup, J. A., jt. auth. see Hall, W. A.

Draeger, jt. auth. see Kiong.

Draeger, Alain. Brazil. LC 78-65839. (Illus.). 196p. 1979. 40.00 o.p. (ISBN 0-87951-091-9). Overlook Pr.

Draeger, D. F. Indonesian Fighting Arts. 12.50x o.p. Wehman.

Draeger, Don. Budo: Classical. 1975. 15.00x. Wehman.
--Bujutso & Budo: Modern. 1974. 17.95 o.s.i. (ISBN 0-685-83520-0). Wehman.
--Bujutso: Classical. 1973. 15.00x (ISBN 0-685-83519-7). Wehman.

Draeger, Donn F. & Nakayama, Masatoshi. Practical Karate, 6 vols. LC 63-11828. (Illus.). 1963-65. Vol. 1. pap. 5.95 (ISBN 0-8048-0481-8); Vol. 2. pap. 5.95 (ISBN 0-8048-0482-6); Vol. 3. pap. 4.75 (ISBN 0-8048-0483-4); Vol. 4. pap. 5.95 (ISBN 0-8048-0484-2); Vol. 5. pap. 4.95 (ISBN 0-8048-0485-0); Vol. 6. pap. 4.75 (ISBN 0-8048-0486-9). C E Tuttle.

Draeger, Donn F. & Otaki, Tadao. Judo Formal Techniques: A Complete Guide to Kodokan Randori No Kata. LC 82-50095. (Illus.). 1983. 35.00 (ISBN 0-8048-1187-3). C E Tuttle.

Draeger, Donn F. & Smith, Robert. Asian Fighting Arts. (Illus.). 1969. 12.50x o.s.i. (ISBN 0-685-21878-3, Pub. by Kodansha). Wehman.

Draf, W. Endoscopy of the Paranasal Sinuses: Technique-Typical Findings-Theraputic Possibilities. Pohl, W. E., tr. from Ger. (Illus.). 112p. 1983. 27.50 (ISBN 0-387-11258-8). Springer-Verlag.

Draffan, I. W. & Poole, F., eds. Distributed Data Bases. LC 80-40399. 400p. 1981. 32.50 (ISBN 0-521-23091-8). Cambridge U Pr.

Drage, Charles, ed. Respiratory Medicine for Primary Care Physicians. LC 82-6870. 222p. 1983. 29.95 (ISBN 0-12-788165-4). Acad Pr.

Drage, Martha O., jt. auth. see Wilson, Richard E.

Draghi, Suzanne C., jt. auth. see Flach, Frederic F.

Dragnich, Alex N. The First Yugoslavia: Search for a Viable Political System. (Publication Ser.: No. 284). (Illus.). 186p. 1983. 24.95 (ISBN 0-8179-7841-0). Hoover Inst Pr.

Drago, Harry S. Canal Days in America: The History & Romance of Old Towpaths & Waterways. (Illus.). 352p. 1972. 10.00 o.p. (ISBN 0-517-50087-6). Crown.

Dragomir, V., jt. ed. see Gheorghiu, A.

Dragomir, V. C., et al. Theory of the Earth's Shape. (Developments in Solid Earth Geophysics Ser.: Vol. 13). 694p. 1982. 110.75 (ISBN 0-444-99705-9). Elsevier.

Dragone, Carol. Out of Absence. Hettich, M. & Ahern, Colleen, eds. 25p. 1978. 1.50 (ISBN 0-686-38057-6). Moons Quilt Pr.

Dragonwagon, Crescent. Stevie Wonder. LC 77-78535. (Illus.). 1977. pap. 3.95 (ISBN 0-8256-3908-5, Quick Fox). Putnam Pub Group.
--When Light Turns into Night. LC 74-2634. (Illus.). 32p. (ps-3). 1975. PLB 10.89 (ISBN 0-06-021740-5, HarpJ). Har-Row.

Dragoo, Alva W. General Shop Metalwork. rev. ed. (gr. 8-9). 1964. pap. text ed. 6.64 (ISBN 0-87345-109-0). McKnight.

Dragoon, M. M., jt. auth. see Mitchell, B. J.

Dragt, Donald, tr. see Chekhov, A. P.

Dragt, Tonke. The Towers of February. LC 75-22154. 224p. (gr. 7-9). 1975. 7.25 o.s.i. (ISBN 0-688-22044-4); PLB 8.59 (ISBN 0-688-32044-9). Morrow.

Drahms, August. Criminal, His Personnel & Environment: A Scientific Study. LC 72-108231. (Criminology, Law Enforcement, & Social Problems Ser.: No. 114). (With intro. added). 1971. Repr. of 1900 ed. lib. bdg. 20.00x (ISBN 0-87585-114-2). Patterson Smith.

Drain, L. E. The Laser Doppler Technique. LC 79-40638. 1980. text ed. 59.95 (ISBN 0-471-27627-8, Pub. by Wiley-Interscience). Wiley.

Drain, Robert H. & Oakley, Neil. Successful Conference & Convention Planning. 205p. 1979. 14.95 o.p. (ISBN 0-07-082609-9). McGraw.

Draine, Betsy. Substance under Pressure: Artistic Coherence & Evolving Form in the Novels of Doris Lessing. LC 82-70556. 240p. 1983. 18.95 (ISBN 0-299-09230-5). U of Wis Pr.

Draisey, T., jt. auth. see Hyde, T. A.

Drakakis, John, ed. British Radio Drama. 300p. 1981. 49.50 (ISBN 0-521-22183-8); pap. 15.95 (ISBN 0-521-29383-9). Cambridge U Pr.

Drakakis-Smith, David. Urbanization, Housing & the Development Process. 256p. 1980. 36.00 (ISBN 0-312-83519-1). St Martin.

Drake, Albert. Returning to Oregon. LC 74-28453. 1975. pap. 1.00 (ISBN 0-914994-07-7). Cider Pr.
--Street was Fun in Fifty-One. 1982. pap. 8.00 (ISBN 0-936892-11-0). Stone Pr MI.

Drake, Alvin W. Fundamentals of Applied Probability Theory. (Illus.). 1967. text ed. 39.95 (ISBN 0-07-017815-1, C). McGraw.

Drake, Alvin W., et al. The American Blood Supply. (Health & Public Policy Ser.). 224p. 1982. 20.00x (ISBN 0-262-04070-0). MIT Pr.

Drake, Alvin W., et al, eds. Analysis of Public Systems. 480p. 1972. 30.00x (ISBN 0-262-04038-7). MIT Pr.

Drake, Barbara, ed. see Webb, Beatrice.

Drake, Bill. Marijuana Cultivation: A Handbook of Essential Techniques. Date not set. cancelled (ISBN 0-686-78527-4). Wingbow Pr.

Drake, Bonnie. Lover from the Sea. (Candlelight Ecstasy Ser.: No. 114). (Orig.). 1983. pap. 1.95 (ISBN 0-440-14888-X). Dell.
--Passion & Illusion. (Candlelight Ecstasy Ser.: No. 146). (Orig.). 1983. pap. 1.95 (ISBN 0-440-16816-3). Dell.
--The Silver Fox. (Candlelight Ecsasy Ser.: No. 132). (Orig.). 1983. pap. 1.95 (ISBN 0-440-18139-9). Dell.

Drake, Charles L. Geodynamics: Progress & Prospects. 1976. pap. 7.50 o.p. (ISBN 0-87590-203-0). Am Geophysical.

Drake, Dana. Don Quijote (1894-1970) A Selective Annotated Bibliography, Vol. 1. (Studies in the Romance Languages & Literatures: No. 138). 267p. 1974. pap. 14.50x (ISBN 0-8078-9138-X). U of NC Pr.

Drake, David. The Dragon Lord. LC 79-10298. 1979. 10.95 o.p. (ISBN 0-399-12380-6). Putnam Pub Group.

--The Dragon Lord. 320p. 1983. pap. 2.95 (ISBN 0-523-48552-2). Pinnacle Bks.

Drake, Don A. You Deserve to be Rich. 110p. (Orig.). 1982. pap. text ed. 9.95 (ISBN 0-89532-009-6); visualization guide 7.00 (ISBN 0-89532-010-X). United Seabears.

Drake, Ellen A., jt. auth. see Cantor, Dorothy W.

Drake, F. R., et al, eds. Recursion Theory: Its Generalisations & Applications, Proceedings of Logic Colloquium '79, Leeds, Aug. 1979. (London Mathematical Society Lecture Notes Ser.: No. 45). 300p. 1980. pap. 25.95 (ISBN 0-521-23543-X). Cambridge U Pr.

Drake, Francis S. Dictionary of American Biography Including Men of the Time. LC 73-11061. 1974. Repr. of 1872 ed. 87.00x (ISBN 0-8103-3731-2). Gale.

--Tea Leaves: Being a Collection of Letters & Documents Relating to the Shipment of Tea to the American Colonies in the Year 1773, by the East India Tea Company. LC 77-95778. (Illus.). 1970. Repr. of 1884 ed. 34.00x (ISBN 0-8103-3577-8). Gale.

Drake, Frank R. Set Theory: An Introduction to Large Cardinals. (Studies in Logic & the Foundation of Mathematics Ser: Vol. 76). 352p. 1974. 53.25 (ISBN 0-444-10535-2, North-Holland). Elsevier.

Drake, George. Complete Handbook of Power Tools. (Illus.). 1977. 17.95 (ISBN 0-87909-150-9); pap. 10.95 (ISBN 0-87909-183-5). Reston.

--Everyone's Book of Hand & Small Power Tools. LC 74-10554. 1974. 14.95 (ISBN 0-87909-260-2); pap. 11.95 (ISBN 0-87909-217-3). Reston.

--Small Gas Engines: Maintenance, Troubleshooting & Repair. 500p. 1981. text ed. 17.95 (ISBN 0-8359-7014-0); pap. text ed. 7.95 o.p. (ISBN 0-8359-7013-2); soln. manual avail. (ISBN 0-8359-7015-9). Reston.

Drake, George R. The Repair & Servicing of Small Appliances. (Illus.). 528p. 1977. ref. ed. 20.95 (ISBN 0-87909-727-2); text ed. 18.95 (ISBN 0-686-96871-9); instructor's manual free (ISBN 0-87909-726-4). Reston.

Drake, H. A. In Praise of Constantine: A Historical Study of Eusebius' Tricennial Orations. LC 75-62009. (Library Reprint Ser.: No. 93). 1978. 18.95x (ISBN 0-520-03694-8). U of Cal Pr.

Drake, Harold L. Humanistic Radio Production. LC 81-40943. 126p. (Orig.). 1982. lib. bdg. 19.50 (ISBN 0-8191-2250-5); pap. text ed. 8.25 (ISBN 0-8191-2251-3). U Pr of Amer.

Drake, James A., jt. auth. see Ponselle, Rosa.

Drake, Julia A. & Orndorff, J. R. From Millwheel to Plowshare: Orndorff Family Genealogy. 271p. 1938. 10.00 (ISBN 0-686-36497-X). Md Hist.

Drake, M., tr. see Sundt, Eilert.

Drake, Maurice & Drake, Wilfred. Saints & Their Emblems. LC 68-18021. xiv, 235p. 1972. Repr. of 1916 ed. 41.00 (ISBN 0-8103-3032-6). Gale.

Drake, Michael. Population & Society in Norway, 1735-1865. LC 69-14393. (Cambridge Studies in Economic History). (Illus.). 1969. 37.50 (ISBN 0-521-07319-7). Cambridge U Pr.

Drake, Michael, ed. Applied Historical Studies. 1973. pap. 9.50x (ISBN 0-416-79110-7). Methuen Inc.

Drake, Michael, jt. ed. see Barker, Theo.

Drake, Miriam A. User Fees: A Practical Perspective. LC 81-6032. 142p. 1981. lib. bdg. 17.50 (ISBN 0-87287-244-0). Libs Unl.

Drake, Phyllis E. How to Succeed in Selling Real Estate: A Guide for Real Estate Rookies. (Illus.). 112p. (Orig.). 1982. pap. 3.50 (ISBN 0-914846-12-4). Golden West Pub.

Drake, R. M., jt. auth. see Eckert, Ernest R.

Drake, Raleigh M. Abnormal Psychology. rev. ed. (Quality Paperback: No. 101). 1972. pap. 3.95 (ISBN 0-8226-0101-X). Littlefield.

Drake, Raymond W. Gods or Spacemen? 1976. pap. 1.50 o.p. (ISBN 0-451-07192-1, W7192, Sig). NAL.

Drake, St. Clair & Cayton, Horace R. Black Metropolis, Vol. 1. LC 73-12271. (Illus.). 1970. pap. 2.85 o.p. (ISBN 0-15-613050-5, H078, Harv). HarBraceJ.

--Black Metropolis, Vol. 2. LC 73-12271. (Illus.). 1970. pap. 2.85 o.p. (ISBN 0-15-613051-3, HO79, Harv). HarBraceJ.

Drake, Samuel A. Book of New England Legends & Folk Lore. LC 69-19881. 1969. Repr. of 1901 ed. 34.00 o.p. (ISBN 0-8103-3829-7). Gale.

--The Heroical Book of American Colonial Homes. (Illus.). 109p. 1983. Repr. of 1894 ed. 89.75 (ISBN 0-89901-104-7). Found Class Reprints.

--Nooks & Corners of the New England Coast. LC 69-19883. 1969. Repr. of 1875 ed. 37.00x (ISBN 0-8103-3827-0). Gale.

--Old Boston Taverns & Tavern Clubs. LC 78-162511. 132p. 1971. Repr. of 1917 ed. 34.00x (ISBN 0-8103-3293-0). Gale.

--Old Landmarks & Historic Personages of Boston. LC 76-99068. (Illus.). 1970. Repr. of 1900 ed. 37.00x (ISBN 0-8103-3582-4). Gale.

Drake, Stiliman. Galileo. Thomas, Keith, ed. (Pastmasters Ser.). 1981. 7.95 (ISBN 0-8090-4850-7); pap. 2.95 (ISBN 0-8090-1416-5). Hill & Wang.

Drake, Stillman. Galileo Studies: Personality, Tradition, & Revolution. LC 73-124427. 1970. 8.50x o.p. (ISBN 0-472-08283-3). U of Mich Pr.

Drake, Stillman, tr. from Lat. Galileo Galilei: "Two New Sciences". 366p. 1974. 25.00 o.p. (ISBN 0-299-06400-X); pap. 7.95 o.p. (ISBN 0-299-06404-2). U of Wis Pr.

Drake, Stillman, tr. see Galilei, Galileo.

Drake, Thelbert L., jt. auth. see Roe, William H.

Drake, W. Homer, Jr. & Herzog, Richard B. Bankruptcy: A Concise Guide for Creditors & Debtors. LC 82-8834. (Illus.). 288p. 1983. 14.95 (ISBN 0-668-05256-2); pap. 9.95 (ISBN 0-668-05261-9). Arco.

Drake, W. Raymond. Gods & Spacemen in the Ancient West. pap. 1.50 o.p. (ISBN 0-451-06055-5, W6055, Sig). NAL.

--Gods & Spacemen of the Ancient Past. 1974. pap. 1.50 o.p. (ISBN 0-451-06140-3, W6140, Sig). NAL.

Drake, Wilfred, jt. auth. see Drake, Maurice.

Drake, William E. Betrayal on Mt. Parnassus. 1983. 21.95 (ISBN 0-8022-2416-4). Philos Lib.

Drake Del Castillo, E. Illustrationes Florae Insularum Maris Pacifici. 1977. Repr. of 1892 ed. 100.00 (ISBN 3-7682-1130-4). Lubrecht & Cramer.

Drakeford, J. W. Psicologia y Religion. 384p. 1980. pap. 10.95 (ISBN 0-311-46035-6, Edit Mundo). Casa Bautista.

Drakeford, John W. The Awesome Power of the Listening Heart. 192p. 1982. pap. 5.95 (ISBN 0-310-70261-5). Zondervan.

--Counseling for Church Leaders. LC 61-12412. 1961. 7.95 (ISBN 0-8054-2405-9). Broadman.

--Hechos el Uno Para el Otro. De Plou, Dafne C., tr. (Sexo en la Vida Cristiana Ser.). 1980. pap. 3.50 (ISBN 0-311-46256-1). Casa Bautista.

--Marriage: How to Keep a Good Thing Growing. 192p. 1982. pap. 5.95 (ISBN 0-310-70081-7). Zondervan.

Drakeford, John W., jt. auth. see Drakeford, Robina.

Drakeford, Robina & Drakeford, John W. In Praise of Women: A Christian Approach to Love, Marriage, & Equality. LC 79-3000. 160p. 1980. 8.95i o.p. (ISBN 0-06-062063-3, HarpR). Har-Row.

Drakontides, Anna B., et al. Anatomy & Physiology: Workbook & Laboratory Manual. (Illus.). 1977. pap. text ed. 12.95 (ISBN 0-02-330050-7, 33005). Macmillan.

Dralse De Grandpierre. Relation de Divers Voyages Faits dans l'Afrique, l'Amerique, et aux Indes Occidentales. (Bibliotheque Africaine Ser.). 366p. (Fr.). 1974. Repr. of 1718 ed. lib. bdg. 94.00x o.p. (ISBN 0-8287-0390-6, 72-2133). Clearwater Pub.

Dramer, Dan. Disasters! (Illus.). 160p. (Orig.). (gr. 6-8). 1982. pap. text ed. 6.00x (ISBN 0-89061-247-1, 760). Jamestown Pubs.

--Literary Tales. 240p. (Orig.). (gr. 9 up). 1980. pap. text ed. 6.00x (ISBN 0-89061-233-1, 761). Jamestown Pubs.

Drane, James. Authority & Institution: A Study in Church Crisis. 1969. 5.95 o.p. (ISBN 0-685-07610-5, 80187). Glencoe.

Drane, James F. Religion & Ethics. LC 76-45935. (Topics in Moral Argument Ser.). 120p. 1977. pap. 2.25 o.p. (ISBN 0-8091-1992-7). Paulist Pr.

Drane, John. The Early Christians: Life in the First Years of the Church, an Illustrated Documentary. LC 81-47835. (Illus.). 144p. (Orig.). 1982. pap. 9.57i (ISBN 0-06-062067-6, RD 378, HarpR). Har-Row.

Dranov, Paula. The Continuing Education Market, Nineteen Seventy-Nine to Nineteen Eighty-Four: Opportunities & Pitfalls for Publishers & Suppliers. 1979. spiral 450.00 (ISBN 0-686-42872-2). Knowledge Indus.

--Inside the Music Publishing Industry. LC 80-13304. (Communications Library Ser.). 185p. 1980. text ed. 29.95x (ISBN 0-914236-40-7). Knowledge Indus.

Dranov, Paula, et al. Video in the Eighties: Emerging Uses for Television in Business, Education, Medication & Government. LC 80-15745. (Video Bookshelf Ser.). 186p. 1980. text ed. 34.95 (ISBN 0-914236-58-X). Knowledge Indus.

--Video in the Eighties: Emerging Uses for Television in Business, Education, Medicine & Government. 186p. 1980. pap. 34.95 (ISBN 0-86729-065-X). Knowledge Indus.

Dranow, Ralph. The Woman Who Knocked Out Sugar Ray. Darlington, Sandy & Reynolds, Julie, eds. LC 81-70081. (Illus.). 192p. (Orig.). 1982. pap. 4.95 (ISBN 0-9604152-5-4). Arrowhead Pr.

Dransfield, P. & Haber, D. F. Introducing Root Locus. (Illus.). 150p. 1973. 13.95x (ISBN 0-521-20118-7). Cambridge U Pr.

Drant, Thomas H., tr. see Horatius Flaccus, Quintus.

Drapela, Victor J. The Counselor as Consultant & Supervisor. (Illus.). 176p. 1983. 17.50x (ISBN 0-398-04789-8). C C Thomas.

--Guidance & Counseling Around the World. LC 79-64966. 344p. 1981. lib. bdg. 22.25 (ISBN 0-8191-1384-0); pap. text ed. 12.00 (ISBN 0-8191-0777-8). U Pr of Amer.

Draper. Caring for Children. 1979. text ed. 17.28 (ISBN 0-87002-281-4); tchr's. guide 10.00 (ISBN 0-87002-286-5); student guide 4.52 (ISBN 0-87002-291-1). Bennett IL.

--Studying Children: Observing & Participating. 1977. pap. text ed. 12.24 (ISBN 0-87002-194-X). Bennett IL.

Draper & Bailey. Steps in Clothing Skills. (gr. 7-9). 1978. text ed. 17.32 (ISBN 0-87002-265-2); tchr's guide free. Bennett IL.

Draper, jt. auth. see Mitchell.

Draper, A. B., jt. auth. see Niebel, B. W.

Draper, C. R., ed. Production of Printed Circuits & Electronics Assemblies & Metal Finishing in the Electronics Industry. LC 77-492006. (Illus.). 468p. 1969. 35.00x (ISBN 0-85218-028-4). Intl Pubns Serv.

Draper, Cena C. Dandy & the Mystery of the Locked Room. (Illus.). (gr. 6 up). 1974. 7.50 o.p. (ISBN 0-8309-0114-0, 15-0118-6). Ind Pr MO.

Draper, E. Linn, Jr., ed. Technology of Controlled Thermonuclear Fusion Experiments & the Engineering Aspects of Fusion Reactors: Proceedings. LC 74-600044. (AEC Symposium Ser.). 1052p. 1974. pap. 34.25 (ISBN 0-87079-221-0, CONF-721111); microfiche 4.50 (ISBN 0-87079-222-9, CONF-721111). DOE.

Draper, Edythe. Cool: How a Kid Should Live. 5.95 (ISBN 0-8423-0435-5). Tyndale.

--In Touch. 1973. deluxe ed. 8.95 (ISBN 0-8423-1711-2); kivar 5.95 (ISBN 0-8423-1710-4). Tyndale.

--Living Light. Incl. Large Print Edition. 1976. kivar 4.95 (ISBN 0-8423-2652-9). 1972. 8.95 (ISBN 0-8423-2651-0); kivar 4.95 (ISBN 0-8423-2650-2). Tyndale.

Draper, Frank D. & Pitsvada, Bernard T. Zero-Base Budgeting for Public Programs Nineteen Seventy-Nine. rev. ed. 154p. 1979. pap. text ed. 8.75 (ISBN 0-8191-0719-0). U Pr of Amer.

Draper, George & Sather, Edgar. It's All in a Day's Work. LC 76-57146. 1977. pap. text ed. 9.95 (ISBN 0-88377-067-9). Newbury Hse.

Draper, Hal. Karl Marx's Theory of Revolution, Part One: The State & Bureaucracy, 2 vols. LC 76-40467. 1977. 28.50 set o.p. (ISBN 0-85345-387-X, CL-387-X). Monthly Rev.

--Karl Marx's Theory of Revolution: The State & Bureaucracy, 2 book set. LC 76-40467. 1978. pap. 9.50 (ISBN 0-85345-461-2, PB-4612). Monthly Rev.

Draper, Henry. The Caring Parent. 1982. text ed. 15.96 (ISBN 0-87002-380-2). Bennett IL.

Draper, James T. The Conscience of a Nation. 1983. pap. 7.95 (ISBN 0-8054-1530-0). Broadman.

Draper, James T., Jr. Discover Joy: Studies in Philippians. 1983. pap. 4.95 (ISBN 0-8423-0606-4); leader's guide 2.95 (ISBN 0-8423-0607-2). Tyndale.

--Ecclesiastes, the Life Without God. 1981. pap. 4.95 (ISBN 0-8423-0681-1). Tyndale.

--Faith that Works: Studies in James. 1983. pap. 5.95 (ISBN 0-686-82693-0, 82-0872-5); Leader's Guide 2.95 (ISBN 0-686-82694-9, 82-0873-3). Tyndale.

--Foundations of Biblical Faith. LC 78-67001. 1979. 6.95 (ISBN 0-8054-1951-9). Broadman.

Draper, Joan E., jt. auth. see Zukowsky, John.

Draper, John W. Orientalia & Shakespeareana. LC 77-20542. 1978. 6.95 o.p. (ISBN 0-533-00608-2). Vantage.

Draper, Lyman C. King's Mountain & Its Heroes: History of the Battle of King's Mountain, October 7th 1780 & the Events Which Led to It. LC 67-25801. (Illus.). 1967. Repr. of 1881 ed. 27.50 (ISBN 0-87152-035-4). Reprint.

Draper, M. W. & Nissenson, R. A., eds. Parathyroid Hormone. (Journal: Mineral & Electrolyte Metabolism: Vol. 8, No. 3-4). (Illus.). vix, 124p. 1982. pap. 46.75 (ISBN 3-8055-3550-3). S Karger.

Draper, Maurice L. Restoration Studies, Vol. II. 1983. pap. 13.00 (ISBN 0-8309-0362-3). Herald Hse.

Draper, N. R. & Smith, H. Applied Regression Analysis. 2nd ed. LC 80-17951. (Probability & Mathematical Statistics Ser.). 709p. 1981. 28.95x (ISBN 0-471-02995-5, Pub. by Wiley-Interscience). Wiley.

Draper, Norman & Smith, H. Applied Regression Analysis. LC 66-17641. (Probability & Mathematical Statistics Ser.). 1966. 21.95 o.p. (ISBN 0-471-22170-8, Pub. by Wiley-Interscience). Wiley.

Draper, Norman R., jt. auth. see Box, George E.

Draper, Ronald P. D. H. Lawrence. LC 74-80241. (Griffin Authors Ser). 200p. 1975. pap. 5.95 o.p. (ISBN 0-312-18095-0). St Martin.

--D. H. Lawrence. (English Authors Ser.). 1964. lib. bdg. 11.95 (ISBN 0-8057-1320-4, Twayne). G K Hall.

Draper, Simon R. Biochemical Analysis in Crop Service. (Illus.). 1976. 39.50x o.p. (ISBN 0-19-854128-7). Oxford U Pr.

Draper, Theodore. The Eighty-Fourth Infantry Division in the Battle of Germany. (Divisional Ser.: No. 24). (Illus.). 260p. 1983. Repr. of 1946 ed. 25.00x (ISBN 0-89839-069-9). Battery Pr.

Draper, Wanetta, jt. auth. see Hunt, Inez.

Drar, M., jt. auth. see Tackholm, V.

Drasdo, Harold, jt. ed. see Tobias, Charles.

Drasgow, Fritz, jt. auth. see Hulin, Charles L.

Draskau, Jennifer, ed. Taw & Other Thai Stories. (Writing in Asia Ser.). 1975. pap. text ed. 6.50x (ISBN 0-686-65344-0, 00215). Heinemann Ed.

Draskovich, Slobodan. Will America Surrender? 480p. 1972. 12.95 (ISBN 0-8159-7211-3). Devin.

Drassler, M. World-Wide Treasures. 5.95 o.p. (ISBN 0-8062-0998-4). Carlton.

Drath, Viola & Moeller, Jack. Noch Dazu! LC 79-64140. (Sequential German Readers Ser.: Bk. II). (gr. 9-12). 1980. pap. text ed. 4.72 (ISBN 0-395-27930-5). HM.

Draudt, Susan B. Food Processor Cookery. (Illus.). 175p. 1981. pap. 5.95 (ISBN 0-89586-122-4). H P Bks.

Drauglis, E., et al. Molecular Processes on Solid Surfaces. (Materials Science & Engineering Ser). 1969. text ed. 74.50 (ISBN 0-07-017827-5, P&RB). McGraw.

Draves, William A. The Free University: A Model for Lifelong Learning. 324p. 1980. 12.95 (ISBN 0-695-81443-5). Follett.

Dravnieks, Dzintar E., et al, eds. IBM Personal Computer Handbook. (Illus.). 448p. (Orig.). 1983. pap. 17.95 (ISBN 0-915904-66-7). And-or Pr.

Drawbaugh, Charles C. & Hull, William L. Agricultural Education: Approaches to Learning & Teaching. LC 71-132866. 1971. text ed. 20.95 (ISBN 0-675-09274-4). Merrill.

Drawbell, Marjorie. Making Pottery Figures. (gr. 9 up). 6.95 o.p. (ISBN 0-85458-080-8); pap. 7.50 o.s.i. (ISBN 0-85458-081-6). Transatlantic.

Draxl, Peter K. Skew Fields. LC 82-22036. (London Mathematical Society Lecture Note Ser.: No. 81). 194p. Date not set. pap. 19.95 (ISBN 0-521-27274-2). Cambridge U Pr.

Draxten, Nina. Kristofer Janson in America. (International Studies & Translations Program). 1976. lib. bdg. 11.95 (ISBN 0-8057-9000-4, Twayne). G K Hall.

Dray, William H. Laws & Explanation in History. LC 78-25936. 1979. Repr. of 1957 ed. lib. bdg. 20.50x (ISBN 0-313-20790-9, DRLE). Greenwood.

--Philosophy of History. (Orig.). 1964. pap. 10.95x ref. ed. (ISBN 0-13-663849-X). P-H.

Dray, William H., ed. Philosophical Analysis & History. LC 77-26206. 1978. Repr. of 1966 ed. lib. bdg. 34.00x (ISBN 0-313-20068-8, DRPA). Greenwood.

Dray, Williams, jt. ed. see Pampa, Leon.

Draycott, A. P. Sugar-Beet Nutrition. 250p. 1972. 35.95x o.p. (ISBN 0-470-22160-7). Halsted Pr.

Drayson, James E. Herd Bull Fertility. (Illus.). 160p. (Orig.). 1982. pap. 9.95 (ISBN 0-934318-08-5). J E Drayson.

Drayton, Grace & Fontana, Frank. Dolly Dingle Coloring Book. (Coloring Bks.). (Illus.). 32p. (Orig.). (gr. 2 up). 1983. pap. 2.00 (ISBN 0-486-24416-4). Dover.

Drayton, Grace G. More Dolly Dingle Paper Dolls. 32p. 1979. pap. 2.75 (ISBN 0-486-23848-2). Dover.

Drayton, Michael. Michael Drayton: Selected Poems. Thomas, Vivien, ed. (Fyfield). 1979. 7.95 o.p. (ISBN 0-85635-225-X, Pub. by Carcanet New Pr England); pap. 4.95 o.p. (ISBN 0-85635-226-8). Humanities.

Draze, Dianne. Design-a-Project. Schnare, Sharon, ed. (Illus.). 48p. (gr. 4-10). 1980. tchrs ed 12.00 (ISBN 0-931724-11-2). Dandy Lion.

--Options: A Guide for Creative Decision Making. Bachelis, Faren, ed. (Illus.). 72p. 1982. 8.00 (ISBN 0-931724-18-X). Dandy Lion.

Drazin, P. & Reid, W. Hydrodynamic Stability. LC 80-40273. (Cambridge Monographs on Mechanics & Applied Mathematics). (Illus.). 600p. 1981. 85.50 (ISBN 0-521-22798-4). Cambridge U Pr.

Drazin, P. G. & Reid, W. H. Hydrodynamic Stability. LC 80-40273. (Cambridge Monographs on Mechanics & Applied Mathematics). (Illus.). 539p. 1982. pap. 24.95 (ISBN 0-521-28980-7). Cambridge U Pr.

Draznin, Boris. Marshmellowterra: The Land of Marshmallow People & Whimsical Animals. (Illus.). 96p. (gr. 7-12). 1982. 6.50 (ISBN 0-682-49914-5). Exposition.

Dreben, Burton & Goldfarb, Warren D. Decision Problem: Solvable Classes of Quantificational Formulas. LC 79-18456. (Illus.). 1980. text ed. 32.50 (ISBN 0-201-02540-X); pap. text ed. o.p. (ISBN 0-201-02539-6). A-W.

Drebin, Allan R. & Chan, James L. Objectives of Accounting & Financial Reporting by Governmental Units: A Research Study, 2 vols. Incl. Vol. I. (Illus.). 128p. pap. no charge; Vol. II. (Illus.). 200p. pap. 7.50 (ISBN 0-686-84260-X). 1981. Municipal.

Drechsel, Robert. Newsmaking in the Trial Courts. LC 81-17202. (Professional Studies in Political Communication & Policy). 224p. 1982. 22.50x (ISBN 0-582-28319-1); pap. 9.95x (ISBN 0-582-28318-3). Longman.

Dreeben, Robert & Thomas, J. Alan, eds. Issues in Microanalysis. LC 79-62118. (Analysis of Educational Productivity Ser.: Vol. 1). 288p. 1980. prof ref 27.50x (ISBN 0-88410-191-6). Ballinger Pub.

Dreele, W. H. Von see Von Dreele, W. H.

Drees, Thomas. Blood Plasma: The Promise & the Politics. LC 82-11617. (Illus.). 1983. 25.00 (ISBN 0-87949-225-2). Ashley Bks.

Dreger, Carol, jt. auth. see Patterson, Barbara.

Dreher, Barbara B. & Gervase, Charles J. Phonetics: Instructional Aid in Language Arts. 1976. perfect bdg. 5.95 (ISBN 0-8403-1310-1). Kendall-Hunt.

Dreher, Denise, ed. see Goodale, Katherine D.

Dreher, E., ed. Schweizerische Gesellschaft fuer Gynaekologie und Geburtshilfe unter Mitkirkung der Schweizerischen Gesellschaft fuer Medizinische Genetik. Bericht ueber die Jahresversammlung, Zuerich, 1982. (Journal-Gynaekologische Rundschau: Vol. 22, Suppl. 3). (Illus.). iv, 104p. 1983. pap. 23.50 (ISBN 3-8055-3656-9). S Karger.

Dreher, G. K., ed. see Peele, George.

Dreier, Patricia, compiled by. The Gold of Friendship: A Bouquet of Special Thoughts. (Illus.). 1980. 5.50 (ISBN 0-8378-1707-2). Gibson.

Dreifus, J. J., jt. ed. see Baertschi, A. J.

Dreifus, Miriam. Brave Betsy. (See & Read Storybooks). (Illus.). (gr. k-3). 1961. PLB 3.96 o.p. (ISBN 0-399-60073-6). Putnam Pub Group.

Dreifuss. Childhood Epilepsy. 1983. text ed. 35.00 (ISBN 0-7236-7039-0). Wright-PSG.

Dreijmanis, John, jt. ed. see Browne, Eric C.

Dreikorn, Kurt, jt. auth. see Marberger, Michael.

Dreikurs, Rudolf. Challenge of Marriage. 1978. pap. 7.95 (ISBN 0-8015-1177-1, 0772-230, Hawthorn). Dutton.

--Challenge of Parenthood. 1979. 9.95 o.p. (ISBN 0-8015-1182-8, Hawthorn); pap. 5.95 o.p. (ISBN 0-8015-1183-6). Dutton.

--Coping with Children's Misbehavior. 1972. pap. 4.95 (ISBN 0-8015-1764-8, 0481-140, Hawthorn). Dutton.

Dreikurs, Rudolf & Grey, Loren. Parent's Guide to Child Discipline. 1970. pap. 3.95 (ISBN 0-8015-5736-4, 0383-120, Hawthorn). Dutton.

Dreikurs, Rudolf & Soltz, Vicki. Children: The Challenge. 1964. 9.95 (ISBN 0-8015-1248-4, Hawthorn); pap. 6.25 (ISBN 0-8015-1249-2, 0607-180, Hawthorn). Dutton.

Dreikurs, Rudolph. Discipline Without Tears. 1974. pap. 5.25 (ISBN 0-8015-2132-7, 0510-150, Hawthorn). Dutton.

Dreisbach, Robert H. Handbook of Poisoning: Prevention, Diagnosis, & Treatment. 11th ed. LC 79-92918. 578p. 1983. lexotone cover 11.00 (ISBN 0-87041-075-X). Lange.

Dreiser, Theodore. An American Tragedy. 832p. 1973. pap. 3.95 (ISBN 0-451-51696-6, CE1696, Sig Classics). NAL.

--Financier. 1967. pap. 3.95 (ISBN 0-451-51719-9, CE1719, Sig Classics). NAL.

--Sister Carrie. (Bantam Classics Ser.). 432p. (gr. 9-12). 1982. pap. 2.25 (ISBN 0-553-21058-0). Bantam.

--Sister Carrie. Salzman, Jack, ed. LC 69-16530. 1970. 5.50 o.p. (ISBN 0-685-91574-3); pap. 5.50 (ISBN 0-672-61014-0). Bobbs.

--Sister Carrie. 1962. pap. 2.25 (ISBN 0-451-51725-3, CE1725, Sig Classics). NAL.

--Titan. pap. 3.95 (ISBN 0-451-51688-5, CE1688, Sig Classics). NAL.

Dreiser, Theodore, et al. Harlan Miners Speak: Report on Terrorism in the Kentucky Coal Fields. LC 70-107410. (Civil Liberties in American History Ser.). 1970. Repr. of 1932 ed. lib. bdg. 32.50 (ISBN 0-306-71889-8). Da Capo.

Dreizen, LaVerne & Audet, Thelma. Medical Assistant's Examination Review Book, Vol. 1. 2nd. ed. 1979. 12.75 (ISBN 0-87488-490-X). Med Exam.

Drell, S. D., jt. auth. see Bjorken, James D.

Dreman, David. The New Contrarian Investment Strategy: The Psychology of Stock Market Sucess. LC 78-21820. Date not set. 16.95 (ISBN 0-394-52364-4). Random.

Drendel, Lou. Air War over Southeast Asia, Vol. I. (Illus.). 80p. 1982. softcover 8.95 (ISBN 0-89747-134-2, 6034). Squad Sig Pubns.

--Air War Over Southeast Asia, Vol. II. (Vietnam Studies Group Ser.). (Illus.). 80p. 1983. 8.95 (ISBN 0-89747-141-5). Squad Sig Pubns.

--F-Sixteeen Falcon in Action. (Aircraft in Action Ser.). (Illus.). 50p. 1982. saddlestitch 4.95 (ISBN 0-89747-133-4). Squad Sig Pubns.

--Phantom II, A Pictorial History of the McDonnell-Douglas F-4 Phantom II. (Illus.). 64p. 1982. 6.95 (ISBN 0-89747-062-1). Squad Sig Pubns.

--SR-Seventy-One Blackbird in Action. (Illus.). 50p. 1982. 4.95 (ISBN 0-89747-136-9, 1055). Squad Sig Pubns.

Drengson, Alan R., jt. ed. see Beehler, Roger.

Drennan, James C., ed. Orthopaedic Management of Neuromuscular Disorders. (Illus.). 384p. 1983. text ed. 39.50 (ISBN 0-397-50469-1, Lippincott Medical). Lippincott.

Drennen, D. A., ed. Modern Introduction to Metaphysics. LC 62-15360. 1962. text ed. 12.25 (ISBN 0-02-907600-5). Free Pr.

Dreosti, Ivor E., jt. ed. see Prasad, Ananda S.

Dreppard, Carl W. A Dictionary of American Antiques. (Illus.). 6.95 o.p. (ISBN 0-686-51542-0, 99013). Wallace-Homestead.

Drescher, Henrik. The Strange Appearance of Howard Cranebill, Jr. LC 82-71. (Illus.). 32p. (ps-3). 1982. 9.50 (ISBN 0-688-00961-1); PLB 9.00 (ISBN 0-688-00962-X). Lothrop.

--The Strange Appearance of Howard Cranebill Jr. (Illus.). (ps-3). 1982. 9.50 (ISBN 0-688-00961-1); PLB 8.59 (ISBN 0-688-00962-X). Morrow.

Drescher, Henrik & Zeit, Calvin. True Paranoid Facts. LC 82-61411. (Illus.). 64p. (Orig.). 1982. pap. 3.95 (ISBN 0-688-01854-8). Quill NY.

Drescher, Joan. I'm in Charge. (Illus.). (gr. 1-3). 1981. 9.95 (ISBN 0-316-19330-5, Pub. by Atlantic Pr). Little.

--Max & Rufus. (Illus.). (gr. k-3). 1982. PLB 9.20 (ISBN 0-395-32435-1); 8.95. HM.

Dresner, Joanne, ed. It's up to You. (English As a Second Language Bk.). (Illus.). 1979. pap. text ed. 4.95x (ISBN 0-582-79727-6); cassette 11.95x (ISBN 0-582-79728-4); plastic tote (book & cassette) 14.95x (ISBN 0-582-79771-3). Longman.

Dresner, Samuel H. God, Man & Atomic War. 6.95 (ISBN 0-87677-007-3). Hartmore.

--Zaddik: The Doctrine of the Zaddik According to the Writings of Rabbi Yaakov Yosef of Polnoy. LC 60-7228. 312p. 1974. pap. 4.95 (ISBN 0-8052-0437-7). Schocken.

Dressel, Paul L. Handbook of Academic Evaluation: Assessing Institutional Effectiveness, Student Progress, & Professional Performance for Decision Making in Higher Education. LC 75-44881. (Higher Education Ser.). (Illus.). 544p. 1976. 25.95x (ISBN 0-87589-276-0). Jossey-Bass.

Dressel, Paul L. & Marcus, Dora. On Teaching & Learning in College: Reemphasizing the Roles of Learners & the Disciplines. LC 82-48077. (Higher Education Ser.). 1982. text ed. 16.95x (ISBN 0-87589-543-3). Jossey Bass.

Dressel, Paul L. & Mayhew, Lewis B. Higher Education as a Field of Study: The Emergence of a Profession. LC 73-21073. (Higher Education Ser). 200p. 1974. 16.95x (ISBN 0-87589-226-4). Jossey-Bass.

Dresser, Christopher. The Art of Decorative Design. LC 76-17751. (Aesthetic Movement Ser.: Vol. 4). (Illus.). 1977. Repr. of 1862 ed. lib. bdg. 44.00x o.s.i. (ISBN 0-8240-2453-2). Garland Pub.

--Japan: Its Art, Architecture, & Art Manufacture. LC 76-17752. (Aesthetic Movement & the Arts & Crafts Movement Ser.: Vol. 5). 1977. Repr. of 1882 ed. lib. bdg. 44.00 o.s.i. (ISBN 0-8240-2454-0). Garland Pub.

--Unity in Variety. Stansky, Peter & Shewan, Rodney, eds. LC 76-17748. (Aesthetic Movement & the Arts & Crafts Movement Ser.). 1978. Repr. of 1859 ed. lib. bdg. 44.00x o.s.i. (ISBN 0-8240-2451-6). Garland Pub.

Dressler, Isidore. Preliminary Mathematics. (Orig.). 1980. pap. text ed. 11.58 (ISBN 0-87720-242-7). AMSCO Sch.

Dressler, Isidore & Rich, Barnett. Modern Algebra Two. (Orig.). (gr. 11-12). 1973. text ed. 14.25 (ISBN 0-87720-233-8); pap. text ed. 7.50 (ISBN 0-87720-232-X). AMSCO Sch.

Dressler, Robert E. & Stromberg, Karl. Techniques of Calculus. (Orig.). (gr. 12 up). 1982. text ed. 25.00 (ISBN 0-87720-979-0); pap. text ed. 17.50 (ISBN 0-87720-978-2). AMSCO Sch.

Dressler, Wofgang U. & Mayerthaler, Willi. Leitmotifs in Natural Morphology. 400p. 1982. 43.00 o.p. (ISBN 0-686-36244-6). Benjamins North Am.

Dressler, Wolfgang U., et al. Leifmotifs in Natural Morphology. (Studies in Language Companion Ser.: No. 10). 400p. (Orig.). 1983. 43.00 (ISBN 90-272-3009-9). Benjamins North Am.

Dretske, Fred I. Knowledge & the Flow of Information. LC 81-21633. (Illus.). 288p. 1981. text ed. 20.00x (ISBN 0-262-04063-8, Pub. by Bradford). MIT Pr.

--Knowledge & the Flow of Information. 288p. 1983. pap. 8.95x (ISBN 0-262-54038-X). MIT Pr.

Drevdahl, Elmer R. Profitable Use of Excavation Equipment. 14.95 (ISBN 0-89741-009-2); pap. 11.25 (ISBN 0-686-96875-1). Roadrunner Tech.

Drever, James I. The Geochemistry of Natural Waters. (Illus.). 400p. 1982. 34.95 (ISBN 0-13-351403-X). P-H.

Drew, Christopher, jt. auth. see Berry, Newton.

Drew, Clifford J. Introduction to Designing & Conducting Research. 2nd. ed. LC 79-25403. (Illus.). 1980. 18.95 (ISBN 0-8016-1460-0). Mosby.

Drew, Clifford J. & Hardman, Michael L. Mental Retardation: Social & Education Perspectives. LC 73-26680. (Illus.). 1977. pap. 12.00 o.p. (ISBN 0-8016-1462-7). Mosby.

Drew, D. R. Traffic Flow Theory & Control. LC 68-13626. (Transportation Ser). (Illus.). 1968. 34.50 o.p. (ISBN 0-07-017831-3, C). McGraw.

Drew, David. Man-Environment Processes. (Processes in Physical Geography Ser.: No. 6). (Illus.). 152p. 1983. pap. text ed. 9.95x (ISBN 0-04-551063-6). Allen Unwin.

Drew, Edwin P. The Complete Light-Pack Camping & Trail-Food Cookbook. (Orig.). 1977. pap. 4.95 (ISBN 0-07-017843-7, SP). McGraw.

Drew, Elizabeth. American Journal: The Events of 1976. (Giant Ser.). pap. 5.95 o.p. (ISBN 0-394-72611-1, V-611, Vin). Random.

--Washington Journal: A Diary of the Events of 1973-1974. 448p. 1975. 12.95 o.p. (ISBN 0-394-49575-6); pap. 4.95 (ISBN 0-394-72091-1). Random.

Drew, George. The Beatitudes: Attitudes for a Better Future. 63p. (Orig.). 1980. pap. 6.95 (ISBN 0-940754-03-7). Ed Ministries.

--The Original Ideas of Jesus That Are Changing the World. 45p. (Orig.). 1980. pap. 5.45 (ISBN 0-940754-05-3). Ed Ministries.

--The Parables in Depth. 55p. (Orig.). 1982. pap. 6.95 (ISBN 0-940754-18-5). Ed Ministries.

--The Prophets Speak to Our Time. 62p. (Orig.). 1981. pap. 6.95 (ISBN 0-940754-09-6). Ed Ministries.

Drew, Jane, jt. auth. see Fry, Maxwell.

Drew, John H. Kenilworth Castle Illustrated. 1981. 39.50x o.p. (ISBN 0-86023-150-X, Pub. by Barracuda England). State Mutual Bk.

--Yesterday's Town: Kenilworth. 1981. 39.50x o.p. (ISBN 0-86023-103-8, Pub. by Barracuda England). State Mutual Bk.

Drew, Jon S. Doing Business in the European Community. (Illus.). 1979. text ed. 34.95 (ISBN 0-408-10631-X). Butterworth.

Drew, L. R. & Stolz, P., eds. Man, Drugs & Society: Current Perspectives. new ed. 474p. (Orig.). 1982. pap. text ed. 25.95 (ISBN 0-909190-12-7, 1242, Pub. by ANUP Australia). Bks Australia.

Drew, Philip. The Architecture of Arata Isozaki. LC 81-48061. (Illus.). 206p. 1982. 33.65i (ISBN 0-06-431550-9, HarpT). Har-Row.

--The Architecture of Arata Isozaki. 216p. 1982. 90.00x o.p. (ISBN 0-246-11254-9, Pub. by Granada England). State Mutual Bk.

--The Meaning of Freedom. 460p. 1982. 35.50 (ISBN 0-08-025743-7). Pergamon.

--Two Towers: Australia Square MLC Centre by Harry Seidler. (Illus.). 56p. 1983. pap. 15.00 (ISBN 0-8390-0307-2). Allanheld & Schram.

Drew, Wayland. Corvette Summer. (Orig.). (RL 9). 1978. pap. 1.95 o.p. (ISBN 0-451-08014-9, J8014, Sig). NAL.

--Dragonslayer. (Orig.). 1981. pap. 2.75 (ISBN 0-345-29694-X, Del Rey). Ballantine.

Drewal, Henry J. & Drewal, Margaret T. Gelede: Art & Female Power among the Yoruba. LC 82-48388. (Traditional Arts of Africa Ser.). (Illus.). 352p. 1983. 32.50x (ISBN 0-253-32569-2). Ind U Pr.

Drewal, Margaret T., jt. auth. see Drewal, Henry J.

Drewett, R., jt. auth. see Drewitt, M.

Drewitt, M. & Drewett, R. Nature of Settle Structure & Change: A European View. 1984. write for info. (ISBN 0-08-028138-9). Pergamon.

Drewnowski, Jan, ed. Crisis in the East European Economy: The Spread of the Polish. LC 82-42560. 1982. 20.00x (ISBN 0-312-17314-8). St Martin.

Drewry, Gavin, jt. auth. see Burton, Ivor.

Drews, Robert. Basileus: The Evidence for Kingship in Geometric Greece. LC 82-10915. (Yale Classical Monographs: No. 4). 160p. 1983. text ed. 18.50x (ISBN 0-300-02831-8). Yale U Pr.

Drews, Toby R. Get Rid of Anxiety & Stress. 1982. pap. 4.95 (ISBN 0-88270-537-7). Bridge Pub.

Drexler, Charles H. The Authority to Teach: A Study in the Ecclesiology of Henry Edward Manning. LC 77-18567. 1978. pap. text ed. 9.00 o.p. (ISBN 0-8191-0410-8). U Pr of Amer.

Drey, Rudolph E. Apothecary Jars: Pharmaceutical Pottery & Porcelain in Europe & the East 1150-1850. (Illus.). 257p. 1978. 49.95 (ISBN 0-571-09965-3). Faber & Faber.

Dreyer, Frederick A. Burke's Politics: A Study in Whig Orthodoxy. 93p. 1979. text ed. 9.75x (ISBN 0-88920-077-7, Pub. by Wilfred Laurier U Pr Canada). Humanities.

Dreyer, Jacob S. Composite Reserve Assets in the International Monetary System, Vol. 2. Altman, Edward I. & Walter, Ingo, eds. LC 76-5757. (Contemporary Studies in Economic and Financial Analysis). 325p. 1977. lib. bdg. 34.50 (ISBN 0-89232-003-6). Jai Pr.

Dreyer, Jacob S., et al, eds. International Monetary System: A Time of Turbulence. 1982. 29.95 (ISBN 0-8447-2228-6); pap. 14.95 (ISBN 0-8447-2227-8). Am Enterprise.

Dreyer, Julie, jt. auth. see Olshan, Neil.

Dreyer, Peter. A Gardener Touched with Genius: The Life of Luther Burbank. LC 75-10477. (Illus.). 256p. 1975. 10.00 o.p. (ISBN 0-698-10691-1, Coward). Putnam Pub Group.

--Martyrs & Fanatics. 1980. 11.95 o.p. (ISBN 0-671-24428-0). S&S.

Dreyer, Sharon, et al. Guide to Nursing Management of Psychiatric Patients. 2nd ed. LC 78-31432. 248p. 1979. pap. text ed. 13.95 (ISBN 0-8016-0832-5). Mosby.

Dreyer, Sharon S. The Bookfinder: A Guide to Children's Literature About the Needs & Problems of Youth Aged 2 to 15, 2 vols. 1981. Set. text ed. 73.50 (ISBN 0-913476-44-7); Vol. 1. text ed. 39.50 (ISBN 0-913476-45-5); Vol. 2. text ed. 39.50 (ISBN 0-913476-46-3). Am Guidance.

Dreyfack, Raymond. Making It In Management the Japanese Way. 228p. 1982. 14.95 (ISBN 0-87863-006-6). Farnswth Pub.

Dreyfus, Alfred & Dreyfus, Pierre. The Dreyfus Case. LC 75-16227. 1977. Repr. of 1937 ed. 22.50 o.s.i. (ISBN 0-86527-046-5). Fertig.

--Dreyfus Case. 1937. text ed. 49.50x (ISBN 0-686-83527-1). Elliots Bks.

Dreyfus, Edward A. Adolescence: Theory & Experience. new ed. 256p. 1976. pap. text ed. 13.50 (ISBN 0-675-08679-5). Merrill.

Dreyfus, Hubert L. What Computers Can't Do: A Critique of Artificial Reason. 1979. pap. 7.50i (ISBN 0-06-090613-8, CN 613, CN). Har-Row.

Dreyfus, M. Bertrand, ed. International Codata Conference on Generation, Compilation, Evaluation & Dissemination of Data for Science & Technology, 4th: Proceedings. 160p. 1975. pap. 34.00 (ISBN 0-08-019850-3). Pergamon.

Dreyfus, Pierre, jt. auth. see Dreyfus, Alfred.

Dreyfuss, Henry, ed. Symbol Sourcebook: An Authoritative Guide to International Graphic Symbols. LC 71-172261. (Illus.). 320p. 1972. 54.95 (ISBN 0-07-017837-2, P&RB). McGraw.

Dreyfuss, Jack R. & Janower, Murray L. Radiology of the Colon. (Golden's Diagnostic Radiology Ser.: Section 21). 616p. 1980. lib. bdg. 65.00 (ISBN 0-683-02652-6). Williams & Wilkins.

Dreyfuss, Jack R. see Squire, Lucy F., et al.

Dreyfuss, P. Poly (Tetrahydrofuran, Vol. 8. (Polymer Monographs Ser.). 320p. 1981. 65.00 (ISBN 0-677-03330-3). Gordon.

Drickamer, H. G. Electron Transitions & the High Pressure Chemistry & Physics of Solids. (Studies in Chemical Physics). 1973. 35.00x (ISBN 0-412-11650-2, Pub. by Chapman & Hall). Methuen Inc.

Drickson, John, jt. ed. see Drillock, David.

Dridzo, Solomon A. Marx & the Trade Unions. LC 75-22758. 1976. Repr. of 1942 ed. lib. bdg. 16.00x (ISBN 0-8371-8352-9, DRMT). Greenwood.

Drier, Patricia, compiled by. The Blessings of Friendship. 1979. pap. 5.50 (ISBN 0-8378-5026-6). Gibson.

Driesen, W., et al, eds. Computerized Tomography-Brain Metabolism-Spinal Injuries. (Advances in Neurosurgery Ser.: Vol. 10). (Illus.). 420p. 1982. pap. 52.00 (ISBN 0-387-11115-8). Springer-Verlag.

Driessen, E. J., jt. auth. see De Boer, S. P.

Driessle, H., jt. auth. see Rognebakke, M.

Driessle, Hannelore, jt. auth. see Rognebakke, Myrtle.

Drifte, R., jt. ed. see Chapman, J. W.

Driggs, Frank & Lewine, Harris. Black Beauty, White Heat: A Pictorial History of Classic Jazz, 1920-1950. LC 82-60449. 360p. 1982. 39.95 (ISBN 0-688-03771-2). Morrow.

Drillock, David & Drickson, John, eds. The Divine Liturgy. 368p. 1982. text ed. 30.00 (ISBN 0-913836-95-8); pap. 20.00 (ISBN 0-913836-93-1). St Vladimirs.

Drimmer, Frederick, compiled by. A Friend Is Someone Special. LC 75-16038. 44p. 1976. boxed 3.95 (ISBN 0-8378-2101-0). Gibson.

Drinan, Robert F. Beyond the Nuclear Freeze. 176p. (Orig.). 1983. pap. 7.95 (ISBN 0-8164-2406-3). Seabury.

--Honor the Promise: America's Commitment to Israel. 250p. 7.95 (ISBN 0-686-95158-1). ADL.

Dring, M. J. The Biology of Marine Plants. 240p. 1983. pap. text ed. 19.95 (ISBN 0-7131-2860-7). E Arnold.

Drinker, Henry S., tr. see Schubert, Franz.

Drinnon, Anna M., ed. see Goldman, Emma.

Drinnon, Richard. Rebel in Paradise. LC 82-8531. (Phoenix). (Illus.). xvi, 350p. 1983. Repr. of 1961 ed. pap. 8.95 (ISBN 0-226-16364-4). U of Chicago Pr.

Drinnon, Richard, ed. see Goldman, Emma.

Dripps, Robert D., et al. Introduction to Anesthesia: The Principles of Safe Practice. 5th ed. LC 76-51011. (Illus.). 1977. text ed. 19.95 o.p. (ISBN 0-7216-3193-2). Saunders.

Driscoll, Clancy. Getting a Mortgage. (Illus.). 160p. 1980. 8.95 o.p. (ISBN 0-07-017852-6). McGraw.

Driscoll, Dennis M., jt. auth. see Griffiths, John F.

Driscoll, Donald C. & Davey, Homer C. The Practice of Real Estate in California. (Illus.). 304p. 1981. 21.95 (ISBN 0-13-693606-7). P-H.

Driscoll, Eileen R. The Selection & Appointment of School Heads. 3rd. ed. 1982. pap. 6.50 (ISBN 0-934338-47-7). NAIS.

Driscoll, F., jt. auth. see Coughlin, R.

Driscoll, F. F., jt. auth. see Coughlin, R. F.

Driscoll, Frederick F. Microprocessor-Microcomputer Technology. 1982. text ed. 24.95 (ISBN 0-534-01326-0, Pub. by Breton Pubs). Wadsworth Pubs.

Driscoll, Frederick F., Jr., jt. auth. see Coughlin, Robert F.

Driscoll, Laura A., jt. auth. see Goodwin, William L.

Driscoll, Lucy & Toda, K. Chinese Calligraphy. (Illus.). 1964. Repr. of 1932 ed. 12.50 o.p. (ISBN 0-8188-0026-7). Paragon.

Drisdale, Tommy & Hanes, Steven. The Ultralight Aviator's Handbook. (Illus.). 1982. pap. 16.95 (ISBN 0-686-38786-4). Skyflight Intl.

Driskill, Frank A. & Casad, Dede. Admiral of the Hills: Biography of Chester W. Nimitz. 1983. 11.95 (ISBN 0-89015-364-7). Eakin Pubns.

Driven, Rene & Goosens, Louis. The Scene of Linguistic Action & its Perspectivization by Speak, Talk, Say, & Tell. 1982. 16.00 (ISBN 90-272-2528-1). Benjamins North Am.

Driver, Clive E. Passing Through: Letters & Documents Written in Philadelphia by Famous Vistors. (Illus.). 144p. 1983. pap. 10.00 (ISBN 0-939084-14-7). Rosenbach Mus Lib.

--A Selection from Our Shelves: Books, Manuscripts & Drawings from the Rosenbach Foundation Museum. 1972. pap. 12.50x (ISBN 0-939084-08-2, Pub by Rosenbach Museum & Library). U Pr of Va.

Driver, Harold, et al. California Indians One: Indians Land Use & Occupancy in California, 3 vols. Beals, Ralph L., ed. (American Indian Ethnohistory Ser: California & Basin-Plateau Indians). (Illus.). Vol. 1 O.s.i. lib. bdg. 42.00 ea. (ISBN 0-8240-0771-9). Garland Pub.

Driver, Harold E. & Massey, William C. Comparative Studies of North American Indians. LC 57-11239. (Transactions Ser.: Vol. 47, Pt. 2). (Illus.). 1957. pap. 8.00 o.p. (ISBN 0-87169-472-7). Am Philos.

Driver, Harold E., ed. Americas on the Eve of Discovery. LC 79-15337. 1979. Repr. of 1964 ed. lib. bdg. 20.75x (ISBN 0-313-22028-X, DRAM). Greenwood.

Driver, Tom F. Romantic Quest & Modern Query: A History of the Modern Theater. LC 80-5756. 510p. 1980. lib. bdg. 20.75 (ISBN 0-8191-1217-8); pap. text ed. 10.75 (ISBN 0-8191-1218-6). U Pr of Amer.

Drivers License Guide Co. Drivers License Guide, 1982. (Illus.). 96p. 1982. pap. 10.95 o.p. (ISBN 0-938964-02-X). Drivers License.

--Drivers License Guide, 1983. (Illus.). 96p. 1983. pap. 12.95 (ISBN 0-938964-04-6). Drivers License.

--U. S. Identification Manual. (Illus.). 700p. 1982. 100.00 o.p. (ISBN 0-938964-03-8). Drivers License.

Drivers License Guide Co. Staff. U. S. Identification Manual. (Illus.). 700p. 1983. text ed. 100.00 (ISBN 0-686-38068-1). Drivers License.

Drizari, Nelo. Spoken & Written Albanian: A Practical Handbook. 1959. 7.50 (ISBN 0-8044-0131-4). Ungar.

Drob, Harold A., jt. auth. see Merrill, Irving R.

Drobinowski, W., et al. Calcium Binding Proteins. 1975. 67.50 (ISBN 0-444-99889-6). Elsevier.

Drobner, Hubertus R. Grefor von Nyssa: Die drei Tage Zwischen Tod und Auferstehung unseres Hern Jesus Christus. (Philosophia Patrum: Vol. 5). x, 252p. 1982. write for info. (ISBN 90-04-06553-9). E J Brill.

Droege, Thomas A. Faith Passages & Patterns. LC 82-48544. (Lead Bks.). 128p. 1983. pap. 3.95 (ISBN 0-8006-1602-2, 1-1602). Fortress.

Droge, Ed. The Honor Legion. 1979. pap. 1.95 o.p. (ISBN 0-451-08657-0, J8657, Sig). NAL.

Drogheda, Lord, et al. The Covent Garden Album: Two Hundred Fifty Years of Theatre, Opera & Ballet. 1982. 30.00 (ISBN 0-686-87366-1); pap. 16.95 (ISBN 0-7100-9336-5). Routledge & Kegan.

Drogin, Richard, jt. auth. see Orkin, Michael.

Drolet, Cindy. Unipix: Universal Language of Pictures. Drolet, Ken, ed. (Illus.). 58p. (Orig.). 1982. pap. 7.95 (ISBN 0-9609464-0-3). Imaginart Pr.

Drolet, Ken, ed. see Drolet, Cindy.

Dromgoole, Dick. The Poor Seekers. LC 70-127121. 1970. 7.95 o.p. (ISBN 0-913632-01-5). Am Univ Artforms.

Dromgoole, Dick, ed. see Stopple, Libby.

Dronenberg, D. H., jt. auth. see Bent, R. K.

Dronke, P. The Medieval Lyric. 1978. 29.95 (ISBN 0-521-21944-2); pap. 9.95x (ISBN 0-521-29319-7). Cambridge U Pr.

Dronke, Ursula, ed. Poetic Edda Vol. 1: Heroic Poems. 1969. 32.50x (ISBN 0-19-811497-4). Oxford U Pr.

Drooyan, Irving & Wooton, William. Beginning Algebra: An Individualized Approach. LC 78-625. 1978. 23.50x (ISBN 0-471-03877-6). Wiley.

--Elementary Algebra for College Students. 5th ed. LC 78-31666. 375p. 1980. text ed. 20.95 (ISBN 0-471-03607-2); solutions manual 8.95 (ISBN 0-471-05868-8). Wiley.

--Elementary Algebra with Geometry. LC 75-35736. 334p. 1976. text ed. 22.95x (ISBN 0-471-22245-3). Wiley.

Drooyan, Irving, jt. auth. see Carico, Charles C.

Drooyan, Irving, et al. Trigonometry: An Analytic Approach. 3rd ed. 1979. text ed. 20.95x o.p. (ISBN 0-02-330240-2); student study guide avail. o.p. (ISBN 0-685-96777-8); instr's. manual avail. o.p. (ISBN 0-685-96778-6). Macmillan.

--Trigonometry: An Analytic Approach. 4th ed. 370p. 1983. text ed. 23.95 (ISBN 0-02-330350-6). Macmillan.

--Introductory Algebra: A Guided Worktext. LC 81-99. 410p. 1982. text ed. 22.95x (ISBN 0-471-06318-5); text suppl. avail. (ISBN 0-471-86591-5). Wiley.

Dropkin, Ruth, ed. Science in the Open Classroom: Approaches to & Samples of Science Teaching in the Elementary School. (Illus.). 50p. 1973. pap. 1.50 o.p. (ISBN 0-918374-14-6). Workshop Ctr.

Dropkin, Stan, et al. Contemporary American Education. 3rd ed. 512p. 1975. pap. text ed. 12.95x (ISBN 0-02-330190-2, 33019). Macmillan.

Dropkin, Victor H. Introduction to Plant Nematology. LC 80-13556. 293p. 1980. 31.50x (ISBN 0-471-05578-6, Pub. by Wiley Interscience). Wiley.

Droque, A. C. Chambre des Pairs de France. (Slave Trade in France Ser., 1744-1848). 154p. (Fr.). 1974. Repr. of 1821 ed. lib. bdg. 47.00 o.p. (ISBN 0-8287-1344-8, TN150). Clearwater Pub.

Dror, Yehezkel. Public Policymaking Reexamined. (Illus.). 420p. 1983. pap. text ed. 19.95 (ISBN 0-87855-928-0). Transaction Bks.

Dror, Yehezkel, jt. auth. see Horowitz, Irving L.

Droske, Susan C. Pediatric Diagnostic Procedures. LC 80-22920. 293p. 1981. pap. 14.95 (ISBN 0-471-04928-X, Pub. by Wiley Med). Wiley.

Drossin, Julius, jt. auth. see Martin, William R.

Drossman, Melvyn, jt. auth. see Belove, Charles.

Droste, R. L., jt. ed. see Schiller, E. J.

Drotar, David L., jt. auth. see Madison, Arnold.

Drotning, Jayne & Masotto, Rosemarie. Creative Woodworking. (Illus.). 1979. 12.95 (ISBN 0-8092-7158-3); pap. 8.95 (ISBN 0-8092-7157-5). Contemp Bks.

Drotning, Phillip T. Putting the Fun in Fund Raising: Five Hundred Ways to Raise Money for Charity. 1979. 10.95 o.p. (ISBN 0-8092-7627-5). Contemp Bks.

Drotning, Phillip T., jt. auth. see Crain, Sharie.

Drott, M. Carl, jt. auth. see Mancall, Jacqueline C.

Drouet, F. Revision of the Nostocaceae with Constricted Trichomes. (Beihefte zur Nova Hedwigia: No. 57). (Illus.). 1978. text ed. 40.00 (ISBN 3-7682-5457-7). Lubrecht & Cramer.

--Revision of the Stigonematacaea: With a Summary of the Classification of Blue-Green Algae. (Nova Hedwigia Beiheft: No. 66). (Illus.). 300p. 1981. lib. bdg. 48.00x (ISBN 3-7682-5466-6). Lubrecht & Cramer.

Drouet, Francais. Summary of the Classification of Blue-Green Algae. (Illus.). 1981. pap. text ed. 8.00x (ISBN 3-7682-1293-9). Lubrecht & Cramer.

Drouet, L. Method of Flute Playing. (The Flute Library: Vol. 17). 1981. Repr. of 1830 ed. write for info. o.s.i. (ISBN 90-6027-390-7, Pub. by Frits Knuf Netherlands); wrappers write for info. o.s.i. (ISBN 90-6027-213-7, Pub. by Frits Knuf Netherlands). Pendragon NY.

Drought, A. Bernard, ed. see Teller, Edward, et al.

Drouillard, Richard, jt. auth. see Raynor, Sherry.

Drover, jt. auth. see Dawson.

Droz, Eugenie, et al, eds. Trois Chansonniers Francais Du XV Siecle. (Music Reprint Ser.). 1978. Repr. of 1927 ed. lib. bdg. 29.50 (ISBN 0-306-77561-1). Da Capo.

Drozd, J. Chemical Derivatization in Gas Chromatography. (Journal of Chromatography Library: Vol. 19). 1981. 51.00 (ISBN 0-444-41917-9). Elsevier.

Drozd, V. N. & Zefirov, N. S. Sigmatropic Additions & Cyclosubstitutions in Five-Membered Heterocyclic Compounds Containing Exocyclic Double Bonds. (Sulfur Reports Ser.). 45p. 1981. pap. 15.00 (ISBN 3-7186-0081-1). Harwood Academic.

Dr. Suess. The Cat in the Hat in English & French. Vallier, Jean, tr. (French Beginner Bks.). (Illus.). (gr. k-3). 1967. PLB 7.00 (ISBN 0-394-81063-5). Random.

Dru, Ricki. The First Blue Jeans. LC 78-14398. (Famous Firsts Ser.). (Illus.). 1978. PLB 10.76 (ISBN 0-89547-059-4). Silver.

Drucker, H. M. Doctrine & Ethos in the Labour Party. 1979. text ed. 19.95x (ISBN 0-04-329026-4); pap. text ed. 8.95x (ISBN 0-04-329027-2). Allen Unwin.

Drucker, Harvey, ed. Biological Implications of Metals in the Environment: Proceedings. Wildung, Raymond E. LC 77-1039. (ERDA Symposium Ser.). 692p. 1977. pap. 25.25 (ISBN 0-87079-104-4, CONF-750929); microfiche 4.00 (ISBN 0-87079-149-4, CONF-750929). DOE.

Drucker, Malka. Hanukkah: Eight Nights, Eight Lights. LC 80-15852. (A Jewish Holidays Book). (Illus.). 96p. (gr. 5 up). 1980. PLB 9.95 (ISBN 0-8234-0377-7). Holiday.

--Passover: A Season of Freedom. LC 80-8810. (A Jewish Holidays Book). (Illus.). 96p. (gr. 5 up). 1981. PLB 9.95 (ISBN 0-8234-0389-0). Holiday.

--Sukkot: A Time to Rejoice, A Jewish Holidays Book. LC 82-80814. (Illus.). 96p. (gr. 5 up). 1982. Reinforced bdg. 10.95 (ISBN 0-8234-0466-8). Holiday.

Drucker, Mark, ed. Urban Decision Making...a Guide to Information Sources. LC 80-19252. (Urban Studies Information Guide Series. Part of the Gale Information Guide Library: Vol. 13). 200p. 1981. 42.00x (ISBN 0-8103-1481-9). Gale.

Drucker, Peter F. Age of Discontinuity. 1978. pap. 5.95xi (ISBN 0-06-131973-2, TB1973, Torch). Har-Row.

--Age of Discontinuity: Guidelines to Our Changing Society. LC 68-28192. 1969. 14.37i (ISBN 0-06-011093-7, HarpT). Har-Row.

--The Concept of the Corporation. LC 72-74. (John Day Bk.). 352p. 1972. 13.41i (ISBN 0-381-98093-6, A16190). T Y Crowell.

--Effective Executive. LC 67-11341. 1967. 12.45i (ISBN 0-06-031825-2, HarpT). Har-Row.

--The Last of All Possible Worlds: A Novel. LC 81-48034. 288p. 1982. 13.41i (ISBN 0-06-014974-4, HarpT). Har-Row.

--Managing for Results. LC 64-12670. 1964. 14.37i (ISBN 0-06-031830-9, HarpT). Har-Row.

--Managing in Turbulent Times. LC 79-33389. 1980. 12.45i (ISBN 0-06-011094-5, HarpT). Har-Row.

--Men, Ideas & Politics. LC 73-138719. 1971. 12.45i (ISBN 0-06-011091-0, HarpT). Har-Row.

--Men, Ideas & Politics. 1977. pap. 4.95xi o.p. (ISBN 0-06-131947-3, TB1947, Torch). Har-Row.

--Toward the Next Economics & Other Essays. LC 80-8370. 256p. 1981. 12.45i (ISBN 0-06-014828-4, HarpT). Har-Row.

--The Unseen Revolution: How Pension Fund Socialism Came to America. LC 75-34795. 160p. 1976. 10.53i (ISBN 0-06-011097-X, HarpT). Har-Row.

Drucker, Peter F., et al. Power & Democracy in America. D'Antonio, William V. & Ehrlich, Howard J., eds. LC 79-28576. xviii, 181p. 1980. Repr. of 1961 ed. lib. bdg. 19.00x (ISBN 0-313-22319-X, PDAM). Greenwood.

Drucker, Philip. Indians of the Northwest Coast. pap. 4.50 (ISBN 0-385-02443-6, B3, AMS). Natural Hist.

Drucker-Brown, Susan, ed. see Malinowski, Bronislaw.

Drud, Arne & Grais, Wafik. Thailand: An Analysis of Structural & Non-Structural Adjustments. LC 82-10890. (World Bank Staff Working Papers: No. 513). (Orig.). 1982. pap. text ed. 5.00 (ISBN 0-8213-0023-7). World Bank.

Drude, O., jt. ed. see Engler, A.

Drudy, P. J., ed. Ireland: Land, Politics & People. LC 81-18044. (Irish Studies Ser.: Vol. 2). (Illus.). 250p. 1982. 49.50 (ISBN 0-521-24577-X). Cambridge U Pr.

Druick, Douglas & Hoog, Michel. Henri Fantin-Latour. (Illus.). 350p. 1983. pap. price not set (56351-0). U of Chicago Pr.

Druist, Miriam. Wildlife on the Farm. 1977. 6.00 (ISBN 0-686-23334-4). Rod & Staff.

Drujan, Boris D. & Laufer, Miguel, eds. The S-Potential. LC 82-20394. (Progress in Clinical & Biological Research Ser.: Vol. 113). 319p. 1982. 60.00 (ISBN 0-8451-0113-7). A R Liss.

Druks, Herbert. Jewish Resistance to the Holocaust. 132p. 1983. text ed. 14.95x (ISBN 0-8290-1295-8). Irvington.

Druley, Ray M. & Ordway, Gerald L. Toxic Substances Control Act. rev. ed. LC 81-12811. 416p. 1981. pap. 19.50 (ISBN 0-87179-362-8). BNA.

Drum, David J. & Figler, Howard E. Outreach in Counseling: Applying the Growth & Prevention Model in Schools & Colleges. LC 77-8091. 1973. pap. 7.50x (ISBN 0-910328-11-0). Carroll Pr.

Drummond, A. M. & Coles-Mogford, A. M. Applied Typing. 4th ed. 240p. 1983. price not set (ISBN 0-07-084650-2). McGraw.

Drummond, David A. & Perkins, G. Dictionary of Russian Obscenities. rev. ed. 79p. (Rus. & Eng.). 1980. pap. text ed. 3.50 (ISBN 0-933884-17-6). Berkeley Slavic.

Drummond, Donald. Mountain. LC 82-72569. 63p. 1971. 5.95 (ISBN 0-8040-0519-2); pap. 3.25 (ISBN 0-8040-0619-9). Swallow.

Drummond, Donald F. Passing of American Neutrality, Nineteen Thirty-Seven-Nineteen Forty-One. LC 68-54416. (Illus.). 1968. Repr. of 1955 ed. lib. bdg. 20.25x (ISBN 0-8371-0394-0, DRAN). Greenwood.

Drummond, G. I., et al, eds. see International Conference on Cyclic Amp, 2nd, July, 1974.

Drummond, Gordon D. The German Social Democrats in Opposition, 1949-1960. 1982. 27.50 (ISBN 0-8061-1730-3). U of Okla Pr.

Drummond, Henry. The Doctrine of Immortality & the Conquest of Eternal Life. (An Essential Knowledge Library Bk.). (Illus.). 137p. 1983. Repr. of 1886 ed. 67.75 (ISBN 0-89901-102-0). Found Class Reprints.

--The Greatest Thing in the World. Bd. with The Skeleton in the Closet. Darrow, Clarence. pap. 3.00 (ISBN 0-8283-1438-1, IPL). Branden.

--Greatest Thing in the World. 1959. 2.50 (ISBN 0-448-01642-7, G&D). Putnam Pub Group.

--Greatest Thing in the World. (Inspirational Classic Ser). 64p. 1968. 4.95 (ISBN 0-8007-1144-0); pap. 2.25 (ISBN 0-8007-8018-3, Spire Bks). Revell.

--The Greatest Thing in the World. 1.95 o.p. (ISBN 0-686-92335-9, 6416). Hazelden.

Drummond, Henry, et al. Inspiration Three, Vol. 2: Three Famous Classics in One Book. LC 73-80032. (Pivot Family Reader Ser.). 128p. 1973. pap. 1.25 o.p. (ISBN 0-87983-042-5). Keats.

Drummond, Ian. The Floating Pound & the Sterling Area, 1931-1939. LC 80-14539. 352p. 1981. 47.50 (ISBN 0-521-23165-5). Cambridge U Pr.

Drummond, Ivor. A Tank of Sacred Eels. LC 75-40785. 1976. 8.95 o.p. (ISBN 0-312-78505-4). St Martin.

Drummond, June. The Trojan Mule. 159p. 1982. 17.50 (ISBN 0-575-03135-2, Pub. by Gollancz England). David & Charles.

Drummond, Lewis A. The Revived Life. LC 82-71217. 1982. pap. 5.95 (ISBN 0-8054-5205-2). Broadman.

Drummond, M. F. Principles of Economic Appraisal in Health Care. (Illus.). 1980. pap. 15.95x (ISBN 0-19-261273-5). Oxford U Pr.

--Studies in Economic Appraisal in Health Care. 224p. 1981. text ed. 35.00x (ISBN 0-19-261274-3). Oxford U Pr.

Drummond, Robert R. Early German Music in Philadelphia. LC 74-125068. (Music Ser). 1970. Repr. of 1910 ed. lib. bdg. 16.50 (ISBN 0-306-70005-0). Da Capo.

Drury, Allen. Advise & Consent. 1972. pap. 3.50 o.s.i. (ISBN 0-380-01007-0, 52340). Avon.

--Capable of Honor. LC 66-20961. 1966. 15.95 (ISBN 0-385-01028-1). Doubleday.

--Come Nineveh, Come Tyre. 1974. pap. 2.95 o.s.i. (ISBN 0-380-00126-8, 52027). Avon.

--Decision. 504p. 1983. 17.95 (ISBN 0-385-18832-3). Doubleday.

--A God Against the Gods. LC 75-41673. 336p. 1976. 14.95 (ISBN 0-385-00199-1). Doubleday.

--Preserve & Protect. LC 68-26725. 1968. 14.95 (ISBN 0-385-01030-3). Doubleday.

--The Promise of Joy. LC 74-18774. 456p. 1975. 14.95 (ISBN 0-385-04396-1). Doubleday.

--A Senate Journal, 1943-1945. LC 76-38824. (FDR & the Era of the New Deal Ser.). 1972. Repr. of 1963 ed. lib. bdg. 59.50 (ISBN 0-306-70448-X). Da Capo.

--Shade of Difference. LC 62-8838. 1962. 15.95 (ISBN 0-385-02389-8). Doubleday.

Drury, Blanche J., jt. auth. see Schmid, Andrea B.

Drury, C. G., ed. Human Reliability in Quality Control. Fox, J. G. LC 75-11695. (Illus.). 315p. 1975. 27.50x (ISBN 0-85066-088-2). Intl Pubns Serv.

Drury, C. G. & Fox, J. G., eds. Human Reliability in Quality Control. LC 75-11695. 315p. 1975. 29.95x o.s.i. (ISBN 0-470-22315-4). Halsted Pr.

Drury, Elizabeth, jt. ed. see Bridgeman, Harriet.

Drury, G. Thorn, ed. see Waller, Edmund.

Drury, George. Facts & Figures about North American Railroads: The Unofficial Guide. Hayden, Bob, ed. (Illus., Orig.). 1983. pap. price not set (ISBN 0-89024-061-2). Kalmbach.

Drury, Ian, intro. by. Hard Lines. (Illus.). 1983. pap. 3.95 (ISBN 0-571-13073-9). Faber & Faber.

Drury, John, ed. & tr. see Bellini, Enzo, et al.

Drury, John, ed. & tr. see Bellini, Enzo.

Drury, John, ed. & tr. see Bellini, Enzo, et al.

Drury, John, tr. see Boff, Leonardo.

Drury, John, tr. see Camps, Arnulf.

Drury, John, tr. see Segundo, Jean L.

Drury, John, tr. see Segundo, Juan L.

Drury, Jolyon, jt. auth. see Falconer, Peter.

Drury, K. This Is the Newfoundland. 17.95 (ISBN 0-87666-340-4, PS666). TFH Pubns.

Drury, M. The Danger of Words. (Studies in Philosophical Psychology). 136p. 1973. text ed. 7.50x (ISBN 0-391-00277-5). Humanities.

Drury, Michael. Every Whit Whole: The Adventure of Spiritual Healing. LC 78-18389. 1978. 5.95 o.p. (ISBN 0-396-07578-9). Dodd.

Drury, Nevill. The Healing Power: A Handbook of Alternative Medicine & Natural Health in Australia & New Zealand. (Illus.). 235p. 1982. pap. 12.95 (ISBN 0-938190-10-5). North Atlantic.

--The Shaman & the Magician: Journeys Between the Worlds. 156p. (Orig.). 1982. pap. 8.95 (ISBN 0-7100-0910-0). Routledge & Kegan.

Drury, P., jt. auth. see Finn, R.

Drury, Rebecca. Bitter Victory. (Women at War Ser.: No. 16). (Orig.). 1983. pap. 3.25 (ISBN 0-440-00648-1). Dell.

--Courage at Sea. (Women at War Ser.: No. 12). (Orig.). 1983. pap. 3.25 (ISBN 0-440-01485-9). Dell.

--Darkness at Dawn. (Women at War Ser.: No. 11). (Orig.). 1983. pap. 3.25 (ISBN 0-440-01663-0, Emerald). Dell.

--Desert Battle. (Women at War Ser.: No. 15). (Orig.). 1983. pap. 3.25 (ISBN 0-440-02065-4). Dell.

--Distant Thunder. (Women at War Ser.: No. 14). (Orig.). 1983. pap. 3.25 (ISBN 0-440-01899-4, Emerald). Dell.

--Splendid Victory. (Woman at War Ser.: No. 10). 352p. (Orig.). 1983. pap. 3.25 (ISBN 0-440-08016-9, Emerald). Dell.

--Valiant Wings. (Women at War Ser.: No. 13). (Orig.). 1983. pap. 3.25 (ISBN 0-440-09243-4). Dell.

Drury, Roger. The Finches Fabulous Furnace. (Illus.). (gr. 4-6). 1971. 8.95 (ISBN 0-316-19348-8). Little.

Druse, Kenneth. Free Things for Gardeners. Osborn, Susan, ed. LC 81-15396. (Free Things! A Bargain Hunter's Bonanza Ser.). 128p. 1982. pap. 4.95 (ISBN 0-399-50604-7, Perige). Putnam Pub Group.

Druskin, Mikhail S. Igor Stravinsky: His Life, Works & Views. Cooper, Martin, tr. 190p. 1982. 24.95 (ISBN 0-521-24590-7). Cambridge U Pr.

Druten, John Van see Van Druten, John.

Drutman, Irving, ed. see Flanner, Janet.

Drvodelic, M. Yugoslavic Dictionary: English-Croata-Serbian. 6th ed. 1981. text ed. 27.50x o.p. (ISBN 0-89918-670-X, Y670). Vanous.

Dryansky, Gerald. The Heirs. LC 78-5222. 1978. 12.50 o.p. (ISBN 0-399-11976-0). Putnam Pub Group.

Dryden. Efficient Use of Energy. 2nd ed. 1982. text ed. 89.95 (ISBN 0-408-01250-1). Butterworth.

Dryden, H. L., et al see Von Mises, Richard & Von Karman, Theodore.

Dryden, I. G., ed. Coal Science, Vol. 1. (Serial Publication). 304p. 1982. 32.50 (ISBN 0-12-150701-7). Acad Pr.

Dryden, John. A Choice of Dryden's Verse. Auden, W. H., ed. 116p. 1973. pap. 3.95 (ISBN 0-571-10255-7). Faber & Faber.

--Four Comedies. Beaurline, L. A. & Bowers, Fredson, eds. LC 67-26813. (Curtain Playwrites Ser.). 1968. 22.50x o.s.i. (ISBN 0-226-16565-5). U of Chicago Pr.
--Poems of John Dryden, 4 Vols. Kinsley, James, ed. (Oxford English Texts Ser.). 1958. Set. 154.00x (ISBN 0-19-811810-4). Oxford U Pr.
--The Works of John Dryden. Incl. Vol. I, Poems, 1649-1680. Hooker, Edward N. & Swedenberg, H. T., eds. 1956. 48.50x (ISBN 0-520-00358-6); Vol. II, Poems, 1681-1684. Swedenberg, H. T., ed. 1973. 48.50x (ISBN 0-520-02118-5); Vol. III, Poems, 1684-1692. Miner, Earl & Dearing, Vinton A., eds. 1970. 48.50x (ISBN 0-520-01625-4); Vol. IV, Poems, 1693-1699. Chambers, A. B., et al, eds. 1974. 50.00x (ISBN 0-520-02120-7); Vol. VIII, Plays, The Wild Gallant, The Rival Ladies, The Indian Ladies. Smith, John H., et al, eds. 1962. 48.50x (ISBN 0-520-00359-4); Vol. IX, Plays; The Indian Emporour, Secret Love, Sir Martin Mar-All. Loftis, John & Dearing, Vinton A., eds. 1966. 48.50x (ISBN 0-520-00360-8); Vol. X, Plays; The Tempest, Tyrannick Love, An Evenings Love. Novak, Maximillan E. & Giuffey, George R., eds. 1970. 48.50x (ISBN 0-520-01589-4); Vol. XI, Plays; The Conquest of Granada, Part I & II, Marriage-a-la Mode, & The Assignation-or, Love in a Nunnery. Loftis, John, et al, eds. 1978. 50.00x (ISBN 0-520-02125-8); Vol. XV, Plays; Albion & Albanios, Don Sebastion, Anphitryon. Miner, Earl, ed. 1976. 25.50x (ISBN 0-520-02129-0); Vol. XVII, Prose, 1668-1691, an Essay of Dramatic Poesie & Shorter Works. Monk, Samuel A. & Maurer, A. E., eds. 1972. 48.50x (ISBN 0-520-01814-1); Vol. XVIII, The History of the League, 1684. Roper, Alan & Vinton, Dearing, eds. 1974. 48.50x (ISBN 0-520-02131-2); Vol. XIX, Prose, The Life of St. Francis Xavier. Roper, Alan & Vinton, Dearing A., eds. 1979. 52.50x (ISBN 0-520-02132-0). U of Cal Pr.

Dryden, John & Shadwell, Thomas. Dryden & Shadwell: The Literary Controversy & MacFlecknoe 1668-1678. Oden, Richard L., ed. LC 77-5952. 1977. lib. bdg. 45.00x (ISBN 0-8201-1289-5). Schol Facsimiles.

Dryden, John, tr. see Plutarch.

Dryden, Pamela. Mask For My Heart. 1982. pap. 1.95 (ISBN 0-451-11943-6, Sig Vista). NAL.

Dryer, R., jt. auth. see Fisher, J.

Dryer, Robert L., jt. auth. see Montogomery, Rex.

Dryfhout, John H. The Work of Augustus Saint-Gaudens. LC 82-7095. (Illus.). 368p. 1982. 60.00 (ISBN 0-87451-243-3). U Pr of New Eng.

Drymon, Kathleen. Wild Desires. 1982. pap. 3.50 (ISBN 0-8217-1103-2). Zebra.

Drysdale, Vera L. & Brown, Joseph E. The Gift of the Sacred Pipe. (Illus.). 128p. 1982. 29.95 (ISBN 0-8061-1806-7). U of Okla Pr.

Dryuk, V. G. The Mechanism of Epoxidation of Olefins by Pelacids. 1977. text ed. write for info. (ISBN 0-08-021586-6). Pergamon.

Drywer, R., jt. ed. see Fisher, J.

D'Silva, Emmanuel H., jt. auth. see Goering, Theodore J.

Duane, Allan. The Hadrian Ransom. LC 78-24411. 1979. 9.95 o.p. (ISBN 0-399-12177-3). Putnam Pub Group.

Duane, Thomas, ed. see Loose Leaf Reference Service.

Duane, Thomas D. & Jaeger, Edward A., eds. Biomedical Foundations of Opthalmology, 3 vols. (Illus.). 1982. 300.00 (ISBN 0-686-97942-7, Harper Medical); revision pages 25.00 (ISBN 0-686-97943-5). Lippincott.

Duarte, Alex. Stop Your Cataract. 1981. 4.00x (ISBN 0-686-32618-0). Cancer Control Soc.

Duarte, R. L., jt. auth. see Duarte, Salvador R.

Duarte, Salvador R. & Duarte, R. L. Electronics Assembly & Fabrication Methods. 2nd ed. Orig. Title: Electronics Assembly Methods. 1973. text ed. 14.95 (ISBN 0-07-017880-1, G); instructors' guide 2.95 (ISBN 0-07-017881-X). McGraw.

Duax, jt. auth. see Griffin.

Dubacher, H., ed. see Ladewig, D. & Hobi, V.

Duban, James. Melville's Major Fiction: Politics, Theology, & Imagination. (Illus.). 250p. 1982. 22.00 (ISBN 0-87580-086-6). N Ill U Pr.

DuBane, Janet & Kuman, Alexandra, eds. Quick & Quilted Projects. (Illus.). 64p. (Orig.). 1981. pap. 2.50 (ISBN 0-918178-26-6). Simplicity.

Dubanevich, Arlene. Hearts in Love. (Illus.). 80p. 1983. cancelled (ISBN 0-02-533600-2). Macmillan.

Dubanevich, Arlene, jt. auth. see Nassisi, Thomas.

DuBarry, Jacques. French Rainbows. LC 81-80155. (Illus.). 512p. 1983. 19.95 (ISBN 0-86666-003-8). GWP.

Du Bartas, Guillaume D. Bartas: His Devine Weekes & Workes. LC 65-10398. 1965. Repr. of 1605 ed. lib. bdg. 70.00x (ISBN 0-8201-1265-8). Schol Facsimiles.

Dubasov, Yu V., jt. auth. see Vdovenko, V. M.

Du Bay, Bill, tr. see Rovin, Jeff.

DuBay, Sandra. Fidelity's Flight. 448p. (Orig.). 1982. pap. cancelled o.p. (ISBN 0-505-51825-2). Tower Bks.

Dubay, Thomas. God Dwells Within Us. 6.95 (ISBN 0-87193-027-7). Dimension Bks.
--Pilgrims Pray. LC 74-533. 1976. pap. 3.95 o.p. (ISBN 0-8189-0335-X). Alba.

Dubbel, S. Earl. Daughter of the Plain Folk. LC 72-95023. 192p. 1975. pap. 3.95 (ISBN 0-8024-1762-0). Moody.

Dubbey, J. M. The Mathematical Work of Charles Babbage. LC 77-71409. (Illus.). 1978. 52.50 (ISBN 0-521-21649-4). Cambridge U Pr.

Dube. Structure & Meaning. 2d ed. 1982. text ed. 19.95 (ISBN 0-686-84579-X, LT26); instr's. manual avail. (LT27). HM.

Dube, Anthony & Franson, J. Earl. Structure & Meaning: An Introduction to Literature. LC 82-83173. 1296p. 1983. text ed. 18.95 (ISBN 0-395-32570-6); write for info. instr's manual (ISBN 0-395-32571-4). HM.

Dube, Anthony, et al. Structure & Meaning: An Introduction to Literature. LC 75-31038. (Illus.). 1152p. 1976. text ed. 18.95 (ISBN 0-395-21967-1); instr's. manual, Teaching Structure & Meaning 1.25 (ISBN 0-395-21968-X). HM.

Dube, H. C. A Textbook of Fungi, Bacteria & Viruses. 1978. 12.50x o.p. (ISBN 0-7069-0587-3, Pub. by Vikas India). Advent NY.

Dube, Normand. Le Nuage de ma Pensee. (Illus.). 91p. (Fr.). (gr. 11-12). 1981. pap. 2.50x (ISBN 0-911409-12-2). Natl Mat Dev.

Dube, Pierre H., et al. A Concordance to Flaubert's Madame Bovary, 2 vols. LC 77-83409. (Library of Humanities Reference Bks.: No. 109). lib. bdg. 120.00 o.s.i. (ISBN 0-8240-9832-3). Garland Pub.

Dube, R. K., jt. auth. see Upadhyaya, G. S.

Dube, S. C. Explanation & Management of Change. 1974. text ed. 3.95 o.p. (ISBN 0-07-096388-6, P&RB). McGraw.

Du'Bellay, Joachim. The Regrets. Sisson, C. H., tr. from Fr. 128p. 1983. pap. text ed. 6.95x (ISBN 0-85635-471-6, Pub. by Carcanet New Pr England). Humanities.

Dubelman, A. J. On the Straight Path. LC 78-65997. 1979. 7.50 o.p. (ISBN 0-533-04131-7). Vantage.

Dubelman, Richard. The Adventures of Holly Hobbie. 1980. 10.95 o.s.i. (ISBN 0-440-00154-4, E Friede). Delacorte.

Duberman, Lucile & Hartjen, Clayton. Sociology: Focus on Society. 1979. text ed. 19.95x o.p. (ISBN 0-673-15287-1); study guide 6.95x o.p. (ISBN 0-673-15294-4). Scott F.

DuBey, R. E., et al. A Practical Guide for Dynamic Conferences. LC 80-6083. (Illus.). 180p. 1982. lib. bdg. 22.25 (ISBN 0-8191-2152-5); pap. text ed. 10.00 (ISBN 0-8191-2153-3). U Pr of Amer.

DuBey, Robert E., et al. Performance-Based Guide to Student Teaching. 2nd ed. 1975. pap. text ed. 6.50x (ISBN 0-8134-1713-9, 1713). Interstate.

Dubey, Vinod & Faruqi, Shakil. Turkey Policies & Prospects for Growth. xxxi, 316p. 1980. pap. 10.00 (ISBN 0-686-36123-7, RC-8003). World Bank.

Dubin, Arthur D. Some Classic Trains. LC 64-14749. (Illus.). 434p. 1964. 30.00 o.p. (ISBN 0-89024-011-6). Kalmbach.

Dubin, F. & Margol, M. It's Time to Talk: Communication Activities for Learning English As a New Language. 1977. pap. text ed. 11.95 (ISBN 0-13-507103-8); tchr's man. o.p. free. P-H.

Dubin, F. & Olshtain, E. Facilitating Language Learning: A Guidebook for the ESL-EFL Teacher. 1977. pap. 5.50 (ISBN 0-07-017877-1). McGraw.

Dubin, F. S., et al. How to Save Energy & Cut Costs in Existing Industrial & Commercial Buildings-an Energy Conservation Manual. LC 76-40570. (Energy Technology Review: No. 10). (Illus.). 1977. 24.00 o.p. (ISBN 0-8155-0638-4). Noyes.

Dubin, Fred S. & Long, Chalmers G., Jr. Energy Conservation Standards. (Illus.). 1978. 32.50 (ISBN 0-07-017883-6, P&RB). McGraw.
--Energy Conservation Standards: For Building Design, Construction & Operation. 432p. 1982. 14.95 (ISBN 0-07-017884-4). McGraw.

Dubin, Robert. Handbook of Work, Organization & Society. 1068p. 1976. 52.95 (ISBN 0-395-30591-8). HM.
--Theory Building. rev. ed. LC 77-90010. (Illus.). 1978. text ed. 19.95 (ISBN 0-02-907620-X). Free Pr.

Dubinin, Y. V., jt. auth. see Borisov, C. B.

Dubiny, Mary J., jt. ed. see Fitch, Grace E.

Dubisch, Roy. Basic Concepts of Mathematics for Elementary Teachers. 2nd ed. LC 80-19446. (Mathematics Ser.). (Illus.). 483p. 1981. 21.95 (ISBN 0-201-03170-1); wkbk. 6.95 (ISBN 0-201-03156-6); instrs' manual 3.50 (ISBN 0-201-03173-6). A-W.

Dubisch, Roy & Hood, Vernon. Elementary Algebra. LC 76-3846. 1977. text ed. 21.95 (ISBN 0-8053-2338-4); instr's guide 4.95 (ISBN 0-8053-2339-2). Benjamin-Cummings.

Dublin, Arthur B., jt. auth. see Dublin, William B.

Dublin, Jack & Dublin, Selma M. Credit Unions in a Changing World: The Tanzania-Kenya Experience. 1983. 18.95 (ISBN 0-8143-1742-1); pap. 9.95 (ISBN 0-8143-1743-X). Wayne St U Pr.

Dublin, Lewis. Business Mathematics. (Blue Books Ser.). 1975. pap. 1.25 o.p. (ISBN 0-671-18123-8). Monarch Pr.

Dublin, Lewis, jt. auth. see Warner, Paul.

Dublin, Selma M., jt. auth. see Dublin, Jack.

Dublin, Thomas, ed. Farm to Factory: Women's Letters, 1830-1860. 191p. 1982. pap. 9.50 (ISBN 0-231-05119-0). Columbia U Pr.

Dublin, William B. Fundamentals of Vestibular Pathology. 380p. 1983. 32.50 (ISBN 0-87527-203-7). Green.

Dublin, William B. & Dublin, Arthur B. Atlas of Neuroanatomy for Radiologists: Surface & Sectional-with CT Scanning Correlation. LC 79-50199. (Illus.). 250p. 1982. 62.50 (ISBN 0-87527-204-5). Green.

Dubner, Ronald see Kawamura, Yojiro.

Dubnick, Mel & Gitelson, Alan, eds. Regulatory Policy Analysis. (Orig.). 1982. pap. 6.00 (ISBN 0-918592-51-8). Policy Studies.

Dubofsky, Melvyn & Theoharis, Alan. Imperial Democracy: The United States Since 1945. (Illus.). 288p. 1983. pap. 14.95 (ISBN 0-13-451740-7). P-H.

Du Bois, Cora. People of Alor: A Social-Psychological Study of an East Indian Island, 2 vols. in 1. LC 60-16359. (Illus.). 1960. 32.50x o.p. (ISBN 0-674-66100-1). Harvard U Pr.
--Social Forces in Southeast Asia. LC 59-2120. 1959. 6.95x o.p. (ISBN 0-674-81330-8). Harvard U Pr.

Dubois, Daniel, jt. auth. see Fronval, George.

Dubois, Diana, ed. & intro. by. My Harvard, My Yale. 292p. 1982. 14.00 (ISBN 0-394-51920-5). Random.

Du Bois, Edward. St. Godwin: A Tale of the Sixteenth, Seventeenth, & Eighteenth Centuries, by Count Reginald De St. Leon. Luria, Gina, ed. (The Feminist Controversy in England, 1788-1810 Ser.). 1974. lib. bdg. 50.00 o.s.i. (ISBN 0-8240-0853-7). Garland Pub.

Dubois, Edward N. Essential Methods in Business Statistics. 1964. text ed. 19.95 (ISBN 0-07-017875-5, C); solutions manual 4.95 (ISBN 0-07-017874-7). McGraw.
--Essential Methods in Business Statistics. (Illus.). 1979. text ed. 24.95 (ISBN 0-07-017889-5, C); instructors manual 7.95 (ISBN 0-07-017890-9). McGraw.

Dubois, J. B., ed. Immunopharmacologic Effects of Radiation Therapy. (European Organization for Research on Treatment of Cancer (EORTC) Monographs: Vol. 8). 568p. 1981. 68.00 (ISBN 0-89004-531-3). Raven.

DuBois, June. William R. Leigh: the Definitive Illustrated Biography. LC 77-15343. 1977. 40.00 (ISBN 0-913504-42-4). Lowell Pr.

Dubois, P. Le Baroque. new ed. (Collection themes et textes). 256p. (Orig., Fr.). 1973. pap. 6.95 (ISBN 2-03-035016-8). Larousse.

Dubois, Philip, ed. Judicial Reform. (Orig.). 1982. pap. 6.00 (ISBN 0-918592-56-9). Policy Studies.

Dubois, Philip L. The Analysis of Judicial Reform. LC 80-8947. (Policy Studies Organization Bk.). 224p. 1982. 24.95x (ISBN 0-669-04480-6). Lexington Bks.

Dubois, Rochelle. The Invisible Dog. 1981. leather bdg. 16.00 (ISBN 0-686-91885-1). Merging Media.
--Timelapse. (Contemporary Poetry Ser.: No. 1). (Illus.). 80p. (Orig.). 1983. pap. 6.50 (ISBN 0-938136-08-9). Lunchroom Pr.
--Timesharing: A Consumer's Guide to a New Vacation. 1982. 3.50 (ISBN 0-686-98387-4). Merging Media.
--The Train in the Rain. 1982. 4.50 (ISBN 0-686-91884-3). Merging Media.

Dubois, Rochelle, ed. Search: Reasons for Relationships. 1981. 0.75 (ISBN 0-686-98389-0). Merging Media.

Dubois, Shirley G. Gamal Abdel Nasser: Son of the Nile. (Illus.). 250p. 1972. 8.95 (ISBN 0-89388-048-5). Okpaku Communications.
--His Day Is Marching on: Memoirs of W. E. B. DuBois. LC 71-146693. 1971. 10.00 (ISBN 0-89388-156-2); pap. 5.95 (ISBN 0-89388-157-0). Okpaku Communications.

Dubois, Theodora & Smith, Dorothy V. Staten Island Patroons. (Illus.). 1961. pap. 1.50 (ISBN 0-686-23393-X). Staten Island.

DuBois, W. Burghardt. Negro. 1970. pap. 5.95 (ISBN 0-19-501262-3, 333, GB). Oxford U Pr.

Du Bois, W. E. B. The Black Flame; a Trilogy. Incl. Bk. 1. The Ordeal of Mansart. 15.00 (ISBN 0-527-25270-0); Bk. 2. Mansart Builds a School. 17.00 (ISBN 0-527-25271-9); Bk. 3. Worlds of Color. 17.00 (ISBN 0-527-25272-7). 1976. Repr. 49.00. Kraus Intl.

Du Bois, William E. The Philadelphia Negro: A Social Study. LC 67-26984. (Sourcebooks in Negro History Ser). 1968. 11.00x o.p. (ISBN 0-8052-3201-X); pap. 6.50 o.p. (ISBN 0-8052-0160-2). Schocken.
--Souls of Black Folk. (Classic Ser). (Orig.). 1969. pap. 2.50 (ISBN 0-451-51674-5, CE1674, Sig Classics). NAL.
--The Suppression of the African Slave Trade to the United States of America 1638-1870. LC 69-20337. (Sourcebooks in Negro History Ser). 1969. 10.00x o.p. (ISBN 0-8052-3256-7). Schocken.
--Suppression of the African Slave Trade, 1638 to 1870. xx, 336p. 1970. pap. text ed. 7.95x (ISBN 0-8071-0149-4). La State U Pr.

Du Bois, William P. Squirrel Hotel. 1980. PLB 6.95 (ISBN 0-8398-2606-0, Gregg). G K Hall.

Du Bois, William Pene see Du Bois, William P.

Du Bois, William Pene see Pene du Bois, William.

Du Bois, William Pene see Pene Du Bois, William.

Dubois, William R. & Nisbet-Snyder Drama Collection, Northern Illinois University Libraries, eds. English & American Stage Productions: An Annotated Checklist of Prompt Books, 1800-1900. 1973. lib. bdg. 22.50 (ISBN 0-8161-1035-2, Hall Reference). G K Hall.

DuBose, Francis M. God Who Sends. 1983. 9.95 (ISBN 0-8054-6331-3). Broadman.

DuBose, LaRocque. For Whom the Bell Tolls Notes. (Orig.). 1967. pap. 2.75 (ISBN 0-8220-0497-6). Cliffs.

Dubost, G. Flat Radiating Dipoles & Applications to Arrays. (Electronic & Electrical Engineering Research Studies: Research Studies on Antennas Ser.). 120p. 1981. 28.95x (ISBN 0-471-10050-1, Pub. by Res Stud Pr). Wiley.

DuBoulay, F. R. H. Germany Thirteen Fifty to Fifteen Hundred. 200p. 1982. text ed. 26.25x (ISBN 0-485-11220-5, Althlone Pr). Humanities.

Du Boulay, G. H. Principles of X-Ray Diagnosis of the Skull. 2nd ed. (Illus.). 384p. 1979. text ed. 115.00x (ISBN 0-407-00117-4). Butterworth.

Dubovik, Alexander. The Photographic Recording of High-Speed Processes. 2nd ed. Aksenov, Arthur, tr. LC 80-17318. 533p. 1981. 79.95x (ISBN 0-471-04204-8, Pub. by Wiley-Interscience). Wiley.

Dubovsky, Steven L. Clinical Psychiatry in Primary Care. 1978. pap. 12.95 o.p. (ISBN 0-683-02671-2). Williams & Wilkins.

Dubovsky, Steven L. & Feiger, Allan D. Psychiatric Decision Making. 300p. 1983. text ed. 30.00 (ISBN 0-941158-16-0, D1483-X). Mosby.

Dubovsky, Steven L. & Weissberg, Michael P. Clinical Psychiatry in Primary Care. 2nd ed. (Illus.). 291p. 1982. pap. text ed. 13.95 (ISBN 0-683-02672-0). Williams & Wilkins.

DuBovy, Joseph L. Introduction to Biomedical Electronics. (Illus.). 1978. text ed. 17.95 (ISBN 0-07-017895-X, G); instructor's manual 2.50 (ISBN 0-07-017896-8). McGraw.

Dubowitz, Victor. Muscle Disorders in Childhood. LC 77-23997. (Major Problems in Clinical Pediatrics Ser.: Vol. 16). (Illus.). 1978. text ed. 15.00 (ISBN 0-7216-3210-6). Saunders.

Duboys, Jacques. Recueil des Reglements, Declarations et Arrets, 2 vols. (Slave Trade in France, 1744-1848, Ser.). 578p. (Fr.). 1974. Repr. of 1745 ed. Set. lib. bdg. 153.00x o.p. (ISBN 0-8287-0281-0, TN102-3). Clearwater Pub.

DuBrin, Andrew. Human Relations: A Job-Oriented Approach. 2nd ed. 300p. 1981. text ed. 19.95 (ISBN 0-8359-3002-5); instr's. manual free (ISBN 0-8359-3003-3). Reston.
--Personnel & Human Resource Management. 1980. text ed. 18.95 (ISBN 0-442-25407-5); instr's. manual 2.00 (ISBN 0-442-25406-7). Van Nos Reinhold.

DuBrin, Andrew J. Bouncing Back: How to Handle Setbacks in Work & Personal Life. 185p. 1982. 11.95 (ISBN 0-13-080366-9); pap. 5.95 (ISBN 0-13-080358-8). P-H.
--Effective Business Psychology. (Illus.). 1979. 18.95 (ISBN 0-8359-1607-3); instrs'. manual avail. (ISBN 0-8359-1608-1). Reston.

Du Brin, Andrew J. Fundamentals of Organizational Behavior: An Applied Perspective. 2nd ed. LC 77-12720. 1978. text ed. 47.00 (ISBN 0-08-022252-8); pap. text ed. 15.00 (ISBN 0-08-022251-X). Pergamon.

Dubrouillet, Jane. Of Such Is the Kingdom of Heaven. pap. 7.95 o.p. (ISBN 0-8091-2078-X). Paulist Pr.

Dubrovin, Vivian. Baseball Just for Fun. LC 74-10867. (Summer Fun, Winter Fun Ser). (gr. 3-6). 1974. PLB 4.95 o.p. (ISBN 0-88436-136-5); pap. 3.95 (ISBN 0-88436-137-3). EMC.
--A Better Bit & Bridle. LC 75-20346. (Saddle up Ser.). (Illus.). 40p. (gr. 4-9). 1975. PLB 6.95 (ISBN 0-88436-201-9); pap. 3.95 (ISBN 0-88436-202-7). EMC.
--A Chance to Win. LC 75-20081. (Saddle up Ser.). (Illus.). 40p. (gr. 4-9). 1975. PLB 6.95 (ISBN 0-88436-203-5); pap. 3.95 (ISBN 0-88436-204-3). EMC.
--The Magic Bowling Ball. LC 74-10869. (Summer Fun, Winter Fun Ser.). (gr. 3-6). 1974. PLB 4.95 o.p. (ISBN 0-88436-130-6); pap. 3.95 (ISBN 0-88436-131-4). EMC.
--Open the Gate. LC 75-20026. (Saddle up Ser.). (Illus.). 40p. (gr. 4-9). 1975. PLB 6.95 (ISBN 0-88436-207-8); pap. 3.95 (ISBN 0-88436-208-6). EMC.
--Rescue on Skis. LC 74-11004. (Summer Fun, Winter Fun Ser). (gr. 3-6). 1974. PLB 4.95 o.p. (ISBN 0-88436-134-9); pap. 3.95 (ISBN 0-88436-135-7). EMC.
--The Track Trophy. LC 74-10931. (Summer Fun, Winter Fun Ser). (gr. 3-6). 1974. PLB 4.95 o.p. (ISBN 0-88436-132-2); pap. 3.95 (ISBN 0-88436-133-0). EMC.
--Trailering Troubles. LC 75-20362. (Saddle up Ser.). (Illus.). 40p. (gr. 4-9). 1975. PLB 6.95 (ISBN 0-88436-205-1); pap. 3.95 (ISBN 0-88436-206-X). EMC.

Dubrow, Eileen, jt. auth. see Dubrow, Richard.

Dubrow, Richard & Dubrow, Eileen. American Furniture of the Nineteenth Century, 1840-1880. LC 82-50615. (Illus.). 224p. 1983. 30.00 (ISBN 0-916838-68-4). Schiffer.

--Furniture Made in America 1875-1905. LC 82-50617. (Illus.). 320p. (Orig.). 1982. pap. 17.95 (ISBN 0-916838-66-8). Schiffer.

DuBrul, E. Lloyd. Sicher's Oral Anatomy. 7th ed. LC 80-15943. (Illus.). 578p. 1980. text ed. 32.95 (ISBN 0-8016-4605-7). Mosby.

DuBrul, E. Lloyd, jt. auth. see Sicher, Harry.

Dubus, Andre. Finding a Girl in America. LC 79-90371. 1981. 12.95 (ISBN 0-87923-311-7); pap. 6.95 (ISBN 0-87923-393-1). Godine.

--Separate Flights. LC 74-25955. 1977. pap. 6.95 (ISBN 0-87923-123-8). Godine.

Dubus, Elizabeth N. Cajun. 496p. 1983. 16.95 (ISBN 0-399-31004-5). Seaview Bks.

Duby, Georges. The Age of the Cathedrals: Art & Society, 980-1420. Levieux, Eleanor & Thompson, Barbara, trs. LC 80-22769. (Illus.). vi, 312p. 1981. 22.50 (ISBN 0-226-16769-0); pap. 9.95 (ISBN 0-226-16770-4). U of Chicago Pr.

--The Three Orders: Feudal Society Imagined. Goldhammer, Arthur, tr. LC 80-13158. 432p. 1980. lib. bdg. 25.00x (ISBN 0-226-16771-2, PHOEN); pap. 9.95 (ISBN 0-226-16772-0). U of Chicago Pr.

Duc, Don R. Le see LeDuc, Don R.

Duca, Anthony Del. New Visualizations in Elementary Physics. LC 82-60821. (Illus.). 65p. (Orig.). 1982. pap. 11.95x (ISBN 0-9609410-0-2). Magnet Pub.

Ducan, J. P. & Mair, S. E. Sculptured Surfaces in Engineering & Medicine. LC 82-1116. (Illus.). 400p. Date not set. price not set (ISBN 0-521-23450-6). Cambridge U Pr.

DuCann, C. G. Adventures in Antiques. 15.00x (ISBN 0-392-10032-0, SpS). Sportshelf.

Ducasse, C. J. Nature, Mind & Death. (Paul Carus Lecture Ser.). xix, 533p. 1951. 27.00 (ISBN 0-87548-102-7). Open Court.

Ducat, jt. auth. see Chase.

Ducat, Craig R. & Chase, Harold W. Constitutional Interpretation. 3rd ed. 1550p. 1983. text ed. 27.95 (ISBN 0-314-69640-7). West Pub.

Du Cellier, Florent. Les Classes Ouvrieres en France depuis 1789. (Conditions of the 19th Century French Working Class Ser.). 96p. (Fr.). 1974. Repr. of 1857 ed. lib. bdg. 34.50 o.p. (ISBN 0-8287-0284-5, 1003). Clearwater Pub.

Ducey, Jean. Out of this Nettle. (Voyager Ser.). (Orig.). 1983. pap. 3.50 (ISBN 0-8010-2927-9). Baker Bk.

Duchac, Joseph. The Poems of Emily Dickinson: An Annotated Guide to Commentary Published in English, 1890-1977. 1979. lib. bdg. 45.00 (ISBN 0-8161-7830-5, Hall Reference). G K Hall.

Duchacek, Ivo D. Nations & Men: An Introduction to International Politics. 3rd ed. LC 81-40916. 608p. 1982. pap. text ed. 20.75 (ISBN 0-8191-2260-2). U Pr of Amer.

--Power Maps: Comparative Politics of Constitutions. LC 72-95265. (Studies in International & Comparative Politics: No. 2). (Illus.). 252p. 1973. pap. text ed. 9.75 o.p. (ISBN 0-87436-115-X). ABC-Clio.

Du Chaillu, Paul. Land of the Long Night. LC 75-159938. (Tower Bks). (Illus.). (gr. 5 up). 1971. Repr. of 1899 ed. 34.00x (ISBN 0-8103-3905-6). Gale.

--Lost in the Jungle. LC 79-159939. 1971. Repr. of 1872 ed. 34.00x (ISBN 0-8103-3766-5). Gale.

Duchan, Judith F., jt. auth. see Lund, Nancy J.

DuCharme, Jerome J. Readers Guide to Proclamation: Cycle B. 140p. 1975. pap. 2.95 o.p. (ISBN 0-8199-0578-X). Franciscan Herald.

Ducharte, P. L. The Italian Comedy. (Illus.). 12.50 (ISBN 0-8446-2002-5). Peter Smith.

Duchatel, M. T. La Charite dans ses Rapports avec l'Etat Moral, et le Bien-Etre des Classes Inferieures de la Societe. (Conditions of the 19th Century French Working Class Ser.). 431p. (Fr.). 1974. Repr. of 1829 ed. lib. bdg. 108.50 o.p. (ISBN 0-8287-0285-3, 1005). Clearwater Pub.

Duchaufour, Philippe. Ecological Atlas of Soils of the World. De Kimpe, C. R., tr. from Fr. LC 77-94822. (Illus.). 178p. 1978. 41.25x (ISBN 0-89352-012-8). Masson Pub.

Duchaufour, R. Pedology. Paton, T. R., tr. from French. (Illus.). 480p. 1982. text ed. 50.00x (ISBN 0-04-631015-0); pap. text ed. 24.95x (ISBN 0-04-631016-9). Allen Unwin.

Duche, Jean, jt. auth. see Bryan, Anne-Marie.

Duchene, A., ed. see ICRP.

Duchesneau, Thomas. Competition in the U. S. Energy Industry. LC 74-22179. (Ford Foundation Energy Policy Project Ser). 1975. prof ref 25.00x (ISBN 0-88410-337-4); pap. 15.00x (ISBN 0-88410-338-2). Ballinger Pub.

Duchin, Faye, jt. auth. see Leontief, Wassily.

Ducis, V. & Rodonvilliers, Le P. Discours Prononces Dans L'academie Francaise, le 4 Mars, 1979. Repr. of 1779 ed. 23.00 o.p. (ISBN 0-8287-0286-1). Clearwater Pub.

Duck, Stephen W. Personal Relationships & Personal Constructs: A Study of Friendship Formation. LC 73-8193. 170p. 1973. 27.00 o.p. (ISBN 0-471-22356-5, Pub. by Wiley-Interscience). Wiley.

Ducker, James H. Men of the Steel Rails: Workers on the Atchison, Topeka, & Santa Fe Railroad, 1869-1900. LC 82-17541. (Illus.). 232p. 1983. 17.95 (ISBN 0-8032-1662-9). U of Nebr Pr.

Duckert, Mary. Help: I'm a Sunday School Teacher. LC 77-83133. (Illus.). 1969. pap. 3.95 (ISBN 0-664-24862-4). Westminster.

Duckert, Mary, ed. see Chenoweth, Linda.

Duckett, Al, jt. auth. see Robinson, Jackie.

Duckett, Alfred. Changing of the Guard: The New Breed of Black Politicians. (Challenge Bk). (Illus.). (gr. 6 up). 1972. 4.00 o.p. (ISBN 0-698-20171-X, Coward). Putnam Pub Group.

Duckett, George, jt. auth. see Burnet, Sir Thomas.

Duckett, J. G., jt. ed. see Amos, W. B.

Duckworth, D., jt. auth. see Philp, M.

Duckworth, Eddie, tr. see Frantzeskakis, Ion F.

Duckworth, Elisabeth, tr. see Kafka, Franz.

Duckworth, J. R., jt. auth. see Northen, E. E.

Duckworth, John, et al. Muhammad & the Arab Empire. Yapp, Malcolm & Killingray, Margaret, eds. (World History Ser.). (Illus.). (gr. 10). 1980. lib. bdg. 6.95 (ISBN 0-89908-036-7); pap. text ed. 2.25 (ISBN 0-89908-011-1). Greenhaven.

Duckworth, Marion. The Strong Place. 1983. pap. 4.95 (ISBN 0-8423-6663-6). Tyndale.

Duckworth, Paul. Creative Photographic Effects Simplified. (Illus.). 96p. 1975. pap. 4.95 o.p. (ISBN 0-8174-0188-1, Amphoto); Spanish Ed. pap. 6.95 o.p. (ISBN 0-8174-0321-3). Watson-Guptill.

Duckworth, Robin. This is the Word of the Lord: Year C. The Year of Luke. 180p. (Orig.). 1982. pap. 9.95 (ISBN 0-19-826666-9). Oxford U Pr.

Duckworth, Sophia, jt. auth. see Reed, Henry H.

Duckworth, Walter E. & Hoyle, G. Electro-Slag Refining. 1969. 30.00 (ISBN 0-412-09670-6, Pub by Chapman & Hall). Methuen Inc.

Duckworth, William. A Creative Approach to Music Fundamentals. 320p. 1981. pap. text ed. 17.95x (ISBN 0-534-00891-7). Wadsworth Pub.

Duconte, C. M. & Sabourud, J. A. Pyrenean Mountain Dogs. 96p. 1982. 14.95 (ISBN 0-7182-2290-3, Pub. by Kaye & Ward). David & Charles.

Ducpetiaux, Edouard. De la Condition Physique et Morale des Jeunes Ouvriers et des Moyens de l'Ameliorer. (Conditions of the 19th Century French Working Class Ser.). 472p. (Fr.). 1974. Repr. of 1843 ed. lib. bdg. 118.00 o.p. (ISBN 0-8287-0287-X, 1161). Clearwater Pub.

--Le Pauperisme en Belgique, Causes et Remedes. (Conditions of the 19th Century French Working Class Ser.). 87p. (Fr.). 1974. Repr. of 1844 ed. lib. bdg. 32.00x o.p. (ISBN 0-8287-0288-8, 1006). Clearwater Pub.

Ducrol, H., et al, eds. Computer Aid to Drug Thearpy & to Drug Monitoring. 1978. 55.50 (ISBN 0-444-85188-7). Elsevier.

Ducsik, Dennis W. Shoreline for the Public: A Handbook of Social, Economic, & Legal Considerations Regarding Public Recreational Use of the Nation's Coastal Shoreline. 1974. 17.50x (ISBN 0-262-04045-X). MIT Pr.

Duczman, Linda. The Baby-Sitter. LC 76-44229. (Moods & Emotions Ser.). (Illus.). (gr. k-3). 1977. PLB 12.85 o.p. (ISBN 0-8172-0065-7, Raintree Editions). Raintree Pubs.

Duda, Richard O. & Hart, Peter E. Pattern Classification & Scene Analysis. LC 72-7008. 482p. 1973. 49.95x (ISBN 0-471-22361-1, Pub. by Wiley-Interscience). Wiley.

Dudden, Arthur P. Joseph Fels & the Single-Tax Movement. LC 77-157738. 308p. 1971. 24.95 (ISBN 0-87722-010-7). Temple U Pr.

Dudden, Faye E. Serving Women: Household Service in Nineteenth-Century America. 352p. 1983. 17.95x (ISBN 0-8195-5072-8). Wesleyan U Pr.

Dudding, Burton, jt. auth. see Cho, Cheng.

Duddington, C. L. Instructions in Biology. (Illus.). (gr. 9 up). 14.50x (ISBN 0-392-03422-0, SpS). Sportshelf.

Duddington, Natalie, tr. see Solov'Ev, Vladimir S.

Dudeck, C. V. Hegel's Phenomenology of Mind: Analysis & Commentary. LC 80-67258. 292p. 1981. lib. bdg. 22.25 (ISBN 0-8191-1406-5); pap. text ed. 11.25 (ISBN 0-8191-1407-3). U Pr of Amer.

Dudek, Gerald, jt. auth. see Ault, Addison.

Dudeney, Charles. A Guide to Executive Re-Employment. 192p. 1972. 29.00 (ISBN 0-7121-1972-8, Pub. by Macdonald & Evans). State Mutual Bk.

Duderstadt, James J. & Hamilton, Louis J. Nuclear Reactor Analysis. LC 75-20389. 650p. 1976. text ed. 47.95 (ISBN 0-471-22363-8). Wiley.

Duderstadt, James J. & Martin, William R. Transport Theory. LC 78-13672. 1979. 55.95x (ISBN 0-471-04492-X, Pub. by Wiley-Interscience). Wiley.

Duderstadt, James J., et al. Principles of Engineering. LC 81-10450. 558p. 1982. text ed. 25.95 (ISBN 0-471-08445-X); study guide 10.95 (ISBN 0-471-09746-2); solns. manual 8.50 (ISBN 0-471-09154-5). Wiley.

Dudewicz, Edward J. & Koo, Joo O. The Complete Categorized Guide to Statistical Selection & Ranking Procedures. LC 80-68288. (The American Sciences Press Ser. in Mathematical & Management Sciences: Vol. 6). 1982. text ed. 85.00 (ISBN 0-935950-03-6). Am Sciences Pr.

Dudick, T. S. & Cornell, R. Inventory Control for the Financial Executive. 251p. 1979. 44.95 (ISBN 0-471-01503-2, Pub. by Wiley-Interscience). Wiley.

Dudick, Thomas S. How to Improve Profitability Through More Effective Planning. LC 75-20445. (Systems & Control for Financial Management Ser). 349p. 1975. 29.95 o.p. (ISBN 0-471-22364-6, Pub. by Wiley-Interscience). Wiley.

--Profile for Profitability: Using Cost Control & Profitability Analysis. LC 72-4353. (Systems & Controls for Financial Management Ser.). 253p. 1972. 33.50 o.p. (ISBN 0-471-22362-X, Pub. by Wiley-Interscience). Wiley.

Dudley, Billy. An Introduction to Nigerian Government & Politics. LC 82-47926. 384p. (Orig.). 25.00 (ISBN 0-253-33104-8); pap. 9.95 (ISBN 0-253-28400-7). Ind U Pr.

Dudley, Billy J. Murtala Muhammed. 1982. cancelled (ISBN 0-7146-3140-X, F Cass Co). Biblio Dist.

Dudley, Brian A. Mathematical & Biological Interrelations. LC 77-7284. 1978. pap. 27.95 (ISBN 0-471-99484-7, Pub. by Wiley-Interscience). Wiley.

Dudley, Carl S. Making the Small Church Effective. LC 78-2221. 1983. pap. 5.95 (ISBN 0-687-23044-6). Abingdon.

Dudley, Carl S., ed. Building Effective Ministry: Theory & Practice in the Local Church. LC 82-48411. 256p. 1983. pap. 8.61 (ISBN 0-06-062102-8, HarpR). Har-Row.

Dudley, Cliff, jt. auth. see Bakker, Tammy.

Dudley, Cliff, jt. auth. see Curtis, Helene.

Dudley, Cliff, jt. auth. see Custodio, Sidney.

Dudley, Cliff, jt. auth. see Kilpatrick, Paula.

Dudley, Cliff, jt. auth. see McLeod, Mary Alice.

Dudley, Cliff, jt. auth. see Steer, John L.

Dudley, Cliff, pref. by. I Gotta Be Me. LC 78-64670. 144p. (Orig.). 1981. pap. 2.95 (ISBN 0-89221-104-0). New Leaf.

Dudley, Cliff, ed. see Godman, Henry.

Dudley, D. R., ed. Neronians & Flavians: Silver Latin I. (Greek & Latin Studies Ser). 1972. 22.50x (ISBN 0-7100-7273-2). Routledge & Kegan.

Dudley, Darle W., ed. Gear Handbook: The Design, Manufacture & Application of Gears. (Illus.). 1962. 69.50 (ISBN 0-07-017902-6, P&RB). McGraw.

Dudley, Donald R. Civilization of Rome. (Orig.). 1960. pap. 3.95 (ISBN 0-451-62149-2, ME2149, Ment). NAL.

Dudley, Edward & Novak, Maximillian E., eds. The Wild Man Within: An Image in Western Thought from the Renaissance to Romanticism. LC 72-77191. (Illus.). 1972. 17.95 (ISBN 0-8229-3246-6). U of Pittsburgh Pr.

Dudley, Guilford A. A History of Eastern Civilizations. LC 72-6744. 733p. 1973. text ed. 26.95 o.p. (ISBN 0-471-22365-4). Wiley.

Dudley, Guilford, 3rd. Religion on Trial: Mircea Eliade & His Critics. LC 77-77644. 191p. 1977. 24.95 (ISBN 0-87722-102-2). Temple U Pr.

Dudley, H. Abdomen. 3rd ed. Rob & Smith, eds. (Operative Surgery Ser.). (Illus.). 1978. 129.95 (ISBN 0-407-00600-1). Butterworth.

Dudley, J. W., ed. Severly Generators of Selection for Oil & Protein in Maize. 1974. 10.00 (ISBN 0-89118-502-X). Crop Sci Soc Am.

Dudley, James R. Living with Stigma: The Plight of Being Mentally Retarded. 110p. 1983. text ed. price not set (ISBN 0-398-04831-2). C C Thomas.

Dudley, L. Architectural Illustration. 1976. 32.95 (ISBN 0-13-044610-6). P-H.

Dudley, Louise & Faricy, Austin. The Humanities. 5th ed. Myers, Bernard S., rev. by. (Illus.). 480p. 1973. text ed. 24.00 (ISBN 0-07-017970-0, C). McGraw.

Dudley, Louise, et al. The Humanities. 6th ed. (Illus.). 1978. text ed. 22.50 (ISBN 0-07-017971-9, C); instructor's manual 15.00 (ISBN 0-07-017972-7); study guide 12.95 (ISBN 0-07-017973-5). McGraw.

Dudley, N. A., jt. ed. see Muramatsu, R.

Dudley, William C. Letters To Our Son: The AG Teacher. 108p. 1983. pap. text ed. 8.95x (ISBN 0-8134-2288-4). Interstate.

Dudley-Evans, Tony see Bates, Martin & Dudley-Evans, Tony.

Dudley-Evans, Tony, jt. ed. see Bates, Martin.

Dudley-Evans, Tony, et al see Bates, Martin & Dudley-Evans, Tony.

Dudman, Helge. Street People. (Illus.). 263p. 1982. 14.95 (ISBN 965-220-039-5, Carta Maps & Guides Pub Isreal). Hippocrene Bks.

Dudman, Jane. International Music Guide 1983. (International Music Guide Ser.). (Illus.). 304p. 1982. pap. 10.95 (ISBN 0-900730-05-6). NY Zoetrope.

Dudzinski, M. L., jt. auth. see Arnold, G. W.

Due, Jean M. Costs, Returns & Repayment Experience of Ujamaa Villages in Tanzania, 1973-1976. LC 80-490. 167p. 1980. text ed. 19.75 (ISBN 0-8191-1019-1); pap. text ed. 9.75 (ISBN 0-8191-1020-5). U Pr of Amer.

Due, John F. & French, Giles. Rails to the Mid Columbia Wheatlands: The Columbia Southern & Great Southern Railroads & the Development of Sherman & Wasco Counties, Oregon. LC 79-89206. (Illus.). 1979. pap. text ed. 15.00 (ISBN 0-8191-0798-0). U Pr of Amer.

Dueber, Julianne, jt. auth. see Holt, Marion P.

Duedall, Iver W., jt. auth. see Park, Kilho P.

Duedney, Daniel. Space: The High Frontier in Perspective. LC 82-50920. (Worldwatch Papers). 1982. pap. 2.00 (ISBN 0-916468-49-6). Worldwatch Inst.

Dueker, Christopher & Dueker, Joyce. The Old Fashioned Home-made Ice-Cream Cookbook. LC 73-11803. 192p. 1974. 8.95 (ISBN 0-672-51765-5); pap. 7.95 (ISBN 0-672-52716-2). Bobbs.

Dueker, David & Albert, Daniel. Foundations of Opthalmology: Glaucoma. Date not set. 50.00tx (ISBN 0-8385-2693-4). ACC.

Dueker, Joyce, jt. auth. see Dueker, Christopher.

Dueland, Joy V. Filled up Full. (Illus.). 32p. (Fr.). (gr. k-2). 1980. pap. 2.50 (ISBN 0-87510-151-8). Chr Science.

Duell, Marie. Countess of Sedgwick. LC 79-9471. 1980. 11.95 o.p. (ISBN 0-07-017976-X). McGraw.

Duelli-Klein, Renata, jt. ed. see Bowles, Gloria.

Duenas. Curso Basico de Correspondencia Comercial. 120p. 1982. 4.56 (ISBN 0-07-017995-6, G). McGraw.

--Curso Basico de Matematicas Comerciales. 172p. 1982. 4.56 (ISBN 0-07-017994-8, G). McGraw.

--Curso Basico de Mecanografia. 84p. 1982. 4.56 (ISBN 0-07-017991-3, G). McGraw.

--Curso Basico de Practicas Secretariales. 120p. 1982. 4.56 (ISBN 0-07-017992-1, G). McGraw.

Duenewald, Doris. Scribble Draw & Color Your Own Pictures. (Elephant Bks.). (Illus.). 128p. (gr. 2-5). 1974. pap. 1.25 (ISBN 0-448-11694-4, G&D). Putnam Pub Group.

Duenewald, Doris, ed. Bad News Bears Go to Japan Activity Book. (Elephant Books Ser.). (Illus.). (gr. k-7). 1978. pap. 1.50 o.s.i. (ISBN 0-448-16175-3, G&D). Putnam Pub Group.

--Close Encounters of the Third Kind Activity Book. (Elephant Books Ser.). (Illus.). 1978. pap. 1.50 (ISBN 0-448-14818-8, G&D). Putnam Pub Group.

--The Play Money Book. (Elephant Bks.). (Illus.). 1978. pap. 1.95 o.s.i. (ISBN 0-448-16163-X, G&D). Putnam Pub Group.

Duenewald, Doris, ed. see Altman, Margery.

Duenewald, Doris, ed. see Anthony, Nina.

Duenewald, Doris, ed. see Benson, Murray & Ladd, Fred.

Duenewald, Doris, ed. see Brown, Michael.

Duenewald, Doris, ed. see Callan, Mallory.

Duenewald, Doris, ed. see Cook, Gladys E.

Duenewald, Doris, ed. see Elliott, Joan.

Duenewald, Doris, ed. see Fujikawa, Guyo.

Duenewald, Doris, ed. see Harvey Famous Name Comics.

Duenewald, Doris, ed. see Hoch, Edward D.

Duenewald, Doris, ed. see Mumford, Thad & Muntean, Michaela.

Duenewald, Doris, ed. see Romagnoli, Robert.

Duenewald, Doris, ed. see Rushnell, Elaine.

Duenewald, Doris, ed. see Stratemeyer Syndicate.

Duenewald, Doris, ed. see Tallarico, Tony.

Duenewald, Doris, ed. see Walt Disney Studios.

Duenk, Lester G., et al. Autobody Repair. 1977. 18.60 (ISBN 0-87002-164-8); student guide 4.76 (ISBN 0-87002-243-1). Bennett IL.

Duenwald, Doris, ed. see Roberts, David.

Duerden, Dennis, jt. ed. see Pieterse, Cosmo.

Duerfeldt, Pryse H., ed. see O'Dell, Richard F.

Duerksen, Christopher J. Dow vs California: A Turning Point in the Envirobusiness Struggle. LC 82-19942. (Illus.). 150p. (Orig.). 1982. pap. 10.00 (ISBN 0-89164-076-2). Conservation Foun.

Duerr, Hans-Peter, jt. auth. see Breitenlohner, Peter.

Duerr, William A., ed. Timber! Problems, Prospects, Policies. LC 72-1160. 252p. 1973. 9.95x (ISBN 0-8138-1700-5). Iowa St U Pr.

Duespohl, T. Audean, ed. Nursing in Transition. LC 82-13946. 259p. 1982. 22.50 (ISBN 0-89443-837-9). Aspen Systems.

Dueuker, R. Sheldon. Tensions in the Connection. 128p. 1983. pap. 3.95 (ISBN 0-687-41243-9). Abingdon.

Dufair. Woman in the Moon. 1982. pap. 3.50 (ISBN 0-686-83906-4). Merging Media.

Dufey, Gunter & Giddy, Ian H. International Money Market. LC 78-1298. (Foundations of Finance Ser.). (Illus.). 1978. ref. ed. o.p. 13.95 (ISBN 0-13-470914-4); pap. 12.95 (ISBN 0-686-96835-2). P-H.

Dufey, Gunter, ed. see Abbey, Augustus.

Dufey, Gunter, ed. see Jilling, Michael.

Dufey, Gunter, ed. see Pence, Christine C.

Dufey, Gunter, ed. see Sanger, Gary C.

Dufey, Gunter, ed. see Schillereff, Ronald L.

Dufey, Gunter, ed. see Yahr, Robert B.

Duff, jt. ed. see Baruth.

Duff, A., jt. auth. see Maley, A.

Duff, Alan, jt. auth. see Maley, Alan.

Duff, Alan, tr. see Touraine, Alain.

Duff, Bill. Getting Married. LC 73-331250. (New Citizen Bks.). (Illus.). 80p. 1973. 7.50x o.p. (ISBN 0-85340-238-8). Intl Pubns Serv.

Duff, Charles. The Basis & Essentials of French. (Quality Paperback: No. 247). 122p. (Orig.). 1972. pap. 2.95 (ISBN 0-8226-0247-4). Littlefield.

--The Basis & Essentials of Spanish. (Quality Paperback: No. 249). 181p. 1972. pap. 1.95 o.p. (ISBN 0-8226-0249-0). Littlefield.

--French for Beginners. 1955. pap. 4.95 (ISBN 0-06-463252-0, EH 252, EH). B&N NY.

--Spanish for Beginners. (Orig.). 1958. pap. 4.95 (ISBN 0-06-463271-7, EH 271, EH). B&N NY.

Duff, Charles & Freund, Richard. The Basis & Essentials of German. (Quality Paperback: No. 248). 117p. 1972. pap. 2.95 (ISBN 0-8226-0248-2). Littlefield.

Duff, Charles & Makaroff, Dmitri. Russian for Beginners. 1962. pap. 5.29i (ISBN 0-06-463287-3, EH 287, EH). B&N NY.

Duff, David. Punch on Children: A Panorama 1845-1865. (Illus.). 228p. 1976. 12.95 o.p. (ISBN 0-584-10230-5). Transatlantic.

--Whisper Louise: Edward the Seventh & Mrs. Cresswell. (Illus.). 1975. 12.00 o.p. (ISBN 0-584-10336-0). Transatlantic.

Duff, G. F., jt. auth. see Del Grande, J. J.

Duff, Gerald. Calling Collect. LC 82-2819. (University of Central Florida Contemporary Poetry Ser.). 1982. 8.95 (ISBN 0-8130-0711-9). U Presses Fla.

Duff, I. S. & Stewart, G. W., eds. Sparse Matrix Proceedings 1978. LC 79-88001. xvi, 334p. 1979. text ed. 23.00 (ISBN 0-89871-160-6). Soc Indus-Appl Math.

Duff, J. D., tr. see Rostovtzeff, Mikhail I.

Duff, James D., ed. see Lucretius.

Duff, Jim. Whiz, the Elf Who Made Christmas Special. (Story Book Ser.). (Illus.). (ps-5). 1980. cancelled o.p. (ISBN 0-89305-030-X); pap. cancelled o.p. (ISBN 0-89305-031-8). Anna Pub.

Duff, John R. & Kaufman, Milton. Alternating Current Fundamentals. 2nd ed. (Electrical Trades Ser.). (gr. 9-10). 1980. 18.00 (ISBN 0-8273-1133-8); pap. 16.00 (ISBN 0-8273-1142-7); instr's. guide 4.75 (ISBN 0-8273-1140-0). Delmar.

Duff, M. J. & Isham, C. J., eds. Quantum Structure of Space & Time: Proceedings of the Nuffield Workshop, Imperial College, London, August 3-21, 1981. LC 82-9732. 420p. Date not set. 49.50 (ISBN 0-521-24732-2). Cambridge U Pr.

Duff, Margaret, tr. see Simenon, Georges.

Duff, Mary K., jt. auth. see Gilmore, John S.

Duff, O. French Reader & Vocabulary. (Illus.). Date not set. 25.00 (ISBN 0-89835-056-5). Abaris Bks.

Duff, Robert A. Spinoza's Political & Ethical Philosophy. LC 71-108858. Repr. of 1903 ed. lib. bdg. 27.50x (ISBN 0-678-00615-6). Kelley.

Duff, Shiela G. The Parting of Ways: A Personal Account of the Thirties. 223p. 1982. 19.95 (ISBN 0-7206-0586-5, Pub. by Peter Owen). Merrimack Bk Serv.

Duff, William. Critical Observations on the Writings of the Most Celebrated Original Geniuses in Poetry (1770) LC 73-9526. 400p. 1973. Repr. lib. bdg. 45.00x (ISBN 0-8201-1119-8). Schol Facsimiles.

--An Essay on Original Genius & Its Various Modes of Exertion in Philosophy & the Fine Arts. LC 64-10669. 1978. Repr. of 1767 ed. 40.00x (ISBN 0-8201-1261-5). Schol Facsimiles.

--Letters on the Intellectual & Moral Character of Women. (The Feminist Controversy in England, 1788-1810 Ser.). 1974. lib. bdg. 50.00 o.s.i. (ISBN 0-8240-0854-5). Garland Pub.

Duff, Wilson. Arts of the Raven: Masterworks by the Northwest Coast Indian. (Illus.). 112p. 1967. pap. 11.50 o.p. (ISBN 0-295-95583-X, Pub. by Vancouver Art Canada). U of Wash Pr.

Duffala, Sharon L. Rocky Mountain Cache: Western Wild Game Cookbook. (Illus.). 72p. (Orig.). 1982. pap. 5.95 (ISBN 0-87108-630-1). Pruett.

Duffee, David, et al. Criminal Justice: Organization, Structure & Analysis. (Criminal Justice Ser.). 1978. ref. 21.95 (ISBN 0-13-193490-2). P-H.

Duffee, David E. Correctional Management: Change & Control in Correctional Organizations. (Criminal Justice Ser.). (Illus.). 1980. text ed. 23.95 (ISBN 0-13-178400-5). P-H.

Duffee, David E. & Meyer, Peter B. Outcomes & Costs of a Prerelease System. 256p. 1983. text ed. 22.50 (ISBN 0-89946-099-2). Oelgeschlager.

Duffer, H. F., Jr., tr. see Maston, T. B.

Duffer, Hiram F., Jr., tr. see Bunyan, Juan & Leavell, L. P.

Duffett, John. Boatowner's Guide to Modern Maintenance: Protecting Your Floating Investment. (Illus.). 1983. 19.95 (ISBN 0-393-03279-5). Norton.

Duffett-Smith, Peter. Practical Astronomy with Your Calculator. 2nd ed. LC 81-6191. 200p. 1981. 32.50 (ISBN 0-521-24059-X); pap. 9.95 (ISBN 0-521-28411-2). Cambridge U Pr.

Duffey, Bernard, jt. ed. see Williams, Kenny J.

Duffey, Eric. Grassland Ecology & Wildlife Management. 1974. 32.00x o.p. (ISBN 0-412-12290-1, Pub. by Chapman & Hall). Methuen Inc.

Duffey, George H. Theoretical Physics: Classical & Modern Views. LC 79-23794. 704p. 1980. Repr. of 1973 ed. lib. bdg. 29.50 (ISBN 0-89874-062-2). Krieger.

Duffey, Rick & Stephenson, Harry. Fifth House. 1979. 1.50 (ISBN 0-942582-01-2). Erie St Pr.

Duffie, J. A. & Beckman, W. A. Solar Energy Thermal Processes. LC 74-12390. 1974. 41.50 (ISBN 0-471-22371-9, Pub. by Wiley-Interscience). Wiley.

--Solar Engineering of Thermal Processes. LC 80-13297. 762p. 1980. 32.50 (ISBN 0-471-05066-0, Pub. by Wiley-Interscience). Wiley.

Duffie, John A., jt. ed. see Boer, Karl W.

Duffield, B. S., jt. auth. see Coppock, J. T.

Duffield, C. G., jt. auth. see Welch, W.

Duffield, Guy P. Handbook of Bible Lands. LC 77-80446. 192p. 1969. pap. 2.95 o.p. (ISBN 0-8307-0073-0, 5001854). Regal.

Duffield, M. H., ed. Exercise in Water. 2nd ed. (Illus.). 1976. pap. text ed. 10.50 (ISBN 0-02-857590-3, Pub. by Bailliere-Tindall). Saunders.

Duffieux, P. M. The Fourier Transform & Its Applications to Optics. 2nd ed. (Pure & Applied Optics Ser.). 264p. 1983. 33.95 (ISBN 0-471-09589-3, Pub. by Wiley-Interscience). Wiley.

Duffus, C. M. & Slaughter, J. C. Seeds & Their Uses. LC 80-40283. 154p. 1980. 36.95x (ISBN 0-471-27799-1, Pub. by Wiley-Interscience); pap. write for info. (ISBN 0-471-27798-3). Wiley.

Duffy, Charles G. Young Ireland: A Fragment of Irish History, 1840-1850. LC 71-127257. (Europe 1815-1945 Ser.). 796p. 1973. Repr. of 1881 ed. lib. bdg. 79.50 (ISBN 0-306-71119-2). Da Capo.

Duffy, Charles G., ed. The Ballad Poetry of Ireland. LC 72-13882. 256p. 1973. Repr. of 1869 ed. lib. bdg. 32.00x (ISBN 0-8201-1116-3). Schol Facsimiles.

Duffy, Christopher. Royal Adversaries: The Armies of Frederick the Great & Maria Theresa. (Illus.). 572p. boxed set 32.00 (ISBN 0-88254-713-5). Hippocrene Bks.

--Siege Warfare: The Fortress in the Early Modern World, 1494-1660. (Illus.). 1979. 30.00 (ISBN 0-7100-8871-X). Routledge & Kegan.

Duffy, Dave, jt. auth. see Lamb, Tony.

Duffy, David M. Hunting Dog Know-How. rev. ed. (Illus.). 208p. 1983. pap. 8.95 (ISBN 0-8329-0287-X, Pub. by Winchester Pr.). New Century.

Duffy, Dick, jt. auth. see Jones, Jeanne.

Duffy, E. A. A Monograph of the Immature Stages of Australasian Timber Beetles - Cerambycidae. (Illus.). 235p. 1963. 35.75x (ISBN 0-565-00577-4, Pub. by Brit Mus Nat Hist England). Sabbot-Natural Hist Bks.

--A Monograph of the Immature Stages of African Timber Beetles (Cerambycidae) (Illus.). vii, 338p. 1957. 43.00x (ISBN 0-565-00094-2, Pub. by Brit Mus Nat Hist). Sabbot-Natural Hist Bks.

--A Monograph of the Immature Stages of Neotropical Timber Beetles (Cerambycidae) (Illus.). v, 327p. 1960. 43.00x (ISBN 0-565-00109-4, Pub. by Brit Mus Nat Hist). Sabbot-Natural Hist Bks.

--A Monograph of the Immature Stages of Oriental Timber Beetles (Cerambycidae) (Illus.). 434p. 1968. 54.00x (ISBN 0-565-00667-3, Pub. by Brit Mus Nat Hist England). Sabbot-Natural Hist Bks.

--A Monograph on the Immature Stage of the African Tumber Beetles (CERAMBYCIDAE) Supplement. (Systematic Monograph of the Commonwealth Institute of Entomology: No. 2). (Illus.). 186p. 1980. pap. 42.00 o.p. (ISBN 0-85198-488-6, CAB). Unipub.

Duffy, Edward. Rousseau in England: The Context for Shelley's Critique of the Enlightenment. LC 78-57307. 1979. 18.95x (ISBN 0-520-03695-6). U of Cal Pr.

Duffy, Frank, ed. see Klein, Judy G.

Duffy, J. I., ed. Treatment, Recovery, & Disposal Processes for Radioactive Wastes: Recent Advances. LC 82-22260. (Pollution Technology Review No.95, Chemical Technology Review No. 216). (Illus.). 287p. 1983. 39.00 (ISBN 0-8155-0922-7). Noyes.

--Vaccine Preparation Techniques. LC 80-10174. 403p. 1980. 48.00 o.p. (ISBN 0-8155-0796-8). Noyes.

Duffy, James P., jt. auth. see Czajka, Peter A.

Duffy, John. A History of Public Health in New York City, 1625-1866, Vol. 1. LC 68-25852. 620p. 1968. 20.00x (ISBN 0-87154-212-9). Russell Sage.

Duffy, John C. Child Psychiatry. 3rd ed. (Medical Examination Review Bks.: Vol. 23). 1977. spiral bdg. 23.00 (ISBN 0-87488-126-9). Med Exam.

Duffy, Joseph. Power: Prime Mover of Technology. rev. ed. (gr. 11-12). 1972. text ed. 21.97 (ISBN 0-87345-420-0). McKnight.

Duffy, Karen L., jt. ed. see Rankin, Sally.

Duffy, Mary E., jt. auth. see Wolf, Margaret S.

Duffy, Patrick G. The Official Mixer's Annual. 7th ed. LC 82-45452. (Illus.). 240p. Date not set. 10.95 (ISBN 0-385-18307-0). Doubleday.

Duffy, Tony. Swimming & Diving. LC 80-50933. (Intersport Ser.). 13.00 (ISBN 0-382-06515-8). Silver.

--Track & Field. LC 80-52507. (Intersport Ser.). 13.00 (ISBN 0-382-06430-5). Silver.

Dufour, Charles P. New Orleans. 1981. english ed. 19.95 (ISBN 0-8071-0799-9); french ed. 22.50 (ISBN 0-8071-0851-0). La State U Pr.

Dufour, Leon. Vocabulario De Teologia Biblica. 9th ed. 976p. 1977. 35.95 (ISBN 84-254-0809-1, S-50205). French & Eur.

Dufrechou, Carole. Neil Young. LC 77-88754. 1978. pap. 5.95 (ISBN 0-8256-3917-4, Quick Fox). Putnam Pub Group.

Dufresne, Ed. The Lawsuitor. 1980. pap. 1.00 o.s.i. (ISBN 0-89274-133-3). Harrison Hse.

Dufresne, Francine. Cooking Fish & Wild Game. LC 75-25760. (Illus.). 144p. 1975. 4.95 o.s.i. (ISBN 0-912238-75-5). One Hund One Prods.

Du Fresne, Jim. Tramping in New Zealand. (Lonely Planet Travel Ser.). (Illus.). 144p. (Orig.). 1982. pap. 6.95 o.s.i. (ISBN 0-88254-675-9, Pub. by Lonely Planet Australia). Hippocrene Bks.

Duft, Ken. Principles of Management in Agribusiness. (Illus.). 1979. text ed. 20.95 (ISBN 0-8359-5595-8); instrs'. manual avail. (ISBN 0-8359-5596-6). Reston.

Dufty, William, jt. auth. see Holiday, Billie.

Dufualt, Paul. Sanatorium. (Novels by Franco-Americans in New England 1850-1940 Ser.). 153p. (Fr.). (gr. 10 up). 1982. pap. 4.50x (ISBN 0-911409-23-8). Natl Mat Dev.

Dugan, Michael, ed. Stuff & Nonsense. LC 76-53610. (gr. 3 up). 1977. 5.95 o.p. (ISBN 0-529-05337-3, A4657, Philomel). Putnam Pub Group.

Dugan, Richard L. Building Christian Commitment. (Trinity Bible Ser.). 107p. (Orig.). 1982. wkbk. 4.50x (ISBN 0-87123-280-4, 240280). Bethany Hse.

Dugan, Thomas. A Modern Bestiary. (Illus.). 64p. (Orig.). 1982. pap. 9.95 (ISBN 0-940170-06-X). Station Hill Pr.

Du Gard, Bertrand. Reproductions in Colors of the Best American Paintings of the 19th Century: A Book for Students, Critics, Collectors & Art Lovers. (Illus.). 1978. 67.75 o.p. (ISBN 0-89266-137-2). Am Classical Coll Pr.

Dugas, Andre, jt. auth. see Paillet, Jean-Pierre.

Du Gas, Beverly W. Introduction to Patient Care. 3rd ed. LC 76-58601. (Illus.). 1977. text ed. 17.95 (ISBN 0-7216-3226-2). Saunders.

Dugdale, S. Electrical Properties of Metals & Alloys. (Structure & Properties of Solids Ser.). 304p. 1977. pap. text ed. 16.95 (ISBN 0-7131-2524-1). E Arnold.

Duggan, Anne S. The Complete Tap Dance Book. 1977. pap. text ed. 8.00 (ISBN 0-8191-0137-0). U Pr of Amer.

Duggan, Curt, jt. auth. see Kriz, Joseph.

Duggan, Hayden A. A Second Chance. LC 77-15814. (Illus.). 1978. 20.95x (ISBN 0-669-02060-5). Lexington Bks.

Duggan, Joseph J. The Song of Roland: Formulaic Style & Poetic Craft. LC 75-186101. 1973. 21.00x o.p. (ISBN 0-520-02201-7). U of Cal Pr.

Duggan, Maurice. Falter Tom & the Water Boy. LC 59-12200. (Illus.). (gr. 3-6). 1959. 8.95 (ISBN 0-87599-027-4). S G Phillips.

Dugger, James G. The New Professional: An Introduction for the Human Service Worker. 2nd ed. LC 80-13324. 200p. 1980. text ed. 17.95 (ISBN 0-8185-0393-9). Brooks-Cole.

Dugger, W. E., et al. Basic Electronic Systems Technology, 8 units. Incl. Unit 1. Electrical Energy; Unit 2. Controlling Electrical Energy (ISBN 0-02-818380-0); Unit 3. Control Devices & Systems (ISBN 0-02-818390-8); Unit 4. Communications (ISBN 0-02-818400-9); Unit 5. Computer Concepts (81841); Unit 6. Measurement & Control (ISBN 0-02-818420-3); Unit 7. Circuit Measurements (81843); Unit 8. Circuit Analysis (ISBN 0-02-818440-8). 1973. pap. text ed. 3.96 ea. o.p.; tchrs' eds 5.28 ea. o.p. Glencoe.

Dugger, W. E., Jr., jt. auth. see Gerrish, H. H.

Dugger, W. E., Jr., jt. auth. see Suess, A. R.

Dugger, W., Jr., jt. auth. see Gerrish, H.

Dugger, William E., Jr., jt. auth. see Gerrish, Howard H.

Dugger, William E., Jr., jt. auth. see Patrick, Dale.

Du Gran, Claurene. Wordsmanship. 95p. 1981. 9.95 (ISBN 0-930454-11-1). Verbatim.

DuGran, Claurene. Wordsmanship: A Dictionary. 1982. Repr. pap. 2.95 (ISBN 0-671-45468-4). WSP.

Du Gue Trapier, E. Ribera in the Collection. (Illus.). 1952. pap. 0.50 (ISBN 0-87535-073-9). Hispanic Soc.

--Valdes Leal: Baroque Concept of Death & Suffering in his Paintings. (Illus.). 1956. pap. 1.50 (ISBN 0-87535-090-9). Hispanic Soc.

Du Halde. Cotton & Silk Making in Manchu China. LC 79-93005. (Illus.). 112p. 1980. pap. 12.50 o.p. (ISBN 0-8478-0306-6). Rizzoli Intl.

Duhamel, P. A., jt. auth. see Hughes, Richard E.

Duhault, J., jt. ed. see Regnault, F.

Duhl, Bunny S. From the Inside Out & Other Metaphors: Thinking Systems Multicentrically. 320p. 1983. 30.00 (ISBN 0-87630-328-9). Brunner-Mazel.

Duignan, P. & Gann, L. H., eds. Colonialism in Africa, 1870-1960, 5 vols. Incl. Vol. 1. History & Politics of Colonialism, 1870-1914. 74.50 (ISBN 0-521-07373-1); Vol. 2. History & Politics of Colonialism, 1914-1960. 74.50 (ISBN 0-521-07732-X); Vol. 3. 1975. 64.50 (ISBN 0-521-07844-X); Vol. 4. The Economics of Colonialism. 1975. 84.50 (ISBN 0-521-08641-8); Vol. 5. Bibliography. 74.50 (ISBN 0-521-07859-8). Cambridge U Pr.

Duignan, Peter & Gann, L. H. The Middle East & North Africa: The Challenge to Western Security. (Publication Ser.: No.239). 180p. 1981. pap. 9.95x o.p. (ISBN 0-8179-7392-3). Hoover Inst Pr.

Duignan, Peter, jt. auth. see Gann, L. H.

Duiker, William. The Communist Road to Power in Vietnam. LC 80-22098. (Westview Special Studies on South & Southeast Asia). 375p. 1982. lib. bdg. 32.50 (ISBN 0-89158-794-2); pap. 12.95 (ISBN 0-86531-505-1). Westview.

Duiker, William J. The Comintern & Vietnamese Communism. LC 75-620112. (Papers in International Studies: Southeast Asia: No. 37). 1975. pap. 4.50x (ISBN 0-89680-023-7, Ohio U Ctr Intl). Ohio U Pr.

--Cultures in Collision: The Boxer Rebellion. LC 77-73550. (Illus.). 1978. 12.95 o.p. (ISBN 0-89141-028-7). Presidio Pr.

--Ts'ai Yuan-P'ei: Educator of Modern China. LC 76-43212. (Penn State Studies: No. 41). 1977. pap. 4.50x (ISBN 0-271-00504-1). Pa St U Pr.

--Vietnam: A Nation in Revolution. (Nations of Contemporary Asia). 135p. 1983. lib. bdg. 16.50 (ISBN 0-86531-336-9). Westview.

--Vietnam Since the Fall of Saigon. LC 80-21166. (Southeast Asia Ser., Ohio University Papers in International Studies: No. 56). (Illus.). 78p. (Orig.). 1981. pap. 9.00 (ISBN 0-89680-106-3, Ohio U Ctr Intl). Ohio U Pr.

Duing, Walter. Monsoon Regime of the Currents in the Indian Ocean. LC 76-104320. (International Indian Ocean Expedition Oceanographic Monographs: No. 1). (Illus.). 1970. 12.00x (ISBN 0-8248-0092-3, Eastwest Ctr). UH Pr.

Du Jardin, Rosamond. Boy Trouble. (gr. 4-9). 1953. 12.95i (ISBN 0-397-30229-0, JBL-J). Har-Row.

--Class Ring. LC 51-9796. (gr. 4-9). 1951. 12.95i (ISBN 0-397-30184-7, JBL-J). Har-Row.

--One of the Crowd. LC 61-15257. (gr. 4-9). 1961. 11.89 (ISBN 0-397-30582-6, JBL-J). Har-Row.

--Practically Seventeen. (gr. 4-9). 1949. 11.89 (ISBN 0-397-30153-7, JBL-J). Har-Row.

Du Jardin, Rosamond see Du Jardin, Rosamond.

Dujarier, Michel. A History of the Catechumenate. 144p. 1982. pap. 4.95 (ISBN 0-8215-9327-7). Sadlier.

--The Rites of Christian Initiation. 244p. 1982. pap. 4.95 (ISBN 0-8215-9328-5). Sadlier.

Duke, Benjamin C. Japan's Militant Teachers: A History of the Left-Wing Teachers' Movement. 192p. 1973. 12.00x (ISBN 0-8248-0237-3, Eastwest Ctr). UH Pr.

Duke, Bill, jt. auth. see Lyon, William.

Duke, Charles R. & Jacobsen, Sally-Ann. Reading & Writing Poetry: Success Approaches for the Student & Teacher. 248p. 1982. pap. text ed. 18.50 (ISBN 0-89774-031-9). Oryx Pr.

Duke, Daniel. Managing Student Behavior Problems. LC 80-10443. 1980. pap. 12.50x (ISBN 0-8077-2583-8). Tchrs Coll.

Duke, Daniel L., ed. Classroom Management: The National Society for the Study of Education, 78th Yearbook, Pt. II. LC 78-66032. (Illus.). xxii, 448p. 1983. lib. bdg. 13.00x o.p. (ISBN 0-226-60127-7); pap. text ed. price not set o.p.; pap. 8.00 o.p. (ISBN 0-226-60096-3). U of Chicago Pr.

Duke, David C. Distant Obligations: Modern Writers & Foreign Causes. 320p. 1983. 27.50 (ISBN 0-19-503221-7). Oxford U Pr.

Duke, James, tr. see Schleiermacher, Friedrich.

Duke, James A. Medicinal Plants of the Bible. (Traditional Healing Ser.: No. 10). (Illus.). 300p. 1983. lib. bdg. 49.95 (ISBN 0-932426-23-9). Trado-Medic.

Duke, Judith S. Children's Books & Magazines: A Market Study. LC 78-24705. (Communications Library Ser.). (Illus.). 1979. text ed. 29.95 (ISBN 0-914236-17-2). Knowledge Indus.

--Religious Publishing & Communications. LC 80-17694. (Communications Library). 275p. 1980. text ed. 29.95x (ISBN 0-914236-61-X). Knowledge Indus.

--The Technical, Scientific & Medical Publishing Market. 1981. spiral 850.00 (ISBN 0-686-42881-1). Knowledge Indus.

Duke, Judith S., ed. The Knowledge Industry Two Hundred: America's Two Hundred Largest Media Companies, 1983. 400p. 1983. pap. 88.00 (ISBN 0-86729-034-X). Knowledge Indus.

Duke, Kenneth L., jt. auth. see Mossman, Harland W.

Duke Law Journal. Medical Malpractice: The Duke Law Journal Symposium. LC 76-49822. 304p. 1977. prof ref 22.50x (ISBN 0-88410-701-9). Ballinger Pub.

Duke, Marshall & Nowicki, Steven. Abnormal Psychology: Perspectives on Being Different. LC 78-7584. (Illus.). 1978. text ed. 25.95 (ISBN 0-8185-0274-6). Brooks-Cole.

Duke, Maurice. James Branch Cabell: A Reference Guide. 1979. lib. bdg. 15.00 (ISBN 0-8161-7838-0, Hall Reference). G K Hall.

Duke, Maurice & Bryer, Jackson R., eds. American Women Writers: Bibliographical Essays. LC 82-6156. 464p. 1983. lib. bdg. 29.95 (ISBN 0-313-22116-2, DAW/). Greenwood.

Duke, Michael S. Lu You. (World Author Ser.). 1977. lib. bdg. 15.95 (ISBN 0-8057-6267-1, Twayne). G K Hall.

Duke Of Bedford. Parrots & Parrot Like Birds. 14.95 (ISBN 0-87666-428-1, H931). TFH Pubns.

Duke of Edinburgh, frwd. by. Harpers Handbook to Edinburgh. 322p. 1982. pap. 12.95 (ISBN 0-907686-01-X, Pub. by Auto Assn-British Tourist Authority England). Merrimack Bk Serv.

Duke, Robert E. How to Lose Weight & Stop Smoking Through Self-Hypnosis (includes audio cassette) 140p. 1983. text ed. 18.95x (ISBN 0-8290-1276-1). Irvington.

--Why Children Fail & How You Can Help Them: Meditation-Therapy. 130p. 1983. 16.95x (ISBN 0-686-84047-X). Irvington.

Duke, Salcacion C. English-Spanish Workbook I: Taller de la Gramatica Espanola I. (Illus.). 237p. (Orig.). 1982. write for info. (ISBN 0-9609446-0-5). Research Lang.

Duke, Thomas S. Celebrated Criminal Cases of America. LC 79-172594. (Criminology, Law Enforcement, & Social Problems Ser.: No. 184). (Illus.). Date not set. 22.50x (ISBN 0-87585-184-3). Patterson Smith.

Duke University. Financing Health Care: Competition vs. Regulation. Yaggy, Duncan & William, Anlyan G., eds. 264p. 1982. prof ref 28.75x (ISBN 0-88410-737-X). Ballinger Pub.

Duke University Center for Commonwealth & Comparative Studies see Kornberg, Allan & Clarke, Harold D.

Duke University Hospital Nursing Services. Quality Assurance: Guidelines for Nursing Care. text ed. 17.50 (ISBN 0-686-97986-9, Lippincott Nursing). Lippincott.

Duke, William J. Themes of Wholeness. 200p. 1981. pap. 7.50 o.s.i. (ISBN 0-686-36896-7). Ideals PA.

Duke-Elder, Stewart, ed. System of Ophthalmology Series. Incl. Vol. 1. The Eye in Evolution. (Illus.). 843p. 1958. 65.50 (ISBN 0-8016-8282-7); Vol. 2. The Anatomy of the Visual System. (Illus.). 901p. 1961. 67.50 (ISBN 0-8016-8283-5); Vol. 3, Pt. 1. Normal & Abnormal Development: Embryology. (Illus.). 330p. 1963. 51.50 (ISBN 0-8016-8285-1); Vol. 3, Pt. 2. Normal & Abnormal Development: Congenital Deformities. (Illus.). 1190p. 1964. 72.50 (ISBN 0-8016-8286-X); Vol. 4. The Physiology of the Eye & of Vision. (Illus.). xx, 734p. 1968. 75.50 (ISBN 0-8016-8296-7); Vol. 5. Ophthalmic Optics & Refraction. (Illus.). xix, 879p. 1970. 65.50 o.p. (ISBN 0-8016-8298-3); Vol. 7. The Foundations of Ophthalmology: Heredity, Pathology, Diagnosis & Therapeutics. (Illus.). 829p. 1962. 69.50 (ISBN 0-8016-8284-3); Vol. 8. Diseases of the Outer Eye: Conjunctiva, Cornea & Sclera, 2 vols. (Illus.). 1242p. 1965. 100.00 (ISBN 0-8016-8287-8); Vol. 9. Diseases of Uveal Tract. (Illus.). xvi, 978p. 1966. 80.00 (ISBN 0-8016-8290-8); **Vol. 10. Diseases of the Retina. (Illus.). xv, 878p. 1967. 85.00 (ISBN 0-8016-8295-9); Vol. 11. Diseases of the Lens & Vitreous: Glaucoma & Hypotony. (Illus.). xx, 779p. 1969. 85.00 (ISBN 0-8016-8297-5); Vol. 12. Neuro-Ophthalmology. (Illus.). xxi, 994p. 1971. 89.50 (ISBN 0-8016-8299-1); Vol. 14. Injuries, 2 vols. 1357p. 1972. Set. 117.00 (ISBN 0-8016-8300-9). Mosby.**

Dukeminier, Jesse & Johanson, Stanley. Family, Wealth Transactions, Wills, Trusts, Future Interests & Estate Planning, 1982 Supplement. 1982. pap. text ed. 6.95 (ISBN 0-316-19513-8). Little.

Dukeminier, Jesse & Krier, James E. Property. LC 80-84030. 1507p. 1981. text ed. 28.00 (ISBN 0-316-19510-3). Little.

Dukeminier, Jesse, Jr. & Johanson, Stanley M. Family Wealth Transactions: Wills, Trusts, Future Interests and Estate Planning. 1978. 29.95 (ISBN 0-316-19507-3). Little.

Duker, Jan, jt. auth. see Gilberstadt, Harold.

Duker, Sam. Individualized Instruction in Mathematics. LC 72-5739. 1972. 14.50 o.p. (ISBN 0-8108-0533-2). Scarecrow.

Duker, William F. A Constitutional History of Habeas Corpus. LC 79-6834. (Contributions in Legal Studies: No. 13). 349p. 1980. lib. bdg. 35.00 (ISBN 0-313-22264-9, DHC/). Greenwood.

Dukert, Joseph M. Nuclear Ships of the World. (Illus.). 192p. (gr. 7-9). 1973. PLB 6.59 o.p. (ISBN 0-698-30501-9, Coward). Putnam Pub Group.

--This Is Antarctica. rev. ed. (Illus.). (gr. 5-8). 1972. PLB 5.49 o.p. (ISBN 0-698-30364-4, Coward). Putnam Pub Group.

Dukes. Side Effect of Drugs, Vol. 9. 1980. 106.50 (ISBN 0-444-90102-7). Elsevier.

--Side Effects of Drugs: Annual 4, 1980. 1980. 70.25 (ISBN 0-444-90130-2). Elsevier.

--Side Effects of Drugs: Annual 6, 1982. 1982. 70.25 (ISBN 0-444-90211-2). Elsevier.

Dukes, David. I Have Never Lived in America. 1978. 6.50 o.p. (ISBN 0-533-03054-4). Vantage.

Dukes, Helen, jt. auth. see Hoffman, Banesh.

Dukes, Hubert N. The Bible: Fact, Fiction, Fantasy, Faith. Carleton, Nancy G., ed. LC 81-17169. 176p. (Orig.). pap. 8.00 o.p. (ISBN 0-89581-040-9). Lancaster-Miller.

Dukes, P. Catherine the Great & the Russian Nobility. 1968. 47.50 (ISBN 0-521-04858-3). Cambridge U Pr.

Dukes, Paul. October & the World: Perspectives on the Russian Revolution. LC 79-15143. 1979. 20.00x (ISBN 0-312-58096-7). St Martin.

--Russia under Catherine the Great, 2 vols. 1978. 24.00 set (ISBN 0-89250-104-9); Vol. 1. 12.00 ea. (ISBN 0-89250-106-5). Vol. 2 (ISBN 0-89250-105-7). pap. set o. p. (ISBN 0-89250-107-3). Orient Res Partners.

Dukhin, S. S. & Shilov, V. N. Dielectric Phenomena & the Double Layer in Disperse Systems & Polyelectrolytes. Greenberg, P., ed. Lederman, D., tr. from Rus. LC 74-13579. 192p. 1974. 43.95 o.s.i. (ISBN 0-470-22415-0). Halsted Pr.

Duk Song Son & Clark, Robert. Black Belt Korean Karate. (Illus.). 256p. 1983. 14.95 (ISBN 0-13-077669-6). P-H.

Dulac, Colette. Shortcut to French. (gr. 9 up). 1977. pap. text ed. 4.75 (ISBN 0-88345-300-2); cassettes 25.00 (ISBN 0-685-79306-0). Regents Pub.

--Spanish Conversation for Students & Travelers. (gr. 7-12). 1983. pap. price not set (ISBN 0-8120-2598-9). Barron.

Dulac, Collette, jt. auth. see Madrigal, Margarita.

Dulcy, Faye & Wilhelm, Irma J., eds. Aquatics: A Revived Approach to Pediatric Management. (Physical & Occupational Therapy in Pediatrics Ser.: Vol. 3, No. 1). 120p. 1983. text ed. 19.95 (ISBN 0-86656-215-X). Haworth Pr.

Duldt, Bonnie W., et al. Interpersonal Communication in Nursing: A Humanistic Approach. 200p. 1983. 10.95 (ISBN 0-8036-2936-2). Davis Co.

Duley, W. W. Laser Processing & Analysis of Materials. 450p. 1982. 59.59x (ISBN 0-306-41067-2, Plenum Pr). Plenum Pub.

Dulieu, Jean. Paulus & the Dragon. Visser, Vivien, tr. LC 77-17090. (Children's Stories Ser.). (Illus.). (gr. 2-5). 1977. PLB 9.95 (ISBN 0-912278-96-X); pap. 3.95 (ISBN 0-912278-97-8). Crossing Pr.

Dulin, John, jt. auth. see Veley, Victory.

Dulin, John J. Modern Electronic Calculations. LC 76-49496. 150p. 1976. pap. text ed. 6.95x o.p. (ISBN 0-915668-27-0). G S E Pubns.

Dulin, John J. & Veley, Victor F. Modern Electronics: A First Course. (Illus.). 640p. 1983. 20.95 (ISBN 0-13-481663-3). P-H.

Dulin, Mark. Fish Diseases. 1979. 4.95 (ISBN 0-87666-524-5, KW-066). TFH Pubns.

Dulin, Mark P. Diseases of Marine Aquarium Fishes. (Illus.). 1976. pap. 7.95 (ISBN 0-87666-787-6, PS731). TFH Pubns.

Dull, Lloyd W. Educational Supervision: A Handbook. (Illus.). 504p. 1981. text ed. 23.95 (ISBN 0-675-08060-6). Merrill.

Duller, H. J. Devlopment Technology. (International Library of Anthropology). 192p. (Orig.). 1982. pap. 11.95 (ISBN 0-7100-0990-9). Routledge & Kegan.

Dulles, Allen. The Craft of Intelligence. LC 76-57671. (Illus.). 1977. Repr. of 1963 ed. lib. bdg. 27.50 (ISBN 0-8371-9452-0, DUCI). Greenwood.

Dulles, Avery. Church Membership As a Catholic & Ecumenical Problem. (Pere Marquette Theology Lectures). 1974. 7.95 (ISBN 0-87462-506-8). Marquette.

--Models of Revelation. LC 82-45243. 360p. 1983. 16.95 (ISBN 0-385-17975-8). Doubleday.

Dulles, Foster R. America in the Pacific. LC 73-86595. (American Scene Ser). 1969. Repr. of 1932 ed. 37.50 (ISBN 0-306-71431-0). Da Capo.

--American Policy Toward Communist China, 1949-1969. LC 70-184974. 1972. pap. 10.95x (ISBN 0-88295-728-7). Harlan Davidson.

--America's Rise to World Power: 1898-1954. (Illus.). pap. 4.75xi o.p. (ISBN 0-06-133021-3, TB3021, Torch). Har-Row.

--History of Recreation: America Learns to Play. 2nd ed. (Illus., Orig.). 1965. pap. text ed. 22.95 (ISBN 0-13-391953-6). P-H.

--Labor in America: A History. 3rd ed. LC 66-19224. 1968. pap. 12.95x (ISBN 0-88295-729-5). Harlan Davidson.

Dulles, John W. Brazilian Communism 1935-1945: Repression during World Upheaval. (Illus.). 311p. 1983. text ed. 25.00x (ISBN 0-292-70741-X). U of Tex Pr.

Dullfield, Robert. Rogue Bull: The Story of Lang Hancock King of the Pilbara. 231p. 1982. 20.95 (ISBN 0-00-216423-X, Pub. by W. Collins Australia); pap. 8.95 (ISBN 0-686-98394-7). Intl Schol Bk Serv.

Dulmatovskaya, G. & Shilova, I. Who's Who in Soviet Cinema. 685p. 1982. 12.50 (ISBN 0-8285-1553-0, Pub. by Progress Pubs USSR). Imported Pubns.

Dulsey, Bernard M., tr. see Icaza, Jorge.

Dumaine, Deborah. Write to the Top. 1982. pap. 7.95 (ISBN 0-394-71226-9). Random.

Duman, Daniel. The English & Colonial Bars in the Nineteenth Century. 256p. 1983. text ed. 30.00x (ISBN 0-85664-468-4, Pub. by Croom Helm Ltd England). Biblio Dist.

--The Judicial Bench in England. (Royal Historical Society-Studies in History: No. 29). 208p. 1982. text ed. 33.75x (ISBN 0-901050-80-6, Pub. by Swiftbks England). Humanities.

Dumarest, Noel. Notes on Cochiti, New Mexico. LC 20-23196. 1919. pap. 12.00 (ISBN 0-527-00526-6). Kraus Repr.

Du Maroussem. Ministere du Commerce, de l'Industrie et des Colonies. Office du Travail. La Petite Industrie. Salaires et Duree du Travail, 2 vols. (Conditions of the 19th Century French Working Class Ser.). (Fr.). 1974. Repr. of 1873 ed. Set. lib. bdg. 251.50x o.p. (ISBN 0-8287-1387-1). Vol. 1 (1127). Vol. 2 (1128). Clearwater Pub.

Du Maroussem, P. La Question Ouvriere, 4 vols. (Conditions of the 19th Century French Working Class Ser.). (Fr.). 1974. Repr. of 1891 ed. Set. lib. bdg. 282.00x o.p. (ISBN 0-8287-0292-6). Vol. 1 (1183). Vol. 2 (1184). Vol. 3 (1185). Vol. 4 (1186). Clearwater Pub.

Dumarsias, Cesar-Chesneau. Analyse de la Religion Chretienne. (Holbach & His Friends Ser). 58p. (Fr.). 1974. Repr. of 1767 ed. lib. bdg. 19.00x o.p. (ISBN 0-8287-0293-4, 1506). Clearwater Pub.

Dumas, Alexandre. The Count of Monte Cristo. abr. ed. Blair, Lowell, tr. from French. (Bantam Classics Ser.). 441p. (gr. 6 up). 1981. pap. 2.75 (ISBN 0-553-21031-9). Bantam.

--Dumas on Food. Davidson, Alan & Davidson, Jane, trs. from Fr. (Illus.). 327p. 1982. 17.50x (ISBN 0-7181-1842-1). U Pr of Va.

--My Memoirs. Bell, A. Craig, ed. & tr. from Fr. LC 75-17781. (Illus.). 257p. 1975. Repr. of 1961 ed. lib. bdg. 16.25x (ISBN 0-8371-8186-0, DUMM). Greenwood.

--Three Musketeers. (Illus.). (gr. 4-6). 1953-59. il. jr. lib. 5.95 (ISBN 0-448-05824-3, G&D); deluxe ed. 8.95 (ISBN 0-448-06024-8). Putnam Pub Group.

--The Three Musketeers. (The Illustrated Junior Library). (Illus.). 288p. 1982. pap. 5.95 (ISBN 0-448-11024-5, G&D). Putnam Pub Group.

Dumas, Alexandre see Eyre, A. G.

Dumas, Alexandre see Swan, D. K.

Dumas, Emma P. Mirbah. (Novels by Franco-Americans in New England 1850-1940 Ser.). 246p. (Fr.). (gr. 10 up). 1979. pap. 4.50x (ISBN 0-911409-20-3). Natl Mat Dev.

Dumas, J. B. Discours et Eloges Academiques. Repr. of 1885 ed. 183.00 o.p. (ISBN 0-8287-1363-4). Clearwater Pub.

Dumas, Lloyd J. The Political Economy of Arms Reduction: Reversing Economic Delay. (AAAS Selected Symposium 80 Ser.). 162p. 1982. lib. bdg. 17.50x (ISBN 0-86531-405-5). Westview.

Dumas, Phillipe. Lucie: A Tale of a Donkey. (Illus.). (ps-2). 1979. 7.95 o.p. (ISBN 0-13-541169-6). P-H.

Du Maurier, Daphne. Echoes from the Macabre. 1978. pap. 1.95 o.p. (ISBN 0-380-01953-1, 38331). Avon.

--Myself When Young: The Shaping of a Writer. 1978. pap. 1.95 o.p. (ISBN 0-380-40485-0, 40485). Avon.

--Rebecca. 1948. 14.95 (ISBN 0-385-04380-5). Doubleday.

Dumaurier, Daphne, jt. auth. see Quiller-Couch, Arthur.

Dumbaugh, Kerry & Serota, Gary. Capitol Jobs: An Insider's Guide to Finding a Job in Congress. LC 82-50885. 120p. (Orig.). 1982. pap. 5.95 (ISBN 0-9605750-4-9). Tilden Pr.

Dumbaugh, Winnifred. William Blake's Vision of America. (Illus.). 58p. 1971. 3.00 o.p. (ISBN 0-910286-16-7). Boxwood.

Dumbleton, J. H. The Tribology of Natural & Artifical Joints. (Tribology Ser.: Vol. 3). 1981. 74.50 (ISBN 0-444-41898-9). Elsevier.

Dumbleton, Susanne. In & Around Albany Calendar & Chronicle of Past Events. (Illus.). 28p. (Orig.). 1982. pap. 8.95 (ISBN 0-9605460-2-2). Wash Park.

Dumbleton, William A. James Cousins. (English Authors Ser.). 1980. 14.95 (ISBN 0-8057-6745-2, Twayne). G K Hall.

Dumery, Henry. Phenomenology & Religion: Structures of the Christian Institution. Barrett, Paul, tr. LC 73-94443. (Hermeneutics Series: Studies in the History of Religion). 1975. 21.00x (ISBN 0-520-02714-0). U of Cal Pr.

Dumesil, Carla D., jt. auth. see Evans, Helen M.

Du Mesnil. L' Hygenie a Paris. l'Habitation du Pauvre. (Conditions of the 19th Century French Working Class Ser.). 233p. (Fr.). 1974. Repr. of 1890 ed. lib. bdg. 65.00x o.p. (ISBN 0-8287-0700-6, 1172). Clearwater Pub.

Du Mesnil & Mangenot. Etude d'Hygiene et d'Economie Sociale. Enquete sur les Logements, Professions, Salaires et Budgets. (Conditions of the 19th Century French Working Class Ser.). 166p. (Fr.). 1974. Repr. of 1899 ed. lib. bdg. 50.00x o.p. (ISBN 0-8287-0295-0, 1114). Clearwater Pub.

Dumestre, G. Atlas Linguistique de Cote d'Ivoire. (Black Africa Ser.). 323p. (Fr.). 1974. Repr. of 1971 ed. lib. bdg. 85.00 o.p. (ISBN 0-8287-0296-9, 71-2009). Clearwater Pub.

Dumezil, Georges. Camillus: A Study of Indo-European Religion As Roman History. Strutynski, Udo, ed. Aronowicz, Annette, et al, trs. from Fr. LC 80-36771. 250p. 1980. 17.95x (ISBN 0-520-02841-4). U of Cal Pr.

--Gods of the Ancient Northmen. Haugen, Einar, ed. & tr. (Study of Comparative Folklore & Mythology, No. 3). 1974. 29.50x (ISBN 0-520-02044-8); CAL 371. pap. 3.95 (ISBN 0-520-03507-0). U of Cal Pr.

--The Stakes of the Warrior. Puhvel, Jaan, ed. Weeks, David, tr. from Fr. LC 82-13384. 128p. 1983. text ed. 14.95 (ISBN 0-520-04834-2). U of Cal Pr.

Dumitriu, Petru. To the Unknown God. Kirkup, James, tr. from Fr. LC 82-5722. 256p. 1982. pap. 11.95 (ISBN 0-8164-2424-1). Seabury.

Dummer, Geoffrey W. Electronic Reliability. Griffin, N. B., ed. 1966. 17.75 o.p. (ISBN 0-08-011448-2); pap. inquire for price o.p. (ISBN 0-08-011447-4). Pergamon.

Dummer, Geoffrey W. & Robertson, J. M., eds. Electronic Connection Techniques & Equipment, 1968-69. 1969. inquire for price (ISBN 0-08-013243-X). Pergamon.

Dummett, Michael. The Game of Tarot. (Illus.). 600p. 1980. 39.95 (ISBN 0-7156-1014-7). US Games Syst.

--Twelve Tarot Games. (Illus.). 242p. 1980. 14.95 (ISBN 0-7156-1485-1); pap. 9.95 (ISBN 0-7156-1488-6). US Games Syst.

Dummett, Nanci L. Self-Paced Business Mathematics. 410p. 1979. pap. text ed. 17.85x o.p. (ISBN 0-534-00616-7); instr's manual avail. o.p. Kent Pub Co.

Dummett, Nancilee. Self-Paced Business Mathematics. 2nd ed. 425p. 1982. pap. text ed. 18.95x (ISBN 0-534-01155-1). Kent Pub Co.

Dumond, Dwight L. Antislavery Origins of the Civil War in the United States. LC 80-12505. vii, 133p. 1980. Repr. of 1959 ed. lib. bdg. 17.00x (ISBN 0-313-22378-5, DUAO). Greenwood.

Dumond, Dwight L., jt. ed. see Barnes, Gilbert H.

Dumond, Michael, ed. Coping with Life after High School. (Personal Adjustment Ser.). 1983. lib. bdg. 7.97 (ISBN 0-8239-0606-X). Rosen Pr.

Dumonde, D. C. & Maini, R. N., eds. Research into Rheumatoid Arthritis & Allied Diseases. Date not set. cancelled o.p. (ISBN 0-8391-1180-0). Univ Park.

Dumont & Nunez, eds. Hormones & Cell Regulation, Vol. 6. 1982. 66.00 (ISBN 0-444-80419-6). Elsevier.

Dumont, A. A. Les Habitations Ouvrieres dans les Grands Centre Industries et Plus Particulierments dans la Region du Nord. (Conditions of the 19th Century French Working Class Ser.). 268p. (Fr.). 1974. Repr. of 1905 ed. lib. bdg. 72.50x o.p. (ISBN 0-8287-0297-7, 1054). Clearwater Pub.

Dumont, Francis M. French Grammar. 2nd ed. 1969. pap. 4.76i (ISBN 0-06-460035-1, CO 35, COS). B&N NY.

Du Mont, J. The Basis of Combination in Chess. (Illus.). 1978. pap. 4.50 (ISBN 0-486-23644-7). Dover.

Du Mont, J., jt. auth. see Tartakower, A.

Dumont, J. & Nunez, J., eds. Hormones & Cell Regulation. (Hormones & Cell Regulation Ser.: Vol. 5). 1981. 55.00 (ISBN 0-444-80322-X). Elsevier.

Dumont, J., ed. see Symposia on Hormones & Cell Regulation (INSERM), France, 1976-79.

Dumont, J. E., jt. ed. see Boeynaems, J. J.

Dumont, Jacques E., jt. ed. see Swillens, Stephane.

Dumont, Jacques E., et al, eds. Fourth International Conference on Cyclic Nucleotides, Brussels, Belgium: Proceedings. (Advances in Cyclic Nucleotide Research: Vol. 14). 756p. 1981. text ed. 87.00 (ISBN 0-89004-546-1). Raven.

Dumont, Jean-Paul. Under the Rainbow: Nature & Supernature among the Panare Indians. LC 75-22049. (Texas Pan American Ser.). 192p. 1976. 13.95x o.p. (ISBN 0-292-78504-6). U of Tex Pr.

Dumont, Lora L. Consonant Articulation Drills. 2nd ed. 268p. 1980. pap. text ed. 6.75x (ISBN 0-8134-2129-2, 2129). Interstate.

Dumont, Louis. Affinity As a Value: Marriage Alliance in South India with Comparative Essays on Austrailia. LC 82-13468. (Illus.). 248p. 1983. lib. bdg. 22.00x (ISBN 0-226-16964-2). U of Chicago Pr.

--From Mandeville to Marx: The Genesis & Triumph of Economic Ideology. LC 76-8087. (Midway Reprint Ser.). 236p. 1977. pap. write for info. (ISBN 0-226-16966-9). U of Chicago Pr.

Dumont, M. A Treatise on Judicial Evidence, Extracted from the Manuscripts of Jeremy Bentham. Dumont, M., ed. xvi, 366p. 1981. Repr. of 1825 ed. lib. bdg. 35.00x (ISBN 0-8377-0318-2). Rothman.

DuMont, Rosemary R. Reform & Reaction: The Big City Public Library in American Life. LC 77-71864. (Contributions in Librarianship & Information Science: No. 21). 1977. lib. bdg. 25.00 (ISBN 0-8371-9540-3, DRR/). Greenwood.

Dumoulin, Heinrich. Christianity Meets Buddhism. Maraldo, John C., tr. from Ger. LC 73-82783. (Religious Encounter: West Meets East Ser., Vol. 1). 212p. 1974. 16.00 (ISBN 0-87548-121-3). Open Court.

Du Moulin-Eckart, Richard. Cosima Wagner, 2 vols. Phillips, Catherine A., tr. from Ger. (Music Ser.). (Illus.). 1981. Repr. of 1930 ed. Set. lib. bdg. 85.00 (ISBN 0-306-76102-5). Da Capo.

Dumpleton, John. Law & Order: The Story of the Police. (Junior Ref. Ser). (Illus.). (gr. 3-7). 1982. Repr. of 1963 ed. 8.95 (ISBN 0-7136-1079-4). Dufour.

Dumur, Guy. Nicolas De Stael. (Q. L. P. Ser.). (Illus.). 1976. 7.95 (ISBN 0-517-52611-5). Crown.

Dumville, David & Lapidge, Michael, eds. The Anglo-Saxon Chronicle Seventeen: The Annals of St. Neots. 108p. 1983. text ed. 30.00x (ISBN 0-85991-117-9, Pub. by Boydell & Brewer). Biblio Dist.

Dun & Bradstreet Intl. Export Documentation Handbook: 1982 Edition. 2nd ed. Murd, Ruth E., compiled by. 125p. Date not set. soft-cover handbook 55.00 (ISBN 0-942526-01-5). Dun & Brad Intl.

Dun, Philip. The Cabal. (Orig.). 1981. pap. 2.25 o.p. (ISBN 0-425-04845-4). Berkley Pub.

Dunas, Jeff, photos by. Captured Women. (Illus.). 96p. pap. 12.95 (ISBN 0-394-62466-1). Grove.

Dunavent, James. How to Draw Airplanes. 1973. 7.95 (ISBN 0-8306-9973-2); pap. 3.95 o.p. (ISBN 0-8306-2216-0, 2216). TAB Bks.

Dunaway, et al. Bragon the Dragon Calendar Capers. (gr. 1-4). 1978. 9.95 o.p. (ISBN 0-916456-36-6, GA93). Good Apple.

--Bragon the Dragon Tells Time. (gr. 1-4). 1978. 9.95 o.p. (ISBN 0-916456-37-4, GA94). Good Apple.

Dunaway, David K. How Can I Keep from Singing: Pete Seeger. (Illus.). 1982. pap. 9.95 (ISBN 0-07-018151-9). McGraw.

Dunaway, Diane. Desire & Conquer. (Candlelight Ecstasy Ser.: No. 158). (Orig.). 1983. pap. 1.95 (ISBN 0-440-11779-8). Dell.

Dunaway, James O., jt. auth. see Sports Illustrated Editors.

Dunaway, John M. Jacques Maritain. (World Authors Ser.). 1978. lib. bdg. 15.95 (ISBN 0-8057-6315-5, Twayne). G K Hall.

Dunaway, Kate A., jt. auth. see Knopf, Howard.

Dunaway, Vic. Modern Saltwater Fishing. (Stoeger Bks). (Illus.). 288p. 1976. pap. 5.95 o.s.i. (ISBN 0-695-80657-2). Follett.

Dunayavskaya, Raya. Rosa Luxemburg, Women's Liberation & Marx's Philosophy of Revolution. 260p. 1982. text ed. 19.95x (ISBN 0-391-02569-4, Pub. by Harvester England); pap. text ed. 10.95x (ISBN 0-391-02793-X). Humanities.

Dunayevskaya, Raya, et al. The Free Speech Movement & the Negro Revolution. (Illus.). 56p. (Orig.). 1965. pap. 0.50x (ISBN 0-686-32888-4). News & Letters MN.

Dunbabin, J. P. Rural Discontent in 19th Century Britain. LC 73-94070. 1975. text ed. 35.00x (ISBN 0-8419-0146-5). Holmes & Meier.

Dunbabin, Thomas J. The Greeks & Their Eastern Neighbours: Studies in the Relations Between Greece & the Countries of the Near East in the Eighth & Seventh Centuries B. C. Boardman, John, ed. LC 78-24477. (Illus.). 1979. Repr. of 1957 ed. lib. bdg. 17.50x (ISBN 0-313-20791-7, DUGR). Greenwood.

Dunbar, Carl O. & Waage, Karl M. Historical Geology. 3rd ed. LC 72-89681. (Illus.). 556p. 1969. text ed. 28.95x (ISBN 0-471-22507-X). Wiley.

Dunbar, Clement. A Bibliography of Shelley Studies: Eighteen Twenty-Three to Nineteen Fifty. LC 75-24093. (Reference Library of the Humanities: Vol. 32). 425p. 1975. lib. bdg. 24.50 o.s.i. (ISBN 0-8240-9980-X). Garland Pub.

Dunbar, David, jt. auth. see Winchester, Kenneth.

Dunbar, Georgia, jt. auth. see Rorabacher, Louise.

Dunbar, Ian. Dog Behavior. (Illus.). 223p. 1979. 12.95 (ISBN 0-87666-671-3, H-1016). TFH Pubns.

Dunbar, M. J., ed. Marine Production Mechanisms. LC 77-88675. (International Biological Programme Ser: No. 20). (Illus.). 1979. 75.00 (ISBN 0-521-21937-X). Cambridge U Pr.

Dunbar, Paul L. Little Brown Baby: Paul Laurence Dunbar Poems for Young People. LC 40-4721. (Illus.). (gr. 4-6). 1940. 5.95 (ISBN 0-396-01993-5). Dodd.

Dunbar, Robert E. Heredity. (First Bks.). (Illus.). (gr. 4 up). 1978. PLB 8.90 s&l (ISBN 0-531-01408-8). Watts.

--Into Jupiter's World. LC 80-25526. (Triumph Bks.). (YA) (gr. 7 up). 1981. PLB 8.90 (ISBN 0-531-04266-9). Watts.

--Mental Retardation. (First Bks). (Illus.). (gr. 4-6). 1978. PLB 8.90 (ISBN 0-531-01491-6). Watts.

Dunbar, Tony & Kravitz, Linda. Hard Traveling: Migrant Farm Workers in America. LC 76-2056. 1976. prof ref 16.50x (ISBN 0-88410-293-9). Ballinger Pub.

Duncalf, Brian. The Focalguide to Slide-Tape. (Focalguide Ser.). (Illus.). 1978. pap. 7.95 (ISBN 0-240-51006-2). Focal Pr.

Duncan, A. A. Scotland: the Making of the Kingdom. LC 75-5386. (Edinburgh History of Scotland Ser.: Vol. 1). (Illus.). 705p. 1975. text ed. 37.50x o.p. (ISBN 0-06-491830-0). B&N Imports.

Duncan, A. S., et al, eds. Dictionary of Medical Ethics. 1977. pap. text ed. 15.50x o.p. (ISBN 0-232-51302-3). Humanities.

Duncan, Alastair. Art Nouveau Furniture. (Illus.). 1982. 25.00 (ISBN 0-517-54786-4, C N Potter Bks). Crown.

--Leaded Glass: A Handbook of Techniques. (Illus.). 216p. 1976. 19.95 o.p. (ISBN 0-8230-2660-4). Watson-Guptill.

Duncan, Bettie N. It's Casimir Pulaski Day! 1979. 4.95 o.p. (ISBN 0-533-03938-X). Vantage.

Duncan, Beverly & Duncan, Otis D. Sex Typing & Social Roles: A Research Report. (Quantitative Studies in Social Relations Ser.). 1978. 29.50 (ISBN 0-12-223850-8). Acad Pr.

Duncan, Bob, ed. see Marder, William & Marder, Estelle.

Duncan, Carol. The Pursuit of Pleasure: the Rococo Revival in French Romantic Art. LC 75-23789. (Outstanding Dissertations in the Fine Arts - 19th Century). (Illus.). 1976. lib. bdg. 31.00 o.s.i. (ISBN 0-8240-1985-7). Garland Pub.

Duncan, Charles. The Art of Classical Guitar Playing. (The Art of Ser.). (Illus.). 132p. (Orig.). 1980. pap. text ed. 13.75 (ISBN 0-87487-079-8). Summy.

Duncan, Colin, et al. Low Pay: Its Causes & the Post-War Trade Union Response. (Social Policy Research Monographs). 159p. 1981. 41.95x (ISBN 0-471-10052-8, Pub. by Res Stud Pr). Wiley.

Duncan, David & Gold, Robert. Drugs & the Whole Person. LC 81-15984. 272p. 1982. pap. text ed. 14.95x (ISBN 0-471-04120-3); test avail. 5.00 (ISBN 0-471-87622-4). Wiley.

Duncan, David D. The World of Allah. 1982. 40.00 (ISBN 0-395-32504-8). HM.

Duncan, David J. The River Why. LC 82-5508. 320p. (Orig.). 1983. 12.95 (ISBN 0-87156-321-5). Sierra.

Duncan, Doris G. & Aviel, S. David. Computers & Remote Computing Services. LC 82-20094. (Illus.). 258p. (Orig.). 1983. lib. bdg. 22.50 (ISBN 0-8191-2881-3); pap. text ed. 11.50 (ISBN 0-8191-2882-1). U Pr of Amer.

Duncan, Edmondstoune. Story of Minstrelsy. LC 69-16802. (Music Story Ser). 1968. Repr. of 1907 ed. 34.00x (ISBN 0-8103-4240-5). Gale.

--Story of the Carol. LC 69-16805. 1968. Repr. of 1911 ed. 31.00 o.p. (ISBN 0-8103-3547-6). Gale.

Duncan, Elmer H., ed. see Reid, Thomas.

Duncan, F. Microprocessor Programming & Software Development. 1980. 31.95 (ISBN 0-13-581405-7). P-H.

Duncan, G. Marx & Mill: Two Views of Social Conflict & Social Harmony. 416p. 1973. 42.50 (ISBN 0-521-20257-4); pap. 11.95 (ISBN 0-521-29130-5). Cambridge U Pr.

Duncan, George B. The Person & Work of the Holy Spirit in the Life of the Believer. LC 74-21900. 87p. 1975. pap. 1.99 (ISBN 0-8042-0681-3). John Knox.

Duncan, Greg J., jt. ed. see Morgan, James N.

Duncan, Helen A. Duncan's Dictionary for Nurses. LC 74-121974. (Illus.). 1971. pap. text ed. 6.25 o.s.i. (ISBN 0-8261-1121-1). Springer Pub.

Duncan, Iain M. Higher Grade Chemistry. 1978. pap. text ed. 9.00x o.p. (ISBN 0-435-65527-2). Heinemann Ed.

Duncan, Isadora. My Life. (Black & Gold Lib). (Illus.). 1955. 10.00 (ISBN 0-87140-942-9); pap. 6.95 (ISBN 0-87140-274-2). Liveright.

Duncan, J. & Derrett, M. Studies in the New Testament, Vol. 13: Midrasn, Haggadah, & the Character of the Community. xxi, 261p. 1982. write for info. (ISBN 90-04-06596-2). E J Brill.

Duncan, J., jt. auth. see Bonsall, F. F.

Duncan, J. R. & Prasse, K. W. Veterinary Laboratory Medicine: Clinical Pathology. (Illus.). 1977. text ed. 16.50x (ISBN 0-8138-1915-6). Iowa St U Pr.

Duncan, Jane. Brave Janet Reachfar. LC 74-8693. 32p. (ps-3). 1975. 7.95 (ISBN 0-8164-3130-2, Clarion). HM.

--My Friends George & Tom. 1977. lib. bdg. 12.50 o.p. (ISBN 0-8161-6456-8, Large Print Bks). G K Hall.

Duncan, Jeffrey L. The Power & Form of Emerson's Thought. LC 73-85043. xiv, 105p. 1974. 9.95x (ISBN 0-8139-0510-9). U Pr of Va.

Duncan, Judith. Tender Rhapsody. (Superromances Ser.). 384p. 1983. pap. 2.50 (ISBN 0-373-70051-2, Pub. by Worldwide). Harlequin Bks.

Duncan, Judith A., illus. The Sermon on the Mount: From the Translation Prepared at Cambridge in 1611 for King James I. LC 81-211201. (Illus.). 1978. 15.00 (ISBN 0-9606844-0-9). Mac Col MN.

Duncan, K. & Rutledge, I., eds. Land & Labour in Latin America. LC 76-11076. (Cambridge Latin American Studies: No. 26). (Illus.). 1978. 59.50 (ISBN 0-521-21206-5). Cambridge U Pr.

Duncan, K. D., et al, eds. Changes in Working Life. LC 80-40129. 1981. 71.95x (ISBN 0-471-27777-0, Pub. by Wiley-Interscience). Wiley.

Duncan, Karen, ed. Information Technology & Health Care: The Critical Issues. 200p. 1980. 25.00 (ISBN 0-88283-031-7). AFIPS Pr.

Duncan, Leonard C. Greek Roots. (Illus.). 82p. (Orig.). (gr. 6-12). 1982. pap. 5.00 (ISBN 0-941414-01-9); pap. text ed. 10.00 (ISBN 0-941414-02-7). LCD.

Duncan, Lois. Chapters: My Growth as a Writer. 276p. (gr. 7 up). 1982. 10.95 (ISBN 0-316-19552-9). Little.

--Down a Dark Hall. (RL 6). 1975. pap. 1.50 o.p. (ISBN 0-451-08326-1, W8326, Sig). NAL.

--Five Were Missing ("Ransom") (RL 7). 1972. pap. 1.75 (ISBN 0-451-11040-4, AE1040, Sig). NAL.

--From Spring to Spring: Poems & Photographs. LC 82-11160. 80p. (gr. 3-7). 1982. 10.95 (ISBN 0-664-32695-1). Westminster.

--Hotel for Dogs. (Illus.). (gr. 1-3). 1972. pap. 1.75 (ISBN 0-380-01258-8, 62133-9, Camelot). Avon.

--Killing Mr. Griffin. (YA) 1980. pap. 2.25 (ISBN 0-440-94515-1, LFL). Dell.

--Summer of Fear. (YA) 1977. pap. 2.25 (ISBN 0-440-98324-X, LFL). Dell.

--They Never Came Home. 192p. 1980. pap. 1.95 (ISBN 0-380-50229-1, 62026X). Avon.

Duncan, MacDonald B. Development of Muslin Theology, Jurisprudence, & Constitutional Theory. LC 65-2183. 386p. 1903. Repr. of 1973 ed. 14.00x (ISBN 0-686-43336-X). Intl Pubns Serv.

Duncan, Otis D., jt. auth. see Duncan, Beverly.

Duncan, Otis D., et al. Statistical Geography: Problems in Analyzing Areal Data. LC 77-7890. (Illus.). 1977. Repr. of 1961 ed. lib. bdg. 17.50x (ISBN 0-8371-9676-0, DUSG). Greenwood.

--Social Change in a Metropolitan Community. LC 73-76764. 136p. 1973. 9.95 o.p. (ISBN 0-686-86716-5); pap. 4.50x (ISBN 0-87154-216-1). Russell Sage.

Duncan, Phillip, ed. Current Topics in Organizational Behavior Management. LC 82-11685. (Journal of Organizational Behavior Management Ser.: Vol. 3, No. 3). 119p. 1982. text ed. 20.00 (ISBN 0-86656-198-6, B198). Haworth Pr.

Duncan, R. & Weston-Smith, M., eds. The Encyclopedia of Ignorance, Vol. 1 & 2. 1977. Combined Ed. text ed. 38.00 o.p. (ISBN 0-08-021238-7). Pergamon.

Duncan, R. M., ed. see Sender, Ramon J.

Duncan, Robert. Dragons at the Gate. 1976. pap. 1.95 o.p. (ISBN 0-451-06984-6, J6984, Sig). NAL.

Duncan, Robert, et al. The Male Muse: Gay Poetry Anthology. LC 73-77318. (Crossing Press Ser. of Contemporary Anthologies). 90p. (Orig.). 1973. 14.95 (ISBN 0-912278-35-8); pap. 4.95 (ISBN 0-912278-34-X). Crossing Pr.

Duncan, Robert C. & Knapp, Rebecca G. Introductory Biostatistics for the Health Sciences. 7th ed. 250p. 1983. 15.95 (ISBN 0-471-07869-7, Wiley Med). Wiley.

Duncan, Robert C., et al. Introductory Biostatistics for the Health Sciences. LC 76-44291. 163p. 1977. 12.50 (ISBN 0-471-01604-7, Pub. by Wiley Medical); avail. solutions (ISBN 0-471-03944-6). Wiley.

Duncan, Robert I. Architectural Graphics & Communication Problems. 144p. 1982. pap. text ed. 11.95 (ISBN 0-8403-2764-1). Kendall-Hunt.

Duncan, Roger F. & Ware, John P. A Cruising Guide to the New England Coast. Rev. ed. (Illus.). 1983. 24.95 (ISBN 0-396-08166-5). Dodd.

Duncan, S. Blackwell. Plumbing with Plastic. (Illus., Orig.). 1980. 15.95 o.p. (ISBN 0-8306-9958-9); pap. 9.95 o.p. (ISBN 0-8306-1214-9, 1214). TAB Bks.

Duncan, Stuart B. The Complete Book of Outdoor Masonry. (Illus.). 1978. 11.95 o.p. (ISBN 0-8306-9904-X); pap. 6.95 (ISBN 0-8306-1080-4, 1080). TAB Bks.

Duncan, T. Exploring Physics, 3 Vols. (gr. 11-12). Vol. 1&2. pap. text ed. 4.95 o.p. (ISBN 0-686-86795-5); Vol. 3. pap. text ed. 4.95 o.p. (ISBN 0-7195-2043-6). Transatlantic.

Duncan, Thomas. A Taxonomic Study of the Ranunculus Hispidus. (U. C. Publications in Botany V Ser.: Vol. 77). 1980. 11.00x (ISBN 0-520-09617-7). U of Cal Pr.

Duncan, W., ed. Clinical Toxicology. (International Congress Ser.: No. 417). (Proceedings). 1977. 44.00 (ISBN 0-444-15248-2). Elsevier.

Duncan, W. C. U. S. - Japan Automobile Diplomacy: A Study in Economic Confrontation. LC 73-12032. 1973. 22.50 o.p. (ISBN 0-88410-255-6). Ballinger Pub.

Duncan, W. Jack. Organizational Behavior. 2nd ed. LC 80-82460. (Illus.). 464p. 1981. text ed. 24.95 (ISBN 0-395-29640-4); instr's manual 1.00 (ISBN 0-395-29641-2). HM.

Duncan-Jones, Arthur S. Struggle for Religious Freedom in Germany. LC 72-136064. 1971. Repr. of 1938 ed. lib. bdg. 16.25x (ISBN 0-8371-5214-3, DURF). Greenwood.

Duncan-Jones, Katherine, ed. see Sidney, Philip.

Duncan-Jones, Richard. The Economy of the Roman Empire: Quantitative Studies. 2nd ed. LC 81-21564. (Illus.). 432p. 1982. 49.50 (ISBN 0-521-24970-8); pap. 17.50 (ISBN 0-521-28793-6). Cambridge U Pr.

Duncanson, Dennis. Changing Qualities of Chinese Life. 100p. 1983. 16.50x (ISBN 0-8448-1404-0). Crane-Russak Co.

Dunckel, E. B., et al. Business Environment of the Seventies: A Trend Analysis for Business Planning. 1970. 3.95 o.p. (ISBN 0-07-018207-8, P&RB). McGraw.

Duncombe, Beverly. A Matter of Love. 1983. 5.95 (ISBN 0-533-05091-X). Vantage.

Duncombe, Frances. Summer of the Burning. new ed. LC 75-42956. (Illus.). 180p. (gr. 5-9). 1976. 7.95 o.p. (ISBN 0-399-20513-6). Putnam Pub Group.

Dundas, Charles. African Crossroads. LC 76-45443. 1977. Repr. of 1955 ed. lib. bdg. 21.00x (ISBN 0-8371-9089-4, DUAF). Greenwood.

Dundas, James L. Heating Service. (Illus.). 1978. text ed. 17.95 (ISBN 0-8403-1866-9). Kendall-Hunt.

Dundes, Alan. German National Character: An Anthropological Study, or Life Is Like a Chicken Coop Ladder. (Illus.). 176p. 1983. 16.00x (ISBN 0-231-05494-7). Columbia U Pr.

--Study of Folklore. (Illus.). 1965. text ed. 17.95 (ISBN 0-13-858944-5). P-H.

Dundes, Alan & Falassi, Alessandro. La Terra in Piazza: An Interpretaion of the Palio of Siena. (Illus.). 325p. 1983. 36.50x (ISBN 0-520-02681-0); pap. 11.95 (ISBN 0-520-04771-0). U of Cal Pr.

Dundes, Alan & Falassi, Allesandro. La Terra in Piazza: An Interpretation of the Palio in Siena. LC 73-91675. (Illus.). 1975. 36.50x (ISBN 0-520-02681-0). U of Cal Pr.

Dundes, Alan, ed. see Samuelson, Sue.

Dundon, H. Dwyer, jt. ed. see Jackson, Elinor.

Dundon, Mary L. & Gay, George A. The Nineteen Seventy-Eight Revision of the U. S. Standard Certificates. Olmstead, Mary, tr. (Ser. 4: No. 23). 45p. 1982. pap. 1.75 (ISBN 0-8406-0268-5). Natl Ctr Health Stats.

Dundy, Elaine. Elvis & Gladys. 320p. 1983. 15.95 (ISBN 0-02-553910-8). Macmillan.

Dunfee, Maxine. Social Studies for the Real World. 1978. pap. text ed. 18.95 (ISBN 0-675-08366-4). Additional supplements may be obtained from publisher. Merrill.

Dunfee, Thomas W. & Bellace, Janice. Business & Its Legal Environment. (Illus.). 688p. 1983. text ed. 24.95 (ISBN 0-13-101006-9). P-H.

Dunfee, Thomas W., et al. Modern Business Law: An Introduction to the Legal Environment of Business. LC 77-71017. (Law Ser.). 346p. 1978. pap. text ed. 15.95 (ISBN 0-471-87018-8); tchr's manual avail. (ISBN 0-471-86987-2). Wiley.

--Modern Business Law: Contracts. Sutton, L., ed. LC 77-91087. (Law Ser.). 448p. 1978. pap. text ed. 20.95x (ISBN 0-471-86989-9); tchr's manual o.p. avail. (ISBN 0-471-86990-2). Wiley.

Dunford, Elizabeth P. The Hawaiians of Old. Rayson, Ann, ed. (Illus.). 220p. (gr. 4 up). 1980. text ed. 12.00 (ISBN 0-935848-00-2); pap. text ed. 10.00 (ISBN 0-935848-01-0); wkbk 4.00 (ISBN 0-935848-02-9); tchr's. manual 5.00 (ISBN 0-935848-09-6). Bess Pr.

Dunford, H. B. & Dolphin, D. The Biological Chemistry of Iron. 1982. 59.50 (ISBN 90-277-1444-4, Pub. by Reidel Holland). Kluwer Boston.

Dungan, David L., jt. auth. see Cartlidge, David R.

Dunham, Aileen. Political Unrest in Upper Canada, 1815-1836. LC 74-3751. 210p. 1975. Repr. of 1927 ed. lib. bdg. 15.50x (ISBN 0-8371-7474-0, DUPU). Greenwood.

Dunham, Arthur & Nusberg, Charlotte. Toward Planning for the Aging in Local Communities: An International Perspective. 49p. (Orig.). 1978. pap. text ed. 4.00 (ISBN 0-910473-05-6). Intl Fed Ageing.

Dunham, Clarence, et al. Contracts, Specifications & Law for Engineers. 3rd ed. (Illus.). 1979. text ed. 29.95 (ISBN 0-07-018236-1, C). McGraw.

Dunham, Harold H. Government Handout: A Study in the Administration of the Public Lands 1875-1891. LC 79-87564. (American Scene Ser). 1970. Repr. of 1941 ed. lib. bdg. 42.50 (ISBN 0-306-71433-7). Da Capo.

Dunham, Judith, jt. auth. see Brown, Christopher.

Dunham, Lowell, tr. see Zea, Leopoldo.

Dunham, Mildred see Leed, Lawrence.

Dunham, Montrew. Margaret Bourke-White: Young Photographer. LC 75-34512. (Childhood of Famous Americans Ser). 200p. 1976. 4.95 o.p. (ISBN 0-672-52225-X). Bobbs.

Dunham, Randall & Smith, Frank J. Organizational Surveys: An Internal Assessment of Organizational Health. 1979. pap. text ed. 10.95x (ISBN 0-673-15143-3). Scott F.

Dunham, Vera S. In Stalin's Time. LC 75-10238. 368p. 1976. 42.50 (ISBN 0-521-20949-8); pap. 11.95 (ISBN 0-521-29650-1). Cambridge U Pr.

Dunham, Wm. H. Fane Fragment of the 1461 Lord's Journal. (Yale Historical Pubs., Manuscripts & Edited Texts: No. XIV). 1935. 39.50x (ISBN 0-685-69813-0). Elliots Bks.

Dunick, Randa K. The Structure of Obscurity: Gertrude Stein & the Limits of Language. (Illus.). 200p. 1983. 18.50 (ISBN 0-252-00909-6). U of Ill Pr.

Dunigan, Opal. Training Budgerigars to Talk. (Illus.). 128p. 1981. 8.95 (ISBN 0-87666-845-7, PS-791). TFH Pubns.

Duniway, Abigail S. Path Breaking: An Autobiographical History of the Equal Suffrage Movement in the Pacific Coast States. 2nd ed. LC 79-162285. (Studies in the Life of Women). 1971. pap. 5.50 (ISBN 0-8052-0322-2). Schocken.

Duniway, David. Glimpses of Historic South Salem. 56p. (Orig.). 1982. pap. 3.95 (ISBN 0-686-42960-5). S Salem News.

Dunkel, Harold B. Herbart & Education. (Western Educational Tradition Ser). (Orig.). 1969. pap. text ed. 2.85x (ISBN 0-685-19732-8). Phila Bk Co.

Dunkel, Patricia, jt. auth. see Pialorsi, Frank.

Dunkel, Patty L. Curriculum for Educators in Health Care Institutions: Proceedings & Recommendations of an Invitational Conference. LC 77-26933. (Illus.). 1978. pap. 10.00 (ISBN 0-87914-046-1, 549620). Hosp Res & Educ.

Dunkell, Samuel. Lovelives: How We Make Love. LC 78-7381. (Illus.). 1978. 8.95 o.p. (ISBN 0-688-03354-7). Morrow.

--Sleep Positions: The Night Language of the Body. (Illus.). 1978. pap. 2.25 o.p. (ISBN 0-451-07875-6, J7875, Sig). NAL.

Dunkerley, David. Occupations & Society. (Students Library of Sociology). 96p. 1975. 16.95x (ISBN 0-7100-8239-8); pap. 8.95 (ISBN 0-7100-8240-1). Routledge & Kegan.

--The Study of Organizations. (Students Library of Sociology). 1972. 8.95x o.p. (ISBN 0-7100-7231-7); pap. 3.00 o.p. (ISBN 0-7100-7232-5). Routledge & Kegan.

Dunkerley, David & Salaman, Graeme, eds. The International Yearbook of Organization Studies, 1980. 1981. 30.00x (ISBN 0-686-71902-6). Routledge & Kegan.

--International Yearbook of Organization Studies, 1981. 240p. 1982. 50.00x (ISBN 0-7100-0996-8). Routledge & Kegan.

Dunkin, Michael J. & Biddle, Bruce J. The Study of Teaching. LC 81-40903. (Illus.). 508p. 1982. pap. text ed. 17.50 (ISBN 0-8191-2259-9). U Pr of Amer.

Dunkin, Naomi. Psychology for Physiotherapists. (Psychology for Professional Groups Ser.). 350p. 1981. text ed. 25.00x (ISBN 0-333-31857-9, Pub. by Macmillan England); pap. text ed. 10.95x (ISBN 0-333-31884-6). Humanities.

Dunkin, Paul S. How to Catalog a Rare Book. 2nd. rev ed. LC 72-6515. 112p. 1973. pap. 6.00 o.p. (ISBN 0-8389-0141-7). ALA.
Dunklin, L see Allen, W. S.
Dunkling, L see Allen, W. S.
Dunkling, Leslie. The Guinness Book of Names. (Illus.). 192p. (Orig.). 1982. pap. 9.95 (ISBN 0-85112-293-0, Pub. by Guinness Superlatives England). Sterling.
--The Nightmare. (Readers Ser.: Stage 1). 1979. pap. text ed. 1.80 o.p. (ISBN 0-88377-135-7). Newbury Hse.
Dunkling, Leslie see Allen, W. S.
Dunkling, Leslie A. First Names First. 290p. 1982. Repr. of 1977 ed. 40.00x (ISBN 0-686-82089-4). Gale.
Dunkman, William E. Money, Credit & Banking. 1970. pap. text ed. 10.95x (ISBN 0-394-30170-6). Phila Bk Co.
Dunlap, A. Basic Cases in Public International Law. 1971. pap. text ed. 14.95x (ISBN 0-686-96143-9). Irvington.
Dunlap, Alice. Hospital Literature Subject Headings. 2nd ed. LC 77-519. 200p. 1977. pap. 31.25 (ISBN 0-87258-202-7, AHA-121006). Am Hospital.
Dunlap, Alice, et al, eds. Hospital Literature Index: 1980 Cumulative Annual, Vol. 36. 704p. 1981. 125.00 (ISBN 0-87258-348-1, AHA-121360). Am Hospital.
Dunlap, Alice, et al, eds. see American Hospital Association.
Dunlap, Carol. California People. (Illus.). 240p. 1982. pap. 16.95 (ISBN 0-87905-091-8). Peregrine Smith.
Dunlap, Jane B., jt. auth. see Pfeiffer, Isobel L.
Dunlap, Knight. Religion: Its Functions in Human Life: A Study of Religion from the Point of View of Psychology. LC 77-100158. Repr. of 1946 ed. lib. bdg. 17.75x (ISBN 0-8371-3716-0, DURE). Greenwood.
Dunlap, L. C. Mental Health Concepts Applied to Nursing. 256p. 1978. 22.50 (ISBN 0-471-04360-5). Wiley.
Dunlap, William. Four Plays, 1789-1812. LC 76-46978. 300p. 1976. lib. bdg. 30.00x (ISBN 0-8201-1283-6). Schol Facsimiles.
--Musical Works. LC 79-24504. 1979. 34.00x (ISBN 0-8201-1348-4). Schol Facsimiles.
Dunlay, Thomas W. Wolves for the Blue Soldiers: Indian Scouts & Auxiliaries with the United States Army, 1860-90. LC 81-16326. (Illus.). xii, 316p. 1982. 21.95x (ISBN 0-8032-1658-0). U of Nebr Pr.
Dunleavy, Aidan O. & Miracle, Andrew W., eds. Studies in the Sociology of Sport. LC 82-16807. 402p. 1982. pap. text ed. 15.00 (ISBN 0-912646-78-0). Tex Christian.
Dunlop, Burton, jt. auth. see Durman, E. C.
Dunlop, Burton D. The Growth of Nursing Home Care. LC 78-14715. 1979. 22.95x (ISBN 0-669-02704-9). Lexington Bks.
Dunlop, Douglas. Arab Civilization to A.D. 1500. (Arab Background Ser.). 1971. 20.00x (ISBN 0-86685-012-0). Intl Bk Ctr.
Dunlop, Fiona, ed. Paris Art Guide. (Art Guide Ser.). (Illus.). 96p. (Orig.). 1981. pap. 5.95 (ISBN 0-9507160-1-4, 50010, Pub. by Art Guide England). Morgan.
Dunlop, I. & Schrand, H. Communication for Business: Materials for Reading Comprehension & Discussion. (Materials for Language Practice Ser.). (Illus.). 110p. 1982. pap. 4.95 (ISBN 0-08-029438-3). Pergamon.
Dunlop, Ian & Schrand, Heinrich. In & About English: Authentic Texts for Developing Reading Skills. LC 80-40438. 96p. 1981. pap. 5.50 (ISBN 0-08-024570-6). Pergamon.
Dunlop, John T. Industrial Relations Systems. LC 77-24354. (Arcturus Books Paperbacks). 412p. 1977. pap. 8.95x o.p. (ISBN 0-8093-0850-9). S Ill U Pr.
Dunlop, John T., jt. auth. see Bok, Derek C.
Dunlop, Philip, tr. see Tibullus.
Dunlop, Sandy. The Golfing Bodymind. 1981. 35.00x o.p. (ISBN 0-7045-3029-5, Pub. by Wildwood House). State Mutual Bk.
Dunlop, Stewart & Adam, Alan. Village, Town & City. (Place & People Ser.). 1976. pap. text ed. 4.95x o.p. (ISBN 0-435-34692-X). Heinemann Ed.
Dunlop, Stewart & MacDonald, Donald. Farming & the Countryside. (Place & People Ser.). 1976. pap. text ed. 4.95x o.p. (ISBN 0-435-34695-4). Heinemann Ed.
--Social Geography. (Place & People Ser.: No. 7). 1977. pap. text ed. 4.95x o.p. (ISBN 0-435-34699-7). Heinemann Ed.
Dunlop, Stewart, jt. auth. see Bell, Evelyn.
Dunlop, Stewart, ed. Place & People: A Guide to Modern Geography Teaching. 1976. text ed. 8.95x o.p. (ISBN 0-435-34697-0). Heinemann Ed.
Dunlop, W. S. Lee's Sharpshooters or Forefront of Battle. 488p. 1982. 30.00 (ISBN 0-686-97672-X). Pr of Morningside.
Dunman, Jack. Agriculture: Capitalist & Socialist. 1975. text ed. 13.00x o.p. (ISBN 0-85315-330-2). Humanities.
Dunmire, Reba. Toys of Early America: You Can Make. (Illus.). 64p. (Orig.). 1983. pap. text ed. 5.40 (ISBN 0-87006-441-X). Goodheart.
Dunmore. The Stalinist Command Economy. LC 79-26712. 224p. 1980. 26.00 (ISBN 0-312-75516-3). St Martin.
Dunmore, Charles W. Selections from Ovid. rev. ed. LC 63-12153. 1969. pap. text ed. 10.50x (ISBN 0-582-28131-8). Longman.
Dunmore, Spencer. Means of Escape. LC 78-26763. 1979. 8.95 o.p. (ISBN 0-698-10976-7, Coward). Putnam Pub Group.
Dunn. Advertising. 5th ed. 1982. 26.95 (ISBN 0-03-060049-9). Dryden Pr.
Dunn, A. J., jt. ed. see Nemeroff, C. B.
Dunn, A. S. Rubber & Rubber Elasticity, No. 48. (Journal of Polymer Science: Polymer Symposia). 232p. 1974. pap. 15.00 (ISBN 0-685-88107-5, Pub. by Wiley). Krieger.
Dunn, Alan. Architecture Observed. LC 75-165515. 144p. 1971. 10.00 o.p. (ISBN 0-07-018305-8, Architectural Rec Bks). McGraw.
Dunn, Angela. Second Book of Mathematical Bafflers. (Puzzles, Amusements, Recreations Ser.). (Illus.). 192p. (Orig.). 1983. pap. 3.50 (ISBN 0-486-24352-4). Dover.
Dunn, C. D. Current Concepts in Erythropoiesis. 1983. 59.00 (ISBN 0-471-90033-8, Pub. by Wiley Med). Wiley.
Dunn, Charles. American Democracy Debated: An Introduction to American Government. 2nd ed. 1982. text ed. 20.95x (ISBN 0-673-15547-1). Scott F.
Dunn, Delmer D. Financing Presidential Campaigns. (Studies in Presidential Selection). 1972. pap. 7.95 (ISBN 0-8157-1961-2). Brookings.
Dunn, Dennis J. Detente & Papal-Communist Relations, 1962-1978. (Westview Replica Edition Ser.). 1979. lib. bdg. 27.50 (ISBN 0-89158-197-9). Westview.
Dunn, Dennis J., ed. Religion & Modernization in the Soviet Union. LC 77-86372. (Illus.). 414p. 1978. 33.00 (ISBN 0-89158-241-X). Westview.
Dunn, Donald J., jt. auth. see Reams, Bernard D., Jr.
Dunn, Douglas, ed. Two Decades of Irish Writing: A Critical Survey. (Essays, Prose, & Scottish Literature). 1979. 10.95 o.p. (ISBN 0-85635-070-2, Pub. by Carcanet New Pr England). Humanities.
Dunn, Edgar S., Jr. Recent Southern Economic Development, as Revealed by the Changing Structure of Employment. LC 62-63139. (U of Fla. Social Sciences Monographs Ser.: No. 14). (Illus.). 1962. pap. 2.75 (ISBN 0-8130-0067-X). U Presses Fla.
--Social Information Processing & Statistical Systems: Change & Reform. LC 74-5289. 246p. 1974. 22.95 o.p. (ISBN 0-471-22747-1, Pub. by Wiley-Interscience). Wiley.
Dunn, Edmond J. Missionary Theology: Foundations in Development. LC 80-67259. 409p. 1980. lib. bdg. 24.25 (ISBN 0-8191-1209-7); pap. text ed. 14.75 (ISBN 0-8191-1210-0). U Pr of Amer.
Dunn, Elizabeth, et al. Guidelines for the Pediatric Nurse Practitioner. (Illus.). 250p. 1982. cancelled 12.50 (ISBN 0-8036-2948-6). Davis Co.
Dunn, F. D. Heat Pipes. 3rd ed. (Illus.). 320p. 1982. 49.50 (ISBN 0-08-029356-5); pap. 20.00 (ISBN 0-08-029355-7). Pergamon.
Dunn, Forrest D. Butte County Place Names. (ANCRR Occasional Paper: No. 3). 122p. 1977. 6.00 (ISBN 0-686-38932-8). Assn NC Records.
Dunn, Frank. Paul's Later Life & Letters. pap. 1.00 (ISBN 0-88027-101-9). Firm Foun Pub.
Dunn, George E., ed. Gilbert & Sullivan Dictionary. LC 72-125070. (Music Ser). 1971. Repr. of 1936 ed. lib. bdg. 17.50 (ISBN 0-306-70007-7). Da Capo.
Dunn, I. S., et al. Fundamentals of Geotechnical Analysis. LC 79-13583. 1980. text ed. 31.50x (ISBN 0-471-03698-6); solutions manual avail. (ISBN 0-471-04997-2). Wiley.
Dunn, J. Political Obligation in Its Historical Context. LC 80-40037. (Illus.). 360p. 1980. 37.50 (ISBN 0-521-22890-5). Cambridge U Pr.
--Western Political Theory in the Face of the Future. LC 78-25625. (Themes in the Social Sciences Ser.). 1979. 27.95 (ISBN 0-521-22619-8); pap. 7.95 (ISBN 0-521-29578-5). Cambridge U Pr.
Dunn, J. & Robertson, A. F. Independence & Opportunity: Political Change in Ahafo. LC 73-79303. (African Studies, No. 8). (Illus.). 420p. 1974. 42.50 (ISBN 0-521-20270-1). Cambridge U Pr.
Dunn, J. D. & Rachel, F. Wage & Salary Administration: Total Compensation Systems. 1970. text ed. 26.95 (ISBN 0-07-018291-4, C). McGraw.
Dunn, J. D. & Stephens, E. C. Management of Personnel. (Management Ser.). (Illus.). 640p. 1972. text ed. 17.95 o.p. (ISBN 0-07-018273-6, C); tchr's manual 4.95 o.p. (ISBN 0-07-018277-9); study guide 6.95 o.p. (ISBN 0-07-018274-4). McGraw.
Dunn, J. D., et al. Management Essentials: Resource. (Illus.). 384p. 1973. 16.30 (ISBN 0-07-018307-4, G); Practicium o.p. 5.90 (ISBN 0-07-018308-2); instructor's manual & key o.p. 6.40 (ISBN 0-07-018309-0). McGraw.
Dunn, James A., jt. auth. see Bergan, John R.
Dunn, James A., Jr. Miles to Go: European & American Transportation Politics. (Transportation Studies). 288p. 1981. 22.50x (ISBN 0-262-04062-X). MIT Pr.
Dunn, James D. Baptism in the Holy Spirit: A Re-Examination of the New Testament Teaching on the Gift of the Spirit in Relation to Pentacostalism Today. LC 77-3995. 1977. pap. 8.95 (ISBN 0-664-24140-9). Westminster.
--Unity & Diversity in the New Testament: An Inquiry into the Character of Earliest Christianity. LC 77-22598. 1977. text ed. 19.50 (ISBN 0-664-21342-1). Westminster.
Dunn, Jane. Moon in Eclipse: A Life of Mary Shelley. LC 78-850. 1978. 20.00 (ISBN 0-312-54692-0). St Martin.
Dunn, Jerry G. Alcoholic Victorious. (Moody Acorn Ser.). pap. 3.00 (ISBN 0-8024-0200-3). Moody.
--God Is for the Alcoholic. LC 65-24232. 1967. pap. 2.95 (ISBN 0-8024-3020-1). Moody.
Dunn, Joan. Retreat from Learning: Why Teachers Can't Teach, a Case History. LC 75-16609. 224p. 1975. Repr. of 1955 ed. lib. bdg. 15.50x (ISBN 0-8371-8252-2, DURL). Greenwood.
Dunn, John. Modern Revolutions: An Introduction to the Analysis of a Political Phenomenon. LC 72-177942. 352p. 1972. 37.50 (ISBN 0-521-08441-5); pap. 11.95 (ISBN 0-521-09698-7). Cambridge U Pr.
--Political Thought of John Locke. 1969. 37.50 (ISBN 0-521-07408-8). Cambridge U Pr.
--The Political Thought of John Locke: An Historical Account of the Argument of the 'Two Treatises of Government' 306p. 1983. pap. 12.95 (ISBN 0-521-27139-8). Cambridge U Pr.
Dunn, John, ed. Gold Smugglers. 10.00x o.p. (ISBN 0-392-03128-0, ABC). Sportshelf.
--West African States. LC 77-80832. (African Studies Ser.). (Illus.). 1978. 39.50 (ISBN 0-521-21801-2); pap. 12.95 (ISBN 0-521-29283-2). Cambridge U Pr.
Dunn, John P. Ornamentation in the Works of Frederick Chopin. LC 78-125069. (Music Ser). (Illus.). 1971. Repr. of 1921 ed. lib. bdg. 15.00 (ISBN 0-306-70006-9). Da Capo.
Dunn, Judy. The Little Duck. LC 75-36467. (Picturebacks Ser). (Illus.). 32p. (ps-1). 1976. pap. 1.50 (ISBN 0-394-83247-7, BYR). Random.
--The Little Goat. LC 77-91658. (Picturebacks Ser.). (Illus.). (ps-1). 1979. PLB 4.99 (ISBN 0-394-93872-0, BYR); pap. 1.50 (ISBN 0-394-83872-6). Random.
--The Little Kitten. LC 82-16711. (Picturebacks Ser.). (Illus.). 32p. (ps-4). 1983. PLB 4.99 (ISBN 0-394-95818-7); pap. 1.50 (ISBN 0-394-85818-2). Random.
--The Little Rabbit. LC 79-5241. (Picturebacks Ser.). (Illus.). 32p. (ps). 1980. PLB 4.99 (ISBN 0-394-94377-5, BYR); pap. 1.50 (ISBN 0-394-84377-0). Random.
Dunn, Judy, jt. auth. see Dunn, Phoebe.
Dunn, Judy, jt. auth. see Shaffer, David.
Dunn, Kenneth & Dunn, Rita. Situational Leadership for Principles: The School Administrator in Action. LC 82-11211. 228p. 1983. 17.50 (ISBN 0-686-84595-1, Parker). P-H.
--Teaching Students Through Their Individual Learning Styles: A Practical Approach. (Illus.). 1978. pap. 18.95 (ISBN 0-87909-808-2). Reston.
Dunn, Kenneth J., jt. auth. see Dunn, Rita.
Dunn, Marsh L. Pre-Writing Skills. (Skill Starters for Motor Development Ser.). 80p. 1982. pap. text ed. 12.95 (ISBN 0-88450-822-6, 2089-B). Communication Skill.
Dunn, Marsha L. Pre-Scissor Skills: Skill Starters for Motor Development. (Illus.). 1979. pap. text ed. 10.95 (ISBN 0-88450-701-7, 3101-B). Communication Skill.
--Pre-Sign Language Motor Skills. (Skill Starters for Motor Development Ser.). 110p. 1982. pap. text ed. 14.95 (ISBN 0-88450-821-8, 2085-B). Communication Skill.
Dunn, Martha D. Fundamentals of Nutrition. (Illus.). 560p. 1982. text ed. 19.95 (ISBN 0-8436-2284-9). CBI Pub.
Dunn, Martin J. Dental Auxiliary Practice. Incl. Module 2. Dentofacial Growth & Development - Orthodontics. pap. 8.95 (ISBN 0-683-02688-7); Module 3. Oral Pathology. pap. 13.95; Module 4. Internal Med. pap. 8.95 (ISBN 0-683-02690-9); Module 5. Pharmacology, Pain Control, Sterile Technique, & Oral Surgery. pap. 10.95 (ISBN 0-683-02691-7); Module 6. Periodontics. pap. 10.95 (ISBN 0-683-02692-5). 1975. pap. Williams & Wilkins.
Dunn, Mary M., ed. Humboldt's Political Essay on the Kingdom of New Spain. 1972. pap. text ed. 3.95x (ISBN 0-394-31510-3). Phila Bk Co.
Dunn, Marylois & Mayhar, Ardath. The Absolutely Perfect Horse. LC 82-47726. 192p. (gr. 5 up). 1983. 9.57i (ISBN 0-06-021773-1, HarpJ); PLB 9.89g (ISBN 0-06-021774-X). Har-Row.
Dunn, Michael J. & Patrono, Carlo, eds. Prostaglandins & the Kidney: Biochemistry, Physiology, Pharmacology, & Clinical Applications. 406p. 1982. 49.50 (ISBN 0-306-41054-0, Plenum Med Bk). Plenum Pub.
Dunn, Nell. Talking to Women. LC 66-2184. (Illus.). 1965. 5.25x o.p. (ISBN 0-8002-2054-4). Intl Pubns Serv.
Dunn, Olive J. Basic Statistics: A Primer for the Biomedical Sciences. 2nd ed. LC 77-9328. (Probability & Mathematical Statistics: Applied Probability & Statistics Section). 1977. 25.95x (ISBN 0-471-22744-7, Pub. by Wiley-Interscience). Wiley.
Dunn, Olive J. & Clark, Virginia A. Applied Statistics: Analysis of Variance & Regression. LC 73-13683. (Probability & Mathematical Statistics Ser.). 387p. 1974. 31.95x (ISBN 0-471-22700-5, Pub. by Wiley-Interscience). Wiley.
Dunn, P. D. & Reay, D. A. Heat Pipes. 2nd ed. 1977. text ed. 48.00 o.s.i. (ISBN 0-08-022127-0); pap. text ed. 17.00 (ISBN 0-08-022128-9). Pergamon.
Dunn, Peter N. Spanish Picaresque Novel. (World Authors Ser.). 1979. lib. bdg. 15.95 (ISBN 0-8057-6399-6, Twayne). G K Hall.
Dunn, Phoebe & Dunn, Judy. The Animals of Buttercup Farm. LC 81-4892. (Illus.). 48p. (ps-1). 1981. 4.95 (ISBN 0-394-84798-9); PLB 5.99 o.p. (ISBN 0-394-94798-3). Random.
Dunn, Richard, ed. The English Novel: Twentieth Century Criticism, Defoe Through Hardy, Vol. 1. LC 82-74110. 202p. 1976. 20.00x (ISBN 0-8040-0742-X). Swallow.
Dunn, Richard, et al, trs. see Freund, Gisele.
Dunn, Richard J. David Copperfield: An Annotated Bibliography. (British Literature Catalogue Ser.). 400p. 1981. lib. bdg. 42.50 o.s.i. (ISBN 0-8240-9322-4). Garland Pub.
Dunn, Richard S. Age of Religious Wars, Fifteen Fifty-Nine to Seventeen Fifteen. 2nd ed. (Illus.). 1979. 18.95x o.p. (ISBN 0-393-05694-5); pap. text ed. 6.95x (ISBN 0-393-09021-3). Norton.
Dunn, Richard S., jt. ed. see Soderlund, Jean R.
Dunn, Rita & Dunn, Kenneth J. Administrator's Guide to New Programs for Faculty Management & Evaluation. 1976. 16.95 (ISBN 0-13-008623-1, Parker). P-H.
Dunn, Rita, jt. auth. see Dunn, Kenneth.
Dunn, Robert & Ullman, Richard. Quality Assurance for Computer Software. (Illus.). 1982. 26.95x (ISBN 0-07-018312-0). McGraw.
Dunn, Stephen. A Circus of Needs. LC 78-59800. (Poetry Ser). 1978. 8.95; pap. 4.95 (ISBN 0-915604-15-9). Carnegie-Mellon.
--The Fall & Rise of the Asiatic Mode of Production. 240p. (Orig.). 1982. pap. 9.95 (ISBN 0-7100-9053-6). Routledge & Kegan.
--Full of Lust & Good Usage. LC 76-12129. (Poetry Ser.). 1976. pap. 3.50 o.p. (ISBN 0-915604-07-8). Carnegie-Mellon.
--Looking for Holes in the Ceiling. LC 73-93172. 72p. 1974. lib. bdg. 7.50x (ISBN 0-87023-154-5); pap. 3.50 (ISBN 0-87023-155-3). U of Mass Pr.
--Work & Love. LC 81-69796. 1981. 12.95 (ISBN 0-915604-60-4); pap. 5.95 (ISBN 0-915604-61-2). Carnegie-Mellon.
Dunn, Stephen P., tr. see Yanov, Alexander.
Dunn, Stuart, jt. auth. see Bickford, Elwood D.
Dunn, Tom, ed. The Pipe Smoker's Ephemeris: Spring, 1965 through Summer-Autumn, 1979. ltd., signed ed. 541p. 40.00 (ISBN 0-686-38920-4). Univ Coterie Pipe.
Dunn, W. Public Policy Analysis: An Introduction. 1981. pap. 23.95 (ISBN 0-13-737957-9). P-H.
Dunn, W. L. Introduction to Digital Computer Problems Using Fortran IV. 1969. text ed. 20.00 o.p. (ISBN 0-07-018285-X, C). McGraw.
Dunn, Waldo H. R. D. Blackmore: The Author of "Lorna Doone"; a Biography. LC 73-19573. (Illus.). 316p. 1974. Repr. of 1956 ed. lib. bdg. 17.75x (ISBN 0-8371-7286-1, DUBL). Greenwood.
Dunn, William, ed. Social Values & Public Policy. (Orig.). 1981. pap. 6.00 (ISBN 0-918592-44-5). Policy Studies.
Dunn, William N., ed. Values, Ethics & the Practice of Policy Analysis. LC 82-47929. (Policy Studies Organization Bk.). 256p. 1982. 27.95X (ISBN 0-669-05707-X). Lexington Bks.
Dunn, William R. Fighter Pilot: The First American Ace of World War II. LC 82-40172. (Illus.). 272p. 1982. 18.00 (ISBN 0-8131-1465-9). U Pr of Ky.
Dunnahoo, Terry. Before the Supreme Court: The Story of Belva Ann Lockwood. LC 73-22057. (Illus.). 192p. (gr. 4-7). 1974. 7.95 o.p. (ISBN 0-395-18520-3). HM.
--This Is Espie Sanchez. (gr. 4-7). 1976. 7.95 o.p. (ISBN 0-525-41130-5). Dutton.
--Who Cares About Espie Sanchez? 144p. (gr. 4-7). 1975. 7.95 o.p. (ISBN 0-525-42690-6). Dutton.
Dunnam, Maxie. The Sanctuary for Lent, 1983. 48p. 1983. pap. 22.00 per 100 (ISBN 0-687-36845-6). Abingdon.
Dunne, Dominick. The Winners: Part II of Joyce Haber's "The Users". 464p. 1983. pap. 3.95 (ISBN 0-446-30221-X). Warner Bks.
Dunne, Gerald T. Hugo Black & the Judicial Revolution. 1978. pap. 6.95 o.p. (ISBN 0-671-24406-X, Touchstone Bks). S&S.
Dunne, Hope. The Art of Teaching Reading: A Language & Self Concept Approach. LC 72-80163. 1972. pap. text ed. 6.95 (ISBN 0-675-09075-X). Merrill.
Dunne, John J. & O'Connor, Lawrence. Haunted Ireland: Her Romantic & Mysterious Ghosts. (Illus.). 115p. pap. 8.95 (ISBN 0-904651-30-4, Pub. by Salem Hse Ltd). Merrimack Bk Serv.
Dunne, John S. The Church of the Poor Devil. 160p. 1982. 14.95 (ISBN 0-02-533960-5). Macmillan.

--The Reasons of the Heart: A Journey into Solitude & Back Again into the Human Circle. 1979. pap. 5.95 (ISBN 0-268-01606-2). U of Notre Dame Pr.
--The Way of All the Earth: Experiments in Truth & Religion. LC 78-1575. 1978. text ed. 15.95x (ISBN 0-268-01927-4); pap. 6.95 (ISBN 0-268-01928-2). U of Notre Dame Pr.
Dunne, Lee. The Ringleader. 1980. 9.95 o.p. (ISBN 0-671-24887-1). S&S.
Dunne, Mary C. Return to Timberlake. (YA) 1981. 6.95 (ISBN 0-686-73949-3, Avalon). Bouregy.
--The Secret of Captives Cave. (gr. 5 up). 1976. 5.95 o.p. (ISBN 0-399-20547-0). Putnam Pub Group.
Dunne, Mary Collins. The Secret of Cliffsedge. (YA) 1979. 6.95 (ISBN 0-685-93874-3, Avalon). Bouregy.
Dunne, Peter M. Black Robes in Lower California. (California Library Reprint Series: No. 3). (Illus.). 1968. Repr. 33.00x (ISBN 0-520-00362-4). U of Cal Pr.
Dunne, Robert L. & Sterman, Donna. Egg Carton Critters. LC 78-4319. (Illus.). (gr. 1-4). 1978. 5.95 o.s.i. (ISBN 0-8027-6334-0); PLB 7.85 (ISBN 0-8027-6335-9). Walker & Co.
Dunne, Thomas L. The Scourge. 1978. 9.95 o.p. (ISBN 0-698-10893-0, Coward). Putnam Pub Group.
Dunnell, Karen & Cartwright, Ann. Medicine Takers, Prescribers & Hoarders. (Social Studies in Medical Care). 1972. 18.00x (ISBN 0-7100-7351-8). Routledge & Kegan.
Dunnell, R. C. Systematics in Prehistory. LC 76-142359. 1971. 8.95 (ISBN 0-02-907800-8). Free Pr.
Dunner, Joseph, ed. Handbook of World History. LC 66-10222. 1968. 20.00 o.p. (ISBN 0-8022-0427-9). Philos Lib.
Dunnet, Walter. Outline of New Testament Survey. (Orig.). 1960. pap. 4.95 (ISBN 0-8024-6245-6). Moody.
Dunnett, Alastair. No Thanks to the Duke. LC 80-1984. (Crime Club Ser.). 192p. 1981. 10.95 o.p. (ISBN 0-385-17389-X). Doubleday.
Dunnett, Dorothy. Disorderly Knights. 334p. 1981. Repr. lib. bdg. 16.95x (ISBN 0-89966-295-1). Buccaneer Bks.
Dunnette, Marvin D. Handbook of Industrial & Organizational Psychology. 1976. 64.95 o.p. (ISBN 0-395-30859-3). HM.
Dunnigan, Ann, tr. see Chekhov, Anton.
Dunnigan, Ann, tr. see Tolstoy, Leo.
Dunnigan, James, ed. The War Against Hitler: Europe, North Africa, Southeast Asia, 1939-1945. (Illus.). 200p. 1983. 22.50 (ISBN 0-88254-631-7). Hippocrene Bks.
Dunnigan, James F. The Complete Wargames Handbook: How to Play, Design, & Find Them. (Illus.). 256p. 1980. pap. 7.95 (ISBN 0-688-08649-7). Quill NY.
--How to Make War: A Comprehensive Guide to Modern Warfare. rev., upd. ed. (Illus.). 444p. 1983. pap. 7.95 (ISBN 0-688-01975-7). Quill NY.
Dunnill, Michael. Pathological Basis of Renal Disease. LC 76-26775. (Illus.). 1976. text ed. 15.00 (ISBN 0-7216-3230-0). Saunders.
Dunnill, Michael, jt. auth. see Aherne, William.
Dunning, Albert. Count Unico Wilhelm van Wassenaar, Sixteen Ninety-Two to Seventeen Sixty-Six: A Master Unmasked or the Pergolesi-Ricciotti Puzzle Solved. Rimmer, Joan, tr. from Dutch. (Illus.). 210p. 65.00 o.s.i. (ISBN 90-6027-400-8, Pub. by Frits Knuf Netherlands); wrappers 47.50 o.s.i. (ISBN 90-6027-399-0, Pub. by Frits Knuf Netherlands). Pendragon NY.
--Pietro Antonio Locatelli, Sixteen Ninety-Five to Seventeen Sixty-Four: Der Virtuose und seine Welt, 2 vols. (Illus.). 500p. 1981. 95.00 o.s.i. (ISBN 90-6027-380-X, Pub. by Frits Knuf Netherlands); wrappers 75.00 o.s.i. (ISBN 90-6027-214-5, Pub. by Frits Knuf Netherlands). Pendragon NY.
Dunning, Brad, jt. auth. see Andrews, Bart.
Dunning, Chester S., ed. & tr. see Margeret, Jacques.
Dunning, D., jt. ed. see Whelan, A.
Dunning, David, jt. auth. see Dunning, Mary.
Dunning, Decla. Simon's Wife. 320p. 1980. 11.95 o.p. (ISBN 0-517-54211-0). Crown.
Dunning, F. B., jt. ed. see Stebbings, R. F.
Dunning, F. W. & Mykura, W., eds. Mineral Deposits of Europe: Vol. 2-Southeast Europe. 304p. 1981. text ed. 100.00x (ISBN 0-900488-63-8). IMM North Am.
Dunning, H. R. Pressure Sensitive Adhesives: Formulations & Technology. 2nd ed. LC 74-75900. (Chemical Technology Review Ser.: No. 95). (Illus.). 1978. 39.00 o.p. (ISBN 0-8155-0672-4). Noyes.
Dunning, H. Ray. Fruit of the Spirit. 1982. pap. 2.95 (ISBN 0-8341-0806-2). Beacon Hill.
Dunning, H. Ray, jt. auth. see Greathouse, William.
Dunning, James B. New Wine: New Wineskins. 128p. (Orig.). 1981. pap. 4.95 (ISBN 0-8215-9807-4). Sadlier.
Dunning, James M. Principles of Dental Public Health. 3rd ed. LC 78-14328. (Illus.). 1979. text ed. 25.00x (ISBN 0-674-70549-1). Harvard U Pr.
Dunning, John H. & Pearce, Robert D. The World's Largest Industrial Enterprises. 1981. 55.00x (ISBN 0-312-89277-2). St Martin.
Dunning, John H., jt. ed. see Stopford, John M.
Dunning, Lawrence. Keller's Bomb. 1978. pap. 1.95 o.p. (ISBN 0-380-40873-2, 40873). Avon.
Dunning, Marcy, jt. auth. see Houghton-Alico, Doann.
Dunning, Mary & Dunning, David. Good Apple & Wonderful Word Games. (gr. 3-7). 1981. 9.95 (ISBN 0-86653-053-3, GA 254). Good Apple.
Dunning, Stephen. Teaching Literature to Adolescents: Poetry. 1966. pap. 9.95x (ISBN 0-673-05544-2). Scott F.
--Teaching Literature to Adolescents: Short Stories. 1968. pap. 9.95x (ISBN 0-673-05843-3). Scott F.
--Walking Home Dead. (Poetry Ser.: No. 12). 40p. (Orig.). 1981. pap. 5.95 (ISBN 0-930020-11-1). Stone Country.
Dunning, Stephen & Howes, Alan B. Literature for Adolescents: Teaching Poems, Stories, Novels, & Plays. 1975. text ed. 7.95x (ISBN 0-673-05841-7). Scott F.
Dunn-Rankin, Patricia. Vocabulary. (Illus.). 1978. pap. text ed. 13.95 (ISBN 0-07-018268-X, C); instructor's manual 12.50 (ISBN 0-07-018269-8). McGraw.
Dunn-Rankin, Peter. Scaling Methods. (Illus.). 400p. 1983. text ed. 36.00 (ISBN 0-89859-203-8). L Erlbaum Assocs.
Dunphy, D. C. & Dick, B. Organizational Change by Choice. 312p. Date not set. 21.00x (ISBN 0-07-072947-6). McGraw.
Dunphy, Jack. Nightmovers. 7.95 (ISBN 0-911660-16-X). Yankee Peddler.
Dunphy, Pat & Wolf, Michael. The Sexy Stomach: How to Get it & How to Keep it. LC 82-83928. (Illus.). 64p. (Orig.). 1983. pap. 4.95 (ISBN 0-88011-096-1). Leisure Pr.
Dunphy, Philip W., ed. Career Development for the College Student. 5th ed. LC 80-20933. 128p. 1981. pap. 6.50x (ISBN 0-910328-02-1). Carroll Pr.
Dunraven, Geraldine. Irish Houses Castles & Gardens: Open to the Public. (Illus.). 34p. 1982. pap. 3.95 (ISBN 0-900346-34-5, Pub. by Salem Hse Ltd.). Merrimack Bk Serv.
Dunsany, Edward see Brown, Edmund R.
Dunsany, Lord. The Lost Silk Hat. Brown, Edmund R., ed. (International Pocket Library). pap. 3.00 (ISBN 0-686-77239-3). Branden.
Dunseath, T. K. Spenser's Allegory of Justice in Book Five of "The Faerie Queene". LC 78-14441. 1979. Repr. of 1968 ed. lib. bdg. 20.50x (ISBN 0-313-21047-0, DUSA). Greenwood.
Dunseth, William B. An Introduction to Annuity, Charitable Remainder Trust & Bequest Programs. 2nd ed. 37p. 1982. 14.50 (ISBN 0-89964-193-8). CASE.
Dunsheath, Percy. History of Electrical Power Engineering. 1969. pap. 6.95x (ISBN 0-262-54007-X). MIT Pr.
Dunsire, Andrew. Control in a Bureaucracy. LC 78-19207. 1979. 27.50 (ISBN 0-312-16897-7). St Martin.
Dunsker, Stewart, ed. Cervical Spondylosis. (Seminars in Neurological Surgery). 229p. 1980. text ed. 27.50 (ISBN 0-89004-421-X). Raven.
Dunsmore, I. R., jt. auth. see Aitchison, J.
Dunson, Josh. Freedom in the Air: Song Movements of the Sixties. LC 80-11678. 127p. 1980. Repr. of 1965 ed. lib. bdg. 16.25x (ISBN 0-313-22393-9, DUFA). Greenwood.
Dunst, Carl J. A Clinical & Educational Manual for Use of the Uzgiris-Hunt Scales. 128p. 1980. pap. text ed. 9.95 (ISBN 0-8391-1571-7). Univ Park.
Dunst, Carl J., ed. Infant & Preschool Assessment Instruments: Relability, Validity & Utility. (Illus.). 1983. text ed. price not set (ISBN 0-8391-1716-7, 17574). Univ Park.
Dunstan. Course in Painting. (Grosset Art Instruction Ser.: No.39). pap. 2.95 (ISBN 0-448-00548-4, G&D). Putnam Pub Group.
Dunstan, Bernard. Painting Methods of the Impressionists. (Illus.). 184p. (Orig.). 1976. 21.95 o.p. (ISBN 0-8230-3710-X). Watson-Guptill.
Dunstan, Bob. The Book of Falmouth & Penryn. 1977. 20.00x o.p. (ISBN 0-86023-002-3). State Mutual Bk.
Dunstan, M., jt. auth. see Garlan, P. W.
Dunstan, Mary J. & Garlan, Patricia. Worlds in the Making: Probes for Students of the Future. 1970. pap. text ed. 12.50 (ISBN 0-13-969048-4). P-H.
Dunstan, Ralph. A Cyclopaedic Dictionary of Music. LC 72-14060. 642p. 1973. Repr. of 1925 ed. lib. bdg. 65.00 (ISBN 0-306-70559-1). Da Capo.
Dunster, David, ed. see Smithson, Alison & Smithson, Peter.
Dunster, Jack. Mao Zedong & China. LC 81-21577. (Cambridge Introduction to the History of Mankind Topic Bk.). 32p. 1982. 3.95 (ISBN 0-521-23148-5). Cambridge U Pr.
Dunster, Mark. Crumwell. (Henry the 8th Ser.: Pt. 4). 41p. (Orig.). 1982. pap. 4.00 (ISBN 0-89642-085-X). Linden Pubs.
--Hollywood Poems. 80p. (Orig.). 1983. pap. 5.00 (ISBN 0-89642-095-7). Linden Pubs.
--Infare. 23p. (Orig.). 1983. pap. 4.00 (ISBN 0-89642-098-1). Linden Pubs.
--Jeff. (Rin Ser.: Pt. 30). 23p. (Orig.). 1983. pap. 4.00 (ISBN 0-89642-096-5). Linden Pubs.
--Lint. 24p. (Orig.). 1983. pap. 4.00 (ISBN 0-89642-100-7). Linden Pubs.
--Miser. 2nd, Rev. ed. 39p. (Orig.). 1982. pap. 4.00 (ISBN 0-89642-093-0). Linden Pubs.
--Postmortem. 19p. (Orig.). 1983. pap. 4.00 (ISBN 0-89642-099-X). Linden Pubs.
--Scrooge. 16p. (Orig.). 1983. pap. 4.00 (ISBN 0-89642-101-5). Linden Pubs.
--Thief. 24p. (Orig.). 1983. pap. 4.00 (ISBN 0-89642-097-3). Linden Pubs.
Dunston, Patricia, jt. ed. see Chunn, Jay, II.
Dunthorne, Gordon. Flower & Fruit Prints of the Eighteenth & Early Nineteenth Centuries. LC 67-25443. (Graphic Art Ser). (Illus.). 1970. Repr. of 1938 ed. lib. bdg. 75.00 o.p. (ISBN 0-306-70958-9). Da Capo.
Dunthorne, Kirstine B. Artists Exhibited in Wales, Nineteen Fourty-Five toNineteen Seventy-Four. 344p. 1980. pap. 18.95 (ISBN 0-9500455-8-6, Pub. by Welsh Art Wales). Intl Schol Bk Serv.
Dunton, John. Teague Land or a Merry Ramble to the Wild Irish. 78p. 1983. Repr. of 1733 ed. 10.00x (ISBN 0-7165-0291-7, Pub. by Irish Academic Pr Ireland). Biblio Dist.
Dunton, Loren. The Vintage Years: Be Glad You're Getting Older. LC 78-70239. 1978. 8.95 o.p. (ISBN 0-913668-76-1); pap. 4.95 o.p. (ISBN 0-913668-77-X). Ten Speed Pr.
Dunton, Sabina & Miller, Kathy A. CounSELFile. McNeely, Richard A., ed. LC 82-50626. (Illus.). 150p. (Orig.). 1982. 25.00 (ISBN 0-943562-50-3); incl. 3-ring notebk. 28.00. Well Aware.
Dunton, Sabina M. & Fanning, Melody S. Smoking: Facilitator's Manual. McNeely, Richard A., ed. (Well Aware About Health Risk Reduction Ser.). (Illus.). 186p. (Orig.). 1982. 29.95 (ISBN 0-943562-51-1). Well Aware.
--Smoking: Workbook. McNeely, Richard A., ed. (Well Aware About Health Risk Redution Ser.). (Illus.). 109p. (Orig.). 1982. pap. 7.95 (ISBN 0-943562-52-X). Well Aware.
Duo Publishing. French Farm & Holiday Guide. 1982. pap. 12.95. Bradt Ent.
Dupain, Max & Johnson, Peter. Leslie Wilkinson: A Practical Idealist. (Illus.). 128p. 1983. 50.00 (ISBN 0-9594202-1-5). Allen Unwin.
Du Pan, Jacques Mallet see Mallet Du Pan, Jacques.
Dupaquier, J., et al, eds. Marriage & Remarriage in Populations of the Past. (Population & Social Structure Ser.). 1981. 72.00 (ISBN 0-12-224660-8). Acad Pr.
Dupee, F. W. see Trotsky, Leon.
Dupetit-Mere, Frederic. La Famille Sirven, Ou Voltaire a Castres. Repr. of 1820 ed. 30.00 o.p. (ISBN 0-8287-0299-3). Clearwater Pub.
Dupeux, Georges. French Society, Seventeen Eighty-Nine to Nineteen Seventy. Wait, Peter, tr. LC 75-46320. 294p. 1976. 25.00x (ISBN 0-416-65250-6). Methuen Inc.
Dupin, Charles. Du Travail des Enfants Qu'Emploient les Ateliers, les Usines, et les Manufactures. (Conditions of the 19th Century French Working Class Ser.). (Fr.). 1974. Repr. of 1847 ed. lib. bdg. 84.00x o.p. (ISBN 0-8287-0301-9, 1118). Clearwater Pub.
--Des Forces Productives et Commerciales De la France. (Conditions of the 19th Century French Working Class Ser.). (Fr.). 1974. Repr. of 1827 ed. lib. bdg. 180.50x o.p. (ISBN 0-8287-0300-0, 1153). Clearwater Pub.
Dupin, Jacques. Giacometti. Ashberry, John, tr. from Fr. (The Maeght Gallerly Art Ser.). (Illus.). Repr. 25.95 o.p. (ISBN 0-8120-5385-0). Barron.
Duplaix, Nicole & Simon, Noel. World Guide to Mammals. 1977. 15.95 o.p. (ISBN 0-517-52920-3). Crown.
Du Plessis, David. Forgiveness: God Has No Grandsons. 1974. 0.95 (ISBN 0-88270-203-3). Bridge Pub.
Du Plessis, Hugo. Fiberglass Boats, Fitting Out, Maintenance & Repair. 3rd ed. LC 72-94973. 1982. 18.50 o.p. (ISBN 0-8286-0091-0). De Graff.
Duplessis, Yves. Surrealism. Capon, Paul, tr. LC 77-17880. 1978. Repr. of 1963 ed. lib. bdg. 18.50x (ISBN 0-313-20110-2, DUSU). Greenwood.
Duplissey, Claude, jt. auth. see Khailany, Asad.
Du Plou, Dafne C., tr. see Edens, David.
Dupoizat, Marie-France, jt. ed. see Young, Carol M.
Du Ponceau, Peter S. A Brief View of the Constitution of the United States. LC 72-124893. (American Constitutional & Legal History Ser.). 1974. Repr. of 1834 ed. lib. bdg. 18.50 (ISBN 0-306-71986-X). Da Capo.
Duponchel, L., jt. auth. see Lamy, A.
Dupont. Les Ouvriers. Histoire Populaire Illustree des Travailleurs au Dix-Neuvieme Siecle. (Conditions of the 19th Century French Working Class Ser.). 600p. (Fr.). 1974. Repr. of 1890 ed. lib. bdg. 146.00x o.p. (ISBN 0-8287-0302-7, 1151). Clearwater Pub.
Dupont, Jacqueline, ed. see Colorado Dietectic Association Conference - 1969.
Dupont, Jacques & Gnudi, Cesare, eds. Gothic Painting: From the Thirteenth Century to Fifteenth Century. LC 79-64728. (Illus.). 1979. pap. 14.95 o.p. (ISBN 0-8478-0226-4). Rizzoli Intl.
DuPont, Robert L., ed. Phobia: A Comprehensive Summary of Modern Treatments. LC 82-9. 300p. 1982. 25.00 (ISBN 0-87630-274-6). Brunner-Mazel.
Dupont-Jones, Louisa. Pierrot-Watteau: A Ninteenth Century Myth. (Etudes Litteraires Francaises Ser.: No. 23). 140p. (Orig.). 1982. pap. 17.00 (ISBN 3-87808-948-1). Benjamins North Am.
Dupont-White, Charles. Essai sur les Relations du Travail avec le Capital. (Conditions of the 19th Century French Working Class Ser.). 444p. (Fr.). 1974. Repr. of 1846 ed. lib. bdg. 111.00 o.p. (ISBN 0-8287-0303-5, 1007). Clearwater Pub.
Dupre, Catherine. John Galsworthy: A Biography. LC 76-13473. (Illus.). 288p. 1976. 12.50 o.p. (ISBN 0-698-10715-2, Coward). Putnam Pub Group.
--Kelston Knoll. 1981. pap. 2.95 o.p. (ISBN 0-451-09895-1, E9895, Sig). NAL.
DuPre, Flint O. Your Career in Federal Civil Service. rev. ed. LC 79-2618. 256p. 1980. 11.49i (ISBN 0-06-011103-8, HarpT). Har-Row.
Dupree, A. Hunter, ed. see Gray, Asa.
Dupree, Louis, et al. Prehistoric Research in Afghanistan. LC 75-184166. (Transactions Ser.: Vol. 62, Pt. 4). (Illus.). 1972. pap. 5.00 (ISBN 0-87169-624-X). Am Philos.
Dupreez, Peter. The Politics of Identity. 1980. 26.00 (ISBN 0-312-62697-5). St Martin.
Dupret, S., jt. auth. see Pauchet, Victor.
Duprey, Kenneth. Old Houses on Nantucket. 15.00 o.s.i. (ISBN 0-8038-0193-9). Architectural.
--Old Houses on Nantucket. (Illus.). 256p. 1983. 16.95 (ISBN 0-8038-5399-8). Hastings.
Du Prey, Pierre De La Ruffiniere. John Soane: The Making of an Architect. LC 81-16453. 1982. 37.50x (ISBN 0-226-17298-8). U of Chicago Pr.
Dupuis, Adrian M., jt. auth. see Craig, Robert C.
Dupuy. Air War in the Pacific: Victory in the Air. 1964. 8.60 (ISBN 0-531-01246-8). Watts.
--Naval War in the Pacific: On to Tokyo. 1963. 8.60 (ISBN 0-531-01244-1). Watts.
--Naval War in the West: The Wolf Pack. 1963. 8.60 (ISBN 0-531-01237-9). Watts.
Dupuy & Crick. Campaigns on the Turkish Front. 1967. 7.90 (ISBN 0-686-94438-0). Watts.
--Decision in West, Nineteen Eighteen. 1967. 7.90 (ISBN 0-686-94474-7). Watts.
Dupuy, Rene-Jean. The Law of the Sea: Current Problems. LC 74-79800. 200p. 1974. lib. bdg. 25.00 o.p. (ISBN 0-379-00217-5). Oceana.
Dupuy, Trevor N. Military History of Civil War Land Battles. (Illus.). (gr. 7 up). 1960. PLB 8.60 (ISBN 0-531-01253-0). Watts.
--Military History of Civil War Naval Action. (Illus.). (gr. 7 up). 1960. PLB 8.60 (ISBN 0-531-01254-9). Watts.
--Military History of Revolutionary War Land Battles. LC 79-110470. (Illus.). (gr. 7 up). 1970. PLB 8.60 (ISBN 0-531-01258-1). Watts.
--Military History of Revolutionary War Naval Battles. LC 72-110471. (Illus.). (gr. 7 up). 1970. PLB 8.60 (ISBN 0-531-01257-3). Watts.
Dupuy, Trevor N., ed. Holidays: Days of Significance for All Americans. LC 65-21633. (gr. 9 up). 1965. PLB 8.90 o.p. (ISBN 0-531-01687-0). Watts.
Dupuy, Trevor Nevitt. The Military History of World War 1, 12 vols. Incl; Vol. 3. Stalemate in the Trenches: November, 1914-March, 1918. (Illus.) (ISBN 0-531-01223-9); Vol. 4. Triumphs & Tragedies in the East: 1915-17. (Illus.) (ISBN 0-531-01224-7); Vol. 5. The Campaigns on the Turkish Fronts. (Illus.) (ISBN 0-531-01225-5); Vol. 6. Campaigns in Southern Europe. (Illus.) (ISBN 0-531-01226-3); Vol. 7. The German Offensives: 1918. (Illus.) (ISBN 0-531-01227-1); Vol. 8. Decision in the West: 1918. (Illus.) (ISBN 0-531-01228-X); Vol. 9. Naval & Overseas War: 1914-15. (Illus.) (ISBN 0-531-01229-8); Vol. 10. Naval & Overseas War: 1916-18. (Illus.) (ISBN 0-531-01230-1); Vol. 11. The War in the Air. (Illus.) (ISBN 0-531-01231-X); Vol. 12. Summation: Strategic & Combat Leadership (ISBN 0-531-01232-8). LC 67-10130. 96p. (gr. 7up). 1967. PLB 8.60 ea. Watts.
Du Puynode, Gustave. De l'Esclavage et des Colonies. (Slave Trade in France, 1744-1848, Ser.). 241p. (Fr.). 1974. Repr. of 1847 ed. lib. bdg. 66.50x o.p. (ISBN 0-8287-0304-3, TN140). Clearwater Pub.
Duquette, Susan. Sunburst Farm Family Cookbook. rev. ed. LC 78-70916. (Illus.). 256p. (Orig.). 1978. pap. 7.95 (ISBN 0-912800-60-7). Woodbridge Pr.
Duquoc, Christian. Gift of Joy. LC 68-59156. (Concilium Ser.: Vol. 39). 172p. pap. 6.95 o.p. (ISBN 0-8091-1578-6). Paulist Pr.
Duquoc, Christian & Floristan, Casiano. Job & the Silence of God. (Concilium 1983: Vol. 169). 128p. (Orig.). 1983. pap. 6.95 (ISBN 0-8164-2449-7). Seabury.
Duquoc, Christian & Floristan, Casiano, eds. Christian Experience. (Concilium Ser.: Vol. 139). 128p. (Orig.). 1980. pap. 5.95 (ISBN 0-8164-2281-8). Seabury.
Duraipandian, P. Textbook of Dynamics. 1967. pap. 3.75x (ISBN 0-210-27140-X). Asia.
Duram, James C. Justice William O. Douglas. (United States Authors Ser.). 1981. lib. bdg. 12.95 (ISBN 0-8057-7334-7, Twayne). G K Hall.
--Norman Thomas. (United States Authors Ser.). 1974. lib. bdg. 12.95 (ISBN 0-8057-0727-1, Twayne). G K Hall.
Duran, Daniel F. Latino Materials: A Multimedia Guide for Children & Young Adults, No. 1. LC 78-18470. (Selection Guide Ser.). 249p. 1979. text ed. 16.50 o.s.i. (ISBN 0-87436-262-8, Co-Pub. by Neal-Schuman). ABC-Clio.
Duran, Gloria & Duran, Manuel, eds. Vivir Hoy. (Span.). 1973. pap. text ed. 10.95 (ISBN 0-15-594947-0, HC). HarBraceJ.

Duran, Helen C. Blonde Chicana Bride's Mexican Cookbook. (Wild & Woolly West Ser.: No. 40). (Illus., Orig.). 1980. 7.00 (ISBN 0-910584-95-8); pap. 2.00 (ISBN 0-910584-96-6). Filter.

Duran, Ignacio, jt. auth. see Decker, David R.

Duran, Manuel. Cervantes. LC 74-7006. (World Author's Ser.). 1974. lib. bdg. 12.95 (ISBN 0-8057-2206-8, Twayne). G K Hall.

Duran, Manuel, jt. ed. see Duran, Gloria.

Duran, Richard P., ed. Latino Language & Communicative Behavior, Vol. 6. 384p. 1981. 35.00x (ISBN 0-89391-038-4); pap. text ed. 17.50x (ISBN 0-89391-093-7). Ablex Pub.

Durand. De la Condition des Ouvriers de Paris de 1789 jusqu'en 1841. (Conditions of the 19th Century French Working Class Ser.). 287p. (Fr.). 1974. Repr. of 1841 ed. lib. bdg. 77.00x o.p. (ISBN 0-8287-0305-1, 1009). Clearwater Pub.

Durand, Douglas E., jt. auth. see Schoen, Sterling H.

Durand, John. Life & Times of Asher Brown Durand. LC 68-8688. (Library of American Art Ser). 1970. Repr. of 1894 ed. lib. bdg. 29.50 (ISBN 0-306-71167-2). Da Capo.

Durand, John & Miller, A. T. The Business of Trading in Stocks. 1967. Repr. of 1933 ed. flexible cover 5.00 (ISBN 0-87034-019-0). Fraser Pub Co.

Durand, Loup. The Angkor Massacre. Lane, Helen R., tr. from Fr. 416p. 1983. 15.95 (ISBN 0-688-00487-3). Morrow.

Durand, Megan. Detective McGruff Sniffs Out a Thief. LC 82-61497. (Sniffy Books-Crime Dog McGruff). (Illus.). 24p. (ps-4). 1983. pap. 3.95 (ISBN 0-394-85819-0). Random.

Durand, P. & O'Brien, J. S., eds. Genetic Errors of Glycoprotein Metabolism. (Illus.). 220p. 1983. 33.50 (ISBN 0-387-12066-1). Springer-Verlag.

Durand, Regis, ed. Myth & Ideology in American Culture. 1976. pap. text ed. 12.00x (ISBN 2-85939-064-2). Humanities.

Durand, Robert. Landscape for Two Figures. (Illus., Orig.). 1975. pap. 4.00 o.p. (ISBN 0-914726-01-3). Mudra.

Durand, T. see Jackson, B. D., et al.

Durang, Christopher. Christopher Durang Explains It All for You. 240p. 1983. pap. 3.95 (ISBN 0-380-82636-4, Bard). Avon.

Durant, Ariel, jt. auth. see Durant, Will.

Durant, Frederick C., jt. auth. see Miller, Ron.

Durant, Jack D. Richard Brinsley Sheridan. (English Authors Ser.). 1975. lib. bdg. 12.95 (ISBN 0-8057-6650-2, Twayne). G K Hall.

--Richard Brinsley Sheridan: A Reference Guide. 1981. lib. bdg. 32.00 (ISBN 0-8161-8146-2, Hall Reference). G K Hall.

Durant, John. The Heavyweight Champions. sixth, rev. & enl. ed. (Illus.). 224p. (gr. 7 up). 1976. PLB 8.95 o.p. (ISBN 0-8038-3034-3). Hastings.

Durant, Mary. Who Named the Daisy? Who Named the Rose? A Roving Dictionary of North American Wildflowers. (Illus.). 224p. 1983. pap. 8.95 (ISBN 0-312-92944-7). Congdon & Weed.

Durant, S. History of Oneida County, 1878. deluxe ed. 1983. Repr. of 1878 ed. deluxe ed. 40.00 (ISBN 0-932334-41-5). Heart of the Lakes.

Durant, Will. The Pleasures of Philosophy. pap. 10.75 (ISBN 0-671-58110-4, Touchstone Bks). S&S.

--Story of Philosophy. (gr. 11-12). 1961. pap. 9.50 (ISBN 0-671-20159-X, Touchstone Bks). S&S.

--Transition: A Mental Autobiography. 1978. pap. 5.95 o.p. (ISBN 0-671-24203-2, Touchstone Bks). S&S.

Durant, Will & Durant, Ariel. A Dual Autobiography. 1977. 14.95 o.p. (ISBN 0-671-22925-7); deluxe ed. 20.00 o.p. (ISBN 0-671-23078-6). S&S.

--Interpretations of Life. 1976. pap. 4.95 o.p. (ISBN 0-671-22424-7, Touchstone Bks). S&S.

Durante, Francesco & Rodino, Walter. Western Europe & the Development of the Law of the Sea, 3 binders. LC 79-55008. 1979. looseleaf 75.00 (ISBN 0-379-20286-7). Oceana.

Durantini, Mary F. Studies in the Role & Function of the Child in 17th Century Dutch Painting. Seidel, Linda, ed. (Studies in Fine Arts: Iconography: No. 7). 1983. write for info (ISBN 0-8357-1292-3, Pub. by UMI Res Pr). Univ Microfilms.

Durbin, Elizabeth, jt. auth. see Allison, R. Bruce.

Durbin, Enoch & McGeer, Patrick L., eds. Methane: Fuel for the Future. 350p. 1982. 42.50x (ISBN 0-306-41122-9, Plenum Pr). Plenum Pub.

Durbin, J. Distribution Theory for Tests Based on the Sample Distribution Function. (CBMS-NSF Regional Conference Ser.: Vol. 9). (Orig.). 1973. pap. text ed. 7.00 (ISBN 0-89871-007-3). Soc Indus-Appl Math.

Durbin, John R. College Algebra. LC 81-11379. 506p. 1982. text ed. 22.95x (ISBN 0-471-03368-5); avail. student solutions. Wiley.

--Modern Algebra: An Introduction. LC 78-15778. 329p. 1979. text ed. 24.50 (ISBN 0-471-02158-X); tchrs. manual 6.00 (ISBN 0-471-03753-2); solutions avail. (ISBN 0-471-86456-0). Wiley.

Durbin, Paul T., ed. Research in Philosophy & Technology, Vol. 1. 350p. (Orig.). 1979. lib. bdg. 45.00 (ISBN 0-89232-022-2). Jai Pr.

--Research in Philosophy & Technology, Vol. 2. (Orig.). 1979. lib. bdg. 45.00 (ISBN 0-89232-101-6). Jai Pr.

--Research in Philosophy & Technology, Vol. 4. 450p. 1981. 47.50 (ISBN 0-89232-181-4). Jai Pr.

Durckheim, Karlfried. The Grace of Zen: Zen Texts for Meditation. 1977. pap. 2.00 (ISBN 0-8164-2151-X). Seabury.

Durden-Smith, Jo & De Simone, Diane. Sex & the Brain. (Illus.). 1983. 16.95 (ISBN 0-87795-484-4). Arbor Hse.

Durdent, R. J. Histoire Litteraire et Philosophique De Voltaire. Repr. of 1818 ed. 87.00 o.p. (ISBN 0-8287-0306-X). Clearwater Pub.

Dureau, Lorena. Lynette. 352p. (Orig.). 1983. pap. 2.95 (ISBN 0-523-41638-5). Pinnacle Bks.

Durell, Gerald. Ark on the Move. 144p. 1983. 14.95 (ISBN 0-698-11211-3, Coward). Putnam Pub Group.

Durell, Julie, illus. Look at the Farm. (Illus.). 14p. (ps). 1982. 2.95 (ISBN 0-448-12312-6, G&D). Putnam Pub Group.

Durer, Albrecht. The Complete Engravings, Etchings & Drypoints of Albrecht Durer. Strauss, Walter L., ed. (Illus.). 12.50 (ISBN 0-8446-4624-5). Peter Smith.

--Durer. Heinzl, Brigitte, ed. (Art Library Ser.: No. 19). (Illus., Orig.). 1969. pap. 2.95 o.p. (ISBN 0-448-00468-2, G&D). Putnam Pub Group.

Durfee, D. A., ed. William H. Harrison, 1773-1841; John Tyler 1790-1862: Chronology, Documents, Bibliographical Aids. LC 76-116058. (Oceana Presidential Chronology Ser.). 144p. 1970. 8.00 (ISBN 0-379-12081-X). Oceana.

Durfee, W. H. Calculus & Analytic Geometry. 1971. text ed. 31.00 (ISBN 0-07-018378-3, C); solutions manual 25.50 (ISBN 0-07-018379-1). McGraw.

Durgant, Raymond. The Crazy Mirror. 1972. pap. 2.45 o.s.i. (ISBN 0-440-51616-1, Delta). Dell.

Durgin, Jean, jt. auth. see Ross, Beverly.

Durgnat, Raymond. Franju. movie ed. LC 68-31139. 1967. 10.95x o.p. (ISBN 0-520-00366-7); pap. 1.95 o.p. (ISBN 0-520-00367-5, CAL171). U of Cal Pr.

--Sexual Alienation in the Cinema. 1972. text ed. 10.00x o.p. (ISBN 0-289-70261-5). Humanities.

--The Strange Case of Alfred Hitchcock, or the Plain Man's Hitchcock. LC 74-7239. 1974. pap. 9.95 (ISBN 0-262-54034-7). MIT Pr.

Durgy, Robert G., ed. see Dostoevsky, Fyodor.

Durham, Carolyn A. L' Art Romanesque de Raymond Roussell. (Fr.). 15.00 (ISBN 0-686-38461-X). French Lit.

Durham, Douglass. Taking Aim. 1977. 7.95 o.p. (ISBN 0-89245-011-8). Seventy Six.

Durham, Frank. Elmer Rice. (U. S. Authors Ser.: No. 167). 12.50 o.p. (ISBN 0-8057-0616-X, Twayne). G K Hall.

Durham, G. Homer. N. Eldon Tanner: His Life & Service. LC 82-9681. (Illus.). 370p. 1982. 8.95 (ISBN 0-87747-913-5). Deseret Bk.

Durham, James. Song of Solomon. 1981. lib. bdg. 17.25 (ISBN 0-86524-075-2, 2201). Klock & Klock.

Durham, James C. To Write, Write: Writing. 240p. (gr. 9-12). 1981. pap. 5.50x (ISBN 0-88334-144-1). Ind Sch Pr.

Durham, Marilyn. Dutch Uncle. LC 73-6601. 1973. 7.50 o.p. (ISBN 0-15-126930-0, HC). HarBraceJ.

--Flambard's Confession. LC 82-2978. 784p. 1982. 17.95 (ISBN 0-15-131453-5). HarBraceJ.

Durham, T. R. Introduction to Benefit-Cost Analysis for Evaluating Public Programs. (Learning Packages in the Policy Sciences Ser.: No. 14). (Illus.). 70p. 1979. pap. text ed. 3.00x (ISBN 0-936826-03-7). Pol Stud Assocs.

Durham, William H. Scarcity & Survival in Central America: Ecological Origins of the Soccer War. LC 78-55318. (Illus.). xx, 209p. 1979. pap. 5.95 (ISBN 0-8047-1154-2, SP5); 14.50x (ISBN 0-8047-1000-7). Stanford U Pr.

Durie, Bruce, jt. auth. see Oldfield, Harry.

Durie, G. M., jt. auth. see Russell, D. H.

Durieux, Caroline & Cox, Richard. Caroline Durieux Lithographs of the Thirties & Forties. LC 77-16525. (Illus.). 1977. 14.95 o.p. (ISBN 0-8071-0372-1). La State U Pr.

Durig, J. R., ed. Vibrational Spectra & Structure. (A Series of Advances: Vol. 11). 362p. 1982. 104.25 (ISBN 0-444-42103-3). Elsevier.

--Vibrational Spectra & Structure: A Series of Advances, Vol. 9. 1981. 104.25 (ISBN 0-444-41943-8). Elsevier.

--Vibrational Spectra & Structure: A Series of Advances, Vol. 10. 1981. 121.50 (ISBN 0-686-80642-5). Elsevier.

Durig, James R. Vibrational Spectra & Structure: A Series of Advances, Vols. 4-7. 1981. Vol. 4. 74.50 (ISBN 0-444-41437-1); Vol. 5. 74.50 (ISBN 0-686-96710-0); Vol. 6. 85.00 (ISBN 0-444-41588-2); 85.00 (ISBN 0-686-85930-8). Elsevier.

Durig, James R., ed. Vibrational Spectra & Structure: A Series of Advances, Vol. 2. 300p. 1975. 69.50 (ISBN 0-8247-6193-6). Dekker.

--Vibrational Spectra & Structure: A Series of Advances, Vol. 3. 344p. 1975. 57.50 (ISBN 0-8247-6220-7). Dekker.

Durin, Bernard. Insects Etc: An Anthology of Arthropods, Featuring a Bounty of Beetles. Zappler, Georg, tr. from Ger. LC 81-6908. (Illus.). 108p. 1981. 50.00 (ISBN 0-933920-25-3). Hudson Hills.

During, H. J. Taxonomical Revision of the Garovaglioideae (Pterobryaceae, Musci) (Bryophytorum Bibliotheca Ser.: No. 12). (Illus.). 1977. lib. bdg. 24.00x (ISBN 3-7682-1161-4). Lubrecht & Cramer.

During, Ingemar. Aristotle's De Partibus Animalium: Critical & Literary Commentaries. LC 78-66548. (Ancient Philosophy Ser.). 223p. 1980. lib. bdg. 22.00 o.s.i. (ISBN 0-8240-9602-9). Garland Pub.

Durio, Alice & Rice, James. Cajun Columbus. LC 75-20484. (Illus.). 40p. (gr. 2 up). 1975. 8.95 (ISBN 0-88289-074-3). Pelican.

Durizch, Mary L., jt. ed. see Littleton, Jesse T.

Durka, Gloria & Smith, Joanmarie. Modeling God: Religious Education for Tomorrow. LC 75-44595. 104p. 1976. pap. 1.95 o.p. (ISBN 0-8091-1933-1). Paulist Pr.

Durkee, Jean K. Tout de Suite: A la Microwave, 2 vols. Incl. Vol. I. French, Acadian & Creole Recipes, Delicious, Nutrious & Colorful. (Illus.). 224p. 1977. write for info; Mexican, Italian & French Recipes Tested & Tasted by the Author. (Illus.). 232p. 1982. write for info.. (Illus.). 224p. 1977. Tout de Suite.

--Tout de Suite a la Microwave I. LC 77-93096. (Illus.). 224p. 1977. plastic comb bdg. 9.95 (ISBN 0-9605362-0-5). Tout de Suite.

--Tout de Suite a la Microwave II. LC 80-53827. (Illus.). 236p. 1980. plastic comb bdg. 9.95 (ISBN 0-9605362-1-3). Tout de Suite.

Durkheim, E. Rules of Sociological Method. 1982. 50.00x (ISBN 0-686-42914-1, Pub. by Macmillan England). State Mutual Bk.

Durkheim, Emile. Pragmatism & Sociology. Allcock, John B., ed. Whitehouse, J. C., tr. LC 82-14630. 184p. Date not set. price not set (ISBN 0-521-24686-5). Cambridge U Pr.

--The Rules of Sociological Method & Selected Texts on Sociology & its Method. Lukes, Steven, ed. Halls, W. D., tr. 1982. pap. text ed. write for info. Free Pr.

--Social Morphology: Contributions to L'Annee Sociologique. Nandan, Yash, ed. French, John, et al, trs. from Fr. (Illus.). 192p. 1983. cancelled (ISBN 0-87855-466-1). Transaction Bks.

Durkin, Andrew R. Sergei Aksakov & Russian Pastoral. 421p. Date not set. 30.00x (ISBN 0-686-82101-7). Rutgers U Pr.

Durkin, Dolores. Children Who Read Early. LC 66-25980. 1966. text ed. 10.95x (ISBN 0-8077-1260-4). Tchrs Coll.

--Phonics, Linguistics, & Reading. LC 72-87115. 1972. pap. 5.50x (ISBN 0-8077-1258-2). Tchrs Coll.

Durkin, Henry P. Forty-Four Hours to Change Your Life: Marriage Encounter. (Orig.). pap. write for info (ISBN 0-515-09442-0). Jove Pubns.

Durkin, James, ed. see Educational Research Council of America, et al.

Durkin, Mary. The Natural Foods Diet Book. (Good Health Books Ser.). (Illus.). 1978. pap. 2.95 (ISBN 0-448-14822-6, G&D). Putnam Pub Group.

Durkin, Mary & Hitchcock, James. Catholic Perspectives: Divorce. (Orig.). 1979. pap. 6.95 (ISBN 0-88347-101-9). Thomas More.

Durkin, Sr. Mary Brian. Dorothy L. Sayers. (English Authors Ser.). 1980. lib. bdg. 11.95 (ISBN 0-8057-6778-9, Twayne). G K Hall.

Durkin, Mary G. The Suburban Woman: Her Changing Role in the Church. 180p. 1975. 2.00 (ISBN 0-8164-1200-6). Seabury.

Durkin, Thomas A., jt. auth. see Polakoff, Murray.

Durlacher, Jennifer, jt. ed. see Blauvelt, Evan.

Durland, William R. & Bruening, William H., eds. Ethical Issues: A Search for Contemporary Conscience. LC 74-33868. 443p. 1975. pap. text ed. 11.95 o.p. (ISBN 0-87484-328-6). Mayfield Pub.

Durling, Allen E., jt. auth. see Childers, Donald G.

Durman, E. C. & Dunlop, Burton. Volunteers in Social Services: Consumer Assessment of Nursing Homes. 48p. 1979. pap. text ed. 7.00 (ISBN 0-87766-261-4). Urban Inst.

Durnbaugh, Donald F., ed. Every Need Supplied: Mutual Aid & Christian Community in Free Churches, 1525-1675. LC 73-94279. (Documents in Free Church History Ser.: No. 1). (Illus.). 258p. 1974. 19.95 (ISBN 0-87722-031-X). Temple U Pr.

Durney, C. H. & Johnson, C. C. Introduction to Modern Electromagnetics. 1969. text ed. 25.50 o.p. (ISBN 0-07-018388-0, C); instructor's solutions manual 3.95 o.p. (ISBN 0-07-018389-9). McGraw.

Durnin, John. Toward Educational Engineering. LC 81-40101. (Illus.). 134p. (Orig.). 1982. PLB 19.00 (ISBN 0-8191-2435-4); pap. text ed. 8.25 (ISBN 0-8191-2436-2). U Pr of Amer.

Durnin, Richard G., ed. Education in America: A Guide to Information Sources. LC 73-17553. (American Studies Information Guide Ser.: Vol. 14). 225p. 1982. 42.00x (ISBN 0-8103-1265-4). Gale.

Durodola, James I. Scientific Insights into Yoruba Traditional Medicine. (Traditional Healing Ser.). 1982. 27.50 (ISBN 0-686-85813-1). Conch Mag.

--Scientific Insights into Yoruba Traditional Medicine. (Traditional Healing Ser.). 1982. 27.50 (ISBN 0-932426-17-4). Trado-Medic.

Duroska, Lud. Tennis for Beginners. new ed. Lundgren, Charles, ed. LC 74-94. (Illus.). 128p. (gr. 3-9). Date not set. 4.95 (ISBN 0-448-11792-4, G&D). Putnam Pub Group. Postponed.

Duroska, Lud, jt. auth. see Schiffer, Don.

Duroska, Lud, ed. see Mazer, Bill.

Durphy. Volleyball. 1976. 4.95 o.p. (ISBN 0-448-12715-6, G&D). Putnam Pub Group.

Durphy, Michael, jt. auth. see Sonkin, Daniel J.

Durr, Frank, jt. auth. see Greene, Orville.

Durr, Karl. The Propositional Logic of Boethius. LC 80-18931. (Studies in Logic & the Foundations of Mathematics). 79p. 1980. Repr. of 1951 ed. lib. bdg. 16.25x (ISBN 0-313-21102-7, DUPL). Greenwood.

Durr, Ruth E. A Shelter from Compassion. LC 56-6375. (Orig.). 1956. pap. 1.50 o.p. (ISBN 0-87574-087-1). Pendle Hill.

Durr, W. Theodore, et al. Baltimore People, Baltimore Places. (Illus.). 64p. 1980. pap. 6.00 (ISBN 0-686-36492-9). Md Hist.

Durrance, E. M. & Laming, D. J. The Geology of Devon. 416p. 1982. 75.00x (ISBN 0-85989-153-4, Pub. by Exeter Univ England). State Mutual Bk.

Durrance, Joan. Armed for Action: The Power of an Informed Citizenry. 250p. lib. bdg. 24.95 (ISBN 0-918212-71-5). Neal-Schuman.

Durrant, A. E. Steam in Africa. LC 81-158557. (Illus.). 208p. 1981. 25.00x (ISBN 0-86977-139-6). Intl Pubns Serv.

Durrant, Geoffrey H. William Wordsworth. (British Authors Ser). 29.95 (ISBN 0-521-07608-0); pap. 9.95 (ISBN 0-521-09584-0). Cambridge U Pr.

--Wordsworth & the Great System: A Study of Wordsworth's Poetic Universe. LC 78-92247. 1970. 34.50 (ISBN 0-521-07704-4). Cambridge U Pr.

Durrant, John H. & Lovrinic, Jean H. Bases of Hearing Science. 1977. pap. 17.50 o.p. (ISBN 0-683-02696-8). Williams & Wilkins.

Durrant, Michael. The Logical Status of God. LC 72-93886. (New Studies in the Philosophy of Religion). 132p. 1973. 17.95 (ISBN 0-312-49455-6). St Martin.

Durrant, Samuel W. & Peirce, Henry B. History of Saint Lawrence County, New York 1749-1878. (Illus.). 914p. 1983. Repr. of 1878 ed. 40.00 (ISBN 0-932334-52-0). Heart of the Lakes.

Durrant, Tom. The Camelia Story. 168p. 1983. 47.95 (ISBN 0-686-83932-3, Pub. by Heinemann Pub New Zealand). Intl Schol Bk Serv.

Durrell, Gerald. Birds, Beasts, & Relatives. 1977. pap. 3.95 (ISBN 0-14-004385-3). Penguin.

--Fillets of Plaice. 1977. pap. 1.95 o.p. (ISBN 0-14-004338-1). Penguin.

--My Family & Other Animals. 1977. pap. 2.95 o.p. (ISBN 0-14-001399-7). Penguin.

--The Picnic, & Other Inimitable Stories. 1980. 10.95 o.p. (ISBN 0-671-25329-8). S&S.

--The Whispering Land. (Illus.). 224p. 1975. pap. 3.50 (ISBN 0-14-002083-7). Penguin.

--A Zoo in My Luggage. 192p. 1976. pap. 3.50 (ISBN 0-14-002084-5). Penguin.

Durrell, L. W., jt. auth. see Harrington, H. D.

Durrell, Laurence. Balthazar. 1961. pap. 4.95 (ISBN 0-525-47081-6, 0481-140). Dutton.

Durrell, Lawrence. Alexandria Quartet. Incl. Justine; Balthazar; Mountolive; Clea. 1961. Boxed set. pap. 19.50 (ISBN 0-525-47795-0, 01893-570). Dutton.

--Bitter Lemons. (Illus.). 1959. pap. 5.75 (ISBN 0-525-47044-1, 0558-170). Dutton.

--Clea. 1961. pap. 4.95 (ISBN 0-525-47083-2, 0481-140). Dutton.

--Constance. LC 81-69998. 365p. 1982. 15.95 (ISBN 0-670-23909-7). Viking Pr.

--Justine. 1957. pap. 4.95 (ISBN 0-525-47080-8, 0481-140). Dutton.

--Monsieur. 320p. 1975. 12.95 (ISBN 0-670-48678-7). Viking Pr.

--Mountolive. 1961. pap. 4.95 (ISBN 0-525-47082-4, 0481-140). Dutton.

--The Plant-Magic Man. new ed. (Capra Chapbook Ser.: No. 5). (Illus.). 1973. pap. 4.00 (ISBN 0-912264-51-9). Capra Pr.

--Pope Joan. LC 72-81088. 176p. 1972. Repr. of 1960 ed. 15.95 (ISBN 0-87951-002-1). Overlook Pr.

--White Eagles Over Serbia. LC 58-7779. 1958. 10.95 (ISBN 0-87599-030-4). S G Phillips.

Durrell, Lawrence, ed. see Lawrence, D. H.

Durrell, Oliver. Official Guide to Platform Tennis. pap. 2.95 o.p. (ISBN 0-448-02485-3, G&D). Putnam Pub Group.

Durrenberger, E. Paul. Agricultural Production & Household Budgets in a Shan Peasant Village in Northwest Thailand: A Quantitative Description. LC 78-13234. (Papers in International Studies: Southeast Asia: No. 49). (Illus.). 1978. pap. 9.50 (ISBN 0-89680-071-7, Ohio U Ctr Intl). Ohio U Pr.

Durrenmatt, Friedrich. Der Besuch der Alten Dame. Ackermann, Paul K., ed. LC 60-3863. (Ger). (gr. 11-12). 1960. pap. text ed. 9.50 (ISBN 0-395-04089-2). HM.

--Die Physiker. Helbling, Robert E., ed. (Illus., Orig., Ger.). 1965. pap. 6.95x (ISBN 0-19-500908-8). Oxford U Pr.

--The Quarry. 1979. pap. 1.95 o.p. (ISBN 0-446-79909-2). Warner Bks.

AUTHOR INDEX

--The Quarry. 2nd ed. Bd. with The Judge & His Hangman. (Double Detective Ser.: No. 2). 256p. 1983. pap. 7.95 (ISBN 0-87923-408-3). Godine.

Durso, Joe, jt. auth. see **Gehrig, Eleanor.**

Durst, H. Dupont & Gokel, George W. Experimental Organic Chemistry. (Illus.). 1980. text ed. 26.00 (ISBN 0-07-018393-7); instr's manual 7.95 (ISBN 0-07-018394-5). McGraw.

Durst, Lorraine S. United States Numismatic Auction Catalogs: A Bibliography. lib. bdg. 35.00 (ISBN 0-915262-44-4). S J Durst.

Durst, Lorriane S., jt. auth. see **Durst, Sanford J.**

Durst, S. J., ed. see **Raymond, W.**

Durst, Sanford J. Comprehensive Guide to American Colonial Coinage. LC 75-32796. (Illus.). 1976. lib. bdg. 20.00 (ISBN 0-915262-02-9). S J Durst.

--Encyclopedia of Values: U. S. Gold Coins. 1983. deluxe ed. 45.00 (ISBN 0-685-91294-9); lib. bdg. 37.50 (ISBN 0-915262-27-4). S J Durst.

Durst, Sanford J. & Durst, Lorriane S. Suncoast Cultural Catalog. (Illus.). 1983. softcover 4.95 (ISBN 0-686-79428-1). S J Durst.

Durst, Sanford J., jt. auth. see **Reisman, Daniel.**

Durst, T., jt. ed. see **Buncel, E.**

Duru, Robert C. The Nigerian Green Revolution: An Analysis of Rural Transformation in Africa. LC 81-40205. (Illus.). 264p. (Orig.). 1982. lib. bdg. 22.50 (ISBN 0-8191-2535-0); pap. text ed. 11.50 (ISBN 0-8191-2536-9). U Pr of Amer.

Durwood, A., jt. auth. see **Porter, T.**

Dury, G. H. Map Interpretation. 25.00x o.p. (ISBN 0-392-08099-0, SpS). Sportshelf.

DuSablon, Mary Anna. Cincinnati Recipe Treasury: Queen City's Culinary Heritage. Browder, Robyn, ed. LC 82-14773. (Regional Cookbook Ser.). (Illus.). 300p. 1983. pap. 8.95 (ISBN 0-89865-247-2). Donning Co.

Duschinsky, Michael P. British Political Finance, 1830-1980. 1981. 17.95; pap. 10.50 (ISBN 0-8447-3452-7). Am Enterprise.

Dusek, Jerome B., jt. auth. see **Meyer, William J.**

Dusen, C. Raymond Van see **Van Dusen, C. Raymond & Van Smith, Howard.**

Dusen, Clarence R. Van. Stroke Prediction & Prevention. (Royal Court Reports: No. 1). (Illus.). 14p. (Orig.). 1981. pap. 2.00x (ISBN 0-941354-00-8). Royal Court.

Dusen, William D. Van see **Van Dusen, William D., et al.**

Dusen, Willian D. Van see **Van Dusen, William D., et al.**

Dushman, S. & Lafferty, J. M. Scientific Foundations of Vacuum Technique. 2nd ed. LC 61-17361. 1962. 69.95x (ISBN 0-471-22803-6, Pub. by Wiley-Interscience). Wiley.

Dussart, Bernard H. Man-Made Lakes As Modified Ecosystems: Scope Report 2. (Scientific Committee on Problems of the Environment Ser.). 76p. 1972. pap. 8.00x (ISBN 0-471-99595-9, Pub. by Wiley-Interscience). Wiley.

Dussault, Jean H., jt. ed. see **Burrow, Gerard N.**

Dussek, Johann L. Collected Works of Johann Ladislaus Dussek, 12 vols. in six. LC 79-5313. (Music Reprint Ser.). 1978. Repr. of 1817 ed. Set. lib. bdg. 55.00 ea.; lib. bdg. 295.00 (ISBN 0-306-77270-1). Da Capo.

Dussel, Enrique. Ethics & the Theology of Liberation. McWilliams, Bernard F, tr. from Sp. LC 77-13397. Orig. Title: Tealogia de la Liberation y etica. 1978. 9.95x o.p. (ISBN 0-88344-115-2); pap. 6.95x o.p. (ISBN 0-88344-116-0). Orbis Bks.

--The History of the Church in Latin America: Colonialism to Liberation. Neely, Alan, tr. 368p. 1981. 21.95 (ISBN 0-8028-3548-1). Eerdmans.

Dustan, Jane, jt. auth. see **Zurcher, Arnold J.**

Dusterville, L. C. Stalky's Reminiscences. 298p. 1982. Repr. of 1928 ed. lib. bdg. 35.00 (ISBN 0-686-98147-2). Darby Bks.

Dustin, Richard & George, Rickey. Action Counseling for Behavior Change. 2nd ed. LC 77-8686. 1977. 7.50x (ISBN 0-910328-20-X). Carroll Pr.

Dutch, R. A., ed. see **Roget, Peter M.**

Dutens, J. M. Essai Comparatif sur la Formation et la Distribution du Revenu de la France en 1815 et 1835. (Conditions of the 19th Century French Working Class Ser.). 182p. (Fr.). 1974. Repr. of 1842 ed. lib. bdg. 53.50x o.p. (ISBN 0-8287-0307-8, 1010). Clearwater Pub.

du Terrage, Marc de Villiers see **De Villiers du Terrage, Marc.**

Duthie, Alexander. The Greek Mythology: A Reader's Handbook. 2nd ed. LC 78-12988. 1979. Repr. of 1949 ed. lib. bdg. 19.75x (ISBN 0-313-21077-2, DUGM). Greenwood.

Duthie, H. C., jt. auth. see **Contant, H.**

Duthie, J. F. The Orchids of the Western Himalaya. (Illus.). 1967. Repr. of 1906 ed. 120.00 (ISBN 3-7682-0465-0). Lubrecht & Cramer.

Duthie, R. B. & Bentley, George, eds. Mercer's Orthopaedic Surgery. (Illus.). 1200p. 1983. 150.00 (ISBN 0-8391-1806-6, 19828). Univ Park.

Dutile, Fernand N. & Foust, Cleon H., eds. Early Childhood Intervention & Juvenile Delinquency: As the Twig Is Bent. LC 81-47973. 224p. 1982. 23.95x (ISBN 0-669-05204-3). Lexington Bks.

Dutka, Anna B., jt. auth. see **Morse, Dean W.**

Du Toit, Brian M. Drug Use & South African Students. LC 78-21910. (Papers in International Studies: Africa: No. 35). (Illus.). 1978. pap. 7.50 (ISBN 0-89680-076-8, Ohio U Ctr Intl). Ohio U Pr.

Du Toit, Brian M., ed. Ethnicity in Modern Africa. LC 78-58295. (Special Studies on Africa Ser.). 1978. lib. bdg. 32.00 o.p. (ISBN 0-89158-314-9). Westview.

Duton, Mark & Owen, David. The Complete Home Video Handbook. 1982. 19.95 (ISBN 0-394-52761-5). Random.

Dutouquet, H. E. De la Condition des Classes Pauvres a la Campagne, des Moyens les plus Efficaces de l'Ameliorer. (Conditions of the 19th Century French Working Class Ser.). 112p. (Fr.). 1974. Repr. of 1846 ed. lib. bdg. 38.00x o.p. (ISBN 0-8287-0308-6, 1011). Clearwater Pub.

Dutra, Francis A. A Guide to the History of Brazil: 1500-1822, the Literature in English. LC 80-10933. 625p. 1980. lib. bdg. 36.75 (ISBN 0-87436-263-6). ABC Clio.

Dutrochet, Henri. Memoires Pour Servir a L'histoire Anatomique et Physiologique Des Animaux et Des Vegetaux. Repr. of 1837 ed. 340.00 o.p. (ISBN 0-8287-0309-4). Clearwater Pub.

Dutt, Ashok K. Southeast Asia: Realm of Contrasts. 3rd rev. ed. 275p. 1983. lib. bdg. 28.50x (ISBN 0-86531-561-2); pap. text ed. 15.00x (ISBN 0-86531-562-0). Westview.

Dutt, Ashok K., ed. Contemporary Perspectives on the Medical Geography of South & Southeast Asia. (Illus.). 78p. 1981. pap. 20.00 (ISBN 0-08-026762-9). Pergamon.

Dutt, N. Buddhist Sects in India. 2nd ed. 1977. 9.00x o.p. (ISBN 0-88386-971-3). South Asia Bks.

Dutta, M. & Hartline, Jessie, eds. Essays in Regional Economic Studies. LC 82-71901. 336p. 1983. 27.50 (ISBN 0-89386-005-0). Acorn NC.

Dutta, Reginald. Beginner's Guide to Tropical Fish: Fish Tanks, Aquarium Fish, Pond Fish, Ponds & Marines. 1977. 14.00 o.p. (ISBN 0-7207-0832-X). Transatlantic.

--Fell's Beginner's Guide to Tropical Fish & Fish Tanks. LC 75-4357. 1975. 9.95 o.s.i. (ISBN 0-8119-0254-4). Fell.

Dutta, Rex. Flying Saucer Viewpoint. 1972. 8.95 o.p. (ISBN 0-7207-0316-6). Transatlantic.

--Reality of the Occult: Yoga, Meditation, Flying Saucers. 199p. 1975. 10.00 o.p. (ISBN 0-7207-0789-7). Transatlantic.

Duttarer, Janet & Edberg, E. Quadriplegia After Spinal Cord Injury: A Treatment Guide for Physical Therapists. LC 72-84793. 50p. 7.00x o.p. (ISBN 0-913590-03-7). Slack Inc.

Dutton, Bertha P. American Indians of the Southwest. (Illus.). 328p. 1982. 24.95x (ISBN 0-8263-0551-2); pap. 12.50x (ISBN 0-8263-0704-3). U of NM Pr.

Dutton, Beth & DeMeo, Victoria. The Little Black Book: A Guide to the One Hundred Most Eligible Bachelors in Washington D.C. 200p. 1983. pap. 5.95 (ISBN 0-312-48821-1). St Martin.

--The Little Black Book: A Guide to the One Hundred Most Eligible Bachelors in Beverly Hills. 200p. 1983. pap. 5.95 (ISBN 0-312-48818-1). St Martin.

Dutton, Brian. Catalogo-Indice de la Poesia Cancioneril del Siglo XV, 2 Vols. in 1. (Bibliographical Ser.: No. 3). 1982. 40.00 (ISBN 0-942260-25-2). Hispanic Seminary.

Dutton, Denis. The Forger's Art: Forgery & the Philosophy of Art. LC 82-11029. (Illus.). 250p. 1983. 22.50 (ISBN 0-520-04341-3). U of Cal Pr.

Dutton, Frederick G. Changing Sources of Power. 1972. pap. 2.95 o.p. (ISBN 0-07-018402-X, SP). McGraw.

Dutton, Gordon. Mental Handicap. (Postgraduate Psychiatry Ser.). 230p. 1975. 16.95 o.p. (ISBN 0-407-00035-6). Butterworth.

Dutton, H. I. & King, J. E. Ten Per Cent & No Surrender: The Preston Strike, 1853-1854. (Illus.). 288p. 1981. 42.50 (ISBN 0-521-23620-7). Cambridge U Pr.

Dutton, Joan P. They Left their Mark. LC 82-83659. (Illus.). 192p. 1983. 15.00 (ISBN 0-937088-05-6); pap. 9.00 (ISBN 0-937088-06-4). Illum Pr.

Dutton, John A. The Ceaseless Wind: An Introduction to the Theory of Atmospheric Motion. (Illus.). 1976. text ed. 47.50 (ISBN 0-07-018407-0, C). McGraw.

Dutton, June & Perl, Susan. Faith, Hope & Charity. LC 77-78293. (Illus.). 5.95 (ISBN 0-915696-46-0). Determined Prods.

Dutton, June, jt. auth. see **Schulz, Charles M.**

Dutton, Nancy C. Civil Defense: From Town Hall to the Pentagon. Smith, Linda H., ed. 1980. pap. 4.95 (ISBN 0-936386-07-X). Creative Learning.

Dutton, Robert R. Saul Bellow. rev. ed. (United States Authors Ser.). 1982. lib. bdg. 11.95 (ISBN 0-8057-7353-3, Twayne). G K Hall.

--Saul Bellow. (U. S. Authors Ser.: No. 181). lib. bdg. 12.50 o.p. (ISBN 0-8057-0044-7, Twayne). G K Hall.

Dutton, Tom. The Hiri in History. new ed. (Pacific Research Monograph: No. 8). 159p. (Orig.). 1982. pap. text ed. 14.95 (ISBN 0-909150-63-X, 1258, Pub. by ANUP Australia). Bks Australia.

Dutton, William H., jt. auth. see **Danziger, James N.**

Dutwin, Phyllis, jt. auth. see **Diamond, Harriet.**

Duty, Guy. Divorcio y Nuevo Matrimonio. 176p. Date not set. 2.50 (ISBN 0-88113-060-5). Edit Betania.

Duursma, E. K. & Dawson, R., eds. Marine Organic Chemistry: Evolution, Composition, Interactions & Chemistry of Organic Matter in Seawater. (Oceanography Ser.: Vol. 31). 1981. 91.50 (ISBN 0-444-41892-X). Elsevier.

Duus, Peter. The Rise of Modern Japan. LC 75-33416. (Illus.). 304p. 1976. text ed. 17.50 (ISBN 0-395-20665-0). HM.

Duval, Arnaud, tr. see **Wolman, Arnold.**

Duval, Edwin M. Poesis & Poetic Tradition in the Early Works of Saint-Amant: Four Essays in Contextual Reading. 18.00 (ISBN 0-917786-23-8). French Lit.

Duval, Evelyn M. Por Que Esperar Hasta el Matrimonio? Deiros, Pablo A., tr. from Eng. Orig. Title: Why Wait till Marriage? 160p. 1979. pap. 2.75 (ISBN 0-311-46044-5, Edit Mundo). Casa Bautista.

DuVal, F. Alan, et al. Moderne Deutsche Sprachlehre. 3rd ed. 672p. 1980. text ed. 22.00 (ISBN 0-394-32345-9); wkbk. 8.00 (ISBN 0-394-32406-4); tapes 200.00 (ISBN 0-394-32407-2); individualized instruction program 5.95 (ISBN 0-394-32434-X). Random.

Duval, Jeanne. The Ravishers. (Orig.). 1980. pap. 2.50 o.p. (ISBN 0-451-09523-5, E9523, Sig). NAL.

Du Val, P. Elliptic Functions & Elliptic Curves. (Condon Mathematical Society Lecture Notes Ser.: No. 9). (Illus.). 200p. 1972. 29.95 (ISBN 0-521-20036-9). Cambridge U Pr.

Duval, Shelley & Duval, Virginia H. Consistency & Cognition: A Theory of Causal Attribution. 176p. 1983. text ed. 18.95 (ISBN 0-89859-220-8). L Erlbaum Assocs.

Duval, Virginia H., jt. auth. see **Duval, Shelley.**

Duvall, Aimee. Halfway There, No. 67. 1982. pap. 1.75 (ISBN 0-515-06678-8). Jove Pubns.

--Lover in Blue, No. 84. 1982. pap. 1.75 (ISBN 0-515-06695-8). Jove Pubns.

Duvall, Betty. Learn to Write Italic Style: A Programmed Workbook for the Older Beginner. 60p. 1981. pap. 7.50 (ISBN 0-686-36653-0). Can Do Pubns.

Duvall, Evelyn. Evelyn Duvall's Handbook for Parents. LC 73-85699. 1974. pap. 3.25 (ISBN 0-8054-5609-0). Broadman.

Duvall, Evelyn M. & Duvall, Sylvanus M. Sense & Nonsense About Sex. 1962. pap. 1.25 o.s.i. (ISBN 0-8096-1770-6, Assn Pr). Follett.

Duvall, Sylvanus M. Men, Women, & Morals. LC 72-12636. 336p. 1973. Repr. of 1952 ed. lib. bdg. 17.50x (ISBN 0-8371-6681-0, DUMW). Greenwood.

Duvall, Sylvanus M., jt. auth. see **Duvall, Evelyn M.**

Duvall, W. L., jt. auth. see **Obert, Leonard.**

Duval Sanadon, David. Discours sur l'Esclavage des Negres et sur l'Idee de Leur Affranchissement dans les Colonies, par un Colon de Saint-Domingue. (Slave Trade in France Ser., 1744-1848). 126p. (Fr.). 1974. Repr. of 1786 ed. lib. bdg. 41.00x o.p. (ISBN 0-8287-0310-8, TN108). Clearwater Pub.

Duval-Thibault, Anna. Les Deux Testaments (Novels by Franco-Americans in New England 1850-1940 Ser.). 204p. (Fr.). (gr. 10 up). pap. 4.50 (ISBN 0-911409-15-7). Natl Mat Dev.

Duverger, Maurice. Political Parties: Their Organization & Activity in the Modern State. 3rd rev. ed. North, Barbara & North, Robert, trs. 1964. pap. 12.50x (ISBN 0-416-68320-7). Methuen Inc.

Duvernet, Abbe. La Vie De Voltaire. Repr. of 1786 ed. 101.00 o.p. (ISBN 0-8287-0311-6). Clearwater Pub.

Du Vernois, Julius A. Von Verdy see **Von Verdy Du Vernois, Julius A.**

Duvignaud, Jean. Change at Shebika: Report from a North African Village. 325p. 1977. pap. text ed. 8.95x o.p. (ISBN 0-292-71041-0). U of Tex Pr.

Duvis, Fritz D. & Schippers, M. E. Document Reproduction Services: Their Efficient Organization & Management. 1961. pap. 2.25 o.p. (ISBN 92-3-100468-9, U170, UNESCO). Unipub.

Duvoisin, Roger. Petunia. (Illus.). (gr. k-3). 1950. PLB 7.99 (ISBN 0-394-90865-1). Knopf.

--Petunia's Christmas. (Illus.). (gr. k-3). 1952. PLB 7.99 (ISBN 0-394-90868-6). Knopf.

--Snowy & Woody. LC 79-897. (Illus.). (ps-2). 1979. PLB 6.99 (ISBN 0-394-94241-8). Knopf.

--Transactions of the American Neurological Association 1981, Vol. 106. 448p. 1982. text ed. 45.00 (ISBN 0-8261-0483-5). Springer pub.

Duvoisin, Roger, ed. see **American Neurological Assoc.**

Dux, John A., ed. A Collection of Letters & Addresses Issued by Great Americans in all Walks of Life at the Time of the Unification of Italy. (An American Culture Library). (Illus.). 167p. 1982. Repr. of 1871 ed. 137.45 (ISBN 0-686-83078-4). Found Class Reprints.

Duxbury, Victor & Wray, Gordon R. Modern Developments in Weaving Machinery. 7.50 o.s.i. (ISBN 0-87245-087-2). Textile Bk.

Duxler, Margot, jt. auth. see **Sala, Andre.**

Duyckinck, Evert A. & Duyckinck, George L. Cyclopaedia of American Literature, 2 vols. Simons, M. Laird, ed. LC 66-31801. 1965. Repr. of 1875 ed. Set. 99.00x (ISBN 0-8103-3021-0). Gale.

Duyckinck, George L., jt. auth. see **Duyckinck, Evert A.**

Duym, A. V. van see **DeJong, Dola.**

Duyn, H. Van see **Cobb, W. A. & Van Duyn, H.**

Duyn, J. Van see **Van Duyn, J.**

Duyn, Janet Van see **Van Duyn, Janet.**

Duyse, Florimond van. De Melodie van het Nederlandsche Lied en hare rhytmische vormen. (Facsimile of Dutch Songbks. Ser.: Vol. 6). 1979. Repr. of 1902 ed. 45.00 o.s.i. (ISBN 90-6027-216-1, Pub. by Frits Knuf Netherlands); wrappers 30.00 o.s.i. (ISBN 90-6027-215-3, Pub. by Frits Knuf Netherlands). Pendragon NY.

Dvorak, Eileen M. NCLEX-LPN Examination. 100p. 1982. pap. 6.95 o.p. (ISBN 0-686-87082-4). Chicago Review.

Dvorak, J. R., jt. auth. see **Rostoker, William.**

Dvorak, Paul F., tr. see **Hermlin, Stephan.**

Dvorine, William. A Dermatologist's Guide to Home Skin Care. 160p. 1983. 12.95 (ISBN 0-686-83863-7, ScribT). Scribner.

Dwan, Lois. Los Angeles Restaurant Guide. LC 76-24713. 189p. 1982. pap. 6.95 (ISBN 0-87477-226-5). J P Tarcher.

Dweck, Carol S., jt. auth. see **Langer, Ellen J.**

Dwek, Joe. Backgammon for Profit. LC 75-37885. (Illus.). 1978. pap. 7.95 (ISBN 0-8128-2313-3). Stein & Day.

Dwiggins, Boyce. Automotive Air Conditioning. 5th ed. 416p. 1983. pap. text ed. 16.80 (ISBN 0-8273-1940-1); write for info. instr's guide (ISBN 0-8273-1942-8). Delmar.

Dwiggins, Boyce H. Automotive Electricity. (Illus.). 352p. 1981. text ed. 20.95 (ISBN 0-8359-0268-4); pap. text ed. 16.95 (ISBN 0-8359-0267-6). Reston.

Dwiggins, Don. Restoration of Antique & Classic Planes. 1975. pap. 3.95 o.p. (ISBN 0-8306-2230-6, 2230). TAB Bks.

Dwight, Beryl M., ed. see **Bennett, Addison C.**

Dwight, Henry Otis, et al, eds. Encyclopedia of Missions: Descriptive, Historical, Biographical, Statistical. 2nd ed. LC 74-31438. 851p. 1975. Repr. of 1904 ed. 71.00x (ISBN 0-8103-3325-2). Gale.

Dwight, John, jt. auth. see **Perkins, Charles.**

Dwight, John A. & Speer, Dana C. How to Write a Research Paper. LC 79-3012. (gr. 11-12). 1979. pap. text ed. 7.50 (ISBN 0-934902-01-1); tchr's ed. 30.00 (ISBN 0-934902-02-X); work pad 1.20 (ISBN 0-934902-03-8). Learn Concepts OH.

Dwight, Jonathan, Jr. The Sequence of Plumages & Moults of the Passerine Birds of New York. (Annals of the New York Academy of Sciences). Repr. of 1900 ed. 10.00x (ISBN 0-89072-004-5). NY Acad Sci.

Dwight, Theodore. History of the Hartford Convention. LC 77-99474. (American Constitutional & Legal History Ser). 1970. Repr. of 1833 ed. 52.50 (ISBN 0-306-71855-3). Da Capo.

--Sketches of Scenery & Manners in the United States. LC 82-10258. 1983. 30.00x (ISBN 0-8201-1383-2). Schol Facsimiles.

Dwight, Timothy. Conquest of Canaan: A Poem in Eleven Books. LC 69-13890. Repr. of 1788 ed. lib. bdg. 16.25x (ISBN 0-8371-3407-2, DWCC). Greenwood.

--Major Poems: 5 Vols. in 1. LC 68-24207. 1969. 55.00x (ISBN 0-8201-1059-0). Schol Facsimiles.

Dwivedi, A. N. T. S. Eliot's Major Poems: An Indian Interpretation. (Salzburg-Poetic Drama: Vol. 61). 145p. 1982. pap. text ed. 25.00x (ISBN 0-391-02731-X, Pub. by Salzburg Austria). Humanities.

Dwivedi, O. P., jt. auth. see **Hodgetts, J. E.**

Dwivedi, T. D., jt. auth. see **Bedford, F. W.**

Dwock, Laureen. Miss Claringdon's Condition. (Candlelight Regency Special Ser.: No. 680). (Orig.). 1981. pap. 1.75 o.s.i. (ISBN 0-440-11467-5). Dell.

Dworetzky, John. Introduction to Child Development. (Illus.). 550p. 1981. pap. text ed. 21.95 (ISBN 0-8299-0368-2). West Pub.

Dwork, Bernard. Lectures on P-Adic Differential Equations. (Grundlehron der Mathematischen Wissenschaften Ser.: Vol. 253). (Illus.). 304p. 1982. 46.00 (ISBN 0-387-90714-9). Springer-Verlag.

Dworkin, Andrea. Our Blood: Prophecies & Discourses on Sexual Politics. LC 76-9187. 144p. 1976. 11.49i (ISBN 0-06-011116-X, HarpT). Har-Row.

--Our Blood: Prophecies & Discourses on Sexual Politics. 128p. 1981. pap. 4.95 (ISBN 0-399-50575-X, Perige). Putnam Pub Group.

--Right-Wing Women: The Politics of Domesticated Females. 256p. 1983. 14.95 (ISBN 0-698-11171-0, Coward). Putnam Pub Group.

--Right-Wing Women: The Politics of Domesticated Females. 256p. 1983. pap. 6.95 (ISBN 0-399-50671-3, Perige). Putnam Pub Group.

--Woman Hating: A Radical Look at Sexuality. 217p. 1976. pap. 6.50 (ISBN 0-525-47423-4, 0631-190). Dutton.

Dworkin, Daniel M. Environmental Sciences in Developing Countries: Scope Report 4. 70p. 1978. pap. 8.00x (ISBN 0-471-99597-5). Wiley.

Dworkin, Daniel M., jt. ed. see **Baumann, Duane D.**

Dworkin, Florence, jt. auth. see **Dworkin, Stanley.**

Dworkin, Floss & Dworkin, Stan. The Apartment Gardener. 1979. pap. 4.95 o.p. (ISBN 0-452-25203-2, Z5203, Plume). NAL.

Dworkin, Floss, jt. auth. see **Dworkin, Stan.**

Dworkin, James B. Owners Versus Players: Baseball & Collective Bargaining. LC 81-3472. 320p. 1981. 21.00 (ISBN 0-86569-072-3). Auburn Hse.

Dworkin, Martin, ed. Dewey on Education: Selections, with an Introduction & Notes. LC 59-15893. (Illus.). 1959. text ed. 9.50 (ISBN 0-8077-1266-3); pap. text ed. 4.50x (ISBN 0-8077-1263-9). Tchrs Coll.

Dworkin, Ronald M., ed. The Philosophy of Law. (Oxford Readings in Philosophy). 1977. pap. 7.95x (ISBN 0-19-875022-6). Oxford U Pr.

Dworkin, Stan & Dworkin, Floss. The Good Goodies: Recipes for Natural Snacks & Sweets. LC 74-22337. 240p. 1974. 11.95 o.p. (ISBN 0-87857-087-X); pap. 11.95 (ISBN 0-87857-107-8). Rodale Pr Inc.

Dworkin, Stan, jt. auth. see Dworkin, Floss.

Dworkin, Stanley & Dworkin, Florence. Bake Your Own Bread. (Illus.). 224p. 1973. pap. 2.25 (ISBN 0-451-11708-5, AE1708, Sig). NAL.

Dworkin, Susan. Making Tootsie: A Film Study With Dustin Hoffman & Sydney Pollack. 192p. 1983. pap. 8.95 (ISBN 0-937858-19-6). Newmarket.

Dworking, Andrea. Pornography: Men Possessing Women. 12.95 (ISBN 0-399-12619-8, Perige); pap. 5.95 (ISBN 0-399-50532-6). Putnam Pub Group.

Dworsky, Lawrence N. Modern Transmission Line Theory & Applications. LC 79-9082. 1979. 28.50x (ISBN 0-471-04086-X, Pub. by Wiley-Interscience). Wiley.

Dwoskin, Stephen. Film Is: The International Free Cinema. LC 75-7685. (Illus.). 272p. 1978. pap. 8.95 (ISBN 0-87951-072-2). Overlook Pr.

--Film Is: The International Free Cinema Paper. LC 75-7685. (Illus.). 272p. 1982. 18.95 (ISBN 0-87951-036-6). Overlook Pr.

Dwyer, David. Ariana Olisvos: Her Last Works & Days. LC 76-8752. 72p. 1976. lib. bdg. 8.00x (ISBN 0-87023-218-5); pap. 3.95 (ISBN 0-87023-219-3). U of Mass Pr.

Dwyer, Edward B., jt. auth. see Dwyer, Jan P.

Dwyer, Francis. On Seats & Saddles, Bits & Bitting, & the Prevention & Cure of Restiveness in Horses. reprint ed. LC 77-3336. (Illus.). 1977. Repr. of 1869 ed. 25.00 (ISBN 0-88427-027-0). North River.

Dwyer, James H. Statistical Models for the Social & Behavioral Sciences. (Illus.). 550p. 1983. text ed. 39.95x (ISBN 0-19-503145-8). Oxford U Pr.

Dwyer, Jan P. & Dwyer, Edward B. Traditional Art of Africa, Oceania & the Americas. LC 73-75844. (Illus.). 1977. 9.95 (ISBN 0-88401-014-7, Pub. by Fine Arts Mus); pap. 4.95 (ISBN 0-88401-013-9). C E Tuttle.

Dwyer, John C. Son of Man & Son of God: A New Language for Faith. 160p. 1983. pap. 7.95 (ISBN 0-8091-2505-6). Paulist Pr.

Dwyer, Margaret A., jt. auth. see Adams, Judith-Anne.

Dwyer, Richard A., jt. ed. see Lingenfelter, Richard E.

Dwyer, Robert J. The Gentile Comes to Utah. 270p. 1971. 7.95 (ISBN 0-914740-05-9). Western Epics.

Dwyer, Thomas & Critchfield, Margot. Bit of Basic. LC 80-11428. 192p. 1980. pap. text ed. 7.95 (ISBN 0-201-03115-9). A-W.

Dwyer, Thomas A. & Critchfield, Margot. CP-M & the Personal Computer: Popular. LC 82-20703. (Microcomputer Bks.). 280p. 1982. pap. 16.95 (ISBN 0-201-10355-9). A-W.

Dwyer-Joyce, Alice. The Master of Jethart. LC 76-2562. 1976. 7.95 o.p. (ISBN 0-312-52010-7). St Martin.

--The Penny-Box. 192p. 1981. 8.95 o.p. (ISBN 0-312-60002-X). St Martin.

Dyadkin, Iosif G. Unnatural Deaths in the U. S. S. R., 1928-1954. Deruguine, Tania, tr. from Rus. (Illus.). 80p. (Orig.). 1983. pap. text ed. 6.95x (ISBN 0-87855-919-1). Transaction Bks.

Dyal, James, et al. Readings in Psychology: The Search for Alternatives. 3rd ed. (Illus.). 420p. 1975. pap. text ed. 15.50 (ISBN 0-07-018537-9, C). McGraw.

Dyball, G. E. Mathematics for Technician Engineers: Levels 4 & 5. 384p. 1983. write for info. (ISBN 0-07-084664-2). McGraw.

Dyche, June. Educational Program Development for Employees in Health Care Agencies. 384p. (Orig.). 1982. pap. text ed. 23.50 (ISBN 0-9609732-0-6). Tri-Oak.

Dychtwald, Ken. Bodymind. 1978. pap. 2.95 (ISBN 0-515-06135-2). Jove Pubns.

Dyck, et al. Computing: An Introduction to Structured Problem Solving Using Pascal. 1981. text ed. 21.95 (ISBN 0-8359-0902-6); instr's. manual free (ISBN 0-8359-0903-4). Reston.

Dyck, J. W. Boris Pasternak. (World Authors Ser.). lib. bdg. 12.95 (ISBN 0-8057-2678-0, Twayne). G K Hall.

Dyck, Peter J., et al, eds. Peripheral Neuropathy. LC 73-81830. (Illus.). 1975. text ed. 80.00 ea. (ISBN 0-686-67128-7). Vol. 1 (ISBN 0-7216-3270-X). Vol. 2 (ISBN 0-7216-3271-8). Saunders.

Dyckman, Katherine M. & Carroll, L. Patrick. Solitude to Sacrament. LC 82-252. 128p. (Orig.). 1982. pap. 2.95 (ISBN 0-8146-1255-5). Liturgical Pr.

Dyckman, Thomas & Thomas, L. Joseph. Algebra & Calculus for Business. (Illus.). 464p. 1974. text ed. 23.95 (ISBN 0-13-021758-1). P-H.

Dyckman, Thomas, et al. Efficient Capital Markets & Accounting: A Critical Analysis. (Comtemporary Topics in Accounting Ser.). (Illus.). 144p. 1975. pap. 12.95 (ISBN 0-13-246967-7). P-H.

Dyckman, Thomas R. & Swieringa, Robert J. Cases in Financial Accounting, Vol. 1. rev. ed. LC 81-67860. (Illus.). 336p. (Orig.). 1981. pap. text ed. 12.95x (ISBN 0-931920-31-0). Dame Pubns.

Dyckman, Thomas R. & Thomas, L. Joseph. Fundamental Statistics for Business & Economics. 1977. 26.95 (ISBN 0-13-344523-2). P-H.

Dyckman, Thomas R., jt. auth. see Bierman, Harold, Jr.

Dycus, Webb. Honeysuckle Whiskers. new ed. (Illus.). (gr. 6-10). 1978. pap. 3.00 (ISBN 0-932044-08-5). M O Pub Co.

Dye & Frankfort. Spectrum One: Teacher's Edition. (Spectrum Ser.). 158p. 1982. pap. text ed. 7.95 (ISBN 0-88345-513-7). Regents Pub.

--Spectrum Two: Teacher's Edition. (Spectrum Ser.). 1983. pap. text ed. 7.95 (ISBN 0-88345-514-5). Regents Pub.

Dye, Charles M., ed. The American Educator: Introductory Readings in the Traditions of the Profession. LC 80-5759. 430p. 1980. pap. text ed. 16.00 (ISBN 0-8191-1221-6). U Pr of Amer.

--Education & American Society. 2nd ed. 1978. pap. text ed. 10.25 o.p. (ISBN 0-8191-0588-0). U Pr of Amer.

Dye, David A., jt. auth. see Tourda, Wayne F.

Dye, Frank & Dye, Margaret. Open-Boat Cruising - Coastal & Inland Waters. (Illus.). 176p. (Orig.). 1982. 17.50 (ISBN 0-7153-8247-0). David & Charles.

Dye, Gerald. Hebrews. (Double Trouble Puzzles Ser.). (Illus.). 64p. 1977. pap. 1.50 o.p. (ISBN 0-87239-154-X, 2825). Standard Pub.

--Writings of John. (Double Trouble Puzzles Ser.). (Illus.). 64p. 1977. pap. 1.50 o.p. (ISBN 0-87239-150-7, 2821). Standard Pub.

Dye, H. Allan & Hackney, Harold. Gestalt Approaches to Counseling. 1975. pap. 2.40 o.p. (ISBN 0-395-20041-5). HM.

Dye, H. Allan, jt. auth. see Diedrich, Richard C.

Dye, Margaret, jt. auth. see Dye, Frank.

Dye, T. Who's Running America: The Carter Years. 2nd ed. 1979. pap. 12.95 (ISBN 0-13-958462-5). P-H.

Dye, Thomas, jt. auth. see Gray, Virginia.

Dye, Thomas R. Politics in States & Communities. 4th ed. (Illus.). 512p. 1981. text ed. 22.95 (ISBN 0-13-685131-2). P-H.

--Power & Society: An Introduction to the Social Sciences. 3rd ed. LC 82-14579. (Political Science Ser.). 400p. 1982. pap. text ed. 15.95 (ISBN 0-534-01237-X). Brooks-Cole.

--Understanding Public Policy. 4th ed. (Illus.). 464p. 1981. text ed. 22.95 (ISBN 0-13-936260-6). P-H.

Dye, Thomas R. & Zeigler, L. Harmon. American Politics in the Media Age. LC 82-17710. (Political Science Ser.). 450p. 1983. text ed. 20.95 (ISBN 0-534-01176-4). Brooks-Cole.

Dye, Thomas R., jt. auth. see DiNitto, Diana M.

Dyen, D. & Aberle, D. F. Lexical Reconstruction. LC 73-92780. (Illus.). 484p. 1974. 64.50 (ISBN 0-521-20369-4). Cambridge U Pr.

Dyer. Introduction to Liquid Scintillation Counting. 1974. 29.95 (ISBN 0-471-25664-1). Wiley.

Dyer, A. Gas Chemistry in Nuclear Reactors & Large Industrial Plants. 1980. 49.95 (ISBN 0-471-25663-3, Pub. by Wiley Heyden). Wiley.

--Liquid Scintillation Counting Practice. 112p. 1980. 29.95 (ISBN 0-471-25664-1, Wiley Heyden). Wiley.

--Liquid Scintillation Counting Practice. 122p. 1980. 29.95 (ISBN 0-471-25664-1, Pub. by Wiley Heyden). Wiley.

Dyer, A., ed. Liquid Scintillation Counting, Vol. 1. 1971. 30.50 o.p. (ISBN 0-85501-053-3). Wiley.

Dyer, B. Personnel Systems & Records. 1979. text ed. 34.00x (ISBN 0-566-02106-4). Gower Pub Ltd.

Dyer, Brainerd. The Public Career of William M. Evarts. LC 72-87565. 279p. 1969. Repr. of 1933 ed. lib. bdg. 35.00 (ISBN 0-686-42966-4). Da Capo.

Dyer, Carole, jt. ed. see Marsh, Judy.

Dyer, Ceil. The Carter Family Favorites Cookbook. 1977. 8.95 o.s.i. (ISBN 0-440-01678-9, E Friede). Delacorte.

--Chicken Cookery. (Illus.). 160p. 1983. pap. 7.95 (ISBN 0-89586-054-6). H P Bks.

--Coffee Cookery. LC 78-6188. (Illus.). 1978. pap. 4.95 (ISBN 0-89586-009-0). H P Bks.

--More Wok Cookery. LC 82-81010. (Illus.). 160p. 1982. 6.95 (ISBN 0-89586-138-0). H P Bks.

--Shape up America! A Diet for the New Era. LC 77-13627. 1978. 9.95 o.p. (ISBN 0-399-12056-4). Putnam Pub Group.

--Wok Cookery. LC 77-83279. (Illus.). 1977. pap. 6.95 (ISBN 0-912656-75-1). H P Bks.

Dyer, D., et al. Measuring & Improving the Efficiency of Boilers. Gyftopoulos, Elias P. & Cohen, Karen C., eds. (Industrial Energy-Conservation Manuals: No. 3). 120p. 1982. loose-leaf 17.50x (ISBN 0-262-04067-0). MIT Pr.

Dyer, Davis, jt. auth. see Lawrence, Paul R.

Dyer, Donita. Bright Promise. 176p. 1983. pap. 5.95 (ISBN 0-310-45751-3). Zondervan.

Dyer, Esther & Berger, Pam, eds. Public, School & Academic Media Centers: A Guide to Information Sources. LC 74-11554. (Books, Publishing & Libraries Information Guide Ser.: Vol. 3). 350p. 1980. 42.00x (ISBN 0-8103-1286-7). Gale.

Dyer, Esther R. Cultural Pluralism & Children's Media. (School Media Centers: Focus on Issues & Trends: No. 1). 1979. pap. 6.00 (ISBN 0-8389-3218-5). ALA.

Dyer, Everett D. The American Family: Variety & Change. (Illus.). 1979. text ed. 22.00 (ISBN 0-07-018540-9, C); instructor's manual 2.95 (ISBN 0-07-018541-7). McGraw.

Dyer, George. Poems, 2 vols. in 1. LC 75-31198. (Romantic Context Ser.: Poetry 1789-1830: Vol. 50). 1978. Repr. of 1802 ed. lib. bdg. 47.00 o.s.i. (ISBN 0-8240-2149-5). Garland Pub.

Dyer, George, ed. An American Catholic Catechism. LC 75-7786. 320p. 1975. 10.00 o.p. (ISBN 0-8164-1196-4); pap. 5.95 (ISBN 0-8164-2588-4). Seabury.

Dyer, Gillian. Advertising as Communication. (Studies in Communication). 1982. 18.95x (ISBN 0-416-74520-2); pap. 7.95x (ISBN 0-416-74530-X). Methuen Inc.

Dyer, Irra & Chyssostomidis, C., eds. Arctic Policy & Technology. (Illus.). 400p. 1983. text ed. 69.95 (ISBN 0-89116-361-1). Hemisphere Pub.

Dyer, J. Applications of Absorption Spectroscopy of Organic Compounds. 1965. pap. 15.95 (ISBN 0-13-038802-5). P-H.

Dyer, James. The Penguin Guide to Prehistoric England & Wales. (Illus.). 400p. 1983. pap. 7.95 (ISBN 0-14-046351-8). Penguin.

Dyer, James, jt. auth. see Dony, John G.

Dyer, James A., jt. auth. see Bernstein, Robert A.

Dyer, James S. & Shapiro, Roy D. Management Science-Operations Reseach: Cases & Readings. LC 81-19703. 388p. 1982. pap. text ed. 19.95x (ISBN 0-471-09757-8); 20.00 (ISBN 0-471-86554-0). Wiley.

Dyer, James S., jt. auth. see Buffa, Elwood S.

Dyer, Jon C. & Mignone, Nicholas A. Handbook of Industrial Residues. LC 82-19082. (Environment Engineering Ser.). (Illus.). 453p. 1983. 54.00 (ISBN 0-8155-0924-3). Noyes.

Dyer, K. F. Challenging the Men: Women in Sport. LC 81-21846. (Illus.). 271p. 1982. text ed. 27.50 (ISBN 0-7022-1652-6); pap. 14.95 (ISBN 0-7022-1921-5). U of Queensland Pr.

Dyer, K. R., ed. Estuarine Hydrography & Sedimentation. LC 78-67308. (Illus.). 1980. 49.50 (ISBN 0-521-22435-7); pap. 17.95 (ISBN 0-521-29496-7). Cambridge U Pr.

Dyer, Keith R. Estuaries: A Physical Introduction. LC 72-8598. 140p. 1973. 25.95 (ISBN 0-471-22905-9, Pub. by Wiley-Interscience). Wiley.

Dyer, Lee & Paulson, Gary D. Project Management: An Annotated Bibliography. LC 76-2085. (ILR Bibliography Ser.: No. 13). 48p. 1976. pap. 2.75 (ISBN 0-87546-059-3); pap. 5.75 special hard bdg. (ISBN 0-87546-286-3). ILR Pr.

Dyer, Lee, ed. Careers in Organizations: Individual Planning & Organizational Development. LC 76-49471. (Illus.). 68p. 1976. pap. 3.25 (ISBN 0-87546-061-5); pap. 6.25 special hard bdg. (ISBN 0-87546-288-X). ILR Pr.

Dyer, Lorna. Ice Dancing Illustrated. Brandt, Harry, ed. (Illus.). 297p. 1980. 29.50 (ISBN 0-9602616-0-5). Moore Pubns.

Dyer, Marilyn, jt. auth. see Dickerson, Thelma M.

Dyer, Mike. Getting into Pro Baseball. (Getting into the Pros Ser.). (Illus.). (gr. 6 up). 1979. PLB 8.40 s&l (ISBN 0-531-01319-7). Watts.

Dyer, Nancy A., jt. auth. see Starr, John B.

Dyer, Pete. Coaching Football's Split Four-Four Multiple Defense. (Illus.). 1980. 11.95 o.p. (ISBN 0-13-139014-7, Parker). P-H.

Dyer, Raymond. Her Father's Daughter: The Work of Anna Freud. LC 82-11334. 332p. 1983. write for info. (ISBN 0-87668-627-7). Aronson.

Dyer, Wayne. Gifts from Eykis. 1983. 12.95 (ISBN 0-671-46066-8). S&S.

--The Sky's the Limit. 1980. 12.95 o.p. (ISBN 0-671-24989-4). S&S.

Dyer, Wayne W. Your Erroneous Zones. 1981. pap. 2.95 (ISBN 0-380-01669-9, 62836-8). Avon.

--Your Erroneous Zones. LC 75-35621. (Funk & W Bk.). 256p. 1976. 12.45i (ISBN 0-308-10228-2). T Y Crowell.

--Your Erroneous Zones. pap. 2.95 o.p. (ISBN 0-686-92422-3, 6697). Hazelden.

Dyer, William G. Contemporary Issues in Management & Organization Development. LC 82-8732. 224p. 1982. text ed. 15.95 (ISBN 0-201-10348-6). A-W.

Dygaard, Thomas. Outside Shooter. LC 78-24002. (gr. 7-9). 1979. o.s.i. 7.50 (ISBN 0-688-22177-7); PLB 8.88 (ISBN 0-688-32177-1). Morrow.

Dygard, Thomas. Running Scared. LC 76-56862. (gr. 7 up). 1977. 8.95 (ISBN 0-688-22103-3); PLB 8.59 (ISBN 0-688-32103-8). Morrow.

Dygard, Thomas J. Point Spread. LC 79-24511. 192p. (gr. 7-9). 1980. 7.95 o.s.i. (ISBN 0-688-22222-6); PLB 9.36 (ISBN 0-688-32222-0). Morrow.

--Soccer Duel. LC 81-883. 192p. (gr. 7-9). 1981. 8.95 (ISBN 0-688-00366-4); PLB 8.59 (ISBN 0-688-00367-2). Morrow.

--Winning Kicker. LC 77-17727. (gr. 7 up). 1978. PLB 8.88 (ISBN 0-688-32140-2). Morrow.

Dygat, Stanislaw. Cloak of Illusion. Welsh, David, tr. 1970. 17.50x (ISBN 0-262-04029-8). MIT Pr.

Dyke, John M. Van see Van Dyke, John M.

Dyke, S. E. Thoughts on the American Flintlock Pistol. LC 74-24435. (Illus.). 52p. 1974. pap. 7.50 (ISBN 0-87387-070-0). Shumway.

Dyke, Van M. & Wehausen, J. V., eds. Annual Review of Fluid Mechanics, Vol. 15. LC 74-80866. (Illus.). 1983. text ed. 28.00 (ISBN 0-8243-0715-1). Annual Reviews.

Dykeman, jt. auth. see Elias, Thomas.

Dykeman, Francis C. Forensic Accounting: The Accountant As Expert Witness. LC 81-13001. 236p. 1982. 39.95x (ISBN 0-471-08395-X, Pub. by Wiley-Interscience). Ronald Pr.

Dyken, Paul R. & Miller, Max D. Facial Features of Neurologic Syndromes. LC 79-17012. (Illus.). 450p. 1979. text ed. 64.50 (ISBN 0-8016-1485-6). Mosby.

Dyker, David A. The Process of Investment in the Soviet Union. LC 82-14600. (Soviet & East European Studies). (Illus.). 240p. Date not set. 39.50 (ISBN 0-521-24831-0). Cambridge U Pr.

--The Soviet Economy. LC 76-2192. (Illus.). 200p. 1976. 15.95 o.p. (ISBN 0-312-74760-8). St Martin.

Dykes, Jeff C. Western High Spots: Reading & Collecting Guides. LC 76-52539. (Illus.). 1977. 12.50 o.p. (ISBN 0-87358-162-8). Northland.

Dykes, Merv. Time Out in New Zealand. (Tourist "Floppy" Ser.). (Illus.). 1979. pap. 6.65 (ISBN 0-589-01135-9, Pub. by Reed Books Australia). C E Tuttle.

Dykes, S. F. The Chemistry of Enamines. 22.95 (ISBN 0-521-08676-0); pap. 10.95x (ISBN 0-521-09731-2). Cambridge U Pr.

Dykhuizen, George. Life & Mind of John Dewey. LC 73-4602. (Illus.). 472p. 1973. 27.50x (ISBN 0-8093-0616-6). S Ill U Pr.

Dykman, Jackson A., jt. auth. see White, Edwin A.

Dykstra, Gerald. Composition: Guided - Free Kit Prog. 1-4. 1973. pap. text ed. 15.30 (ISBN 0-8077-2521-8). Tchrs Coll.

Dykstra, Gerald, et al. Composition: Guided - Free Kit Prog. 5-8. 1978. pap. text ed. 17.95 (ISBN 0-8077-2515-3). Tchrs Coll.

--Composition: Guided Free Manual, Programs 5-8. 1978. pap. text ed. 3.95 (ISBN 0-8077-2388-6). Tchrs Coll.

--Composition: Guided Free Program 5. 1978. pap. text ed. 3.50 (ISBN 0-8077-2389-4). Tchrs Coll.

--Composition: Guided Free Program 6. 1978. pap. text ed. 3.50 (ISBN 0-8077-2390-8). Tchrs Coll.

--Composition: Guided Free Program 7. 1978. pap. text ed. 3.50 (ISBN 0-8077-2391-6). Tchrs Coll.

--Composition: Guided Free Program 8. 1978. pap. text ed. 3.50 (ISBN 0-8077-2392-4). Tchrs Coll.

Dykstra, Gerald, et al, eds. Composition: Guided-Free. LC 73-76064. (gr. 1-6). 1974. Program 1. pap. text ed. 2.95 (ISBN 0-8077-2384-3); Program 2. pap. text ed. 2.95 (ISBN 0-8077-2385-1); Program 3. pap. text ed. 2.95 (ISBN 0-8077-2386-X); Program 4. pap. text ed. 2.75x (ISBN 0-8077-2387-8); tchrs. manual 2.75x (ISBN 0-8077-2383-5). Tchrs Coll.

Dylan, Bob. Tarantula. 1977. pap. 3.95 (ISBN 0-14-004572-4). Penguin.

Dyller, Fran, jt. auth. see Mason, David.

Dym, Joseph B. Product Design with Plastics: A Practical Manual. (Illus.). 288p. 1982. 27.95 (ISBN 0-8311-1141-0). Indus Pr.

Dymax & Inman. TRS-80 Color Computer Graphics. 1982. text ed. 20.95 (ISBN 0-8359-7865-6); pap. text ed. 14.95 (ISBN 0-8359-7864-8). Reston.

Dyment, Alan R., ed. The Literature of the Film: A Bibliographical Guide to the Film As Art & Entertainment 1936-1970. 1975. 59.00 o.p. (ISBN 0-685-70659-1). Gale.

Dymsza, W. Multinational Business Strategy. 1971. pap. text ed. 12.00 (ISBN 0-07-018570-0, C). McGraw.

Dyne, Susan Van see Van Dyne, Susan.

Dynes, Russell R., jt. ed. see Freeman, Howard E.

Dynkin, E. B. Markov Processes & Related Problems of Analysis. LC 81-38438. (London Mathematical Society Lecture Note Ser.: No. 54). 300p. 1982. pap. 24.95 (ISBN 0-521-28512-7). Cambridge U Pr.

Dyos, H. J. Exploring the Urban Past: Essays in Urban History. Cannadine, David & Reeder, David, eds. LC 82-1209. (Illus.). 320p. 1982. 39.50 (ISBN 0-521-24624-5); pap. 12.95 (ISBN 0-521-28848-7). Cambridge U Pr.

--Study of Urban History. LC 68-29379. (Illus.). 1968. 25.00 (ISBN 0-312-77280-7). St Martin.

Dyrek, K. & Haber, J., eds. Reactivity of Solids: Proceedings of the 9th International Symposium, Cracow, Sept. 1980, 2 vols. (Materials Science Monographs: No. 10). 1500p. 1982. 189.50 (ISBN 0-444-99707-5). Elsevier.

Dyrness, William A. Christian Apologetics in a World Community. LC 82-21383. 180p. 1983. pap. 5.95 (ISBN 0-87784-399-6). Inter-Varsity.

Dyson, A. E. & Lovelock, Julian, eds. Education & Democracy. (Birth of Modern Britain Ser). 308p. 1975. 22.50x (ISBN 0-7100-8016-6). Routledge & Kegan.

Dyson, H. V. Emergence of Shakespeare's Tragedy. (Studies in Shakespeare, No. 24). 1950. pap. 11.95x o.p. (ISBN 0-8383-0023-5). Haskell.

Dyson, R. H., jt. auth. see Porada, Edith.

Dyson, S. L. The Stories of the Trees. LC 78-175735. (Illus.). 272p. 1974. Repr. of 1890 ed. 34.00x (ISBN 0-8103-3033-4). Gale.

Dyson, Verne. Land of the Yellow Spring. LC 38-122. 1937. 30.00 o.p. (ISBN 0-686-25962-9). J G Stanoff.

Dyson-Hudson, Rada & Little, Michael A. Rethinking Human Adaptation. (Special Study). 200p. 1982. lib. bdg. 20.00 (ISBN 0-86531-511-6). Westview.

Dywasuk, Colette T., rev. by see Raymond, Louise.

Dzama, Mary Ann. Ready to Read: A Parents Guide. Gilstrap, Robert, ed. (Parent Education Ser.). 287p. 1983. pap. text ed. 8.95 (ISBN 0-471-86637-7). Wiley.

Dziak, John J. Soviet Perceptions of Military Power: The Interaction of Theory & Practice. LC 81-3260. (NSIC Strategy Paper Ser.: No. 36). 1981. pap. text ed. 5.95x (ISBN 0-8448-1389-3). Crane-Russak Co.

Dziech, Billie W. & Faaborg, Linda. The Lecherous Professor: Sexual Harassment on Campus. LC 82-73960. 320p. 1983. 14.37 (ISBN 0-8070-3100-3). Beacon Pr.

Dziedzic, Stan. National Wrestling Syllabus. LC 81-85635. (Illus.). 208p. 1983. pap. 11.95 (ISBN 0-88011-014-7). Leisure Pr.

Dziewanowski, M. K. A History of Soviet Russia. LC 78-133392. (Illus.). 1979. pap. text ed. 20.95 (ISBN 0-13-392159-X). P-H.

Dziewonski, A. Physics & the Earth's Interior. (Enrico Fermi Summer School Ser.: No. 78). 1980. 140.50 (ISBN 0-686-95265-0). Elsevier.

Dzubay, Thomas G., ed. X-Ray Fluorescence Analysis of Environmental Samples. LC 76-22238. 1982. 39.95 o.p. (ISBN 0-250-40134-7). Ann Arbor Science.

E

E. W. Classey Ltd., ed. Butterflies of the Oriental Region. 288p. 1982. 155.00x (ISBN 0-686-82393-1, Pub. by E W Classey England). State Mutual Bk.

--The Leipodoptera of America North of Mexico. 1982. 135.00x (ISBN 0-86096-016-1, Pub. by E W Classey England). State Mutual Bk.

Eachus, Irving. Raid on the Bremerton. 252p. 1980. 12.95 o.p. (ISBN 0-670-58912-8). Viking Pr.

Eacker, Jay N. Problems of Metaphysics & Psychology. LC 82-8053. 260p. 1983. text ed. 19.95x (ISBN 0-88229-685-X); pap. text ed. 9.95x (ISBN 0-88229-814-3). Nelson-Hall.

Eade, Alfred T. Expanded Panorama Bible Study Course. (Illus.). 192p. 9.95 (ISBN 0-8007-0086-4). Revell.

--Panorama De la Biblia. Orig. Title: New Panorama Bible Study Course. Repr. of 1982 ed. pap. 3.75 (ISBN 0-311-03657-0). Casa Bautista.

Eade, D., jt. ed. see Hodgson, J. T.

Eades, J. S. The Yoruba Today. LC 79-50236. (Changing Cultures Ser.). (Illus.). 1980. 27.95 (ISBN 0-521-22656-2); pap. 9.95 (ISBN 0-521-29602-1). Cambridge U Pr.

Eadie & Kline. Interpersonal Communication. rev ed. Applbaum, Ronald & Hart, Roderick, eds. (MODCOM Modules in Speech Communication Ser.). 1982. pap. text ed. 2.75 (ISBN 0-574-22589-7, 13-5589). SRA.

Eadie, Donald. Minicomputers: Theory & Operation. (Illus.). 1979. 22.95 (ISBN 0-8359-4387-9). Reston.

--A User's Guide to Computer Peripherals. (Illus.). 224p. 1982. 19.95 (ISBN 0-13-939660-8). P-H.

Eadie, John. Colossians. 1981. 10.50 (ISBN 0-86524-067-1, 5103). Klock & Klock.

Eadie, Mervyn J., jt. auth. see Tyrer, John H.

Eadie, W. T., et al. Statistical Methods in Experimental Physics. LC 75-157034. 1972. 42.00 (ISBN 0-444-10117-9, North-Holland). Elsevier.

Eadis, M. J. & Tyrer, J. H., eds. Biochemical Neourology. LC 82-22859. 278p. 1983. 48.00 (ISBN 0-8451-3009-9). A R Liss.

Eagan, Andrea B. Why Am I So Miserable If These Are the Best Years of My Life? 1979. pap. 2.25 (ISBN 0-380-46136-6, 63024-9). Avon.

--Why Am I So Miserable If These Are the Best Years of My Life? LC 75-43726. (gr. 8 up). 1976. 10.53i (ISBN 0-397-31655-0, JBL-J). Har-Row.

Eagan, Eileen. Class, Culture, & the Classroom: The Student Peace Movement of the 1930s. (American Civilization Ser.). 319p. 1982. 27.95 (ISBN 0-87722-236-3). Temple U Pr.

Eagar, Patrick. Test Decade. (Illus.). 224p. 1982. 32.50 (ISBN 0-437-04050-X, Pub. by World's Work). David & Charles.

Eager, Edward. Half Magic. LC 54-5153. (Illus.). (gr. 4-6). 1954. 8.95 (ISBN 0-15-233078-X, HJ). HarBraceJ.

--Half Magic. LC 54-5153. (Illus.). (gr. 3-7). 1970. pap. 2.95 (ISBN 0-15-637990-2, VoyB). HarBraceJ.

--Knight's Castle. LC 56-5234. (Illus.). (gr. 3-7). 1956. 6.75 o.p. (ISBN 0-15-243102-0, HJ). HarBraceJ.

--Knight's Castle. LC 56-5234. (gr. 3-7). 1965. pap. 2.95 (ISBN 0-15-647350-X, VoyB). HarBraceJ.

--Magic or Not? LC 78-71152. (gr. 3-7). 1979. pap. 3.95 (ISBN 0-15-655121-7, VoyB). HarBraceJ.

Eager, Fred. Italic Way to Beautiful Handwriting. 128p. 1974. pap. 5.95 (ISBN 0-02-079990-X, Collier). Macmillan.

Eager, George B. How to Succeed in Winning Children to Christ. 190p. 1979. pap. 3.95 (ISBN 0-9603752-0-1). Mailbox.

Eager, Renee. Dining In: Phoenix. (Dining In Ser.). 200p. (Orig.). 1982. pap. 8.95 (ISBN 0-89716-035-5). Peanut Butter.

Eagle, Audrey. Eagle's Trees & Shrubs of New Zealand in Colour. (Illus.). 311p. 1983. Repr. of 1975 ed. 95.00 (ISBN 0-686-84831-4, Pub. by W Collins Australia). Intl Schol Bk Serv.

Eagle, D. J. & Caverly, D. J. Diagnosis of Herbicide Damage to Crops. (Illus.). 1981. 35.00 (ISBN 0-8206-0294-9). Chem Pub.

Eagle, Dorothy & Carnell, Hilary. The Oxford Literary Guide to the British Isles. LC 76-47430. (Illus.). 1977. 19.95 (ISBN 0-19-869123-8). Oxford U Pr.

Eagle, Dorothy, jt. ed. see Harvey, Paul.

Eagle, John. Becoming a Runner. 1983. 10.00 (ISBN 0-533-05612-8). Vantage.

Eagle, Robert & Dickey, Lawrence D. Eating & Allergy. LC 80-1860. 216p. 1981. 11.95 (ISBN 0-385-17361-X). Doubleday.

Eaglefield-Hull, A., ed. Dictionary of Modern Music & Musicians. LC 78-139192. (Music Ser). 1971. Repr. of 1924 ed. lib. bdg. 55.00 (ISBN 0-306-70086-7). Da Capo.

Eaglefield-Hull, A., ed. see Beethoven, Ludwig Van.

Eagleman, Joe R. Severe & Unusual Weather Discussion Guide. 96p. 1982. pap. text ed. 7.95 (ISBN 0-8403-2777-3). Kendall-Hunt.

Eagleman, Joe R., et al. Thunderstorms, Tornadoes & Building Damage. LC 74-30674. 320p. 1975. 27.95x (ISBN 0-669-98137-0). Lexington Bks.

Eagles, Charles W. Jonathan Daniels & Race Relations: The Evolution of a Southern Liberal. LC 82-2756. (Twentieth-Century American Ser.). 254p. 1982. text ed. 24.50x (ISBN 0-87049-356-6); pap. text ed. 11.95x (ISBN 0-87049-357-4). U of Tenn Pr.

Eagles, Douglas A. Your Weight. (First Bks). (Illus.). 72p. (gr. 4 up). 1982. PLB 8.90 (ISBN 0-531-04395-9). Watts.

Eagles, Juanita, et al. Mary Swartz Rose, Eighteen Seventy Four to Nineteen Forty One: Pioneer in Nutrition. LC 79-4342. 1979. text ed. 10.95 (ISBN 0-8077-2556-0). Tchrs Coll.

Eagleson, Mike, jt. auth. see Ziel, Ron.

Eagleson, P. Dynamic Hydrology. 1970. text ed. 35.00 (ISBN 0-07-018596-4, C). McGraw.

Eagleson, P. S. Land Surface Processes in Atmospheric General Circulation Models. LC 82-9740. 572p. 59.50 (ISBN 0-521-25222-9). Cambridge U Pr.

Eagleson, Robert D., ed. English in the Eighties. 176p. (Orig.). 1982. pap. text ed. 10.25 (ISBN 0-909955-40-9). Boynton Cook Pubs.

Eagleton, Terry. Criticism & Ideology: A Study in Marxist Literary Theory. 1978. 10.00x o.p. (ISBN 0-902308-92-0, Pub by NLB); pap. 6.50 (ISBN 0-8052-7047-7). Schocken.

--Marxism & Literary Criticism. LC 76-6707. 1976. 11.95x o.p. (ISBN 0-520-03237-3); pap. 3.75 (ISBN 0-520-03243-8, CAL 337). U of Cal Pr.

--The Rape of Clarissa: Writing, Sexuality & Class-Struggle in Richardson. 128p. 1983. 25.00x (ISBN 0-8166-1204-8); pap. 9.95 (ISBN 0-8166-1209-9). U of Minn Pr.

Eakin, Frank E. Religion & Culture of Israel: Selected Issues. 1977. pap. 11.75 (ISBN 0-8191-0208-3). U Pr of Amer.

--Religion & Western Culture: Selected Issues. 1977. 12.00 (ISBN 0-8191-0256-3). U Pr of Amer.

Eakin, Lucille. Nuevo Destino: The Life Story of a Shipibo Bilingual Educator. LC 79-91447. (Museum of Anthropology Ser.: No. 9). (Illus.). 26p. (Orig.). 1980. pap. 2.95x (ISBN 0-88312-159-X); microfiche 1.50x (ISBN 0-88312-246-4). Summer Inst Ling.

Eakin, Richard M. Great Scientists Speak Again. LC 74-22960. (Illus.). 128p. 1982. 12.95 (ISBN 0-520-04768-0). U of Cal Pr.

--Vertebrate Embryology. 3rd ed. LC 77-88420. (Campus Ser.: No. 208). 1978. pap. 8.50x (ISBN 0-520-03593-3). U of Cal Pr.

Eakins, Barbara & Eakins, R. Gene. Sex Differences in Human Communication. LC 77-77660. (Illus.). 1978. pap. text ed. 9.95 (ISBN 0-395-25510-4). HM.

Eakins, Pamela S. Mothers in Transition. 224p. 1983. 18.95 (ISBN 0-87073-475-X); pap. 8.95 (ISBN 0-87073-476-8). Schenkman.

Eakins, R. Gene, jt. auth. see Eakins, Barbara.

Eakle, Arlene H. American Census Schedules. (How-to Ser.). 1983. pap. text ed. 5.50x (ISBN 0-940764-13-X). Genealog Inst.

Eales, Majorie. An Annotated Guide to Pre-Union Government Publications of the Orange Free State: 1854-1910. 1976. lib. bdg. 22.00 (ISBN 0-8161-7959-X, Hall Reference). G K Hall.

Ealy, Lawrence O. Yanqui Politics & the Isthmian Canal. LC 74-127385. 1971. 17.95x (ISBN 0-271-01126-2). Pa St U Pr.

Eames, A. J. Morphology of the Angiosperms. LC 76-57780. 532p. 1977. Repr. of 1961 ed. 29.50 (ISBN 0-88275-527-7). Krieger.

Eames, Arthur J. Morphology of Vascular Plants: Lower Groups. LC 76-40217. 452p. 1977. Repr. of 1936 ed. 24.50 (ISBN 0-88275-459-9). Krieger.

Eames, Edwin & Goode, Judith G. Anthropology of the City: An Introduction to Urban Anthropology. LC 76-57696. 1977. pap. text ed. 15.95 (ISBN 0-13-038414-3). P-H.

Eames, Edwin, jt. auth. see Cohen, Eugene N.

Eames, Edwin, jt. ed. see Saran, Parmatma.

Eames, Marian. Dancing in Prints, 1634-1870: A Portfolio Assembled from the Archives of the Dance Collection. (Illus.). 1964. 25.00 (ISBN 0-87104-060-3). NY Pub Lib.

Eames, Wilberforce. Early New England Catechisms. LC 68-31081. 1969. Repr. of 1898 ed. 30.00x (ISBN 0-8103-3478-X). Gale.

Earechson, Joni & Musser, Joe. Joni. (General Ser.). 1979. lib. bdg. 12.95 (ISBN 0-8161-6775-3, Large Print Bks). G K Hall.

Eareckson, Joni. Joni. Arcangeli, Gianfranco, ed. 203p. (Ital.). 1981. pap. 1.60 (ISBN 0-8297-1022-1). Life Pubs Intl.

Eareckson, Joni & Estes, Steve. Un Paso Mas. Mercado, Ben, ed. Romanenghi de Powell, Elsie, tr. 222p. (Span.). 1979. pap. 2.80 (ISBN 0-8297-0663-1). Life Pubs Intl.

--A Step Further. 192p. 1982. mass market pb 3.95 (ISBN 0-310-23972-9). Zondervan.

--Um Passo Mais. 1980. 1.80 (ISBN 0-8297-0981-9). Life Pubs Intl.

Earhart, Amelia. The Fun of It. LC 77-16052. (Illus.). 1977. lib. bdg. 11.95 (ISBN 0-915864-56-8); pap. 5.00 (ISBN 0-915864-55-X). Academy Chi Ltd.

--The Fun of It: Random Records of My Own Flying & of Women in Aviation. LC 71-159945. 1975. Repr. of 1932 ed. 34.00x (ISBN 0-8103-4078-X). Gale.

Earhart, Robert L., jt. auth. see Raup, Omer B.

Earl, Boyd. Introduction to Probability: A Programmed Unit in Modern Mathematics. 1963. pap. 11.00 o.p. (ISBN 0-07-018773-8, C). McGraw.

Earl, Ethel M. Professionalism, Legal Considerations, & Office Management. 3rd ed. (Dental Assisting Manuals: No. 1). ix, 85p. 1980. 6.00x (ISBN 0-8078-1375-3). U of NC Pr.

Earl, Gloria. The Book. 1981. cancelled 6.75 (ISBN 0-8062-1572-0). Carlton.

Earl, James. Cassette Tape Recorders. 1977. 12.50x o.p. (ISBN 0-85242-510-4). Intl Pubns Serv.

Earl, John. How to Choose & Use Tuners & Amplifiers. 1970. 12.50x o.p. (ISBN 0-85242-330-6). Intl Pubns Serv.

Earl, Peter E., jt. auth. see Dow, Sheila C.

Earl, R., jt. ed. see Horeker, Bernard.

Earle, Alice M. Child Life in Colonial Days. (Illus.). 420p. 1982. Repr. of 1909 ed. 40.00x (ISBN 0-8103-4272-3). Gale.

--China Collecting in America. LC 78-142764. (Illus.). 1971. pap. 7.75 (ISBN 0-8048-0958-5). C E Tuttle.

--China Collecting in America. LC 77-99044. 1970. Repr. of 1892 ed. 34.00x (ISBN 0-8103-3579-4). Gale.

--Colonial Days in Old New York. LC 68-21767. 1968. Repr. of 1896 ed. 30.00x (ISBN 0-8103-3428-3). Gale.

--Costume of Colonial Times. LC 75-159946. xiv, 264p. 1975. Repr. of 1924 ed. 37.00x (ISBN 0-8103-3965-X). Gale.

--Curious Punishments of Bygone Days. LC 68-31516. (Illus.). 1968. Repr. of 1896 ed. 30.00x (ISBN 0-8103-3504-2). Gale.

--Curious Punishments of Bygone Days. LC 69-14922. (Criminology, Law Enforcement, & Social Problems Ser.: No. 33). (Illus.). 1969. Repr. of 1896 ed. 6.00x (ISBN 0-87585-033-2). Patterson Smith.

--Customs & Fashions in Old New England. LC 71-142765. 1971. pap. 5.95 (ISBN 0-8048-0960-7). C E Tuttle.

--Customs & Fashions in Old New England. LC 68-17959. 1968. Repr. of 1893 ed. 30.00x (ISBN 0-8103-0155-5). Gale.

--Home Life in Colonial Days. LC 74-11507. 470p. 1974. pap. 8.00 (ISBN 0-912944-23-4). Berkshire Traveller.

--Old Time Gardens, Newly Set Forth. LC 68-31219. (Illus.). 1968. Repr. of 1901 ed. 30.00x (ISBN 0-8103-3429-1). Gale.

--Sabbath in Puritan New England. LC 68-17961. 1968. Repr. of 1891 ed. 27.00 o.p. (ISBN 0-8103-3430-5). Gale.

--Stage-Coach & Tavern Days. LC 68-17962. (Illus.). 1968. Repr. of 1900 ed. 37.00x (ISBN 0-8103-3431-3). Gale.

--Sun Dials & Roses of Yesterday. LC 79-75790. 1969. Repr. of 1902 ed. 37.00x (ISBN 0-8103-3830-0). Gale.

Earle, Allic M., ed. see Winslow, Anna G.

Earle, Anitra. How to Live Fairly Elegantly on Virtually Nothing...in Los Angeles. LC 82-161492. 100p. (Orig.). 1982. pap. 7.95 (ISBN 0-910795-00-2). Ondine Pr.

Earle, Edward W., ed. Points of View: The Stereograph in America - A Cultural History. LC 79-4836. (Illus.). 120p. 1979. pap. 15.00x (ISBN 0-89822-006-8). Visual Studies.

Earle, George, jt. ed. see Anderson, Eric A.

Earle, J. H. Drafting Technology. 1982. 27.95 (ISBN 0-201-10233-1). A-W.

Earle, James H. Descriptive Geometry. 2nd ed. LC 76-55640. (Illus.). 384p. 1978. text ed. 21.95 (ISBN 0-201-01776-8). A-W.

--Engineering Design Graphics. 3rd ed. LC 76-2931. 1977. text ed. 27.95 (ISBN 0-201-01774-1). A-W.

--Engineering Design Graphics. 4th ed. LC 82-6709. 704p. 1983. text ed. 27.95 (ISBN 0-201-11318-X). A-W.

Earle, Jean. A Trial of Strength. (Carcanet New Poetry Ser.). (Orig.). 1981. pap. 6.95 o.p. (ISBN 0-85635-298-5, Pub. by Carcanet New Pr England). Humanities.

Earle, Joe. Japanese Prints. (The Victoria & Albert Museum Introduction to the Decorative Arts Ser.). (Illus.). 48p. 1982. 9.95 (ISBN 0-88045-003-7). Stemmer Hse.

--Netsuke. (The Victoria & Albert Museum Introduction to the Decorative Arts Ser.). (Illus.). 48p. 1982. 9.95 (ISBN 0-88045-004-5). Stemmer Hse.

Earle, Joe, tr. see Soto, Kanzan.

Earle, John. Microcosmographie, 1628. Arber, Edward, ed. 125p. pap. 12.50x (ISBN 0-87556-083-0). Saifer.

Earle, Kenneth M. & Rubinstein, Lucien J. Central Nervous System. (Anatomic Pathology Seminars). (Illus.). 1976. text & slides 55.00 o.p. (ISBN 0-89189-052-1, 15-1-015-00); proceedings 5.00 o.p. (ISBN 0-89189-003-3, 50-1-040-00). Am Soc Clinical.

Earle, Olive L. Camels & Llamas. (Illus.). (gr. 3-7). 1961. PLB 8.16 (ISBN 0-688-31138-5). Morrow.

--State Birds & Flowers. (Illus.). (gr. 3-7). 1961. Repr. of 1951 ed. PLB 8.16 (ISBN 0-688-31536-4). Morrow.

Earle, Olive L. & Kantor, Michael. Animals & Their Ears. LC 73-13047. (Illus.). 64p. (gr. 3-7). 1974. PLB 8.16 (ISBN 0-688-30106-1). Morrow.

--Nuts. LC 74-26800. (Illus.). 64p. (gr. 3-7). 1975. 8.50 (ISBN 0-688-22025-8); PLB 7.20 o.s.i. (ISBN 0-688-32025-2). Morrow.

Earle, P. D. Guide to Country Living: Your Questions Answered. rev. ed. (Illus.). 320p. 1973. 6.50 o.p. (ISBN 0-7153-5789-1). David & Charles.

Earle, Patty, et al. Child Development: An Observation Manual. 256p. 1982. pap. 13.95 (ISBN 0-13-130427-5). P-H.

Earle, Peter. The Life & Times of Henry V. (Kings & Queens of England Ser.). (Illus.). 224p. 1972. text ed. 17.50x (ISBN 0-297-99428-X, Pub. by Weidenfeld & Nicolson England). Biblio Dist.

--Monmouth's Rebels: The Road to Sedgamoor 1685. LC 77-84928. (Illus.). 1977. 17.95x (ISBN 0-312-54512-6). St Martin.

Earle, R. L. Unit Operations in Food Processing. 2nd ed. (Illus.). 220p. 1983. 40.00 (ISBN 0-08-025537-X); pap. 19.95 (ISBN 0-08-025536-1). Pergamon.

Earle, Ralph. How We Got Our Bible. 1972. 1.50 (ISBN 0-8341-0226-9). Beacon Hill.

--Mark: Gospel of Action. LC 73-15084. (Everyman's Bible Commentary). 1970. pap. 4.50 (ISBN 0-8024-2041-9). Moody.

--Peloubet's Notes 1981-82. 408p. (Orig.). 1981. pap. 5.95 o.p. (ISBN 0-8010-3363-2). Baker Bk.

--Peloubet's Notes: 1983-1984. 408p. (Orig.). 1983. pap. 6.95 (ISBN 0-8010-3389-6). Baker Bk.

--Word Meanings in the New Testament, Vol. 2. 1982. text ed. 9.95 (ISBN 0-8341-0776-7). Beacon Hill.

--Word Meanings in the New Testament, Vol. 1: Matthew, Mark, Luke. (Word Meanings in the New Testament Ser.). 285p. 1980. 9.95 (ISBN 0-8341-0683-3). Beacon Hill.

Earle, Timothy, jt. ed. see Ericson, Jonathan.

Earle, W. Hubert. Cacti of the Southwest. (Illus.). 210p. 1982. 17.50 (ISBN 0-935810-05-6); pap. 11.00 (ISBN 0-686-97701-7). Primer Pubs.

Earle, William, tr. see Jaspers, Karl.

Earlley, Elsie C., jt. auth. see Cook, J. E.

Earl Of Harewood, ed. The New Kobbe's Complete Opera Book. new rev. ed. LC 76-12106. 663p. 1976. 25.00 (ISBN 0-399-11633-8). Putnam Pub Group.

Earls, Michael. Manuscripts & Memories: Chapters in Our Literary Tradition. 275p. 1982. Repr. of 1935 ed. lib. bdg. 45.00 (ISBN 0-686-81683-8). Century Bookbindery.

Early, Eileen. Joy in Exile. LC 79-5429. 1980. pap. text ed. 8.25 (ISBN 0-8191-0878-2). U Pr of Amer.

Early, James G., et al, eds. Time-Dependent Failure Mechanisms & Assessment Methodologies. (Illus.). 344p. Date not set. price not set (ISBN 0-521-25375-6). Cambridge U Pr.

Early, Paul J., jt. auth. see Sodee, D. Bruce.

Earn, Josephine. Looking at Canada. LC 76-8481. (Looking at Other Countries Ser.). (Illus.). 1977. 10.53i (ISBN 0-397-31704-2, JBL-J). Har-Row.

Earnest, Adele. The Art of the Decoy: American Bird Carving. (Illus.). 1982. pap. 14.95 (ISBN 0-916838-58-7); 25.00 (ISBN 0-916838-62-5). Schiffer.

--The Art of the Decoy: American Bird Carvings. (Illus.). 208p. 1965. 10.00 o.p. (ISBN 0-517-09733-8, C N Potter Bks). Crown.

Earnest, Ernest. Expatriates & Patriots: American Scholars, Artists & Writers in Europe. LC 68-19469. (Illus.). 1968. 16.25 o.p. (ISBN 0-8223-0051-6). Duke.

Earney, Fillmore C. Petroleum & Hard Minerals from the Sea. LC 80-17653. (Scripta Series in Geography). 291p. 1980. 39.95x o.p. (ISBN 0-470-27009-8, Pub. by Halsted Pr). Wiley.

Earnshaw, Judith, ed. Sprouts on Helicon. (gr. 9 up). 5.95 o.p. (ISBN 0-233-95784-7). Transatlantic.

Earp, T. W. Frank Dobson, Sculptor. (Illus.). 2.50 o.p. (ISBN 0-685-20585-1). Transatlantic.

Earp, Wyatt S. Wyatt Earp: His Autobiography. Boyer, Glenn G., ed. (Illus., Orig.). 1981. leather 300.00 (ISBN 0-686-36171-7). Y V Bissette.

Earthday X Colloquium, University of Denver, April 21-24, 1980. Ecological Consciousness: Essays from the Earthday X Colloquium. Schultz, Robert C. & Hughes, J. Donald, eds. LC 80-6084. 510p. 1981. lib. bdg. 28.25 (ISBN 0-8191-1496-0); pap. text ed. 17.50 (ISBN 0-8191-1497-9). U Pr of Amer.

Eary, Donald F. & Johnson, G. E. Process Engineering: For Manufacturing. (Illus.). 1962. text ed. 29.95 (ISBN 0-13-723122-9). P-H.

Eary, Donald F. & Reed, Edward A. Techniques of Pressworking Sheet Metal: An Engineering Approach to Die Design. 2nd ed. 1974. ref. ed. 32.95 (ISBN 0-13-900696-6). P-H.

Eash, Dianne, ed. see Wilson, Arthur N.

Eash, Nancy Greene see West, Betty M.

Easley, Eddie, et al. Contemporary Business: Challenges & Opportunities. (Illus.). 1978. pap. text ed. 18.95 (ISBN 0-8299-0166-3); study guide 8.50 (ISBN 0-8299-0218-X); instrs.' manual avail. (ISBN 0-8299-0476-X); transparency masters avail. (ISBN 0-8299-0477-8). West Pub.

Easley, Grady M. Primer for Small Systems Management. 1978. text ed. 22.95 (ISBN 0-316-20360-2). Little.

Easley, Wayne & Creech, Kenneth. Communication: A Configurative Approach. 1979. pap. text ed. 7.95 (ISBN 0-8403-2059-0). Kendall-Hunt.

Easlon, Steven. The Los Angeles Railway Through the Years. (Illus.). 6.95 (ISBN 0-933506-00-7). Darwin Pubns.

Easmon, C. S. & Jeljaszewicz, J., eds. Medical Microbiology, Vol. I. 1983. 59.50 (ISBN 0-12-228001-6). Acad Pr.

Eason, Helena. Bristol's Historic Inns. 80p. 1982. 30.00x (ISBN 0-905459-30-X, Pub. by Redcliffe England). State Mutual Bk.

Eason, Helena, jt. auth. see Shipsides, Frank.

Eason, Robert, ed. Adapted Physical Activity: From Theory to Implementation. Proceedings of the 3rd International Symposium on Adapted Physical Activities. 1983. text ed. price not set (ISBN 0-931250-40-4). Human Kinetics.

Eason, Thomas, jt. auth. see Fitzgerald, Jerry.

Eason, Thomas S. & Webb, Douglas. Nine Steps to Effective EDP Loss Control. 240p. 1983. 21.00 (ISBN 0-932376-25-8). Digital Pr.

Eason, Tom, jt. auth. see Fitzgerald, Jerry.

Easson, A. J. Tax Law & Policy in the EEC. LC 80-41430. (European Practice Ser.). 284p. 1980. lib. bdg. 50.00 (ISBN 0-379-20711-7). Oceana.

Easson, Eric C. Cancer of the Uterine Cervix. LC 72-88847. (Illus.). 1973. text ed. 9.00 (ISBN 0-7216-3303-X). Saunders.

Easson, Roger R. & Essick, Robert N. William Blake: Book Illustrator, Vol. I. LC 72-82993. 1972. pap. 20.00 (ISBN 0-913130-01-X, American Blake Foundation). St Luke TN.

--William Blake: Book Illustrator, Vol. II. 1979. 125.00 (ISBN 0-913130-07-9, American Blake Foundation); pap. 45.00 (ISBN 0-913130-08-7). St Luke TN.

East African Law Reports. Court of Appeals for Eastern Africa Nineteen Thirty-Four to Nineteen Fifty-Six, 23 Vols. 1967. Set. 287.50 o.s.i. (ISBN 0-379-20100-3); 15.00 ea. o.s.i. Oceana.

East, Ben & Nentl, Jerolyn. Danger in the Air. Schroeder, Howard, ed. LC 79-53774. (Survival Ser.). (Illus., Orig.). (gr. 3 up). 1979. PLB 6.95 (ISBN 0-89686-047-7); pap. 3.50 (ISBN 0-89686-055-8). Crestwood Hse.

--Desperate Search. Schroeder, Howard, ed. LC 79-5186. (Survival Ser.). (Illus., Orig.). (gr. 3 up). 1979. PLB 6.95 (ISBN 0-89686-043-4); pap. 3.50 (ISBN 0-89686-051-5). Crestwood Hse.

--Forty Days Lost. Schroeder, Howard, ed. LC 79-5185. (Survival Ser.). (Illus., Orig.). (gr. 3 up). 1979. PLB 6.95 (ISBN 0-89686-042-6); pap. 3.50 (ISBN 0-89686-050-7). Crestwood Hse.

--Found Alive. Schroeder, Howard, ed. LC 79-53749. (Survival Ser.). (Illus., Orig.). (gr. 3 up). 1979. PLB 6.95 (ISBN 0-89686-044-2); pap. 3.50 (ISBN 0-89686-052-3). Crestwood Hse.

--Frozen Terror. Schroeder, Howard, ed. LC 79-53747. (Survival Ser.). (Illus., Orig.). (gr. 3 up). 1979. PLB 6.95 (ISBN 0-89686-049-3); pap. 3.50 (ISBN 0-89686-057-4). Crestwood Hse.

--Grizzly. Schroeder, Howard, ed. LC 79-53748. (Survival Ser.). (Illus., Orig.). (gr. 3 up). 1979. PLB 6.95 (ISBN 0-89686-045-0); pap. 3.50 (ISBN 0-89686-053-1). Crestwood Hse.

--Mistaken Journey. Schroeder, Howard, ed. LC 79-53775. (Survival Ser.). (Illus., Orig.). (gr. 3 up). 1979. PLB 6.95 (ISBN 0-89686-046-9); pap. 3.50 (ISBN 0-89686-054-X). Crestwood Hse.

--Trapped in Devil's Hole. Schroeder, Howard, ed. LC 79-53773. (Survival Ser.). (Illus., Orig.). (gr. 3 up). 1979. PLB 6.95 (ISBN 0-89686-048-5); pap. 3.50 (ISBN 0-89686-056-6). Crestwood Hse.

East, G. C., jt. auth. see Margerison, D.

East, Robert. John Adams. (World Leaders Ser.). 1979. lib. bdg. 13.95 (ISBN 0-8057-7723-7, Twayne). G K Hall.

East, Robert A; see Weaver, Glenn.

East, W. Gordon. Geography Behind History. (Illus.). 1967. pap. 5.95 (ISBN 0-393-00419-8, Norton Lib). Norton.

East-West Foundation, jt. auth. see Kushi, Michio.

Eastaugh, Kenneth. The Carry-on Book. 1978. 10.95 o.p. (ISBN 0-7153-7403-6). David & Charles.

Eastcott, R. Sketches of the Origin, Process & Effects of Music. LC 70-159680. (Music Ser). 1971. Repr. of 1793 ed. lib. bdg. 29.50 (ISBN 0-306-70184-7). Da Capo.

Easter, Deb, jt. auth. see Eppenbach, Sarah.

Easter, Robert S. The Sword of Solomon. 1962. text ed. 3.50 o.p. (ISBN 0-88053-055-3, M-318). Macoy Pub.

Easterbrook, David L. African Book Reviews, 1885-1945: An Index to Books Reviewed in Selected English-Language Publications. 1979. lib. bdg. 27.00 (ISBN 0-8161-8003-2, Hall Reference). G K Hall.

Easterbrook, Don J. Principles of Geomorphology. LC 69-13207. (Illus.). 1969. text ed. 23.00 o.p. (ISBN 0-07-018780-0, C). McGraw.

Easterbrook, Frank H., jt. auth. see Posner, Richard A.

Easterby, J. H., ed. South Carolina Rice Plantation. Repr. of 1945 ed. lib. bdg. 27.50x (ISBN 0-678-01350-0). Kelley.

Easterby, Ronald & Zwaga, Harm. Visual Presentation of Information: The Design & Evaluation of Signs & Printed Material. 1983. write for info. (ISBN 0-471-10431-0, Pub. by Wiley-Interscience). Wiley.

Easterlin, Richard A. Birth & Fortune: The Impact of Numbers on Personal Welfare. LC 79-56369. 205p. 1980. 13.95 (ISBN 0-465-00688-4). Basic.

Easterlin, Richard A. & Ward, David. Immigration. (Dimensions of Ethnicity Ser.). 176p. 1982. pap. text ed. 5.95x (ISBN 0-674-44439-6). Harvard U Pr.

Easterling, P. E., ed. see Sophocles.

Easterly, Lane, ed. Great Bible Stories for Children. 6.95 (ISBN 0-8407-4988-0). Nelson.

Eastgate, Robert J. Master Guide to Creative Financing of Real Estate Investments. LC 82-9313. 246p. 1982. text ed. 89.50 (ISBN 0-87624-366-9). Inst Busn Plan.

Eastham. Biochemical Values in Clinical Medicine. 6th ed. 266p. 1978. pap. 13.50 (ISBN 0-7236-0502-5). Wright-PSG.

--Pocket Guide to Differential Diagnosis. 474p. 1980. pap. 16.50 (ISBN 0-7236-0542-4). Wright-PSG.

Eastham, M. S. & Kalf, H. Schrodinger Type Operators with Continuous Spectra. (Research Notes in Mathematics Ser.: No. 65). 208p. 1982. pap. text ed. 27.50 (ISBN 0-273-08526-3). Pitman Pub MA.

Easther, Michael, jt. auth. see Maddock, Shirley.

Easthope, Gary. Community, Heirarchy & Open Education. 128p. 1975. 12.00x (ISBN 0-7100-8210-X); pap. 6.00 (ISBN 0-7100-8211-8). Routledge & Kegan.

Easthope, Jean, jt. auth. see McCullough, Colleen.

Eastlick, John T., jt. auth. see Stueart, Robert D.

Eastman, Addison J. A Handful of Pearls: The Epistle of James. LC 78-5797. 1978. pap. 5.50 (ISBN 0-664-24202-2). Westminster.

Eastman, Arthur, et al, eds. The Norton Reader. 5th ed. 1980. pap. 12.95x (ISBN 0-393-95109-X); pap. text ed. 10.95x shorter ed.0438085xx (ISBN 0-393-95113-8); guide to norton reader 3.95x (ISBN 0-393-95116-2). Norton.

Eastman, Arthur M., et al, eds. Norton Anthology of Poetry. rev. ed. 1975. text ed. 19.95x o.p. (ISBN 0-393-09240-2); pap. text ed. 16.95x complete ed. (ISBN 0-393-09245-3); pap. text ed. 12.95x shorter ed. (ISBN 0-393-09251-8). Norton.

Eastman, Carol, jt. ed. see Miller, Jay.

Eastman, Carol M. Language Planning: An Introduction. Langness, L. L. & Edgerton, Robert B., eds. (Publications in Anthropology & Related Fields Ser.). (Illus.). 288p. (Orig.). 1983. pap. text ed. 9.95x (ISBN 0-88316-552-X). Chandler & Sharp.

--Markers in English-Influenced Swahili Conversation. LC 70-632593. (African Ser.). (Illus.). 1970. pap. 2.00x o.s.i. (ISBN 0-89680-041-5, Ohio U Ctr Intl). Ohio U Pr.

Eastman, Charles A. Indian Boyhood. (Illus.). 8.50 (ISBN 0-8446-0085-7). Peter Smith.

Eastman, H. C. & Stykolt, S. Tariff & Competition in Canada. (Illus.). 1968. 26.00 (ISBN 0-312-78540-2). St Martin.

Eastman Kodak. Kodak's Pocket Field Guide to 35mm Photography. 1983. pap. price not set (ISBN 0-671-46833-2). S&S.

Eastman Kodak Co., jt. auth. see American Photographic Book Publishing Co.

Eastman Kodak Company. Analysis, Treatment & Disposal of Ferricyanide in Photographic Effluents. LC 79-57024. 72p. 1980. pap. 5.75 (ISBN 0-87985-244-5, J-54). Eastman Kodak.

--Basic Chemistry of Photographic Processing, Pts. 1 & 2. 1971. 5.00 o.s.i. (ISBN 0-87985-194-5, Z-23-ED). Eastman Kodak.

--Cinematographer's Field Guide (H-2) (Illus.). 1982. 8.95 (ISBN 0-87985-310-7). Eastman Kodak.

--A Collection of Articles from the Kodak Compass, No. 2. (Kodax Publication). 1977. pap. 3.75 o.p. (ISBN 0-87985-207-0, G-50-C2). Eastman Kodak.

--A Collection of Articles from the Kodak Compass, No. 1. (Illus.). 1976. pap. 2.50 o.p. (ISBN 0-87985-184-8, G-50-C1). Eastman Kodak.

--Designing for People at Work. (Engineering Ser.). (Illus.). 600p. 1983. 49.95 (ISBN 0-686-82248-X). Lifetime Learn.

--Kodak Color Darkroom Dataguide. 7th ed. (Illus.). 34p. 1982. pap. 20.00 spiral bound (ISBN 0-87985-086-8, R-19). Eastman Kodak.

--Photographic Studio Management. 1977. pap. 4.00 o.p. (ISBN 0-87985-191-0, O-1). Eastman Kodak.

--Presenting Yourself: S-60. 160p. (Orig.). 1982. pap. text ed. 12.95 (ISBN 0-87985-258-5). Eastman Kodak.

--Quality Enlarging with Kodak B-W Papers (G-1) (Illus.). 156p. Date not set. pap. 10.95 (ISBN 0-87985-279-8). Eastman Kodak.

--Using Photography to Preserve Evidence. (Illus.). 48p. 1976. pap. 4.50 (ISBN 0-87985-166-X, M-2). Eastman Kodak.

Eastman Kodak Company, ed. Basic Production Techniques for Motion Pictures. 2nd ed. LC 76-16716. (Illus.). 62p. (Orig.). 1976. pap. 5.00 o.p. (ISBN 0-87985-004-3, P18). Eastman Kodak.

--Basic Titling & Animation for Motion Pictures. 3rd ed. (Illus.). 60p. (Orig.). 1976. pap. 2.50 o.p. (ISBN 0-87985-003-5, S21). Eastman Kodak.

--Cinematographer's Field Guide, (H-2) 3rd rev. ed. (Illus.). 100p. 1980. text ed. 6.95 o.p. (ISBN 0-87985-276-3). Eastman Kodak.

--Close-up Photography & Photomacrography. LC 77-88930. (Illus.). 1977. pap. 8.00 o.s.i. (ISBN 0-87985-206-2, N-12). Eastman Kodak.

--Contacting Procedures for the Graphic Arts. (Illus.). 1974. pap. 3.95 o.p. (ISBN 0-87985-099-X, Q-4). Eastman Kodak.

--Continuous-Tone Processor Control for the Graphic Arts. 1975. pap. 1.00 o.p. (ISBN 0-87985-208-9, Q-37). Eastman Kodak.

--The Joy of Photography. Bd. with More Joy of Photography. 288p. (Illus.). 312p. 1982. Set. pap. 27.90 (ISBN 0-201-99239-6). A-W.

--Photography Through the Microscope. LC 79-54858. (Illus.). 96p. 1980. pap. 9.95 (ISBN 0-87985-248-8, P-2). Eastman Kodak.

--Processing & Process Monitoring of Kodak Black & White Films. 2nd ed. (Illus.). 1982. pap. 5.00 (ISBN 0-87985-059-0, Z-126). Eastman Kodak.

--Using Process C-41 (Kodak Publication No. Z-121) 3rd ed. 1982. 60.00 (ISBN 0-87985-151-1). Eastman Kodak.

Eastman Kodak Company Editors. The Joy of Photography. (Illus.). 312p. Date not set. pap. 10.00 o.p. (ISBN 0-87985-313-1). Eastman Kodak.

Eastman Kodak Company Staff, ed. Images, Images, Images: The Book of Programmed Multi-Image Production (S-12) 3rd ed. (Illus.). 264p. 1983. pap. 19.95 (ISBN 0-87985-327-1). Eastman Kodak.

Eastman, Margaret, jt. auth. see Eastman, Wilbur F.

Eastman, Max. The Young Trotsky. 104p. 1982. pap. 20.00x (ISBN 0-902030-92-2, Pub by New Park Pubns England). State Mutual Bk.

Eastman, P. D. Cat in the Hat Beginner Book Dictionary. LC 64-1157. (Illus.). (gr. k-6). 1964. 5.95 (ISBN 0-394-81009-0); PLB 6.99 o.p. (ISBN 0-394-91009-5). Beginner.

--Cat in the Hat Beginner Book Dictionary in French & English. LC 65-22650. (Illus., Fr. & Eng.). (gr. 2-3). 1965. 8.95 (ISBN 0-394-81063-5). Beginner.

Eastman, Philip D. Big Dog, Little Dog: A Bedtime Story. (Illus.). (ps-1). 1973. pap. 1.50 (ISBN 0-394-82669-8, BYR). Random.

Eastman, Philip D., jt. auth. see McKie, Roy.

Eastman, Sheila & McGee, Timothy J. Barbara Pentland. (Canadian Composers Ser.). 284p. 1983. 30.00x (ISBN 0-8020-5562-1). U of Toronto Pr.

Eastman, Susan T. & Head, Sidney W. Broadcast Programming: Strategies for Winning Television & Radio Audiences. 400p. 1980. text ed. 18.95x (ISBN 0-534-00882-8). Wadsworth Pub.

Eastman, Susan Tyler & Klein, Robert. Strategies in Broadcast & Cable Promotion: Commercial Television, Radio, Cable, Pay Television, Public Television. 352p. 1982. pap. text ed. 13.95x (ISBN 0-534-01156-X). Wadsworth Pub.

Eastman, Terry R. Radiographic Fundamentals & Technique Guide. LC 78-31461. (Illus.). 176p. 1979. pap. text ed. 13.95 (ISBN 0-8016-1493-7). Mosby.

Eastman, Wilbur F. & Eastman, Margaret. Planning & Building Your Fireplace. (Illus.). 144p. 1976. 11.95 o.p. (ISBN 0-88266-084-5); pap. 5.95 o.p. (ISBN 0-88266-083-7). Garden Way Pub.

Eastmann, C. R., ed. see Von Zittel, K. A.

Easton, A. S. Chemical Analysis of Silicate Rocks: Methods in Geochemistry & Geophysics, Vol. 6. 1972. 68.50 (ISBN 0-444-40985-8). Elsevier.

Easton, Allan. Decision Making: A Short Course in Problem Solving for Professionals. (Professional Development Programs Ser.). 352p. 1976. Set. text ed. 29.95x (ISBN 0-471-01700-0). Wiley.

--The Design of Health Maintenance Organization: A Handbook for Practitioners. LC 74-17893. (Illus.). 532p. 1975. text ed. 31.95 o.p. (ISBN 0-275-05460-8). Praeger.

--This Is the Shih Tzu. rev. ed. 1969. 12.95 (ISBN 0-87666-389-7, PS661). TFH Pubns.

Easton, Allen, jt. auth. see Brearley, Joan M.

Easton, Brian & Thomson, Norman. An Introduction to the New Zealand Economy. LC 81-19737. (Illus.). 339p. 1983. text ed. 25.00x (ISBN 0-7022-1920-7); pap. 13.50x (ISBN 0-7022-1940-1). U of Queensland Pr.

Easton, Burton S., tr. The Apostolic Tradition of Hippolytus. 112p. 1962. pap. 10.50 o.p. (ISBN 0-208-01575-2, Archon). Shoe String.

Easton, Carol. The Search for Sam Goldwyn. LC 75-28167. 1976. 8.95 o.p. (ISBN 0-688-03007-6). Morrow.

Easton, M. G. Baker's Illustrated Bible Dictionary. (Baker's Paperback Reference Library). 760p. 1983. pap. 15.95 (ISBN 0-8010-3386-1). Baker Bk.

Easton, Malcolm & Holroyd, Michael. Art of Augustus John. LC 74-84335. (Illus.). 1975. 35.00 (ISBN 0-87923-113-0). Godine.

Easton, Nina, jt. ed. see Brownstein, Ronald.

Easton, Richard J. & Graham, George P. Intermediate Algebra. LC 72-4744. (Illus.). 258p. 1973. text ed. 22.95x (ISBN 0-471-22939-3); student wkbk. 12.95x (ISBN 0-471-22943-1). Wiley.

Easton, Robert. This Promised Land. (The Saga of California Trilogy: Vol. I). 320p. (Orig.). 1982. pap. 9.95 (ISBN 0-88496-183-4). Capra Pr.

Easton, S., jt. auth. see Lamb, D.

Easton, Stewart, ed. see Steiner, Rudolf.

Easton, Thomas A. How to Write a Readable Business Report. LC 82-73624. 275p. 1983. 14.95 (ISBN 0-87094-393-6). Dow Jones-Irwin.

Easton, Thomas A. & Rischer, Carl E. Bioscope. LC 78-71612. 592p. 1979. text ed. 19.95 o.p. (ISBN 0-87484-417-7); instructors manual avail. o.p. Mayfield Pub.

Eastwick, Ivy O. Seven Little Popovers. (gr. 2up). PLB 4.65 (ISBN 0-695-41291-4, Dist. by Caroline Hse). Follett.

Eastwood, F. W., et al. Organic Chemistry: A First University Course in Twelve Programs. 2nd ed. 1970. text ed. 15.95x (ISBN 0-521-07951-9). Cambridge U Pr.

Easu & Rodehaver, Gladys K., eds. Book II of Revelations for the Aquarian Age. 1983. pap. 6.95 (ISBN 0-930208-14-5). Mangan Bks.

Easwaran, Eknath. Gandhi the Man. 2nd ed. LC 77-25976. (Illus.). 1978. 10.50 (ISBN 0-915132-13-3); pap. 7.95 (ISBN 0-915132-14-1). Nilgiri Pr.

--Meditation: Commonsense Directions for an Uncommon Life. LC 78-10935. 1978. pap. 6.00 (ISBN 0-915132-16-8). Nilgiri Pr.

Eaton, jt. auth. see Ho.

Eaton, Allen, jt. auth. see Adriani, John.

Eaton, Charles E. The Thing King. 104p. 1982. 9.95 (ISBN 0-8453-4743-8). Cornwall Bks.

Eaton, Clement. The Growth of Southern Civilization, 1790-1860. (New American Nation Ser.). (Illus.). 1963. 17.26xi (ISBN 0-06-011150-X, HarpT). Har-Row.

--Henry Clay & the Art of American Politics. (The Library of American Biography). 209p. 1962. pap. 5.95 (ISBN 0-316-20412-9). Little.

Eaton, David. Shale Oil Technology: Status of the Industry. (Working Paper Ser.: No. 7). 1977. 2.50 (ISBN 0-686-10611-3). LBJ Sch Public Affairs.

Eaton, Elizabeth. Cook & Bake. (Make & Play Ser.). (Illus.). 48p. (gr. k-6). 1976. pap. 1.50 o.p. (ISBN 0-263-05934-0). Transatlantic.

Eaton, Evelyn. Snowy Earth Comes Gliding. 1974. pap. 5.00 (ISBN 0-686-30737-2). Bear Tribe.

Eaton, Harriette G. Bunya-Bunya Magic. (Orig.). pap. 2.00 (ISBN 0-685-08696-8). Creative Pr.

Eaton, J. Electric Power Transmission Systems. 1972. ref. ed. 23.95 (ISBN 0-13-247338-0). P-H.

Eaton, J. H. Psalms. (Student Christian Movement Press-Torch Bible Ser.). (Orig.). 1967. pap. 7.95 (ISBN 0-19-520296-1). Oxford U Pr.

Eaton, J. Robert & Cohen, Edwin. Electric Power Transmission Systems. 2nd ed. (Illus.). 432p. 1983. 24.95 (ISBN 0-13-247304-6). P-H.

Eaton, Jeanette. Lone Journey: The Life of Roger Williams. LC 44-8239. (Illus.). (gr. 10 up). 1966. pap. 0.75 (ISBN 0-15-652985-8, VoyB). HarBraceJ.

Eaton, Jeffrey C. The Logic of Theism: An Analysis of the Thought of Austin Farrer. LC 80-67260. 288p. 1980. lib. bdg. 20.50 (ISBN 0-8191-1337-9); pap. text ed. 11.00 (ISBN 0-8191-1338-7). U Pr of Amer.

Eaton, Jeffrey C., ed. For God & Clarity: New Essays in Honor of Austin Ferrer. Loades, Ann. (Pittsburgh Theological Monographs New Series: No. 4). 1983. pap. write for info. (ISBN 0-915138-52-2). Pickwick.

Eaton, Jerome A. & Calkins, Carroll C. How to Garden. LC 78-13121. (Illus.). 1979. 12.50 (ISBN 0-394-49383-4); pap. 6.95 o.p. (ISBN 0-394-73531-5). Knopf.

Eaton, John. Grant, Lincoln & the Freedman. LC 70-78763. (Illus.). Repr. of 1907 ed. 17.50x o.p. (ISBN 0-8371-1388-1, Pub. by Negro U Pr). Greenwood.

Eaton, John P. & Kurnitz, Julie. The Disgusting Despicable Cat Cookbook. (Illus.). 96p. (Orig.). 1982. pap. 3.95 (ISBN 0-8329-0143-1). New Century.

Eaton, Jonathan & Gersovitz, Mark. Poor-Country Borrowing in Private Financial Markets & the Repudiation Issue. LC 81-2925. (Princeton Studies in International Finance: No. 47). 1981. pap. text ed. 4.50x (ISBN 0-88165-218-0). Princeton U Int Finan Econ.

Eaton, K. J. & Eaton, K. J., eds. Proceedings of International Conference on Wind Effects on Buildings & Structures: Heathrow Nineteen Seventy-Five. LC 75-2730. 650p. 1976. 110.00 (ISBN 0-521-20801-7). Cambridge U Pr.

Eaton, Marge. Flower Pressing. LC 72-13340. (Early Craft Bks). (Illus.). 36p. (gr. 1-4). 1973. PLB 3.95g (ISBN 0-8225-0855-9). Lerner Pubns.

Eaton, Mick, ed. Screen Reader Two: Cinema & Semiotics. Neale, Stephen. 197p. 1982. 17.95 (ISBN 0-900676-08-6). NY Zoetrope.

Eaton, Peggy & Eiring, Leslie. Joy of Learning. 7.35 (ISBN 0-86575-027-0). Dormac.

Eaton, Quaintance. The Miracle of the Met. (Music Reprint Ser.). (Illus.). xii, 490p. 1982. Repr. of 1968 ed. lib. bdg. 45.00 (ISBN 0-306-76168-8). Da Capo.

--Opera Caravan. LC 78-9128. (Music Reprint 1978 Ser.). (Illus.). 1978. lib. bdg. 32.50 (ISBN 0-306-77596-4); pap. 6.95 (ISBN 0-306-80089-6). Da Capo.

--Opera Production One: A Handbook. LC 73-20232. (Music Ser.). 266p. 1974. Repr. of 1961 ed. lib. bdg. 25.00 (ISBN 0-306-70635-0). Da Capo.

Eaton, Randall L. The Cheetah: The Biology, Ecology, & Behavior of an Endangered Species. LC 81-18556. 192p. 1982. Repr. lib. bdg. 13.95 (ISBN 0-89874-451-2). Krieger.

Eaton, William E., jt. ed. see Dennis, Lawrence J.

Eatwell, David. Steam Locomotives. (Illus.). 64p. 1983. pap. 4.95 (ISBN 0-7134-1835-4, Pub. by Batsford England). David & Charles.

Eatwell, John, jt. auth. see Robinson, Joan.

Eaves, Thomas F., jt. auth. see Johnson, Paul R.

Eayrs, James. In Defence of Canada, Vol. IV: Growing up Allied. LC 72-7513. (Studies in the Structure of Power). 1979. 27.50x (ISBN 0-8020-2345-2). U of Toronto Pr.

--In Defence of Canada, Vol. 5: Indochina - Roots of Complicity. (Studies in the Structure of Power Ser.). 352p. 1983. 45.00x (ISBN 0-8020-2460-2); pap. 17.50 (ISBN 0-8020-6473-6). U of Toronto Pr.

Ebadi, M. & Costa, E., eds. Role of Vitamin B-Six in Neurobiology. LC 73-84113. (Advances in Biochemical Psychopharmacology Ser.: Vol. 4). (Illus.). 248p. 1972. 27.00 (ISBN 0-911216-18-9). Raven.

Ebbatson, Roger. The Evolutionary Self: Hardy, Forster, Lawrence. LC 82-8769. 142p. 1983. text ed. 24.50x (ISBN 0-389-20297-5). B&N Imports.

Ebbert, Mary K. By the Way. (Contemporary Poets of Dorrance Ser.). 36p. 1983. 4.95 (ISBN 0-8059-2843-X). Dorrance.

Ebbighausen, E. G. Introductory Astronomy. LC 73-89492. 1974. pap. 14.95x o.p. (ISBN 0-675-08843-7). Merrill.

Ebbighausen, Edward G. Astronomy. 4th ed. (Physics & Physical Science Ser.). 168p. 1980. pap. text ed. 9.95 (ISBN 0-675-08184-X). Merrill.

Ebbitt, David R., jt. auth. see Ebbitt, Wilma R.

Ebbitt, Wilma R. & Ebbitt, David R. Index to English. 7th ed. pap. 8.95 (ISBN 0-673-15541-2). Scott F.

--Writer's Guide. 7th ed. 1981. pap. 13.50x (ISBN 0-673-15540-4). Scott F.

--Writer's Guide & Index to English. 7th ed. 1981. pap. text ed. 16.95x (ISBN 0-673-15542-0). Scott F.

Ebdon, John. Ebdon's Iliad. (Illus.). 192p. 1983. 17.50 (ISBN 0-434-22196-1, Pub. by Heineman England). David & Charles.

--Edbon's Odyssey. 1979. 14.95 (ISBN 0-686-84206-5, Pub. by W Heinemann). David & Charles.

Ebel, Hans F., ed. see Dehmlow, Eckhard & Dehmlow, Sigrid.

Ebel, Hans F., ed. see Schmid, Roland & Sapunov, Valentin N.

Ebel, Henry, jt. ed. see DeMause, Lloyd.

Ebel, Holly. Christmas in the Air: A New Fashioned Book for an Old Fashioned Christmas. (Illus.). 96p. (Orig.). 1982. pap. 6.95 (ISBN 0-943786-00-2). HollyDay.

Ebel, Robert D. & Kamins, Robert M. Who Pays Hawaii's Taxes? A Study of the Incidence of State & Local Taxes in Hawaii for 1970. 1975. pap. 4.00x (ISBN 0-8248-0403-1). UH Pr.

Ebel, Robert L. Essentials of Educational Measurement. 3rd ed. LC 78-13392. 1979. ref. ed. 24.95 (ISBN 0-13-286013-9). P-H.

--Practical Problems in Educational Measurement. (Orig.). 1980. pap. text ed. 10.95 (ISBN 0-669-03164-X). Heath.

Ebeling, Doug. Industrial Innovation in Australia. 45p. (Orig.). 1981. pap. text ed. 18.75x (ISBN 0-85825-161-2, Pub. by Inst Engineering Australia). Renouf.

Ebeling, Gerhard. Introduction to a Theological Theory of Language. Wilson, R. A., tr. from Ger. LC 72-87057. 224p. 1973. 6.50 o.p. (ISBN 0-8006-0256-0, 1-256). Fortress.

Ebeling, Gerhard, et al. The Bible As a Document of the University. Betz, H. D., ed. 1981. pap. 10.00 (ISBN 0-89130-422-3, 00-03-03). Scholars Pr CA.

Ebeling, Nancy B. & Hill, Deborah A., eds. Child Abuse & Neglect: A Guide for Treating the Child & Family. 400p. 1982. text ed. 27.50 (ISBN 0-7236-7040-4). Wright-PSG.

Ebeling, Walter. The Fruited Plain: The Story of American Agriculture. LC 78-62837. 1980. 30.00x (ISBN 0-520-03751-0). U of Cal Pr.

Ebelke, John F., jt. auth. see Homberger, Conrad P.

Ebenstein, W. & Fogelman, E. Today's Isms. 8th ed. 1980. 18.95 (ISBN 0-13-924399-2); pap. 13.95 (ISBN 0-13-924381-X). P-H.

Eber, Christine E. Just Momma & Me. LC 75-30308. (Illus.). 40p. (Orig.). (ps-3). 1975. pap. 3.25 (ISBN 0-914996-09-6). Lollipop Power.

Eber, Dorothy, ed. see Pitseolak, Peter.

Eber, Jose. Shake Your Head, Darling. LC 82-50639. (Illus.). 208p. (Orig.). 1983. 17.50 (ISBN 0-446-51250-8). Warner Bks.

Eber, Victor I. Up Your Equity: Build up Your Personal Net Worth. LC 72-95079. (Illus.). 9.95 (ISBN 0-686-05084-3). Financial Pr.

Eberhard, Wolfram. China's Minorities: Yesterday & Today. 192p. 1982. pap. text ed. 8.95x (ISBN 0-534-01080-6). Wadsworth Pub.

--A History of China. rev.,4th ed. LC 76-7758. 1977. 30.00x (ISBN 0-520-03227-6); pap. 8.95x (ISBN 0-520-03268-3). U of Cal Pr.

--Life & Thought of Ordinary Chinese: Collected Essays. (East Asian Folklore & Social Life Monographs: Vol. 106). 230p. 1982. 18.00 (ISBN 0-89986-337-X). Oriental Bk Store.

--Studies in Chinese Folklore & Related Essays. (Folklore Monographs Ser: Vol. 23). 1970. pap. text ed. 12.00x o.p. (ISBN 0-87750-147-5). Res Ctr Lang Semiotic.

Eberhardt, Isabelle. The Oblivion Seekers & Other Writings. Bowles, Paul, tr. from Fr. LC 75-12962. (Illus.). 88p. (Orig.). 1975. pap. 3.50 (ISBN 0-87286-082-5). City Lights.

Eberhardt, Lorraine, jt. auth. see Sanborn, Laura.

Eberhardt, Louise. A Woman's Journey, Vol. I. 1976. pap. 7.00 (ISBN 0-934698-00-7). New Comm Pr.

--A Woman's Journey, Vol. II. 1978. pap. 7.00 (ISBN 0-934698-01-5). New Comm Pr.

Eberhart, Dikkon. Paradise. 256p. (YA) 1983. 14.50 (ISBN 0-916144-52-6). Stemmer Hse.

Eberhart, George M., compiled By. A Geo-Bibliography of Anomalies: Primary Access to Observations of UFOs, Ghosts, & Other Mysterious Phenomena. LC 79-6183. xl, 1114p. 1980. lib. bdg. 65.00 (ISBN 0-313-21337-2, EBA/). Greenwood.

Eberhart, Mignon. Another Man's Murder. 160p. 1983. pap. 2.50 (ISBN 0-446-31180-4). Warner Bks.

--Postmark Murder. 208p. 1983. pap. 2.50 (ISBN 0-446-31181-2). Warner Bks.

Eberhart, Mignon G. Next of Kin: A Suspense Novel. 1982. 10.50 (ISBN 0-394-52433-0). Random.

Eberhart, Perry. Treasure Tales of the Rockies. 3rd ed. LC 82-72080. (Illus.). 315p. 1969. 14.95 (ISBN 0-8040-0295-9). Swallow.

Eberhart, Perry & Schmuck, Philip. Fourteeners: Colorado's Great Mountains. LC 82-70761. (Illus.). 128p. 1970. 15.00 (ISBN 0-8040-0122-7, SB); pap. 8.95 (ISBN 0-8040-0123-5, SB). Swallow.

Eberhart, Philip. Guide to the Colorado Ghost Towns & Mining Camps. 4th ed. LC 82-70860. (Illus.). 496p. 1969. pap. 13.95 (ISBN 0-8040-0140-5). Swallow.

Eberhart, Richard. Ways of Light. 1980. pap. 15.95 (ISBN 0-19-502737-X). Oxford U Pr.

Eberhart, Richard & Rodman, Selden, eds. War & the Poet. LC 73-19574. 240p. 1974. Repr. of 1945 ed. lib. bdg. 17.25x (ISBN 0-8371-7287-X, EBWP). Greenwood.

Eberhart, Stephen, tr. see Adams, George.

Eberle, Bob. Chip In. (gr. 3-8). 1982. 7.95 (ISBN 0-86653-050-9, GA 416). Good Apple.

Eberle, Gerda. Studien und Berufsberatung Aus der Sicht Von Maturanden. 236p. (Ger.). 1982. write for info. (ISBN 3-261-05022-5). P Lang Pubs.

Eberle, Irmengarde. Koalas Live Here. LC 67-17779. (gr. 1-3). 1967. 9.95 o.p. (ISBN 0-385-08719-5). Doubleday.

Eberle, Jean F. The Incredible Owen Girls. (YA) 1977. pap. 4.50 (ISBN 0-932114-00-8). Boars Head.

Eberle, Luke, tr. see Heufelder, Emmanuel.

Eberle, Paul see Swan Egan De Butz, pseud.

Eberle, Sarah. What Is Love? Sparks, Judith, ed. (A Happy Day Book). (Illus.). 24p. (Orig.). (gr. k-2). 1980. 1.29 (ISBN 0-87239-410-7, 3642). Standard Pub.

Eberlein, H. D. & Van Dyke Hubbard, Cortlandt. American Georgian Architecture. LC 76-22726. (Architecture & Decorative Arts Ser.). (Illus.). 1976. Repr. of 1952 ed. 32.50 (ISBN 0-306-70796-9). Da Capo.

Eberly, David. What Has Been Lost. 1982. pap. 4.95 (ISBN 0-914852-10-8). Good Gay.

Eberly, J. H., jt. auth. see Allen, A.

Ebershoff-Coles, Susan & Leibenguth, Charla, eds. Motorsports: A Guide to Information Sources. LC 79-13736. (Sports, Games, & Pastimes Information Guide Ser.: Vol. 5). 1979. 42.00x (ISBN 0-8103-1446-0). Gale.

Ebersole, Frank B. Language & Perception: Essays in the Philosophy of Language. LC 79-88305. 1979. pap. text ed. 12.25 (ISBN 0-8191-0776-X). U Pr of Amer.

--Meaning & Saying: Essays in the Philosophy of Language. LC 79-88304. 1979. pap. text ed. 11.25 (ISBN 0-8191-0775-1). U Pr of Amer.

Ebersole, Priscilla & Hess, Patricia. Toward Healthy Aging: Human Needs & Nursing Response. LC 80-26668. (Illus.). 697p. 1981. text ed. 23.95 (ISBN 0-8016-1491-0). Mosby.

Ebersole, Priscilla, jt. auth. see Burnside, Irene.

Eberstadt, Isabel. Natural Victims. LC 82-48730. 1983. 14.95 (ISBN 0-394-52951-0). Knopf.

Eberstein, Arthur, jt. auth. see Goodgold, Joseph.

Ebert, Alan & Rotchstein, Janice. Traditions. 1983. pap. 3.95 (ISBN 0-671-22838-2). Bantam.

Ebert, Friedrich A. General Bibliographical Dictionary, 4 vols. LC 68-19956. 1968. Repr. of 1837 ed. 191.00x (ISBN 0-8103-3304-X). Gale.

Ebert, H., et al, eds. Radiation Protection Optimization-Present Experience & Methods: Proceedings of the European Scientific Seminar, Luxembourg, Oct. 1979. LC 80-41671. (Illus.). 330p. 1981. 50.00 (ISBN 0-08-027291-6). Pergamon.

Ebert, Hilmar, jt. auth. see Dickins, Anthony S.

Ebert, M. & Howard, A., eds. Current Topics in Radiation Research, Vols. 1-8. 1965. Vol. 1. 24.50 (ISBN 0-444-10179-9, North-Holland); Vol. 2. 35.00 (ISBN 0-444-10180-2); Vol. 3. 27.75 (ISBN 0-444-10181-0); Vol. 4. 40.75 (ISBN 0-7204-4154-4); Vol. 5. 35.00 (ISBN 0-444-10183-7); Vol. 6. 43.25 (ISBN 0-444-10184-5); Vol. 7. 51.75 (ISBN 0-444-10599-9); Vol. 8. 51.75 (ISBN 0-7204-4158-7). Elsevier.

--Current Topics in Radiation Research, Vol. 11. 1979. 85.00 (ISBN 0-444-85183-6, North Holland). Elsevier.

--Current Topics in Radiation Research, Vol. 13. 1978. 55.50 (ISBN 0-444-85164-X, North-Holland). Elsevier.

Ebert, Paul A. see Zuidema, G. D. & Skinner, D. B.

Ebert, Richard. Lawrence of Arabia. LC 78-31450. (Raintree Great Adventures). (Illus.). (gr. 3-6). 1979. PLB 12.85 (ISBN 0-8393-0150-2). Raintree Pubs.

Ebert, Robert, ed. Northwest Energy Resource Manual. (Illus.). 96p. 1983. pap. 3.95 (ISBN 0-942886-01-1). Periwinkle Pubns.

--Solar Design: A Handbook for Solar Homebuilders. 1983. pap. write for info. (ISBN 0-942886-02-X). Periwinkle Pubns.

--Solar Home Plan Book. 1983. pap. 3.95 (ISBN 0-942886-03-8). Periwinkle Pubns.

Eberwein, Jane D. Early American Poetry: Bradstreet, Taylor, Dwight, Freneau & Bryant. LC 77-91051. 398p. 1978. 25.00 (ISBN 0-299-07440-4); pap. 12.50 (ISBN 0-299-07444-7). U of Wis Pr.

Ebihara, May & Gianutsos, Rosamond, eds. Papers in Anthropology & Linguistics. (Annals of the New York Academy of Sciences: Vol. 318). (Orig.). 1978. pap. 21.00x (ISBN 0-89072-077-0). NY Acad Sci.

Ebin, D. G., jt. auth. see Cheeger, J.

Ebinger, Charles & Center for Strategic & International Studies. The Critical Link: Energy & National Security. 296p. 1982. prof ref 29.75x (ISBN 0-88410-645-4). Ballinger Pub.

Ebison, Maurice, ed. see Mackay, Alan L.

Eble, Kenneth. F. Scott Fitzgerald. rev ed. (United States Authors Ser.). 1977. lib. bdg. 9.95 (ISBN 0-8057-7183-2, Twayne). G K Hall.

--William Dean Howells. 2nd ed. (United States Authors Ser.). 1982. lib. bdg. 13.95 (ISBN 0-8057-7372-X, Twayne). G K Hall.

Ebner, James H. God Present As Mystery: A Search for Personal Meaning in Contemporary Theology. LC 76-13750. 1976. pap. 5.95 (ISBN 0-88489-084-8). St Marys.

Ebon, M. Psychic Warfare: Threat of Illusion? 304p. 1983. 15.95 (ISBN 0-07-018860-2). McGraw.

Ebon, Martin. Cloning of Man: A Brave New Hope--or Horror? (Orig.). 1978. pap. 1.95 o.p. (ISBN 0-451-08526-4, J8526, Sig). NAL.

--Demon Children. (Orig.). 1978. pap. 1.75 o.p. (ISBN 0-451-07986-8, E7986, Sig). NAL.

--The Evidence for Life After Death. (Orig.). 1977. pap. 1.50 o.p. (ISBN 0-451-07543-9, W7543, Sig). NAL.

--The Signet Handbook of Parapsychology. (Orig.). 1978. pap. 2.95 (ISBN 0-451-09500-6, E9500, Sig). NAL.

--Test Your ESP. 1971. pap. 1.95 (ISBN 0-451-11297-0, AJ1297, Sig). NAL.

Ebon, Martin, ed. The Amazing Uri Geller. (Orig.). 1975. pap. 1.50 o.p. (ISBN 0-451-06475-5, W6475, Sig). NAL.

--Exorcism: Fact Not Fiction. pap. 1.25 o.p. (ISBN 0-451-05701-5, Y5701, Sig). NAL.

--Mysterious Pyramid Power. 1976. pap. 1.75 o.p. (ISBN 0-451-08110-2, E8110, Sig). NAL.

--The Riddle of the Bermuda Triangle. (Orig.). 1975. pap. 1.75 o.p. (ISBN 0-451-08261-3, E8063, Sig.). NAL.

--True Experiences with Ghosts. Date not set. pap. 1.50 o.p. (ISBN 0-451-09622-3, W9622, Sig). NAL.

Ebrey, Patricia B. The Aristocratic Families of Early Imperial China. LC 76-40836. (Cambridge Studies in Chinese History, Literature & Institutions). (Illus.). 1978. 32.50 (ISBN 0-521-21484-X). Cambridge U Pr.

Ebsworth, E. A., et al, eds. New Pathways in Inorganic Chemistry. (Illus.). 1969. 49.50 (ISBN 0-521-07254-9, 68-26984). Cambridge U Pr.

Eby, Cecil D., Jr. Porte Crayon: The Life of David Hunter Strother. LC 72-11235. (Illus.). 258p. 1973. Repr. of 1960 ed. lib. bdg. 15.00x o.p. (ISBN 0-8371-6638-1, EBPC). Greenwood.

Eby, Ray. Bakers Bible Atlas Study Guide. 1977. 4.60 (ISBN 0-686-25535-6); test 1.55 (ISBN 0-686-31725-4); map 1.55 (ISBN 0-686-31726-2). Rod & Staff.

Eby, Richard E. The Amazing Lamb of God: Bedtime Stories to be Read to Children. (Illus.). 160p. 1983. 12.95 (ISBN 0-8007-1336-2). Revell.

--Tell Them I Am Coming. 1980. pap. 4.95 (ISBN 0-8007-5045-4, Power Bks). Revell.

Eca de Queiroz. The Illustrious House of Ramires. Stevens, Ann, tr. from Port. LC 68-29766. 310p. (Port). 1969. 15.00x (ISBN 0-8214-0044-4, 82-80489). Ohio U Pr.

Eccles. The Inhibitory Pathways of the Central Nervous System. 140p. 1982. 50.00x (ISBN 0-85323-050-1, Pub. by Liverpool Univ England). State Mutual Bk.

Eccles, George S. The Politics of Banking. Hyman, Sidney, ed. 320p. 1982. 20.00 (ISBN 0-87480-208-3); pap. 13.00 (ISBN 0-87480-209-1). U of Utah Pr.

Eccles, John, ed. Mind & Brain: The Many-Faceted Problems. (Illus.). 370p. 1982. 24.95 (ISBN 0-89226-016-5). ICF Pr.

Eccles, John C. The Understanding of the Brain. 2nd ed. (Illus.). 1976. pap. text ed. 14.50 (ISBN 0-07-018865-3, HP). McGraw.

Eccles, John C. & Schade, J. P. Physiology of Spinal Neurons. (Progress in Brain Research: Vol. 12). 1964. 61.00 o.p. (ISBN 0-444-40187-3). Elsevier.

Eccles, M. J. & Sim, M. E. Low Light Level Detectors in Astronomy. LC 82-12881. (Cambridge Astrophysics Ser.: No. 3). (Illus.). 200p. Date not set. price not set (ISBN 0-521-24088-3). Cambridge U Pr.

Eccles, Mark, ed. see Shakespeare, William.

Eccles, Marriner S. Economic Balance & a Balanced Budget. LC 72-2367. (FDR & the Era of the New Deal Ser). 328p. 1973. Repr. of 1940 ed. lib. bdg. 39.50 (ISBN 0-306-70479-X). Da Capo.

Eccles, Robert G., jt. auth. see Schlesinger, Leonard.

Eccles, W. J. Canadian Frontier, 1534-1821. LC 70-81783. (Histories of the American Frontier Ser.). (Illus.). 234p. 1974. pap. 9.95x (ISBN 0-8263-0311-0). U of NM Pr.

Ecclestone, Alan. The Night Sky of the Lord. LC 82-5514. 240p. 1982. 14.95 (ISBN 0-8052-3810-7). Schocken.

Echard, William E. Napoleon III & the Concert of Europe. LC 82-12660. 325p. 1983. text ed. 32.50x (ISBN 0-8071-1056-6). La State U Pr.

Echau, Robustiano. Sketches of the Island of Negros. Hart, Donn V., tr. LC 78-13403. (Papers in International Series: Southeast Asia: No. 50). (Illus.). 1978. pap. 10.00x (ISBN 0-89680-070-9, Ohio U Ctr Intl). Ohio U Pr.

Echeruo, Michael. Joyce Cary & the Novel of Africa. LC 72-76609. 200p. 1973. text ed. 19.50x (ISBN 0-8419-0131-7, Africana). Holmes & Meier.

Echols, John M. & Shadily, Hassan. An English-Indonesian Dictionary. LC 72-5638. 660p. 1975. 49.50x (ISBN 0-8014-0728-1); softcover 25.00x (ISBN 0-8014-9859-7). Cornell U Pr.

Echols, John M., ed. & tr. see Teselkin, A. S.

Eck, B. Fans: Design & Operation of Centrifugal, Axial Flow & Cross Flow Fans. LC 72-137613. 612p. 1974. 115.00 o.s.i. (ISBN 0-08-015872-2); write for info. xerox copyflo avail. Pergamon.

Eck, Diana L. Darsan: Seeing the Divine Image in India. 64p. 1981. pap. 3.00 (ISBN 0-89012-024-2). Anima Pubns.

Eck, Ellen, tr. from Eng. Himnos de la Vida Cristiana. 1980. words only 3.25 (ISBN 0-87509-277-2); pap. 3.25 (ISBN 0-87509-275-6); words & music 4.50. Chr Pubns.

Eck, G. H. van, Jr. Handboek der Nederlandsche Muziekliteratuur, 2 pts. in 1. (Dictionarium Musicum Ser.: Vol. 4). 1978. Repr. of 1890 ed. Set. 45.00 o.s.i. (ISBN 90-6027-218-8, Pub. by Frits Knuf Netherlands); Set. wrappers 30.00 o.s.i. (ISBN 90-6027-217-X, Pub. by Frits Knuf Netherlands). Pendragon NY.

Eck, Laurence, jt. auth. see Buzzard, Lynn.

Eckardt, A. R., ed. Your People, My People: The Meeting of Jews & Christians. 212p. 7.95 (ISBN 0-686-95188-3). ADL.

Eckardt, A. Roy. Elder & Younger Brothers: The Encounter of Jews & Christians. LC 67-23687. (Illus.). 216p. 1973. pap. 4.95 (ISBN 0-8052-0379-6). Schocken.

Eckardt, A. Roy & Eckardt, Alice L. Long Night's Journey into Day - Life & Faith After the Holocaust. LC 81-14788. 206p. 1982. 16.50 (ISBN 0-8143-1692-1). Wayne St U Pr.

Eckardt, Alice L., jt. auth. see Eckardt, A. Roy.

Eckardt, F. E., ed. see Symposium on Functioning of Terrestrial Ecosystems at Primary Production Level, Copenhagen, 1968.

Eckardt, Wolf Von see Von Eckardt, Wolf.

Eckart, Richard, ed. Letters of Hans Von Bulow. Waller, Hannah, tr. LC 72-183503. 434p. Date not set. Repr. of 1931 ed. price not set. Vienna Hse.

Eckblad, Edith. God Listens & Knows. (Illus.). pap. 3.50 (ISBN 0-686-73866-7, 10-258). Augsburg.

Eckbo, Garrett. Art of Home Landscaping. 1956. 16.95 o.p. (ISBN 0-07-018878-5, P&RB). McGraw.

--Home Landscape: The Art of Home Landscaping. rev. & enl. ed. (Illus.). 1978. 24.95 (ISBN 0-07-018879-3, P&RB). McGraw.

--Landscape We See. 1967. 28.50 o.p. (ISBN 0-07-018882-3, P&RB). McGraw.

--Urban Landscape Design. (Illus.). 1964. 41.50 (ISBN 0-07-018880-7, P&RB). McGraw.

Eckbo, Paul L. The Future of World Oil. LC 76-16809. 160p. 1976. prof ref 25.00x (ISBN 0-88410-455-9). Ballinger Pub.

Ecke, Gustav. Chinese Painting in Hawaii: In the Honolulu Academy of Arts & in Private Collections, 3 vols. 1965. Set. boxed 250.00 (ISBN 0-87022-205-8). UH Pr.

Ecke, Tseng Yu-Ho. Chinese Folk Art. (Illus.). 1977. pap. text ed. 14.00x (ISBN 0-8248-0572-0). UH Pr.

Ecke, Wolfgang. The Castle of the Red Gorillas. (Illus.). 96p. (gr. 5 up). 1983. 8.95 (ISBN 0-13-120360-6). P-H.

Eckel, Edwin B. The Geographical Society of America: Life History of a Learned Society. LC 82-15412. (Memoir Ser.: No. 155). (Illus.). 1982. 24.50x (ISBN 0-8137-1155-X). Geol Soc.

Eckel, Lorelei & Schoyer, Maxine. One Thousand-One Broadways: Hometown Talent on Stage. 160p. 1982. 12.95 (ISBN 0-686-83955-2). Iowa St U Pr.

Eckelman, W. C., ed. Technetium Ninety-nine-M: Generators, Chemistry, & Preparation of Radiopharmaceuticals. (Illus.). 168p. 1983. 25.00 (ISBN 0-08-029144-9). Pergamon.

Eckenfelder, W. W., Jr., jt. ed. see Wanielista, Martin P.

Eckenrode, Hamilton J. Separation of Church & State in Virginia. LC 75-122164. (Civil Liberties in American History Ser). 1971. Repr. of 1910 ed. lib. bdg. 22.50 (ISBN 0-306-71969-X). Da Capo.

Eckenstein, Lina. Comparative Studies in Nursery Rhymes. LC 68-23469. 1968. Repr. of 1906 ed. 30.00x (ISBN 0-8103-3479-8). Gale.

--Spell of Words: Studies in Language Bearing on Custom. LC 68-23153. 1969. Repr. of 1932 ed. 30.00x (ISBN 0-8103-3892-0). Gale.

Ecker, B. A. Independence Day. 208p. pap. 2.25 (ISBN 0-380-82990-8, Flare). Avon.

Ecker, Martin. Radiation & All You Need to Know about It. 1981. 4.95x (ISBN 0-394-74650-3). Cancer Control Soc.

Ecker, Tom & Calloway, Bill. Athletic Journal's Encyclopedia of Football. (Illus.). 1978. 12.95 o.p. (ISBN 0-13-050047-X, Parker). P-H.

Eckermann, R., ed. see Gmehling, J., et al.

Eckermann, R., ed. see Gmehling, J. & Onken, U.

Eckermann, R., ed. see Knapp, H. & Doring, R.

Eckermann, R., ed. see Sorensen, J. M. & Arlt, W.

Eckermann, Reiner, ed. see Gmehling, J., et al.

Eckermann, Reiner, ed. see Sorenson, J. M. & Arlt, W.

Eckert, Allan. Whattizit? Nature Pun Quizzes. (Illus.). 48p. (Orig.). 1981. pap. 2.95 (ISBN 0-913428-30-2). Landfall Pr.

Eckert, Allan W. Gateway to Empire. 1982. 20.00 (ISBN 0-316-20861-2). Little.

--Song of the Wild. 252p. 1980. 10.95 (ISBN 0-316-20877-9). Little.

Eckert, Allan W., jt. auth. see Karalus, Karl E.

Eckert, Ernest R. & Drake, R. M. Analysis of Heat & Mass Transfer. LC 73-159305. (Mechanical Engineering Ser). (Illus.). 832p. 1971. text ed. 46.50 (ISBN 0-07-018925-0, C). McGraw.

Eckert, Ernest R. & Goldstein, Richard J., eds. Measurement in Heat Transfer. (McGraw-Hill Hemisphere Series in Thermal & Fluids Engineering). (Illus.). 1976. text ed. 33.95 o.p. (ISBN 0-07-018926-9, C). McGraw.

Eckert, Helen M., jt. auth. see Espenschade, Anna S.

Eckert, John E. & Shaw, Frank R. Beekeeping. (Illus.). 1960. 19.95 (ISBN 0-02-534910-4). Macmillan.

Eckert, Sidney W., jt. auth. see Garman, E. Thomas.

Eckert, William G. Introduction to Forensic Sciences. LC 80-10864. (Illus.). 240p. 1980. pap. text ed. 13.95 (ISBN 0-8016-1489-9). Mosby.

Eckhardt, Caroline D. & Stewart, David H. The Wiley Reader: Designs for Writing. brief ed. LC 78-15326. 1979. pap. 12.50x (ISBN 0-673-15669-9). Scott F.

Eckhardt, Caroline D., ed. The Phopheta Merlini of Geoffrey of Monmouth: A Fifteenth-Century English Commentary. 1983. 12.50X (ISBN 0-910956-73-1); pap. 5.00x (ISBN 0-910956-74-X). Medieval Acad.

Eckhardt, Caroline D., et al. The Wiley Reader: Designs for Writing. LC 75-29499. 592p. 1976. 14.50x (ISBN 0-673-15668-0). Scott F.

Eckhardt, Robert B. The Study of Human Evolution. (Illus.). 1979. text ed. 28.00 (ISBN 0-07-018902-1, C). McGraw.

Eckhart, J., ed. Sepsis unter besonderer Beruecksichtigung der Ernaehrungsprobleme. (Beitraege zu Infusionstherapie und klinische Ernaehrung: Vol. 10). (Illus.). viii, 200p. 1983. pap. 30.00 (ISBN 3-8055-3677-1). S Karger.

Eckhart, Wolfgang. Der Boden Als Anlargeobjekt und Produktionsfaktor. 173p. (Ger.). 1982. write for info. (ISBN 3-8204-7222-3). P Lang Pubs.

Eckhaus, W. Asymptotic Analysis of Singular Perturbations. (Studies in Mathematics & Its Applications: Vol. 9). 286p. 1979. 55.50 (ISBN 0-686-65900-7, North Holland). Elsevier.

Eckhaus, W. & Van Harten, A. The Inverse Scattering Transformation & the Theory of Solitons: An Introduction. (North Holland Mathematics Studies: Vol. 50). 1981. 40.50 (ISBN 0-444-86166-1). Elsevier.

Eckhaus, W., jt. auth. see Scheveningen Conference on Differential Equations, 2nd, the Netherlands, 1975.

Eckhaus, W. & De Jager, E. M., eds. Theory & Applications of Singular Perturbations, Oberwolfach, Germany 1981: Proceedings. (Lecture Note in Mathematics: Vol. 942). 372p. 1982. pap. 18.50 (ISBN 0-387-11584-6). Springer-Verlag.

Eckhaus, Wiktor. Matched Asymptotic Expansions & Singular Perturbations. LC 72-96145. (Mathematics Studies: Vol. 6). 146p. 1973. pap. text ed. 32.00 (ISBN 0-444-10438-0, North-Holland). Elsevier.

Eckholm, Erik P. The Picture of Health: Environmental Sources of Disease. 1977. 9.95 o.p. (ISBN 0-393-06434-4); pap. 5.95 (ISBN 0-393-06440-9). Norton.

Eckhouse, Moe. Day-by-Day in Cleveland Indians History. LC 82-83939. (Illus.). 300p. (Orig.). 1983. pap. 9.95 (ISBN 0-88011-107-0). Leisure Pr.

Eckhouse, Morris, jt. auth. see Graeff, Burt.

Eckhouse, Richard H., Jr. & Morrison, L. Robert. Minicomputer Systems: Organization, Programming & Applications (PDP-11) 2nd ed. (Illus.). 1979. text ed. 30.00 (ISBN 0-13-583914-9). P-H.

Ecklein, J. L. & Lauffer, A. Community Organizers & Social Planners: A Volume of Cases & Illustrative Materials. LC 75-171912. (Community Organization Ser.). 378p. 1972. pap. 21.95x (ISBN 0-471-22980-6). Wiley.

Eckles, Clarence H., et al. Milk & Milk Products. 4th ed. (Agricultural Sciences Ser). (Illus.). 1951. text ed. 19.95 o.p. (ISBN 0-07-018959-5, C). McGraw.

Eckles, Robert W. & Carmichael, Ronald L. Supervisory Management. 2nd ed. LC 80-21684. (Management Ser.). 524p. 1981. text ed. 24.95 (ISBN 0-471-05947-1). Wiley.

--Supervisory Management: A Short Course in Supervision. 2nd ed. LC 82-17553. (Professional Development Programs Ser.). 288p. 1983. text ed. 55.95 (ISBN 0-471-87492-2). Wiley.

Eckles, Robert W., et al. Supervisory Management: A Short Course in Supervision. LC 74-31815. (Professional Development Programs). 293p. 1975. 49.95x (ISBN 0-471-23005-7). Wiley.

--Essentials of Management for First-Line Supervision. LC 73-17037. 642p. 1974. text ed. 23.95 o.p. (ISBN 0-471-23000-6, Pub. by Wiley Hamilton). Wiley.

Eckley, Grace. Benedict Kiely. (English Authors Ser.). lib. bdg. 14.95 (ISBN 0-8057-1304-2, Twayne). G K Hall.

--Finley Peter Dunne. (United States Authors Ser.). 1981. lib. bdg. 11.95 (ISBN 0-8057-7295-2, Twayne). G K Hall.

Eckley, Mary & Norton, Mary J. McCall's Cooking School. 1982. pap. 7.95 (ISBN 0-394-73281-2). Random.

Eckley, Mary, ed. see McCall's Food Staff.

Eckley, Wilton. Harriette Arnow. (United States Authors Ser.). 1974. lib. bdg. 13.95 (ISBN 0-8057-0023-4, Twayne). G K Hall.

--Herbert Hoover. (United States Authors Ser.). 1980. lib. bdg. 12.95 (ISBN 0-8057-7285-5, Twayne). G K Hall.

--T. S. Stribling. LC 75-1096. (United States Authors Ser.). 1975. lib. bdg. 13.95 (ISBN 0-8057-7151-4, Twayne). G K Hall.

Eckman, Fred R., ed. Current Themes in Linguistics: Bilingualism, Experimental Linguistics, & Language Typologies. LC 77-5934. 277p. 1977. 19.95x o.s.i. (ISBN 0-470-99171-2). Halsted Pr.

Eckman, Fred R. & Hastings, Ashley, eds. Studies in First & Second Language Acquisition. 1979. pap. text ed. 14.95 (ISBN 0-88377-119-5). Newbury Hse.

Eckmann, M., jt. auth. see Jeger, M.

Eckols, Steve. Report Writer. Oppliger, Jeannie, ed. LC 80-82868. (Illus.). 106p. (Orig.). 1980. pap. text ed. 13.50 (ISBN 0-911625-07-0). M Murach & Assoc.

Eckols, Steve, ed. see Clary, Wayne.

Eckols, Steve, ed. see Lowe, Doug.

Eckschlager, Karel & Stepanek, Vladimir. Information Theory As Applied to Chemical Analysis. LC 79-1405. (A Series of Monographs on Analytical Chemistry & Its Applications: Vol. 53). 1979. 32.50 (ISBN 0-471-04945-X, Pub. by Wiley-Interscience). Wiley.

Eckstein, A. China's Economic Revolution. LC 76-9176. (Illus.). 1977. 54.50 (ISBN 0-521-21283-9); pap. 14.95 (ISBN 0-521-29189-5). Cambridge U Pr.

Eckstein, Artis A. How to Make Treasures from Trash. (Illus.). 1972. 8.95 (ISBN 0-8208-0348-0). Hearthside.

Eckstein, Daniel G., jt. auth. see Baruth, Leroy G.

Eckstein, Everett E. Sunrise on the Mohican. (Illus.). 64p. 1982. 6.00 (ISBN 0-682-49918-8). Exposition.

Eckstein, Harry & Gurr, Ted R. Patterns of Authority: A Structural Basis for Political Inquiry. LC 75-19003. (Comparative Studies in Behavioral Science Ser). 488p. 1975. 31.95 o.p. (ISBN 0-471-23076-6, Pub. by Wiley-Interscience). Wiley.

Eckstein, J. & Gleit, J. The Best Joke Book for Kids. (Illus.). (gr. 7-12). 1977. pap. 1.95 (ISBN 0-380-01734-2, 82032-3, Camelot). Avon.

Eckstein, Jerome. Platonic Method: An Interpretation of the Dramatic-Philosophic Aspects of the Meno. LC 68-58747. 1968. lib. bdg. 25.00 (ISBN 0-8371-1499-3, ECP/). Greenwood.

Eckstein, O. Parameters & Policies in the U. S. Economy. (Data Resources Ser.: Vol. 2). 1976. 59.75 (ISBN 0-444-10939-0, North-Holland). Elsevier.

Eckstein, Otto. Core Inflation. (Illus.). 128p. 1981. 14.95 (ISBN 0-13-172643-9); pap. 10.95 (ISBN 0-13-172635-8). P-H.

Eckstein, Peter, jt. auth. see Sichel, Werner.

Eckstein, Shlomo. Land Reform in Latin America: Bolivia, Chile, Mexico, Peru & Venezuela. (Working Paper: No. 275). v, 187p. 1978. 5.00 (ISBN 0-686-36069-9, WP-O275). World Bank.

Eckstorm, Fanny. Minstrelsy of Maine. LC 79-152248. 1971. Repr. of 1927 ed. 37.00x (ISBN 0-8103-3707-X). Gale.

Eckstrom, Jack D. Time of the Hedrons. (YA) 6.95 (ISBN 0-685-07461-7, Avalon). Bouregy.

Eckstrom, Lawrence J. Licensing in Foreign & Domestic Operations, 3 vols. rev. ed. LC 58-13380. 1980. looseleaf in post binders pages 210.00 (ISBN 0-87632-075-2). Boardman.

Eclov, Lee. The Church: Pictures of Christ's Body. (Fisherman Bible Studyguides). 64p. 1981. saddle stitched 2.50 (ISBN 0-87788-155-3). Shaw Pubs.

Eco, Umberto. Looking for a Logic of Culture. (Orig.). 1975. pap. 1.00x o.p. (ISBN 90-316-0012-1). Humanities.

--The Name of the Rose. Weaver, William, tr. 512p. 15.95 (ISBN 0-15-144647-4). HarBraceJ.

Ecodyne Corporation. Weather Data Handbook. Orig. Title: Evaluated Weather Data for Cooling Equipment Design. 320p. 1980. 37.50 (ISBN 0-07-018960-9, P&RB). McGraw.

Ecole Biblique et Archeologique Francaise. Jerusalem. Catalogue De la Bibliotheque De L'ecole Biblique et Archeologique Francaise (Catalog of the Library of the French Biblical & Archaeological School, 13 vols. 1975. lib. bdg. 1350.00 (ISBN 0-8161-1154-5, Hall Library). G K Hall.

Ecole Freudienne, jt. auth. see Lacan, Jacques.

Ecological Analysts. The Sources Chemistry Fate & Effects of Chromium in Aquatic Environments. LC 82-71261. (Orig.). 1982. pap. 8.10 (ISBN 0-89364-046-8, 847-89600). Am Petroleum.

Economic & Foreign Affairs Research Association (Tokyo), ed. Statistical Survey of Japan's Economy, 1982. LC 54-43626. (Illus.). 83p. (Orig.). 1982. pap. 20.00x (ISBN 0-8002-3040-X). Intl Pubns Serv.

Economic & Social Committee of the European Communities - General Secretariat, ed. Community Advisory Committees for the Representation of Socio-Economic Interest. 240p. 1980. text ed. 24.75x (ISBN 0-566-00328-7). Gower Pub Ltd.

Economic & Social Committee of the European Community, General Secretariat. European Interest Groups & Their Relationship to the Economic & Social Committee. 464p. 1980. text ed. 74.50x (ISBN 0-566-00365-1). Gower Pub Ltd.

Economic Behavior Program Staff see Morgan, James N.

Economic Information Systems, ed. The Second Fifteen Hundred Companies, 1982. LC 82-73379. 325p. 1982. 120.00 (ISBN 0-86692-016-1). Econ Info Syst.

--The Top Fifteen Hundred Companies, 1982. LC 82-73380. 350p. 1982. 120.00 (ISBN 0-86692-015-3). Econ Info Syst.

--Top Fifteen Hundred Private Companies, 1982. LC 82-73381. 350p. 1982. 120.00 o.p. (ISBN 0-86692-017-X). Econ Info Syst.

--Zip Code Business Patterns, 1982. LC 82-73378. 546p. 1982. 140.00 (ISBN 0-86692-018-8). Econ Info Syst.

Economics & National Security Council. Strategic Minerals: A Resource Crisis. (Illus.). 105p. 1980. pap. text ed. 5.95x (ISBN 0-87855-913-2). Transaction Bks.

Economics & Research Division of the National Association of Realtors, jt. auth. see Society of Industrial Realtors.

Economos, Paul. Seventh Sense. (Illus.). 24p. 1981. pap. 3.00 (ISBN 0-932662-36-6). St Andrews NC.

Economou, George. Ameriki: Book One, & Selected Earlier Poems. LC 77-3612. 1977. pap. 5.00 (ISBN 0-915342-20-0). SUN.

Economy, James, ed. New & Specialty Fibers. (Applied Polymer Symposia: No. 29). 1976. 24.00 o.p. (ISBN 0-471-02302-7, Pub. by Wiley-Interscience). Wiley.

Ecorcheville, Jules A., ed. Catalogue du Fonds de Musique Ancienne de la Bibliotheque Nationale, 8 vols. in 4. LC 79-166103. (Music Ser). (Illus.). 1973. Repr. of 1914 ed. Set. lib. bdg. 195.00 (ISBN 0-306-70280-0). Da Capo.

Ecroyd, Donald & Wagner, Hilda S. Communicate Through Oral Reading. 1979. pap. text ed. 17.50x (ISBN 0-07-018970-6). McGraw.

Ecroyd, Donald H., et al. Voice & Articulation: A Handbook. 1966. pap. 9.95x (ISBN 0-673-05722-4). Scott F.

--Voice & Articulation: Programmed Instruction. 1966. pap. 9.95x (ISBN 0-673-05720-8). Scott F.

Ed Dufresne Ministries. Praying God's Word. 1979. pap. 1.50 (ISBN 0-89274-126-0). Harrison Hse.

Edades, Jean, jt. auth. see Hashimoto, Yasuko.

Edberg, E., jt. auth. see Duttarer, Janet.

Edding, Friedrich & Berstecher, Dieter. International Developments of Educational Expenditure, 1950-1965. (Statistical Reports & Studies, No. 14). (Illus., Orig.). 1970. pap. 4.00 o.p. (ISBN 92-3-100766-1, U322, UNESCO). Unipub.

Eddingfield, June. The Gate & the Lamp. Ranck, Joyce H., ed. 108p. 1982. pap. 4.95 (ISBN 0-9606006-1-2). Ranck.

Eddington, Arthur. Nature of the Physical World. 1958. pap. 4.95 o.p. (ISBN 0-472-06015-5, 15, AA). U of Mich Pr.

Eddington, Arthur S. The Mathematical Theory of Relativity. 3rd ed. LC 74-1458. ix, 270p. 1975. text ed. 13.95 (ISBN 0-8284-0278-7). Chelsea Pub.

--Space, Time & Gravitation. 27.95 (ISBN 0-521-04865-6). Cambridge U Pr.

Eddington, Thomas. Contemporary Artistic & the Metaphysics of the Art Expression. (An Essential Knowledge Library Bk.). (Illus.). 137p. 1983. 43.55 (ISBN 0-86650-051-0). Gloucester Art.

Eddins, John M., jt. auth. see Peters, G. David.

Eddison, E. R., tr. Egil's Saga, Skallagrimssonar: Done into English Out of the Icelandic. LC 69-10087. Repr. of 1930 ed. lib. bdg. 19.25x (ISBN 0-8371-0402-5, EGSS). Greenwood.

Eddleman, H. Leo. Hail Mary, Are You Heeding the Blessed Virgin? (Orig.). 1982. pap. 3.95 (ISBN 0-682-49899-8). Exposition.

Eddowes, Michael. The Oswald File. (Illus.). 1977. 10.00 o.p. (ISBN 0-517-53055-4). Crown.

Edds, John A. Management Auditing: Concepts & Practice. 432p. 1980. text ed. 21.95 (ISBN 0-8403-2209-7). Kendall-Hunt.

Eddy, D. Screening for Cancer: Theory, Analysis & Design. 1980. 31.95 (ISBN 0-13-796789-6). P-H.

Eddy, Donald D. Samuel Johnson-Book Reviewer in the Literary Magazine: Or Universal Review 1756-1758. LC 78-53000. 170p. 1979. lib. bdg. 17.00 o.s.i. (ISBN 0-8240-3425-2). Garland Pub.

Eddy, Edward D. Colleges for Our Land & Time. LC 73-13456. 328p. 1974. Repr. of 1957 ed. lib. bdg. 17.25x (ISBN 0-8371-7138-5, EDCO). Greenwood.

Eddy, Jackie. Slicing, Hooking & Cooking. (Illus.). 192p. 1981. 10.95 (ISBN 0-920510-06-X, Pub. by Personal Lib). Dodd.

Eddy, James M. & Alles, Wesley F. Death Education. (Illus.). 383p. 1982. pap. text ed. 12.95 (ISBN 0-8016-1497-X). Mosby.

Eddy, John, et al. Counseling Methods: Developing Counselors. LC 80-6315. 285p. 1981. lib. bdg. 20.75 o.p. (ISBN 0-8191-1474-X); pap. text ed. 10.75 o.p. (ISBN 0-8191-1475-8). U Pr of Amer.

--Counseling Theories: Developing Counselors. LC 80-6316. 138p. 1981. lib. bdg. 17.50 o.p. (ISBN 0-8191-1476-6); pap. text ed. 7.75 o.p. (ISBN 0-8191-1477-4). U Pr of Amer.

Eddy, John, et al, eds. College Student Personnel Development, Administration, & Counseling. 2nd ed. 538p. 1980. lib. bdg. 29.50 (ISBN 0-8191-1230-5); pap. text ed. 19.25 (ISBN 0-8191-1231-3). U Pr of Amer.

Eddy, John A., ed. The New Solar Physics. LC 78-66338. (AAAS Selected Symposium Ser.: No. 17). 1978. lib. bdg. 22.00 o.p. (ISBN 0-89158-444-7). Westview.

Eddy, Junius. The Music Came from Deep Inside: A Story of Artists & Severely Handicapped Children. 1982. 16.95 (ISBN 0-07-018971-4). McGraw.

Eddy, Mary B. Christ & Christmas, Poem. (Illus.). 12.50 (ISBN 0-87952-091-4). First Church.

--The First Church of Christ, Scientist, & Miscellany. German Ed. pap. 7.00 (ISBN 0-87952-155-4). First Church.

--Manual of the Mother Church, The First Church of Christ, Scientist, in Boston, Massachusetts. standard ed. 7.00 (ISBN 0-87952-061-2); century ed. 7.00 (ISBN 0-87952-063-9); leather 25.00 (ISBN 0-87952-064-7). First Church.

--Miscellaneous Writings, 1883-1896. 2.30; pap. 7.00; pap. 4.50 span. (ISBN 0-87952-229-1). First Church.

--The People's Idea of God, Christian Healings No & Yes. pap. 2.00 (ISBN 0-87952-042-6). First Church.

--Poems. 11.00 (ISBN 0-87952-090-6). First Church.

--Prose Works. new type ed. 35.00 (ISBN 0-87952-074-4); garnet new type ed. o.p. 60.00 (ISBN 0-87952-076-0); standard ed. 22.00 (ISBN 0-87952-070-1); new type bonded lea. ed. 47.00 (ISBN 0-87952-075-2). First Church.
--Pulpit & Press. pap. 2.50 (ISBN 0-87952-046-9). First Church.
--Retrospection & Introspection. pap. 2.00 (ISBN 0-87952-044-2). First Church.
--Retrospection & Introspection. French 10.00 (ISBN 0-87952-122-8); German 10.00 (ISBN 0-87952-157-0); Italian 7.00 (ISBN 0-87952-182-1); Portugese 7.00 (ISBN 0-87952-207-0); Spanish 7.00 (ISBN 0-87952-231-3); Swedish 8.00 (ISBN 0-87952-252-6). First Church.
--Rudimental Divine Science & No & Yes. Danish 8.00 (ISBN 0-87952-105-8); German 8.00 (ISBN 0-87952-158-9); Italian 5.00 (ISBN 0-87952-183-X); Portugese 5.00 (ISBN 0-87952-208-9); Swedish 6.00 (ISBN 0-87952-253-4); Spanish 5.00 (ISBN 0-87952-232-1). First Church.
--Science & Health with Key to the Scriptures. standard ed. 9.00 (ISBN 0-87952-001-9); new type ed. 17.50 (ISBN 0-87952-010-8); new type lea. bdg. 45.00 (ISBN 0-87952-015-9); readers ed. 30.00 (ISBN 0-87952-019-1); lea. bdg. 75.00 (ISBN 0-87952-020-5); Century ed. brown lea. bdg 32.50 (ISBN 0-87952-007-8); pap. 3.50 (ISBN 0-87952-000-0); new type bonded lea. ed. 35.00 (ISBN 0-87952-012-4). First Church.
--Science & Health with Key to the Scriptures. (Polish.). 20.00 (ISBN 0-87952-200-3). First Church.
--Science & Health with Key to the Scriptures. pap. 7.00 Spanish ed. (ISBN 0-87952-225-9); pap. 9.00 German ed. (ISBN 0-87952-150-3); pap. 9.00 French ed. (ISBN 0-87952-116-3). First Church.
--Science & Health with Key to the Scriptures. Indonesian 20.00 (ISBN 0-87952-175-9); Japanese 20.00 (ISBN 0-87952-190-2). First Church.
--Seven Messages to The Mother Church. pap. 2.00 (ISBN 0-87952-045-0). First Church.
--Unity of Good, Rudimental Divine Science. pap. 2.00 (ISBN 0-87952-043-4). First Church.
--Unity of Good, Two Sermons. Danish 10.00 (ISBN 0-87952-106-6); Norwegian 7.00 (ISBN 0-87952-197-X); German 6.00 (ISBN 0-87952-159-7). First Church.
Eddy, Mary Baker. Unity of Good. Indonesian ed. 8.00 (ISBN 0-87952-177-5); French Ed. 5.50 (ISBN 0-87952-123-6). First Church.
Eddy, S., et al. Atlas of Drawings for Vertebrate Anatomy. 3rd ed. 176p. 1964. text ed. 14.95x (ISBN 0-471-23168-1). Wiley.
Eddy, Samuel, et al. Taxonomic Keys to the Common Animals of the North Central States. 4th. ed. 1982. spiral bdg. 12.95x (ISBN 0-8087-2210-7). Burgess.
Eddy, William B. Public Organization Behavior & Development. 1981. text ed. 13.95 (ISBN 0-316-21050-1); pap. text ed. 9.95 (ISBN 0-316-21052-8). Little.
Eddy, William B. & Burke, W. Warner, eds. Behavioral Science & the Manager's Role. 2nd, rev. & enl. ed. LC 79-67692. 375p. 1980. pap. 19.50 (ISBN 0-88390-123-4). Univ Assocs.
Ede, D. A., et al, eds. Vertebrate Limb & Somite Morphogenesis: The Third Symposium of the British Society for Developmental Biology. LC 76-50312. (British Society for Developmental Biology Symposium: No. 3). 1978. 80.00 (ISBN 0-521-21552-8). Cambridge U Pr.
Edeiken, Jack. Roentgen Diagnosis of Diseases of the Bone. 3rd ed. (Golden's Diagnostic Radiology Ser.: Section No. 6). (Illus.). 1752p. 1981. 135.00 (ISBN 0-686-77386-1, 2744-1). Williams & Wilkins.
Edel, Leon. Henry James: The Master 1901-1916. LC 76-163225. (Henry James Ser). (Illus.). 1972. 13.41i (ISBN 0-397-00733-7). Har-Row.
Edel, Leon, ed. & intro. by see Wilson, Edmund.
Edel, Leon, et al. Telling Lives: The Biographer's Art. Pachter, Marc, ed. LC 79-698. 1979. 9.95 (ISBN 0-915220-54-7). New Republic.
Edel, Matthew & Rothenberg, Jerome. Readings in Urban Economics. (Illus.). 544p. 1972. pap. text ed. 17.95 (ISBN 0-02-331480-X, 33148). Macmillan.
Edelberg, Cynthia D. Robert Creeley's Poetry: A Critical Introduction. LC 78-55700. 216p. 1978. 11.95x o.p. (ISBN 0-8263-0479-6). U of NM Pr.
Edelhart & Lindenmann. Interferon. 1981. 11.95x (ISBN 0-201-03943-5). Cancer Control Soc.
Edelhart, Michael. Breaking Through the Job Barrier: Real Life Stories on the Career Trail. LC 80-2047. 240p. 1980. pap. 6.95 (ISBN 0-385-15581-6, Anch). Doubleday.
--College Knowledge. LC 78-1193. (Illus.). 1979. pap. 10.95 o.p. (ISBN 0-385-13386-3, Anch). Doubleday.
Edelhart, Mike. America the Quotable. 640p. 1983. 29.95x (ISBN 0-87196-331-0). Facts on File.
--Getting from Twenty to Thirty: Surviving Your First Decade in the Real World. 240p. 1983. 10.95 (ISBN 0-87131-381-2); pap. 6.95 (ISBN 0-87131-382-0). M Evans.
--Living on a Shoestring. LC 79-6535. (Illus.). 216p. 1980. pap. 5.95 o.p. (ISBN 0-385-15580-8, Anch). Doubleday.
Edelhertz, Herbert & Walsh, Marilyn. The White-Collar Challenge to Nuclear Safeguards. LC 77-15816. (Human Affairs Research Center Ser.). (Illus.). 128p. 1978. 15.95x (ISBN 0-669-02058-3). Lexington Bks.
Edelhertz, Herbert & Overcast, Thomas D., eds. White-Collar Crime: An Agenda for Research. LC 81-47451. (The Battelle Human Affairs Research Centers Ser.). 256p. 1981. 18.95x (ISBN 0-669-04649-3). Lexington Bks.
Edelhertz, Herbert & Rogovin, Charles, eds. A National Strategy for Containing White-Collar Crime. LC 79-2373. (Human Affairs Research Center Ser.). 160p. 1980. 17.95x (ISBN 0-669-03166-6). Lexington Bks.
Edelman, Chester M., jt. auth. see Gauthier, Bernard.
Edelman, Gerald M. & Mountcastle, Vernon B. The Mindful Brain: Cortical Organization & the Group - Selective Theory of Higher Brain Function. 1978. text ed. 10.00x o.p. (ISBN 0-262-05020-X). MIT Pr.
--The Mindful Brain: Cortical Organization & the Group-Selective Theory of Higher Brain Function. 128p. 1978. pap. text ed. 5.95x (ISBN 0-262-55007-5). MIT Pr.
Edelman, Gerald M., ed. Cellular Selection & Regulation in the Immune Response. LC 73-93857. (Society of General Physiologists Ser.: Vol. 29). 299p. 1974. 38.00 (ISBN 0-911216-71-5). Raven.
Edelman, Lily, ed. see Goodman, Lenn E.
Edelman, M. & Hallick, R. B., eds. Methods in Chloroplast Molecular Biology. 1152p. 1982. 183.00 (ISBN 0-444-80368-8, Biomedical Pr). Elsevier.
Edelman, Murray J., jt. auth. see Dolbeare, Kenneth M.
Edelman, Sandra A. Summer People--Winter People. LC 79-17113. (Illus.). 48p. (Orig.). 1979. pap. 2.25 (ISBN 0-913270-44-X). Sunstone Pr.
Edelman, Sandra P., ed. see Nusbaum, Rosemary.
Edelson. Federal Income Tax. 1982 ed. 1982. text ed. 12.95 (ISBN 0-8359-1875-0); instr's. manual o.p. free (ISBN 0-8359-1876-9). Reston.
Edelson, Edward. Great Animals of the Movies. LC 79-8015. (Illus.). 144p. (gr. 6-9). 1980. 8.95a o.p. (ISBN 0-385-14728-7); PLB 8.95a (ISBN 0-385-14729-5). Doubleday.
--Great Kids of the Movies. LC 78-14697. 1979. PLB 6.95 o.p. (ISBN 0-385-14128-9). Doubleday.
--Great Monsters of the Movies. LC 72-87499. 128p. (gr. 6 up). 1973. 8.95a (ISBN 0-385-00668-3); PLB (ISBN 0-385-00857-0). Doubleday.
Edelson, Edward, jt. auth. see Boikess, Robert S.
Edelstein, Arthur, ed. Images & Ideas in American Culture: The Functions of Criticism - Essays in Memory of Philip Rahv. LC 78-63584. 232p. 1979. text ed. 15.00x (ISBN 0-87451-164-X); pap. 8.00x (ISBN 0-87451-218-2). U Pr of New Eng.
Edelstein, Barbara. The Woman Doctor's Diet for Teen-Age Girls. LC 79-26546. 1980. 8.95 o.p. (ISBN 0-13-961631-4). P-H.
--The Woman Doctor's Diet for Women: Balanced Deficit Dieting & the Brand New Re-Start Diet. LC 77-2804. (Illus.). 1977. 8.95 o.p. (ISBN 0-13-961623-3). P-H.
--The Woman Doctor's Medical Guide for Women: How to Look Better, Feel Great, & Get the Most Out of Life. LC 82-8025. 256p. 1982. 13.95 (ISBN 0-688-01318-X). Morrow.
Edelstein, C. D. & Wicks, R. J. An Introduction to Criminal Justice. 1977. text ed. 17.95 (ISBN 0-07-018980-3); instr's manual & key avail. McGraw.
Edelstein, J., jt. ed. see Chilcote, R.
Edelstein, J. D. & Warner, M. A Comparative Union Democracy: Organization & Opposition in British & American Unions. LC 75-25204. 378p. 1976. 34.95x o.s.i. (ISBN 0-470-23268-4). Halsted Pr.
Edelstein, Joel C., jt. ed. see Chilcote, Ronald H.
Edelstein, Michael. Overseas Investment in the Age of High Imperialism. LC 82-1329. 480p. 1982. 35.00x (ISBN 0-686-86966-4); pap. 15.00x (ISBN 0-231-04439-9). Columbia U Pr.
Edelstein, Sidney M. & Borghetty, H. C., trs. Plictho of Gioanventura Rosetti. 1969. 50.00x (ISBN 0-262-18030-8); deluxe ed. 200.00x (ISBN 0-262-18038-3). MIT Pr.
Edelstein, Stewart L., jt. auth. see Medsker, Leland L.
Edelstein, Tilden G. Strange Enthusiasm: A Life of Thomas Wentworth Higginson, 1823-1911. LC 68-27752. (Studies in American Negro Life). 1970. pap. 3.95 o.p. (ISBN 0-689-70241-8, NL25). Atheneum.
Edelwich, Jerry & Brodsky, Archie. Burn-Out: Stages of Disillusionment in the Helping Professions. LC 79-27412. 255p. 1980. text ed. 26.95 (ISBN 0-87705-507-6); pap. 12.95 (ISBN 0-89885-035-5). Human Sci Pr.
--Sexual Dilemmas for the Helping Professional. LC 82-9491. 250p. 1982. 17.50 (ISBN 0-87630-314-9). Brunner-Mazel.
Eden, Alvin N. & Heilman, Joan. Dr. Eden's Diet & Nutrition Program for Children. 1981. 11.95 o.p. (ISBN 0-8015-3180-2, Hawthorn); pap. 6.95 o.p. (ISBN 0-8015-3181-0, Hawthorn). Dutton.
Eden, D. Mental Handicap: An Introduction. LC 75-34375. 122p. 1975. 10.50 (ISBN 0-470-01373-7). Krieger.
Eden, Dorothy. An Afternoon Walk. 1971. 6.95 (ISBN 0-698-10017-4, Coward). Putnam Pub Group.
--The American Heiress. 252p. 1980. 11.95 (ISBN 0-698-11058-7, Coward). Putnam Pub Group.
--An Important Family. 352p. 1983. pap. 3.50 (ISBN 0-380-63297-7). Avon.
--The Millionaire's Daughter. 1974. 8.95 (ISBN 0-698-10607-5, Coward). Putnam Pub Group.
--The Salamanca Drum. 320p. 1977. 8.95 (ISBN 0-698-10823-X, Coward). Putnam Pub Group.
--Speak to Me of Love. 1972. 7.95 (ISBN 0-698-10462-5, Coward). Putnam Pub Group.
--The Storrington Papers. LC 78-11782. 1978. 9.95 (ISBN 0-698-10962-7, Coward). Putnam Pub Group.
--The Time of the Dragon. LC 15-22243. 288p. 1975. 8.95 (ISBN 0-698-10699-7, Coward). Putnam Pub Group.
--The Vines of Yarrabee. LC 78-6654. 1978. 10.95 o.s.i. (ISBN 0-698-10942-2, Coward). Putnam Pub Group.
Eden, Douglas & Short, Frederick. Political Change in Europe. 1981. 25.00x (ISBN 0-312-62202-3). St Martin.
Eden, Horatia K. Juliana Horatia Ewing & Her Books. LC 71-77001. (Library of Lives & Letters). (Illus.). 1969. Repr. of 1896 ed. 34.00x (ISBN 0-8103-3897-1). Gale.
Eden, Jerome. Animal Magnetism & the Life Energy. 1974. 8.50 o.p. (ISBN 0-682-48045-2). Exposition.
--View from Eden: Talks to Students of Orgonomy. 1976. 8.00 o.p. (ISBN 0-682-48570-5). Exposition.
Eden, Michael. Rain Forests. (Illus.). 24p. (gr. 1-4). 1982. 5.95 (ISBN 0-370-30369-5, Pub. by Chatto-Bodley-Jonathan). Merrimack Bk Serv.
--Weather. (Illus.). 24p. (gr. 1-4). 1982. 5.95 (ISBN 0-370-30454-3, Pub. by Chatto-Bodley-Jonathan). Merrimack Bk Serv.
Eden, Murray, jt. auth. see Rutstein, David D.
Eden, Richard, tr. & compiled by see Arber, E.
Eden, Richard J., et al. Energy Economics: Growth, Resources & Policies. LC 80-40858. (Illus.). Date not set. pap. 12.95 (ISBN 0-521-28160-1). Cambridge U Pr.
--Energy Economics: Growth, Resources & Policies. LC 80-40858. (Illus.). 445p. 1981. 44.50 (ISBN 0-521-23685-1). Cambridge U Pr.
Eden, William, ed. see Butterworth, Neal.
Edens, Cooper. Emily & the Shadow Shop. (Illus.). 40p. 1982. pap. 8.95 o.s.i. (ISBN 0-914676-63-6, Star & Eleph Bks). Green Tiger Pr.
--Inevitable Papers. (Illus.). 40p. 1982. pap. 5.95 (ISBN 0-914676-94-6, Star & Eleph Bks). Green Tiger Pr.
Edens, Cooper, compiled by. Weird & Wonderful. (Illus., Orig.). pap. 10.01 o.s.i. (ISBN 0-914676-66-0, Star & Eleph Bks). Green Tiger Pr.
Edens, David. Estoy Creciendo Estoy Cambiando. Du Plou, Dafne C., tr. (Sexo en la Vida Cristiana Ser). (Illus.). 1981. pap. 1.60 (ISBN 0-311-46252-9). Casa Bautista.
--Marriage: How to Have It the Way You Want It. 170p. 1981. 11.95 (ISBN 0-13-558510-4); pap. 5.95 (ISBN 0-13-558502-3). P-H.
Eder, G. What's Behind Inflation & How to Beat It. 1979. 9.95 o.p. (ISBN 0-13-952143-7). P-H.
Eder, Joseph M. Ausfuhrliches Handbuch der Photographie: 1891-93, 4 Vols. (Illus.). 476p. Set. pap. 250.00 (ISBN 0-686-82589-6). Saifer.
Eder, Phanor J. American-Colombian Private International Law. LC 56-8273. 95p. 1956. 15.00 (ISBN 0-379-11405-4). Oceana.
Ederer, Rupert J. The Social Teachings of Wilhelm Emmanuel Von Ketteler: Bishop of Mainz (1811-1877) LC 80-5556. 622p. 1982. lib. bdg. 35.25 (ISBN 0-8191-1831-1); pap. text ed. 22.50 (ISBN 0-8191-1832-X). U Pr of Amer.
Edersheim, Alford. Practical Truths From Elisha. 368p. 1983. Repr. of 1882 ed. 11.95 (ISBN 0-8254-2511-5). Kregel.
Edes, Shirley & Philipson, Julia. Peter Christian's Recipes. (Illus.). 192p. (Orig.). 1983. pap. 12.00 (ISBN 0-936988-09-6). Tompson & Rutter.
Edewar, J. O., ed. see Benn, F. R.
Edey, H. C., jt. auth. see Yamey, B. S.
Edey, Harold C. Accounting Queries. LC 82-82487. (Accountancy in Transition Ser.). 296p. 1982. lib. bdg. 40.00 (ISBN 0-8240-5335-4). Garland Pub.
--Business Budgets & Accounts. 3rd ed. 1966. pap. text ed. 2.75x o.p. (ISBN 0-09-022422-1, Hutchinson U Lib). Humanities.
Edey, Maitland. The Northeast Coast. LC 70-187925. (American Wilderness Ser). (Illus.). (gr. 6 up). 1972. lib. bdg. 15.96 (ISBN 0-8094-1149-0, Pub. by Time-Life). Silver.
Edgar, Josephine. Duchess. 1978. pap. 2.25 o.p. (ISBN 0-446-82423-2). Warner Bks.
--Margaret Normanby. 448p. 1983. 13.95 (ISBN 0-312-51444-1). St Martin.
Edgar, Ken. Mirrors. 1980. 9.95 o.p. (ISBN 0-458-93390-2). Methuen Inc.
Edgar, Neal L. & Ma, Wendy Y., eds. Travel in Asia: A Guide to Information Sources. (Geography & Travel Information Guide Ser.: Vol. 6). 350p. 1982. 42.00x (ISBN 0-8103-1470-3). Gale.
Edgar, P. Study of Shelley. LC 70-116792. (Studies in Shelley, No. 25). 1970. Repr. of 1899 ed. lib. bdg. 29.95x (ISBN 0-8383-1034-6). Haskell.
Edgar, Thomas F. Coal Processing & Population Control Handbook. 1983. text ed. 45.00 (ISBN 0-87201-122-4). Gulf Pub.
Edgar, William J. Evidence. LC 80-67262. 471p. 1980. lib. bdg. 25.50 (ISBN 0-8191-1292-5); pap. text ed. 14.50 (ISBN 0-8191-1293-3). U Pr of Amer.
--The Problem Solver's Guide to Logic. LC 82-20285. 106p. (Orig.). 1983. pap. text ed. 6.50 (ISBN 0-8191-2876-7). U Pr of Amer.
Edgcumbe, Richard. Musical Reminiscences of the Earl of Mount Edgecumbe. LC 76-125071. 294p. 1973. Repr. of 1834 ed. lib. bdg. 29.50 (ISBN 0-306-70008-5). Da Capo.
Edge, David & Mulkay, Michael J. Astronomy Transformed: The Emergence of Radio Astronomy in Britain. LC 76-13532. (Science, Culture & Society Ser.). 482p. 1976. 48.95 (ISBN 0-471-23273-4, Pub. by Wiley-Interscience). Wiley.
Edge, Findley B. Metodologia Pedagogica. Mendoza, Celia & Molina, Sara P., trs. from Eng. Orig. Title: Helping the Teacher. 155p. 1982. pap. 3.75 (ISBN 0-311-11026-6). Casa Bautista.
--Pedagogia Fructifera. Lopez, Alberto, tr. from Eng. 192p. (Span.). 1982. pap. 3.75 (ISBN 0-311-11025-8). Casa Bautista.
Edge, Henry T. The Astral Light: Nature's Amazing Picture Gallery. Small, W. Emmett & Todd, Helen, eds. (Theosophical Manual: No. 10). 62p. 1975. pap. 2.00 (ISBN 0-913004-20-0). Point Loma Pub.
--Design & Purpose: A Study in the Drama of Evolution. (Study Ser.: No. 4). 1980. 1.25 (ISBN 0-913004-37-5). Point Loma Pub.
--Esoteric Keys to the Christian Scriptures. rev. 2nd ed. Small, W. Emmett & Todd, Helen, eds. Bd. with The Universal Mystery-Language of Myth & Symbol. Orig. Title: The Universal Mystery-Language & Its Interpretations. Orig. Title: Theosophical Light on the Christian Bible. 1973. pap. 2.50 (ISBN 0-913004-12-X, 913004-12). Point Loma Pub.
--Evolution: Who & What Is Man. Small, W. Emmett & Todd, Helen, eds. (Theosophical Manual: No. 6). 78p. 1975. pap. 2.00 (ISBN 0-913004-22-7, 913004-22). Point Loma Pub.
--Theosophy & Christianity. rev. ed. Small, W. Emmett & Todd, Helen, eds. (Theosophical Manual: No. 12). 80p. 1974. pap. 2.00 (ISBN 0-913004-17-0). Point Loma Pub.
Edge, Henry T., et al. Mirrors of the Hidden Wisdom: Threads of Theosophy in Literature - I. (Study Ser.: No. 7). 122p. 1981. pap. 6.50 (ISBN 0-913004-42-1). Point Loma Pub.
Edge, Nellie. May I Have That Recipe? Martin, Paul J., ed. LC 82-61483. (Illus.). 132p. (Orig.). 1982. pap. 7.95 (ISBN 0-918146-24-0). Peninsula WA.
Edge, Nellie & Leitz, Pierr M. Kids in the Kitchen. (Illus.). 165p. (gr. k-6). 1979. pap. 7.95 (ISBN 0-918146-18-6). Peninsula WA.
Edge, Sylviac., jt. auth. see Fielo, Sandra B.
Edgerton, F., ed. Panchatantra Reconstructed, 2 Vols. 1924. Set. pap. 56.00 (ISBN 0-527-02677-8). Kraus Repr.
Edgerton, Franklin, ed. Buddhist Hybrid Sanscrit Reader. 1953. 39.50x (ISBN 0-685-69814-9). Elliots Bks.
Edgerton, Franklin, tr. see Apadeva.
Edgerton, Harold E. & Killian, James R., Jr. Moments of Vision: The Stroboscopic Revolution in Photography. (Illus.). 1979. 27.50 (ISBN 0-262-05022-6); deluxe ed. 100.00 (ISBN 0-262-05023-4). MIT Pr.
Edgerton, Robert B. Alone Together: Social Order on an Urban Beach. LC 78-59448. 1979. 13.95x (ISBN 0-520-03738-3). U of Cal Pr.
--The Individual in Cultural Adaptation: A Study of Four East African Peoples. LC 73-117948. 1971. 30.00x (ISBN 0-520-01730-7). U of Cal Pr.
Edgerton, Robert B., ed. see Eastman, Carol M.
Edgerton, Robert B., ed. see Kearney, Michael.
Edgerton, Robert H. Available-Energy & Environmental Economics. LC 81-47624. 480p. 1982. 36.95x (ISBN 0-669-04699-X). Lexington Bks.
Edgerton, William B., ed. Indiana Slavic Studies, Vol. 4. (Russian & East European Ser.: No. 36). 268p. 1967. pap. 6.95x o.p. (ISBN 0-253-39036-2). Ind U Pr.
Edgerton, William L. Nicholas Udall. (English Authors Ser.). 14.95 (ISBN 0-8057-1552-5, Twayne). G K Hall.
Edgeworth, Maria. Letters for Literary Ladies. (The Feminist Controversy in England, 1788-1810 Ser.). 1974. lib. bdg. 50.00 o.s.i. (ISBN 0-8240-0855-3). Garland Pub.
--Moral Tales for Young People, 3 vols. (The Feminist Controversy in England, 1788-1810 Ser.). 1974. lib. bdg. 50.00 ea. o.s.i. (ISBN 0-8240-0856-1). Garland Pub.
Edgin, Charles A. General Welding. LC 81-1882. 325p. 1982. text ed. 15.95 (ISBN 0-471-08001-2); tchrs. manual avail. (ISBN 0-471-09188-X). Wiley.
Edginton, C. R. & Williams, J. G. Productive Management of Leisure Service Organizations: A Behavioral Approach. 530p. 1978. 22.95x (ISBN 0-471-01574-1). Wiley.
Edginton, Chris, jt. ed. see Neal, Larry.

Edginton, J. K. & Sherman, H. J. Physical Science for Biologists. 1971. text ed. 6.25x o.p. (ISBN 0-09-107860-1, Hutchinson U Lib); pap. text ed. 3.50x o.p. (ISBN 0-09-107861-X, Hutchinson U Lib). Humanities.

Edgmand, Michael R. Macroeconomics: Theory & Policy. 2nd ed. (Illus.). 576p. 1983. 24.95 (ISBN 0-13-542688-X). P-H.

Edholm. Man: Hot & Cold. (Studies in Biology: No. 97). 1978. 5.95 o.p. (ISBN 0-7131-2694-9). Univ Park.

Edholm, Felicity, tr. see Meillassoux, C.

Edholm, Otto & Weiner, Joe, eds. Principles & Practice of Human Physiology. LC 80-40831. 1981. 88.50 (ISBN 0-12-231650-9). Acad Pr.

Edie, C., et al, eds. Vehicular Traffic Science. (Proceedings). 1967. 17.50 (ISBN 0-444-00015-1). Elsevier.

Edie, James M., et al. Russian Philosophy, 3 vols. LC 64-10928. 1976. Vol. 1. pap. 7.95x (ISBN 0-87049-200-4); Vol. 2. pap. 6.95x (ISBN 0-686-91542-9); Vol. 3. pap. 8.95x (ISBN 0-686-77174-5). U of Tenn Pr.

Edie, Lionel D. Dollars. 1934. 32.50x (ISBN 0-686-25727-8). Elliots Bks.

--Easy Money: A Study of Low Interest Rates, Their Bearing on the Outlook for the Gold Standard & on the Problem of Curbing a Boom. 1937. 29.50x (ISBN 0-686-51374-6). Elliots Bks.

Edinburgh University Library. First Supplement to Manuscripts, Edinburgh University Library. (Library Catalogs-Supplements). lib. bdg. 115.00 (ISBN 0-8161-0319-4, Hall Library). G K Hall.

--Index to Manuscripts, 2 vols. 1964. Set. 165.00 (ISBN 0-8161-0706-8, Hall Library). G K Hall.

Edinger, Claudio. Chelsea Hotel. (Illus.). 160p. (Orig.). 1983. 29.95 (ISBN 0-89659-368-1); pap. 14.95 (ISBN 0-89659-338-X). Abbeville Pr.

Edinger, Lewis J. Politics in West Germany. 2nd ed. (Ser. in Comparative Politics). 375p. 1977. pap. 10.95 (ISBN 0-316-21081-1). Little.

Edington, D. W. Biological Awareness: Statements for Self-Discovery. Cunningham, Lee N., tr. (Illus.). 224p. 1975. 18.95x (ISBN 0-13-077180-5). P-H.

Edington, George, jt. auth. see Wilson, Bradford.

Edinin, M. & Johnson, M. H., eds. Immunobiology of Gametes. LC 76-49952. (Clinical & Experimental Immunoreproduction Ser.: No. 4). (Illus.). 1977. 67.50 (ISBN 0-521-21441-6). Cambridge U Pr.

Edison, Nancy, jt. ed. see Ciesielski, Stephen D.

Editions des Belles Images Staff, tr. from Fr. The Butterfly Book of Birds. (Butterfly Bks). (Illus.). 16p. (Orig.). (ps-2). 1976. pap. 1.50 o.p. (ISBN 0-8467-0226-6, Pub. by Two Continents). Hippocrene Bks.

Editions les Belles Images Staff, ed. Hidden in the Woods. (Butterfly Bks). (Illus., Orig.). (gr. 2-6). 1977. pap. 1.50 o.p. (ISBN 0-8467-0332-7, Pub. by Two Continents). Hippocrene Bks.

Editions les Belles Images Staff, tr. from Fr. Butterfly Books: The Catnip Family. (Illus., Orig.). (gr. 1-2). 1977. pap. 1.50 o.p. (ISBN 0-8467-0330-0, Pub. by Two Continents). Hippocrene Bks.

--In My Garden: Learning to Count. (Butterfly Bks). (Illus.). 16p. (Orig.). (ps-2). 1976. pap. 1.50 o.p. (ISBN 0-8467-0219-3, Pub. by Two Continents). Hippocrene Bks.

Editions les Belles Images Staff, tr. Mother Goose Rhymes. (Butterfly Bks). (Illus., Orig.). (gr. 1-2). 1977. pap. 1.50 o.p. (ISBN 0-8467-0331-9, Pub. by Two Continents). Hippocrene Bks.

Editorial Board see Langs, Robert.

Editorial Board, ed. Poetry Index Annual Nineteen Eighty Two. 372p. 1982. 49.99 (ISBN 0-89609-223-2). Granger Bk.

Editorial Board, Grange Book Co., ed. The World's Best Poetry: Supplement One: Twentieth Century English & American Verse, 1900-1929. (The Granger Anthology Ser.: No. I). 400p. 1983. 39.50 (ISBN 0-89609-236-4). Granger Bk.

Editorial Board, Granger Book Co., ed. American Poetry Index, Vol. 1. 1983. price not set (ISBN 0-89609-238-0). Granger Bk.

--Poetry Index Annual 1983. 1983. price not set (ISBN 0-89609-237-2). Granger Bk.

Editorial Experts, Inc, ed. Directory of Editorial Resources, 1983-84. 50p. 1983. 9.50 (ISBN 0-935012-05-2). Edit Experts.

Editorial Staff. Yokley's Law of Subdivisions. 2nd ed. 1981. with 1980 suppl. 60.00 (ISBN 0-87215-061-5); 1980 suppl 25.00 (ISBN 0-87215-344-4). Michie-Bobbs.

Editorial Staff, ed. Beautiful Crafts Book. LC 76-21846. (Illus.). (YA) 1976. 16.95 (ISBN 0-8069-5366-7); PLB 14.99 o.p. (ISBN 0-8069-5367-5). Sterling.

Editorial Staff of Francis Hodgson. Who's Who in World Agriculture, 2 vols. LC 79-40830. 831p. Set. 220.00x (ISBN 0-686-75644-4, Pub. by Longman). Gale.

Editors, Change Magazine, ed. In the Public Interest: The Governmental Role in Academic Institutions. LC 78-64964. Date not set. cancelled (ISBN 0-915390-19-1). Change Mag.

Editors of Consumer Guide, ed. see Dickinson, Peter A.

Editors of Curtin & London, Inc., ed. The Book of 35mm Photography: A Complete Guide for Creative Photographers. (Illus.). 176p. 1983. pap. 15.95 (ISBN 0-930764-41-2). Curtin & London.

Editors of Gun Digest. Gun Digest's Book of Gun Accessories. Schroeder, Joseph J., ed. (Illus.). 288p. 1979. pap. 8.95 o.s.i. (ISBN 0-695-81313-7). Follett.

Editors of Hamlyn Publishing Group. Instant Metric Conversion Tables. LC 75-24712. 144p. 1979. 2.50 o.p. (ISBN 0-89196-001-5, Domus Bks). Quality Bks IL.

Editors of Hudson Home Magazine. Practical Guide to Home Restoration. 144p. 1980. 12.95 o.p. (ISBN 0-442-25400-8). Van Nos Reinhold.

Editors of Time-Life Books. Boutique Attire. LC 75-7826. (The Art of Sewing). (Illus.). (gr. 6 up). 1975. PLB 11.97 o.p. (ISBN 0-8094-1751-0, Pub. by Time Life). Silver.

--The Custom Look. LC 73-87766. (The Art of Sewing). (Illus.). (gr. 6 up). 1973. PLB 11.97 o.p. (ISBN 0-8094-1707-3, Pub. by Time-Life). Silver.

--Making Home Furnishings. LC 75-15877. (The Art of Sewing). (Illus.). (gr. 6 up). 1975. PLB 11.97 o.p. (ISBN 0-8094-1755-3, Pub. by Time-Life). Silver.

--Seven Centuries of Art: Survey & Index. LC 77-133188. (Time-Life Library of Art). (Illus.). (gr. 6 up). 1970. 19.92 (ISBN 0-8094-0288-2, Pub. by Time-Life). Silver.

Editors of Who's Who in America, compiled by. Who Was Who During the American Revolution. LC 75-34514. (Illus.). 448p. 1976. 19.95 o.p. (ISBN 0-672-52216-0). Bobbs.

Editura Tehnica. Dictionar Tehnic Poliglot. 1233p. (Rumanian, Rus., Eng., Ger., Fr. & Span.). 1982. Repr. of 1967 ed. text ed. 98.50x (ISBN 0-8290-0987-6). Irvington.

Edkins, Anthony & Harris, Derek, eds. The Poetry of Luis Cernuda. LC 74-173878. 1971. 17.50x o.p. (ISBN 0-8147-2151-6). NYU Pr.

Edkins, David. The Prussian Orden Pourle Merite: History of the Blue Max. LC 81-65302. (Illus.). 1981. softcover 10.95 (ISBN 0-939440-05-9). AJAY Ent.

Edkins, Diana. Vanity Fair: Portrait of an Age. LC 82-7682. 224p. 1982. 35.00 (ISBN 0-517-54625-6, Pub. by Potter). Crown.

Edlin, Herbert L. & Huxley, Anthony. Atlas of Plant Life. LC 73-734361. (John Day Bk.). (Illus.). 128p. 1973. 14.37i (ISBN 0-381-98245-9). T Y Crowell.

Edlund, Calvin V. How Human Behavior Is Learned: A Handbook for Parents & Professional Workers with Children. LC 79-170092. (Orig.). 1972. pap. 5.00x o.p. (ISBN 0-87562-033-7). Spec Child.

Edman, Irwin. Philosopher's Quest. LC 72-7973. 275p. 1973. Repr. of 1947 ed. lib. bdg. 18.00x (ISBN 0-8371-6559-8, EDPQ). Greenwood.

Edman, Irwin, ed. see Dewey, John.

Edman, Marion, ed. The Horizons of Man. LC 62-16348. (Leo M. Franklin Memorial Lectures in Human Relations Ser: Vol. 11). 1963. 6.95x o.p. (ISBN 0-8143-1206-3). Wayne St U Pr.

Edman, Polly, jt. auth. see Jensen, Virginia A.

Edman, V. E. & Laidlaw, R. A. The Fullness of the Spirit. 36p. pap. 0.85 (ISBN 0-87509-083-4). Chr Pubns.

Edman, V. Raymond. But God! 1980. large print 6.95 (ISBN 0-310-24047-6). Zondervan.

--The Disciplines of Life. LC 81-84813. 254p. 1982. pap. 3.25 (ISBN 0-89081-276-4, 2764). Harvest Hse.

Edmands, Allan, jt. auth. see Edmands, Dodie.

Edmands, Dodie & Edmands, Allan. Child Signs: Understanding Your Child Through Astrology. LC 82-45630. (Illus.). 200p. 1983. pap. 6.95 (ISBN 0-916360-19-9). CRCS Pubns NV.

Edminister, J. Schaum's Outline of Electric Circuits. 2nd ed. (Schaum Outline Ser.). 304p. 1983. pap. 6.95 (ISBN 0-07-018984-6, SP). McGraw.

Edminister, Joseph. Schaum's Outline of Electromagnetics. (Schaum's Outline Ser). (Illus.). 1979. pap. 6.95 (ISBN 0-07-018990-0, SP). McGraw.

Edminister, Joseph A. Electric Circuits. (Schaum's Outline Ser). (Orig.). 1965. pap. 6.95 (ISBN 0-07-018974-9, SP). McGraw.

Edmister, Robert O. Financial Institutions Management. (Financial Ser.). 560p. 1980. text ed. 24.95 (ISBN 0-07-018995-1, C); instr's manual 16.95 (ISBN 0-07-018996-X). McGraw.

Edmister, Wayne C. & Lee, Byung I. Applied Hydrocarbon Thermodynamics, Vol. 1. 2nd ed. 400p. 1983. 59.95x (ISBN 0-87201-855-5). Gulf Pub. Postponed.

Edmond, Carolyn E., jt. auth. see Washington, Allyn J.

Edmond, J. B., et al. Fundamentals of Horticulture. 4th ed. (Illus.). 576p. 1975. text ed. 31.50 (ISBN 0-07-018985-4, C). McGraw.

Edmonds, Dean, jt. auth. see Cioffari, Bernard.

Edmonds, Dean S., Jr. Cioffari's Experiments in College Physics, 7th ed. 456p. pap. 16.95 (ISBN 0-669-04492-X). Heath.

Edmonds, G. A. & Howe, F. G., eds. Roads & Resources: Appropriate Technology in Road Construction in Developing Countries. (Illus.). 200p. (Orig.). 1980. pap. 11.50x (ISBN 0-903031-69-8, Pub. by Intermediate Tech England). Intermediate Tech.

Edmonds, I. G. Automotive Tune-Ups for Beginners. (Illus.). 224p. (gr. 9 up). 1974. 7.25 (ISBN 0-8255-3020-2). Macrae.

--Buddhism. (First Books Ser.). (Illus.). (gr. 5-8). 1978. PLB 8.90 s&l (ISBN 0-531-01349-9). Watts.

--China's Red Rebel: The Story of Mao Tse-Tung. (Illus.). 176p. (gr. 7 up). 1973. 6.50 (ISBN 0-8255-3017-2). Macrae.

--Drag Racing for Beginners. LC 72-75894. (gr. 6-10). 6.50 o.p. (ISBN 0-672-51596-2). Bobbs.

--Hinduism. (First Bks.). (Illus.). (gr. 4 up). 1979. PLB 8.90 s&l (ISBN 0-531-02943-3). Watts.

--Hot Rodding for Beginners. LC 76-127427. (Illus.). (gr. 7 up). 1970. 6.71 (ISBN 0-8255-3000-8); PLB 6.71 (ISBN 0-8255-3001-6). Macrae.

--Islam. LC 77-2664. (First Bks.). (gr. 5-8). 1977. PLB 8.90 s&l (ISBN 0-531-01288-3). Watts.

--Jet & Rocket Engines: How They Work. new ed. (How It Works Ser.). (Illus.). 96p. (gr. 5-9). 1973. PLB 4.89 o.p. (ISBN 0-399-60816-8). Putnam Pub Group.

--The Magic Dog. (Illus.). 128p. (gr. 5-9). 1982. 9.95 (ISBN 0-525-66757-1, 0966-290). Lodestar Bks.

--Mao's Long March. LC 72-12337. (Illus.). 128p. (gr. 7 up). 1973. 6.50 (ISBN 0-8255-3004-0). Macrae.

--Micronesia: Pebbles in the Sea. LC 73-22689. 1974. 6.95 o.p. (ISBN 0-672-51815-5). Bobbs.

--Minibikes & Minicycles for Beginners. LC 72-11099. (Illus.). 168p. (gr. 4 up). 1973. PLB 7.61 (ISBN 0-8255-3003-2). Macrae.

--The Miser's Guide to More Miles-per-Gallon. LC 74-7666. (Illus.). 192p. Date not set. 5.95 (ISBN 0-8255-3025-3). Macrae. Postponed.

--Motorcycling for Beginners. LC 74-183864. (Illus.). 192p. (gr. 7 up). 1972. PLB 7.61 (ISBN 0-8255-3007-5). Macrae.

--Second Sight: People Who Saw the Future. LC 77-9881. (gr. 7 up). 1977. 7.95 o.p. (ISBN 0-525-66566-8). Lodestar Bks.

Edmonds, James E., ed. Short History of World War One. LC 68-54989. (Illus.). 1968. Repr. of 1951 ed. lib. bdg. 44.50x o.p. (ISBN 0-8371-0405-X, EDWW). Greenwood.

Edmonds, Michael. Lytton Strachey: A Bibliography. LC 80-8493. (Illus.). 250p. 1981. lib. bdg. 30.00 o.s.i. (ISBN 0-8240-9494-8). Garland Pub.

Edmonds, Paul. Microbiology: An Environmental Perspective. (Illus.). 1978. text ed. 23.95x (ISBN 0-02-333580-7). Macmillan.

Edmonds, Peggy, jt. ed. see Harris, Beatrice.

Edmonds, Robert L., ed. Aerobiology: The Ecological Systems Approach. LC 78-23769. (US-IBP Synthesis Ser.: Vol. 10). 386p. 1979. 36.00 (ISBN 0-87933-346-4). Hutchinson Ross.

--Analysis of Coniferous Forest Ecosystems in the Western United States. LC 80-26699. (US-IBP Synthesis Ser.: Vol. 14). 448p. 1982. 44.00 (ISBN 0-87933-382-0). Hutchinson Ross.

Edmonds, Ronald R., jt. ed. see Willie, Charles V.

Edmonds, Rosemary, tr. see Tolstoy, Leo.

Edmonds, S. J., jt. auth. see Stephen, A. C.

Edmonds, Thomas P. & McKinnon, Sharon M. Financial Accounting: An Elements Approach. LC 81-70862. 652p. 1983. text ed. 24.95x (ISBN 0-931920-36-1). Dame Pubns.

Edmonds, Walter D. Beaver Valley. (Illus.). (gr. 4-6). 1971. 5.50g o.p. (ISBN 0-316-21164-8). Little.

--Seven American Stories. LC 69-10657. (gr. 7 up). 1970. 8.95 o.p. (ISBN 0-316-21150-8). Little.

--The Story of Richard Storm. (Illus.). 32p. (gr. k-3). 1974. 6.95g o.p. (ISBN 0-316-21165-6). Little.

Edmonds, Willa M. Realistic Reflections in Poetry. 1978. 4.50 o.p. (ISBN 0-533-03590-2). Vantage.

Edmondson, Madeleine. Anna Witch. LC 81-43653. (Illus.). 64p. (gr. 3-5). 1982. 8.95a (ISBN 0-385-17393-8); PLB (ISBN 0-385-17394-6). Doubleday.

Edmondson, W. T., et al. Freshwater Biology. 2nd ed. LC 59-6781. (Illus.). 1248p. 1959. 79.95x (ISBN 0-471-23298-X). Wiley.

Edmonson, A. S. & Crenshaw, A. H. Campbell's Operative Orthopaedics, 2 Vols. 6 ed. LC 80-14731. 2592p. 1980. Set. 199.50 (ISBN 0-8016-1071-0). Mosby.

Edmonson, Harold A., ed. Journey to Amtrak. LC 76-182034. (Illus.). 104p. 1972. 9.00 o.p. (ISBN 0-89024-023-X). Kalmbach.

Edmonston, William E. Hypnosis & Relaxation: Modern Verification of an Old Equation. LC 80-22506. (Personality Processes Ser.). 255p. 1981. 28.95 (ISBN 0-471-05903-X, Pub. by Wiley-Interscience). Wiley.

Edmonston, William E., Jr., ed. Conceptual & Investigative Approaches to Hypnosis & Hypnotic Phenomena, Vol. 296. (Annals of the New York Academy of Sciences). 619p. 1977. 24.00x (ISBN 0-89072-042-8). NY Acad Sci.

Edmundo, jt. auth. see Desnoes.

Edmunds, Charles P. Essentials of Personal Finance. LC 78-26740. (Illus.). 1979. text ed. 20.95x (ISBN 0-673-16084-X). study guide 9.95x (ISBN 0-673-16083-1). Scott F.

Edmunds, E. Pope & His Poetry. LC 73-18098. (English Biography Ser., No. 31). 1974. lib. bdg. 31.95x (ISBN 0-8383-1735-9). Haskell.

Edmunds, L. Francis. Anthroposophy, a Way of Life. 1982. 35.00x (ISBN 0-903580-65-9, Pub. by Element Bks). State Mutual Bk.

--Anthroposophy as a Healing Force. 14p. Date not set. pap. 2.25 (ISBN 0-88010-037-0, Pub.by Steinerbooks). Anthroposophic.

Edmunds, Lowell. The Silver Bullet: The Martini in American Civilization. LC 80-1196. (Contributions in American Studies: No. 52). (Illus.). 199p. 1981. lib. bdg. 25.00 (ISBN 0-313-22225-8, ESB/). Greenwood.

Edmunds, Stahrl W. Alternative U. S. Futures. LC 77-28093. 1978. pap. text ed. 12.50x (ISBN 0-673-16255-9). Scott F.

--Basics of Private & Public Management. LC 77-9147. 1978. 24.95x (ISBN 0-669-01679-9). Lexington Bks.

Edmundson & Burnap. Athletics for Boys & Girls. 12.50x (ISBN 0-392-08958-0, SpS). Sportshelf.

Edmundson, Joseph. New Art of Keeping Fit: Modern Methods for Men. rev. ed. LC 63-13393. (Illus.). 1978. 8.95 (ISBN 0-87523-144-6). Emerson.

Edney, A. T., ed. Dog & Cat Nutrition: A Handbook for Students, Veterinarians, Breeders & Owners. (Illus.). 124p. 1982. 24.00 (ISBN 0-08-028891-X); pap. 12.00 (ISBN 0-08-028890-1). Pergamon.

Edry, Carol F., ed. The West Virginia Edition of the Woman's Yellow Pages: Original Sourcebook for Women. Gerstein, Rosalyn. (Illus.). 1979. pap. 7.95 o.p. (ISBN 0-918556-02-3). Public Works.

Edry, Carol F. & Gerstein, Rosalyn, eds. The New England Women's Yellow Pages: Original Sourcebook for Women. 4th ed. (Illus.). 1978. pap. 9.95x (ISBN 0-918556-01-5). Public Works.

Edsall, Marian S. Library Promotion Handbook. (Neal-Schuman Professional Bk.). 1980. lib. bdg. 32.50x (ISBN 0-912700-15-7); pap. 25.00x (ISBN 0-912700-12-2); of 4 cassettes 67.50 set. Oryx Pr.

Edson, Gary. Mexican Market Pottery. (Illus.). 1979. 24.50 o.p. (ISBN 0-8230-3048-2). Watson-Guptill.

Edson, J. T. The Bad Bunch. (Orig.). 1982. pap. 1.95 o.p. (ISBN 0-425-05228-1). Berkley Pub.

--The Bad Bunch. 1979. pap. 1.75 o.p. (ISBN 0-425-03956-0). Berkley Pub.

--Cuchilo. (Orig.). 1981. pap. 1.95 o.p. (ISBN 0-425-04836-5). Berkley Pub.

--The Fast Gun. (Orig.). 1981. pap. 1.95 o.p. (ISBN 0-425-04802-0). Berkley Pub.

--Forty-Four Caliber Man. 1980. pap. 1.75 o.p. (ISBN 0-425-04620-6). Berkley Pub.

--Go Back to Hell. (Orig.). 1979. pap. 1.75 o.p. (ISBN 0-425-04110-7). Berkley Pub.

--Goodnight's Dream. (Orig.). 1980. pap. 1.75 o.p. (ISBN 0-425-04633-8). Berkley Pub.

--The Half Breed. (Orig.). 1981. pap. 1.95 o.p. (ISBN 0-425-04736-9). Berkley Pub.

--The Half Breed. 192p. 1983. pap. 2.25 (ISBN 0-425-05966-9). Berkley Pub.

--Hell in the Palo Duro. 1979. pap. 1.75 o.p. (ISBN 0-425-04096-8). Berkley Pub.

--The Hide & Tallow Men. 1978. pap. 1.95 (ISBN 0-425-05069-6). Berkley Pub.

--The Hooded Riders. (Orig.). 1980. pap. 1.75 o.p. (ISBN 0-425-04622-2). Berkley Pub.

--A Horse Called Mogollon. 1980. pap. 1.75 o.p. (ISBN 0-425-04632-X). Berkley Pub.

--Quiet Town. 1980. pap. 1.95 o.p. (ISBN 0-425-04623-0). Berkley Pub.

--Rangeland Hercules. 192p. (Orig.). 1983. pap. 2.25 (ISBN 0-425-05965-0). Berkley Pub.

--The Rio Hondo Kid. 192p. (Orig.). 1983. pap. 2.25 (ISBN 0-425-05939-1). Berkley Pub.

--Set Texas Back on Her Feet. 1980. pap. 1.75 o.p. (ISBN 0-425-04413-0). Berkley Pub.

--The South Will Rise Again. 1980. pap. 1.75 o.p. (ISBN 0-425-04491-2). Berkley Pub.

--The Texan. 192p. (Orig.). 1983. pap. 2.25 (ISBN 0-425-05858-1). Berkley Pub.

--To Arms! to Arms, in Dixie! 1980. pap. 1.75 o.p. (ISBN 0-425-04162-X). Berkley Pub.

--Trail Boss. 192p. 1982. pap. 1.95 (ISBN 0-686-83166-7). Berkley Pub.

--Wagons to Backsight. (Orig.). 1980. pap. 1.95 o.p. (ISBN 0-425-04625-7). Berkley Pub.

--Wagons to Backsight. 192p. (Orig.). 1982. pap. 2.25 (ISBN 0-425-05951-0). Berkley Pub.

Edson, Lee. How We Learn. LC 74-33050. (Human Behavior Ser.). (Illus.). 1975. lib. bdg. 13.28 (ISBN 0-8094-1917-3). Silver.

Edson, Russell. The Falling Sickness: A Book of Plays. LC 74-23986. 96p. 1975. 7.95 o.p. (ISBN 0-8112-0561-4); pap. 3.75 (ISBN 0-8112-0562-2, NDP389). New Directions.

--What a Man Can See & Other Fables. LC 60-9954. pap. 6.00 (ISBN 0-912330-13-9, Dist. by Inland Bk). Jargon Soc.

Edstrom, A. E., jt. auth. see Levens, A. S.

Education & Public Welfare Division, jt. ed. see Congressional Research Service.

Education & Training Comm. Oregon Association of Milk, Food & Environment Sanitarians, Inc. HTST Pasteurizer Operation Manual. (Illus.). 6.50 (ISBN 0-88246-057-9). Oreg St U Bkstrs.

Educational Challenges, Inc. Map Skills. Hayes, Heidi, ed. Incl. Book C (ISBN 0-8372-3505-7). tchr's. ed. (ISBN 0-8372-9195-X); Book D (ISBN 0-8372-3506-5). tchr's. ed. (ISBN 0-8372-9196-8); Book E (ISBN 0-8372-3507-3). tchr's. ed. (ISBN 0-8372-9197-6); Book F (ISBN 0-8372-3508-1). tchr's. ed. (ISBN 0-8372-9198-4). (Elementary Skills Ser). 1977. tchr's. eds. 1.47 ea. Bowmar-Noble.

Educational Research Council of America.
Accountant. Ferris, Theodore N. & Marchak, John P., eds. (Real People at Work Ser.: S). (Illus.). 36p. 1977. 2.45 (ISBN 0-89247-141-7). Changing Times.
--Actress. rev. ed. Ferris, Theodore N. & Marchak, John P., eds. (Real People at Work Ser: C). (Illus.). 36p. 1977. pap. text ed. 2.45 (ISBN 0-89247-023-2). Changing Times.
--Advertising Copy Writer. Ferris, Theodore N. & Marchak, John P., eds. (Real People at Work Ser.: Q). (Illus.). 36p. 1977. 2.45 (ISBN 0-89247-122-0). Changing Times.
--Airplane Machinist. Ferris, Theodore N. & Marchak, John P., eds. (Real People at Work Ser.: R). (Illus.). 36p. 1977. 2.45 (ISBN 0-89247-136-0). Changing Times.
--Analytical Testing Manager. Ferris, Theodore N. & Marchak, John P., eds. (Real People at Work: Series N). (Orig.). 36p. (gr. 5). 1976. pap. text ed. 2.45 (ISBN 0-89247-094-1). Changing Times.
--Architect. rev. ed. Ferris, Theodore N., et al, eds. (Real People at Work Ser: K). (Illus.). 36p. 1980. pap. text ed. 2.45 (ISBN 0-89247-083-6). Changing Times.
--Assistant Bank Manager. rev. ed. Ferris, Theodore N. & Marchak, John P., eds. (Real People at Work Ser: F). (Illus.). 36p. 1976. pap. text ed. 2.45 (ISBN 0-89247-042-9). Changing Times.
--Astrophysicist. Ferris, Theodore N. & Marchak, John P., eds. (Real People at Work: Series O). (Illus.). 36p. (Orig.). (gr. 5). 1976. pap. text ed. 2.45 (ISBN 0-89247-101-8). Changing Times.
--Auto Body Repairman. rev. ed. Ferris, Theodore N. & Marchak, John P., eds. (Real People at Work Ser: E). (Illus.). 36p. 1976. pap. text ed. 2.45 (ISBN 0-89247-037-2). Changing Times.
--Baker. Ferris, Theodore N. & Marchak, John P., eds. (Real People at Work Ser.: Q). (Illus.). 36p. 1977. 2.45 (ISBN 0-89247-124-7). Changing Times.
--Beautician. rev. ed. Engle, Jacqueline & Marchak, John P., eds. (Real People at Work Ser: C). (Illus.). 36p. 1976. pap. text ed. 2.45 (ISBN 0-89247-025-9). Changing Times.
--Blacksmith. Ferris, Theodore N. & Marchak, John P., eds. (Real People at Work Ser.: S). (Illus.). 36p. 1977. 2.45 (ISBN 0-89247-146-8). Changing Times.
--Boat Builders. Ferris, Theodore N. & Marchak, John P., eds. (Real People at Work Ser.: R). (Illus.). 36p. 1977. 2.45 (ISBN 0-89247-135-2). Changing Times.
--Boot Maker. Ferris, Theodore N., et al, eds. (Real People at Work Ser: I). (Illus.). 36p. 1975. pap. text ed. 2.45 (ISBN 0-89247-060-7). Changing Times.
--Building Maintenance Worker. rev. ed. Ferris, Theodore N., ed. (Real People at Work Ser: I). (Illus.). 36p. 1980. pap. text ed. 2.45 (ISBN 0-89247-061-5). Changing Times.
--Cabinetmaker. Ferris, Theodore N. & Marchak, John P., eds. (Real People at Work: Series M). (Illus.). 36p. (Orig.). (gr. 5). 1976. pap. text ed. 2.45 (ISBN 0-89247-090-9). Changing Times.
--Camera Technician. Ferris, Theodore N. & Marchak, John P., eds. (Real People at Work Ser.: S). (Illus.). 36p. 1977. 2.45 (ISBN 0-89247-142-5). Changing Times.
--Carpenter. rev. ed. Ferris, Theodore N. & Marchak, John P., eds. (Real People at Work Ser: A). (Illus.). 36p. 1976. pap. text ed. 2.45 (ISBN 0-89247-001-1). Changing Times.
--Carpet Maker. Ferris, Theodore N. & Marchak, John P., eds. (Real People at Work Ser.: Q). (Illus.). 36p. 1977. 2.45 (ISBN 0-89247-129-8). Changing Times.
--Cellist. Ferris, Theodore N. & Marchak, John P., eds. (Real People at Work: Series N). (Illus., Orig.). (gr. 5). 1976. pap. text ed. 2.45 (ISBN 0-89247-097-6). Changing Times.
--Ceramic Worker. rev. ed. Ferris, Theodore N., et al, eds. (Real People at Work Ser: I). (Illus.). 36p. 1980. pap. text ed. 2.45 (ISBN 0-89247-067-4). Changing Times.
--Chef. rev. ed. Ferris, Theodore N. & Marchak, John P., eds. (Real People at Work Ser: B). (Illus.). 36p. 1976. pap. text ed. 2.45 (ISBN 0-89247-015-1). Changing Times.
--Chemical Technicians. Ferris, Theodore N. & Marchak, John P., eds. (Real People at Work Ser: F). (Illus.). 36p. 1974. pap. text ed. 2.45 (ISBN 0-89247-049-6). Changing Times.
--Child-Care Attendants. Ferris, Theodore N. & Marchak, John P., eds. (Real People at Work Ser.: R). (Illus.). 36p. 1977. 2.45 (ISBN 0-89247-134-4). Changing Times.
--Children's Librarian. Keck, Florence & Marchak, John P., eds. (Real People at Work Ser: A). (Illus.). 36p. 1974. pap. text ed. 2.45 (ISBN 0-89247-003-8). Changing Times.
--Citrus Grower. Ferris, Theodore N. & Marchak, John P., eds. (Real People at Work Ser.: B). (Illus.). 36p. 1974. pap. text ed. 2.45 (ISBN 0-89247-014-3). Changing Times.
--Civil Engineers. Ferris, Theodore N. & Marchak, John P., eds. (Real People at Work: Series N). (Illus.). 36p. (Orig.). (gr. 5). 1976. pap. text ed. 2.45 (ISBN 0-89247-091-7). Changing Times.
--Coal Miner. rev. ed. Ferris, Theodore N., et al, eds. (Real People at Work Ser: I). (Illus.). 36p. 1980. pap. text ed. 2.45 (ISBN 0-89247-064-X). Changing Times.
--Coast Guard Petty Officer. Ferris, Theodore N. & Marchak, John P., eds. (Real People at Work Ser.: Q). (Illus.). 36p. 1977. 2.45 (ISBN 0-89247-127-1). Changing Times.
--Commercial Airline Pilot. Ferris, Theodore N. & Marchak, John P., eds. (Real People at Work Ser.: Q). (Illus.). 36p. 1977. pap. 2.45 (ISBN 0-89247-121-2). Changing Times.
--Computer Operator. rev. ed. Ferris, Theodore N., et al, eds. (Real People at Work Ser: I). (Illus.). 36p. 1980. pap. text ed. 2.45 (ISBN 0-89247-062-3). Changing Times.
--Congresswoman. Ferris, Theodore N. & Marchak, John P., eds. (Real People at Work: Series M). (Illus.). 36p. (Orig.). (gr. 5). 1976. pap. text ed. 2.45 (ISBN 0-89247-111-5). Changing Times.
--Contract Cleaner. rev. ed. Ferris, Theodore N., et al, eds. (Real People at Work Ser: J). (Illus.). 36p. 1980. pap. text ed. 2.45 (ISBN 0-89247-071-2). Changing Times.
--Corporate Lawyer. Ferris, Theodore N. & Marchak, John P., eds. (Real People at Work Ser: I). (Illus.). 36p. 1975. pap. text ed. 2.45 (ISBN 0-89247-068-2). Changing Times.
--Corrugated Box Worker. Ferris, Theodore N. & Marchak, John P., eds. (Real People at Work Ser.: Q). (Illus.). 36p. 1977. 2.45 (ISBN 0-89247-123-9). Changing Times.
--Costume Maker. Ferris, Theodore N. & Marchak, John P., eds. (Real People at Work: Series O). (Illus.). 36p. (Orig.). (gr. 5). 1976. pap. text ed. 2.45 (ISBN 0-89247-119-0). Changing Times.
--Dentist. rev. ed. Kunze, Linda J. & Marchak, John P., eds. (Real People at Work Ser: G). (Illus.). 36p. 1976. pap. text ed. 2.45 (ISBN 0-89247-055-0). Changing Times.
--Dredge Operator. Ferris, Theodore N. & Marchak, John P., eds. (Real People at Work Ser.: Q). (Illus.). 36p. 1977. 2.45 (ISBN 0-89247-125-5). Changing Times.
--Dressmaker. rev. ed. Ferris, Theodore N. & Marchak, John P., eds. (Real People at Work Ser: C). (Illus.). 36p. 1976. pap. text ed. 2.45 (ISBN 0-89247-020-8). Changing Times.
--Dry Cleaners. rev. ed. Ferris, Theodore N. & Marchak, John P., eds. (Real People at Work Ser: G). (Illus.). 36p. 1976. pap. text ed. 2.45 (ISBN 0-89247-050-X). Changing Times.
--Ecologist. rev. ed. Ferris, Theodore N., et al, eds. (Real People at Work Ser: J). (Illus.). 36p. 1980. pap. text ed. 2.45 (ISBN 0-89247-078-X). Changing Times.
--Economist. Ferris, Theodore N. & Marchak, John P., eds. (Real People at Work: Series M). (Illus.). 36p. (Orig.). (gr. 5). 1976. pap. text ed. 2.45 (ISBN 0-89247-093-3). Changing Times.
--Electrician. Ferris, Theodore N., et al, eds. (Real People at Work Ser: K). (Illus.). 36p. 1981. pap. text ed. 2.45 (ISBN 0-89247-081-X). Changing Times.
--Electronic Repairer. Ferris, Theodore N. & Marchak, John P., eds. (Real People at Work Ser.: Q). (Illus.). 36p. 1977. 2.45 (ISBN 0-89247-128-X). Changing Times.
--Employee Counselor. Ferris, Theodore N. & Marchak, John P., eds. (Real People at Work: Series O). (Illus.). 36p. (Orig.). (gr. 5). 1976. pap. text ed. 2.45 (ISBN 0-89247-104-2). Changing Times.
--Estimator. rev. ed. Ferris, Theodore N. & Marchak, John P., eds. (Real People at Work Ser: F). (Illus.). 36p. 1976. pap. text ed. 2.45 (ISBN 0-89247-041-0). Changing Times.
--Executive Housekeeper. rev. ed. Marchak, John P., ed. (Real People at Work Ser: B). (Illus.). 36p. 1976. pap. text ed. 2.45 (ISBN 0-89247-011-9). Changing Times.
--Fashion Designer. Ferris, Theodore N. & Marchak, John P., eds. (Real People at Work: Series N). (Illus.). 36p. (Orig.). (gr. 5). 1976. pap. text ed. 2.45 (ISBN 0-89247-118-2). Changing Times.
--FDA Investigator. rev. ed. Kunze, Linda J. & Marchak, John P., eds. (Real People at Work Ser: E). (Illus.). 36p. 1976. pap. text ed. 2.45 (ISBN 0-89247-038-0). Changing Times.
--Firearms Examiner. Ferris, Theodore N. & Marchak, John P., eds. (Real People at Work Ser.: R). (Illus.). 36p. 1977. 2.45 (ISBN 0-89247-137-9). Changing Times.
--Firefighters. rev. ed. Muesegaes, Mary & Marchak, John P., eds. (Real People at Work Ser: A). (Illus.). 36p. 1976. pap. text ed. 2.45 (ISBN 0-89247-008-9). Changing Times.
--Fish Biologist. Kunze, Linda J. & Marchak, John P., eds. (Real People at Work Ser: G). (Illus.). 36p. 1974. pap. text ed. 2.45 (ISBN 0-89247-056-9). Changing Times.
--Fisher. rev. ed. Braverman, Jack R. & Marchak, John P., eds. (Real People at Work Ser: A). (Illus.). 36p. 1977. pap. text ed. 2.45 (ISBN 0-89247-006-2). Changing Times.
--Florist. rev. ed. Ferris, Theodore N. & Marchak, John P., eds. (Real People at Work Ser: A). 36p. 1976. pap. text ed. 2.45 (ISBN 0-89247-004-6). Changing Times.
--Food Technologist. Ferris, Theodore N. & Marchak, John P., eds. (Real People at Work: Series M). (Illus.). 36p. (Orig.). (gr. 5). 1976. pap. text ed. 2.45 (ISBN 0-89247-102-6). Changing Times.
--Forester. rev. ed. Ferris, Theodore N. & Marchak, John P., eds. (Real People at Work Ser: C). (Illus.). 36p. 1976. pap. text ed. 2.45 (ISBN 0-89247-028-3). Changing Times.
--Furniture Maker. rev. ed. Ferris, Theodore N. & Marchak, John P., eds. (Real People at Work Ser: C). (Illus.). 36p. 1976. pap. text ed. 2.45 (ISBN 0-89247-021-6). Changing Times.
--Furrier. rev. ed. Ferris, Theodore N. & Marchak, John P., eds. (Real People at Work Ser: E). (Illus.). 36p. 1976. pap. text ed. 2.45 (ISBN 0-89247-030-5). Changing Times.
--General Store Owner. rev. ed. Ferris, Theodore N. & Marchak, John P., eds. (Real People at Work Ser: E). (Illus.). 36p. 1976. pap. text ed. 2.45 (ISBN 0-89247-032-1). Changing Times.
--Graphic Artist. rev. ed. Ferris, Theodore N. & Marchak, John P., eds. (Real People at Work Ser: B). (Illus.). 36p. 1977. pap. text ed. 2.45 (ISBN 0-89247-013-5). Changing Times.
--Hand Weaver. Ferris, Theodore N. & Marchak, John P., eds. (Real People at Work Ser: A). (Illus.). 36p. 1974. pap. text ed. 2.45 (ISBN 0-89247-000-3). Changing Times.
--Hardrock Miner. Ferris, Theodore N. & Marchak, John P., eds. (Real People at Work Ser: F). (Illus.). 36p. 1974. pap. text ed. 2.45 (ISBN 0-89247-044-5). Changing Times.
--Helicopter Pilot. Kunze, Linda J. & Marchak, John P., eds. (Real People at Work Ser: K). (Illus.). 36p. 1976. pap. text ed. 2.45 (ISBN 0-89247-082-8). Changing Times.
--Home Economist. rev. ed. Ferris, Theodore N. & Marchak, John P., eds. (Real People at Work Ser: J). (Illus.). 36p. 1980. pap. text ed. 2.45 (ISBN 0-89247-073-9). Changing Times.
--Horticulturist. Ferris, Theodore N. & Marchak, John P., eds. (Real People at Work Ser.: R). (Illus.). 36p. 1977. 2.45 (ISBN 0-89247-133-6). Changing Times.
--Housing Consultant. Ferris, Theodore N. & Marchak, John P., eds. (Real People at Work Ser.: S). (Illus.). 36p. 1977. 2.45 (ISBN 0-89247-147-6). Changing Times.
--Industrial Film Maker. rev. ed. Ferris, Theodore N. & Marchak, John P., eds. (Real People at Work Ser: G). (Illus.). 36p. 1976. pap. text ed. 2.45 (ISBN 0-89247-053-4). Changing Times.
--Industrial Nurse. Ferris, Theodoe N., et al, eds. (Real People at Work Ser: I). (Illus.). 36p. 1975. pap. text ed. 2.45 (ISBN 0-89247-065-8). Changing Times.
--Instrument Repairer. Ferris, Theodore N. & Marchak, John P., eds. (Real People at Work: Series O). (Illus.). 36p. (Orig.). (gr. 5). 1976. pap. text ed. 2.45 (ISBN 0-89247-110-7). Changing Times.
--Insulation Knitter. Ferris, Theodore N., et al, eds. (Real People at Work Ser: K). (Illus.). 36p. 1975. pap. text ed. 2.45 (ISBN 0-89247-080-1). Changing Times.
--Ironworker. Ferris, Theodore N. & Marchak, John P., eds. (Real People at Work: Series O). (Illus.). 36p. (Orig.). (gr. 5). 1976. pap. text ed. 2.45 (ISBN 0-89247-092-5). Changing Times.
--Judge. rev. ed. Ferris, Theodore N. & Marchak, John P., eds. (Real People at Work Ser: G). (Illus.). 36p. 1976. pap. text ed. 2.45 (ISBN 0-89247-058-5). Changing Times.
--Laser Project Engineer. Ferris, Theodore N. & Marchak, John P., eds. (Real People at Work: Series N). (Illus.). 36p. (Orig.). (gr. 5). 1976. pap. text ed. 2.45 (ISBN 0-89247-115-8). Changing Times.
--Leather Worker. Ferris, Theodore & Marchak, John P., eds. (Real People at Work Ser: B). (Illus.). 36p. 1974. pap. text ed. 2.45 (ISBN 0-89247-010-0). Changing Times.
--Lock Master. Braverman, Jack R. & Marchak, John P., eds. (Real People at Work Ser: E). (Illus.). 36p. 1974. pap. text ed. 2.45 (ISBN 0-89247-036-4). Changing Times.
--Luggage Maker. Ferris, Theodore N. & Marchak, John P., eds. (Real People at Work Ser.: R). (Illus.). 36p. 1977. 2.45 (ISBN 0-89247-139-5). Changing Times.
--Lumber Worker. rev. ed. Ferris, Theodore N. & Marchak, John P., eds. (Real People at Work Ser.: K). (Illus.). 36p. 1980. pap. text ed. 2.45 (ISBN 0-89247-084-4). Changing Times.
--Machinist. rev. ed. Kunze, Linda J. & Marchak, John P., eds. (Real People at Work Series G). (Illus.). 36p. 1976. pap. text ed. 2.45 (ISBN 0-89247-057-7). Changing Times.
--The Making of Our America. LC 80-67910. (Concepts & Understanding Ser.). (gr. 5). 1982. 15.32 (ISBN 0-205-06791-3); write for info. dupl. masters (ISBN 0-205-06793-X); write for info. wrkbk dup. masters; write for info. tests, black-line masters (ISBN 0-205-07766-8). Allyn.
--Managing Editor. Ferris, Theodore N. & Marchak, John P., eds. (Real People at Work: Series O). (Illus.). 36p. (Orig.). (gr. 5). 1976. pap. text ed. 2.45 (ISBN 0-89247-098-4). Changing Times.
--Manufacturing Optician. Ferris, Theodore N. & Marchak, John P., eds. (Real People at Work Ser: B). (Illus.). 36p. 1974. pap. text ed. 2.45 (ISBN 0-89247-019-4). Changing Times.
--Marine Engineer. Ferris, Theodore N., ed. (Real People at Work Ser: K). (Illus.). 36p. 1975. pap. text ed. 2.45 (ISBN 0-89247-086-0). Changing Times.
--Market Researcher. Kunze, Linda J. & Marchak, John P., eds. (Real People at Work Ser: J). (Illus.). 36p. 1975. pap. text ed. 2.45 (ISBN 0-89247-072-0). Changing Times.
--Mechanic-Attendant. rev. ed. Kunze, Linda A. & Marchak, John P., eds. (Real People at Work Ser.: Pt. A). (Illus.). 36p. 1976. pap. text ed. 2.45 (ISBN 0-89247-007-0). Changing Times.
--Medical Technologist. rev. ed. Kunze, Linda J. & Marchak, John P., eds. (Real People at Work Ser: E). (Illus.). 36p. 1976. pap. text ed. 2.45 (ISBN 0-89247-035-6). Changing Times.
--Metal Molder. rev. ed. Braverman, Jack R. & Marchak, John P., eds. (Real People at Work Ser: B). (Illus.). 36p. 1976. pap. text ed. 2.45 (ISBN 0-89247-017-8). Changing Times.
--Metallurgical Technician. rev. ed. Ferris, Theodore N. & Marchak, John P., eds. (Real People at Work Ser: C). 36p. 1976. pap. text ed. 2.45 (ISBN 0-89247-029-1). Changing Times.
--Meteorologist. rev. ed. Kunze, Linda J. & Marchak, John P., eds. (Real People at Work Ser: G). (Illus.). 36p. 1976. pap. text ed. 2.45 (ISBN 0-89247-054-2). Changing Times.
--Natural Science Chemist. Ferris, Theodore N., et al, eds. (Real People at Work Ser: J). (Illus.). 36p. 1975. pap. text ed. 2.45 (ISBN 0-89247-074-7). Changing Times.
--Nuclear Plant Designer. Ferris, Theodore N., et al, eds. (Real People at Work Er: J). (Illus.). 36p. 1976. pap. text ed. 2.45 (ISBN 0-89247-079-8). Changing Times.
--Nuclear Reactor Operator. Ferris, Theodore N. & Marchak, John P., eds. (Real People at Work Ser: G). (Illus.). 36p. 1974. pap. text ed. 2.45 (ISBN 0-89247-059-3). Changing Times.
--Nursery Worker. Ferris, Theodore N. & Marchak, John P., eds. (Real People at Work: Series M). (Illus.). 36p. (Orig.). (gr. 5). 1976. pap. text ed. 2.45 (ISBN 0-89247-099-2). Changing Times.
--Oceanographers. Ferris, Theodore N. & Marchak, John P., eds. (Real People at Work: Series M). (Illus.). 36p. (Orig.). (gr. 5). 1976. pap. text ed. 2.45 (ISBN 0-89247-105-0). Changing Times.
--Office Worker. Ferris, Theodore N., et al, eds. (Real People at Work Ser: G). (Illus.). 36p. 1974. pap. text ed. 2.45 (ISBN 0-89247-052-6). Changing Times.
--Oil Driller. Ferris, Theodore N. & Marchak, John P., eds. (Real People at Work Ser: C). (Illus.). 36p. 1974. pap. text ed. 2.45 (ISBN 0-89247-024-0). Changing Times.
--Operating Engineer. Ferris, Theodore N. & Marchak, John P., eds. (Real People at Work Ser.: S). (Illus.). 36p. 1977. 2.45 (ISBN 0-89247-140-9). Changing Times.
--Paint Chemist. Ferris, Theodore N. & Marchak, John P., eds. (Real People at Work Ser.: S). (Illus.). 36p. 1977. 2.45 (ISBN 0-89247-148-4). Changing Times.
--Painter Apprentices. Ferris, Theodore N. & Marchak, John P., eds. (Real People at Work Ser.: R). (Illus.). 36p. 1977. 2.45 (ISBN 0-89247-130-1). Changing Times.
--Paper Makers. rev. ed. Braverman, Jack R. & Marchak, John P., eds. (Real People at Work Ser: E). (Illus.). 36p. 1976. pap. text ed. 2.45 (ISBN 0-89247-034-8). Changing Times.
--Pest Controller. rev. ed. Kunze, Linda J. & Marchak, John P., eds. (Real People at Work Ser: G). (Illus.). 36p. 1976. pap. text ed. 2.45 (ISBN 0-89247-051-8). Changing Times.

Educational Research Council of America, et al.
Pharmacist. Durkin, James, ed. (Real People at Work Ser: A). (Illus.). 36p. 1974. pap. text ed. 2.45 (ISBN 0-89247-005-4). Changing Times.

Educational Research Council of America.
Photographer. Ferris, Theodore N. & Marchak, John P., eds. (Real People at Work: Series M). (Illus.). 36p. (Orig.). (gr. 5). 1976. pap. text ed. 2.45 (ISBN 0-89247-096-8). Changing Times.
--Physical Therapists. rev. ed. Ferris, Theodore N., et al, eds. (Real People at Work Ser: K). (Illus.). 1980. pap. text ed. 2.45 (ISBN 0-89247-085-2). Changing Times.
--Plant Guard. Ferris, Theodore N. & Marchak, John P., eds. (Real People at Work: Series O). (Illus.). 36p. (Orig.). (gr. 5). 1976. pap. text ed. 2.45 (ISBN 0-89247-113-1). Changing Times.
--Plumber. rev. ed. Ferris, Theodore N. & Marchak, John P., eds. (Real People at Work Ser: E). (Illus.). 36p. 1976. pap. text ed. 2.45 (ISBN 0-89247-031-3). Changing Times.
--Police Team. rev. ed. Ferris, Theodore N. & Marchak, John P., eds. (Real People at Work Ser: B). (Illus.). 36p. 1976. pap. text ed. 2.45 (ISBN 0-89247-018-6). Changing Times.
--Power Line Worker. rev. ed. Ferris, Theodore N., et al, eds. (Real People at Work Ser: I). (Illus.). 36p. 1980. pap. text ed. 2.45 (ISBN 0-89247-069-0). Changing Times.

--Power Plant Worker. Ferris, Theodore H., et al, eds. (Real People at Work Ser. K). (Illus.). 36p. (gr. 3). 1975. pap. text ed. 2.45 (ISBN 0-89247-089-5). Changing Times.
--Power Transformer Assembler. Ferris, Theodore N., et al, eds. (Real People at Work Ser: J). (Illus.). 36p. 1975. pap. text ed. 2.45 (ISBN 0-89247-077-1). Changing Times.
--Pro Basketball Player. rev. ed. Ferris, Theodore N. & Marchak, John P., eds. (Real People at Work Ser: F). (Illus.). 36p. 1976. pap. text ed. 2.45 (ISBN 0-89247-045-3). Changing Times.
--Production Planner. Ferris, Theodore N. & Marchak, John P., eds. (Real People at Work Ser.: Q). (Illus.). 36p. 1977. 2.45 (ISBN 0-89247-126-3). Changing Times.
--Protective Clothing Maker. rev. ed. Ferris, Theodore N., et al, eds. (Real People at Work Ser: J). (Illus.). 36p. 1980. pap. text ed. 2.45 (ISBN 0-89247-070-4). Changing Times.
--Public Relations Writers. Kunze, Linda J. & Marchak, John P., eds. (Real People at Work Ser: F). (Illus.). 36p. 1974. pap. text ed. 2.45 (ISBN 0-89247-043-7). Changing Times.
--Quality Control Engineer. rev. ed. Ferris, Theodore N. & Marchak, John P., eds. (Real People at Work Ser: E). (Illus.). 36p. 1976. pap. text ed. 2.45 (ISBN 0-89247-039-9). Changing Times.
--Real Estate Broker. Ferris, Theodore N. & Marchak, John P., eds. (Real People at Work Ser.: R). (Illus.). 36p. 1977. 2.45 (ISBN 0-89247-131-X). Changing Times.
--Recreation Leader. Ferris, Theodore N. & Marchak, John P., eds. (Real People at Work Ser.: S). (Illus.). 36p. 1977. 2.45 (ISBN 0-89247-144-1). Changing Times.
--Research Scientist. Ferris, Theodore N. & Marchak, John P., eds. (Real People at Work: Series O). (Illus.). 36p. (Orig.). (gr. 5). 1976. pap. text ed. 2.45 (ISBN 0-89247-116-6). Changing Times.
--Safety Engineer. rev. ed. Ferris, Theodore N. & Marchak, John P., eds. (Real People at Work Ser: F). (Illus.). 36p. 1976. pap. text ed. 2.45 (ISBN 0-89247-048-8). Changing Times.
--Sales Representative. Ferris, Theodore N. & Marchak, John P., eds. (Real People at Work: Series O). (Illus.). 36p. (Orig.). (gr. 5). 1976. pap. text ed. 2.45 (ISBN 0-89247-095-X). Changing Times.
--Seafood Processor. Ferris, Theodore N. & Marchak, John P., eds. (Real People at Work: Series N). (Illus.). 36p. (gr. 5). 1976. pap. text ed. 2.45 (ISBN 0-89247-106-9). Changing Times.
--Seaman. rev. ed. Braverman, Jack R. & Marchak, John P., eds. (Real People at Work Ser: B). (Illus.). 36p. 1977. pap. text ed. 2.45 (ISBN 0-89247-016-X). Changing Times.
--Sheetmetal Worker. rev. ed. Eppert, M. R. & Marchak, John P., eds. (Real People at Work Ser: C). (Illus.). 36p. 1976. pap. text ed. 2.45 (ISBN 0-89247-027-5). Changing Times.
--Shipfitter. Braverman, Jack R. & Marchak, John P., eds. (Real People at Work Ser: C). (Illus.). 36p. 1974. pap. text ed. 2.45 (ISBN 0-89247-026-7). Changing Times.
--Ship's Engineer. Kunze, Linda J. & Marchak, John P., eds. (Real People at Work Ser: J). (Illus.). 36p. 1975. pap. text ed. 2.45 (ISBN 0-89247-076-3). Changing Times.
--Shipyard Workers. Ferris, Theodore N. & Marchak, John P., eds. (Real People at Work: Series O). (Illus.). 36p. (Orig.). (gr. 5). 1976. pap. text ed. 2.45 (ISBN 0-89247-107-7). Changing Times.
--Shoe Repairer. rev. ed. Ferris, Theodore N. & Marchak, John P., eds. (Real People at Work Ser: F). (Illus.). 36p. 1976. pap. text ed. 2.45 (ISBN 0-89247-040-2). Changing Times.
--Solar Cell Scientist. Ferris, Theodore N. & Marchak, John P., eds. (Real People at Work Ser.: S). (Illus.). 36p. 1977. 2.45 (ISBN 0-89247-143-3). Changing Times.
--Sound Engineer. Ferris, Theodore N. & Marchak, John P., eds. (Real People at Work Ser.: R). (Illus.). 36p. 1977. 2.45 (ISBN 0-89247-132-8). Changing Times.
--Space Technologist. Ferris, Theodore N. & Marchak, John P., eds. (Real People at Work Ser.: R). (Illus.). 36p. 1977. 2.45 (ISBN 0-89247-138-7). Changing Times.
--Special Education Teacher. rev. ed. Kunze, Linda J. & Marchak, John P., eds. (Real People at Work Ser: E). (Illus.). 36p. 1977. pap. text ed. 2.45 (ISBN 0-89247-033-X). Changing Times.
--Steelworker. Ferris, Theodore N. & Marchak, John P., eds. (Real People at Work: Series M). (Illus.). 36p. (Orig.). (gr. 5). 1976. pap. text ed. 2.45 (ISBN 0-89247-108-5). Changing Times.
--Supermarket Cashier. rev. ed. McCabe, Bernard & Marchak, John P., eds. (Real People at Work Ser: B). 36p. 1976. pap. text ed. 2.45 (ISBN 0-89247-012-7). Changing Times.
--Supervisor Trainee. rev. ed. Ferris, Theodore N. & Marchak, John P., eds. (Real People at Work Ser.: A). 36p. 1976. pap. text ed. 2.45 (ISBN 0-89247-002-X). Changing Times.
--Tailor. Ferris, Theodore N. & Marchak, John P., eds. (Real People at Work Ser.: S). (Illus.). 36p. 1977. 2.45 (ISBN 0-89247-149-2). Changing Times.
--Telephone Repairman. rev. ed. Spinell, Donald & Marchak, John P., eds. (Real People at Work Ser: A). (Illus.). 36p. 1976. pap. text ed. 2.45 (ISBN 0-89247-009-7). Changing Times.
--Television News Broadcaster. rev. ed. Ferris, Theodore N, et al, eds. (Real People at Work Ser: I). (Illus.). 36p. 1980. pap. text ed. 2.45 (ISBN 0-89247-063-1). Changing Times.
--Test Room Engineer. Ferris, Theodore N. & Marchak, John P., eds. (Real People at Work: Series M). (Illus.). 36p. (Orig.). (gr. 5). 1976. pap. text ed. 2.45 (ISBN 0-89247-114-X). Changing Times.
--Textile Designer. Ferris, Theodore N. & Marchak, John P., eds. (Real People at Work: Series M). (Illus.). 36p. (Orig.). (gr. 5). 1976. pap. text ed. 2.45 (ISBN 0-89247-117-4). Changing Times.
--Tool & Die Apprentice. Ferris, Theodore N. & Marchak, John P., eds. (Real People at Work: Series N). (Illus.). 36p. (Orig.). (gr. 5). 1976. pap. text ed. 2.45 (ISBN 0-89247-109-3). Changing Times.
--Tour Director. Ferris, Theodore N. & Marchak, John P., eds. (Real People at Work: Series N). (Illus.). 36p. (Orig.). (gr. 5). 1976. pap. text ed. 2.45 (ISBN 0-89247-103-4). Changing Times.
--Towboat Pilot. Ferris, Theodore N., et al, eds. (Real People at Work Ser: I). (Illus.). 36p. 1975. pap. text ed. 2.45 (ISBN 0-89247-066-6). Changing Times.
--Truck Driver. rev. ed. McCabe, Bernard & Marchak, John P., eds. (Real People at Work Ser: C). (Illus.). 36p. 1976. pap. text ed. 2.45 (ISBN 0-89247-022-4). Changing Times.
--Truck Mechanic. rev. ed. Ferris, Theodore N., et al, eds. (Real People at Work Ser: K). (Illus.). 36p. 1980. pap. text ed. 2.45 (ISBN 0-89247-087-9). Changing Times.
--Tugboat Pilot. rev. ed. Ferris, Theodore N. & Marchak, John P., eds. (Real People at Work Ser: F). (Illus.). 36p. 1977. pap. text ed. 2.45 (ISBN 0-89247-046-1). Changing Times.
--Union Representative. Ferris, Theodore N. & Marchak, John P., eds. (Real People at Work: Series N). (Illus.). 36p. (Orig.). (gr. 5). 1976. pap. text ed. 2.45 (ISBN 0-89247-112-3). Changing Times.
--Violin Maker. Ferris, Theodore N. & Marchak, John P., eds. (Real People at Work Ser.: Q). (Illus.). 36p. 1977. 2.45 (ISBN 0-89247-120-4). Changing Times.
--Water Analyst. Ferris, Theodore N, et al, eds. (Real People at Work Ser: J). (Illus.). 36p. 1975. pap. text ed. 2.45 (ISBN 0-89247-075-5). Changing Times.
--Welders. rev. ed. Braverman, Jack R. & Marchak, John P., eds. (Real People at Work Ser: F). (Illus.). 36p. 1976. pap. text ed. 2.45 (ISBN 0-89247-047-X). Changing Times.
--Wheat Farmer. Ferris, Theodore N. & Marchak, John P., eds. (Real People at Work: Series N). (Illus.). 36p. (Orig.). (gr. 5). 1976. pap. text ed. 2.45 (ISBN 0-89247-100-X). Changing Times.
--Yacht Broker. Ferris, Theodore N. & Marchak, John P., eds. (Real People at Work Ser.: S). (Illus.). 36p. 1977. pap. text ed. 2.45 (ISBN 0-89247-145-X). Changing Times.
Educational Research Council or America. Watch Engineer. Ferris, Theodore N., et al, eds. (Real People at Work Ser: K). (Illus.). 36p. 1975. pap. text ed. 2.45 (ISBN 0-89247-088-7). Changing Times.
Educational Systems Corp. Skills in Mathematics, Bks. 1-2. (Cambridge Skill Power Ser.). 192p. (gr. 10-12). Bk. 1. pap. text ed. 6.15 (ISBN 0-8428-2108-2); Bk. 2. pap. text ed. 6.00 (ISBN 0-8428-2110-4); Key Bk. 1. 1.33 (ISBN 0-8428-2109-0). Cambridge Bk.
Educational Systems, Inc. Skills in Reading, 2 bks. (Cambridge Skill Power Ser.). (gr. 9-12). Bk.1. pap. text ed. 6.00 (ISBN 0-8428-9004-1); Bk. 2. pap. text ed. 4.15 (ISBN 0-8428-9013-0); 1.33 (ISBN 0-8428-9200-1); 1.33 (ISBN 0-8428-9201-X). Cambridge Bk.
EDUCOM Fall Conference, Oct. 1977. Closing the Gap Between Technology & Application: Proceedings. Emery, James C., ed. 1978. lib. bdg. 28.00 o.p. (ISBN 0-89158-167-7). Westview.
Edward, Ernest. Kate Greenaway Treasury. LC 67-23363. (Illus.). 1977. 19.95 o.s.i. (ISBN 0-529-00313-9, Philomel). Putnam Pub Group.
Edward, Karl. The Year's Best Horror Stories. (Series X). 1982. pap. 2.50 (ISBN 0-87997-757-4, UE1757). DAW Bks.
Edward, Page, Jr. The Mules That Angels Ride. LC 70-188737. 1972. 5.95 (ISBN 0-87955-900-4). O'Hara.
Edwardes, Michael. Ralph Fitch: Elizabethan in the Indies. (Great Travellers Ser.). (Illus.). 1973. 6.95 o.p. (ISBN 0-571-10133-X). Faber & Faber.
Edwards. Evolution in Modern Biology. (Studies in Biology: No. 87). 1978. 5.95 o.p. (ISBN 0-7131-2651-5). Univ Park.
--Family & Change. pap. text ed. 5.95x (ISBN 0-685-69590-5). Phila Bk Co.
Edwards, A. Water Gardens, Rock Gardens & Alpine Gardens. 312p. Date not set. 13.95 (ISBN 0-686-82963-8); pap. 8.95 (ISBN 0-89496-029-6). Ross Bks.
Edwards, A. & Wohl, G. The Picture Life of Muhammad Ali. 1977. pap. 1.75 o.p. (ISBN 0-380-01904-3, 51623, Camelot). Avon.
Edwards, A. S. Stephen Hawes. (English Authors Ser.: No. 354). 152p. 1983. lib. bdg. 18.95 (ISBN 0-8057-6840-8, Twayne). G K Hall.
Edwards, A. W. Foundations of Mathematical Genetics. LC 76-9168. (Illus.). 1977. 32.50 (ISBN 0-521-21325-8). Cambridge U Pr.
--Likelihood: An Account of the Statistical Concept of Likelihood & Its Application to Scientific Inference. LC 70-163060. (Illus.). 1972. 34.50 (ISBN 0-521-08299-4). Cambridge U Pr.
Edwards, Andrea. Now Come the Spring. 240p. 1983. pap. 2.95 (ISBN 0-380-83329-8). Avon.
Edwards, Anne. The Great Houdini. LC 76-8472. (See & Read Biographies). (Illus.). (gr. k-3). 1977. PLB 5.99 o.p. (ISBN 0-399-61020-0). Putnam Pub Group.
--P. T. Barnum. LC 76-52993. (See & Read Biographies). (Illus.). (gr. k-4). 1977. PLB 5.99 o.p. (ISBN 0-399-61083-9). Putnam Pub Group.
--The Road to Tara: The Life of Margaret Mitchell. LC 82-19520. (Illus.). 384p. 1983. 15.95 (ISBN 0-89919-169-X). Ticknor & Fields.
--Sonya: The Life of Countess Tolstoy. 1981. 15.95 o.s.i. (ISBN 0-671-24040-4). S&S.
Edwards, Barbara J. & Brilhart, John K. Communications in Nursing Practice. LC 81-1960. (Illus.). 245p. 1981. pap. text ed. 12.95 (ISBN 0-8016-0786-8). Mosby.
Edwards, Betty, jt. auth. see Coleman, Emily.
Edwards, Bruce & Fudge, Edward. A Journey Toward Jesus. 1.50 (ISBN 0-686-12687-4). Providential Pr.
Edwards, C. A. & Lofty, J. R. Biology of Earthworms. (Illus.). pap. 7.95 (ISBN 0-916302-20-2). Bookworm NY.
Edwards, C. H. Advanced Calculus of Several Variables. 1973. 21.00 (ISBN 0-12-232550-8). Acad Pr.
Edwards, C. H. & Penney, David E. Calculus & Analytic Geometry. 1120p. 1982. 33.95 (ISBN 0-13-111609-6). P-H.
Edwards, C. H., Jr. The Historical Development of the Calculus. (Illus.). 351p. (Corrected Second Printing). 1983. 29.40 (ISBN 0-387-90436-0). Springer-Verlag.
Edwards, Candy. The Reference Point. LC 82-83712. (Illus.). 80p. (gr. 3-6). 1983. pap. text ed. 5.95 (ISBN 0-86530-042-9, IP 42-9). Incentive Pubns.
Edwards, Cassie. Forbidden Embrace. 1982. pap. 3.50 (ISBN 0-8217-1105-9). Zebra.
--Heart Strings, No. 3. (First Romance Ser.). 192p. (gr. 6-12). 1982. pap. 1.95 o.s.i. (ISBN 0-8439-1153-0, Leisure Bks). Nordon Pubns.
--Secrets of the Heart. 400p. (Orig.). 1982. pap. 3.50 o.s.i. (ISBN 0-8439-1142-5, Leisure Bks). Nordon Pubns.
Edwards, Charles. John Knox, Bold One for God. LC 78-61733. (Destiny Ser.). 1979. pap. 4.95 o.p. (ISBN 0-8163-0238-3). Pacific Pr Pub Assn.
Edwards, Charles M., Jr. & Lebowitz, Carl R. Retail Advertising & Sales Promotion. (Illus.). 576p. 1981. text ed. 21.95 (ISBN 0-13-775098-6); pap. 24.95 (ISBN 0-13-775080-3). P-H.
Edwards, Chris. Developing Microcomputer-Based Business Systems. (Illus.). 224p. 1983. pap. 14.95 (ISBN 0-13-204552-4). P-H.
Edwards, Corwin D. Big Business & the Policy of Competition. LC 79-26189. 180p. 1980. Repr. of 1956 ed. lib. bdg. 19.00x (ISBN 0-313-22256-8, EDBB). Greenwood.
Edwards, D. K., et al. Transfer Processes. (Illus.). 1976. Repr. of 1973 ed. text ed. 18.00 o.p. (ISBN 0-07-019040-2, C). McGraw.
--Transfer Processes. 2nd ed. LC 78-7883. (Series in Thermal and Fluids Engineering). (Illus.). 1979. text ed. 39.95 (ISBN 0-07-019041-0, C). McGraw.
Edwards, Dan W. Communication Skills for the Helping Professions. 112p. 1983. 16.75x (ISBN 0-398-04766-9). C C Thomas.
Edwards, Dan W. & Letman, Sloan T. Aging in the Urban Community. 120p. 1983. pap. text ed. 12.50 (ISBN 0-934872-05-8). Carlinshar.
Edwards, David. The American Political Experience: An Introduction to Government. 2nd ed. (Illus.). 704p. 1982. text ed. 22.95 (ISBN 0-13-028308-8). P-H.
Edwards, David L. Christian England: Its Story to the Reformation. (Illus.). 1981. 22.50x (ISBN 0-19-520229-5). Oxford U Pr.
Edwards, David V. The American Political Experience: An Introduction to Government. 2nd ed. 256p. 1982. learning guide 7.95 (ISBN 0-13-028282-0). P-H.
Edwards, Donald E. & Kettering, Ronald C. Computer Assisted Practice Set in Financial Accounting: Cook's Solar Energy Systems. LC 82-83660. 96p. 1983. pap. 9.95 (ISBN 0-395-33492-6); write for info. instr's. manual (ISBN 0-395-33493-4). HM.
Edwards, Dorothy. A Wet Monday. LC 76-12405. (Illus.). (ps-1). 1976. PLB 8.16 (ISBN 0-688-32081-3); pap. 2.95 o.p. (ISBN 0-688-27081-6). Morrow.
--The Witches & the Grinnygog. 176p. (gr. 5-8). 1983. 10.95 (ISBN 0-571-11720-1). Faber & Faber.
Edwards, E. Hartley. All About Horses & Ponies. 1976. 7.95 o.p. (ISBN 0-491-01726-X). Transatlantic.
Edwards, Edgar O. & Bell, Philip W. The Theory & Measurement of Business Income. 1961. 18.95x (ISBN 0-520-00376-4). U of Cal Pr.
Edwards, Edward B. Pattern & Design with Dynamic Symmetry. Orig. Title: Dynamarhythmic Design, li. pap. 4.00 (ISBN 0-486-21756-6). Dover.
Edwards, Eleanor M. Making Music with the Hearing Impaired. 1982. pap. cancelled (ISBN 0-914562-13-4). Merriam-Eddy.
Edwards, Eliezer E. Words, Facts & Phrases: A Dictionary of Curious, Quaint, & Out-of-the-Way Matters. LC 68-21768. 1968. Repr. of 1881 ed. 42.00x (ISBN 0-8103-3087-3). Gale.
Edwards, Elwyn & Lees, Frank P. The Human Operator in Process Control. (Illus.). 480p. 1974. 35.00x (ISBN 0-85066-069-6). Intl Pubns Serv.
Edwards, Elwyn H. & Geddes, Candida, eds. The Complete Book of the Horse. LC 82-81528. (Illus.). 344p. 17.95 (ISBN 0-686-83103-9, 8220). Larousse.
Edwards, Ernest P. A Coded Workbook of Birds of the World: Vol. 1-Non-Passerines. 2nd ed. LC 82-82891. (Illus.). xxi, 134p. 1982. pap. 10.00 plastic ring bdg. (ISBN 0-911882-07-3). E P Edwards.
Edwards, Everett E. Bibliography of the History of Agriculture in the U. S. LC 66-27834. 1967. Repr. of 1930 ed. 34.00x (ISBN 0-8103-3102-0). Gale.
Edwards, F. H. Life & Ministry of Jesus. 1982. pap. 13.50 (ISBN 0-686-95353-3). Herald Hse.
Edwards, Florence. The Tizzy Stories. 1979. 6.95 o.p. (ISBN 0-533-04097-3). Vantage.
Edwards, Frederick H. The Principles of Switching Circuits. 352p. 1973. 25.00x (ISBN 0-262-05011-0). MIT Pr.
Edwards, G. Franklin. The Negro Professional Class. LC 82-11990. 224p. 1982. Repr. of 1959 ed. lib. bdg. 25.00x (ISBN 0-313-22330-0, EDNP). Greenwood.
Edwards, Gabrielle. Coping with V. D. rev. ed. (Coping with Ser.). (Illus.). 1983. lib. bdg. 7.97 (ISBN 0-8239-0512-8). Rosen Pr.
Edwards, Gabrielle I., ed. Barron's Regents Exams & Answers Biology. rev. ed. LC 58-19074. 300p. (gr. 9-12). 1982. pap. text ed. 4.50 (ISBN 0-8120-3110-5). Barron.
Edwards, Gareth. Labor & the Constitution 1972-5: The Whitlam Years in Australian Government. 1977. text ed. 58.50x o.p. (ISBN 0-435-83250-6). Heinemann Ed.
Edwards, Gene. Our Mission. (Orig.). 1983. pap. 4.95 (ISBN 0-940232-11-1). Christian Bks.
Edwards, Gene, ed. see Brother Lawerance & Laubach, Frank.
Edwards, Gene, ed. see Fenelon.
Edwards, Gene, ed. see Molinos, Michael.
Edwards, Geoffrey, jt. ed. see Arbuthnott, Hugh.
Edwards, George C., III. Public Policy Implementation. (Politics & Public Policy Ser.). 300p. (Orig.). 1980. pap. text ed. 6.95 (ISBN 0-87187-155-6). Congr Quarterly.
Edwards, George C., III & Wayne, Stephen J., eds. Studying the Presidency. LC 82-17472. 320p. 1983. text ed. 19.95x (ISBN 0-87049-378-7); pap. text ed. 9.95 (ISBN 0-87049-379-5). U of Tenn Pr.
Edwards, George T. Music & Musicians of Maine. (Illus.). 542p. 1928. 15.00 (ISBN 0-686-05799-6). O'Brien.
Edwards, Gerald M., ed. see Homer.
Edwards, Griffith, jt. auth. see Orford, Jim.
Edwards, Griffith & Grant, Marcus, eds. Alcoholism Treatment in Transition. 336p. 1980. pap. 18.95 (ISBN 0-8391-4132-7). Univ Park.
Edwards, H., jt. auth. see Katzeff, I. E.
Edwards, H. E., et al, eds. see Association for Radiation Research, Winter Meeting Jan.3-5, 1979.
Edwards, H. L., tr. see Stendhal.
Edwards, H. Sutherland. History of the Opera: From Monteverdi to Donizetti, 2 vols. in one. LC 77-5587. 1977. Repr. of 1862 ed. lib. bdg. 55.00 (ISBN 0-306-77416-X). Da Capo.
--The Prima Donna: Her History & Surroundings from the 17th to the 19th Century, 2 vols, Vol. 1. LC 77-17875. (Music Reprint Ser.). 1978. Repr. of 1888 ed. Set. lib. bdg. 55.00 (ISBN 0-306-77558-1). Da Capo.
Edwards, Hardy M., jt. auth. see Lassiter, J. W.
Edwards, Harold M. Advanced Calculus. LC 79-23792. 524p. 1980. Repr. of 1969 ed. lib. bdg. 21.50 (ISBN 0-89874-047-9). Krieger.
Edwards, Harry. The Struggle That Must Be: An Autobiography. 350p. 1980. 14.95 o.p. (ISBN 0-02-535040-4). Macmillan.
Edwards, Harry J., Jr. Automatic Controls for Heating & Air Conditioning: Pneumatic-Electric Control Systems. (Illus.). 1980. 20.75 (ISBN 0-07-019046-1). McGraw.
Edwards, Harry T. & Nordin, Virginia D. Cumulative Supplement, 1982: Higher Education & the Law. LC 79-88195. 180p. (Orig.). 1982. pap. text ed. 8.50x (ISBN 0-934222-06-1). Inst Ed Management.
--Higher Education & the Law: 1981, Cumulative Supplement. LC 79-88195. 186p. (Orig.). 1981. pap. text ed. 8.50x o.p. (ISBN 0-934222-05-3); pap. 2.50x o.p. (ISBN 0-934222-05-3). Inst Ed Management.

--Nineteen Eighty Cumulative Supplement Higher Education & the Law. LC 80-82432. 136p. (Orig.). 1980. pap. text ed. 5.95x o.p. (ISBN 0-934222-03-7); pap. 2.50x o.p. (ISBN 0-934222-03-7). Inst Ed Manage.

Edwards, Herbert W., jt. auth. see Horton, Rod W.

Edwards, Holly. Patterns & Precision: The Arts & Sciences of Islam. (Illus.). 56p. pap. 6.50 (ISBN 0-87474-399-0). Smithsonian.

Edwards, I. E. Tutankhamun's Jewelry. LC 76-41859. (Illus.). 1976. pap. 3.95 o.s.i. (ISBN 0-87099-155-8). Metro Mus Art.

Edwards, Ifor. Davies Brothers Gatesmiths. (Illus.). 111p. 1980. pap. 9.50 (ISBN 0-905171-22-5, Pub. by Welsh Art Wales). Intl Schol Bk Serv.

Edwards, India. Pulling No Punches: Memoirs of a Woman in Politics. 1977. 8.95 o.p. (ISBN 0-399-11574-9). Putnam Pub Group.

Edwards, J. B. & Owens, D. H. Analysis & Control of Multipass Process. (Control Theory & Applications Ser.). 298p. 1982. 43.95 (ISBN 0-471-10163-X, Pub. by Res Studies). Wiley.

Edwards, J. H. Human Genetics. 1978. pap. 6.50x (ISBN 0-412-13170-6, Pub. by Chapman & Hall). Methuen Inc.

Edwards, James & MacDonald, Douglass. Occasions for Philosophy. 1979. pap. text ed. 18.95 (ISBN 0-13-629287-9). P-H.

Edwards, James, jt. ed. see Cole, E. R.

Edwards, James C. Ethics Without Philosophy: Wittgenstein & the Moral Life. LC 82-2830. xiv, 274p. 1982. 20.00 (ISBN 0-8130-0706-2). U Presses Fla.

Edwards, James D. History of Public Accounting in the United States. Previts, Gary J., ed. LC 66-63369. 1978. pap. 11.95 o.s.i. (ISBN 0-8173-8903-2). U of Ala Pr.

Edwards, James D. & Hermanson, Roger H. How Accounting Works: A Guide for the Perplexed. LC 82-73625. 190p. 1983. 14.95 (ISBN 0-87094-394-4). Dow Jones-Irwin.

Edwards, James D. & Black, Homer A., eds. The Modern Accountant's Handbook. LC 76-2112. (Illus.). 1976. 45.00 (ISBN 0-87094-121-6). Dow Jones-Irwin.

Edwards, James D., jt. ed. see Black, Homer A.

Edwards, James Don, jt. auth. see Benke, Ralph L., Jr.

Edwards, James W., et al. Interim Financial Reporting. 17.95 (ISBN 0-86641-023-6, 7253). Natl Assn Accts.

Edwards, Jerome E. Pat McCarran: Political Boss of Nevada. LC 82-8576. (History & Political Science: No. 17). (Illus.). 237p. (Orig.). 1982. pap. 8.75x (ISBN 0-87417-071-0). U of Nev Pr.

Edwards, Jim L., jt. auth. see Ottaway, Hal N.

Edwards, John. Christian Cordoba: The City & its Region in the Late Middle Ages. LC 81-24213. (Cambridge, Iberian & Latin American Studies). 256p. 1982. 47.50 (ISBN 0-521-24320-3). Cambridge U Pr.

--The Seventies. LC 80-54638. (History of the Modern World Ser.). 13.00 (ISBN 0-382-06448-8). Silver.

Edwards, John & Batley, Richard. The Politics of Positive Discrimination: An Evaluation of the Urban Programme, 1967-1977. 1978. 27.00x (ISBN 0-422-76660-7, Pub. by Tavistock). Methuen Inc.

Edwards, John, jt. auth. see Weiss, Ulrich.

Edwards, John A., jt. ed. see Gale, Anthony.

Edwards, John B. Combustion: Formation & Emission of Trace Species. LC 73-93952. (Illus.). 256p. 1974. 49.95 (ISBN 0-250-40054-5). Ann Arbor Science.

Edwards, John C. Patriots in Pinstripe: Men of the National Security League. LC 81-40869. (Illus.). 248p. (Orig.). 1982. lib. bdg. 23.00 (ISBN 0-8191-2349-8); pap. text ed. 10.75 (ISBN 0-8191-2350-1). U Pr of Amer.

Edwards, John H. & Vasse, William W. Annotated Index to the Cantos of Ezra Pound. LC 57-10500. 1980. 29.50x (ISBN 0-520-01923-7). U of Cal Pr.

Edwards, Jonathan. Charity & Its Fruits. 1978. 8.95 (ISBN 0-85151-351-4). Banner of Truth.

--Life & Diary of David Brainerd. (Wycliffe Classic Ser.). 384p. 1980. pap. 8.95 (ISBN 0-8024-4772-4). Moody.

Edwards, Joseph W. Integral Calculus, 2 Vols. LC 55-234. 45.00 ea. Vol. 1 (ISBN 0-8284-0102-0). Vol. 2 (ISBN 0-8284-0105-5). Chelsea Pub.

Edwards, Judson. A Matter of Choice. Date not set. 3.25 (ISBN 0-8054-5204-4). Broadman.

Edwards, Junius. If We Must Die. (Howard University Press Library of Contemporary Literature). 124p. 1983. pap. 6.95 (ISBN 0-88258-117-1). Howard U Pr.

Edwards, Katherine, jt. auth. see Amato, Antony.

Edwards, Kenneth N., ed. Urethane Chemistry & Applications. (ACS Symposium Ser.: No. 172). 1981. write for info. Am Chemical.

Edwards, Lauton. Industrial Arts Plastics. rev. ed. (gr. 10-12). 1974. 15.96 (ISBN 0-87002-146-X). Bennett IL.

Edwards, Lawrence. The Field of Form. 1982. pap. 19.95 (ISBN 0-903540-50-9). St George Bk Serv.

Edwards, Lee H. You Can Make the Difference. 1980. 12.95 o.p. (ISBN 0-87000-471-9, Arlington Hse). Crown.

Edwards, Lee R. & Diamond, Arlyn, eds. American Voices, American Women. 1973. pap. 1.95 o.p. (ISBN 0-380-01017-8, 17871, Bard). Avon.

Edwards, Linda S. The Downtown Day. LC 82-4645. (Illus.). 48p. (gr. k-3). 1983. 9.95 (ISBN 0-394-85407-1); PLB 9.99 (ISBN 0-394-95407-6). Pantheon.

Edwards, Lovitt F. Yugoslavia. (Batsford Countries of Europe Ser.). 1971. 9.95 o.p. (ISBN 0-8038-8594-6). Hastings.

Edwards, Malcolm, jt. auth. see Holdstock, Robert.

Edwards, Marie & Hoover, Eleanor. The Challenge of Being Single. 1975. pap. 2.95 (ISBN 0-451-09903-6, E9903, Sig). NAL.

Edwards, Mark U., Jr. Luther's Last Battles: Politics & Polemics, 1531-46. 272p. 1983. 19.95x (ISBN 0-8014-1564-0). Cornell U Pr.

Edwards, Mark U., Jr., ed. see Moeller, Bernd.

Edwards, Mary F., ed. How to Recognize & Handle Recreational Liability Cases: Sports Torts. 271p. 1980. pap. 25.00 (ISBN 0-941916-04-9). Assn Trial Ed.

--Settlement & Plea Bargaining. 388p. 1981. pap. 35.00 (ISBN 0-941916-02-2). Assn Trial Ed.

Edwards, Mary I. & Morrow, Margot D., eds. The Cross-Cultural Study of Women: A Complete Guide to Methods & Materials. 192p. (Orig.). 1983. pap. 7.95 (ISBN 0-935312-02-1). Feminist Pr.

Edwards, Mary L. In Woods & Meadows. 1978. 7.95 o.p. (ISBN 0-533-03698-4). Vantage.

Edwards, Mona, jt. auth. see Tate, Sharon.

Edwards, Nancy M., ed. Office Automation: A Glossary & Guide. LC 82-47140. (Information & Communications Management Guides Ser.). 275p. 1982. text ed. 59.50 (ISBN 0-86729-012-9). Knowledge Indus.

Edwards, Nick H. The Inevitable. (Illus.). 1980. 5.00 o.p. (ISBN 0-682-49523-9). Exposition.

Edwards, O. C. The Living & Active Word: A Way to Preach from the Bible Today. 166p. 1975. 1.50 (ISBN 0-8164-0265-5). Seabury.

Edwards, O. C., jt. auth. see Abbey, Merrill R.

Edwards, O. C., jt. auth. see Bennett, Robert A.

Edwards, O. C., Jr. Elements of Homiletic. 110p. (Orig.). 1982. pap. 7.95 (ISBN 0-916134-55-5). Pueblo Pub CO.

Edwards, Owen D., jt. ed. see Doyle, David N.

Edwards, Owen D., jt. ed. see Shepperson, George A.

Edwards, P., jt. ed. see Muir, Kenneth.

Edwards, P., ed. see Muir, Kenneth.

Edwards, P. D. Anthony Trollope's Son in Australia: The Life & Letters of F.J.A. Trollope (1847-1910) LC 82-4928. 69p. 1983. text ed. 16.50x (ISBN 0-7022-1891-X). U of Queensland Pr.

Edwards, P. K. & Scullion, Hugh. The Social Organization of Industrial Conflict: Control & Resistance in the Workplace. (Warwick Studies in Industrial Relations). 328p. 1982. text ed. 35.00x (ISBN 0-631-13127-2, Pub. by Basil Blackwell England). Biblio Dist.

Edwards, Paul, jt. ed. see Walvin, James.

Edwards, Perry. Flowcharting & Fortran IV. (Illus.). 132p. 1973. pap. text ed. 10.55 (ISBN 0-07-019042-9, G). McGraw.

Edwards, Perry & Broadwell, Bruce. Data Processing: Computers in Action. 1979. pap. text ed. 20.95x o.p. (ISBN 0-534-00615-9); wkbk. 8.95x o.p. (ISBN 0-534-00723-6). Wadsworth Pub.

--Data Processing: Computers in Action. 2nd ed. 608p. 1982. text ed. 22.95x (ISBN 0-534-01063-6); study guide 8.95x (ISBN 0-534-01064-4). Wadsworth Pub.

Edwards, Perry, ed. see Weissberger, A.

Edwards, Peter & Wratten, Stephen D. Ecology of Insect-Plant Interaction. (Studies in Biology: No. 121). 64p. 1980. pap. text ed. 8.95 (ISBN 0-7131-2803-8). E Arnold.

Edwards, Philip. Shakespeare & the Confines of Art. (Methuen Library Reprint Ser.). 176p. 1981. 25.00x (ISBN 0-416-32200-X). Methuen Inc.

--Threshold of a Nation. LC 78-72085. (Illus.). 1980. 29.95 (ISBN 0-521-22463-2). Cambridge U Pr.

Edwards, Philip, ed. see Massinger, Philip.

Edwards, Philip, et al. Shakespeare's Styles. LC 79-51226. 1980. 34.50 (ISBN 0-521-22764-X). Cambridge U Pr.

Edwards, Philip, et al, eds. The Revels History of Drama in English: 1613-1660, Vol. 4. (Illus.). 1982. 53.00x (ISBN 0-416-13050-X). Methuen Inc.

Edwards, R., et al. Target Usage: Guides for Capitalization, Punctuation. 1976. tchr's. ed. 11.64 (ISBN 0-201-46622-8, Sch Div); target usage kit 325.00 (ISBN 0-201-46621-X, 46600); dupe masters avail.; target mechanics avail. (ISBN 0-201-46576-0). A-W.

Edwards, R. A. Physics for O.N.C. Courses. LC 71-82381. 1970. 21.00 o.s.i. (ISBN 0-08-013432-7); pap. 9.75 (ISBN 0-08-013431-9). Pergamon.

Edwards, R. E., ed. Integration & Harmonic Analysis on Compact Groups. LC 77-190412. (London Mathematical Society Lecture Notes Ser.: No. 8). 228p. 1972. 22.95 (ISBN 0-521-09717-7). Cambridge U Pr.

Edwards, R. G. & Purdy, J. M. Human Conception In Vitro. LC 82-71006. 1982. 37.00 (ISBN 0-12-232740-3). Acad Pr.

Edwards, R. G. & Johnson, M. H., eds. Physiological Effects of Immunity Against Reproductive Hormones. LC 75-12470. (Clinical & Experimental Immunoreproduction Ser.: No. 3). (Illus.). 300p. 1976. 49.50 (ISBN 0-521-20914-5). Cambridge U Pr.

Edwards, R. G., et al, eds. Immunobiology of Trophoblast. LC 74-31800. (Clinical & Experimental Immunoreproduction Ser.: No. 1). (Illus.). 300p. 1975. 45.00 (ISBN 0-521-20636-7). Cambridge U Pr.

Edwards, R. W. & Brooker, M. P. The Ecology of the Wye. 1982. text ed. 41.50 (ISBN 90-6193-103-7, Pub. by Junk Pubs Netherlands). Kluwer Boston.

Edwards, R. W., ed. see Zoological Society of London - 29th Symposium.

Edwards, Ralph. Sheraton Furniture Design. (Illus.). 1974. pap. 6.95 o.s.i. (ISBN 0-85458-909-0). Transatlantic.

Edwards, Reese. The Middle School Experiment. (Students Library of Education). 112p. 1972. 9.95x (ISBN 0-7100-7329-1). Routledge & Kegan.

Edwards, Rem B. Reason & Religion: An Introduction to the Philosophy of Religion. LC 78-66278. 1979. pap. text ed. 12.25 (ISBN 0-8191-0690-9). U Pr of Amer.

--A Return to Moral & Religious Philosophy in Early America. LC 81-43488. (Illus.). 288p. (Orig.). 1982. PLB 23.00 (ISBN 0-8191-2479-6); pap. text ed. 11.00 (ISBN 0-8191-2480-X). U Pr of Amer.

Edwards, Rem B., ed. Psychiatry & Ethics: Insanity, Rational Autonomy, & Mental Health Care. 350p. 1982. 29.95 (ISBN 0-87975-178-9); pap. 12.95 (ISBN 0-87975-179-7). Prometheus Bks.

Edwards, Renee, jt. auth. see Barker, Larry.

Edwards, Rice. Topical Reviews in Neurosurgery, Vol. I. 202p. 1982. 36.50 (ISBN 0-7236-0576-9). Wright-PSG.

Edwards, Richard A. The Sign of Jonah: In the Theology of the Evangelists & Q. (Student Christian Movement Press-Studies in Biblical Theology). 134p. (Orig.). 1971. pap. 6.95x (ISBN 0-19-520375-5). Oxford U Pr.

Edwards, Richard C., et al. The Capitalist System: A Radical Analysis of American Society. 2nd ed. LC 77-1495. (Illus.). 1978. pap. 15.95 ref. ed. (ISBN 0-13-113597-X). P-H.

Edwards, Robert. Australian Aboriginal Art: The Art of the Alligator Rivers Region Northern Territory. (AIAS New Ser.: No. 15). (Illus.). 1979. text ed. 21.50x (ISBN 0-391-01610-5); pap. text ed. 13.75x (ISBN 0-391-01611-3). Humanities.

--The Montecassino Passion & the Poetics of Medieval Drama. LC 75-22655. 1977. 30.00x (ISBN 0-520-03102-4). U of Cal Pr.

Edwards, Robert D. & Magee, John. Technical Analysis of Stock Trends. 5th ed. (Illus.). 50.00 (ISBN 0-910944-00-8). Magee.

Edwards, Ronald J. In-Service Training in British Libraries: Its Development & Present Practice. 1978. pap. 10.00 o.p. (ISBN 0-85365-219-8, 6508). Gaylord Prof Pubns.

Edwards, Ross. Fiddledust. LC 82-70670. 102p. 1965. 4.95 (ISBN 0-8040-0109-X). Swallow.

Edwards, Roy, tr. see Penrose, Valentine.

Edwards, Ruth. Answer Me. (Illus., Orig.). 1983. pap. 5.56 (ISBN 0-89390-042-7); pap. text ed. 6.95. Resource Pubns.

Edwards, Ruth D. An Atlas of Irish History. 2nd ed. (Illus.). 180p. 1981. 19.95x (ISBN 0-416-74820-1); pap. 8.95x (ISBN 0-416-74050-2). Methuen Inc.

Edwards, Sally. The Man Who Said No. LC 75-106925. (Illus.). (gr. 6-8). 1970. 4.95 o.p. (ISBN 0-698-20086-1, Coward). Putnam Pub Group.

--Triathlon: A Triple Fitness Sport. (Illus.). 224p. (Orig.). 1983. pap. 6.95 (ISBN 0-8092-5555-3). Contemp Bks.

Edwards, Samuel. The Vidocq Dossier: The Story of the World's First Detective. 1977. 7.95 o.p. (ISBN 0-395-25176-1). HM.

Edwards, Sherman, jt. auth. see Stone, Peter.

Edwards, T., jt. auth. see Hicks, Tyler G.

Edwards, T. C. Foundations for Microstrip Circuit Design. LC 80-41687. 304p. 1981. 34.95 (ISBN 0-471-27944-7, Pub. by Wiley-Interscience). Wiley.

Edwards, Ted L., Jr. & Lau, Barbara. Weight Loss to Super Wellness. (Illus.). 176p. (Orig.). 1982. pap. text ed. 7.95 (ISBN 0-686-38849-6). Hills Med.

Edwards, Thomas C. A Commentary on the First Epistle to the Corinthians. 1979. 18.00 (ISBN 0-86524-013-2, 4602). Klock & Klock.

Edwards, Tilden. Spiritual Friend: Reclaiming the Gift of Spiritual Direction. LC 79-91408. 272p. 1980. pap. 8.95 (ISBN 0-8091-2288-X). Paulist Pr.

Edwards, W. Burke. Second Life or Second Death. 1980. 5.75 o.p. (ISBN 0-8062-1402-3). Carlton.

Edwardss, Marcia & McDonnell, Unity, eds. Symposium Zoological Society London, No. 50. (Serial Publication). 336p. 1982. 49.00 (ISBN 0-12-613350-6). Acad Pr.

Eeden, Frederik Van see Van Eeden, Frederik.

Eel Pie, pseud. The Clash: Before & After. (Illus.). 160p. (gr. 7 up). 1982. 8.95g o.p. (ISBN 0-316-80169-0). Little.

Eells, Ellery T. Rational Decision & Causality. LC 81-18001. (Cambridge Studies in Philosophy). (Illus.). 240p. 1982. 29.50 (ISBN 0-521-24213-4). Cambridge U Pr.

Eells, George. Ginger, Loretta & Irene Who? LC 76-20806. (Illus.). 1976. 9.95 o.p. (ISBN 0-399-11822-5). Putnam Pub Group.

Eells, George, jt. auth. see O'Day, Anita.

Eells, J., ed. Complex Analysis Trieste: Proceedings, 1981. (Lecture Notes in Mathematics Ser.: Vol. 950). 428p. 1983. pap. 20.50 (ISBN 0-387-11596-X). Springer-Verlag.

Eells, Robert & Nyberg, Bartell. Lonely Walk: The Life of Senator Mark Hatfield. 201p. 1979. 8.95 (ISBN 0-915684-49-7). Multnomah.

Eells, Walter C. & Haswell, Harold A. Academic Degrees. LC 70-128397. Repr. of 1960 ed. 30.00x (ISBN 0-8103-3015-6). Gale.

Eells, Walter C., jt. auth. see Anderson, H. D.

EerNisse, E. P., jt. auth. see Holland, Richard.

Effinger, George A. The Wolves of Memory. 228p. 1981. 14.95 (ISBN 0-399-12652-X). Putnam Pub Group.

Effler, Roy R. John Duns Scotus & the Principle "Omne Quod Movetur Ab Alio Movetur. (Philosophy Ser). 1962. 10.00 (ISBN 0-686-11545-7). Franciscan Inst.

Effron, Benjamin, ed. see Karp, Deborah.

Efird, James M. The New Testament Writings: History, Literature, Interpretation. LC 79-87750. (Biblical Foundation Ser.). 1980. pap. 5.95 (ISBN 0-8042-0246-X). John Knox.

--These Things Are Written: An Introduction to the Religious Ideas of the Bible. LC 77-15749. (Biblical Foundations Ser.). 1978. pap. 5.95 (ISBN 0-8042-0073-4). John Knox.

Efron, B. The Jackknife, the Bootstrap & Other Resampling Plans. LC 81-84856. (CBMS-NSF Regional Conference Ser.: No. 38). viii, 92p. 1982. 12.50 (ISBN 0-89871-179-7). Soc Indus Appl Math.

Efron, Daniel, et al, eds. Ethnopharmacologic Search for Psychoactive Drugs: Proceedings. LC 79-3955. 488p. 1979. Repr. of 1967 ed. text ed. 28.50 softcover (ISBN 0-89004-047-8). Raven.

Efron, Daniel H., ed. Psychotomimetic Drugs. LC 73-89388. (Illus.). 365p. 1970. 30.00 (ISBN 0-911216-07-3). Raven.

Efron, Marshall & Olsen, Alfa B. Bible Stories You Can't Forget. 1979. pap. 1.25 o.p. (ISBN 0-440-41382-6, YB). Dell.

--Bible Stories You Can't Forget. (Illus.). 1976. 9.95 (ISBN 0-525-26500-7, 0966-290). Dutton.

Efron, Vera see Keller, Mark.

Efvergren, Carl J. Names of Places in a Transferred Sense in English: A Sematological Study. LC 68-17922. 1969. Repr. of 1909 ed. 30.00x (ISBN 0-8103-3233-7). Gale.

Egami, Nobuo. Radiation Effects on Aquatic Organisms. 308p. 1980. text ed. 49.95 o.p. (ISBN 0-8391-4125-4). Univ Park.

Egan, Carol B. Body Buddies. (ps-2). 1982. 5.95 (ISBN 0-86653-060-6, GA 420). Good Apple.

Egan, Clifford L. Neither Peace nor War: Franco-American Relations, 1803 to 1812. LC 82-17272. (Illus.). 288p. 1983. text ed. 30.00 (ISBN 0-8071-1076-0). La State U Pr.

Egan, D. F. & Illingworth, R. S., eds. Developmental Screening Zero to Five Years. (Clinics in Developmental Medicine Ser.: Vol. 30). 70p. 1969. text ed. 17.00 o.p. (ISBN 0-686-97934-6, Pub. by Spastics Intl England). Lippincott.

Egan, David R. & Egan, Melinda A. V. I. Lenin: An Annotated Bibliography of English-Language Sources to 1980. LC 82-659. 516p. 1982. 32.50 (ISBN 0-8108-1526-5). Scarecrow.

Egan, E. W., tr. see Cherrier, Francois.

Egan, E. W., tr. see Fronval, George & Dubois, Daniel.

Egan, E. W., tr. see Riviere, Marie-Claude.

Egan, E. W., et al, eds. Kings, Rulers & Statesmen. LC 67-16020. (Illus.). 1976. 20.00 o.p. (ISBN 0-8069-0050-4); lib. bdg. 17.59 o.p. (ISBN 0-8069-0051-2). Sterling.

Egan, Gerard. Exercises in Helping Skills. 2nd ed. 1981. pap. 8.45 (ISBN 0-8185-0480-3). Brooks-Cole.

--Interpersonal Living: A Skills - Contract Approach to Human Relations Training in Groups. LC 76-6651. 1976. pap. text ed. 13.95 (ISBN 0-8185-0189-8). Brooks-Cole.

--The Skilled Helper: A Model for Systematic Helping & Interpersonal Relating. 2nd ed. LC 74-82756. (Illus.). 1982. text ed. 17.95 (ISBN 0-8185-0479-X); test items avail. (ISBN 0-685-52374-8). Brooks-Cole.

--You & Me: The Skills of Communicating & Relating to Others. LC 77-6475. (Illus.). 1977. pap. text ed. 13.95 (ISBN 0-8185-0238-X); instructor's manual free (ISBN 0-685-79911-5). Brooks-Cole.

Egan, Gerard & Cowan, Michael A. Moving into Adulthood: Themes & Variations in Self--Directed Development for Effective Living. LC 80-15876. 288p. (Orig.). 1980. pap. text ed. 13.95 (ISBN 0-8185-0406-4). Brooks-Cole.

Egan, Jack. Your Complete Guide to IRAs & Keoghs: The Simple, Safe Tax Deferred Way to Future Financial Security. LC 81-48152. 224p. 1982. 13.41i (ISBN 0-06-014975-2, HarpT). Har-Row.

Egan, John, et al. Housing & Public Policy: A Role for Mediating Structures. 144p. 1981. prof ref 19.00x (ISBN 0-88410-827-9). Ballinger Pub.

Egan, John P. & Colford, Paul D. Baptism of Resistance - Blood & Celebration: A Road to Wholeness in the Nuclear Age. 1983. pap. 5.95 (ISBN 0-89622-164-4). Twenty-Third Pubns.

Egan, John W. Economics of the Pharmaceutical Industry. 218p. 1982. 25.95 (ISBN 0-03-061803-7). Praeger.

Egan, Kieran. Education & Psychology: Plato, Paiget & Scientific Psychology. (Orig.). 1983. 18.95x. Tchrs Coll.

--Educational Development. 1979. text ed. 10.95x (ISBN 0-19-502458-3); pap. text ed. 6.95x (ISBN 0-19-502459-1). Oxford U Pr.

Egan, M. Mark Twain's "Huckleberry Finn". Race, Class & Society. 15.00x (ISBN 0-686-97014-4, Pub. by Scottish Academic Pr Scotland). State Mutual Bk.

Egan, M. David. Concepts in Architectural Acoustics. (Illus.). 192p. 1972. text ed. 42.50 (ISBN 0-07-019053-4, P&RB). McGraw.

--Concepts in Building Fire Safety. LC 77-12184. 1978. 34.95x (ISBN 0-471-02229-2, Pub. by Wiley-Interscience). Wiley.

--Concepts in Thermal Comfort. (Illus.). 224p. 1975. 19.95 (ISBN 0-13-166447-6). P-H.

Egan, M. David & Klas, Rodger H. Concepts in Lighting for Architecture. (Illus.). 224p. 1983. 23.95 (ISBN 0-07-019054-2, C). McGraw.

Egan, Melinda A., jt. auth. see Egan, David R.

Egan, Robert L. Technologist Guide to Mammography. 2nd ed. 170p. 1977. 19.95 o.p. (ISBN 0-683-02767-0). Williams & Wilkins.

Egan, William F. Frequency Synthesis by Phase-Lock. LC 80-16917. 279p. 1981. text ed. 32.50x (ISBN 0-471-08202-3, Pub. by Wiley-Interscience). Wiley.

Egbert, Barbara. Cheerleading & Songleading. LC 80-52322. (Illus.). 128p. (gr. 8 up). 1980. 13.95 (ISBN 0-8069-4626-1); PLB 16.79 (ISBN 0-8069-4627-X); pap. 8.95 (ISBN 0-8069-8950-5). Sterling.

Egbert, Lawrence D. Multilingual Law Dictionary: English, French, Spanish, German. LC 77-25072. 551p. 1978. lib. bdg. 50.00 (ISBN 0-379-00589-1); pap. 37.00 o.p. (ISBN 0-379-00598-0). Oceana.

Egdahl, Richard H., et al, eds. Core Textbook of Surgery. LC 72-3715. 480p. 1972. pap. 32.50 o.p. (ISBN 0-8089-0772-7); cloth 42.25 o.p. (ISBN 0-8089-0762-X). Grune.

Egdaul, Richard H. & Walsh, Diana C., eds. Corporate Medical Departments: A Changing Agenda. (Industry & Health Care Ser.: Vol. 1). 272p. 1983. prof ref 35.00x. Ballinger Pub.

Egede, H. P. A Description of Greenland. Repr. of 1818 ed. 25.00 o.s.i. (ISBN 0-527-26550-0). Kraus Repr.

Egejuru, Phanuel A. Towards African Literary Independence: A Dialogue with Contemporary African Writers. LC 79-6188. (Contributions in Afro-American & African Studies: No. 53). vii, 173p. 1980. lib. bdg. 27.50 (ISBN 0-313-22310-6, EAL/). Greenwood.

Egelstaff, P. A. & Poole, M. J. Experimental Neutron Thermalization. LC 79-86201. 1969. 65.00 (ISBN 0-08-006533-3). Pergamon.

Egelston, Roberta. Career Planning Materials. 190p. 1981. text ed. 20.00 (ISBN 0-8389-0343-6). ALA.

Egenter, Nold. Gottersitze Aus Schilf und Bambus. (Illus.). 152p. (Ger.). 1982. write for info. (ISBN 3-261-04821-2). P Lang Pubs.

--Sacred Symbols of Reed & Bamboo. (Illus.). 152p. 1982. write for info. (ISBN 3-261-04821-2). P Lang Pubs.

Eger, Edmond I. Anesthetic Uptake & Action. 383p. 1974. 28.00 o.p. (ISBN 0-683-02771-9). Williams & Wilkins.

Eger, J. D. & Hughes, J. S., eds. Marine Affairs Journal, No. 4. 110p. 1976. 1.00 (ISBN 0-686-36974-2, P532). URI Mas.

Egerer, Marlene M. & Frank, Myra G. Holiday Articulation Activities. 1974. text ed. 9.95x (ISBN 0-8134-1630-2). Interstate.

Egermeier, Elsie E. Picture Story Bible ABC Book. rev. ed. (Illus.). (gr. k-6). 1963. 5.95 (ISBN 0-87162-262-9, D1703). Warner Pr.

Egerton, F. Clement. Angola in Perspective: Endeavour. LC 73-9706. 288p. 1973. Repr. of 1967 ed. 29.00 o.s.i. (ISBN 0-527-26600-0). Kraus Repr.

Egerton, Frank N., ed. see Greene, Edward L.

Egerton, Frank N., 3rd, ed. see Forel, Francois A.

Egerton, John. Generations: An American Family. LC 82-40465. (Illus.). 272p. 1983. 19.50 (ISBN 0-8131-1482-9). U Pr of Ky.

Egerton, Judy & Snelgrove, Dudley. British Sporting & Animal Drawings & Paintings, 2 vols. (From the Paul Mellon Collection Ser.). 1980. two volumes 70.00 ea. Vol. 1 (ISBN 0-8120-5390-7). Vol. 2 (ISBN 0-8120-5391-5). Barron.

Eggan, Fred. The American Indian: Perspectives for the Study of Social Change. LC 80-67926. (Lewis Henry Morgan Lectures). 192p. 1981. 27.95 (ISBN 0-521-23752-1); pap. 8.95 (ISBN 0-521-28210-1). Cambridge U Pr.

Eggan, Lawrence C. & Vanden Eynden, Charles. Mathematics: Models & Applications. 1979. text ed. 20.95x (ISBN 0-669-01051-0); instr's manual 1.95 (ISBN 0-669-01052-9). Heath.

Egge, Ruth S. Recycled with Flair: How to Remodel Old Furniture & Flea Market Finds. (Illus.). 1980. 10.95 o.p. (ISBN 0-698-11024-2, Coward); pap. 5.95 o.s.i. (ISBN 0-698-11031-5). Putnam Pub Group.

Eggebrecht, Hans H., jt. auth. see Dahlhaus, Carl.

Eggeling, Julius. The Satapatha Brahmana. (Sacred Bks. of the East: Vols. 12, 26, 41, 43, 44). 5 vols. 55.00 (ISBN 0-686-97483-2); 11.00 ea. Lancaster-Miller.

Eggen, Paul, jt. auth. see Kauchak, Donald P.

Eggen, Paul, et al. Strategies for Teachers: Information Processing Models in the Classroom. (Curriculum & Teaching Ser.). (Illus.). 1979. ref. ed. 23.95 (ISBN 0-13-851162-4). P-H.

Egger, Rowland. The President of the United States. 2nd ed. (Foundations of the American Government & Political Science). 208p. 1972. text ed. 8.95 o.p. (ISBN 0-07-019064-X, C). McGraw.

Eggermont, P. H. L. & Hoftijzer, J., eds. The Moral Edicts of King Asoka: Includes the Greco-Aramaic Inscription of Kandahar & Further Inscriptions of the Maurian Period. (Textus Minores in Usum Academicum Ser.: Vol. 29). 48p. 1962. gilded 3.25 (ISBN 90-04-02251-1). E J Brill.

Eggert, Jim. Invitation to Economics. (Illus.). 300p. Date not set. pap. 9.95 (ISBN 0-86576-046-2). W Kaufmann. Postponed.

Eggleston. Applied Sensitometry. 1983. write for info. (ISBN 0-240-51144-1). Focal Pr.

Eggleston, Edward. The Hoosier Schoolmaster. rev. ed. Dixson, Robert J., ed. (American Classics Ser.: Bk. 6). (gr. 9 up). 1974. pap. text ed. 3.25 (ISBN 0-88345-202-2, 18125); cassettes 40.00 (ISBN 0-685-38929-4); 40.00 o.p. tapes (ISBN 0-685-38930-8). Regents Pub.

Eggleston, George C. Rebel's Recollections. LC 58-12205. (Indiana University Civil War Centennial Ser.). 1968. Repr. of 1959 ed. 10.00 o.s.i. (ISBN 0-527-26640-X). Kraus Repr.

Eggleston, George T. Roosevelt, Churchill, & the World War II Opposition. LC 79-1727. (Illus.). 1979. text ed. 12.95 (ISBN 0-8159-5311-9). Devin.

Eggleston, H. G. Convexity. (Cambridge Tracts in Mathematics & Mathematical Physics: No. 47). 1958. 23.95 (ISBN 0-521-07734-6). Cambridge U Pr.

Eggleston, John, ed. Contemporary Research in the Sociology of Education. 1974. pap. 12.95x (ISBN 0-416-78790-8). Methuen Inc.

--Work Experience in Secondary Schools. (Routledge Education Books Ser.). 192p. 1983. 18.50 (ISBN 0-7100-9219-9). Routledge & Kegan.

Eggleston, Suzie, ed. see Sexias, Frank A.

Eggleston, Wilfrid. The Road to Nationhood: A Chronicle of Dominion-Provincial Relations. LC 70-147218. 337p. 1972. Repr. of 1946 ed. lib. bdg. 17.75x (ISBN 0-8371-5983-0, EGRN). Greenwood.

Eghishe. Vasn Vardanay Ew Hayots Paterazmin: On Vardan & the Armenian War. Sanjian, Avedis K., ed. (Classical Armenian Texts). Date not set. write for info. (ISBN 0-88206-034-1). Caravan Bks.

Egidy, T. von see Von Egidy, T. & Gonnenweir, F.

Eglamour. Sir Eglamour. Cook, Albert S., ed. 1911. 19.50x (ISBN 0-685-69803-3). Elliots Bks.

Eglash, Albert. Died on the Fourth of July: A Jewish Unitarian Psychologist Flees a Fascist Fellowship. LC 80-53581. (Illus.). 200p. (Orig.). 1982. pap. cancelled (ISBN 0-935320-22-9). San Luis Quest.

Eglesfield, Robert, tr. see Simenon, Georges.

Egleton, Clive. The Mills Bomb. LC 78-55207. 1978. 8.95 o.p. (ISBN 0-689-10910-5). Atheneum.

--The Russian Enigma. LC 82-45170. 256p. 1982. 12.95 (ISBN 0-689-11303-X). Atheneum.

Eglinton. Chemsyn: The Organic Chemistry Teaching Aid. 9.95 (ISBN 0-471-25666-8). Wiley.

Egloff, Brian J. Wreck Bay: An Aboriginal Fishing Community. (AIAS New Ser.: No. 28). 52p. 1981. pap. text ed. 7.00x (ISBN 0-391-02240-7, Pub. by Australian Inst Australia). Humanities.

Egloff, Fred R. El Paso Lawman: G. W. Campbell. (The Early West Ser.). (Illus.). 144p. 1982. 12.95 (ISBN 0-932702-22-8); pap. 7.95 (ISBN 0-932702-24-4); leatherbound collectors ed. 75.00 (ISBN 0-932702-23-6). Creative Texas.

Egly. Fringe Benefits for Classified Employees in Cities of 100,000 Population or Greater. (Research Bulletin: No. 19). pap. 0.69 (ISBN 0-685-57189-0). Assn Sch Busn.

Egmond, J. Van see Van Egmond, J., et al.

Egner, Robert E., ed. see Russell, Bertrand.

Egoff, Sheila, et al, eds. Only Connect: Readings on Children's Literature. 2nd ed. (Illus.). 1980. pap. text ed. 10.95x (ISBN 0-19-540309-6). Oxford U Pr.

Egoff, Sheila A. Thursday's Child. LC 81-8066. 340p. 1981. text ed. 15.00 (ISBN 0-8389-0327-4). ALA.

Egolf, Donald B., jt. auth. see Shame, George H.

Egoville, Barbara B., jt. auth. see Strong, Jo Ann.

Egypt, Ophelia S. James Weldon Johnson. LC 73-9521. (Biographies Ser). (Illus.). 40p. (gr. 2-5). 1974. PLB 10.89 (ISBN 0-690-00215-7, TYC-J). Har-Row.

Eheart, Brenda & Martan, Susan. The Fourth Trimester: On Becoming a Mother. 1983. 13.95 (ISBN 0-686-43210-X); pap. 7.50 (ISBN 0-686-43211-8). ACC.

Ehle, John. The Winter People. 1982. pap. 3.95 (ISBN 0-440-39770-7, LE). Dell.

Ehlers, Anita, tr. see Ferris, Timothy.

Ehlers, Eckart, ed. Iran: A Bibliographic Research Survey, Vol. 2. (Bibliographies on Regional Geography & Area Studies Ser.). 441p. 1980. 50.00x (ISBN 0-686-98304-1, K G Saur). Gale.

Ehlers, F. Edward, et al see Heat Transfer & Fluid Mechanics Institute.

Ehlers, J., ed. Isolated Gravitating Systems in General Relativity. (Enrico Fermi Ser.: Vol. 67). 1979. 100.00 (ISBN 0-444-85329-4, North Holland). Elsevier.

Ehlers, Jurgen, et al, eds. Texas Symposium on Relativistic Astrophysics, 9th. LC 80-11614. (Annals of the New York Academy of Sciences: Vol. 336). 599p. 1980. 107.00x (ISBN 0-89766-045-5). NY Acad Sci.

Ehlers, Victor M. & Steel, E. W. Municipal & Rural Sanitation. 6th ed. (Sanitary & Water Resources Engineering Ser.). 1965. text ed. 36.50 (ISBN 0-07-019089-5, C). McGraw.

Ehlers, Walter H., et al. Administration for the Human Services: An Introductory Programmed Text. (Harper Ser. in Social Work). 416p. 1976. pap. text ed. 16.50 scp o.p. (ISBN 0-06-041868-0, HarpC). Har-Row.

--Mental Retardation & Other Developmental Disabilities: A Programmed Introduction. 3rd ed. 520p. 1982. pap. 16.95 (ISBN 0-675-09816-5). Merrill.

Ehlert, Lois. Designs. (Paint by Number: No. 1481). (Illus.). 32p. (gr. 1 up). 1983. pap. 1.99 (ISBN 0-307-21481-8). Western Pub.

Ehlich, Konrad & Rehbein, Jochen. Augenkommunikation. Methodenreflexion und Beispielanalyse. (Linguistik Aktuell Ser.: No. 2). viii, 150p. 1982. 18.00 (ISBN 9-0272-2722-5). Benjamins North Am.

Ehling, Bill. Twenty-Five Walks in the Finger Lakes Region of New York. LC 78-71718. (Twenty-Five Walks Ser.). (Illus.). 160p. 1979. pap. 5.95 (ISBN 0-89725-004-4). Backcountry Pubns.

Ehling, William P. Canoeing Central New York. LC 82-4018. (Illus.). 176p. (Orig.). 1982. pap. 8.95 (ISBN 0-942440-01-3). Backcountry Pubns.

Ehman, Lee & Mehlinger, Howard. Toward Effective Instruction in Secondary Social Studies. LC 82-21894. (Illus.). 476p. 1983. pap. text ed. 18.75 (ISBN 0-8191-2916-X). U Pr of Amer.

Ehninger, Douglas. Influence, Belief, & Argument: An Introduction to Responsible Persuasion. 192p. 1974. pap. 7.95x (ISBN 0-673-07867-1). Scott F.

Ehninger, Douglas, et al. Principles & Types of Speech Communication. 9th ed. 1981. 16.50x (ISBN 0-673-15538-2). Scott F.

--Principles of Speech Communication. 8th ed. 1980. pap. text ed. 12.50x (ISBN 0-673-15276-6). Scott F.

Ehrardt, Roy. American Railroad Watches: George Townsend 1977. 1982. 8.00 (ISBN 0-913902-40-3). Heart Am Pr.

Ehre, Milton, tr. see Gogol, Nikolay.

Ehrenberg, A. S. Data Reduction: Analyzing & Interpreting Statistical Data. LC 74-3724. 391p. 1975. 55.95 (ISBN 0-471-23399-4, Pub. by Wiley-Interscience); pap. 21.00x (ISBN 0-471-23398-6). Wiley.

Ehrenberg, Miriam & Ehrenberg, Otto. Brain Power: A Total Program for Increasing Your Intelligence. 256p. 1983. 15.95 (ISBN 0-89479-121-4, A & W Visual Library). A & W Pubs.

Ehrenberg, Otto, jt. auth. see Ehrenberg, Miriam.

Ehrenberg, Ralph E. Archives & Manuscripts: Maps & Architectural Drawings. 64p. 1982. pap. 5.00 member o.p. (ISBN 0-686-95749-0); pap. 7.00 non-member o.p. (ISBN 0-686-99602-X). Soc Am Archivist.

Ehrenberg, Ronald & Smith, Robert S. Modern Labor Economics: Analysis & Public Policy. 1982. text ed. 24.50x (ISBN 0-673-15365-7). Scott F.

Ehrenberg, Ronald, ed. Research in Labor Economics, Vol. 2. 381p. 1979. 42.50 (ISBN 0-89232-097-4). Jai Pr.

--Research in Labor Economics, Vol. 3. 410p. 1980. lib. bdg. 45.00 (ISBN 0-89232-157-1). Jai Pr.

Ehrenberg, Ronald G. & Schumann, Paul L. Longer Hours or More Jobs? An Investigation of Amending Hours Legislation to Create Employment. LC 81-11284. (Cornell Studies in Industrial & Labor Relations: No. 22). 190p. 1982. 22.50 (ISBN 0-87546-090-9); pap. 12.95 (ISBN 0-87546-091-7). ILR Pr.

Ehrenberg, Ronald G., ed. Research in Labor Economics, Vol. 1. (Orig.). 1977. lib. bdg. 42.50 (ISBN 0-89232-017-6). Jai Pr.

Ehrenberg, Victor. The Greek State. 2nd ed. 1974. pap. 12.95x o.p. (ISBN 0-416-70110-8). Methuen Inc.

--Man, State & Deity: Essays in Ancient History. LC 74-7695. 170p. 1974. pap. 11.95x (ISBN 0-416-79610-9). Methuen Inc.

Ehrenburg, Ilya. Julio Jurenito. Bostok, Anna & Kapp, Yvonne, trs. from Russ. LC 76-9856. 1976. Repr. of 1958 ed. lib. bdg. 20.75x (ISBN 0-8371-8889-X, BOJJ). Greenwood.

Ehrenburg, Ilya & Grossman, Vasily, eds. The Black Book. 595p. 19.95 o.p. (ISBN 0-686-87398-X). Schocken.

--The Black Book. Glad, John, tr. from Rus. (Illus.). 576p. 19.95 (ISBN 0-686-95057-7); pap. 9.95 (ISBN 0-686-99455-8). ADL.

Ehrenburg, Ilya G. Love of Jeanne Ney. Matheson, Helen C., tr. LC 68-8060. (Illus.). 1968. Repr. of 1930 ed. lib. bdg. 18.75x (ISBN 0-8371-0069-0, EHJN). Greenwood.

Ehrenfeld, Alfred, tr. see Lefebvre, Henri.

Ehrenfeld, David W. The Arrogance of Humanism. (A Galaxy Bk.: No. 637). 1981. pap. 7.95 (ISBN 0-19-502890-2, GB). Oxford U Pr.

--The Arrogance of Humanism. LC 78-1664. 1978. 14.95 (ISBN 0-19-502415-X). Oxford U Pr.

Ehrenfeld, William K., jt. auth. see Wylie, Edwin J.

Ehrenhardt, Alan, ed. see Congressional Quarterly Inc.

Ehrenkrantz Group, et al. Solar Energy Performance History Information Series: Vol. 1 Active Solar Energy Systems; Preliminary Design Practice Manual Based on Field Experience, Vol. 2 Solar Domestic Hot Water; A Reference Manual, Vol. 3 Architectural & Engineering Concerns in Solar System Design, Installation, & Operation, 3 vols. 398p. 1982. pap. 59.50x (ISBN 0-89934-158-6, H-07). Solar Energy Info.

Ehrenkranz, Lois B. & Kahn, Gilbert R. Public Relations-Publicity: A Key Link in Communications. (Illus.). 270p. 1983. text ed. 14.50 (ISBN 0-87005-449-X). Fairchild.

Ehrenpreis, Irvin. Acts of Implication: Suggestion & Covert Meaning in the Works of Dryden, Swift, Pope & Austen. (The Beckman Lectures Ser.). 150p. 1981. 29.50x (ISBN 0-520-04047-3). U of Cal Pr.

--The Types Approach to Literature. LC 73-19263. 1945. lib. bdg. 15.00 (ISBN 0-685-44515-1). Folcroft.

Ehrenpreis, Leon. Fourier Analysis in Several Complex Variables. (Pure & Applied Mathematics Ser.). 1970. 54.95x (ISBN 0-471-23400-1, Pub. by Wiley-Interscience). Wiley.

Ehrenpreis, Seymour & Kopin, Irwin J., eds. Reviews of Neuroscience, Vol. 1. LC 74-80538. 361p. 1974. 38.00 (ISBN 0-911216-84-7). Raven.

--Reviews of Neuroscience, Vol. 3. LC 74-80538. 238p. 1978. 27.00 (ISBN 0-89004-168-7). Raven.

Ehrenreich, Barbara. Hearts of Men: American Dreams & the Flight from Commitment. LC 82-45104. 264p. 1983. 13.95 (ISBN 0-385-17614-7, Anchor Pr). Doubleday.

Ehrenreich, Barbara & English, Deirdre. For Her Own Good: 150 Years of Expert's Advice to Women. LC 77-76234. (Illus.). 1978. pap. 5.95 (ISBN 0-385-12651-4, Anch). Doubleday.

Ehrenstein, David & Reed, Bill. Rock on Film. (Illus.). 384p. 1981. pap. 9.95 (ISBN 0-933328-12-5). Delilah Bks.

Ehrenzweig, Albert A. Private International Law, 3 vols. LC 67-28516. 1973. 112.50 set (ISBN 0-379-00353-8); 37.50 ea. Oceana.

Ehrenzweig, Albert A., et al. American-Greek Private International Law. LC 56-8413. 111p. 1957. 15.00 (ISBN 0-379-11406-2). Oceana.

--American-Japanese Private International Law. LC 63-19600. (Bilateral Studies in Private International Law: No. 12). 173p. 1964. 15.00 (ISBN 0-379-11412-7). Oceana.

Ehresmann, Donald L. Fine Arts: A Bibliographic Guide to Basic Reference Works, Histories & Handbooks. 2nd ed. LC 79-9051. 1979. lib. bdg. 27.50 (ISBN 0-87287-201-7). Libs Unl.

Ehret, Charles F. & Scanlon, Lynne W. Overcoming Jet Lag. 192p. (Orig.). 1983. pap. 4.95 (ISBN 0-425-05877-8). Berkley Pub.

Ehret, Christopher & Posnansky, Merrick. The Archaeological & Linguistic Reconstruction of African History. LC 82-8431. 216p. 1982. 28.50x (ISBN 0-520-04593-9). U of Cal Pr.

Ehret, Walter, jt. auth. see Trusler, Ivan.

Ehrfeld, W. Elements of Flow & Diffusion Processes in Separation Nozzles. (Springer Tracts in Modern Physics Ser.: Vol. 97). (Illus.). 160p. 1983. 26.00 (ISBN 0-387-11924-8). Springer-Verlag.

Ehrhardt, Larry. Encyclopedia of Pocket Knives, Bk. 3: Winchester-Marbles-Knives & Hardware. (Illus.). 1974. plastic ring bdg. 6.95 o.p. (ISBN 0-913902-08-X). Heart Am Pr.

Ehrhardt, Roy. Hamilton Watch Company Identification & Price Guide, with Serial Numbers. rev. ed. (Illus.). 1981. plastic ring bdg. 10.00 (ISBN 0-913902-12-8). Heart Am Pr.

Ehrhardt, Roy, illus. American Pocket Watches Encyclopedia & Price Guide, Vol. 1. 1982. plastic ring bdg 25.00x (ISBN 0-913902-33-0). Heart Am Pr.

Ehrhart & Evans. Channel Fever. 64p. 1982. handbound 5.00 (ISBN 0-943018-01-3). Backstreet.

Ehrich, Robert W. & Pleslova-Stikova, Emilie. Homolka: An Eneolithic Site in Bohemia. LC 79-16861. (American School of Prehistoric Research Bulletins: Vol. 24). (Orig.). 1968. pap. text ed. 18.50x (ISBN 0-87365-525-7). Peabody Harvard.

Ehrlich, Amy. Annie: The Storybook Based on the Movie. LC 81-15416. (Movie Storybooks Ser.). (Illus.). 64p. (gr. 5 up). 1982. 5.95 (ISBN 0-394-85087-4); PLB 6.99 o.p. (ISBN 0-394-95087-9). Random.

Ehrlich, Ann. Business Administration for the Dental Assistant. 2nd ed. LC 75-21039. (Illus.). 1981. 10.95 (ISBN 0-940012-16-2). Colwell Co.

--Cavity Classification & Related Terminology. (Illus.). 1978. 4.25 (ISBN 0-940012-04-9). Colwell Co.

--Dental Hand Instruments Identification. (Illus.). 1978. 4.25 (ISBN 0-940012-05-7). Colwell Co.
--Dental Office Procedures Manual. (Illus.). 164p. 1974. 19.95 (ISBN 0-940012-06-5). Colwell Co.
--Ethics & Jurisprudence. 1978. 4.25 (ISBN 0-940012-07-3). Colwell Co.
--Introduction to Dental Charting. (Illus.). 1978. 4.25 (ISBN 0-940012-08-1). Colwell Co.
--Introduction to Dental Instrument Sterilization & Disinfection. (Illus.). 1978. 3.95 (ISBN 0-940012-09-X). Colwell Co.
--Introduction to Dental Terminology. (Illus.). 1978. 3.95 (ISBN 0-940012-10-3). Colwell Co.
--Introduction to the Auxiliary's Role in Oral Surgery. (Illus.). 1978. 4.25 (ISBN 0-940012-11-1). Colwell Co.
--Psychology in the Dental Office. (Illus.). 1978. 4.95 (ISBN 0-940012-15-4). Colwell Co.
--Role of Computers on Medical Practice Management. LC 81-69069. (Illus.). 8.95. Colwell Co.

Ehrlich, Anne H., jt. auth. see Ehrlich, Paul R.

Ehrlich, Edith, jt. auth. see Heller, Peter.

Ehrlich, Eugene. How to Study Better & Get Higher Marks. 2nd, rev. ed. LC 76-41684. (Illus.). 1976. 12.45i (ISBN 0-690-01181-4). T Y Crowell.
--Schaum's Outline of Punctuation Capitalization & Spelling. (Schaum's Outline Ser.). 1977. pap. 4.95 (ISBN 0-07-019095-X, SP). McGraw.

Ehrlich, Eugene & Carruth, Gorton. The Oxford Illustrated Literary Guide to the United States. LC 82-8034. (Illus.). 450p. 1982. 29.95 (ISBN 0-19-503186-5). Oxford U Pr.

Ehrlich, Eugene & Murphy, Daniel. Basic Vocabulary Builder. (McGraw-Hill Paperbacks). 192p. (Orig.). 1975. pap. 3.95 (ISBN 0-07-019105-0, SP). McGraw.
--English Grammar. (Schaum's Outline Ser.). 224p. 1976. pap. 4.95 (ISBN 0-07-019098-4, SP). McGraw.

Ehrlich, Everett M., jt. auth. see Scheppach, Raymond C.

Ehrlich, Howard J., ed. see Drucker, Peter F., et al.

Ehrlich, Margarete. Emploi de Films Detecteurs pour la Protection du Personnel. (Safety Ser.: No. 8). (Illus.). 192p. (Eng. & Rus. eds. also avail.). 1962. pap. write for info. o.p. (ISBN 92-0-223262-8, STI/PUB/43, IAEA). Unipub.

Ehrlich, Paul R. & Ehrlich, Anne H. Extinction: The Causes & Consequences of the Disappearance of Species. 400p. 1983. pap. 4.50 (ISBN 0-345-28895-5). Ballantine.

Ehrlich, Paul R. & Holm, R. W. Evolution. (Biocore Ser: Unit 22). 1974. 17.50 o.p. (ISBN 0-07-005353-7, C). McGraw.

Ehrlich, Paul R., et al. Biology & Society. (Illus.). 1976. text ed. 25.95 o.p. (ISBN 0-07-019147-6, C); instructor's manual 4.00 o.p. (ISBN 0-07-019148-4). McGraw.
--The Process of Evolution. 2nd ed. (Population Biology Ser.). (Illus.). 416p. 1974. text ed. 32.50 (ISBN 0-07-019133-6, C). McGraw.

Ehrlich, Richard L., ed. & intro. by. Immigrants in Industrial America: 1850-1920. LC 76-56376. 1977. 13.95x (ISBN 0-8139-0678-4, Eleutherian Mills -Hagley Foundation). U Pr of Va.

Ehrlich, Ruth A. & Givens, Ellen M. Patient Care in Radiography. LC 80-39489. (Illus.). 191p. 1981. pap. text ed. 15.95 (ISBN 0-8016-1507-0). Mosby.

Ehrlich, S. Pluralism on & off Course. (Illus.). 276p. 1982. pap. 40.00 (ISBN 0-08-027936-8); 19.50 (ISBN 0-08-028114-1). Pergamon.

Ehrlich, Thomas & Hazard, Geoffrey C., Jr. Going to Law School? Readings on a Legal Career. 252p. 1975. 8.95 (ISBN 0-316-22287-9); pap. 9.95 (ISBN 0-316-22288-7). Little.

Ehrlich, Walter. Presidential Impeachment. 1974. pap. text ed. 2.95x. Forum Pr IL.
--They Have No Rights. 266p. 1979. pap. 7.95 (ISBN 0-686-95751-2). Jefferson Natl.
--They Have No Rights: Dred Scott's Struggle for Freedom. LC 78-22135. (Contributions in Legal Studies: No. 9). (Illus.). 1979. lib. bdg. 29.95 (ISBN 0-313-20819-0, ETH/). Greenwood.

Ehrlichman, John. Whole Truth. 1979. 10.95 o.p. (ISBN 0-671-24358-6). S&S.
--Witness to Power: The Nixon Years. 1982. pap. 3.95 (ISBN 0-671-45995-3). PB.

Ehrman, Edith & Morehouse, Ward. Students, Teachers & the 3rd World in the American College Curriculum. (Occasional Publication). 96p. 1972. pap. 2.00 o.p. (ISBN 0-89192-140-0). Interbk Inc.

Ehrman, John. The Younger Pitt: The Reluctant Transition. LC 82-42859. (Illus.). 736p. 1983. 49.50x (ISBN 0-8047-1184-4). Stanford U Pr.
--The Younger Pitt: The Years of Acclaim. (Illus.). 650p. 1969. text ed. 45.00x (ISBN 0-8047-1186-0). Stanford U Pr.

Ehrman, Lee & Parsons, Peter. Behavior Genetics & Evolution. (Illus.). 448p. 1981. text ed. 38.50 (ISBN 0-07-019276-6, C). McGraw.

Ehrmann, Henry W. Comparative Legal Cultures. 176p. 1976. pap. text ed. 10.95 (ISBN 0-13-153858-6). P-H.
--Politics in France. 4th ed. (Ser. in Comparative Politics). 1976. pap. text ed. 10.95 (ISBN 0-316-22289-5). Little.

Ehrmann, Jacques. Un Paradis Desespere: L'Amour, L'Illusion. (Yale Romantic Studies). 1963. pap. 37.50x (ISBN 0-685-69816-5). Elliots Bks.

Ehrmann, Lee & Omenn, Gilbert S., eds. Genetics, Environment & Behavior: Implications for Educational Policy. 1972. 49.50 (ISBN 0-12-233450-7). Acad Pr.

Eichberger, J., jt. auth. see Siebert, H.

Eichborn, Reinhart Von see Von Eichborn, Reinhart.

Eichelberger, Clayton L. Published Comment on William Dean Howells Through 1920: A Research Bibliography. 1976. lib. bdg. 29.00 o.p. (ISBN 0-8161-1078-6, Hall Reference). G K Hall.

Eichelberger, James W., jt. ed. see Budde, William L.

Eichelberger, Rosa K. Big Fire in Baltimore. (Illus.). 204p. 1979. pap. 6.95 (ISBN 0-686-36722-7). Md Hist.

Eichelman, Burr & Soskis, David A., eds. Terrorism: Interdisciplinary Perspectives. LC 82-24393. (Illus.). 186p. 1983. text ed. 22.50x (ISBN 0-89042-109-9). Am Psychiatric.

Eichenbaum, J., et al. Seattle. LC 76-4491. (Contemporary Metropolitan Analysis Ser.). (Illus.). 1976. pap. 8.95x prof ref (ISBN 0-88410-437-0). Ballinger Pub.

Eichenbaum, Luise & Orbach, Susie. Understanding Women: A Feminist Psychoanalytic Approach. 1983. 15.50 (ISBN 0-465-08864-3). Basic.
--What Do Women Want. LC 82-14150. 288p. 1983. 13.95 (ISBN 0-698-11210-5, Coward). Putnam Pub Group.

Eichenberg, Fritz. Ape in a Cape: An Alphabet of Odd Animals. LC 52-6908. (Illus.). (ps-3). 6.95 o.p. (ISBN 0-15-203722-5, HJ). HarBraceJ.
--Ape in a Cape: An Alphabet of Odd Animals. LC 52-6908. (Illus.). 32p. (ps-3). 1973. pap. 3.95 (ISBN 0-15-607830-9, VoyB). HarBraceJ.
--The Art of the Print: Masterpieces, History, Techniques. LC 74-18024. (Illus.). 608p. 1976. 55.00 (ISBN 0-8109-0103-X). Abrams.
--Dance of Death. (Illus.). 136p. 1983. 25.95 (ISBN 0-89659-339-8). Abbeville Pr.
--Dancing in the Moon: Counting Rhymes. LC 55-8674. (Illus.). (gr. k-3). 1956. 7.95 o.p. (ISBN 0-15-221443-7, HJ). HarBraceJ.
--Dancing in the Moon: Counting Rhymes. LC 75-8514. (Illus.). 32p. (gr. k-1). 1975. pap. 1.85 (ISBN 0-15-623811-X, VoyB). HarBraceJ.
--The Wood & the Graver. (Illus.). 1977. limited ed. 45.00 o.p. (ISBN 0-517-52927-0, C N Potter Bks); 22.50 o.p. (ISBN 0-517-52910-6, C N Potter). Crown.

Eichenberg, Fritz, retold by. & illus. Poor Troll: The Story of Ruebezahl & the Princess. (Illus.). 48p. 1982. 9.95 (ISBN 0-686-91966-1). Stemmer Hse.

Eichenberger, Shirley. Mother's Day Out. LC 82-42762. 1983. 12.95 (ISBN 0-911391-25-8); pap. 10.95 (ISBN 0-911391-26-6). Oak Hill KS.

Eichengreen, Barry J. Sterling & the Tariff, 1929-32. LC 81-6673. (Princeton Studies in International Finance Ser.: No. 48). 1981. pap. text ed. 4.50x (ISBN 0-88165-219-9). Princeton U Int Finan Econ.

Eicher, David J., ed. Deep-Sky Observing with Small Telescopes. (Illus.). 256p. 1983. pap. 15.95 (ISBN 0-89490-075-7). Enslow Pubs.

Eicher, Don & McAlester, Lee. History of the Earth. (Illus.). 1980. text ed. 28.95 (ISBN 0-13-390047-9). P-H.

Eicher, Don L. Geologic Time. 2nd ed. (Foundations of Earth Sciences Ser.). (Illus.). 160p. 1976. pap. 11.95 (ISBN 0-13-352484-1). P-H.

Eicher, George J. The Enviromental Control Department in Industry & Government: It's Organization & Operation. 165p. 1982. 38.50 (ISBN 0-9607390-0-9). Words Pr.

Eichholz, Alice & Rose, James M., eds. Free Black Heads of Households in the New York State Federal Census, 1790 to 1830. (Genealogy & Local History Ser: Vol. 14). 301p. 42.00x (ISBN 0-8103-1468-1). Gale.

Eichholz, Alice, jt. ed. see Rose, James M.

Eichholz, Geoffrey G. & Poston, John W. Principles of Nuclear Radiation Detection; & Laboratory Manual. LC 79-88897. (Illus.). 1979. 29.95 (ISBN 0-250-40263-7); lab manual 14.95 (ISBN 0-250-40264-5). Ann Arbor Science.

Eichhorn, G. L., ed. Advances in Inorganic Biochemistry. (Vol. 1). 1979. 32.95 (ISBN 0-444-00323-1). Elsevier.

Eichler, A. W. Bluethendiagramme, 2 vols. (Illus.). 1954. 66.00 (ISBN 3-87429-003-4). Lubrecht & Cramer.

Eichler, Edward P. & Kaplan, Marshall. The Community Builders. LC 67-13601. (California Studies in Urbanization & Environmental Design). 1967. 22.50x (ISBN 0-520-00380-2). U of Cal Pr.

Eichler, Margrit. The Double Standard: A Feminist Critique of the Social Sciences. 1979. 18.95 (ISBN 0-312-21823-0). St Martin.
--Martin's Father. 2nd ed. LC 77-81779. 31p. (ps-1). 1977. pap. 3.25 (ISBN 0-914996-16-9); 6.50 o.p. (ISBN 0-914996-17-7). Lollipop Power.

Eichler, Margrit & Scott, Hilda, eds. Women in Futures Research. (Women's Studies Quarterly: Vol. 4, No. 1). (Illus.). 124p. 1982. 19.00 (ISBN 0-08-028100-1). Pergamon.

Eichler, Martin. Introduction to the Theory of Algebraic Numbers & Functions. (Pure & Applied Mathematics: Vol. 23). 1966. 63.00 (ISBN 0-12-233650-X). Acad Pr.

Eichler, Ned. The Merchant Builders. (Illus.). 296p. 1982. text ed. 24.95x (ISBN 0-262-05026-9). MIT Pr.

Eichler, Victor B. Atlas of Comparative Embryology: A Laboratory Guide to Invertebrate & Vertebrate Embryos. LC 77-16023. (Illus.). 202p. 1978. pap. text ed. 11.50 o.p. (ISBN 0-8016-1492-9). Mosby.

Eichling, Jeanne. Dogs, 3 Vols. (Illus.). 48p. 1982. 20.00 ea. (ISBN 0-686-82187-4). Vol. I (ISBN 0-88014-051-8). Vol. II (ISBN 0-686-82187-4). Vol. III (ISBN 0-88014-053-4). Mosaic Pr OH.

Eichner, A. S. The Megacorp & Oligopoly. LC 75-17115. (Illus.). 450p. 1976. 44.50 (ISBN 0-521-20885-8). Cambridge U Pr.

Eichner, Alfred S. The Megacorp & Oligopoly. LC 79-92295. 365p. 1980. pap. 10.95 (ISBN 0-87332-168-5). M E Sharpe.

Eicholz, R. & O'Daffer, P. Mathematics in Our Modern World: Spanish Editions. (gr. 4-6). 1982. Grade 4. 12.84 (ISBN 0-201-09734-6, Sch Div); Grade 5. 12.84 (ISBN 0-201-09735-4); Grade 6. 12.84 (ISBN 0-201-09736-2). A-W.

Eicholz, R. E., ed. Skillseekers, 3 kits. (gr. 3-8). 1977. Kit I. 227.55 (ISBN 0-201-23026-7, Sch Div); Kit II. 236.43 (ISBN 0-201-23080-1); 227.55 (ISBN 0-201-23200-6); tchr's ed. 8.00 (ISBN 0-201-23027-5); dup. master 6.72 (ISBN 0-201-23030-5). A-W.

Eicholz, Robert & O'Daffer, Phares. Mathematics In Our World. rev. ed. (gr. 1). 1982. 18.75 (ISBN 0-201-18111-8, Sch Div); team package, with tchr's. ed. 56.25 (ISBN 0-201-18112-6, Sch Div). A-W.

Eicholz, Robert E., et al. Investigating School Mathematics Primer. (Investigating School Math Ser.). (gr. 1-6). 1973. pap. text ed. 4.72 (ISBN 0-201-01290-1, Sch Div); tchr's. ed. 18.20 (ISBN 0-201-01291-X). A-W.
--Mathematics in Our World. Incl. Bk. 1. (gr. 1). text ed. 4.72 kindergarten (ISBN 0-201-09800-8); text ed. 7.64 (ISBN 0-201-09810-5); tchr's. ed. 20.00 (ISBN 0-201-09811-3); wkbk. 3.44 (ISBN 0-201-09813-X); wkbk. tchr's. ed. 3.64 (ISBN 0-201-09814-8); duplicator masters 49.68 (ISBN 0-201-09812-1); enrichment wkbk. 3.44 (ISBN 0-201-09815-6); tchr's. enrichment wkbk. 3.64 (ISBN 0-201-09816-4); Bk. 2. (gr. 2). text ed. 7.64 (ISBN 0-201-09820-2); tchr's ed. 20.00 (ISBN 0-201-09821-0); wkbk. 3.44 (ISBN 0-201-09823-7); wkbk. tchr's ed. 3.64 (ISBN 0-201-09824-5); duplicator masters 49.68 (ISBN 0-201-09822-9); enrichment wkbk. 3.44 (ISBN 0-201-09825-3); tchr's enrichment wkbk 3.64 (ISBN 0-201-09826-1); Bk. 3. (gr. 3). text ed. 12.84 (ISBN 0-201-09830-X); tchr's ed. 20.00 (ISBN 0-201-09831-8); dup. masters 49.68 (ISBN 0-201-16039-0); wkbk 4.64 (ISBN 0-201-09833-4); wkbk 4.56 (ISBN 0-201-09835-0); wkbk tchr's ed. 4.88 (ISBN 0-201-09836-9); Bk. 4. (gr. 4). text ed. 12.84 (ISBN 0-201-09840-7); tchr's ed. 20.00 (ISBN 0-201-09841-5); wkbk. tchr's. ed. 5.12 (ISBN 0-201-09844-X); Bk. 5. (gr. 5). text ed. 12.84 (ISBN 0-201-09850-4); tchr's ed. 20.00 (ISBN 0-201-09851-2); duplicator masters 49.68 (ISBN 0-201-16059-5); wkbk. 4.36; wkbk. tchr's. ed. 5.12 (ISBN 0-201-09854-7); Bk. 6. (gr. 6). text ed. 12.84 (ISBN 0-201-09860-1); tchr's ed. 20.00 (ISBN 0-201-09861-X); duplicator masters 49.68 (ISBN 0-201-09862-8); wkbk. 4.36 (ISBN 0-201-16063-3); wkbk. tchr's ed. 5.12 (ISBN 0-201-09864-4); Bk. 7. (gr. 7). 1980. text ed. 15.08 (ISBN 0-201-09870-9); tchr's ed. 20.00 (ISBN 0-201-09871-7); sch div. 40.00 (ISBN 0-201-09875-X); Bk. 8. (gr. 8). 1978. text ed. 15.08 (ISBN 0-201-09880-6); tchr's ed. 20.00 (ISBN 0-201-09881-4); wkbk. 4.36 (ISBN 0-201-09883-0); tchr's ed. wkbk 5.12 (ISBN 0-201-09884-9). (gr. 1-6). 1978. duplicator masters 52.52 ea. (ISBN 0-201-09882-2, Sch Div). A-W.
--Mathematics in Our World: Spanish Edition. 2nd ed. (gr. 1-6). 1981. Bk. 1. text ed. 7.64 (ISBN 0-201-09700-1, Sch Div); Bk. 2. text ed. 7.64 (ISBN 0-201-09701-X); Bk. 3. text ed. 9.04 (ISBN 0-201-09702-8). A-W.

Eichorn, G. L. & Marzilli. Advances in Inorganic Chemistry, Vol. 4. 1982. 54.50 (ISBN 0-444-00680-X). Elsevier.

Eichorn, W. & Henn, R., eds. Economic Theory of Natural Resources. 592p. 1982. pap. text ed. 42.50 (ISBN 3-7908-0274-3). Birkhauser.
--Qualitative Studies on Production & Prices. 304p. 1982. text ed. 23.95x (ISBN 3-7908-0275-1). Birkhauser.

Eichrodt, Walther. Ezekiel: A Commentary. LC 71-117646. (Old Testament Library). 1970. 18.95 (ISBN 0-664-20872-X). Westminster.
--Theology of the Old Testament, 2 Vols. Baker, J., tr. LC 61-11867. (Old Testament Library). 1967. 17.95 ea. Vol. 1 (ISBN 0-664-20352-3). Vol. 2 (ISBN 0-664-20769-3). Westminster.

Eichstaedt, Carl B., jt. auth. see Kalakian, Leonard H.

Eickelman, Dale F. The Middle East: An Anthropological Approach. (Ser. in Anthropology). (Illus.). 368p. 1981. text ed. 14.95 (ISBN 0-13-581629-7). P-H.

Eickenberg, H. U., ed. The Influence of Antibiotics on the Host-Parasite Relationship. (Illus.). 270p. 1982. pap. 25.00 (ISBN 0-387-11680-X). Springer-Verlag.

Eicoff, Alvin. Or Your Money Back: How to Make a Fortune Merchandise Your Product on Radio, TV, & Cable. LC 82-5020. 192p. 1982. 14.95 (ISBN 0-517-54739-2). Crown.

Eide, Arvid R., et al. Engineering Fundamentals & Problem Solving. (Illus.). 1979. text ed. 24.50 (ISBN 0-07-019123-9, C); solutions manual 17.50 (ISBN 0-07-019124-7). McGraw.

Eide, Asbjorn & Thee, Marek, eds. Problems of Contemporary Militarism. LC 79-3379. 1980. 30.00x (ISBN 0-312-64744-1). St Martin.

Eide, Ingrid, ed. Students As Links Between Cultures. 1971. 15.00 (ISBN 92-3-100800-5, U641, UNESCO). Unipub.

Eidelberg, Paul. Beyond Detente: Toward an American Foreign Policy. 1977. 12.95 (ISBN 0-89385-000-4); pap. 6.95 (ISBN 0-686-82978-6). Sugden.

Eidenier, Elon G. Sonnets to Eurydice. LC 75-22876. 1976. 5.00 (ISBN 0-911838-46-5). Windy Row.

Eidlin, Fred. Constitutional Democracy: Essays in Comparative Politics. (Replica Edition Ser.). 350p. 1983. softcover 20.00x (ISBN 0-86531-948-0). Westview.

Eidlitz, Leopold. The Nature & Function of Art, More Especially of Architecture. LC 77-4765. (Architecture & Decorative Art Ser.). 1977. Repr. of 1881 ed. lib. bdg. 39.50 (ISBN 0-306-70898-1). Da Capo.

Eidt, Mary B. & Gandy, Joan W., eds. The Complete Guide to Natchez. LC 76-56980. (Illus.). 111p. 1982. pap. text ed. 5.00 (ISBN 0-9609728-0-3). Myrtle Bank.

Eidus, J., et al. Atlas of Electronic Spectra of Five-Nitrofuran Compounds. 153p. 1972. 29.95x o.s.i. (ISBN 0-470-23430-X). Halsted Pr.

Eiduson, Bernice T. & Beckman, Linda, eds. Science As a Career Choice: Theoretical & Empirical Studies. LC 72-83833. 752p. 1973. 25.00x (ISBN 0-87154-230-7). Russell Sage.

EIFAC Consultation on Eel Fishing Gear & Techniques, Hamburg, 1970. Report & Document. (FAO-EIFAC Technical Papers: No. 14). 192p. 1971. pap. 12.75 (ISBN 0-686-93086-X, F757, FAO). Unipub.

EIFAC, IUNS & ICES Working Group on Standardization of Methodology in Fish Nutrition Research. Report. (FAO-EIFAC Technical Papers: No. 36). 24p. 1980. pap. 8.25 (ISBN 0-686-92849-0, F2048, FAO). Unipub.

Eifer, Bert. Developing the Creative Edge in Photography. (Illus.). 160p. (Orig.). 1983. pap. 14.95 (ISBN 0-89879-110-3). Writers Digest.

Eifert, Virginia S. Essays on Nature. 274p. 1967. pap. 3.50 (ISBN 0-89792-033-3). Ill St Museum.

Eige, Lillian E. The Kidnapping of Mr. Huey. LC 82-48610. 160p. (gr. 6 up). 1983. 9.57i (ISBN 0-06-021798-7, HarpJ); PLB 9.89g (ISBN 0-06-021799-5). Har-Row.

Eigen, Manfred & Winkler, Ruthild. Laws of the Game. LC 81-47550. (Illus.). 368p. 1982. pap. 8.61i (ISBN 0-06-090971-4, CN-971, CN). Har-Row.

Eigenfeld, Neil, jt. auth. see Darlington, C. LeRoy.

Eighmy, John L. Churches in Cultural Captivity: A History of the Social Attitudes of Southern Baptists. LC 70-111047. 1972. 16.50x (ISBN 0-87049-115-6). U of Tenn Pr.

Eighmy, Judith B., jt. auth. see Will, Connie A.

Eigler, G. Studien Zur Gliederung der Flechtengattung Lecanora. (Illus.). 12.00 (ISBN 3-7682-0628-9). Lubrecht & Cramer.

Eigner, Edwin M. The Metaphysical Novel in England & America: Dickens, Bulwer, Hawthorne, Melville. LC 76-50246. 1978. 23.75x (ISBN 0-520-03382-5). U of Cal Pr.

Eigner, Larry. Waters, Places, a Time. Grenier, Robert, ed. 140p. (Orig.). 1983. pap. 7.50 (ISBN 0-87685-497-8); signed cloth ed. 20.00 (ISBN 0-87685-498-6). Black Sparrow.

Eigsti, jt. auth. see Clemen.

Eigsti, Mary S., tr. see Marbot, Bernard.

Eikner, Allen V., ed. Religious Perspectives & Problems: An Introduction to the Philosophy of Religion. LC 80-67265. 368p. 1980. lib. bdg. 23.50 (ISBN 0-8191-1215-1); pap. text ed. 13.50 (ISBN 0-8191-1216-X). U Pr of Amer.

Eikum, A. S. & Seabloom, R. W. Alternative Wastewater Treatment. 1982. 45.00 (ISBN 90-277-1430-4, Pub. by Reidel Holland). Kluwer Boston.

Eiler, Lyntha S. & Eiler, Terry, eds. Blue Ridge Harvest: A Region's Folklife in Photographs. LC 80-607940. (Illus.). vi, 116p. 1981. pap. 6.00 (ISBN 0-8444-0341-5). Lib Congress.

Eiler, Terry, jt. ed. see Eiler, Lyntha S.

Eilon, S., et al. Exercises in Industrial Management. 1966. 10.00 o.p. (ISBN 0-312-27440-8). St Martin.

Eilon, Samuel. Aspects of Management. 1978. text ed. 13.75 o.p. (ISBN 0-08-020969-6); pap. text ed. 5.50 o.p. (ISBN 0-08-020968-8). Pergamon.

Eimerl, Sarel. World of Giotto. LC 67-23024. (Library of Art Ser.). (Illus.). (gr. 6 up). 1967. 19.92 (ISBN 0-8094-0268-8, Pub. by Time-Life). Silver.

Eimerl, Sarel & DeVore, Irven. The Primates. (Young Readers Library). (Illus.). 1977. PLB 6.80 (ISBN 0-8094-1385-X). Silver.

Eimermann, Thomas E. Fundamentals of Paralegalism. (Illus.). 420p. 1980. pap. text ed. 19.95 (ISBN 0-316-23120-7); instuctor's manual avail. (ISBN 0-316-23121-5). Little.

Eimers, Robert & Aitchison, Robert. Effective Parents - Responsible Children. LC 76-44340. 1977. pap. 5.95 (ISBN 0-07-019108-5, GB). McGraw.

Eimert, Herbert & Stockhausen, Karlheinz, eds. Anton Webern. Black, Leo & Smith, Eric, trs. from Ger. (Die Reihe: No. 2). 1958. pap. 12.00 (ISBN 3-7024-0151-2, 47-26102). Eur-Am Music.

--Electronic Music. (Die Reihe: No. 1). 1958. pap. 14.00 (ISBN 0-900938-10-2, 47-26101). Eur-Am Music.

--Form Space. Cardew, Cornelius, tr. from Ger. (Die Reihe: No. 7). 1965. pap. 14.00 (ISBN 3-7024-0142-3, 47-26107). Eur-Am Music.

--Musical Craftsmanship. Cardew, Cornelius & Black, Leo, trs. from Ger. (Die Reihe: No. 3). 1959. pap. 14.00 (ISBN 0-900938-11-0, 47-26103). Eur-Am Music.

--Reports, Analyses. Black, Leo & Koenig, Ruth, trs. from Ger. (Die Reihe: No. 5). 1961. pap. 14.00 (ISBN 0-900938-13-7, 47-26105). Eur-Am Music.

--Retrospective. Cardew, Cornelius & Koenig, Ruth, trs. (Die Reihe: No. 8). 1968. pap. 6.25 (ISBN 3-7024-0152-0, 50-26108). Eur-Am Music.

--Speech & Music. Shenfield, Margaret & Koenig, Ruth, trs. from Ger. (Die Reihe: No. 6). 1964. pap. 4.75 (ISBN 0-900938-14-5, 50-26106). Eur-Am Music.

--Young Composers. (Die Reihe: No. 4). 1960. pap. 14.00 (ISBN 0-900938-13-7, 47-26104). Eur-Am Music.

Eims, Leroy. Be a Motivational Leader. 144p. 1981. pap. 4.50 (ISBN 0-89693-008-4). Victor Bks.

--Be the Leader You Were Meant to Be. 132p. 1975. pap. 4.50 (ISBN 0-88207-723-6). Victor Bks.

--Prayer: More Than Words. LC 82-61301. 1983. pap. 3.95 (ISBN 0-89109-493-8). NavPress.

--Wisdom from Above. 1978. pap. 4.95 (ISBN 0-88207-761-9). Victor Bks.

Einaudi, Karen & Bragantini, Irene, eds. Ancient Roman Architecture: A Text-Fiche, 2 Vols. (Illus.). 1982. Vol. I, 40p. ring binder 800.00x (ISBN 0-686-97828-5, 69041-5); Vol. II, 24p. ring binder 800.00x (ISBN 0-686-97829-3, 69040-7). U of Chicago Pr.

Einaudi, Paula F. A Grammar of Biloxi. LC 75-25114. (American Indian Linguistics Ser.). 1976. lib. bdg. 42.00 o.s.i. (ISBN 0-8240-1965-2). Garland Pub.

Einberg, Elizabeth. The Kennedys Abroad: Ann & Peter in Southern Germany. 10.50 (ISBN 0-392-08619-0, SpS). Sportshelf.

Ein-Dor, Philip & Segev, Eli. Managing Management Information Systems. LC 77-10001. (Illus.). 1978. 24.95x (ISBN 0-669-01642-X). Lexington Bks.

Einem, Herbert Von. Michelangelo. 2nd ed. 1973. 43.00x (ISBN 0-416-15140-X); pap. 19.95x (ISBN 0-416-18050-7). Methuen Inc.

Einhard. Life of Charlemagne. 1960. pap. 4.95 (ISBN 0-472-06035-X, 35, AA). U of Mich Pr.

Einhorn, et al. Effective Employment Interviewing: Unlocking Human Potential. 1981. pap. text ed. 9.95x (ISBN 0-673-15321-5). Scott F.

Einhorn, E. C. Old French: A Concise Handbook. 210p. 1975. 32.50 (ISBN 0-521-20343-0); pap. 12.95 (ISBN 0-521-09838-6). Cambridge U Pr.

Einhorn, Eric & Logue, John. Welfare States in Hard Times: Denmark & Sweden in the 1970's. (Illus.). 1980. pap. 2.95 o.p. (ISBN 0-933522-03-7). Kent Popular.

Einhorn, Lawrence H., ed. Testicular Tumors: Management & Treatment. LC 79-89999. (Cancer Management Series: Vol. 3). (Illus.). 224p. 1980. 43.75 (ISBN 0-89352-078-0). Masson Pub.

Einhorn, Vibeke, tr. see Jackins, Harvey.

Einspahr, Bruce, compiled by. Index to the Brown, Driver & Briggs Hebrew Lexicon. LC 76-25479. 1976. 23.95 (ISBN 0-8024-4082-7). Moody.

Einspruch, Norman, ed. VLSI Electronics: Microstructure Science. 1982. Vol. 4. write for info. (ISBN 0-12-234104-X); Vol. 6. write for info. (ISBN 0-12-234106-6). Acad Pr.

Einspruch, Norman G., ed. VLSI Electronics Microstructure Science, Vol. 5. 1982. 54.00 (ISBN 0-12-234105-8). Acad Pr.

Einstein. Willie's Time: A Memoir. pap. 2.50 o.p. (ISBN 0-425-04658-3). Berkley Pub.

Einstein, Albert. Einstein on Peace. Nathan, Otto & Norden, Heinz, eds. LC 68-28903. 1968. pap. 5.95 o.p. (ISBN 0-8052-0191-2). Schocken.

--Essays in Humanism. 130p. 1983. pap. 4.95 (ISBN 0-8022-2417-2). Philos Lib.

--Ideas & Opinions. 1954. 6.95 o.p. (ISBN 0-517-00393-7). Crown.

--Relativity: The Special & General Theory. Lawson, Robert W., tr. 1961. pap. 2.95 (ISBN 0-517-02530-2). Crown.

Einstein, Alfred. Essays on Music. 1962. pap. 8.95 (ISBN 0-393-00177-6, Norton Lib). Norton.

--Greatness in Music. LC 70-87527. 1972. Repr. of 1941 ed. lib. bdg. 27.50 (ISBN 0-306-71441-8). Da Capo.

Einstein, C. The Baseball Reader: Favorites from the Fireside Book of Baseball. 384p. 1983. pap. 8.95 (ISBN 0-07-019531-5, GB). McGraw.

Einstein, Charles. The Baseball Reader. 384p. 1980. 14.37i (ISBN 0-690-01898-3). T Y Crowell.

--Willie Mays: Coast to Coast Giant. (Putnam Sports Shelf). (Illus.). (gr. 5-9). 1963. PLB 4.97 o.p. (ISBN 0-399-60673-4). Putnam Pub Group.

Einstein, Charles, jt. auth. see Marichal, Juan.

Einstein, Charles, jt. auth. see Mays, Willie.

Einstein, Elizabeth R. Proteins of the Brain & CSF in Health & Disease. (Illus.). 326p. 1982. 37.50x (ISBN 0-398-04657-3). C C Thomas.

Einstein, Stanley. Use & Misuse of Drugs. 1970. pap. 6.95x o.p. (ISBN 0-534-00257-9). Wadsworth Pub.

Einstein, Susan, jt. auth. see Selz, Peter.

Einzig, Barbara. Color. 1976. pap. 3.00 (ISBN 0-87924-020-2). Membrane Pr.

Einzig, Barbara, ed. see Kuwayama, George.

Einzig, P. Primitive Money. (Illus.). 1983. Repr. of 1949 ed. lib. bdg. 40.00 (ISBN 0-942666-13-5). S J Durst.

Einzig, Paul. Case Against Joining the Common Market. 144p. 1971. 27.50 (ISBN 0-312-12320-5). St Martin.

--The Destiny of Gold. LC 72-85830. 1972. 25.00 (ISBN 0-312-19565-6). St Martin.

--Dynamic Theory of Forward Exchange. 2nd ed. 1969. 22.50 o.p. (ISBN 0-312-22365-X). St Martin.

--Euro-Bond Market. 1969. 22.50 (ISBN 0-312-26705-3). St Martin.

--Foreign Exchange Crises. 2nd ed. LC 68-10638. 1970. 25.00 (ISBN 0-312-29855-2). St Martin.

--History of Foreign Exchange. 2nd ed. LC 74-124951. 1970. 27.50 (ISBN 0-312-37835-1). St Martin.

--Leads & Lags. 1968. 22.50 (ISBN 0-312-47670-1). St Martin.

--Roll-Over Credits: The System of Adaptable Interest Rates. LC 73-87565. 114p. 1974. 22.50 (ISBN 0-312-68950-0). St Martin.

--Textbook of Foreign Exchange. 1966. 22.50 (ISBN 0-312-79380-4). St Martin.

Einzig, Paul & Quinn, Brian S. The Euro-Dollar System: Practice & Theory of International Interest Rates. 6th ed. LC 77-78988. 1977. 22.50x (ISBN 0-312-26741-X). St Martin.

Eirinberg, Estelle, tr. see Thomas, Edith.

Eiring, Leslie, jt. auth. see Eaton, Peggy.

Eis, Ruth. Torah Binders of the Judah L. Magnes Museum. LC 79-83877. 80p. 1979. pap. 18.00 (ISBN 0-686-30820-4). Magnes Mus.

Eisberg, John F. Medical Malpractice Litigation. Mason Editorial Staff, ed. 225p. 1982. pap. write for info. (ISBN 0-86678-015-7). Mason Pub.

Eisberg, Robert & Resnick, Robert. Quantum Physics of Atoms, Molecules, Solids, Nuclei & Particles. LC 74-1195. 791p. 1974. text ed. 34.95x (ISBN 0-471-23464-8); avail. solutions (ISBN 0-471-05438-0). Wiley.

Eisberg, Robert M. Applied Mathematical Physics with Programmable Pocket Calculators. (Illus.). 1976. pap. text ed. 13.95 (ISBN 0-07-019109-3, C). McGraw.

--Fundamentals of Modern Physics. LC 61-6770. (Illus.). 1961. 33.95 (ISBN 0-471-23463-X). Wiley.

Eisberg, Robert M. & Lerner, Lawrence S. Physics, Foundations & Applications, 2 Vols. 720p. 1981. Vol. 1. text ed. 24.95x (ISBN 0-07-019091-7, C); Vol. 2. text ed. 24.95x (ISBN 0-07-019092-5); Vol. 1. solutions manual 15.00 (ISBN 0-07-019119-0); Vol. 2. solutions manual 20.00 (ISBN 0-07-019112-3). McGraw.

--Physics: Foundations & Applications, Combined Vol. (Illus.). 1552p. 1981. 36.50x (ISBN 0-07-019110-7). numerical calculation supplement avail. (ISBN 0-07-019120-4). McGraw.

Eischen, Martha. Compu-Guide: The Consumer's Guide to Small Business Computers. LC 81-22120. (Illus.). 180p. 1982. pap. 14.95 o.p. (ISBN 0-918398-69-X). Dilithium Pr.

Eisdorfer, C. & Fann, W. E., eds. Psychopharmacology of Aging. (Illus.). 327p. 1980. text ed. 45.00 (ISBN 0-89335-117-2). Spectrum Pub.

Eisdorfer, Carl & Cohen, Donna. Mental Health Care of the Aging: A Multidisciplinary Curriculum for Professional Training. 1982. text ed. 23.95 (ISBN 0-8261-4090-4). Springer Pub.

Eisdorfer, Carl, ed. Annual Review of Gerontology & Geriatrics, Vol. 3. 352p. 1982. text ed. 42.00 (ISBN 0-8261-3082-8). Springer Pub.

Eisdorfer, Carl & Fann, William E., eds. Treatment of Psychopathology in the Aging. (Springer Psychiatry Ser.: Vol. 2). 1982. text ed. 31.95 (ISBN 0-8261-3810-1). Springer Pub.

Eisele, J. A. & Mason, R. M. Applied Matrix & Tensor Analysis. LC 71-114916. 729p. 1970. 25.50 o.p. (ISBN 0-471-23465-6, Pub. by Wiley-Interscience). Wiley.

Eiseley, Loren. Darwin & the Mysterious Mr. X: New Light on the Evolutionists. LC 80-24833. 1981. pap. 6.95 (ISBN 0-15-623949-3, Harv). HarBraceJ.

--Firmament of Time. rev. ed. LC 60-11032. 1960. pap. 5.95 (ISBN 0-689-70068-7, 95). Atheneum.

--Immense Journey. 1957. pap. 2.95 (ISBN 0-394-70157-7, Vin). Random.

--The Unexpected Universe. LC 67-20308. 239p. 1972. pap. 3.50 (ISBN 0-15-692850-7, Harv). HarBraceJ.

Eiseman, Ben & Wotkyns, Roger S. Surgical Decision Making. LC 77-84668. (Illus.). 1978. text ed. 39.00 (ISBN 0-7216-3343-9). Saunders.

Eiseman, Ben & Steele, Glen, eds. Follow-Up of the Cancer Patient. LC 81-84767. (Illus.). 320p. 1982. text ed. 38.00 (ISBN 0-86577-021-2). Thieme-Stratton.

Eisemann, Fred, tr. see Chekhov, Anton.

Eisemon, Thomas O. The Science Profession in the Third World: Studies from India & Kenya. Altbach, Philip G., ed. (Special Studies in Comparative Education). 186p. 1982. 22.95 (ISBN 0-03-062023-6). Praeger.

Eisen, Carole, jt. auth. see Eisen, Martin.

Eisen, G. Enchytroids. Bd. with Tubicolous Annelids. Bush, K. J. (Harriman Alaska Expedition, 1899). (Illus.). 1904. 28.00 (ISBN 0-527-38172-1). Kraus Repr.

Eisen, Gail, jt. auth. see Friedman, Philip.

Eisen, Glen P., jt. auth. see Barlow, C. W.

Eisen, Herman N. Immunology. 2nd ed. (Illus.). 259p. 1980. pap. text ed. 18.00x (ISBN 0-06-140781-X, Harper Medical). Lippincott.

Eisen, Jeffrey. Get the Right Job Now! (Illus.). 1978. 10.00i (ISBN 0-397-01349-3, LP-137); pap. 5.95i (ISBN 0-397-01311-6). Har-Row.

Eisen, Martin & Eisen, Carole. Finite Mathematics. 1978. text ed. 22.95 (ISBN 0-02-472450-5). Macmillan.

Eisen, Sydney & Lightman, Bernard. Victorian Science & Religion: A Bibliography of Works on Ideas & Institutions with Emphasis on Evolution, Belief & Unbelief, Published from c.1900 to 1975. 1983. price not set (ISBN 0-208-02010-1, Archon Bks). Shoe String.

Eisenbach, Rina. Calculating & Administering Medications. rev. ed. LC 78-711. (Illus.). 131p. 1978. 7.50x (ISBN 0-8036-3080-8). Davis Co.

Eisenbacher, Mario. Programming Your Timex-Sinclair 1000 in BASIC. (Illus.). 160p. 1983. 17.95 (ISBN 0-13-729871-4); pap. 9.95 (ISBN 0-13-729863-3). P-H.

Eisenbarth, George, jt. ed. see Fellows, Robert.

Eisenbeis, Walter. The Key Ideas of Martin Heidegger's Treatise, Being & Time. LC 82-23874. 172p. (Orig.). 1983. lib. bdg. 20.75 (ISBN 0-8191-3009-5); pap. text ed. 10.00 (ISBN 0-8191-3010-9). U Pr of Amer.

--The Key Ideas of P ul Tillich's Systematic Theology. LC 82-21834. 268p. (Orig., Ger. & Eng.). 1983. lib. bdg. 21.75 (ISBN 0-8191-2948-8); pap. text ed. 11.50 (ISBN 0-8191-2949-6). U Pr of Amer.

Eisenberg, jt. auth. see Patterson.

Eisenberg, A. Technical Communication. 1982. 19.50 (ISBN 0-07-019096-8); 13.50 (ISBN 0-07-019097-6). McGraw.

Eisenberg, A. & Globe, Leah A. Secret Weapon & Other Stories of Faith & Valor. (Illus.). (gr. 4-6). 1971. 9.95x (ISBN 0-685-01035-X). Bloch.

Eisenberg, Abne M. Living Communication. (Speech Communications Ser.). (Illus.). 336p. 1975. pap. text ed. 16.95 (ISBN 0-13-538900-3). P-H.

--Speech Communication in Business & Professions. (Illus.). 1978. pap. text ed. 13.95 (ISBN 0-02-331850-3); pap. text ed. 6.95 o.p. (ISBN 0-686-67729-3). Macmillan.

Eisenberg, Abne M. & Gamble, Teri K. Painless Public Speaking. (Illus.). 288p. 1982. pap. text ed. 13.95x (ISBN 0-02-331830-9). Macmillan.

Eisenberg, Abne M. & Ilardo, Joseph A. Argument: A Guide to Formal & Informal Debate. 2nd ed. (Speech Communication Ser.). (Illus.). 1980. pap. 14.95 (ISBN 0-13-045989-5). P-H.

Eisenberg, Adi & Yeager, Howard L., eds. Perfluorinated Ionomer Membranes. (ACS Symposium Ser.: No. 180). 1982. write for info. (ISBN 0-8412-0698-8). Am Chemical.

Eisenberg, Anne. Reading Technical Books. LC 78-672. (Illus.). 1978. pap. 11.95 ref. ed. (ISBN 0-13-762138-8). P-H.

Eisenberg, Arlene, jt. auth. see Eisenberg, Howard.

Eisenberg, Arlene, et al. The Special Guest Cookbook: Elegant Menus & Recipes for Those Who Are -- Allergic to Certain Foods, Bland Dieters, Calorie Counters, Cholesterol Conscious, Diabetic, Hypoglycemic, Kosher, Milk Sensitive, Pritikin Porselytes, Salt-Avoiding, Strictly Vegetarian. LC 81-17106. 400p. 1982. 19.95 (ISBN 0-8253-0090-8). Beaufort Bks NY.

Eisenberg, Azriel. The Book of Books: The Story of the Bible Text. 1976. 9.95x (ISBN 0-685-84453-6). Bloch.

--Witness to the Holocaust. 672p. 1983. pap. 12.95 (ISBN 0-8298-0614-8). Pilgrim NY.

Eisenberg, Azriel & Arian, Philip. The Story of the Prayer Book. pap. 5.95x (ISBN 0-87677-017-0). Hartmore.

Eisenberg, Azriel, jt. auth. see Arian, Phillip.

Eisenberg, C. G. History of the First Dakota-District of the Evangelical-Lutheran Synod of Iowa & Other States. Richter, Anton H., tr. from Ger. LC 82-17645. 268p. (Orig.). 1983. lib. bdg. 23.25 (ISBN 0-8191-2798-1); pap. text ed. 12.00 (ISBN 0-8191-2799-X). U Pr of Amer.

Eisenberg, David & Crothers, Donald M. Physical Chemistry with Applications to the Life Sciences. 1979. 29.95 (ISBN 0-8053-2402-X); instrs'. guide 4.95 (ISBN 0-8053-2403-8). Benjamin-Cummings.

Eisenberg, Dennis, et al. The Mossad: Israel's Secret Intelligence Service--Inside Stories. (Illus.). 1979. pap. 2.95 (ISBN 0-451-11816-2, AE1816, Sig). NAL.

--Operation Uranium Ship: A True Story. (RL 6). 1978. pap. 1.75 o.p. (ISBN 0-451-08001-7, E8001, Sig). NAL.

Eisenberg, Frank, Jr., jt. ed. see Wells, William W.

Eisenberg, Gerson G. Learning Vacations. 4th ed. (Illus.). 330p. 1982. pap. 7.95 (ISBN 0-686-36752-9). Md Hist.

--Learning Vacations Nineteen Eighty-Two: A Guide to All Season Worldwide Educational Travel. 4th ed. LC 81-21002. 246p. (Orig.). 1982. write for info. (ISBN 0-930080-04-1). Eisenberg Ed.

Eisenberg, Helen & Eisenberg, Larry. Handbook of Skits & Stunts. 1953. 5.95 o.s.i. (ISBN 0-8096-1086-8, Assn Pr). Follett.

Eisenberg, Hershey. The Reinhard Action. LC 79-19446. 1980. 8.95 o.p. (ISBN 0-688-03583-3). Morrow.

Eisenberg, Howard & Eisenberg, Arlene. Alive & Well: Decisions in Health. 1979. text ed. 24.50 (ISBN 0-07-019113-1, C); instructor's manual 15.00 (ISBN 0-07-019114-X); study guide 11.95 (ISBN 0-07-019136-0); test bank 15.00 (ISBN 0-07-019137-9). McGraw.

Eisenberg, Howard, jt. auth. see Kantrowitz, Walter.

Eisenberg, Howard, jt. auth. see Sehnert, Keith.

Eisenberg, Howard, jt. auth. see Sehnert, Keith W.

Eisenberg, J. F. & Kleiman, D. G., eds. Advances in the Study of Mammalian Behavior. (American Society of Mammalogists Special Publication Ser.: No.7). 753p. 1983. 45.00, 36.00 members (ISBN 0-943612-06-3). Am Soc Mammalogists.

Eisenberg, J. M. & Greiner, W. Nuclear Theory, Vol. 1: Nuclear Models. 2nd ed. 1976. pap. 42.75 (ISBN 0-444-10790-8, North-Holland). Elsevier.

--Nuclear Theory, Vol. 3: Microscopic Theory of the Nucleus. 2nd ed. 1976. pap. 47.00 (ISBN 0-7204-0484-3, North-Holland). Elsevier.

Eisenberg, James & Kafka, Francis J. Silk Screen Printing. rev. ed. (Illus.). (gr. 9 up). 1957. pap. 6.00 (ISBN 0-87345-205-4). McKnight.

Eisenberg, John F. The Mammalian Radiations: An Analysis of Trends in Evolution, Adaption & Behavior. LC 80-27940. (Illus.). 640p. 1982. 45.00x (ISBN 0-226-19537-6); pap. 20.00 (ISBN 0-226-19538-4). U of Chicago Pr.

Eisenberg, John M. & Williams, Sarkey V. The Physicians Practice. LC 80-13691. 274p. 1980. 30.50 (ISBN 0-471-05469-0, Pub. by Wiley Med). Wiley.

Eisenberg, Judah & Greiner, Walter. Nuclear Theory, Vol. 2: Excitation Mechanisms of the Nucleus. 2nd ed. LC 78-97200. 1976. pap. 42.75 (ISBN 0-7204-0158-5, North-Holland). Elsevier.

Eisenberg, Judah M. & Koltun, Daniel S. Theory of Meson Interactions with Nuclei. LC 79-24653. 1980. 59.50 (ISBN 0-471-03915-2, Pub. by Wiley-Interscience). Wiley.

Eisenberg, Larry, jt. auth. see Eisenberg, Helen.

Eisenberg, Lee, jt. auth. see Levi, Vicki G.

Eisenberg, Lisa. Killer Music. LC 79-52657. (Laura Brewster Bks.). 1980. pap. 4.24 (ISBN 0-8224-1085-0). Pitman Learning.

Eisenberg, M. G. Psychological Aspects of Physical Disability: A Guide for the Health Care Educator. (League Exchange Ser.: No. 114). 38p. 1977. 3.95 (ISBN 0-686-38192-0, 20-1692). Natl League Nurse.

Eisenberg, Martin A. Introduction to the Mechanics of Solids. LC 78-74682. (Illus.). 1980. text ed. 29.95 (ISBN 0-201-01934-5). A-W.

Eisenberg, Melvin A. Structure of the Corporation. 1977. pap. text ed. 9.95 (ISBN 0-316-22542-8). Little.

Eisenberg, Mickey & Bergner, Lawrence, eds. Cardiopulmonary Resuscitation: Evaluating Performance & Potential. (Emergency Health Services Quarterly Ser.: Vol. 1, No. 3). 94p. 1982. pap. text ed. 15.00 (ISBN 0-917724-58-5, B58). Haworth Pr.

Eisenberg, Mickey S. & Copass, Michael. Manual of Emergency Medical Therapeutics. new ed. (Illus.). 1978. pap. text ed. 12.95 o.p. (ISBN 0-7216-5048-1). Saunders.

Eisenberg, Mickey S., et al. Manual of Antimicrobial Therapy & Infectious Diseases. (Illus.). 282p. 1981. 18.50 (ISBN 0-7216-3347-1); pap. text ed. 14.95 o.p. (ISBN 0-7216-3348-X). Saunders.

Eisenberg, Myron G., et al. Disabled People As Second Class Citizens. (Springer Ser. on Rehabilitation: Vol. 2). 1982. text ed. 26.95 (ISBN 0-8261-3220-0); textbk. quanties 21.95 (ISBN 0-8261-3221-9). Springer Pub.

Eisenberg, Nancy, ed. The Development of Prosocial Behavior. (Developmental Psychology Ser.). 416p. 1982. 35.00 (ISBN 0-12-234980-6). Acad Pr.

Eisenberg, Peter L. The Sugar Industry in Pernambuco, 1840-1910: Modernization Without Change. LC 75-117340. 1974. 33.00x (ISBN 0-520-01731-5). U of Cal Pr.

Eisenberg, Ronald L. Gastrointestinal Radiology: A Pattern Approach. (Illus.). 1056p. 1982. text ed. 95.00 (ISBN 0-397-52113-8, Lippincott Medical). Lippincott.

Eisenberg, Sheldon & Delaney, Daniel J. The Counseling Process. 2nd ed. 1977. pap. 13.50 (ISBN 0-395-30796-1). HM.

Eisenberg, Sheldon & Patterson, Lewis P. Helping Clients with Special Concerns. LC 81-85322. 1979. pap. 15.50 (ISBN 0-395-30592-6). HM.

Eisenbud, Jule. Parapsychology & the Unconscious. 250p. 1983. cloth 19.95 (ISBN 0-938190-07-5); pap. 9.95 (ISBN 0-938190-08-3). North Atlantic.
Eisenhart, E. J., jt. ed. see Hills, M. T.
Eisenhauer, Laurel A., jt. auth. see Asperheim, Mary K.
Eisenhower, Dwight D. Crusade in Europe. LC 76-25037. (Politics & Strategy of World War II Ser.). 1977. 45.00 (ISBN 0-306-70768-3); pap. 8.95 (ISBN 0-306-80109-4). Da Capo.
--White House Years: Waging Peace, 1956-1961. LC 65-19046. 7.95 o.p. (ISBN 0-385-03868-2). Doubleday.
Eisenhower, Julie, ed. Great Love Stories from the Saturday Evening Post. LC 76-41559. 320p. 1976. 5.95 (ISBN 0-89387-003-X, Co-Pub by Sat Eve Post). Curtis Pub Co.
--Great Westerns from the Saturday Evening Post. LC 76-41560. 320p. 1976. 5.95 (ISBN 0-89387-004-8, Co-Pub by Sat Eve Post). Curtis Pub Co.
--Mystery & Suspense: Great Stories from the Saturday Evening Post. LC 76-41561. 320p. 1976. 5.95 (ISBN 0-89387-005-6, Co-Pub by Sat Eve Post). Curtis Pub Co.
Eisenhower, Julie N. Special People. 1977. 9.95 o.p. (ISBN 0-671-22708-4). S&S.
Eisenkramer, Henry E. Classroom Music. LC 78-60416. (Illus.). 1978. pap. 10.95 (ISBN 0-916656-11-X). Mark Foster Mus.
Eisenman, et al. Five Architects: Eisenman, Graves, Gwathmey Hejduk, Meiser. 1975. 29.50 o.p. (ISBN 0-19-519794-1); pap. 18.95 (ISBN 0-19-519795-X). Oxford U Pr.
Eisenman, G., ed. Glass Electrodes for Hydrogen & Other Cations: Principles & Practice. 1967. 75.00 (ISBN 0-8247-1170-X). Dekker.
Eisenman, Peter. Giuseppe Terragni: Transformations, Decompositions, Critiques. Date not set. price not set (ISBN 0-262-05017-X). MIT Pr.
--House X. LC 80-51622. (Illus.). 176p. 1983. 35.00 (ISBN 0-8478-0355-4); pap. 19.95 (ISBN 0-686-63413-6). Rizzoli Intl.
Eisenman, Peter & Rossi, Aldo. Aldo Rossi in America: 1976-1979. (IAUS Exhibition Catalogs). (Illus.). 1980. pap. 12.00 (ISBN 0-262-59012-3). MIT Pr.
Eisenmann, Charles. The University Teaching of Social Sciences: Law. LC 72-95476. (Teaching in the Social Sciences Ser.). 182p. (Orig.). 1973. pap. 7.50 o.p. (ISBN 92-3-101035-2, UNESCO). Unipub.
Eisenmann, L. Le Compromis Austro-Honqrois De 1867: Etude Sur le Dualisme. (Central & East European Ser.: Vol. 1). 1904. 25.00 o.p. (ISBN 0-87569-018-1). Academic Intl.
Eisenreich, G. & Sube, R. Dictionary of Mathematics, 2 vols. (Eng. & Fr. & Ger. & Rus.). 1982. Set. 159.75 (ISBN 0-444-99706-7). Elsevier.
Eisenreich, Steven J. Atmospheric Pollutants in Natural Waters. LC 80-65504. 1981. text ed. 49.95 (ISBN 0-250-40369-2). Ann Arbor Science.
Eisenson, J. Adult Aphasia: Assessment & Treatment. 1973. 21.95 (ISBN 0-13-038646-4). P-H.
Eisenson, Jon. Voice & Diction: A Program for Improvement. 4th ed. (Illus.). 1979. pap. text ed. 14.95 (ISBN 0-02-331950-X). Macmillan.
Eisenson, Jon & Boase, Paul H. Basic Speech. 3rd ed. (Illus.). 448p. 1975. text ed. 20.95x (ISBN 0-02-331870-8, 33187). Macmillan.
Eisenson, Jon & Ogilvie, Mardel. Communication Disorders in Children. 5th ed. 480p. 1983. text ed. 21.95 (ISBN 0-02-332100-8). Macmillan.
Eisenstadt, Abraham S., ed. American History: Recent Interpretations. 2nd ed. Incl. Vol 1. To 1877 (ISBN 0-88295-731-7); Vol 2. Since 1865 (ISBN 0-88295-732-5). LC 69-13256. 1969. pap. text ed. 11.95. Harlan Davidson.
Eisenstadt, S. N. The Absorption of Immigrants. LC 74-31867. 275p. 1975. Repr. of 1954 ed. lib. bdg. 15.75x (ISBN 0-8371-7947-5, EIAI). Greenwood.
--Tradition, Change, & Modernity. LC 73-7560. 367p. 1973. 33.95x o.p. (ISBN 0-471-23471-0, Pub. by Wiley-Interscience). Wiley.
Eisenstadt, S. N. & Curelaru, M. The Form of Sociology: Paradigms & Crises. LC 76-7602. 386p. 1976. 38.50 (ISBN 0-471-23472-9, Pub. by Wiley-Interscience). Wiley.
Eisenstadt, S. N., ed. Post-Traditional Societies. 257p. 1974. pap. text ed. 5.95x o.s.i. (ISBN 0-393-09303-4). Norton.
--Readings in Social Evolution & Development. LC 78-96463. 1969. 27.00 o.p. (ISBN 0-08-006813-8); pap. 13.25 (ISBN 0-08-006812-X). Pergamon.
Eisenstadt, Samuel N. Political Systems of Empires. LC 63-7656. 1969. pap. text ed. 5.95 (ISBN 0-02-909460-7). Free Pr.
Eisenstadt, Samuel N. & Bar-Yosef, Rivkah. Integration & Development in Israel. 720p. 1971. casebound 24.95 o.p. (ISBN 0-87855-178-6). Transaction Bks.
Eisenstein, Elizabeth. The Printing Press As an Agent of Change, 2 vols. LC 77-91083. 1979. Vol. 1. 54.50 (ISBN 0-521-21967-1); Vol. 2. 44.50 (ISBN 0-521-21969-8); Set. 89.50 (ISBN 0-521-22044-0). Cambridge U Pr.
--The Printing Press As an Agent of Change, 2 vols. in 1. LC 77-91083. 852p. 1980. pap. 18.95 (ISBN 0-521-29955-1). Cambridge U Pr.
Eisenstein, Hester & Jardine, Alice. The Future of Difference: The Scholar & the Feminist Conference Series, Vol. 1. 1980. lib. bdg. 25.00 (ISBN 0-8161-9029-1, Univ Bks). G K Hall.
Eisenstein, James & Jacob, Herbert. Felony Justice: An Organizational Analysis of Criminal Courts. 1977. 14.95 (ISBN 0-316-22551-7); pap. text ed. 10.95 (ISBN 0-316-22552-5). Little.
Eisenstein, Sergei. Film Form. LC 49-8349. 1969. pap. 4.95 (ISBN 0-15-630920-3, HB153, Harv). HarBraceJ.
Eisenstein, Sergei M. Ivan the Terrible. (Film Scripts-Classic Ser.). 1969. 3.25 o.p. (ISBN 0-671-20447-5, Touchstone Bks). S&S.
Eisenthal, K. B., et al, eds. Picosecond Phenomena III, Garmisch Partenkirchen, FRG, 1982: Proceedings. (Springer Series in Chemical Physics: Vol. 23). (Illus.). 401p. 1983. 30.00 (ISBN 0-387-11912-4). Springer-Verlag.
Eiser, J. Richard. Cognitive Social Psychology. (Illus.). 368p. 1980. pap. text ed. 29.50 (ISBN 0-07-084103-9). McGraw.
--Social Psychology & Behavioral Medicine. LC 80-42062. 608p. 1981. 41.95x (ISBN 0-471-27994-3, Pub. by Wiley-Interscience). Wiley.
Eisey, Neil. Golf. LC 80-52506. (Intersport Ser.). 13.00 (ISBN 0-382-06429-1). Silver.
Eisiminger, Sterling, jt. auth. see Idol, John L.
Eisinger, Erica M. & McCarty, Mari, eds. Colette: The Woman, the Writer. LC 81-47169. 230p. 1981. 17.95x (ISBN 0-271-00286-7). Pa St U Pr.
Eisinger, Peter K. American Politics: The People & the Polity. 2nd ed. 1982. 15.95 (ISBN 0-316-22564-9); tchrs. manual avail. (ISBN 0-316-22565-7). Little.
Eisinger, Peter K., et al. American Politics: People & the Polity. 1978. pap. text ed. 14.95 o.p. (ISBN 0-316-22562-2); tchr's manual free o.p. (ISBN 0-316-22563-0). Little.
Eisler, ed. Trace Metal Concentrations in Marine Organisms. 3500p. 1981. 120.00 (ISBN 0-08-025975-8). Pergamon.
Eisler, Hanns. A Rebel in Music. LC 76-55331. 250p. 1978. pap. 1.95 (ISBN 0-7178-0486-0). Intl Pub Co.
Eisler, Paul A. California Uninsured Motorist Law Handbook. 3rd ed. 756p. 1979. 1982 suppl. incl. 68.00 (ISBN 0-911110-27-5). Parker & Son.
Eisler, Paul E. World Chronology of Music History, 5 vols. plus index. LC 72-4354. (Illus.). 512p. 1972. lib. bdg. 45.00 ea. (ISBN 0-379-16080-3). Oceana.
Eisler, Riane. Dissolution. LC 76-41416. 1977. 8.95 o.p. (ISBN 0-07-019142-5, GB); pap. 4.95 (ISBN 0-07-019150-6). McGraw.
Eisler, Richard M., jt. ed. see Hersen, Michel.
Eisman, Philip, jt. auth. see Gehlmann, John.
Eisner, Elliot. The Educational Imagination: On the Design & Evaluation of School Programs. 1979. text ed. 19.95x (ISBN 0-02-332130-X). Macmillan.
Eisner, Elliot W. Cognition & Curriculum: A Basis for Deciding What to Teach. LC 81-11804. 96p. 1982. 12.95 (ISBN 0-686-37781-8). Longman.
--Educating Artistic Vision. (Illus.). 352p. 1972. text ed. 22.95x (ISBN 0-02-332120-2). Macmillan.
Eisner, Elliot W. & Vallance, Elizabeth. Conflicting Conceptions of Curriculum. LC 73-17616. 1974. 19.00x (ISBN 0-8211-0411-X); text ed. 17.25x (ISBN 0-685-42630-0). McCutchan.
Eisner, Jack. The Survivor. 272p. 1982. pap. 3.50 (ISBN 0-553-20092-5). Bantam.
Eisner, Lotte. The Haunted Screen: Expressionism in the German Cinema & the Influence of Max Reinhardt. Greaves, Roger, tr. LC 68-8719. Orig. Title: Ecran Demoniaque. 1969. pap. 6.50 o.s.i. (ISBN 0-520-02479-6). U of Cal Pr.
--Murnau. LC 72-82222. 1973. 26.50x (ISBN 0-520-02285-8). U of Cal Pr.
Eisner, Robert. Factors in Business Investment. LC 78-7548. (National Bureau of Economic Research Ser.: No. 102). 256p. 1978. prof ref 29.00x (ISBN 0-88410-484-2). Ballinger Pub.
Eisner, Simon, jt. auth. see Gallion, Arthur B.
Eisner, Vivien & Shisler, William. Crafting with Newspapers. LC 76-19771. (Little Craft Bk.). (gr. 5up). 1976. 6.95 (ISBN 0-8069-5368-3); PLB 8.99 (ISBN 0-8069-5369-1). Sterling.
Eisner, Will. Spirit Color Album, Vol. II. Agger, Jens P., ed. (Illus.). 110p. 1983. Repr. 13.95 (ISBN 0-87816-010-8). Kitchen Sink.
Eison, Irving L. Strategic Marketing in Food Service: Planning for Change. LC 80-16264. 1980. 20.95 (ISBN 0-86730-231-3). Lebhar Friedman.
Eissfeldt, Otto. Old Testament, an Introduction. LC 65-15399. 1965. 14.95i (ISBN 0-06-062171-0, RD162, HarpR). Har-Row.
Eissner, W. B., jt. ed. see Burke, P. G.
Eitel, Wilhelm, ed. Silicate Science: A Treatise, 5 vols. Incl. Vol. 1. Silicate Structures. 1964 (ISBN 0-12-236301-9); Vol. 2. Glasses, Enamels, Slags. 1965 (ISBN 0-12-236302-7); Vol. 3. Dry Silicate Systems. 1965 (ISBN 0-12-236303-5); Vol. 4. Hydrothermal Silical Systems. 1966 (ISBN 0-12-236304-3); Vol. 5. Ceramics & Hydraulic Binders. 1966 (ISBN 0-12-236305-1). 82.50 ea.; by subscription 71.00 ea. Acad Pr.
Eiteman, David K. & Stonehill, Arthur. Multinational Business Finance. 3rd ed. LC 81-17580. (Business Ser.). (Illus.). 469p. 1982. text ed. 26.95 (ISBN 0-201-03824-2). A-W.
Eiteman, David K. & Stonehill, Arthur I. Multinational Business Finance. 2nd ed. LC 78-55818. 1979. text ed. 25.95 (ISBN 0-201-01744-X). A-W.
--Multinational Business Finance. 108p. Date not set. pap. text ed. price not set Instrs' Manual (ISBN 0-201-03835-8). A-W.
Eiteman, W. J., et al. Stock Market. 4th ed. 1966. text ed. 32.95 (ISBN 0-07-019139-5, C). McGraw.
Eitinger, Leo. Psychological & Medical Effects on Concentration Camps. 122p. 1982. lib. bdg. 15.00 (ISBN 0-8482-0747-5). Norwood Edns.
Eitner, Lorenz. Neoclassicism & Romanticism: 1750-1850, 2 vols. Incl. Vol. 1. Enlightenment-Revolution. 1970 (ISBN 0-13-610907-1); Vol. 2. Restoration-the Twilight of Humanism. (Illus.). 1970 (ISBN 0-13-610915-2). pap. 13.95 ea. ref. ed. P-H.
Eizenstat, Stuart E. & Barutio, William H. Andrew Young: The Path to History. 1973. 5.00 (ISBN 0-686-38000-2). Voter Ed Proj.
Ejiogu, Lem O. Effective Structured Programming. (Illus.). 292p. 1983. 24.95 (ISBN 0-89433-205-8). Petrocelli.
Ek, J. A. Van see Van Ek, J. A.
Ekdahl, Janis K., ed. American Sculpture: A Guide to Information Sources. LC 74-11544. (Art & Architecture Information Guide Ser.: Vol. 5). 1977. 42.00x (ISBN 0-8103-1271-9). Gale.
Ekeland, I. & Temam, R. Convex Analysis & Variational Problems. (Applied Mathematics & Its Applications: Vol. 1). 1976. 64.00 (ISBN 0-444-10898-X, North Holland). Elsevier.
Ekelof, Gunnar. Guide to the Underworld. Lesser, Rika, tr. from Swedish. LC 80-13181. 112p. 1980. 10.00x (ISBN 0-87023-306-8). U of Mass Pr.
Ekelund, R. B. & Hebert, R. H. A History of Economic Theory & Method. 1975. 32.95 (ISBN 0-07-019143-3, C). McGraw.
Ekelund, Robert B. & Herbert, Robert E. History of Economic Theory & Method. (Illus.). 624p. 1983. text ed. 27.95 (ISBN 0-07-019239-1, C). McGraw.
Ekelund, Robert B., jt. auth. see Auernheimer, Leonardo.
Ekern, Doris. Suits to Fit Your Man. LC 80-50504. (Illus.). 56p. 1980. pap. 4.00 (ISBN 0-933956-05-3). Sew-Fit.
Ekert, Henry. Clinical Paediatric Haematology & Oncology. (Illus.). 248p. 1982. text ed. 34.50 (ISBN 0-632-00777-X, B 1510-0). Mosby.
Ekert-Rotholz, Alice. The Sydney Circle. Hutter, Catherine, tr. from Ger. 416p. 1983. 15.95 (ISBN 0-88064-009-X). Fromm Intl Pub.
Ekgren, William. Out of Six Attitudes: A Collection of Poems. 1983. 7.95 (ISBN 0-533-05653-5). Vantage.
Ekiel, J., jt. auth. see Morecki, A.
Ekin, Cemal A., jt. auth. see Mecca, Stephen J.
Ekins, R. & Fagalia, G. Free Thyroid Hormones. (International Congress Ser.: Vol. 479). 1980. 53.00 (ISBN 0-444-90105-1). Elsevier.
Ekins, R. P., jt. ed. see Albertini, A.
Eklund, Bo-Lennart. Modern Greek: Verbal Aspect & Compound Nouns. (Acta Regiae Societatis Scientiarm et Litterarum Gothoburgensis, Humaniora: No. 11). 1976. pap. text ed. 7.00x (ISBN 91-85252-08-5). Humanities.
Eklund, C. E., jt. auth. see Wyss, Orville.
Eklund, Dara, ed. see Judge, William Q.
Eklund, Gordon & Anderson, Poul. Inheritors of Earth. 1979. pap. 1.75 o.s.i. (ISBN 0-515-04496-2). Jove Pubns.
Eklund, Stephen A., jt. auth. see Landis, J. Richard.
Ekman, Kerstin. The Witches' Circles. Schenck, Linda, tr. from Swedish. Orig. Title: Haexringarna. 256p. (Orig.). 1983. pap. 7.95 (ISBN 0-940242-05-2). Fjord Pr.
Ekman, Paul, ed. Emotion in the Human Face. 2nd ed. LC 81-21621. (Studies in Emotion & Social Interaction: No. 2). (Illus.). 416p. 1983. 39.50 (ISBN 0-521-23992-3); pap. 14.95 (ISBN 0-521-28393-0). Cambridge U Pr.
Ekman-Nilsson. COBOL Programming: An Introduction. (Studentlitteratur Ser). (Illus.). 100p. 1975. pap. 8.50 o.p. (ISBN 0-442-80303-6). Van Nos Reinhold.
Ekoko, A. E. British Defence Strategy in Western Africa 1880-1914. 200p. 1983. text ed. 30.00x (ISBN 0-7146-3219-8, F Cass Co). Biblio Dist.
Ekpo, Monday U., ed. Bureaucratic Corruption in Sub-Saharan Africa: Toward a Search for Causes & Consequences. LC 79-66150. 1979. pap. text ed. 16.50 (ISBN 0-8191-0796-4). U Pr of Amer.
Ekrutt, Joachim W. Star Gazer. Kellner, Hugo M., tr. from Ger. (gr. 9-12). Date not set. pap. cancelled (ISBN 0-8120-2043-X). Barron.
Ekse, Martin, jt. auth. see Hennes, Robert G.
Ekstrom, Jan. Deadly Reunion. Tate, Joan, tr. 256p. 1982. 12.95 (ISBN 0-684-17765-X, ScribT). Scribner.
Ekstrom, M. P., jt. ed. see Mitra, S. K.
Ekundare, R. O. Economic History of Nigeria 1860-1960. LC 72-94209. 480p. 1973. text ed. 35.00x (ISBN 0-8419-0135-X, Africana). Holmes & Meier.
Ekvall, Robert B. Tiendas en las Cumbres. Carrodeguas, Andy & Marosi, Esteban, eds. Powell, Elsa A., tr. from Span. Orig. Title: Tents Against the Sky. 252p. 1982. pap. 2.75 (ISBN 0-8297-1253-4). Life Pubs Intl.
Ekwall, Eldon. Psychological Factors in Teaching Reading. LC 72-96688. 1973. text ed. 19.95 o.p. (ISBN 0-675-08965-4). Merrill.
Ekwall, Eldon E. Diagnosis & Remediation in Reading: Teacher's Handbook. new ed. (Orig.). 1977. pap. text ed. 21.95 (ISBN 0-205-05628-8). Allyn.
--Locating & Correcting Reading Difficulties. 3rd ed. (Illus.). 192p. 1981. pap. text ed. 10.95 (ISBN 0-675-08062-2). Merrill.
Ekwensi, Cyprian O. Drummer Boy. 1960. text ed. 3.50x (ISBN 0-521-04882-6). Cambridge U Pr.
--Passport of Mallam Ilia. 1960. text ed. 3.50x (ISBN 0-521-04883-4). Cambridge U Pr.
--Trouble in Form Six. 1966. text ed. 3.50x (ISBN 0-521-04884-2). Cambridge U Pr.
El-Aasser, M. S. Emulsion Polymerisation of Vinyl Acetate. 1981. 53.50 (ISBN 0-85334-971-1, Pub. by Applied Sci England). Elsevier.
El-Abiad, Ahmed H., jt. auth. see Stagg, Glenn W.
Elagin, Ivan. V Zale Vselennoi. 214p. (Rus.). 1982. pap. 7.50 (ISBN 0-938920-24-3). Hermitage MI.
El-Agra, A. M. & Jones, A. J. Theory of Customs Unions. 1981. 30.00 (ISBN 0-312-79737-0). St Martin.
El-Agraa, A. M. The Economics of the European Community. 1980. 39.00 (ISBN 0-312-23285-3). St Martin.
El-Agraa, Ali M. International Economic Integration. LC 81-21261. 1982. 30.00 (ISBN 0-312-42085-4). St Martin.
Elaine. Thank God It's Friday. 1983. 13.95 (ISBN 0-686-82678-7). Vantage.
Elais, E. Pocket Arabic Dictionary: Arabic-English. (Illus.). 949p. 1981. 14.95 o.s.i. (ISBN 0-88254-509-4). Hippocrene Bks.
Elam, J. O., jt. ed. see Safar, P.
Elam, Richard M., ed. Teen-Age Suspense Stories. (gr. 6-10). 1963. PLB 6.19 o.p. (ISBN 0-8313-0047-7). Lantern.
Elam, Stanley, compiled by. A User's Index to the Phi Delta Kappan, 1970-81. LC 82-61909. 150p. 1982. pap. 7.00 (ISBN 0-87367-785-4). Phi Delta Kappa.
Elamatha, K. T. Extravaganza. LC 79-63831. 129p. 1982. 10.00 (ISBN 0-533-04281-X). Vantage.
Eland, J. H. Photoelectron Spectroscopy. LC 73-17763. 239p. 1974. 35.95x o.s.i. (ISBN 0-470-23485-7). Halsted Pr.
Elandt-Johnson, Regina C. Probability Models & Statistical Methods in Genetics. LC 75-140177. (Ser. in Probability & Mathematical Statistics). 1971. 59.95x (ISBN 0-471-23490-7, Pub. by Wiley-Interscience). Wiley.
Elandt-Johnson, Regina C. & Johnson, Norman L. Survival Models & Data Analysis. LC 79-22836. (Wiley Series in Probability & Mathematical Statistics: Applied Probability & Statistics). 457p. 1980. 46.50x (ISBN 0-471-03174-7, Pub. by Wiley-Interscience). Wiley.
Elazar, Daniel J. Jewish Communities in Frontier Societies. 250p. 1983. text ed. 29.00x (ISBN 0-8419-0449-9). Holmes & Meier.
--Kinship & Consent: The Jewish Political Tradition & Its Contemporary Uses. LC 82-21851. 412p. 1983. lib. bdg. 24.75 (ISBN 0-8191-2800-7, Co-pub. by Ctr Jewish Comm Studies); pap. text ed. 13.75 (ISBN 0-8191-2801-5). U Pr of Amer.
--Politics of Belleville: A Profile of the Civil Community. LC 70-182890. 100p. 1972. 19.95 (ISBN 0-87722-013-1). Temple U Pr.
Elazar, Daniel J., ed. Governing Peoples & Territories. LC 81-20298. (Illus.). 368p. 1982. text ed. 25.00x (ISBN 0-89727-034-7). Inst Study Human.
Elazar, Daniel J., ed. see Grodzins, Morton.
El-Baz, Farouk. Say It in Arabic. pap. 2.50 (ISBN 0-486-22026-5). Dover.
Elbaz, Freema. Teacher Thinking: A Study of Practical Knowledge. LC 82-14418. 224p. 1983. 24.50 (ISBN 0-89397-144-8). Nichols Pub.
Elbaz, Jean S. & Flageul, G. Plastic Surgery of the Abdomen. Keavy, William T., tr. LC 79-84907. (Illus.). 120p. 1979. 36.75x (ISBN 0-89352-036-5). Masson Pub.
Elbe, Guenther Von see Lewis, Bernard & Von Elbe, Guenther.
Elbert, Joyce. Crazy Ladies. 1970. pap. 2.95 (ISBN 0-451-11005-6, AE1005, Sig). NAL.
--Crazy Lovers. 1979. pap. 3.50 (ISBN 0-451-12041-8, AE2041, Sig). NAL.
--Red Eye Blues. 1982. pap. 3.50 (ISBN 0-451-11505-8, AE1505, Sig). NAL.
--The Three of Us. 1974. pap. 1.75 o.p. (ISBN 0-451-07323-1, E7323, Sig). NAL.
Elbert, R. & Luggr, J., eds. Practice in Software Adaption & Maintenance. 1980. 68.00 (ISBN 0-444-85449-5). Elsevier.
Elbert, Samuel H. Dictionary of the Language of Rennell & Bellona: Part One: Rennellese & Bellonese to English. 1975. 35.00x (ISBN 0-8248-0490-2). UH Pr.
--Spoken Hawaiian. LC 77-98134. (Illus., Orig.). 1970. pap. 5.00 (ISBN 0-87022-216-3). UH Pr.
Elbert, Samuel H. & Pukui, Mary K. Hawaiian Grammar. LC 78-21692. 1979. text ed. 12.95x (ISBN 0-8248-0494-5). UH Pr.
Elbert, Samuel H., jt. auth. see Pukui, Mary K.

Elbert, Samuel H., ed. Selections from Fornander's Hawaiian Antiquities & Folk-Lore. (Illus.). 297p. 1959. pap. 9.50x (ISBN 0-87022-213-9). UH Pr.

Elbert, Samuel H. & Mahoe, Noelani K., eds. Na Mele O Hawaii Nei: One Hundred & One Hawaiian Songs. (Orig., Hawaiian & Eng, Bi-Lingual Ed). 1970. pap. 3.95 (ISBN 0-87022-219-8). UH Pr.

Elbing, Alvar. Behavioral Decisions in Organizations. 2nd ed. 1978. text ed. 23.50x (ISBN 0-673-15025-9). Scott F.

Elborn, Geoffrey. Edith Sitwell: A Biography. LC 80-1985. 336p. 1981. 15.95 o.p. (ISBN 0-385-13467-3). Doubleday.

Elbow, Margaret. Patterns in Family Violence. LC 80-527850. 160p. 1980. pap. 9.95 (ISBN 0-87304-185-2). Family Serv.

Elbow, Peter. Writing with Power: Techniques for Mastering the Writing Process. 396p. 1981. 22.50x (ISBN 0-19-502912-7). Oxford U Pr.

--Writing Without Teachers. LC 72-96608. 1975. pap. 4.95 (ISBN 0-19-501679-3, GB435, GB). Oxford U Pr.

Elcan, Ruth V. Elements of College Writing. 2nd ed. 1980. pap. text ed. 11.95 (ISBN 0-316-23132-0); instructor's manual avail. (ISBN 0-316-23133-9). Little.

Elcano, Barrett W., jt. auth. see Bullough, Vern L.

Elcock, Howard. Political Behaviour. 1976. 39.95x (ISBN 0-416-81790-4); pap. 15.95x (ISBN 0-416-81800-5). Methuen Inc.

Elcock, Howard, ed. What Sort of Society? (Economic & Social Policy in Modern Britain). (Illus.). 256p. 1982. text ed. 27.50x (ISBN 0-85520-523-7, Pub. by Martin Robertson England); pap. text ed. 9.95x (ISBN 0-85520-524-5). Biblio Dist.

Eldefonso, Edward. Law Enforcement & the Youthful Offender. 3rd ed. LC 77-13331. 363p. 1978. 22.95 (ISBN 0-471-03234-4); tchrs.' manual 5.00 (ISBN 0-471-03769-9). Wiley.

Eldefonso, Edward & Coffey, Alan. Process & Impact of the Juvenile Justice System. 1976. pap. 11.95x (ISBN 0-02-472490-4). Macmillan.

Eldefonso, Edward, jt. auth. see Coffey, Alan R.

Eldefonso, Edward, et al. Principles of Law Enforcement: Overview of the Justice System. 3rd ed. LC 80-70901. 383p. 1982. text ed. 19.95x (ISBN 0-471-05509-3); tchr's manual (law) avail. (ISBN 0-471-86651-2). Wiley.

Eldelman, A. I., jt. ed. see Freier, S.

Elder, Ann & Kiser, George. Governing American States & Communities: Constraints & Opportunities. 1983. text ed. 20.95x (ISBN 0-673-15358-4). Scott F.

Elder, Arlene A. The Hindered Hand: Cultural Implications of Early African-American Fiction. LC 77-95358. (Contributions in Afro-American & African Studies: No. 39). 1978. lib. bdg. 27.50 (ISBN 0-313-20323-7, EHH/). Greenwood.

Elder, Charles D. & Cobb, Roger W. The Political Uses of Symbols. Rockwood, Irving, ed. (Professional Studies in Political Communication). (Illus.). 192p. 1983. text ed. 22.50x (ISBN 0-582-28392-2); pap. text ed. 9.95x (ISBN 0-582-28393-0). Longman.

Elder, Crawford. Appropriating Hegel. Brennan, Andrew & Lyons, William, eds. (Scots Philosophical Monographs: Vol. 3). 116p. 1981. 12.00 (ISBN 0-08-025729-1). Pergamon.

Elder, Gary. Hold Fire: Selected Poems. 96p. (Orig.). pap. cancelled (ISBN 0-931896-02-9). Cove View.

Elder, Gary, ed. see Tedlock, Ernest.

Elder, Glen H., Jr. Children of the Great Depression: Social Charge in Life Experience. LC 73-87301. (Illus.). 1977. pap. 6.95 o.s.i. (ISBN 0-226-20263-1, P713, Phoen). U of Chicago Pr.

--Children of the Great Depression: Social Change in Life Experience. LC 73-87301. 384p. 1974. 10.00x (ISBN 0-226-20262-3). U of Chicago Pr.

Elder, H. Y. & Trueman, E. R., eds. Aspects of Animal Movement. LC 79-8520. (Society for Experimental Biology Seminar Ser.: No. 5). (Illus.). 250p. 1980. 47.50 (ISBN 0-521-23086-1); pap. 17.95 (ISBN 0-521-29795-8). Cambridge U Pr.

Elder, H. Y., jt. ed. see Meek, G. A.

Elder, Jane, tr. see Seneca, L.

Elder, John. Belief in God in the Twentieth Century. LC 82-81671. 70p. 1982. pap. 3.25 (ISBN 0-686-36314-0). Nur Pubns.

--The Bowels of the Earth. (Illus.). 1978. 19.95x (ISBN 0-19-854412-X); pap. 6.95x (ISBN 0-19-854413-8). Oxford U Pr.

Elder, Lonne, 3rd. Ceremonies in Dark Old Men. LC 70-87212. (Orig.). 1969. pap. 6.25 (ISBN 0-374-50792-9, N372). FS&G.

Elder, M. G. & Hawkins, D. F. Human Fertility Control: The Theory & Practice. 1979. text ed. 61.95 o.p. (ISBN 0-407-00127-1). Butterworth.

Elder, Michael. For Those in Peril. 6.50 o.p. (ISBN 0-685-20584-3). Transatlantic.

Elder, Neil & Thomas, Alastair H. The Consensual Democracies? The Government & Politics of the Scandinavian States. 256p. 1982. text ed. 35.00x (ISBN 0-85520-423-0, Pub. by Martin Robertson England). Biblio Dist.

Elder, Norman. This Thing of Darkness. LC 79-67678. (Illus.). 1980. 17.95 (ISBN 0-89696-086-2, An Everest House Book). Dodd.

Elder, Shirley, jt. auth. see Ornstein, Norman J.

Elder, William V., III. Baltimore Painted Furniture, Eighteen Hundred to Eighteen-Forty. (Illus.). 132p. 1972. pap. 8.50 (ISBN 0-686-36472-4). Md Hist.

Elderfield, John. Henri Matisse-Cut-Outs. LC 78-56503. 1978. 22.50 (ISBN 0-8076-0885-8); pap. 14.95 (ISBN 0-8076-0886-6). Braziller.

Elderton, W. P. & Johnson, N. L. Systems of Frequency Curves. LC 69-10571. Orig. Title: Frequency Curves & Correlation. (Illus.). 1969. 37.50 (ISBN 0-521-07369-3). Cambridge U Pr.

Eldred, Patricia M. What Do We Do When We're Asleep? (Creative's Questions & Answers Ser.). (Illus.). 32p. (gr. 3-4). 1981. PLB 5.95 (ISBN 0-87191-752-1). Creative Ed.

Eldred, Vince. Tennis Without Mistakes. LC 74-16589. (Illus.). 224p. 1975. 8.95 o.p. (ISBN 0-399-11309-6). Putnam Pub Group.

Eldredge, Niles & Tattersall, Ian. The Myths of Human Evolution. LC 82-1118. 192p. 1982. 16.95 (ISBN 0-231-05144-1). Columbia U Pr.

Eldren, R., et al. Calendaring of Plastics. 1971. 12.50 (ISBN 0-444-19609-9). Elsevier.

Eldridge, Benjamin P. & Watts, William B. Our Rival, the Rascal: A Faithful Portrayal of the Conflict Between the Criminals of This Age & the Defenders of Society, the Police. LC 79-172578. (Criminology, Law Enforcement, & Social Problems Ser.: No. 166). (Illus., With intro. added). 1973. Repr. of 1897 ed. 16.00x (ISBN 0-87585-166-5). Patterson Smith.

Eldridge, F. P. Wind Machines. pap. cancelled o.p. (ISBN 0-930978-98-6). Solar Energy Info.

Eldridge, Hope T. The Materials of Demography: A Selected & Annotated Bibliography. LC 75-16843. 222p. 1975. Repr. of 1959 ed. lib. bdg. 16.00x (ISBN 0-8371-8166-6, ELMD). Greenwood.

Eldridge, Paul. Kingdom Without God. 15p. 1951. pap. 1.00 (ISBN 0-686-95273-1). Am Atheist.

Eldridge, Paul, jt. auth. see Viereck, George S.

Eldridge, Roswell & Fahn, Stanley, eds. Dystonia. LC 75-25112. (Advances in Neurology Ser: Vol. 14). 510p. 1976. 53.00 (ISBN 0-89004-070-2). Raven.

Eldridge, Winfield H., jt. auth. see Brown, Curtis M.

Electric Power Research Institute. Electricity: Today's Technologies, Tomorrow's Alternatives. (Illus.). 128p. (Orig.). 1981. pap. 7.95 (ISBN 0-86576-003-9). Pub Serv Ctr.

Electric Power Research Institute & Jepperson. The Kaiparowits Coal Project & the Environment. LC 80-53420. 1981. text ed. 16.95 (ISBN 0-250-40399-4). Ann Arbor Science.

Electronic Industries Association & Zbar, Paul B. Industrial Electronics: A Text-Lab Manual. 3rd ed. (Illus.). 320p. 1981. 14.50x (ISBN 0-07-072793-7, G); instr's guide 3.00 (ISBN 0-07-072794-5). McGraw.

Electronic Industries Association, jt. auth. see Zbar, Paul B.

Electronics Magazine. Applying Microprocessors. 1977. 29.50 (ISBN 0-07-019160-3, P&RB). McGraw.

--Basics of Data Communications. Karp, Harry R., ed. LC 76-16475. (Illus.). 303p. 1976. text ed. 35.75 (ISBN 0-07-019159-X, R-603). McGraw.

--Circuits for Electronic Engineers. 1977. 39.90 (ISBN 0-07-019157-3). McGraw.

--Design Techniques for Electronics Engineers. 1978. 39.90 (ISBN 0-07-019158-1, P&RB). McGraw.

--Large Scale Integration. 1976. 28.50 (ISBN 0-07-019187-5). McGraw.

--McGraw-Hill's Leader in Electronics. 1979. 43.50 (ISBN 0-07-019149-2, P&RB). McGraw.

--Memory Design: Microcomputers to Mainframes. 1978. 29.00 (ISBN 0-07-019154-9). McGraw.

--Microelectronics Interconnection & Packaging. (Electronics Book Ser.). (Illus.). 1980. 29.50 (ISBN 0-07-019184-0). McGraw.

--Microprocessors. Altman, Laurence, ed. (Illus.). 1975. pap. text ed. 32.50 (ISBN 0-07-019171-9, R-520). McGraw.

--Microprocessors & Microcomputers: One-Chip Controllers to High-End Systems. Capece, Raymond P. & Posa, John G., eds. LC 80-11816. (Illus.). 484p. 1980. 31.25 (ISBN 0-07-019141-7, R-011). McGraw.

--New Product Trends in Electronics Number One. (Electronic Book Ser.). 1978. 35.75 (ISBN 0-07-019152-2, P&RB). McGraw.

--Personal Computing: Hardware & Software Basics. 1979. 26.95 (ISBN 0-07-019151-4). McGraw.

Eleen, Luba. The Illustration of the Pauline Epistles in French & English Bibles of the Twelfth & Thirteenth Century. (Illus.). 356p. 1982. 89.00x (ISBN 0-19-817344-X). Oxford U Pr.

Elegant, Robert. Hong Kong. (The Great Cities Ser.). (Illus.). 1977. lib. bdg. 14.94 o.p. (ISBN 0-686-51003-8). Silver.

Elementary Science Study. Animal Activity. (gr. 4-6). 1969. experiment student bk. 5.80 (ISBN 0-07-017519-5, W); tchr's guide 8.44 (ISBN 0-07-017518-7); wheel 72.60 (ISBN 0-07-017520-9). McGraw.

--Animals in the Classroom: A Book for Teachers. 1970. 11.36 (ISBN 0-07-017706-6, W). McGraw.

--Balloons & Gases. 1971. tchr's. guide 11.48 (ISBN 0-07-017714-7, W). McGraw.

--Batteries & Bulbs Two: Student's Book. (gr. 5-9). 1971. text ed. 23.64 (ISBN 0-07-017713-9, W). McGraw.

--Behavior of Mealworms. 2nd ed. 1975. tchr's. guide 13.16 (ISBN 0-07-018576-X, W). McGraw.

--Bones. (gr. 4-6). 1967. picture bk. 7.48 (ISBN 0-07-018496-8, W); tchr's guide 13.80 (ISBN 0-07-018516-6). McGraw.

--Brine Shrimp. 1975. tchr's. guide 8.04 (ISBN 0-07-018577-8, W). McGraw.

--Changes. 2nd ed. 1975. tchr's. guide 8.08 (ISBN 0-07-018578-6, W). McGraw.

--Clay Boats. 2nd ed. 1975. tchr's. guide 6.76 (ISBN 0-07-018579-4, W). McGraw.

--Crayfish. 2nd ed. 1975. tchr's. guide 7.68 (ISBN 0-07-018580-8, W). McGraw.

--Daytime Astronomy. 1971. tchr's guide 13.56 o.p. (ISBN 0-07-017717-1, W). McGraw.

--Drops, Streams, & Containers. 1971. tchr's. guide 15.48 (ISBN 0-07-017692-2, W). McGraw.

--Earthworms. 1971. tchr's. guide 11.48 (ISBN 0-07-017707-4, W). McGraw.

--Gases & Airs. 1975. tchr's. guide 14.96 (ISBN 0-07-018519-0, W). McGraw.

--Geo Blocks. 1975. tchr's guide 7.08 (ISBN 0-07-018520-4, W). McGraw.

--Growing Seeds. 1975. tchr's. guide 10.92 (ISBN 0-07-018521-2, W). McGraw.

--Heating & Cooling. (gr. 3-8). 1971. tchr's. guide 12.52 (ISBN 0-07-017709-0, W). McGraw.

--Ice Cubes. 1975. tchr's. guide 14.56 (ISBN 0-07-018522-0, W). McGraw.

--Kitchen Physics. 2nd ed. 1975. tchr's. guide 14.40 (ISBN 0-07-018523-9, W). McGraw.

--Life of Beans & Peas. 2nd ed. 1975. 7.60 (ISBN 0-07-018581-6, W). McGraw.

--Light & Shadows. 2nd ed. 1975. tchr's. guide 9.44 (ISBN 0-07-018582-4, W). McGraw.

--Mapping. (gr. 3-8). 1971. tchr's guide 16.44 (ISBN 0-07-017718-X, W); wkbk. 5.64 (ISBN 0-07-017719-8). McGraw.

--Match & Measure. (gr. 3-8). 1971. tchr's. guide 15.20 (ISBN 0-07-017721-X, W). McGraw.

--Microgardening. 2nd ed. 1975. tchr's. guide 24.00 (ISBN 0-07-018583-2, W). McGraw.

--Mirror Cards. 1975. tchr's guide 12.28 (ISBN 0-07-018524-7, W). McGraw.

--Mobiles. 2nd ed. 1975. tchr's. guide 7.60 (ISBN 0-07-018584-0, W). McGraw.

--Mosquitoes. (gr. 3-8). 1971. resource bk for the classroom 7.04 (ISBN 0-07-017723-6, W). McGraw.

--Musical Instruments Recipe Book. (gr. 3-8). 1971. tchr's resource bk. 13.84 (ISBN 0-07-017730-9, W). McGraw.

--Optics. (gr. 3-8). 1971. tchr's guide 16.44 (ISBN 0-07-017694-9, W). McGraw.

--Pattern Blocks. (gr. 3-8). 1970. tchr's guide 8.24 (ISBN 0-07-017586-1, W). McGraw.

--Peas & Particles. 1975. tchr's. guide 10.20 (ISBN 0-07-018526-3, W). McGraw.

--Pendulums. 2nd ed. 1975. tchr's guide 10.16 (ISBN 0-07-018585-9, W). McGraw.

--Pond Water. 2nd ed. 1975. tchr's guide 10.44 (ISBN 0-07-018586-7, W). McGraw.

--Rocks & Charts. 1975. tchr's guide 7.44 (ISBN 0-07-018527-1, W). McGraw.

--Sand. (gr. 3-8). 1970. tchr's guide 12.52 (ISBN 0-07-017683-3, W). McGraw.

--Senior Balancing. 1970. tchr's guide 9.92 (ISBN 0-07-017588-8, W). McGraw.

--Sink or Float. (gr. 3-8). 1971. tchr's guide 11.32 (ISBN 0-07-017724-4, W). McGraw.

--Spinning Tables. 1971. tchr's guide 7.00 (ISBN 0-07-017699-X, W). McGraw.

--Starting from Seeds. 1971. tchr's guide 9.60 (ISBN 0-07-017726-0, W). McGraw.

--Structures. 1970. tchr's guide 9.80 (ISBN 0-07-017696-5, W). McGraw.

--Tangrams. 1968. tchr's guide 3.96 o.p. (ISBN 0-07-017444-X, W). McGraw.

--Tangrams. 1975. tchr's guide 6.20 (ISBN 0-07-018587-5, W). McGraw.

--Tracks. 1971. tchr's guide 11.32 (ISBN 0-07-017701-5, W); picture bk. 10.36 (ISBN 0-07-017702-3). McGraw.

--Water Flow. 1971. tchr's guide 13.16 (ISBN 0-07-017733-3, W). McGraw.

--Whistles & Strings. 1971. tchr's. guide 12.36 (ISBN 0-07-017728-7, W). McGraw.

Elenkin, A. A., jt. auth. see Gaidukov, N.

Elesh, James, ed. James Ensor: The Complete Graphic Work, 2 vols. LC 79-50679. (Illustrated Bartsch: Vol. 141: Pts. A & B). 1982. Set. 190.00 (ISBN 0-89835-000-X). Abaris Bks.

Eley, D. D. & Pines, H., eds. Advances in Catalysis, Vol. 31. (Serial Publication). 1983. 52.50 (ISBN 0-12-007831-7); 68.50 (ISBN 0-12-007888-0). Acad Pr.

Eley, D. D., et al see Frankenburg, W. G., et al.

Eley, Glen D. Improve Your Softball Program, H.S. & College. (Illus.). 60p. 1983. pap. 5.95 (ISBN 0-940934-04-3). GDE Pubns OH.

--Softball-The Game of the Eighties: Slowpitch-How to-Guide. 75p. 1983. pap. price not set. GDE Pubns OH.

Elf-Aquitaine, et al. Exploration for Carbonate Petroleum Reservoirs. LC 81-13144. 232p. 1982. 39.95x (ISBN 0-471-08603-7, Pub. by Wiley-Interscience). Wiley.

El Fathaly, Omar I. & Palmer, Monte. Political Development & Social Change in Libya. LC 77-712. 240p. 1980. 24.95x (ISBN 0-669-01427-3). Lexington Bks.

El Fathaly, Omar I., et al. Political Development & Bureaucracy in Libya. LC 77-713. 1977. 18.95x (ISBN 0-669-01426-5). Lexington Bks.

Elfenbein, Julien. Business Journalism. 2nd ed. LC 72-91759. Repr. of 1960 ed. lib. bdg. 18.75x (ISBN 0-8371-2433-6, ELBJ). Greenwood.

Elfenbein, Julien, ed. Businesspaper Publishing Practice. Repr. of 1952 ed. lib. bdg. 17.00x (ISBN 0-8371-3090-5, ELBU). Greenwood.

Elford, Homer J. Guide to Church Ushering. (Orig.). 1961. pap. 1.50 o.p. (ISBN 0-687-16242-4). Abingdon.

--A Guide to Church Ushering. 64p. (Orig.). 1983. pap. 4.50 (ISBN 0-687-16243-2). Abingdon.

Elfrey, Priscilla. The Hidden Agenda: Recognizing What Really Matters at Work. LC 82-8500. (Contemporary Issues in Business Ser.). 208p. 1982. 16.95 (ISBN 0-471-86529-X). Wiley.

Elger, C. E., jt. ed. see Speckmann, E. J.

Elgerd, O. I. Electric Energy Systems Theory: An Introduction. 2nd ed. (McGraw-Hill Ser. in Electrical Engineering). 576p. 1982. 38.00x (ISBN 0-07-019230-8). McGraw.

Elgerd, Olle I. Basic Electric Power Engineering. LC 76-1751. (Electrical Engineering Ser.). 1977. text ed. 30.95 (ISBN 0-201-01717-2); sol. man. avail. (ISBN 0-201-01918-3). A-W.

Elgers, Pieter T., jt. auth. see Bloom, Robert.

Elgin, Catherine Z. With Reference to Reference. LC 82-15488. 208p. 1982. lib. bdg. 27.50 (ISBN 0-915145-52-9); pap. text ed. 12.75 (ISBN 0-915145-53-7). Hackett Pub.

Elgin, Duane. Voluntary Simplicity: Toward a Way of Life That Is Outwardly Simple, Inwardly Rich. LC 81-643. (Illus.). 312p. 1981. 10.95 (ISBN 0-688-00322-2); pap. 5.95 (ISBN 0-686-82943-3). Morrow.

Elgin, Robert. The Tiger Is My Brother. LC 79-25876. (Illus.). 1980. pap. 10.95 o.p. (ISBN 0-688-03575-2). Morrow.

Elgin, S. What Is Linguistics? 2nd ed. 1979. pap. 12.95 (ISBN 0-13-952333-2). P-H.

Elgin, Suzette H. A Primer of Transformational Grammar: For Rank Beginners. 25p. 1975. pap. 3.00 (ISBN 0-8141-3693-1); pap. 2.00 members (ISBN 0-686-86451-4). NCTE.

--Twelve Fair Kingdoms. LC 80-2837. (The Ozark Fantasy Trilogy Ser.: Bk. 1). 1981. 10.95 (ISBN 0-385-15876-9). Doubleday.

--Twelve Fair Kingdoms. (Ozark Fantasy Ser.: No. 1). 208p. 1983. pap. 2.50 (ISBN 0-425-05850-6). Berkley Pub.

Elgood, Chris. Handbook of Management Games. 2nd ed. 246p. 1981. text ed. 44.00x (ISBN 0-566-02229-X). Gower Pub Ltd.

El Guindi, Fadwa. Religion in Culture. (Elements in Anthropology). 80p. 1977. pap. text ed. write for info. o.p. (ISBN 0-697-07549-4). Wm C Brown.

El Guindy, M. I., ed. Precious Metals 1982: Proceedings of the 6th International Precious Metals Institute Conference, Newport Beach, California, June 7-11, 1982. 600p. 1983. 125.00 (ISBN 0-08-025396-2). Pergamon.

Elhart, Dorothy, et al. Scientific Principles in Nursing. 8th ed. LC 77-23961. (Illus.). 690p. 1978. pap. text ed. 17.95 o.p. (ISBN 0-8016-1953-X). Mosby.

El-Hawary, Mohamed. Electric Power Systems: Design & Analysis. 1982. text ed. 22.95 (ISBN 0-8359-1627-8); instrs'. manual avail. (ISBN 0-8359-1628-6). Reston.

El-Helbawy, Kamal, tr. see Ali-Nadawi, Abul H.

El-Hinnawi, E. E. Energy & the Environment. write for info (ISBN 0-685-83146-9). Elsevier.

Elhmann, Paul W., jt. auth. see White, Trentwell M.

Elia, Annibale. La Syntaxe du Verbe Italien: Les Constructions a Completives des Verbes a un Complement, Vol. 1. 250p. (Fr.). 1982. 28.00 o.p. (ISBN 90-272-3117-6). Benjamins North Am.

--La Syntaxe du verbe italien: Vol. I, Les constructions a completives des verbes a un complement. (Lingvisticae Investigationes Supplementa: 7). 250p. (Fr.). 1983. text ed. 28.00 (ISBN 90-272-3117-6). Benjamins North Am.

Eliach, Yaffa. Hasidic Tales of the Holocaust. 1982. 15.95 (ISBN 0-19-503199-7). Oxford U Pr.

Eliach, Yaffa & Gurewitsch, Brana. The Liberators: Eyewitness Accounts of the Liberation of Concentration Camps, Liberation Day Vol. I. LC 81-70261. (The Liberators Ser.). (Illus.). 59p. (Orig.). 1981. pap. 8.95 (ISBN 0-9609970-1-6). Ctr For Holo.

Eliade, Marcea. No Souvenirs: Journals 1957-1969. 368p. 1982. pap. 7.64i (ISBN 0-06-062143-5, RD-405, HarpT). Har-Row.

Eliade, Mircea. The Forge & the Crucible: The Origins & Structures of Alchemy. 2nd ed. Corrin, Stephen, tr. LC 78-55040. 1979. pap. 6.95 (ISBN 0-226-20390-5, P780, Phoen). U of Chicago Pr.

--From Medicine Men to Muhammad. LC 73-20404. 224p. 1974. pap. 3.50xi o.p. (ISBN 0-06-062138-9, RD-079, HarpR). Har-Row.

--From Primitives to Zen: A Thematic Sourcebook in the History of Religions. LC 66-20775. 1978. 10.52xi (ISBN 0-06-062134-6, RD 249, HarpR). Har-Row.

--Gods, Goddesses, & Myths of Creation. LC 73-20949. 176p. 1974. pap. 3.50xi o.p. (ISBN 0-06-062136-2, RD-76, HarpR). Har-Row.
--Myths, Rites, Symbols: A Mircea Eliade Reader, 2 vols. Beane, Wendell C. & Doty, William G., eds. 1976. Vol. 1. pap. 5.95i o.p. (ISBN 0-06-131955-4, TB 1955, Torch); Vol. 2. pap. 4.95i o.p. (ISBN 0-06-090511-5, CN511). Har-Row.
--Patanjali & Yoga. LC 75-10785. (Illus.). 224p. 1975. pap. 5.95 (ISBN 0-8052-0491-1). Schocken.
--Patterns in Comparative Religion. pap. 8.95 (ISBN 0-452-00609-0, F609, Mer). NAL.
--Quest: History & Meaning in Religion. LC 68-19059. xii, 180p. 1975. pap. 3.95 o.s.i. (ISBN 0-226-20397-2, P625, Phoen). U of Chicago Pr.
Elial, Ernest L., jt. auth. see Geoffroy, Gregory.
Elias. Elias English-Arabic & Arabic-English Pocket Dictionary. pap. 15.95 (ISBN 0-686-18361-4). Kazi Pubns.
Elias, Arthur W., ed. Key Papers in Information Science. LC 78-162999. (Key Papers Ser). 1971. 10.00 (ISBN 0-87715-101-6). Am Soc Info Sci.
Elias, E. A. English-Arabic; Arabic-English Dictionary. 12.00x (ISBN 0-86685-173-9). Intl Bk Ctr.
Elias, E. A. & Elias, E. E. Arabic: Egyptian-Arabic Manual for Self-Study. pap. 7.50 (ISBN 0-685-58558-1). Heinman.
Elias, E. E., jt. auth. see Elias, E. A.
Elias, Elias. Elias' English-Arabic Dictionary. 1979. 30.00x (ISBN 0-86685-288-3). Intl Bk Ctr.
Elias, H. & Hyde, D. M. A Guide to Practical Stereology. (Karger Continuing Education Ser.: Vol. 1). (Illus.). viii, 192p. 1983. 59.00 (ISBN 3-8055-3466-3). S Karger.
Elias, Hans, et al. Histology & Human Microanatomy. 4th ed. LC 78-9108. 1978. 31.95 (ISBN 0-471-04929-8, Pub. by Wiley Medical). Wiley.
Elias, Horace J. The Flintstone Storybook. LC 77-94035. (Illus.). (ps-2). 1978. 4.95 (ISBN 0-448-14744-0, G&D). Putnam Pub Group.
Elias, Judith. Los Angeles: Dream to Reality, Eighteen Eighty-Five to Nineteen Fifteen. (Santa Susana Pr California Masters Ser.: No. 5). (Illus.). 112p. 1983. 70.00 (ISBN 0-937048-33-X). CSUN.
Elias, Merrill F. & Streeten, David H., eds. Hypertension & Cognitive Processes. LC 80-22618. 165p. 1980. 20.00 o.p. (ISBN 0-933786-04-2); pap. text ed. 10.00 (ISBN 0-933786-03-4). Beech Hill.
Elias, Norbert. Power & Civility: The Civilizing Process, Vol. II. Jephcott, Edmund, tr. LC 82-8157. 376p. 1982. 22.50 (ISBN 0-394-52769-0). Pantheon.
Elias, Robert. Victims of the System: Crime Victims & Compensation in American Politics & Criminal Justice. (Illus.). 352p. 1983. 24.95 (ISBN 0-87855-470-X). Transaction Bks.
Elias, T. O. The Modern Law of Treaties. LC 73-94064. 350p. 1974. lib. bdg. 25.00 (ISBN 0-379-00230-2). Oceana.
--New Horizons in International Law. LC 73-94064. 272p. 1979. lib. bdg. 36.00 (ISBN 0-379-20499-1). Oceana.
Elias, Thomas & Dykeman. Field Guide to North American Edible Wild Plants. 288p. 1983. 22.95 (ISBN 0-442-22200-9). Van Nos Reinhold.
Elias, Thomas S. & Whittaker, David M. A Report on the City of Poughkeepsie: A Master Plan for the Planning, Planting & Maintenance of Trees & Other Woody Plants on Public Property. (Illus.). 1976. pap. 10.00 o.p. (ISBN 0-89327-218-3). NY Botanical.
Elias-Olivares, Lucia, jt. ed. see Amastae, Jon.
Eliason, Alan. Business Information Processing. 496p. 1979. text ed. 20.95 (ISBN 0-574-21235-3, 13-4235); instr's guide avail. (ISBN 0-574-21236-1, 13-4236). SRA.
Eliason, Alan & Kitts, Kent D. Business Computer Systems & Applications. 2nd ed. LC 78-18447. 384p. 1979. 12.95 (ISBN 0-574-21215-9, 13-4215); instructor's guide 2.25 (ISBN 0-574-21216-7, 13-4216). SRA.
Eliason, Alan L. Mason Oaks: An Online Case Study in Business Systems Design. 128p. 1981. pap. text ed. 7.95 (ISBN 0-574-21310-4, 13-4310); instr's guide avail. (ISBN 0-574-21311-2, 13-4311). SRA.
--Online Business Computer Applications. 336p. 1983. pap. text ed. write for info. (ISBN 0-574-21405-4, 13-4405); write for info. instr's. guide (ISBN 0-574-21406-2, 13-4406). SRA.
Eliason, Claudia & Jenkins, Loa T. A Practical Guide to Early Childhood Curriculum. 2nd ed. LC 80-39694. (Illus.). 389p. 1981. pap. text ed. 14.95 (ISBN 0-8016-1511-9). Mosby.
Eliason, Karine, et al. Make-A-Mix Cookery. LC 78-50687. (Illus.). 1978. pap. 6.95 (ISBN 0-89586-007-4). H P Bks.
--More Make-A-Mix Cookery. LC 80-82533. (Orig.). 1980. pap. 6.95 (ISBN 0-89586-055-4). H P Bks.
Eliasson, Gunnar. Business Economic Planning: Theory, Practice & Comparison. LC 76-5895. 1977. 28.00 o.p. (ISBN 0-471-01813-9, Pub. by Wiley-Interscience). Wiley.
Eliasson, Rune, jt. ed. see Von Euler, Ulf S.
Eliasson, Sven G., et al, eds. Neurological Pathophysiology. 2nd ed. (Pathophysiology Ser.). 1978. text ed. 24.95x (ISBN 0-19-502337-4); pap. text ed. 15.95x (ISBN 0-19-502338-2). Oxford U Pr.
Eliastam. Medical of Surgical Emergencies. 1983. 19.95 (ISBN 0-8151-3058-9). Year Bk Med.
Eliav-Feldon, Miriam. Realistic Utopias: The Ideal Imaginary Societies of the Renaissance 1516-1630. (Oxford Historical Monographs). 1982. 41.00 (ISBN 0-19-821889-3). Oxford U Pr.
Elich, C. J. & Elich, J. College Algebra with Calculator Applications. 1982. text ed. 20.95 (ISBN 0-201-13340-7). A-W.
Elich, Carletta J., jt. auth. see Elich, Joseph.
Elich, Carlotta J. & Elich, Joseph. Trigonometry Using Calculators. LC 79-18934. (Illus.). 1980. text ed. 18.95 (ISBN 0-201-03186-8); instrs' manual avail. A-W.
Elich, J., jt. auth. see Elich, C. J.
Elich, Joseph & Elich, Carletta J. Precalculus with Caculator Applications. (Math-Mallion Ser.). (Illus.). 576p. 1981. text ed. 21.95x (ISBN 0-201-13345-8); Instr's. manual 321 0-201-13346-6 avail. A-W.
Elich, Joseph, jt. auth. see Elich, Carlotta J.
Elieff, De Anne. Andy the Real "Live" Toy Airplane. (Illus.). 24p. (ps-5). 1983. pap. 2.95 (ISBN 0-86666-099-2). GWP.
Eliel, E. L. Stereochemistry of Carbon Compounds. (Advanced Chemistry Ser.). 1962. text ed. 38.00 (ISBN 0-07-019177-8, C). McGraw.
Eliel, E. L. & Basolo, F. Elements of Stereochemistry: With a Section on Coordination Compounds. 98p. 1969. 6.95x (ISBN 0-471-23745-0). Wiley.
Eliel, E. L. & Allinger, N. L., eds. Topics in Stereochemistry Ser., Vol. 5. 1970. 28.50 (ISBN 0-471-23750-7, Pub. by Wiley). Krieger.
Eliel, Ernest L. & Allinger, Norman L. Topics in Stereochemistry. (Topics in Stereochemistry Ser.). 35.95_o.p. (ISBN 0-470-23747-3, Pub. by Wiley-Interscience); Vol. 10, 1978. 70.95_o.s.i. (ISBN 0-471-04344-3). Wiley.
Eliel, Ernest L., jt. auth. see Allinger, Norman L.
Eliel, Ernest L. & Otsuka, Sei, eds. Asymmetric Reactions & Processes in Chemistry. (ACS Symposium Ser.: No. 185). 1982. write for info. (ISBN 0-8412-0717-8). Am Chemical.
Eliel, Ernest L., jt. ed. see Allinger, Norman L.
Eliel, Ernest L., et al, eds. Conformational Analysis. LC 65-14028. 1965. 45.00 o.p. (ISBN 0-470-23742-2, Pub. by Wiley-Interscience). Wiley.
Elifson, Kirk, et al. Fundamentals of Social Statistics. (Statistics Ser.). (Illus.). 416p. 1982. text ed. 19.95 (ISBN 0-201-10430-X). A-W.
Elijah the Prophet. The Time of the End. 1983. 6.95 (ISBN 0-533-05402-8). Vantage.
Elimelech, Baruch. A Tonal Grammar of Etsako. (Publications in Linguistics Ser.: Vol. 87). 1979. 14.50x (ISBN 0-520-09576-6). U of Cal Pr.
Elingson, Marnie. Jessica Windom. (Orig.). 1980. pap. 1.50 o.s.i. (ISBN 0-440-14633-X). Dell.
Elins, Roberta, jt. auth. see Alexander, Jerome.
Eliot, Alistair, tr. see Heine, Heinrich.
Eliot, Charles see Brown, Edmund R.
Eliot, Charles W. The Religion of the Future. Brown, Edmund R., ed. (International Pocket Library). pap. 3.00 (ISBN 0-686-77240-7). Branden.
Eliot, Charles W., ed. Epic & Saga. 438p. Repr. of 1938 ed. lib. bdg. 30.00 (ISBN 0-89984-187-2). Century Bookbindery.
Eliot, George. Adam Bede. pap. 2.95 (ISBN 0-451-51578-1, CE1578, Sig Classics). NAL.
--Adam Bede. (English Library). 1980. pap. 4.95 (ISBN 0-14-043121-7). Penguin.
--Middlemarch. (Orig.). pap. 4.95 (ISBN 0-451-51750-4, CE1750, Sig Classics). NAL.
--Mill on the Floss. pap. 3.50 (ISBN 0-451-51543-9, CE1543, Sig Classics). NAL.
--Romola. (World's Classics Ser: No. 178). 15.95 (ISBN 0-19-250178-X). Oxford U Pr.
--Scenes of Clerical Life. 1976. 8.95x (ISBN 0-460-00468-9, Evman); pap. 2.95x (ISBN 0-460-01468-4, Evman). Biblio Dist.
--Scenes of Clerical Life. Lodge, David, ed. (English Library). (Orig.). 1973. pap. 4.95 (ISBN 0-14-043087-3). Penguin.
--Silas Marner. (RL 10). pap. 1.75 (ISBN 0-451-51678-8, CE1678, Sig Classics). NAL.
Eliot, George see Allen, W. S.
Eliot, George, tr. see Feuerbach, Ludwig.
Eliot, J. N. & Kawazoe, A. Blue Butterflies of the Lycaenopsis-group. (Illus.). 300p. 1983. 62.50x (ISBN 0-565-00860-9, Pub. by Brit Mus Nat Hist England). Sabbot-Natural Hist Bks.
Eliot, Jessica. A Vintage Year. (Candlelight Romance Ser.: No. 689). 224p. 1981. pap. 1.75 o.s.i. (ISBN 0-440-19383-4). Dell.
Eliot, John. John Eliot's Indian Dialogues: A Study in Cultural Interaction. Bowden, Henry W. & Ronda, James P., eds. LC 80-542. (Contributions in American History: No. 88). (Illus.). 173p. 1980. lib. bdg. 27.50 (ISBN 0-313-21031-4, RID/). Greenwood.
Eliot, John see Allen, W. S.
Eliot, Marc. Burt! The Unauthorized Biography. 224p. (Orig.). 1982. pap. 3.95 (ISBN 0-440-00876-X). Dell.
--Death of a Rebel: Phil Ochs & a Small Circle of Friends. LC 77-25586. 1979. pap. 6.95 o.p. (ISBN 0-385-13610-2, Anch). Doubleday.
--Televisions: One Season of American Television. LC 82-17015. 208p. 1983. 14.95 (ISBN 0-312-79076-7). St Martin.
Eliot, Philip. Serpent on the Hill. LC 81-69383. 249p. 1982. 12.95 (ISBN 0-941282-00-7). Dallas Pub.
Eliot, Susan B., jt. auth. see May, Frank B.
Eliot, T. S. Cats: The Book of the Musical, Based on Old Possum's Book of Practical Cats. LC 82-48026. Date not set. pap. 12.95 (ISBN 0-15-615582-6, Harv). HarBraceJ. Postponed.
--The Complete Poems & Plays, 1909-1950. LC 52-11346. 1952. 17.95 (ISBN 0-15-121185-X). HarBraceJ.
--Knowledge & Experience in the Philosophy of F. H. Bradley. 1964. 4.50 o.p. (ISBN 0-374-18176-4). FS&G.
--Old Possum's Book of Practical Cats. Gorey, Edward, ed. (Illus.). 1982. 8.95 (ISBN 0-15-168656-4); pap. 4.95 (ISBN 0-15-168657-2, Harv). HarBraceJ.
--Sacred Wood. 7th ed. 171p. 1960. pap. 9.95x (ISBN 0-416-67610-3). Methuen Inc.
--Selected Poems. LC 67-23064. (gr. 7-12). 1967. pap. 2.50 (ISBN 0-15-680647-9, Harv). HarBraceJ.
Eliot, T. S., tr. see Perse, St. John.
Eliot, T. S., et al, trs. see Perse, Saint-John.
Eliot-Hurst, M. E. Transportation Geography: Comments & Readings. 1973. pap. 28.50 (ISBN 0-07-019190-5, C). McGraw.
Eliot Hurst, Michael. I Came to the City: Essays & Comments on the Urban Scene. 1975. pap. text ed. 13.50 o.p. (ISBN 0-395-17016-8). HM.
Eliott, John E. Marx & Engels on Economics, Politics, & Society: Essential Readings with Editorial Commentary. 1981. pap. text ed. 16.50x (ISBN 0-673-16034-3). Scott F.
Elisco, Ben. On Any Given Sunday. 384p. 1982. pap. 3.25 (ISBN 0-441-62674-2, Pub. by Charter Bks). Ace Bks.
Elishakoff, Isaac. Probabilistic Methods in the Theory of Structures. 430p. 1983. 44.95 (ISBN 0-471-87572-4, Pub. by Wiley Interscience). Wiley.
Elison, Craig, ed. Modifying Man: Implications & Ethics. 12.50 (ISBN 0-8191-0302-0). U Pr of Amer.
Elison, George & Smith, Bardwell L., eds. Warlords, Artists, & Commoners: Japan in the Sixteenth Century. LC 80-24128. (Illus.). 372p. 1981. 20.00x (ISBN 0-8248-0692-1). UH Pr.
Elithorn, A. Artificial & Human Intelligence. Date not set. price not set (ISBN 0-444-86545-4). Elsevier.
Elithorn, A. & Jones, D., eds. Artificial & Human Thinking. 1973. 12.50 (ISBN 0-444-41023-6). Elsevier.
Elizabeth, Laura. What Happened to Love? 1978. 4.95 o.p. (ISBN 0-533-03785-9). Vantage.
Elizondo, Virgil & Greinacher, Norbert, eds. Church & Peace. (Concilium 1983: Vol. 164). 128p. (Orig.). 1983. pap. 6.95 (ISBN 0-8164-2444-6). Seabury.
Elizondo, Virgilio. Galilean Journey: The Mexican-American Promise. LC 82-18852. 144p. (Orig.). 1983. pap. 6.95 (ISBN 0-88344-151-9). Orbis Bks.
Elizur, Dov. Job Evaluation: A Systematic Approach. 165p. 1980. text ed. 37.25 (ISBN 0-566-02120-X). Gower Pub Ltd.
Elkan, E. & Reichenbach-Klinke, H. Color Atlas of the Diseases of Fishes, Amphibians, & Reptiles. (Illus.). 256p. 1974. 29.95 (ISBN 0-87666-028-6, H-948). TFH Pubns.
Elkan, E., jt. auth. see Reichenbach-Klinke, H.
Elkana, Yehuda, et al, eds. Toward a Metric of Science: The Advent of Science Indicators. LC 77-24513. (Science, Culture & Society. Wiley-Interscience Ser.). 1978. 35.95x (ISBN 0-471-98435-3, Pub. by Wiley-Interscience). Wiley.
Elkayam, Uri & Gleicher, Norbert, eds. Cardiac Problems in Pregnancy: Diagnosis & Management of Maternal & Fetal Disease. LC 82-9938. 638p. 1982. 85.00 (ISBN 0-8451-0216-8). A R Liss.
Elkeles, R. D. & Tavill, A. S. Biochemical Aspects of Human Disease. (Illus.). 704p. 1982. text ed. 58.00 (ISBN 0-632-00012-0, B1521-6). Mosby.
El Khashab, A. G. Heating Ventilating & Air-Conditioning Systems Estimating Manual. 2nd ed. 320p. 1983. 37.50 (ISBN 0-07-034536-8, P&RB). McGraw.
El-Khawas, Mohamed A., jt. auth. see Serapiao, Luis B.
El-Khawas, Mohamed A. & Kornegay, Francis A., eds. American-Southern African Relations: Bibliographic Essays. LC 75-25331. (African Bibliographic Ser.: No. 1). 188p. 1975. lib. bdg. 27.50 (ISBN 0-8371-8398-7, EA/A01). Greenwood.
Elkin, A. P. Aboriginal Men of High Degree. 2nd ed. LC 77-87170. (Illus.). 1978. 18.95x (ISBN 0-312-00167-3). St Martin.
Elkin, Benjamin. Big Jump & Other Stories. LC 58-13127. (Illus.). (gr. 1-2). 1958. PLB 5.99 (ISBN 0-394-90004-9). Beginner.
--King's Wish & Other Stories. LC 60-13491. (Illus.). (gr. 1-2). 1960. PLB 5.99 (ISBN 0-394-90014-6). Beginner.
Elkin, Frederick, jt. auth. see Handel, Gerald.
Elkin, Ginny, jt. auth. see Yalom, Irvin D.
Elkin, Robert, jt. auth. see Cornick, Delroy L.
Elkind, Arnold B., jt. auth. see Cotchett, Joseph W.
Elkind, David. Children & Adolescents. 3rd ed. 1981. text ed. 17.95x (ISBN 0-19-502820-1); pap. text ed. 7.95x (ISBN 0-19-502821-X). Oxford U Pr.
Elkind, David & Weiner, Irving B. Development of the Child. LC 77-14214. 728p. 1978. text ed. 28.50 (ISBN 0-471-23785-X); study guide 9.95 (ISBN 0-471-03435-5); tchrs. manual avail. (ISBN 0-471-04049-5). Wiley.
Elkind, David, jt. auth. see Lovell, K.
Elkind, David, jt. auth. see O'Connor, Kathleen.
Elkind, David, jt. auth. see Weiner, Irving B.
Elkind, David, jt. auth. see Carnine, Douglas.
Elking, Henry. A View of the Greenland Trade & Whale Fishery, 1722. 1981. 35.00x (ISBN 0-686-98239-8, Pub. by Caedmon of Whitby). State Mutual Bk.
Elkins, A. Management: Structures, Functions, & Practices. 1980. 23.95 (ISBN 0-201-01517-X). A-W.
Elkins, Arthur & Callaghan, Dennis W. Managerial Odyssey: Problems in Business & Its Enviroment. 600p. 1981. text ed. 21.95 (ISBN 0-201-03962-1); instrs' manual avail. A-W.
Elkins, Carolyn. Community Health Nursing in Action. (Illus.). 512p. 1983. text ed. 18.95 (ISBN 0-89303-264-6). R J Brady.
Elkins, Chris. What Do You Say to a Moonie? 80p. 1981. 2.50 (ISBN 0-8423-7867-7). Tyndale.
Elkins, Deborah. Teaching Literature: Designs for Cognitive Development. new ed. (Secondary Education Ser.). 384p. 1976. text ed. 15.95 (ISBN 0-675-08653-1). Merrill.
Elkins, Don, jt. auth. see McCarty, James A.
Elkins, Donald M., jt. auth. see Metcalf, Darrel S.
Elkins, Elizabeth A., jt. auth. see Morris, Jacquelyn M.
Elkins, Garland, jt. ed. see Warren, Thomas B.
Elkins, Jerry W. Ransom from a Poet. LC 81-50913. 116p. 1981. 7.95 (ISBN 0-938232-01-0); pap. 5.95 (ISBN 0-938232-02-9). Winston-Derek.
Elkins, R., jt. ed. see Albertini, A.
Elkins, Richard E. Major Grammatical Patterns of Western Bukidnon Manobo. (Publications in Linguistics & Related Fields Ser.: No. 26). 76p. 1970. pap. 2.00x (ISBN 0-88312-028-3); microfiche 1.50 (ISBN 0-88312-486-6). Summer Inst Ling.
--Manobo-English Dictionary. LC 68-63364. (Oceanic Linguistics Special Publications: No. 3). 1968. pap. text ed. 8.50x (ISBN 0-87022-225-2). UH Pr.
Elkins, Stanley M. Slavery: A Problem in American Institutional & Intellectual Life. 3rd ed. LC 76-615. 1976. 16.00x (ISBN 0-226-20476-6); pap. text ed. 7.50 (ISBN 0-226-20477-4). U of Chicago Pr.
Elkins, William R., et al. Literary Reflections. 3rd ed. (Illus.). 1975. pap. text ed. 15.95 (ISBN 0-07-019182-4, C). McGraw.
Elkins, William R., et al, eds. Literary Reflections. 4th ed. (Illus.). 544p. 1982. pap. 15.50x (ISBN 0-07-019232-4). McGraw.
Elkins, Wilson H. & Callcott, George H. Forty Years As a College President. 130p. 1981. cancelled o.p. (ISBN 0-686-64814-5). Carrollton Pr.
Elkoff, Marvin. After the Race. 1983. price not set (ISBN 0-671-47033-7). S&S.
Elkouri, Edna A., jt. auth. see Elkouri, Frank.
Elkouri, Frank & Elkouri, Edna A. How Arbitration Works. 3rd ed. LC 72-95857. 845p. 1973. 30.00 (ISBN 0-87179-180-3). BNA.
--Legal Status of Federal-Sector Arbitration: Supplement to Third Ed. of How Arbitration Works. 32p. 1980. 4.00 (ISBN 0-87179-331-8). BNA.
Elkow, J. D., jt. auth. see Stack, Herbert.
Ell Ell Diversified, Inc., jt. auth. see Usher, Harlan.
Ell, P. J. & Walton, S. Radionuclide Ventricular Function Studies: Correlation with ECG, Echo & X-ray Data. 1982. text ed. 99.50 (ISBN 90-247-2639-5, Pub. by Martinus Nijhoff Netherlands). Kluwer Boston.
Ell, P. J. & Holman, B. L., eds. Computed Emission Tomography. (Illus.). 562p. 1982. 75.00 (ISBN 0-19-261347-2). Oxford U Pr.
Ellakim, M., et al, eds. Recurrent Polyserositis: Familial Mediterranean Fever, Periodic Disease. 1981. 64.25 (ISBN 0-444-80331-9). Elsevier.
Ellam, Patrick. Yacht Cruising. (Illus.). 1983. 19.50 (ISBN 0-393-03280-9). Norton.
Ellebracht, Mary P. Easter Passage: The RCIA Experience. 204p. 1983. pap. 11.95 (ISBN 0-86683-693-4). Winston Pr.
Ellefson, Ashley C. The Higher Schooling in the United States. LC 77-94531. (Orig.). 1978. pap. 4.95 o.p. (ISBN 0-8467-0455-2, Pub. by Two Continents). Hippocrene Bks.
Ellegard, Alvar. The Syntactic Structure of English Texts. (Gothenburg Studies in English: No. 43). 1978. pap. text ed. 19.75x o.p. (ISBN 91-7346-051-6). Humanities.
--Who Was Junius? LC 78-12218. 1979. Repr. of 1962 ed. lib. bdg. 16.00x (ISBN 0-313-21114-0, ELWJ). Greenwood.
Elleman, Barbara. Popular Reading for Children: A Collection of the Booklist Columns. 60p. 1981. pap. 5.00 (ISBN 0-8389-0322-3). ALA.
Ellen, Roy. Environment, Subsistence & System. LC 81-18035. (Themes in the Social Sciences). (Illus.). 340p. 1982. 39.50 (ISBN 0-521-24458-7); pap. 12.95 (ISBN 0-521-28703-0). Cambridge U Pr.
Ellenberg, H., et al, eds. Progress in Botany, Vol. 44. (Illus.). 450p. 1983. 65.00 (ISBN 0-387-11840-3). Springer-Verlag.

Ellenberg, Heinz, jt. auth. see Mueller-Dombois, Dieter.

Ellenberg, Jonas H., jt. ed. see Nelson, Karin B.

Ellenberg, Max & Rifkin, Harold. Diabetes Mellitus: Theory & Practice. 3rd ed. 1982. 95.00 (ISBN 0-87488-606-6). Med Exam.

Ellenberger, Carl, Jr. Perimetry: Principles, Techniques, & Interpretations. 128p. 1980. text ed. 15.50 (ISBN 0-89004-504-6). Raven.

Ellenbogen, Eileen, tr. see Simenon, Georges.

Ellenbrook, Edward C. Outdoor & Trail Guide to the Wichita Mountains of Southwest Oklahoma. (Illus.). 102p. 1983. pap. 5.95 (ISBN 0-941634-01-9). In Valley Wichita.

Ellendorf, F., et al, eds. Physiology & Control of Parturition in Domestic Animals. LC 79-14408. (Developments in Animal & Veterinary Sciences Ser.: Vol. 5). 348p. 1979. 74.50 (ISBN 0-444-41808-3). Elsevier.

Ellentuck, Albert B. Year End Tax Planning Manual 1982. 384p. 1982. perfect bd. 46.50 (ISBN 0-88262-807-0). Warren.

Eller, Ronald. Miners, Millhands, & Mountaineers: Industrialization of the Appalachian South, 1880-1930. LC 81-16020. (Twentieth Century America Ser.). (Illus.). 304p. 1982. 23.50x (ISBN 0-87049-340-X); pap. 12.50 (ISBN 0-87049-341-8). U of Tenn Pr.

Eller, Vernard. The Mad Morality. pap. 1.50 (ISBN 0-451-09402-6, Sig). NAL.

--A Pearl of Christian Counsel for the Brokenhearted. LC 82-20028. 152p. (Orig.). 1983. lib. bdg. 18.75 (ISBN 0-8191-2850-3); pap. text ed. 8.25 (ISBN 0-8191-2851-1). U Pr of Amer.

--Thy Kingdom Come: A Blumhardt Reader. 160p. (Orig.). 1980. 9.95 o.p. (ISBN 0-8028-3544-9). Eerdmans.

Ellerbach, Richard. Tax Reduction Strategies for Small Business: Planning Techniques for Wealth Accumlation in the Eighties. (Illus.). 145p. 1982. 17.95 (ISBN 0-13-885228-6); pap. 8.95 (ISBN 0-13-885210-3). P-H.

Ellerbeck, Rosemary. Rose, Rose Where Are You? LC 77-12133. 1978. 8.95 o.p. (ISBN 0-698-10869-8, Coward). Putnam Pub Group.

Ellerbusch, Fred, jt. auth. see Cheremisinoff, Paul N.

Ellerbusch, Fred, jt. ed. see Cheremisinoff, Paul N.

Ellerby, Leona. King Tut's Game Board. LC 79-91279. (Adult & Young Adult Bks.). (YA) (gr. 5 up). 1980. 8.95g (ISBN 0-8225-0765-X). Lerner Pubns.

Ellerhorst, Winfred. Handbuch der Orgelkunde: Die mathematischen und akustischen, technischen und kunstlerischen Grundlagen sowie die Geschichte und Pflege der Modernen Orgel, 2 vols. (Bibliotheca Organologica Ser.: Vol. 7). 1976. Repr. of 1936 ed. 102.50 o.s.i. (ISBN 90-6027-024-X, Pub. by Frits Knuf Netherlands); wrappers 77.50 o.s.i. (ISBN 90-6027-219-6, Pub. by Frits Knuf Netherlands). Pendragon NY.

Ellerman, David P. Economics, Accounting, & Property Theory. LC 82-47648. 224p. 1982. 27.95x (ISBN 0-669-05552-2). Lexington Bks.

Ellerstein, Norman S. Child Abuse & Neglect: A Medical Reference. LC 81-2978. 355p. 1981. 38.00 (ISBN 0-471-05877-7, Pub. by Wiley Med). Wiley.

Ellery, John B. John Stuart Mill. (English Authors Ser.: No. 5). 1964. lib. bdg. 11.95 o.p. (ISBN 0-8057-1392-1, Twayne). G K Hall.

Ellery Queen. Cop Out. Bd. with Last Woman in His Life. 1982. pap. 2.50 (ISBN 0-451-11562-7, AE1562, Sig). NAL.

--Face to Face. Bd. with The House of Brass. 1982. pap. 2.75 (ISBN 0-451-11464-7, AE1464, Sig). NAL.

Ellfeldt, Lois. Primer for Choreographers. LC 67-20074. (Illus.). 121p. 1967. pap. 7.95 (ISBN 0-87484-192-5). Mayfield Pub.

Ellfeldt, Lois & Morton, Virgil L. This Is Ballroom Dance. LC 73-84770. (Illus.). 114p. 1974. pap. 5.95 (ISBN 0-87484-244-1). Mayfield Pub.

Ellfeldt, Lois E. Dance: From Magic to Art. 248p. 1976. pap. text ed. write for info. o.p. (ISBN 0-697-07129-4). Wm C Brown.

--Folk Dance. (Physical Education Activities Ser.). 72p. 1969. pap. text ed. write for info. (ISBN 0-697-07012-3); tchrs.' manual avail. (ISBN 0-697-07218-5). Wm C Brown.

Ellicott, Charles J. Ellicott's Bible Commentary. Bowdle, Donald, ed. 960p. 1971. 18.95 o.p. (ISBN 0-310-24120-0). Zondervan.

Ellict, George R. Dramatic Providence in Macbeth: A Study of Shakespeare's Tragic Theme of Humanity & Grace, with a Supplementary Essay on King Lear. LC 70-90501. Repr. of 1960 ed. lib. bdg. 25.00x (ISBN 0-8371-3091-3, ELMA). Greenwood.

Ellig, Bruce R. Executive Compensation - A Total Pay Perspective. 343p. 1981. 27.50 (ISBN 0-07-019144-1). McGraw.

Elliman, David, jt. auth. see Challis, James.

Ellin, Joseph & Pritchard, Michael S., eds. Profits & Professional Essays in Business & Professional Ethics. (Contemporary Biomedicine, Ethics, & Society Ser.). 336p. 1983. 29.50 (ISBN 0-89603-039-3). Humana.

Ellin, Stanley. The Dark Fantastic. LC 82-60902. 300p. 1983. 13.95 (ISBN 0-89296-059-0); write for info. limited ed. (ISBN 0-89296-060-4). Mysterious Pr.

--The Eighth Circle. 1979. lib. bdg. 9.95 (ISBN 0-8398-2532-3, Gregg). G K Hall.

--Kindly Dig Your Grave & Other Wicked Stories. Queen, Ellery, ed. LC 78-82628. 1977. pap. 1.50 o.s.i. (ISBN 0-89559-008-5). Davis Pubns.

Elling, Ray H., ed. Cross National Study of Health Systems by Countries & World Region, & Special Problems: A Guide to Information Sources. LC 79-26099. (Health Affairs Information Guide Ser.: Vol. 3). 1980. 42.00x (ISBN 0-8103-1453-3). Gale.

--Cross National Study of Health Systems: Concepts, Methods, & Data Sources: a Guide to Information Sources. LC 79-24028. (Health Affairs Information Guide Ser.: Vol. 2). 1980. 42.00x (ISBN 0-8103-1449-5). Gale.

Ellinger, Charles W., et al, eds. Synopsis of Complete Dentures. LC 74-23703. (Illus.). 348p. 1975. text ed. 16.50 o.p. (ISBN 0-8121-0399-8). Lea & Febiger.

Ellinger, Herb. Automechanics. 3rd ed. (Illus.). 592p. 1983. text ed. 19.95 (ISBN 0-13-054767-0); wkbk. 8.95 (ISBN 0-13-054775-1). P-H.

Ellinger, Herbert E. Automechanics. 2nd ed. LC 76-18687. (Illus.). 1977. 20.95 (ISBN 0-13-055145-7); wkbk. 7.95 (ISBN 0-13-054965-7). P-H.

--Automotive Engines: Theory & Servicing. 432p. 1981. text ed. 18.95 (ISBN 0-13-054999-1); 6.95 (ISBN 0-13-054890-1). P-H.

Ellinger, Herbert E. & Hathaway, Richard B. Automotive Suspension, Steering & Brakes. (Transportation & Technology Ser.). (Illus.). 1980. text ed. 16.95 (ISBN 0-13-054288-1). P-H.

Ellingham, Mark. A Rough Guide to Greece. (Illus.). 224p. (Orig.). 1982. pap. 8.95 (ISBN 0-7100-9206-7). Routledge & Kegan.

Ellingsen, Mark. Doctrine & Word. LC 82-21311. 192p. 1983. pap. 8.95 (ISBN 0-8042-0533-7). John Knox.

Ellingson, Marnie. Dolly Blanchard's Fortune. 192p. 1983. 11.95 (ISBN 0-8027-0728-9). Walker & Co.

Ellingsworth, Huber W., jt. auth. see Welden, Terry A.

Ellington, C. D. Professional Apartmenteering. 348p. 1979. pap. 20.00 (ISBN 0-86718-086-2). Natl Assn Home Builders.

Ellington, Duke. Great Music of Duke Ellington. pap. 9.95 (ISBN 0-486-20757-9). Dover.

--Music Is My Mistress. LC 73-83189. (Illus.). 544p. 1973. 14.95 (ISBN 0-385-02235-2). Doubleday.

Ellington, Henry. Dictionary of Instructional Technology. 200p. 1983. 23.50 (ISBN 0-89397-149-9). Nichols Pub.

Ellington, Henry, jt. auth. see Percival, Fred.

Ellington, Henry, et al. A Handbook of Game Design. 150p. 1982. 25.00 (ISBN 0-89397-134-0). Nichols Pub.

Ellington, J. W., ed. see Kant, Immanuel.

Ellington, James W., tr. see Kant, Immanuel.

Ellington, Marnie. Double Folly. (Orig.). 1980. pap. 1.50 o.s.i. (ISBN 0-440-12473-5). Dell.

--Unwilling Bride. (Orig.). 1980. pap. 1.50 o.s.i. (ISBN 0-440-19743-0). Dell.

Ellingworth, P. & Nida, E. A. Translator's Handbook on Paul's Letter to the Thessalonians. (Helps for Translators Ser.). 1982. Repr. of 1975 ed. soft cover 2.10x (ISBN 0-8267-0146-9, 08526). United Bible.

Ellinwood, L. & Porter, K. Bio-Biographical Index of Musicians in the United States of America Since Colonial Times. LC 76-159677. (Music Ser). 1971. Repr. of 1956 ed. lib. bdg. 39.50 (ISBN 0-306-70183-9). Da Capo.

Ellinwood, Leonard. History of American Church Music. LC 69-12683. (Music Reprint Ser.). 1970. Repr. of 1953 ed. lib. bdg. 25.00 (ISBN 0-306-71233-4). Da Capo.

Elliot. A Zoological Triology of the Performing Arts. 1983. 31.95 (ISBN 0-87645-113-X). Gambit.

Elliot, A. M., tr. see Vidali, Vittorio.

Elliot, Alfred & Outka, Darryl E. Zoology. 5th ed. (Illus.). 1976. 21.95 o.p. (ISBN 0-13-984021-4). P-H.

Elliot, Alfred M. Biology of Tetrahymena. LC 73-12911. 508p. 1973. text ed. 62.00 (ISBN 0-87933-013-9). Hutchinson Ross.

Elliot, Alison J. Child Language. (Cambridge Textbooks in Linguistics). 180p. 1981. text ed. 32.95 (ISBN 0-521-22518-3); pap. text ed. 9.95 (ISBN 0-521-29556-4). Cambridge U Pr.

Elliot, Carolyn M., jt. ed. see Kelly, Gail P.

Elliot, Curtis M., jt. auth. see Vaughan, Emmett J.

Elliot, D. H., jt. ed. see Bennett, P. B.

Elliot, Dan. Ernie's Little Lie. LC 82-7574. (Sesame Street Start-to-Read Bks.). (Illus.). 40p. (ps-3). 1983. PLB 4.99 (ISBN 0-394-95440-8); pap. 3.95 (ISBN 0-394-85440-3). Random.

Elliot, Elisabeth. Discipline: The Glad Surrender. 160p. 1983. 8.95 (ISBN 0-8007-1318-4). Revell.

--Facing the Death of Someone You Love. 16p. 1980. pap. 0.95 (ISBN 0-89107-196-2). Good News.

--Let Me Be a Woman. 1976. 5.95 (ISBN 0-8423-2160-8); pap. 4.95 (ISBN 0-8423-2161-6). Tyndale.

--Notes on Prayer. 1982. pap. 0.95 (ISBN 0-89107-254-3). Good News.

--Through Gates of Splendor. (Spire Bks). (Illus.). 208p. 1975. pap. 2.50 o.p. (ISBN 0-8007-8062-0); pap. 0.39 o.p. (ISBN 0-8007-8514-2, Spire Comic). Revell.

--Through Gates of Splendor. 1981. 3.50 (ISBN 0-8423-7151-6). Tyndale.

--What God Has Joined. 32p. 1983. Repr. 1.50 (ISBN 0-89107-276-4). Good News.

Elliot, F. Language Is You, Bk. 2. rev. ed. (gr. 7-8). 1982. pap. text ed. 5.83 (ISBN 0-201-20173-9, Sch Div); tchr's. ed. 6.19 (ISBN 0-201-20174-7). A-W.

Elliot, Geraldine. The Long Grass Whispers: A Book of African Folk Tales. LC 68-21826. (Illus.). (gr. 3-7). 1970. pap. 2.95 o.p. (ISBN 0-8052-0260-9). Schocken.

--The Singing Chameleon: A Book of African Stories Based on Local Custom, Proverbs & Folk-Lore. (Illus.). 1971. Repr. of 1957 ed. 11.95 o.p. (ISBN 0-7100-1326-4). Routledge & Kegan.

--Where the Leopard Passes: A Book of African Folk Tales. LC 68-21827. (Illus.). (gr. 3-7). 1970. pap. 2.95 o.p. (ISBN 0-8052-0259-5). Schocken.

Elliot, Hugh S. Herbert Spencer. LC 79-98219. Repr. of 1917 ed. lib. bdg. 16.25x (ISBN 0-8371-3741-1, ELHS). Greenwood.

Elliot, Jeffrey M. Black Voices, No. 1: Interviews with Prominent Afro-Americans. LC 81-21644. (Borgo Bioviews Ser.: Vol. 1). 64p. 1983. lib. bdg. 9.95x (ISBN 0-89370-153-X); pap. text ed. 3.95x (ISBN 0-89370-253-6). Borgo Pr.

--Fantasy Voices, No. 1: Interviews with Fantasy Authors. LC 80-22575. (Milford Series: Popular Writers of Today: Vol. 31). 64p. (Orig.). 1982. lib. bdg. 9.95x (ISBN 0-89370-146-7); pap. text ed. 3.95x (ISBN 0-89370-246-3). Borgo Pr.

--The Future of the Space Program--Large Corporations & Society: Discussions with 22 Science-Fiction Writers. LC 80-19754. (Great Issues of the Day Ser.: Vol. 1). 64p. (Orig.). 1981. lib. bdg. 9.95x (ISBN 0-89370-140-8); pap. text ed. 3.95x (ISBN 0-89370-240-4). Borgo Pr.

--Literary Voices One. LC 80-12768. (The Milford Ser.: Popular Writers of Today: Vol. 27). 1980. lib. bdg. 9.95x (ISBN 0-89370-139-4); pap. 3.95x (ISBN 0-89370-239-0). Borgo Pr.

--Political Voices, No. 1: Interviews with Prominent American Politicians. LC 81-21643. (Borgo Bioviews: Vol. 2). 64p. 1983. lib. bdg. 9.95x (ISBN 0-89370-154-8); pap. text ed. 3.95x (ISBN 0-89370-254-4). Borgo Pr.

--Pulp Voices or Science Fiction Voices: Interviews with Pulp Magazine Writers & Editors, No. 6. LC 81-21632. (The Milford Series-Popular Writers of Today: Vol. 37). (Illus.). 64p. 1983. lib. bdg. 9.95x (ISBN 0-89370-157-2); pap. text ed. 3.95x (ISBN 0-89370-257-9). Borgo Pr.

--Reader's Guide to A. E. van Vogt. Schlobin, Roger C., ed. (Reader's Guides to Contemporary Science Fiction & Fantasy Authors Ser.: Vol. 17). (Illus., Orig.). 1983. 10.95x (ISBN 0-916732-46-0); pap. text ed. 4.95x (ISBN 0-916732-45-2). Starmont Hse.

--Science Fiction Voices: No. 2. LC 79-1396. (The Milford Ser.: Popular Writers of Today: Vol. 25). 1979. lib. bdg. 9.95x (ISBN 0-89370-137-8); pap. 3.95x (ISBN 0-89370-237-4). Borgo Pr.

--Science Fiction Voices: No. 3. LC 79-1396. (The Milford Ser.: Popular Writers of Today: Vol. 29). 1980. lib. bdg. 9.95x (ISBN 0-89370-143-2); pap. 3.95x (ISBN 0-89370-243-9). Borgo Pr.

--Science-Fiction Voices, No. 4: Interviews with Science-Fiction Authors. LC 80-22580. (Milford Series: Popular Writers of Today: Vol. 33). 64p. (Orig.). 1982. lib. bdg. 9.95x (ISBN 0-89370-148-3); pap. text ed. 3.95x (ISBN 0-89370-248-X). Borgo Pr.

Elliot, Jeffrey M. & Reginald, R. The Analytical Congressional Directory. LC 81-21587. (Borgo Reference Library: Vol. 12). 256p. (Orig.). 1983. lib. bdg. 19.95x (ISBN 0-89370-141-6); pap. text ed. 9.95x (ISBN 0-89370-241-2). Borgo Pr.

Elliot, Jeffrey M. & Shieh, Francis. Keys to Economic Understanding. LC 76-13795. 1976. pap. text ed. 9.95 (ISBN 0-8403-1483-3). Kendall-Hunt.

Elliot, Jeffrey M., jt. auth. see Brasfield, Philip.

Elliot, Jeffrey M., jt. auth. see Reginald, R.

Elliot, Jeffrey M., jt. auth. see Weeks, John.

Elliot, Jessica. Home to the Highlands. (Orig.). 1980. pap. 1.25 o.s.i. (ISBN 0-440-13104-9). Dell.

Elliot, Len & Kelly, Barbara. Who's Who in Golf. 1976. 8.95 o.p. (ISBN 0-87000-225-2, Arlington Hse). Crown.

Elliot, Mai Van, tr. No Other Road to Take: Memoir of Mrs. Nguyen Thi Dinh. 1976. 5.00 o.p. (ISBN 0-87727-102-X, DP 102). Cornell SE Asia.

Elliot, Mark R. Pawns of Yalta: Soviet Refugees & America's Role in Their Repatriation. LC 81-7599. (Illus.). 300p. 1982. 18.95 (ISBN 0-252-00897-9). U of Ill Pr.

Elliot, Nem & Elliot, Percy. The Complete German Shepherd Dog. (Illus.). 304p. 1983. 22.50 (ISBN 0-7182-2350-0, Pub. by Kaye & Ward). David & Charles.

Elliot, Percy, jt. auth. see Elliot, Nem.

Elliot, R. J. Stochastic Calculus & Applications. (Applications of Mathematics Ser.: Vol. 18). 302p. 1983. 42.00 (ISBN 0-387-90763-7). Springer-Verlag.

Elliot, Ralph N. Natue's Law & its Application for the Mastering of the Stock Market. (Illus.). 157p. 1983. 145.15 (ISBN 0-86654-068-7). Inst Econ Finan.

Elliot, Sharon. The Busy People's Naturally Nutritious Decidedly Delicious Fast Food Book. LC 83-3055. (Illus.). 120p. (Orig.). 1983. pap. 6.95 (ISBN 0-8069-7732-9). Sterling.

Elliot, Sharon A. & Haight, Sandy. The Busy People's Naturally Nutritious, Decidedly Delicious, Fast Foodbook. LC 77-77054. (Illus.). 120p. (Orig.). 1977. pap. 4.95 (ISBN 0-9601398-1-8). Fresh Pr.

Elliot-Binns, Christopher. Too Much Tenderness: An Autobiography of Childhood & Youth. 224p. 1983. 17.50 (ISBN 0-7100-9418-3). Routledge & Kegan.

Elliott, A. M., tr. see Campannella, Thomas.

Elliott, A. M., tr. see Carrillo, Santiago.

Elliott, Alan C. On Sunday the Wind Came. LC 79-19083. (Illus.). 32p. (gr. k-3). 1980. 8.75 o.s.i. (ISBN 0-688-22218-8); PLB 9.36 (ISBN 0-688-32218-2). Morrow.

Elliott, Alfred M. & Sloat, Barbara F. Laboratory Guide for Zoology. 6th ed. 1979. pap. text ed. 11.95x (ISBN 0-8087-0522-9). Burgess.

Elliott, Bette. The Clockwatcher's Cookbook. 1968. 9.50 (ISBN 0-87716-003-1, Pub. by Moore Pub Co). F Apple.

Elliott, Brad. Surf's Up: The Beach Boys on Record, 1961-1981. LC 81-80190. (Rock & Roll Reference Ser.: No. 6). 512p. 1981. individuals 17.95 (ISBN 0-87650-118-8); institutions 24.95. Pierian.

Elliott, Brian & McCrone, David. The City: Patterns of Domination & Conflict. LC 81-51614. 220p. 1982. 25.00 (ISBN 0-312-13984-5). St Martin.

Elliott, Bruce & Champion, Nigel. Squash: For Players, Coaches & Teachers. 80p. 1982. 30.00x (ISBN 0-85950-368-2, Pub. by Thornes England). State Mutual Bk.

Elliott, C. M. & Ockendon, J. R. Weak & Variational Methods for Free & Moving Boundary Problems. (Research Notes in Mathematics Ser.: No. 59). 220p. 1982. pap. text ed. 27.50 (ISBN 0-273-08503-4). Pitman Pub MA.

Elliott, Charles. Care of Game Meat & Trophies. LC 74-33570. (Funk & W Bk.). (Illus.). 160p. 1975. 7.50i (ISBN 0-308-10206-1); pap. 4.50i (ISBN 0-308-10207-X, TYC-T). T Y Crowell.

--Mr. Anonymous: Robert W. Woodruff of Coca-Cola. (Illus.). 316p. 1982. 14.95 (ISBN 0-87797-062-9). Cherokee.

--Turkey Hunting with Charlie Elliott. (Illus.). xi, 275p. 1982. 14.95 (ISBN 0-87797-063-7). Cherokee.

Elliott, Cheri. The Digest Book of Bowhunting. (The Sports & Leisure Library). (Illus.). 96p. 1979. pap. 2.95 o.s.i. (ISBN 0-695-81317-X). Follett.

Elliott, Clark A. Biographical Dictionary of American Science: The Seventeenth Through the Nineteenth Centuries. LC 78-4292. 1979. lib. bdg. 55.00x (ISBN 0-313-20419-5, EAS/). Greenwood.

Elliott, Curtis M., jt. auth. see Vaughan, Emmett J.

Elliott, David. Thailand: Origins of Military Rule. 190p. 1978. 20.00 (ISBN 0-905762-10-X, Pub. by Zed Pr England); pap. 7.95 (ISBN 0-905762-11-8, Pub. by Zed Pr England). Lawrence Hill.

Elliott, David W. Listen to the Silence. (RL 10). pap. 1.25 o.p. (ISBN 0-451-06588-3, Y6588, Sig). NAL.

Elliott, David W., ed. The Third Indochina Conflict. (Westview Replica Edition Ser.). 250p. 1981. lib. bdg. 18.50 (ISBN 0-89158-739-X). Westview.

Elliott, Douglas F. & Rao, K. Ramamohan. Fast Transforms: Algorithms, Analyses, Applications. LC 79-8852. (Computer Science & Applied Mathematical Ser.). 1981. 69.00 (ISBN 0-12-237080-5). Acad Pr.

Elliott, Ebenezer. Night, a Descriptive Poem, Pt. 1, 4 Bks., Repr. Of 1813. Bd. with Love, a Poem in Three Parts. To Which Is Added, the Giaour, a Satirical Poem. Repr. of 1823 ed. LC 75-31200. (Romantic Context Ser.: Poetry 1789-1830: Vol. 52). 1978. lib. bdg. 47.00 o.s.i. (ISBN 0-8240-2151-7). Garland Pub.

--The Vernal Walk; a Poem, Repr. Of 1801 Ed. Bd. with Peter Faultless to His Brother Simon, Tales of Night, in Rhyme, & Other Poems. Repr. of 1820 ed. LC 75-31199. (Romantic Context Ser.: Poetry 1789-1830: Vol. 51). 1978. lib. bdg. 47.00 o.s.i. (ISBN 0-8240-2150-9). Garland Pub.

--The Village Patriarch; a Poem, Repr. Of 1829 Ed. Reiman, Donald H., ed. Bd. with The Corn-Law Rhymes. Repr. of 1831 ed. LC 75-31202. (Romantic Context Ser.: Poetry 1789-1830). 1979. lib. bdg. 47.00 o.s.i. (ISBN 0-8240-2152-5). Garland Pub.

Elliott, Edwin B. Algebra of Quantics. 2nd ed. LC 63-11320. 14.95 (ISBN 0-8284-0184-5). Chelsea Pub.

Elliott, Emily. Portrait of My Love. (Candlelight Ecstasy Ser.: No. 140). (Orig.). 1983. pap. 1.95 (ISBN 0-440-16719-1). Dell.

Elliott, F. Language is You, Bk. 1. rev. ed. 1982. pap. text ed. 5.83 (ISBN 0-201-20148-8, Sch Div); tchr's ed. 6.19 (ISBN 0-201-20149-6). A-W.

Elliott, Fred T. Language Is You, Bks. 1 & 2. 2nd ed. (gr. 7-8). 1977. pap. text ed. (Sch Div); Bk. 1. pap. text ed. 5.84 (ISBN 0-201-41511-9); Bk. 2. pap. text ed. 6.48 (ISBN 0-201-41513-5); tchr's eds. 6.88 ea.; Bk. 1 Tchr's Ed. (ISBN 0-201-41512-7); Bk. 2 Tchr's Ed. 6.88 (ISBN 0-201-41514-3). A-W.

Elliott, Gerald. Grand Rapids: Renaissance on the Grand. Silvey, Kitty & Flagg, Marie, eds. LC 81-86569. (American Portrait Ser.). (Illus.). 240p. 1982. 29.95 (ISBN 0-932986-22-6). Continent Herit.
Elliott, Harley. The Tiger's Spots. LC 76-45383. (The Crossing Press Childresn's Stories Ser.). (Illus.). 64p. 1977. 10.95 (ISBN 0-912278-79-X); pap. 3.95 (ISBN 0-912278-80-3). Crossing Pr.
Elliott, J. F. The New Police. 88p. 1973. 9.75x (ISBN 0-398-02680-7). C C Thomas.
Elliott, J. H. Imperial Spain 1469-1716. 1977. pap. 8.95 (ISBN 0-452-00614-7, F614, Mer). NAL.
Elliott, James P. & Dawber, P. G. Symmetry in Physics, 2 vols. 608p. 1979. 28.50x ea. o.p. Vol. 1 o.p (ISBN 0-19-520161-2). Vol. 2 (ISBN 0-19-520162-0). Oxford U Pr.
Elliott, Joan. Cats. Duenewald, Doris, ed. (Illus.). 1978. 2.95 (ISBN 0-448-16263-6, G&D). Putnam Pub Group.
--Dogs. LC 78-58087. (Illus.). 1978. 2.95 (ISBN 0-448-16262-8, G&D). Putnam Pub Group.
Elliott, John E. & Grey, Arthur. Economic Issues & Policies: Readings in Introductory Economics. 3rd ed. 1975. pap. text ed. 14.50 (ISBN 0-395-19824-0). HM.
Elliott, John F., ed. Steelmaking: The Chipman Conference. 1965. 30.00x (ISBN 0-262-05003-X). MIT Pr.
Elliott, John H. & Martin, R. A. Augsburg Commentary on the New Testament. LC 82-70962. 192p. (Orig.). 1982. 7.50 (ISBN 0-8066-1937-6, 10-9042). Augsburg.
Elliott, Judith, tr. Tivadar Csontvary Kosztka. (Illus.). 206p. 1981. 55.00 (ISBN 0-89893-173-8). CDP.
Elliott, Kitt. African School. LC 78-111128. 1970. 24.95x (ISBN 0-521-07722-2). Cambridge U Pr.
Elliott, Lawrence. Little Flower: The Life & Times of Fiorello La Guardia. (Illus.). 256p. 1983. 13.95 (ISBN 0-688-02057-7). Morrow.
Elliott, Lloyd H., jt. auth. see Goodpoaster, Andrew J.
Elliott, Lloyd h. & Goodpaster, Andrew J., eds. Toward a Consensus on Military Service: Report of the Atlantic Council's Working Group on Military Service. (Illus.). 300p. 1982. 32.50 (ISBN 0-08-029399-9, K125); pap. 13.95 (ISBN 0-08-029398-0). Pergamon.
Elliott, Lynn C., jt. auth. see Weinhold, Barry.
Elliott, Martin A., ed. Chemistry of Coal Utilization: Supplementary Volume 2. LC 80-13296. 2374p. 1981. 195.00 (ISBN 0-471-07726-7, Pub. by Wiley-Interscience). Wiley.
Elliott, Maude H., jt. auth. see Richards, Laura E.
Elliott, May. Extraordinary Blessings of an Ordinary Christian. LC 73-90493. 1974. 6.00 o.p. (ISBN 0-8309-0113-2). Herald Hse.
Elliott, Norman F. & Kustra, Mary E., eds. Patterson's American Education, Vol. 78. 1981. 42.50x o.p. (ISBN 0-910536-29-5). Ed Direct.
Elliott, Norman F. & Moody, Douglas C., eds. Patterson's American Education, Vol. 79. 780p. 1982. 42.50x (ISBN 0-910536-31-7). Ed Direct.
Elliott, Norman F. & Stair, Joan, eds. Patterson's Schools Classified. 1979. pap. 4.75x o.p. (ISBN 0-910536-24-4). Ed Direct.
Elliott, Orrin L. The Tariff Controversy in the United States, 1789-1833. (Perspectives in American History Ser.: No. 58). 272p. Repr. of 1892 ed. lib. bdg. 22.50x (ISBN 0-87991-097-6). Porcupine Pr.
Elliott, Patricia L. see Lind, Carolyn P., pseud.
Elliott, Paul M. Eskimos of the World. LC 76-25964. (Illus.). 128p. (gr. 4-6). 1976. PLB 7.29 o.p. (ISBN 0-671-32767-4). Messner.
Elliott, Paul R., jt. auth. see Fox, L. Raymond.
Elliott, R. W. Runes. 1959. pap. 6.50 (ISBN 0-7190-0787-9). Manchester.
Elliott, Ralph N. The Ralph Nelson Elliott's Understanding of the Intimate Life of the Stock Market & Its Speculative Expression. Dietrich, Emerson, ed. (Illus.). 187p. 1982. 135.45 (ISBN 0-86654-024-5). Inst Econ Finan.
Elliott, Raymond. Fundamentals of Music. 3rd ed. LC 76-139599. (Illus.). 1971. pap. text ed. 14.95 (ISBN 0-13-341305-5). P-H.
Elliott, Rex R. Hawaiian Bottles of Long Ago. 3rd ed. LC 78-134504. (Illus.). 1971. pap. 4.95 o.p. (ISBN 0-930492-13-7). Hawaiian Serv.
Elliott, Robert C., ed. see Bellamy, Edward.
Elliott, Robert K. & Willingham, John J. Management Fraud: Detection & Deterrence. 300p. 1980. 25.00 o.p. (ISBN 0-07-091072-3). McGraw.
Elliott, Sumner L. Water Under the Bridge. 1977. 9.95 o.p. (ISBN 0-671-22823-4). S&S.
Elliott, Thomas G. Ammianus Marcellinus & Fourth Century History. 277p. 1983. 35.00x (ISBN 0-686-84471-8). Samuel Stevens.
Elliott, William D. Henry Handel Richardson. (World Authors Ser.: No. 366). 1975. lib. bdg. 15.95 (ISBN 0-8057-6217-5, Twayne). G K Hall.
Elliott, William M., Jr. Cure for Anxiety. LC 64-18326. (Orig.). 1964. pap. 2.45 o.p. (ISBN 0-8042-3388-8). John Knox.
Elliotts, R., jt. ed. see Schreiber, J.
Ellis. Carpet Substrates. 17.95x (ISBN 0-87245-511-4). Textile Bk.
--Nursing in Today's World: Challenges, Issues & Trends. pap. text ed. 9.95 (ISBN 0-686-97981-8, Lippincott Nursing). Lippincott.
Ellis, jt. auth. see Barton.
Ellis, jt. auth. see Martin.
Ellis, jt. auth. see Thompson, Harwood.
Ellis, et al. Base. (A vocabulary enrichment program). (gr. 4-12). pap. 3.39 student bk. (ISBN 0-8372-4253-3); tchr's handbk. 3.39 (ISBN 0-8372-4254-1); tapes avail. Bowmar-Noble.
--Introduction to the Foundations of Education. 1981. 22.95 (ISBN 0-13-484105-0). P-H.
Ellis, A., jt. auth. see Ard, B.
Ellis, A. E. British Freshwater Bivalve Mollusca: Keys & Notes for the Identification of the Species. (A Volume in the Synopses of the British Fauna Ser.). 1978. pap. 8.50 o.s.i. (ISBN 0-12-236950-5). Acad Pr.
Ellis, A. J. College Algebra & Geometry. 200p. 1982. write for info. (ISBN 0-471-10174-5, Pub. by Wiley-Interscience); pap. 24.95x (ISBN 0-471-10175-3). Wiley.
Ellis, Albert. The Art & Science of Love. pap. 2.75 (ISBN 0-686-36803-7). Inst Rat Liv.
--A Garland of Rational Songs. pap. 3.50 (ISBN 0-686-36738-3). Inst Rat Liv.
--How To Live With-& Without-Anger. 7.95 (ISBN 0-686-36756-1). Inst Rat Liv.
--How to Master Your Fear of Flying. pap. 3.95 (ISBN 0-686-36759-6). Inst Rat Liv.
--Humanistic Psychotherapy: The Rational-Emotive Approach. Sagarin, Edward, ed. LC 72-94222. 320p. 1974. 12.50 o.p. (ISBN 0-517-52779-0). Crown.
--Humanistic Psychotherapy: The Rational-Emotive Approach. 12.50 (ISBN 0-686-36760-X); pap. 4.95 (ISBN 0-686-37353-7). Inst Rat Liv.
--The Intelligent Woman's Guide to Dating & Mating. 7.95 (ISBN 0-686-36806-1). Inst Rat Liv.
--Reason & Emotion in Psychotherapy. 15.00 (ISBN 0-686-36795-2); pap. 6.95 (ISBN 0-686-37356-1). Inst Rat Liv.
--Sex & the Liberated Man. 7.95 (ISBN 0-686-36809-6). Inst Rat Liv.
--Sex Without Guilt. pap. 5.00 (ISBN 0-87980-145-X). Wilshire.
--Sex Without Guilt. pap. 3.00 (ISBN 0-686-36810-X). Inst Rat Liv.
Ellis, Albert & Abrahms, Eliot. Brief Psychotherapy in Medical & Health Practice. pap. 13.95 (ISBN 0-686-36685-9). Inst Rat Liv.
Ellis, Albert & Abrahms, Eliot R. Brief Psychotherapy in Medical & Health Practice. LC 78-12947. 1978. pap. 19.95 (ISBN 0-8261-2641-3). Springer Pub.
Ellis, Albert & Becker, Irving. Guide to Personal Happiness. Date not set. pap. 5.00 (ISBN 0-87980-395-9). Wilshire.
Ellis, Albert & Harper, Robert A. A Guide to Successful Marriage. pap. 5.00 (ISBN 0-686-36804-5). Inst Rat Liv.
--A New Guide to Rational Living. 3.00 o.p. (ISBN 0-686-92385-5, 6420). Hazelden.
--A New Guide to Rational Living. 8.95 (ISBN 0-686-36770-7); pap. 3.00 (ISBN 0-686-37354-5). Inst Rat Liv.
Ellis, Albert & Knaus, William. Overcoming Procrastination. 1979. pap. 2.95 (ISBN 0-451-12046-9, AE2046, Sig). NAL.
Ellis, Albert & Knaus, william J. Overcoming Procrastination. pap. 4.95 (ISBN 0-686-36781-2). Inst Rat Liv.
Ellis, Albert & Whiteley, John. Theoretical & Empirical Foundations of Rational-Emotive Therapy. pap. 12.95 (ISBN 0-686-36801-0). Inst Rat Liv.
Ellis, Albert & Whiteley, John M. Theoretical & Empirical Foundations of Rational-Emotive Therapy. LC 79-11083. (Orig.). 1979. pap. text ed. 12.95 o.p. (ISBN 0-8185-0336-X). Brooks-Cole.
Ellis, Albert & Wolfe, Janet L. How to Raise an Emotionally Healthy, Happy Child. pap. 3.00 (ISBN 0-686-36818-5). Inst Rat Liv.
Ellis, Albert, jt. ed. see Grieg, Russell.
Ellis, Alexander J. & Mendel, Arthur. Studies in the History of Musical Pitch. (Music Ser.). 238p. 1981. lib. bdg. 25.00 (ISBN 0-306-76020-7). Da Capo.
Ellis, Alfred B. A History of the Gold Coast of West Africa. 400p. 1971. Repr. of 1893 ed. 15.00x o.p. (ISBN 0-87471-034-0). Rowman.
Ellis, Allan B. The Computer in Education. (Illus.). 240p. 1973. text ed. 17.95 o.p. (ISBN 0-07-019236-7, C). McGraw.
Ellis, Anne. The Life of an Ordinary Woman. LC 80-138. (Illus.). xxiv, 301p. 1980. pap. 6.95 (ISBN 0-8032-6704-5, BB 736, Bison). U of Nebr Pr.
Ellis, Audrey. All About Home Freezing. 1971. pap. 2.95 (ISBN 0-600-30227-X). Transatlantic.
--French Family Cooking. 1976. 8.95 o.p. (ISBN 0-600-38091-2). Transatlantic.
--Home Guide to Food Freezing. 1974. 7.50 o.p. (ISBN 0-600-34469-X). Transatlantic.
--Meals to Enjoy from Your Freezer. (Illus.). 1971. pap. 2.95 o.p. (ISBN 0-600-31645-9). Transatlantic.
Ellis, Bettie H. Word Processing. (Concepts & Applications). (Illus.). 48p. 1980. 10.24 (ISBN 0-07-019242-1, G). McGraw.
Ellis, C. Hamilton. British Trains of Yesteryear. (Illus.). 19.50x (ISBN 0-392-02397-0, SpS). Sportshelf.
--Midland Railway. (Illus.). pap. 8.50x (ISBN 0-392-03937-0, SpS). Sportshelf.
Ellis, Charles, retold by. Shakespeare & the Bible, a Reading from Shakespeare's Merchant of Venice, Shakespeariana Sonnets with Their Scriptural Harmonies. 288p. Repr. of 1982 ed. lib. bdg. 50.00 (ISBN 0-89987-218-2). Darby Bks.
Ellis, Chris. How to Go Plastic Modeling. rev ed. (Illus.). 1976. 13.95 (ISBN 0-85059-247-X). Aztex.
Ellis, Chris, jt. auth. see Chamberlain, Peter.
Ellis, David. Let's Look at Indonesia. 1973. pap. 1.25 o.p. (ISBN 0-85363-077-1). OMF Bks.
Ellis, David B. Survival Tools for College: Techniques, Skills, Hints, Aids, Resources, Ideas, Procedures, Illustrations, Examples, Instructions, Methods, & Suggestions for College Success. 2nd ed. LC 81-71530. (Illus.). 226p. 1982. pap. 19.65 (ISBN 0-942456-02-5); pap. text ed. 19.65 (ISBN 0-686-86979-6). Coll Survival.
--Survival Tools For Students Instuctor's Guide. LC 82-71713. (Illus.). 159p. 1982. 30.00 (ISBN 0-686-91895-9). Coll Survival.
--Survival Tools for Students: Techniques, Skills, Hints, Aids, Resources, Ideas, Procedures, Illustrations, Examples, Instructions, Methods & Suggestions for Success. 3rd ed. (Illus.). 226p. 1982. pap. 19.65 (ISBN 0-686-91909-2); pap. text ed. 19.65 (ISBN 0-686-98409-9). Coll Survival.
Ellis, Derek V., ed. Marine Tailings Disposal. LC 82-73416. (Illus.). 368p. 1982. 37.50 (ISBN 0-250-40614-4). Ann Arbor Science.
Ellis, Don. Creative Photography with Front Projection. (Illus.). 1979. cancelled (ISBN 0-8174-2466-0, Amphoto); pap. cancelled (ISBN 0-8174-2139-4). Watson-Guptill.
Ellis, Dorsey D. Look Unto the Rock: A History of the Presbyterian Church, U.S. in West Virginia from 1719 to 1974. LC 82-60889. (Illus.). 372p. (Orig.). 1982. pap. 14.95 (ISBN 0-9609076-0-2). McClain.
Ellis, E. Earle. Eschatology in Luke. Reumann, John, ed. LC 72-75649. (Facet Bks.). 48p. 1972. pap. 0.50 (ISBN 0-8006-3070-X, 1-3070). Fortress.
Ellis, Edward R. Echoes of Distant Thunder: Life in the United States 1914-1918. LC 73-93767. 1975. 15.00 o.p. (ISBN 0-698-10583-4, Coward). Putnam Pub Group.
Ellis, Ella T. Celebrate the Morning. LC 72-75269. (gr. 5-9). 1972. 7.95 o.p. (ISBN 0-689-30051-4). Atheneum.
--Hugo & the Princess Nena. LC 82-16315. 204p. (gr. 5-8). 1983. 10.95 (ISBN 0-689-30953-8). Atheneum.
Ellis, F. R., ed. Inherited Disease & Anaesthesia. (Monographs in Anaesthesiology: Vol. 9). 1981. 98.75 (ISBN 0-444-80266-5). Elsevier.
Ellis, Florence H. Navajo Indians, Vol. 1: Anthropological Study of the Navajo Indians. (American Indian Ethnohistory Ser: Indians of the Southwest). (Illus.). lib. bdg. 42.00 o.s.i. (ISBN 0-8240-0703-4). Garland Pub.
Ellis, Frank H., ed. Poems on Affairs of State: Augustan Satirical Verse, 1660-1714, Vol. 6, 1697-1704. (Illus.). 1970. 60.00x (ISBN 0-300-01194-6). Yale U Pr.
Ellis, Franklin. History of Columbia County, New York 1878. (Illus.). 550p. 1983. Repr. of 1878 ed. deluxe ed. price not set (ISBN 0-932334-57-1). Heart of the Lakes.
Ellis, G. F., jt. auth. see Hawking, Steven.
Ellis, G. P. Chromenes, Chromanones, & Chromones: Chemistry of Heterocyclic Compounds-A Series of Monographs. (Vol. 31). 1196p. 1977. 212.95x (ISBN 0-471-38212-4). Wiley.
Ellis, G. P. & West, G. B. Progress in Medicinal Chemistry, Vol. 19. Date not set. 93.75 (ISBN 0-444-80415-3, North-Holland). Elsevier.
Ellis, G. P., jt. auth. see Criddle, W. J.
Ellis, G. P. & West, G. B., eds. Progress in Medicinal Chemistry, Vol. 3. 360p. 1963. 93.25 (ISBN 0-7204-7403-5, North-Holland). Elsevier.
--Progress in Medicinal Chemistry, Vols. 8-15. LC 73-86078. 298p. 1973-78. Vol. 8. 76.00 o.p. (ISBN 0-444-10555-7, North-Holland); Vol. 9. 66.50; Vol. 10. 75.75 (ISBN 0-444-10538-7); Vol. 11. 75.75 (ISBN 0-7204-7409-4); Vol. 12. 108.50 (ISBN 0-444-10880-7); Vol. 13. 86.00 (ISBN 0-7204-0650-1); Vol. 14. 75.75 (ISBN 0-7204-0645-5); 105.75 (ISBN 0-7204-0655-2). Elsevier.
--Progress in Medicinal Chemistry, Vols. 8 & 9. 1971-75. Vol. 8, Pt. 1. pap. 14.75 (ISBN 0-7204-7408-6); Vol. 8, Pt. 2. pap. 40.50 o.p. (ISBN 0-686-42999-0); Vol. 9, Pt. 1. pap. 12.25 (ISBN 0-7204-7409-4); Vol. 9, Pt. 2. pap. 23.25 (ISBN 0-444-10578-6). Elsevier.
--Progress in Medicinal Chemistry, Vol. 16. LC 62-2712. 292p. 1979. 90.00 (ISBN 0-7204-0667-6, North Holland). Elsevier.
--Progress in Medicinal Chemistry, Vol. 17. 1980. 78.50 (ISBN 0-7204-0669-2, North-Holland). Elsevier.
--Progress in Medicinal Chemistry, Vol. 18. 252p. 1981. 69.00 (ISBN 0-444-80345-9, North Holland). Elsevier.
Ellis, Geoffrey. Napoleon's Continental Blockade: The Case of Alsace. (Oxford Historical Monographs). (Illus.). 368p. 1981. 49.95x (ISBN 0-19-821881-8). Oxford U Pr.
Ellis, George A. Inside Folsom Prison: The TM-Sidhi Program. 1979. 13.95 o.p. (ISBN 0-88280-058-2); pap. 8.95 o.p. (ISBN 0-88280-059-0). ETC Pubns.
Ellis, Gerald C. Blood, Sweat, Toil & Tears. (Orig.). 1980. pap. 2.95 o.p. (ISBN 0-89260-171-X). Hwong Pub.
Ellis, Gwynn P. & Lockhart, Ian M. Chromans & Tocopherols. LC 80-16902. (The Chemistry of Heterocyclic Compounds: Vol. 36). 1980. 125.00x o.p. (ISBN 0-471-03038-4, Pub. by Wiley-Interscience). Wiley.
Ellis, H. B., jt. auth. see Todd, J. P.
Ellis, H. D., jt. auth. see Shepherd, J. W.
Ellis, Hamilton. The Pictorial Encyclopedia of Railways. 1968. 10.00 o.p. (ISBN 0-517-01305-3). Crown.
Ellis, Harold. Varicose Veins: How They are Treated, & What You Can Do to Help. LC 82-3975. (Positive Health Guides Ser.). (Illus.). 108p. 1983. 12.95 (ISBN 0-668-05334-8, 5334). Arco.
Ellis, Harry B. Israel: One Land, Two Peoples. LC 73-175104. (Illus.). 210p. 1972. 10.95i o.p. (ISBN 0-690-45028-1). T y Crowell.
Ellis, Havelock. Criminal. 5th, rev. & enl ed. LC 74-172610. (Criminology, Law Enforcement, & Social Problems Ser.: No. 200). (Illus., With intro added 1973). 1973. Repr. of 1914 ed. 15.00x (ISBN 0-87585-200-9). Patterson Smith.
--The Genius of Europe. LC 74-10374. 1974. Repr. of 1951 ed. lib. bdg. 21.00x (ISBN 0-8371-7680-8, ELGE). Greenwood.
--The World of Dreams. LC 75-43879. (Illus.). 1976. Repr. of 1922 ed. 40.00x (ISBN 0-8103-3780-0). Gale.
Ellis, Henry C. Fundamentals of Human Learning, Memory & Cognition. 2nd ed. (Fundamentals of Psychology Ser.). 240p. 1978. pap. text ed. write for info. o.p. (ISBN 0-697-06623-1); tchrs.' manual avail. o.p. (ISBN 0-697-06650-9). Wm C Brown.
Ellis, Henry C. & Hunt, R. Reed. Fundamentals of Human Memory & Cognition. 3rd ed. 350p. 1983. pap. text ed. write for info. (ISBN 0-697-06554-5); instr's. manual avail. (ISBN 0-697-06555-3). Wm C Brown.
Ellis, Herbert. The Mystery of the Wax Museum. LC 79-19627. (Unsolved Mysteries of the World Ser.). PLB 11.96 (ISBN 0-89547-084-5). Silver.
Ellis, Howard S. Exchange Control in Central Europe. LC 69-13892. Repr. of 1941 ed. lib. bdg. 17.75x (ISBN 0-8371-4462-0, ELEX). Greenwood.
Ellis, Howard S., ed. The Economy of Brazil. LC 69-16737. 1969. 33.00x (ISBN 0-520-01520-7). U of Cal Pr.
Ellis, Iris. S. O. S.-Save on Shopping. (Orig.). Date not set. pap. price not set (ISBN 0-440-58398-5, Dell Trade Pbks). Dell. Postponed.
--Save on Shopping. 8th ed. LC 81-50395. 400p. 1981. pap. 7.95 (ISBN 0-448-12153-0, G&D). Putnam Pub Group.
--Save on Shopping. 9th ed. (Illus.). 400p. 1982. pap. 7.95 (ISBN 0-448-12154-9, G&D). Putnam Pub Group.
Ellis, J. Introduction to the Real Estate Profession: Guide to Real Estate License Examination. 1981. pap. 8.24 o.p. (ISBN 0-13-494005-9). P-H.
Ellis, J., compiled by. Three Hundred Sermon Outlines & Suggestions. (Pocket Pulpit Library). 1979. pap. 2.95 (ISBN 0-8010-3355-1). Baker Bk.
Ellis, J. C., jt. auth. see Murray, M. A.
Ellis, J. M. Narration in the German Novelle. LC 78-73602. (Anglica Germanica Ser.: No. 2). 1979. pap. 12.95 (ISBN 0-521-29592-0). Cambridge U Pr.
Ellis, Jack C. A History of Film. (Illus.). 1979. pap. 18.95 ref. ed. (ISBN 0-13-389460-6). P-H.
Ellis, James, ed. see Gilbert, W. S.
Ellis, Janice R. & Nowlis, Elizabeth A. Nursing: A Human Needs Approach. 2nd ed. LC 80-82841. (Illus.). 528p. 1981. text ed. 24.50 (ISBN 0-395-29642-0); instr's manual 0.50 (ISBN 0-395-29643-9); test bank 2.00 (ISBN 0-395-29644-7). HM.
Ellis, Janice R., et al. Modules for Basic Nursing Skills, 2 vols. 2nd ed. LC 79-89521. (Illus.). 1980. Vol. 1. pap. text ed. 15.95 (ISBN 0-395-28654-9); Vol. 2. pap. text ed. 12.50 (ISBN 0-395-28655-7). HM.
Ellis, Jody. ABC's of Successful Living. 1974. pap. 3.95 (ISBN 0-913270-26-1). Sunstone Pr.
Ellis, John. The Cavalry: The History of Mounted Warfare. LC 78-53441. (Illus.). 1978. 20.00 o.p. (ISBN 0-399-12179-X). Putnam Pub Group.
--Visible Fictions. (Illus.). 232p. 1983. pap. 10.50 (ISBN 0-7100-9304-7). Routledge & Kegan.
Ellis, John T. Guide to Real Estate License Examinations. LC 73-22125. (Illus.). 304p. 1974. 11.95 o.p. (ISBN 0-13-371005-X); pap. 3.95 North Carolina suppl. o.p. (ISBN 0-13-371054-8). pap. 3.50 Maryland suppl. o.p. (ISBN 0-13-371039-4); pap. 3.50 Virginia suppl. o.p. (ISBN 0-13-371062-9). P-H.
Ellis, John T. & Beam, Victoria R. Mastering Real Estate Math in One Day. 1983. pap. 7.95 (ISBN 0-13-559666-1). P-H.
Ellis, John T. & Trisco, Robert. A Guide to American Catholic History. 2nd ed. LC 81-17585. 265p. 1982. text ed. 29.85 (ISBN 0-87436-318-7); pap. 19.95 (ISBN 0-87436-315-2). ABC-Clio.
Ellis, Joseph A. Latin America: Its Peoples & Institutions. 2nd ed. 1975. pap. text ed. 15.95x (ISBN 0-02-474200-7, 47420). Macmillan.
Ellis, Joseph J. After the Revolution: Profiles of Early American Culture. (Illus.). 1979. 19.95 o.p. (ISBN 0-393-01253-0); pap. write for info. Norton.

Ellis, Josephy & Moore, Robert. School for Soldiers: An Inquiry into West Point. 240p. 1974. 16.95x (ISBN 0-19-501843-5). Oxford U Pr.
Ellis, Joyce. The Big Split. rev. ed. 128p. 1983. pap. 4.95 (ISBN 0-8024-0190-2). Moody.
Ellis, Judith M., jt. auth. see Ellis, Peter F.
Ellis, Julie. East Wind. 1983. 15.95 (ISBN 0-87795-498-4). Arbor Hse.
--The Hampton Heritage. 1978. 10.95 o.p. (ISBN 0-671-23072-7). S&S.
--The Hampton Women. 1980. 14.95 o.p. (ISBN 0-671-24138-9). S&S.
--Savage Oaks. 1977. 10.00 o.p. (ISBN 0-671-22874-9). S&S.
Ellis, Leigh. Green Lady. 208p. 1981. pap. 2.25 o.p. (ISBN 0-380-77701-0, 77701). Avon.
Ellis, Loudell O. Church Treasurer's Handbook. LC 77-10433. 1978. 7.95 (ISBN 0-8170-0762-8); pap. 6.95 (ISBN 0-8170-0780-6). Judson.
Ellis, Loudell O. & Thacker, Ronald J. Intermediate Accounting. 1980. text ed. 29.95 (ISBN 0-07-019252-9); study guide 11.95 (ISBN 0-07-019254-5); instructor's manual 38.50 (ISBN 0-07-019253-7); working papers A 9.95 (ISBN 0-07-019255-3); working papers B 9.95 (ISBN 0-07-019256-1); practice set 7.95 (ISBN 0-07-019257-X); tests 29.95 (ISBN 0-07-019258-8); overhead transparencies 325.00 (ISBN 0-07-074798-9). McGraw.
Ellis, M. Leroy, ed. Prose Classique. LC 65-14565. 280p. 1966. pap. text ed. 13.50 o.p. (ISBN 0-471-00151-1). Wiley.
Ellis, Michael J. Why People Play. (Illus.). 192p. 1973. 14.95 (ISBN 0-13-958991-0). P-H.
Ellis, Norman, ed. International Review of Research in Mental Retardation, Vol. II. 412p. 1982. 37.50 (ISBN 0-12-366211-7). Acad Pr.
Ellis, P. B. The Cornish Language & Its Literature. 1974. 16.95x (ISBN 0-7100-7928-1); pap. 12.95 (ISBN 0-7100-9070-6). Routledge & Kegan.
Ellis, P. E., jt. auth. see Ashall, C.
Ellis, Patricia D. & Billings, Diane. Cardiopulmonary Resusitation: Procedures for Basic & Advanced Life Support. LC 79-19356. 240p. 1979. pap. text ed. 13.95 (ISBN 0-8016-1557-7). Mosby.
Ellis, Paul. Aircraft of the Royal Navy. (Illus.). 192p. 1982. 17.95 (ISBN 0-86720-556-3). Sci Bks Intl.
--Aircraft of the USAF. (Illus.). 192p. 1980. 19.95 (ISBN 0-86720-576-8); pap. 12.95 (ISBN 0-86720-577-6). Sci Bks Intl.
Ellis, Peter. Permanent Press-Pre or Post Cure? 1975. 19.95x (ISBN 0-87245-543-2). Textile Bk.
Ellis, Peter B. The Boyne Water: The Battle of the Boyne, 1690. LC 76-6753. 175p. 1976. text ed. 18.95x o.p. (ISBN 0-312-09415-9). St Martin.
--Hell or Connaught: The Cromwellian Colonization of Ireland. LC 74-24650. 288p. 1975. 22.50 (ISBN 0-312-36715-5). St Martin.
Ellis, Peter F. Seven Pauline Letters. LC 82-15252. (Orig.). 1982. pap. 8.95 (ISBN 0-8146-1245-8). Liturgical Pr.
Ellis, Peter F. & Ellis, Judith M. Access Guide for Scripture Study: John. manuaul 3.95 (ISBN 0-8215-5936-2); guide 2.95 (ISBN 0-8215-5918-4). Sadlier.
Ellis, Philip P. Ocular Therapeutics & Pharmacology. 6th ed. LC 81-9632. (Illus.). 320p. 1981. text ed. 37.50 (ISBN 0-8016-1518-6). Mosby.
Ellis, Richard. The Book of Sharks. LC 76-578. (Illus.). 1976. 12.95 (ISBN 0-448-12457-2, G&D). Putnam Pub Group.
--The Book of Sharks: A Complete Illustrated Natural History of the Sharks of the World. (Illus.). 256p. 29.95 (ISBN 0-15-113462-6). HarBraceJ.
--The Book of Sharks: A Complete Illustrated Natural History of the Sharks of the World. (Illus.). 256p. pap. 14.95 (ISBN 0-15-613552-3, Harv). HarBraceJ.
--Dolphins & Porpoises. LC 82-47823. 1982. 25.00 (ISBN 0-394-51800-4). Knopf.
Ellis, Richard B. Statistical Inference: Basic Concepts. (Illus.). 272p. 1975. text ed. 19.95 (ISBN 0-13-844621-0). P-H.
Ellis, Richard E. Jeffersonian Crisis: Courts & Politics in the Young Republic. 1971. 17.95x (ISBN 0-19-501390-5). Oxford U Pr.
Ellis, Richard N., ed. New Mexico, Past & Present: A Historical Reader. LC 71-153941. 140p. 1971. 9.95xo.p. (ISBN 0-8263-0210-6); pap. 7.95 (ISBN 0-8263-0215-7). U of NM Pr.
Ellis, Robert & Gulick, Denny. College Algebra. 473p. 1981. text ed. 20.95 (ISBN 0-15-507905-0, HC); 2.00 (ISBN 0-15-507906-9). HarBraceJ.
--College Algebra & Trigonometry. 661p. 1981. text ed. 21.95 (ISBN 0-15-507907-7, HC); answer manual 2.00 (ISBN 0-15-507908-5). HarBraceJ.
Ellis, Robert L. & Lipetz, Marcia J. Essential Sociology. 1979. pap. text ed. 13.95x o.p. (ISBN 0-673-15112-3). Scott F.
Ellis, S. M., ed. The Hardman Papers: A Further Selction (1865-1868) from the Letters & Memoirs of Sir Francis Hardman. 357p. 1982. Repr. of 1930 ed. lib. bdg. 45.00 (ISBN 0-89760-213-7). Telegraph Bks.
Ellis, Susan J., ed. Children As Volunteers. (Volunteer Energy Ser.: No. 3). (Illus.). 65p. 1983. pap. 7.50x (ISBN 0-940576-05-8). Energize.
Ellis, T. M. & Semenkov, O. I. Advances in CAD-CAM. Date not set. price not set (ISBN 0-444-86549-7). Elsevier.
Ellis, W. Ashton, tr. Family Letters of Richard Wagner. LC 71-163796. 307p. Date not set. price not set. Vienna Hse.
--Letters of Richard Wagner to Mathilde Wesendonck. LC 74-163794. 386p. Date not set. Repr. of 1905 ed. price not set. Vienna Hse.
--Letters of Richard Wagner to Minna Wagner, 2 vols. LC 75-163797. Date not set. Repr. of 1909 ed. price not set. Vienna Hse.
Ellis, Wesley. Lone Star & the Border Bandits, No. 3. 192p. 1982. pap. 2.25 (ISBN 0-515-06228-6). Jove Pubns.
--Lone Star & the Hardrock Payoff, No. 9. 192p. 2.25 (ISBN 0-515-06234-0). Jove Pubns.
--Lone Star & the Land Grabbers, No. 6. 192p. 1982. pap. 2.25 (ISBN 0-515-06231-6). Jove Pubns.
--Lone Star & the Opium Rustlers, No. 2. 192p. 1982. pap. 2.25 (ISBN 0-515-06227-8). Jove Pubns.
--Lone Star & the Renegade Comanches. 192p. 1983. pap. 2.25 (ISBN 0-515-06235-9). Jove Pubns.
--Lone Star & the Showdowners, No. 8. 192p. 1983. pap. 2.25 (ISBN 0-515-06233-2). Jove Pubns.
--Lone Star & the Timber Pirates, No. 5. 192p. 1983. pap. 2.25 (ISBN 0-515-06232-4). Jove Pubns.
--Lone Star & the Utah Kid, No. 5. 192p. 1982. pap. 2.25 (ISBN 0-515-06230-8). Jove Pubns.
--Lone Star on Outlaw Mountain, No. 11. 192p. 1983. pap. 2.25 (ISBN 0-515-06236-7). Jove Pubns.
--Lone Star on the Treachery Trail, No. 1. 192p. 1982. pap. 2.25 (ISBN 0-515-06226-X). Jove Pubns.
Ellis, William & Seidel, Frank. How to Win the Conference. 214p. 1982. 6.95 (ISBN 0-13-439489-5). P-H.
Ellis, William A. & Glassenapp, C. F. Life of Richard Wagner: Being an Authorized English Version of das Leben Richard Wagner, 6 vols. (Music Reprint Ser.). 1977. Repr. of 1902 ed. lib. bdg. 42.50 ea.; Set. lib. bdg. 220.00 (ISBN 0-306-70887-6). Vol. 1 (ISBN 0-306-70881-7). Vol. 2 (ISBN 0-306-70882-5). Vol. 3 (ISBN 0-306-70883-3). Vol. 4 (ISBN 0-306-70884-1). Vol. 5 (ISBN 0-306-70885-X). Vol. 6 (ISBN 0-306-70886-8). Da Capo.
Ellis, William T. Billy Sunday. (Golden Oldies Ser.). 1959. pap. 3.95 (ISBN 0-8024-0042-6). Moody.
Ellisen, Stanley A. Divorce & Remarriage in the Church. 1977. pap. 4.95 (ISBN 0-310-35561-3). Zondervan.
Ellis-Femor, Una, tr. see Ibsen, Henrik.
Ellis-Fermor, U. Shakespeare, the Dramatist. (Methuen Library Reprints Ser.). 188p. 1973. 28.00x (ISBN 0-416-18830-3). Methuen Inc.
Ellison, Constance M. Gropings & Hopings. LC 73-79845. 72p. 1973. 4.00 (ISBN 0-911838-30-9). Windy Row.
Ellison, Craig. The Urban Mission. LC 74-8744. 1974. pap. 3.95 o.p. (ISBN 0-8028-1560-X). Eerdmans.
--The Urban Mission: Essays on the Building of a Comprehensive Model for Evangelical Urban Ministry. LC 82-23764. 230p. 1983. pap. text ed. 10.75 (ISBN 0-8191-2968-2). U Pr of Amer.
Ellison, Craig W. Loneliness: The Search for Intimacy. LC 79-55681. 1980. 8.95 (ISBN 0-915684-57-8, HarpR). Har-Row.
Ellison, Craig W., ed. Your Better Self: Christianity, Psychology, & Self-Esteem. LC 82-47742. 224p. (Orig.). 1982. pap. 8.61i (ISBN 0-686-97230-9, HarpR). Har-Row.
Ellison, Curtis W. & Metcalf, E. W., Jr. Charles W. Chesnutt: A Reference Guide. (Reference Publications Ser.). 1977. lib. bdg. 19.00 (ISBN 0-8161-7825-9, Hall Reference). G K Hall.
Ellison, Curtis W. & Metcalf, E. W., eds. William Wells Brown & Martin R. Delany: A Reference Guide. 1978. lib. bdg. 29.00 (ISBN 0-8161-8025-3, Hall Reference). G K Hall.
Ellison, Darlene. Saying Goodbye. (Illus.). 138p. (Orig.). 1981. pap. 6.95 (ISBN 0-9604344-6-1). Sunrise Pub OR.
Ellison, David L. The Bio-Medical Fix: Human Dimensions of Bio-Medical Technologies. LC 77-91104. 1978. lib. bdg. 25.00 (ISBN 0-313-20038-6, ELB/). Greenwood.
Ellison, Fred P. Brazil's New Novel: Four Northeastern Masters: Jose Lins do Rego, Jorge Amado, Graciliano, Rachel de Queiroz. LC 78-9880. 1979. Repr. of 1954 ed. lib. bdg. 18.50x (ISBN 0-313-21237-6, ELBN). Greenwood.
Ellison, H. L. Exodus. Gibson, John C., ed. LC 81-12917. (Daily Study Bible Old Testament Ser.). 224p. 1982. 12.95 (ISBN 0-664-21803-2); pap. 6.95 (ISBN 0-664-24570-6). Westminster.
Ellison, Harlan. Approaching Oblivion. 176p. (RL 7). 1976. pap. 1.95 (ISBN 0-451-09683-5, J9683, Sig). NAL.
--The Beast That Shouted Love at the Heart of the World. 256p. 1974. pap. 1.75 o.p. (ISBN 0-451-08590-6, E8590, Sig). NAL.
--The Fantasies of Harlan Ellison. (Science Fiction Ser.). 1979. lib. bdg. 15.00 o.p. (ISBN 0-8398-2411-4, Gregg). G K Hall.
--Gentleman Junkie. (The Ace Ellison Ser.: No. 6). 256p. 1983. pap. 2.50 (ISBN 0-441-27938-4). Ace Bks.
--The Glass Teat. 1983. pap. 2.95 (ISBN 0-441-28988-6, Pub. by Ace Science Fiction). Ace Bks.
--Partners in Wonder. (Harlan Ellison Ser.: No. 4). 1982. pap. 2.95 (ISBN 0-441-65204-2, Pub. by Ace Science Fiction). Ace Bks.
--Shatterday. 304p. 1982. pap. 2.95. Berkley Pub.
Ellison, Harlan, ed. Again, Dangerous Visions, Vol. 1. (RL 7). pap. 2.25 o.p. (ISBN 0-451-07580-3, E7580, Sig). NAL.
--Again, Dangerous Visions, Vol. 2. (RL 7). pap. 2.25 o.p. (ISBN 0-451-07635-4, E7635, Sig). NAL.
--Dangerous Visions. (Illus.). (RL 7). 1975. pap. 2.50 o.p. (ISBN 0-451-08502-7, E8502, Sig). NAL.
Ellison, Jack S., jt. auth. see Kirk, Robert H.
Ellison, Jerome. Life's Second Half. 1978. 10.95 (ISBN 0-8159-6116-2). Devin.
--Life's Second Half: The Pleasures of Aging. (General Ser.). 1979. lib. bdg. 13.95 (ISBN 0-8161-6766-4, Large Print Bks). G K Hall.
Ellison, Joseph. California & the Nation, Eighteen Fifty to Eighteen Sixty-Nine. LC 78-87529. (American Scene Ser.). 1969. Repr. of 1927 ed. lib. bdg. 32.50 (ISBN 0-306-71443-4). Da Capo.
Ellison, Marvin M. The Center Cannot Hold: The Search for a Global Economy of Justice. LC 82-23795. 330p. (Orig.). 1983. lib. bdg. 24.75 (ISBN 0-8191-2963-1); pap. text ed. 13.75 (ISBN 0-8191-2964-X). U Pr of Amer.
Ellison, Neil M., jt. ed. see Newell, Guy R.
Ellison, Ralph. Invisible Man. 1963. 3.95 o.s.i. (ISBN 0-394-60338-9, M338). Modern Lib.
--Invisible Man: Thirtieth Anniversary Edition. 1982. 15.95 (ISBN 0-394-52549-3). Random.
Ellison, T. Cotton Trade of Great Britain. 355p. 1968. Repr. of 1886 ed. 30.00x (ISBN 0-7146-1391-6, F Cass Co). Biblio Dist.
Ellison, William H. A Self-Governing Dominion: California, 1849-1860. (Library Reprint Ser.: Vol. 95). 1978. 27.50x (ISBN 0-520-03713-8). U of Cal Pr.
Elliston, Frederick & Feldberg, Michael, eds. Moral Issues in Police Work. 180p. 1983. text ed. 25.00x (ISBN 0-8476-7191-7); pap. 9.95x (ISBN 0-8476-7192-5). Rowman.
Elliston, Frederick, jt. ed. see Baker, Robert.
Elliston, Frederick A. & Bowie, Norman E., eds. Ethics, Public Policy & Criminal Justice. LC 82-7974. 512p. 1982. text ed. 30.00 (ISBN 0-89946-138-7). Oelgeschlager.
El Liwaru, Maisha Z., jt. auth. see El Liwaru, Saidi J.
El Liwaru, Saidi J. & El Liwaru, Maisha Z. The Muslim Family Reader. Quinlan, Hamid, ed. LC 82-74126. 130p. 1983. pap. 4.00 (ISBN 0-89259-028-9). Am Trust Pubns.
Ellman, Edgar S. Put it in Writing: A Complete Guide for Preparing Employee Personnel Handbooks. 160p. 1982. Comb-bound 59.95 (ISBN 0-8436-0884-6). CBI Pub.
Ellman, Michael. Socialist Planning. LC 78-57757. (Modern Cambridge Economics Ser.). 1979. 47.50 (ISBN 0-521-22229-X); pap. 14.95 (ISBN 0-521-29409-6). Cambridge U Pr.
--Soviet Planning Today, Proposals for an Optimally Functioning Economic System. LC 72-145613. (Department of Applied Economics, Occasional Papers: No. 25). (Illus.). 1971. 23.95 (ISBN 0-521-08156-4); pap. 11.95x (ISBN 0-521-09648-0). Cambridge U Pr.
Ellman, Richard. Ulysses on the Liffey. 1972. 17.95 (ISBN 0-19-519665-1). Oxford U Pr.
Ellman, Richard, ed. see Wilde, Oscar.
Ellmann, Richard. The Consciousness of Joyce. 1981. pap. 6.95 (ISBN 0-19-502898-8, GB 636). Oxford U Pr.
--The Consciousness of Joyce. 1977. 17.95 (ISBN 0-19-519950-2). Oxford U Pr.
--Golden Codgers: Biographical Speculations. 1973. 16.95x (ISBN 0-19-211827-7). Oxford U Pr.
--Identity of Yeats. 2nd ed. 1964. 18.95x (ISBN 0-19-501233-X). Oxford U Pr.
--James Joyce. 1959. 29.95 o.p. (ISBN 0-19-500541-4). Oxford U Pr.
--James Joyce. pap. 12.95 o.p. (ISBN 0-19-500723-9, GB). Oxford U Pr.
--Ulysses on the Liffey. (Illus.). 230p. 1973. pap. 6.95 (ISBN 0-19-501663-7, GB). Oxford U Pr.
Ellmann, Richard, ed. The New Oxford Book of American Verse. LC 75-46354. 1976. 27.50 (ISBN 0-19-502058-8); deluxe ed. 65.00 leatherbound (ISBN 0-19-502194-0). Oxford U Pr.
Ellmann, Richard & O'Clair, Robert, eds. Modern Poems: An Introduction to Poetry. 500p. 1976. pap. text ed. 11.95x (ISBN 0-393-09187-2). Norton.
--Norton Anthology of Modern Poetry. 1400p. 1973. 28.95 (ISBN 0-393-09357-3); pap. 21.95x (ISBN 0-393-09348-4). Norton.
Ellmann, Richard, ed. see Joyce, James.
Ellmann, Richard, ed. see Wilde, Oscar.
Ellner, Carolyn L. & Barnes, Carol P. Studies in Post-Secondary Teaching: Experimental Results, Theoretical Interpretations, & New Perspectives. LC 82-47853. 1982. write for info. (ISBN 0-669-05656-1). Lexington Bks.
Ellory, J. C. & Young, T. Red Cell Membranes: A Methodological Approach. (Biological Techniques Ser.). 1982. 55.50 (ISBN 0-12-237140-2). Acad Pr.
Ellos, William J. Thomas Reid's Newtonian Realism. LC 81-40524. 76p. (Orig.). 1981. lib. bdg. 16.75 (ISBN 0-8191-1774-9); pap. text ed. 7.00 (ISBN 0-8191-1775-7). U Pr of Amer.
Ellrodt, Robert, ed. Essays & Studies-1975. (Essays & Studies: Vol. 28). 122p. 1975. text ed. 15.00x (ISBN 0-7195-3232-9, Pub. by Murray England). Humanities.
Ellroy, James. Clandestine. 352p. 1982. pap. 2.75 (ISBN 0-380-81141-3, 81141-3). Avon.
Ellsberg, Robert, ed. By Little by Little: The Selected Writings of Dorothy Day. LC 82-48887. 1983. 17.95 (ISBN 0-394-52499-3); pap. 9.95 (ISBN 0-394-71432-6). Knopf.
Ellsworth, A. Eugene. Aural Harmony. LC 72-138243. 1970. spiral bdg. 19.95 (ISBN 0-910842-00-0, GE9, Pub. by GWM); 34 tapes 134.50 set (ISBN 0-8497-6325-8, GE9T). Kjos.
Ellsworth, Edward W. Liberators of the Female Mind: The Shirreff Sisters, Educational Reform, & the Women's Movement. LC 78-67910. (Contributions in Women's Studies: No. 7). (Illus.). 1979. lib. bdg. 29.95 (ISBN 0-313-20644-9, ELL). Greenwood.
Ellsworth, Gerald C. The Inflexible Pressure of the Elliot Waves upon the Stock Market & Prediction of Major Future Price Movements. (Illus.). 143p. 1983. 71.85 (ISBN 0-86654-064-4). Inst Econ Finan.
Ellsworth, J. W. & Stahnke, A. A. Politics & Political Systems. 1976. text ed. 21.00x (ISBN 0-07-019250-2, C); instructor's manual 3.95 (ISBN 0-07-019251-0). McGraw.
Ellsworth, Leon W., jt. auth. see Burril, Claude W.
Ellsworth, Liz. Frederick Wiseman: A Guide to References & Resources. 1979. lib. bdg. 28.00 (ISBN 0-8161-8066-0, Hall Reference). G K Hall.
Ellsworth, Paul T. Chile: An Economy in Transition. LC 78-10217. (Illus.). 1979. Repr. of 1945 ed. lib. bdg. 17.00x (ISBN 0-313-20739-9, ELCH). Greenwood.
Ellsworth, Paul T. & Leith, J. Clark. The International Economy. 5th ed. (Illus.). 608p. 1975. text ed. 23.95x (ISBN 0-02-332760-X, 33276). Macmillan.
Ellsworth, S. George. Utah's Heritage. LC 72-85712. (Illus.). 350p. (gr. 7-12). 1977. text ed. 16.00x (ISBN 0-87905-006-3). Peregrine Smith.
Ellsworth, Scott, jt. ed. see Reeves, Clyde H.
Ellul, Jacques. Meaning of the City. 1970. pap. 4.95 o.p. (ISBN 0-8028-1555-3). Eerdmans.
--Prayer & Modern Man. Hopkins, C. Edward, tr. from Fr. 192p. 1973. pap. 6.95 (ISBN 0-8164-2081-5). Seabury.
--Presence of the Kingdom. 1967. pap. 4.95 (ISBN 0-8164-2058-0, SP41). Seabury.
Ellul, Jacques, et al. Jacques Ellul: Interpretive Essays. Christians, Clifford G. & Van Hook, Jay M., eds. LC 80-12342. 340p. 1981. 24.95 o.p. (ISBN 0-252-00812-X); pap. 8.95 o.p. (ISBN 0-252-00890-1). U of Ill Pr.
Ellwanger, Joseph W. Let My People Go. pap. 3.50 (ISBN 0-933350-01-5). Morse Pr.
Ellwood, John W., ed. Reductions in U. S. Domestic Spending: How They Affect State & Local Governments. LC 82-10975. (Illus.). 401p. 1982. 19.95 (ISBN 0-87855-472-6); pap. 9.95 (ISBN 0-87855-923-X). Transaction Bks.
Ellwood, L. W. Ellwood Tables For Real Estate Appraising & Financing. 4th ed. LC 77-4874. 656p. 1977. ref 22.50 (ISBN 0-88410-587-3). Ballinger Pub.
Ellwood, Robert S., Jr. Introducing Religion: From Inside & Outside. (Illus.). 1978. pap. text ed. 12.95 ref. (ISBN 0-13-477505-8). P-H.
--Introducing Religion: From Inside & Outside. (Illus.). 240p. 1983. pap. text ed. 11.95 (ISBN 0-13-477497-3). P-H.
--Many Peoples, Many Faiths. 2nd ed. (Illus.). 416p. 1982. 20.95 (ISBN 0-13-556001-2). P-H.
--Mysticism & Religion. 1980. text ed. 13.95 (ISBN 0-13-608810-4); pap. text ed. 10.95 (ISBN 0-13-608802-3). P-H.
--Religious & Spiritual Groups in Modern America. 352p. 1973. pap. 15.95 (ISBN 0-13-773309-7). P-H.
--Words of the World's Religion. 1977. pap. text ed. 15.95x (ISBN 0-13-965004-0). P-H.
Ellwood, Robert S., Jr., ed. Readings on Religion: From Inside & Outside. 1978. pap. text ed. 16.95 (ISBN 0-13-760942-6). P-H.
Ellyson, Mary H. Mud & Money. 5.95 o.p. (ISBN 0-533-00446-2). Vantage.
Ellzey, Roy. Data Structures for Computer Information Systems. 288p. 1982. pap. 21.95 (ISBN 0-574-21400-3, 13-4400); 4.95 (ISBN 0-574-21402-X). SRA.
Elmaghraby, F. E. Activity Networks: Project Planning & Control by Network Models. LC 77-9501. 443p. 1977. 49.95x (ISBN 0-471-23861-9, Pub. by Wiley-Interscience). Wiley.
El Mallakh, Dorothea H., jt. ed. see El Mallakh, Ragaei.
El Mallakh, Dorthea & Mallakh, Ragaei El, eds. U. S. & World Energy Resources: Prospects & Priorities. LC 77-88785. (Illus.). 1977. pap. 12.50x (ISBN 0-918714-03-6). Intl Res Ctr Energy.
El Mallakh, Ragaei. Qatar: Development of an Oil Economy. LC 78-12167. (Illus.). 1979. 25.00 (ISBN 0-312-65751-X). St Martin.
El Mallakh, Ragaei & McGuire, Carl. Energy & Development. LC 74-21511. 1975. pap. 12.00x (ISBN 0-918714-00-1). Intl Res Ctr Energy.

El Mallakh, Ragaei & El Mallakh, Dorothea H., eds. Heavy Versus Light Oil: Technical Issues & Economic Considerations. LC 82-84233. (Illus.). 1983. pap. 32.00x (ISBN 0-918714-07-9). Intl Res Ctr Energy.

--New Policy Imperatives for Energy Producers. LC 80-81017. (Illus.). 1980. pap. 16.50x (ISBN 0-918714-06-0). Intl Res Ctr Energy.

El-Mallakh, Ragaei, et al. Capital Investment in the Middle East: The Use of Surplus Funds for Regional Development. LC 77-7806. (Praeger Special Studies). 1977. text ed. 27.95 o.p. (ISBN 0-03-021986-8). Praeger.

El Mallakh, Ragael E., jt. ed. see Mallakh, Ragael E.

El Mallakh, Ragai & Atta, Jacob K. The Absorptive Capacity of Kuwait: Domestic & International Perspectives. LC 81-47026. (Illus.). 224p. 1981. 23.95x (ISBN 0-669-04541-1). Lexington Bks.

Elman, jt. auth. see Peterson.

Elman, Richard. The Breadfruit Lotteries. LC 79-20725. 1980. 9.95 o.p. (ISBN 0-416-00541-1). Methuen Inc.

--The Menu Cypher: A Novel. 224p. 1982. 12.95 (ISBN 0-02-535390-X). Macmillan.

Elman, Robert. The Hunter's Field Guide to the Game Birds & Animals of North America. LC 73-7289. 1982. 12.95 (ISBN 0-394-71260-9). Knopf.

--The Living World of Audubon Mammals. (Illus.). 272p. 1976. 12.95 (ISBN 0-448-12459-9, G&D). Putnam Pub Group.

Elman, Robert & Rees, Clair. The Hiker's Bible. rev. ed. LC 81-43776. (Outdoor Bible Ser.). (Illus.). 160p. 1982. pap. 4.95 (ISBN 0-385-17505-1). Doubleday.

Elmasry, M. I. Digital MOS Integrated Circuits. LC 81-6522. 489p. 1981. 38.95x (ISBN 0-471-86202-9, Pub. by Wiley Interscience); pap. 25.50 (ISBN 0-471-86203-7). Wiley.

Elmasy, Mohamed, ed. Digital MOS Integrated Circuits. LC 81-6522. 1981. 38.95 (ISBN 0-87942-151-7). Inst Electrical.

Elmendorf, Mary. Nine Mayan Women: A Village Faces Change. 1976. 10.00 (ISBN 0-470-23862-3); pap. 9.95 (ISBN 0-470-23864-X). Schenkman.

Elmentary Science Study. The Balance Book: A Guide for Teachers. 2nd ed. 1975. 16.88 o.p. (ISBN 0-07-018575-1, W). McGraw.

Elmer, Irene. Anthony's Father. (Illus.). (gr. 3-5). 1972. PLB 4.39 o.p. (ISBN 0-399-60741-2). Putnam Pub Group.

Elmer, Irene & Mathews. Boy Who Ran Away. LC 63-23143. (Arch Bks: Set 1). (Illus.). (gr. 3-5). 1964. laminated bdg. 0.89 (ISBN 0-570-06001-X, 59-1104). Concordia.

Elmer, William B. The Optical Design of Reflectors. 2nd ed. LC 79-14206. (Wiley Ser. in Pure & Applied Optics). 1980. 36.50x (ISBN 0-471-05310-4, Pub. by Wiley-Interscience). Wiley.

Elmes, David G. Readings in Experimental Psychology. 1978. pap. 13.95 (ISBN 0-395-30797-X). HM.

Elmes, David G., et al. Methods in Experimental Psychology. 1981. 20.95 (ISBN 0-395-30798-8); instr's manual 1.25 (ISBN 0-395-30799-6). HM.

Elmes, Frank. The Police As a Career. 14.50x (ISBN 0-392-08281-0, SpS). Sportshelf.

Elmo, Francis, tr. from Span. I in Christ Arisen. LC 81-85745. Orig. Title: Yo en Cristo Resucitado. 100p. Date not set. pap. price not set (ISBN 0-9607590-0-X). F Elmo.

Elmont, Nancy. Bradley's Complete Gas Grill Cookbook: A Barbeque Cookbook. LC 81-69074. (Illus.). 144p. 1982. 10.95 (ISBN 0-916752-52-6). Dorison Hse.

Elmore, D. T. Peptides & Proteins. LC 68-21392. (Cambridge Chemistry Texts Ser). (Illus.). 1968. 29.95 (ISBN 0-521-07107-0); pap. 9.95x (ISBN 0-521-09535-2). Cambridge U Pr.

Elmore, Richard. Insight. LC 76-56712. 1977. 12.95 (ISBN 0-87716-072-4, Pub. by Moore Pub Co). F Apple.

Elmore, Richard F., jt. auth. see Rand Corporation.

Elmore, Richard F., jt. ed. see Williams, Walter.

Elmore, W. C. & Heald, M. A. Physics of Waves. (International Pure & Applied Physics Ser). 1969. text ed. 42.00 (ISBN 0-07-019260-X, C). McGraw.

Elmslie, Kenward. Communications Equipment. (Burning Deck Poetry Ser.). 1979. pap. 3.00 (ISBN 0-930900-71-5); pap. 20.00 signed handmade (ISBN 0-930900-72-3). Burning Deck.

--Moving Right Along. 1980. 10.00 (ISBN 0-915990-21-0); pap. 5.00 (ISBN 0-915990-20-2). Z Pr.

--Tropicalism. LC 75-26459. 80p. (Orig.). 1976. pap. 5.00 (ISBN 0-915990-00-8). Z Pr.

Elmslie, Kenward, ed. see Ashbery, Elmslie J., et al.

Elmslie, Kenward, ed. see Burckhardt, Rudy.

Elmslie, Kenward, ed. see Koch, Kenneth & Berrigan, Ted.

Elmslie, Kenward, ed. see Padgett, Ron.

Elmslie, Kenward, ed. see Schuyler, James, et al.

Elmslie, Kenward, ed. see Welt, Bernard.

El-Namaki, M. S. Problems of Management in a Developing Environment: The Case of Tanzania (State Enterprises Between 1967 & 1975) 1979. 38.50 (ISBN 0-444-85303-0, North Holland). Elsevier.

Elon, Amos. Flight into Egypt. LC 79-6165. (Illus.). 264p. 1980. 11.95 o.p. (ISBN 0-385-15796-7). Doubleday.

--Flight into Egypt. 288p. 1981. pap. 3.50 o.p. (ISBN 0-523-41623-7). Pinnacle Bks.

--Israelis: Founders & Sons. 1983. pap. 5.95 (ISBN 0-14-022476-9, Pelican). Penguin.

Elonka, S. M. Standard Basic Math & Applied Plant Calculations. 1977. text ed. 25.95 (ISBN 0-07-019297-9). McGraw.

Elonka, Stephen M. Marmaduke Surfaceblow's Salty Technical Romances. LC 79-14107. 320p. 1979. lib. bdg. 18.00 (ISBN 0-88275-967-1). Krieger.

--Standard Plant Operators Manual. 3rd ed. LC 79-22089. (Illus.). 416p. 1980. 27.50 (ISBN 0-07-019298-7). McGraw.

Elonka, Stephen M. & Bernstein, J. L. Standard Electronics Questions & Answers, 2 vols. Incl. Vol. 1. Basic Electronics. 28.50 o.p. (ISBN 0-07-019283-9); Vol. 2. Industrial Applications. 24.50 o.p. (ISBN 0-07-019284-7). 1964 (P&RB). McGraw.

Elonka, Stephen M. & Johnson, O. H. Standard Industrial Hydraulics Questions & Answers. (Illus.). 1967. 41.50 (ISBN 0-07-019280-4, P&RB). McGraw.

Elonka, Stephen M. & Kohan, A. Standard Boiler Operators' Questions & Answers. 1969. 39.95 (ISBN 0-07-019275-8, P&RB). McGraw.

Elonka, Stephen M. & Minich, Quaid. Standard Refrigeration & Air Conditioning: Questions & Answers. 2nd ed. 1973. 32.50 (ISBN 0-07-019291-X, P&RB). McGraw.

Elonka, Stephen M. & Minich, Quaid W. Standard Refrigeration & Air Conditioning Questions & Answers. (Illus.). 416p. 1983. 34.00 (ISBN 0-07-019317-7, P&RB). McGraw.

Elonka, Stephen M. & Robinson, Joseph R. Standard Plant Operator's Questions & Answers, 2 vols. 2nd ed. 1981. Set. 36.50 (ISBN 0-07-079191-0); Vol. 1. 19.50 (ISBN 0-07-019315-0); Vol. 2. 19.50 (ISBN 0-07-019316-9). McGraw.

Elonka, Stephen M., jt. auth. see Higgins, Alex.

Elonka, Stephen M., jt. auth. see Moore, Arthur H.

Elorza. Matematicas para Ciencias del Comportamiento. 300p. (Span.). 1983. pap. text ed. write for info. (ISBN 0-06-310700-7, Pub. by HarLA Mexico). Har-Row.

Elphick, jt. ed. see Walters, A.

El-Rayyes, Riad. Guerrillas for Palestine. LC 76-15869. 1976. 22.50 (ISBN 0-312-35280-8). St Martin.

Elrod, J. McRee. Choice of Main & Added Entries: Updated for Use with AACR2. 3rd ed. LC 80-23724. (Modern Library Practices Ser.: No. 4). 90p. 1980. pap. text ed. 6.50 (ISBN 0-8108-1339-4); pap. text ed. 32.50, 5 Vol. Set. Scarecrow.

--Choice of Subject Headings. 3rd ed. LC 80-23719. (Modern Library Practices Ser.: No. 5). 1980. pap. text ed. 6.50 (ISBN 0-686-86726-2); pap. text ed. 32.50, 5 Vol. Set. Scarecrow.

--Classification: For Use with LC or Dewey. 3rd ed. LC 80-23718. (Modern Library Practices Ser.: No. 3). 87p. 1980. pap. text ed. 6.50 (ISBN 0-8108-1338-6); pap. text ed. 32.50, 5 Vol. Set. Scarecrow.

--Construction & Adaption of the Unit Card. 3rd ed. LC 80-18903. (Modern Library Practices Ser.: No. 1). 80p. 1980. pap. text ed. 6.50 (ISBN 0-8108-1336-X); pap. text ed. 32.50, 5 Vol. Set. Scarecrow.

--Filing in the Public Catalogue & Shelf List. 3rd ed. LC 80-23723. (Modern Library Practices Ser.: No. 2). 89p. 1981. pap. text ed. 13.50 (ISBN 0-8108-1337-8); pap. text ed. 32.50, 5 Vol. Set. Scarecrow.

Elrod, Mavis. American Colonial Life. (Social Studies). 24p. (gr. 5-9). 1979. wkbk. 5.00 (ISBN 0-8209-0248-9, SS-15). ESP.

Elrod, Mavis S. Energy & Man. (Science Ser.). 24p. (gr. 5-9). 1976. wkbk. 5.00 (ISBN 0-8209-0148-2, S-10). ESP.

ELS International. New Ways to English, 3 bks. 1974. pap. text ed. 4.75 ea.; Student Text I. pap. text ed. Avail. (ISBN 0-89318-001-7); Student Text II. pap. text ed. Avail (ISBN 0-89318-002-5); Student Text III. pap. text ed. avail (ISBN 0-89318-003-3); 5.50 (ISBN 0-89318-000-9); Cassettes I 60.00 (ISBN 0-89318-004-1); Cassettes 2 60.00 (ISBN 0-89318-005-X); Cassettes 3 60.00 (ISBN 0-89318-006-8). ELS Intl.

El-Sadat, Anwar. My Testament. LC 81-47672. (A Cornelia & Michael Bessie Bk.). 368p. Date not set. price not set (ISBN 0-06-039004-2, HarpT). Har-Row. Postponed.

Elsasser, Albert B., jt. auth. see Heizer, Robert F.

Elsbree, Langdon, et al. The Heath Handbook of Composition. 10th ed. 560p. 1981. text ed. 11.95 (ISBN 0-669-03352-9); pap. text ed. 8.95 (ISBN 0-669-03353-7); instr's guide with tests 1.95 (ISBN 0-669-03356-1); wkbk. 6.95 (ISBN 0-669-03456-8); answer key to wkbk. avail. (ISBN 0-669-04701-5); diagnostic achievementtests avail. (ISBN 0-669-03355-3). Heath.

--Heath's Brief Handbook of Usage. 9th ed. 1977. pap. text ed. 8.95x (ISBN 0-669-00588-6). Heath.

Elsby, F. H. Marketing Cases. LC 70-122006. 1970. o.s.i 27.00 (ISBN 0-08-015784-X); pap. text ed. 13.25 (ISBN 0-08-015783-1). Pergamon.

Else, Gerald F., tr. see Aristotle.

Elsen, Albert E. The Partial Figure in Modern Sculpture, from Rodin to 1969. LC 73-106903. (Illus.). 1969. pap. 10.00 (ISBN 0-912298-03-0); pap. 8.00 (ISBN 0-912298-04-9). Baltimore Mus.

Elsen, Albert E., ed. Rodin Rediscovered. LC 81-9576. (Illus.). pap. 14.95 (ISBN 0-686-81955-1). Natl Gallery Art.

Elsgolc, L. E. Calculus of Variations. 1962. text ed. write for info. o.p. (ISBN 0-08-009554-2). Pergamon.

El-Shaarawi, A. H., ed. Time Series Methods in Hydrosciences: Proceedings of the International Conference, Burlington, Ontario, Canada, October 6-8, 1981. (Developments in Water Science Ser.: No. 17). 614p. 1982. 85.00 (ISBN 0-444-42102-5). Elsevier.

El-Shafie, Mahmoud A., jt. ed. see Dorner, Peter.

El-Shakhs, Salah S., jt. auth. see Lutz, Jesse G.

El-Shamy, Hasan M., ed. Folktales of Egypt. LC 79-9316. (Folktales of the World Ser.). 1980. lib. bdg. 25.00x (ISBN 0-226-20624-6); pap. 8.95 (ISBN 0-226-20625-4). U of Chicago Pr.

El Shazly, E. M., compiled by. Geology of Uranium & Thorium. (Bibliographical Ser.: No. 4). 134p. 1962. pap. write for info. (ISBN 92-0-044062-2, STI/PUB/21/4, IAEA). Unipub.

Elson, Alex, et al. Illinois & Federal Civil Practice Forms, 2 Vols. rev. ed. 1965. Set. 47.50 o.p. (ISBN 0-672-81433-1, Bobbs-Merrill Law). Michie-Bobbs.

Elson, C. M., tr. see Rozanov, Y. A.

Elson, Charles L., jt. auth. see Ray, Charles M.

Elson, Diane. A Christmas Book. (Illus.). 104p. (gr. 6 up). 1982. 11.00 (ISBN 0-437-37703-2, Pub. by World's Work). David & Charles.

--A Country Book. (Illus.). 104p. 1983. 13.95 (ISBN 0-437-37704-0, Pub. by World's Work). David & Charles.

Elson, Lawrence. Its Your Body. (Illus.). 576p. 1973. text ed. 32.50 (ISBN 0-07-019299-5, C); instructor's manual 15.00 (ISBN 0-07-019303-7). McGraw.

Elson, Lawrence, jt. auth. see Kapit, Wynn.

Elson, Louis C. Elson's Music Dictionary. LC 70-173097. xii, 306p. 1972. Repr. of 1905 ed. 37.00x (ISBN 0-8103-3268-X). Gale.

--The National Music of America & Its Sources. LC 70-159950. (Illus.). 1975. Repr. of 1911 ed. 37.00x (ISBN 0-8103-4039-9). Gale.

Elson, Mark. Concepts of Programming Languages. LC 72-94972. (Illus.). 333p. 1973. text ed. 22.95 (ISBN 0-574-17922-4, 13-0922); instr's guide avail. (ISBN 0-574-17923-2, 13-0923). SRA.

--Data Structures. LC 75-1451. 450p. 1975. text ed. 23.95 (ISBN 0-574-18020-6, 13-4020). SRA.

Elson, Robert, et al. Prelude to War. LC 76-10024. (World War II). (Illus.). (gr. 6 up). 1976. PLB 19.92 (ISBN 0-8094-2451-7, Pub by Time-Life). Silver.

Elspass, Margy L. Tips & Notes for the Artist, Bk. 1. Elspass, Ralph W., ed. LC 79-93059. (Illus.). 100p. 1980. pap. 10.00 (ISBN 0-935798-00-5). RaMar.

Elspass, Ralph W., ed. see Elspass, Margy L.

Elstein, Max & Sparks, Richard. Intrauterine Contraception, Vol. 1. Briggs, Michael, ed. (Annual Research Reviews Ser.). 1978. 12.00 (ISBN 0-88831-021-8). Eden Pr.

Elster, J. Ulysses & the Sirens. LC 78-15444. 1979. 29.95 (ISBN 0-521-22388-1). Cambridge U Pr.

Elster, Jon. Explaining Technical Change: A Case Study in the Philosophy of Science. LC 82-9702. (Studies in Rationality & Social Change). (Illus.). 304p. Date not set. 39.50 (ISBN 0-521-24920-1); pap. 11.95 (ISBN 0-521-27072-3). Cambridge U Pr.

--Logic & Society: Contradictions & Possible Worlds. LC 77-9550. 1978. 49.95 (ISBN 0-471-99549-5, Pub. by Wiley-Interscience). Wiley.

Elstob & Barber, trs. Russian Folktales. 213p. 1974. 12.95 o.p. (ISBN 0-7135-1653-4). Transatlantic.

Elston, C. A., jt. auth. see Whitson, M. E.

Elstun, Esther N. Richard Beer-Hoffmann: His Life & Work. Strelka, Joseph P., ed. LC 82-14990. (Penn State Studies in German Literature). 225p. 1983. 17.95x (ISBN 0-271-00335-9). Pa St U Pr.

Eltherington, L. G., jt. auth. see Barnes, C. D.

Elting, John R. Battle for Scandinavia. LC 81-5698. (World War II Ser.). 19.92 (ISBN 0-8094-3396-6). Silver.

Elting, John R. & Cragg, Dan. A Dictionary of Soldier Talk. 480p. 1983. 24.95 (ISBN 0-686-83680-4, ScribT). Scribner.

Elting, Mary. Answer Book. (Illus.). (gr. 4-6). 1959. 5.95 (ISBN 0-448-02864-6, G&D). Putnam Pub Group.

--Answers & More Answers. (Illus.). (gr. 4-6). 1961. 5.95 (ISBN 0-448-04410-2, G&D). Putnam Pub Group.

--Gorilla Mysteries. (Illus.). 64p. (gr. 1-9). 1981. 5.95 (ISBN 0-448-47488-3, G&D). Putnam Pub Group.

Elting, Mary & Folsom, Franklin. Still More Answers. (Illus.). (gr. 4-6). 1970. 5.95 (ISBN 0-448-02812-3, G&D). Putnam Pub Group.

Elting, Mary & Goodman, Ann. Dinosaur Mysteries. (Illus.). 64p. (gr. 1-7). 1980. write for info. (ISBN 0-448-47487-5, G&D). Putnam Pub Group.

Elting, Mary & Wyler, Rose. The Answer Book about You. (Illus.). 1980. 6.95 (ISBN 0-448-16566-X, G&D); PLB 11.95 (ISBN 0-448-13191-9). Putnam Pub Group.

--A New Answer Book. LC 77-71531. (Illus.). (gr. 3-8). 1977. 6.95 (ISBN 0-448-12899-3, G&D); PLB 11.85 (ISBN 0-448-13418-7). Putnam Pub Group.

Eltis, W. A. Economic Growth: Analysis & Policy. (Orig.). 1966. text ed. 5.50x o.p. (ISBN 0-09-079462-1, Hutchinson U Lib); pap. text ed. 2.75x o.p. (ISBN 0-09-079463-X, Hutchinson U Lib). Humanities.

Eltis, Walter, jt. auth. see Bacon, Robert.

El Tom, M. E. Developing Mathematics in Third World Countries. (North Holland Mathematics Studies: Vol. 33). 1979. 40.50 (ISBN 0-444-85260-3, North Holland). Elsevier.

Elton, C. S. The Ecology of Animals. 3rd ed. 1977. pap. 6.95 (ISBN 0-412-20390-1, Pub. by Chapman & Hall). Methuen Inc.

Elton, E. J. & Gruber, M. J. Portfolio Analysis a Practical Approach. LC 80-19517. 450p. 1981. text ed. 29.95 o.p. (ISBN 0-471-04690-6). Wiley.

Elton, Edwain J. & Gruber, Martin J. Finance As a Dynamic Process. (Foundations of Finance Ser.). (Illus.). 176p. 1975. ref. ed. 14.95 o.p. (ISBN 0-13-314690-1); pap. text ed. 11.95 o.p. (ISBN 0-13-314682-0). P-H.

Elton, Edwin J. & Gruber, Martin J. Modern Portfolio Theory & Investment Analysis. LC 80-19517. (Illus.). 553p. 1981. 26.50 (ISBN 0-471-04690-6). Wiley.

Elton, G., ed. Annual Bibliography of British & Irish History 1981. 196p. 1982. text ed. 37.50x (ISBN 0-391-02728-X, Pub. by Harvester England). Humanities.

Elton, G. R. England: Twelve Hundred to Sixteen Forty. LC 69-63003. (Sources of History Ser.). 255p. 1969. pap. 4.95x (ISBN 0-8014-9123-1, CP123). Cornell U Pr.

--England under the Tudors. 2nd ed. (Illus.). 1974. text ed. 29.95x o.p. (ISBN 0-416-78720-7); pap. 15.95x (ISBN 0-416-70690-8). Methuen Inc.

--Essays on Tudor & Stuart Politics & Government: Vol. 3, Papers & Reviews 1973-1981. LC 73-79305. 512p. Date not set. 49.50 (ISBN 0-521-24893-0). Cambridge U Pr.

--Reformation Europe, 1517-1559. (History of Europe Ser.). 1968. pap. 6.95xi o.p. (ISBN 0-06-131270-3, TB1270, Torch). Har-Row.

Elton, Gelfrey R. Renaissance & Reformation, Thirteen Hundred to Sixteen Forty-Eight. 3rd ed. (Ideas & Institutions in Western Civilization: Vol. 3). 1976. pap. text ed. 12.95x (ISBN 0-02-332840-1). Macmillan.

Elton, Geoffrey R. Policy & Police: The Enforcement of the Reformation in the Age of Cromwell. LC 79-172831. 400p. 1972. 47.50 (ISBN 0-521-08383-4). Cambridge U Pr.

--Reform & Renewal, Thomas Cromwell & the Common Weal. (Wiles Lectures, 1972). 230p. 1973. 29.50 o.p. (ISBN 0-521-20054-7); pap. 9.95 (ISBN 0-521-09809-2). Cambridge U Pr.

--Tudor Constitution: Documents & Commentary. (Orig.). 1960. 49.50 (ISBN 0-521-04891-5); pap. 19.95 (ISBN 0-521-09120-9, 120). Cambridge U Pr.

--The Tudor Constitution: Documents & Commentary. 2nd ed. LC 81-15216. 522p. 1982. 59.50 (ISBN 0-521-24506-0); pap. 17.50 (ISBN 0-521-28757-X). Cambridge U Pr.

Elton, Martin C., et al see Lazer, Ellen A.

Elton, O. Tennyson & Matthew Arnold. LC 75-163127. (Studies in Comparative Literature, No. 35). 1971. Repr. of 1924 ed. lib. bdg. 48.95x (ISBN 0-8383-1305-1). Haskell.

Elton, W. R. & Neuschloss, G. Shakespeare's World: Renaissance Intellectual Contexts: a Selective Annotated Guide. LC 76-52681. (Reference Library of the Humanities Ser.: Vol. 83). 1979. lib. bdg. 40.00 o.s.i. (ISBN 0-8240-9890-0). Garland Pub.

Elton, William. Aesthetics & Language. 1967. 5.75 o.p. (ISBN 0-8022-0451-1). Philos Lib.

Elton, Y. R., ed. see Loades, D. M.

El Torky, Mohamed A., jt. auth. see Correa, Hector.

Elvander, Nile, jt. ed. see Heidenheimer, Arnold J.

Elvee, Richard Q., ed. Mind in Nature: New Concepts of Mind in Science & Philosophy; The Nobel Conference XVII. LC 82-48155. 176p. (Orig.). 1983. pap. 7.64i (ISBN 0-06-250285-9, HarpR). Har-Row.

Elvin, Charles N. Hand-Book of Mottoes: Borne by the Nobility, Gentry, Cities, Public Companies. LC 79-122638. (Illus.). 1971. Repr. of 1860 ed. 30.00x (ISBN 0-8103-3387-2). Gale.

Elvin, Lionel. The Place of Commonsense in Educational Thought. (Unwin Educational Books). 1977. text ed. 22.50x (ISBN 0-04-370078-0); pap. text ed. 8.95x (ISBN 0-04-370079-9). Allen Unwin.

Elvin, Margo, jt. auth. see McLean, Gary N.

Elving, P., jt. auth. see Kolthoff, I.

Elving, P. J., jt. auth. see Kolthoff, I. M.

Elving, Philip J., jt. auth. see Kolthoff, I. M.

Elvin-Lewis, P. F., jt. auth. see Lewis, Walter H.

El-Wakil, M. M. Nuclear Power Engineering. (Nuclear Engineering Ser). 1962. text ed. 40.00 (ISBN 0-07-019300-2, C). McGraw.

Elward, James, jt. auth. see Van Slyke, Helen.

Elward, Margaret & Whiteway, Catherine E. Encyclopedia of Guinea Pigs. (Illus.). 224p. 1980. 12.95 (ISBN 0-87666-916-X, H-975). TFH Pubns.

Elwell, Ellen S. & Levenson, Edward R., eds. Jewish Women's Studies Guide (College Level) 112p. (Orig.). 1982. pap. 6.95 (ISBN 0-9602036-5-6). Biblio NY.

Elwell, Walter, intro. by. Bagster's Bible Handbook. 264p. 1983. Repr. 9.95 (ISBN 0-8007-1334-6). Revell.

Elwell-Sutton, L. P., ed. Bibliographical Guide to Iran. LC 82-22748. 300p. 1983. text ed. 35.00x (ISBN 0-389-20339-4). B&N Imports.

Elwin, Malcolm. Life of Llewelyn Powys. 300p. 1982. 39.00x (ISBN 0-686-82400-8, Pub. by Redcliffe England). State Mutual Bk.

Elwood, J. Harold, jt. auth. see Elwood, J. Mark.

Elwood, J. Mark & Elwood, J. Harold. Epidemiology of Anencephalus & Spina Bifida. (Illus.). 1980. text ed. 75.00x (ISBN 0-19-261220-4). Oxford U Pr.

Elwood, Roger. The Other Side of Tomorrow: Original Science Fiction Stories About Young People of the Future. (gr. 6 up). 1973. 3.95 o.p. (ISBN 0-394-82468-7); PLB 5.99 (ISBN 0-394-92468-1). Random.

Elwood, Roger, ed. The Extraterrestrials. LC 74-7667. 160p. Date not set. 5.95 (ISBN 0-8255-3054-7). Macrae. Postponed.

--Night of the Sphinx & Other Stories. LC 73-21482. (Science Fiction Bks). Orig. Title: When the Cold Came & Other Stories. (Illus.). (gr. 4-8). 1974. PLB 3.95g (ISBN 0-8225-0954-7). Lerner Pubns.

Elwood, Roger & Ghidalia, Vic, eds. Androids, Time Machines, & Blue Giraffes. 384p. 1973. 6.95 o.s.i. (ISBN 0-695-80369-7). Follett.

Elwood, Roger, ed. see Binder, Eando, et al.

Elwood, Roger, ed. see Giles, Gordon, et al.

Elwood, Roger, ed. see Holly, J. Hunter, et al.

Elwood, Roger, ed. see Lytle, B. J., et al.

Elwood, Roger, ed. see Orgill, Michael, et al.

Elwood, Roger, ed. see Zebrowski, George, et al.

Elwork, Amiram & Sales, Bruce D. Making Jury Instructions Understandable. 300p. 1982. 35.00 (ISBN 0-87215-450-5). Michie-Bobbs.

Elworthy, K. D. Stochastic Differential Equations on Manifolds. LC 82-4426. (London Mathematical Society Lecture Note Ser.: No. 70). 326p. 1982. pap. 27.50 (ISBN 0-521-28767-7). Cambridge U Pr.

Ely, Barbara R. The Gypsum Throne. (Shield Romance Ser.). 1983. pap. 6.95 (ISBN 0-932906-11-7). Pan-Am Publishing Co.

Ely, Evelyn & Hughes, Phyllis. Ojos de Dios. (Illus.). 1972. pap. 2.25 (ISBN 0-89013-056-6). Museum NM Pr.

Ely, R. L., jt. auth. see Gardner, R. P.

Ely, Ralph L., Jr., jt. auth. see Gardner, Robin P.

Ely, Silas J., jt. auth. see Betts, Richard M.

Ely, V. K. Organization for Marketing. (Occupational Manuals & Projects in Marketing). 1971. 5.96 o.p. (ISBN 0-07-019305-3, G); teacher's manual 3.00 o.p. (ISBN 0-07-019306-1). McGraw.

Ely, Vivian & Barnes, Michael. Starting Your Own Marketing Business. 2nd ed. Dorr, Eugene, ed. (Occupational Manuals & Projects Marketing Ser.). (Illus.). (gr. 11-12). 1978. pap. text ed. 7.32 (ISBN 0-07-019307-X, G); teacher's manual & key 4.50 (ISBN 0-07-019308-8). McGraw.

Elyot, Thomas. Bibliotheca Eliotae. Cooper, Thomas, ed. LC 74-23334. 1170p. 1975. Repr. of 1548 ed. lib. bdg. 100.00x o.p. (ISBN 0-8201-1146-5). Schol Facsimiles.

--The Book Named the Governor. 1975. Repr. of 1962 ed. 9.95x (ISBN 0-460-00227-9, Evman). Biblio Dist.

--Castel of Helthe. LC 37-11679. Repr. of 1541 ed. 30.00x (ISBN 0-8201-1176-7). Schol Facsimiles.

--Four Political Treatises, Fifteen Thirty-Three to Fifteen Forty-One. LC 67-10273. 1967. 50.00x (ISBN 0-8201-1015-9). Schol Facsimiles.

Elytis, Odysseus. The Sovereign Sun: Selected Poems. Friar, Kimon, tr. from Greek. LC 74-77777. 200p. 1974. 19.95 (ISBN 0-87722-019-0). Temple U Pr.

--The Sovereign Sun: Selected Poems. Friar, Kimon, tr. from Greek. 200p. 1979. pap. 9.95 (ISBN 0-87722-113-8). Temple U Pr.

Elze, Karl. William Shakespeare: A Literary Biography. Schmitz, L. Dora, tr. 587p. 1982. Repr. of 1888 ed. lib. bdg. 50.00 (ISBN 0-89760-214-5). Telegraph Bks.

El Zeini, Hanny, jt. auth. see Sety, Omm.

Elzey, Freeman F. A First Reader in Statistics. 2nd ed. LC 74-83225. 1974. pap. text ed. 6.95 (ISBN 0-8185-0140-5). Brooks-Cole.

--An Introduction to Statistical Methods in the Behavioral Sciences. LC 76-9924. (Brooks-Cole Series in Statistics). 1976. pap. text ed. 12.95 (ISBN 0-8185-0194-4); solutions manual avail. (ISBN 0-685-67086-4). Brooks-Cole.

--A Programmed Introduction to Statistics. 2nd ed. LC 79-161489. 385p. (Orig.). 1971. pap. text ed. 13.95 (ISBN 0-8185-0018-2); test items avail. (ISBN 0-685-23470-3); instructor's manual avail. (ISBN 0-685-23471-1). Brooks-Cole.

Elzinga, Kenneth G., jt. auth. see Breit, William.

Elzinga, Kenneth G., ed. Economics: A Reader. 3rd ed. 1978. pap. text ed. 12.50 scp (ISBN 0-06-041912-1, HarpC). Har-Row.

Elzinga, Richard J. Fundamentals of Entomology. 2nd ed. (Illus.). 464p. 1981. text ed. 24.95 (ISBN 0-13-338194-3). P-H.

Eman, Virginia, ed. see Conference on Communication, Language & Sex, 1st Annual.

Emans, S. J. & Goldstein, Donald P. Pediatric & Adolescent Gynecology. 1977. text ed. 17.95 o.p. (ISBN 0-316-23400-1). Little.

Emans, S. Jean & Goldstein, Donald P. Pediatric & Adolescent Gynecology. 2nd ed. (Little, Brown Clinical Pediatrics Ser.). 1982. text ed. 28.00 (ISBN 0-316-23402-8). Little.

Emants, Marcellus. A Posthumous Confession. Coetzee, J. M., tr. (International Studies & Translations Program). 1975. lib. bdg. 9.95 (ISBN 0-8057-8152-8, Twayne). G K Hall.

Emanuel, Edward F. Action & Idea: The Roots of Entertainment. 120p. 1982. pap. text ed. 9.95 (ISBN 0-8403-2845-1). Kendall-Hunt.

Emanuel, James A. Langston Hughes. (United States Authors Ser.). 1967. lib. bdg. 11.95 (ISBN 0-8057-0388-8, Twayne). G K Hall.

Emanuel, N. M. & Evseenko, D. S. Clinical Oncology: A Quantitative Approach. Abramson, J. H., ed. Kaner, N., tr. from Rus. LC 73-16436. 272p. 1974. 64.95x o.s.i. (ISBN 0-470-23891-7). Halsted Pr.

Emanuel, N. M. & Knorre, D. G. Chemical Kinetics (Homogenous Reactions) Slutzkin, D., ed. Kondor, R., tr. from Rus. LC 73-12689. 447p. 1973. text ed. 43.95 o.s.i. (ISBN 0-470-23890-9). Halsted Pr.

Emanuel, N. M., et al. Oxidation of Organic Compounds: Solvent Effects in Radical Reactions. 350p. 1983. 58.01 (ISBN 0-08-022067-3). Pergamon.

Emanuel, Pericles & Leff, Edward. Introduction to Feedback Control Systems. (Electrical Engineering). (Illus.). 1979. text ed. 29.95 (ISBN 0-07-019310-X, C); solutions manual 17.00 (ISBN 0-07-019311-8). McGraw.

Emanuel, W. D. Asahi Pentax Guide. 21st ed. (Camera Guide Ser.). (Illus.). 1979. pap. 3.95 (ISBN 0-240-44874-X). Focal Pr.

--Canon Reflex Guide. 7th ed. (Camera Guide Ser.). (Illus.). 1981. pap. 3.95 (ISBN 0-240-50659-6). Focal Pr.

--Canonet Guide. 7th ed. (Camera Guide Ser.). (Illus.). 1979. pap. 3.95 (ISBN 0-240-44974-6). Focal Pr.

--Exacta 35mm Guide. 12th ed. (Camera Guide Ser.). 1974. pap. 3.95 (ISBN 0-240-44780-8). Focal Pr.

--Konica Reflex Guide. 6th ed. (Camera Guide Ser.). (Illus.). 80p. 1978. pap. 3.95 (ISBN 0-240-50690-1). Focal Pr.

--Konica 35 Millimeter Compact Guide. 2nd ed. (Camera Guide Ser.). (Illus.). 100p. 1978. pap. 3.95 (ISBN 0-240-50828-9). Focal Pr.

--Leica Guide. 45th ed. (Illus.). 130p. 1979. pap. 3.95 (ISBN 0-240-44848-0). Focal Pr.

--Mamiya Sekor Guide. 4th ed. (Camera Guide Ser.). 70p. 1980. pap. 3.95 o.p. (ISBN 0-240-50734-7). Focal Pr.

--Mamiya Sekor Guide. 5th ed. (Camera Guide Ser.). (Illus.). 1980. pap. 3.95 o.p. (ISBN 0-240-51063-1). Focal Pr.

--Minolta SLR Guide. 12th ed. (Camera Guide Ser.). (Illus.). 80p. 1979. pap. 3.95 (ISBN 0-240-38788-0). Focal Pr.

--Minox Guide. 10th ed. (Camera Guide Ser.). (Illus.). 90p. 1979. pap. 3.95 (ISBN 0-240-44864-2). Focal Pr.

--Nikkormat Guide. 8th ed. (Camera Guide Ser.). (Illus.). 96p. 1977. pap. 3.95 (ISBN 0-240-50672-3). Focal Pr.

--Nikon F Guide. 7th ed. (Camera Guide Ser.). (Illus.). 80p. 1979. pap. 3.95 (ISBN 0-240-50666-9). Focal Pr.

--Olympus Compact 35mm Guide. 3rd ed. (Camera Guide Ser.). 1980. 3.95 (ISBN 0-240-50827-0). Focal Pr.

--Olympus OM-One Guide. 5th ed. (Camera Guide Ser.). (Illus.). 96p. 1979. pap. 3.95 (ISBN 0-240-50792-4). Focal Pr.

--Praktica-Prakticamat Guide. 7th ed. (Illus.). 1974. pap. 3.95 (ISBN 0-240-44777-8). Focal Pr.

--Rollei 35mm Guide. 4th ed. (Camera Guide Ser.). (Illus.). 75p. 1979. pap. 3.95 (ISBN 0-240-50696-0). Focal Pr.

--Rolleiflex Twin Lens Guide. 41st ed. (Camera Guide Ser.). 1978. pap. 3.95 (ISBN 0-240-44910-X). Focal Pr.

--Toda la Fotografia En un Solo Libro. Cuni, Antonio, tr. from Eng. 228p. (Span.). 1975. 8.95 o.p. (ISBN 0-240-51098-4, Pub. by Ediciones Spain). Focal Pr.

--Yashica Twin Lens Reflex Guide. 8th ed. (Camera Guide Ser.). 1979. pap. 3.95 (ISBN 0-240-50653-7). Focal Pr.

--Yashica 35mm Guide. 5th ed. (Camera Guide Ser.). 72p. 1978. pap. 3.95 (ISBN 0-240-38817-8). Focal Pr.

Emanuels, George. Ygnacio Valley Eighteen Thirty-Four to Nineteen Seventy. (Illus.). 1982. 14.95. Diablo Bks.

Emanuelsen, Kathy L. & Densmore, Mary J. Acute Respiratory Care. LC 81-50072. (Series in Critical Care Nursing). (Illus.). 216p. (Orig.). 1981. pap. text ed. 12.95. Wiley.

Emark, Donald R., jt. ed. see Erickson, Joan G.

Emary, A. B. Handbook of Carpentry & Joinery. LC 81-50984. (Illus., Orig.). 1981. pap. 9.95 (ISBN 0-8069-7536-9). Sterling.

Ember, Carol R. & Ember, Melvin. Anthropology. 3rd ed. (Illus.). 592p. 1981. text ed. 22.95 (ISBN 0-13-037002-9). P-H.

--Cultural Anthropology. 3rd ed. (Illus.). 416p. 1981. pap. text ed. 17.95 (ISBN 0-13-195230-7); workbook 8.95 (ISBN 0-13-195263-3). P-H.

Ember, Melvin. Marriage, Family, & Kinship: Comparative Studies of Social Organization. LC 82-83702. 425p. 1983. 30.00 (ISBN 0-87536-113-7); pap. 15.00 (ISBN 0-87536-114-5). HRAFP.

Ember, Melvin, jt. auth. see Ember, Carol R.

Emberley, Barbara. Drummer Hoff. (Illus.). (ps-3). 1967. PLB 9.95x (ISBN 0-13-220822-9); pap. 3.95 (ISBN 0-13-220855-5). P-H.

Emberley, Ed. Drawing Book of Animals. (Illus.). 32p. (gr. 1-3). 1970. 6.95 (ISBN 0-316-23597-0). Little.

--Ed Emberley's Drawing Book: Make a World. LC 70-154962. (gr. 2 up). 1972. 6.95g (ISBN 0-316-23598-9). Little.

--Ed Emberley's Drawing Book of Animals. LC 75-107232. (Illus.). (gr. 2 up). 1970. 6.95 (ISBN 0-316-23597-0). Little.

--Ed Emberley's Great Thumbprint Drawing Book. (Illus.). (gr. 1 up). 1977. 6.95g (ISBN 0-316-23613-6). Little.

--Ed Emberley's Science Flip books: Six Nature Adventures. (Illus.). 128p. (gr. k-5). 1983. of 3 7.95 set (ISBN 0-316-23616-0); 6-copy counter display 47.70 (ISBN 0-316-23403-6). Little.

Embery, Joan & Demong, Denise. My Wild World. 1980. 14.95 o.s.i. (ISBN 0-440-05742-6). Delacorte.

Embery, Joan & Lucaire, Ed. Joan Embery's Collection of Amazing Animal Facts. (Illus.). 224p. 1983. 14.95 (ISBN 0-440-04224-0). Delacorte.

Embleton, C. & King, C. A. Glacial & Periglacial Morphology, 2 vols. 2nd ed. Incl. Vol. 1. Glacial Geomorphology. LC 75-14188. pap. 24.95x o.s.i. (ISBN 0-470-23893-3); Vol. 2. Periglacial Geomorphology. LC 75-14187. pap. 17.95x o.s.i. (ISBN 0-470-23895-X). 1975. pap. Halsted Pr.

Embleton, Clifford & Thornes, John, eds. Process in Geomorphology. LC 79-18747. 436p. 1979. 54.95x o.s.i. (ISBN 0-470-26807-7); pap. 24.95x o.s.i. (ISBN 0-470-26808-5). Halsted Pr.

Emblidge, David, ed. The Third Berkshire Anthology. (Illus.). 208p. (Orig.). 1982. pap. 7.50 (ISBN 0-9609540-0-7). Berkshire Writ.

Embree, Ainslie, ed. Pakistan's Western Borderlands: The Transformation of a Political Order. LC 76-43386. 1977. 11.95 (ISBN 0-89089-074-9). Carolina Acad Pr.

Embree, Ainslie T., ed. The Hindu Tradition. 448p. 1972. pap. 4.95 (ISBN 0-394-71702-3, V696, Vin). Random.

Embree, Harland D. Organic Chemistry: Brief Course. 1983. text ed. 23.95x (ISBN 0-673-15435-1). Scott F.

Embree, John F. Acculturation Among the Japanese of Kona, Hawaii. LC 43-1209. (American Anthropological Association Memoirs). pap. 20.00 (ISBN 0-527-00558-4). Kraus Repr.

--The Japanese Nation, a Social Survey. LC 75-8766. (Illus.). 308p. 1975. Repr. of 1945 ed. lib. bdg. 20.00x (ISBN 0-8371-8117-8, EMJN). Greenwood.

Embry, Joan. My Wild World. 1981. pap. 3.50 (ISBN 0-440-15941-5). Dell.

Embry, Lynn. Motivation Marvels. (gr. k-6). 1981. 6.95 (ISBN 0-916456-99-4, GA 242). Good Apple.

--Super Sheets III. (gr. 3-6). 1982. 5.95 (ISBN 0-86653-055-X, GA 408). Good Apple.

--Super Sheets IV. (gr. 3-8). 1982. 5.95 (ISBN 0-86653-075-4, GA 409). Good Apple.

Embry, Mike. Basketball in the Blue Grass State: The Championship Teams. LC 82-83924. (Illus.). 192p. (Orig.). 1983. pap. 7.95 (ISBN 0-88011-120-8). Leisure Pr.

Embry, P. G., jt. auth. see Hey, M. H.

Embury, David A. Fine Art of Mixing Drinks. rev. ed. LC 58-5572. (Illus.). 1948. pap. 4.95 (ISBN 0-385-09683-6, Dolp). Doubleday.

Emden, Cecil S. Pepys Himself. LC 80-17177. xi, 146p. 1980. Repr. of 1963 ed. lib. bdg. 18.50x (ISBN 0-313-22607-5, EMPH). Greenwood.

Emecheta, Buchi. In the Ditch. 128p. 1980. pap. 4.95 (ISBN 0-8052-8010-3, Pub. by Allison & Busby England). Schocken.

--The Joys of Motherhood. LC 78-24640. 1979. 8.95 (ISBN 0-8076-0914-5); pap. 4.95 (ISBN 0-8076-0950-1). Braziller.

--The Moonlight Bride. LC 82-17816. 77p. (gr. 6-10). 1983. 7.95 (ISBN 0-8076-1062-3); pap. 4.95 (ISBN 0-8076-1063-1). Braziller.

--Nowhere to Play. LC 80-40596. 72p. (gr. 3-8). 1980. 6.95 (ISBN 0-8052-8058-8, Pub. by Allison & Busby England). Schocken.

--Second-Class Citizen. 175p. 1983. pap. 4.95 (ISBN 0-8076-1066-6). Braziller.

--The Wrestling Match. LC 82-177750. 74p. (gr. 6-10). 7.95 (ISBN 0-8076-1060-7); pap. 4.95 (ISBN 0-8076-1061-5). Braziller.

Emeleus, H. J. & Sharpe, A. G., eds. Advances in Inorganic Chemistry & Radiochemistry, Vol. 25. 340p. 1982. 56.00 (ISBN 0-12-023625-7); lib ed. 73.00 (ISBN 0-12-023690-7); microfiche 39.50 (ISBN 0-12-023691-5). Acad Pr.

Emeleus, H. J., jt. ed. see Sharpe, A. G.

Emelus, K. G. & Woolsey, G. A., eds. Discharges in Electronegative Gases. 162p. 1970. write for info. (ISBN 0-85066-035-1, Pub. by Taylor & Francis). Intl Pubns Serv.

Emeneau, Murray B & Van Nooten, B. A. Sanskrit Sandhi & Exercises. rev. ed. 1952. pap. 2.75x o.p. (ISBN 0-520-00384-5, CAMPUS13). U of Cal Pr.

Emeneau, Murray B., compiled by. Union List of Printed Indic Texts & Translations in American Libraries. 1935. pap. 40.00 (ISBN 0-527-02681-6). Kraus Repr.

Emerick, Lon L. A Casebook of Diagnosis & Evaluation in Speech Pathology. (Illus.). 224p. 1981. pap. text ed. 14.95 (ISBN 0-13-117358-8). P-H.

Emerick, Lon L. & Hatten, John T. Diagnosis & Evaluation in Speech Pathology. 2nd ed. (Illus.). 1979. ref. ed. 23.95 (ISBN 0-13-208512-7). P-H.

Emerick, Robert H. Handbook of Mechanical Specifications for Buildings & Plants. 1966. 27.50 o.p. (ISBN 0-07-019313-4, P&RB). McGraw.

--Heating Handbook: A Manual of Standards, Codes & Methods. (Illus.). 1964. 7.95 o.p. (ISBN 0-07-019312-6, P&RB). McGraw.

--Troubleshooters Handbook for Mechanical Systems. LC 68-28413. (Illus.). 1969. 45.00 o.p. (ISBN 0-07-019314-2, P&RB). McGraw.

Emerson & Johnson, G. M., eds. The Journals & Miscellaneous Notebooks of Ralph Waldo Emerson: 1866-1882, Vol. 16. (Illus.). 624p. 1982. text ed. 45.00x (ISBN 0-674-48479-7). Harvard U Pr.

Emerson, et al. Political & Civil Rights in the United States: Student Edition, Vol. 1. 1980. pap. 8.95 suppl. o.p. (ISBN 0-316-19051-9). Little.

Emerson, Barbara. Leopold II of the Belgians: King of Colonialism. 1979. 26.00x (ISBN 0-312-48012-1). St Martin.

Emerson, Caryl, tr. see Bakhtin, M. M.

Emerson, Connie. How to Make Money Writing Fillers. 252p. 1983. 12.95 (ISBN 0-89879-104-9). Writers Digest.

Emerson, Edward W. Emerson in Concord. LC 79-78149. (Library of Lives & Letters). (Illus.). 1970. Repr. of 1889 ed. 39.00x (ISBN 0-8103-3601-4). Gale.

Emerson, Ellen T. The Life of Jackson Emerson. Hall, G. K., ed. LC 80-14908. (Twayne's American Literary Manuscript Ser.). (Illus.). 269p. 1981. 25.00 o.p. (ISBN 0-8057-9651-7, Twayne). G K Hall.

Emerson, Everett. Puritanism in America. (World Leaders Ser.). 1977. lib. bdg. 11.95 (ISBN 0-8057-7692-3, Twayne). G K Hall.

Emerson, Everett, ed. American Literature, Seventeen Sixty-Four to Seventeen Eighty-Nine: The Revolutionary Years. 320p. 1977. 27.50 (ISBN 0-299-07270-3). U of Wis Pr.

Emerson, Everett H. Captain John Smith. (United States Authors Ser.). lib. bdg. 12.95 (ISBN 0-8057-0676-3, Twayne). G K Hall.

--English Puritanism from John Hooper to John Milton. LC 68-29664. 1968. 18.50 o.p. (ISBN 0-8223-0052-4). Duke.

--John Cotton. (United States Author Ser.). 13.95 (ISBN 0-8057-0160-5, Twayne). G K Hall.

Emerson, James C., ed. The Life of Christ in the Conception & Expression of Chinese & Oriental Artists. (The Great Art Masters of the World Ser.). (Illus.). 117p. 1983. 61.75 (ISBN 0-86650-054-5). Gloucester Art.

Emerson, Julie. The Collectors: Early European Ceramics & Silver. LC 82-60159. (Illus.). 94p. (Orig.). 1982. pap. 12.95 (ISBN 0-932216-08-0). Seattle Art.

Emerson, Kathy L. Wives & Daughters: The Women of Sixteenth Century England. 150p. 1983. price not set (ISBN 0-87875-246-3). Whitston Pub.

Emerson, Nathaniel B. Pele & Hiiaka: A Myth from Hawaii. LC 77-83040. (Illus.). 1978. 15.00 (ISBN 0-8048-1251-9). C E Tuttle.

--Unwritten Literature of Hawaii: The Sacred Songs of the Hula. LC 65-12971. (Illus.). 1965. Repr. pap. 5.50 (ISBN 0-8048-1067-2). C E Tuttle.

Emerson, Oliver F. History of the English Language. LC 70-145520. 1971. Repr. of 1909 ed. 45.00x (ISBN 0-8103-3666-9). Gale.

Emerson, Ralph W. Essays: Second Series. Ferguson, Alfred R. & Carr, Jean F., eds. (Collected Works of Ralph Waldo Emerson Ser.: Vol. III) (Illus.). 320p. 1983. text ed. 25.00x (ISBN 0-674-13990-9, Belknap Pr). Harvard U Pr.

--Journals & Miscellaneous Notebooks of Ralph Waldo Emerson, 16 Vols. Incl. Vol. 1. 1819-1822. Gilman, W. H., et al, eds. 1960. 25.00x (ISBN 0-674-48450-9); Vol. 2. 1822-1826. Gilman, W. H., et al, eds. 1961. 25.00x (ISBN 0-674-48451-7); Vol. 4. 1832-1834. Ferguson, Alfred R., ed. 1964. o.p. (ISBN 0-674-48453-3); Vol. 5. 1835-1838. Sealts, M. M., Jr., ed. 1965. 25.00x (ISBN 0-674-48454-1); Vol. 6. 1824-1838. Orth, Ralph W., ed. 1966. 22.50x (ISBN 0-674-48456-8); Vol. 7. 1838-1842. Plumstead, A. W. & Hayford, Harrison, eds. 1969. 25.00x (ISBN 0-674-48457-6); Vol. 8. 1841-1843. Gilman, W. H. & Parsons, J. E., eds. 1970. 27.50x (ISBN 0-674-48470-3); Vol. 9. 1843-1847. Orth, Ralph H. & Ferguson, Alfred R., eds. 1971. 25.00x (ISBN 0-674-48471-1); Vol. 10. 1847-1848. Sealts, Merton M., Jr., ed. 1973. 30.00x (ISBN 0-674-48473-8); Vol. 11. 1848-1851. Gilman, William H. & Plumstead, A. W., eds. 1975. text ed. 35.00x (ISBN 0-674-48474-6); Vol. 12. 1835-1862. Allardt, Linda, ed. 1976. 37.50x (ISBN 0-674-48475-4); Vol. 13. 525p. 1977. text ed. 35.00 (ISBN 0-674-48476-2); Vol. 14. 523p. 1978. text ed. 37.50x (ISBN 0-674-48477-0); Vol. 15. 1860-1866. 608p. 1982. text ed. 40.00x (ISBN 0-674-48478-9). LC 60-11554. (Illus., Belknap Pr). Harvard U Pr.

--The Portable Emerson. new ed. Bode, Carl & Cowley, Malcolm, eds. 664p. 1981. pap. 6.95 (ISBN 0-14-015094-3). Penguin.

--Selected Writings. 1981. pap. 3.95x (ISBN 0-394-30914-6, T14, Mod LibC). Modern Lib.

--Selected Writings of Ralph Waldo Emerson. Gilman, William H., ed. (Orig.). pap. 3.50 (ISBN 0-451-51720-2, CE1720, Sig Classics). NAL.

--Sound of Trumpets. Daugherty, James, ed. & illus. (Illus.). (gr. 7 up). 1971. 8.95 o.p. (ISBN 0-670-65846-4). Viking Pr.

Emerson, Ralph Waldo. Five Essays on Man & Nature. Spiller, Robert E., ed. LC 54-9979. (Crofts Classics Ser). 128p. 1954. pap. 3.50x (ISBN 0-88295-034-7). Harlan Davidson.

--The Selected Writings of Ralph Waldo Emerson. Atkinson, Brooks, ed. 9.95 (ISBN 0-394-60418-0). Modern Lib.

--Self Reliance. 2nd ed. Dekovic, Gene, ed. LC 75-12544. (Illus.). 96p. 1983. 12.00 (ISBN 0-937088-07-2); pap. 8.00 (ISBN 0-937088-08-0). Illum Pr.

Emerson, Robert & Grumbach, Jane, eds. Monologues: Men. LC 76-1027. 56p. 1976. pap. 3.95x (ISBN 0-910482-78-0). Drama Bk.

--Monologues: Women. LC 76-1965. 56p. 1976. pap. 3.95x (ISBN 0-910482-79-9). Drama Bk.

Emerson, Robert, jt. ed. see Grumbach, Jane.

Emerson, Robert L. Fast Food: The Endless Shakeout. LC 79-17145. 1979. 21.95 (ISBN 0-86730-235-6). Lebhar Friedman.

Emerson, Sally. Second Sight of Jennifer Hamilton. LC 80-1722. 312p. 1981. 11.95 o.p. (ISBN 0-385-15815-7). Doubleday.

Emerson, W. A., jt. auth. see Irwin, James B., Jr.

Emerson, W. W., et al. Modification of Soil Structure. 1978. 84.95x (ISBN 0-471-99530-4, Pub. by Wiley-Interscience). Wiley.

Emerson, William K. Chevrons: Illustrated History & Catalog of U. S. Army Insignia. LC 82-600002. (Illus.). 350p. 1983. text ed. 49.50 (ISBN 0-87474-412-1). Smithsonian.

Emert, George H., jt. ed. see Klass, Donald L.

Emerton, J. A. Congress Volume: Vienna, 1980. (Vetus Testamentum Ser.: Vol. 32, Suppl.). (Illus.). xii, 483p. 1981. write for info. (ISBN 90-04-06514-8). E J Brill.

Emerton, J. A. & Reif, Stefan C., eds. Interpreting the Hebrew Bible. LC 81-21668. (University of Cambridge Oriental Publication Ser.: No. 32). 1982. 44.50 (ISBN 0-521-24424-2). Cambridge U Pr.

Emerton, Wolseley P. An Abridgment of Adam Smith's Inquiry into the Nature & Causes of the Wealth of Nations. 406p. Repr. of 1881 ed. lib. bdg. 65.00 (ISBN 0-89987-217-4). Darby Bks.

Emery. Modern Trends in Human Genetics, Vol. 2. 1975. 54.95 o.p. (ISBN 0-407-00028-3). Butterworth.

Emery, Anne. Dinny Gordon, Freshman. (gr. 4-6). 1959. PLB 5.97 (ISBN 0-8255-3107-1). Macrae.

--Dinny Gordon, Junior. (gr. 4-9). 1964. PLB 5.97 (ISBN 0-8255-3110-1). Macrae.

--Dinny Gordon, Senior. (gr. 9 up). 1965. PLB 5.97 (ISBN 0-8255-3113-6). Macrae.

--Dinny Gordon, Sophomore. (gr. 7-10). 1961. PLB 5.97 (ISBN 0-8255-3115-2). Macrae.

--First Love, True Love. (gr. 7-10). 1956. 8.95 (ISBN 0-664-32140-2). Westminster.

--Going Steady. (gr. 5-9). 1950. 8.95 (ISBN 0-664-32066-X). Westminster.

--Scarlet Royal. LC 76-23407. 1976. 6.50 o.s.i. (ISBN 0-664-32604-8). Westminster.

--Senior Year. (Illus.). (gr. 5-9). 1949. 4.95 o.s.i. (ISBN 0-664-32051-1). Westminster.

--Spy in Old Philadelphia. LC 58-8953. (Illus.). (gr. 3-7). 1958. pap. 1.50 o.p. (ISBN 0-528-87647-3). Rand.

--Sweet Sixteen. (gr. 6-9). 1956. 6.25 (ISBN 0-8255-3145-4). Macrae.

Emery, Ashley F. see Heat Transfer & Fluid Mechanics Institute.

Emery, C. F. Horny. LC 68-17304. (Illus.). (gr. 2 up). 1967. PLB 6.75x (ISBN 0-87783-017-7); pap. 2.75x deluxe ed. o.p. (ISBN 0-87783-094-0). Oddo.

Emery, D. A. The Compleat Manager: Combining the Humanistic & Scientific Approaches to the Management Job. 1970. 21.95 (ISBN 0-07-019336-3). McGraw.

Emery, D. W., jt. auth. see Pence, R. W.

Emery, Donald W., et al. English Fundamentals: Form B. 7th ed. 1981. pap. text ed. 12.95x (ISBN 0-02-333560-2). Macmillan.

--English Fundamentals: Form A. 7th ed. 1979. pap. text ed. 12.95x (ISBN 0-02-333490-8). Macmillan.

--English Fundamentals: Form C. 7th ed. 1982. text ed. 12.95x (ISBN 0-02-333610-2). Macmillan.

Emery, Edwin & Emery, Michael. The Press & America. 4th ed. (Illus.). 1978. ref. 23.95 (ISBN 0-13-697979-3). P-H.

Emery, F. E., ed. Systems Thinking. (Education Ser). (Orig.). 1970. pap. 4.95 o.s.i. (ISBN 0-14-080071-9). Penguin.

Emery, Frederic B. Violin Concerto. LC 75-93979. (Music Ser). 1969. Repr. of 1928 ed. lib. bdg. 55.00 (ISBN 0-306-71822-7). Da Capo.

Emery, Gary. A New Beginning. 1981. 13.95 o.p. (ISBN 0-671-24866-9). S&S.

--Own Your Own Life: How the New Cognitive Therapy Can Make You Feel Wonderful. 1982. 15.95 (ISBN 0-453-00428-8, H428). NAL.

Emery, Henry C. Politician, Party & People. 1913. 24.50x (ISBN 0-685-89771-0). Elliots Bks.

Emery, James C. Planning for Computing in Higher Education. (EDUCOM Series in Computing & Telecommunications in Higher Education: No. 5). 218p. 1980. lib. bdg. 27.50 (ISBN 0-86531-025-4). Westview.

Emery, James C. see Bernard, Dan, et al.

Emery, James C., ed. The Reality of National Computer Networking for Higher Education: Proceedings of the 1978 EDUCOM Fall Conference. LC 79-10565. (EDUCOM Series in Computing & Telecommunications in Higher Education: No. 2). 1979. lib. bdg. 17.50 (ISBN 0-89158-553-2). Westview.

Emery, James C., ed. see EDUCOM Fall Conference, Oct. 1977.

Emery, Jared M. & Jacobson, Adrienne C. Current Concepts in Cataract Surgery: Selected Proceedings of the Sixth Biennial Cataract Surgical Congress. LC 80-24694. (Illus.). 466p. 1980. text ed. 69.50 o.p. (ISBN 0-8016-1527-5). Mosby.

Emery, Jared M., ed. Current Concepts in Cataract Surgery: Selected Proceedings of the Fifth Biennial Cataract Surgical Congress. 5th ed. LC 78-23408. (Illus.). 588p. 1978. text ed. 66.50 o.p. (ISBN 0-8016-1524-0). Mosby.

Emery, Joy S. Stage Costume Techniques. (Ser. in Theatre & Drama). (Illus.). 368p. 1981. 24.95 (ISBN 0-13-840330-9). P-H.

Emery, Laura. George Eliot's Creative Conflict: The Other Side of Silence. LC 75-3768. 1976. 24.50x (ISBN 0-520-02979-8). U of Cal Pr.

Emery, Leslie, et al. Horseshoeing Theory & Hoof Care. LC 76-16742. (Illus.). 271p. 1977. text ed. 15.50 o.p. (ISBN 0-8121-0574-5). Lea & Febiger.

Emery, Lucilius A. Concerning Justice. 1914. 29.50x (ISBN 0-685-69818-1). Elliots Bks.

Emery, Michael & Smythe, Ted C. Readings in Mass Communication: Concept & Issues in the Mass Media. 5th ed. 550p. 1982. pap. text ed. write for info. (ISBN 0-697-04215-4). Wm C Brown.

Emery, Michael, jt. auth. see Emery, Edwin.

Emery, Michael C. & Smythe, Ted C. Readings in Mass Communications: Concepts & Issues in the Mass Media. 4th ed. 550p. 1980. pap. text ed. write for info. o.p. (ISBN 0-697-04167-0). Wm C Brown.

Emery, Noemie. Alexander Hamilton: An Intimate Portrait. 288p. 1982. 13.95 (ISBN 0-399-12681-3). Putnam Pub Group.

--Washington: A Biography. 1976. 12.95 o.p. (ISBN 0-399-11617-6). Putnam Pub Group.

Emery, Richard D., jt. auth. see Ennis, Bruce J.

Emes, John H. & Nowak, Thomas J. Introduction to Pathophysiology: Basic Principles of the Disease Process. (Illus.). 1983. text ed. 24.95 (ISBN 0-8391-1775-2, 16594). Univ Park.

Emig, C. C. British & Other Phoronids: Keys & Notes for the Identification of the Species. (Synopses of the British Fauna Ser.). 1979. pap. 9.00 o.s.i. (ISBN 0-12-238750-3). Acad Pr.

Emig, Janet. The Web of Meaning: Essays on Writing, Teaching, Learning, & Thinking. Goswami, Dixie & Butler, Maureen, eds. 192p. (Orig.). 1983. pap. text ed. 8.50x (ISBN 0-86709-047-2). Boynton Cook Pubs.

Emiohe, Matthew O. Search for Love. 224p. 1983. 11.00 (ISBN 0-682-49954-4). Exposition.

Emlen, John T. Land Bird Communities of Grand Bahama Island: The Structure & Dynamics of an Avifauna. 129p. 1977. 9.00 (ISBN 0-943610-24-9). Am Ornithologists.

Emley, Alban M. Song of a Soul. 96p. Date not set. pap. 4.95 (ISBN 0-911336-45-1). Sci of Mind.

Emley, E. F. Principles of Magnesium Technology. 1966. inquire for price o.p. (ISBN 0-08-010673-0). Pergamon.

Emmanouilides, George C., jt. auth. see Adams, Forrest H.

Emmanuel, Arghiri. Appropriate or Underdeveloped Technology? (Wiley-IRM Series on Multinationals). 186p. 1982. 25.95 (ISBN 0-471-10467-1, Pub. by Wiley-Interscience). Wiley.

--Unequal Exchange: A Study of the Imperialism of Trade. Pearce, Brian, tr. from Fr. LC 78-158920. (Illus.). 1972. 16.50 o.p. (ISBN 0-85345-152-4, CL-1524); pap. 6.95 (ISBN 0-85345-188-5, PB-1885). Monthly Rev.

Emmanuel, E. Stephen, jt. auth. see Freudberg, Frank.

Emme, Eugene M., ed. Science Fiction & Space Futures: Past & Present. (AAS History Ser.: Vol. 5). (Illus.). 278p. 1982. lib. bdg. 35.00x (ISBN 0-87703-172-X); pap. text ed. 25.00 (ISBN 0-87703-173-8). Am Astronaut.

Emmel, Thomas, ed. Global Perspectives on Ecology. LC 76-56504. 522p. 1977. pap. 13.95 (ISBN 0-87484-338-3). Mayfield Pub.

Emmel, Victor E. & Cowdry, E. V. Laboratory Technique in Biology & Medicine. 4th ed. LC 64-13546. 1970. Repr. of 1964 ed. 22.00 (ISBN 0-88275-016-X). Krieger.

Emmelkamp, Paul M., jt. auth. see Foa, Edna B.

Emmelot, P. & Muhlbach, O., eds. Cellular Control Mechanisms & Cancer. 1964. 34.25 (ISBN 0-686-43080-8). Elsevier.

Emmens, C. W. Guppy Handbook. (Illus.). pap. 6.95 (ISBN 0-87666-084-7, PS668). TFH Pubns.

Emmens, C. W. & Axelrod, Herbert. Catfishes for the Advanced Hobbyist. 9.95 (ISBN 0-87666-018-9, PS650). TFH Pubns.

--Fancy Guppies for the Advanced Hobbyist. 1968. pap. 7.95 (ISBN 0-87666-086-3, M526). TFH Pubns.

Emmens, Carol A. Album of the Sixties. LC 80-21295. (Picture Albums Ser.). (Illus.). (gr. 5 up). 1981. 9.60 (ISBN 0-531-04199-9). Watts.

--Short Stories on Film. LC 78-13488. 1978. lib. bdg. 25.00 (ISBN 0-87287-146-0). Libs Unl.

--Stunt Work & Stunt People. (Triumph Bks). (Illus.). 96p. 1982. lib. bdg. 8.90 (ISBN 0-531-04411-4). Watts.

Emmens, Cliff W. The Marine Aquarium in Theory & Practice. (Illus.). 208p. 1975. 19.95 (ISBN 0-87666-446-X, PS-735). TFH Pubns.

Emmens, Clifford W. Keep Tropical Fish. (Illus.). (YA) (gr. 7-10). 9.95 (ISBN 0-87666-091-X, H910). TFH Pubns.

Emmer, Rae. Dictionary Skills. Hasinbiller, Dolly, ed. Incl. Book C. Purcell, Darryle & Moore, Madeleine, illus. (ISBN 0-8372-3510-3). tchr's ed (ISBN 0-8372-9200-X); Book D. Christianson, David, illus. (ISBN 0-8372-3511-1); tchr's ed. (ISBN 0-8372-9201-8); Book E. Purcell, Darryle, illus. (ISBN 0-8372-3512-X); tchr's ed. (ISBN 0-8372-9202-6); Book F. Christianson, David, illus. (ISBN 0-8372-3513-8); tchr's ed. (ISBN 0-8372-9203-4). (Elementary Skills Ser.). (Illus.). (gr. 3-6). pap. text ed. 1.47 ea. (ISBN 0-686-96682-1); tchr's ed. ea. 1.47 (ISBN 0-685-81574-9). Bowmar-Noble.

Emmerich, Andre. Art Before Columbus. (Illus.). 1983. pap. price not set (ISBN 0-671-47073-6, Touchstone Bks). S&S.

Emmerich, Janet. Anthony Trollope: His Perception of Character & the Traumatic Experience. LC 79-3734. 1980. text ed. 14.00 (ISBN 0-8191-0918-5); pap. text ed. 6.50 (ISBN 0-8191-0919-3). U Pr of Amer.

Emmerichs, J. Superurimpus. 1978. pap. 6.00 (ISBN 0-07-019342-8). McGraw.

Emmerichs, Jack. How to Build a Program. 190p. (Orig.). 1983. pap. 19.95 (ISBN 0-88056-068-1). Dilithium Pr.

--Superwumpus. LC 78-7537. 1978. pap. 6.00 o.p. (ISBN 0-07-582017-X, BYTE Bks). McGraw.

--Tiny Assembler 6800: Version 3.1. LC 78-7997. 1978. pap. 9.00 (ISBN 0-07-019341-X, BYTE Bks). McGraw.

Emmerling, Mary & Trask, Richard. Collecting American Country: A Style & Source Book. (Illus.). 1983. 35.00 (ISBN 0-517-54957-3, C N Potter Bks). Crown.

Emmerling, Mary E. American Country. (Illus.). 292p. 1980. 30.00 (ISBN 0-686-36473-2). Md Hist.

--American Country: A Style & Source Book. 1980. 30.00 (ISBN 0-517-53846-6, C N Potter Bks). Crown.

Emmers, Carol A. Album of Television. LC 79-22778. (gr. 5 up). 1980. PLB 8.90 (ISBN 0-531-01503-3, A15). Watts.

Emmers, Raimond. Pain: A Spike-Interval Coded Message in the Brain. 144p. 1981. text ed. 27.50 (ISBN 0-89004-650-6). Raven.

Emmers, Raimond & Tasker, Ronald R. The Human Somesthetic Thalamus: With Maps for Physiological Target Localization During Stereotactic Neurosurgery. LC 74-80534. 112p. 1975. 77.00 (ISBN 0-911216-72-3). Raven.

Emmerson, A. M. The Microbiology & Treatment of Life-Threatening Infections. (Antimicrobial Chemotherapy Ser.). 175p. 1982. 31.95 (ISBN 0-471-90049-4, Pub. by Res Stud Pr). Wiley.

Emmerson, Bryan T. Hyperuricaemia & Gout in Clinical Practice. 120p. 1982. text ed. 16.00 (ISBN 0-86792-006-8). Wright-PSG.

Emmerson, Donald K. Rethinking Artisanal Fisheries Development: Western Concepts, Asian Experiences. (Working Paper: No. 423). x, 97p. 1980. 5.00 (ISBN 0-686-36074-5, WP-0423). World Bank.

Emmerson, Joan S., compiled by. Catalogue of the Pybus Collection of Medical Books, Letters & Engravings from the 15th-20th Centuries Held in the University Library, Newcastle upon Tyne. 280p. 1982. 60.00 (ISBN 0-7190-1295-3). Manchester.

Emmerson, John K. A View from Yenan. LC 79-1019. 15p. 1979. 1.50 (ISBN 0-934742-02-2, Inst Study Diplomacy). Geo U Sch For Serv.

Emmert, Philip & Donaghy, William. Human Communication: Elements & Contexts. LC 80-17595. (Speech Ser.). (Illus.). 46p. 1981. text ed. 16.95 (ISBN 0-201-03597-9); instrs' manual avail. A-W.

Emmet, Dorothy. Function, Purpose & Powers: Some Concepts in the Study of Individuals & Societies. LC 70-180877. 300p. 1972. 29.95 (ISBN 0-87722-007-7). Temple U Pr.

--The Moral Prism. LC 78-31396. 1979. 22.50x (ISBN 0-312-54782-X). St Martin.

Emmet, E. R. Diversity of Puzzles: Not Only for Experts. pap. 2.95 o.p. (ISBN 0-06-463463-9, EH 463, EH). B&N NY.

--The Island of Imperfection Puzzle Book. 160p. (Orig.). 1980. pap. 2.95 o.p. (ISBN 0-06-463512-0, EH 512). B&N NY.

Emmet, Eric. Mind Tickling Brain Teasers. LC 77-90769. (Illus.). 1978. 10.95 (ISBN 0-87523-192-6). Emerson.

Emmet, Eric E. Puzzles for Pleasure. LC 71-189618. (Illus.). 256p. 1972. 11.95 (ISBN 0-87523-178-0). Emerson.

Emmett, Robert. Actaeon Homeward. 1979. 8.95 o.p. (ISBN 0-686-15534-3); pap. 4.50 o.p. (ISBN 0-686-15535-1). Writers West.

--American Avenger, No. 3: The Devil's Finger. 1982. pap. 2.50 (ISBN 0-451-11458-2, AE1458, Sig). NAL.

--American Avenger, No. 5: Trojan Horses. 208p. 1982. pap. 2.50 (ISBN 0-451-11825-1, Sig). NAL.

Emmett, Victor J., Jr. Ms. Murphy's Theater. 32p. 1975. pap. 1.25 (ISBN 0-914994-04-2, CB-005). Cider Pr.

Emmichoven, F. W. The Anthroposophical Understanding of the Soul. Schwarzkopf, Friedemann, tr. from Ger. 170p. (Orig.). 1983. pap. 8.95 (ISBN 0-88010-019-2). Anthroposophic.

Emmitt, Robert. The Last War Trail: The Utes & the Settlement of Colorado. (Civilization of the American Indian Ser.: Vol. 40). (Illus.). 352p. 1954. 14.95 (ISBN 0-685-25209-4); pap. 7.95 (ISBN 0-8061-1043-0). U of Okla Pr.

Emmons, Michael L., jt. auth. see Alberti, Robert E.

Emmons, Shirlee & Sonntag, Stanley. The Art of the Song Recital. LC 78-66978. 1979. pap. text ed. 15.95 (ISBN 0-02-870530-0). Schirmer Bks.

Emmons, Terence. Russian Landed Gentry & the Peasant Emancipation of 1861. LC 68-29654. 1968. 47.50 (ISBN 0-521-07340-5). Cambridge U Pr.

Emmons, Terrence. The Formation of Political Parties & the First National Elections in Russia. (Illus.). 576p. 1983. text ed. 42.50x (ISBN 0-674-30935-9). Harvard U Pr.

Emmons, Vicki. Simply Seafood. (Illus.). 224p. (Orig.). 1983. pap. 4.95 (ISBN 0-89933-043-6). DeLorme Pub.

Emmott, Robert. Ride the Tiger. (American Avenger Ser.: No. 2). (Orig.). 1982. pap. 2.50 (ISBN 0-451-11268-7, AE1268, Sig). NAL.

Emory University Law & Economics Center, jt. auth. see Federal Reserve Bank of Atlanta.

Emotions Anonymous International. Emotions Anonymous. LC 79-103619. 251p. 1982. 6.00 (ISBN 0-9607356-0-7, RA790.A1E5633). Emotions Anony Intl.

Empedocles. The Fragments of Empedocles. Leonard, William E., tr. from Gr. & intro. by. LC 73-85282. 100p. 1973. 12.00 (ISBN 0-87548-300-3); pap. 5.00 (ISBN 0-87548-301-1). Open Court.

Empey, LaMar T. The Future of Childhood & Juvenile Justice. LC 79-15129. xi, 422p. 1979. 20.00x (ISBN 0-8139-0832-9). U Pr of Va.

Empie, Paul C., et al, eds. Teaching Authority & Infallibility in the Church, No. 6. LC 79-54109. (Lutherans & Catholics in Dialogue). 352p. (Orig.). 1979. pap. 5.95 (ISBN 0-8066-1733-0, 10-6222). Augsburg.

Employee Benefit Research Institute. Retirement Income Opportunities in an Aging America: Income Levels & Adequacy, Vol. 2. LC 81-5494. 121p. (Orig.). 1982. pap. 10.00 (ISBN 0-86643-014-8). Employee Benefit.

Emre, Yunus. The Wandering Fool: Sufi Poems. Roditi, Edouard, tr. from Turkish. LC 79-114869. (Inklings: No. 4). 36p. 1982. pap. cancelled (ISBN 0-930012-34-8). Mudborn.

Emrich, D. & Weinheimer, B., eds. Thyroid, 1979. 1980. 48.00 (ISBN 0-444-80280-0). Elsevier.

Emrick, Roy, jt. ed. see Tomizuka, Carl.

EMSA Annual Meeting, 41st, 1983. Electron Microscopy Society of America: Proceedings. 1983. 45.00 (ISBN 0-911302-47-6). San Francisco Pr.

Emshoff, James R. & Sisson, Roger L. Design & Use of Computer Simulation Models. (Illus.). 1970. 22.95 (ISBN 0-02-333720-6, 33372). Macmillan.

Emsley. Visual Optics, 2 vols. 5th ed. (Illus.). 1976. Vol. 1. 39.00 (ISBN 0-407-93415-4); Vol. 2. 39.00 (ISBN 0-407-93414-6). Butterworth.

Emsley & Miyazawa, T. NMR Analyses of Molecular Conformations & Conformational Equilibria with the Lanthanide Probe Method. (Illus.). 45p. 1981. pap. 23.00 (ISBN 0-08-027104-9). Pergamon.

Emurian, Ernest K. Forty Stories of Famous Gospel Songs. (Interlude Bks). 1972. pap. 4.50 (ISBN 0-8010-3267-9). Baker Bk.

--Stories of Christmas Carols. (Paperback Program Ser). 1969. pap. 4.50 (ISBN 0-8010-3265-2). Baker Bk.

Emy, H. V. Liberals, Radicals & Social Politics, 1892-1914. LC 72-85435. 320p. 1973. 42.50 (ISBN 0-521-08740-6). Cambridge U Pr.

Encarnacao, J., ed. File Structures & Data Bases for CAD: Proceedings of the IFIP-WG 5-2 Working Conference, Seeheim, Federal Republic of Germany, September 14-16, 1981. 372p. 1982. 51.25 (ISBN 0-444-86462-8, North Holland). Elsevier.

Encarnacao, J. L., ed. Eurographics Eighty-One. 1982. 42.75 (ISBN 0-444-86284-6). Elsevier.

Encarnacas, J. & Torres, F. F., eds. CAD-CAM as a Basis for Development of Technology in Developing Nations: Proceedings. 1982. 76.75 (ISBN 0-444-86320-6). Elsevier.

Encel, Sol, jt. ed. see Bell, Colin.

Ench, J. R. Not of This Generation. 1983. 10.95 (ISBN 0-533-05565-2). Vantage.

Enchi, Fumiko. Masks. Carpenter, Juliet W., tr. from Japanese. LC 82-48726. 1983. 11.95 (ISBN 0-394-50945-5). Knopf.

Encyclopaedia Judaica Editors. Encyclopaedic Dictionary of Judaica. (Illus.). 700p. 1974. 29.95 o.p. (ISBN 0-7065-1412-2). L Amiel Pub.

Endacott, G. B. A History of Hong Kong. (Illus.). 1974. pap. 14.50x o.p. (ISBN 0-19-519776-3). Oxford U Pr.

Endacott, G. B. & Hinton, A. Fragrant Harbour: A Short History of Hong Kong. LC 76-57678. 1977. Repr. of 1962 ed. lib. bdg. 18.50x (ISBN 0-8371-9456-3, ENFH). Greenwood.

Endacott, Geoffrey. Fine Furniture-Making & Woodworking. LC 81-85026. (Illus.). 168p. 1982. 14.95 (ISBN 0-8069-5458-2); lib. bdg. 17.79 (ISBN 0-8069-5459-0); pap. 9.95 (ISBN 0-8069-7610-1). Sterling.

Endak, Maurice, intro. by. Maxfield Parrish Poster Book. (Illus.). 48p. 1974. pap. 8.95 (ISBN 0-517-51402-8, Harmony). Crown.

Endean, Robert. Australia's Great Barrier Reef. (Illus.). 348p. 1983. text ed. 29.95x (ISBN 0-7022-1678-X). U of Queensland Pr.

Endell, Fritz A. Old Tavern Signs: An Excursion into the History of Hospitality. LC 68-26572. (Illus.). 1968. Repr. of 1916 ed. 34.00x (ISBN 0-8103-3505-0). Gale.

Enderle, Judith. Cheer Me On! (A Caprice Romance Ser.). 192p. 1982. pap. 1.95 (ISBN 0-441-06980-0, Pub. by Tempo). Ace Bks.

Enderle, Judith A. Good Junk. 32p. (ps-3). 1982. 5.95 (ISBN 0-525-66720-2). Dandelion Pr.

Endersby, Frank. The Boy & the Horse. (Illus.). 16p. 1980. 5.50 (ISBN 0-85953-098-1, Pub. by Child's Play England). Playspaces.

Enderton, Herbert B. A Mathematical Introduction to Logic. 1972. 17.75 (ISBN 0-12-238450-4). Acad Pr.

Endfield, Cy. Zulu Dawn. 288p. 1980. pap. 2.50 o.p. (ISBN 0-523-41148-0). Pinnacle Bks.

Endicott, John E. & Heaton, William P. The Politics of East Asia: China, Japan, Korea. LC 77-1346. 1978. lib. bdg. 30.00 (ISBN 0-89158-127-8); pap. text ed. 11.00 (ISBN 0-89158-128-6). Westview.

Endicott, K. M. An Analysis of Malay Magic. 1970. pap. 11.50x (ISBN 0-19-582513-6). Oxford U Pr.

Endicott, Kirk. Batek Negrito Religion: The World-View & Rituals of a Hunting & Gathering People of Peninsular Malaysia. (Illus.). 1979. 39.00x (ISBN 0-19-823197-0). Oxford U Pr.

Endicott, Stephen. James G. Endicott: Rebel Out of China. 1980. 18.95 (ISBN 0-8020-2377-0); pap. 9.95 (ISBN 0-8020-6409-4). U of Toronto Pr.

Endler, Norman S. Holiday of Darkness: A Psychologist's Personal Journey Out of His Depression. LC 81-16179. 169p. 1982. 14.95 (ISBN 0-471-86250-9, Pub. by Wiley-Interscience). Wiley.

Endler, Norman S., jt. auth. see Magnusson, David.

Endlicher, S., jt. auth. see Poeppig, E.

Endo, Russell, jt. ed. see Munoz, Faye U.

Endo, Shusaku. A Life of Jesus. Schuchert, Richard, tr. from Japanese. LC 78-61721. 192p. 1979. 9.95 (ISBN 0-8091-0269-2); pap. 2.95 (ISBN 0-8091-2319-3). Paulist Pr.

--The Samurai. Gessel, Van C., tr. from Japanese. LC 82-57851. 272p. 1982. 12.95 (ISBN 0-06-859852-1, HarpT). Har-Row.

Endrenyi, J. Reliability Modeling in Electric Power Systems. LC 78-6222. 1978. 69.95 (ISBN 0-471-99664-5, Pub. by Wiley-Interscience). Wiley.

Endres, Dieter. Die Besteuerung Fesellschaftsrechtlicher Vermogensubertragunsgen. xiv, 340p. (Ger.). 1982. write for info. (ISBN 3-8204-7205-3). P Lang Pubs.

Endres, H., et al see Von Wiesner, J. & Von Regel, C.

Endres, Jeannette & Rockwell, Robert E. Food, Nutrition, & the Young Child. LC 80-10848. (Illus.). 312p. 1980. pap. text ed. 13.95 (ISBN 0-8016-4139-X). Mosby.

Eneberg, Kaa, tr. see Bjorkegren, Hans.

Enehjelm, Curt A. Australian Finches. Friese, U. Erich, tr. from Ger. Orig. Title: Australische Prachtfinken. (Illus.). 1979. 4.95 (ISBN 0-87666-987-9, KW-O27). TFH Pubns.

Enehjelm, Curt Af see Af Enehjelm, Curt.

Enelow, Allen J. Elements of Psychotherapy. 1977. text ed. 18.95x (ISBN 0-19-502205-X); pap. text ed. 8.95x (ISBN 0-19-502206-8). Oxford U Pr.

Enelow, Allen J. & Swisher, Scott N. Interviewing & Patient Care. 2nd ed. 1979. text ed. 18.95x (ISBN 0-19-502545-8); pap. text ed. 8.95x (ISBN 0-19-502546-6). Oxford U Pr.

Eneneau-Meneau, Murray B. Toda Grammar & Texts. LC 82-72155. (Memoirs Ser.: Vol. 155). 1983. 35.00 (ISBN 0-87169-155-8); pap. 29.00. Am Philos.

Energlyn, L. & Brealey, L. Analytical Geochemistry. LC 76-103358. (Methods in Geochemistry & Geophysics Ser.: Vol. 5). (Illus.). 441p. 1971. 76.75 (ISBN 0-444-40826-6). Elsevier.

Energy Development International & Heffner, G. Potential Markets for U.S. Solar & Conservation Technologies in Thailand: Supplement. (Progress in Solar Energy Ser.). 224p. 1983. pap. text ed. 18.00 (ISBN 0-89553-116-X). Am Solar Energy.

Energy Development International & Weingart, J. Potential Markets for U.S. Solar & Conservation Technologies in Indonesia: Supplement. (Progress in Solar Energy Ser.). 204p. 1983. pap. text ed. 18.00 (ISBN 0-89553-115-1). Am Solar Ener.

Energy, Environment, & Resource Center, the University of Tennessee see Bohm, Robert A., et al.

Energy, Environment, & Resources Center, the University of Tennessee see Bohm, Robert A., et al.

Energy, Environment, & Resources Center,the University of Tennessee see Bohm, Robert A., et al.

Energy Policy Project Staff. A Time to Choose: America's Energy Future. LC 74-14787. (Ford's Foundation's Energy Policy Project Ser.). 528p. 1974. prof ref 19.00x (ISBN 0-88410-023-5); pap. 11.95x prof ref (ISBN 0-88410-024-3). Ballinger Pub.

Energy Resources Center. Illustrated Guide to Home Retrofitting for Energy Savings. Knight, et al, eds. LC 80-23568. (Illus.). 384p. 1981. 16.50 (ISBN 0-07-019490-4, P&RB). McGraw.

Energyworks Inc., jt. auth. see Berkeley Planning Associates Inc.

Engberg, Robert, ed. John Muir to Yosemite & Beyond: Writings from the Years 1863-1875. Wesling, Donald. (Illus.). 194p. 1980. 20.00 (ISBN 0-299-08270-9); pap. 6.95t (ISBN 0-299-08274-1). U of Wis Pr.

Engberg, Susan. Pastorale. LC 82-4730. (Illinois Short Fiction Ser.). 160p. 1982. 11.95 (ISBN 0-252-00993-2); pap. 4.95 (ISBN 0-252-00994-0). U of Ill Pr.

Engdahl, David. Color Printing Materials. 1977. 9.95 o.p. (ISBN 0-8174-2420-2, Amphoto). Watson-Guptill.

Engdahl, Sylvia L. Enchantress from the Stars. LC 74-98609. 1970. sparton bdg. 9.95 (ISBN 0-689-20508-2). Atheneum.

Engel & Hansen, Rosanna. Gymnastics: The New Era. LC 79-55009. (Illus.). 96p. 1982. 10.15 (ISBN 0-448-13614-7, G&D); pap. 5.95 (ISBN 0-448-16581-3). Putnam Pub Group.

Engel, A., et al. Justice Game. 1974. pap. 7.95x (ISBN 0-02-472590-0, 47259). Macmillan.

Engel, A. J. From Clergyman to Don: The Rise of the Academic Profession in Nineteenth-Century Oxford. 336p. 1983. 55.00 (ISBN 0-19-822606-3). Oxford U Pr.

Engel, Barbara A. Mothers & Daughters: Women of the Intelligentsia in Nineteenth Century Russia. LC 82-14611. (Illus.). 224p. 1983. 39.50 (ISBN 0-521-25125-7). Cambridge U Pr.

Engel, Barbara A. & Rosenthal, Clifford N., eds. Five Sisters: Women Against the Tsar. LC 76-48814. (Illus.). 1977. pap. 6.95 o.p. (ISBN 0-8052-0561-6). Schocken.

Engel, Beth B. Big Words. (Illus.). 160p. (gr. 5-9). 1982. 11.50 (ISBN 0-525-66779-2, 01117-330). Lodestar Bks.

Engel, Carl & Howard, John T., eds. Music from the Days of George Washington: A Collection of Patriotic & Military Tunes, Piano & Dance Music, Songs & Operatic Airs. (Music Reprint Ser.). 103p. 1983. Repr. of 1931 ed. lib. bdg. 25.00 (ISBN 0-306-76086-X). Da Capo.

Engel, David M. Law & Kingship in Thailand During the Reign of King Chulalongkorn. LC 74-20343. (Michigan Papers on South & Southeast Asia: No. 9). x, 131p. (Orig.). 1975. pap. 6.50x (ISBN 0-89148-009-9). Ctr S&SE Asian.

Engel, Dolores. Voyage of the Kon-Tiki. LC 78-26766. (Raintree Great Adventures). (Illus.). (gr. 3-6). 1979. PLB 12.85 (ISBN 0-8393-0151-0). Raintree Pubs.

Engel, Heinrich. Japanese House: A Tradition for Contemporary Architecture. LC 63-20587. (Illus.). 1964. 65.00 (ISBN 0-8048-0304-8). C E Tuttle.

Engel, Herbert. Handbook of Creative Learning Exercises. (Building Blocks of Human Potential Ser.). (Illus.). 1973. 17.95 (ISBN 0-87201-162-3). Gulf Pub.

Engel, J. Ronald. Sacred Sands: The Struggle for Community in the Indiana Dunes. (Illus.). 288p. 1983. 19.95 (ISBN 0-8195-5073-6). Wesleyan U Pr.

Engel, Jack. Advertising: The Process & Practice. (Marketing Ser.). (Illus.). 1980. text ed. 23.95x (ISBN 0-07-019511-0); instr's manual 24.30x (ISBN 0-07-019512-9). McGraw.

Engel, James F. How Can I Get Them to Listen? 1977. pap. 4.95 o.p. (ISBN 0-310-24171-5). Zondervan.

Engel, Lehman. Getting the Show On. 1983. 14.95 (ISBN 0-02-870680-3). Schirmer Bks.

Engel, Leonard. The Sea. rev. ed. LC 80-52121. (Life Nature Library). 13.40 (ISBN 0-8094-3887-9). Silver.

--The Sea. (Young Readers Library). (Illus.). 1977. PLB 6.80 (ISBN 0-8094-1393-0). Silver.

Engel, Lothar, et al. An Atlas of Polymer Damage. (Illus.). 1981. reference 68.00 (ISBN 0-13-050013-5). P-H.

Engel, Louis, jt. auth. see Boyd, Brendan.

Engel, M., jt. ed. see Fulleborn, U.

Engel, M., jt. ed. see Hodson, H. V.

Engel, Marian. Inside the Easter Egg. (Anansi Fiction Ser.: No. 33). 172p. 1975. 16.95 o.p. (ISBN 0-88784-436-7, Pub. by Hse Anansi Pr Canada). U of Toronto Pr.

--The Year of the Child. 192p. 1981. 9.95 o.p. (ISBN 0-312-89627-1). St Martin.

Engel, P., jt. ed. see Hossfeld, D. K.

Engel, P. C. Enzyme Kinetics: The Steady-State Approach. 2nd ed. (Outline Studies in Biology). 96p. 1982. pap. 6.50x (ISBN 0-412-23970-1, Pub. by Chapman & Hall England). Methuen Inc.

Engel, Paul, jt. auth. see Childs, Marquis.

Engel, Peter A. Impact Wear of Materials. (Tribology Ser.: Vol. 2). 1976. 68.00 (ISBN 0-444-41533-5). Elsevier.

Engel, S. Analyzing Informal Fallacies. 1980. pap. 10.95 (ISBN 0-13-032854-5). P-H.

Engel, S. Morris. With Good Reason: An Introduction to Informal Fallacies. LC 75-33579. 224p. 1976. 15.95 o.p. (ISBN 0-312-88480-X); pap. text ed. 4.95 o.p. (ISBN 0-312-88515-6). St Martin.

Engelbourg, Saul. Power & Morality: American Business Ethics, 1840-1914. LC 79-8288. (Contributions in Economics & Economic History: No. 28). 1980. lib. bdg. 25.00 (ISBN 0-313-20871-9, ENP/). Greenwood.

Engelbrecht, Helmuth C., jt. auth. see Hanifhen, Frank C.

Engelbrecht, Ted D., et al. Federal Taxation of Estates, Gifts, & Trusts. (Illus.). 528p. 1981. 35.95 (ISBN 0-13-313858-5). P-H.

Engelder, Theodore, et al, trs. see Pieper, Francis.

Engelhardt, W. V., et al. Sedimentary Petrology: The Origin of Sediments & Sedimentary Rocks, Part III. Johns, William D., tr. LC 67-28575. 359p. 1977. 89.95 o.p. (ISBN 0-470-99142-9). Halsted Pr.

Engelken, David & Huth, Tricia. Undiscovered Denver Dining. (Illus.). 84p. 1982. pap. 3.95 (ISBN 0-9610064-0-4). Undiscovered.

Engelken, Ralph & Engelken, Rita. The Art of Natural Farming & Gardening. 1981. 9.95 (ISBN 0-686-97057-8). Barrington IA.

Engelken, Rita, jt. auth. see Engelken, Ralph.

Engelkes, James R. & Vandergoot, David. Introduction to Counseling. 1982. 22.95 (ISBN 0-395-30800-3). HM.

Engelking, R. Dimension Theory. (Mathematical Library Ser.: Vol. 19). 1979. 59.75 (ISBN 0-444-85176-3, North Holland). Elsevier.

Engelman, Matylda. End of the Journey. 320p. 1980. pap. 2.50 o.p. (ISBN 0-523-41060-3). Pinnacle Bks.

Engelmann, Arthur, et al. History of Continental Civil Procedure. (Continental Legal History Ser.: Vol. 7). lxiii, 948p. 1969. Repr. of 1927 ed. 27.50x o.p. (ISBN 0-8377-2101-6). Rothman.

Engelmann, R. J. & Slinn, W. G., eds. Precipitation Scavenging (1970) Proceedings. LC 70-609397. (AEC Symposium Ser.). 508p. 1970. pap. 20.75 (CONF-700601); microfiche 4.50 (ISBN 0-87079-308-X, CONF-700601). DOE.

Engelmann, Rudolf J., ed. Atmosphere-Surface Exchange of Particulate & Gaseous Pollutants (1974) Proceedings. Sehmel, George A. LC 75-38716. (ERDA Symposium Ser.). 1000p. 1976. pap. 33.00 (ISBN 0-87079-138-9, CONF-740921); microfiche 4.50 (ISBN 0-87079-139-7, CONF-740921). DOE.

Engelmann, Siegfried. Preventing Failure in the Primary Grades. 1969. text ed. 14.95 (ISBN 0-574-50050-2, 5-0050); pap. text ed. 12.95 (ISBN 0-574-50051-0, 5-0051). SRA.

Engelmann, Siegfried & Colvin, Geoffrey. Generalized Compliance Training. (Illus.). 250p. (Orig.). Date not set. pap. text ed. price not set (ISBN 0-936104-31-7, 0375). Pro Ed.

Engelmayer, Sheldon D. & Wagman, Robert J. Tax Revolt Nineteen Eighty. 1980. 12.95 o.p. (ISBN 0-87000-469-7, Arlington Hse). Crown.

Engeln, Oscar D. Von see Von Engeln, Oscar D.

Engeln, Oscar Dedrich Von & Urquhart, Jane M. The Story Key to Geographic Names. LC 74-13855. 279p. 1976. Repr. of 1924 ed. 37.00x (ISBN 0-8103-4062-3). Gale.

Engels, Donald W. Alexander the Great & the Logistics of the Macedonian Army. LC 76-52025. 1978. 24.75x (ISBN 0-520-03433-3); pap. 5.95 (ISBN 0-520-04272-7, CAL 472). U of Cal Pr.

Engels, F., jt. auth. see Marx, K.

Engels, Frederick. Anti-Duhring: Herr Eugen Duhring's Revolution in Science. LC 66-21950. 1966. 6.95 o.p. (ISBN 0-7178-0009-1); pap. 2.85 o.p. (ISBN 0-7178-0008-3). Intl Pub Co.

Engels, Frederick, jt. auth. see Marx, Karl.

Engels, Friedrich, jt. auth. see Marx, Karl.

Engels, John. Blood Mountain. LC 76-26854. (Pitt Poetry Ser.). 1977. 9.95 (ISBN 0-8229-3338-1); ltd. ed. 20.00x (ISBN 0-8229-3289-X); pap. 4.50 (ISBN 0-8229-5277-7). U of Pittsburgh Pr.

--Signals from the Safety Coffin. LC 74-17525. (Pitt Poetry Ser.). 1975. 9.95 (ISBN 0-8229-3291-1); pap. 4.50 (ISBN 0-8229-5255-6). U of Pittsburgh Pr.

--Studies in Paterson. 1971. pap. text ed. 2.50x o.p. (ISBN 0-675-09212-4). Merrill.

--Vivaldi in Early Fall. LC 80-24571. (Contemporary Poetry Ser.). 88p. 1981. 8.95 (ISBN 0-8203-0543-X); pap. 4.95 (ISBN 0-8203-0552-9). U of Ga Pr.

--Weather-Fear: New & Selected Poems, 1958-1982. LC 82-8373. (Contemporary Poetry Ser.). 144p. 1983. text ed. 12.50x (ISBN 0-8203-0654-1); pap. 6.95x (ISBN 0-8203-0655-X). U of Ga Pr.

Engels, W. & Pohl, H., eds. German Yearbook on Business History, 1982. (Illus.). 186p. 1983. 15.00 (ISBN 0-387-11892-6). Springer-Verlag.

Engelsman, Coert. Engelsman's General Construction Cost Guide 1983. 1982. 34.50 (ISBN 0-442-26677-4). Van Nos Reinhold.

--Heavy Construction Cost File, 1982: Unit Prices. 256p. 1981. pap. text ed. 24.50 (ISBN 0-442-26507-7). Van Nos Reinhold.

--Heavy Construction Cost File 1983: Unit Prices. 260p. 1982. pap. text ed. 27.50 (ISBN 0-442-26676-6). Van Nos Reinhold.

--Residential Construction Cost Guide 1983. 382p. 1982. pap. text ed. 32.50 (ISBN 0-442-26675-8). Van Nos Reinhold.

--Watch It, Mr. Contractor. Date not set. price not set (ISBN 0-442-22314-5). Van Nos Reinhold.

Engelsohn, Harold S. Trigonometry: A Complete & Concrete Approach. (Illus.). 1981. text ed. 20.95 (ISBN 0-07-019419-X); instructor's manual avail. (ISBN 0-07-019420-3). McGraw.

Engelsohn, Harold S. & Feit, J. Basic Mathematics: Algebra with Arithmetic. LC 79-21287. 532p. 1980. text ed. 23.95 (ISBN 0-471-24145-8). Wiley.

Engelstein, Laura. Moscow, 1905: Working-Class Organization & Political Conflict. LC 81-50786. 320p. 1982. 29.50x (ISBN 0-8047-1118-6). Stanford U Pr.

Engeman, Richard H. The Jacksonville Story. (Illus.). 1980. 10.00x (ISBN 0-943388-01-5); pap. 2.95 (ISBN 0-943388-02-3). South Oregon.

--Preliminary Guide to Local History Materials: Jacksonville Museum Library. (Illus.). 86p. 1978. 5.00x (ISBN 0-943388-00-7). South Oregon.

Engeman, Thomas S., et al, eds. The Federalist Concordance. LC 80-10406. 630p. 1980. 48.75 (ISBN 0-8195-5045-0, IS-00106, Pub. by Wesleyan U Pr). Univ Microfilms.

Engemann, Joseph G. & Hegner, Robert W. Invertebrate Zoology. 3rd ed. 1981. text ed. 25.95 (ISBN 0-02-333780-X). Macmillan.

Engen, Gavin. Kit Cars. LC 77-6203. (Superwheels & Thrill Sports Bks.). (Illus.). (gr. 3-9). 1977. PLB 7.95g (ISBN 0-8225-0417-0). Lerner Pubns.

Engen, Rodney. Kate Greenaway: A Biography. LC 80-14850. (Illus.). 240p. 1981. 29.95 (ISBN 0-8052-3775-5). Schocken.

Engen, S. Stochastic Abundance Models: With Emphasis on Biological Communities & Species Diversity. 126p. 1978. 17.95x (ISBN 0-412-15240-1, Pub. by Chapman & Hall England). Methuen Inc.

Engestrom, Melissa, ed. see Lamb, Samuel H.

Engestrom, Melissa, ed. see Ortiz Y Pino, Jose.

Enggass, Catherine, tr. see Manetti, Antonio.

Enggass, Catherine, tr. see Puppi, Lionello.

Enggass, Robert & Brown, Jonathan. Italy & Spain: 1600-1750. (Sources & Documents in the History of Art Ser.). 1970. pap. 13.95 ref. ed. (ISBN 0-13-508101-7). P-H.

Engie, A., jt. auth. see Martins, R. E.

Engineer, Asghar A. The Origin & Development of Islam: An Essay on Its Socio-Economic Growth. 248p. 1980. text ed. 18.95 (ISBN 0-86131-174-4, Pub. by Orient Longman Ltd India). Apt Bks.

Engineering & Mineral Journal Editors, compiled by. E-MJ Operating Handbook of Mineral Processing, Vol. II. 500p. 1980. 26.90 (ISBN 0-07-019527-7). McGraw.

Engineering Concepts Curriculum Project - State University of New York. Man & His Technology. (Illus.). 256p. 1973. text ed. 24.00 (ISBN 0-07-019510-2, C); 13.00 o.p. wkbk. (ISBN 0-07-049914-4). McGraw.

Engineering Equipment Users Association Staff. Systematic Fault Diagnosis. (Illus.). 168p. 1982. text ed. 38.00x (ISBN 0-7114-5739-5). Longman.

Engineering Foundation Conference. Innovative Management of the Technical Information Function: Proceedings. 190p. 1978. 36.95x o.p. (ISBN 0-931690-11-0). GE Tech Marketing.

Engineering Management Conference, Melbourne, Australia, March 1979. Engineering Management Update. 78p. (Orig.). 1979. pap. text ed. 24.00x (ISBN 0-85825-105-1, Pub. by Inst Engineering Australia). Renouf.

Engineering Manpower Commission. Demand for Engineers, 1981. (Illus.). 1982. 35.00x (ISBN 0-87615-112-8, 231-82). AAES.

--Professional Income of Engineers, 1982. (Illus.). 1982. 35.00 (ISBN 0-87615-134-9, 302-82). AAES.

Engineering Mining Journal Magazine. Operating Handbook of Mineral Underground Mining, Vol. III. (Library of Operating Handbooks). 1979. 26.90 (ISBN 0-07-019521-8, P&RB). McGraw.

Engineering Research Associates, Inc. High Speed Computing Devices. (The Charles Babbage Institute Reprint Series for the History of Computing: Vol. 4). (Illus.). 1982. Repr. of 1950 ed. write for info. set ltd. ed. (ISBN 0-938228-02-1). Tomash Pubs.

Engineering Societies Library, New York. Classed Subject Catalog of the Engineering Societies Library, New York City, 1st Supplement. 1965. 105.00 (ISBN 0-8161-0700-9, Hall Library). G K Hall.

--Classed Subject Catalog of the Engineering Societies Library, New York City, 2nd Supplement. 1966. 105.00 (ISBN 0-8161-0752-1, Hall Library). G K Hall.

--Classed Subject Catalog of the Engineering Societies Library, New York City, 3rd Supplement. 1967. 105.00 (ISBN 0-8161-0756-4, Hall Library). G K Hall.

--Classed Subject Catalog of the Engineering Societies Library, New York City, 4th Supplement, 1968 & 5th Supplement, 1969. Fourth Suppl. 105.00 (ISBN 0-8161-0817-X, Hall Library); Fifth Suppl. 105.00 (ISBN 0-8161-0836-6). G K Hall.

--Classed Subject Catalog of the Engineering Societies Library, New York City, 8th Supplement. 1972. lib. bdg. 105.00 (ISBN 0-8161-0982-6, Hall Library). G K Hall.

--Classed Subject Catalog of the Engineering Societies Library, New York City, 9th Supplement. 1973. lib. bdg. 105.00 (ISBN 0-8161-1050-6, Hall Library). G K Hall.

--Classed Subject Catalog of the Engineering Societies Library, New York City, 10th Supplement. 1974. 105.00 (ISBN 0-8161-1123-5, Hall Library). G K Hall.

Engineering Societies. New York. Classed Subject Catalog of the Engineering Societies Library, New York City, 6th Supplement. 1970. 105.00 (ISBN 0-8161-0883-8, Hall Library). G K Hall.

--Classed Subject Catalog of the Engineering Societies Library, New York City, 7th Supplement. 1971. lib. bdg. 95.00 (ISBN 0-8161-0913-3, Hall Library). G K Hall.

--Classed Subject Catalog of the Engineering Societies Library, New York City, 12 vols. 1140.00, incl. index (ISBN 0-8161-0653-3, Hall Library); index alone 95.00 (ISBN 0-8161-0237-6). G K Hall.

Engineering Staff of Archive. Streaming. (Illus.). 196p. (Orig.). pap. 14.95 (ISBN 0-9608810-0-X). Archive Corp.

Engineering Staff of Texas Instruments. The Bipolar Microcomputer Components Data Book. 3rd, rev. ed. LC 81-51167. 560p. 1981. pap. 12.50 (ISBN 0-89512-110-7, LCC5831). Tex Instr Inc.

--The M O S Memory Data Book for Design Engineers, 1980. LC 79-93268. 192p. pap. 3.75 o.p. (ISBN 0-89512-105-0, LCC4782). Tex Instr Inc.

--The MOS Memory Data Book for Design Engineers, 1982. Rev. ed. 296p. pap. 8.35 (ISBN 0-89512-112-3, LCC7061). Tex Instr Inc.

Engineering Staff of Texas Instruments Inc. T T L Data Book for Design Engineers: 1981 Supplement. 2nd. rev. ed. LC 81-50954. 380p. pap. 8.75 (ISBN 0-89512-108-5, LCC 5772). Tex Instr Inc.

Engineers Joint Council Editors. Thesaurus of Engineering & Scientific Terms. rev. ed. LC 68-6569. 1967. flexible cover 50.00 (ISBN 0-87615-163-2). AAES.

England, jt. ed. see Vanselow.

England, G. A. Out of the Abyss. (YA) 6.95 (ISBN 0-685-07451-X, Avalon). Bouregy.

England, George A. Darkness & Dawn. LC 75-13253. (Classics of Science Fiction Ser.). (Illus.). 690p. 1973. 16.50 (ISBN 0-88355-108-X); pap. 5.95 (ISBN 0-88355-137-3). Hyperion Conn.

England, J. M., jt. auth. see Assendelft, Van.

England, J. W., jt. auth. see Martin, N. F. G.

England, Martha W. Garrick & Stratford. LC 62-17403. (Illus., Orig.). 1962. pap. 8.00 (ISBN 0-87104-084-0). NY Pub Lib.

England, Martha W. & Sparrow, John. Hymns Unbidden: Donne, Herbert, Blake, Emily Dickinson & the Hymnographers. LC 66-28617. 1966. 15.00 (ISBN 0-87104-092-1). NY Pub Lib.

England, Nora C. A Gammar of Mam Mayan Language: A Mayan Language. (Texas Linguistics Ser.). 365p. 1983. text ed. 25.00x (ISBN 0-292-72726-7). U of Tex Pr.

England, Paul. Favorite Operas by German & Russian Composers. LC 79-96409. Orig. Title: Fifty Favorite Operas. 269p. 1973. pap. 2.50 o.p. (ISBN 0-486-22933-5). Dover.

--Favorite Operas by Italian & French Composers. LC 72-96410. Orig. Title: Fifty Favorite Operas. 320p. 1973. pap. 2.50 o.p. (ISBN 0-486-22932-7). Dover.

England, William L., jt. ed. see Roberts, Stephen D.

Englander, W., jt. auth. see Saxon, J.

Engle, jt. auth. see Hyde, Sarah.

Engle, Eloise. National Governments Around the World. LC 72-179013. (Around the World Ser). (Illus.). (gr. 5 up). 1973. 9.50 (ISBN 0-8303-0117-8). Fleet.

Engle, Jacqueline, ed. see Educational Research Council of America.

Engle, Joanna. Cap'n Kid Goes to the South Pole. LC 82-61013. (Sea World Mini-Storybooks). (Illus.). 32p. (gr. 1-6). 1983. pap. 1.25 saddlestitched (ISBN 0-394-85643-0). Random.

Engle, John D., Jr. Modern Odyssey. LC 79-175151. 80p. 1971. 4.00 o.p. (ISBN 0-8233-0171-0). Golden Quill.

Engle, Mary A., ed. Pediatric Cardiology. (Cardiovascular Clinics Ser: Vol. 4, No. 3). (Illus.). 366p. 1972. text ed. 15.00x o.p. (ISBN 0-8036-3200-2). Davis Co.

Engle, Tom, jt. auth. see Shugart, Cooksey.

Englebardt, Leland S. Living Together: What's the Law? 1981. 10.95 o.p. (ISBN 0-517-54072-X, Michelman Books). Crown.

Englebardt, Stanley L. The Nibbling Diet: The Natural Way to Lose Weight & Keep It Off. LC 77-25210. 1978. 7.95 o.p. (ISBN 0-399-12057-2). Putnam Pub Group.

Englekirk, John E., et al, eds. Anthology of Spanish-American Literature, 2 vols. 2nd ed. (Span.). 1968. Vol. 1. pap. text ed. 15.95 (ISBN 0-13-038786-X); Vol. 2. pap. text ed. 15.95 (ISBN 0-13-038794-0). P-H.

Englekirk, Robert & Hart, Gary. Earthquake Design of Concrete & Masonry Buildings: Response Spectrual Analysis & General Earthquake Modeling Considerations, Vol. I. (Illus.). 160p. 1982. 28.95 (ISBN 0-13-223065-8). P-H.

Engleman, R., ed. Nonradiative Decay of Ions & Molecules in Solids. 1979. 68.00 (ISBN 0-444-85244-1, North Holland). Elsevier.

Engler, A. Hochgebirgsflora Des Tropischen Afrikas. (Akad. D. Wissenschaften, Berlin Ser.). 461p. (Ger.). 1975. pap. text ed. 70.40x (ISBN 3-87429-088-3). Lubrecht & Cramer.

--Versuch Einer Entwicklungsgeschichte der Pflanzenwelt Insbesondere der Florengebiete Seit der Tertiaerperiode. 1971. 72.00 (ISBN 3-7682-0749-8). Lubrecht & Cramer.

Engler, A. & Drude, O., eds. Vegetation der Erde. Repr. of 1976 ed. of 13 vols. 800.00 set (ISBN 3-7682-0984-9). Lubrecht & Cramer.

Engler, Barbara O. Personality Theories: An Introduction. LC 78-69596. (Illus.). 1979. text ed. 22.50 (ISBN 0-395-26772-2); instr's. manual 1.00 (ISBN 0-395-26773-0). HM.

Engles, Friedrich, jt. auth. see Marx, Karl.

English. Basic Guide to Dog Training & Obedience. Date not set. pap. price not set (ISBN 0-448-16329-2, G&D). Putnam Pub Group.

English, Deirdre, jt. auth. see Ehrenreich, Barbara.

English, Dori, jt. auth. see Wiggins, James D.

English, Fenwick W. & Sharpes, Donald K. Strategies for Differentiated Staffing. LC 75-190058. 1972. 23.50x (ISBN 0-8211-0409-8); text ed. 21.25x (ISBN 0-685-24962-X). McCutchan.

English, Fenwick W., jt. auth. see Steeves, Frank L.

English, Gerald, ed. see Loose Leaf Reference Services.

English, Gerald M., ed. Otolaryngology, 5 vols. (Illus.). 4900p. 1982. 375.00 (ISBN 0-686-97946-X, Harper Medical); revision pages 55.00 (ISBN 0-686-97947-8). Lippincott.

English, H. Edward, ed. Canada-U. S. Relations. LC 76-38067. (Special Studies). 1976. text ed. 24.95 o.p. (ISBN 0-275-23300-6). Praeger.

English, James, Jr., et al. Principles of Organic Chemistry. 4th ed. 1971. text ed. 28.00 (ISBN 0-07-019520-X, C). McGraw.

English, Jane. Sex Equality. LC 76-53000. (Illus.). 256p. 1977. text ed. 14.95 (ISBN 0-13-807594-8); pap. text ed. 11.95 (ISBN 0-13-807586-7). P-H.

English, Jean. The Devices of Darkness. 1978. pap. 1.50 o.p. (ISBN 0-523-40259-7). Pinnacle Bks.

English, John W., jt. auth. see Cardiff, Gray E.

English Language Institute. English Conversation Practices. (Intensive Course in English Ser.). 1968. pap. 4.95x (ISBN 0-472-08306-6). U of Mich Pr.

--English Pattern Practices: Establishing the Patterns As Habits. rev. 3rd ed. (Intensive Course in English Ser.). (Illus., Orig.). (gr. 9 up). 1958. pap. 6.95x (ISBN 0-472-08302-3). U of Mich Pr.

--English Pronunciation: Exercises in Sound Segments, Intonation & Rhythm. rev. 2nd ed. (Intensive Course in English Ser.). (Orig.). (gr. 9 up). 1958. pap. 5.95x (ISBN 0-472-08303-1). U of Mich Pr.

--Vocabulary in Context. (Intensive Course in English Ser). 1964. pap. 5.95x (ISBN 0-472-08305-8). U of Mich Pr.

English Language Institute & Krohn, Robert. English Sentence Structure. rev. 4th ed. (Intensive Course in English Ser). 1971. pap. 6.95x (ISBN 0-472-08307-4). U of Mich Pr.

English Language Services. Readings & Conversations: About the United States, Its People, Its History & Its Customs, 2 vols. rev. ed. 1976. text ed. 4.50 ea.; Vol. 1. (ISBN 0-87789-195-8); Vol. 2. (ISBN 0-87789-196-6); Set. cassette tapes 95.00 (ISBN 0-87789-201-6). Cassettes 1. Cassettes 2 (ISBN 0-87789-202-4). Eng Language.

English, Margaret. A Basic Guide to Dog Training & Obedience. LC 74-27943. (Illus.). 196p. 1975. pap. 4.95 o.p. (ISBN 0-448-11862-9, G&D). Putnam Pub Group.

English, Mary P. Medical Mycology. (Studies in Biology: No. 119). 64p. 1980. pap. text ed. 8.95 (ISBN 0-7131-2795-3). E Arnold.

English, Maurice. Midnight in the Century. LC 82-71363. 69p. 1964. 5.00 (ISBN 0-8040-0204-5). Swallow.

English, Michael. Three-D Eye. (Paper Tiger Ser.). (Illus.). 127p. (Orig.). 1980. pap. 6.98 (ISBN 0-399-50497-4, Perige). Putnam Pub Group.

English, Paul W. World Regional Geography: A Question of Place. 1977. text ed. 23.50 scp o.p. (ISBN 0-06-167401-X, HarpC); inst. manual avail. o.p. (ISBN 0-06-167410-9). Har-Row.

English, Peter C. Shock, Physiological Surgery & George Washington Crile: Medical Innovation in the Progressive Era. LC 79-8579. (Contributions in Medical History: No. 5). xi, 271p. 1980. lib. bdg. 29.95 (ISBN 0-313-21490-5, EMI/). Greenwood.

English, R. William & Oberle, Judson B., eds. Rehabilitation Counselor Supervision: A National Perspective. 1980. 2.00 (ISBN 0-686-36377-9); 2.75 (ISBN 0-686-37296-4). Am Personnel.

English, Raymond, jt. auth. see Lefever, Ernest W.

English, Richard A., jt. ed. see Hasenfeld, Yeheskel.

English, Sandal. Fruits of the Desert. 181p. (Orig.). 1981. pap. 6.75 (ISBN 0-9607758-0-3). Ariz Daily Star.

English, W. E. & Lien, David A. Complete Guide for Easy Car Care. (Illus.). 384p. 1975. 17.95 (ISBN 0-13-160226-8). P-H.

Englman, R. The Jahn-Teller Effect in Molecules & Crystals. LC 77-37113. (Monographs in Chemical Physics Ser.). 370p. 1972. 74.95x (ISBN 0-471-24168-7, Pub. by Wiley-Interscience). Wiley.

Englund, Sr. Sergia, tr. see Lubac, Henri De.

Engs, Ruth & Wantz, Molly. Teaching Health Education in the Elementary School. LC 77-79371. (Illus.). 1978. text ed. 22.95 (ISBN 0-395-25483-3); instr's manual 1.00 (ISBN 0-395-25484-1). HM.

Engs, Ruth C. Responsible Drug & Alcohol Use. (Illus.). text ed. 12.95 (ISBN 0-02-333760-5). Macmillan.

Engs, Ruth C., et al. Health Games Students Play: Creative Strategies for Health Education. 1976. perfect bdg. 8.50 (ISBN 0-8403-1238-5). Kendall-Hunt.

Engstead, John. Star Shots: Fifty Years of Pictures & Stories by One of Hollywood's Greatest Photographers. (Illus.). 256p. 1980. 14.95 (ISBN 0-525-20950-6); pap. 6.95 (ISBN 0-525-47653-9). Dutton.

Engstrand, Iris H. Serra's San Diego: Father Junipero Serra & California's Beginnings. (Illus.). 1982. 2.95 (ISBN 0-918740-02-9). San Diego Hist.

Engstrom, A. X-Ray Microscopy & X-Ray Microanalysis. 1962. 5.80 (ISBN 0-444-40192-X). Elsevier.

Engstrom, A., et al, eds. X-Ray Microscopy & X-Ray Microanalysis. (Proceedings). 1961. 34.25 (ISBN 0-444-40193-8). Elsevier.

Engstrom, Albert. Twelve Tales. Borland, Harold, tr. from Swedish. (Bilingual Ser.). 1949. 5.00 (ISBN 0-911268-47-2). Rogers Bk.

Engstrom, Barbie. Egypt & a Nile Cruise. (Engstrom's Travel Experience Guides Ser.). (Illus.). 400p. (Orig.). 1983. pap. 15.50 (ISBN 0-916588-05-X). Kurios Pr.

--Paris to See & Enjoy: A Travel Enrichment Book. LC 76-7857. (Illus., Orig.). 1976. 3.95 o.p. (ISBN 0-916588-02-5). Kurios Pr.

Engstrom, J. Eric. The Medallic Portraits of Sir Winston Churchill. 1977. 12.00 (ISBN 0-685-51522-2, Pub by Spink & Son England). S J Durst.

Engstrom, Karen M. Consent Manual: Policies, Laws, Procedures, 2nd ed. 115p. pap. write for info (ISBN 0-87125-078-0). Catholic Health.

Engstrom, Paul F., jt. ed. see Sutnick, Alton I.

Engstrom, Ted W. Un Lider No Nace, Se Hace. 256p. Date not set. 3.50 (ISBN 0-88113-330-2). Edit Betania.

Engstrom, Ted W., jt. auth. see Dayton, Edward R.

Engstrom, Y., jt. auth. see Sumption, Merle R.

Enguang, Wang, jt. ed. see Renyong, Wu.

Engvick, William, ed. Lullabies & Night Songs. LC 65-22880. (Illus.). (ps-3). 1965. 22.50 (ISBN 0-06-021820-7, HarpJ); PLB 21.89 (ISBN 0-06-021821-5). Har-Row.

Engwall, Lars. Newspapers As Organisations. 1979. text ed. 34.00x (ISBN 0-566-00262-0). Gower Pub Ltd.

Enis, Ben. Marketing Principles. 3rd ed. 1980. 24.50x (ISBN 0-673-16110-2). study guide 9.95 (ISBN 0-673-16111-0). Scott F.

--Personal Selling: Foundations, Process, & Management. LC 78-12171. (Illus.). 1979. text ed. 23.50x (ISBN 0-673-16132-3). Scott F.

Enk, Gordon A. & Hornick, William F. Value Issues in Technology Assessment. (Special Studies in Science, Technology, & Public Policy). 180p. Date not set. lib. bdg. 20.00 (ISBN 0-89158-973-2). Westview. Postponed.

Enk, Gordon A., jt. auth. see Hart, Stuart L.

Enk, Mary J. & Hendricks, Marjorie E. Lighten Your Load with Volunteers. (Illus.). 1976. pap. 3.98 (ISBN 0-686-21679-2). Lyl Inc.

Enlow, D. K., compiled by. We Drive an Eighteen Wheeler. LC 81-67320. 136p. (Orig.). 1981. pap. 2.95 (ISBN 0-87509-305-1). Chr Pubns.

Enlow, David, ed. see Meloon, Walter.

Enlow, David R. Church Usher: Servant of God. LC 80-66769. 64p. (Orig.). 1980. pap. 2.50 (ISBN 0-87509-284-5). Chr Pubns.

Enlow, Donald H. A Handbook of Facial Growth. LC 75-293. (Illus.). 423p. 1975. 25.00 o.p. (ISBN 0-7216-3385-4). Saunders.

Enlow, Harold L. Carving Figure Caricatures in the Ozark Style. (Illus.). 8.50 (ISBN 0-8446-5183-4). Peter Smith.

Enna, S. J. & Yamamura, H. D., eds. Neurotransmitter Receptors, 2 pts. (Receptors & Recognition Ser. B: Vols. 9 & 10). 1980. Set. 90.00x (ISBN 0-686-80428-7, Pub by Chapman & Hall England); Pt. 1: Amino Acids, Peptides & Benzodiazepines. 49.95x ea. (ISBN 0-412-16250-4). Pt. 2: Biogenic Amines (ISBN 0-412-23130-1). Methuen Inc.

Enna, S. J., et al, eds. Brain Neurotransmitters & Receptors in Aging & Age-Related Disorders. (Aging Ser.: Vol. 17). 292p. 1981. text ed. 35.00 (ISBN 0-89004-643-3). Raven.

Enna, Salvatore J., jt. ed. see Coyle, Joseph T.

Enna, Salvatore J., et al, eds. Antidepressants: Neurochemical, Behavioral, & Clinical Perspectives. (Central Nervous System Pharmacology Ser.: Vol. 1). 275p. 1981. 35.00 (ISBN 0-89004-534-8). Raven.

Ennen, E. The Medieval Town. (Europe in the Middle Ages Selected Studies Ser.: Vol. 8). 1978. 44.00 (ISBN 0-444-85133-X, North-Holland). Elsevier.

Ennever, Len & Harlen, Wynne. With Objectives in Mind. LC 77-82993. (Science 5-13 Ser.). (Illus.). 1977. pap. text ed. 12.85 (ISBN 0-356-04009-7). Raintree Pubs.

Ennew, Judith. The Western Isles Today. LC 79-13643. (Changing Cultures Ser.). (Illus.). 1980. 27.95 (ISBN 0-521-22590-6); pap. 8.95 (ISBN 0-521-29572-6). Cambridge U Pr.

Ennis. Vascular Radionuclide Imaging. 1981. 75.00x (ISBN 0-471-25670-6, Wiley Heyden). Wiley.

Ennis, Bruce J. & Emery, Richard D. The Rights of Mental Patients. 1972. pap. 2.50 o.p. (ISBN 0-380-01859-4, 77024, Discus). Avon.

Ennis, Daniel & Mullen, Kenneth. The Operating Characteristic Curves Manual: Infinite Lot Size, Single Sampling Plans. 1980. lib. bdg. 25.00 (ISBN 0-8161-2208-3, Hall Medical). G K Hall.

Ennis, Joseph T. & Dowsett, David J. Vascular Radionuclide Imaging: A Clinical Atlas. 256p. 1982. 75.00 (ISBN 0-471-25670-6). Wiley.

Enns, Paul P. Ruth: A Bible Study Commentary. 96p. (Orig.). 1982. pap. 3.95 (ISBN 0-310-44061-0). Zondervan.

Eno, Arthur L., Jr., ed. see Lowell Historical Society.

Enoch, M. D. & Trethowan, W. H. Uncommon Psychiatric Syndromes. 1979. 28.75 o.p. (ISBN 0-8151-3124-0). Year Bk Med.

Enochson, L., jt. auth. see Otnes, R. K.

Enochson, Loren, jt. auth. see Otnes, Robert K.

Enock, Esther. Missionary Heroine of Calabar (Mary Slessor) 1973. pap. 1.95 o.p. (ISBN 0-87508-613-6). Chr Lit.

Enos, Chris. Gar-baj. LC 81-70289. (Illus.). 54p. (Orig.). 1982. pap. 5.00 (ISBN 0-89822-025-4). Visual Studies.

Enos, Darryl & Sultan, Paul. The Sociology of Health Care: Social, Economic & Political Perspectives. LC 76-17250. 1977. 15.95 o.p. (ISBN 0-275-56970-5). Praeger.

Enos, John L. Petroleum Progess & Profits: A History of Process Innovation. (Illus.). 1962. 22.50x o.p. (ISBN 0-262-05002-1). MIT Pr.

Enrick, N. L. Management Planning. 1967. 21.50x (ISBN 0-87245-097-X). Textile Bk.

--Quality Control & Reliability. 1969. 28.50x (ISBN 0-87245-098-8). Textile Bk.

Enrick, Norbert L. Experimentation & Statistical Validation. LC 81-20928. 1983. pap. write for info. (ISBN 0-89874-445-8). Krieger.

--Management Control Manual for the Textile Industry. 19.95x (ISBN 0-87245-095-3). Textile Bk.

--Management Planning: A Systems Approach. 1967. 24.95 o.p. (ISBN 0-07-019524-2, P&RB). McGraw.

Enrico Fermi Course 63, Vareno, Italy 1974. New Directions in Physical Acoustics: Proceedings. Sette, D., ed. 1976. 106.50 (ISBN 0-7204-0489-4, North-Holland). Elsevier.

Enrico Fermi Course 64, Vareno, Italy, 1975. Nonlinear Spectroscopy: Proceedings. Bloembergen, N., ed. 1977. 89.50 (ISBN 0-7204-0568-8, North-Holland). Elsevier.

Enright, D. J. The Apothecary's Shop. LC 75-15663. 236p. 1975. Repr. of 1957 ed. lib. bdg. 15.50x (ISBN 0-8371-8222-0, ENAS). Greenwood.

--The Typewriter Revolution & Other Poems. LC 73-158612. 143p. 1971. 12.00x (ISBN 0-912050-07-1, Library Pr). Open Court.

Enright, D. J., ed. The Oxford Book of Death. 320p. 1983. 19.95 (ISBN 0-19-214129-5). Oxford U Pr.

Enright, Elizabeth. Gone-Away Lake. LC 57-5172. (Illus.). (gr. 4-6). 1966. pap. 3.95 (ISBN 0-15-636460-3, VoyB). HarBraceJ.

--Return to Gone-Away. LC 61-6113. (Illus.). 191p. (gr. 3-7). 1973. pap. 1.15 (ISBN 0-15-676900-X, AVB74, VoyB). HarBraceJ.

--Thimble Summer. (gr. 2-6). 1976. pap. 2.25 (ISBN 0-440-48681-5, YB). Dell.

Enright, T. J. Lectures on Representations of Complex Semi-Simple Lie Groups. (Tata Institute Lectures on Mathematics Ser.). 91p. 1982. pap. 7.20 (ISBN 0-387-10829-7). Springer-Verlag.

Enriques, Federigo. The Problems of Science. Royce, Katherine, tr. from It. xvi, 408p. 1914. 24.50 (ISBN 0-87548-214-7). Open Court.

Enroth, Ronald, et al. A Guide to Cults & New Religions. 200p. (Orig.). 1983. pap. 5.95 (ISBN 0-87784-837-8). Inter-Varsity.

Enser, A. G. Filmed Books & Plays Nineteen Twenty-Eight to Nineteen Seventy-Four. 552p. 1975. 26.50 (ISBN 0-233-96676-5, 05784-3, Pub. by Gower Pub Co England). Lexington Bks.

--A Subject Bibliography of the First World War: Books in English, 1914-1978. LC 76-54230. 1979. lib. bdg. 48.00 (ISBN 0-89158-722-5). Westview.

--A Subject Bibliography of the First World War: Books in English 1914-1978. 488p. 1979. 39.00 (ISBN 0-233-96742-7, 05782-7, Pub. by Gower Pub Co England). Lexington Bks.

--A Subject Bibliography of the Second World War: Books in English 1939-1974. 567p. 1977. 39.00 (ISBN 0-233-96742-7, 05783-5, Pub. by Gower Pub Co England). Lexington Bks.

Enser, A. G. S. Filmed Books & Plays: 1975-1981. 1983. write for info (ISBN 0-566-03475-1, 05786-X, Pub. by Gower Pub Co England). Lexington Bks.

Ensko, Stephen G. American Silversmiths & Their Marks: The Definitive Edition, 1948. 2nd ed. (Illus.). 287p. 1983. pap. 6.00 (ISBN 0-486-24428-8). Dover.

Enslein, Kurt, et al. Statistical Methods for Digital Computers. LC 60-6509. (Mathematical Methods for Digital Computers Ser.: Vol. 3). 1977. 56.50 (ISBN 0-471-70690-6, Pub. by Wiley-Interscience). Wiley.

Enslin, Morton S. The Prophet from Nazareth. LC 68-27322. 1969. 6.00x o.p. (ISBN 0-8052-3210-9); pap. 1.95 o.p. (ISBN 0-8052-0184-X). Schocken.

Enslin, Theodore. The Fifth Direction. (Orig.). 1980. 35.00 o.p. (ISBN 0-915316-81-1); pap. 5.00 (ISBN 0-915316-80-3). Pentagram.

Enslin, Theodore, ed. F. P. 1982. pap. 1.95 (ISBN 0-917488-12-1). Ziesing Bros.

Enslow, D. H., ed. see Comtre Corp.

Ensminger, A. H. & Ensminger, M. E. Foods & Nutrition Encyclopedia, 2 vols. (Illus.). 2432p. 1983. Set. 99.00x (ISBN 0-941218-05-8). Pegus Pr.

Ensminger, Louise, ed. Commencement Addresses & Talks to Students 1982. LC 81-85784. 103p. 1982. spiral bdg. 12.95 (ISBN 0-918214-09-2). F E Peters.

Ensminger, M. E. Beef Cattle Science. 5th ed. LC 74-29763. (Illus.). 1976. 36.50 (ISBN 0-8134-1752-X, 1752); text ed. 27.50x. Interstate.

--Dairy Cattle Science. 2nd ed. LC 78-78193. (Illus.). 640p. 1980. 32.50 (ISBN 0-8134-2079-2, 2079); text ed. 24.50x. Interstate.

--Horses & Horsemanship. 5th ed. LC 76-45238. (Illus.). 1977. 26.50 (ISBN 0-8134-1888-7); text ed. 19.95x. Interstate.

--Poultry Science. 2nd ed. (Illus.). (gr. 9-12). 1980. 28.00 (ISBN 0-8134-2087-3, 2087); text ed. 21.00x. Interstate.

--The Stockman's Handbook. 5th ed. LC 76-58206. 1978. 36.50 (ISBN 0-8134-1943-3, 1943); text ed. 27.50x. Interstate.

Ensminger, M. E., jt. auth. see Ensminger, A. H.

Ensminger, M. Eugene. Animal Science. 7th ed. LC 76-1512. (Illus.). 1977. 36.50 (ISBN 0-8134-1798-8, 1798); text ed. 27.50x (ISBN 0-686-86130-2). Interstate.

Ensor, Allison. Mark Twain & the Bible. LC 76-80092. 144p. 1969. 9.00x o.p. (ISBN 0-8131-1181-1). U Pr of Ky.

Ensor, Bill. News at Six & Other Stories & Essays. 1982. 6.95 (ISBN 0-533-05377-3). Vantage.

Ensor, H. Blaine see Oakley, Carey.

Ensor, James. The Prints of James Ensor. LC 76-184012. 1972. Repr. of 1952 ed. lib. bdg. 29.50 (ISBN 0-306-70439-0). Da Capo.

Ensor, Wendy-Ann. Heroes & Heroines in Music. (Illus.). 1982. pap. 5.00 (ISBN 0-19-321105-X); cassette 18.00. Oxford U Pr.

--More Heroes & Heroines in Music. (Illus.). 48p. 1983. pap. 5.00 laminated (ISBN 0-19-321106-8); cassette 18.00 (ISBN 0-19-321107-6). Oxford U Pr.

Ensrud, Barbara. The Pocket Guide to Cheese. 144p. 1981. pap. 4.95 (ISBN 0-399-50518-0, Perige). Putnam Pub Group.

--The Pocket Guide to Wine. rev. ed. 144p. 1982. pap. 5.95 (ISBN 0-399-50483-4, Perige). Putnam Pub Group.

Enstice, Andrew. Thomas Hardy: Landscapes of the Mind. (Illus.). 1979. 22.50x (ISBN 0-312-80153-X). St Martin.

Enstrom, Robert. Beta Colony. LC 78-22315. (Science Fiction Ser.). 1980. 10.95 o.p. (ISBN 0-385-14644-2). Doubleday.

Enteen, George M. The Soviet Scholar-Bureaucrat: M. N. Pokrovskii & the Society of Marxist Historians. LC 78-50002. 1978. 22.50x (ISBN 0-271-00548-3). Pa St U Pr.

Enteen, George M., et al. Soviet Historians & the Study of Russian Imperialism. LC 78-27563. (Penn State Studies: No. 45). 1979. pap. text ed. 3.50x (ISBN 0-271-00211-5). Pa St U Pr.

Enteen, Shellie & Jacobs, Judy. Passion Planets: The Astrology of Relationships. 288p. (Orig.). 1980. pap. 2.50 o.s.i. (ISBN 0-515-05269-8). Jove Pubns.

Entelis, S. G. & Tiger, R. P. Reaction Kinetics in the Liquid Phase. Kondor, R., tr. from Rus. LC 75-17857. 362p. 1976. 74.95 o.s.i. (ISBN 0-470-24330-9). Halsted Pr.

Enters, Angna. First Person Plural. (Ser. in Dance). (Illus.). 1978. Repr. of 1937 ed. lib. bdg. 25.00 (ISBN 0-306-77594-8). Da Capo.

Enthoven, A. J. Accountancy & Economic Development Policy. 300p. 1973. pap. 42.75 (ISBN 0-7204-3072-0, North-Holland). Elsevier.

--Accountancy Systems in Third World Economies. 1977. 51.00 (ISBN 0-7204-0721-4, North-Holland). Elsevier.

--Accounting Education in Economic Development Management. 1981. 34.00 (ISBN 0-444-86195-5). Elsevier.

Entrekin, Dee. Make Your Own Silk Flowers. LC 74-31705. (Illus.). 80p. 1981. pap. 7.95 (ISBN 0-8069-8994-7). Sterling.

--Make Your Own Silk Flowers. LC 74-31705. (Illus.). 80p. 1975. 12.95 (ISBN 0-8069-5318-7); PLB 11.69 o.p. (ISBN 0-8069-5319-5). Sterling.

Entrikin, John B., jt. auth. see Cheronis, Nicholas D.

Entwisle, E. A. French Scenic Wallpapers, Eighteen Hundred to Eighteen Sixty. 40.00x (ISBN 0-87245-610-2). Textile Bk.

Entwistle, Beverly M., jt. auth. see Lange, Brian M.

Entwistle, Harold. Political Education in a Democracy. (Students Library of Education). 1970. 12.95x (ISBN 0-7100-7132-9). Routledge & Kegan.

Entwistle, Noel. Styles of Learning & Teaching: An Integrated Outline of Educational Psychology for Students, Teachers, & Lecturers. LC 80-41172. 1981. 52.95 (ISBN 0-471-27901-3, Pub. by Wiley-Interscience); pap. 22.95 (ISBN 0-471-10013-7). Wiley.

Entwistle, W. J. & Morison, W. A. Russian & the Slavonic Languages. 407p. 1982. Repr. of 1949 ed. lib. bdg. 65.00 (ISBN 0-8495-1429-0). Arden Lib.

Environmental Action Foundation. Accidents Will Happen. LC 79-2435. (Illus., Orig.). 1979. pap. 2.50i o.p. (ISBN 0-06-080505-6, P505, PL). Har-Row.

Environmental Engineering Conference, Canberra Australia, 1979. The Status of the National Environment. 110p. (Orig.). 1979. pap. text ed. 24.00x (ISBN 0-85825-115-9, Pub. by Inst Engineering Australia). Renouf.

Environmental Protection Agency. Toxic Substances Control Act Inspection Manual. 350p. 1982. pap. 35.00 (ISBN 0-86587-056-X). Gov Insts.

Environmental Resources Ltd., ed. The Law & Practice Relating to Pollution Control in the Member States of the European Communities, 10 vols. 1982. Set. 850.00 (ISBN 0-686-82384-2, Pub. by Graham & Trotman England); 90.00x ea. State Mutual Bk.

Enyeart, James L. Jerry N. Uelsmann, -Twenty-Five Years: A Retrospective. LC 82-12736. 231p. 1982. 39.95 (ISBN 0-8212-1519-1, 477400). NYGS.

Enyedi, Gyorgy & Volgyes, Ivan, eds. The Effect of Modern Agriculture on Rural Developement. LC 80-25232. (Pergamon Policy Studies on International Developement Comparative Rural Transformations Ser.). (Illus.). 256p. 1982. 32.50 (ISBN 0-08-027179-0). Pergamon.

Enz, C. P., ed. see Pauli, Wolfgang.

Enz, Jacob J. The Christian & Warfare: The Old Testament, War & the Christian. (Christian Peace Shelf Ser.). 104p. 1972. pap. 2.95 (ISBN 0-8361-1684-4). Herald Pr.

Enzel, Hajnalka V., ed. see Enzel, Robert G.

Enzel, Robert G. The White Book of Ski Areas. Enzel, Hajnalka V., ed. (Illus.). 348p. 1982. write for info. Inter-Ski.

Enzer, Selwyn, et al. Neither Feast nor Famine. LC 78-3128. (Illus.). 1978. 17.95x (ISBN 0-669-02317-5). Lexington Bks.

Enzinger, Franz M. & Weiss, Sharon W. Soft Tissue Tumors. LC 82-50823. (Illus.). 840p. 1983. text ed. 99.95 (ISBN 0-8016-1499-6). Mosby.

Eoff, S. H., ed. see Rodrìruez, Mario B., et al.

Eoff, Sherman, et al. Zalacain el Aventurero. Babcock, U. C. & Ramirez-Araujo, Alejandro, eds. LC 49-8551. (Graded Spanish Readers, Bk. 4). (Span). 1954. pap. text ed. 4.95 (ISBN 0-395-04127-9). HM.

Eoff, Sherman H. & Ramirez-Aranjo, Alejandro. Pio Bargjca's Zalacain el Aventurereo, Bk. 4. (Graded Spanish Readers (Span.)). 1954. pap. text ed. 5.50 (ISBN 0-395-04127-9). HM.

Eolis, Wendeen. How to Write Effective Resumes for Professionals & Executives. 1983. pap. 3.95 (ISBN 0-8120-0872-3). Barron.

EORTC, see European Organization for Research & Treatment of Cancer.

Eoyang, Eugene C., ed. see Qing, Ai.

Epachin, Betty C., jt. auth. see Paul, James L.

Epanchin, Betty C. & Paul, James L. Casebook for Educating the Emotionally Disturbed. 288p. 1982. pap. text ed. 9.95 (ISBN 0-675-20018-0). Merrill.

Ephremides, A. Random Processes, Pt. 1: Poisson & Jump Point Processes. LC 75-1287. (Benchmark Papers in Electrical Engineering & Computer Science Ser: No. 11). 352p. 1973. Vol. 1. 54.50 o.p. (ISBN 0-12-786431-8); Pt. 2,1975. 54.50 (ISBN 0-12-786432-6). Acad Pr.

Ephron, Delia. Teenage Romance: Or How to Die of Embarrassment. 1982. pap. 5.95 (ISBN 0-345-30457-8). Ballantine.

Ephron, Nora. Heartburn. LC 82-48999. 1983. 12.95 (ISBN 0-394-53180-9). Knopf.

Epictetus see Aurelius, Marcus.

Epigraphic Survey. The Temple of Khonsu: Vol. 2, Scenes & Inscriptions in the Court & the First Hypostyle Hall. LC 80-82999. (Oriental Institute Publications Ser.: Vol. 103). 1981. pap. 95.00x incl. 96 plates in portfolio (ISBN 0-918986-29-X). Oriental Inst.

Epilepsy International Symposium, 10th. Advances in Epileptology: Proceedings. Wada, Juhn & Penry, J. Kiffin, eds. 594p. 1980. text ed. 72.00 (ISBN 0-89004-511-9). Raven.

Epilepsy International Symposium, 11th., et al. Advances in Epileptology: Proceedings. Canger, Raffaele & Penry, J. Kiffin, eds. 510p. 1980. text ed. 61.50 (ISBN 0-89004-510-0). Raven.

Epilepsy International Symposium, 12th. Copenhagen, Denmark, et al. Advances in Epileptology: Proceedings. Dam, Mogens, ed. 724p. 1981. 82.50 (ISBN 0-89004-611-5). Raven.

Epilepsy International Symposium, 13th., et al. Advances in Epileptology: Proceedings. Akimoto, H., ed. 750p. 1982. text ed. 95.00 (ISBN 0-89004-798-7). Raven.

Episcopal Church. Prayer Book Guide to Christian Education. 224p. 1983. pap. 9.95 (ISBN 0-8164-2422-5). Seabury.

Episcopal Church Center. The Work You Give Us to Do: A Mission Study. 179p. (Orig.). 1982. pap. 4.95 (ISBN 0-8164-7116-9); study guide 1.25 (ISBN 0-8164-7117-7). Seabury.

Episcopal Churchwomen of All Saints. La Bonne Cuisine: Cooking New Orleans Style. (Illus.). pap. 9.95 (ISBN 0-9606880-0-5). Mercury Print.

Epker, Bruce N. & Wolford, Larry M. Dentofacial Deformities: Surgical-Orthodontic Correction. LC 80-12405. (Illus.). 490p. 1980. text ed. 77.50 (ISBN 0-8016-1606-9). Mosby.

Epley, Donald R. & Millar, James A. Basic Real Estate Finance & Investments. LC 79-19530. 633p. 1980. text ed. 28.50 (ISBN 0-471-03635-8). Wiley.

Epley, Donald R. & Rabianski, Joseph. Principles of Real Estate Decisions. LC 80-21354. 1981. text ed. 23.95 (ISBN 0-201-03188-4); instrs' manual 9.95 (ISBN 0-201-03189-2). A-W.

Epp, C. D., jt. auth. see Bernard, C. H.

Epp, Donald J. & Malone, John W., Jr. Introduction to Agricultural Economics. 1981. text ed. 25.95x (ISBN 0-02-333940-3). Macmillan.

Epp, Eldon J. & Gordon, Fee D., eds. New Testament Textual Criticism: Its Significance for Exegesis. (Illus.). 438p. 94.00x (ISBN 0-19-826175-6). Oxford U Pr.

Epp, Frank H. Mennonites in Canada, 1786-1920, Vol. I. (Illus.). 480p. 1982. text ed. 12.95x (ISBN 0-8361-1254-7). Herald Pr.

--Mennonites in Canada, 1920-1940, Vol. II. 640p. 1982. text ed. 21.95x (ISBN 0-8361-1255-5). Herald Pr.

Epp, Michael, tr. see Krussman, Gerd.

Epp, Robert. Kinoshita Yuji. (World Authors Ser.). 168p. 1982. lib. bdg. 18.95 (ISBN 0-8057-6505-0, Twayne). G K Hall.

Eppard, Philip, jt. auth. see Monteiro, George.

Eppen, Gary D. & Gould, F. J. Quantitative Concepts for Management Decision Making Without Algorithms. 1979. 28.95 (ISBN 0-13-746602-1). P-H.

Eppenbach, Sarah & Easter, Deb. Alaska's Southeast: Touring the Inside Passage. (Illus.). 223p. (Orig.). 1983. pap. 9.95 (ISBN 0-914718-79-7). Pacific Search.

Epperson, Arlin. Private & Commercial Recreation: A Text & Reference. LC 76-56453. 385p. 1977. text ed. 23.95 (ISBN 0-471-24335-3). Wiley.

Eppert, M. R., ed. see Educational Research Council of America.

Epple, Anne O. Amphibians of New England. LC 82-73602. (Illus.). 1983. pap. 8.95t (ISBN 0-89272-159-6). Down East.

Epple, Dennis. Petroleum Discoveries & Government Policy: An Econometric Study of Supply. LC 75-25626. 160p. 1975. prof ref 25.00x (ISBN 0-88410-420-6). Ballinger Pub.

Epps, Charles H., ed. Complications in Orthopaedic Surgery, 2 vols. LC 78-17997. 1978. Set. 112.00x (ISBN 0-397-50382-2, Lippincott Medical). Lippincott.

Epps, Edgar G. Cultural Pluralism. LC 73-17617. 1974. 19.00x (ISBN 0-8211-0412-8); text ed. 17.25x (ISBN 0-685-42631-9). McCutchan.

Epps, Edgar G., jt. auth. see Gurin, Patricia.

Epps, Garrett. The Shad Treatment. LC 76-20493. 1977. 9.95 o.p. (ISBN 0-399-11829-2). Putnam Pub Group.

Epps, Louvella, jt. auth. see Harris, Teresa.

Epps, Preston H., tr. see Aristotle.

Eppstein, John. The Cult of Revolution in the Church. LC 73-18470. 160p. 1975. pap. 2.50 o.p. (ISBN 0-87973-795-6). Our Sunday Visitor.

Epstein. Kidney in Liver Disease. 1982. 75.00 (ISBN 0-444-00655-9). Elsevier.

Epstein & Troy. Barron's Guide to Law Schools. 5th ed. LC 80-11446. 1982. pap. 6.95 (ISBN 0-8120-2436-2). Barron.

Epstein, A. J. & Conwell, E. M., eds. Low-Dimensional Conductors. (Molecular Crystals & Liquid Crystals Ser.: Vols. 77, 79, 81, 83, 85, & 86). 2078p. 1982. 620.00 (ISBN 0-677-16405-X). Gordon.

Epstein, A. L. Ethos & Identity. 1982. pap. 6.50x (ISBN 0-422-76370-5, Pub. by Tavistock England). Methuen Inc.

Epstein, A. N., et al, eds. Neuropsychology of Thirst. LC 73-10257. 357p. 1973. 17.50x o.s.i. (ISBN 0-470-24350-3). Halsted Pr.

Epstein, Abraham & White, Morris. Shorthand, Typewriting & Secretarial Training. 1958. pap. 2.95 (ISBN 0-448-01506-4, G&D). Putnam Pub Group.

Epstein, Alan, jt. ed. see Sprague, James.

Epstein, Alan N., jt. ed. see Sprague, James M.

Epstein, Arthur J., jt. ed. see Miller, Joel S.

Epstein, Benjamin & Forster, Arnold. Some of My Best Friends... LC 75-2694. 274p. 1975. Repr. of 1962 ed. lib. bdg. 17.25x (ISBN 0-8371-8027-9, EPBF). Greenwood.

Epstein, Benjamin R., jt. auth. see Forster, Arnold.

Epstein, Beryl & Epstein, Samuel. Dr. Beaumont & the Man with the Hole in His Stomach. LC 77-8236. (Science Discovery Bk. Ser.). (Illus.). (gr. 3-5). 1978. PLB 5.99 (ISBN 0-698-30680-5, Coward). Putnam Pub Group.

--Mister Peale's Mammoth. LC 76-49644. (Science Discovery Bk.). (Illus.). (gr. 3-5). 1977. 5.95 o.p. (ISBN 0-698-20402-6, Coward). Putnam Pub Group.

--Who Says You Can't? (gr. 7 up). 1969. 7.95 o.p. (ISBN 0-698-20165-5, Coward). Putnam Pub Group.

Epstein, Beryl, jt. auth. see Epstein, Sam.

Epstein, Beryl, jt. auth. see Epstein, Samuel.

Epstein, Cathleen, tr. see Wandruszka, Adam.

Epstein, Charlotte. Classroom Management & Teaching: Persistent Problems & Rational Solutions. 1979. text ed. 18.95 (ISBN 0-8359-0824-0). Reston.

--An Introduction to the Human Services: Developing Knowledge, Skills, & Sensitivity. (Illus.). 368p. 1981. text ed. 22.95 (ISBN 0-13-484501-3). P-H.

--The Nurse Leader: Philosophy & Practice. 304p. 1982. text ed. 17.95 (ISBN 0-8359-5027-1); pap. text ed. 14.95 (ISBN 0-8359-5026-3). Reston.

Epstein, Cynthia F. Woman's Place: Options & Limits in Professional Careers. LC 75-98139. 1970. 18.95x (ISBN 0-520-01581-9); pap. 3.95 (ISBN 0-520-01870-2, CAL227). U of Cal Pr.

--Women in Law. LC 80-68954. 382p. 1981. 18.50 (ISBN 0-465-09205-5). Basic.

--Women in Law. LC 82-45611. 456p. 1983. pap. 10.95 (ISBN 0-385-18431-X, Anch). Doubleday.

Epstein, Daniel M. The Book of Fortune. LC 81-18907. 64p. 1982. 10.95 (ISBN 0-87951-146-X); deluxe ed. 40.00 (ISBN 0-87951-151-6). Overlook Pr.

Epstein, David. Beyond Orpheus: Studies in Musical Structure. 1979. 27.50x (ISBN 0-262-05016-1). MIT Pr.

Epstein, David G. Brasilia-Plan & Reality: A Study of Planned & Spontaneous Urban Settlement. LC 72-186103. 1973. 30.00x (ISBN 0-520-02203-3). U of Cal Pr.

Epstein, David G. & Landers, Jonathan M. Debtors & Creditors, Cases & Materials. 2nd ed. LC 82-7088. (American Casebook Ser.). 725p. 1982. 20.95 (ISBN 0-314-66044-5). West Pub.

Epstein, David G. & Martin, James A. Basic Uniform Commercial Code Teaching Materials. 2d ed. (American Casebook Ser.). 589p. 1983. text ed. write for info. (ISBN 0-314-71764-1). West Pub.

Epstein, E. Common Skin Disorders: A Physician's Illustrated Manual with Patient Instruction Sheets. (Illus.). 1983. pap. 25.95 (ISBN 0-87489-308-9). Med Economics.

Epstein, Edmund L. Language & Style. (New Accents Ser.). 1978. 14.95x (ISBN 0-416-83270-9); pap. 7.95x (ISBN 0-416-83280-6). Methuen Inc.

Epstein, Edmund L., ed. see Joyce, James.

Epstein, Edward & Votaw, Dow. Rationality, Legitimacy, Responsibility: Search for New Directions in Business & Society. LC 78-18302. 1978. pap. 17.95x (ISBN 0-673-16135-8). Scott F.

Epstein, Edward J. Agency of Fear: Opiates & Political Power in America. LC 76-14443. 1977. 9.95 o.p. (ISBN 0-399-11656-7). Putnam Pub Group.
--Between Fact & Fiction: The Problem of Journalism. (Orig.). 1975. pap. 4.95 (ISBN 0-394-71396-6, Vin). Random.
--Cartel. LC 78-7490. 1978. 9.95 o.p. (ISBN 0-399-12086-6). Putnam Pub Group.
--The Legend: Secret World of Lee Harvey Oswald. 1978. 12.95 o.p. (ISBN 0-07-019539-0, GB). McGraw.
Epstein, Ellen R. & Mendelsohn, Rona. Record & Remember. LC 78-1411. 1978. pap. 2.95 o.p. (ISBN 0-671-18356-7). Monarch Pr.
Epstein, Ellen R., jt. auth. see Lewit, Jane.
Epstein, Emanuel. Mineral Nutrition of Plants: Principles & Perspectives. LC 75-165018. 412p. 1972. 24.95x (ISBN 0-471-24340-X). Wiley.
Epstein, Ervin & Epstein, Ervin, Jr. Skin Surgery, 2 vols. 5th ed. (Illus.). 1276p. 1982. Set. 215.00x (ISBN 0-398-04540-2). C C Thomas.
Epstein, Fritz T. German Source Materials in American Libraries. 1958. pap. 1.95 o.p. (ISBN 0-87462-409-6). Marquette.
Epstein, George, et al, eds. Kevlar Composites. LC 80-53544. (Illus.). 93p. 1980. 32.00 (ISBN 0-938648-02-0). T-C Pubns CA.
Epstein, Gerald, ed. Studies in Non-Deterministic Psychology. LC 80-13820. (New Directions in Psychotheraphy Ser.: Vol. V). 294p. (Series editor Paul T. Olsen). 1980. 29.95 (ISBN 0-87705-654-4). Human Sci Pr.
Epstein, H. Domestic Animals of China. LC 73-152339. (Illus.). 1971. 39.50x (ISBN 0-8419-0073-6). Holmes & Meier.
Epstein, Hans, tr. see Wandruszka, Adam.
Epstein, Helen. Children of the Holocaust: Conversations with Sons & Daughters of Survivors. LC 78-23429. 1979. 10.95 o.p. (ISBN 0-399-12316-4). Putnam Pub Group.
Epstein, Henry F. & Wolf, Stewart, eds. Genetic Analysis of the Chromosome: Studies of Duchenne Muscular Dystrophy & Related Disorders, Vol. 154. (Advances in Experimental Medicine & Biology). 222p. 1982. 37.50x (ISBN 0-306-41129-6, Plenum Pr). Plenum Pub.
Epstein, Henry F., jt. ed. see Pearson, Mark L.
Epstein, Herman T. Strategy for Education. LC 71-124614. 1970. 11.95x (ISBN 0-19-501261-5). Oxford U Pr.
Epstein, I. Ivan. Basic Physics in Anesthesiology. (Illus.). 1976. pap. 19.95 o.p. (ISBN 0-8151-3135-6). Year Bk Med.
Epstein, Isidore. Faith of Judaism. pap. 8.75x (ISBN 0-900689-13-7). Bloch.
--Step by Step in the Jewish Religion. PLB 4.95x (ISBN 0-900689-12-9). Bloch.
Epstein, James & Thompson, Dorothy, eds. The Chartist Experience-Studies in Working-Class Radicalism & Culture 1830 to 1860. 416p. 1982. text ed. 28.00x (ISBN 0-333-32971-6, 41403, Pub. by Macmillan England); pap. text ed. 12.50x (ISBN 0-333-32972-4, 41424). Humanities.
Epstein, Jane & Magnus, Laury. Common Ground: A Thematic Reader. 1981. pap. text ed. 12.50x (ISBN 0-673-15505-6). Scott F.
Epstein, Jerome & Gaines, John. Clinical Respiratory Care of the Adult Patient. (Illus.). 448p. 1983. pap. text ed. 21.95 (ISBN 0-89303-209-3). R J Brady.
Epstein, Joseph. Ambition: The Secret Passion. 320p. 1981. 13.95 o.p. (ISBN 0-525-05280-1). Dutton.
--Familiar Territory: Observations on American Life. 1979. 15.95x (ISBN 0-19-502604-7). Oxford U Pr.
Epstein, Joyce L., ed. The Quality of School Life. LC 80-5350. 320p. 1981. 29.95x (ISBN 0-669-03869-5). Lexington Bks.
Epstein, Joyce L. & Karweit, Nancy L., eds. Friends in School: Patterns of Selection & Influence in Secondary Schools. LC 82-22822. Date not set. price not set (ISBN 0-12-240540-4). Acad Pr.
Epstein, Judy. Keeping Score. 33p. 1975. 2.00 (ISBN 0-87886-067-3). Ithaca Hse.
Epstein, Laura. Helping People: The Task-Centered Approach. LC 79-21084. (Illus.). 266p. 1980. pap. text ed. 12.95 (ISBN 0-8016-1509-7). Mosby.
Epstein, Lawrence J. Samuel Goldwyn. (Filmmakers Ser.). 1981. lib. bdg. 14.95 (ISBN 0-8057-9282-1, Twayne). G K Hall.
Epstein, Leon D. Governing the University: The Campus & the Public Interest. LC 73-20967. (Higher Education Ser). 264p. 1974. 18.95x (ISBN 0-87589-215-9). Jossey-Bass.
Epstein, Leon J., jt. ed. see Simon, Alexander.
Epstein, Leslie. King of the Jews. LC 78-14558. 1979. 10.95 o.s.i. (ISBN 0-698-10955-4, Coward). Putnam Pub Group.
--Regina. 288p. 1982. 13.95 (ISBN 0-698-11203-2, Coward). Putnam Pub Group.
Epstein, Lewis C. Relativity Visualized. LC 82-84280. (Illus.). 250p. 1983. pap. 12.95 (ISBN 0-935218-03-3). Insight Pr CA.
Epstein, M. A., jt. ed. see Richter, G. W.
Epstein, Marc J. & Flamholtz, Eric G. Corporate Social Performance: The Measurement of Product & Service Contributions. 133p. pap. 12.95 (ISBN 0-86641-050-3, 7792). Natl Assn Accts.
Epstein, Marc J., jt. auth. see Book, Stephen A.
Epstein, Michael, jt. auth. see Cullinan, Douglas.
Epstein, Michael, jt. auth. see Cullinhan, Douglas.
Epstein, Mortimer. Early History of the Levant Company. LC 68-24162. 1968. Repr. of 1908 ed. 25.00x (ISBN 0-678-00416-1). Kelley.
Epstein, Natalie, jt. auth. see Oppenheimer, Lillian.
Epstein, R. B., tr. see Hua, Ch'an Master.
Epstein, Rhoda & Conley, Virginia. Developing a Master's Program in Nursing. 37p. 1978. 3.95 (ISBN 0-686-38262-5, 15-1747). Natl League Nurse.
Epstein, Rhoda B. & Millsap, Margaret. Coping with Change through Assessment & Evaluation. 102p. 1976. 5.50 (ISBN 0-686-38248-X, 23-1618). Natl League Nurse.
Epstein, Robert, ed. see Skinner, B. F.
Epstein, Robert S. Query Processing Techniques for Distributed, Relational Data Base Systems. Stone, Harold, ed. LC 82-6949. (Computer Science: Distributed Database Systems Ser.: No. 13). 106p. 1982. 34.95 (ISBN 0-8357-1341-5, Pub. by UMI Res Pr). Univ Microfilms.
Epstein, Roslyn. American Indian Needlepoint Designs for Pillows, Belts, Handbags & Other Projects. (Illus.). 48p. (Orig.). 1973. pap. 1.95 (ISBN 0-486-22973-4). Dover.
Epstein, S. & Somers, R., eds. Weldability of Steels. 1971. 18.00 o.p. (ISBN 0-685-65960-7). Am Welding.
Epstein, S., ed. see Stout, R. D. & Doty, W. D.
Epstein, Sam & Epstein, Beryl. All About Engines & Power. (Allabout Ser.: No. 46). (Illus.). (gr. 5-9). 1962. PLB 5.39 o.p. (ISBN 0-394-90245-9). Random.
--Charles De Gaulle: Defender of France. LC 72-6254. (Century Biographies Ser.). (Illus.). (gr. 4-8). 1973. PLB 3.98 (ISBN 0-8116-4756-0). Garrard.
--The First Book of Electricity. LC 76-41317. (First Bks.). (Illus.). 72p. (gr. 4-6). 1977. PLB 7.90 (ISBN 0-531-00522-4). Watts.
--Game of Baseball. LC 65-10098. (Sports Library Ser). (Illus.). (gr. 3-6). 1965. PLB 7.12 (ISBN 0-8116-6651-4). Garrard.
--Harriet Tubman: Guide to Freedom. LC 68-22638. (Americans All Ser). (Illus.). (gr. 3-6). 1968. PLB 7.12 (ISBN 0-8116-4550-9). Garrard.
--Henry Aaron: Home-Run King. LC 75-9966. (Sports Library Ser.). (Illus.). 96p. (gr. 3-6). 1975. PLB 7.12 (ISBN 0-8116-6674-3). Garrard.
--Jackie Robinson: Baseball's Gallant Fighter. LC 74-4499. (Sports Library). (Illus.). 96p. (gr. 3-6). 1974. PLB 7.12 (ISBN 0-8116-6668-9). Garrard.
--Mexico. rev. ed. (First Bk.). (Illus.). 72p. (gr. 4 up). 1983. PLB 8.90 (ISBN 0-531-04530-7). Watts.
--Saving Electricity. LC 76-46986. (Good Earth). (Illus.). (gr. 2-6). 1977. PLB 6.57 o.p. (ISBN 0-8116-6107-5). Garrard.
--Secret in a Sealed Bottle. LC 78-1494. (Science Discovery Bks). (Illus.). (gr. 3-5). 1979. PLB 5.99 (ISBN 0-698-30700-3, Coward). Putnam Pub Group.
--She Never Looked Back: Margaret Mead in Samoa. LC 78-31821. (Science Discovery Ser.). (Illus.). (gr. 3-7). 1980. PLB 5.99 (ISBN 0-698-30715-1, Coward). Putnam Pub Group.
--Washington, D. C. LC 30-25022. (First Books About Washington Ser.). (gr. 4 up). 1981. PLB 8.90 (ISBN 0-531-04253-7). Watts.
--Willie Mays: Baseball Superstar. LC 74-20954. (Sports Library). (Illus.). 96p. (gr. 2-6). 1975. PLB 7.12 (ISBN 0-8116-6671-9). Garrard.
--A Year of Japanese Festivals. LC 73-22045. (Around the World Holidays Ser). (Illus.). 96p. (gr. 4-7). 1974. PLB 7.12 (ISBN 0-8116-4954-7). Garrard.
Epstein, Samuel & De Armand, David W. How to Develop, Print & Enlarge Your Own Pictures. rev. ed. pap. 3.95 (ISBN 0-448-00670-7, G&D). Putnam Pub Group.
Epstein, Samuel & Epstein, Beryl. Spring Holidays. LC 64-12340. (Holiday Bks.). (gr. 2-5). 1964. PLB 7.56 (ISBN 0-8116-6553-4). Garrard.
Epstein, Samuel & Legator, Marvin. Mutagenicity of Pesticides: Concepts & Evaluation. 1971. 17.50x (ISBN 0-262-05008-0). MIT Pr.
Epstein, Samuel, jt. auth. see Epstein, Beryl.
Epstein, Samuel & Lederberg, Joshua, eds. Drugs of Abuse: Their Genetic & Other Chronic Nonpsychiatric Hazards. 1971. 20.00x (ISBN 0-262-05009-9). MIT Pr.
Epstein, Samuel S. & Grundy, Richard D., eds. Consumer Health & Product Hazards: Cosmetics & Drugs, Pesticides, Food Additives Vol. 2 of the Legislation of Product Safety, Vol. 2. 1974. 20.00x (ISBN 0-262-05015-3). MIT Pr.
--Consumer Health & Product Hazards: Chemicals, Electronic Products, Radiation Vol. 1 of the Legislation of Product Safety. 1974. 20.00x (ISBN 0-262-05013-7). MIT Pr.
Epstein, Sherrie S. Penny the Medicine Maker: The Story of Penicillin. LC 60-14006. (Medical Bks for Children). (Illus.). (gr. k-5). 1960. PLB 3.95g (ISBN 0-8225-0006-X). Lerner Pubns.
Epstein, Stephan B., jt. auth. see Lynch, Peter J.
Epstein, W. Stability & Constancy in Visual Perception: Mechanisms & Processes. 463p. 1977. 39.50x (ISBN 0-471-24355-8). Wiley.
Epstein, Yakov M., jt. ed. see Baum, Andrew.
Epting, Franz R. & Neimeyer, Robert A., eds. Personal Meanings of Death. (Death Education, Aging & Health Care Ser.). (Illus.). 200p. 1983. text ed. 24.95 (ISBN 0-89116-363-8). Hemisphere Pub.
Epton, Arli, jt. ed. see Cumming, Marsue.
Equal Rights Amendment Project, compiled by. The Equal Rights Amendment: A Bibliographic Study. Miller, Anita & Greenberg, Hazel, eds. LC 76-24999. 400p. 1976. lib. bdg. 35.00 (ISBN 0-8371-9058-4, ERA/). Greenwood.
Eral, Bill, jt. auth. see Barns, R. E.
Eranko, E. O., ed. Histochemistry of Nervous Transmission. LC 70-168912. (Progress in Brain Research Ser.: Vol. 34). 541p. 1971. 131.50 (ISBN 0-444-40951-3). Elsevier.
Eranko, Olavi, et al, eds. Histochemistry & Cell Biology of Autonomic Neurons: Sif Cells, & Paraneurons. (Advances in Biochemical Psychopharmacology: Vol. 25). (Illus.). 410p. 1980. text ed. 49.50 (ISBN 0-89004-495-3). Raven.
Erasmus, D. A. Electron Probe Microanalysis in Biology. 248p. 1978. 42.00x (ISBN 0-412-15010-7, Pub. by Chapman & Hall England). Methuen Inc.
Erasmus, Desiderius. The Complaint of Peace. Paynell, T., tr. 86p. 1974. 12.00 (ISBN 0-87548-276-7); pap. 4.50 (ISBN 0-87548-195-7). Open Court.
--De Contemptu Mundi. Paynell, Thomas, tr. LC 67-18715. 1967. 25.00x (ISBN 0-8201-1016-7). Schol Facsimiles.
--The Correspondence of Erasmus, Vol. 1, Letters 1-141: 1484-1500. Corrigan, Beatrice, ed. LC 72-97422. (Collected Works of Erasmus). (Illus.). 1974. 75.00x o.p. (ISBN 0-8020-1981-1). U of Toronto Pr.
--The Correspondence of Erasmus, Vol. 6: Letters 842-992 (May 1518 - June 1519) Mynors, R. A. & Thomson, D. F., trs. (Collected Works of Erasmus). 1981. 75.00x (ISBN 0-8020-5500-1). U of Toronto Pr.
--The Praise of Folly. Miller, Clarence H., intro. by. LC 78-13575. 1979. text ed. 22.50 (ISBN 0-300-02279-4); pap. 6.95x (ISBN 0-300-02373-1). Yale U Pr.
--Tudor Translations of the Colloquies of Erasmus, 1536-1568, 7 vols. in one. LC 74-161931. 384p. 1972. 43.00x (ISBN 0-8201-1097-3). Schol Facsimiles.
Erastov, Konstantin, tr. see Bogomolov, Yu. G. & Zhabin, V. F.
Erastov, Konstantin, tr. see Kalashnikov, N. P. & Remizovich, V. S.
Eraut. Fundamentals of Arithmetic: A Program for Self-Instruction. (Basic Skills System). 1970. text ed. 14.95 (ISBN 0-07-051401-1). McGraw.
--Fundamentals of Elementary Algebra: A Program for Self-Instruction. (Basic Skills System). 1970. text ed. 14.95 (ISBN 0-07-051402-X). McGraw.
--Fundamentals of Intermediate Algebra: A Program for Self-Instruction. (Basic Skills System). 1970. text ed. 14.95 (ISBN 0-07-051403-8). McGraw.
Erb, Gary E. & Severance, Tom. People on Peace: What We All Can Do Rather Than Have a Nuclear War. LC 82-83102. (Illus.). 68p. (Orig.). 1982. pap. 2.50 (ISBN 0-939634-01-5). Laughing Waters.
Erb, Glenora, jt. auth. see Kozier, Barbara.
Erb, Glenora L., jt. auth. see Kozier, Barbara B.
Erb, Joanna S., jt. auth. see Hufbauer, Gary C.
Erb, Peter C., ed. The Pietists. (Classics of Western Spirituality Ser.). 1983. 11.95 (ISBN 0-8091-0334-6); pap. 7.95 (ISBN 0-8091-2509-9). Paulist Pr.
Erb, Richard D. & Ross, Stanely R., eds. United States Relations with Mexico. 1981. pap. 7.25 (ISBN 0-8447-1343-0). Am Enterprise.
Erber, Thomas & Fowler, Clarence M., eds. Francis Bitter: Selected Papers & Commentaries. 1969. 27.50x (ISBN 0-262-05006-4). MIT Pr.
Erc Editorial Staff. The ERC Guide to Slashing Payroll Costs. LC 81-17267. 272p. 1981. 99.50 (ISBN 0-13-283747-1). Exec Reports.
Ercolano, N. Review of Medical Nursing. 1978. text ed. 12.50 (ISBN 0-07-019541-2). McGraw.
ERDA Technical Information Center. Controlled Fusion & Plasma Research: A Literature Search. 848p. 1977. pap. 56.50 (ISBN 0-87079-170-2, TID-3557-S12); microfiche 4.50 (ISBN 0-87079-413-2, TID-3557-S12). DOE.
--Nuclear Medicine: A Bibliography January 1975 through June 1976. 503p. 1976. pap. 37.00 (ISBN 0-87079-364-0, TID-3319-S7); microfiche 4.50 (ISBN 0-87079-432-9, TID-3319-S7). DOE.
Erdahl, Carol, jt. auth. see Erdahl, Lowell.
Erdahl, Lowell & Erdahl, Carol. Be Good to Each Other-An Open Letter on Marriage. 1976. 5.95 o.p. (ISBN 0-8015-0584-4, Hawthorn). Dutton.
--Be Good to Each Other: An Open Letter on Marriage. LC 80-8893. 96p. 1981. pap. 4.95i (ISBN 0-06-062248-2, RD358, HarpR). Har-Row.
Erdahl, Sivert, tr. see Rolvaag, Ole E.
Erdall, Lowell. Better Preaching. (Preacher's Workshop Ser.). 1981. pap. text ed. 2.50 (ISBN 0-570-07408-8, 12-2680). Concordia.
Erdberg, Eleanor Von see Von Erdberg, Eleanor.
Erdelyi, A. Higher Transcendental Functions, 3 vols. Incl. Vol. 1. 328p. Repr. of 1953 ed. 22.50 (ISBN 0-89874-206-4); Vol. 2. 414p. Repr. of 1953 ed. 28.50 (ISBN 0-89874-069-X); Vol. 3. 310p. Repr. of 1955 ed. 22.50 (ISBN 0-89874-207-2). LC 79-26544. 1981. Repr. lib. bdg. write for info. Krieger.
Erdelyi, Arthur, ed. Higher Transcendental Functions, 3 Vols. text ed. 21.50 ea. o.p. (P&RB). Vol. 1 (ISBN 0-07-019545-5). Vol. 2 (ISBN 0-07-019546-3). Vol. 3 O.p (ISBN 0-07-019547-1). McGraw.
--Tables of Integral Transforms, Vol. 1. (Illus.). 1954. text ed. 32.50 o.p. (ISBN 0-07-019549-8, P&RB). McGraw.
Erdelyi, I., ed. Operator Theory & Functional Analysis. LC 79-18548. (Research Notes in Mathematics Ser.: No. 38). 176p. (Orig.). 1979. pap. text ed. 20.95 (ISBN 0-273-08450-X). Pitman Pub MA.
Erdman, Charles R. The Book of Deuteronomy. 96p. 1982. pap. 3.50 (ISBN 0-8010-3379-9). Baker Bk.
--The Book of Exodus. 144p. 1982. pap. 4.50 (ISBN 0-8010-3376-4). Baker Bk.
--The Book of Isaiah. 160p. 1982. pap. 4.50 (ISBN 0-8010-3380-2). Baker Bk.
--The Book of Leviticus. 144p. 1982. pap. 4.50 (ISBN 0-8010-3377-2). Baker Bk.
--The Book of Numbers. 144p. 1982. pap. 4.50 (ISBN 0-8010-3378-0). Baker Bk.
--Commentaries on the New Testament Books: Corinthians 1 & 2, 2 Vols. 1983. pap. 4.95 ea. Vol. 1 (ISBN 0-664-24715-6). Vol. 2 (ISBN 0-664-24716-4). Westminster.
Erdman, David V., ed. The Complete Poetry & Prose of William Blake. LC 79-7196. (Illus.). 1024p. 1982. 19.95 (ISBN 0-385-15213-2, Anchor Pr). Doubleday.
--The Romantic Movement: A Selective & Critical Bibliography. LC 82-48435. (English Language Notes Ser.). 400p. 1982. lib. bdg. 45.00 o.s.i. (ISBN 0-8240-9508-1). Garland Pub.
--Selected Poetry of William Blake. pap. 2.95 o.p. (ISBN 0-451-51373-8, CE1373, Sig Classics). NAL.
Erdman, Loula G. The Edge of Time. (Westerns Ser.). 1981. lib. bdg. cancelled o.s.i. (ISBN 0-8398-2675-3, Gregg). G K Hall.
--Life Was Simpler Then. LC 63-12211. 1974. 5.95 o.p. (ISBN 0-396-04843-9). Dodd.
--The Years of the Locust. 1979. lib. bdg. 10.95 (ISBN 0-8398-2595-1, Gregg). G K Hall.
Erdman, Paul. The Last Days of America. 1981. 13.95 o.p. (ISBN 0-671-24248-2). S&S.
Erdman, V. R. Signs of Christ's Second Coming. 29p. pap. 0.85 (ISBN 0-87509-130-X). Chr Pubns.
Erdmann, Erika. Realism & Human Values. 1978. 5.95 o.p. (ISBN 0-533-03403-5). Vantage.
Erdmann, Kurt. Oriental Carpets. 1982. 90.00x (ISBN 0-903580-35-7, Pub. by Element Bks). State Mutual Bk.
Erdoes, Richard. The Native Americans: Navajos. LC 78-57885. (Illus.). (gr. 5 up). 1978. 16.95 (ISBN 0-8069-2740-2); PLB 19.99 (ISBN 0-8069-2741-0). Sterling.
--Native Americans: The Sioux. LC 81-85036. (Illus.). 96p. (gr. k up). 1982. 16.95 (ISBN 0-8069-2742-9); lib. bdg. 19.99 (ISBN 0-686-97813-7). Sterling.
Erdoes, Richard, jt. auth. see John Lame Deer.
Erdos, Paul L. Professional Mail Surveys. Rev. ed. LC 82-10024. 304p. 1983. lib. bdg. 29.50 (ISBN 0-89874-530-6). Krieger.
Erdsneker, Barbara. Mathematics Simplified & Self-Taught. 6th ed. LC 81-14912. 224p. 1982. pap. 6.95 (ISBN 0-668-05357-7, 5357). Arco.
Erdsneker, Barbara & Saunders, Brigitte. Mathematics Workbook for the Act. LC 82-4097. 304p. 1982. pap. 6.95 (ISBN 0-668-05443-3, 5443). Arco.
Erdstein, Erich & Bean, Barbara. Inside the Fourth Reich. pap. 1.95 o.s.i. (ISBN 0-515-04897-6). Jove Pubns.
--Inside the Fourth Reich: The Real Story of the Boys from Brazil. LC 77-9153. 1978. 8.95 o.p. (ISBN 0-312-41885-X). St Martin.
Erdy, Miklos. The Sumerian, Ural-Altaic, Magyar Relationship: A History of Research, Pt. 1, the 19th Century. LC 72-112303. (Studia Sumiro-Hungarica: Vol. 3). (Illus.). 530p. (Bilingual text). 1974. 18.00 (ISBN 0-914246-53-4). Gilgamesh Pub.
Erdy, Miklos, ed. Studia Sumiro-Hungarica, 3 vols. 1968-1974. Set. 44.00 (ISBN 0-914246-50-X). Gilgamesh Pub.
Erdy, Miklos, jt. ed. see Feher, Matyas.
Ereira, Alan. Invergordon Mutiny. 160p. 1981. 14.95 (ISBN 0-7100-0930-5). Routledge & Kegan.
Erenberg, Lewis A. Steppin' Out: New York Nightlife & the Transformation of American Culture, 1890-1930. LC 80-930. (Contributions in American Studies Ser.: No. 50). (Illus.). xix, 291p. 1981. lib. bdg. 29.95 (ISBN 0-313-21342-9, EUN/). Greenwood.
Erevan University Press. A Polyglot Dictionary of Plant Names. 180p. 1981. pap. 40.00x (ISBN 0-686-82330-3, Pub. by Collets). State Mutual Bk.
Erfft, Shirley. Little Things Mean a Lot. 1982. 5.95 (ISBN 0-8062-1897-5). Carlton.
Erfurt, John C. & Foote, Andrea. Blood Pressure Control Programs in Industrial Settings. 83p. 1979. pap. 5.00 (ISBN 0-87736-334-X). U of Mich Inst Labor.

Erfurt, John C., jt. auth. see Foote, Andrea.
Ergang, Robert & Rohr, Donald G. Europe from the Renaissance to Waterloo. 3rd ed. 1967. pap. text ed. 21.95 (ISBN 0-669-04354-0). Heath.
--Europe Since Waterloo. 3rd ed. 1967. text ed. 21.95x (ISBN 0-669-22830-3). Heath.
Ergood, Bruce & Kuhre, Bruce E., eds. Appalachia: Social Context, Past & Present. 2nd ed. 1982. pap. text ed. 19.95 (ISBN 0-8403-2805-2). Kendall-Hunt.
Erhard, Ludwig. Germany's Comeback in the World Market. Johnston, W. H., tr. LC 76-15289. (Illus.). 1976. Repr. of 1954 ed. lib. bdg. 18.50x (ISBN 0-8371-8948-9, ERGC). Greenwood.
--Prosperity Through Competition. Roberts, Edith T. & Wood, John B., trs. LC 75-27681. 260p. 1976. Repr. of 1958 ed. lib. bdg. 17.50x (ISBN 0-8371-8457-6, ERPC). Greenwood.
Erhardt, Rhoda P. Developmental Hand Dysfunctions. (Illus.). 152p. 1982. pap. text ed. 24.50 (ISBN 0-943596-01-7). Ramsco Pub.
Erhardt, Roy. Set of Price Guides to Townsend Books. 1982. 5.00 (ISBN 0-913902-47-0). Heart Am Pr.
Erh-Soon Tay, Alice, jt. ed. see Kamenka, Eugene.
Ericcson, Samuel, jt. auth. see Buzzard, Lynn.
Erichsen, Heino, jt. auth. see Erichsen, Jean.
Erichsen, Jean & Erichsen, Heino. The Adoption Kit: U. S. Adoptions. 2nd ed. (How to Adopt: No. 3). 40p. (Orig.). 1982. pap. 6.95 (ISBN 0-935366-22-9). Los Ninos.
Ericksen, Donald H. Oscar Wilde. (English Authors Ser.). 1977. lib. bdg. 11.95 (ISBN 0-8057-6680-4, Twayne). G K Hall.
Ericksenn, Lief & Sincebaugh, Els. Adventures in Close-Up Photography: Rediscovering Familiar Environments Through Details. 144p. 1983. 22.50 (ISBN 0-8174-3501-8, Amphoto). Watson-Guptill.
Erickson, Arvel B. Edward T. Cardwell: Peelite. LC 59-8893. (Transactions Ser.: Vol. 49, Pt. 2). 1959. pap. 1.00 o.p. (ISBN 0-87169-492-1). Am Philos.
Erickson, Carlton W. Fundamentals of Teaching with Audiovisual Technology. 2nd ed. (Illus.). 416p. 1972. text ed. 19.95 (ISBN 0-02-334030-4, 33403). Macmillan.
Erickson, Carolly. Civilization & Society in the West. 1978. pap. 16.50x (ISBN 0-673-15123-9). Scott F.
--The First Elizabeth. 464p. 1983. 19.95 (ISBN 0-671-41746-0). Summit Bks.
Erickson, Clint, jt. ed. see Teague, Robert.
Erickson, Donald A., ed. Educational Organization & Administration. LC 76-18037. (Readings in Educational Research Ser.). 1977. 30.75 (ISBN 0-8211-0415-2); text ed. 28.00 10 or more copies (ISBN 0-685-71413-6). McCutchan.
Erickson, Donald A. & Reller, Theodore L., eds. The Principal in Metropolitan Schools. new ed. LC 78-62641. (Contemporary Educational Issues Ser.). 1978. 21.75 (ISBN 0-8211-0417-9); text ed. 19.50 ten or more copies (ISBN 0-686-52389-X). McCutchan.
Erickson, Edsel L., et al. Child Abuse & Neglect: A Guidebook for Educators & Community Leaders. LC 78-59726. 1979. lib. bdg. 9.95x (ISBN 0-918452-08-2). Learning Pubns.
Erickson, Frances G., jt. auth. see Cornell, Dale D.
Erickson, Gerald D. & Hogan, Terrence P. Family Therapy: An Introduction to Theory & Technique. 2nd ed. LC 80-28686. 448p. (Orig.). 1981. pap. text ed. 16.95 (ISBN 0-8185-0437-4). Brooks-Cole.
Erickson, Helen & Tomlin, Evelyn. Modeling & Role Modeling: A Theory & Paradigm for Nursing. (Illus.). 240p. 1983. text ed. 17.95 (ISBN 0-13-586198-5); pap. 13.95 (ISBN 0-13-586180-2). P-H.
Erickson, J. Gunnar & Hearn, Edward R. Musician's Guide to Copyright. rev. ed. 160p. 12.95 (ISBN 0-686-83667-7, ScribT). Scribner.
Erickson, Joan G. & Emark, Donald R., eds. Communication Assessment of the Bilingual - Bicultural Child. 392p. 1981. 19.95 (ISBN 0-8391-1599-7). Univ Park.
Erickson, John. The Road To Berlin. (Illus.). 700p. 1983. 30.00 (ISBN 0-89158-795-0). Westview.
Erickson, John D. Nommo: African Fiction in French. (Francophone Studies: Black Africa). 17.00 (ISBN 0-917786-08-4). French Lit.
Erickson, John R. The Devil in Texas. LC 82-90172. (Illus.). 104p. (gr. 5-12). 1982. pap. 5.95 (ISBN 0-9608612-0-3). Maverick Bks.
--The Devil in Texas & Other Cowboy Tales. LC 82-90172. (Illus.). 96p. 1982. pap. 5.95 (ISBN 0-9608612-0-3). Maverick Bks.
--Hank the Cowdog. (Illus.). 105p. (Orig.). 1983. pap. 5.95 (ISBN 0-9608612-2-X). Maverick Bks.
--Panhandle Cowboy. LC 79-24929. (Illus.). xiv, 213p. 1980. pap. 4.95 (ISBN 0-8032-6702-9, BB 777, Bison). U of Nebr Pr.
--Through Time & the Valley. (Illus.). 260p. 1983. pap. 7.95 (ISBN 0-9608612-1-1). Maverick Bks.
Erickson, Jon J. & Rollo, F. David, eds. Digital Nuclear Medicine. (Illus.). 274p. 1982. pap. text ed. 19.50 (ISBN 0-397-50532-9, Lippincott Medical). Lippincott.
Erickson, K. Please, Lord, Untie My Tongue. 1983. pap. 2.25 (ISBN 0-570-03881-2). Concordia.
Erickson, Kenneth P. The Brazilian Corporative State & Working-Class Politics. 1978. 30.00x (ISBN 0-520-03162-8). U of Cal Pr.
Erickson, Lynn. High Country Pride. (Tapestry Romance Ser.). 320p. (Orig.). 1982. pap. 2.50 (ISBN 0-671-46137-0). PB.
Erickson, Marcene L., jt. auth. see Barnard, Kathryn E.
Erickson, Marilyn T. Child Psychopathology: Behavior Disorders & Developmental Disabilities. 2nd ed. (Illus.). 368p. 1982. reference 23.95 (ISBN 0-13-131094-1). P-H.
Erickson, Millard J. Relativism in Contemporary Christian Ethics. 1974. pap. 3.95 o.p. (ISBN 0-8010-3315-2). Baker Bk.
Erickson, Milton H. Hypnotic Alteration of Sensory, Perceptual & Psychophysiological Processes, Vol. II. Rossi, Ernest L., ed. (The Collected Papers of Milton H. Erickson on Hypnosis). 368p. 1980. text ed. 29.95x (ISBN 0-8290-0543-9). Irvington.
--The Hypnotic Investigation of Psychodynamic Processes, Vol. III. Rossi, Ernest L., ed. (The Collected Papers of Milton H. Erickson on Hypnosis Ser.). 368p. 1980. text ed. 29.95 (ISBN 0-8290-0544-7). Irvington.
--Innovative Hypnotherapy, Vol. IV. Rossi, Ernest L., ed. (The Collected Papers of Milton H. Erickson on Hypnosis Ser.). 570p. 1980. text ed. 34.95x (ISBN 0-8290-0545-5). Irvington.
--The Nature of Hypnosis & Suggestion, Vol. I. Rossi, Ernest L., ed. (The Collected Papers of Milton H. Erickson on Hypnosis Ser.). 570p. 1980. text ed. 34.95 (ISBN 0-8290-0542-0). Irvington.
Erickson, Robert. Sound Structure in Music. LC 72-9352. (Illus.). 1975. 26.50x (ISBN 0-520-02376-5). U of Cal Pr.
--The Structure of Music: a Listener's Guide: A Study of Music in Terms of Melody & Counterpoint. LC 75-31361. 1977. Repr. of 1955 ed. lib. bdg. 20.25x (ISBN 0-8371-8519-X, ERSM). Greenwood.
Erickson, Russel E. A Toad for Tuesday. 64p. (gr. 2-5). 1975. pap. 0.95 o.p. (ISBN 0-440-48669-6, YB). Dell.
Erickson, Russell E. Warton & the Castaways. (gr. k-4). 1982. 9.00 (ISBN 0-688-41939-9). Lothrop.
Erickson, V. Lois & Whiteley, John M. Developmental Counseling & Teaching. LC 79-20598. (Counseling Ser.). 1980. pap. text ed. 14.95 (ISBN 0-8185-0327-0). Brooks-Cole.
Ericksson, C. Maillard Reactions in Food: Proceedings of the International Symposium, Uddevalla, Sweden, September 1979. (Progress in Food & Nutrition Science Ser.: Vol. 5). (Illus.). 500p. 1982. 100.00 (ISBN 0-08-025496-9). Pergamon.
Erickstad, H. G. The Prophecies of Nostradamus in Historical Sequence from A.D. 1550-2005. LC 80-53660. 218p. 1982. 10.00 (ISBN 0-533-04862-1). Vantage.
Ericson, Carolyn & Ingmire, Frances, eds. First Settlers of the Louisiana Territory, 2 Vols, Vols. I & II. Incl. Vol. II. 243p. pap. 19.50 (ISBN 0-911317-13-9). LC 82-84532. 1983. Set. pap. 30.00 (ISBN 0-911317-14-7). Ericson Bks.
--First Settlers of the Louisiana Territory, 2 vols, Vol. 1. LC 82-84532. 235p. (Orig.). pap. 19.50 (ISBN 0-911317-09-0). Ericson Bks.
--First Settlers of the Mississippi Territory, 2 vols. LC 82-83848. 110p. (Orig.). pap. 19.50 (ISBN 0-911317-07-4). Ericson Bks.
--First Settlers of the Missouri Territory, Vol. I. Incl. Vol. II. 185p. pap. 15.00 (ISBN 0-911317-11-2); Vols. I & II, 2 Vols. Set. pap. 25.00 (ISBN 0-911317-12-0). LC 82-84533. 182p. 1983. pap. 15.00 (ISBN 0-911317-10-4). Ericson Bks.
Ericson, Carolyn, ed. see Harris, Ollie K. & Slover, Elizabeth.
Ericson, Carolyn R., ed. First Settlers of the Republic of Texas, Vol. 1. 278p. 1982. pap. 19.95 (ISBN 0-911317-00-7). Ericson Bks.
--First Settlers of the Republic of Texas, Vol. 2. 273p. 1982. pap. 19.95 (ISBN 0-911317-01-5). Ericson Bks.
Ericson, David. The Money Game. LC 77-81593. (Pacesetters Ser.). (Illus.). 64p. (gr. 4 up). 1978. PLB 8.65 (ISBN 0-516-02156-7). Childrens.
Ericson, E. E., jt. auth. see Andrews, Robert.
Ericson, Edward E., Jr. Solzhenitsyn: The Moral Vision. 1982. pap. 6.95 (ISBN 0-8028-1718-1, 1718-1). Eerdmans.
Ericson, Eric. The Woman Who Slept with Demons. 224p. 1980. 9.95 o.p. (ISBN 0-312-88645-4). St Martin.
Ericson, Georgia. Aunt Hank's Rock House Kitchen: A Cookbook with a Story. 1977. 14.69x (ISBN 0-686-31816-1). Crosby County.
Ericson, Jack T. Genealogy & Local History: Title List, Parts 2 & 3. 85p. 1981. write for info. Microfilming Corp.
Ericson, Joe E. Judges of the Republic of Texas, Eighteen Thirty-Six through Eighteen Forty-Six. (Illus.). 350p. 1980. 20.00 (ISBN 0-911317-04-X). Ericson Bks.
Ericson, Jon. Motion by Motion: A Commentary on Parlimentary Procedure. 130p. 1983. pap. text ed. 9.95x (ISBN 0-8290-1272-9). Irvington.
Ericson, Jon M., jt. auth. see Murphy, James J.
Ericson, Jonathan & Earle, Timothy, eds. Contexts for Prehistoric Exchange. (Studies in Archaeology Ser.). 1982. 34.50 (ISBN 0-12-241580-9). Acad Pr.
Ericson, Jonathon E., et al, eds. Peopling of the New World. LC 81-22800. (Anthropological Papers: No. 23). (Illus.). 364p. 1982. 19.95 (ISBN 0-87919-095-7). Ballena Pr.
Ericson, Virginia, jt. auth. see Townsend, Sallie.
Ericsson, Dag. Materials Administration. 1974. 21.50 o.p. (ISBN 0-07-084441-0, P&RB). McGraw.
Ericsson, Mary K. Flying Feathers. (Apple Bks.). (Illus.). (gr. 5 up). 1978. pap. 3.50 o.p. (ISBN 0-570-07901-2, 56-1601). Concordia.
Ericsson, Ronald J., jt. auth. see Glass, Robert H.
Eriksen, Arthur. Nature's Arthritis Breakthrough. 200p. (Orig.). 1982. pap. cancelled (ISBN 0-942922-01-8). Renner Pub.
Eriksen, Karin. Human Services Today. 2nd ed. 192p. 1981. text ed. 16.95 (ISBN 0-8359-3004-1). Reston.
Erikson, Alvar, ed. Letters from Erik Benzelius the Younger from Learned Foreigners, 2 vols. Orig. Title: Acta Regiae Societatis Scientiarum et Literarum. (Orig.). 1980. 31.00x set (ISBN 91-85252-22-0). Vol. 1, 1697-1722. Vol. 2, 1723-1743. Humanities.
Erikson, Erik H. Childhood & Society. 1964. 14.95x o.p. (ISBN 0-393-01075-9, NortonC); pap. 3.95x (ISBN 0-393-09622-X). Norton.
--Gandhi's Truth: On the Origins of Militant Nonviolence. 1969. 10.00 o.p. (ISBN 0-393-01049-X, Norton Lib). Norton.
--Identity: Youth & Crisis. 1968. 12.95 o.p. (ISBN 0-393-01069-4); pap. 5.95x o.s.i. (ISBN 0-393-09786-2). Norton.
--The Life Cycle Completed: A Review. 1982. 10.95 (ISBN 0-393-01622-6). Norton.
--Young Man Luther. 1958 o.p. 6.50 (ISBN 0-393-07365-3); pap. 5.95 (ISBN 0-393-00170-9). Norton.
Erikson, Erik H., ed. Adulthood. 1978. 11.95 o.p. (ISBN 0-393-01165-8); pap. 8.95x (ISBN 0-393-09086-8). Norton.
Erikson, K. T. Wayward Puritans: A Study in the Sociology of Deviance. LC 66-16140. 228p. 1966. pap. text ed. 11.95x (ISBN 0-471-24427-9). Wiley.
Erikson, Kai T. Everything in Its Path. 1978. pap. 6.75 (ISBN 0-671-24067-6, Touchstone Bks). S&S.
Erikson, Kate, jt. auth. see Best, Joan.
Erikson, Paul. The Dynast. LC 78-12194. 1979. 8.95 o.p. (ISBN 0-688-03418-7). Morrow.
Erikson, Rika, ed. Flowers & Plants of Western Australia. rev. ed. (Illus.). 231p. 1979. 33.75 (ISBN 0-589-50116-X, Dist. by C E Tuttle). Reed.
Erikson, Robert S., et al. American Public Opinion: Its Origins, Content, & Impact. 2nd ed. LC 79-17806. 337p. 1980. pap. text ed. 14.95 (ISBN 0-471-03139-9). Wiley.
Eriksson & Furberg, eds. Swimming Medicine IV. (International Series on Sport Sciences). 1978. 34.50 o.p. (ISBN 0-8391-1214-9). Univ Park.
Eriksson, A., jt. auth. see Astroms, P.
Eriksson, Ejnar. Illustrated Handbook in Local Anaesthesia. 2nd ed. LC 79-65870. (Illus.). 159p. 1980. text ed. 45.00 o.p. (ISBN 0-7216-3399-4). Saunders.
Eringen, A. C., ed. Recent Advances in Engineering Science, 5 Vols. (Orig.). 1967-69. Vol. 1,878. 144.00x (ISBN 0-677-10790-0); Vol. 2,456. 103.00x (ISBN 0-677-10800-1); Vol. 3,568. 114.00x (ISBN 0-677-11880-5); Vol. 4,362. 81.00x (ISBN 0-677-13100-3); Vol. 5,862. 172.00 (ISBN 0-677-13780-X). Gordon.
Eringer, Robert. Strike for Freedom! The Story of Lech Walesa & Polish Solidarity. LC 82-12978. 320p. 1982. 11.95 (ISBN 0-396-08065-0). Dodd.
Erk, Rien Van see Van Erk, Rien.
Erlandson. Diagnostic Transmission Electron Miscroscopy of Human Tumors: The Interpretation of Submicroscopic Structures in Neoplastic Cells. LC 81-11717. (Masson Monographs in Diagnostic Pathology: Vol. 3). (Illus.). 208p. 1981. 47.25x (ISBN 0-89352-138-8). Masson Pub.
Erlanger, Philippe. St. Bartholomew's Night: The Massacre of Saint Bartholomew. O'Brian, Patrick, tr. from Fr. LC 75-17191. (Illus.). 285p. 1975. Repr. of 1962 ed. lib. bdg. 19.00x (ISBN 0-8371-8288-3, ERBN). Greenwood.
Erlanger, Rachel. Lucretia Borgia: A Biography. LC 75-39117. (Illus.). 1978. 13.95 o.p. (ISBN 0-8015-4725-3, Hawthorn); pap. 7.95 o.p. (ISBN 0-8015-4724-5). Dutton.
Erlewein, David L., et al. Instructions for Veterinary Clients. LC 74-12908. (Illus.). 380p. 1975. pap. 42.00 o.p. (ISBN 0-7216-3400-1). Saunders.
Erlich, et al. Business Administration for the Medical Assistant. 2nd ed. LC 81-67045. (Illus.). 1981. 10.95 (ISBN 0-940012-01-4). Colwell Co.
Erlich, Ann. The Role of Computers in Dental Practice Management. LC 81-67044. (Illus.). 8.95 (ISBN 0-940012-00-6). Colwell Co.
Erlich, Haggai. The Struggle Over Eritrea, 1962-1978: War & Revolution in the Horn of Africa. (Publication Ser.: No. 260). 150p. 1982. pap. 9.95 (ISBN 0-8179-7602-7). Hoover Inst Pr.
Erlich, Lillian. What Jazz Is All About. rev. ed. LC 74-30486. (Illus.). 256p. (gr. 7 up). 1975. PLB 8.29 o.p. (ISBN 0-671-32731-3). Messner.
Erlich, Shelley. How the Rooted Travel. pap. 3.00 (ISBN 0-686-84327-4, JB41). Juniper Pr WI.
Erman, Adolf. Life in Ancient Egypt. Tirard, H. M., tr. (Illus.). pap. 7.95 (ISBN 0-486-22632-8). Dover.
Erman, Adolph. Life in Ancient Egypt. 11.50 (ISBN 0-8446-0090-3). Peter Smith.
Ermarth, Elizabeth. Realism & Consensus in the English Novel. LC 82-61360. 304p. 1983. 25.00x (ISBN 0-691-06560-8). Princeton U Pr.
Ernest, Charlotte, jt. auth. see Ernest, John.
Ernest, J. T., ed. Year Book of Ophthalmology, 1982. (Illus.). 385p. 1982. 37.00 (ISBN 0-8151-3136-4). Year Bk Med.
--Year Book of Ophthalmology, 1983. 1983. 40.00 (ISBN 0-8151-3137-2). Year Bk Med.
Ernest, Jeanette. Lover's Lair. (Rapture Romance Ser.: No. 3). 1983. pap. 1.95 (ISBN 0-451-12005-1, AJ2005). NAL.
Ernest, John & Ashmun, Richard. Selling Principles & Practices. 5th ed. LC 79-17748. (Illus.). 1980. text ed. 14.36 (ISBN 0-07-019620-6); student activity guide 7.32 (ISBN 0-07-019621-4); tchrs. manual & key 5.00 (ISBN 0-07-019622-2). McGraw.
Ernest, John & Ernest, Charlotte. Basic Business Mathematics. 1977. text ed. 20.95 (ISBN 0-02-472610-9). Macmillan.
Ernest, John, jt. auth. see Haas, Kenneth B.
Ernest, John W. & Ashmun, Richard D. Salesmanship Fundamentals. 4th ed. (Illus.). 480p. (gr. 9-12). 1792. text ed. 15.48 (ISBN 0-07-019590-0, G); tchr's manual & key 5.95 (ISBN 0-07-019592-7); student activity guide 7.32 (ISBN 0-07-019591-9). McGraw.
Ernest, John W. & DaVall, G. M. Salesmanship Fundamentals: Creative Selling for Today's Market. 3rd ed. 1965. text ed. 13.96 o.p. (ISBN 0-07-019608-7, G); tchrs. manual o.p. 3.50 o.p. (ISBN 0-07-019597-8). McGraw.
Ernest, John W. & Dorr, E. L. Basic Salesmanship. (Occupational Manuals & Projects in Marketing). 1969. 5.96 o.p. (ISBN 0-07-019595-1, G). McGraw.
--Creative Selling. (Occupational Manuals & Projects in Marketing). 1971. text ed. 6.96 o.p. (ISBN 0-07-019596-X, G); tchr's manual 3.50 o.p. (ISBN 0-07-019598-6). McGraw.
Ernest, P. Edward, ed. Family Album of Favorite Poems. (Illus.). (gr. 7-9). 1959. 7.95 (ISBN 0-448-01279-0, G&D). Putnam Pub Group.
Ernest, Verleigh. Typing. college ed. LC 72-142516. 1971. 15.95 (ISBN 0-672-96001-X); pap. 12.50 (ISBN 0-672-96002-8); tchrs' manual o.p. 7.95 (ISBN 0-672-96003-6); wkbk. 11.50 (ISBN 0-672-96004-4). Bobbs.
Ernst. Aged Patient: Source Book Allied Health Professional. 1982. 29.95 (ISBN 0-8151-3133-X). Year Bk Med.
--Programming with Assembler Language ASS 300. 1980. 35.95 (ISBN 0-471-25671-4, Wiley Heyden). Wiley.
Ernst, ed. Dictionary of Engineering & Technology, Vol. 1. 4th ed. 1981. 68.00x (ISBN 0-19-520269-4). Oxford U Pr.
Ernst, et al, eds. Random House Readers in American History: Essays on the National Past, Vol. 2, 1860-present. pap. text ed. 5.95x (ISBN 0-685-39878-1). Phila Bk Co.
Ernst, C. & Angst, J. Birth Order: Its Influence on Personality. (Illus.). 370p. 1983. 29.80 (ISBN 0-387-11248-0). Springer-Verlag.
Ernst, David. The Evolution of Electronic Music. LC 76-41624. (Illus.). 1977. pap. text ed. 14.95 (ISBN 0-02-870880-6). Schirmer Bks.
Ernst, Earle. The Kabuki Theatre. (Illus.). 368p. 1974. pap. 4.95 (ISBN 0-8248-0319-1, Eastwest Ctr). UH Pr.
Ernst, Edgar. Fahrplanerstellung und Umlaufdisposition Im Containerschiffsverkehr. 136p. (Ger.). 1982. write for info. (ISBN 3-8204-5822-0). P Lang Pubs.
Ernst, Edward A., jt. auth. see Lowe, Harry J.
Ernst, Ervin. International Commodity Agreements. 1982. lib. bdg. 29.00 (ISBN 90-247-2648-4, Pub. by Martinus Nijhoff Netherlands). Kluwer Boston.
Ernst, Franklin H., Jr. Bad Guys & Psychological Racketeers: Workbook. 1982. 17.00x (ISBN 0-916944-25-5). Addressoset.
Ernst, Frederic. New French Self-Taught. 390p. (Fr.). 1982. pap. text ed. 4.76i (ISBN 0-06-463614-3, EH 614). B&N NY.
Ernst, Frederic & Bashour, Dora. New French Self-Taught. 1982. pap. 4.76i (ISBN 0-06-463614-3, EH-614). Har-Row.
Ernst, George. New England Miniature: A History of York, Maine. LC 61-14421. 1961. 10.00 (ISBN 0-87027-063-X). Cumberland Pr.
Ernst, J. Escape King: The Story of Harry Houdini. (Illus.). (gr. 3-7). 1975. 5.95 (ISBN 0-13-283416-2); pap. 1.50 (ISBN 0-13-283424-3). P-H.
Ernst, Joseph A., ed. Forming of a Nation, 1607-1781. (Readings in American History Ser.). (Orig.). 1970. pap. text ed. 3.95 (ISBN 0-685-19728-X). Phila Bk Co.
Ernst, Joseph A., et al, eds. Essays on the National Past, 2 vols. (Readings in American History Ser.). (Orig.). 1970. Vol. 1. pap. text ed. 5.95x (ISBN 0-685-47632-4); Vol. 2. pap. text ed. 5.95 (ISBN 0-685-47633-2). Phila Bk Co.
Ernst, Kathryn. Mr. Tamarin's Trees. LC 76-3648. (Illus.). (gr. k-2). 1976. reinforced lib. bdg. 5.95 o.p. (ISBN 0-517-52615-8). Crown.
Ernst, Kathryn F. Indians: The First Americans. LC 78-13742. (Easy-Read Fact Bk.). (Illus.). (gr. 2-4). 1979. PLB 8.60 s&l (ISBN 0-531-02273-0). Watts.

Ernst, Klaus. Tradition & Progress in the African Village: Non-Capitalist Reform of Rural Communities in Mali - The Sociological Problems. LC 74-22292. 350p. 1977. 32.50x (ISBN 0-312-81235-3). St Martin.

Ernst, M. L. The First Freedom. LC 73-166324. (Civil Liberties in American History Ser.). 316p. 1971. Repr. of 1946 ed. lib. bdg. 39.50 (ISBN 0-306-70242-8). Da Capo.

Ernst, M. L. & Lindey, A. The Censor Marches on. LC 73-164512. (Civil Liberties in American History Ser.). 346p. 1971. Repr. of 1940 ed. lib. bdg. 39.50 (ISBN 0-306-70295-9). Da Capo.

Ernst, Mary O. A Guide Through the Dissertation Process. LC 81-22301. 56p. 1982. pap. 6.95x soft cover (ISBN 0-88946-626-2). E Mellen.

Ernst, Max. A Little Girl Dreams of Talking the Veil. Tanning, Dorothea, tr. from Fr. LC 82-9700. Orig. Title: Reve d'une petite fille qui voulut entrer au Carmel. (Illus.). 176p. (Bilingual ed.). 1982. 30.00 (ISBN 0-8076-1051-8); pap. 14.95 (ISBN 0-8076-1052-6). Braziller.

Ernst, Morris & Lorentz, Pare. Censored: The Private Life of the Movies. LC 72-160230. (Moving Pictures Ser). xvi, 199p. 1971. Repr. of 1930 ed. lib. bdg. 12.95x (ISBN 0-89198-031-8). Ozer.

Ernst, Morris L. Utopia Nineteen Seventy-Six. LC 73-90502. Repr. of 1955 ed. lib. bdg. 15.00x o.p. (ISBN 0-8371-2325-9, ERUT). Greenwood.

Ernst, Morris L. & Schwartz, Alan U. Privacy: The Right to Be Let Alone. LC 77-10983. 1977. Repr. of 1962 ed. lib. bdg. 20.50x (ISBN 0-8371-9805-4, ERPR). Greenwood.

Ernst, Morris L., jt. auth. see Loth, David.

Ernst, Nora S. & West, Helen L. Nursing Home Staff Development. 1983. text ed. 15.95 (ISBN 0-8261-3860-8). Springer Pub.

Ernst, Richard. Comprehensive Dictionary of Engineering & Technology: French-English. 1982. 69.00 (ISBN 0-19-520414-X). Oxford U Pr.

--Dictionary of Engineering & Technology: With Extensive Treatment of the Most Modern Techniques & Processes, Vol. 2, English-German. 4th, rev. & enl. ed. 1178p. 1975. text ed. 69.00x (ISBN 0-19-520109-4). Oxford U Pr.

Ernst, W. G. Earth Materials. (gr. 10 up). 1969. pap. text ed. 11.95 (ISBN 0-13-222604-9). P-H.

Ernst, W. G., ed. The Geotectonic Development of California, Vol. 1. (Illus.). 720p. 1981. text ed. 39.95 (ISBN 0-13-353938-5). P-H.

Ernster, L., ed. see Lee, C. P., et al.

Erny, Pierre. The Child & His Environment in Black Africa: An Essay on Traditional Education. Wanjohi, Gerald, tr. (Illus.). 1982. 29.00x (ISBN 0-19-572509-3). Oxford U Pr.

Erofeev, Benedict. Moscow Circles. Dorell, J. R., tr. (Russian.). 1982. 12.95 (ISBN 0-906495-26-1). Writers & Readers.

Erpenback, William J., jt. auth. see Heddesheimer, Janet.

Errera, Maurice & Forssberg, Arne, eds. Mechanisms in Radiobiology, 2 vols. Incl. Vol. 1. General Principles. 1961. 55.50 o.p. (ISBN 0-12-241101-3); Vol. 2. Multicellular Organisms. 1960. 55.00 o.p. (ISBN 0-12-241102-1). Acad Pr.

Erridge. Self Assessment Questions & Answers for Dental Assistants. 128p. 1979. pap. 10.95 (ISBN 0-7236-0524-6). Wright-PSG.

Errington, Paul L. Muskrats & Marsh Management. LC 77-14177. (Illus.). x, 183p. 1978. 13.50x o.p. (ISBN 0-8032-0975-4); pap. 3.25 o.p. (ISBN 0-8032-5892-5, BB 664, Bison). U of Nebr Pr.

--The Red Gods Call. (Illus.). 127p. 1973. 8.50 (ISBN 0-8138-1340-9). Iowa St U Pr.

Ersevim, Ismail. Untitled - Short Stories. 96p. 1983. 6.50 (ISBN 0-682-49974-9). Exposition.

Ershkowitz, Herbert. The Origin of the Whig & Democratic Parties, New Jersey Politics, 1820-1837. LC 82-17652. (Illus.). 300p. (Orig.). 1983. lib. bdg. 23.00 (ISBN 0-8191-2769-8); pap. text ed. 11.50 (ISBN 0-8191-2770-1). U Pr of Amer.

Ershov. A. P. Ershov: The British Lectures. 1980. 25.95 (ISBN 0-471-25672-2, Pub. by Wiley Heyden). Wiley.

Ershov, V. V. & Nikiforov, G. A. Quinonediazides. (Studies in Organic Chemistry: Vol. 7). 1981. 74.50 (ISBN 0-444-42008-8). Elsevier.

Erskine, Albert, jt. ed. see Warren, Robert P.

Erskine, Jim. Fold a Banana: & 146 Other Things to Do When You're Bored. (Illus.). 1978. pap. 5.95 (ISBN 0-517-53503-3, C N Potter Bks). Crown.

Erskine, Jim & Moran, George. Lie Down & Roll Over: & 156 Other Ways to Say I Love You. 96p. 1981. 5.95 (ISBN 0-517-54524-1, C N Potter Bks). Crown.

--Throw a Tomato. (Illus.). 1979. 5.95 (ISBN 0-517-53865-2, C N Potter Bks); ten copy prepack 59.50 (ISBN 0-517-53971-3). Crown.

Erskine, Jim & Moran, George. Hug a Teddy. 1980. 5.95 (ISBN 0-517-54215-3, C N Potter Bks) (ISBN 0-517-54239-0). Crown.

Erskine, John. My Life in Music. LC 73-8158. (Illus.). 283p. 1973. Repr. of 1950 ed. lib. bdg. 15.75x (ISBN 0-8371-6950-X, ERLM). Greenwood.

Erskine, John, et al. Early Histories of the New York Philharmonic, 3 vols. in one. Incl. The Philharmonic Society of New York, a Memorial; The Philharmonic Society of New York & Its Seventy-Fifth Anniversary, a Retrospect; The Philharmonic Society of New York, Its First Hundred Years. (Music Reprint Ser., 1978). (Illus.). 1979. Repr. of 1943 ed. lib. bdg. 49.50 (ISBN 0-306-77537-9). Da Capo.

Erskine, Thomas L. & Finnie, W. Bruce, eds. Words on Words: A Language Reader. 1971. pap. text ed. 3.50x (ISBN 0-685-04764-4). Phila Bk Co.

Erskine-Hill, Howard. The Augustan Idea in English Literature. 400p. 1983. text ed. write for info. (ISBN 0-7131-6373-9). E Arnold.

Ersley, Allan J. & Gabuzda, Thomas G. Pathophysiology of Blood. 2nd ed. LC 78-24813. (Illus.). 1979. pap. text ed. 16.95 (ISBN 0-7216-3403-6). Saunders.

Erte. Erte: Things I Remember. (Illus.). 208p. 1983. 22.50 (ISBN 0-7206-0124-X, Pub by Peter Owen). Merrimack Bk Serv.

Ertel, Kenneth & Walsh, Lawrence. Wholesaling & Physical Distribution. Dorr, Eugene L., ed. (Occupational Manuals & Projects in Marketing). 1978. pap. text ed. 7.32 (ISBN 0-07-019627-3, G); teacher's manual & key 4.50 (ISBN 0-07-019628-1). McGraw.

Ertl, John, jt. auth. see Konrad, Patricia.

Erven, Lawrence. Techniques of Fire Hydraulics. (Fire Science Ser). 1972. text ed. 22.95x (ISBN 0-02-473000-9, 47300). Macmillan.

Erven, Lawrence W. Handbook of Emergency Care & Rescue. rev. ed. 1976. text ed. 21.95x (ISBN 0-02-472630-3). Macmillan.

Ervin, David E, et al. Land Use Control: Evaluating Economic & Political Effects. LC 76-51214. 208p. 1977. prof ref 19.50x (ISBN 0-88410-062-6). Ballinger Pub.

Ervin-Tripp, Susan M. Language Acquisition & Communicative Choice: Essays by Susan M. Ervin-Tripp. Dil, A. S., ed. LC 72-97206. (Language Science & National Development Ser). xvi, 384p. 1973. 18.75x (ISBN 0-8047-0831-2). Stanford U Pr.

Erway, E. Listening: A Programmed Approach. 1969. text ed. 7.95 o.p. (ISBN 0-07-019655-9, C); tchr's. guide 4.95 o.p. (ISBN 0-07-019656-7); cassettes 115.00 o.p. (ISBN 0-07-075008-4). McGraw.

Erway, E. A. Listening: A Programmed Approach. 1979. pap. 13.95 (ISBN 0-07-019660-5); instr's manual avail. McGraw.

Erwin, Bette J. & Dinwiddie, Elza. Test Without Trauma: How to Overcome Test Anxiety & Score Higher on Every Test. LC 82-82312. 192p. (Orig.). 1983. pap. 7.95 (ISBN 0-448-16607-0, G&D). Putnam Pub Group.

Erwin, Betty K. Behind the Magic Line. LC 69-10658. (Illus.). (gr. 4-6). 1969. 7.95 o.p. (ISBN 0-316-24945-9). Little.

Erwin, D. C. & Garcia, Bartnicki, eds. Phytophthora: It's Biology, Taxanomy, Ecology & Pathology. 400p. 1983. text ed. 68.00 (ISBN 0-89054-050-0); text ed. 76.00 nonmember (ISBN 0-686-82684-1). Am Phytopathological Soc.

Erwin, Dell & Erwin, John. The Man Who Keeps Going to Jail. (Illus.). 1980. pap. 2.50 (ISBN 0-89191-107-3). Cook.

Erwin, E. Behavior Therapy: Scientific, Philosophical & Moral Foundations. 1978. 36.50 (ISBN 0-521-22293-1); pap. 10.95 (ISBN 0-521-29439-8). Cambridge U Pr.

Erwin, John, jt. auth. see Erwin, Dell.

Erwin, Mabel D., et al. Clothing for Moderns. 6th ed. (Illus.). 1979. text ed. 21.95x (ISBN 0-02-334220-X). Macmillan.

Erwin, Paul, ed. see Parry, Clive.

Erwin, Wallace M. A Basic Course in Iraqi Arabic. (Richard Slade Harrell Arabic Ser). 411p. 1969. pap. 8.95 o.p. (ISBN 0-87840-001-X); cassettes 107.00 o.p. (ISBN 0-87840-011-7). Georgetown U Pr.

Erwitt, Elliott. Recent Developments. (Illus.). 1978. 17.95 o.p. (ISBN 0-671-24645-3); pap. 9.95 o.p. (ISBN 0-671-24646-1). S&S.

Esau, Helmut, et al. Language & Communication. 1980. pap. 8.75 (ISBN 0-917496-15-9). Hornbeam Pr.

Esau, Katherine. Anatomy of Seed Plants. 2nd ed. LC 76-41191. 550p. 1977. text ed. 29.95 (ISBN 0-471-24520-8). Wiley.

--Plant Anatomy. 2nd ed. LC 65-12713. 767p. 1965. 32.95x (ISBN 0-471-24455-4). Wiley.

Esau, Theodore. Complete Real Estate Listings Handbook. 265p. 18.95 o.p. (ISBN 0-13-162404-0, Busn). P-H.

Esbensen, Barbara. Swing Around the Sun. LC 65-19583. (General Juvenile Bks). (Illus.). (gr. 5-11). 1965. PLB 3.95g (ISBN 0-8225-0253-4). Lerner Pubns.

Escamilla, Roberto. Prisoners de la Esperanza. 1983. 4.50 (ISBN 0-8358-0438-0). Upper Room.

--Prisoners of Hope. 1982. 4.50 (ISBN 0-8358-0437-2). Upper Room.

Escandon, R. Como Llegar a Ser Vencedor. 128p. (Span.). 1982. pap. write for info (ISBN 0-311-46092-5, Edit Mundo). Casa Bautista.

Esch, Gerald W. & McFarlane, Robert W., eds. Thermal Ecology II: Proceedings. LC 76-28206. (ERDA Symposium Ser.). 414p. 1976. pap. 18.25 (ISBN 0-87079-223-7, CONF-750425); microfiche 4.00 (ISBN 0-87079-224-5, CONF-750425). DOE.

Esch, Robert & Walker, Roberta. Art of Styling Paragraphs. (gr. 9-12). 1984. pap. text ed. 2.75 (ISBN 0-8120-2360-9). Barron.

Eschenbach, Vilfred. The Wall Street Maximal Physical Fitness Handbook. (Illus.). 109p. 1983. 55.85 (ISBN 0-86654-065-2). Inst Econ Finan.

Eschenbach, Wolfram Von. Parzival. 1961. pap. 5.95 (ISBN 0-394-70188-7, V-188, Vin). Random.

Eschenburg, jt. auth. see Russell.

Escher, M. C. & Locher, J. C. World of M. C. Escher. pap. 9.95 (ISBN 0-451-79970-4, G9961, Abrams Art Bks). NAL.

Escherich, Peter. Social Biology of the Bushy-Tailed Woodrat, Neotoma Cinerea. (U.C. Publications in Zoology: Vol. 110). 1981. pap. 11.00x (ISBN 0-520-09595-2). U of Cal Pr.

Escherny, Francois L. De. De l'Egalite Ou Principes Generaux sur les Institutions Civiles, Politiques et Religieuses. (Rousseauism, 1788-1797). 1978. Repr. lib. bdg. 244.00x o.p. (ISBN 0-8287-0317-5). Clearwater Pub.

Eschholz, Paul & Rosa, Alfred, eds. Language Awareness. 3rd ed. LC 81-51837. 332p. 1982. pap. text ed. 9.95 (ISBN 0-312-46693-5); Instr's. manual avail. St Martin.

Eschholz, Paul, jt. ed. see Rosa, Alfred.

Eschholz, Paul A., jt. ed. see Biddle, Arthur W.

Eschholz, Paul A., jt. ed. see Rosa, Alfred F.

Escholz, Paul A. & Rosa, Alfred F. Subject & Strategy: A Rhetoric Reader. 2nd ed. 400p. 1981. pap. text ed. 9.95x (ISBN 0-312-77473-7); instr's. manual avail. (ISBN 0-312-77474-5). St Martin.

Eschwege, E., ed. Advances in Diabetes Epidemiology: Proceedings of the International Symposium on the Advances in Diabetes Epidemiology, Abbaye de Fontevraud, France, 3-7 May 1982. (INSERM Symposium Ser.: No. 22). 408p. Date not set. 81.00 (ISBN 0-444-80453-6, Biomedical Pr). Elsevier.

Escobar, Alice. Art Lessons from Around the World. LC 82-7952. 224p. 1982. 14.50 (ISBN 0-13-047399-5, Busn). P-H.

Escobar, Javier I., jt. ed. see Becerra, Rosina M.

Escoffier, Auguste. Ma Cuisine. LC 77-83670. 884p. 1978. 12.50 o.s.i. (ISBN 0-89479-012-9). A & W Pubs.

Escot, Pozzi, jt. auth. see Cogan, Robert.

Escott, Colin & Hawkins, Martin. Elvis Presley: An Illustrated Discography. (Illus.). 136p. 1981. pap. 4.95 (ISBN 0-8256-3955-7, Quick Fox). Putnam Pub Group.

Escott, Paul D. Slavery Remembered: A Record of Twentieth Century Slave Narratives. LC 78-12198. xv, 221p. 1979. 15.00x (ISBN 0-8078-1340-0); pap. 7.00x (ISBN 0-8078-1343-5). U of NC Pr.

Escott, Thomas H. Masters of English Journalism: A Study of Personal Forces. LC 74-98834. Repr. of 1911 ed. lib. bdg. 17.75x (ISBN 0-8371-3020-4, ESME). Greenwood.

Escoula, Yvonne. Six Blue Horses. LC 70-103044. (gr. 5-9). 1970. 10.95 (ISBN 0-87599-162-9). S G Phillips.

Escreet, P. K. Introduction to the Anglo-American Cataloging Rules. (Grafton Books on Library Science). 1977. lib. bdg. 19.75 o.p. (ISBN 0-233-96033-7). Westview.

--Introduction to the Anglo-American Cataloguing Rules. 384p. 1971. 18.00 (ISBN 0-233-96033-3, 05787-8, Pub. by Gower Pub Co England). Lexington Bks.

Escribano, Jose. Por Aqui. tchrs. guide & cassettes 72.00 (ISBN 0-686-82067-3); student textbook 6.50 (ISBN 0-88436-911-0, 40289). EMC.

Esedebe, P. Olisanwuche. Pan-Africanism. 271p. 1983. 12.95 (ISBN 0-88258-124-4); pap. 6.95 (ISBN 0-88258-125-2). Howard U Pr.

Esenin, Sergei. Confessions of a Hooligan. Thurley, Geoffrey, tr. from Rus. 107p. 1973. text ed. 8.50x (ISBN 0-902145-48-7, Pub. by Carcanet New Pr England). Humanities.

Esenwein, J. Berg & Chambers, Mary D. The Art of Story-Writing. 210p. 1982. Repr. of 1913 ed. lib. bdg. 40.00 (ISBN 0-89984-186-4). Century Bookbindery.

Eshbach, Ovid W. & Souders, Mott. Handbook of Engineering Fundamentals. 3rd ed. LC 74-7467. (Wiley Engineering Handbook Ser.). 1562p. 1975. 49.95x (ISBN 0-471-24553-4, Pub. by Wiley-Interscience). Wiley.

Eshelman, James A. Interpreting Solar Returns. 1983. pap. 9.95 (ISBN 0-917086-40-6, Pub. by Astro Comp Serv). Para Res.

Eshenbach, Benson, jt. auth. see Frush, James, Jr.

Esherick, Joseph W. Reform & Revolution in China: The 1911 Revolution in Hunan & Hubei. LC 75-17297. 1976. 30.00x (ISBN 0-520-03084-2). U of Cal Pr.

Eshleman, Clayton. Fracture. 140p. 1983. 14.00 (ISBN 0-87685-580-X); pap. 7.50 (ISBN 0-87685-579-6); (signed cloth edition) 25.00 (ISBN 0-87685-581-8). Black Sparrow.

--Hades in Manganese. 100p. (Orig.). 1981. pap. 5.00 (ISBN 0-87685-472-2); signed cloth ed. o.p. 20.00 (ISBN 0-87685-473-0). Black Sparrow.

--The Lich Gate. 16p. 1980. ltd., signed ed. 10.00 (ISBN 0-930794-29-X); pap. 2.50 (ISBN 0-930794-20-6). Station Hill Pr.

--Visions of the Fathers of Lascaux. 40p. (Orig.). 1983. pap. 4.50 (ISBN 0-915572-70-2). Panjandrum.

Eshleman, Clayton, tr. see Vallejo, Cesar.

Eshmeyer, R. E. Ask Any Vegetable. (Illus.). (gr. 7 up). 1975. 7.95 o.p. (ISBN 0-13-049759-2); pap. 4.95 (ISBN 0-13-049742-8). P-H.

Esin, Emel. A History of Pre-Islamic & Early-Islamic Turkish Culture. (Supplementy to the Handbook of Turkish Culture Series II: Vol. 1-b). (Illus.). 400p. 1980. pap. 35.00x (ISBN 0-8002-3050-7). Intl Pubns Serv.

Eskanazi, Gerald, jt. auth. see Esposito, Phil.

Eskelin, Neil. Vida Positiva, Em Um Mundo Negative. Batista, Joao, ed. Ferreira, Ruth V., tr. from Eng. 173p. (Port.). 1981. pap. 1.60 (ISBN 0-8297-1203-8). Life Pubs Intl.

--Yes Yes Living in a No No World. LC 80-80914. 187p. 1982. pap. 4.95 (ISBN 0-943338-00-X). Executive Pub.

Eskes, T. K., jt. auth. see Fairweather, D. V.

Eskes, T. K., et al, eds. Aspects of Obstetrics Today. 448p. 1975. 132.00 (ISBN 0-444-15151-6, Excerpta Medica). Elsevier.

Es'Kia, Mphahlele. Chirundu. 168p. cancelled (ISBN 0-88208-121-7); pap. 7.95 (ISBN 0-88208-122-5). Lawrence Hill.

Eskin, Bernard A., ed. The Menopause: Comprehensive Management. LC 80-80302. (Illus.). 224p. 1980. 31.75x (ISBN 0-89352-085-3). Masson Pub.

Eskin, Gerald & Montgomery, David. Computer Models in Marketing: Data Analysis. 128p. 1977. pap. 13.75x (ISBN 0-89426-002-2). Scientific Pr.

Esko, Edward & Esko, Wendy. Macrobiotic Cooking for Everyone. LC 79-89344. (Illus., Orig.). 1980. pap. 14.50 (ISBN 0-87040-469-5). Japan Pubns.

Esko, Edward, ed. The Cancer Prevention Diet: Macrobiotics. 1981. 7.95 (ISBN 0-686-36338-8). Cancer Control Soc.

Esko, Wendy. Introducing Macrobiotic Cooking. LC 79-1957. (Illus.). 1979. pap. 9.95 (ISBN 0-87040-458-X). Japan Pubns.

Esko, Wendy, jt. auth. see Esko, Edward.

Eskow, John. Smokestack Lightning. 1980. 10.95 o.s.i. (ISBN 0-440-07688-9); pap. 4.95 o.s.i. (ISBN 0-440-07689-7). Delacorte.

Esler, Anthony. The Youth Revolution: The Conflict of Generations in Modern History. 1975. pap. 5.50 (ISBN 0-669-90928-9). Heath.

Esler, Mary K., jt. auth. see Esler, William K.

Esler, William K. & Esler, Mary K. Teaching Elementary Science. 3rd ed. 512p. 1980. text ed. 23.95x (ISBN 0-534-00913-1). Wadsworth Pub.

Esmay, Merle L., et al. Rice Postproduction Technology in the Tropics. LC 79-15428. (An East-West Center Book). (Illus., Orig.). 1979. pap. text ed. 7.00x (ISBN 0-8248-0638-7). UH Pr.

Esmond, Truman H., Jr. Budgeting Procedures for Hospitals: 1982 Edition. LC 82-13852. (Illus.). 208p. 1982. manual 38.75 (ISBN 0-87258-376-7, AHA-061140). Am Hospital.

Esnol, A., jt. auth. see Cook, V. J.

Espada, Martin. The Immigrant Iceboy's Bolero. (Illus.). 28p. (Orig.). 1982. pap. 4.00 (ISBN 0-941160-05-X). Ghost Pony Pr.

Espejel, Carlos. Mexican Folk Ceramics. (Illus.). 220p. 1982. 35.00 (ISBN 84-7031-222-7, Pub. by Editorial Blume Spain). Intl Schol Bk Serv.

--Mexican Folk Crafts. (Illus.). 237p. 1982. 35.00 (ISBN 84-7031-058-5, Pub. by Editorial Blume Spain). Intl Schol Bk Serv.

Espeland, Pamela. How to Play Word Games. (Creative Activities, Games, Projects Ser.). (Illus.). 32p. (gr. 4-8). Date not set. PLB 5.95 cancelled (ISBN 0-87191-797-1); pap. 2.75 (ISBN 0-89812-249-X). Creative Ed. Postponed.

Espeland, Pamela, ed. see Rossi, Emilio, et al.

Espenschade, Anna S. & Eckert, Helen M. Motor Development. 2nd ed. (Special Education Ser.). 368p. 1980. pap. text ed. 9.95 (ISBN 0-675-08142-4). Merrill.

Espenshade, Edward B. & Morrison, Joel L., eds. The World Book Atlas. LC 80-51751. (Illus.). 445p. (gr. 6-12). 1980. lib. bdg. 21.90 (ISBN 0-7166-3108-3). World Bk.

Espenshade, Edward B., Jr., ed. Goode's World Atlas. 16th ed. Morrison, Joel. LC 73-21108. 1978. text ed. 19.95 (ISBN 0-528-83125-9); pap. text ed. 10.95 (ISBN 0-528-63007-5). Rand.

Espenshade, Edward B., Jr. & Morrison, Joel L., eds. The World Book Atlas. LC 76-57897. (Illus.). 1977. text ed. 15.95 o.p. (ISBN 0-7166-2026-X). World Bk.

--The World Book Atlas. LC 78-58583. (Illus.). 1979. text ed. 19.95 o.p. (ISBN 0-7166-2029-4). World Bk.

Espenshade, Jean E. Staff Manual for Teaching Patients about Diabetes Mellitus. (Illus.). 1982. 52.50 (ISBN 0-87258-373-2, AHA-070121). Am Hospital.

Espenson, James H. Chemical Kinetics & Reaction Mechanisms. (Advanced Chemistry Ser.). (Illus.). 240p. 1981. text ed. 26.95 (ISBN 0-07-019667-2, C). McGraw.

Esper, E. J. Icones Fucorum Cum Characteribus Systematicis Synonymis Auctorum & Descriptionibus Novarum Specierum. 1966. Repr. of 1797 ed. 96.00 (ISBN 3-7682-0262-3). Lubrecht & Cramer.

Esperet, Eric. Langage et Origine Sociale Des Eleves. 2nd ed. 281p. (Fr.). 1982. write for info. (ISBN 3-261-04754-2). P Lang Pubs.

Esperti, Robert A. & Peterson, Renno L. The Handbook of Estate Planning. (Illus.). 288p. 1983. 29.95 (ISBN 0-07-019668-0, P&RB). McGraw.

Espinosa, Aurelio M. & Wonder, John P. Gramatica Analitica. 400p. 1975. text ed. 21.95 (ISBN 0-669-82941-2). Heath.

Espinosa, Aurelio M., Jr., jt. auth. see Turk, Laurel H.

Espinosa, Mayra C., tr. see LaBrucherie, Roger A.

Espinoza, Luis R. & Osterland, C. Kirk, eds. Circulating Immune Complexes. LC 82-83042. (Illus.). 1983. pap. 37.50 (ISBN 0-87993-188-4). Futura Pub.

Esposito, Anthony. Fluid Power with Applications. (Illus.). 1980. text ed. 21.95 (ISBN 0-13-322701-4). P-H.

--Kinematics for Technology. LC 72-96341. 1973. text ed. 23.95 (ISBN 0-675-09005-9). Additional supplements may be obtained from publisher. Merrill.

Esposito, Barbara, et al. Prison Slavery. Bardsley, Kathryn, ed. (Illus., Orig.). pap. 12.95 (ISBN 0-910007-00-4). Comm Abol Prison.

Esposito, John L., ed. Islam & Development: Religion & Sociopolitical Change. LC 80-25119. (Contemporary Issues in the Middle East Ser.). 292p. 1980. pap. text ed. 9.95x (ISBN 0-8156-2230-9). Syracuse U Pr.

Esposito, Joseph L. Evolutionary Metaphysics: The Development of Peirce's Theory of Catagories. LC 80-15736. (Illus.). x, 252p. 1980. 17.95x (ISBN 0-8214-0551-9, 82-83442). Ohio U Pr.

Esposito, Phil & Eskanazi, Gerald. Hockey Is My Life. LC 72-3927. (Illus.). 240p. 1972. 5.95 o.p. (ISBN 0-396-06700-X). Dodd.

Esposito, R., ed. see Doll, John P. & Orazem, Frank.

Espy, Rosalie & Martin, Clyde I. Fun with Dusty. (Illus.). (gr. k-1). 1958. text ed. 4.00 (ISBN 0-87443-031-3). Benson.

Espy, Willard. Children's Almanac of Words at Play. (Illus.). 256p. 1982. 15.95 (C N Potter Bks); pap. 8.95. Crown.

--Espygrams. 96p. 1982. pap. 3.95 (ISBN 0-517-54598-5, C N Potter Bks). Crown.

--Have a Word on Me. 1981. 13.95 o.p. (ISBN 0-671-25255-0). S&S.

Espy, Willard R. An Almanac of Words at Play. (Illus.). 352p. 1975. 12.95 o.p. (ISBN 0-517-52090-7, C N Potter Bks); pap. 7.95 o.p. (ISBN 0-517-52463-5, C N Potter). Crown.

--Another Almanac of Words at Play. (Illus.). 384p. 1980. 14.95 (ISBN 0-517-53187-9, C N Potter); pap. 8.95 (ISBN 0-517-53188-7, C N Potter Bks). Crown.

--Oysterville: Roads to Grandpa's Village. 1977. 12.95 (ISBN 0-517-52196-2, C N Potter Bks). Crown.

Espy, William. Espygrams Two. 1983. pap. 3.95 o.p. (ISBN 0-517-54757-0, C N Potter). Crown.

Espy, William R. An Almanac of Words at Play for Older Children. (Illus.). (gr. 3-9). 1982. 19.95 (ISBN 0-517-54660-4, C N Potter); pap. 9.95 (ISBN 0-517-54666-3). Crown.

Espy, Williard R. O, Thou Improper, Thou Uncommon Noun. (Illus.). 1978. 12.95 (ISBN 0-517-53511-4, C N Potter); pap. 7.95 (ISBN 0-517-53081-3, C N Potter Bks). Crown.

Esquivel, Adolfo P. Christ in a Poncho: Witnesses to the Nonviolent Struggle in Latin America. Barr, Robert R., tr. from Span. LC 82-28760. 160p. (Orig.). 1983. pap. 6.95 (ISBN 0-88344-104-7). Orbis Bks.

Esquivel, Julia. Threatened with Resurrection: Amenazado de Resurreccion. 128p. (Span.). 1982. pap. 4.95 (ISBN 0-87178-844-6). Brethren.

Ess, Donald H. Van see Van Ess, Donald H.

Ess, Dorothy Van see Van Ess, Dorothy.

Essa, Eva. A Practical Guide to Solving Preschool Behavior Problems. LC 82-70426. (Illus.). 288p. (Orig.). 1983. pap. text ed. 10.20 (ISBN 0-8273-2082-5). Delmar.

Essen, Juliet & Wedge, Peter. Continuities in Childhood Disadvantage, No. 6. (SSRC DHSS Studies in Deprivation & Disadvantage). 200p. 1982. text ed. 27.00x (ISBN 0-435-82283-7). Heinemann Ed.

Essenfeld, Bernice & Kormondy, Edward. Biology. (gr. 10-12). 1983. text ed. price not set (ISBN 0-201-03816-1, School Div); tchrs. ed. avail. (ISBN 0-201-03817-X, Sch Div); lab manual, stud. ed. avail. (ISBN 0-201-03818-8, Sch Div); lab manual, tchr. ed. avail. (ISBN 0-201-03819-6, Sch Div); tests avail. (ISBN 0-201-03823-4, Sch Div). A-W.

Essenwanger, O. M. Applied Statistics in Atmospheric Science Part A: Frequencies & Curve Fitting. (Developments in Atmospheric Science: Vol. 4A). 1976. 85.00 (ISBN 0-444-41327-8). Elsevier.

Esser, Karl. Cryptogams: Cyanobacteria, Algae, Fungi, Lichens, Textbook & Practical Guide. Hackston, Michael G. & Webster, John, trs. LC 80-41070. 624p. 1982. text ed. 74.50 (ISBN 0-521-23621-5). Cambridge U Pr.

Esser, Peter & Sorenson, James, eds. Digital Imaging: Clinical Advances in Nuclear Medicine. (Illus.). 304p. 1983. members 27.50 (ISBN 0-932004-13-X); 35.00. Soc Nuclear Med.

Esser, Peter O., et al. Functional Mapping of Organ Systems & Other Computer Topics & Other Computer Topics. LC 81-51827. (Illus.). 272p. 1981. 28.00 (ISBN 0-932004-09-1). Soc Nuclear Med.

Esser, William L. Dictionary of Hygienic Food. (Illus.). 1982. pap. 3.50 (ISBN 0-686-84404-1). Natural Hygiene.

Essers, J. A., ed. Computational Methods for Turbulent, Transonic, & Viscous Flows. (A von Karman Institute Bk.). 350p. 1983. text ed. 49.50 (ISBN 0-89116-273-9). Hemisphere Pub.

Esses, Michael. Michael, Michael, Why Do You Hate Me? The Story of a Rabbi Who Has Had a Damascus Road Experience. LC 73-85241. 1973. pap. 4.95 o.p. (ISBN 0-88270-047-2, Pub. by Logos). Bridge Pub.

Essick, Edward. RPG-Two Programming. 304p. 1981. pap. text ed. 18.95 (ISBN 0-574-21315-5, 13-4315); instr's. guide avail. (ISBN 0-574-21316-3, 13-4316). SRA.

Essick, Edward, jt. auth. see Dock, V. Thomas.

Essick, Robert N. The Separate Plates of William Blake: A Catalogue. LC 82-7588. (Illus.). 310p. 1983. 75.00x (ISBN 0-691-04011-7). Princeton U Pr.

Essick, Robert N., jt. auth. see Easson, Roger R.

Essig, Alvin, jt. auth. see Caplan, S. Roy.

Essig, James. The Bonds of Wickedness: American Evangelicals Against Slavery, 1770-1808. 224p. 1982. 24.95 (ISBN 0-87722-282-7). Temple U Pr.

Esslen, Rainer. The Complete Book of International Investing: How to Buy Foreign Securities & Who's on the International Investment Scene. 1977. 38.50 (ISBN 0-07-019665-6, P&RB). McGraw.

Esslin, Martin. The Theatre of the Absurd. rev. ed. LC 72-94410. 448p. 1973. Repr. of 1961 ed. 22.50 (ISBN 0-87951-005-6). Overlook Pr.

--Theatre of the Absurd. 1983. pap. 5.95 (ISBN 0-14-020929-8, Pelican). Penguin.

Esslinger, Dean R. Immigrants & the City: Ethnicity & Mobility in a 19th Century Midwestern City. 1975. 15.95 (ISBN 0-8046-9108-8, Natl U). Kennikat.

Essman, W. B. & Valzelli, L., eds. Neuropharmacology: Clinical Applications. (Illus.). 500p. 1982. text ed. 55.00 (ISBN 0-89335-154-7). SP Med & Sci Bks.

Essman, Walter B., ed. Hormonal Actions in Non-Endocrine Systems. 300p. 1983. text ed. 30.00 (ISBN 0-89335-170-9). SP Med & Sci Bks.

Essoe, Gabe. The Book of Movielists. (Illus.). 256p. 1982. pap. 8.95 (ISBN 0-517-54802-X, Arlington Hse). Crown.

--The Offical Book of Movie Lists. (Illus.). 256p. 1981. 12.95 o.p. (ISBN 0-87000-496-4, Arlington Hse); pap. 8.95 o.p. (ISBN 0-87000-520-0). Crown.

Essrig, Harry. Judaism. (gr. 11 up). 1984. pap. text ed. 2.25 (ISBN 0-8120-0309-8). Barron.

Essrig, Harry & Segal, Abraham. Israel Today. rev. ed. LC 77-7536. (Illus.). (YA) (gr. 8-10). 1977. text ed. 8.50 (ISBN 0-8074-0007-6, 142601); tchr's guide o.p. 5.00 (ISBN 0-686-83000-8, 202601). UAHC.

Estabrook, Ronald W., jt. ed. see Srere, Paul A.

Estabrooks, George H. Hypnotism. rev. ed. 1959. pap. 6.50 (ISBN 0-525-47038-7, 0631-190). Dutton.

Estadella, Victor, tr. see Spitzing, Gunter.

Estarellas, Juan. Spanish One Two-One: From Sound to Letter. (gr. 9-12). 1975. pap. 6.95 (ISBN 0-88345-239-1); cassettes 105.00 (ISBN 0-685-65048-0); 110.00 o.p. tapes (ISBN 0-686-77136-2). Regents Pub.

Esteban, Claude. Transparent God. Cloutier, David, tr. from Fr. LC 80-84603. (Modern Poets in Translation Ser.: Vol. II). ix, 107p. 1983. 13.00x (ISBN 0-916426-07-6); pap. 6.95 (ISBN 0-916426-08-4). KOSMOS.

Esten, John, jt. auth. see White, Nancy.

Estep, Samuel D., jt. auth. see Stason, Edwin B.

Esterik, Penny Van see Van Esterik, Penny.

Estermann, Carlos. Ethnography of Southwestern Angola: The Hero People, Vol. 3. LC 75-8794. (Illus.). 1981. text ed. 29.50x (ISBN 0-8419-0206-2, Africana). Holmes & Meier.

Esterno, F. C. De la Misere, de ses Causes, de ses Remedies. (Conditions of the 19th Century French Working Class Ser.). 259p. (Fr.). 1974. Repr. of 1842 ed. lib. bdg. 83.00x o.p. (ISBN 0-8287-0319-1, 1012). Clearwater Pub.

Estes. Models of Learning, Memory & Choice. 410p. 1982. 29.95 (ISBN 0-03-059266-6). Praeger.

Estes, Bill & Generghty, John. RX for RV Performance & Fuel Economy. 360p. 1983. 14.95 (ISBN 0-934798-06-0). TL Enterprises.

Estes, Eleanor. Ginger Pye. LC 51-10446. (Illus.). (gr. 3-7). 10.95 (ISBN 0-15-230930-6, HJ). HarBraceJ.

--Ginger Pye. LC 51-10446. (Illus.). (gr. 4-8). 1972. pap. 2.95 (ISBN 0-15-634750-4, VoyB). HarBraceJ.

--The Hundred Dresses. LC 73-12940. (Illus.). 80p. (gr. k-3). 1974. pap. 3.95 (ISBN 0-15-642350-2, VoyB). HarBraceJ.

--The Middle Moffat. LC 79-11970. (Illus.). (gr. 4-7). 1979. pap. 2.95 (ISBN 0-15-659536-2, VoyB). HarBraceJ.

--Moffats. LC 41-51893. (Illus.). (gr. 4-6). 1968. pap. 4.95 (ISBN 0-15-661850-8, VoyB). HarBraceJ.

--Pinky Pye. LC 75-31581. (Illus.). 192p. (gr. 4-6). 1976. pap. 1.75 (ISBN 0-15-671840-5, VoyB). HarBraceJ.

--Witch Family. LC 60-11250. (Illus.). (gr. 3-7). 1960. 10.95 (ISBN 0-15-298571-9, HJ). HarBraceJ.

--Witch Family. LC 60-11250. (Illus.). (gr. 4-6). 1965. pap. 2.95 (ISBN 0-15-697645-5, VoyB). HarBraceJ.

Estes, Glenn E., jt. ed. see Hannigan, Jane A.

Estes, J. Worth. Hall Jackson & the Purple Foxglove: Medical Practice & Research in Revolutionary America, 1760-1820. LC 79-63083. (Illus.). 309p. 1979. text ed. 25.00x (ISBN 0-87451-173-9). U Pr of New Eng.

Estes, Jack C. Compound Interest & Annuity Tables. 240p. (Orig.). 1976. pap. 4.95 (ISBN 0-07-019683-4, SP). McGraw.

--Handbook of Interest & Annuity Tables. 1976. 38.50 (ISBN 0-07-019681-8, P&RB). McGraw.

--Handbook of Loan Payment Tables. 1976. 38.50 (ISBN 0-07-019682-6, P&RB). McGraw.

--Interest Amortization Tables. (McGraw-Hill Paperbacks). 224p. (Orig.). 1976. pap. 5.95 (ISBN 0-07-019680-X, SP). McGraw.

Estes, Jack C. & Kokus, J. Real Estate License Preparation Course for the Uniform Examinations: For Salesmen & Brokers. (Illus.). 224p. 1976. 22.95 (ISBN 0-07-019670-2, P&RB). McGraw.

Estes, James M. Christian Magistrate & State Church: The Reforming Career of Johannes Brenz. 208p. 1982. 27.50x (ISBN 0-8020-5589-3). U of Toronto Pr.

Estes, John E. & Senger, Leslie W. Remote Sensing: Techniques for Environmental Analysis. LC 73-8601. 340p. 1974. 24.95x (ISBN 0-471-24595-X). Wiley.

Estes, Nada J. & Heinemann, M. Edith. Alcoholism: Development, Consequences & Interventions. 2nd ed. LC 81-14036. (Illus.). 385p. 1982. pap. text ed. 14.95 (ISBN 0-8016-1500-3). Mosby.

Estes, R. W. Corporate Social Accounting. 166p. 1976. 23.50x o.p. (ISBN 0-471-24592-5, Pub. by Wiley-Interscience). Wiley.

Estes, Ralph W. Corporate Social Accounting. LC 75-42445. 1976. 23.50x o.p. (ISBN 0-471-24592-5). Ronald Pr.

--A Dictionary of Accounting. 176p. 1981. text ed. 16.50x (ISBN 0-262-05024-2); pap. 4.95 (ISBN 0-262-55009-1). MIT Pr.

Estes, Steve, jt. auth. see Eareckson, Joni.

Estes, Winston M. Another Part of the House. LC 70-91674. 1970. 9.57i (ISBN 0-397-00632-2). Har-Row.

Estess, Sybil P., jt. auth. see Schwartz, Lloyd.

Estess, Ted L. Elie Wiesel. LC 80-5337. (Literature and Life Ser.). 160p. 1980. 11.95 (ISBN 0-8044-2184-6). Ungar.

Esteva, Gustavo. The Struggle for Rural Mexico. Orig. Title: La Batalla En el Mexico Rural. (Illus.). 320p. 1983. text ed. 25.95x (ISBN 0-89789-025-6). J F Bergin.

Estey, Dale. The Bonner Deception. 352p. 1983. 13.95 (ISBN 0-312-08780-2). St Martin.

Estey, Marten. The Unions: Structure, Development, & Management. 3rd ed. 153p. 1981. pap. text ed. 7.95 (ISBN 0-15-592952-6, HC). HarBraceJ.

Estey, Martin, jt. auth. see Blum, Albert.

Esthus, Raymond A. Theodore Roosevelt & Japan. LC 66-19567. 339p. 1966. 11.50 o.p. (ISBN 0-295-74040-X). U of Wash Pr.

--Theodore Roosevelt & the International Rivalries. LC 71-102172. 165p. Repr. of 1970 ed. text ed. 15.95x (ISBN 0-941690-04-0); pap. text ed. 6.95x (ISBN 0-941690-05-9). Regina Bks.

Estienne, H. Traite de la Confirmite du Francais avec le Grec. (Linguistics 13th-18th Centuries Ser.). 190p. (Fr.). 1974. Repr. of 1565 ed. lib. bdg. 55.00x o.p. (ISBN 0-8287-0320-5, 71-5006). Clearwater Pub.

Estleman, Loren D. Aces & Eights. LC 80-2447. (Double D Western Ser.). 192p. 1981. 10.95 (ISBN 0-385-17469-1). Doubleday.

--Mister St. John. LC 82-45869. (D. D. Western Ser.). 192p. 1983. 11.95 (ISBN 0-385-18713-0). Doubleday.

Estner, Lois J., jt. auth. see Cohen, Nancy Wainer.

Estrada, Jose R. Dias Sin Gloria. 64p. (Span.). 1980. pap. 1.75 (ISBN 0-311-08213-0, Edit Mundo). Casa Bautista.

Estrada, Leo, jt. auth. see Kitchens, James A.

Estrada, Leobardo. Grandes Hombres de la Biblia. 235p. 1975. pap. 5.25 (ISBN 0-311-04656-8). Casa Bautista.

Estrada, Rita. With Time & Tenderness. (Candlelight Ecstasy Ser.: No. 133). (Orig.). 1983. pap. 1.95 (ISBN 0-440-19587-X). Dell.

Estrella, Gregorio. Cuentos Del Hombre Cacataibo (Cashibo) II. (Comunidades y Culturas Peruanas: No. 11). 1977. 4.25x (ISBN 0-88312-745-8); microfiche 1.50x (ISBN 0-686-77053-6). Summer Inst Ling.

Estrello, Francisco E. En Comunion Con Lo Eterno. pap. 1.75 o.s.i. (ISBN 0-8358-0415-1). Upper Room.

Estrello, Francisco E., tr. see White, D. M.

Estrin, Herman A., jt. ed. see Cunningham, Donald H.

Estrin, Mark. Lillian Hellman: A Reference Guide. 1980. lib. bdg. 26.00 (ISBN 0-8161-7907-7, Hall Reference). G K Hall.

Estrin, Saul & Holmes, Peter. French Planning in Theory & Practice. 224p. 1983. text ed. 29.50x (ISBN 0-04-339028-5). Allen Unwin.

Estrin, Y. B. & Glaskov, I. B. Play the King's Gambit: King's Gambit Accepted, Vol. 1. Neat, K. P., tr. (Illus.). 200p. 1982. 22.00 (ISBN 0-08-026873-0); pap. 13.95 (ISBN 0-08-026872-2). Pergamon.

--Play the King's Gambit: King's Gambit Declined, Vol. 2. Neat, K. P., tr. (Pergamon's Chess Openings Ser.). (Illus.). 130p. 1982. 20.00 (ISBN 0-08-026875-7); pap. 11.95 (ISBN 0-08-026874-9). Pergamon.

Esty, John, Jr. Choosing a Private School. LC 73-11550. 250p. 1974. 6.95 o.p. (ISBN 0-396-06861-8). Dodd.

ET D Staff. Color TV Trouble Factbook: Problems & Solutions. 3rd ed. LC 76-21178. 1976. pap. 9.95 (ISBN 0-8306-1119-3). Tab Bks.

ETA Offshore Seminars, Inc. Technology of Offshore Drilling: Completion & Production 1976. LC 75-21903. 434p. 1976. 44.95x (ISBN 0-87814-066-2). Pennwell Book Division.

Etcheberry, O. A. American-Chilean Private International Law. LC 60-16610. (Bilateral Studies in Private International Law: No. 10). 96p. 1960. 15.00 (ISBN 0-379-11410-0). Oceana.

Etchemendy, Nancy. The Watchers of Space. (Illus.). (gr. 3-7). 1980. pap. 1.75 (ISBN 0-380-75374-X, 78220-0, Camelot). Avon.

Etchinson, Dennis. The Dark Country. (Illus.). 232p. 1983. 15.00 (ISBN 0-910489-00-9). Scream Pr.

Eterovich, Francis H. Aristotle's Nicomachean Ethics: Commentary & Analysis. LC 80-5202. 331p. 1980. text ed. 22.25 (ISBN 0-8191-1056-6); pap. text ed. 12.50 (ISBN 0-8191-1057-4). U Pr of Amer.

Etgen, William M. & Reaves, Paul M. Dairy Cattle Feeding & Management. 6th ed. LC 63-20646. 638p. 1978. text ed. 34.95 (ISBN 0-471-71199-3). Wiley.

Ethell, Jeff, jt. auth. see Ohlrich, Walter.

Ethell, Jeffrey. Mustang: A Documentary History. (Illus.). 160p. 1981. 18.95 (ISBN 0-86720-561-X). Sci Bks Intl.

Ethell, Jeffrey & Price, Alfred. The German Jets in Combat. (Illus.). 160p. 1980. 17.95 (ISBN 0-86720-582-2). Sci Bks Intl.

--Target Berlin: Mission Two Hundred Fifty: Sixth of March Nineteen Forty-Four. (Illus.). 224p. 1982. 19.95 (ISBN 0-86720-551-2). Sci Bks Intl.

Etheredge, Lloyd S. A World of Men: The Private Sources of American Foreign Policy. 1978. text ed. 16.00x (ISBN 0-262-05019-6). MIT Pr.

Etheredge, Randall & Etheridge, Warren. The Football Quiz Book. 124p. 1980. pap. 3.50 (ISBN 0-8015-2720-1, Hawthorn). Dutton.

Etherege, George. The Plays of Sir George Etherege. Cordner, Michael, ed. LC 82-1180. (Plays by Renaissance & Restoration Dramatists Ser.). (Illus.). 384p. 1982. 39.50 (ISBN 0-521-24654-7); pap. 14.95 (ISBN 0-521-28879-7). Cambridge U Pr.

Etherege, Sir George. Letters of Sir George Etherege. Bracher, Frederick, ed. LC 70-187870. 1974. 36.00x (ISBN 0-520-02218-1). U of Cal Pr.

Etheridge, Christina. The Cranshaw Inheritance. 1979. pap. 1.95 o.s.i. (ISBN 0-515-05148-9). Jove Pubns.

Etheridge, David E. Mozart's Clarinet Concerto: The Clarinetists' View. LC 82-20420. 1983. 19.95 (ISBN 0-88289-372-6). Pelican.

Etheridge, Elizabeth W. The Butterfly Caste: A Social History of Pellagra in the South. LC 70-176431. (Contributions in American History: No. 17). 278p. 1972. lib. bdg. 27.50 (ISBN 0-8371-6276-9, EHP/). Greenwood.

Etheridge, Lloyd S. Can Governments Learn? 200p. 1983. 22.50 (ISBN 0-08-027218-5). Pergamon.

Etheridge, Warren, jt. auth. see Etheredge, Randall.

Etherington. Plant Physiological Ecology. (Studies in Biology: No. 98). 1978. 5.95 o.p. (ISBN 0-7131-2690-6). Univ Park.

Etherington, H. Nuclear Engineering Handbook. 1958. 55.00 o.p. (ISBN 0-07-019720-2, P&RB). McGraw.

Etherington, John R. Environment & Plant Ecology. 2nd ed. LC 81-16167. 487p. 1982. 59.95 (ISBN 0-471-10136-2, Pub. by Wiley-Interscience); pap. 27.95 (ISBN 0-471-10146-X, Pub. by Wiley-Interscience). Wiley.

--Wetland Ecology. (Studies in Biology: No. 154). 64p. 1983. pap. text ed. 8.95 (ISBN 0-7131-2865-8). E Arnold.

Etherton, Michael. The Development of African Drama. (Orig.). 1983. text ed. write for info. (ISBN 0-8419-0812-5); pap. text ed. write for info. (ISBN 0-8419-0813-3). Holmes & Meier.

Ethier, Wilfred J. Modern International Economics. 550p. 1982. text ed. 22.95x. Norton.

Ethridge, E. C., jt. auth. see Hench, L. L.

Ethridge, James M., ed. Directory of Directories: An Annotated Guide to Business & Industrial Directories, Professional & Scientific Rosters, & Other Lists & Guides of All Kinds. 1980. 72.00 o.p. (ISBN 0-8103-0270-5, Pub. by Information Ent); 64.00 o.p. (ISBN 0-8103-0271-3). Gale.

Ethridge, Marcus E., jt. auth. see Bingham, Richard D.

Ethridge, Willie S. Mark Ethridge: The Life & Times of a Great Newspaperman. (Illus.). 484p. Date not set. cancelled (ISBN 0-8149-0852-7). Vanguard. Postponed.

Etienne, Mona, jt. ed. see Gailey, Christine W.

Etier, A. Faborn & Etier, Betty A. Individualized Typing. 176p. (Orig.). 1983. pap. text ed. 12.95 (ISBN 0-672-97934-9); instr's. guide 3.33 (ISBN 0-672-97935-7); tapes 125.00 (ISBN 0-672-97939-X). Bobbs.

Etier, Betty A., jt. auth. see Etier, A. Faborn.

Etier, F., jt. auth. see Rowe, John L.

Etier, Faborn, jt. auth. see Rowe, John L.

Etkin, Bernard. Dynamics of Atmospheric Flight. LC 73-165946. (Illus.). 579p. 1972. text ed. 39.95x (ISBN 0-471-24620-4). Wiley.

--Dynamics of Flight Stability & Control. 2nd ed. LC 81-13058. 370p. 1982. text ed. 29.95x (ISBN 0-471-08936-2). Wiley.

Etkin, Ruth. Playing & Composing on the Recorder. LC 74-31711. (Illus.). 64p. (gr. 2 up). 1975. 7.95 o.p. (ISBN 0-8069-4528-1); PLB 7.49 o.p. (ISBN 0-8069-4529-X). Sterling.

--The Rhythm Band Book. LC 78-57886. (Illus.). (gr. 2 up). 1978. 9.95 (ISBN 0-8069-4570-2); PLB 13.29 (ISBN 0-8069-4571-0). Sterling.

Etkind, Efim. Notes of a Non-Conspirator. 1978. 12.50x (ISBN 0-19-211739-4). Oxford U Pr.

Etlin, Walter. Wordstar Made Easy. 2nd ed. (Orig.). 1982. pap. 11.95 (ISBN 0-931988-90-X). Osborne-McGraw.

Etnier, Elizabeth L., jt. ed. see Travis, Curtis C.

Etons, Ursula. Angel Dusted: A Family's Nightmare. 1981. 8.95 o.p. (ISBN 0-02-002600-5); pap. 4.95 (ISBN 0-686-96782-8). Macmillan.

Ets, Marie H. Elephant in a Well. (Viking Seafarer Ser). (Illus.). (gr. k). 1973. pap. 2.50 o.p. (ISBN 0-670-05084-9, Puffin). Penguin.

--Gilberto & the Wind. LC 63-8527. (gr. k-3). 1969. pap. 3.50 (ISBN 0-14-050276-9, Puffin). Penguin.

Etsujin see Shan, Han.

Ettema, James S. Working Together: A Study of Cooperation among Producers, Educators & Researchers to Create Educational Television. 220p. 1980. pap. 14.00x (ISBN 0-87944-251-4). Inst Soc Res.

Ettenson, Herb, ed. The Puzzle Lover's Daily Crossword, No. 5. 128p. 1983. pap. 1.75 (ISBN 0-686-83164-0). Berkley Pub.

--The Puzzle Lover's Daily Crossword, No. 6. 128p. (Orig.). 1983. pap. 1.75 (ISBN 0-425-05857-3). Berkley Pub.

Etter, D. M. Structured FORTRAN 77 for Engineers & Scientists. 1982. 19.95 (ISBN 0-8053-2520-4, 32520). Benjamin-Cummings.

Etter, Dave. Strawberries. 1979. pap. 3.00 (ISBN 0-686-61860-2). Juniper Pr WI.

Etter, Don D., jt. auth. see West, William A.

Etter, Jane. Alliance, Illinois. 256p. 1983. 14.95 (ISBN 0-933180-43-8). Spoon Riv Poetry.

Etter, Les. Basketball Superstars: Three Great Pros. LC 73-9659. (Sports Ser.). (Illus.). 96p. (gr. 3-6). 1974. PLB 7.12 (ISBN 0-8116-6667-0). Garrard.

--The Game of Hockey. LC 77-4720. (Sports Ser.). (Illus.). (gr. 3-6). 1977. PLB 7.12 (ISBN 0-8116-6682-4). Garrard.

--Hockey's Masked Men: Three Great Goalies. LC 75-28413. (Sports Series). (Illus.). 80p. (gr. 3-6). 1976. lib. bdg. 7.99 (ISBN 0-8116-6676-X). Garrard.

--Vince Lombardi: Football Legend. LC 74-18076. (Sports Library Ser.). (Illus.). 96p. (gr. 3-6). 1975. PLB 7.12 (ISBN 0-8116-6670-0). Garrard.

Etter, Lewis E. Glossary of Words & Phrases Used in Radiology, Nuclear Medicine & Ultrasound. 2nd ed. 384p. 1970. ed. spiral 32.50xphotocopy (ISBN 0-398-00526-5). C C Thomas.

Ettesvold, Paul M. The Eighteenth-Century Woman. Cone, Poly, et al, eds. (Illus., Orig.). 1982. pap. 2.95 (ISBN 0-87099-296-1). Metro Mus Art.

Ettinger, Andrew, ed. see Freedman, Melvin H. & Silver, Samuel M.

Ettinger, Elzbieta, ed. see Luxemburg, Rosa.

Ettinger, P., jt. auth. see Caussinus, H.

Ettinger, P., jt. ed. see Caussinus, H.

Ettinger, Richard P. & Golieb, D. E. Credits & Collections. 5th ed. 1962. text ed. 21.00 (ISBN 0-13-192641-1). P-H.

Ettinger, Stephen J. & Suter, Peter F. Canine Cardiology. LC 77-97547. (Illus.). 1970. 42.00 (ISBN 0-7216-3437-0). Saunders.

Ettinger, Stephen J., ed. Textbook of Veterinary Internal Medicine: Diseases of the Dog and Cat. LC 74-4559. (Illus.). 1767p. 1975. Vol. 1. 43.00 (ISBN 0-7216-3424-9); Vol. 2. 50.00 (ISBN 0-7216-3425-7); Set. 90.00 (ISBN 0-7216-3422-2). Saunders.

Ettinghausen, Richard & Yarshater, Ehsan, eds. Highlights of Persian Art. LC 79-4746. (Persian Art Ser.). 1983. 75.00x (ISBN 0-89158-295-9). Caravan Bks.

Ettl, H. Die Gattung Chloromonas Gobi Emend Wille. 1970. pap. 48.00 (ISBN 3-7682-5434-8). Lubrecht & Cramer.

--Die Gattungen Carteria und Provasoliella. (Nova Hedwigia: Suppl. 60). 1979. lib. bdg. 40.00x (ISBN 3-7682-5460-7). Lubrecht & Cramer.

Ettlinger, John R. & Spirit, Diana. Choosing Books for Young People. LC 82-11659. 238p. 1982. text ed. 25.00 (ISBN 0-8389-0366-5). ALA.

Ettlinger, Lester A., et al. High-Temperature Plasma Technology Applications. LC 80-65507. (Electrotechnology Ser.: Vol. 6). (Illus.). 163p. 1980. 39.95 (ISBN 0-250-40376-5). Ann Arbor Science.

Ettre, L. S. & Zlatkis, A. Seventy-Five Years of Chromatography - an Historical Dialogue. (Journal of Chromatography Ser.: Vol. 17). 1979. 53.25 (ISBN 0-444-41754-0). Elsevier.

Etulain, Richard W. A Bibliographical Guide to the Study of Western American Literature. LC 82-8579. xviii, 317p. 1982. 22.50x (ISBN 0-8032-1801-X). U of Nebr Pr.

Etulain, Righard W., jt. ed. see Douglass, William A.

Etzell, Paul S., jt. auth. see Everson, Lloyd K.

Etzioni, A. An Immodest Agenda: Rebuilding America Before the 21st Century. (New Press Ser.). 464p. 1982. 26.95 (ISBN 0-07-019723-7). McGraw.

--Modern Organizations. 1964. pap. 9.95 (ISBN 0-13-596049-5). P-H.

Etzioni, Amitai. Genetic Fix: The Next Technological Revolution. 272p. 1975. pap. 3.95i o.p. (ISBN 0-06-090428-3, CN428, CN). Har-Row.

--Social Problems. (Foundations of Modern Sociology Ser.). 192p. 1976. pap. text ed. 9.95 (ISBN 0-13-817403-2). P-H.

Etzioni, Amitai & Remp, Richard. Technological Shortcuts to Social Change. LC 72-83834. 236p. 1973. 10.95x (ISBN 0-87154-236-6). Russell Sage.

Etzkowitz, Henry. Is America Possible? Social Problems from Conservative, Liberal, & Socialist Perspectives. 2nd ed. 400p. 1980. pap. text ed. 16.95 (ISBN 0-8299-0329-1). West Pub.

Etzler, John A. Collected Works of John Adolphus Etzler. LC 77-7124. 1977. Repr. 48.00x (ISBN 0-8201-1290-9). Schol Facsimiles.

Etzold, Thomas H. & Davison, Will, eds. Aspects of Sino-American Relations Since 1784. LC 78-10227. 1978. 10.00 o.p. (ISBN 0-531-05399-7); pap. 5.95 o.p. (ISBN 0-531-05609-0). Watts.

Eubank, Keith. Origins of World War Two. LC 73-77338. (Europe Since 1500 Ser.). 1969. pap. 7.95x (ISBN 0-88295-733-3). Harlan Davidson.

Eubank, Mary G. When I Grow Up. (Scribbler Play Bks.). (Illus.). 20p. (ps). 1983. pap. write for info. (ISBN 0-307-20327-1). Western Pub.

Eubanks, David, jt. auth. see Wasserberger, Jonathan.

Eubanks, David H., jt. auth. see Wasserberger, Jonathan.

Euclid. The Elements, 3 vols. Heath, Thomas L., ed. 1926. Vol. 1. pap. 6.50 (ISBN 0-486-60088-2); Vol. 2. pap. 6.50 (ISBN 0-486-60089-0); Vol. 3. pap. 6.50 (ISBN 0-486-60090-4). Dover.

Eudaly, Maria S. De. El Cuidado De Dios. Villasenor, Emma Z., tr. (gr. 1-3). Date not set. pap. price not set (ISBN 0-311-38555-9). Casa Bautista.

Eudes, Abbot J. The Abbey Psalter: The Book of Psalms Used by the Trappist Monks of Genesee Abbey. LC 81-80871. 368p. 1981. 24.95 (ISBN 0-8091-0316-8). Paulist Pr.

Eugene, P. M. I Am a Daughter of the Church. Clare, M. V., Sr., tr. 667p. 1982. pap. 15.00 (ISBN 0-87061-050-3). Chr Classics.

--I Want to See God. Clare, M. V., Sr., tr. 549p. 1982. pap. 15.00 (ISBN 0-87061-051-1). Chr Classics.

Eugenics Society, 9th Symposium. Resources & Population: Proceedings. Benjamin, B., et al, eds. 1973. 25.00 o.p. (ISBN 0-12-088350-3). Acad Pr.

Eugenie. Jenny's Surprise Summer. (Little Golden Bks.). (Illus.). 24p. (ps). 1981. 1.49 (ISBN 0-307-02047-9, Golden Pr); PLB 5.77 (ISBN 0-307-60247-8). Western Pub.

Eugster, Carla. Peter & the Guru. 16p. 1979. pap. 1.00 o.p. (ISBN 0-686-28230-2). Samisdat.

--Rural Water. 16p. 1981. pap. 1.00 o.p. (ISBN 0-686-30664-3). Samisdat.

Eulalie, illus. Mother Goose Rhymes. (Illus.). 48p. (ps-3). Date not set. price not set (ISBN 0-448-40114-2, G&D). Putnam Pub Group.

Eulau, H. & Czudnowski, M. M., eds. Elite Recruitment in Democratic Politics: Comparative Studies Across the Nations. LC 76-2698. 299p. 1976. 19.95x o.s.i. (ISBN 0-470-15056-4). Halsted Pr.

Eulau, Heinz. Behaviorial Persuasion in Politics. 1963. pap. text ed. 3.50x (ISBN 0-685-69587-5). Phila Bk Co.

--Political Behavior in America. 1966. pap. text ed. 7.95 (ISBN 0-685-41969-X). Phila Bk Co.

Eulau, Heinz, jt. auth. see Wahlke, John.

Eulenburg, Milton D., et al. Introductory Algebra. 3rd ed. LC 74-24338. 360p. 1975. text ed. 21.95x (ISBN 0-471-24686-7); avail. answers (ISBN 0-471-24687-5). Wiley.

Euler, Manfred. Physikunterricht: Anspruch und Realitat. 254p. (Ger.). 1982. write for info. (ISBN 3-8204-7103-0). P Lang Pubs.

Euler, Ulf S. Von see Von Euler, Ulf S. & Eliasson, Rune.

Euler, Von see Von Euler.

Eulo, Ken. The Deathstone. (Orig.). 1982. pap. 3.95 (ISBN 0-686-82447-4). PB.

Eun, Lee & Blyth, R. H. First Book of Korean. 1962. pap. 9.95 o.p. (ISBN 0-89346-026-5, Pub. by Hokuseido Pr). Heian Intl.

Eurich, Alvin C., ed. Major Transitions in the Human Life Cycle. LC 81-47067. 544p. 1981. 25.95x (ISBN 0-669-04559-4). Lexington Bks.

Eurich, Nell P. Science in Utopia: A Mighty Design. LC 67-14339. 1967. 16.50x o.p. (ISBN 0-674-79440-0). Harvard U Pr.

Euripides. Alcestis. Arrowsmith, William, tr. (Greek Tragedy in New Translations Ser). 1973. 12.95x (ISBN 0-19-501861-3). Oxford U Pr.

--The Bacchae. Cacoyannis, Michael, tr. (Orig.). 1982. pap. 1.95 (ISBN 0-451-62058-5, MJ2058, Ment). NAL.

--Euripides Five: Three Tragedies. Grene, David & Lattimore, Richard, eds. Incl. Electra. Vermeule, Emily T., tr; The Phoenician Women. Wyckoff, Elizabeth, tr; The Bacchae. Arrowsmith, William, tr. LC 55-5787. 228p. 1959. pap. 4.95 (ISBN 0-226-30784-0, P312, Phoen). U of Chicago Pr.

--Heracles: With Introduction & Commentary. Bond, Godfrey W., ed. 1982. 62.00x (ISBN 0-19-814012-6). Oxford U Pr.

--Iphigeneia in Tauris. Lattimore, Richmond, tr. (Greek Tragedy in New Translations Ser.). 1973. 12.95x (ISBN 0-19-501736-6). Oxford U Pr.

Euripides see Hadas, Moses.

Eurodata Analysts. The Pulp, Paper & Paperbound Industry: Profits, Future Development & Investment Risk, Long & Short Term-A Global Scenario. (Illus.). 150p. 1982. pap. 495.00 (ISBN 0-87930-141-4, 526). Miller Freeman.

EUROMICRO Symposium on Microprocessing & Microprogramming, 8th, 1982. Microsystems: Architecture, Integration & Use. Van Spronsen, C. J. & Richter, L., eds. 375p. 1982. 59.75 (ISBN 0-444-86470-9, North Holland). Elsevier.

European Chemoreception Research Organisation, Symposium, Netherlands, 1979. Preference Behaviour & Chemoreception: Proceedings. Kroeze, J. H., ed. (ECRO Minisymposium Ser.). 400p. 1979. 26.00 (ISBN 0-904147-12-6). IRL Pr.

European Chemoreception Research Organisation, 2nd Interdisciplinary Symposium, Switzerland, 1975. Structure-Activity Relationships in Chemoreception: Proceedings. 197p. 20.00 o.p. (ISBN 0-904147-03-7). IRL Pr.

European Commission on Agricultural Working Party on Water Resources & Irrigation, Romania, 1972. Drainage Machinery. (Irrigation & Drainage Papers: No. 15). 126p. 1973. pap. 8.50 (ISBN 92-5-100006-9, F984, FAO). Unipub.

European Commission on Agriculture Working Party on Water Resources & Irrigation, Tel Aviv, 1970. Drainage Materials. (Irrigation & Drainage Papers: No. 9). 126p. 1972. pap. 8.50 (ISBN 0-686-93183-1, F978, FAO). Unipub.

European Commission on Agriculture Working Party on Water Resources & Irrigation, Bucharest, 1972. Drainage of Salty Soils. (Irrigation & Drainage Papers: No. 16). 87p. 1973. pap. 6.00 o.p. (ISBN 0-686-93187-4, F985, FAO). Unipub.

European Commission on Agriculture, Working Party on Water Resources & Irrigation, Tel Aviv, 1970. Village Irrigation Programmes: A New Approach in Water Economy. (Irrigation & Drainage Papers: No. 6). 114p. 1971. pap. 7.50 (ISBN 0-686-93057-6, F973, FAO). Unipub.

European Conference of Ministers of Transport. Trends in Transport Investment & Expediture in 1979: Statistical Report on Road Accidents in 1980. 108p. (Orig.). 1982. pap. 10.00x (ISBN 0-686-37603-X). OECD.

European Congress on Molecular Spectroscopy, 12th, Strasbourg, 1975, et al. Molecular Spectroscopy of Dense Phases: Proceedings. Grosmann, M., et al, eds. 1976. 117.00 (ISBN 0-444-41409-6). Elsevier.

European Consultation on the Economic Evaluation of Sport & Commercial Fisheries, 2nd Gothenburg, Sweden, 1975. Report & Technical Papers. (FAO-EIFAC Technical Papers: No. 26). 190p. 1977. pap. 12.75 (ISBN 92-5-000256-4, F767, FAO). Unipub.

European Geophysical Symposium, August 1980, Budapest. Geomagnetic Pulsations. Orr, D., ed. 100p. 1982. pap. 27.50 (ISBN 0-08-026508-1). Pergamon.

European Heating & Ventilating Associations, ed. The International Dictionary of Heating, Ventilating, & Air Conditioning. LC 79-41714. 416p. 1982. 79.95x (ISBN 0-419-11650-8, E&FN Spon England). Methuen Inc.

European Meeting of Statisticians, Sept. 6-11 1976, Grenoble, France, et al. Recent Developments in Statistics: Proceedings. 1977. 95.75 (ISBN 0-7204-0751-6, North-Holland). Elsevier.

European Organization for Research & Treatment of Cancer. Treatment of Neoplastic Lesions of the Nervous System: Proceedings of a Symposium Sponsored by the European Organization for Research & Treatment of Cancer (EORTC), Brussels, April, 1980. Hildebrand, J. & Gangji, D., eds. (Illus.). 178p. 1982. 50.00 (ISBN 0-08-027989-9). Pergamon.

European Peptide Symposium, 9th, France, 1968. Peptides: Proceedings. Bricas, E., ed. 1968. 24.50 (ISBN 0-444-10156-X, North-Holland). Elsevier.

European Society for Opinion & Marketing Research Congress-24th-Helsinki, Aug. 22-26, 1971, ed. Proceedings: From Experience to Innovation, 2 vols. 1182p. 1973. Set. pap. 62.50x o.p. (ISBN 0-8002-1878-7). Intl Pubns Serv.

European Symposium on Thermal Analysis & Dollimore. Thermal Analysis: Proceedings. 1981. 61.95 (ISBN 0-471-25664-1, Wiley Heyden). Wiley.

Eusden, John D., ed. & tr. see Ames, William.

Eustace, E. J. The King of the Mountains: A Play in Five Acts. LC 74-25360. 88p. 1975. 7.00 o.p. (ISBN 0-87104-257-6). NY Pub Lib.

Eustice, James S., jt. auth. see Bittker, Boris I.

Eustis, Alvin, tr. see Chevalier, Francois.

Eustis, O. B. Notes from the North Country. 248p. 1983. pap. 8.95 (ISBN 0-472-06346-4). U of Mich Pr.

Euwe, Max. Bobby Fischer-the Greatest? LC 78-66270. (Illus.). 1979. 9.95 o.p. (ISBN 0-8069-4950-3); lib. bdg. 9.29 o.p. (ISBN 0-8069-4951-1). Sterling.

Evan, Paul. Gunsmoke Over Sabado. 256p. (YA) 1974. 6.95 (ISBN 0-685-49199-4, Avalon). Bouregy.

Evan, W. M. Organization Theory: Structures, Systems, & Environments. LC 76-22742. 312p. 1976. 31.95x (ISBN 0-471-01512-1). Wiley.

Evangelical Sisterhood of Mary, tr. see Schlink, Basilea.

Evanoff, Vlad. Fresh-Water Fisherman's Bible. rev. ed. LC 79-7684. (Outdoor Bible Ser.). (Illus.). 1980. pap. 4.95 (ISBN 0-385-14405-9). Doubleday.

Evanovich, Peter & Kerner, Martin. Precalculus: A Functional Approach to Algebra & Trigonometry. 1981. text ed. 21.95x (ISBN 0-8162-2715-2); study guide & instr's manual avail. Holden-Day.

Evans. Breaking Up Bell: Essays on Industrial Organization & Regulation. Date not set. price not set (ISBN 0-444-00734-2). Elsevier.

Evans & Roberts. Clinical Radiology: For Medical Students. 1982. text ed. 18.50 (ISBN 0-407-00177-8). Butterworth.

Evans, jt. auth. see Ehrhart.

Evans, A. J. Reading & Thinking, 2 vols. 1979. pap. text ed. 9.00 set (ISBN 0-8077-2576-5). Tchrs Coll.

Evans, A. J. & Palmer, Marilyn. More Writing about Pictures: Using Pictures to Develop Language & Writing Skills. (gr. 1-3). 1982. Bk. 1: Familiar Places. pap. 3.95 (ISBN 0-8077-6037-4); Bk. 2: Action & Activity. pap. 3.95 (ISBN 0-8077-6038-2); Bk. 3: Supplement-Fables. pap. 3.95 (ISBN 0-8077-6039-0); Tchrs' Manual 2.95 (ISBN 0-8077-6040-4). Tchrs Coll.

--Writing About Pictures: Using Pictures to Develop Language & Writing Skills, 6 bks. (gr. 1-3). 1982. Bk. 1: Completing Sentences. pap. text ed. 3.50 (ISBN 0-8077-5994-5); Bk. 2: Writing Sentences. pap. text ed. 3.50 (ISBN 0-8077-6031-5); Bk. 3: Getting At The Story. pap. text ed. 3.50x (ISBN 0-8077-6032-3); Bk. 4: Linking Story Ideas. pap. text ed. 3.50 (ISBN 0-8077-6033-1); Bk. 5: Writing Your Story, I. pap. text ed. 3.50 (ISBN 0-8077-6034-X); Bk. 6: Writing Your Story, II. pap. text ed. 3.50 (ISBN 0-8077-6035-8); tchrs. manual 2.95x (ISBN 0-8077-6036-6). Tchrs Coll.

Evans, A. M. Metallization Associated with Acid Magmatism. LC 76-366369. (International Geological Correlation Programme Ser.: Vol. 6). 385p. 1982. 52.50x (ISBN 0-471-09995-3, Pub. by Wiley-Interscience). Wiley.

Evans, A. R., ed. see Markley, Rayner W.

Evans, A. R., ed. see Sheeler, W. D., et al.

Evans, A. R., ed. see Sheeler, W. D. & Bayley, S. C.

Evans, A. W., tr. see France, Anatole.

Evans, Alan W. The Economics of Residential Location. LC 73-88176. (Illus.). 274p. 1974. 19.95 o.p. (ISBN 0-312-23520-8). St Martin.

Evans, Alfred S. & Feldman, Harry A., eds. Bacterial Infections of Humans Epidemiology & Control. 744p. 1982. 59.50x (ISBN 0-306-40967-4, Plenum Pr). Plenum Pub.

Evans, Alice F., jt. auth. see Evans, Robert A.

Evans, Alona E. & Murphy, John F., eds. Legal Aspects of International Terrorism. new ed. LC 78-404. 736p. 1978. 38.95x (ISBN 0-669-02185-7). Lexington Bks.

Evans, Ambrose see Manley, Mary D.

Evans, Anthony. Aquariums. (Foyle's Handbks). 1973. 3.95 (ISBN 0-685-55811-8). Palmetto Pub.

--Glossary of Molecular Biology. LC 74-26571. 55p. 1975. 17.95 o.s.i. (ISBN 0-470-24740-1). Halsted Pr.

--Goldfish. Foyle, Christina, ed. (Foyle's Handbks). 1973. 3.95 (ISBN 0-685-55819-3). Palmetto Pub.

--Your Book of Aquaria. (gr. 7 up). 1971. 4.50 o.p. (ISBN 0-571-04764-5). Transatlantic.

Evans, Archibald, jt. auth. see Waterlow, Charlotte.

Evans, Arthur. Palace of Minos, 4 Vols. in 7. LC 63-18048. 1921. 750.00x (ISBN 0-8196-0129-2). Vol. 1 (ISBN 0-8196-0130-6). Vol. 2, Pt. 1 (ISBN 0-8196-0131-4). Vol. 2, Pt. 2 (ISBN 0-8196-0141-1). Vol. 3 (ISBN 0-8196-0132-2). Vol. 4, Pt. 1 (ISBN 0-8196-0133-0). Vol. 4, Pt. 2 (ISBN 0-8196-0134-9). Index (ISBN 0-8196-0135-7). Biblo.

Evans, Audrey E., ed. Advances in Neuroblastoma Research. (Progress in Cancer Research & Therapy Ser.: Vol. 12). 360p. 1980. 42.00 (ISBN 0-89004-459-7, 516). Raven.

Evans, Barbara L., ed. see Evans, Gareth L.

Evans, Barry, ed. Prayer Book Renewal: Worship & the New Book of Common Prayer. 1978. pap. 1.00 (ISBN 0-8164-2157-9). Seabury.

Evans, Benjamin. Daylight in Architecture. LC 80-26066. (Illus.). 204p. 1982. 34.50x (ISBN 0-07-019768-7). McGraw.

Evans, Benjamin I. A Short History of English Drama. LC 77-27446. 1978. Repr. of 1950 ed. lib. bdg. 17.00x (ISBN 0-8371-9072-X, EVED). Greenwood.

Evans, Bertrand. Shakespeare's Tragic Practice. 1980. 34.50x (ISBN 0-19-812094-X). Oxford U Pr.

Evans, Bertrand, jt. auth. see Knapton, James.

Evans, Bertrand, ed. The College Shakespeare: Fifteen Plays & the Sonnets. 736p. 1973. pap. text ed. 17.95x (ISBN 0-02-334440-7, 33444). Macmillan.

Evans, C. F. Resurrection & the New Testament. (Student Christian Movement Press Ser.). (Orig.). 1970. pap. 10.95x (ISBN 0-19-520316-X). Oxford U Pr.

Evans, C. S. Cinderella. (Illus.). 1982. 14.95 (ISBN 0-434-95862-X, Pub. by Heinemann). David & Charles.

--Preserving the Person: A Look at the Human Sciences. 178p. 1982. pap. 5.95 (ISBN 0-8010-3385-3). Baker Bk.

--Sleeping Beauty. (Illus.). 1982. 14.95 (ISBN 0-686-84338-X, Pub. by W Heinemann). David & Charles.

Evans, C. W. Powdered & Particulate Rubber Technology. (Illus.). 1978. 24.75 (ISBN 0-85334-773-5, Pub. by Applied Sci England). Elsevier.

--Practical Rubber Compounding & Processing. 1981. 39.00 (ISBN 0-85334-901-0, Pub. by Applied Sci England). Elsevier.

Evans, C. W., ed. Developments in Rubber & Rubber Composites, Vol. 1. 1980. 35.00 (ISBN 0-85334-892-8, Pub. by Applied Sci England). Elsevier.

--Developments in Rubber & Rubber Composites, Vol. 2. Date not set. 45.00 (ISBN 0-85334-173-7, Pub. by Applied Sci England). Elsevier.

Evans, Charles H. Electronic Amplifiers: Theory, Design, & Use. LC 76-3950. 1979. pap. text ed. 17.00 (ISBN 0-8273-1626-7); instr's. manual 5.50 (ISBN 0-8273-1627-5). Delmar.

--Electronic Amplifiers: Theory, Design & Use. 1979. 15.50 o.p. (ISBN 0-442-22341-2). Van Nos Reinhold.

Evans, Christopher. Capella's Golden Eye. 256p. 1982. pap. 2.50 (ISBN 0-686-98013-1, Pub. by Ace Science Fiction). Ace Bks.

--The Micro Millenium. 256p. 1980. 10.95 (ISBN 0-686-98078-6). Telecom Lib.

--Understanding Yourself. LC 77-73786. 1977. 12.95 o.s.i. (ISBN 0-89104-100-1, A & W Visual Library); pap. 4.95 o.s.i. (ISBN 0-89104-084-6). A & W Pubs.

--Understanding Yourself. (Illus.). 160p. 1983. pap. 6.95 (ISBN 0-89104-084-6, A & W Visual Library). A & W Pubs.

Evans, Claire. Apollo's Dream. 192p. 1982. pap. 1.75 (ISBN 0-686-81838-5). Jove Pubns.

Evans, Clifford, jt. ed. see Meggers, Betty.

Evans, Colin W. Hose Technology. 2nd ed. (Illus.). 1979. 41.00x (ISBN 0-85334-830-8, Pub. by Applied Sci England). Elsevier.

Evans, Colleen. The Vine Life. 120p. 1980. pap. 4.95 (ISBN 0-912376-97-X). Chosen Bks Pub.

Evans, Colleen T. Love Is an Everyday Thing. 1977. pap. 1.50 (ISBN 0-8007-8271-2, Spire Bks). Revell.

--A New Joy. (Orig.). pap. write for info (ISBN 0-515-09500-1). Jove Pubns.

Evans, Craig. On Foot Through Europe: A Trail Guide to Europe's Long-Distance Footpaths. 7.00 (ISBN 0-688-01156-X). Morrow.

--On Foot Through Europe: A Trail Guide to France & the Benelux Nations. 1982. 10.50 (ISBN 0-688-01171-3). Morrow.

--On Foot Through Europe: A Trail Guide to Scandinavia. 1982. 12.50 o.p. (ISBN 0-686-95249-9). U of Ill Pr.

--On Foot Through Europe: A Trail Guide to Spain & Portugal. 1982. 9.50 (ISBN 0-688-01195-0). Morrow.

Evans, Craynne, ed. see Shakespeare, William.

Evans, D. J., et al, eds. International Laterite Symposium. LC 78-73974. (Illus.). 1979. text ed. 33.00x (ISBN 0-89520-255-7). Soc Mining Eng.

Evans, D. MacLean & Bowen Jones, John. Introduction to Medical Chemistry. 288p. 1976. text ed. 25.50 scp (ISBN 0-06-041921-0, HarpC). Har-Row.

Evans, D. P. Backache. 280p. 1982. text ed. 24.50 (ISBN 0-8391-1739-6). Univ Park.

Evans, D. R., et al. Essential Interviewing: A Programmed Approach to Effective Communication. LC 79-13719. 1979. pap. text ed. 14.95 (ISBN 0-8185-0342-4). Brooks-Cole.

Evans, D. S. Observation in Modern Astronomy. 1968. 28.95 o.p. (ISBN 0-444-19941-1). Elsevier.

Evans, D. S., ed. see International Astronomical Union Symposium, 44th, Uppsala, Sweden, 1970.

Evans, David. As Mad as a Hatter. 224p. 1982. text ed. 16.75x (ISBN 0-904387-90-9, Pub. by Sutton England). Humanities.

--A Bibliography of Stained Glass. 214p. 1983. text ed. 75.00x (ISBN 0-85991-087-3, Pub by Boydell & Brewer). Biblio Dist.

--The Ingenious Mr. Pedersen. 132p. 1979. Repr. of 1978 ed. text ed. 10.25x (ISBN 0-904387-29-1, Pub. by Alan Sutton England). Humanities.

Evans, David & Hoxeng, James, eds. The Eucador Project. Clason, Carla & Massee, Robin, trs. from Eng. & Fr. (Technical Notes Ser.: No.1). 20p. (Orig.). 1972. pap. 1.00 (ISBN 0-932288-03-0). Eng. Fr (ISBN 0-932288-05-7). Span (ISBN 0-932288-04-9). Ctr Intl Ed U of MA.

Evans, David A. Train Windows. LC 75-36977. 56p. 1976. 6.95 (ISBN 0-8214-0204-8, 82-82113); pap. 2.50 o.s.i. (ISBN 0-8214-0213-7). Ohio U Pr.

--What the Tallgrass Sats? 120p. pap. 6.95 (ISBN 0-931170-17-6). Ctr Western Studies.

Evans, David A., jt. auth. see Sharp, William R.

Evans, David E. Dursley & Cam. 125p. 1981. text ed. 8.25x (ISBN 0-904387-88-7, Pub. by Alan Sutton England). Humanities.

Evans, David J. Geographical Perspectives in Juvenile Delinquency. 132p. 1980. text ed. 27.75x (ISBN 0-566-00351-1). Gower Pub Ltd.

Evans, David J., ed. Preconditioning Methods: Analysis & Application. (Topics in Computer Mathematics Ser.: Vol. 1). 1982. write for info. (ISBN 0-677-16320-7). Gordon.

Evans, Don A. Texas Business Law Workbook. LC 80-17836. 256p. (Orig.). 1982. pap. text ed. 12.95 (ISBN 0-88289-305-X); Answer Bk. & Teacher Guide avail. (ISBN 0-88289-356-4). Pelican.

Evans, Dorinda. Mather Brown: Early American Artist in England. (Illus.). 1982. 32.50 (ISBN 0-8195-5069-8). Wesleyan U Pr.

Evans, Doris P. Mr. Charley's Chopsticks. (Break-of-Day Bk). (Illus.). 64p. (gr. 1-3). 1972. PLB 4.69 o.p. (ISBN 0-698-30421-7, Coward). Putnam Pub Group.

Evans, Douglas. Western Energy Policy. LC 78-23315. 1979. 25.00x (ISBN 0-312-86392-6). St Martin.

Evans, E. A. Tritium & Its Compounds. 441p. 1966. 21.50 (ISBN 0-442-02339-1, Pub. by Van Nos Reinhold). Krieger.

Evans, Edward G. Developing Library Collections. LC 78-27303. (Library Science Text Ser.). 340p. 1979. lib. bdg. 28.00 (ISBN 0-87287-145-2); pap. text ed. 20.00 (ISBN 0-87287-247-5). Libs Unl.

Evans, Elizabeth. Eudora Welty. LC 81-2812. (Literature and Life Ser.). 180p. 1981. 11.95 (ISBN 0-8044-2187-0). Ungar.

--Ring Lardner. LC 79-4829. (Literature and Life Ser.). 1980. 11.95 (ISBN 0-8044-2185-4). Ungar.

Evans, Ellen. Convention Girls. 224p. 1982. pap. 2.50 o.p. (ISBN 0-505-51850-3). Tower Bks.

Evans, Elwood. Puget Sound. facs. ed. (Shorey Historical Ser.). 16p. Repr. of 1869 ed. pap. 1.95 (ISBN 0-8466-0051-X, SJS51). Shorey.

Evans, Emory G. Thomas Nelson of Yorktown: Revolutionary Virginian. LC 74-83323. (Williamsburg in America Ser.: Vol. 10). 1975. 3.95x o.p. (ISBN 0-8139-0515-X). U Pr of Va.

Evans, Eric J. The Contentious Tithe: The Tithe Problem & English Agriculture, 1750-1850. (Studies in Economic History). 1976. 16.95x (ISBN 0-7100-8324-6). Routledge & Kegan.

Evans, Ernest. Calling a Truce to Terror: The American Response to International Terrorism. LC 78-22722. (Contributions in Political Science Ser: No. 29). (Illus.). 1979. lib. bdg. 25.00 (ISBN 0-313-21140-X, EIT/). Greenwood.

Evans, Evelyn J. A Tropical Library Service: The Story of Ghana's Libraries. 256p. 1964. 15.00 (ISBN 0-233-95719-7, 05788-6, Pub. by Gower Pub Co England). Lexington Bks.

Evans, F. C. A First Geography of Jamaica. 2nd ed. (Illus.). 48p. (gr. 5-8). 1973. 5.95x (ISBN 0-521-20252-3). Cambridge U Pr.

--A First Geography of the Eastern Caribbean. (Illus.). 48p. (gr. 5 up). 1972. text ed. 5.95x (ISBN 0-521-08312-5). Cambridge U Pr.

--A First Geography of the West Indies. (gr. 5 up). 1974. 6.95x (ISBN 0-521-20112-8). Cambridge U Pr.

--A First Geography of Trinidad & Tobago. 2nd ed. LC 67-21957. (Illus.). text ed. 5.95x (ISBN 0-521-20180-2). Cambridge U Pr.

Evans, F. C. & Young, N. The Bahamas. LC 76-16133. (Illus.). 1977. 5.95x (ISBN 0-521-21292-8). Cambridge U Pr.

Evans, F. Gaynor. Mechanical Properties of Bone. (Illus.). 336p. 1973. 32.75x (ISBN 0-398-02775-7). C C Thomas.

Evans, Francis L., III. Ozone in Water & Wastewater Treatment. LC 72-78476. 200p. 1972. 29.50 o.p. (ISBN 0-250-97523-8). Ann Arbor Science.

Evans, Frank L. Equipment Design Handbook for Refineries & Chemical Plants, Vol. 1. 2nd ed. 196p. 1980. 37.95x (ISBN 0-87201-254-9). Gulf Pub.

--Equipment Design Handbook for Refineries & Chemical Plants, Vol. 2. 2nd ed. 370p. 1980. 41.95x (ISBN 0-87201-255-7). Gulf Pub.

Evans, G. Blakemore, et al, eds. see Shakespeare, William.

Evans, G. C., et al, eds. Light As an Ecological Factor 2: Proceedings. LC 76-921. 616p. 1976. 68.95x o.s.i. (ISBN 0-470-15043-2). Halsted Pr.

Evans, G. Edward, jt. auth. see Bloomberg, Marty.

Evans, G. Owen, et al. The Terrestrial Acari of the British Isles: an Introduction to Their Morphology, Biology & Classification, Vol. 1: Introduction & Biology. (Illus.). 219p. 1961. Repr. of 1968 ed. 12.50x (ISBN 0-565-00696-7, Pub. by Brit Mus Nat Hist England). Sabbot-Natural Hist Bks.

Evans, G. Russell & Singer, C. Gregg. The Church & the Sword. LC 82-50234. 128p. 1982. pap. text ed. 6.95 (ISBN 0-686-81950-0). St Thomas.

Evans, Gareth. The Varieties of Reference. McDowell, John, ed. (Illus.). 432p. 1982. 34.95 (ISBN 0-19-824685-4); pap. 10.95x (ISBN 0-19-824686-2). Oxford U Pr.

Evans, Gareth L. The Upstart Crow: An Introduction to Shakespeare's Plays. Evans, Barbara L., ed. 414p. 1982. text ed. 24.95x (ISBN 0-460-10256-7, Pub. by J. M. Dent England); pap. text ed. 11.95x (ISBN 0-460-11256-2, Pub. by J. M. Dent England). Biblio Dist.

Evans, Gary. Environmental Stress. LC 82-1336. (Illus.). 400p. 1983. 34.50 (ISBN 0-521-24636-9). Cambridge U Pr.

Evans, Gary T. & Hayes, Richard E. Equipping God's People. (Church's Teaching Ser.: Introductory). 80p. 1979. pap. 1.25 (ISBN 0-8164-2238-9). Seabury.

Evans, George E. The Pattern Under the Plough. (Illus.). 270p. 1966. pap. 5.95 (ISBN 0-571-08977-1). Faber & Faber.

Evans, George E., jt. auth. see Thomson, David.

Evans, George W. & Perry, C. L. Programming & Coding for Automatic Digital Computers. 1961. 39.50 (ISBN 0-07-019755-5, P&RB). McGraw.

Evans, Gillian. Learning in Medieval Times. Reeves, Marjorie, ed. (Then & There Ser.). (Illus.). 112p. (Orig.). (gr. 7-12). 1974. pap. text ed. 3.10 (ISBN 0-582-20535-2). Longman.

Evans, Gillian, ed. St. Anselm, Archbishop of Canterbury: A Concordance to the Works of St. Anselm, 4 vols. LC 82-48973. (Orig.). 1983. Set. lib. bdg. 325.00 (ISBN 0-527-03661-7). Kraus Intl.

Evans, Graig. On Foot Through Europe: A Trail Guide to the British Isles. 1982. 9.50 (ISBN 0-688-01164-0). Morrow.

Evans, Harold, jt. auth. see Jackman, Brian.

Evans, Harry B. Publica Carmina: Ovid's Books from Exile. LC 82-10899. 224p. 1983. 23.50x (ISBN 0-8032-1806-0). U of Nebr Pr.

Evans, Hazel & Kumm, Alan. Woman's Own Pot Plant Doctor-a Guide to Coping with Pot Plant Ailments. (Illus.). 1978. pap. 4.95 o.p. (ISBN 0-600-37150-6). Transatlantic.

Evans, Helen M. & Dumesil, Carla D. Invitation to Design. 2nd ed. 1982. text ed. 25.95 (ISBN 0-02-334540-3). Macmillan.

Evans, Humphrey. The Mystery of the Pyramids. LC 79-7085. (Illus.). 1979. 19.95i o.p. (ISBN 0-690-01842-8, TYC-T). T Y Crowell.

Evans, Hywell. Governmental Regulation of Industrial Relations: A Comparative Study of United States & British Experience. 128p. 1961. pap. 2.50 (ISBN 0-87546-016-X). ILR Pr.

Evans, Idella M. & Murdoff, Ron. Psychology for a Changing World. 2nd ed. LC 77-13677. 596p. 1978. text ed. 23.95 (ISBN 0-471-24872-X); tchrs. manual 4.00 (ISBN 0-471-03754-0). Wiley.

Evans, Irene & Paradise, Paul. All About Canaries. rev ed. (Illus.). 96p. 1976. 3.95 (ISBN 0-87666-753-1, PS315). TFH Pubns.

Evans, Ivor H., ed. Brewer's Dictionary of Phrase & Fable. 1248p. 1982. 50.00x (ISBN 0-304-30706-8, Pub. by Cassell England). State Mutual Bk.

Evans, J. Adolescent & Pre-Adolescent Psychiatry. LC 81-71578. 1982. write for info (ISBN 0-8089-1473-1). Grune.

Evans, J., jt. auth. see Bell, P.

Evans, J. A. Herodotus. (World Authors Ser.). 1982. lib. bdg. 15.95 (ISBN 0-8057-6488-7, Twayne). G K Hall.

--Procopius. (World Authors Ser.). lib. bdg. 15.95 (ISBN 0-8057-2722-1, Twayne). G K Hall.

Evans, J. D. Aristotle's Concept of Dialectic. LC 76-22982. 1977. 24.95 (ISBN 0-521-21425-4). Cambridge U Pr.

Evans, J. Grimley, jt. ed. see Caird, F. I.

Evans, J. Harvey. Ship Structural Design Concepts: Second Cycle. LC 82-23436. (Illus.). 528p. 1983. text ed. 45.00 (ISBN 0-87033-303-8). Cornell Maritime.

Evans, J. L. Knowledge & Infallibility. 1979. 22.50 (ISBN 0-312-45906-8). St Martin.

Evans, J. M. Paradise Lost & the Genesis Tradition. 1968. 24.95x o.p. (ISBN 0-19-811665-9). Oxford U Pr.

Evans, Jack M., jt. auth. see Cain, Sandra E.

Evans, Jack M., jt. auth. see Cain, Sandra G.

Evans, Jacque, jt. auth. see Leptich, Anne.

Evans, James S. An Uncommon Gift. LC 82-25930. (A Bridgebooks Publication). 180p. 1983. write for info. (ISBN 0-664-27009-3). Westminster.

Evans, Jay. The Kayaking Book. (Illus.). 224p. 1983. pap. 8.95 (ISBN 0-8289-0501-0). Greene.

Evans, Joel R. & Berman, Barry. Marketing. 656p. 1982. text ed. 26.95 (ISBN 0-02-334500-4). Macmillan.

Evans, John, ed. see White, Eric W.

Evans, John C. The Environment of Early Man in the British Isles. LC 74-29803. 256p. 1975. 30.00x (ISBN 0-520-02973-9). U of Cal Pr.

Evans, John M. An Introduction to Clinical Scotometry. 1938. 49.50x (ISBN 0-685-89759-1). Elliots Bks.

Evans, Joseph, tr. see Maritain, Jacques.

Evans, Joyce. Practical Problems in Mathematics for Cosmetologists. LC 81-71649. (Illus.). 128p. 1983. pap. text ed. 7.00 (ISBN 0-8273-1380-2); instr's. guide 3.25 (ISBN 0-8273-1381-0). Delmar.

Evans, Judith L. Children in Africa: A Review of Psychological Research. LC 71-113095. 1970. pap. 6.50x (ISBN 0-8077-1297-3). Tchrs Coll.

Evans, K. M. Attitudes & Interests in Education. 1965. pap. 7.95 (ISBN 0-7100-7166-3). Routledge & Kegan.

Evans, K. T. & Gravelle, I. H. Mammography, Thermography & Ultrasonography in Breast Disease. Trapnell, David H., ed. (Radiology in Clinical Diagnosis Ser.). (Illus.). 1973. 16.95 o.p. (ISBN 0-407-26450-7). Butterworth.

Evans, Ken. Cycling. LC 80-51146. (Intersport Ser.). 13.00 (ISBN 0-382-06427-5). Silver.

Evans, Kenneth L. A Feast for Spiders. 1980. pap. 1.95 o.p. (ISBN 0-451-09484-0, J9484, Sig). NAL.

--A Feast for Spiders. LC 78-22458. 1979. 9.95i o.p. (ISBN 0-690-01805-3). T Y Crowell.

Evans, L. Convergent Strabismus. 1982. 72.00 (ISBN 90-619-3806-6, Pub. by Junk Pubs Netherlands). Kluwer Boston.

Evans, L. T., ed. Crop Physiology. LC 73-91816. (Illus.). 384p. 1975. 49.50 (ISBN 0-521-20422-4); pap. 19.95x (ISBN 0-521-29390-1). Cambridge U Pr.

Evans, L. T. & Peacock, W. J., eds. Wheat Science-Today & Tomorrow. LC 80-41871. (Illus.). 300p. 1981. 42.50 (ISBN 0-521-23793-9). Cambridge U Pr.

Evans, Lansing B., jt. auth. see Freedman, M. David.

Evans, Larry. Chess: Beginner to Expert. (Illus.). 8.95 (ISBN 0-910872-15-5). Lee Pubns.

--Space Maze. (Posterbook Ser.). (Illus.). 1978. pap. 1.50 (ISBN 0-912300-87-6). Troubador Pr.

--Three-D Mazes, Vol. 1. (Illus.). 40p. 1976. pap. 2.95 (ISBN 0-912300-66-3). Troubador Pr.

--Three-D Mazes, Vol. 2. (Illus.). 40p. 1977. pap. 2.95 (ISBN 0-912300-79-5). Troubador Pr.

--Three-D Monster Mazes. (Illus.). 40p. 1976. pap. 2.25 (ISBN 0-912300-74-4). Troubador Pr.

--Three-D Optical Illusions. 32p. 1977. pap. 4.95 (ISBN 0-912300-78-7). Troubador Pr.

--What's the Best Move? 1974. pap. 3.95 o.p. (ISBN 0-671-21758-5, Fireside). S&S.

Evans, Laurence, ed. see Wilmington, Martin W.

Evans, Len. Love, Love, Love. 1978. 3.95 (ISBN 0-88270-366-8, Pub. by Logos). Bridge Pub.

Evans, Leonard A., ed. see Kaplan, Barbara J.

Evans, Lionel. Total Communication: Structure & Strategy. LC 81-85672. (Illus.). xiv, 162p. 1982. 10.95 (ISBN 0-913580-75-9). Gallaudet Coll.

Evans, Llewelyn. Sources of Radiant Living. (Orig.). pap. 2.00 (ISBN 0-685-08705-0). Creative Pr.

Evans, Louis H. Your Thrilling Future. 1982. pap. 4.95 (ISBN 0-8423-8573-8). Tyndale.

Evans, M. S., jt. auth. see Wood, J. M.

Evans, Malcolm, ed. see Hill, Don.

Evans, Marchsll C., jt. auth. see Chamblee, Ronald F.

Evans, Mari. Jim Flying High. LC 78-22628. (Illus.). (gr. 6). 1979. PLB 9.95 o.p. (ISBN 0-385-14130-0). Doubleday.

--Nightstar. Keys, Romey T., ed. LC 79-54308. (Special Publications Ser.). (Illus.). 78p. (Orig.). 1981. pap. 5.25x (ISBN 0-934934-07-X). Ctr Afro-Am Stud.

Evans, Mari, ed. Black Women Writers, 1950-1980: A Critical Perspective. LC 81-43914. (Illus.). 432p. 1983. 22.50 (ISBN 0-385-17124-2, Anchor Pr). Doubleday.

Evans, Mark. The Morality Gap. 2nd, rev. ed. LC 76-6702. 1976. pap. 1.85 o.p. (ISBN 0-8189-1132-8, Pub. by Alba Bks). Alba.

--Pepito: The Little Dancing Dog. LC 78-65354. (Illus.). (gr. k-4). 1979. 5.95 (ISBN 0-87592-063-2). Scroll Pr.

Evans, Mary. Garden Books, Old & New. LC 71-162512. 1971. Repr. of 1926 ed. 30.00x (ISBN 0-8103-3743-6). Gale.

--How to Make Historic American Costumes. LC 78-159952. (Illus.). xii, 178p. 1976. Repr. of 1942 ed. 40.00x (ISBN 0-8103-4141-7). Gale.

--Woman in the Bible. 192p. (Orig.). Date not set. pap. text ed. 9.50 (ISBN 0-85364-337-7). Attic Pr.

Evans, Mary & Morgan, David. Work on Women: A Guide to Literature. viii, 84p. 1979. 10.95x (ISBN 0-422-77130-9, Pub. by Tavistock England); pap. 6.95x (ISBN 0-422-77140-6). Methuen Inc.

Evans, Mary, et al. Feminist Review: Spring '82 Issue. 1982. pap. text ed. 5.00 ea. No. 10 (ISBN 0-86104-409-6). No. 2 (ISBN 0-86104-401-0). No. 9 (ISBN 0-86104-408-8). Pluto Pr.

Evans, Maurice. Spenser's Anatomy of Heroism: A Commentary on the Faerie Quenne. LC 74-96087. 1970. 44.50 (ISBN 0-521-07662-5). Cambridge U Pr.

Evans, Max. The Hi Lo Country. 1980. lib. bdg. 10.95 (ISBN 0-8398-2685-0, Gregg). G K Hall.

--Mountain of Gold. LC 65-3985. (Illus.). 1965. 4.95 o.p. (ISBN 0-910220-11-5). Berg.

--The Rounders. 1980. lib. bdg. 10.95 (ISBN 0-8398-2686-9, Gregg). G K Hall.

--Shadow of Thunder. LC 82-71934. 78p. 1969. 6.50 (ISBN 0-8040-0274-6). Swallow.

--The White Shadow. LC 77-85861. 1977. 7.95 (ISBN 0-89325-006-6). Joyce Pr.

Evans, Michael K. The Truth About Supply-Side Economics. 230p. 1983. 17.95 (ISBN 0-465-08778-7). Basic.

Evans, Myron W., et al. Molecular Dynamics. LC 81-11592. 880p. 1982. 115.00x (ISBN 0-471-05977-3, Pub. by Wiley-Interscience). Wiley.

Evans, N. Dean, jt. auth. see Neagley, Ross L.

Evans, Nancy, jt. auth. see Appelbaum, Judith.

Evans, Nigel. The Architect & the Computer, a Guide Through the Jungle. (Illus.). 40p. 1982. pap. 6.00 (ISBN 0-900630-77-9, Pub. by RIBA). Intl Schol Bk Serv.

Evans, Norma P., compiled by. Pontiff Paths: Two Hundred Years in Louisiana. LC 82-82598. (Illus.). 300p. (Orig.). 1982. write for info. (ISBN 0-686-81969-1); pap. 30.00. N P Evans.

Evans, Norman. Preliminary Evaluation of the In-Service B.Ed Degree. (General Ser.). 168p. 1981. pap. text ed. 26.25x (ISBN 0-85633-221-6, NFER). Humanities.

Evans, Owen, ed. see International Congress of Acarology-2nd.

Evans, P. L., jt. auth. see Long, W. E.

Evans, Patricia & Blandford, Linda. Supreme Court of the United States 1789-1980: An Index to Opinions Arranged by Justice. LC 82-48981. (Orig.). 1983. lib. bdg. 85.00 (ISBN 0-527-27952-8). Kraus Intl.

Evans, Patricia L., jt. auth. see Deichman, Elizabeth S.

Evans, Patrick. Janet Frame. (World Authors Ser.). 1977. 9.95 o.p. (ISBN 0-8057-6254-X, Twayne). G K Hall.

Evans, Paul. Outlaws of Lost River. 256p. (YA) 1974. 6.95 (ISBN 0-685-39180-9, Avalon). Bouregy.

Evans, Peter. Caring for the Elderly. 192p. 1982. 29.00x o.p. (ISBN 0-246-11136-4, Pub. by Granada England). State Mutual Bk.

--The Englishman's Daughter. LC 82-16532. 256p. 1983. 13.95 (ISBN 0-394-53036-5). Random.

--Mastering Your Migraine. 1978. pap. 12.95x o.s.i. (ISBN 0-8464-1230-6). Beekman Pubs.

--Peter Sellers: The Mask Behind the Mask. 1980. pap. 2.50 o.p. (ISBN 0-451-09758-0, E9758, Sig). NAL.

Evans, R. D., jt. auth. see Wagner, C. F.

Evans, R. D., jt. auth. see Wagner, Charles F.

Evans, Ralph M. Eye, Film & Camera in Color Photography. LC 78-21990. 1979. Repr. of 1959 ed. lib. bdg. 23.50 (ISBN 0-88275-798-9). Krieger.

--The Perception of Color. LC 74-10812. 264p. 1974. 26.50 o.p. (ISBN 0-471-24785-5, Pub. by Wiley-Interscience). Wiley.

Evans, Rhys, jt. auth. see Hoetzsch, Otto.

Evans, Richard. The Making of Psychology. 1976. text ed. 8.95x o.p. (ISBN 0-394-31153-1). Random.

Evans, Richard I. Carl Rogers: The Man & His Ideas. 192p. 1975. pap. 3.95 o.p. (ISBN 0-525-47396-3). Dutton.

--Dialogue with C. G. Jung. 256p. 1981. 26.95 (ISBN 0-03-059927-X). Praeger.

--Dialogue with Erik Erikson. 1969. pap. 3.45 (ISBN 0-525-47246-0). Dutton.

Evans, Richard J. The Feminists: Women's Emancipation Movements in Europe, America & Australasia 1840-1920. LC 77-77490. 1977. text ed. 22.50x o.p. (ISBN 0-06-492037-2); pap. text ed. 8.50x (ISBN 0-06-492044-5). B&N Imports.

Evans, Robert see Kirkland, Douglas W.

Evans, Robert, tr. see Polisensky, J. V.

Evans, Robert A. & Evans, Alice F. Human Rights: A Dialogue Between the First & Third Worlds. LC 82-18780. 272p. (Orig.). 1983. pap. 19.95 (ISBN 0-88344-194-2). Orbis Bks.

Evans, Robert C. Introduction to Crystal Chemistry. 2nd ed. (Illus.). 1964. pap. text ed. 24.95 (ISBN 0-521-09367-8). Cambridge U Pr.

Evans, Robert G., jt. auth. see Humphrey, Clifford C.

Evans, Robert J. Paintings by G. P. A. Healy. (Handbook of Collections Ser.: No. 2). (Illus.). 26p. 1974. pap. 0.75 (ISBN 0-89792-056-2). Ill St Museum.

Evans, Robert O., ed. see Borges, Jorge L. & De Torres, Esther Z.

Evans, Robert O., tr. see Borges, Jorge L. & De Torres, Esther Z.

Evans, Robin. The Fabrication of Virtue: English Prison Architecture, 1750-1840. LC 81-18105. (Illus.). 380p. 1982. 69.50 (ISBN 0-521-23955-9). Cambridge U Pr.

Evans, Robley D. Atomic Nucleus. 1955. text ed. 31.95 o.p. (ISBN 0-07-019750-4, C). McGraw.

Evans, Roger. How to Play Guitar. 1980. 9.95 (ISBN 0-312-39608-2); pap. 5.95 (ISBN 0-312-39609-0). St Martin.

--How to Read Music. 1979. 9.95 (ISBN 0-517-53897-0). Crown.

Evans, Rowland & Novak, Robert. The Reagan Revolution: An Inside Look at the Transformation of the U. S. Government. 288p. 1981. 12.75 o.p. (ISBN 0-525-18970-X, 01238-370). Dutton.

Evans, Rupert & Herr, Edward. Foundations of Vocational Education. 3rd ed. Taylor, Robert E., ed. (Merrill Series in Career Programs). 1978. text ed. 21.95 (ISBN 0-675-08442-3). Merrill.

Evans, S. The Slow Rapprochement: Britain & Turkey in the Age of Kemal Atatürk, 1919-38. 123p. 1982. pap. text ed. 8.00x (ISBN 0-906719-04-6, Pub. by Eothen Pr England). Humanities.

Evans, S. M. Behaviour of Birds, Mammals & Fish. (Investigation in Biology Ser.). 1970. pap. text ed. 3.95x o.p. (ISBN 0-435-60281-0). Heinemann Ed.

Evans, Sabastian, tr. High History of the Holy Graal. (Illus.). 395p. 1969. 16.95 (ISBN 0-227-67727-7). Attic Pr.

Evans, Stephens. Subjectivity & Religious Belief. LC 82-40062. 238p. 1982. pap. text ed. 10.75 (ISBN 0-8191-2665-9). U Pr of Amer.

Evans, Susan H., jt. auth. see Clarke, Peter.

Evans, T. The Challenge of Change. LC 71-104788. 1970. 17.25 o.p. (ISBN 0-08-015825-0); pap. 7.75 o.p. (ISBN 0-08-015824-2). Pergamon.

Evans, T. N., jt. ed. see Hafez, E. S.

Evans, Tabor. Longarm & the Buckskin Rogue, No. 53. 192p. pap. 2.25 (ISBN 0-515-06254-5). Jove Pubns.

--Longarm & the Calico Kid. 192p. 1983. pap. 2.25 (ISBN 0-515-06255-3). Jove Pubns.

--Longarm & the Eastern Dudes, No. 49. 192p. 1982. pap. 2.25 (ISBN 0-515-06250-2). Jove Pubns.

--Longarm & the French Actress, No. 55. 192p. 1983. pap. 2.25 (ISBN 0-515-06256-1). Jove Pubns.

--Longarm & the Great Train Robbery. (Longarm Ser.). 192p. 1982. pap. 2.25 (ISBN 0-515-05602-2). Jove Pubns.

--Longarm & the Lone Star Legend. 1982. pap. 2.75 (ISBN 0-515-06225-1). Jove Pubns.

--Longarm & the Snake Dancers. (Longarm Ser.: No. 51). 192p. 1983. pap. 2.25 (ISBN 0-515-06252-9). Jove Pubns.

--Longarm in the Badlands, No. 47. 192p. 1982. pap. 2.25 (ISBN 0-515-05603-0). Jove Pubns.

--Longarm in the Big Bend. (Longarm Ser.: No. 50). 192p. 1982. pap. 2.25 (ISBN 0-515-06251-0). Jove Pubns.

--Longarm on the Great Divide, No. 52. 192p. 1983. pap. 2.25 (ISBN 0-515-06253-7). Jove Pubns.

Evans, Ted R. Applications of Lasers to Chemical Problems. LC 82-1904. (Techniques of Chemistry Ser.). 291p. 1982. text ed. 55.00 (ISBN 0-471-04949-2, Pub. by Wiley-Interscience). Wiley.

Evans, Thomas G., jt. auth. see Granof, Michael H.

Evans, Tony & Green, Candide L. English Cottages. (Illus.). 160p. 1983. 25.00 (ISBN 0-670-29670-8, Studio). Viking Pr.

Evans, Tony, jt. auth. see Rice, Brian.

Evans, W. Bryce. Improving Your Speech: "Here's How". 1976. perfect bdg. 9.95 (ISBN 0-8403-1404-3). Kendall Hunt.

Evans, W. Glyn. Daily with the King. LC 79-21970. 1979. pap. 5.95 (ISBN 0-8024-1739-6). Moody.

Evans, W. H. A Catalogue of the American Hesperiidae Indictating the Classification & Nomenclature Adopted in the British Museum (Natural History), Pt. I: Pyrrhopyginae. (Illus.). x, 92p. 1951. 16.50x o.p. (ISBN 0-565-00180-9, Pub. by Brit Mus Nat Hist England). Sabbot-Natural Hist Bks.

--A Catalogue of the American Hesperiidae Indicating the Classification & Nomenclature Adopted in the British Museum (Natural History), Pt. II: Pyrginae, Sect. 1. (Illus.). v, 178p. 1952. 26.75x (ISBN 0-565-00181-7, Pub. by Brit Mus Nat Hist England). Sabbot-Natural Hist Bks.

--A Catalogue of the American Hesperiidae Indicating the Classification & Nomenclature Adopted in the British Museum (Natural History), Pt. III: Pyrginae, Sect. 2. (Illus.). v, 246p. 1953. 30.00x (ISBN 0-565-00208-2, Pub. by Brit Mus Nat Hist England). Sabbot-Natural Hist Bks.

--A Catalogue of the American Hesperiidae Indicating the Classification & Nomenclature Adopted in the British Museum (Natural History), Pt. IV: Hesperiinae & Megathyminae, Pt. IV. (Illus.). v, 499p. 1955. 34.50x (ISBN 0-565-00182-5, Pub. by Brit Mus Nat Hist England). Sabbot-Natural Hist Bks.

--Preparation & Characterisation of Mammalian Plasma Membranes. (Techniques in Biochemistry & Molecular Biology Ser.: Vol. 7, Pt. 1). 1978. pap. 28.00 (ISBN 0-7204-4222-2, 7:1). Elsevier.

Evans, Walker. Walker Evans at Work. LC 79-1661. 256p. 1982. 18.22i (ISBN 0-06-011104-6, HarpT). Har-Row.

--Walker Evans: Photographs for the Farm Security Admininistration, 1935-1938. LC 74-149598. (Photography Ser.). 1974. Repr. of 1970 ed. lib. bdg. 32.50 (ISBN 0-306-70099-9). Da Capo.

Evans, Walter. Short Stories & Tall Tales. 1980. 4.50 o.p. (ISBN 0-8062-1334-5). Carlton.

Evans, Webster. Encyclopedia of Golf. 2nd ed. LC 72-165470. (Illus.). 352p. 1973. 10.95 o.p. (ISBN 0-312-24850-4). St Martin.

Evans, Wilbur & Little, Bill. Texas Baseball: The Longhorns. 1983. 13.95 (ISBN 0-87397-234-1). Strode.

Evans, Wilbur & McElroy, H. B. Texas A&M Football. 1982. 10.95 o.p. (ISBN 0-87397-217-1). Strode.

--The Twelfth Man: A Story of Texas A & M Football. LC 74-81347. (College Sports Ser.). Orig. Title: Texas A & M Football. 1982. 10.95 (ISBN 0-87397-217-1). Strode.

Evans, Wilbur, jt. auth. see Stowers, Carlton.

Evans, Willa M. Ben Jonson & Elizabethan Music. 2nd ed. LC 65-18503. (Music Ser). 1965. Repr. of 1929 ed. 17.50 (ISBN 0-306-70907-4). Da Capo.

Evans, William. How to Prepare Sermons. 1964. 9.95 (ISBN 0-8024-3725-7). Moody.

--Journey to Harley Street. 15.00 (ISBN 0-392-16316-0, SpS). Sportshelf.

Evans, William E., jt. auth. see Coerr, Eleanor.

Evans, William J. The Scott, Foresman Robert's Rules of Order. rev. ed. 1981. 15.95x (ISBN 0-673-15472-6); leather ed. 39.95x (ISBN 0-673-15473-4); spiral bdg. 29.95x (ISBN 0-673-15581-1). Scott F.

Evans, William R. Robert Frost & Sidney Cox: Forty Years of Friendship. LC 80-54464. 315p. 1981. 22.50x (ISBN 0-87451-195-X). U Pr of New Eng.

Evanson, John M., jt. auth. see Woolley, David E.

Evanson, Roy. Illustrating Your Newsletter. (Illus.). 1982. pap. 3.95 (ISBN 0-916068-19-6). Groupwork Today.

Evans-Pritchard, Edward E. Nuer Religion. 1956. pap. 6.95x (ISBN 0-19-874003-4). Oxford U Pr.

--Witchcraft Oracles, & Magic among the Azande. abr. ed. Gillies, Eva, ed. 1976. pap. text ed. 9.95x (ISBN 0-19-874029-8). Oxford U Pr.

Evanston Conference, Oct. 11-15, 1975. Brauer Groups: Proceedings. Zelinsky, D., ed. (Lecture Notes in Mathematics: Vol. 549). 1976. soft cover 11.00 (ISBN 0-387-07989-0). Springer-Verlag.

Evans-Wentz, W. Y. Cuchama & Sacred Mountains. Waters, Frank & Adams, Charles L., eds. LC 82-75554. (Illus.). xxxii, 196p. 1982. 22.95 (ISBN 0-8040-0411-0). Swallow.

Evans-Wentz, W. Y., ed. Tibetan Book of the Dead. 1957. 21.95x (ISBN 0-19-501435-9). Oxford U Pr.

--Tibetan Book of the Dead. (Illus.). 1960. Repr. of 1957 ed. pap. 6.95 (ISBN 0-19-500223-7, GB). Oxford U Pr.

--Tibetan Book of the Great Liberation. 1954. 18.95x (ISBN 0-19-501437-5). Oxford U Pr.

--Tibetan Book of the Great Liberation. (Illus.). 1968. pap. 8.95 (ISBN 0-19-500293-8, GB). Oxford U Pr.

--Tibetan Yoga & Secret Doctrines. (Illus.). 1967. pap. 10.95 (ISBN 0-19-500278-4, GB). Oxford U Pr.

--Tibet's Great Yogi, Milarepa. 2nd ed. (Illus.). 1951. 18.95x (ISBN 0-19-501436-7). Oxford U Pr.

--Tibet's Great Yogi, Milarepa. 2nd ed. (Illus.). 1969. pap. 8.95 (ISBN 0-19-500301-2, 294, GB). Oxford U Pr.

Evan-Wanowski, R. Resonance Oscillations in Mechanical Systems. 1976. 64.00 (ISBN 0-444-41474-6). Elsevier.

Eva Of Friedenshort, Sr. The Working of the Holy Spirit in Daily Life. 76p. 1974. pap. 1.25 (ISBN 0-87123-647-8, 200647). Bethany Hse.

Evarts, C. M. see Hip Society.

Evarts, Susan. The Art & Craft of Greeting Cards. 1982. pap. 13.95 (ISBN 0-89134-048-3). North Light Pub.

Evatt, B. L., et al, eds. Megakaryocyte Biology & Precursors: In Vitro Cloning & Cellular Properties. 1981. 75.00 (ISBN 0-444-00585-4). Elsevier.

Evatt, Cris & Feld, Bruce. The Givers & the Takers. (Illus.). 256p. 1983. 12.95 (ISBN 0-02-536690-4). Macmillan.

Eveleigh, Virgil. Introduction to Control Systems Design. (Electrical & Electronic Engineering Ser.). 1971. text ed. 38.50 (ISBN 0-07-019773-3, C); solutions manual 7.95 (ISBN 0-07-019774-1). McGraw.

Eveleth, P. B. & Tanner, J. M. World-Wide Variation in Human Growth. LC 75-10042. (International Biological Programme Ser.: No. 8). (Illus.). 544p. 1977. 90.00 (ISBN 0-521-20806-8). Cambridge U Pr.

Evely, Louis. In the Face of Death. 112p. 1979. 7.95 (ISBN 0-686-83909-9). Seabury.

--Suffering. 120p. 1974. pap. 1.45 (ISBN 0-385-02996-9, Im). Doubleday.

--We Are All Brothers. 120p. 1975. pap. 2.25 o.p. (ISBN 0-385-04830-0, Im). Doubleday.

Evelyn & Marie. Pick Your Own Strawberries. (Illus.). 32p. (gr. k-3). 1983. 4.95 (ISBN 0-8062-1892-4). Carlton.

Evelyn, John see Lodge, James P., Jr.

Even-Shosan, Abraham, ed. Condensed Hebrew Dictionary. (Illus.). 824p. (Hebrew.). 1982. text ed. 35.00 (ISBN 0-686-38120-3). K Sefer.

Even-Shoshan, Abraham, ed. The Complete Hebrew Dictionary in Seven Volumes. (Illus.). 3236p. (Eng. & Hebrew.). text ed. 70.00 (ISBN 0-686-42964-8). K Sefer.

--The Complete Hebrew Dictionary in Three Volumes. (Illus.). 1664p. (Eng. & Hebrew.). text ed. 70.00 (ISBN 0-686-42959-1). K Sefer.

--The Dictionary for School. (Illus.). 728p. (Hebrew.). 1982. text ed. 10.00 (ISBN 0-686-38116-5). K Sefer.

--The New Biblical Concordance in Three Volumes. (Illus.). 2384p. (Hebrew.). 1982. text ed. 79.00 (ISBN 0-686-42965-6). K Sefer.

--The New Biblical Conmcordance in Two Volumes. (Illus.). 1304p. (Hebrew.). 1981. text ed. 54.00 (ISBN 0-686-42969-9). K Sefer.

--The Student's Dictionary. (Illus.). 592p. (Hebrew.). 1982. text ed. 12.00 (ISBN 0-686-38121-1). K Sefer.

Even-Shoshan, Avraham, ed. A New Concordance of the Bible. 1288p. 1982. text ed. 39.00 (ISBN 965-17-0098-X). Ridgefield Pub.

Evenson. Paris: A Century of Change, Eighteen Seventy-Eight to Nineteen Seventy-Eight. LC 78-10257. 1979. 40.00x (ISBN 0-300-02210-7); pap. 14.95 (ISBN 0-300-02667-6). Yale U Pr.

Evenson, Flavis, ed. see Music Education National Conference.

Everaerts, E. M., ed. see Deyl, Z., et al.

Everaerts, F. M., et al. Isotachophoresis: Theory, Instrumentation & Applications. (Journal of Chromatography Library: Vol. 6). 1976. 85.00 (ISBN 0-444-41430-4). Elsevier.

Everaerts, F. M., et al, eds. Analytical Isotachophoresis. (Analytical Chemistry Symposia Ser.: Vol. 6). 1981. 55.50 (ISBN 0-444-41957-8). Elsevier.

Everard & Tanner, J. L. Reinforced Concrete Design. (Schaum Outline Ser.). 1966. text ed. 7.95 (ISBN 0-07-019770-9, SP). McGraw.

Everest, Allan S. Morgenthau, The New Deal & Silver. LC 72-2368. (FDR & the Era of the New Deal Ser.). 209p. 1973. Repr. of 1950 ed. lib. bdg. 32.50 (ISBN 0-306-70469-2). Da Capo.

Everest, Anne, ed. see Media Publications Staff.

Everest, F. A. How to Build a Small Budget Recording Studio from Scratch: With 12 Tested Designs. (Illus.). 1979. 12.95 o.p. (ISBN 0-8306-9787-X); pap. 9.95 (ISBN 0-8306-1166-5, 1166). TAB Bks.

Everest, F. Alton. Acoustic Techniques for Home & Studio. LC 73-78198. (Illus.). 224p. 1973. pap. 7.95 o.p. (ISBN 0-8306-2646-8, 646). TAB Bks.

Everest, Gordon, jt. auth. see Davis, Gordon B.

Everett, B. Auden. (Writers & Critics Ser.). 1980. 19.75 (ISBN 0-686-82879-8). Chips.

Everett, B., ed. see Shakespeare, William.

Everett, Betty S. Who Am I, Lord? LC 82-72645. 112p. (Orig.). (gr. 3-6). 1983. pap. 3.50 (ISBN 0-8066-1951-1, 10-7072). Augsburg.

Everett, David. Works of David Everett. LC 82-3390. 1983. Repr. of 1811 ed. write for info. (ISBN 0-8201-1378-6). Schol Facsimiles.

Everett, Graham. Strange Coast. (Illus., Orig.). 1979. pap. 5.00 (ISBN 0-918092-15-9). Tamarack Edns.

Everett, Jana M. Women & Social Change in India. 1979. 18.95 (ISBN 0-312-88731-0). St Martin.

Everett, Michael. Birds of Prey. LC 75-18596. (Illus.). 128p. 1976. 12.95 o.p. (ISBN 0-399-11675-3). Putnam Pub Group.

Everett, Michael W., jt. ed. see Waddell, Jack O.

Everett, Susanne. The Slaves. LC 78-52985. (Illus.). 1978. 20.00 o.p. (ISBN 0-399-12180-3). Putnam Pub Group.

Everett, Thomas H. The New York Botanical Garden Illustrated Encyclopedia of Horticulture, Vols. 7-10. LC 80-65941. 1468p. 1982. 210.00 o.p. (ISBN 0-686-82042-8). Garland Pub.

Everett, William W. & Bachmeyer, T. J. Disciplines in Transformation: A Guide to Theology & the Behavioral Sciences. LC 78-68570. 1979. pap. text ed. 10.75 (ISBN 0-8191-0692-5). U Pr of Amer.

Everhart, Marion E. Land Classification for Rural & Urban Uses, Management & Valuation. LC 82-74565. (Illus.). 190p. 1983. 23.50 (ISBN 0-935988-23-8). Todd Pub.

Everhart, Robert, ed. The Public School Monopoly: Education & State in American Society. (Pacific Institute for Public Policy Research Ser.). 608p. 1982. prof ref 35.00x (ISBN 0-88410-383-8). Ballinger Pub.

Everhart, Thomas E., jt. auth. see Angelakos, Diogenes J.

Everhart, William. The National Park Service. (Westview Library of Federal Departments, Agencies, & Systems). (Illus.). 250p. 1982. lib. bdg. 23.50 (ISBN 0-86531-130-7); pap. text ed. 10.95 (ISBN 0-86531-498-5). Westview.

Everitt, B. S. The Analysis of Contingency Tables. 1977. 15.00x (ISBN 0-412-14970-2, Pub. by Chapman & Hall). Methuen Inc.

Everitt, B. S. & Hand, D. J. Finite Mixture Distributions. (Monographs in Applied Probability & Statistics). 1981. 17.50x (ISBN 0-412-22420-8, Pub. by Chapman & Hall). Methuen Inc.

Everitt, N., ed. see Akheizer, N. I.

Everitt, N., ed. see Akheizer, N. I. & Glazman, I. M.

Everly, George & Girdano, Daniel. The Stress Mess Solution. LC 79-14652. 174p. 1980. text ed. 12.95 (ISBN 0-87619-666-0); pap. 6.95 (ISBN 0-87619-434-X). P-H.

Everly, George S., Jr., jt. auth. see Girdano, Daniel A.

Everman, W. D. Orion. (Ithaca House Fiction Ser.). 93p. 1975. 4.50 (ISBN 0-87886-055-X). Ithaca Hse.

Evers, Dora, jt. auth. see Feingold, S. Norman.

Evers, Ona C. Everybody's Dowser Book. LC 77-76983. (Illus.). 1977. pap. 3.95 (ISBN 0-918900-01-8). Onaway.

Eversaul, George A. Clinical Nutrition. 1983. 85.00 (ISBN 0-9601978-2-6, 0-9601-7826). G A Eversaul.

--Dental Kinesiology. LC 78-66982. 1978. 57.50x (ISBN 0-9601978-1-8). G A Eversaul.

Everse, Johannes, et al, eds. The Pyridine Nucleotide Coenzymes. 416p. 1982. 46.00 (ISBN 0-12-244750-6). Acad Pr.

Eversen, H. J., et al. Compendium of Case Law Relating to the European Communities, 1973. LC 74-23454. 304p. 1975. 85.00 (ISBN 0-444-10794-0, North-Holland). Elsevier.

Eversley, David. Social Theories of Fertility & the Malthusian Debate. LC 74-9219. 313p. 1975. Repr. of 1959 ed. lib. bdg. 18.25x (ISBN 0-8371-7628-X, EVST). Greenwood.

Eversley, David & Kollmann, Wolfgang. Population Change & Social Planning. 600p. 1982. text ed. 98.50 (ISBN 0-7131-6345-3). E Arnold.

Eversley, George J. Gladstone & Ireland: The Irish Policy of Parliament from 1850-1894. LC 74-114520. 1971. Repr. of 1912 ed. lib. bdg. 15.75x (ISBN 0-8371-4795-6, EVGI). Greenwood.

Eversole, James, jt. auth. see Sacher, Jack.

Everson. American Political Parties. 1980. 15.00 o.p. (ISBN 0-531-05628-7, BB17, New Viewpoints); pap. 7.95 o.p. (ISBN 0-531-05628-7, BB20). Watts.

Everson, David H., jt. ed. see David, Paul T.

Everson, H. J., et al, eds. Compendium of Case Law Relating to the European Communities, 1975. 1977. 89.50 (ISBN 0-7204-0579-3, North-Holland). Elsevier.

Everson, Jennie. Tidewater Ice of the Kennebec River. LC 68-11102. (Maine Heritage Ser.: No. 1). (Illus.). 1971. 9.95 o.p. (ISBN 0-913764-03-5). Maine St Mus.

Everson, Lloyd K. & Etzell, Paul S. Hematologic Diseases: Focus on Clinical Diagnosis. 1982. 30.00 (ISBN 0-87488-837-9). Med Exam.

Everson, Mary, jt. auth. see Everson, Ralph.

Everson, Ralph & Everson, Mary. Everson's Best Farm Manual & Helpful Hints. LC 80-68664. (Illus.). 300p. (Orig.). 1980. pap. 9.95 o.p. (ISBN 0-89708-027-0). And Bks.

Everson, Robert F., Jr. Trick & Ballet Skiing. (Illus., Orig.). 1975. pap. 6.95 (ISBN 0-917602-00-5). Fotoflip Bk.

Everson, William. Residual Years. rev. ed. LC 68-25585. 1968. pap. 3.95 (ISBN 0-8112-0273-9). New Directions.

Everson, William K. American Silent Film. LC 77-25188. (Illus.). 1978. 25.00x (ISBN 0-19-502348-X). Oxford U Pr.

--Bad Guys: A Pictorial History of the Movie Villain. (Photos). 1968. pap. 8.95 (ISBN 0-8065-0198-7, C264). Citadel Pr.

Everstine, Carl N. The General Assembly of Maryland: Sixteen Thirty-four to Seventeen Seventy-six. 550p. 1980. 12.00 o.s.i. (ISBN 0-87215-312-6). Michie-Bobbs.

Everstine, Diana S. & Everstine, Louis. People in Crisis: Strategic Therapeutic Interventions. 256p. 1983. 20.00 (ISBN 0-87630-286-X). Brunner-Mazel.

Everstine, Louis, jt. auth. see Everstine, Diana S.

Evert, Judi. Introduction to Hospitality: Recreation Careers. (gr. 7-10). 1975. pap. text ed. 7.33 activity ed. (ISBN 0-87345-185-6). McKnight.

Everton, Clive. Better Billiards & Snooker. new ed. (Better Sports Ser). (Illus.). 90p. (gr. 7 up). 1976. text ed. 16.95x o.p. (ISBN 0-7182-1441-2, SpS). Sportshelf.

Everton, Ian. Alienation: A Novel on British Gay Movement. 216p. (Orig.). 1982. pap. 7.50 (ISBN 0-907040-10-1). Gay Mens Pr.

Evertts, Eldonna L., ed. Explorations in Children's Writing. LC 70-120182. (Illus., Orig.). 1970. pap. 6.00 (ISBN 0-8141-1658-2); pap. 4.25 members (ISBN 0-686-86411-5). NCTE.

Everwine, Peter & Yasny-Starkman, Shulamit, trs. from Hebrew. The Static Element: Selected Poems of Natan Zach. LC 82-71257. 72p. 1982. 12.95 (ISBN 0-689-11318-8); pap. 7.95 (ISBN 0-689-11319-6). Atheneum.

Every, Dale Van see Van Every, Dale & Messner, Julian.

Every, Edward Van see Van Every, Edward.

Every Frost, Joan van see Van Every Frost, Joan.

Evett, Elisa. The Critical Reception of Japanese Art in Late Nineteenth Century Europe. Foster, Stephen C., ed. LC 82-13702. (Studies in Fine Arts: The Avant-Garde: No. 36). 182p. 1982. 39.95 (ISBN 0-8357-1368-7, Pub. by UMI Res Pr). Univ Microfilms.

Evett, Jack B., tr. see Liu, Cheng.

Evgrafov, M. A. Analytic Functions. 1978. pap. text ed. 6.50 (ISBN 0-486-63648-8). Dover.

Evison, Lilian, jt. auth. see James, A.

Evison, Vera I., et al, eds. Medieval Pottery from Excavations. LC 74-82134. (Illus.). 278p. 1975. 18.95 o.p. (ISBN 0-312-52745-4). St Martin.

Evler, R. C. & Gummerman, G. S., eds. Investigations of the Southwestern Anthropological Research Group: An Experiment in Archaeological Cooperation. (MNA Bulletin Ser.: No. 50). 1978. pap. 5.95 (ISBN 0-89734-018-3). Mus Northern Ariz.

Evola, Julius. Metaphysics of Sex. Ormrod, J. A., tr. from Ital. (Illus.). 384p. 1983. pap. 9.95 (ISBN 0-89281-025-4). Inner Tradit.

Evory, Ann, ed. Contemporary Authors: A Bio-Bibliographical Guide to Current Writers in Fiction, General Nonfiction, Poetry, Journalism, Drama, Motion Pictures, Television & Other Fields. rev. ed. (Vol. 7). 570p. 1982. 74.00x (ISBN 0-8103-1936-5). Gale.

--Contemporary Authors New Revision Series, 6 vols. Incl. Vol. 1. 1980 (ISBN 0-8103-1930-6); Vol. 2. 1980 (ISBN 0-8103-1931-4); Vol. 3. 1981 (ISBN 0-8103-1932-2); Vol. 4. 1981 (ISBN 0-8103-1933-0); Vol. 5. 1982 (ISBN 0-8103-1934-9); Vol. 6. 1982 (ISBN 0-8103-1935-7). LC 81-640179. 1982. 74.00x. Gale.

--Contemporary Authors New Revision Series, Vol. 8. 600p. 1983. 74.00x (ISBN 0-8103-1937-3). Gale.

Evory, Ann, jt. ed. see Locher, Frances C.

Evrard, Gwen. Homespun Crafts from Scraps. (Illus.). 168p. 1983. 17.95 (ISBN 0-8329-0253-5). New Century.

Evseenko, D. S., jt. auth. see Emanuel, N. M.

Evual, Thomas, jt. auth. see Cheffers, John T.

EW Engineering Inc., ed. see Van Brunt, Leroy B.

Ewald, Helen R. Writing As Process: Invention & Convention. 1983. 9.95 (ISBN 0-675-20014-8). Additional supplements may be obtained from publisher. Merrill.

Ewald, Peter K. Encyclopedia of Finance & Investment Terms. 1983. pap. price not set (ISBN 0-8120-2522-9). Barron.

Ewalt, Norma & Huth, Tom. Decadent Dinners & Lascivious Lunches. LC 82-71880. (Illus.). 320p. 1982. 10.95 (ISBN 0-686-82435-0). Clear Creek.

Ewalt, Patricia L., ed. Toward a Definition of Clinical Social Work. LC 80-81821. 104p. 1980. pap. 7.50x (ISBN 0-87101-086-0, CBP-086-C). Natl Assn Soc Wkrs.

Ewan, Dale & Heaton, Leroy. Physics for Technical Education. (Illus.). 720p. 1981. text ed. 24.95 (ISBN 0-13-674127-4). P-H.

Ewan, J. Introduction to the Reprint of Pursh's Flora Americae Septentrionalis. 118p. 1980. pap. text ed. 10.00 (ISBN 3-7682-1272-6). Lubrecht & Cramer.

Ewan, J. & Ewan, N. D. Biographical Dictionary of Rocky Mountain Naturalists. 1982. 42.00 (ISBN 90-313-0415-8, Pub. by Junk Pubs Netherlands). Kluwer Boston.

Ewan, Joseph, ed. Short History of Botany in the United States. 174p. 1969. lib. bdg. 8.50 (ISBN 0-686-37870-9). Lubrecht & Cramert.

Ewan, N. D., jt. auth. see Ewan, J.

Ewans, Michael. Wagner & Aeschylus: The "Ring" & The "Oresteia". LC 82-12762. 272p. Date not set. price not set (ISBN 0-521-25073-0). Cambridge U Pr.

Ewans, Michael C. Haytor Granite Tramway & Stover Canal. LC 66-80. (Illus.). 1964. 9.95x (ISBN 0-678-05665-X). Kelley.

Ewart, Gavin. No Fool Like an Old Fool. (Gollancz Poets Ser.). 1977. pap. 6.75 o.p. (ISBN 0-575-02152-7). Transatlantic.

--Or Where a Penguin Lies Screaming. 1978. pap. 7.95 o.p. (ISBN 0-575-02342-2). Transatlantic.

Ewart, Nei. Unsafe As Houses: A Guide to Home Safety. (Illus.). 160p. 1981. 12.50 o.p. (ISBN 0-7137-1090-X, Pub. by Blandford Pr England). Sterling.

Ewart, Neil & O'Connell, Nina. The Lore of Flowers. 192p. 1983. 19.95 (ISBN 0-7137-1176-0, Pub. by Blandford Pr England). Sterling.

Ewart, Neil, jt. auth. see Hill, Graham.

Ewart, Park J., et al. Probability for Statistical Decision Making. (Illus.). 400p. 1974. ref. ed. 27.95 (ISBN 0-13-711614-4). P-H.

Ewart, W., jt. auth. see Norris, G.

Ewegen, Robert, jt. auth. see Johnson, Byron L.

Ewel, Katherine C. & Odum, Howard T., eds. Cypress Swamps. (Center for Wetlands Research Bks.). 1982. 29.00 (ISBN 0-8130-0714-3). U Presses Fla.

Ewen, Alfred. Shakespeare. 126p. 1982. Repr. of 1904 ed. lib. bdg. 20.00 (ISBN 0-89760-215-3). Telegraph Bks.

Ewen, Cecil H. Guide to the Origin of British Surnames. LC 68-30596. 1969. Repr. of 1938 ed. 34.00x (ISBN 0-8103-3123-3). Gale.

--History of Surnames of the British Isles: A Concise Account of Their Origin, Evolution, Etymology & Legal Status. LC 68-30597. 1968. Repr. of 1931 ed. 37.00x (ISBN 0-8103-3124-1). Gale.

Ewen, Dale & Schurter, Neil. Physics for Career Education. 2nd ed. (Illus.). 448p. 1982. 18.95 (ISBN 0-13-672329-2). P-H.

Ewen, Dale & Topper, Michael A. Mathematics for Technical Education. 2nd ed. (Illus.). 496p. 1983. text ed. 23.95 (ISBN 0-13-565168-9). P-H.

--Technical Calculus. (Illus.). 1977. 20.95 (ISBN 0-13-898122-1). P-H.

Ewen, David. American Composers: A Biographical Dictionary. 1982. 50.00 (ISBN 0-399-12626-0). Putnam Pub Group.

--The Book of European Light Opera. LC 77-1795. 1977. Repr. of 1962 ed. lib. bdg. 34.50x (ISBN 0-8371-9520-9, EWBE). Greenwood.

--Composers of Tomorrow's Music: A Non-Technical Introduction to the Musical Avant-Garde Movement. LC 79-18514. (Illus.). 1980. Repr. of 1971 ed. lib. bdg. 19.75x (ISBN 0-313-22107-3, EWCT). Greenwood.

Ewen, David, ed. From Bach to Stravinsky: The History of Music by Its Foremost Critics. LC 68-54419. (Illus.). 1968. Repr. of 1933 ed. lib. bdg. 16.25x (ISBN 0-8371-0411-4, EWBS). Greenwood.

--Great Composers: Thirteen Hundred-Nineteen Hundred. (Illus.). 429p. 1966. 18.00 (ISBN 0-8242-0018-7). Wilson.

--Musicians Since Nineteen Hundred. 970p. 1978. 40.00 (ISBN 0-8242-0565-0). Wilson.

--Popular American Composers. (Illus.). 1962. 11.00 (ISBN 0-8242-0040-3). Wilson.

--Popular American Composers First Supplement. (Illus.). 121p. 1972. 8.00 (ISBN 0-8242-0436-0). Wilson.

Ewen, Doris & Ewen, Mary. An ABC of Children's Names. (Illus.). 30p. (ps-4). pap. 8.95 o.s.i. (ISBN 0-914676-41-5, Star & Eleph Bks). Green Tiger Pr.

Ewen, Mary, jt. auth. see Ewen, Doris.

Ewen, Robert B. An Introduction to Theories of Personality. 1980. 19.25 (ISBN 0-12-245150-3). Acad Pr.

Ewen, Stuart. Captains of Consciousness. LC 75-34432. 1976. 10.00 o.p. (ISBN 0-07-019845-4, GB); pap. 5.95 o.p. (ISBN 0-07-019846-2). McGraw.

Ewens, James M. Pass It on. (Orig.). pap. 1.50 o.s.i. (ISBN 0-89129-051-6). Jove Pubns.

Ewens, Jim & Herrington, Pat. The Hospice Handbook. Kubler-Ross, Elisabeth, ed. LC 82-73364. (Illus.). 264p. (Orig.). (gr. 11-12). 1982. pap. 8.95 (ISBN 0-939680-10-6). Bear & Co.

Ewens, Thomas. Think Piece on CBE & Liberal Education. Woditsch, Gary, ed. LC 77-72212. (CUE Project Occasional Paper Ser.: No. 1). 1977. pap. 2.50 (ISBN 0-89372-001-1). General Stud Res.

Ewens, W. Price, et al. Elementary School Career Education & System-Wide Programs. LC 74-1198. (Guidance Monograph). 1975. pap. 2.40 o.p. (ISBN 0-395-20055-5). HM.

Ewenstein, Neal, jt. auth. see Wade, Alex.

Ewer, J. R. & Latorre, G. A Course in Basic Scientific English. (English As a Second Language Bk.). 199p. 1969. pap. text ed. 6.25x (ISBN 0-582-52009-6); teacher's bk. 3.25x (ISBN 0-582-52059-2). Longman.

Ewer, T. K. Practical Animal Husbandry. (Illus.). 265p. 1982. text ed. 25.00 (ISBN 0-7236-0635-8). Wright-PSG.

Ewers, John C. Blackfeet: Raiders on the Northwestern Plains. (Civilization of the American Indian Ser.: No. 49). (Illus.). 1976. Repr. of 1958 ed. 19.95 (ISBN 0-8061-0405-8). U of Okla Pr.

--Chippewa Indians VI. Horr, David A., ed. (American Indian Ethnohistory Ser.). 1978. lib. bdg. 42.00 o.s.i. (ISBN 0-8240-0813-8). Garland Pub.

Ewers, William L. Solar Energy: A Biased Guide. LC 76-55551. (International Library of Ecology Ser.). (Illus.). 1977. pap. 4.95 o.p. (ISBN 0-89196-013-9, Domus Bks). Quality Bks IL.

Ewert, David. The Holy Spirit in the New Testament. LC 82-95089. 328p. (Orig.). 1983. pap. 11.95 (ISBN 0-8361-3309-9). Herald Pr.

Ewert, Jorg-Peter, jt. ed. see Capranica, Robert.

Ewing. The Brownies & Other Stories. (Childrens Illustrated Classics Ser). (Illus.). 250p. 1975. Repr. of 1954 ed. 11.00x o.p. (ISBN 0-460-05025-7, Pub. by J. M. Dent. England). Biblio Dist.

--Lob Lie-by-the Fire & the Story of a Shore Life: Childrens Illustrated Classics Ser. (Illus.). 184p. 1964. 9.00x o.p. (ISBN 0-460-05063-X, Pub. by J. M. Dent England). Biblio Dist.

Ewing, A. C. Fundamental Questions of Philosophy. 260p. 1980. pap. 7.95 (ISBN 0-7100-0586-5). Routledge & Kegan.

--Idealism: A Critical Survey. 454p. 1974. Repr. of 1934 ed. text ed. 19.50x o.p. (ISBN 0-416-80950-2). Methuen Inc.

Ewing, A. F. Planning & Policies in the Textile Finishing Industry. 10.00x (ISBN 0-87245-494-0). Textile Bk.

Ewing, Alfred C. Morality of Punishment. LC 70-108233. (Criminology, Law Enforcement, & Social Problems Ser.: No. 116). (With new intro. added). 1970. Repr. of 1929 ed. 20.00x (ISBN 0-87585-116-9). Patterson Smith.

Ewing, Barbara. Strangers. LC 77-15348. 1978. 6.95 o.p. (ISBN 0-689-10855-9). Atheneum.

Ewing, Channing L., et al. Impact Injury of the Head & Spine. (Illus.). 688p. 1983. 88.50x (ISBN 0-398-04702-2). C C Thomas.

Ewing, Charles P. Crisis Intervention As Psychotherapy. 1978. pap. 8.95x (ISBN 0-19-502271-8). Oxford U Pr.

Ewing, Cortez A. Presidential Elections from Abraham Lincoln to Franklin D. Roosevelt. LC 70-142857. (Illus.). 226p. 1972. Repr. of 1940 ed. lib. bdg. 18.00x (ISBN 0-8371-5956-3, EWPE). Greenwood.

--Primary Elections in the South: A Study in Uniparty Politics. LC 80-12616. (Illus.). xii, 112p. 1980. Repr. of 1953 ed. lib. bdg. 16.25x (ISBN 0-313-22452-8, EWPR). Greenwood.

Ewing, David W. Do it My Way or You're Fired: Employee Rights & the Changing Role of Management Perogatives. (Contemporary Issues on Business Ser.). 408p. 1983. 17.95 (ISBN 0-471-86843-4, Pub. by Wiley-Interscience). Wiley.

--Writing for Results in Business, Government, the Sciences & the Professions. 2nd ed. LC 79-11756. 448p. 1979. 24.95 (ISBN 0-471-05036-9). Wiley.

Ewing, Elizabeth. Dress & Undress: A History of Women's Underwear. LC 78-16819. (Illus.). 192p. 1978. text ed. 16.95x (ISBN 0-89676-000-6). Drama Bk.

Ewing, Galen W. Instrumental Methods of Chemical Analysis. 4th ed. (Illus.). 576p. 1975. text ed. 35.00 (ISBN 0-07-019853-5, C); solutions manual 15.00 (ISBN 0-07-019854-3). McGraw.

Ewing, Galen W., jt. auth. see Vassos, Basil H.

Ewing, George M. Living on a Shoestring: A Scrounge Manuel for the Hobbyist. Heid, Jim, ed. (Illus.). 1983. write for info. Green.

Ewing, Juliana H. Six to Sixteen. LC 75-32179. (Classics of Children's Literature, 1621-1932: Vol. 42). (Illus.). 1977. Repr. of 1875 ed. PLB 38.00 o.s.i. (ISBN 0-8240-2291-2). Garland Pub.

Ewing, Kathryn. A Private Matter. LC 74-23673. (gr. 4-8). 1975. 7.95 (ISBN 0-15-263576-9, HJ). HarBraceJ.

Ewing, Kenneth D. Trade Unions, the Labor Party, & the Law. 224p. 1982. 25.00 (ISBN 0-686-83097-0, Pub. by Edinburgh U Pr Scotland). Columbia U Pr.

Ewing, Steve. U. S. S. Enterprise (CV-Six), the Most Decorated Ship of World War II: A Pictorial History. (Illus.). 132p. 1982. 7.95. Pictorial Hist.

Ewing, Ward B. Job: A Vision of God. 1976. 2.00 (ISBN 0-8164-0285-X). Seabury.

Ewy, Donna & Ewy, Rodger. Preparation for Childbirth. 224p. 1974. pap. 3.95 (ISBN 0-451-11921-5, AE1921, Sig). NAL.

Ewy, Donna, jt. auth. see Ewy, Rodger.

Ewy, Donna, jt. auth. see Ewy, Roger.

Ewy, Rodger & Ewy, Donna. Preparation for Breastfeeding. LC 74-33606. (Illus.). 144p. 1975. pap. 5.50 (ISBN 0-385-08962-7, Dolp). Doubleday.

Ewy, Rodger, jt. auth. see Ewy, Donna.

Ewy, Roger & Ewy, Donna. Preparation for Childbirth: A Lamaze Guide. 1982. pap. 3.95 (ISBN 0-451-11921-5, Pub. by NAL). Formur Intl.

Execucom Systems Corp. IFPS User's Manual, Release 9.0. 550p. 1983. pap. 24.95 (ISBN 0-911941-00-2). Execucom Sys Corp.

Exell, Joseph S. Practical Truths from Jonah. 240p. 1983. Repr. of 1874 ed. 8.95 (ISBN 0-8254-2525-5). Kregel.

Exely, Richard, jt. auth. see Exley, Helen.

Exley, D., jt. ed. see Vermeulen, A.

Exley, Helen & Exely, Richard. Dear World. LC 78-20852. 1979. 9.95 o.p. (ISBN 0-416-00211-0). Methuen Inc.

Exley, Helen, ed. Love: A Celebration. (Illus.). 80p. 1982. 7.95 (ISBN 0-448-12328-2, G&D). Putnam Pub Group.

Exley, Helen, jt. ed. see Exley, Richard.

Exley, Richard & Exley, Helen, eds. To Dad: Written by Children. 1978. pap. 2.95 o.p. (ISBN 0-395-26472-3). HM.

--To Grandma & Grandpa. 1979. pap. 3.95 o.p. (ISBN 0-395-27502-4). HM.

--To Mom: Written by Children. 1978. pap. 2.95 o.p. (ISBN 0-395-26478-2). HM.

--What Is a Husband? LC 78-4012. (Illus.). 1979. 5.95 o.p. (ISBN 0-312-86599-6). St Martin.

Exline, Christopher H., et al. The City: Patterns & Processes in the Urban Ecosystem. (Illus.). 300p. (Orig.). 1981. lib. bdg. 30.00 (ISBN 0-89158-904-X); pap. 14.75 (ISBN 0-89158-905-8). Westview.

Exner. Fondues. 1983. cancelled (ISBN 0-8120-5404-0). Barron.

Exner, J. E. & Weiner, I. B. The Rorschach: A Comprehensive System, Assessment of Children & Adolescents, Vol. 3. 449p. 1982. text ed. 42.50x (ISBN 0-471-09364-5). Wiley.

Exner, John E. The Rorschach: A Comprehensive System. (Personality Processes Ser.: Current Research & Advanced Interpretation: Vol 2). 1978. 49.95x (ISBN 0-471-04166-1, Pub. by Wiley-Interscience). Wiley.

Exner, John E., Jr., jt. auth. see London, Harvey.

Exner, John, Jr. The Rorschach: A Comprehensive System. LC 74-8888. (Personality Processes Ser: Vol. 1). 512p. 1974. 49.95x (ISBN 0-471-24964-5, Pub. by Wiley-Interscience). Wiley.

Exner, Jurgen H., ed. Detoxication of Hazardous Waste. LC 82-70696. (Illus.). 350p. 1982. 37.50 (ISBN 0-250-40521-0). Ann Arbor Science.

Experience & the Future Discussion Group, compiled by. Poland Today: The State of the Republic. Vale, Michel, et al, trs. from Polish. LC 81-8782. 256p. 1981. 20.00 (ISBN 0-87332-201-0); pap. 7.95 (ISBN 0-87332-205-3). M E Sharpe.

Experimental Technology Incentives Program. Toward Competitive Provision of Public Record Message Services. 1981. 75.00 (ISBN 0-686-37963-2). Info Gatekeepers.

Expert Consultation on Selective Shrimp Trawls, the Netherlands, 1973. Report. (FAO Fisheries Reports: No. 139). 71p. 1973. pap. 7.50 (ISBN 0-686-93970-0, F784, FAO). Unipub.

Expert Consultation on Small-Scale Fisheries Development, Rome, 1975. Report. (Fao Fisheries Reports: No. 169). 16p. 1975. pap. 7.50 (ISBN 0-686-93987-5, F816, FAO). Unipub.

Expert Group on Rural Industrialization. Report. pap. 1.50 (ISBN 0-686-94407-0, UN74/4/4, UN). Unipub.

Expert Working Group on the Use of Solar & Wind Energy. Proceedings. (Energy Resources Development Ser.: No. 16). pap. 11.00 (ISBN 0-686-92909-8, UN76/2F13, UN). Unipub.

Experts Group Meeting, National Institute of Urban Affairs, & Town & Country Planning, India, April, 1977. Urban Perspectives: Two Thousand & One. Chandrasekhara, C. S. & Raj, Deva, eds. 1979. text ed. 15.00x o.p. (ISBN 0-210-40615-1). Asia.

Expose General. Expose General des Resultats du Patronage des Esclaves dans les Colonies Francaises. (Slave Trade in France Ser., 1744-1848). 668p. (Fr.). 1974. Repr. of 1844 ed. lib. bdg. 161.00x o.p. (ISBN 0-8287-0324-8, TN 160). Clearwater Pub.

Exton-Smith, A. N. Geriatrics. 352p. 1979. text ed. 27.95 (ISBN 0-8391-1456-7). Univ Park.

Extraordinary Session, Budapest 1976. Regional Association Six, Europe: Abridged Final Report. (Illus.). 1977. pap. 25.00 (ISBN 92-63-10456-5, W422, WMO). Unipub.

Exum, Wallace L. Battleship. LC 80-22891. 1981. pap. 4.95 o.p. (ISBN 0-89865-093-3). Donning Co.

Eyde, Donna R. & Rich, Jay. Psychological Distress in Aging: A Family Management Model. LC 82-164440. 254p. 1982. 26.50 (ISBN 0-89443-667-8). Aspen Systems.

Eyde, Pamela. Inuit Games. 1983. write for info. U of Wash Pr.

Eye, Glen G., et al. Supervision of Instruction. 2nd ed. (Fowlkes Ser). (Illus.). 1971. text ed. 29.50 scp o.p. (ISBN 0-06-041951-2, HarpC). Har-Row.

Eyer, Dianne W., jt. auth. see Gonzalez-Mena, Janet.

Eyerly, Jeanenette. Bonnie Jo, Go Home. LC 72-1863. (gr. 7 up). 1972. 10.53i (ISBN 0-397-31390-X, JBL-J). Har-Row.

--Goodbye to Budapest. LC 74-4347. (gr. 5 up). 1974. 10.53i (ISBN 0-397-31496-5, JBL-J). Har-Row.

Eyerly, Jeannette. Drop-Out. LC 63-19125. (gr. 7-9). 1963. PLB 10.95i o.p. (ISBN 0-397-30654-7, JBL-J). Har-Row.

--The Girl Inside. 1980. pap. 1.75 o.p. (ISBN 0-425-04522-6). Berkley Pub.

--Good-Bye to Budapest. 1980. pap. 1.75 o.p. (ISBN 0-425-04523-4). Berkley Pub.

--He's My Baby Now. LC 77-23189. 1977. 10.35i o.p. (ISBN 0-397-31744-1, JBL-J). Har-Row.

--If I Loved You Wednesday. LC 80-7772. 128p. (gr. 7up). 1980. 10.53i (ISBN 0-397-31913-4, JBL-J); PLB 10.89 (ISBN 0-397-31914-2). Har-Row.

--More Than a Summer Love. LC 62-15512. (gr. 7-9). 1962. 8.95 o.p. (ISBN 0-397-30618-0, JBL-J). Har-Row.

--See Dave Run. LC 78-8139. (gr. 6-12). 1978. 9.57i (ISBN 0-397-31819-7, JBL-J). Har-Row.

--The Seeing Summer. LC 81-47440. (Illus.). 128p. (gr. 4-6). 1981. 9.13i (ISBN 0-397-31965-7, JBL-J); PLB 9.89g (ISBN 0-397-31966-5). Har-Row.

--Seth & Me & Rebel Make Three. LC 82-48463. 128p. (YA) (gr. 7 up). 1983. 9.57i (ISBN 0-397-32042-6, JBL-J); PLB 9.89g (ISBN 0-397-32043-4). Har-Row.

--World of Ellen March. LC 64-19039. (gr. 7-9). 1964. 10.53i o.p. (ISBN 0-397-30793-4, JBL-J). Har-Row.

Eyestone, Robert. From Social Issues to Public Policy. LC 78-13334. (Viewpoints on American Politics Ser.). 197p. 1978. pap. text ed. 11.95 (ISBN 0-471-24978-5). Wiley.

Eyken, Willem van der see Van der Eyken, Willem.

Eykhoff, P. System: Identification, Parameter & State Estimation. LC 73-2781. 1974. 107.95 (ISBN 0-471-24980-7, Pub. by Wiley-Interscience). Wiley.

Eykhoff, P., ed. see Pugachev.

Eyles, Allen. John Wayne & the Movies. pap. 7.95 o.p. (ISBN 0-448-14076-4, G&D). Putnam Pub Group.

Eyles, John, jt. auth. see Jones, Emrys.

Eyman, William, jt. auth. see Gerald, Mark.

Eynden, Charles Vanden see Eggan, Lawrence C. & Vanden Eynden, Charles.

Eynon, Dana. Adventures Through the Bible. rev. ed. LC 79-1031. 176p. (gr. 3-6). 1980. pap. 6.95 (ISBN 0-87239-378-X, 3234). Standard Pub.

Eyo, Ekpo, jt. auth. see Willet, Frank.

Eyre, A. G see Allen, W. S.

Eyre, A. G., ed. Longman Simplified English Series, 27 bks. Incl. The Adventures of Huckleberry Finn. new ed. Twain, Mark (ISBN 0-582-52840-2); The Adventures of Tom Sawyer. Twain, Mark (ISBN 0-582-52816-X); Best Stories of Thomas Hardy. Hardy, Thomas (ISBN 0-582-52598-5); Call for the Dead. Le Carre, John (ISBN 0-582-53546-8); Castle of Danger. Stewart, Mary (ISBN 0-582-52688-4); The Coral Island. Ballantyne, R. M. (ISBN 0-582-52803-8); Far from the Madding Crowd. Hardy, Thomas (ISBN 0-582-52597-7); Hound of the Baskervilles. Conan Doyle, Arthur (ISBN 0-582-52910-7); Jane Eyre. new ed. Bronte, Charlotte (ISBN 0-582-52825-9); Journey to the Center of the Earth. Verne, Jules. o.p. (ISBN 0-582-52877-1); Kidnapped. new ed. Stevenson, Robert L (ISBN 0-582-52914-X); Moby Dick. Melville, Herman (ISBN 0-582-52855-0); Pride & Prejudice. new ed. Austen, Jane (ISBN 0-582-52913-1); The Prisoner of Zenda. Hope, Anthony (ISBN 0-582-52841-0); Round the World in Eighty Days. Verne, Jules (ISBN 0-582-52806-2); **Sherlock Holmes Short Stories. Conan Doyle, Arthur (ISBN 0-582-52911-5); Spinechillers (ISBN 0-582-52672-8); The Strange Case of Dr. Jekyll & Mr. Hyde. new ed. Stevenson, Robert L (ISBN 0-582-52547-0); A Summer Romance & Other Short Stories. Cave, Hugh (ISBN 0-582-52647-7); A Tale of Two Cities. Dickens, Charles (ISBN 0-582-52821-6); Tales of Mystery & Imagination. Poe, Edgar A (ISBN 0-582-52891-7); Tales from Shakespeare. Lamb, Charles & Lamb, Mary. (ISBN 0-582-52851-8); The Thirty-Nine Steps. new ed. Buchan, John (ISBN 0-582-52798-8); Three Men in a Boat. new ed. Jerome, Jerome K (ISBN 0-582-52635-3); The Three Musketeers. Dumas, Alexandre (ISBN 0-582-52827-5); Vanity Fair. Thackeray, W. M. o.p. (ISBN 0-582-52869-0); Wuthering Heights. new ed. Bronte, Emily (ISBN 0-582-52318-4). (English As a Second Language Bk.). (Suitable for intermediate secondary school & adult students). 1956-81. pap. 2.15x ea. Longman.**

Eyre, A. G., ed. see Twain, Mark.

Eyre, Linda & Eyre, Richard. Teaching Children Responsibility. LC 82-12842. (Illus.). 247p. 1982. 7.95 (ISBN 0-87747-918-6). Deseret Bk.

Eyre, Richard, jt. auth. see Eyre, Linda.

Eyre, S. R. The Real Wealth of Nations. LC 77-93019. 1978. 27.50x (ISBN 0-312-66525-3). St Martin.

Eyre, S. R. & Jones, C. R. Geography As Human Ecology. (Illus.). 1966. 17.95 o.p. (ISBN 0-312-32165-1). St Martin.

Eyre, V. Journal of an Afghanistan Prisoner. 1976. 20.00 o.p. (ISBN 0-7100-8349-1). Routledge & Kegan.

Eyres, Alfred, jt. auth. see Pearson, Charles.

Eyre-Todd, George, ed. Early Scottish Poetry: Thomas the Rhymer, John Barbour, Andrew of Wyntown, Henry the Minstrel. LC 77-98753. Repr. of 1891 ed. lib. bdg. 15.00x o.p. (ISBN 0-8371-3094-8, EYES). Greenwood.

--Mediaeval Scottish Poetry: King James the First, Robert Henryson, William Dunbar, Gavin Douglas. LC 70-98754. 1971. Repr. of 1892 ed. lib. bdg. 15.00x o.p. (ISBN 0-8371-3095-6, EYMS). Greenwood.

--Scottish Poetry of the Sixteenth Century. LC 78-98756. Repr. of 1892 ed. lib. bdg. 15.00x o.p. (ISBN 0-8371-3097-2, EYSC). Greenwood.

Eyring, H., jt. auth. see Krausz, A. S.

Eyring, H., et al. Basic Chemical Kinetics. LC 79-26280. 1980. 44.50x (ISBN 0-471-05496-8, Pub. by Wiley-Interscience). Wiley.

Eyring, H., et al, eds. Physical Chemistry: An Advanced Treatise in Eleven Volumes. Incl. Vol. 1. Thermodynamics. Jost, W., ed. 1971. 78.50, by subscription 89.50 (ISBN 0-12-245601-7); Vol. 2. Statistical Mechanics. Eyring, H., ed. 63.50, by subscription 72.50 (ISBN 0-12-245602-5); Vol. 3. Electronic Structure of Atoms & Molecules. Henderson, D., ed. 78.50, by subscription 89.50 (ISBN 0-12-245603-3); Vol. 4. Molecular Properties. Henderson, D., ed. 88.50, by subscription 101.00 (ISBN 0-12-245604-1); Vol. 5. Valency. Eyring, H., ed. 78.50, by subscription 89.50 (ISBN 0-12-245605-X); Vol. 6A. General Introduction & Gas Reactions. Jost, W., ed. Pt. A. 74.00, subscription 84.50 (ISBN 0-12-245606-8); Pt. B. 78.50 (ISBN 0-686-76948-1); Vol. 7. Reactions in Condensed Phases. Eyring, H., ed. 91.00, subscription 91.00 (ISBN 0-12-245607-6); Vol. 8. Liquid State. Henderson, D., ed. Pt. A. by subscription 55.00 50.00 (ISBN 0-12-245608-4); Pt. B. by subscription 72.50 63.50 (ISBN 0-12-245658-0); Vol. 9. Electrochemistry. **Eyring, H., ed. Pt. A. 63.50, by subscription 72.50 (ISBN 0-12-245609-2); Pt. B. 63.50, by subscription 72.50 (ISBN 0-12-245659-9). Pt. B; Vol. 10. Solid State Chemistry. Jost, W., ed. 78.50, by subscription 89.50 (ISBN 0-12-245610-6); Vol. 11 Pt. A. Mathematical Applications. Henderson, D., ed. 78.50, by subscription 89.50 (ISBN 0-12-245611-4); Pt. B. 74.00 (ISBN 0-12-245661-0). Acad Pr.**

Eyring, Henry & Jhon, Mu S. Significant Liquid Structures. 1969. text ed. 11.00 o.p. (ISBN 0-471-24982-3, Pub. by Wiley). Krieger.

Eyring, Henry & Henderson, Douglas, eds. Theoretical Chemistry: Advances in Perspectives, Vol. 2. 1976. 60.00 (ISBN 0-12-681902-5); lib. ed 76.50 (ISBN 0-12-681972-6); microfiche 43.50 (ISBN 0-12-681973-4). Acad Pr.

Eyring, Henry, et al. Quantum Chemistry. 394p. 1944. 26.95x (ISBN 0-471-24981-5). Wiley.

--Statistical Mechanics & Dynamics. 2nd ed. LC 78-1073. 29.95 o.p. (ISBN 0-471-37042-8, Pub. by Wiley-Interscience). Wiley.

Eyring, Henry, et al, eds. Annual Review of Physical Chemistry, Vol. 24. LC 51-1658. (Illus.). 1973. text ed. 17.00 (ISBN 0-8243-1024-1). Annual Reviews.

Eyring, L., jt. ed. see Gschneider, K. A., Jr.

Eyring, L., jt. ed. see Gschneidner, K. A.

Eys, Jan Van see Van Eys, Jan & Sullivan, Margaret P.

Eysenck, H. Intelligence Controversy: H. J. Eysenck vs Leon Kamin. LC 80-28571. 192p. 1981. 14.95 (ISBN 0-471-08884-6, Pub. by Wiley-Interscience). Wiley.

Eysenck, H. J. Crime & Personality. 3rd, rev. ed. 222p. 1977. 18.95 (ISBN 0-7100-8487-0). Routledge & Kegan.

--The Dynamics of Anxiety & Hysteria: An Experimental Application of Modern Learning Theory to Psychiatry. (Illus.). 1967. Repr. of 1957 ed. 32.95x (ISBN 0-7100-1354-X). Routledge & Kegan.

--Eysenck on Extraversion. LC 73-4503. 174p. 1973. pap. 8.50 (ISBN 0-470-24995-1). Krieger.

--The Measurement of Intelligence. 488p. 1973. 26.00 (ISBN 0-686-86258-9, Pub. by W & W). Krieger.

--Psychology Is About People. LC 73-39003. 385p. 1972. 24.50x (ISBN 0-912050-19-5, Library Pr). Open Court.

Eysenck, H. J. & Nias, D. K. Astrology: Science or Superstition. 1982. 45.00x (ISBN 0-85117-214-8, Pub. by M Temple Smith). State Mutual Bk.

--Sex, Violence & the Media. LC 78-69824. 1978. 10.95x o.p. (ISBN 0-312-71340-1). St Martin.

Eysenck, H. J. & Wilson, Glenn. The Psychology of Sex. (Illus.). 208p. 1979. 17.50x (ISBN 0-460-04332-3, Pub. by J. M. Dent England). Biblio Dist.

Eysenck, H. J., ed. see Galton, Francis.

Eysenck, Hans J. Mindwatching. LC 81-43734. (Illus.). 400p. 1983. 19.95 (ISBN 0-385-17843-3, Anchor Pr). Doubleday.

Eyton, Audrey. The F-Plan Diet. LC 82-17969. 256p. 1983. 12.95 (ISBN 0-517-54934-4). Crown.

Eze, Osita C. Human Rights in Africa: Some Selected Problems. LC 82-16809. 310p. 1982. 22.50x (ISBN 0-312-39962-6). St Martin.

Ezekiel, Mordecai. Twenty-Five Hundred Dollars a Year: From Scarsity to Abundance. LC 72-2369. (FDR & the Era of the New Deal Ser). 348p. 1973. Repr. of 1936 ed. lib. bdg. 39.50 (ISBN 0-306-70468-4). Da Capo.

Ezekiel, Mordecai & Fox, Karl A. Methods of Correlation & Regression Analysis: Linear & Curvilinear. 3rd ed. LC 59-11993. (Illus.). 1959. 49.95 (ISBN 0-471-25014-7, Pub. by Wiley-Interscience). Wiley.

Ezekiel, S. & Arditty, H. J., eds. Fiber-Optic Rotation Sensors, Cambridge, MA: Proceedings, 1981. (Springer Series in Optical Sciences Ser.: Vol. 32). (Illus.). 440p. 1983. 33.00 (ISBN 0-387-11791-1). Springer-Verlag.

Ezell, Gene, jt. auth. see Anspaugh, David.

Ezell, Hazel. Closeness. 1981. 5.75 (ISBN 0-8062-1791-X). Carlton.

Ezell, John S., ed. see Miranda, Francisco De.

Ezorsky, Gertrude, ed. Philosophical Perspectives on Punishment. LC 72-37999. 1972. 44.50x (ISBN 0-87395-212-X); pap. 11.95x (ISBN 0-87395-213-8). State U NY Pr.

Ezra, Derek. Coal & Energy: The Need to Exploit the World's Most Abundant Fossil Fuel. LC 78-5785. 182p. 1978. 24.95x o.p. (ISBN 0-470-26339-3). Halsted Pr.

Ezra, Kate, tr. see Zahan, Dominique.

Ezzati, Ali. World Energy Markets & OPEC Stability. LC 77-14615. 1978. 23.95 o.p. (ISBN 0-669-01950-X). Lexington Bks.

Ezzell, Marilyn. The Clue in Witchcrest Well. (Susan Sand Mystery Ser.). (Orig.). (gr. 3-9). 1982. pap. 1.95 (ISBN 0-523-41742-X). Pinnacle Bks.

--The Mystery of Hollowhearth House. (Susan Sand Mystery Ser.: No. 1). (Orig.). (gr. 3-9). 1982. pap. 1.95 (ISBN 0-523-41701-2). Pinnacle Bks.

--The Phantom of Featherford Falls. (Susan Sand Mystery: No. 5). 192p. 1983. pap. 1.95 (ISBN 0-523-41744-6). Pinnacle Bks.

--The Secret of Clovercrest Castle. (Susan Sand Mystery Ser.: No. 2). (Orig.). (gr. 3-9). 1982. pap. 1.95 (ISBN 0-523-41741-1). Pinnacle Bks.

F

F & S Press Book, jt. auth. see Siafaca, Katie.

F & S Press Book, ed. see Bernstein, Joan Z.

F & S Press Book, jt. ed. see Gingerich, Duane.

F & S Press Book, ed. see Turk, Michael H.

F. W. Dodge. Dodge Construction Systems Costs, 1982. 292p. 1982. 46.65x o.p. (ISBN 0-07-017392-3). McGraw.

--Dodge Guide to Public Works & Heavy Construction Costs, 1982. 224p. 1982. 34.90x o.p. (ISBN 0-07-017391-5). McGraw.

--Dodge Manual for Building Construction Pricing & Scheduling, 1982. 310p. 1982. 32.90x o.p. (ISBN 0-07-017393-1). McGraw.

F. W. Faxon Co. Cumulated Dramatic Index. 1909-1949, 2 vols. 1965. lib. bdg. 590.00 (ISBN 0-8161-0402-6, Hall Library). G K Hall.

--Cumulated Magazine Subject Index. 1907-1949, 2 Vols. 1964. Set. 590.00 (ISBN 0-8161-0401-8, Hall Library). G K Hall.

F.A.A. How to Become a Pilot: The Step by Step Guide to Flying. LC 74-8723. (Illus.). pap. 8.95 (ISBN 0-8069-8386-8). Sterling.

Faaborg, Linda, jt. auth. see Dziech, Billie W.

Faaland, Just. Population & the World Economy in the 21st Century. LC 82-10579. 272p. 1982. 32.50x (ISBN 0-312-63123-5). St Martin.

Faaland, Just & Parkinson, John R. Bangladesh: The Test Case for Development. LC 76-851. 1976. lib. bdg. 30.00 o.p. (ISBN 0-89158-546-X). Westview.

Faaland, Just, ed. Aid & Influence: The Case of Bangladesh. LC 80-13481. 1980. 27.50 (ISBN 0-312-01492-9). St Martin.

Faas, Ekbert. Young Robert Duncan: Portrait of the Poet as Homosexual in Society. 300p. (Orig.). 1983. 20.00 (ISBN 0-87685-489-7); pap. 10.00 (ISBN 0-87685-488-9); signed cloth 40.00. Black Sparrow.

Faas, Larry A. Children with Learning Problems: A Handbook for Teachers. LC 79-89741. (Illus.). 1980. text ed. 19.95 (ISBN 0-395-28352-3); instr's. manual 1.00 (ISBN 0-395-28353-1). HM.

--Learning Disabilities: A Competency-Based Approach. 2nd ed. (Illus.). 480p. 1981. pap. text ed. 20.50 (ISBN 0-395-29699-4); instr's. manual 1.00 (ISBN 0-395-29700-1). HM.

Faase, Thomas P. Making the Jesuits More Modern. LC 81-40388. (Illus.). 478p. (Orig.). 1981. lib. bdg. 26.50 (ISBN 0-8191-1761-7); pap. text ed. 16.50 (ISBN 0-8191-1762-5). U Pr of Amer.

Fabbro, Mârio Dal see Dal Fabbro, Mario.

Fabel, Arthur. Cosmic Genesis. (Tielherd Studies). 1981. 2.00 (ISBN 0-89012-028-5). Anima Pubns.

Fabella, Virginia & Torres, Sergio, eds. Irruption of the Third World: Challenge to Theology. LC 82-18851. 304p. (Orig.). 1983. pap. 10.95 (ISBN 0-88344-216-7). Orbis Bks.

Faber, Adele & Mazlish, Elaine. Liberated Parents-Liberated Children. 1975. pap. 2.95 (ISBN 0-380-00466-6, 54965). Avon.

Faber, Arlene, jt. auth. see Potter, William G.

Faber, Donald & Korn, Henri, eds. Neurobiology of the Mauthner Cell. LC 78-66351. 302p. 1978. 34.50 (ISBN 0-89004-233-0). Raven.

Faber, Doris. Enough! The Revolt of the American Consumer. LC 72-81486. 192p. (gr. 7 up). 1972. 8.95 o.p. (ISBN 0-374-32193-0). FS&G.

--Lucretia Mott: Foe of Slavery. LC 70-151992. (Discovery Ser.). (Illus.). (gr. 2-5). 1971. PLB 6.69 o.p. (ISBN 0-8116-6306-X). Garrard.

--The Miracle of Vitamins. (Science Survey Ser.). (Illus.). (gr. 5 up). 1964. PLB 5.29 o.p. (ISBN 0-399-60466-9). Putnam Pub Group.

Faber, Doris & Faber, Howard. The Assassination of Martin Luther King, Jr. LC 78-1726. (Focus Bks.). (Illus.). 1978. lib. bdg. 7.90 s&l (ISBN 0-531-02465-2). Watts.

Faber, Doris, jt. auth. see Faber, Harold.

Faber, Gail & Lasagna, Michele. Whispers from the First Californians. 2nd ed. (California History Ser.). (Illus.). 1981. permabound 10.95 (ISBN 0-936480-00-9); pap. text ed. 7.95 student's ed., 223pgs. (ISBN 0-686-86316-X); Tchr's ed., 240p. 3-ring binder 14.95 (ISBN 0-936480-01-7). Magpie Pubns.

Faber, Harold & Faber, Doris. American Heroes of the 20th Century. (Landmark Giant Ser.). (Illus.). (gr. 5-9). 1967. 4.95 o.p. (ISBN 0-394-80296-9, BYR); PLB 5.99 o.p. (ISBN 0-394-90296-3). Random.

Faber, Heije. Pastoral Care in the Modern Hospital. De Waal, Hugo, tr. LC 70-168632. 1972. 10.95 (ISBN 0-664-20922-X). Westminster.

Faber, Howard, jt. auth. see Faber, Doris.

Faber, J., jt. auth. see Chandebois, Rosine.

Faber, John, Jr., ed. see AIP Conference, 89th, Argonne National Laboratory, 1981.

Faber, M. D. Culture & Consciousness: The Social Meaning of Altered Awareness. LC 80-36683. 296p. 1981. text ed. 29.95x (ISBN 0-87705-505-X); professional 29.95 (ISBN 0-686-96741-0). Human Sci Pr.

Faber, Marilyn M. & Reinhardt, Adina M. Promoting Health Through Risk Reduction. 1982. text ed. 22.95 (ISBN 0-02-334850-X). Macmillan.

Faber, Marion, tr. see Hildesheimer, Wolfgang.

Faber, Marion, et al, trs. see Reich, Wilhelm.

Faber, Richard. The Brave Courtier: Sir William Temple. 176p. 1983. 29.95 (ISBN 0-571-11982-4). Faber & Faber.

Faber, Rodney B. Applied Electricity & Electronics for Technology. LC 77-15037. (Electronics Technology Ser.). 348p. 1978. text ed. 21.95 (ISBN 0-471-25022-8); avail. solutions (ISBN 0-471-03699-4). Wiley.

Faber, Stuart J. Handbook of Guardianships & Conservatorships. 3rd, rev. ed. 1981. pap. text ed. 27.50 (ISBN 0-686-37115-1). Lega Bks.

Faber, T. E. Introduction to the Theory of Liquid Metals. LC 76-184903. (Cambridge Monographs in Physics). (Illus.). 600p. 1972. 79.50 (ISBN 0-521-08477-6). Cambridge U Pr.
Fabian, Erika, jt. auth. see Moldavy, Albert.
Fabian, Erika, jt. auth. see Moldvay, Albert.
Fabian, Erika, jt. auth. see Wanderer, Dr. Zev.
Fabian, Johannes. Time & the Other. 224p. 1983. text ed. 28.00 (ISBN 0-231-05590-0); pap. 14.00 (ISBN 0-231-05591-9). Columbia U Pr.
Fabian, Leonard. Fishing. (Monarch Illustrated Guide Ser.). (Illus.). 1977. pap. 2.95 o.p. (ISBN 0-671-18761-9). Monarch Pr.
Fabian, Leonard W. Decade of Clinical Progress. (Illus.). 1971. text ed. 15.00x o.p. (ISBN 0-8036-3315-7). Davis Co.
Fabian, M. E. Semiconductor Laser Diodes: A User's Handbook. 1981. 125.00x (ISBN 0-686-71789-9, Pub. by Electrochemical Scotland). State Mutual Bk.
Fabian, Monroe. The Pennsylvania German Decorated Chest, Vol. XII. 1978. 25.00 o.p. (ISBN 0-686-79897-X). Penn German Soc.
Fabian, P., tr. see Breuer, Georg.
Fabio, Anthony di see Di Fabio, Anthony.
Fable, Edmund. The True Life of Billy the Kid. LC 80-18408. 75p. (Orig.). 1980. Repr. 19.95 o.p. (ISBN 0-932702-11-2); collector's edition 75.00 (ISBN 0-932702-12-0). Creative Texas.
Fabos, Julius G. Planning the Total Landscape: A Guide to Intelligent Land Use. (Illus.). 1979. lib. bdg. 21.00 (ISBN 0-89158-172-3). Westview.
Fabozzi, Frank J. & Zarb, Frank G. The Handbook of Financial Markets: Securities, Options and Futures. LC 80-70448. 825p. 1981. 45.50 (ISBN 0-87094-216-6). Dow Jones-Irwin.
Fabozzi, Frank J. & Pollack, Irving M., eds. The Handbook of Fixed Income Securities. LC 82-71874. 850p. 1983. 45.00 (ISBN 0-87094-306-5). Dow Jones-Irwin.
Fabozzi, Frank J., jt. ed. see Chrystie, Thomas L.
Fabre, Genevieve E., et al, eds. Afro-American Poetry & Drama, Seventeen Sixty to Nineteen Seventy-Five: A Guide to Information Sources. LC 74-11518. (American Literature, English Literature, & World Literature in English Information Guide Ser.: Vol. 17). 1979. 42.00x (ISBN 0-8103-1208-5). Gale.
Fabre, J., jt. ed. see McMichael, A.
Fabre, Jean H. Social Life in the Insect World. LC 72-164264. 1974. Repr. of 1912 ed. 42.00x (ISBN 0-8103-3967-6). Gale.
Fabre, Michel & Davis, Charles T. Richard Wright: A Primary Bibliography. 1982. lib. bdg. 34.50 (ISBN 0-8161-8410-0, Hall Reference). G K Hall.
Fabre, Michel, ed. see Wright, Richard.
Fabreau, Donald F. & Gillespie, Joseph E. Modern Police Administration. (P-H Ser. in Criminal Justice). (Illus.). 1978. ref. 20.95 (ISBN 0-13-597229-9). P-H.
Fabrega, Horacio, Jr. Disease & Social Behavior: An Elementary Exposition. 1974. pap. 9.95x (ISBN 0-262-56020-8). MIT Pr.
Fabri, Charles. Indian Dress. 1977. Repr. of 1960 ed. 4.00x o.p. (ISBN 0-8364-0114-X). South Asia Bks.
Fabri, Felix. The Wanderings of Felix Fabri: Circa 1480-1483 A.D, 2 Vols. Stewart, Aubrey, tr. LC 74-141802. Set. 65.00 (ISBN 0-404-09140-7); Vol. 9-10 (Vol. 2, Pts. 1-2) 32.50 (ISBN 0-686-81995-0); 32.50 (ISBN 0-686-81996-9). AMS Pr.
Fabri, Ralph. Color: A Complete Guide for Artists. (Illus.). 176p. 1967. 22.50 (ISBN 0-8230-0700-6); pap. 9.95 o.p. (ISBN 0-686-83005-9). Watson-Guptill.
Fabricant, Carole. Swift's Landscape. LC 82-165. 336p. 1982. text ed. 25.00x (ISBN 0-8018-2721-3). Johns Hopkins.
Fabricant, Michael. Juvenile Injustice: Dilemmas of the Family Court System. 198p. (Orig.). 1981. pap. 7.00 (ISBN 0-88156-003-0). Comm Serv Soc NY.
--Juveniles in the Family Courts. LC 82-47927. 176p. 1982. 21.95x (ISBN 0-669-05706-1). Lexington Bks.
Fabricant, S. The Trend of Government Activity in the United States Since 1900. LC 52-7402. (National Bureau of Economic Research. General Ser.). 18.00 o.s.i. (ISBN 0-527-03017-1). Kraus Repr.
Fabricant, Solomon. Studies in Social & Private Accounting. LC 82-82488. (Accountancy in Transition Ser.). 300p. 1982. lib. bdg. 40.00 (ISBN 0-8240-5337-0). Garland Pub.
Fabricating Manufacturers Association, jt. ed. see Society of Manufacturing Engineers.
Fabricio, Robert, jt. auth. see Dorschner, John.
Fabrick, Martin N. & O'Rourke, Joseph J. Environmental Planning for Design & Construction. LC 81-23070. (Construction Management & Engineering Ser.). 304p. 1982. 41.95x (ISBN 0-471-05848-3, Pub. by Wiley-Interscience). Wiley.
Fabris, Alfred C. A Prosecutor's Guide for California Peace Officers. LC 76-45963. 1977. text ed. 9.95 o.p. (ISBN 0-8465-1519-9); pap. text ed. 11.95 (ISBN 0-8465-1520-2). Benjamin-Cummings.
Fabry, Joseph. Swing Shift: Building the Liberty Ships. LC 81-14449. (Illus.). 224p. (Orig.). 1982. pap. 7.95 (ISBN 0-89407-049-5). Strawberry Hil.
Fabrycky, W., jt. auth. see Blanchard, B.
Fabrycky, W. J. & Thuesen, G. J. Engineering Economy. 5th ed. (Illus.). 1977. text ed. 27.95 (ISBN 0-13-277491-7). P-H.
Fabrycky, W. J., et al. Industrial Operations Research. (Illus.). 592p. 1972. ref. ed. 29.95 (ISBN 0-13-464263-5). P-H.
Fabrycky, Walter J. & Thuesen, G. J. Economic Decision Analysis. 2nd ed. 1980. text ed. 25.95 (ISBN 0-13-223248-0). P-H.
Fabun, Don. Communications: The Transfer of Meaning. (Illus.). 1983. 4.50 (ISBN 0-686-84070-4). Intl Gen Semantics.
--Dimensions of Change. 1971. text ed. 9.95x (ISBN 0-02-475500-1, 47550). Macmillan.
Facaros, Dana & Pauls, Michael. New England. (The American Traveler). 250p. 1982. 19.95 (ISBN 0-89526-645-8); pap. 12.95 (ISBN 0-89526-857-4). Regnery-Gateway.
Facchetti, S., ed. Applications of Mass Spectrometry to Trace Analysis. 1982. 78.75 (ISBN 0-444-42042-8). Elsevier.
Face, J. D., jt. ed. see Oliver, Roland.
Facione, Peter & Scherer, Donald. Logic & Logical Thinking. LC 77-24173. (Illus.). 1977. pap. text ed. 24.95 (ISBN 0-07-019884-5, C); instructor's manual 15.00 (ISBN 0-07-019885-3). McGraw.
Facione, Peter A., et al. Values & Society: An Introduction to Ethics & Social Philosophy. 1978. pap. text ed. 15.95 (ISBN 0-13-940338-8). P-H.
Facius, Johannes & Noer, Johny. El Pequeno Libro Blanco Para Jovenes. Orig. Title: The Little White Book. Date not set. cancelled (ISBN 0-311-46057-7). Casa Bautista.
Fackenheim, Emil L. Metaphysics & Historicity. (Aquinas Lecture). 1961. 7.95 (ISBN 0-87462-126-7). Marquette.
Fackenhein, Emil L. To Mend the World: Foundations of Future Jewish Thought. LC 81-16614. 352p. (Orig.). 1982. 22.50x (ISBN 0-8052-3795-X); pap. 12.95 (ISBN 0-8052-0699-X). Schocken.
Facklam, R. Recent Developments in Laboratory Identification Techniques. (International Congress Ser.: Vol. 519). 1980. 42.25 (ISBN 0-444-90152-3). Elsevier.
Fackler, Fern. A Women's Directory for the Cedar Rapids & Iowa City Area. 2nd ed. (Women's Directories-Cedar Rapids Iowa City-1983). 1983. pap. text ed. 3.50 (ISBN 0-910757-01-1). P R N Corp.
--A Women's Guide for the Cedar Rapids & Iowa City Area. (Women's Directories Cedar Rapids-Iowa City, 1982). 96p. 1982. pap. text ed. 3.50 (ISBN 0-910757-00-3). P R N Corp.
Fackler, John P. Inorganic Syntheses, Vol. 21. LC 39-23015. (Inorganic Synthesis Ser.). 215p. 1982. 37.50 (ISBN 0-471-86520-6, Pub. by Wiley-Interscience). Wiley.
Fackre, Gabriel. The Religious Right & the Christian Faith. 1982. 8.95 (ISBN 0-8028-3566-X). Eerdmans.
Facos, James. Morning's Come Singing. Topham, J., ed. LC 81-65570. 40p. (Orig.). 1981. pap. 3.95 (ISBN 0-933486-22-7). Am Poetry Pr.
--Silver Wood. 1977. pap. 1.50 (ISBN 0-686-38383-4). Eldridge Pub.
Facter, Dolly. Doctrine of the Buddha. LC 65-11949. 1965. 4.75 o.p. (ISBN 0-8022-0465-1). Philos Lib.
Factory Mutual System. Handbook of Industrial Loss Prevention. 2nd ed. (Insurance Ser). 1967. 67.50 o.p. (ISBN 0-07-019888-8, P&RB). McGraw.
Faculty of Lynchburg College, ed. Series One: Poverty & Wealth, Vol. IV. LC 82-45155. (Classical Selections on Great Issues, Symposium Readings Ser.). 532p. (Orig.). 1982. lib. bdg. 18.50 (ISBN 0-8191-2468-0); pap. text ed. 8.50 (ISBN 0-8191-2469-9). U Pr of Amer.
--Tyranny & Freedom: Series One, Volume III. LC 82-45156. (Classical Selections on Great Issues, Symposium Readings Ser.). 538p. (Orig.). 1982. lib. bdg. 18.75 (ISBN 0-8191-2466-4); pap. text ed. 8.50 (ISBN 0-8191-2467-2). U Pr of Amer.
Fadala, Sam. The Complete Black Powder Handbook. (Illus.). 288p. 1979. pap. 7.95 o.s.i. (ISBN 0-695-81311-0). Follett.
Fadanelli, R. Dizionario Italiano-Russo, Russo-Italiane. 286p. (Ital. & Rus.). leatherette 5.95 (ISBN 0-686-92582-3). French & Eur.
Faddah, Mohammad I. The Middle East in Transition: A Study of Jordan's Foreign Policy. 1974. 15.95x (ISBN 0-210-22387-1). Asia.
Fadely, Jack L. & Hosler, Virginia N. Case Studies in Left & Right Hemisheric Functioning. (Illus.). 136p. 1983. 16.75x (ISBN 0-398-04792-8). C C Thomas.
--Developmental Psychometrics: A Resource Book for Mental Health Workers & Educators. (Illus.). 168p. 1980. 13.75x (ISBN 0-398-04056-7); pap. 9.75x (ISBN 0-398-04057-5). C C Thomas.
--Understanding the Alpha Child at Home & School: Left & Right Hemispheric Function in Relation to Personality & Learning. (Illus.). 256p. 1979. photocopy ed. spiral 24.75x (ISBN 0-398-03862-7). C C Thomas.
Faden, Arnold M. Economics of Space & Time: The Measure Theoretic Foundations of Social Science. 1977. 22.50x (ISBN 0-8138-0500-7). Iowa St U Pr.
Fader, Bruce. Industrial Noise Control. LC 81-2158. 251p. 1981. 30.95x (ISBN 0-471-06007-0, Pub. by Wiley-Interscience). Wiley.
Faderman, Lillian. Scotch Verdict. (Illus.). 388p. 1983. 17.50 (ISBN 0-688-01559-X). Morrow.
--Scotch Verdict. (Illus.). 388p. 1983. pap. 8.95 (ISBN 0-688-02054-2). Quill NY.
Faderman, Lillian & Bradshaw, Barbara. Speaking for Ourselves: American Ethnic Writing. 2nd ed. 1975. pap. 9.95x (ISBN 0-673-07925-2). Scott F.
Fadia, Babu L. State Politics in India, 2 Vols. 1125p. 1983. Set. text ed. 55.00x (ISBN 0-391-02827-8, Pub. by Radiant Pub India). Humanities.
Fadia, Babulal. Pressure Groups in Indian Politics. (Illus.). 295p. 1980. text ed. 22.50x (ISBN 0-391-01795-0). Humanities.
Fadiman, Clifton. The Lifetime Reading Plan. new, rev. ed. LC 77-14289. 1978. 11.49i (ISBN 0-690-01499-6). T Y Crowell.
Fadiman, James & Kewman, Donald. Exploring Madness: Experience, Theory, & Research. 2nd ed. LC 78-16543. (Psychology Ser.). 1979. pap. text ed. 10.95 (ISBN 0-8185-0281-9). Brooks-Cole.
Fadiman, Jeffery. Mountain Warriors: The Precolonial Meru of Mt. Kenya. LC 75-620140. (Papers in International Studies, Africa Ser.: No. 27). (Orig.). 1980. pap. 8.50 o.p. (ISBN 0-89680-060-1, Ohio U Ctr Intl). Ohio U Pr.
Fadiman, Jeffrey. Mountain Warrior: The Pre-Colonial Meru of Mt. Kenya. LC 75-620140. (Papers in International Studies: Africa: No. 27). (Illus.). 1976. pap. 4.75 (ISBN 0-89680-060-1, Ohio U Ctr Intl). Ohio U Pr.
Fadiman, Jeffrey A. The Moment of Conquest: Meru, Kenya, 1907. LC 79-10870. (Papers in International Studies: Africa: No. 36). 1979. pap. 5.50 (ISBN 0-89680-081-4, Ohio U Ctr Intl). Ohio U Pr.
--An Oral History of Tribal Warfare: The Meru of Mt. Kenya. LC 81-16940. 194p. 1982. text ed. 20.95x (ISBN 0-8214-0632-9, 82-83277); pap. 7.95x (ISBN 0-8214-0633-7, 82-84663). Ohio U Pr.
Faensen, Hubert & Ivanov, Vladimir. Early Russian Architecture. LC 73-87578. (Illus.). 542p. 1975. 42.50 o.p. (ISBN 0-399-11293-6). Putnam Pub Group.
Fagalia, G., jt. auth. see Ekins, R.
Fagan, B. M., jt. auth. see Oliver, Roland.
Fagan, Brian M. People of the Earth: An Introduction to World Prehistory. 3rd ed. (Illus.). 412p. 1980. pap. text ed. 13.95 (ISBN 0-316-25993-4). Little.
Fagan, Ted & Moran, William, eds. The Encyclopedic Discography of Victor Recordings. LC 82-9343. (Discographies Ser.: No. 7). (Illus.). 488p. 1982. lib. bdg. 49.95 (ISBN 0-313-23003-X, FPM/). Greenwood.
Fage, J. D. History of West Africa. 4th ed. LC 71-85742. (Illus.). 1969. 29.95 (ISBN 0-521-07406-1); pap. 9.95x (ISBN 0-521-09579-4). Cambridge U Pr.
Fage, J. D. & Oliver, Roland A. Papers in African Prehistory. LC 74-77286. (Illus.). 1970. 42.50 (ISBN 0-521-07470-3); pap. 12.95 (ISBN 0-521-09566-2). Cambridge U Pr.
Fage, John. Supreme Court Practice & Procedure. 1980. 30.00x (ISBN 0-686-97116-7, Pub. by Fourmat England). State Mutual Bk.
Fagen, Richard R. & Tuohy, William S. Politics & Privilege in a Mexican City. xiv, 210p. 1972. 5.95 (ISBN 0-8047-0809-6); pap. 2.95 o.p. (ISBN 0-8047-0879-7, SP135). Stanford U Pr.
Fagen, Richard R. & Pellicer, Olga, eds. The Future of Central America: Policy Choices for the U.S. & Mexico. LC 82-62447. 224p. 1983. text ed. 20.00x (ISBN 0-8047-1177-1); pap. text ed. 11.95x (ISBN 0-8047-1190-9). Stanford U Pr.
Fagen, Stanly, et al. Teaching Children Self-Control: Preventing Emotional & Learning Problems in the Elementary School. new ed. (Special Education Ser.). 288p. 1975. pap. text ed. 14.95 (ISBN 0-675-08783-X). Merrill.
Fagerlind, I. & Saha, L. Education & National Development: A Comparative Perspective. (Illus.). 200p. 1983. 32.00 (ISBN 0-08-028915-0); pap. 13.00 (ISBN 0-08-030202-5). Pergamon.
Fagerstrom, Stan. Catch More Steelhead. LC 75-425000047. 1981. pap. 11.95 (ISBN 0-939116-00-6). Creative Comm.
Fagg, John E. Pan Americanism: Its Meaning & History. LC 81-17176. (Anvil Ser.). 218p. 1982. pap. text ed. 5.95 (ISBN 0-89874-258-7). Krieger.
Faggiolo. Bernini. pap. 12.50 (ISBN 0-935748-42-3). ScalaBooks.
Fagley, Richard M. Population Explosion & Christian Responsibility. 1960. 16.95x (ISBN 0-19-501166-X). Oxford U Pr.
Fagnon, Michael, tr. from Ger. Werwolf Combat Instruction Manual. LC 82-6286. (Illus.). 200p. 1982. 16.95 (ISBN 0-87364-248-1). Paladin Ent.
Fagothey, Austin. Right & Reason: Ethics in Theory & Practice. 6th ed. LC 75-33045. (Illus.). 488p. 1976. text ed. 18.95 o.p. (ISBN 0-8016-1545-3). Mosby.
Faheem, Ahmed D., jt. auth. see Favazza, Armando R.
Faherty, Ruth. Westies: From Head to Tail. (Illus.). 232p. 1981. 19.00 (ISBN 0-931866-08-1). Alpine Pubns.
Faherty, William B. Wide River Wide Land. new ed. LC 75-37091. (Illus.). 200p. 1976. lib. bdg. 6.95 (ISBN 0-913656-15-1, Piraeus). Forum Pr IL.
Fahey, Charles J. The Infirm Elderly: Their Care is an Agenda Item for All Segments of Society. (Vital Issues Ser.: Vol. XXXI, No. 10). 0.80 (ISBN 0-686-84151-4). Ctr Info Am.
Fahey, Frank & Fahey, Maria. Chapters from the American Experience, Vol. 2. (American History Ser). (Illus.). 1971. pap. text ed. 13.95 (ISBN 0-13-128124-0). P-H.
Fahey, Frank & Fahey, Marie, eds. Chapters from the American Experience, Vol. 1. (American History Ser). (Illus.). 1971. pap. text ed. 13.95 (ISBN 0-13-128108-9). P-H.
Fahey, Maria, jt. auth. see Fahey, Frank.
Fahey, Marie, jt. ed. see Fahey, Frank.
Fahey, Sheila M. Charismatic Social Action: Reflection-Resource Manual. LC 77-70633. 192p. 1977. pap. 4.95 o.p. (ISBN 0-8091-2014-3). Paulist Pr.
Fahey, William A., jt. auth. see Richardson, Ben.
Fahien, R. Fundamentals of Transport Phenomena. (Chemical Engineering Ser.). 640p. 1983. 32.50x (ISBN 0-07-019891-8, C); write for info. solutions manual (ISBN 0-07-019892-6). McGraw.
Fahim, Hussein M. Egyptian Nubians: Resettlement & Years of Coping. (Illus.). xiv, 197p. 1983. 20.00x (ISBN 0-87480-215-6). U of Utah Pr.
Fahlbusch, Rudolf & Von Werder, Klaus, eds. Treatment of Pituitary Adenomas. LC 77-99148. (Illus.). 458p. 1978. pap. 42.50 o.p. (ISBN 0-88416-236-2). Wright-PSG.
Fahn, A. Plant Anatomy. 3rd ed. LC 81-13813. (Illus.). 528p. 1982. 60.00 (ISBN 0-08-028030-7); pap. 27.00 (ISBN 0-08-028029-3). Pergamon.
Fahn, Stanley, jt. ed. see Eldridge, Roswell.
Fahn, Stanley, et al, eds. Cerebral Hypoxia & Its Consequences. LC 78-57236. (Advances in Neurology Ser.: Vol. 26). 366p. 1979. text ed. 40.00 (ISBN 0-89004-296-9). Raven.
Fahnestock, Jeanne, jt. auth. see Secor, Marie.
Fahnestock, Lee, tr. see Ponge, Francis.
Fahrenbruch, Alan & Bube, Richard. Fundamentals of Solar Cells. LC 82-13919. Date not set. price not set (ISBN 0-12-247680-8). Acad Pr.
Fahrettin, Iskender. English-Turkish Dictionary. LC 54-11387. 20.00 o.p. (ISBN 0-8044-0140-3). Ungar.
Fahrney, Ralph R. Horace Greeley & the Tribune in the Civil War. LC 77-135663. (American Scene Ser). 1970. Repr. of 1936 ed. lib. bdg. 29.50 (ISBN 0-306-71120-6). Da Capo.
Fahs, Sophia L. Uganda's White Man of Work. 185p. 5.80 (ISBN 0-686-05597-7). Rod & Staff.
Fahy, Benen, ed. see Francis of Assisi, Saint.
Fahy, Carole. Cooking with Beer. 7.00 (ISBN 0-8446-5683-6). Peter Smith.
Fahy, Everett. Metropolitan Flowers. Allison, Ellyn, ed. (Illus.). 112p. 1982. 14.95 (ISBN 0-87099-310-0). Metro Mus Art.
--Metropolitan Flowers. Allison, Ellyn, ed. (Illus.). 112p. (Orig.). 1982. 29.50 (ISBN 0-8109-1317-8). Abrams.
Fahy, Everett & Watson, Francis B. The Wrightsman Collection, Vol. 5: Paintings, Drawings, Sculpture. LC 66-10181. (Illus.). 469p. 1973. 40.00 o.p. (ISBN 0-87099-012-8, Pub. by Metro Mus Art). NYGS.
Faibisoff, Sylvia G., jt. ed. see Bonn, George S.
Faid, Mary. No Stars So Bright. (Aston Hall Romances Ser.: No. 108). 192p. (Orig.). 1980. pap. 1.50 o.p. (ISBN 0-523-41120-0). Pinnacle Bks.
Faig, Kenneth W., Jr. Love Craft: The Notes & Commonplace Book. 2.95 (ISBN 0-686-31244-9). Necronomicon.
Faiguiet De Villeneuve, Joachim. L' Economie Politique, Project pour Enricluir et pour Perfectionner 1,Espece Humaine. Repr. of 1763 ed. 23.00 o.p. (ISBN 0-8287-0327-2). Clearwater Pub.
Failing, George E. Did Christ Die for All? 1.25 (ISBN 0-937296-02-3, 222-B). Presence Inc.
--Secure & Rejoicing. 0.95 (ISBN 0-937296-03-1, 223-A). Presence Inc.
Fain, Stephen M., et al. Teaching in America. 1979. pap. text ed. 13.50x (ISBN 0-673-15056-9). Scott F.
Fain, V. M. & Khanin, Ya. Quantum Electronics-Vol. 2: Maser Amplifiers & Oscillators. 1969. inquire for price o.p. (ISBN 0-08-012238-8). Pergamon.
Fainstein, Norman I. & Fainstein, Susan S. Urban Political Movements: The Search for Power by Minority Groups in American Cities. LC 73-21876. 352p. 1974. ref. ed. 15.95 (ISBN 0-13-939330-7); pap. 13.95 ref. ed. (ISBN 0-13-939322-6). P-H.
Fainstein, Susan S., jt. auth. see Fainstein, Norman I.
Faiola, Theodora & Pullen, Jo A. McGraw-Hill Guide to Clothing. MacGowan, Sandra, ed. (Illus.). 384p. 1981. text ed. 18.56 (ISBN 0-07-019855-1, W); tchrs. activity manual 6.16 (ISBN 0-07-019856-X, W). McGraw.
Fair, D. E. & De Juvigny, F. Leonard. Bank Management in a Changing Domestic & International Environment. 1982. lib. bdg. 57.00 (ISBN 90-247-2606-9, Pub. by Martinus Nijhoff Netherlands). Kluwer Boston.
Fair, G. M., et al. Water & Wastewater Engineering: Water Purification & Wastewater Treatment & Disposal. LC 66-16139. 668p. 1968. 43.95x (ISBN 0-471-25131-3). Wiley.

--Water & Wastewater Engineering: Water Supply & Wastewater Removal, Vol. 1. LC 66-16139. 489p. 1966. 39.95x (ISBN 0-471-25130-5). Wiley.

Fair, Gordon M., et al. Elements of Water Supply & Waste Water Disposal. 2nd ed. LC 72-151032. (Illus.). 752p. 1971. 43.95x (ISBN 0-471-25115-1). Wiley.

Fair, Harold L. Class Devotions. 128p. (Orig.). 1983. pap. 4.95 (ISBN 0-687-08623-X). Abingdon.

Fair, Jan. Electric Drill-Decimals. (Electric Drill Set Ser.). (Illus.). (gr. 5-12). 1977. tchrs. ed. 27.50 (ISBN 0-88488-078-8). Creative Pubns.

--Electric Drill-Fractions. (Electric Drill Set Ser.). (Illus.). (gr. 5-12). 1977. tchrs. ed. 27.50 (ISBN 0-88488-077-X). Creative Pubns.

--Electric Drill-Per Cents. (Electric Drill Set Ser.). (Illus.). (gr. 5-12). 1977. tchrs. ed. 27.50 (ISBN 0-88488-079-6). Creative Pubns.

--Electric Drill-Whole Numbers. (Electric Drill Set Ser.). (gr. 5-12). 1977. 27.50 (ISBN 0-88488-076-1). Creative Pubns.

Fair, Jan & Rand, Ken. Handy Math: Focus on Purchasing. (gr. 7-9). 1979. 7.25 (ISBN 0-88488-126-1). Creative Pubns.

--Handy Math: Focus on Sports. (gr. 7-9). 1979. 7.25 (ISBN 0-88488-128-8). Creative Pubns.

--Handy Math: Focus on Travel. (gr. 7-9). 1979. 7.25 (ISBN 0-88488-127-X). Creative Pubns.

Fair, Martha H. Tools for Survival: A Positive Action Plan for Minorities & Women. (Illus.). 160p. (Orig.). Date not set. pap. 12.95 (ISBN 0-911181-00-8). Harris Learning.

Fair, Marvin L. & Guandolo, John. Transportation Regulation. 9th ed. 500p. 1983. text ed. write for info. (ISBN 0-697-08515-5). Wm C Brown.

Fair, Ray C. A Model of Macroeconomic Activity: Vol. II: the Empirical Model. LC 74-12199. 316p. 1976. text ed. 20.00 o.p. (ISBN 0-88410-295-5). Ballinger Pub.

Fair, Sylvia. The Bedspread. LC 81-11152. (Illus.). 32p. (gr. k-3). 1982. 10.50 (ISBN 0-688-00877-1). Morrow.

--The Ivory Anvil. 1974. 12.50 o.p. (ISBN 0-575-01809-7, Pub. by Gollancz England). David & Charles.

Fairbairn, Douglas. Down & Out in Cambridge. 348p. 1982. 14.95 (ISBN 0-698-11089-7, Coward). Putnam Pub Group.

Fairbairn, James. Fairbairn's Crests of the Families of Great Britain & Ireland. LC 68-25887. (Illus.). 800p. 1968. 32.30 (ISBN 0-8048-0177-0). C E Tuttle.

Fairbairn, Patrick. An Exposition of Ezekiel. 1979. 18.50 (ISBN 0-86524-002-7, 2601). Klock & Klock.

Fairbairns, Zoe. Benefits. 224p. pap. 2.95 (ISBN 0-380-63164-4, Bard). Avon.

--Stand We at Last. 1983. 15.95 (ISBN 0-395-33124-2). HM.

Fairbank, Alfred. A Book of Scripts. 2nd ed. (Illus.). 48p. 1977. pap. 7.50 (ISBN 0-571-11080-0). Faber & Faber.

Fairbank, J. K., ed. The Cambridge History of China: Late Ch'ing, 1800-1911, Vol. 10: 1800-1911, Part 1. LC 76-29852. (Cambridge History of China). 89.50 (ISBN 0-521-21447-5). Cambridge U Pr.

Fairbank, John K. & Kwang-Ching, Lui. Cambridge History of China: Late Ch'ing, Vol. 11:1800-1911, Part 2. LC 76-29852. (Cambridge History of China). (Illus.). 1980. 89.50 (ISBN 0-521-22029-7). Cambridge U Pr.

Fairbank, John K. & Reischauer, Edwin O. China: Tradition & Transformation. LC 77-77980. (Illus.). 1978. text ed. 18.95 (ISBN 0-395-25813-8). HM.

Fairbank, John K., ed. Ch'ing Documents: An Introductory Syllabus, 2 Vols. 3rd ed. LC 65-3942. (East Asian Monographs Ser: No. 8). 1970. Set. pap. 6.00x o.p. (ISBN 0-674-12750-1). Harvard U Pr.

Fairbank, John K., et al. East Asia: Tradition & Transformation. 2nd ed. LC 77-77994. (Illus.). 1978. text ed. 25.50 (ISBN 0-395-25812-X). HM.

Fairbanks, Charles H. Florida Indians III. Horr, David A., ed. (American Indian Ethnohistory Ser.). 1978. lib. bdg. 42.00 o.s.i. (ISBN 0-8240-0759-X). Garland Pub.

Fairbanks, Henry G. Louise Imogen Guiney. (United States Authors Ser.). 1973. lib. bdg. 13.95 (ISBN 0-8057-0342-X, Twayne). G K Hall.

Fairbanks, Jonathan & Bates, Elizabeth B. American Furniture Sixteen Twenty to the Present. (Illus.). 576p. 1981. 50.00 (ISBN 0-399-90096-9, Marek). Putnam Pub Group.

Fairbanks, Jonathan L., intro. by. Copley, Stuart, West in America & England. (Illus.). 48p. 1976. pap. 5.95 (ISBN 0-87846-101-9). Mus Fine Arts Boston.

Fairbanks, Jonathan L., jt. auth. see Department of American Decorative Arts & Sculpture.

Fairbanks, LeBron. Philippians, Colossians, Experiencing His Peace. (Beacon Small-Group Bible Studies). 72p. 1982. pap. 2.25 (ISBN 0-8341-0778-3). Beacon Hill.

Fairbanks, Virgil. Current Hematology, Vol. 2. (Current Hematology Ser.). 480p. 1983. 55.00 (ISBN 0-471-09557-5, Pub. by Wiley Med). Wiley.

Fairbanks, Virgil F. Current Hematology, Vol. 1. 640p. 1981. 60.00 (ISBN 0-471-09504-4, Pub. by Wiley Med). Wiley.

Fairbridge, R. W. & Bourgeois, J., eds. The Encyclopedia of Sedimentology. LC 78-18259. (Encyclopedia of Earth Sciences Ser.: Vol. VI). 901p. 1978. 98.00 (ISBN 0-87933-152-6). Hutchinson Ross.

Fairbridge, R. W. & Finkl, C. W., Jr., eds. The Encyclopedia of Soil Science: Part 1, Physics, Chemistry, Biology, Fertility, & Technology. LC 78-31233. (Encyclopedia of Earth Sciences Ser.: Vol. XII). 700p. 1979. 76.00 (ISBN 0-87933-176-3). Hutchinson Ross.

Fairbridge, R. W. & Jablonski, D., eds. The Encyclopedia of Paleontology. LC 79-11468. (Encyclopedia of Earth Sciences Ser.: Vol. VII). 886p. 1979. 98.00 (ISBN 0-87933-185-2). Hutchinson Ross.

Fairbridge, Rhodes W., jt. auth. see Michel, Jean-Pierre.

Fairbrook, Paul. College & University Food Service Manual. LC 79-50956. (Illus.). 1979. pap. 17.50x (ISBN 0-9602456-0-X). Colman Pubs.

Fairchild Book Division Research Staff. Electronic News Financial Fact Book & Directory: 1981. 20th ed. 578p. 1981. pap. 90.00 o.s.i. (ISBN 0-87005-383-3). Fairchild.

--Electronic News Financial Fact Book & Directory: 1980. (Illus.). 640p. 1980. pap. text ed. 90.00 o.s.i. (ISBN 0-87005-360-4). Fairchild.

--Electronic News Financial Fact Book & Directory: 1979. (Illus.). 616p. 1979. pap. text ed. 80.00 o.s.i. (ISBN 0-87005-308-6). Fairchild.

--Electronic News Financial Fact Book & Directory: 1978. 670p. 1978. pap. 80.00 o.p. (ISBN 0-87005-235-7). Fairchild.

--Fairchild's Financial Manual of Retail Stores: 1980. (Illus.). 324p. 1980. pap. text ed. 50.00 (ISBN 0-87005-362-0). Fairchild.

--Fairchild's Financial Manual of Retail Stores: 1979. (Illus.). 1979. pap. text ed. 40.00 o.p. (ISBN 0-87005-310-8). Fairchild.

--Fairchild's Financial Manual of Retail Stores. 400p. 1978. pap. 45.00 o.p. (ISBN 0-87005-236-5). Fairchild.

--Fairchild's Textile & Apparel Financial Directory. 300p. 1978. pap. 40.00 o.p. (ISBN 0-87005-237-3). Fairchild.

--Fairchild's Textile & Apparel Financial Directory: 1980. 260p. 1980. text ed. 45.00 (ISBN 0-87005-361-2). Fairchild.

--Fairchild's Textile & Apparel Financial Directory: 1979. (Illus.). 230p. 1979. pap. text ed. 40.00 o.p. (ISBN 0-87005-309-4). Fairchild.

--SN Distribution Study Grocery Store Sales - 1980. 1980. pap. text ed. 27.50 (ISBN 0-87005-313-2). Fairchild.

--SN Distribution Study of Grocery Store Sales - 1981. 250p. 1981. pap. 30.00 (ISBN 0-87005-370-1). Fairchild.

Fairchild Book Research Division. Electronic News Financial Fact Book & Directory: 1982. 580p. 1982. pap. 100.00 (ISBN 0-87005-414-7). Fairchild.

Fairchild Books Special Projects Division. SN Distribution Study of Grocery Store Sales 1983. (Illus.). 300p. 1983. pap. 35.00 (ISBN 0-87005-444-9). Fairchild.

Fairchild, David. Logic: A First Course. 201p. 1977. pap. text ed. 10.00 (ISBN 0-8191-0117-6). U Pr of Amer.

Fairchild, Effie L. & Neal, Larry L., eds. Common-Unity in the Community: A Forward-Looking Program of Recreation & Leisure Service for the Handicapped. 114p. 1975. pap. 4.50 (ISBN 0-686-84031-3). U OR Ctr Leisure.

Fairchild, Johnson E., ed. Personal Problems & Psychological Frontiers. 8.50x (ISBN 0-911378-18-9). Sheridan.

--Women, Society & Sex. 255p. 1952. 8.50x (ISBN 0-911378-28-6). Sheridan.

Fairchild, Johnson E. & Landman, David, eds. America Faces the Nuclear Age. 1961. 8.50 o.p. (ISBN 0-911378-01-4). Sheridan.

Fairchild Market Research Division. Department Store Sales. (Fairchild Fact File Ser.). 1979. pap. 12.50 o.p. (ISBN 0-87005-327-2). Fairchild.

--Department Store Sales, Pt. 1. (Fact File Ser). 1978. pap. 10.00 o.p. (ISBN 0-87005-220-9). Fairchild.

--Department Store Sales, Pt. 2. (Fact File Ser). 1978. pap. 10.00 o.p. (ISBN 0-87005-254-3). Fairchild.

--Department Store Sales, 1980. (Fairchild Fact Files Ser.). (Illus.). 80p. 1980. pap. 12.50 o.p. (ISBN 0-87005-355-8). Fairchild.

--Fashion Accessories. (Fact File Ser). (Orig.). 1979. pap. 12.50 o.p. (ISBN 0-87005-319-1). Fairchild.

--Fashions Accessories (Men's & Women's) (Fact File Ser.). (Illus.). 55p. 1983. pap. text ed. 12.50 (ISBN 0-87005-456-2). Fairchild.

--Floor Coverings. (Fact File Ser). 1978. pap. 10.00 o.p. (ISBN 0-87005-255-1). Fairchild.

--Footwear (Men's, Women's, Children's) Includes Detail Information on the FN Magazine Survey. special ed. (Fact File Ser.). (Illus.). 50p. 1983. pap. text ed. 15.00 (ISBN 0-87005-460-0). Fairchild.

--Home Electronics. (Fairchild Fact File Ser.). 1979. pap. 12.50 o.p. (ISBN 0-87005-320-5). Fairchild.

--Home Textiles. (Fairchild Fact Files Ser.). 90p. 1980. pap. 12.50 o.p. (ISBN 0-87005-353-1). Fairchild.

--Household Furniture & Bedding. (Fact File Ser.). (Illus.). 60p. 1980. pap. 12.50 o.p. (ISBN 0-87005-346-9). Fairchild.

--Household Furniture & Bedding. (Fact Files Ser). 1978. pap. 10.00 o.p. (ISBN 0-87005-222-5). Fairchild.

--Infants', Girls', & Boys' Wear. (Fairchild Fact File Ser.). 1979. pap. 12.50 o.p. (ISBN 0-87005-326-4). Fairchild.

--Infants', Girls', & Boys' Wear. (Fact File Ser.). (Orig.). 1977. pap. 9.50 o.p. (ISBN 0-87005-194-6). Fairchild.

--Infants' Toddlers' Girls' & Boys' (Fact File Ser.). (Illus.). 1983. pap. text ed. 12.50 (ISBN 0-87005-457-0). Fairchild.

--Major Appliances & Electric Housewares. (Fairchild Fact File Ser.). 1979. pap. 12.50 o.p. (ISBN 0-87005-324-8). Fairchild.

--Major Appliances & Electric Housewares. (Fact File Ser.). 1977. pap. 9.50 o.p. (ISBN 0-87005-192-X). Fairchild.

--Men's & Women's Hosiery & Legwear. (Fact File Ser). 1978. pap. 12.50 o.p. (ISBN 0-87005-223-3). Fairchild.

--Men's Clothing, Tailored Sportswear, Rainwear. (Fairchild Fact File Ser.). 1979. pap. 12.50 o.p. (ISBN 0-87005-325-6). Fairchild.

--Men's Clothing, Tailored Sportswear, Rainwear. (Fact File Ser). (Orig.). 1977. pap. 9.50 o.p. (ISBN 0-87005-193-8). Fairchild.

--Men's Furnishings & Work Wear. (Fairchild Fact Files Ser.). (Illus.). 56p. 1981. pap. text ed. 12.50 (ISBN 0-87005-455-4). Fairchild.

--Men's Furnishings, Career - Work Wear. (Fairchilds Fact File Ser.). 1979. pap. 12.50 o.p. (ISBN 0-87005-318-3). Fairchild.

--Men's Sportswear & Casual Wear. (Fact File Ser). 1978. pap. 10.00 o.p. (ISBN 0-87005-251-9). Fairchild.

--Men's Sportswear, Casual Wear, Jeans & Active Wear. (Fact File Ser.). (Illus.). 100p. 1980. pap. 12.50 o.p. (ISBN 0-87005-351-5). Fairchild.

--Men's, Women's & Children's Bodywear, Legwear-Hosiery. (Fact File Ser.). (Illus.). 100p. 1980. pap. 12.50 o.p. (ISBN 0-87005-348-5). Fairchild.

--Men's, Women's & Children's Footwear. (Fairchild Fact File Ser.). 1979. pap. 12.50 o.p. (ISBN 0-87005-322-1). Fairchild.

--Men's, Women's & Children's Footwear. (Fact File Ser.). 1978. pap. 9.50 o.s.i. (ISBN 0-87005-189-X). Fairchild.

--Men's, Women's & Children's Footwear, 1980. (Fact File Ser.). (Illus.). 100p. 1980. pap. 12.50 o.p. (ISBN 0-87005-349-3). Fairchild.

--Personal Electronics. special ed. (Fact File Ser.). (Illus.). 50p. 1983. pap. text ed. 15.00 (ISBN 0-87005-458-9). Fairchild.

--Textile - Apparel Industries. (Fairchild Fact File Ser.). 1979. pap. 12.50 o.p. (ISBN 0-87005-321-3). Fairchild.

--Textile-Apparel Industries. (Fact File Ser). 1977. pap. 9.50 o.p. (ISBN 0-87005-190-3). Fairchild.

--Toiletries, Beauty Aids & Cosmetics. (Fact File Ser). 35p. 1978. pap. 10.00 o.p. (ISBN 0-87005-221-7). Fairchild.

--Toiletries, Beauty Aids, Cosmetics, Fragrances. (Fact File Ser.). (Illus.). 100p. 1980. pap. 12.50 o.p. (ISBN 0-87005-347-7). Fairchild.

--Women's Coats, Suits, Rainwear, Furs. (Fairchild Fact File Ser.). 1979. pap. 12.50 o.p. (ISBN 0-87005-328-0). Fairchild.

--Womens' Coats, Suits, Rainwear, Furs. (Fact File Ser). (Orig.). 1977. pap. 9.50 o.p. (ISBN 0-87005-195-4). Fairchild.

--Women's Coats, Suits, Rainwear, Furs. (Fact File Ser.). (Illus.). 50p. 1983. pap. text ed. 12.50 (ISBN 0-87005-459-7). Fairchild.

--Women's Dresses. (Fact File Ser). 1978. pap. 12.50 o.p. (ISBN 0-87005-256-X). Fairchild.

--Women's Dresses. (Fairchild Fact Files). (Illus.). 50p. 1980. pap. 12.50 o.p. (ISBN 0-87005-356-6). Fairchild.

--Women's Inner Fashions: Lingerie, Loungewear, Foundations. (Fact File Ser). (Orig.). 1977. pap. 9.50 o.p. (ISBN 0-87005-191-1). Fairchild.

--Women's Inner Fashions: Nightwear & Daywear. (Fairchild Fact File Ser.). 1979. pap. 12.50 o.p. (ISBN 0-87005-323-X). Fairchild.

--Women's Sportswear, Separates, Jeans & Active Wear. (Fact File Ser.). (Illus.). 100p. 1980. pap. 12.50 o.p. (ISBN 0-87005-352-3). Fairchild.

--Women's Sportwear & Casual Wear. (Fact File Ser). 1978. pap. 12.50 o.p. (ISBN 0-87005-252-7). Fairchild.

Fairchild Research Staff. Fairchild's Market Directory of Women's & Children's Apparel. 2nd ed. 96p. 1979. pap. 9.50 (ISBN 0-87005-311-6). Fairchild.

Fairchild, Roy W. Christians in Families. (Orig.). 1964. pap. 2.49 (ISBN 0-8042-9612-X). John Knox.

Fairchild, Thomas N., et al. Kindergarten Primer. 1975. 3.75 o.p. (ISBN 0-89301-023-5). U Pr of Idaho.

Fairchild, William. Astrology for Dogs (& Owners) (Illus.). 95p. 1981. 8.95 o.p. (ISBN 0-241-10380-0, Pub. by Hamish Hamilton England). David & Charles.

--Catsigns: An Astrological Guide to Your Cat's Innerself. (Illus.). 1981. 5.95 (ISBN 0-517-54434-2, C N Potter Bks). Crown.

Faircloth, Marjorie A., jt. auth. see Faircloth, Samuel R.

Faircloth, Mary E., et al. Mosby's Review of Practical Nursing. 8th ed. LC 81-14105. (Illus.). 352p. 1982. pap. text ed. 13.95 (ISBN 0-8016-3538-1). Mosby.

Faircloth, Rudy & Carter, W. Horace. Ernie Pyle-Typewriter Soldier. (Illus.). 76p. (Orig.). 1982. pap. 1.95 o.p. (ISBN 0-937866-04-0). Atlantic Pub Co.

Faircloth, Samuel R. & Faircloth, Marjorie A. Phonetic Science: A Program of Instruction. (Illus.). 144p. 1973. pap. text ed. 15.95 (ISBN 0-13-664565-8). P-H.

Fairclough, A. Cornwall's Railway's: A Pictorial Survey. 96p. 1981. 35.00x (ISBN 0-686-97152-3, Pub. by D B Barton England). State Mutual Bk.

Fairclough, Chris. Take a Trip to England. (Take a Trip Ser.). (Illus.). 32p. (gr. 1-3). 1982. PLB 8.40 (ISBN 0-531-04416-5). Watts.

--Take a Trip to Holland. (Take a Trip Ser.). (Illus.). 32p. 1982. PLB 8.40 (ISBN 0-531-04417-3). Watts.

--Take a Trip to Italy. (Take a Trip to Ser.). (Illus.). 32p. (gr. 1-3). 1981. lib. bdg. 8.40 (ISBN 0-531-04319-3). Watts.

--Take a Trip to West Germany. (Take a Trip to Ser.). (Illus.). 32p. (gr. 1-3). 1981. lib. bdg. 8.40 (ISBN 0-531-04320-7). Watts.

Faire, Ulf De see De Faire, Ulf & Theorell, Tores.

Faire, Zabrina. Wicked Cousin. (Orig.). 1980. pap. 1.75 o.p. (ISBN 0-446-94104-2). Warner Bks.

Faires, Barbara, jt. auth. see Faires, Douglas.

Faires, Douglas & Faires, Barbara. Calculus & Analytic Geometry. 1104p. 1982. text ed. write for info. (ISBN 0-87150-323-9, 33L 2571). Prindle.

Faires, Virgil M. Design of Machine Elements. 4th ed. 1965. text ed. 31.95 (ISBN 0-02-335950-1, 33595). Macmillan.

Faires, Virgil M. & Keown, Robert. Mechanism. 5th ed. 1960. text ed. 18.95 o.p. (ISBN 0-07-019899-3, C). McGraw.

Faires, Virgil M. & Keown, Robert M. Mechanism. 5th ed. LC 80-13135. 346p. 1980. Repr. of 1960 ed. lib. bdg. 19.50 (ISBN 0-89874-182-3). Krieger.

Faires, Virgil M. & Simmang, Clifford M. Problems on Thermodynamics. 6th ed. 1978. pap. 9.95x (ISBN 0-02-335230-2, 33523). Macmillan.

--Thermodynamics. 6th ed. (Illus.). 1978. text ed. 31.95x (ISBN 0-02-335530-1, 33553). Macmillan.

Faires, Virgil M. & Wingren, Roy M. Problems on the Design of Machine Elements. 4th ed. 1965. text ed. 8.95x (ISBN 0-02-335960-9, 33596). Macmillan.

Fairfax, Ann. Henrietta. (Orig.). 1979. pap. 1.75 o.s.i. (ISBN 0-515-05128-4). Jove Pubns.

--My Dear Duchess. 1979. pap. 1.75 o.s.i. (ISBN 0-515-05129-2). Jove Pubns.

Fairfax, Kate. Sweet Fire. 272p. pap. 2.95 (ISBN 0-441-79119-0). Ace Bks.

Fairfax, Lynn. Guarded Moments. (Second Chance at Love Ser.: No. 96). 192p. 1983. pap. 1.75 (ISBN 0-515-06860-8). Jove Pubns.

Fairfax, Sally K., jt. auth. see Dana, Samuel T.

Fairfield, Gail. Choice Centered Tarot. rev. ed. 160p. (Orig.). 1981. pap. 6.95 (ISBN 0-9609650-1-7). Choice Astro.

Fairfield, Roy P. Person-Centered Graduate Education. LC 77-77206. 270p. 1977. 15.95 (ISBN 0-87975-069-3). Prometheus Bks.

Fairholt, Frederick W. Costume in England, 2 vols. 4th ed. LC 68-21769. 1968. Repr. of 1885 ed. 42.00x (ISBN 0-8103-3506-9). Gale.

--Tobacco: Its History & Associations. LC 68-21770. 1968. Repr. of 1859 ed. 27.00 o.p. (ISBN 0-8103-3507-7). Gale.

Fairholt, Frederick W., ed. Dictionary of Terms in Art. LC 68-30630. (Illus.). 1969. Repr. of 1854 ed. 37.00x (ISBN 0-8103-3071-7). Gale.

Fairless, Michael. The Roadmender. 122p. 1982. 30.00x o.p. (ISBN 0-7045-0431-6, Pub. by Wildwood House). State Mutual Bk.

Fairley, Barker. A Study of Goethe. LC 76-56253. 1977. Repr. of 1947 ed. lib. bdg. 18.75x (ISBN 0-8371-9330-3, FASG). Greenwood.

Fairley, Barker, tr. see Goethe, Johann W.

Fairley, John, jt. auth. see Welfare, Simon.

Fairley, Michael. With Friends Like That. LC 80-22068. 1983. 15.95 (ISBN 0-87949-194-9). Ashley Bks.

Fairlie, Henry. The Seven Deadly Sins Today. LC 78-3646. (Illus.). 1978. 10.00 (ISBN 0-915220-41-5). New Republic.

Fairman, Charles & Morrison, Stanley. Fourteenth Amendment & the Bill of Rights: The Incorporation Theory. LC 71-25622. (American Constitutional & Legal History Ser). 1970. Repr. of 1949 ed. lib. bdg. 35.00 (ISBN 0-306-70029-8). Da Capo.

Fairman, H. W., ed. & tr. The Triumph of Horus: An Ancient Egyptian Sacred Drama. LC 73-84383. 1974. 27.50x (ISBN 0-520-02550-4). U of Cal Pr.

Fairman, Paula. Forbidden Destiny. 1977. pap. 1.95 o.p. (ISBN 0-685-79858-5, 40-105-1). Pinnacle Bks.

--The Fury & the Passion. (Orig.). 1979. pap. 2.95 (ISBN 0-523-41798-5). Pinnacle Bks.

--In Savage Splendor. 1978. pap. 2.25 o.p. (ISBN 0-523-40181-7). Pinnacle Bks.

--Jasmine Passion. 288p. (Orig.). 1981. pap. 2.95 (ISBN 0-523-41783-7). Pinnacle Bks.

--Passion's Promise. 352p. 1983. pap. 3.25 (ISBN 0-523-41750-0). Pinnacle Bks.
--Southern Rose. 384p. (Orig.). 1980. pap. 2.95 (ISBN 0-523-41800-0). Pinnacle Bks.
--Storm of Desire. 1979. pap. 2.95 (ISBN 0-523-41797-7). Pinnacle Bks.
--Wildest Passion. 304p. (Orig.). 1982. pap. 3.25 (ISBN 0-523-42034-X). Pinnacle Bks.
Fairmont Press. Economic Thickness for Industrial Insulation. (Illus.). 191p. 1983. text ed. 24.00 (ISBN 0-915586-72-X). Fairmont Pr.
--Process Energy Conservation Manual. 154p. 1983. text ed. 22.00 (ISBN 0-915586-73-8). Fairmont Pr.
Fairservis, Walter A., Jr. Asia: Traditions & Treasures. 1981. 50.00 o.p. (ISBN 0-8109-0695-3). Am Mus Natl Hist.
Fairservis, Walter A., Jr., ed. see Setti, Umm.
Fairthorne, S., jt. auth. see Meek, B. L.
Fairweather, Brenda C. & Haun, Donna H. Communication Systems for Severely Handicapped Persons: . (Illus.). 110p. 1983. text ed. 15.75x (ISBN 0-398-04809-6). C C Thomas.
Fairweather, D., ed. Some Metabolic Considerations of Oral Contraceptive Usage: Proceedings of the 2nd International Norgestral Symposium. (International Congress Ser.: No. 34). 1975. pap. 18.75 (ISBN 0-444-15159-1). Elsevier.
Fairweather, D. V. & Eskes, T. K. Amniotic Fluid: Research & Clinical Applications. 2nd ed. 1978. 110.25 (ISBN 90-219-2111-1). Elsevier.
Fairweather, George W., et al. Creating Change in Mental Health Organizations. 200p. 1974. text ed. 21.00 o.s.i. (ISBN 0-08-017833-2); pap. text ed. 10.75 (ISBN 0-08-017832-4). Pergamon.
Fairweather, Janet. Seneca the Elder. (Cambridge Classical Studies). 384p. 1981. 49.50 (ISBN 0-521-23101-9). Cambridge U Pr.
Fairweather, Owen. Practice & Procedure in Labor Arbitration. 2nd ed. 750p. 1983. 35.00 (ISBN 0-87179-365-2). BNA.
Fairweather, William. Background of the Epistles. 1977. 16.50 (ISBN 0-86524-118-X, 8002). Klock & Klock.
--Background of the Gospels. 1977. 17.00 (ISBN 0-86524-117-1, 8001). Klock & Klock.
Faison, Edmund W. Advertising: A Behavioral Approach for Managers. LC 79-21379. (Marketing Ser.). 783p. 1980. text ed. 28.95 (ISBN 0-471-04956-5); avail. tchrs. manual (ISBN 0-471-07768-2). Wiley.
Faison, S. L. Art Museums of New England: Connecticut & Rhode Island, Vol. 1. 160p. 1982. pap. 8.95 (ISBN 0-87923-373-7). Godine.
Faison, S. L., Jr. Art Museums of New England: Massachussettes, Vol. 2. 256p. 1982. pap. 9.95 (ISBN 0-87923-432-6). Godine.
--Art Museums of New England: New Hampshire, Vermont, Maine, Vol. 3. 128p. 1982. pap. 8.95 (ISBN 0-87923-433-4). Godine.
Faiss, Fritz W. Hackney Jade & the War Horse. LC 76-15322. (Illus.). 64p. 1977. ltd. ed. signed 18.50x (ISBN 0-916678-00-8); hand-colored, signed ltd. ed. 200.00x (ISBN 0-916678-01-6). Green Hut.
--Modern Art & Man's Search for the Self. (Illus.). 30p. 1974. pap. 9.00x ltd. ed. signed (ISBN 0-916678-12-1); pap. 75.00x hand-colored, signed ltd. ed. (ISBN 0-916678-13-X). Green Hut.
--Out of Loneliness. (Illus.). 71p. 1972. pap. 8.00x ltd ed, signed o.p. (ISBN 0-916678-05-9); pap. 10.00x ltd ed (ISBN 0-916678-06-7). Green Hut.
Faiss, Fritz W., ed. Lenticle: Two Radio Interviews with Fritz Faiss. (Illus.). 63p. 1972. deluxe ed. 50.00x ltd ed. signed o.p. (ISBN 0-916678-07-5); pap. 15.00x ltd ed., signed (ISBN 0-916678-08-3); pap. 9.00x single interview, ltd. ed., signed (ISBN 0-916678-09-1). Green Hut.
Faith, C., jt. auth. see Cozzens, J.
Faith, Nicholas. Safety in Numbers: The Mysterious World of Swiss Banking. LC 82-70121. 384p. 1982. 15.95 (ISBN 0-670-61463-7). Viking Pr.
Faith, William R. Bob Hope: A Life in Comedy. LC 81-22716. (Illus.). 467p. 1982. 15.95 (ISBN 0-399-12627-9). Putnam Pub Group.
Faithorne, W. Art of Graveing & Etching. Mayor, A. Hyatt, ed. LC 68-54841. (Graphic Art Ser.: Vol. 9). 1970. Repr. of 1662 ed. lib. bdg. 25.00 o.p. (ISBN 0-306-71049-8). Da Capo.
Faizi, Gloria. The Baha'i Faith: An Introduction. rev. ed. LC 72-84825. 1972. pap. 1.95 (ISBN 0-87743-051-9, 231-059). Baha'i.
Fajardo, Luis F. Pathology of Radiation Injury. LC 82-15373. (Masson Monographs in Diagnostic Pathology: Vol. 6). (Illus.). 300p. 1982. 66.50 (ISBN 0-89352-182-5). Masson Pub.
Fajardo, Roque. Helping Your Alcoholic Before He or She Hits Bottom. 9.95 o.p. (ISBN 0-686-92097-X). Hazelden.
Fajardo, Salvador J. & Wilcox, John, eds. At Home & Beyond: New Essays on Spanish Poets of the Twenties. LC 82-60341. 150p. (Orig.). 1983. pap. 18.00 (ISBN 0-89295-022-6). Society Sp & Sp-Am.
Fakhry, Majid. A History of Islamic Philosophy. 2nd ed. 450p. 1982. text ed. 27.50x (ISBN 0-231-05532-3). Columbia U Pr.
Fakhry, Tamir. The Gospel Unified. 1983. 11.00 (ISBN 0-533-05126-6). Vantage.
Fakkema, Robert, jt. auth. see Bannerman, Glenn.
Falace, jt. auth. see Little, James W.
Falassi, Alessandro, jt. auth. see Dundes, Alan.
Falassi, Allesandro, jt. auth. see Dundes, Alan.
Falb, Lewis. American Drama in Paris, 1945-1970: A Study of its Critical Reception. (Studies in Comparative Literature Ser.: No. 54). ix, 181p. 1973. 13.00x (ISBN 0-8078-7054-4). U of NC Pr.
Falb, Lewis W. Jean Anouilh. LC 72-79928. (Literature and Life Ser.). 140p. 1977. 11.95 (ISBN 0-8044-2189-7). Ungar.
Falb, P., jt. auth. see Athans, Michael.
Falbe, Jurgen. Chemical Feedstocks from Coal. LC 81-3022. 647p. 1982. 91.00 (ISBN 0-471-05291-4, Pub. by Wiley-Interscience). Wiley.
Falcaro, Joe & Goodman, M. Bowling for All. 3rd ed. (Illus.). 123p. 1966. 14.95x (ISBN 0-471-07141-2). Wiley.
Falck, Robert & Rice, Timothy, eds. Cross-Cultural Perspectives on Music. 288p. 1982. 27.50x (ISBN 0-8020-5510-9). U of Toronto Pr.
Falco, Maria J. Bigotry: Ethnic, Machine, & Sexual Politics in a Senatorial Election. LC 79-7468. (Contributions in Political Science: No. 34). 1980. lib. bdg. 27.50 (ISBN 0-313-20726-7, FBI/). Greenwood.
--Truth & Meaning in Political Science: An Introduction to Political Inquiry. LC 73-75328. 1973. pap. text ed. 7.50 o.p. (ISBN 0-675-08934-4). Merrill.
--Truth & Meaning in Political Science: An Introduction to Political Inquiry. 2nd ed. LC 82-25095. 160p. 1983. pap. text ed. 9.75 (ISBN 0-8191-3048-6). U Pr of Amer.
Falco, Maria J., ed. Through the Looking Glass: Epistemology & the Conduct of Inquiry, an Anthology. LC 79-66471. 1979. pap. text ed. 15.50 (ISBN 0-8191-0841-3). U Pr of Amer.
Falcon Press Staff. Hi Mom. 64p. 1982. pap. 3.95 (ISBN 0-941404-24-2). Falcon Pr Az.
Falcon, William D., jt. auth. see Cannavale, Frank J.
Falconer, Douglas S. Introduction to Quantitative Genetics. (Illus.). 1960. 22.50 o.p. (ISBN 0-471-06771-7). Wiley.
Falconer, Mary W. Patient Studies in Pharmacology: A Guidebook. LC 75-44608. 160p. 1976. pap. text ed. 7.00 o.p. (ISBN 0-7216-3545-8). Saunders.
Falconer, Mary W., et al. The Drug, the Nurse, the Patient. 6th ed. LC 77-84669. (Illus.). 1978. text ed. 19.95 o.p. (ISBN 0-7216-3549-0). Saunders.
Falconer, Peter & Drury, Jolyon. Building & Planning for Industrial Storage & Distribution. LC 75-28387. 1975. 54.95x o.p. (ISBN 0-470-25355-X). Halsted Pr.
Falconnet, Paulette, jt. auth. see D'Assaily, Gisele.
Faldi, Italo. Pittori Viterbesi Di Cinque Secoli. LC 77-106770. (Illus., It.). 1970. 69.50x (ISBN 0-271-00119-4). Pa St U Pr.
Faler, Paul G. Mechanics & Manufacturers in the Early Industrial Revolution: Lynn, Massachusetts 1780-1860. LC 80-21619. (American Social History Ser.). 310p. 1981. 39.50x (ISBN 0-87395-504-8); pap. 10.95x (ISBN 0-87395-505-6). State U NY Pr.
Fales, Frederick F. Spanish Grammar. (College Outlines Ser.). pap. 4.95 o.p. (ISBN -0671-08033-4). Monarch Pr.
Fales, Frederick F., jt. auth. see Nebel, Cecile.
Fales, James, et al. Manufacturing: A Basic Text for Industrial Arts. (Illus.). 1980. 17.96 (ISBN 0-87345-586-X, B82088); instr's guide 5.68 (ISBN 0-87345-587-8); activities 6.00 (ISBN 0-87345-588-6). McKnight.
Fales, John T. Functional Housekeeping in Hotels & Motels. LC 72-142508. 1971. text ed. 17.50 (ISBN 0-672-96080-X); tchr's manual 6.67 (ISBN 0-672-96082-6); wkbk. 7.95 (ISBN 0-672-96081-8). Bobbs.
Faletto, Enzo, jt. auth. see Cardoso, Fernando E.
Falicov, L. M., et al, eds. Valence Fluctuations in Solids. 1981. 70.25 (ISBN 0-444-86204-8). Elsevier.
Falk, Byron A. & Falk, Valerie R. Personal Name Index to the New York Times Index: Eighteen Fifty-One to Nineteen Seventy-Four, Vol. 21. 421p. 1982. lib. bdg. 61.00 (ISBN 0-89902-121-2). Roxbury Data.
Falk, Cathy. God's Care. Bennett, Marian, ed. (Bible Activities for Little People Ser.: Bk. 1). 24p. (Orig.). (ps-k). 1983. pap. 1.25 (ISBN 0-87239-676-2, 2451). Standard Pub.
--God's Friends. Bennett, Marian, ed. (Bible Activities for Little People Ser.: BK. 2). 24p. (Orig.). (ps-k). 1983. pap. 1.29 (ISBN 0-87239-677-0, 2452). Standard Pub.
--God's Son. Bennett, Marian, ed. (Bible Activities for Little People Ser.: Bk. 3). 24p. (Orig.). (ps-k). 1983. pap. 1.29 (ISBN 0-87239-678-9, 2453). Standard Pub.
--We Love God. Bennett, Marian, ed. (Bible Lessons for Little People Ser.: Bk. 2). 144p. (Orig.). (ps-k). 1983. pap. 6.95 (ISBN 0-87239-613-4, 3360). Standard Pub.
--We Please God. Bennett, Marian, ed. (Bible Activities Ser.: Bk. 4). 24p. (Orig.). (ps-k). 1983. pap. 1.29 (ISBN 0-87239-679-7, 2454). Standard Pub.
--Year-Round Preschool Activity Patterns. Bennett, Marian, ed. 48p. (Orig.). (ps-k). 1983. pap. 4.50 (ISBN 0-87239-680-0, 2141). Standard Pub.
Falk, Doris V. Lillian Hellman. LC 78-4299. (Literature and Life Ser.). 1978. 11.95 (ISBN 0-8044-2194-3); pap. 4.95 (ISBN 0-8044-6144-9). Ungar.
Falk, Edwin A. From Perry to Pearl Harbor: The Struggle for Supremacy in the Pacific. LC 73-21285. (Illus.). 362p. 1974. Repr. of 1943 ed. lib. bdg. 20.00x (ISBN 0-8371-6161-4, FAPP). Greenwood.
Falk, Edwin A. & Abel, Charles. Practical Portrait Photography for Home & Studio. (Illus.). 1967. 13.95 o.p. (ISBN 0-8174-0489-9, Amphoto). Watson-Guptill.
Falk, Isidore Sydney. Security Against Sickness: A Study of Health Insurance. LC 79-38822. (FDR & the Era of the New Deal Ser.). 424p. 1972. Repr. of 1936 ed. lib. bdg. 49.50 (ISBN 0-306-70447-1). Da Capo.
Falk, Julia S. Linguistics & Language: A Survey of Basic Concepts & Implications. 2nd ed. LC 77-22927. 1978. pap. text ed. 20.95x (ISBN 0-673-15670-2). Scott F.
Falk, Kathryn. The Complete Doll House Building Book. LC 81-66315. 1981. 16.95 (ISBN 0-672-52339-6); pap. 9.95 (ISBN 0-672-52694-8). Bobbs.
--How to Write a Romance & Get it Published: With Intimate Advice form the World's Most Popular Romance Writers. 1983. 14.95 (ISBN 0-517-54944-1). Crown.
Falk, Mervyn L., jt. auth. see Wicka, Donna K.
Falk, Nicholas & Lee, James. Planning the Social Services. 1978. 19.95 o.p. (ISBN 0-347-01135-7, 00559-2, Pub. by Saxon Hse England). Lexington Bks.
Falk, R. A. Aftermath of Sabbatino. LC 65-19486. (Hammarskjold Forum Ser.: No. 7). 228p. 1965. 12.50 (ISBN 0-379-11807-6); pap. o.p. Oceana.
Falk, Richard. The End of World Order. 340p. 1982. 39.50 (ISBN 0-8419-0739-0). Holmes & Meier.
Falk, Richard, jt. auth. see Lifton, Robert J.
Falk, Richard & Kratochwil, Friedrich V., eds. International Law & a Just World Order, Vol. 2. (Studies on a Just World Order). 500p. 1983. lib. bdg. 36.50X o.p. (ISBN 0-86531-241-9); pap. text ed. 15.00X o.p. (ISBN 0-86531-252-4). Westview.
Falk, Richard A. A World Order Perspective on Authoritarian Tendencies. 67p. 1980. pap. 1.50 (ISBN 0-686-64552-9). Transaction Bks.
Falk, Richard A. & Kim, Samuel S., eds. The War System: An Interdisciplinary Approach. LC 79-19566. (Westview Special Studies in Peace, Conflict, & Conflict Resolution). 500p. 1980. lib. bdg. 37.00 (ISBN 0-89158-569-9); pap. text ed. 15.00 (ISBN 0-86531-042-4). Westview.
Falk, Robert, jt. auth. see Radin, Sheldon.
Falk, Robert, ed. Literature & Ideas in America: Essays in Memory of Harry Hayden Clark. LC 74-27708. xi, 243p. 1975. 15.00x (ISBN 0-8214-0180-7, 82-81784). Ohio U Pr.
Falk, S. Uno & Salkind, A. J. Alkaline Storage Batteries. LC 77-82980. (Electrochemical Society Ser.). 1969. 72.50x (ISBN 0-471-25362-6, Pub. by Wiley-Interscience). Wiley.
Falk, Signi L. Tennessee Williams. 2nd ed. (United States Authors Ser.). 1978. lib. bdg. 10.95 (ISBN 0-8057-7202-2, Twayne). G K Hall.
Falk, Valerie R., jt. auth. see Falk, Byron A.
Falkbeer, Ernest, tr. see Lange, Max.
Falkenberg, P. Die Rhodomelaceen Des Golfes Von Neapel und der Angrenzenden Meenesabschnitte. (Fauna & Flor d. Golfes v. Neapel). (Illus., Ger.). 1979. Repr. of 1901 ed. lib. bdg. 130.00x (ISBN 3-87429-143-X). Lubrecht & Cramer.
Falkenmark, Malin & Lindh, Gunnar. Water for a Starving World. LC 76-45475. 1977. lib. bdg. 19.75 o.p. (ISBN 0-89158-211-8); pap. 8.50 o.p. (ISBN 0-89158-212-6). Westview.
Falkin, Gregory R. Reducing Delinquency. (Illus.). 240p. 1979. 23.95 (ISBN 0-669-02318-3). Lexington Bks.
Falkner, Frank & Macy, Christopher. Pregnancy & Birth: Pleasure & Problems. (Life Cycle Ser.). 1980. pap. text ed. 4.95 scp o.p. (ISBN 0-06-384741-8, HarpC). Har-Row.
Falkner, Meade see Bleiler, E. F.
Falkow, S. Infectious Multiple Drug Resistance. (Advanced Biochemistry Ser.). 300p. 1975. 26.50x (ISBN 0-85086-049-0, Pub. by Pion England). Methuen Inc.
Falkowski, Lawrence. Presidents, Secretaries of State & Crisis Management in U.S. Foreign Relations: A Model & Predictive Analysis. LC 77-27049. (Westview Special Studies in International Relations & U.S. Foreign Policy Ser.). (Illus.). 1978. lib. bdg. 25.00 (ISBN 0-89158-072-7); pap. text ed. 10.00 (ISBN 0-89158-073-5). Westview.
Falkowski, Lawrence S., ed. Psychological Models in International Politics. (Special Studies in International Relations). 1979. lib. bdg. 30.00 (ISBN 0-89158-377-7); pap. text ed. 13.00 (ISBN 0-86531-043-2). Westview.
Falkson, Joseph L. HMOs & the Politics of Health System Reform. LC 79-21932. 224p. (Orig.). 1980. casebound 15.00 (ISBN 0-87258-288-4, AHA-073183); pap. 12.50 (ISBN 0-87258-276-0, AHA-073182). Am Hospital.
Falkus, Christopher. The Life & Times of Charles II. (Kings & Queens of England Ser.). (Illus.). 224p. 1973. text ed. 17.50x (ISBN 0-297-99427-1, Pub. by Weidenfeld & Nicolson England). Biblio Dist.
Falkus, Hugh. Master of Cape Horn: W. A. Nelson 1839-1929. (Illus.). 196p. 1982. 32.50 (ISBN 0-575-03089-5, Pub. by Gollancz England). David & Charles.
Falkus, Hugh & Kerr, Joan. From Sydney Cove to Duntroon: An Australian Family Album. (Illus.). 128p. 1982. 24.95 (ISBN 0-575-03039-9, Pub. by Gollancz England). David & Charles.
Fall, Bernard B. Last Reflections on a War. Fall, Dorothy, ed. LC 67-28638. 288p. 1972. pap. 3.95 o.p. (ISBN 0-8052-0329-X). Schocken.
Fall, Dorothy, ed. see Fall, Bernard B.
Fall, S. M. & Lynden-Bell, D., eds. The Structure & Evolution of Normal Galaxies. LC 80-42026. (Illus.). 280p. 1981. 35.00 (ISBN 0-521-23907-9). Cambridge U Pr.
Fall, Thomas. Jim Thorpe. LC 72-94793. (Crocodile Paperback Ser.). (Illus.). (gr. 2-5). 1970. pap. 2.95 (ISBN 0-690-46219-0, TYC-J); lib. bdg. 10.89 (ISBN 0-690-46218-2). Har-Row.
Falla & Sibson. A New Guide to the Birds of New Zealand. 39.95 (ISBN 0-686-42760-2, Collins Pub England). Greene.
Falla, R. A. & Sibson, R. B. The New Guide to the Birds of New Zealand. (Illus.). 247p. 1983. 17.95 (ISBN 0-00-216928-2, Pub. by W Collins Australia). Intl Schol Bk Serv.
Fallaci, Oriana. Interview with History. 1977. pap. 7.95 (ISBN 0-395-25223-7). HM.
--Letter to a Child Never Born. 1982. pap. 2.95 (ISBN 0-671-45162-6). WSP.
--A Man: A Novel. 1980. 16.95 o.p. (ISBN 0-671-25241-0). S&S.
Fallen, Nancy & McGovern, Jill. Young Children with Special Needs. (Special Education Ser.). 1978. text ed. 20.95 (ISBN 0-675-08382-6). study guide 3.95 (ISBN 0-675-08383-4). Merrill.
Fallen-Bailey, Darrel G. & Byer, Trevor A. Energy Options & Policy Issues in Developing Countries. (Working Paper: No.350). vi, 107p. 1979. 5.00 (ISBN 0-686-36157-1, WP-0350). World Bank.
Faller, Kathleen C. Social Work with Abused & Neglected Children. 256p. 1981. text ed. 16.95. Free Pr.
Faller, Rosalie. Polli & Woggy Capers: The Polka Dot Frogs. 1979. 4.50 o.p. (ISBN 0-533-03845-6). Vantage.
Fallet, E. M. La Vie Musicale au Pays de Neuchatel du XIIIe a la fin du XVIIIe siecle: Contribution a l'histoire de la Musique en Suisse. (Sammlung Mw. Abh. 20-1936 Ser.). xx, 322p. 47.50 o.s.i. (ISBN 90-6027-222-6, Pub. by Frits Knuf Netherlads). Pendragon NY.
Fallig, Ralph L. Practical Guide to Bookkeeping & Accounting. 1972. pap. 2.95 (ISBN 0-448-01504-8, G&D). Putnam Pub Group.
Fallis, A. M., ed. Ecology & Physiology of Parasites: A Symposium. LC 70-151365. 1971. 30.00x o.p. (ISBN 0-8020-1730-4). U of Toronto Pr.
Fallis, William J. Points for Emphasis, 1983-1984. (Orig.). 1983. pap. 2.50 (ISBN 0-8054-1475-4); pap. 3.25 large type ed. (ISBN 0-8054-1476-2). Broadman.
Fallon. Electric Wiring: Domestic. 8th ed. 1983. text ed. price not set (ISBN 0-408-00392-8). Butterworth.
Fallon, Ann C. Katharine Tynan. (English Authors Ser.). 1979. 14.95 (ISBN 0-8057-6754-1, Twayne). G K Hall.
Fallon, Beth C. Training Leaders for Family Life Education. LC 82-10200. (Workshop Models for Family Life Education Ser.). 124p. 1982. plastic comb 12.95 (ISBN 0-87304-188-7). Family Serv.
Fallon, Daniel. The German University: A Heroic Ideal in Conflict with the Modern World. LC 80-66184. 120p. 1980. 9.50x (ISBN 0-87081-088-X). Colo Assoc.
Fallon, Jack. All About Surf Fishing. (Illus.). 288p. pap. 5.95 o.p. (ISBN 0-88317-029-9). Stoeger Pub Co.
Fallon, John F. & Caplan, Arnold I., eds. Limb Development & Regeneration, Pt. A. LC 82-20391. (Progress in Clinical & Biological Research Ser.: Vol. 110A). 639p. 1982. 68.00 (ISBN 0-8451-0170-6). A R Liss.
Fallon, Padraic. Poems & Versions. 96p. 1982. pap. text ed. 8.50x (ISBN 0-85635-431-7, 51363, Pub. by Carcanet Pr England). Humanities.
Fallon, William K. AMA Management Handbook. 2nd ed. 1872p. 1983. 69.95 (ISBN 0-8144-0100-7). Am Mgmt.
Fallows, Marjorie R. Irish Americans: Identity & Assimilation. (Ethnic Groups in American Life Ser.). 1979. ref. ed. 12.95 (ISBN 0-13-506261-6); pap. text ed. 10.95 (ISBN 0-13-506253-5). P-H.
Falls, C. B. ABC Book. (ps). 1957. 8.95a (ISBN 0-385-07663-0); PLB (ISBN 0-385-07698-3); pap. 1.95 (ISBN 0-385-08097-2, Zephyr). Doubleday.
Falls, Leota K. The Birthright with Love. LC 78-65168. (Illus.). 1978. 9.95 (ISBN 0-87716-096-1, Pub. by Moore Pub Co). F Apple.
Falls, William R. Investigations in the College Physical Sciences. 1977. pap. text ed. 8.95 (ISBN 0-8403-1752-2). Kendall-Hunt.
Falls, William R., jt. auth. see Payne, Charles A.
Falmagne, Rachel J., ed. Reasoning: Representation & Process in Children & Adults. 275p. 1975. 18.00x o.s.i. (ISBN 0-470-25369-X). Halsted Pr.
Falstein, L. D. Basic Mathematics for College Students (You Can Count on Yourself) 1982. pap. text ed. 20.95 (ISBN 0-201-13361-X); test bklt 4.00 (ISBN 0-201-13362-8). A-W.

Falster, P. & Rolstadas, A., eds. Production Management Systems. 1981. 32.00 (ISBN 0-444-86176-9). Elsevier.

Falusi, A. O. & Williams, L. B. Nigeria Fertilizer Sector Present Situation & Future Prospects. (Technical Bulletin Ser.: T-18). (Illus.). 93p. (Orig.). 1981. pap. 4.00 (ISBN 0-88090-017-2). Intl Fertilizer.

Falzone, Mary G. Elder Tastes. 1983. 5.95 (ISBN 0-533-05094-4). Vantage.

Falzone, Vincent J. Terence V. Powderly: Middle Class Reformer. 1978. pap. text ed. 9.75x o.p. (ISBN 0-8191-0393-4). U Pr of Amer.

Family Law Reporter Editorial Staff. Desk Guide to the Uniform Marriage & Divorce Act. 106p. 1982. pap. text ed. 10.00 (ISBN 0-87179-378-4). BNA.

Family Service Association of America. Using Results of a Time Analysis, Vol. 4. (Time & Cost Analysis Ser.). 1969. pap. 5.50 o.p. (ISBN 0-87304-076-7). Family Serv.

Family Welfare Association. Guide to the Social Services (U.K.) 1982. 70th ed. LC 55-33805. 326p. (Orig.). 1982. pap. 16.50x (ISBN 0-900954-15-9). Intl Pubns Serv.

Famularo, Joseph J. Handbook of Modern Personnel Administration. (Illus.). 1280p. 1972. 59.95 (ISBN 0-07-019912-4, P&RB). McGraw.

Fanaroff, Avroy & Martin, Richard J. Behrman's Neonatal-Perinatal Medicine: Diseases of the Fetus & Infant. 3rd ed. LC 82-6371. (Illus.). 1216p. 1983. text ed. 69.95 (ISBN 0-8016-0580-6). Mosby.

Fanburg. Sacoidosis & Other Granulatons Diseases of the Lung. (Lung & Biology in Health & Disease Ser.: Vol. 19). 544p. 1983. 59.75 (ISBN 0-8247-1866-6). Dekker.

Fancher, Raymond E. Pioneers of Psychology. 1979. 15.95x o.p. (ISBN 0-393-01161-5); instrs' manual avail. (ISBN 0-393-95076-X). Norton.

Fancher, Terry & Shay, Arthur. Forty Common Errors in Racquetball & How to Correct Them. LC 77-23707. 1978. 9.95 o.p. (ISBN 0-8092-7704-2); pap. 7.95 (ISBN 0-8092-7703-4). Contemp Bks.

Fandel, G. & Gal, T., eds. Multiple Criteria Decision Making: Theory & Application. Proceedings. (Lecture Notes in Economics & Mathematical Systems: Vol. 177). (Illus.). 570p. 1980. 48.00 (ISBN 0-387-09963-8). Springer-Verlag.

Fandozzi, Phillip R. Nihilism & Technology: A Heideggerian Investigation. LC 82-17337. 158p. (Orig.). 1983. lib. bdg. 19.25 (ISBN 0-8191-2825-2); pap. text ed. 8.75 (ISBN 0-8191-2826-0). U Pr of Amer.

Fane, Julian. Gentleman's Gentleman. 148p. 1981. 17.50 (ISBN 0-241-10434-3, Pub. by Hamish Hamilton England). David & Charles.

Fanelli. Brunelleschi. pap. 12.50 (ISBN 0-935748-01-6). ScalaBooks.

Fanelli, Maresa. Aujourd'hui. 2nd ed. 1980. text ed. 19.95 (ISBN 0-669-02503-8); wkbk. 7.95 (ISBN 0-669-02504-6); tapes-reels 75.00 (ISBN 0-669-02506-2); cassettes cancelled (ISBN 0-669-02507-0); demo tape (ISBN 0-669-02508-9); tapescript (ISBN 0-669-02505-4). Heath.

Fang. Modern Publishing & Librarianship. 1983. write for info. (Pub. by K G Saur). Shoe String.

Fang, Chaoying. The Asami Library: A Descriptive Catalogue. Huff, Elizabeth, ed. LC 69-16505. (Illus.). 1969. 48.50x (ISBN 0-520-01521-5). U of Cal Pr.

Fang, Fu-An. Chinese Labour: An Economic & Statistical Survey of the Labour Conditions & Labour Movements in China. LC 78-22780. (The Modern Chinese Economy Ser.: Vol. 34). 185p. 1980. lib. bdg. 20.00 o.s.i. (ISBN 0-8240-4282-4). Garland Pub.

Fang, L. S. Manual of Clinical Nephrology. 231p. 1982. 13.95 (ISBN 0-07-019901-9). McGraw-Pretest.

Fanger, P. O. Thermal Comfort. 256p. 1973. text ed. 27.00 o.p. (ISBN 0-07-019915-9, C). McGraw.

Fang-Kuei, Li see Li, Fang-Kuei.

Fang Yu-Wang, Fred. Character Text for Chinese Dialogues. 4.75 (ISBN 0-686-11095-1); tapes avail. (ISBN 0-686-11096-X). Far Eastern Pubns.

Fann, K. T. Wittgenstein's Conception of Philosophy. LC 65-24178. 1969. 15.95x o.p. (ISBN 0-520-01615-7); pap. 6.50x (ISBN 0-520-01837-0, CAMPUS 171). U of Cal Pr.

Fann, K. T., ed. Symposium on J. L. Austin. (International Library of Philosophy & Scientific Method). (Illus.). 1979. Repr. of 1969 ed. text ed. 25.00x o.p. (ISBN 0-391-00981-8); pap. text ed. 32.50x o.p. (ISBN 0-391-00981-8). Humanities.

Fann, K. T. & Hodges, Donald C., eds. Readings in U. S. Imperialism. LC 78-133507. (Extending Horizons Ser). 1971. pap. 4.95 o.p. (ISBN 0-87558-054-8). Porter Sargent.

Fann, W. E., jt. ed. see Eisdorfer, C.

Fann, William, et al, eds. Phenomonology & Treatment of Psychosexual Disorders. 192p. 1983. text ed. 25.00 (ISBN 0-89335-184-9). SP Med & Sci Bks.

Fann, William E. & Maddox, George. Drug Issues in Geropsychiatry. 125p. 1974. pap. 9.50 o.p. (ISBN 0-683-03002-7). Williams & Wilkins.

Fann, William E., jt. ed. see Eisdorfer, Carl.

Fannin, Allen. Handloom Weaving Technology. 1979. 26.50 o.p. (ISBN 0-442-22370-6). Van Nos Reinhold.

Fannin County Historical Commission. Tempting Traditions. Jones, Barbara C., ed. 280p. (Orig.). 1982. pap. 11.95 (ISBN 0-686-38456-3). Fannin County.

Fannin, James. Tennis & Kids-The Family Connection: The S.C.O.R.E. - Self-Discipline, Concentration, Optimism, Relaxation, Enjoyment--Way to Great Tennis That the Pros Use. LC 78-22317. (Illus.). 1979. 8.95 (ISBN 0-385-14378-8). Doubleday.

Fanning, Anthony E. Planets, Stars & Galaxies: Descriptive Astronomy for Beginners. (Illus.). 9.00 (ISBN 0-8446-2042-4). Peter Smith.

Fanning, David. Marketing Company Shares. 270p. 1982. text ed. 42.00x (ISBN 0-566-02174-9). Gower Pub Ltd.

--The Narrative of Colonel David Fanning (a Tory in the Revolutionary War with Great Britain) LC 73-2736. 112p. 1973. Repr. of 1865 ed. 10.50 o.p. (ISBN 0-87152-132-6). Reprint.

Fanning, Kent A. & Manheim, Frank T. The Dynamic Environment of the Ocean Floor. LC 78-24651. 512p. 1981. 41.95x (ISBN 0-669-02809-6). Lexington Bks.

Fanning, Melody S., jt. auth. see Dunton, Sabina M.

Fanning, Ralph & Myron, Robert. Italian Renaissance. (Pitman Art Ser.: Vol. 53). pap. 1.50 o.p. (ISBN 0-448-00562-X, G&D). Putnam Pub Group.

Fanning, Robbie. One Hundred Butterflies. LC 79-14776. (gr. 4-6). 1979. 8.95 (ISBN 0-664-32654-4). Westminster.

Fanqin, Yu, tr. see Lanyun, Liu.

Fanshawe, Elizabeth. Rachel. 28p. (ps-2). 1983. bds. 3.95 (ISBN 0-370-10783-7, Pub by The Bodley Head). Merrimack Bk Serv.

Fanshawe, Richard, tr. see Guarini, Battista.

Fanshel, David. On the Road to Permanency: An Expanded Data Base for Service to Children in Foster Care. (Orig.). 1982. pap. text ed. 18.95 (ISBN 0-87868-141-8, AM-34). Child Welfare.

Fanshel, David, ed. Future of Social Work Research. LC 79-92733. 198p. 1980. pap. 12.95 (ISBN 0-87101-084-4, CBQ-084-C). Natl Assn Soc Wkrs.

Fanshell, D., jt. auth. see Labov, W.

Fant, Clyde. Preaching for Today. 1977. pap. 6.98i (ISBN 0-06-062332-2, RD-204, HarpR). Har-Row.

Fant, David J., Jr. A. W. Tozer: A Twentieth Century Prophet. LC 64-21945. (Illus.). 180p. 1964. pap. 4.50 (ISBN 0-87509-048-6). Chr Pubns.

Fant, Gunnar. Speech Sounds & Features. (Current Studies in Linguistics Ser: No. 4). 224p. 1974. 20.00x (ISBN 0-262-06051-5). MIT Pr.

Fant, Gunnar, ed. Speech Communication, 4 Vols. Incl. Vol. 1: Speech Wave Processing & Transmission. 058p (ISBN 0-470-25425-4); Vol. 2: Speech Production & Synthesis by Rules. 332p (ISBN 0-470-25426-2); Vol. 3: Speech Perception & Automatic Recognition. 425p (ISBN 0-470-25427-0); Speech & Hearing Defects & Aids, Language Acquisition. 157p (ISBN 0-470-25428-9). 1976. Set. 160.50 (ISBN 0-470-25429-7). Krieger.

Fant, Jesse E., et al. Report Four-Metes & Bounds Descriptions. rev. ed. (Illus.). 161p. (Orig.). 1980. 21.10 (ISBN 0-87518-207-0). Fant-Freeman-Madson.

Fanta, Ladd & Lewis, Jack. Airgun Digest. (DBI Bks). 1977. pap. 6.95 o.s.i. (ISBN 0-695-80764-1). Follett.

Fante, John. Wait Until Spring, Bandini. (Orig.). 1983. 17.50 (ISBN 0-87685-555-9); signed ed. 25.00 (ISBN 0-87685-556-7); pap. 8.50 (ISBN 0-87685-554-0). Black Sparrow.

Fantel, Hans. Better Listening. 192p. 1983. pap. 6.95 (ISBN 0-686-83792-4, ScribT). Scribner.

Fantham, Elaine. Seneca's Troades: A Literary Introduction with Text, Translation, & Commentary. LC 82-47592. (Illus.). 465p. 1982. 42.50x (ISBN 0-691-03561-X). Princeton U Pr.

Fantin-Latour, Victoria. Catalogue De L'qeuve Comblet De Fantin Latour. (Graphic Art Ser.). 320p. (Fr.). 1970. Repr. of 1911 ed. 47.50 o.p. (ISBN 0-306-71924-X). Da Capo.

FAO. Assessment of Logging Costs from Forest Inventories in the Tropics, 2 vols. Swedish International Development Authority, tr. Incl. Vol. 1. Principles & Methodology. 56p; Vol. 2. Data Collections & Calculations. 74p. (Forestry Papers: No. 1Q, Pts. 1&2). 1978. Set. pap. 13.00 (ISBN 0-686-93608-6, F1492, FAO). Unipub.

FAO Conference, 3rd Special Session, Rome, 1956. Report. 36p. 1956. pap. 4.50 (ISBN 0-686-92780-X, F385, FAO). Unipub.

FAO Expert Consultation of Fishery Education & Training, Rome, 1972. Report. (FAO Fisheries Reports: No. 127). 16p. 1972. pap. 7.50 (ISBN 0-686-93085-1, F1708, FAO). Unipub.

FAO Expert Panel for Facilitation of Tuna Research, 3rd Session, 1969. Report. (FAO Fisheries Reports: No. 80). 97p. 1969. pap. 7.50 (ISBN 0-686-93036-3, F1683, FAO). Unipub.

FAO Expert Panel for the Facilitation of Tuna Research, 4th Session, LA Jolla, 1971. Report. (FAO Fisheries Reports: No. 118). 26p. 1972. pap. 7.50 (ISBN 0-686-93074-6, F1701, FAO). Unipub.

FAO Fisheries Department. FAO Fisheries Department List of Publications & Documents 1948-1978. 3rd, rev. ed. (Fisheries Circular: No. 100). 241p. 1979. pap. 7.50 (ISBN 0-686-93225-0, F2053, FAO). Unipub.

FAO Fisheries Technology Service & Hamabe, Mototsugu, eds. Squid Jigging from Small Boats. 84p. 1982. 42.95x (ISBN 0-85238-122-0, Pub. by Fishing News England). State Mutual Bk.

FAO-ILO-WHO Joint Symposium of Industrial Feeding & Canteen Management in Europe, Rome, 1963. Report. (FAO Nutrition Meetings Report Ser.: No. 36). 44p. 1965. pap. 4.50 (ISBN 0-686-92864-4, F375, FAO). Unipub.

FAO In-Service Consultation on Middle-Level Training in Agricultural Marketing in African & Near East Countries, Nairobi, Kenya, 1974. Training in Agricultural & Food Marketing at Middle Level: Report. (FAO Developmental Documents: No. 12). 99p. 1974. pap. 7.50 (ISBN 0-686-92717-6, F1228, FAO). Unipub.

FAO-NORAD Round Table Discussion on Expanding the Utilization of Marine Fishery Resources for Human Consumption, Svany, Norway, 1975. Report. (FAO Fisheries Reports: No. 175). 53p. 1975. pap. 7.50 (ISBN 0-686-93990-5, F825, FAO). Unipub.

FAO-Norway Expert Consultation on International Cooperation in Fishery Development in Developing Countries, Svany, Norway, 1977. Report. (FAO Fisheries Reports: No. 201). 52p. 1977. pap. 7.50 (ISBN 0-686-93998-0, F1414, FAO). Unipub.

FAO Regional Seminar on Rainfed Agriculture in the Near East & North Africa, Amman, Jordan, 1979. Rainfed Agriculture in the Near East & North Africa: Proceedings. 409p. 1980. pap. 28.75 (ISBN 0-686-92795-8, F2174, FAO). Unipub.

FAO-SIDA-ARCN Regional Seminar, Ibadan, Nigeria, 1973. Shifting Cultivation & Soil Conservation in Africa: Papers. (Soils Bulletins: No. 24). 254p. 1974. pap. 17.00 (ISBN 0-686-92698-6, F1166, FAO). Unipub.

FAO-SIDA Consultation, Rome, 1972. Effects of Intensive Fertilizers Used on the Human Environment: Report. (Soils Bulletins: No. 16). 368p. 1972. pap. 26.50 (ISBN 92-5-100657-1, F1158, FAO). Unipub.

FAO-SIDA Experts Consultation on Policies & Institutions for Integrated Rural Development, Naerobi, Kenya, 1976. Report. (FAO Development Documents: No. 30). 1976. Set. pap. 13.00 (ISBN 0-686-92832-6, F1205, FAO); Vol. 1, 43p. pap. Vol. 2, 95p. Unipub.

FAO Technical Conference of Fishery Representatives of the Near East Countries, Kuwait, 1966. Report. (FAO Fisheries Reports: No. 39). 36p. 1966. pap. 7.50 (ISBN 0-686-92934-9, F1660, FAO). Unipub.

FAO Technical Conference on Fish Inspection & Quality Control, Halifax, 1969. Report. (FAO Fisheries Reports: No. 81). 73p. 1969. pap. 7.50 (ISBN 0-686-93041-X, F1684, FAO). Unipub.

FAO Technical Conference on Fishery Research Craft, Seattle, 1968. Proceedings. (FAO Fisheries Reports: No. 64). 56p. 1968. pap. 7.50 (ISBN 0-686-92946-2, F1675, FAO). Unipub.

FAO Technical Conference on the Freezing & Irradiation of Fish, Madrid, 1967. Report. (FAO Fisheries Reports: No. 53). 60p. 1968. pap. 7.50 (ISBN 0-686-93012-6, F1669, FAO). Unipub.

FAO-UNAFPA Seminar on Agricultural Planning & Population, Rome, 1974. Report. (FAO Development Documents: No. 18). 250p. 1975. pap. 17.00 (ISBN 0-686-92806-7, F1138, FAO). Unipub.

FAO-UNDP Regional Seminar on Effective Use of Irrigation Water at the Farm Level, Damascuc, 1971. Water Use Seminar: Report. (Irrigation & Drainage Papers: No. 13). 316p. 1972. pap. 20.50 (ISBN 0-686-92947-0, F982, FAO). Unipub.

FAO-UNDP Regional Seminar on Reclamation & Management of Calcareous Soils, Cairo, 1972. Calcareous Soils: Report. (Soils Bulletins: No. 21). 276p. 1973. pap. 18.00 (ISBN 92-5-100276-2, F1162, FAO). Unipub.

FAO-UNDP Seminar on Measures to Accelerate Benefits from Water Development Projects by Improved Irrigation Drainage & Water Use at the Farm Level, Manila, 1970. Farm Water Management Seminar: Report. (Irrigation & Drainage Papers: No. 12): 350p. 1972. pap. 19.00 o.p. (ISBN 0-686-92753-2, F981, FAO). Unipub.

FAO-WHO Expert Group, Rome, 1961. Calcium Requirements: Report. (FAO Nutrition Meetings Report Ser.: No. 30). 54p. 1962. pap. 4.75 (ISBN 0-686-93129-7, F86, FAO). Unipub.

FAO-WHO Joint Conference on Food Additives, Geneva, 1955. Report. (FAO Nutrition Meetings Report Ser.: No. 11). 14p. 1956. pap. 4.50 (ISBN 0-686-92802-4, F246, FAO). Unipub.

FAO-WHO Joint Conference on Food Additives, 2nd, Rome, 1963. Report: FAO-WHO Joint Conference on Food Additives. (FAO Nutrition Meetings Report Ser.: No. 34). 12p. 1973. pap. 4.50 (ISBN 0-686-92845-8, F381, FAO). Unipub.

FAO-WHO Joint Expert Committee on Food Additives, Rome, 1974. Evaluation of Certain Food Additives, 18th Report. (FAO Nutrition Meetings Report Ser.: No. 54). 36p. 1974. pap. 3.50 o.p. (ISBN 0-686-92844-X, F128, FAO). Unipub.

FAO-WHO Joint Expert Committee on Food Additives, Geneva, 1975. Evaluation of Certain Food Additives, 19th Report. (FAO Nutrition Meetings Report Ser.: No. 55). 23p. 1975. pap. 4.25 (ISBN 0-686-92846-6, F129, FAO). Unipub.

FAO-WHO Joint Expert Committee on Food Additives, Geneva, 1971. Evaluation of Food Additives: Some Enzymes, Modified Starches, & Certain other Substances, 15th Report. (FAO Nutrition Meetings Report Ser.: No. 50). 41p. 1972. pap. 3.50 o.p. (ISBN 0-686-92838-5, F138, FAO). Unipub.

FAO-WHO Joint Expert Committee on Food Additives. Evaluation of the Carcinogenic Hazards of Food Additives: Report, No. 5. (FAO Nutrition Meetings Report Ser.: No. 29). 33p. 1961. pap. 3.00 (ISBN 0-686-92852-0, F134, FAO). Unipub.

FAO-WHO Joint Expert Committee on Food Additives, Geneva, 1961. Evaluation of Toxicity of a Number of Antimicrobials & Antioxidants, 6th Report. (FAO Nutrition Meetings Report Ser.: No. 31). 104p. 1962. pap. 4.25 (ISBN 0-686-92854-7, F133, FAO). Unipub.

FAO-WHO Joint Expert Committee on Food Additives, 1st Session, Rome, 1956. General Principles Governing the Use of Food Additives: Report. (FAO Nutrition Meetings Ser.: No. 15). 22p. 1957. pap. 4.50 (ISBN 0-686-92890-3, F376, FAO). Unipub.

FAO - WHO Joint Expert Committee on Food Additives, Geneva, 1957. Procedures for the Testing of International Food Additives to Establish Their Society for Use: 2nd Report. (FAO Nutrition Meetings Report Ser.: No. 17). 19p. 1958. pap. 4.50 (ISBN 0-686-92907-1, F336, FAO). Unipub.

FAO-WHO Joint Expert Committee on Food Additives, Rome, 1969. Specifications for the Identity & Purity of Food Additives & Their Toxicological Evaluation, 13th Report: Some Food Colours, Emulsifiers, Stabilizers, Anticaking Agents, & Certain Other Substances. (FAO Nutrition Meeting Reports Ser.: No. 46). 31p. 1970. pap. 4.50 (ISBN 0-686-92740-0, F434, FAO). Unipub.

FAO-WHO Joint Expert Committee on Milk Hygeine. Report, No. 3. (FAO Agricultural Studies: No. 83). (Illus., Orig.). 1971. pap. 4.25 o.p. (ISBN 0-685-00275-6, FAO). Unipub.

FAO-WHO Joint Expert Committee on Veterinary Public Health, Geneva, 1974. The Veterinary Contribution to Public Health Practice: Report. (FAO Agricultural Studies Ser.: No. 96). 79p. 1975. pap. 9.50 (ISBN 0-686-93052-5, F491, FAO). Unipub.

FAO-WMO Joint Technical Meeting on Methods of Planning & Evaluation in Applied Nutrition Programs, Rome, 1965. Report. (FAO Nutrition Meetings Report Ser.: No. 39). 77p. 1966. pap. 4.50 (ISBN 0-686-92875-X, F377, FAO). Unipub.

FAO Working Party of Experts & the WHO Expert Committee on Pesticide Residues in a Joint Meeting, Geneva, 1971. Pesticide Residues in Food: Report. (FAO Agricultural Studies: No. 88). (Orig.). 1972. pap. 4.50 (ISBN 0-685-36313-9, F311, FAO). Unipub.

FAO Working Party on Pesticide Residues & WHO Expert Committee on Pesticide Residues. Pesticide Residues in Food: Report of the 1974 Joint Meeting, Rome. (FAO Agricultural Studies: No. 97). 37p. 1975. pap. 4.50 (ISBN 0-686-92789-3, F134, FAO). Unipub.

--Pesticides Residues in Food: Joint Report, Geneva, 1966. (FAO Agricultural Studies: No. 73). 19p. 1967. pap. 2.75 o.p. (ISBN 0-686-92792-3, F1917, FAO). Unipub.

--Pesticides Residues in Food: Report of the 1968 Joint Meeting, Geneva. (FAO Agricultural Studies Ser.: No. 78). 40p. 1969. pap. 4.25 (ISBN 0-686-92791-5, F309, FAO). Unipub.

FAO World Symposium on Warm-Water Pond Fish Culture, Rome, 1966. Proceedings, 2 Vols. (FAO Fisheries Reports: No. 44, Vols. 3-4). 1967-68. Vol. 3, 426p. pap. 25.50 (ISBN 0-686-92950-0, F1395, FAO); Vol. 4, 495p. pap. 29.25 (ISBN 0-686-98807-8, F1664). Unipub.

Fapso, Richard J. Norwegians in Wisconsin. (Illus.). 1977. pap. 2.00 (ISBN 0-87020-171-9). State Hist Soc Wis.

Faqih, I. Glimpses of Islamic History. 14.95 (ISBN 0-686-63900-6). Kazi Pubns.

Far Eastern Economic Review Staff, ed. All Asia Guide. new ed. (Illus.). 688p. 1982. pap. 9.95 (ISBN 0-8048-1363-9, Pub. by Far Eastern Economic Review Hong Kong). C E Tuttle.

Farabee, Barbara. Erotic Love Poems. LC 74-9755. (Illus.). 1974. pap. 5.95 o.p. (ISBN 0-912310-72-3). Celestial Arts.

Farace, Richard V., et al. Communicating & Organizing. LC 76-12794. 1976. text ed. 18.95 (ISBN 0-201-01980-9); instr's guide 3.50 (ISBN 0-201-01981-7). A-W.

Faraday, Ann. The Dream Game. 1976. pap. 4.33i (ISBN 0-06-080371-1, P371, PL). Har-Row.

--Dream Power. 1981. pap. 3.35 (ISBN 0-425-06232-5). Berkley Pub.

Faraday, M. M. The Sharing. 304p. 1982. pap. 3.50 (ISBN 0-553-22579-0). Bantam.

Faraday, Michael. Chemical Manipulation. (Illus.). ix, 656p. 1974. 24.75 (ISBN 0-85334-596-1, Pub. by Applied Sci England). Elsevier.

Farag, M. M. Materials & Process Selection in Engineering. (Illus.). 1979. 63.75 (ISBN 0-85334-824-3, Pub. by Applied Sci England). Elsevier.

Faraggi, H. & Ricci, R. A. Nuclear Spectroscopy & Nuclear Reactions with Heavy Ions. 1976. 115.00 (ISBN 0-7204-0450-9, North-Holland). Elsevier.

Farago, Ladislas. Burn After Reading. 320p. (YA) 1978. pap. 1.95 o.p. (ISBN 0-523-40345-3). Pinnacle Bks.

Farah, Caesar E. Islam: Beliefs & Observances. 3rd ed. 306p. (gr. 11-12). 1983. pap. text ed. 4.50 (ISBN 0-8120-2358-7). Barron.

Farah, Nuruddin. Sardines. 256p. 1982. 13.95 (ISBN 0-8052-8126-6, Pub. by Allison & Busby England). Schocken.

Farah, Tawfic E., ed. Political Behavior in the Arab States. 240p. 1983. lib. bdg. 20.00 (ISBN 0-86531-524-8); pap. text ed. 9.95 (ISBN 0-86531-525-6). Westview.

Farah, Victor W., jt. auth. see Horn, Frederick F.

Fararo, Thomas J. Mathematical Sociology: An Introduction to Fundamentals. LC 78-2379. 830p. 1978. Repr. of 1973 ed. lib. bdg. 36.50 (ISBN 0-88275-664-8). Krieger.

Farb, Milton H. & Singer, David, eds. American Jewish Year Book, Vol. 83. 450p. 1982. 23.50 (ISBN 0-8276-0221-9). Jewish Pubn.

Farb, Peter. Ecology. rev. ed. LC 80-52123. (Life Nature Library). PLB 13.40 (ISBN 0-8094-3899-2). Silver.

--The Forest. rev. ed. LC 80-52496. (Life Nature Library). PLB 13.40 (ISBN 0-8094-3883-6). Silver.

--The Insects. rev. ed. LC 80-52117. (Life Nature Library). PLB 13.40 (ISBN 0-8094-3883-6). Silver.

--The Land & Wildlife of North America. rev. ed. LC 80-52262. (Life Nature Library). 13.40 (ISBN 0-8094-3919-0). Silver.

Farb, Peter & Armelagos, George. Consuming Passions: The Anthropology of Eating. 1983. pap. 4.95 (ISBN 0-671-43420-9). WSP.

Farb, Stanley N. Otolaryngology. 4th ed. LC 70-94388. (Medical Examination Review Bk.: Vol. 16). 1977. spiral bdg. 22.00 o.p. (ISBN 0-87488-116-1). Med Exam.

--Otolaryngology. 5th ed. (Medical Exam Review Bks.: Vol. 16). 1982. pap. text ed. 22.00 (ISBN 0-87488-116-1). Med Exam.

Farber, jt. auth. see Knoepfel.

Farber, Anne & Rogler, LLoyd H. Unitas: Hispanic & Black Children in a Healing Community. 144p. 1982. 13.95 (ISBN 0-87073-505-5); pap. 8.95 (ISBN 0-87073-506-3). Schenkman.

Farber, Barry A., ed. Stress & Burnout in the Human Service Professions. (Pergamon General Psychology Ser.). (Illus.). 272p. 1983. 25.00 (ISBN 0-08-028801-4). Pergamon.

Farber, David J., jt. auth. see Uhlig, Ronald P.

Farber, Donald C. & Baumgarten, Paul. Producing, Financing, & Distributing Film. LC 72-87054. 224p. 1973. 15.95 (ISBN 0-910482-31-4); pap. 15.95 (ISBN 0-89676-075-8). Drama Bk.

Farber, Evan, intro. by. Combined Retrospective Index to Book Reviews in Scholarly Humanities Journals 1802-1974, 2 Vols. 1983. 1165.00 (ISBN 0-89235-061-X). Res Pubns Conn.

Farber, Evan I. Combined Retrospective Index to Book Reviews in Scholarly Journals, 1886-1974, 15 vols. LC 79-89137. 1979. lib. bdg. 1540.00 (ISBN 0-8408-0172-6). Res Pubns Conn.

Farber, Jerry. Field Guide to the Aesthetic Experience. LC 82-83129. 284p. (Orig.). 1982. pap. 5.95x (ISBN 0-943292-15-8). Foreworks.

Farber, Joseph C. Thomas Jefferson Redivivus. 1971. 25.00 o.p. (ISBN 0-517-14158-2). Crown.

Farber, Marvin. Foundation of Phenomenology: Edmund Husserl & the Quest for a Rigorous Science of Philosophy. 3rd ed. LC 67-25983. 1967. 55.50x (ISBN 0-87395-023-2); pap. 12.00x o.p. (ISBN 0-87395-037-2). State U NY Pr.

--Naturalism & Subjectivism. LC 59-11896. 1959. pap. 17.95x (ISBN 0-87395-036-4). State U NY Pr.

Farber, Marvin, ed. Philosophical Essays in Memory of Edmund Husserl. LC 68-19270. Repr. of 1968 ed. lib. bdg. 18.25x (ISBN 0-8371-0071-2, FAPE). Greenwood.

Farber, Norma. How the Hibernators Came to Bethlehem. LC 80-7685. (Illus.). 32p. (gr. k-3). 1980. 6.95 o.p. (ISBN 0-8027-6352-9); PLB 7.85 (ISBN 0-8027-6353-7). Walker & Co.

--Mercy Short: A Winter Journal, North Boston, 1692-1693. 160p. (YA) 1982. 11.95 (ISBN 0-525-44014-3, 01160-350, Unicorn Bk). Dutton.

--Small Wonders. LC 78-31282. (Illus.). (gr. 2-5). 1979. 6.50 o.p. (ISBN 0-698-20484-0, Coward). Putnam Pub Group.

Farber, Robert. The Fashion Photographer. (Illus.). 192p. 1981. 24.95 (ISBN 0-8174-3850-5, Amphoto). Watson-Guptill.

--Images of Woman. rev. ed. (Illus.). 1979. 19.95 o.p. (ISBN 0-8174-2483-0, Amphoto); pap. 9.95 o.s.i. (ISBN 0-8174-2155-6). Watson-Guptill.

--Moods. (Illus.). 136p. 1980. 19.95 o.p. (ISBN 0-8174-4900-0, Amphoto). Watson-Guptill.

--Professional Fashion Photography. (Illus.). 1978. 19.95 (ISBN 0-8174-2440-7, Amphoto). Watson-Guptill.

--Professional Fashion Photography: New, Updated Edition of an AMPHOTO Bestseller. Rev. ed. 1983. pap. 14.95 (ISBN 0-8174-5549-3, Amphoto). Watson-Guptill.

Farber, Shereen D. Neurorehabilitation: A Multisensory Approach. (Illus.). 282p. 1982. 19.50 (ISBN 0-7216-3571-7). Saunders.

Farber, Thomas. Who Wrote the Book of Love? 1977. 6.95 o.p. (ISBN 0-393-08799-9). Norton.

Farber, William. Business Letters Simplified & Self-Taught. LC 82-3890. 160p. 1982. 11.95 (ISBN 0-668-05554-5); pap. 4.95 (ISBN 0-668-05394-1). Arco.

Farberman, Harvey A., jt. auth. see Stone, Gregory P.

Farberow, N. Suicide in Different Cultures. (Illus.). 1975. 24.50 o.p. (ISBN 0-8391-0843-5). Univ Park.

Farberow, Norman L., jt. auth. see Reynolds, David K.

Farberow, Norman L., ed. The Many Faces of Suicide: Indirect Self-Destructive Behavior. LC 79-18797. (Illus.). 1979. 23.95 (ISBN 0-07-019944-2). McGraw.

Fardo, Stephen W., jt. auth. see Patrick, Dale R.

Fardy, Paul S., et al. Cardiac Rehabilitation: Implications for the Nurse & Other Health Professionals. LC 80-16296. (Illus.). 283p. 1980. pap. text ed. 19.95 (ISBN 0-8016-1610-7). Mosby.

Fareed, George C. & Linke, Hawley K. Molecular Biology of Polyomaviruses & Herpesviruses. 175p. 1983. 30.00 (ISBN 0-471-05058-X, Pub. by Wiley Interscience). Wiley.

Farelle, F. F. De La see De La Farelle, F. F.

Farfan, H. F. Mechanical Disorders of the Low Back. LC 73-3348. (Illus.). 247p. 1973. text ed. 17.50 o.p. (ISBN 0-8121-0418-8). Lea & Febiger.

Farge, Henry A. La see Pischel, Gina, et al.

Farge, John La see La Farge, John.

Farge, Oliver La see La Farge, Oliver.

Farge, Sheila La see Beskow, Elsa.

Farge, Sheila La see Bodker, Cecil.

Farge, Sheila La see Gripe, Maria.

Farge, Sheila La see La Farge, Sheila.

Fargo, Gail B. Talks to Truth Searchers. LC 74-75082. 64p. 1974. 4.75 o.p. (ISBN 0-8022-2138-6). Philos Lib.

Farguharson, J. B. & Holt, S. C. Europe from Below: An Assessment of Franco-German Popular Contacts. LC 75-591. 224p. 1975. 22.50 (ISBN 0-312-26915-3). St Martin.

Farhady, Hossein, jt. auth. see Hatch, Evelyn.

Farhar-Pilgrim, Barbara & Unseld, Charles T. America's Solar Potential: A National Consumer Study. Shama, Avraham, ed. (Studies in Energy Conservation & Solar Energy). 464p. 1982. 35.00 (ISBN 0-03-061696-4). Praeger.

Farhat, Nabil H., ed. Advances in Holography, Vol. 1. 192p. 1975. 29.00 o.p. (ISBN 0-8247-6277-0). Dekker.

--Advances in Holography, Vol. 2. 200p. 1976. 34.00 o.p. (ISBN 0-8247-6313-0). Dekker.

--Advances in Holography, Vol. 3. 1976. 42.00 o.p. (ISBN 0-8247-6389-0). Dekker.

Farhi, Moris. The Last of Days: A Novel. 1983. 16.95 (ISBN 0-517-54908-5). Crown.

Faria, I. E. & Cavanagh, P. R. The Physiology & Biomechanics of Cycling. 179p. 1978. 17.95x (ISBN 0-471-25490-8). Wiley.

Faricy, Austin, jt. auth. see Dudley, Louise.

Faricy, Robert. The End of the Religious Life. 96p. 1983. pap. 6.96 (ISBN 0-86683-690-X). Winston Pr.

Farina, A. Abnormal Psychology. LC 75-22136. (Personality Ser.). 240p. 1976. pap. 11.95 o.p. (ISBN 0-13-001164-9). P-H.

Farina, John E. Quantum Theory of Scattering Processes, Pt. 1: General Principles & Advanced Topics. McWeeny, R., ed. LC 74-22357. 144p. 1975. text ed. 37.00 (ISBN 0-08-018130-9). Pergamon.

Farina, Mario V. Flowcharting. 1970. pap. 12.95 ref. ed. (ISBN 0-13-322750-2). P-H.

--Fortran IV Self-Taught. 1966. pap. 16.95 (ISBN 0-13-329722-5). P-H.

--Programming in BASIC: The Time-Sharing Language. (Orig.). 1968. pap. 14.95 ref. ed. (ISBN 0-13-730424-2). P-H.

Farina, Richard. Been Down So Long It Looks Like Up to Me. 1983. pap. 4.95 (ISBN 0-14-006536-9). Penguin.

--Been Down So Long It Looks Like Up to Me. 1983. 14.75 (ISBN 0-670-15476-8). Viking Pr.

Farington, Joseph. The Diary of Farington, Joseph, R. A, 6 vols. Garlick, Kenneth, et al, eds. Incl. Vols. 1 & 2. Set. text ed. 95.00x (ISBN 0-300-02314-6); text ed. 47.50x ea. Vol. 1 (ISBN 0-300-02294-8). Vol. 2 (ISBN 0-300-02295-6); Vols. 3 & 4. Set. text ed. 95.00x (ISBN 0-300-02371-5); text ed. 45.00x ea. Vol. 3 (ISBN 0-300-02369-3). Vol. 4 (ISBN 0-300-02370-7); Vols. 5 & 6. Set. text ed. 95.00x (ISBN 0-300-02418-5); text ed. 45.00x ea. Vol. 5 (ISBN 0-300-02416-9). Vol. 6 (ISBN 0-300-02417-7). LC 78-7056. (Studies in British Art Ser.). 1979. Yale U Pr.

--The Diary of Joseph Farington: Volumes 9 & 10: January 1808 Through December 1810, 2 Vols. Cave, Kathryn, ed. LC 78-7056. (Studies in British Art Ser.). 1000p. 1982. Set. text ed. 95.00x (ISBN 0-300-02859-8); Vol. 9. text ed. 47.50 ea. (ISBN 0-300-02890-3). Vol. 10 (ISBN 0-300-02857-1). Yale U Pr.

Fariq, K. A. Ziyad-B-Abih. 1968. 8.00x o.p. (ISBN 0-210-22510-6). Asia.

Faris, Ellsworth, et al, eds. Intelligent Philanthropy. LC 69-16231. (Criminology, Law Enforcement, & Social Problems Ser.: No. 82). 1969. Repr. of 1930 ed. 15.00x (ISBN 0-87585-082-0). Patterson Smith.

Faris, N. A. The Book of Knowledge. 8.95 (ISBN 0-686-18617-6). Kazi Pubns.

--The Mysteries of Almsgiving. pap. 4.00 (ISBN 0-686-18616-8). Kazi Pubns.

--The Mysteries of Purity. pap. 4.00 (ISBN 0-686-18614-1). Kazi Pubns.

Faris, Ralph, ed. Crisis & Consciousness. (Philosophical Currents Ser.: 20). 1977. pap. text ed. 23.00x o.p. (ISBN 90-6032-093-X). Humanities.

Faris, Wendy B. Carlos Fuentes. LC 82-40281. (Literature & Life Ser.). 220p. 1983. 14.50 (ISBN 0-8044-2193-5). Ungar.

Farish, Hunter D. Circuit Rider Dismounts, a Social History of Southern Methodism 1865-1900. LC 77-87534. (American Scene Ser). 1969. Repr. of 1938 ed. 45.00 (ISBN 0-306-71450-7). Da Capo.

Farish, Kay, jt. auth. see Hutchison, Becky.

Faristzaddi, Millard. Itations of Jamaica & I Rastafari. LC 82-82460. (Illus.). 192p. (Orig.). 1982. 9.95 (ISBN 0-394-62435-1, E836, Ever). Grove.

Fariz, Husni see Allen, W. S.

Farjam, Farideh. The Crystal Flower & the Sun. new & rev. ed. Jabbari, Ahmad, ed. & tr. from Persian. (Illus.). 24p. (Orig.). (gr. k up). 1983. pap. 5.95 (ISBN 0-939214-16-4). Mazda Pubs.

Farjam, Farideh & Azaad, Meyer. Uncle Noruz (Uncle New Year) Jabbari, Ahmad, ed. & tr. from Persian. (Illus.). 24p. (Orig.). (gr. k up). 1983. pap. 5.95 (ISBN 0-939214-14-8). Mazda Pubs.

Farkas. Qualitative Theory of Differential Equations, 2 vols. (Colloquia Mathematica Ser.: Vol. 30). 1982. Set. 159.75 (ISBN 0-444-86173-4). Elsevier.

Farkas, Emil & Corcoran, John. The Illustrated Encyclopedia of Martial Arts. (Illus.). 480p. Date not set. 24.95 (ISBN 0-8317-5805-8). Smith Pubs. Postponed.

Farkas, Emil, jt. auth. see Corcoran, John.

Farkas, F. Flavonoids & Bioflavonoids, 1981. (Studies in Organic Chemistry: Vol. 11). 1982. 95.75 (ISBN 0-444-99694-X). Elsevier.

Farkas, Lucien L. Management of Technical Field Operations. 1970. 27.50 o.p. (ISBN 0-07-019956-6, P&RB). McGraw.

Farkas, M., ed. Differential Equations. (Colloquia Mathematica Societatis Janos Bolyai: Vol. 15). 1977. 74.50 (ISBN 0-7204-0496-7, North-Holland). Elsevier.

Farkas, Philip. Art of French Horn Playing. (Illus.). 1956. pap. 10.95 (ISBN 0-87487-021-6). Summy.

Farkas, Sandor B. Journey in North America, 1831. Kadarkay, Arpad, tr. from Hung. LC 77-19145. 230p. 1978. text ed. 24.75 o.p. (ISBN 0-87436-270-9). ABC-Clio.

Farkas, Susan, ed. see Journalism Reseach Fellows of 1982.

Farkas, Tiber. Introduction to Criminal Justice. 1977. pap. text ed. 14.50 (ISBN 0-8191-0184-2). U Pr of Amer.

Farkasfalvy, Denis, jt. auth. see Farmer, William R.

Farley, Alice R., jt. auth. see Farley, Eugene J.

Farley, Carol. Mystery of the Fiery Message. (Illus.). 108p. 1983. pap. 1.95 (ISBN 0-380-81927-9, 81927-9, Camelot). Avon.

Farley, Edward. Theologia: The Fragmentation & Unity of Theological Education. LC 82-48621. 224p. 1983. pap. text ed. 14.50 (ISBN 0-8006-1705-3). Fortress.

Farley, Eugene J. Barron's How to Prepare for the High School Equivalency Examination: The Reading Skills Test. LC 79-28101. 1980. pap. text ed. 4.95 (ISBN 0-8120-2057-X). Barron.

Farley, Eugene J. & Farley, Alice R. Barron's How to Prepare for the High School Equivalency Examination (GED) The Science Test. (gr. 11-12). 1982. pap. text ed. 5.95 (ISBN 0-8120-2055-3). Barron.

--Developing Reading Skills for the High School Equivalency Examination (Ged) in Social Studies, Science, & Literature: In 26 Lessons. LC 72-84413. 1972. pap. text ed. 6.95 (ISBN 0-8120-0487-6). Barron.

Farley, Frank & Gordon, Neal J., eds. Psychology & Education: The State of the Union. LC 80-82902. (National Society for the Study of Education Series on Contemporary Educational Issues). 400p. 1981. 23.00 (ISBN 0-8211-0506-X); text ed. 20.75 (ISBN 0-686-77730-1). McCutchan.

Farley, James A. Behind the Ballots: A Personal History of a Politician. LC 72-2370. (FDR & the Era of the New Deal Ser). (Illus.). 402p. 1973. Repr. of 1938 ed. lib. bdg. 45.00 (ISBN 0-306-70475-7). Da Capo.

--Behind the Ballots: The Personal History of a Politician. LC 78-114521. (Illus.). 392p. 1972. Repr. of 1938 ed. lib. bdg. 19.00x (ISBN 0-8371-4738-7, FABB). Greenwood.

Farley, Jennie. Academic Women & Employment Discrimination: A Critical Annotated Bibliography. LC 82-3570. (ILR Bibliography Ser.: No. 16). 112p. 1982. pap. 8.95 (ISBN 0-87546-092-5). ILR Pr.

Farley, Jennie, ed. Sex Discrimination in Higher Education: Strategies for Equality. LC 81-9604. 168p. 1981. pap. 7.50 (ISBN 0-87546-089-5). ILR Pr.

--The Woman in Management: Career & Family Issues. (Orig.). 1983. pap. price not set (ISBN 0-87546-100-X). ILR Pr.

Farley, Lauren, jt. auth. see Farley, Michael.

Farley, Lauren, jt. auth. see Hall, Howard.

Farley, Lin. Sexual Shakedown: The Sexual Harassment of Women on the Job. 1978. 9.95 o.p. (ISBN 0-07-019957-4, GB). McGraw.

Farley, M. Foster. Indian Summer: An Account of a Visit to India. 211p. 1977. pap. text ed. 10.00 (ISBN 0-8191-0051-X). U Pr of Amer.

Farley, Michael. Scuba Equipment Care & Maintenance. (Illus.). 176p. 1980. pap. text ed. 9.95 (ISBN 0-932248-01-2). Marcor Pub.

Farley, Michael & Farley, Lauren. Diving Mexico's Baja California. (Illus.). 176p. 1978. pap. text ed. 9.95 (ISBN 0-686-43074-3). Marcor Pub.

Farley, Philip J., et al. Arms Across the Sea. LC 77-91804. 1978. 14.95 (ISBN 0-8157-2746-1); pap. 5.95 (ISBN 0-8157-2745-3). Brookings.

Farley, Reuben W., et al. Trigonometry: A Unitized Approach. (Illus.). 1975. pap. text ed. 20.95 (ISBN 0-13-930909-8). P-H.

Farley, Venner M. An Evaluative Study of an Open Curriculum: Career Ladder Nursing Program. (League Exchange Ser.: No. 118). 65p. 1978. 5.95 (ISBN 0-686-38181-5, 19-1728). Natl League Nurse.

--First Level Nursing-Study Modules. (Nursing-Registered Ser.). 1981. pap. 11.00 (ISBN 0-8273-1873-1); 5.50 (ISBN 0-8273-1875-8). Delmar.

Farley, Walter. Black Stallion. LC 41-21882. (Illus.). (gr. 3-7). 1944. 3.95 o.p. (ISBN 0-394-80601-8, BYR); PLB 6.99 (ISBN 0-394-90601-2); pap. 1.95 o.p. (ISBN 0-394-83609-X). Random.

--Black Stallion & Flame. (Illus.). (gr. 5 up). 1960. 3.95 o.p. (ISBN 0-394-80615-8, BYR); PLB 7.99 (ISBN 0-394-90615-2); pap. 1.95 o.p. (ISBN 0-394-84372-X). Random.

--Black Stallion & Satan. (Illus.). (gr. 4-6). 1949. 3.95 o.p. (ISBN 0-394-80605-0, BYR); PLB 6.99 (ISBN 0-394-90605-5); pap. 1.95 o.p. (ISBN 0-394-83914-5). Random.

--The Black Stallion & the Girl. (gr. 4 up). 1971. 3.95 o.p. (ISBN 0-394-82145-9, BYR); PLB 6.99 (ISBN 0-394-92145-3); pap. 1.95 o.p. (ISBN 0-394-83614-6). Random.

--Black Stallion Challenged. (Illus.). (gr. 5-9). 1964. 3.95 o.p. (ISBN 0-394-80617-4, BYR); PLB 6.99 (ISBN 0-394-90617-9); pap. 1.95 o.p. (ISBN 0-394-84371-1). Random.

--The Black Stallion Mystery. (gr. 4-6). 1957. 3.95 o.p. (ISBN 0-394-80613-1, BYR); PLB 6.99 (ISBN 0-394-90613-6); pap. 1.95 o.p. (ISBN 0-394-83611-1). Random.

--The Black Stallion Returns. LC 45-8763. (gr. 4-9). 1977. 3.95 o.p. (ISBN 0-394-80602-6, BYR); PLB 6.99 (ISBN 0-394-90602-0); pap. 1.95 o.p. (ISBN 0-394-83610-3). Random.

--The Black Stallion Returns: Movie Storybooks. Spinner, Stephanie, ed. LC 82-3861. (Illus.). 64p. (gr. 2-7). 1982. 5.95 (ISBN 0-394-85412-8); PLB 6.99 (ISBN 0-394-95412-2). Random.

--The Black Stallion Revolts. LC 49-6117. (gr. 4-9). 1977. 3.95 o.p. (ISBN 0-394-80609-3, BYR); PLB 6.99 (ISBN 0-394-90609-8); pap. 1.95 o.p. (ISBN 0-394-83613-8). Random.

--Black Stallion's Ghost. (Illus.). (gr. 5-9). 1969. 3.95 (ISBN 0-394-80618-2, BYR); PLB 6.99 (ISBN 0-394-90618-7); pap. 1.95 (ISBN 0-394-83919-6). Random.

--Black Stallion's Sulky Colt. (Illus.). (gr. 4-6). 1954. 3.95 o.p. (ISBN 0-394-80610-7, BYR); PLB 8.99 (ISBN 0-394-90610-1); pap. 1.95 o.p. (ISBN 0-394-83917-X). Random.

--Island Stallion Races. (Illus.). (gr. 4-6). 1965. 3.95 o.p. (ISBN 0-394-80611-5, BYR); PLB 6.99 (ISBN 0-394-90611-X); pap. 1.95 o.p. (ISBN 0-394-84375-4). Random.

--Island Stallion's Fury. (Illus.). (gr. 5-6). 1951. 3.95 o.p. (ISBN 0-394-80607-7, BYR); PLB 6.99 (ISBN 0-394-90607-1); pap. 1.95 o.p. (ISBN 0-394-84373-8). Random.

--Little Black, a Pony. LC 61-7789. (Illus.). (gr. 1-2). 1961. 4.95 o.p. (ISBN 0-394-80021-4); PLB 5.99 (ISBN 0-394-90021-9). Beginner.

--Little Black Goes to the Circus. LC 63-13866. (Illus.). (gr. k-3). 1963. 3.95 o.p. (ISBN 0-394-80033-8); PLB 5.99 (ISBN 0-394-90033-2). Beginner.

--Little Black Pony Races. (Illus.). (ps-1). 1968. 2.95 o.p. (ISBN 0-394-81349-9, BYR); PLB 5.99 (ISBN 0-394-91349-3). Random.

--Son of the Black Stallion. (Illus.). (gr. 4-6). 1947. 3.95 o.p. (ISBN 0-394-80603-4, BYR); PLB 7.99 (ISBN 0-394-90603-9); pap. 1.95 (ISBN 0-394-83612-X). Random.

--Walter Farley's How to Stay Out of Trouble with Your Horse: Some Basic Safety Rules to Help You Enjoy Riding. LC 79-8922. (Illus.). 80p. (gr. 4-8). 1981. 7.95a (ISBN 0-385-15480-1); PLB o.p. (ISBN 0-385-15481-X). Doubleday.

Farlie, Barbara & Abell, Vivian. Flower Craft. LC 78-55664. (Illus.). 1978. 14.95 (ISBN 0-685-53358-1); pap. 10.95 (ISBN 0-686-96678-3). Bobbs.

Farlie, Barbara L., jt. auth. see Abell, Vivian.

Farlie, Dennis, jt. auth. see Budge, Ian.

Farlow, George. How to Successfully Sell Information by Mail. 120p. 1982. pap. 10.00 (ISBN 0-936300-05-1). Pr Arden Park.

Farlow, Helen. Publicizing & Promoting Programs. 1979. 18.95x (ISBN 0-07-019947-7). McGraw.

Farlow, W. C. The Marine Algae of New England & Adjacent Coast. (Illus.). 1969. Repr. of 1881 ed. 40.00 (ISBN 3-7682-0582-7). Lubrecht & Cramer.

Farlow, W. G. Mushroom Hunters Guide & Common Poisonous Plants. LC 82-72605. (Illus.). 100p. (Orig.). 1982. pap. 4.95 (ISBN 0-89708-084-X). And Bks.

Farm Journal. Farm Journal's Complete Cake Decorating Book. LC 82-45540. (Illus.). 160p. 1983. 15.95 (ISBN 0-385-18376-3). Doubleday.

Farm Journal Editors. America's Best Vegetable Recipes. LC 74-89068. (Illus.). 1970. 14.95 (ISBN 0-385-03155-6). Doubleday.

Farm Journal Editors & Nichols, Nell B. Homemade Candy. LC 79-121953. (Illus.). 1972. 9.95 (ISBN 0-385-01893-2). Doubleday.

Farm Journal Food Editors. America's Best Vegetable Recipes. LC 74-89068. 352p. 7.95 o.p. (ISBN 0-686-79502-4); pap. 3.95 o.p. (ISBN 0-06-463442-6). Har-Row.

Farm Journal's Food Editors. Chicken Twice a Week. LC 76-12306. 128p. (Orig.). 1976. pap. 2.95 (ISBN 0-89795-019-4). Farm Journal.

--Farm Journal's Country-Style Microwave Cookbook 2. LC 82-12025. 128p. (Orig.). 1982. pap. 3.95 (ISBN 0-89795-014-3). Farm Journal.

--Farm Journal's Ground Beef Roundup. LC 82-12107. 128p. (Orig.). 1982. pap. 3.95 (ISBN 0-686-84082-8). Farm Journal.

--Farm Journal's Molded Salads, Desserts. LC 76-10410. 128p. (Orig.). 1976. pap. 3.95 (ISBN 0-89795-017-8). Farm Journal.

Farmakides, Anne. Advanced Modern Greek. LC 82-48914. 400p. 1983. pap. text ed. 22.50x (ISBN 0-300-03023-1). Yale U Pr.

--A Manual of Modern Greek, Vol. I. LC 82-48915. 304p. 1983. pap. text ed. 16.95x (ISBN 0-300-03019-3). Yale U Pr.

--A Manual of Modern Greek, Vol. II. LC 82-48916. 304p. 1983. pap. text ed. 14.95x (ISBN 0-300-03020-7). Yale U Pr.

--Modern Greek Reader, No. I. LC 82-48913. 278p. 1983. pap. text ed. 14.95x (ISBN 0-300-03021-5). Yale U Pr.

--Modern Greek Reader, No. II. LC 82-48913. 260p. 1983. pap. text ed. 14.95 (ISBN 0-300-03022-3). Yale U Pr.

Farman, J. V. & Hall, Leslie. Cardiac Output. (Major Problems in Anaesthesia Ser.: Vol. 4). (Illus.). 1973. text ed. write for info. o.p. (ISBN 0-7216-3573-3). Saunders.

Farmer & Anderson. Business Transcription. 192p. 1973. text ed. 11.20x (ISBN 0-7715-0740-2); Section A, Units 1-10, 6 Cassettes. 112.00x (ISBN 0-7715-0742-9); Section B, Units 11-20, 6 Cassettes. 119.64x (ISBN 0-7715-0743-7); Section C, Units 21-30, 6 Cassettes. 119.64x (ISBN 0-7715-0744-5). Forkner.

Farmer & Lyvely. Tits & Clits, No. 2. (Women's Humor Ser.). (Illus.). 1976. 1.25 (ISBN 0-918440-03-3). Nanny Goat.

Farmer, jt. auth. see Chevli.

Farmer, jt. auth. see Lyvely.

Farmer, et al. Business Applications in Typewriting. 368p. 1976. text ed. 16.75x (ISBN 0-7715-0878-6); tchr's. manual 7.80 (ISBN 0-7715-0879-4); stationery & business forms 7.50x (ISBN 0-7715-0880-8); Set Of 26 Cassettes. 336.00x (ISBN 0-7715-0882-4); book of resource materials 44.95x (ISBN 0-7715-0832-8); certificate of proficiency (business, 1 per student) free (ISBN 0-7715-0866-2). Forkner.

--Personal Applications in Typewriting. 272p. 1976. text ed. 14.30x (ISBN 0-7715-0875-1); tchr's. manual 7.80x (ISBN 0-7715-0876-X); Set Of 26 Cassettes. 336.00x (ISBN 0-7715-0882-4); book of resource materials 39.95x (ISBN 0-7715-0831-X); typing facts & tips o.p. 3.56x ea. (ISBN 0-7715-0889-1); typing facts & tips, package of 10 o.p. 24.48x (ISBN 0-7715-0896-4); certificate of proficiency (personal, 1 per student) free (ISBN 0-7715-0865-4); roll of honor for production efficiency (1 per classroom) free (ISBN 0-7715-0864-6). Forkner.

--Professional Applications in Typewriting. 260p. 1977. text ed. 16.75x (ISBN 0-7715-0886-7); tchr's. manual 7.80x (ISBN 0-7715-0887-5); stationery & business forms 7.50x (ISBN 0-7715-0888-3); book of resource materials 44.95x (ISBN 0-7715-0833-6); typing facts & tips o.p. 3.56x ea. (ISBN 0-7715-0889-1); typing facts & tips, package of 10 o.p. 24.48x (ISBN 0-7715-0896-4); certificate of proficiency (professional, 1 per student) free (ISBN 0-7715-0867-0); roll of honor for production efficiency (1 per classroom) free (ISBN 0-7715-0864-6). Forkner.

Farmer, B. H. Green Revolution. LC 76-51278. (Cambridge Commonwealth Ser.). (Illus.). 1977. lib. bdg. 36.00x o.p. (ISBN 0-89158-709-8). Westview.

Farmer, Charles. The Digest Book of Canoeing. (Sports & Leisure Library). (Illus.). 1979. pap. 2.95 o.s.i. (ISBN 0-695-81287-4). Follett.

--The Digest Book of Outdoor Cooking. (Sports & Leisure Library). (Illus.). 1979. pap. 2.95 o.s.i. (ISBN 0-695-81285-8). Follett.

Farmer, Charles J. The Digest Book of Canoes, Kayaks, & Rafts. (DBI Bks). (Illus.). 1977. pap. 5.95 o.p. (ISBN 0-695-80719-6). Follett.

Farmer, D. H., ed. The Oxford Dictionary of Saints. 1978. 25.00 (ISBN 0-19-869120-3). Oxford U Pr.

Farmer, David. Flannery O'Connor: A Descriptive Bibliography. LC 80-8480. 1981. lib. bdg. 20.00 o.s.i. (ISBN 0-8240-9493-X). Garland Pub.

Farmer, David, jt. auth. see Bailey, Peter.

Farmer, David, jt. auth. see Baily, Peter.

Farmer, David & Taylor, Bernard, eds. Corporate Planning & Procurement. LC 74-19369. 272p. 1975. 34.95x o.p. (ISBN 0-470-25499-8). Halsted Pr.

Farmer, David H., ed. The Oxford Dictionary of Saints. 440p. 1978. pap. 7.95 (ISBN 0-19-283036-8). Oxford U Pr.

Farmer, Edward L., et al. Comparative History of Civilization in Asia, Vols. 1 & 2. LC 75-12095. (History Ser.). (Illus.). 1977. Vol. 1. text ed. 20.95 (ISBN 0-201-01998-1); Vol. 2. text ed. 20.95 (ISBN 0-201-01999-X). A-W.

Farmer, F. M. Original Boston Cooking School Cookbook. pap. 6.95 (ISBN 0-452-25314-4, Z5314, Plume). NAL.

Farmer, Frances, ed. Wilson Reader. (Docket Ser.: Vol. 4). 286p. (Orig.). 1956. 7.50 o.p.; pap. 7.50 (ISBN 0-379-11304-X). Oceana.

Farmer, Geraldine M. & Brown, Muriel J. Machine Transcription: A Brief Course. LC 81-65398. (Illus.). 72p. (gr. 10-12). 1981. pap. text ed. 3.16x (ISBN 0-912036-48-6); tchr's resource manual 3.96x (ISBN 0-912036-49-4); instructional narrative 240.00x (ISBN 0-912036-50-8). Forkner.

Farmer, Helen S. & Backer, Thomas E. New Career Options for Women: A Three-Part Series for Counselors, Counselor Trainers & Women Thinking About Careers, 3 pts. 1977. Set. 39.95 (ISBN 0-87705-266-2); Pt. 1, 349 p. 29.95 (ISBN 0-87705-297-2); Pt. 2, 60p. 6.95 (ISBN 0-87705-272-7); Pt. 3, 144pp. 19.95 (ISBN 0-87705-273-5). Human Sci Pr.

Farmer, Henry G. History of Music in Scotland. LC 70-100613. (Music Ser). (Illus.). 1970. Repr. of 1947 ed. lib. bdg. 35.50 (ISBN 0-306-71865-0). Da Capo.

Farmer, Herbert H. Servant of the Word. LC 64-20405. 128p. (Orig.). 1964. pap. 2.75 o.p. (ISBN 0-8006-4001-2, 1-4001). Fortress.

Farmer, I. W. Strata Mechanics. (Developments in Geotechnical Engineering Ser.: Vol. 32). 1982. 85.00 (ISBN 0-444-42086-X). Elsevier.

Farmer, Ian, jt. auth. see Attwell, Peter.

Farmer, James, jt. auth. see Lippert, Frederick G., III.

Farmer, John N. The Protozoa: Introduction to Protozoology. LC 80-10817. (Illus.). 718p. 1980. pap. text ed. 31.95 (ISBN 0-8016-1550-X). Mosby.

Farmer, John S. Americanisms: Old & New. LC 75-44079. 1976. Repr. of 1889 ed. 56.00 o.p. (ISBN 0-8103-3746-0). Gale.

--Public School Word-Book. LC 68-17988. 1968. Repr. of 1900 ed. 30.00x (ISBN 0-8103-3280-9). Gale.

Farmer, Mary A. Barnyard Beauties. (Illus.). 10p. 1981. pap. 4.00 (ISBN 0-943574-04-8). That Patchwork.

--Be an Angel. (Illus.). 10p. 1981. pap. 4.00 (ISBN 0-943574-07-2). That Patchwork.

--Calico Critters. (Illus.). 10p. 1981. pap. 4.00 o.p. (ISBN 0-943574-05-6). That Patchwork.

--Special Santas. (Illus.). 18p. 1981. pap. 4.00 (ISBN 0-943574-08-0). That Patchwork.

Farmer, Mary Ann. Always Ride a White Horse. (Illus.). 12p. 1982. 4.00 (ISBN 0-686-82697-3). That Patchwork.

--Pilots, Partners & Pals. (Illus.). 12p. 1982. 4.00 (ISBN 0-943574-16-1). That Patchwork.

Farmer, MaryAnn. Warmest Witches To You. (Illus.). 12p. 1982. 4.00 (ISBN 0-943574-18-8). That Patchwork.

Farmer, Philip J. The Cache. rev. ed. 288p. 1981. pap. 2.75 (ISBN 0-523-48534-4). Pinnacle Bks.

--Dare. 1980. lib. bdg. 11.95 (ISBN 0-8398-2621-4, Gregg). G K Hall.

--The Dark Design. LC 77-5138. (Riverworld Ser.). (YA) 1977. pap. 2.75 (ISBN 0-425-05546-9, Dist. by Putnam). Berkley Pub.

--The Fabulous Riverboat. (Science Fiction Ser.). 1980. lib. bdg. 13.50 o.p. (ISBN 0-8398-2619-2, Gregg). G K Hall.

--The Green Odyssey. (Science Fiction Ser.). 1978. lib. bdg. 9.00 o.p. (ISBN 0-8398-2414-9, Gregg). G K Hall.

--Hadon of Ancient Opar. (Science Fiction Ser.). 1981. pap. 2.50 o.p. (ISBN 0-87997-637-3, UE 1637). DAW Bks.

--Inside-Outside. 1979. pap. 1.75 o.p. (ISBN 0-425-04041-0). Berkley Pub.

--Inside Outside. 1980. lib. bdg. 11.95 (ISBN 0-8398-2622-2, Gregg). G K Hall.

--Lord Tyger. 1972. pap. 1.50 o.p. (ISBN 0-451-07577-3, W7577, Sig). NAL.

--The Magic Labyrinth. LC 80-144. 1980. 11.95 (ISBN 0-399-12381-4). Putnam Pub Group.

--Riverworld & Other Stories. 1981. lib. bdg. 15.95 (ISBN 0-8398-2618-4, Gregg). G K Hall.

--Strange Relations. 1978. pap. 1.75 o.p. (ISBN 0-380-00095-4, 41418). Avon.

--To Your Scattered Bodies Go. 1980. lib. bdg. 12.95 (ISBN 0-8398-2620-6, Gregg). G K Hall.

--The Unreasoning Mask. 300p. 1981. 12.95 (ISBN 0-399-12673-2); limited deluxe boxed 40.00 (ISBN 0-399-12676-7). Putnam Pub Group.

Farmer, Philip Jose, intro. by see Upfield, Arthur W.

Farmer, R. D., jt. auth. see Miller, D. L.

Farmer, Richard & Kowalewski, Victor. Law Enforcement & Community Relations. 160p. 1976. 14.95 (ISBN 0-87909-434-6). Reston.

Farmer, Richard, ed. see Hawes, Jon M.

Farmer, Richard N. & Hogue, W. Dickerson. Corporate Social Responsibility. LC 72-96061. (Illus.). 223p. 1973. pap. text ed. 12.95 (ISBN 0-574-17930-5, 13-0930); instr's guide avail. (ISBN 0-574-17931-3, 13-0931). SRA.

Farmer, Richard N., ed. see Bartlett, Roger W.

Farmer, Richard N., ed. see Bindon, Kathleen R.

Farmer, Richard N., ed. see Joo, Jalaleddin S.

Farmer, Richard N., ed. see Magann, Julia H.

Farmer, Silas. History of Detroit & Wayne County & Early Michigan: A Chronological Cyclopedia of the Past & Present. LC 68-26178. 1969. Repr. of 1890 ed. 60.00x (ISBN 0-8103-3326-0). Gale.

Farmer, Silas, jt. auth. see Hall, Theodore P.

Farmer, Thomas W. Pediatric Neurology. 3rd ed. (Illus.). 768p. 1982. text ed. 67.50 (ISBN 0-06-140802-6, Harper Medical). Lippincott.

Farmer, V. C., jt. ed. see Mortland, M. M.

Farmer, W. D. Homes for Pleasant Living. 27th ed. (Illus.). 1977. pap. 2.50 o.p. (ISBN 0-931518-04-0). W D Farmer.

--Homes for Pleasant Living. 26th ed. (Illus.). 1977. pap. 2.50 o.p. (ISBN 0-931518-03-2). W D Farmer.

--Homes for Pleasant Living. 39th ed. (Orig.). 1982. pap. 4.50 (ISBN 0-931518-16-4). W D Farmer.

--Homes for Pleasant Living: Country & Victorian Style Homes. (Illus.). 113p. (Orig.). 1982. pap. 5.00 (ISBN 0-931518-15-6). W D Farmer.

Farmer, Walter A., jt. auth. see Sipe, H. Craig.

Farmer, Wesley M. Sea-Slug Gastropods. (Illus.). 177p. (Orig.). 1980. pap. 9.57 (ISBN 0-937772-00-3). Farmer Ent.

Farmer, William R. & Farkasfalvy, Denis. The Formation of the New Testament: An Ecumenical Approach. LC 82-62417. (Theological Inquiries Ser.). 1983. pap. 8.95 (ISBN 0-8091-2495-5). Paulist Pr.

Farmer, William R., et al. Christian History & Interpretation. 1967. 47.50 (ISBN 0-521-04981-4). Cambridge U Pr.

Farnay, Josie & Soleillant, Claude. Egypt: Activities & Projects in Color. LC 78-66309. (Illus.). 1979. 10.95 (ISBN 0-8069-4554-0); PLB 13.29 (ISBN 0-8069-4555-9). Sterling.

Farness, Jay, jt. auth. see Jones, Peter.

Farnham, Charles H. Life of Francis Parkman. LC 69-13894. Repr. of 1901 ed. lib. bdg. 17.50x (ISBN 0-8371-4463-9, FAFP). Greenwood.

Farnham, Rebecca & Link, Irene. Effects of the Works Program on Rural Relief. LC 73-165682. (Research Monograph Ser.: Vol. 13). 1971. Repr. of 1938 ed. lib. bdg. 19.50 (ISBN 0-306-70345-9). Da Capo.

Farnham, Thomas J. Travels in the Great Western Prairies, 2 vols. in 1. LC 68-16231. (The American Scene Ser.). 612p. 1973. Repr. of 1843 ed. lib. bdg. 75.00 (ISBN 0-306-71012-9). Da Capo.

Farnham-Diggory, Sylvia. Cognitive Processeing in Education: A Psychological Preparation for Teaching & Curriculum Development. 1972. text ed. 25.50 scp o.p. (ISBN 0-06-041999-7, HarpC); instructors' manual avail. o.p. (ISBN 0-06-361975-X). Har-Row.

Farnsworth, Allan. Contracts. LC 81-84829. 1982. text ed. 25.00 (ISBN 0-316-27461-5). Little.

Farnsworth, E. Allan & Honnold, John O. Cases & Materials on the Law of Sales & Sales Financing 4th Ed., & Cases & Material on Commercial Law, 3rd Ed. 1982 Supplement. 58p. 1982. pap. text ed. write for info. (ISBN 0-88277-098-5). Foundation Pr.

Farnsworth, Edward A. An Introduction to the Legal System of the United States. 2nd, rev. ed. LC 74-29388. 184p. Date not set. lib. bdg. 10.00 (ISBN 0-379-00255-8). Oceana.

Farnsworth, Kirk E. Integrating Psychology & Theology: Elbows Together but Hearts Apart. LC 81-40100. 94p. 1982. lib. bdg. 18.50 (ISBN 0-8191-1851-6); pap. text ed. 7.00 (ISBN 0-8191-1852-4). U Pr of Amer.

Farnsworth, M. W. Genetics. 1978. text ed. 29.50 scp (ISBN 0-06-042003-0, HarpC). Har-Row.

Farnsworth, Paul R. Social Psychology of Music. 2nd ed. 1969. 15.00x (ISBN 0-8138-1547-9). Iowa St U Pr.

Farnsworth, Robert. Three or Four Hills & A Cloud: Wesleyan Poetry, Vol. 106. LC 82-4934. 1982. 12.00x (ISBN 0-8195-2108-6); pap. 6.95 (ISBN 0-8195-1108-0). Wesleyan U Pr.

Farnsworth, Robert M., ed. see Tolson, Melvin B.

Farnsworth, Terry. On the Way up. 1976. 17.50 o.p. (ISBN 0-07-084471-2, P&RB). McGraw.

Farny, Michael. New England Over the Handlebars: A Cyclist's Guide. (Illus., Orig.). 1975. pap. 6.95 (ISBN 0-316-27465-8). Little.

Farouk, Brimah K. Georgia State Senate District Thirty-Five Democratic Primaries of 1982. 1982. 1.00 (ISBN 0-686-38025-8). Voter Ed Proj.

--Profile of Mississippi Black Voting Strength & Political Representation. 1982. 1.00 (ISBN 0-686-38028-2). Voter Ed Proj.

Farouk, Brimah K. & Hudlin, Richard A. Population Trends in Majority Black Counties in Eleven Southern States: 1900 to 1980. 1981. 1.00 (ISBN 0-686-38018-5). Voter Ed Proj.

Farouk, Brimah K., jt. auth. see Hudlin, Richard A.

Farquhar, Francis P., ed. see Brewer, William H.

Farquhar, John W. The American Way of Life Need Not Be Hazardous to Your Health. (Illus.). 208p. 1979. 12.95 o.p. (ISBN 0-393-06443-3); pap. 6.95 (ISBN 0-393-00963-7). Norton.

Farquhar, Judith & Gajdusek, D. Carleton, eds. Kuru: Early Letters & Field Notes from the Collection of D. Carleton Gajdusek. 366p. 1981. text ed. 44.00 (ISBN 0-89004-359-0). Raven.

Farquhar, Judith, jt. ed. see Murata, Alice K.

Farquhar, Roger B. Old Homes & History of Montgomery County, Maryland. (Illus.). 1981. 35.00 (ISBN 0-910086-06-0). Am Hist Res.

Farquharson, Robin. Theory of Voting. LC 70-81417. 1969. 15.00x (ISBN 0-300-01121-0). Yale U Pr.

Farr, Alan. Storm Warnings. 1979. pap. 4.95 (ISBN 0-686-25037-0). Whitmer Pub Co.

Farr, Carolina. House of Dark Illusions. Incl. Secret of the Chateau. 1977. pap. 2.50 (ISBN 0-451-11691-7, AE1691, Sig). NAL.

Farr, Caroline. Castle in Spain. Bd. with So Near & Yet... 1978. pap. 2.50 (ISBN 0-451-11694-1, AE1694, Sig). NAL.

--Castle on the Rhine. (Orig.). 1979. pap. 1.50 o.p. (ISBN 0-451-08615-5, W8615, Sig). NAL.

--Dark Citadel. 1975. pap. 1.25 o.p. (ISBN 0-451-07552-8, Y7552, Sig). NAL.

--House of Illusions. Bd. with Secret of the Chateau. 1982. pap. 2.50 (ISBN 0-451-11691-7, AE1691, Sig). NAL.

--Sinister House. (Orig.). 1978. pap. 1.50 o.p. (ISBN 0-451-07892-6, W7892, Sig). NAL.

--Witch's Hammer. Bd. with Granite Folly. 1978. pap. 2.50 (ISBN 0-451-11699-2, AE1699, Sig). NAL.

Farr, D. F., jt. auth. see Miller, O. K., Jr.

Farr, Dennis. The Oxford History of English Art, Vol. XI: English Art 1870-1940. (History of English Art Ser.). (Illus.). 1979. 54.00x (ISBN 0-19-817208-7). Oxford U Pr.

Farr, Finis. Margaret Mitchell of Atlanta. 1976. pap. 1.75 o.p. (ISBN 0-380-00810-6, 20594). Avon.

--Rickenbacker's Luck: An American Life. 1979. 12.95 o.p. (ISBN 0-395-27102-9). HM.

Farr, Gerald G. Biology Illustrated. (Illus.). 117p. 1979. pap. text ed. 5.95x (ISBN 0-89641-054-4). American Pr.

--Botany Illustrated. (Illus.). 52p. 1979. pap. text ed. 3.95x (ISBN 0-89641-055-2). American Pr.

--Zoology Illustrated. (Illus.). 65p. 1979. pap. text ed. 3.95x (ISBN 0-89641-056-0). American Pr.

Farr, James A. & Wright, Jackson. Estate Planner's Handbook, 1982: Supplement. LC 79-88997. 1982. pap. 17.50 (ISBN 0-316-27475-5). Little.

Farr, Michael. The Work Book. 1982. 10.00 (ISBN 0-686-36295-0); instr's. guide 5.28 (ISBN 0-686-37286-7). McKnight.

Farr, Naunerle, ed. see Poe, Edgar Allan.

Farr, Naunerle C. Babe Ruth - Jackie Robinson. (Pendulum Illustrated Biography Ser.). (Illus.). (gr. 4-12). 1979. text ed. 5.00 (ISBN 0-88301-371-1); pap. text ed. 1.95 (ISBN 0-88301-359-2); wkbk 1.25 (ISBN 0-88301-383-5). Pendulum Pr.

Farr, Sidney S. More than Moonshine: Appalachian Recipes & Recollections. LC 82-13524. 176p. 1983. 11.95 (ISBN 0-8229-3475-2); pap. 4.95 (ISBN 0-8229-5347-1). U of Pittsburgh Pr.

Farrall, Arthur W. Engineering for Dairy & Food Products. 2nd ed. LC 79-1171. (Illus.). 1980. lib. bdg. 31.00 (ISBN 0-88275-859-4). Krieger.

Farran, Christopher. Infant Colic: What It Is & What You Can Do About It. 106p. 1982. 10.95 (ISBN 0-684-17779-X, ScribT). Scribner.

Farrand, John, jt. auth. see Bull, John.

Farrand, John, Jr., ed. The Audubon Society Encyclopedia of Animal Life. LC 82-81466. (Illus.). 600p. 1982. 45.00 (ISBN 0-517-54657-4, Pub. by Potter). Crown.

Farrand, John, Jr., ed. see Audubon Society.

Farrand, Max. Fathers of the Constitution. 1921. text ed. 8.50x (ISBN 0-686-83547-6). Elliots Bks.
Farrant, Smith J., jt. auth. see Ashwood, M. J.
Farrar, Becky. Centennial Clairette Eighteen Eighty to Nineteen Eighty. 333p. 1980. 20.00 (ISBN 0-9609406-0-X). Greens Creek.
Farrar, C. L. & Leeming, D. W. Military Ballistics: A Basic Manual. 225p. 1983. 26.00 (ISBN 0-08-028342-X); pap. 13.00 (ISBN 0-08-028343-8). Pergamon.
Farrar, D., jt. auth. see Meyer, J.
Farrar, Estelle S. H. P. Sinclaire, Jr., Glassmaker, Vol. 1: The Years Before 1920. (Illus.). viii, 152p. 1974. pap. 10.95 (ISBN 0-686-09327-5). Corning.
--H. P. Sinclaire, Jr., Glassmaker, Vol. 2: The Manufacturing Years. (Illus.). viii, 119p. 1975. pap. 10.95 (ISBN 0-686-10549-4). Corning.
Farrar, F. W. The First Book of Kings. 1981. 19.00 (ISBN 0-86524-035-3, 1101). Klock & Klock.
--The Life & Work of St. Paul. 1980. 2 vol. set 43.95 (ISBN 0-86524-055-8, 8402). Klock & Klock.
--The Second Book of Kings. 1981. 19.00 (ISBN 0-86524-036-1, 1201). Klock & Klock.
Farrar, Frederic W. Life of Christ. 1982. lib. bdg. 24.95 (ISBN 0-86524-089-2, 9508). Klock & Klock.
Farrar, Frederick W. Eric, or Little by Little. LC 75-32199. (Classics of Children's Literature, 1621-1932: Vol. 60). (Illus.). 1976. Repr. of 1892 ed. PLB 38.00 o.s.i. (ISBN 0-8240-2309-9). Garland Pub.
Farrar, G. E., Jr., jt. auth. see Dean, W. B.
Farrar, Geraldine. Such Sweet Compulsion, the Autobiography of Geraldine Farrar. LC 70-100656. (Music Ser). 1970. Repr. of 1938 ed. lib. bdg. 29.50 (ISBN 0-306-71863-4). Da Capo.
Farrar, Kenneth G. Hurry Gringo. Ashton, Sylvia, ed. LC 78-31374. 1983. 14.95 (ISBN 0-87949-143-4). Ashley Bks.
Farrar, Margaret. The Funk & Wagnall's-Los Angeles Crossword Treasury, 3 vols. (Funk & W Bk.). 1978. pap. 3.95i ea. (TYC-T); Vol. 1. (ISBN 0-308-10311-4); Vol. 2. (ISBN 0-308-10312-2); Vol. 3. o.p. (ISBN 0-308-10313-0). T Y Crowell.
Farrar, Richard. The Birds' Woodland: What Lives There. new ed. LC 75-28034. (What Lives There Ser.). (Illus.). 32p. (gr. 3-5). 1976. PLB 4.99 o.p. (ISBN 0-698-30608-2, Coward). Putnam Pub Group.
--The Hungry Snowbird. (Break-of-Day Bk.). (Illus.). 48p. (gr. 1-3). 1975. PLB 6.59 o.p. (ISBN 0-698-30557-4, Coward). Putnam Pub Group.
Farrell, B. A. see Smith, B. Babington.
Farrell, Bryan H. Hawaii, the Legend That Sells. LC 81-16177. (Illus.). 420p. 1982. text ed. 20.00x (ISBN 0-8248-0766-9). UH Pr.
Farrell, Catharine H. & Nessel, Denise D. Effects of Storytelling: An Ancient Art for Modern Classrooms. 36p. (Orig.). 1982. write for info. (ISBN 0-936434-04-X). Zellerbach.
Farrell, Cliff. Comanch: Ride the Wild Trail. 1982. pap. 2.50 (ISBN 0-451-11565-1, AE1565, Sig). NAL.
--The Devil's Playground. 1978. pap. 1.50 o.p. (ISBN 0-451-08260-5, W8260, Sig). NAL.
--Patchsaddle Drive. Bd. with Shootout at Sioux Wells. 1980. pap. 2.50 (ISBN 0-451-11603-8, Sig). NAL.
--Return of the Long Riders. Bd. with Terror in Eagle Basin. 1982. pap. 2.75 (ISBN 0-451-11839-1, AE1839, Sig). NAL.
Farrell, David. Collegiate Book Arts Presses: A New Census of Printing Presses in American Colleges & Universities. LC 81-17387. 46p. (Orig.). 1982. pap. 7.50x (ISBN 0-9607290-0-3). Fine Print.
Farrell, Edward. Can You Drink This Cup? pap. 4.95 (ISBN 0-87193-179-6). Dimension Bks.
Farrell, Edward, jt. auth. see Ghani, Noordin.
Farrell, Gerald J., jt. auth. see Kosicki, George W.
Farrell, Gordon H., jt. auth. see Briscall, C. M.
Farrell, J. G. The Singapore Grip. 1980. pap. 2.75 o.p. (ISBN 0-425-04503-X). Berkley Pub.
Farrell, Jack, jt. auth. see Grossman, William.
Farrell, James J. Inventing the American Way of Death, 1830-1920. Davis, Allen F., ed. (American Civilization Ser.). 287p. 1980. 27.95 (ISBN 0-87722-180-4). Temple U Pr.
Farrell, James L. Guide to Portfolio Management. (McGraw-Hill Guide Series in Finance). (Illus.). 368p. 1983. text ed. 19.95 (ISBN 0-07-019970-1, C). McGraw.
Farrell, James T. Sam Holman. 246p. 1983. 15.95 (ISBN 0-87975-202-5). Prometheus Bks.
--When Time Was Born. LC 66-16296. 1966. 3.50 (ISBN 0-912292-04-0); signed ltd. ed. 25.00 (ISBN 0-912292-05-9). The Smith.
Farrell, Jane. Illustrated Guide to Orthopedic Nursing. LC 77-3920. 1977. pap. text ed. 14.75x o.p. (ISBN 0-397-54205-4, Lippincott Nursing). Lippincott.
--Illustrated Guide to Orthopedic Nursing. 2nd ed. (Illus.). 400p. 1982. pap. text ed. 14.75 (ISBN 0-397-54274-7, Lippincott Nursing). Lippincott.
Farrell, Kate, jt. auth. see Koch, Kenneth.
Farrell, M. J., ed. Readings in Welfare Economics. LC 72-85152. 308p. 1973. 26.00 (ISBN 0-312-66500-8). St Martin.
Farrell, Michael, jt. auth. see Greer, Gaylon E.
Farrell, Nigel, jt. auth. see Parker, Bruce.
Farrell, Patricia & Lundegren, Herberta M. The Process of Recreation Programming: Theory & Technique. LC 78-17100. 315p. 1978. text ed. 21.95x (ISBN 0-471-01709-4). Wiley.
--The Process of Recreation Programming: Theory & Technique. 2nd ed. LC 82-17626. 296p. 1983. text ed. 21.95 (ISBN 0-471-86181-2). Wiley.
Farrell, Paul V., jt. auth. see Heinritz, Stuart F.
Farrell, Paul V., ed. see National Association of Purchasing Management.
Farrell, Philip, ed. Lung Development: Biological & Clinical Perspectives, 2 vols. LC 82-1616. 1982. Vol. 1: Biochemistry & Physiology. 28.00 (ISBN 0-12-249780-5); Vol. 2: Neonatal Respiratory Distress. 37.50 (ISBN 0-12-249702-3). Acad Pr.
Farrell, R. B. Dictionary of German Synonyms. 3rd ed. LC 75-36175. 1977. 54.50 (ISBN 0-521-21189-1); pap. 14.95 (ISBN 0-521-29068-6). Cambridge U Pr.
Farrell, R. T., ed. Daniel & Azarias. LC 74-31590. (Old English Library). 1974. 20.00x (ISBN 0-416-78130-6). Methuen Inc.
Farrell, Robert, jt. ed. see Hammond, Thomas T.
Farrell, Ronald A. & Swigert, Victoria L. Deviance & Social Control. 1981. pap. text ed. 9.95x o.p. (ISBN 0-673-15268-5). Scott F.
Farrell, William R. The U. S. Government Response to Terrorism, 1972-1980: In Search of an Effective Strategy. (National & International Terrorism Ser.). 200p. 1982. lib. bdg. 20.00 (ISBN 0-86531-402-0). Westview.
Farrelly, M. Natalena. Thomas Francis Meehan Eighteen Fifty-Four to Nineteen Forty-Two: A Memoir. LC 44-8793. (Monograph: No. 20). (Illus.). 1944. 10.00x (ISBN 0-930060-02-4). US Cath Hist.
Farren, Fick, jt. auth. see Carr, Roy.
Farren, Mick & Snow, George. Rock 'n' Roll Circus. LC 77-87150. (Illus.). 120p. 1978. 14.95 o.s.i. (ISBN 0-89104-088-9); pap. 7.95 o.s.i. (ISBN 0-89104-091-9, A & W Visual Library). A & W Pubs.
Farren, Mick, jt. auth. see Dalton, David.
Farren, Mike, compiled by. Elvis Presley in His Own Words. (Illus.). 128p. 1981. pap. 4.95 (ISBN 0-8256-3921-2, Quick Fox). Putnam Pub Group.
Farrenc, Louise. Trio in E Minor: Opus Forty Five for Piano, Flute, (Violin) & Cello. (Women Composers Ser.: No. 3). 1979. Repr. of 1862 ed. 22.50 (ISBN 0-306-79553-1). Da Capo.
Farrer, Austin. Finite & Infinite: A Philosophical Essay. 312p. (Orig.). 1979. pap. 8.95 (ISBN 0-8164-2001-7). Seabury.
Farrer, James A. Literary Forgeries. LC 68-23156. 1969. Repr. of 1907 ed. 30.00x (ISBN 0-8103-3305-8). Gale.
--Military Manners & Customs. LC 68-21771. 1968. Repr. of 1885 ed. 30.00x (ISBN 0-8103-3510-7). Gale.
Farrer-Meschan, R. M. F., jt. auth. see Meschan, Isadore.
Farrington, B. Samuel Butler & the Odyssey. LC 73-21626. (English Literature Ser., No. 33). 1974. lib. bdg. 46.95x (ISBN 0-8383-1777-4). Haskell.
Farrington, Brian. Industrial Purchase Price Management. 208p. 1980. text ed. 43.25x (ISBN 0-566-02186-2). Gower Pub Ltd.
Farrington, David P., jt. auth. see Gunn, John.
Farrington, G. H., jt. auth. see Scorer, C. G.
Farrington, S. Kip. Fishing with Hemingway & Glassel. 7.95 (ISBN 0-911660-23-2). Yankee Peddler.
Farrington, William, et al. Fertilizer, Chemicals & Seed. (Illus.). 144p. 1980. pap. text ed. 6.96 (ISBN 0-07-019965-5, G). McGraw.
Farris, Edmond J. Art Students' Anatomy. 2nd ed. (Illus.). 1953. pap. 3.50 (ISBN 0-486-20744-7). Dover.
Farris, Jack. Me & Gallagher. 1982. 13.95 (ISBN 0-671-45697-0). S&S.
Farris, John. Catacombs. 1981. 13.95 o.s.i. (ISBN 0-440-01120-5). Delacorte.
Farris, Martin T. & McElhiney, Paul T. Modern Transportation: Selected Readings. 2nd ed. LC 72-6891. 1973. pap. text ed. 9.95 o.p. (ISBN 0-395-14034-X). HM.
Farris, Martin T. & Sampson, Roy J. Public Utilities: Regulation, Management, & Ownership. LC 72-85908. 420p. 1973. text ed. 24.50 (ISBN 0-395-13884-1). HM.
Farris, Martin T., jt. auth. see Sampson, Roy.
Farris, Mayme. Mayme Farris Cook Book. 192p. 1980. pap. 8.95 o.p. (ISBN 0-87706-112-2). Branch-Smith.
Farris, Paul, jt. auth. see Albion, Mark S.
Farrokhzad, Forugh. Another Birth. Javadi, Hasan & Sallee, Susan, trs. from Farsi. 144p. (Orig.). 1981. pap. 7.00 (ISBN 0-686-97509-X). Three Continents.
Farrow, Anthony. George Moore. (English Authors Ser.). 1978. 13.95 (ISBN 0-8057-6685-5, Twayne). G K Hall.
Farrugia & Gammons. Carrying British Mails. 6.50. StanGib Ltd.
Farrukhzad, Furugh. Bride of Acacias. Kessler, Jascha, tr. LC 82-1156. 1983. 25.00x (ISBN 0-88206-050-3). Caravan Bks.
Farthing, Geoffrey. Theosophy: What's It All About. 1967. 5.25 o.p. (ISBN 0-8356-5075-8). Theos Pub Hse.
Farudi, Daryush, jt. auth. see Robinson, Ruth E.
Faruqee, F., jt. auth. see Amin, R.
Faruqee, Rashid. Integrating Family Planning with Health Services: Does it Help? LC 82-8405. (World Bank Staff Working Papers: No. 515). (Orig.). 1982. pap. 3.00 (ISBN 0-8213-0003-2). World Bank.
--Kenya: Population & Development. xii, 213p. 1980. pap. 15.00 (ISBN 0-686-36110-5, RC-8010). World Bank.
Faruqi, Lois I. Al see Al Faruqi, Lois I.
Faruqi, Shakil, jt. auth. see Dubey, Vinod.
Farvour, James L. TRSDOS 2.3 Decoded & Other Mysteries. (TRS-80 Information Ser.: Vol. VI). 300p. (Orig.). 1982. pap. 29.95 (ISBN 0-936200-07-3). IJG Inc.
Farwell, Byron. The Man Who Presumed: A Biography of Henry M. Stanley. LC 73-15205. (Illus.). 334p. 1974. Repr. of 1957 ed. lib. bdg. 19.25x (ISBN 0-8371-7160-1, FAMW). Greenwood.
Farwell, L. C., jt. auth. see Leffler, G. L.
Farwell, R. F., jt. auth. see Schmitt, N. M.
Farzan, Satter, et al. A Concise Handbook of Respiratory Diseases. (Illus.). 1978. text ed. 23.95 (ISBN 0-87909-180-0). Reston.
Farzin, Yeganeh. The Effect of Discount Rate & Substitute Technology on Depletion of Exhaustible Resources. LC 82-8612. (World Bank Staff Working Papers: No. 516). (Orig.). 1982. pap. 5.00 (ISBN 0-8213-0004-0). World Bank.
Fasan, Ernst. Relations with Alien Intelligences. the Scientific Basis of Metalaw. LC 76-463957. 110p. 1970. 10.00x (ISBN 3-87061-021-2). Intl Pubns Serv.
Fasana, Paul, jt. auth. see Malinconico, S. Michael.
Fasier, Gil. Big Ear & the Albino: Two Stories. LC 81-86420. 160p. 1983. pap. 5.95 (ISBN 0-86666-040-2). GWP.
Fasman, G., jt. ed. see Timasheff, S.
Fasman, G. D., ed. Poly-Alpha-Amino Acids: Protein Models for Conformational Studies. (Biological Macromolecules Ser: Vol. 1). 1967. 79.50 o.p. (ISBN 0-8247-1186-6). Dekker.
Fasman, G. D., jt. ed. see Timasheff, S. N.
Fasman, Gerald D. & Timasheff, Serge, eds. Subunits in Biological Systems, Pt. B. (Biological Macromolecules Ser: Vol. 6). 336p. 1973. 55.00 o.p. (ISBN 0-8247-6041-7). Dekker.
Fasnacht, H. D., et al. How to Use Business Machines. 3rd ed. 1969. text ed. 7.96 (ISBN 0-07-019972-8, G); tchr's manual & key 4.50 (ISBN 0-07-019973-6). McGraw.
Faso, La see Flynn, Elizabeth W. & La Faso, John F.
Faso La, see Flynn, Elizabeth & La Faso, John.
Fasold, Ralph W., jt. auth. see Walfman, Walt.
Fasolo. Titian. pap. 12.50rite for info. (ISBN 0-935748-09-1). ScalaBooks.
Fass, Arnold L. & Newman, Claire M. Unified Mathematics: Content, Methods, Materials for Elementary School Teachers. 448p. 1975. text ed. 16.95x o.p. (ISBN 0-669-89359-5). Heath.
Fass, Paula S. The Damned & the Beautiful: American Youth in the 1920s. LC 76-42644. 1977. 29.50x (ISBN 0-19-502148-7). Oxford U Pr.
--The Damned & the Beautiful: American Youth in the 1920's. LC 76-42644. 1979. pap. 8.95 (ISBN 0-19-502492-3, GB567, GB). Oxford U Pr.
Fass, Peter M., jt. auth. see Haft, Robert J.
Fassbender, William. You & Your Health. 2nd ed. LC 79-12472. 479p. 1980. text ed. 16.95 (ISBN 0-471-04936-0); tchrs' manual 7.00 (ISBN 0-471-06384-3). Wiley.
Fassett, Norman C. Spring Flora of Wisconsin. 4th ed. LC 74-27307. (Illus.). 430p. 1976. 15.00 (ISBN 0-299-06750-5); pap. 8.50 (ISBN 0-299-06754-8). U of Wis Pr.
Fassler, D. & Lay, N. Encounter with a New World: A Reading-Writing Text for Speakers of English As a Second Language. 1979. pap. 11.95 (ISBN 0-13-274910-6). P-H.
Fassman, Paula & Tavares, Suzanne. Gallery. (Illus.). 1982. pap. 6.95x (ISBN 0-19-503132-6). Oxford U Pr.
Fassnacht, C. Theory & Practice of Observing Behavior. (Behavioural Development Monographs). 1982. 28.00 (ISBN 0-12-249780-5). Acad Pr.
Fassnacht, Karl. Unternehmungsplanung und Mitbestimmung Nach Dem Betriebsverfassungsgesetz. 248p. (Ger.). 1982. write for info. (ISBN 3-8204-5846-8). P Lang Pubs.
Fast, Barry, ed. The Catfish Cookbook. LC 82-11253. 105p. (Orig.). 1982. pap. 5.95 (ISBN 0-914788-61-2). East Woods.
Fast, Franziska, jt. ed. see Nusberg, Charlotte.
Fast, Howard. April Morning. (YA) 1961. 8.95 (ISBN 0-517-50681-5). Crown.
--Citizen Tom Paine. 2nd ed. 360p. 1983. pap. 6.95 (ISBN 0-394-62464-5, Ever). Grove.
--Conceived in Liberty: A Novel of Valley Forge. 208p. 1974. pap. 1.25 o.p. (ISBN 0-451-05604-3, Y5604, Sig). NAL.
--The Establishment. (General Ser.). 1979. lib. bdg. 16.95 (ISBN 0-8161-3003-5, Large Print Bks). G K Hall.
--Freedom Road. 1944. 5.95 o.p. (ISBN 0-517-50689-0); pap. 1.95 (ISBN 0-517-05039-0). Crown.
--Max. (General Ser.). 1983. lib. bdg. 18.95 (ISBN 0-8161-3495-2, Large Print Bks). G K Hall.
--Time & the Riddle. 15.00 o.p. (ISBN 0-517-53769-9, Pub. by Ward Ritchie). Crown.
Fast, J. D. Entropy. 2nd ed. 332p. 1970. 81.00x (ISBN 0-677-61260-5). Gordon.
Fast, Jonathan. Mortal Gods. (RL 7). 1979. pap. 1.75 o.p. (ISBN 0-451-08573-6, E8573, Sig). NAL.
--The Secrets of Synchronicity. (Orig.). (RL 5). 1977. pap. 1.50 o.p. (ISBN 0-451-07556-0, W7556, Sig). NAL.
Fast, Julius. Body Language. LC 72-106592. (Illus.). 192p. 1970. 9.95 (ISBN 0-87131-391-X). M Evans.
--The Body Language of Sex, Power & Aggression. 1978. pap. 2.75 (ISBN 0-515-06487-4). Jove Pubns.
Fast, R. W. Advances in Cryogenic Engineering, Vol.27. 1252p. 1982. 95.00 (ISBN 0-306-41103-2, Plenum Pr). Plenum Pub.
Fasteau, Marc F. The Male Machine. LC 74-9858. (Illus.). 240p. 1974. 8.95 o.p. (ISBN 0-07-019985-X, GB). McGraw.
Fata, Frank J., tr. see Ilardi, Vincent.
Fatehally, Laeeq, ed. Women in the Third World. 155p. 1980. pap. 7.95x (ISBN 0-86590-016-7, Jaico Books India). Apt Bks.
Father. The Language of Flowers. 1976. 5.00 o.p. (ISBN 0-517-52555-0, Harmony). Crown.
Father of Candor. An Enquiry into the Doctrine, Lately Propagated, Concerning Libels, Warrants, & the Seizure of Papers. facsimile ed. LC 76-121100. (Civil Liberties in American History Ser.). 136p. 1970. Repr. of 1764 ed. 22.50 (ISBN 0-306-71970-3). Da Capo.
Father Powell. Ox'zem: Boxelder & His Sacred Lance. (Indian Culture Ser.). 1.95 o.p. (ISBN 0-89992-030-6). MT Coun Indian.
Father Power. Issiwin: Boxelder & His Sacred Lance. (Indian Culture Ser.). 2.00 o.p. (ISBN 0-686-22329-2). MT Coun Indian.
Fathman, Ann K., et al. Science Discoveries for Language Learning: Ideas for Physical Science. (The Teacher IDEA Ser.). 64p. (Orig.). 1983. pap. text ed. write for info. (ISBN 0-88499-628-X). Inst Mod Lang.
Fathman, C. Garrison, ed. Isolation, Characterization & Utilization of T Lymphocyte Clones. 1982. 59.50 (ISBN 0-12-249920-4). Acad Pr.
Fathy, Hassan. Architecture for the Poor. LC 72-95133. 1973. 17.50x (ISBN 0-226-23915-2). U of Chicago Pr.
--Architecture for the Poor. LC 72-95133. (Illus.). xviii, 234p. 1973. pap. 9.95 (ISBN 0-226-23916-0, P660, Phoen). U of Chicago Pr.
Fatio. The Happy Lioness. 113p. 1980. PLB 8.95 (ISBN 0-07-020069-6). McGraw.
Fatio, Louise. Happy Lion & the Bear. (gr. k-3). 1964. PLB 8.95 (ISBN 0-07-020060-2, GB). McGraw.
--Happy Lion in Africa. (Illus.). (gr. k-3). 1955. PLB 8.95 o.p. (ISBN 0-07-020043-2, GB). McGraw.
--Happy Lion's Quest. (Illus.). (gr. k-3). 1961. PLB 8.95 o.p. (ISBN 0-07-020054-8, GB). McGraw.
--Happy Lion's Treasure. (Illus.). (gr. k-3). 1970. PLB 7.95 o.p. (ISBN 0-07-020064-5, GB). McGraw.
--Hector & Christina. (Illus.). (ps-3). 1977. 8.95 o.p. (ISBN 0-07-020072-6, GB); PLB 7.95 o.p. (ISBN 0-07-020073-4). McGraw.
Fator, Sue. The Adventures of Tomoteo. pap. 1.25 (ISBN 0-89985-992-5). Christ Nations.
Fatrell, Jon, jt. auth. see Gill, Chris.
Fatt, Irving. Polarographic Oxygen Sensor: Its Theory of Operation & Its Application in Biology, Medicine & Technology. LC 82-6581. 290p. (Orig.). 1982. Repr. of 1976 ed. 59.95 (ISBN 0-89874-511-X). Krieger.
Fattoross, Camille, jt. auth. see Scarpato, Maria.
Fattorusso, J., ed. Wonders of Italy. 16th rev. ed. 1974. 55.00 (ISBN 0-685-12054-6). Heinman.
Fau, Margaret E., compiled by. Gabriel Garcia Marquez: An Annotated Bibliography, 1947-1979. LC 80-784. x, 198p. 1980. lib. bdg. 35.00 (ISBN 0-313-22224-X, FGM/). Greenwood.
Faucett, Beth. Mighty Mouth. 48p. (gr. k-8). 1981. tchr's. ed. 4.95 (ISBN 0-86653-016-9, GA 245); wkbk. 4.95 (GA246). Good Apple.
Faucher, Philippe, jt. auth. see Bruneau, Thomas C.
Fauchet, Claude & Bonneville, Nicolas De, eds. La Bouche De Fer. (Le Cercle Social). (Fr.). 1978. lib. bdg. 615.25x o.p. (ISBN 0-8287-1335-9). Clearwater Pub.
Fauchet, Joseph. Le Despotisme Decrete Par L'assemblee Nationale. (Rousseauism, 1788-1797). 1978. Repr. lib. bdg. 26.00x o.p. (ISBN 0-8287-0332-9). Clearwater Pub.
Fauci, A. S. & Ballieux, R., eds. Human B Lymphocyte Function: Activation & Immunoregulation. 384p. 1982. text ed. 55.00 (ISBN 0-89004-620-4). Raven.
Fauci, Anthony S., jt. auth. see Cupps, Thomas R.
Fauci, Anthony S., jt. auth. see Lichtenstein, Lawrence M.
Fauci, Anthony S., jt. ed. see Gallin, John I.
Faucon, Bernard. Summer Camp. (Illus.). 100p. 1982. 22.50 (ISBN 0-937950-00-9). Xavier-Moreau.
Faude, Bill & Friedland, Joan W. Connecticut Firsts. LC 78-51226. (Illus.). (gr. 5-12). 1978. pap. 4.95 o.p. (ISBN 0-87106-095-7). Globe Pequot.
Faulder, Carolyn. Breast Cancer: A Guide to It's Early Detection & Treatment. 186p. 1983. pap. 7.95 (ISBN 0-86068-287-0, Virago Pr). Merrimack Bk Serv.

Faulk, John H. Fear on Trial. rev. ed. 256p. 1983. 17.50 (ISBN 0-292-72443-8); pap. 7.95 (ISBN 0-292-72442-X). U of Tex Pr.

Faulk, Odie B. Destiny Road: The Gila Trail & the Opening of the Southwest. (Illus.). 1973. 15.95x (ISBN 0-19-501710-2). Oxford U Pr.

--Geronimo Campaign. LC 72-83042. (Illus.). 1969. 15.95x (ISBN 0-19-500544-9). Oxford U Pr.

Faulk, Odie B. & Stout, Joseph A., Jr., eds. The Mexican War: Changing Interpretations. LC 82-73484. 243p. 1973. 12.95x (ISBN 0-8040-0642-3, SB); pap. 5.95x (ISBN 0-8040-0643-1, SB). Swallow.

Faulke, Patricia, jt. auth. see Faulke, Robert.

Faulke, Robert & Faulke, Patricia. Budget Vacations & Daytrips in New England. 224p. 1983. pap. 8.95 (ISBN 0-87106-978-4). Globe Pequot.

Faulkenberry, Luces M. An Introduction to Operational Amplifiers. LC 76-53778. (Electronic Technology Ser.). 257p. 1977. text ed. 22.95 o.p. (ISBN 0-471-01548-2); solutions manual avail. o.p. (ISBN 0-471-02531-3). Wiley.

--An Introduction to Operational Amplifiers with Linear Applications. 2nd ed. LC 81-13043. (Electronic Technology Ser.). 560p. 1982. text ed. 22.95x (ISBN 0-471-05790-8); solutions manual 5.00 (ISBN 0-471-86319-X). Wiley.

Faulkenstein, Dezmon A. Faulkenstein's Theories are Loose on the Earth. 1982. 7.95. Vantage.

Faulker, John. Dollar Cotton. 1975. Repr. of 1942 ed. 12.50 (ISBN 0-916242-06-4). Yoknapatawpha.

Faulkes, Anthony, ed. Snorri Sturluson - Edda: Prologue & Gylfaginning. (Illus.). 1981. 29.95x (ISBN 0-19-811175-4). Oxford U Pr.

Faulkner. More Money in Your Pocket. 2.50 (ISBN 0-448-06980-6, G&D). Putnam Pub Group.

Faulkner, Charles H. & McCollough, C. R., eds. Fifth Report of the Normandy Archaeological Project. (Orig.). 1978. pap. text ed. 23.95x (ISBN 0-87049-286-1, Pub. by U of TN Dept. of Anthropology). U of Tenn Pr.

--Fourth Report of the Normandy Archaeological Project. (Orig.). 1977. pap. text ed. 14.95x (ISBN 0-87049-247-0, Pub. by U of TN Dept. of Anthropology). U of Tenn Pr.

Faulkner, Christopher. Jean Renoir: A Guide to References & Resources. 1979. lib. bdg. 45.00 (ISBN 0-8161-7912-3, Hall Reference). G K Hall.

Faulkner, Chuck. Seven Hundred & Fifty Helpful Household Hints. Friedman, Robert S., ed. LC 82-19820. 160p. (Orig.). 1983. pap. 6.95 (ISBN 0-89865-262-6). Donning Co.

Faulkner, D., et al. Integrity of Offshore Structures. 1981. 90.25 (ISBN 0-85334-989-4, Pub. by Applied Sci England). Elsevier.

Faulkner, Ed & Weymuller, Fred. Ed Faulkner's Tennis: How to Play It, How to Teach It. (Illus.). 294p. 1970. 8.95 o.p. (ISBN 0-686-37460-6). USTA.

Faulkner, Florence. A Challenge for Two. 1982. 6.95 (ISBN 0-686-84158-1, Avalon). Bouregy.

--Clue to Romance. 192p. (YA) 1976. 6.95 (ISBN 0-685-59252-9, Avalon). Bouregy.

--House of Hostile Women. (YA) 1978. 6.95 (ISBN 0-685-05589-2, Avalon). Bouregy.

--Season of Deception. 1981. pap. 6.95 (ISBN 0-686-84675-3, Avalon). Bouregy.

Faulkner, Harold U. The Decline of Laissez Faire 1897-1917. LC 76-48800. (The Economic History of the United States Ser.). 1977. pap. 10.95 (ISBN 0-87332-102-2). M E Sharpe.

--Politics, Reform & Expansion: 1890-1900. (New American Nation Ser.). 1959. 17.26xi (ISBN 0-06-011210-7, HarpT). Har-Row.

Faulkner, Harold V. From Versailles to the New Deal. 1951. text ed. 8.50x (ISBN 0-686-83555-7). Elliots Bks.

Faulkner, Janette & Henderson, Robbin. Ethnic Notions: Black Images in the White Mind. (Illus.). 80p. (Orig.). pap. 11.00x (ISBN 0-686-42913-3). Berkeley Art.

Faulkner, Joseph. Religion's Influence in Contemporary Society: Readings in the Sociology of Religion. LC 72-76586. 608p. 1972. text ed. 13.95 (ISBN 0-675-09105-5). Merrill.

Faulkner, Larry R., jt. auth. see Bard, Allen J.

Faulkner, Peter. Against the Age: An Introduction to William Morris. (Illus.). 192p. 1980. text ed. 28.50x (ISBN 0-04-809012-3). Allen Unwin.

--Robert Bage. (English Authors Ser.). 1979. lib. bdg. 14.95 (ISBN 0-8057-6739-8, Twayne). G K Hall.

Faulkner, Peter, ed. & intro. by see Holcroft, Thomas.

Faulkner, R. O. The Ancient Egyptian Coffin Texts: Vol. II, Spells 355-787. 308p. 1977. text ed. 29.00x (ISBN 0-85668-051-6, Pub. by Aris & Phillips England). Humanities.

Faulkner, Robert K. Richard Hooker & the Politics of a Christian England. LC 79-65776. 195p. 1981. 24.50x (ISBN 0-520-03993-9). U of Cal Pr.

Faulkner, Robert R. Music on Demand: Composers & Careers in the Hollywood Film Industry. (Illus.). 250p. 1982. 24.95 (ISBN 0-87855-403-3). Transaction Bks.

Faulkner, Waldron. Architecture & Color. LC 80-22370. 170p. 1983. Repr. of 1972 ed. text ed. 22.50 (ISBN 0-89874-223-4). Krieger.

Faulkner, William. Absalom, Absalom. 1951. 3.95 o.s.i. (ISBN 0-394-60271-4, M271). Modern Lib.

--As I Lay Dying. 1967. 3.95 o.s.i. (ISBN 0-394-60378-8, M378). Modern Lib.

--The Faulkner Reader. LC 59-5911. 8.95 (ISBN 0-394-60399-0). Modern Lib.

--Flags in the Dust. Day, Douglas, ed. LC 74-3315. 1974. pap. 3.95 (ISBN 0-394-71239-0, V-239, Vin). Random.

--Go Down, Moses. 1955. pap. 4.95 o.s.i. (ISBN 0-394-60175-0, M175). Modern Lib.

--Helen: A Courtship (ISBN 0-916242-11-0). limited edition, deluxe box & binding 155.00 (ISBN 0-686-63443-8). Yoknapatawpha.

--Intruder in the Dust. 1964. 3.95 o.s.i. (ISBN 0-394-60351-6, M351). Modern Lib.

--Light in August. 1931. 3.95 o.s.i. (ISBN 0-394-60088-6, M88). Modern Lib.

--The Mansion. 1959. pap. 4.95 (ISBN 0-394-70282-4). Random.

--The Marionettes. Polk, Noel, ed. LC 77-8994. (Bibliographical Society of the University of Va.). (Illus.). xxxii, 106p. 1978. 9.95x (ISBN 0-8139-0734-9). U Pr of Va.

--Portable Faulkner. rev. ed. Cowley, Malcolm, ed. (Viking Portable Library: No. 18). (gr. 10 up). 1977. pap. 6.95 (ISBN 0-14-015018-8). Penguin.

--Sanctuary. 1962. pap. 10.00 o.p. (ISBN 0-394-44368-3); pap. 3.95 (ISBN 0-394-70381-2). Random.

--Selected Short Stories. 1962. 3.95 o.s.i. (ISBN 0-394-60324-9, M324). Modern Lib.

--Selected Short Stories of William Faulkner. 5.95 (ISBN 0-394-60456-3). Modern Lib.

--Sound & the Fury. (YA) 1966. 3.95 o.s.i. (ISBN 0-394-60187-4, 60187). Modern Lib.

--Sound & the Fury. 1966. 14.00 (ISBN 0-394-44640-2). Random.

--Three Famous Short Novels. Incl. Spotted Horses; Old Man; Bear. 1958. pap. 3.95 (ISBN 0-394-70149-6, V-149, Vin). Random.

--The Unvanquished. 1965. pap. 3.95 (ISBN 0-394-70351-0). Random.

--Wild Palms. 1964. pap. 4.95 (ISBN 0-394-70262-X, V262, Vin). Random.

Faulkner, William J. The Days When the Animals Talked: Black American Folktales & How They Came to Be. LC 76-50315. (Illus.). (gr. 6 up). 1977. PLB 5.31 (ISBN 0-695-40755-4, Dist. by Caroline Hse). Follett.

Faulkner Hudson, T. Vanadium Toxicology. 1964. 9.75 (ISBN 0-444-40207-1). Elsevier.

Faulks, Yvonne M., ed. Texas Appellate Practice Manual-1982 Cumulative Supplement. 153p. 1982. pap. 20.00 (ISBN 0-938160-05-2, 6230). State Bar TX.

Faullkner, Edward A. Guide to Efficient Boiler Operation: Gas, Oil, Dual Fuel. 1981. text ed. 32.00 (ISBN 0-915586-35-5). Fairmont Pr.

Faulstich, H. & Kommerell, B. Amanita Toxins & Poisoning: International Amanita Symposium, Heidelberg 1978. (Illus.). 246p. 1980. pap. text ed. 42.50x. Lubrecht & Cramer.

Fauman, Beverly J. & Fauman, Michael. Emergency Psychiatry for the House Officer. (House Officer Ser.). (Illus.). 184p. 1981. soft cover 9.95 (ISBN 0-683-03046-9, 3046-9). Williams & Wilkins.

Fauman, Michael, jt. auth. see Fauman, Beverly J.

Faunce, William. Problems of an Industrial Society. 2nd ed. Munson, Eric M., ed. 256p. 1981. pap. text ed. 11.95 (ISBN 0-07-020105-6, C). McGraw.

Fauntleroy, Fran, ed. Houston Epicure 1982-83. (Epicure Ser.). 160p. 1982. pap. 5.95 (ISBN 0-89716-114-9). Peanut Butter.

Faupel, J. H. & Fisher, F. E. Engineering Design: A Synthesis of Stress Analysis & Materials Engineering. 2nd ed. LC 80-16727. 1056p. 1981. 45.50x (ISBN 0-471-03381-2, Pub. by Wiley-Interscience). Wiley.

Faure, Gunter. Principles of Isotope Geology. LC 77-4479. (Intermediate Geology Ser.). 464p. 1977. text ed. 36.95 (ISBN 0-471-25665-X). Wiley.

Faurot, Ruth M. Jerome K. Jerome. LC 73-15938. (English Authors Ser.: No. 164). 1974. lib. bdg. 12.95 o.p. (ISBN 0-8057-1291-7, Twayne). G K Hall.

Fausboll, V., jt. auth. see Muller, F. Max.

Fausold, Martin L. Gifford Pinchot, Bull Moose Progressive. LC 73-7672. (Illus.). 270p. 1973. Repr. of 1961 ed. lib. bdg. 15.50x (ISBN 0-8371-6943-7, FAGP). Greenwood.

Fausold, Martin L. & Mazuzan, George T., eds. The Hoover Presidency: A Reappraisal. LC 74-13876. (Illus.). 1974. 29.50x (ISBN 0-87395-280-4). State U NY Pr.

Fausset, Hugh I'Anson. Tennyson: A Modern Portrait. 309p. 1982. Repr. of 1923 ed. lib. bdg. 30.00 (ISBN 0-89760-235-8). Telegraph Bks.

Faust, A. B. Guide to the Materials for American History in Swiss & Austrian Archives. 1916. pap. 26.00 (ISBN 0-527-00695-5). Kraus Repr.

Faust, Aly. Chemistry of Natural Waters. LC 80-70322. 400p. 1981. text ed. 40.00 (ISBN 0-250-40387-0). Ann Arbor Science.

Faust, Frederic L. & Brantingham, Paul J. Juvenile Justice Philosophy: Readings, Cases & Comments. 2nd ed. (Criminal Justice Ser.). 1978. pap. text ed. 19.50 (ISBN 0-8299-0179-5). West Pub.

Faust, Harriet. Enough of Christmas. (Orig.). 1980. pap. 2.00 (ISBN 0-937172-08-1). JLJ Pubs.

Faust, Joan L. New York Times Book of House Plants. 274p. 1975. pap. 6.95 o.s.i. (ISBN 0-89104-002-1, A & W Visual Library). A & W Pubs.

--New York Times Book of Vegetable Gardening. LC 75-37082. (Illus.). 282p. 1976. pap. 5.95 o.s.i. (ISBN 0-89104-030-7, A & W Visual Library). A & W Pubs.

Faust, Langdon L., ed. American Women Writers: A Critical Reference Guide from Colonial Times to the Present, Vol. 1, A-L. Abr. ed. LC 82-40286. 445p. 1983. pap. 14.95 (ISBN 0-8044-6164-3). Ungar.

--American Women Writers: A Critical Reference Guide from Colonial Times to the Present, Vol. 2, M-Z. Abr. ed. LC 82-40286. 445p. 1983. pap. 14.95 (ISBN 0-8044-6165-1). Ungar.

Faust, Norma. Lecciones para el Aprendizage del Idioma Shipibo-Conibo. (Documento del Trabajo (Peru) Ser.: No. 1). 160p. 1973. pap. 3.00x (ISBN 0-88312-783-0); microfiche 2.25x (ISBN 0-88312-353-3). Summer Inst Ling.

Faust, Norma W. Gramatica Cocama: Lecciones para el Apprendizaje del Idioma Cocama. (Peruvian Linguistic Ser.: No. 6). 173p. 1972. pap. 3.00x (ISBN 0-88312-766-0); 2.25 (ISBN 0-88312-388-6). Summer Inst Ling.

Faust, Ron. Snowkill. 208p. 1981. pap. 2.25 (ISBN 0-686-97418-2, Leisure Bks). Nordon Pubns.

Faust, Samuel D. & Aly, Osman M. Chemistry of Water Treatment. LC 82-72854. 1983. text ed. 40.00 (ISBN 0-250-40388-9). Ann Arbor Science.

Faust, V., ed. see Ladewig, D. & Hobi, V.

Faust, Verne. Establishing Guidance Programs in Elementary Schools. (Guidance Monograph). 1968. pap. 2.60 o.p. (ISBN 0-395-09904-8). HM.

Faustos of Buzand. Patmowtiwn Hayots: History of the Armenians. Garsoian, Nina G., ed. (Classical Armenian Texts). 1983. write for info. (ISBN 0-88206-033-3). Caravan Bks.

Fauver, L. B. Exonumia Symbolism & Classification: A Catalogue of Kettle Pieces & an Examination of the Symbolism & Classification of Kettle Pieces & of American Exonumia of the Hard Times, Compromise, & Civil War Periods. (Illus.). 368p. 1982. 0.60.00 (ISBN 0-9607162-0-3). Oak Grove Pubns.

Faux, Ian. Modern Lithography. 2nd ed. (Illus.). 1979. pap. 20.00 o.s.i. (ISBN 0-7121-1294-4). Transatlantic.

Faux, Marian. Resumes for Professional Nurses. (Job Finders Ser.). 144p. (Orig.). 1982. pap. 6.95 (ISBN 0-671-43452-7). Monarch Pr.

--Successful Free-Lancing: The Complete Guide to Establishing & Running Any Kind of Free-Lance Business. LC 82-5595. 256p. 1982. 11.95 (ISBN 0-312-77478-8). St Martin.

Faux, Marian, jt. auth. see Stewart, Marjabelle.

Faux, Ronald. Everest: Goddess of the Wind. (Illus.). 1978. 13.95 o.p. (ISBN 0-550-20361-3, Pub. by Two Continents); pap. 7.95 o.p. (ISBN 0-550-20351-6). Hippocrene Bks.

Favazza, Armando R. & Faheem, Ahmed D. Themes In Cultural Psychiatry: An Annoted Bibliography 1975-1980. LC 82-2738. 208p. 1982. 30.00 (ISBN 0-8262-0377-9). U of MO Pr.

Fave, L. J. La see La Fave, L. J., et al.

Favero, Giampaolo Bordignon see Bordignon Favero, Giampaolo.

Favish, Melody. Christmas in Scandinavia. (Illus.). 160p. 1982. write for info. Trollpost.

Favorite, F. G., ed. see C.O.S.P.A.R International Space Science Symposium, 7th, Vienna, 1966.

Favorite, F. G., ed. see C.O.S.P.A.R., 11th Plenary Meeting, Tokyo, 1968.

Favorite, F. G., ed. see C.O.S.P.A.R., 12th Meeting, Prague, 1969.

Favre, David S. Wildlife: Cases, Law & Policy. LC 82-71698. 240p. (Orig.). 1983. pap. text ed. 16.00x (ISBN 0-86733-023-6). Assoc Faculty Pr.

Favre, David S. & Loring, Murray, eds. Animal Law. LC 82-23130. 296p. 1983. lib. bdg. 35.00 (ISBN 0-89930-021-9, LAL/, Quorum). Greenwood.

Favreau, Donald F. Fire Service Management. (Illus.). 1969. 8.00 o.p. (ISBN 0-686-12260-7). Fire Eng.

Favre de Vaugelas, Cl. Nouvelles Remarques sur la Langue Francaise. (Linguistics 13th-18th Centuries Ser.). 651p. (Fr.). 1974. Repr. lib. bdg. 173.00x o.p. (ISBN 0-8287-0335-3, 71-5014). Clearwater Pub.

--Remarques sur la Langue Francaise. (Linguistics 13th-18th Centuries Ser.). 664p. (Fr.). 1974. Repr. of 1647 ed. lib. bdg. 160.50x o.p. (ISBN 0-8287-0336-1, 71-5013). Clearwater Pub.

Favret-Saada, Jeanne. Deadly Words. Cullen, Catherine, tr. from Fr. LC 79-41607. (Illus.). 1981. 49.50 (ISBN 0-521-22317-2); pap. text ed. 13.95 (ISBN 0-521-29787-7). Cambridge U Pr.

Favretti, Joy P., jt. auth. see Favretti, Rudy J.

Favretti, Rudy J. & Favretti, Joy P. Landscapes & Gardens for Historic Buildings: A Handbook for Reproducing & Creating Authentic Landscape Settings. LC 78-17200. (Illus.). 1979. pap. 12.00 (ISBN 0-910050-34-1). AASLH.

Faw, Marc. A Verdi Discography. 201p. 1983. 14.95 (ISBN 0-937664-63-4). Pilgrim Bks OK.

Faw, Terry. Schaum's Outline of Child Psychology. (Illus., Orig.). 1979. pap. 5.95 (ISBN 0-07-020110-2). McGraw.

Fawcett & Sandberg. Grassroots. 2d ed. 1982. pap. text ed. 11.95 (ISBN 0-686-84574-9, RM96); instr's. annotated ed. 12.95 (ISBN 0-686-84575-7, RM95). HM.

Fawcett, Anthony. California Rock, California Sound. LC 78-51060. (Illus.). 1979. 19.95 (ISBN 0-89169-507-9); pap. 9.95 (ISBN 0-89169-506-0). Reed Bks.

Fawcett, B., jt. auth. see Siegel, A.

Fawcett, Bradly K. The Z Eight Thousand Microprocessor: A Design Handbook. (Illus.). 320p. 1982. text ed. 23.95 (ISBN 0-13-983742-6); pap. text ed. 16.95 (ISBN 0-13-983734-5). P-H.

Fawcett, Claude W. School Personnel Systems. LC 78-57240. (Illus.). 192p. 1979. 22.95x (ISBN 0-669-02375-2). Lexington Bks.

Fawcett, David M. & Callander, Lee A. Native American Painting: Selections from the Museum of the American Indian. 96p. 1982. pap. 15.95x (ISBN 0-934490-40-6). Mus Am Ind.

Fawcett, Don W. & Newberne, J. W. Workshop on Cellular & Molecular Toxicology. (Illus.). 300p. 1980. lib. bdg. 20.00 o.p. (ISBN 0-683-03047-7). Williams & Wilkins.

Fawcett, Edmund & Thomas, Tony. The American Condition. LC 81-48033. 448p. 1982. 18.22i (ISBN 0-06-038030-6, HarpT). Har-Row.

Fawcett, H. H. & Wood, W. S. Safety & Accident Prevention in Chemical Operations. 2nd ed. LC 82-2623. 910p. 1982. 80.00 (ISBN 0-471-02435-X, Pub. by Wiley-Interscience). Wiley.

Fawcett, Harold & Cummins, Kenneth. Teaching of Mathematics: From Counting to Calculus. LC 69-19768. 1970. text ed. 15.95 (ISBN 0-675-09512-3). Merrill.

Fawcett, Henry. Pauperism: Its Causes & Remedies. LC 74-1334. Repr. of 1871 ed. lib. bdg. 19.50x (ISBN 0-678-01067-6). Kelley.

Fawcett, Hilary & Strang, Jeanne. The Good Cook's Guide: More Recipes from Restaurants in the Good Food Guide. (Illus.). 208p. 1975. 3.95 o.p. (ISBN 0-7153-6901-6). David & Charles.

Fawcett, Howard H. & Wood, W. S., eds. Safety & Accident Prevention in Chemical Operations. LC 65-12712. (Illus.). 1965. 61.50x o.p. (ISBN 0-470-25678-8, Pub. by Wiley-Interscience). Wiley.

Fawcett, Jacqueline. Conceptual Models in Nursing: Evaluation & Analysis. 1983. write for info. (ISBN 0-8036-3409-9). Davis Co.

Fawcett, James T. see Arnold, Fred, et al.

Fawcett, Jane, ed. Seven Victorian Architects. LC 76-42090. (Illus.). 1977. 18.50x (ISBN 0-271-00500-9). Pa St U Pr.

Fawcett, John. Christ Precious to Those That Believe. 1979. 10.00 (ISBN 0-86524-026-4, 8901). Klock & Klock.

Fawcett Publications Editors. Manual of Home Repairs, Remodeling and Maintainance. 1969. 10.95 o.p. (ISBN 0-448-01753-9, G&D). Putnam Pub Group.

Fawcett, Stephen B., jt. auth. see Borck, Leslie E.

Fawcett, Susan & Sandberg, Alvin. Grassroots: The Writer's Handbook. 2d ed. 288p. 1982. pap. text ed. 11.95 (ISBN 0-395-32572-2); instr's. annotated ed. 12.95 (ISBN 0-395-32573-0). HM.

--Grassroots: The Writer's Workbook, Form B. LC 80-68139. 272p. 1981. pap. text ed. 11.95 (ISBN 0-395-29726-5); instr's. manual 0.50 (ISBN 0-395-29727-3). HM.

Fawcett, Susan C. & Sandberg, Alvin. Evergreen: A Guide to Basic Writing. LC 79-89001. 1980. pap. text ed. 12.95 (ISBN 0-395-28694-8); instrs' manual 0.50 (ISBN 0-395-28695-6). HM.

Fawdry, Marguerite & Brown, Deborah. The Book of Samplers. (Illus.). 160p. 1980. 9.98 o.p. (ISBN 0-312-09006-4). St Martin.

Fawkner, Harold W. Animation & Reification in Dickens' Vision of the Life-Denying Society. (Studia Anglistice Upsaliensia: Vol. 31). 1977. pap. text ed. 17.25x o.p. (ISBN 91-554-0630-0). Humanities.

Faxon, Alicia, jt. auth. see Brayer, Yves.

Fay, Allen, jt. auth. see Lazarus, Arnold.

Fay, Amy. Music Study in Germany. (Music Reprint Ser.: 1979). 1979. Repr. of 1880 ed. lib. bdg. 35.00 (ISBN 0-306-79541-8). Da Capo.

Fay, Ann, ed. see Anderson, Leone C.

Fay, Ann, ed. see Aylesworth, Jim.

Fay, Ann, ed. see Heide, Florence P. & Heide, Roxanne.

Fay, Ann, ed. see Lapp, Elaenor.

Fay, Ann, ed. see Smith, Carole.

Fay, Bertrand. Church at Eucharist. LC 67-29589. 1967. 3.95 o.p. (ISBN 0-685-07620-2, 80217). Glencoe.

Fay, C. E. see Marton, L.

Fay, Charles H., jt. auth. see Wallace, Marc J., Jr.

Fay, Charles R. Life & Labour in the Nineteenth Century. LC 73-90143. Repr. of 1920 ed. lib. bdg. 15.75x (ISBN 0-8371-2165-5, FALL). Greenwood.

Fay, Clifford T., Jr., jt. auth. see Tarr, Stanley B.

Fay, Clifford T., Jr., et al. Managerial Accounting for the Hospitality Service Industries. 2nd ed. 616p. 1976. text ed. write for info (ISBN 0-697-08406-X); instrs.' manual avail. (ISBN 0-697-08415-9). Wm C Brown.

--Basic Financial Accounting for the Hospitality Industry. rev. ed. 1982. 26.95 (ISBN 0-86612-010-6). Educ Inst Am Hotel.

Fay, Cornelius R. & Tiblier, Henry. Epistemology. 1967. pap. text ed. 3.95 o.p. (ISBN 0-02-827300-1). Glencoe.

Fay, Loren V. Broome County, N. Y. Genealogical Research Secrets. 25p. 1982. pap. 5.00 (ISBN 0-942238-04-4). L V Fay.

--Delaware County, N. Y. Genealogical Research Secrets. 30p. 1982. pap. 5.00 (ISBN 0-942238-13-3). L V Fay.

--Fulton County, N. Y. Genealogical Research Secrets. (Illus.). 25p. 1982. pap. 5.00 (ISBN 0-942238-18-4). L V Fay.

--Genesee County, N. Y. Genealogical Research Secrets. 25p. 1982. pap. 5.00 (ISBN 0-942238-19-2). L V Fay.

--Montgomery County, N. Y. Genealogical Research Secrets. 25p. 1982. pap. 5.00 (ISBN 0-942238-29-X). L V Fay.

--New York State Area Key. Bd. with New York State Area Key Corrections. 1p. 1982 (ISBN 0-942238-99-0). 200p. 1979. pap. 12.00 (ISBN 0-942238-98-2). L V Fay.

--Oswego County, New York. (New York Genealogical Secrets Ser.). (Illus.). 25p. 1982. pap. 5.00 (ISBN 0-942238-38-9). L V Fay.

--Otsego County, New York. (New York Genealogical Research Secrets Ser.). 20p. 1982. pap. 5.00 (ISBN 0-942238-39-7). L V Fay.

--Rensselaer County, N. Y. Genealogical Research Secrets. 30p. 1982. pap. 5.00 (ISBN 0-942238-42-7). L V Fay.

--Saratoga County, N. Y. Genealogical Research Secrets. 25p. 1982. pap. 5.00 (ISBN 0-942238-46-X). L V Fay.

--Schenectady County, N. Y. Genealogical Research Secrets. 25p. 1982. pap. 5.00 (ISBN 0-942238-47-8). L V Fay.

--Schoharie County, N. Y. Genealogical Research Secrets. 25p. 1982. pap. 5.00 (ISBN 0-942238-48-6). L V Fay.

--Tioga County, N. Y. Genealogical Research Secrets. 25p. 1982. pap. 5.00 (ISBN 0-942238-54-0). L V Fay.

--Wayne County, N. Y. Genealogical Research Secrets. 30p. 1982. pap. 5.00 (ISBN 0-942238-59-1). L V Fay.

--Yates County, N. Y. Genealogical Research Secrets. 25p. 1982. pap. 5.00 (ISBN 0-942238-62-1). L V Fay.

Fay, Peter W. The Opium War, 1840-1842. (Illus.). 432p. 1976. pap. 7.95x (ISBN 0-393-00823-1). Norton.

Fay, Stephan. Beyond Greed. 1983. pap. 6.95 (ISBN 0-14-006688-8). Penguin.

Fayemi, A. Olusegun, jt. auth. see Ali, Majid.

Fayen, E. G., jt. auth. see Lancaster, F. W.

Fayen, Emily G. The Era of Online Public Access Catalogs. 150p. 1983. 34.50 (ISBN 0-86729-054-4); pap. 27.50 (ISBN 0-86729-053-6). Knowledge Indus.

Fayers, F. J. Enhanced Oil Recovery. (Developments in Petroleum Science Ser.: Vol. 13). 1981. 72.50 (ISBN 0-444-42033-9). Elsevier.

Fayers, Heather. Divorce Guide for Manitoba & Saskatchewan. 96p. 1979. 7.95 (ISBN 0-88908-502-1); Manitoba forms 8.50 (ISBN 0-686-35997-6); Saskatchewan forms 12.50 (ISBN 0-686-37246-8). Self Counsel Pr.

Fayers, Heather, jt. auth. see James, Jack.

Fayerweather, John. International Business Strategy & Administration. 2nd ed. LC 82-1784. 568p. 1982. text ed. 27.50x (ISBN 0-88410-889-9). Ballinger Pub.

--International Business Strategy & Administration. LC 78-5675. 608p. 1978. text ed. 22.50x (ISBN 0-88410-669-1). Ballinger Pub.

--International Marketing. 2nd ed. (Foundations of Marketing Ser). 1970. pap. 10.95 ref. ed. (ISBN 0-13-473124-7). P-H.

Fayerweather, John & Kapoor, Ashok. Strategy & Negotiation for the International Corporation: Guidelines & Cases. LC 76-10537. 480p. 1976. prof ref 25.00x (ISBN 0-88410-299-8). Ballinger Pub.

Fayerweather, John, ed. International Business-Government Affairs: Toward an Era of Accommodation. LC 73-12445. 152p. 1973. prof ref 18.50x (ISBN 0-88410-256-4). Ballinger Pub.

Fayle, H. & Newham, A. T. The Waterford & Tramore Railway. (Illus.). 56p. 1972. 7.50 (ISBN 0-7153-5518-X). David & Charles.

Fayman, Danah. The Photographic Art of Lynn G. Fayman. (Illus.). 22p. 1969. 3.00x (ISBN 0-686-99831-6). La Jolla Mus Contemp Art.

Fazal-E-Rab, Syed. The JP Movement & Emergence of Janata Party: A Select Bibliography, Vol. 1: Pre-Emergency. 1977. 12.50x o.p. (ISBN 0-8364-0097-6). South Asia Bks.

Fazio, Joe. Emergency Road Service Guide, 3 vols. 1977. Set. pap. 2.95 o.p. (ISBN 0-910684-06-5). Hagstrom Map.

Fazzolare, Rocco & Smith, C. B., eds. Energy Use Management: Proceedings of the International Conference, 4 vols. LC 77-86455. Date not set. Set. write for info. (ISBN 0-08-021723-0); xerox copy avail. Pergamon.

Fe, Lu. God Bless Our HUD Home: Downtowner Congregate Housing. 1983. 7.95 (ISBN 0-533-05597-0). Vantage.

Fea, Allan. Secret Chambers & Hiding-Places. rev. ed. 3rd ed. LC 79-155739. 1971. Repr. of 1901 ed. 37.00x (ISBN 0-8103-3385-6). Gale.

Feachem, Richard. Guide to Prehistoric Scotland. 1977. 8.95 o.p. (ISBN 0-7134-3264-0, Pub. by Batsford England). David & Charles.

Feachem, Richard, et al, eds. Water, Wastes & Health in Hot Climates. LC 76-18946. 1977. 54.95 (ISBN 0-471-99410-3, Pub. by Wiley-Interscience). Wiley.

Feachem, Richard G. & Bradley, David J. Sanitation & Disease: Health Aspects of Excreta & Wastewater Management. Garelick, Hemda & Mara, D. Duncan, eds. 1983. write for info. (ISBN 0-471-90094-X, Pub. by Wiley-Interscience). Wiley.

Feagans, Lynne & Garvey, Catherine. The Origins & Growth of Communication. 432p. 1983. 37.50 (ISBN 0-89391-164-X). Ablex Pub.

Feagans, Lynne, jt. ed. see McKinney, James D.

Feagin, Joe R. Racial & Ethnic Relations. LC 77-27306. (P-H Ser. in Sociology). (Illus.). 1978. ref. 22.95 (ISBN 0-13-749887-X). P-H.

--Social Problems: A Critical Power - Conflict Perspective. (Illus.). 432p. (Orig.). 1982. pap. 18.95 (ISBN 0-13-817338-9). P-H.

Feagin, Joe R. & Hahn, Harlan. Ghetto Revolt. 1974. pap. 14.95x (ISBN 0-02-336550-1, 33655). Macmillan.

Feagin, Joe R., jt. auth. see Benokraitis, Nijole V.

Feagles, Anita M. The Year the Dreams Came Back. (gr. 7-9). 1978. pap. 1.25 o.p. (ISBN 0-671-29875-5). Archway.

Fear, David E. Technical Communication. 2nd ed. 1981. pap. text ed. 14.50x (ISBN 0-673-15401-7). Scott F.

Fear, David E. & Schiffhorst, Gerald J. Short English Handbook. 2nd ed. pap. 9.95x (ISBN 0-673-15545-5). Scott F.

Fear, David E., jt. auth. see Schiffhorst, Gerald J.

Fear, Gene. Fundamentals of Outdoor Enjoyment: Text or Teaching Guide for Coping with Outdoor Environments, All Seasons. (Illus.). 1976. pap. 5.00 (ISBN 0-913724-09-2). Survival Ed Assoc.

Fear, Richard. The Evaluation Interview. rev. 2nd ed. (Illus.). 1978. 24.95 (ISBN 0-07-020201-X, P&RB). McGraw.

Fear, Richard A. McGraw-Hill Course in Effective Interviewing. 1973. 52.50 (ISBN 0-07-079484-7, P&RB). McGraw.

Fearey, Robert A. The Occupation of Japan, Second Phase, 1948-50. LC 72-176133. 239p. 1972. Repr. of 1950 ed. lib. bdg. 17.75x (ISBN 0-8371-6271-8, FEOJ). Greenwood.

Fearing, Kelly, et al. The Creative Eye, 2 Vols. (Illus.). (gr. 7-8). 1979. Vol. 1. text ed. 21.32 gr. 7 (ISBN 0-87443-009-7); Vol. 2. text ed. 21.32 gr. 8 (ISBN 0-87443-010-0); tchr's manual for both vols. 3.00 (ISBN 0-87443-011-9). Benson.

Fearn, Leif. The First First I Think. 91p. (gr. 1-3). 1981. 6.50 (ISBN 0-940444-14-3). Kabyn.

--First I Think: Then I Write My Think. 160p. (gr. 3-12). 1981. 6.50 (ISBN 0-940444-13-5). Kabyn.

--Geocabulary Cards. (gr. 3-9). 1978. card pack 8.40 (ISBN 0-686-36308-6). Kabyn.

Fearn, Leif & Garner, Irene A. Maneras de Divertirme con Mi Mente. (Illus.). 182p. (gr. 3-9). 1982. 6.50 (ISBN 0-940444-16-X). Kabyn.

Fearn, Leif & Goldman, Elizabeth. Writing Kabyn: Assessment & Editing. 96p. (gr. 2-9). 1981. classroom kit 25.00 (ISBN 0-940444-11-9). Kabyn.

--Writing Kabyn: Products. 148p. (gr. 2-9). 1982. classroom kit 45.00 (ISBN 0-940444-09-7). Kabyn.

--Writing Kabyn: Sentences-Paragraphs. 125p. (gr. 2-9). 1982. classroom kit 60.00 (ISBN 0-940444-08-9). Kabyn.

--Writing Kabyn: Technology. 76p. (gr. 2-9). 1981. classroom Kit 40.00 (ISBN 0-940444-10-0). Kabyn.

Fearn, Leif & Golisz-Benson, Ursula. Seventy-Two Ways to Have Fun with My Mind. (Illus.). 80p. (Orig.). 1976. 3.00 (ISBN 0-940444-03-8). Kabyn.

Fearn, Robert M. Labor Economics: The Emerging Synthesis. 1981. text ed. 19.95 (ISBN 0-316-27636-7). Little.

Fearnley, Bernard. Child Photography. 2nd ed. 1979. 19.95 (ISBN 0-240-51021-6). Focal Pr.

Fearnside, W. Ward. About Thinking. 1980. pap. text ed. 13.95 (ISBN 0-13-000844-3). P-H.

Fearon, et al. Fundamentals of Production Operations Management. 171p. 1979. pap. text ed. 9.95 (ISBN 0-8299-0269-4); instrs.' manual avail. (ISBN 0-8299-0478-6). West Pub.

Fearon, George, jt. auth. see Brown, Ivor J.

Fearon, Harold E. Fundamentals of Production-Operations Management. 2nd ed. (Illus.). 1982. pap. text ed. 9.95 (ISBN 0-314-69647-4); tchrs.' manual avail. (ISBN 0-314-71089-2). West Pub.

Fearon, Henry B. Sketches of America. (The Americas Collection Ser.). (Illus.). 454p. 1982. pap. 24.95 (ISBN 0-936332-16-6). Falcon Hill Pr.

Fearon, Mary & Hirstein, Sandra J. Celebrating the Gift of Forgiveness. 64p. 1982. pap. 2.75 (ISBN 0-697-01792-3); program manual 6.95 (ISBN 0-697-01793-1). Wm C Brown.

--Celebrating the Gift of Jesus. 64p. 1982. pap. 2.75 (ISBN 0-697-01794-X); program manual 6.95 (ISBN 0-697-01795-8). Wm C Brown.

--The Eucharist Makes Us One. box set 79.95 (ISBN 0-697-01843-1); program dir. manual 4.50 (ISBN 0-697-01844-X); write for info. study leaflets; write for info. tchr's. manual. Wm C Brown.

--Wonder-Filled. 1983. pap. write for info. Wm C Brown.

Fearon, Peter, jt. auth. see Aldcroft, Derek.

Fearon, Peter, jt. ed. see Aldcroft, Derek H.

Fears, J. Wayne. Trout Fishing the Southern Appalachians. LC 79-1277. (Illus.). 192p. 1979. pap. 7.95 (ISBN 0-914788-10-8). East Woods.

Feast, W. J., jt. auth. see Clark, D. T.

Feather, Leonard. Inside Jazz. LC 77-23411. (Roots of Jazz Ser.). (Illus.). 1977. lib. bdg. 22.50 (ISBN 0-306-77437-2); pap. 5.95 (ISBN 0-306-80076-4). Da Capo.

--The Pleasures of Jazz. 1977. pap. 3.95 o.s.i. (ISBN 0-440-56946-X, Delta). Dell.

Feather, Leonard G., tr. see Goffin, Robert.

Featherstone, David. Photographs by Marsha Burns. Alinder, James, ed. LC 81-71995. (Untitled Ser.: No. 28). (Illus.). 56p. (Orig.). 1982. pap. 15.00 (ISBN 0-933286-25-2). Friends Photography.

Featherstone, Donald F. Advanced War Games. 18.50x o.p. (ISBN 0-392-00441-0, SpS). Sportshelf.

Featherstone, Vaughn G. Purity of Heart. LC 82-72728. 103p. 1982. 5.95 (ISBN 0-87747-914-3). Deseret Bk.

Feaver, J. Clayton & Horosz, William. Religion in Philosophical & Cultural Perspectives. 520p. 1967. 16.50 (ISBN 0-442-02378-2, Pub. by Van Nos Reinhold). Krieger.

Feaver, Vicki. Close Relatives. 1981. 11.50 (ISBN 0-686-84223-5, Pub. by W Heinemann). David & Charles.

FEBS Meeting, Eighth. Analysis & Simulation of Biochemical Systems: Proceedings, Vol. 25. Hemker, A. H. & Hess, B., eds. 1973. 32.00 (ISBN 0-444-10417-8, North-Holland). Elsevier.

Febvre, Lucien. The Problem of Unbelief in the Sixteenth Century: The Religion of Rabelais. Gottlieb, Beatrice, tr. from Fr. (Illus.). 528p. 1982. text ed. 35.00x (ISBN 0-674-70825-3). Harvard U Pr.

Fecher, Amrei. I Am a Little Lion. (Little Animal Stories Ser.). (Illus.). 24p. (ps). 1983. 5.95 (ISBN 0-8120-5516-0). Barron.

Fecher, Charles A. Philosophy of Jacques Maritain. LC 70-90705. Repr. of 1953 ed. lib. bdg. 17.75x (ISBN 0-8371-2287-2, FEJM). Greenwood.

Fecher, Vincent J. Religion & Aging: An Annotated Bibliography. LC 82-81019. 119p. 1982. 16.00 (ISBN 0-911536-96-5); pap. 9.00 (ISBN 0-911536-97-3). Trinity U Pr.

Fechner, Amrei. I Am a Little Dog. (Little Animal Stories Ser.). (Illus.). 24p. (ps). 1983. 5.95 (ISBN 0-8120-5514-4). Barron.

Fechner, Amrel. I Am a Little Elephant. (Little Animal Stories Ser.). (Illus.). 24p. 1983. 5.95 (ISBN 0-8120-5515-2). Barron.

Fecht, Gerald. The Complete Parent's Guide to Soccer. (Illus.). 1979. pap. 9.95x (ISBN 0-673-16184-6). Scott F.

Feda, J. Mechanics of Particulate Materials: The Principles. (Development in Geotechnical Materials Ser.: Vol. 30). 440p. 1982. 78.75 (ISBN 0-444-99713-X). Elsevier.

Fedden, Robin. Chantemesle. LC 66-15543. 1966. 4.00 o.s.i. (ISBN 0-8076-0349-X). Braziller.

Fedden, Robin, ed. Treasures of the National Trust. (Illus.). 1976. 24.00 o.p. (ISBN 0-224-01241-X). Transatlantic.

Fedder, Norman, ed. Wrestling with God: An Anthology of Contemporary Religious Drama. Date not set. pap. 16.00 (ISBN 0-87602-018-X). Anchorage.

Fedder, Ruth. Girl Grows Up. 4th ed. (Illus.). (gr. 9 up). 1967. 5.95 o.p. (ISBN 0-07-020294-X, GB). McGraw.

--You, the Person You Want to Be. (Illus.). (gr. 10 up). 1957. 3.83 o.p. (ISBN 0-07-020335-0, GB). McGraw.

Fedder, Ruth & Gabaldon, Jacqueline. No Longer Deprived: Using Minority Cultures & Languages in Educating Disadvantaged Children & Their Teachers. LC 78-76318. 1970. pap. text ed. 8.50x (ISBN 0-8077-1312-0). Tchrs Coll.

Feder & Burrell. Impact of Seafood Cannery Waste on the Benthic Biota & Adjacent Waters at Dutch Harbor Alaska. (IMS Report Ser.: No. R82-1). write for info. U of AK Inst Marine.

Feder, Georg, jt. auth. see Larsen, Jens P.

Feder, Gersgon & Just, Richard. Adoption of Agricultural Innovations in Developing Countries: A Survey. (Working Paper: No. 444). 67p. 1981. 3.00 (ISBN 0-686-36056-7, WP-0444). World Bank.

Feder, Jack & Merrick, Kathryn W. Zen of Cubing: In Search of the Seventh Side. LC 82-72610. (Illus.). 110p. (Orig.). 1982. pap. 4.95 (ISBN 0-89708-103-X). And Bks.

Feder, Jan. The Life of a Cat. LC 82-12795. (Animal Lives Ser.). (Illus.). (gr. 2-4). 1982. PLB 9.25g (ISBN 0-516-08931-5). Childrens.

--The Life of a Dog. LC 82-9752. (Animal Lives Ser.). (Illus.). (gr. 2-4). 1982. PLB 9.25g (ISBN 0-516-08932-3). Childrens.

--The Life of a Hamster. LC 82-12768. (Animal Lives Ser.). (Illus.). (gr. 2-4). 1982. PLB 9.25g (ISBN 0-516-08933-1). Childrens.

--The Life of a Rabbit. LC 82-9750. (Animal Lives Ser.). (Illus.). (gr. 2-4). 1982. PLB 9.25g (ISBN 0-516-08934-X). Childrens.

Feder, R. F. & Taylor, G. J. Junior Body Building: Growing Strong. LC 82-50552. (Illus.). 144p. (gr. 4 up). 1982. 8.95 (ISBN 0-8069-4168-5); lib. bdg. 10.99 (ISBN 0-8069-4169-3); pap. 4.95 (ISBN 0-8069-7676-4). Sterling.

Feder, W. A., jt. auth. see Manning, W. J.

Federal Administration, Dept. of Transportation. Pilot's Federal Aviation Regulations: (Composite Edition) 1983. 252p. 1982. pap. 5.95 (ISBN 0-686-81816-4). Astro Pubs.

Federal Architecture Project Staff & Craig, Lois A. The Federal Presence: Architecture, Politics, & Symbols in U. S. Government Building. (Illus.). 1978. 45.00 (ISBN 0-262-03057-8). MIT Pr.

Federal Aviation Administration. Airframe & Powerplant Mechanics Written Exam Airfram (AC-65-22) 1978. pap. text ed. 5.50 (ISBN 0-939158-21-3, Pub. by Natl Flightshops). Aviation.

--Airframe & Powerplant Mechanics Written Exam (AC-65-21) 1978. pap. text ed. 5.50 (ISBN 0-939158-20-5, Pub. by Natl Flightshops). Aviation.

--Airline Transport Pilot, Airplane, Practical Test Guide (Ac 61-77) 1974. pap. text ed. 1.75 o.p. (ISBN 0-686-74081-5, Pub. by Astro). Aviation.

--Commercial Pilot Flight Test Guide. 2nd ed. (Pilot Training Ser.: Pilot Training Ser.). 70p. 1975. pap. 1.75 (ISBN 0-89100-172-7, EA-AC61-55A). Aviation Maintenance.

--Federal Aviation Regulations fo Pilots, 1982. 7th ed. Winner, Walter P., ed. 160p. 1983. pap. 4.00w (ISBN 0-911721-95-9). Aviation.

--Flight Test Guide: Private & Commericial Pilots (Helicopter) Ac 61-59A. 1977. pap. 2.50 o.p. (ISBN 0-686-74530-2, Pub. by Astro). Aviation.

--Instrument Rating Written Test Guide: FAA AC 61-8D. Winner, Walter P., ed. (Illus.). 1978. pap. 4.25 (ISBN 0-911721-03-7). Aviation.

--Pilot's Handbook of Aeronautical Knowledge. (Illus.). 384p. 1974. pap. 6.00 o.p. (ISBN 0-668-03479-3). Arco.

--VFR Pilot Exam-O-Grams. Aviation Book Company Staff, ed. (Illus.). 120p. 1982. pap. 3.50 (ISBN 0-911721-78-9). Aviation.

Federal Aviation Administration. Department of Transportation. Pilot's Federal Aviation Regulations: 1983 Composite Edition. 256p. 1983. pap. text ed. 6.00 (ISBN 0-686-82514-4). Astro Pubs.

Federal Aviation Administration, Dept. of Transportation. Airman's Information Manual & ATC Procedures. (Illus.). 260p. (Orig.). 1983. pap. text ed. 8.00 (ISBN 0-686-81817-2). Astro Pubs.

Federal Aviation Agency. Pilot Instruction Manual. 1961. 8.95 (ISBN 0-385-01046-X). Doubleday.

Federal Communications Commission. Competitive Impact Statement on the AT&T Anti-Trust Case. 1982. 50.00 (ISBN 0-686-37962-4). Info Gatekeepers.

Federal Communications Commission Planning Conference November 8 & 9, 1976 & Hopewell, Lynn. Computers & Communications: Proceedings. (Illus.). 197p. 1976. pap. 11.50 (ISBN 0-88283-022-8). AFIPS Pr.

Federal Council of the Churches of Christ in America. The Public Relations of the Motion Picture Industry: A Report by the Department of Research & Education. LC 76-160231. (Moving Pictures Ser). 156p. 1971. Repr. of 1931 ed. lib. bdg. 11.95x (ISBN 0-89198-032-6). Ozer.

Federal Electric Corporation. A Programmed Introduction to PERT: Program Evaluation & Review Technique. 1963. pap. 22.95x (ISBN 0-471-25680-3, Pub. by Wiley-Interscience). Wiley.

Federal Judicial Center - Board Of Editors. Manual of Complex Litigation. LC 77-27536. 1981. looseleaf with 1978 rev. pages 45.00 (ISBN 0-87632-089-2). Boardman.

Federal Reserve Bank of Atlanta & Emory University Law & Economics Center. Supply-Side Economics in the Nineteen Eighties: Conference Proceedings. LC 82-15025. (Illus.). 572p. 1982. lib. bdg. 35.00 (ISBN 0-89930-045-6, FSU/, Quorum). Greenwood.

Federal Reserve Bank of Kansas City. Western Water Resources: Coming Problems & the Policy Alternatives. LC 80-14142. 376p. 1980. lib. bdg. 30.00 (ISBN 0-86531-036-X). Westview.

Federal Writer's Project. American Stuff. (FDR & the Era of the New Deal Ser.). 1976. Repr. of 1937 ed. lib. bdg. 39.50 (ISBN 0-306-70806-X). Da Capo.

Federal Writers Project. Idaho: A Guide in Word & Picture. 2nd ed. (American Guide Ser). 1950. 19.95x (ISBN 0-19-500589-9). Oxford U Pr.

--New York: Guide to the Empire State. (American Guide Ser). 1940. 19.95x (ISBN 0-19-500038-2). Oxford U Pr.

--North Dakota: Guide to the Northern Prairie State. 2nd ed. (American Guide Ser). 1950. 19.95x (ISBN 0-19-500043-9). Oxford U Pr.

--These Are Our Lives. 448p. 1975. pap. 6.95 (ISBN 0-393-00763-4, Norton Lib). Norton.

Federal Writers' Project. The WPA Guide to New York City. 1982. 20.00 (ISBN 0-394-52792-5); pap. 8.95 (ISBN 0-394-71215-3). Pantheon.

Federation Internationale de la Precontrainte. Multi-Lingual Dictionary of Concrete. 1976. 89.50 (ISBN 0-444-41237-9). Elsevier.

Federation of American Scientists. Seeds of Promise: The First Real Hearing on Nuclear Freeze. 192p. 1983. pap. 9.95 (ISBN 0-686-84755-5). Brick Hse Pub.

Federation of Feminist Women's Health Centers. A New View of a Woman's Body. 1981. 17.95 o.p. (ISBN 0-671-41214-0, Touchstone Bks); pap. 9.50 (ISBN 0-671-41215-9). S&S.

Federation of Feminist's Women's Health Centers. How to Stay Out of the Gynecologist's Office. LC 81-2983. (Illus.). 136p. 1981. pap. 7.95 (ISBN 0-915238-51-9). Peace Pr.

Federation of Societies for Coatings Technology, Educational Committee, ed. see Fuller, W. R.

Federation of Societies for Coatings Technology, Definitions Committee, ed. Paint-Coatings Dictionary. 632p. case-bound 30.00 (ISBN 0-686-95495-5); nonmembers 50.00 (ISBN 0-686-99513-9). Fed Soc Coat Tech.

Federici, Silvia, jt. auth. see Cox, Nicole.

Federico, Helen. ABC. (Golden Sturdy Bks). (Illus.). (ps). 1969. 3.95 (ISBN 0-307-12131-3, Golden Pr). Western Pub.

--Counting. (Golden Sturdy). (Illus.). (ps). 1969. 3.95 (ISBN 0-307-12132-1, Golden Pr). Western Pub.

Federico, P. J. Descartes on Polyhedra: A Study of the "De Solidorum Elementis". (Sources in the History of Mathematics & Physical Sciences: Vol. 4). (Illus.). 144p. 1983. 36.00 (ISBN 0-387-90760-2). Springer-Verlag.

Federico, Pat A., et al. Management Information Systems & Organizational Behavior. Brun, Kim & McCalla, Douglas B., eds. LC 80-15174. 204p. 1980. 26.95 (ISBN 0-03-057021-2). Praeger.

Federico, Ronald C. An Introduction to the Social Welfare Institution. 3rd ed. 1980. text ed. 19.95x o.p. (ISBN 0-669-97287-8). Heath.

--The Social Welfare Institution: An Introduction. 3rd ed. 1980. text ed. 19.95x (ISBN 0-669-01916-X); instr's manual 1.95 (ISBN 0-669-03219-0). Heath.

Federico, Ronald C. & Schwartz, Janet. Sociology. 3rd ed. LC 82-11375. 640p. 1983. text ed. 20.95 (ISBN 0-201-12030-5). A-W.

Federico, Ronald C., jt. ed. see Baer, Betty.

Federico, Ronald C., jt. ed. see Baer, Betty L.

Federle, Michael P. & Brandt-Zawadzki, Michael. Computed Tomography in the Evaluation of Trauma. (Illus.). 280p. 1982. lib. bdg. 39.95 (ISBN 0-683-03101-5). Williams & Wilkins.

Federlin, Konrad & Pfeifeer, Ernst F. Islet Pancreas Transplantation & Artificial Pancreas. 315p. 39.95 (ISBN 0-86577-062-X). Thieme-Stratton.

Federman, Raymond. Double or Nothing: A Novel. LC 82-72983. 203p. 1971. 8.95x (ISBN 0-8040-0543-5); pap. 4.95x (ISBN 0-8040-0544-3). Swallow.

--Journey into Chaos: Samuel Beckett's Early Fiction. LC 65-25284. 1965. 28.50x (ISBN 0-520-00398-5). U of Cal Pr.

Federman, Raymond, ed. Surfiction: Fiction Now & Tomorrow. LC 82-73559. 294p. 1973. 18.00x (ISBN 0-8040-0651-2). Swallow.

--Surfiction: Fiction Now & Tomorrow. 2nd ed. LC 82-73567. viii, 316p. 1981. pap. 8.95x (ISBN 0-8040-0652-0). Swallow.

Federn, Karl. Materialist Conception of History: A Critical Analysis. LC 75-114523. 1971. Repr. of 1939 ed. lib. bdg. 22.25x (ISBN 0-8371-4789-1, FECH). Greenwood.

Federoff, S. & Hertz, L., eds. Advances in Cellular Neurobiology, Vol. 3. (Serial Publication). 448p. 1982. 56.00 (ISBN 0-12-008303-5). Acad Pr.

Fedida, Sam & Malik, Rex. The Viewdata Revolution. LC 79-23869. 186p. 1979. 38.95x o.s.i. (ISBN 0-470-26879-4). Halsted Pr.

--The Viewdata Revolution. LC 79-23869. 186p. 1980. 38.95x o.s.i. (ISBN 0-470-26879-4). Wiley.

Fedigan, Linda M. Primate Paradigms: Sex Roles & Social Bonds. (Illus.). 1982. (ISBN 0-920792-03-0); pap. write for info. Eden Pr.

Fedler, Fred. Reporting for the Print Media. 2nd ed. 342p. 1979. pap. text ed. 14.95 (ISBN 0-15-576613-9, HC); instructor's manual avail. (ISBN 0-15-576614-7). HarBraceJ.

Fedoroff, S. & Hertz, L., eds. Advances in Cellular Neurobiology, Vol. 4. (Serial Publication). 420p. 1983. price not set (ISBN 0-12-008304-3). Acad Pr.

Fedorov, A., ed. Chromosome Numbers of Flowering Plants. 926p. 1969. Repr. of 1974 ed. lib. bdg. 88.00x (ISBN 3-87429-067-0). Lubrecht & Cramer.

Fedorov, E. S. Symmetry of Crystals. 4.50 (ISBN 0-686-60371-0). Polycrystal Bk Serv.

Fedorowicz, J. K., ed. & tr. A Republic of Nobles: Studies in Polish History to 1864. LC 81-12284. (Illus.). 310p. 1982. 37.50 (ISBN 0-521-24093-X). Cambridge U Pr.

Fedoseyev, P. & Timofeyev, T. Social Problems of Man's Enviornment: Where We Live & Work. 334p. 1981. 8.50 (ISBN 0-8285-2273-1, Pub. by Progress Pubs USSR). Imported Pubns.

Fedoseyev, P., ed. What Is "Democratic Socialism"? 143p. 1980. pap. 3.50 (ISBN 0-8285-2051-8, Pub. by Progress Pubs USSR). Imported Pubns.

Fedtschenko, O. Eremurus: Kritische Uebersicht Ueber Die Gattung. (Plant Monography Ser.: No.3). 1968. pap. 20.00 (ISBN 3-7682-0560-6). Lubrecht & Cramer.

Feduccia, Alan. Evolutionary Trends in the Neotropical Ovenbirds & Woodhewers. 69p. 1973. 3.50 (ISBN 0-943610-13-3). Am Ornithologists.

Feduccia, Alan, jt. auth. see Torrey, Theodore W.

Feduchi, L. Spanish Folk Architecture, Vol. 1. (Illus.). 389p. 1982. 59.95 (ISBN 84-7031-017-8, Pub. by Editorial Blume Spain). Intl Schol Bk Serv.

Fedyszyn, Stan. The Chauvinist Guide to Gourmet Entertaining. LC 79-24600. (Orig.). 1980. pap. 5.95 o.p. (ISBN 0-89865-018-6). Donning Co.

Fee, A. L. Memoires sur la Famille des Fougeres: 1844-66, 11parts in 1 vol. (Illus.). 1966. 280.00 (ISBN 3-7682-0447-2). Lubrecht & Cramer.

Fee, Elizabeth, ed. Women & Health: The Politics of Sex in Medicine. (Baywood Policy, Politics, Health & Medicine Ser.: Vol. 4). 264p. (Orig.). 1983. pap. text ed. 14.50 (ISBN 0-89503-034-9). Baywood Pub.

Fee, Gordon D. New Testament Exegesis: A Handbook for Students & Pastors. LC 82-24829. (Illus.). 180p. (Orig.). 1983. pap. price not set (ISBN 0-664-24469-6). Westminster.

Fee, Roger D. Basic Ideas About Singing: The Teaching of Theodore Harrison, an American Maestro. LC 78-63254. pap. text ed. 6.50 (ISBN 0-8191-0614-3). U Pr of Amer.

Feegel, John R. Autopsy. 304p. 1982. pap. 2.95 o.s.i. (ISBN 0-380-00269-8, 79681). Avon.

--Death Sails the Bay. 1978. pap. 1.95 o.s.i. (ISBN 0-380-01972-8, 38570). Avon.

--Malpractice. 1982. pap. 3.50 (ISBN 0-451-11821-9, AE1821, Sig). NAL.

Feeley, Falk. A Swarm of WASPS: A Guide to the Manners (Lovely), Mores (Traditional), Morals (Well...), & Way of Life of the Fortunate Few Who Have Always Had Money. (Illus.). 132p. (Orig.). 1983. 11.95 (ISBN 0-688-01927-7). Morrow.

Feeley, Mrs. Falk. A Swarm of Wasps: A Guide to the Manners (Lovely), Mores (Traditional), Morals (Well...), & Way of Life of the Fortunate Few Who Have Always Had Money. (Illus.). 132p. 1983. pap. 4.95 (ISBN 0-688-02048-8). Quill NY.

Feeley, Kathleen. Flannery O'Connor: Voice of the Peacock. 2nd ed. xviii, 198p. 1982. pap. 9.00 (ISBN 0-8232-1093-6). Fordham.

Feeley, Malcolm M. Court Reform On Trial: Why Simple Solutions Fail (A Twentieth Century Fund Report) 200p. 1983. 14.95 (ISBN 0-465-01437-2). Basic.

--The Process Is the Punishment: Handling Cases in a Lower Criminal Court. LC 79-7349. (Illus.). 330p. 1979. 12.95x (ISBN 0-87154-253-6). Russell Sage.

Feeley, Malcolm M., jt. ed. see Becker, Theodore L.

Feeling, Durbin, tr. see Ziegenfuss, Mary Lou.

Feely, Margot, ed. see O'Neill, John P.

Feely, T. J. Embrace Tomorrow. 352p. Date not set. pap. 2.95 (ISBN 0-686-97484-0). PB.

Feeney, Floyd, Jr. The Police & Pretrial Release. LC 79-9629. 240p. 1982. 23.95x (ISBN 0-669-03597-1). Lexington Bks.

Feeney, Leonard. Survival Till Seventeen. LC 79-25067. 1980. 6.95 (ISBN 0-932506-08-9). St Bedes Pubns.

Feeney, Robert E. & Allison, R. G. Evolutionary Biochemistry of Proteins. LC 69-19099. 290p. 1969. text ed. 15.75 o.p. (ISBN 0-471-25685-4, Pub. by Wiley). Krieger.

Feeney, Stephanie. A Is for Aloha. LC 80-5462. (Illus.). 64p. (ps-k). 1980. 7.95 (ISBN 0-8248-0722-7). UH Pr.

Feeney, Stephanie & Christensen, Doris. Who Am I in the Lives of Children? An Introduction to Early Childhood Education. (Early Childhood Education Ser.). 1978. text ed. 18.50 (ISBN 0-675-08391-5). Additional supplements may be obtained from publisher (ISBN 0-685-86845-1). Merrill.

--Who Am I in the Lives of Children? An Introduction to Teaching Young Children. 416p. 1983. text ed. 19.95 (ISBN 0-675-20056-3). Additional supplements may be obtained from publisher. Merrill.

Feeney, William, ed. Lost Plays of the Irish Renaissance, Vol. 2. 10.00x (ISBN 0-912262-70-2). Proscenium.

Feenstra, jt. auth. see Spanoghe.

Feeny, Bill, jt. auth. see Robinson, Dorothy N.

Feeny, Mary, tr. see Israel, Lucien.

Feeny, Maura. A La Mode: Womens Fashion in French Art, 1850-1900. 44p. 1982. pap. 4.00 (ISBN 0-686-37427-4). S & F Clark.

Feerick, Amalie P., jt. auth. see Feerick, John D.

Feerick, John D. & Feerick, Amalie P. The Vice-Presidents of the United States. (First Books). (Illus.). (gr. 4-6). 1977. PLB 8.90 s&l (ISBN 0-531-02907-7). Watts.

Feerick, John D., jt. auth. see Barbash, Joseph.

Fefer, Alexander & Goldstein, Allan, eds. The Potential Role of T-Cells in Cancer Therapy. (Progress in Cancer Research & Therapy Ser.: Vol. 22q). 311p. 1982. text ed. 41.00 (ISBN 0-89004-747-2). Raven.

Fegan, Patrick W. Vineyards & Wineries of America: A Traveler's Guide. 1982. pap. 9.95 (ISBN 0-8289-0489-8). Greene.

Feher, K. Digital Communications: Microwave Applications. 1981. 34.00 (ISBN 0-13-214080-2). P-H.

Feher, Matyas & Erdy, Miklos, eds. Studia Sumiro-Hungarica, 2 vols. Incl. A Sumir Kerdes (the Sumerian Question) Galgoczy, Janos. LC 79-7359. (Vol. 1). 270p (ISBN 0-914246-51-8); Szumirok Es Magyarok (Sumerians & Magyars) Somogyi, Ede. LC 70-7362. (Vol. 2). 270p (ISBN 0-914246-52-6). (Illus.). 1968. Repr. 13.00 ea. Gilgamesh Pub.

Feher, Zsuzsa D., intro. by. Twentieth Century Hungarian Painting. Bodoczky, Caroline & Bodoczky, Istvan, trs. (Illus.). 83p. 1980. 55.00 (ISBN 0-89893-162-2). CDP.

Feherdy, Imre, tr. see Feuer-Toth, Rozsa.

Fehl, Fred. Stars of the Ballet & Dance in Performance Photographs. (Illus.). 144p. (Orig.). (gr. 6 up). 1983. pap. 8.95 (ISBN 0-486-24492-X). Dover.

--Stars of the Broadway Stage, 1940-1970. (Illus.). 144p. (Orig.). pap. 8.95 (ISBN 0-486-24398-2). Dover.

Fehl, Jim, ed. Standard Lesson Commentary, 1983-84. (Illus.). 456p. pap. 6.50 (ISBN 0-87239-616-9). Standard Pub.

Fehlauer, Adolph F. Bible Reader's Guide. 1981. 5.95 (ISBN 0-8100-0146-2, 06N0558). Northwest Pub.

Fehr, Howard F., et al. Unified Mathematics Series, 4 levels. (gr. 7-9). 1971-74. Level 1. text ed. 14.80 (ISBN 0-201-01833-0, Sch Div); Level 2. text ed. 14.80 (ISBN 0-201-01836-5); Level 3. text ed. 13.56 o.p. (ISBN 0-201-01838-1); Level 4. text ed. 13.64 o.p. (ISBN 0-201-02251-6); tchrs' commentaries for levels 1-3 o.p. 7.04 ea. A-W.

Fehr, Lawrence A. Introduction to Personality. 576p. 1983. text ed. 25.95 (ISBN 0-02-336700-8). Macmillan.

Fehr, Terry, jt. auth. see Mangan, Doreen.

Fehr, Terry, jt. auth. see Petersen, W. P.

Fehrenbach, T. R. Lonestar: History of Texas & the Texans. 1983. 9.98 (ISBN 0-517-40280-7). Crown.

--Seven Keys to Texas. 120p. 1983. 15.00 (ISBN 0-87404-069-8). Tex Western.

Fehrenbacher, Don E. The Dred Scott Case: Its Significance in American Law & Politics. LC 78-4665. (Illus.). 1978. 35.00x (ISBN 0-19-502403-6). Oxford U Pr.

--The Era of Expansion: 1800-1848. LC 68-8713. (American Republic Ser.). 165p. 1969. pap. text ed. 11.95x (ISBN 0-471-25691-9). Wiley.

--The Leadership of Abraham Lincoln. LC 77-114013. (Problems in American History Ser.). 194p. 1970. pap. text ed. 11.50 (ISBN 0-471-25689-7). Wiley.

--Prelude to Greatness: Lincoln in the 1850's. 1962. 12.50x (ISBN 0-8047-0119-9); pap. 4.95x (ISBN 0-8047-0120-2, SX109). Stanford U Pr.

--Slavery, Law, & Politics: The Dred Scott Case in Historical Perspective. (Illus.). 1981. 17.95 (ISBN 0-19-502882-1). Oxford U Pr.

--Slavery, Law & Politics: The Dred Scott Case in Historical Perspective. (Illus.). 1981. pap. 7.95 (ISBN 0-19-502883-X, GB639, GB). Oxford U Pr.

Fehrman, Cherie. The Complete School Secretary's Desk Book. LC 82-3782. 356p. 1982. 24.50 (ISBN 0-13-163352-X, Busn). P-H.

Feia, Marian R., jt. auth. see Christenson, Toni.

Feibleman, James K. Aesthetics: A Study of the Fine Arts in Theory & Practice. 1968. text ed. 12.50x o.p. (ISBN 0-391-00483-2). Humanities.

--Introduction to the Philosophy of Charles S. Peirce. 1970. pap. 5.95x o.p. (ISBN 0-262-56008-9). MIT Pr.

--The New Cosmology. LC 77-81794. 224p. 1983. 14.50 (ISBN 0-87527-171-5). Green.

--Religious Platonism. LC 78-161628. 236p. Repr. of 1959 ed. lib. bdg. 22.25x (ISBN 0-8371-6184-3, FERP). Greenwood.

Feibleman, Peter. The Bayous. LC 73-84544. (American Wilderness Ser). (Illus.). (gr. 6 up). 1973. lib. bdg. 15.96 (ISBN 0-8094-1189-X, Pub. by Time-Life). Silver.

Feibleman, Peter S. Cooking of Spain & Portugal. LC 70-82142. (Foods of the World Ser.). (Illus.). (gr. 6 up). 1969. PLB 17.28 (ISBN 0-8094-0066-9, Pub. by Time-Life). Silver.

Feichtinger, G., ed. Optimal Control Theory & Economic Analysis: Proceedings of the Viennese Workshop on Economic Applications of Control Theory, First, Vienna, Austria, October 28-30, 1981. 414p. 1982. 68.00 (ISBN 0-444-86428-8, North Holland). Elsevier.

Feichtinger, Gustav & Kall, Peter. Operations Research in Progress. 1982. 56.50 (ISBN 90-277-1464-9, Pub. by Reidel Holland). Kluwer Boston.

Feier, John L. The Woodworker's Reference Guide & Sourcebook. (Illus.). 368p. 1983. 35.00 (ISBN 0-686-83663-4, ScribT). Scribner.

Feierabend, Ivo, et al. Political Events Project, 1948-1965. 1976. write for info. codebk. (ISBN 0-89138-017-5). ICPSR.

Feierman, Steven. The Shambaa Kingdom: A History. LC 72-7985. 250p. 1974. 27.50 (ISBN 0-299-06360-7). U of Wis Pr.

Feifel, Herman. New Meanings of Death. 1st ed. (Illus.). 1977. 18.95 (ISBN 0-07-020350-4, HP); pap. 11.95 (ISBN 0-07-020349-0). McGraw.

Feifel, Herman, ed. Meaning of Death. 1959. pap. 4.95 (ISBN 0-07-020347-4, SP). McGraw.

Feifelder, David. Molecular Biology: A Comprehensive Introduction to Prokaryotes & Eukaryotes. (Illus.). 876p. 1983. text ed. 33.50 (ISBN 0-86720-012-X). Sci Bks Intl.

Feifer, George, jt. auth. see Panov, Valery.

Feiffer, Jules. Ackroyd. LC 76-558872. 1977. 8.95 o.p. (ISBN 0-671-22502-2). S&S.

--Feiffer: Jules Feiffer's America From Eisenhower to Reagan. Heller, Steve, ed. 1982. 25.00 (ISBN 0-394-52846-8); pap. 12.95 (ISBN 0-394-71279-X). Knopf.

--Little Murders. 1983. pap. 4.95 (ISBN 0-14-048118-4). Penguin.

Feig, Stephen A. & McLelland, Robert, eds. Breast Carcinoma: Diagnostic Imaging & Current Therapeutic Update. (Illus.). 556p. 1983. write for info. (ISBN 0-89352-178-7). Masson Pub.

Feigel, William & Zamzow, Dennis. Foot Care Book. (Illus.). 1982. 9.95 (ISBN 0-89037-245-4). Anderson World.

Feigenbaum, ed. see Kohavi, Zvi.

Feigenbaum, Armand V. Total Quality Control. 3rd ed. (Illus.). 768p. 39.50 (ISBN 0-07-020353-9, P&RB). McGraw.

--Total Quality Control: Engineering & Management. 1961. 42.00 o.p. (ISBN 0-07-020352-0, P&RB). McGraw.

Feigenbaum, E., ed. see Hamacher, V. C., et al.

Feigenbaum, Edward, ed. see Katzan, Harry.

Feiger, Allan D., jt. auth. see Dubovsky, Steven L.

Feighner, John, jt. auth. see Damlouji, Namir F.

Feighner, John P., ed. see Schuckit, Marc A.

Feigl, Dorothy M., jt. auth. see Hill, John W.

Feigl, F. Spot Tests in Inorganic Analysis. 6th ed. 1972. 106.50 (ISBN 0-444-40929-7). Elsevier.

Feigl, Fritz. Spot Tests in Organic Analysis. 7th ed. 1966. 106.50 (ISBN 0-444-40209-8). Elsevier.

Feigl, Herbert & Sellars, Wilfrid, eds. Readings in Philosophical Analysis. x, 593p. 1981. lib. bdg. 25.00 (ISBN 0-917930-29-0); pap. text ed. 15.00x (ISBN 0-917930-09-6). Ridgeview.

Feigs, Wolfgang. Deskriptive Edition Auf Allograph-, Wort- und Satzniveau, Demonstriert An Handschriftlich Uberlieferten, Deutschsprachigen Briefen Von H. Steffens. ix, 699p. (Ger.). 1982. write for info. (ISBN 3-261-04938-3). P Lang Pubs.

Feild, Lance. Exploring Nova Scotia. LC 79-4903. (Illus.). 192p. 1978. pap. 7.95 (ISBN 0-914788-16-7). East Woods.

--Map User's Sourcebook. LC 81-18941. 194p. 1982. lib. bdg. 17.50 (ISBN 0-379-20717-6). Oceana.

Feild, Reshad. The Last Barrier. LC 75-9345. 1977. pap. 6.45i (ISBN 0-06-062586-4, RD 202, HarpR). Har-Row.

Feild, Tracey, jt. auth. see Gutowski, Michael.

Feilden. The Conservation of Historic Buildings. 1982. text ed. 124.00 (ISBN 0-408-10782-0). Butterworth.

Feilen, John. Dirt Track Speedsters. LC 76-5639. (Winners Circle Ser.). (gr. 4-5). 1976. PLB 7.95 (ISBN 0-913940-39-9). Crestwood Hse.

--Motocross. LC 78-17436. (Winners Circle Ser.). (Illus.). (gr. 4). 1978. PLB 6.95 o.p. (ISBN 0-913940-79-8). Crestwood Hse.

--Winter Sports. LC 76-5640. (Winners Circle Ser.). (gr. 4-5). 1976. PLB 7.95 (ISBN 0-913940-43-7). Crestwood Hse.

Fein, Alan & Szuts, Ete Z. Photoreceptors: Their Role in Vision. LC 81-24209. (International Union of Pure & Applied Physics Biophysics Ser.: No. 5). (Illus.). 1982. 34.50 (ISBN 0-521-24433-1); pap. 13.95 (ISBN 0-521-28684-0). Cambridge U Pr.

Fein, Barbara. The New Medical College Admission Test. 1982. pap. 6.68 (ISBN 0-06-463549-X, EH-549). Har-Row.

Fein, Bill. They all Depend on You. LC 82-81044. (Illus.). 50p. 1983. pap. 3.95 (ISBN 0-86666-097-6). GWP.

Fein, Cheri. New York: Open to the Public. LC 81-21468. (Illus.). 224p. 1982. 24.95 (ISBN 0-941434-00-1, 8001). Stewart Tabori & Chang.

Fein, Greta. Child Development. (Illus.). 1978. text ed. 23.95 (ISBN 0-13-132571-X); study guide & wkbk. 8.95 (ISBN 0-13-132555-8). P-H.

Fein, Greta G. & Clarke-Stewart, K. Alison. Day Care in Context. LC 72-8588. 359p. 1973. 40.95 (ISBN 0-471-25695-1, Pub. by Wiley-Interscience). Wiley.

Fein, Helen. Accounting for Genocide: Victims-& Survivors-of the Holocaust. 468p. Repr. 17.95 (ISBN 0-686-95049-6). ADL.

--Imperial Crime & Punishment: The Massacre at Jallianwala Bagh & British Judgment, 1919-1920. LC 77-2930. 1977. text ed. 15.00x (ISBN 0-8248-0506-2). UH Pr.

Fein, Lois, jt. auth. see Gonzalez, Harvey J.

Fein, Mitchell. Improshare: An Alternative to Traditional Managing. 1981. pap. text ed. 15.00 (ISBN 0-89806-031-1); pap. text ed. 7.50 members. Inst Indus Eng.

--Motivation for Work. 1974. pap. text ed. 12.00 o.p. (ISBN 0-89806-028-1, 86). Inst Indus Eng.

--Rational Approaches to Raising Productivity. 1974. pap. text ed. 12.00 (ISBN 0-89806-029-X, 26); pap. text ed. 6.00 members. Inst Indus Eng.

--Wage Incentive Plans. 1970. pap. text ed. 12.00 (ISBN 0-89806-026-5, 42); pap. text ed. 6.00 members. Inst Indus Eng.

Fein, Rashi, jt. auth. see Lewis, Charles E.

Fein, Richard J. Robert Lowell. (U. S. Authors Ser.: No. 176). lib. bdg. 8.50 o.p. (ISBN 0-8057-0464-7, Twayne). G K Hall.

--Robert Lowell. 2nd ed. (United States Authors Ser.). 1979. lib. bdg. 11.95 (ISBN 0-8057-7279-0, Twayne). G K Hall.

Fein, Sylvia. Heidi's Horse. LC 74-76077. (Illus.). 1976. 15.00 (ISBN 0-917388-01-1). Exelrod Pr.

Feinberg, Barry. Bertrand Russell's America: 1945-1970. 1982. 20.00 (ISBN 0-89608-157-5); pap. 8.00 (ISBN 0-89608-156-7). South End Pr.

Feinberg, Barry, ed. see Russell, Betrand.

Feinberg, Charles L. Jeremiah. 320p. 1982. 13.95 (ISBN 0-310-45330-5). Zondervan.

--Millenialism: The Two Major Views. LC 80-12818. 1980. pap. 9.95 (ISBN 0-8024-6816-0). Moody.

--The Minor Prophets. rev ed. LC 76-44088. 384p. 1976. 13.95 (ISBN 0-8024-5306-6). Moody.

--Prophecy of Ezekiel. 1969. 14.95 (ISBN 0-8024-6900-0). Moody.

Feinberg, Gerald & Schapiro, Robert. Life Beyond Earth: The Intelligent Earthling's Guide to Extraterrestrial Life. (Illus.). 480p. 1980. pap. 9.95 (ISBN 0-688-08642-X). Quill NY.

Feinberg, Gerald, et al, eds. A Festschrift for Maurice Goldhaber. new ed. LC 80-20599. (Transaction Ser.: Vol. 40). 293p. 1980. 27.00x (ISBN 0-89766-086-2). NY Acad Sci.

Feinberg, Harold S., jt. auth. see Ryder, Joanne.

Feinberg, Joel. Reason & Responsibility. 5th ed. 640p. 1980. text ed. 21.95x (ISBN 0-534-00924-7). Wadsworth Pub.

--Social Philosophy. 1973. pap. 8.95 ref. ed. (ISBN 0-13-817254-4). P-H.

Feinberg, John S. Theologies & Evil. LC 79-66474. 1979. text ed. 18.00 (ISBN 0-8191-0838-3); pap. text ed. 9.50 (ISBN 0-8191-0839-1). U Pr of Amer.

Feinberg, John S. & Feinberg, Paul D. Tradition & Testament. LC 81-11223. 1982. 12.95 (ISBN 0-8024-2544-5). Moody.

Feinberg, Karen. Crown Jewels. LC 82-60559. (Illus.). 64p. 1982. 24.00 (ISBN 0-88014-055-0). Mosaic Pr OH.

Feinberg, Lillian O. Applied Business Communications. 585p. 1982. text ed. 15.95 (ISBN 0-88284-125-4); instructor's manual avail. Alfred Pub.

Feinberg, Mortimer R. Effective Psychology for Managers. 1975. 14.95 o.p. (ISBN 0-13-244855-6, Reward); pap. 4.95 (ISBN 0-13-244848-3). P-H.

Feinberg, Paul. Friends. (Illus.). 96p. 1980. pap. 5.95 (ISBN 0-8256-3184-X, Quick Fox). Putnam Pub Group.

Feinberg, Paul D., jt. auth. see Feinberg, John S.

Feinberg, R., ed. Modern Power Transformer Practice. LC 78-5608. 359p. 1979. 64.95x o.p. (ISBN 0-470-26344-X). Halsted Pr.

Feinberg, Renee. Women, Education & Employment: A Bibliography of Periodical Citations, Pamphlets, Newspapers & Government Documents, 1970-1980. 274p. 1982. 25.00 (ISBN 0-208-01967-7, Lib Prof Pubns). Shoe String.

Feinberg, Richard E. The Intemperate Zone: The Third World Challenge to U.S. Foreign Policy. 1983. 17.50 (ISBN 0-393-01712-5). Norton.

--The Triumph of Allende. pap. 1.25 o.p. (ISBN 0-451-61134-9, MY1134, Ment). NAL.

Feinberg, Richard E., ed. Central America: International Dimensions of the Crisis. 300p. 1982. 29.50 (ISBN 0-8419-0737-4); pap. 12.50 (ISBN 0-8419-0738-2). Holmes & Meier.

Feinberg, Walter. Reason & Rhetoric: The Intellectual Foundations of Twentieth Century Liberal Educational Policy. LC 74-16009. 287p. 1975. text ed. 24.95 o.p. (ISBN 0-471-25697-8). Wiley.

Feinberg, Walter, jt. ed. see Bredo, Eric.

Feinberg, William J., ed. Directory of Real Estate Investors 1983. 1983. pap. 98.00 (ISBN 0-938184-07-5). Whole World.

Feinberg, Wm. J., ed. The Whole World Oil Directory, 1983, 2 vols. 1983. Set. pap. 97.00 (ISBN 0-938184-10-5); Vol. 1. pap. (ISBN 0-938184-08-3); Vol. 2. pap. (ISBN 0-938184-09-1). Whole World.

Feineman, Neil. Nicolas Roeg. (Filmmakers Ser.). 1978. 12.95 (ISBN 0-8057-9258-9, Twayne). G K Hall.

Feinendegen, L. E. & Tisljarlentulis, G., eds. Molecular & Microdistribution of Radioisotopes & Biological Consequences: Proceedings Held in Julich, Federal Republic of Germany, October 1975. (Current Topics in Radiator Research: Vol. 12). 1978. Repr. 138.50 (ISBN 0-444-85142-9, North-Holland). Elsevier.

Feinerman, R. P. & Newman, D. J. Polynomial Approximation. 156p. 1974. 13.50 o.p. (ISBN 0-683-03077-9, Pub. by W & W). Krieger.

Feingold, Ben F. Why Your Child Is Hyperactive. LC 74-9078. 1974. 10.50 (ISBN 0-394-49343-5, Co-Pub by Bookworks). Random.

Feingold, Carl. Fundamentals of Structured COBOL Programming. 3rd ed. 690p. 1978. pap. text ed. write for info. o.p. (ISBN 0-697-08128-1); avail. o.p. Wm C Brown.

--Fundamentals of Structured COBOL Programming. 4th ed. 720p. 1983. pap. text ed. write for info. (ISBN 0-697-08173-7); write for info. (ISBN 0-697-08185-0); write for info. (ISBN 0-697-08186-9). Wm C Brown.

Feingold, Henry L. Zion in America. (Immigrant Heritage of America Ser). 1974. lib. bdg. 14.50 o.p. (ISBN 0-8057-3298-5, Twayne). G K Hall.

Feingold, Marie, jt. auth. see Feingold, S. Norman.

Feingold, S. Norman & Evers, Dora. Your Future in Exotic Occupations. LC 76-182515. (Careers in Depth Ser.). (Illus.). 160p. (gr. 7 up). 1980. PLB 7.97 (ISBN 0-8239-0260-9). Rosen Pr.

Feingold, S. Norman & Feingold, Marie. Scholarships, Fellowships & Loans, Vol. 7. LC 49-49180. 804p. 1982. 75.00x (ISBN 0-87442-007-5). Bellman.

Feingold, S. Norman & Hansard-Winkler, Glenda A. Nine-Hundred Thousand Plus Jobs Annually: Published Sources of Employment Listings. 196p. 1982. 10.95. Impact VA.

Feininger, Andreas. Andreas Feininger: Experimental Work. (Illus.). 1978. 14.95 o.p. (ISBN 0-8174-2441-5, Amphoto); pap. 9.95 o.p. (ISBN 0-8174-2116-5). Watson-Guptill.

--Andreas Feininger: Total Photography. (Illus.). 252p. 1982. 14.95 (ISBN 0-8174-3531-X, Amphoto). Watson-Guptill.

--Light & Lighting in Photography. (Illus.). 296p. 1976. 12.95 o.p. (ISBN 0-8174-0585-2, Amphoto). Watson-Guptill.

--Perfect Photograph. (Illus.). 196p. 1974. 12.95 (ISBN 0-8174-0565-8, Amphoto). Watson-Guptill.

--Principles of Composition in Photography. (Illus.). 136p. 1973. 12.95 (ISBN 0-8174-0552-6, Amphoto). Watson-Guptill.

--Shells: Forms & Designs of the Sea. (Illus.). 128p. 1983. pap. 8.95 (ISBN 0-486-24498-9). Dover.

--Successful Photography. rev. ed. LC 74-23537. 1975. 12.95 o.p. (ISBN 0-13-864603-1). P-H.

--Total Picture Control. (Illus.). 1970. write for info o.p. (ISBN 0-8174-0465-1, Amphoto). Watson-Guptill.

Feininger, T. Lux, tr. see Rudolph, Wolfgang.

Feinman, Jeffrey. The Catalogue of Magic. 1979. 12.50 o.p. (ISBN 0-671-23107-3); pap. 4.95 o.p. (ISBN 0-671-24650-X). S&S.

--How You Can Profit from Today's Gold Rush. LC 80-7786. 94p. 1980. pap. 4.95 o.p. (ISBN 0-385-17196-X, Dolp). Doubleday.

--U. S. Gardening Catalog. 1979. 14.95 o.p. (ISBN 0-671-24026-9); pap. 6.95 o.p. (ISBN 0-671-24861-8). S&S.

Feinman, Max L. & Wilson, Josleen. Live Longer. 1982. pap. 2.75 (ISBN 0-515-06537-4). Jove Pubns.

--Live Longer - Control Your Blood Pressure. LC 76-43300. (Illus.). 1977. 7.95 o.p. (ISBN 0-698-10768-3, Coward). Putnam Pub Group.

Feinsilber, Mike & Mead, William B. American Averages: Amazing Facts of Everyday Life. LC 79-8567. 1980. pap. 8.95 (ISBN 0-385-15176-4, Dolp). Doubleday.

Feinstein, C. H. Domestic Capital Formation in the United Kingdom. (Publications of the National Institute of Economic & Social Research & Cambridge Department of Applied Economics: No. 4). 49.00 (ISBN 0-521-04986-5). Cambridge U Pr.

--National Income, Expenditure & Output of the United Kingdom, 1855-1965. LC 71-163055. (Studies in the National Income & Expenditure of the United Kingdom: Vol. 6). (Illus.). 1972. 79.50 (ISBN 0-521-07230-1). Cambridge U Pr.

--Statistical Tables of National Income Expenditure & Output of the U. K. 1855-1965. LC 76-19627. 1976. limp bdg. 22.95x (ISBN 0-521-21396-7). Cambridge U Pr.

Feinstein, C. H., jt. auth. see Pajestka, Josef.

Feinstein, Charles. The Managed Economy: Essays in British Economic Policy & Performance Since 1929. 310p. 1983. 39.95 (ISBN 0-19-828289-3); pap. 17.95 (ISBN 0-19-828290-7). Oxford U Pr.

Feinstein, Elaine, tr. see Aliger, Margarita, et al.

Feinstein, Elaine, tr. see Tsvetayeva, Marina.

Feinstein, Ellen, jt. auth. see Harris, L. C.

Feinstein, George W. Programmed College Vocabulary Three Thousand Six Hundred. 2nd ed. 1979. pap. text ed. 12.95 (ISBN 0-13-729806-4). P-H.

--Programmed Spelling Demons. 240p. 1973. pap. text ed. 11.95 (ISBN 0-13-730135-9). P-H.

Feinstein, Lloyd, jt. auth. see Kline, Linda.

Feinstein, R. Dermatology. (Clinical Monographs). (Illus.). 1975. pap. 7.95 o.p. (ISBN 0-87618-066-7). R J Brady.

Feinstein, Sherman C. & Looney, John G., eds. Adolescent Psychiatry, Vol. X. LC 70-147017. (Adolescent Psychiatry Ser.). 624p. 1983. lib. bdg. 30.00x (ISBN 0-226-24056-8). U of Chicago Pr.

Feintuch, Abraham & Saeks, R. System Theory: A Hilbert Space Approach. LC 82-1816. (Pure & Applied Mathematics Ser.). 1982. 39.50 (ISBN 0-12-251750-4). Acad Pr.

Feirer. Bench Woodwork. (gr. 7-9). 1978. text ed. 13.00 (ISBN 0-87002-201-6); student guide 4.40 (ISBN 0-87002-203-2). Bennett IL.

--Furniture & Cabinet Making. 1983. price not set (ISBN 0-87002-388-8). Bennett Il.

--Guide to Residential Carpentry. 1983. text ed. price not set (ISBN 0-87002-383-7). Bennett Il.

--Industrial Arts Woodworking. rev. ed. (gr. 9-12). 1982. text ed. 15.96 (ISBN 0-87002-340-3). Bennett IL.

--Woodworking for Industry. 1979. text ed. 22.60 (ISBN 0-87002-242-3); student guide 6.88 (ISBN 0-87002-300-4); tchr's. ed. 3.32 (ISBN 0-87002-352-7). Bennett IL.

Feirer & Hutchings. Advanced Woodwork & Furniture Making. rev. ed. (gr. 9-12). 1982. text ed. 19.56 (ISBN 0-87002-341-1). Bennett IL.

--Advanced Woodwork & Furniture Making. 1978. text ed. 17.28 o.p. (ISBN 0-87002-205-9); student guide 4.36 (ISBN 0-87002-366-7); visual masters 14.40 (ISBN 0-87002-148-6); tchr's. guide 3.52 (ISBN 0-87002-348-9). Bennett IL.

--Carpentry & Building Construction. rev. ed. 1981. text ed. 26.60 (ISBN 0-87002-327-6); student guide 4.36 (ISBN 0-87002-370-5); tchrs'. guide 3.96 (ISBN 0-87002-377-2). Bennett IL.

Feirer & Lindbeck. Basic Drafting. (gr. 9-12). 1978. 6.60 (ISBN 0-87002-287-3); pap. 4.76 (ISBN 0-87002-273-3); Activities for Basic Drafting 3.96 (ISBN 0-87002-306-3). Bennett IL.

--Metalwork S.I. Metric Edition. 1979. text ed. 14.60 (ISBN 0-87002-292-X); student guide 6.00 (ISBN 0-87002-316-0). Bennett IL.

Feirer, John. Cabinetmaking & Millwork. 1982. text ed. 23.96 (ISBN 0-87002-374-8); student guide 4.20 (ISBN 0-87002-176-1); tchr's. guide 3.32 (ISBN 0-87002-349-7). Bennett IL.

Feirer, John L. General Metals. rev. 5th ed. (Industrial Education Ser.). (Illus.). 480p. (gr. 9-10). 1980. text ed. 20.88 (ISBN 0-07-020380-6, W); study guide 5.68 (ISBN 0-07-020382-2); tchrs. resource guide 5.80 (ISBN 0-07-020381-4). McGraw.

--Industrial Arts Woodworking. (gr. 9-12). 1977. text ed. 13.96 o.p. (ISBN 0-87002-195-8); wkbk 3.96 (ISBN 0-87002-284-9); tchr's. ed. 3.32 (ISBN 0-87002-350-0). Bennett IL.

--Machine Tool Metalworking. 2nd ed. Gilmore, D. E., ed. LC 72-10166. (Illus.). 568p. (gr. 10-12). 1973. text ed. 20.50 (ISBN 0-07-020369-5). McGraw.

--Wood: Materials & Processes. rev. ed. (gr. 7-12). 1980. text ed. 19.32 (ISBN 0-87002-307-1); student guide 5.28 (ISBN 0-87002-179-6); tchr's. ed. 3.32 (ISBN 0-87002-351-9). Bennett IL.

Feirer, John L. & Lindbeck, John R. Metalwork. rev. ed. (gr. 7-9). 1970. 14.00 (ISBN 0-87002-017-X); student guide 4.56 (ISBN 0-87002-048-X). Bennett IL.

Feirer, John L., jt. auth. see Groneman, Chris H.

Feirstein, Bruce, ed. see Redman, Scott.

Feirstein, Frederick. Fathering. 55p. 1982. pap. 4.95 (ISBN 0-918222-33-8). Apple Wood.

Feirtag, Michael, jt. ed. see Brecher, Kenneth.

Feis, Herbert. Nineteen Thirty-Three: Characters in Crisis. (FDR & the Era of the New Deal Ser.). 1976. Repr. of 1966 ed. lib. bdg. 39.50 (ISBN 0-306-70807-8). Da Capo.

Feisenberger, H. A. Sale Catalogues of Libraries of Eminent Persons: Scientists, Vol. 11. 302p. 1975. 23.00 o.p. (ISBN 0-7201-0450-5, Pub. by Mansell England). Wilson.

Feisner, Edith A. Needlepoint & Beyond: 27 Lessons in Advanced Canvas Work. (Illus.). 176p. 1983. pap. 10.95 (ISBN 0-686-83716-9, ScribT). Scribner.

Feist, Raymond E. The Magician. LC 80-2957. 552p. 1982. 19.95 (ISBN 0-385-17580-9). Doubleday.

Feistritzer, W. P., ed. Cereal Seed Technology: A Manual of Cereal Seed Production, Quality Control & Distribution. (FAO Agricultural Development Paper, No. 98; FAO Plant Production & Protection Ser.: No. 10). 238p. 1975. pap. 17.00 (ISBN 0-686-93146-7, F94, FAO). Unipub.

Feit, Edward. Governments & Leaders: An Approach to Comparative Politics. LC 77-77977. (Illus.). 1978. text ed. 24.50 (ISBN 0-395-25367-5). HM.

Feit, Eugene D. & Wilkins, Cletus, Jr., eds. Polymer Materials for Electronic Applcations. (ACS Symposium Ser.: No. 184). 1982. write for info. (ISBN 0-8412-0715-1). Am Chemical.

Feit, J., jt. auth. see Engelsohn, Harold S.

Feit, W. Representation Theory of Finite Groups. (Mathematical Library: Vol. 25). Date not set. 55.00 (ISBN 0-444-86155-6, North Holland). Elsevier.

Feitis, Rosemary. Ida Rolf Talks About Rolfing & Physical Reality. LC 78-2126. 1979. pap. 5.95i o.p. (ISBN 0-06-090665-0, CN 665, CN). Har-Row.

Feito, Francisco E., jt. auth. see Alba-Buffill, Elio.

Feitz, Frank J. Bum Connection. 204p. 1980. 4.95 (ISBN 0-686-98047-6). Telecom Lib.

Feiveson, Harold A., et al, eds. Boundaries of Analysis: An Inquiry into the Tocks Island Dam Controversy. Sinden, Frank W. & Socolow, Robert H. LC 76-3773. (American Academy of Arts & Sciences Ser). 440p. 1976. prof ref 17.50x (ISBN 0-88410-430-3). Ballinger Pub.

Fejto, Francois. French Communist Party & the Crisis of International Communism. (Studies in Communism, Revisionism & Revolution). 1967. 20.00x (ISBN 0-262-06017-5). MIT Pr.

Fekete, Francois, jt. auth. see Nahum, Henri.

Fekete, Janos. Back to the Realities: Reflections of a Hungarian Banker. 359p. 1982. text ed. 42.00x (ISBN 963-05-2987-4, 41219, Pub. by Kultura Pr Hungary). Humanities.

Fekety, Robert. Reviews of Clinical Infectious Diseases, 1982. 1982. 24.95. Acad Pr.

Felber, Stanley B. & Koch, Arthur. What Did You Say? A Guide to Communications Skills. 2nd ed. (Illus.). 1978. pap. text ed. 12.95 (ISBN 0-13-951996-3). P-H.

Feld, Barry & Levy, Robert J. Standards Relating to Rights of Minors. LC 77-1684. (IJA-ABA Juvenile Justice Standards Project Ser.). 114p. 1980. prof ref 20.00x (ISBN 0-88410-243-2); pap. 10.00x (ISBN 0-88410-810-4). Ballinger Pub.

Feld, Barry C. Neutralizing Inmate Violence: Juvenile Offenders in Institutions. LC 77-21389. (CCJ Series on Massachusetts Youth Correctional Reform). 1977. prof ref 18.50x (ISBN 0-88410-790-6). Ballinger Pub.

Feld, Bernard T., ed. see Szilard, Leo.

Feld, Bruce, jt. auth. see Evatt, Cris.

Feld, E. S., et al. Anfang und Fortschritt: An Introduction to German. 2nd ed. 1973. 21.95x (ISBN 0-02-336760-1); wkbk. 6.95x (ISBN 0-02-336740-7). Macmillan.

Feld, Ellen. Zielsprache Deutsch: Deutsch. Feld, Von Nardroff, ed. 1981. text ed. 21.95x (ISBN 0-02-336810-1). Macmillan.

Feld, J. Construction Failure. LC 68-30908. (Practical Construction Guides Ser.). 1968. 42.95 (ISBN 0-471-25700-1, Pub. by Wiley-Interscience). Wiley.

Feld, Ross. Philip Guston. LC 79-27425. (Illus.). 152p. 1980. 25.00 (ISBN 0-8076-0975-7); pap. 14.95 (ISBN 0-8076-0962-5). Braziller.

--Plum Poems. LC 79-137210. 1971. pap. 3.00 (ISBN 0-912330-06-6, Dist. by Inland Bk). Jargon Soc.

Feld, Stuart P., jt. auth. see Gardner, Albert T.

Feld, Stuart P., intro. by. American Paintings & Historical Prints from the Middendorf Collection. LC 67-26582. (Illus.). 1967. pap. 2.95 (ISBN 0-87099-116-7). Metro Mus Art.

Feld, Von Nardroff, ed. see Feld, Ellen.

Feld, Werner J. & Wilgen, John K. Domestic Political Realities of European Unification: A Study of Mass Public & Elites in the European Community Countries. new ed. LC 76-28703. (Westview Replica Editions). 1977. PLB 25.00 (ISBN 0-89158-149-9). Westview.

Feldacker, Bruce S. Labor Guide to Labor Law. (Illus.). 1980. ref. ed. 24.95 (ISBN 0-8359-3921-9); text ed. 19.50. Reston.

Feldbaum, Eleanor G., jt. auth. see Levitt, Morris J.

Feldbausch, Friedrich K. Finance Dictionary, German-English, English-German. 205p. 1972. 18.75x (ISBN 0-900537-02-7, Dist. by Hippocrene Books Inc.). Leviathan Hse.

Feldberg, Michael. The Philadelphia Riots of Eighteen Forty-Four: A Study of Ethnic Conflict. LC 75-65. (Contributions in American History: No. 43). (Illus.). 209p. 1975. lib. bdg. 27.50 (ISBN 0-8371-7876-2, FGC/). Greenwood.

--The Turbulent Era: Riot & Disorder in Jacksonsian America. 1980. text ed. 9.95x (ISBN 0-19-502677-2); pap. text ed. 4.95x (ISBN 0-19-502678-0). Oxford U Pr.

Feldberg, Michael, jt. ed. see Elliston, Frederick.

Feldbrugge, F. J., ed. Encyclopedia of Soviet Law, 2 vols. LC 73-85236. 900p. 1974. Set. lib. bdg. 120.00 (ISBN 0-379-00481-X). Oceana.

Feldbrugge, J. T. & Von Elgg, Y. A., eds. Involuntary Institutionalization: Changing Concepts in the Treatment of Delinquency. (International Congress Ser.: No. 562). 1981. 23.00 (ISBN 0-444-90233-3). Elsevier.

Felder, David W. The Best Investment: Land In a Loving Community. LC 86-61882. (Illus.). 176p. 1983. pap. 8.50 (ISBN 0-910959-00-5). Wellington Pr.

Felder, Dell, ed. Professionalizing Social Studies: Teaching Through Competency Based Teacher Education. LC 78-58629. (Bulletin Ser.: No. 56). 1978. pap. 6.95 (ISBN 0-87986-020-0, 498-15272). Coun Soc Studies.

Felder, Eleanor. X Marks the Spot. (Illus.). (gr. k-3). 1972. gb 3.69 o.p. (ISBN 0-698-30412-8, Coward); GB 3.69 o.p. (ISBN 0-685-92700-8). Putnam Pub Group.

Felder, Richard M. & Rousseau, Ronald W. Elementary Principles of Chemical Processes. LC 77-12043. 571p. 1978. text ed. 30.95x (ISBN 0-471-74330-5); solutions manual 10.95 (ISBN 0-471-03680-3). Wiley.

Feldman. Nutrition in the Middle & Later Years. (Illus.). 352p. 1982. text ed. 29.50 (ISBN 0-7236-7046-3). Wright-PSG.

Feldman, jt. auth. see Scurr.

Feldman, jt. ed. see Newman.

Feldman, A. Bronson. The Unconscious in History. 1959. 4.75 o.p. (ISBN 0-8022-0482-1). Philos Lib.

Feldman, Alan. Frank O'Hara. (United States Authors Ser.). 1979. lib. bdg. 12.95 (ISBN 0-8057-7277-4, Twayne). G K Hall.

Feldman, Annette. The Big Book of Small Needlework Gifts. 160p. 1980. 15.95 (ISBN 0-8437-3360-8). Hammond Inc.

Feldman, B., jt. auth. see Hyatt, H. R.

Feldman, Ben & Feldman, Richard. Selling Your Way to a Million Dollars. LC 82-82308. 1982. pap. 8.95 (ISBN 0-448-07366-8, G&D). Putnam Pub Group.

Feldman, Charles F., ed. Executive Compensation Planning. 181p. 1982. text ed. 30.00 (ISBN 0-686-97765-3, J3-1437). PLI.

Feldman, Daniel & Arnold, Hugh J. Managing Individual & Group Behavior in Organizations. (Illus.). 560p. 1983. text ed. 24.95x (ISBN 0-07-020386-5, C); 9.95 (ISBN 0-07-020389-X). McGraw.

Feldman, David H. Beyond Universals in Cognitive Development. LC 79-24338. (Publications for the Advancement of Theory & History in Psychology). (Illus.). 1980. 24.50x (ISBN 0-89391-029-5). Ablex Pub.

Feldman, David H., ed. Gifted & Talented Children. LC 80-84258. 1982. 7.95x (ISBN 0-87589-876-9, CD-16). Jossey-Bass.

Feldman, David M. Marital Relations, Birth Control, & Abortion in Jewish Law. LC 68-15338. 336p. 1974. pap. 7.95 (ISBN 0-8052-0438-5). Schocken.

Feldman, Edmund B. The Artist. 200p. 1982. text ed. 14.95 (ISBN 0-13-049031-8); pap. text ed. 10.95 (ISBN 0-13-049023-7). P-H.

Feldman, Edwin B. Building Design for Maintainability. (Illus.). 256p. 1975. 27.95 o.p. (ISBN 0-07-020385-7, P&RB). McGraw.

--How to Use Your Time to Get Things Done. LC 68-18138. 273p. 1968. 12.95 (ISBN 0-8119-0110-6). Fell.

Feldman, Edwin B. & Wright, George B. The Supervisor's Handbook. LC 82-71741. 420p. 1982. 29.95 (ISBN 0-8119-0449-0). Fell.

Feldman, Egal. The Dreyfus Affair & the American Conscience, 1895-1906. 184p. 1981. 17.95 (ISBN 0-8143-1677-8). Wayne St U Pr.

Feldman, Ellen. A.K.A. Katherine Wilson. 1983. pap. 3.50 (ISBN 0-440-10219-7). Dell.

Feldman, Elliot J. A Practical Guide to the Conduct of Field Research in the Social Sciences. 120p. 1981. lib. bdg. 16.00 (ISBN 0-89158-980-5); pap. text ed. 6.95 (ISBN 0-89158-981-3). Westview.

Feldman, Elliot J. & Milch, Jerome. The Politics of Canadian Airport Development: Lessons for Federalism. (Duke Press Policy Studies: No. 47). 288p. 1983. 28.50 (ISBN 0-8223-0479-1). Duke.

Feldman, Ethel K. Cook Your Way Thin. (Illus.). 1974. lib. bdg. 5.95 o.p. (ISBN 0-668-02925-0). Arco.

Feldman, Eugene, ed. see Kahn, Louis I.

Feldman, Frances L. The Family in Today's Money World. 2nd ed. LC 75-279660. 1976. 12.95 (ISBN 0-87304-130-5); pap. 7.95 (ISBN 0-87304-131-3). Family Serv.

Feldman, Fred. Introductory Ethics. 1978. text ed. 13.95 (ISBN 0-13-501783-1). P-H.

Feldman, Fredric J., jt. auth. see Christian, Gary D.

Feldman, Gerald D., jt. ed. see Barnes, Thomas G.

Feldman, Harry A., jt. ed. see Evans, Alfred S.

Feldman, Harvey W., et al, eds. Angel Dust: An Ethnographic Study of Phencyclidine Users. LC 79-8319. 240p. 1979. 17.95x (ISBN 0-669-03379-0). Lexington Bks.

Feldman, Howard, jt. auth. see Lopez, Martita A.

Feldman, Irving. New & Selected Poems. 1979. 15.00 o.p. (ISBN 0-670-50648-6). Viking Pr.

--Teach me, Dear Sister. 80p. 1983. 14.75 (ISBN 0-670-31135-9). Viking Pr.

--Teach Me, Dear Sister: Poems. 1983. pap. 7.95 (ISBN 0-14-042302-8). Penguin.

Feldman, J., et al, eds. Intercellular Junctions & Synapses. (Receptors & Recognition Series B: Vol. 2). 1976. 49.95x (ISBN 0-412-14820-X, Pub. by Chapman & Hall). Methuen Inc.

Feldman, James M. The Physics & Circuit Properties of Transistors. LC 71-39722. 600p. 1972. 34.95 o.p. (ISBN 0-471-25706-0). Wiley.

Feldman, Julian, jt. auth. see Tonge, Frederic M.

Feldman, Kenneth A., ed. College & Student: Selected Readings in the Social Psychology of Higher Education. 502p. 1972. text ed. 29.00 o.s.i. (ISBN 0-08-016785-3); pap. text ed. 12.75 (ISBN 0-08-016788-8). Pergamon.

Feldman, Laurence P. Consumer Protection: Problems & Prospects. 2nd ed. (Illus.). 1980. pap. 14.95 (ISBN 0-8299-0301-1). West Pub.

Feldman, Leonard, et al. Materials Analysis by Channeling: Submicron Crystallography. 1982. 42.00 (ISBN 0-12-252680-5). Acad Pr.

Feldman, M. Basic Principles of Genetics. (Biocore Ser: Unit 7). 1974. 15.00 o.p. (ISBN 0-07-005337-5, C). McGraw.

Feldman, M. Philip. Criminal Behaviour: A Psychological Analysis. LC 76-13229. 1977. 49.95 (ISBN 0-471-99401-4, Pub. by Wiley-Interscience). Wiley.

Feldman, Nans A. How to Prepare a Personal Policy Manual. rev. ed. Cobb, Norman B., ed. 252p. 1982. 3-ring looseleaf binder 42.95 (ISBN 0-910053-00-6). Angus Downs.

Feldman, P. & MacCulloch, M. Human Sexual Behavior. LC 79-41220. 226p. 1980. 39.95 (ISBN 0-471-27676-6, Pub. by Wiley-Interscience). Wiley.

Feldman, Paula R. & Pugh, Diana, eds. The Shelley Journals, 2 vols. (Illus.). 1982. 125.00x (ISBN 0-19-812571-2). Oxford U Pr.

Feldman, Phil, jt. auth. see Rugg, Tom.

Feldman, Philip. Developments in the Study of Criminal Behavior: The Prevention & Control of Offending, Vol. 1. 250p. 1982. 41.95 (ISBN 0-471-10176-1, Pub. by Wiley-Interscience). Wiley.

--Developments in the Study of Criminal Behaviour: Violence, Vol. 2. LC 81-21946. 238p. 1982. 34.95 (ISBN 0-471-10373-X, Pub. by Wiley-Interscience). Wiley.

Feldman, Richard, jt. auth. see Feldman, Ben.

Feldman, Richard S., jt. auth. see Salzinger, Kurt.

Feldman, Robert A., tr. see Nakamura, Takafusa.

Feldman, Robert S. & Quenzer, Linda F. Fundamentals of Neuropsychopharmacology. (Illus.). 650p. 1983. price not set (ISBN 0-87893-178-3). Sinauer Assoc.

Feldman, Robert S., ed. Development of Nonverbal Behavior in Children. (Illus.). 315p. 1983. 27.50 (ISBN 0-387-90716-5). Springer-Verlag.

Feldman, Ron, ed. see Arendt, Hannah.

Feldman, Ruth, tr. see Cattafi, Bartolo.

Feldman, Ruth D. Whatever Happened to the Quiz Kids? Perils & Profits of Growing Up Gifted. (Illus.). 375p. 1982. 12.95 (ISBN 0-914091-17-4). Chicago Review.

Feldman, S. Shirley, jt. ed. see Sears, Robert R.

Feldman, Samuel. Home Health Record Book. (Illus.). 128p. (Orig.). 1982. pap. 5.95 (ISBN 0-89893-307-2). CDP.

Feldman, Sandy, jt. auth. see Ulene, Art.

Feldman, Sari & Feldman, Sharon A. Drugs: A Multimedia Sourcebook for Young Adults. (Selection Guide Ser.: No. 4). 256p. 1980. 16.50 o.s.i. (ISBN 0-87436-281-4, Co-Pub. by Neal-Schuman). ABC-Clio.

Feldman, Saul D., ed. Deciphering Deviance. 1978. pap. text ed. 11.95 (ISBN 0-316-27757-6). Little.

Feldman, Seth R. Dziga Vertov: A Guide to References & Resources. 1979. lib. bdg. 32.00 (ISBN 0-8161-8085-7, Hall Reference). G K Hall.

Feldman, Shai. Israeli Nuclear Deterrence: A Strategy for the 1980's. LC 82-9679. 314p. 1983. 25.00x (ISBN 0-231-05546-3); pap. 9.95 (ISBN 0-231-05547-1). Columbia U Pr.

Feldman, Sharon A., jt. auth. see Feldman, Sari.

Feldman, Shirley C. & Merrill, Kathleen K. Learning Ways to Read Words, 4 bks. Incl. Bk. 1. Ways to Read Words (ISBN 0-8077-2509-9); Bk. 2. More Ways to Read Words (ISBN 0-8077-2516-1); Bk. 3. Learning About Words (ISBN 0-8077-2517-X); Bk. 4. Learning More About Words (ISBN 0-8077-2518-8). 1978. pap. 14.00 set (ISBN 0-8077-2505-6); 3.50 ea. Tchrs Coll.

Feldman, Silvia. Choices in Childbirth. LC 77-95181. 1978. 14.95 o.p. (ISBN 0-448-14524-3, G&D). Putnam Pub Group.

--Choices in Childbirth. LC 77-95181. (Illus.). 288p. 1979. Repr. of 1978 ed. pap. 8.95 (ISBN 0-448-14525-1, G&D). Putnam Pub Group.

--Choices in Childbirth. rev. ed. (Illus.). 288p. 1982. pap. 8.95 (ISBN 0-448-00953-6, G&D). Putnam Pub Group.

Feldman, Stephen, jt. auth. see Barnes, Leo.

Feldman, Stephen J. Vocational Training for the Mentally Retarded. (Special Education Ser.). (Illus., Orig.). 1978. pap. text ed. 15.00 (ISBN 0-89568-084-X). Spec Learn Corp.

Feldman, Stephen L. & Wirtshafter, Robert M., eds. On the Economics of Solar Energy: The Public Utility Interface. LC 79-5442. 272p. 1980. 28.95x (ISBN 0-669-03449-5). Lexington Bks.

Feldman, Steven A., jt. auth. see Denhoff, Eric.

Feldmann, H. Kompendium der Medizinischen Psychologie. (Illus.). viii, 264p. 1983. pap. 12.00 (ISBN 3-8055-3673-9). S Karger.

Feldmann, Rodney M. & Heimlich, Richard A. Geology Field Guide: The Black Hills. 208p. (Orig.). 1980. pap. 9.95 (ISBN 0-8403-2193-7). Kendall-Hunt.

Feldmann-Mazoyer, Genevieve. Recherches sur les Ceramiaceae de la Mediterranee. 1977. pap. text ed. 70.40x (ISBN 3-87429-120-0). Lubrecht & Cramer.

Feldon, Leah. Dressing Rich: A Guide to Classic Chic for Women with More Taste Than Money. (Illus.). 160p. 1982. 14.95 (ISBN 0-399-12684-8). Putnam Pub Group.

--Womanstyle. (Illus.). 1979. 14.95 o.p. (ISBN 0-517-53871-7, C N Potter); pap. 8.95 o.p. (ISBN 0-517-53747-8, C N Potter Bks). Crown.

Feldscher, Sharla. Help! The Kid Is Bored. LC 79-53122. (Illus.). 224p. (Orig.). 1979. pap. 7.95 o.s.i. (ISBN 0-89104-158-3, A & W Visual Library). A & W Pubs.

Feldstein, Donald, jt. auth. see Dolgoff, Ralph.

Feldstein, Leonard C. Choros: The Orchestrating Self. 300p. 1983. 30.00 (ISBN 0-8232-1075-8). Fordham.

Feldstein, M. S., jt. auth. see International Economic Association, Conference, Turin, Italy.

Feldstein, Martin. The American Economy in Transition. LC 80-17450. (National Bureau of Economic Research Ser.). 1980. 25.00x (ISBN 0-226-24081-9, PHOEN); pap. 10.00 (ISBN 0-226-24082-7). U of Chicago Pr.

--Behavioral Simulation Methods in Tax Policy Formation. LC 82-21766. (National Bureau of Economic Research-Project Report). 1983. lib. bdg. price not set (ISBN 0-226-24084-3). U of Chicago Pr.

--Capital Taxation. (Illus.). 96p. 1983. text ed. 40.00x (ISBN 0-674-09482-4). Harvard U Pr.

--Inflation: Tax Rules & Capital Formation. LC 82-10854. (National Bureau of Economic Research-Monograph). 304p. 1983. lib. bdg. 31.00x (ISBN 0-226-24085-1). U of Chicago Pr.

Feldstein, Paul J. Health Care Economics. LC 79-14268. (Health Services Ser.). 1979. 25.95x (ISBN 0-471-05361-9, Pub. by Wiley Medical). Wiley.

Feldstein, Ronald F., tr. see Illich-Svitych, Vladislav M.

Feldstein, Stuart. Home, Inc. LC 81-47700. 256p. 1981. 12.95 (ISBN 0-448-12021-6, G&D). Putnam Pub Group.

Feldt, Robert H., ed. Atrioventricular Canal Defects. LC 76-8574. (Illus.). 1976. text ed. 22.00 o.p. (ISBN 0-7216-3615-2). Saunders.

Feldzaman, A. N., jt. auth. see Rosenberg, Harold.

Felgar, Robert. Richard Wright. (United States Authors Ser.). 1980. lib. bdg. 10.95 (ISBN 0-8057-7320-7, Twayne). G K Hall.

Felger, Donna, ed. Doll Catalog. 3rd ed. 254p. 1982. pap. 8.95 (ISBN 0-87588-188-2). Hobby Hse.

Felger, Donna H., jt. auth. see Rainwater, Dorothy T.

Felheim, Marvin. Theater of Augustin Daly. LC 77-90503. Repr. of 1956 ed. lib. bdg. 15.75x (ISBN 0-8371-2209-0, FETD). Greenwood.

Felheim, Marvin & Traci, Philip. Realism in Shakespeare's Romantic Comedies: "O Heavenly Mingle". LC 80-5580. 239p. 1980. lib. bdg. 20.00 (ISBN 0-8191-1282-8); pap. text ed. 10.75 (ISBN 0-8191-1283-6). U Pr of Amer.

Felicetti, Daniel A. Mental Health & Retardation Politics: The Mind Lobbies in Congress. LC 74-14042. (Illus.). 218p. 1975. text ed. 23.95 o.p. (ISBN 0-275-09930-X). Praeger.

Feliciano, Margarita. Window on the Sea Ventana sobre el Mar. Miller, Yvette E., ed. 69p. 1981. pap. 7.95 (ISBN 0-686-83751-7). Lat Am Lit Rev Pr.

Felig, P., et al. Endocrinology & Metabolism. 1981. 79.00 (ISBN 0-07-020387-3). McGraw.

Felins, Yehuda. Nature & Man in the Bible: Chapters in Biblical Ecology. 1982. 25.00x (ISBN 0-900689-19-6). Bloch.

Felitia, Frank De see De Felitta, Frank.

Felitta, Frank De see De Felitta, Frank.

Felix, David. Marx as Politician. 288p. 1983. write for info (ISBN 0-8093-1073-2). S Ill U Pr.

Felix, Glenn H., jt. auth. see Riggs, James L.

Felix, James V. Accounting Career Strategies: The Comprehensive Career Planning Guide for Accounting & Financial Professionals. LC 82-73146. (Illus.). 225p. 1982. 19.95 (ISBN 0-910595-00-3). Career Plan.

Felix, Lucienne. Modern Mathematics & the Teacher. (Orig.). 1966. 17.95 (ISBN 0-521-04989-X); pap. 7.95x (ISBN 0-521-09385-6). Cambridge U Pr.

Felix, Monique. The Story of a Little Mouse Trapped in a Book. (Illus.). 6.95 (ISBN 0-914676-52-0). Green Tiger Pr.

--Yum, Yum: I'll Be My Own Cook. (Illus.). 32p. 1982. 6.95 o.p. (ISBN 0-914676-81-4, Star & Eleph Bks). Green Tiger Pr.

Felix, Monique, illus. If I Were a Sheep. (Illus.). 12p. (Orig.). 1982. pap. 2.50 (ISBN 0-914676-67-9, Pub. by Envelope Bks). Green Tiger Pr.

Felix, Pal, tr. see Kadar, Bela.

Felix, R. E. & Wegner, O. H., eds. Contrast Media in Computed Tomography. (International Congress Ser.: No. 561). 1981. 55.50 (ISBN 0-444-90225-2). Elsevier.

Felix, Sascha W. Psycholinguistische Aspekte des Zweitsprachenerwerbs. (Language Development (LD) Ser.: 2). 340p. (Ger.). 1982. 42.00 (ISBN 3-87808-252-5); pap. 22.00 (ISBN 3-87808-543-5). Benjamins North Am.

Felix, Sascha W., jt. ed. see Wode, Henning.

Felkenes, George. Constitutional Law for Criminal Justice. (Criminal Justice Ser.). 1978. ref. 20.95 (ISBN 0-13-167833-7). P-H.

Felkenes, George T. Criminal Law & Procedure: Text & Cases. LC 75-5735. 480p. 1976. text ed. 22.95 (ISBN 0-13-193441-4). P-H.

--Michigan Criminal Justice Law Manual. (Criminal Justice Ser.). 300p. 1981. pap. text ed. 18.95 (ISBN 0-8299-0369-0). West Pub.

Felkenes, George T., ed. Effective Police Supervision: A Behavioral Approach. (Administration of Justice Ser.: Vol. 5). 1977. pap. text ed. 12.95 (ISBN 0-914526-04-9). Justice Sys.

Felker, Charles A. Machine Shop Technology. rev. ed. (gr. 9-12). 1962. text ed. 8.96 o.p. (ISBN 0-02-816210-2); ans. bk. 1.36 o.p. (ISBN 0-02-816230-7). Glencoe.

--Shop Mathematics. rev. ed. (gr. 9-12). 1965. text ed. 7.60 o.p. (ISBN 0-02-816250-1); ans. bk. 1.60 o.p. (ISBN 0-02-816270-6). Glencoe.

Felker, Evelyn H. Foster Parenting Young Children: Guidelines from a Foster Parent. LC 73-93885. 1974. pap. 5.25 (ISBN 0-87868-119-1, F-51). Child Welfare.

Felknor, Bruce L. Dirty Politics. LC 75-37917. 295p. 1976. Repr. of 1966 ed. lib. bdg. 19.25x (ISBN 0-8371-8148-8, FEDP). Greenwood.

Fell, Dereck. House Plants & Crafts: For Fun & Profit. (Fun & Profit Ser.). (Illus.). 1978. 7.95 (ISBN 0-916302-16-4); pap. 5.50 (ISBN 0-916302-04-0). Bookworm NY.

Fell, John L. Film Before Griffith. 352p. 1983. pap. 12.95 (ISBN 0-520-04758-3, CAL 578). U of Cal Pr.

Fell, Joseph P. Heidegger & Sartre: An Essay on Being & Place. 517p. 1983. pap. 15.00 (ISBN 0-231-04555-7). Columbia U Pr.

Fell, Marie L. The Foundations of Nativism in American Textbooks, 1783-1860. LC 76-145480. (The American Immigration Library). ix, 259p. 1971. Repr. of 1941 ed. lib. bdg. 15.95x (ISBN 0-89198-011-3). Ozer.

Felleman, Hazel, ed. Best Loved Poems of the American People. 1936. 12.95 (ISBN 0-385-00019-7). Doubleday.

Feller, G., et al, eds. Peace & World Order Studies: A Curriculum Guide. 1981. pap. 8.00 (ISBN 0-686-26990-X). Inst World Order.

Feller, Steven, jt. auth. see Kasper, Joseph.

Feller, William. Introduction to Probability Theory & Its Applications, Vol. 1. 3rd ed. LC 68-11708. (Probability & Mathematical Statistics Ser.). 509p. 1968. 29.95x (ISBN 0-471-25708-7). Wiley.

--An Introduction to Probability Theory & Its Applications, Vol. 2. 2nd ed. LC 57-10805. (Probability & Mathematical Statistics Ser). 669p. 1971. 32.95x (ISBN 0-471-25709-5). Wiley.

Fellerer, K. G. Beitrage zur Choralbegleitung und Choralverarbeitung in der Orgelmusik des ausgehenden 18en und beginnenden 19en Jahrhunderts. (Sammlung Mw. Abh. 6-1932 Bibliotheca Organologica Ser.: Vol. 40). viii, 132p. 35.00 o.p. (ISBN 90-6027-225-0, Pub. by Frits Knuf Netherlands). Pendragon NY.

--Studien zur Orgelmusik des ausgehenden Eighteen und fruhen Nineteen Jahrhunderts. (Bibliotheca Organologica Ser.: Vol. 48). 1980. Repr. of 1932 ed. 47.50 o.s.i. (ISBN 90-6027-224-2, Pub. by Frits Knuf Netherlands); wrappers 32.50 o.s.i. (ISBN 90-6027-223-4, Pub. by Frits Knuf Netherlands). Pendragon NY.

Fellerer, Karl G. The History of Catholic Church Music. Brunner, Francis A., tr. LC 78-21637. 1979. Repr. of 1951 ed. lib. bdg. 20.75x (ISBN 0-313-21147-7, FECC). Greenwood.

Fellers, Frederick P., jt. ed. see Meyers, Betty.

Fellig, Arthur see Weegee, pseud.

Fellin, Phillip, jt. auth. see Tripodi, Tony.

Fellman, David. The Defendant's Rights Today. 462p. 1976. 30.00 (ISBN 0-299-07200-2); pap. 12.50 (ISBN 0-299-07204-5). U of Wis Pr.

Fellman, David, ed. Supreme Court & Education. 3rd ed. LC 76-14495. 1976. pap. text ed. 7.50x (ISBN 0-8077-2511-0). Tchrs Coll.

Fellman, Len. Merchandising by Design. 1981. 20.95 (ISBN 0-86730-237-2). Lebhar Friedman.

Fellman, Michael. The Unbounded Frame: Freedom & Community in Nineteenth Century American Utopianism. LC 72-797. 203p. 1973. lib. bdg. 25.00 (ISBN 0-8371-6369-2, FUF/). Greenwood.

Fellmeth, Robert. Interstate Commerce Omission: The Report on the Interstate Commerce Commission & Transportation. LC 70-112514. (Ralph Nader Study Group Reports). 1970. 12.95 o.p. (ISBN 0-670-40019-X, Grossman). Viking Pr.

Fellows, Donald K. Our Environment: An Introduction to Physical Geography. 2nd ed. LC 79-18159. 532p. 1980. text ed. 23.95 (ISBN 0-471-05755-X). Wiley.

Fellows, E. Barrett Prettyman. Preliminary Hearing, D. C. Work, C. R., ed. 1967. 6.50 o.p. (ISBN 0-685-14185-3). Lerner Law.

Fellows, Hugh & Ikeda, Fusaye. Business Speaking & Writing. (Illus.). 352p. 1982. text ed. 21.95 (ISBN 0-13-107854-2). P-H.

Fellows, Julian R., jt. auth. see Severns, William H.

Fellows, Len, jt. auth. see Bragdon, Allen.

Fellows, Otis. Diderot. (World Authors Ser.). 1977. lib. bdg. 13.95 (ISBN 0-8057-6265-5, Twayne). G K Hall.

Fellows, Otis, et al. A Livre Ouvert: Premieres Lectures En Francais. 1970. text ed. 8.95x (ISBN 0-02-336860-8). Macmillan.

Fellows, Otis E. Buffon. (World Authors Ser.). lib. bdg. 15.95 (ISBN 0-8057-2184-3, Twayne). G K Hall.

Fellows, Otis E. & Torrey, Norman L. Age of Enlightenment. 2nd ed. LC 73-147121. 1971. text ed. 21.95 (ISBN 0-13-018465-9). P-H.

Fellows, Reginald B. Railways to Cambridge Actual & Proposed. (Cambridge Town, Gown & County Ser.: Vol. 2). (Illus.). 32p. 1976. Repr. of 1948 ed. pap. 4.00 (ISBN 0-902675-62-1). Oleander Pr.

Fellows, Robert & Eisenbarth, George, eds. Monoclonal Antibodies in Endocrine Research. 212p. 1981. text ed. 25.50 (ISBN 0-89004-687-5). Raven.

Fellowship of Catholic Scholars. Christian Faith & Freedom: Proceedings. Williams, Paul L., ed. LC 82-81072. 128p. (Orig.). 1982. pap. text ed. 4.50 (ISBN 0-686-97454-9). NE Bks.

Fellucci, Mario. The Masterpieces of the Vatican. (A Science of Man Library Bk). (Illus.). 40p. 1975. 67.00 (ISBN 0-913314-54-4). Am Classical Coll Pr.

Felman, Alvin H. The Pediatric Chest: Radiological, Clinical, & Pathological Observations. (Illus.). 552p. 1983. 56.50x (ISBN 0-398-04730-8). C C Thomas.

Felman, Shoshana, et al. Discours et Pouvoi, Vol. II. Chambers, Ross, ed. LC 81-50963. (Michigan Romance Studies Ser.). 262p. (Orig.). 1982. pap. 8.00 (ISBN 0-939730-01-4). Mich Romance.

Felmeister, Charles J. & Tulman, Michael M. Personalized Guide to Financial Planning. Snyder, Thomas L., ed. (Dental Practice Management Ser.). 136p. 1982. pap. text ed. 12.95 (ISBN 0-8016-4713-4). Mosby.

Felmeister, Charles J., ed. see Bosmajian, C. Perry & Bosmajian, Linda S.

Felmeister, Charles J., ed. see Domer, Larry R. & Bauer, Jeffrey C.

Felmeister, Charles J., ed. see Haver, Jurgen F.

Felmeister, Charles J., ed. see Snyder, Thomas L. & Domer, Larry R.

Felner, Robert D. & Jason, Leonard A., eds. Preventive Psychology: Theory, Research & Practice. 475p. 1983. 19.50 (ISBN 0-08-026340-2). Pergamon.

Fels, et al. Staff Notes to Accompany a Casebook of Economic, Microeconomic Problems & Policies: Practice in Thinking. 4th ed. 112p. 1978. 5.95 o.s.i. (ISBN 0-8299-0479-4). West Pub.

Fels, George. Mastering Pool. LC 77-75726. (Mastering Ser.). (Illus.). 1977. 9.95 o.p. (ISBN 0-8092-7896-0); pap. 8.95 (ISBN 0-8092-7895-2). Contemp Bks.

Fels, Gerhard, jt. ed. see Corden, W. M.

Fels, Rendig, et al. Macroeconomic Problems & Policies. 4th ed. 1979. pap. text ed. 6.95 (ISBN 0-8299-0191-4). West Pub.

--Microeconomic Problems & Policies. 4th ed. 1978. pap. text ed. 6.95 (ISBN 0-8299-0192-2). West Pub.

Felsen, Henry G. Here Is Your Hobby: Car Customizing. (Here Is Your Hobby Ser.). (Illus.). (gr. 5 up). 1965. PLB 5.29 o.p. (ISBN 0-399-60244-5). Putnam Pub Group.

Felsen, Jerry. How to Earn Investment Returns of Fifty Percent to One Hundred Percent A Year: A Guide to Finding the Best Investment Managers, Advisory Services & Trading Systems. (Illus.). 160p. 1982. pap. 20.00 (ISBN 0-916376-08-7). CDS Pub.

Felsen, L. B., jt. auth. see Marcuvitz, Nathan.

Felsenstein, Frank, ed. see Smollett, Tobias.

Felsenthal, Carol, jt. auth. see Giffin, Mary.

Felsenthal, Norman. Orientations to Mass Communication. rev. ed. Applbaum, Ronald & Hart, Roderick, eds. (Modcom, Modules in Speech Communication Ser.). 1980. pap. text ed. 2.75 (ISBN 0-574-22569-2, 13-5569). SRA.

Felson, Benjamin. Chest Roentgenology. LC 73-188387. (Illus.). 1973. text ed. 32.50 (ISBN 0-7216-3591-1). Saunders.

Felson, Benjamin, ed. Roentgenology of the Gallbladder & Biliary Tract. (Seminars in Roentgenology Reprint). (Illus.). 160p. 1976. Repr. 29.50 o.p. (ISBN 0-8089-0999-1). Grune.

Felson, Henry G. Living with Your First Motorcycle. LC 75-29401. (Illus.). 96p. (gr. 6-8). 1976. 7.95 o.p. (ISBN 0-399-20488-1). Putnam Pub Group.

Felt, W. Mark. FBI Pyramid: From the Inside. LC 78-24257. (Illus.). 1980. 12.95 o.p. (ISBN 0-399-11904-3). Putnam Pub Group.

Feltenburg, E. J. Vrysi: A Subterranean Settlement in Cyprus - Excavations of Ayios Epiktitos, 1969-1973. (Illus.). 132p. 1983. pap. text ed. 31.50x (ISBN 0-85668-217-9, Pub. by Aris & Phillips England). Humanities.

Feltner, Charles E. & Feltner, Jeri B. Great Lakes Maritime History: Bibliography & Sources of Information. LC 82-51175. 124p. 1982. 14.95 (ISBN 0-9609014-1-8); pap. 9.95 (ISBN 0-9609014-0-X). Seajay.

Feltner, Helen A., jt. auth. see Smith, Ruth E.

Feltner, Jeri B., jt. auth. see Feltner, Charles E.

Felton, Bruce & Fowler, Mark. Felton & Fowler's Best, Worst & Most Unusual. LC 75-9895. 288p. (YA) 1975. 12.45i (ISBN 0-690-00569-5). T Y Crowell.

Felton, Craig & Jordan, William B., eds. Jusepe de Ribera: Lo Spagnoletto (1591-1652) 246p. 1982. 50.00 (ISBN 0-912804-09-2, Dist by U of Wash Pr); pap. text ed. 24.95 (ISBN 0-912804-10-6). Kimbell Art.

Felton, Elizabeth N., jt. auth. see Short, Max H.

Felton, Harold W. Big Mose: Hero Fireman. LC 69-11774. (American Folktales Ser.). (Illus.). (gr. 2-5). 1969. PLB 6.69 (ISBN 0-8116-4017-5). Garrard.

Felton, Randall G., jt. auth. see Chapin, June R.

Felton, Sidney. Masters of Equitation. (Illus.). 12.50 o.p. (ISBN 0-87556-088-1). Saifer.

Felts, William J. & Harrison, Richard J., eds. International Review of General & Experimental Zoology, 4 vols. 1964-70. Vol. 1. 55.50, by subscription 46.00 (ISBN 0-12-368101-4); Vol. 2. 55.50, by subscription 46.00 (ISBN 0-12-368102-2); Vol. 3. 55.00, by subscription 46.00 (ISBN 0-12-368103-0); Vol. 4. by subscription 46.00 o.p. 55.50 (ISBN 0-12-368104-9). Acad Pr.

Feltskog, E. N., ed. see Cooper, James Fenimore.

Feltskog, E. N., ed. see Parkman, Frances.

Feltskog, E. N., jt. ed. see Pochman, Henry A.

Feltwell, Ray. Small-Scale Poultry Keeping. 176p. 1980. pap. 9.50 (ISBN 0-571-11557-8). Faber & Faber.

Feminist Press. Black Foremothers: Three Lives. (Women's Lives-Women's Work). (Illus.). (gr. 10-12). 1979. pap. text ed. 7.44 (ISBN 0-07-020433-0, W); tchr's. ed. 6.04 (ISBN 0-07-020434-9). McGraw.

--Out of the Bleachers: Writings on Women & Sport. (Women's Lives-Women's Work). (Illus.). (gr. 10-12). 1979. pap. 9.12 (ISBN 0-07-020429-2, W); tchr's guide 6.04 (ISBN 0-07-020430-6). McGraw.

--Women Working: An Anthology of Stories & Poems. (Women's Lives-Women's Work). (Illus.). (gr. 10-12). 1979. pap. text ed. 10.52 (ISBN 0-07-020431-4, W); tchrs' ed. 6.04 (ISBN 0-07-020432-2). McGraw.

Feminist Press, et al. Rights & Wrongs: Women's Struggle for Legal Equality. (Women's Lives-Women's Work). (Illus.). (gr. 10-12). 1979. pap. text ed. 6.52 (ISBN 0-07-020423-3, W); tchrs' ed. 6.04 (ISBN 0-07-020424-1). McGraw.

Fenby, Eric. Delius As I Knew Him. LC 75-25255. (Illus.). 234p. 1976. Repr. of 1948 ed. lib. bdg. 17.25x (ISBN 0-8371-8394-4, FEDE). Greenwood.

Fencl, Shirley & Jager, Susan G. The Two R's: Paragraph to Essay. LC 78-16026. 1979. pap. text ed. 14.50x (ISBN 0-673-15723-7). Scott F.

Fendler, Dolores T., jt. auth. see Becker, Betty G.

Fendler, E. J., jt. ed. see Mittal, K. L.

Fendler, Eleanor J., jt. auth. see Fendler, Janos H.

Fendler, J. Membrane Mimetic Agents: Characterizations & Applications of Micelles, Micro-Emulsions, Monolayers, Bilayers, Vesicles, Host-Guest Systems & Polyions. LC 82-2583. 522p. 1982. 59.95x (ISBN 0-471-07918-9, Pub. by Wiley-Interscience). Wiley.

Fendler, Janos H. & Fendler, Eleanor J. Catalysis in Micellar & Macromolecular Systems. 1975. 76.00 (ISBN 0-12-252850-6). Acad Pr.

Fenelon. Fenelon's Spiritual Letters. Edwards, Gene, ed. 139p. pap. 4.95 (ISBN 0-940232-09-X). Christian Bks.

--Let Go! 1973. pap. 2.50 (ISBN 0-88368-010-6). Whitaker Hse.

Fenelon, Archbishop. The Royal Way of the Cross. Helms, Hal M., ed. 1982. 3.95 (ISBN 0-941478-00-9). Paraclete Pr.

Feng. Joy of Chinese Cooking. 2.95 (ISBN 0-448-01370-3, G&D). Putnam Pub Group.

Feng Meng-Lung. Stories from a Ming Collection: Translations of Chinese Short Stories Published in the 17th Century. Birch, Cyril, tr. LC 77-26340. (UNESCO Collection of Representative Works: Chinese Ser.). (Illus.). 1978. Repr. of 1959 ed. lib. bdg. 19.25x (ISBN 0-313-20067-X, FESM). Greenwood.

Fenhagen, James. Mutual Ministry: New Vitality for the Local Church. 1977. 9.95 (ISBN 0-8164-0332-5). Seabury.

Fenhagen, James C. More Than Wanderers: Spiritual Disciplines for Christian Ministry. LC 77-17974. 1978. 9.95 (ISBN 0-8164-0386-4). Seabury.

Fenhagen, James C. & Hahn, Celia A. Congregations in Change: Study Guide. LC 73-17894. 1974. 1.45 o.p. (ISBN 0-8164-2093-9). Seabury.

Fenichel, Carol, ed. Changing Patterns in Information Retrieval: Proceeding of the Tenth National Information Retrieval Colloquium. LC 66-29616. 1974. pap. 1.00 (ISBN 0-87715-106-7). Am Soc Info Sci.

Fenick, Barbara. Collecting the Beatles. (Rock & Roll Reference Ser.: Vol. 7). 1982. individuals 15.95 (ISBN 0-87650-147-1); institutions 19.95. Pierian.

Fenlon, D. Heresy & Obedience in Tridentine Italy: Cardinal Pole & the Counter-Reformation. LC 72-87177. 336p. 1973. 52.50 (ISBN 0-521-20005-9). Cambridge U Pr.

Fenlon, Iain. Music & Patronage in Sixteenth-Century Mantua 2. LC 79-41377. (Cambridge Studies in Music). 220p. Date not set. price not set (ISBN 0-521-23587-1); pap. price not set (ISBN 0-521-28603-4). Cambridge U Pr.

Fenlon, Iain, ed. Cambridge Music Manuscripts 900-1700. LC 81-17059. 174p. 1982. 54.50 (ISBN 0-521-24452-8). Cambridge U Pr.

Fenn, Dan H., Jr., jt. auth. see Bauer, Raymond A.

Fenn, Elizabeth A. & Wood, Peter H. Natives & Newcomers: The Way We Lived in North Carolina Before 1770. Nathans, Sydney, ed. LC 82-20128. (The Way We Lived in North Carolina Ser.). (Illus.). viii, 98p. 1983. 11.95 (ISBN 0-8078-1549-7); pap. 6.95 (ISBN 0-8078-4101-3). U of NC Pr.

Fenn, H. C. & Tewksbury, M. G. Read Chinese, Vol. 1. 236p. Date not set. includes 4 cassettes 55.00x (ISBN 0-88432-090-1, M300). J Norton Pubs.

--Read Chinese, Vol. 2. 267p. Date not set. includes 3 cassettes 45.00x (ISBN 0-88432-091-X, M310). J Norton Pubs.

Fenn, Henry, et al. Speak Mandarin. Tewksbury, M. Gardner, ed. 238p. 1979. 7 audio cassettes incl. 125.00x (ISBN 0-88432-027-8, M201); 7 audio cassettes incl. J Norton Pubs.

Fenn, Henry C. & Tewksbury, M. Gardner. Speak Mandarin. (Yale Linguistic Ser). 1967. text ed. 20.00x o.p. (ISBN 0-300-00453-2); pap. text ed. 10.95x (ISBN 0-300-00084-7); wkbk. 17.50x (ISBN 0-300-00454-0); 8.95x (ISBN 0-300-00085-5); teacher's manual, text ed. o.p. 10.00x (ISBN 0-300-00455-9). Yale U Pr.

Fenn, Richard K. Liturgies & Trials: The Seculariztion of Religious Language. 1982. cancelled (ISBN 0-312-48873-4). St Martin.

Fenn, Ross S., jt. auth. see Karolevitz, Robert F.

Fennell, Dorothy I., jt. auth. see Raper, Kenneth B.

Fennell, Francis. Writing Now: A College Handbook. 1980. pap. text ed. 9.95 (ISBN 0-574-22050-X, 13-5050); instr's guide avail. (ISBN 0-574-22051-8, 13-5051). SRA.

Fennell, Geraldine C. A Little Bit of War. 1983. 6.95 (ISBN 0-533-05415-X). Vantage.

Fennell, J. L., tr. Correspondence Between Prince A. M. Kurbsky & Tsar Ivan Fourth of Russia, 1564-1579. 1956. 49.50 (ISBN 0-521-05501-6). Cambridge U Pr.

Fennell, J. L., jt. ed. see Foote, I. P.

Fennell, John & Stokes, Antony. Early Russian Literature. LC 72-89799. 1974. 36.00x (ISBN 0-520-02343-9). U of Cal Pr.

Fennell, John, ed. Nineteenth-Century Russian Literature: Studies of Ten Russian Writers. (Library Reprint Ser.). 1976. 33.00x (ISBN 0-520-03203-9). U of Cal Pr.

Fennelly. Handbook of Loss Prevention & Crime Prevention. 1982. text ed. 59.95 (ISBN 0-409-95047-5); 59.95 (ISBN 0-686-34339-5). Butterworth.

Fennelly, Catherine see Weaver, Glenn.

Fennelly, Lawrence J. Museum, Archive, & Library Security. new ed. 866p. 1982. text ed. 55.00 (ISBN 0-409-95058-0). Butterworth.

Fennema, Elizabeth, ed. Mathematics Education Research: Implications for the 80's. LC 81-67144. 182p. 1981. 6.75 (ISBN 0-87353-196-5). NCTM.

Fennema, M. International Networks of Banks & Industry. 1982. lib. bdg. 34.50 (ISBN 90-247-2620-4, Pub. by Martinus Nijhoff Netherlands). Kluwer Boston.

Fenner, Ball. Raising the Veil, or, Scenes in the Courts. LC 77-172580. (Criminology, Law Enforcement, & Social Problems Ser.: No. 168). (Illus.). Date not set. 12.50x (ISBN 0-87585-168-1). Patterson Smith.

Fenner, Carol. Gorilla Gorilla. (gr. 2 up). 1973. 4.95 o.p. (ISBN 0-394-82069-X, BYR); PLB 6.99 (ISBN 0-394-92069-4). Random.

Fenner, Edward T. Rasayana Siddhi: Medicine & Alchemy in the Buddhist Tantras. (Traditional Healing Ser.). 300p. 1983. 39.95 (ISBN 0-932426-28-X). Trado-Medic.

Fenner, Frank & Ratcliffe, F. N. Myxomatosis. 1966. 69.50 (ISBN 0-521-04991-1). Cambridge U Pr.

Fenner, Phyllis, compiled by. Where Speed Is King: Stories of Racing Adventure. LC 78-39618. (Illus.). 192p. (gr. 7 up). 1972. 8.95 (ISBN 0-688-21772-9). Morrow.

Fenner, Phyllis R., compiled by. Consider the Evidence, Stories of Mystery & Suspense. LC 73-792. (Illus.). 192p. (gr. 7 up). 1973. 8.75 (ISBN 0-688-20080-X). Morrow.

--A Dog's Life: Stories of Champions, Hunters, & Faithful Friends. (Illus.). (gr. 7-9). 1978. 9.75 (ISBN 0-688-22156-4); PLB 9.36 (ISBN 0-688-32156-9). Morrow.

--The Endless Dark: Stories of Underground Adventure. LC 77-5494. (Illus.). (gr. 7 up). 1977. 9.95 (ISBN 0-688-22122-X); PLB 9.55 (ISBN 0-688-32122-4). Morrow.

--Gentle Like a Cyclone: Stories of Horses & Their Riders. LC 74-2499. (Illus.). 192p. (gr. 7 up). 1974. 7.25 o.p. (ISBN 0-688-21821-0); PLB 9.55 (ISBN 0-688-31821-5). Morrow.

Fenner, Phyllis R., ed. Keeping Christmas: Stories of the Joyous Season. LC 79-15590. (Illus.). 224p. (gr. 7-9). 1979. 9.75 (ISBN 0-688-22206-4); PLB 9.36 (ISBN 0-688-32206-9). Morrow.

--Wide-Angle Lens: Stories of Time & Space. LC 80-16992. (Illus.). 224p. (gr. 7-9). 1980. 9.36 (ISBN 0-688-22241-2); PLB 9.75 (ISBN 0-688-32241-7). Morrow.

Fenner, Sal. Sea Machines. LC 79-28586. (Machine World Ser.). (Illus.). (gr. 2-4). 1980. PLB 13.85 (ISBN 0-8172-1334-1). Raintree Pubs.

Fennimore, Keith J. Booth Tarkington. (U. S. Authors Ser.: No. 238). 1974. lib. bdg. 10.95 o.p. (ISBN 0-8057-0715-8, Twayne). G K Hall.

Fenno, Richard F., Jr. Congressmen in Committees. (The Study of Congress Ser.). 320p. 1973. 9.95 o.p. (ISBN 0-316-27808-4); pap. text ed. 8.95 (ISBN 0-316-27807-6). Little.

--Home Style: House Members in Their Districts. 1978. pap. text ed. 9.95 (ISBN 0-316-27809-2). Little.

Fenoaltea, Doranne. Si Haulte Architecture: The Design of Sceve's Delie. LC 81-71432. (French Forum Monographs: No. 35). 246p. (Orig.). 1982. pap. 15.00x (ISBN 0-917058-34-8). French Forum.

Fenocketti, Mary. Coping with Pain. 80p. 1982. pap. 1.95 (ISBN 0-89243-166-0). Liguori Pubns.

Fenoglio. Progress in Surgical Pathology, Vol. III. LC 80-80334. 1981. 62.50x (ISBN 0-89352-122-1). Masson Pub.

Fenoglio, Cecilia M. & Wolff, Marianne, eds. Progress in Surgical Pathology, Vol. IV. LC 80-80334. 312p. 1981. 62.50x (ISBN 0-89352-143-4). Masson Pub.

--Progress in Surgical Pathology, Vol. I. LC 80-80334. (Illus.). 296p. 1980. 62.50x (ISBN 0-89352-087-X). Masson Pub.

--Progress in Surgical Pathology, Vol. II. LC 80-80334. (Illus.). 304p. 1980. 62.50x (ISBN 0-89352-090-X). Masson Pub.

Fenoglio, Cecilia M., jt. auth. see King, Donald W.

Fenollosa, Ernest. Chinese Written Character As a Medium for Poetry. Pound, Ezra, ed. 1963. pap. 2.00 o.s.i. (ISBN 0-87286-014-0). City Lights.

Fenollosa, Ernest F. Epochs of Chinese & Japanese Art. 2 Vol. (Illus.). 1921. pap. 6.00 ea.; Vol. 1. (ISBN 0-486-20364-6); Vol. 2. 6.00 (ISBN 0-486-20365-4). Dover.

Fensham, F. Charles. The Books of Ezra & Nehemiah. (The New International Commentary on the Old Testament Ser.). 256p. 1983. 12.95 (ISBN 0-8028-2362-9). Eerdmans.

Fensterheim, H. & Baer, J. Stop Running Scared. 1978. pap. 3.95 (ISBN 0-440-17734-0). Dell.

Fensterheim, Herbert & Baer, Jean. Don't Say Yes When You Want to Say No. 2.50 o.p. (ISBN 0-686-92314-6, 6378). Hazelden.

Fensterheim, Herbert & Glazer, Howard I., eds. Behavioral Psychotherapy: Basic Principles & Case Studies in an Integrative Clinical Model. 220p. 1983. 20.00 (ISBN 0-87630-325-4). Brunner-Mazel.

Fensterheim, Robert J., jt. ed. see Lederer, William H.

Fenstermacher, Gary D. & Goodlad, John I., eds. Individual Differences in the Common Curriculum: National Society for the Study of Education 82nd Yearbook, Pt. 1. LC 82-62381. 350p. 1983. lib. bdg. 18.00x (ISBN 0-226-60135-8). U of Chicago Pr.

Fenstermaker, John J. Charles Dickens, 1940-1975: An Analytical Subject Index to Periodical Criticism of the Novels & Christmas Books. 1979. lib. bdg. 30.00 (ISBN 0-8161-8064-4, Hall Reference). G K Hall.

Fenten, Barbara & Fenten, D. X. Tourism & Hospitality: Careers Unlimited. LC 78-19108. (Illus.). (gr. 7 up). 1978. 06667855x 8.95 (ISBN 0-664-32634-X). Westminster.

Fenten, D. Better Photography for Amateurs. 1975. 10.95 o.p. (ISBN 0-13-075929-5, Spec). P-H.

Fenten, D. X. Better Photography for Amateurs. (Illus.). 96p. 1975. pap. 4.95 o.p. (ISBN 0-8174-0183-0, Amphoto). Watson-Guptill.

--Ms-Architect. LC 77-7498. (Illus.). (gr. 7 up). 1977. 7.95 (ISBN 0-664-32615-3). Westminster.

--Ms.-Attorney. LC 74-4492. (Illus.). (gr. 9 up). 1974. 7.50 (ISBN 0-664-32552-1). Westminster.

--Strange Differences. LC 74-21074. (Illus.). (gr. 6-8). 1975. 5.75 o.p. (ISBN 0-399-20439-3). Putnam Pub Group.

--The Weekend Gardener. 1976. pap. 1.50 o.p. (ISBN 0-451-06953-6, W6953, Sig). NAL.

Fenten, D. X., jt. auth. see Fenten, Barbara.

Fenton, Ann D., jt. auth. see Peterson, Carolyn S.

Fenton, Barb, jt. auth. see Fenton, Don.

Fenton, Carroll L. & Kitchen, Hermine B. Plants We Live On: The Story of Grains & Vegetables. rev. ed. LC 78-89322. (Illus.). (gr. 3-6). 1971. PLB 10.89 (ISBN 0-381-99819-3, A61600, JD-J). Har-Row.

Fenton, Don & Fenton, Barb. Behind the Circus Scene. Schroeder, Howard, ed. LC 80-14521. (Behind the Scenes Ser.). (Illus.). (gr. 4). 1980. PLB 6.95 (ISBN 0-89686-059-0); pap. 3.50 (ISBN 0-89686-064-7). Crestwood Hse.

--Behind the Newspaper Scene. Schroeder, Howard, ed. LC 80-14593. (Behind the Scenes Ser.). (Illus.). (gr. 4). 1980. PLB 6.95 (ISBN 0-89686-058-2); pap. 3.50 (ISBN 0-89686-063-9). Crestwood Hse.

--Behind the Radio Scene. Schroeder, Howard, ed. LC 80-14594. (Behind the Scenes Ser.). (Illus.). (gr. 4). 1980. PLB 6.95 (ISBN 0-89686-061-2); pap. 3.50 (ISBN 0-89686-066-3). Crestwood Hse.

--Behind the Sports Scene. Schroeder, Howard, ed. LC 80-14070. (Behind the Scenes Ser.). (Illus.). (gr. 4). 1980. PLB 6.95 (ISBN 0-89686-060-4); pap. 3.50 (ISBN 0-89686-065-5). Crestwood Hse.

--Behind the Television Scene. Schroeder, Howard, ed. LC 80-14151. (Behind the Scenes Ser.). (Illus.). (gr. 4). 1980. PLB 6.95 (ISBN 0-89686-062-0); pap. 3.50 (ISBN 0-89686-067-1). Crestwood Hse.

Fenton, Edward. Anne of the Thousand Days. (Orig.). (RL 7). 1970. pap. 1.95 (ISBN 0-451-09864-1, J9864, Sig). NAL.

Fenton, G. L., tr. see Jellinek, S.

Fenton, Irene, ed. see Darwin, Gary.

Fenton, J. C. Saint Matthew. LC 77-81620. (Westminster Pelican Commentaries Ser.). 1978. 14.95 (ISBN 0-664-21343-X). Westminster.

Fenton, Joan, ed. Directory of Member Agencies, 1983. rev. ed. 104p. 1983. pap. 11.00 (ISBN 0-87304-200-X). Family Serv.

Fenton, Judith A. & Lifchez, Aaron S. The Fertility Handbook. (Orig.). 1980. 12.95 (ISBN 0-517-53991-8, C N Potter); pap. 5.95 (ISBN 0-517-54125-4, C N Potter Bks). Crown.

Fenton, Judith A., jt. auth. see Hindler, Nelson H.

Fenton, N. Brock. Just Bats. (Illus.). 176p. 1983. 25.00x (ISBN 0-8020-2452-1); pap. 10.00 (ISBN 0-8020-6464-7). U of Toronto Pr.

Fenton, Robert, ed. see Darwin, Gary.

Fenton, Robert S. Chess for You: The Easy Book for Beginners. (Illus.). 80p. 1975. pap. 0.99 (ISBN 0-448-11863-7, G&D). Putnam Pub Group.

Fenton, William N., ed. see Parker, Arthur C.

Fenves, Steven J., et al. STRESS: A Reference Manual. 1965. 27.50x (ISBN 0-262-06007-8). MIT Pr.

--STRESS: User's Manual. 1964. pap. 14.00x (ISBN 0-262-06029-9). MIT Pr.

Fenwick, Benedict J. Memoirs to Serve for the Future Ecclesiastical History of the Diocese of Boston. McCarthy, Joseph M., ed. LC 78-64366. (Monograph: No. 35). (Illus.). 270p. 1979. 10.95 (ISBN 0-686-65388-2). US Cath Hist.

Fenwick, Charles G. Foreign Policy & International Law. LC 68-57015. 142p. 1968. 8.50 (ISBN 0-379-00366-X). Oceana.

Fenwick, Deman C. The Master Handbook of Boat & Marine Repair. (Illus.). 1979. 14.95 o.p. (ISBN 0-8306-9794-2); pap. 9.95 o.p. (ISBN 0-8306-1061-8, 1061). TAB Bks.

Fenwick, Eliza. Visits to the Juvenile Library, Repr. Of 1805 Ed. Bd. with The Adventures of Ulysses. Lamb, Charles. Repr. of 1808 ed. LC 75-32152. (Classics of Children's Literature, 1621-1932: Vol. 18). 1976. PLB 38.00 o.s.i. (ISBN 0-8240-2266-1). Garland Pub.

Fenwick, Hubert. Architect Royal. 1980. 21.00x o.p. (ISBN 0-900093-12-9, Pub. by Roundwood). State Mutual Bk.

Fenwick, Jill. Moon. LC 80-52523. (Starters Ser.). PLB 8.00 (ISBN 0-382-06489-5). Silver.

Fenyo, S. Modern Mathematical Methods in Technology, Vol. 2. LC 69-16400. (Applied Mathematics & Mechanics Ser.: Vol. 17). 326p. 1975. 40.50 (ISBN 0-444-10565-4, North-Holland). Elsevier.

Fenyvesi, Charles. Splendor in Exile: The Ex-Majesties of Europe. LC 79-20707. (Illus.). 1979. 12.95 (ISBN 0-915220-55-5). New Republic.

Fenzi, Jewell. Netherlands Antilles Cookbook. 1972. 7.50 (ISBN 0-911268-23-5). Rogers Bk.

Fer, F. Thermodynamique Macroscopique, 2 Vols. (Fr). 1970. Vol. 1,300. 70.00x (ISBN 0-677-50300-8); Vol. 2,248. 60.00x (ISBN 0-677-50310-5). Gordon.

Feravolo, Rocco V. Electricity. LC 60-6464. (Junior Science Books Ser.). (Illus.). (gr. 2-5). 1960. PLB 6.69 (ISBN 0-8116-6151-2). Garrard.

--Light. LC 61-5489. (Junior Science Ser.). (Illus.). (gr. 2-5). 1961. PLB 6.69 (ISBN 0-8116-6156-3). Garrard.

--Magnets. LC 60-12079. (Junior Science Bks.). (Illus.). (gr. 2-5). 1960. PLB 6.69 (ISBN 0-8116-6155-5). Garrard.

Ferber, Edna. Ice Palace. LC 58-5936. 1958. 6.95 (ISBN 0-385-04799-1). Doubleday.

--One Basket. LC 57-5531. 1957. 3.95 (ISBN 0-686-67637-8). Doubleday.

--A Peculiar Treasure. LC 60-8865. (Illus.). 1971. 5.95 (ISBN 0-385-00563-6). Doubleday.

Ferber, Ellen, jt. ed. see Fulton, Len.

Ferber, Linda S. Tokens of a Friendship: Miniature Watercolors by William T. Richards. Hochfield, Sylvia, ed. (Illus.). 118p. (Orig.). 1982. pap. 14.95 (ISBN 0-87099-319-4). Metro Mus Art.

Ferber, Robert. Handbook of Marketing Research. (Illus.). 1344p. 1974. 67.50 (ISBN 0-07-020462-4, P&RB). McGraw.

Ferber, Robert & Hirsch, Werner Z. Social Experimentation & Economic Policy. LC 81-6146. (Cambridge Surveys of Economic Literature Ser.). (Illus.). 224p. 1981. 37.50 (ISBN 0-521-24185-5); pap. 12.95 (ISBN 0-521-28507-0). Cambridge U Pr.

Ferch, Arthur J. The Son of Man in Daniel Seven. (Andrews University Seminary Doctoral Dissertation Ser.: Vol. 6). x, 237p. 1983. pap. 8.95 (ISBN 0-943872-38-3). Andrews Univ Pr.

Ferdico, John M. Criminal Procedure for the Law Enforcement Officer. 2nd ed. (Criminal Justice Ser.). (Illus.). 1979. text ed. 21.95 (ISBN 0-8299-0188-4). West Pub.

Ferdinand. Typologies of Delinquency. pap. text ed. 3.95 (ISBN 0-685-39879-X). Phila Bk Co.

Ferdinand, Theodore N., jt. auth. see Cavan, Ruth S.

Ferdinand, W. The Enzyme Molecule. LC 76-7530. 1976. 46.95 (ISBN 0-471-01822-8, Pub. by Wiley-Interscience); pap. 23.95 (ISBN 0-471-01821-X). Wiley.

Fere, Maud. Does Diet Cure Cancer. 5.96x o.p. (ISBN 0-7225-0170-6). Cancer Control Soc.

Ferebee, Ann, ed. Education for Urban Design. (Urban Design Selections Ser.). 183p. 1982. pap. 20.00 (ISBN 0-942468-00-7). Inst Urban Des.

Ferencz, B., jt. auth. see Mohilla, R.

Ferencz, Ben. Enforcement of International Law, 2 vols. 1983. lib. bdg. 90.00 set (ISBN 0-379-12147-6); Vol. 1, 500p. lib. bdg. 45.00 (ISBN 0-379-12148-4); Vol. 2, 500p. lib. bdg. 45.00 (ISBN 0-379-12149-2). Oceana.

Ferencz, Benjamin. An International Criminal Court: A Step Toward World Peace, 2 vols. LC 80-10688. 1212p. 1980. Vol. 1. lib. bdg. 75.00 set (ISBN 0-379-20389-8). Oceana.

Ferenczi, Sandor. Theory & Technique of Psychoanalysis. 1952. text ed. 10.95x o.s.i. (ISBN 0-465-08472-9). Basic.

Ferenczy, Alex & Richart, Ralph M. Female Reproductive System: Dynamics of Scanning & Transmission Electron Microscopy. LC 73-17486. 401p. 1974. 74.95 o.p. (ISBN 0-471-25730-3, Pub. by Wiley-Medical). Wiley.

Ferge, Zsusza, tr. from Hungarian. A Society in the Making: Hungarian Social & Societal Policy 1945-75. LC 80-80116. 1980. 27.50 (ISBN 0-87332-155-3). M E Sharpe.

Fergersen, Lorraine, jt. auth. see Matthew, Marie-Louise.

Fergus, Patricia M. Spelling Improvement: A Program for Self-Improvement. 4th ed. 256p. 1983. pap. text ed. 11.95 (ISBN 0-07-020476-4, C); instr's. manual 5.00 (ISBN 0-07-020477-2). McGraw.

Fergus, Robert A. Some Stuff. 1978. 4.50 o.p. (ISBN 0-533-03641-0). Vantage.

Ferguson. Readings on Concepts of Criminal Law. (Criminal Justice Ser.). 1975. pap. text ed. 14.95 o.s.i. (ISBN 0-8299-0619-3). West Pub.

Ferguson & King. Guide to Antique Shops in Britain 1983. (Illus.). 1980. 16.00 o.p. (ISBN 0-902028-87-1). Apollo.

--Guide to Antique Shops in Britain 1983. (Illus.). 1983. 16.00. Apollo.

Ferguson, A. Angular Correlation Methods in Gamma Ray Spectroscopy. 1965. 19.50 (ISBN 0-444-10194-2). Elsevier.

Ferguson, A., ed. Natural Philosophy Through the 18th Century & Allied Topics. 172p. 1972. write for info. (ISBN 0-85066-055-6, Pub. by Taylor & Francis). Intl Pubns Serv.

Ferguson, Adam. An Essay on the History of Civil Society. LC 79-64856. (Social Science Classic Ser.). 327p. 1980. 29.95 (ISBN 0-87855-314-2); pap. text ed. 6.95 (ISBN 0-87855-696-6). Transaction Bks.

Ferguson, Albert. Orthopaedic Surgery in Infancy & Childhood. 5th ed. (Illus.). 960p. 1981. 81.00 (ISBN 0-683-03167-8, 3167-8). Williams & Wilkins.

Ferguson, Alfred R., ed. see Emerson, Ralph W.

Ferguson, Alfred R. see Emerson, Ralph W.

Ferguson, Allen R., ed. see Public Interest Economics Foundation.

Ferguson, Allen R., ed. see Public Interest Economics Foundation, et al.

Ferguson, Barbara J., ed. see Ortho Books Staff.

Ferguson, C., jt. auth. see Snow, Catherine.

Ferguson, C. A., et al, eds. Language in the U. S. A. 650p. 1981. 42.50 (ISBN 0-521-23140-X); pap. 15.95 (ISBN 0-521-29834-2). Cambridge U Pr.

Ferguson, C. E. Neoclassical Theory of Production & Distribution. (Illus.). 1969. 29.95 (ISBN 0-521-07453-3). Cambridge U Pr.

Ferguson, Charles W., et al. El Mundo De Rotary. McCleary, Elliott, ed. Rubiano, Alfonso & Orellana, Ramon, trs. from Eng. (Illus.). 144p. 1975. 7.00 o.p. (ISBN 0-915062-04-6). Rotary Intl.

--Rotary No Mundo. McCleary, Elliott, ed. Cazao, Alayde, tr. from Eng. (Illus.). 144p. 1975. 7.00 o.p. (ISBN 0-915062-03-8). Rotary Intl.

--The World of Rotary. McCleary, Elliott, ed. LC 74-18334. (Illus.). 144p. 1975. 7.00 o.p. (ISBN 0-915062-00-3). Rotary Intl.

Ferguson, Dale V., jt. auth. see Buffaloe, Neal D.

Ferguson, Donald N. Image & Structure in Chamber Music. LC 77-5586. (Music Reprint Ser.). 1977. Repr. of 1964 ed. lib. bdg. 32.50 (ISBN 0-306-77415-1). Da Capo.

Ferguson, E. James. The American Revolution: A General History, 1763-1790. rev. ed. 1979. pap. text ed. 13.50x o.p. (ISBN 0-256-02195-3). Dorsey.

Ferguson, E. James & Catanzariti, John, eds. The Papers of Robert Morris, 1781-1784, Vol. 1: February 7 - July 31, 1781. LC 72-91107. (Robert Morris Papers Ser.). (Illus.). 1973. 22.50x (ISBN 0-8229-3267-9). U of Pittsburgh Pr.

--The Papers of Robert Morris, 1781-1784, Vol. 2: August-September 1781. LC 72-91107. (Robert Morris Papers Ser.). (Illus.). 1975. 22.50x (ISBN 0-8229-3297-0). U of Pittsburgh Pr.

--The Papers of Robert Morris, 1781-1784, Vol. 3: October 1, 1781-January 10, 1782. LC 72-91107. (Robert Morris Papers Ser). (Illus.). 1977. 23.50x (ISBN 0-8229-3324-1). U of Pittsburgh Pr.

--The Papers of Robert Morris, 1781-1784, Vol. 4: January 11-April 15, 1782. LC 72-91107. (Robert Morris Papers Ser). 1978. 25.00x (ISBN 0-8229-3352-7). U of Pittsburgh Pr.

Ferguson, Estelle & Barbaresi, Sara M. How to Raise & Train a Chihuahua. pap. 2.95 (ISBN 0-87666-266-1, DS1008). TFH Pubns.

Ferguson, Eva D. Motivation: An Experimental Approach. LC 82-6559. 470p. 1982. Repr. of 1976 ed. 24.50 (ISBN 0-89874-485-7). Krieger.

Ferguson, George. Signs & Symbols in Christian Art. (Illus.). 1959. 19.95x (ISBN 0-19-501168-6). Oxford U Pr.

Ferguson, George A. Statistical Analysis in Psychology & Education. 5th, rev. ed. (Psychology Ser.). (Illus.). 560p. 1981. text ed. 25.50x (ISBN 0-07-020482-9, C); instructor's manual 10.95 (ISBN 0-07-020483-7). McGraw.

Ferguson, H. L. & Znamensky, V. A., eds. Methods of Computation of the Water Balance of Large Lakes & Reservoirs: Vol. 1, Methodology. (Studies & Reports in Hydrology: No. 31). (Illus.). 120p. 1981. pap. write for info. (ISBN 92-3-101906-6, U385, UNESCO). Unipub.

Ferguson, I. K. & Muller, J., eds. The Evolutionary Significance of the Exine. (Linnean Society Symposia Ser.: No. 1). 1976. 86.50 (ISBN 0-12-253650-9). Acad Pr.

Ferguson, J. G., jt. auth. see Berry, C.

Ferguson, J. M. Advertising & Competition: Theory, Measurement, Fact. LC 74-20592. 208p. 1975. prof ref 17.50 (ISBN 0-88410-253-X). Ballinger Pub.

Ferguson, J. Ray, ed. see Reams, Bernard J., Jr.

Ferguson, James & Taylor, Craig, eds. The Comprehensive Handbook of Behavioral Medicine, 3 vols. Incl. Vol. 1: Systems Intervention. 364p. 1980 (ISBN 0-89335-078-8); Vol. 2: Syndromes & Special Areas. 308p. 1981 (ISBN 0-89335-111-3); Vol. 3: Extended Applications & Issues. (Illus.). 361p. 1980. text ed. 30.00 ea. (ISBN 0-89335-112-1); 80.00 set (ISBN 0-686-86752-1). LC 79-24021. (Illus.). text ed. 30.00 ea.; 75.00 set (ISBN 0-686-86752-1). Spectrum Pub.

Ferguson, James E., et al. Essays on the National Past: 1607 to the Present. (Readings in American History Ser.). 1970. pap. text ed. 6.95x (ISBN 0-394-30494-2). Phila Bk Co.

Ferguson, Jeanne & Miller, Maria B. You're Speaking-Who's Listening? 1980. pap. text ed. 10.95 (ISBN 0-574-22560-9, 13-5560); instr's guide avail. (ISBN 0-574-22561-7, 13-5561). SRA.

Ferguson, Jerry T., ed. see Beaton, William R., et al.

Ferguson, John. Aristotle. (World Authors Ser.). lib. bdg. 12.95 (ISBN 0-8057-2064-2, Twayne). G K Hall.

--Bibliographical Notes on Histories & Inventions & Books of Secrets, 2 vols. in 1. Date not set. 75.00 (ISBN 0-87556-494-1). Saifer.

--Biblioteca Chimica; Catalog of the Alchemical & Pharmaceutical Books in the Library of James Young, 2 vols. 1100p. 150.00 (ISBN 0-87556-493-3). Saifer.

--Callimachus. (World Authors Ser.). 1980. lib. bdg. 15.95 (ISBN 0-8057-6431-3, Twayne). G K Hall.

--Clement of Alexandria. (World Authors Ser.). 1974. lib. bdg. 15.95 (ISBN 0-8057-2231-9, Twayne). G K Hall.

--Death Comes to Perigord. 292p. 1983. pap. 5.95 (ISBN 0-486-24434-2). Dover.

--Disarmament: The Unanswerable Case. 112p. 1982. pap. 8.95 (ISBN 0-434-25707-9, Pub by Heinemann, England). David & Charles.

--Gods Many, Lords Many. 128p. 1982. 39.00x (ISBN 0-7188-2496-2, Pub. by Lutterworth Pr England). State Mutual Bk.

--Greek & Roman Religion: A Source Book. LC 79-23009. (Classical Studies Ser.). 1980. 12.00 o.p. (ISBN 0-8155-5055-3, NP). Noyes.

--An Illustrated Encyclopedia of Mysticism & Mystery Religions. LC 76-55812. (Illus.). 1976. 14.95 o.p. (ISBN 0-8264-0115-5). Continuum.

--The Place of Suffering. 137p. 1972. 11.50 (ISBN 0-227-67803-6). Attic Pr.

--War & Peace in the World's Religions. 1978. 12.95x (ISBN 0-19-520073-X); pap. 5.95 (ISBN 0-19-520074-8, GB 557). Oxford U Pr.

Ferguson, John & McHenry, Dean. The American Federal Government. 14th ed. Munson, Eric M., ed. 592p. 1981. text ed. 18.95 (ISBN 0-07-020527-2); instr's. manual 22.50 (ISBN 0-07-020529-9). McGraw.

Ferguson, John, jt. auth. see Chisolm, Kitty.

Ferguson, John & Nelson, William, eds. The Hymnal of the United Church of Christ. LC 74-12571. 1974. 7.00x (ISBN 0-8298-0300-9). Pilgrim NY.

Ferguson, John H. & McHenry, Dean E. The American System of Government. 14th ed. Munson, Eric M., ed. (Illus.). 688p. 1981. text ed. 24.50 (ISBN 0-07-020528-0). McGraw.

Ferguson, Kathy E. Self, Society, & Womankind: The Dialectic of Liberation. LC 79-6831. (Contributions in Women's Studies: No. 17). xii, 200p. 1980. lib. bdg. 25.00 (ISBN 0-313-22245-2, FSS/). Greenwood.

Ferguson, Larry & Lister, Priscilla, eds. The Outdoor Epicure. new ed. (Illus.). 1979. pap. 2.95 o.s.i. (ISBN 0-913140-40-6). Signpost Bk Pub.

Ferguson, Leland, ed. Historical Archaeology & the Importance of Material Things, No. 2. 1977. pap. 5.00 (ISBN 0-686-36591-7). Am Anthro Assn.

Ferguson, Lucy R., jt. auth. see Young, Harben B.

Ferguson, M. Carr, et al. Federal Income Taxation of Estates & Beneficiaries. 749p. (Orig.). 1970. text ed. 45.00 (ISBN 0-316-27889-0); text ed. 12.50 1979 supplement o.p. (ISBN 0-316-27899-8). Little.

--Federal Income Taxation of Estates & Beneficiaries. 20.00; 1982 supplement avail. (ISBN 0-316-27879-3). Little.

Ferguson, Margaret W. Trials of Desire: Renaissance Defenses of Poetry. LC 82-8525. (Illus.). 280p. 1983. pap. text ed. 22.50x (ISBN 0-300-02787-7). Yale U Pr.

Ferguson, Mary Anne. Images of Women in Literature. 3rd ed. LC 80-82761. (Illus.). 528p. 1981. pap. text ed. 13.95 (ISBN 0-395-29113-5). HM.

Ferguson, Norman B. Neuropsychology Laboratory Manual. rev. ed. 1982. 5.95 (ISBN 0-87735-630-0). Freeman C.

Ferguson, Phil M. Reinforced Concrete Fundamentals. 4th ed. LC 78-21555. 724p. 1979. text ed. 35.95x (ISBN 0-471-01459-1). Wiley.

--Reinforced Concrete Fundamentals: SI Version. 4th ed. LC 80-24409. 694p. 1981. text ed. 36.95 (ISBN 0-471-05897-1). Wiley.

Ferguson, R. Comparative Risks of Electricity Generating Fuel Systems in the UK. 216p. 1981. 66.00 (ISBN 0-906048-66-4). Inst Elect Eng.

Ferguson, R. Fred, jt. auth. see Whisenand, Paul M.

Ferguson, Robert H. Cost-of-Living Adjustments in Union-Management Agreements. LC 76-21445. (ILR Bulletin: No. 65). 76p. 1976. pap. 2.50 (ISBN 0-87546-214-6). ILR Pr.

Ferguson, Robert W. Nature of Vice Control in the Administration of Justice. (Criminal Justice Ser.). 1974. text ed. 18.95 o.s.i. (ISBN 0-8299-0618-5). West Pub.

Ferguson, Robert W. & Stokke, Allan H. Legal Aspects of Evidence. (HBJ Criminal Justice Ser.). 139p. 1979. pap. text ed. 10.95 o.p. (ISBN 0-15-516100-8, HC); instructor's manual avail. o.p. (ISBN 0-15-550490-8). HarBraceJ.

Ferguson, Roger. Experiencing Fullness in Christian Living: Studies in Colossians. 36p. 1982. pap. 3.50 (ISBN 0-939298-08-2). J M Prods.

Ferguson, Rosemary & King, Stella, eds. Guide to the Antique Shops of Britain, 1982. 1116p. 1981. 16.00 o.p. (ISBN 0-902028-87-1). Antique Collect.

--Guide to the Antique Shops of Britain 1983. 1983. 16.00 (ISBN 0-907462-03-0). Antique Collect.

Ferguson, Sara K., jt. ed. see Moore, Julie.

Ferguson, Sheila. Village & Town Life. (History in Focus Ser.). (Illus.). 72p. (gr. 7-12). 1983. 14.95 (ISBN 0-7134-4301-4, Pub. by Batsford England). David & Charles.

Ferguson, Sinclair. Man Overboard. 1982. pap. 3.95 (ISBN 0-8423-4015-7). Tyndale.

Ferguson, Suzanne. Critical Essays on Randall Jarrell. (Critical Essays in American Literature Ser.). 313p. 1983. lib. bdg. 35.00 (ISBN 0-8161-8486-0). G K Hall.

Ferguson, Sybil. The Diet Center Program: Lose Weight Fast & Keep It Off Forever. 424p. 1983. 14.45i (ISBN 0-316-27901-3). Little.

Ferguson, W. Keene. History of the Bureau of Economic Geology, Nineteen Nine to Nineteen Sixty. (Illus.). 329p. 1981. 11.00 (ISBN 0-686-36604-2); pap. 6.00 (ISBN 0-686-37333-2). Bur Econ Geology.

Ferguson, Wallace K. & Bruun, Geoffrey. A Survey of European Civilization. 4th ed. Incl. Pt. 1. To 1660. text ed. 21.95 (ISBN 0-395-04427-8); Complete. 1969. 23.50 (ISBN 0-395-04425-1); instr's manual o.p. 4.00 (ISBN 0-395-04432-4). HM.

Ferguson, William S. Greek Imperialism. LC 63-18045. 1941. 10.00x (ISBN 0-8196-0127-6). Biblo.

Ferguson, Y. H., jt. auth. see Mansbach, R. W.

Fergusson, Erna. Mexican Cookbook. LC 46-214. (Illus.). 120p. 1982. Repr. of 1967 ed. pap. 4.95 (ISBN 0-8263-0035-9). U of NM Pr.

Fergusson, Harvey. The Blood of the Conquerors. 1978. lib. bdg. 9.95 (ISBN 0-8398-2470-X, Gregg). G K Hall.

--In Those Days: An Impression of Change. 1978. lib. bdg. 9.95 (ISBN 0-8398-2472-6, Gregg). G K Hall.

--Wolf Song. 1978. lib. bdg. 9.95 (ISBN 0-8398-2471-8, Gregg). G K Hall.

Fergusson, Harvey, Jr., tr. see Silone, Ignazio.

Fergusson, I. L., et al. Records & Curiosities in Obstetrics & Gynecology. 1982. pap. text ed. 19.95x o.p. (ISBN 0-02-857650-0, Bailliere-Tindall). Saunders.

Fergusson, J. E. Inorganic Chemistry & the Earth: Chemical Resources, Their Extraction, Use & Environmental Impact. LC 82-15096. (Pergamon Series on Environmental Science: Vol. 6). (Illus.). 409p. 1982. 40.00 (ISBN 0-08-023995-1); pap. 19.95 (ISBN 0-08-023994-3). Pergamon.

Fergusson, James. Balloon Tytler. (Illus.). 160p. 1973. 12.00 o.p. (ISBN 0-571-09986-6). Transatlantic.

--An Historical & Illustrated Vision of German Architecture. (Illus.). 127p. 1983. Repr. of 1885 ed. 89.75 (ISBN 0-89901-105-5). Found Class Reprints.

--The Man Behind Macbeth. (Illus.). 192p. 1969. 6.95 o.p. (ISBN 0-571-08909-7). Faber & Faber.

Ferholt, Deborah L. Clinical Assessment of Children: A Comprehensive Approach to Primary Pediatric Care. (Illus.). 331p. 1980. text ed. 19.50 o.p. (ISBN 0-397-54329-8, Lippincott Medical). Lippincott.

Ferlatte, William J. A Flora of the Trinity Alps. LC 72-635566. (Illus.). 1974. 23.75x (ISBN 0-520-02089-8). U of Cal Pr.

Ferlazzo, Paul J. Emily Dickinson. (United States Authors Ser.). 1976. lib. bdg. 12.50 (ISBN 0-8057-7180-8, Twayne). G K Hall.

Ferlin, Guy R. Techniques du Reboisement dans les Zones Subdesertiques d'Afrique. 48p. 1981. pap. 3.50 o.p. (ISBN 0-88936-295-5, IDRC-169F, IDRC). Unipub.

Ferling, John E. The Loyalist Mind: Joseph Galloway & the American Revolution. LC 77-22369. 1977. 16.50x (ISBN 0-271-00514-9). Pa St U Pr.

--A Wilderness of Miseries: War & Warriors in Early America. LC 79-8951. (Contributions in Military History: No. 22). (Illus.). xiv, 227p. 1980. lib. bdg. 27.50 (ISBN 0-313-22093-X, FWW/). Greenwood.

Ferlinghetti, Lawrence. Endless Life: The Selected Poems. LC 80-29127. 224p. 1981. 14.95 (ISBN 0-8112-0796-X); pap. 4.95 (ISBN 0-8112-0797-8, NDP516). New Directions.

--Northwest Ecolog. LC 78-2627. 1978. pap. 2.00 o.p. (ISBN 0-87286-102-3). City Lights.

--Secret Meaning of Things. LC 69-17826. 1969. 3.95 (ISBN 0-8112-0275-5); pap. 1.00 (ISBN 0-8112-0045-0, NDP268). New Directions.

--Who Are We Now? LC 76-1061. 1976. 4.95 (ISBN 0-8112-0628-9). New Directions.

Ferlinghetti, Lawrence, jt. ed. see Lettau, Reinhard.

Ferlita, Ernest & May, John R. Film Odyssey: The Art of Film As Search for Meaning. pap. 4.95 o.p. (ISBN 0-8091-1931-5). Paulist Pr.

--Parables of Lina Wertmuller. pap. 3.95 o.p. (ISBN 0-8091-2048-8). Paulist Pr.

Ferm, Dean W. Alternative Lifestyles Confront the Church. 144p. 1983. pap. 8.95 (ISBN 0-8164-2394-6). Seabury.

Ferm, Deane W. Contemporary American Theologies II: A Book of Readings. 214p. (Orig.). 1982. pap. 15.95 (ISBN 0-8164-2407-1). Seabury.

Ferm, Vergilius. Cross-Currents in the Personality of Martin Luther. LC 71-189362. 192p. 1972. 6.50 o.p. (ISBN 0-8158-0277-3). Chris Mass.

Ferm, Vergilius, ed. Encyclopedia of Religion. LC 62-18535. 1962. 19.95 (ISBN 0-8022-0490-2). Philos Lib.

--History of Philosophical Systems. (Quality Paperback: No. 130). 1968. pap. 3.45 o.p. (ISBN 0-8226-0130-3). Littlefield.

Fermadig, Mac. Your Michigan Outdoors: An Educational Coloring Book. 1982. pap. 2.00 (ISBN 0-933112-09-2). Mich United Conserv.

Ferman, Edward L., ed. Best from Fantasy & Science Fiction: A Special Twenty-Fifth Anniversary Anthology. LC 73-9024. 336p. 1974. 10.95 (ISBN 0-385-08221-5). Doubleday.

--The Best from Fantasy & Science Fiction. 24th ed. 2.95 (ISBN 0-441-05485-4, Pub. by Ace Science Fiction). Ace Bks.

--The Best from Fantasy & Science Fiction: Twenty-Third Series. LC 79-7685. (Science Fiction Ser.). 1980. 10.95 o.p. (ISBN 0-385-15225-6). Doubleday.

Ferman, G. S. & Levin, J. Social Science Research: A Handbook for Students. rev. ed. LC 73-22223. 138p. 1977. pap. text ed. 5.95x o.p. (ISBN 0-470-99291-3). Halsted Pr.

Ferman, Louis A. Evaluating the War on Poverty. Lambert, Richard D., ed. LC 73-92365. (The Annals of the American Academy of Political & Social Science: No. 385). 1969. 15.00 (ISBN 0-87761-120-3); pap. 7.95 (ISBN 0-87761-119-X). Am Acad Pol Soc Sci.

Fernadez, Rafael. A Scene of Light & Glory: Approaches to Venice. (Illus.). 48p. 1982. pap. 4.00 (ISBN 0-686-37429-0). S & F Clark.

Fernald, Grace M. Remedial Techniques in Basic School Subjects. 1943. text ed. 27.50 o.p. (ISBN 0-07-020540-X, C). McGraw.

Fernald, James. English Grammar Simplified. Gale, Cedric, rev. by. 320p. (Orig.). 1979. pap. 3.95 (ISBN 0-06-463484-1, EH 484, EH). B&N NY.

Fernald, James C. Funk & Wagnall's Standard Handbook of Synonyms, Antonyms & Prepositions. rev. ed. LC 47-11924. (Funk & W Bk.). (gr. 9-12). 1947. 13.41i (ISBN 0-308-40024-0, 420140). T y Crowell.

Fernald, L. Dodge & Fernald, Peter S. Introduction to Psychology. 4th ed. LC 77-78911. (Illus.). 1978. text ed. 23.95 (ISBN 0-395-25815-4); instr's. manual 4.00 (ISBN 0-395-25816-2); student guidebk. 9.50 (ISBN 0-395-25817-0); test item manual 2.40 (ISBN 0-395-25818-9); write for info. suppl. test manual (ISBN 0-395-28656-5). HM.

Fernald, Mabel R., et al. Study of Women Delinquents in New York State. LC 68-55770. (Criminology, Law Enforcement, & Social Problems Ser.: No. 23). 1968. Repr. of 1920 ed. 20.00x (ISBN 0-87585-023-5). Patterson Smith.

Fernald, Peter S., jt. auth. see Fernald, L. Dodge.

Fernandes, Florestan. Reflections on the Brazilian Counterrevolution. Dean, Warren, pref. by. Vale, Michel & Hughes, Patrick M., trs. from Portuguese. LC 80-5456. 200p. 1981. 27.50 (ISBN 0-87332-177-4). M E Sharpe.

Fernandes, Judi N. & Ashley, Ruth. CP-M Eighty-Six for the IBM Personal Computer. (A Self-Teaching & Wiley IBM PC Ser.). 331p. 1983. pap. text ed. 14.95 (ISBN 0-471-89719-1). Wiley.

Fernandez, Alejandro M. International Law in Philippine Relations: 1898-1946. 1971. 7.00x (ISBN 0-8248-0439-2). UH Pr.

Fernandez, D. S. Los Falsos Testigos De Jehova. 46p. 1981. pap. 1.25 (ISBN 0-311-06351-9). Casa Bautista.

Fernandez, Domingo. Por Que Guardamos el Domingo? 87p. 1981. pap. 2.00 (ISBN 0-311-05603-2). Casa Bautista.

Fernandez, Domingo S. Una Interpretacion Del Apocalipsis. 234p. (Span.). 1981. pap. 3.50 (ISBN 0-311-04312-7). Casa Bautista.

Fernandez, Doreen G. The Iloilo Zarzuela: Nineteen Hundred & Three to Nineteen Thirty. (Illus.). 1979. 22.25x (ISBN 0-686-24651-9, Pub. by Ateneo Univ Pr); pap. 16.75x. Cellar.

Fernandez, Eduardo B., et al. Database Security & Integrity. LC 80-15153. (IBM Systems Programming Ser.). (Illus.). 288p. 1981. text ed. 22.95 (ISBN 0-201-14467-0). A-W.

Fernandez, Gaston J., jt. auth. see Zayas-Bazan, Eduardo.

Fernandez, J., jt. auth. see Fitzgibbons, R.

Fernandez, Jack E. Organic Chemistry: An Introduction. (Illus.). 528p. 1982. text ed. 25.95 (ISBN 0-13-640417-0); solutions manual 6.95 (ISBN 0-13-640425-1). P-H.

Fernandez, John P. Black Managers in White Corporations. LC 75-6820. 308p. 1975. 31.50 o.p. (ISBN 0-471-25764-8, Pub. by Wiley-Interscience). Wiley.

Fernandez, Judi, jt. auth. see Ashley, Ruth.

Fernandez, Judi N. Using CPM. Ashley, Ruth, ed. LC 80-36673. (Self-Teaching Guides Ser.). 243p. 1980. pap. text ed. 12.95 (ISBN 0-471-08011-X). Wiley.

Fernandez, Judi N., jt. auth. see Ashley, Ruth.

Fernandez, Judi N., et al. Assembly Language Programming 6502. (Wiley Self-Teaching Guides Ser.). 256p. 1968. pap. 12.95 (ISBN 0-471-86120-0). Wiley.

Fernandez, Laura B., jt. auth. see Sallese, Nicholas F.

Fernandez, Ronald. The Future As a Social Problem: A Reader. LC 76-8150. (Illus.). 1977. pap. text ed. 12.95 o.p. (ISBN 0-673-16306-7). Scott F.

Fernandez, Sergio, tr. see Ziglar, Zig.

Fernandez-Armesto, Felip. Sadat & His Statecraft. 1983. 15.95 (ISBN 0-686-38874-7, Pub. by Salem Hse Ltd). Merrimack Bk Serv.

Fernandez-Armesto, Felipe. The Canary Islands after the Conquest: The Making of a Colonial Society in the Early Sixteenth Century. (Historical Monographs). (Illus.). 258p. 1982. 44.00x (ISBN 0-19-821888-5). Oxford U Pr.

Fernandez-Caballero, Carlos & Fernandez-Caballero, Marianne, eds. Emergency Medical Services Systems: A Guide to Information Sources. (Health Affairs Information Guide Series, Gale Information Guide Library: Vol. 9). 250p. 1981. 42.00x (ISBN 0-8103-1503-3). Gale.

Fernandez-Caballero, Marianne, jt. ed. see Fernandez-Caballero, Carlos.

Fernandez-Santamaria, J. A. The State, War & Peace. LC 76-27903. (Studies in Early Modern History). 1977. 49.50 (ISBN 0-521-21438-6). Cambridge U Pr.

Fernando, Enrique M. The Bill of Rights. 338p. 1970. lib. bdg. 15.00 (ISBN 0-379-00087-3). Oceana.

--The Constitution of the Philippines. 739p. 1974. 32.50 (ISBN 0-379-00295-7). Oceana.

Fernando, Quintas & Ryan, Michael D. Calculations in Analytical Chemistry. 256p. (Orig.). 1982. pap. text ed. 10.95 (ISBN 0-15-505710-3). HarBraceJ.

Fernando, Tissa. Sri Lanka: An Island Republic. 128p. 1983. lib. bdg. 16.50x (ISBN 0-89158-926-0). Westview.

Fernando, Tissa & Kearney, Robert N., eds. Modern Sri Lanka: A Society in Transition. LC 79-13077. (Foreign & Comparative Studies: South Asian Ser.: No. 4). (Illus.). 297p. 1979. pap. text ed. 8.00x (ISBN 0-915984-80-6). Syracuse U Foreign Comp.

Fernbach, David, tr. see Lukacs, Georg.

Fernea, Elizabeth W. Guests of the Sheik: An Ethnology of an Iraqi Village. LC 65-13098. 1969. pap. 5.50 (ISBN 0-385-01485-6, A693, Anch). Doubleday.

Ferner, Helmut & Staubesand, Jochen, eds. Sobotta's Atlas of Human Anatomy, 2 vols. 10th ed. Incl. Vol. 1. Head, Neck, Upper Extremities (ISBN 0-8067-1710-6); Vol. 2. Thorax, Abdomen, Pelvis, Lower Extremities, Skin. 1983 (ISBN 0-8067-1720-3). (Illus.). Date not set. text ed. 42.50 ea. Urban & S.

Ferner, Helmut, ed. see Pernkopf, Eduard.

Ferner, Jack D. Successful Time Management. LC 79-13680. (Self-Teaching Guide Ser.). 296p. 1980. pap. text ed. 9.95 (ISBN 0-471-03911-X); leaders' guide 5.00 (ISBN 0-471-07773-9). Wiley.

Ferneti, Casper & Lent, James. Shaving Your Face. (Project MORE Daily Living Skills Ser.). 68p. (Orig.). 1978. pap. text ed. 9.50 (ISBN 0-8331-1236-8). Hubbard Sci.

Ferneti, Casper, jt. auth. see Ingenthron, Donita.

Ferneti, Casper, jt. auth. see Lewis, Patricia.

Ferneti, Casper, jt. auth. see Stevens, Crystal.

Fernholz, H. & Krause, E., eds. Three-Dimensional Turbulaent Boundry Layers, Berlin FRG 1982: Proceedings. (International Union of Theoretical & Applied Mechanics Ser.). (Illus.). 389p. 1982. 39.00 (ISBN 0-387-11772-5). Springer-Verlag.

Fernie, William T. The Occult & Curative Powers of Precious Stones. LC 80-8894. (The Harper Library of Spiritual Wisdom Ser.). 496p. 1981. pap. 8.95 (ISBN 0-06-062360-8, CN4009, HarpR). Har-Row.

Ferns, H. S. The Disease of Government. LC 78-17637. 1978. 14.95 (ISBN 0-312-21256-9). St Martin.

Ferns, John. A. J. M. Smith. (World Authors Ser.). 1979. lib. bdg. 15.95 (ISBN 0-8057-6377-5, Twayne). G K Hall.

Ferntheil, Carol, ed. Baby Jesus ABC Storybook. (Happy Day Bk.). (Illus.). 24p. (gr. k-3). 1979. 1.29 (ISBN 0-87239-354-2, 3624). Standard Pub.

--Garden of Cheer. (Illus.). 16p. (Orig.). 1979. pap. 0.85 (ISBN 0-87239-343-7, 7946). Standard Pub.

--Psalms of Cheer. (Illus.). 16p. (Orig.). 1979. pap. 0.85 (ISBN 0-87239-342-9, 7945). Standard Pub.

--Songs of Cheer. (Illus.). 16p. (Orig.). 1979. pap. 0.85 (ISBN 0-87239-345-3, 7948). Standard Pub.

--Words of Cheer. (Illus.). 16p. (Orig.). 1979. pap. 0.85 (ISBN 0-87239-344-5, 7947). Standard Pub.

Ferracuti, Franco & Wolfgang, Marvin E. Criminological Diagnosis: An International Perspective, 2 vols. LC 77-2686. 1983. Vol. 1. 320p 31.95x (ISBN 0-669-01624-1); Vol. 2. 336p 33.95x (ISBN 0-669-05971-4); 60.00x set (ISBN 0-669-06434-3). Lexington Bks.

Ferrair, Antoine & Thoret, Jacques. Atiekwa: Un Village de Cote d'Ivoire. (Black Africa Ser.). 99p. (Fr.). 1974. Repr. of 1970 ed. lib. bdg. 35.00 o.p. (ISBN 0-8287-1331-6, 71-2021). Clearwater Pub.

Ferrar, Terry A., et al. Electric Energy Policy Issues. LC 77-93384. 1979. 27.00 o.p. (ISBN 0-250-40237-8). Ann Arbor Science.

Ferrar, W. L. A Textbook of Convergence. (Illus.). 200p. 1980. Repr. of 1938 ed. 15.95x (ISBN 0-19-853176-1). Oxford U Pr.

Ferrar, William L. Advanced Mathematics for Science: A Sequel to Mathematics for Science. 1969. 10.25x o.p. (ISBN 0-19-853143-5); pap. 5.00x o.p. (ISBN 0-19-853144-3). Oxford U Pr.

Ferrara, Peter. East vs West in the Middle East. (Impact Ser.). 96p. (gr. 7 up). 1983. PLB 8.90 (ISBN 0-531-04543-9). Watts.

Ferrara, S. & Taylor, J. G., eds. Supergravity Nineteen Eighty One. LC 82-1204. 512p. 1982. 44.50 (ISBN 0-521-24738-1). Cambridge U Pr.

Ferrara, William L. The Lease Purchase Decision: How Some Companies Make It. 49p. pap. 4.95 (ISBN 0-86641-038-4, 7899). Natl Assn Accts.

Ferrara, William L. & Thies, James B. The Lease-Purchase Decision. 126p. pap. 12.95 (ISBN 0-86641-011-2, 80117). Natl Assn Accts.

Ferrari, D., ed. The Performance of Computer Installations. 1979. 64.00 (ISBN 0-444-85186-0, North Holland). Elsevier.

Ferrari, D. & Spadoni, H., eds. Experimental Computer Performance Evaluation. 1981. 47.00 (ISBN 0-444-86129-7). Elsevier.

Ferrari, Domenico. Computer Systems Performance Evaluation. LC 77-15096. (Illus.). 1978. ref. ed. 34.95x (ISBN 0-13-165126-9). P-H.

Ferrari, Domenico & Serazzi, Guiseppe. Measurement & Tuning of Computer Systems. (Illus.). 624p. 1983. text ed. 35.00 (ISBN 0-13-568519-2). P-H.

Ferrari, Guy. How to Profit from Future Technology: A Guide to Success in the Eighties & Beyond. Adams, Mary, ed. LC 82-73571. 300p. 1983. pap. 14.95 (ISBN 0-686-37897-0). Windsor Hse.

Ferrari, R. Repertorio dei Sinonimi della Lingua Italiana. 463p. (Ital.). 1980. Leatherette 5.95 (ISBN 0-686-97415-3, M-9181). French & Eur.

Ferrari, R. L. & Jonscher, A. K., eds. Problems in Physical Electronics. 1973. 26.50x (ISBN 0-85086-038-5, Pub. by Pion England). Methuen Inc.

Ferrari, T. J. Elements of System-Dynamic Simulation: A Textbook with Exercises. LC 78-10505. 188p. 1978. pap. text ed. 22.95x o.p. (ISBN 0-470-26548-5). Halsted Pr.

--Elements of System-Dynamics Simulation. 93p. 1978. pap. 19.95 (ISBN 0-686-93160-2, PDC143, Pudoc). Unipub.

Ferrario, C. M., jt. auth. see Buckley, J. P.

Ferrario, Carlos, jt. ed. see Buckley, Joseph P.

Ferraro, Douglas P., jt. auth. see Logan, Frank A.

Ferraro, J. R., jt. auth. see Rao, C. N.

Ferraro, Rose M. Giudizi Critici E Criteri Estetici Nei "Poetices Libri Septem" (1561) Di Giulio Cesare Scaligero: Rispetto alla Teoria Letteraria del Rinascimento. (Studies in Comparative Literature Ser.: No. 52). vii, 202p. 1971. 13.50x (ISBN 0-8078-7052-8). U of NC Pr.

Ferrars, E. X. Death of a Minor Character. LC 82-23479. (Crime Club Ser.). 192p. 1983. 11.95 (ISBN 0-385-18839-0). Doubleday.

--Witness Before the Fact. (General Ser.). 1980. lib. bdg. 11.95 (ISBN 0-8161-3126-0, Large Print Bks). G K Hall.

Ferrater Mora, Jose. Unamuno: A Philosophy of Tragedy. Silver, Philip, tr. from Span. LC 81-20162. Orig. Title: Unamuno: Bosquejo De una Filosofia. xx, 136p. 1982. Repr. of 1962 ed. lib. bdg. 20.75x (ISBN 0-313-23341-1, FMUN). Greenwood.

Ferrato, Philip. The Porter Family. (Illus.). 23p. 1980. catalogue 1.00. Parrish Art.

Ferre, Frederick. Language, Logic, & God. LC 77-9060. 1977. Repr. of 1961 ed. lib. bdg. 20.25x (ISBN 0-8371-9716-3, FELL). Greenwood.

Ferre, John P. Merrill Guide to the Research Paper. 1983. pap. text ed. 7.95 (ISBN 0-675-20029-6). Additional supplements may be obtained from publisher. Merrill.

Ferre, Rosario. Medio Pollito. (Illus.). 54p. (gr. 6). 1977. pap. 4.00 o.p. (ISBN 0-940238-04-7). Ediciones Huracan.

Ferreira, Linda. Notion by Notion. 96p. (Orig.). 1981. pap. text ed. 6.95 (ISBN 0-88377-199-3). Newbury Hse.

--Verbs in Action. LC 77-10886. 1978. pap. text ed. 7.95 (ISBN 0-88377-097-0). Newbury Hse.

Ferreira, Linda A. & Vai, Marjorie. Read on, Speak Out. LC 79-314. 1979. pap. text ed. 8.95 (ISBN 0-88377-133-0). Newbury Hse.

Ferreira, Ruth V., tr. see Eskelin, Neil.

Ferreiro, Emilia & Teberosky, Ana. Literacy Before Schooling. Castro, Karen G., tr. from Span. 324p. text ed. 16.00x (ISBN 0-686-97784-X). Heinemann Ed.

Ferrel, O. C. & Pride, William. Fundamentals of Marketing. LC 81-82558. 1981. 22.95 (ISBN 0-395-31696-0); instr's manual 2.50 (ISBN 0-395-31697-9); study guide 8.50 (ISBN 0-395-31698-7); test bank manual 3.50 (ISBN 0-395-31699-5); color transparencies 95.00 set (ISBN 0-395-32025-9). HM.

Ferrell, jt. auth. see Pride.

Ferrell, D. T., Sr., ed. Memorial Edition of the Poems of the Late George Washington Ferrell. 1978. 6.50 o.p. (ISBN 0-533-03170-2). Vantage.

Ferrell, Keith. H. G. Wells: First Citizen of the Future. 192p. 1983. text ed. 9.95 (ISBN 0-87131-403-7). M Evans.

Ferrell, O. C., jt. auth. see Luck, David J.

Ferrell, O. C., jt. auth. see Pride, William M.

Ferrell, Robert H. Harry S. Truman & the Modern American Presidency. 1983. 13.00i (ISBN 0-316-27480-1). Little.

Ferrell, Robert H., ed. The Diary of James C. Hagerty: Eisenhower in Mid-Course, 1954-1955. LC 82-48477. (Illus.). 256p. 1983. 17.50x (ISBN 0-253-11625-2). Ind U Pr.

Ferrell, Robert H., ed. see Truman, Harry S.

Ferrell, William R., jt. auth. see Sheridan, Thomas B.

Ferren, William P., jt. auth. see Jensen, J. T.

Ferrer, Claire R., ed. see American Ethnological Society.

Ferrer, Edward B. Operation Puma: The Air Battle of the Bay of Pigs. (Illus.). 242p. 1982. pap. 11.50 (ISBN 0-9609000-0-4). Intl Av Consult.

Ferrer, Esteban A., jt. ed. see Holland, Susan S.

Ferrer, M. Irene, ed. Current Cardiology, Vol. 1. (Current Ser.). 363p. 1979. 50.00 (ISBN 0-471-09478-1, Pub. by Wiley Med). Wiley.

Ferrero, Guglielmo. The Nastiest Imperial Women in Ancient Rome. (Illus.). 1979. Repr. of 1903 ed. 47.50 o.p. (ISBN 0-89266-210-7). Am Classical Coll Pr.

--The Nastiest Women in Ancient Rome. (Illus.). 1979. deluxe ed. 47.85 o.p. (ISBN 0-930582-48-9). Gloucester Art.

Ferrers Howell, A. G. see Dante Alighieri.

Ferres, John H. Arthur Miller: A Reference Guide. 1979. lib. bdg. 29.00 (ISBN 0-8161-7822-4, Hall Reference). G K Hall.

Ferretti, Fred. The Year the Big Apple Went Bust. LC 75-44452. 1976. 10.00 o.p. (ISBN 0-399-11643-5). Putnam Pub Group.

Ferretti, Paolo A. Estetica Gregoriana. LC 77-5498. (Music Reprint Ser.). 1977. Repr. of 1934 ed. lib. bdg. 39.50 (ISBN 0-306-77414-3). Da Capo.

Ferretti, Val S. & Scott, David L. Death in Literature. (Patterns in Literary Art Ser). (gr. 10-12). 1977. pap. text ed. 9.16 (ISBN 0-07-020633-3, W). McGraw.

Ferri, Robert & Silverberg, Barry. The Tax Organizer. (McGraw-Hill Paperbacks Ser.). 1977. pap. 2.95 o.p. (ISBN 0-07-020639-2, SP). McGraw.

Ferrier, Ronald W. The History of the British Petroleum Company: The Developing Years 1901-1932, Vol. 1. LC 81-18019. 696p. 1982. 64.50 (ISBN 0-521-24647-4). Cambridge U Pr.

Ferrigno, Lou & Hall, Douglas K. The Incredible Lou Ferrigno. 1981. 14.50 (ISBN 0-671-42863-2). S&S.

Ferrigno, Lou, jt. auth. see Reynolds, Bill.

Ferrigno, Peter, jt. auth. see Besner, Edward.

Ferril, Thomas H. Anvil of Roses. Burmaster, Orvis C., ed. LC 82-73829. (Ahsahta Press Modern & Contemporary Poetry of the West Ser.). 50p. (Orig.). 1983. pap. 3.00 (ISBN 0-916272-20-6). Ahsahta Pr.

Ferris, Byron, jt. auth. see Nelson, Roy P.

Ferris, Elizabeth G. & Lincoln, Jennie I., eds. Latin American Foreign Policies: Global & Regional Dimensions. (Special Studies on Latin America Ser.). 350p. 1981. lib. bdg. 26.50 (ISBN 0-86531-208-7); pap. text ed. 10.95 (ISBN 0-86531-284-2). Westview.

Ferris, Elvira & Fong, Elizabeth. Microbiology for Health Careers. 2nd ed. LC 81-66764. (Allied Health Ser.). (Illus.). 192p. 1982. pap. text ed. 10.00 (ISBN 0-8273-1901-0); instr's guide 2.75 (ISBN 0-8273-1902-9). Delmar.

Ferris, Elvira & Skelley, Esther G. Body Structures & Functions. LC 77-83347. 160p. 1979. pap. 10.80 (ISBN 0-8273-1322-5); instructor's guide 2.75 (ISBN 0-8273-1323-3); slide packet 39.50 (ISBN 0-8273-1821-9). Delmar.

Ferris, George. Fly Fishing in New Zealand. (Illus.). 116p. 1976. 6.95 (ISBN 0-686-42803-X, Pub. by Heinemann Pubs New Zealand). Intl Schol Bk Serv.

--Flycasting: Techniques for the Flyfisherman. (Illus.). 56p. 1977. pap. 3.95 (ISBN 0-686-42805-6, Pub. by Heinemann Pubs New Zealand). Intl Schol Bk Serv.

Ferris, George D. Glory & Beauty in the Land of the Pilgrims. (Illus.). 109p. 1983. Repr. of 1899 ed. 79.15 (ISBN 0-89901-106-3). Found Class Reprints.

Ferris, Harry B. Indians of Cuzco & the Apurimac. LC 18-6196. 1916. pap. 16.00 (ISBN 0-527-00513-4). Kraus Repr.

Ferris, James J. Inflation: The Ultimate Craven Image. 192p. (Orig.). 1982. pap. 4.95 (ISBN 0-89221-087-7). New Leaf.

Ferris, Norman B. Desperate Diplomacy: William H. Seward's Foreign Policy, 1861. LC 75-5509. 1976. 16.50x (ISBN 0-87049-170-9). U of Tenn Pr.

--The Trent Affair: A Diplomatic Crisis. LC 76-28304. 1977. 17.95x (ISBN 0-87049-169-5). U of Tenn Pr.

Ferris, Paul. High Places. 1977. 7.95 o.p. (ISBN 0-698-10799-3, Coward). Putnam Pub Group.

--Richard Burton: An Arm's Length Biography. 1981. 13.95 (ISBN 0-698-11106-0, Coward). Putnam Pub Group.
--Talk to Me About England. LC 78-26797. 1979. 8.95 o.p. (ISBN 0-698-10969-4, Coward). Putnam Pub Group.
Ferris, Robert G. & Morris, Richard E. The Signers of the Declaration of Independence. LC 82-82219. (Illus.). 180p. 1982. 19.95 (ISBN 0-936478-06-3); pap. 4.95 (ISBN 0-936478-07-1). Interpretive Pubns.
Ferris, Roxana S. Native Shrubs of the San Francisco Bay Region. (California Natural History Guides Ser.: No. 24). (Illus.). 1968. 14.95x o.p. (ISBN 0-520-03090-7); pap. 2.85 (ISBN 0-520-00405-1). U of Cal Pr.
Ferris, Roxana S. see Abrams, LeRoy.
Ferris, Theodoe N., et al, eds. see Educational Research Council of America.
Ferris, Theodore, ed. see Educational Research Council of America.
Ferris, Theodore H., et al, eds. see Educational Research Council of America.
Ferris, Theodore N. Spectrum. 64p. 4.00 o.p. (ISBN 0-682-49638-3). Exposition.
Ferris, Theodore N., ed. see Educational Research Council of America.
Ferris, Theodore N., et al, eds. see Educational Research Council of America.
Ferris, Theodore N, et al, eds. see Educational Research Council of America.
Ferris, Theodore N., et al, eds. see Educational Research Council of America.
Ferris, Theodore N, et al, eds. see Educational Research Council of America.
Ferris, Theodore N., et al, eds. see Educational Research Council or America.
Ferris, Thomas F., jt. auth. see Burrow, Gerard N.
Ferris, Timothy. Galaxien. Ehlers, Anita, tr. from Eng. 184p. (Ger.). 1981. 94.00 (ISBN 3-7643-1250-5). Birkhauser.
--The Red Limit: The Search for the Edge of the Universe. rev. ed. (Illus.). 288p. 1983. pap. 14.95 (ISBN 0-688-01836-X). Quill NY.
Ferris, William. Afro-American Folk Art & Crafts. (Illus.). 444p. 1983. lib. bdg. 39.95 (ISBN 0-8161-9045-3, Univ Bks). G K Hall.
--Blues from the Delta. (Roots of Jazz Ser.). (Illus.). 226p. 1983. Repr. of 1979 ed. lib. bdg. 25.00 (ISBN 0-306-76215-3). Da Capo.
--Local Color: A Sense of Place in Folk Art. 272p. 1983. 19.95 (ISBN 0-07-020652-X); pap. 11.95 (ISBN 0-07-020651-1). McGraw.
Ferriss, Abbott L. Indicators of Change in the American Family. LC 76-102385. 170p. 1970. pap. 5.50x (ISBN 0-87154-250-1). Russell Sage.
--Indicators of Trends in American Education. LC 76-92860. 454p. 1969. pap. 6.95x (ISBN 0-87154-251-X). Russell Sage.
--Indicators of Trends in the Status of American Women. LC 76-153996. 452p. 1971. pap. 8.50x (ISBN 0-87154-252-8). Russell Sage.
Ferriss, Lloyd. Secrets of a Mountain. Jack, Susan, ed. (Secrets of Ser.). (Illus.). 76p. (Orig.). 1982. pap. 5.95 (ISBN 0-930096-18-5). G Gannett.
Ferro, Beatriz. Caught in the Rain. LC 79-2513. (gr. 2). 1980. 7.95a o.p. (ISBN 0-385-15624-3); PLB 7.95a (ISBN 0-385-15625-1). Doubleday.
Ferro Milone, A. & Giacomo, P. Metrology & Fundamental Constants. (Enrico Fermi Summer School Ser.: No. 68). 1980. 153.25 (ISBN 0-444-85467-3). Elsevier.
Ferrone, J., ed. see Calvino, Italo.
Ferrone, Soldano & David, Chella S. IA Antigens. 1982. Vol. I, Mice. 73.50 (ISBN 0-8493-6461-2); Vol. II, Man & Other Species. 55.00 (ISBN 0-8493-6462-0). CRC Pr.
Ferrone, Soldano & Solheim, Bjarte G., eds. HLA Typing: Methodology & Clinical Aspects, 2 vols. 208p. 1982. 59.00 ea. Vol. I (ISBN 0-8493-6410-8). Vol. II (ISBN 0-8493-6411-6). CRC Pr.
Ferronsky, V. I. & Polyakov, V. A. Environmental Isotopes in the Hydrosphere. 466p. 1982. 71.00 (ISBN 0-471-10114-1, Pub. by Wiley-Interscience). Wiley.
Ferrucci, Joseph T. & Wittenberg, Jack. Interventional Radiology of the Abdomen. (Illus.). 264p. 1981. lib. bdg. 39.00 (ISBN 0-683-03174-0). Williams & Wilkins.
Ferry, Anne. All in War with Time: Love Poetry in Shakespeare, Donne, Jonson, Marvell. LC 74-31995. 304p. 1975. text ed. 16.50x o.p. (ISBN 0-674-01630-0). Harvard U Pr.
Ferry, Charles. Raspberry One. LC 82-25476. 224p. (gr. 7 up). 1983. 10.95 (ISBN 0-395-34069-1). HM.
Ferry, Diane L., jt. auth. see Van de Ven, Andrew H.
Ferry, John D. Viscoelastic Properties of Polymers. 3rd ed. LC 79-2866. 641p. 1980. 57.50x (ISBN 0-471-04894-1, Pub. by Wiley-Interscience). Wiley.
Ferry, Ted S. Modern Accident Investigation & Analysis: An Executive Guide to Accident Investigation. LC 80-21046. 273p. 1981. 29.95x (ISBN 0-471-07776-3, Pub. by Wiley-Interscience). Wiley.
Ferry, W. Hawkins. Buildings of Detroit: A History. rev. ed. LC 80-15976. (Illus.). 1980. 40.00 (ISBN 0-8143-1665-4). Wayne St U Pr.
Fersch, Ellsworth A. Psychology & Psychiatry in Courts & Corrections: Controversy & Change. LC 80-11726. (Wiley Series on Personality Processes). 370p. 1980. 29.95x (ISBN 0-471-05604-9, Pub. by Wiley-Interscience). Wiley.
Ferszt, R. see Cervos-Navarro, J.
Fertis, Demeter G. Dynamics & Vibrations of Structures. LC 72-11788. 485p. 1973. 48.95 (ISBN 0-471-25777-X, Pub. by Wiley-Interscience). Wiley.
Fertl, W. H. Abnormal Formation Pressures. (Developments in Petroleum Science: Vol. 2). 1976. 42.75 (ISBN 0-444-41328-6). Elsevier.
Ferziger, Joel H. Numerical Methods for Engineering Application. LC 81-1260. 288p. 1981. 29.95x (ISBN 0-471-06336-3, Pub. by Wiley-Interscience). Wiley.
Feschenko, S., et al, eds. Asymptotic Methods in the Theory of Linear Differential Equations. 1968. 17.50 (ISBN 0-444-00026-7). Elsevier.
Fesharaki, Fereidum & Isaak, David T. OPEC, The Gulf & the World Petroleum Market: A Study in Government Policy & Downstream Operations. (Special Studies in International Economics & Business). 250p. 1983. lib. bdg. 27.50x (ISBN 0-86531-305-9). Westview.
Fesharaki, Fereidun. Development of the Iranian Oil Industry: International & Domestic Aspects. LC 75-19782. (Special Studies). (Illus.). 346p. 1976. text ed. 32.95 o.p. (ISBN 0-275-55600-X). Praeger.
Feshbach, Ann, tr. see Gourfinkel, Nina.
Feshbach, H., jt. auth. see Morse, Philip M.
Feshbach, Norma & Feshbach, Seymour. Learning to Care: Classroom Activities for Social & Affective Development. 1983. pap. text ed. 9.95 (ISBN 0-673-15804-7). Scott F.
Feshbach, Seymour, jt. auth. see Feshbach, Norma.
Feshback, Norma D., et al. Early Schooling in England & Israel. (IDEA Reports on Schooling). 224p. 1973. 3.20 (ISBN 0-07-020635-X, P&RB). McGraw.
Fesler, James. Public Administration: Theory & Practice. (Illus.). 1980. text ed. 22.95 (ISBN 0-13-737320-1). P-H.
Fesler, James W., ed. American Public Administration: Pattern of the Past. (PAR Classics Ser.: Vol. IV). 1982. write for info. (ISBN 0-936678-05-4). Am Soc Pub Admin.
Fess, Elaine, et al. Hand Splinting: Principles & Methods. LC 80-17398. (Illus.). 318p. 1980. text ed. 39.50 (ISBN 0-8016-1569-0). Mosby.
Fessenden, Francis, ed. see Fessenden, William P.
Fessenden, William P. Life & Public Services of William Pitt Fessenden, 2 Vols. Fessenden, Francis, ed. LC 70-87532. (American Public Figures Ser). (Illus.). 1970. Repr. of 1907 ed. Set. lib. bdg. 85.00 (ISBN 0-306-71446-9). Da Capo.
Fessler, Edward A. Directed-Energy Weapons: A Juridical Analysis. LC 79-65950. 204p. 1980. 24.95 (ISBN 0-03-053511-5). Praeger.
Fessler, Stella L. Chinese Poultry Cooking. (Illus.). 288p. 1982. 7.95 (ISBN 0-452-25365-9, Z5365, Plume). NAL.
Fessler, Stella L., tr. see Hatano, Sumi.
Fest, Wilfried. Peace or Partition: The Habsburg Monarchy & British Policy, 1914-1918. LC 77-92396. 1978. 20.00x (ISBN 0-312-59935-8). St Martin.
Festa-McCormick, Diane. Honore De Balzac. (World Authors Ser.). 1979. lib. bdg. 12.95 (ISBN 0-8057-6383-X, Twayne). G K Hall.
Festing, Michael F. Inbred Strains in Biomedical Research. 1980. text ed. 55.00x (ISBN 0-19-520111-6). Oxford U Pr.
Festinger, Leon, ed. Retrospections on Social Psychology. (Illus.). 1980. text ed. 16.95x (ISBN 0-19-502751-5). Oxford U Pr.
Fetsko, J. M., ed. see Walker, W. C., et al.
Fetter, Alexander L. & Walecka, J. Dirk. Theoretical Mechanics of Particles & Continua. (Illus.). 1980. text ed. 31.50 (ISBN 0-07-020658-9). McGraw.
Fetter, B., et al. Mycoses of the Central Nervous System. 219p. 1967. 14.25 o.p. (ISBN 0-683-03185-6, Pub. by Williams & Wilkins). Krieger.
Fetter, Bruce, ed. Colonial Rule in Africa: Readings from Primary Sources. LC 78-65020. 238p. 1979. 25.00 (ISBN 0-299-07780-2); pap. 9.95 (ISBN 0-299-07784-5). U of Wis Pr.
Fetter, Charles W., Jr. Applied Hydrogeology. (Physics & Physical Science Ser.). 448p. 1980. text ed. 34.95 (ISBN 0-675-08126-2). Merrill.
Fetter, Richard. Frontier Boulder. (Illus.). 80p. (Orig.). 1983. pap. write for info. (ISBN 0-933472-72-2). Johnson Bks.
Fetterman, Elsie & Klamkin, Charles. Consumer Education in Practice. LC 75-38976. 1976. text ed. 12.00 o.p. (ISBN 0-471-25780-X); pap. text ed. 15.95 (ISBN 0-471-25781-8). Wiley.
Fettes, E. M. Chemical Reactions of Polymers, Vol. 19. (High Polymers Ser.). 1304p. 1964. 102.00 o.p. (ISBN 0-470-39305-X). Wiley.
Fettes, Edward M., ed. Macromolecular Synthesis, Vol.7. LC 63-18627. (Macromolecular Synthesis Ser.). 1980. 35.95 (ISBN 0-471-05891-2, Pub. by Wiley-Interscience). Wiley.
Fettic, Muriel E. Stories of Cherry Creek, Nevada, & Surrounding Country. 1979. 4.95 o.p. (ISBN 0-533-03857-X). Vantage.
Fettig, Art. How to Hold an Audience in the Hollow of Your Hand: Seven Techniques for Starting Your Speech, Eleven Techniques for Keeping It Rolling. LC 79-14145. 192p. 1979. 9.95 o.p. (ISBN 0-8119-0322-2). Fell.
--Mentor: Secrets of the Ages. LC 80-70956. (Illus.). 96p. 1981. 9.95 o.p. (ISBN 0-8119-0333-8). Fell.
--Remembering. LC 81-90188. (Illus.). 96p. 1982. 4.00 (ISBN 0-9601334-2-9). Growth Unltd.
--Selling Lucky. LC 81-1150. 130p. 1978. 9.95 o.p. (ISBN 0-8119-0306-0). Fell.
Fettke, Steven M. Messages to a Nation in Crisis: An Introduction to the Prophecy of Jeremiah. LC 82-19997. (Illus.). 72p. (Orig.). 1983. pap. text ed. 6.75 (ISBN 0-8191-2839-2). U Pr of Amer.
Fettweis, G. B. World Coal Resources: Methods of Assessment & Results. (Developments in Economic Geology Ser.: Vol. 10). 425p. 1979. 78.75 (ISBN 0-444-99779-2). Elsevier.
Fetyko, David F. Financial Accounting: Concepts & Principles. 746p. 1980. text ed. 21.95x o.p. (ISBN 0-534-00753-8, Kent Pub.); guide 6.95xstudy o.p. (ISBN 0-534-00851-8); papers 6.95xworking o.p. (ISBN 0-534-00846-1). Kent Pub Co.
Fetyko, David F., et al. CPA Review, 1981-82: Volume II: Problems & Solutions. (Business Ser.). 1088p. 1981. text ed. 23.95x (ISBN 0-534-00967-0). Kent Pub Co.
Fetzer, John. Clemens Brentano. (World Authors Ser.). 15.95 (ISBN 0-8057-6457-7, Twayne). G K Hall.
Fetzer, John F. Romantic Orpheus: Profiles of Clemens Brentano. LC 72-85527. 1974. 30.00x (ISBN 0-520-02312-9). U of Cal Pr.
Fetzer, Leland, tr. see Tolstoi, Alexei N.
Feucht, Oscar, ed. Christians Worship. LC 76-161192. (Discipleship Ser). (Orig.). 1971. pap. 4.25 o.p. (ISBN 0-570-06308-6, 20-1051); tchrs. manual 3.35 o.p. (ISBN 0-570-06309-4, 20-1052). Concordia.
Feucht, Oscar E. Learning to Use Your Bible. LC 77-76228. 1969. pap. text ed. 4.25 (ISBN 0-570-06300-0, 14-1531); tchr's manual 3.35 (ISBN 0-570-06301-9, 14-1532). Concordia.
Feucht, Oscar E., ed. see Norden, Rudolph F.
Feuchtwanger, E. J. Gladstone. LC 75-7712. (British Political Biography Ser.). 250p. 1975. 22.50 (ISBN 0-312-32760-9). St Martin.
Feuchtwanger, E. J., ed. Upheaval & Continuity: A Century of German History. LC 73-17691. 1974. 10.95 o.p. (ISBN 0-686-82998-0); pap. 4.95x (ISBN 0-685-39229-5). U of Pittsburgh Pr.
Feuchtwanger, E. J. & Nailor, E. J., eds. The Soviet Union & the Third World. 1981. 26.00x (ISBN 0-312-74909-0). St Martin.
Feuchtwanger, Lion. Power. Muir, Willa & Muir, Edwin, trs. 424p. 1982. Repr. of 1927 ed. lib. bdg. 20.00 (ISBN 0-89760-238-2). Telegraph Bks.
Feuer, Henry, ed. The Chemistry of the Nitro & Nitroso Groups: Part 1. LC 80-21491. 996p. 1981. Repr. of 1969 ed. text ed. (ISBN 0-89874-271-4); text ed. (ISBN 0-89874-272-2); Pts. 1 & 2. text ed. 76.00 (ISBN 0-686-86251-1). Krieger.
Feuerbach, Ludwig. Essence of Christianity. Eliot, George, tr. 1958. 12.00 (ISBN 0-8446-2055-6). Peter Smith.
--Thoughts on Death & Immortality. Massey, James A., tr. from Ger. LC 80-25259. 263p. 1981. 26.50x (ISBN 0-520-04051-1); pap. 6.95 (ISBN 0-520-04062-7, CAL 486). U of Cal Pr.
Feuerbacher, B., et al. Photoemission & the Electronic Properties of Surfaces. 540p. 1978. 86.00x (ISBN 0-471-99555-X). Wiley.
Feuerlicht, Ignace. Alienation: From the Past to the Future. LC 77-87940. (Contributions in Philosophy: No. 11). 1978. lib. bdg. 29.95 (ISBN 0-313-20055-6, FEA/). Greenwood.
--Thomas Mann. (World Authors Ser.). 1969. lib. bdg. 12.95 (ISBN 0-8057-2584-9, Twayne). G K Hall.
Feuerstein, G. Bhagavad Gita: A Critical Rendering. 170p. 1981. text ed. 10.75x (ISBN 0-391-02191-5, Pub. by Arnold Heinemann India). Humanities.
Feuerstein, Georg. Bhagavad Gita: An Introduction. LC 82-42702. 191p. 1983. pap. 6.75 (ISBN 0-8356-0575-2, Quest). Theos Pub Hse.
Feuerstein, R. Instrumental Enrichment. 462p. 1979. text ed. 28.95 (ISBN 0-8391-1509-1). Univ Park.
Feuer-Toth, Rozsa. Renaissance Architecture in Hungary. Feherdy, Imre, tr. from Hungarian. (Illus.). 243p. 1981. 27.50x (ISBN 963-207-592-7). Intl Pubns Serv.
Feuerwerger, Marvin C. Congress & Israel: Foreign Aid Decision-Making in the House of Representatives, Nineteen Sixty-Nine to Ninety Seventy-Six. LC 78-74654. (Contributions in Political Science Ser.: No. 28). (Illus.). 1979. lib. bdg. 27.50 (ISBN 0-313-21240-6, FCO/). Greenwood.
Feuillerat, A., ed. see Sidney, Philip.
Feuillerat, Albert. Baudelaire et la Belle aux Cheveux D'or. 1941. text ed. 32.50x (ISBN 0-686-83483-6). Elliots Bks.
--French Life & Ideals. 1925. 42.50x (ISBN 0-685-89753-2). Elliots Bks.
Feurerstein, George. The Philosophy of Classical Yoga. LC 80-507. 160p. 1980. 25.00 (ISBN 0-312-60665-6). St Martin.
Feutchwant & Hussain. The Chinese Economic Reforms. LC 82-10703. 384p. 1982. 32.50x (ISBN 0-312-13385-5). St Martin.
Feutry, Michel, et al, eds. Dictionary of Industrial Technology: English-French-German-Portuguese-Spanish. 90.00 (ISBN 2-85608-000-6). Heinman.
Fewell, Rebecca R., jt. auth. see Garwood, S. Gray.
Fewings, David R. Corporate Growth & Common Stock Risk, Vol. 12. Altman, Edward I. & Walter, Ingo, eds. LC 76-52014. (Contemporary Studies in Economic & Financial Analysis). (Orig.). 1979. lib. bdg. 36.50 (ISBN 0-89232-053-2). Jai Pr.
Fey, James T. Patterns of Verbal Communication in Mathematics Classes. LC 74-103135. (Illus.). 1970. text ed. 9.50x (ISBN 0-8077-1342-2). Tchrs Coll.
Fey, Marshall. The Slot Machine Story. (Illus.). 1983. 35.00 (ISBN 0-913814-53-9). Nevada Pubns.
Fey, Willard R., jt. auth. see Gutierrez, Luis T.
Feydeau, Georges. Four Farces. Shapiro, Norman R., ed. & tr. LC 78-125164. 1972. pap. 8.50 (ISBN 0-226-24477-6, P474, Phoen). U of Chicago Pr.
Feydel, Gabriel. Un Cahier D'Histoire Litteraire. Repr. of 1818 ed. 28.00 o.p. (ISBN 0-8287-0341-8). Clearwater Pub.
Feyerabend, Cessa. Budgerigar Diseases. pap. 7.95 (ISBN 0-87666-791-4, PS671). TFH Pubns.
Feyerabend, Cessa & Vriends, Matthew M. Taming & Training Budgerigars. rev. ed. Orig. Title: The Budgerigar As a Pet. (Illus.). 1978. pap. 7.95 (ISBN 0-87666-960-7, AP-1880). TFH Pubns.
Feyerabend, Cessa, jt. auth. see Vriends, Matthew M.
Feyerabend, Cessa & Vriends, Matthew M., eds. Feeding Budgerigars. (Illus.). 1978. pap. 6.95 (ISBN 0-87666-971-2, AP-400). TFH Pubns.
Feyerabend, P. K. Problems of Empiricism: Philosophical Papers, Vol. 2. LC 80-41931. 260p. 1981. 39.50 (ISBN 0-521-23964-8). Cambridge U Pr.
--Realism, Rationalism & Scientific Method: Philosophical Papers, Vol. 1. LC 80-41931. (Illus.). 360p. 1981. 49.50 (ISBN 0-521-22897-2). Cambridge U Pr.
Feyerabend, Paul. Against Method. (Illus.). 1978. pap. 7.95 (ISBN 0-8052-7008-6, Pub by NLB). Schocken.
--Science in a Free Society. 1979. 16.00 (ISBN 0-8052-7043-4, Pub by NLB). Schocken.
Feyman, P & Hibbs, A. R. Quantum Mechanics & Path Integrals. (International Earth & Planetary Sciences Ser). 1965. text ed. 37.50 (ISBN 0-07-020650-3, C). McGraw.
Feynman, Carl, jt. auth. see Leighton, Ralph.
Feynman, R. P., et al. Feynman Lectures on Physics, 3 Vols. Vol. 1. text ed. 19.95 (ISBN 0-201-02010-6); Vol. 2. text ed. 19.95 (ISBN 0-201-02011-4); Vol. 3. text ed. 19.95 (ISBN 0-201-02014-9); Set. pap. 36.95 (ISBN 0-201-02115-3); exercises for vols 2 & 3 2.95 (ISBN 0-685-03072-5). Vol. 2 Excercises (ISBN 0-201-02017-3). Vol. 3 Excercises (ISBN 0-201-02019-X). excercises for vol. 1 2.50 (ISBN 0-686-66303-9). A-W.
Feys, J. The Yogi & the Mystic. LC 76-902829. 1976. 11.00x o.p. (ISBN 0-8364-0480-7). South Asia Bks.
Ffolliott, Rosemary. De Bever Hall. (Illus.). 75p. 1976. 8.95 (ISBN 0-7156-1018-X, Pub. by Duckworth England). Biblio Dist.
Ffrench, Florence F. Music & Musicians in Chicago. (Music Reprint Ser.). 1979. Repr. of 1899 ed. lib. bdg. 29.50 (ISBN 0-306-79542-6). Da Capo.
Fiarotta, Noel, jt. auth. see Fiarotta, Phyllis.
Fiarotta, Phyllis & Fiarotta, Noel. Pin It, Tack It, Hang It. LC 75-20211. (Illus.). 288p. (gr. 1 up). 1975. 9.95 (ISBN 0-911104-61-5); pap. 4.95 o.s.i. (ISBN 0-911104-63-1). Workman Pub.
Fiber, Larry, jt. auth. see Huffman, Harry.
FIBERARTS Magazine Staff. The FIBERARTS Design Book II. LC 82-84032. (Illus.). 208p. (Orig.). 1983. 27.95 (ISBN 0-937274-06-2); pap. 18.95 (ISBN 0-937274-07-0). Lark Bks.
Fiberarts Magazine Staff, ed. The Fiberarts Design Book. LC 80-67315. (Illus.). 176p. (Orig.). 1980. 24.95 (ISBN 0-937274-00-3); pap. 15.95 (ISBN 0-937274-01-1). Lark Bks.
Ficarra. Medicolegal Handbook: A Guide for Winning. 328p. 1983. price not set (ISBN 0-8247-7005-6). Dekker.
Ficat & Philippe, eds. Contrast Arthography of the Synovial Joints. LC 81-12391. 184p. 1981. 39.50x (ISBN 0-89352-135-3). Masson Pub.
Ficat, R. Paul, et al. Ischemia & Necroses of Bone. 200p. 1980. lib. bdg. 35.00 o.p. (ISBN 0-683-03199-6). Williams & Wilkins.
Ficek. Real Estate Principles & Practices. 2nd ed. 1976. text ed. 22.95 (ISBN 0-675-08104-1). Additional supplements may be obtained from publisher. Merrill.
Ficek, Edmund. Comprehensive CPA Business Law Review. 1st ed. (Illus.). 640p. 1983. text ed. 23.95 (ISBN 0-07-020671-6, C); instr's. manual 10.95 (ISBN 0-07-020672-4). McGraw.
Ficek, Edmund F. & Johnson, Ross H. Real Estate: Principles & Practices. 3rd ed. 1983. 21.95 (ISBN 0-675-20016-4); study guide 8.95 (ISBN 0-675-20064-4). Additional supplements may be obtained from publisher. Merrill.
Fich, S., jt. auth. see Potter, James L.
Fichera, G. Numerical & Quantitative Analysis. (Surveys & References Ser.: No. 3). 218p. 1978. text ed. 46.00 (ISBN 0-273-00284-8). Pitman Pub MA.

--Trends in Applications of Pure Mathematics to Mechanics, Vol. 1. (Mongraphs & Studies: No. 2). 459p. 1976. text ed. 49.50 (ISBN 0-273-00129-9). Pitman Pub MA.

Fichman, Martin. Alfred Russel Wallace. (English Author Ser.). 1981. lib. bdg. 13.95 (ISBN 0-8057-6797-5, Twayne). G K Hall.

Fichte, J. G. Fichte's Critique of All Revelation. Green, G. D., tr. LC 77-77756. 1978. 29.95 (ISBN 0-521-21707-5). Cambridge U Pr.

--The Science of Knowledge: With First & Second Introductions. Heath, Peter & Lachs, John, eds. Heath, Peter & Lachs, John, trs. LC 82-4536. (Texts in German Philosophy Ser.). 298p. 1982. 37.50 (ISBN 0-521-25018-8); pap. 12.50 (ISBN 0-521-27050-2). Cambridge U Pr.

Fichte, Johann G. Vocation of Man. Smith, William, tr. from Ger. xii, 190p. 1965. 16.00 (ISBN 0-87548-074-8); pap. 6.00 (ISBN 0-87548-075-6). Open Court.

Fichtel, Carl E. & McDonald, Frank B., eds. High Energy Particles & Quanta in Astrophysics. 1974. 30.00x (ISBN 0-262-06048-5). MIT Pr.

Fichtenau, Heinrich. The Carolingian Empire. Munz, Peter, tr. (Mediaeval Academy Reprints for Teaching Ser.). 1979. pap. 7.25 (ISBN 0-8020-6367-5). U of Toronto Pr.

Fichter, George. Bicycles & Bicycling. LC 77-16511. (First Books Ser.). (Illus.). (gr. 4-6). 1978. PLB 8.90 s&l (ISBN 0-531-01403-7). Watts.

--Iraq. (First Bks). (Illus.). (gr. 4-6). 1978. PLB 8.90 s&l (ISBN 0-531-02236-6). Watts.

Fichter, George S. Comets & Meteors. (First Bks). (Illus.). 72p. (gr. 4 up). 1982. PLB 8.90 (ISBN 0-531-04382-7). Watts.

--Disastrous Fires. LC 81-2448. (First Bks.). (Illus.). 72p. (gr. 4 up). 1981. lib. bdg. 8.90 (ISBN 0-531-04325-8). Watts.

--Florida-In Pictures. LC 78-66310. (Visual Geography Ser.). (Illus.). (gr. 5 up). 1979. PLB 6.69 (ISBN 0-8069-1221-9); pap. 2.95 (ISBN 0-8069-1220-0). Sterling.

--The Future Sea. LC 78-57790. (Illus.). 1978. 14.95 o.p. (ISBN 0-8069-3106-X); lib. bdg. 13.29 o.p. (ISBN 0-8069-3107-8). Sterling.

--Karts & Karting. (First Bks). (Illus.). 72p. (gr. 4 up). 1982. PLB 8.90 (ISBN 0-531-04394-0). Watts.

--Keeping Amphibians & Reptiles As Pets. (First Bks.). (Illus.). (gr. 4-6). 1979. PLB 8.90 s&l (ISBN 0-531-02257-9). Watts.

--Poisonous Snakes. (First Bks.). (Illus.). 72p. (gr. 4 up). 1982. PLB 8.90 (ISBN 0-531-04349-5). Watts.

--Racquetball. (First Bks.). (Illus.). (gr. 4 up). 1979. PLB 8.90 s&l (ISBN 0-531-04078-X). Watts.

--Snakes Around the World. LC 78-9774. (Easy Read Fact Bks.). (Illus.). (gr. 2-4). 1980. PLB 8.60 s&l (ISBN 0-531-02275-7). Watts.

--The Space Shuttle. (First Bks.). (Illus.). 72p. (gr. 4 up). 1981. lib. bdg. 8.90 (ISBN 0-531-04354-1). Watts.

--Working Dogs. (First Bks.). (Illus.). (gr. 4-6). 1979. PLB 8.90 s&l (ISBN 0-531-02887-9). Watts.

Fichter, Joseph H. The Rehabilitation of Clergy Alcoholics: Ardent Spirits Subdued. LC 80-28447. 203p. 1982. 24.95x (ISBN 0-89885-009-6). Human Sci Pr.

Fichter, Joseph H., ed. Alternatives to American Mainline Churches. LC 82-50819. (Conference Ser.: No. 14). (Orig.). 1982. pap. text ed. 9.95 (ISBN 0-932894-14-3). Unif Theol Seminary.

Fichtner, Hans & Garff, Michael. How to Build Sailboards: Step-by-Step Custom-Made Designs. (Illus.). 126p. 1983. pap. 10.00 (ISBN 0-915160-28-5). Seven Seas.

Ficino, Marsilio. The Letters of Marsilio Ficino, Vol. 2. School of Economic Science, London, Language Dept., tr. from Lat. 121p. 1978. 16.00 (ISBN 0-85683-036-4). Spring Pubns.

--The Letters of Marsilio Ficino, Vol. 3. School of Economic Science, London, Language Dept., tr. from Lat. 162p. 1981. 16.00 (ISBN 0-85683-045-3). Spring Pubns.

--The Letters of Marsilo Ficino, Vol. 1. School of Economic Science, London, Language Dept., tr. from Lat. 248p. 1975. 16.00 (ISBN 0-85683-010-0). Spring Pubns.

Fick, G. & Sprague, R. H., Jr., eds. Decision Support Systems-Issues & Challenges: Proceedings of an International Task Foce Meeting, June 23-25, 1980. (IIASA Proceedings: Vol. 11). (Illus.). 190p. 1980. 32.00 (ISBN 0-08-027321-1). Pergamon.

Fickeisen, D. H. & Schneider, M. J., eds. Gas Bubble Disease: Proceedings. LC 75-619327. (AEC Technical Information Center Ser.). 123p. 1967. pap. 11.00 (ISBN 0-87079-023-4, CONF-741033); microfiche 4.00 (ISBN 0-87079-213-X, CONF-741033). DOE.

Ficker, Victor B. & Graves, Herbert S. Social Science & Urban Crisis: Introductory Readings. 2nd ed. 1978. pap. text ed. 13.95 (ISBN 0-02-337170-6, 33717). Macmillan.

Fickett, Harold. The Holy Fool. 360p. 1983. pap. 7.95 (ISBN 0-89107-227-6, Crossway Bks). Good News.

Fickett, Lewis P., Jr. The Major Socialist Parties of India: A Study in Leftist Fragmentation. LC 76-20536. (Foreign & Comparative Studies-South Asian Ser.: No. 2). 1976. pap. text ed. 4.50x o.p. (ISBN 0-915984-76-8). Syracuse U Foreign Comp.

Fidanza, F., jt. ed. see Somogyi, J. C.

Fiddian, Robin. Ignacio Aldecoa. (World Authors Ser.). 1979. 15.95 (ISBN 0-8057-6370-8, Twayne). G K Hall.

Fideler, Raymond & Kvande, Carol. South America. rev. ed. LC 76-17680. (World Cultures Ser). (Illus.). (gr. 5 up). 1978. text ed. 11.20 1-4 copies o.s.i. (ISBN 0-88296-103-9); text ed. 8.96 5 or more o.s.i. (ISBN 0-686-96719-4); tchrs' ed 6.96 o.s.i. (ISBN 0-88296-353-8). Fideler.

Fidell, Estelle A. see Cook, Dorothy E. & Monro, Isabel S.

Fidell, Linda S., jt. auth. see Tabachnick, Barbara G.

Fidell-Beaufort, Madeleine & Bailly-Herzberg, Janine. Daubigny. (Illus.). 1975. 90.00x o.p. (ISBN 2-85787-001-9). Kent St U Pr.

Fidillino, Tony, ed. see Martinez, Maria.

Fidler, Gail S. & Fidler, Jay W. Occupational Therapy. 1963. text ed. 15.95 o.p. (ISBN 0-02-337190-0). Macmillan.

Fidler, Jay W., jt. auth. see Fidler, Gail S.

Fiebelman, Walter A. Rails to Pittsburgh: A Train Watchers Collection. LC 79-12058. (Illus.). 1979. 19.95 o.s.i. (ISBN 0-87564-531-3). Superior Pub.

Fiebig, Susan L. With Every Falling Star. 1978. 4.50 o.p. (ISBN 0-533-03560-0). Vantage.

Fiechter, A. Space & Terrestrial Biotechnology. (Advances in Biochemical Engineering Ser.: Vol. 22). (Illus.). 230p. 1982. 39.00 (ISBN 0-387-11464-5). Springer-Verlag.

Fiechter, A., ed. Chromatography. (Advances in Biochemical Engineering Ser.: Vol. 25). (Illus.). 145p. 1983. 25.00 (ISBN 0-387-11829-2). Springer-Verlag.

Fieck, G. Symmetry of Polycentric Systems: The Polycentric Tensor Algebra for Molecules. (Lecture Notes in Physics: Vol. 167). 137p. 1983. pap. 7.50 (ISBN 0-387-11589-7). Springer-Verlag.

Fiedler, Conrad. On Judging Works of Visual Art. Schaefer-Simmern, Henry, tr. from Ger. (Library Reprint Ser.: Vol. 88). 1978. 17.95x (ISBN 0-520-03597-6). U of Cal Pr.

Fiedler, F. Theory of Leadership Effectiveness. 1967. text ed. 22.50 o.p. (ISBN 0-07-020675-9, C). McGraw.

Fiedler, Fred E., et al. Improving Leadership Effectiveness: The Leader Match Concept. LC 76-20632. (Self-Teaching Guides). 229p. 1976. pap. text ed. 9.95 (ISBN 0-471-25811-3). Wiley.

Fiedler, Jean & Mele, Jim. Isaac Asimov. LC 81-70122. (Recognitions Ser.). 180p. 1982. 11.95 (ISBN 0-8044-2203-6); pap. 5.95 (ISBN 0-8044-6147-3). Ungar.

Fiedler, Leslie. The Inadvertant Epic. 1980. postponed 6.95 o.p. (ISBN 0-686-60924-7, 25371, Touchstone Bks); pap. 2.95 o.p. (ISBN 0-671-25372-7). S&S.

--Love & Death in the American Novel. LC 66-14948. 1975. pap. 12.95 (ISBN 0-8128-1799-0). Stein & Day.

Fiedler, Leslie A. Olaf Stapledon: A Man Divided. (Science Fiction Writers Ser.). (Illus.). 256p. 1983. pap. 4.95 (ISBN 0-19-503087-7, GB 682, GB). Oxford U Pr.

--Olaf Stapledon: A Man Divided. LC 82-8168. (Science Fiction Writers Ser.). 256p. 1983. 19.95 (ISBN 0-19-503086-9). Oxford U Pr.

--What Was Literature? 1982. 14.95 (ISBN 0-671-24983-5). S&S.

Fiedorek, Mary B. & Jewell, Diana L. Executive Style: Looking It... Living It. (Illus.). 256p. 1983. 12.95 (ISBN 0-8329-0254-3). New Century.

Fieg, John. InterAct: Thailand-U. S. Renwick, George W., ed. LC 80-83909. (Country Orientation Ser.). 82p. 1980. pap. text ed. 10.00 (ISBN 0-933662-15-7). Intercult Pr.

Field & Cameron. The Dusty Universe. 1975. 15.00 (ISBN 0-07-020685-6). McGraw.

Field, Andrew. Nabokov: A Bibliography. LC 72-10473. 276p. 1973. 15.00 o.p. (ISBN 0-07-020680-5, GB). McGraw.

Field, Annita T. Fingerprint Handbook. (Illus.). 196p. 1976. photocopy ed. spiral 22.75x (ISBN 0-398-00562-1). C C Thomas.

Field, Barry C. & Willis, Cleve E., eds. Environmental Economics: A Guide to Information Sources. (Man & the Environment Information Guide Ser.: Vol. 8). 1979. 42.00x (ISBN 0-8103-1433-9). Gale.

Field, Barry C., jt. ed. see Berndt, Ernst R.

Field, C. Al-Ghazzali's Al-Chemy of Happiness. 2.50 (ISBN 0-686-18621-4). Kazi Pubns.

Field, Claud H. Dictionary of Oriental Quotations. LC 68-23157. 1969. Repr. of 1911 ed. 38.00x (ISBN 0-8103-3183-7). Gale.

Field, D. M. Step-by-Step Guide to Tracing Your Ancestors. 64p. 1983. 9.95 (ISBN 0-7095-1228-7, Pub. by Auto Assn-British Tourist Authority England). Merrimack Bk Serv.

Field, D. R., et al. Water & Community Development: Social & Economic Perspectives. LC 73-86058. (Man, the Community & Natural Resources: No. 1). (Illus.). 1978. pap. text ed. 12.50 o.p. (ISBN 0-250-40260-2). Ann Arbor Science.

Field, Daniel. The End of Serfdom: Nobility & Bureaucracy in Russia, 1855-1861. LC 75-32191. (Russian Research Center Studies: No. 75). 496p. 1976. 25.00x o.p. (ISBN 0-674-25240-3). Harvard U Pr.

Field, Dick & Newick, John, eds. The Study of Education & Art. 1973. 12.95x o.p. (ISBN 0-7100-7648-7); pap. 9.50 (ISBN 0-7100-7775-0). Routledge & Kegan.

Field, Edwin & Field, Selma. How to Get Rich Through OPN. 1978. 14.95 (ISBN 0-13-409508-1, Busn). P-H.

Field Enterprises, jt. auth. see Armstrong, Tom.

Field, Ernest R. Rich Man's Tax Guide. LC 76-153543. 1971. 10.00 (ISBN 0-8208-0341-3). Hearthside.

Field, Evan. What Nigel Knew. 224p. 1981. 10.95 o.p. (ISBN 0-517-54468-7, C N Potter Bks). Crown.

Field, F. Three French Writers & the Great War. LC 35-22982. 1975. 27.50 (ISBN 0-521-20916-1). Cambridge U Pr.

Field, Faye. Walk & Pray. 1982. pap. 3.50 (ISBN 0-8341-0785-6). Beacon Hill.

Field, Frances, jt. auth. see Clancy, John.

Field, Frances, jt. auth. see Field, Michael.

Field, Frank. Dr. Frank Field's Weather Book. 208p. 1981. 13.95 (ISBN 0-399-12634-1). Putnam Pub Group.

--Take It off with Frank! LC 77-13448. 1977. 6.95 o.p. (ISBN 0-688-03263-X). Morrow.

Field, Frank, ed. The Conscript Army: A Study of Britain's Unemployed. (Inequality & Society Ser.). (Orig.). 1978. pap. 8.95 o.p. (ISBN 0-7100-8779-9). Routledge & Kegan.

--Education & the Urban Crisis. 1976. 14.00 (ISBN 0-7100-8535-4); pap. 8.95 (ISBN 0-7100-8536-2). Routledge & Kegan.

--The Wealth Report Two. (Inequality in Society Ser.). 200p. (Orig.). 1983. pap. price not set (ISBN 0-7100-9452-3). Routledge & Kegan.

Field, Frederick Vanderbilt. From Right to Left: An Autobiography. Davidson, Donald J., ed. 228p. 1983. 14.95 (ISBN 0-88208-162-4); pap. 8.95 (ISBN 0-88208-161-6). Lawrence Hill.

Field, G. C. Plato & His Contemporaries. LC 74-30008. (Studies in Philosophy, No. 40). 1974. lib. bdg. 49.95x o.p. (ISBN 0-8383-1992-0). Haskell.

Field, George W. Hermann Hesse. (World Authors Ser.). lib. bdg. 12.95 (ISBN 0-8057-2424-9, Twayne). G K Hall.

Field, Henrey. The Track of Man, Adventures of an Anthropologist: Volume 2: The White House Years, 1941-1945. 134p. 10.95 (ISBN 0-686-84234-0). Banyan Bks.

Field, Hyman H., jt. auth. see Hilliard, Robert L.

Field, Isobel. This Life I've Loved. 353p. 1982. lib. bdg. 35.00 (ISBN 0-89760-233-1). Telegraph Bks.

Field, James A., jt. ed. see Hohman, Helen F.

Field, John. English Field Names. (Illus.). 291p. 1983. Repr. of 1975 ed. 19.95 (ISBN 0-7153-5710-7). David & Charles.

--English Field-Names: A Dictionary. LC 76-148407. (Illus.). xxx, 120p. 1973. 25.00 o.p. (ISBN 0-8103-2010-X). Gale.

Field, John P. & Weiss, Robert H. Cases for Composition. 1979. pap. text ed. 7.95 (ISBN 0-316-28173-5); tchr's manual avail. (ISBN 0-316-28174-3). Little.

Field, Joyce W., jt. ed. see Field, Leslie A.

Field, Kent A. Test Your Salvation. 1.00 (ISBN 0-89137-531-7). Quality Pubns.

Field, Lance. Godzilla Search a Word Shapes. (Illus.). (gr. 3-6). 1979. pap. 0.95 (ISBN 0-448-15920-1, G&D). Putnam Pub Group.

Field, Laurence W. Ab Thatcher's Mistress. 1978. pap. 3.00 (ISBN 0-932044-16-6). M O Pub Co.

Field, Leslie, ed. see Wolfe, Thomas.

Field, Leslie A. & Field, Joyce W., eds. Bernard Malamud & His Critics. LC 70-133016. 1970. 20.00x o.p. (ISBN 0-8147-2552-X); pap. 10.00x o.p. (ISBN 0-8147-2553-8). NYU Pr.

Field, Louise F. Child & His Book. 2nd ed. LC 67-23937. 1968. Repr. of 1892 ed. 34.00x (ISBN 0-8103-3480-1). Gale.

Field, Michael & Field, Frances. Quintet of Cuisines. LC 72-130359. (Foods of the World Ser.). (Illus.). (gr. 6 up). 1970. PLB 17.28 o.s.i. (ISBN 0-8094-0075-8, Pub. by Time-Life). Silver.

Field Newspaper Syndicate Editors. Boggle Challenge. 1982. pap. 1.95 (ISBN 0-451-11937-1, AJ1937, Sig). NAL.

Field, Norma M., tr. see Soseki, Natsume.

Field, O. P. Effect of an Unconstitutional Statute. LC 74-146273. (American Constitutional & Legal History Ser). 1971. Repr. of 1935 ed. lib. bdg. 42.50 (ISBN 0-306-70118-9). Da Capo.

Field, R. M. A Glossary of Office Automation Terms. 32p. 1982. pap. text ed. 15.00 (ISBN 0-914548-42-5). Soc Tech Comm.

Field, Richard S. Paul Gauguin: The Paintings of the First Voyage to Tahiti. LC 76-23617. (Outstanding Dissertations in the Fine Arts Ser.). 1977. lib. bdg. 63.00 o.s.i. (ISBN 0-8240-2688-8). Garland Pub.

Field, Sandra. Jamais Plus de Secrets. (Collection Harlequin). 192p. 1983. pap. 1.95 (ISBN 0-373-49322-3). Harlequin Bks.

--Walk by My Side. (Harlequin Presents Ser.). 192p. 1983. pap. 1.75 (ISBN 0-373-10568-1). Harlequin Bks.

Field, Selma, jt. auth. see Field, Edwin.

Field, Stephen J. Personal Reminiscences of Early Days in California. LC 68-29601. (American Scene Ser). 1968. Repr. of 1893 ed. lib. bdg. 45.00 (ISBN 0-306-71157-5). Da Capo.

Field, Syd. Screenplay. 1979. pap. 5.95 o.s.i. (ISBN 0-440-58273-3, Delta). Dell.

Field, Thomas W. Essay Towards an Indian Bibliography. LC 67-14026. 1967. Repr. of 1873 ed. 31.00 o.p. (ISBN 0-8103-3327-9). Gale.

Field, Tiffany & Sostek, Anita, eds. High Risk Infants: Perceptual & Physiological Processes. write for info (ISBN 0-8089-1563-0). Grune.

Field, Tiffany, et al, eds. High-Risk Infants & Children: Adult & Peer Interactions. (Developmental Psychology Ser.). 1980. 29.50 (ISBN 0-12-255550-3). Acad Pr.

Field, Tiffany M. & Fogel, Alan, eds. Emotion & Early Interactions. 320p. 1982. text ed. 29.95 (ISBN 0-89859-241-0). L Erlbaum Assocs.

Field, Tiffany M., jt. ed. see Lipsitt, Lewis P.

Field, Tiffany M., et al. Review of Human Development. LC 81-21886. 736p. 1982. 45.00x (ISBN 0-471-08116-7, Pub. by Wiley-Interscience). Wiley.

Field, Xenia. Window Box Gardening. (Illus.). 139p. 1975. 8.95 o.p. (ISBN 0-7137-0656-2). Transatlantic.

Fielden, Rosemary, jt. auth. see Rosen, Arnold.

Fielder, Erica, jt. auth. see Shaffer, Carolyn.

Fielder, Gilbert & Wilson, Lionel, eds. Volcanoes of the Earth, Moon, & Mars. LC 74-19887. (Illus.). 1975. 25.00 o.p. (ISBN 0-312-85120-0). St Martin.

Fielder, Mildred. Wild Fruits: An Illustrated Field Guide & Cookbook. (Illus.). 288p. (Orig.). 1983. pap. 9.95 (ISBN 0-8092-5614-2). Contemp Bks.

Fieldhouse, D. K. Colonialism Eighteen Seventy to Nineteen Forty-Five: An Introduction. 1981. 22.50 (ISBN 0-312-15074-1). St Martin.

Fieldhouse, David K., jt. ed. see Madden, Frederick.

Fieldhouse, Harry. Everyman's Good English Guide. 283p. 1983. 15.95 (ISBN 0-686-38410-5, Pub. by Evman England). Biblio Dist.

Fielding, Dodge. Fielding's Favorites: Hotels & Inns, Europe 1982. (Illus.). 480p. 1981. 5.95 (ISBN 0-688-00659-0). Morrow.

Fielding, Gordon J. Geography As Social Science. 1974. text ed. 24.50 scp o.p. (ISBN 0-06-042051-0, HarpC); inst. manual avail. o.p. (ISBN 0-06-362080-4). Har-Row.

--Programmed Case Studies in Geography. 299p. 1974. pap. text ed. 9.95 scp o.p. (ISBN 0-06-042052-9, HarpC). Har-Row.

Fielding, Henry. Adventures of Joseph Andrews. (World's Classics Ser.). 6.95 o.p. (ISBN 0-19-250334-0). Oxford U Pr.

--Amelia, 2 vols. in 1. 1978. Repr. of 1974 ed. 16.95x (ISBN 0-460-10852-2, Evman). Biblio Dist.

--Amelia. 1983. write for info. Wesleyan U Pr.

--An Enquiry into the Causes of the Late Increase of Robbers. 2nd ed. (Criminology, Law Enforcement, & Social Problems Ser.). Date not set. o. p. 10.00 (ISBN 0-87585-210-6). Patterson Smith.

--Jonathan Wild. pap. 3.50 (ISBN 0-451-51706-7, CE1706, Sig Classics). NAL.

--Jonathan Wild. Nokes, David, ed. (Penguin English Library). 1982. pap. 3.95 (ISBN 0-14-043151-9). Penguin.

--Joseph Andrews. (YA) 1950. pap. 3.50 o.p. (ISBN 0-394-30916-2, T16, Mod LibC). Modern Lib.

--Joseph Andrews. Brissenden, R. F., ed. (English Library). 1977. pap. 2.95 (ISBN 0-14-043114-4). Penguin.

--The Life of Mr. Jonathan Wild. LC 74-17291. (Novel in England, 1700-1775 Ser). 1974. Repr. of 1754 ed. lib. bdg. 50.00 o.s.i. (ISBN 0-8240-1108-2). Garland Pub.

--Tom Jones, 2 Vols. 1974. Repr. of 1909 ed. Vol. 1. 9.95x (ISBN 0-460-00355-0, Evman); Vol. 2. 8.95x (ISBN 0-460-00356-9). Biblio Dist.

--Tom Jones. (YA) 1950. pap. 4.50x (ISBN 0-394-30915-4, T15, Mod LibC). Modern Lib.

--Tom Jones. pap. 2.95 (ISBN 0-451-51634-6, CE1634, Sig Classics). NAL.

Fielding, Henry see Swan, D. K.

Fielding, Joy. Kiss Mommy Goodbye. 1982. pap. 3.50 (ISBN 0-451-11544-9, AE1544, Sig). NAL.

Fielding, Kathy. Having Your Baby at Home. 1980. softcover 3.95 o.p. (ISBN 0-912216-23-9). Angel Pr.

Fielding, Leslie. Handheld Calculator Programs for Rotating Equipment Design. LC 82-9962. (Illus.). 480p. 1983. 39.95 (ISBN 0-07-020695-3, P&RB). McGraw.

Fielding, Mantle. Dictionary of American Painters, Sculptors & Engravers. (Illus.). 25.00 (ISBN 0-913274-03-8). Wallace-Homestead.

--Dictionary of American Painters, Sculptors & Engravers. 1974. 30.00 (ISBN 0-913274-03-8). Apollo.

Fielding, Mantle, jt. auth. see Biddle, Edward.

Fielding, Meral, et al. Fundamentals of College Accounting. LC 72-186146. 1972. text ed. 14.00 o.p. (ISBN 0-89702-027-8); wkbk. 6.20 o.p. (ISBN 0-89702-028-6); 7.40 o.p. (ISBN 0-89702-026-X). PAR Inc.

Fielding, Nancy, jt. auth. see Fielding, Temple.

Fielding, Raymond. The March of Time: 1935-1951. (Illus.). 1978. 25.00 (ISBN 0-19-502212-2). Oxford U Pr.

--The Technique of Special Effects Cinematography. 3rd rev. & enl. ed. (Library of Communication Techniques). 426p. 1972. 26.95 o.p. (ISBN 0-240-50616-2). Focal Pr.

Fielding, Raymond, compiled by. A Technological History of Motion Pictures & Television. 1967. 40.00x (ISBN 0-520-03981-5). U of Cal Pr.

Fielding, Sarah. The History of Ophelia. Shugrue, Michael F., ed. (Flowering of the Novel Ser.: 1740-1775). Repr. of 1760 ed. lib. bdg. 50.00 o.s.i. (ISBN 0-8240-1154-6). Garland Pub.

--The History of the Countess of Dellwyn, 1759, 2 vols. in 1. (The Flowering of the Novel, 1740-1775 Ser: Vol. 53). 1974. lib. bdg. 50.00 o.s.i. (ISBN 0-8240-1152-X). Garland Pub.

Fielding, Temple. Fielding's Europe, 1981. 34th, rev. ed. 1030p. 1980. Fieldingflex bdg. 10.95 o.p. (ISBN 0-688-03776-3). Morrow.

--Fielding's Europe 1982. 1981. 12.95 (ISBN 0-688-00658-2). Morrow.

--Fielding's Europe 1983. 1982. 12.95 (ISBN 0-688-01346-5). Morrow.

Fielding, Temple & Fielding, Nancy. Fielding's Low-Cost Europe, 1981. 15th, rev. ed. (Illus.). 872p. 1980. Fieldingflex bdg. o.s.i. 5.95 o.p. (ISBN 0-688-03777-1). Morrow.

--Fielding's Low-Cost Europe 1983. 17th, rev. ed. (Illus.). 860p. 1982. pap. 7.50 (ISBN 0-688-01340-6). Morrow.

--Fielding's Low-Cost Europe 1983. 17th rev. ed. (Illus.). 875p. 1982. pap. 7.00 (ISBN 0-688-01340-6). Fielding.

--Fielding's Selective Shopping Guide to Europe Annual, 1983. 27th, rev. ed. 310p. (Orig.). 1982. pap. 5.50 (ISBN 0-688-01344-9). Morrow.

--Fielding's Selective Shopping Guide to Europe 1983. 27th rev. ed. 320p. 1982. pap. 4.95 (ISBN 0-688-01344-9). Fielding.

Fielding, Waldo L. Pregnancy: The Best State of the Union. LC 72-153881. (Illus.). 1971. pap. 6.95 o.s.i. (ISBN 0-87027-147-4). Cumberland Pr.

Fields. The Sun. (gr. 2-4). 1980. PLB 8.60 (ISBN 0-531-03243-4, G23). Watts.

Fields, jt. auth. see Campbell.

Fields, Alice. Insects. (gr. 2-4). 1980. PLB 8.60 o.p. (ISBN 0-531-03244-2). Watts.

--Pets. LC 80-20281. (Easy-Read Fact Bks.). (gr. 2-4). 1981. PLB 8.60 (ISBN 0-531-04188-3). Watts.

--Racing Cars. LC 80-15697. (gr. 2-4). 1981. PLB 8.60 (ISBN 0-531-03245-0). Watts.

--Satellites. (Easy Read Fact Bks.). (gr. 2-4). 1981. PLB 8.60 (ISBN 0-531-03246-9). Watts.

--Seals. (gr. 2-4). 1980. PLB 8.60 (ISBN 0-531-03242-6). Watts.

--Television. LC 79-26891. (Easy-Read Fact Bks.). (gr. 2-4). 1981. PLB 8.60 (ISBN 0-531-03248-5). Watts.

Fields, Annie. Life & Letters of Harriet Beecher Stowe. LC 77-102057. (Library of Lives & Letters). (Illus.). 1970. Repr. of 1897 ed. 34.00 o.p. (ISBN 0-8103-3602-2). Gale.

Fields, Annie, ed. James T. Fields: Biographical Notes & Personal Sketches with Unpublished Fragments & Tributes from Men & Women of Letters. LC 73-157501. 1971. Repr. of 1881 ed. 37.00x (ISBN 0-8103-3724-X). Gale.

Fields, Francis R. & Horwitz, Rudy J., eds. Psychology & Professional Practice: The Interface of Psychology & the Law. LC 81-19899. (Illus.). 248p. 1982. lib. bdg. 29.95 (ISBN 0-89930-015-4, FIH/, Quorum). Greenwood.

Fields, Gary S. How Segmented is the Bogota Labor Market? (Working Paper: No. 434). 99p. 1980. 5.00 (ISBN 0-686-36146-6, WP-0434). World Bank.

--Poverty, Inequality, & Development. LC 79-21017. (Illus.). 256p. 1980. 37.50 (ISBN 0-521-22572-8); pap. 9.95 (ISBN 0-521-29852-0). Cambridge U Pr.

Fields, Howard. High Crimes & Misdemeanors: The Untold & Dramatic Story of the Rodino Committee. 1978. 10.95 o.p. (ISBN 0-393-05681-3). Norton.

Fields, Kenneth, jt. ed. see Winters, Yvor.

Fields, Louis W. Bookkeeping Made Simple. 1956. pap. 4.95 (ISBN 0-385-01205-5, Made). Doubleday.

Fields, Nora. New Ideas for Christmas Decorations with Greens, Pods & Cones. (Illus.). 4.95 (ISBN 0-8208-0049-X). Hearthside.

Fields, P. Computer Assisted Home Energy Management. Date not set. pap. 15.95 (ISBN 0-686-82319-2). Sams.

Fields, Paul E. Fields Teaching Tests. rev. ed. (Prog. Bk.). 1971. pap. 5.95x o.p. (ISBN 0-673-07794-2). Scott F.

Fields, Rick. How the Swans Came to the Lake: A Narrative History of Buddhism in America. LC 81-50971. (Illus.). 480p. 1981. pap. 12.95 (ISBN 0-394-74883-2). Shambhala Pubns.

Fields, Robert R. Survival Primer: The Single Sourcebook for Coping with Crisis. (Illus.). 192p. 1983. pap. 7.95 (ISBN 0-89651-704-7). Icarus.

Fields, Rona M. Northern Ireland: Society under Siege. LC 80-80316. 267p. 1980. pap. 5.95 (ISBN 0-87855-806-3). Transaction Bks.

--Society under Siege: A Psychology of Northern Ireland. LC 76-21895. 283p. 1977. 24.95 (ISBN 0-87722-074-3). Temple U Pr.

Fields, Sylvia K., jt. ed. see Sherman, Jacques L., Jr.

Fields, Uriah J. How Lovers Can Become Friends. 26p. 1982. pap. 2.95 (ISBN 0-938844-04-0). Am Mutuality.

--The Montgomery Story. 26p. 1982. pap. 7.95 (ISBN 0-938844-05-9). Am Mutuality.

Fields, W. C. Drat! Anobile, Richard J., ed. (Illus.). 152p. 1973. pap. 1.25 o.p. (ISBN 0-451-06887-4, Y6887, Sig). NAL.

Fieler, Frank B. The David McCandless McKell Collection: A Descriptive Catalog of Manuscripts, Early Printed Books & Children's Books. 1973. lib. bdg. 45.00 (ISBN 0-8161-0993-1, Hall Reference). G K Hall.

Fielo, S. B. A Summary of Integrated Nursing Theory. 1975. 8.50 o.p. (ISBN 0-07-020715-1, HP). McGraw.

Fielo, Sandra B. & Edge, Sylviac. Technical Nursing of the Adult: Medical, Surgical & Psychiatric Approaches. 2nd ed. 1974. 22.95 (ISBN 0-02-337280-X, 33728). Macmillan.

Fienberg, S. Studies in Bayesian Econometrics & Statistics. LC 73-86697. (Contributions to Economic Analysis: Vol. 86). 677p. 1975. Repr. of 1977 ed. 85.00 (ISBN 0-444-10579-4, North-Holland). Elsevier.

Fienberg, S. E. & Zellner, A., eds. Studies in Bayesian Econometrics & Statistics: In Honor of Leonard J. Savage, 2 vols. 1977. Set. pap. 42.75 (ISBN 0-7204-0765-6, North-Holland); Vol. 1. pap. 42.75 (ISBN 0-7204-0562-9); Vol. 2. pap. 42.00 (ISBN 0-7204-0563-7). Elsevier.

Fienberg, Stephen. The Analysis of Cross-Classified Categorical Data. 2nd ed. 1980. text ed. 15.00x (ISBN 0-262-06071-X). MIT Pr.

Fiennes, G. F. I Tried to Run a Railway. pap. text ed. 16.50x (ISBN 0-392-07972-0, SpS). Sportshelf.

Fiennes, R. N. The Environment of Man. LC 77-26881. (Biology & Environment Ser.). 1978. 16.95x o.p. (ISBN 0-312-25699-X). St Martin.

Fiennes, Ranulph. To the Ends of the Earth: The Transglobe Expedition, the First Polo-to Pole Circumnavigation of the Globe. (Illus.). 1983. 14.50 (ISBN 0-87795-490-9). Arbor Hse.

Fiennes, Richard N. Ecology & Earth History. LC 75-32938. (Biology & Environment Ser.). 1976. text ed. 17.95 o.p. (ISBN 0-312-22610-1). St Martin.

Fiennes, T. W. Infectious Cancers of Animals & Man. 1982. 20.50 (ISBN 0-12-256040-X). Acad Pr.

Fiering, Myron B. & Jackson, Barbara B., eds. Synthetic Streamflows. LC 77-172418. (Water Resources Monograph: Vol. 1). (Illus.). 1971. pap. 10.00 (ISBN 0-87590-300-2). Am Geophysical.

Fiero, Gloria K. The Humanistic Tradition: Chapters in the History of Culture to 1650. LC 81-40631. (Illus.). 510p. (Orig.). 1981. lib. bdg. 29.25 (ISBN 0-8191-1755-2); pap. text ed. 18.75 (ISBN 0-8191-1756-0). U Pr of Amer.

Fierro, Robert D. Tax Shelters in Plain English. 1983. pap. 4.95 (ISBN 0-14-006362-5). Penguin.

Fierst, John, jt. auth. see Fried, Lewis.

Fierstein, Jeff. Kid Contracts. (gr. 4-8). 1982. 3.95 (ISBN 0-86653-091-6, GA 442). Good Apple.

Fierz, Markus, ed. Girolamo Cardano (1501-1576) Physician, Natural Philosopher, Mathematician, Astrologer & Interpreter of Dreams. Niman, Helga, tr. from Ger. 242p. Date not set. price not set (ISBN 3-7643-3057-0). Birkhauser.

Fieser, Louis F. & Fieser, Mary. Reagents for Organic Synthesis, 8 vols. Set. 265.00 (ISBN 0-471-08070-5); Vol. 1, 1967. 65.00x (ISBN 0-471-25875-X); Vol. 2, 1969. 44.95x (ISBN 0-471-25876-8); Vol. 3, 1972. 42.95x (ISBN 0-471-25879-2); Vol. 4, 1974. 45.00x (ISBN 0-471-25881-4); Vol. 5, 1975. 48.50x (ISBN 0-471-25882-2); Vol. 6, 1977. 46.50x (ISBN 0-471-25873-3); Vol. 7, 1979. 44.95x (ISBN 0-471-02918-1); Vol. 8, 1980. 46.95x (ISBN 0-471-04834-8). Wiley.

--Style Guide for Chemists. LC 60-11201. 122p. 1972. pap. 6.95 o.p. (ISBN 0-88275-018-6). Krieger.

Fieser, Louis F. & Williamson, Kenneth L. Organic Experiments. 4th ed. 1979. text ed. 22.95x (ISBN 0-669-01688-8); instr's manual 1.95 (ISBN 0-669-01689-6). Heath.

--Organic Experiments. 448p. 1983. 24.95 (ISBN 0-669-05890-4). Heath.

Fieser, Mary. Fieser & Fieser's Reagents for Organic Synthesis, Vol. 10. (Reagents for Organic Synthesis Ser.). 528p. 1982. 39.50 (ISBN 0-471-86636-9, Pub. by Wiley-Interscience). Wiley.

Fieser, Mary, jt. auth. see Fieser, Louis F.

Fieser, Mary, et al. Reagents for Organic Synthesis, Vol. 9. (Reagents for Organic Synthesis Ser.). 596p. 1981. 44.95 (ISBN 0-471-05631-6, Pub. by Wiley-Interscience). Wiley.

Fiesta, Janine. The Law & Liability: A Guide for Nurses. 300p. 1982. 13.95 (ISBN 0-471-07879-4, Pub. by Wiley Med). Wiley.

Fieve, Ronald. Moodswing: The Third Revolution in Psychology. LC 75-15624. 1975. 8.95 o.p. (ISBN 0-688-02938-8). Morrow.

Fifadara, Haresh, jt. auth. see Hollo, Reuven.

Fife, Dale. Adam's ABC. (Illus.). (gr. k-2). 1971. PLB 5.49 o.p. (ISBN 0-698-30002-5, Coward). Putnam Pub Group.

--Follow That Ghost! LC 79-11370. (Illus.). (gr. 1-5). 1979. 9.75 (ISBN 0-525-30010-4, 0947-280, Unicorn Bk). Dutton.

--The Little Park. LC 73-7322. (Self Starter Ser.). (Illus.). 32p. (gr. k-2). 1973. 7.75g o.p. (ISBN 0-8075-4634-8). A Whitman.

--Ride the Crooked Wind. (Illus.). 96p. (gr. 5-10). 1973. 5.95 o.p. (ISBN 0-698-20249-X, Coward). Putnam Pub Group.

--What's the Prize, Lincoln? (Illus.). (gr. 2-6). 1971. PLB 5.59 o.p. (ISBN 0-698-30396-2, Coward). Putnam Pub Group.

--Who Goes There Lincoln? LC 74-83016. (Illus.). 64p. (gr. 2-5). 1975. PLB 5.99 (ISBN 0-698-30565-5, Coward). Putnam Pub Group.

--Who'll Vote for Lincoln? (Illus.). 64p. (gr. 3-6). 1977. PLB 5.99 (ISBN 0-698-30665-1, Coward). Putnam Pub Group.

--Who's in Charge of Lincoln? LC 65-13286. (Illus.). 61p. (gr. 2-4). 1965. 5.99 (ISBN 0-698-30406-3, Coward). Putnam Pub Group.

Fifer, Bill. Metal Projects, Book 2. 96p. 1981. 5.40 (ISBN 0-87006-172-0). Goodheart.

Fifer, C. N. The Correspondence of James Boswell with Certain Members of the Club. 1976. 22.50 (ISBN 0-07-020750-X, P&RB). McGraw.

Fifer, Ken. Falling Man. LC 79-15032. 75p. 1979. 4.00 (ISBN 0-87886-105-X). Ithaca Hse.

Fifield, Sarah A. Train Whistles. LC 81-51156. (Collaboration of Southwest Writers & Artists Ser.). 53p. 1981. pap. 10.00 (ISBN 0-686-96957-X). SarSan Pub.

Fifield, William. In Search of Genius. LC 82-8193. 1982. 13.95 (ISBN 0-688-03717-8). Morrow.

Fifth International Symposium on Organic Solid State Chemistry, Brandeis Univ., June 1978. Molecular Crystals & Liquid Crystals Special Topics: Proceedings, 2 pts. Adler, G., ed. 632p. 1979. 460.00x (ISBN 0-677-40265-1). Gordon.

Fifth Symposium, Nov. 19-22, 1977. Toward Human Dignity: Social Work in Practice. Hanks, John W., ed. LC 78-65076. 269p. 1978. pap. 12.95x (ISBN 0-87101-079-8, CBO-079-C). Natl Assn Soc Wkrs.

Figes, E. Sex & Subterfuge: Women Novelists to 1850. 1982. 50.00x (ISBN 0-333-29208-1, Pub. by Macmillan England). State Mutual Bk.

Figge, Frank H., ed. see Sobotta, Johannes.

Figler, Homer R. Overcoming Executive Midlife Crisis. LC 77-29206. 1978. 16.95x o.p. (ISBN 0-471-04147-5, Pub. by Wiley-Interscience). Wiley.

Figler, Howard E. Path: A Career Workbook for Liberal Arts Students. LC 74-12041. 1979. 6.75x (ISBN 0-910328-07-2). Carroll Pr.

Figler, Howard E., jt. auth. see Drum, David J.

Figley, Charles R. & McCubbin, Hamilton I., eds. Stress & the Family: Coping with Catastrophe, Vol. II. 300p. 1983. price not set (ISBN 0-87630-332-7). Brunner-Mazel.

Figley, Charles R., jt. ed. see McCubbin, Hamilton I.

Figliuzzi, Richard M. An Aircraft in Trouble. 1983. 7.95 (ISBN 0-533-05401-X). Vantage.

Figner, Vera N. Memoirs of a Revolutionist. Daniels, Camilla-Chapin, et al, trs. LC 68-30820. (Illus.). 1968. Repr. of 1927 ed. lib. bdg. 17.00x (ISBN 0-8371-0418-1, FIRE). Greenwood.

Figueiredo, D. G. de see De Figueiredo, D. G.

Figueiredo, J. L. Progress in Catalyst Deactivation. 1982. lib. bdg. 49.50 (ISBN 90-247-2690-5, Pub. by Martinus Nijhoff Netherlands). Kluwer Boston.

Figueras, J., ed. Skiing Safety II. (International Series on Sport Sciences). 336p. 1978. text ed. 24.95 o.p. (ISBN 0-8391-1209-2). Univ Park.

Figueroa, Gonzalo, jt. auth. see Mulloy, William.

Figueroa, John J. Ignoring Hurts. LC 76-16342. (Orig.). 1976. 14.00 o.s.i. (ISBN 0-914478-43-5); pap. 7.00 o.s.i. (ISBN 0-914478-44-3). Three Continents.

--Society, Schools & Progress in the West Indies. 1971. inquire for price o.p. (ISBN 0-08-016174-X). Pergamon.

Figueroa, Jose. A Manifesto to the Mexican Republic. Hutchinson, C. Alan, tr. LC 76-47992. 1978. 24.50 (ISBN 0-520-03347-7). U of Cal Pr.

Figulla, H. H. Business Documents of the New Babylonian Period. (Ur Excavations: Texts No.4). (Illus.). 1949. 25.00x (ISBN 0-686-17773-8). Univ Mus of U PA.

Figurski, Leszek. Finality & Intelligence. LC 78-62252. 1978. pap. text ed. 9.75 (ISBN 0-8191-0565-1). U Pr of Amer.

Fike, J. L. & Friend, G. E. Understanding Telephone Electronics. (Understanding Ser.). (Illus.). 272p. 1983. pap. 6.95 (ISBN 0-686-84797-0, 7141). Tex Instr Inc.

Fikrig, Senih M., ed. Handbook of Immunology for Students & House Staff. LC 82-6878. (Illus.). 216p. 1982. pap. 28.50x (ISBN 0-89573-111-8). Verlag Chemie.

Filby, D. E., jt. auth. see Cox, S. W.

Filby, P. William. American & British Genealogy & Heraldry: A Selected List of Books. 2nd ed. LC 75-29383. 1976. 25.00 o.p. (ISBN 0-8389-0203-0). ALA.

Filby, P. William, ed. Passenger & Immigration Lists Bibliography (1538-1900) Being a Guide to Published Lists of Arrivals in the United States & Canada. 200p. 1981. 56.00x (ISBN 0-8103-1098-8). Gale.

--Passenger & Immigration Lists Index: A Reference Guide to Published Lists of About 500,000 Passengers Who Arrived in America in the Seventeenth, Eighteenth & Nineteenth Centuries, 3 vols. 1981. Set. 285.00x (ISBN 0-8103-1099-6). Gale.

--Philadelphia Naturalization Records, 1789-1880: Index to Records of Aliens' Declarations of Intention and - or Oaths of Allegiance. 700p. 1982. 170.00x (ISBN 0-8103-1116-X). Gale.

Filby, P. William, jt. ed. see Meyer, Mary K.

Filek, Werner Von see Von Filek, Werner.

Filey, Michael. Toronto Album: Glimpses of the City That Was. LC 70-19204. (Illus.). 1970. pap. 10.95 o.p. (ISBN 0-8020-6350-0). U of Toronto Pr.

Filing Committee of the Resources & Technical Services Division American Library Association. ALA Filing Rules. LC 80-22186. 62p. 1980. pap. 5.00 (ISBN 0-8389-3255-X). ALA.

Filipiniana Book Guild & Scott, William H., eds. German Travelers on the Cordillera (1860-1890, Vol. 23. 1975. 16.50x (ISBN 0-686-18669-9). Cellar.

Filipovic, R. Croatian-English, English-Croatian Small Pocket Dictionary. 1977. pap. 10.00x (ISBN 0-89918-727-7, Y-727). Vanous.

Filipovic, R., et al. English-Croatian or Serbian Dictionary. 11th ed. 1980. 60.00x (ISBN 0-89918-779-X, Y-779). Vanous.

Filipovitch, Anthony & Reeves, Earl, eds. Urban Community: A Guide to Information Sources. LC 78-13171. (The Urban Studies Information Guide Ser.: Vol. 4). 1978. 42.00x (ISBN 0-8103-1429-0). Gale.

Filippo, Eduardo De see De Filippo, Eduardo.

Filippone, Samuel R. & Williams, Michael Z. Elementary Mathematics: A Fundamentals & Techniques Approach. LC 75-19539. (Illus.). 448p. 1976. text ed. 23.50 (ISBN 0-395-20028-8); instr's. manual 3.50 (ISBN 0-395-20029-6). HM.

Filippov, V. V. Quality Control Procedures for Meteorological Use. (World Weather Watch Planning Report Ser.: No. 26). 1968. pap. 12.00 (ISBN 0-685-22334-5, W238, WMO). Unipub.

Fillard, J. P. & Van Turnhout, J., eds. Thermally Stimulated Processes in Solids - New Prospects: Proceedings of an International Workshop, Montpellier, June, 1976. 1978. 68.00 (ISBN 0-444-41652-8). Elsevier.

Filler, Louis. Appointment at Armageddon: Muckraking & Progressivism in American Life. LC 75-23865. (Contributions in American Studies: No. 20). (Illus.). 476p. 1976. lib. bdg. 29.95 (ISBN 0-8371-8261-1, FAR/). Greenwood.

--Dictionary of American Social Change. rev. ed. LC 82-10036. 266p. 1982. 16.50 (ISBN 0-89874-242-0); pap. 10.50 (ISBN 0-89874-564-0). Krieger.

--The Muckrakers. rev. ed. LC 75-27152. Orig. Title: Crusaders for American Liberalism. (Illus.). 466p. 1975. 20.00x (ISBN 0-271-01212-9); pap. 10.75 (ISBN 0-271-01213-7). Pa St U Pr.

--The Rise & Fall of Slavery in America. ix, 165p. 1981. lib. bdg. 10.95x (ISBN 0-89198-122-5); pap. text ed. 6.95x (ISBN 0-89198-123-3). Ozer.

--Voice of the Democracy: A Critical Biography of David Graham Phillips, Journalist, Novelist, Progressive. LC 77-13893. 1978. 18.75x (ISBN 0-271-00528-9). Pa St U Pr.

Filler, Louis, ed. The President in the Twentieth Century, Vol. I: The Ascendant President: From William McKinley to Lyndon B. Johnson. rev. ed. 424p. 1983. lib. bdg. 22.95 (ISBN 0-89198-127-6); pap. text ed. 10.95 (ISBN 0-89198-128-4). Ozer.

Filler, Louis, ed. see Phillips, Wendell.

Filley, Alan C. Interpersonal Conflict Resolution. 180p. 1975. pap. 10.95x (ISBN 0-673-07589-3). Scott F.

Filley, Dorothy M. Recapturing Wisdom's Valley: The Watervliet Shaker Heritage, 1775-1975. Richmond, Mary L., ed. LC 75-27133. (Illus.). 128p. 1975. 10.00 o.p. (ISBN 0-89062-010-5, Pub by Albany Institute of History & Art); pap. 5.00 o.p. (ISBN 0-89062-029-6). Pub Ctr Cult Res.

Filley, Richard D. & Szoka, Kathryn. Communicating with Graphics: A Series from Industrial Engineering. 1982. pap. text ed. 19.50 (ISBN 0-89806-036-2); pap. text ed. 15.00 members. Inst Indus Eng.

Fillian, Barbia & Livingston, Lida. Eat Yourself Thin. 1979. pap. text ed. 3.95 o.p. (ISBN 0-448-16800-6, G&D). Putnam Pub Group.

Fillingham, Patricia. Progress Notes on a State of Mind. 64p. 1980. pap. 2.00 (ISBN 0-686-36234-9). Warthog Pr.

Fillmore, Donna. Leading Children In Worship, Vol. 2. 216p. 1982. pap. 7.95 (ISBN 0-8341-0767-8). Beacon Hill.

Filmer, Edward. A Defence of Plays: The Stage Vindicated from...Mr. Collier's Short View. LC 70-170449. (The English Stage Ser.: Vol. 36). lib. bdg. 50.00 o.s.i. (ISBN 0-8240-0619-4). Garland Pub.

Filmer, Paul, et al. New Directions in Sociological Theory. 246p. 1974. 17.50x (ISBN 0-262-06050-7); pap. 5.95 o.p. (ISBN 0-262-56014-3). MIT Pr.

Filov, V. A., et al. Quantitative Toxicology (Selected Topics) LC 78-12530. (Environmental Science & Technology Ser.). 1980. 73.95 (ISBN 0-471-02109-1, Pub. by Wiley-Interscience). Wiley.

Filsinger, Cheryl. Locus. 4th ed. 192p. 1982. pap. 35.00 (ISBN 0-916754-02-2). Filsinger & Co.

Filskov, Susan B. & Boll, Thomas J. Handbook of Clinical Neuropsychology. LC 80-15392. (Personality Processes Ser.). 806p. 1981. 39.95x (ISBN 0-471-04802-X, Pub. by Wiley-Interscience). Wiley.

Filson, F. V., jt. ed. see Wright, G. Ernest.

Filson, Floyd V. John. LC 59-10454. (Layman's Bible Commentary Ser: Vol. 19). 1963. pap. 3.95 (ISBN 0-8042-3079-X). John Knox.

--A New Testament History: The Story of the Emerging Church. LC 64-15360. 1964. 12.95 (ISBN 0-664-20525-9). Westminster.
Filson, John. Discovery, Settlement & Present State of Kentucke. 8.00 (ISBN 0-8446-2058-0). Peter Smith.
Filson, Sidney. How to Protect Yourself & Survive: From One Woman to Another. (Illus.). 1979. 8.95 o.p. (ISBN 0-531-09905-9). Watts.
Filstead, William, jt. ed. see Mayer, John E.
Filstead, William J., et al, eds. Alcohol & Alcohol Problems: New Thinking & New Directions. LC 76-7401. 320p. 1976. prof ref 22.00x (ISBN 0-88410-115-0). Ballinger Pub.
Filstrup, Chris & Filstrup, Janie. China: From Emperors to Communes. Schneider, Tom, ed. (Discovering Our Heritage Ser.). (Illus.). 144p. (gr. 5 up). 1982. PLB 9.95 (ISBN 0-87518-227-5). Dillon.
Filstrup, Janie, jt. auth. see Filstrup, Chris.
Filtzer, Donald A., ed. see Preobrazhensky, E. A.
Fimbres, Eric C. Approaching Re-Creation: A Form for Seeing the Delicate Threads. LC 82-90184. (Illus.). 208p. (Orig.). 1982. pap. 5.95 (ISBN 0-9608946-0-8). Life Sustaining.
Finaly, Patrick, ed. Jane's Freight Containers, 1982. (Jane's Yearbooks). (Illus.). 640p. 1982. 140.00 (ISBN 0-86720-613-6). Sci Bks Intl.
Finan, John J. & Child, John, eds. Latin America: International Relations: A Guide to Information Sources. LC 73-117508. (International Relations Information Guide Ser.: Vol.11). 250p. 1981. 42.00x (ISBN 0-8103-1325-1). Gale.
Finance, Charles. Buffet Catering. (Illus.). text ed. 26.95x (ISBN 0-911202-02-1). Radio City.
Financial Accounting Standards Board. Accounting Standards: Vol. 1: Original Pronouncements as of June 1, 1982. 1800p. 22.50x (ISBN 0-07-020821-2). McGraw.
--Accounting Standards: Vol. 2: Current Text As of June 1, 1982. 1800p. 1982. 24.50 (ISBN 0-07-020822-0). McGraw.
--Financial Accounting Standards Board Current Text 1982-1984. 1800p. 1982. loose leaf ed.-domestic 210.00 (ISBN 0-07-020901-4). McGraw.
--Financial Accounting Standards Board Current Text 1982-1984: International. 1800p. 1982. loose leaf ed.-international 300.00 (ISBN 0-07-020902-2). McGraw.
Financial Times Business Publishing Ltd., ed. British Banking Directory. 1982. 125.00x (ISBN 0-902998-42-0, Pub. by Finan Times England). State Mutual Bk.
--Japanese Banking & Capital Markets. 1982. 150.00x (ISBN 0-686-82306-0, Pub. by Finan Times England). State Mutual Bk.
--Offshore Financial Centres. 1982. 159.00x (ISBN 0-902998-41-2, Pub. by Finan Times England). State Mutual Bk.
Financial Times Staff, ed. Financial Times Who's Who in World Oil & Gas: 1982-83. 600p. 1982. text ed. 75.00x (ISBN 0-582-90313-0). Longman.
--World Hotel Directory 1982-83. 900p. 1982. 50.00 (ISBN 0-582-90314-9). Longman.
--World Insurance Yearbook 1982. 500p. 1982. 90.00 (ISBN 0-582-90312-2). Longman.
Finar, I. L. Stereochemistry & the Chemistry of Natural Products. 2nd ed. (Organic Chemistry Ser.: Vol. 2). 834p. 1959. 24.95x o.s.i. (ISBN 0-471-25888-1). Halsted Pr.
Finberg, H. P., jt. auth. see Beresford, Maurice W.
Finberg, H. P., ed. Agrarian History of England & Wales, Vol. 1, Pt. 2: A.D. 43-1042. LC 66-19763. (Illus.). 600p. 1972. 79.50 (ISBN 0-521-08423-7). Cambridge U Pr.
Finberg, Harris J., ed. Case Studies in Diagnostic Ultrasound, Vol. 9. (Clinics in Diagnostic Ultrasound Ser.). (Illus.). 260p. 1981. 22.00 (ISBN 0-686-37166-6). Churchill.
Finberg, Joscelyne. Exploring Villages. 12.50 (ISBN 0-392-15845-0, SpS). Sportshelf.
Finby, Malcolm E., jt. ed. see Pitts, John D.
Finby, N., jt. auth. see Chynn, K. Y.
Finch, A. F., ed. Yearbook Nineteen, 1983. (Theilheimer's Synthetic Methods of Organic Chemistry: Vol. 37). 540p. 1983. 298.25 (ISBN 3-8055-3600-3). S Karger.
Finch, Bill, jt. auth. see Finch, Elizabeth.
Finch, C. A., ed. Polyvinyl Alcohol. LC 72-8599. 622p. 1973. 106.75 o.p. (ISBN 0-471-25892-X, Pub. by Wiley-Interscience). Wiley.
Finch, Christopher. Making of the Dark Crystal. (Illus.). 96p. 1983. pap. 10.95 (ISBN 0-686-84850-0). HR&W.
--Norman Rockwell. LC 79-57405. (Abbeville Library of Art: No. 5). (Illus.). 112p. 1980. pap. 4.95 o.p. (ISBN 0-89659-090-9). Abbeville Pr.
--Rainbow: The Stormy Life of Judy Garland. LC 74-5632. (Illus.). 256p. 1975. pap. 4.95 (ISBN 0-448-11731-2, G&D); pap. 7.95 (ISBN 0-448-12142-5). Putnam Pub Group.
Finch, Christopher & Ramachandran, Srinivasa. Matchmaking: Science Technology & Manufacturing. 220p. 1983. 65.00x (ISBN 0-470-27371-2). Halsted Pr.
Finch, Curtis R. & McGough, Robert C. Administering & Supervising Vocational Education. 352p. 1982. 19.95 (ISBN 0-13-004838-0). P-H.
Finch, Elizabeth & Finch, Bill. Photo-Chromotherapy. 3.50 (ISBN 0-686-97350-X). Esoteric Pubns.
Finch, F. E., et al. Managing for Organizational Effectiveness: An Experiential Approach. (Management Ser). 1975. text ed. 18.95 (ISBN 0-07-020899-9, C). McGraw.
Finch, Frank. Concise Encyclopedia of Management Techniques. 1976. 18.95 (ISBN 0-434-90240-3, Pub. by Heinemann). David & Charles.
Finch, Henry L. Wittgenstein, the Early Philosophy: An Exposition of the Tractatus. LC 73-135985. 1982. text ed. 17.50x (ISBN 0-391-00123-X). Humanities.
--Wittgenstein-the Later Philosophy: An Exposition of the Philosophical Investigations. LC 76-46421. 1977. text ed. 17.50x (ISBN 0-391-00680-0). Humanities.
Finch, I. J. General Studies: First Handbook for Technical Students. 1965. 16.25 o.p. (ISBN 0-08-011106-8); pap. 7.00 o.p. (ISBN 0-08-011105-X). Pergamon.
Finch, Janet. Married to the Job: Wives' Incorporation in Men's Work. 170p. 1983. text ed. 18.95x (ISBN 0-04-301149-7). Allen Unwin.
Finch, Jay S., jt. auth. see DeKornfeld, Thomas J.
Finch, Jeremiah S. Sir Thomas Browne: A Doctor's Life of Science & Faith. 319p. 1982. Repr. of 1950 ed. lib. bdg. 40.00 (ISBN 0-89760-237-4). Telegraph Bks.
Finch, Philip. Storm Front. (Fic). 1977. 7.95 o.p. (ISBN 0-698-10830-2, Coward). Putnam Pub Group.
Finch, Phillip. Birthright. 1981. pap. 2.75 o.p. (ISBN 0-425-04590-0). Berkley Pub.
--Toxin L. 240p. 1981. pap. 2.50 o.p. (ISBN 0-425-04927-2). Berkley Pub.
Finch, R., jt. auth. see Reed, Jeanne.
Finch, Richard C. A Study Guide to Putnam's Geology. 4th ed. (Illus.). 200p. 1982. text ed. 25.95x (ISBN 0-19-503002-8); tchr's manual avail. (ISBN 0-19-503004-4); wkbk. 7.95x (ISBN 0-19-503003-6). Oxford U Pr.
Finch, Robert. The Primal Place. 1983. 14.50x (ISBN 0-393-01623-4). Norton.
Fincham, J. R. A Study of Genetic Recombination. rev. ed. Head, J. J., ed. LC 77-75593. (Biology Readers Ser.). (Illus.). 16p. (gr. 11 up). 1983. pap. 1.60 (ISBN 0-89278-202-1, 45-9602). Carolina Biological.
Fincham, W. H. & Freeman, M. H. Optics. 8th ed. 29.95 o.p. (ISBN 0-407-93421-9). Butterworth.
Fincher, Beatrice, ed. Funds for Hispanics. LC 81-90470. 36p. (Orig.). 1981. pap. 15.00 (ISBN 0-9607386-0-6). Spanish Pub.
Fincher, E. B. The Bill of Rights. LC 77-10890. (First Books Ser.). (Illus.). (gr. 4-6). 1978. PLB 8.90 s&l (ISBN 0-531-01347-2). Watts.
--Mexico & the United States: Their Linked Destinies. LC 82-45581. (Illus.). 224p. (YA) (gr. 7 up). 1983. 10.10i (ISBN 0-690-04310-4, TYC-J); PLB 10.89g (ISBN 0-690-04311-2). Har-Row.
--The War in Korea. (First Bks.). (Illus.). 72p. (gr. 4 up). 1981. lib. bdg. 8.90 (ISBN 0-531-04330-4). Watts.
Fincher, Ernest B. Government of the United States. 3rd ed: (Illus.). 384p. 1976. pap. 15.95 (ISBN 0-13-361881-1). P-H.
Fincher, Jack. Lefties: The Origins & Consequences of Being Left-Handed. 1980. pap. 4.95 (ISBN 0-399-50460-5, Perigee). Putnam Pub Group.
--Sinister People: The Looking-Glass World of the Left-Hander. 1977. 7.95 o.p. (ISBN 0-399-11839-X). Putnam Pub Group.
Finck, H. T. My Adventures in the Golden Age of Music. LC 70-87496. (Music Ser.). 462p. 1971. Repr. of 1926 ed. lib. bdg. 45.00 (ISBN 0-306-71448-5). Da Capo.
Finck, Henry T. Musical Laughs: Jokes, Tittle-Tattle, & Anecdotes, Mostly Humorous, About Musical Celebrities. LC 79-159955. 1971. Repr. of 1924 ed. 34.00x (ISBN 0-8103-3397-X). Gale.
Fincke, Gary. Victims. 64p. 1974. 4.00 (ISBN 0-911838-36-8). Windy Row.
Finckenauer, James O. Scared Straight: & the Panacea Phenomenon. (Prentice Hall Criminal Justice Ser.). (Illus.). 288p. 1982. pap. 15.95 (ISBN 0-13-791558-6). P-H.
Finckh, E. & Clayton-Jones, E., eds. Anatomical & Clinical Pathology. (International Congress Ser.: No. 369). (Abstracts). 1977. pap. 31.25 (ISBN 0-686-43410-2). Elsevier.
Findeisen, W., et al. Control & Coordination in Hierarchical Systems. (IIASA International Ser. on Applied Systems Analysis: No. 9). 469p. 1980. 63.95x (ISBN 0-471-27742-8). Wiley.
Finder, Joseph. Red Carpet. (A New Republic Bk.). (Illus.). 336p. Date not set. 16.95 (ISBN 0-03-060484-2). HR&W.
Finder, Morris. Reason & Art in Teaching Secondary-School English. LC 76-9554. 217p. 1976. text ed. 19.95 (ISBN 0-87722-071-9). Temple U Pr.
Findhorn Community. The Findhorn Garden. 1976. pap. 6.97i (ISBN 0-06-090520-4, CN520, CN). Har-Row.
Findlay, Allan M., et al. Tunisia. (World Bibliographical Ser.: Vol. 33). 249p. 1982. 36.00 (ISBN 0-903450-63-1). ABC-Clio.
Findlay, Elsa. Rhythm & Movement: Applications of Dalcroze Eurhythmics. LC 71-169706. 1971. pap. 10.95 (ISBN 0-87487-078-X). Summy.
Findlay, J. N. Hegel: A Re-Examination. LC 76-12155. 372p. 1976. pap. 6.95 (ISBN 0-19-519879-4, 473, GB). Oxford U Pr.
Findlay, John N. Psyche & Cerebrum. (Aquinas Lecture, 1972). 52p. 1972. 7.95 (ISBN 0-87462-137-2). Marquette.
Findlay, L. M., ed. see Swinburne, Algernon C.
Findlay, M. C., jt. ed. see Whitmore, G. A.
Findlay, Michael. Kittens & Cats. LC 80-52200. (Whizz Kids Ser.). 8.00 (ISBN 0-382-06456-9). Silver.
Findlay, R., jt. auth. see Brockett, O.
Findlay, Ted & Beasley, Conger, Jr., eds. Above the Thunder. LC 82-72730. (Orig.). 1982. pap. 9.95 (ISBN 0-89334-039-1). Humanics Ltd.
--Above the Thunder: A Collection of Personal Experiences from Concern Counts. LC 82-72730. (Illus.). 255p. (Orig.). 1982. pap. 6.95 (ISBN 0-686-38089-4). Concern Counts.
Findlay, William & Watt, David A. PASCAL: An Introduction to Methodical Programming. 2nd ed. (Illus.). 1982. pap. text ed. 16.95x (ISBN 0-914894-73-0). Computer Sci.
Findler, N. & Meltzer. Artificial Intelligence & Heuristic Programming. 1971. 23.50 (ISBN 0-444-19597-1). Elsevier.
Findley, Timothy. Famous Last Words. 1983. pap. 3.95 (ISBN 0-440-32543-9, LE). Dell.
--The Wars. 1983. pap. 3.95 (ISBN 0-440-39239-X, LE). Dell.
Findley, W., et al. Creep & Relaxation of Nonlinear Viscoelastic Materials. 1976. 72.50 (ISBN 0-444-10775-4). Elsevier.
Findling, John E. Dictionary of American Diplomatic History. LC 79-7730. (Illus.). 1980. lib. bdg. 45.00 (ISBN 0-313-22039-5, FDD/). Greenwood.
Findlow, Virginia H. Hysterical Histories. LC 77-189519. 88p. 1972. 5.00 (ISBN 0-911838-19-8). Windy Row.
Fine, David M. The City, the Immigrant, & American Fiction, 1880-1920. LC 77-6297. 1977. 11.00 o.p. (ISBN 0-8108-1038-7). Scarecrow.
Fine, Ellen S. Legacy of Night: The Literary Universe of Elie Wiesel. LC 81-14601. (Modern Jewish Literature & Culture Ser.). 276p. 1982. 33.50x (ISBN 0-87395-589-7); pap. 10.95x (ISBN 0-87395-590-0). State U NY Pr.
Fine, Elsa H. The Afro-American Artist. LC 81-82922. (Illus.). 300p. 1983. Repr. of 1973 ed. lib. bdg. 35.00 (ISBN 0-87817-287-4). Hacker.
Fine, John V. The Early Medieval Balkans: A Critical Survey from the Sixth to the Late Twelfth Century. LC 82-8452. (Illus.). 368p. 1983. text ed. 29.95x (ISBN 0-472-10025-4). U of Mich Pr.
Fine, Jonathan & Freedle, Roy O. Developmental Issues in Discourse. (Advances in Discourse Processes Ser.: Vol. 10). 336p. 1983. text ed. 32.50 (ISBN 0-686-82457-1); pap. text ed. 16.50 (ISBN 0-89391-161-5). Ablex Pub.
Fine, Leonard W. Chemistry Decoded. (Illus.). 1976. text ed. 13.95x o.p. (ISBN 0-19-501886-9). Oxford U Pr.
Fine, Linda. How to Make the Most of the New You. LC 80-27861. 208p. 1981. 11.95 o.p. (ISBN 0-668-04919-7); pap. 6.95 o.p. (ISBN 0-668-04923-5). Arco.
Fine, Marvin J. Parents V. Children: Making the Relationship Work. 1979. 9.95t (ISBN 0-13-649947-3, Spec); pap. 3.95 o.p. (ISBN 0-13-649939-2). P-H.
Fine, Morris, et al, eds. American Jewish Year Book, 1980, Vol. 80. 650p. 1980. 15.00 o.p. (ISBN 0-8276-0173-5, 454). Jewish Pubn.
Fine, Reuben. The Healing of the Mind. 416p. 1982. text ed. 39.95. Free Pr.
--Lessons From My Games: A Passion for Chess. (Illus.). 256p. 1983. pap. 4.95 (ISBN 0-486-24429-6). Dover.
--The Logic of Psychology: A Dynamic Approach. LC 82-21983. 232p. (Orig.). 1983. lib. bdg. 20.50 (ISBN 0-8191-2891-0); pap. text ed. 10.50 (ISBN 0-8191-2892-9). U Pr of Amer.
--Middle Game in Chess. 1952. pap. 8.95 (ISBN 0-679-14021-2, Tartan). McKay.
Fine, Reuben, jt. ed. see Reinfeld, Fred.
Fine, Ruth E. Lessing J. Rosenwald: Tribute to a Collector. LC 81-14133. (Illus.). pap. 19.95 (ISBN 0-89468-004-8). Natl Gallery Art.
Fine, Sidney. Laissez Faire & the General-Welfare State: A Study of Conflict in American Thought, 1865-1901. 1964. pap. 9.95 (ISBN 0-472-06086-4, 86, AA). U of Mich Pr.
Fine, Stuart. Retinal Vascular & Macular Disorders. (Illus.). 390p. 1983. lib. bdg. price not set (ISBN 0-683-03212-7). Williams & Wilkins.
Fine, Stuart L. & Patz, Arnall. Sights & Sounds in Ophthalmology: Vol. 4, Diabetic Retinopathy. (Illus.). 64p. 1980. pap. 199.00 (ISBN 0-8016-3767-8). Mosby.
Fine, Stuart L., ed. see Miller, Neil R.
Fine, Stuart L., et al. Sights & Sounds in Ophthalmology: Retinal Vascular Disorders, Diagnosis & Management, Vol 2. LC 76-46869. (Illus.). 1976. pap. 199.00 (ISBN 0-8016-3762-7). Mosby.
Fine Woodworking Magazine Editors. Fine Woodworking Design Book Two. LC 78-68950. (Illus.). 288p. 1979. 15.95 (ISBN 0-918804-08-6, Dist. by Van Nostrand Reinhold); pap. 11.95 (ISBN 0-918804-07-8). Taunton.
--Fine Woodworking Techniques 3. LC 81-50953. (Illus.). 232p. 1981. 16.95 (ISBN 0-918804-10-8, Dist. by Van Nostrand Reinhold). Taunton.
--Fine Woodworking Techniques 4. LC 78-58221. (Illus.). 232p. 1982. 16.95 (ISBN 0-918804-13-2, Dist. by Van Nostrand Reinhold). Taunton.
Fine Woodworking Magazine Staff, ed. Fine Woodworking Techniques Five. (Illus.). 232p. 1983. 16.95 (ISBN 0-918804-17-5). Taunton.
Finean, J. B. & Michell, R. H., eds. Membrane Structure. (New Comprehensive Biochemistry Ser.: Vol. 1). 1981. 64.25 (ISBN 0-444-80304-1). Elsevier.
Fineberg, Harvey, jt. auth. see Neustadt, Richard.
Fineberg, Keith S., et al. Obstetrics-Gynecology & the Law. 650p. 1983. text ed. price not set (ISBN 0-914904-85-X). Health Admin Pr.
Finegan, Edward. Attitudes Toward English Usage: A History of the War of Words. 1980. pap. 10.95x (ISBN 0-8077-2581-1). Tchrs Coll.
Finegan, Jack. Archaeological History of the Ancient Middle East. (Illus.). 1979. lib. bdg. 40.00 (ISBN 0-89158-164-2, Dawson). Westview.
Finegold, jt. auth. see Seitz.
Finelli, Pasquale F. Diagnostic Reference Index of Clinical Neurology: A Problem-Oriented Approach. 380p. 1980. lib. bdg. 35.00 o.p. (ISBN 0-683-03215-1). Williams & Wilkins.
Fineman, Mark. The Home Darkroom. 2nd ed. LC 72-79608. (Illus.). 96p. 1976. pap. 5.95 (ISBN 0-8174-0555-0, Amphoto); Spanish Ed. pap. 6.95 o.p. (ISBN 0-8174-0325-6). Watson-Guptill.
--The Inquisitive Eye. (Illus.). 1981. pap. text ed. 9.95x (ISBN 0-19-502773-6). Oxford U Pr.
Fineman, Stephen. White Collar Unemployment. (Organizational Change & Development Ser.). 180p. 1982. 29.95 (ISBN 0-471-10490-6, Pub. by Wiley-Interscience). Wiley.
Finer, Herman. Road to Reaction. LC 77-9010. 1977. Repr. of 1945 ed. lib. bdg. 19.25x (ISBN 0-8371-9726-0, FIRR). Greenwood.
--The T. V. A. Lessons for International Application. LC 77-172008. (FDR & the Era of the New Deal Ser.). (Illus.). 1972. Repr. of 1944 ed. lib. bdg. 39.50 (ISBN 0-306-70378-5). Da Capo.
Finer, S. E., ed. Five Constitutions: Contrasts & Comparisons. (Orig.). 1979. pap. 5.95 (ISBN 0-14-022203-0, Pelican). Penguin.
Fineran, J. M. A Taxonomic Revision of the Genus Entorrhiza C. Weber (Ustilaginales) (Nova Hedwigia Ser.). (Illus.). 1979. pap. text ed. 10.00 (ISBN 3-7682-1211-4). Lubrecht & Cramer.
Finestone, Albert J., ed. Evaluation & Clinical Management of Dizziness & Vertigo. (Illus.). 268p. 1982. casebound 25.00 (ISBN 0-7236-7003-X). Wright-PSG.
Finestone, Harold. Victims of Change: Juvenile Delinquents in American Society. LC 76-5327. (Contributions in Sociology: No. 20). (Illus.). 256p. 1976. lib. bdg. 27.50 (ISBN 0-8371-8897-0, FTD/). Greenwood.
Finetti, Bruno De see De Finetti, Bruno.
Fingado, Dorothy & McMillen, Loretta. Richmondtown Receipts-Three Centuries of Staten Island Cookery. (Illus.). 1976. spiral bdg. 5.00 (ISBN 0-686-20333-X). Staten Island.
Fingar, Elmer L., et al. New York Wills & Trusts: Laws, Forms & Taxes, 2 vols. rev. 2nd ed. LC 61-9883. 1971. losseleaf with 1979 suppl. 110.00 (ISBN 0-87632-062-0). Boardman.
Fingar, Thomas, ed. China's Quest for Independence: Policy Evolution in the Nineteen Seventy's. (Westview Special Studies on China & East Asia). 245p. 1980. 27.00 (ISBN 0-89158-570-2). Westview.
Fingard, Judith. Jack in Port: Sailortowns of Eastern Canada. (Social History in Canada Ser.). (Illus.). 292p. 1982. 35.00x (ISBN 0-8020-2458-0); pap. 12.50 (ISBN 0-8020-6467-1). U of Toronto Pr.
Fingarette, Herbert. The Meaning of Criminal Insanity. LC 70-165223. 300p. 1972. 30.00x (ISBN 0-520-02082-0); pap. 6.95x (ISBN 0-520-02631-4). U of Cal Pr.
--The Self in Transformation: Psychoanalysis, Philosophy & the Life of the Spirit. LC 63-12846. 1977. pap. 6.95x (ISBN 0-06-131177-4, TB1177, Torch). Har-Row.
Fingarette, Herbert & Hasse, Ann F. Mental Disabilities & Criminal Responsibilities. LC 77-91756. 1979. 28.50x (ISBN 0-520-03630-1). U of Cal Pr.
Finger, Ellis, jt. auth. see Bergethon, K. Roald.
Finger, Larry W., jt. auth. see Hazen, Robert M.
Finger, Seymour M. & Harbert, Joseph R., eds. U. S. Policy in International Institutions: Defining Reasonable Options in an Unreasonable World. rev. & updated ed. (Special Studies in International Relations). 200p. (Orig.). 1982. lib. bdg. 22.00; pap. 10.00 (ISBN 0-86531-106-4). Westview.
--U. S. Policy in International Institutions: Defining Reasonable Options in an Unreasonable World. LC 78-4335. (Special Studies in International Relations & U.S. Foreign Policy Ser.). (Illus.). 1978. lib. bdg. 38.50 (ISBN 0-89158-077-8); pap. text ed. 15.00 (ISBN 0-89158-078-6). Westview.
Finger, Stanley & Stein, Donald. Brain Damage & Recovery: Research & Clinical Perspectives. (Historical & Contemporary Issues Ser.). 352p. 1982. 39.50 (ISBN 0-12-256780-3). Acad Pr.

Finger, William R., ed. The Tobacco Industry in Transition: Policies for the Nineteen Eighties. LC 81-47064. 352p. 1981. 24.95x (ISBN 0-669-04552-7). Lexington Bks.

Fingerhut, Astri & Baker, Carol, eds. The Book of Festivals in the Midwest, 1983 & 1984. (Illus.). 1983. pap. 9.95 (ISBN 0-89651-056-5). Icarus.

Fingerhut, Bruce M. & Haskin, Steve. Read That Label: How to Tell What's Inside a Wine Bottle from What's on the Outside. (Illus.). 100p. (Orig.). 1983. pap. 4.95 (ISBN 0-89651-652-0). Icarus.

Fingerhut, Eugene R. Survivor: Cadwallader Colden II in Revolutionary America. LC 82-20092. (Illus.). 200p. (Orig.). 1983. lib. bdg. 21.75 (ISBN 0-8191-2868-6); pap. text ed. 10.50 (ISBN 0-8191-2869-4). U Pr of Amer.

Fingleton, David. Kiri Te Kanawa: A Biography. LC 82-73013. 188p. 1983. 13.95 (ISBN 0-689-11345-5). Atheneum.

Finigan, Robert. Finigan on Wine: A Complete Guide to Buying, Tasting, & Enjoying American & European Wines. LC 78-64561. (Illus.). cancelled (ISBN 0-89169-541-9). Reed Bks.

--Robert Finigan's Guide to Distinctive Dining--San Francisco. LC 79-51793. (Illus.). 1980. pap. cancelled o.s.i. (ISBN 0-89169-526-5). Reed Bks.

Finizio, Norman & Ladas, Gerasimons. An Introduction to Differential Equations. 608p. 1981. text ed. 25.95x (ISBN 0-534-00960-3). Wadsworth Pub.

--Ordinary Differential Equations with Modern Applications. 2nd ed. 432p. 1981. text ed. 25.95x (ISBN 0-534-00898-4). Wadsworth Pub.

Fink, Arlene, jt. auth. see Kosecoff, Jacqueline.

Fink, Augusta. I-Mary: A Biography of Mary Austin. 320p. 1983. 17.50 (ISBN 0-8165-0789-9). U of Ariz Pr.

Fink, B. Raymond. The Human Larynx: A Functional Study. LC 74-80536. 207p. 1975. 21.00 (ISBN 0-911216-86-3). Raven.

Fink, B. Raymond, ed. Molecular Mechanisms of Anesthesia. (Progress in Anesthesiology Ser.: Vol. 2). (Illus.). 528p. 1980. text ed. 64.00 (ISBN 0-89004-456-2). Raven.

--Molecular Mechanisms of Anesthesia. LC 74-14474. (Progress in Anesthesiology Ser: Vol. 1). 672p. 1975. 53.00 (ISBN 0-911216-94-4). Raven.

Fink, Diane D. Speedreading for Executives. (Self-Teaching Guides Ser.). 256p. 1981. pap. 9.95 (ISBN 0-471-08407-7). Wiley.

Fink, Donald G. Electronics Engineers' Handbook. 2000p. 1975. 59.95 (ISBN 0-07-020980-4, P&RB). McGraw.

Fink, Donald G. & Beaty, H. Wayne. Standard Handbook for Electrical Engineers. 11th ed. (Illus.). 1978. 65.95 (ISBN 0-07-020974-X, P&RB). McGraw.

Fink, Gary & Reed, Merl E., eds. Essays in Southern Labor History: Selected Papers, Southern Labor History Conference, 1976. LC 77-85. (Contributions in Economics & EconomicHistory: No. 16). 1977. lib. bdg. 27.50 (ISBN 0-8371-9528-4, FES/). Greenwood.

Fink, Gary M. Labor Unions. LC 76-8734. (Greenwood Encyclopedia of American Institutions). 544p. 1977. lib. bdg. 45.00 (ISBN 0-8371-8938-1, FLU/). Greenwood.

--Prelude to the Presidency: The Political Character & Legislative Leadership Style of Governor Jimmy Carter. LC 79-7725. (Contributions in Political Science: No. 40). (Illus.). 1980. lib. bdg. 27.50 (ISBN 0-313-22055-7, FPP/). Greenwood.

Fink, Gary M. & Cantor, Milton, eds. Biographical Dictionary of American Labor Leaders. LC 74-9322. 1974. lib. bdg. 35.00 (ISBN 0-8371-7643-3, FAL/). Greenwood.

Fink, Hans. Social Philosophy. 128p. 1981. 14.50x (ISBN 0-416-71990-2); pap. 6.50x (ISBN 0-416-72000-5). Methuen Inc.

Fink, Howard. The Apartment Carpenter. LC 74-28708. (Illus.). 144p. (Orig.). 1976. pap. 3.95 o.p. (ISBN 0-8256-3053-3, Quick Fox). Putnam Pub Group.

Fink, John W., jt. auth. see Kirkham, E. Bruce.

Fink, Joseph & Sealy, Lloyd G. The Community & the Police: Conflict or Cooperation? LC 74-1144. 216p. 1974. 27.95 o.s.i. (ISBN 0-471-25894-6, Pub. by Wiley-Interscience). Wiley.

--The Community & the Police: Conflict or Cooperation? 216p. Repr. 9.95 o.p. (ISBN 0-686-95017-8). ADL.

Fink, Karl J. & Marchand, James W., eds. The Quest for the New Science: Language & Thought in Eighteenth-Century Science. LC 79-889. 110p. 1979. 7.95x o.p. (ISBN 0-8093-0917-3). S Ill U Pr.

Fink, Kevin. California Corporation Start-Up Package & Minute Book. LC 82-81322. 190p. 1982. 3 ring binder 33.95 (ISBN 0-916378-18-7). PSI Res.

Fink, Leon. Workingmen's Democracy: The Knights of Labor & American Politics. LC 82-6902. (Working Class in American History Ser.). (Illus.). 1983. 19.95 (ISBN 0-252-00999-1). U of Ill Pr.

Fink, Max. Convulsive Therapy: Theory & Practice. LC 77-74618. 319p. 1979. text ed. 28.50 (ISBN 0-89004-221-7). Raven.

Fink, Max, ed. see Symposium on Anticholinergic Drugs & Brain Functions in Animals & Man - 6th - Washington D. C., 1968.

Fink, Max, et al, eds. Psychobiology of Convulsive Therapy. LC 73-21990. 312p. 1974. 11.95x o.s.i. (ISBN 0-470-25901-9). Halsted Pr.

Fink, Michael, jt. auth. see Lofland, John.

Fink, Norman S. & Metzler, Howard C. The Costs & Benefits of Deferred Giving. 24.50 (ISBN 0-686-38899-2). Public Serv Materials.

Fink, Richard H., intro. by. Supply-Side Economics: A Critical Appraisal. LC 82-51294. (Illus.). 488p. 1982. lib. bdg. 27.50 (ISBN 0-89093-460-6, Aletheia Bks); pap. 12.00. U Pubns Amer.

Fink, Robert R. & Ricci, Robert. The Language of Twentieth-Century Music. LC 74-13308. 1975. 15.50 (ISBN 0-02-870600-5). Schirmer Bks.

Fink, William B. Getting to Know New York State. (Getting to Know Ser.). (Illus.). (gr. 3-4). 1971. PLB 3.97 o.p. (ISBN 0-698-30138-2, Coward). Putnam Pub Group.

Finke, Blythe F. Assassination: Case Studies. Rahmas, Sigurd C., ed. (Topics of Our Times Ser.: No. 17). 32p. (Orig.). 1982. 2.95x (ISBN 0-87157-318-0); pap. text ed. 1.95 (ISBN 0-87157-818-2). SamHar Pr.

--Howard R. Hughes, Twentieth Century Multi-Millionaire & Recluse. Rahmas, D. Steve, ed. (Outstanding Personalities Ser.: No. 69). 32p. (Orig.). (gr. 7-12). 1974. lib. bdg. 2.95 incl. catalog cards (ISBN 0-87157-569-8); pap. 1.95 vinyl laminated covers (ISBN 0-87157-069-6). SamHar Pr.

--Our Besieged Environment: The Pollution Problem. new ed. Rahmas, D. Steve, ed. (Topics of Our Times Ser.). 32p. 1975. lib. bdg. 2.95 incl. catalog cards (ISBN 0-87157-815-8); pap. 1.95 vinyl laminated covers (ISBN 0-87157-315-6). SamHar Pr.

Finkel, Ashner J. Hamilton & Hardy's Industrial Toxicology. 432p. 1982. text ed. 42.50 (ISBN 0-7236-7027-7). Wright-PSG.

Finkel, Bruria, tr. see Abulafia, Abraham Ben Samuel.

Finkel, Jules. Computer-Aided Experimentation: Interfacing to Minicomputers. LC 74-22060. 422p. 1975. 42.50x o.p. (ISBN 0-471-25884-9, Pub. by Wiley-Interscience). Wiley.

Finkel, L. Learning Word Processing Concepts Using Apple Writer. 80p. 1982. 7.00 (ISBN 0-07-020986-3, G); instr's manual & key 2.50 (ISBN 0-07-020987-1). McGraw.

Finkel, Lawrence S. & Krawitz, Ruth. Learning English As a Second Language, 3 vols, Level 1, 2, 3. LC 75-132280. (Learning English Ser). (Illus., Orig.). 1970-71. level 1 5.00 o.p. (ISBN 0-379-14250-3); pap. 3.95 ea. o.p. Oceana.

Finkel, Lawrence S. & Krawltz, Ruth. How to Study & Improve Test-Taking Skills. 2nd ed. LC 76-48196. Orig. Title: How to Study. (Illus.). 96p. (gr. 4-7). 1976. pap. text ed. 4.00 o.p. (ISBN 0-379-00157-8). Oceana.

Finkel, LeRoy & Brown, Jerald R. Apple BASIC Data File Programming. LC 81-13100. (Wiley Self-Teaching Guides Ser.). 303p. 1982. pap. text ed. 14.95 (ISBN 0-471-09157-X). Wiley.

--Data File Programming in BASIC. LC 80-39790. (Self-Teaching Guide Ser.). 338p. 1981. pap. text ed. 12.95 (ISBN 0-471-08333-X). Wiley.

Finkel, LeRoy, jt. auth. see Bove, Tony.

Finkel, LeRoy, jt. auth. see Brown, Jerald R.

Finkel, Maurice. Fresh Hope in Cancer. 7.95x o.p. (ISBN 0-85032-159-X). Cancer Control Soc.

Finkel, Norman J. Mental Illness & Health: Its Legacy Tensions, & Changes. 128p. 1976. pap. text ed. 9.95 (ISBN 0-02-337700-3, 33770). Macmillan.

Finkelhor, David & Gelles, Richard J., eds. The Dark Side of Families: Current Family Violence Research. 384p. 1983. 29.95 (ISBN 0-8039-1934-4); pap. 14.95 (ISBN 0-8039-1935-2). Sage.

Finkelman, Paul. An Imperfect Union: Slavery, Federalism, & Comity. LC 79-27526. (Studies in Legal History). xii, 378p. 1981. 22.00x (ISBN 0-8078-1438-5); pap. 8.95x (ISBN 0-8078-4066-1). U of NC Pr.

Finkelpearl, Philip J. John Marston of the Middle Temple: An Elizabethan Dramatist in His Social Setting. LC 69-12722. (Illus.). 1969. 15.00x o.p. (ISBN 0-674-47860-6). Harvard U Pr.

Finkelstein, L. & Carson, E. R. Mathematical Modeling of Dynamic Biological Systems. 329p. 1979. 44.95 (ISBN 0-471-27890-4, Research Studies Pr). Wiley.

Finkelstein, Louis, ed. The Jews, Vol. 1: Their History. 4th ed. LC 74-107615. 1970. pap. 6.95 o.p. (ISBN 0-8052-0271-4). Schocken.

--The Jews, Vol. 2: Their Religion & Culture. 4th ed. LC 74-107615. 1971. pap. 7.95 o.p. (ISBN 0-8052-0272-2). Schocken.

Finkelstein, Milton, jt. auth. see Basch, Lester D.

Finkelstein, Norman, tr. see Amin, Samir.

Finkelstein, Sidney. Jazz: A People's Music. LC 74-23386. (Roots of Jazz Ser.). ix, 278p. 1975. Repr. of 1948 ed. lib. bdg. 25.00 (ISBN 0-306-70659-8). Da Capo.

Finkenaur, Robert G. COBOL for Students: A Programmer Primer. (Orig.). 1977. pap. text ed. 16.95 (ISBN 0-316-28320-7); tchrs'. manual avail. (ISBN 0-316-28321-5). Little.

Finkl, C. W., Jr., jt. ed. see Fairbridge, R. W.

Finkl, Charles, Jr., ed. Soil Classification. LC 81-6214. (Benchmark Papers in Soil Science: Vol. 1). 416p. 1982. 45.00 (ISBN 0-87933-399-5). Hutchinson Ross.

Finkle, J. L. & Gable, R. W. Political Development & Social Change. LC 72-149769. 685p. 1971. pap. text ed. 24.50x (ISBN 0-471-25891-1). Wiley.

Finkle, Robert B. & Jones, William S. Assessing Corporate Talent: A Key to Managerial Manpower Planning. LC 71-120702. 1970. 23.95 o.p. (ISBN 0-471-25896-2, Pub. by Wiley-Interscience). Wiley.

Finland, Maxwell. Drugs Useful vs Infectious Diseases. LC 74-21394. (Principles & Techniques of Human Research & Therapeutics Ser: Vol. 7). (Illus.). 132p. 1975. 13.50 o.p. (ISBN 0-87993-051-9). Futura Pub.

Finland, Maxwell & McCabe, William R., eds. Contemporary Standards for Antimicrobial Usage. LC 76-27216. (Principles & Techniques of Human Research & Therapeutics: Vol. 13). (Illus.). 1977. monograph 13.50 o.p. (ISBN 0-87993-085-3). Futura Pub.

Finlay, Ian H. & Bann, Stephen. Heroic Emblems. (Illus.). 1978. pap. 5.00 (ISBN 0-915990-10-5). Z Pr.

Finlay, John L. Canada in the North Atlantic Triangle: Two Centuries of Social Change. 348p. 1975. pap. 12.50x o.p. (ISBN 0-19-540237-5). Oxford U Pr.

Finlay, M. H. The Lim Family of Singapore. 1982. 6.25 (ISBN 0-686-36254-3). Rod & Staff.

Finlay, Patrick, ed. Jane's Freight Containers 1983. 15th ed. (Jane's Yearbooks). (Illus.). 640p. 1983. 140.00x (ISBN 0-86720-642-X). Sci Bks Intl.

Finlay, Roger A. Population & Metropolis: The Demography of London, 1580-1650. LC 78-20956. (Cambridge Geographical Studies: No. 12). 224p. 1981. 47.50 (ISBN 0-521-22535-3). Cambridge U Pr.

Finlay, Winifred. Danger at Black Dyke. LC 68-31174. (Illus.). (gr. 7-10). 1968. 10.95 (ISBN 0-87599-150-5). S G Phillips.

Finlayson, A. N. International Wind Energy Symposium. 1982. 60.00 (100153). ASME.

Finlayson, Ann. Champions at Bat: Three Power Hitters. LC 74-113838. (Sports Ser.). (Illus.). (gr. 3-6). 1970. PLB 7.12 o.p. (ISBN 0-8116-6661-1). Garrard.

--Runaway Teen. LC 63-8739. (gr. 6-9). 1970. 7.95 o.p. (ISBN 0-385-05123-9). Doubleday.

--The Silver Bullet. LC 78-6575. (gr. 7 up). 1978. 7.50 o.p. (ISBN 0-525-66586-2). Lodestar Bks.

Finlayson, B., ed. see International Urinary Stone Conference, Australia, 1979, et al.

Finlayson, Birdwell, jt. auth. see Roth, Robert A.

Finlayson, Roderick. D'Arcy Cresswell. (World Authors Ser.). lib. bdg. 15.95 (ISBN 0-8057-2248-3, Twayne). G K Hall.

Finletter, Thomas K. Power & Policy. LC 74-159718. 408p. 1972. Repr. of 1954 ed. lib. bdg. 19.75x (ISBN 0-8371-6189-4, FIPP). Greenwood.

Finley, Blanche. The Structure of the United Nations General Assembly: Its Committees & Other Organisms, 1946-1973, 3 vols. LC 77-72373. 1463p. 135.00 (ISBN 0-379-10240-4); Vol. 1. o.p. Oceana.

Finley, Diane E. End of the Rainbow. 192p. (YA) 1975. 6.95 (ISBN 0-685-50845-5, Avalon). Bouregy.

Finley, Gerald. George Heriot: Postmaster Painter of the Canadas. 288p. 1983. 35.00 (ISBN 0-8020-5584-2). U of Toronto Pr.

Finley, Glenna. Affairs of Love. 1980. pap. 1.95 (ISBN 0-451-11174-5, AJ1174, Sig). NAL.

--Beware My Heart. (Orig.). 1978. pap. 1.95 (ISBN 0-451-11323-3, AJ1323, Sig). NAL.

--Bridal Affair. 1972. pap. 1.95 (ISBN 0-451-11496-5, AJ1496, Sig). NAL.

--Dare to Love. 1977. pap. 1.95 (ISBN 0-451-09992-3, J9992, Sig). NAL.

--Holiday for Love. 1976. pap. 1.95 (ISBN 0-451-09951-6, J9951, Sig). NAL.

--Journey to Love. 1971. pap. 1.95 (ISBN 0-451-11495-7, AJ1495, Sig). NAL.

--Kiss a Stranger. 1972. pap. 1.95 (ISBN 0-451-11228-8, AJ1228, Sig). NAL.

--Love for a Rogue: Highwayman No. 16. pap. 1.95 (ISBN 0-451-11315-2, AJ1315, Sig). NAL.

--Love's Hidden Fire. pap. 1.95 (ISBN 0-451-11498-1, AJ1498, Sig). NAL.

--Love's Magic Spell. 1974. pap. 1.95 (ISBN 0-451-11489-2, AJ1489, Sig). NAL.

--The Marriage Merger. (Orig.). 1978. pap. 1.95 (ISBN 0-451-11718-2, AJ1718, Sig). NAL.

--Master of Love. (Orig.). 1978. pap. 1.75 (ISBN 0-451-09442-5, E9442, Sig). NAL.

--Midnight Encounter. (Orig.). 1981. pap. 1.95 (ISBN 0-451-12095-7, AJ2095, Sig). NAL.

--One Way to Love, No. 30. 1982. pap. 1.95 (ISBN 0-451-11426-4, AJ1426, Sig). NAL.

--Reluctant Maiden. (Orig.). 1975. pap. 1.75 (ISBN 0-451-09863-3, E9863, Sig). NAL.

--Return Engagement. 1981. pap. 2.25 (ISBN 0-451-12323-9, AE2323, Sig). NAL.

--The Romantic Spirit. 1973. pap. 1.95 (ISBN 0-451-11493-0, AJ1493, Sig). NAL.

--Stateroom for Two. (Orig.). 1980. pap. 1.95 (ISBN 0-451-11497-3, AJ1497, Sig). NAL.

--Storm of Desire. 1977. pap. 1.95 (ISBN 0-451-11800-6, AJ1800, Sig). NAL.

--Taken by Storm, No. 31. 1982. pap. 2.25 (ISBN 0-451-11784-0, AE1784, Sig). NAL.

--Timed for Love. (Orig.). 1979. pap. 1.95 (AJ1494, Sig). NAL.

--To Catch a Bride. (Orig.). 1977. pap. 1.95 (ISBN 0-451-11500-7, AJ1500, Sig). NAL.

--When Love Speaks. 1973. pap. 1.95 (ISBN 0-451-11799-9, AJ1799, Sig). NAL.

--Wildfire of Love. 1979. pap. 1.95 (ISBN 0-451-11491-4, AJ1491, Sig). NAL.

Finley, John, jt. auth. see Sehlinger, Bob.

Finley, K. T. Tnazoles of One Two Three, Vol. 19. 349p. 1980. 141.95 (ISBN 0-471-07827-1, Pub. by Wiley-Interscience). Wiley.

--Triazoles. (Chemistry of Heterocyclic Compounds, Series of Monographs: Vol. 39). 349p. 1980. 126.50x (ISBN 0-471-07827-1). Wiley.

Finley, Lorraine N. John Comes First. 1968. 4.00 o.p. (ISBN 0-8233-0124-9). Golden Quill.

Finley, M. I. The Ancient Economy. (Sather Classical Lectures: Vol. 43). 1973. 23.00x (ISBN 0-520-02436-2); pap. 3.95 (ISBN 0-520-02564-4). U of Cal Pr.

--Ancient Slavery & Modern Ideology. 1983. pap. 6.95 (ISBN 0-14-022500-5, Pelican). Penguin.

--Atlas of Classical Archaeology. LC 76-16761. 1977. 22.50 o.p. (ISBN 0-07-021025-X, GB). McGraw.

--Early Greece: The Bronze & Archaic Ages. LC 78-95884. (Ancient Culture & Society Ser). 1970. pap. 4.95 o.p. (ISBN 0-393-00541-0, Norton Lib). Norton.

--Economy & Society in Ancient Greece. 1983. pap. 7.95 (ISBN 0-14-022520-X). Penguin.

Finley, M. I., ed. The Legacy of Greece: A New Appraisal. (Illus.). 1981. 22.50x (ISBN 0-19-821915-6). Oxford U Pr.

--Studies in Roman Property. (Classical Studies). (Illus.). 192p. 1976. 17.50 (ISBN 0-521-21115-8). Cambridge U Pr.

Finley, M. I., ed. see Garlan, Yvon.

Finley, M. I., ed. see Lloyd, G. E.

Finley, Martha. Elsie at Nantucket. 301p. 1981. Repr. PLB 15.95x (ISBN 0-89966-333-8). Buccaneer Bks.

--Elsie Dinsmore. 332p. Repr. PLB 15.95x (ISBN 0-89966-332-X). Buccaneer Bks.

--Elsie Dinsmore. Lurie, Alison & Schiller, Justin G., eds. LC 75-32168. (Classics of Children's Literature Ser.: 1621-1932). PLB 38.00 o.s.i. (ISBN 0-8240-2281-5). Garland Pub.

Finley, Merrill. Christ & Colonel. 120p. 1948. pap. 5.00 (ISBN 0-686-96411-X). Am Atheist.

Finley, R. J. & Gustavson, T. C. Climatic Controls on Erosion in the Rolling Plains along the Caprock Escarpment of the Texas Panhandle: Geological Circular 80-11. (Illus.). 50p. 1980. 1.75 (ISBN 0-686-36578-X). Bur Econ Geology.

Finley, Tom. Diabolus Seeks Revenge. (Illus.). 96p. (gr. 7 up). 1982. pap. 3.95 (ISBN 0-8307-0839-1, 5416704). Regal.

Finley, Virginia, jt. auth. see Mason, Beverly.

Finn, Bernard, jt. ed. see Coates, Vary T.

Finn, Chester E., jt. ed. see Breneman, David W.

Finn, Chester E., Jr. Scholars, Dollars, & Bureaucrats. LC 78-13363. (Studies in Higher Education Policy). 1978. 18.95 (ISBN 0-8157-2828-X); pap. 7.95 (ISBN 0-8157-2827-1). Brookings.

Finn, Daniel P. Managing the Ocean Resources of the United States: The Role of the Federal Marine Sanctuary Program. (Lecture Notes in Coastal & Estuarine Studies: Vol. 2). (Illus.). 193p. 1982. pap. 16.00 (ISBN 0-387-11583-8). Springer-Verlag.

Finn, David & Moore, Henry. Henry Moore: Sculpture & Environment. LC 76-12588. (Illus.). 1977. 65.00 o.p. (ISBN 0-8109-1313-5). Abrams.

Finn, David, photos by. The Florence Baptistery Doors. LC 80-5365. 328p. 1980. 50.00 o.p. (ISBN 0-670-31997-X, Studio). Viking Pr.

--Large Two Forms: A Sculpture by Henry Moore. 80p. 1981. 19.95 o.s.i. (ISBN 0-89659-269-3). Abbeville Pr.

Finn, F. C. History of Chelsea. 15.00x (ISBN 0-392-07888-0, SpS). Sportshelf.

Finn, James, ed. Global Economics & Religion. 277p. 1983. 26.95 (ISBN 0-87855-477-7). Transaction Bks.

Finn, James D. Extending Education Through Technology: Selected Writings by James D. Finn on Instructional Technology. McBeath, Ronald J., ed. LC 72-87833. 1972. 11.95 o.p. (ISBN 0-89240-013-7, 205); pap. 9.95 o.p. (ISBN 0-89240-012-9, 203). Assn Ed Comm Tech.

Finn, Jeremy D. Multivariance Six: Univariate & Multivariate Analysis of Variance, Covariance, Regression & Repeated Measures. pap. 14.25 (ISBN 0-89498-003-3). Natl Ed Res.

Finn, Jeremy D. & Mattsson, Ingrid. Multivariate Analysis in Educational Research. pap. 14.25 (ISBN 0-89498-001-7). Natl Ed Res.

Finn, Matia. Fundraising for Early Childhood Programs: Getting Started & Getting Results. 1982. pap. text ed. 3.50 (ISBN 0-912674-81-4, 120). Natl Assn Child Ed.

Finn, Molly. Summer Feasts. 1979. 11.50 o.p. (ISBN 0-671-24056-0). S&S.

Finn, Nancy B. The Electronic Office. (Illus.). 144p. 1983. pap. 12.95 (ISBN 0-13-251819-8). P-H.

Finn, P. Irish Coin Values. pap. 4.00 (ISBN 0-686-43400-5, Pub. by Spink & Son England). S J Durst.

Finn, R. & Drury, P. A Guide to the Intensive Therapy Unit. 1974. 6.95 o.p. (ISBN 0-407-72755-8). Butterworth.

Finn, William J. Art of the Choral Conductor, 2 vols. (Illus.). 1960. Vol. 1. pap. text ed. 15.00 (ISBN 0-87487-037-2); Vol. 2. pap. text ed. 10.85 (ISBN 0-87487-038-0). Summy.

Finne, Geir, jt. auth. see Kirkwood, Thomas.

Finnegan, David J. Bacterial Conjugation. 48p. 1976. 39.00x (ISBN 0-686-96975-8, Pub. by Meadowfield Pr England). State Mutual Bk.

Finnegan, Edward G., ed. New Webster's Dictionary of the English Language (College Edition) LC 75-18559. (Illus.). 1975. 14.95 (ISBN 0-8326-0035-0, 6602). Delair.

Finnegan, Edward G., ed. see Carter, Linda & Culinary Arts Institute Staff.

Finnegan, Frances. Poverty & Prostitution. LC 78-68123. (Illus.). 1979. 32.50 (ISBN 0-521-22447-0). Cambridge U Pr.

Finnegan, John P. Against the Specter of a Dragon: The Campaign for American Military Preparedness, 1914-1917. LC 74-288. (Contributions in Military History: No. 7). (Illus.). 1975. lib. bdg. 27.50 (ISBN 0-8371-7376-0, FSD/). Greenwood.

Finnegan, Marcus B. & Goldscheider, Robert. The Law & Business of Licensing, 4 vols. LC 75-22337. 1977. Set. looseleaf with 1981 suppl. 250.00 (ISBN 0-87632-136-8). Boardman.

Finnegan, Marcus B., ed. Licensing Law Handbook. 1980. cancelled (ISBN 0-87632-326-3). Boardman.

Finnegan, Michael, jt. ed. see Skal, David J.

Finnegan, Richard B. Ireland: A Nation in the Currents of Change. (Profiles-Nations of Contemporary Western Europe Ser.). (Illus.). 185p. 1983. lib. bdg. 18.50x (ISBN 0-89158-924-4). Westview.

Finnegan, Richard B., et al. Law & Politics in the International System: Case Studies in Conflict Resolution. LC 79-66153. (Illus.). 1979. pap. text ed. 9.50 (ISBN 0-8191-0793-X). U Pr of Amer.

Finneken, Wouter Van see Van Ginneken, Wouter.

Finneran, Richard J. The Prose Fiction of W. B. Yeats: The Search for Those Simple Forms. (New Yeats Papers Ser.: Vol. 4). 1973. pap. text ed. 3.75x o.p. (ISBN 0-85105-217-7, Dolmen Pr). Humanities.

Finneran, Richard J., et al. Recent Research on Anglo-Irish Writers: A Supplement to "Anglo-Irish Literature: A Review of Research". (Reviews of Research Ser.). 450p. 1983. 25.00x (ISBN 0-87352-259-1). Modern Lang.

Finneson, Bernard E. Low Back Pain. 2nd ed. (Illus.). 598p. 1981. text ed. 45.00 (ISBN 0-686-97923-0, Lippincott Medical). Lippincott.

Finneson, Bernard E. & Freese, Arthur. Dr. Finneson on Low Back Pain. LC 75-15342. 224p. 1975. 7.95 o.p. (ISBN 0-399-11537-4). Putnam Pub Group.

Finney, Ben. Once a Marine, Always a Marine. (Illus.). 1978. 6.95 o.p. (ISBN 0-517-53275-1). Crown.

Finney, Ben R. Big-Men & Business: Entrepreneurship & Economic Growth in the New Guinea Highlands. LC 72-93151. (Illus.). 250p. 1973. 12.00x (ISBN 0-8248-0262-4, Eastwest Ctr). UH Pr.

--Hokule'a: The Way to Tahiti. LC 79-9410. 1979. 17.50 o.p. (ISBN 0-396-07719-6). Dodd.

Finney, Ben R., compiled by. Pacific Navigation & Voyaging. (Illus.). 1976. text ed. 12.50x (ISBN 0-8248-0584-4). UH Pr.

Finney, Brian. Christopher Isherwood: A Critical Biography. (Illus.). 1979. 18.95x (ISBN 0-19-520134-5). Oxford U Pr.

Finney, Charles & Parkhurst, L. B. Principles of Liberty. rev. ed. (Finney's Sermons on Romans Ser.). 192p. (Orig.). 1983. pap. 4.95 (ISBN 0-87123-475-0). Bethany Hse.

Finney, Charles G. The Old China Hands. LC 73-429. (Illus.). 258p. 1973. Repr. of 1961 ed. lib. bdg. 17.75x (ISBN 0-8371-6772-8, FIOC). Greenwood.

Finney Company. Occupational Guidance, 5 units. Incl. Unit 1D. 1979 (ISBN 0-912486-41-4); Unit 2D. 1980 (ISBN 0-912486-44-9); Unit 3D. 1981 (ISBN 0-912486-48-1); Unit 4D. 1982 (ISBN 0-912486-51-1); Unit 5C. 1978 (ISBN 0-912486-36-8). LC 75-20074. (gr. 7 up). Set. 330.00 (ISBN 0-912486-16-3); 66.00 ea. Finney Co.

Finney, D. J. Probit Analysis. 3rd ed. LC 78-134618. (Illus.). 1971. 59.50 (ISBN 0-521-08041-X). Cambridge U Pr.

Finney, David. The Power Thyristor & Its Applications. (Illus.). 320p. 1980. 34.95 (ISBN 0-07-084533-6, P&RB). McGraw.

Finney, H. A. Consolidated Statements. LC 82-48362. (Accountancy in Transition Ser.). 242p. 1982. lib. bdg. 25.00 (ISBN 0-8240-5313-3). Garland Pub.

Finney, Jack. The Body Snatchers. (Science Fiction Ser.). (Illus.). 224p. 1976. Repr. of 1955 ed. lib. bdg. 12.50 o.p. (ISBN 0-8398-2332-0, Gregg). G K Hall.

--Forgotten News: The Crime of the Century & Other Lost Stories. LC 81-43561. (Illus.). 312p. 1983. 14.95 (ISBN 0-385-17721-6). Doubleday.

Finney, Joseph. Culture Change, Mental Health & Poverty. 1970. pap. 2.95 o.p. (ISBN 0-671-20548-X, Touchstone Bks). S&S.

Finney, Patricia. The Crow Goddess. LC 79-1322. 1979. 11.95 o.p. (ISBN 0-399-12315-6). Putnam Pub Group.

--A Shadow of Gulls. LC 77-5733. 1977. 8.95 o.p. (ISBN 0-399-11979-5). Putnam Pub Group.

Finney, R., jt. auth. see Thomas, G.

Finney, Ross L. & Ostberg, Donald E. Elementary Differential Equations with Linear Algebra. 2nd ed. LC 75-12096. (Mathematics Ser.). 704p. 1976. text ed. 25.95 (ISBN 0-201-05515-5). A-W.

Finney, Ross L., jt. auth. see Thomas, George B., Jr.

Finney, Shan. Cheerleading & Baton Twirling. (First Bks). (Illus.). 72p. 1982. PLB 8.90 (ISBN 0-531-04391-6). Watts.

--Dance. (First Bks.). (Illus.). 72p. (gr. 4 up). 1983. PLB 8.90 (ISBN 0-531-04525-0). Watts.

Finnie, Nancy. Handling the Young Cerebral Palsied Child at Home. rev. ed. (Illus.). 1975. 9.95 (ISBN 0-87690-174-7); pap. 6.50 (ISBN 0-87690-175-5, 0631-190). Dutton.

Finnie, W. Bruce, jt. ed. see Erskine, Thomas L.

Finnis, John. Natural Law & Natural. (Clarendon Law Ser.). text ed. 45.00x (ISBN 0-19-876098-1); pap. text ed. 14.95x (ISBN 0-19-876110-4). Oxford U Pr.

Finny, D. J. Statistics for Biologists. 1980. pap. 9.95x (ISBN 0-412-21540-3, Pub by Chapman & Hall England). Methuen Inc.

Finocchiaro, Mary. English As a Second Language: From Theory to Practice. 1981. 20.00x o.p. (ISBN 0-686-75662-2, Pub. by European Schoolbks England). State Mutual Bk.

Finocchiaro, Mary & Brumfit, Christopher. The Functional-Notional Approach: From Theory to Practice. (Illus.). 320p. (Orig.). 1983. pap. text ed. 10.95x (ISBN 0-19-502744-2). Oxford U Pr.

Finocchiaro, Mary & Sako, Sydney. Foreign Language Testing: A Practical Approach. 1983. pap. text ed. 9.95 (ISBN 0-88345-362-2). Regents Pub.

Finsand, Mary J. Caring & Cooking for the Hyperactive Child. LC 80-54335. 192p. 1981. 12.95 (ISBN 0-8069-5560-0); lib. bdg. 15.69 (ISBN 0-8069-5561-9); pap. 6.95 (ISBN 0-8069-8980-7). Sterling.

--Diabetic Candy, Cookie & Dessert Cookbook. LC 81-85024. (Illus.). 160p. 1982. 15.69 (ISBN 0-8069-5568-6); lib. bdg. 11.69 (ISBN 0-8069-5569-4); pap. 6.95 (ISBN 0-8069-7586-5). Sterling.

--The Town that Moved. LC 82-9703. (Carolrhoda on my Own Bks). (Illus.). 48p. (gr. 1-4). 1983. PLB 6.95g (ISBN 0-87614-200-5). Carolrhoda Bks.

Finsand, Mary Jane. Complete Diabetic Cookbook. LC 79-91382. (Illus.). 160p. 1980. 12.95 (ISBN 0-8069-5554-6); lib. bdg. 15.69 (ISBN 0-8069-5555-4); pap. 6.95 (ISBN 0-8069-8908-4). Sterling.

Finster, Jerome, ed. The National Archives & Urban Research. LC 73-92905. (National Archives Conferences Ser.: Vol. 6). xii, 164p. 1974. 15.00x (ISBN 0-8214-0154-8, 82-81578). Ohio U Pr.

Finsterbusch, Kurt & Wolf, Charles P., eds. Methodology of Social Impact Assessment. 2nd ed. LC 81-2400. (Community Development Ser.: Vol. 32). 386p. 1981. 32.00 (ISBN 0-87933-401-0). Hutchinson Ross.

Finston, Charles, jt. auth. see Ragen, Joseph E.

Finston, Harmon L. & Rychtman, Allen C. A New View of Current Acid-Base Theories. LC 81-16030. 216p. 1982. 50.00 (ISBN 0-471-08472-7, Pub. by Wiley-Interscience). Wiley.

Finton, Esther. Math Bulletin Boards. (gr. 3-6). 1981. 5.95 (ISBN 0-86653-015-0, GA 244). Good Apple.

Finzer, K. H., tr. see Frangenheim, H.

Fiore, jt. auth. see Streitmatter.

Fiore, Albie. Shaping Rubik's Snake. 128p. 1981. pap. 1.95 (ISBN 0-14-006181-9). Penguin.

Fiore, E., jt. auth. see Glatzle, M.

Fiore, Edith. You Have Been Here Before. 1978. 8.95 (ISBN 0-686-91905-X, Coward). Putnam Pub Group.

--You Have Been Here Before: A Psychologist Looks at Past Lives. LC 77-20211. 1978. 8.95 o.p. (ISBN 0-698-10883-3, Coward). Putnam Pub Group.

Fiore, Evely. YWCA Way to Tropical Fitness. LC 82-445639. 192p. 1983. pap. 9.95 (ISBN 0-385-18472-7). Doubleday.

Fiore, Evelyn L., ed. Low Carbohydrate Diet. (Orig.). 1965. pap. 1.95 (ISBN 0-448-01298-7, G&D). Putnam Pub Group.

Fiore, Kyle, jt. auth. see Weigle, Marta.

Fiore, M. V. & Strauss, P. S. How to Develop Dynamic Leadership: A Short Course for Professionals. (Wiley Professional Development Programs). 274p. 1977. 24.95x (ISBN 0-471-02314-0). Wiley.

Fiore, Peter A. Milton & Augustine: Patterns of Augustinian Thought in Milton's Paradise Lost. LC 80-17854. 144p. 1981. 15.75x (ISBN 0-271-00269-7). Pa St U Pr.

Fiore, Peter A., ed. Just So Much Honor: Essays Commemorating the Four-Hundredth Anniversary of the Birth of John Donne. LC 79-157768. 1972. 18.95x (ISBN 0-271-00554-8). Pa St U Pr.

Fiorenza, Elisabeth S. In Memory of Her: A Feminist Theological Reconstruction of Christian Origins. 275p. 1983. 17.50 (ISBN 0-8245-0493-3). Crossroad NY.

Fiorenza, Francis S. Foundational Theology: Jesus & the Church. 175p. 1983. 12.95 (ISBN 0-8245-0494-1). Crossroad NY.

Fiorenza, Francis S., tr. see Schleiermacher, Friedrich.

Fioretti, Sandra & Magarian, Judy. The Georule in Action. (gr. k-4). 1979. 3.95 (ISBN 0-88488-131-8). Creative Pubns.

Fiori, Vito, jt. auth. see Streitmatter, Gene.

Fiorini, S. & Wilson, R. J. Edge-Colourings of Graphs. (Research Notes in Mathematics Ser.: No. 16). 154p. (Orig.). 1977. pap. text ed. 20.95 (ISBN 0-273-01129-4). Pitman Pub MA.

Fiorito, Len, jt. auth. see Marazzi, Rich.

Firby, P. A. & Gardiner, C. F. Surface Topology. (Mathematics & its Applications Harwood Ser.). 190p. 1982. 54.95X (ISBN 0-470-27528-6). Halsted Pr.

Firchow, Evelyn S., jt. tr. see Firchow, Peter E.

Firchow, Peter E. & Firchow, Evelyn S., trs. East German Short Stories: An Introductory Anthology. (International Studies & Translations Program). 1979. lib. bdg. 15.00 (ISBN 0-8057-8159-5, Twayne). G K Hall.

Firdawsi. Suhrab & Rustam: A Poem from the Shah Namah of Firdausi. Atkinson, James, tr. from Persian. LC 72-3772. Orig. Title: Soohrab, a Poem. (Eng. & Persian.). 1972. Repr. of 1814 ed. 25.00x (ISBN 0-8201-1103-1). Schol Facsimiles.

Fire & Casualty Bulletin Editors. Agent's & Buyer's Guide: Annual Edition 1981. rev. ed. LC 77-92759. 550p. 1981. pap. 11.50 o.p. (ISBN 0-87218-309-2). Natl Underwriter.

Fire, Casualty & Surety Bulletins Editors. Non-Resident & Surplus Line Laws. LC 78-58858. 60p. 1981. pap. 5.50 o.p. (ISBN 0-87218-312-2). Natl Underwriter.

Firebaugh, Morris, jt. ed. see Ruedisili, Lon C.

Firebaugh, Morris W., jt. ed. see Ruedisili, Lon C.

Fireman, Bert M. Arizona: Historic Land. LC 82-47807. (Illus.). 305p. 1982. 16.95 (ISBN 0-394-50797-5). Knopf.

Fireman, Judy, ed. The Cat Catalog. LC 76-25473. (Illus.). 354p. 1976. 12.50 o.s.i. (ISBN 0-911104-81-X); pap. 8.95 (ISBN 0-911104-82-8). Workman Pub.

Fireside, Harvey. Soviet Psychoprisons. (Illus.). 1979. 17.50 o.p. (ISBN 0-393-01266-2); pap. write for info. Norton.

Firestein, Cecily. Rubbing Craft. LC 76-56570. (Illus., Orig.). 1977. pap. 4.95 (ISBN 0-8256-3062-2, Quick Fox). Putnam Pub Group.

Firestein, Gary S., jt. auth. see Harrell, Robert A.

Firestein, Stephen, jt. auth. see Applebaum, Eleanor G.

Firestone, David B. & Reed, Frank C. Environmental Law for Non-Lawyers. LC 82-70697. (Illus.). 300p. 1983. 36.00 (ISBN 0-250-40529-6). Ann Arbor Science.

Firestone, Philip, jt. ed. see McGrath, Patrick J.

Firestone, Robert & Catlett, Joyce. The Truth: A Psychological Cure. 234p. 1982. pap. 7.95 (ISBN 0-89696-167-2, An Everest House Book). Dodd.

Firestone, Ross, jt. auth. see Crosby, Gary.

Firestone, Shulamith. The Dialectic of Sex. LC 70-123149. 288p. 1974. pap. 5.95 (ISBN 0-688-06454-X). Morrow.

Firkin, Barry G., et al. Progress in Transfusion & Transplantation, 1972. Schmidt, Paul J., ed. 365p. 1972. 7.50 o.p. (ISBN 0-914404-04-0). Am Assn Blood.

Firmage, D. A., jt. auth. see Heins, C. P.

Firmage, D. Allan. Fundamental Theory of Structures. LC 76-28518. 1971. Repr. of 1963 ed. 14.50 o.p. (ISBN 0-88275-019-4). Krieger.

--Fundamental Theory of Structures. LC 76-28518. 584p. 1980. 18.00 (ISBN 0-88275-443-2). Krieger.

Firmage, David A. Modern Engineering Practice: Ethical, Professional & Legal Aspects. LC 79-23450. 256p. 1980. lib. bdg. 24.50 o.s.i. (ISBN 0-8240-7108-5). Garland Pub.

Firmage, George J. & Kennedy, Richard S., eds. Etcetera: The Unpublished Poems of E. E. Cummings. 1983. 16.95 (ISBN 0-87140-644-6); pap. 6.95 (ISBN 0-87140-128-2). Liveright.

Firmage, George J., ed. see Kennedy, Richard S.

Firmin, jt. auth. see Portgate.

Firmin, Joe. Sea Birds. LC 81-83998. (Fact Finders Ser.). PLB 8.00 (ISBN 0-382-06620-0). Silver.

Firmin, Peter. Basil Brush Goes Flying. (Illus.). 48p. (gr. 3-7). 1983. pap. 3.95 (ISBN 0-13-066985-7). P-H.

--Chicken Stew - With a Dash of Vinegar: Life with the Badd-Wolfe Family. (Illus.). 32p. 1982. pap. 6.95 (ISBN 0-7207-1299-8, Pub. by Michael Joseph). Merrimack Bk Serv.

--The Winter Diary of a Country Rat. (Illus.). 144p. (gr. 2-5). 1983. 11.00 (ISBN 0-7182-2541-4, Pub. by Kaye & Ward). David & Charles.

Firmin, Phillippe. Dissertation sur la Question: S'il Est Permis d'Avoir En sa Possession des Esclaves et de S'en Servir Comme Tels, dans les Colonies de l'Amerique. (Slave Trade in France Ser., 1744-1848). 88p. (Fr.). 1974. Repr. of 1770 ed. lib. bdg. 32.50x o.p. (ISBN 0-8287-0342-6, TN105). Clearwater Pub.

Firminger, Walter K., ed. see Great Britain. Parliament. House of Commons.

Firpo, Patrick, et al. Copy Art: The First Complete Guide to the Copy Machine. LC 78-15827. (Illus.). 1978. pap. 7.95 o.s.i. (ISBN 0-399-90016-0, Marek). Putnam Pub Group.

First. Move Over Beethoven. 1978. 8.90 (ISBN 0-686-94473-9). Watts.

First, Julia. Look Who's Beautiful. (gr. 5 up). 1980. PLB 8.90 (ISBN 0-531-04109-3, B21). Watts.

First, Ruth & Scott, Ann. Olive Schreiner. LC 80-13190. (Illus.). 384p. 1980. 20.00 (ISBN 0-8052-3749-6). Schocken.

Firth, Charles H. American Garland, Being a Collection of Ballads Relating to America, 1536-1759. LC 68-20123. 1969. Repr. of 1915 ed. 30.00x (ISBN 0-8103-3411-9). Gale.

Firth, Grace. A Natural Year. 1973. 6.95 o.p. (ISBN 0-671-21205-2). S&S.

Firth, Norene. A Bowl of Cherries: Looking at Life Through Homespun Homilies. 1980. 3.95 (ISBN 0-8378-2025-1). Gibson.

Firth, R. J. Viewdata Systems: A Practical Evaluation Guide. (Office Technology in the Eighties Ser.). (Illus.). 114p. (Orig.). 1982. pap. 15.00x (ISBN 0-85012-370-4). Intl Pubns Serv.

Firth, Raymond. History & Traditions of Tikopia. 1961. text ed. 8.20x (ISBN 0-8248-0585-2). UH Pr.

Firth, Raymond, ed. Man & Culture: An Evaluation of the Work of Bronislaw Malinowski. 1957. 26.00x (ISBN 0-7100-1376-0). Routledge & Kegan.

--Themes in Economic Anthropology. (Illus.). 1970. pap. 13.95x (ISBN 0-422-72540-4, Pub by Tavistock England). Methuen Inc.

Firth, Robert E., jt. ed. see Phillips, Harold R.

Firth, Susanna. The Overlord. (Harlequin Romances Ser.). 192p. 1982. pap. 1.50 (ISBN 0-373-02493-2). Harlequin Bks.

--Prince of Darkness. (Romances Ser.). 192p. (Orig.). 1980. pap. text ed. 1.25 (ISBN 0-373-02344-8). Harlequin Bks.

Firth, Suzanna. Dark Encounter. (Harlequin Romances Ser.). (Orig.). 1980. pap. 1.25 (ISBN 0-373-02307-3). Harlequin Bks.

Firtz, Jean. Will You Sign Here, John Hancock? (Illus.). (gr. 2-6). 1982. pap. 4.95 (ISBN 0-698-20539-1, Coward). Putnam Pub Group.

Fiscalini, Janet. Evasions. 1972. 3.00 (ISBN 0-913270-01-6). Sunstone Pr.

Fisch, Allan E., jt. auth. see Redman, Helen C.

Fisch, H. Zionist Revolution. LC 78-424. 1978. 17.95x (ISBN 0-312-89886-X). St Martin.

Fisch, Harold. S. Y. Agnon. LC 74-76126. (Literature and Life Ser.). 124p. 1975. 11.95 (ISBN 0-8044-2197-8). Ungar.

Fisch, Max H., ed. Classic American Philosophers. (Orig.). 1966. pap. text ed. 17.95 (ISBN 0-13-135186-9). P-H.

Fisch, Max H. & Kloesel, Christian J., eds. Writings of Charles S. Peirce: A Chronological Edition, Vol. 1, 1857-1866. LC 79-1993. 738p. 1982. 32.50 (ISBN 0-253-37201-1). Ind U Pr.

Fischbach. Manual of Laboratory Diagnostic Tests. pap. text ed. 14.75 (ISBN 0-686-97967-2, Lippincott Nursing). Lippincott.

Fischbach, David P. & Fogdall, Richard P. Coagulation: The Essentials. (Illus.). 280p. 1981. soft cover 19.00 (ISBN 0-683-03312-3). Williams & Wilkins.

Fischel, Walter J. Ibn Khaldun in Egypt: His Public Functions & His Historical Research, (1382-1406); A Study in Islamic Historiography. LC 67-11200. 1967. 30.00x (ISBN 0-520-00414-0). U of Cal Pr.

Fischer, A., ed. Current Directions in Anthropology. 1970. pap. 2.50 (ISBN 0-686-36560-7). Am Anthro Assn.

Fischer, Al, jt. auth. see Fischer, Mildred.

Fischer, Al & Fischer, Mildred, eds. Arizona Cook Book. 1974. plastic 3.50 (ISBN 0-914846-00-0). Golden West Pub.

Fischer, Carol & Terry, Ann. Children's Language & the Language Arts. 1976. 22.50 (ISBN 0-07-021107-8). McGraw.

Fischer, Charlotte F. The Hartree-Fock Method for Atoms: A Numerical Approach. LC 76-50115. 1977. 55.50x o.p. (ISBN 0-471-25990-X, Pub. by Wiley-Interscience). Wiley.

Fischer, Claude S., et al. Human Aggression & Conflict: Interdisciplinary Perspectives. (Illus.). 352p. 1975. pap. 16.95 ref. ed. (ISBN 0-13-444620-8). P-H.

Fischer, David H. Growing Old in America: The Bland-Lee Lectures Delivered at Clark University. Expanded Edition. 1978. pap. 7.95 (ISBN 0-19-502366-8, GB532, GB). Oxford U Pr.

--Historian's Fallacies: Toward a Logic of Historical Thought. 1970. pap. 5.95xi (ISBN 0-06-131545-1, TB1545, Torch). Har-Row.

Fischer, David W. North Sea Oil: An Environment Interface. 332p. (Orig.). 1982. pap. 38.00 (ISBN 82-00-05832-8). Universitet.

Fischer, Donald E. & Jordan, Ronald J. Security Analysis & Portfolio Management. 2nd ed. 1979. 24.95 (ISBN 0-13-798850-8). P-H.

--Security Analysis & Portfolio Management. 3rd ed. (Illus.). 672p. 1983. 24.95 (ISBN 0-13-798876-1). P-H.

Fischer, E. Intermediate Real Analysis. (Undergraduate Texts in Mathematics Ser.). (Illus.). 770p. 1983. 28.00 (ISBN 0-387-90721-1). Springer-Verlag.

Fischer, Edward. Light in the Far East: Archbishop Harold Henry's Forty-Two Years in Korea. 1976. 3.00 (ISBN 0-8164-0307-4). Seabury.

--Mindanao Mission: Archbishop Patrick Cronin's Forty Years in the Phillipines. 1979. 3.00 (ISBN 0-8164-0412-7). Seabury.

Fischer, Eileen, jt. auth. see Vollmar, Karen.

Fischer, Frank. Politics, Values, & Public Policy. (Westview Special Study Ser.). 275p. 1980. lib. bdg. 24.75x (ISBN 0-89158-799-3); pap. 12.00 (ISBN 0-86531-214-1). Westview.

Fischer, Frederic E. Fundamental Statistical Concepts. LC 72-3309. 1973. text ed. 22.95 scp o.p. (ISBN 0-06-382662-3, HarpC). Har-Row.

Fischer, George. American Research on Soviet Society. (Occasional Publication Ser.). 1967. pap. 2.00 o.p. (ISBN 0-89192-144-3). Interbk Inc.

Fischer, Georges, jt. ed. see Morris-Jones, W. H.

Fischer, Gerald C., jt. auth. see Hoffman, Margaret A.

Fischer, Hal. Gay Semiotics. LC 77-93056. (Illus.). 1978. pap. 25.00x (ISBN 0-917986-03-2). NFS Pr.

Fischer, Helmut, tr. see Mehnert, Klaus.

Fischer, Helmut, tr. see Meinecke, Friedrich.

Fischer, Henry L., et al. Sex Education for the Developmentally Disabled: A Guide for Parents, Teachers & Professionals. 60p. 1976. pap. text ed. 11.95 (ISBN 0-8391-0750-1). Univ Park.

Fischer, Inge. Christophe in Egypt: The Odyssey of Pharaoh's Cat. LC 68-9214. (Illus.). 154p. (gr. 3-7). 1981. pap. 7.95 (ISBN 0-9610238-0-5, 111). I Fischer.

Fischer, Joel. Effective Casework Practice: An Eclectic Approach. LC 77-4069. (Illus.). 1977. 23.00 (ISBN 0-07-021085-3, C). McGraw.

Fischer, Joel, jt. auth. see Bloom, Martin.

Fischer, John. Dark Horse. 100p. 1983. price not set (ISBN 0-88070-016-5). Multnomah.

--From the High Plains: An Account of the Hard Men, High-Spirited Women -- & a Few Rascals -- Who Settled the Last Frontier of the Old West. LC 78-437. (Illus.). 1978. 12.45i (ISBN 0-06-011269-7, HarpT). Har-Row.

Fischer, John, jt. ed. see Greenspan, Kalman.

Fischer, John L., et al. Annotations to the Book of Luelen. LC 76-50498. (Pacific History Ser.: No. 9). 1978. text ed. 8.50x o.p. (ISBN 0-8248-0533-X). UH Pr.

Fischer, John L., et al, eds. see Bernart, Luelen.

Fischer, Josef E. Total Parenteral Nutrition. LC 75-30283. 1976. text ed. 32.50 (ISBN 0-316-28370-3). Little.

Fischer, K. H., jt. auth. see Bass, J.

Fischer, Kathleen R. The Inner Rainbow: The Imagination in Christian Life. 160p. 1983. pap. 5.95 (ISBN 0-8091-2498-X). Paulist Pr.

Fischer, Klaus. History & Prophecy: Oswald Spengler & the Decline of the West. LC 76-57812. 1977. 12.95 (ISBN 0-87716-080-5, Pub. by Moore Pub Co). F Apple.

Fischer, L. Introduction to Gel Chromatography. (Lab Techiques in Biochemistry & Molecular Biology Vol. 1, Pt. 2). 1969. pap. 21.00 (ISBN 0-444-10197-7, North-Holland). Elsevier.

--Introduction to Gel Filtration Chromatography. rev. ed. (Laboratory Techniques in Biochemistry & Molecular Biology Ser.: Vol. 1, Pt. 2). 1980. 23.50 (ISBN 0-444-80223-1, North Holland). Elsevier.

Fischer, Louis. The Essential Gandhi. LC 82-48890. 1983. pap. 4.95 (ISBN 0-394-71466-0, Vin). Random.

--Gandhi: His Life & Message for the World. pap. 2.95 (ISBN 0-451-62142-5, ME2142, Ment). NAL.

--The Life of Mahatma Gandhi. 1983. pap. 8.95 (ISBN 0-06-091038-0, CN1038, CN). Har-Row.

--Soviet Journey. LC 72-136529. (Illus.). 308p. 1973. Repr. of 1935 ed. lib. bdg. 15.75x (ISBN 0-8371-5450-2, FISJ). Greenwood.

Fischer, Louis & Schimmel, David. The Rights of Students & Teachers: Resolving Conflicts in the School Community. 447p. 1982. pap. text ed. 12.50 scp (ISBN 0-06-042075-8, HarpC). Har-Row.

Fischer, Lucy. Jacques Tati: A Guide to References & Resources. 1983. lib. bdg. 25.00 (ISBN 0-8161-8000-8, Hall Reference). G K Hall.

Fischer, Ludwig, jt. ed. see Daviau, Donald G.

Fischer, Malcolm R. Economic Analysis of Labour. 1972. 22.50 (ISBN 0-312-22680-2). St Martin.

Fischer, Michael W. Verheissungen des Glucks. 251p. (Ger.). 1982. write for info. (ISBN 3-8204-6251-1). P Lang Pubs.

Fischer, Mildred & Fischer, Al. Chili-Lovers' Cook Book. 1978. pap. 3.50 plastic (ISBN 0-914846-06-X). Golden West Pub.

Fischer, Mildred, jt. ed. see Fischer, Al.

Fischer, N. & Georgopoulos, N., eds. Continuity & Change in Marxism. 249p. 1982. text ed. 19.95x (ISBN 0-391-02564-3, Pub. by Macmillan England). Humanities.

Fischer, Norman. Economy & Self: Philosophy & Economics from the Mercantilists to Marx. LC 78-73799. (Contributions in Economics & Economic History: No. 24). 1979. lib. bdg. 29.95 (ISBN 0-313-20888-3, FIE/). Greenwood.

Fischer, O., jt. ed. see Maple, M. B.

Fischer, P. Applications of Technical Devices in Archaeology. (Studies in Mediterranean Archaeology Ser.: Vol. LXIII). 64p. 1981. pap. text ed. 30.00x (ISBN 91-85058-33-5, Pub. by Paul Astroms Sweden). Humanities.

Fischer, Peter, ed. A Collection of International Concessions & Related Instruments. LC 81-11268. (Contemporary Ser.). 1981. lib. bdg. 50.00 (ISBN 0-379-20665-X); index 30.00. Oceana.

--A Collection of International Concessions & Related Instruments, Vols. 1-11. LC 75-43707. 1976. text ed. write for info. (ISBN 0-379-10075-4); Set. text ed. write for info. Oceana.

Fischer, Robert. Stocks or Options: Programs for Profits. LC 80-11669. 1979. 39.95 (ISBN 0-471-05599-9, Pub. by Wiley-Interscience). Wiley.

Fischer, Robert & Architectural Record Magazine, eds. Engineering for Architecture. (Architectural Record Book Ser.). (Illus.). 224p. 1980. 32.50 (ISBN 0-07-002353-0, P&RB). McGraw.

Fischer, Ruth. Stalin & German Communism: A Study in the Orgins of the State Party. LC 81-3418. (Social Science Classics). 700p. 1982. pap. 19.95 (ISBN 0-87855-822-5). Transaction Bks.

Fischer, S. Principles of General Psychopathology. 4.75 o.p. (ISBN 0-8022-0507-0). Philos Lib.

Fischer, S. & Dornbusch, R. Introduction to Macroeconomics. 608p. 1983. 15.95 (ISBN 0-07-021005-5). McGraw.

--Introduction to Microeconomics. 640p. 1983. 15.95 (ISBN 0-07-021006-3). McGraw.

Fischer, Stanley, jt. auth. see Dornbusch, Rudiger.

Fischer, Steven R. The Complete Medieval Dreambook: A Multilingual, Alphabetical "Somnia Danielis" Collation. 172p. 1982. write for info. (ISBN 3-261-05001-2). P Lang Pubs.

Fischer, Susan K., jt. auth. see Siegel, Carole.

Fischer, W., jt. auth. see Chodat, R.

Fischer, W., jt. auth. see Sessions, K. W.

Fischer, William A. Fischtale Enterprises. 1981. pap. text ed. 9.95x (ISBN 0-673-15414-9). Scott F.

Fischer, William C. & Lohmann, Christopher K. Selected Letters of W. D. Howells: Vol. 5, 1902-1911. (Critical Editions Program). 494p. 1983. lib. bdg. 40.00 (ISBN 0-8057-8531-0, Twayne). G K Hall.

Fischer-Galati, Stephen, ed. Eastern Europe in the Nineteen Eighties. 384p. (Orig.). 1981. lib. bdg. 27.50 (ISBN 0-89158-198-7); pap. 11.50 (ISBN 0-86531-122-6). Westview.

Fischer-Galati, Stephen A. New Rumania: From People's Democracy to Socialist Republic. (Studies in Communism, Revisionism & Revolution). 1967. 20.00x (ISBN 0-262-06019-1). MIT Pr.

Fischer-Munstermann, Uta. Jazz Dance & Jazz Gymnastics. Williamson, Liz, ed. LC 78-57794. (Illus.). 1978. 13.95 (ISBN 0-8069-4618-0); lib. bdg. 16.79 (ISBN 0-8069-4619-9); pap. 6.95 (ISBN 0-8069-4620-2). Sterling.

Fischer-Williams, Mariella, et al. A Textbook of Biological Feedback. LC 80-15235. 576p. 1981. 39.95 (ISBN 0-89885-014-2). Human Sci Pr.

Fischle, Willy H. The Way to the Centre. Nevill, Tim, tr. from Ger. Orig. Title: Der Weg zur Mitte. (Illus.). 80p. 1982. 17.90 (ISBN 0-7224-0209-0). Robinson & Wat.

Fischler. Uptown & Downtown. pap. 8.95 (ISBN 0-8015-8196-6, 0869-260, Hawthorn). Dutton.

Fischler, Shirley, jt. auth. see Fischler, Stan.

Fischler, Stan. The Great Gretzky. (Illus.). 160p. (Orig.). 1982. pap. 8.95 (ISBN 0-688-01695-2). Quill NY.

--Hockey's One Hundred: A Personal Ranking of the Best Players in Hockey History. (Illus.). 350p. 1983. pap. 9.95 (ISBN 0-89104-304-7, A & W Visual Library). A & W Pubs.

--The New Breed. LC 82-60969. (Illus.). 160p. (Orig.). 1982. pap. text ed. 8.95 (ISBN 0-688-01696-0). Quill NY.

Fischler, Stan & Fischler, Shirley. The Best, Worst & Most Unusual in Sports. LC 77-4099. (Illus.). 1977. 12.45i (ISBN 0-690-01457-0). T Y Crowell.

Fischler, Stan & Friedman, Richard. Getting into Pro Soccer. (Getting into the Pros Ser.). (Illus.). (gr. 6 up). 1979. PLB 8.40 s&l (ISBN 0-531-02280-3). Watts.

Fischler, Stan, jt. auth. see Mazer, Bill.

Fischler, Stan, jt. auth. see Potvin, Denis.

Fischler, Stan, jt. auth. see Schultz, Dave.

Fischman, Bernard. The Man Who Rode His Ten-Speed Bicycle to the Moon. LC 78-23730. 1979. 7.95 o.p. (ISBN 0-399-90038-1, Marek). Putnam Pub Group.

Fischman, Joyce. Holiday Work & Play. 1961. pap. 3.00 o.p. (ISBN 0-685-02011-8, 101960). UAHC.

--Let's Learn About Jewish Symbols. LC 68-9347. (Illus.). (ps-k). 1969. pap. text ed. 5.50 (ISBN 0-8074-0144-7, 101035). UAHC.

Fischman, Sheila, tr. see Carrier, Roch.

Fischman, Walter, jt. auth. see Grinims, Mark.

Fischoff, Ephraim, tr. see Weber, Max.

Fiscina, Salvatore F. Medical Law for the Attending Physician: A Case-Oriented Analysis. (Medical Humanities Ser.). 424p. 1983. 40.00x (ISBN 0-8093-1045-7). S Ill U Pr.

Fiscus, Edward D. & Mandell, Colleen J. Developing Individualized Education Programs (IEP) (Illus.). 350p. 1983. pap. text ed. 9.95 (ISBN 0-314-69648-2); write for info. instr's. manual (ISBN 0-314-72292-0). West Pub.

Fiscus, Edward D., jt. auth. see Mandell, Colleen J.

Fiscus, J. Walter. Let's Take a Happiness Break. 1978. 4.95 o.p. (ISBN 0-533-03195-8). Vantage.

Fiser, Robert H., Jr., ed. see National Foundation-March of Dimes Symposium, April, 1976, New York City.

Fiser, Webb S. Mastery of the Metropolis. LC 80-23244. x, 168p. 1981. Repr. of 1962 ed. lib. bdg. 19.25x (ISBN 0-313-22732-2, FIMAM). Greenwood.

Fisera, Vladimir. Workers' Councils in Czechoslovakia. LC 78-25995. 1979. 25.00x (ISBN 0-312-88959-3). St Martin.

Fish, C. R. Guide to the Materials for American History in Roman & Other Italian Archives. 1911. pap. 26.00 (ISBN 0-527-00693-9). Kraus Repr.

Fish, Carl R. Path of Empire. 1919. text ed. 8.50x (ISBN 0-686-83685-5). Elliots Bks.

Fish, Debra, ed. Home-Based Training Resouce Handbook. 2nd rev. ed. (Illus.). 392p. 1980. pap. text ed. 24.95 (ISBN 0-934140-13-8). Toys N Things.

Fish, Enrica. Cat in Art. LC 71-84406. (Fine Art Books). (Illus.). 50p. (gr. 5-11). 1970. PLB 4.95g (ISBN 0-8225-0164-3). Lerner Pubns.

Fish, Gertrude S., ed. The Story of Housing. (Illus.). 1979. text ed. 25.95 (ISBN 0-02-337920-0). Macmillan.

Fish, Hamilton. Masters of Terrorism. 1982. 14.95 (ISBN 0-686-81786-9). Devin.

--Tragic Deception: FDR & America's Involvement in World War II. 1983. 12.95 (ISBN 0-8159-6917-1). Devin.

Fish, Harriet U. Creative Lace-Making with Thread & Yarn. LC 72-81039. (Little Craft Book Ser.). (Illus.). 50p. 1972. 5.95 o.p. (ISBN 0-8069-5216-4); lib. bdg. 6.69 o.p. (ISBN 0-8069-5217-2). Sterling.

Fish, Helen D. When the Root Children Wake Up. (Illus.). scroll 7.95 (ISBN 0-914676-06-7). Green Tiger Pr.

Fish, Kenneth L. Conflict & Dissent in American High Schools. 1970. 6.95 o.p. (ISBN 0-685-07623-7, 80220). Glencoe.

Fish, Mary, jt. auth. see Williams, Vergil L.

Fish Protein Conference. Economics, Marketing, & Technology of Fish Protein Concentrate: Proceedings. Tannenbaum, Steven, et al, eds. 1974. 30.00x (ISBN 0-262-20029-5). MIT Pr.

Fish, Roy J. Every Member Evangelism for Today. rev. ed. LC 75-12289. 128p. 1976. pap. 5.72i (ISBN 0-06-061551-6, RD125, HarpR). Har-Row.

--The Master Plan of Evangelism: Study Guide. 64p. 1972. pap. 1.25 o.p. (ISBN 0-8007-0479-7). Revell.

Fish, Sharon & Shelly, Judith A. Spiritual Care: The Nurse's Role. LC 77-27688. (Illus.). 1978. 8.95 o.p. (ISBN 0-87784-509-3); pap. text ed. 5.95 (ISBN 0-87784-506-9). Inter-Varsity.

Fish, Sharon, jt. auth. see McCormick, Thomas.

Fish, Stanley E. The Living Temple: George Herbert & Catechizing. LC 73-90664. (Quantum Bks.). 1978. 24.50x (ISBN 0-520-02657-8). U of Cal Pr.

--Surprised by Sin: The Reader in Paradise Lost. 1971. pap. 8.95 (ISBN 0-520-01897-4, CAL228). U of Cal Pr.

Fishbane, Michael. Text & Texture: Close Readings of Selected Biblical Texts. LC 79-14083. 154p. 1982. pap. 7.95 (ISBN 0-8052-0726-0). Schocken.

Fishbein, Harold. Evolution, Development & Children's Learning. Siegal, Alex, ed. LC 75-13478. 320p. 1976. text ed. 19.95x (ISBN 0-673-16188-9). Scott F.

Fishbein, L. Chromatography of Environmental Hazards Vol. 1: Carcinogens, Mutagens & Teratogens. 1972. 80.50 (ISBN 0-444-40948-3). Elsevier.

--Chromatography of Environmental Hazards, Vol. 2: Metals, Gaseous & Industrial Pollutants. LC 78-180000. 654p. 1974. 106.50 (ISBN 0-444-41059-7). Elsevier.

--Chromatography of Environmental Hazards, Vol. 4: Drugs of Abuse. 1982. 95.75 (ISBN 0-444-42024-X). Elsevier.

--Potential Industrial Carcinogens & Mutagens. (Studies in Environmental Science: Vol. 4). 1979. 95.75 (ISBN 0-444-41777-X). Elsevier.

Fishbein, L., ed. Chromatography of Enviromental Hazards, Vol. 3: Pesticides. 1975. 123.50 (ISBN 0-444-41158-5). Elsevier.

Fishbein, Martin & Ajzen, Icek. Belief, Attitude, Intention, & Behavior: An Introduction to Theory & Research. 544p. 1975. 24.95 (ISBN 0-201-02089-0). A-W.

--Understanding Attitudes & Predicting Social Behavior. (Illus.). 1980. text ed. 18.95 (ISBN 0-13-936443-9); pap. text ed. 11.95 (ISBN 0-13-936435-8). P-H.

Fishbein, Meyer H. The National Archives & Statistical Research. LC 72-85545. (National Archives Conferences Ser.: Vol. 2). xiv, 255p. 1973. 15.00x (ISBN 0-8214-0104-1, 82-81099). Ohio U Pr.

Fishbein, Morris. Dr. Fishbein's Popular Illustrated Medical Encyclopedia. LC 78-18133. (Illus.). 1979. 24.95 (ISBN 0-385-14190-4). Doubleday.

Fishberg, Maurice. Materials for the Physical Anthropology of the Eastern European Jews. LC 6-2111. 1905. pap. 15.00 (ISBN 0-527-00500-2). Kraus Repr.

Fishbone, Leslie, tr. see Zel'Dovich, Ya. B. & Novikov, I. D.

Fishburn, Angela. The Complete Home Guide to Making Pillows, Draperies, Lampshades, Quilts & Slipcovers. LC 78-54046. (Illus.). 1978. 10.95 o.p. (ISBN 0-88332-090-8, 8039). Larousse.

--Making Lampshades. LC 77-7729. (Illus.). 1977. pap. 5.95 o.p. (ISBN 0-8069-8494-5). Sterling.

Fishburn, Peter C. Les Mathematiques De la Decision: Traduit De L'anglais Par Elliot Cohen. (Mathematiques et Sciences De L'homme Ser.: No. 17). 1973. pap. 9.45x (ISBN 90-2797-233-8). Mouton.

Fishelis, Avraham. Bastion of Faith. 3rd ed. 256p. 1980. 9.00 (ISBN 0-9605560-1-X). A Fishelis.

--Kol Rom, Vol. I. 3rd ed. 208p. (Hebrew.). 5.50 (ISBN 0-9605560-0-1). A Fishelis.

--Kol Rom, Vol. II. 292p. (Hebrew.). 6.50 (ISBN 0-9605560-2-8). A Fishelis.

--Kol Rom, Vol. III. 431p. (Hebrew.). 12.00 (ISBN 0-9605560-3-6). A Fishelis.

Fishelson, Lev. Tilapia in Aquaculture. (Illus.). 600p. pap. 69.00 (ISBN 0-86689-018-1). Balaban Intl Sci Serv.

Fisher. Reading to Discover Organization. (Basic Skills System). 1969. text ed. 13.50 (ISBN 0-07-051381-3). McGraw.

Fisher, A. Security for Business & Industry. 1979. 21.95 (ISBN 0-13-798967-9). P-H.

Fisher, A. S., jt. auth. see Russell, J. G. B.

Fisher, Aileen. All on a Mountain Day. 127p. 5.80 (ISBN 0-686-05600-0). Rod & Staff.

--Going Barefoot. LC 60-6238. (Illus.). (gr. k-3). 1960. 10.89 o.p. (ISBN 0-690-33331-5, TYC-J). Har-Row.

--Ways of Animals, 10 bks. Incl. Animal Disguises (ISBN 0-8372-0860-2); Animal Houses (ISBN 0-8372-0859-9); Animal Jackets (ISBN 0-8372-0861-0); Filling the Bill (ISBN 0-8372-0864-5); Going Places (ISBN 0-8372-0865-3); No Accounting for Taste (ISBN 0-8372-0868-8); Now That Days Are Colder (ISBN 0-8372-0862-9); Sleepy Heads (ISBN 0-8372-0866-1); Tail Twisters (ISBN 0-8372-0863-7); You Don't Look Like Your Mother, Said the Robin to the Fawn (ISBN 0-8372-0867-X). (Nature Ser.). (ps-6). 1973. 7.98 ea.; Set. 79.80 (ISBN 0-8372-0880-7); resource guide 3.21 (ISBN 0-8372-0869-6); filmstrips, cassettes, & records avail. Bowmar-Noble.

--The Ways of Plants, 10 Bks. Incl. Plant Magic (ISBN 0-8372-2391-1); Mysteries in the Garden (ISBN 0-8372-2392-X); Swords & Daggers (ISBN 0-8372-2393-8); And a Sunflower Grew (ISBN 0-8372-2394-6); Petals Yellow & Petals Red (ISBN 0-8372-2395-4); Now That Spring Is Here (ISBN 0-8372-2396-2); As the Leaves Fall Down (ISBN 0-8372-2397-0); Prize Performances (ISBN 0-8372-2398-9); A Tree with a Thousand Uses (ISBN 0-8372-2399-7); Seeds on the Go (ISBN 0-8372-2400-4). (Nature Ser.). 1977. 7.98 ea.; tchr's. guide 3.21 (ISBN 0-8372-5440-X); 10 bks., 10 filmstrips, tchr's guide record ed. 270.81 (ISBN 0-8372-3318-6); cassette ed. 270.81 (ISBN 0-8372-3317-8). Bowmar-Noble.

Fisher, Alan. Country Walks Near Baltimore. (Illus.). 214p. 1982. pap. 6.95 (ISBN 0-910146-36-5). Appalach Mtn.

--Country Walks Near Philadelphia. (Country Walks Ser.). (Illus.). 224p. (Orig.). 1983. pap. 6.95 (ISBN 0-910146-47-0). Appalach Mtn.

Fisher, Alec. Formal Number Theory & Computability: A Workbook. (Oxford Logic Guides). 1982. 37.50x (ISBN 0-19-853178-8). Oxford U Pr.

Fisher, Allan G. Clash of Progress & Security. LC 66-21369. Repr. of 1935 ed. 19.50x (ISBN 0-678-00158-8). Kelley.

Fisher, Anthony. Must History Repeat Itself? 155p. 1974. 6.00 o.p. (ISBN 0-685-50126-4). Transatlantic.

Fisher, Arthur. The Healthy Heart. LC 80-21587. (Library of Health). PLB 18.60 (ISBN 0-686-79854-6). Silver.

Fisher, B. A. Small Group Decision Making: Communication & the Group Process. 2nd ed. Wright, Richard R., ed. (Illus.). 1980. text ed. 21.50x (ISBN 0-07-021091-8); instr's manual 15.00 (ISBN 0-07-021097-7). McGraw.

Fisher, B. Aubrey. Perspectives on Human Communication. (Illus.). 1978. text ed. 20.95x (ISBN 0-02-337990-1). Macmillan.

--Small Group Decision Making: Communication & the Group Process. (Illus.). 288p. 1974. text ed. 14.95 o.p. (ISBN 0-07-021090-X, C). McGraw.

Fisher, Barbara. Breathing Room. Pinar, William F., ed. 350p. (Orig.). 1982. pap. 8.00 (ISBN 0-9609642-0-7). Brighton St Pr.

Fisher, Bill. How to Hotrod Volkswagen Engines. LC 72-28084. (Illus.). 1970. pap. 5.95 o.p. (ISBN 0-912656-01-8). H P Bks.

Fisher, Bill & Waar, Bob. How to Hotrod Big-Block Chevys. LC 72-159282. (Illus.). 1971. pap. 7.95 (ISBN 0-912656-04-2). H P Bks.

Fisher, Bruce. When Your Relationship Ends. 1981. pap. text ed. 6.00 (ISBN 0-9607250-0-8). Family Relations.

Fisher, Bruce D. & Phillips, Michael J. The Legal Environment of Business. (Illus.). 850p. 1982. text ed. 22.95 (ISBN 0-314-63172-0); write for info. study guide (ISBN 0-314-71141-4). West Pub.

Fisher, Carol & Terry, Ann. Children's Language & the Language Arts. 2nd ed. (Illus.). 368p. 1982. text ed. 21.50x (ISBN 0-07-021108-6). McGraw.

Fisher, Charles. South-East Asia. 2nd ed. 1966. 65.00x (ISBN 0-416-42480-5). Methuen Inc.

Fisher, Charles O. & Murray, Richard C. Guide to Maryland Negligence Cases. 200p. 1982. 25.00 (ISBN 0-87215-472-6). Michie-Bobbs.

Fisher, Clarence S. The Minor Cemetery at Giza. (Eckley B. Coxe Foundation Ser.: Vol. 1). (Illus.). 170p. 1924. 20.00X (ISBN 0-686-11902-9). Univ Mus of U PA.

Fisher, D. A. & Burrow, G. N., eds. Perinatal Thyroid Physiology & Disease. LC 75-14333. 291p. 1975. 30.00 (ISBN 0-89004-044-3). Raven.

Fisher, Dalmar. Communication in Organizations. (Illus.). 480p. 1980. text ed. 21.95 (ISBN 0-8299-0374-7). West Pub.

Fisher, David. The Pack. LC 75-45467. 1976. 7.95 o.p. (ISBN 0-399-11632-X). Putnam Pub Group.

--Teachings. (Illus.). 40p. lib. bdg. 8.95 (ISBN 0-918510-02-3); pap. 2.95 (ISBN 0-686-63535-3); signed cloth ed. 10.95 (ISBN 0-686-96877-8). Ross-Back Roads.

--The War Magician. 256p. 1983. 17.95 (ISBN 0-698-11140-0, Coward). Putnam Pub Group.

Fisher, David & Bragonier, Reg. What's What: A Visual Glossary to the Physical World. 1982. pap. write for info. (ISBN 0-345-30302-4). Ballantine.

Fisher, David, jt. auth. see Luciano, Ron.

Fisher, David, jt. auth. see Read, Anthony.

Fisher, David W., jt. ed. see Dixon, Frank J.

Fisher, Dennis F., et al, eds. Eye Movements: Cognition & Visual Perception. LC 80-27876. (Eye Movements Ser.). 368p. 1981. text ed. 39.95x (ISBN 0-89859-084-1). L Erlbaum Assocs.

Fisher, Desmond. Broadcasting in Ireland. (Case Studies on Broadcasting Systems). (Orig.). 1978. pap. 15.50 (ISBN 0-7100-8885-X). Routledge & Kegan.

Fisher, Diana, jt. auth. see McDermott, Vern.

Fisher, Douglas. Monetary Theory & the Demand for Money. LC 77-15504. 278p. 1980. pap. 24.95x (ISBN 0-470-27023-3). Halsted Pr.

Fisher, Eddie. Eddie: My Life, My Loves. LC 81-47226. 360p. 1981. 14.38 (ISBN 0-06-014907-8, HarpT). Har-Row.

Fisher, Edward C. & Reeder, Robert H. Vehicle Traffic Law. LC 74-77463. 352p. 1974. 22.50 (ISBN 0-912642-00-9). Traffic Inst.

Fisher, Elaine F. Aesthetic Awareness & the Child. LC 77-83352. 1978. text ed. 18.95 (ISBN 0-87581-222-8). Peacock Pubs.

Fisher, Ernest C. & Werner, H. Metal Pi-Complexes: Vol 1: Complexes with Di- & Oligo-Olefinic Ligands, Vol. 1. 1966. 36.75 (ISBN 0-444-40211-X). Elsevier.

Fisher, Esther O., ed. Impact of Divorce on the Extended Family. LC 81-20207. (Journal of Divorce Ser.: Vol. 5, Nos. 1 & 2). 181p. 1982. text ed. 30.00 (ISBN 0-917724-43-7, B43). Haworth Pr.

--Therapists, Lawyers, & Divorcing Spouses. (Journal of Divorce Ser.: Vol. 6, Nos. 1-2). 148p. 1982. text ed. 30.00 (ISBN 0-86656-169-2, B169). Haworth Pr.

Fisher, Eugene & Jensen, C. W. PET-CBM & the IEEE Four Eighty-Eight Bus (GPIB) 2nd ed. 322p. 1982. pap. 15.99 (ISBN 0-931988-78-0). Osborne-McGraw.

Fisher, Eugene J. & Polish, Daniel F., eds. Liturgical Foundations of Social Policy in the Catholic & Jewish Traditions. LC 82-40378. 180p. 1982. text ed. 16.95 (ISBN 0-268-01267-9); pap. text ed. 9.95 (ISBN 0-268-01268-7). U of Notre Dame Pr.

Fisher, Eugenia M., jt. auth. see Fisher, Maurice D.

Fisher, F. A Priori Information & Time Series Analysis. 1966. 17.00 (ISBN 0-7204-3110-7, North Holland). Elsevier.

Fisher, F. E., jt. auth. see Faupel, J. H.

Fisher, G. H. Cost Considerations in Systems Analysis. 1970. 18.95 (ISBN 0-444-00087-9). Elsevier.

Fisher, G. Lawrence, jt. ed. see Gordon, Gerald.

Fisher, Gail T., jt. auth. see Volhard, Joachim J.

Fisher, Glen. American Communication in a Global Society. LC 79-9331. (Communication & Information Science Ser.). 1979. 21.50x (ISBN 0-89391-025-2). Ablex Pub.

--International Negotiation: A Cross Cultural Perspective. LC 81-85716. 69p. (Orig.). 1982. pap. text ed. 6.50 (ISBN 0-933662-24-6). Intercult Pr.

Fisher, Glen W. Financing Local Improvements by Special Assessment. LC 74-18143. (Illus.). 59p. 1974. pap. 6.00 (ISBN 0-686-84375-4). Municipal.

Fisher, Harrison. U. H. F. O. 60p. (Orig.). 1982. pap. 4.50 (ISBN 0-933442-05-X). Dianas Bimonthly.

Fisher, Harwood, ed. Developments in High School Psychology. LC 73-20023. (High School Behavioral Science Ser.: Vol. 1). 292p. 1974. 26.95 (ISBN 0-87705-111-9). Human Sci Pr.

Fisher, Helen E. The Sex Contract. LC 82-18126. (Illus.). 256p. 1983. Repr. pap. 6.95 (ISBN 0-688-01599-9). Quill NY.

Fisher, Herbert A. Studies in Napoleonic Statesmanship: Germany. LC 69-13897. Repr. of 1903 ed. lib. bdg. 20.75 (ISBN 0-8371-1302-4, FINS). Greenwood.

Fisher, Hilda B. Improving Voice & Articulation. 2nd ed. 1975. text ed. 20.95 (ISBN 0-395-19232-3). HM.

Fisher, Irving. The Rate of Interest: With a New Introduction by Donald Dewey. LC 82-48363. (Accountancy in Transition Ser.). 472p. 1982. lib. bdg. 50.00 (ISBN 0-8240-5314-1). Garland Pub.

--The Theory of Interest: As Determined by Impatience to Spend Income & Opportunity to Invest It. LC 77-22591. (Illus.). Repr. of 1930 ed. pap. 9.95x (ISBN 0-87991-864-0). Porcupine Pr.

Fisher, J. & Downey, J. U. S. Studies Program. Irvin, J. L., ed. 15p. 1980. tchrs guide 5.00 (ISBN 0-943068-13-4). Graphic Learning.

Fisher, J. & Dryer, R. California Map Studies Program. Yockstick, M. L., ed. Martinas-Miller, Orlando, tr. 56p. (Spanish.). (gr. 4). 1980. 49.00 o.p. (ISBN 0-943068-21-5). Graphic Learning.

--California Studies Program. Yockstick, M. L., ed. 56p. (gr. 4). 1980. 49.00 o.p. Graphic Learning.

--California Studies Program: Activity Manual. Combs, Eunice A., ed. (Illus.). 133p. (gr. 4). 1982. 49.00 (ISBN 0-943068-23-1); tchrs guide 5.00. Graphic Learning.

--Los Estrados Unidos: Programa de Estudios Sociales. Yockstick, Elizabeth, ed. Olivares, Angelina S., tr. 126p. (Spanish.). (gr. 5). 1981. 49.00 (ISBN 0-943068-17-7). Graphic Learning.

--World Studies Program: Activity Manual. Irvin, J. L. & Yockstick, Elizabeth, eds. Orlando & Miller, M., trs. (Illus.). 126p. (Spanish.). (gr. 6). 1981. 49.00 (ISBN 0-943068-08-8). Graphic Learning.

Fisher, J. & Drywer, R., eds. United States Studies Program: Activity Manual. Olivares, Angelina S., tr. 126p. (Spanish.). (gr. 5). 1980. 49.00 o.p. (ISBN 0-943068-15-0). Graphic Learning.

Fisher, J. Patrick. Basic Medical Terminology. 2nd ed. 288p. 1983. pap. text ed. 14.95 (ISBN 0-672-61573-8); cassettes 150.00 (ISBN 0-672-61575-4); instr's guide 3.33 (ISBN 0-672-61574-6). Bobbs.

Fisher, Jacob. The Response of Social Work to the Depression. 1980. lib. bdg. 23.95 (ISBN 0-8161-8413-5, Univ Bks). G K Hall.

Fisher, Jamer E., jt. auth. see Christensen, James E.

Fisher, James R., Jr. Confident Selling. LC 77-137885. 1971. pap. 4.95 o.p. (ISBN 0-13-167510-9, Reward). P-H.

Fisher, James W., jt. auth. see Germann, Donald R.

Fisher, Jeffery. King Henry Fifth Notes. (Orig.). 1981. pap. 2.95 (ISBN 0-8220-0029-6). Cliffs.

Fisher, Jeffrey. The Fish Book: How to Buy, Clean, Catch, Cook & Preserve Them. (Illus.). 128p. 1981. 9.95 (ISBN 0-87523-196-9). Emerson.

Fisher, Jeffrey D. & Nadler, Arie, eds. New Directions in Helping: Vol. 1: Recipient Reactions to Aid. Date not set. price not set (ISBN 0-12-257301-3). Acad Pr.

Fisher, Joanne, jt. auth. see Nortman, Dorothy.

Fisher, John. The Alice in Wonderland Cookbook. (Illus.). 1976. 6.95 o.p. (ISBN 0-517-52484-8, C N Potter Bks). Crown.

Fisher, John, ed. Essays on Aesthetics: Perspectives on the Work of Monroe C. Beardsley. 1983. write for info. (ISBN 0-87722-287-8). Temple U Pr.

--Perceiving Artworks. (Philosophical Monographs: 3rd Ser.). 246p. 1980. 27.95 (ISBN 0-87722-164-2). Temple U Pr.

Fisher, John, jt. ed. see Wiener, Philip P.

Fisher, John J. Cancer Was My Copilot. 160p. 1983. 11.95 (ISBN 0-682-49978-1). Exposition.

Fisher, John J., III, jt. auth. see Rubin, Richard R.

Fisher, John W. & Struik, John H. Guide to Design Criteria for Bolted & Riveted Joints. LC 73-17158. 314p. 1974. 51.50 (ISBN 0-471-26140-8, Pub. by Wiley-Interscience). Wiley.

Fisher, Jon. Escape! Strange Places Where You Can Live Free: Antarctica, Blimps, Treehouses, Etc. Date not set. pap. cancelled (ISBN 0-686-23958-X). Loompanics.

Fisher, Karen, jt. auth. see Von Furstenberg, Egon.

Fisher, Lani. A Shadow at Winter's Fall. 1978. 4.50 o.p. (ISBN 0-533-03835-9). Vantage.

Fisher, Leonard E. The Factories. LC 79-2092. (Nineteenth Century America Bk.). (Illus.). 64p. (gr. 5 up). 1979. PLB 9.95 (ISBN 0-8234-0367-X). Holiday.

--Noonan: A Novel About Baseball, ESP & Time Warps. LC 77-80887. 1978. 7.95 o.p. (ISBN 0-385-11693-4). Doubleday.

--The Railroads. LC 79-1458. (A Nineteenth Century America Bk.). (Illus.). 64p. (gr. 5 up). 1979. PLB 9.95 (ISBN 0-8234-0352-1). Holiday.

--The Schools. LC 82-18710. (Nineteenth Century America Ser.). (Illus.). 64p. (gr. 5 up). 1983. reinforced binding 10.95 (ISBN 0-8234-0477-3). Holiday.

--The Unions Nineteenth Century America Bk. LC 81-6632. (The Unions Ser.). (Illus.). 64p. (gr. 5 up). 1982. PLB 9.95 (ISBN 0-8234-0434-X). Holiday.

Fisher, Lillian E. Violet Richardson Ward: Founder-President of Soroptimist. 1983. 10.95 (ISBN 0-533-05563-6). Vantage.

Fisher, Lois. A Literary Gazetteer of England. (Illus.). 1980. 49.95 (ISBN 0-07-021098-5). McGraw.

--A Peking Diary. LC 78-21424. 1979. 10.95 (ISBN 0-312-59997-8). St Martin.

Fisher, Lois I. Puffy P. Pushycat, Problem Solver. LC 82-19833. (Illus.). 128p. (gr. 4 up). 1983. PLB 8.95 (ISBN 0-396-08119-3). Dodd.

Fisher, Louis. Politics of Shared Power: Congress & the Executive. LC 81-5442. 232p. (Orig.). 1981. pap. 8.95 (ISBN 0-87187-163-7). Congr Quarterly.

Fisher, M., jt. ed. see Battaglia, J.

Fisher, M. B., ed. see Pliny.

Fisher, M. F. The Art of Eating. 1976. pap. 9.95 (ISBN 0-394-71399-0, Vin). Random.

--As They Were. LC 82-40427. 272p. 1983. pap. 5.95 (ISBN 0-686-43019-0, Vin). Random.

--Cooking of Provincial France. LC 67-20204. (Foods of the World Ser.). (Illus.). (gr. 6 up). 1968. PLB 17.28 (ISBN 0-8094-0056-1, Pub. by Time-Life). Silver.

--A Cordiall Water: A Garland of Odd & Old Receipts to Assuage the Ills of Man & Beast. LC 80-28409. 160p. 1981. 12.50 (ISBN 0-86547-035-9); pap. 6.00 (ISBN 0-86547-036-7). N Point Pr.

--Not Now, But Now. New ed. LC 82-81499. 264p. 1982. pap. 9.25 (ISBN 0-86547-072-3). N Point Pr.

--Sister Age. LC 82-48880. 1983. 12.95 (ISBN 0-394-53066-7). Knopf.

--With Bold Knife & Fork. LC 79-15562. 1979. pap. 4.95 (ISBN 0-399-50397-8, Perige). Putnam Pub Group.

Fisher, M. F., jt. auth. see Clancy, Judith.

Fisher, M. F., tr. see Brillat-Savarin.

Fisher, Margaret. Palm Leaf Patterns: A New Approach to Clothing Design. LC 76-57189. (Illus.). 1977. pap. 5.95 (ISBN 0-915572-20-6). Panjandrum.

Fisher, Margaret, jt. ed. see Withington, W. A.

Fisher, Marquita O. Jacqueline Cochran: First Lady of Flight. LC 72-14368. (Americans All Ser.). (Illus.). 96p. (gr. 3-6). 1973. PLB 7.12 (ISBN 0-8116-4580-0). Garrard.

Fisher, Maurice D. & Fisher, Eugenia M. The Early Education Connection: An Instructional Resource for Teachers & Parents of Preschool & Kindergarten Children. 54p. (Orig.). 1981. pap. text ed. 7.50 (ISBN 0-910609-01-2). Reading Tutor.

--Gifted Education: Critical Evaluations of Important Books on Identification, Program Development & Research. 40p. (Orig.). 1982. pap. text ed. 7.50 (ISBN 0-910609-02-0). Reading Tutor.

--Identifying & Teaching the Gifted, American Education's Stepchildren. 42p. (Orig.). 1981. pap. text ed. 6.50 (ISBN 0-910609-00-4). Reading Tutor.

Fisher, Milton. Intuition: How to Use It for Success & Happiness. 192p. 1981. 12.75 (ISBN 0-525-93111-2, 01238-370). Dutton.

Fisher, Muriel. A Touch of Nature. (Illus.). 91p. 1982. 29.95 (ISBN 0-00-216979-7, Pub. by W Collins Australia). Intl Schol Bk Serv.

Fisher, P. S. & Slonim, Jacob. Advances in Distributed Processing Management, Vol. 2. (Advances in Library EDP Management Ser.). 200p. 1983. price not set (ISBN 0-471-26232-3, Pub. by Wiley Heyden). Wiley.

Fisher, Patricia, ed. see Considine, Tim.

Fisher, Pete. Dreamlovers. LC 81-97. 224p. (Orig.). 1982. pap. 8.95x (ISBN 0-933322-07-0). Sea Horse.

Fisher, Peter. Prescription for National Health Insurance. LC 72-77266. (Illus.). 158p. 1972. 10.00 (ISBN 0-88427-007-6). North River.

Fisher, Philip. Making Up Society: The Novels of George Eliot. LC 81-50639. 252p. 1981. 19.95 (ISBN 0-8229-3800-6). U of Pittsburgh Pr.

Fisher, R. Digital Applications in Television Receivers. 1983. text ed. price not set (ISBN 0-408-01149-1). Butterworth.

Fisher, Richard B. & Christie, George A. A Dictionary of Drugs: The Medicines You Use. rev. ed. LC 76-12241. 1976. 7.95x (ISBN 0-8052-3638-4); pap. 2.75 (ISBN 0-8052-0552-7). Schocken.

Fisher, Richard H., jt. auth. see Davis, William S.

Fisher, Robert A. An Introduction to RPG: RPG II Programming. LC 74-9537. 393p. 1975. pap. 29.95 (ISBN 0-471-26001-0). Wiley.

--Optical Phase Conjugation. (Quantum Electronics Princples & Applications Ser.). 612p. 1983. write for info (ISBN 0-12-257740-X). Acad Pr.

Fisher, Robert C. & Ziebur, Allen D. Calculus & Analytic Geometry. 3rd ed. (Illus.). 784p. 1975. text ed. 33.95 (ISBN 0-13-112227-4). P-H.

--Integrated Algebra, Trigonometry & Analytic Geometry. 4th ed. (Illus.). 560p. 1982. 23.95 (ISBN 0-13-468967-4). P-H.

Fisher, Robert M. Twenty Years of Public Housing. LC 75-29075. (Illus.). 303p. 1975. Repr. of 1959 ed. lib. bdg. 21.00x (ISBN 0-8371-8411-8, FIPH). Greenwood.

Fisher, Robin, ed. see Walker, Alexander.

Fisher, Roger. International Conflicts for Beginners. (Illus.). 1970. pap. 4.95xi (ISBN 0-06-131911-2, TB1911, Torch). Har-Row.

Fisher, Roger & Ury, William. Getting to Yes: Negotiating Agreement Without Giving In. 1983. pap. 4.95 (ISBN 0-14-006534-2). Penguin.

Fisher, Ronald. The Genetical Theory of Natural Selection. 2nd ed. 1958. pap. 6.00 (ISBN 0-486-60466-7). Dover.

Fisher, Ronald J. Social Psychology: An Applied Approach. LC 81-51855. 712p. 1982. text ed. 20.95 (ISBN 0-312-73473-5); instr's. manual; study guide 6.95 (ISBN 0-312-73475-1). St Martin.

Fisher, S. & Freedman, A. M., eds. Opiate Addiction: Origins & Treatment. LC 73-19073. (Series in General Psychiatry). 247p. 1974. 11.95x o.s.i. (ISBN 0-470-26153-6). Halsted Pr.

Fisher, Seymour & Greenberg, Roger P. The Scientific Credibility of Freud's Theories & Therapy. LC 76-7685. (Illus.). 1977. text ed. 22.50x o.s.i. (ISBN 0-465-07385-9). Basic.

Fisher, Seymour & Greenberg, Roger, eds. The Scientific Evaluation of Freud's Theories & Therapy: A Book of Readings. LC 77-90537. 1978. text ed. 25.00x o.s.i. (ISBN 0-465-07388-3). Basic.

Fisher, Sidney G. Quaker Colonies. 1919. text ed. 8.50x (ISBN 0-686-83720-7). Elliots Bks.

--Trial of the Constitution. LC 70-164511. (American Constitutional & Legal History Ser.). 1972. Repr. of 1864 ed. lib. bdg. 45.00 (ISBN 0-306-70281-9). Da Capo.

Fisher, Stanley. Standards Relating to Pretrial Court Proceedings. (Juvenile Justice Standards Project Ser.). 160p. Date not set. 20.00x (ISBN 0-88410-227-0); pap. 10.00x (ISBN 0-88410-811-2). Ballinger Pub.

Fisher, Stanley W. Collector's Progress. rev. ed. 1972. 9.50 o.p. (ISBN 0-7181-0941-4). Transatlantic.

Fisher, Stephen D. Function Theory on Planar Domains: A Second Course in Complex Analysis. (Pure & Applied Mathematics Series of Texts, Monographs). 400p. 1983. 37.50 (ISBN 0-471-87314-4, Pub. by Wiley-Interscience). Wiley.

Fisher, Sydney G. Men, Women & Manners in Colonial Times, 2 Vols. LC 70-95776. 1969. Repr. of 1897 ed. Set. 45.00x (ISBN 0-8103-3567-0). Gale.

Fisher, Sydney N. The Middle East: A History. 3rd ed. 1978. text ed. 24.00x (ISBN 0-394-32098-0). Knopf.

Fisher, T. Richard. Workbook & Manual Introduction to Horticulture. 3rd ed. 1982. pap. text ed. 11.25x (ISBN 0-89917-002-1). TIS Inc.

Fisher, T. W. & Orth, Robert. The Marsh Flies of California: Diptera, Sciomyzidae. (The California Insect Survey Ser.: Vol. 24). 128p. 1982. 23.50x (ISBN 0-520-09665-7). U of Cal Pr.

Fisher, Terry. International Students' Guide to Cooking Without Getting Caught. Carr, Sally B., ed. LC 76-18503. 1976. pap. 8.95 (ISBN 0-87949-055-1). Ashley Bks.

Fisher, W. B. The Middle East: A Physical, Social, & Regional Geography. 7th ed. (Illus.). 1978. 49.95x (ISBN 0-416-71510-9); pap. 25.00x (ISBN 0-416-71520-6). Methuen Inc.

Fisher, W. B., jt. auth. see Clarke, J. I.

Fisher, W. R., tr. see Schimper, A. F.

Fisher, Wallace E. Because God Cares: Messages 1980. LC 80-67791. 112p. (Orig.). 1980. pap. 4.75 (ISBN 0-8066-1852-3, 10-0566). Augsburg.

Fisher, Walter D. Statistics Economized: Basic Statistics for Economics & Business. LC 81-40114. (Illus.). 282p. (Orig.). 1981. pap. text ed. 11.25 (ISBN 0-8191-1745-5). U Pr of Amer.

Fisher, Wesley A., jt. ed. see Yanowitch, Murray.

Fisher, William P., ed. Creative Marketing for the Foodservice Industry: A Practitioner's Handbook. 288p. 1982. 29.95x (ISBN 0-471-08111-6, Pub. by Wiley-Interscience). Wiley.

Fishery Committee for the Eastern Central Atlantic (CECAF) Working Party on Resources Evaluation, Rome, 1976. Report. (Illus.). 92p. 1976. pap. 9.00 (ISBN 0-685-66351-5, F831, FAO). Unipub.

Fishery Committee for the Eastern Central Atlantic (CECAF), 1st Session, Accra, Ohana, 1969. Report. (FAO Fisheries Reports: No. 69). 42p. 1969. pap. 7.50 (ISBN 0-686-93019-3, F1676, FAO). Unipub.

Fishery Committee for the Eastern Central Atlantic (CECAF), 2nd Session, Casablanca, 1971. Report. (FAO Fisheries Reports: No. 107). 25p. 1971. pap. 7.50 (ISBN 0-686-93061-4, F1697, FAO). Unipub.

Fishery Committee for the Eastern Central Atlantic (CECAF) Working Party on Regulatory Measures for Demersal Stocks, 2nd Session, Rome 1971. Report. (FAO Fisheries Reports: No. 109). 113p. 1971. pap. 8.00 (ISBN 0-686-93066-5, F1698, FAO). Unipub.

Fishery Committee for the Eastern Central Atlantic (CECAF) Sub-Committee on Implementation of Management Measures, 1st Session, Rome, 1972. Report. (FAO Fisheries Reports: No. 125). 14p. 1972. pap. 7.50 (ISBN 0-686-93080-0, F1706, FAO). Unipub.

Fishery Committee for the Eastern Central Atlantic (CECAF), 3rd Session, Canary Islands, 1972. Report. (FAO Fisheries Reports: No. 132). 26p. 1973. pap. 7.50 (ISBN 0-686-93089-4, F1710, FAO). Unipub.

Fishery Committee for the Eastern Central Atlantic (CECAF) Working Party on Resource Evaluation, Rome, 1972. Report. (FAO Fisheries Report: No. 136). 73p. 1973. pap. 7.50 (ISBN 0-686-93095-9, F782, FAO). Unipub.

Fishery Committee for the Eastern Central Atlantic (CECAF), Sub-Committee on Fishery Development, 1st Session, Dakar, Senegal, 1974. Report. (FAO Fisheries Reports: No. 145). 40p. 1974. pap. 7.50 (ISBN 0-686-93973-5, F1713, FAO). Unipub.

Fishery Committee for the Eastern Central Atlantic (CEVAF), 4th Session, Rome, 1974. Report. (FAO Fisheries Reports: No. 151). 28p. 1974. pap. 7.50 (ISBN 0-686-93978-6, F1714, FAO). Unipub.

Fishery Committee for the Eastern Central Atlantic (CECAF), Working Party on Resources Evaluation, 2nd Session, Rome, 1973. Report. (FAO Fisheries Reports: No. 158). 95p. 1975. pap. 7.50 (ISBN 0-686-93981-6, F800, FAO). Unipub.

Fishery Committee for the Eastern Central Atlantic (CECAF), Working Party on Resource Evaluation, 5th Session, Dakar, Senegal, 1980. Report. (FAO Fisheries Reports: No. 244). 127p. 1981. pap. 9.75 (ISBN 0-686-94016-4, F2169, FAO). Unipub.

Fishery Committee for the Eastern Central Atlantic (CECAF), Sub-Committee on Management of Resources Within the Limits of National Jurisdiction, 3rd Session, Dakar, Senegal, 1981. Report. (FAO Fisheries Reports: No. 250). 47p. 1981. pap. 7.50 (ISBN 0-686-94017-2, F2170, FAO). Unipub.

Fishkin, James S. Justice, Equal Opportunity & the Family. LC 82-10939. 208p. 1983. text ed. 18.95x (ISBN 0-300-02865-2). Yale U Pr.

Fishkin, Lois & Dimarco, Susan. The Not-Strictly Vegetarian Cookbook. (Illus., Orig.). 1982. pap. 8.95 (ISBN 0-916870-49-9). Creative Arts Bk.

Fishler, Stan, jt. auth. see Stamm, Laura.

Fishlock, D. A Guide to Earth Satellites. LC 79-167624. 1972. 29.95 (ISBN 0-444-19581-5). Elsevier.

Fishlow, Albert. The Mature Neighbor Policy: A New United States Economic Policy for Latin America. (Policy Papers in International Affairs: No. 3). 1977. pap. 3.95x (ISBN 0-87725-503-2). U of Cal Intl St.

Fishman, Alfred, ed. see American Physiological Society.

Fishman, Alfred P. Pulmonary Diseases & Disorders, 2 vols. (Illus.). 1696p. 1979. Set. text ed. 140.00 (ISBN 0-07-021116-7). McGraw.

Fishman, Alfred P., ed. Heart Failure. (Illus.). 1978. text ed. 29.95 (ISBN 0-07-021118-3, HP). McGraw.

Fishman, Alfred P. & Renkin, Eugene M., eds. Pulmonary Edema. (Clinical Physiology Ser. - American Physiological Society). (Illus.). 269p. 1979. 30.00 o.p. (ISBN 0-683-03245-3). Williams & Wilkins.

Fishman, David. Shopping Centers & the Accessibility Codes. 1979. 14.00 (ISBN 0-913598-12-7). Intl Coun Shop.

Fishman, George S. Principles of Discrete Event Simulation. LC 78-17555. (Systems Engineering & Analysis Ser.). 1978. 37.95x (ISBN 0-471-04395-8, Pub. by Wiley-Interscience). Wiley.

Fishman, Hal, jt. auth. see Schiff, Barry.

Fishman, Isidore. Gateway to the Mishnah. (gr. 10-12). 1970. text ed. 6.95x (ISBN 0-685-29098-0). Prayer Bk.

Fishman, Jack. And the Walls Came Tumbling Down. (Illus.). 384p. 1983. 17.95 (ISBN 0-02-538470-8). Macmillan.

Fishman, James J., jt. auth. see Kalodner, Howard I.

Fishman, Joan, et al. Something's Got to Taste Good: The Cancer Patient's Cookbook. 1982. pap. 3.50 (ISBN 0-451-11362-4, AE1362, Sig). NAL.

Fishman, Joseph F. Crucibles of Crime: The Shocking Story of the American Jail. LC 69-14923. (Criminology, Law Enforcement, & Social Problems Ser.: No. 35). 1969. Repr. of 1923 ed. 10.00x (ISBN 0-87585-035-9). Patterson Smith.

Fishman, Joshua & Cooper, Robert L. The Spread of English. LC 77-1068. 1977. pap. 14.95 (ISBN 0-88377-087-3). Newbury Hse.

Fishman, Joshua A. Bilingual Education: An International Sociological Perspective. 1976. pap. text ed. 12.95 o.p. (ISBN 0-88377-056-3). Newbury Hse.

--Guide to Non-English Language Broadcasting. LC 82-225306. (Language Resources in the United States Ser.). 144p. (Orig.). 1982. pap. 14.50 (ISBN 0-89763-064-5). Natl Clearinghse Bilingual Ed.

--Guide to Non-English-Language Print Media. (Language Resources in the United States Ser.). 80p. (Orig.). 1981. pap. 7.50 (ISBN 0-89763-062-9). Natl Clearinghse Bilingual Ed.

--Guide to Non-English-Language Schools. (Language Resources in the United States Ser.). (Orig.). 1982. pap. 15.00 o.p. (ISBN 0-89763-065-3). Natl Clearinghse Bilingual Ed.

--Hungarian Language Maintenance in the United States. LC 66-63012. (Uralic & Altaic Ser: Vol. 62). (Orig.). 1966. pap. text ed. 5.00x o.p. (ISBN 0-87750-021-5). Res Ctr Lang Semiotic.

--Language & Nationalism. LC 72-149036. 1973. pap. 11.95 o.p. (ISBN 0-912066-15-6). Newbury Hse.

Fishman, Joshua A., frwd. by. Never Say Die! A Thousand Years of Yiddish in Jewish Life & Letters. LC 81-3957. (Contributions to the Sociology of Language Ser.: No. 30). 763p. 1981. 47.50 (ISBN 0-686-37011-2). Mouton.

Fishman, Judith. Responding to Prose: A Reader for Writers. (Illus.). 480p. (Orig.). 1982. pap. text ed. 9.95 (ISBN 0-672-61569-X); instr's. guide 3.33 (ISBN 0-672-61566-5). Bobbs.

Fishman, Judith, jt. auth. see Schor, Sandra.

Fishman, Lew & Golf Magazine Editors, eds. Golf Magazine's Shortcuts to Better Golf. LC 78-19559. (Illus.). 1979. 13.41i (ISBN 0-06-011273-5, HarpT). Har-Row.

Fishman, M. E., jt. auth. see Glasscote, R. M.

Fishman, M. E., jt. auth. see Glasscote, Raymond M.

Fishman, Meryl & Horwich, Kathleen. Living with Your Teenage Daughter & Liking it. 1983. 7.95 (ISBN 0-671-46880-4, Fireside). S&S.

Fishman, P. A. Assessment of Pulmonary Function. 1980. text ed. 25.95 (ISBN 0-07-021117-5). McGraw.

Fishman, Richard, ed. Housing for All Under Law: New Directions in Housing, Land Use & Planning Law. LC 77-810. 720p. 1977. prof ref 25.00x (ISBN 0-88410-751-5). Ballinger Pub.

Fishman, W. J. & Breach, N. The Streets of East London. (Illus.). 1980. pap. 20.00 (ISBN 0-7156-1416-9). Heinman.

Fishman, William H., ed. Metabolic Conjugation & Metabolic Hydrolysis, 3 vols. LC 79-107556. 1970-73. Vol. 1. 68.50 (ISBN 0-12-257601-2); Vol. 2. 93.50 (ISBN 0-12-257602-0); Vol. 3. 67.00 (ISBN 0-12-257603-9); Set. 173.50 (ISBN 0-685-03086-5). Acad Pr.

Fishwick, Francis. Multinational Companies & Economic Concentration in Europe. 120p. 1983. 26.95 (ISBN 0-03-059124-4). Praeger.

Fishwick, Marshall W. American Heroes, Myth & Reality. LC 72-10695. 242p. 1975. Repr. of 1954 ed. lib. bdg. 18.50x (ISBN 0-8371-6610-1, FIAH). Greenwood.

--Lee After the War. LC 73-7102. (Illus.). 242p. 1973. Repr. of 1963 ed. lib. bdg. 16.25x (ISBN 0-8371-6911-9, FILW). Greenwood.

Fishwick, Olive, tr. see Kyber, Manfred.

Fisiak, Jacek, ed. Theoretical Issues in Contrastive Linguistics. (Current Issues in Linguistic Theory Ser.). x, 430p. 1980. 44.00 (ISBN 90-272-3502-3, 12). Benjamins North Am.

Fisichella, Anthony J. Just What Is Metaphysics, Anyway? Friedman, Robert, ed. (Illus.). 224p. (Orig.). 1983. pap. 6.95 (ISBN 0-89865-182-4). Donning Co.

Fisk, E. K. & Rani, Osman, eds. The Political Economy of Malaysia. 350p. 1982. 55.00x (ISBN 0-19-582501-2). Oxford U Pr.

Fisk, E. K., jt. ed. see Young, E. A.

Fisk, E. R. Construction Project Administration. 434p. 1982. text ed. 28.95 (ISBN 0-471-09186-3). Wiley.

Fisk, Edward R. Construction Project Administration. LC 77-16455. 316p. 1978. text ed. 22.50 o.p. (ISBN 0-471-02312-4). Wiley.

--Fields Engineer's Form Book. LC 80-22395. 624p. 1981. text ed. 54.95 (ISBN 0-471-06307-X). Wiley.

Fisk, Frank S., ed. see Thiers, Adolphe.

Fisk, Jim & Barron, Robert. Buzzwords: The Official MBA Dictionary. 1983. pap. 5.95 (ISBN 0-671-47006-X, Wallaby). S&S.

--The Official MBA Handbook. 1982. 4.95 (ISBN 0-686-93901-8, Wallaby). S&S.

Fisk, Leonard W., Jr., jt. auth. see Lindgren, Henry C.

Fisk, Loretta Z. & Lindgren, Henry C. A Survival Guide for Teachers. LC 73-11269. 176p. 1973. pap. text ed. 14.50 (ISBN 0-471-26190-4). Wiley.

Fisk, Lori & Lindgren, Henry C. Learning Centers. 1974. pap. 6.95 (ISBN 0-914420-54-2). Exceptional Pr Inc.

Fisk, Mary B. Baby Gourmet Cookbook. (Illus.). 1978. pap. 3.95 (ISBN 0-915696-09-6). Determined Prods.

Fisk, Michael D. Treason with Glory: Or, What Happened at Paradise, Nevada? 1983. 10.95 (ISBN 0-533-05234-3). Vantage.

Fisk University Library (Nashville) Dictionary Catalog of the Negro Collection of the Fisk University Library, 6 vols. 1974. Set. lib. bdg. 490.00 (ISBN 0-8161-1055-7, Hall Library). G K Hall.

Fiske, David. Theory of Cosmology. 1979. 13.00 o.p. (ISBN 0-533-03981-9). Vantage.

Fiske, Donald W., jt. auth. see Kelly, Everett L.

Fiske, Frank S., tr. see Thiers, Adolphe.

Fiske, John. Introduction to Communication Studies. (Studies in Communication). 1982. 18.95x (ISBN 0-416-74560-1); pap. 7.50x (ISBN 0-416-74570-9). Methuen Inc.

Fiske, John & Hartley, John. Reading Television. (New Accents Ser.). 1978. 14.95x o.p. (ISBN 0-416-85580-6); pap. 6.95x (ISBN 0-416-85560-1). Methuen Inc.

Fiske, Majorie. Book Selection & Censorship: A Study of School & Public Libraries in California. LC 59-10464. (California Library Reprint: No. 1). 1968. 24.50x (ISBN 0-520-00418-3). U of Cal Pr.

Fiske, Richard, jt. auth. see Simkin, Tom.

Fiske, Susan T., jt. auth. see Clark, Margaret S.

Fison, J. E. Understanding the Old Testament: The Way of Holiness. LC 78-21116. 1979. Repr. of 1952 ed. lib. bdg. 20.50x (ISBN 0-313-20839-5, FIUO). Greenwood.

Fisz, Marek. Probability Theory & Mathematical Statistics. 3rd ed. LC 80-12455. 704p. 1980. lib. bdg. 36.50 (ISBN 0-89874-179-3). Krieger.

Fiszdon, W., ed. Rarefied Gas Flows: Theory & Experiment. (CISM-International Centre for Mechanical Sciences, Courses & Lectures: Vol. 224). (Illus.). 524p. 1982. pap. 45.60 (ISBN 0-387-81595-3). Springer-Verlag.

Fit Magazine Editors. Aloe Vera: The Miracle Plant. 64p. 1983. pap. 3.95 (ISBN 0-89037-261-6). Anderson World.

--Breast Care. (Fit Self-Improvement Ser.). 96p. 1983. pap. 7.95 (ISBN 0-89037-259-4). Anderson World.

--Figure Maintenance. (Fit Self-Improvement Ser.). 96p. 1983. pap. 7.95 (ISBN 0-89037-255-1). Anderson World.

--Legs & Thifgs. (Fit Self-Improvement Ser.). 96p. 1983. pap. 7.95 (ISBN 0-89037-260-8). Anderson World.

Fitch, A. A., ed. Developments in Geographic Exploration Methods, Vol. 4. Date not set. 37.00 (ISBN 0-85334-174-5, Pub. by Applied Sci England). Elsevier.

--Developments in Geophysical Exploration Methods, Vol. 1. (Illus.). 1979. 51.80x (ISBN 0-85334-835-9, Pub. by Applied Sci England). Elsevier.

--Developments in Geophysical Exploration Methods, Vol. 2. 1981. 41.00 (ISBN 0-85334-930-4, Pub. by Applied Sci England). Elsevier.

--Developments in Geophysical Exploration Methods, Vol. 3. (Illus.). 320p. 1982. 57.50 (ISBN 0-85334-126-5, Pub. by Applied Sci England). Elsevier.

Fitch, Asa. Their Own Voices: Oral Accounts of Early Settlers in Washington County, New York. Adler, Winston, ed. 135p. 1983. 12.95 (ISBN 0-932334-59-8); pap. 8.95 (ISBN 0-932334-60-1). Heart of the Lakes.

Fitch, Canon J. see Birkby, Elizabeth.

Fitch, E. C. & Surjaatmadja, J. B. Introduction to Fluid Logic. (McGraw-Hill-Hemisphere in Fluids & Thermal Engineering Ser.). (Illus.). 1978. text ed. 35.00 (ISBN 0-07-021126-4, C). McGraw.

Fitch, Frank, jt. auth. see Booth, Basil.

Fitch, Frederick B. Symbolic Logic: An Introduction. 238p. 1952. 15.95x (ISBN 0-471-07001-7). Wiley.

Fitch, Grace E. & Larson, Margaret A. Basic Arithmetic Review & Drug Therapy for Practical-Vocational Nurses. 4th ed. (Illus.). 192p. 1977. pap. text ed. 13.95 (ISBN 0-02-338010-1, 33801). Macmillan.

Fitch, Grace E. & Dubiny, Mary J., eds. Macmillan Dictionary for the Practical & Vocational Nurse. 1966. 8.95 o.p. (ISBN 0-02-338160-4, 33816). Macmillan.

Fitch, Henry S. Autecology of the Copperhead, Vol. 13, No. 4. 2nd ed. Hall, Raymond E. & Wilson, Robert W., eds. (Illus.). 203p. 1980. pap. 12.00 (ISBN 0-89338-016-4). U of KS Mus Nat Hist.

Fitch, James M. American Building: The Environmental Forces That Shape It, Vol. II. 2nd ed. LC 75-10857. (Illus.). 368p. 1975. pap. 9.95 (ISBN 0-8052-0503-9). Schocken.

Fitch, Janet. Foreign Devil: Reminiscences of a China Missionary Daughter, 1909-1935. (Asian Library Ser.: No. 39). 1982. 28.75x (ISBN 0-686-37543-2). Oriental Bk Store.

Fitch, Noel R. Sylvia Beach & the Lost Generation: A History of Literary Paris in the Twenties & Thirties. (Illus.). 1983. 25.00 (ISBN 0-393-01713-3). Norton.

Fitch, Raymond E. The Poison Sky: Myth & Apocalypse in Ruskin. LC 70-122097. (Illus.). xii, 722p. 1982. 35.00x (ISBN 0-8214-0090-8, 82-80943). Ohio U Pr.

Fitch, Richard D. & Porter, Edward A. Accidental or Incendiary. 224p. 1975. photocopy ed.spiral 22.75x (ISBN 0-398-00582-6). C C Thomas.

Fitch, Robert M. & Svengalis, Cordell M. Futures Unlimited: Teaching about Worlds to Come. LC 79-52124. (Bulletin Ser.: No. 1). 86p. (Orig.). 1979. pap. 7.25 (ISBN 0-87986-023-5). Coun Soc Studies.

Fitch, William D. Study of the Oboe. 13.00 (ISBN 0-685-21807-4). Wahr.

Fitchen, F. C., jt. auth. see Motchenbacher, C. D.

Fitchen, Franklin C. Electronic Integrated Circuits & Systems. LC 79-23338. 432p. 1980. lib. bdg. 25.00 (ISBN 0-89874-027-4). Krieger.

Fitchen, Janet M. Poverty in Rural America: A Cast Study. (Special Studies in Contemporary Social Issues). 266p. (Orig.). 1981. lib. bdg. 23.50 (ISBN 0-89158-868-X); pap. text ed. 10.00 (ISBN 0-89158-901-5). Westview.

Fitcher. Bulge of Africa. 1981. 8.90 (ISBN 0-531-04270-7). Watts.

Fite, Emerson D. Social & Industrial Conditions in the North During the Civil War. LC 74-22742. 328p. 1982. Repr. of 1910 ed. 32.50 (ISBN 0-404-58493-4). AMS Pr.

Fite, Gilbert C. Farmers' Frontier, 1865-1900. LC 66-15477. (Histories of the American Frontier Ser.). (Illus.). 286p. 1977. pap. 9.95x (ISBN 0-8263-0312-9). U of NM Pr.

Fite, Gilbert C. & Graebner, Norman A. Recent United States History. (Illus.). 901p. 1972. 18.95 (ISBN 0-8260-3110-2). Wiley.

Fite, Gilbert C., ed. Elmer Ellis: Teacher, Scholar, & Administrator. LC 61-10289. 1961. 7.50x o.p. (ISBN 0-8262-0010-9). U of Mo Pr.

Fite, R., jt. auth. see Blair, T.

Fitt, A. P. Life of D. L. Moody. pap. 2.95 (ISBN 0-8024-4727-9). Moody.

Fitt, Yann, et al. The World Economic Crisis: American Imperialism at Bay. 224p. (Orig.). 1980. 31.00 (ISBN 0-905762-53-3, Pub. by Zed Pr England); pap. 8.50 (ISBN 0-905762-54-1, Pub. by Zed Pr England). Lawrence Hill.

Fitter. Collins Pocket Guide to Bird Watching. 29.95 (ISBN 0-686-42749-1, Collins Pub England). Greene.

--Finding Wild Flowers. 29.95 (ISBN 0-686-42765-3, Collins Pub England). Greene.

Fitter & Blamey. The Wild Flowers of Britain & Northern Europe. pap. 14.95 (ISBN 0-686-42738-6, Collins Pub England). Greene.

Fitter & Richardson. Collins Pocket Guide to British Birds. 26.95 (ISBN 0-686-42750-5, Collins Pub England). Greene.

--Collins Pocket Guide to Nests & Eggs. 26.95 (ISBN 0-686-42751-3, Collins Pub England). Greene.

Fitter, jt. auth. see Arlott.

Fitter, jt. auth. see Heinzel.

Fitter, jt. auth. see McClintock.

Fitter, Richard, jt. ed. see Robinson, Eric.

Fitton, Mary, tr. see Lanez, Manual M.

Fitts, Donald D. Vector Analysis in Chemistry. (Advanced Chemistry Ser.). (Illus.). 192p. 1974. text ed. 25.95 (ISBN 0-07-021130-2, C). McGraw.

Fitts, Dudley, tr. see Anthologia Graeca Selections.

Fitts, Leroy. Lott Carey: First Black Missionary to Africa. 1978. pap. 6.95 (ISBN 0-8170-0820-9). Judson.

Fitts, Paul M. & Posner, Michael I. Human Performance. LC 79-4253. (Illus.). 1979. Repr. of 1967 ed. lib. bdg. 19.75x (ISBN 0-313-21245-7, FIHP). Greenwood.

Fitz, Franklin H. A Gardener's Guide to Propagating Food Plants. (Illus.). 160p. 1983. 10.95 (ISBN 0-684-17655-6, ScribT). Scribner.

Fitzell, Lincoln. Selected Poems. LC 82-71884. 88p. 1955. 5.95 (ISBN 0-8040-0269-X). Swallow.

Fitzell, Philip B. Private Labels. (Illus.). 1982. lib. bdg. 25.00 (ISBN 0-87055-415-8). AVI.

Fitzgerald, A. E., et al. Basic Electrical Engineering. 1981. text ed. 34.95 (ISBN 0-07-021154-X); instr's manual avail. McGraw.

--Electric Machinery. 4th ed. (McGraw-Hill Series in Electrical Engineering). (Illus.). 640p. 1983. text ed. 32.50x (ISBN 0-07-021145-0, C); solutions manual 8.00 (ISBN 0-07-021146-9). McGraw.

FitzGerald, Ann, jt. ed. see McPhee, Carol.

Fitzgerald, Arthur E., et al. Basic Electrical Engineering. 4th ed. (Electrical & Electronic Engineering Ser.). 1975. text ed. 31.50 (ISBN 0-07-021152-3, C); solutions manual 4.00 (ISBN 0-07-021153-1). McGraw.

--Electric Machinery. 3rd ed. 1971. text ed. 32.50 (ISBN 0-07-021140-X, C). McGraw.

Fitzgerald, Bob. Practical Sign Shop Operation. (Illus.). 1982. 25.00 (ISBN 0-911380-58-2). Signs of Times.

Fitzgerald, Brigid, jt. auth. see Young, Lynne.

Fitzgerald, Don, jt. auth. see Roy, Mike.

FitzGerald, E. V. The Political Economy of Peru Nineteen Fifty-Six to Seventy-Seven. LC 78-72086. (Illus.). 1980. 52.50. Cambridge U Pr.

--The State & Economic Development: Peru Since 1968. LC 75-30443. (Department of Applied Economics, Occasional Papers Ser.: No. 49). (Illus.). 140p. 1976. pap. 12.95x (ISBN 0-521-29054-6). Cambridge U Pr.

Fitzgerald, Edward & Hemmant, Lynette. Rubaiyat of Omar Khayam. 1979. 8.95 (ISBN 0-437-40120-0, Pub. by World's Work). David & Charles.

Fitzgerald, Edward, tr. Rubaiyat of Omar Khayaam. (Illus.). 8.95 (ISBN 0-385-00146-0); pap. 2.95 (ISBN 0-385-09499-X, Dolp). Doubleday.

Fitzgerald, Edward T. & Hughes, Robert E. Effective Written Communication in Criminal Justice. LC 78-57263. 1978. 15.95. Benjamin-Cummings.

Fitzgerald, Elisa B., ed. see Leroe, Ellen.

Fitzgerald, Ernest A. Diamonds Everywhere: Appreciating God's Gifts. 112p. (Orig.). 1983. pap. 5.95 (ISBN 0-687-10734-2). Abingdon.

Fitzgerald, F. Scott. The Beautiful & Damned. 464p. 1983. pap. 4.95 (ISBN 0-686-83691-X, ScribT). Scribner.

--Tender is the Night. 320p. 1982. pap. 3.95 (rack size) (ISBN 0-686-83693-6, ScribT). Scribner.

FitzGerald, G. M. Sixth Century Monastery at Beth-Shan (Scythopolis) (Publications of the Palestine Section Ser.: Vol. 6). (Illus.). 1939. 15.00x (ISBN 0-686-24094-4). Univ Mus of U.

FitzGerald, Gerald F., jt. auth. see Bloomfield, Louis M.

Fitzgerald, Hiram & McGreal, Cathieen E., eds. Fathers & Infants: A Special Issue of Infant Mental Health Journal, Vol. 2, No. 4. LC 81-82739. 88p. 1981. pap. 9.95 (ISBN 0-89885-121-1). Human Sci Pr.

Fitzgerald, Hiram E. & Gage, Patricia, eds. Child Nurturance, Vol. 3: Studies of Development in Nonhuman Primates. 288p. 1982. 29.50x (ISBN 0-306-41176-8, Plenum Pr). Plenum Pub.

Fitzgerald, Hiram E. & Lester, Barry M., eds. Theory & Research in Behavioral Pediatrics, Vol. 1. 300p. 1982. 29.50x (ISBN 0-306-40851-1, Plenum Pr). Plenum Pub.

Fitzgerald, J. J. Applied Radiation Protection & Control, 2 vols. LC 65-27846. 1018p. 1969. 62.70 o.p. (ISBN 0-685-58267-1, 450009). Am Nuclear Soc.

--Mathematical Theory of Radiation Dosimetry. LC 65-27846. 747p. 1967. 38.00 o.p. (ISBN 0-685-58265-5, 450008). Am Nuclear Soc.

Fitzgerald, Jack D., jt. auth. see Cox, Steven M.

Fitzgerald, James A. & Fitzgerald, Patricia G. Fundamentals of Reading Instruction. (Illus., Orig.). 1967. pap. 2.50x o.p. (ISBN 0-02-816440-7). Glencoe.

--Learning & Using Words. 1959. 3.96 o.p. (ISBN 0-02-816400-8). Glencoe.

--Teaching Reading & the Language Arts. 1965. 7.95 o.p. (ISBN 0-02-816420-2). Glencoe.

Fitzgerald, Janet A. Alfred North Whitehead's Early Philosophy of Space & Time. LC 79-63849. (Illus.). 1979. 10.50 (ISBN 0-8191-0747-6). U Pr of Amer.

FitzGerald, Jerry. Internal Controls for Computerized Systems. LC 78-69677. (Illus.). 93p. 1978. pap. text ed. 14.95 (ISBN 0-932410-04-9). FitzGerald & Assocs.

Fitzgerald, Jerry & Eason, Thomas. Fundamentals of Data Communications. LC 77-20842. 260p. 1978. text ed. 23.95 (ISBN 0-471-26254-4, Pub. by Wiley-Hamilton). Wiley.

Fitzgerald, Jerry & Eason, Tom. Fundamentals of Data Communications. 260p. 1978. 23.95 (ISBN 0-686-98098-0). Telecom Lib.

Fitzgerald, Jerry, et al. Fundamentals of Systems Analysis. 2nd ed. LC 80-11769. 500p. 1980. text ed. 29.95 (ISBN 0-471-04968-9, Pub. by Wiley Heyden); write for info. (ISBN 0-471-08117-5). Wiley.

Fitzgerald, Joe, jt. auth. see Auerbach, Arnold Red.

Fitzgerald, John & Murcer, Bill. Building New Families: Through Adoption & Fostering. (The Practice of Social Work Ser.: No. 10). 44p. 1982. text ed. 25.00x (ISBN 0-631-13148-5, Pub. by Basil Blackwell England); pap. text ed. 9.95x (ISBN 0-631-13193-0, Pub. by Basil Blackwell England). Biblio Dist.

Fitzgerald, John D. Brave Buffalo Fighter (Waditaka Tatahka Kisisohitika) LC 73-80213. (Illus.). 192p. (gr. 5-7). 1973. PLB 7.50 o.p. (ISBN 0-8309-0100-0). Ind Pr MO.

--Great Brain. (Illus.). (gr. 7 up). 1971. pap. 2.50 (ISBN 0-440-40307-3, YB). Dell.

--Great Brain at the Academy. 176p. (gr. 3-7). 1973. pap. 2.25 (ISBN 0-440-43113-1, YB). Dell.

--Great Brain Reforms. 176p. 1975. pap. 2.25 (ISBN 0-440-44841-7, YB). Dell.

--Me & My Little Brain. (gr. 4-7). 1972. pap. 1.95 (ISBN 0-440-45533-2, YB). Dell.

--More Adventures of the Great Brain. 1971. pap. 2.25 (ISBN 0-440-45822-6, YB). Dell.

--The Return of the Great Brain. (gr. 3-5). 1975. pap. 2.25 (ISBN 0-440-45941-9, YB). Dell.

Fitzgerald, John D., jt. auth. see Meredith, Robert C.

Fitzgerald, Louise S. & Kearney, Elizabeth I. The Continental Novel: A Checklist of Criticism in English 1967-1980. LC 82-20454. 510p. 1983. 29.50 (ISBN 0-8108-1598-2). Scarecrow.

FitzGerald, Mary, ed. Selected Plays of Lady Gregory. (Irish Drama Selections Ser.: No. 3). 1983. 27.95 (ISBN 0-8132-0582-4); pap. 7.95 (ISBN 0-8132-0583-2). Cath U Pr.

Fitzgerald, Michael G. American Movies: The Forties, Vol. 1: 1940-1944. 1979. cancelled o.p. (ISBN 0-87000-424-7, Arlington Hse). Crown.

Fitzgerald, Michael R., jt. auth. see Watson, Richard A.

Fitzgerald, Nancy. Chelsea. LC 78-60290. 1979. 10.95 o.p. (ISBN 0-385-12686-7). Doubleday.

--Down Into the Water. 52p. 1981. 1.95 (ISBN 0-89900-143-2). College Pr Pub.

Fitzgerald, Patricia G., jt. auth. see Fitzgerald, James A.

Fitzgerald, Penelope. At Freddie's. 182p. 1983. 12.95 (ISBN 0-87923-439-3). Godine.

--The Knox Brothers. LC 77-22621. (Illus.). 1978. 10.95 o.p. (ISBN 0-698-10860-4, Coward). Putnam Pub Group.

Fitzgerald, Percy. Bozland: Dickens' Places & People. LC 70-141754. 1971. Repr. of 1895 ed. 34.00 o.p. (ISBN 0-8103-3616-2). Gale.

--Chronicles of a Bow Street Police-Office, 2 vols. in 1. LC 78-129313. (Criminology, Law Enforcement, & Social Problems Ser.: No. 136). (Illus.). 816p. (With intro. & index added). 1972. Repr. of 1888 ed. 30.00x (ISBN 0-87585-136-3). Patterson Smith.

Fitzgerald, R. S. Liverpool Road Station, Manchester. 1980. 20.00 (ISBN 0-7190-0765-8); pap. 9.50 (ISBN 0-7190-0790-9). Manchester.

Fitzgerald, R. W. Mechanics of Materials. 2nd ed. LC 81-4737. 1982. 29.95 (ISBN 0-201-04073-5); solutions manual avail. (ISBN 0-201-04573-7). A-W.

Fitzgerald, Richard. Art & Politics: Cartoonists of the "Masses" & "Liberator". LC 72-609. (Contributions in American Studies: No. 8). 288p. 1973. lib. bdg. 29.95 (ISBN 0-8371-6006-5, FRI/). Greenwood.

Fitzgerald, Robert, ed. see O'Connor, Flannery.

Fitzgerald, Robert, tr. see Homer.

Fitzgerald, Ross, ed. Comparing Political Thinkers. 320p. 1980. 31.00 (ISBN 0-08-024800-4); pap. 17.50 (ISBN 0-08-024799-7). Pergamon.

--Human Needs & Politics. 1978. text ed. 27.50 (ISBN 0-08-021402-9); pap. text ed. 17.50 (ISBN 0-08-021401-0). Pergamon.

Fitzgerald, S. China & the Overseas Chinese: A Study of Peking's Changing Policy, 1949-1970. LC 77-177938. (Cambridge Studies in Chinese History, Literature & Institutions). (Illus.). 250p. 1972. 44.50 (ISBN 0-521-08410-5); pap. 14.95 (ISBN 0-521-29810-5). Cambridge U Pr.

Fitzgerald, S. J. The Story of the Savoy Opera in Gilbert & Sullivan Days. (Music Reprint Ser.). 1979. Repr. of 1925 ed. lib. bdg. 27.50 (ISBN 0-306-79543-4). Da Capo.

Fitzgerald, Sally, ed. see O'Connor, Flannery.

FitzGerald, Susan. Reading Your Way to English, Bk. 3. 1975. pap. text ed. 5.95 o.p. (ISBN 0-88377-032-6). Newbury Hse.

--Reading Your Way to English, Bk. 4. 1976. pap. text ed. 5.95 o.p. (ISBN 0-88377-033-4). Newbury Hse.

Fitzgerald, T. H. Money Market Directory of Pension Funds & Their Investment Managers: 1983. 1982. 385.00 (ISBN 0-939712-02-4). Money Mkt.

Fitzgerald, Theodore C. The Coturnix Quail: Anatomy & Histology. (Illus.). 1970. 11.95x (ISBN 0-8138-0356-X). Iowa St U Pr.

Fitzgerald, Tom. Chocolate Charlie Comes Home. 1978. pap. 1.95 o.p. (ISBN 0-446-89243-2). Warner Bks.

Fitz-Gerald, William. The Harness Maker's Illustrated Manual. 16.95 o.p. (ISBN 0-88427-014-9). Green Hill.

--The Harness Makers' Illustrated Manual. (Illus.). 1977. Repr. of 1875 ed. 16.95x o.s.i. (ISBN 0-88427-014-9). North River.

Fitzgerald, Zelda. Save Me the Waltz. 208p. 1974. pap. 1.25 o.p. (ISBN 0-451-05603-5, Y5603, Sig). NAL.

--Save Me the Waltz. LC 32-30021. (Arcturus Books Paperbacks). 224p. 1967. pap. 8.95 (ISBN 0-8093-0255-1). S Ill U Pr.

--Scandalabra. limited ed. 1980. 35.00x (ISBN 0-89723-022-1). Bruccoli.

Fitzgibbon, Constantine. Drink. LC 78-22757. 1979. 8.95 o.p. (ISBN 0-385-14830-5). Doubleday.

Fitzgibbon, Dan, jt. auth. see Carlson, Dale.

Fitzgibbon, Russell H. Cuba & the United States, 1900-1935. LC 64-16466. (Illus.). 1964. Repr. of 1935 ed. 8.50x o.p. (ISBN 0-8462-0449-5). Russell.

Fitzgibbon, Russell H., ed. & Brazil: A Chronology & Fact Book. LC 73-17058. (World Chronology Ser.). 150p. 1974. lib. bdg. 8.50 (ISBN 0-379-16309-8). Oceana.

Fitzgibbon, W. E. & Walker, H. F., eds. Nonlinear Diffusion. (Research Notes in Mathematics Ser.: No. 14). 232p. 1977. pap. text ed. 20.95 (ISBN 0-273-01066-2). Pitman Pub MA.

Fitzgibbon, W. E., jt. ed. see Walker, H. F.

Fitzgibbons, R. & Fernandez, J. Latin America: Political Culture & Development. 2nd ed. 1981. pap. 14.95 (ISBN 0-13-524348-3). P-H.

Fitzgibbons, Robert E. Making Educational Decisions: An Introduction to Philosophy of Education. 261p. 1981. pap. text ed. 12.95 (ISBN 0-15-554621-X, HC). HarBraceJ.

Fitzhenry, Robert I., ed. Barnes & Noble Book of Quotations. 340p. 1983. pap. 4.76i (ISBN 0-06-463571-6, EH 571). B&N NY.

Fitzhugh, Hank A. & Bradford, G. Eric, eds. Hair Sheep of West Africa & the Americas: A Genetic Resource for the Tropics. (Winrock International Studies). 280p. 1982. lib. bdg. 25.00 (ISBN 0-86531-370-9). Westview.

Fitzhugh, Louise. Harriet the Spy. 240p. (gr. 3-9). 1975. pap. 2.75 (ISBN 0-440-43447-5, YB). Dell.

--I Am Five. LC 78-50404. (Illus.). (ps-2). 1978. 5.95 o.s.i. (ISBN 0-440-03952-5); PLB 5.47 o.s.i. (ISBN 0-440-03953-3). Delacorte.

--The Long Secret. 224p. (gr. 3-7). 1975. pap. 1.75 (ISBN 0-440-44977-4, YB). Dell.

--Long Secret. LC 65-23370. (Illus.). (gr. 5 up). 1965. 12.45i (ISBN 0-06-021410-4, HarpJ); PLB 12.89 (ISBN 0-06-021411-2). Har-Row.

--Sport. (gr. k-6). 1982. pap. 2.25 (ISBN 0-440-48221-6, YB). Dell.

Fitzhugh, Louise & Scoppettoone, Sandra. Bang Bang You're Dead. LC 69-14440. 32p. (ps-3). 1969. PLB 12.89 (ISBN 0-06-021914-9, HarpJ). Har-Row.

Fitzhugh, William W. & Kaplan, Susan. Inua: Spirit World of the Bering Sea Eskimo. (Illus.). 296p. 1982. 35.00 (ISBN 0-87474-429-6); pap. 15.00 (ISBN 0-87474-430-X). Smithsonian.

Fitzig, Irving. Leicaflex & Leicaflex SL Guide. pap. 2.95 o.p. (ISBN 0-8174-0172-5, Amphoto). Watson-Guptill.

Fitzmaurice, George & Guinan, John. The Wonderful Wedding. (Lost Play Ser.). pap. 1.95x (ISBN 0-912262-52-4). Proscenium.

Fitzmaurice-Kelly, Julia. Antonio Perez. 1922. pap. 4.00 (ISBN 0-87535-011-9). Hispanic Soc.

Fitzmyer, Joseph F. Pauline Theology: A Brief Sketch. (Orig.). 1967. pap. text ed. 8.95 (ISBN 0-13-654525-4). P-H.

Fitzpatrick, Eva & Stubbs, Joanna. Kirsty at the Lodge. (Illus.). (ps-5). Date not set. write for info. o.p. (ISBN 0-571-09769-3). Faber & Faber.

Fitzpatrick, J. Puerto Rican Americans: The Meaning of Migration to the Mainland. 1971. pap. 10.95 ref. ed. (ISBN 0-13-740100-0). P-H.

Fitzpatrick, Joseph F., Jr. How to Know the Freshwater Crustacea. (Pictured Key Nature Ser.). 300p. 1982. write for info wire coil (ISBN 0-697-04783-0). Wm C Brown.

Fitzpatrick, Joyce & Whall, Ann. Conceptual Models of Nursing & Analysis Evaluation: Applications. (Illus.). 352p. 1982. pap. text ed. 21.95 (ISBN 0-89303-233-6). R J Brady.

Fitzpatrick, Joyce, et al. Nursing Models & Their Psychiatric Mental Health Applications. (Illus.). 128p. 1981. pap. text ed. 9.95 (ISBN 0-89303-026-0). R J Brady.

Fitzpatrick, M. Louise. The National Organization for Public Health Nursing 1912-1952: Development of a Practice Field. 226p. 1975. 10.95 (ISBN 0-686-38315-X, 11-1510). Natl League Nurse.

--Prologue to Professionalism. 320p. 1983. pap. text ed. 15.95 (ISBN 0-89303-773-7). R J Brady.

Fitzpatrick, Malcolm S. Environmental Health Planning: Community Development Based on Environmental & Health Precepts. LC 77-11692. 288p. 1978. prof ref 18.50x (ISBN 0-88410-517-2). Ballinger Pub.

Fitzpatrick, Mariana, jt. auth. see Cunningham, Ann Marie.

Fitzpatrick, Mariana, tr. see Berrondo, Marie.

Fitzpatrick, Mary C., tr. see Thomas Aquinas, Saint.

Fitzpatrick, Philip M. Principles of Celestial Mechanics. 1970. text ed. 17.00 (ISBN 0-12-257950-X). Acad Pr.

Fitzpatrick, Sheila. Commissariat of Enlightenment. (Soviet & East European Studies). (Illus.). 1971. 49.50 (ISBN 0-521-07919-5). Cambridge U Pr.

--Education & Social Mobility in the Soviet Union: 1921-1934. LC 78-58788. (Soviet & East European Studies). 1979. 42.50 (ISBN 0-521-22325-3). Cambridge U Pr.

--The Russian Revolution. 250p. 1983. 19.95 (ISBN 0-19-219162-4). Oxford U Pr.

Fitzpatrick, Sheila, ed. Cultural Revolution in Russia, 1928-1931. LC 77-74439. (Studies of the Russian Institute, Columbia University Ser.). 352p. 1978. 17.50 o.p. (ISBN 0-253-31591-3). Ind U Pr.

Fitzpatrick, T. B., et al. Dermatology in General Medicine. 2nd ed. LC 78-9850. (Illus.). 1979. text ed. 110.00 (ISBN 0-07-021196-5, HP). McGraw.

Fitzpatrick, Thomas B. & Polano, Machiel K. Color Atlas & Synopsis of Clinical Dermatology. (Illus.). 352p. 1982. pap. text ed. 29.95 (ISBN 0-07-021197-3, HP). McGraw.

Fitzsimmons, J. A. & Sullivan, R. S. Service Operations Management. 464p. 1982. 25.95x (ISBN 0-07-021215-5). McGraw.

Fitzsimmons, S. J., et al. Guidance Manual to Providing Neighborhood Services. LC 77-5225. 1977. PLB 13.50 o.p. (ISBN 0-89158-242-8). Westview.

--Social Assessment Manual: A Guide to the Preparation of the Social Well-Being Account for Planning Water Resource Projects. LC 76-58332. 1977. lib. bdg. 25.00 (ISBN 0-89158-228-2). Westview.

Fitzsimons. A Field Guide to the Snakes of Southern Africa. 29.95 (ISBN 0-686-42782-3, Collins Pub England). Greene.

Fitzsimons, Christopher. Early Warning. 256p. 1981. pap. 2.25 o.p. (ISBN 0-380-50179-1, 50179). Avon.

Fitzsimons, J. T. The Physiology of Thirst & Sodium Appetite. LC 78-16212. (Physiological Society Monographs: No. 35). 1979. 85.00 (ISBN 0-521-22292-3). Cambridge U Pr.

Fitzsimons, M. A. The Past Recaptured: Great Historians & the History of History. 1983. price not set. U of Notre Dame Pr.

Fitzsimons, Virginia, jt. auth. see Forbes, Elizabeth.

Fitzwarren. The Nature of Nature from Alpha to Zeta. 1981. 1.50 (ISBN 0-942788-07-9). Marginal Med.

Fitzwilliam Museum. All for Art: The Ricketts & Shannon Collection. Darracott, J., ed. LC 79-51597. (Illus.). 1979. 39.50 (ISBN 0-521-22841-7); pap. 11.95 (ISBN 0-521-29674-9). Cambridge U Pr.

--Drawings & Watercolours by Peter De Wint. LC 79-4652. (Illus.). 34.50 (ISBN 0-521-22745-3); pap. 9.95 (ISBN 0-521-29631-5). Cambridge U Pr.

Fivaz, Derek & Scott, Patricia E., eds. African Languages: A Genetic & Decimalised Classification for Bibliographic & General Reference. 1977. lib. bdg. 32.00 o.p. (ISBN 0-8161-8026-1, Hall Reference). G K Hall.

Fix, James A., jt. auth. see Becker, R. Frederick.

Fix, Theodore. Observations sur l'Etat des Classes Ouvrieres. (Conditions of the 19th Century French Working Class Ser.). 416p. (Fr.). 1974. Repr. of 1846 ed. lib. bdg. 105.50 o.p. (ISBN 0-8287-0343-4, 1013). Clearwater Pub.

Fixel, Lawrence. Time to Destroy-To Discover. 1972. regular ed 3.00 (ISBN 0-915572-58-3); ltd. signed, numbered ed 5.00 (ISBN 0-686-96843-3). Panjandrum.

Fixler, Alvin. Family River Rafting Guide. 1979. LC 79-83686. (Illus.). 1979. pap. cancelled o.p. (ISBN 0-89803-006-4). Caroline Hse.

Fixler, Michael, ed. The Mentor Literary Bible. 1973. pap. 1.95 o.p. (ISBN 0-451-61251-5, MJ1251, Ment). NAL.

Fixx, James. Games for the Super Intelligent. 128p. 1982. pap. 2.75 (ISBN 0-446-31032-8). Warner Bks.

--More Games for the Super-Intelligent. 144p. 1982. pap. 2.75 (ISBN 0-446-31044-1). Warner Bks.

--Solve It. 128p. 1982. pap. 2.95 (ISBN 0-446-31080-8). Warner Bks.

Fixx, James F. The Complete Book of Running. (Illus.). 1977. 12.95 (ISBN 0-394-41159-5). Random.

--The Complete Runner's Day-by-Day Log & Calendar, 1982. (Illus.). 168p. 1981. 6.95 (ISBN 0-394-73940-X). Random.

--Games for the Superintelligent. LC 73-180074. (Illus.). 120p. 1972. 9.95 (ISBN 0-385-05768-7). Doubleday.

--Jackpot! 1982. 12.50 (ISBN 0-394-50899-8). Random.

--Solve It. LC 77-25589. (gr. 4-9). 1978. 6.95 o.p. (ISBN 0-385-13039-2); PLB (ISBN 0-385-13040-6). Doubleday.

Fizdale, Robert, jt. auth. see Gold, Arthur.

Fjeld, Per-Olaf. Sverere Fehn: On the Thought of Construction. LC 82-42845. (Illus.). 168p. 1983. pap. 25.00 (ISBN 0-8478-0471-2). Rizzoli Intl.

Fjelde, Rolf, tr. see Gibson, Henrik.

Fjelde, Rolf, tr. see Ibsen, Henrik.

Flaceliere, Robert. Love in Ancient Greece. Cleugh, James, tr. LC 72-13866. (Illus.). 224p. 1973. Repr. of 1962 ed. lib. bdg. 17.50x (ISBN 0-8371-6758-2, FLLA). Greenwood.

Flach, Frederic F. & Draghi, Suzanne C. The Nature & Treatment of Depression. LC 74-28265. 448p. 1975. 55.00 o.p. (ISBN 0-471-26271-4, Pub. by Wiley Medical). Wiley.

Flach, George W., jt. auth. see Osborn, Richard W.

Flachmann, Kim. Focus: A College English Handbook. LC 80-82699. (Illus.). 448p. 1981. pap. text ed. 10.95 (ISBN 0-395-29728-1); instr's. manual 1.00 (ISBN 0-395-29729-X). HM.

Flachmann, Michael, jt. auth. see Appel, Libby.

Flack, Elmer E., ed. see Melanchthon, Philipp.

Flack, J. A. Douglas. Bird Populations of Aspen Forests in Western North America. 97p. 1976. 7.50 (ISBN 0-943610-19-2). Am Ornithologists.

Flack, J. Ernest. Urban Water Conservation. LC 82-70113. 112p. 1982. pap. text ed. 13.25 (ISBN 0-87262-296-7). Am Soc Civil Eng.

Flack, Marjorie. Angus & the Ducks. (ps-k). 7.95 (ISBN 0-385-07213-9); PLB o.p. (ISBN 0-385-07600-2); pap. 1.95 (ISBN 0-385-01026-5). Doubleday.

--Walter the Lazy Mouse. LC 62-16500. (gr. 2-5). 6.95a (ISBN 0-385-02772-9); PLB (ISBN 0-385-03771-6); pap. 2.50 (ISBN 0-385-01078-8, Zephyr). Doubleday.

Flackes, W. D. Northern Ireland: A Political Directory 1968-79. 1980. 26.00 (ISBN 0-686-60013-4). St Martin.

Flacks, Niki & Rasberry, Robert W. Power Talk: How to Win Your Audience with Theater Techniques. LC 81-69632. 256p. 1982. text ed. 12.95 (ISBN 0-02-910390-8). Free Pr.

Flader, Susan L., ed. The Great Lakes Forest: An Environmental & Social History. (Illus.). 416p. 1983. 29.50x (ISBN 0-8166-1089-4). U of Minn Pr.

Flagel, Clarice. Avoiding Burnout: Time Management for D. R. E.'s. 60p. (Orig.). 1981. pap. 5.95 (ISBN 0-697-01782-6). Wm C Brown.

Flageul, G., jt. auth. see Elbaz, Jean S.

Flagg, Fanny. Coming Attraction. 1982. pap. text ed. 2.95 (ISBN 0-451-11507-4, AE1507, Sig). NAL.

Flagg, Jared B. Life & Letters of Washington Allston. LC 68-27719. (Library of American Art Ser). 1969. Repr. of 1892 ed. lib. bdg. 45.00 (ISBN 0-306-71168-0). Da Capo.

Flagg, Marie, ed. see Elliott, Gerald.

Flagg, William G. The Clam Lover's Cookbook. 2nd ed. LC 80-10619. (Illus., Orig.). 1980. pap. 5.95 o.p. (ISBN 0-88427-041-6). North River.

--The Clam Lover's Cookbook. 3rd ed. (Illus.). 160p. (Orig.). 1983. pap. 6.95 (ISBN 0-88427-054-8, Dist. by Everest Hse). North River.

--The Mushroom Lover's Cookbook. LC 80-39496. (Illus.). 160p. (Orig.). 1983. pap. 6.95 (ISBN 0-88427-044-0, Dist. by Everest Hse). North River.

Flagler, John J. Labor Movement in the U. S. LC 75-84423. (Real World of Economics Ser). (Illus.). (gr. 5-11). 1970. PLB 4.95g (ISBN 0-8225-0620-3). Lerner Pubns.

--Modern Trade Unionism. LC 79-84424. (Real World of Economics Ser). (Illus.). (gr. 5-11). 1970. PLB 4.95g (ISBN 0-8225-0621-1). Lerner Pubns.

Flahault, C., jt. auth. see Bornet, E.

Flaherty, Daniel, jt. auth. see Ciszek, Walter J.

Flaherty, Daniel L., jt. auth. see Ciszek, Walter J.

Flaherty, David H., ed. see Strachey, William.

Flaherty, Doug. A Love-Tangle of Roots. LC 77-3018. 65p. 1977. 3.50 (ISBN 0-87886-080-0). Ithaca Hse.

Flaherty, M. Josephine, jt. auth. see Curtin, Leah.

Flaherty, Patricia, jt. ed. see Davis, Bernard D.

Flaherty, Patrick F. & Ziegler, Richard. Estate Planning for Everyone. rev. ed. LC 80-8314. 160p. 1981. 14.37i (ISBN 0-690-01943-2, HarpT). Har-Row.

Flaim, Stephen & Zelis, Robert F., eds. Calcium Blockers: Mechanisms of Action & Clinical Applications. LC 82-8548. (Illus.). 313p. 1982. text ed. 44.50 (ISBN 0-8067-0611-2). Urban & S.

Flaim, T. A User's Guide to SERICOST: A Computer Program for Estimating Electric Utility Avoided Cost Rates. (Progress in Solar Energy Supplements SERI Ser.). 40p. 1983. pap. text ed. 7.50x (ISBN 0-89553-075-9). Am Solar Energy.

--A User's Guide to SERICPAC: A Computer Program for Calculating Electric Utility Avoided Cost Rates. (Progress in Solar Energy Supplements SERI Ser.). 140p. 1983. pap. text ed. 13.50x (ISBN 0-89553-074-0). Am Solar Energy.

Flaim, T. & Sulliven, R. L. WECS Value Analysis: A Comparative Assessment of Four Methods. (Progress in Solar Energy Supplements SERI Ser.). 70p. 1982. pap. text ed. 9.00 (ISBN 0-89553-073-2). Am Solar Energy.

Flake, Raymond, ed. Index of Papers Read Before the Bucks County Historical Society, Vols. 1-8. 262p. 1972. pap. 12.50 (ISBN 0-910302-05-7). Bucks Co Hist.

Flake-Hobson, Carol & Robinson, Bryan E. Child Development & Relationships. (Illus.). 608p. 1983. text ed. 15.95 (ISBN 0-201-04092-1). A-W.

Flam, Jack D., ed. Matisse on Art. 1978. pap. 9.95 (ISBN 0-525-47490-0, 0966-290). Dutton.

Flamenbaum, Walter. Nephrology: An Approach to the Patient with Renal Disease. (Illus.). 640p. 1982. text ed. 37.50 (ISBN 0-397-50533-7, Lippincott Medical). Lippincott.

Flamholtz, Eric G., jt. auth. see Epstein, Marc J.

Flamigni, C. & Givens, J. R., eds. The Gonadotropins. (Serono Symposium Ser.: No. 42). 512p. 1982. 58.50 (ISBN 0-12-258550-X). Acad Pr.

Flamini, Roland. Ava. (Illus.). 352p. 1983. 14.95 (ISBN 0-698-11123-0, Coward). Putnam Pub Group.

Flamm, D. & Schoberl, F. Introduction to the Quark Model of Elementary Particles. (Quantum Numbers, Gauge Theories & Hadron Spectroscopy Ser.: Vol. 1). 384p. 1982. 73.50 (ISBN 0-677-16270-7). Gordon.

Flamm, Steven, jt. auth. see Miller, Ed.

Flammanc, Solveng, tr. see McDowell, Josh.

Flammarion, Camille. Haunted Houses. LC 76-159957. (Tower Bks). 1971. Repr. of 1924 ed. 37.00x (ISBN 0-8103-3911-0). Gale.

Flammer, A. & Kintsch, W., eds. Discourse Processing: An Edited Selection of Papers Presented at the International Symposium, Fribourg, Switzerland. (Advances in Psychology Ser.: Vol. 8). 614p. 1982. 66.00 (ISBN 0-444-86515-2, North Holland). Elsevier.

Flammonde, Paris. UFO Exist! LC 75-42925. (Illus.). 384p. 1976. 12.95 o.p. (ISBN 0-399-11538-2). Putnam Pub Group.

Flanagan. School Food Purchasing Guide. (Research Bulletin: No. 7). pap. 1.00 o.p. (ISBN 0-685-57182-3). Assn Sch Busn.

Flanagan, F. Spitalfields Silks of the Eighteenth & Nineteenth Centuries. 22.50x (ISBN 0-87245-104-6). Textile Bk.

Flanagan, G. T. Feed Water Systems & Treatment. (Marine Engineering Ser.). 144p. 1978. pap. 9.95x (ISBN 0-540-07343-1). Sheridan.

--Marine Boilers: Questions & Answers. 2nd ed. (Marine Engineering Ser.). 102p. 1980. pap. 9.95x (ISBN 0-540-07348-2). Sheridan.

Flanagan, Geraldine L. The First Nine Months of Life. 1982. 14.95 (ISBN 0-671-45974-0, Touchstone Bks); pap. 6.95 (ISBN 0-671-45975-9). S&S.

Flanagan, Henry E., Jr. & Gardner, Robert. Basic Lacrosse Strategy: An Introduction for Young Players. (Illus.). 1979. 7.95 o.p. (ISBN 0-385-14001-0); PLB (ISBN 0-385-14002-9). Doubleday.

Flanagan, J. L. & Rabiner, L. R., eds. Speech Synthesis. LC 73-9728. (Benchmark Papers in Acoustics: Vol. 3). 511p. 1973. text ed. 55.00 (ISBN 0-87933-044-9). Hutchinson Ross.

Flanagan, Joan. The Grass Roots Fund Raising Book. 1981. 12.00 (ISBN 0-686-31965-6). Public Serv Materials.

Flanagan, Martin J. The Passing Parade: The Story of Somersworth, NH, 1910-1981. LC 82-62138. (Illus.). 285p. 1983. 10.00 (ISBN 0-89725-036-2). NE History.

Flanagan, Neal M. The Gospel According to John 7 the Johannine Epistles, No. 4. Karris, Robert J., ed. LC 82-22908. (Collegeville Bible Commentary Ser.). 128p. 1983. pap. 2.50 (ISBN 0-8146-1304-7). Liturgical Pr.

Flanagan, Robert J., et al. National Incomes Policies in Industrial Countries in the 1970s. 1983. 34.95 (ISBN 0-8157-2856-5); pap. 16.95 (ISBN 0-8157-2855-7). Brookings.

Flanagan, W., jt. auth. see Gugler, J.

Flanagan, William G. How to Beat the (Financial) Squeeze: Don't Just Get Mad, Get Even. LC 79-7814. 240p. 1980. 10.95 o.p. (ISBN 0-385-14836-4). Doubleday.

Flanary, David A. Champfleury: The Realist Writer As Art Critic. Kuspit, Donald B., ed. LC 80-17475. (Studies in Fine Arts: Criticism: No. 1). 96p. 1980. 34.95 (ISBN 0-8357-1087-4, Pub. by UMI Res Pr). Univ Microfilms.

Flanders, Dennis. The Great Livery Companies of the City of London. 120p. 1982. 75.00x (ISBN 0-284-98512-0, Pub. by C Skilton Scotland). State Mutual Bk.

Flanders, H. Calculus. 1970. text ed. 29.50 o.p. (ISBN 0-12-259640-4); ans. manual 3.50 o.p. (ISBN 0-12-259642-0). Acad Pr.

Flanders, H. & Price, J. Calculus with Analytic Geometry. 1041p. 1978. text ed. 31.50 o.p. (ISBN 0-12-259672-2); instr's. manual 3.50 o.p. (ISBN 0-12-259673-0). Acad Pr.

Flanders, H. J. & Cresson, B. C. Introduction to the Bible. 558p. 1973. 22.95 (ISBN 0-471-07012-2). Wiley.

Flanders, Harley & Price, Justin J. A Second Course in Calculus. 1974. text ed. 21.75 o.p. (ISBN 0-12-259662-5); instrs' manual 3.50 o.p. (ISBN 0-12-259663-3). Acad Pr.

Flanders, Harley, et al. A First Course in Calculus with Analytic Geometry. 1973. 21.75 o.p. (ISBN 0-12-259657-9); instrs' manual 3.50 o.p. (ISBN 0-12-259658-7). Acad Pr.

Flanders, Helen H. & Brown, George. Vermont Folk-Songs & Ballads. LC 68-20768. iv, 256p. 1968. Repr. of 1931 ed. 34.00x (ISBN 0-8103-5010-6). Gale.

Flanders, Henry J., Jr., et al. People of the Covenant: An Introduction to the Old Testament. 2nd ed. (Illus.). 539p. 1973. 22.50 (ISBN 0-471-07011-4). Wiley.

Flanders, Jane. The Students of Snow. LC 82-8461. 68p. 1982. lib. bdg. 8.00x (ISBN 0-87023-378-5); pap. 4.00 (ISBN 0-87023-379-3). U of Mass Pr.

Flanders, Peter. A Thematic Index to the Works of Benedetto Pallavicino. (Music Indexes & Bibliographies: No. 11). 1974. pap. 9.00 (ISBN 0-913574-11-2). Eur-Am Music.

Flanders, Rebecca. A Matter of Trust. (American Romance Ser.). 192p. 1983. pap. 2.25 (ISBN 0-373-16006-2). Harlequin Bks.

Flanders, Robert G. Learn to Type. LC 78-54788. (Illus.). 1978. pap. 6.95 (ISBN 0-89709-036-5). Liberty Pub.

Flandrin, J. L. Families in Former Times. LC 78-18095. (Themes in the Social Sciences Ser.). (Illus.). 1979. 42.50 (ISBN 0-521-22323-7); pap. 11.95 (ISBN 0-521-29449-5). Cambridge U Pr.

Flanigan, Francis J. Complex Variables: Harmonic & Analytic Functions. (Illus.). 353p. 1983. pap. 8.00 (ISBN 0-486-61388-7). Dover.

Flanigan, Michael G. & Boone, Robert S. Using Media in the Language Arts. LC 76-9550. (Language Arts for Children Ser). 1977. pap. text ed. 6.50 (ISBN 0-87581-194-9). Peacock Pubs.

Flanigan, William & Zingale, Nancy. American Voting Behavior: Presidential Elections from 1952-1976. 1978. codebook write for info. o.p. (ISBN 0-89138-999-7). ICPSR.

Flanigan, William H. & Zingale, Nancy H. American Voting Behavior: Presidential Elections from 1952 to 1980. LC 82-83324. 1982. write for info. (ISBN 0-89138-920-2, ICPSR 7581). ICPSR.

Flannagan, Roy C. Paradise Lost Notes. 1970. pap. 2.50 (ISBN 0-8220-0977-3). Cliffs.

Flanner, Hildegarde. Hearkening Eye. Trusky, Tom, ed. LC 79-51631. (Modern & Contemporary Poets of the West Ser.). 1979. pap. 3.00 (ISBN 0-916272-12-5). Ahsahta Pr.

Flanner, Janet, pseud. Paris Was Yesterday: Nineteen Twenty Five - Nineteen Thirty Nine. Drutman, Irving, ed. 1979. pap. 3.95 (ISBN 0-14-005068-X). Penguin.

Flanner, Janet, tr. see Leblanc, Georgette.

Flannery, Edward H. The Anguish of the Jews. 332p. pap. 3.95 o.p. (ISBN 0-686-95105-0). ADL.

Flannery, Kent V., ed. The Early Mesoamerican Village. LC 82-6737. 250p. 1982. pap. 17.50 (ISBN 0-12-259852-0). Acad Pr.

Flannery, Kent V. & Marcus, Joyce, eds. The Cloud People: The Divergent Evolution of the Zapotic & Mixte Civilizations. Date not set. price not set (ISBN 0-12-259860-1). Acad Pr.

Flannery, Sean. False Prophets. Date not set. pap. price not set (Pub. by Charter Bks). Ace Bks.

Flannigan, Arthur. Les Desordres De L'Amour: Madame De Villedieu: A Critical Edition. LC 82-16138. (Illus.). 130p. 1983. lib. bdg. 19.00 (ISBN 0-8191-2730-2); pap. text ed. 8.25 (ISBN 0-8191-2731-0). U Pr of Amer.

--Me De Villedieu's Les Desordres Del L'amour: History, Literature & the Nouvelle Historique. LC 81-43835. 206p. 1983. lib. bdg. 22.50 (ISBN 0-8191-2696-9); pap. text ed. 10.75 (ISBN 0-8191-2697-7). U Pr of Amer.

Flanz, Gisbert H. Comparative Women's Rights & Political Participation in Europe. (Comparative Women's Rights). 542p. 1982. text ed. 45.00 (ISBN 0-941320-02-2); pap. 19.50. Transnatl Pubs.

Flanz, Gisbert H., jt. ed. see Blaustein, Albert P.

Flanzer, Jerry P. The Many Faces of Family Violence. 142p. 1982. 22.75x (ISBN 0-398-04612-3). C C Thomas.

Flasch, Joy. Melvin B. Tolson. (United State Authors Ser.). lib. bdg. 12.95 (ISBN 0-8057-0736-0, Twayne). G K Hall.

Flaschka, H. A. & Barnard, A. J., Jr., eds. Chelates in Analytical Chemistry: A Collection of Monographs, Vol. 4. 1972. 49.50 o.p. (ISBN 0-8247-1198-X). Dekker.

Flaschner, Alan B., jt. auth. see Spitz, A. Edward.

Flashka, H. A. & Barnard, A. J., Jr., eds. Chelates in Analytical Chemistry: A Collection of Monographs, Vol. 5. 1976. 49.50 o.p. (ISBN 0-8247-1194-7). Dekker.

Flaste, Richard, jt. auth. see Franey, Pierre.

Flaster, Donald J. Malpractice: A Guide to the Legal Rights of Doctors & Patients. 256p. 1983. 15.95 (ISBN 0-686-83840-8, ScribT). Scribner.

Flatauer, S., tr. see Levy, J.

Flatauer, Susanne, tr. see Schneede, Uwe M., et al.

Flatauer, Susanne, tr. see Von Goethe, J. W.

Flathman, R. The Practice of Rights. LC 75-38185. 1977. 29.95 (ISBN 0-521-21170-0). Cambridge U Pr.

Flatt, Adrian E. The Care of Congenital Hand Anomalies. LC 77-5932. (Illus.). 372p. 1977. text ed. 40.50 o.p. (ISBN 0-8016-1586-0). Mosby.

--The Care of Minor Hand Injuries. 4th ed. LC 79-12082. (Illus.). 340p. 1979. text ed. 49.50 (ISBN 0-8016-1581-X). Mosby.

--The Care of the Arthritic Hand. 4th ed. (Illus.). 305p. 1983. text ed. 39.50 (ISBN 0-8016-1585-2). Mosby.

Flatt, Bill & Flatt, Dowell. Counseling the Homosexual. 9.95 (ISBN 0-934916-49-7). Natl Christian Pr.

Flatt, Dowell, jt. auth. see Flatt, Bill.

Flatt, Lilyan J. Merely Musing. 1978. 4.95 o.p. (ISBN 0-533-03309-8). Vantage.

Flatte, S. M., ed. Sound Transmission Through a Fluctuating Ocean. LC 77-88676. (Cambridge Monographs on Mechanics & Applied Mathematics). (Illus.). 1979. 48.50 (ISBN 0-521-21940-X). Cambridge U Pr.

Flatter, Charles H., jt. auth. see Rice, Mary F.

Flatto, Edwin. The Restoration of Health: Nature's Way. 1970. 9.95 o.p. (ISBN 0-935540-03-2). Plymouth Pr.

Flaubert, Gustave. The First Sentimental Education. Garman, Douglas, tr. LC 77-149947. 275p. 1972. 27.50x (ISBN 0-520-01967-9). U of Cal Pr.

--The Letters of Gustave Flaubert, 1857-1880, Vol. II. Steegmuller, Francis, ed. & tr. from Fr. (Illus.). 336p. 1982. 15.00 (ISBN 0-674-52640-6, Belknap Pr). Harvard U Pr.

--Madame Bovary. Bersani, Leo & Bair, Lowell, eds. (Bantam Classics Ser.). 424p. (gr. 9-12). 1981. pap. 2.50 (ISBN 0-553-21033-5). Bantam.

--Madame Bovary. Steegmuller, Francis, tr. (YA) 1981. pap. 3.50 (ISBN 0-394-30917-0, T17, Mod LibC). Modern Lib.

--Madame Bovary. Marmur, Mildred, tr. (Orig.). 1964. pap. 1.95 (ISBN 0-451-51681-8, CJ1681, Sig Classics). NAL.

--Salammbo. Krailsheimer, A. J., tr. (Classics Ser.). 1977. pap. 3.95 (ISBN 0-14-044328-2). Penguin.

--Sentimental Education. Date not set. pap. 3.50 (ISBN 0-451-51692-3, CE 1692, Sig Classics). NAL.

--Temptation of St. Anthony. 1983. pap. 4.95 (ISBN 0-14-044410-6). Penguin.

Flavell, John & Ross, Lee, eds. Social Cognitive Development: Frontiers & Possible Futures. (Cambridge Studies in Social & Emotional Development). (Illus.). 336p. 1981. 36.50 (ISBN 0-521-23687-8); pap. 13.95 (ISBN 0-521-28156-3). Cambridge U Pr.

Flavell, John H. Cognitive Development. (Illus.). 1977. 18.95x (ISBN 0-13-139774-5); pap. 12.95 (ISBN 0-13-139766-4). P-H.

Flavell, R. B., jt. ed. see Dover, G. A.

Flavin, Christopher. Electricity from Sunlight: The Future of Photovoltaics. LC 82-62631. (Worldwatch Papers). 1982. pap. 2.00 (ISBN 0-916468-50-X). Worldwatch Inst.

--The Future of Synthetic Materials: The Petroleum Connection. LC 80-51137. (Worldwatch Papers Ser.). 1980. pap. 2.00 (ISBN 0-916468-35-6). Worldwatch Inst.

--Wind Energy: A Turning Point. LC 81-52516. (Worldwatch Papers). 1981. pap. 2.00 (ISBN 0-916468-44-5). Worldwatch Inst.

Flavin, Christopher, jt. auth. see Deudney, Daniel.

Flavin, Martin. Journey in the Dark. LC 78-104220. Repr. of 1943 ed. lib. bdg. 19.75x (ISBN 0-8371-3337-8, FLJD). Greenwood.

Flavin, Matt. Fundamental Concepts of Information Modeling. (Illus.). 136p. (Orig.). 1981. pap. 15.00 (ISBN 0-917072-22-7). Yourdon.

Flax, Zena, ed. The Old Fashioned Children's Storybook. LC 82-80875. (Illus.). 64p. 1982. 6.95 (ISBN 0-448-12537-4, G&D). Putnam Pub Group.

Flaxman, Ruth. Health Hints. 160p. 1981. pap. 4.95 (ISBN 0-8256-3238-2, Quick Fox). Putnam Pub Group.

--Home Remedies for Common Ailments. 1982. 4.95 (ISBN 0-399-50685-3, Perige). Putnam Pub Group.

Flayderman, Norm. Flayderman's Guide to Antique American Firearms & Their Values. 480p. 1977. pap. 12.95 o.s.i. (ISBN 0-695-80650-5). Follett.

--Flayderman's Guide to Antique American Firearms & Their Value. 2nd ed. 288p. 1980. pap. 15.95 o.s.i. (ISBN 0-695-81414-1). Follett.

Flayhart, William J., III, jt. auth. see Shaum, John H., Jr.

Fleagle, Robert G. & Businger, J. A. Introduction to Atmospheric Physics. (International Geophysics Ser.: Vol. 5). 1963. 26.25 o.p. (ISBN 0-12-260350-8). Acad Pr.

Fleck, Henrietta. Introduction to Nutrition. 4th ed. 1981. text ed. 24.95x (ISBN 0-02-338280-5). Macmillan.

--Toward Better Teaching of Home Economics. 3rd ed. (Illus.). 1980. text ed. 21.95x (ISBN 0-02-338240-6). Macmillan.

Fleck, Raymond F. & Hollaender, Alexander, eds. Genetic Toxicology: An/Agricultural Perspective, Vol.21. (Basic Life Sciences). 560p. 1982. 65.00x (ISBN 0-686-83967-6, Plenum Pr.). Plenum Pub.

Fleck, Richard F. Cottonwood Moon. 4.00 (ISBN 0-936204-06-0). Jelm Mtn.

Fleck, Robert & Honess, C. Brian. Data Processing & Computers: An Introduction. (Business C11 Ser.). 1978. pap. text ed. 18.95 (ISBN 0-675-08412-1); media pkg. 595.00 (ISBN 0-675-08413-X). Additional supplements may be obtained from publisher. Merrill.

Fleckenstein, Albrect. Calcium-Antagonism in Heart & Smooth Muscle: Experimental Facts & Therapeutic Prospects. 350p. 1982. 50.00 (ISBN 0-471-05435-6, Pub. by Wiley-Interscience). Wiley.

Fleckenstein, Henry, Jr New Jersey Decoys. (Illus.). 240p. 1983. text ed. 37.50 (ISBN 0-916838-75-7). Schiffer.

Fleckenstein, J. Early Medieval Germany. (Europe in the Middle Ages, Selected Studies: Vol. 16). 1978. 47.00 (ISBN 0-444-85134-8, North-Holland). Elsevier.

Fleckles, David, jt. auth. see Alvarez, Charles.

Fleenor, Juliann, ed. The Female Gothic. 250p. (Orig.). Date not set. pap. price not set (ISBN 0-920792-06-5). Eden Pr.

Fleet, Anne. Children's Libraries. 160p. 1973. 17.00 (ISBN 0-233-96229-8, 05789-4, Pub. by Gower Pub Co England). Lexington Bks.

Fleet, Robert R. Red-tailed Tropicbird on Kure Atoll. 64p. 1974. 5.50 (ISBN 0-943610-16-8). Am Ornithologists.

Fleetwood, Hugh. Fictional Lives. 166p. 1981. 15.95 (ISBN 0-241-10434-3, Pub. by Hamish Hamilton England). David & Charles.

--The Redeemer. LC 79-55598. 1980. 8.95 o.p. (ISBN 0-689-11037-5). Atheneum.

--Roman Magic. LC 77-12547. 1978. 7.95 o.p. (ISBN 0-689-10839-7). Atheneum.

--A Young Fair God. 224p. 1982. 16.95 (ISBN 0-241-10715-6, Pub. by Hamish Hamilton England). David & Charles.

Flefenheimer, Walter V. Techniques of Brief Psychotherapy. LC 82-13891. 224p. 1982. write for info. (ISBN 0-87668-460-6). Aronson.

Fleg, Edmond. The Jewish Anthology. Samuel, Maurice, tr. LC 72-142934. 399p. 1975. Repr. of 1925 ed. lib. bdg. 17.50x (ISBN 0-8371-5824-9, FLJA). Greenwood.

Flegg, Graham. Numbers: Their History & Meaning. LC 82-19134. (Illus.). 288p. 1983. 14.95 (ISBN 0-8052-3847-6). Schocken.

Flegmann, Vilma. Called to Account: The Public Accounts Committee of the House of Commons. 328p. 1980. text ed. 34.25x (ISBN 0-566-00371-6). Gower Pub Ltd.

Fleichits, Ye & Makovsky, A. The Civil Codes of the Soviet Republics. 1976 ed. 288p. 14.95 (ISBN 0-686-37387-1). Beekman Pubs.

Fleischauer, Paul, jt. ed. see Adamson, Authur W.

Fleischauer, Paul D., jt. auth. see Adamson, Arthur W.

Fleischer, Alan S., jt. auth. see Cooper, Paul R.

Fleischer, Arthur, et al, eds. Ninth Annual Institute on Securities Regulation: A Multi-Authored Text. 1978. 25.00 (ISBN 0-685-65703-5, B2-1253). PLI.

Fleischer, Arthur C. & James, A. Everette. Introduction to Diagnostic Sonography. LC 79-19065. 1980. 38.50 (ISBN 0-471-05473-9, Pub. by Wiley-Medical). Wiley.

Fleischer, Arthur, Jr. & Lipton, Martin, eds. Annual Institute on Securities Regulation, 13th. LC 70-125178. 472p. 1982. text ed. 50.00 (ISBN 0-686-82490-3, B2-1281). PLI.

Fleischer, Arthur, Jr., et al, eds. Eleventh Annual Institute on Securities Regulation. LC 70-125178. 593p. 1980. text ed. 30.00 (ISBN 0-686-69167-9, B2-1275). PLI.

--Tenth Annual Institute on Securities Regulation. LC 70-125178. 1979. text ed. 25.00 (ISBN 0-686-58549-6, B2-1266). PLI.

--Twelfth Annual Institute on Securities Regulation. 611p. 1981. text ed. 40.00 (ISBN 0-686-76238-X, B2-1280). PLI.

Fleischer, D. Digital Logic Elements. 29.95 (ISBN 0-471-25675-7, Pub. by Wiley Heyden). Wiley.

Fleischer, David & Freedman, David M. Death of an American: The Killing of John Singer. (Illus.). 248p. 1983. 14.95 (ISBN 0-8264-0231-3). Crossroad NY.

Fleischer, Eugene B. A Style Manual for Citing Microform & Nonprint Media. LC 78-9375. 1978. pap. 6.00 (ISBN 0-8389-0268-5). ALA.

Fleischer, Lenore. The Cat's Pajamas. LC 82-47907. (Illus.). 192p. 1982. pap. 6.68i (ISBN 0-06-090974-9, CN 974, CN). Har-Row.

Fleischer, Leonore. Breathless. 1983. pap. 2.95 (ISBN 0-440-10804-7). Dell.

--John Denver. LC 76-8065. 1976. pap. 3.95 o.p. (ISBN 0-8256-3909-3, Quick Fox). Putnam Pub Group.

--Joni Mitchell. LC 75-29868. (Illus.). 96p. (Orig.). 1976. pap. 3.95 (ISBN 0-8256-3907-7, Quick Fox). Putnam Pub Group.

--Running. (Orig.). 1979. pap. 2.25 o.s.i. (ISBN 0-515-05114-4). Jove Pubns.

Fleischer, Nathaniel S. Fifty Years at Ringside. LC 77-90144. Repr. of 1958 ed. lib. bdg. 18.25x (ISBN 0-8371-2164-7, FLFY). Greenwood.

Fleischer, Robert L., et al. Nuclear Tracks in Solids. LC 73-90670. 1975. 57.50x (ISBN 0-520-02665-9); pap. 17.50x (ISBN 0-520-04096-1). U of Cal Pr.

Fleischmajer, P. & Billingham, R. Epithelial Mesenchymal Interactions. 340p. 1968. 17.50 o.p. (ISBN 0-683-03260-7, Pub. by Williams & Wilkins). Krieger.

Fleischmajer, Paul, jt. auth. see Wagner, Bernard M.

Fleischman, Charles & Helberg, Kristin. The Victorian Seaside Hotel Coloring Book. (Illus.). 48p. (gr. 3 up). 1983. pap. 2.50 (ISBN 0-486-24399-0). Dover.

Fleischman, Marjorie R. Dosage Calculation: Method & Workbook. (League Exchange Ser.: No. 106). 106p. 1975. 5.95 (ISBN 0-686-38188-2, 20-1560). Natl League Nurse.

Fleischman, Matthew J. & Horne, Arthur M. Troubled Families: A Treatment Program. 250p. (Orig.). 1983. pap. text ed. price not set (ISBN 0-87822-296-0). Res Press.

Fleischman, Paul. The Animal Hedge. LC 82-2404. (Illus.). 32p. (gr. 2-5). 1983. 9.95 (ISBN 0-525-44002-X, 0966-290). Dutton.

--The Birthday Tree. LC 78-22155. (Illus.). (gr. k-3). 1979. 9.57i (ISBN 0-06-021915-7, HarpJ); PLB 8.89 o.p. (ISBN 0-06-021916-5). Har-Row.

--Graven Images. LC 81-48649. (A Charlotte Zolotow Bk.). (Illus.). 96p. (gr. 6 up). 1982. 9.57i (ISBN 0-06-021906-8, HarpJ); PLB 9.89g (ISBN 0-06-021907-6). Har-Row.

--The Half-a-Moon Inn. LC 79-2010. (Illus.). 96p. (gr. 5 up). 1980. 8.95 o.p. (ISBN 0-06-021917-3, HarpJ); PLB 9.89 (ISBN 0-06-021918-1). Har-Row.

--Path of the Pale Horse. LC 82-48611. 160p. (gr. 6 up). 1983. 9.57i (ISBN 0-06-021904-1, HarpJ); PLB 9.89g (ISBN 0-06-021905-X). Har-Row.

Fleischman, Sid. The Bloodhound Gang's Secret Code Book. LC 82-3682. (A Three-Two-One Contact Bk.). (Illus.). 64p. (gr. 3-7). 1983. pap. 3.95 (ISBN 0-394-85231-1). Random.

--By the Great Horn Spoon. (Illus.). (gr. 4-6). 8.95 (ISBN 0-316-28577-3, Pub. by Atlantic Monthly Pr). Little.

--Chauncy & the Grand Rascal. (Illus.). (gr. 4-6). 1966. 7.95 (ISBN 0-316-28575-7, Pub. by Atlantic Monthly Pr). Little.

--The Ghost on Saturday Night. (Illus.). 64p. (gr. 4-6). 1974. 7.95 (ISBN 0-316-28583-8, Pub. by Atlantic Monthly Pr.). Little.

--Humbug Mountain. LC 78-9419. (Illus.). (gr. 4-6). 1978. 8.95 (ISBN 0-316-28569-2, Pub. by Atlantic Monthly Pr). Little.

--Jingo Django. (gr. 4-6). 1971. 9.95 (ISBN 0-316-28580-3, Pub. by Atlantic Monthly Pr). Little.

--Kate's Secret Riddle Book. (Easy-Read Story Books). (Illus.). (gr. k-3). 1977. PLB 7.90 s&l o.p. (ISBN 0-531-00377-9). Watts.

--McBroom & the Big Wind. (Illus.). 48p. (gr. 3 up). 1982. 8.95 (ISBN 0-316-28543-9, Pub. by Atlantic Monthly Pr); pap. 3.95 (ISBN 0-316-28544-7). Little.

--McBroom the Rainmaker. (Illus.). 48p. (gr. 3 up). 1982. 8.95 (ISBN 0-316-28541-2, Pub. by Atlantic Monthly Pr); pap. 3.95 (ISBN 0-316-28542-0). Little.

--McBroom's Zoo. (Illus.). 48p. (gr. 3 up). 1982. 8.95g (ISBN 0-316-28536-6, Pub. by Atlantic Monthly Pr); pap. 3.95 (ISBN 0-316-28538-2). Little.

--Mr. Mysterious & Company. (Illus.). (gr. 4-6). 1962. 8.95 (ISBN 0-316-28578-1, Pub. by Atlantic Monthly Pr). Little.

--Mr. Mysterious's Secrets of Magic. (Illus.). 96p. (gr. 4-6). 1975. 6.95 (ISBN 0-316-28584-6, Pub. by Atlantic Monthly Pr). Little.

Fleischmann, Paul. Phoebe Danger, Detective, in the Case of the Two-Minute Cough. LC 82-15616. (Illus.). 64p. (gr. 2-5). 1983. 8.95 (ISBN 0-395-33226-5). HM.

Fleisher, Belton M. & Kniesner, Thomas J. Labor Economics: Theory, Evidence & Policy. 2nd ed. (Illus.). 1980. text ed. 24.95 (ISBN 0-13-517433-3). P-H.

Fleisher, Gary & Ludwig, Stephen. Pediatric Emergency Medicine. (Illus.). 1109p. 1983. text ed. write for info (ISBN 0-683-03253-4). Williams & Wilkins.

Fleisher, Michael. The Great Superman Book. (Illus., Orig.). 1978. pap. 8.95 o.p. (ISBN 0-446-87494-9). Warner Bks.

Fleisher, Michael L. The Great Superman Book. 1979. 15.95 o.p. (ISBN 0-517-53677-3, Harmony). Crown.

Fleisher, Wilfrid. Sweden, the Welfare State. LC 72-10696. (Illus.). 255p. 1973. Repr. of 1956 ed. lib. bdg. 19.25x (ISBN 0-8371-6611-X, FLSW). Greenwood.

Fleishman, Avrom. Figures of Autobiography: The Language of Self-Writing in Victorian & Modern England. LC 81-23163. 512p. 1983. text ed. 29.50x (ISBN 0-520-04666-8). U of Cal Pr.

Fleishman, Joel L. Future of Postal Service. 336p. 1983. 33.95 (ISBN 0-03-059921-0); pap. 4.00 (ISBN 0-03-063562-4). Praeger.

Fleishman, L. & Raevskaia-Hughes, eds. Russkii Berlin: Nineteen Twenty-One to Nineteen Twenty-Three Iz Arkhiva Zhurnala Novaia Russkaia Kniga. 350p. 1982. write for info. (ISBN 0-89830-056-8); pap. write for info. (ISBN 0-89830-057-6). Russica Pubs.

Fleiss, Joseph L. Statistical Methods for Rates & Proportion. LC 72-8521. (Probability & Statistics Ser: Applied Section). (Illus.). 223p. 1973. 28.95 o.p. (ISBN 0-471-26370-2, Pub. by Wiley-Interscience). Wiley.

--Statistical Methods for Rates & Proportions. 2nd ed. LC 80-26382. (Probability & Statistics Ser.: Applied Probability & Statistics). 336p. 1981. 32.95x (ISBN 0-471-06428-9, Pub. by Wiley-Interscience). Wiley.

Fleiszar, Kathleen, jt. auth. see Daniel, William.

Fleitzer, Mark H., jt. auth. see Budlong, Ware.

Flek, J., jt. auth. see Sedivec, V.

Flemans, R. J., jt. auth. see Hayhoe, F. G.

Fleming, A. William & Bloom, Joel A. Paddleball & Raquetball. 1st ed. LC 72-90984. (Physical Education Ser.). 1973. pap. text ed. 7.95x (ISBN 0-673-16193-5). Scott F.

Fleming, Alice. Hosannah the Home Run: Poems About Sports. (Illus.). (gr. 7 up). 1972. 8.95 (ISBN 0-316-28588-9). Little.

--Something for Nothing: A History of Gambling. LC 77-86341. (Illus.). (gr. 5 up). 1978. 7.95 o.s.i. (ISBN 0-440-08036-3); PLB 7.45 o.s.i. (ISBN 0-440-08037-1). Delacorte.

Fleming, Berry. Country Wedding4. 128p. 1983. 8.95 (ISBN 0-932298-29-X). Copple Hse.

Fleming, C. M. The Social Psychology of Education: An Introduction & Guide to Its Study. 2nd ed. (International Library of Sociology). 1967. 12.00x (ISBN 0-7100-3215-3); pap. 5.95 (ISBN 0-7100-4639-1). Routledge & Kegan.

Fleming, David L. A Contemporary Reading of the Spiritual Exercises: A Companion to St. Ignatius' Text. 2nd ed. Ganss, George E., ed. LC 80-81812. (Study Aids on Jesuit Topics Ser.: No. 2). 112p. 1980. pap. 3.00 (ISBN 0-912422-47-5); smyth sewn 4.00 (ISBN 0-912422-48-3). Inst Jesuit.

--The Spiritual Exercises of St. Ignatius: A Literal Translation & a Contemporary Reading. Ganss, George E., ed. LC 77-93429. (Study Aids on Jesuit Topics Ser.: No. 7). 290p. 1978. 12.00 (ISBN 0-912422-32-7); smythe sewn 8.50 (ISBN 0-912422-31-9); pap. 7.00 o.s.i. (ISBN 0-912422-28-9). Inst Jesuit.

Fleming, Don A. How to Stop the Battle with Your Child. LC 82-90682. 144p. Date not set. pap. 7.95 (ISBN 0-9609264-0-2). D Fleming Sem.

Fleming, Esther, jt. auth. see Fleming, Robert E.

Fleming, Farold, ed. see Krause, Tina.

Fleming, Gladys A. Creative Rhythmic Movement: Boys & Girls Dancing. (Illus.). 432p. 1976. 17.95 o.p. (ISBN 0-13-191114-7); pap. 17.95 (ISBN 0-13-191106-6). P-H.

Fleming, Harold. English Grammar: Forms & Structures. 1971. pap. cancelled o.p. (ISBN 0-87835-012-8). Boyd & Fraser.

--A Needed Path. (Black Willow Poetry Chapbook Ser.). 20p. (Orig.). 1982. pap. 2.50 (ISBN 0-910047-00-6). Black Willow.

Fleming, Harold, ed. see DeFoe, Mark.

Fleming, Harold, ed. see McCcane, Kenneth A.

Fleming, Howard A. Canada's Artic Outlet: A History of the Hudson Bay Railway. LC 78-5665. (Illus.). 129p. 1978. Repr. of 1957 ed. lib. bdg. 18.75x (ISBN 0-313-20392-X, FLCA). Greenwood.

Fleming, I. Frontier Orbitals & Organic Chemical Reactions. LC 76-3800. 249p. 1976. 43.50x (ISBN 0-471-01820-1); pap. 17.50 (ISBN 0-471-01819-8, Pub. by Wiley-Interscience). Wiley.

Fleming, I., jt. auth. see Williams, D. H.

Fleming, Ian. Casino Royale. 192p. 1983. pap. 2.75 (ISBN 0-425-05825-5). Berkley Pub.

--Diamonds Are Forever. 224p. 1980. pap. 2.50 (ISBN 0-515-06060-7). Jove Pubns.

--Doctor No. 240p. 1980. pap. 2.25 o.s.i. (ISBN 0-515-06163-8). Jove Pubns.

--Doctor No. 1959. pap. 1.50 o.p. (ISBN 0-451-08195-1, W8195, Sig). NAL.

--Doctor No. 240p. 1982. pap. 2.75 (ISBN 0-425-05365-2). Berkley Pub.

--For Your Eyes Only. (James Bond Ser.). 192p. 1981. pap. 2.25 o.s.i. (ISBN 0-515-06074-7). Jove Pubns.

--From Russia with Love. 256p. 1980. pap. 2.25 o.s.i. (ISBN 0-515-06061-5). Jove Pubns.

--Goldfinger. (James Bond Ser.). 272p. (Orig.). 1980. pap. 2.25 o.s.i. (ISBN 0-515-05839-4). Jove Pubns.

--Live & Let Die. 224p. 1980. pap. 2.25 o.s.i. (ISBN 0-515-05889-0). Jove Pubns.

--Live & Let Die. 224p. 1983. pap. 2.75 (ISBN 0-425-05369-5). Berkley Pub.

--Man with the Golden Gun. pap. 2.50 (ISBN 0-451-12106-6, AE2106, Sig). NAL.

--On Her Majesty's Secret Service. pap. 2.50 (ISBN 0-451-12107-4, AE2107, Sig). NAL.

--Selected Organic Syntheses: A Guidebook for Organic Chemists. LC 72-615. 227p. 1973. 45.95x (ISBN 0-471-26390-7); pap. 24.95 (ISBN 0-471-26391-5, Pub. by Wiley-Interscience). Wiley.

--You Only Live Twice. pap. 2.50 (ISBN 0-451-12108-2, AE2108, Sig). NAL.

Fleming, James E. The Blacksmith's Source Book: An Annotated Bibliography. LC 80-18560. 120p. 1981. 19.95x (ISBN 0-8093-0989-0). S Ill U Pr.

Fleming, Joan. The Day of the Donkey Derby. LC 78-9376. 1978. 8.95 o.p. (ISBN 0-399-12263-X). Putnam Pub Group.

--Every Inch a Lady: A Murder of the Fifties. LC 77-10423. 1978. 7.95 o.p. (ISBN 0-399-12087-4). Putnam Pub Group.

Fleming, John G. An Introduction to the Law of Torts. (Clarendon Law Ser.). 1978. pap. 11.95x (ISBN 0-19-876079-5). Oxford U Pr.

Fleming, John K. The Cowans from County Down. 440p. 1971. pap. 11.00. Synod NC Church.

--History of the Third Creek Presbyterian Church. 1967. 8.00 (ISBN 0-686-37869-5). Synod NC Church.

Fleming, John V. From Bonaventure to Bellini: An Essay in Franciscan Exegesis. LC 82-47593. (Princeton Essays on the Arts Ser.: No. 14). (Illus.). 192p. 1982. 25.00x (ISBN 0-691-07270-1). Princeton U Pr.

Fleming, Laurence & Gore, Alan. The English Garden. (Illus.). 256p. 1983. pap. 10.95 (ISBN 0-7181-2191-0, Pub by Michael Joseph). Merrimack Bk Serv.

Fleming, Macklin. Of Crimes & Rights. 1978. 11.95x o.p. (ISBN 0-393-05650-3). Norton.

Fleming, Malcolm L. & Hutton, Deane W., eds. Mental Imagery & Learning. 160p. 1983. 24.95 (ISBN 0-87778-185-0). Educ Tech Pubns.

Fleming, Margaret. Language All Around Us. 84p. 6.00 (ISBN 0-686-95312-6); members 5.00 (ISBN 0-686-99492-2). NCTE.

Fleming, N. C., jt. ed. see Masters, P. M.

Fleming, Paul. Principles of Switching, Vol. X. 1979. 15.00 (ISBN 0-686-98066-2). Telecom Lib.

Fleming, Peter. Bayonets to Lhasa. LC 73-16737. (Illus.). 1974. Repr. of 1961 ed. lib. bdg. 19.00x (ISBN 0-8371-7216-0, FLBL). Greenwood.

Fleming, Quentin W. How to Put "Earned Value" into Your Management Control System: A Special Edition Describing the Government's Cost-Schedule Control System Criteria. (Illus.). 350p. (Orig.). 1983. 29.95x (ISBN 0-942280-04-0); pap. 15.95x (ISBN 0-942280-03-2). Pub Horizons.

Fleming, R. F., tr. see Kratzsch, H.

Fleming, Robert, jt. auth. see Saunders, Leonard.

Fleming, Robert E. Willard Motley. (United States Authors Ser.: No. 302). 1978. lib. bdg. 13.95 o.p. (ISBN 0-8057-7207-3, Twayne). G K Hall.

Fleming, Robert E. & Fleming, Esther. Sinclair Lewis: A Reference Guide. 1980. lib. bdg. 20.00 (ISBN 0-8161-8094-6, Hall Reference). G K Hall.

Fleming, Robert E., ed. James Weldon Johnson & Arna Wendell Bontemps: A Reference Guide. 1978. lib. bdg. 16.00 (ISBN 0-8161-7932-8, Hall Reference). G K Hall.

Fleming, Ronald L. Facade Stories: The Saving & Renovation of Fifty American Commercial Buildings & Shop Fronts. (Illus.). 128p. 1982. pap. 13.50 (ISBN 0-8038-2398-3). Hastings.

Fleming, Ronald L. & Von Tsharner, Renata. Place Makers. (Illus.). 128p. (Orig.). 1981. pap. 9.95 (ISBN 0-8038-5894-9). Hastings.

Fleming, Spencer. How to Develop the Creative Powers of your Imagination. (Human Development Library Book). (Illus.). 63p. (Orig.). 1983. pap. 6.95 (ISBN 0-89266-388-X). Am Classical Coll Pr.

--Power Anatomy of the Economic Forces Dominating the Business & the Political World. (Illus.). 137p. 1983. 49.75 (ISBN 0-86722-032-5). Inst Econ Pol.

Fleming, Stuart, et al. The Egyptian Mummy: Secrets & Science. (University Museum Handbook Ser.: No. 1). (Illus.). x, 93p. (Orig.). 1980. pap. 8.00x (ISBN 0-934718-38-5). Univ Mus of U Pa.

Fleming, Susan. Countdown at Thirty-Seven Pinecrest Drive. LC 82-8337. (gr. 3-5). 1982. 9.95 (ISBN 0-664-32694-3). Westminster.

--Trapped on the Golden Flyer. LC 77-15941. 1978. 8.95 (ISBN 0-664-32627-7). Westminster.

Fleming, Thomas. Dreams of Glory. 496p. 1983. pap. 3.95 (ISBN 0-446-80655-2). Warner Bks.

--Living Land of Lincoln. 1980. 20.00 o.p. (ISBN 0-07-021297-X). Readers Digest Pr.

Fleming, W. H. & Rishel, R. W. Deterministic & Stochastic Optimal Control. LC 75-28391. (Applications of Mathematics Ser.: Vol. 1). (Illus.). xi, 222p. 1975. 35.00 (ISBN 0-387-90155-8). Springer-Verlag.

Fleming, W. H. & Riskel, R. W. Deterministic & Stochastic Optional Control. ix, 222p. (Corrected Second Printing 1982). 1983. 36.00 (ISBN 0-387-90155-8). Springer-Verlag.

Fleming, W. H. & Gorostiza, L. G., eds. Advances in Filtering & Optimal Stochastic Control: Proceedings; Cocoyoc, Mexico 1982. (Lecture Notes in Control & Information Science: Vol. 42). 392p. 1983. pap. 17.50 (ISBN 0-387-11936-1). Springer-Verlag.

Fleming, Walter & Varberg, Dale. Algebra & Trigonometry. (Illus.). 1980. text ed. 23.95 (ISBN 0-13-021824-3); study guide 7.95 (ISBN 0-13-021881-2). P-H.

Fleming, Walter & Varberg, Dale E. College Algebra. (Illus.). 1980. text ed. 23.95 (ISBN 0-13-141606-5). P-H.

--Plane Trigonometry. 1980. text ed. 20.95 (ISBN 0-13-679043-7). P-H.

Fleming, Walter L. Sequel of Appomattox. 1919. text ed. 8.50x (ISBN 0-686-83736-3). Elliots Bks.

Flemings, Merton. Solidification Processing. (Materials Sciences Ser). (Illus.). 1974. text ed. 38.50 (ISBN 0-07-021283-X, C). McGraw.

Flemion, Philip F. Historical Dictionary of El Salvador. LC 78-189546. (Latin American Historical Dictionaries Ser.: No. 5). 1972. 11.00 (ISBN 0-8108-0471-9). Scarecrow.

Flemming & Mansbach. Reading for Results. 2d ed. pap. text ed. 11.95 (ISBN 0-686-84576-5, RM98); instr's manual avail. (RM99). HM.

Flemming, Bonnie M. & Hamilton, Darlene S. Resources for Creative Teaching in Early Childhood Education. (Illus.). 636p. (Orig., Songs & Parodies by Joanne D. Hicks). 1977. pap. text ed. 20.95 (ISBN 0-15-576624-4, HC). HarBraceJ.

Flemming, Donald N. & Mowry, Robert G. Sobre Heroes y Rumbos: Modelo Para Explicar. LC 81-40620. 240p. (Orig.). 1982. lib. bdg. 21.25 (ISBN 0-8191-2027-8); pap. text ed. 10.75 (ISBN 0-8191-2028-6). U Pr of Amer.

Flemming, John. Inflation. (Illus.). 1976. 14.95x o.p. (ISBN 0-19-877085-5); pap. 7.95x (ISBN 0-19-877086-3). Oxford U Pr.

Flemming, Laraine. Reading for Results. LC 77-76422. (Illus.). 1978. pap. text ed. 11.95 (ISBN 0-395-25419-1); instr's. manual 0.50 (ISBN 0-395-25430-2). HM.

--Reading for Results. 2d ed. 468p. 1983. pap. text ed. 12.95 (ISBN 0-395-32605-2); write for info. instr's. manual (ISBN 0-395-32606-0). HM.

Flender, Harold. Rescue in Denmark. (Illus.). 280p. pap. 5.95 (ISBN 0-686-95083-6). ADL.

Flenley, David C. Respiratory Diseases. (Illus.). 276p. (Orig.). 1981. pap. text ed. 17.95x (ISBN 0-02-857710-8, Bailliere-Tindall). Saunders.

Flenley, J. R. The Equatorial Rain Forest: A Geological History. (Illus.). 1979. text ed. 74.95 (ISBN 0-408-71305-4). Butterworth.

Fleron, Frederic J., Jr., ed. Technology & Communist Culture: The Socio-Cultural Impact of Technology Transter Under Socialism. LC 77-7810. (Praeger Special Studies). 1977. 49.95 o.p. (ISBN 0-03-021821-7). Praeger.

Flesch, Carl. The Memoirs of Carl Flesch. (Music Reprint Ser.). 1979. Repr. of 1957 ed. lib. bdg. 35.00 (ISBN 0-306-77574-3). Da Capo.

--Violin Fingering: It's Theory & Practice. (Music Reprint Ser.). Repr. of 1960 ed. lib. bdg. 39.50 (ISBN 0-306-79573-6). Da Capo.

Flesch, Janos. Planning in Chess. (Illus.). 96p. 1983. pap. 11.50 (ISBN 0-7134-1597-5, Pub. by Batsford England). David & Charles.

Flesch, Rudolf. The Art of Clear Thinking. (Illus.). 212p. 1973. pap. 3.95 (ISBN 0-06-463369-1, EH 369, EH). B&N NY.

--The Art of Clear Thinking. 1951. 12.45i (ISBN 0-06-001440-7, HarpT). Har-Row.

--The Art of Readable Writing, 25th Anniversary Edition. rev. & enl. ed. LC 73-14260. (Illus.). 288p. (YA) 1974. 13.41i (ISBN 0-06-011293-X, HarpT). Har-Row.

--How to Write Plain English: A Book for Lawyers & Consumers. LC 76-26225. 1979. 10.53i (ISBN 0-06-011278-6, HarpT). Har-Row.

--How to Write, Speak & Think More Effectively. 1964. pap. 3.50 (ISBN 0-451-12168-6, AE2168, Sig). NAL.

--Johnny Still Can't Read: A New Look at the Scandal of Our Schools. LC 80-8686. 224p. 1983. pap. 4.76i (ISBN 0-06-091031-3, CN 1031, CN). Har-Row.

--Look It up: A Deskbook of American Spelling & Style. LC 75-23880. 1977. 13.41i (ISBN 0-06-011292-1, HarpT). Har-Row.

--Rudolf Flesch on Business Communications: How to Say What You Mean in Plain English. pap. 4.50 (ISBN 0-06-463393-4, EH 393, EH). B&N NY

--Say What You Mean. LC 72-79664. 256p. (YA) 1972. 13.41i (ISBN 0-06-011291-3, HarpT). Har-Row.

--Why Johnny Still Can't Read: A New Look at the Scandal of Our Schools. LC 80-8686. 192p. 1981. 12.45i (ISBN 0-06-014842-X, HarpT). Har-Row.

Flesch, Rudolf & Lass, A. H. A New Guide to Better Writing. 1982. pap. 2.50 (ISBN 0-446-31091-3). Warner Bks.

Flesher, Dale L., jt. auth. see Flesher, Tonya K.

Flesher, Tonya K. & Flesher, Dale L. Accounting Principles for Midmanagement. LC 78-62620. (Accounting Ser.). 454p. 1980. text ed. 19.60 (ISBN 0-8273-1628-3); instructor's guide 6.50 (ISBN 0-8273-1629-1). Delmar.

Fleshman, Robert, jt. auth. see Fryrear, Jerry L.

Flesner, David E. & Freed, Edwin D., eds. Aging & the Aged: Problems, Opportunities, Challenges. LC 80-5869. 368p. 1980. lib. bdg. 22.00 o.p. (ISBN 0-8191-1267-4); pap. text ed. 13.75 o.p. (ISBN 0-8191-1268-2). U Pr of Amer.

Fletcher, Aaron. The Microwave Factor. 304p. 1982. pap. 3.25 cancelled (ISBN 0-505-51857-0). Tower Bks.

Fletcher, Adele. Mystery of Blue Star Lodge. LC 65-14020. (Signal Bks.). 7.95 (ISBN 0-385-04912-9). Doubleday.

Fletcher, Alan. Advertising & Society. 256p. 1983. text ed. write for info. (ISBN 0-87251-082-4). Crain Bks.

Fletcher, Alan D. & Bowers, Thomas A. Fundamentals of Advertising Research. 2nd ed. LC 82-24217. (Grid Series in Advertising & Journalism). 334p. 1983. price not set. Grid Pub.

Fletcher, Alan M. The Land & People of the Guianas. rev. ed. LC 78-37743. (Portraits of the Nations Ser.). (Illus.). (gr. 6 up). 1972. 9.57i o.p. (ISBN 0-397-31541-4, HarpJ). Har-Row.

Fletcher, Angus. Allegory: The Theory of a Symbolic Mode. LC 64-11415. (Illus.). 464p. 1982. 9.95x (ISBN 0-8014-9238-6). Cornell U Pr.

Fletcher, Anthony. Tudor Rebellions. 2nd rev. ed. (Seminar Studies in History). (Illus.). 176p. 1973. pap. text ed. 5.95x (ISBN 0-582-35205-3). Longman.

Fletcher, Betsy J. Quick Reference to Critical Care Nursing. (Quick References for Nurses Ser.). (Illus.). 400p. 1982. pap. text ed. 14.50 (ISBN 0-397-54367-0, Lippincott Nursing). Lippincott.

Fletcher, C. & Thompson, M., eds. Issues in Community Education. 214p. 1980. write for info. (ISBN 0-905273-09-5, Pub. by Taylor & Francis); pap. write for info. (ISBN 0-905273-08-7). Intl Pubns Serv.

Fletcher, C., et al. The Natural History of Chronic Bronchitis & Emphysema. (Illus.). 1976. text ed. 35.00x o.p. (ISBN 0-19-261119-4). Oxford U Pr.

Fletcher, C. M. Communication in Medicine: Rock Carling Fellowship. 130p. 1973. 25.00x (ISBN 0-686-97003-9, Pub. by Nuffield England). State Mutual Bk.

Fletcher, Colin. Beneath the Surface: An Account of Three Styles of Sociological Research. 1974. 17.50 (ISBN 0-7100-7978-8); pap. 8.95 o.p. (ISBN 0-7100-7979-6). Routledge & Kegan.

--The Man Who Walked Through Time. 1972. pap. 3.95 (ISBN 0-394-71852-6, V852, Vin). Random.

Fletcher, D. L., jt. auth. see Rhodes, A.

Fletcher, D. S. & Nye, I. W. The Generic Names of Moths of the World, Vol. IV: Bombycoidea, Castnioidea, Cossoidea, Mimallonoidea, Sesioidea, Sphingoidea, Zygaenoidea, Vol. IV. (Illus.). xiv, 192p. 1982. 56.50 (ISBN 0-565-00848-X). Sabbot-Natural Hist Bks.

Fletcher, David. Henry VIII. LC 77-188. (History Makers Ser.). (Illus.). (YA) 1977. 6.95 o.p. (ISBN 0-312-36802-X). St Martin.

--Raffles. 1977. 7.95 o.p. (ISBN 0-399-11948-5). Putnam Pub Group.

Fletcher, David B. Social & Political Perspectives in the Thought of Soren Kierkegaard. LC 81-43716. 88p. 1983. lib. bdg. 18.00 (ISBN 0-8191-2689-6); pap. text ed. 7.00 (ISBN 0-8191-2690-X). U Pr of Amer.

Fletcher, David E., jt. auth. see Garrison, Joe.

Fletcher, Dirk. Rocky Mountain Vamp. (Spur Ser.: No. 4). 224p. (Orig.). 1982. pap. 2.50 o.s.i. (ISBN 0-8439-1180-8, Leisure Bks). Nordon Pubns.

--St. Louis Jezebel. (Spur Ser.: No. 3). 208p. (Orig.). 1983. pap. 2.50 o.s.i. (ISBN 0-8439-1157-3, Leisure Bks). Dorchester Pub Co.

Fletcher, Edward. Rock & Gem Polishing. (Illus.). 1973. 4.95 o.p. (ISBN 0-7137-0617-1, Pub by Blandford Pr England). Sterling.

Fletcher, Elizabeth H. The Iron Man of the Hoh the Man, not the Myth. LC 79-55972. (Illus.). 173p. (gr. 6). 1979. pap. 15.95 (ISBN 0-939116-03-0). Creative Comm.

Fletcher, G. G. The Begg Appliance & Technique. (Dental Practitioner Handbook Ser.: No. 28). (Illus.). 180p. 1981. text ed. 34.50 (ISBN 0-7236-0570-X). Wright-PSG.

Fletcher, Geoffrey. Popular Art in England. 10.00x (ISBN 0-392-05977-0, LTB). Sportshelf.

--Town's Eye View. 10.00x (ISBN 0-392-06028-0, LTB). Sportshelf.

Fletcher, George P. Rethinking Criminal Law. 1978. 25.00 (ISBN 0-316-28592-7). Little.

Fletcher, Gerald F., et al. Exercise in the Practice of Medicine. LC 82-71096. (Illus.). 416p. 1982. 39.50 (ISBN 0-87993-177-9). Futura Pub.

Fletcher, Gilbert & Nervi, Carlo, eds. Biological Bases & Clinical Implications of Tumor Radioresistance. LC 82-14819. (Illus.). 400p. 1983. write for info. (ISBN 0-89352-179-5). Masson Pub.

Fletcher, Gilbert H. History of Radiotherapy. (Illus.). 450p. cancelled o.s.i. (ISBN 0-87527-145-6). Green.

Fletcher, Giles & Fletcher, Phineas. Poetical Works, 2 Vols. Boas, F. S., ed. 1970. 59.50 ea. Vol. 1. (ISBN 0-521-07773-7). Vol. 2 (ISBN 0-521-07827-X). Cambridge U Pr.

Fletcher, Gordon A. & Smoots, Vernon A. Construction Guide for Soils & Foundations. LC 73-21789. (Practical Construction Guides Ser). 420p. 1974. 43.50 (ISBN 0-471-26400-8, Pub. by Wiley-Interscience). Wiley.

Fletcher, H. & Howell, A. A. Mathematics with Understanding. Vol. 1. 21.00 o.s.i. (ISBN 0-08-015657-6); Vol. 2. 20.00 (ISBN 0-08-016745-4); Vol. 1. pap. 9.75 (ISBN 0-08-015656-8). Pergamon.

Fletcher, Hans. Paintings from the Royal Academy. Walker, Janet M., ed. LC 82-82937. (Illus.). 52p. (Orig.). 1982. pap. 13.00 (ISBN 0-88397-043-0). Intl Exhibit Foun.

Fletcher, Harris F. Milton's Rabbinical Readings. LC 67-30701. 1967. Repr. of 1930 ed. 9.00x (ISBN 0-87752-034-8). Gordian.

Fletcher, Helen J. Put on Your Thinking Cap. LC 68-13231. (Illus.). (gr. 3-7). 1968. PLB 10.89 (ISBN 0-200-72009-0, B67201, AbS-J). Har-Row.

--Puzzles & Quizzles. LC 78-132191. (Illus.). (gr. 1 up). 1971. PLB 10.89 (ISBN 0-200-71771-5, B67311, AbS-J). Har-Row.

Fletcher, Hugo F. see Morely-Fletcher, Hugo.

Fletcher, I. F. Conflicts of Law & European Community Law. Date not set. 68.00 (ISBN 0-444-86376-1). Elsevier.

Fletcher, Ian, ed. The Collected Poems of Lionel Johnson. LC 80-8987. 475p. 1982. lib. bdg. 60.00 (ISBN 0-8240-9400-X). Garland Pub.

--Meredith Now: Some Critical Essays. 1971. 25.00 o.p. (ISBN 0-7100-7061-6). Routledge & Kegan.

--Romantic Mythologies. 297p. 1973. 9.00 (ISBN 0-7100-1368-X). Routledge & Kegan.

Fletcher, Ian, ed. see Allen, Grant.

Fletcher, Ian, ed. see Brookfield, Charles & Glover, J. M.

Fletcher, Ian, ed. see Davidson, John.

Fletcher, Ian, ed. see Dowson, Ernest & Moore, Arthur.

Fletcher, Ian, ed. see Hichens, Robert S.

Fletcher, Ian, ed. see Lee, Vernon.

Fletcher, Ian, ed. see Moore, George.

Fletcher, Ian, ed. see O'Shaughnessy, Arthur.

Fletcher, Ian, ed. see O'Sullivan, Vincent.

Fletcher, Inglis. Bennett's Welcome. 451p. 1976. Repr. of 1950 ed. lib. bdg. 18.95x (ISBN 0-89244-001-5). Queens Hse.

--Cormorant's Brood. 324p. 1976. Repr. of 1959 ed. lib. bdg. 18.95x (ISBN 0-89244-002-3). Queens Hse.

--Lusty Wind for Carolina. LC 44-8968. 1973. 13.95 (ISBN 0-910220-50-6). Berg.

--Lusty Wind for Carolina. 1976. Repr. of 1944 ed. lib. bdg. 18.95x (ISBN 0-89244-003-1). Queens Hse.

--Men of Albemarle. 500p. 1976. Repr. of 1942 ed. lib. bdg. 18.95x (ISBN 0-89244-004-X). Queens Hse.

--Queen's Gift. 448p. 1976. Repr. of 1952 ed. lib. bdg. 17.95x (ISBN 0-89244-005-8). Queens Hse.

--Raleigh's Eden. 1976. Repr. of 1940 ed. lib. bdg. 18.95x (ISBN 0-89244-006-6). Queens Hse.

--Red Jasmine. 320p. 1976. Repr. of 1932 ed. lib. bdg. 16.95x (ISBN 0-89244-012-0). Queens Hse.

--Roanoke Hundred. 501p. 1976. Repr. of 1948 ed. lib. bdg. 18.95x (ISBN 0-89244-007-4). Queens Hse.

--Toil of the Brave. 548p. 1976. Repr. of 1946 ed. lib. bdg. 17.95x (ISBN 0-89244-010-4). Queens Hse.

--The White Leopard. 304p. 1976. Repr. of 1931 ed. lib. bdg. 16.95x (ISBN 0-89244-013-9). Queens Hse.

--Wicked Lady. 245p. 1976. Repr. of 1962 ed. lib. bdg. 16.95x (ISBN 0-89244-009-0). Queens Hse.

--The Wind in the Forest. 448p. 1976. Repr. of 1957 ed. lib. bdg. 17.95x (ISBN 0-89244-011-2). Queens Hse.

Fletcher, J. Use of Economics Literature. 1971. 19.95 o.p. (ISBN 0-408-70171-4). Butterworth.

Fletcher, Jerry, ed. Rural Education. LC 82-80482. (Dialogue Bks.). 368p. (Orig.). 1982. pap. 15.75 (ISBN 0-89881-009-4). Intl Dialogue Pr.

Fletcher, John, jt. auth. see Beaumont, Francis.

Fletcher, John, ed. see Boos-Hamberger, Hilde.

Fletcher, John, ed. see Groddeck, Marie.

Fletcher, John, ed. see Schindler, Maria.

Fletcher, Joseph. Humanhood: Essays in Biomedical Ethics. LC 79-1756. (Impact Ser.). 204p. 1979. 14.95 (ISBN 0-87975-112-6); pap. 9.95 (ISBN 0-87975-123-1). Prometheus Bks.

--Situation Ethics: The New Morality. 1966. 7.95 o.s.i. (ISBN 0-664-20700-6); pap. 4.95 o.s.i. (ISBN 0-664-24691-5). Westminster.

Fletcher, Joseph, jt. ed. see Cox, Harvey.

Fletcher, L. S. & Shoup, T. E. Introduction to Engineering Including FORTRAN Programming. (Illus.). 1978. pap. 18.95 ref. ed. (ISBN 0-13-501858-7). P-H.

Fletcher, L. S., ed. ASME Conference on Mechanical Engineering Education-1980: Proceedings. 181p. 1982. 15.00 (I00145). ASME.

Fletcher, Leon. How to Speak Like a Pro. 272p. (Orig.). 1983. pap. 2.95 (ISBN 0-345-30171-4). Ballantine.

Fletcher, Max E. Economics & Social Problems. LC 78-69590. (Illus.). 1979. pap. text ed. 16.50 (ISBN 0-395-26508-8); instr's. manual 1.00 (ISBN 0-395-26509-6). HM.

Fletcher, Mike & Ross, Bob. Tuning a Racing Yacht. (Illus.). 128p. 1974. 8.50 o.p. (ISBN 0-393-03176-4). Norton.

Fletcher, Miles. The Search for a New Order: Intellectuals & Fascism in Prewar Japan. LC 81-16198. x, 226p. 1982. 24.00x (ISBN 0-8078-1514-4). U of NC Pr.

Fletcher, N. E. & Ladd, J. D. Family Sports Boating. (Illus.). 242p. 1972. 12.00 o.p. (ISBN 0-7207-0601-7). Transatlantic.

Fletcher, Neville H. Chemical Physics of Ice. LC 74-75825. (Monographs on Physics). (Illus.). 1970. 44.50 (ISBN 0-521-07597-1). Cambridge U Pr.

Fletcher, Paul & Garman, Michael, eds. Language Acquisition. LC 78-67305. 1980. 64.50 (ISBN 0-521-22521-3); pap. 17.95x (ISBN 0-521-29536-X). Cambridge U Pr.

Fletcher, Phineas, jt. auth. see Fletcher, Giles.

Fletcher, R. Practical Methods of Optimization: Unconstrained Optimization, Vol. 1. LC 79-41486. 120p. 1980. 26.95x (ISBN 0-471-27711-8, Pub. by Wiley-Interscience). Wiley.

--Practical Methods of Optimization, Vol. 2: Constrained Optimization. 224p. 1981. 31.95x (ISBN 0-471-27828-9, Pub. by Wiley Interscience). Wiley.

Fletcher, Robert, et al. Clinical Epidemiology: The Essentials. (Illus.). 232p. 1982. 16.00 (ISBN 0-683-03252-6). Williams & Wilkins.

Fletcher, Ronald. Biography of a Victorian Village. 1979. 19.95 o.p. (ISBN 0-7134-0787-5, Pub. by Batsford England). David & Charles.

Fletcher, Sarah. My Stories About God's People. (Illus.). 32p. (ps-3). 1974. pap. 1.10 (ISBN 0-570-03426-4, 56-1181). Concordia.

--My Stories About Jesus. (Illus.). 32p. (ps-3). 1974. 5.50 (ISBN 0-570-03428-0, 56-1183); pap. 1.10 (ISBN 0-570-03427-2, 56-1182). Concordia.

--Prayers for Little People. (Illus.). 32p. (ps-3). 1974. pap. 1.10 (ISBN 0-570-03429-9, 56-1184). Concordia.

Fletcher, Sheila. Feminists & Bureaucrats. LC 79-20630. 1980. 34.50 (ISBN 0-521-22880-8). Cambridge U Pr.

Fletcher, Susanne. The Other Anne Fletcher. 1981. pap. 2.95 o.p. (ISBN 0-451-09805-6, E9805, Sig). NAL.

Fletcher, Sybil M., jt. auth. see Keane, Claire B.

Fletcher, Sydney E. Big Book of Cowboys. (Illus.). (gr. 4-6). 1964. 1.50 o.p. (ISBN 0-448-00334-1, G&D). Putnam Pub Group.

Fletcher, T. J. Some Lessons in Mathematics. pap. 12.95x (ISBN 0-521-09248-5). Cambridge U Pr.

Fletcher, Tyler, jt. auth. see Braswell, Michael C.

Fletcher, W., jt. auth. see Richardson, G.

Fletcher, W. K. Analytical Methods in Geochemical Prospecting, Vol. 1. (Handbook of Exploration Geochemistry: Vol. 1). 1981. 59.75 (ISBN 0-444-41930-6). Elsevier.

Fletcher, W. W. The Pest War. LC 74-11440. 218p. 1978. pap. 15.95x o.s.i. (ISBN 0-470-26345-8). Halsted Pr.

Fletcher, W. W. & Kirkwood, R. C. Herbicide Plant Growth Regulation. 1982. 49.95x (ISBN 0-412-00271-X, Pub. by Chapman & Hall England). Methuen Inc.

Fletcher, William, jt. ed. see Lenihan, John.

Fletcher, William I. An Engineering Approach to Digital Design. (Illus.). 1980. text ed. 31.95 (ISBN 0-13-277699-5). P-H.

Fletcher, William W., jt. auth. see Lenihan, John.

Fletcher, William W., jt. ed. see Lenihan, John.

Fletcher, Winston. Teach Yourself Advertising. (Teach Yourself Ser.). 1978. pap. 2.95 o.p. (ISBN 0-679-10450-X). McKay.

Flett, M. Characteristic Frequencies of Chemical Groups in the Infra-Red. 1963. 14.75 (ISBN 0-444-40212-8). Elsevier.

Flett, T. M. Differential Analysis. Pym, J. S., ed. LC 78-67303. (Illus.). 1980. 52.50 (ISBN 0-521-22420-9). Cambridge U Pr.

Flett, Una. Falling From Grace: My Early Years in Ballet. 194p. 1982. 12.95 (ISBN 0-86241-011-8, Pub. by Salem Hse Ltd.). Merrimack Bk Serv.

Fleure, H. F. & Peake, Harold. Priests & Kings. (Corridors of Time Ser.: No. 4). 1927. text ed. 24.50x (ISBN 0-686-83710-X). Elliots Bks.

Fleure, H. J. & Peake, Harold. Hunters & Artists. (Corridors of Time Ser.: No. 2). 1927. text ed. 24.50x (ISBN 0-686-83573-5). Elliots Bks.

--Merchant Ventures in Bronze. (Corridors of Time Ser.: No. 7). 1931. text ed. 24.50x (ISBN 0-686-83625-1). Elliots Bks.

--Peasants & Potters. (Corridors of Time Ser.: No. 3). 1927. text ed. 24.50x (ISBN 0-686-83689-8). Elliots Bks.

--Steppe & the Sown. (Corridors of Time Ser.: No.5). 1928. text ed. 24.50x (ISBN 0-686-83785-1). Elliots Bks.

--Way of the Sea. (Corridors of Time Ser.: No. 6). 1929. text ed. 24.50x (ISBN 0-686-83850-5). Elliots Bks.

Fleure, H. J., jt. auth. see Peake, Harold.

Fleury, P. J., ed. Advances in Non-Communicative Ring-Theory, Plattsburg, 1981. (Lecture Notes in Mathematics Ser.: Vol. 951). 142p. 1983. pap. 8.50 (ISBN 0-387-11597-8). Springer-Verlag.

Flew, Anthony. A Rational Animal: & Other Philosophical Essays on the Nature of Man. 1978. 24.95x (ISBN 0-19-824576-9). Oxford U Pr.

Flew, Antony. A Dictionary of Philosophy. 1980. pap. 8.95 (ISBN 0-312-20922-3). St Martin.

--Philosophy: An Introduction. LC 79-93076. 194p. 1980. pap. text ed. 7.95 (ISBN 0-87975-127-4). Prometheus Bks.

Flew, Antony, ed. Dictionary of Philosophy. LC 78-68699. 1979. 20.00 (ISBN 0-312-20921-5). St Martin.

Flew, R. Newton. Idea of Perfection in Christian Theology: An Historical Study of the Christian Ideal for the Present Life. 1968. Repr. of 1934 ed. pap. text ed. 15.00x o.p. (ISBN 0-391-00507-3). Humanities.

Flew, Robert N. & Davies, Rupert E., eds. The Catholicity of Protestantism: Being a Report Presented to His Grace the Archbishop of Canterbury by a Group of Free Churchmen. LC 80-29108. 159p. 1981. Repr. of 1950 ed. lib. bdg. 19.25x (ISBN 0-313-22825-6, FLCAT). Greenwood.

Flewett, H. W. & Pantin, William E. First Book of Latin Poetry with Vocabulary. (Illus., Lat.). 1977. pap. text ed. 10.95 (ISBN 0-312-29226-0). St Martin.

Flexner, Abraham. Prostitution in Europe. LC 69-14924. (Criminology, Law Enforcement, & Social Problems Ser.: No. 30). 1969. Repr. of 1914 ed. 18.00x (ISBN 0-87585-030-8). Patterson Smith.

Flexner, Helen T. Quaker Childhood. 1940. text ed. 29.50x (ISBN 0-686-83718-5). Elliots Bks.

Flexner, James. World of Winslow Homer. LC 66-27562. (Library of Art Ser.). (Illus.). (gr. 6 up). 1966. 19.92 (ISBN 0-8094-0264-5, Pub. by Time-Life). Silver.

Flexner, James T. The Traitor & the Spy: Benedict Arnold & John Andre. (Illus.). 1975. 15.00 (ISBN 0-316-28606-0). Little.

--Washington: The Indispensable Man. 1979. pap. 3.95 (ISBN 0-451-62213-8, ME2213, Ment). NAL.

Flexner, James T., et al. Institute to University: A Seventy-Fifth Anniversary Colloquim. LC 77-24825. 1977. pap. 3.00x (ISBN 0-87470-025-6). Rockefeller.

Flexner, Stuart B. I Hear America Talking. 1979. 8.95 o.p. (ISBN 0-671-24994-0, Touchstone Bks). S&S.

--Listening to America. 1982. 24.95 (ISBN 0-671-24895-2). S&S.

Flexner, Stuart B., jt. auth. see Wentworth, Harold.

Flexner, William, et al. Strategic Planning in Health Care Management. LC 81-2488. 408p. 1981. text ed. 34.50 (ISBN 0-89443-298-2). Aspen Systems.

Flicek, Barbara D., jt. auth. see Gross, John A.

Flick, Art. Art Flicks New Streamside Guide to Naturals & Their Imitations. (Illus.). 176p. 1970. 7.50 o.p. (ISBN 0-517-50783-8). Crown.

Flick, Art, et al, eds. Art Flick's Master Fly-Tying Guide. (Illus.). 220p. 1972. 10.95 o.p. (ISBN 0-517-50023-X); pap. 8.95 o.p. (ISBN 0-517-52135-0). Crown.

Flicker, Barbara. Standards for Juvenile Justice: A Summary & Analysis. (Juvenile Justice Standards Project Ser.). 336p. 1982. prof ref 29.00x (ISBN 0-88410-758-2); pap. 15.00x prof ref (ISBN 0-88410-831-7). Ballinger Pub.

Flieger, Verlyn. Splintered Light: Logos & Languages in Tolkien's World. 144p. 1983. pap. 6.95 (ISBN 0-8028-1955-9). Eerdmans.

Flier, Michael S., jt. auth. see Stepanoff, N. C.

Flinchum, Betty M. Motor Development in Early Childhood: A Guide for Movement Education with Ages 2-6. LC 74-13129. 130p. 1975. text ed. 9.45 o.p. (ISBN 0-8016-1587-9). Mosby.

Flinder, Peter, jt. auth. see Barchilon, Jacques.

Fling, Paul N. & Puterbaugh, Donald L. The Basic Manual of Fly Tying. LC 77-80194. (Illus.). 1979. pap. 8.95 (ISBN 0-8069-8146-6). Sterling.

--Expert Fly-Tying. LC 81-85025. (Illus.). 160p. (Orig.). 1982. pap. 8.95 (ISBN 0-8069-7580-6). Sterling.

Flink, James J. America Adopts the Automobile, 1895-1910. 1970. 17.50 (ISBN 0-262-06036-1). MIT Pr.

--The Car Culture. LC 74-31191. 280p. 1975. 20.00x (ISBN 0-262-06059-0); pap. 4.95 (ISBN 0-262-56015-1). MIT Pr.

Flink, Salomon J. & Grunewald, Donald. Managerial Finance. LC 68-8714. 639p. 1969. 22.50 (ISBN 0-471-26420-2, Pub. by Wiley). Krieger.

Flinn, E., ed. Scientific Results of Viking Project. 1977. 15.00 (ISBN 0-87590-207-3). Am Geophysical.

Flinn, Frank K., ed. Hermeneutics & Horizons: The Shape of the Future. LC 82-50053. (Conference Ser.: No. 11). xvii, 445p. (Orig.). 1982. pap. text ed. 11.95 (ISBN 0-932894-11-9). Unif Theol Seminary.

Flinn, John J. History of the Chicago Police: From the Settlement of the Community to the Present Time. LC 75-172577. (Criminology, Law Enforcement, & Social Problems Ser.: No. 164). (Illus.). 750p. (With intro. & index added). 1973. Repr. of 1887 ed. lib. bdg. 20.00x (ISBN 0-87585-164-9). Patterson Smith.

Flinn, M. W. & Smout, T. C., eds. Essays in Social History. (Illus.). 1974. pap. 15.95x (ISBN 0-19-877017-0). Oxford U Pr.

Flinn, Michael W. Scottish Population History: From the Seventeenth Century to the 1930s. LC 76-11060. (Illus.). 1978. 72.50 (ISBN 0-521-21173-5). Cambridge U Pr.

Flinn, Richard A. & Trojan, Paul K. Engineering Materials & Their Applications. 2nd ed. (Illus.). 753p. 1981. text ed. 28.95 (ISBN 0-395-29645-5); solutions manual 3.95 (ISBN 0-395-29646-3). HM.

Flinn, Thomas A. Local Government & Politics: Analyzing Decision-Making Systems. 1970. pap. 9.95x (ISBN 0-673-05562-0). Scott F.

Flint, Austin. Insights: A Contemporary Reader. 192p. (Orig.). 1981. pap. text ed. 8.95 (ISBN 0-88377-185-3). Newbury Hse.

Flint, Emily, ed. see Schaafsma, Polly.

Flint, Emily, ed. see Stone, Doris.

Flint, Harrison. The Country Journal Book of Hardy Trees & Shrubs. (Illus.). 176p. (Orig.). 1983. pap. 8.95 (ISBN 0-918678-02-1). Country Journ.
Flint, Harrison L. Landscape Plants for Eastern North America: Exclusive of Florida & the Immediate Gulfcoast. 750p. 1983. 59.95 (ISBN 0-471-86905-8, Pub. by Wiley-Interscience). Wiley.
Flint, Helen, ed. see Beckley, John L.
Flint, Mary L., et al, eds. Integrated Pest Management for Rice. (Illus.). 85p. (Orig.). 1983. pap. text ed. 15.00x (ISBN 0-931876-61-3). Ag Sci Pubns.
Flint, Richard F. Glacial & Quaternary Geology. LC 74-141198. (Illus.). 892p. 1971. 40.95x (ISBN 0-471-26435-0). Wiley.
Flint, Richard F. & Skinner, Brian J. Physical Geology. 2nd ed. LC 76-23206. 671p. 1977. text ed. 26.95 (ISBN 0-471-26442-3); study guide 7.50 (ISBN 0-471-02593-3); tchrs.' manual avail. (ISBN 0-471-03075-9). Wiley.
Flint, Thomas, Jr. & Cain, Harvey D. Emergency Treatment & Management. 5th ed. LC 74-9433. (Illus.). 800p. 1975. text ed. 15.75 o.p. (ISBN 0-7216-3728-0). Saunders.
Flint, Timothy. Condensed Geography & History of the Western States or the Mississippi Valley 1828, 2 Vols. LC 70-119865. 1970. Repr. of 1828 ed. 120.00x set (ISBN 0-8201-1076-0). Schol Facsimiles.
--Recollections of the Last Ten Years in the Valley of the Mississippi. 2nd ed. LC 68-24891. (American Scene Ser). 1968. Repr. of 1826 ed. lib. bdg. 49.50 (ISBN 0-306-71136-2). Da Capo.
Flippo, Chet. Your Cheatin' Heart: A Biography of Hank Williams. 1981. 13.95 o.p. (ISBN 0-671-24114-1). S&S.
Flippo, Edwin B. Principles of Personnel Management. 5th, rev. ed. (Illus.). 1980. text ed. 23.95 (ISBN 0-07-021319-4). McGraw.
--Principles of Personnel Management. 1976. 23.95 (ISBN 0-07-021316-X, C); instructor's manual 4.95 (ISBN 0-07-021317-8). McGraw.
Fliss, Tiffany, tr. see Bazin, Andre.
Flisser, Ana, et al, eds. Cysticercosis: Symposium. 1982. 55.00 (ISBN 0-12-260740-6). Acad Pr.
Floan, Howard R. William Saroyan. (U. S. Authors Ser.: No. 100). 1966. lib. bdg. 10.95 o.p. (ISBN 0-8057-0652-6, Twayne). G K Hall.
Flock, Warren L. Electromagnetics & the Environment: Remote Sensing & Telecommunications. (Illus.). 1979. ref. 34.95 (ISBN 0-13-248997-X). P-H.
Flodin, N. W. Vitamin - Trace Mineral - Protein Interactions, Vol. 1. Horrobin, D. F., ed. (Annual Research Reviews). 1979. 26.40 (ISBN 0-88831-042-0). Eden Pr.
--Vitamin - Trace Mineral - Protein Interactions, Vol. 2. Horrobin, D. F., ed. (Annual Research Reviews). 1980. 30.00 (ISBN 0-88831-062-5, Dist. by Pergamon). Eden Pr.
Flodin, Nestor W. Vitamin-Trace Mineral-Protein Interactions. (Annual Research Reviews Ser.: Vol. 4). 386p. 1981. 38.00 (ISBN 0-88831-114-1). Eden Pr.
--Vitamin-Trace Mineral-Protein Interactions, Vol. 3. Horribin, David F., ed. (Annual Research Reviews). 362p. 1980. 38.00 (ISBN 0-88831-085-4). Eden Pr.
Floegel, Ekkehard, jt. auth. see Hofacker, Winfried.
Flohn, H. Investigations on the Climatic Conditions of the Advancement of the Tunisian Sahara. (Technical Note Ser.). 55p. (Orig.). 1972. pap. 10.00 (ISBN 0-685-25260-4, W92, WMO). Unipub.
Flood, C. R., jt. auth. see Parkin, N.
Flood, J. The Moth Hunters: Aboriginal Prehistory of the Australian Alps. (AIAS New Ser.). (Illus.). 1980. text ed. 25.00x (ISBN 0-391-00993-1); pap. text ed. 17.50x (ISBN 0-391-00994-X). Humanities.
Flood, James, jt. auth. see Lapp, Diane.
Flood, James E. & Lapp, Diane. Language-Reading Instruction for the Young Child. (Illus.). 1981. text ed. 20.95x (ISBN 0-02-338470-0). Macmillan.
Flood, Kenneth U. & Callson, Oliver G. Transportation Management. 4th ed. 550p. 1983. text ed. write for info. (ISBN 0-697-08514-7). Wm C Brown.
Flood, Kenneth U., ed. Research in Transportation: Legal-Legislative & Economic Sources & Procedures. LC 72-118792. (Management Information Guides Ser.: No. 20). 1970. 42.00x (ISBN 0-8103-0820-7). Gale.
Flood, Robert. Graduation: A New Start. LC 80-27606. 128p. 1981. pap. 8.95 (ISBN 0-8024-3298-0). Moody.
Flood, Robert G. The Christian's Vacation & Travel Guide. 224p. 1982. pap. 9.95 (ISBN 0-8423-0260-3). Tyndale.
Flood, William G. The Story of the Bagpipe. LC 76-22332. (Illus.). 1976. Repr. of 1911 ed. lib. bdg. 25.00 (ISBN 0-89341-009-8). Longwood Pr.
Flook, E. Evelyn & Sanazaro, Paul J., eds. Health Services Research & R & D in Perspective. LC 73-86625. 311p. 1973. 10.00 (ISBN 0-914904-00-0). Health Admin Pr.
Flora, James. The Day the Cow Sneezed. LC 75-8746. (Illus.). 42p. (gr. k-1). 1975. pap. 1.95 (ISBN 0-15-624213-3, VoyB). HarBraceJ.
--Grandpa's Farm. LC 65-19989. (Illus.). (gr. 1-4). 1965. 6.95 o.p. (ISBN 0-15-232340-6, HJ). HarBraceJ.
--Grandpa's Withched-Up Christmas. LC 81-12843. (Illus.). 32p. (ps-4). 10.95 (ISBN 0-689-50232-X, McElderry Bk). Atheneum.
--Leopold, the See-Through Crumbpicker. LC 61-6114. (Illus.). (gr. k-3). 1961. 6.95 o.p. (ISBN 0-15-244892-6, HJ). HarBraceJ.
--My Friend Charlie. LC 64-16265. (Illus.). (gr. 1-4). 1972. pap. 1.25 (ISBN 0-15-662330-7, VoyB). HarBraceJ.
Flora, Joseph M. Vardis Fisher. (United States Authors Ser.). 1965. lib. bdg. 14.95 (ISBN 0-8057-0252-0, Twayne). G K Hall.
--William Ernest Henley. (English Authors Ser.). 14.95 (ISBN 0-8057-1252-6, Twayne). G K Hall.
Flora, Peter & Heidenheimer, Arnold J., eds. Development of Welfare States in Europe & America. LC 79-65227. 420p. 1981. 19.95 (ISBN 0-87855-357-6). Transaction Bks.
Flora, Philip C., ed. Robotics Industry Directory, 1983. (Illus.). 250p. 1983. pap. 50.00 (ISBN 0-910747-02-4). Tech Data Corp.
Florance, Cheri L., jt. auth. see Shames, George H.
Florczyk, Sandra E., jt. auth. see Bednarski, Mary W.
Flore, Ron Le see Le Flore, Ron & Hawkins, Jim.
Florea, J. H. ABC of Poultry Raising: A Complete Guide for the Beginner or Expert. (Illus.). 9.00 (ISBN 0-8446-5186-9). Peter Smith.
Florea, Vasile. Romanian Painting. (Illus.). 176p. 1983. 13.50 (ISBN 0-8143-1731-6). Wayne St U Pr.
Floren, Lee. Guns of Montana. 192p. 1981. pap. 1.95 (ISBN 0-8439-0965-X, Leisure Bks). Nordon Pubns.
--Smoky River. 1980. lib. bdg. 10.95 o.p. (ISBN 0-8161-3027-2, Large Print Bks). G K Hall.
Florence, A. T. & Attwood, D. Physicochemical Principles of Pharmacy. 1982. 29.95x (ISBN 0-412-00131-4). Methuen Inc.
Florence, A. T., jt. auth. see Attwood, D.
Florence, D. & Hegedus, Frank. Coping with Chronic Pain: A Patient's Guide to Wellness. 1982. 5.25 (ISBN 0-686-84598-6). Sis Kenny Inst.
Florence, Gene. Elegant Glassware of the Depression Era. 160p. Date not set. 17.95 (ISBN 0-89145-220-6). Collector Bks.
--Pocket Guide to Depression Glass. 3rd ed. 160p. Date not set. 9.95 (ISBN 0-89145-209-5). Collector Bks.
Florence, Philip S. Economics of Fatigue & Unrest & the Efficiency of Labour in English & American Industry. LC 77-136530. 426p. Repr. of 1924 ed. lib. bdg. 19.75x (ISBN 0-8371-5451-0, FLEF). Greenwood.
Florens, J. P., et al, eds. Specifying Statistical Models, From Parametric to Non-Parametric, Using Bayesian or Non-Bayesian Approaches: Proceedings, Louvain-la-Neuve, Belgium, 1981. (Lecture Notes in Statistics Ser.: Vol. 16). (Illus.). 204p. 1983. pap. 14.00 (ISBN 0-387-90809-9). Springer-Verlag.
Florentz, C. So Wild a Dream. LC 77-77158. (Pacesetters Ser.). (Illus.). 64p. (gr. 4 up). 1978. PLB 8.65 (ISBN 0-516-02172-9). Childrens.
Flores, A. & Anderson, H. Masterpieces of Latin-American Literature, 2 vols. 1973. Vol. 1. 18.95x (ISBN 0-02-338320-8); Vol. 2. 19.95x (ISBN 0-02-338330-5). Macmillan.
Flores, Evelina V. El Yugo De los Infieles. 116p. (Sp.). 1981. pap. 2.20 (ISBN 0-311-37008-X). Casa Bautista.
Flores, F., jt. auth. see Garcia-Moliner, F.
Flores, Ivan. Data Structure & Management. 2nd ed. 1977. 26.95 (ISBN 0-13-197335-5). P-H.
Flores, Janis. High Dominion. (Orig.). 1981. pap. 3.50 o.p. (ISBN 0-686-73353-3, AE1106, Sig). NAL.
Flores, Rhode, tr. see Bennett, Gordon H.
Flores D'Arcais, G. B. & Levelt, W. J., eds. Advances in Psycholinguistics. 1971. pap. 35.25 o.p. (ISBN 0-444-10071-7, North-Holland); pap. 29.50 o.p. (ISBN 0-444-10064-4). Elsevier.
Floret, C., jt. ed. see Mabbutt, J. A.
Florey, Francis G. Elementary Linear Algebra with Applications. LC 78-9412. (Illus.). 1979. ref. ed. 23.95 (ISBN 0-13-258251-1). P-H.
Florey, Kitty B. Chez Cordelia. 1982. pap. 2.50 o.p. (ISBN 0-451-11266-0, AE1266, Sig). NAL.
--The Garden Path. 304p. 1983. 16.95 (ISBN 0-399-31019-3). Seaview Bks.
Florey, Klaus, ed. Analytical Profiles of Drug Subsubstances, Vol. II. LC 70-187259. 1982. 39.00 (ISBN 0-12-260811-9). Acad Pr.
Flor-Henry. Cerebral Bases of Psychopathology. 1983. text ed. 40.00 (ISBN 0-7236-7034-X). Wright-PSG.
Flor-Henry, P., jt. auth. see Gruizelier, J. H.
Florian, Doug. People Working. LC 82-45188. (Illus.). 32p. (ps-3). 1983. 9.57i (ISBN 0-690-04263-9, TYC-J); PLB 9.89g (ISBN 0-690-04264-7). Har-Row.
Florian, John, ed. Puerto Rico Living, Vol. 20. rev ed. 166p. 1982. pap. 2.95 (ISBN 0-936216-28-X). NE Outdoors.
Florian, M. A., ed. Traffic Equilibrium Methods. (Lecture Notes in Economics & Mathematical Systems: Vol. 118). 1976. pap. 21.00 o.p. (ISBN 0-387-07620-4). Springer-Verlag.
Florida Atlantic University Conference. Management Problems in Serials Work: Proceedings. Spyers Duran, Peter & Gore, Daniel, eds. LC 73-10775. 1974. lib. bdg. 25.00 (ISBN 0-8371-7050-8, SSW/). Greenwood.
Florida Flair Books Staff. The Everglades Coloring Book. (Illus.). 32p. Date not set. pap. 1.95 (ISBN 0-686-84290-1). Banyan Bks.
Florida State University, Dept. of Philosophy, ed. see Kaelin, E. F.
Floridi, Alexis. Moscow & the Vatican. 365p. 1983. 23.50 (ISBN 0-88233-647-9). Ardis Pubs.
Florin, John W., jt. auth. see Birdsall, Stephen S.
Florin, Lambert F. Arizona Ghost Towns. LC 74-160181. (Illus.). 1971. pap. 4.95 o.s.i. (ISBN 0-87564-325-6). Superior Pub.
--Montana-Idaho-Wyoming Ghost Towns. LC 75-160184. (Illus.). 1971. pap. 4.95 o.s.i. (ISBN 0-87564-328-0). Superior Pub.
--Washington Ghost Towns. LC 72-160178. (Illus.). 1971. pap. 4.95 o.s.i. (ISBN 0-87564-322-1). Superior Pub.
Florinsky, Michael T. Integrated Europe? LC 78-712. 1978. Repr. of 1955 ed. lib. bdg. 19.00x (ISBN 0-313-20279-6, FLIE). Greenwood.
--Russia: A History & Interpretation, 2 vols. 1954. Vol. 1. 14.95x (ISBN 0-02-338350-X, 33835); Vol. 2. 12.95 o.p. (ISBN 0-02-338420-4, 33842). Macmillan.
Florio, A. E. & Alles. Safety Education. 4th, rev. ed. (Illus.). 1979. text ed. 27.50 (ISBN 0-07-021371-2, C). McGraw.
Florio, A. E. & Stafford, George T. Safety Education. 3rd ed. LC 69-13219. (Illus.). 1969. text ed. 15.95 (ISBN 0-07-021370-4, C). McGraw.
Florio, C., jt. auth. see Cross, W.
Florio, P. L., jt. auth. see Salvadori, F. B.
Florisha, Barbara L. Sex Roles & Personal Awareness. 1978. pap. text ed. 12.50x (ISBN 0-673-15307-X). Scott F.
Floristan, Casiano, jt. auth. see Duquoc, Christian.
Floristan, Casiano, jt. ed. see Duquoc, Christian.
Florit, Eugenio. Obras Completas, Vol. 2. LC 82-60407. (Illus.). 150p. (Orig.). 1983. pap. 25.00 (ISBN 0-89295-021-8). Society Sp & Sp-Am.
Florkin, M. & Stotz, E. H. Comprehensive Biochemistry, Section 6: History of Biochemistry, Vols. 30-32. Incl. Vol. 30, Pt. 1. Proto-Biochemistry; Vol. 30, Pt. 2. Proto-Biochemistry to Biochemistry; Vol. 31. History of Identification of Sources of Free Energy in Organisms. 1975; Vol. 32. Early Studies in Biosynthesis. 1972-77. Vol. 30, Pts. 1 & 2. 82.75 (ISBN 0-444-41024-4, North Holland); Vol. 31. 119.75 (ISBN 0-444-41145-3); Vol. 32. 73.75 (ISBN 0-444-41544-0). Elsevier.
Florkin, M. & Dollfus, A., eds. Life Sciences & Space Research, Vol. 2. (Cospar Ser.), 1964. 38.50 (ISBN 0-444-10198-5, North-Holland). Elsevier.
Florkin, M. & Neuberger, A., eds. Comprehensive Biochemistry, Vol. 19B, Pt. 1: Protein Metabolism. 1980. 101.50 (ISBN 0-444-80171-5, North Holland). Elsevier.
Florkin, M. & Stotz, eds. Comprehensive Biochemistry, Vol. 19: Metabolism of Amino Acids, Proteins, Purines & Pyrimidines. 1981. 103.50 (ISBN 0-444-80257-6, North Holland). Elsevier.
--Comprehensive Biochemistry, Vol. 33A: Unravelling of Biosynthetic Pathways. 1979. 96.75 (ISBN 0-444-80067-0, North Holland). Elsevier.
--Comprehensive Biochemistry, Vol. 33B: Biosynthetic Pathways of Amino Acids & Their Extensions. 1979. 78.50 (ISBN 0-444-80068-9, North Holland). Elsevier.
Florkin, M., & Stotz, E. H., eds. Comprehensive Biochemistry, Vol. 18S: Pyruvates & Fatty Acid Metabolism. LC 62-10359. (Illus.). 125p. 1971. 39.25 (ISBN 0-444-40950-5, North Holland). Elsevier.
Florkin, M. & Van Deenen, L. L., eds. Comprehensive Biochemistry, Vol. 19B, Pt. 2: Protein Metabolism. 1982. 74.50 (ISBN 0-444-80346-7, North Holland). Elsevier.
Florman, Samuel. Blaming Technology: The Irrational Search for Scapegoats. 224p. pap. 6.95 (ISBN 0-312-08363-7). St Martin.
--The Existential Pleasures of Engineering. LC 75-9480. 1977. pap. 4.95 (ISBN 0-312-27546-3). St Martin.
Flory, Charles, ed. Managers for Tomorrow. 1971. pap. 2.75 (ISBN 0-451-61938-2, ME1938, Ment). NAL.
Flory, David, jt. auth. see Van Name, Frederick W.
Flory, E., jt. auth. see Bradbury, Ellen.
Flory, Esther V. see Cook, Dorothy E. & Monro, Isabel S.
Flory, Jane. Miss Plunkett to the Rescue. LC 82-15797. (Illus.). 96p. (gr. 3-6). 1983. 7.95 (ISBN 0-395-33072-6). HM.
Flory, Joan, jt. auth. see Walne, Damien.
Flory, M. A. A Book about Fans: The History of Fans & Fan-Painting. LC 72-174940. (Illus.). xiv, 141p. 1975. Repr. of 1895 ed. 37.00x (ISBN 0-8103-4049-6). Gale.
Flory, P. J. Statistical Mechanics of Chain Molecules. LC 68-21490. 1969. 47.95 (ISBN 0-470-26495-0, Pub. by Wiley-Interscience). Wiley.
Flothius, Marius. Notes on Notes: Selected Essays. (Illus.). 178p. 1974. 35.00 o.s.i. (ISBN 90-6027-227-7, Pub. by Frits Knuf Netherlands); wrappers 20.00 o.s.i. (ISBN 90-6027-226-9, Pub. by Frits Knuf Netherlands). Pendragon NY.
Floud, J. E., et al. Social Class & Educational Opportunity. LC 73-7195. (Illus.). 152p. 1973. Repr. of 1957 ed. lib. bdg. 19.00x (ISBN 0-8371-6918-6, FLSC). Greenwood.
Floud, Roderick. The British Machine-Tool Industry, 1850-1914. LC 75-46205. (Illus.). 180p. 1976. 34.50 (ISBN 0-521-21203-0). Cambridge U Pr.
--Introduction to Quantitative Methods for Historians. 2nd ed. 1980. 24.95x (ISBN 0-416-71660-1); pap. 12.95x (ISBN 0-416-71670-9). Methuen Inc.
Flourney, Sheryl. Flames of Passion. (Tapestry Romance Ser.). (Orig.). 1982. pap. 2.50 (ISBN 0-686-83758-4). PB.
Flournoy, Fran. The Very Best Book of All. Mahany, Patricia, ed. LC 82-80032. (Happy Day Bk.). (Illus.). 24p. (Orig.). (ps-3). 1982. pap. 1.29 (ISBN 0-87239-545-6, 3591). Standard Pub.
Flower, Dean. Henry James in Northhampton: Vision & Revision. 28p. 1971. pap. 3.00 (ISBN 0-87391-027-3). Smith Coll.
Flower, Dean, ed. see James, Henry.
Flower, Elizabeth & Murphey, Murrary G. A History of Philosophy in America, 2 vols. 1977. Set. 30.00 o.p. (ISBN 0-685-80671-5); Vol. I. (ISBN 0-399-11650-8); Vol. II. (ISBN 0-399-11743-1). Putnam Pub Group.
Flower, Elizabeth & Murphey, Murray G. A History of Philosophy in America, 2 vols. LC 75-40254. Vol. 1 488pp. 17.50 (ISBN 0-399-11650-8); Vol. 2. 544pp. 17.50 (ISBN 0-399-11743-1). Vols. 1 & 2. Hackett Pub.
Flower Essence Society. The Flower Essence Journal, Issue 1. rev. ed. Katz, Richard A., ed. (Illus.). 36p. 1982. pap. 3.00 (ISBN 0-943986-01-X). Gold Circle.
--The Flower Essence Journal, Issue 2. rev. ed. Katz, Richard A., ed. (Illus.). 36p. 1983. pap. 3.00 (ISBN 0-943986-02-8). Gold Circle.
--The Flower Essence Journal, Issue 3. rev. ed. Katz, Richard A., ed. (Illus.). 48p. 1982. pap. 3.00 (ISBN 0-943986-03-6). Gold Circle.
--The Flower Essence Journal, Issue 4. Katz, Richard A. & Kaminski, Patricia A., eds. (Illus.). 80p. (Orig.). 1982. pap. 7.00 (ISBN 0-943986-04-4). Gold Circle.
Flower, John E. Literature & the Left in France. LC 76-2895. 1983. text ed. 28.50x (ISBN 0-06-492135-2). B&N Imports.
Flower, Linda. Problem-Solving Strategies for Writing. 210p. 1981. pap. text ed. 9.95 (ISBN 0-15-571983-1, HC); instr's. manual 1.95 (ISBN 0-15-571984-X). HarBraceJ.
Flower, Milton E. James Parton, the Father of Modern Biography. LC 68-29742. (Illus.). 1968. Repr. of 1951 ed. lib. bdg. 16.75x o.p. (ISBN 0-8371-0420-3, FLJP). Greenwood.
--John Dickinson: Conservative Revolutionary. LC 82-11151. 360p. 1983. 27.50x (ISBN 0-8139-0966-X). U Pr of Va.
Flower, Raymond & Jones, Michael W. Lloyd's of London: An Illustrated History. (Illus.). 1974. 16.50 o.p. (ISBN 0-8038-4290-2). Hastings.
Flower, Robin, tr. see O Crohan, Tomas.
Flower, Sybilla J., compiled by. Debrett's Stately Homes of Great Britain. (Illus.). 240p. 1982. 24.45 (ISBN 0-03-061993-9). HR&W.
FLowerdew, Robin, ed. Institutions & Geographical Patterns. LC 82-42541. 352p. 1982. 27.50x (ISBN 0-312-41886-8). St Martin.
Flowers, B. H. & Mendoza, E. Properties of Matter. LC 70-11815. (Manchester Physics Ser.). 1970. 41.95x (ISBN 0-471-26497-0, Pub. by Wiley-Interscience). Wiley.
Flowers, Charles M., jt. ed. see Callaway, Cason J., Jr.
Flowers, H. D. Speech As an Art. 1978. pap. text ed. 9.95 (ISBN 0-8403-1939-8). Kendall-Hunt.
Flowers, James L. A Complete Preparation for the New MCAT: Knowledge & Comprehension of Science, Vol. 1. (Illus.). 456p. 1982. pap. text ed. 15.00 (ISBN 0-941406-01-6). Betz Pub Co Inc.
Flowers, James L. & Jenkins-Murphy, Andrew. A Complete Preparation for the Health Professions: Dentistry, Optometry, Pharmacy, Veterinary Medicine. (Illus.). 500p. (Orig.). 1983. pap. text ed. 15.00 (ISBN 0-941406-04-0). Betz Pub Co Inc.
Flowers, James L., et al. A Complete Preparation for the New MCAT: Knowledge & Comprehension of Science & Skills Development in Reading & Quantitative. Set. pap. 27.00 (ISBN 0-941406-03-2). Betz Pub Co Inc.
Flowers, John V., et al. Help Your Children Be Self-Confident. LC 78-16705. 1978. 8.95 o.p. (ISBN 0-13-386219-4). P-H.
Flowers, Ronald B., jt. auth. see Miller, Robert T.
Flowers, T. H. Introduction to Exchange Systems. LC 76-13447. 1976. 69.95 (ISBN 0-471-01865-1, Pub. by Wiley-Interscience). Wiley.
Flowers, T. J., jt. auth. see Hall, J. L.
Floy, Michael. The Diary of Michael Floy Jr., Bowery Village, Eighteen Thirty-Three to Eighteen Thirty-Seven. Brooks, R. A., ed. 1941. 49.50 (ISBN 0-686-51371-1). Elliots Bks.

Floyd, Ann. Cognitive Development in the School Years. LC 78-9155. 383p. 1979. 29.95x o.s.i. (ISBN 0-470-26429-2). Halsted Pr.

Floyd, Barry. Jamaica: An Island Microcosm. (Illus.). 1979. 18.95x (ISBN 0-312-43953-9). St Martin.

Floyd, Beth, jt. ed. see Floyd, Steve.

Floyd, Bryan A. The Long War Dead: An Epiphany. 1976. pap. 1.50 o.p. (ISBN 0-380-00524-7, 27615, Bard). Avon.

Floyd, Charles F. Real Estate Principles. 592p. 1981. text ed. 25.00 (ISBN 0-394-32263-0). Random.

Floyd, Dale E. Actions with Indians. 1979. pap. 4.95 o.p. Old Army.

Floyd, Dale R. Actions With Indians. 1983. pap. 4.95 (ISBN 0-88342-248-4). Old Army.

Floyd, Robert A., ed. Free Radicals & Cancer. (Illus.). 552p. 1982. 69.75 (ISBN 0-8247-1551-9). Dekker.

Floyd, Samuel A., Jr. & Reisser, Marsha J. Black Music in the United States: An Annotated Bibliography of Selected Reference & Research Materials. LC 82-49044. 420p. 1983. lib. bdg. 30.00 (ISBN 0-527-30164-7). Kraus Intl.

Floyd, Steve & Floyd, Beth, eds. Handbook of Interactive Video. (Video Bookshelf Ser.). 168p. 1982. text ed. 34.95 (ISBN 0-86729-019-6). Knowledge Indus.

Floyd, Thomas L. Digital Fundamentals. 2nd ed. Orig. Title: Digital Logic Fundamentals. 624p. 1982. text ed. 23.95 (ISBN 0-675-09876-9). Additional Supplements May Be Obtained From Publisher. Merrill.

--Digital Logic Fundamentals. (Electronics Technology Ser.). 1977. text ed. 23.95 (ISBN 0-675-08495-4). Additional supplements may be obtained from publisher. Merrill.

--Electric Circuits: Electron Flow Version. 1983. text ed. 24.95 (ISBN 0-675-20037-7). Additional supplements may be obtained from publisher. Merrill.

--Essentials of Electronic Devices. 1983. pap. text ed. 7.95 (ISBN 0-675-20062-8). Merrill.

--Principles of Electric Circuits. (Illus.). 768p. 1981. text ed. 24.95 (ISBN 0-675-08081-9). Additional supplements may be obtained from publisher. Merrill.

Floyd, Virginia H., jt. ed. see Doyle, Esther M.

Floyd, Wanita, jt. auth. see Meins, Betty.

Fltting, M. Fundamentals of Generalized Recursion Theory. (Studies in Logic & the Foundations of Mathematics: Vol. 105). 1982. 64.00 (ISBN 0-444-86171-8). Elsevier.

Flubacher, Joseph F. The Concept of Ethics in the History of Economics. 460p. Repr. of 1950 ed. lib. bdg. 27.50x (ISBN 0-87991-069-0). Porcupine Pr.

Fluchere, Henri, tr. see Giono, Jean.

Fluck, Sandra. Experiential English. 288p. 1973. pap. text ed. 5.95x o.p. (ISBN 0-02-473620-1). Glencoe.

Flude, Michael, jt. ed. see Ahier, John.

Fluegelman, Andrew & Hewes, Jeremy J. Writing in the Computer Age: A Guide to Skills & Styles for Word Processing. LC 81-43852. (Headlands Press Bks.). 256p. 1983. 19.95 (ISBN 0-385-18124-8, Anchor Pr); pap. 10.95 (ISBN 0-385-18125-6, Anch). Doubleday.

Fluegge, E., ed. Encyclopedia of Physics, 54 vols, Vols. 46-49, 51-54. Incl. Vol. 46, Pt. 1. Cosmic Rays One. 1961. 97.40 (ISBN 0-387-02689-4); Vol. 46, Pt. 2. Cosmic Rays Two. Sitte, K., ed. 1967. 159.30 (ISBN 0-387-03855-8); Vol. 47. Geophysics One. 1956. 116.90 (ISBN 0-387-02046-2); Vol. 48. Geophysics Two. 1957. 194.70 (ISBN 0-387-02174-4); Vol. 49. Geophysics Three, 4 pts. Bartels, J. & Rower, K., eds. (Illus.). Pt. 1, 1966. 112.10 (ISBN 0-387-03549-4); Pt. 2, 1967. 112.10 (ISBN 0-686-96891-3); Pt. 3, 537p, 1971. 159.30 (ISBN 0-387-05570-3); Pt. 4, 592p, 1972. 140.50 (ISBN 0-387-05583-5); Vol. 51. Astrophysics Two: Stellar Structure. (Illus.). 1958. 171.10 (ISBN 0-387-02299-6); Vol. 52. Astrophysics Three: The Solar System. (Illus.). 1959. 141.60 (ISBN 0-387-02416-6); Vol. 53. Astrophysics Four: Stellar Systems. (Illus.). 1959. 141.60 (ISBN 0-387-02417-4); Vol. 54. Astrophysics Five: Miscellaneous. (Illus.). 1962. 97.40 (ISBN 0-387-02844-7). Springer-Verlag.

Fluegge, S. Encyclopedia of Physics, Vol. 49, Pt. 5: Geophysics 3, Pt. 5. LC 56-2942. (Illus.). 420p. (Eng, Fr, & Ger.). 1976. 116.90 (ISBN 0-387-07512-7). Springer-Verlag.

Fluegge, S., ed. Geophysics Three, Part Six. (Encyclopedia of Physics Ser.: Vol. 49, Pt. 6). (Illus.). 429p. 1982. 118.60 (ISBN 0-387-07080-X). Springer-Verlag.

Flueler, Niklaus. Werner Bischof. (Illus.). 1976. pap. 6.95 o.p. (ISBN 0-8174-0318-3, Amphoto). Watson-Guptill.

Flugel, Karl H. Salons Success Society. LC 78-73478. 330p. 1981. lib. bdg. 50.00 (ISBN 0-933136-00-5). Academie Pr.

Flugge, Wilhelm, ed. Handbook of Engineering Mechanics. 1962. 75.00 o.p. (ISBN 0-07-021392-5, P&RB). McGraw.

Fluharty, Vernon L. Dance of the Millions: Military Rule & the Social Revolution in Colombia. LC 75-26918. (Illus.). 336p. 1975. Repr. of 1957 ed. lib. bdg. 19.25x (ISBN 0-8371-8368-5, FLDM). Greenwood.

Fluiani, Carlo M. The Elliot Wave Theory Flow of Speculative Matter into the Active Cylinder Theory Stream. (The Recondite Sources of Stock Market Action Library). (Illus.). 137p. 1983. 81.45 (ISBN 0-86654-043-1). Inst Econ Finan.

Fluke, Joanne. The Other Child. (Orig.). 1983. pap. 2.95 (ISBN 0-440-16767-1). Dell.

Flukinger, Roy, jt. auth. see Downs, Fane.

Flume, Violet S. The Last Mountain: The Life of Robert Wood. 1983. 19.95 (ISBN 0-8283-1739-9); pap. 10.50 (ISBN 0-8283-1878-6). Branden.

Flumiani, C. M. The Best Critical Stock Market Studies of the Fibonacci-Elliot Research Foundation, 3 vols. (Illus.). 418p. 1983. Set. 575.00 (ISBN 0-86654-070-9). Inst Econ Finan.

--The Collapse of Gold & the Tragic Dilemma of the Swiss Banks. (Illus.). 205p. 1976. 49.50 (ISBN 0-918968-18-6). Am Classical Coll Pr.

--The Hidden & Mysterious Life of Stock Market Syndicates. (A New Stock Market Library Bk.). (Illus.). 116p. 1983. 49.85 (ISBN 0-86654-057-1). Inst Econ Finan.

--How to Gain Exposure to the Possibility of Gaining Thousands upon Thousands of Dollars in the Stock Market by Following a Simple Method Recently Discovered. (A New Stock Market Library Bk.). (Illus.). 77p. 1983. pap. 6.95 (ISBN 0-89266-393-6). Am Classical Coll Pr.

--The Work Efficiency Organizer & Life Perfector. (Illus.). 80p. 1974. 27.50 o.p. (ISBN 0-913314-32-3). Am Classical Coll Pr.

Flumiani, C. M., ed. Collection of the Best Critical Studies Which Have Appeared in the Catholic Activist, 2 vols. (Illus.). 1980. Set. deluxe ed. 59.85 o.p. (ISBN 0-89266-236-0). Am Classical Coll Pr.

Flumiani, Carlo M. How to Select a Stock with the Power to make you Wealthy Almost Overnight. (New Stock Market Library Book). (Illus.). 61p. (Orig.). 1983. pap. 6.95 (ISBN 0-89266-390-1). Am Classical Coll Pr.

--The Technical Wall Street Encyclopedia. (The Library). 198p. 1982. 68.15 (ISBN 0-86654-041-5). Inst Econ Finan.

--Three Ways for an Investor with very Little Money to make a Killing in the Stock Market. 04/1983 ed. (New Stock Market Library Book). (Illus.). 69p. (Orig.). pap. 6.95 (ISBN 0-89266-391-X). Am Classical Coll Pr.

--Your Financial I. Q. Personal Test. (A New Stock Market Library Bk). 91p. 1983. 21.75 (ISBN 0-86654-044-X). Inst Econ Finan.

Flurry, Robert L., Jr. Symmetry Groups: Theory & Chemical Applications. (Illus.). 1980. text ed. 36.95 (ISBN 0-13-880013-8). P-H.

Flurscheim, C. H., ed. Power Circuit Breaker Theory & Design. (IEE Power Ser.: No. 1). 602p. 1982. 61.00 (ISBN 0-906048-70-2). Inst Elect Eng.

Flusser, David. Die Rabbinischen Gleichnisse und der Gleichniserzahler Jesus. 322p. (Ger.). 1981. write for info. (ISBN 3-261-04778-X). P Lang Pubs.

Fly, J. Mark, jt. auth. see Marans, Robert W.

Flygare, W. H. Molecular Structure & Dynamics. LC 77-16786. (Illus.). 1978. ref. 38.95 (ISBN 0-13-599753-4). P-H.

Flying Armadillo Staff, jt. ed. see Singer, Michael.

Flynn, Bernice, jt. auth. see Flynn, Leslie.

Flynn, Carolyn. Washed in the Blood. LC 81-84525. 352p. 1983. 16.95 (ISBN 0-399-31018-5). Seaview Bks.

Flynn, Cleta. The Parable: A Story of Jesus, Son of Joseph. LC 79-14062. 1979. 7.95 o.p. (ISBN 0-915442-81-7, Unilaw); pap. 4.95 o.p. (ISBN 0-915442-76-0). Donning Co.

Flynn, David H. & Pancheri, Michael. The IRA Handbook. (Illus.). 224p. 1983. 12.95 (ISBN 0-8329-0263-2). New Century.

Flynn, Don. Murder Isn't Enough. 192p. 1983. 12.95 (ISBN 0-8027-5495-3). Walker & Co.

Flynn, Edward J. You're the Boss. LC 82-24156. x, 244p. 1983. Repr. of 1947 ed. lib. bdg. 29.75x (ISBN 0-313-23627-5, FLYB). Greenwood.

Flynn, Elizabeth & La Faso, John. Group Discussion As Learning Process: Sourcebook, Student Edition. LC 74-170013. 272p. 1972. pap. 8.95 o.p. (ISBN 0-8091-1589-1). Paulist Pr.

Flynn, Elizabeth G. The Rebel Girl: An Autobiography. new ed. LC 72-94154. 352p. 1973. pap. 5.95 (ISBN 0-7178-0368-6). Intl Pub Co.

Flynn, Elizabeth W. & LaFaso, John F. Designs in Affective Education: A Teacher Resource Program for Junior & Senior High. LC 73-90085. 360p. 1974. pap. 10.00 o.p. (ISBN 0-8091-1811-4). Paulist Pr.

Flynn, Elizabeth W. & La Faso, John F. Group Discussion As Learning Process, a Guide Book: Teacher's Edition. LC 74-170013. 120p. 5.95 o.p. (ISBN 0-8091-0172-6); pap. 4.95 o.p. (ISBN 0-8091-1737-1). Paulist Pr.

Flynn, Errol. Beam Ends. 1976. Repr. of 1937 ed. lib. bdg. 16.95 (ISBN 0-89966-092-4). Buccaneer Bks.

Flynn, George Q. The Mess in Washington: Manpower Mobilization in World War II. LC 78-4027. (Contributions in American History: No. 76). xi, 294p. 1979. lib. bdg. 29.95 (ISBN 0-313-20418-7, FMW/). Greenwood.

--Roosevelt & Romanism: Catholics & American Diplomacy, 1937-1945. LC 75-35343. (Contributions in American History: No. 47). 272p. 1976. lib. bdg. 29.95 (ISBN 0-8371-8581-5, FRR/). Greenwood.

Flynn, Gerard. Manuel Breton de los Herreros. (World Authors Ser.). 1978. lib. bdg. 15.95 (ISBN 0-8057-6328-7, Twayne). G K Hall.

--Manuel Tamayo y Baus. (World Authors Ser.). 1973. lib. bdg. 15.95 (ISBN 0-8057-2880-5, Twayne). G K Hall.

Flynn, Gregory, ed. Economic Interests in the Nineteen Eighties: Convergence or Divergence? (Atlantic Papers Ser.: No. 44-45). 126p. 1982. pap. text ed. 13.00x (ISBN 0-86598-103-5). Allanheld.

Flynn, J. Edward. Hand Surgery. 2nd ed. 850p. 1975. 53.00 o.p. (ISBN 0-683-03267-4). Williams & Wilkins.

Flynn, J. M. Danger Zone. (Inflation Fighters Ser.). 192p. 1982. pap. cancelled o.s.i. (ISBN 0-8439-1139-5, Leisure Bks). Nordon Pubns.

Flynn, Jay. Bannerman. 192p. 1982. pap. 2.25 o.s.i. (ISBN 0-8439-1119-0, Leisure Bks). Nordon Pubns.

Flynn, Jean. Jim Bowie: A Texas Legend. (Stories for Young Americans Ser.). 1980. 5.95 (ISBN 0-89015-241-1). Eakin Pubns.

Flynn, Jean P., jt. auth. see Mahoney, Elizabeth A.

Flynn, Joe B. The Design of Executive Protection Systems. (Illus.). 100p. 1979. 12.75x (ISBN 0-398-03894-5). C C Thomas.

Flynn, John T. While You Slept: Our Tragedy in Asia & Who Made It. 1951. 6.50 (ISBN 0-8159-7207-5). Devin.

Flynn, John Thomas. Country Squire in the White House. LC 77-167846. (FDR & the Era of the New Deal Ser). 122p. 1972. Repr. of 1940 ed. lib. bdg. 22.50 (ISBN 0-306-70324-6). Da Capo.

Flynn, Kathleen, jt. auth. see Marram, Gwen.

Flynn, Leslie. Joseph: God's Man in Egypt. 1979. pap. 4.50 (ISBN 0-88207-788-0). Victor Bks.

--The Twelve. 156p. 1982. pap. 4.50 (ISBN 0-88207-310-9). Victor Bks.

Flynn, Leslie & Flynn, Bernice. God's Will: You Can Know It. 1979. pap. 3.95 (ISBN 0-88207-779-1). Victor Bks.

Flynn, Leslie B. Man: Ruined & Restored. 1978. pap. 3.95 o.p. (ISBN 0-88207-762-7). Victor Bks.

--Nineteen Gifts of the Spirit. LC 74-91027. 204p. 1974. pap. 5.95 (ISBN 0-88207-701-5). Victor Bks.

--What Is Man? 132p. 1983. pap. 4.50 (ISBN 0-88207-104-1). Victor Bks.

--Worship: Together We Celebrate. 132p. 1983. pap. 4.50 (ISBN 0-88207-608-6). Victor Bks.

Flynn, M. J., et al. Operating Systems: An Advanced Course. (Springer Study Editions). 593p. 1980. pap. 16.00 (ISBN 0-387-09812-7). Springer-Verlag.

Flynn, Owen. Fifty Trout Ponds in Massachusetts: Where to Find Them, How to Fish Them. LC 78-71717. (Illus.). 1979. pap. 5.95 (ISBN 0-89725-005-2). Backcountry Pubns.

Flynn, Patricia, jt. auth. see Burbach, Roger.

Flynn, Patricia A. Holistic Health: The Art & Science of Care. (Illus.). 259p. 1980. pap. text ed. 15.95 (ISBN 0-87619-626-1). R J Brady.

Flynn, Peter. Brazil: A Political Analysis. (Nations of the Modern World Ser.). (Illus.). 1979. pap. 14.00 (ISBN 0-89158-694-6). Westview.

Flynn, Richard B., jt. ed. see Coates, Edward.

Flynn, Rose. Quicksilver Love. (YA) 1980. 6.95 (ISBN 0-686-73941-8, Avalon). Bouregy.

Flynt, Wayne. Duncan Upshaw Fletcher: Dixie's Reluctant Progressive. LC 73-149954. 213p. 1971. 10.00 (ISBN 0-8130-0426-8). U Presses Fla.

Fo, Dario. Gli Imbianchini Non Hanno Ricordi. (Easy Readers a). 1977. pap. 2.95 (ISBN 0-88436-296-5). EMC.

Foa, Edna B. & Emmelkamp, Paul M. Failures in Behavior Therapy. (Personality Processes Ser.). 450p. 1983. 39.95 (ISBN 0-471-09238-X, Pub. by Wiley-Interscience). Wiley.

Foa, Edna B., jt. auth. see Foa, Uriel G.

Foa, Edna B., jt. auth. see Goldstein, Alan.

Foa, Piero P., jt. ed. see Cohen, Margo P.

Foa, Uriel G. & Foa, Edna B. Societal Structures of the Mind. (Illus.). 468p. 1974. pap. 37.50x o.p. (ISBN 0-398-02932-6). C C Thomas.

Foad, John, jt. auth. see Davies, Brinley.

Foakes, R. A. Shakespeare, the Dark Comedies to the Last Plays: From Satire to Celebration. LC 70-146536. 200p. 1971. 12.50x (ISBN 0-8139-0327-0). U Pr of Va.

Foakes, R. A., ed. see Shakespeare, William.

Fobel, Jim & Boleach, Jim. The Stencil Book. 200p. 1983. pap. 9.95 (ISBN 0-442-22661-6). Van Nos Reinhold.

Fobes, James & King, James, eds. Primate Behavior. (Communication & Behavior Ser.). 385p. 1982. 27.50 (ISBN 0-12-261320-1). Acad Pr.

Fochs, Arnold. The Very Idea: A Collection of Unusual Retail Advertising Ideas, Vol. 2. rev. ed. 272p. (Orig.). 1980. pap. 13.50 (ISBN 0-914190-02-4). A J Pub.

Fochs, Arnold, ed. Best Local-Retail Ads. rev. ed. 248p. 1981. pap. 14.92 (ISBN 0-685-99089-3). A J Pub.

Fochs, Arnold, compiled by. Prize-Winning Ads Used by Night Clubs, Cafes, Drive-Ins, & Hotels-Motels. rev. ed. 1982. pap. 14.92 (ISBN 0-685-58280-9). A J Pub.

Fochtman, Edward G., ed. see Stockham, John J.

Fodaski, Martha. George Barker. (English Authors Ser.). 14.95 (ISBN 0-8057-1028-0, Twayne). G K Hall.

Foderaro, Anthony. Elements of Neutron Interaction Theory. LC 79-103896. 1971. text ed. 40.00x (ISBN 0-262-06033-7). MIT Pr.

Fodere, F. E. Essai Historique et Moral sur la Pauvrete des Nations, la Population, la Mendicite, les Hospitaux et les Enfants Trouves. (Conditions of the 19th Century French Working Class Ser.). 628p. (Fr.). 1974. Repr. of 1825 ed. lib. bdg. 152.50x o.p. (ISBN 0-8287-0347-7, 1014). Clearwater Pub.

Fodor, D. The Neutrals. (World War II Ser.). 1982. lib. bdg. 19.92 (ISBN 0-8094-3432-6, Pub. by Time-Life). Silver.

--Victory in Europe. LC 81-18315. (World War II Ser.). lib. bdg. 19.92 (ISBN 0-8094-3404-0, Pub. by Time-Life). Silver.

Fodor, J. A., et al. The Psychology of Language. (Illus.). 512p. 1974. text ed. 33.00 (ISBN 0-07-021412-3, C). McGraw.

Fodor, Janet D. The Linguistic Description of Opaque Contexts. Hankamer, Jorge, ed. LC 78-66537. (Outstanding Dissertations in Linguistics Ser.). 1979. lib. bdg. 42.00 (ISBN 0-8240-9686-X). Garland Pub.

Fodor, Jerry A. Representations: Philosophical Essays on the Foundations of Cognitive Science. LC 81-24313. (Illus.). 384p. 1981. 22.50x (ISBN 0-262-06079-5, Pub. by Bradford). MIT Pr.

--Representations: Philosophical Essays on the Foundations of Cognitive Science. 356p. 1983. pap. 9.95x (ISBN 0-262-56027-5). MIT Pr.

Fodor, R. V. Chiseling the Earth: How Erosion Shapes the Land. LC 82-18227. (Illus.). 96p. (gr. 7-12). 1983. PLB 9.95 (ISBN 0-89490-074-9). Enslow Pubs.

--Competitive Weightlifting. LC 77-93307. (Illus.). 1979. pap. 6.95 (ISBN 0-8069-8836-3). Sterling.

--Earth in Motion: The Concept of Plate Tectonics. LC 77-12568. (Illus.). (gr. 3-7). 1978. 8.75 (ISBN 0-688-22135-1); PLB 8.40 (ISBN 0-688-32135-6). Morrow.

--Nickels, Dimes & Dollars, How Currency Works. LC 79-22539. (Illus.). 96p. (gr. 4-6). 1980. 8.75 (ISBN 0-688-22220-X); PLB 8.40 (ISBN 0-688-32220-4). Morrow.

Fodor, Ronald V. Competitive Weightlifting. LC 77-93307. (Illus.). 1978. 12.95 o.p. (ISBN 0-8069-4124-3); lib. bdg. 11.69 o.p. (ISBN 0-8069-4125-1). Sterling.

--Frozen Earth: Explaining the Ice Ages. LC 80-21588. (Illus.). 64p. (gr. 7-12). 1981. PLB 8.95 (ISBN 0-89490-036-6). Enslow Pubs.

--What to Eat & Why: The Science of Nutrition. LC 78-24086. (Illus.). (gr. 4-6). 1979. 8.25 (ISBN 0-688-22189-0); PLB 7.92 (ISBN 0-688-32189-5). Morrow.

Foell, W. K. Management of Energy Environment Systems: National & Regional Perspectives. 320p. 1982. 44.50x (ISBN 0-471-10022-6, Pub. by Wiley-Interscience). Wiley.

Foell, Wesley K. Management of Energy-Environment Systems: Methods & Case Studies. LC 78-13617. (International Institute Series on Applied Systems Analysis). 487p. 1979. 49.95x (ISBN 0-471-99721-8, Pub. by Wiley-Interscience). Wiley.

Foelsch, D. & Vestergaard, K. Das Verhalten von Huehnern. (Animal Management Ser.: 12). 176p. 1981. 16.45x (ISBN 3-7643-1240-8). Birkhauser.

Foerst, W. Newer Methods of Preparative Organic Chemistry, 3 vols. LC 48-6233. 1968. Vol. IV. 43.60x (ISBN 3-527-25087-5); Vol. V. 43.60x (ISBN 3-527-25088-3); Vol. VI. 53.00x (ISBN 3-527-25338-6). Verlag Chemie.

Foerster, Iris, tr. see Wodehouse, P. G.

Foerster, Norman, et al, eds. American Poetry & Prose, 3 Vols. 5th ed. LC 70-137981. 1970. pap. 16.50 ea. o.p.; Vol. 1. pap. 17.50 (ISBN 0-395-04460-X); Vol. 2. pap. 17.50 (ISBN 0-395-04461-8); Vol. 3. pap. (ISBN 0-395-04462-6). HM.

--American Poetry & Prose, 2 pts. 5th ed. LC 70-137981. 1970. pap. 19.95 ea. Pt. 1 (ISBN 0-395-04458-8). Pt. 2 (ISBN 0-395-04459-6). pap. 22.50 one-vol. ed. (ISBN 0-395-30471-7). HM.

--Introduction to American Poetry & Prose. LC 72-140999. 1971. text ed. 21.50 (ISBN 0-395-04457-X). HM.

Foerster, P., et al. Algebra: The Language of Math, Bk. 2. (gr. 10-12). 1977. text ed. 17.60 (ISBN 0-201-14308-9, Sch Div); tchr's. ed. 22.20 (ISBN 0-201-14309-7). A-W.

Foerster, Paul A. Algebra & Trigonometry: Functions & Applications. (gr. 11-12). 1980. pap. text ed. 20.80 (ISBN 0-201-02475-6, Sch Div); tchrs' commentary 7.25 (ISBN 0-201-02476-4, Sch Div); solutions manual avail. A-W.

Foerster, Paul A., et al. Trigonometry: Functions & Applications. (gr. 9-12). 1977. pap. text ed. 17.04 (ISBN 0-201-01996-5, Sch Div); tchr's ed. 11.08 (ISBN 0-201-01997-3). A-W.

Foerster, Rolf, tr. see Wodehouse, P. G.

Foerstner, U., et al. Metal Pollution in the Aquatic Environment. (Illus.). 1979. 56.70 o.p. (ISBN 0-387-09307-9). Springer-Verlag.

Fogarty, Michael, ed. Retirement Policy: The Next Fifty Years, No. 5. (NIESR, PSI, RII A Joint Studies in Public Policy Ser.). viii, 216p. 1982. text ed. 28.00x (ISBN 0-435-83320-0). Heinemann Ed.

Fogarty, Michael P. The Just Wage. LC 75-29076. 309p. 1975. Repr. of 1961 ed. lib. bdg. 18.00x (ISBN 0-8371-8404-5, FOJW). Greenwood.

Fogarty, Robert S. Dictionary of American Communal & Utopian History. LC 79-7476. 320p. 1980. lib. bdg. 35.00 (ISBN 0-313-21347-X, FDA/). Greenwood.

Fogarty, Robert S., ed. American Utopianism. LC 75-174161. (AHM Primary Sources in American History Ser.). 1972. pap. text ed. 6.95x (ISBN 0-88295-785-6). Harlan Davidson.

Fogdall, Alberta B. Royal Family of the Columbia: Dr. John McLoughlin & His Family. LC 78-17170. (Illus.). 1982. 16.95 (ISBN 0-8323-0413-1). Binford.

Fogdall, Richard P., jt. auth. see Fischbach, David P.

Foged, N. Diatoms Found in a Bottom Sediment Sample from a Small Deep Lake in the Northern Slope, Alaska. 1971. pap. text ed. 12.00 (ISBN 3-7682-0824-9). Lubrecht & Cramer.

--Diatoms in Eastern Australia. (Bibliotheca Phycologica Ser.: No. 41). (Illus.). 1979. pap. text ed. 24.00 (ISBN 3-7682-1203-3). Lubrecht & Cramer.

--Diatoms in New Zealand, the North Island. (Bibliotheca Phycologica: No. 47). (Illus.). 1979. pap. text ed. 24.00x (ISBN 3-7682-1253-X). Lubrecht & Cramer.

--Freshwater Diatoms in Ireland. (Bibliotheca Phycologica Ser.: No. 34). (Illus.). 1977. lib. bdg. 20.00x (ISBN 3-7682-1155-X). Lubrecht & Cramer.

Foged, Niels. Diatoms in Alaska. (Bibliotheca Phycologica). (Illus.). 318p. 1981. text ed. 32.00x (ISBN 3-7682-1303-X). Lubrecht & Cramer.

--Diatoms in Bornholm, Denmark. (Bibliotheca Phyc. 59). (Illus.). 104p. 1982. pap. text ed. 20.00 (ISBN 0-686-37597-1). Lubrecht & Cramer.

--Diatoms in Oland, Sweden. (Bibliotheca Phycologica Ser.: No. 49). (Illus.). 194p. 1980. pap. 20.00 (ISBN 3-7682-1269-6). Lubrecht & Cramer.

Fogel, Alan, jt. ed. see Field, Tiffany M.

Fogel, Daniel. Africa in Struggle: National Liberation & Proletarian Revolution. LC 82-82655. (Illus.). 428p. (Orig.). 1982. pap. 8.00 (ISBN 0-910383-00-6). Ism Pr.

Fogel, Daniel M. A Trick of Resilience. 55p. 1975. 3.50 (ISBN 0-87886-063-0). Ithaca Hse.

Fogel, Joshua A. & Rowe, William T., eds. Perspectives on a Changing China: Essays in Honor of Prof. C. Martin Wilbur. (Westview Special Studies on China & East Asia). 1979. lib. bdg. 30.00 (ISBN 0-89158-091-3, Dawson). Westview.

Fogel, Seymour, jt. ed. see Gabriel, Mordecai L.

Fogelman, E., jt. auth. see Ebenstein, W.

Fogelman, Morris J., jt. auth. see Vanatta, John C.

Fogg Art Museum, ed. see Harvard University.

Fogg, G. E. Algal Cultures & Phytoplankton Ecology. 2nd ed. LC 74-27308. 192p. 1975. 22.50 (ISBN 0-299-06760-2). U of Wis Pr.

Fogg, H. Witham. Salad Crops all Year Round. (Illus.). 200p. 1983. 19.95 (ISBN 0-7153-8411-2). David & Charles.

Fogg, Stephen. Imperial Sportswear, Inc. An Audit Case Problem. 65p. 1980. pap. text ed. 14.95scp (ISBN 0-06-042107-X, HarpC); solution manual avail. (ISBN 0-06-362205-X). Har-Row.

Fogg, Walter. One Thousand Sayings of History, Presented As Pictures in Prose. LC 79-143634. 1971. Repr. of 1929 ed. 47.00x (ISBN 0-8103-3779-7). Gale.

Fogle, French see Milton, John.

Fogle, Richard H. Idea of Coleridge's Criticism. LC 77-26232. (Perspectives in Criticism: No. 9). 1978. Repr. of 1962 ed. lib. bdg. 19.00x (ISBN 0-313-20086-6, FOIC). Greenwood.

Fogler, H. Scott. The Elements of Chemical Kinetics & Reactor Calculations: A Self-Paced Approach. (Illus.). 512p. 1974. pap. 28.95 ref. ed. (ISBN 0-13-263442-2). P-H.

Fogler, H. Scott, ed. Chemical Reactors: ACS Symposium Ser. (No. 168). 1981. write for info. (ISBN 0-8412-0658-9). Am Chemical.

Foglio, Frank. Ehi, Dio! Arcangeli, Gianfranco, ed. (Ital.). 1972. pap. 1.90 (ISBN 0-8297-0753-0). Life Pubs Intl.

Fohl, F. C. A Microprocessor Course. 1979. 15.00 o.p. (ISBN 0-07-091039-1, P&RB). McGraw.

Fohl, Mark E. An Assembly Course. (Illus.). 216p. 1982. 17.50 (ISBN 0-89433-149-3). Petrocelli.

Foigny, Gabriel De. Les Aventures de Jacques Sadeur dans la Decouvert et le Voyage de la Terre Australe. (Utopias in the Enlightenment Ser.). 359p. (Fr.). 1974. Repr. of 1692 ed. lib. bdg. 92.50 o.p. (ISBN 0-8287-0348-5, 049). Clearwater Pub.

Foin, Theodore C., Jr. Ecological Systems & the Environment. LC 75-25010. (Illus.). 640p. 1976. text ed. 24.50 o.p. (ISBN 0-395-20666-9); instr's. manual 1.10 o.p. (ISBN 0-395-20667-7). HM.

Fokkelman, J. P. Narrative Art & Poetry in the Books of Samuel: King David, Vol. 1. 536p. 1981. text ed. 45.00x (ISBN 90-232-1852-3, Pub. by Van Gorcum Holland). Humanities.

Fokkema, D. W. & Kunne-Ibsch, Elrud. Theories of Literature in the Twentieth Century. LC 77-608292. 1978. 18.95x o.p. (ISBN 0-312-79643-9). St Martin.

Fol, Monique, jt. auth. see Barrette, Paul.

Folan, William J., et al. Coba: A Classical Maya Metropolis. (Studies in Archaeology). 224p. 1983. write for info (ISBN 0-12-261880-7). Acad Pr.

Folda, Jaroslav, et al, eds. see Buchthal, Hugo.

Foldeak, Arpad. Chess Olympiads. (Illus.). 1966. 10.00 (ISBN 0-8283-1175-7). Branden.

Foldes, Joseph. Everybody's Photo Course. 1966. pap. 3.95 o.p. (ISBN 0-8174-0957-2, Amphoto). Watson-Guptill.

Foldiak, G. Radiation Chemistry of Hydrocarbons. (Studies in Physical & Theoretical Chemistry: Vol. 14). 1982. 83.00 (ISBN 0-444-99746-6). Elsevier.

Folejewski, Zsiginew. Maria Dabrowska. (World Authors Ser.: No. 16). 15.95 o.p. (ISBN 0-8057-2260-2, Twayne). G K Hall.

Folena, G., ed. see Palazzi, F.

Foley. The Gazelle & the Hunter. LC 79-18880. (Folk Tales Ser.). (Illus.). 64p. (gr. 2-6). 1980. PLB 7.95 (ISBN 0-516-06480-0). Childrens.

Foley, Albert S. Dream of an Outcaste: Patrick F. Healy. 1983. 12.50 (ISBN 0-916620-31-X). Portals Pr.

Foley, Bernice W. A Walk Among Clouds. LC 79-18295. (Folk Tales Ser.). (Illus.). 32p. (gr. 2-6). 1980. 7.95g (ISBN 0-516-06484-3). Childrens.

--Why the Cock Crows Three Times. LC 79-19088. (Folk Tales Ser.). (Illus.). 32p. (gr. 2-6). 1980. 7.95g (ISBN 0-516-06485-1). Childrens.

Foley, Daniel J. Ground Covers for Easier Gardening. (Illus.). 224p. 1972. pap. 5.00 (ISBN 0-486-20124-4). Dover.

Foley, Donald L. Governing the London Region: Reorganization & Planning in the 1960's. LC 76-157822. (Institute of Governmental Studies, UC Berkeley & Lane Studies in Regional Environment). 1972. 27.50x (ISBN 0-520-02040-5); pap. 7.95x (ISBN 0-520-02248-3, CAMPUS81). U of Cal Pr.

Foley, Helene P. Reflections of Women in Antiquity. 420p. 1982. 40.00 (ISBN 0-677-16370-3). Gordon.

Foley, Henry A. & Sharfstein, Steven. Madness & Government. 330p. 1983. 19.95x (ISBN 0-88048-001-7). Am Psychiatry.

Foley, J. & Maneker, M. National Service & the American Future. 1983. pap. 7.95 (ISBN 0-8159-6315-7). Devin.

Foley, James. Foundations of Theoretical Phonology. LC 76-27904. (Cambridge Studies in Linguistics Monographs: No. 2). 1977. 29.95 (ISBN 0-521-21466-1). Cambridge U Pr.

Foley, James W., jt. auth. see Hunter, John M.

Foley, Joseph E. British Stamps Overprinted by Irish Republican Philatelic Office. (Illus.). 1972. 1.25 o.p. (ISBN 0-686-09671-1). Am Philatelic.

Foley, June. It's No Crush, I'm in Love. (Young Love Romance Ser.). (YA) (gr. 7-12). 1983. pap. 2.50 (ISBN 0-440-94212-8, LFL). Dell.

--Love by Any Other Name. LC 82-72752. 224p. (gr. 7 up). 1983. 13.95 (ISBN 0-440-04865-6). Delacorte.

--Love by Any Other Name. (Young Love Romance Ser.). (YA) (gr. 7-12). 1983. pap. 2.50 (ISBN 0-440-94738-3, LFL). Dell.

Foley, June, ed. see Rafferty, Robert.

Foley, Kathryn, et al. The Good Apple Guide to Creative Drama. (gr. 2-6). 1981. 8.95 (ISBN 0-86653-030-4, GA 258). Good Apple.

Foley, Louise M. Tackle Twenty-Two. LC 78-50425. (Illus.). (gr. 1-3). 1978. 6.95 o.s.i. (ISBN 0-440-08464-4); PLB 6.46 o.s.i. (ISBN 0-440-08465-2). Delacorte.

--Tackle Twenty-Two. (gr. k-6). 1981. pap. 1.75 (ISBN 0-440-48484-7, YB). Dell.

Foley, Martha & Burnett, David, eds. Fifty Best American Short Stories 1915-1965. 1965. 15.00 o.p. (ISBN 0-395-07687-0). HM.

Foley, Mary M. The American House. LC 79-1662. (Illus.). 304p. 1981. pap. 14.37i (ISBN 0-06-090831-9, CN 831, CN). Har-Row.

Foley, Rae. Girl on a High Wire. LC 79-91277. 1983. pap. 2.95 (ISBN 0-396-08163-0). Dodd.

Foley, Rita. Create! 2nd ed. (Catechist Training Ser.). 1982. 3.95 (ISBN 0-8215-1230-7). Sadlier.

Foley, Theresa S. & Davies, Marilyn A. Rape: Nursing Care of Victims. (Illus.). 512p. 1983. pap. text ed. 12.95 (ISBN 0-8016-1620-4). Mosby.

Foley, W. T. Advances in the Management of Cardiovascular Disease, Vol. 3. 1982. 39.95 (ISBN 0-8151-3256-5). Year Bk Med.

Folger, John K., et al. Human Resources & Higher Education: Staff Report on the Commission on Human Resources & Advanced Education. LC 68-58129. 476p. 1970. 20.00x (ISBN 0-87154-258-7). Russell Sage.

Folger Shakespeare Library, Washington, D. C. Catalog of Manuscripts of the Folger Shakespeare Library, 3 vols. (Library Catalogs). 1970. Set. lib. bdg. 260.00 (ISBN 0-8161-0888-9, Hall Library). G K Hall.

--Catalog of Printed Books of the Folger Shakespeare Library, 28 vols. 1970. Set. lib. bdg. 2250.00 (ISBN 0-8161-0887-0, Hall Library). G K Hall.

--Folger Shakespeare Library: Catalog of the Shakespeare Collection, 2 vols. 1972. Set. 45.00 (ISBN 0-8161-1009-3, Hall Library). G K Hall.

Foligno, Cesare, tr. see Malaparte, Curzio.

Foligno, Cesare, tr. see Malparte, Curzio.

Folio Magazine Editors, ed. Handbook of Magazine Publishing. 1977. 59.95 o.p. (ISBN 0-918110-00-9). Folio.

Folk, Edgar E., jt. auth. see Shaw, Bynum.

Folk, Ernest L., III. The Delaware General Corporation Law: A Commentary & Analysis. 1972. 55.00 (ISBN 0-316-28780-6). Little.

Folk, G. Edgar, Jr. Hamster Guide. rev. ed. (Illus.). 1958. pap. 4.95 o.p. (ISBN 0-87666-203-3, AP7200). TFH Pubns.

Folk, Jerry. Worldly Christians. LC 82-72652. 144p. 1983. pap. 6.50 (10-7343). Augsburg.

Folkers, K., jt. auth. see Wagner, A. F.

Folkers, K., et al, eds. see International Symposium on Coenzyme Q, Lake Yamanaka, Japan, 1976 & 1979.

Folkerts-Landau, O. F. Intertemporal Planning, Exchange, & Macroeconomics. LC 81-38501. (Illus.). 308p. 1982. 32.50 (ISBN 0-521-23067-5). Cambridge U Pr.

Folkes, M. J. Short Fibre Reinforced Thermoplastics. (Polymer Engineering Research Studies Ser.). 186p. 1982. 32.95x (ISBN 0-471-10209-1, Pub. by Res Stud Pr). Wiley.

Folkners, K. Biomedical & Clinical Aspects of Coenzyme Q: Proceedings, Vol. 3. 1981. 69.50 (ISBN 0-444-80319-X, North Holland). Elsevier.

Folkow, Bjoern & Neil, Eric. Circulation. (Illus., Orig.). 1971. text ed. 35.00x (ISBN 0-19-501343-3). Oxford U Pr.

Folks, Homer. The Care of Destitute, Neglected & Delinquent Children. LC 78-51849. (NASW Classics Ser.). 262p. 1978. pap. 5.95x (ISBN 0-87101-076-3, CBC-076-C). Natl Assn Soc Wkrs.

Folks, J. Leroy. Ideas of Statistics. LC 80-14723. 368p. 1981. text ed. 19.95 (ISBN 0-471-02099-0). study guide avail. (ISBN 0-471-07972-3); tchrs.' manual avail. (ISBN 0-471-07969-3). Wiley.

Folk St. John, Wylly. The Secrets of the Pirate Inn. (gr. 2-7). 1976. pap. 1.75 o.p. (ISBN 0-380-00629-4, 51979, Camelot). Avon.

Follain, James, et al. Place to Place Indexes of the Price of Housing. 98p. 1979. pap. text ed. 5.50 (ISBN 0-87766-265-7). Urban Inst.

Follain, James R., Jr. & Malpezzi, S. Dissecting Housing Value & Rent. 132p. (Orig.). pap. text ed. 8.50 (ISBN 0-87766-276-2). Urban Inst.

Follain, Jean. Canisy. Guiney, Louise & Follain, Madeleine, trs. from Fr. 96p. 1981. text ed. 10.00 (ISBN 0-937406-06-6); pap. 5.00 (ISBN 0-937406-05-8); ltd. ed. 50.00 (ISBN 0-937406-07-4). Logbridge-Rhodes.

Follain, Madeleine, tr. see Follain, Jean.

Folland, H. F., jt. auth. see Adamson, J. H.

Follett, Barbara Lee. Checklist for a Perfect Wedding. rev. ed. LC 72-97272. 120p. 1973. pap. 2.25 (ISBN 0-385-04251-5, Dolp). Doubleday.

Follett, Ken. Eye of the Needle. movie ed. (Illus.). 1981. pap. 3.50 o.p. (ISBN 0-451-09913-3, E9913, Sig). NAL.

--Eye of the Needle. (RL 6). 1979. pap. 3.95 (ISBN 0-451-11970-3, AE1970, Sig). NAL.

--Triple. (General Ser.). 1979. lib. bdg. 15.95 (ISBN 0-8161-3005-1, Large Print Bks). G K Hall.

--Triple. 1980. pap. 3.95 (ISBN 0-451-12429-4, AE2429, Sig). NAL.

Follett, Muriel. New England Year: A Journal of Vermont Farm Life. LC 73-145711. 1971. Repr. of 1939 ed. 30.00x (ISBN 0-8103-3393-7). Gale.

Follett, Wilson. Modern American Usage. 1974. pap. 2.50 o.p. (ISBN 0-446-81529-2). Warner Bks.

--Modern American Usage: A Guide. Barzun, Jacques, ed. 443p. 1966. 12.95 (ISBN 0-8090-6950-4); pap. 9.95 (ISBN 0-8090-0139-X). Hill & Wang.

Follette, P. La see Hunter, W. F. & La Follette, P.

Folley, R. R. Intensive Crop Economics. 1973. text ed. 30.00x o.p. (ISBN 0-435-62991-3). Heinemann Ed.

Folley, T. Spanish Aide-Memoire: English-Spanish Vocabulary. pap. 6.50x (ISBN 0-392-08443-0, SpS). Sportshelf.

Follie. Voyages dans les Deserts du Sahara. (Bibliotheque Africaine Ser.). 168p. (Fr.). 1974. Repr. of 1792 ed. lib. bdg. 50.00x o.p. (ISBN 0-8287-0349-3, 72-2100). Clearwater Pub.

Follis, Joan J., jt. auth. see Fordney, Marilyn T.

Follis, Richard H., Jr. The Pathology of Nutritional Disease: Physiological & Morphological Changes Which Result from Deficiencies of the Essential Elements, Amino Acids, Vitamins, & Fatty Acids. (Illus.). 306p. 1948. photocopy ed. spiral 24.50x (ISBN 0-398-04255-1). C C Thomas.

Folmar, J. Kent. United States History to 1877: An Outline & Workbook. 104p. 1975. pap. 5.50 o.p. (ISBN 0-910042-24-1). Allegheny.

Folmsbee, Stanley J. Sectionalism & Internal Improvements in Tennessee 1796-1845. (Perspectives in American History Ser.: No. 57). (Illus.). vi, 293p. Repr. of 1939 ed. lib. bdg. 25.00x (ISBN 0-87991-098-4). Porcupine Pr.

Folomkina, S. & Weiser, H. Learner's English-Russian Dictionary. 1963. pap. 9.95 (ISBN 0-262-56002-X). MIT Pr.

Folon, Jean-Michel. Folon: The Eyewitness. (Illus.). 64p. 1980. 55.00 o.s.i. (ISBN 0-8109-0906-5, 0906-5); limited edition aquatint with signed book 500.00 o.s.i. (ISBN 0-686-62700-8, 84909-1). Abrams.

Folsch, D. W. & Nabholz, A., eds. Ethologische Aussagen zur Artgerechten Nutztierhaltung. (Animal Management Ser.: Vol. 13). 184p. 1982. pap. 15.50 (ISBN 3-7643-1338-2). Birkhauser.

Folse, Keith S. English Structure Practices. 384p. 1983. pap. text ed. 6.95x (ISBN 0-472-08034-2). U of Mich Pr.

Folse, Lois J., jt. auth. see Ingram, Marilyn W.

Folsom, Franklin. The Life & Legend of George McJunkin: Black Cowboy. LC 73-6446. (Illus.). 160p. (gr. 5 up). 1973. 8.95 o.p. (ISBN 0-525-66326-6). Lodestar Bks.

--Red Power on the Rio Grande. 2.95 (ISBN 0-686-43411-0, Dist. by Caroline Hse); lib. bdg. 3.96. Follett.

Folsom, Franklin, jt. auth. see Elting, Mary.

Folsom, James K. & Slotkin, Richard, eds. So Dreadful a Judgement: Puritan Responses to King Philip's War, 1676-77. LC 77-14847. 25.00x (ISBN 0-686-82883-6, Pub. by Wesleyan U Pr); pap. 10.00x (ISBN 0-686-82884-4). Columbia U Pr.

Folsom, M. M. & Kirschner, L. H. By Women. 1975. pap. text ed. 12.95 (ISBN 0-395-20500-X); instr's. resource bk. 5.32 (ISBN 0-395-20494-1). HM.

Folsom, Michael B. & Lubar, Steven D., eds. The Philosophy of Manufactures: Early Debates Over Industrialization in the United States. (Documents in American Industrial History Ser.). 512p. 1982. 45.00x (ISBN 0-262-06076-0). MIT Pr.

Folsor, DeFrancias. Our Police: A History of the Baltimore Police from the First Watchman to the Latest Appointee. LC 75-172585. (Criminology, Law Enforcement, & Social Problems Ser.: No. 175). (Illus.). Date not set. Repr. of 1888 ed. o. p. 17.50 (ISBN 0-87585-175-4). Patterson Smith.

Folta, J. & Deck, E. Sociological Framework for Patient Care. 2nd ed. LC 78-12073. 1979. pap. 17.95 (ISBN 0-471-04496-2, Pub. by Wiley Medical). Wiley.

Foltin, L. B. Aus Nah und Fern. 2nd ed. 1976. pap. text ed. 8.75 o.p. (ISBN 0-395-04464-2). HM.

Foltman, Felician F. Manpower Information for Effective Management, 2 pts. Incl. Pt. 1. Collecting & Managing Employee Information (ISBN 0-87546-217-0); Pt. 2. Skills Inventories & Manpower Planning (ISBN 0-87546-218-9). (Key Issues Ser.: Nos. 10 & 14). 1973. pap. 2.00 ea. ILR Pr.

--White & Blue-Collars in a Mill Shutdown: A Case Study in Relative Redundancy. LC 68-63931. (Paperback Ser.: No. 6). 136p. 1968. pap. 3.00 (ISBN 0-87546-031-3); pap. 5.00 special hard bdg. o.s.i (ISBN 0-87546-272-3). ILR Pr.

Foltman, Felician F., jt. ed. see Briggs, Vernon M., Jr.

Folts. Logic Design with TTL. (McGraw-Hill Course in Continuing Education for Electronics Engineers: Lesson 6). 1976. 6.50 o.p. (ISBN 0-07-045166-4, P&RB). McGraw.

Folts, Franklin E. Introduction to Industrial Management. LC 77-22994. 686p. 1979. Repr. of 1963 ed. 29.75 (ISBN 0-88275-566-8). Krieger.

Folts, Harold C. & Karp, Harry R. McGraw-Hill's Compilation of Data Communications Standards. LC 78-17191. (Illus.). 1133p. 1978. text ed. 165.00 o.p. (ISBN 0-07-099782-9). McGraw.

Foltz, Floyd M., jt. auth. see Matzke, Howard A.

Folz, Robert. Coronation of Charlemagne. 1975. 21.95 (ISBN 0-7100-7847-1). Routledge & Kegan.

Fomin, S. V., jt. auth. see Gelfand, Izrail M.

Fomon, Samuel & Bell, Julius. Rhinoplasty: New Concepts, Evaluation & Application. (Illus.). 332p. 1970. photocopy ed. spiral 37.75x (ISBN 0-398-00592-3). C C Thomas.

Fonagy, Ivan. Situation et Signification. 160p. 1982. pap. 18.00 o.p. (ISBN 90-272-2504-4). Benjamins North Am.

Fonda, Jane. Jane Fonda's Workout Book. 1981. 17.95 (ISBN 0-686-86722-X). S&S.

Fonda, Peter & Harper, Dennis. Easy Rider. (Film Ser). (Illus., Orig.). (RL 10). 1970. pap. 1.50 o.p. (ISBN 0-451-06045-8, W6045, Sig). NAL.

Fondation des Sciences Politiques, Paris, France. Bibliographie Courante D'Articles de Periodiques Posterieurs a 1944 Sur les Problems Politiques, Economiques et Sociaux: Dixieme Supplement, 2 vols. (Library Catalogs Bib.Guides). Orig. Title: Index to Post-1944 Periodical Articles on Political Economic & Social Problems - Tenth Supplement. 1979. Set. lib. bdg. 275.00 (ISBN 0-8161-0298-8, Hall Library). G K Hall.

Fondation Le Corbusier & Architectural History Foundation. Le Corbusier Sketchbooks: Vol. 1: 1914-1948. LC 80-28987. (Architectural History Foundation Ser.). (Illus.). 456p. 1981. 150.00x (ISBN 0-262-03078-0). MIT Pr.

Fondation Le Corbusier & Architectural History Foundation, eds. Le Corbusier Sketchbooks: Volume 4, 1957-1964. (Illus.). 520p. (Fr. & Eng.). 1982. 150.00x (ISBN 0-262-12093-3). MIT Pr.

--Le Corbusier Sketchbooks: Vol. 3, 1954-1957. (Illus.). 520p. (Fr. & Eng.). 1982. 150.00x (ISBN 0-262-12092-5). MIT Pr.

Fondation Le Corbusier & the Architectural History Foundation, ed. Le Corbusier Sketchbooks: 1950-1954, Vol. 2. (Illus.). 444p. (Fr. & Eng.). 1981. 150.00x (ISBN 0-262-12090-9). MIT Pr.

Fondation Nationale Des Sciences Politique, Paris. Bibliographie Courante D' Articles De Periodiques Posterieurs a 1944 Sur les Problems Poliiques, Economiques, et Sociaux, Suppl 6, 2 vols. 1974. Set. lib. bdg. 215.00 (ISBN 0-8161-1171-5, Hall Library). G K Hall.

Fondation Nationale des Sciences Politiques. Bibliographie Courante d'Articles de Periodiques Posterieurs a 1944 sur les Problemes Politiques. Economiques et Sociaux, 17 Vols. 1968. Set. lib. bdg. 1615.00 (ISBN 0-8161-0769-6, Hall Library); first suppl., 1969, 2 vols. 215.00 (ISBN 0-8161-0803-X); second suppl., 1970, 2 vols. 215.00 (ISBN 0-8161-0917-6); third suppl., 1971, 2 vols. 215.00 (ISBN 0-8161-0981-8); fourth suppl., 1972, 2 vols. 215.00 (ISBN 0-8161-1056-5). G K Hall.

Fondation Nationale Des Sciences Politiques, Paris. Bibliographie Courante D'Articles De Periodiques Posterieurs a, 1944 Sur les Problems, Economiques et Sociaux, Fifth Supplement, 2 vols. 1345p. 1973. Set. lib. bdg. 215.00 (ISBN 0-8161-1122-7, Hall Library). G K Hall.

Fondation Nationale Des Sciences Politiques (Paris) Bibliographie Courante d'Articles de Periodiques Posterieurs a 1944 Sur les Problemes Politiques, Economiques et Sociaux: Seventh Supplement, 2 vols. 1976. Set. lib. bdg. 215.00 (ISBN 0-8161-0035-7, Hall Library). G K Hall.

Fondation Nationale Des Sciences Politiques. Index to Post-Nineteen Forty-Four Periodical Articles on Political, Economic & Social Problems, Supplement Eleven. 1981. lib. bdg. 275.00 (ISBN 0-8161-0357-7, Hall Library). G K Hall.

Fondiller, Harvey V., ed. The Best of Popular Photography. (Illus.). 1979. 29.95 (ISBN 0-87165-037-1); deluxe ed. 35.00 (ISBN 0-686-96927-8); deluxe ed. 100.00 signed (ISBN 0-685-96576-7). Ziff-Davis Pub.

Fondu, M. Food Additives Tables, Two: Classes V-VIII. updated ed. Date not set. 138.50 (ISBN 0-444-42069-X). Elsevier.

Fondu, M. H., et al, eds. Food Additives Tables: Updated Edition, Classes I-IV. 1981. 106.50 (ISBN 0-444-41937-3). Elsevier.

Foner, Anne, jt. auth. see Riley, Matilda W.

Foner, Eric. Politics & Ideology in the Age of the Civil War. 256p. 1981. pap. 6.95 (ISBN 0-19-502926-7, GB 646, GB). Oxford U Pr.

--Tom Paine & Revolutionary America. LC 75-25456. (Illus.). 1977. pap. 8.95 (ISBN 0-19-502182-7). Oxford U Pr.

Foner, Eric, ed. see Kaestle, Carl.

Foner, Nancy. Jamaica Farewell: Jamaican Migrants in London. LC 77-80471. 1978. 28.50x (ISBN 0-520-03544-5). U of Cal Pr.

--Status & Power in Rural Jamaica: A Study of Educational & Political Change. LC 72-5943. (Illus.). 1973. text ed. 11.50x (ISBN 0-8077-2366-5); pap. text ed. 7.95x (ISBN 0-8077-2408-4). Tchrs Coll.

Foner, Philip, ed. see Marti, Jose.

Foner, Philip S. American Socialism & Black Americans: From the Age of Jackson to World War II. LC 77-71858. (Contributions in Afro-American & African Studies: No. 33). 1977. lib. bdg. 35.00 (ISBN 0-8371-9545-4, FAS/). Greenwood.

--Case of Joe Hill. LC 65-26742. (Illus.). 1965. pap. 2.50 o.p. Intl Pub Co.

--Essays in Afro American History. LC 78-16944. 1978. 24.95 (ISBN 0-87722-140-5). Temple U Pr.

--First Facts of American Labor. 260p. 1983. 29.50x (ISBN 0-8419-0742-0). Holmes & Meier.

--Frederick Douglass on Women's Rights. LC 76-5326. (Contributions in Afro-American & African Studies: No. 25). (Orig.). 1976. lib. bdg. 27.50 (ISBN 0-8371-8895-4, FFD/). Greenwood.

--History of Black Americans: From Africa to the Emergence of the Cotton Kingdom, 4 vols, Vol. 1. LC 74-5987. (Contributions in American History: Vol. 1, No. 40). 680p. 1975. lib. bdg. 45.00 (ISBN 0-8371-7529-1, FBA/1). Greenwood.

--History of the Labor Movement in the U. S. On the Eve of America's Entry into World War I, 1915-1916, Vol. 6. 300p. 1982. 17.00 (ISBN 0-7178-0602-2); pap. 5.75 (ISBN 0-7178-0595-6). Intl Pub Co.

--History of the Labor Movement in the United States: The AFL in the Progressive Era (1910-1915, Vol. 5. 17.00 (ISBN 0-7178-0570-0); pap. 4.95 (ISBN 0-7178-0562-X). Intl Pub Co.

--Political & Economic Struggles of the AFL in the Progressive Era, Nineteen Hundred & Ten to Nineteen Hundred & Thirteen. (History of the Labor Movement in the United States Ser.: Vol. 5). 1979. 17.00 (ISBN 0-7178-0570-0); pap. 4.95 (ISBN 0-7178-0562-X). Intl Pub Co.

Foner, Philip S., ed. The Black Worker: The Era of Post-War Prosperity & the Great Depression, 1920 to 1936, Vol. VI. Lewis, Ronald L. 632p. 1981. 29.95 (ISBN 0-87722-196-0). Temple U Pr.

--Black Worker: The Era of the AFL, the Railroad Brotherhood & the UMW, 1880-1903, Vol. IV. Lewis, Ronald L. LC 78-2875. 416p. 1979. 29.95 (ISBN 0-87722-139-1). Temple U Pr.

--The Democratic-Republican Societies, 1790-1800: A Documentary Sourcebook. LC 76-5260. (Orig.). 1976. lib. bdg. 39.95 (ISBN 0-8371-8907-1, FLT/). Greenwood.

--Wilhelm Liebknecht: Letters to the Chicago Workingmen's Advocate (1870-1871) 190p. 1983. text ed. 24.50x (ISBN 0-8419-0743-9). Holmes & Meier.

Foner, Philip S. & Chamberlin, Brewster, eds. Friedrich A. Sorge's Labor Movement in the United States: A History of the American Working Class from Colonial Times to 1890. LC 76-15319. (Illus.). 1977. lib. bdg. 35.00 (ISBN 0-8371-9028-2, FLM/). Greenwood.

Foner, Philip S. & Lewis, Ronald L., eds. The Black Worker: A Documentary History from Colonial Times to the Present: The Era from World War II to the AFL-CIO Merger, 1937-1954, Vol. VII. 1983. 29.95 (ISBN 0-87722-197-9). Temple U Pr.

--The Black Worker: From Colonial Times to 1869, Vol. 1. LC 78-2875. 432p. 1978. 29.95 (ISBN 0-87722-136-7). Temple U Pr.

--The Black Worker: From Nineteen Hundred to Nineteen Nineteen, Vol. V. 450p. 1980. 29.95 (ISBN 0-87722-184-7). Temple U Pr.

--Black Worker: The Era of the Knights of Labor, Vol. III. LC 78-2875. 416p. 1979. 29.95 (ISBN 0-87722-138-3). Temple U Pr.

--The Black Worker: The Era of the National Labor Union, Vol. II. LC 78-2875. 416p. 1978. 29.95 (ISBN 0-87722-137-5). Temple U Pr.

Foner, Philip S. & Walker, George E., eds. Proceedings of the Black State Conventions, Eighteen Forty to Eighteen Sixty-Five, 2 vols. 34.95 ea.; Vol. 1, 1979, 387p. (ISBN 0-87722-145-6); Vol. 2, 1980, 336p. (ISBN 0-87722-149-9). Temple U Pr.

Foner, Philip S., ed. see Brawley, Benjamin.

Foner, Philip S., ed. see Douglass, Frederick.

Foner, Philip S., ed. see Marti, Jose.

Foner, Philip S., ed. see Mother Jones.

Foner, Phillip S. History of Black Americans: From the Compromise of 1850 to the End of the Civil War, Vol. III. LC 82-11702. (Contributions in American History Ser.: No. 103). 528p. 1983. lib. bdg. 39.95 (ISBN 0-8371-7967-X, E449). Greenwood.

--History of Black Americans: From the Emergence of the Cotton Kingdom to the Eve of the Compromise of 1850, Vol II. LC 74-5987. (Contributions in American History Ser.: No. 102). 600p. 1983. lib. bdg. 45.00 (ISBN 0-8371-7966-1, FBA/2). Greenwood.

--Labor & the American Revolution. LC 76-18034. 1976. lib. bdg. 27.50 (ISBN 0-8371-9003-7, FLA/). Greenwood.

Foner, Phillip S., ed. Karl Marx Remembered: Comments at the Time of His Death. 2nd. rev. ed. 282p. (Orig.). 1983. pap. 6.95 (ISBN 0-89935-020-8). Synthesis Pubns.

Fong, Elizabeth, jt. auth. see Ferris, Elvira.

Fong, Francis K. Theory of Molecular Relaxation Applications in Chemistry & Biology. LC 75-17814. 314p. 1975. 31.95 o.p. (ISBN 0-471-26555-1, Pub. by Wiley-Interscience). Wiley.

Fong, H. G. Bond Portfolio Analysis & Management. LC 82-73626. 225p. 1983. 32.50 (ISBN 0-87094-245-X). Dow Jones-Irwin.

Fong, Leo. Modified Wing Chun, Vol. One: Basic Techniques. Date not set. pap. 5.95 (ISBN 0-86635-009-8). Koinonia Prods.

Fong, Leo T. Sil Lum Kung-Fu: The Chinese Art of Self Defense. Alston, Pat, ed. LC 76-157045. (Ser. 304). (Illus.). 1971. pap. text ed. 6.95 (ISBN 0-89750-032-6). Ohara Pubns.

Fong, Paul, ed. see Brauer, Richard.

Fong, Peter. Statistical Theory of Nuclear Fission. (Documents on Modern Physics Ser.). 228p. (Orig.). 1969. 60.00x (ISBN 0-677-01850-9). Gordon.

Fong, Wen, ed The Great Bronze Age of China: An Exhibition from the People's Republic of China. (Illus.). xviii, 404p. 1980. 18.50 (ISBN 0-87099-226-0). Metro Mus Art.

Fontaine, J. R. Le see Le Fontaine, J. R.

Fontaine, J. S. La see La Fontaine, J. S.

Fontaine, Jean de la see La Fontaine, Jean de.

Fontaine, Leni. Astrology: Order of the Portal. (Illus., Orig.). Date not set. pap. price not set (ISBN 0-86649-056-6). Twentieth Century.

Fontaine, P. Basic Formal Structures in Music. 1967. text ed. 20.95 o.p. (ISBN 0-13-061416-5). P-H.

Fontaine, Pierre-Michel, jt. ed. see Alpers, Edward A.

Fontaine, Thomas D., III & Bartell, Steven M., eds. Dynamics of Lotic Ecosystems. LC 82-48641. (Illus.). 450p. 1983. 24.50 (ISBN 0-250-40612-8). Ann Arbor Science.

Fontana, David. Psychology for Teachers. (Psychology for Professional Groups Ser.). 350p. 1981. text ed. 25.00x (ISBN 0-333-31858-7, Pub. by Macmillan England); pap. text ed. 10.95x (ISBN 0-333-31880-3). Humanities.

Fontana, Frank, jt. auth. see Drayton, Grace.

Fontana, Mars G. & Greene, Norbert D. Corrosion Engineering. 2nd ed. (Materials Sciences & Engineering). (Illus.). 1978. text ed. 39.50 (ISBN 0-07-021461-1, C); solutions manual 7.95 (ISBN 0-07-021462-X). McGraw.

Fontana, Peter. Atomic Radiative Processes. (Pure & Applied Physics Ser.). 1982. 32.50 (ISBN 0-12-262020-8). Acad Pr.

Fontanay, Elisabeth de see De Fontenay, Elisabeth.

Fontanetta, John & Heller, Al. The Passive Solar Dome Greenhouse Book. LC 81-7083. Orig. Title: Building & Using a Solar Heated Geodesic Greenhouse. (Illus.). pap. 9.95 o.p. (ISBN 0-88266-161-2). Garden Way Pub.

Fontein, Jan & Pal, Pratapaditya. Museum of Fine Arts, Boston: Oriental Art. LC 73-93137. (Illus.). 1970. 27.50 o.p. (ISBN 0-87846-028-4, Pub. by Boston Museum of Fine Arts). NYGS.

Fontenay, Charles L. Estes Kefauver: A Biography. LC 79-28299. (Illus.). 432p. 1980. 19.95 (ISBN 0-87049-262-4). U of Tenn Pr.

Fontenelle, Don H. Understanding & Managing Overactive Children: A Guide for Parents & Teachers. 200p. 1983. 13.95 (ISBN 0-13-936765-9); pap. 6.95 (ISBN 0-13-936757-8). P-H.

Fontenelle, Don, 2nd, jt. auth. see Collins, Mallary M.

Fontenilles, Alfred & Heimerdinger, Mark C. Le Francais des Affaires. 1981. pap. text ed. 11.95x (ISBN 0-02-338700-9). Macmillan.

Fontenot, Mary A. Clovis Crawfish & the Orphan Zozo. LC 81-17740. (Clovis Crawfish Ser.). (Illus.). 32p. (gr. k-6). 1983. 9.95 (ISBN 0-88289-312-2). Pelican.

Fontenrose, Joseph. The Delphic Oracle: Its Responses & Operations. LC 76-47969. 1978. 40.00x o.p. (ISBN 0-520-03360-4); pap. 10.95 (ISBN 0-520-04359-6, CAL 490). U of Cal Pr.

--Python. 1959. 25.00x (ISBN 0-8196-0285-X). Biblo.

Fontes, J. C., jt. auth. see Fritz, P.

Fonteyn, Margot. The Magic of Dance. LC 79-2221. (Illus.). 1979. 22.95 (ISBN 0-394-50778-9). Knopf.

Fonvizin, Dennis. Political Writings. Gleason, Walter, tr. from Rus. 170p. Date not set. 22.50 (ISBN 0-88233-799-8). Ardis Pubs.

Fonyam, John, ed. see Kopf, Ebs Dumm.

Food & Drug Administration. FDA Executive Information Manual. Hadley, Richard D., ed. 294p. 1982. pap. text ed. 35.00 (ISBN 0-914176-19-6). Wash Busn Info.

Food & Nutrition Group. Feed, Need, Greed. Tafler, Sue & Phillips, Connie, eds. (Illus.). 108p. (Orig.). 1980. pap. 5.00 (ISBN 0-9607314-0-7); tchr's. ed. 5.00 (ISBN 0-686-84488-2). Sci People.

Food Editors of Farm Journal, jt. auth. see Manning, Elsie.

Food Processors Institute. Canned Foods: Principles of Thermal Process Control, Acidification & Container Closure Evaluation. rev. 3rd ed. 224p. 1979. pap. 15.00 (ISBN 0-937774-02-2). Food Processors.

--Canned Foods: Principles of Thermal Process Control, Acidification & Container Closure Evaluation. 4th, rev. ed. 256p. 1982. pap. 40.00 (ISBN 0-937774-07-3). Food Processors.

--Guide for Waste Management in the Food Processing Industry, 2 vols, Vol. 1. Katsuyama, Allen M., ed. Incl. Vol. II. Warrick, Louis F., ed. 555p. pap. text ed. 15.00 (ISBN 0-937774-01-4). LC 79-115086. 276p. 1979. pap. text ed. 50.00 (ISBN 0-937774-00-6). Food Processors.

Food Products & Drink Industries, Second Tripartite Technical Meeting, Geneva, 1978. Appropriate Technology for Employment Creation in the Food Processing & Drink Industries of Developing Countries: Report III. 88p. 1978. 8.55 (ISBN 92-2-101880-6, FAD/2/III). Intl Labour Office.

Food Safety Council, Columbia, U. S. A., ed. Proposed System for Food Safety Assessment: A Comprehensive Report on the Issues of Food Ingredient Testing. new ed. LC 78-40901. (Illus.). 1979. 25.00 (ISBN 0-08-023752-5). Pergamon.

Fookes, P. J. & Collis, L. Concrete in the Middle East, Pt. I. 1982. pap. 4.00 (ISBN 0-86310-001-5). Scholium Intl.

Fookes, P. J. & Pollock, D. J. Concrete in the Middle East, Pt. II. 1982. pap. 15.00 (ISBN 0-86310-007-4). Scholium Intl.

Fookien Times (Manila), ed. Philippines Yearbook, 1980. (Illus.). 384p. (Orig.). 1980. pap. 20.00x o.p. (ISBN 0-8002-2832-4). Intl Pubns Serv.

Foon, Chew S. & MacDougall, John A. Forever Plural: The Perception & Practice of Inter-Communal Marriage in Singapore. LC 77-620031. (Papers in International Studies: Southeast Asia: No. 45). (Illus.). 1977. pap. 6.00 (ISBN 0-89680-030-X, Ohio U Ctr Intl). Ohio U Pr.

Fooner, Michael. Inside Interpol: Combatting World Crime Through Science & International Police Cooperation. new ed. LC 75-4252. (Illus.). 48p. (gr. 3 up). 1975. PLB 4.99 o.p. (ISBN 0-698-30576-0, Coward). Putnam Pub Group.

--Smuggling Drugs: The World-Wide Connection. (Illus.). 48p. 1977. PLB 5.59 o.p. (ISBN 0-698-30664-3, Coward). Putnam Pub Group.

--Women in Policing: Fighting Crime Around the World. LC 76-15571. (Illus.). (gr. 5 up). 1976. PLB 5.59 o.p. (ISBN 0-698-30630-9, Coward). Putnam Pub Group.

Foord, J. Decorative Plant & Flower Studies for Artists & Craftsmen. (Illus.). 144p. 1982. pap. 5.50 (ISBN 0-486-24276-5). Dover.

Foose, Marlin E., ed. The Heritage Cookbook. LC 79-10606. 1979. pap. 5.95 o.p. (ISBN 0-915442-86-8). Donning Co.

Fooshee, George, Jr. & Fooshee, Marjean. You Can Beat the Money Squeeze. pap. 4.95 (ISBN 0-8007-5030-6). Revell.

Fooshee, Marjean, jt. auth. see Fooshee, George, Jr.

Foot, David, jt. auth. see Richards, Viv.

Foot, Hugh C., jt. auth. see Chapman, Antony J.

Foot, Hugh C., jt. ed. see Chapman, Anthony J.

Foot, Hugh C., et al. Friendship & Social Relations in Children. LC 79-40637. 1980. 61.95 (ISBN 0-471-27628-6, Pub. by Wiley-Interscience). Wiley.

Foot, Isaac. John Milton, Selections from His Works & Tributes to His Genius. 151p. 1982. Repr. of 1935 ed. lib. bdg. 65.00 (ISBN 0-89987-279-4). Darby Bks.

Foot, Philippa, ed. Theories of Ethics. 1967. pap. 8.95x (ISBN 0-19-875005-6). Oxford U Pr.

Foote, ed. Thesaurus of Entomology. 1977. 15.00 (ISBN 0-686-22689-5). Entomol Soc.

Foote, Andrea & Erfurt, John C. Cost Effectiveness of Occupational Employee Assistance Programs: Test of an Evaluation Method. 110p. 1978. 6.00 (ISBN 0-87736-328-5). U of Mich Inst Labor.

Foote, Andrea, jt. auth. see Erfurt, John C.

Foote, Arthur. Quintet for Piano & Strings in A Minor, Opus 38. (Earlier American Music Ser.: No.26). 108p. 1983. Repr. of 1898 ed. lib. bdg. 22.50 (ISBN 0-306-76145-9). Da Capo.

--Suite in E Major, Op. Sixty-Three & Serenade in E Major, Op. 25. (Earlier American Music Ser.: No.24). 58p. 1983. Repr. of 1909 ed. lib. bdg. 18.50 (ISBN 0-306-76091-6). Da Capo.

Foote, Caleb, et al. Cases & Materials on Family Law. 2nd ed. 1975. 27.50 (ISBN 0-316-28850-0); pap. 5.97 1980 suppl. (ISBN 0-316-28852-7). Little.

Foote, Darby. Baby Love & Casey Blue. LC 74-16597. 320p. 1975. 6.95 o.p. (ISBN 0-399-11436-X). Putnam Pub Group.

Foote, G. W. & Wheeler, J. M., eds. Sepher Tolduth Jeshu: The Jewish Life of Christ. (Illus.). 49p. 1982. pap. 3.00 (ISBN 0-910309-02-7). Am Atheist.

Foote, Henry W. John Smilbert, Painter. LC 78-87537. (Library of American Art Ser). 1969. Repr. of 1930 ed. lib. bdg. 32.50 (ISBN 0-306-71453-1). Da Capo.

--Robert Feke, Colonial Portrait Painter. LC 72-75357. (Library of American Art Ser). 1969. Repr. of 1950 ed. lib. bdg. 32.50 (ISBN 0-306-71319-5). Da Capo.

Foote, Henry W., jt. auth. see Clarke, Herman F.

Foote, I. P. & Fennell, J. L., eds. Oxford Slavonic Papers: New Series, Vol. 15. 144p. 1982. 38.50 (ISBN 0-19-815658-8). Oxford U Pr.

Foote, I. P., ed. see Saltykov-Shchedrin, M. E.

Foote, Paul, tr. see Lermontov.

Foote, R. B. Prehistory & Protohistoric Antiquities of India. 1979. text ed. 22.50x (ISBN 0-391-01865-5). Humanities.

Foote, Shelby. Shiloh. 1976. 11.95 (ISBN 0-394-40873-X). Random.

Foote, Timothy. The Great Ringtail Garbage Caper. (Illus.). (gr. 3-6). 1980. 6.95 (ISBN 0-395-28759-6). HM.

--World of Bruegel. LC 68-31677. (Library of Art Ser.). (Illus.). (gr. 6 up). 1968. 19.92 (ISBN 0-8094-0275-0, Pub. by Time-Life). Silver.

Foote, Warren E., jt. auth. see Pedde, Lawrence D.

Foote, William H. Sketches of North Carolina. 3rd ed. 593p. 1965. 12.00. Synod NC Church.

Foote-Smith, Elizabeth. Gentle Albatross. LC 75-44098. 1976. 6.95 o.p. (ISBN 0-399-11730-X). Putnam Pub Group.

Footman, David. The Alexander Conspiracy: A Life of A. I. Zhelybov. LC 74-57. Orig. Title: Red Prelude. (Illus.). 370p. 1974. Repr. of 1944 ed. 21.00x (ISBN 0-912050-47-0, Library Pr). Open Court.

--Civil War in Russia. LC 75-17470. (Illus.). 328p. 1975. Repr. of 1962 ed. lib. bdg. 18.25x (ISBN 0-8371-8306-5, FOCW). Greenwood.

Footner, Hulbert. Maryland Main & the Eastern Shore. LC 67-1719. 1967. Repr. of 1942 ed. 27.00 o.p. (ISBN 0-8103-5034-3). Gale.

Foott, Bethia. Dismissal of a Premier: The Philip Game Papers. 16.50x (ISBN 0-392-02674-0, ABC). Sportshelf.

Foran, Thomas J. Puerto Rico: Pupil's Edition. LC 76-40992. (gr. k-3). 1976. pap. text ed. 5.16 (ISBN 0-07-021477-8, W); tchr's manual 3.20 (ISBN 0-07-021478-6). McGraw.

Forbes, A. Dean, jt. auth. see Andersen, Francis.

Forbes, Andrew F., jt. auth. see Bartholomew, David J.

Forbes, C. D. Unresolved Problems in Haemophilia. (Illus.). 245p. 1981. text ed. 29.95 (ISBN 0-85200-388-9, Pub. by MTP Pr England). Kluwer Boston.

Forbes, C. D., jt. ed. see Barvenel, J. C.

Forbes, Calvin. From the Book of Shine. (Burning Deck Poetry Ser.). 1979. pap. 10.00 signed ed. (ISBN 0-930900-70-7). Burning Deck.

Forbes, Cheryl. The Religion of Power. 176p. 1983. 9.95 (ISBN 0-310-45770-X). Zondervan.

Forbes, Colin. The Stockholm Syndicate. 320p. 1982. 13.95 (ISBN 0-525-24102-7, 01354-410). Dutton.

Forbes, Crosby H. Chinese Export Silver, Seventeen Eighty-Five to Eighteen Eighty-Five. LC 85-12401. (Illus.). 1975. 100.00 (ISBN 0-937650-02-1); deluxe ed. 85.00 o.p. (ISBN 0-686-77324-1). Mus Am China Trade.

--Hills & Streams: Landscape Decoration on Chinese Export Blue & White Porcelain. Walker, Janet, ed. LC 82-81634. 20p. (Orig.). 1982. pap. 5.00x (ISBN 0-88397-041-4). Intl Exhibit Foun.

Forbes, D., ed. see Hegel, Georg W.

Forbes, Daniel. The Rapist. 1977. 7.95 o.p. (ISBN 0-698-10803-5, Coward). Putnam Pub Group.

Forbes, David C. Successful Sea Angling. (Illus.). 156p. 1971. 3.50 o.p. (ISBN 0-7153-5116-8). David & Charles.

Forbes, Duncan. Life Before Man: The Story of Fossils. 2nd ed. (Illus.). 64p. (gr. 4-9). 1974. 6.95 o.p. (ISBN 0-7136-1300-9). Transatlantic.

Forbes, Elizabeth & Fitzsimons, Virginia. The Older Adult: A Process for Wellness. LC 80-39513. 333p. 1981. pap. text ed. 15.95 (ISBN 0-8016-1631-X). Mosby.

Forbes, Elizabeth, jt. auth. see Litwack, Lawrence L.

Forbes, Eric G. & Pacela, Allan F. A Source Book of Government-Owned Biomedical Inventions. LC 77-88370. (Illus.). 1978. looseleaf 82.50x o.p. (ISBN 0-930844-02-5). Quest Pub.

Forbes, Eric G., ed. The Gresham Lectures of John Flamsteed. LC 76-358799. (Illus.). 467p. 1975. 64.00x o.p. (ISBN 0-7201-0518-8, Pub. by Mansell England). Wilson.

Forbes, Esther. Johnny Tremain. 1969. pap. 2.50 (ISBN 0-440-94250-0, LFL). Dell.

--Johnny Tremain. (Illus.). (gr. 2-6). pap. 2.95 (ISBN 0-440-44150-1, YB). Dell.

Forbes, Harold M. West Virginia History: Bibliography & Guide to Studies. 359p. 1981. 9.00 (ISBN 0-686-92647-1). West Va U Pr.

Forbes, J. A., jt. auth. see Clark, Ewen M.

Forbes, Jean & Ross, James. Communications & Networks. (Place & People Ser.: No. 3). (Illus.). 1977. pap. text ed. 4.95x o.p. (ISBN 0-435-34694-6). Heinemann Ed.

--Landscapes in Towns. (Place & People Ser.: No. 2). 1976. pap. text ed. 4.95x o.p. (ISBN 0-435-34693-8). Heinemann Ed.

Forbes, John Douglas. Stettinius, Senior: Portrait of a Morgan Partner. LC 73-89906. 368p. 1974. 15.95x o.p. (ISBN 0-8139-0517-6). U Pr of Va.

Forbes, Judy, jt. auth. see Johnson, Mary M.

Forbes, Kathryn. Mama's Bank Account. (gr. 10 up). 1968. pap. 2.50 (ISBN 0-15-656377-0, Harv). HarBraceJ.

Forbes, Mary J. Word Processing: Procedures for Today's Office. 250p. 1983. 22.00 (ISBN 0-932376-23-1). Digital Pr.

Forbes, Patrick. Champagne: The Wine, the Land & the People. 1981. 40.00x o.p. (ISBN 0-575-00948-9, Pub. by Gollancz England). State Mutual Bk.

Forbes, Reginald D., et al, eds. Forestry Handbook. (Illus.). 1955. 42.50x (ISBN 0-471-06829-2, Pub. by Wiley-Interscience). Wiley.

Forbes, Rosalind. Corporate Stress: How to Manage Stress & Make It Work for You. LC 78-55849. 1979. pap. 4.95 o.p. (ISBN 0-385-14440-7, Dolp). Doubleday.

Forbes, T. W., ed. Human Factors in Highway Traffic Safety Research. LC 80-15240. 442p. 1981. Repr. of 1972 ed. lib. bdg. 23.00 (ISBN 0-89874-231-5). Krieger.

Forbes, Thomas R. The Midwife & the Witch. LC 79-8099. (Satanism Ser.). 224p. 1982. Repr. of 1966 ed. 28.00 (ISBN 0-404-18411-1). AMS Pr.

Forbes, Tom. Quincy's Harvest. LC 76-24807. (gr. 5-8). 1976. 9.57i (ISBN 0-397-31688-7, JBL-J). Har-Row.

Forbin, A. Catalogue de Timbres-Fiscaux. LC 80-50908. (Illus.). 800p. (Fr.). Date not set. Repr. of 1915 ed. lib. bdg. 35.00x (ISBN 0-88000-116-X). Quarterman. Postponed.

Forbis, W. The Cowboys. LC 72-87680. (Old West Ser). (Illus.). (gr. 5 up). 1973. 17.28 (ISBN 0-8094-1451-1, Pub. by Time-Life). Silver.

Forbush, Gabrielle. Puppies. (Illus.). 4.95 (ISBN 0-87666-674-8, KW-023). TFH Pubns.

Force, Lorraine M. Tess of the D'Urbervilles Notes. (Orig.). 1966. pap. 2.50 (ISBN 0-8220-1273-1). Cliffs.

Force, Rich, ed. I-C Test Equipment. (Seventy-Three Test Equipment Library: Vol. 4). 136p. 1977. pap. text ed. 4.95 o.p. (ISBN 0-88006-013-1, LB7362). Green Pub Inc.

Force, Rich, ed. see Lee, James, et al.

Force, Rich, ed. see Leventhal, Lawrence A., et al.

Forcese, D. & Richter, S. Social Research Methods. (Illus.). 1973. text ed. 20.95 (ISBN 0-13-818237-X). P-H.

Forch, Carolyn. Undetermined. Wright, C. D. & Gander, Forrest, eds. (Lost Roads Ser.: No. 24). 55p. (Orig.). 1982. pap. 5.95 (ISBN 0-686-83488-7). Lost Roads.

Forche, Carolyn. Undisclosed, No. 24. LC 82-84509. 55p. 1983. pap. 5.95 (ISBN 0-918786-27-4). Lost Roads.

Forche, Carolyn, tr. see Alegria, Claribel.

Ford, ed. see Symposium, New York, 1972.

Ford, Aaron N. & Turpin, Waters. Extending Horizons. 1969. pap. text ed. 3.95x (ISBN 0-685-55622-0, 30181). Phila Bk Co.

Ford, Alice E. Edward Hicks, Painter of the Peaceable Kingdom. LC 52-13392. (Illus.). 1973. Repr. of 1952 ed. 39.00 o.s.i. (ISBN 0-527-30400-X). Kraus Repr.

Ford, Alphonse. The Cleaning, Repairing, Lining & Restoring of Oil Paintings: A Practical Guide for Their Better Care & Preservation. (Library of the Arts). (Illus.). 1977. Repr. of 1867 ed. 65.25 (ISBN 0-89266-074-0). Am Classical Coll Pr.

Ford, Amasa B. Urban Health in America. (Illus.). 275p. 1976. 18.95x (ISBN 0-19-502003-0); pap. 9.95x (ISBN 0-19-502002-2). Oxford U Pr.

Ford, Anne. Davy Crockett. (Beginning Biographies Ser.). (Illus.). (gr. k-3). 1961. PLB 5.99 o.p. (ISBN 0-399-60120-1). Putnam Pub Group.

Ford, Arthur L. Joel Barlow. (United States Authors Ser.). 13.95 (ISBN 0-8057-0036-6, Twayne). G K Hall.

--Robert Creeley. (United States Authors Ser.). 1978. lib. bdg. 12.95 (ISBN 0-8057-7220-0, Twayne). G K Hall.

Ford, Arthur M., jt. ed. see Heilbroner, Robert L.

Ford, Audrey, jt. auth. see Wallace, Arthur.

Ford, Barbara. Alligators, Raccoons, & Other Survivors: The Wildlife of the Future. LC 80-28193. (Illus.). 160p. (gr. 4-6). 1981. 10.95 (ISBN 0-688-00369-9); PLB 10.32 (ISBN 0-688-00370-2). Morrow.

--Animals That Use Tools. LC 78-16895. (Illus.). 96p. (gr. 4-6). 1978. PLB 7.29 o.p. (ISBN 0-671-32950-2). Messner.

--The Island Ponies: An Environmental Study of Their Life on Assateague. LC 79-11026. (Illus.). (gr. 4-6). 1979. 9.25 (ISBN 0-688-22179-3); PLB 8.88 (ISBN 0-688-32179-8). Morrow.

--Why Does a Turtle Live Longer Than a Dog? A Report on Animal Longevity. LC 79-28159. (Illus.). (gr. 4-6). 1980. 8.75 (ISBN 0-688-22229-3); PLB 8.40 (ISBN 0-688-32229-8). Morrow.

Ford, Beryl I. Health Education: A Source Book for Teaching. 1978. text ed. 23.00 (ISBN 0-08-021327-8); pap. text ed. 16.50 (ISBN 0-08-021326-X). Pergamon.

Ford, Betty & Chase, Chris. The Times of My Life. LC 78-2131. 1978. 14.37i (ISBN 0-06-011298-0, HarpT). Har-Row.

Ford, Boris, ed. The Age of Shakespeare. (Guide to English Literature Ser.: Vol. 2). 512p. 1982. pap. 5.95 (ISBN 0-14-022265-0, Pelican). Penguin.

--From Blake to Byron. 1983. pap. 5.95 (ISBN 0-14-022268-5). Penguin.

--From Dickens to Hardy. 1983. pap. 5.95 (ISBN 0-14-022269-3, Pelican). Penguin.

--Medieval Literature, Pt. 2. 1983. pap. 5.95 (ISBN 0-14-022272-3, Pelican). Penguin.

Ford, Brian, jt. auth. see McCartney, Kevin.

Ford, Charles H. The Super Executive's Guide to Getting Things Done. 272p. 1983. 14.95 (ISBN 0-8144-5724-X). Am Mgmt.

Ford, Charles W. & Morgan, Margaret K. Teaching in Health Professions. LC 75-37571. (Illus.). 290p. 1976. text ed. 18.95 o.p. (ISBN 0-8016-1622-0). Mosby.

Ford, Colin & Harrison, Brian. A Hundred Years Ago: Britain in the 1880s in Words & Photographs. (Illus.). 344p. 1983. text ed. 25.00x (ISBN 0-674-42626-6). Harvard U Pr.

Ford, D. H., et al. Atlas of the Human Brain. 3rd ed. 1978. 37.25 (ISBN 0-444-80008-5). Elsevier.

Ford, Daniel. The Country Northward: A Hiker's Journal. LC 76-11306. (Illus.). 1976. 12.50 (ISBN 0-912274-60-3); pap. 6.95. Backcountry Pubns.

--The Cult of the Atom. 1982. 13.95 (ISBN 0-671-25301-8). S&S.

Ford, Daniel, jt. auth. see Ford, Sally.

Ford, Daniel, ed. see Carter, Robert.

Ford, Daniel, et al. Beyond the Freeze: The Road to Nuclear Sanity. LC 82-72504. (Orig.). 1982. pap. 4.76 (ISBN 0-8070-0484-7, BP646). Beacon Pr.

Ford, Desmond. The Abomination of Desolation in Biblical Eschatology. LC 79-64195. 1979. pap. text ed. 12.50 (ISBN 0-8191-0757-3). U Pr of Amer.

Ford, Donald H. & Urban, Hugh B. Systems of Psychotherapy: A Comparative Study. LC 63-20630. 712p. 1963. 42.95x (ISBN 0-471-26580-2). Wiley.

Ford, Donald H., jt. auth. see Kaplan, Harry.

Ford, Donald H., jt. ed. see Lajtha, A.

Ford, Doug. Start Golf Young. LC 77-93324. (gr. 5 up). 1978. 8.95 (ISBN 0-8069-4126-X); PLB 10.99 (ISBN 0-8069-4127-8). Sterling.

Ford, E. B. Genetics & Adaptation. (Studies in Biology: No. 69). 64p. 1976. pap. text ed. 8.95 (ISBN 0-7131-2563-2). E Arnold.

Ford, Edsel. Looking for Shiloh: Poems. LC 68-9420. 64p. 1969. pap. 5.95 (ISBN 0-8262-8012-9). U of Mo Pr.

Ford, Edward E. Choosing to Love: A New Way to Respond. 192p. 1983. pap. 7.95 (ISBN 0-86683-695-0). Wilton Pr.

Ford, Eileen, ed. More Beautiful You in Twenty-One Days. 1972. 10.95 o.p. (ISBN 0-671-21191-9). S&S.

Ford, Elaine. Missed Connections. 1983. 13.95 (ISBN 0-394-52980-4). Random.

Ford, Emma. Birds of Prey. (Illus.). 1982. pap. 8.95 (ISBN 0-686-98031-X). Branford.

Ford, Ford. The Soul of London. LC 72-91. (English Literature Ser., No. 33). 1972. Repr. of 1911 ed. lib. bdg. 33.95x (ISBN 0-8383-1407-4). Haskell.

Ford, Ford M. Critical Writings of Ford Madox Ford. MacShane, Frank, ed. LC 64-11356. (Regents Critics Ser). xiv, 168p. 1964. 13.95x (ISBN 0-8032-0455-8); pap. 3.95x (ISBN 0-8032-5454-7, BB 401, Bison). U of Nebr Pr.

--Portraits from Life. LC 74-2553. (Illus.). 227p. 1974. Repr. of 1937 ed. lib. bdg. 17.25x (ISBN 0-8371-7405-8, FOPL). Greenwood.

--The Rash Act. 348p. 1982. text ed. 14.75x (ISBN 0-85635-399-X, Pub. by Carcanet Pr England). Humanities.

Ford, Ford Madox. Return to Yesterday. 416p. 1983. 12.95 (ISBN 0-87140-563-6); pap. 7.95 (ISBN 0-87140-271-8). Liveright.

Ford, Ford Madox, jt. auth. see Pound, Ezra.

Ford Foundation & Atwater, James D. Better Testing, Better Writing: A Report to the Ford Foundation. LC 81-15136. (Papers on Research About Learning Ser.). 36p. (Orig.). 1981. pap. text ed. 3.50 (ISBN 0-916584-20-8). Ford Found.

Ford Foundation & Lynton, Ernest. A Tale of Three Cities: Boston, Birmingham, Hartford. LC 81-9790. (Ford Foundation Series on Higher Education in the Cities). 80p. (Orig.). 1981. pap. text ed. 4.00 (ISBN 0-916584-18-6). Ford Found.

Ford Foundation & Orfield, Gary. Toward a Strategy for Urban Integration: Lessons in School & Housing Policy from Twelve Cities: A Report to the Ford Foundation. LC 81-19447. 87p. (Orig.). 1982. pap. text ed. 4.50 (ISBN 0-916584-19-4). Ford Found.

Ford, Frank B; see Lion, Eugene & Ball, David.

Ford, Franklin L. Strasbourg in Transition, 1648-1789. (Illus.). 1966. pap. 1.85x o.p. (ISBN 0-393-00321-3, Norton Lib). Norton.

Ford, G. B., jt. auth. see Black, James M.

Ford, George A. & Ford, Kathleen H. Analysis of Sex Role Traits. 1982. programmed wkbk. 1.95 (ISBN 0-934698-15-5). New Comm Pr.

Ford, George A. & Lippitt, Gordon L. Planning Your Future: A Workbook for Personal Goal Setting. LC 76-11357. Orig. Title: Life Planning Workbook for Guidance in Planning & Personal Goal Setting. 50p. 1976. 7.00 (ISBN 0-88390-120-X). Univ Assocs.

Ford, George A., jt. auth. see Hall, Anna H.

Ford, Gerald R. A Time to Heal: The Autobiography of Gerald R. Ford. LC 78-20162. (Illus.). 1979. 14.37i (ISBN 0-06-011297-2, HarpT). Har-Row.

Ford, Henry J. Cleveland Era. 1919. text ed. 8.50x (ISBN 0-686-83504-2). Elliots Bks.

--Rise & Growth of American Politics. 2nd ed. LC 67-23377. (Law, Politics, & History Ser). 1967. Repr. of 1898 ed. lib. bdg. 35.00 (ISBN 0-306-70946-5). Da Capo.

--Washington & His Colleagues. 1918. text ed. 8.50x (ISBN 0-686-83847-5). Elliots Bks.

Ford, High & Alexander, J. M. Advanced Mechanics of Materials. 2nd ed. 672p. 1977. 44.95x o.p. (ISBN 0-470-99065-1). Halsted Pr.

Ford, Hildegard. My Go to Bed Book. (Illus.). 1976. 5.50 (ISBN 0-8054-4151-4). Broadman.

Ford, Hildegarde. Baby's Animal Book. (Illus.). 1976. 5.50 (ISBN 0-8054-4150-6). Broadman.

Ford, Ira W. Traditional Music of America. (Music Reprint Ser., 1978). 1978. Repr. of 1940 ed. lib. bdg. 39.50 (ISBN 0-306-77588-3). Da Capo.

Ford, J. Massyngberde, tr. Revelation. LC 74-18796. (Anchor Bible Ser.: Vol. 38). (Illus.). 504p. 1975. 18.00 (ISBN 0-385-00895-3). Doubleday.

Ford, James L. & Ford, Mary K., eds. Every Day in the Year: A Political Epitome of the World's History. LC 68-17941. 1969. Repr. of 1902 ed. 34.00x (ISBN 0-8103-3105-5). Gale.

Ford, James M. & Monroe, James E. Living Systems: Principles & Relationships. 3rd ed. 640p. 1977. text ed. 25.50 scp o.p. (ISBN 0-06-382697-6, HarpC); instructor's manual avail. o.p.; scp lab manual 10.50 o.p. (ISBN 0-06-382699-2); scp study guide 8.50 o.p. (ISBN 0-06-382698-4). Har-Row.

Ford, Jeremiah D. Main Currents of Spanish Literature. LC 68-13689. 1968. Repr. of 1919 ed. 10.00x (ISBN 0-8196-0213-2). Biblo.

Ford, Jill. Human Behavior: Towards a Practical Understanding Library of Social Work. 160p. 1983. pap. 7.95 (ISBN 0-7100-9218-0). Routledge & Kegan.

Ford, Jo Ann G., et al. Applied Decision Making for Nurses. LC 78-15713. (Illus.). 140p. 1979. pap. text ed. 12.50 (ISBN 0-8016-1624-7). Mosby.

Ford, John. Role of the Trypanosomiases in African Ecology: A Study of the Tsetse-Fly Problem. (Illus.). 1971. 41.00x o.p. (ISBN 0-19-854375-1). Oxford U Pr.

Ford, John G. Chinese Snuff Bottles: The Edward Choate O'Dell Collection. LC 82-83402. (Illus.). 80p. 1982. Casebound 22.50x (ISBN 0-9609668-0-3). Intl Chi Snuff.

Ford, John K. A Framework for Financial Analysis. 176p. 1981. pap. text ed. 12.95 (ISBN 0-13-330241-5). P-H.

Ford, John M. The Princes of the Air. 175p. 1982. pap. 2.50 (ISBN 0-686-82235-8, Timescape). PB.

Ford, Julienne. Paradigms & Fairy Tales: An Introduction to the Science of Meanings, 2 vols. 1975. Vol. 1. 18.50 (ISBN 0-7100-8068-9); Vol. 2. 18.50 (ISBN 0-7100-8215-0); Set. 36.00 (ISBN 0-7100-8216-9); Vol. 1. pap. 7.95 (ISBN 0-7100-8248-7); Vol. 2. pap. 7.95 (ISBN 0-7100-8249-5); Set. pap. 15.00 (ISBN 0-7100-8250-9). Routledge & Kegan.

Ford, Julienne, et al. Special Education & Social Control: Invisible Disasters. 192p. 1982. pap. 18.95 (ISBN 0-7100-0951-8). Routledge & Kegan.

Ford, Kathleen H., jt. auth. see Ford, George A.

Ford, Kenneth. Classical & Modern Physics, 3 vols. Incl. Vol. 1. 1972. text ed. 22.50x o.p. (ISBN 0-471-00723-4); Vol. 2. text ed. 24.95x (ISBN 0-471-00724-2); answer manual 7.50 (ISBN 0-471-00945-8); Vol. 3. 1974. text ed. 26.95x (ISBN 0-471-00878-8); answer manual o.p. 6.95 (ISBN 0-471-00946-6). LC 76-161385. 1973. combined ed. for vols. 1 & 2 35.95 (ISBN 0-471-00666-1). Wiley.

Ford, Kristina, ed. Remote Sensing for Planners. LC 78-31594. (Illus.). 1979. text ed. 25.00 (ISBN 0-88285-058-X). Ctr Urban Pol Res.

Ford, Lee E., ed. Women of the Eighties: Vol. 6: the Political Woman. 100p. (Orig.). 1982. pap. 12.00 (ISBN 0-686-31644-4). Ford Assocs.

Ford, LeRoy. Capacitese Como Lider. Blair, Guillermo, tr. 64p. (Span.). 1982. pap. 3.75 (ISBN 0-311-17023-4, Edit Mundo). Casa Bautista.

--La Conferencia en la Ensenanza. Orig. Title: Using the Lecture in Teaching & Training. 136p. (Span.). pap. 0.00 cancelled (ISBN 0-311-11027-4). Casa Bautista.

--Pedagogia Ilustrada: Tomo I Principios Generales. Orig. Title: A Primer for Teachers & Leaders. (Illus.). 144p. 1982. pap. 2.75 (ISBN 0-311-11001-0, Edit Mundo). Casa Bautista.

--Sugerencias Para Ayudas Visuales. Campbell, Viola D., tr. from Eng. Orig. Title: Tool for Teaching & Training. (Illus.). 72p. (Span.). 1980. pap. 1.45 o.p. (ISBN 0-311-24302-9). Casa Bautista.

Ford, Lester R. Automorphic Functions. LC 52-8647. 17.50 (ISBN 0-8284-0085-7). Chelsea Pub.

--Differential Equations. 2nd ed. (Illus.). 1955. text ed. 14.50 o.p. (ISBN 0-07-021509-X, C). McGraw.

Ford, Madox B. The Diary of Madox Brown Ford. Surtees, Virginia, ed. LC 81-51344. (Paul Mellon Centre for Studies in British Art). (Illus.). 320p. 1981. 30.00x (ISBN 0-300-02743-5). Yale U Pr.

Ford, Madox F. The Benefactor. LC 82-73429. 349p. Repr. of 1905 ed. lib. bdg. 25.00 (ISBN 0-88116-003-2). Brenner Bks.

--A Call. LC 82-73428. 304p. Repr. of 1910 ed. lib. bdg. 25.00 (ISBN 0-88116-004-0). Brenner Bks.

Ford, Madox F., jt. auth. see Conrad, Joseph.

Ford, Marcia. The Sycamores. (YA) 1972. 6.95 (ISBN 0-685-25148-9, Avalon). Bouregy.

Ford, Mary K., jt. ed. see Ford, James L.

Ford, Miriam A. de see De Ford, Miriam A. & Jackson, Joan S.

Ford, Newell F., intro. by see Shelley, Percy B.

Ford, Nick A., ed. Black Insights: Significant Literature by Black-Americans, 1760 to the Present. LC 77-127525. (Orig.). 1971. pap. text ed. 15.95 o.p. (ISBN 0-471-00168-6). Scott F.

--Language in Uniform: A Reader on Propaganda. LC 67-18746. (Orig.). 1967. pap. 4.25 (ISBN 0-672-63054-0). Odyssey Pr.

Ford, P. L., ed. see Dickinson, John.

Ford, P. R. J. The Oriental Carpet: A History & Guide to Traditional Motifs, Patterns, & Symbols. (Illus.). 352p. 1981. 75.00 (ISBN 0-8109-1405-0). Abrams.

Ford, Patrick K. The Poetry of Llywarch Hen: Introduction, Text & Translation. LC 73-87249. 1974. 22.50x (ISBN 0-520-02601-2). U of Cal Pr.

Ford, Patrick K., ed. Mabinogi & Other Medieval Welsh Tales. LC 76-3885. 1977. 20.00x (ISBN 0-520-03205-5); pap. 3.95 (ISBN 0-520-03414-7). U of Cal Pr.

Ford, Paul. Companion to Narnia, a Complete Illustrated Guide to the Themes, Characters & Events of C. S. Lewis Imaginary World. LC 80-7734. (Illus.). 304p. 1980. 14.95i o.p. (ISBN 0-06-250340-5, HarpR). Har-Row.

Ford, Paul F. Companion to Narnia: A Complete, Illustrated Guide to the Themes, Characters, & Events of C. S. Lewis's Imaginary World. LC 80-7734. (Illus.). 512p. 1983. pap. 6.68 (ISBN 0-06-250341-3, HarpR). Har-Row.

Ford, Paul L. Pamphlets on the Constitution of the United States. LC 68-22228. (American History, Politics & Law Ser). 1968. Repr. of 1888 ed. lib. bdg. 35.00 (ISBN 0-306-71144-3). Da Capo.

Ford, Paul L., ed. New England Primer. LC 62-20977. (Orig.). 1962. pap. text ed. 4.50x (ISBN 0-8077-1368-6). Tchrs Coll.

Ford, Peter, jt. auth. see Howell, Michael.

Ford, Phyllis. Eco-Acts. rev. 2nd ed. 200p. 1982. 10.00 (ISBN 0-686-84023-2). U OR Ctr Leisure.

--Provocative Facts. 120p. 1982. 7.00 (ISBN 0-686-84025-9). U OR Ctr Leisure.

Ford, Phyllis M. Principles & Practices of Outdoor-Environment Education. LC 80-23200. 348p. 1981. text ed. 20.95 (ISBN 0-471-04768-6). Wiley.

Ford, Phyllis M., jt. auth. see Rodney, Lynn S.

Ford, Richard. Children in the Cinema. LC 70-160232. (Moving Pictures Ser). viii, 232p. 1971. Repr. of 1939 ed. lib. bdg. 16.95x (ISBN 0-89198-033-4). Ozer.

Ford, Richard K., jt. auth. see Lewis, Bruce R.

Ford, Robert. Children's Rhymes, Children's Games, Children's Songs, Children's Stories. LC 69-16067. 1968. Repr. of 1904 ed. 31.00 o.p. (ISBN 0-8103-3526-3). Gale.

Ford, Robert C. & Heaton, Cherrill P. Principles of Management: A Decision-Making Approach. (Illus.). 1980. text ed. 21.95 (ISBN 0-8359-5593-1); instr's manual avail. (ISBN 0-8359-5594-X); study guide 9.95 (ISBN 0-8359-5597-4). Reston.

Ford, Robert S. Stale Food vs. Fresh Food: Cause & Cure of Choked Arteries. 6th ed. 48p. 1977. pap. 6.00 (ISBN 0-686-09051-9). Magnolia Lab.

Ford, Sally & Ford, Daniel. Twenty-Five Ski Tours in the Green Mountains. LC 78-56097. (Twenty-Five Ski Tours Ser.). (Illus.). 128p. 1978. pap. 4.95 (ISBN 0-912274-93-X). Backcountry Pubns.

--Twenty-Five Ski Tours in the White Mountains. LC 77-78189. (Twenty-Five Ski Tours Ser.). (Illus.). 128p. 1977. pap. 4.95 (ISBN 0-912274-75-1). Backcountry Pubns.

Ford, Stephen. Acquisition of Library Materials. LC 73-9891. 350p. 1973. text ed. 20.00 (ISBN 0-8389-0145-X). ALA.

Ford, Tamara De see De Ford, Tamara.

Ford, Thomas W. A. B. Guthrie, Jr. (United States Authors Ser.). 1981. 11.95 (ISBN 0-8057-7327-4, Twayne). G K Hall.

Ford, W. Herschel. Simple Sermons on Grace & Glory. 1977. pap. 3.95 o.p. (ISBN 0-310-24751-9). Zondervan.

--Simple Sermons on Great Christian Doctrines. (Simple Sermons Ser.). 144p. 1976. pap. 3.95 o.p. (ISBN 0-310-24471-4). Zondervan.

--Simple Sermons on Old Testament Texts. 112p. 1975. pap. 3.95 o.p. (ISBN 0-310-24561-3). Zondervan.

--Simple Sermons on the Old Time Religion. pap. 3.95 o.p. (ISBN 0-310-24571-0). Zondervan.

Ford, Wendell H. Public Papers of Governor Wendell H. Ford, Nineteen Seventy-One to Nineteen Seventy-Four. Jones, W. Landis, ed. LC 77-73702. (The Public Papers of the Governors of Kentucky Ser.). 722p. 1978. 28.00x o.p. (ISBN 0-8131-0602-8). U Pr of Ky.

Ford, Worthington C., ed. Defences of Philadelphia in 1777. LC 71-146145. (Era of the American Revolution Ser). 1971. Repr. of 1897 ed. lib. bdg. 39.50 (ISBN 0-306-70140-5). Da Capo.

Forde, C. Daryll. Ancient Mariners: The Story of Ships & Sea Routes. 88p. 1982. Repr. of 1928 ed. lib. bdg. 20.00 (ISBN 0-89760-236-6). Telegraph Bks.

Forde, M. J. & Boggis, J. G. Electricity Rates & Economics of Supply. 1983. text ed. cancelled (ISBN 0-08-020859-2); pap. cancelled (ISBN 0-08-021277-8). Pergamon.

Forde, Nels W. Cato the Censor. LC 74-28128. (World Leaders Ser). 1975. lib. bdg. 13.95 (ISBN 0-8057-3017-6, Twayne). G K Hall.

Forde-Johnston. Hillforts of the Iron Age in England & Wales. 370p. 1982. 90.00x (ISBN 0-85323-381-0, Pub. by Liverpool Univ England). State Mutual Bk.

Forde-Johnston, J. Castles & Fortifications of Britain & Ireland. (Illus.). 192p. 1977. 12.50x o.p. (ISBN 0-460-04195-9, J M Dent England). Biblio Dist.

Forder, Anthony. Concepts in Social Administration: A Framework for Analysis. 200p. 1974. 14.95 (ISBN 0-7100-7869-2); pap. 8.95 (ISBN 0-7100-7870-6). Routledge & Kegan.

Forder, Henry G. Calculus of Extension. LC 59-1178. 25.00 (ISBN 0-8284-0135-7). Chelsea Pub.

Fordham, jt. auth. see Cooper, W. F.

Fordham, Derek. Eskimos. LC 79-65843. (Surviving Peoples Ser.). PLB 12.68 (ISBN 0-382-06305-8). Silver.

Fordham, Ernest W. & Ali, Amjad, eds. Atlas of Total Body Radionuclide Imaging, 2 vols. (Illus.). 1000p. 1982. Set. text ed. 175.00x (ISBN 0-06-140848-4, Harper Medical). Lippincott.

Fordham, Jefferson B. Larger Concept of Community. LC 56-6198. (Edward Douglass White Lectures). viii, 118p. 1956. 8.95x o.p. (ISBN 0-8071-0450-7). La State U Pr.

Fordham, Michael, ed. Jungian Psychotherapy: A Study in Analytical Psychology. LC 77-26331. (Wiley Series on Methods in Psychotherapy). 1978. 38.00x (ISBN 0-471-99617-3, Pub. by Wiley-Interscience); pap. 17.50 o.p. (ISBN 0-471-99618-1). Wiley.

Fordham, Morva, jt. auth. see Wilson-Barnett, J.

Fordham, Sheldon L. & Leaf, Carol A. Physical Education & Sports: An Introduction to Alternative Careers. LC 77-19115. 385p. 1978. text ed. 25.95x (ISBN 0-471-26622-1). Wiley.

Fordney, Marilyn T. Insurance Handbook for the Medical Office. 2nd ed. (Illus.). 475p. 1981. pap. text ed. 19.95 (ISBN 0-7216-3814-7). Saunders.

Fordney, Marilyn T. & Follis, Joan J. Administrative Medical Assisting. LC 81-2141. 668p. 1982. 19.95 (ISBN 0-471-06380-0, Pub. by Wiley Med); instructors manual avail. Wiley.

Fordney, Marilyn T., jt. auth. see Diehl, Marcy O.

Fordtran, John S., jt. auth. see Sleisenger, Marvin H.

Fordyce, Edward, jt. ed. see Beach, Charles.

Fordyce, M. W., jt. auth. see Fordyce, Wodehouse.

Fordyce, Rachel. Children's Theatre & Creative Dramatics: An Annotated Bibliography of Critical Works. 1975. lib. bdg. 26.00 (ISBN 0-8161-1161-8, Hall Reference). G K Hall.

Fordyce, Rachel, ed. Caroline Drama: A Bibliographic History of Criticism. 1978. lib. bdg. 27.00 (ISBN 0-8161-7952-2, Hall Reference). G K Hall.

Fordyce, Wilbert E., jt. auth. see Berni, Rosemarian.

Fordyce, Wodehouse & Fordyce, M. W. GRC in Buildings. 1983. text ed. 39.95 (ISBN 0-408-00395-2). Butterworth.

Forehand, G. A., et al. Psychology for Living. 4th ed. 1977. 19.12 (ISBN 0-07-021520-0, W); tchr's manual 5.80 (ISBN 0-07-021521-9); Webstermasters 46.64 (ISBN 0-07-021522-7); work & study guide 5.80 (ISBN 0-07-021523-5). McGraw.

Forehand, Garlie A., ed. Applications of Time Series Analysis to Evaluation. LC 81-48580. 1982. 7.95x (ISBN 0-87589-918-8, PE-16). Jossey-Bass.

Foreign Affairs & Bundy, William P., eds. America & the World 1982. 300p. 1983. 30.00 (ISBN 0-08-030132-0); pap. 7.95 (ISBN 0-08-030131-2). Pergamon.

Foreign & Commonwealth Office, London. Catalogue of the Colonial Office Library: Third Supplement, 4 vols. 1979. Set. lib. bdg. 520.00 (ISBN 0-8161-0010-1, Hall Library). G K Hall.

--Catalogue of the Foreign Office Library, 1926-1968, 8 vols. 6208p. 1972. lib. bdg. 760.00 (ISBN 0-8161-0998-2, Hall Library). G K Hall.

Foreign & Commowealth Office, London. Catalogue of the Colonial Office Library, London, 15 vols. 1964. Set. 1425.00 (ISBN 0-8161-0688-6, Hall Library); First Suppl. 1963-67. 130.00 (ISBN 0-8161-0729-7); Second Suppl. 1972. 2 Vols. 210.00 (ISBN 0-8161-0843-9). G K Hall.

Foreign Policy Research Institute Staff. The Three Percent Solution & the Future of NATO. 118p. (Orig.). 1981. pap. 6.95 (ISBN 0-910191-02-6). For Policy Res.

Foreign Service Institute. Advanced German Course. 375p. 1980. plus 18 audio-cassettes 185.00x (ISBN 0-88432-043-X, G160). J Norton Pubs.

--Advanced Spanish, Pt. C. 472p. Date not set. includes 18 cassettes 185.00x (ISBN 0-88432-102-9, S170). J Norton Pubs.

--Advanced Spanish, Part B. 614p. 1980. plus 12 audio-cassettes 145.00x (ISBN 0-88432-058-8, S 153). J Norton Pubs.

--Advanced Spanish, Pt. A. 699p. 1980. plus 16 audio cassettes 175.00x (ISBN 0-88432-057-X, S 131). J Norton Pubs.

--Basic Korean Course, Vol. 2. 560p. 1980. plus 16 audio-cassettes 175.00x (ISBN 0-88432-048-0, Q850). J Norton Pubs.

--Basic Swedish Course. 261p. 1980. plus 28 audio-cassettes 245.00x (ISBN 0-88432-045-6, K381). J Norton Pubs.

--Basic Thai Course, Vol. 1. 383p. 1980. plus 19 audio-cassettes 195.00x (ISBN 0-88432-050-2, D300). J Norton Pubs.

--Basic Turkish Course, Vol. 1. 385p. 1980. plus 14 audio-cassettes 175.00x (ISBN 0-88432-049-9, T700). J Norton Pubs.

--Basic Vietnamese Course, Vol. 1. 328p. 1980. plus 22 audio-cassettes 225.00x (ISBN 0-88432-051-0, V401). J Norton Pubs.

--Bulgarian Basic Course. 487p. Date not set. with 23 cassettes 225.00x (ISBN 0-88432-089-8, L450). J Norton Pubs.

--Cantonese Basic Course, Vol. I. (Chinese.). 1979. 8 audio cassettes incl. 135.00x (ISBN 0-88432-020-0, C131-C138). J Norton Pubs.

--Cantonese Basic Course, Vol. 2. 320p. (Chinese.). 1980. 175.00 (ISBN 0-88432-033-2, C140); 15 audio cassettes incl. J Norton Pubs.

--French & Spanish Testing Kit. 140p. Date not set. with 8 cassettes 95.00x (ISBN 0-88432-060-X, X100). J Norton Pubs.

--French Basic Course, 2 pts. (Fr.). 1979. Vol. 1, Pt. A, 194p. 12 audio cassettes incl. 125.00x (ISBN 0-88432-021-9, F170); Vol. 1, Pt. B, 290p. 18 audio cassettes incl. 149.00x (ISBN 0-88432-022-7, F181). J Norton Pubs.

--French Basic Course, Vol. 2, Pts. A & B. 572p. (Fr.). 1980. Pt. A. 18 audio cassettes & text 185.00x (ISBN 0-88432-023-5, F260); Pt. B. 18 audio cassettes & text 185.00x (ISBN 0-88432-024-3). J Norton Pubs.

--French Phonology. 394p. (Fr.). 1980. 85.00x (ISBN 0-88432-032-4, F250); 8 audiocassettes incl. J Norton Pubs.

--Greek Basic Course, Vol. 1. 328p. (Gr.). 1980. 12 cassettes plus text 145.00x (ISBN 0-88432-034-0, R301, Audio-Forum). J Norton Pubs.

--Greek Basic Course, Vol. 2. 200p. (Gr.). 12 cassettes plus text 145.00x (ISBN 0-88432-035-9, R318, Audio-Forum). J Norton Pubs.

--Greek Basic Course, Vol. 3. 201p. (Gr.). 1980. 6 cassettes plus text 75.00x (ISBN 0-88432-036-7, R338, Audio-Forum). J Norton Pubs.

--Hausa Basic Course. 420p. Date not set. with 15 cassettes 175.00x (ISBN 0-88432-109-6, HA1). J Norton Pubs.

--Hebrew Basic Course. 552p. (Hebrew.). 1980. 195.00x (ISBN 0-88432-040-5, H345); 24 audiocassettes incl. J Norton Pubs.

--Hungarian, Vol. 1. 266p. 1980. plus 24 audio-cassettes 195.00 (ISBN 0-88432-046-4, U500). J Norton Pubs.

--Khmer Basic Course, 2 vols. Date not set. Vol. 1. with 19 cassettes 185.00x (ISBN 0-88432-097-9, KH1); Vol. 2. with 29 cassettes 175.00x (ISBN 0-88432-098-7, KH50). J Norton Pubs.

--Modern Written Arabic, Vol. 1. 419p. (Arabic.). 1980. 185.00x (ISBN 0-88432-039-1, A269); 18 audiocassettes incl. J Norton Pubs.

--Modern Written Arabic, Vol. 2. 385p. Date not set. with 8 cassettes 125.00x (ISBN 0-88432-088-X, A320). J Norton Pubs.

--Programmatic German, 2 vols. (Ger.). 1978. Vol. 1. 10 audio cassettes incl. 125.00x (ISBN 0-88432-017-0, G140-G147); Vol. 2. 8 audio cassettes incl. 110.00x (ISBN 0-88432-018-9, G151-G158). J Norton Pubs.

--Programmatic Portuguese, Vol. I. (Port.). 1982. 16 audio cassettes incl. 149.00x (ISBN 0-88432-019-7, P151-P164). J Norton Pubs.

--Programmatic Portuguese, Vol. II. 600p. Date not set. with 22 cassettes 190.00x (ISBN 0-88432-100-2, P180). J Norton Pubs.

--Programmatic Spanish, 2 vols. (Span.). 1978. Vol. 1. 12 audio cassettes incl. 125.00x (ISBN 0-88432-015-4, S101); Vol. 2. 8 audio cassettes incl. 110.00x (ISBN 0-88432-016-2, S120-S127). J Norton Pubs.

--Saudi Arabic Basic Course: Urban Hijazi Dialect. 287p. (Arabic.). 1980. 135.00x (ISBN 0-88432-037-5, A234); 10 audiocassettes incl. J Norton Pubs.

--Serbo-Croatian Basic Course, Vol. 1. 633p. (Serbo-Croatian.). 1980. 185.00x (ISBN 0-88432-042-1, Y601); 22 audiocassettes incl. J Norton Pubs.

--Serbo-Croatian Basic Course, Vol. 2. 677p. Date not set. includes 24 cassettes 195.00x (ISBN 0-88432-101-0, Y650). J Norton Pubs.

--Spanish to Portugese. 91p. 1980. 2 cassettes incl. 35.00x (ISBN 0-88432-059-6). J Norton Pubs.

--Swahili: An Active Introduction-Conversation. 159p. Date not set. with 2 cassettes 39.00x (ISBN 0-88432-110-X, W300). J Norton Pubs.

--Swahili Basic Course. 560p. (Swahili.). 1980. 215.00x (ISBN 0-88432-041-3, W426); 20 audiocassettes incl. J Norton Pubs.

--Thai Basic Course, Vol. 2. 411p. Date not set. with 17 cassettes 185.00x (ISBN 0-88432-104-5, D350). J Norton Pubs.

--Turkish Basic Course, Vol. 2. 358p. Date not set. with 13 cassettes 175.00x (ISBN 0-88432-105-3, T750). J Norton Pubs.

--Twi Basic Course. 240p. Date not set. with 9 cassettes 125.00x (ISBN 0-88432-111-8, TW1). J Norton Pubs.

--Vietnamese Basic Course, Vol. 2. 325p. Date not set. with 10 cassettes 185.00x (ISBN 0-88432-108-8, V450). J Norton Pubs.

--Yoruba Basic Course. 381p. Date not set. with 36 cassettes 295.00x (ISBN 0-88432-112-6, YR1). J Norton Pubs.

Foreign Service Institute Staff. Levantine Arabic: Introduction to Pronunciation. 100p. (Arabic.). 1980. 10 cassettes incl. 85.00x (ISBN 0-88432-038-3, A244); 10 audiocassettes incl. J Norton Pubs.

Forel, Francois A. Handbuch der Seenkunde, Allgemeine Limnologie: Handbook of Lake Studies. Egerton, Frank N., 3rd, ed. LC 77-74225. (History of Ecology Ser.). 1978. Repr. of 1901 ed. lib. bdg. 15.00x (ISBN 0-405-10395-6). Ayer Co.

Forell, Betty & Wind, Betty. Little Benjamin & the First Christmas. (Arch Bks: Set 1). (Illus.). (ps-3). 1964. laminated bdg. 0.89 (ISBN 0-570-06005-2, 59-1113). Concordia.

Forell, George W. Christian Lifestyle: Reflections on Romans 12-15. LC 75-13033. 96p. (Orig.). 1975. pap. 1.00 o.p. (ISBN 0-8006-1200-0, 1-1200). Fortress.

Foreman, Dave & Koehler, Bart, eds. Don't Fence Me in: A Wilderness Campfire Anthology. Spurs, Jackson. (A Ned Ludd Book). (Illus.). 400p. (Orig.). Date not set. pap. price not set (ISBN 0-942688-03-1). Dream Garden.

Foreman, Gail H., jt. auth. see Zollers, Frances E.

Foreman, George C., jt. auth. see O'Neill, Barbara T.

Foreman, Grant, ed. see Marcy, Randolph B. & McClellan, G. B.

Foreman, Ken. Coaching Track & Field Techniques for Girls & Women. 4th ed. 250p. 1982. pap. write for info. o.p. (ISBN 0-697-07187-1). Wm C Brown.

--Track & Field. 2nd ed. (Physical Education Ser.). 112p. 1983. pap. text ed. write for info. (ISBN 0-697-07213-4); tchr's manual avail. Wm C Brown.

Foreman, Kenneth E. & Husted, Virginia M. Track & Field Techniques for Girls & Women. 3rd ed. 304p. 1977. plastic comb avail. o.p. (ISBN 0-697-07139-1). Wm C Brown.

Foreman, Kenneth J. Romans, First & Second Corinthians. LC 59-10454. (Layman's Bible Commentary Ser: Vol. 21). 1961. 4.25 o.p. (ISBN 0-8042-3021-8); pap. 3.95 (ISBN 0-8042-3081-1). John Knox.

Foreman, Kenneth J., et al. Introduction to the Bible. Kelly, Balmer H., et al, eds. LC 59-10454. (Layman's Bible Commentary, Vol. 1). 1959. pap. 3.95 (ISBN 0-8042-3061-7). John Knox.

Foreman, L. L. The Silver Flame. 192p. 1982. pap. 1.95 (ISBN 0-441-76592-0, Pub. by Charter Bks). Ace Bks.

Foreman, Max L. Rx from the Pulpit. 1982. 20.00 (ISBN 0-8197-0490-3). Bloch.

Foreman, Michael. Land of Dreams. LC 82-11889. (Illus.). 32p. (gr. k-3). 1982. 11.45 (ISBN 0-03-062053-8). HR&W.

--Trick a Tracker: The Zaniest Animal Fable Ever. (Illus.). (gr. 1-4). 1981. 9.95 (ISBN 0-399-20820-8, Philomel); lib. bdg. 9.99 (ISBN 0-399-61185-1). Putnam Pub Group.

--Winter's Tales. LC 79-1862. 1979. 7.95a o.p. (ISBN 0-385-15460-7); PLB 7.95a (ISBN 0-385-15461-5). Doubleday.

Foreman-Peck, James. A History of the World Economy: Economic Relations Since 1850. LC 82-24295. 320p. 1983. text ed. 27.50 (ISBN 0-389-20337-8). B&N Imports.

Forest, David, jt. auth. see Stone, Michael H.

Forest History Society. Encyclopedia of American Forest & Conservation History, 2 vols. Davis, Richard C., ed. 1983. lib. bdg. 150.00X (ISBN 0-02-919750-3). Macmillan.

Forest Industries Commission on Timber Valuation & Taxation. Timber Tax Journal, Vol. 18. 335p. 1982. 30.00 (ISBN 0-686-43165-0, Pub. by FICTVT). Intl Schol Bk Serv.

Forest, John W. De see De Forest, John W.

Forestell, J. T. Targumic Traditions & the New Testament. LC 79-19293. (Society of Biblical Literature Aramaic Studies: No. 4). pap. 12.00 (ISBN 0-686-29277-4, 06-13-04). Scholars Pr CA.

Forester, C. S. Admiral Hornblower in the West Indies. (Hornblower Saga Ser.: No. 10). 320p. 1980. pap. 2.50 (ISBN 0-523-41395-5). Pinnacle Bks.

--Age of a Fighting Sail. pap. 1.75 o.p. (ISBN 0-451-08003-3, E8003, Sig). NAL.

--Beat to Quarters. (Hornblower Saga Ser.: No. 5). 224p. 1980. pap. 2.50 (ISBN 0-523-41390-4). Pinnacle Bks.

--Commodore Hornblower. (Hornblower Saga Ser.: No. 8). 320p. 1980. pap. 2.50 (ISBN 0-523-41393-9). Pinnacle Bks.

--Flying Colors. (Hornblower Saga Ser.: No. 7). 224p. 1980. pap. 2.50 (ISBN 0-523-41392-0). Pinnacle Bks.

--The Good Shepherd. 1979. pap. 2.50 (ISBN 0-523-41861-2). Pinnacle Bks.

--Hornblower & the Hotspur. (Hornblower Saga Ser.: No. 3). 352p. 1980. pap. 2.75 (ISBN 0-523-41790-X). Pinnacle Bks.

--The Hornblower Companion. 192p. 1980. pap. 1.95 o.p. (ISBN 0-523-25440-7). Pinnacle Bks.

--Hornblower, No. 6: Ship of the Line. 192p. 1975. pap. 2.50 (ISBN 0-523-41391-2, 00220386-7). Pinnacle Bks.

--Lord Hornblower. (Hornblower Saga Ser.: No. 9). 256p. 1980. pap. 2.50 (ISBN 0-523-41394-7). Pinnacle Bks.

--Mr. Midshipman Hornblower. (Hornblower Saga Ser.: No. 1). 172p. 1980. pap. 2.50 (ISBN 0-523-41672-5). Pinnacle Bks.

--The Nightmare. (C. S. Forester Ser.). 1979. pap. 1.95 o.p. (ISBN 0-523-40607-X). Pinnacle Bks.

--Payment Deferred. 1979. pap. 1.95 o.p. (ISBN 0-523-40619-3). Pinnacle Bks.

Forester, C. S see Swan, D. K.

Forester, Cecil S. African Queen. 1940. 3.95 o.s.i. (ISBN 0-394-60102-5, M102). Modern Lib.

Forester, John. Effective Cycling: Instructors Manual. (Illus.). 158p. 1982. pap. 6.00 (ISBN 0-940558-02-5). CCF.

Forester, Tom, ed. The Microelectronics Revolution: The Complete Guide to the New Technology & Its Impact on Society. (Illus.). 608p. 1981. 27.50x (ISBN 0-262-06075-2); pap. 12.50 (ISBN 0-262-56021-6). MIT Pr.

Forey, P. L., ed. The Evolving Biosphere. (Chance, Change & Challenge Ser.). (Illus.). 350p. 1981. 79.50 (ISBN 0-521-23811-0); pap. 27.95 (ISBN 0-521-28230-6). Cambridge U Pr.

Foreyt, John P., jt. ed. see Williams, Ben J.

Forgacs, S. Bones & Joints in Diabetes Mellitus. 1982. lib. bdg. 34.00 (ISBN 90-247-2395-7, Pub. by Martinus Nijhoff Netherlands). Kluwer Boston.

Forgan, Harry W. Read All About It! Using Interests & Hobbies to Motivate Young Readers. LC 78-27598. 1979. pap. text ed. 11.95 o.p. (ISBN 0-673-16418-7). Scott F.

--Reading Skillbuilder: Comprehension Skills. 1982. pap. text ed. 5.95x (ISBN 0-673-16549-3). Scott F.

--Reading Skillbuilder: Functional Reading Skills. 1982. pap. text ed. 5.95x (ISBN 0-673-16550-7). Scott F.

--Reading Skillbuilder: Prereading Skills. 1982. pap. text ed. 5.95x (ISBN 0-673-16547-7). Scott F.

--Reading Skillbuilder: Word Recognition Skills. 1982. pap. text ed. 5.95x (ISBN 0-673-16548-5). Scott F.

Forgan, Harry W. & Mangrum, Charles T. Teaching Content Area Reading Skills. 2nd ed. (Illus.). 336p. 1981. pap. text ed. 16.50 (ISBN 0-675-08037-1). Additional supplements may be obtained from publisher. Merrill.

--Teaching Content Area Reading Skills: A Modular Preservice & Inservice Program. new ed. (Elementary Education Ser.). 384p. 1976. pap. text ed. 15.95 (ISBN 0-675-08597-7). Additional supplements may be obtained from publisher. Merrill.

Forgan, Harry W., jt. auth. see Mangrum, Charles T.

Forgan, Ruth A., jt. auth. see Striebel, Bonnie.

Forgatsch, Olive H. A World of Wonder: Poetry for Children. LC 82-90106. (Illus.). 60p. (gr. 2-5). 1982. lib. bdg. 18.95 (ISBN 0-9608784-0-8). Rainbow Child Bks.

Forgays, Donald G., ed. Environmental Influences & Strategies in Primary Prevention. LC 77-95398. (Primary Prevention Psychopathology Ser.: Vol. 2). (Illus.). 277p. 1978. text ed. 25.00x (ISBN 0-87451-153-4). U Pr of New Eng.

Forge, P. G. La see La Forge, P. G.

Forge, Suzanne. Victorian Splendour: Australian Interior Decoration, 1837-1901. (Illus.). 162p. 1981. 65.00x (ISBN 0-19-554299-1). Oxford U Pr.
Forgus, Ronald, jt. auth. see Shulman, Bernard H.
Forgus, Ronald H. & Melamed, Lawrence E. Perception: A Cognitive-Stage Approach. 2nd ed. 1976. text ed. 27.50 (ISBN 0-07-021620-7, C). McGraw.
Forisha, Barbara. Experience of Adolescence: Development in Context. 1983. text ed. 21.95x (ISBN 0-673-15353-3). Scott F.
Forkel, Johann N. Johann Sebastian Bach: His Life, Art, & Work. LC 75-125044. (Music Ser). 1970. Repr. of 1920 ed. lib. bdg. 32.50 (ISBN 0-306-70010-7). Da Capo.
Forker, Dom. The Ultimate Pro-Basketball Quiz Book. 1982. pap. 2.95 (ISBN 0-451-11842-1, AE1842, Sig). NAL.
--The Ultimate World Series Quiz Book. 1982. pap. 1.95 (ISBN 0-451-11788-3, AJ1788, Sig). NAL.
--Ultimate Yankee Baseball Quiz Book. 1982. pap. 2.50 (ISBN 0-451-11429-9, AE1429, Sig). NAL.
Forkner, Hamden L., jt. auth. see Brown, Frances A.
Forkner, Hamden L., jt. auth. see Brown, Francis A.
Forkner, Hamden L., et al. Forkner Shorthand. 4th ed. 206p. 8.96x (ISBN 0-912036-10-9); pap. 7.48x (ISBN 0-912036-11-7); tchr's. manual 1.28 (ISBN 0-912036-14-1). Forkner.
--Forkner Shorthand: Study Guide. 4th ed. 121p. 1968. pap. 5.36x (ISBN 0-912036-12-5). Forkner.
Forkner, Irvine, jt. auth. see McLeod, Raymond.
Forkner, Irvine F. Basic Programming for Business. (Illus.). 288p. 1978. pap. text ed. 16.95x (ISBN 0-13-066423-5). P-H.
Forkosch, Morris D. Outer Space & Legal Liability. 1982. lib. bdg. 43.50 (ISBN 90-247-2582-8, Pub. by Martinus Nijhoff Netherlands). Kluwer Boston.
Forland, Marvin. Concise Textbook of Nephrology. 1982. pap. text ed. 30.00 (ISBN 0-87488-177-3). Med Exam.
--Nephrology-A Review of Clinical Nephrology. 1977. pap. 20.50 o.p. (ISBN 0-87488-622-8). Med Exam.
Forlini, Gary, jt. auth. see Leo, Miriam.
Forliti, John E. Reverence for Life & Family Program. write for info.. Wm C Brown.
Form, William H., jt. auth. see Huber, Joan.
Formaad, William. Articulation Therapy Through Play. 1974. pap. 6.95 (ISBN 0-914420-51-8). Exceptional Pr Inc.
Formacek, V. & Kubeczka, K. H. Essential Oils Analysis by Capillary Gas Chromatography & Carbon-13 NMR Spectroscopy. 400p. 1982. 89.95x (ISBN 0-471-26218-8, Pub. by Wiley Heyden). Wiley.
Forman, Brenda & Kiernan, Thomas. B-Fifteen: The Miracle Vitamin. LC 78-73322. (Illus.). 1979. pap. 4.95 o.p. (ISBN 0-448-15172-3, G&D). Putnam Pub Group.
Forman, Chandlee. Early Manor & Plantation Houses of Maryland: Arch History. (Illus.). 272p. 1982. Repr. 35.00 (ISBN 0-686-98032-8). Bodine.
Forman, George E. & Kuschner, David S. The Child's Construction of Knowledge. LC 77-8676. (Illus.). 1977. text ed. 17.95 (ISBN 0-8185-0231-2). Brooks-Cole.
Forman, H. B. The Books of William Morris. 45.00x (ISBN 0-87556-290-6). Saifer.
Forman, H. Chandlee. Maryland Architecture. (Illus.). 102p. 10.00 (ISBN 0-686-36808-8). Md Hist.
Forman, Harrison. Report from Red China. LC 74-28417. (China in the 20th Century Ser). (Illus.). iv, 250p. 1975. Repr. of 1945 ed. lib. bdg. 29.50 (ISBN 0-306-70676-8). Da Capo.
Forman, James. Code Name Valkyrie: Count Claus von Stauffenberg & the Plot to Kill Hitler. LC 72-12581. (Illus.). 256p. (gr. 9-12). 1973. PLB 12.95 (ISBN 0-87599-188-2). S G Phillips.
--Communism. 1976. pap. 1.95 (ISBN 0-440-94611-5, LFL). Dell.
--Ring the Judas Bell. (gr. 6). 1977. pap. 1.25 o.p. (ISBN 0-440-97488-7, LFL). Dell.
--So Ends This Day. LC 78-125148. 256p. (gr. 7 up). 1970. 4.50 o.p. (ISBN 0-374-37120-2). FS&G.
Forman, James D. Call Back Yesterday. pap. 1.95 (ISBN 0-451-11851-0, AJ1851, Sig). NAL.
Forman, Joan & Strongman, Harry. The Romans. LC 77-86188. (Peoples of the Past Ser.). (Illus.). 1977. PLB 12.68 (ISBN 0-686-51160-3). Silver.
Forman, Michael L. Kapampangan Dictionary. McKaughan, Howard P., ed. LC 75-152464. (PALI Language Texts: Philippines). (Orig.). 1971. pap. text ed. 6.50x o.p. (ISBN 0-87022-266-X). UH Pr.
--Kapampangan Grammar Notes. McKaughan, Howard P., ed. LC 79-152465. (PALI Language Texts: Philippines). (Orig.). 1971. pap. text ed. 5.00x o.p. (ISBN 0-87022-267-8). UH Pr.
Forman, Rachel Z. Let Us Now Praise Obscure Women: A Comparative Study of Publicly Supported Unmarried Mothers in Government Housing in the United States & Britain. LC 82-17579. 240p. (Orig.). 1983. lib. bdg. 22.00 (ISBN 0-8191-2813-9); pap. text ed. 10.75 (ISBN 0-8191-2814-7). U Pr of Amer.
Forman, Robert. How to Control Your Allergies. 256p. (Orig.). 1979. pap. 3.25 (ISBN 0-915962-29-2). Larchmont Bks.
Forman, Werner, jt. auth. see Bancroft-Hunt, Norman.
Forman, Werner, jt. auth. see Storry, Richard.
Forman, William & Gavurin, Lester L. Elements of Arithmetic, Algebra & Geometry. LC 78-159159. 318p. 1972. text ed. 20.95x (ISBN 0-471-00654-8). Wiley.
Formanek, Ruth, jt. auth. see Gurian, Anita.
Formento, Dan. Rock Chronicle: Today in Rock History. (Illus.). 372p. (Orig.). 1982. pap. 9.95 (ISBN 0-933328-41-9). Delilah Bks.
Formisano, Ronald P. The Transformation of Political Culture: Massachusetts Parties, 1790s-1840s. (Illus.). 599p. 1983. 35.00 (ISBN 0-19-503124-5). Oxford U Pr.
Fornara, Charles W., ed. Archaic Times to the End of the Peloponnesian War: Translated Documents of Greece & Rome, No. 1. LC 79-54018. 232p. Date not set. price not set (ISBN 0-521-25019-6); pap. price not set (ISBN 0-521-29946-2). Cambridge U Pr.
Fornatale, Peter & Mills, Joshua E. Radio in the Television Age. LC 79-67675. 240p. 1983. pap. 7.95 (ISBN 0-87951-172-9). Overlook Pr.
Fornell. A Second Generation of Multivariate Analysis, 2 Vols. 444p. 1982. 44.50 ea. Vol. 1 (ISBN 0-03-062632-3). Vol. 2 (ISBN 0-03-062627-7). 79.50 set. Praeger.
Fornell, Claes. Consumer Input for Marketing Decisions: A Study of Corporate Departments for Consumer Affairs. LC 76-14397. 1976. 22.95 o.p. (ISBN 0-275-23480-0). Praeger.
Fornes & Hauptman. Wordplays: New American Drama. LC 80-83855. 1981. 14.95 (ISBN 0-933826-10-9); pap. 6.95 (ISBN 0-933826-11-7). Performing Arts.
Forney, J. W. Anecdotes of Public Men, 2 Vols. in 1. LC 70-87540. (American Scene Ser). 1970. Repr. of 1873 ed. lib. bdg. 95.00 (ISBN 0-306-71456-6). Da Capo.
Fornoff, Frederick, tr. see Alban, Laureano.
Forrer, Gordon R. Adventure of Tangerine Island. LC 81-81615. 1982. 7.95 (ISBN 0-87212-148-8). Libra.
Forrest, Anthony. Captain Justice: Secret Agent Against Napoleon. LC 82-60691. 320p. 1983. pap. 3.25 (ISBN 0-86721-234-9). Playboy Pbks.
--The Pandora Secret: A Captain Justice Story. 285p. 1982. 15.50 (ISBN 0-8090-7504-0). Hill & Wang.
Forrest, E. & Johnson, R. H. CAE, CAD, CAD-CAM Service Bureaus: Directory, Review, & Outlook, 1983. (Illus.). 130p. 1983. spiral bdg. 150.00 (ISBN 0-938484-09-5). Daratech.
Forrest, Earle R. The Snake Dance of the Hopi Indians. LC 61-15835. (Illus.). 8.95 (ISBN 0-87026-018-9). Westernlore.
Forrest, Gary G. Alcoholism & Human Sexuality. 390p. 1982. 34.50x (ISBN 0-398-04691-3). C C Thomas.
--The Diagnosis & Treatment of Alcoholism. 2nd ed. 364p. 1978. 22.50x (ISBN 0-398-03779-5); pap. 15.75x (ISBN 0-398-03780-9). C C Thomas.
--How to Cope with a Teenage Drinker: New Alternatives & Hope for Parents & Families. LC 82-73023. 128p. 1983. 9.95 (ISBN 0-689-11346-3). Atheneum.
Forrest, Helen & Libby, Bill. I Had the Craziest Dream: Helen Forrest & the Big Band Era. LC 81-7756. 256p. 1982. 13.95 (ISBN 0-698-11096-X, Coward). Putnam Pub Group.
Forrest, Irene S., et al, eds. Phenothiazines & Structurally Related Drugs. LC 73-88571. (Advances in Biochemical Psychopharmacology Ser.: Vol. 9). 840p. 1974. 67.50 (ISBN 0-911216-61-8). Raven.
Forrest, James F. & Greaves, Richard L. John Bunyan: A Reference Guide. 1982. lib. bdg. 50.00 (ISBN 0-8161-8267-1, Hall Reference). G K Hall.
Forrest, James T. Bill Gollings: The Man & His Art. LC 78-71374. (Illus.). 1979. 17.00 o.p. (ISBN 0-87358-182-2); pap. 10.00 o.p. (ISBN 0-87358-192-X). Northland.
Forrest, Jane & Watson, Margaret. Practical Nursing & Anatomy for Pupil Nurses. 272p. 1981. pap. text ed. 12.95 (ISBN 0-7131-4392-4). E Arnold.
Forrest, John F. Explorations in Australia, 3 vols. in 1. Incl. Vol. 1. Explorations in Search of Dr. Leichardt & Party; Vol. 2. From Perth to Adelaide, Around the Great Australian Bight; Vol. 3. From Champion Bay, Across the Desert to the Telegraph & to Adelaide. LC 68-55186. 1968. Repr. of 1875 ed. lib. bdg. 17.75x (ISBN 0-8371-1648-1, FOAU). Greenwood.
Forrest, Lewis C., Jr. Training for the Hospitality Industry: Techniques to Improve. Harless, Marjorie, ed. 1983. text ed. 34.95 (ISBN 0-86612-009-2). Educ Inst Am Hotel.
Forrest, Mary & Olson, Margot. Exploring Speech Communication: An Introduction. 433p. 1981. pap. text ed. 14.95 (ISBN 0-8299-0381-X). West Pub.
Forrest, Ray & Henderson, Jeff. Urban Political Economy & Social Theory. 220p. 1982. text ed. 32.00x (ISBN 0-566-00493-3). Gower Pub Ltd.
Forrest, Richard. Death Through the Looking Glass. LC 77-15438. 1977. 7.95 o.p. (ISBN 0-672-52379-5). Bobbs.
Forrestal, Dan. Faith, Hope & Five Thousand Dollars: Story of Monsanto. 1977. 12.95 o.p. (ISBN 0-671-22784-X). S&S.
Forrestal, Dan J. The Kernel & the Bean: The 75-Year Story of the A. E. Staley Corp. 1982. 15.95 (ISBN 0-671-45825-6). S&S.
Forrester, A. R., et al. Organic Chemistry of Stable Free Radicals. 1968. 55.50 (ISBN 0-12-262050-X). Acad Pr.
Forrester, D. A., jt. ed. see Wanless, P. T.
Forrester, D. M., et al. The Radiology of Joint Disease. 2nd ed. LC 77-27747. 1978. text ed. 47.50 (ISBN 0-7216-3822-8). Saunders.
Forrester, David. Listening with the Heart. LC 78-70822. 96p. 1979. pap. 3.50 (ISBN 0-8091-2183-2). Paulist Pr.
Forrester, James & Gray, Douglas M. Man in His World Series, 10 bks. Incl. China (ISBN 0-672-71058-7); Eskimo (ISBN 0-672-71060-9); Gifts of the Nile (ISBN 0-672-71062-5); Grassland Safari (ISBN 0-672-71064-1); Indians of the Plains (ISBN 0-672-71066-8); Kings of Peru. o.p. (ISBN 0-637-11119-2); Mexico Emerges (ISBN 0-672-71068-4); The Navigators. (Incl. atlas) (ISBN 0-672-71072-2); Nomadic Journey. o.p.; Greeks: From Longhouse to Blast Furnace. o.p. (ISBN 0-672-71305-5). (gr. 4-8). text ed. 2.40 ea. o.p.; tchrs' guide 0.80 ea. o.p. Bobbs.
Forrester, Jay W. Collected Papers of Jay W. Forrester. LC 73-89547. (Illus.). 1975. 47.50x (ISBN 0-262-06065-5). MIT Pr.
--Principles of Systems. 2nd ed. 1968. pap. 15.00x (ISBN 0-262-56017-8). MIT Pr.
--Urban Dynamics. 1969. 27.50x (ISBN 0-262-06026-4). MIT Pr.
Forrester, Nathan B. The Life Cycle of Economic Development. LC 73-86760. (Illus.). 1972. 27.50x (ISBN 0-262-06067-1). MIT Pr.
Forrester, Victoria. The Magnificent Moo. LC 82-13781. (Illus.). 40p. (ps-1). write for info. (ISBN 0-689-30954-6). Atheneum.
Forrest-Thompson, Veronica. Poetic Artifice: A Theory of Twentieth Century Poetry. 1979. 26.00 (ISBN 0-312-61798-4). St Martin.
Forristal, Desmond. Kolbe: A Saint in Auschwitz. (Patron Bk.). Orig. Title: Maximillian of Auschwitz. 191p. (Orig.). Date not set. pap. 2.95 (ISBN 0-89944-066-5, P066-5). D Bosco Multimedia.
Forristal, Desmond & O'Fiaich, Tomas. Oliver Plunkett. LC 76-5978. 1976. pap. 3.95 o.p. (ISBN 0-87973-681-X). Our Sunday Visitor.
Forry, John I. A Practical Guide to Foreign Investment in the United States, Suppl. 2nd ed. 350p. 1983. text ed. 80.00 (ISBN 0-906524-05-9); pap. text ed. 30.00 (ISBN 0-906524-06-7). BNA.
Forsberg, Foy. Beginner's Guide to Shorecasting. (Illus.). 183p. 1975. 10.95 o.s.i. (ISBN 0-7207-0753-6). Transatlantic.
Forsberg, Gerald. Salvage from the Sea. (Illus.). 179p. 1978. 14.95 (ISBN 0-7100-8698-9). Routledge & Kegan.
Forsberg, Ray. Sea Angling from the Shore. (Illus.). 192p. 1982. 19.95 (ISBN 0-7153-8147-4). David & Charles.
Forsberg, Roberta J. Antoine De Saint-Exupery & David Beaty: Poets of a New Dimension. lib. bdg. 11.95 o.p. (ISBN 0-8057-9001-2, Twayne). G K Hall.
--The World of David Beaty: The Place of Images. lib. bdg. 9.95 o.p. (ISBN 0-8057-5789-9, Twayne). G K Hall.
Forsdale, Louis. Perspectives on Communication. LC 80-16616. (Speech Ser.). (Illus.). 400p. 1981. text ed. 14.95 (ISBN 0-201-04571-0); tchrs' manual avail. A-W.
Forshall, Josiah & Madden, Frederic, eds. The Holy Bible: John Wycliffe's English Bible, 4 vols. LC 78-63193. (Heresies of the Early Christian & Medieval Era: Second Ser.). 1982. Repr. of 1850 ed. 475.00 set (ISBN 0-404-16240-1). AMS Pr.
Forshaw, Joseph. Birds of Paradise & Bower Birds. LC 79-51036. (Illus.). 1979. 200.00 (ISBN 0-87923-291-9). Godine.
Forshaw, Joseph M. Parrots of the World. (Illus.). 1977. Repr. of 1973 ed. 34.95 (ISBN 0-87666-959-3, PS-753). TFH Pubns.
Forsky, V., ed. see Romen, A. S.
Forsling, Mary. Anti-Diuretic Hormone, Vol. 3. Horrobin, D. F., ed. (Annual Research Reviews Ser.). 1979. 26.00 (ISBN 0-88831-044-7). Eden Pr.
Forsling, Mary L. Anti-Diuretic Hormone, Vol. 1. (Annual Research Reviews Ser.). 1977. 19.20 (ISBN 0-904406-51-2). Eden Pr.
--Anti-Diuretic Hormone, Vol. 2. LC 78-309279. (Annual Research Reviews). 1978. 24.00 (ISBN 0-88831-016-1). Eden Pr.
--Antidiuretic Hormone, Vol. 4. Horrobin, D. F., ed. (Annual Research Reviews Ser.). 165p. 1980. 26.00 (ISBN 0-88831-072-2). Eden Pr.
Forsman, John, ed. Recipe Index, Nineteen Seventy-One: The Eater's Guide to Periodical Literature. LC 72-884. 1972. 35.00x (ISBN 0-8103-0526-7). Gale.
--Recipe Index, Nineteen Seventy: The Eater's Guide to Periodical Literature. LC 72-884. 1972. 35.00x (ISBN 0-8103-0525-9). Gale.
Forssberg, Arne, jt. ed. see Errera, Maurice.
Forst, Martin L., ed. Sentencing Reform: Experiments in Reducing Disparity. (Sage Criminal Justice System Annuals: Vol. 17). (Illus.). 288p. 1982. 25.00 (ISBN 0-8039-1858-5); pap. 12.00 (ISBN 0-8039-1859-3). Sage.
Forste, L. H, jt. ed. see Schmidt, H. L.
Forstel, H, jt. ed. see Schmidt, H. L.
Forster, A. S., tr. see Crouzet, Francois.
Forster, Arnold & Epstein, Benjamin R. Cross-Currents. LC 72-591. 382p. 1956. Repr. lib. bdg. 16.25x (ISBN 0-8371-5993-8, FOCC). Greenwood.
--The New Anti-Semitism. 324p. Repr. 5.00 o.p. (ISBN 0-686-95109-3). ADL.
Forster, Arnold, jt. auth. see Epstein, Benjamin.
Forster, C. Oxidation Ditches. (Water Resources Engineering Ser.). 300p. 1983. text ed. 60.00 (ISBN 0-273-08527-1). Pitman Pub MA.
Forster, C., jt. auth. see Calleley, A.
Forster, D. F. see Pickersgill, J. W.
Forster, E. M. Albergo Empedocle & Other Early Writings. Thomson, George H., ed. LC 79-162435. 1971. 7.95 o.s.i. (ISBN 0-87140-540-7). Liveright.
--Alexandria: A History & A Guide. new ed. LC 74-78549. 243p. 1974. 14.95 o.p. (ISBN 0-87951-023-4). Overlook Pr.
--Aspects of the Novel. LC 27-23181. 1956. pap. 2.95 (ISBN 0-15-609180-1, Harv). HarBraceJ.
--E. M. Forster's Letters to Donald Windham. 1975. wrappers, ltd. ed. 35.00x o.p. (ISBN 0-917366-04-2). S Campbell.
--The Hill of Devi & Other Indian Writings. Stalybrass, Oliver, ed. (The Abinger Edition of E. M. Forster Ser.). 400p. 1983. text ed. 55.00 (ISBN 0-8419-5828-9). Holmes & Meier.
--The Hill of Devl. LC 53-9224. (Illus.). 1971. pap. 3.95 (ISBN 0-15-640265-3, HB204, Harv). HarBraceJ.
--Howards End. Stallybrass, Oliver, ed. (Abinger Edition of E. M. Forster Ser.). 1978. text ed. 22.50x (ISBN 0-8419-5806-8). Holmes & Meier.
--Longest Journey. 1922. 5.95 o.p. (ISBN 0-394-70040-6). Knopf.
--Maurice. 1975. pap. 4.95 o.p. (ISBN 0-452-25195-8, Z5195, Plume). NAL.
--Only Connect: Letters to Indian Friends. Husain, Syed H., ed. 104p. 1981. text ed. 5.50x o.p. (ISBN 0-391-02425-6). Humanities.
--A Passage to India. LC 43-1812. (Modern Classic Ser). 1949. 11.95 (ISBN 0-15-171141-0). HarBraceJ.
--Room with a View. (YA) 1923. 6.75 o.s.i. (ISBN 0-394-70187-9). Knopf.
Forster, Elborg, tr. see Furet, Francois M.
Forster, John. The Life & Adventures of Oliver Goldsmith: A Biography, 4 bks. 704p. 1982. Repr. of 1848 ed. Set. lib. bdg. 100.00 (ISBN 0-89984-209-7). Century Bookbindery.
Forster, Kurt. New West Coast Architecture. LC 82-42533. (Illus.). 120p. 1983. pap. 18.50 (ISBN 0-8478-0463-1). Rizzoli Intl.
Forster, Leonard, ed. Penguin Book of German Verse. (Poets Ser.). (Orig., Ger., With prose translations). (YA) (gr. 9 up). 1957. pap. 4.95 (ISBN 0-14-042036-3). Penguin.
Forster, Leonard W. Icy Fire: Four Studies in European Petrarchism. LC 71-77288. (Illus.). 1969. 29.50 (ISBN 0-521-07495-9); pap. 9.95x (ISBN 0-521-29521-1). Cambridge U Pr.
--Poet's Tongues: Multilingualism in Literature. LC 76-112469. 1971. text ed. 29.95 (ISBN 0-521-07766-4). Cambridge U Pr.
Forster, M. C., jt. auth. see Beck, P. G.
Forster, O. Analysis: Differential & Integralrechnung einer Veranderlichen. 2nd ed. Incl. No. 1. Differential & Integralrechnung Einer Veranderlichen. 208p. 1976 (ISBN 3-528-07224-5); No. 2. Differentialrechnung im Rn Gewohnliche Differentialgleichungen. 1977. (Mathematik Grundkurs Ser.: No. 1). 208p. (Ger., No. 2. differentialrechnung im Rn Gewognliche Differentialgleichungen). 1977. pap. 9.50. Birkhauser.
Forster, Peter G. The Esperanto Movement. (Contributions to the Sociology of Language Ser.: No. 32). xiv, 413p. 1982. 60.00 (ISBN 90-279-3399-5). Mouton.
Forster, R. R. Small Land Animals of New Zealand. rev ed. (Illus.). 175p. 1975. pap. 13.55x (ISBN 0-8002-0482-4). Intl Pubns Serv.
Forster, Walter. Numerical Solution of Highly Nonlinear Problems. 1980. 59.75 (ISBN 0-444-85427-4). Elsevier.
Forstner, H., jt. ed. see Gnaiger, E.
Forsyth, Anne. Cheap & Cheerful: Homemaking on a Budget. (Illus.). 104p. 1973. 6.95 o.p. (ISBN 0-263-05236-2). Transatlantic.
Forsyth, Benjamin. Unified Design of Reinforced Concrete Members. LC 80-16123. 656p. 1980. Repr. of 1971 ed. 31.50 (ISBN 0-89874-189-0). Krieger.
Forsyth, Donelson R. An Introduction to Group Dynamics. LC 82-12783. (Psychology Ser.). 512p. 1982. text ed. 24.95 (ISBN 0-534-01225-6). Brooks-Cole.
Forsyth, Elizabeth H., jt. auth. see Hyde, Margaret O.
Forsyth, Frederick. The Dogs of War. LC 73-19103. 416p. 1974. 11.95 (ISBN 0-670-27753-3). Viking Pr.
Forsyth, J., ed. see Vinokur, G. O.
Forsyth, J. B., jt. auth. see Brown, P. Jane.
Forsyth, Patrick. Running an Effective Sales Office. 142p. 1980. text ed. 37.25x (ISBN 0-566-02185-4). Gower Pub Ltd.
Forsyth, Richards. Pascal at Work & Play. 1982. 21.00x (ISBN 0-412-23370-3, Pub. by Chapman & Hall); pap. 13.95 (ISBN 0-412-23380-0). Methuen Inc.

Forsyth, Roger, et al. Family Pactice Self Assessment & Review. 3rd ed. 1982. 27.50 (ISBN 0-87488-261-3). Med Exam.

Forsyth, William. Hortensius the Advocate: An Historical Essay on the Office & Duties of an Advocate. xvii, 404p. 1982. Repr. of 1882 ed. lib. bdg. 35.00x (ISBN 0-8377-0617-3). Rothman.

Forsythe, A. I., et al. Computer Science: A First Course. 2nd ed. LC 74-34244. 876p. 1975. pap. text ed. 31.95 (ISBN 0-471-26681-7); tchrs.' manual avail. (ISBN 0-471-26682-5). Wiley.

Forsythe, Alan B., ed. Control Language Summary. (BMDP Statistical Software). 56p. (Orig.). 1980. pap. 3.00 (ISBN 0-935386-01-7). BMDP Stat.

Forsythe, Alexander I., et al. Computer Science: Programming in BASIC. 148p. 1976. pap. 11.95x (ISBN 0-471-26684-1). Wiley.

Forsythe, Alexandra I., et al. Computer Science: Programming in FORTRAN IV with WATFOR-WATFIV. LC 74-96044. 210p. 1975. pap. 9.50x (ISBN 0-471-26685-X). Wiley.

Forsythe, George, ed. see Sammet, Jean E.

Forsythe, George E. & Moler, C. Computer Solution of Linear Algebraic Systems. 1967. ref. ed. 21.95 (ISBN 0-13-165779-8). P-H.

Forsythe, George E., et al. Computer Methods for Mathematical Computations. (Illus.). 1977. ref. ed. 29.95x (ISBN 0-13-165332-6). P-H.

Forsythe, J. M., ed. see World Conference on First Medical Informatics, Aug. 5-10, 1974.

Fort, Joel. Alcohol: Our Biggest Drug Problem. (Illus.). 180p. 1973. 23.50 (ISBN 0-07-021598-7, C); pap. 16.50 (ISBN 0-07-021599-5). McGraw.

Fort, Joel & Salin, Lothar. To Dream the Perfect Organization. LC 80-53829. (Illus.). 144p. 1981. text ed. 14.95 (ISBN 0-89914-005-X); pap. text ed. 7.95. Third Party Pub.

Forte, Allen. The Compositional Matrix. LC 73-4337. 1974. Repr. of 1961 ed. lib. bdg. 16.50 (ISBN 0-306-70577-X). Da Capo.

Forte, Allen & Gilbert, Steven E. Introduction to Schenkerian Analysis: Form & Content in Tonal Music. 350p. 1982. text ed. 24.95x (ISBN 0-393-95192-8); inst. manual avail. (ISBN 0-393-95230-4). Norton.

Forte, David F. The Supreme Court. (American Government Ser.). (Illus.). (gr. 7 up). 1979. PLB 8.90 s&l (ISBN 0-531-02267-6). Watts.

Forte, Francesco, ed. see International Institute of Public Finance, 35th Congress, 1979.

Forte, Imogene. The Kids' Stuff Book of Patterns, Projects, & Plans to Perk Up Early Learning Programs. LC 82-83051. (Illus.). 200p. (ps-1). 1982. pap. text ed. 9.95 (ISBN 0-86530-054-2, IP 54-2). Incentive Pubs.

--The Me I'm Learning to Be. (Illus.). 80p. (gr. 4-6). 1983. pap. text ed. 5.95 (ISBN 0-86530-061-5). Incentive Pubns.

--Read About It! Beginning Readers. LC 82-81720. (Read About It Ser.). (Illus.). 80p. (gr. k-1). 1982. pap. text ed. 5.95 (ISBN 0-86530-005-4, IP 05-4). Incentive Pubns.

--Write about It Series, 3 vols. Incl. Beginning Readers. 80p. (gr. k-1). pap. text ed. 5.95 (ISBN 0-86530-044-5); Primary. 80p. (gr. 2-4). pap. text ed. 5.95 (ISBN 0-86530-045-3); Middle Grades. 80p. (gr. 4-6). 1983. pap. text ed. 5.95 (ISBN 0-86530-046-1). (Illus.). (gr. k-6). 1983. pap. text ed. 16.95 set (ISBN 0-86530-043-7, IP 43-7). Incentive Pubns.

Forte, Imogene & MacKenzie, Joy. For the Love of Ladybug. LC 77-83783. (Days of Wonder Paper). (Illus.). (ps). 1979. pap. 2.95 (ISBN 0-913916-89-7, IP89-7). Incentive Pubns.

--Of Rhinoceros Wings & More Usual Things. LC 77-83784. (Days of Wonder Paper Set Ser.). (Illus.). 64p. (ps). 1979. pap. 2.95 (ISBN 0-913916-92-7, IP92-7). Incentive Pubns.

Forte, Imogene, et al. Kids' Stuff: Reading & Language Experiences, Intermediate-Jr High. LC 77-670152. (The Kids' Stuff Set). (Illus.). 368p. (gr. 4-8). 1973. 10.95 (ISBN 0-913916-02-1, IP 02-1). Incentive Pubns.

Forte, M. Cecile, jt. auth. see Lewis, Stephen C.

Forte, Nancy. Warrior in Art. LC 65-29039. (Fine Art Books). (Illus.). (gr. 5-11). 1966. PLB 4.95g (ISBN 0-8225-0162-7). Lerner Pubns.

Fortenbaug, Doris & Knust, Louise H. The Flea Market Cookbook. 59p. 1971. pap. 2.00 (ISBN 0-686-36730-8). Md Hist.

Fortenbaugh, William W., ed. On Stoic & Peripatetic Ethics: The Work of Arius Didymus. (Rutgers University Studies in Classical Humanities: Vol. 1). (Illus.). 352p. 1983. text ed. 29.95 (ISBN 0-87855-462-9). Transaction Bks.

Forter, Elizabeth T., ed. see Shaw, George B.

Fortes, Meyer. Time & Social Structure & Other Essays. (Monographs on Social Anthropology: No.40). (Illus.). 1970. text ed. 26.25x (ISBN 0-391-00112-4, Athlone Pr). Humanities.

Fortescue-Foulkes, J. Seasonal Breeding & Migrations of the Desert Locust (Schistocerca Gregaria Forskal) in South-Western Asia. 1953. 35.00x (ISBN 0-85135-015-1, Pub. by Centre Overseas Research). State Mutual Bk.

Fortey, Richard. Fossils: The Key to the Past. LC 82-8371. (Illus.). 169p. 1982. 24.95 (ISBN 0-442-22615-2). Van Nos Reinhold.

Forth, Inc. & Brodie, Leo. Starting Forth: An Introduction to the FORTH Language & Operating Systems for Beginners & Professionals. LC 81-11837. (P-H Software Ser.). (Illus.). 384p. 1982. text ed. 21.95 (ISBN 0-13-842930-8); pap. text ed. 17.95 (ISBN 0-13-842922-7). P-H.

Forth, W. & Rummel, W., eds. Pharmacology of Intestinal Absorption: Gastrointestinal Absorption of Drugs. 1975. text ed. 150.00 (ISBN 0-08-016210-X). Pergamon.

Forthofer, Ronald N. & Lehnen, Robert G. Public Program Analysis: A New Categorical Data Approach. (Illus.). 225p. 1981. 29.95 (ISBN 0-534-97974-2); solutions manual 4.95 (ISBN 0-534-01133-0). Lifetime Learn.

Fortier, Ed. One Survived. LC 78-10530. (Illus.). 1979. pap. 2.95 (ISBN 0-88240-118-1). Alaska Northwest.

Fortiner, Virginia J. Science-Hobby Book of Archaeology. rev. ed. LC 62-11633. (Science Hobby Bks). (Illus.). (gr. 5-10). 1968. PLB 4.95g (ISBN 0-8225-0552-5). Lerner Pubns.

Fortino, Denise, jt. auth. see Haberman, Fredric.

Fortman, E. J., tr. see De Margerie, Bertrand.

Fortman, Edmund J. Theology of Man & Grace: Commentary. 1966. pap. 4.95 o.p. (ISBN 0-02-816630-2). Glencoe.

Fortman, Jan. First to Sail the World Alone: Joshua Slocum. LC 78-13720. (Famous Firsts Ser.). (Illus.). 1978. PLB 10.76 (ISBN 0-89547-054-3). Silver.

Fortner, Ethel. Nervous on the Curves. Bayes, Ronald H., ed. LC 82-62748. 60p. (Orig.). 1982. pap. 7.00 (ISBN 0-932662-40-4). St Andrews NC.

Fortson, James C., jt. auth. see Clutter, Jerome L.

Fortun, Michael, jt. ed. see Nader, Ralph.

Fortunato, Donald J. Two Thousand Miles on the Appalachian Trail. 1983. 6.00 (ISBN 0-686-26176-3). D J Fortunato.

Fortunato, Pat. All American Foozles. (Orig.). (gr. 7-12). 1980. pap. 1.25 o.p. (ISBN 0-440-90090-5, LFL). Dell.

--Dino-Mite Foozles. (YA) (gr. 6 up). 1979. pap. 1.25 o.p. (ISBN 0-440-91950-9, LFL). Dell.

--Spaced Out Foozles. (YA) 1979. pap. 1.25 o.p. (ISBN 0-440-97766-5, LFL). Dell.

Fortunato, Peter. A Bell or a Hook. LC 77-22186. 45p. 1977. 3.50 (ISBN 0-87886-087-8). Ithaca Hse.

Fortune, Dion, ed. The Esoteric Orders & Their Work. 144p. 1983. pap. 7.95 (ISBN 0-85030-310-9). Newcastle Pub.

Fortune Editorial Staff. The Exploding Metropolis. LC 76-5781. (Illus.). 193p. 1976. Repr. of 1958 ed. lib. bdg. 17.50x (ISBN 0-8371-8823-7, FMEM). Greenwood.

Fortune, Marie M. Sexual Violence: The Unmentionable Sin: An Ethical & Pastoral Perspective. 256p. (Orig.). 1983. pap. 8.95 (ISBN 0-8298-0652-0). Pilgrim NY.

Fortune, Nigel, ed. see Cross, Eric.

Fortune, Richard. Alexander Sukhovo-Kobylin. (World Authors Ser.). 1982. lib. bdg. 18.95 (ISBN 0-8057-6515-8, Twayne). G K Hall.

Fortune, Stephen A. Merchants & Jews: The Struggle for British West Indian Commerce, 1650-1750. 1983. write for info (ISBN 0-8130-0735-6). U Presses Fla.

Forty, George & Batchelor, John. United States Tanks of World War II in Action. (Illus.). 160p. 1983. 16.95 (ISBN 0-7137-1214-7, Pub. by Blandford Pr England). Sterling.

Forve, Guy. Alexander MacKenzie: Lone Courage. (American Explorers Ser.: No. 12). (Orig.). 1983. pap. 2.95 (ISBN 0-440-00066-1, Emerald). Dell.

Fosdick, Harry E. The Meaning of Prayer. 1982. pap. 2.95 (ISBN 0-687-23960-5, Festival). Abingdon.

--The Meaning of Service. 224p. 1983. pap. 3.75 (ISBN 0-687-23961-3). Abingdon.

--On Being a Real Person. LC 76-49749. 1977. pap. 3.95i o.p. (ISBN 0-06-062790-5, RD 205, HarpR). Har-Row.

Fosdick, L., ed. Performance Evaluation of Numerical Software. 1979. 42.75 (ISBN 0-444-85330-8, North Holland). Elsevier.

Fosdick, Raymond B. American Police Systems. LC 69-14925. (Criminology, Law Enforcement, & Social Problems Ser.: No. 53). (With intro. added). 1969. o. p. 18.00 (ISBN 0-87585-053-7); pap. 8.50x (ISBN 0-87585-909-7). Patterson Smith.

--European Police Systems. LC 69-14926. (Criminology, Law Enforcement, & Social Problems Ser.: No. 54). (With intro. added). 1969. 18.00x (ISBN 0-87585-054-5); pap. 8.50 (ISBN 0-87585-910-0). Patterson Smith.

FOSECO, see Foundry Services Ltd.

Foseco Minsep Group. The Business Traveller's Handbook: How to Get along with People in 100 Countries. 300p. 1983. 14.95 (ISBN 0-13-107797-X); pap. 7.95 (ISBN 0-13-107789-9). P-H.

Foshay, Arthur W., ed. Professional As Educator. LC 73-120602. 1970. pap. text ed. 7.50x (ISBN 0-8077-1378-3). Tchrs Coll.

Foskett, A. C. The Subject Approach to Information. 3rd ed. xvi, 476p. 1977. 17.50 o.p. (ISBN 0-208-01546-9, Linnet). Shoe String.

--The Subject Approach to Information. 4th ed. 480p. 1982. 31.50 (ISBN 0-85157-313-4, Pub. by Bingley England); pap. 20.50 (ISBN 0-85157-339-8, Pub. by Bingley England). Shoe String.

Foskett, D. J. Classification & Indexing in the Social Sciences. 2nd ed. 1975. 17.95 o.p. (ISBN 0-408-70644-9). Butterworth.

Foskett, Daphne. Samuel Cooper (Sixteen Nine to Sixteen Seventy-Two) (Illus.). 151p. 1974. 17.95. Faber & Faber.

Fosler, Scott & Berger, Renee A. Public-Private Partnership in American Cities: Seven Case Studies. LC 82-48016. 368p. 1982. 24.95x (ISBN 0-669-05834-3). Lexington Bks.

Foss, Arthur. Country House Treasures of Britain. (Illus.). 352p. 1980. 25.00 o.p. (ISBN 0-399-12549-3). Putnam Pub Group.

--Ionian Islands. 1970. 12.00 o.p. (ISBN 0-571-08944-5). Transatlantic.

Foss, Christopher. Jane's World Armoured Fighting Vehicles. LC 76-57887. 1977. 25.00 o.p. (ISBN 0-312-44047-2). St Martin.

Foss, Christopher, ed. Jane's Military Vehicles & Ground Support Equipment, 1983. (Jane's Yearbooks Ser.). (Illus.). 700p. 1983. 140.00x (ISBN 0-86720-647-0). Sci Bks Intl.

Foss, Clive. Ephesus After Antiquity. LC 78-1152. (Illus.). 1980. 37.50 (ISBN 0-521-22086-6). Cambridge U Pr.

Foss, Donald J. & Hakes, David T. Psycholinguistics: An Introduction to the Psychology of Language. LC 77-27826. (Experimental Psychology Ser.). (Illus.). 1978. ref. 23.95 (ISBN 0-13-732446-4). P-H.

Foss, F. F. Ragweed the Pixie, the Pixies & the Great Flood: Ragweed & the Coldest Winter. (Illus.). 48p. 1982. pap. 4.00 (ISBN 0-682-49923-4). Exposition.

Foss, Hubert. Ralph Vaughan Williams: A Study. LC 74-9042. (Illus.). 219p. 1974. Repr. of 1950 ed. lib. bdg. 18.00x (ISBN 0-8371-7610-7, FORW). Greenwood.

Foss, Merle L. & Garrick, James G. Ski Conditioning. LC 77-24553. (American College of Sports Medicine Ser.). 179p. 1978. text ed. 18.50x (ISBN 0-471-26764-3). Wiley.

Foss, Murray F. The U. S. National Income & Product Accounts: Selected Topics. LC 82-11081. (National Bureau of Economic Research-Studies in Income & Wealth: No. 47). (Illus.). 1983. lib. bdg. 43.00x (ISBN 0-226-25728-2). U of Chicago Pr.

Foss, Phillip, Jr. Somata. (Illus.). 1982. 34.50 (ISBN 0-931460-18-2). Bieler.

Foss, Phillip O., ed. see Western Resources Conference - 1968.

Foss, William, jt. auth. see Bergaust, Erik.

Foss, William O. Here Is Your Hobby: Skiing. (Here Is Your Hobby Ser.). (Illus.). (gr. 5 up). 1964. PLB 5.29 o.p. (ISBN 0-399-60253-4). Putnam Pub Group.

Fossard, Esta de, jt. auth. see Rinsky, Lee A.

Fossum, Timothy V. & Gatterdam, Ronald W. Calculus & the Computer: An Approach to Problem Solving. 1980. pap. text ed. 12.50x (ISBN 0-673-15158-1). Scott F.

Foster. Cryptanalysis for Microcomputers. Date not set. 14.95 (ISBN 0-686-82007-X, 5174). Hayden.

--Introduction to Earth Science. 1982. 24.95 (ISBN 0-8053-2660-X); instr's manual 4.95 (ISBN 0-8053-2661-8). Benjamin-Cummings.

Foster, A. Durwood. God Who Loves. (Faith & Life Bk). 1971. pap. 3.50 o.p. (ISBN 0-02-802360-9). Glencoe.

Foster, Alan D. Clash of the Titans. 1981. pap. 3.25 (ISBN 0-446-96675-4). Warner Bks.

--For Love of Mother-Not. 256p. (Orig.). 1983. pap. 2.95 (ISBN 0-345-30511-6, Del Rey). Ballantine.

--Krull. 240p. 1983. pap. 2.95 (ISBN 0-446-30642-8). Warner Bks.

--Spellsinger. 288p. 1983. pap. 2.95 (ISBN 0-446-90352-3). Warner Bks.

--The Thing. 1982. pap. 2.75 (ISBN 0-553-20477-7). Bantam.

Foster, Anthony M. The Book of Hitchin. 1981. 39.50x o.p. (ISBN 0-86023-138-0, Pub. by Barracuda England). State Mutual Bk.

Foster Associates. Energy Prices, 1960-73. LC 74-9503. (Ford Foundation Energy Policy Project Ser.). 280p. 1974. prof ref 25.00 (ISBN 0-88410-327-7); pap. text ed. 15.00 (ISBN 0-88410-330-7). Ballinger Pub.

Foster, Blanche F. East Central Africa. LC 80-2684. (First Bks.). (gr. 4 up). 1981. PLB 8.90 (ISBN 0-531-04272-3). Watts.

Foster, Brian. Commerce & Ethnic Differences: The Case of the Mons in Thailand. 100p. 1982. pap. 11.00 (ISBN 0-89680-112-8, Ohio U Ctr Intl). Ohio U Pr.

Foster, Bruce D., jt. auth. see Stark, Rodney.

Foster, C. A., et al. Introduction to the Administration of Justice. 2nd ed. (Administration of Justice Ser.). 1979. text ed. 21.95 o.p. (ISBN 0-471-04079-7). Wiley.

Foster, Carrie W. The Different World & Other Stories. 1979. 4.95 o.p. (ISBN 0-533-04084-1). Vantage.

Foster, Catharine O. The Organic Gardener. 1972. 10.95 (ISBN 0-394-47210-1); pap. 8.95 (ISBN 0-394-71785-6). Knopf.

Foster, Catherine O. The Organic Gardener. pap. 8.95 (ISBN 0-394-71785-6, V-785, Vin). Random.

Foster, Charles. First Steps: Bible Stories for Children. (Illus.). (gr. 5-8). 1960. pap. 2.50 o.p. (ISBN 0-8024-0023-X). Moody.

Foster, Clifford E., jt. auth. see Jarolimek, John.

Foster, Daniel. A Layman's Guide to Modern Medicine. 1980. 14.95 o.p. (ISBN 0-671-24366-7). S&S.

Foster, Daniel W. Modern Medicine: A Doctor Explains to the Layman. 1981. 11.95 o.p. (ISBN 0-671-24366-7). S&S.

Foster, Dave, ed. Jerusalem: The Christian Herald Photoguide. LC 79-57167. (Illus.). 128p. 1980. 14.95 o.p. (ISBN 0-915684-60-8). Christian Herald.

Foster, David. A Primer for Writing Teachers: Theories, Theorists, Issues, Problems. 192p. (Orig.). 1983. pap. text ed. 8.50x (ISBN 0-86709-053-7). Boynton Cook Pubs.

Foster, David, ed. Latin American Government Leaders. LC 75-15809. 1975. 8.00x (ISBN 0-87918-021-8); pap. 5.50x (ISBN 0-686-96665-1). ASU Lat Am St.

Foster, David & Stern, Jossi, eds. People of the Book. 120p. 9.95 o.p. (ISBN 0-529-05639-9, 53405). Cook.

Foster, David W. Augusto Roa Bastos. (World Authors Ser.). 1978. lib. bdg. 15.95 (ISBN 0-8057-6348-1, Twayne). G K Hall.

--The Early Spanish Ballad. (World Authors Ser.). lib. bdg. 13.95 (ISBN 0-8057-2288-2, Twayne). G K Hall.

--The Marques de Santillana. (World Authors Ser.: Spain: No. 154). lib. bdg. 7.95 o.p. (ISBN 0-8057-2790-6, Twayne). G K Hall.

--Puerto Rican Literature: A Bibliography of Secondary Sources. LC 82-6198. 256p. 1982. lib. bdg. 35.00 (ISBN 0-313-23419-1, FPR/). Greenwood.

Foster, David W. & Foster, Virginia R. Luis de Gongora. (World Authors Ser.). 1973. lib. bdg. 15.95 (ISBN 0-8057-2386-2, Twayne). G K Hall.

--Research Guide to Argentine Literature. LC 70-9731. 1970. 11.00 o.p. (ISBN 0-8108-0298-8). Scarecrow.

Foster, David W., ed. Chilean Literature: A Working Bibliography of Secondary Sources. (Reference Publications). 1978. lib. bdg. 31.00 (ISBN 0-8161-8180-2, Hall Reference). G K Hall.

Foster, David W. & Reis, Roberto, eds. A Dictionary of Contemporary Brazilian Authors. LC 79-29686. 152p. 1982. 18.95x (ISBN 0-87918-051-X); pap. 11.95x (ISBN 0-686-97323-2). ASU Lat Am St.

Foster, Dorothy F. The Life of Christ Visualized. LC 77-75501. (Illus.). (gr. 3-7). 1977. pap. 5.95 (ISBN 0-87239-155-8, 3005). Standard Pub.

Foster, Edward H. Catharine Maria Sedgwick. (U. S. Authors Ser.). 1974. lib. bdg. 13.95 (ISBN 0-8057-0658-5, Twayne). G K Hall.

--Richard Brautigan. (United States Authors Ser.). 176p. 1983. lib. bdg. 14.95 (ISBN 0-8057-7378-9, Twayne). G K Hall.

--Susan & Anna Warner. (United States Authors Ser.). 1978. lib. bdg. 13.95 (ISBN 0-8057-7232-4, Twayne). G K Hall.

Foster, Elizabeth. Lyrico: The Only Horse of His Kind. LC 79-114000. (Illus.). (gr. 3-7). 1970. 10.95 (ISBN 0-87645-027-3). Gambit.

Foster, Elizabeth R. The Painful Labour of Mr. Elsyng. LC 72-89400. (Transactions Ser.: Vol. 62, Pt. 8). 1972. pap. 3.00 (ISBN 0-87169-628-2). Am Philos.

Foster, Eugene S. Understanding Broadcasting. 2nd ed. (Illus.). 512p. 1982. text ed. 21.95 (ISBN 0-201-10106-8). A-W.

Foster, Frances S., ed. Witnessing Slavery: The Development of the Ante-Bellum Slave Narratives. LC 78-22137. (Contributions in African & Afro-American Studies: No. 46). lib. bdg. 25.00 (ISBN 0-313-20821-2, FWS/). Greenwood.

Foster, George. Financial Statement Analysis. (Illus.). 1978. 25.95 (ISBN 0-13-316273-7). P-H.

Foster, George M. Problems in Intercultural Health Programs. LC 58-10873. 1958. pap. 5.00 (ISBN 0-527-03300-6). Kraus Repr.

Foster, George M. & Anderson, Barbara G. Medical Anthropology. LC 78-18449. 354p. 1978. text ed. 23.95 (ISBN 0-471-04342-7). Wiley.

Foster, Gregory D., jt. auth. see Yarmolinsky, Adam.

Foster, Hal. Prince Valiant: Adventures in Two Worlds. 1977. 14.95 o.p. (ISBN 0-517-53018-X). Crown.

--Prince Valiant-An American Epic. LC 82-17919. (Prince Valiant Ser.). 56p. 1982. 100.00 (ISBN 0-936414-04-9). Manuscript Pr.

--Prince Valiant in the Days of King Arthur. (Illus.). 160p. (YA) 1974. 14.95 o.p. (ISBN 0-517-51584-9). Crown.

--Prince Valiant in the New World. 1976. 6.95 o.p. (ISBN 0-517-52565-8). Crown.

--Prince Valiant: Queen of the Misty Isles. 1977. 14.95 o.p. (ISBN 0-517-53019-8). Crown.

Foster, Hal & Trell, Max. Prince Valiant & the Golden Princess. 1976. 6.95 o.p. (ISBN 0-517-52564-X). Crown.

--Prince Valiant's Perilous Voyage. 1976. 6.95 o.p. (ISBN 0-517-52563-1). Crown.

Foster, Henry & Fox, James, eds. The Mouse in Biomedical Research: Vol. 3, Normative Biology, Immunology & Husbandry. 390p. 1983. 83.00 (ISBN 0-12-262503-X); subscription 71.00 (ISBN 0-686-83144-6). Acad Pr.

Foster, Henry L., et al, eds. The Mouse in Biomedical Research: Vol. 4, Experimental Biology & Oncology. 545p. 1982. 85.00 (ISBN 0-12-262504-8); subscription 72.50. Acad Pr.

Foster, Herbert L. Ribbin', Jivin', & Playin' the Dozens: The Unrecognized Dilemma of Inner-City Schools. LC 74-7393. 304p. 1974. text ed. 16.50 o.s.i. (ISBN 0-88410-150-9); pap. 10.95x (ISBN 0-88410-163-0). Ballinger Pub.

Foster, Hope S., jt. auth. see Halper, H. Robert.

Foster, J. R., tr. see Stifter, Adalbert.

Foster, Jane. An Unamerican Lady. (Illus.). 254p. 1983. pap. 7.95 (ISBN 0-686-38853-4, Pub by Sidgwick & Jackson). Merrimack Bk Serv.

Foster, Jerry, jt. auth. see Berkeley, William D.

Foster, John. The Case for Idealism: International Library of Philosophy. 280p. 1982. 25.00x (ISBN 0-7100-9019-6). Routledge & Kegan.

--Class Struggle & the Industrial Revolution. LC 74-19888. 352p. 1975. 26.00 (ISBN 0-312-14280-3). St Martin.

--Napoleon's Marshal: The Life of Michel Ney. (Illus.). (gr. 7 up). 1968. 9.50 (ISBN 0-688-21606-4). Morrow.

--The Sea Miners. (Illus.). 128p. (gr. 7 up). 1977. reinforced bdg. 8.50 o.p. (ISBN 0-8038-6723-9). Hastings.

Foster, John & Goldsborough, June. Christian ABC Book. (Illus.). 1982. 6.95 (ISBN 0-911346-05-8). Christianica.

Foster, John L. A Fourth Poetry Book. (Poetry Anthologies). (Illus.). 144p. (gr. 4-7). 1983. 9.95 (ISBN 0-19-918152-7, Pub by Oxford U Pr Childrens); pap. 4.95 (ISBN 0-19-918151-9). Merrimack Bk Serv.

--A Third Poetry Book. (Poetry Anthologies). (Illus.). 144p. (gr. 3-6). 1983. 9.95 (ISBN 0-19-918140-3, Pub by Oxford U Pr Childrens); pap. 4.95 (ISBN 0-19-918139-X). Merrimack Bk Serv.

Foster, John L., jt. auth. see Henderson, Thomas A.

Foster, John L., ed. A First Poetry Book. (Illus.). (gr. 1-3). 1980. pap. 7.95 (ISBN 0-19-918112-8). Oxford U Pr.

Foster, John L., et al. National Policy Game: A Simulation of the American Political Process. LC 74-3411. 108p. 1975. text ed. 13.50x (ISBN 0-471-26775-9). Wiley.

Foster, John W. American Diplomacy in the Orient. LC 74-112309. (Law, Politics, & History Ser). 1970. Repr. of 1903 ed. lib. bdg. 55.00 (ISBN 0-306-71915-0). Da Capo.

--Century of American Diplomacy. LC 79-87542. (American History, Politics & Law Ser). 1970. Repr. of 1900 ed. lib. bdg. 55.00 (ISBN 0-306-71458-2). Da Capo.

Foster, Joseph G., tr. see Glissant, Edouard.

Foster, K. Minoan Ceramic Relief. (Studies in Mediterranean Archaeology: No. LXIV). 196p. 1982. pap. text ed. 69.00x (ISBN 91-86098-08-X, Pub. by Astroms Sweden). Humanities.

Foster, K. Neill. The Discerning Christian. 104p. (Orig.). 1982. 6.75 (ISBN 0-87509-312-4); pap. 4.95 (ISBN 0-87509-316-7). Chr Pubns.

--Revolucion del Amor. 120p. Date not set. 1.25 (ISBN 0-88113-260-8). Edit Betania.

Foster, Kenelm. The Two Dantes & Other Studies. LC 76-24581. 1978. 30.00x (ISBN 0-520-03326-4). U of Cal Pr.

Foster, L. Sheila, jt. auth. see Sandler, Reuben.

Foster, Lee. Making the Most of the Peninsula: A California Guide to San Mateo, Santa Clara, & Santa Cruz Counties. (Illus.). 304p. (Orig.). 1983. pap. 8.95 (ISBN 0-89141-164-X). Presidio Pr.

Foster, Lewis. The Only Way. LC 77-83658. 96p. (Orig.). 1978. pap. 1.95 (ISBN 0-87239-193-0, 40048). Standard Pub.

--The True Life. LC 77-83656. 96p. (Orig.). 1978. pap. 1.95 (ISBN 0-87239-192-2, 40047). Standard Pub.

Foster, Lewis & Stedman, Jon. Selecting a Translation of the Bible. Korth, Bob, ed. (Illus.). 128p. (Orig.). 1983. pap. price not set (ISBN 0-87239-645-2). Standard Pub.

Foster, Lowell W. Geo-Metrics II: The Application of Geometric Tolerancing Techniques (Using Customary System) Rev. ed. LC 82-11655. (Illus.). 320p. 1983. pap. text ed. 18.95 (ISBN 0-201-11520-4). A-W.

Foster, M. A. The Gameplayers of Zan. (Science Fiction Ser.). 1977. pap. 2.25 o.p. (ISBN 0-87997-287-4, UE1497). DAW Bks.

Foster, M. W., ed. Recent Antarctic & Subantarctic Brachiopods. LC 74-9234. (Antarctic Research Ser.: Vol. 21). (Illus.). 1974. 39.00 (ISBN 0-87590-121-2). Am Geophysical.

Foster, Marcia S. OJT Payroll Clerk Resource Materials. 2nd ed. (Gregg Office Job Training Program). (Illus.). 112p. (gr. 11-12). 1980. soft cover 5.60 (ISBN 0-07-021641-X); training manual 4.16 (ISBN 0-07-021642-8). McGraw.

Foster, Mark. The Denver Bears: From Sandlots to Sellouts. (Illus.). 1983. price not set (ISBN 0-87108-643-3). Pruett.

Foster, Mark S. From Streetcar to Superhighway: American City Planners & Urban Transportation, 1900-1940. LC 80-27202. (Technology & Urban Growth Ser.). (Illus.). 263p. 1981. 29.95 (ISBN 0-87722-210-X). Temple U Pr.

Foster, Marshall E. & Swanson, Mary E. The American Covenant: The Untold Story. (Illus.). 117p. (Orig.). 1982. pap. text ed. 6.95 (ISBN 0-941370-00-3); write for info. study leader's guide (ISBN 0-941370-01-1). Foun Chr Self Gov.

Foster, Martha. Medical Office Practice. LC 75-4051. (Allied Health Ser). 1975. pap. 6.25 (ISBN 0-672-61381-6). Bobbs.

Foster, Michael J. Energy in Law Enforcement. LC 81-67133. 327p. 1981. lib. bdg. 19.95 (ISBN 0-917882-14-8). Maryland Hist Pr.

Foster, Michael S., jt. auth. see Dawson, E. Yale.

Foster, Myles B. Anthems & Anthem Composers. LC 76-125047. (Music Ser). 1970. Repr. of 1901 ed. lib. bdg. 22.50 (ISBN 0-306-70012-3). Da Capo.

Foster, Norman. Construction Estimates from Take Off to Bid. 2nd ed. (Modern Structure Ser.). (Illus.). 288p. 1973. 42.50 (ISBN 0-07-021632-0, P&RB). McGraw.

--Practical Tables for Building Construction. 1963. 22.50 (ISBN 0-07-021628-2, P&RB). McGraw.

Foster, Pearl B. Mrs. Foster's Creative American Cookery. (Illus.). Date not set. 17.50 (ISBN 0-671-44303-8). S&S.

Foster, Phillips. Plaid for Introduction to Environmental Science. 1977. pap. 5.95 o.p. (ISBN 0-256-01262-8, 08-0313-00). Dow Jones-Irwin.

Foster, R. C. Studies in the Life of Christ. 1979. Repr. 29.95 (ISBN 0-8010-3452-3). Baker Bk.

Foster, R. F. Lord Randolph Churchill: A Political Life. (Illus.). 1982. 29.95x (ISBN 0-19-822679-9). Oxford U Pr.

--Lord Randolph Churchill: A Political Life. (Illus.). 448p. 1983. pap. 15.95 (ISBN 0-19-822756-6). Oxford U Pr.

Foster, R. W. & Cox, Barry. Basic Pharmacology. LC 80-49873. (Illus.). 296p. 1980. text ed. 19.95 (ISBN 0-407-00170-0). Butterworth.

Foster, Raymond. The Garden in Autumn & Winter. (Illus.). 192p. 1983. 24.95 (ISBN 0-7153-8416-3). David & Charles.

--The Gardener's Guide to Rare, Exotic, & Difficult Plants. (Illus.). 208p. 1983. 27.50 (ISBN 0-7153-8293-4). David & Charles.

Foster, Richard J. Celebration of Discipline Study Guide. LC 77-20444. 96p. (Orig.). 1983. pap. 3.80i (ISBN 0-06-062833-2, HarpR). Har-Row.

Foster, Rick, ed. West Coast Plays, No. 11-12. (Illus.). 369p. (Orig.). 1982. pap. 9.95 (ISBN 0-934782-11-3). West Coast Plays.

--West Coast Plays Ten: Hotel Universe & Ghosts, the Day Roosevelt Died, An Evening in Our Century, & Inching Through the Everglaglades. (Illus.). 186p. (Orig.). 1981. pap. 6.00 (ISBN 0-934782-09-1). Cal Theatre.

Foster, Robert D. The Navigator: Experiences & Teachings of Dawson Trotman. 1983. pap. 3.95 (ISBN 0-89109-495-4). NavPress.

Foster, Robert J. General Geology. 4th ed. 672p. 1983. text ed. 26.95 (ISBN 0-675-20020-2). Merrill.

--Geology. 4th ed. (Physics & Physical Science Ser.). 192p. 1980. pap. text ed. 9.95 (ISBN 0-675-08183-1). Merrill.

--Physical Geology. 3rd ed. (Science Ser.). 1979. text ed. 24.95 (ISBN 0-675-08312-5); study guide 8.95 (ISBN 0-675-08258-7). Merrill.

--Physical Geology. 4th ed. 460p. 1983. text ed. 24.95 (ISBN 0-675-20021-0). Additional supplments may be obtained from publisher. Merrill.

Foster, Ronald S., jt. auth. see Beckman, Theodore N.

Foster, Ruel E. Jesse Stuart. LC 68-24298. (United States Author Ser: No. 140). 1968. lib. bdg. 10.95 o.p. (ISBN 0-8057-0704-2, Twayne). G K Hall.

Foster, Stephanie. Star Light, Star Bright. (First Romance: No. 4). 192p. (gr. 6-12). 1982. pap. 1.95 o.s.i. (ISBN 0-8439-1144-1, Leisure Bks). Nordon Pubns.

Foster, Stephen. Household Songs: Eighteen Forty-Four to Eighteen Sixty-Four. LC 76-169647. (Earlier American Music Ser.: No. 12). (Illus.). 1973. Repr. of 1862 ed. lib. bdg. 21.50 (ISBN 0-306-77312-0). Da Capo.

--The Social Orchestra for Flute or Violin: A Collection of Popular Melodies Arranged As Duets, Trios, & Quartets. Hitchcock, H. Wiley, ed. LC 79-169645. (Earlier American Music Ser: Vol. 13). (Illus.). 96p. 1973. Repr. of 1854 ed. lib. bdg. 21.50 (ISBN 0-306-77313-9). Da Capo.

--Stephen Foster Song Book. 224p. (Orig.). 1974. 8.95 (ISBN 0-486-23086-4); pap. 6.00 (ISBN 0-486-23048-1). Dover.

Foster, Stephen, ed. see Allen, Roy F.

Foster, Stephen, ed. see Bantens, Robert J.

Foster, Stephen, ed. see Boyle-Turner, Caroline.

Foster, Stephen, ed. see Buckberrough, Sherry A.

Foster, Stephen, ed. see Chadwick, Whitney.

Foster, Stephen, ed. see Cox, Annette.

Foster, Stephen, ed. see Dittmann, Reidar.

Foster, Stephen, ed. see Howe, Jeffery W.

Foster, Stephen, ed. see Isdebsky-Pritchard, Aline.

Foster, Stephen, ed. see Kaplan, Julius D.

Foster, Stephen, ed. see Santomasso, Eugene A.

Foster, Stephen, ed. see Slatkin, Wendy.

Foster, Stephen C., ed. see Evett, Elisa.

Foster, Stephen C., ed. see Ross, Novelene.

Foster, Stephen C., ed. see Teilhet-Fisk, Jehane.

Foster, Sunny & Billionis, Cynthia. Using a Sanitary Napkin. (Project MORE Daily Living Skills Ser.). 48p. 1978. Repr. of 1976 ed. pap. text ed. 7.95 (ISBN 0-8331-1245-7). Hubbard Sci.

Foster, Thomas E. Tangram Patterns. (gr. k-12). 1977. wkbk. 9.60 (ISBN 0-88488-081-8). Creative Pubns.

Foster, Timothy. You & God: The Abba Relationship. 120p. 1980. pap. 3.95 (ISBN 0-88207-221-8). Victor Bks.

Foster, Vanda. Bags & Purses. (Illus.). 96p. 1982. text ed. 13.95x (ISBN 0-7134-3772-3). Drama Bk.

Foster, Virginia R. Baltasar Gracian. (World Authors Ser.). 1975. lib. bdg. 12.95 (ISBN 0-8057-2398-6, Twayne). G K Hall.

Foster, Virginia R., jt. auth. see Foster, David W.

Foster, W. H., jt. auth. see Walker, P. D.

Foster, W. S. Handbook of Municipal Administration & Engineering. 1977. 34.95 (ISBN 0-07-021630-4). McGraw.

Foster, William L. Vicksburg: Southern City Under Siege. Urquhart, Kenneth T., ed. LC 80-84685. 82p. 1982. pap. text ed. 6.95 (ISBN 0-917860-12-8). Historic New Orleans.

Foster, William Z. Great Steel Strike & Its Lessons. LC 70-139202. (Civil Liberties in American History Ser). (Illus.). 1971. Repr. of 1920 ed. lib. bdg. 37.50 (ISBN 0-306-70079-4). Da Capo.

--Negro People in American History. 1970. 8.50 (ISBN 0-7178-0275-2); pap. 4.95 (ISBN 0-7178-0276-0). Intl Pub Co.

--Pages from a Worker's Life. LC 72-130864. 1970. 7.50 (ISBN 0-7178-0297-3); pap. 3.50 (ISBN 0-7178-0149-7). Intl Pub Co.

Fostieris, Andonis. The Devil Sang in Tune. Friar, Kimon, tr. from Gr. (Contemporary Poets Ser.: No. 3). (Illus.). 48p. (Orig.). 1983. pap. 3.95 (ISBN 0-916982-28-9, RL228). Realities.

Foth, Henry & Schafer, John. Soil Geography & Land Use. LC 79-27731. 484p. 1980. text ed. 32.95 (ISBN 0-471-01710-8). Wiley.

Foth, Henry D. Fundamentals of Soil Science. 6th ed. LC 77-86509. 436p. 1978. 28.95 (ISBN 0-471-26792-9). Wiley.

Foth, Henry D., et al. Laboratory Manual for Introductory Soil Science. 5th ed. 145p. 1980. write for info. wire coil o.p. (ISBN 0-697-05854-9). Wm C Brown.

Fothergill, Richard & Butchart, Ian. Non-Book Materials in Libraries: A Practical Guide. 2nd ed. 288p. 1983. write for info (ISBN 0-85157-345-2, Pub By Bingley England). Shoe String.

Fotheringham, John & Morris, Joan. Understanding the Preschool Retarded Child. 1976. pap. 4.25 o.p. (ISBN 0-8077-8006-5). Tchrs Coll.

Fotinis, Athanasios P. The De Anima of Alexander of Aphrodisias: A Translation & Commentary. LC 80-5062. 362p. 1980. text ed. 22.75 (ISBN 0-8191-1032-9); pap. text ed. 13.50 (ISBN 0-8191-1033-7). U Pr of Amer.

Foucault, Michel. The Archaeology of Knowledge. Smith, A. Sheridan, tr. 1982. pap. 6.95 (ISBN 0-686-37779-6). Pantheon.

--Mental Illness & Psychology. Smith, A. M., tr. 1976. pap. 3.95i o.p. (ISBN 0-06-131801-9, TB 1801, Torch). Har-Row.

--Order of Things: An Archaeology of the Human Sciences. 1973. pap. 5.95 (ISBN 0-394-71935-2, V935, Vin). Random.

--This is Not a Pipe. Harkness, James, tr. 66p. 14.95 (ISBN 0-686-42856-0). U of Cal Pr.

--This Is Not a Pipe: With Illustrations & Letters by Rene Magritte. Harkness, James, tr. LC 80-26627. (Art Quantum). (Illus.). 112p. 1982. 16.50 (ISBN 0-520-04232-8). U of Cal Pr.

Foucault, Michel, ed. I, Pierre Riviere, Having Slaughtered My Mother, My Sister, & My Brother: A Case Of Parricide in the Nineteenth Century. Jellinek, Frank, tr. from Fr. xiv, 289p. 1982. pap. 7.50 (ISBN 0-8032-6857-2, BB 819, Bison). U of Nebr Pr.

Fouchier, J. & Billet, F. Chemical Dictionary. 3rd ed. (Fr., Ger., & Eng.). 1972. 106.50 (ISBN 0-444-41090-2). Elsevier.

Fougereau, M. & Dausset, J., eds. Immunology Eighty: Fourth International Congress of Immunology. 1981. 110.00 o.p. (ISBN 0-686-74510-8). Acad Pr.

Fought, Catherine A. Rabble's Curse. 1980. 10.00 o.p. (ISBN 0-453-00381-8, H381). NAL.

Foulet, Lucien see Roach, William.

Foulger, R. J. Programming Embedded Microprocessors: A High-Level Language Solution. (Illus.). 240p. (Orig.). 1982. pap. 28.00x (ISBN 0-85012-336-4). Intl Pubns Serv.

Foulis, David, jt. auth. see Munem, Mustafa.

Foulis, David J., jt. auth. see Munem, Mustafa.

Foulis, David J., jt. auth. see Munem, Mustafa A.

Foulke, Adrienne, tr. see Malaurie, Jean.

Foulke, Adrienne, tr. see Masi, Edoarda.

Foulke, D., ed. Electroplaters' Process Control Handbook. rev. ed. LC 74-13010. 444p. 1975. Repr. of 1963 ed. 24.50 (ISBN 0-88275-213-8). Krieger.

Foulke, Jan. Blue Book of Dolls & Values. 5th ed. 364p. 1982. pap. 12.95 (ISBN 0-87588-189-0). Hobby Hse.

--Kestner: King of Dollmakers. 5th ed. 236p. 1982. 19.95 (ISBN 0-87588-185-8). Hobby Hse.

Foulke, R. A. Practical Financial Statement Analysis. 6th ed. (Accounting Ser.). 1968. text ed. 30.95 (ISBN 0-07-021655-X, C); solutions to theory & problems 5.50 (ISBN 0-07-021652-5). McGraw.

Foulkes, A. Peter & Lohner, Edgar, eds. Das Deutsche Drama von Kleist bis Hauptmann. LC 76-185793. 680p. 1973. text ed. 27.50 (ISBN 0-395-12742-4). HM.

Foulkes, David. Children's Dreams: Longitudinal Studies. LC 81-11478. 477p. 1982. 35.00 (ISBN 0-471-08181-7, Pub. by Wiley-Interscience). Wiley.

Foulkes, E. C., ed. Biological Roles of Metallothionein. (Developments in Toxicology & Environmental Sciences: Vol. 9). 1981. 60.00 (ISBN 0-444-80013-1). Elsevier.

Foulkes, F. Personnel Policies in Large Nonunion Companies. 1980. 25.00 (ISBN 0-13-660308-4). P-H.

Foulkes, Fred K. & Livernash, E. Robert. Human Resources Management: Text & Cases. (Illus.). 456p. 1982. text ed. 23.95 (ISBN 0-13-446310-2); pap. text ed. 17.95 (ISBN 0-13-446302-1). P-H.

Found, James. Basic Greek in Thirty Minutes A Day. 128p. 1983. pap. 4.95 (ISBN 0-87123-285-5). Bethany Hse.

Found, Peter, ed. International Literary Market Place, 1981-1982. 15th ed. LC 77-70295. 516p. 1981. pap. 45.00 o.p. (ISBN 0-8352-1345-5). Bowker.

Foundation Center. COMSEARCH: Geographic. (COMSEARCH Printouts Ser.). 1981. pap. 25.00 (ISBN 0-87954-057-5). Foundation Ctr.

--COMSEARCH: Special Topics. (COMSEARCH Printouts Ser.). 1980. pap. 12.00 (ISBN 0-87954-044-3). Foundation Ctr.

--Corporate Foundation Profiles. rev. ed. LC 80-69622. 512p. (Orig.). 1981. pap. 50.00 o.p. (ISBN 0-87954-038-9). Foundation Ctr.

--Corporate Foundation Profiles. 512p. (Orig.). 1983. pap. text ed. 50.00 (ISBN 0-87954-075-3). Foundation Ctr.

--Foundation Grants Index. 12th ed. 540p. (Orig.). 1983. pap. 35.00 (ISBN 0-87954-078-8). Foundation Ctr.

--National Data Book. 6th ed. 1982. pap. 45.00 o.p. (ISBN 0-87954-052-4). Foundation Ctr.

--Source Book Profiles 1983. (Source Book Profiles Ser.). (Orig.). 1983. pap. 200.00 (ISBN 0-87954-076-1). Foundation Ctr.

Foundation Center, ed. National Data Book, 2 vols. 7th ed. (Orig.). 1983. pap. 50.00 (ISBN 0-87954-077-X). Foundation Ctr.

Foundation of the Dramatists Guild Editors. The Young Playwrights Festival Collection. 256p. 1983. pap. 3.95 (ISBN 0-380-83642-4, Bard). Avon.

Foundry Services Ltd. Foundryman's Handbook. 8th ed. 1975. text ed. 15.00 (ISBN 0-08-018020-5). Pergamon.

Foundyller, Charles M. CAD-CAM Computer Graphics: 1982 Survey & Buyer's Guide. Rev. ed. Murphy, Jane A., ed. (U. S. Directory of Vendors: Part 3). (Illus.). 294p. 1982. spiral 185.00 (ISBN 0-938484-07-9). Daratech.

--CAD-CAM Minisystem Report: A Guide to Ready-to-Use Design & Drafting Systems Under 100,000 Dollars. (Illus.). 275p. 1983. spiral 225.00x (ISBN 0-938484-05-2). Daratech.

--Turnkey CAD-CAM Computer Graphics: A Survey & Buyers' Guide for Manufacturers, Pt. 3, US Directory of Vendors. (Illus.). 156p. 1981. spiral with laminated covers 99.00x o.p. (ISBN 0-938484-07-9). Daratech.

--U. S. Directory of Systems & Vendors, 1982: CAD-CAM Computer Graphics: Survey & Buyers Guide. rev. ed. Murphy, Jane A., ed. (Illus.). 374p. 1982. spiral 185.00 (ISBN 0-938484-08-7). Daratech.

Fountain, Clara G. Danville: A Pictorial History. LC 79-10603. (Illus.). 1979. 16.95 o.p. (ISBN 0-915442-87-6). Donning Co.

Fountain, Helen. A Cage of Birds. 1970. 4.00 o.p. (ISBN 0-8233-0159-1). Golden Quill.

Fountain, Robert L. Chemistry for Operators. LC 81-68897. (Illus.). 148p. 1981. pap. text ed. 16.95 (ISBN 0-250-40504-0). Ann Arbor Science.

Fountain, Sarah M. On Wings of Thought. (Illus.). 158p. 1982. 6.50 (ISBN 0-942078-02-0). R Tanner Assocs Inc.

Fountain, Thomas. Claves De Interpretacion Biblica. pap. 2.75 (ISBN 0-311-03653-8). Casa Bautista.

Fountaine, George La see La Fountaine, George.

Fourah Bay College, Library University of Sierra Leone. Catalog of the Sierra Leone Collection. 1979. lib. bdg. 55.00 (ISBN 0-8161-8227-2, Hall Reference). G K Hall.

Fouraker, Lawrence E., jt. auth. see Siegel, Sidney.

Fourcard, Bruno. Courbet. (Q.L.P. Ser.). (Illus.). 1978. 7.95 (ISBN 0-517-53285-9). Crown.

Fourel, M. Exercices de Verbes. Incl. No. 1. 60p. 1969 (ISBN 0-87774-031-3); No. 2. 86p. 1969; No. 3. 102p. 1969 (ISBN 0-87774-033-X); No. 4. 75p. 1967 (ISBN 0-87774-034-8). (Fr.). pap. text ed. 2.75 ea. Schoenhof.

Fourez, Gerard. Liberation Ethics. LC 82-799. 236p. 1982. 19.95 (ISBN 0-87722-254-1). Temple U Pr.

Fourier, Charles. Design for Utopia: Selected Writings of Charles Fourier. Gide, Charles, ed. Franklin, Julia, tr. from Fr. LC 70-148712. (Studies in the Libertarian & Utopian Tradition Ser). 1971. pap. 4.95 o.p. (ISBN 0-8052-0303-6). Schocken.

Fourier, Francois M. Theory of Social Organization, 2 vols. in 1. 1972. Repr. of 1876 ed. cancelled (ISBN 0-86527-192-5). Fertig.

Fournet, Beauregard A., Jr. Strategic Planning in Health Services Management. LC 82-8796. 330p. 1982. 29.95 (ISBN 0-89443-660-0). Aspen Systems.

Fournier. Le Grand Meaulnes. (Easy Reader, B). pap. 3.95 (ISBN 0-88436-110-1, 40272). EMC.

Fournier, Felix A. Playing Cards: Fournier Musuem. (Illus.). 344p. 1982. 45.00 (ISBN 0-88079-026-1). US Games Syst.

Fournier, Priscilla. American Wok Cookery. LC 82-50569. 64p. (Orig.). 1982. pap. 2.98 (ISBN 0-686-82681-7). WRC Pub.

Fournier, Ron. Metal Fabricator's Handbook: Race & Custom Car. 176p. 1982. pap. 9.95 (ISBN 0-89586-171-2). H P Bks.

Fournies, Ferdinand F. Performance Appraisal: Design Manual. (Illus.). 326p. 1983. 96.45 (ISBN 0-917472-09-8). F Fournies.

Fourquin, G. The Anatomy of Popular Rebellion in the Middle Ages. (Europe in the Middle Ages - Selected Studies: Vol. 9). 1978. 42.75 (ISBN 0-444-85006-6, North-Holland). Elsevier.

Fourquin, Guy. Lordship & Feudalism in the Middle Ages. LC 75-11141. 1976. 12.50x o.p. (ISBN 0-87663-718-7, Pica). Universe.

Fourth Budapest Conference on Soil Mechanics & Foundation Engineering. Proceedings. Kezdi, A., ed. Incl. 3rd Conference, 1968. 685p. 25.00x (ISBN 0-685-29786-1); 4th Conference, 1971. 861p. 1971. 60.00x (ISBN 0-8002-2392-6). (Illus.). Intl Pubns Serv.

Fousek, Marianka S. Church in a Changing World. LC 77-139331. (Church in History Ser). 1980. pap. 4.95 (ISBN 0-570-06279-9, 12-2729). Concordia.

Foust, A. S., et al. Principles of Unit Operations. 2nd ed. 768p. 1980. 41.95x (ISBN 0-471-26897-6). Wiley.

Foust, Brady, jt. auth. see DeSouza, Anthony.

Foust, Cleon H. & Webster, D. Robert, eds. An Anatomy of Criminal Justice: A System Overview. LC 79-3908. 352p. 1980. 27.95x (ISBN 0-669-02854-1). Lexington Bks.

Foust, Cleon H., jt. ed. see Dutile, Fernand N.

Foust, Juana. Searching for Fifth Mesa. Smith, James C., Jr., ed. LC 78-31284. (Orig.). 1979. pap. text ed. 4.95 (ISBN 0-913270-81-4). Sunstone Pr.

Foust, O. J., ed. Sodium-Nak Engineering Handbook, Vol. 3 & 4. (U.S. Atomic Energy Commission Monograhs). (Illus.). Vol. 3,348. 81.00 (ISBN 0-677-03040-1); Vol. 4,298. 81.00 (ISBN 0-677-03050-9). Vol. 5. Gordon.

Fout, John C., jt. ed. see Riemer, Eleanor S.

Fowke, Edith. Sally Go Round the Sun. (Illus.). (gr. 4 up). 1970. PLB 9.95 (ISBN 0-385-02956-X). Doubleday.

Fowke, Edith F. Traditional Singers & Songs from Ontario. LC 65-26777. (Illus.). x, 210p. Repr. of 1965 ed. 34.00x (ISBN 0-8103-5011-4). Gale.

Fowkes, Charles, ed. see Donne, John.

Fowkes, Virginia K., jt. auth. see Andreoli, Kathleen G.

Fowler, A., ed. see Lewis, Clive S.

Fowler, Alastair. Triumphal Forms, Structural Patterns in Elizabethan Poetry. LC 75-105498. (Illus.). 1970. 44.50 (ISBN 0-521-07747-8). Cambridge U Pr.

Fowler, Arlen L. The Black Infantry in the West, 1869-1891. LC 78-105985. (Contributions in Afro-American & African Studies: No. 6). (Illus.). 1971. 25.00 (ISBN 0-8371-3313-0, Pub. by Negro U Pr). Greenwood.

Fowler, Cary. Graham Center Seed Directory: A Guide to Old-Timey Varieties. 1.00 (ISBN 0-686-95948-5). Alternatives.

Fowler, Charles B. Dance As Education. 1977. pap. text ed. 4.95 (ISBN 0-88314-051-9, 243-26106). AAHPERD.

Fowler, Charles W. & Smith, Tim D. Dynamics of Large Mammal Populations. LC 81-115. 477p. 1981. 42.50x (ISBN 0-471-05160-8, Oub. by Wiley-Interscience). Wiley.

Fowler, Clarence M., jt. ed. see Erber, Thomas.

Fowler, Cynthia, jt. auth. see Donne, Michael.

Fowler, Douglas. Reading Nabokov. LC 82-17342. 224p. 1983. pap. text ed. 10.25 (ISBN 0-8191-2721-3). U Pr of Amer.

--S. J. Perelman. (United States Authors Ser.). 192p. 1983. lib. bdg. 12.95 (ISBN 0-8057-7376-2, Twayne). G K Hall.

Fowler, E. P., tr. see Benedikt, Moriz.

Fowler, Elaine, jt. auth. see Wright, Louis B.

Fowler, Elaine W., jt. ed. see Wright, Louis B.

Fowler, F. G., jt. auth. see Fowler, Henry W.

Fowler, F. Parker, Jr. Basic Mathematics for Administration. 358p. 1983. text ed. price not set (ISBN 0-89874-613-2). Krieger.

Fowler, Floyd J. Citizen Attitudes Toward Local Government, Services & Taxes. LC 74-9976. 180p. 1974. prof ref 20.00 (ISBN 0-88410-408-7). Ballinger Pub.

Fowler, Frank P. & Sandberg, E. W. Basic Mathematics for Administration. LC 62-15189. 339p. 1962. text ed. 26.95x (ISBN 0-471-26976-X); supp. mat. avail. (ISBN 0-471-26978-6); test avail. (ISBN 0-471-26985-9). Wiley.

Fowler, Gene. Lady Scatterly's Lovers. LC 72-86170. 160p. 1973. 5.95 o.p. (ISBN 0-8184-0048-X). Lyle Stuart.

--Return of the Shaman. 64p. (Orig.). 1981. pap. 4.00 (ISBN 0-915016-29-X). Second Coming.

Fowler, Gus. Getting What You Pay For. LC 82-74187. (Illus.). 248p. 1983. 10.95 (ISBN 0-9610432-1-0); pap. 9.95 (ISBN 0-9610432-0-2). Amistad Brands.

Fowler, H. R. The Fishes of Oceania: With Supplements 1-3. 1967. Repr. of 1881 ed. 120.00 (ISBN 3-7682-0444-8). Lubrecht & Cramer.

Fowler, H. Ramsey & Little, Brown Editors. The Little, Brown Handbook. 555p. 1980. text ed. 10.95 (ISBN 0-316-28961-2); 7.95 (ISBN 0-316-28964-7); teachers manual avail.; supplementary materials avail. Little.

Fowler, H. Seymour, jt. auth. see Palmer, E. Lawrence.

Fowler, H. W. A Dictionary of Modern English Usage. 2nd ed. Gowers, Ernest, ed. 748p. 1983. pap. 8.95 (ISBN 0-19-281389-7, GB 725, GB). Oxford U Pr.

Fowler, Henry W. Dictionary of Modern English Usage. 2nd ed. Gowers, Ernest, ed. (YA) (gr. 9 up). 1965. 15.95 (ISBN 0-19-500153-2); with thumb index 18.50 (ISBN 0-19-500154-0). Oxford U Pr.

Fowler, Henry W. & Fowler, F. G. King's English. 3rd ed. 1931. 15.95x (ISBN 0-19-869105-X); pap. 3.95x (ISBN 0-19-881330-9, GB 418). Oxford U Pr.

Fowler, James W. Stages of Faith: The Psychology of Human Development & the Quest for Meaning. LC 80-7757. 224p. 1981. 16.95i (ISBN 0-06-062840-5, HarpR). Har-Row.

Fowler, John M. Energy & the Environment. (Illus.). 480p. 1975. pap. text ed. 22.00 (ISBN 0-07-021720-3, C); instructors' manual 11.00 (ISBN 0-07-021721-1). McGraw.

Fowler, Kenneth. Jackal's Gold. LC 79-7797. (Double D Western Ser.). 1980. 10.95 o.p. (ISBN 0-385-15683-9). Doubleday.

Fowler, Laurence H. & Baer, Elizabeth, eds. The Fowler Architectural Collection of the Johns Hopkins University. 1982. 15.20. Res Pubns Conn.

Fowler, Mark, jt. auth. see Felton, Bruce.

Fowler, Murray E., ed. see Morris Animal Foundation.

Fowler, N., tr. see Raudive, Konstantin.

Fowler, Nathaniel C. The Story of Story Writing: Facts & Information about Literary Work of Practical Value to Both Amateur & Professional Writers. 255p. 1982. Repr. of 1913 ed. lib. bdg. 40.00 (ISBN 0-89984-207-0). Century Bookbindery.

Fowler, Noble O., ed. Noninvasive Diagnostic Methods in Cardiology. (Cardiovascular Clinics: Vol.13, No. 3). (Illus.). 440p. 1983. 50.00 (ISBN 0-8036-3712-8). Davis Co.

Fowler, Ralph H. Statistical Mechanics. rev., 2nd ed. (Illus.). 875p. 1980. 99.50 (ISBN 0-521-05025-1); pap. 39.50 (ISBN 0-521-09377-5). Cambridge U Pr.

Fowler, Richard J. Electricity: Principles & Applications. Schuler, Charles, ed. (Basic Skills in Electricity & Electronics). (Illus.). 1979. text ed. 21.96 (ISBN 0-07-021704-1, G); activities manual 10.96 (ISBN 0-07-021705-X); tchr's manual 2.00 (ISBN 0-07-021706-8). McGraw.

Fowler, Robert B. Believing Skeptics: American Political Intellectuals, 1945-1964. LC 77-87967. (Contributions in Political Science Ser.: No. 5). 1978. lib. bdg. 29.95 (ISBN 0-313-20026-2, FAP/). Greenwood.

--A New Engagement: Evangelical Political Thought, 1966-1976. 320p. (Orig.). 1983. pap. 13.95 (ISBN 0-8028-1929-X). Eerdmans.

Fowler, Robert B. & Orenstein, Jeffrey R. Contemporary Issues in Political Theory. LC 76-7410. 168p. 1977. pap. text ed. 12.50 o.p. (ISBN 0-471-27032-6). Wiley.

Fowler, Roe. Christmas Was. 88p. 1982. pap. 6.95 (ISBN 0-686-38093-2). Fig Leaf Pr.

Fowler, Roger. Essays on Style & Language: Linguistic & Critical Approaches to Literary Style. 1970. text ed. 9.50x o.p. (ISBN 0-7100-1391-4); pap. text ed. 8.75x o.p. (ISBN 0-7100-6870-0); pap. 9.75x o.p. (ISBN 0-7100-6870-0). Humanities.

--Introduction to Transformational Syntax. 1971. 9.95x (ISBN 0-7100-6975-8); pap. 10.95x (ISBN 0-7100-6976-6). Routledge & Kegan.

--Linguistics & the Novel. (New Accents Ser.). 160p. 1977. 6.95 (ISBN 0-416-83820-0); pap. 6.95x (ISBN 0-416-83830-8). Methuen Inc.

Fowler, Ron. Pre-Flight Planning. (Illus.). 320p. 1983. 17.95 (ISBN 0-02-540300-1). Macmillan.

Fowler, Ruth, ed. see Soon Man Rhim.

Fowler, Stewart H. Beef Production in the South. LC 78-55815. (Illus.). (gr. 9-12). 1979. 32.50 (ISBN 0-8134-2035-0); text ed. 24.50x (2035). Interstate.

Fowler, Thomas B., Jr., tr. see Zubiri, Xavier.

Fowler, William. Potentials of Childhood: An Historical View of Early Experience, Vol. I. LC 80-8839. 1983. price not set (ISBN 0-669-04387-7). Lexington Bks.

Fowler, William & Ogston, Karen. Potentials of Childhood: Studies in Early Developmental Learning, Vol. II. LC 80-8839. 1983. write for info. (ISBN 0-669-06433-5). Lexington Bks.

Fowler, William A. Nuclear Astrophysics. LC 67-18204. (Memoirs Ser.: Vol. 67). (Illus.). 1967. 5.00 (ISBN 0-87169-067-5). Am Philos.

Fowler, William L. Take Another Look at the Keyboard. LC 82-90364. (Illus.). 100p. 1982. pap. text ed. 15.00 (ISBN 0-943894-00-X). Fowler Music.

Fowler, William M. & Coyle, Wallace, eds. The American Revolution: Changing Perspectives. LC 79-88424. (Illus.). 231p. 1979. 20.95x (ISBN 0-930350-03-0). NE U Pr.

Fowler, William M., Jr. William Ellery: A Rhode Island Politico & Lord of Admiralty. LC 72-12673. (Illus.). 1973. 11.00 o.p. (ISBN 0-8108-0576-6). Scarecrow.

Fowler, William W. Woman on the American Frontier. LC 73-12867. 1974. Repr. of 1878 ed. 50.00x (ISBN 0-8103-3702-9). Gale.

Fowler, Zinita. Monster Magic: A Reading Activities Idea Book for Use with Children. (A Fun with Reading Bk.). (Illus.). 78p. (Orig.). 1983. pap. text ed. 14.50 (ISBN 0-89774-044-0). Oryx Pr.

Fowles, jt. auth. see Cartmell.

Fowles, A. J. Complex Sequencing by Programmable Logic Controller, 1977. 1981. 35.00x (ISBN 0-686-97049-7, Pub. by W Spring England). State Mutual Bk.

Fowles, Jib, ed. Handbook of Futures Research. LC 77-84767. (Illus.). 1978. lib. bdg. 55.00x (ISBN 0-8371-9885-2, FHF/). Greenwood.

Fowles, John. The Aristos. 1975. pap. 5.95 (ISBN 0-452-25354-3, Z5354, Plume). NAL.

--Daniel Martin. 1978. pap. 4.50 (ISBN 0-451-12210-0, AE2210, Sig). NAL.

--The Ebony Tower. 320p. 1975. pap. 3.50 (ISBN 0-451-12354-9, AE2354, Sig). NAL.

--French Lieutenant's Woman. 1971. pap. 2.95 o.p. (ISBN 0-451-08535-3, E9003, Sig). NAL.

--A Short History of Lime Regis. (Illus.). 56p. 1983. 13.00 (ISBN 0-316-28987-6). Little.

Fowles, John & Huffaker, Robert. Fowles John. (English Authors Ser.). 1980. 11.95 (ISBN 0-8057-6785-1, Twayne). G K Hall.

Fowles, John V. Lecture Notes in Surgical Anatomy & General Surgical Pathology for Orthopaedic Surgeons. 401p. 1983. lib. bdg. 37.00 (ISBN 0-683-03317-4). Williams & Wilkins.

Fowles, Robert B. Mass Advertising As Social Forecast: A Method for Futures Research. LC 75-35344. (Illus.). 160p. 1976. lib. bdg. 25.00 (ISBN 0-8371-8595-5, FMA/). Greenwood.

Fowlie, Wallace. Characters from Proust: Poems. 65p. 1983. text ed. 13.95 (ISBN 0-8071-1070-1); pap. 5.95 (ISBN 0-8071-1071-X). La State U Pr.

--Lautreamont. (World Authors Ser.). 1974. lib. bdg. 15.95 (ISBN 0-8057-2511-3, Twayne). G K Hall.

--Mid-Century French Poets. (International Studies & Translations Ser.). 1980. 15.00 o.p. (ISBN 0-8057-5822-4, Twayne). G K Hall.

--Pantomime, a Journal of Rehearsals. LC 74-29632. 246p. 1975. Repr. of 1951 ed. lib. bdg. 17.00x (ISBN 0-8371-7981-5, FOPA). Greenwood.

Fowlkes, Frank. The Peruvian Contracts. LC 75-34217. 1976. 8.95 o.p. (ISBN 0-399-11710-5). Putnam Pub Group.

Fox. Great Racing Cars & Drivers. 9.95 o.p. (ISBN 0-448-01150-6, G&D). Putnam Pub Group.

Fox, A. F. World of Oil. 1964. 13.25 (ISBN 0-08-010687-0); pap. 7.00 (ISBN 0-08-010686-2). Pergamon.

Fox, Alistair. Thomas More: History & Providence. LC 82-11178. 288p. 1983. text ed. 19.95x (ISBN 0-300-02951-9). Yale U Pr.

Fox, Annie & Fox, David. Armchair BASIC: An Absolute Beginner's Guide to Programming in BASIC. 272p. (Orig.). 1982. pap. 11.95 (ISBN 0-931988-92-6). Osborne-McGraw.

Fox, Arturo A. Espana: Ida y Vuelta. 224p. 1981. pap. text ed. 9.95 (ISBN 0-15-522868-4, HC). HarBraceJ.

Fox, B. W., ed. Techniques of Sample Preparation for Liquid Scintillation Counting. (Laboratory Techniques in Biochemistry & Molecular Biology: Vol. 5, Pt. 1). 1976. pap. 27.75 (ISBN 0-444-11056-9, North-Holland). Elsevier.

Fox, Barbara. Popsicles & Pennies. new ed. (Illus.). 40p. 1977. pap. 2.00 (ISBN 0-932044-04-2). M O Pub Co.

Fox, Betsy. Visions of Sugar Plums. 1980. 6.95 o.p. (ISBN 0-935746-00-5). Green Hill.

Fox, Brian A. & Cameron, Allan G. Food Science: A Chemical Approach. 3rd ed. 380p. 1977. pap. 10.50x o.s.i. (ISBN 0-8448-0938-1). Crane-Russak Co.

--Food Science: A Chemical Approach. 382p. 1982. pap. 13.50x (ISBN 0-8448-1451-2). Crane-Russak Co.

Fox, C. Fred & Chabner, Bruce A., eds. Rational Basis for Chemotherapy. LC 82-24921. (UCLA Symposium on Molecular & Cellular Biology Ser.: Vol. 4). 524p. 1983. 54.00 (ISBN 0-8451-2603-2). A R Liss.

Fox, C. J., ed. see Lewis, Wyndham.

Fox, C. J., Jr. C. J. Understanding. 261p. 1982. 10.95 (ISBN 0-89962-286-0). Todd & Honeywell.

Fox, Caroline. Sea Spell. 222p. 1980. 10.95 o.s.i. (ISBN 0-698-11060-9, Coward). Putnam Pub Group.

Fox, Charles. The Noble Enemy. LC 78-22770. 1980. 12.50 (ISBN 0-385-14526-8). Doubleday.

Fox, Charles J. Speeches During the French Revolution. 415p. 1982. Repr. of 1924 ed. lib. bdg. 20.00 (ISBN 0-89984-210-0). Century Bookbindery.

Fox, Charles P. Circus Baggage Stock: A Tribute to the Percheron Horse. (Illus.). 250p. 1983. write for info (ISBN 0-87108-625-5). Pruett.

--When Summer Comes. (Illus.). (gr. k-3). 1966. 4.50 o.p. (ISBN 0-8092-8768-4). Contemp Bks.

Fox, Charles P. & Kelley, Beverly F. The Great Circus Street Parade in Pictures. LC 77-11234. (Illus.). 1978. pap. 5.00 o.s.i. (ISBN 0-486-23571-8). Dover.

Fox, Charles P. & Parkinson, Tom. Billers, Banners & Bombast: The Story of Circus Advertising. (Illus.). 300p. 1983. price not set (ISBN 0-87108-609-3). Pruett.

Fox, Claire R. Syndicating Single-Family Homes. Golomb, Patricia C., ed. LC 81-86370. (Illus.). 256p. 1982. pap. 16.95 (ISBN 0-9601530-6-3, Dist. by Har-Row). Impact Pub.

Fox, Clayton. Prairie Empire. 192p. 1982. pap. 2.25 o.p. (ISBN 0-505-51823-6). Tower Bks.

Fox, Clement A. & Snider, Ray S. Cerebellum. (Progress in Brain Research: Vol. 25). 1967. 91.00 (ISBN 0-444-40243-8). Elsevier.

Fox, D., et al. Physics & Chemistry of the Organic Solid State, Vol. 1. 1963. 39.50 o.p. (ISBN 0-470-27042-X). Krieger.

--Physics & Chemistry of the Organic Solid State, Vol. 2. 975p. cancelled o.p. (ISBN 0-470-27045-4). Krieger.

--Physics & Chemistry of the Organic Solid State, Vol. 3. 520p. cancelled o.p. (ISBN 0-470-27046-2). Krieger.

Fox, D. R. Theory of Stochastic Processes. 1965. 20.00x (ISBN 0-412-15170-7, Pub. by Chapman & Hall). Methuen Inc.

Fox, Daniel E., ed. Traces of Texas History. (Illus.). 1983. 16.95 (ISBN 0-931722-24-1); pap. 9.95 (ISBN 0-931722-23-3). Corona Pub.

Fox, Danny, jt. auth. see Minish, Gary.

Fox, David & Waite, Mitch. Computer Animation Primer. (Illus.). 208p. 1982. pap. 18.95 (ISBN 0-07-021742-4, BYTE Bks). McGraw.

Fox, David & Waite, Mitchell. PASCAL Primer. 1981. pap. 16.95 (ISBN 0-672-21793-7, 21793). Sams.

Fox, David, jt. auth. see Fox, Annie.

Fox, David S. Mediterranean Heritage. (Illus.). 1978. 22.00 (ISBN 0-7100-8840-X). Routledge & Kegan.

Fox, Denis. Animal Biochromes & Structural Colours. LC 72-89801. 1976. 45.00x (ISBN 0-520-02347-1). U of Cal Pr.

Fox, Denis L. Biochromy: Natural Coloration of Living Things. LC 78-57309. (Illus.). 1979. 35.00x (ISBN 0-520-03699-9). U of Cal Pr.

Fox, Denton, ed. The Poems of Robert Henryson. (Oxford English Texts Ser.). 1980. 105.00x (ISBN 0-19-812703-0). Oxford U Pr.

Fox, Donald H., ed. see Fox, Frederic E.

Fox, Edward J. & Wheatley, Edward W. Modern Marketing: Principles & Practice. 1978. text ed. 20.95x (ISBN 0-673-15045-3). Scott F.

Fox, Eleanor M. W. L. Esquire. 1978. 5.35 (ISBN 0-932518-00-1). Marando Pr.

Fox, Elliot M. & Urwick, L., eds. Dynamic Administration: The Collected Papers of Mary Parker Follett. 1982. pap. 8.95 (ISBN 0-88254-452-7); 16.95 (ISBN 0-88254-703-8). Hippocrene Bks.

Fox, Emmet. Alter Your Life. 1950. 8.45i (ISBN 0-06-062850-2, HarpR). Har-Row.

--Sermon on the Mount. 1934. 9.57i (ISBN 0-06-062950-9, HarpR). Har-Row.

Fox, Eugene R., jt. auth. see Sysler, Barry.

Fox, Frederic E. Seven Sermons & One Eulogy as Preached in the Chapel of Princeton University from 1965 to 1980. Fox, Donald H., ed. LC 82-90693. 88p. (Orig.). 1982. pap. 5.95 (ISBN 0-910521-02-6). Fox Head.

Fox, Frederick & Miller, Richard. Earthman Come Home. LC 81-85707. 273p. 1983. pap. 6.95 (ISBN 0-86666-054-2). GWP.

Fox, George. Amok. 1978. 8.95 o.p. (ISBN 0-671-22681-9). S&S.

--Warlord's Hill. 1982. 13.95 (ISBN 0-8129-1022-2). Times Bks.

Fox, Gerald, jt. auth. see Chandler, Tertius.

Fox, Harland. Top Experience Compensation 1982. (Report No. 827). (Illus.). ix, 66p. (Orig.). pap. text ed. 45.00 (ISBN 0-8237-0266-9). Conference Bd.

Fox, Harrison W., Jr. & Schnitzer, Martin. Doing Business in Washington: How to Win Friends & Influence Governemnt. LC 80-2313. (Illus.). 1981. 14.95 (ISBN 0-02-910460-2). Free Pr.

Fox, Harry W., Jr. Master OP Amp Applications Handbook. (Illus.). 1977. 17.95 o.p. (ISBN 0-8306-7856-5); pap. 13.95 (ISBN 0-8306-6856-X, 856). TAB Bks.

Fox, Hugh. The Guernica Cycle: The Year Franco Died. 64p. 1983. 12.00x (ISBN 0-916156-60-5); pap. 4.00x (ISBN 0-916156-61-3). Cherry Valley.

--Keep It Peaking. cancelled (ISBN 0-930012-17-8, 79-87598, Erasmus); pap. cancelled (ISBN 0-930012-16-X). Bandanna Bks.

--Leviathan. LC 80-39823. 1981. pap. 5.95x (ISBN 0-914140-10-8). Carpenter Pr.

Fox, J., ed. Microwave Research Institute Symposia. Incl. Vol. 1. Modern Network Synthesis. 1952. 23.00 o.p. (ISBN 0-470-27093-4); Vol. 4. Modern Advances in Microwave Techniques. LC 55-12897. 1955. o.p. (ISBN 0-470-27192-2); Vol. 5. Modern Network Synthesis. LC 56-2590. 1956. o.p. (ISBN 0-470-27225-2); Vol. 6. Nonlinear Circuit Analysis. LC 55-3575. 1956. o.p. (ISBN 0-470-27258-9); Vol. 9. Millimeter Waves. LC 60-10073. 1960. o.p. (ISBN 0-470-27357-7); Vol. 11. Electromagnetics & Fluid Dynamics of Gaseaous Plasma. LC 62-13174. 1962. 38.95 (ISBN 0-470-27423-9); Vol. 13. Optical Lasers. LC 63-22084. o.p. (ISBN 0-470-27428-X); Vol. 15. System Theory. LC 65-28522. 1965. 36.00 (ISBN 0-470-27430-1); Vol. 17. Modern Optics. LC 67-31757. 1967. o.p. (ISBN 0-470-27433-6); Vol. 19. Computer Processing in Communications. LC 77-122632. 1970. o.p. (ISBN 0-471-27436-4); Vol. 20. Submillimeter Waves. 1971. o.p. (ISBN 0-471-27437-2); Vol. 21. Computers & Automata. 1972. 42.95 (ISBN 0-471-27438-0); Vol. **22. Computer Communications. 1972. 46.95 (ISBN 0-471-27439-9); Vol. 24. Computer Software Engineering. 1977. 44.95 o.p. (ISBN 0-470-98948-3). Pub. by Wiley-Interscience). Wiley.**

Fox, J. A. Introduction to Engineering Fluid Mechanics. 1975. 29.50 (ISBN 0-07-021750-5, C). McGraw.

Fox, J. C., jt. ed. see Singleton, W. T.

Fox, J. D., jt. ed. see Robson, D.

Fox, J. G. see Drury, C. G.

Fox, J. G., jt. ed. see Drury, C. G.

Fox, J. Ronald. Arming America: How the U. S. Buys Weapons. LC 73-93774. (Illus.). 500p. 1974. 22.50x (ISBN 0-87584-108-2). Harvard Busn.

Fox, Jack & Hungness, Carl, eds. Indianapolis Five Hundred Yearbook, 1982. 224p. 1982. 16.95 (ISBN 0-915088-32-0); pap. 10.95 (ISBN 0-915088-31-2). C Hungness.

Fox, James. Comeback: An Actor's Direction. 224p. 1983. 9.95 (ISBN 0-8028-3585-6). Eerdmans.

--White Mischief. LC 82-42800. (Illus.). 299p. 1983. 15.95 (ISBN 0-394-50918-8). Random.

Fox, James, jt. ed. see Foster, Henry.

Fox, James A. Forecasting Crime Data. LC 77-8720. (Illus.). 1978. 18.95x (ISBN 0-669-01639-X). Lexington Bks.

Fox, James G. Organizational & Racial Conflict in Maximum-Security Prisons. LC 81-47710. (Illus.). 288p. 1982. 25.95x (ISBN 0-669-04727-9). Lexington Bks.

Fox, James M. A Shroud for Mr. Bundy. (Raven House Mysteries Ser.). 224p. 1983. pap. cancelled (ISBN 0-373-63049-2, Pub. by Worldwide). Harlequin Bks.

Fox, John. The Poetry of Villon. LC 76-43255. 1976. Repr. of 1962 ed. lib. bdg. 16.00x (ISBN 0-8371-9291-9, FOPV). Greenwood.

Fox, John, jt. auth. see Anderson, Carl.

Fox, John C., jt. auth. see Murg, Gary E.

Fox, John P., et al. Epidemiology: Man & Disease. (Illus.). 1970. text ed. 19.95 (ISBN 0-02-339170-7). Macmillan.

Fox, K. A., et al. Theory of Quantitative Economic Policy: With Applications to Economic Growth, Stabilization & Planning. 2nd rev. ed. (Studies in Mathematical & Managerial Economics: Vol. 5). (Illus.). 290p. 1974. 42.75 (ISBN 0-444-10544-1, North-Holland). Elsevier.

Fox, Karl A. Social Indicators & Social Theory: Elements of an Operational System. LC 74-16255. (Urban Research Ser). 328p. 1974. 27.50 o.p. (ISBN 0-471-27060-1, Pub. by Wiley-Interscience). Wiley.

Fox, Karl A. & Kaul, Tej K. Intermediate Economic Statistics, 2 vols. 2nd ed. Incl. Vol. 1. An Integration of Economic Theory & Statistical Methods. 584p. 1980. Repr. of 1968 ed. 25.50 (ISBN 0-88275-521-8); Vol. 2. A Guide to Recent Developments & Literature, 1968-1978. 186p. 1980. 12.50 (ISBN 0-88275-987-6). LC 76-30914. 584p. 1980. 33.00 set, vol's 1 & 2 (ISBN 0-686-86255-4). Krieger.

Fox, Karl A., jt. auth. see Ezekiel, Mordecai.

Fox, Kenneth P. Better City Government: Innovation in American Urban Politics, 1850-1937. LC 77-71957. 244p. 1977. 27.95 (ISBN 0-87722-099-9). Temple U Pr.

Fox, L., ed. Advances in Programming Non-Numerical Applications to Computing Machines. 1965. inquire for price o.p. (ISBN 0-08-011356-7). Pergamon.

Fox, L. Raymond & Elliott, Paul R. Heredity & You. LC 76-51113. 1978. pap. text ed. 5.95 (ISBN 0-8403-1691-7). Kendall-Hunt.

Fox, Larry. Illustrated History of Basketball. LC 72-90847. 288p. 1974. Repr. 3.95 (ISBN 0-448-11622-7, G&D). Putnam Pub Group.

Fox, Leslie. Introduction to Numerical Linear Algebra. (Monographs on Numerical Analysis Ser.). 1965. 19.95x (ISBN 0-19-500325-X). Oxford U Pr.

Fox, Lorene, jt. auth. see Brogan, Peggy.

Fox, Mary V. Barbara Walters: The News Her Way. LC 79-21900. (Taking Part Ser.). (Illus.). (gr. 3 up). 1980. PLB 7.95 o.p. (ISBN 0-87518-190-2). Dillon.

--Justice Sandra Day O'Connor. LC 82-8857. (Illus.). 96p. (gr. 5-11). 1983. PLB 9.95 (ISBN 0-89490-073-0). Enslow Pubs.

Fox, Matt & Swimme, Brian. Manifesto for a Global Civilization. LC 82-71450. 64p. (Orig.). 1982. pap. 3.50 (ISBN 0-939680-05-X). Bear & Co.

Fox, Matt, jt. auth. see Doyle, Brendan.

Fox, Matthew. Meditations with TM Meister Eckhart. LC 82-71451. (Meditations with TM Ser.). (Illus.). 128p. (Orig.). 1982. pap. 6.95 (ISBN 0-939680-04-1). Bear & Co.

--On Becoming a Musical Mystical Bear: Spirituality American Style. LC 75-34842. 192p. 1976. pap. 3.95 (ISBN 0-8091-1913-7). Paulist Pr.

--Western Spirituality: Historical Roots, Ecumenical Routes. 440p. pap. 10.95 (ISBN 0-939680-01-7). Bear & Co.

Fox, Matthew, intro. By. Breakthrough: Meister Eckhart's Creation Spirituality. LC 80-909. 600p. 1980. 15.95 (ISBN 0-385-17045-9, Dolp); pap. 8.95 (ISBN 0-385-17034-3). Doubleday.

Fox, Matthew, frwd. by. Whee! We, Wee All the Way Home: A Guide to a Sensual Prophetic Spirituality. 264p. pap. 8.95 (ISBN 0-686-42950-8). Bear & Co.

Fox, Matthew H., jt. auth. see Barker, Carol M.

Fox, Michael. Whitepaws: A Coyote-Dog. LC 78-11312. (Illus.). (gr. 6-8). 1979. 7.50 o.p. (ISBN 0-698-20478-6, Coward). Putnam Pub Group.

Fox, Michael W. Between Animal & Man. LC 76-4952. (Illus.). 256p. 1976. 8.95 o.p. (ISBN 0-698-10710-1, Coward). Putnam Pub Group.

--Farm Animals: Husbandry, Behavior, & Veterinary Practice. 288p. 1983. pap. 24.95 (ISBN 0-8391-1769-8). Univ Park.

--The Healing Touch. Orig. Title: Dr. Michael Fox's Massage Program for Cats & Dogs. 152p. 1983. pap. 6.95X (ISBN 0-937858-18-8). Newmarket.

--How to Be Your Pet's Best Friend. 1981. 12.95 (ISBN 0-698-11070-6, Coward). Putnam Pub Group.

--Love is a Happy Cat. LC 82-14216. (Illus.). 112p. 1982. 7.95 (ISBN 0-937858-16-1). Newmarket.

--One Earth, One Mind. LC 79-25811. 1980. 11.95 (ISBN 0-698-10997-X, Coward). Putnam Pub Group.

--Ramu & Chennai: Brothers of the Wild. (Illus.). 96p. (gr. 5-8). 1975. 6.95 o.p. (ISBN 0-698-20338-0, Coward). Putnam Pub Group.

--Sundance Coyote. new ed. (Illus.). 96p. (gr. 5-11). 1974. 5.95 o.p. (ISBN 0-698-20284-8, Coward). Putnam Pub Group.

--Understanding Your Cat. (Illus.). 220p. 1974. 9.95 (ISBN 0-698-10603-2). Putnam Pub Group.

--Understanding Your Dog. (Illus.). 288p. 1972. 9.95 o.s.i. (ISBN 0-698-10382-3, Coward). Putnam Pub Group.

--Understanding Your Pet: Pet Care & Humane Concerns. LC 78-4959. (Illus.). 1978. 9.95 (ISBN 0-698-10851-5, Coward). Putnam Pub Group.

--Vixie: The Story of a Little Fox. new ed. (Illus.). 96p. (gr. 3-7). 1973. 5.95 o.p. (ISBN 0-698-20275-9, Coward). Putnam Pub Group.

--Wild Dogs Three. (Illus.). (gr. 5-8). 1977. 6.95 o.p. (ISBN 0-698-20400-X, Coward). Putnam Pub Group.

--The Wolf. (Illus.). 96p. (gr. 6-10). 1973. 6.95 o.p. (ISBN 0-698-20200-7, Coward). Putnam Pub Group.

Fox, Michael W. & Gates, Wende D. What Is Your Cat Saying? LC 81-4884. (Illus.). 80p. 1982. 9.95 (ISBN 0-698-20443-3, Coward). Putnam Pub Group.

--What Is Your Dog Saying ? LC 76-20784. (Illus.). (gr. 6-8). 1977. 7.95 (ISBN 0-698-20367-4, Coward). Putnam Pub Group.

Fox, Micheal & McDonough, Kathleen. Wisconsin Municipal Records Manual. 102p. pap. 1.50 o.s.i. (ISBN 0-686-31607-X). State Hist Soc Wis.

Fox, Nell N. How to Raise & Train an Australian Terrier. (Orig.). pap. 2.00 o.p. (ISBN 0-87666-238-6, DS1050). TFH Pubns.

Fox, Norman. Fossils: Hard Facts from the Earth. LC 81-68315. 1981. pap. 3.95 (ISBN 0-89051-077-6); tchr's guide 2.95x (ISBN 0-686-33037-4). CLP Pubs.

Fox, P. F., ed. Developments in Dairy Chemistry, Vol. 1: Proteins. (Illus.). x, 405p. 1982. 90.25 (ISBN 0-85334-142-7, Pub. by Applied Sci England). Elsevier.

Fox, P. F. & Condon, J. J., eds. Food Proteins. (Illus.). xi, 358p. 1982. 78.00 (ISBN 0-85334-143-5, Pub. by Applied Sci England). Elsevier.

Fox, P. W. Politics: Canada. 5th ed. 672p. 1982. 12.95 (ISBN 0-07-548024-7). McGraw.

Fox, Paula. Blowfish Live in the Sea. LC 75-122740. 128p. (gr. 5-7). 1970. 8.95 (ISBN 0-02-735610-8). Bradbury Pr.

--How Many Miles to Babylon? LC 79-25802. (Illus.). 128p. (gr. 5-7). 1980. 8.95 (ISBN 0-02-735590-X). Bradbury Pr.

--King's Falcon. LC 69-13322. (Illus.). 64p. (gr. 4-7). 1969. 6.95 (ISBN 0-02-735580-2). Bradbury Pr.

--Portrait of Ivan. LC 74-93085. (Illus.). 144p. (gr. 5-7). 1969. 8.95 (ISBN 0-02-735550-0). Bradbury Pr.

--The Slave Dancer. LC 73-80642. (Illus.). 192p. (gr. 5-8). 1973. 10.95 (ISBN 0-02-735560-8). Bradbury Pr.

--Stone-Faced Boy. LC 68-9053. (Illus.). 128p. (gr. 4-7). 1968. 8.95 (ISBN 0-02-735570-5). Bradbury Pr.

Fox, Peter. The Trail of the Reaper. 224p. 1983. 11.95 (ISBN 0-312-81366-X). St Martin.

Fox, R. The Tory Islanders. LC 77-83992. (Illus.). 1978. 32.50 (ISBN 0-521-21870-5); pap. 9.95 (ISBN 0-521-29298-0). Cambridge U Pr.

Fox, Renee C. Essays in Medical Sociology: Journeys into the Field. LC 79-10413. (Health, Medicine & Society: a Wiley Interscience Ser.). 1979. 32.95 (ISBN 0-471-27040-7, Pub. by Wiley-Interscience). Wiley.

Fox, Renee C. & Lambert, Richard D., eds. The Social Meaning of Death. LC 79-53669. (Annals of the American Academy of Political & Social Science: No. 447). 1980. 15.00 (ISBN 0-87761-246-3); pap. 7.95 (ISBN 0-87761-247-1). Am Acad Pol Soc Sci.

Fox, Richard G. Kin, Clan, Raja, & Rule: State-Hinterland Relations in Preindustrial India. LC 76-129614. (Center for South & Southeast Asia Studies, UC Berkeley). 1971. 27.50x (ISBN 0-520-01807-9). U of Cal Pr.

Fox, Richard W. So Far Disordered in Mind: Insanity in California, 1870-1930. LC 77-93479. 1979. 17.95x (ISBN 0-520-03653-0). U of Cal Pr.

Fox, Robert, jt. auth. see Rotatori, Anthony F.

Fox, Robert & Weisz, George, eds. The Organisation of Science & Technology in France 1808-1914. LC 80-40227. (La Maison Des Sciences De L'homme). (Illus.). 336p. 1980. 39.50 (ISBN 0-521-23234-1). Cambridge U Pr.

Fox, Robert, et al. Diagnosing Classroom Learning Environments. LC 65-29237. 131p. 1966. pap. text ed. 5.95 (ISBN 0-574-17133-9, 13-0133). SRA.

Fox, Robert J. A Catholic Prayer Book. LC 74-75133. 128p. 1980. 4.95 (ISBN 0-87973-671-2, 671). Our Sunday Visitor.

--A Catholic Prayer Book. LC 74-75133. 128p. 1974. pap. 3.95 (ISBN 0-87973-771-9). Our Sunday Visitor.

--A Prayer Book for Young Catholics. LC 76-47869. 1977. deluxe ed. 4.95 o.p. (ISBN 0-87973-638-0); pap. 3.50 o.p. (ISBN 0-87973-370-5). Our Sunday Visitor.

--A Prayer Book for Young Catholics. LC 82-81318. 168p. (gr. 4-8). 1982. pap. 4.95 Leatherette (ISBN 0-87973-637-2, 637). Our Sunday Visitor.

--Prayerbook for Catholics. 112p. (Orig.). 1982. 6.00 (ISBN 0-931888-08-5); pap. 2.95. Christendom Pubns.

--Rediscovering Fatima. LC 82-60667. (Illus.). 144p. (Orig.). 1982. pap. 4.50 (ISBN 0-87973-657-7, 657). Our Sunday Visitor.

Fox, Robert W. & McDonald, Alan T. Introduction to Fluid Mechanics. 2nd ed. LC 77-20839. 684p. 1978. text ed. 30.95x (ISBN 0-471-01909-7). Wiley.

Fox, Robin. The Red Lamp of Incest: What the Taboo Can Tell Us About Who We Are & How We Got That Way. (Illus.). 288p. 1980. 12.95 o.p. (ISBN 0-525-18943-2). Dutton.

Fox, Ronald F. Biological Energy Transduction: The Uroboros. LC 81-11556. 279p. 1982. 36.95 (ISBN 0-471-09026-3, Pub. by Wiley-In terscience). Wiley.

Fox, Ruth. The Tangled Chain: The Structure of Disorder in the Anatomy of Melancholy. LC 75-17296. 1976. 23.50x (ISBN 0-520-03085-0). U of Cal Pr.

Fox, S. L. Industrial & Occupational Ophthalmology. (Illus.). 224p. 1973. photocopy ed. spiral 16.25x (ISBN 0-398-02827-3). C C Thomas.

Fox, Sandra S., jt. auth. see Bassuk, Ellen L.

Fox, Sanford. Economic Control & Free Enterprise. LC 63-19700. 1963. 4.50 o.p. (ISBN 0-8022-0526-7). Philos Lib.

Fox, Sidney. Labor Law. 124p. 1968. pap. 4.00x (ISBN 0-87526-042-X). Gould.

Fox, Sidney A. Surgery of Ptosis. (Illus.). 176p. 1980. lib. bdg. 35.00 (ISBN 0-683-03315-8). Williams & Wilkins.

Fox, Sonny. Funnier Than the First One: Another Joke Book. (Illus.). (gr. 4-9). 1972. PLB 4.49 o.p. (ISBN 0-399-60770-6). Putnam Pub Group.

--Jokes & How to Tell Them. (Illus.). (gr. 5 up). 1965. PLB 4.99 o.p. (ISBN 0-399-60328-X). Putnam Pub Group.

--Jokes & Tips for the Joke Teller. LC 75-2535. (Illus.). 96p. (gr. 3-5). 1976. PLB 4.96 o.p. (ISBN 0-399-60947-4). Putnam Pub Group.

Fox, Steve, ed. see Parsons, James.

Fox, Theron. Utah Treasure Hunter's Ghost Town Guide. (Illus.). 1983. pap. 2.50. Nevada Pubns.

Fox, Valerie. Abigail to Zachariah. LC 82-7681. 1983. pap. write for info. (ISBN 0-86628-021-9). Ridgefield Pub.

Fox, Vernon. Correctional Institutions. (Illus.). 336p. 1983. 21.95 (ISBN 0-13-178228-2). P-H.

--Introduction to Criminology. (Illus.). 416p. 1976. 22.95 (ISBN 0-13-480053-2). P-H.

--Violence Behind Bars. LC 73-13414. 317p. 1973. Repr. of 1956 ed. lib. bdg. 20.00x (ISBN 0-8371-7131-8, FOVB). Greenwood.

Fox, Vernon B. Introduction to Corrections. 2nd ed. (Illus.). 1977. text ed. 22.95 (ISBN 0-13-479485-0). P-H.

Fox, Virgil. A Basic Book of Self-Instruction on How to Draw & Paint Successfully Both in the Fine & in the Commercial Art. (Illus.). 201p. 1982. 47.85 (ISBN 0-86650-035-9). Gloucester Art.

Fox, W. J., jt. auth. see McBirnie, S. C.

Fox, William & Stein, Emanuel. Cardiac Rhythm Disturbances: A Step by Step Approach. LC 82-12727. (Illus.). 250p. 1982. text ed. write for info (ISBN 0-8121-0838-8). Lea & Febiger.

Fox, William T. & Lambert, Richard D., eds. How Wars End. LC 70-130999. (Annals of the American Academy of Political & Social Science: No. 392). 1970. 15.00 (ISBN 0-87761-132-7); pap. 7.95 (ISBN 0-87761-131-9, 87761). Am Acad Pol Soc Sci.

Foxall, Gordon. Marketing Behavior: Issues in Managerial & Buyer Decision Making. 200p. 1981. text ed. 35.50x (ISBN 0-566-00434-8). Gower Pub Ltd.

Foxall, Gordon R. Co-Operative Marketing in European Agriculture. 116p. 1982. text ed. 29.50x (ISBN 0-566-00512-3). Gower Pub Ltd.

Foxall, Raymond. Highwayman No. One: Society of the Dispossessed. pap. 1.25 o.p. (ISBN 0-451-07216-2, Y7216, Sig). NAL.

--Highwayman No. 2: Amorous Rogue. pap. 1.25 o.p. (ISBN 0-451-07616-8, 47616, Sig). NAL.

Foxcroft, jt. auth. see Cole.

Foxcroft, Thomas. The Sermons of Thomas Foxcroft of Boston: 1697-1769. LC 82-10457. 1982. 50.00x (ISBN 0-8201-1387-5). Schol Facsimiles.

Foxe, John. The English Sermons of John Foxe. LC 77-29100. 1978. Repr. of 1578 ed. 45.00x (ISBN 0-8201-1267-4). Schol Facsimiles.

Foxe, Sonja & Miles, Barbara. Essential Chicago: An Astrological Portrait of the Windy City. (Illus.). 1982. pap. 3.80 (ISBN 0-933646-21-6). Aries Pr.

Fox-Genovese, Elizabeth & Genovese, Eugene D. Fruits of Merchant Capital: Slavery & Bourgeois Property in the Rise & Expansion of Capitalism. 1983. 29.95 (ISBN 0-19-503157-1); pap. 10.95 (ISBN 0-19-503158-X). Oxford U Pr.

Foxhall, William B. Professional Construction Management & Project Administration. 2nd ed. LC 76-4483. 1976. 24.75 (ISBN 0-07-021755-6, Architectural Rec Bks). McGraw.

Foxley, A., ed. Income Distribution in Latin America. LC 75-20835. 1976. 37.50 (ISBN 0-521-21029-1). Cambridge U Pr.

Foxman, S. Classified Love: A Guide to the Personals. 120p. 1982. pap. 5.95 (ISBN 0-07-021756-4). McGraw.

Foxworth, Jo. Wising up. 1980. 9.95 o.s.i. (ISBN 0-440-09605-7). Delacorte.

Foxworth, Thomas & Laurence, Michael. Passengers. LC 79-7227. 432p. 1983. 17.95 (ISBN 0-385-12843-6). Doubleday.

Foxworth, Thomas, ed. see Matt, Paul, et al.

Foxworth, Thomas G., ed. see Matt, Paul R.

Foxx, Jack. Wildfire. LC 78-51082. 1978. 8.95 o.p. (ISBN 0-672-52214-4). Bobbs.

Foxx, Reginald. Journey to Delta Centaurus. LC 81-86213. 112p. 1983. pap. 4.95 (ISBN 0-86666-044-5). GWP.

Foxx, Richard M. Decreasing Behaviors of Severely Retarded & Autistic Persons. LC 82-60088. 191p. (Orig.). 1982. pap. text ed. 9.95 1-9 copies (ISBN 0-87822-264-2, 2642); pap. text ed. 8.95 ea.; pap. text ed. 17.90 set of decreasing & increasing (ISBN 0-686-83082-2). Res Press.

--Increasing Behaviors of Severely Retarded & Autistic Persons. LC 82-60087. 227p. (Orig.). 1982. pap. text ed. 9.95 (ISBN 0-87822-263-4, 2634). Res Press.

Foxx, Richard M., jt. auth. see Azrin, Nathan H.

Foy, Charles. Pigeons for Pleasure & Profit. (Illus.). 1972. pap. 3.50 o.p. (ISBN 0-911466-19-3). Swanson.

Foy, Elizabeth. Decoupage, the Ancient Art of Surface Finishing & Antiquing. new ed. LC 73-185673. (Handicraft Ser.). (Illus.). 32p. (Orig.). (gr. 7-12). 1971. lib. bdg. 2.45 incl. catalog cards o.p. (ISBN 0-87157-905-7); pap. 1.25 vinyl laminated covers o.p. (ISBN 0-87157-405-5). SamHar Pr.

Foy, Elizabeth & Schurer, John. Construction of Assemblages. new ed. Rahmas, D. Steve, ed. (Handicraft Ser.: No. 7). (Illus.). 32p. (Orig.). (gr. 7-12). 1973. lib. bdg. 2.45 incl. catalog cards o.p. (ISBN 0-87157-907-3); pap. 1.25 vinyl laminated covers o.p. (ISBN 0-87157-407-1). SamHar Pr.

Foy, Felician A., ed. Catholic Almanac, 1982. 1982. roncote 10.95 (ISBN 0-87973-252-0, 252). Our Sunday Visitor.

--Catholic Almanac, 1983. LC 73-641001. 1982. roncote 12.95 (ISBN 0-87973-253-9, 253). Our Sunday Visitor.

Foy, Frank E. The Painful Road Back. 1979. 7.95 o.p. (ISBN 0-533-04050-7). Vantage.

Foy, Nancy. The Yin & Yang of Organizations. LC 80-18558. 1980. 11.95 o.p. (ISBN 0-688-03769-0). Morrow.

Foy, Sally & Oxford Scientific Films. The Grand Design: Form & Color in Animals. (Illus.). 192p. 1983. 24.95 (ISBN 0-13-362574-5). P-H.

Foy, Whitfield. Man's Religious Quest: A Reader. LC 77-12266. 1978. 30.00 (ISBN 0-312-51254-6). St Martin.

Foye, Raymond, jt. auth. see Poe, Edgar Allan.

Foyle, Christina, ed. see Beak, Linda.

Foyle, Christina, ed. see Birchall, M. Joyce.

Foyle, Christina, ed. see Casperz, D. A.

Foyle, Christina, ed. see Daglish, E. Fitch.

Foyle, Christina, ed. see Evans, Anthony.

Foyle, Christina, ed. see Genders, Roy.

Foyle, Christina, ed. see Gill, Joan.

Foyle, Christina, ed. see Gordon, John F.

Foyle, Christina, ed. see Gore, Catherine.

Foyle, Christina, ed. see Harmar, Hilary.

Foyle, Christina, ed. see Hayes, Irene E.

Foyle, Christina, ed. see Hill, Frank W.

Foyle, Christina, ed. see Hill, Herminie W.

Foyle, Christina, ed. see Keeling, Jill A.

Foyle, Christina, ed. see Pond, Grace.

Foyle, Christina, ed. see Rogers, Cyril H.

Foyle, Christina, ed. see Shelton, Margaret R., et al.

Foyle, Christina, ed. see Stenning, Eiliah M.

Foyle, Christina, ed. see Trevisick, Charles.

Foyle, Christina, ed. see Wiley, Constance & Wiley, Wilson.

Foyle, W. G., ed. see Chenuz, Frida J.

Foyles, Christina, ed. see Noel-Hume, Ivor & Noel-Hume, Audrey.

Fraade, David J., ed. Automation of Pharmaceutical Operations. 400p. 1983. 57.50 (ISBN 0-943330-02-5). Pharm Tech.

Fraas, Arthur P. & Ozisik, M. N. Heat Exchanger Design. LC 65-21441. 1965. 54.95 (ISBN 0-471-27432-1, Pub. by Wiley-Interscience). Wiley.

Fraas, John W. & Newman, Isadore. Educational Statistics for Beginners: A Workbook. LC 79-64246. 1979. pap. text ed. 11.75 (ISBN 0-8191-0758-1). U Pr of Amer.

Frabey, Pierre, jt. auth. see Claiborne, Craig.

Frable, William J., jt. auth. see Johnston, William W.

Fraccaroli, Aldo. Italian Warships of World War Two. 15.50x o.p. (ISBN 0-392-09124-0, SpS). Sportshelf.

Fracchia, Charles A. Junk Bonds. (Illus.). 1983. 10.95 (ISBN 0-07-021766-1). McGraw.

--Second Spring: U. S. Catholicism in the 1980s. LC 79-3599. 208p. 1980. 9.95i o.p. (ISBN 0-06-063012-4, HarpR, HarpR). Har-Row.

Fracht, J. A. Violin First Handbook. (Illus.). 1979. 24.50 (ISBN 0-8206-0256-6). Chem Pub.

Fradenburg, Leo G. United States Airlines: Trunk & Regional Carriers, Their Operations & Management. (Orig.). 1980. pap. text ed. 20.95 (ISBN 0-8403-2128-7). Kendall-Hunt.

Fradin, Dennis. Fires, Disaster! LC 82-9404. (Illus.). (gr. 3 up). 1982. PLB 10.00g (ISBN 0-516-00855-2); pap. 3.95 (ISBN 0-516-40855-0). Childrens.

--Floods, Disaster! LC 82-9402. (Illus.). (gr. 3 up). 1982. PLB 10.00g (ISBN 0-516-00856-0); pap. 3.95 (ISBN 0-516-40856-9). Childrens.

--Georgia: In Words & Pictures. LC 80-26768. (Young People's Stories of Our States Ser.). (Illus.). 48p. (gr. 2-5). 1981. PLB 9.25 (ISBN 0-516-03910-5). Childrens.

--Hurricanes, Disaster! LC 81-38553. (Illus.). (gr. 3 up). 1982. PLB 10.00g (ISBN 0-516-00852-8); pap. 3.95 (ISBN 0-516-40852-6). Childrens.

Frado, John, et al. Twenty-Five Ski Tours in Western Massachusetts: Cross Country Trails from Worcester to the New York Border. LC 78-59804. (Illus.). 128p. 1978. pap. 4.95 (ISBN 0-912274-94-8). Backcountry Pubns.

Frady, Marshall. Southerners: A Journalist's Odyssey. 1981. pap. 6.95 (ISBN 0-452-00566-3, F566, Mer). NAL.

Fraenkel, A. A. Abstract Set Theory. 4th rev. ed. (Studies in Logic & the Foundation of Mathematics: Vol. 22). 1976. text ed. 32.00 (ISBN 0-444-11032-1, North-Holland). Elsevier.

Fraenkel, C. E., ed. see Grass, Gunter.

Fraenkel, Eduard. Horace. 1957. 34.00x o.p. (ISBN 0-19-814310-9). Oxford U Pr.

Fraenkel, Heinrich, jt. auth. see Manvell, Roger.

Fraenkel, J. Helping Students Think & Value: Strategies for Teaching the Social Studies. 1973. 17.95 o.p. (ISBN 0-13-386557-6). P-H.

Fraenkel, Jack R. How to Teach About Values: An Analytic Approach. (Illus.). 176p. 1977. text ed. 14.95x (ISBN 0-13-435446-X); pap. text ed. 14.95x (ISBN 0-13-435453-2). P-H.

Fraenkel, Pierre, jt. ed. see Augustijn, Cornelis.

Fraenkel, Richard, et al, eds. American Agriculture & U. S. Foreign Policy. LC 78-19761. 270p. 1979. 26.95 (ISBN 0-03-043101-8). Praeger.

Fraenkel-Conrat, Heinz & Kimball, Paul. Virology. (Illus.). 432p. 1982. 35.95 (ISBN 0-13-942144-0). P-H.

Fraga, S. & Muszynska, J. Atoms in External Fields: Physical Sciences Data Ser. (Vol. 8). 1981. 104.25 (ISBN 0-444-41936-5). Elsevier.

Fraga, S., et al. Biomolecular Information Theory. (Studies in Physical & Theoretical Chemistry: Vol. 4). 1978. 59.75 (ISBN 0-444-41736-2). Elsevier.

--Handbook of Atomic Data. 1976. 98.00 (ISBN 0-444-41461-4). Elsevier.

--Atomic Energy Levels: Data for Parametric Calculations, Vol. 4. (Physical Sciences Data Ser.). 1979. 98.00 (ISBN 0-444-41838-5). Elsevier.

Fragiacomo, C., jt. auth. see Noseda, G. F.

Fraginals, Manuel M., ed. Africa in Latin America. Blum, Leonor, tr. 400p. 1983. 39.50X (ISBN 0-8419-0748-X). Holmes & Meier.

Fragomen, Austin L., ed. see Annual Legal Conference on the Representation of Aliens 1978-1981.

Fragomen, Austin T., ed. Fourteenth Annual Immigration & Naturalization Institute. (Litigation & Administrative Practice Ser.). 524p. 1981. 30.00 (ISBN 0-686-80141-5, H4-4864). PLI.

Fragomen, Austin T., Jr., ed. Tenth Annual Immigration & Naturalization Institute. LC 79-53161. 1979. text ed. 25.00 (ISBN 0-686-58199-7, H2-2947). PLI.

Fraiberg, Selma. Every Child's Birthright. LC 77-74574. 1977. 10.95 o.s.i. (ISBN 0-465-02132-8). Basic.

Frailey, Lester E. Handbook of Business Letters. rev. ed. 918p. 1965. 32.50 (ISBN 0-13-375972-5, Busn). P-H.

Frain Du Tremblay. Traite des Langues Ou L'on donne des Principes et des Regles pour Juger du Merite et de l'Excellence de Chaque Langue et en particulier de la Langue Francaise. (Linguistics 13th-18th Centuries Ser.). 288p. (Fr.). 1974. Repr. of 1703 ed. lib. bdg. 77.00x o.p. (ISBN 0-8287-0353-1, 71-5015). Clearwater Pub.

Frair, John & Ardoin, Birthney. Effective Photography. (Illus.). 496p. 1982. 23.95 (ISBN 0-13-244459-3); pap. 16.95 (ISBN 0-13-244442-9). P-H.

Fraire, Isabel. Poems in the Lap of Death. Miller, Yvette E., ed. Hoeksema, Thomas, tr. 99p. 1980. pap. 8.50 (ISBN 0-935480-02-1). Lat Am Lit Rev Pr.

--Poems in the Lap of Death: English & Spanish. Hoekema, Thomas, tr. (Discoveries Ser.). 9.50 (ISBN 0-935480-04-8). Lat Am Lit Rev Pr.

Fraisse, jt. auth. see Groner.

Frajese, G., et al, eds. Oligozoospermia: Recent Progress in Andrology. 469p. 1981. text ed. 54.00 (ISBN 0-89004-589-5). Raven.

Frajndlich, Abe. Lives I've Never Lived: A Portrait of Minor White. (Illus.). 80p. (Orig.). 1981. write for info. (ISBN 0-9600884-3-1). ARC Pr.

Frakes, James R. & Traschen, Isadore. Short Fiction: A Critical Collection. 2nd ed. LC 69-11382. 1968. pap. text ed. 13.95 (ISBN 0-13-809178-1). P-H.

Frakes, L. A. Climates Throughout Geologic Time. 1980. 30.00 (ISBN 0-444-41925-X). Elsevier.

Fraleigh, J. B. A First Course in Abstract Algebra. 3rd ed. 1982. text ed. 24.95 (ISBN 0-201-10405-9). A-W.

Fraleigh, John B. Calculus with Analytic Geometry. LC 79-18693. (Illus.). 1980. text ed. 32.95 (ISBN 0-201-03041-1); student supplement avail.; avail. solutions manual 8.95. A-W.

Fraleigh, John B., jt. auth. see Beauregard, Raymond A.

Fraleigh, Patrick W., jt. auth. see Gilmore, Susan K.

Fraley, Lawrence E., ed. Behavioral Analysis of Issues in Higher Education. (Illus.). 224p. 1980. pap. text ed. 11.00 (ISBN 0-8191-1715-3). U Pr of Amer.

Fraley, P., jt. auth. see Weston, P.

Fraley, Ruth A., jt. ed. see Katz, Bill.

Fram, Eugene H. What You Should Know About Small Business Credit & Finance. LC 65-27748. (Business Almanac Ser.: No. 5). 90p. 1966. 5.95 (ISBN 0-379-11205-1). Oceana.

--What You Should Know About Small Business Marketing. LC 67-28902. (Business Almanac Ser: No. 11). 90p. 1968. 5.95 (ISBN 0-379-11211-6). Oceana.

Frame, Donald, tr. see De Voltaire, Francois M.

Frame, Donald M. & McKinley, Mary B., eds. Columbia Montaigne Conference Papers. LC 80-70811. (French Forum Monographs: No. 27). 134p. (Orig.). 1981. pap. 9.50x (ISBN 0-917058-26-7). French Forum.

Frame, Donald M., tr. see Moliere, Jean.

Frame, Donald M., tr. see Moliere, Jean B.

Frame, George & Frame, Lory. Swift & Enduring: Cheetahs & Wild Dogs of the Serengeti. (Illus.). 1981. 16.50 o.p. (ISBN 0-525-93060-4, 01602-480). Dutton.

Frame, J. Davidson. International Business & Global Technology. LC 82-48480. 224p. 1982. 24.95 (ISBN 0-669-06156-5). Lexington Bks.

Frame, Janet. To the Is-Land. LC 82-1350. 253p. 1982. 10.95 (ISBN 0-8076-1042-9). Braziller.

Frame, Lory, jt. auth. see Frame, George.

Frame, Paul. Drawing Dogs & Puppies. LC 78-5289. (How to Draw Ser.). (Illus.). (gr. 4-6). 1978. PLB 8.90 s&l (ISBN 0-531-01452-5). Watts.

--Drawing Sharks, Whales, Dolphins & Seals. (How-to-Draw Ser.). (Illus.). 64p. (gr. 4-6). 1983. PLB 8.90 (ISBN 0-531-04541-2). Watts.

--Drawing the Big Cats. LC 81-2966. (How to Draw Ser.). (Illus.). 72p. (gr. 4 up). 1981. lib. bdg. 8.90 (ISBN 0-531-04321-5). Watts.

Frame, Paul, jt. auth. see McCreight, Ruby E.

Frame, R., jt. auth. see Jedamus, Paul.

Frame, Robert, jt. auth. see Curry, Dudley.

Frame, Robin. English Lordship in Ireland, Thirteen Nineteen to Thirteen Sixty-One. (Illus.). 1982. 52.00x (ISBN 0-19-822673-X). Oxford U Pr.

Framery, Nicolas E., et al. Encyclopedie Methodique: Musique, 2 vols. LC 73-125049. (Music Ser.). 1971. Repr. of 1791 ed. Set. lib. bdg. 150.00 (ISBN 0-306-70014-X). Da Capo.

Framo Publishers. Tele-Fontos. 96p. 1983. 3.00 (ISBN 0-936398-15-9). Framo Pub.

Frampton, David, jt. auth. see Chaikin, Miriam.

Frampton, George, Jr., jt. auth. see Ben-Veniste, Richard.

Frampton, Hollis. Circles of Confusion: Texts 1968-1981, Film, Photography, Video. LC 82-70152. (Illus.). 200p. 1983. pap. 12.95 (ISBN 0-89822-020-3). Visual Studies.

Frampton, Kenneth. Hans Hollein. LC 82-50625. (Illus.). 120p. 1983. pap. 18.50 (ISBN 0-8478-0452-6). Rizzoli Intl.

Frampton, Kenneth, ed. Scolari: Beyond Memory & Hope. (IAUS Catalogs). (Illus.). 1980. pap. 12.00 (ISBN 0-262-59011-5). MIT Pr.

Frampton, P. H. & Van Dam, H., eds. Third Workshop on Grand Unification. (Progress in Physics Ser.: Vol. 6). 384p. 1982. text ed. 22.50 (ISBN 3-7643-3105-4). Birkhauser.

Frampton, Susan, jt. auth. see Cole, Michael.

France, Anatole. Le Jongleu de Notre Dame & Other Stories. Weale, Margaret, tr. from French. 102p. 1955. 5.00 (ISBN 0-911268-51-0); pocket size edition avail. Rogers Bk.

--Le Livre de Mon Ami. (Easy Readers, A). 1976. pap. text ed. 2.95 (ISBN 0-88436-289-2). EMC.

--Penguin Island. Evans, A. W., tr. LC 81-80108. 1981. pap. 6.95 (ISBN 0-918172-09-8). Leetes Isl.

France, Anna K. Boris Pasternak's Translations of Shakespeare. LC 76-52027. 1978. 26.50x (ISBN 0-520-03432-5). U of Cal Pr.

France, Anne E., jt. auth. see France, Ghollean T.

France, Ghollean T. & France, Anne E. Amazon Forest & River. (Illus.). Date not set. pap. cancelled (ISBN 0-8120-5330-3). Barron.

France, Kenneth. Crisis Intervention: A Handbook of Immediate Person-to-Person Help. 252p. 1982. 23.75x (ISBN 0-398-04535-6). C C Thomas.

France, P. W. Experiments in Elementary Physics. 2nd ed. 1981. pap. text ed. 12.95 (ISBN 0-89917-311-X). TIS Inc.

France, R. T. & Wenham, David, eds. Gospel Perspectives: Studies of History & Tradition in the Four Gospels, Vol. II. 375p. 1981. text ed. 16.95x (ISBN 0-905774-31-0, Pub. by JSOT Pr England). Eisenbrauns.

--Gospel Perspectives: Studies of History & Tradition in the Four Gospels, Vol. 1. 263p. 1980. text ed. 16.95x (ISBN 0-905774-21-3, Pub. by JSOT Pr England). Eisenbrauns.

Francello, Joseph A. The Seneca World of Ga-No-Say-Yeh (Peter Crouse, White Captive) LC 80-1358. 227p. 1980. pap. text ed. 10.50 (ISBN 0-8191-1141-4). U Pr of Amer.

Frances, Carol. College Enrollment Trends: Testing the Conventional Wisdom Against the Facts. 64p. 1980. 12.50 o.p. (ISBN 0-8268-1235-X). ACE.

--The Short-Run Economic Outlook for Higher Education. 64p. 1980. 7.95 o.p. (ISBN 0-8268-1395-X). ACE.

Frances, Jack. Tribal Rugs from Afghanistan. 1982. 50.00x (ISBN 0-903580-25-X, Pub. by Element Bks). State Mutual Bk.

Frances, Michael, jt. ed. see Pinner, R.

Francesco, Henry De see De Francesco, Henry.

Franchere, Hoyt C. Edwin Arlington Robinson. (United States Authors Ser.). 1968. lib. bdg. 11.95 (ISBN 0-8057-0632-1, Twayne). G K Hall.

Franchere, Ruth. Cesar Chavez. LC 78-101927. (Crocodile Paperbacks Ser). (Illus.). 48p. (gr. 2-6). 1973. pap. 2.95 (ISBN 0-690-18385-2, TYC-J); lib. bdg. 10.89 (ISBN 0-690-18384-4). Har-Row.

--The Wright Brothers. LC 70-158689. (Biography Ser). (Illus.). (gr. 1-5). 1972. PLB 10.89 (ISBN 0-690-90701-X, TYC-J). Har-Row.

Franchet, A. R. Plantae Davidianae Ex Sinarum Imperio, 2 pts. (Illus.). 1970. Repr. of 1884 ed. 120.00 (ISBN 3-7682-0670-X). Lubrecht & Cramer.

Franchi, Eda. The Long Road Back. (Orig.). 1975. pap. 1.50 o.p. (ISBN 0-451-06360-0, W6360, Sig). NAL.

Franchi, G., jt. ed. see Garattini, S.

Francia, Arthur J. & Strawser, Robert H. Accounting for Managers. LC 82-71152. 1982. text ed. 24.95x (ISBN 0-931920-38-8). Dame Pubns.

--Managerial Accounting. 4th ed. (Illus.). 651p. 1980. pap. text ed. 24.95 (ISBN 0-931920-39-6); practice problems 4.95x (ISBN 0-931920-53-1); study guide 5.95x (ISBN 0-931920-55-8); work papers 7.95x (ISBN 0-686-70446-0). Dame Pubns.

Francia, G. Toraldo Di see International School of Physics.

Francin, Rudy. The Turbulent History of North Adriatic Archipelago. 304p. 1983. 13.00 (ISBN 0-682-49977-3). Exposition.

Francis, Andre. Jazz. LC 76-6983. (Roots of Jazz Ser.). 1976. Repr. of 1960 ed. lib. bdg. 22.50 (ISBN 0-306-70812-4). Da Capo.

Francis, Austin. Catskill Rivers. (Illus.). 224p. 1983. 24.95 (ISBN 0-8329-0282-9). Winchester Pr.

Francis, C. W. Radiostrontium Movement in Soils & Uptake in Plants. LC 78-19051. (DOE Critical Review Ser.). 139p. 1978. pap. 11.50 (ISBN 0-87079-110-9, TID-27564); microfiche 4.50 (ISBN 0-87079-332-2, TID-27564). DOE.

Francis, Carl C. & Martin, Alexander H. Introduction to Human Anatomy. 7th ed. LC 75-2455. (Illus.). 1975. text ed. 19.95 o.p. (ISBN 0-8016-1646-8). Mosby.

Francis, Charles E. Tuskegee Airmen: The Story of the Negro in the U. S. Air Force. 12.00 (ISBN 0-8283-1386-5). Branden.

Francis, Chester & Auerbach, Stanley I., eds. Environment & Solid Wastes: Characterization, Treatment, & Disposal. LC 82-71528. (Illus.). 450p. 1983. 49.95 (ISBN 0-250-40583-0). Ann Arbor Science.

Francis, Clark & Archer, Stephen H. Portfolio Analysis. 2nd ed. (Foundations of Finance Ser.). (Illus.). 1979. text ed. 24.95 (ISBN 0-13-686675-1). P-H.

Francis, Dale, ed. see Seeley, Burns K.

Francis, Daniel & Morantz, Toby. Partners in Furs: A History of the Fur Trade in Eastern James Bay, 1600-1870. 200p. 1983. 25.00x (ISBN 0-7735-0385-4); pap. 9.95 (ISBN 0-7735-0386-2). McGill-Queens U Pr.

Francis, Dave & Young, Don. Improving Work Groups: A Practical Manual for Team Building. LC 78-64978. 261p. 1979. pap. 19.50 (ISBN 0-88390-149-8). Univ Assocs.

Francis, David. The First Peninsular War: Seventeen-Two to Seventeen-Thirteen. LC 74-23033. 390p. 1975. 19.95 o.p. (ISBN 0-312-29260-0). St Martin.

Francis, Deak. American International Law Cases: 1971-1978, Vols. 1-20. Incl. Vols. 21- Ruddy, F. 1980. LC 78-140621. 50.00 ea. (ISBN 0-379-20075-9). Oceana.

Francis, Dick. Banker. 288p. 1983. 14.95 (ISBN 0-399-12778-X). Putnam Pub Group.

--Knockdown. LC 74-15870. (Harper Novel of Suspense). (Illus.). 224p. 1975. 11.49i (ISBN 0-06-011339-1, HarpT). Har-Row.

--Reflex. 288p. 1981. 11.95 (ISBN 0-399-12598-1). Putnam Pub Group.

--Risk. LC 77-11786. 1978. 11.49i (ISBN 0-06-011302-2, HarpT). Har-Row.

--Slayride. Bd. with Forfeit. LC 82-48488. 512p. 1983. 13.41i (ISBN 0-06-015126-9, HarpT). Har-Row.

--Trial Run. LC 78-20204. (Harper Novel of Suspense). 1979. 11.49i (ISBN 0-06-011383-9, HarpT). Har-Row.

--Twice Shy. 307p. 1982. 13.95 (ISBN 0-399-12707-0). Putnam Pub Group.

--Twice Shy. (General Ser.). 1982. lib. bdg. 14.95 (ISBN 0-8161-3445-6, Large Print Bks). G K Hall.

--Twice Shy. 320p. 1983. pap. 3.50 (ISBN 0-449-20053-1, Crest). Fawcett.

Francis, Dorothy B. Blink of the Mind. (Twilight Ser.). (gr. 5 up). 1982. pap. 1.95 (ISBN 0-440-90496-X, LFL). Dell.

--Captain Morgana Mason. 160p. (gr. 5-9). 1982. 9.95 (ISBN 0-525-66764-4, 0966-290). Lodestar Bks.

Francis, Edward P., jt. auth. see De Angelis, George.

Francis, Elizabeth A. Tennyson: A Collection of Critical Essays. (Twentieth Century Views Ser.). 224p. 1980. text ed. 12.95 o.p. (ISBN 0-13-902353-4, Spec); pap. text ed. 3.95 o.p. (ISBN 0-13-902346-1). P-H.

Francis, F. J., jt. auth. see Clydesdale, Fergus S.

Francis, Frank. Natasha's New Doll. LC 73-935. (Illus.). 32p. (ps-3). 1974. cancelled 4.95 o.p. (ISBN 0-87955-199-2). O'Hara.

Francis, Frank, ed. Treasures of the British Museum. rev. & enl. ed. (The World of Art Library Ser.: Galleries). (Illus.). 360p. 1975. pap. 8.50 o.p. (ISBN 0-500-20119-6). Transatlantic.

Francis, Fred O. Conflict at Colossae: A Problem in the Interpretation of Early Christianity, Illustrated by Selected Modern Studies. LC 75-15737. (Society of Biblical Literature. Sources for Biblical Study). 1975. pap. 11.95 (ISBN 0-89130-009-0, 06-03-04). Scholars Pr Ca.

Francis, Frederick J., jt. auth. see Clydesdale, Fergus M.

Francis, Gloria A. & Lozynsky, Artem, eds. Whitman at Auction: 1899-1972. LC 77-16647. (Authors at Auction Ser.). (Illus.). 444p. 1978. 40.00x (ISBN 0-8103-0921-1, Bruccoli Clark). Gale.

Francis, Hazel. Language in Childhood: Form & Function in Language Learning. LC 75-4393. 200p. 1975. 26.00 (ISBN 0-312-46725-7). St Martin.

Francis, J. C. Readings in Investments. 1980. 17.95 (ISBN 0-07-019963-9). McGraw.

Francis, Jack C. Investments: Analysis & Management. 2nd ed. 1976. 25.95 (ISBN 0-07-021789-0, C); solutions manual 4.95 (ISBN 0-07-021788-2). McGraw.

Francis, Leslie J. Experience of Adulthood: A Profile of 26-39 Year Olds. 221p. 1982. text ed. 32.00x (ISBN 0-566-00562-X). Gower Pub Ltd.

--Youth in Transit: A Profile of 16-25 year olds. 189p. 1982. text ed. 32.00x (ISBN 0-566-00530-1). Gower Pub Ltd.

Francis, Linda & Hartzel, John. What's in a Name? (Orig.). 1982. pap. write for info. (ISBN 0-8423-7935-5). Tyndale.

Francis, Mary. Beginner's Guide to Flying. (Illus.). 1970. 9.50 o.p. (ISBN 0-7207-0245-3). Transatlantic.

--Blessed Are You. (Spirit & Life Ser). 1976. 3.50 o.p. (ISBN 0-686-17961-7). Franciscan Inst.

Francis, Nelle & Smith, J. Warren. Patterns for Prose Writing: From Notes to Theme. 1969. pap. 9.95x (ISBN 0-673-05679-1). Scott F.

Francis, Philip see Callahan, Parnell J.

Francis, R. Mabel. Filled with the Spirit-Then What? 1974. 1.50 (ISBN 0-87509-082-6). Chr Pubns.

Francis, Ray, jt. ed. see Pons, Valdo.

Francis, Robert. Pot Shots at Poetry. (Poets on Poetry Ser.). 1980. pap. 7.95 (ISBN 0-472-06318-9). U of Mich Pr.

Francis, Roy G. The Complete Chi-Square. 256p. 1983. 15.95 (ISBN 0-87073-211-0). Schenkman.

--Sociology in a Different Key: Essays in Non-Linear Sociology. LC 82-72534. 170p. 1983. text ed. 15.95 (ISBN 0-88105-000-8). Cap & Gown.

Francis, Valerie, jt. auth. see MacDonald, Janet.

Francis, W. W., et al, eds. Bibliotheca Osleriana. 1969. 85.00 (ISBN 0-7735-9050-1). McGill-Queens U Pr.

Francis, Wayne L., jt. auth. see Leege, David C.

Francisca, Beverly. Love, a Symposium. 1976. pap. 2.95 o.p. (ISBN 0-685-77530-5). New Age.

Franciscan Educational Conference - 43rd. Holy Eucharist & Christian Unity. 1962. pap. 4.50 o.p. (ISBN 0-8199-0300-0, L38270). Franciscan Herald.

Franciscan Educational Conference - 44th. Elements of Franciscan Formation. 1963. 4.50 o.p. (ISBN 0-685-10964-X, L38134). Franciscan Herald.

Francis Clare, Sr. Wow God. new ed. LC 75-32009. 1978. pap. 2.95 (ISBN 0-89221-057-5). New Leaf.

Francisco, Al, et al. Cost Accounting: Study Guide. (Illus.). 1977. pap. 8.95 (ISBN 0-8299-0145-0). West Pub.

Francisco, C. T. Introduccion Al Antiguo Testamento. Lacue, Juan J., tr. from Eng. 350p. (Span.). 1964. pap. 4.95 (ISBN 0-311-04010-1). Casa Bautista.

Francisco, Clyde T. Un Varon Llamado Job. Glaze, Jack A., tr. from Eng. (Reflexiones Teologicas Ser.). Orig. Title: A Man Called Job. 64p. 1981. pap. 1.95 (ISBN 0-311-04659-2). Casa Bautista.

Francisco, Garcia & Pavon. Las Hermanas Coloradas. (Easy Readers, C Ser.). 1977. pap. 3.95 (ISBN 0-88436-295-7). EMC.

Francisco, Llach. Renal Vein Thrombosis. LC 82-83041. (Illus.). 1983. pap. 29.50 monograph (ISBN 0-87993-186-8). Futura Pub.

Francisco, Ronald A. & Laird, Betty A. Agricultural Policies in the USSR & Eastern Europe. (Westview Special Studies on the Soviet Union & Eastern Europe Ser.). (Illus.). 332p. 1980. lib. bdg. 32.00 (ISBN 0-89158-687-3). Westview.

Francis of Assisi, Saint Writings of Saint Francis. Fahy, Benen & Hermann, Placid, eds. 1964. 4.95 o.p. (ISBN 0-8199-0106-7, L39025). Franciscan Herald.

Franck, Cesar. Selected Piano Compositions. D'Indy, Vincent, ed. LC 75-27672. 192p. 1976. pap. 6.50. (ISBN 0-486-23269-7). Dover.

Franck, Frederick. The Book of Angelus Silesius. 1976. 10.00 o.p. (ISBN 0-394-71641-8). Knopf.

--Messenger of the Heart: The Book of Angelus Silesius. (Illus.). 192p. 1982. pap. 9.95 (ISBN 0-8245-0495-X). Crossroad NY.

--The Supreme Koan: An Artist's Spiritual Journey. LC 81-22037. (Illus.). 1982. pap. 12.95 (ISBN 0-8245-0430-5). Crossroad NY.

Franck, Marga, jt. ed. see Afflerbach, Lois.

Franck, Susana see Mehler, Jacques & Walker, Edward.

Franck, T. M. & Carey, J. The Legal Aspects of the United Nations in the Congo. LC 63-14451. (Hammarskjold Forum Ser: No. 2). 137p. 1963. 10.00 (ISBN 0-379-11802-5); pap. 1.75 o.p. (ISBN 0-686-96823-9). Oceana.

Franck, Thomas M. Human Rights in Third World Perspective, Vol. 1-3. 1982. 150.00 (ISBN 0-379-20725-7). Set. Oceana.

--Race & Nationalism: The Struggle for Power in Rhodesia-Nyasaland. LC 73-11853. 369p. 1973. Repr. of 1960 ed. lib. bdg. 20.00x (ISBN 0-8371-7074-5, FRRN). Greenwood.

Franck, Thomas M. & Weisband, Edward. Foreign Policy by Congress. 1979. 22.50 (ISBN 0-19-502635-7). Oxford U Pr.

Franck, Thomas M. & Weisband, Edward, eds. Secrecy & Foreign Policy. 1974. 27.50x (ISBN 0-19-501746-3). Oxford U Pr.

Francke, Arthur E. Coacoochee, Made from the Sands of Florida: An Account of a Once Free Seminole Chief Presented in Free Verse. LC 82-62492. (Historic Byways of Florida Ser.: Vol. XI). (Illus.). 60p. (Orig.). 1982. pap. 5.95 (ISBN 0-686-38771-6, 32). St Johns Oklawaha.

Francke, Elizabeth. The Make-Your-Own Cosmetic & Fragrance Book. 180p. 1980. pap. 20.95 (ISBN 0-589-01319-X, Pub. by Reed Books Australia). C E Tuttle.

Francke, Linda B. Growing Up Divorced: Children of the Eighties. 1983. 16.50 (ISBN 0-671-25516-9, Linden). S&S.

Francke, O. F., jt. auth. see Moody, J. V.

Franco, Jean. Introduction to Spanish-American Literature. LC 69-12927. 1969. 42.50 (ISBN 0-521-07374-X); pap. 11.95 (ISBN 0-521-09891-2). Cambridge U Pr.

Franco, Jean, ed. Spanish Short Stories. (gr. 9 up). 1966. pap. 3.95 (ISBN 0-14-002500-6). Penguin.

Franco, Marjorie. Genevieve & Alexander. LC 81-69147. (Illus.). 256p. 1982. 12.95 (ISBN 0-689-11259-9). Atheneum.

Franco, Sylvia, et al. The World of Cosmetology: A Professional Text. LC 79-20678. (Illus.). 512p. 1980. text ed. 17.96 (ISBN 0-07-021791-2); student activities manual 9.96 (ISBN 0-07-021792-0); instr's planning manual 17.00 (ISBN 0-686-82938-7). McGraw.

Francoeur, A., jt. ed. see Francoeur, R.

Francoeur, R. & Francoeur, A., eds. Future of Sexual Relations. 1974. pap. 2.95 o.p. (ISBN 0-13-345900-4, Spec). P-H.

Francoeur, Robert T. Becoming a Sexual Person. LC 81-19782. 840p. 1982. text ed. 21.95 (ISBN 0-471-07848-4); 7.95 (ISBN 0-471-09893-0). Wiley.

--Eve's New Rib. 1973. pap. 2.65 o.s.i. (ISBN 0-440-52340-0, Delta). Dell.

Francois, Carlo. Raison et Deraison dans le Theatre de Pierre Corneille. (Fr.). 15.00 (ISBN 0-917786-17-3). French Lit.

Francois, D., jt. ed. see Sih, G. C.

Francois, J., ed. see International Society for Paediatric Ophthalmology, 2nd Meeting.

Francois, Louis. The Right to Education: From Proclamation to Achievement, 1948-1968. 1968. pap. 2.25 (ISBN 92-3-100700-9, U558, UNESCO). Unipub.

Francois, Michal & Keul, Michael, eds. International Bibliography of Historical Sciences, Vol. 47-48. 458p. (Ital.). 1982. 90.00x (ISBN 0-686-82086-X, Pub. by K G Saur). Gale.

Francois, Victor E. Two Deaf Men. (Silver Series of Puppet Plays). pap. 1.00 (ISBN 0-8283-1243-5). Branden.

Francois-Poncet, Andre. The Fateful Years: Memoirs of a French Ambassador in Berlin, 1931-1938. LC 76-80549. 295p. 1973. Repr. of 1949 ed. 25.00x (ISBN 0-86527-066-X). Fertig.

Francombe, Maurice H. see Hass, Georg, et al.

Francombe, Maurice H., jt. ed. see Hass, Georg.

Francovich, Allan, tr. see Salles Gomes, P. E.

Francuch, Peter D. Four Concepts of the Spiritual Structure of Creation. LC 82-62630. 150p. 1983. pap. 5.00 (ISBN 0-939386-05-4). Spiritual Advisory.

--Messages From Within. LC 82-60513. 220p. 1982. pap. 8.00 (ISBN 0-939386-03-8). Spiritual Advisory.

--Principles of Spiritual Hypnosis. LC 81-50059. 240p. 1981. cancelled (ISBN 0-939386-00-3). Spiritual Advisory.

Francuch, Peter D. & Jones, Arthur E. Intensive Spiritual Hypnotherapy. LC 82-62015. 450p. 1983. 25.00 (ISBN 0-939386-04-6). Spiritual Advisory.

Franda, Marcus. Bangladesh: The First Decade. 1982. 22.00x (ISBN 0-8364-0891-8). South Asia Bks.

--Punjabis, War & Women: The Short Stories of Gulzar Singh Sandhu. 1983. 17.00x (ISBN 0-8364-0936-1, Pub. by Heritage India). South Asia Bks.

Franda, Marcus F. Radical Politics in West Bengal. (Studies in Communism, Revisionism, & Revolution). 1971. 20.00x (ISBN 0-262-06040-X). MIT Pr.

Franda, Marcus F., jt. ed. see Brass, Paul R.

Frandsen & Benson. Nonverbal Communication. rev. ed. Applbaum, Ronald & Hart, Roderick, eds. (MODCOM Modules in Speech Communication Ser.). 1982. pap. text ed. 2.75 (ISBN 0-574-22585-4, 13-5585). SRA.

Frandsen, Asger, ed. Dental Health Care in Scandinavia. (Illus.). 260p. (Orig.). 1982. 14.00 (ISBN 0-931386-46-2). Quint Pub Co.

Frandsen, Kathryn J., jt. auth. see Hafen, Brent Q.

Franey, Pierre. The New York Times More 60-Minute Gourmet. 1983. pap. 7.95 (ISBN 0-449-90038-X, Columbine). Fawcett.

Franey, Pierre & Flaste, Richard. Pierre Franey's Kitchen. (Illus.). 304p. 16.95 (ISBN 0-8129-1023-0). Times Bks.

Franey, Pierre, jt. auth. see Claiborne, Craig.

Frangenheim, H. Laparoscopy & Culdoscopy in Gynecology: Textbook & Atlas. Finzer, K. H., tr. from Ger. (Illus.). 114p. 1972. 19.95 o.p. (ISBN 0-407-90100-0). Butterworth.

Frangia, George W., jt. auth. see Wolf, Harvey J.

Frangsmyr, Tore, ed. see Lindroth, Stan, et al.

Frank, A. G. Mexican Agriculture: Fifteen Twenty-One to Sixteen Thirty. LC 78-6201. (Studies in Modern Capitalism Ser.). 1979. 22.95 (ISBN 0-521-22209-5). Cambridge U Pr.

Frank, A. L. A Guide for Software Entrepreneurs. (Illus.). 208p. 1982. text ed. 29.00 (ISBN 0-13-370726-1). P-H.

Frank, Adolph F. Animated Scale Models Handbook. LC 80-22858. (Illus.). 160p. 1982. pap. 9.95 (ISBN 0-668-05120-5, 5120). Arco.

Frank, Alan. The Science Fiction & Fantasy Film Handbook. LC 82-8802. (Illus.). 194p. 1982. 24.95 (ISBN 0-389-20319-X). B&N Imports.

Frank, Alan R. & McFarland, Thomas. Coin Skills Curriculum. (Illus.). 100p. (Orig.). 1983. pap. text ed. write for info. (ISBN 0-936104-28-7, 0360). Pro Ed.

Frank, Alfred L. & Abou-Rass, Marwan, eds. Clinical & Surgical Endodontics: Concepts in Practice. (Illus.). 288p. 1983. text ed. price not set (ISBN 0-397-50567-1, Lippincott Medical). Lippincott.

Frank, Allan D. Communicating on the Job. 1981. text ed. 17.95x (ISBN 0-673-15275-8). Scott F.

Frank, Amin P. Kenneth Burke. (U. S. Authors Ser.: No. 160). 12.50 o.p. (ISBN 0-8057-0116-8, Twayne). G K Hall.

Frank, Andre G. Reflections on the World Economic Crisis. LC 80-29270. 192p. 1981. 13.50 (ISBN 0-85345-563-5); pap. 5.50 (ISBN 0-85345-564-3, PB5643). Monthly Rev.

--World Accumulation, 1492-1789. LC 77-91746. 1978. 16.50 (ISBN 0-85345-442-6, CL4426). Monthly Rev.

Frank, Anne. Anne Frank: The Diary of a Young Girl. rev. ed. (YA) 1967. 15.95a (ISBN 0-385-04019-9); PLB (ISBN 0-385-09190-7). Doubleday.

--Diary of a Young Girl. LC 58-11474. 1958. 5.95 (ISBN 0-394-60298-6). Modern Lib.

--The Works of Anne Frank. LC 73-16643. (Illus.). 332p. 1974. Repr. of 1959 ed. lib. bdg. 29.75x (ISBN 0-8371-7206-3, FRWO). Greenwood.

Frank, Barbara, jt. auth. see Frank, Jerome.

Frank, Beryl. A Pictorial History of Pikesville, Maryland. (Baltimore County Heritage Publication). (Illus.). 140p. 1982. 9.95 (ISBN 0-937076-02-3). Baltimore Co Pub Lib.

Frank, Charles R., Jr. Foreign Trade & Domestic Aid. LC 76-51821. 1977. 14.95 (ISBN 0-8157-2914-6). Brookings.

Frank, Charles R., Jr. & Webb, Richard C., eds. Income Distribution & Growth in the Less-Developed Countries. LC 77-86494. 1977. pap. 15.95 (ISBN 0-8157-2915-4). Brookings.

Frank, Clyde, jt. auth. see Pietrzyk, Donald J.

Frank, Daniel B. Deep Blue Funk & Other Stories: Portraits of Teenage Parents. 1983. pap. 3.95 (ISBN 0-686-83916-1, 25994-3). U of Chicago Pr.

Frank, Dorothy. Cooking with Nuts. 1979. 12.95 (ISBN 0-517-53727-3, C N Potter Bks). Crown.

Frank, Dorothy C. The Peanut Cookbook. 1977. 3.95 o.p. (ISBN 0-685-76360-9, C N Potter Bks). Crown.

Frank, Elke, jt. auth. see Irish, Marion D.

Frank, Ellen, jt. auth. see Boller, Francois.

Frank, Ellen E. Literary Architecture: Essays Toward a Tradition-Walter Pater, Gerard Manley Hopkins, Marcel Proust, Henry James. (Illus.). 328p. 1982. 15.95 (ISBN 0-520-03352-3); pap. 8.95 (ISBN 0-520-03352-3). U of Cal Pr.

Frank, Erich. Philosophical Understanding & Religious Truth. LC 82-8476. 220p. 1982. pap. text ed. 10.75 (ISBN 0-8191-2510-5). U Pr of Amer.

Frank, Ernest. Electrical Measurement Analysis. LC 77-3508. (Electrical & Electronic Engineering Ser.). (Illus.). 458p. 1977. Repr. of 1959 ed. lib. bdg. 25.00 (ISBN 0-88275-554-4). Krieger.

Frank, Gary. Juan Peron vs. Spruille Braden: The Story Behind the Blue Book. LC 80-1359. 184p. 1980. lib. bdg. 17.75 o.p. (ISBN 0-8191-1157-0); pap. text ed. 9.00 o.p. (ISBN 0-8191-1158-9). U Pr of Amer.

Frank, Gerold. Boston Strangler. 1971. pap. 2.50 (ISBN 0-451-09553-7, E9553, Sig). NAL.

Frank, Harriet, Jr. Single. 1978. pap. 2.50 o.p. (ISBN 0-446-81543-8). Warner Bks.

--Special Effects. 1979. 8.95 o.p. (ISBN 0-395-27219-X). HM.

Frank, Harry T., ed. Atlas of the Bible Lands. new ed. 1979. pap. 6.95 (ISBN 0-8054-1136-4). Broadman.

Frank, Harvey. My Reservoir of Dreams. 1978. 4.50 o.p. (ISBN 0-533-03068-4). Vantage.

Frank, Helmut & Schanz, John T. U.S.-Canadian Energy Trade Relationships: Past Perspectives & Future Opportunities. (Westview Special Studies in Natural Resources & Energy Management). 1978. lib. bdg. 16.50 o.p. (ISBN 0-89158-250-9). Westview.

Frank, Howard & Frisch, Ivan T. Communication, Transmission, & Transportation Networks. LC 78-119666. (Engineering Ser). 1971. text ed. 30.95 (ISBN 0-201-02081-5). A-W.

Frank, Isaiah. Trade Policy Issues for the Developing Countries in the 1980's. (Working Paper Ser.: No. 478). 52p. 1981. 5.00 (ISBN 0-686-36203-9, WP-0478). World Bank.

Frank, Jerome & Frank, Barbara. Not Guilty. LC 72-138495. (Civil Liberties in American History Ser.). 1971. Repr. of 1957 ed. lib. bdg. 32.50 (ISBN 0-306-70072-7). Da Capo.

Frank, John P. Marble Palace: The Supreme Court in American Life. LC 79-163538. (Illus.). 301p. 1958. Repr. lib. bdg. 17.00x (ISBN 0-8371-6204-1, FRMP). Greenwood.

Frank, Joseph. Cromwell's Press Agent: A Critical Biography of Marchamont Nedham, 1620-1678. LC 80-5637. 213p. 1980. lib. bdg. 19.75 (ISBN 0-8191-1193-7); pap. text ed. 10.00 (ISBN 0-8191-1194-5). U Pr of Amer.

--The Widening Gyre: Crisis & Mastery in Modern Literature. LC 68-27360. (Midland Bks.: No. 120). 296p. 1968. pap. 2.65x o.p. (ISBN 0-253-20120-9). Ind U Pr.

Frank, Josette, adapted by see Barrie, J. M.

Frank, Lawrence. The Importance of Infancy. 1966. pap. text ed. 3.25x (ISBN 0-394-30892-1). Phila Bk Co.

Frank, M. Modern English: Exercises for Non Native Speakers, 2 pts. Incl. Pt. 1. Parts of Speech. 1972. pap. text ed. 11.95 (ISBN 0-13-593806-6); Pt. 2. Sentences & Complex Structures (ISBN 0-13-593814-7). 1972. pap. text ed. 10.95 (ISBN 0-686-86555-3). P-H.

Frank, Marcella. Modern English: A Practical Reference Guide. (Illus.). 1972. pap. text ed. 14.95 (ISBN 0-13-594002-8). P-H.

Frank, Marge. Fraction Action. (Choose-a-Card Ser.). (Illus.). 32p. (gr. 3-6). 1981. pap. text ed. 5.95 (ISBN 0-86530-015-1, IP 15-1). Incentive Pubns.

Frank, Marjorie, ed. see Ozaeta, Pablo.

Frank, Martha. Liberating Thoughts. 84p. 1946. 1.50 o.p. (ISBN 0-87516-406-4). De Vorss.

Frank, Martin J. & Alvarez-Mena, Sergio C. Cardiovascular Physical Diagnosis. 2nd ed. (Illus.). 1982. 25.00 (ISBN 0-8151-3331-6). Year Bk Med.

Frank, Mary, ed. Children & Families of Newcomers to the United States. (Journal of Children in Contemporary Society, Vol. 15, No. 3). 128p. text ed. 19.95 (ISBN 0-86656-181-1, B181). Haworth Pr.

--Children of Exceptional Parents. LC 82-25481. (Journal of Children in Contemporary Society Ser.: Vol. 15, No. 1). 104p. 1983. text ed. 20.00 (ISBN 0-917724-96-8, B96). Haworth Pr.

--Primary Prevention for Children & Families. LC 81-17858. (Journal of Children in Contemporary Society Ser.: Vol. 14, Nos. 2 & 3). 127p. 1982. text ed. 20.00 (ISBN 0-86656-107-2, B107). Haworth Pr.

--The Puzzling Child: From Recognition to Treatment. LC 82-11692. (Journal of Children in Contemporary Society Ser.: Vol. 14, No. 4). 119p. 1982. text ed. 20.00 (ISBN 0-86656-119-6, B119). Haworth Pr.

--Young Children in a Computerized Environment. LC 81-20028. (Journal of Children in Contemporary Society Ser.: Vol. 14, No. 1). 104p. 1982. text ed. 20.00 (ISBN 0-86656-108-0, B108). Haworth Pr.

Frank, Mel & Rosenthal, Ed. Marijuana Grower's Guide. LC 77-82452. 1978. deluxe ed. 12.95 (ISBN 0-915904-26-8); spiral bdg. 14.95 (ISBN 0-686-96657-0). And-or Pr.

Frank, Michael. My Autograph Book. 48p. (Orig.). 1982. pap. 1.75 (ISBN 0-8431-0912-2). Price Stern.

Frank, Michael B., ed. see Blair, Walter.

Frank, Myra G. Speech Activity Card File. 1972. text ed. 12.50x (ISBN 0-8134-1427-X). Interstate.

--Switch, R Sound. 1978. 3.75x (ISBN 0-8134-2005-9). Interstate.

--Switch, S Sound. 1976. text ed. 3.75x (ISBN 0-8134-1790-2, 1790). Interstate.

Frank, Myra G., jt. auth. see Egerer, Marlene M.

Frank, Neil A., jt. auth. see Kram, Shirley W.

Frank, Phil & Frank, Susan. Subee Lives on a Houseboat. LC 79-26354. (Illus.). 64p. (gr. 4 up). 1980. PLB 6.97 o.p. (ISBN 0-671-33055-1). Messner.

Frank, R. I., tr. see Bengtson, Hermann.

Frank, R. M. & Leach, S. A., eds. Surface & Colloid Phenomena in the Oral Cavity: Methodological Aspects. Proceedings of Workshop of the Research Group. (Illus.). 274p. 1981. pap. 24.00 (ISBN 0-904147-36-3). IRL Pr.

Frank R. Walker Company, ed. see Bourgeois, G. Patrick, et al.

Frank R. Walker Company, ed. see Crespin, Vick S., et al.

Frank, Robert & Model, Lisette. Charles Pratt: Photographs. LC 82-71396. (Illus.). 88p. Date not set. pap. 25.00 (ISBN 0-89381-111-4). Aperture.

Frank, Robert G., Jr. Harvey & the Oxford Physiologists: Scientific Ideas & Social Interaction. LC 79-63553. (Illus.). 1981. 30.00x (ISBN 0-520-03906-8). U of Cal Pr.

Frank, Ronald E. & Greenberg, Marshall G. Audiences for Public Television. (Illus.). 224p. 1982. 25.00 (ISBN 0-8039-0764-8). Sage.

Frank, Ronald E. & Massy, William F. An Economic Approach to a Marketing Decision Model. 1971. 25.00x (ISBN 0-262-06037-X). MIT Pr.

Frank, S. L. Go with Us. 1946. text ed. 29.50x (ISBN 0-686-83560-3). Elliots Bks.

Frank, S. L., ed. see Solov'Ev, Vladimir S.

Frank, Samuel B. & Schonfeld, Josef. The Impressed Duty Stamps of Great Britain. LC 81-131530. (Illus.). 360p. 1981. pap. 17.00 (ISBN 0-686-36297-7). Barber W A.

Frank Schaffer Publications. Addition. (Help Your Child Learn Ser.). (Illus.). 24p. (gr. 1-3). 1978. workbook 1.29 (ISBN 0-86734-007-X, FS 3008). Schaffer Pubns.

--The Alphabet. (Help Your Child Learn Ser.). (Illus.). 24p. (ps-2). 1978. workbook 1.29 (ISBN 0-86734-001-0, FS 3002). Schaffer Pubns.

--Beginning Activities with Numbers. (Getting Ready for Kindergarten Ser.). (Illus.). 24p. (ps-k). 1980. workbook 1.29 (ISBN 0-86734-014-2, FS 3027). Schaffer Pubns.

--Beginning Activities with Pencil & Paper. (Getting Ready for Kindergarten Ser.). (Illus.). 24p. (ps-k). 1980. workbook 1.29 (ISBN 0-86734-017-7, FS 3030). Schaffer Pubns.

--Beginning Activities with Shapes. (Getting Ready for Kindergarten Ser.). (Illus.). 24p. (ps-k). 1980. workbook 1.29 (ISBN 0-86734-013-4, FS 3026). Schaffer Pubns.

--Beginning Activities with the Alphabet. (Getting Ready for Kindergarten Ser.). (Illus.). 24p. (ps-k). 1980. workbook 1.29 (ISBN 0-86734-015-0, FS 3028). Schaffer Pubns.

--Following Directions. (Helping Your Child Learn Ser.). (Illus.). 24p. (gr. 2-4). 1978. workbook 1.29 (ISBN 0-86734-008-8, FS 3009). Schaffer Pubns.

--Getting Ready for Kindergarten. (Help Your Child Learn Ser.). (Illus.). 24p. (ps-k). 1978. workbook 1.29 (ISBN 0-86734-000-2, FS 3001). Schaffer Pubns.

--Getting Ready for Math. (Getting Ready for Kindergarten Ser.). (Illus.). 24p. (ps-k). 1980. 1.29 (ISBN 0-86734-020-7, FS 3033). Schaffer Pubns.

--Getting Ready for Phonics. (Getting Ready for Kindergarten Ser.). (Illus.). 24p. (ps-k). 1980. workbook 1.29 (ISBN 0-86734-018-5, FS 3031). Schaffer Pubns.

--Getting Ready for Reading. (Getting Ready for Kindergarten Ser.). (Illus.). 24p. (ps-k). 1980. workbook 1.29 (ISBN 0-86734-019-3, FS 3032). Schaffer Pubns.

--Getting Ready for Science. (Getting Ready for Kindergarten). (Illus.). 24p. (ps-k). 1980. workbook 1.29 (ISBN 0-86734-021-5, FS 3034). Schaffer Pubns.

--Getting Ready for Writing. (Getting Ready for Kindergarten Ser.). (Illus.). 24p. (ps-k). 1980. workbook 1.29 (ISBN 0-86734-016-9, FS 3029). Schaffer Pubns.

--Handwriting with Harvey Hippo. (Help Your Child Learn Ser.). (Illus.). 24p. (gr. 2-4). 1978. workbook 1.29 (ISBN 0-86734-009-6, FS 3010). Schaffer Pubns.

--Kindergarten Skills. (Getting Ready for Kindergarten Ser.). (Illus.). 24p. (ps-k). 1980. workbook 1.29 (ISBN 0-86734-012-6, FS 3025). Schaffer Pubns.

--Multiplication. (Help Your Child Learn Ser.). (Illus.). 24p. (gr. 3-5). 1978. workbook 1.29 (ISBN 0-86734-010-X, FS 3011). Schaffer Pubns.

--My First Words. (Help Your Child Learn Ser.). (Illus.). 24p. (gr. 1-3). 1978. workbook 1.29 (ISBN 0-86734-005-3, FS 3006). Schaffer Pubns.

--Phonics: Consonants. (Help Your Child Learn Ser.). (Illus.). 24p. (ps-2). 1978. workbook 1.29 (ISBN 0-86734-003-7, FS 3004). Schaffer Pubns.

--Reading Comprehension. (Help Your Child Learn Ser.). (Illus.). 24p. (gr. 3-5). 1978. workbook 1.29 (ISBN 0-86734-011-8, FS 3012). Schaffer Pubns.

Frank Schaffer Publications, Inc. Numbers. (Help Your Child Learn Ser.). (Illus.). 24p. (ps-2). 1978. workbook 1.29 (ISBN 0-86734-002-9, FS 3003). Schaffer Pubns.

--Phonics: Vowels. (Help Your Child Learn Ser.). (Illus.). 24p. (gr. 1-3). 1978. workbook 1.29 (ISBN 0-86734-004-5, FS 3005). Schaffer Pubns.

--Printing with Peter Possum. (Help Your Child Learn Ser.). (Illus.). 24p. (gr. k-2). 1978. workbook 1.29 (ISBN 0-86734-006-1, FS 3007). Schaffer Pubns.

Frank, Stuart M. & Webb, Robert L. M. V. Brewington: A Bibliography & Catalogue of the Brewington Press. 36p. 1982. commemorative & numbered ed. 6.00 (ISBN 0-686-83948-X); pap. 4.00 (ISBN 0-686-83949-8). Kendall Whaling.

Frank, Susan, jt. auth. see Frank, Phil.

Frank, Ted & Ray, David. Basic Business & Professional Speech Communication. (Speech Communication Ser.). (Illus.). 1979. pap. text ed. 24.95 (ISBN 0-13-057273-X). P-H.

Frank, Thomas. Introduction to the PDP11 & its Assembly Language. (P-H Software Ser.). (Illus.). 512p. 1983. text ed. 24.95 (ISBN 0-13-491704-9). P-H.

Frank, Victor C. Rainbow in My Church. pap. 0.50 o.p. (ISBN 0-8100-0068-7, 18-0220). Northwest Pub.

Frank, Werner L. Critical Issues in Software: A Guide to Software Economics, Strategy & Profitability. 288p. 1983. 25.00x (ISBN 0-471-87293-8, Pub. by Wiley Interscience). Wiley.

Frank, William L. Sherwood Bonner (Catherine McDowell) (United States Authors Ser.). 1976. lib. bdg. 13.95 (ISBN 0-8057-7169-7, Twayne). G K Hall.

Franke, Lois & Udell, William L. Handwrought Jewelry. (gr. 7 up). 1962. text ed. 19.96 (ISBN 0-87345-175-9). McKnight.

Franke, Monte, jt. auth. see Coughlan, Bill.

Frankel & Richard. Be Alive As Long As You Live: The Older Person's Guide to Exercise for Joyful Living. 1980. 14.37i (ISBN 0-690-01892-4). Har-Row.

Frankel, A., jt. auth. see Bernays, P.

Frankel, Aaron. Writing the Broadway Musical. LC 76-58925. 1977. pap. text ed. 8.00x (ISBN 0-910482-82-9). Drama Bk.

Frankel, Charles, ed. Controversies & Decisions: The Social Sciences & Public Policy. LC 75-28514. 310p. 1976. 10.00x (ISBN 0-87154-262-5). Russell Sage.

Frankel, Edward. DNA: The Ladder of Life. 2nd ed. (Illus.). (gr. 7 up). 1978. 9.95 (ISBN 0-07-021883-8, GB). McGraw.

Frankel, Godfrey, jt. auth. see Frankel, Lillian.

Frankel, Hans H., compiled by. Catalogue of Translations from the Chinese Dynastic Histories for the Period 220-960. LC 74-9395. (Chinese Dynastic Studies. Translations. U of Cal Pr). 295p. 1974. Repr. of 1957 ed. lib. bdg. 17.25x (ISBN 0-8371-7661-1, FRDH). Greenwood.

Frankel, Haskel, jt. auth. see Hagen, Uta.

Frankel, Jack B. Helping Students Think & Value: Strategies for Teaching Social Studies. 2nd ed. 1980. text ed. 22.95 (ISBN 0-13-386375-1). P-H.

Frankel, Jonathan. Prophecy & Politics: Socialism, Nationalism, & the Russian Jews, 1862-1917. LC 80-14414. (Illus.). 816p. 1981. 54.50 (ISBN 0-521-23028-4). Cambridge U Pr.

Frankel, Jonathan, ed. Vladimir Akimov on the Dilemmas of Russian Marxism 1895-1903: Two Texts in Translation. (Cambridge Studies in the History & Theory of Politics). (Illus.). 1969. 54.50 (ISBN 0-521-05029-4). Cambridge U Pr.

Frankel, Joseph. International Relations in a Changing World. rev. ed. 1980. 14.50x (ISBN 0-19-219147-0); pap. text ed. 6.95x (ISBN 0-19-289128-6). Oxford U Pr.

Frankel, Julie, jt. auth. see Scheier, Michael.

Frankel, Lillian & Frankel, Godfrey. Bikeways: One Hundred One Things to Do with a Bike. rev. ed. LC 61-15857. (Illus.). 128p. (gr. 8 up). 1972. 6.95 o.p. (ISBN 0-8069-4004-2); PLB 7.49 o.p. (ISBN 0-8069-4005-0). Sterling.

Frankel, Linda, jt. auth. see Bart, Pauline B.

Frankel, Lionel H. & McDonnell, Julian B. Commercial Transactions: Payment Systems. (Contemporary Legal Education Ser.). 322p. 1982. pap. text ed. 11.00 (ISBN 0-686-84215-4). Michie-Bobbs.

--Commercial Transactions: Sales. (Contemporary Legal Education Ser.). 463p. pap. text ed. 15.00 (ISBN 0-87215-470-X). Michie-Bobbs.

--Commercial Transactions: Secured Financing. (Contemporary Legal Education Ser.). 389p. 1982. pap. text ed. 14.00 (ISBN 0-87215-468-8). Michie-Bobbs.

Frankel, M., jt. auth. see Levy, Alex.

Frankel, Mark, jt. auth. see Rudestam, Kjell E.

Frankel, Martin R. Inference from Survey Samples: An Empirical Investigation. LC 72-161550. 173p. 1971. 12.00x (ISBN 0-87944-013-9). Inst Soc Res.

Frankel, O. H. & Soule, M. E. Conservation & Evolution. LC 80-40528. (Illus.). 300p. 1981. 52.50 (ISBN 0-521-23275-9); pap. 18.95 (ISBN 0-521-29889-X). Cambridge U Pr.

Frankel, O. H. & Hawkes, J. G., eds. Crop Genetic Resources for Today & Tomorrow. LC 74-82586. (International Biological Programme Ser.: Vol. 2). (Illus.). 544p. 1975. 80.00 (ISBN 0-521-20575-1). Cambridge U Pr.

Frankel, Paul. Essentials of Petroleum. LC 74-96375. Repr. of 1946 ed. lib. bdg. 19.50x o.p. (ISBN 0-678-05103-8). Kelley.

Frankel, R., ed. Heterosis. (Monographs on Theoretical & Applied Genetics: Vol. 6). (Illus.). 320p. 1983. 33.50 (ISBN 0-387-12125-0). Springer-Verlag.

Frankel, Robert. Radiation Protection for Radiologic Technologists. (Illus.). 1976. text ed. 21.50 (ISBN 0-07-021875-7, HP). McGraw.

Frankel, S. Herbert. Two Philosophies of Money: The Conflict of Trust & Authority. LC 77-9211. 1977. 20.00x (ISBN 0-312-82698-2). St Martin.

Frankel, Tamar. The Regulation of Money Managers, 4 vols. LC 77-1577. 1980. Vol. 1. 32.00 (ISBN 0-316-29191-9); Vol. 2. text ed. 32.00 (ISBN 0-316-29192-7); text ed. 32.00 (ISBN 0-316-29193-5); Vol. 4. text ed. 50.00 ea. (ISBN 0-316-29194-3); 215.00 set (ISBN 0-316-29190-0); 1982 supplement avail. (ISBN 0-316-29195-1). Little.

Frankel, Theodore. Tables for Traffic Management & Design. 1977. 8.95 (ISBN 0-686-98071-9). Telecom Lib.

Franken, Peter, et al. Queues & Point Processes. (Probability & Mathematical Statistics Ser.). 230p. 1983. 35.95x (ISBN 0-471-10074-9, Pub. by Wiley-Interscience). Wiley.

Franken, Robert E. Human Motivation. LC 81-9937. 512p. 1981. text ed. 19.95 (ISBN 0-8185-0461-7). Brooks-Cole.

Frankena, William K. Ethics. 2nd ed. (Foundations of Philosophy Ser). 144p. 1973. pap. text ed. 8.95 (ISBN 0-13-290478-0). P-H.

--Philosophy of Education. 1965. pap. 12.95x (ISBN 0-02-339490-0, 33949). Macmillan.

Frankena, William K. & Granrose, John T. Introductory Readings in Ethics. 496p. 1974. text ed. 24.95 (ISBN 0-13-502112-X). P-H.

Frankenberg, Lloyd, ed. Invitation to Poetry: A Round of Poems from John Skelton to Dylan Thomas. LC 68-8061. (Illus.). 1968. Repr. of 1956 ed. lib. bdg. 39.75 (ISBN 0-8371-0077-1, FRIP). Greenwood.

Frankenberg, Ronald, ed. Custom & Conflict in British Society. 361p. 1982. text ed. 21.00x (ISBN 0-7190-0855-7, 40671, Pub. by Manchester England). Humanities.

Frankenburg, W. G., et al. Advances in Catalysis & Related Subjects, 28 vols. Incl. Vol. 1. 1948 (ISBN 0-12-007801-5); Vol. 2. 1950 (ISBN 0-12-007802-3); Vol. 3. 1951 (ISBN 0-12-007803-1); Vol. 4. 1952 (ISBN 0-12-007804-X); Vol. 5. 1953. (ISBN 0-12-007805-8); Vol. 6. 1954 (ISBN 0-12-007806-6); Vol. 7. 1955 (ISBN 0-12-007807-4); Vol. 8. 1956 (ISBN 0-12-007808-2); Vol. 9. Proceedings. International Congress on Catalysis - Philadelphia - 1956. Eley, D. D., et al, eds. 1957 (ISBN 0-12-007809-0); Vol. 10. 1958 (ISBN 0-12-007810-4); Vol. 11. Eley, D. D., et al, eds. 1959 (ISBN 0-12-007811-2); Vol. 12. 1960 (ISBN 0-12-007812-0); Vol. 13. 1962 (ISBN 0-12-007813-9); Vol. 14. Eley, D. D., et al, eds. 1963 (ISBN 0-12-007814-7); Vol. 15. 1964 (ISBN 0-12-007815-5); Vol. 16. 1966 (ISBN 0-12-007816-3); Vol. 17. 1967 (ISBN 0-12-007817-1); Vol. 18. 1968 (ISBN 0-12-007818-X); Vol. 19. 1969 (ISBN 0-12-007819-8); Vol. 20. 1969. (ISBN 0-12-007820-1); Vol. 21. 1970 (ISBN 0-12-007821-X); Vol. 22. 1972 (ISBN 0-12-007822-8); **Vol. 24. 1975. 67.00 (ISBN 0-12-007824-4); lib. ed. 85.50 (ISBN 0-12-007874-0); microfiche 48.00 (ISBN 0-12-007875-9); Vol. 25. 1976. 67.00 (ISBN 0-12-007825-2); lib. ed. 85.00 (ISBN 0-12-007876-7); microfiche 48.00 (ISBN 0-12-007877-5); Vol. 26. 1977. 67.00 (ISBN 0-12-007826-0); lib. ed. 85.50 (ISBN 0-12-007878-3); microfiche 48.00 (ISBN 0-12-007879-1); Vol. 27. 1979. 58.00 (ISBN 0-12-007827-9); lib. ed. 73.00 (ISBN 0-12-007880-5); microfiche 42.00 (ISBN 0-12-007881-3); Vol. 28. 1979. 56.00 (ISBN 0-12-007828-7); lib. ed. 67.50 (ISBN 0-12-007882-1); microfiche 37.00 (ISBN 0-12-007883-X). Vols. 1-16. 59.50 ea.; Vols 17-18. 59.50 ea.; Vols. 19-22. 59.50 ea.; Vol. 23. 59.50 (ISBN 0-12-007823-6). Acad Pr.**

--Advances in Catalysis & Related Subjects, Vol. 29. 1980. 51.50 (ISBN 0-12-007829-5); lib. ed. 67.00 (ISBN 0-12-007884-8); microfiche ed. 36.00 (ISBN 0-12-007885-6). Acad Pr.

Frankenstein, Alfred. After the Hunt. LC 68-31417. (Illus.). 1975. 57.50x (ISBN 0-520-02936-4). U of Cal Pr.

--The Reminiscent Object: Paintings by William Michael Harnett, John Frederick Peto & John Haberle. (Illus.). 68p. 1965. 3.00x (ISBN 0-686-99840-5). La Jolla Mus Contemp Art.

--World of Copley. LC 74-113381. (Library of Art Ser.). (Illus.). (gr. 6 up). 1970. 19.92 (ISBN 0-8094-0284-X, Pub. by Time-Life). Silver.

Frankenstein, Marilyn. Basic Algebra. (Illus.). 1979. pap. text ed. 20.95 (ISBN 0-13-056788-4). P-H.

Frankfather, Dwight L., et al. Family Care of the Elderly: Public Initiatives & Private Obligations. LC 80-7577. 144p. 1981. 19.95x (ISBN 0-669-03759-1). Lexington Bks.

Frankfort, jt. auth. see Dye.

Frankfort, Hans, tr. see Schafer, Harald.

Frankfort, Henri. Ancient Egyptian Religion: An Interpretation. 10.00 (ISBN 0-8446-2084-X). Peter Smith.

Frankfort, Henri, et al. The Intellectual Adventure of Ancient Man: An Essay on Speculative Thought in the Ancient Near East. LC 47-1318. 1977. pap. 8.95 (ISBN 0-226-26008-9, P725, Phoen); 13.50x o.s.i. (ISBN 0-226-26009-7). U of Chicago Pr.

Frankfurter, Felix. Case of Sacco & Vanzetti. 1962. pap. 3.95 o.p. (ISBN 0-448-00110-1, G&D). Putnam Pub Group.

Frankfurter, Felix, ed. Mr. Justice Brandeis. LC 73-37766. (American Constitutional & Legal History Ser). (Illus.). 232p. 1972. Repr. of 1932 ed. lib. bdg. 27.50 (ISBN 0-306-70430-7). Da Capo.

--Mr. Justice Brandeis. 1932. 24.50x (ISBN 0-686-51416-5). Elliots Bks.

Frankfurter, Felix, ed. see Cleveland Foundation.

Frankl, Paul T. Form & Reform: Practical Handbook of Modern Interiors. LC 72-143347. (Illus.). 1972. Repr. of 1930 ed. 15.00 o.s.i. (ISBN 0-87817-067-7). Hacker.

--New Dimensions: The Decorative Arts of Today in Words & Pictures. LC 75-15851. (Architecture and Decorative Arts Ser.). (Illus.). 122p. 1975. Repr. of 1928 ed. lib. bdg. 39.50 (ISBN 0-306-70741-1). Da Capo.

Frankl, Victor E. Man's Search for Meaning: An Introduction to Logotherapy. 1970. pap. 4.95 (ISBN 0-671-20782-2, Touchstone Bks). S&S.

Frankl, Viktor E. The Doctor & the Soul: From Psychotherapy to Logotherapy. 320p. 1973. pap. 3.95 (ISBN 0-394-71866-6, Vin). Random.

Frankland, Barry, jt. auth. see Kendrick, Richard.

Frankland, J. C., et al. Decomposer Basidiomycetes: Their Biology & Ecology. LC 81-18145. (British Mycological Society Symposium Ser.: No. 4). (Illus.). 250p. 1982. 74.50 (ISBN 0-521-24634-2). Cambridge u Pr.

Frankland, Thomas W. Pipe Fitter's & Welder's Handbook. (Illus., Orig.). 1955. pap. 6.95 (ISBN 0-02-802490-7). Glencoe.

--Pipe Template Layout. (Illus., Orig.). 1967. pap. 6.95 (ISBN 0-02-802400-1). Glencoe.

--Pipe Trades Pocket Manual. (Illus., Orig.). 1969. pap. 7.25 (ISBN 0-02-802410-9). Glencoe.

Frankle, John T., jt. auth. see Klapper, Jacob.

Frankle, Reva T. & Owen, Anita Y. Nutrition in the Community: The Art of Delivering Services. LC 78-9144. 396p. 1978. text ed. 21.95 (ISBN 0-8016-1666-2). Mosby.

Franklin, ed. Clinical Immunology Update, 1981: Reviews for Physicians. 1980. 34.95 (ISBN 0-444-00416-5). Elsevier.

--Clinical Immunology Update, 1983. 1982. 42.50 (ISBN 0-444-00711-3). Elsevier.

Franklin, A. White, ed. see Royal Society of Medicine.

Franklin, Allan. The Principle of Inertia in the Middle Ages. LC 76-10515. 100p. (Orig.). 1976. pap. 5.95x (ISBN 0-87081-069-3). Colo Assoc.

Franklin, Anderson J. see Boykin, A. Wade, et al.

Franklin, Aubrey A. Teatime. LC 80-70953. (Illus.). 224p. 1981. 10.95 o.p. (ISBN 0-8119-0414-8). Fell.

Franklin, Barbara A., tr. see Glissant, Edouard.

Franklin, Benjamin. Autobiography & Other Writings. 1961. pap. 2.75 (ISBN 0-451-51625-7, CE1625, Sig Classics). NAL.

--Autobiography & Selected Writings. (YA) 1981. pap. 3.95 (ISBN 0-394-30918-9, T18, Mod LibC). Modern Lib.

--Autobiography of Benjamin Franklin. (Classics Ser.). (gr. 8 up). pap. 1.50 (ISBN 0-8049-0071-X, CL-71). Airmont.

--Boston Printers, Publishers & Booksellers: 1640-1800. 1980. lib. bdg. 30.00 (ISBN 0-8161-8472-0, Hall Reference). G K Hall.

--Essays on General Politics, Commerce & Political Economy. Sparks, Jared & Phillips, W., eds. LC 66-21673. Repr. of 1836 ed. 22.50 (ISBN 0-678-00292-4). Kelley.

--The Papers of Benjamin Franklin: March 23, 1775 Through October 27, 1776, Vol. 22. Willcox, William B., ed. LC 59-12697. 768p. 1982. 45.00x (ISBN 0-300-02618-8). Yale U Pr.

--The Papers of Benjamin Franklin, Vol. 23: October Twenty-Seventh, Seventeen Seventy-Six, Through April Thirtieth, Seventeen Seventy-Seven. Willcox, William B. & Arnold, Douglas M., eds. LC 59-12697. 752p. 1983. text ed. 45.00x (ISBN 0-300-02897-0). Yale U Pr.

--The Whistle. LC 72-12487. (Seedling Bks). (Illus.). 32p. (gr. 2-6). 1974. text ed. 4.95g (ISBN 0-8225-0282-8). Lerner Pubns.

Franklin, Benjamin & Schneider, Duane. Anais Nin: An Introduction. LC 79-10635. 309p. 1980. pap. 10.00x (ISBN 0-8214-0432-6, 82-82857). Ohio U Pr.

--Anais Nin: An Introduction. LC 79-10635. 1980. 17.50x (ISBN 0-8214-0395-8, 82-82865). Ohio U Pr.

Franklin, Benjamin, ed. Poetry of the Minor Connecticut Wits, 1791-1818. LC 68-17015. 1970. 90.00x (ISBN 0-8201-1066-3). Schol Facsimiles.

--The Prose of the Minor Connecticut Wits, 3 vols. LC 74-11124. 1500p. 1974. Repr. 200.00x set (ISBN 0-8201-1132-5). Schol Facsimiles.

Franklin, Carolyn, jt. auth. see Rubey, Jane A.

Franklin, Clay. Anybody We Know. 4.50 (ISBN 0-573-60080-5). French.

--Skits for the Young in Heart. 1977. pap. 3.00 (ISBN 0-686-38386-9). Eldridge Pub.

--Skits for the Young in Heart. 1977. pap. 3.00 (ISBN 0-686-38753-8). Eldridge Pub.

Franklin, Clyde W., jt. auth. see Martin, James G.

Franklin, Doris R. Selective & Nonselective Admissions Criteria in Junior College Nursing Programs. (League Exchange Ser.: No. 104). 68p. 1975. 5.50 (ISBN 0-686-38369-9, 23-1561). Natl League Nurse.

Franklin, Douglas & Jankowski, Thaddeus. Understanding Property Revaluation: A Massachusetts Handbook. 176p. (Orig.). 1983. pap. write for info. (ISBN 0-88063-030-2). Butterworth Legal Pubs.

Franklin, E. C., ed. Clinical Immunology Update 1979: Reviews for Physicians. (1979 Update). 1979. 35.00 (ISBN 0-444-00312-6). Elsevier.

Franklin, Francis, ed. see Bowers, Claude G. & Browder, Earl.

Franklin, Gene F. & Powell, J. David. Digital Control of Dynamic Systems. LC 79-16377. 1980. text ed. 27.95 (ISBN 0-201-02891-3); solution manual 2.00 (ISBN 0-201-02892-1). A-W.

Franklin, Grace A., jt. ed. see Ripley, Randall B.

Franklin, H. Bruce. American Prisoners & Ex-Prisoners: Their Writings: An Annotated Bibliography of Published Works, 1798-1981. LC 82-11682. 64p. 1982. pap. 5.95 (ISBN 0-88208-147-0). Lawrence Hill.

--Future Perfect: American Science Fiction of the Nineteenth Century. rev. ed. 1978. pap. 8.95 (ISBN 0-19-502323-4, GB241, GB). Oxford U Pr.

--Prison Literature in America: The Victim As Criminal & Artist. 303p. 1982. pap. 8.95 (ISBN 0-88208-146-2). Lawrence Hill.

--The Victim As Criminal & Artist: Literature from the American Prison. 1978. 19.95x (ISBN 0-19-502244-0). Oxford U Pr.

Franklin, H. Bruce, ed. Future Perfect: American Science Fiction of the Nineteenth Century. 1978. 22.50x (ISBN 0-19-502322-6). Oxford U Pr.

Franklin, H. Bruce, ed. see Melville, Herman.

Franklin, Howard. A Flowers Arrangers Guide to Showing. 1979. 14.95 (ISBN 0-7134-3321-3, Pub by Batsford, England). David & Charles.

Franklin Institute Gmbh, ed. see Gillespie, Paul D.

Franklin, Jack L. & Thrasher, Jean H. An Introduction to Program Evaluation. LC 76-4789. 1976. 20.50x o.p. (ISBN 0-471-27519-0, Pub. by Wiley-Interscience). Wiley.

Franklin, James. New German Cinema. (Filmmakers Ser.). 248p. 1983. lib. bdg. 19.95 (ISBN 0-8057-9288-0, Twayne). G K Hall.

Franklin, Jerome L., jt. auth. see Bowers, David G.

Franklin, Jerome L., ed. Human Resource Development in the Organization: A Guide to Information Sources. LC 76-28289. (Management Information Guide Ser.: No. 35). 1978. 42.00x (ISBN 0-8103-0835-5). Gale.

Franklin, Joel N. Matrix Theory. 1968. ref. ed. 24.95 (ISBN 0-13-565648-6). P-H.

Franklin, John H. From Slavery to Freedom: A History of Negro Americans. 5th ed. 554p. 1980. pap. text ed. 12.50 (ISBN 0-394-32256-8); wkbk. 4.95 (ISBN 0-394-32474-9). Knopf.

Franklin, John H. & Meier, August, eds. Black Leaders of the Twentieth Century. 1983. pap. 7.95 (ISBN 0-252-00939-8). U of Ill Pr.

Franklin, Jon & Doelp, Alan. Not Quite a Miracle: Brain Surgeons & Their Patients on the Frontier of Medicine. LC 82-45461. 288p. 1983. 16.95 (ISBN 0-385-17495-0). Doubleday.

Franklin, Julia, tr. see Fourier, Charles.

Franklin, Julian H. Jean Bodin & the Rise of Absolutist Theory. (Cambridge Studies in the History & Theory of Politics). 1973. 19.95 (ISBN 0-521-20000-8). Cambridge U Pr.

--John Locke & the Theory of Sovereignty. LC 77-80833. (Studies in the History & Theory of Politics). 1978. 27.95 (ISBN 0-521-21758-X). Cambridge U Pr.

Franklin, Justin D. & Bouchard, Robert F., eds. Guidebook to the Freedom of Information & Privacy Acts. LC 79-27406. 1980. 45.00 (ISBN 0-87632-310-7). Boardman.

Franklin, Karl, et al. Tolai Language Course. (Asian-Pacific Ser., No. 7). 140p. 1974. pap. 4.25x o. p. (ISBN 0-88312-207-3); microfiche 2.25x (ISBN 0-88312-307-X). Summer Inst Ling.

Franklin, Linda C. Album. (Old Fashioned Keepbook Photo Albums Ser.). (Illus.). 32p. 1982. 17.50 (ISBN 0-934504-14-8). Tree Comm.

--Baby Pictures. (Old Fashioned Keepbook Photo Albums Ser.). (Illus.). 32p. 1982. 17.50 (ISBN 0-934504-15-6). Tree Comm.

--Good Home Cooking: Breads & Biscuits. LC 81-51420. (Old Fashioned Keepbook Ser.). (Illus.). 128p. 1981. Tree Comm.

--Our Old Fashioned Country Diary for 1984. (Old Fashioned Keepbk.). (Illus.). 144p. 1982. 10.00 (ISBN 0-934504-17-2). Tree Comm.

--Three Hundred Years of Kitchen Collectibles: Identification & Values for Collectors. (Illus.). 400p. 1981. pap. 9.95 o.p. (ISBN 0-517-54410-5, Americana). Crown.

--Three Hundred Years of Kitchen Collectibles: Identification & Value Guide. (Illus.). 286p. (Orig.). 1981. pap. 9.95 o.p. (ISBN 0-89689-020-1). Bks Americana.

--Three Hundred Years of Kitchen Collectables: Identification & Value Guide. 2nd ed. 340p. 1983. pap. 10.95 (ISBN 0-89689-041-4). Bks Americana.

--Travel Diary. (Old Fashioned Keepbook Ser.). 96p. 1983. pap. 7.50 (ISBN 0-934504-19-9). Tree Comm.

--Wedding Album. (Old Fashioned Keepbook Photo Albums Ser.). (Illus.). 32p. 1982. 17.50 (ISBN 0-934504-16-4). Tree Comm.

Franklin, Lynn & Harrison, Shirley. Psychic Search. 280p. 1981. 12.95 (ISBN 0-930096-22-3). G Gannett.

Franklin, M. J. British Biscuit Tins, 1868-1939: An Aspect of Decorative Packaging. 1980. 99.95 (ISBN 0-904568-11-3, Pub. by New Cavendish). Methuen Inc.

Franklin, Max. Baby Blue Marine. 1976. pap. 1.50 o.p. (ISBN 0-451-06895-5, W6895, Sig). NAL.

--Good Guys Wear Black. (Illus., Orig.). 1978. pap. 1.75 o.p. (ISBN 0-451-07972-8, E7972, Sig). NAL.

Franklin, Miles. My Brilliant Career. 272p. 1981. pap. 3.95 (ISBN 0-671-45915-5). WSP.

--On Dearborn Street. LC 81-11570. 224p. (YA) 1982. 14.95 (ISBN 0-7022-1636-4). U of Queensland Pr.

Franklin, Miriam A. Rehearsal: The Principles & Practice of Acting for the Stage. 5th ed. (Illus.). 256p. 1972. pap. 17.95 ref. ed. (ISBN 0-13-771592-7). P-H.

Franklin, N. L., jt. auth. see Bennett, Carl A.

Franklin, P., ed. see Bauer-Lechner, Natalie.

Franklin, Paul L. The Comprehensive Employment & Training Act: A Guide for Educators. 1979. pap. 6.50 o.p. (ISBN 0-87447-112-5, 219011). College Bd.

Franklin, Paula & Franklin, Richard. Tomorrow's Track. 1976. pap. 6.95 (ISBN 0-934698-09-0). New Comm Pr.

Franklin, Richard, jt. auth. see Franklin, Paula.

Franklin, Shirley A. Perilous Homecoming. 192p. (YA) 1975. 6.95 (ISBN 0-685-53497-9, Avalon). Bouregy.

Franklin, Steven C., jt. auth. see Fulmer, Robert M.

Franklin, Vincent P. & Anderson, James D., eds. New Perspectives on Black Educational History. 1978. lib. bdg. 18.00 (ISBN 0-8161-8114-4, Hall Reference). G K Hall.

Franklin, William M. Protection of Foreign Interests, a Study in Diplomatic and Consular Practice. Repr. of 1947 ed. lib. bdg. 18.00x (ISBN 0-8371-0426-2, FRFI). Greenwood.

Franklin, Woodman B. Guatemala. (World Bibliographical Ser.: No. 9). 109p. 1981. text ed. 21.00 (ISBN 0-903450-24-0). ABC-Clio.

Franklyn, Julian, ed. A Dictionary of the Occult. Repr. of 1935 ed. 34.00x (ISBN 0-685-32596-2). Gale.

Franko, David A. & Wetzel, Robert G. To Quench Our Thirst. (Illus.). 176p. 1983. text ed. 20.00 (ISBN 0-472-10032-7); pap. text ed. 8.50 (ISBN 0-472-08037-7). U of Mich Pr.

Franko, Ivan. Ivan Franko, the Poet of the Western Ukraine, Selected Poems. Manning, Clarence A., ed. Cundy, Percival, tr. Repr. of 1948 ed. lib. bdg. 15.75x (ISBN 0-8371-0078-X, FRSP). Greenwood.

Franks, A. H. Svetlana Beriosova: A Biography. (Series in Dance). 1978. Repr. of 1958 ed. 19.50 (ISBN 0-306-79537-X). Da Capo.

Franks, Alan. Boychester's Bugle. 245p. 1983. 16.95 (ISBN 0-434-27060-1, Pub. by Heinemann England). David & Charles.

Franks, Arthur. Dancing As a Career. (Illus.). (gr. 9 up). 14.50x (ISBN 0-392-02643-0, SpS). Sportshelf.

Franks, C. Behavior Therapy Appraisal & Status. 1969. text ed. 32.00 o.p. (ISBN 0-07-021903-6, C). McGraw.

Franks, C. M., jt. ed. see Rubin, R. D.

Franks, C. S. The Fiction of Radclyffe Hall. 1982. 50.00x o.p. (ISBN 0-686-79108-8, Pub. by Avebury Pub England). State Mutual Bk.

Franks, Cyril M. & Wilson, Terence G. Annual Review of Behavior Therapy, Vol. 8. LC 76-126864. 417p. 1982. text ed. 27.50 (ISBN 0-89862-612-9). Guilford Pr.

Franks, Cyril M., ed. The New Developments in Behavior Therapy: From Research to Clinical Application. (Supplement to Child & Family Behavior Therapy Ser.: Vol. 4). 525p. 1983. pap. text ed. 20.00 (ISBN 0-86656-178-1, B178). Haworth Pr.

Franks, Cyril M., jt. ed. see Wilson, G. Terence.

Franks, Felix. Biophysics of Water: Proceedings of a Working Conference Held at Girton College Cambridge, June 29 - July 3, 1981. 300p. 1982. 62.95 (ISBN 0-471-10229-6, Pub. by Wiley-Interscience). Wiley.

--Polywater. (Illus.). 200p. 1981. 15.00x (ISBN 0-262-06073-6). MIT Pr.

Franks, J. R. & Broyles, J. E. Modern Managerial Finance. LC 79-83955. 376p. 1979. 45.95 (ISBN 0-471-99751-X); pap. 21.00x (ISBN 0-471-27563-8, Pub. by Wiley-Interscience). Wiley.

Franks, John M. Homology & Dynamical Systems. LC 82-8897. (Conference Board of the Mathematical Sciences Ser.: Vol. 49). 14.00 (ISBN 0-8218-1700-0). Am Math.

Franks, Kenny A. & Lambert, Paul F. Early Louisana & Arkansas Oil: A Photographic History, 1901-1946. LC 82-40313. (The Montague History of Oil Ser.: No. 3). (Illus.). 260p. 1982. 27.95 (ISBN 0-89096-134-4). Tex A&M Univ Pr.

Franks, Laurie. All the Stamps of New Zealand. rev. ed. (Illus.). 172p. 1981. 20.00 (ISBN 0-589-01008-5, Pub. by Reed Books Australia). C E Tuttle.

Franks, Lloyd W. The Journal of Elder William Conrad: Pioneer Preacher. 1976. pap. text ed. 6.50x o.p. (ISBN 0-8191-0054-4). U Pr of Amer.

Franks, Maurice R. How to Avoid Alimony. 1976. pap. 2.50 (ISBN 0-451-11302-0, AE1302, Sig). NAL.

--Winning Custody. LC 82-24114. 185p. 1983. 16.95 (ISBN 0-13-961011-1, Busn); pap. 7.95 (ISBN 0-13-961003-0). P-H.

Franks, Norman L. The Battle of the Airfields. 1982. 40.00x (ISBN 0-686-82339-7, Pub. by W Kimber). State Mutual Bk.

Franks, Ray. What's in a Nickname? LC 82-90195. (Illus.). 208p. (Orig.). 1982. pap. 12.95 (ISBN 0-943976-00-6). R Franks Ranch.

Franks, Roger G. Modeling & Simulation in Chemical Engineering. LC 72-39717. 411p. 1972. 40.50x (ISBN 0-471-27535-2, Pub. by Wiley-Interscience). Wiley.

Franks, Ronald & Dowd, Thomas. The Will, a Modern Day Treasure Hunt. 2nd ed. Date not set. pap. text ed. 6.95 (ISBN 0-9607132-0-4). Tricore Assoc.

Franks, Violet. The Stereotyping of Women: Its Effects on Mental Health. (Springer Series-Focus on Women: No. 5). 1982. 23.95 (ISBN 0-8261-3820-9). Springer Pub.

Franks, Violet & Burtle, Vasanti, eds. Women in Therapy: New Psychotherapies. LC 73-91875. 1974. pap. 10.95 o.p. (ISBN 0-87630-113-8). Brunner-Mazel.

Franks, Violet, jt. ed. see Gomberg, Edith S.

Frankson, Carl & Benson, Kenneth R. Crafts Activities: Featuring Sixty-Five Holiday Ideas. 1970. 15.50 (ISBN 0-13-188755-6, Parker). P-H.

Fransecky, Roger B. & Debes, John L. Visual Literacy: A Way to Learn, a Way to Teach. 1972. pap. 5.95 (ISBN 0-89240-024-2, 904). Assn Ed Comm Tech.

Fransella, F. & Bannister, D. A Manual for Repertory Grid Technique. 1977. 31.00 (ISBN 0-12-265450-1); pap. 12.00 o.s.i. (ISBN 0-12-265456-0). Acad Pr.

Fransella, F., jt. auth. see Bannister, D.

Fransella, Fay. On Being a Woman. (Tavistock Women's Studies). 1977. pap. 9.95 (ISBN 0-422-76080-3, Pub. by Tavistock England). Methuen Inc.

--Psychology for Occupational Therapists. Chapman, Antony & Gale, Anthony, eds. (Psychology for Professional Groups Ser.). 300p. 1982. 49.00x (ISBN 0-333-31859-5, Pub. by Macmillan England). State Mutual Bk.

--Psychology for Occupational Therapists. (Psychology for Professional Groups Ser.). 320p. 1982. text ed. 25.00x (ISBN 0-333-31859-5, Pub. by Macmillan England); pap. text ed. 10.95x (ISBN 0-333-31883-8). Humanities.

Franson, J. Earl, jt. auth. see Dube, Anthony.

Franson, Robert W. The Shadow of the Ship. 304p. (Orig.). 1983. pap. 2.75 (ISBN 0-345-30688-0, Del Rey). Ballantine.

Franssen, Herman, et al. World Energy Supply & International Security. (Special Reports Ser.). 96p. 1983. 7.50 (ISBN 0-89549-048-X). Inst Foreign Policy Anal.

Fransson, Peter. Att Radas Prov Och Att Vilja Veta (Fear of Examinations in Educations & the Will to Learn) (Gotebog Studies in Educational Sciences: No. 24). 1978. pap. text ed. write for info. o.p. (ISBN 91-7346-047-8). Humanities.

Franta, Gregory E. & Glenn, Barbara H., eds. Twenty-five Years of the Sun at Work: Proceedings of the Annual Meeting of the American Section of the International Solar Energy Society, 2 vols. 1980. pap. 150.00x (ISBN 0-89553-021-X). Am Solar Energy.

Franta, Gregory E. & Haggard, Keith W., eds. Progress in Solar Energy: Vol. 5, The Renewable Challenge. 1982. pap. text ed. 175.00x (ISBN 0-89553-034-1). Am Solar Energy.

Franta, Gregory E. & Olson, Kenneth R., eds. Solar Architecture. LC 77-91356. 1978. 28.00 (ISBN 0-250-40233-5). Ann Arbor Science.

Franta, Gregory E., ed. see International Solar Energy Society American Section Annual Meeting, Phoenix, 1980.

Franta, Gregory E., ed. see International Solar Energy Society, American Section, Annual Meeting, Denver, 1978.

Franta, Gregory E., ed. see National Passive Solar Conference, 4th, Kansas City, 1979.

Franta, Gregroy E., ed. see International Solar Energy Society, American Section, Annual Meeting, Philadelphia, 1981.

Franta, W. R. The Process View of Simulation. (Operating & Programming Systems Ser.: Vol. 4). 1977. 12.95 (ISBN 0-444-00221-9, North Holland); pap. text ed. 25.95 (ISBN 0-444-00223-5). Elsevier.

Franta, W. R. & Chlamtac, Imrich. Local Networks: Motivation, Technology, & Performance. LC 80-7725. (Illus.). 512p. 1981. 41.95x (ISBN 0-669-03779-6). Lexington Bks.

Frantz, Adolf I. Water from the Well. 420p. 1978. 10.00 o.p. (ISBN 0-8059-2469-8). Dorrance.

Frantz, Charles, ed. Ideas & Trends in World Anthropology. (ICAES Ser.: No. 4). 278p. 1981. pap. text ed. 14.25x (ISBN 0-391-02280-6, Pub. by Concept India). Humanities.

Frantz, Donald G. Toward a Generative Grammar of Blackfoot. (Publications in Linguistics & Related Fields Ser.: No. 34). 151p. 1971. pap. 3.25x o.p. (ISBN 0-88312-036-4); microfiche 2.25 (ISBN 0-88312-436-X). Summer Inst Ling.

Frantz, Forest H. Successful Small Business Management. LC 77-14385. 1978. text ed. 21.95 (ISBN 0-13-872119-X). P-H.

Frantzen, Allen J. The Literature of Penance in Anglo-Saxon England. 395p. Date not set. 27.50x (ISBN 0-8135-0955-6). Rutgers U Pr.

Frantzeskakis, Ion F., ed. Zygos. Cullen, Timothy & Duckworth, Eddie, trs. from Greek. (Illus.). 216p. 1982. pap. 9.95 (ISBN 0-686-83954-4, Pub. by Zygos Greece). Intl Schol Bk Serv.

Frantzich, Stephen. Setups: Presidential Popularity in America. 1982. pap. 5.00 (ISBN 0-915654-53-9). Am Political.

Frantzich, Stephen E. Computers in Congress: The Politics of Information. (Managing Information Ser.: Vol. 4). (Illus.). 288p. 1982. 24.00 (ISBN 0-686-97289-9). Sage.

Franz, David R., jt. auth. see Jacobson, Morris K.

Franz, Marie-Louise von see Von Franz, Marie-Louise.

Franz, Marie-Louise Von see Von Franz, Marie-Louise.

Franz, Mary-Louise Von see Von Franz, Mary-Louise.

Franz, Philip. Gogol Bibliography. 300p. 1983. 30.00 (ISBN 0-88233-809-9). Ardis Pubs.

Franz, Thomas R. Remaking Reality in Galdos: A Writer's Interactions with His Context. LC 82-80783. 114p. 1982. pap. 22.00 (ISBN 0-942858-00-X). Strathmore Pr.

Franzen, Carl G. Foundations of Secondary Education. Repr. of 1955 ed. lib. bdg. 19.75x (ISBN 0-8371-2878-1, FRSF). Greenwood.

Franzen, Greta. Great Ship Vasa. LC 72-150019. (Illus.). 96p. (gr. 7 up). 1971. 7.95g o.p. (ISBN 0-8038-2647-8). Hastings.

Franzen, H. F. Second-Order Phase Transitions & the Irreducible Representation of Space Groups. (Lecture Notes in Chemistry Ser.: Vol. 32). 98p. 1983. pap. 11.00 (ISBN 0-387-11958-2). Springer-Verlag.

Franzen, Sixten, jt. ed. see Linsk, Joseph A.

Franzen, William L., jt. auth. see Bonaparte, T. H.

Franzini, Joseph, jt. auth. see Linsley, Ray K.

Franzini, Joseph B., jt. auth. see Daugherty, Robert L.

Franz Joseph, I. Incredible Friendship: Letters of Emperor Franz Joseph to Frau Katharina Schratt. De Bourgoing, Jean, ed. LC 66-63789. 1966. 39.50x (ISBN 0-87395-019-4). State U NY Pr.

Franzke, Andreas. Dubuffet. Wolf, Robert E., tr. (Illus.). 340p. 1982. 95.00 (ISBN 0-686-81035-X). Abrams.

Franzmann, Martin H. The Revelation to John. 136p. 1976. 6.95 (ISBN 0-570-03728-X, 12-2630). Concordia.

Franzmeyer, Fritz. Approaches to Industrial Policy Within the EC & Its Impact on European Integration. 167p. 1982. text ed. 40.00x (ISBN 0-566-00358-9). Gower Pub Ltd.

Franzoni, T. & Vesentini, E. Holomorphic Maps & Invariant Distances. (Mathematics Studies Ser.: Vol. 40). 1980. 38.50 (ISBN 0-444-85436-3, North Holland). Elsevier.

Franzwa, Gregory, ed. see Haines, Aubrey L.

Franzwa, Gregory M. Maps of the Oregon Trail. North, Arielle, ed. LC 82-675039. (Illus.). 299p. 1982. 24.95 (ISBN 0-935284-23-0). Patrice Pr.

Franzwa, Gregory M., ed. see Hanson, William L.

Franzwa, Gregory M., ed. see Kelley, F. Beverly.

Frappier, Jean. Chretien De Troyes: The Man & His Work. Cormier, Raymond J., tr. from Fr. LC 81-9475. (Illus.). xx, 241p. 1982. lib. bdg. 21.95 (ISBN 0-8214-0603-5, 82-83889). Ohio U Pr.

Frary, Michael & Owens, William A. Impressions of the Big Thicket. (Illus.). 112p. 1983. pap. 12.95 (ISBN 0-292-73831-5). U Of Tex Pr.

Frascina & Harrison. Modern Art & Modernism. 320p. 1982. text ed. 20.00 (ISBN 0-06-318234-3, Pub. by Har-Row Ltd England); pap. text ed. 9.95 (ISBN 0-06-318233-5, Pub. by Har-Row Ltd England). Har-Row.

Frascina, Francis & Harrison, Charles. Modern Art & Modernism: An Anthology of Critical Texts from Manet to Pollock. LC 82-48153. (Icon Editions). (Illus.). 352p. 1983. 19.23i (ISBN 0-06-433215-2, HarpT). Har-Row.

Frascino, Edward. Avocado Is Not Your Color: And Other Scenes of Married Bliss. (Illus.). 112p. 1983. pap. 3.95 (ISBN 0-14-006364-1). Penguin.

--Eddie Spaghetti. LC 77-11850. (Illus.). 1978. 9.57i (ISBN 0-06-021908-4, HarpJ); PLB 9.89 (ISBN 0-06-021909-2). Har-Row.

Frascogna, X. M., Jr. & Hetherington, H. Lee. Successful Artist Management. 224p. 1978. 17.50 (ISBN 0-8230-5000-9, Billboard Bks). Watson-Guptill.

Frasconi, Antonio. House That Jack Built: A Picture Book in Two Languages. LC 58-8625. (Illus.). (gr. k-4). 6.95 (ISBN 0-15-236300-9, HJ). HarBraceJ.

--See & Say. LC 55-8675. (Illus.). (gr. 1 up). 1972. pap. 1.35 (ISBN 0-15-680350-X, VoyB). HarBraceJ.

Frasconi, Antonio, jt. auth. see Neruda, Pablo.

Frase, Richard S., jt. auth. see Zimring, Franklin E.

Fraser, Alexander C., ed. see Locke, John.

Fraser, Amy S., ed. Dae Ye Min Langsyne. (Illus.). 224p. 1975. 14.95 (ISBN 0-7100-8233-9). Routledge & Kegan.

Fraser, Andrew F. Farm Animal Behaviour. 2nd ed. (Illus.). 291p. 1980. pap. 14.75 o.p. (ISBN 0-8121-0739-X). Lea & Febiger.

Fraser, Anthea. Home Through the Dark. (General Ser.). 1977. lib. bdg. 10.95 o.p. (ISBN 0-8161-6442-8, Large Print Bks). G K Hall.

Fraser, Antonia. Cool Repentance: A Jemima Shore Mystery. 1983. 12.95 (ISBN 0-393-01625-0). Norton.

--Mary Queen of Scots. 1978. 17.95 o.s.i. (ISBN 0-440-05261-0). Delacorte.

--Quiet as a Nun. 1982. pap. 3.95 (ISBN 0-393-30120-6). Norton.

Fraser, Antonia, ed. Heroes & Heroines. (Illus.). 272p. Date not set. pap. 9.95 (ISBN 0-89104-305-5, A & W Visual Library). A & W Pubs. Postponed.

--Oxford & Oxfordshire in Verse. 96p. 1983. 13.95 (Pub. by Secker & Warburg). David & Charles.

Fraser, Antonia, ed. see Judd, Denis.

Fraser, Antonia, ed. see Marshall, Dorothy.

Fraser, Antonia, ed. see Miller, John.

Fraser, Antonia, ed. see Senior, Michael.

Fraser, Antonia, ed. see Watson, D. R.

Fraser, Antonio, ed. see Lacey, Robert.

Fraser Associates. PAC Handbook: Political Action for Business. 432p. 1982. prof ref 27.50x (ISBN 0-88410-879-1). Ballinger Pub.

Fraser, B. Kay. Decorative Tole Painting: A Basic Course in Folk Art for Beginners & Craftsmen. (Arts & Crafts Ser). (Illus.). 96p. 1972. 5.95 o.p. (ISBN 0-517-50130-9); pap. 5.95 (ISBN 0-517-50373-5). Crown.

Fraser, Beverly A. & Hensinger, Robert N. Managing Physical Handicaps: A Practical Guide for Parents, Care Providers, & Educators. LC 82-19716. (Illus.). 256p. 1983. text ed. 17.95 (ISBN 0-933716-30-3). P H Brookes.

Fraser, Colin. Tractor Pioneer: The Life of Harry Ferguson. LC 73-85451. (Illus.). vi, 294p. 1973. 15.00x (ISBN 0-8214-0134-3, 82-81370). Ohio U Pr.
Fraser, Colin & Scherer, Klaus R., eds. Advances in the Social Psychology of Language. LC 81-15551. (European Studies in Social Psychology). (Illus.). 280p. 1982. 39.50 (ISBN 0-521-23192-2); pap. 12.95 (ISBN 0-521-29857-1). Cambridge U Pr.
Fraser, D., jt. auth. see Yuen, C. K.
Fraser, D. A. The Physics of Semiconductor Devices. 2nd ed. (Oxford Physics Ser.). 1979. 39.50x o.p. (ISBN 0-19-851850-1); pap. 12.95x o.p. (ISBN 0-19-851851-X). Oxford U Pr.
--The Physics of Semiconductor Devices. 3rd ed. (Oxford Physics Ser.). 1982. 35.00x (ISBN 0-19-851859-5); pap. text ed. 12.95 (ISBN 0-19-851860-9). Oxford U Pr.
Fraser, D. R., jt. auth. see Cooper, S. K.
Fraser, Derek. Power & Authority in the Victorian City. LC 79-10895. 1979. 22.50x (ISBN 0-312-63366-1). St Martin.
--The Pursuit of Urban History. 512p. 1983. text ed. 69.50 (ISBN 0-7131-6383-6). E Arnold.
--Urban Politics in Victorian England: The Structure of Politics in Victorian Cities. 320p. 1976. text ed. 30.00x o.p. (ISBN 0-7185-1145-X, Leicester). Humanities.
Fraser, Derek, ed. A History of Modern Leeds. 488p. 1982. 25.00 (ISBN 0-7190-0747-X); pap. 8.50 (ISBN 0-7190-0781-X). Manchester.
--The New Poor Law in the Nineteenth Century. LC 75-43484. (Problems in Focus Ser.). 250p. 1976. 25.00 (ISBN 0-312-56910-6). St Martin.
Fraser, Edward & Gibbons, John. Soldier & Sailor Words & Phrases. LC 68-30635. 1968. Repr. of 1925 ed. 40.00x (ISBN 0-8103-3281-7). Gale.
Fraser, G. S. Metre, Rhyme, & Free Verse. (Critical Idiom Ser.). 1970. pap. 4.95x (ISBN 0-416-17300-4). Methuen Inc.
--A Short History of English Poetry. 396p. 1981. 28.50x (ISBN 0-389-20174-X); pap. 11.95x (ISBN 0-389-20175-8). B&N Imports.
Fraser, George M. Flashman. 1971. pap. 2.50 (ISBN 0-451-11658-5, AE1658, Sig). NAL.
--Flashman in the Great Game. 1977. pap. 2.50 (ISBN 0-451-09688-6, E9688, Sig). NAL.
--Flashman's Lady. 1979. pap. 2.95 (ISBN 0-451-11660-7, AE1660, Sig). NAL.
--Mr. American. 1981. 16.95 o.s.i. (ISBN 0-671-42571-4). S&S.
Fraser, Gordon. Bill Brandt: Nudes 1945-1980. 132p. 1982. 55.00x (ISBN 0-86092-064-X, Pub. by Fraser Bks). State Mutual Bk.
Fraser, Hugh, jt. ed. see Barnett, Herbert E.
Fraser, Hugh, jt. ed. see Barnett, Hert E.
Fraser, J. H. British Pelagic Tunicates. LC 80-42174. (Synopses of the British Fauna Ser.: No. 20). 65p. 1982. pap. 12.95 (ISBN 0-521-28367-1). Cambridge U Pr.
Fraser, J. T. The Genesis & Evolution of Time: A Critique of Interpretation in Physics. LC 82-8622. (Illus.). 224p. 1982. lib. bdg. 20.00x (ISBN 0-87023-370-X). U of Mass Pr.
Fraser, J. T., et al, eds. Study of Time I: 1st Conference of the International Society for the Study of Time. LC 72-80472. (Illus.). 558p. 1972. 33.00 o.p. (ISBN 0-387-05824-9). Springer-Verlag.
Fraser, James, jt. ed. see Scott, Ronald B.
Fraser, James F. Dr. Jimmy: Some Reminiscences by James Fowler Fraser 1893-1979. 150p. 1982. pap. 10.90 (ISBN 0-08-025737-2). Pergamon.
Fraser, James H., ed. Society & Children's Literature. LC 77-94110. 1978. pap. 8.00 o.p. (ISBN 0-8389-3213-4). ALA.
Fraser, James L. The Art of Selling Stocks. 1982. 2.00 (ISBN 0-87034-066-2). Fraser Pub Co.
--P. S. What Do You Think of the Market. (Orig.). 1966. Repr. of 1920 ed. 4.00 (ISBN 0-87034-023-9). Fraser Pub Co.
--Ten Rules for Investing. 1964. 2.00 (ISBN 0-87034-030-1). Fraser Pub Co.
--Ten Ways to Become Rich. (Illus.). 1967. flexible cover 2.00 (ISBN 0-87034-031-X). Fraser Pub Co.
Fraser, Janet, jt. auth. see May, Ernest R.
Fraser, Janet, jt. ed. see Moore, Jonathan.
Fraser, John. Violence in the Arts. LC 73-84319. 208p. 1976. 27.00 o.p. (ISBN 0-521-20331-7); pap. 9.95 (ISBN 0-521-29029-5). Cambridge U Pr.
Fraser, John W. Tips on Having a Successful Sale, etc. LC 82-60525. 125p. (Orig.). 1983. pap. 4.95 (ISBN 0-88247-679-3). R & E Res Assoc.
Fraser, Julius T. Time As Conflict: A Scientific & Humanistic Study. (Science & Culture Ser.: No. 35). 356p. 1978. 24.95x (ISBN 3-7643-0950-4). Birkhauser.
Fraser, Lisa, ed. see Graham, Winifred.
Fraser, Louise W. A Cup of Kindness. LC 72-75224. (Illus., Orig.). 1973. pap. 5.50x o.p. (ISBN 0-87562-037-X). Spec Child.
Fraser, M. J. & Sleet, R. J. Resource Book on Chemical Education in the United Kingdom. 1975. 29.95 (ISBN 0-471-26116-5, Pub. by Wiley Heyden). Wiley.
Fraser, Marshall. College Algebra & Trigonometry: A Functions Approach. 1978. 21.95 (ISBN 0-8053-2590-5); instr's guide 6.95 (ISBN 0-8053-2591-3). Benjamin-Cummings.
Fraser, Mitchell W. English Pulpit Oratory from Andrews to Tillotson: A Study of Its Literary Aspects. 516p. 1982. Repr. of 1932 ed. lib. bdg. 85.00 (ISBN 0-89760-564-0). Telegraph Bks.
Fraser, Morris. E. C. T. A Clinical Guide. LC 82-2666. 200p. 1982. pap. 18.00 (ISBN 0-471-10416-7, Pub. by Wiley Med). Wiley.
Fraser, N. M., jt. auth. see Bates, R. W.
Fraser, P. M., tr. see Lofstedt, Einar.
Fraser, Peter. Vanessa. (The Portrait Ser.). 176p. (Orig.). 1983. pap. 2.50 (ISBN 0-523-41817-5). Pinnacle Bks.
Fraser, Phyllis, jt. ed. see Wise, Herbert.
Fraser, Richard G. Marketing One & Two. 1977. No. 1, 224p. text ed. 14.30x (ISBN 0-7715-0870-0); No. 2, 208p. text ed. 14.30x (ISBN 0-7715-0872-7); tchr's. guide 6.54x (ISBN 0-7715-0871-9). Forkner.
Fraser, Robert G. & Pare, J. A. Diagnosis of Diseases of the Chest, Vol. 1. 2nd ed. LC 76-20932. (Illus.). 1977. text ed. 40.00 (ISBN 0-7216-3852-X). Saunders.
--Diagnosis of Diseases of the Chest, Vol. 2. 2nd ed. LC 76-20932. (Illus.). 1978. pap. 45.00 (ISBN 0-7216-3853-8). Saunders.
--Diagnosis of Diseases of the Chest, Vol. 3. LC 76-20932. (Illus.). 1979. 45.00 (ISBN 0-7216-3854-6). Saunders.
--Diagnosis of Diseases of the Chest, Vol. 4. 2nd. ed. LC 76-20932. (Illus.). 1979. text ed. 35.00 (ISBN 0-7216-3855-4). Saunders.
Fraser, Russel A. & Rabkin, Norman. Drama of the English Renaissance: The Tudor Period, Vol. 1. 1976. 21.95x (ISBN 0-02-339570-2, 33957). Macmillan.
--Drama of the English Renaissance: The Stuart Period, Vol. 2. 736p. 1976. pap. text ed. 21.95x (ISBN 0-02-339580-X, 33958). Macmillan.
Fraser, Russell, ed. see Shakespeare, William.
Fraser, Russell A., ed. Essential Shakespeare: Nine Major Plays & the Sonnets. (Illus.). 544p. 1972. pap. text ed. 15.95x (ISBN 0-02-339550-8). Macmillan.
Fraser, Sylvia. The Emperor's Virgin. LC 80-1064. 408p. 1980. 12.95 o.p. (ISBN 0-385-17237-0). Doubleday.
Fraser, T. G. The Middle East: 1914-1979. 1980. 22.50 (ISBN 0-312-53181-8). St Martin.
Fraser, T. M. Human Stress, Work & Job Satisfaction: A Critical Approach. International Labour Office, ed. (Occupational Safety & Health Ser.: No. 50). 72p. (Orig.). 1982. pap. 8.55 (ISBN 92-2-103042-3). Intl Labour Office.
Fraser, Theodore P., jt. auth. see Kopp, Richard D.
Fraser, Theodore P., jt. auth. see Kopp, Richard L.
Fraser, Vera, tr. see Maurois, Andre.
Fraser, W. R. Reforms & Restraints in Modern French Education. (World Education Ser). 1971. 18.95x (ISBN 0-7100-7174-4). Routledge & Kegan.
Fraser, William I., jt. auth. see Hallas, Charles H.
Frassanito, Elaine, jt. auth. see Arias, Toby.
Frassanito, William. Antietam. (Illus.). 304p. 1982. pap. 11.95 (ISBN 0-684-17645-9, ScribT). Scribner.
Frassanito, William A. Grant & Lee: The Virginia Campaigns, 1864-1865. (Illus.). 448p. 1983. 19.95 (ISBN 0-686-83857-2, ScribT). Scribner.
Frassica, Pietro & Carrara, Antonio. Per Modo Di Dire: A First Course in Italian. 544p. 1981. text ed. 21.95 (ISBN 0-669-02068-0); wkbk. 8.95 (ISBN 0-669-02069-9); cassette 20.00 (ISBN 0-669-02073-7); tapes-reels 40.00 (ISBN 0-669-02072-9); instr's guide 1.95 (ISBN 0-686-82918-2); tapescript (ISBN 0-669-02074-5); demo tape (ISBN 0-669-02075-3). Heath.
Frasure, David W. Bluebirds. 1978. pap. 4.95 (ISBN 0-932298-08-7). Copple Hse.
--Mary. 1982. pap. 5.95 o.p. (ISBN 0-686-34665-3). Caroline Hse.
Frasure, E. P. My Garden of Thoughts. 1978. 6.95 o.p. (ISBN 0-533-03476-0). Vantage.
Frasure, William W., jt. auth. see Rossell, James H.
Frasw, Marianne, jt. auth. see Hunt, Linda.
Fratangelo, Robert A., jt. auth. see Connelly, James F.
Frate, FRank. Bridgewalker. 12p. 1982. pap. 1.00 (ISBN 0-686-37934-9). Samisdat.
--Investigations, Pt. 1. 24p. 1980. pap. 1.00 o.p. (ISBN 0-686-30662-7). Samisdat.
Frater Albertus. Alchemist's Handbook. LC 74-21127. 1981. 12.50 (ISBN 0-87728-181-5). Weiser.
Frates, Jeffrey & Moldrup, William. Introduction to the Computer: An Integrative Approach. (Illus.). 1980. text ed. 21.95 (ISBN 0-13-480301-9); pap. 7.95 study guide (ISBN 0-13-480285-3). P-H.
Frates, Jeffrey E., jt. auth. see Potter, George B.
Frauchimont, Paul, jt. auth. see Odell, William.
Frauenfelder, Hans & Henley, Ernest M. Subatomic Physics. (Illus.). 544p. 1974. 36.95 (ISBN 0-13-859082-6). P-H.
Frauenglas, Robert A., ed. see Houston, Lee.
Fraunfelder, F. T. Drug-Induced Ocular Side Effects & Drug Interactions. 2nd ed. LC 82-146. 544p. 1982. text ed. 30.00 (ISBN 0-8121-0850-7). Lea & Febiger.
Fraunfelder, F. T. & Roy, F. Hampton. Current Ocular Therapy. 600p. 1980. text ed. 55.00 (ISBN 0-7216-3860-0). Saunders.
Fraunhofer, J. A. Von see Von Fraunhofer, J. A.
Frauwallner, Erich. History of Indian Philosophy, 2 vols. Bedekar, V. M., tr. from Ger. 500p. 1974. text ed. 23.50x (ISBN 0-391-00337-2). Humanities.
Frawley, William, ed. Linguistics & Literacy. (Topics in Language & Linguistics). 495p. 1982. 55.00x (ISBN 0-306-41174-1, Plenum Pr). Plenum Pub.
Frayer, William C., ed. Lancaster Course in Ophthalmic Histopathology. (Illus.). 320p. 1980. Text, Slides, Cassette tapes & Fourteen Units with Lectures. 936.00x (ISBN 0-8036-3827-2). Davis Co.
Frazee, Charles A. Catholics & Sultans: The Church & the Ottoman Empire 1453-1923. LC 82-4562. 384p. Date not set. price not set (ISBN 0-521-24676-8). Cambridge U Pr.
--Orthodox Church in Independent Greece 1821-52. LC 69-10488. 1969. 39.50 (ISBN 0-521-07247-6). Cambridge U Pr.
Frazer, A., ed. Biochemical Problems of Lipids. 1963. 34.25 (ISBN 0-444-40244-6). Elsevier.
Frazer, F. W., ed. Rehabilitation Within the Community. 208p. 1983. pap. 7.95 (ISBN 0-571-11901-8). Faber & Faber.
Frazer, Felix J. Parallel Paths to the Unseen Worlds. 1967. pap. 5.50 (ISBN 0-87516-298-3). De Vorss.
Frazer, J. Ronald. Business Decision Simulation: A Time Sharing Approach. LC 74-28036. 1975. pap. 7.95 (ISBN 0-87909-113-4); free instrs'. manual o.p. Reston.
--Introduction to Business Simulation. 1977. pap. 8.95 (ISBN 0-87909-387-0); instrs'. manual avail. (ISBN 0-87909-386-2). Reston.
Frazer, James. The New Golden Bough. rev. ed. Gaster, Theodore, ed. 832p. 1975. pap. 5.95 (ISBN 0-451-62208-1, ME2208, Ment). NAL.
Frazer, James G. Golden Bough. abr ed. 19.95 (ISBN 0-02-095560-X); pap. 8.95 (ISBN 0-685-15196-4). Macmillan.
--New Golden Bough. abridged ed. Gaster, Theodor H., ed. LC 59-6125. 1959. 21.95 (ISBN 0-87599-036-3). S G Phillips.
Frazer, Joan, jt. auth. see Blockcolsky, Valeda.
Frazer, Joan, et al. Thirty-Thousand Selected Words Organized by Letter, Sound & Syllable. 1978. text ed. 15.95 (ISBN 0-88450-799-8, 3083-B); pap. text ed. 10.95 (ISBN 0-88450-798-X, 2506-B). Communication Skill.
Frazer, Joan, jt. auth. see Blockcolsky, Valeda.
Frazer, Joan M. & Smith, Cynthia J. Shape up your Language. 1982. 3-ring binder 75.00 (ISBN 0-88450-828-5, 2071-B). Communication Skill.
Frazer, John. Artificially Arranged Scenes: The Films of Georges Meiles. 1979. lib. bdg. 28.00 (ISBN 0-8161-8368-6, Hall Reference). G K Hall.
Frazer, R. M., tr. The Poems of Hesiod. LC 82-40451. (Illus.). 160p. 1983. 14.95x (ISBN 0-8061-1837-7); pap. 4.95x (ISBN 0-8061-1846-6). U of Okla Pr.
Frazer, Ray & Kelling, Harold D., eds. Literature in Four Aspects. 1965. pap. text ed. 14.95x o.p. (ISBN 0-669-20628-8). Heath.
Frazer, William. Expectations, Forecasting & Control: A Provisional Textbook of Macroeconomics, Vol. I: Monetary Matters, Keynesian & Other Models. LC 80-1361. 493p. 1980. lib. bdg. 28.25 (ISBN 0-8191-1144-9); pap. text ed. 17.50 (ISBN 0-8191-1145-7). U Pr of Amer.
Frazer, Winifred L. Love As Death in "The Iceman Cometh: A Modern Treatment of an Ancient Theme. LC 67-65495. (U of Fla. Humanities Monographs: No. 27). 1967. pap. 3.00 o.p. (ISBN 0-8130-0081-5). U Presses Fla.
Frazer Clark, C. E., Jr., ed. The Nathaniel Hawthorne Journal 1976. (Illus.). 1976. 22.00 o.p. (ISBN 0-685-77416-3). Bruccoli.
Frazier, Alexander. Values, Curriculum & the Elementary School. LC 79-87862. 1980. pap. text ed. 12.95 (ISBN 0-395-26739-0). HM.
Frazier, Allie M. Issues in Religion: A Book of Readings. 2nd ed. 1975. pap. 10.95x (ISBN 0-442-21680-7). Van Nos Reinhold.
Frazier, Allie M., ed. Readings in Eastern Religious Thought, 3 vols. Incl. Vol. 1. Hinduism. (ISBN 0-664-24846-2); Vol. 2. Buddhism. (ISBN 0-664-24847-0); Vol. 3. Chinese & Japanese Religions. (ISBN 0-664-24848-9). LC 69-14197. 1969. pap. 4.95 ea. Westminster.
Frazier, Carla. To the South Pole. LC 78-26274. (Raintree Great Adventures). (Illus.). (gr. 3-6). 1979. PLB 12.85 (ISBN 0-8393-0153-7). Raintree Pubs.
Frazier, Claude A. Annual Review of Allergy 1977-1978. 1978. spiral bdg. 22.50 o.p. (ISBN 0-87488-329-6). Med Exam.
--Bi-Annual Review of Allergy, 1983. 1983. write for info. (ISBN 0-87488-294-X). Med Exam.
--Insect Allergy: Allergic & Toxic Reactions to Insects & Other Arthropods. 2nd ed. LC 67-30896. (Illus.). 508p. 1983. 42.50 (ISBN 0-87527-010-7). Green.
--Parents' Guide to Allergy in Children. 1978. pap. 3.95 o.p. (ISBN 0-448-16180-X, G&D). Putnam Pub Group.
--Self-Assessment of Current Knowledge in Allergy & Clinical Immunology. 1981. pap. 22.00 (ISBN 0-87488-296-6). Med Exam.
Frazier, David. Around the House. (Illus.). 1979. pap. 6.95 (ISBN 0-8256-3143-2, Quick Fox). Putnam Pub Group.
Frazier, E. Franklin. Negro Family in the United States. rev. & abr ed. LC 66-13868. 1966. pap. 8.00x (ISBN 0-226-26141-7). U of Chicago Pr.
Frazier, Gregory, jt. auth. see Collins, Al J.
Frazier, Lois E., jt. auth. see Moon, Harry R.
Frazier, Lois E., ed. see Frye, Marianne E., et al.
Frazier, Richard H., et al. Magnetic & Electric Suspensions. (Monographs in Modern Electrical Technology). 416p. 1974. 37.50x (ISBN 0-262-06054-X). MIT Pr.
Frazier, Robert C., et al. The Humanities: A Quest for Meaning in Twentieth Century America. 352p. 1982. pap. text ed. 19.95 (ISBN 0-686-98355-6). Kendall-Hunt.
Frazier, Shervert, ed. Aggression. (ARNMD Research Publications Ser.: Vol. 52). 360p. 1974. 38.00 (ISBN 0-683-00246-5). Raven.
Frazier, Thomas. Do You Pray with Your Spirit? 1978. pap. 0.50 mini o.s.i. (ISBN 0-89274-088-4, HH-088). Harrison Hse.
Frazier, William A. & Glaser, Luis, eds. Cellular Recognition. LC 82-6555. (UCLA Symposia on Molecular & Cellular Biology Ser.: Vol. 3). 966p. 1982. 152.00 (ISBN 0-8451-2602-4). A R Liss.
Frazier, William C. Food Microbiology. 2nd ed. 1967. text ed. 18.00 o.p. (ISBN 0-07-021916-8, C). McGraw.
Frazier, William C. & Westhoff, Dennis. Food Microbiology. 3rd ed. (Illus.). 1978. text ed. 35.00 (ISBN 0-07-021917-6, C). McGraw.
Frazzetta, Thomas H. Complex Adaptations in Evolving Populations. LC 74-24359. (Illus.). 288p. 1975. text ed. 6.95x o.p. (ISBN 0-87893-194-5). Sinauer Assoc.
Freakley, P. K. & Payne, A. R. Theory & Practice of Engineering with Rubber. (Illus.). 1978. text ed. 98.50x (ISBN 0-85334-772-7, Pub. by Applied Sci England). Elsevier.
Frears, J. R. Parties & Elections in the French Fifth Republic. LC 77-82033. (Illus.). 1977. 17.95 o.p. (ISBN 0-312-59750-9). St Martin.
--Political Parties & Elections in the French 5th Republic. LC 77-82043. 1978. 25.00 (ISBN 0-312-62331-3). St Martin.
Freas, Kelly, ed. see Adams, Robert.
Freas, Kelly, ed. see Asprin, Robert.
Freas, Kelly, ed. see Bone, J. F.
Freas, Kelly, ed. see Bradley, Marion Z.
Freas, Kelly, ed. see Budrys, Algis.
Freas, Kelly, ed. see Garrett, Randall.
Freas, Kelly, ed. see Lovin, Roger.
Freas, Kelly, ed. see Maclean, Katherine.
Freas, Kelly, ed. see Moore, Raylyn.
Freas, Kelly, ed. see Silverberg, Robert.
Freas, Kelly, ed. see Warren, George.
Freas, Kelly, ed. see Whelan, Michael.
Freas, Polly, ed. see Adams, Robert.
Freas, Polly, ed. see Asprin, Robert.
Freas, Polly, ed. see Bone, J. F.
Freas, Polly, ed. see Bradley, Marion Z.
Freas, Polly, ed. see Budrys, Algis.
Freas, Polly, ed. see Garrett, Randall.
Freas, Polly, ed. see Lovin, Roger.
Freas, Polly, ed. see Maclean, Katherine.
Freas, Polly, ed. see Moore, Raylyn.
Freas, Polly, ed. see Silverberg, Robert.
Freas, Polly, ed. see Warren, George.
Freas, Polly, ed. see Whelan, Michael.
Frech, Mary, jt. ed. see Swindler, William F.
Frechet, Alec. John Galsworthy: A Reassessment. Mahaffey, Denis, tr. from French. LC 81-22900. 242p. 1982. text ed. 27.50x (ISBN 0-389-20277-0). B&N Imports.
Frechtling, Douglas C., jt. auth. see Goeldner, C. R.
Frechtman, Bernard, tr. see Genet, Jean.
Frechtman, Bernard, tr. see Gide, Andre.
Fred Astaire Dance Studios & Monte, John. Fred Astaire Dance Book. 1978. 10.95 o.p. (ISBN 0-671-23064-6). S&S.
Freddoso, Alfred J., ed. The Existence & Nature of God. 1983. price not set. U of Notre Dame Pr.
Fredeman, William D., ed. see Rossetti, William M.
Freden, Lars. Psychosocial Aspects of Depression. 240p. 1982. 34.95x (ISBN 0-471-10023-4, Pub. by Wiley-Interscience). Wiley.
Fredenberg, D. Van. Wills for Washington. 3rd ed. 72p. 1982. pap. 3.95 (ISBN 0-88908-719-9). Self Counsel Pr.
Fredenberg, D. van see Van Fredenberg, D.
Fredenslund, et al. Vapor-Liquid Equilibria Using UNIFAC: A Group Contribution Method. 1977. 83.00 (ISBN 0-444-41621-8). Elsevier.
Frederic, Harold. The Market-Place. Garner, Stanton & Dodge, Charlyne, eds. LC 81-8853. (Harold Frederic Edition Ser.: Vol. II). 1981. 25.00x (ISBN 0-912646-60-8); pap. 12.00 (ISBN 0-912646-74-8). Tex Christian.
Frederick. Origins & Evolution of Eukaryotic Intracellular Organalles, Vol. 361. 1981. 101.00 (ISBN 0-89766-111-7); pap. write for info. (ISBN 0-89766-112-5). NY Acad Sci.
--Psycho-Nutrition. (Health, Nutrition & Well Being Bks). 5.95 (ISBN 0-448-14479-4, G&D). Putnam Pub Group.
Frederick, A. Bruce. Gymnastics for Men. (Physical Education Activities Ser.). 80p. 1969. pap. text ed. write for info. (ISBN 0-697-07014-X); tchr's manual (ISBN 0-697-07219-3). Wm C Brown.

--Gymnastics for Women. (Physical Education Activities Ser.). 94p. 1966. pap. text ed. write for info. (ISBN 0-697-07015-8); write for info. tchr's. manual (ISBN 0-697-07220-7). Wm C Brown.

Frederick, Daniel, jt. auth. see Pletta, Dan H.

Frederick, Dean K. & Carlson, A. Bruce. Linear Systems in Communication & Control. LC 71-155118. 575p. 1971. 36.95x (ISBN 0-471-27721-5). Wiley.

Frederick, Dean K., jt. auth. see Close, Charles M.

Frederick, Donald. That Crazy, Mixed-up Cube. rev. ed. (Illus.). 72p. 1981. pap. 1.95 o.p. (ISBN 0-9607180-0-1). Frederick Ent.

Frederick, Gary E., jt. auth. see Weaver, Betsy.

Frederick, Guy. One Hundred One Best Magic Tricks. 1979. pap. 2.50 (ISBN 0-451-12163-5, AE2163, Sig). NAL.

Frederick, J. George. The Long Island Seafood Cookbook. Joyce, Jean, ed. 1971. pap. 4.50 (ISBN 0-486-22677-8). Dover.

Frederick, John T. William Henry Hudson. (English Authors Ser.: No. 130). 10.95 o.p. (ISBN 0-8057-1276-3, Twayne). G K Hall.

Frederick, Kenneth D. Water for Western Agriculture. LC 82-47985. (A Resources for the Future Research Paper). (Illus.). 256p. (Orig.). 1982. pap. text ed. 15.00x (ISBN 0-8018-2832-5). Resources Future.

Frederick, M. T. & Smith, R. T. Bolivia Fertilizer Situation & Recommendations. (Technical Bulletin Ser.: No. T-15). (Illus., Orig.). 1979. pap. 4.00 (ISBN 0-88090-014-8). Intl Fertilizer.

Frederick, Portia M. & Kinn, Mary E. The Medical Office Assistant: Administrative & Clinical. 5th ed. (Illus.). 707p. 1981. text ed. 24.95 (ISBN 0-7216-3863-5). Saunders.

--Medical Office Assistant: Administrative & Clinical. 4th ed. LC 73-89176. (Illus.). 735p. 1974. text ed. 17.95 o.p. (ISBN 0-7216-3862-7). Saunders.

Frederick, William, jt. auth. see McGlynn, John.

Frederick Of Prussia. The Refutation of Machiavelli's Prince or Anti-Machiavel. Sonnino, Paul, tr. LC 80-15801. viii, 174p. 1981. 14.95x (ISBN 0-8214-0559-4, 82-83541); pap. 5.95x (ISBN 0-8214-0598-5, 82-83558). Ohio U Pr.

Fredericks, jt. auth. see Gould.

Fredericks, Carlton. Arthritis: Don't Learn to Live with It. LC 80-85373. 224p. 1981. 12.95 (ISBN 0-448-14028-4, G&D). Putnam Pub Group.

--Breast Cancer: A Nutritional Approach. LC 76-50870. 1979. pap. 8.95 o.p. (ISBN 0-448-12985-X, G&D). Putnam Pub Group.

--The Carlton Fredericks No-Nonsense Nutrition Guide. 1980. 9.95 (ISBN 0-448-12258-8, G&D). Putnam Pub Group.

--Carlton Frederick's Nutrition Guide for Prevention & Cure of Common Ailments & Disease. 1982. 8.95x. Cancer Control Soc.

--Carlton Frederick's Nutrition Guide for the Prevention & Cure of Common Ailments & Diseases. LC 82-10705. (Illus.). 194p. Date not set. pap. 8.95 (ISBN 0-671-44509-X, Fireside). S&S.

--Eat Well, Get Well, Stay Well. LC 79-91618. 1980. 9.95 (ISBN 0-448-12258-8, G&D); pap. 5.95 (ISBN 0-448-12023-2). Putnam Pub Group.

--Look Younger, Feel Healthier. 2.95x o.p. (ISBN 0-448-11933-1). Cancer Control Soc.

--Look Younger, Feel Healthier. Orig. Title: Eating Right for You. 320p. 1975. pap. 3.95 o.p. (ISBN 0-448-11933-1, G&D). Putnam Pub Group.

--New & Revised Carlton Fredericks Cook Book for Good Nutrition. LC 73-15132. 304p. 1974. 3.95 (ISBN 0-448-11665-0, G&D). Putnam Pub Group.

--Psycho-Nutrition. 224p. 1976. pap. 5.95 (ISBN 0-448-14479-4, G&D). Putnam Pub Group.

--Winning the Fight Against Breast Cancer. 196p. Date not set. pap. price not set (ISBN 0-448-16527-9, G&D). Putnam Pub Group.

Fredericks, Carlton & Goodman, Herman. Low Blood Sugar & You. 1969. pap. 4.95 (ISBN 0-448-12246-4, G&D, Today Press). Putnam Pub Group.

Fredericks, Lee & Wells, R. G. Rice Processing in Malaysia. (Illus.). 1982. 19.95 (ISBN 0-19-582522-5); pap. 9.95x (ISBN 0-19-582523-3). Oxford U Pr.

Fredericksen, Alan. Red Roe Run. LC 82-82810. 258p. 1983. 12.95 (ISBN 0-910783-00-4). Green Key Pr.

Frederickson, F. M., ed. Snubber Design Applications & Minimization Methods. (PVP Ser.: Vol. 55). 75p. 1981. 14.00 (ISBN 0-686-34515-0, H00191). ASME.

Frederickson, G., jt. auth. see Pettigrew, T.

Frederickson, H. George & Wise, Charles, eds. Administering Public Policy. 1976. pap. 6.00 (ISBN 0-918592-16-X). Policy Studies.

--Public Administration & Public Policy. LC 76-14280. (Policy Studies Organization Bk.). (Illus.). 1977. 22.95x (ISBN 0-669-00738-2). Lexington Bks.

Frederickson, Robert S. Hjalmar Hjorth Boyesen. (United States Authors Ser.). 1980. lib. bdg. 13.95 (ISBN 0-8057-7290-1, Twayne). G K Hall.

Frederick The Great. Musical Works of Frederick the Great, 4 Vols. in 3. Spitta, Philip, ed. LC 67-27453. (Music Ser). 1967. Repr. of 1889 ed. Set. lib. bdg. 125.00 (ISBN 0-306-70980-5). Da Capo.

Frederiksen, Christian P. Budgeting for Nonprofits. 57.50 (ISBN 0-686-82267-6, 42A). Public Management.

--Nonprofit Financial Management. 57.50 (ISBN 0-686-82266-8, 41A). Public Management.

Frederiksen, D. W., jt. ed. see Colowick, Sidney P.

Frederiksen, Lee W. Handbook of Organizational Behavior Management. LC 82-4741. 604p. 1982. 32.95 (ISBN 0-471-09109-X, Pub. by Wiley-Interscience). Wiley.

Frederiksen, N., et al. Prediction of Organizational Behavior. 344p. 1973. text ed. 29.00 (ISBN 0-08-016967-8); pap. text ed. 14.50 (ISBN 0-08-017189-3). Pergamon.

Fredette, Jean. Fiction Writer's Market 1983-84. 2nd ed. 672p. 1983. 17.95 (ISBN 0-89879-108-1). Writers Digest.

Fredette, Jean, ed. Fiction Writer's Market, 1982-83. annual 672p. 1982. 16.95 o.p. (ISBN 0-89879-073-5). Writers Digest.

Fredgant, Don. Collecting Art Nouveau, Identification & Values. (Illus.). 300p. (Orig.). 1982. pap. 10.95 (ISBN 0-89689-036-8). Bks Americana.

Fredriksson, Don. Plumbing for Dummies: A Guide to the Maintenance & Repair of Everything Including the Kitchen Sink. (Illus.). 256p. 1983. pap. 10.95 (ISBN 0-672-52738-3). Bobbs.

Fredland, Richard A. Africa Faces the World. LC 80-81101. (Scholarly Monograph Ser.). 212p. 1980. pap. 15.00 o.p. (ISBN 0-8408-0502-0); pap. text ed. 15.00 o.p. (ISBN 0-686-64869-2). Carrollton Pr.

Fredland, Richard A., jt. ed. see Potholm, Christian P.

Fredman, Lionel E. James Madison, American President & Constitutional Author. Rahmas, D. Steve, ed. LC 74-14592. (Outstanding Personalities Ser.). 32p. 1974. lib. bdg. 2.95 incl. catalog cards (ISBN 0-87157-578-7); pap. 1.95 vinyl laminated covers (ISBN 0-87157-078-5). SamHar Pr.

--John Dickinson, American Revolutionary Statesman. new ed. LC 74-14599. (Outstanding Personalities Ser.). 32p. 1974. lib. bdg. 2.95 incl. catalog cards (ISBN 0-87157-575-2); pap. 1.95 vinyl laminated covers (ISBN 0-87157-075-0). SamHar Pr.

Fredman, Lionel E & Kurland, Gerald. John Adams, American Revolutionary Leader & President. Rahmas, D. Steve, ed. LC 73-87627. (Outstanding Personalities Ser.: No. 65). 32p. (Orig.). (gr. 7-12). 1973. lib. bdg. 2.95 incl. catalog cards (ISBN 0-87157-565-5); pap. 1.95 vinyl laminated covers (ISBN 0-87157-065-3). SamHar Pr.

Fredman, Ruth G. The Passover Seder. 1982. pap. 5.95 (ISBN 0-452-00606-6, Mer). NAL.

--The Passover Seder: Afikoman in Exile. 192p. 15.00 (ISBN 0-686-95143-3). ADL.

Fredman, Stephen, tr. see Alegria, Fernando.

Fredrick, David & Fredrick, Donna. Death Education in Counseling. 147p. 1978. softcover 9.95 (ISBN 0-932930-01-8). Pilgrimage Inc.

Fredrick, Donna, jt. auth. see Fredrick, David.

Fredrick, Laurence & Baker, Robert. An Introduction to Astronomy. 9th ed. 1980. text ed. 22.95 (ISBN 0-442-22422-2); instr's. manual 3.95 (ISBN 0-442-22421-4). Van Nos Reinhold.

Fredrick, Laurence W. & Baker, Robert H. Introduction to Astronomy. 8th ed. 1974. pap. text ed. 16.95 (ISBN 0-442-22436-2); instructors' manual 2.00x (ISBN 0-442-22437-0); study guide 4.95x (ISBN 0-442-22438-9). Van Nos Reinhold.

Fredrick, Peter. Creative Sunprinting. (Illus.). 192p. 1980. 29.95 (ISBN 0-240-51045-3). Focal Pr.

Fredricks, Simon & Brody, Garry S., eds. Symposium on the Neurologic Aspects of Plastic Surgery. LC 78-7355. (Symposia of the Educational Foundaion of the American Society of Plastic & Reconstructive Surgeons, Inc. Ser.: Vol. 17). 1978. text ed. 60.00 o.p. (ISBN 0-8016-1679-4). Mosby.

Fredrickson, George, ed. William Lloyd Garrison. (Great Lives Observed Ser). 1968. 8.95 (ISBN 0-13-346858-5, Spec); pap. 1.95 (ISBN 0-13-346841-0, Spec). P-H.

Fredrikson, Roger L. The Communicator's Commentary-John, Vol. 4. Ogilvie, Lloyd J., ed. (The Communicator's Commentaries Ser.). 1983. 14.95 (ISBN 0-8499-0157-X). Word Pub.

Free, Anne R. Social Usage. 2nd ed. (Illus.). 1969. pap. text ed. 14.95 (ISBN 0-13-819607-9). P-H.

Free, James L. Training Your Retriever. 7th rev. ed. (Illus.). 1980. 12.95 (ISBN 0-698-11009-9, Coward). Putnam Pub Group.

--Training Your Retriever. rev. 6th ed. LC 76-30660. (Illus.). 336p. 1977. 9.95 o.p. (ISBN 0-698-10821-3, Coward). Putnam Pub Group.

Free, John B. Social Organization of Honeybees. (Studies in Biology: No. 81). 74p. 1977. pap. text ed. 8.95 (ISBN 0-7131-2655-8). E Arnold.

Free, John Da see Da Free, John.

Free Library Of Philadelphia. Catalog of the Hampton L. Carson Collection Illustrative of the the Growth of the Common Law, 2 Vols. 1962. Set. 190.00 (ISBN 0-8161-0490-5, Hall Library). G K Hall.

Free, Lloyd A. & Cantril, Hadley. Political Beliefs of Americans: A Study of Public Opinion. 1968. pap. 2.95 o.p. (ISBN 0-671-20057-7, Touchstone Bks). S&S.

Free, Montague. Plant Propagation in Pictures. rev. ed. Dietz, Marjorie J., ed. LC 76-56290. (Illus.). 1957. 9.95 (ISBN 0-385-12986-6). Doubleday.

Free Stuff Editors. Free Stuff for Kids. rev. ed. LC 81-2416. (Illus.). 120p. pap. 2.95 (ISBN 0-915658-90-9). Meadowbrook Pr.

--Free Things for Seniors. LC 82-2217. (Illus.). 64p. (Orig.). 1982. pap. 2.00 (ISBN 0-915658-76-3). Meadowbrook Pr.

Free Stuff Editors, ed. Free Stuff for Cooks. rev. ed. LC 80-15462. (Illus.). 110p. 1981. pap. 2.95 o.p. (ISBN 0-915658-23-2). Meadowbrook Pr.

--Free Stuff for Home & Garden. rev. ed. LC 80-39692. (Illus.). 130p. 1981. pap. 2.95 o.p. (ISBN 0-915658-27-5). Meadowbrook Pr.

--Free Stuff for Parents. rev. ed. LC 80-25596. (Illus.). 110p. 1981. pap. 2.95 o.p. (ISBN 0-915658-25-9). Meadowbrook Pr.

--Free Stuff for Travelers. LC 81-2305. (Illus.). 130p. (Orig.). 1981. pap. 2.95 o.p. (ISBN 0-915658-29-1). Meadowbrook Pr.

Free, Woodrow W. A Short History of the Metric System of Weights & Measures. 1977. 4.50 o.p. (ISBN 0-533-02208-8). Vantage.

Freebairen-Smith, S. J. & Littlejohn, G. N. Winner Take All: From Trial to Triumph, Vol. 1. 1977. pap. text ed. 6.50x o.p. (ISBN 0-435-36320-4). Heinemann Ed.

Freebairn-Smith, S. J. & Littlejohn, G. N. Chief Factors for the Gods: From Trial to Triumph, Vol. 2. 1977. pap. text ed. 6.50x o.p. (ISBN 0-435-36321-2). Heinemann Ed.

Freeborn, Richard. The Russian Revolutionary Novel: Turgenev to Pasternak. LC 82-4259. (Cambridge Studies in Russian Literature). 220p. Date not set. price not set (ISBN 0-521-24442-0). Cambridge U Pr.

Freeborn, Richard, tr. see Turgenev, Ivan.

Freeborn, Richard, et al, eds. Russian & Slavic Literature. 1976. soft cover 17.95 (ISBN 0-89357-038-9). Slavica.

Freed, Daniel J. & Terrell, Timothy P. Standards Relating to Interim Status: The Release, Control & Detention of Accused Juvenile Offenders Between Arrest & Disposition. LC 77-2318. (IJA-ABA Juvenile Justice Standards Project Ser.). 144p. 1980. prof ref 20.00x (ISBN 0-88410-244-0); pap. 10.00x prof ref (ISBN 0-88410-812-0). Ballinger Pub.

Freed, Debbie, jt. auth. see Darling, Kathy.

Freed, Edwin D., jt. ed. see Flesner, David E.

Freed, Harvey G. Chapel Talks, Sermons & Debates. 1983. pap. 6.95 (ISBN 0-89225-269-3). Gospel Advocate.

Freed, Lewis. T. S. Eliot: Aesthetics & History. LC 61-11289. xvi, 251p. 1962. pap. 7.50 (ISBN 0-87548-011-X). Open Court.

Freed, Lynn. Heart Change. 1982. pap. 2.95 (ISBN 0-451-11916-9, AE1916, Sig). NAL.

Freed, Ray. Moom. (Backstreet Editions Ser.). 16p. 1980. pap. 3.00 (ISBN 0-935252-13-4); op 10.00 (ISBN 0-686-61077-6). Street Pr.

Freed, Rita E. Egypt's Golden Age: A Picture Book. (Illus.). 68p. (Orig.). 1982. pap. 4.95 (ISBN 0-87846-208-2). Mus Fine Arts Boston.

Freed, Stanley A., ed. Anthropology & the Climate of Opinion, Vol. 293. (Annals of the New York Academy of Sciences). 274p. 1977. 23.00x (ISBN 0-89072-039-8). NY Acad Sci.

Freedberg, S. J. Circa Sixteen Hundred: A Revolution of Style in Italian Painting. (Illus.). 176p. 1983. text ed. 25.00x (ISBN 0-674-13156-8). Harvard U Pr.

Freedberg, Sydney J., ed. see Fuseli, Henry.

Freedland, Mark R. The Contract of Employment. 1975. 42.00x (ISBN 0-19-825306-0). Oxford U Pr.

Freedland, Michael. Gregory Peck. LC 80-82359. (Illus.). 320p. 1980. 10.95 o.p. (ISBN 0-688-03619-8). Morrow.

Freedland, R. A. & Briggs, S. A Biochemical Approach to Nutrition. 1977. pap. 6.50x (ISBN 0-412-13040-8, Pub. by Chapman & Hall). Methuen Inc.

Freedle, R. O., jt. auth. see Hall, W. S.

Freedle, Roy O., jt. auth. see Fine, Jonathan.

Freedle, Roy O., ed. Discourse Production & Comprehension. (Discourse Processes: Advances in Research & Theory Ser.: Vol. 1). (Illus.). 1977. text ed. 32.50 (ISBN 0-89391-001-5); pap. text ed. 16.50. Ablex Pub.

Freedle, Roy O., ed. see Beaugrande, Robert de.

Freedle, Roy O., ed. see Pelligrini, Anthony D. & Yawkey, Thomas D.

Freedley, George & Reeves, John A. History of the Theatre. rev. ed. (Illus.). (YA) (gr. 9 up). 1968. 10.00 o.p. (ISBN 0-517-50958-X). Crown.

Freedley, George, ed. Three Plays about Crime & Criminals. Incl. Arsenic & Old Lace. Kesselring, Joseph; Detective Story. Kingsley, Sidney; Kind Lady. Chodorov, Edward. 279p. Date not set. pap. 2.95 (ISBN 0-671-44138-8). WSP.

Freedman. Israel in the Begin Era. 288p. 1982. 29.95 (ISBN 0-03-059376-X). Praeger.

Freedman, A. M., jt. ed. see Fisher, S.

Freedman, Alan. The Computer Glossary: It's Not Just a Glossary. 3rd ed. (Illus.). 320p. Date not set. price not set (ISBN 0-941878-02-3). Computer Lang.

Freedman, Alan & Morrison, Irma L. The Computer Glossary: It's Not Just a Glossary. 320p. 1983. pap. 14.95 (ISBN 0-686-38832-1). P. H.

Freedman, Alan & Morrison, Irma Lee. The Computer Coloring Book: It's Not Just a Coloring Book. 80p. 1983. pap. 6.95 (ISBN 0-13-164632-X). P-H.

Freedman, Alfred M. & Kaplan, Harold I. Comprehensive Textbook of Psychiatry. 3rd ed. (Illus.). 4000p. 1980. 100.00 o.p. (ISBN 0-683-04520-2). Williams & Wilkins.

Freedman, Ariva & Pringle, Ian, eds. Reinventing the Rhetorical Tradition. 197p. 11.40 (ISBN 0-686-95317-7); members 9.95 (ISBN 0-686-99494-9). NCTE.

Freedman, B. Markov Chains. (Illus.). 382p. 1983. Repr. of 1971 ed. 28.00 (ISBN 0-387-90808-0). Springer-Verlag.

Freedman, Benedict & Freedman, Nancy. Mrs. Mike. (Illus.). 1947. 8.95 o.s.i. (ISBN 0-698-10260-6, Coward). Putnam Pub Group.

Freedman, D. Approximating Countable Markov Chains. (Illus.). 140p. 1983. Repr. of 1972 ed. 20.00 (ISBN 0-387-90804-8). Springer-Verlag.

--Brownian Motion & Diffusion. (Illus.). 231p. 1983. Repr. of 1971 ed. 24.00 (ISBN 0-387-90805-6). Springer-Verlag.

Freedman, D. X., ed. see Association for Research in Nervous & Mental Disease.

Freedman, Daniel X., ed. Year Book of Psychiatry & Applied Mental Health 1983. 1983. 45.00 (ISBN 0-686-83776-2). Year Bk Med.

Freedman, David, ed. see Morton, A. Q., et al.

Freedman, David, et al. Statistics. (Illus.). 1978. 21.95x (ISBN 0-393-09076-0); instr.s bk. 2.95 (ISBN 0-393-09041-8). Norton.

Freedman, David M., jt. auth. see Fleischer, David.

Freedman, David N., ed. Archaeological Reports from the Tabqa Dam Project--Euphrates Valley, Syria. LC 78-12251. (American Schools of Oriental Research Ser.: Vol. 44). 182p. 1979. text ed. 20.00x (ISBN 0-89757-044-8, Am Sch Orient Res). Eisenbrauns.

--The Biblical Archaeologist Reader, Vol. 4. 1983. text ed. price not set (ISBN 0-89757-509-1, Pub. by Am Sch Orient Res); pap. text ed. price not set (ISBN 0-89757-506-7). Eisenbrauns.

--Preliminary Excavation Reports: Bab edh-Dhra, Sardis, Meiron, Tell el-Hesi, Carthage. LC 77-13341. (American Schools of Oriental Research Ser.: Vol. 43). 190p. 1978. pap. text ed. 17.50x (ISBN 0-89757-043-X, Am Sch Orient Res). Eisenbrauns.

Freedman, David N. & Campbell, Edward F., eds. The Biblical Archaeologist Reader, Vol. 2. LC 75-9592. 420p. 1975. pap. text ed. 6.00x (ISBN 0-89757-502-4, Am Sch Orient Res). Eisenbrauns.

Freedman, David N., ed. see Morton, A. Q. & Michaelson, S.

Freedman, David N., jt. ed. see Wright, G. Ernest.

Freedman, David Noel, ed. see Andersen, Francis & Forbes, A. Dean.

Freedman, James O. Crisis & Legitimacy. LC 78-51683. 1978. 32.50 (ISBN 0-521-22063-7); pap. 11.95 (ISBN 0-521-29380-4). Cambridge U Pr.

Freedman, Jill. Circus Days. (Illus.). 126p. 1975. 12.95 o.p. (ISBN 0-517-52008-7, Harmony). Crown.

Freedman, Johnathan, jt. auth. see Goleman, Dan.

Freedman, Jonathan, et al. Readings in Social Psychology. (Personality, Clinical & Social Psychology Ser). 1971. pap. text ed. 16.95 (ISBN 0-13-761072-6). P-H.

--Social Psychology. 4th ed. (Illus.). 656p. 1981. text ed. 23.95 (ISBN 0-13-817783-X). P-H.

Freedman, Jonathan L. Introductory Psychology. 2nd ed. LC 81-17600. (Psychology Ser.). (Illus.). 672p. 1982. text ed. 23.95 (ISBN 0-201-05772-7); study guide 6.95 (ISBN 0-201-05774-3); Instr's. manual 2.50 (ISBN 0-201-05773-5). A-W.

Freedman, Lawrence. The Evolution of Nuclear Strategy. 473p. 1982. pap. 10.95 (ISBN 0-312-27270-7). St Martin.

Freedman, Lawrence R. Infective Endocarditis & Other Intravascular Infections. (Current Topics in Infectious Diseases Ser.). (Illus.). 250p. 1982. 35.00x (ISBN 0-306-40937-2, Plenum Med Bk). Plenum Pub.

Freedman, Lawrence Z., intro. by. By Reason of Insanity: Essays on Psychiatry & the Law. 250p. 1983. PLB 24.95 (ISBN 0-8420-2203-1). Scholarly Res Inc.

Freedman, Lawrence Z. & Alexander, Yonah, eds. Perspectives on Terrorism. 225p. 1983. PLB 24.95 (ISBN 0-8420-2201-5). Scholarly Res Inc.

Freedman, Leonard. Power & Politics in America. 4th ed. LC 82-12867. 500p. 1982. pap. text ed. 15.95 (ISBN 0-534-01252-3). Brooks-Cole.

Freedman, M. & Perl, T. A Source for Substitutes... & Other Teachers. 1974. 11.80 (ISBN 0-201-05786-7, Sch Div); dupe masters avail. A-W.

Freedman, M. David & Evans, Lansing B. Designing Systems with Microcomputers: A Systematic Approach. (Illus.). 320p. 1983. text ed. 26.00 (ISBN 0-13-201350-9). P-H.

Freedman, Matt & Hoffman, Paul. What WASP Do Instead. pap. 3.95 (ISBN 0-312-86581-3). ST Martin.

--What Wasps Say After Sex. (Illus.). 80p. 1982. pap. 3.95 (ISBN 0-312-86585-6). St Martin.

Freedman, Matthew. Radiology of the Postoperative Hip. LC 79-12411. 1979. 57.50 o.p. (ISBN 0-471-04416-4, Pub. by Wiley Medical). Wiley.

Freedman, Maurice, tr. see Granet, Marcel.

Freedman, Melvin H. & Silver, Samuel M. How to Enjoy This Moment. rev. ed. Ettinger, Andrew & Bafaro, Johanna, eds. 192p. pap. 8.95 (ISBN 0-911665-00-5, EN982). Entre Prods.

Freedman, Monroe. Lawyers' Ethics in an Adversary System. 1975. 15.00 o.p. (ISBN 0-672-82065-X, Bobbs-Merrill Law). Michie-Bobbs.

Freedman, Morris. American Drama in Social Context. LC 79-156787. (Crosscurrents-Modern Critiques Ser). 158p. 1971. 6.95 o.p. (ISBN 0-8093-0526-7). S Ill U Pr.

Freedman, Nancy, jt. auth. see Freedman, Benedict.

Freedman, Paul H. The Diocese of Vic: Tradition & Regeneration in Medieval Catalonia. 232p. 1983. 20.00 (ISBN 0-8135-0970-X). Rutgers U Pr.

Freedman, Philip, et al. Nephrology. 2nd ed. (Medical Examination Review Book: Vol. 34). 1981. 26.50 (ISBN 0-87488-176-5). Med Exam.

Freedman, Ralph, ed. & intro. by. Virginia Woolf: Revaluation & Continuity, a Collection of Essays. 1980. 14.95 o.s.i. (ISBN 0-520-03625-5); pap. 4.95 (ISBN 0-520-03980-7). U of Cal Pr.

Freedman, Richard. The Novel. LC 74-84890. (World of Culture Ser.). (Illus.). 192p. 1975. 12.95 o.p. (ISBN 0-88225-115-5). Newsweek.

Freedman, Robert, ed. Marx on Economics. LC 61-7691. (Orig.). 1961. pap. 4.95 (ISBN 0-15-657479-9, Harv). HarBraceJ.

Freedman, Robert O., ed. Soviet Jewry in the Decisive Decade, 1971-1980. (Duke Press Policy Studies). 135p. 1983. lib. bdg. 18.75 (ISBN 0-8223-0544-5); pap. 9.75 (ISBN 0-8223-0555-0). Duke.

Freedman, Russell. Farm Babies. LC 81-2898. (Illus.). 40p. (gr. k-3). 1981. PLB 9.95 (ISBN 0-8234-0426-9). Holiday.

--Immigrant Kids. LC 79-20060. 64p. (gr. 3-7). 1980. 11.95 (ISBN 0-525-32538-7, 01160-350). Dutton.

--Killer Fish. LC 81-85089. (Illus.). 40p. (gr. 1-4). 1982. PLB 8.95 (ISBN 0-8234-0449-8). Holiday.

--Killer Snakes. LC 82-80821. (Illus.). 40p. (gr. 1-4). 1982. Reinforced bdg. 9.95 (ISBN 0-8234-0460-9). Holiday.

Freedman, Samuel O. & Gold, Phil. Clinical Immunology. 2nd ed. (Illus.). 1976. 42.00 (ISBN 0-06-140834-4, Harper Medical). Lippincott.

Freedy, Amos see Hopple, Gerald W. & Andriole, Stephen J.

Freehafer, Ruth W. R. B. Stewart & Purdue University. 140p. 1983. 10.00 (ISBN 0-931682-14-2). Purdue Univ Bks.

FreeHand, Julianna. A Seafaring Legacy. LC 81-40240. 192p. 1981. 18.50 (ISBN 0-394-51771-7). Random.

Freehling, Alison G. Drift Toward Dissolution: The Virginia Slavery Debate of 1831-1832. 360p. 1982. text ed. 30.00x (ISBN 0-8071-1035-3). La State U Pr.

Freehling, William. Prelude to Civil War: The Nullification Controversy in South Carolina, 1816-1836. (Illus.). 1968. pap. 7.95xi (ISBN 0-06-131359-9, TB1359, Torch). Har-Row.

Freehling, William H., ed. see Rose, Willie L.

Freehling, William W., ed. see Rose, Willie L.

Freeland, Jeanne H., jt. auth. see Peckham, Gladys C.

Freeland, Richard M. The Truman Doctrine & the Origins of McCarthyism: Foreign Policy, Domestic Politics, & Internal Security, 1946-1948. LC 71-142958. 444p. 1974. pap. 4.95 o.p. (ISBN 0-8052-0439-3). Schocken.

Freelander, Iris see Carr, Clare.

Freeley, Austin J. Argumentation & Debate. 5th ed. 432p. 1981. text ed. 18.95x (ISBN 0-534-00944-1). Wadsworth Pub.

Freeling, Nicholas. Gadget. LC 77-24130. 1977. 8.95 o.p. (ISBN 0-698-10810-8, Coward). Putnam Pub Group.

Freeling, Nicolas. Wolfnight. LC 82-40427. (Henri Castang Ser.). 288p. 1983. pap. 2.95 (ISBN 0-394-71381-8, Vin). Random.

Freelove, William F. Victorian Horses & Carriages: Personal Sketch Book. 1980. 35.40 (ISBN 0-517-54057-6, C N Potter Bks). Crown.

Freely, John. Boston & Environs. (Blue Guides Ser.). 1983. write for info (ISBN 0-393-01560-2); pap. price not set (ISBN 0-393-30012-9). Norton.

--Istanbul. (Blue Guides Ser.). 400p. 1983. 25.95 (ISBN 0-393-01558-0); pap. 14.95 (ISBN 0-393-30010-2). Norton.

Freeman, A. J., ed. Proceedings of the Arbeitsgemeinschaft Magnetismus Conference, 1974. 503p. 1975. 59.75 (ISBN 0-444-10900-5, North-Holland). Elsevier.

Freeman, A. J. & Schuler, D., eds. Proceedings of the Arbeitsgemeinschaft Magnetismus Conference, 1976: Held at Bad Nauheim, Ger., Mar. 1976. (Journal of Magnetism & Magnetic Materials: Vol. 4). 1977. 93.00 (ISBN 0-7204-0576-9, North-Holland). Elsevier.

Freeman, A. J. & Schuler, K., eds. Proceedings of the Arbeitsgemeinschaft Magnetismus Conference, 1977: Munster, Federal Republic of Germany, March 1977. 1978. Repr. 83.75 (ISBN 0-444-85090-2, North-Holland). Elsevier.

Freeman, A. J., et al, eds. International Conference on Magnetic Alloys & Oxides: Haifa, Israel, August 1977. 1978. 89.50 (ISBN 0-444-85162-3, North-Holland). Elsevier.

Freeman, A. Myrick. Air & Water Pollution Control: A Benefit Cost Assessment. LC 82-8409. (Environmental Science & Technology Monographs). 186p. 1982. 32.00 (ISBN 0-471-08985-0, Pub. by Wiley-Interscience). Wiley.

Freeman, A. Myrick, et al. The Economics of Environmental Policy. LC 72-7249. 184p. 1973. pap. text ed. 12.95x (ISBN 0-471-27786-X). Wiley.

Freeman, Allen G. Railways: Past, Present, & Future. LC 82-60816. (Illus.). 304p. 1982. 39.50 (ISBN 0-688-00636-1). Morrow.

Freeman, Arnold. Boy Life & Labour: The Manufacture of Inefficiency. LC 79-56956. (The English Working Class Ser.). 1980. lib. bdg. 25.00 o.s.i. (ISBN 0-8240-0110-9). Garland Pub.

Freeman, Arnold, tr. see Steiner, Rudolf.

Freeman, Arthur. Apollonian Poems. LC 61-9254. (Orig.). 1961. pap. 1.65 o.p. (ISBN 0-689-10091-4). Atheneum.

Freeman, B. M., ed. Physiology & Biochemistry of the Domestic Fowl, Vol. 4. Date not set. price not set (ISBN 0-12-267104-X). Acad Pr.

Freeman, C. E., jt. ed. see Lowe, W. D.

Freeman, Charles. Defence. (Today's World Ser.). (Illus.). 72p. (gr. 7-12). 1983. 14.95 (ISBN 0-7134-0969-X, Pub. by Batsford England). David & Charles.

Freeman, Christopher. The Economics of Industrial Innovation. 2nd ed. 320p. 1983. 25.00 (ISBN 0-262-06083-3). MIT Pr.

Freeman, Cynthia. No Time for Tears. 448p. 1982. pap. 3.95 (ISBN 0-553-22656-8). Bantam.

Freeman, Dan. Elephants: The Vanishing Giants. (Illus.). 192p. 1981. 20.00 (ISBN 0-399-12567-1). Putnam Pub Group.

--The Great Apes. LC 79-84552. 1979. 15.95 o.p. (ISBN 0-399-12399-7). Putnam Pub Group.

Freeman, Derek. Margaret Mead & Samoa: The Making & Unmaking of an Anthropological Byth. (Illus.). 416p. 1983. 25.00 (ISBN 0-674-54830-2). Harvard U Pr.

Freeman, Don. Beady Bear. (Illus.). (gr. 3-6). 1977. pap. 2.95 (ISBN 0-14-050197-5, Puffin). Penguin.

--Corduroy. (Picture Puffin Ser). (Illus.). (gr. k-1). 1976. pap. 3.50 (ISBN 0-14-050173-8, Puffin). Penguin.

--Dandelion. (gr. k-3). 1982. incl. cassette 17.95 (ISBN 0-941078-11-6); pap. 11.95 incl. cassette (ISBN 0-941078-09-4); user's guide incl. 6 pbs. & cassette 29.95 (ISBN 0-941078-10-8). Live Oak Media.

--Eyes As Big As Cantaloupes. new ed. 1978. 9.95 (ISBN 0-89325-013-9). Joyce Pr.

--Mop Top. (Picture Puffins Ser.). 1978. pap. 2.95 (ISBN 0-14-050326-9, Puffin). Penguin.

--A Rainbow of My Own. 32p. (ps-2). 1978. pap. 3.50 (ISBN 0-14-050328-5, Puffin). Penguin.

--Rainbow of My Own. (Illus.). (gr. k-3). 1966. PLB 9.95 (ISBN 0-670-58928-4). Viking Pr.

--Seal & the Slick. (Illus.). 32p. (gr. k-3). 1974. PLB 8.95 o.p. (ISBN 0-670-62659-7). Viking Pr.

--Space Witch. (Picture Puffins Ser.). (Illus.). (gr. k-3). 1979. pap. 3.95 (ISBN 0-14-050346-3, Puffin). Penguin.

--Tilly Witch. (Illus.). (gr. k-3). 1969. 9.95 (ISBN 0-670-71303-1). Viking Pr.

Freeman, Don, jt. auth. see Wills, Maury.

Freeman, Donald C., ed. Essays in Modern Stylistics. 424p. 1981. 32.00x (ISBN 0-416-74420-6); pap. 13.95x (ISBN 0-416-74430-3). Methuen Inc.

Freeman, E. M., ed. Campfire Chillers. LC 79-28318. (Illus.). 192p. (Orig.). 1980. pap. 7.95 (ISBN 0-914788-23-X). East Woods.

Freeman, Eugene, ed. The Abdication of Philosophy: Essays in Honor of Paul A. Schilpp. LC 72-93357. 328p. 1976. 21.00 (ISBN 0-87548-274-0). Open Court.

Freeman, Eugene & Mandelbaum, Maurice, eds. Spinoza: Essays in Interpretation. LC 72-84079. (The Monist Library of Philosophy Ser.). 329p. 1974. pap. 8.50 (ISBN 0-87548-196-5). Open Court.

Freeman, Eugene & Sellars, Wilfrid, eds. Basic Issues in the Philosophy of Time. LC 73-128197. (The Monist Library of Philosophy Ser.). 241p. 1971. 16.00 (ISBN 0-87548-078-0). Open Court.

Freeman, Eugene, jt. ed. see Reese, William L.

Freeman, G. W., ed. The Masters of Eventing. LC 78-3772. 1978. 14.95 (ISBN 0-668-04639-2, 4639). Arco.

Freeman, Gail. Alien Thunder. LC 82-9578. 192p. (gr. 7 up). 1982. 10.95 (ISBN 0-02-735620-5). Bradbury Pr.

--Out from Under. LC 81-18154. 192p. (YA) (gr. 7 up). 1982. 9.95 (ISBN 0-02-735400-8). Bradbury Pr.

Freeman, Gillian. An Easter Egg Hunt. 272p. 1982. pap. 2.95 (ISBN 0-441-18152-X). Ace Bks.

Freeman, Grace. Midnight to Dawn. (Illus.). 46p. (Orig.). 1981. pap. 6.95 (ISBN 0-932662-37-4). St Andrews NC.

Freeman, Grace & Sugarman, Joan G. Inside the Synagogue. LC 62-19996. (Illus.). (gr. 3-5). 1963. 5.00 (ISBN 0-8074-0041-6, 301782). UAHC.

Freeman, Grace B. Children Are Poetry. 3rd ed. (Illus.). 16p. 1982. pap. 2.00 (ISBN 0-9607730-3-7). Johns Pr.

--Children of Laughter & Tears. (Illus., Orig.). 1982. pap. write for info. Johns Pr.

--No Costumes Or Masks. (Red Clay Reader Ser.: Vol. 10, No. 2). 48p. 1983. pap. 4.95 (ISBN 0-9607730-2-9). Johns Pr.

Freeman, H. Nahum Zeph Hab. (Everyman's Bible Commentary Ser.). 1973. pap. 4.50 o.p. (ISBN 0-8024-2034-6). Moody.

Freeman, Harold. Toward Socialism in America. 2nd ed. LC 79-12410. 256p. 1982. text ed. 16.50x (ISBN 0-87073-911-5); pap. text ed. 8.50x (ISBN 0-87073-912-3). Schenkman.

Freeman, Harold, Jr., jt. auth. see Richardson, Ellis.

Freeman, Harrop A. & Freeman, Norman D. Tax Practice Desk Book. 1973. 47.50 (ISBN 0-88262-061-4). Warren.

Freeman, Harvey A., jt. auth. see Bray, Olin H.

Freeman, Henry P. The Unjust & Deceitful Man: An Autobiography, 1 vol. 304p. (Orig.). 1979. 9.95 (ISBN 0-686-38721-X); pap. 5.95 (ISBN 0-9609920-1-4). Freeman Sr.

Freeman, Hobart. Introduction to the Old Testament Prophets. 14.95 o.p. (ISBN 0-8024-4145-9). Moody.

Freeman, Howard E. & Jones, Wyatt C. Social Problems. 3rd ed. 1979. 22.95 (ISBN 0-395-30594-2); Instr's. manual 1.25 (ISBN 0-395-30595-0). HM.

Freeman, Howard E., jt. auth. see Bernstein, Ilene N.

Freeman, Howard E. see Brim, Orville G., Jr., et al.

Freeman, Howard E. & Dynes, Russell R., eds. Applied Sociology: Roles & Activities of Sociologists in Diverse Setting. LC 82-49035. (Social & Behavioral Science Ser.). 1983. text ed. 23.95x (ISBN 0-87589-563-8). Jossey-Bass.

Freeman, Howard E., et al. Handbook of Medical Sociology. 3rd ed. 1979. 26.95 (ISBN 0-13-380253-1). P-H.

Freeman, Ira, jt. auth. see Freeman, Mae.

Freeman, Ira M. Science of Sound & Ultrasonics. (Science Library Ser.: No. 5). (Illus.). (gr. 5-8). 1968. PLB 4.99 o.p. (ISBN 0-394-90942-9, BYR). Random.

Freeman, Ira M., jt. auth. see Freeman, Mae.

Freeman, Ira M., jt. auth. see Freeman, Mae B.

Freeman, James A. & Beeler, Myrton F., eds. Laboratory Medicine-Urine Analysis & Medical Microscopy. 2nd ed. LC 82-17254. (Illus.). 405p. 1983. text ed. write for info (ISBN 0-8121-0822-1). Lea & Febiger.

Freeman, James D. Tu Puedes! LC 82-70490. 256p. 1982. 4.95 (ISBN 0-87159-158-8). Unity Bks.

Freeman, James M. Scarcity & Opportunity in an Indian Village. LC 76-4423. (Kiste-Ogan Social Change Ser.). 1976. pap. text ed. 9.95 (ISBN 0-8465-2115-6). Benjamin-Cummings.

Freeman, Jean K., jt. ed. see Haikalis, Peter D.

Freeman, Jim. California Steelhead Fishing. (Illus.). 96p. 1971. pap. 1.95 o.p. (ISBN 0-87701-032-3). Chronicle Bks.

--California Trout. (Illus.). 224p. 1983. pap. 6.95 (ISBN 0-87701-251-2). Chronicle Bks.

--Shasta Lake Fishing. (Illus.). 80p. 1971. pap. 1.95 o.p. (ISBN 0-87701-033-1). Chronicle Bks.

Freeman, Jim, jt. auth. see Best, Don.

Freeman, Jo, ed. Social Movements of the 60's & 70's. (Illus.). 480p. (Orig.). 1982. pap. text ed. 14.95x (ISBN 0-582-28091-5). Longman.

Freeman, John. Creative Writing. (gr. 9-12). pap. 3.95 o.p. (ISBN 0-584-62006-3). Transatlantic.

Freeman, John A. Survival Gardening: Enough Nutrition from 1000 Square Feet to Live On--Just in Case. LC 90-7966. (Illus.). 88p. (Orig.). 1982. pap. 6.95 (ISBN 0-9607730-0-2). Johns Pr.

Freeman, John M. Practical Management of Meningomyelocele. (Illus.). 1974. 29.50 o.p. (ISBN 0-8391-0639-4). Univ Park.

Freeman, Joy. The Suitable Match. 1982. pap. 2.25 (ISBN 0-451-11773-5, AE1773, Sig). NAL.

Freeman, Kenneth J., ed. Schools of Hellas. LC 73-7994. (Illus.). 1969. text ed. 11.00 (ISBN 0-8077-1391-0); pap. text ed. 6.00x (ISBN 0-8077-1390-2). Tchrs Coll.

Freeman, Leonard, ed. Nuclear Medicine Annual, 1980. Weissmann, Heidi. 440p. 1980. text ed. 47.00 (ISBN 0-89004-472-4). Raven.

Freeman, Leonard M. & Blaufox, M. Donald, eds. Radionuclide Studies of the Gastrointestinal System. LC 72-10097. 232p. 1973. Repr. 49.00 o.s.i. (ISBN 0-8089-0796-4). Grune.

Freeman, Leonard M. & Weissman, Heidi S., eds. Nuclear Medicine Annual, 1982. 425p. 1982. text ed. 54.00 (ISBN 0-89004-726-X). Raven.

Freeman, Leonard M. & Weissmann, Heidi S., eds. Nuclear Medicine Annual, 1981. 357p. 1981. text ed. 43.00 (ISBN 0-89004-581-X). Raven.

Freeman, Leslie G., jt. ed. see Butzer, Karl.

Freeman, Linton C. Elementary Applied Statistics: For Students in Behavioral Science. LC 65-14256. 298p. 1965. text ed. 19.95x o.p. (ISBN 0-471-27780-0). Wiley.

Freeman, Lory. What Would You Do If? A Children's Guide to First Aid. (ps-3). 1983. PLB 9.95 (ISBN 0-943990-00-9); pap. 4.95 (ISBN 0-943990-01-7). Parenting Pr.

Freeman, Louis. Guide to Typewriting. (Orig.). (gr. 7-12). 1974. wkbk 5.00 o.p. (ISBN 0-87720-401-2). AMSCO Sch.

Freeman, Lucy. Fight Against Fears. 368p. 1983. pap. 3.50 (ISBN 0-446-30329-1). Warner Bks.

--The Murder Mystique: Crime Writers on Their Art. (Recognitions Ser.). 200p. 1982. 11.95 (ISBN 0-8044-2212-5); pap. 6.95 (ISBN 0-8044-6162-7). Ungar.

Freeman, Lucy, jt. auth. see Schlossberg, Harvey.

Freeman, M. A., jt. ed. see Swanson, S. A.

Freeman, M. H., jt. auth. see Fincham, W. H.

Freeman, M. Herbert, jt. auth. see Logan, William B.

Freeman, Mae & Freeman, Ira. Fun with Light. (Learning with Fun Ser.). (Illus.). (gr. 5 up). 1971. 13.50x o.p. (ISBN 0-7182-0070-5, SpS). Sportshelf.

Freeman, Mae & Freeman, Ira M. You Will Go to the Moon. LC 75-158389. (gr. 1-2). 1971. PLB 5.99 (ISBN 0-394-92340-5). Beginner.

Freeman, Mae B. Finding Out About the Past. (Gateway Ser.: No. 44). (Illus.). (gr. 4-8). 1967. 2.95 o.p. (ISBN 0-394-80144-X, BYR); PLB 5.99. o.p. (ISBN 0-394-90144-4). Random.

--Fun with Ballet. (Illus.). (gr. 4-6). 1952. 5.95 (ISBN 0-394-80276-4, BYR); PLB 4.99 o.p. (ISBN 0-394-90276-9). Random.

--Fun with Cooking. rev ed. (Illus.). (gr. 4-6). 1947. 3.95 o.p. (ISBN 0-394-80278-0, BYR); PLB 4.99 (ISBN 0-394-90278-5). Random.

--Stars & Stripes: The Story of the American Flag. (Gateway Ser.: No. 34). (Illus.). (gr. 3-7). 1964. PLB 5.99 o.p. (ISBN 0-394-90134-7, BYR). Random.

--Story of Albert Einstein. (Illus.). (gr. 5-9). 1958. 2.95 (ISBN 0-394-81680-3, BYR); PLB 5.39 (ISBN 0-394-91680-8). Random.

Freeman, Mae B. & Freeman, Ira M. Fun with Scientific Experiments. (Illus.). (gr. 4-7). 1960. 3.95 o.p. (ISBN 0-394-80281-0, BYR); PLB 4.99 o.p. (ISBN 0-394-90281-5). Random.

--You Will Go to the Moon. rev. ed. (Illus.). 60p. (gr. 1-3). 1971. 3.95 o.p. (ISBN 0-394-82340-0, BYR); PLB 5.99 (ISBN 0-394-92340-5). Random.

Freeman, Margaret B. The St. Martin Embroideries. LC 68-21564. (Illus.). 1968. 2.95 o.p. (ISBN 0-87099-071-3). Metro Mus Art.

--The Unicorn Tapestries. LC 76-2466. 246p. 1976. 45.00 o.s.i. (ISBN 0-87099-147-7, Dist. by E. P. Dutton). Metro Mus Art.

Freeman, Marian, ed. California Legal Secretary's Handbook. 12th ed. LC 76-52065. 974p. 1980. incl. 1981 suppl. 60.00 (ISBN 0-911110-22-4). Parker & Son.

Freeman, Martin. Forecasting by Astrology. 160p. 1983. pap. 7.95 (ISBN 0-85030-297-8). Newcastle Pub.

Freeman, Max H., et al. Accounting Ten-Twelve, 4 pts. Incl. Pt. 1. Elements of Financial Records. text ed. 5.04 o.p. (ISBN 0-07-022021-2); comprehensive problems, study guides & working papers 2.88 o.p. (ISBN 0-07-022025-5); Pt. 2. Accounting Systems & Procedures. text ed. 5.04 o.p. (ISBN 0-07-022022-0); 3.48 o.p. comprehensive problems, study guides & working papers (ISBN 0-07-022026-3); Pt. 3. Special Accounting Procedures. text ed. 5.04 o.p. (ISBN 0-07-022023-9); comprehensive problems, study guides & working papers 3.48 o.p. (ISBN 0-07-022027-1); Pt. 4. Business Data Processing Fundamentals. text ed. 5.04 o.p. (ISBN 0-07-022024-7); comprehensive problems, study guides & working papers 3.48 o.p. (ISBN 0-07-022028-X); 4.25 o.p. general suggestions & key (ISBN 0-07-022030-1). 1968. text ed. 4.56 o.p. (ISBN 0-07-022018-2, G); comprehensive problems, study guides & working papers 4.88 o.p. (ISBN 0-07-022019-0); complete program 14.64 o.p. (ISBN 0-07-022017-4); comprehensive test free o.p. (ISBN **0-07-022029-8); source bk. & key 14.50 o.p. (ISBN 0-07-022020-4). McGraw.**

Freeman, Michael. Manual of Indoor Photography. (Illus.). 1981. 14.95 (ISBN 0-87165-111-4, Amphoto). Watson-Guptill.

--The Manual of Indoor Photography. (Illus.). 14.95 (ISBN 0-07-083742-2, Amphoto). Watson-Guptill.

--Photo School: A Step by Step Course in Photography. (Illus.). 224p. 1982. 24.95 (ISBN 0-8174-5402-0, Amphoto). Watson-Guptill.

--The Thirty-Five Millimeter Handbook. (Illus.). 320p. 1980. 25.00 (ISBN 0-87165-093-2, Amphoto). Watson-Guptill.

Freeman, N. T. & Whiteman, J. Introduction to Safety in the Chemical Laboratory. 1982. write for info. (ISBN 0-12-267220-8). Acad Pr.

Freeman, Neil J., jt. auth. see Waite, Thomas D.

Freeman, Norman D., jt. auth. see Freeman, Harrop A.

Freeman, Paul & De Meillon, Botha. Simuliide of the Ethiopian Region. (Illus.). vii, 224p. 1953. Repr. of 1968 ed. 23.50x (ISBN 0-565-00194-9, Pub. by Brit Mus Nat Hist). Sabbot-Natural Hist Bks.

Freeman, Peter. Software Systems Principles: A Survey. LC 75-1440. (Computer Science Ser). (Illus.). 600p. 1975. text ed. 26.95 (ISBN 0-574-18000-1, 13-4000). SRA.

Freeman, R. & Pescar, S. Safe Delivery: Your Baby During High Risk Pregnancy. 320p. 1983. 7.95 (ISBN 0-07-022048-4, GB). McGraw.

Freeman, R. R., ed. see AIP Conference, 90th, Boulder, 1982.

Freeman, Richard. How to Study Effectively. 94p. 1978. 15.00x (ISBN 0-686-81992-6, Pub. by Macdonald & Evans). State Mutual Bk.

Freeman, Richard B. & Medoff, James L. What Do Unions Do? 350p. 1983. 20.95 (ISBN 0-465-09133-4). Basic.

Freeman, Robert J., jt. auth. see Lynn, Edward S.

Freeman, Robert R., et al, eds. Information in the Language Sciences. (Mathematical Linguistics & Automatic Language Processing Ser.: Vol. 5). 1969. 27.95 (ISBN 0-444-00036-4, North Holland). Elsevier.

Freeman, Roger. Telecommunication System Engineering: Analog & Digital Network. LC 79-26661. 1980. 39.95 (ISBN 0-471-02955-6, Pub. by Wiley-Interscience). Wiley.

Freeman, Roger & Garite, Thomas. Fetal Monitoring. (Illus.). 187p. 1981. lib. bdg. 27.00 (ISBN 0-683-03378-6). Williams & Wilkins.

Freeman, Roger A. Mighty Eigth War Diary. (Illus.). 240p. 1981. 29.50 (ISBN 0-86720-560-1). Sci Bks Intl.

Freeman, Roger L. Telecommunication Transmission Handbook. 2nd ed. LC 81-7499. 706p. 1981. 53.50 (ISBN 0-471-08029-2, Pub. by Wiley-Interscience). Wiley.

--Telecommunications Transmission Handbook. LC 75-1134. 587p. 1975. 43.00 o.p. (ISBN 0-471-27789-4, Pub. by Wiley-Interscience). Wiley.

--Telecommunications Transmission Handbook. 700p. 1980. 49.50 (ISBN 0-686-98109-X). Telecom Lib.

Freeman, S. H. Basic Baseball Strategy. LC 65-15666. 7.95a o.p. (ISBN 0-385-00872-4); PLB o.p. (ISBN 0-385-04737-1). Doubleday.

Freeman, S. T. & Walters, L. R. Europeanist Social Anthropologists in North America: A Directory. 1975. pap. 1.50 (ISBN 0-686-36564-X). Am Anthro Assn.

Freeman, Sarah. Isabella & Sam: The Story of Mrs. Beeton. LC 77-11157. 1978. 9.95 o.p. (ISBN 0-698-10711-X, Coward). Putnam Pub Group.

Freeman, Stephen W. Does Your Child Have a Learning Disability? Questions Answered for Parents. 128p. 1974. photocopy ed. spiral 12.75x (ISBN 0-398-03073-1). C C Thomas.

Freeman, T. L. Optimization of Solar Heating & Cooling Systems. (Progress in Solar Energy Supplements IEA Ser.). 1983. pap. text ed. 15.00x (ISBN 0-89553-050-3). Am Solar Energy.

Freeman, T. M. & Gregg, O. W, eds. Sodium Intake: Dietary Concerns. LC 81-71372. 168p. 1982. 20.00 (ISBN 0-913250-26-0). Am Assn Cereal Chem.

Freeman, T. W., et al, eds. Geographers Biobibliographical Studies, Vol. 1. (Illus.). 138p. 1977. pap. 26.00 (ISBN 0-7201-0637-0, Pub. by Mansell England). Wilson.

Freeman, W. H. & Bracegirdle, Brian. An Atlas of Histology. 2nd ed. (Heinemann Biology Atlases Ser.). 1967. pap. 12.50x (ISBN 0-435-60319-1). Heinemann Ed.

--An Atlas of Invertebrate Structure. (Heinemann Biology Atlases Ser.). 1971. pap. 12.50x (ISBN 0-435-60319-1). Heinemann Ed.

Freeman, Warren S., jt. auth. see Barbour, Harriet.

Freeman, Warren S., jt. auth. see Barbour, Harriot B.

Freeman, William. Incredible Defoe. LC 77-159085. 1971. Repr. of 1950 ed. 15.00 o.p. (ISBN 0-8046-1627-2). Kennikat.

Freeman, William H. Physical Education & Sports in a Changing Society. 2nd ed. LC 81-67688. 1982. text ed. 13.95x (ISBN 0-8087-0690-X). Burgess.

Freemand, Michael & Robertson, David, eds. Frontiers of Political Theory: Essays in a Revitalized Discipline. LC 79-27449. 224p. 1980. 32.50x (ISBN 0-312-30920-1). St Martin.

Freeman-Grenville, G. S. P., ed. Memoirs of An Arabian Princess. (Illus.). 308p. 1982. 17.95 (ISBN 0-85692-062-2, Pub. by Salem Hse Ltd.). Merrimack Bk Serv.

Freeman-Moir, John D., jt. auth. see Broughton, John M.

Freemantle, Brian. Charlie M. 1979. pap. 1.95 o.p. (ISBN 0-345-28336-8). Ballantine.

--Charlie M. 192p. 1982. pap. 2.25 (ISBN 0-345-30611-2). Ballantine.

--Charlie Muffin U. S. A. 208p. 1982. pap. 2.50 (ISBN 0-345-29440-8). Ballantine.

--Good-Bye to an Old Friend. 1973. 6.95 o.p. (ISBN 0-399-11084-4). Putnam Pub Group.

--KGB. LC 81-23205. (Illus.). 192p. 1982. 14.95 (ISBN 0-03-062458-4). HR&W.

Freemantle, James S. The Psalms of David. LC 82-60816. (Illus.). 352p. 1982. 17.50 (ISBN 0-688-01312-0). Morrow.

Freer, Harold W. & Hall, Francis B. Two or Three Together. LC 54-5849. 1954. pap. 3.95i o.p. (ISBN 0-06-063030-2, RD210, HarpR). Har-Row.

Freese, Arthur, jt. auth. see Finneson, Bernard E.

Freese, Arthur J. The Miracle of Vision. LC 76-26226. 1977. 12.45i (ISBN 0-06-011371-5, HarpT). Har-Row.

Freese, Arthur S. The Bionic People Are Here. LC 78-8253. (Illus.). (gr. 7-9). 1979. 7.95 (ISBN 0-07-022133-2, GB). McGraw.

--Headaches: The Kinds & the Cures. LC 74-10152. 192p. 1974. pap. 2.75 o.p. (ISBN 0-8052-0467-9). Schocken.

--Stroke: The New Help & the New Life. 1980. 10.95 o.p. (ISBN 0-394-50179-9). Random.

Freese, Doris. Children's Church: A Complete How-to. LC 81-22426. 128p. 1982. pap. 8.95 (ISBN 0-8024-1250-5). Moody.

Freethy, Ron. The Naturalist's Guide to the British Coastline. (Illus.). 192p. 1983. 22.50 (ISBN 0-7153-8342-6). David & Charles.

Freeze, Allan see Back, William.

Freeze, Gregory. The Parish Clergy in Nineteenth-Century Russia: Crisis, Reform, Counter-Reform. LC 82-61361. 552p. 1983. 50.00x (ISBN 0-691-05381-2). Princeton U Pr.

Freeze, R. A. & Back, W., eds. Physical Hydrogeology. LC 82-2976. (Benchmark Papers in Geology: Vol. 72). 448p. 1983. 48.00 (ISBN 0-87933-431-2). Hutchinson Ross.

Freeze, R. Allan & Cherry, John A. Groundwater. (Illus.). 1979. text ed. 38.95 (ISBN 0-13-365312-9). P-H.

Freeze, R. Allan, jt. ed. see Narasimhan, T. N.

Freezer, Cyril. Building Model Railways. (Illus.). 122p. (Orig.). 1982. pap. 10.50x (ISBN 0-85242-778-6). Intl Pubns Serv.

--Model Railways. LC 80-53614. (Whizz Kids Ser.). 8.00 (ISBN 0-382-06463-1). Silver.

Frege, Gottlob. The Basic Laws of Arithmetic: Exposition of the System. Furth, Montgomery, ed. & tr. (gr. 9-12). 1965. 14.00x (ISBN 0-520-00432-9). U of Cal Pr.

--The Basic Laws of Arithmetic: Exposition of the System. Furth, Montgomery, ed. (California Library Reprint Ser.: No. 116). 208p. 1982. 17.95x (ISBN 0-520-04761-3). U of Cal Pr.

Fregier, H. A. Des Classes Dangereuses De la Societe Dans les Grandes Villes et Des Moyens De les Rendre Meilleures, 2 vols. (Conditions of the 19th Century French Working Class Ser.). (Fr.). 1974. Repr. of 1840 ed. Set. lib. bdg. 115.00 o.p. (ISBN 0-8287-0354-X, 1015, 1037). Clearwater Pub.

Fregly, Melvin & Kare, Morley. The Role of Salt in Cardiovascular Hypertension. (Nutrition Foundation Ser.). 473p. 1982. 39.50 (ISBN 0-12-267280-1). Acad Pr.

Fregosi, Claudia. The Pumpkin Sparrow. LC 76-13027. (Illus.). (gr. k-3). 1977. 9.12 (ISBN 0-688-80060-2); PLB 8.16 (ISBN 0-688-84060-4). Greenwillow.

--Snow Maiden. (Illus.). (gr. 1-4). 1979. 6.95g o.p. (ISBN 0-13-815340-X). P-H.

Frehland, E. Stochastic Transport Processes in Discrete Biological Systems. (Lecture Notes in Biomathematics Ser.: Vol. 47). 169p. 1983. pap. 11.00 (ISBN 0-387-11964-7). Springer-Verlag.

Frehse, J. & Pallaschke, D. Special Topics of Applied Mathematics: Functional Analysis, Numerical Analysis & Optimization. 1980. 51.00 (ISBN 0-444-86035-5). Elsevier.

Frei, Daniel. Managing International Crisis. (Advances in Political Science: An International Ser.: Vol. 2). 1982. 22.50 (ISBN 0-8039-1849-6). Sage.

Frei, Daniel & Catrina, Christian. Risks of Unintentional Nuclear War. LC 82-16333. 255p. 1983. pap. text ed. 10.95 (ISBN 0-86598-106-X). Allanheld.

Frei, Daniel & Ruloff, Dieter. East-West Relations: Vol. 1, A Systematic Survey. LC 81-22356. 380p. 1983. 30.00 (ISBN 0-89946-136-0). Oelgeschlager.

--East-West Relations: Vol. 2, Methodology & Data. LC 81-22356. 300p. 1983. 30.00 (ISBN 0-89946-137-9). Oelgeschlager.

Frei, Eduardo. The Mandate of History & Chile's Future. Walker, Thomas W., ed. D'Escoto, Miguel, tr. from Sp. LC 77-620018. (Papers in International Studies: Latin America: No. 1). (Illus.). 1977. pap. 8.00x (ISBN 0-89680-066-0, Ohio U Ctr Intl). Ohio U Pr.

Freiberg, Karen L. Human Development: A Life-Span Approach. 2nd ed. LC 82-24736. 600p. 1983. text ed. 20.95 (ISBN 0-534-01413-5). Brooks-Cole.

Freiberg, Marcos. Snakes of South America. (Illus.). 192p. 1982. 14.95 (ISBN 0-87666-912-7, PS-758). TFH Pubns.

--Turtles of South America. (Illus.). 128p. 1981. 14.95 (ISBN 0-87666-913-5, PS-757). TFH Pubns.

Freiberger, Nancy & Vy Thi Be. Nung Fan Slihng Vocabulary. 353p. 1976. pap. 9.00x (ISBN 0-88312-793-8); microfiche 3.75 (ISBN 0-88312-337-1). Summer Inst Ling.

Freiberger, W. & Grenander, U. A Course in Computational Probability & Statistics. LC 76-176272. (Applied Mathematical Sciences: Vol. 6). 168p. 1971. pap. 18.00 o.p. (ISBN 0-387-90029-2). Springer-Verlag.

Freidberg, Ardy. Fully Fit in Sixty Minutes a Week: The Complete Shape-Up Program for Men. (Illus.). 64p. 1983. pap. 2.95 (ISBN 0-943392-06-3). Tribeca Comm.

Freidel, Frank. America in the Twentieth Century. 5th, rev. ed. 1982. text ed. 9.95x o.p. (ISBN 0-394-31995-8); pap. text ed. 14.95 (ISBN 0-394-32780-2). Knopf.

Freidel, Frank, ed. see Carlisle, Rodney P.

Freidel, Frank, ed. see Dizikes, John.

Freidel, Frank, ed. see Hand, Samuel B.

Freidel, Frank, ed. see James, Janet W.

Freidel, Frank, ed. see Mulder, Ronald A.

Freidel, Frank, ed. see Nordhauser, Norman.

Freidel, Frank, ed. see Smith, Glenn H.

Freidel, Frank, ed. see Walker, Forrest A.

Freiden, R., jt. auth. see Rosen, A.

Freides, Thelma K. Literature & Bibliography of the Social Sciences. LC 73-10111. (Information Sciences Ser). 284p. 1973. 33.95x (ISBN 0-471-27790-8, Pub. by Wiley-Interscience). Wiley.

Freidewald, Vincent E., Jr. Textbook of Echocardiography. LC 76-4247. (Illus.). 1977. text ed. 19.50 o.p. (ISBN 0-7216-3919-4). Saunders.

Freidheim, Elizabeth A. From Types to Theory: A Natural Method for an Unnatural Science. LC 82-17401. (Illus.). 188p. (Orig.). 1983. lib. bdg. 21.50 (ISBN 0-8191-2831-7); pap. text ed. 9.75 (ISBN 0-8191-2832-5). U Pr of Amer.

Freidheim, Robert L., ed. Managing Ocean Resources: A Primer. LC 79-53772. (Westview Special Studies in Natural Resources & Energy Management). 1979. lib. bdg. 25.00 (ISBN 0-89158-572-9). Westview.

Freidin, John S. Twenty Bicycle Tours in Vermont: Including Eight-Hundred Miles of Sights, Delights, & Special Events for Every Traveler. LC 78-71715. (Twenty Bicycle Tours Ser.). (Illus.). 160p. 1982. pap. 6.95 (ISBN 0-942440-07-2). Backcountry Pubns.

Freidlin, Gershon, tr. see Mark, Ber.

Freidman, D. Z., jt. auth. see Van Nieuwenhuizen, P.

Freidman, Robert, ed. see DeBolt, Margaret W.

Freidrich, Heinz, ed. Man & Animal: Studies in Behavior. LC 76-179704. 1972. 17.95 o.p. (ISBN 0-312-50960-X). St Martin.

Freidrich, Otto. Going Crazy. 1976. pap. 1.95 o.p. (ISBN 0-380-00888-2, 47779). Avon.

Freidus, Alberta J. Sumatran Contributions to the Development of Indonesian Literature, 1920-1942. (Asian Studies at Hawaii Ser.: No. 19). 1977. pap. text ed. 5.75x (ISBN 0-8248-0462-7). UH Pr.

Freier, S. & Eldelman, A. I., eds. Human Milk: Its Biological & Social Value. (International Congress Ser.: No. 518). 1981. 69.00 (ISBN 0-444-90183-3). Elsevier.

Freifeld, Karen, jt. auth. see Gross, Joy.

Freifeld, Wilbur & Taddeo, Frank. The Legal Facts of Life: How the Courts Have Ruled in Hundreds of Everyday Situations. 224p. 1982. 13.50 o.p. (ISBN 0-525-93221-6, 01311-390); pap. 8.25 o.p. (ISBN 0-525-93220-8, 0801-240). Dutton.

Freifelder, David. Problems in Molecular Biology. 272p. 1982. pap. text ed. 8.95 (ISBN 0-86720-013-8). Sci Bks Intl.

Freifelder, Leonard R. A Decision Theoretic Approach to Insurance Ratemaking. LC 75-26414. (S. S. Huebner Foundation Monographs: No. 4). (Illus.). 1976. pap. 9.95 (ISBN 0-918930-04-9). Huebner Foun Insur.

Freifelder, Morris. Catalytic Hydrogenation in Organic Synthesis: Procedures & Commentary. LC 78-9458. 1978. 29.95x (ISBN 0-471-02945-9, Pub. by Wiley-Interscience). Wiley.

Freilich, Morris, ed. Marginal Natives at Work: Anthropologists in the Field. 325p. 1977. text ed. 16.25x o.p. (ISBN 0-470-99306-5); pap. text ed. 7.95x (ISBN 0-470-99307-3). Halsted Pr.

Freiman, Jane S. The Art of Food Processor Cooking. 1980. pap. 7.95 (ISBN 0-8092-7004-8). Contemp Bks.

Freimann, Aron. Union Catalog of Hebrew Manuscripts & Their Location, 2 vols. LC 66-7594. 1964-1973. Set. 100.00 o.s.i. (ISBN 0-527-02372-8). Kraus Repr.

Freire. Cultural Action for Freedom. (Monograph Ser.: No. 1). 3.50 (ISBN 0-916690-11-3). Harvard Educ Rev.

Freire, Paulo, frwd. by see Giroux, Henry A.

Freis. Treatment of Hypertension. 1978. 19.95 o.p. (ISBN 0-8391-1316-1). Univ Park.

Freis, jt. auth. see Sleigh.

Freis, Edward, jt. auth. see Sleight, Peter.

Freisem, Deborah, jt. auth. see Peacock, Nancy W.

Freisem, Deborah K., jt. auth. see Peacock, Nancy W.

Freisner, Arlyne, jt. auth. see Conley, Virginia.

Freitag, Alfred H. The Most Powerful Instruments of Economic Prediction, with Special Attention to the Stock Market. (Illus.). 165p. 1983. 87.65 (ISBN 0-86654-066-0). Inst Econ Finan.

Frejus, Roland. Relation d'un Voyage Fait dans la Mauritanie, en Afrique, de Marseille En 1666. (Bibliotheque Africaine Ser.). 300p. (Fr.). 1974. Repr. of 1670 ed. lib. bdg. 79.50x o.p. (ISBN 0-8287-0355-8, 72-2132). Clearwater Pub.

Frel, Jiri. The Getty Bronze. rev. ed. LC 82-81305. 58p. 1982. 10.00 (ISBN 0-89236-053-4); pap. 5.00 (ISBN 0-89236-039-9). J P Getty Mus.

Frel, Jiri, ed. The J. Paul Getty Museum Journal: No. 5. (Illus.). 1977. pap. 13.50 (ISBN 0-686-96758-5). J P Getty Mus.

Freligh, H. M. Studies in Revelation, 4 Vols. Schroeder, E. H., ed. 327p. 1969. pap. text ed. 1.50 ea.; Vol. 1. (ISBN 0-87509-139-3); Vol. 2. (ISBN 0-87509-140-7); Vol. 3. (ISBN 0-87509-141-5); Vol. 4. (ISBN 0-87509-142-3). Chr Pubns.

Freligh, H. M., ed. see Pardington, G. P.

Freligh, Harold M. Job. pap. 1.75 (ISBN 0-87509-097-4). Chr Pubns.

--Say unto This Mountain. 40p. 1966. pap. 1.00 (ISBN 0-87509-128-8). Chr Pubns.

Fremantel, Ann. Age of Faith. LC 66-22782. (Great Ages of Man Ser.). PLB 19.96 (ISBN 0-8094-0365-X). Silver.

Fremantle, Anne, ed. Age of Belief: The Medieval Philosophers. (Orig.). 1955. pap. 2.75 (ISBN 0-451-62111-5, ME2111, Ment). NAL.

Fremantle, Francesca & Trungpa, Chogyam. Tibetan Book of the Dead. (Illus.). 144p. 1982. deluxe ed. 30.00 deluxe ed. o.p. (ISBN 0-87773-073-3). Great Eastern.

Fremes, Marvin. Historic Inns of Ontario. rev. ed. 167p. 1982. pap. 8.95 (ISBN 0-88879-079-1, Pub By Deneau Publishers). Berkshire Traveller.

Fremes, Ruth & Sabry, Z. Nutriscore: The Rate Yourself Plan for Better Nutrition. 268p. 1976. 12.95 o.p. (ISBN 0-8467-0189-8); pap. 7.95 o.p. (ISBN 0-416-00391-5). Methuen Inc.

Fremgen, James M. & Liao, Shu S. The Allocation of Corporate Indirect Costs. 103p. pap. 12.95 (ISBN 0-86641-006-6). Natl Assn Accts.

Fremlin, D. H. Topological Riesz Spaces & Measure Theory. LC 72-95410. 300p. 1974. 48.50 (ISBN 0-521-20170-5). Cambridge U Pr.

Fremlin-Key, Hermyone. Toys with a Theme. (Illus.). 79p. 1975. 8.50 o.p. (ISBN 0-263-05483-7). Transatlantic.

Fremon, George & Fremon, Suzanne. Why Trade It In? How to Keep Your Car Running Almost Indefinitely. 2nd ed. LC 76-42603. (Illus.). 176p. 1982. pap. 5.95 (ISBN 0-89709-039-X). Liberty Pub.

--Your First Car. LC 81-80572. (Illus.). 176p. 1981. pap. 4.95 (ISBN 0-89709-024-1). Liberty Pub.

Fremon, Suzanne, jt. auth. see Fremon, George.

Fremont, Robert A., ed. Favorite Songs of the Nineties. (Illus.). 416p. (Orig.). 1973. pap. 10.95 (ISBN 0-486-21536-9). Dover.

Fremont-Smith, Marion R. Foundations & Government: State & Federal Law & Supervision. LC 65-22280. 564p. 1965. 13.95x (ISBN 0-87154-278-1). Russell Sage.

--Philanthropy & the Business Corporation. LC 72-83835. 110p. 1972. pap. 4.50x (ISBN 0-87154-279-X). Russell Sage.

Fremouw, W. J., jt. ed. see Golann, S.

Frenaye, Frances, tr. see Mussolini, Benito.

French, A. L. Shakespeare & the Critics. LC 75-183221. 224p. 1972. 44.50 (ISBN 0-521-08470-9). Cambridge U Pr.

French, A. P. Principles of Modern Physics. 355p. 1958. 15.00 (ISBN 0-471-27885-8, Pub by Wiley). Krieger.

--Vibrations & Waves. (M.I.T. Introductory Physics Ser). (Illus.). 1971. 6.75 o.p. (ISBN 0-393-09924-5); pap. text ed. 9.95x (ISBN 0-393-09936-9). Norton.

French, A. P. & Taylor, Edwin F. Introduction to Quantum Physics. (M. I. T. Introductory Physics Ser.). (Illus.). 500p. 1978. text ed. 17.95x o.p. (ISBN 0-393-09015-9); pap. text ed. 13.95x (ISBN 0-393-09106-6). Norton.

French, Alfred. The Growth of the Athenian Economy. LC 75-31363. 208p. 1976. Repr. of 1964 ed. lib. bdg. 19.75x (ISBN 0-8371-8506-8, FRAC). Greenwood.

French, Alfred & Berlin, Irving. Depression in Children & Adolescents. LC 79-13481. 298p. 1979. 29.95 (ISBN 0-87705-390-1). Human Sci Pr.

French, Allen. General Gage's Informers: New Material upon Lexington & Concord, Benjamin Thompson As Loyalist & the Treachery of Benjamin Church, Jr. LC 68-54420. (Illus.). 1968. Repr. of 1932 ed. lib. bdg. 15.75x (ISBN 0-8371-0431-9, FRGI). Greenwood.

French, Anthony P. Special Relativity. (M. I. T. Introductory Physics Ser). 1968. pap. 8.95x (ISBN 0-393-09793-5). Norton.

French, Bevan M. The Moon Book. 1977. pap. 5.95 (ISBN 0-14-004340-3). Penguin.

French, Blaire A. The Presidential Press Conference: Its History & Role in the American Political System. LC 81-40883. 54p. (Orig.). 1982. pap. text ed. 5.75 (ISBN 0-8191-2064-2). U Pr of Amer.

French, Chester D. Papaya: The Melon of Health. LC 75-29904. 128p. 1976. pap. 1.50 o.p. (ISBN 0-668-03918-3). Arco.

French Colonial Historical Society. Proceedings of the French Colonial Historical Society Annual Meetings, Sixth & Seventh, 1980-1981. Cooke, James J., ed. LC 76-644752. 160p. (Orig.). 1982. lib. bdg. 22.25 (ISBN 0-8191-2333-1); pap. text ed. 10.25 (ISBN 0-8191-2334-X). U Pr of Amer.

French Colonial Historical Society, 5th Meeting. Proceedings. Cooke, James J., ed. LC 80-5683. 125p. lib. bdg. 18.00 (ISBN 0-8191-1146-5); pap. text ed. 8.25 (ISBN 0-8191-1147-3). U Pr of Amer.

French, David & French, Elena. Working Communally: Patterns & Possibilities. LC 74-25854. 288p. 1975. 11.95x (ISBN 0-87154-291-9). Russell Sage.

French, David N. Metallurgical Failures in Fossil Fired Boilers. 228p. 1983. 32.50 (ISBN 0-471-89841-4, Pub. by Wiley-Interscience). Wiley.

French, Elena, jt. auth. see French, David.

French, Frances. OJT Mail Clerk Resource Materials. 2nd ed. (Gregg Office Job Training Program Ser.). (Illus.). 112p. (gr. 11-12). 1980. soft cover 5.60 (ISBN 0-07-022190-1); training manual 4.16 (ISBN 0-07-022191-X). McGraw.

French, Giles, jt. auth. see Due, John F.

French, H. W. Art & Artists in Connecticut. LC 70-87543. (Library of American Art Ser). 1970. Repr. of 1879 ed. lib. bdg. 22.50 (ISBN 0-306-71459-0). Da Capo.

French, Hollis. Jacob Hurd & His Sons, Nathaniel & Benjamin. LC 70-175722. (Architecture & Decorative Art Ser.: Vol. 39). 158p. 1972. Repr. of 1939 ed. lib. bdg. 35.00 (ISBN 0-306-70406-4). Da Capo.
--Silver Collector's Glossary & a List of Early American Silversmiths & Their Marks. LC 67-27454. (Architecture & Decorative Art Ser). 1967. lib. bdg. 19.50 (ISBN 0-306-70979-4). Da Capo.
French Institute Of Black Africa, ed. International Atlas of West Africa, Pts. 1-2. (Illus., Eng. & Fr.). 55.00x ea. Pt. 1, 1968 (ISBN 0-8002-1571-0). Pt. 2 (ISBN 0-8002-2372-1). Intl Pubns Serv.
French, J. H. Historical & Statistical Gazetteer of New York State. (Illus.). 782p. 1980. Repr. of 1860 ed. deluxe ed. 25.00 (ISBN 0-932334-31-8); pap. 17.50 (ISBN 0-686-96738-0). Heart of the Lakes.
French, Jack. Up the EDP Pyramid: The Complete Job Hunting Manual for Computer Professionals. LC 81-11605. 19.95x. 1981. 19.95x (ISBN 0-471-08925-7, Pub. by Wiley-Interscience); pap. write for info. (ISBN 0-471-87117-6). Wiley.
French, Jennie. Design for Stained Glass. 168p. 1982. pap. 9.95 (ISBN 0-442-22449-4). Van Nos Reinhold.
French, Jere S. Urban Space: A Brief History of the City Square. (Illus.). 1978. pap. 11.95 (ISBN 0-8403-1861-8). Kendall Hunt.
French, John. Electrics & Electronics for Small Craft. 2nd ed. (Illus.). 255p. 1981. 30.00 (ISBN 0-229-11612-4, Pub. by Adlard Coles). Sheridan.
French, John, et al, trs. see Durkheim, Emile.
French, Michael. Flyers. LC 82-15032. (Movie Storybooks). (Illus.). 64p. (gr. 4-7). 1983. 6.95 (ISBN 0-394-85535-3); PLB 7.99 (ISBN 0-394-95535-8). Random.
--Rhythms. LC 79-6650. 1980. 12.95 o.p. (ISBN 0-385-14358-3). Doubleday.
French, Paul C. We Won't Murder: Being the Story of Men Who Followed Their Conscientious Scruples & Helped Give Life to Democracy. LC 79-137541. (Peace Movement in America Ser.). 189p. 1972. Repr. of 1940 ed. lib. bdg. 13.95x (ISBN 0-89198-068-7). Ozer.
French, Peter. Social Skills for Nursing Practice. 260p. 1983. pap. text ed. 17.50x (ISBN 0-7099-1009-6, Pub. by Croom Helm Ltd England). Biblio Dist.
French, Peter & MacLure, Margaret, eds. Adult-Child Conversation: Studies in Structure & Process. 1981. 30.00 (ISBN 0-312-00515-6). St Martin.
French, Peter A. Ethics in Government. 176p. 1983. pap. 8.95 (ISBN 0-13-290908-1). P-H.
French, Peter A. & Uehling, Theodore E., Jr., eds. Contemporary Perspectives on the History of Philosophy. (Midwest Studies in Philosophy: Vol. 8). 550p. 1983. 45.00x (ISBN 0-8166-1207-2); pap. 18.95x (ISBN 0-8166-1212-9). U of Minn Pr.
French Petroleum Institute Staff. Drilling Mud & Cement Slurry Rheology Manual. 152p. 1983. 27.95x (ISBN 0-87201-780-X). Gulf Pub.
French, Philip, ed. Three Honest Men: Edmund Wilson, F. R. Leavis, Lionel Trilling, A Critical Mosaic. 120p. 1980. 18.95x (ISBN 0-85635-299-3, Pub. by Carcanet New Pr England). Humanities.
French, R. A. & Hamilton, F. Ian. The Socialist City: Spatial Structure & Urban Policy. LC 78-16828. 1979. 61.95 (ISBN 0-471-99689-0, Pub. by Wiley-Interscience). Wiley.
French, R. J., jt. auth. see Carleton, A. J.
French, R. M., tr. see Berdiaev, Nikolai A.
French, Reginald M., tr. from Rus. Way of a Pilgrim. (Illus.). 242p. 1974. 7.50 (ISBN 0-8164-0259-0); pap. 5.95 (ISBN 0-8164-2069-6, SP18). Seabury.
French, Richard. A Guide to the Birds of Trinidad & Tobago. rev. ed. LC 76-25609. (Illus.). 1976. Repr. of 1973 ed. 25.00 (ISBN 0-915180-03-0). Harrowood Bks.
French, Richard F., tr. see Asafiev.
French, Robert D. Memorial Quadrangle (Yale University) 1929. text ed. 49.50x (ISBN 0-686-83624-3). Elliots Bks.
French, Ronald & Jansma, Paul. Special Physical Education. 416p. 1982. 21.95 (ISBN 0-675-09829-7). Additional Supplements May Be Obtained From Publisher. Merrill.
French, Ruth. Dynamics of Health Care. 3rd ed. (Illus.). 1979. pap. text ed. 12.50 (ISBN 0-07-022143-X, HP). McGraw.
--Guide to Diagnostic Procedures. 1980. text ed. 21.50 (ISBN 0-07-022146-4); pap. text ed. 14.50 (ISBN 0-07-022147-2). McGraw.
French, Ruth M. Nurse's Guide to Diagnostic Procedures. 4th ed. (Illus.). 384p. 1975. text ed. 11.95 o.p. (ISBN 0-07-022141-3, HP); pap. text ed. 8.95 o.p. (ISBN 0-07-022140-5). McGraw.
French, Seth, ed. Semi-Tropical Florida: Its Climate, Soil & Productions, with a Sketch of Its History, Natural Features & Social Condition, Being a Manual of Reliable Information Concerning the Resources of the State, & the Inducements Which It Offers to Persons. LC 82-62496. (Historic Byways of Florida Ser.: Vol. VII). (Illus.). 60p. 1982. pap. 5.95 (ISBN 0-941948-07-2). St Johns-Oklawaha.
French, Thomas, jt. auth. see Gibson, John.
French, Thomas E. & Svensen, C. L. Familiar Problems in Mechanical Drawing. 1973. 7.84 (ISBN 0-07-022312-2, W). McGraw.
French, Thomas E. & Vierck, Charles J. Engineering Drawing & Graphic Technology. 11th ed. LC 70-38135. Orig. Title: Manual of Engineering Drawing for Students & Draftsmen. (Illus.). 984p. 1972. text ed. 27.00 (ISBN 0-07-022157-X, C); tchrs' manual & solutions 8.50 (ISBN 0-07-067427-2); problems 14.00 (ISBN 0-07-067435-3). McGraw.
--Engineering Drawing & Graphic Technology. 12th ed. (Illus.). 1978. text ed. 29.50 (ISBN 0-07-022158-8, C); problems 22.50 (ISBN 0-07-022160-X); tchr. manual 4.50 (ISBN 0-07-022159-6). McGraw.
--Graphic Science & Design. 3rd ed. (Engineering Drawing Ser). 1970. text ed. 29.95 (ISBN 0-07-022301-7, C); problems 18.50 (ISBN 0-07-067443-4). McGraw.
French, Warren. J. D. Salinger. 2nd rev. ed. (United States Author Ser.). 1976. lib. bdg. 10.95 (ISBN 0-8057-7163-8, Twayne). G K Hall.
--John Steinbeck. 2nd ed. (United States Authors Ser.). 1975. lib. bdg. 12.95 (ISBN 0-8057-0693-3, Twayne). G K Hall.
French, Warren A., et al. Views of Marketing: A Reader. (Illus.). 1979. pap. text ed. 11.50 scp o.p. (ISBN 0-06-042187-8, HarpC). Har-Row.
French, Wendell. The Personnel Management Process: Cases in Human Resources Administration. 5th ed. LC 81-86540. 1982. 23.95; instr's manual 2.25. HM.
French, Wendell I., et al. The Personnel Management Process: Cases on Human Resources Administration. 2d ed. (Illus.). 1982. 12.50; instr's. manual 1.00. HM.
French, William B. & Martin, Stephen J. Real Estate Review's Guide to Real Estate Licensing Examinations for Salespersons & Brokers. 2nd ed. LC 81-10331. 367p. 1982. text ed. 20.95 (ISBN 0-471-87754-9); write for info. tchr's manual (ISBN 0-471-89519-9). Wiley.
French, William B., et al. Real Estate Review's Guide to Real Estate Licensing Examinations for Salespersons & Brokers. 2nd. ed. 1981. text ed. 17.95x o.p. (ISBN 0-88262-628-0). Warren.
French, William J. & Criley, J. Michael. Practical Cardiology: Ischemic & Valvular Heart Disease. 328p. 1982. 32.50 (ISBN 0-471-09551-6, Pub. by Wiley Med). Wiley.
Frenchak, David & Keyes, Sharrel, eds. Metro-Ministry. LC 78-72935. 1979. pap. 6.95 (ISBN 0-89191-101-4). Cook.
French-Lazovik, Grace, ed. Practical Approaches to Evaluating Faculty Performance. LC 81-48584. 1982. 7.95x (ISBN 0-87589-925-0, TL-11). Jossey-Bass.
Frend, W. H. The Rise of the Monophysite Movement: Chapters in the History of the Church in the Fifth & Sixth Centuries. LC 72-75302. (Illus.). 400p. 1972. 74.50 (ISBN 0-521-08130-0). Cambridge U Pr.
Freneau, Philip M. A Collection of Poems on American Affairs & Variety of Other Subjects. LC 76-15581. 1976. Repr. of 1815 ed. lib. bdg. 42.00x (ISBN 0-8201-1174-0). Schol Facsimiles.
--Poems Written Between the Years 1768 & 1794. LC 76-11752. 480p. 1976. Repr. of 1795 ed. lib. bdg. 53.00x (ISBN 0-8201-1172-4). Schol Facsimiles.
--Poems, 1786 & Miscellaneous Works (1788) of Philip Freneau, 2 vols. in one. LC 74-31251. 880p. 1975. Repr. lib. bdg. 90.00x (ISBN 0-8201-1151-1). Schol Facsimiles.
Freney, J. R., jt. auth. see Ivanov, M. V.
Freney, J. R., jt. ed. see Calbally, E. I.
Frenkel, M., jt. ed. see Arias, I. M.
Frenkel, Robert E. Ruderal Vegetation along Some California Roadsides. (California Library Reprint Ser.: No. 92). 1978. Repr. of 1970 ed. 18.95x (ISBN 0-520-03589-5). U of Cal Pr.
Frenkiel, F. N. see Landsberg, H. E.
Frenkiel, F. N., ed. see Symposium on Fundamental Problems in Turbulence & Their Relation to Geophysics.
Frenkiel, Francois N. & Goodall, David W. Simulation Modeling of Environmental Problems: Scope Report 9. LC 77-92369. (Scientific Committee on Problems of the Environment). 112p. 1978. 15.00x (ISBN 0-471-99580-0, Pub. by Wiley-Interscience). Wiley.
Frenkiel, J. Evaporation Reduction: Physical & Chemical Principles & Review of Experiments. (Arid Zone Research Ser.: No. 27). 79p. 1965. pap. 4.00 (ISBN 92-3-100600-2, U234, UNESCO). Unipub.
Frenz, Horst. Eugene O'Neill. Sebba, Helen, tr. LC 79-143188. (Literature and Life Ser.). 1971. 11.95 (ISBN 0-8044-2211-7); pap. 4.95 (ISBN 0-8044-6159-7). Ungar.
Frenz, Horst, jt. ed. see Hibbard, Addison.
Frenz, Horst, ed. see Nobel Foundation.
Frenzel, Louis E. Digital Counter Handbook. 1981. pap. 10.95 (ISBN 0-672-21758-9). Sams.
Frere, John H. Prospectus & Specimen of an Intended National Work by William & Robert Whistlecraft of Stowmarket. Reiman, Donald H., ed. LC 75-31204. (Romantic Context Ser.: Poetry 1789-1830: Vol. 55). 1978. lib. bdg. 47.00 o.s.i. (ISBN 0-8240-2154-1). Garland Pub.
Freret. Recherches sur les Miracles. (Holbach & His Friends Ser.). 173p. (Fr.). 1974. Repr. of 1773 ed. lib. bdg. 51.00x o.p. (ISBN 0-8287-1407-X, 1555). Clearwater Pub.
Freret, Nicolas. Lettre de Thrasibule a Leucippe. (Holbach & His Friends Ser). 310p. (Fr.). 1974. Repr. of 1766 ed. lib. bdg. 82.00x o.p. (ISBN 0-8287-0356-6, 1527). Clearwater Pub.
Freris, T., jt. auth. see Laithwaite, L.
Freschet, Berniece. Biography of a Buzzard. LC 76-16584. (Nature Biography Ser.). (Illus.). (gr. 3-5). 1977. PLB 6.59 o.p. (ISBN 0-399-60991-1). Putnam Pub Group.
--Black Bear Baby. (See & Read Book). (Illus.). 48p. (gr. 6-9). 1981. PLB 6.99 (ISBN 0-399-61151-7). Putnam Pub Group.
--Moose Baby. LC 79-4337. (See & Read Nature Story Ser.). (Illus.). (gr. 1-4). 1979. 6.99 (ISBN 0-399-61146-0). Putnam Pub Group.
--Porcupine Baby. (See & Read Nature Bks.). (Illus.). (gr. 1-4). 1978. 6.99 (ISBN 0-399-61101-0). Putnam Pub Group.
--Possum Baby. LC 77-21000. (See & Read Nature Bks.). (Illus.). (gr. k-3). 1978. 6.99 (ISBN 0-399-61105-3). Putnam Pub Group.
--Where's Henrietta's Hen? LC 78-11158. (Illus.). 32p. (gr. 3-7). 1980. 7.95 (ISBN 0-399-20669-8). Putnam Pub Group.
--Wufu: The Story of the Little Brown Bat. new ed. (Illus.). 48p. (gr. k-4). 1975. 5.95 o.p. (ISBN 0-399-20482-2). Putnam Pub Group.
Frese, Wolfgang, jt. auth. see Howell, Frank M.
Fresenius, W., ed. Reviews on Analytical Chemistry. (Illus.). 256p. 1977. text ed. 45.50x (ISBN 2-225-46860-5). Masson Pub.
Freshman, Phil, ed. see Maeder, Edward, et al.
Freshney, Ian R., ed. Culture of Animal Cells: A Manual of Basic Technique. LC 82-24960. 280p. 1983. write for info. (ISBN 0-8451-0223-0). A R Liss.
Freshwater Biological Association, Cumbria England. Catalogue of the Library of the Freshwater Biological Association. 1979. lib. bdg. 630.00 (ISBN 0-8161-0289-9, Hall Library). G K Hall.
Fresne, Jim Du see Du Fresne, Jim.
Fretheim, Terence E. Interpreting Biblical Texts: Deuteronomic History. Bailey, Lloyd R. & Furnish, Victory P., eds. 160p. (Orig.). 1983. pap. 7.95. Abingdon.
Fretheim, Terrence. Deuteronomic History. 160p. 1983. pap. 7.00 (ISBN 0-687-10497-1). Abingdon.
Fretz, Bruce R. & Stang, David J. Preparing for Graduate Study: Not for Seniors Only! 1980. 9.00x (ISBN 0-912704-12-8). Am Psychol.
Freuchen, Peter. Arctic Adventure: My Life in the Frozen North. 467p. 1982. Repr. of 1935 ed. lib. bdg. 35.00 (ISBN 0-89987-269-7). Darby Bks.
Freud, Anna. Psychoanalysis for Teachers & Parents. Low, Barbara, tr. 1935. 7.95 (ISBN 0-87523-011-3). Emerson.
Freud, Anna, ed. see Freud, Sigmund.
Freud, Sigmund. The Basic Writings of Sigmund Freud. Brill, A. A., ed. & intro. by. 12.95 (ISBN 0-394-60400-8). Modern Lib.
--Beyond the Pleasure Principle. Strachey, James, ed. & tr. 96p. 1975. 6.95 o.p. (ISBN 0-393-01118-6, Norton Lib); pap. 3.95 (ISBN 0-393-00769-3). Norton.
--The Collected Papers of Sigmund Freud, 5 vols. Freud, Anna & Jones, Ernest, eds. Incl. Vol. 1. Early Papers. 36.00x (ISBN 0-686-91728-6); Clinical Papers. 36.00x (ISBN 0-686-91729-4); Case Histories. 36.00 (ISBN 0-686-91730-8); Papers on Metapsychology. 36.00x (ISBN 0-686-91731-6); Miscellaneous Papers. 36.00x (ISBN 0-686-91732-4). Set. 175.00x (ISBN 0-686-98009-3). Basic.
--Creativity & the Unconscious: Papers on the Psychology of Art, Literature, Love, Religion. pap. 6.95i o.p. (ISBN 0-06-130045-4, TB 45, Torch). Har-Row.
--Dora: An Analysis of a Case of Hysteria. 1963. pap. 2.95 o.p. (ISBN 0-02-076250-X, Collier). Macmillan.
--General Psychological Theory. 1963. pap. 3.95 (ISBN 0-02-076350-6, Collier). Macmillan.
--Inhibitions, Symptoms & Anxiety. Strachey, James, ed. Strachey, Alix, tr. 1977. 6.95 (ISBN 0-393-01166-6); pap. 3.95 (ISBN 0-393-00874-6). Norton.
--Moses & Monotheism. Jones, Katherine, ed. 1955. pap. 3.95 (ISBN 0-394-70014-7, V14, Vin). Random.
--On the History of the Psychoanalytic Movement. Strachey, James, ed. Riviere, Joan, tr. (Standard ed.). 1966 10.95 (ISBN 0-393-01022-8); pap. 3.95, 1967 (ISBN 0-393-00150-4). Norton.
--Origins of Psycho-Analysis: Letters to Wilhelm Fliess, Drafts & Notes, 1887-1902. Bonaparte, Marie, et al, eds. Mosbacher, Eric & Strachey, James, trs. LC 54-8148. 1954. 20.00x (ISBN 0-465-05351-3); pap. 7.95x (ISBN 0-465-09711-1, CN 5011). Basic.
--Psychopathology of Everyday Life. 1952. pap. 3.50 (ISBN 0-451-62137-9, ME2137, Ment). NAL.
--Sexual Enlightenment of Children. 1963. pap. 3.95 (ISBN 0-02-076500-2, Collier). Macmillan.
--Three Contributions to the Theory of Sex. Brill, A. A., tr. from Ger. 118p. 1982. Repr. of 1925 ed. lib. bdg. 40.00 (ISBN 0-89984-211-9). Century Bookbindery.
--Three Essays in Sexuality. Strachey, James, tr. LC 62-11202. 1962. 6.95x (ISBN 0-465-08607-1). Basic.
--Three Essays on the Theory of Sexuality. Strachey, James, tr. LC 62-11202. 1982. 17.50x (ISBN 0-465-08607-1); pap. 6.95x (ISBN 0-465-09708-1). Basic.
Freud, Sigmund, jt. auth. see Breuer, Josef.
Freudberg, Frank & Emmanuel, E. Stephen. Herpes: A Complete Guide to Relief & Reassurance. (Illus.). 160p. (Orig.). 1982. 12.95 (ISBN 0-89471-193-8); lib. bdg. 15.90 (ISBN 0-89471-187-3); pap. 12.95 (ISBN 0-89471-188-1). Running Pr.
Freudenberg, K. & Neish, A. C. Constitution & Biosynthesis of Lignin. (Molecular Biology, Biochemistry & Biophysics: Vol. 2). 1968. 20.40 o.p. (ISBN 0-387-04274-1). Springer-Verlag.
Freudenheim, Yehoshua. Government in Israel. LC 66-17246. 309p. 1967. 15.00 (ISBN 0-379-00248-5). Oceana.
Freudenthal, Alfred M. Introduction to the Mechanics of Solids. LC 66-17638. 1966. text ed. 19.50 o.p. (ISBN 0-471-27960-9, Pub. by Wiley). Krieger.
Freudenthal, Alfred M., et al, eds. Structural Safety & Reliability: Proceedings of the International Conference. 1972. write for info. (ISBN 0-08-016566-4). Pergamon.
Freudenthal, Juan R. & Katz, Jeffrey. Index to Anthologies of Latin American Literature in English Translation. 1977. lib. bdg. 19.00 (ISBN 0-8161-7861-5, Hall Reference). G K Hall.
Freudenthal, Ralph I. & Jones, Peter, eds. Polynuclear Aromatic Hydrocarbons: Chemistry, Metabolism, & Carcinogenesis. LC 75-43194. 465p. 1976. 54.00 (ISBN 0-89004-103-2). Raven.
Freudenthal, Ralph I., ed. see International Symposium on Analysls, Chemistry, & Biology, No. 2.
Freudiger, Ullrich D., jt. auth. see Keller, Peter D.
Freund, E. Hans, jt. ed. see Mourant, John A.
Freund, Gisele. Photography & Society. Dunn, Richard, et al, trs. from Fr. LC 78-58502. Orig. Title: Photographie et Societe. (Illus.). 248p. 1982. 15.00 (ISBN 0-87923-250-1); pap. 8.95 (ISBN 0-686-85996-0). Godine.
Freund, J., jt. auth. see Miller, I.
Freund, John E. College Mathematics with Business Applications. 2nd ed. (Illus.). 720p. 1975. ref. ed. 24.95 (ISBN 0-13-146464-7). P-H.
--Modern Elementary Statistics. 5th ed. 1979. text ed. 26.95 (ISBN 0-13-593491-5); pap. 5.95 study guide (ISBN 0-13-593517-2). P-H.
Freund, John E. & Perles, Benjamin M. Business Statistics: A First Course. (Quantitative Analysis for Business Ser.). 368p. 1974. text ed. 19.95 (ISBN 0-13-107714-7). P-H.
Freund, John E. & Walpole, Ronald E. Mathematical Statistics. 3rd ed. 1980. text ed. 28.95 (ISBN 0-13-562066-X). P-H.
Freund, John E. & Williams, Frank J. Elementary Business Statistics: The Modern Approach. 4th ed. (Illus.). 576p. 1982. text ed. 25.95 (ISBN 0-13-253120-8). P-H.
Freund, John E. & Williams, Thomas A. College Mathematics with Business Applications. 3rd ed. (Illus.). 464p. 1983. text ed. 24.95 (ISBN 0-13-146498-1). P-H.
Freund, Paul A., et al. Constitutional Law: Cases & Other Problems. 4th ed. 1977. 30.00 (ISBN 0-316-29333-4); pap. 7.95 (ISBN 0-316-57823-1). Little.
Freund, Peter E. The Civilized Body: Social Domination, Control & Health. LC 82-10787. 166p. 1983. text ed. 15.95x (ISBN 0-87722-285-1). Temple U Pr.
Freund, Philip. Three Poetic Plays: Jocasta, Flame & Cedar, the Bacchae. 216p. 1973. 5.75 o.p. (ISBN 0-693-01607-8); pap. 4.95 o.p. (ISBN 0-693-01608-6). Transatlantic.
Freund, Richard, jt. auth. see Duff, Charles.
Freund, Ronald. What One Christian Can Do to Help Prevent Nuclear War. LC 82-15584. xiv, 185p. (Orig.). 1982. pap. 7.95 (ISBN 0-8190-0650-5, FC 144). Fides Claretian.
Frevert, Patricia. Patrick, Yes You Can. (Everyday Heroes Ser). (Illus.). 48p. 1983. lib. bdg. 7.95 (ISBN 0-87191-891-9). Creative Ed.
Frevert, Patricia D. Beatrix Potter, Children's Storyteller. Redpath, Ann, ed. (People to Remember Ser.). (Illus.). 32p. (gr. 5-9). 1981. PLB 7.95 (ISBN 0-87191-801-3). Creative Ed.
--Margaret Mead Herself. Redpath, Ann, ed. (People to Remember Ser.). (Illus.). 32p. (gr. 5-9). 1981. PLB 7.95 (ISBN 0-87191-799-8). Creative Ed.
--Mark Twain, an American Voice. Redpath, Ann, ed. (People to Remember Ser.). (Illus.). 32p. (gr. 5-9). 1981. PLB 7.95 (ISBN 0-87191-802-1). Creative Ed.
--Pablo Picasso, Twentieth Century Genius. Redpath, Ann, ed. (People to Remember Ser.). (Illus.). 32p. (gr. 5-9). 1981. PLB 7.95 (ISBN 0-87191-800-5). Creative Ed.
--Patty Gets Well. (Everyday Heroes Ser.). (Illus.). 48p. 1983. lib. bdg. 7.95 (ISBN 0-87191-890-0). Creative Ed.
Frevert, Richard K., jt. auth. see Schwab, Glenn O.
Frew, David R., jt. auth. see Frew, Mary A.

Frew, Mary A. & Frew, David R. Comprehensive Medical Assisting: Administrative & Clinical Procedures. LC 81-9820. 756p. 1983. 24.95x (ISBN 0-8036-3858-2); wkbk. 11.95 (ISBN 0-8036-3864-7). Davis Co.
--Medical Office Administrative Procedures. LC 81-17435. (Illus.). 343p. 1983. pap. 14.95x (ISBN 0-8036-3861-2); instrs. guide avail.; wkbk. 11.95 (ISBN 0-8036-3864-7). Davis Co.
Frewin, Leslie, ed. Parnassus Near Piccadilly. 15.00 (ISBN 0-392-16445-0, SpS). Sportshelf.
Frey, jt. auth. see Kummerly.
Frey, Albert R. Sobriquets & Nicknames. LC 66-22671. 1966. Repr. of 1888 ed. 34.00x (ISBN 0-8103-3003-2). Gale.
Frey, Albert W. & Halterman, Jean C. Advertising. 4th ed. 594p. 1970. 30.95x (ISBN 0-471-06597-8, 33291). Wiley.
Frey, C. F., jt. auth. see Jelenko, C.
Frey, Charles H., jt. auth. see Griffith, John W.
Frey, David G., ed. Limnology in North America. (Illus.). 752p. 1963. 35.00x o.p. (ISBN 0-299-02760-0). U of Wis Pr.
Frey, David H. & Heslet, Frederick E. Existential Theory for Counselors. LC 74-11964. (Guidance Monograph). 1975. pap. 2.40 o.p. (ISBN 0-395-20039-3). HM.
Frey, Deborah A., ed. The Organic Gardening 1984 Planning Guide & Country Calendar. (Illus.). 96p. pap. 5.95 (ISBN 0-87857-459-X, 01-171-1). Rodale Pr Inc.
Frey, Diane & Carlock, Charlene. Enhancing Self Esteem. 280p. 1983. pap. text ed. price not set. Accel Devel.
Frey, James H. An Organizational Analysis of University Environment Relations. 1977. pap. text ed. 9.25 (ISBN 0-8191-0335-7). U Pr of Amer.
Frey, James H. & Ginsberg, Ralph B., eds. Contemporary Issues in Sport. LC 80-50267. (Annals of the American Academy of Political & Social Science: No. 445). 1979. pap. 7.95 (ISBN 0-87761-243-9). Am Acad Pol Soc.
Frey, Jean M. Communautes Syriaques en Iran et Irak Des Origines A 1552. 382p. 1979. 70.00x (ISBN 0-686-97648-7, Pub. by Variorum). State Mutual Bk.
Frey, John, ed. Common Dilemmas in Family Medicine. 420p. 1982. 25.80 (ISBN 0-942068-04-1). Bogden & Son.
Frey, John W. see Kavass, Igor I. & Sprudzs, Adolf.
Frey, Leonard H., ed. Readings in Early English Language History. LC 66-13894. (Orig.). 1966. pap. 5.50 (ISBN 0-672-63100-8). Odyssey Pr.
Frey, Lucius J. Philosophie Sociale Dediee Au Peuple Francais...Par un Citoyen De la Section De la Republique Francaise, Ci-Devant Du Roule. (Rousseauism, 1788-1797). 1978. Repr. lib. bdg. 73.00x o.p. (ISBN 0-8287-0357-4). Clearwater Pub.
Frey, P. W., ed. Chess Skill in Man & Machine. rev ed. (Texts & Monographs in Computer Science). (Illus.). 1979. 17.00 o.p. (ISBN 0-387-07957-2). Springer-Verlag.
Frey, R., et al, eds. Mobile Intensive Care Units: Advanced Emergency Care Delivery Systems. (Anaesthesiology & Resuscitation: Vol. 95). 1976. pap. 29.00 o.p. (ISBN 0-387-07561-5). Springer-Verlag.
Frey, R. G. Interests & Rights: The Case Against Animals. (Clarendon Library of Logic & Philosophy Ser.). 1980. 26.50x (ISBN 0-19-824421-5). Oxford U Pr.
Frey, R. W., ed. The Study of Trace Fossils: A Synthesis of Principles, Problems, & Procedures in Ichnology. LC 74-30164. (Illus.). xxiii, 570p. 1975. 66.50 o.p. (ISBN 0-387-06870-8). Springer-Verlag.
Frey, Thomas L. & Behrens, Robert H. Lending to Agricultural Enterprises. LC 81-12874. 475p. 1981. 30.00 (ISBN 0-87267-037-6). Bankers.
Freyberger, H., jt. ed. see Wise, T. N.
Freycinet, Charles L. De. Souvenirs, Eighteen Seventy-Eight to Eighteen-Ninety-Three. LC 73-258. (Europe 1815-1945 Ser.). 524p. 1973. Repr. of 1913 ed. lib. bdg. 65.00 (ISBN 0-306-70560-5). Da Capo.
Freyer, Grattan. W. B. Yeats & the Anti-Democratic Tradition. 1982. 45.00x (ISBN 0-686-99819-7, Pub. by Gill & Macmillan Ireland). State Mutual Bk.
Freyer, Grattan, ed. Bishop Stock's "Narrative" of the Year of the French: 1798. LC 82-71112. (Illus.). 118p. 1982. 9.00 (ISBN 0-906462-07-X, Pub. by Irish Humanities Ireland); pap. 5.00 (ISBN 0-906462-08-8). Dufour.
Freyhardt, H. C. Analytical Methods: High-Melting Metals. (Crystals, Growth, Properties, & Applications Ser.: Vol. 7). (Illus.). 150p. 1982. 42.00 (ISBN 0-387-11790-3). Springer-Verlag.
Freyhardt, H. C., ed. Silicon-Chemical Etching. (Crystals-Growth, Properties & Applications Ser.: Vol. 8). (Illus.). 255p. 1983. 55.00 (ISBN 0-387-11862-4). Springer-Verlag.
Freymann, Sara J. Season's Greetings. 1974. 2.50 o.p. (ISBN 0-517-51649-7). Crown.
Freyne, Sean. Galilee from Alexander the Great to Hadrian, 232 BCE to 135 CE. 506p. 1980. 27.50 o.p. (ISBN 0-268-01002-1). U of Notre Dame Pr.
Freystatter, Wilhelm. Die Musikalischen Zeitschriften seit ihrer Entstenhung bis zur Gegenwart 1722-1884. 1971. Repr. of 1884 ed. wrappers 20.00 o.s.i. (ISBN 90-6027-139-4, Pub. by Frits Knuf Netherlands). Pendragon NY.
Freytag, Fredericka F. The Body Image in Gender Orientation Disturbances. 1977. 12.50 o.p. (ISBN 0-533-02660-1). Vantage.
Friar, John G. & Kelly, George W. Practical Spanish Grammar. 1960. pap. 4.95 (ISBN 0-385-00977-1). Doubleday.
Friar, Kimon, ed. Modern Greek Poetry: Translation, Introduction, an Essay on Translation, & Notes by Kimon Friar. LC 70-171604. 1973. 20.00 o.p. (ISBN 0-671-21025-4). S&S.
Friar, Kimon, tr. see Elytis, Odysseus.
Friar, Kimon, tr. see Fostieris, Andonis.
Friar, Kimon, tr. see Kazantzakis, Nikos.
Friar, Kimon, tr. see Ritsos, Yannis.
Friar, Wayne & Davis, Percival. A Case for Creation. 3rd ed. (Illus.). 1983. pap. 5.95 (ISBN 0-8024-0176-7). Moody.
Fribance, Austin E. Industrial Instrumentation Fundamentals. 1962. text ed. 23.95 (ISBN 0-07-022370-X, G); answers 1.00 (ISBN 0-07-022371-8). McGraw.
Friberg, L., et al, eds. Handbook of the Toxicology of Metals. Vouk, V. 700p. 1980. 142.75 (ISBN 0-444-80075-1, North Holland). Elsevier.
Frich, Elisabeth. Matt Mattox Book of Jazz Dance. (Illus.). 128p. 1983. 19.95 (ISBN 0-8069-7048-0); pap. 12.95 (ISBN 0-8069-7662-4). Sterling.
Frick, C. H. Patch. LC 57-6559. (gr. 7 up). 5.25 (ISBN 0-15-259570-8, HJ). HarBraceJ.
Frick, Frank S. The City in Ancient Israel. LC 77-21984. (Society of Biblical Literature. Dissertation Ser.: No. 36). 1977. pap. 7.50 (ISBN 0-89130-149-6, 06-01-36). Scholars Pr Ca.
Frick, G. William. Environmental Compliance Audits Manuel. 99p. 1982. Wkbk. 38.00 (ISBN 0-86587-099-3). Gov Insts.
--Environmental Glossary. 2nd ed. LC 82-83908. 310p. 1982. text ed. 28.00 (ISBN 0-686-38762-7). Gov Insts.
Frick, G. William, jt. auth. see Arbuckle, J. Gordon.
Frick, G. William, ed. Environmental Glossary. LC 80-67274. 225p. 19.50 o.p. (ISBN 0-86587-080-2). Gov Insts.
Frick, H. C., II, jt. auth. see Gusberg, S. B.
Frick, P., et al, eds. Advances in Internal Medicine & Pediatrics, Vol. 49. (Illus.). 172p. 1982. 45.00 (ISBN 0-387-11444-0). Springer-Verlag.
--Advances in Internal Medicine & Pediatrics, Vol. 50. (Illus.). 190p. 1983. 39.00 (ISBN 0-387-11445-9). Springer-Verlag.
Frick, Paul. Blood & Bone Marrow Morphology Blood Coagulation. 3rd ed. (Illus.). 64p. 1981. pap. text ed. 18.00 (ISBN 0-397-58279-X, Lippincott Medical). Lippincott.
Fricke, Charles W. California Criminal Law. 11th ed. Alarcon, Arthur L., ed. LC 75-32437. 1977. 18.00x o.p. (ISBN 0-910874-37-9). Legal Bk Co.
--Criminal Investigation & the Law. 7th ed. Payton, George T., ed. LC 74-110781. 1974. 15.00x (ISBN 0-910874-32-8). Legal Bk Co.
--Five Thousand Criminal Definitions Terms & Phrases. 5th ed. 1968. 7.00x (ISBN 0-910874-10-7). Legal Bk Co.
--Sentence & Probation, the Imposition of Penalties upon Convicted Criminals. 1960. 3.50x (ISBN 0-910874-11-5). Legal Bk Co.
Fricke, Charles W. & Alarcon, Arthur L. California Criminal Evidence. 9th ed. LC 77-94992. 1978. 18.00x o.p. (ISBN 0-910874-44-1). Legal Bk Co.
--California Criminal Procedure. 9th ed. LC 73-80491. 1974. 18.00x o.p. (ISBN 0-910874-26-3). Legal Bk Co.
Fricke, Charles W. & Payton, George T. One Thousand Police Questions & Answers. 7th ed. LC 75-32086. 1978. 8.00 (ISBN 0-910874-36-0). Legal Bk Co.
Fricke, Ronald. Revision of the Genus Synchiropus (Teleostei: Callionymidae) (Theses Zoologicae: Vol. 1). (Illus.). 194p. 1981. text ed. 20.00x (ISBN 3-7682-1306-4). Lubrecht & Cramer.
Fricke, W. & Teleki, G., eds. Sun & Planetary System. 1982. 65.00 (ISBN 90-277-1429-0, Pub. by Reidel Holland). Kluwer Boston.
Frickelton, Annelise & Dierrsen, Gunther. It's Fun to Speak Danish. 48p. Date not set. includes 5 cassettes 75.00 (ISBN 0-88432-092-8, DAI). J Norton Pubs.
Fricker, Francois. Einfuhrung in die Gitterpunktlehre. (LMW - MA: 73). 256p. (Ger.). 1981. text ed. 49.50x (ISBN 3-7643-1236-X). Birkhauser.
Frid, Tage. Tage Frid Teaches Woodworking--Joinery, Tools & Techniques. LC 78-65178. (Illus.). 224p. 1979. 17.95 (ISBN 0-918804-03-5, Dist. by Van Nostrand Reinhold). Taunton.
--Tage Frid Teaches Woodworking--Shaping, Veneering, Finishing. LC 78-65178. (Illus.). 224p. 1981. 17.95 (ISBN 0-918804-11-6, Dist. by Van Nostrand Reinhold). Taunton.
Friday, James R., jt. ed. see Porter, George.
Friday, Nancy. Men in Love, Male Sexual Fantasies: The Triumph of Love Over Rage. 1981. pap. 3.75 (ISBN 0-440-15404-9). Dell.
--Men in Love: Men's Sexual Fantasies: The Triumph of Love Over Rage. 1980. 12.95 o.s.i. (ISBN 0-440-05264-5). Delacorte.
--My Mother, My Self: The Daughter's Search for Identity. 1977. 12.95 o.s.i. (ISBN 0-440-06006-0). Delacorte.
Friddell, Guy. Colgate Darden: Conversations with Guy Friddell. LC 78-7026. xi, 256p. 1978. 12.95 (ISBN 0-8139-0744-6). U Pr of Va.
--What Is It About Virginia? (Illus.). 1966. 4.25 o.p. (ISBN 0-685-09021-3). Dietz.
Fridkin, V. M. & Grekov, A. A., eds. Ferroelectric Semiconductors Symposium, 4th, Rostov-on-Don, USSR, June 1981: Proceedings. (Ferroelectrics Ser.: Vol. 43, Nos. 3-4, & Vol. 45, Nos. 1-2). 280p. 1982. 203.50 (ISBN 0-686-83423-2). Gordon.
Fridriksson, S. Surtsey: Evolution of Life on a Volcanic Island. LC 74-30850. 198p. 1975. 34.95x o.s.i. (ISBN 0-470-28000-X). Halsted Pr.
Friebert, Stuart & Young, David. Longman Anthology of Poetry: Contemporary American. LC 81-15630. 1982. text ed. 22.50x tent. (ISBN 0-582-28267-5); pap. text ed. 14.95tx (ISBN 0-582-28263-2). Longman.
Fried, Albert. The Prescott Chronicles. LC 76-9116. 1976. 9.95 o.p. (ISBN 0-399-11711-3). Putnam Pub Group.
Fried, Benjamin S., ed. Film Index of Work Measurement & Methods Engineering Subjects. 1980. 10.00 (ISBN 0-89806-027-3); members 5.00. Inst Indus Eng.
Fried, Charles. Contract As Promise: A Theory of Contractual Obligation. LC 80-26548. 176p. 1982. text ed. 14.00x (ISBN 0-674-16925-5); pap. text ed. 5.95x (ISBN 0-674-16930-1). Harvard U Pr.
Fried, Edward R. & Schultze, Charles L., eds. Higher Oil Prices & the World Economy: The Adjustment Problem. 1975. 18.95 (ISBN 0-8157-2932-4); pap. 7.95 (ISBN 0-8157-2931-6). Brookings.
Fried, Emanuel. Meshugah & Other Stories. Walsh, Joy, ed. 40p. (Orig.). 1982. pap. 2.95 (ISBN 0-938838-09-1). Textile Bridge.
Fried, Erich. On Pain of Seeing. Rapp, Georg, tr. LC 82-71603. (Poetry Europe Ser.: No. 11). 72p. 1969. 7.95 (ISBN 0-8040-0234-7). Swallow.
Fried, J. J. Groundwater Pollution. LC 74-29680. (Developments in Water Science: Vol. 4). 330p. 1976. 70.25 (ISBN 0-444-41316-2). Elsevier.
Fried, Jacob. Crawley: New Town. 350p. (Orig.). 1983. pap. 10.95 (ISBN 0-913244-60-0). Hapi Pr.
Fried, Jonathan L. & Gettlemen, Marvin, eds. Guatemala in Rebellion: Unfinished History. 360p. (Orig.). 1983. pap. 7.95 (ISBN 0-394-62455-6, Ever). Grove.
Fried, Lewis & Fierst, John. Jacob A. Riis: A Reference Guide. 1977. lib. bdg. 25.00 (ISBN 0-8161-7862-3, Hall Reference). G K Hall.
Fried, Michael. Absorption & Theatricality: Painting & Beholder in the Age of Diderot. LC 78-62843. 249p. 1980. 30.00x (ISBN 0-520-03758-8); pap. 11.50 (ISBN 0-520-04339-1, 489). U of Cal Pr.
Fried, Peter A., ed. Readings in Perception. 1974. pap. text ed. 10.95 o.p. (ISBN 0-669-89367-6). Heath.
Fried, Rainer, ed. Methods of Neurochemistry, Vol. 1. 1971. 57.75 o.p. (ISBN 0-8247-1215-3). Dekker.
--Methods of Neurochemistry, Vol. 2. 1972. 57.75 o.p. (ISBN 0-8247-1216-1). Dekker.
--Methods of Neurochemistry, Vol. 4. 252p. 1973. 57.75 o.p. (ISBN 0-8247-6024-7). Dekker.
--Methods of Neurochemistry, Vol. 5. 296p. 1973. 57.75 o.p. (ISBN 0-8247-6073-5). Dekker.
Fried, Robert C. & Rabinovitz, Frances F. Comparative Urban Politics: A Performance Approach. 240p. 1980. pap. text ed. 13.95 (ISBN 0-13-154351-2). P-H.
Fried, Vojtech, et al. Physical Chemistry. 1977. 29.95x (ISBN 0-02-339760-8, 33976). Macmillan.
Friedan, Betty. The Feminine Mystique. 1963. 10.00 o.p. (ISBN 0-393-08436-1). Norton.
--The Second Stage. 352p. 1982. pap. 5.95 (ISBN 0-671-45951-1). Summit Bks.
Friedan, Leon, compiled by. The Law of War: A Documentary History, 2 vols. LC 72-765. 1972. Set. lib. bdg. 95.00 (ISBN 0-313-20133-1). Greenwood.
Friedberg & Hanawalt. DNA Repair. 296p. 1983. price not set (ISBN 0-8247-1805-4). Dekker.
--DNA Repair: A Laboratory Manual of Research Procedures, Vol. 1 Pts. A & B. 424p. 1981. Pt. A. 34.75 (ISBN 0-8247-1093-2); Pt. B. 46.25 (ISBN 0-8247-1184-X). Dekker.
Friedberg, Ardy. Fully Fit in Sixty Minutes a Week: The Complete Shape-Up Program for Women. (Illus.). 64p. 1983. pap. 2.95 (ISBN 0-943392-07-1). Tribeca Comm.
Friedberg, Ardy, jt. auth. see Mentzer, Mike.
Friedberg, Ardy, jt. auth. see Research & Forecasts, Inc.
Friedberg, Charles K., ed. Congestive Heart Failure. LC 58-8981. (Illus.). 320p. 1970. 57.00 o.p. (ISBN 0-8089-0670-4). Grune.
--Physical Diagnosis in Cardiovascular Disease. (Illus.). 368p. 1969. 56.00 o.p. (ISBN 0-8089-0143-5). Grune.
Friedberg, Charles K. & Donoso, Ephraim, eds. Pathophysiology & Differential Diagnosis in Cardiovascular Disease. LC 58-8981. (Illus.). 352p. 1971. 44.50 o.p. (ISBN 0-8089-0694-1). Grune.
Friedberg, Robert. Gold Coins of the World: An Illustrated Standard Catalogue with Valuations. 5th ed. LC 68-18787. (Illus.). 467p. 1980. 29.50 o.p. (ISBN 0-8069-6056-6); lib. bdg. 24.99 o.p. (ISBN 0-8069-6057-4). Sterling.
Friedberg, Stephen, et al. Linear Algebra. (Illus.). 1979. ref. ed. 26.95 (ISBN 0-13-537019-1). P-H.
Frieddrich Ebert Foundation, ed. Towards One World? International Responses to the Brandt Report. 1981. 33.00x (ISBN 0-85117-218-0, Pub. by M Temple Smith). State Mutual Bk.
Friede, Goldie, et al. The Beatles A-Z: John Lennon, Paul McCartney, George Harrison & Ringo Starr. (Illus.). 1981. pap. 8.95 (ISBN 0-413-48380-0). Methuen Inc.
Friedel, Richard. The Movie Lover. 1981. 12.95 o.s.i. (ISBN 0-698-11068-4, Coward). Putnam Pub Group.
Friedel, Robert. Pioneer Plastic: The Making & Selling of Celluloid. LC 81-69818. (Illus.). 176p. 1983. 19.95 (ISBN 0-299-09170-8). U of Wis Pr.
Frieden, B. R. Probability, Statistical Optics, & Data Analysis. (Springer Series in Information Sciences: Vol. 10). (Illus.). 404p. 1983. 39.00 (ISBN 0-387-11769-5). Springer-Verlag.
Frieden, Bernard J. The Environmental Protection Hustle. (Joint Center for Urban Studies). (Illus.). 1979. 17.50 (ISBN 0-262-06068-X); pap. 5.95 (ISBN 0-262-56022-4). MIT Pr.
Frieden, Bernard J. & Kaplan, Marshall. The Politics of Neglect: Urban Aid from Model Cities to Revenue Sharing. LC 75-6792. (MIT-Harvard Joint Center for Urban Studies). 386p. 1975. 20.00 (ISBN 0-262-06061-2); pap. 5.95 (ISBN 0-262-56016-X). MIT Pr.
Frieden, Carl & Nichol, Lawrence. Protein-Protein Interactions. LC 80-29424. 403p. 1981. 55.95 (ISBN 0-471-04979-4, Pub. by Wiley-Interscience). Wiley.
Frieden, Earl & Lipner, Harry. Biochemical Endocrinology of the Vertebrates. (Modern Biochemistry Ser). 1971. pap. text ed. 13.95 (ISBN 0-13-076489-2). P-H.
Frieden, Earl, jt. auth. see Bennett, Thomas P.
Friedenberg, Edgar Z. Coming of Age in America. 1965. pap. 2.25 (Vin). Random.
--Deference to Authority: The Case of Canada. LC 79-55935. 192p. 1980. 12.50 (ISBN 0-87332-167-7). M E Sharpe.
Friedenberg, Joan E., jt. auth. see Bradley, Curtis H.
Friedenhain, Paula. Write & Reveal. 1973. Repr. of 1959 ed. text ed. 9.25x o.p. (ISBN 0-7206-0102-9). Humanities.
Friedenreich, Kenneth. Henry Vaughan. (English Authors Ser.). 1978. lib. bdg. 14.95 (ISBN 0-8057-6697-9, Twayne). G K Hall.
Friedenwald, Herbert. The Declaration of Independence: An Interpretation & an Analysis. LC 77-166325. (American Constitutional & Legal History Ser.). xii, 299p. 1974. Repr. of 1904 ed. lib. bdg. 35.00 (ISBN 0-306-70230-4). Da Capo.
Friederichsen, Kay. God's Word Made Plain. (Span). 1958. pap. 3.95 (ISBN 0-8024-3041-4). Moody.
Friederichsen, Mrs. P. Profundas Verdades De La Biblia. Orig. Title: Great Truths of the Bible. 1958. pap. 3.95 (ISBN 0-8024-4875-5). Moody.
Friedhoff, Arnold H. & Chase, Thomas N., eds. Gilles de la Tourette Syndrome. (Advances in Neurology Ser.: Vol. 35). 590p. 1982. text ed. 47.50 (ISBN 0-89004-761-8). Raven.
Friedhoff, Herman & Lenthall, Ben. The University Desk Encyclopedia. 59.95 o.p. (ISBN 0-525-93001-9). Gaylord Prof Pubns.
Friedhoff, Herman, ed. Encyclopedia of the Animal World. (Illus.). 2000p. 1980. lib. bdg. 159.95 (ISBN 0-85835-427-6). M Cavendish Corp.
Friedjung, M. & Viotti, R., eds. The Nature of Symbiotic Stars. 1982. 43.50 (ISBN 0-686-37436-3, Pub. by Reidel Holland). Kluwer Boston.
Friedl, Ernestine, jt. ed. see Dimen, Muriel.
Friedl, J. & Chrisman, N. J. City Ways: A Selective Reader in Urban Anthology. 1975. pap. text ed. 12.50 scp o.p. (ISBN 0-690-00152-5, HarpC). Har-Row.
Friedl, John. The Human Portrait: An Introduction to Cultural Anthropology. (Illus.). 464p. 1981. pap. text ed. 16.95 (ISBN 0-13-445353-0); pap. 8.95 (ISBN 0-13-445387-5). P-H.
Friedlaender, Ann F. & Spady, Richard H. Freight Transport Regulation: Equity, Efficiency & Competition in the Rail & Trucking Industries. 400p. 1981. 35.00x (ISBN 0-262-06072-8). MIT Pr.
Friedlaender, Ann F., ed. Approaches to Controlling Air Pollution. LC 77-25484. (MIT Bicentennial Ser.: Vol. 3). 1978. 35.00x (ISBN 0-262-06064-7). MIT Pr.
Friedlaender, Jonathan S., jt. ed. see Giles, Eugene.
Friedlaender, Walter. Caravaggio Studies. LC 72-86848. (Illus.). 1970. 15.00x o.p. (ISBN 0-8052-3028-9). Schocken.
--Mannerism & Anti-Mannerism in Italian Painting. LC 57-8295. (Illus.). 1965. pap. 5.50 (ISBN 0-8052-0094-0). Schocken.
Friedland, Ann, ed. U. S. Information Moscow: Spring 1981 to Winter 1982. rev. ed. (Illus.). 507p. 1981. pap. 9.95 o.p. (ISBN 0-934192-03-0). Dimes Group.
Friedland, B., jt. auth. see Schwarz, Ralph.
Friedland, Bea. Louise Farrenc, 1804-1875: Composer, Performer, Scholar. Buelow, George, ed. LC 80-22465. (Studies in Musicology: No. 32). 284p. 1980. 44.95 (ISBN 0-8357-1111-0, Pub. by UMI Res Pr). Univ Microfilms.

Friedland, Dion, et al. People Productivity in Retailing: A Manpower Development Plan. LC 80-23109. 1980. 19.95 (ISBN 0-86730-519-3). Lebhar Friedman.

Friedland, Edward P. Antique Houses: Their Construction & Restoration. (Illus.). 288p. 1983. 20.75 (ISBN 0-525-93076-0, 02015-600); pap. 13.50 (ISBN 0-525-47707-1, 01311-390). Dutton.

Friedland, Joan W., jt. auth. see Faude, Bill.

Friedland, Joyce & Gross, Irene. Reading for Mathematics. 1977. pap. 2.75x (ISBN 0-88323-129-8, 218); tchrs answer key 3.00x (ISBN 0-88323-142-5, 231). Richards Pub.

Friedland, Louis S., ed. see Chekhov, Anton.

Friedland, Robert P., ed. Selected Papers of Morris B. Bender. 350p. 1982. text ed. write for info. (ISBN 0-89004-710-3). Raven.

Friedland, Robert P., jt. ed. see Weinstein, Edwin A.

Friedland, Roger. Power & Crisis in the City, Corporations, Unions & Urban Policy. LC 82-10368. 292p. 1983. 19.95 (ISBN 0-8052-3838-7). Schocken.

Friedland, Ronnie & Kort, Carol, eds. The Mother's Book. 384p. 1981. 14.95 (ISBN 0-395-30527-6); pap. 9.95 (ISBN 0-395-31134-9). HM.

Friedland, Seymour & Lawson, William M. Principles of Financial Management: Corporate Finance, Investments, & Macrofinance. 1978. text ed. 18.95 (ISBN 0-316-29311-3); tchr's ed. avail. (ISBN 0-316-29312-1). Little.

Friedland, William H., et al. Manufacturing Green Gold: Capital, Labor, & Technology in the Lettuce Industry. (American Sociological Association Rose Monograph). (Illus.). 1981. 27.95 (ISBN 0-521-24284-3); pap. 8.95 (ISBN 0-521-28584-4). Cambridge U Pr.

Friedlander. Introduction to the Mathematical Theory of Geophysical Fluid Dynamics. (Mathematics Studies: Vol. 41). 1980. 34.00 (ISBN 0-444-86032-0). Elsevier.

Friedlander, et al. Concepts & Methods of Social Work. 2nd ed. LC 75-45164. (Illus.). 288p. 1976. text ed. 21.95 (ISBN 0-13-166488-3). P-H.

Friedlander, Anna F. Solar Economics. Date not set. cancelled (ISBN 0-88410-646-2). Ballinger Pub.

Friedlander, F. G. Introduction to the Theory of Distributions. LC 82-4504. 150p. 1983. 34.50 (ISBN 0-521-24300-9); pap. 14.95 (ISBN 0-521-28591-7). Cambridge U Pr.

--The Wave Equation on a Curved Space-Time. LC 74-14435. (Cambridge Monographs on Mathematical Physics). (Illus.). 328p. 1976. 69.50 (ISBN 0-521-20567-0). Cambridge U Pr.

Friedlander, Gerhart, et al. Nuclear & Radiochemistry. 3rd ed. LC 81-1000. 684p. 1981. 47.50 (ISBN 0-471-28021-6, Pub. by Wiley-Interscience); pap. 29.50 (ISBN 0-471-86255-X, Pub. by Wiley-Interscience). Wiley.

Friedlander, Henry & Milton, Sybil, eds. The Holocaust: Ideology, Bureaucracy & Genocide. LC 80-16913. 1981. lib. bdg. 45.00 (ISBN 0-527-63807-2). Kraus Intl.

Friedlander, Melvin A. Sadat & Begin: The Domestic Politics of Peacemaking. 350p. 1983. softcover 23.50x (ISBN 0-86531-949-9). Westview.

Friedlander, Peter. The Emergence of a UAW Local, 1936-1939: A Study in Class & Culture. LC 74-26020. 1975. 10.95 (ISBN 0-8229-3295-4). U of Pittsburgh Pr.

Friedlander, Robert A. Terror-Violence: Aspects of Social Control. 350p. 1982. text ed. 35.00 (ISBN 0-379-20748-6). Oceana.

--Terrorism: Documents of International & Local Control 1977-1978, 3 vols. LC 78-26126. 1979. 120.00 set (ISBN 0-379-00690-1). Oceana.

Friedlander, Robert A., jt. ed. see Alexander, Yonah.

Friedlander, S. K. Smoke, Dust & Haze: Fundamentals of Aerosol Behavior. LC 76-26928. 317p. 1977. 35.50 (ISBN 0-471-01468-0, Pub. by Wiley Interscience). Wiley.

Friedlander, Saul. History & Psychoanalysis. Suleiman, Susan, tr. 175p. 1978. 29.50 (ISBN 0-8419-0339-5); pap. 15.50 (ISBN 0-686-43335-1, 0-8419-061). Holmes & Meier.

--Reflections on Nazism. Weyr, Thomas, tr. from Fr. LC 82-48117. 160p. 1983. 11.49i (ISBN 0-06-015097-1, HarpT). Har-Row.

--When Memory Comes. 1980. pap. 2.75 o.p. (ISBN 0-380-50807-9, 50807, Discus). Avon.

Friedlander, Saul, et al, eds. The End of the World: Images of Apocalypse in Western Civilization. 300p. 1983. 24.50x (ISBN 0-8419-0673-4); pap. 12.50x (ISBN 0-8419-0755-2). Holmes & Meier.

Friedlander, W., ed. Current Reviews. LC 75-14572. (Advances in Neurology Ser.: Vol. 13). 404p. 1975. 40.00 (ISBN 0-89004-000-1). Raven.

Friedlander, Walter A. & Apte, Robert Z. Introduction to Social Welfare. 5th ed. (Illus.). 1980. text ed. 23.95 (ISBN 0-13-497032-2). P-H.

Friedman, jt. ed. see Beschner.

Friedman, A. Variational Principles & Free-Boundary Problems. (Pure & Applied Mathematics Ser.). 710p. 1982. text ed. 52.50x (ISBN 0-471-86849-3, Pub. by Wiley-Interscience). Wiley.

Friedman, Aileen R., jt. auth. see Lee, Karen.

Friedman, Alan H., et al. Diagnosis & Management of Uveitis: An Atlas Approach. (Illus.). 136p. 1982. lib. bdg. 95.00 (ISBN 0-683-03379-4). Williams & Wilkins.

Friedman, Albert B., ed. The Penguin Book of Folk Ballads of the English-Speaking World. 1982. pap. 6.95 (ISBN 0-14-006112-6). Penguin.

Friedman, Arthur & Menon, Premachandran R. Theory & Design of Switching Circuits. LC 75-15888. (Illus.). 581p. 1975. 28.95x (ISBN 0-914894-52-8). Computer Sci.

Friedman, Arthur, ed. see Goldsmith, Oliver.

Friedman, Arthur D., jt. auth. see Breuer, Melvin A.

Friedman, Avner. Differential Games. LC 75-155119. (Pure & Applied Mathematics Ser.). 1971. 46.95x (ISBN 0-471-28049-6, Pub. by Wiley-Interscience). Wiley.

Friedman, B. Economic Stabilization Policy: Methods in Optimization. LC 73-86080. (Studies in Mathematical & Managerial Economics: Vol. 15). 375p. 1975. 59.75 (ISBN 0-444-10566-2, North-Holland). Elsevier.

Friedman, B. H. Coming Close. 224p. 1982. 11.95 (ISBN 0-914590-70-7); pap. 5.95 (ISBN 0-914590-71-5). Fiction Coll.

--Whispers. (Ithaca House Fiction Ser.). 154p. 1972. 3.95 (ISBN 0-87886-021-5). Ithaca Hse.

Friedman, Benjamin M., ed. New Challenges to the Role of Profit: The Fourth Series of the John Diebold Lectures. 1978. 16.95x (ISBN 0-669-02171-7). Lexington Bks.

Friedman, Bernard. Smuts: A Reappraisal. LC 75-21835. 200p. 1976. 25.00 (ISBN 0-312-73045-4). St Martin.

Friedman, Bill. Casino Games. (Golden Guide Ser). 160p. 1973. pap. 2.95 (ISBN 0-307-24358-3, Golden Pr). Western Pub.

Friedman, Bruce. Stern. Bd. with A Mother's Kisses. 1966. pap. 2.25 o.p. (ISBN 0-671-68830-8, Touchstone Bks). S&S.

Friedman, Bruce Jay. The Lonely Guys Book of Life. 1978. 8.95 o.p. (ISBN 0-07-022432-3, GB). McGraw.

Friedman, Carol A. & Meade, Andre T. Reading & Writing Skills Workbook for the GED Test. LC 82-18400. (Arco's Preparation for the GED Examination Ser.). 256p. 1983. pap. 5.95 (ISBN 0-668-05540-5). Arco.

Friedman, Charles N., jt. auth. see Dollard, John D.

Friedman, Charles P. & Purcell, Elizabeth, eds. The New Biology & Medical Education: Merging the Biological, Information, & Cognitive Sciences. (Illus.). 300p. 1983. pap. 15.00 (ISBN 0-914362-40-2). J Macy Foun.

Friedman, Daniel P. The Little Lisper. LC 73-91284. 64p. 1974. pap. text ed. 4.95 (ISBN 0-574-19165-8, 13-2165). SRA.

Friedman, David. The Machinery of Freedom: A Guide to Radical Capitalism. 1978. 10.00 o.p. (ISBN 0-87000-420-4, Arlington Hse). Crown.

Friedman, David, jt. auth. see Christy, John.

Friedman, Donna R., ed. see Boss, Judith A.

Friedman, Donna R., ed. see Clark, Nancy.

Friedman, Donna R., ed. see Conley, Patrick T.

Friedman, Donna R., ed. see Hoffman, Roslyn.

Friedman, Donna R., ed. see Kirkman, Kay & Stinnett, Roger.

Friedman, Donna R., ed. see Walker, Carroll.

Friedman, Donna R., ed. see Willoughby, Larry.

Friedman, Donna R., ed. see Woodward, Sandra K.

Friedman, E. J., et al. Stationary Lead-Acid Batteries: Applications & Performance. LC 79-56111. (Electrotechnology Ser.: Vol. 3). (Illus.). 1980. 29.95 o.p. (ISBN 0-250-40258-0). Ann Arbor Science.

Friedman, Eitan, et al, eds. Depression & Antidepressants. Date not set. price not set (ISBN 0-89004-573-9). Raven.

Friedman, Eli A. Strategy in Renal Failure. LC 77-11003. (Nephrology & Hypertension Ser.). 1978. 60.00 (ISBN 0-471-01597-0, Pub. by Wiley Medical). Wiley.

Friedman, Eli A., ed. Diabetic Renal-Retinal Syndrome II: Prevention & Management. Date not set. price not set (ISBN 0-8089-1539-8). Grune.

Friedman, Eli A., ed. see International Society for Artificial Organs, 2nd, New York, April 18-19, 1979, et al.

Friedman, Ellen G. Joyce Carol Oates. LC 79-4828. (Literature and Life Ser.). 1980. 14.50 (ISBN 0-8044-2221-4). Ungar.

Friedman, Emanuel, tr. see Reiffenstuhl, Gunther & Platzer, Werner.

Friedman, Emanuel A. Obstetrical Decision Making. 222p. 1982. 34.00 (ISBN 0-941158-01-2, D1680-8). Mosby.

Friedman, Emanuel A., jt. auth. see Greenhill, J. P.

Friedman, Emanuel A., jt. ed. see Cohen, Wayne R.

Friedman, Estelle. Ben Franklin. (See & Read Biographies). (Illus.). (gr. k-3). 1961. PLB 4.97 o.p. (ISBN 0-399-60051-5). Putnam Pub Group.

Friedman, F. L. & Koffman, E. B. Problem Solving & Structured Programming in FORTRAN. 2nd ed. 1981. pap. 18.95 (ISBN 0-201-02461-6); wkbk. 5.95 (ISBN 0-201-02465-9). A-W.

Friedman, Frank & Koffman, Elliot. Problem Solving & Structured Programming in WATFIV. LC 81-20598. (Illus.). 480p. Date not set. pap. text ed. 15.95 (ISBN 0-201-10482-2). A-W.

Friedman, Frank L., jt. auth. see Koffman, Elliot B.

Friedman, Frieda. Dot for Short. (Illus.). (gr. 4-6). 1947. 9.95 (ISBN 0-688-21242-5). Morrow.

Friedman, Gene. Your Husband is Cheating When... 96p. (Orig.). 1982. pap. 2.25 (ISBN 0-523-41901-5). Pinnacle Bks.

Friedman, Gerald M. & Sanders, John E. Principles of Sedimentology. LC 78-5355. 792p. 1978. text ed. 35.95 (ISBN 0-471-75245-2). Wiley.

Friedman, Gerald M., jt. ed. see Bhattacharyya, Ajit.

Friedman, H. Harold. Diagnostic Electrocardiography & Vectorcardiography. 2nd ed. (Illus.). 1976. text ed. 40.00 (ISBN 0-07-022424-2, HP). McGraw.

Friedman, Hal. Tunnel: A Nightmare Come True. LC 78-32072. 1979. 10.95 o.p. (ISBN 0-688-03439-X). Morrow.

Friedman, Herbert. Introduction to Statistics. 1972. text ed. 12.95 o.p. (ISBN 0-394-31337-2); wkbk. 3.95 o.p. (ISBN 0-394-31338-0). Random.

Friedman, Herman, ed. Subcellular Factors Immunity. LC 79-24875. (Annals of the New York Academy of Sciences: Vol. 332). 625p. 1979. 112.00x (ISBN 0-89766-035-8). NY Acad Sci.

--Thymus Factors in Immunity. (Annals of the New York Academy of Sciences: Vol. 249). 547p. 1975. 65.00x (ISBN 0-89072-003-7). NY Acad Sci.

Friedman, Herman & Southam, Chester, eds. International Conference on Immunobiology of Cancer, Vol. 276. (Annals of the New York Academy of Sciences). 1976. 47.00x (ISBN 0-89072-055-X). NY Acad Sci.

Friedman, Herman, jt. ed. see Southam, Chester.

Friedman, Howard, ed. Interpersonal Issues in Health Care. 301p. 1982. 24.50 (ISBN 0-12-268340-4). Acad Pr.

Friedman, Howard M. Securities & Commodities Enforcement: Criminal Prosecutions & Civil Injunctions. LC 79-9685. 256p. 1981. 36.95x (ISBN 0-669-03617-X). Lexington Bks.

Friedman, I. Edward. How to Prepare for & Pass a High School Equivalency Exam. 1966. pap. 5.95 (ISBN 0-385-04537-9). Doubleday.

Friedman, Ina, tr. see Golan, Matti.

Friedman, Irving M., jt. auth. see Viscardi, Henry, Jr.

Friedman, J., et al. A Computer Model of Transformational Grammar. (Mathematical Linguistics & Automatic Language Processing: No. 9). 1971. 29.95 (ISBN 0-444-00084-4). Elsevier.

Friedman, Jack & Ordway, Nicholas. Income Property Appraisal & Analysis. 300p. 1981. text ed. 22.95 (ISBN 0-8359-3057-2); instr's. manual free (ISBN 0-8359-3058-0). Reston.

Friedman, James T. The Divorce Handbook: Your Basic Guide to Divorce. 1982. 12.50 (ISBN 0-394-52357-1). Random.

Friedman, Jean E., jt. ed. see Shade, William G.

Friedman, Jerome. The Most Ancient Testimony: Sixteenth-Century Christian-Hebraica in the Age of Renaissance Nostalgia. LC 82-18830. x, 279p. 1983. text ed. 24.95 (ISBN 0-8214-0700-7, 82-84697). Ohio U Pr.

Friedman, Jessie J. A New Air Transport Policy for the North Atlantic. LC 76-15035. 1976. 5.95 o.p. (ISBN 0-689-10761-7). Atheneum.

Friedman, Joel Wm. & Strickler, George M., Jr. Cases & Materials on the Law of Employment Discrimination. LC 82-21016. (University Casebook Ser.). 865p. 1982. text ed. write for info. (ISBN 0-88277-096-9). Foundation Pr.

Friedman, Joseph & Weinberg, Daniel. The Economics of Housing Vouchers. (Studies in Urban Economics). 215p. 1982. 27.50 (ISBN 0-12-268360-9). Acad Pr.

Friedman, Joy T. The Important Thing About. LC 80-83936. (Illus.). 96p. (gr. k-2). 1981. PLB 10.15 (ISBN 0-448-13947-2, G&D); pap. 3.95 (ISBN 0-448-14754-8). Putnam Pub Group.

--Sounds All Around. LC 80-83935. Orig. Title: Look Around & Listen. (Illus.). 80p. (gr. k-2). 1981. PLB 10.15 (ISBN 0-448-13945-6, G&D); pap. 3.95 (ISBN 0-448-14755-6). Putnam Pub Group.

--What's So Important About ? (Illus.). 96p. (ps-4). 1972. 3.50 o.p. (ISBN 0-448-02498-5, G&D). Putnam Pub Group.

Friedman, Judi. The Eels Strange Journey. LC 75-20136. (A Let's Read & Find Out Science Bk). (Illus.). 40p. (gr. k-3). 1976. PLB 10.89 (ISBN 0-690-01007-9, TYC-J). Har-Row.

--Puffins, Come Back! LC 80-2786. (Illus.). 80p. (gr. 3-7). 1981. PLB 7.95 o.p. (ISBN 0-396-07940-7). Dodd.

Friedman, Judith & Sonnenblick, Carol. Attack Pack. 128p. (gr. 4-12). 1982. write for info. (ISBN 0-9609616-0-7). New Dir Pr.

Friedman, Judith, tr. see Reiffenstuhl, Gunther & Platzer, Werner.

Friedman, Judith C. Jelly Jam, the People Preserver. rev. ed. (Illus.). 70p. (gr. 2-5). 1983. write for info wkbk. (ISBN 0-910812-27-6). Johnny Reads.

Friedman, L. Jeanne, jt. auth. see Inmon, William H.

Friedman, Laura, jt. auth. see Coryell, Julie.

Friedman, Lawrence M. A History of American Law. 1974. pap. 10.75 (ISBN 0-671-21742-9, Touchstone Bks). S&S.

--Introduction to American Law. 1983. write for info (ISBN 0-393-95251-7). Norton.

--Law & Society: An Introduction. 192p. 1977. text ed. 11.95 o.p. (ISBN 0-13-526616-5); pap. text ed. 9.85 (ISBN 0-13-526608-4). P-H.

--The Legal System: A Social Science Perspective. LC 74-25855. 338p. 1975. text ed. 13.50x (ISBN 0-87154-296-X). Russell Sage.

Friedman, Lawrence M. & Percival, Robert V. The Roots of Justice: Crime & Punishment in Alameda County, California, 1870-1910. (Studies in Legal History). xvi, 335p. 1981. 27.50x (ISBN 0-8078-1476-8). U of NC Pr.

Friedman, Lawrence M., et al. Fundamentals of Clinical Trials. 236p. 1981. 26.00 (ISBN 0-88416-296-6). Wright-PSG.

Friedman, Lee M. Zola & the Dreyfus Case. (World History Ser., No. 48). (Illus.). 1970. pap. 12.95x o.p. (ISBN 0-8383-0092-8). Haskell.

Friedman, Lenemaja. Shirley Jackson. (United States Authors Ser.). 1975. lib. bdg. 11.95 (ISBN 0-8057-0402-7, Twayne). G K Hall.

Friedman, Leon, ed. Southern Justice. LC 75-33296. 306p. 1976. Repr. of 1965 ed. lib. bdg. 19.25x (ISBN 0-8371-8489-4, FRSJ). Greenwood.

Friedman, Leonard R., ed. The Russian Winter, the American Fall, the Chinese Spring & Summer: A Historian's Fairy Tale. 1979. 6.95 o.p. (ISBN 0-533-02957-0). Vantage.

Friedman, Leslie. Sex Role Stereotyping in the Mass Media: An Annotated Bibliography. LC 76-52685. (Reference Library of Social Science Ser.). lib. bdg. 34.50 o.s.i. (ISBN 0-8240-9865-X). Garland Pub.

Friedman, Lynne, jt. auth. see Heckens, Gertrude.

Friedman, M. A Beginner's Guide to Sightsinging & Musical Rudiments. 1981. pap. 15.95 (ISBN 0-13-074088-8). P-H.

Friedman, M., et al, eds. Diagnosis & Treatment of Upper Gastrointestinal Tumors. (International Congress Ser.: No. 542). 1981. 98.75 (ISBN 0-444-90189-2). Elsevier.

Friedman, Marilyn. Consider Consignments: How to Own, Open, & Operate Your Town's Permanent Garage Sale. 1979. 4.95 o.p. (ISBN 0-533-03919-3). Vantage.

Friedman, Martin. Martin Buber's Life & Work: The Early Years, 1878-1923. (Illus.). 480p. 1982. 25.75 (ISBN 0-525-15325-X, 02500-750). Dutton.

Friedman, Maurice. The Hidden Human Image. 1974. pap. 3.45 o.s.i. (ISBN 0-440-53511-5, Delta). Dell.

--Martin Buber's Life & Work: The Middle Years, 1923-1945. (Illus.). 416p. 1983. 29.95 (ISBN 0-525-24176-0, 02908-870). Dutton.

Friedman, Maurice, ed. & tr. see Buber, Martin.

Friedman, Maurice, jt. ed. see Schilpp, Paul A.

Friedman, Maurice S., ed. & tr. see Buber, Martin.

Friedman, Michael. Foundations of Space-Time Theories: Relativistic Physics & Philosophy of Science. LC 82-61362. 400p. 1983. 35.00 (ISBN 0-691-07239-6). Princeton U Pr.

Friedman, Mickey. Hurricane Season: A Novel with Murder. 1983. 14.95 (ISBN 0-525-24175-2, 01354-410). Dutton.

Friedman, Milton. An Adult Guide to Beginning Piano & Basic Musicianship. (Illus.). 1979. pap. 14.95 ref. (ISBN 0-13-008797-1). P-H.

--Bright Promises, Dismal Performance: An Economist's Protests. 272p. 16.95 (ISBN 0-15-114152-5). HarBraceJ.

--Bright Promises, Dismal Performance: An Economist's Protest. 272p. pap. 5.95 (ISBN 0-15-614161-2, Harv). HarBraceJ.

--Capitalism & Freedom. LC 62-19619. 1962. 13.00x o.s.i. (ISBN 0-226-26400-9). U of Chicago Pr.

--There's No Such Thing as a Free Lunch. 330p. 18.50 (ISBN 0-87548-310-0). Open Court.

Friedman, Milton, et al. Milton Friedman's Monetary Framework: A Debate with His Critics. Gordon, Robert J., ed. LC 73-92599. xii, 192p. 1975. pap. 5.95 (ISBN 0-226-26408-4, P619, Phoen). U of Chicago Pr.

Friedman, Milton R. The Cumulative Supplement to Contracts & Conveyances of Real Property, 1982. 3rd ed. 444p. 1982. 45.00 (ISBN 0-686-96167-6, N6-1340); pap. 30.00 (ISBN 0-686-99716-6, N5-1338). PLI.

--Cumulative Supplement to Friedman on Leases, 1982, 3 Vols. 694p. 1982. 45.00 (ISBN 0-686-96175-7, N6-1339). PLI.

Friedman, Morton P., jt. ed. see Carterette, Edward C.

Friedman, Murray, ed. Jewish Life in Philadelphia, 1830-1940. (Illus.). 320p. 1983. 19.95 (ISBN 0-89727-050-9). Inst Study Human.

Friedman, Murray, et al, eds. New Perspectives on School Integration. LC 78-21715. 192p. 1979. pap. 6.50 o.p. (ISBN 0-8006-1359-7, 1-1359). Fortress.

Friedman, Myles I. & Willis, Martha R. Human Nature & Predictability. LC 81-47582. 368p. 1981. 28.95x (ISBN 0-669-04684-1). Lexington Bks.

Friedman, Nathalie S., jt. auth. see Rogers, Theresa F.

Friedman, Norman. E. E. Cummings: The Growth of a Writer. LC 80-17081. (Arcturus Books Paperbacks Ser.). 218p. 1980. pap. 7.95 (ISBN 0-8093-0978-5). S Ill U Pr.

--U. S. Naval Weapons. LC 82-61473. (Illus.). 256p. 1982. 24.95 (ISBN 0-87021-735-6). Naval Inst Pr.

Friedman, Norman, ed. E. E. Cummings: A Collection of Critical Essays. LC 74-163857. (Twentieth Century Views). 192p. 1972. 10.95 o.p. (ISBN 0-13-195552-7, Spec). P-H.

Friedman, Paul. Computer Programs in BASIC. 1981. 10.95 (ISBN 0-13-165217-6); pap. 19.95 (ISBN 0-13-165225-7). P-H.

Friedman, Philip. Their Brothers' Keepers: The Christian Heroes & Heroines Who Helped the Oppressed Escape the Nazi Terror. LC 57-8773. 1978. pap. 3.95 (ISBN 0-8052-5002-6, Pub. by Holocaust Library). Schocken.

--Their Brothers' Keepers: The Christian Heroes & Heroines Who Helped the Oppressed Escaper the Nazi Terror. 232p. Repr. 4.95 (ISBN 0-686-95090-9). ADL.

Friedman, Philip & Eisen, Gail. The Pilates Method of Physical & Mental Conditioning. (Illus.). 1983. pap. 6.95 (ISBN 0-446-97859-0). Warner Bks.

Friedman, Ralph. Oregon for the Curious. LC 75-151057. (Illus.). 1972. pap. 5.95 (ISBN 0-87004-222-X). Caxton.

--This Side of Oregon. LC 79-57241. (Illus., Orig.). 1983. pap. 7.95 (ISBN 0-87004-284-X). Caxton.

Friedman, Richard, jt. auth. see Fischler, Stan.

Friedman, Richard C., ed. Behavior & the Menstrual Cycle. (Sexual Behavior Ser.). (Illus.). 480p. 1982. 55.00 (ISBN 0-8247-1852-6). Dekker.

Friedman, Richard E., ed. The Creation of Sacred Literature: Composition & Redaction of the Biblical Text. Vol. 22. (U.C. Publications in Near Eastern Studies). 1981. pap. 16.50x (ISBN 0-520-09637-1). U of Cal Pr.

Friedman, Robert, ed. see Fisichella, Anthony J.

Friedman, Robert, ed. see Stearn, Jess & Thompson, Alec.

Friedman, Robert E. & Schweke, William, eds. Expanding the Opportunity to Produce: Revitalizing the American Economy Through New Enterprise Development. LC 81-66853. 570p. (Orig.). 1981. pap. 19.95x (ISBN 0-9605804-0-9). Corp Ent Dev.

Friedman, Robert M., jt. ed. see Merigan, Thomas C.

Friedman, Robert S., ed. see Culbert, Michael L.

Friedman, Robert S., ed. see Faulkner, Chuck.

Friedman, Robert S., ed. see Kincaid, Jim.

Friedman, Robert S., ed. see Payne, Daniel H.

Friedman, Robert S., ed. see Reichel, Aaron.

Friedman, Ronald. Pennsylvania Guide Real Estate Licensing. LC 79-48053. 124p. 1981. pap. text ed. 7.95 o.p. (ISBN 0-88262-415-6). Warren.

Friedman, Ronald & Henszey, Benjamin. Protecting Your Sales Commission: Professional Liability in Real Estate. 1982. 32.95 o.p. (ISBN 0-686-34649-1). Caroline Hse.

Friedman, Ronald, jt. auth. see Henszey, Benjamin.

Friedman, Ronald M. Pennsylvania Guide to Real Estate Licensing Examinations for Salespersons & Brokers. LC 79-48053. 124p. 1982. pap. 9.95 (ISBN 0-471-87758-1). Wiley.

Friedman, Ronald M., jt. auth. see Henszey, Benjamin N.

Friedman, Saul S. Amcha: An Oral Testament of the Holocaust. LC 79-67054. 1979. pap. text ed. 15.50 (ISBN 0-8191-0867-7). U Pr of Amer.

--Land of Dust: Palestine at the Turn of the Century. LC 81-43466. (Illus.). 256p. (Orig.). 1982. lib. bdg. 23.00 (ISBN 0-8191-2403-6); pap. text ed. 11.50 (ISBN 0-8191-2404-4). U Pr of Amer.

Friedman, Scarlet & Sarah, Elizabeth. On the Problem of Men: Two Feminist Conferences. 288p. 1982. pap. 10.95 (ISBN 0-7043-3887-4, Pub. by Quartet Bks). Merrimack Bk Serv.

Friedman, Sonya. Men Are Just Desserts. 256p. 1983. 14.50 (ISBN 0-446-51255-9). Warner Bks.

Friedman, Thomas, jt. auth. see Solman, Paul.

Friedman, V. S., tr. see Alpatov, M. V.

Friedman, Victor A. The Grammatical Categories of the Macedonian Indicative. 1977. pap. 11.95 (ISBN 0-89357-042-7). Slavica.

Friedman, Walter F. & Kipnees, Jerome J. Distribution Packaging. LC 75-22096. 558p. 1977. 29.50 (ISBN 0-88275-950-7); pap. text ed. 12.50 o.p. (ISBN 0-88275-222-7). Krieger.

Friedmann & Pile. Interior Design. 3rd ed. 1982. 27.50 (ISBN 0-444-00670-2). Elsevier.

Friedmann, Herbert, ed. Enzymes. LC 79-22573. (Benchmark Papers in Biochemistry: Vol. 1). 736p. 1981. 68.00 (ISBN 0-87933-367-7). Hutchinson Ross.

Friedmann, J., et al. Fortran IV. 2nd ed. (Self Teaching Guide Ser.). 499p. 1980. pap. 12.95 (ISBN 0-471-07771-2). Wiley.

Friedmann, John. The Good Society. 1979. 15.00x (ISBN 0-262-06070-1). MIT Pr.

Friedmann, John & Weaver, Clyde. Territory & Function. 1979. 33.00x (ISBN 0-520-03928-9); pap. 7.95x (ISBN 0-520-04105-4). U of Cal Pr.

Friedmann, John & Alonso, William, eds. Regional Policy: Readings in Theory & Applications. rev. ed. 1975. 25.00x (ISBN 0-262-06057-4). MIT Pr.

Friedman-Weiss, Jeffrey, jt. auth. see Wise, Herbert H.

Friedrich, et al. Experiments in Atomic Physics. (gr. 12). text ed. 6.95 o.p. (ISBN 0-7195-0467-8). Transatlantic.

Friedrich, David. Crime & Justice: Perspectives from the Past. 1977. pap. text ed. 6.00 o.p. (ISBN 0-8191-0068-4). U Pr of Amer.

Friedrich, Engels see Marx, Karl & Engels, Friedrich.

Friedrich, Ernst, jt. auth. see Kraus, Frederick T.

Friedrich, Gerhard, jt. ed. see Kittel, Gerhard.

Friedrich, Gus, et al. Classroom Communication: Context, Roles & Process. (Interpersonal Communication Ser.). (Illus.). 1976. pap. text ed. 6.95 (ISBN 0-675-08644-2). Merrill.

Friedrich, Johannes. Extinct Languages. Gaynor, Frank, tr. from Ger. LC 74-139132. (Illus.). 1971. Repr. of 1957 ed. lib. bdg. 20.25x (ISBN 0-8371-5748-X, FREL). Greenwood.

Friedrich, Klaus. International Economics. (Illus.). 375p. 1974. text ed. 16.95 o.p. (ISBN 0-07-022435-8, C). McGraw.

Friedrich, Lawrence W., ed. Nature of Physical Knowledge. 1960. 7.95 (ISBN 0-87462-420-7). Marquette.

Friedrich, M. H. Adoleszentenpsychosen. (Bibliotheca Psychiatrica: No. 163). (Illus.). vi, 140p. 1983. pap. 41.50 (ISBN 3-8055-3640-2). S Karger.

Friedrich, Otto. Clover: A Love Story. 1979. 12.95 o.p. (ISBN 0-671-22509-X). S&S.

--The End of the World: A History. LC 82-2401. 384p. 1982. 19.95 (ISBN 0-698-11128-1, Coward). Putnam Pub Group.

Friedrich, Otto, jt. auth. see Friedrich, Priscilla.

Friedrich, Paul. Bastard Moons. 2nd rev. ed. LC 79-115523. 1979. 3.00 (ISBN 0-934528-02-0). B & M Waite Pr.

Friedrich, Pia. Pier Paolo Pasolini. (World Authors Ser.). 1982. lib. bdg. 17.95 (ISBN 0-8057-6500-X, Twayne). G K Hall.

Friedrich, Priscilla & Friedrich, Otto. The Easter Bunny That Overslept. LC 82-13013. (Illus.). 32p. (gr. k-3). 1983. 10.50 (ISBN 0-688-01540-9); PLB 10.08 (ISBN 0-688-01541-7). Lothrop.

Friedrich, Ralph, ed. see Mizuno, Kogen.

Friedrich, Ralph, ed. see Mori, Masahiro.

Friedrich, Ralph, ed. see Nikkyo, Niwano.

Friedrich, Ralph, ed. see Niwano, Nikkyo.

Friedrich, Robert A. Energy Conservation for American Agriculture. LC 78-11473. (Energy Law Institute State & Local Energy Conservation Project: Vol. 8). 192p. 1979. prof ref 22.50x (ISBN 0-88410-058-8). Ballinger Pub.

Friedrichsmeyer, Erhard. Die Satirische Kurzprosa Heinrich Bolls. (Studies in the Germanic Languages & Literatures: No. 97). xiv, 223p. 1981. 20.00x (ISBN 0-8078-8097-3). U of NC Pr.

Friedson, Anthony M., ed. New Directions in Biography. (Biography Monographs: No. 2). 100p. 1982. pap. text ed. 7.95x (ISBN 0-8248-0783-9). UH Pr.

Frielink, A. Auditing Automatic Data Processing. 1961. 9.75 (ISBN 0-444-40249-7). Elsevier.

Friend, Charles E. The Law of Evidence in Virginia. 2nd ed. 1983. pns (ISBN 0-87215-578-1). Michie-Bobbs.

Friend, Diane & Nicholson, Dale. Bridal Sewing & Crafts. (Illus.). 72p. 1983. pap. 2.50 (ISBN 0-918178-31-2). Simplicity.

Friend, G. E., jt. auth. see Fike, J. L.

Friend, Hilderic. The Flowers & Their Story. LC 78-175751. (Illus.). 300p. 1972. Repr. of 1907 ed. 31.00 o.p. (ISBN 0-8103-3868-8). Gale.

Friend, I., et al. Mutual Funds & Other Institutional Investors: A New Perspective. 1970. 21.95 (ISBN 0-07-022456-0, P&RB). McGraw.

Friend, Irwin, jt. auth. see Blume, Marshall E.

Friend, Irwin, jt. auth. see Burme, Marshall E.

Friend, J. A., ed. Australian Conference on Electrochemistry, 1st. 1964. inquire for price o.p. (ISBN 0-08-010501-7). Pergamon.

Friend, Jewell A. Traditional Grammar: A Short Summary. rev. ed. LC 75-30861. 134p. 1976. 10.00x (ISBN 0-8093-0742-1); pap. text ed. 5.95x (ISBN 0-8093-0752-9); tchrs. manual 1.00 (ISBN 0-8093-0847-9). S Ill U Pr.

Friend, John, et al. Public Planning: The Inter-Corporate Dimension. LC 74-7696. 450p. 1974. 33.00x (ISBN 0-422-74450-6, Pub. by Tavistock England). Methuen Inc.

Friend, Llerena B., ed. see Webb, Walter P.

Friend, Oscar. Lobo Brand. 256p. (YA) 1973. 6.95 (ISBN 0-685-32414-1, Avalon). Bouregy.

Friend, Paul D. The Great Frame-Up: The Consumer's Guide to Eyeglasses. Hammond, Debbie, ed. LC 80-11261. 1983. 14.95 (ISBN 0-87949-181-7). Ashley Bks.

Friend, Robert, jt. tr. see Gigliesi, Primerose.

Friend, Robert C., tr. see Qing, Ai.

Friend, Wayne Z. Corrosion of Nickel & Nickel-Base Alloys. LC 79-11524. (Corrosion Monographs). 1980. 57.50x (ISBN 0-471-28285-5, Pub. by Wiley-Interscience). Wiley.

Friendly, Alfred & Goldfarb, Ronald L. Crime & Publicity. LC 67-15891. 1975. Repr. of 1967 ed. 19.00 o.s.i. (ISBN 0-527-02804-5). Kraus Repr.

Friendly, Fred. The Good Guys, the Bad Guys & the First Amendment: Free Speech Vs. Fairness in Broadcasting. 1976. 3.95 (ISBN 0-394-72320-1). Random.

Friends of the Earth Editors. Ronald Reagan & the American Environment: An Indictment, Alternate Budget Proposal, & Citizen's Guide to Action. 144p. 1982. pap. 8.95 (ISBN 0-913890-55-3). Brick Hse Pub.

Frier, John P. & Frier, Mary E. Industrial Lighting Systems. (Illus.). 336p. 1980. 25.90 (ISBN 0-07-022457-9). McGraw.

Frier, Mary E., jt. auth. see Frier, John P.

Frier, William T. Elementary Metallurgy. 2nd ed. (Illus.). 1952. text ed. 24.95 (ISBN 0-07-022419-6, G). McGraw.

Friermood, Elisabeth H. Promises in the Attic. LC 60-12790. (gr. 5-9). 1975. pap. 4.95 (ISBN 0-913428-14-0). Landfall Pr.

Frierson, Eleanor, tr. see Loti, Pierre.

Frierson, Wright, tr. see Loti, Pierre.

Fries, Adelaide L., ed. The Road to Salem. x, 316p. 1980. Repr. of 1944 ed. 12.50 (ISBN 0-8078-0932-2). U of NC Pr.

Fries, Albert C., jt. auth. see Nanassy, Louis C.

Fries, Albert C., et al. Applied Secretarial Procedures. 7th ed. (Illus.). 544p. (gr. 12). 1973. text ed. 16.40 (ISBN 0-07-022450-1, G); tchr's. manual & key 8.15 (ISBN 0-07-022452-8); wkbk. 7.44 (ISBN 0-07-022451-X). McGraw.

Fries, Charles C. Teaching & Learning English As a Foreign Language. (Orig.). 1945. pap. 8.50x (ISBN 0-472-08347-3). U of Mich Pr.

Fries, Jakob F. Dialogues on Morality & Religion. Phillips, D. Z., et al, eds. LC 82-13787. (Values & Philosophical Inquiry Ser.). 272p. 1982. text ed. 28.95x (ISBN 0-389-20326-2). B&N Imports.

Fries, James F. & Holman, Halsted R. Systematic Lupus Erythematosus: A Clinical Analysis, Vol. 6. LC 74-31837. (Major Problems in Internal Medicine Ser.). (Illus.). 199p. 1975. text ed. 20.00 o.p. (ISBN 0-7216-3917-8). Saunders.

Fries, Peter H. Tagmeme Sequences in the English Noun Phrase. (Publications in Linguistics & Related Fields Ser.: No. 36). 247p. 1972. pap. 5.00x (ISBN 0-88312-038-0); microfiche 3.00x (ISBN 0-88312-438-6). Summer Inst Ling.

Fries, Robert F., jt. auth. see Hughes, Paul L.

Fries, Sylvia D. Urban Idea in Colonial America. LC 77-81333. (Illus.). 236p. 1977. 29.95 (ISBN 0-87722-103-0). Temple U Pr.

Friese, U. Erich. Aquarium Fish. (Illus.). 96p. 1980. 4.95 (ISBN 0-87666-512-1, KW026). TFH Pubns.

--Marine Invertebrates in the Home Aquarium. (Illus.). 240p. (Orig.). 1973. pap. 14.95 (ISBN 0-87666-105-3, PS-658). TFH Pubns.

--Sea Anemones. (Illus.). 1973. 14.95 (ISBN 0-87666-140-1, H-943). TFH Pubns.

Friese, U. Erich, tr. see Af Enehjelm, Curt.

Friese, U. Erich, tr. see Enehjelm, Curt A.

Friese, U. Erich, tr. see Nicolai, Jurgen.

Friese, U. Erich, tr. see Radtke, Georg A.

Friesen, Connie M. The Political Economy of East-West Trade. LC 76-14395. 1976. text ed. 25.95 o.p. (ISBN 0-275-56920-9). Praeger.

Friesen, Delores. Living More with Less Study-Action Guide. 112p. (Orig.). 1981. pap. 5.95 (ISBN 0-8361-1968-1). Herald Pr.

Friesen, Garry & Maxson, Robin. Decision Making & the Will of God: Study Guide. (Critical Concern Ser.). 1983. pap. price not set (ISBN 0-88070-021-1). Multnomah.

Friesen, John W., jt. auth. see Carson, Robert B.

Friesner, Arlyne. Maternity Nursing. 3rd ed. Raff, Beverly, ed. LC 77-80106. (Nursing Outline Ser.). 1982. pap. 13.50 (ISBN 0-87488-377-6). Med Exam.

Friesner, Arlyne, jt. auth. see Yura, Helen.

Frietzsche, Arthur H. Disraeli's Religion: The Treatment of Religion in Disraeli's Novels. 62p. 1982. Repr. of 1961 ed. lib. bdg. 10.00 (ISBN 0-8495-1718-4). Arden Lib.

--The Monstrous Clever Young Man: The Novelist Disraeli & His Heroes. 60p. 1982. Repr. of 1959 ed. lib. bdg. 10.00 (ISBN 0-8495-1735-4). Arden Lib.

Frigerio, A., ed. Recent Developments in Mass Spectrometry in Biochemistry. (Medicine & Environmental Research Ser.: Vol. 7). 1981. 81.00 (ISBN 0-444-42029-0). Elsevier.

Frigerio, A. & Castagnoli, N., Jr., eds. Mass Spectrometry in Biochemistry & Medicine. LC 73-91164. (Monographs of the Mario Negri Institute for Pharmacological Research). 379p. 1974. 53.00 (ISBN 0-911216-53-7). Raven.

Frigerio, A. & McCamisch, M., eds. Recent Developments in Chromatography & Electrophoresis. (Analytical Chemistry Symposia Ser.: Vol. 3). 1980. 68.00 (ISBN 0-444-41871-7). Elsevier.

Friggens, Myriam. Tales, Trails & Tommyknockers: Stories from Colorado's Past. LC 79-84876. 1979. pap. 6.95 (ISBN 0-933472-01-3). Johnson Bks.

Friggens, Paul. Gold & Grass: The Black Hills Story. (Illus.). 1983. price not set (ISBN 0-87108-648-4). Pruett.

Frigidaire. Microwave Cooking in Multiple Speeds. 256p. 1980. 15.95 o.p. (ISBN 0-385-17042-4). Doubleday.

Friguglietti, James, tr. see De Bertier de Sauvigny, G. & Pinkney, David H.

Frigyesi, T., et al, eds. Corticothalamic Projections & Sensorimotor Activities. LC 74-181303. (Illus.). 601p. 1972. 48.00 (ISBN 0-911216-35-9). Raven.

Friis, Babbis. Kristy's Courage. McKinnon, Lise S., tr. LC 65-18728. (Illus.). (gr. 4-6). 1965. 5.95 (ISBN 0-15-243370-8, HJ). HarBraceJ.

--Wanted! A Horse! McKinnon, Lise S., tr. from Norwegian. LC 72-153952. 192p. (gr. 8-12). 1972. 5.95 (ISBN 0-15-294750-7, HJ). HarBraceJ.

Friis, Erick J., tr. see Heinesen, William.

Friis, Erick J., tr. see Nordraa, Olaf.

Friis, Erik J., tr. see Ingstad, Helge.

Friis, Erik J., et al see Allardt, Erik & Andre, Nils.

Friis, Herman R., Jr. & Bale, Shelby G., eds. United States Polar Exploration. LC 70-141379. (National Archives Conferences Ser.: Vol. 1). (Illus.). xvii, 199p. 1972. 15.00x (ISBN 0-8214-0093-2, 82-80984). Ohio U Pr.

Friis, Robert, jt. auth. see Taff, Gail A.

Frimmer, Steven. Stone That Spoke & Other Clues to the Decipherment of Lost Languages. (Science Explorer Ser.). (Illus.). (gr. 6-8). 1969. PLB 3.89 o.p. (ISBN 0-399-60607-6). Putnam Pub Group.

Frings, Virginia S. Fashion: From Concept to Consumer. (Illus.). 320p. 1982. 25.95 (ISBN 0-13-306605-3). P-H.

Fripiat, J., ed. Advanced Techniques for Clay Mineral Analysis. (Developments in Sedimentology Ser.: Vol. 34). 1982. 42.75 (ISBN 0-444-42002-9). Elsevier.

Frisancho, A. Roberto. Human Adaptation: A Functional Interpretation. LC 78-31913. (Illus.). 210p. 1979. text ed. 14.95 o.p. (ISBN 0-8016-1693-X). Mosby.

Frisbee, Lucy P. John F. Kennedy: America's Youngest President. (Childhood of Famous Americans Ser.). (gr. 3-8). 1983. pap. 3.95 (ISBN 0-686-95260-X). Bobbs.

Frisbee-Houde, Cornelia H. Not Just Another Pretty Dress: Two Centuries of Clothing & Textiles from Cherry Hill. LC 82-18738. (Illus., Orig.). 1983. pap. 5.00 (ISBN 0-943366-05-4). Hist Cherry Hill.

Frisbie, Charlotte J., jt. ed. see Bruggee, David M.

Frisby, David, tr. see Simmel, Georg.

Frisch, Ann & Frisch, Paul. Discovering Your Hidden Self. (RL 10). 1976. pap. 1.75 o.p. (ISBN 0-451-06994-3, E6994, Sig). NAL.

Frisch, B., jt. auth. see Bartl, R.

Frisch, D. H. Arms Reduction: Program & Issues. LC 61-11253. (Twentieth Century Fund Ser.). Repr. of 1961 ed. pap. 5.00 (ISBN 0-527-02817-7). Kraus Repr.

Frisch, Ivan T., jt. auth. see Frank, Howard.

Frisch, K. C., jt. auth. see Saunders, J. H.

Frisch, Max. Biedermann und Die Brandstifter. Ackermann, Paul K., ed. (gr. 10-12). 1963. pap. text ed. 9.50 (ISBN 0-395-04090-6). HM.

--Bluebeard. Skelton, Geoffrey, tr. 96p. 1982. 10.95 (ISBN 0-15-113200-3). HarBraceJ.

--Gantenbein. Bullock, Michael, tr. LC 82-48033. Orig. Title: Wilderness of Mirrors. 304p. 1982. Repr. of 1965 ed. 7.95 o.p. (ISBN 0-15-634407-6, Harv). HarBraceJ.

--Homo Faber. Ackermann, Paul K., ed. LC 72-9379. 300p. (Orig.). 1973. pap. text ed. 10.50 (ISBN 0-395-14402-7). HM.

--I'm Not Stiller. 1958. pap. 4.50 o.p. (ISBN 0-394-42983-4); pap. 2.95 (ISBN 0-394-70219-0). Random.

--Sketchbook, Nineteen Forty-Six to Nineteen Forty-Nine. Skelton, Geoffrey, tr. 320p. pap. 8.95 (ISBN 0-15-682746-8, Harv). HarBraceJ.

--Sketchbook, Nineteen Sixty-Six to Nineteen Seventy-One. Skelton, Geoffrey, tr. 343p. pap. 8.95 (ISBN 0-15-682747-6, Harv). HarBraceJ.

--Sketchbook 1946-1949. Skelton, Geoffrey, tr. LC 76-54706. (Helen & Kurt Wolff Bk). 1977. 12.95 o.p. (ISBN 0-15-182893-8). HarBraceJ.

Frisch, Michael H. & Walkowitz, Daniel J., eds. Working-Class America: Essays on Labor, Community, & American Society. LC 81-23971. (Working Class in American History Ser.). 368p. 1983. 29.50 (ISBN 0-252-00953-3); pap. 8.95 (ISBN 0-252-00954-1). U of Ill Pr.

Frisch, Morton J. Franklin D. Roosevelt. LC 74-16425. (World Leaders Ser.: No. 43). 1975. lib. bdg. 9.95 o.p. (ISBN 0-8057-3708-1, Twayne). G K Hall.

Frisch, Morton J. & Stevens, Richard G., eds. The Political Thought of American Statesmen: Selected Writings & Speeches. LC 72-89723. 350p. 1973. 13.50 o.p. (ISBN 0-87581-141-8); pap. text ed. 12.95 (ISBN 0-87581-142-6). Peacock Pubs.

Frisch, Otto R. What Little I Remember. LC 78-18096. (Illus.). 227p. 1980. pap. 11.95 (ISBN 0-521-28010-9). Cambridge U Pr.

Frisch, Paul, jt. auth. see Frisch, Ann.

Frisch, Robert A. ESOP for the Eighties: The Fabulous New Instrument of Corporate Finance Comes of Age. 1982. 24.95 (ISBN 0-87863-003-1). Farnswth Pub.

Frisch, Vern A. & Handal, Joan S. Applied Office Typewriting. 4th ed. (Illus.). (gr. 11-12). 1977. text ed. 8.48 (ISBN 0-07-022504-4, G); teacher's manual & key 3.50 (ISBN 0-07-022505-2). McGraw.

Frisch, Vern A. & Handel, J. S. Applied Office Typewriting: A Practice Set in Clerical Typing. 3rd ed. 1968. text ed. 8.48 (ISBN 0-07-022485-4, G). McGraw.

Frisell, Wilhelm R. Human Biochemistry. 1982. text ed. 35.00x (ISBN 0-02-339820-5). Macmillan.

Frishkoff, Patricia A., jt. auth. see Gibson, Charles H.

Frishman, Austin M. & Schwartz, Arthur P. The Cockroach Combat Manual. (Illus.). 1980. pap. 4.95 (ISBN 0-688-03613-9). Quill NY.

Frishman, Bernard L. & Loshak, Lionel. Metric Architectural Drawing: A Manual for Designers & Draftsmen. LC 80-39805. 191p. 1981. 36.00 (ISBN 0-471-07724-0, Pub. by Wiley-Interscience). Wiley.

Frisinger, Nellie. Jeff & Jenny & the Kidnapping. LC 78-55337. (The Jeff & Jenny Adventure Ser.). (Illus.). (gr. 2-6). 1978. pap. 2.95 (ISBN 0-89636-005-9). Accent Bks.

--Jeff & Jenny on the Chinchilla Ranch. LC 77-75132. (Jeff & Jenny Adventure Ser.). (Illus.). (gr. 2-6). 1977. pap. 2.95 (ISBN 0-916406-73-3). Accent Bks.

--Jeff & Jenny Winter in Alaska. LC 77-81775. (The Jeff & Jenny Adventure Ser.). (Illus.). (gr. 2-6). 1977. pap. 2.95 (ISBN 0-916406-82-2). Accent Bks.

Frisk, Peter D., jt. auth. see Gustafson, R. D.

Frisk, Peter D., jt. auth. see Gustafson, R. David.

Friskey, Margaret. Birds We Know. LC 81-7745. (The New True Books). (Illus.). 48p. (gr. k-4). 1981. PLB 9.25 (ISBN 0-516-01609-1). Childrens.

--Indian Two Feet & His Eagle Feather. LC 67-20101. (Illus.). 64p. (gr. k-3). 1967. PLB 9.25 (ISBN 0-516-03503-7). Childrens.

--Indian Two Feet & the Grizzly Bear. LC 74-7481. (Illus.). 32p. (gr. k-2). 1974. PLB 9.25 (ISBN 0-516-03508-8). Childrens.

--Indian Two Feet & the Wolf Cubs. (Easy Reading Picture Story Bks). (Illus.). (gr. k-3). 1971. PLB 9.25 (ISBN 0-516-03506-1). Childrens.

Friskney, Tom. Thirteen Lessons on I & II Thessalonians. LC 82-71253. (Bible Student Study Guide Ser.). 122p. 1982. pap. 2.95 (ISBN 0-89900-172-6). College Pr Pub.

Frison, George & Stanford, Dennis. The Agate Basin Site: A Record of the Paleoindian Occupation of the Northwestern High Plains. (Studies in Archaeology Ser.). 440p. 1982. 74.50 (ISBN 0-12-268570-9). Acad Pr.

Fristrom, James W. & Spieth, Philip T. Principles of Genetics. LC 80-65757. (Illus.). 687p. 1980. text ed. 27.95x (ISBN 0-913462-05-5). Chiron Pr.

Fritchie, G. Edward & Ooi, Wan H. Biology: A Laboratory Experience. 2nd ed. (Illus.). 236p. 1982. pap. text ed. 14.95 (ISBN 0-89641-082-X). American Pr.

Fritchie, G. Edward, et al. Biology: A Laboratory Experience. (Illus.). 1979. lab manual 9.95 o.p. (ISBN 0-89641-012-9). American Pr.

Fritchman, June & Solomon, Karey. Living Lean off the Fat of the Land. 224p. (Orig.). 1983. pap. 8.95 (ISBN 0-943914-03-5). Larson Pubns Inc.

Frith, Francis. Egypt & the Holy Land in Historic Photographs. White, Jon. E., selected by. 12.50 (ISBN 0-8446-5887-1). Peter Smith.

Frith, H. J. Waterfowl in Australia. (Illus.). 1967. 17.50 (ISBN 0-8248-0063-X, Eastwest Ctr). UH Pr.

Frith, Henry. Graphology: The Science of Handwriting. LC 80-80536. (Illus.). 128p. 1980. pap. 5.00 (ISBN 0-89345-205-X, Steinerbks). Garber Comm.

Frith, Uta, ed. Cognitive Processes in Spelling. LC 79-10788. 1980. 45.50 o.s.i. (ISBN 0-12-268660-8). Acad Pr.

Frith, William P. John Leech: His Life & Work, 2 Vols. LC 69-17491. 1969. Repr. of 1891 ed. Set. 56.00x (ISBN 0-8103-3831-9). Gale.

Fritsch, Bruno. Growth Limitation & Political Power. LC 75-45497. 152p. 1976. prof ref 15.00x (ISBN 0-88410-294-7). Ballinger Pub.

Fritsch, Charles T. Genesis. LC 59-10454. (Layman's Bible Commentary Ser: Vol. 2). 1959. pap. 3.95 (ISBN 0-8042-3062-5). John Knox.

Fritsch, Charles T., ed. Studies in the History of Caesarea Maritima: The Joint Expedition to Caesarea Maritima Vol. 1. LC 75-29059. (American Schools of Oriental Research, Supplement Ser.: Vol.19). 122p. 1975. text ed. 6.00x (ISBN 0-89757-319-6, Am Sch Orient Res). Eisenbrauns.

Fritsche, Felix E. Structure & Reproduction of the Algae, 2 Vols. Vol. 1. 80.00 (ISBN 0-521-05041-3); Vol. 2. 95.00 (ISBN 0-521-05042-1). Cambridge U Pr.

Fritschka, E., jt. ed. see Cervos-Navarro, J.

Fritschler, A. Lee. Smoking & Politics: Policy Making & the Federal Bureaucracy. 2nd ed. LC 74-12381. 208p. 1975. pap. text ed. 10.95 (ISBN 0-13-815019-2). P-H.

--Smoking & Politics: Policy Making & the Federal Bureaucracy. 3rd ed. 208p. 1983. pap. 10.95 (ISBN 0-13-815027-3). P-H.

Fritschler, A. Lee & Ross, Bernard H. Business Regulation & Government Decision-Making. 1980. pap. text ed. 11.95 (ISBN 0-316-29362-8). Little.

--Executive's Guide to Government: How Washington Works. 1980. text ed. 17.95 (ISBN 0-316-29363-6). Little.

Fritts, Susan R., tr. see Colleta, Anthony.

Fritz & Lebovitz. Random Fields, 2 vols. (Colloquia Mathematica Ser.: Vol. 27). 1982. Set. 170.25 (ISBN 0-444-85441-X). Elsevier.

Fritz, Dorothy B. Christian Teaching of Kindergarten Children. (Illus., Orig.). 1964. pap. 2.49 (ISBN 0-8042-9503-4). John Knox.

Fritz, George J., jt. auth. see Noggle, G. Ray.

Fritz, Irving, ed. see Symposium on Insulin Action, Toronto, 1971.

Fritz, Jack. Small & Mini Hydropower Systems: Resource Assessment & Project Feasibility. Allen-Browne, Patricia, ed. (Illus.). 448p. 1983. 31.95 (ISBN 0-07-022470-6, P&RB). McGraw.

Fritz, Jan & Billson, Janet M., eds. Clinical Sociology Review. 143p. 1982. pap. 10.50 (ISBN 0-942756-00-2). GU Clin Soc.

Fritz, Jean. And Then What Happened, Paul Revere? (Illus.). 48p. (gr. 2-6). 1973. 8.95 (ISBN 0-698-20274-0, Coward). Putnam Pub Group.

--The Animals of Doctor Schweitzer. (Illus.). (gr. 3-5). 1958. PLB 3.86 o.p. (ISBN 0-698-30013-0, Coward). Putnam Pub Group.

--Brady. (Illus.). (gr. 4-8). 1960. 7.95 (ISBN 0-698-20014-4, Coward). Putnam Pub Group.

--Brendan the Navigator. LC 78-13247. (Illus.). (gr. 2-5). 1979. 7.95 (ISBN 0-698-20473-5). Putnam Pub Group.

--The Cabin Faced West. (Illus.). (gr. 4-7). 1958. 8.95 (ISBN 0-698-20016-0, Coward). Putnam Pub Group.

--Can't You Make Them Behave, King George? (Illus.). 48p. 1982. pap. 4.95 (ISBN 0-698-20542-1, Coward). Putnam Pub Group.

--Early Thunder. (Illus.). (gr. 7-11). 1967. 9.95 (ISBN 0-698-20036-5, Coward). Putnam Pub Group.

--George Washington's Breakfast. (Illus.). (gr. 2-6). 1969. PLB 5.99 (ISBN 0-698-30099-8, Coward). Putnam Pub Group.

--The Good Giants & The Bad Pukwudgies. (Illus.). 40p. 1982. 10.95 (ISBN 0-399-20870-4); pap. 5.95 (ISBN 0-399-20871-2). Putnam Pub Group.

--Homesick: My Own Story. (Illus.). 176p. 1982. 9.95 (ISBN 0-399-20933-6). Putnam Pub Group.

--The Man Who Loved Books. (Illus.). 48p. (gr. 7-11). 1981. 8.95 (ISBN 0-399-20715-5). Putnam Pub Group.

--Stonewall. (Illus.). 1979. 8.95 (ISBN 0-399-20698-1); pap. 3.95 (ISBN 0-399-20699-X). Putnam Pub Group.

--Traitor: The Case of Benedict Arnold. (Illus.). 1981. 9.95 (ISBN 0-399-20834-8). Putnam Pub Group.

--What's the Big Idea, Ben Franklin? (Illus.). 48p. (gr. 2-6). 1982. pap. 4.95 (ISBN 0-698-20543-X, Coward). Putnam Pub Group.

--Where Do You Think You're Going, Christopher Columbus? (Illus.). (gr. 3-7). 1980. 8.95 (ISBN 0-399-20723-6); pap. 3.95 (ISBN 0-399-20734-1). Putnam Pub Group.

--Where Was Patrick Henry on the Twenty-ninth of May? (Illus.). 48p. 1982. pap. 4.95 (ISBN 0-698-20544-8, Coward). Putnam Pub Group.

--Where Was Patrick Henry on the 29th of May? (Illus.). 48p. (gr. 3-5). 1975. 8.95 (ISBN 0-698-20307-0, Coward). Putnam Pub Group.

--Where Was Patrick Henry on the 29th of May? (Illus.). (gr. 3-5). 1982. pap. 4.95 (ISBN 0-698-20544-8, Coward). Putnam Pub Group.

--Who's That Stepping on Plymouth Rock? LC 74-30593. (Illus.). 32p. (gr. 2-6). 1975. 8.95 (ISBN 0-698-20325-9, Coward). Putnam Pub Group.

--Why Don't You Get a Horse, Sam Adams? (Illus.). 48p. (gr. 2-6). 1974. 8.95 (ISBN 0-698-20292-9, Coward). Putnam Pub Group.

--Why Don't You Get a Horse, Sam Adams? (Illus.). 48p. 1982. pap. 4.95 (ISBN 0-698-20545-6, Coward). Putnam Pub Group.

--Why Don't You Get a Horse, Sam Adams? (Illus.). (gr. 2-6). 1982. pap. 4.95 (ISBN 0-698-20545-6, Coward). Putnam Pub Group.

--Will You Sign Here, John Hancock? LC 75-33243. (Illus.). 48p. (gr. 2-6). 1976. 8.95 (ISBN 0-698-20308-9, Coward). Putnam Pub Group.

Fritz, Leah. Dreamers & Dealers: An Intimate Appraisal of the Women's Movement. LC 78-73852. 350p. 1979. pap. 5.95 (ISBN 0-8070-3793-1, BP-604). Beacon Pr.

Fritz, N. Business Record-keeping Practice Set. 2nd ed. 1974. text ed. 5.48 o.p. (ISBN 0-07-022482-X, G); tchr's. manual & key 2.50 o.p. (ISBN 0-07-022487-0). McGraw.

--Service Station Recordkeeping: A Practice Set. 1968. 11.16 (ISBN 0-07-022474-9, G); tchr's manual & key 4.95 (ISBN 0-07-022476-5). McGraw.

Fritz, N. & Hoffman, F. Accounting Fundamentals Text-Kit. 2nd ed. 1971. 19.10 (ISBN 0-07-022498-6, G). McGraw.

Fritz, N. & Wirth, R. H. Supersonic Sounds: A Business Record-Keeping Practice Set. 3rd ed. 1981. text ed. 5.96 (ISBN 0-07-022562-1); tchr's manual & key avail. McGraw.

Fritz, P. & Fontes, J. C. Terrestrial Environment. (Handbook of Environmental Isotope Geochemistry Ser.: Vol. 1). 1980. 85.00 (ISBN 0-444-41780-X). Elsevier.

Fritz, Robert E., jt. auth. see Saxon, James A.

Fritzhand, James. The Innocent Dark. (Orig.). 1983. pap. 3.75 (ISBN 0-440-03852-9). Dell.

--Natural Acts. 1979. pap. 2.50 o.p. (ISBN 0-451-08603-1, E8603, Sig). NAL.

--Third Avenue. (Orig.). 1979. pap. 2.75 o.s.i. (ISBN 0-515-05787-8). Jove Pubns.

Fritzhand, James & Glickman, Frank. The Unicorn Affair. (Orig.). 1981. pap. 2.50 o.p. (ISBN 0-451-09605-3, E9605, Sig). NAL.

Fritzsch, Harald. Quarks: The Stuff of Matter. (Illus.). 1983. 19.00 (ISBN 0-465-06781-6). Basic.

Fritzsch, Karl E. & Bachmann, Manfred. An Illustrated History of German Toys. (Illus.). 1978. 22.50 o.p. (ISBN 0-8038-3417-9). Hastings.

Frizen, Edwin L., Jr., jt. auth. see Coggins, Wade T.

Frizzell-Smith, Dorothy B. & Andrews, Eva L., eds. Subject Index to Poetry for Children & Young People 1957-1975. LC 77-3296. 1977. 45.00 (ISBN 0-8389-0242-1). ALA.

Frizzi, Richard J., jt. auth. see Crinklaw, Frances.

Frobel, Folker, et al. The New International Division of Labour: Structural Unemployment in Industrialised Countries & Industrialisation in Developing Countries. LC 78-72087. (Studies in Modern Capitalism). (Illus.). 448p. 1982. pap. 17.95 (ISBN 0-521-28720-0). Cambridge U Pr.

--The New International Division of Labour. Burgess, P., tr. from Ger. LC 78-72087. (Studies in Modern Capitalism). (Illus.). 1980. 69.50 (ISBN 0-521-22319-9). Cambridge U Pr.

Frobenius, Lore. Ferner Als der Fernste Stern. 1968. pap. text ed. 3.00x o.p. (ISBN 0-435-38320-5). Heinemann Ed.

--Das Safarikleid. 1968. pap. text ed. 3.00x o.p. (ISBN 0-435-38321-3). Heinemann Ed.

Frobish, Dieter & Lamprecht, Hartmut. Graphic Photo Design. LC 77-81319. (Illus.). 1978. 14.95 o.p. (ISBN 0-8174-2434-2, Amphoto). Watson-Guptill.

Frocht, M. M. Photoelasticity, Vol. 2. 1948. 57.95x o.p. (ISBN 0-471-28281-2, Pub. by Wiley-Interscience). Wiley.

Frodsham, J. D., tr. The First Chinese Embassy to the West: The Journals of Kuo Sung-Tao, Liu Hsi-Hung & Chang Te-Yi. (Illus.). 1974. 24.00x o.p. (ISBN 0-19-821555-X). Oxford U Pr.

Frodsham, J. D., tr. see He, Li.

Froe, Otis D. & Otyce, B. The Easy Way to Better Grades. LC 73-76959. 176p. 1959. 4.95 (ISBN 0-668-03353-3); pap. 2.95 (ISBN 0-668-03352-5). Arco.

Froebe, Doris J. & Bain. Quality Assurance Programs & Controls in Nursing. LC 76-165. (Illus.). 161p. 1976. pap. 9.95 o.p. (ISBN 0-8016-1695-6). Mosby.

Froehlich, A. Gelois Module Structure of Algebraic Integers. (Ergebnisse der Mathematik und Ihrer Grenzgebiete Ser. 3. Folge.: Vol. 1). 280p. 1983. 32.00 (ISBN 0-387-11920-5). Springer-Verlag.

Froehlich, Allan F. Managing the Data Center. (Data Processing). (Illus.). 298p. 1982. 28.00 (ISBN 0-534-97942-4). Lifetime Learn.

Froehlich, John P. TRS-80 More than BASIC. 1981. pap. 10.95 (ISBN 0-672-21813-5). Sams.

Froehlich, Margaret W. Hide Crawford Quick. LC 82-21184. 176p. (gr. 5 up). 1983. 9.95 (ISBN 0-395-33884-0). HM.

Froehlich, Werner & Smith, Gudmund, eds. Psychological Processes in Cognition & Personality. LC 82-21230. (Clinical & Community Psychology Ser.). (Illus.). 425p. 1983. text ed. 39.95 (ISBN 0-89116-243-7). Hemisphere Pub.

Froelich, Robert E., et al. Communication in the Dental Office: A Programmed Manual for the Dental Professional. (Illus.). 152p. 1976. pap. 11.95 o.p. (ISBN 0-8016-1698-0). Mosby.

Froese, Paraskeras. Structures & Function of FC Receptors. (Receptors Ser.). 376p. 1983. price not set (ISBN 0-8247-1814-3). Dekker.

Froese, Victor & Straw, Stanley B., eds. Research in the Language Arts. 336p. 1981. pap. text ed. 19.95 (ISBN 0-8391-1609-8). Univ Park.

Froger, Francois. Relation d'un Voyage Fait en 1695, 1696, et 1697 aux Cotes d'Afrique Detroit de Magellan, Brezil, Cayenne, et Antilles. (Bibliotheque Africaine Ser.). 260p. (Fr.). 1974. Repr. of 1698 ed. lib. bdg. 70.50x o.p. (ISBN 0-8287-0358-2, 72-2122). Clearwater Pub.

Frohlich, Edward D., et al, eds. Cardiovascular Drugs. LC 74-12714. (Principles & Techniques of Human Research & Therapeutics Ser.: Vol. 5). (Illus.). 256p. 1974. 15.00 o.p. (ISBN 0-87993-047-0). Futura Pub.

Frohlich, Margaret, jt. auth. see Niederhauser, Hans R.

Frohlichstein, Jack. Mathematical Fun, Games & Puzzles. (Illus., Orig.). 1962. pap. 4.50 (ISBN 0-486-20789-7). Dover.

Frohock, Fred M. Public Policy: Scope & Logic. LC 78-8382. 1979. 22.95 (ISBN 0-13-737932-3). P-H.

Frohock, Wilbur M. French Literature: An Approach Through Close Reading. 4th ed. 1970. 4.95 (ISBN 0-87774-000-3). Schoenhof.

Frohr. Introduction to Electronic Control Engineering. 1981. 42.95 (ISBN 0-471-26200-5, Wiley Heyden). Wiley.

Froiland, Sven G. Natural History of the Black Hills. LC 78-55071. (Illus.). pap. 5.95 (ISBN 0-931170-06-0); pap. 8.95 2d printing. Ctr Western Studies.

Frolich, J. C., ed. Methods in Prostaglandin Research. LC 78-66346. (Advances in Prostaglandin & Thromboxane Research: Vol. 5). 256p. 1978. 32.00 (ISBN 0-89004-204-7). Raven.

Frolick, N. J. & Oppenheimer, J. Modern Political Economy. 1978. pap. 9.95 (ISBN 0-13-597120-9). P-H.

Frolick, S. J. Once There Was a President. rev. ed. LC 80-69972. (Once There Was... Ser.). 64p. (gr. 3-7). 1980. pap. 6.95 (ISBN 0-9605426-0-4). Black Star Pub.

Frolkis, V. V. Aging & Life-Prolonging Processes. (Illus.). 380p. 1983. 39.20 (ISBN 0-387-81685-2). Springer-Verlag.

From, Lester D. & Staver, Allen E. Fundamentals of Weather: A Workbook Approach. 1979. pap. text ed. 15.95 (ISBN 0-8403-2023-X). Kendall-Hunt.

Froman, Katherine. Chance to Grow. 1983. 13.95 (ISBN 0-89696-192-3). Dodd.

--The Chance to Grow. 224p. 1983. 13.95 (ISBN 0-89696-192-3). Everest Hse.

Froman, Robert. Angles Are Easy As Pie. LC 75-6608. (Young Math Ser). (Illus.). 40p. (gr. k-3). 1976. PLB 10.89 (ISBN 0-690-00916-X, TYC-J). Har-Row.

--Arithmetic for Human Beings. 1974. 5.95 o.s.i. (ISBN 0-671-21617-1, Fireside). S&S.

--A Game of Functions. LC 74-2266. (Young Math Ser.). (Illus.). 40p. (gr. k-3). 1974. 6.95 o.p. (ISBN 0-690-00544-X, TYC-J); PLB 10.89 (ISBN 0-690-00545-8). Har-Row.

--The Greatest Guessing Game. LC 77-5463. (A Young Math Book). (Illus.). (gr. 1-3). 1978. PLB 10.89 (ISBN 0-690-01376-0, TYC-J). Har-Row.

--Less Than Nothing Is Really Something. LC 72-7546. (Young Math Ser). (Illus.). (gr. 1-5). 1973. 10.53i (ISBN 0-690-48862-9, TYC-J). Har-Row.

--Mushrooms & Molds. LC 71-187936. (A Let's-Read-&-Find-Out Science Book). (Illus.). (gr. k-3). 1972. PLB 10.89 (ISBN 0-690-56603-4, TYC-J). Har-Row.

--Rubber Bands, Baseballs & Doughnuts: A Book About Topology. LC 74-158690. (Young Math Ser). (Illus.). (gr. 1-4). 1972. 9.57i (ISBN 0-690-71353-3, TYC-J); PLB 10.89 (ISBN 0-690-71354-1). Har-Row.

--Seeing Things: A Book of Poems. LC 73-18494. 64p. (gr. 5-9). 1974. 9.57i (ISBN 0-690-00291-2, TYC-J). Har-Row.

--Venn Diagrams. LC 75-187937. (Young Math Ser). (Illus.). (gr. 1-5). 1972. 4.50 o.p. (ISBN 0-690-85996-1, TYC-J); PLB 10.89 (ISBN 0-690-85997-X). Har-Row.

Frome, Michael. The Forest Service. (Federal Departments, Agencies, & Systems). 300p. 1983. lib. bdg. 25.00 (ISBN 0-86531-177-3). Westview.

--Hosteling U. S. A. The Offical American Youth Hostels Handbook. rev. ed. LC 80-27546. (Illus.). 250p. (Orig.). 1981. pap. 6.95 o.p. (ISBN 0-914788-33-7). East Woods.

--National Park Guide, LC 77-4075. 1983. pap. 8.95 (ISBN 0-528-84277-3). Rand.

Froment, G., jt. auth. see Delman, B.

Froment, G. F., ed. Large Chemical Plants. (Chemical Engineering Monographs: Vol. 10). 190p. 1979. 47.50 (ISBN 0-444-41837-7). Elsevier.

Froment, Gilbert F. & Bischoff, Kenneth B. Chemical Reactor Analysis & Design. LC 78-12465. 765p. 1979. text ed. 43.95x (ISBN 0-471-02447-3). Wiley.

Fromer, Margaret & Keyes, Sharrel. Genesis 1-25: Walking with God. rev. ed. (Fisherman Bible Studyguides). 1979. saddle-stitched 2.50 (ISBN 0-87788-297-5). Shaw Pubs.

--Genesis 26-50: Called by God. rev. ed. (Fisherman Bible Studyguides). 1979. pap. 2.50 saddle-stitched (ISBN 0-87788-298-3). Shaw Pubs.

--Let's Pray Together. LC 74-76160. (Fisherman Bible Studyguide Ser.). 1974. saddle-stitched 2.25 (ISBN 0-87788-801-9). Shaw Pubs.

--Letters to the Thessalonians. LC 75-33441. (Fisherman Bible Studyguides). 1975. saddle-stitched 2.50 (ISBN 0-87788-489-7). Shaw Pubs.

--Letters to Timothy: Discipleship in Action. LC 74-19763. (Fisherman Bible Study Guides). 1974. saddle-stitched 2.50 (ISBN 0-87788-490-0). Shaw Pubs.

Fromer, Margaret & Nystrom, Carolyn. James: Roadmap for Down-to-Earth Christians. (Young Fisherman Bible Studyguides). (Illus.). 96p. 1982. saddle-stiched tchr's. ed. 3.95 (ISBN 0-87788-420-X); student ed. 2.95 (ISBN 0-87788-419-6). Shaw Pubs.

Fromer, Margaret, jt. auth. see Nystrom, Carolyn.

Fromer, Margot J. Community Health Care & the Nursing Process. 2nd ed. (Illus.). 498p. 1983. pap. text ed. 21.95 (ISBN 0-8016-1725-1). Mosby.

--Ethical Issues in Sexuality & Reproduction. 320p. 1983. pap. text ed. 13.95 (ISBN 0-8016-1708-1). Mosby.

Fromer, Margot J., jt. auth. see Conn, Frances G.

Fromhold, A., Jr. Theory of Metal Oxidation Vol. 2: Space Charge. (Defects in Crystalline Solids Ser.: Vol. 12). 70.25 (ISBN 0-444-85381-2, North-Holland). Elsevier.

Fromhold, A. T. Theory of Metal Oxidation, Vol. 1: Fundamentals. LC 75-23121. (Defects in Crystalline Solids: Vol. 9). (Illus.). 106.50 (ISBN 0-444-10957-9, North-Holland). Elsevier.

Fromm, David. Complications of Gastric Surgery. LC 77-9313. (Clinical Gastroenterology Monographs). 1977. 47.50x (ISBN 0-471-28291-X, Pub. by Wiley Medical). Wiley.

Fromm, Erich. The Art of Loving. 128p. 1974. pap. 3.80i (ISBN 0-06-080291-X, P291, PL). Har-Row.

--Art of Loving: An Enquiry into the Nature of Love. LC 56-8750. (World Perspectives Ser.). 1956. 11.49i (ISBN 0-06-011375-8, HarpT). Har-Row.

--The Greatness & Limitations of Freud's Thought. LC 79-2730. 1980. 11.49i (ISBN 0-06-011389-8, HarpT). Har-Row.

--To Have or to Be? LC 73-130449. (World Perspectives). 1976. 13.41i (ISBN 0-06-011379-0, HarpT). Har-Row.

Fromm, Erich, et al. Zen Buddhism & Psychoanalysis. LC 60-5293. 1970. pap. 4.76i (ISBN 0-06-090175-6, CN175, CN). Har-Row.

Fromm, Gary, ed. Studies in Public Regulation. (Regulation of Economic Activity Ser.). (Illus.). 400p. 1981. 49.50x (ISBN 0-262-06074-4). MIT Pr.

Fromm, Hermann. Deutschland in der Offentlichen Kriegszieldiskussion Grossbritanniens 1939-1945. 167p. 1982. write for info. P Lang Pubs.

Fromme, Allan. The Book for Normal Neurotics. LC 78-68156. Date not set. cancelled (ISBN 0-686-58202-0, G&D). Putnam Pub Group.

Frommer. New York on Ten & Fifteen Dollars a Day. reev. ed. (Frommer Travel Guides). (Illus.). 1976. 3.95 (ISBN 0-671-10851-4, Fireside). S&S.
--New Zealand & Austrailia on Ten Dollars a Day: 1976-1977. (Frommer Travel Guides). (Illus.). 1976. pap. 3.95 o.s.i. (ISBN 0-671-10955-3, Fireside). S&S.
--Turkey on Ten Dollars a Day: 1976-1977. rev. ed. (Frommer Travel Guides). (Illus.). 1976. 3.95 o.p. (ISBN 0-671-10947-2, Fireside). S&S.
--Washington, D.C. on Ten & Fifteen Dollars a Day: 1976-1977. rev. ed. (Frommer Travel Guides). (Illus.). 1976. 3.95 o.p. (ISBN 0-671-10948-0, Fireside). S&S.
Frommer & Pasmantier. England on Fifteen Dollars a Day. pap. 4.50 o.p. (ISBN 0-671-22719-X, Fireside). S&S.
--Mexico & Guatemala on Ten Dollars a Day. 1977. pap. 4.95 (ISBN 0-671-10893-X, Fireside). S&S.
--South America on Ten Dollars a Day. 1976. pap. 3.95 o.p. (ISBN 0-671-10898-0, Fireside). S&S.
--The Whole World Handbook. 4th rev. ed. (Illus.). 1976. 2.95 o.p. (ISBN 0-671-10950-2, Fireside). S&S.
Frommer & Pastmantier. Scandinavia on Twenty Dollars a Day. 1977. pap. 4.50 o.p. (ISBN 0-671-22717-3, Fireside). S&S.
Frommer, Arthur. Athens. 1977. pap. 1.95 o.p. (ISBN 0-686-67673-4, Fireside). S&S.
--Boston. 1977. write for info. o.p. (ISBN 0-685-76249-1, Fireside); pap. 1.95 o.p. (ISBN 0-686-66172-9). S&S.
--Dollar-Wise Guide to California (with Las Vegas) 1977. pap. 4.50 o.p. (ISBN 0-671-22724-6, Fireside). S&S.
--Dollar-Wise Guide to Germany: 1976-1977. (Illus.). 1976. 3.95 o.p. (ISBN 0-671-10957-X, Fireside). S&S.
--Dollar-Wise Guide to Italy. 1977. pap. 4.50 o.p. (ISBN 0-671-22725-4, Fireside). S&S.
--Dollar-Wise Guide to Japan & Hong Kong. 1976-1977. (Illus.). 1976. 3.95 o.p. (ISBN 0-671-10958-8, Fireside). S&S.
--Dollar-Wise Guide to Portugal: 1976-1977. (Frommer Travel Guides). (Illus.). 1976. pap. 3.95 o.p. (ISBN 0-671-10956-1, Fireside). S&S.
--Honolulu. 1977. pap. 1.95 o.p. (ISBN 0-671-22734-3, Fireside). S&S.
--Ireland on Ten Dollars a Day. 1977. 3.95 o.p. (ISBN 0-671-10894-8, Fireside). S&S.
--Las Vegas. 1977. pap. 1.95 o.p. (ISBN 0-671-22731-9, Fireside). S&S.
--Lisbon-Madrid-Costa Del Sol. 1977. pap. 1.95 o.p. (ISBN 0-686-67674-2, Fireside). S&S.
--London. 1977. pap. 1.95 o.p. (ISBN 0-671-22736-X, Fireside). S&S.
--Los Angeles. 1977. pap. 1.95 o.p. (ISBN 0-671-22733-5, Fireside). S&S.
--New York. 1977. pap. 1.95 o.p. (ISBN 0-671-22728-9, Fireside). S&S.
--Rome. 1977. pap. 1.95 o.p. (ISBN 0-671-22737-8, Fireside). S&S.
--San Francisco. 1977. pap. 1.95 o.p. (ISBN 0-685-76253-X, Fireside). S&S.
--Spain on Ten Dollars a Day. 1977. pap. 4.50 o.p. (ISBN 0-671-22726-2, Fireside). S&S.
--Washington D.C. 1977. pap. 1.95 o.p. (ISBN 0-686-67671-8, Fireside). S&S.
Frommer, E., tr. see Boos-Hamberger, Hilde.
Frommer, E. A., et al, trs. see Steiner, Rudolf.
Frommer, Harvey. Baseball's Greatest Records, Streaks & Feats. LC 82-45939. 208p. 1983. 13.95 (ISBN 0-689-11385-4). Atheneum.
--Sports Lingo: A Dictionary of the Language of Sports. LC 82-12130. 312p. 1983. pap. 7.95 (ISBN 0-689-70640-5, 289). Atheneum.
Frommer, Herbert H. Radiology in Dental Practice. LC 81-38411. (Illus.). 303p. 1981. text ed. 34.50 (ISBN 0-8016-1709-X). Mosby.
Frommer, L., ed. see Kalimtgis, Konstandinos, et al.
Frompovich, Catherine J. The Fox in Shangri-La. 32p. (ps-2). 1978. tchr's. ed. 0.69 (ISBN 0-935322-01-9). C J Frompovich.
--Kids Cooking Naturally. (Illus.). 32p. (gr. 2-5). 1979. pap. 1.50 (ISBN 0-935322-04-3). C J Frompovich.
--Natural & Nutritious Cooking Course. 94p. 1982. lab manual 50.00 (ISBN 0-935322-21-3). C J Frompovich.
--Upgrading Decision Making. Koppenhaver, April M., ed. (Illus.). 24p. 1982. pap. text ed. 4.00 (ISBN 0-935322-16-7). C J Frompovich.
Frompovich, Catherine J., jt. auth. see Hoffman, Taryn.
Frondel, Judith W. Lunar Mineralogy. LC 75-9786. 323p. 1975. 37.50 o.p. (ISBN 0-471-28289-8, Pub. by Wiley-Interscience). Wiley.
Frondizi, Risieri. What Is Value? An Introduction to Axiology. 2nd ed. Lipp, Solomon, tr. from Sp. LC 70-128196. xi, 183p. 1971. 16.00 (ISBN 0-87548-076-4); pap. 6.00 (ISBN 0-87548-077-2). Open Court.
Front, D., jt. auth. see Penning, L.
Frontado, Jose R. Alejandro E Isabel. 96p. (Span.). 1981. pap. 2.75 (ISBN 0-311-37024-1, Edit Mundo). Casa Bautista.
Fronval, George & Dubois, Daniel. Indian Signs & Signals. Egan, E. W., tr. LC 78-57792. (Illus.). (gr. 3 up). 1978. 16.95 (ISBN 0-8069-2720-8); PLB 19.99 (ISBN 0-8069-2721-6). Sterling.
Fronza, G., ed. Mathematical Models for Planning & Controlling Air Quality: Proceedings, Vol. 17. 255p. 1982. 50.00 (ISBN 0-08-029950-4). Pergamon.
Froomkin, Joseph & Jamison, Dean T., eds. Education As an Industry. LC 76-29631. (National Bureau Conference Ser.: No. 28). 504p. 1977. prof ref 28.00x (ISBN 0-88410-476-1). Ballinger Pub.
Frosch, John. The Psychotic Process. 1983. write for info (ISBN 0-8236-5690-X). Intl Univs Pr.
Frosch, P. J., jt. auth. see Wendt, H.
Frosch, Peter J., tr. see Nasemann, Theodor.
Frossart, Benjamin-Sigismond. La Cause des Esclaves Negres et des Habitants de la Guinee, 2 vols. (Slave Trade in France, 1744-1848, Ser.). 359p. (Fr.). 1974. Repr. of 1789 ed. Set. lib. bdg. 189.50 o.p. (ISBN 0-8287-0359-0, TN111-2). Clearwater Pub.
Frost, Carol. The Fearful Child. LC 82-25861. 59p. (Orig.). 1983. pap. 5.00 (ISBN 0-87886-121-1). Ithaca Hse.
--Liar's Dice. LC 78-16125. 72p. 1978. 3.50 (ISBN 0-87886-098-3). Ithaca Hse.
Frost, Carolyn O. Cataloging Nonbook Materials: Problems in Theory & Practice. Dowell, Arlene T., ed. 350p. 1983. 28.50 (ISBN 0-87287-329-3). Libs Unl.
Frost, Charles. Viennese Waltz. pap. 3.00x (ISBN 0-392-16820-0, SpS). Sportshelf.
Frost, D. L., ed. Selected Plays of Thomas Middleton. LC 77-23339. (Plays by Renaissance & Restoration Dramatists Ser.). 1978. 47.50 (ISBN 0-521-21698-2); pap. 12.95 (ISBN 0-521-29236-0). Cambridge U Pr.
Frost, David & Deakin, Michael. David Frost's Book of the World's Worst Decisions. (Illus.). 1983. 9.95 (ISBN 0-517-54977-8). Crown.
Frost, E. L., jt. auth. see Hoebel, Edward A.
Frost, Everett L. Archaeological Excavations of Fortified Sites on Taveuni, Fiji. (Social Science & Linguistics Institute Special Publications). (Illus.). 1974. pap. 6.00x (ISBN 0-8248-0266-7). UH Pr.
Frost, Gavin & Frost, Yvonne. Meta Psychometry: Key to Power & Abundance. (Illus.). 1977. 9.95 o.p. (ISBN 0-13-578583-9, Parker). P-H.
--Power Secrets from a Sorcerer's Private Magnum Arcanum. (Illus.). 1980. 14.95 o.p. (ISBN 0-13-687251-4, Parker). P-H.
--A Witch's Guide to Life. 1982. 5.00 (ISBN 0-686-97352-6). Esoteric Pubns.
Frost, Gerhard E. Bless My Growing: For Parents, Teachers, & Others Who Learn. LC 74-77680. (Illus.). 96p. 1975. pap. 4.50 (ISBN 0-8066-1431-5, 10-0770). Augsburg.
--Color of the Night: Reflections on the Book of Job. LC 77-72458. 1977. pap. 4.50 (ISBN 0-8066-1583-4, 10-1520). Augsburg.
Frost, H. J. & Ashby, M. F. Deformation-Mechanism Maps: The Plasticity & Creep of Metals & Ceramics. (Illus.). 184p. 1982. 45.00 (ISBN 0-08-029338-7); pap. 25.00 (ISBN 0-08-029337-9). Pergamon.
Frost, H. M., jt. ed. see De Luca, Hector F.
Frost, J. M., ed. World Radio & TV Handbook: A Complete Directory of International Radio & Television. 500p. 1978. pap. 14.95 o.p. (ISBN 0-8230-5904-9, Billboard Bks). Watson-Guptill.
Frost, J. William see Weaver, Glenn.
Frost, Jack, jt. auth. see Potter, Neil.
Frost, Jane C. Your Future As a Dental Assistant. rev. ed. LC 70-114128. (Career Guidance Ser.). 160p. 1976. pap. 4.50 (ISBN 0-668-02238-8). Arco.
Frost, Jens. World Radio TV Handbook: 1982. (Illus.). 600p. 1983. pap. 17.50 (ISBN 0-8230-5910-3, Billboard Bks). Watson-Guptill.
--World Radio TV Handbook 1983. 600p. 1983. pap. 17.50 (ISBN 0-8230-5910-3, Billboard Pub). Watson-Guptill.
Frost, Jens M., ed. World Radio TV Handbook. 33rd ed. 1979. pap. 14.95 o.p. (ISBN 0-8230-5905-7, Billboard Bks). Watson-Guptill.
Frost, Joan van Every see Van Every Frost, Joan.
Frost, Joe L. & Hawkes, Glenn R. Disadvantaged Child: Issues & Innovations. 2nd ed. LC 70-16422. (Illus., Orig.). 1970. pap. text ed. 17.50 (ISBN 0-395-04475-8). HM.
Frost, John E. Maine Genealogy: A Bibliographical Guide. 1976. pap. 4.00 o.p. (ISBN 0-915592-25-8). Maine Hist.
Frost, Lawrence A. Court-Martial of General George Armstrong Custer. Rev. ed. LC 67-24614. (Illus.). 1982. 7.95 (ISBN 0-8061-1608-0). U of Okla Pr.
--General Custer's Libbie. ltd. ed. LC 76-2682. (Illus.). 450p. 1976. deluxe ed. 24.95 o.s.i. (ISBN 0-87564-806-1). Superior Pub.
Frost, Lesley. New Hampshire's Child: Derry Journals of Lesley Frost. LC 69-12099. (Illus.). 1969. 44.50x (ISBN 0-87395-043-7). State U NY Pr.
Frost, Marie. Adventures with Peter Panda. (gr. k-3). 1978. pap. 1.69 (ISBN 0-87239-184-1, 42044). Standard Pub.
--Characteristics of Preschoolers. (Peter Panda Ser.). 1977. pap. 1.75 (ISBN 0-87239-143-4, 42035). Standard Pub.
--Crafts for Preschoolers. (Peter Panda Ser.). 1977. pap. 1.75 (ISBN 0-87239-144-2, 42036). Standard Pub.
--Effective Visitation. (Peter Panda Ser.). 1977. pap. 1.75 (ISBN 0-87239-145-0, 42037). Standard Pub.
--Fun with Peter Panda. (Illus.). (gr. k-3). 1978. pap. 1.69 (ISBN 0-87239-185-X, 42045). Standard Pub.
--Peter Panda Christian Curriculum for Nursery Schools & Day Care Centers. (Peter Panda Ser.). (Illus.). 144p. 1977. pap. 24.95 (ISBN 0-87239-141-8, 42031). Standard Pub.
--Songs for Preschoolers. (Peter Panda Ser.). 32p. 1977. pap. 1.75 (ISBN 0-87239-146-9, 42038). Standard Pub.
Frost, Marjorie, ed. The Gift of Hymns. 1979. pap. 1.95 o.p. (ISBN 0-916642-12-7). Hope Pub.
Frost, Paul, et al. Managers in Focus. 184p. 1982. text ed. 35.50x (ISBN 0-566-00468-2). Gower Pub Ltd.
Frost, Peter. Exploring Cuzco. (Illus.). 139p. 1981. pap. 7.95 o.p. (ISBN 0-933982-05-4). Bradt Ent.
Frost, Peter J., et al. Organizational Reality: Reports from the Firing Line. 2nd ed. 1982. pap. text ed. 16.50x (ISBN 0-673-16004-1). Scott F.
Frost, Phillip & Horwitz, Steven N. Principles of Cosmetics for the Dermatologist. LC 81-18816. (Illus.). 367p. 1982. pap. text ed. 49.50 (ISBN 0-8016-1713-8). Mosby.
Frost, Reuben B. Physical Education: Foundations, Principles, & Practices. LC 74-10351. 528p. 1975. text ed. 20.95 (ISBN 0-201-02107-2). A-W.
Frost, Richard. The Circus Villains: Poems. LC 65-24647. 55p. 1965. 5.95 (ISBN 0-8214-0010-X, 82-80117). Ohio U Pr.
--Getting Drunk with the Birds. LC 72-141385. 49p. 1971. 5.95 (ISBN 0-8214-0088-6, 82-80927). Ohio U Pr.
Frost, Robert. Set My Spirit Free. LC 73-84475. 234p. 1973. pap. 4.95 (ISBN 0-88270-058-8, Pub. by Logos). Bridge Pub.
--Stopping by Woods on a Snowy Evening. LC 78-8134. (Illus.). 1978. 10.75 (ISBN 0-525-40115-6, 01044-310). Dutton.
--A Swinger of Birches: Poems of Robert Frost for Young People. (Illus.). (gr. 4 up). 1982. 17.95 (ISBN 0-916144-92-5); pap. 9.95 (ISBN 0-916144-93-3). Stemmer Hse.
Frost, S. E. Masterworks of Philosophy, Vol. 3. (Masterworks Ser.). 192p. 1972. Pts. 1-2. pap. 2.45 (ISBN 0-07-040803-3, SP). McGraw.
Frost, S. E., Jr., ed. The Sacred Writings of the Worlds Great Religions. 416p. 1972. pap. 5.95 (ISBN 0-07-022520-6, SP). McGraw.
Frost, T. H. Technical Aspects of Renal Dialysis. LC 78-40089. 1978. 47.95 (ISBN 0-471-04524-1, Pub. by Wiley Medical). Wiley.
Frost, T. W. Price Guide to Old Sheffield Plate. (Illus.). 1978. 22.50 (ISBN 0-902028-07-3). Apollo.
Frost, William P. Transcendental Ethics. 1978. pap. text ed. 6.00 (ISBN 0-8191-0576-7). U Pr of Amer.
--Visions of the Divine. 1977. pap. text ed. 6.50 o.p. (ISBN 0-8191-0310-1). U Pr of Amer.
Frost, Yvonne, jt. auth. see Frost, Gavin.
Frostick, Michael. Aston Martin & Lagonda. 196p. 1981. 50.00x (ISBN 0-686-97069-1, Pub. by D Watson England). State Mutual Bk.
--BMW the Bavarian Motor Works. 207p. 1981. 50.00x (ISBN 0-686-97072-1, Pub. by D Watson England). State Mutual Bk.
--The Mighty Mercedes. 208p. 1981. 50.00x (ISBN 0-686-97073-X, Pub. by D Watson England). State Mutual Bk.
Frothingham, A. W. Hispanic Glass. (Illus.). 1941. pap. 3.00 (ISBN 0-87535-052-6). Hispanic Soc.
--Prehistoric Pottery in the Collection from El Acebuchal: site near Carmona, Province of Sevilla. (Illus.). 1953. pap. 0.60 (ISBN 0-87535-075-5). Hispanic Soc.
Frothingham, R. Life & Times of Joseph Warren. LC 72-146148. (Era of the American Revolution Ser). 1971. Repr. of 1865 ed. lib. bdg. 59.50 (ISBN 0-306-70133-2). Da Capo.
Frothingham, Richard. History of the Siege of Boston & of the Battles of Lexington, Concord & Bunker Hill. LC 77-115680. (Era of the American Revolution Ser). 1970. Repr. of 1903 ed. lib. bdg. 49.50 (ISBN 0-306-71932-0). Da Capo.
Froud, Brian & Llewelyn, J. J. World of the Dark Crystal. LC 81-47572. (Illus.). 128p. 1982. 25.00 (ISBN 0-394-52168-4); pap. 14.95 (ISBN 0-394-71280-3). Knopf.
Froud, Nina, ed. see Montagne, Prosper.
Froude, James A. The Nemesis of Faith, 1849. Wolff, Robert L., ed. Bd. with Shadows of the Clouds, 1847. LC 75-1519. (Victorian Fiction Ser.). 1975. lib. bdg. 66.00 o.s.i. (ISBN 0-8240-1592-4). Garland Pub.
Froula, Christine. A Guide to Ezra Pound's Selected Poems. LC 82-18776. 256p. 1983. 16.50 (ISBN 0-8112-0856-7); pap. 7.25 (ISBN 0-8112-0857-5, NDP548). New Directions.
Frowen, S. F., et al, eds. Monetary Policy & Economic Activity in West Germany. LC 77-2403. 268p. 1977. 64.95x o.s.i. (ISBN 0-470-99131-3). Halsted Pr.
FRS Associates. Pension Asset Management: The Corporate Decision. LC 80-69793. 1980. 6.20 (ISBN 0-910586-36-5). Finan Exec.
Frucht, Richard, ed. Black Society in the New World. 1971. pap. text ed. 3.95 (ISBN 0-685-55623-9, 30181). Phila Bk Co.
Frucht, Richard C. Dunarea Noastra: Romania, the Great Powers, & the Danube Question, 1914-1921. (East European Monographs: No. 113). 256p. 1982. 22.50x (ISBN 0-88033-007-4). East Eur Quarterly.
Fruchtenbaum, Arnold G. Hebrew Christianity. pap. 2.95 o.p. (ISBN 0-8010-3472-8). Baker Bk.
Fruchter, Benjamin, jt. auth. see Guilford, Joy P.
Frueh, Alfred J. Frueh on the Theatre: Theatrical Caricatures, 1906-1962. Silverman, Maxwell, ed. LC 72-83887. (Illus.). 128p. 1972. pap. 12.00 (ISBN 0-87104-235-5). NY Pub Lib.
Fruehling. Relacciones Humanas. 141p. 6.32 (ISBN 0-07-022540-0). McGraw.
Fruehling, James A. Sourcebook on Death & Dying. LC 82-82013. 788p. 1982. write for info. (ISBN 0-8379-5801-6). Marquis.
Fruehling, R. T., jt. auth. see Poe, Roy W.
Fruehling, Rosemary T. Working at Human Relations. Herr, Edwin L., ed. (Cooperative Work Experience Education for Careers Program). (Illus.). (gr. 11-12). 1976. pap. text ed. 7.96 (ISBN 0-07-028331-1, G); tchr's manual & key 3.50 (ISBN 0-07-028332-X). McGraw.
Fruehling, Rosemary T. & Bouchard, Sharon. Art of Writing Effective Letters. 1972. 12.95 (ISBN 0-07-022345-9, GB). McGraw.
--Business Correspondence-Thirty. rev. ed. Tinervia, Joseph, ed. (Illus.). 192p. (gr. 10-12). 1981. pap. text ed. 7.96 (ISBN 0-07-022513-3); tchrs. manual & key 6.12 (ISBN 0-07-022514-1). McGraw.
--Business Correspondence Thirty. 1971. pap. 7.24 o.p. (ISBN 0-07-022340-8, G). McGraw.
--Business Corresopndence Thirty. 2nd ed. (Illus.). (gr. 11-12). 1976. pap. 7.96 o.p. (ISBN 0-07-022342-4, G); tchr's manual & key 6.56 o.p. (ISBN 0-07-022343-2). McGraw.
Fruehling, Rosemary T., jt. auth. see Poe, Roy W.
Fruhan, William E., Jr. The Fight for Competitive Advantage: A Study of the United States Domestic Trunk Air Carriers. LC 71-187108. (Illus.). 200p. 1972. 9.00x (ISBN 0-87584-097-3). Harvard Busn.
Frumkin, Gene. Clouds & Red Earth. LC 82-75683. viii, 67p. 1982. 15.95x (ISBN 0-8040-0418-8); pap. 6.95 (ISBN 0-8040-0375-0). Swallow.
Frush, James, Jr. & Eshenbach, Benson. The Retirement Residence: An Analysis of the Architecture & Management of Life-Care Housing. 116p. 1968. photocopy ed. spiral 11.75x (ISBN 0-398-00626-1). C C Thomas.
Fruton, Joseph S. A Bio-Bibliography for the History of the Biochemical Sciences Since 1800. LC 82-72158. 1982. 20.00 (ISBN 0-87169-983-4). Am Philos.
--Molecules & Life: Historical Essays on the Interplay of Chemistry & Biology. LC 72-3095. 579p. 1972. 17.00 o.p. (ISBN 0-471-28448-3, Pub. by Wiley-Interscience). Wiley.
Fruzetti, Lina, jt. auth. see Ostor, Akos.
Fruzzetti, Lina M. The Gift of a Virgin: Women, Marriage & Ritual in a Bengali Society. (Illus.). 170p. Date not set. 22.50 (ISBN 0-8135-0939-4). Rutgers U Pr.
Fry. Data Processing. 1983. text ed. price not set (ISBN 0-408-01171-8). Butterworth.
--Further Computer Appreciation. 1977. 15.95 (ISBN 0-408-00239-5). Butterworth.
--Ultrasound: Its Applications in Biology & Medicine, 2 Vols. (Methods & Phenomena Ser.: Vol. 3). 1978. Set. 110.75 (ISBN 0-444-41641-2). Elsevier.
Fry, Alan. Survival in the Wilderness: A Practical, All-Season Guide to Traditional Woodlore & Survival Techniques. (Illus.). 288p. Date not set. pap. 9.50 (ISBN 0-525-93248-8, 0922-280). Dutton. Postponed.
--The Wilderness Survival Handbook: A Practical, All-Season Guide to Short Trip Preparation & Survival Techniques for Hikers, Skiers, Backpackers, Canoeists, Travelers in Light Aircraft & Anyone Stranded in the Bush. (Illus.). 304p. 1982. 15.95 (ISBN 0-312-87951-2); pap. 8.95 (ISBN 0-312-87952-0). St Martin.
Fry, Bernard M. & White, Herbert S. Publishers & Libraries: The Study of Scholarly & Research Journals. (Illus.). 1976. 19.95x (ISBN 0-669-00886-9). Lexington Bks.
Fry, C. George, jt. auth. see Arnold, Duane W.
Fry, Charles R. Art Deco Interiors in Color. LC 77-75887. (Illus.). 1977. pap. 6.00 (ISBN 0-486-23527-0). Dover.
Fry, Christine, ed. Aging in Culture & Society: Comparative Viewpoints & Strategies. (Illus.). 336p. 1980. 29.95x (ISBN 0-686-75097-7); pap. text ed. 12.95x (ISBN 0-89789-001-9). J F Bergin.
Fry, Christine L., ed. Aging in Culture & Society: Comparative Viewpoints & Strategies. LC 79-13198. 1980. 33.95 (ISBN 0-03-052726-0). Praeger.
Fry, Christopher. Dark Is Light Enough. 1954. 7.95x (ISBN 0-19-500155-9). Oxford U Pr.
--The Lady's Not for Burning, A Phoenix Too Frequent, & an Essay, "An Experience of Critics". 1977. pap. 6.95 (ISBN 0-19-519916-2, 507, GB). Oxford U Pr.
--Venus Observed. 1950. 7.95x (ISBN 0-19-500395-0). Oxford U Pr.
Fry, Christopher, tr. see Anouilh, Jean.
Fry, Christopher see Ibsen, Henrik.

Fry, Dennis B. Acoustic Phonetics: A Course of Basic Reading. (Illus.). 1976. 44.50 (ISBN 0-521-21393-2). Cambridge U Pr.
--Homo Loquens. LC 77-5134. (Illus.). 1977. 27.95 (ISBN 0-521-21705-9); pap. 7.95x (ISBN 0-521-29239-5). Cambridge U Pr.
--The Physics of Speech. LC 78-56752. (Textbooks in Linguistics Ser.). (Illus.). 1979. 29.95 (ISBN 0-521-22173-0); pap. 9.95x (ISBN 0-521-29379-0). Cambridge U Pr.
Fry, E. A., jt. auth. see Phillimore, William P.
Fry, Earl H. Canadian Government & Politics in Comparative Perspective. LC 78-61913. (Illus.). 1978. pap. text ed. 10.75 o.p. (ISBN 0-8191-0627-5). U Pr of Amer.
--Financial Invasion of the U. S. A. A Threat to American Society? (Illus.). 1979. 15.95 (ISBN 0-07-022591-5). McGraw.
--The Politics of International Investment. 224p. 1983. 24.95 (ISBN 0-07-022610-5, P&RB). McGraw.
Fry, Earl H. & Raymond, Gregory A. The Other Western Europe: A Political Analysis of the Smaller Democracies. 2nd ed. Merkl, Peter H., ed. (Studies in International & Comparative Politics Ser.: No. 14). 275p. 1982. lib. bdg. 19.75 (ISBN 0-87436-345-4); pap. text ed. 9.95 (ISBN 0-87436-346-2). Abc-Clio.
Fry, Edmund. Pantographia: Excerpts form the Original Work. 37p. 1982. pap. 2.95 (ISBN 0-912526-31-9). Lib Res.
Fry, Edward. Reading Instruction for Classroom & Clinic. (Illus.). 448p. 1972. text ed. 22.50 (ISBN 0-07-022604-0, C). McGraw.
--Skimming & Scanning. (Illus.). (gr. 7-10). 1978. pap. text ed. 6.00x (ISBN 0-89061-123-8, 781). Jamestown Pubs.
Fry, Edward, jt. auth. see Sakiey, Elizabeth.
Fry, Edward B. Barco de Vela en el Viento: Sailboat in the Wind. Gunning, Monica, tr. (Storybooks for Beginners Ser.: Bk. 4). (Illus.). 15p. (Eng. & Span.). (gr. 1). 1980. pap. 12.00 (ISBN 0-89061-215-3, 432). Jamestown Pubs.
--Dictionary Drills. 128p. (gr. 7-10). 1980. pap. text ed. 6.00x (ISBN 0-89061-206-4, 752). Jamestown Pubs.
--The Emergency Reading Teacher's Manual. 107p. (Orig.). 1979. pap. text ed. 10.00 (ISBN 0-89061-207-2, 752S). Jamestown Pubs.
--Graphical Comprehension: How to Read & Make Graphs. (Illus.). 160p. (Orig.). (gr. 9-12). 1981. pap. text ed. 6.00x (ISBN 0-89061-240-4, 782). Jamestown Pubs.
--Ninety-Nine Phonics Charts. 1971. pap. text ed. 6.00x (ISBN 0-87673-006-3, 425). Jamestown Pubs.
--Reading Diagnosis: Informal Reading Inventories. 153p. (Orig.). 1981. pap. text ed. 20.00x (ISBN 0-89061-217-X, 754S). Jamestown Pubs.
--Reading Drills. (Illus.). 192p. (gr. 9 up). 1975. pap. text ed. 6.00x (ISBN 0-89061-039-8, 751). Jamestown Pubs.
--Reading Drills, Middle Level. (Illus.). 224p. (Orig.). (gr. 4-6). 1982. pap. text ed. 6.00x (ISBN 0-89061-245-5, 750). Jamestown Pubs.
--Skimming & Scanning Middle Level. (Illus.). 160p. (Orig.). (gr. 4-6). 1982. pap. text ed. 6.00x (ISBN 0-89061-246-3, 780). Jamestown Pubs.
Fry, Edward F. & McClintic, Miranda. David Smith: Painter, Sculptor, Draftsman. (Illus.). 144p. 1982. 30.00 (ISBN 0-8076-1056-9); pap. 15.00 (ISBN 0-8076-1057-7). Braziller.
Fry, Elizabeth & Cresswell, Rachel L. Memoir of the Life of Elizabeth Fry: With Extracts from Her Journals & Letters, 2 vols. in one. 2nd, rev. & enl. ed. LC 70-172597. (Criminology, Law Enforcement, & Social Problems Ser.: No. 187). (Genealogical charts & with index added). 1974. Repr. of 1848 ed. 45.00x (ISBN 0-87585-187-8). Patterson Smith.
Fry, Eric C. The Book of Knots & Ropework: Practical & Decorative. (Illus.). 176p. 1983. 10.95 (ISBN 0-517-54885-2); pap. 4.95 (ISBN 0-517-54886-0). Crown.
--The Combined Book of Knots. 1983. 10.95 o.p. (ISBN 0-517-54885-2); pap. 4.95 o.p. (ISBN 0-517-54886-0). Crown.
Fry, Eric C. & Wilson, Peter. Shell Book of Practical & Decorative Ropework. (Illus.). 1979. 12.95 o.p. (ISBN 0-7153-7615-2). David & Charles.
Fry, Fiona S., jt. auth. see Fry, Plantagenet.
Fry, J., ed. The Beecham Manual for Family Practice. 300p. 1982. text ed. 29.00 (ISBN 0-85200-456-7, Pub. by MTP Pr England). Kluwer Boston.
Fry, J., ed. see Glasspool, Michael G.
Fry, J., ed. see Ratnesar, Padnam.
Fry, J., ed. see Tatford, E. Patrick.
Fry, J., ed. see Williams, Kenneth G. & Lancaster-Smith, Michael J.
Fry, John. Limits of the Welfare State. 240p. 1979. text ed. 29.00x o.p. (ISBN 0-566-00235-3). Gower Pub Ltd.
Fry, John & Hunt. The Royal College of General Practitioners: The First 25 Years. (Illus.). 350p. 1982. text ed. 29.00 (ISBN 0-85200-360-9, Pub. by MTP Pr England). Kluwer Boston.
Fry, Joseph A. Henry S. Sanford: Diplomacy & Business in 19th Century America. LC 82-8360. (History & Political Science Ser.: No. 16). (Illus.). 226p. (Orig.). 1982. pap. 9.25 (ISBN 0-87417-070-2). U of Nev Pr.
Fry, Maxwell & Drew, Jane. Tropical Architecture in the Dry & Humid Zones. 2nd ed. LC 80-20394. 1982. lib. bdg. 22.50 (ISBN 0-89874-126-2). Krieger.
Fry, Minerva. Letting Grow. 64p. 1982. pap. 4.00x (ISBN 0-918342-17-1). Cambric.
Fry, N., jt. ed. see Adkinson, A. Wyle.
Fry, Nicholas, tr. see Von Buttlar, Johannes.
Fry, P. Spirits of Protest. LC 75-20832. (Cambridge Studies in Social Anthropology: No. 14). 134p. 1976. 21.95 (ISBN 0-521-21052-6). Cambridge U Pr.
Fry, P. Eileen, jt. auth. see Irvine, Betty J.
Fry, Patricia B. & Rubinstein, Ronald A. Of a Homosexual Teacher: Beneath the Mainstream of Constitutional Equalities. (Scholarly Monographs). 180p. 1981. pap. 15.00 o.p. (ISBN 0-8408-0508-X). Carrollton Pr.
Fry, Plantagenet & Fry, Fiona S. The History of Scotland. 200p. 1982. 17.95 (ISBN 0-7100-9001-3). Routledge & Kegan.
Fry, Roger. Vision & Design. Bullen, J. B., ed. (Paperback Books). (Illus., Orig.). pap. 12.50x (ISBN 0-19-281317-X). Oxford U Pr.
Fry, Ronald E., jt. auth. see Plovnick, Mark S.
Fry, William E. Principles of Plant Disease Management. 366p. 1982. 24.50 (ISBN 0-12-269180-6). Acad Pr.
Fryburger, Vernon. The New World of Advertising. LC 75-21745. 1976. pap. 7.95x (ISBN 0-87251-021-2). Crain Bks.
Fryde, Natalie. The Tyranny & Fall of Edward II: 1321-1326. LC 78-56179. 1979. 37.50 (ISBN 0-521-22201-X). Cambridge U Pr.
Frydman, Maurice, tr. see Nisargadatta Maharaj.
Frye, Albert M. & Levi, Albert W. Rational Belief: An Introduction to Logic. Repr. of 1941 ed. lib. bdg. 19.75x (ISBN 0-8371-2142-6, FRRB). Greenwood.
Frye, Charles. The Impact of Black Studies on the Curricula of Three Univerisities. 109p. 1977. pap. text ed. 10.25 (ISBN 0-8191-0223-7). U Pr of Amer.
Frye, Charles A. Values in Conflict: Blacks & the American Ambivalence Toward Violence. LC 79-5516. 1980. pap. text ed. 9.50 (ISBN 0-8191-0899-5). U Pr of Amer.
Frye, Charles A., ed. Level Three: A Black Philosophy Reader. LC 80-5801. 217p. 1980. lib. bdg. 19.00 o.p. (ISBN 0-8191-1241-0); pap. text ed. 10.50 (ISBN 0-8191-1242-9). U Pr of Amer.
Frye, Eldon C. Out of the Back Woods. 1982. 8.95 (ISBN 0-8062-1906-8). Carlton.
Frye, Ellen. The Marble Threshing Floor: A Collection of Greek Folksongs. (American Folklore Society Memoir Ser.: No. 57). (Illus.). 343p. 1973. 18.50x o.p. (ISBN 0-292-75005-6). U of Tex Pr.
Frye, Keith. Modern Minerology. (Illus.). 336p. 1973. ref. ed. 27.95 (ISBN 0-13-595686-2). P-H.
Frye, Keith, ed. The Encyclopedia of Mineralogy. (Encylopedia of Earth Sciences Ser.: Vol. 4B). 816p. 1981. 95.00 (ISBN 0-686-82844-5). Hutchinson Ross.
Frye, Marianne E., et al. Medical Secretary-Receptionist Simulation Project. Frazier, Lois E., ed. LC 78-78187. 1979. pap. text ed. 5.70 student manual (ISBN 0-87350-313-9); tchr's ed. 21.35 (ISBN 0-87350-316-3); forms wkbk. 16.95 (ISBN 0-87350-319-8). Milady.
Frye, Marilyn. The Politics of Reality: Essays in Feminist Theory. 150p. 1983. 14.95 (ISBN 0-89594-100-7); pap. 6.95 (ISBN 0-89594-099-X). Crossing Pr.
Frye, Northrop. Fables of Identity: Studies in Poetic Mythology. LC 63-20974. (Orig.). 1963. pap. 4.95 (ISBN 0-15-629730-2, Harv). HarBraceJ.
--The Myth of Deliverance: Reflections on Shakespeare's Problem Comedies. 128p. 1983. pap. 5.95 (ISBN 0-8020-6503-1). U of Toronto Pr.
--A Natural Perspective. LC 65-17458. 1969. pap. 2.45 (ISBN 0-15-665414-8, Harv). HarBraceJ.
--The Return of Eden: Five Essays on Milton's Epics. 1975. 15.00x (ISBN 0-8020-1353-8); pap. 5.00 o.p. (ISBN 0-8020-6281-4). U of Toronto Pr.
--Spiritus Mundi: Essays on Literature, Myth, & Society. LC 76-12364. (Midland Bks.: No. 289). 320p. 1983. pap. 7.95 (ISBN 0-253-20289-2). Ind U Pr.
--Stubborn Structure. (Methuen Library Reprints). 1980. 38.00x (ISBN 0-416-74400-1). Methuen Inc.
--A Study of English Romanticism. viii, 180p. 1983. pap. 5.95 (ISBN 0-226-26651-6). U of Chicago Pr.
Frye, Northrop, ed. see Blake, William.
Frye, Northrop, et al. The Practical Imagination: An Introduction to Poetry. 468p. 1982. pap. text ed. 10.95 scp (ISBN 0-06-042219-X, HarpC). Har-Row.
Frye, Northrup. Study of English Romanticism. 1968. pap. text ed. 3.95x (ISBN 0-394-30739-9). Phila Bk Co.
Frye, Roland M. Shakespeare: The Art of the Dramatist. 288p. 1981. text ed. 19.50x (ISBN 0-04-822043-4); pap. 6.95 (ISBN 0-04-822044-2). Allen Unwin.
Frye, Tom. Scratching on the Eight Ball. 351p. 1982. pap. 4.95 (ISBN 0-939644-04-5). Media Prods & Mktg.
Fryer, Bob & Hunt, Alan, eds. Law, State & Society. 234p. 1981. 31.00x (ISBN 0-7099-1004-5, Pub. by Croom Helm LTD England). Biblio Dist.
Fryer, G. & Iles, T. D. The Cichlid Fishes of the Great Lakes of Africa, Their Biology & Evolution. (Illus.). 641p. 1982. Repr. of 1972 ed. lib. bdg. 85.50x cancelled (ISBN 3-87429-169-3). Lubrecht & Cramer.
Fryer, Geoffrey & Iles, T. D. Cichlids of the Great Lakes of Africa. (Illus.). 1972. 29.95 (ISBN 0-87666-030-8, PS-680). TFH Pubns.
Fryer, Judith. The Faces of Eve: Women in the Nineteenth Century American Novel. LC 75-32345. (Illus.). 1976. 19.95x (ISBN 0-19-502025-1). Oxford U Pr.
--How We Hear: The Story of Hearing. LC 61-13575. (Medical Bks for Children). (Illus.). (gr. 3-9). 1961. PLB 3.95g (ISBN 0-8225-0012-4). Lerner Pubns.
Fryer, Lee. The Bio-Gardener's Bible: Building Super-Fertile Soil. (Illus.). 288p. 1982. 14.95 (ISBN 0-686-82061-4); pap. 9.95 (ISBN 0-8019-7289-2). Chilton.
Fryer, Russell G. Recent Conservative Political Thought: American Perspectives. LC 78-68568. 1979. pap. text ed. 13.25 (ISBN 0-8191-0694-1). U Pr of Amer.
Fryklund, Verne C. Occupational Analysis. rev. ed. 1970. 10.95 o.p. (ISBN 0-02-816950-6). Glencoe.
Fryklund, Verne C. & Kepler, Frank R. General Drafting. 4th ed. LC 78-81375. (Illus.). (gr. 9-10). 1969. text ed. 14.63 (ISBN 0-87345-095-7). McKnight.
Fryklund, Verne C. & LaBerge, Armand J. General Shop Bench Woodworking. rev. ed. (Illus.). (gr. 9-10). 1955. pap. 6.64 (ISBN 0-87345-001-9). McKnight.
--General Shop Woodworking. rev. ed. (gr. 9-10). 1972. text ed. 15.28 (ISBN 0-87345-031-0). McKnight.
Fryling, Alice, jt. auth. see Fryling, Robert.
Fryling, Robert & Fryling, Alice. Handbook for Engaged Couples. LC 77-11363. 1978. pap. text ed. 2.95 (ISBN 0-87784-363-5). Inter-Varsity.
Frym, Gloria. Second Stories. LC 79-9390. (Illus.). 1980. pap. 7.95 o.p. (ISBN 0-87701-152-4). Chronicle Bks.
Frymier, Jack R. School for Tomorrow. LC 72-10647. 286p. 1973. 21.75x (ISBN 0-8211-0505-1); text ed. 19.50x (ISBN 0-685-28804-8). McCutchan.
Fryrear, Jerry L. & Fleshman, Robert. Videotherapy in Mental Health. (Illus.). 352p. 1981. pap. 29.75x (ISBN 0-398-04117-2). C C Thomas.
Fryxell, Greta A., ed. Survival Strategies of the Algae. LC 82-12865. (Illus.). 176p. Date not set. price not set (ISBN 0-521-25067-6). Cambridge U Pr.
Ft. Myer School Staff. Instant Pep for Language. 1983. 5.50 (ISBN 0-686-84077-1). Intl Gen Semantics.
Fu, K. S. & Yu, T. S. Statistical Pattern Classification Using Contextual Information. LC 80-40949. (Patterns Recognition & Image Processing Ser.). 191p. 1980. 54.95 (ISBN 0-471-27859-9, Research Studies Press). Wiley.
Fu, K. S. & Kunii, T. L., eds. Picture Engineering. (Springer Series in Information Sciences: Vol. 6). (Illus.). 320p. 1982. 29.50 (ISBN 0-387-11822-5). Springer-Verlag.
Fu, King-Sun, jt. ed. see Zadeh.
Fuchs, Arthur W. Principles of Radiographic Exposure & Processing. 2nd ed. (Illus.). 302p. 1979. 23.75x (ISBN 0-398-00627-X). C C Thomas.
Fuchs, Daniel. Saul Bellow: Vision & Revision. 350p. 1983. text ed. 35.00 (ISBN 0-8223-0503-8). Duke.
Fuchs, E. & Mattson, K. Allergology & Clinical Immunology: Proceedings of the Ketotifen Workshop. (International Congress Ser.: No. 523). 1981. 24.00 (ISBN 0-444-90151-5). Elsevier.
Fuchs, Esther. Encounters with Israeli Authors. LC 82-62086. (Illus.). 104p. 1983. pap. 7.50 (ISBN 0-916288-14-5). Micah Pubns.
Fuchs, Fritz & Klopper, Arnold, eds. Endocrinology of Pregnancy. 2nd ed. (Illus.). 490p. 1977. text ed. 35.00x o.p. (ISBN 0-06-140841-7, Harper-Medical). Lippincott.
--Endocrinology of Pregnancy. 3rd ed. (Illus.). 400p. 1983. write for info (ISBN 0-06-140845-X, Harper Medical). Lippincott.
Fuchs, Gordon E. Evaluating Educational Research. LC 80-5480. 160p. 1980. pap. text ed. 8.25 (ISBN 0-8191-1104-X). U Pr of Amer.
Fuchs, H. O. & Stephens, R. I. Metal Fatigue in Engineering. LC 80-294. 1980. 36.95x (ISBN 0-471-05264-7, Pub. by Wiley-Interscience). Wiley.
Fuchs, H. P. Nomenklatur, Taxonomie & Systematik der Gattung Isoetes Linnaeus in geschichtlicher Entwicklung. (Illus.). 1962. pap. 16.00 (ISBN 3-7682-5403-8). Lubrecht & Cramer.
Fuchs, Hans-Ulrich. Zur Lehre Vom Allgemeinen Bankvertrag. xxi, 212p. (Ger.). 1982. write for info. (ISBN 3-8204-7120-0). P Lang Pubs.
Fuchs, Lawrence H. The Political Behavior of American Jews. LC 79-28711. (Illus.). 220p. 1980. Repr. of 1956 ed. lib. bdg. 21.00x (ISBN 0-313-22282-7, FUPB). Greenwood.
Fuchs, Lucy. Dangerous Splendor. (YA) 1978. 6.95 (ISBN 0-685-05584-1, Avalon). Bouregy.
--Pictures of Fear. (YA) 1981. 6.95 (ISBN 0-686-73951-5, Avalon). Bouregy.
--Wild Winds of Mayaland. (YA) 1978. 6.95 (ISBN 0-685-85784-0, Avalon). Bouregy.
Fuchs, P. L. & Bunnell, C. A. Carbon-Thirteen NMR Based Organic Spectral Problems. LC 78-20668. 309p. 1979. pap. text ed. 14.95 (ISBN 0-471-04907-7). Wiley.
Fuchs, Roland J. & Street, John M., eds. Geography in Asian Universities. 525p. 1975. pap. 7.00x o.p. (ISBN 0-8248-0376-0). UH Pr.
Fuchs, Stephen. The Aboriginal Tribes of India. LC 76-27186. 1977. 18.95 (ISBN 0-312-00175-4). St Martin.
--Rebellious Prophets: A Study of Messianic Movements in Indian Religions. 1965. 12.50x (ISBN 0-210-27136-1). Asia.
Fuchs, Victor. How We Live. (Illus.). 320p. 1983. 17.50 (ISBN 0-674-41225-7). Harvard U Pr.
--Who Shall Live? LC 74-79283. 1975. 12.95x (ISBN 0-465-09185-7). Basic.
Fuchs, Victors R. Who Shall Live? 1983. pap. 8.25 (ISBN 0-465-09186-5). Basic.
Fuchshuber, Annegert. The Wishing Hat. Crawford, Elizabeth D., tr. (ps-3). 1977. 8.95 (ISBN 0-688-22100-9); PLB 8.59 (ISBN 0-688-32100-3). Morrow.
Fuchssteiner, B. & Lusky, W. Convex Cones. (North-Holland Mathematics Studies: Vol. 56). 1981. 53.25 (ISBN 0-444-86290-0). Elsevier.
Fuchtbauer, H. & Peryt, T., eds. The Zechstein Basin with Emphasis on Carbonate Sequences. (Contributions to Sedimentology Ser.: No. 9). (Illus.). 328p. 1980. 72.50x (ISBN 3-510-57009-X). Intl Pubns Serv.
Fuchtbauer, Hans & Muller, G. Sediments & Sedimentary Rocks, Vol. 2, Pt. 1. LC 67-28575. (Sedimentary Petrology Ser.). (Illus.). 464p. 1974. 79.95 o.p. (ISBN 0-471-28500-5). Halsted Pr.
Fucik, S. & Kufner, A. Nonlinear Differential Equations. (Studies in Applied Mechanics: Vol. 2). 1980. 81.00 (ISBN 0-444-99771-7). Elsevier.
Fuckel, L. Symbolae Mycologicae & Supplements. (Illus.). 1966. Repr. of 1877 ed. 80.00 (ISBN 3-7682-0358-1). Lubrecht & Cramer.
Fuda, George E. & Nelson, Edwin L. The Display Specialist. (Illus.). (gr. 10-12). 1976. pap. text ed. 10.04 (ISBN 0-07-022607-5, G); tchr's manual & key 4.95 (ISBN 0-07-022609-1). McGraw.
Fudenberg, H. Hugh, et al. Evaluation of Gastrointestinal, Pulmonary, Anti-Inflammatory and Immunological Agents. LC 74-21396. (Principles & Techniques of Human Research & Therapeutics Ser.: Vol. 9). (Illus.). 230p. 1975. 14.50 o.p. (ISBN 0-87993-053-5). Futura Pub.
--Basic Immunogenetics. 2nd ed. (Illus.). 1978. text ed. 21.95x (ISBN 0-19-502054-5); pap. text ed. 13.95x (ISBN 0-19-502055-3). Oxford U Pr.
Fudge, Colin, jt. ed. see Barrett, Susan.
Fudge, Don. Hi-Res Secrets. 270p. 1981. 3 ring binder 50.00 (ISBN 0-930182-21-9). Avant Garde CR.
--Hi-Res Secrets Graphics Applications System. (Illus.). 240p. 1982. binder 50.00 (ISBN 0-930182-33-2). Avant Garde CR.
Fudge, Edward. Christianity Without Ulcers. pap. 4.50 (ISBN 0-686-12686-6). Providential Pr.
--The Church That Pleases God. 1.50 o.p. (ISBN 0-686-12690-4). Providential Pr.
--Expository Outlines on Ephesians. 2.00 (ISBN 0-686-12688-2). Providential Pr.
--Ezekiel: Prophet of Jehovah's Glory. 1.25 (ISBN 0-686-12692-0). Providential Pr.
--The Fire that Consumes: A Biblical & History Study of Final Punishment. Date not set. 19.95 (ISBN 0-89890-018-2). Providential Pr.
--Gold from the Gospels. pap. 2.00 (ISBN 0-686-12679-3). Providential Pr.
--Helps on Romans. 2.00 (ISBN 0-686-12691-2). Providential Pr.
--Preaching with Power. pap. 2.00 (ISBN 0-686-12680-7). Providential Pr.
--Sermons That Demand a Decision. pap. 2.00 (ISBN 0-686-12681-5). Providential Pr.
--Sermons That Strengthen. pap. 1.50 (ISBN 0-686-12682-3). Providential Pr.
--Sermons to Grow on. pap. 2.00 (ISBN 0-686-12683-1). Providential Pr.
--Simple Sermons That Demand a Decision. 2.00 (ISBN 0-686-12689-0). Providential Pr.
--Simple Sermons That Say Something. pap. 1.50 (ISBN 0-686-12684-X). Providential Pr.
--Sunday Night Sermons. pap. 2.00 (ISBN 0-686-12685-8). Providential Pr.
Fudge, Edward, jt. auth. see Edwards, Bruce.
Fudge, Samuel R. Living with Today's Teenagers. LC 78-99142. 1970. 9.95 (ISBN 0-87716-015-5, Pub. by Moore Pub Co). F Apple.
Fuegi, John, ed. see International Brecht Society.
Fuell, A. J. see Von Wiesner, J. & Von Regel, C.
Fuente, Julio De La see Malinowski, Bronislaw.
Fuente, Tomas De La see Cowan, Marvin W.
Fuentes, Carlos. Aura. bi-lingual ed. Kemp, Lysander, tr. from Sp. 160p. 1975. 7.95 (ISBN 0-374-10701-7); pap. 6.95 (ISBN 0-374-51171-3). FS&G.
--A Change of Skin. Hileman, Sam, tr. 462p. 1968. pap. 5.95 o.p. (ISBN 0-374-51427-5). FS&G.
--The Death of Artemio Cruz. Hileman, Sam, tr. 306p. 1964. pap. 6.25 (ISBN 0-374-50540-3, N307). FS&G.

--The Good Conscience. Hileman, Sam, tr. 148p. 1961. pap. 6.25 (ISBN 0-374-50736-8, N357). FS&G.

Fuentes, Epifanio. Knowledge Versus the College Mind. 1983. 5.95 (ISBN 0-686-84437-8). Vantage.

Fuentes, Ernesto F., et al. Nonwood Plant Fiber Pulping: Progress Report, No. 11. (TAPPI PRESS Reports). (Illus.). 99p. 1981. pap. 38.95 (ISBN 0-89852-391-5, 01 01 R091). TAPPI.

Fuermann, George. Houston: The Once & Future City. LC 73-150578. (Illus.). 1971. deluxe ed. 25.00 o.p. (ISBN 0-385-02949-7). Doubleday.

Fuerst, J. S., ed. Public Housing in Europe & America. LC 73-10890. 216p. 1974. 24.95 o.s.i. (ISBN 0-470-28515-X). Halsted Pr.

Fuerstenau, M. C., ed. Flotation, 2 Vols. LC 76-19745. 1976. 39.00x (ISBN 0-89520-032-5). Soc Mining Eng.

Fuess, Claude M. Daniel Webster, 2 Vols. 2nd ed. LC 68-8722. (American Scene Ser). (Illus.). 1968. Repr. of 1930 ed. Set. lib. bdg. 85.00 (ISBN 0-306-71186-9). Da Capo.

Fugate, Howard. Cardiac Rehabilitation: The Road to a Healthy Heart. McCavitt, William E., ed. 92p. 1980. pap. 5.00 (ISBN 0-935648-06-2). Halldin Pub.

Fugate, Wilbur. Foreign Commerce & Antitrust Laws. 3rd ed. LC 81-83240. 973p. 1982. 100.00set (ISBN 0-316-29534-5). Little.

Fugate, Wilbur L. Foreign Commerce & the Antitrust Laws. 2nd ed. 1973. 45.00 o.p. (ISBN 0-316-29532-9). Little.

Fugitt, Eva D. He Hit Me Back First! Creative Visualization Activities for Parenting & Teaching. LC 82-83063. (Illus.). 106p. (Orig.). 1982. pap. 9.95 (ISBN 0-915190-36-2). Jalmar Pr.

Fugitt, Glenn V., jt. auth. see Johansen, Harley.

Fugitt, Jack. The Big J Handbook for Artists & Cartoonists. 1983. 19.95 (ISBN 0-686-84441-6). Vantage.

Fuglesang, Andreas, ed. About Understanding: Ideas & Observations on Cross Cultural Communication. 232p. 1983. pap. text ed. 10.95 (ISBN 0-910365-01-6). Decade Media.

Fuglsby, Glen O., et al. General Mechanical Drawing. rev. ed. (gr. 7-9). 1966. text ed. 6.60 o.p. (ISBN 0-02-820580-4). Glencoe.

Fuhlrott, Rolf, ed. Library Interior Layout & Design. (IFLA Publications: No. 24). 1983. price not set (ISBN 3-598-20386-1, Pub. by K G Saur). Shoe String.

Fuhr, Sr. Mary T. Clinical Experience Record & Nursing Care Planning: A Guide for Student Nurses. 2nd ed. LC 77-22532. 206p. 1978. pap. text ed. 9.50 o.p. (ISBN 0-8016-1711-1). Mosby.

Fuhrman, Joseph T. Tsar Alexis, His Reign & His Russia. (Russian Ser.: No. 34). 1981. 16.50 (ISBN 0-87569-040-8). Academic Intl.

Fuhrman, Noah. Seven Keys for Doubling Your Standard of Living (Without Increasing Your Income) 224p. 1982. pap. 6.95 (ISBN 0-02-008190-1). Macmillan.

Fuhrmann, Barbara, jt. auth. see Curwin, Richard.

Fuhrmann, P. A. Linear Operators & Systems: Operator Theory, Mathematical Systems Theory, Control Process. 1981. 47.50 (ISBN 0-07-022589-3). McGraw.

Fuhrmann, W. & Vogel, F. Genetic Counseling. 3rd ed. Kurth-Scherer, S., tr. from Ger. (Illus.). 188p. 1983. pap. 15.95 (ISBN 0-387-90715-7). Springer-Verlag.

Fujikawa, Guyo. Millie's Secret. Duenewald, Doris, ed. (Fujikawa Board Books Ser.). (Illus.). (gr. k-3). 1978. PLB 3.50 (ISBN 0-448-14726-2, G&D). Putnam Pub Group.

--My Favorite Thing. Duenewald, Doris, ed. (Fujikawa Board Books Ser.). (Illus.). 1978. 3.50 (ISBN 0-448-14727-0, G&D). Putnam Pub Group.

Fujikawa, Gyo. Betty Bear's Birthday. (Fujikawa Board Books). (Illus.). (ps-2). 1977. 3.50 (ISBN 0-448-14369-0, G&D). Putnam Pub Group.

--Can You Count. (Fujikawa Board Bks.). 1977. 3.50 (ISBN 0-448-12893-4, G&D). Putnam Pub Group.

--Come Follow Me...to the Secret World of Elves & Fairies & Gnomes & Trolls. LC 78-22746. (Illus.). (gr. k-5). 1979. 6.95 (ISBN 0-448-16545-7, G&D); PLB 11.85 (ISBN 0-448-13603-1). Putnam Pub Group.

--Come Out & Play. (Gyo Fujikawa Tiny Board Books). (Illus.). 14p. (ps-k). 1981. 1.95 (ISBN 0-448-15115-4, G&D). Putnam Pub Group.

--Dreamland. (Tiny Board Bks.). (Illus.). 14p. (ps). 1981. 2.25 (ISBN 0-448-15081-6, G&D). Putnam Pub Group.

--Fairy Tales. (Platt & Munk Pandabacks Ser.). (Illus.). 24p. (ps-3). Date not set. pap. price not set (ISBN 0-448-49615-1, G&D). Putnam Pub Group.

--Fairyland. (Gyo Fujikawa Tiny Board Books). (Illus.). 14p. (ps-k). 1981. 1.95 (ISBN 0-448-15139-1, G&D). Putnam Pub Group.

--Faraway Friends. (Gyo Fujikawa Tiny Board Books). (Illus.). 14p. (ps-k). 1981. 1.95 (ISBN 0-448-15103-0, G&D). Putnam Pub Group.

--The Flyaway Kite. LC 80-3353. (Gyo Fujikawa Ser.). (Illus.). 32p. (gr. k-3). 1981. 3.95 (ISBN 0-448-11747-9, G&D); PLB 9.30 (ISBN 0-448-13652-X). Putnam Pub Group.

--Fraidy Cat. LC 81-84015. (Illus.). 32p. (gr. k-3). 1982. 3.95 (ISBN 0-448-11753-3, G&D). Putnam Pub Group.

--Good Morning! (Tiny Board Bks.). (Illus.). 14p. (ps). 1981. 2.25 (ISBN 0-448-15084-0, G&D). Putnam Pub Group.

--Gyo Fujikawa Board Books. Incl. Can You Count (ISBN 0-448-12893-4); Babes of the Wild (ISBN 0-448-12894-2). (Illus.). 1977. 3.50 ea. (G&D). Putnam Pub Group.

--Gyo Fujikawa's A to Z Book. (Illus.). 12p. (gr. k-3). 1981. 3.95 (ISBN 0-448-46827-1, G&D). Putnam Pub Group.

--Gyo Fujikawa's Night Before Christmas. (ps-7). Date not set. price not set (ISBN 0-448-02935-9, G&D). Putnam Pub Group.

--Here I Am. (Tiny Board Bks.). (Illus.). 14p. (ps). 1981. 2.25 (ISBN 0-448-15082-4, G&D). Putnam Pub Group.

--Jenny & Jupie. LC 81-80652. (Gyo Fujikawa Ser.). (Illus.). 32p. (ps-1). 1981. 3.95 (ISBN 0-448-11751-7, G&D). Putnam Pub Group.

--Jenny & Jupie to the Rescue. LC 82-80870. (Checkerboard Bks.). (Illus.). 32p. (gr. k-2). 1982. 3.95 (ISBN 0-448-11754-1, G&D). Putnam Pub Group.

--Jenny Learns a Lesson. (Fujikawa Storybooks). (Illus.). 32p. (ps-2). 3.95 (ISBN 0-448-11746-0, G&D). Putnam Pub Group.

--Let's Eat. 1975. 3.50 (ISBN 0-448-11922-6, 0-448-11922). Putnam Pub Group.

--Let's Grow a Garden. (Fujikawa Board Books). (Illus.). (gr. k-3). 1978. 3.50 (ISBN 0-448-14613-4, G&D). Putnam Pub Group.

--Let's Play. (Fujikawa Board Bks.). 1975. 3.50 (ISBN 0-448-11958-7, G&D). Putnam Pub Group.

--The Magic Show. LC 81-80651. (Gyo Fujikawa Ser.). (Illus.). 32p. (ps-1). 1981. 3.95 (ISBN 0-448-11750-9, G&D). Putnam Pub Group.

--Make-Believe. (Gyo Fujikawa Tiny Board Books). (Illus.). 14p. (ps-k). 1981. 1.95 (ISBN 0-448-15127-8, G&D). Putnam Pub Group.

--Me Too! LC 81-84014. (Illus.). 32p. (gr. k-3). 1982. 3.95 (ISBN 0-448-11752-5, G&D). Putnam Pub Group.

--Mother Goose. (Platt & Munk Pandabacks Ser.). (Illus.). 24p. (ps-3). Date not set. pap. price not set (ISBN 0-448-49618-6, G&D). Putnam Pub Group.

--Mother Goose. (Gyo Fujikawa Tiny Board Books). (Illus.). 14p. (ps-k). 1981. 1.95 (ISBN 0-448-15091-3, G&D). Putnam Pub Group.

--My Animal Friend. (Gyo Fujikawa Tiny Board Books). (Illus.). 14p. (ps-k). 1981. 1.95 (ISBN 0-448-15079-4, G&D). Putnam Pub Group.

--The Night Before Christmas. (Platt & Munk Pandabacks Ser.). (Illus.). 24p. (ps-3). Date not set. pap. price not set (ISBN 0-448-49619-4, G&D). Putnam Pub Group.

--One, Two, Three, A Counting Book. (Tiny Board Bks.). (Illus.). 14p. (ps). 1981. 2.25 (ISBN 0-448-15085-9, G&D). Putnam Pub Group.

--Our Best Friends. (Fujikawa Board Books). (Illus.). (ps-2). 1977. 3.50 (ISBN 0-448-14343-7, G&D). Putnam Pub Group.

--Poems for Children. (Platt & Munk Pandabacks Ser.). (Illus.). 24p. (ps-3). Date not set. pap. price not set (ISBN 0-448-49616-X, G&D). Putnam Pub Group.

--Puppies, Pussycats & Other Friends. 1975. 3.50 (ISBN 0-448-11920-X, G&D). Putnam Pub Group.

--Sam's All-Wrong Day. LC 82-80869. (Checkerboard Bks.). (Illus.). 32p. (Orig.). (gr. k-2). 1982. 3.95 (ISBN 0-448-11755-X, G&D). Putnam Pub Group.

--Shags Has a Dream. LC 80-3352. (Gyo Fujikawa Ser.). (Illus.). (gr. k-3). 1981. 3.95 (ISBN 0-448-11749-5, G&D); PLB 9.30 (ISBN 0-448-13653-8). Putnam Pub Group.

--Sleepy Time. 1975. 3.50 (ISBN 0-448-11921-8, 0-448-11921, G&D). Putnam Pub Group.

--Surprise! Surprise! (Fujikawa Board Books). (Illus.). (gr. k-3). 1978. 3.50 (ISBN 0-448-14557-X, G&D). Putnam Pub Group.

--A Tiny Word Book. (Tiny Board Bks.). (Illus.). 14p. (ps). 1981. 2.25 (ISBN 0-448-15083-2, G&D). Putnam Pub Group.

--Welcome Is a Wonderful Word. (Fujikawa Storybooks). (Illus.). 32p. (ps-2). 3.95 (ISBN 0-448-11748-7, G&D). Putnam Pub Group.

--Year in, Year Out. (Tiny Board Bks.). (Illus.). 14p. (ps). 1981. 1.95 (ISBN 0-448-15080-8, G&D). Putnam Pub Group.

Fujikawa, Gyo, illus. Babies. (ps). 1963. bds. 2.95 (ISBN 0-448-03084-5, G&D). Putnam Pub Group.

--Baby Animals. (Illus.). (ps). 1963. bds. 2.95 (ISBN 0-448-03083-7, G&D). Putnam Pub Group.

--Child's Book of Poems. LC 75-86696. (Illus.). (gr. k-4). 1969. 5.95 (ISBN 0-448-01876-4, G&D); pap. 2.95 abr. ed. (ISBN 0-448-14341-0). Putnam Pub Group.

--Fairy Tales & Fables. (Illus.). (gr. k-3). 1970. 5.95 (ISBN 0-448-02814-X, G&D). Putnam Pub Group.

--Gyo Fujikawa's A to Z Picture Book. LC 73-16655. (Illus.). 80p. (gr. k-3). 1974. 6.95 (ISBN 0-448-11741-X, G&D). Putnam Pub Group.

--Mother Goose. (Illus.). (ps-2). 1968. 5.95 (ISBN 0-448-01810-1, G&D); pap. 2.95 abr. ed. (ISBN 0-448-14340-2). Putnam Pub Group.

--Oh, What a Busy Day. (Illus.). 80p. (gr. k-3). 1976. 5.95 (ISBN 0-448-12511-0, G&D). Putnam Pub Group.

Fujimura, Faith N., ed. Groundwater in Hawaii: A Century of Progress. 270p. 1981. text ed. 20.00x (ISBN 0-8248-0788-X, Water Resources Res Ctr). UH Pr.

Fujimura, Thomas H. The Restoration Comedy of Wit. LC 78-13942. 1978. Repr. of 1952 ed. lib. bdg. 20.00x (ISBN 0-313-21232-5, FURC). Greenwood.

Fujinori, Y. Modern Analysis of Value Theory. (Lecture Notes in Economics & Mathematical Systems: Vol. 207). (Illus.). 165p. 1983. pap. 12.00 (ISBN 0-387-11949-3). Springer-Verlag.

Fujioka, Michio. Japanese Residences & Gardens: A Tradition of Integration. Horton, H. Mack, tr. LC 82-48793. (Great Japanese Art Ser.). (Illus.). 48p. 1983. 18.95 (ISBN 0-87011-561-8). Kodansha.

Fujisawa, K., jt. ed. see Yamaguchi, N.

Fujita, Hiroshi, tr. see Kurata, Michio.

Fujita, Shigeji. Introduction to Non-Equilibrium Quantum Statistical Mechanics. LC 82-23209. 178p. 1983. Repr. of 1966 ed. lib. bdg. write for info. (ISBN 0-89874-593-4). Krieger.

Fujita, T., jt. auth. see Tanaka, K.

Fujita, T., jt. ed. see Coupland, R. E.

Fujita, T., et al. Atlas of Scanning Electron Microscopy in Medicine. 1971. 70.00 (ISBN 0-444-40908-4, North Holland). Elsevier.

Fujiwara, Shizuo & Mark, Harry B., Jr., eds. Information Chemistry: Computer Assisted Chemical Research Design. (Illus.). 1976. 65.00x (ISBN 0-86008-150-8, Pub. by Japan Sci Soc). Intl Schol Bk Serv.

Fujiwara, Yoichi. The Sentence Structure of Japanese: Viewed in the Light of Dialectology. Brannen, Noah & Baird, Scott, trs. from Japanese. LC 73-78976. 156p. 1973. text ed. 10.00x (ISBN 0-8248-0275-6). UH Pr.

Fujiwara no Nagako. The Emperor Horikawa Diary: Sanuki no Suke Nikki. Brewster, Jennifer, tr. from Japanese. LC 77-89194. 1978. text ed. 14.00x (ISBN 0-8248-0605-0). UH Pr.

Fuks, Alexander. Ancestral Constitution: Four Studies in Athenian Party Politics at the End of the Fifth Century B. C. LC 72-138235. 1971. Repr. of 1953 ed. lib. bdg. 15.00x (ISBN 0-8371-5592-4, FUAC). Greenwood.

Fukui, Eiichir O. The Climate of Japan. LC 76-44473. (Developments in Atmospheric Science: Vol. 8). 1977. 81.00 (ISBN 0-444-99818-7). Elsevier.

Fukui, Hotsuaki. Low Noise Microwave Transistors & Amplifiers. 461p. 1981. 33.95x (ISBN 0-471-86589-3, Pub. by Wiley-Interscience); pap. 22.00x (ISBN 0-471-86588-5, Pub. by Wiley-Interscience). Wiley.

Fukui, Saburo, jt. ed. see Chibata, Ichiro.

Fukushima, E. & Roeder, S. B. W. Experimental Pulse NMR: A Nuts & Bolts Approach. 1981. 36.50 (ISBN 0-201-10403-2). A-W.

Fukushima, H. Index Guide to Rational Drug Therapy. 1982. 70.25 (ISBN 0-444-90273-2). Elsevier.

Fukushima, H., et al. Index Guide to Drug Information Retrieval. 1979. 63.50 (ISBN 0-444-80139-1, North Holland). Elsevier.

Fukushima, M. Dirichlet Forms & Markov Processes. (Mathematical Library Ser.: Vol. 23). 1980. 47.00 (ISBN 0-686-95002-X, North Holland). Elsevier.

Fukutake, Tadashi. Japanese Social Structure, 1870-1980. Dore, Ronald P., tr. 180p. 1982. text ed. 14.50x (ISBN 0-86008-316-0, Pub. by U of Tokyo Japan). Columbia U Pr.

Fukuyama. Child Neurology: Proceedings of the Tokyo Meeting, 1981. (International Congress Ser.: Vol. 579). 1982. 93.75 (ISBN 0-444-90257-0). Elsevier.

Fukuyama, Yoshio. The Ministry in Transition: A Case Study of Theological Education. LC 72-1395. 200p. 1973. 16.95x (ISBN 0-271-01129-7). Pa St U Pr.

Fulbright, J. William. Old Myths & New Realities: And Other Commentaries. 1964. 8.95 o.p. (ISBN 0-394-43741-1); pap. 1.45 (ISBN 0-394-70264-6). Random.

Fulcher, Derick H. Medical Care Systems: Public and Private Health Insurance in Selected Industrialised Countries. 1974. 10.00 (ISBN 92-2-101160-7). Intl Labour Office.

Fulco, William J. Maranatha: The Mystical Theology of John the Evangelist. LC 73-82225. 96p. (Orig.). 1973. pap. 1.95 o.p. (ISBN 0-8091-1778-9, Deus). Paulist Pr.

Fuld, G., jt. auth. see Fuld, M.

Fuld, George & Fuld, Melvin. U. S. Civil War Store Cards. rev. ed. LC 75-1785. (Illus.). 704p. 1975. 50.00x (ISBN 0-88000-135-6). Quarterman.

Fuld, Leonhard Felix. Police Administration: A Critical Study of Police Organizations in the United States and Abroad. LC 70-152105. (Criminology, Law Enforcement, & Social Problems Ser.: No. 141). (Illus.). 583p. (With intro. added). 1971. Repr. of 1909 ed. 18.00x (ISBN 0-87585-141-X). Patterson Smith.

Fuld, M. & Fuld, G. Guide to Civil War Store Cards. (Illus.). 1982. Repr. of 1971 ed. softcover 10.00 (ISBN 0-915262-97-5). S J Durst.

Fuld, Melvin, jt. auth. see Fuld, George.

Fulder, Stephen. An End to Aging: Remedies for Life Extensions. 111p. 1983. pap. 5.95 (ISBN 0-89281-044-0). Destiny Bks.

--Tao of Medicine: Ginseng, Oriental Remedies & the Pharmacology of Harmony. (Illus.). 328p. 1982. text ed. 9.95 (ISBN 0-89281-027-0). Destiny Bks.

Fulep, Ferenc, ed. The Hungarian National Museum. Hoch, Elizabeth, tr. (Illus.). 251p. 1980. 15.95 (ISBN 0-89893-161-4). CDP.

Fulford, M. G., jt. ed. see Cunliffe, B. W.

Fulghum, Thomas. Tommy: The Comeback Kid. 1983. text ed. 8.95 (ISBN 0-88207-649-3). Victor Bks.

Fulginiti, Vincent A. Pediatric Clinical Problem Solving. (Illus.). 200p. 1981. lib. bdg. 15.95 (ISBN 0-683-03383-2). Williams & Wilkins.

Fulginiti, Vincent A., jt. auth. see Stiehm, E. Richard.

Fulker, Edmund N. A Model & Checklist for Administrator, Manager & Executive Career Training & Development. 1980. 2.00 (ISBN 0-87771-018-X). Grad School.

Fulker, Mary, jt. auth. see Fulker, Wilber H.

Fulker, Wilber H. & Fulker, Mary. Techniques with Tangibles: A Manual for Teaching the Blind. 84p. 1968. photocopy ed. spiral 9.50x (ISBN 0-398-00628-8). C C Thomas.

Fulkerson, Katherine. The Merchandise Buyers' Game. 1981. pap. text ed. 4.95 (ISBN 0-933836-13-9). Simtek.

Fulkerson, W. J. Hormonal Control of Lactation, Vol. 1. Horrobin, D. F., ed. (Annual Research Reviews). 1980. 18.00 (ISBN 0-88831-061-7). Eden Pr.

Fulkerson, William J. Hormonal Control of Lactation: Vol. 2. Horrobin, David F., ed. (Annual Research Reviews). 84p. 1981. 14.00 (ISBN 0-88831-087-0). Eden Pr.

Fulks, Clay. Christianity: A Continuing Calamity. 31p. Date not set. pap. 3.00 (ISBN 0-686-83977-3). Am Atheist.

Fulks, Danny G. Informal Learning in Elementary Schools. LC 78-61303. 1978. pap. text ed. 8.25 (ISBN 0-8191-0606-2). U Pr of Amer.

Fulks, Watson. Advanced Calculus: An Introduction to Analysis. 3rd ed. LC 78-5268. 731p. 1978. text ed. 31.95 (ISBN 0-471-02195-4); avail. solutions (ISBN 0-471-05125-X). Wiley.

Fullam, Everett L. Facets of the Faith. 133p. 1982. pap. 4.95 (ISBN 0-310-60061-8). Chosen Bks Pub.

Fullard, Harold, jt. auth. see Ginsburg, Norton.

Fullard, Harold, ed. Philips' New World Atlas. LC 79-670343. (Illus.). 1978. 17.50x o.p. (ISBN 0-540-05316-3). Intl Pubns Serv.

Fullard, Harold, ed. see Muir, Ramsey.

Fullard, Harold, et al. Aldine University Atlas. 1969. text ed. 8.95x o.p. (ISBN 0-673-05995-2). Scott F.

Fulleborn, U. & Engel, M., eds. Materialien Zu Rilkes "Duineser Elegien". (Taschenbucher Ser.). 398p. (Orig.). 1980. pap. text ed. 5.20 (ISBN 3-518-37074-X, Pub. by Suhrkamp Verlag Germany). Suhrkamp.

Fullenwider, Malcolm A. Hydrogen Entry & Action in Metals. (Illus.). 125p. 1983. 29.50 (ISBN 0-08-027526-5). Pergamon.

Fuller, Andrew R. Psychology & Religion: Eight Points of View. 143p. 1977. pap. text ed. 8.25 (ISBN 0-8191-0143-5). U Pr of Amer.

Fuller, B. Frank, jt. auth. see Fuller, Benjamin J.

Fuller, Benjamin J. & Fuller, B. Frank. Physician or Magician: The Myths & Realities of Patient Care. (Illus.). 1979. pap. text ed. 12.95 (ISBN 0-07-022617-2, HP). McGraw.

Fuller, Buckminster see Bush, George, et al.

Fuller, C. J. The Nayars Today. LC 76-11078. (Changing Cultures Ser.). (Illus.). 1977. 27.95 (ISBN 0-521-21301-0); pap. 10.95 (ISBN 0-521-29091-0). Cambridge U Pr.

Fuller, David O., ed. see Spurgeon, Charles H.

Fuller, Dean. Passage. 1983. 13.95 (ISBN 0-396-08134-7). Dodd.

Fuller, Dudley D. Theory & Practice of Lubrication for Engineers. LC 36-6483. 1956. 49.95x o.p. (ISBN 0-471-28710-5, Pub. by Wiley-Interscience). Wiley.

Fuller, Dwain & Hutton, William, eds. Presurgical Evaluation of Eyes with Opaque Media. Date not set. 39.50 (ISBN 0-8089-1470-7). Grune.

Fuller, E. G. & Hayward, E., eds. Photonuclear Reactions. (Benchmark Papers in Nuclear Physics: Vol. 2). 1976. 60.50 (ISBN 0-12-786495-4). Acad Pr.

Fuller, Edward C. Chemistry & Man's Environment. 464p. 1974. text ed. 25.95 (ISBN 0-395-17086-9); instr's. manual 1.35 (ISBN 0-395-17865-7); slides 15.95 (ISBN 0-395-18185-2, 3-17136). HM.

Fuller, Elizabeth. Having Your First Baby after Thirty. LC 82-23548. 1983. 10.95 (ISBN 0-396-08154-1). Dodd.

--Poor Elizabeth's Almanac. 1980. 9.95 o.p. (ISBN 0-399-12392-X). Putnam Pub Group.

Fuller, Eugene T. Pricelsee Possesion of a Few. 1974. 10.00 (ISBN 0-913902-41-1). Heart Am Pr.

Fuller, Frank. Engineering of Pile Installations. (Illus.). 320p. 1983. 37.50 (ISBN 0-07-022618-0, P&RB). McGraw.

Fuller, George W., ed. A Bibliography of Bookplate Literature. LC 72-178635. 151p. 1971. Repr. of 1926 ed. 42.00x (ISBN 0-8103-3190-X). Gale.

Fuller, Gordon. Algebra & Trigonometry. 1971. text ed. 23.50 (ISBN 0-07-022605-9, C); instructor's manual 4.95 (ISBN 0-07-022606-7). McGraw.

--Analytic Geometry. 5th ed. LC 78-55820. 1979. text ed. 18.95 (ISBN 0-201-02414-4); ans bk. 13.95 (ISBN 0-201-02415-2). A-W.

--Plane Trigonometry with Tables. 4th ed. (Illus.). 1971. text ed. 21.50 (ISBN 0-07-022608-3, C); instructor's manual 10.00 (ISBN 0-07-022611-3). McGraw.

--Plane Trigonometry with Tables. 5th ed. (Illus.). 1978. text ed. 22.50 (ISBN 0-07-022612-1, C); instructor's manual 15.00 (ISBN 0-07-022613-X). McGraw.

Fuller, Harry J. & Ritchie, Donald D. General Botany. 5th ed. (Illus.). 1967. pap. 5.50 (ISBN 0-06-460033-5, CO 33, COS). B&N NY.

Fuller, Iola. Loon Feather. LC 40-27210. 1967. pap. 3.95 (ISBN 0-15-653200-X, Harv). HarBraceJ.

Fuller, J. F. Grant & Lee: A Study in Personality & Generalship. LC 57-10723. (Midland Bks Ser.: No. 288). (Illus.). 336p. 1982. 25.00 (ISBN 0-253-13400-5); pap. 10.95x (ISBN 0-253-20288-4). Ind U Pr.

Fuller, J. L. & Simmel, E. C., eds. Behavior Genetics: Principles & Application. 496p. 1982. text ed. write for info. (ISBN 0-89859-211-9). L Erlbaum Assocs.

Fuller, Jack. Convergence. LC 81-43483. 384p. 1982. 16.95 (ISBN 0-385-18023-3). Doubleday.

Fuller, Jean O. Shelley; a Biography. 10.00 o.p. (ISBN 0-87556-161-6). Saifer.

--Sir Francis Bacon: A Biography. 384p. 1982. 20.00 (ISBN 0-85692-069-X, Pub. by Salem Hse Ltd.). Merrimack Bk Serv.

--Swinburne: A Biography. LC 79-146790. (Illus.). 1971. 8.00x o.p. (ISBN 0-8052-3388-1). Schocken.

Fuller, John. Beautiful Inventions. 64p. 1983. 12.50 (ISBN 0-436-16811-1, Pub. by Secker & Warburg). David & Charles.

--Poems & Epistles. LC 74-81511. 128p. 1973. 12.95 (ISBN 0-87923-103-3); pap. 5.95 (ISBN 0-87923-116-5). Godine.

--The Sonnet. (Critical Idiom Ser.). 1972. pap. 4.95x (ISBN 0-416-65690-0). Methuen Inc.

Fuller, John & Renold, Edward. Chef's Compendium of Professional Recipes. 1972. 14.95 (ISBN 0-434-90583-6, Pub. by Heinemann). David & Charles.

Fuller, John, jt. ed. see Sargeant, Howard.

Fuller, John G. The Airmen Who Would Not Die. 1980. pap. 2.50 o.p. (ISBN 0-425-04273-1). Berkley Pub.

--The Airmen Who Would Not Die. LC 78-13728. 1979. 10.95 o.p. (ISBN 0-399-12264-8). Putnam Pub Group.

Fuller, John L. Motivation: A Biological Perspective. (Orig.). 1962. pap. text ed. 2.95 (ISBN 0-685-19747-6). Phila Bk Co.

Fuller, John L. & Thompson, William R. Foundations of Behavior Genetics. LC 78-4199. (Illus.). 534p. 1978. text ed. 24.95 o.p. (ISBN 0-8016-1712-X). Mosby.

Fuller, Joseph V. Bismarck's Diplomacy at Its Zenith. 1922. 27.50x (ISBN 0-86527-011-2). Fertig.

Fuller, K. J., jt. auth. see Aiken, D. W.

Fuller, Kpamma R. Surgical Technology: Principles & Practice. (Illus.). 535p. 1981. 32.00 (ISBN 0-7216-3957-7). Saunders.

Fuller, Lyndon. This One's About the ACC. 100p. 1982. pap. 5.95 (ISBN 0-89089-027-7). Carolina Acad Pr.

Fuller, Margaret. Trails of the Sawtooth & White Cloud Mountains. new ed. LC 78-68661. (Illus., Orig.). 1979. pap. 8.95 (ISBN 0-913140-29-5). Signpost Bk Pub.

--Trails of Western Idaho. LC 82-5621. (Illus.). 280p. pap. 10.25 (ISBN 0-913140-44-9). Signpost Bk Pub.

Fuller, Miriam M. Phillis Wheatley: America's First Black Poetess. LC 77-154858. (Americans All Ser). (Illus.). (gr. 3-6). 1971. PLB 7.12 (ISBN 0-8116-4569-X). Garrard.

Fuller, Muriel, ed. More Junior Authors. (Illus.). 235p. 1963. 12.00 (ISBN 0-8242-0036-5). Wilson.

Fuller, Myron. New Madrid Earthquake. 4.00 o.p. (ISBN 0-911208-11-9). Ramfre.

Fuller, Nathan C., ed. The Down East Reader: Selections from the Magazine of Maine. (Illus.). 256p. 1975. pap. 4.75 (ISBN 0-89272-001-8, 050). Down East.

Fuller, Neil, ed. Rush. (Australian Theatre Workshop Ser.). 1975. pap. text ed. 6.00x o.p. (ISBN 0-85859-127-8, 00537). Heinemann Ed.

Fuller, Nelson & Miller, Rex. Experiments for Electricity & Electronics. 2nd ed. LC 78-7708. 1978. pap. 8.95 (ISBN 0-672-97260-3); tchr's guide 3.33 (ISBN 0-672-97261-1). Bobbs.

Fuller, Persis, jt. auth. see Miller, Amy B.

Fuller, Peter. Robert Natkin. (Illus.). 348p. 1981. 65.00 o.p. (ISBN 0-8109-1355-0). Abrams.

Fuller, R. Buckminster. Grunch of Giants. 120p. 1983. 8.95 (ISBN 0-312-35193-3). St Martin.

--Intuition. 2nd ed. 1983. pap. 6.95 (ISBN 0-915166-20-8). Impact Pubs Cal.

--Operating Manual for Spaceship Earth. 1977. pap. 5.75 (ISBN 0-525-47433-1, 0558-170). Dutton.

--Operating Manual for Spaceship Earth. 1970. pap. 2.95 (ISBN 0-671-20783-0, Touchstone Bks). S&S.

Fuller, R. Buckminster & Applewhite, Edgar J. Synergetics II: Further Explorations in the Geometry of Thinking. (Illus.). 624p. 1979. pap. 13.95 (ISBN 0-02-092640-5). Macmillan.

Fuller, Reginald & Perkins, Pheme. Who Is This Christ? Gospel Christology & Contemporary Faith. LC 82-48590. 176p. 1983. pap. 8.95 (ISBN 0-8006-1706-1, 1-1706). Fortress.

Fuller, Reginald H. Interpreting the Miracles. (Student Christian Movement Press). (Orig.). 1963. pap. 5.95x o.p. (ISBN 0-19-520291-0). Oxford U Pr.

Fuller, Reginald H., et al. Hebrews, James, 1 & 2 Peter, Jude, Revelation. Krodel, Gerhard, ed. LC 76-7864. (Proclamation Commentaries). 132p. 1977. pap. 3.95 (ISBN 0-8006-0584-5, 1-584). Fortress.

Fuller, Robert. Amazement 1. (gr. 3-6). 1978. 6.50 (ISBN 0-88488-106-7). Creative Pubns.

--Amazement 2. (gr. 4-9). 1978. 6.50 (ISBN 0-88488-107-5). Creative Pubns.

Fuller, Roy. Owls & Artificers: Oxford Lectures on Poetry. LC 70-158611. 137p. 1971. 12.00 (ISBN 0-912050-06-3); pap. 3.50 o.p. (ISBN 0-686-57679-9). Open Court.

--Professors & Gods. LC 74-75010. 176p. 1974. 20.00 (ISBN 0-312-64785-9). St Martin.

Fuller, Roy, ed. Fellow Mortals: An Anthology of Animal Verse. 304p. 1981. 45.00x (ISBN 0-7121-0635-9, Pub. by Macdonald & Evans). State Mutual Bk.

Fuller, Russell. In a Family Way. (Illus.). 240p. (Orig.). Date not set. pap. 22.00 (ISBN 0-933280-12-2). Island CA. Postponed.

Fuller, Samuel. The Dark Page. 256p. 1983. pap. 2.95 (ISBN 0-380-62117-7). Avon.

Fuller, Tony, jt. auth. see Goldman, Peter.

Fuller, W. H., jt. auth. see Cope, C. B.

Fuller, W. R. Formation & Structure of Paint Films. Federation of Societies for Coatings Technology, Educational Committee, ed. 1965. 2.50 (ISBN 0-686-95499-8). Fed Soc Coat Tech.

Fuller, Wayne A. Introduction to Statistical Time Series. LC 76-6954. (Probability & Mathematical Statistics Ser.). 1976. 43.95 (ISBN 0-471-28715-6, Pub. by Wiley-Interscience). Wiley.

Fuller-Maitland, J. A. English Music in the 19th Century. 328p. 1983. pap. 6.95 (ISBN 0-88072-003-4). Tanager Bks.

Fullerton, Brian, tr. see Holt-Jensen, Arild.

Fullerton, Herbert H. & Prescott, James R. Economic Simulation Model for Regional Development Planning. LC 74-14426. 1975. 12.50 o.p. (ISBN 0-250-40074-X). Ann Arbor Science.

Fullerton, James H. Ice Hockey! Playing & Coaching. (Illus.). 1978. 10.95 o.p. (ISBN 0-686-82915-8); pap. 5.95 (ISBN 0-8038-3406-3). Hastings.

Fullerton, Ralph O. & Ray, John B. Tennessee: Geographical Patterns & Regions. (Illus.). 1977. pap. text ed. 8.95 (ISBN 0-8403-1686-0). Kendall-Hunt.

Fullerton, Timothy T., compiled by. Triviata. (Illus.). 240p. (Orig.). 1975. pap. 4.95 o.s.i. (ISBN 0-89104-169-9, A & W Visual Library). A & W Pubs.

Fullerton, W. Y. Charles Spurgeon. (Golden Oldies Ser.). 288p. 1980. pap. 4.50 (ISBN 0-8024-1236-X). Moody.

Fullick, Roy, jt. auth. see Powell, Geoffery.

Fullman, Everett L. Living the Lord's Prayer. (Epiphany Ser.). 128p. 1983. pap. 2.50 (ISBN 0-345-30432-2). Ballantine.

Fullman, James B., jt. auth. see Shuldener, Henry L.

Fullmer, Daniel W. Counseling: Group Theory & System. 2nd ed. LC 78-9058. 1978. 27.00x (ISBN 0-910328-12-9); pap. 16.50 (ISBN 0-910328-13-7). Carroll Pr.

Fullmer, Hareld M., jt. auth. see Lillie, Ralph D.

Fullner, Bernd. Heinrich Heine In Deutschen Literaturgeschichten. 340p. (Ger.). 1982. write for info. (ISBN 3-8204-7016-6). P Lang Pubs.

Fulmer, Constance M. George Eliot: A Reference Guide. 1977. lib. bdg. 25.00 (ISBN 0-8161-7859-3, Hall Reference). G K Hall.

Fulmer, Robert M. The New Management. 3rd ed. 544p. 1983. text ed. 20.95 (ISBN 0-02-339740-3). Macmillan.

Fulmer, Robert M. & Franklin, Steven C. Supervision: Principles of Professional Management. 2nd ed. 1982. text ed. 22.95x (ISBN 0-02-479660-3). Macmillan.

Fulmer, Robert M. & Herbert, Theodore T. Exploring the New Management. 3rd ed. 320p. 1983. text ed. 9.95 (ISBN 0-02-340080-3). Macmillan.

Fulmer, William E. Union Organizing: Management & Labor Conflict. 240p. 1982. 24.95 (ISBN 0-03-062603-X). Praeger.

Fulrath, R. M. & Pask, Joseph A., eds. Ceramic Microstructures: Their Analysis, Significance & Production. LC 74-32351. 1028p. 1976. Repr. of 1966 ed. 49.50 (ISBN 0-88275-262-6). Krieger.

Fulrath, Richard M., ed. Ceramic Microstructures 1976: With Emphasis on Energy Related Applications. Pask, Joseph A. LC 77-5232. 1977. lib. bdg. 75.00 o.p. (ISBN 0-89158-307-6). Westview.

Fulsher, Keith & Krom, Charles. Hair Wing Atlantic Salmon Flies. 1st ed. Surette, Dick, ed. (Illus.). 184p. (Orig.). 1981. 25.00 (ISBN 0-9607522-0-X); pap. 15.00 (ISBN 0-686-99460-4). Fly Tyer.

Fulton. The Frontal Lobes & Human Behaviour. 30p. 1982. 50.00x (ISBN 0-85323-311-X, Pub. by LIverpool Univ England). State Mutual Bk.

Fulton & Gordon. Diving West. rev. ed. (Updated Every 2 to 4 Years Ser.). (Illus.). 110p. (Orig.). 1983. pap. 7.00 (ISBN 0-938206-01-X). ChartGuide.

Fulton, Alvenia M., ed. see Gregory, Dick.

Fulton, Charles C. Modern Microcrystal Tests for Drugs: The Identification of Organic Compounds by Microcrystalloscopic Chemistry. LC 68-54599. 1969. 49.95 o.p. (ISBN 0-471-28732-6, Pub. by Wiley-Interscience). Wiley.

Fulton, Eleanor & Smith, Pat. Let's Slice the Ice. (Illus.). (gr. 3 up). 1978. pap. text ed. 5.50 (ISBN 0-918812-02-X). Magnamusic.

Fulton, George A., jt. auth. see Shapiro, Harold T.

Fulton, George P., jt. auth. see Shepro, David.

Fulton, James E. & Black, Elizabeth. Dr. Fulton's Step-By-Step Program for Clearing Acne. LC 82-47522. (Illus.). 256p. 1983. 12.45i (ISBN 0-06-038020-9, HarpT). Har-Row.

Fulton, John F. & Thomson, Elizabeth H. Benjamin Silliman, 1779-1864, Pathfinder in American Science. LC 69-10095. 1969. Repr. of 1947 ed. lib. bdg. 19.25x (ISBN 0-8371-0080-1, FUBS). Greenwood.

Fulton, Len & Ferber, Ellen, eds. Directory of Small Magazine-Press Editors & Publishers. 200p. 1983. pap. 12.95 (ISBN 0-913218-65-0). Dustbooks.

--International Directory of Little Magazines & Small Presses: 19th Annual. 600p. 1983. 25.95 (ISBN 0-913218-64-2); pap. 17.95 (ISBN 0-913218-63-4). Dustbooks.

--Small Press Record of Books in Print: 12th Annual. 750p. 1983. 25.95 (ISBN 0-913218-61-8). Dustbooks.

Fulton, Martin W. A Chronology of Substances of Abuse. LC 78-62253. 1978. pap. text ed. 9.00 (ISBN 0-8191-0566-X). U Pr of Amer.

Fulton, O. & Gordon, A. Higher Education & Manpower Planning: A Comparative Study of Planned & Market Economies. 127p. 1982. 11.40 (ISBN 92-2-102973-5). Intl Labour Office.

Fulton, Robert B. Adam Smith Speaks to Our Times. 1963. 4.50 o.p. (ISBN 0-8158-0096-7). Chris Mass.

--Original Marxism - Estranged Offspring. 1960. 4.50 o.p. (ISBN 0-8158-0097-5). Chris Mass.

Fulton, Robert J. & Bendiksen, Robert. Death & Identity. rev. ed. 1978. text ed. 21.95 o.p. (ISBN 0-913486-78-7). Charles.

Fults, John L. Magic Squares. LC 73-23041. (Illus.). 124p. 1974. 12.00 (ISBN 0-87548-317-8); pap. 4.00 (ISBN 0-87548-198-1). Open Court.

Fulves, Karl. Self Working Number Magic. (Magic Ser.). (Illus.). 128p. (Orig.). 1983. pap. 2.95 (ISBN 0-486-24391-5). Dover.

Fulwiler, Toby & Young, Art, eds. The Language Connection: Writing & Reading Across the Curriculum. 190p. 1982. 10.75 o.p. (ISBN 0-686-95292-8); members 9.50 o.p. (ISBN 0-686-99487-6). NCTE.

Fulwood, Robinson & Johnson, Clifford L. Hematological & Nutritional Biochemistries References Data of Persons 6 Months-74 Years of Age: United States, 1976-1980. Cox, Klaudia, tr. (Ser. 11: No. 232). 60p. 1982. pap. 1.95 (ISBN 0-8406-0267-7). Natl Ctr Health Stats.

Fumagalli, ed. Drugs Affecting Lipid Metabolism. (Giovanni Lorenzini Foundation Symposia Ser.: Vol. 7). 1981. 71.00 (ISBN 0-444-80283-5). Elsevier.

Fumi, F. G. Physics of Semiconductors: Proceedings of the 13th International Conference, Rome, 1976. 1976. 138.50 o.p. (ISBN 0-7204-0571-8, North-Holland). Elsevier.

Funck, J. L., ed. see International Society for Artificial Organs.

Funck, R. Recent Developments in Regional Science. (Karlsruhe Papers in Regional Science). 153p. 1974. pap. 10.00x (ISBN 0-85086-034-2, Pub. by Pion England). Methuen Inc.

Funck, R. & Parr, J. B., eds. The Analysis of Regional Structure: Essays in Honour of August Losch. (Karlsruhe Papers in Regional Science). 168p. 1978. pap. 12.50x (ISBN 0-85086-068-7, Pub. by Pion England). Methuen Inc.

Funcken, Fred, jt. auth. see Funcken, Liliane.

Funcken, Fred, jt. auth. see Funcken, Lilliane.

Funcken, Liliane & Funcken, Fred. Ancient Egypt to the Eighteenth Century. (Arms & Uniforms: Vol. 1). (Illus.). 155p. (gr. 6-10). 1972. 11.95x o.p. (ISBN 0-7063-1814-5). Intl Pubns Serv.

--Arms & Uniforms: Lace Wars, Pt. 1. 1978. 17.95 o.p. (ISBN 0-685-87389-7). Hippocrene Bks.

--Arms & Uniforms: Lace Wars, Pt. 2. 1978. 17.95 o.p. (ISBN 0-7063-5566-0). Hippocrene Bks.

--Arms & Uniforms: The Age of Chivalry, 3 vols. 112p. 1983. 17.95 set (ISBN 0-686-84587-0). Vol. I (ISBN 0-13-046284-5). Vol. II (ISBN 0-13-046318-3). Vol. III (ISBN 0-13-046334-5). pap. 8.95 set (ISBN 0-686-84588-9). Vol. I (ISBN 0-13-046276-4). Vol. II (ISBN 0-13-046292-6). Vol. III (ISBN 0-13-046326-4). P-H.

--The Lace Wars, 2 pts. LC 78-305993. (Arms & Uniforms Ser.). (Illus.). 1977. 17.50x ea. (ISBN 0-7063-3562-7). Pt. 1. Pt. 2 (ISBN 0-7063-5566-0). Intl Pubns Serv.

Funcken, Lilliane & Funcken, Fred. British Infantry Uniforms from Marlborough to Wellington. (Illus.). pap. 14.95x o.p. (ISBN 0-8464-0213-0). Beekman Pubs.

Fundaburk, Emma L. Reference Materials & Periodicals in Economics: An International List, Agriculture. LC 78-142232. 1971. 23.00 (ISBN 0-8108-0349-6). Scarecrow.

Funder, jt. auth. see Cumming.

Fung, K. K., tr. see Muqiao, Xue.

Fung, K. K., tr. see Yefung, Sun.

Fung, Raymond, ed. Households of God on China's Soil. LC 82-18974. 96p. (Orig.). 1983. pap. 5.95 (ISBN 0-88344-189-6). Orbis Bks.

Fung, Y., jt. ed. see Greenwood, Donald T.

Fung, Y. C. Foundations of Solid Mechanics. 1965. ref. ed. 34.95 (ISBN 0-13-329912-0). P-H.

Fung, Y. C., ed. see Biomechanics Symposium, 1973.

Fung, Yuan-Cheng. A First Course in Continuum Mechanics. 2nd ed. (International Series in Dynamics). (Illus.). 1977. 33.95 (ISBN 0-13-318311-4). P-H.

Funk, Arthur L. The Politics of Torch: The Allied Landings & the Algiers Putsch, 1942. LC 74-2020. (Illus.). viii, 322p. 1974. 17.95x (ISBN 0-7006-0123-6). Univ Pr KS.

Funk, Berverley M., jt. auth. see Schatz, Anne E.

Funk, Beverley M., jt. auth. see Schatz, Anne E.

Funk, Beverly M., jt. auth. see Schatz, Anne E.

Funk, Edward R. Welding: An Introduction. 1984. text ed. 25.95 (ISBN 0-534-01074-1, Breton Pubs). Wadsworth Pub. Postponed.

Funk, Georg. Die Algenvegetation Des Golfes Von Neapel. (Pubbl. d. Stazione Zool. di Napoli). (Illus., Ger.). Repr. of 1927 ed. lib. bdg. 72.00 (ISBN 3-87429-142-1). Lubrecht & Cramer.

--Beitraege zur Kenntnis der Meeresalgen von Neapel, zugleich mikrophotographischer Atlas. (Pubbl. d. Stazione Zool. di Napoli). (Illus., Ger.). 1978. Repr. of 1935 ed. lib. bdg. 53.60 (ISBN 3-87429-146-4). Lubrecht & Cramer.

Funk, Hal D. & Olberg, Robert T., eds. Learning to Teach in the Elementary School: Introductory Readings. 1971. pap. text ed. 17.50 scp o.p. (ISBN 0-06-042216-5, HarpC). Har-Row.

Funk, Merle M. Shootout at Clearwater. (YA) 1979. 6.95 (ISBN 0-685-59936-1, Avalon). Bouregy.

--Wes Weatherby, Gunfighter. (YA) 1979. 6.95 (ISBN 0-685-93883-2, Avalon). Bouregy.

Funk, Peter & Tarshis, Barry. Word Memory Power in Thirty Days. 1981. 12.95 o.s.i. (ISBN 0-440-08624-8). Delacorte.

Funk, Robert W. A Beginning-Intermediate Grammar of Hellenistic Greek, 3 vols. 2nd, rev. ed. Incl. Vol. 1. Morphology; Vol. 2. Syntax; Vol. 3. Appendices. LC 72-88769. (Society of Biblical Literature. Sources for Biblical Studies). (Orig.). 1977. Set. pap. text ed. 19.50 (ISBN 0-89130-148-8, 06-03-02). Scholars Pr Ca.

--Christopher Isherwood: A Reference Guide. 1979. lib. bdg. 26.00 (ISBN 0-8161-8072-5, Hall Reference). G K Hall.

Funk, Robert W., tr. Greek Grammar of the New Testament & Other Early Christian Literature. 24.00 (ISBN 0-310-24780-2). Zondervan.

Funk, Tom. I Read Signs. (Illus.). 40p. (gr. k-3). 1962. reinforced bdg. 5.95 o.p. (ISBN 0-8234-0058-1). Holiday.

Funk, Vicki Ann. The Systematics of Montanoa (Asteraceae-Heliantheae) (Memoirs of the New York Botanical Garden Ser.: Vol. 36). (Illus.). 1982. pap. 21.00 (ISBN 0-89327-243-4). NY Botanical.

Funk, Wilfred & Lewis, Norman. Thirty Days to a More Powerful Vocabulary. LC 72-94340. (Funk & W Bk.). (gr. 9-12). 1970. text ed. 12.45 (ISBN 0-308-40079-8, 430180). T Y Crowell.

Funke, Gail S., et al. Assets & Liabilities of Correctional Industries. LC 81-47029. 176p. 1981. 19.95x (ISBN 0-669-04542-X). Lexington Bks.

Funkenstein, Daniel H. Medical Students, Medical Schools & Society During Five Eras: Factors Affecting the Career Choices of Physicians, 1958-1976. LC 77-19063. 1978. prof ref 22.00x (ISBN 0-88410-704-3). Ballinger Pub.

Funkhouser, Erica. Natural Affinities. 68p. 1983. 12.95 (ISBN 0-914086-43-X); pap. 4.95 (ISBN 0-914086-42-1). Alicejamesbooks.

Funkhouser, Robert. IBM BASIC for Business & Home. 1982. text ed. 19.95 (ISBN 0-8359-3019-X); pap. text ed. 14.95 (ISBN 0-8359-3018-1). Reston.

Funnell, Charles E. By the Beautiful Sea: The Rise & High Times of That Great American Resort, Atlantic City. 1983. 7.95 (ISBN 0-8135-0986-6). Rutgers U Pr.

Funston, R. Y. Constitutional Counterrevolution: The Warren Court & the Burger Court-Judicial Policy Making in Modern America. 399p. 1977. pap. 8.95x (ISBN 0-470-99023-6, Pub. by Wiley-Interscie). Wiley.

Funt, Peter & Shatzkin, Mike. Gotcha! LC 79-84769. (Illus.). 1979. 7.95 o.p. (ISBN 0-448-15703-9, G&D). Putnam Pub Group.

Fuori, W. M. Introduction to American National Standard Cobol. 1975. 18.50 o.p. (ISBN 0-07-022623-7, G); instructor's manual & key 5.95 o.p. (ISBN 0-07-022624-5). McGraw.

Fuori, William, et al. Introduction to Computer Operations. 1973. text ed. 18.50 o.p. (ISBN 0-07-022619-9, G); instructors' manual 5.95 o.p. (ISBN 0-07-022620-2). McGraw.

Fuori, William M. Introduction to the Computer: The Tool of Business. 3rd ed. (Illus.). 720p. 1981. text ed. 19.95 (ISBN 0-13-480343-4); pap. 7.95 study guide (ISBN 0-13-480368-X). P-H.

Fuori, William M. & Tedesco, Dominick. Introduction to Information Processing: Study Guide. (Illus.). 80p. 1983. pap. 2.95 (ISBN 0-13-484659-1). P H.

Fuoss, D. E. & Troppman, R. J. Creative Management Techniques in Interscholastic Athletics. LC 76-46500. 494p. 1977. 25.50x (ISBN 0-471-28815-2). Wiley.

Fuoss, Donald E. & Troppmann, Robert J. Effective Coaching: A Psychological Approach. LC 81-7624. 348p. 1981. text ed. 21.95 (ISBN 0-471-03233-6). Wiley.

Fuqua, Paul. Drug Abuse: Investigation & Control. LC 77-5809. (Illus.). 1977. text ed. 19.95 (ISBN 0-07-022665-2, G); teacher's manual & key 4.50 (ISBN 0-07-022666-0). McGraw.

Fuqua, Paul & Wilson, Jerry. Security Investigators Handbook. 232p. 1979. 16.95 (ISBN 0-87201-398-7). Gulf Pub.

Fuqua, Paul, jt. auth. see Wilson, Jerry.

Fuquay, jt. auth. see Maddox.

Fuquay, John W. & Bearden, H. Joe. Applied Animal Reproduction. (Illus.). 352p. 1980. text ed. 20.95 (ISBN 0-8359-0249-8); instr's. manual free (ISBN 0-8359-0250-1). Reston.

Fuquay, Robert F., jt. auth. see Maddox, Russell W.

Furan Illustrators see Reece, Collen L.

Furay, Conal & Salevouris, Michael J. History: A Workbook of Skill Development. 1979. pap. 8.95 (ISBN 0-531-05620-1). Watts.

Furbank, P. N. Italo Svevo: The Man & the Writer. LC 66-29426. 1966. 18.50x o.p. (ISBN 0-520-00436-1). U of Cal Pr.

Furbank, P. N., tr. see Svevo, Italo.

Furberg, jt. ed. see Eriksson.

Furcha, E. J., ed. Spirit within Structure: Essays in Honor of George Johnston on the Occasion of his Seventieth Birthday. (Pittsburgh Theological Monographs: No. 3). xvi, 194p. 1983. pap. 12.50 (ISBN 0-915138-53-0). Pickwick.

Furdson, Edward. The European Defense Community: A History. LC 79-21220. 1980. 26.00x (ISBN 0-312-26927-7). St Martin.

Furer, Howard B. Harry S. Truman, 1884-1972: Chronology, Documents, Bibliographical Aids. LC 75-83749. 155p. 1970. 8.00 (ISBN 0-379-12067-4). Oceana.

--New York: A Chronological & Documentary History, 1524-1970. LC 74-3044. (American Cities Chronology Ser.). 153p. 1974. 8.50 (ISBN 0-379-00610-3). Oceana.

Furer, Howard B., ed. & compiled by. The British in America, 1578-1970: A Chronology & Factbook. LC 72-8683. (Ethnic Chronology Ser.: No. 7). 153p. 1972. 8.50 (ISBN 0-379-00507-7). Oceana.

Furer, Howard B., ed. James A. Garfield, 1831-1881; Chester A. Arthur 1830-1886: Chronology, Documents, Bibliographical Aids. Incl. Chester A. Arthur: 1830-1886. LC 74-111214. (Oceana Presidential Chronology Ser.). 148p. 1970. 8.00 (ISBN 0-379-12065-8). Oceana.

Furer, Howard B., ed. & compiled by. The Scandinavians in America, Nine Hundred Eighty-Six to Nineteen Seventy: A Chronology & Fact Book. LC 72-10257. (Ethnic Chronology Ser.: No. 6). 152p. 1972. 8.50 (ISBN 0-379-00505-0). Oceana.

Furer-Haimendorf, Christop Von see Von Furer-Haimendorf, Christoph.

Furer-Haimendorf, Christoph Von see Von Furer-Haimendorf, Christoph.

Furer-Haimendorf, Christoph Von, ed. Caste & Kin in Nepal, India & Ceylon: Anthropological Studies in Hindu-Buddhist Contact Zones. (Illus.). 1978. text ed. 20.00x (ISBN 0-391-01073-5). Humanities.

Furer-Haimendorf, Christopher von see Von Furer-Haimendorf, Christopher.

Furet, Francois M. Interpreting the French Revolution. Forster, Elborg, tr. LC 80-42290. 224p. 1981. 32.50 (ISBN 0-521-23574-X); pap. 9.95 (ISBN 0-521-28049-4). Cambridge U Pr.

Furgis, Ellen V. & Valentine, D. Eugene. Greek Cooking at Its American Best. (Illus.). spiral bdg., softcover 8.95 (ISBN 0-941968-01-4, An Everest House Book). Dodd.

Furler, Rene, jt. auth. see Thurlimann, Bruno.

Furley, Peter A., et al. Geography of Biosphere. (Illus.). 1982. text ed. 82.50 (ISBN 0-408-70801-8). Butterworth.

Furlong, Charles W. Let'er Buck: A Story of the Passing of the Old West. LC 77-159961. 280p. 1971. Repr. of 1921 ed. 34.00x (ISBN 0-8103-3405-4). Gale.

Furlong, Michael, jt. auth. see Nutt-Powell, Thomas E.

Furlong, Monica. Merton: A Biography. LC 79-3588. (Illus.). 320p. 1980. 12.95i o.p. (ISBN 0-06-063079-5, HarpR). Har-Row.

--Puritan's Progress. (Illus.). 224p. 1976. 8.95 o.p. (ISBN 0-698-10688-1, Coward). Putnam Pub Group.

Furlong, William B., jt. auth. see Diamond, Seymour.

Furlonge, Geoffrey. Lands of Barbary. (Illus.). 1968. 9.95 o.p. (ISBN 0-7195-0470-8). Transatlantic.

Furlow, Malcolm. Building the San Juan Central: An Hon 3 Project Railroad. (Illus., Orig.). 1984. pap. price not set (ISBN 0-89024-058-2). Kalmbach.

Furman, A. L., ed. Ghost Stories. (gr. 5-8). 1964. pap. 1.95 (ISBN 0-671-43613-9). Archway.

--More Horse Stories. (gr. 5-7). 1966. pap. 1.95 (ISBN 0-671-43951-0). Archway.

Furman, Abraham L., ed. Teen-Age Ghost Stories. (Illus.). (gr. 6-10). 1961. PLB 6.19 o.p. (ISBN 0-8313-0058-2). Lantern.

--Teen-Age Haunted Stories. (gr. 6-10). PLB 6.19 o.p. (ISBN 0-8313-0045-0). Lantern.

--Teen-Age Secret Agent Stories. (Teen-Age Library). (gr. 5-10). PLB 6.19 o.p. (ISBN 0-8313-0042-6). Lantern.

Furman, Gabriel. Antiquities of Long Island. 9.50 (ISBN 0-911660-15-1). Yankee Peddler.

Furman, Laura. The Shadow Line. LC 81-24089. 288p. 1982. 14.95 (ISBN 0-670-63764-5). Viking Pr.

Furnas, J. C. The Americans: A Social History of the United States (1587-1914) (Illus.). 1969. 12.95 o.p. (ISBN 0-399-10032-6). Putnam Pub Group.

--Great Times: An Informal Social History of the U. S. 1914-1929. LC 74-79645. 640p. 1974. 15.00 o.p. (ISBN 0-399-11381-9). Putnam Pub Group.

--Stormy Weather: Crosslights on the Nineteen Thirties: an Informal Social History, Vol. III. LC 77-6467. (Illus.). 1977. 15.00 o.p. (ISBN 0-399-11842-X). Putnam Pub Group.

Furneaux, Henry, et al, eds. see Tacitus.

Furneaux, Philip. The Palladium of Conscience. LC 74-122161. (Civil Liberties in American History Ser). 267p. 1974. Repr. of 1773 ed. lib. bdg. 35.00 (ISBN 0-306-71972-X). Da Capo.

Furneaux, Rupert. Buried Treasure. LC 79-64159. (Adventures in History Ser.). PLB 12.68 (ISBN 0-382-06298-1). Silver.

Furneaux Jordan, Robert. Concise History of Western Architecture. 1969. pap. text ed. 13.95 o.p. (ISBN 0-15-512950-3, HC). HarBraceJ.

Furness, Eric L. Money & Credit in Developing Africa. LC 75-27161. 1976. 30.00 (ISBN 0-312-54495-2). St Martin.

Furness, Horace H., ed. see Shakespeare, William.

Furness, Pauline. Role-Play in the Elementary School. 224p. (Orig.). 1976. pap. 6.95 (ISBN 0-89104-248-2, A & W Visual Library). A & W Pubs.

Furness, Raymond. Wagner & Literature. LC 81-14391. 1982. 26.00 (ISBN 0-312-85347-5). St Martin.

Furnish, Victor P. Theology & Ethics in Paul. LC 68-17445. 1978. pap. 11.95 (ISBN 0-687-41499-7). Abingdon.

Furnish, Victor P., ed. see Murphy, Roland E.

Furnish, Victory P., ed. see Fretheim, Terence E.

Furniss, W. Todd. Reshaping Faculty Careers. 171p. 1981. 8.95 (ISBN 0-8268-1449-2). Impact VA.

--Steady-State Staffing in Tenure-Granting Institutions. 1973. 3.00 o.p. (ISBN 0-8268-1385-2). ACE.

Furniss, W. Todd, ed. American Universities & Colleges. 11th ed. LC 28-5598. 2000p. 1973. lib. bdg. 59.50 o.p. (ISBN 0-8268-1211-2). ACE.

--Higher Education for Everybody? 1971. 9.00 o.p. (ISBN 0-8268-1319-4). ACE.

Furniss, W. Todd & Gardner, David P., eds. Higher Education & Government. 1979. 15.00 o.p. (ISBN 0-8268-1327-5). ACE.

Furniss, W. Todd & Graham, Patricia A., eds. Women in Higher Education. 325p. 1974. 12.00 o.p. (ISBN 0-8268-1421-2). ACE.

Furnival, Frederick J., ed. Early English Meals & Manners. LC 73-81154. 1969. Repr. of 1868 ed. 53.00 o.p. (ISBN 0-8103-3853-X). Gale.

Furntratt, Ernst & Moller, Christine. Lernprinzip Erfolg. viii, 235p. (Ger.). 1982. write for info. (ISBN 3-8204-5836-0). P Lang Pubs.

Furrer, P. J. Art Therapy Activities & Lesson Plans for Individual & Groups: A Practical Guide for Teachers, Therapists, Parents & those Interested in Promoting Personal Growth in Themselves & Others. (Illus.). 144p. 1982. pap. 12.75x spiral (ISBN 0-398-04799-5). C C Thomas.

Furriack, William de see Reppy, William A. & Samuel, Cynthia A.

Furrow, Barry R. Malpractice in Psychotherapy. LC 79-3253. 176p. 1980. 21.95x (ISBN 0-669-03399-5). Lexington Bks.

Furse, John. Michelangelo & His Art. (The Artist & His Art Ser.). (Illus.). 128p. 1981. 9.98 o.p. (ISBN 0-89196-094-5, Bk Value Intl). Quality Bks IL.

Furst, Alan. The Caribbean Account. 1981. 11.95 o.s.i. (ISBN 0-440-01393-3). Delacorte.

--The Caribbean Account. 1983. pap. 3.95 (ISBN 0-440-11105-6). Dell.

--The Paris Drop. LC 79-7615. 240p. 1980. 8.95 o.p. (ISBN 0-385-14889-5). Doubleday.

Furst, Bruno. Stop Forgetting. rev. ed. Furst, Lotte & Storm, Gerrit, eds. LC 75-164727. (Illus.). 1979. pap. 8.95 (ISBN 0-385-15401-1). Doubleday.

Furst, Jill L., jt. auth. see Furst, Peter T.

Furst, Lilian R. Romanticism. 2nd ed. (Critical Idiom Ser.). 1976. pap. 4.95x (ISBN 0-416-83920-7). Methuen Inc.

--Romanticism in Perspective. 2nd ed. 1979. text ed. 20.00x (ISBN 0-391-00003-9). Humanities.

Furst, Lillian R. & Skrine, Peter N. Naturalism. (Critical Idiom Ser.). 1971. pap. 4.95x (ISBN 0-416-65670-6). Methuen Inc.

Furst, Lotte, ed. see Furst, Bruno.

Furst, Peter T. & Furst, Jill L. North American Indian Art. LC 82-40343. (Illus.). 264p. 1982. 45.00 (ISBN 0-8478-0461-5). Rizzoli Intl.

Furst, Peter T., ed. LAAG Contributions to Afro-American Ethnohistory in Latin America & the Caribbean, Vol. 1. 1976. pap. 2.75 (ISBN 0-686-36583-6). Am Anthro Assn.

Furstenau, E. Dicionario de Temos Tecnicos Ingles-Portugues. 1157p. (Eng. & Port.). 1980. 95.00 (ISBN 0-686-97635-5, M-9211). French & Eur.

Furstenberg, Egon Von see Von Furstenberg, Egon & Fisher, Karen.

Furstenberg, George M. Von see Von Furstenberg, George M.

Furstenberg, George M. von see Von Furstenberg, George M.

Furstenberg-Forbes, Lynn. Hanover Heritage. 352p. 1983. pap. 2.95 (ISBN 0-523-41342-4). Pinnacle Bks.

Furtado, C. Economic Development of Latin America. 1970. 11.95 o.p. (ISBN 0-521-07828-8). Brown Bk.

--Economic Development of Latin America. 2nd ed. LC 74-121365. (Latin American Studies: No.8). (Illus.). 280p. 1977. 42.50 (ISBN 0-521-21197-2); pap. 11.95 (ISBN 0-521-29070-8). Cambridge U Pr.

Furtado, J. I. & Mori, S. Tasek Bera: The Ecology of a Freshwater Swamp. 1982. text ed. 79.00 (ISBN 90-6193-100-2, Pub. by Junk Pubs Netherlands). Kluwer Boston.

Furter, Pierre. Possibilities & Limitations of Functional Literacy: The Iranian Experiment. LC 73-781021. (Educational Studies & Documents, No. 9). (Illus.). 59p. (Orig.). 1973. pap. 2.50 o.p. (ISBN 92-3-101075-1, U472, UNESCO). Unipub.

Furth, Anna J. Lipids & Polysaccharides in Biology. (Studies in Biology: No. 125). 72p. 1980. pap. text ed. 8.95 (ISBN 0-7131-2805-4). E Arnold.

Furth, Hans D. & Wachs, Harry. Thinking Goes to School: Piaget's Theory in Practice. (Illus.). 1974. 17.95 o.p. (ISBN 0-19-501729-3). Oxford U Pr.

Furth, Montgomery, ed. & tr. see Frege, Gottlob.

Furth, Montgomery, ed. see Frege, Gottlob.

Furth, R. Van see Van Furth, R.

Furthmayr, Heinz, ed. Immunochemistry of the Extracellular Matrix, 2 Vols. 1982. Vol. I, 272 pp. 75.00 (ISBN 0-8493-6196-6); Vol. II, 280 pp. 59.50 (ISBN 0-8493-6197-4). CRC Pr.

Furukawa, Chiyoko & Shomaker, Diana. Community Health Services for the Aged: Promotion & Maintenance. LC 81-19105. 372p. 1982. text ed. 31.95 (ISBN 0-89443-382-2). Aspen Systems.

Furukawa, James, jt. auth. see Tosh, Dennis S.

Furuseth, Owen J. & Pierce, John T. Agricultural Land in an Urban Society. Knight, C. Gregory, ed. (Resource Publications in Geography Ser.). (Orig.). 1982. pap. 5.00 (ISBN 0-89291-149-2). Assn Am Geographers.

Fusaro, A. Daniel, ed. Rules of the U.S. Courts in New York. rev. ed. LC 65-16452. 1978. with 1979 rev. pages 45.00 (ISBN 0-87632-070-1). Boardman.

Fusch, Otto. Building Cost Composites. (Orig.). pap. write for info. o.p. (ISBN 0-910460-79-5). Craftsman.

Fusco, Peter, et al. The Romantics to Rodin: French Nineteenth-Century Sculpture from North American Collections. LC 79-27101. (Illus.). 1980. pap. 11.95 o.p. (ISBN 0-87587-091-0). LA Co Art Mus.

Fuse, Katsuji. Soviet Policy in the Orient. LC 75-39027. (China Studies). (Illus.). Repr. of 1927 ed. 25.00 o.p. (ISBN 0-88355-383-X). Hyperion Conn.

Fuseli, Henry. The Lectures of Henry Fuseli- in "Lectures on Paintings by the Royal Academicians". Freedberg, Sydney J., ed. LC 77-19376. (Connoisseurship Criticism & Art History Ser.: Vol. 10). 450p. 1979. lib. bdg. 40.00 o.s.i. (ISBN 0-8240-3268-3). Garland Pub.

Fusfeld, Daniel. Economics: Principles of Political Economy. 1982. text ed. 24.50x (ISBN 0-673-15350-9). Scott F.

Fusfeld, Daniel R. Age of the Economist. 4th ed. 1982. pap. text ed. 9.95x (ISBN 0-673-15500-5). Scott F.

Fusfeld, Herbert I. & Haklisch, Carmela S., eds. Science & Technology Policy: Perspectives for the Nineteen-Eighties. LC 79-28295. (Annals of the New York Academy of Sciences: Vol. 334). 285p. 1979. 52.00x (ISBN 0-89766-037-4); pap. 42.00x (ISBN 0-89766-036-6). NY Acad Sci.

Fusfeld, Herbert I. & Langlois, Richard N., eds. Understanding R&D Productivity. 200p. 19.50 (ISBN 0-686-84787-3). Work in Amer.

Fusino, S. A Neo-Keynesian Theory of Inflation & Economic Growth. (Lecture Notes in Economics & Mathematical Systems Ser.: Vol. 104). v, 96p. 1974. pap. 9.90 o.p. (ISBN 0-387-06964-X). Springer-Verlag.

Fuson, Robert H. Introduction to World Geography: Regions & Cultures. LC 75-46351. 1978. pap. 10.95 (ISBN 0-8403-1413-2). Kendall-Hunt.

Fusonie, Alan & Moran, Leila, eds. International Agricultural Librarianship: Continuity & Change. LC 78-67916. lib. bdg. 25.00 (ISBN 0-313-20640-6, AIA/). Greenwood.

Fuss, M., jt. auth. see McFadden, D.

Fuss, Peter, jt. ed. see Wheelwright, Philip.

Fussell, Edwin, tr. & intro. by see Pavese, Cesare.

Fussell, J. B. & Burdick, G. R., eds. Nuclear Systems Reliability Engineering & Risk Assessment. LC 77-91478. (Illus.). xi, 849p. 1977. text ed. 45.00 (ISBN 0-89871-041-3). Soc Indus-Appl Math.

Fussell, Paul. Abroad: British Literary Traveling Between the Wars. (Illus.). 1980. 17.95 (ISBN 0-19-502767-1). Oxford U Pr.

--The Great War & Modern Memory. (Illus.). 352p. 1975. 17.95 o.p. (ISBN 0-19-501918-0). Oxford U Pr.

Fussell, Paul, ed. English Augustan Poetry. 7.50 o.p. (ISBN 0-8446-4416-1). Peter Smith.

Fussell, Paul, Jr. Poetic Meter & Poetic Form. rev. ed. 1979. pap. text ed. 6.50x (ISBN 0-394-32120-0, RanC). Random.

Fussner, F. Smith, ed. Glimpses of Wheeler County's Past: An Early History of North Central Oregon. LC 75-11035. (Illus.). 1975. pap. 4.95 o.p. (ISBN 0-8323-0249-X). Binford.

Fuster, Joaquin M. The Prefrontal Cortex. 232p. 1980. text ed. 28.00 (ISBN 0-89004-524-0). Raven.

Futagawa, Yukio, jt. auth. see Itoh, Teiji.

Futas, Elizabeth. The Library Forms Illustrated Handbook. (Illus.). 550p. 1983. lib. bdg. 49.95 (ISBN 0-918212-69-3). Neal-Schuman.

Futas, Elizabeth, ed. Library Acquisition Policies. 2nd ed. 1983. price not set (ISBN 0-89774-024-6). Oryx Pr.

Futcher, W. G. Descriptive Statistics for Introductory Measurement. (Andrews University Monographs, Studies in Education: Vol. 1). viii, 96p. 1976. text ed. 6.50 (ISBN 0-943872-50-2). Andrews Univ Pr.

Futrell, Mynga, jt. auth. see Geisert, Paul.

Futrelle, Jacques. Best Thinking Machine Detective Stories. Bleiler, E. F., ed. (Orig.). 1973. pap. 4.00 (ISBN 0-486-20537-1). Dover.

Future Systems, Inc. Electronic Mail: Systems, Developments & Opportunities. (Illus.). 147p. (Orig.). 1982. pap. 385.00x (ISBN 0-940520-49-4). Monegon Ltd.

--Optical Fiber Communications: Current Systems & Future Developments. (Illus.). 135p. (Orig.). 1982. pap. 445.00x (ISBN 0-940520-47-8). Monegon Ltd.

--Teleconferencing: An Enhanced Communications Service. rev. ed. (Illus.). 207p. 1982. pap. 525.00x (ISBN 0-940520-17-6). Monegon Ltd.

Futuyma, Douglas. Science on Trial: The Case for Evolution. (Illus.). 16.50 (ISBN 0-686-35958-5); pap. 6.95 (ISBN 0-686-37223-9). Pantheon.

Futuyma, Douglas J. & Slatkin, Montgomery, eds. Coevolution. LC 82-19496. (Illus.). 400p. 1983. text ed. write for info. (ISBN 0-87893-228-3); pap. text ed. write for info. (ISBN 0-87893-229-1). Sinauer Assoc.

Fyfe, Christopher. Africanus Horton, Eighteen Thirty-Five to Eighteen Eighty-Three. 1972. pap. 4.95x o.p. (ISBN 0-19-501500-2). Oxford U Pr.

Fyfe, T. Who's Who in Dickens: A Complete Dickens Repertory in Dickens Own Words. LC 75-152551. (Studies in Dickens, No. 52). 1971. Repr. of 1913 ed. lib. bdg. 37.95x (ISBN 0-8383-1236-5). Haskell.

Fyfe, Thomas A. Who's Who in Dickens. LC 73-142011. 1971. Repr. of 1912 ed. 39.00 o.p. (ISBN 0-8103-3630-8). Gale.

Fyfe, Thomas A., compiled by. Who's Who in Dickens: A Complete Dickens Repertory in Dickens' Own Words. 355p. 1982. Repr. of 1912 ed. lib. bdg. 45.00 (ISBN 0-89987-278-6). Darby Bks.

Fyfe, W. S. Geochemistry of Solids: An Introduction. 1964. text ed. 16.95 o.p. (ISBN 0-07-022645-8, C). McGraw.

Fyfe, W. S., et al. Fluids in the Earth's Crust: Their Significance in Metamorphic, Tectonic, & Chemical Transport Process. (Developments in Geochemistry Ser.: Vol. 1). 1978. 66.00 (ISBN 0-444-41636-6). Elsevier.

Fyffe, David E., jt. auth. see Clifton, David S., Jr.

Fyleman, Rose, ed. Here We Come A'piping. LC 77-94813. (Granger Poetry Library). (Illus.). (gr. 2-3). 1978. Repr. of 1937 ed. 14.50x o.p. (ISBN 0-89609-085-X). Granger Bk.

Fyler, Donald C., jt. auth. see Nadas, Alexander S.

Fymat, A. L. & Zuev, V. E., eds. Remote Sensing of the Atmosphere: Inversion Methods & Applications. (Developments in Atmospheric Science Ser.: Vol. 9). 1978. 70.25 (ISBN 0-444-41748-6). Elsevier.

Fyodorov, B. & Bartene, I. North Russian Architecture. (Illus.). 322p. 1975. 20.00x o.p. (ISBN 0-8464-0675-6). Beekman Pubs.

Fyre, H. R., jt. auth. see Minor, E. O.

Fyson, Anthony, jt. auth. see Ward, Colin.

Fyvel, T. R. George Orwell: A Personal Memoir. (Illus.). 224p. 1982. 14.95 (ISBN 0-02-542040-2). Macmillan.

--Intellectuals Today: Problems in a Changing Society. LC 68-16655. 1968. 6.95x o.p. (ISBN 0-8052-3115-3). Schocken.

G

G-Jo Institute. Pathways from Cancer: A Directory. 1980. pap. 3.00 o.p. (ISBN 0-916878-08-2). Falkynor Bks.

G. K. Hall & Co., compiled by. Cumulated Subject Index to Psychological Abstracts, 1927-1960, 2 Vols. 1966. 715.00 (ISBN 0-8161-0570-7, Pub. byHall Library); first suppl. 1961-1965 295.00 (ISBN 0-8161-0730-0); second suppl. 1966-1968 390.00 (ISBN 0-8161-0776-9). G K Hall.

G, Laimons Juris. I. E. (New Years: Return of the Life Force) 1975. pap. 12.00 (ISBN 0-9600288-7-0). Poet Papers.
--A Man Without a Gun. 1983. pap. 10.00 (ISBN 0-9600288-6-2). The Forest Library.
G. Peabody College for Teachers. Free & Inexpensive Learning Materials. 21st ed. LC 53-2471. 1983. pap. 4.95 (ISBN 0-686-84844-6). Incentive Pubns.
Gaafar, S. M. Economic Impact & Control of Veterinary Parasitisms. Date not set. 54.00 (ISBN 0-686-94131-4). Elsevier.
Gaal, Lisl. Classical Galois Theory. 3rd ed. LC 73-649. viii, 248p. 1979. text ed. 11.95 (ISBN 0-8284-1268-5). Chelsea Pub.
Gaal, O., et al. Electrophoresis in the Separation of Biological Macromolecules. LC 77-28502. 422p. 1980. 80.00x (ISBN 0-471-99602-5, Pub. by Wiley-Interscience). Wiley.
Gaan, Margaret. Last Moments of a World. (Illus.). 1978. 9.95 o.p. (ISBN 0-393-05657-0). Norton.
--Little Sister. 300p. 1983. 12.95 (ISBN 0-396-08096-0). Dodd.
Gaarder, Kenneth. Eye Movements, Vision & Behavior: A Hierarchical Visual Information Processing Model. LC 74-14710. 156p. 1975. 14.95 o.s.i. (ISBN 0-470-28895-7). Halsted Pr.
Gaarder, Kenneth R. & Montgomery, Penelope S. Clinical Biofeedback: A Procedural Manual for Behavioral Medicine. 2nd ed. (Illus.). 288p. 1981. pap. 24.95 (ISBN 0-683-03401-4). Williams & Wilkins.
Gabain, Marjorie, tr. see Oliver Brachfeld, F.
Gabaldon, Jacqueline, jt. auth. see Fedder, Ruth.
Gaballa, G. A. The Memphite Tomb: Chapel of Mose. 40p. 1977. text ed. 42.00x (ISBN 0-686-86101-9, Pub. by Aris & Phillips England). Humanities.
Gabano, J. B., ed. Lithium Batteries. Date not set. price not set (ISBN 0-12-271180-7). Acad Pr.
Gabard, E. C. & Kenney, John P. Police Writing. 106p. 1957. photocopy ed. spiral 9.75x (ISBN 0-398-04261-6). C C Thomas.
Gabay, Sabit, jt. ed. see Grenell, Robert.
Gabba, Emilio. Republican Rome, the Army & the Allies. Cuff, P. J., tr. LC 76-14307. 1977. 42.50x (ISBN 0-520-03259-4). U of Cal Pr.
Gabbard-Alley, Anne & Porter, M. Erin. An Interpersonal Approach to Business & Professional Speech Communication. 262p. 1977. pap. text ed. 9.95x (ISBN 0-89641-001-3). American Pr.
Gabbay, S. M. Elementary Mathematics for Basic Chemistry & Physics. 128p. (Orig.). 1980. pap. 11.95 (ISBN 0-9604722-0-7). Basic Science Prep Ctr.
Gabel, D. L. & Kagan, M. H. A Summary of Research in Science Education 1978. 578p. 1980. pap. 16.95 (ISBN 0-471-08869-2). Ronald Pr.
Gabel, Katherine. Correctional Institutions for Women in the United States. LC 74-27753. Date not set. cancelled (ISBN 0-669-97733-0). Lexington Bks.
Gabel, Leona C. From Slavery to the Sorbonne & Beyond: The Life & Writings of Anna J. Cooper. LC 80-53219. (Smith College Studies in History: Vol. 49). (Illus.). 98p. 1982. pap. 12.00 (ISBN 0-87391-028-1). Smith Coll.
Gabel, Medard. Energy, Earth & Everyone. LC 77-92213. (Illus.). 1979. 14.95 (ISBN 0-385-14081-9, Anch). Doubleday.
--Ho-Ping Food for Everyone. LC 77-92214. 1979. pap. 14.95 o.p. (ISBN 0-385-14082-7, Anch). Doubleday.
Gabel, Robert A. & Roberts, Richard A. Signals & Linear Systems. 2nd ed. LC 80-14811. 492p. 1980. text ed. 36.95 (ISBN 0-471-04958-1); solns. manual 26.00x (ISBN 0-471-09880-9). Wiley.
Gabelko, Nina H. & Michaelis, John U. Reducing Adolescent Prejudice: A Handbook. 226p. pap. 14.95 (ISBN 0-686-95038-0). ADL.
Gabella, G. Structure of the Automatic Nervous System. 1976. 75.00x (ISBN 0-412-13620-1, Pub. by Chapman & Hall). Methuen Inc.
Gaber, Susan. Ready-to-Use Food & Drink Spot Illustrations. (Clip Art Ser.). 1981. pap. 2.95 (ISBN 0-486-24139-4). Dover.
Gabiou, Alfrieda. Gordon Lightfoot. 1979. pap. 4.95 (ISBN 0-8256-3148-3, Quick Fox). Putnam Pub Group.
Gabka, J. & Vaubel, E. Plastic Surgery: Past & Present. (Illus.). viii, 160p. 1983. 176.75 (ISBN 3-8055-3651-8). S Karger.
Gabl, F., jt. ed. see Kaiser, E.
Gable, R. W., jt. auth. see Finkle, J. L.
Gabor, M. Hungarian Textiles. (Survey of World Textiles). (Illus.). 22.50x (ISBN 0-87245-329-4). Textile Bk.
Gabor, Mark. Art of the Calendar. (Illus.). 128p. 1976. 15.00 o.p. (ISBN 0-517-52540-2). Crown.
Gabor, intro. by see Marton, L.
Gabre-tsadick, Marta. Sheltered by the King. 176p. 1983. 9.95 (ISBN 0-310-60400-1). Chosen Bks Pub.
Gabriel, Barbra L. Biological Electron Microscopy. 240p. 1982. text ed. 29.50 (ISBN 0-442-22923-2). Van Nos Reinhold.
Gabriel, Cynthia, jt. auth. see Gabriel, Roger.
Gabriel, D., jt. auth. see Milwidsky, B.
Gabriel, Daniel. Sacco & Vanzetti: A Narrative Longpoem. (Illus.). 80p. 1983. pap. 5.00 (ISBN 0-940584-05-0). Gull Bks.
Gabriel, Ingrid. Herb Identifier & Handbook. LC 74-31698. (Identifier Ser.). (Illus.). 192p. 1975. 9.95 (ISBN 0-8069-3068-3); lib. bdg. 12.49 (ISBN 0-8069-3069-1). Sterling.
Gabriel, J. W., tr. see Speis, Werner.
Gabriel, Judy M., jt. auth. see Sack, John.
Gabriel, Michael R. & Roselle, William C. The Microform Revolution in Libraries, Vol. 3. Stueart, Robert D., ed. LC 76-5646. (Foundations in Library & Information Science Ser.). 1980. lib. bdg. 37.50 (ISBN 0-89232-008-7). Jai Pr.
Gabriel, Mordecai L. & Fogel, Seymour, eds. Great Experiments in Biology. 1955. pap. text ed. 14.95x o.p. (ISBN 0-13-363549-X). P-H.
Gabriel, P., jt. auth. see Demazure, M.
Gabriel, Peter & Gabriel, Rosemarie. Game Techniques in Applesoft B A S I C. 1983. pap. 12.95 (ISBN 0-8159-5617-7). Devin.
Gabriel, Ralph H. American Values: Continuity & Change. LC 74-24. (Contributions in American Studies: No. 15). 230p. 1974. lib. bdg. 25.00 (ISBN 0-8371-7355-8, GAV/). Greenwood.
--The Course of American Democratic Thought. 2nd ed. 508p. (gr. 10-12). 1956. text ed. 23.95 o.p. (ISBN 0-471-07047-5). Wiley.
--Lure of the Frontier. 1929. text ed. 22.50x (ISBN 0-686-83610-3). Elliots Bks.
--Toilers of Land & Sea. 1926. text ed. 22.50x (ISBN 0-686-83829-7). Elliots Bks.
Gabriel, Ralph H., ed. Christianity & Modern Thought. 1924. 39.50x (ISBN 0-685-89742-7). Elliots Bks.
Gabriel, Ralph H., ed. see Royce, Sarah.
Gabriel, Richard A. The New Red Legions: An Attitudinal Portrait of the Soviet Soldier. LC 79-8956. (Contributions in Political Science: No. 44). (Illus.). xiv, 246p. 1980. lib. bdg. 29.95 (ISBN 0-313-21496-4, GAO/). Greenwood.
Gabriel, Richard A. & Savage, Paul L. Crisis in Command: Mismanagement in the Army. 1978. 10.00 (ISBN 0-8090-3711-4); pap. 6.95 (ISBN 0-8090-0140-3). Hill & Wang.
Gabriel, Richard F. Insider Leverage Techniques: The Fastest Way to Build a Fortune in Real Estate. LC 80-39810. 288p. 1981. deluxe duotang binder 79.50 (ISBN 0-13-467506-1, 45). Exec Reports.
Gabriel, Roger. A Patient's Guide to Dialysis & Transplantation. 175p. 1982. 10.95 (ISBN 0-85200-355-2, Pub. by MTP Pr England). Kluwer Boston.
--Renal Medicine: Concise Medical Textbook. 2nd ed. (Illus.). 288p. 1981. pap. text ed. 11.95 (ISBN 0-02-857780-9, Bailliere-Tindall). Saunders.
Gabriel, Roger & Gabriel, Cynthia. Medical Data Interpretation for MRCP. 2nd ed. 1982. text ed. 11.95 (ISBN 0-407-00217-0). Butterworth.
--Medical Data Interpretation for MRCP. 1978. pap. 6.95 o.p. (ISBN 0-407-00134-4). Butterworth.
Gabriel, Rosemarie, jt. auth. see Gabriel, Peter.
Gabriel, Teshome H. Third Cinema in the Third World: The Aesthetics of Liberation. Kirkpatrick, Diane, ed. LC 82-8641. (Studies in Cinema: No. 21). 160p. 1982. 39.95 (ISBN 0-8357-1359-8, Pub. by UMI Res Pr). Univ Microfilms.
Gabriel, Yiannis. Freud & Society. (International Library of Group Psychotherapy & Group Process). 330p. 1983. price not set (ISBN 0-7100-9410-8). Routledge & Kegan.
Gabriele, Rosemarie. Game Techniques in Applesoft BASIC. 1983. pap. 12.95 (ISBN 0-686-83945-5). Devin.
Gabrieli, Francesco, ed. Arab Historians of the Crusades. LC 68-23783. (The Islamic World Ser.). 1978. 32.50x (ISBN 0-520-03616-6). U of Cal Pr.
Gabrielle, Vincent. Ernest & Celestine. (ps-3). 1982. 9.50 (ISBN 0-688-00855-0); PLB 8.59 (ISBN 0-688-00856-9). Morrow.
--Ernest & Celestine's Picnic. (ps-3). 1982. 9.50 (ISBN 0-688-01250-7); PLB 8.59 (ISBN 0-688-01252-3). Morrow.
--Smile, Ernest & Celestine. (ps-3). 1982. 9.50 (ISBN 0-688-01247-7); PLB 8.59 (ISBN 0-688-01249-3). Morrow.
Gabriels, D. see De Boodt, M.
Gabriels, D., jt. auth. see DeBoodt, M.
Gabrielsen, Milton A., et al. Aquatics Handbook. 2nd ed. 1968. ref. ed. 20.95 (ISBN 0-13-043943-6). P-H.
Gabrielson, Ira N., jt. auth. see Zim, Herbert S.
Gabrovsek, John. The Host, Dental Caries & Concepts of Prevention. 200p. 1983. 26.50 (ISBN 0-87527-209-6). Green.
Gabry, Gyorgy. Old Musical Instruments. 2nd rev. ed. (Illus.). 1969. 7.50x o.p. (ISBN 0-568-00087-0). Intl Pubns Serv.
Gaburo, K. Music in Beckett's: Play. (Paperplay Ser. Mini-Bks.: Vol. 6). 12p. 1976. saddle stitched 2.75 (ISBN 0-939044-06-4). Lingua Pr.
Gaburo, Kenneth. C---ls. (Paperplay Ser. Mini-Bks.: Vol. 2). 12p. 1976. saddle-stitched 2.75 (ISBN 0-939044-02-1). Lingua Pr.
--Lingua Three: In the Can: A Dialectic Mix in Three Rounds. (Illus.). 220p. Date not set. cancelled 25.98 (ISBN 0-939044-18-8). Lingua Pr.
--Murmur. (Paperplay Ser. Mini-Bks.: Vol. 3). 8p. 1976. saddle stitched 2.25 (ISBN 0-939044-03-X). Lingua Pr.
--Non-Scatological Set of Preliminary Remarks. (Paperplay Ser. Mini-Bks.: Vol. 5). 12p. 1976. saddle stitched 2.60 (ISBN 0-939044-05-6). Lingua Pr.
--Privacy One: Words Without Song. (Illus.). 48p. 1977. saddle stitched 10.00 (ISBN 0-939044-25-0). Lingua Pr.
--Privacy Two: My, My, My What a Wonderful Fall. (Illus.). 22p. 1976. saddle stitched 8.00 (ISBN 0-939044-12-9). Lingua Pr.
--Twenty Sensing (Instruction) Compositions. (Illus.). 40p. 1977. saddle stitched 7.00 (ISBN 0-939044-11-0). Lingua Pr.
--Whole Language. (Illus.). 41p. Date not set. softcover 8.75 (ISBN 0-939044-21-8). Lingua Pr.
Gaburo, Kenneth, ed. see Lingua Press.
Gaburo, Virginia. Who Is Bruce Simonds. 44p. 1978. saddle stitched plus boxed recording 13.95 (ISBN 0-939044-22-6). Lingua Pr.
Gabuzda, Thomas G., jt. auth. see Ersley, Allan J.
Gaby, F. J. Relation de la Nigritie. (Bibliotheque Africaine Ser.). 104p. (Fr.). 1974. Repr. of 1689 ed. lib. bdg. 36.00x o.p. (ISBN 0-8287-0360-4, 72-2162). Clearwater Pub.
Gach, Michael & Marco, Carolyn. ACU-Yoga: Self Help Techniques to Relieve Tension. (Illus., Orig.). 1981. pap. 12.95 (ISBN 0-87040-489-X). Japan Pubns.
Gackenbach, Dick. Binky Gets a Car. (Illus.). 32p. (ps-2). 1983. 9.95 (ISBN 0-89919-144-4, Clarion). HM.
--Claude the Dog. LC 74-3403. (Illus.). 32p. (ps-2). 1982. pap. 3.45 (ISBN 0-89919-124-X, Clarion). HM.
--Claude the Dog. 32p. (ps-2). 1974. 7.95 (ISBN 0-395-28792-8, Clarion). HM.
--McGoogan Moves the Mighty Rock. LC 80-8455. (Illus.). 48p. (gr. 1-4). 1981. 8.95 (ISBN 0-06-021967-X, HarpJ); PLB 9.89g (ISBN 0-06-021968-8). Har-Row.
--Mr. Wink & His Shadow, Ned. LC 82-47711. (Illus.). 32p. (gr. 1-4). 1983. 9.57i (ISBN 0-06-021969-6, HarpJ); PLB 9.89g (ISBN 0-06-021974-2). Har-Row.
Gackenbush, Dick. Annie & the Mud Monster. (gr. 1-4). 1982. 9.50 (ISBN 0-688-00791-0); PLB 8.59 (ISBN 0-688-00792-9). Morrow.
Gad, Carl. Johan Bojer, the Man & His Works. Macintire, Elizabeth J., tr. LC 73-17656. (Illus.). 260p. 1974. Repr. of 1920 ed. lib. bdg. 15.75x (ISBN 0-8371-7263-2, GAJB). Greenwood.
Gadamer, Hans-Georg. Dialogue & Dialectic: Eight Hermeneutical Studies on Plato. LC 79-18887. 1980. 25.00x (ISBN 0-300-02126-7). Yale U Pr.
--Dialogue & Dialectic: Eight Hermeneutical Studies on Plato. Smith, P. Christopher, tr. LC 79-18887. 224p. 1983. pap. text ed. 7.95x (ISBN 0-300-02983-7). Yale U Pr.
--Essays in Philosophical Hermeneutics. LC 74-30519. (Cal Ser: No. 363). 1977. pap. 7.95 (ISBN 0-520-03475-9). U of Cal Pr.
--Hegel's Dialectic: Five Hermeneutical Studies. Smith, P. Christopher, tr. from Ger. 130p. 1982. 15.00x (ISBN 0-300-01909-2); pap. 4.95x (ISBN 0-300-02842-3, Y-418). Yale U Pr.
Gaddie, Ronald E. & Douglas, Donald. Earthworms for Ecology & Profit: Earthworms & the Ecology, Vol. II. (Illus.). 1977. pap. 6.95 (ISBN 0-916302-01-6). Bookworm NY.
--Earthworms for Ecology & Profit: Scientific Earthworm Farming, Vol. 1. (Illus.). 192p. 1975. 9.95 (ISBN 0-916302-11-3); pap. 6.95 (ISBN 0-916302-05-9). Bookworm NY.
Gaddis, Ben. How to Repair Home Laundry Appliances. LC 76-8630. 1976. 8.95 o.p. (ISBN 0-8306-6855-1); pap. 5.95 o.p. (ISBN 0-8306-5855-6, 855). TAB Bks.
Gaddis, John L. Russia, the Soviet Union & the United States: An Interpretive History. LC 77-12763. (America & the World Ser.). 309p. 1978. pap. text ed. 11.50x (ISBN 0-471-28911-6). Wiley.
--Strategies of Containment: A Critical Appraisal of Postwar American National Security Policy. LC 81-772. 416p. 1982. 27.50x (ISBN 0-19-502944-5). Oxford U Pr.
--Strategies of Containment: A Critical Appraisal of Postwar American National Security Policy. 1982. pap. 10.95 (ISBN 0-19-503097-4, GB690). Oxford U Pr.
Gaddis, Robert S., jt. ed. see Coker, Lawrence T.
Gaddis, Woody. Basic Photography. LC 77-6190. (Illus.). 1979. pap. 6.95 (ISBN 0-8069-8152-0). Sterling.
Gaddum, John. Pharmacology. 8th ed. Mitchell, J. F. & Burgen, A. S., eds. (Illus.). 1978. 17.95x (ISBN 0-19-261307-3). Oxford U Pr.
Gade, D. New Dimensions in Creativity. LC 74-78396. 1974. pap. 4.00 (ISBN 0-686-14991-2, 261-08418). Home Econ Educ.
Gadler, Steve & Adamson, Wendy. Sun Power: Facts About Solar Energy. LC 77-92290. (Real World, Crisis & Conflict Ser.). (Illus.). (gr. 5 up). 1978. PLB 6.95g (ISBN 0-8225-0643-2). Lerner Pubns.
Gadney, Reg. The Cage. LC 77-4924. 1977. 7.95 o.p. (ISBN 0-698-10833-7, Coward). Putnam Pub Group.
Gadoffre, G., ed. see Descartes, Rene.
Gadol, E. T., ed. Rationality & Sciences: A Memorial Volume for Moritz Schlick. (Illus.). 228p. 1983. 21.00 (ISBN 0-387-81721-2). Springer-Verlag.
Gadourek, Ivan. The Political Control of Czechoslovakia. LC 74-2841. 285p. 1974. Repr. of 1953 ed. lib. bdg. 17.25x (ISBN 0-8371-7437-6, GACZ). Greenwood.
Gadow, Kenneth D. & Bialer, Irv., eds. Advances in Learning & Behavioral Disabilities, Vol. 1. 450p. 1981. 47.50 (ISBN 0-89232-209-8). Jai Pr.
Gadow, Kenneth D. & Loney, Jan, eds. Psychosocial Aspects of Drug Treatment for Hyperactivity. (AAAS Selected Symposium: No. 44). 460p. 1981. lib. bdg. 34.00 (ISBN 0-89158-834-5). Westview.
Gadow, Sandy. All About Escrow: Or How to Buy the Brooklyn Bridge & Have the Last Laugh. Rev. ed. LC 81-65603. 184p. 1982. pap. text ed. 8.95 (ISBN 0-932956-04-1). Express.
Gadsby, Oliver E., tr. see Gautschen, Ivan.
Gadsen, J. A. Infrared Spectra of Minerals & Related Inorganic Compounds. 288p. 1975. 37.95 o.p. (ISBN 0-408-70665-1). Butterworth.
Gadzuk, Marilyn W., tr. see Lionel, Frederic.
Gaebelein, Frank. Letters of Samuel Rutherford. (Wycliff Classic Ser.). 480p. 1980. pap. 9.95 (ISBN 0-8024-4892-5). Moody.
Gaebelein, Frank E. Pattern of God's Truth. LC 54-6908. 1968. pap. 5.95 (ISBN 0-8024-6450-5). Moody.
Gaeddert, Lou Ann. Noisy Nancy Norris. LC 65-10180. (ps-1). 1971. Repr. of 1965 ed. PLB 8.95 o.p. (ISBN 0-385-04749-5). Doubleday.
Gaeddert, LouAnn. The Kid with the Red Suspenders. LC 82-18210. (Illus.). 80p. (gr. 2-4). 1983. 9.95 (ISBN 0-525-44046-1, 0966-290). Dutton.
--Too Many Girls. (Break-of-Day Bk). (Illus.). 48p. (gr. 1-3). 1972. PLB 4.49 o.p. (ISBN 0-698-30422-5, Coward). Putnam Pub Group.
Gaede, Jane T. Clinical Pathology for the House Officer. (House Officer Ser.). (Illus.). 189p. 1982. pap. 9.95 (ISBN 0-683-03403-0). Williams & Wilkins.
Gaede, Sarah R. The Pirate's House Cookbook. (Illus.). 224p. 1982. pap. 10.95 (ISBN 0-939114-61-5). Wimmer Bks.
Gaedeke, Ralph M. & Tootelian, Dennis H. Marketing: Principles & Applications. (Illus.). 700p. 1983. text ed. 19.95 (ISBN 0-314-69649-0); tchrs.' manual avail. (ISBN 0-314-71091-4); student guide avail. (ISBN 0-314-71142-2). West Pub.
Gaedeke, Ralph M., jt. auth. see Tootelain, Dennis H.
Gaedeke, Ralph M., ed. Marketing in Private & Public Nonprofit Organizations: Perspectives & Illustrations. LC 76-23034. 1977. text ed. 18.95x (ISBN 0-673-16509-4). Scott F.
Gaedeke, Ralph M. & Tootelian, Dennis, eds. Marketing Management Cases & Readings. 1980. pap. 23.50x (ISBN 0-673-16105-6). Scott F.
Gael, Sidney. Job Anaysis: A Guide to Assessing Work Activities. LC 82-49036. (Management & Social & Behavioral Science Ser.). 1983. text ed. price not set (ISBN 0-87589-564-6). Jossey-Bass.
Gaenssien, R. E., jt. auth. see DeForest, P. R.
Gaer, Felice D. Scholarly Exchange Programs with Countries Abroad: Should Learning & Politics Mix? (Vital Issues, Vol. XXIX 1979-80: No. 10). 0.50 (ISBN 0-686-81615-3). Ctr Info Am.
Gaer, Joseph. How the Great Religions Began. rev. ed. pap. 1.75 o.p. (ISBN 0-451-07764-4, E7764, Sig). NAL.
--What the Great Religions Believe. pap. 2.95 (ISBN 0-451-11978-9, AE1978, Sig). NAL.
Gaetschenberger, Richard. Grundzuge einer Psychologie des Zeichens. (Foundations of Semiotics: 3). 135p. 1983. 16.00 (ISBN 90-272-3273-3). Benjamins North Am.
Gaff, Jerry G. General Education Today: A Critical Analysis of Controversies, Practices & Reforms. LC 82-49037. 1983. text ed. price not set (ISBN 0-87589-560-3). Jossey-Bass.
Gaffikin, Michael & Aitken, Michael, eds. The Development of Accounting Theory: Significant Contributors to Accounting Thought in the 20th Century. LC 82-82489. (Accountancy in Transition Ser.). 284p. 1982. lib. bdg. 40.00 (ISBN 0-8240-5336-2). Garland Pub.
Gaffin. The Nurse & the Welfare State. 11.95 (ISBN 0-471-25713-3, Wiley Heyden). Wiley.
Gaffney, D. J. & Skadden, D. H. Principles of Federal Income Taxation. 1982. 25.00 (ISBN 0-07-057781-1); instr's manual 20.00 (ISBN 0-07-057782-X); study guide 9.95x (ISBN 0-07-057784-6). McGraw.
--Principles of Federal Income Taxation, 1983-84. 608p. 1983. 25.00 (ISBN 0-07-022631-8, C); price not set instr's manual (ISBN 0-07-022632-6); 10.00 (ISBN 0-07-022633-4). McGraw.
Gaffney, Edward M. & Moots, Philip R. Government & Campus: Federal Regulation of Religiously Affiliated Higher Education. LC 80-53164. 210p. 1981. 15.95 (ISBN 0-268-01003-X); pap. text ed. 8.95 (ISBN 0-268-01005-6). U of Notre Dame Pr.
Gaffney, James. Newness of Life: A Modern Introduction to Catholic Ethics. LC 79-84404. 360p. 1979. pap. 5.95 (ISBN 0-8091-2202-2). Paulist Pr.
--Sin Reconsidered. LC 82-61424. 96p. (Orig.). 1983. pap. 3.95 (ISBN 0-8091-2516-1). Paulist Pr.
Gaffney, M. Mason. Property Taxes & the Frequency of Urban Renewal. 14p. 1964. pap. 0.00 free (ISBN 0-911312-39-0). Schalkenbach.

Gaffney, Maureen & Laybourne, Gerry B. What to Do When the Lights Go On: A Comprehensive Guide to Sixteen Millimeter Films & Related Activities for Children. 268p. 1981. 28.50x (ISBN 0-912700-65-3); pap. 19.50x (ISBN 0-912700-69-6). Oryx Pr.

Gaffney, Maureen, ed. More Films Kids Like. LC 77-12174. 1977. pap. 12.00 (ISBN 0-8389-0250-2). ALA.

Gaffney, Sean & Cashman, Seamus, eds. Proverbs & Sayings of Ireland. (Illus.). 124p. 1978. Repr. of 1974 ed. 10.00x o.p. (ISBN 0-8476-6127-X). Rowman.

Gaffney, Thomas E., et al, eds. Pharmacokinetics, Drug Metabolism & Drug Interactions. LC 74-13905. (Principles & Techniques of Human Research & Therapeutics Ser: Vol. 3). (Illus.). 214p. 1974. 14.00 o.p. (ISBN 0-87993-046-2). Futura Pub.

Gaffney, Walter J., jt. auth. see Nouwen, Henri J.

Gafney, Leo & Beers, John C. Essential Math Skills. Devine, Peter, ed. 224p. 1980. pap. text ed. 6.48 (ISBN 0-07-010260-0, W); tchr's ed. 7.56 (ISBN 0-07-010261-9); Webstermasters tests 5.64 (ISBN 0-07-010262-7). McGraw.

Gafney, Leo, ed. see Belstock, Alan & Smith, Gerald.

Gafney, Leo, ed. see Gurau, Peter K. & Lieberthal, Edwin M.

Gafney, Leo, ed. see Maher, Carolyn.

Gafney, Leo, ed. see Maher, Carolyn A., et al.

Gag, Wanda. The ABC Bunny. LC 33-27359. (Illus.). (gr. k-2). 1978. pap. 2.95 (ISBN 0-698-20465-4, Coward). Putnam Pub Group.

--ABC Bunny. (Illus.). (gr. k-2). 1933. 6.95 (ISBN 0-698-20000-4, Coward); gb 6.99 (ISBN 0-698-30000-9). Putnam Pub Group.

--The Funny Thing. (Illus.). (gr. 1-3). 1929. PLB 6.99 (ISBN 0-698-30097-1, Coward). Putnam Pub Group.

--Gone Is Gone. (Illus.). (gr. k-3). 1933. PLB 5.99 (ISBN 0-698-30179-X, Coward). Putnam Pub Group.

--Millions of Cats. (Illus.). (gr. k-3). 1977. pap. 2.95 (ISBN 0-698-20434-4, Coward). Putnam Pub Group.

--Millions of Cats. (Illus.). (gr. k-3). 1928. 7.95 (ISBN 0-698-20091-8, Coward); 6.99 (ISBN 0-698-30236-2). Putnam Pub Group.

--The Millions of Cats Day Book. (Illus.). 112p. (gr. k-2). 1977. 2.95 (ISBN 0-698-20434-4, Coward); pap. 3.95 o.p. (ISBN 0-698-20520-0); prepak 47.40 (ISBN 0-698-20521-9). Putnam Pub Group.

--More Tales from Grimm. 1981. pap. 5.95 (ISBN 0-698-20533-2, Coward). Putnam Pub Group.

--More Tales from Grimm. (Illus.). (gr. 3-5). 1947. 6.95 o.s.i. (ISBN 0-698-20093-4, Coward). Putnam Pub Group.

--Nothing at All. (Illus.). (gr. 1-3). 1941. PLB 6.99 (ISBN 0-698-30264-8, Coward). Putnam Pub Group.

--Snippy & Snappy. (Illus.). (gr. 1-3). 1931. PLB 5.99 (ISBN 0-698-30319-9, Coward). Putnam Pub Group.

--Snow White & the Seven Dwarfs. (Illus.). (gr. 2-4). 1938. PLB 6.99 (ISBN 0-698-30320-2, Coward). Putnam Pub Group.

--Tales from Grimm. 1981. pap. 5.95 (ISBN 0-698-20534-0, Coward). Putnam Pub Group.

--Tales from Grimm. (Illus.). (gr. 3-5). 1936. 7.95 o.s.i. (ISBN 0-698-20139-6, Coward). Putnam Pub Group.

Gag, Wanda & Tomes, Margot. Jorinda & Joringel. (Illus., Fic). 1978. 6.95 (ISBN 0-698-20440-9, Coward). Putnam Pub Group.

--The Sorcerer's Apprentice. LC 78-23990. (Illus.). (gr. k-3). 1979. 6.95 (ISBN 0-698-20481-6, Coward). Putnam Pub Group.

Gagala, Kenneth. Economics of Minorities: A Guide to Information Sources. LC 73-17573. (Economics Information Guide Ser: Vol. 2). 339p. 1976. 42.00x (ISBN 0-8103-1294-8). Gale.

Gagarin, Michael. Aeschylean Drama. LC 74-30520. 1976. 26.50x (ISBN 0-520-02943-7). U of Cal Pr.

Gage, Joy. Lord, Can We Talk This Over? 96p. 1980. pap. 3.95 (ISBN 0-8024-4011-8). Moody.

Gage, Michael & Vandenberg, M. Hard Landscape in Concrete. LC 75-31700. 167p. 1975. 32.95 o.s.i. (ISBN 0-470-28913-9). Halsted Pr.

Gage, Michael, jt. auth. see Murphy, Ian.

Gage, N. L. & Berliner, David C. Educational Psychology. 2nd ed. 1979. 20.95 (ISBN 0-395-30802-X); instr's. manual 1.25 (ISBN 0-395-30804-6); study guide 11.50 (ISBN 0-395-30803-8). HM.

Gage, Patricia, jt. ed. see Fitzgerald, Hiram E.

Gage, Richard L., tr. see Mizuno, Kogen.

Gage, Richard L., tr. see Niwano, Nichiko.

Gage, Richard L., tr. see Niwano, Nikkyo.

Gage, Thomas. Correspondence of General Thomas Gage: Reprint of 1931-33 Eds, 2 Vols. Carter, Clarence E., ed. LC 73-85914. 1969. Set. 37.50 o.p. (ISBN 0-208-00812-8, Archon). Shoe String.

Gage, Wilson, pseud. Cully Cully & the Bear. LC 82-11715. (Illus.). 32p. (gr. k-3). 1983. 9.00 (ISBN 0-688-01767-3); PLB 8.59 (ISBN 0-688-01769-X). Greenwillow.

Gage, Wilson. The Ghost of Five Owl Farm. (gr. 4-8). 1969. pap. 1.75 (ISBN 0-671-56085-9). Archway.

--Ghost of Five Owl Farm. LC 75-20088. (Illus.). (gr. 4-6). 1966. PLB 6.99 o.s.i. (ISBN 0-529-03889-7, Philomel). Putnam Pub Group.

--Miss Osborne-the-Mop. LC 63-8912. (Illus.). (gr. 4-6). 1963. PLB 6.99 o.s.i. (ISBN 0-529-03735-1, Philomel). Putnam Pub Group.

--Miss Osborne the Mop, No. 10. (Pickerell Ser.). (Illus.). (gr. 4-6). 1975. pap. 1.75 o.s.i. (ISBN 0-671-43136-6). Archway.

Gagen, T. M. Topics in Finite Groups. LC 75-17116. (London Mathematical Society Lecture Note Ser.: No. 16). 80p. 1976. 12.95 (ISBN 0-521-21002-X). Cambridge U Pr.

Gager, John G. Kingdom & Community: The Social World of Early Christianity. 160p. 1975. pap. text ed. 11.50 (ISBN 0-13-516203-3). P-H.

Gager, Nancy & Schurr, Cathleen. Sexual Assault, Confronting Rape in America. LC 73-18531. Orig. Title: Rape. (Illus.). 1976. 2.95 o.p. (ISBN 0-685-59199-9, 11527-1, G&D). Putnam Pub Group.

Gagey, Edmond M. San Francisco Stage: a History. Repr. of 1950 ed. lib. bdg. 15.50x (ISBN 0-8371-3927-9, GAFS). Greenwood.

Gagliano, Felix, jt. auth. see Baum, Edward.

Gagliardi, Gary. How to Make Your Microcomputer Pay Off. (Data Processing Ser.). (Illus.). 300p. 1983. 21.95 (ISBN 0-534-97926-2). Lifetime Learn.

Gagliardi, Richard L. & Valenza, Samuel W., Jr., eds. The Mathematics of the Energy Crisis. LC 78-53592. 96p. (gr. 7-12). 1978. pap. 7.95 (ISBN 0-936918-01-2). Intergalactic NJ.

Gagliardi, Robert. Introduction to Communications Engineering. LC 77-18531. 508p. 1978. 40.00x (ISBN 0-471-03099-6, Pub. by Wiley-Interscience). Wiley.

Gagliardi, Robert M. & Karp, Sherman. Optical Communications. LC 75-26509. 432p. 1976. 54.50x (ISBN 0-471-28915-9, Pub. by Wiley-Interscience). Wiley.

Gagliardo, John G. Enlightened Despotism. LC 67-14301. (AHM Europe Since 1500 Ser.). (Orig.). 1967. pap. 7.95x (ISBN 0-88295-735-X). Harlan Davidson.

Gaglione, Anthony M., jt. auth. see Artino, Ralph A.

Gagne, Danai A. & Thomas, Judith. Dramas in Elemental Scales: A Collection of Mini-Dramas for Voice & Orff Instruments. 1982. pap. 7.50 (ISBN 0-918812-19-4). Magnamusic.

Gagne, Eve E. School Behavior & School Discipline: Coping with Deviant Behavior in the Schools. LC 82-15912. 176p. 1983. lib. bdg. 20.75 (ISBN 0-8191-2748-5); pap. text ed. 10.00 (ISBN 0-8191-2749-3). U Pr of Amer.

Gagnepain, J. Du Vouloir Dire: Traite D'Epistemolgie des Sciences Humaines. (Language & Communication Library: Vol. 3). 256p. 1982. cancelled (ISBN 0-08-027079-4). Pergamon.

Gagnepain, J. J. & Meeker, Thrygve R., eds. Piezoelectricity. (Ferroelectrics Ser.: Vols. 40, Nos. 3-4; 41; & 42, Nos. 1-2). 782p. 1982. 300.00 (ISBN 0-677-16415-7). Gordon.

Gagnon, Constance. Help! for Preschoolers. (ps). 1982. 3.95 (ISBN 0-86653-061-4, GA 412). Good Apple.

Gagnon, J. P., jt. auth. see Berger, B. A.

Gagnon, John H. & Greenblat, Cathy S. Life Designs: Individuals, Marriages & Families. 1978. text ed. 18.95x o.p. (ISBN 0-673-07911-2). Scott F.

Gagnon, John H. & Smith, Barbara. Human Sexualities. 1977. pap. 16.50x (ISBN 0-673-15033-X); study guide 5.50x (ISBN 0-673-15034-8). Scott F.

Gagnon, John H. & Simon, William, eds. The Sexual Scene. rev. 2nd ed. LC 72-87668. 150p. 1973. pap. 4.95 (ISBN 0-87855-541-2); 9.95 (ISBN 0-87855-048-8). Transaction Bks.

Gahart, Betty L. Intravenous Medications: A Handbook for Nurses & Other Allied Health Personnel. 3rd ed. LC 81-4027. 258p. 1981. pap. text ed. 15.50 (ISBN 0-8016-1719-7). Mosby.

Gahl, G., et al, eds. Advances in Peritoneal Dialysis. (International Congress Ser.: No. 567). 1982. 82.75 (ISBN 0-444-90246-5). Elsevier.

Gaida, Davida. Twenty Eighty-Four, Vol. 1. LC 82-62540. (Orig.). 1983. pap. 6.95 (ISBN 0-88100-022-1). Ringa Pr.

Gaidar. Cyk i Gek. (Easy Reader, A). pap. 3.95 (ISBN 0-88436-051-2, 65250). EMC.

Gaidukov, N & Elenkin, A. A. Algological Bibliography of the USSR from Beginning to 1960. (Collectanea Bibliographia Ser.: No. 3). 1976. Repr. lib. bdg. 96.00x (ISBN 3-87429-105-7). Lubrecht & Cramer.

Gaier, Claude. Four Centuries of Liege Gunmaking. (Illus.). 1977. 80.00 o.p. (ISBN 0-686-20478-6). Arma Pr.

Gaige, Frederick H. Regionalism & National Unity in Nepal. LC 74-30520. 1975. 30.00x (ISBN 0-520-02728-0). U of Cal Pr.

Gail, Marzieh, tr. see Baha'u'llah.

Gail, Marzieh, tr. see Muhammad-'Aliy-Salmani, Ustad.

Gailey, Christine W. & Etienne, Mona, eds. Women & the State in Pre-Industrial Societies: Anthropological Perspectives. 336p. 1983. 27.95x (ISBN 0-686-76465-X); pap. 12.95x (ISBN 0-686-76466-8). J F Bergin.

Gailey, Harry A. Africa: Troubled Continent-A Problem Approach. 160p. (Orig.). 1983. pap. 6.50 (ISBN 0-89874-342-7). Krieger.

--Clifford: Imperial Proconsul. 215p. (Orig.). 1982. pap. text ed. 11.50 (ISBN 0-86036-189-6). Krieger.

Gailey, Harry A., Jr. History of Africa Vol. 1: From Earliest Times to 1800. LC 80-15898. (Illus.). 302p. (Orig.). 1981. pap. text ed. 9.95 (ISBN 0-89874-032-0). Krieger.

--History of Africa Vol 2: From 1800 to Present. rev. ed. LC 80-15898. 502p. (Orig.). 1981. pap. text ed. 12.95 (ISBN 0-89874-033-9). Krieger.

Gailey, James H., Jr. Micah-Malachi. LC 59-10454. (Layman's Bible Commentary Ser: Vol. 15). 1962. pap. 3.95 (ISBN 0-8042-3075-7). John Knox.

Gaillard, Dawson. Dorothy L. Sayers. LC 80-5344. (Recognitions Ser.). 180p. 1980. 11.95 (ISBN 0-8044-2222-2); pap. 5.95 (ISBN 0-8044-6169-4). Ungar.

Gaillard, Dawson & Mosier, John. Women & Men Together: An Anthology of Short Fiction. (Illus., LC 77-078566). 1977. pap. text ed. 12.95 (ISBN 0-395-25032-3); instr's. manual 0.55 (ISBN 0-395-25033-1). HM.

Gaillard, Frye. Race, Rock & Religion. LC 82-11325. (Illus.). 192p. 1982. 12.95 (ISBN 0-914788-59-0). East Woods.

Gaillard, P. J., ed. Comparative Endocrinology. (Proceedings). 1978. 84.75 (ISBN 0-444-80071-9). Elsevier.

Gaillardet, Frederic. Sketches of Early Texas & Louisiana. Shepherd, James L., tr. from Fr. (Texas History Paperbacks Ser.: No. 13). 191p. 1966. 7.95 o.p. (ISBN 0-292-73628-2); pap. 5.95x (ISBN 0-292-70102-0). U of Tex Pr.

Gain, D. B., ed. The Aratus Ascribed to Germanicus Caesar. (University of London Classical Studies Ser.: No. 8). (Illus.). 200p. 1976. text ed. 36.50x o.p. (ISBN 0-485-13708-9, Athlone Pr). Humanities.

Gainer, Harold N. & Stark, Sandra L. Choice or Chance: A Guidebook to Career Planning. (Illus.). 1978. pap. text ed. 10.20 (ISBN 0-07-022672-5, G); instr's manual 3.50 (ISBN 0-07-022673-3). McGraw.

Gainer, Patrick W. Folk Songs from the West Virginia Hills. LC 75-38967. 236p. 1982. pap. 8.98 (ISBN 0-686-84022-4). Seneca Bks.

Gaines, Charles. Dangler. 1980. 12.95 o.p. (ISBN 0-671-25281-X). S&S.

Gaines, Charles & Butler, George. Pumping Iron. (Illus.). 1974. 17.95 o.s.i. (ISBN 0-671-21898-0); pap. 9.95 (ISBN 0-671-21922-7). S&S.

Gaines, Edith & Jenkins, Dorothy H. Woman's Day Dictionary of Antique Furniture. (Illus.). 1979. pap. 4.95 o.p. (ISBN 0-8015-8792-1, Hawthorn). Dutton.

Gaines, Ernest J. Bloodline. 256p. 1976. pap. 5.95 (ISBN 0-393-00798-7, Norton Lib). Norton.

--Catherine Carmier. LC 80-27402. 256p. 1981. pap. 9.25 (ISBN 0-86547-022-7). N Point Pr.

Gaines, George, Jr & Coleman, David S. Real Estate Math. 145p. (Orig.). 1980. pap. text ed. 8.95 (ISBN 0-89787-902-3). Gorsuch Scarisbrick.

Gaines, Helen F. Cryptanalysis: A Study of Ciphers & Their Solutions. (Illus.). 1939. pap. text ed. 4.50 (ISBN 0-486-20097-3). Dover.

Gaines, J. H., jt. auth. see Volterra, Enrico.

Gaines, Jack. Fritz Perls: Here & Now. (Illus.). 1979. 12.95 (ISBN 0-89087-186-8); pap. 8.95. Integrated Pr.

Gaines, James R. The Lives of the Piano. LC 82-48228. (Illus.). 215p. 1983. pap. 10.53i (ISBN 0-06-090997-8, CN 997, CN). Har-Row.

--Wit's End: Days & Nights of the Algonquin Round Table. LC 79-10464. (Illus.). 1979. pap. 6.95 o.p. (ISBN 0-15-697651-X, Harv). HarBraceJ.

Gaines, John, jt auth. see Epstein, Jerome.

Gaines, Larry K. & Ricks, Truett A. Managing the Police Organization: Selected Readings. (Criminal Justice Ser.). (Illus.). 1978. pap. text ed. 17.50 (ISBN 0-8299-0163-9). West Pub.

Gaines, Linda, et al. TOSCA: The Total Social Cost of Coal & Nuclear Power. LC 78-26240. 144p. 1979. prof ref 25.00x (ISBN 0-88410-086-3). Ballinger Pub.

Gaines, Price, ed. Life Financial Reports. 1982 ed. 784p. 1982. pap. 29.00 (ISBN 0-87218-023-9). Natl Underwriter.

--Life Financial Reports, 1981. LC 76-6785. 778p. 1981. pap. 26.50 o.p. (ISBN 0-87218-018-2). Natl Underwriter.

--Life Rates & Data. 1982 ed. LC 76-7124. 730p. 1982. pap. 13.50 (ISBN 0-87218-022-0). Natl Underwriter.

--Life Rates & Data, 1981. LC 76-7124. 768p. 1981. pap. 12.25 o.p. (ISBN 0-87218-015-8). Natl Underwriter.

--Time Saver for Health Insurance. LC 76-6783. 141p. 1981. pap. 13.25 o.p. (ISBN 0-87218-017-4). Natl Underwriter.

--Who Writes What - 1982. rev. ed. LC 76-6787. 490p. 1981. plastic bind 11.50 o.p. (ISBN 0-87218-020-4). Natl Underwriter.

--Who Writes What, 1983. 432p. 1982. spirial bdg. 12.60 (ISBN 0-87218-027-1). Natl Underwriter.

Gaines, Richard L. Interior Plantscaping. (Illus.). 1977. 34.50 (ISBN 0-07-022678-4, Architectural Record). McGraw.

Gaines, Steve, jt auth. see Cooper, Alice.

Gaines, William M. Good 'n' Mad. (Illus., Orig.). 1969. pap. 0.95 o.p. (ISBN 0-451-06342-2, Q6342, Sig). NAL.

Gaines, Xerpha M. An Annotated Catalogue of Glen Canyon Plants. (MNA Technical Ser.: No. 4). 1960. pap. 1.00 o.p. (ISBN 0-685-76470-2). Mus Northern Ariz.

Gainesborough, Thomas. Gainsborough. Gatt, Giuseppe, ed. (Art Library Ser.: Vol. 23). (Illus., Orig.). 1969. pap. 2.95 o.p. (ISBN 0-448-00472-0, G&D). Putnam Pub Group.

Gair, Diana. Jungle Antagonist. (Harlequin Romances Ser.). 192p. 1983. pap. 1.50 (ISBN 0-373-02530-0). Harlequin Bks.

Gair, Reavley. The Children of Paul's: The Story of a Theatre Company, 1553-1608. LC 82-4185. (Illus.). 232p. 1982. 34.50 (ISBN 0-521-24360-2). Cambridge U Pr.

Gairdner, James. The Early Chronicles of England. 328p. 1982. Repr. lib. bdg. 50.00 (ISBN 0-8495-2133-5). Arden Lib.

--History of the Life & Reign of Richard the Third, to Which Is Added the Story of Perkin Warbeck. Repr. of 1898 ed. lib. bdg. 19.00x (ISBN 0-8371-1061-0, GART). Greenwood.

Gaito, J. & Nobrega, Jose N. Introduction to Analysis of Variance Procedures. rev. ed. 250p. 1983. text ed. 19.50x (ISBN 0-8290-1287-7). Irvington.

Gaja, Giorgio, ed. International Commercial Arbitration: Cases Under the New York Convention, 2 binders, Vol. 3. LC 78-991. (International Commercial Arbitration Ser.). 1978. write for info. looseleaf (ISBN 0-379-00599-9); Suppl. 1979. 37.50 o.p. (ISBN 0-686-67495-2); Set. 150.00 (ISBN 0-686-77172-9). Oceana.

Gajate, Comandante, ed. see Gerardo, Machado.

Gajda, Patricia A. Postscript to Victory: British Policy & the German-Polish Borderlands, 1919-1925. LC 81-40634. (Illus.). 246p. (Orig.). 1982. lib. bdg. 23.00 (ISBN 0-8191-2203-3); pap. text ed. 10.75 (ISBN 0-8191-2204-1). U Pr of Amer.

Gajda, Robert J., jt. auth. see Dominguez, Richard H.

Gajda, Walter J., Jr & Biles, William E. Engineering: Modeling & Computation. LC 77-74378. (Illus.). 1978. text ed. 26.50 (ISBN 0-395-25585-6); solutions manual 8.50 (ISBN 0-395-25584-8). HM.

Gajdusek, D. Carleton, jt. ed. see Farquhar, Judith.

Gajek, Bernhard & Wedel, Erwin. Gebrauchsliteratur-Interferenz-Kontrastivitat Beitrage Zur Polnischen und Deutschen Literatur-und Sprachwissenschaft. 390p. (Ger.). 1982. write for info. (ISBN 3-8204-7089-1). P Lang Pubs.

Gajendra, Verna K., jt. auth. see Stenhouse, Lawrence.

Gakenheimer, Ralph. Transportation Planning As Response to Controversy: Participation & Conflict in the Boston Case. LC 75-35905. 432p. 1975. 25.00x (ISBN 0-262-07065-0). MIT Pr.

Gakenheimer, Ralph, compiled by see Organization for Economic Cooperation & Development.

Gal, E. & Gal, I. Human Congenital Malformations: The Design of a Computer-Aided Study. 1975. 17.95 o.p. (ISBN 0-407-10003-2). Butterworth.

Gal, Hans, ed. see Brahms, Johannes.

Gal, I., jt. auth. see Gal, E.

Gal, M. Le see Le Gal, M.

Gal, T., jt. ed. see Fandel, G.

Gal, Tomas. Postoptimal Analyses, Parametric Programming, & Related Topics. 1979. text ed. 65.50 (ISBN 0-07-022679-2, C). McGraw.

Galai, Chaya, tr. see Steinsaltz, Adin.

Galambos. Gastroenterology Appraisal for Patient Care. text ed. write for info (ISBN 0-409-95024-6). Butterworth.

Galambos, Janos. The Asymptotic Theory of Extreme Order Statistics. LC 78-1916. (Probability & Mathematical Staistics Ser.). 352p. 1978. 47.95x (ISBN 0-471-02148-2, Pub. by Wiley-Interscience). Wiley.

Galambos, Joht T., tr. see Bruguera, Miquel, et al.

Galambos, Nancy L., jt. auth. see Garbarino, James.

Galamian, Ivan. Principles of Violin Playing & Teaching. 1962. text ed. 17.95 (ISBN 0-13-710780-3). P-H.

Galana, Laurel, jt. ed. see Covina, Gina.

Galand, Rene. Saint-John Perse. (World Authors Ser.). lib. bdg. 13.95 (ISBN 0-8057-2690-X, Twayne). G K Hall.

Galanin, M. D., jt. auth. see Agranovitch, V. M.

Galanoy, Terry. Charge It: Inside the Credit Card Conspiracy. 264p. 1981. 11.95 (ISBN 0-399-12555-8). Putnam Pub Group.

Galante, Pierre. Operation Valkyrie. 1983. pap. 3.95 (ISBN 0-440-17544-5). Dell.

Galanter, Eugene. Kids & Computers: The Parent's Micro-Computer Handbook. LC 82-82310. 192p. (Orig.). 1983. pap. 7.95 (ISBN 0-448-16612-7, G&D). Putnam Pub Group.

--Kids & Computers: The Parent's Microcomputer Handbook; How to Write & Run Your Own BASIC Programs. LC 82-82310. 192p. 1983. pap. 7.95 (ISBN 0-399-50749-3, Perigee). Putnam.

Galanti, Marie E. Lectures et Fantaisies. 1979. 10.95 (ISBN 0-395-30979-4). HM.

Galanti, Marie E., jt. auth. see Curcio, Louis L.

Galantiere, Lewis, tr. see Cocteau, Jean.

Galantiere, Lewis, tr. see Saint-Exupery, Antoine De.

Galarza, Ernesto & Gallegos, Herman. Mexican Americans in the Southwest. (Illus.). 160p. pap. 4.00 (ISBN 0-686-95031-3). ADL.

Galassi, Jonathan, ed. Understand the Weapon Understand the Wound: Selected Writings of John Cornford. (Essays, Prose, & Scottish Literature). 1979. 12.50 o.p. (ISBN 0-85635-152-0, Pub. by Carcanet New Pr England). Humanities.

Galasso, George J., et al, eds. Antivirals & Virus Diseases of Man. LC 78-67025. 731p. 1979. 69.00 (ISBN 0-89004-222-5). Raven.

Galaty, John G. & Salzman, Philip C., eds. Change & Development in Nomadic & Pastoral Societies. (International Studies in Sociology & Social Anthropology: Vol. 33). v, 173p. 1982. pap. write for info. (ISBN 90-04-06587-3). E J Brill.

Galatzer, A., jt. ed. see Laron, Z.

Galaway, Burt & Hudson, Joe, eds. Offender Restitution in Theory & Action. LC 78-54700. 1978. 21.95 (ISBN 0-669-02328-0). Lexington Bks.

Galaway, Burt, jt. ed. see Hudson, Joe.

Galaway, Burton & Hudson, Hamilton C. Perspectives on Crime Victims. LC 80-19922. (Illus.). 435p. 1980. pap. 21.95 (ISBN 0-8016-1733-2). Mosby.

Galbis, Ignacio R. De Mio Cid Alfonso Reyes: Perspectivas Criticas. LC 80-53519. (Senda de Estudios y Ensayos). 139p. (Orig., Span.). 1981. pap. 9.95 (ISBN 0-918454-22-0). Senda Nueva.

Galbo, H. Hormonal & Metabolic Adaption to Exercise. (Illus.). 120p. 1982. 21.00 (ISBN 0-86577-065-4). Thieme-Stratton.

Galbraith. Building Law Four Checkbook. 1982. 22.50 (ISBN 0-408-00677-3); pap. 9.95 (ISBN 0-408-00583-1). Butterworth.

--A Field Guide to the Wild Flowers of South-East Australia. 39.95 (ISBN 0-686-42773-4, Collins Pub England). Greene.

Galbraith, ed. An Outline for the Young Rider. (gr. 7 up). 12.50 (ISBN 0-392-04103-0, SpS). Sportshelf.

Galbraith, Catherine A. & Mehta, Rama. India Now & Through Time. (gr. 6 up). 1980. 7.95 (ISBN 0-395-29207-7). HM.

Galbraith, Ian A., jt. auth. see Connell, Stephen.

Galbraith, J. K. China Passage. 1973. pap. 1.50 o.p. (ISBN 0-451-05654-X, W5654, Sig). NAL.

Galbraith, J. S. Mackinnon & East Africa, 1878-1895: A Study in the New Imperialism. LC 70-168895. (Commonwealth Ser.). (Illus.). 250p. 1972. 34.50 (ISBN 0-521-08344-3). Cambridge U Pr.

Galbraith, Jay. Organization Design. LC 76-10421. (Illus.). 1977. text ed. 23.95 (ISBN 0-201-02558-2). A-W.

Galbraith, Jay R. & Nathanson, Daniel A. Strategy Implementation: The Role of Structure & Process. (West Ser. in Business Policy & Planning). (Illus.). 1978. pap. text ed. 11.95 (ISBN 0-8299-0214-7). West Pub.

Galbraith, John K. The Affluent Society. 3rd rev. ed. 1976. 15.95 (ISBN 0-395-24375-0); pap. 2.95 (ISBN 0-395-12689-4). HM.

--Affluent Society. 3rd rev. ed. 1978. pap. 2.95 (ISBN 0-451-61684-7, ME1684, Ment). NAL.

--Ambassador's Journal: A Personal Account of the Kennedy Years. LC 69-15012. 1969. 10.00 o.s.i. (ISBN 0-395-07708-7). HM.

--American Capitalism: The Concept of Countervailing Power. LC 80-65363. 224p. 1980. 25.00 (ISBN 0-87332-178-2). M E Sharpe.

--Economics & the Public Purpose. 1975. pap. 2.95 (ISBN 0-451-61864-5, ME1864, Sig). NAL.

--Economics, Peace, & Laughter. 1981. pap. 7.95 (ISBN 0-452-00567-1, F567, Mer). NAL.

--Economics, Peace & Laughter. 288p. 1972. pap. 1.75 o.p. (ISBN 0-451-04954-3, E4954, Sig). NAL.

--The Great Crash, Nineteen Twenty-Nine. 50th Anniv. ed. 1979. 10.95 (ISBN 0-395-28420-1); pap. 3.45 o.p. (ISBN 0-395-08359-1). HM.

--The New Industrial State. 3rd, rev. ed. 1979. pap. 3.95 (ISBN 0-451-62029-1, ME2029, Ment). NAL.

--The Scotch. 1964. 6.95 o.s.i. (ISBN 0-395-07715-X). HM.

--Scotch. 1970. pap. 2.95 o.p. (ISBN 0-452-25019-6, Z5019, Plume). NAL.

--The Voice of the Poor: Essays in Economic & Political Persuasion. 96p. 1983. 8.95 (ISBN 0-674-94295-7). Harvard U Pr.

Galbraith, John S. Crown & Charter: The Early Years of the British South Africa Company. LC 73-93050. (Perspectives on Southern Africa Ser.). 1974. 30.00x (ISBN 0-520-02693-4). U of Cal Pr.

Galbraith, Judy. The Gifted Kids Survival Guide. (Illus., Orig.). (gr. 6-12). 1983. pap. price not set (ISBN 0-936750-07-3). Wetherall.

Galbraith, Judy & Karn, George. Romance Novel Madness. (Illus.). 72p. 1982. pap. 3.95 (ISBN 0-936750-03-0). Wetherall.

Galbraith, Judy, ed. see Wetherall, Charles F.

Galbraith, Kathryn O. Katie Did. LC 82-3981. (Illus.). 32p. (ps-2). 1982. 8.95 (ISBN 0-689-50237-0, McElderry Bk). Atheneum.

Galbraith, Thistle. Outline for the Young Rider. 1971. 5.00 o.p. (ISBN 0-600-43346-3). Transatlantic.

Galbraith, V. H., ed. The Anonimalle Chronicle, 1333-1381. 1927. 22.00 (ISBN 0-7190-0398-9). Manchester.

Galbraith, Vivian H. Domesday Book: Its Place in Administrative History. 1975. 32.50x (ISBN 0-19-822424-9). Oxford U Pr.

Galbreath, Donald L. Papal Heraldry. 2nd ed. (Illus.). 156p. 1972. 45.00x (ISBN 0-685-29193-6). Gale.

Galdone, P., jt. auth. see Armour, Richard.

Galdone, P., illus. Hansel & Gretel. 40p. (gr. 4-6). 1982. 11.95 (ISBN 0-07-022727-6). McGraw.

Galdone, Paul. Cinderella. (Illus.). (gr. k-3). 1978. 9.95 (ISBN 0-07-022684-9, GB). McGraw.

--The Gingerbread Boy. (Illus.). 40p. (gr. 3). 1983. pap. 3.45 (ISBN 0-89919-163-5, Clarion). HM.

--House That Jack Built. (Illus.). (gr. k-3). 1961. PLB 8.95 o.p. (ISBN 0-07-022719-5, GB). McGraw.

--King of the Cats. LC 79-16659. (Illus.). 32p. (ps-3). 1980. 9.95 (ISBN 0-395-29030-9, Clarion). HM.

--The Little Red Hen. LC 72-97770. (Illus.). 32p. (ps-2). 1973. 9.95 (ISBN 0-395-28803-7, Clarion). HM.

--Old Woman & Her Pig. (gr. k-3). 1961. PLB 9.95 (ISBN 0-07-022721-7, GB). McGraw.

--Three Little Pigs. LC 75-123456. (Illus.). (ps-3). 1970. 9.95 (ISBN 0-395-28813-4, Clarion). HM.

--Three Wishes. (Illus.). (gr. k-3). 1961. PLB 8.95 (ISBN 0-07-022714-4, GB). McGraw.

--The Turtle & the Monkey. (Illus.). 32p. (ps-3). 1982. 11.50 (ISBN 0-89919-145-2, Clarion). HM.

Galdone, Paul, jt. auth. see Titus, E.

Galdone, Paul, jt. auth. see Titus, Eve.

Galdone, Paul, jt. auth. see Ziner, Feenie.

Galdone, Paul, illus. The Little Red Hen. LC 72-97770. (Illus.). 40p. (ps-2). 1973. 6.95 o.p. (ISBN 0-8164-3099-3). Seabury.

--Little Red Riding Hood. LC 74-6426. (Illus.). 32p. (gr. k-3). 1974. 10.95 o.p. (ISBN 0-07-022731-4, GB); PLB 10.95 (ISBN 0-07-022732-2). McGraw.

Galdos, Benito P. The Shadow. Austin, Karen O., tr. from Sp. LC 80-10549. Orig. Title: La Sombra. xiv, 58p. 1980. 10.95x (ISBN 0-8214-0553-5, 82-83467). Ohio U Pr.

--Tristana. (Easy Readers, Ser. B). 96p. (Span.). 1976. pap. text ed. 3.95 (ISBN 0-88436-279-5, 70269). EMC.

Galdos, Benito Perez see Rodgers, Eamon J.

Galdston, Olive. Play with Puppets. rev. ed. (Illus.). 52p. (Orig.). 1971. pap. 1.25x (ISBN 0-686-01100-7); pap. text ed. 1.50x (ISBN 0-936426-07-1). Play Schs.

Gale, A., jt. auth. see Chapman, A.

Gale, Alice T., jt. auth. see Mancini, Marguerite R.

Gale, Anthony & Edwards, John A., eds. Physiological Correlates of Human Behaviour, Vol. 1. Date not set. Vol. 1. price not set (ISBN 0-12-273901-9); Vol. 2. price not set (ISBN 0-12-273902-7); Vol. 3. price not set (ISBN 0-12-273903-5). Acad pr.

Gale, Anthony, ed. see Fransella, Fay.

Gale, Anthony, ed. see Hall, John.

Gale, Anthony, ed. see Holdsworth, Ruth.

Gale, Anthony, ed. see Purser, Harry.

Gale, Barbara, jt. auth. see Wechsler, Henry.

Gale, Barry & Gale, Linda. Discover What You're Best At: The National Career Aptitude Test. (Orig.). 1982. pap. 8.50 (ISBN 0-671-41754-1). S&S.

Gale, Cedric. Building an Effective Vocabulary. LC 79-1496. (Orig.). 1979. pap. 4.95 (ISBN 0-8120-2041-3); answer bklet, 1 for every 25 ordered avail. (ISBN 0-8120-2167-3). Barron.

Gale, Cedric, jt. auth. see Hopper, Vincent F.

Gale, Cedric, rev. by see Fernald, James.

Gale, D. & Moone, Eric. The Manipulated City. 366p. 1980. 9.95x (ISBN 0-416-60111-1). Methuen Inc.

Gale, David. Theory of Linear Economic Models. 1960. 34.50 (ISBN 0-07-022728-4, P&RB). McGraw.

Gale, Douglas. Money: In Equilibrium. (Cambridge Economic Handbooks). 364p. 1982. 39.50 (ISBN 0-521-24694-6); pap. 14.95 (ISBN 0-521-28900-9). Cambridge U Pr.

Gale, E. F., et al. The Molecular Basis of Antibiotic Action. 2nd ed. LC 80-41380. 672p. 1981. 89.95 (ISBN 0-471-27915-3, Pub. by Wiley-Interscience). Wiley.

Gale, Elizabeth W. Children Together, Vol. 2. 128p. 1982. pap. 11.95 (ISBN 0-8170-0974-4). Judson.

Gale, George. Theory of Science. (Illus.). 1979. text ed. 19.50 (ISBN 0-07-022680-6, C). McGraw.

Gale, Jack L. Listing Real Estate Successfully. 1981. text ed. 20.95 (ISBN 0-8359-4124-8). Reston.

Gale, James S., tr. see Bang, Im & Ryuk, Yi.

Gale, Janice & Gale, Stephen. Guide to Fairs, Festivals & Fun Events. (Illus.). 190p. Date not set. pap. 6.95 (ISBN 0-686-84245-6). Banyan Bks.

Gale, Joseph. I Sang for Diaghilev: Michel Pavloff's Merry Life. LC 82-71166. (Illus.). 120p. 1983. pap. 14.95 (ISBN 0-87127-132-X). Dance Horiz.

Gale, Linda, jt. auth. see Gale, Barry.

Gale, M. T. Surface-Relief Images for Color Reproduction. (Illus.). 200p. 1980. pap. 27.95 (ISBN 0-240-51068-2). Focal Pr.

Gale Research Co. Library of Congress & National Union Catalogue Author Lists, 1942-1962: A Master Cummulation, 152 vols. LC 73-82135. 1969. Set. 3250.00x (ISBN 0-8103-0950-5); fiche only 1650.00x (ISBN 0-686-85981-2); U.S. vols. only 140.00x (ISBN 0-8103-0951-3). Gale.

Gale Research Company, jt. auth. see United States. Nautical Almanac Office.

Gale, Roberson G., jt. auth. see Smith, Len Young.

Gale, Robert L. Francis Parkman. (U. S. Authors Ser.: No. 220). 1973. lib. bdg. 10.95 o.p. (ISBN 0-8057-0582-1, Twayne). G K Hall.

--John Hay. (United States Authors Ser.). 1978. lib. bdg. 13.95 (ISBN 0-8057-7199-9, Twayne). G K Hall.

--Luke Short. (United States Authors Ser.). 1981. 11.95 (ISBN 0-8057-7307-X, Twayne). G K Hall.

--Plots & Characters in the Fiction & Poetry of Edgar Allan Poe. LC 76-113809. (Plots & Characters Ser.). xxiii, 191p. 1970. 16.00 o.p. (ISBN 0-208-00974-4, Archon). Shoe String.

--Plots & Characters in the Fiction & Sketches of Nathaniel Hawthorne. (Plots & Characters Ser.). xxii, 259p. 1968. 17.50 o.p. (ISBN 0-208-00649-4, Archon). Shoe String.

--Plots & Characters in the Fiction of Henry James. (Plots & Characters Ser.). xxi, 207p. 1965. 16.00 o.p. (ISBN 0-208-00500-5, Archon). Shoe String.

--Plots & Characters-James. 280p. 1972. pap. 2.95 o.p. (ISBN 0-262-57031-9). MIT Pr.

--Richard Henry Dana. LC 68-24301. (U. S. Authors Ser.: No. 143). 1969. lib. bdg. 10.95 o.p. (ISBN 0-8057-0184-2, Twayne). G K Hall.

Gale, Roger W. The Americanization of Micronesia: A Study of the Consolidation of the U. S. Role in the Pacific. LC 78-68800. 1979. pap. text ed. 13.50 (ISBN 0-8191-0703-4). U Pr of Amer.

Gale, Stephen, jt. auth. see Gale, Janice.

Gale, Stephen & Moore, Eric G., eds. The Manipulated City: Perspectives on Spatial Structure & Social Issues in Urban America. LC 74-25445. (Maaroufa Press Geography Ser.). (Illus.). 1975. pap. text ed. 6.95x (ISBN 0-88425-003-2). Maaroufa Pr.

Gale, Stephen H. Harold Pinter: An Annotated Bibliography. (Reference Publications). 1978. lib. bdg. 28.00 (ISBN 0-8161-8014-8, Hall Reference). G K Hall.

Gale, Steven H. Readings for Todays Writers. LC 79-21312. 1980. pap. text ed. 13.50x (ISBN 0-673-15672-9); tchrs' manual 1.40 (ISBN 0-471-07846-8). Scott F.

Gale, Zona. Miss Lulu Bett. LC 76-26895. 1976. Repr. of 1920 ed. lib. bdg. 20.50x (ISBN 0-8371-9021-5, GALB). Greenwood.

Galeano, Eduardo. Days & Nights of Love & War. Brister, Judith, tr. from Span. LC 82-48034. 224p. 1982. 16.00 (ISBN 0-85345-620-8, CL6208); pap. 8.00 (ISBN 0-85345-621-6, PB6216). Monthly Rev.

Galen, Nina. Eden Motel & To Love Flaminio. 275p. (Orig.). 1982. pap. 4.95 (ISBN 0-943628-00-8). East Palace.

Galen, P. S. & Gambino, S. R. Beyond Normality: The Predictive Value & Efficiency of Medical Diagnosis. LC 75-25915. 237p. 1975. 32.95x (ISBN 0-471-29047-5, Pub. by Wiley Medical). Wiley.

Galenson, David. White Servitude in Colonial America. LC 81-7682. (Illus.). 320p. 1982. 29.95 (ISBN 0-521-23686-X). Cambridge U Pr.

Galenson, Eleanor & Call, Justin D., eds. Frontiers of Infant Psychiatry. 1982. 37.50 (ISBN 0-465-02585-4). Basic.

Galenson, Walter. Labor Productivity in Soviet & American Industry. LC 76-49596. 1977. Repr. of 1955 ed. lib. bdg. 20.00x (ISBN 0-8371-9370-2, GALPS). Greenwood.

--Primer on Employment & Wages. 1970. pap. text ed. 3.25x (ISBN 0-394-30720-8). Phila Bk Co.

Galenson, Walter, ed. Incomes Policy: What Can We Learn from Europe? LC 72-619695. (Pierce Ser.: No. 3). 120p. 1973. 7.50 (ISBN 0-87546-048-8). ILR Pr.

--Labor in Developing Economics. LC 76-3786. 299p. 1976. Repr. of 1962 ed. lib. bdg. 20.50x (ISBN 0-8371-8817-2, GALD). Greenwood.

Gales, D. V., intro. by. London Inhabitants Within the Walls, Sixteen Ninety-Five. 1966. 50.00x (ISBN 0-686-96617-1, Pub by London Rec Soc England). State Mutual Bk.

Galgoczy, Janos see Feher, Matyas & Erdy, Miklos.

Galich, Alexander. Songs & Poems. Smith, Gerry, tr. from Rus. 188p. 1973. 20.00 (ISBN 0-88233-784-X); pap. 9.50 (ISBN 0-88233-785-8). Ardis Pubs.

Galiegue, B. F. Service Management in the Retail Motor Industry in Britain. (Illus.). 160p. (Orig.). 1982. pap. 14.95 (ISBN 0-434-90650-6, Pub. by W Heinemann). David & Charles.

Galilei, Galileo. Dialogue Concerning the Two Chief World Systems-Ptolemaic & Copernican. 2nd rev. ed. Drake, Stillman, tr. 1967. 37.50x (ISBN 0-520-00449-3); pap. 8.95x (ISBN 0-520-00450-7, CAL66). U of Cal Pr.

--Dialogues Concerning Two New Sciences. (Illus.). 1914. pap. text ed. 5.50 (ISBN 0-486-60099-8). Dover.

--On Motion & on Mechanics. Drabkin, I. E., ed. Drake, Stillman, tr. Bd. with On Mechanics. (Medieval Science Publication Ser). 204p. 1960. 14.00x (ISBN 0-299-02030-4). U of Wis Pr.

Galin, Saul, jt. auth. see Johnson, Norman H.

Galinkin, George B., ed. Readings on Social Services in the Health Professions. 1976. pap. text ed. 10.00 o.p. (ISBN 0-8191-0083-8). U Pr of Amer.

Galinsky, Ellen. The Baby Cardinal. LC 77-5083. (Illus.). (gr. k-4). 1977. 5.95 o.p. (ISBN 0-399-20596-9). Putnam Pub Group.

Galinsky, Ellen & Hooks, William. The New Extended Family: Day Care Programs That Work. 1977. 11.95 o.s.i. (ISBN 0-395-25934-7); pap. 6.95 (ISBN 0-395-25945-2). HM.

Galinsky, G. Karl. Ovid's Metamorphoses: An Introduction to Its Basic Aspects. LC 74-84146. 1975. 30.00x (ISBN 0-520-02848-1). U of Cal Pr.

Galinsky, M. David, jt. auth. see Shaffer, John B.

Galishoff, Stuart. Safeguarding the Public Health. LC 75-66. (Illus.). 191p. 1975. lib. bdg. 25.00 (ISBN 0-8371-7956-4, GPH/). Greenwood.

Galjaard, H. Genetic Metabolic Diseases: Early Diagnosis & Prenatal Analysis. 1980. 142.75 (ISBN 0-444-80143-X). Elsevier.

Gall, J. C. Ancient Sedimentary Environments & the Habitats of Living Organisms: Introduction to Paleoecology. Wallace, P., tr. from Fr. (Illus.). 230p. 1983. 24.00 (ISBN 0-387-12137-4). Springer-Verlag.

Gall, Pirie M., et al. Municipal Development Programs in Latin America: An Intercountry Evaluation. LC 76-23401. (Illus.). 1976. 24.95 o.p. (ISBN 0-275-23280-8). Praeger.

Gall, Sally M., jt. auth. see Rosenthal, M. L.

Gall, Sally M., ed. see Guthrie, Ramon.

Gallager, Nancy E. & Wilson, Dunning S. Haudlist of Arabic Medical Manuscripts at UCLA. LC 82-50985. 28p. 1983. price not set (ISBN 0-89003-128-2). Undena Pubns.

Gallager, R. G. Information Theory & Reliable Communication. LC 68-26850. 588p. 1968. 41.95x (ISBN 0-471-29048-3). Wiley.

Gallager, Robert G. Low-Density Parity-Check Codes. (Press Research Monographs: No. 21). (Illus.). 1963. 12.00x o.p. (ISBN 0-262-07007-3). MIT Pr.

Gallagher. Handbook of Counseling in Higher Education. 348p. 1983. 37.95 (ISBN 0-03-063216-1). Praeger.

Gallagher, A. P. Coordinating Australian University Development: A Study of the Australian Universities Commission, 1959-1970. LC 82-1973. (Scholars Library). 244p. 1983. text ed. 34.50x (ISBN 0-7022-1657-7). U of Queensland Pr.

Gallagher, Bernard J. & Palazzolo, Charles S. The Social World of Occupations. LC 76-41981. 1976. pap. text ed. 11.95 (ISBN 0-8403-1620-8). Kendall-Hunt.

Gallagher, Bernard J., III. Sociology of Mental Illness. (Ser. in Sociology). (Illus.). 1980. text ed. 20.95 (ISBN 0-13-820928-6). P-H.

Gallagher, C. A. & Watson, H. J. Quantitative Methods for Business Decisions. 1980. text ed. 27.95 (ISBN 0-07-022751-9); supplementary materials avail. McGraw.

Gallagher, Charles C. & Helm, Eugene E., eds. Carl Philip Emanuel Bach, Six Symphonies. (The Symphony 1720-1840 Series C: Vol. 8). 1982. lib. bdg. 90.00 (ISBN 0-8240-3821-5). Garland Pub.

Gallagher, Chuck. Call to Healing. 1983. 3.95 (ISBN 0-8215-9873-2). Sadlier.

--Hurrah for Parents. 1980. 3.95 (ISBN 0-8215-6467-6). Sadlier.

--Love Is a Couple. 1978. pap. 3.50 (ISBN 0-385-13595-5, Im). Doubleday.

--Love is a Couple. 1980. 3.95 (ISBN 0-8215-6464-1). Sadlier.

--Love Takes Greatness. 1980. 3.95 (ISBN 0-8215-6465-X). Sadlier.

--Parents are Lovers. 1980. 3.95 (ISBN 0-8215-6466-8). Sadlier.

Gallagher, Donald, ed. see Maritain, Jacques.

Gallagher, Donald A., ed. Some Philosophers on Education: Papers Concerning the Doctrines of Augustine, Aristole, Aquinas & Dewey. 2nd ed. 1961. 6.95 (ISBN 0-87462-403-7). Marquette.

Gallagher, Dorothy. Hannah's Daughters: Six Generations of An American Family. LC 75-38557. (Illus.). 352p. 1976. 10.95i o.p. (ISBN 0-690-01103-2). T Y Crowell.

Gallagher, Edward & Mistichelli, Judith A. Jules Verne: A Primary & Secondary Bibliography. 1980. lib. bdg. 32.00 (ISBN 0-8161-8106-3, Hall Reference). G K Hall.

Gallagher, Edward J. A Critical Edition of the "Passion Nostre Seigneur" f r om Manuscript 1131 from the Bibliotheque Saint-Genevieve, Paris. (Studies in the Romance Languages & Literatures Ser: No. 179). 292p. 1976. pap. 15.50x (ISBN 0-8078-9179-7). U of NC Pr.

Gallagher, Edward J. & Werge, Thomas. Early Puritan Writers, William Bradford, John Cotton, Thomas Hooker, Edward Johnson, Richard Mather, Thomas Sheperd: A Reference Guide. 1976. lib. bdg. 25.00 (ISBN 0-8161-1196-0, Hall Reference). G K Hall.

Gallagher, Elizabeth & Peroni, Carlo. Irish Songs & Airs. 10.00 (ISBN 0-8159-5817-X). Devin.

Gallagher, Eugene B. Infants, Mothers, & Doctors. LC 78-2071. 1978. 21.95x (ISBN 0-669-02269-1). Lexington Bks.

Gallagher, Frank. The Indivisible Island: The Story of the Partition of Ireland. LC 74-5772. (Illus.). 316p. 1974. Repr. of 1957 ed. lib. bdg. 20.00x (ISBN 0-8371-7515-1, GAII). Greenwood.

Gallagher, Idella, ed. see Maritain, Jacques.

Gallagher, J. A. The Decline, Revival & Fall of the British Empire. LC 82-4291. 250p. 1982. 29.50 (ISBN 0-521-24642-3). Cambridge U Pr.

Gallagher, J. Roswell & Harris, Herbert I. Emotional Problems of Adolescents. 3rd ed. 1976. text ed. 17.95x (ISBN 0-19-501972-5). Oxford U Pr.

Gallagher, James J. Leadership Unit: The Use of Teacher-Scholar Teams to Develop Units for the Gifted. (Illus.). 138p. 1982. pap. 12.50 tchr's ed (ISBN 0-89824-036-0). Trillium Pr.

Gallagher, James J., jt. auth. see Haskins, Ron.

Gallagher, James J., jt. auth. see Kirk, Samuel A.

Gallagher, James J., ed. Gifted Children: Reaching their Potential. 440p. (Orig.). 1979. pap. 14.00 (ISBN 0-89824-012-3). Trillium Pr.

Gallagher, James J., jt. ed. see Haskins, Ron.

Gallagher, Janice, jt. auth. see Harrington, John W.

Gallagher, Jeanette & Reid, D. Kim. The Learning Theory of Piaget & Inhelder. LC 80-24410. (Orig.). 1981. pap. text ed. 10.95 (ISBN 0-8185-0343-2). Brooks-Cole.

Gallagher, John S., jt. auth. see Haar, Lester.

Gallagher, Mark. Day-by-Day in New York Yankee History. LC 82-83934. (Illus.). 300p. (Orig.). 1983. pap. 9.95 (ISBN 0-88011-102-X). Leisure Pr.

Gallagher, Mary. Quicksilver. 264p. 1982. 12.95 (ISBN 0-399-12697-X). Putnam Pub Group.

--Spend It Foolishly. LC 77-23661. 1978. 10.95 o.p. (ISBN 0-689-10859-1). Atheneum.

Gallagher, Matthew P. The Soviet History of World War II: Myths, Memories & Realities. LC 75-32458. 1976. Repr. of 1963 ed. lib. bdg. 21.00x (ISBN 0-8371-8551-3, GASH). Greenwood.

Gallagher, Maureen. The Cathedral Book. LC 82-60592. (gr. 3-6). 1983. pap. 2.95 (ISBN 0-8091-2485-8). Paulist Pr.

Gallagher, Michael. The Irish Labor Party in Transition, 1957-82. 1982. 79.00x (ISBN 0-7171-1250-0, Pub. by Gill & Macmillan Ireland). State Mutual Bk.

--The Irish Labour Party in Transition, 1957-81. 351p. 1983. 25.00 (ISBN 0-7190-0866-2). Manchester.

Gallagher, Miriam. Let's Help Our Children Talk. (Illus.). 1978. 10.50 o.p. (ISBN 0-905140-20-6); pap. 6.50 o.p o.p. (ISBN 0-905140-21-4). Transatlantic.

Gallagher, Patricia. Echoes & Embers. 1983. pap. 3.50 (ISBN 0-380-80929-X, 80929). Avon.

--Mystic Rose. 1977. pap. 3.50 (ISBN 0-380-82560-0, 79467). Avon.

--Summer of Sighs. 1977. pap. 1.75 o.p. (ISBN 0-380-01645-1, 33035). Avon.

Gallagher, R. H. Optimum Structural Design: Theory & Applications. LC 72-8600. (Numerical Methods in Engineering Ser.). 358p. 1973. 53.95x (ISBN 0-471-29050-5, Pub. by Wiley-Interscience). Wiley.

Gallagher, R. H., jt. ed. see Ashwell, D. G.

Gallagher, R. H., et al. Finite Elements in Biomechanics. LC 81-13084. (Wiley Series in Numerical Methods in Engineering). 404p. 1982. 49.95x (ISBN 0-471-09996-1, Pub. by Wiley-Interscience). Wiley.

Gallagher, R. H., jt. auth. see Atluri, S. N.

Gallagher, R. H., et al, eds. Finite Elements in Fluids, 3 vols. Incl. Vol. 1. Viscous Flow & Hydrodynamics. 290p. 1975. 67.00x (ISBN 0-471-29045-9); Vol. 2. Mathematical Foundations, Aerodynamics, & Lubrication. 287p. 1975. 67.00x (ISBN 0-471-29046-7); Vol. 3. 1978. 67.00x (ISBN 0-471-99630-0). LC 74-13573 (Pub. by Wiley-Interscience). Wiley.

Gallagher, Richard H. Finite Element Analysis: Fundamentals. (Civil Engr. & Engr. Mechanics Ser.). (Illus.). 416p. 1975. 33.95 (ISBN 0-13-317248-1). P-H.

Gallagher, Richard H., jt. auth. see McGuire, William.

Gallagher, S. F., ed. Woman in Irish Legend, Life & Literature. LC 82-22792. (Irish Literary Studies: No. 14). 154p. 1983. text ed. 28.50x (ISBN 0-389-20361-0). B&N Imports.

Gallagher, Stephen. Chimera. 320p. 1982. 13.95 (ISBN 0-312-13387-1). St Martin.

Gallagher, Tess. Instructions to the Double. LC 76-378309. 76p. 1975. 0. p. 12.00 (ISBN 0-915308-04-5); pap. 5.00 (ISBN 0-915308-03-7). Graywolf.

Gallagher, Thomas. Assault in Norway. 1975. Repr. lib. bdg. 11.95 o.p. (ISBN 0-8161-6289-1, Large Print Bks). G K Hall.

--The X-Craft Raid. 1978. pap. 1.75 o.p. (ISBN 0-523-40454-9). Pinnacle Bks.

Gallagher, Tom. Portugal: A Twentieth Century Interpretation. 256p. 1982. 25.00 (ISBN 0-7190-0876-X). Manchester.

Gallagher, Tom, jt. ed. see O'Connell, James.

Gallagher, Vera. Hearing the Cry of the Poor: The Story of the St. Vincent de Paul Society. 64p. 1983. pap. 1.50 (ISBN 0-89243-174-1). Liguori Pubns.

Gallagher, William D., ed. Selections from the Poetical Literature of the West. LC 68-29083. 1968. Repr. of 1841 ed. 34.00x (ISBN 0-8201-1019-1). Schol Facsimiles.

Gallaher, John G. The Students of Paris & the Revolution of Eighteen Forty-Eight. LC 79-27580. 150p. 1980. 9.95x o.p. (ISBN 0-8093-0953-X). S Ill U Pr.

Gallahue, David L. Enchancing Motor Development in Children Through Movement Experiences. LC 81-16424. 397p. 1982. text ed. 16.95 (ISBN 0-471-08778-5). Wiley.

--Motor Development & Movement Experiences for Young Children. LC 75-37676. 413p. 1976. text ed. 25.50x (ISBN 0-471-29042-4). Wiley.

--Understanding Motor Development in Children Pre-School Through the Elementary Grades. 455p. 1982. text ed. 19.95 (ISBN 0-471-08779-3). Wiley.

Gallahue, David L. & Meadors, William J. Let's Move: A Physical Education Program for Elementary School Teachers. 2nd ed. 1979. pap. 9.95 (ISBN 0-8403-2029-9). Kendall-Hunt.

Gallahue, David L., et al. A Conceptual Approach to Moving & Learning. LC 75-2369. 423p. 1975. text ed. 25.95x (ISBN 0-471-29043-2); tchrs.' resource bk. 6.00x (ISBN 0-471-29039-4). Wiley.

Gallais, Pierre. Dialectique du Recit Medieval. (Faux Titre Ser.: Band 9). 322p. (Fr.). 1982. pap. text ed. 30.00x (ISBN 90-6203-744-5, Pub. by Rodopi Holland). Humanities.

Galland, Frank J. Dictionary of Computing: Data Communications, Hardware & Software Basics, Digital Electronics. 330p. 1982. 34.95 (ISBN 0-471-10468-X, Pub. by Wiley-Interscience); pap. 19.95 (ISBN 0-471-10469-8). Wiley.

Gallant, Ann. Cosmetic Camouflage: The Practice & Techniques. 352p. 1982. 35.00x (ISBN 0-85950-489-1, Pub. by Thornes England). State Mutual Bk.

Gallant, Claire B. Mediation in Special Education Disputes. LC 82-60764. 104p. (Orig.). 1982. pap. 6.95 (ISBN 0-87101-105-0, NASW CODE: CBS-097-C). Natl Assn Soc Wkrs.

Gallant, Edward & Gallant, K. B. Handbook of Connecticut Workers' Compensation Law. 384p. Date not set. price not set (ISBN 0-88063-019-1). Butterworth Legal Pubs.

Gallant, K. B., jt. auth. see Gallant, Edward.

Gallant, Roy A. A B C's of Astronomy. LC 61-5048. (gr. 7 up). 1962. 8.95a o.p. (ISBN 0-385-00116-9); PLB 8.95a (ISBN 0-385-06714-3). Doubleday.

--Astrology: Sense or Nonsense? LC 73-15340. (Illus.). 256p. (gr. 7-9). 1974. PLB 9.95 o.p. (ISBN 0-385-08673-3). Doubleday.

Gallardo, Jose. The Way of Biblical Justice. LC 82-83386. (Mennonite Faith Ser.: Vol. 11). 80p. (Orig.). 1983. pap. 0.95 (ISBN 0-8361-3321-8). Herald Pr.

Gallati, Mary. Mary Gallati's Hostess Dinner Book. 13.50 (ISBN 0-392-07065-0, LTB). Sportshelf.

Gallatin, Judith E. Abnormal Psychology. 1982. text ed. 26.95x (ISBN 0-02-475510-9). Macmillan.

Gallaudet College Library, Washington, D. C. Dictionary Catalog on Deafness & the Deaf, 2 vols. 1970. Set. lib. bdg. 190.00 (ISBN 0-8161-0877-3, Hall Library). G K Hall.

Gallavotti, G. The Elements of Mechanics. (Texts & Monographs in Physics). (Illus.). 528p. 1983. 48.00 (ISBN 0-387-11753-9). Springer-Verlag.

Gallaway, Ira. Drifted Astray: Returning the Church to Witness & Ministry. 160p. (Orig.). 1983. pap. 6.95 (ISBN 0-687-11186-2). Abingdon.

Galle, Emile. Ecrits Pour L'Art Floriculture Art Decoratif, Notices D'Exposition, 1884-89. vi, 382p. (Fr.). 1981. Repr. of 1908 ed. lib. bdg. 150.00 o.p. (ISBN 0-8287-0026-5). Clearwater Pub.

Gallegos, Frederick, jt. auth. see Dawson, Peter P.

Gallegos, Herman, jt. auth. see Galarza, Ernesto.

Gallegos, J. A. What's the Problem? 1979. 5.95 o.p. (ISBN 0-533-03934-7). Vantage.

Gallegue, B. F. Service Management in the Retail Motor Industry. 160p. 1982. pap. 38.00x (Pub. by Heinemann England). State Mutual Bk.

Gallen, Richard, et al. The Unmarried Couple's Legal Handbook: The Questions You Should Ask, The Answers You Should Know. (Orig.). pap. 6.95 o.s.i. (ISBN 0-440-59219-4, Delta). Dell.

Galler & Perlis. A View of Programming Languages. 1976. 26.95 (ISBN 0-201-02324-5). A-W.

Gallery, Daniel V. U-Five Hundred Five. 1967. pap. 2.25 (ISBN 0-446-32012-9). Warner Bks.

Gallessich, June. The Profession & Practice of Consultation: A Handbook for Consultants, Trainers of Consultants, & Consumers of Consultation Services. LC 82-8948. (Social & Behavioral Science Ser.). 1982. text ed. 25.95x (ISBN 0-87589-527-1). Jossey Bass.

Gallet De Kulture, Achille. Le Tsar Nicolas et la Sainte Russie. (Nineteenth Century Russia Ser.). 306p. (Fr.). 1974. Repr. of 1855 ed. lib. bdg. 81.00x o.p. (ISBN 0-8287-0362-0, R8). Clearwater Pub.

Galley, Howard, ed. Morning & Evening Prayer. 300p. 1983. 19.95 (ISBN 0-8164-0117-9). Seabury.

Gallhager, Roy. Smoke Rings Over the Valley. 1970. 6.95 (ISBN 0-932052-32-0). North Country.

Galli, et al, eds. Chemical Toxicology of Food. (Developments in Toxicology Ser.: Vol. 3). (Proceedings). 1978. 76.75 (ISBN 0-444-80074-3). Elsevier.

Galli, C., et al, eds. Dietary Lipids & Postnatal Development. LC 73-79580. (Illus.). 286p. 1973. 30.00 (ISBN 0-911216-50-2). Raven.

Galli, C. L. & Paoletti, R. Principles & Methods in Modern Toxicology. (Giovanni Lorrenzini Foundation Symposia Ser.: Vol. 6). 1980. 68.00 (ISBN 0-444-80230-4). Elsevier.

Galli, Claudio, et al, eds. Phospholipases & Prostaglandins. LC 77-87457. (Advances in Prostaglandin & Thromboxane Research Ser.: Vol. 3). 218p. 1978. 30.00 (ISBN 0-89004-201-2). Raven.

Galli, Nicholas. Foundations & Principles of Health Education. LC 77-21586. 389p. 1978. text ed. 23.95x (ISBN 0-471-29065-3). Wiley.

Gallick, S. Lies to Live By. (Orig.). 1983. pap. 2.95 (ISBN 0-440-04786-2). Dell.

Gallico, Paul. Beyond the Poseidon Adventure. 1978. 10.95 o.s.i. (ISBN 0-440-00453-5). Delacorte.

--The House That Wouldn't Go Away. LC 79-53599. 1980. 8.95 o.s.i. (ISBN 0-440-03496-5); PLB 8.44 o.s.i. (ISBN 0-440-03497-3). Delacorte.

--Snow Goose. (YA) (gr. 9 up). 1941. 7.50 (ISBN 0-394-44593-7). Knopf.

--Thomasina. 256p. 1981. pap. 2.25 (ISBN 0-380-51524-5, 59980-5). Avon.

Gallie, D. In Search of the New Working Class. LC 77-80834. (Studies in Sociology: No. 9). (Illus.). 1978. 42.50 (ISBN 0-521-21771-7); pap. 12.95 (ISBN 0-521-29275-1). Cambridge U Pr.

Gallie, W. B. Peirce & Pragmatism. LC 75-25534. 247p. 1975. Repr. of 1966 ed. lib. bdg. 17.75x (ISBN 0-8371-8342-1, GAPE). Greenwood.

--Philosophers of Peace & War. LC 77-23553. 1979. pap. 7.95 (ISBN 0-521-29651-X). Cambridge U Pr.

--Philosophers of Peace & War. LC 77-23553. (Wiles Lectures Ser.: 1976). 1978. 24.95 (ISBN 0-521-21779-2). Cambridge U Pr.

--Philosophy & the Historical Understanding. 2nd ed. LC 68-26656. 1969. pap. 2.45 o.p. (ISBN 0-8052-0187-4). Schocken.

Gallieni, Thomas M. The Unrelenting Advance of the Financial Collapse of the World. (Illus.). 121p. 1983. 86.45 (ISBN 0-86722-037-6). Inst Econ Pol.

Gallienne, Eva Le see Andersen, Hans C.

Gallier, James. Autobiography of James Gallier, Architect. LC 69-13715. (Architecture & Decorative Art Ser.). 1973. Repr. of 1864 ed. lib. bdg. 29.50 (ISBN 0-306-71247-4). Da Capo.

Galliher, John & Cross, John. Morals Legislation Without Morality: The Case of Nevada. (Crime, Law & Deviance Ser.). 140p. 1983. 15.00 (ISBN 0-8135-0983-1). Rutgers U Pr.

Gallimore, J. G. Transverse Paraphysics: The New Science of Space, Time & Gravity Control. LC 82-50843. (Illus.). 359p. (Orig.). 1982. pap. text ed. 35.00 (ISBN 0-9603536-4-X). Tesla Bk Co.

Gallimore, R., jt. ed. see Boggio, G.

Gallin, D. Intensional & Higher-Order Model Logic. (North-Holland Mathematics Studies: Vol. 19). 1976. text ed. 38.50 (ISBN 0-444-11002-X, North-Holland). Elsevier.

Gallin, John I. & Fauci, Anthony S., eds. Phagocytic Cells, Vol. 1. (Advances in Host Defense Mechanisms: Vol. 1). 318p. 1982. text ed. 35.00 (ISBN 0-89004-574-7). Raven.

Gallin, John I. & Quie, Paul G., eds. Leukocyte Chemotaxis: Methods, Physiology, & Clinical Implications. LC 76-58053. 442p. 1978. 47.00 (ISBN 0-89004-198-9). Raven.

Gallion, Arthur B. & Eisner, Simon. The Urban Pattern, City Planning & Design. 4th ed. 528p. 1980. text ed. 19.95x (ISBN 0-442-26261-2). Van Nos Reinhold.

--The Urban Pattern: City Planning & Design. 4th ed. 464p. 1982. pap. 14.95 (ISBN 0-442-22926-7). Van Nos Reinhold.

Gallistel, C. R. The Organization of Action: A New Synthesis. LC 79-22565. 432p. 1980. 29.95x o.s.i. (ISBN 0-470-26912-X). Halsted Pr.

Gallix, Francois, ed. see White, T. H. & Potts, L. J.

Gallman, Robert E., ed. Recent Developments in the Study of Economic & Business History: Essays in Memory of Herman E. Krooss. LC 76-13956. (Research in Economic History: Suppl. 1). 450p. 1977. lib. bdg. 40.00 (ISBN 0-89232-035-4). Jai Pr.

Gallo & Sedwick. French for Careers: Conversational Perspectives. (Illus., Orig.). 1980. pap. text ed. 8.95 (ISBN 0-442-23883-5). Van Nos Reinhold.

Gallo, Barbara G., jt. auth. see Smith, George P.

Gallo, D. M. & Porter, R. M., eds. Kleinian Groups & Related Topics: Proceedings, Oaxtepec, Mexico, 1981. (Lecture Notes in Mathematics Ser.: Vol. 971). 117p. 1983. pap. 8.50 (ISBN 0-387-11975-2). Springer-Verlag.

Gallo, Ezequiel. Farmers in Revolt: The Revolutions of 1893 in the Province of Santa Fe, Argentina. (Institute of Latin American Studies Monograph: No. 7). (Illus.). 108p. 1976. text ed. 21.00x o.p. (ISBN 0-485-17707-2, Athlone Pr). Humanities.

Gallo, Joseph. Thoughts in Verse. 1980. 4.50 o.p. (ISBN 0-8062-1344-2). Carlton.

Gallo, Michael & Kiehl, Charles. Basic Arithmetic. 1981. pap. text ed. 19.95x (ISBN 0-673-16223-0). Scott F.

Gallo, Phillip S., Jr., jt. auth. see Linton, Marigold.

Gallo, Robert C., jt. ed. see Marchesi, Vincent T.

Gallo, Rose A. F. Scott Fitzgerald. LC 76-15650. (Literature and Life Ser.). 1978. 11.95 (ISBN 0-8044-2225-7). Ungar.

Gallon, Arthur J. Coaching: Ideas & Ideals. 2nd ed. LC 79-90061. (Illus.). 1980. text ed. 14.95 (ISBN 0-395-28693-X). HM.

Gallop, J. Feminism & Psychoanalysis: The Daughters Seduction. 1982. 55.00x (ISBN 0-333-29471-8, Pub. by Macmillan England). State Mutual Bk.

Gallopin, Giberte. Planning Methods & the Human Environment. (Socio-Economic Studies: No. 4). 68p. 1981. pap. 7.50 (ISBN 92-3-101894-9, U1106, UNESCO). Unipub.

Galloway. Twelve Ways to Develop a Positive Attitude. 1975. pap. 1.95 (ISBN 0-8423-7550-3). Tyndale.

Galloway & Ball. Schools & Disruptive Pupils. LC 81-15601. 1982. pap. 10.95x (ISBN 0-582-49707-8). Longman.

Galloway, Charles G. Psychology for Learning & Teaching. 1976. text ed. 21.50 (ISBN 0-07-022737-3, C); instructors' manual 12.00 (ISBN 0-07-022738-1). McGraw.

Galloway, Dale E. Expect a Miracle. 1982. pap. 4.95 (ISBN 0-8423-0822-9). Tyndale.

Galloway, David. Edward Lewis Wallant. (United States Authors Ser.). 1979. lib. bdg. 13.95 (ISBN 0-8057-7250-2, Twayne). G K Hall.

--The Public Prodigals. LC 77-373743. (Illus.). 1976. 15.00x o.p. (ISBN 0-85117-113-3). Intl Pubns Serv.

--Tamsen. 448p. 15.95 (ISBN 0-15-187992-3). HarBraceJ.

Galloway, David & Sabisch, Christian, eds. Calamus: Male Homosexuality in Twentieth Century Literature: An International Anthology. 480p. 1982. pap. 9.50 (ISBN 0-688-00606-X). Quill NY.

Galloway, George B. History of the House of Representatives. 2nd, rev. ed. LC 75-35894. (Illus.). 1976. 12.45i (ISBN 0-690-01101-6). T Y Crowell.

Galloway, Howard P., jt. auth. see Bullwinkle, Alice.

Galloway, Howard P., ed. New Dimensions in Youthwork, Vol. 1. LC 72-96322. 1973. 10.95 (ISBN 0-87874-007-4). Galloway.

--New Dimensions in Youthwork: Challenges to Youth Organizations, Vol. 2. LC 74-15245. 224p. 1974. 10.95 (ISBN 0-87874-014-7). Galloway.

Galloway, John T., Jr. The Gospel According to Superman. 1973. pap. 2.25 (ISBN 0-87981-137-4). Omega Pubns Or.

Galloway, Joseph. Selected Tracts, 3 vols. LC 70-166326. (Era of the American Revolution Ser.). 1974. Set. lib. bdg. 155.00 (ISBN 0-306-70222-3). Da Capo.

Galloway, Patricia K., ed. La Salle & His Legacy: Frenchmen & Indians in the Lower Mississippi Valley. LC 82-17498. 274p. 1982. 20.00x (ISBN 0-87805-171-6). U Pr of Miss.

Galloway, Russell. The Rich & the Poor in Supreme Court History. Aigner, Hal, ed. 230p. 1983. pap. 7.95 (ISBN 0-937572-01-2). Paradigm Pr.

Galloway, W. E. & Brown, L. F., Jr. Report of Investigations No. Seventy-Five: Depositional Systems & Shelf-Slope Relationships in Upper Pennsylvania Rocks, North-Central Texas, No. 75. (Illus.). 62p. 1972. 3.00 (ISBN 0-686-36606-9). Bur Econ Geology.

Galloway, William E. & Henry, Christopher D. Report of Investigations No. 113: Depositional Framework, Hydrostratigraphy, & Uranium Mineralization of the Oakville Sandstone (Miocene), Texas Coastal Plain. (Illus.). 51p. 1982. 2.50 (ISBN 0-686-37542-4). U of Tex Econ Geology.

Gallucci, Vincenzo, jt. ed. see Cohn, Lawrence H.

Gallup, Donald. Ezra Pound: A Bibliography. LC 82-15995. 528p. 1983. write for info. U Pr of Va.

Gallup, Donald, ed. see Wilder, Thornton.

Gallup, George H. The Gallup International Public Opinion Polls, France: 1939, 1944-1975, 2 Vols. 1976. lib. bdg. 47.50 ea. Vol. 1 (ISBN 0-313-20156-0). Vol. 1 (ISBN 0-313-20157-9). Set. lib. bdg. 95.00 (ISBN 0-313-20155-2, GAINF). Greenwood.

Gallup, George H., ed. The Gallup International Public Opinion Polls, Great Britain: 1937-1975, 2 vols. 1976. lib. bdg. 47.50 ea. Vol. 1 (ISBN 0-313-20153-6). Vol. 2 (ISBN 0-313-20154-4). Set. lib. bdg. 95.00 (ISBN 0-313-20152-8, GAING). Greenwood.

--The Gallup Poll: Public Opinion, Nineteen Seventy-Nine. LC 79-56557. 325p. 1980. lib. bdg. 49.50 (ISBN 0-8420-2170-1). Scholarly Res Inc.

--The International Gallup Polls: Public Opinion, Nineteen Seventy-Eight. LC 79-3844. 1980. lib. bdg. 49.50 (ISBN 0-8420-2162-0). Scholarly Res Inc.

Gallwey, W. Timothy. The Inner Game of Golf. 1981. 13.95 (ISBN 0-394-50534-4). Random.

--Inner Tennis: Playing the Game. 1976. 12.95 (ISBN 0-394-40043-7). Random.

Galnoor, Itzhak, ed. Government Secrecy in Democracies. (Orig.). 1977. pap. 5.95i,o.p. (ISBN 0-06-090440-2, CN 440, CN). Har-Row.

Galnoor, Itzhal & Lambert, Richard D., eds. Social Information for Developing Countries. LC 72-148004. (Annals of the American Academy of Political & Social Science: No. 393). 1971. 15.00 (ISBN 0-87761-135-1); pap. 7.95 (ISBN 0-87761-134-3). Am Acad Pol Soc Sci.

Galonska, Michael. Connecticut Supplement. 2nd ed. 196p. 1980. pap. 7.95 o.s.i. (ISBN 0-695-81499-0). Follett.

Galouye, Daniel F. Dark Universe. (Science Fiction Ser). 176p. 1976. Repr. of 1961 ed. lib. bdg. 9.95 o.p. (ISBN 0-8398-2333-9, Gregg). G K Hall.

Galper, Jeffrey. The Politics of Social Services. 272p. 1975. pap. text ed. 14.95 (ISBN 0-13-685214-9). P-H.

--Social Work Practice: A Radical Perspective. (P-H Ser. Sociology & Social Work). 1980. pap. text ed. 14.95 (ISBN 0-13-819508-0). P-H.

Galphin, Bruce, jt. auth. see Shavin, Norman.

Galpin, A. M. & Milligan, E. E. French Prose: An Intermediate Reader. 1965. text ed. 12.95x (ISBN 0-02-340250-4). Macmillan.

Galpin, A. M., et al. Beginning Readings in Italian. 1966. text ed. 13.95x (ISBN 0-02-340200-8). Macmillan.

Galpin, Frances W. A Textbook of European Musical Instruments. LC 75-36509. (Illus.). 256p. 1976. Repr. of 1956 ed. lib. bdg. 18.25x (ISBN 0-8371-8648-X, GAEM). Greenwood.

Galpin, W. Freeman. Pioneering for Peace: A Study of American Peace Efforts to 1846. LC 73-143429. (Peace Movement in America Ser). x, 237p. 1972. Repr. of 1933 ed. lib. bdg. 16.95x (ISBN 0-89198-069-5). Ozer.

Galston, A., et al. Life of the Green Plant. 3rd ed. 1980. 21.95 (ISBN 0-13-536326-8); pap. 16.95 (ISBN 0-13-536318-7). P-H.

Galston, Arthur W. & Davies, Peter J. Control Mechanisms in Plant Development. (Foundations of Developmental Biology Ser). 1970. pap. 13.95x ref. ed. (ISBN 0-13-171801-0). P-H.

Galsworthy, Ada, tr. see De Maupassant, Guy.

Galsworthy, John. Captures. Date not set. Repr. of 1923 ed. cancelled o.p. (ISBN 0-678-02762-5). Kelley.

Galt, Alfreda S., ed. see Burrow, Trigant.

Galt, Denham. The Bear That Had No Bump of Locality. (Illus.). 1983. 4.95 (ISBN 0-533-05290-4). Vantage.

Galt, John. The Life of Benjamin West. LC 60-5041. 1979. Repr. of 1820 ed. lib. bdg. 50.00x (ISBN 0-8201-1251-8). Schol Facsimiles.

--The Provost. Gordon, Ian A., ed. (The World's Classics Ser.). 192p. 1983. pap. 4.95 (ISBN 0-19-281629-2, GB). Oxford U Pr.

Galton, Francis. Finger Prints. 2nd ed. LC 63-23401. 1966. Repr. of 1892 ed. lib. bdg. 27.50 (ISBN 0-306-70910-4). Da Capo.

--Hereditary Genius. (Classics in Psychology Ser.). 1979. Repr. of 1869 ed. 29.95x (ISBN 0-312-36989-1). St Martin.

--Hereditary Genius. Eysenck, H. J., ed. (Classics in Psychology & Psychiatry Ser.). 432p. 1983. Repr. of 1869 ed. write for info. (ISBN 0-904014-40-1). F Pinter Pubs.

Galton, Lawrence. Don't Give up on an Aging Parent. 240p. 1974. 6.95 o.p. (ISBN 0-517-51627-6). Crown.

--The Silent Disease. 192p. 1973. 6.95 o.p. (ISBN 0-517-50357-3). Crown.

--The Silent Disease: Hypertension. 1974. pap. 2.95 (ISBN 0-451-12098-1, AE2098, Sig). NAL.

Galton, Lawrence, jt. auth. see Barnes, Broda.

Galton, Lawrence, jt. auth. see Missildine, W. Hugh.

Galton, Lawrence, jt. auth. see Roth, Oscar.

Galton, Maurice & Willcocks, John, eds. Moving from the Primary Classroom. 260p. (Orig.). 1983. pap. price not set (ISBN 0-7100-9343-8). Routledge & Kegan.

Galton, Maurice, et al. Inside the Primary Classroom. 1980. 25.00x o.p. (ISBN 0-7100-0423-0); pap. 11.95 (ISBN 0-7100-0530-X). Routledge & Kegan.

Galtsoff, Paul S., compiled by. Bibliography of Oysters & Other Marine Organisms Associated with Oyster Bottoms & Estuarine Ecology. 1972. lib. bdg. 85.00 (ISBN 0-8161-0945-1, Hall Reference). G K Hall.

Galtung, Johan. Peace & War Defense. (Essays in Peace Research Ser.: Vol. II). 1976. pap. text ed. 20.50x o.p. (ISBN 87-7241-369-7). Humanities.

--Peace, Research, Education, Action. (Essays in Peace Research Ser.: Vol. I). (Illus., Orig.). 1975. pap. text ed. 17.50x o.p. (ISBN 87-7241-368-9). Humanities.

Galutier, M. W. & Underdown, B. Basic Accounting Practice. 2nd ed. 448p. 1980. 42.00x (ISBN 0-273-01597-4, Pub. by Pitman Bks England). State Mutual Bk.

Galvin, Brendan. Winter Oysters: Contemporary Poetry. LC 82-13367. 88p. 1983. 9.95x (ISBN 0-8203-0643-6); pap. 5.95x (ISBN 0-8203-0644-4). U of Ga Pr.

Galvin, Kathleen M. & Brommel, Bernard J. Family Communication: Cohesion & Change. 1981. pap. text ed. 10.95x (ISBN 0-673-15380-0). Scott F.

Galvin, Patrick J. Finishing off: Additional Rooms. 96p. 1981. pap. 3.95 (ISBN 0-8249-6111-0). Ideals.

Galvin, Thomas J. Current Problems in Reference Service. LC 77-162527. (Bowker Series in Problem-Centered Approaches to Librarianship). 166p. 1971. 16.25 o.p. (ISBN 0-8352-0425-1). Bowker.

Galvin, Thomas J. & Lynch, Beverly P., eds. Priorities for Academic Libraries. LC 81-48572. 1982. 7.95x (ISBN 0-87589-898-X, HE-40). Jossey-Bass.

Galvin, Thomas J., jt. ed. see Kent, Allen.

Galvin, Thomas J., et al, eds. Excellence in School Media Programs: Essays Honoring Elizabeth T. Fast. LC 79-26944. 238p. 1980. 15.00 (ISBN 0-8389-3239-8). ALA.

Galzin, A., jt. auth. see Bourdot, H.

Gama, Bosco Da see Phantom, D. S. & Da Gama, Bosco.

Gama, Roberto, tr. from Eng. Diccionario Biblico Arqueologico. Pfeiffer, Charles F., ed. 768p. (Span.). 1982. 29.95 (ISBN 0-8119-3667-8). Casa Bautista.

Gamache, H. Eighth, Ninth & Tenth Books of Moses. 4.00x o.p. (ISBN 0-685-21888-0). Wehman.

Gamache, Henri. Candle Burning, Master Book. 2.95 (ISBN 0-685-70674-5). Wehman.

--Magic of Herbs. 3.95x o.s.i. (ISBN 0-685-22021-4). Wehman.

Gamage, Arthur W. Mr. Gamage's Great Toy Bazaar 1902-1906. (Illus.). 160p. (Orig.). 1983. 35.00 (ISBN 0-8038-4745-9). Hastings.

Gamal-Eldin, E. Revision der Gattung Pulicaria (Compositae Inuleae) fuer Afrika, Makaronesien und Arabian. (Phanerogamarum Monographiae: No. 14). (Illus.). 406p. (Ger.). 1981. text ed. 40.00x (ISBN 3-7682-1294-7). Lubrecht & Cramer.

Gambaccini, Paul. Paul McCartney: In His Own Words. LC 76-8068. 1976. pap. 5.95 (ISBN 0-8256-3910-7, Quick Fox). Putnam Pub Group.

--Paul McCartney in his own Words. (Illus.). 112p. (Orig.). 1983. pap. 6.95 (ISBN 0-399-41008-2). Delilah Bks.

--The Rock Critic's Choice: The Top 200 Albums. (Illus.). 1978. pap. 4.95 (ISBN 0-8256-3927-1, Quick Fox). Putnam Pub Group.

Gambaccini, Paul, ed. Elton John & Bernie Taupin. (Illus.). 104p. 1975. pap. 3.95 (ISBN 0-8256-3063-0, Quick Fox). Putnam Pub Group.

Gambaccini, Peter. Bruce Springsteen. 1979. pap. 4.95 (ISBN 0-8256-3935-2, Quick Fox). Putnam Pub Group.

--Bruce Springsteen: A Photo Bio. 1979. pap. 2.25 o.s.i. (ISBN 0-515-05220-5). Jove Pubns.

--Photographer's Assistant. (Illus.). 224p. 1981. pap. 12.95 (ISBN 0-8256-3201-3, Quick Fox). Putnam Pub Group.

--The Photographer's Assistant. (Illus.). 224p. 1982. pap. 12.95 (ISBN 0-399-50684-5, Perige). Putnam Pub Group.

Gambaryan, P. R. How Mammals Run: Anatomical Adaptations. Hardin, H., tr. from Rus. LC 74-16190. 367p. 1974. 48.95 o.s.i. (ISBN 0-470-29059-5). Halsted Pr.

Gambell, Ray. The Life of Sea Mammals. LC 78-56582. (Easy Reading Edition of Introduction to Nature Ser.). (Illus.). 1978. PLB 12.68 (ISBN 0-382-06186-1). Silver.

Gamberg, Ruth. Red & Expert: Education in the People's Republic of China. LC 75-34876. (Illus.). 1977. 13.50x o.p. (ISBN 0-8052-3616-3); pap. 6.95 (ISBN 0-8052-0531-4). Schocken.

Gambetta, Vern. Track Technique Annual, 1983. (Illus.). 128p. (Orig.). 1982. pap. 8.50 (ISBN 0-911521-08-9). Tafnews.

Gambhirananda, tr. from Sanskrit. Sruti Gita: The Song of the Srutis. 99p. 1982. pap. 4.95x (ISBN 0-87481-211-9). Vedanta Pr.

Gambhirananda, Swami. Holy Mother, Sri Sarada Devi. (Illus.). 8.95 (ISBN 0-87481-434-0). Vedanta Pr.

Gambhirananda, Swami, tr. see Shankara.

Gambill, Henrietta. Happy Times with the Lollipop Dragon. Sparks, Judith, ed. LC 81-86701. (Happy Day Bks.). (Illus.). 24p. (Orig.). (ps-3). 1982. pap. 1.29 (ISBN 0-87239-538-3, 3584). Standard Pub.

--How God Gives Us Chocolate. Mahany, Patricia, ed. LC 82-80027. (Happy Day Bks.). (Illus.). 24p. (Orig.). (ps-3). 1982. pap. 1.29 (ISBN 0-87239-539-1, 3585). Standard Pub.

--Self-Control. LC 82-1210. (What Does the Bible Say? Ser.). (Illus.). 32p. (gr. k-3). 1982. PLB 4.95 (ISBN 0-89565-223-4, 4941, Pub. by Childs World). Standard Pub.

--Self-Control. LC 82-1201. (What is It? Ser.). 32p. (gr. k-3). 1982. PLB 6.50 (ISBN 0-89565-225-0). Childs World.

Gambill, Henrietta, ed. see Hayes, Wanda.

Gambill, Henrietta, ed. see Howard, E.

Gambill, Henrietta, ed. see Shelton, Ingrid.

Gambill, Henriette, ed. see Shelton, Ingrid.

Gambino, Anthony J. The Make-or-Buy Decision. 128p. pap. 12.95 (ISBN 0-86641-000-7, 80120). Natl Assn Accts.

--Planning & Control in Higher Education. 114p. pap. 12.95 (ISBN 0-86641-027-9, 79111). Natl Assn Accts.

Gambino, Anthony J. & Gartenberg, Morris. Industrial R & D Management. 132p. pap. 12.95 (ISBN 0-86641-028-7, 78109). Natl Assn Accts.

Gambino, Anthony J. & Palmer, John R. Management Accounting in Colonial America. 40p. pap. 4.95 (ISBN 0-86641-052-X, 7685). Natl Assn Accts.

Gambino, Anthony J. & Reardon, Thomas. Financial Planning & Evaluation for the Nonprofit Organization. 170p. pap. 14.95 (ISBN 0-86641-003-1, 81125). Natl Assn Accts.

Gambino, Richard. Blood of My Blood, the Dilemma of the Italian-Americans. LC 73-11705. 400p. 1975. pap. 6.50 (ISBN 0-385-07564-2, Anch). Doubleday.

Gambino, S. R., jt. auth. see Galen, P. S.

Gamble, Allan. The University of Sydney: Pen Sketches. 1982. 26.00 (ISBN 0-909798-25-7, Pub. by Sydney U Pr). Intl Schol Bk Serv.

Gamble, Andrew. Britain in Decline: Economic Policy, Political Strategy, & the British State. LC 81-683554. 312p. 1983. pap. 8.61 (ISBN 0-8070-4701-5, BP649). Beacon Pr.

--The Conservative Nation. 320p. 1974. 26.95x (ISBN 0-7100-8008-5). Routledge & Kegan.

--The Politics of Decline. (Critical Social Studies). 1980. text ed. write for info. o.p. (ISBN 0-391-01179-0); pap. text ed. write for info. o.p. (ISBN 0-391-01180-4). Humanities.

Gamble, Andrew & Walton, Paul. Capitalism in Crisis: Inflation & the State. 1977. text ed. 16.50x o. p. (ISBN 0-391-00592-8); pap. text ed. 7.50x (ISBN 0-391-00593-6). Humanities.

Gamble, David P. A General Bibliography of the Gambia, up to 31 December, 1977. Sterling, Louise J., ed. 1979. lib. bdg. 49.00 (ISBN 0-8161-8177-2, Hall Reference). G K Hall.

Gamble, Geoffrey. Wikchamni Grammar. LC 77-8566. (Publications in Linguistics Ser.: Vol. 89). 1978. 15.00x (ISBN 0-520-09589-8). U of Cal Pr.

Gamble, James L. Chemical Anatomy, Physiology & Pathology of Extracellular Fluid: A Lecture Syllabus. 6th ed. LC 55-4627. (Illus.). 1954. pap. 4.95x o.p. (ISBN 0-674-11350-0). Harvard U Pr.

Gamble, John K., Jr., ed. see Law of the Sea Institute, 10th Annual Conference.

Gamble, Teri K., jt. auth. see Eisenberg, Abne M.

Gamble, Teri K., ed. Intermedia: Communication & Society. LC 79-63912. (Illus.). 1979. pap. text ed. 8.95 (ISBN 0-87716-103-8, Pub. by Moore Pub Co). F Apple.

Gamble, W. L., jt. auth. see Park, R.

Gamble, William. Music Engraving & Printing: Historical & Technical Treatise. LC 70-155576. (Music Ser). 1971. Repr. of 1923 ed. lib. bdg. 27.50 (ISBN 0-306-70168-5). Da Capo.

Gambrill, Eileen. Casework: A Competency-Based Approach. (Illus.). 448p. 1983. 20.95 (ISBN 0-13-119446-1). P-H.

Gambs, John S. John Kenneth Galbraith. (World Leaders Ser.). 1975. lib. bdg. 12.95 (ISBN 0-8057-3681-6, Twayne). G K Hall.

Gamelin, T. W. Uniform Algebras & Jensen Measures. LC 78-16213. (London Mathematical Society Lecture Note Ser.: No. 32). 1979. pap. 20.95 (ISBN 0-521-22280-X). Cambridge U Pr.

Games, Paul A. & Klare, G. R. Elementary Statistics: Data Analysis for the Behavioral Sciences. 1967. text ed. 27.50 (ISBN 0-07-022743-8, C); instructor's manual 10.00 (ISBN 0-07-022744-6). McGraw.

Gamett, James & Paner, Stanley W. Nevada Post Offices: An Illustrated History. 1982. 30.00 (ISBN 0-913814-40-7). Nevada Pubns.

Gammage, Allen Z. Basic Police Report Writing. 2nd ed. (Illus.). 344p. 1978. 15.75x (ISBN 0-398-03204-1). C C Thomas.

Gammage, Allen Z. & Hemphill, Charles F., Jr. Basic Criminal Law. 2nd ed. 1979. text ed. 19.95 (ISBN 0-07-022756-X, G); study guide 10.95 (ISBN 0-07-022757-8); instructor's manual & key 4.50 (ISBN 0-07-022758-6). McGraw.

Gammage, Philip. Teacher & Pupil: Some Socio-Psychological Aspects. (Students Library of Education). 1971. 12.95x (ISBN 0-7100-7135-3); pap. 4.50 (ISBN 0-7100-7136-1). Routledge & Kegan.

Gammell, Alice. Polly Prindle's Book of American Patchwork Quilts. (Illus.). 260p. 1981. pap. 6.95 (ISBN 0-448-12181-6, G&D). Putnam Pub Group.

Gammell, Stephen. Git along, Old Scudder. LC 82-13996. (Illus.). 32p. (gr. k-3). 1983. 10.50 (ISBN 0-688-01674-X); PLB 10.08 (ISBN 0-688-01677-4). Lothrop.

Gammell, Stephen, tr. see McHargue, Georgess.

Gammie, John G., ed. Israelite Wisdom: Theological & Literary Essays in Honor of Samuel Terrien. LC 77-17862. 1978. pap. 18.00 (ISBN 0-89130-208-5, 00-16-03). Scholars Pr Ca.

Gammon, Margaret, compiled by. Normal Diet. 1976. pap. 1.95 o.p. (ISBN 0-87604-010-5). ARE Pr.

Gammon, Samuel R. Presidential Campaign of Eighteen Thirty-Two. LC 79-114532. ix, 180p. Repr. of 1922 ed. lib. bdg. 15.00x o.p. (ISBN 0-8371-4827-8, GAPC). Greenwood.

Gammon, Samuel R., Jr. Presidential Campaign of Eighteen Thirty-Two. LC 78-96952. (Law, Politics & History Ser). 1969. Repr. of 1922 ed. lib. bdg. 25.00 (ISBN 0-306-71830-8). Da Capo.

Gammond, Peter. The Magic Flute. LC 79-67162. (Master Works of Opera Ser.). 15.96 (ISBN 0-382-06312-0). Silver.

Gammond, Peter, jt. auth. see Clayton, Peter.

Gammond, Peter, ed. Duke Ellington: His Life & Music. LC 77-1927. (The Roots of Jazz Ser.). 1977. Repr. of 1958 ed. lib. bdg. 25.00 (ISBN 0-306-70874-4). Da Capo.

Gammons, jt. auth. see Farrugia.

Gamon, Richard Louis. The Thoughts of Thomas Robert Malthus As They Apply to the Economic Complexities of Our Present Age. (The Living Thoughts of the Great Economists Ser.). (Illus.). 127p. 1981. 57.55 (ISBN 0-918968-87-9). Inst Econ Finan.

Gamow, George. Mister Tompkins in Paperback. (Illus., Orig.). 1967. bds. 24.95 (ISBN 0-521-06905-X); pap. 7.95 (ISBN 0-521-09355-4). Cambridge U Pr.

Gamsey, Robert. Ingathering. 1961. 4.50 (ISBN 0-87315-020-1); pap. 1.50x (ISBN 0-87315-021-X). Golden Bell.

Gamson, William A. & Modigliani, Andre. Conceptions of Social Life: A Text-Reader for Social Psychology. LC 79-89925. 1979. pap. 15.25 (ISBN 0-8191-0854-5). U Pr of Amer.

Ganchrow, J. R., jt. ed. see Steiner, J. E.

Ganci, Dave. Hiking the Desert. 1979. 12.95 o.p. (ISBN 0-8092-7617-8); pap. 6.95 o.p. (ISBN 0-8092-7615-1). Contemp Bks.

--Hiking the Southwest: Arizona, New Mexico, & West Texas. LC 82-19418. (A Sierra Club Totebook). (Illus.). 384p. (Orig.). 1983. pap. 8.95 (ISBN 0-87156-338-X). Sierra.

Ganczarczyk. Activated Sludge Processes. (Pollution Engineering Ser.). 288p. 1983. 59.95 (ISBN 0-8247-1758-9). Dekker.

Gande, Anthony, jt. auth. see Gande, Maureen.

Gande, Maureen & Gande, Anthony. L' Affaire Du Pneu Degonfle. (Fr.). 1969. pap. 2.50x o.p. (ISBN 0-435-37351-X). Heinemann Ed.

--La Clef. (Fr.). 1969. pap. text ed. 2.50x o.p. (ISBN 0-435-37352-8). Heinemann Ed.

--Mystere au Bois de Boulogne. 1969. pap. text ed. 2.50x o.p. (ISBN 0-435-37350-1). Heinemann Ed.

Gander, Forrest, ed. see Forch, Carolyn.

Gander, Mary J. & Gardiner, Harry W. Child & Adolescent Development. 1981. text ed. 22.95 (ISBN 0-316-30322-4); tchrs'. manual free (ISBN 0-316-30319-4); study guide 7.95 (ISBN 0-316-30318-6). Little.

Gander, Terry. The Modern British Army. (Illus.). 280p. 1980. 37.95 o.p. (ISBN 0-85059-435-9). Aztex.

Gander, Terry, jt. auth. see Chamberlain, Peter.

Gandert, Slade R. Protecting Your Collection: A Handbook, Survey, & Guide for the Security of Rare Books, Manuscripts, Archives & Works of Art. LC 81-7004. (Library & Archival Security Ser.: Vol. 4, Nos. 1 & 2). 158p. 1982. text ed. 19.95 (ISBN 0-917724-78-X, B78). Haworth Pr.

Gandhi, Indira. India & Bangla Desh: Selected Speeches & Statements, March-December, 1971. 200p. 1972. text ed. 4.75x (ISBN 0-391-00508-1). Humanities.

Gandhi, Kishore. Aldous Huxley: Vedantic & Buddhistic Influences. 256p. 1980. text ed. 13.00x (ISBN 0-391-02024-2). Humanities.

Gandhi, Kishore, ed. Contemporary Relevance of Sri Aurobundo. 1973. text ed. 11.00x (ISBN 0-391-00497-2). Humanities.

Gandhi, M. K. Delhi Diary: Daily Talks at a Prayer Meeting, 1947-8. 426p. 4.00 (ISBN 0-686-87460-9). Greenlf Bks.

--The Health Guide. LC 78-2592. 1978. 15.95 (ISBN 0-89594-005-1); pap. 6.95 (ISBN 0-89594-002-7). Crossing Pr.

--The Law & the Lawyers. Kher, S. B., ed. 261p. pap. 5.00 (ISBN 0-686-87427-7); 8.50 (ISBN 0-686-91570-4). Greenlf Bks.

--Satyagraha in South Africa. Desai, V. G., tr. 1980. 10.00 (ISBN 0-934676-15-1). Greenlf Bks.

--Satyagraha in South Africa. Desai, V. G., tr. from Gujarati. 1979. pap. 5.00 (ISBN 0-934676-03-8). Greenlf Bks.

Gandhi, Mahatma. All Men Are Brothers: Life & Thoughts of Mahatma Gandhi As Told in His Own Words. 186p. pap. 6.95 (ISBN 0-8264-0003-5). Continuum.

Gandhi, Mohandas K. Collected Works of Mahatma Gandhi, Vols. 1-82. LC 58-36286. 1958-81. 10.00x ea. Intl Pubns Serv.

--Collected Works of Mahatma Gandhi, Vols. 83-85. Incl. Vol. 83 (January 20, 1946-April 13, 1946) 476p. 1981 (ISBN 0-8002-2895-2); Vol. 84 (April 14-July 15, 1946) 532p. 1981 (ISBN 0-8002-2896-0); Vol. 85 (July 16-October 20, 1946) 550p. 1982 (ISBN 0-8002-2897-9). LC 58-36286. 10.00x ea. Intl Pubns Serv.

--Non-Violent Resistance. Kumarappa, Bharatan, ed. LC 61-16650. 416p. (YA) 1983. pap. 8.95 (ISBN 0-8052-0017-7). Schocken.

Gandin, L. S., et al. Design of Optimum Networks for Aerological Observing Stations. (World Weather Watch Planning Report Ser.: No. 21). 1969. pap. 12.00 (ISBN 0-685-22301-9, W234, WMO). Unipub.

Gandolfo, G. Qualitative Analysis & Econometric Estimation of Continuous Time Dynamic Models. (Contributions to Economic Analysis Ser.: Vol. 136). 1981. 34.00 (ISBN 0-444-86025-8). Elsevier.

Gandy, Joan W. & Gandy, Thomas H. Norman's Natchez: An Early Photographer & His Town. LC 78-15570. (Illus.). 1978. 25.00 o.p. (ISBN 0-87805-078-7). U Pr of Miss.

Gandy, Joan W., jt. ed. see Eidt, Mary B.

Gandy, Oscar, et al, eds. see Telecommunications Policy Research Conference, Annual 10th.

Gandy, Oscar H., Jr. Beyond Agenda Setting: Information Subsidies & Public Policy. (Communication & Information Science Ser.). 1982. text ed. 27.50 (ISBN 0-89391-096-1); pap. text ed. 13.95x (ISBN 0-89391-194-1). Ablex Pub.

Gandy, R. D. & Hyland, M. Logic Colloquium 1976. (Studies in Logic: Vol. 87). 1977. 64.00 (ISBN 0-7204-0691-9, North-Holland). Elsevier.

Gandy, Ross, jt. auth. see Hodges, Donald.

Gandy, Thomas H., jt. auth. see Gandy, Joan W.

Gandy, Tilly H. Of Cabbages & Kings. 1983. 6.50 (ISBN 0-8062-2138-0). Carlton.

Gane, C. & Sarson, T. Structured Systems Analysis: Tools & Techniques. 1979. 30.00 (ISBN 0-13-854547-2). P-H.

Gane, Chris & Sarson, Trish. Structured Systems Analysis: Tools & Techniques. 373p. (Orig.). 1977. 22.50 (ISBN 0-930196-00-7); pap. 15.00 (ISBN 0-686-37676-5). P F Mallon.

Ganesan, A. T., et al. Molecular Cloning & Gene Regulation in Bacilli. 392p. 1982. 29.50 (ISBN 0-12-274150-1). Acad Pr.

Ganesan, K., tr. see Muhaiyaddeen, Bawa.

Ganesan, R., tr. see Muhaiyaddeen, Bawa.

Gangarosa, Louis P. Iontophoresis in Dental Practice. (Illus.). 144p. 1983. text ed. 48.00 (ISBN 0-931386-52-7). Quint Pub Co.

Gangel, Kenneth O. Building Leaders for Church Education. 1981. 16.95 (ISBN 0-8024-1592-X). Moody.

--Competent to Lead: A Guide to Management in Christian Organizations. 160p. 1974. 4.95 o.p. (ISBN 0-8024-1614-4). Moody.

--The Family First. pap. 3.50 (ISBN 0-88469-106-3). BMH Bks.

--So You Want to Be a Leader. pap. 3.25 (ISBN 0-87509-131-8); leaders guide 2.50 (ISBN 0-87509-298-5). Chr Pubns.

--Understanding Teaching. LC 68-24579. 1979. pap. text ed. 4.25 (ISBN 0-910566-14-3); Perfect bdg. instr's. guide 4.25 (ISBN 0-910566-26-7). Evang Tchr.

--Unwrap Your Spiritual Gifts. 120p. 1983. pap. 4.50 (ISBN 0-88207-102-5). Victor Bks.

Gangel, Kenneth O. & Benson, Warren S. Christian Education: Its History & Philosophy. 1983. 16.95 (ISBN 0-8024-3561-0). Moody.

Gangji, D., ed. see European Organization for Research & Treatment of Cancer.

Gangopadhyaya, Mrinalkanti. Indian Atomosm: History & Sources. 384p. 1980. pap. text ed. 20.50x (ISBN 0-391-02177-X). Humanities.

Gangstad, John E. The Great Pyramid: Signs in the Sun. (Pyramid Design & Prophecy) LC 76-24077. (Illus.). 200p. 1976. lib. bdg. 9.95 (ISBN 0-9603374-0-7); pap. 5.95 (ISBN 0-9603374-1-5); 1980-82 supplement 2.50 (ISBN 0-9603374-2-3). Di-Tri Bks.

Gangulee, N., ed. see Mazzini, Giuseppe.

Ganguli, B. N. Emma Goldman: Portrait of a Rebel Woman. 1979. 7.00x (ISBN 0-8364-0452-1). South Asia Bks.

Ganguly, SN. Tradition, Modernity & Development. 1977. 10.00 o.p. (ISBN 0-333-90144-4). South Asia Bks.

Gangwu, Wang. The Use of History. LC 72-63123. (Papers in International Studies: Southeast Asia: No. 4). 1968. pap. 3.00x (ISBN 0-89680-002-4, Ohio U Ctr Intl). Ohio U Pr.

Gani, J. The Making of Statisticians. (Illus.). 263p. 1982. 19.80 (ISBN 0-387-90684-3). Springer-Verlag.

Gani, J., et al, eds. Progress in Statistics, 2 vols. (Colloquia Mathematica Societatis Janos Bolyai: No. 9). 912p. 1975. Set. 76.75 (ISBN 0-444-10702-9, North-Holland). Elsevier.

Ganiel, Uri, ed. Physics Teaching. 608p. 1980. pap. text ed. write for info. (ISBN 0-86689-000-9). Balaban Intl Scie Serv.

Ganikos, Mary & Grady, Kathleen, eds. A Handbook for Conducting Workshops on the Counseling Needs of the Elderly, 1979. 47p. 1979. 3.75 (ISBN 0-686-36388-4); nonmembers 4.75 (ISBN 0-686-37300-6). Am Personnel.

Ganikos, Mary L., ed. Counseling the Aged: A Training Syllabus for Educators, 1979. 1979. 9.25 (ISBN 0-686-36386-8); 10.50 (ISBN 0-686-37299-9). Am Personnel.

--Work Life Counseling for Older People. 1980. 2.50 (ISBN 0-686-36385-X). Am Personnel.

Ganley, James P. & Roberts, Jean. Eye Conditions & Related Need for Medical Care among Persons One to Seventy-four Years, United States: Series 11, No. 228. Cox, Klaudia, ed. 60p. 1982. pap. text ed. 1.95 (ISBN 0-686-97508-1). Natl Ctr Health Stats.

Ganmaster. Food Irradiation Now. 1982. 22.00 (ISBN 90-247-2763-4, Pub. by Martinus Nijhoff Netherlands). Kluwer Boston.

Gann, Ernest K. Antagonists. 1978. pap. 1.95 o.p. (ISBN 0-451-07899-3, J7899, Sig). NAL.

--Band of Brothers. 1973. 7.95 o.p. (ISBN 0-671-21630-9). S&S.

--Fate Is the Hunter. (gr. 9 up). 1960. 17.95 o.p. (ISBN 0-671-24680-1). S&S.

--Gentlemen of Adventure. 1983. 15.95 (ISBN 0-87795-465-8). Arbor Hse.

Gann, L. H. & Duignan, Peter. Burden of Empire: An Appraisal of Western Colonialism in Africa South of the Sahara. LC 67-26216. (Publications Ser.: No. 69). (Illus.). 435p. 1967. pap. 6.95 o.p. (ISBN 0-8179-1692-X). Hoover Inst Pr.

Gann, L. H., jt. auth. see Duignan, Peter.

Gann, L. H., jt. ed. see Duignan, P.

Gann, William D. The Commodity Writings. (Illus.). 93p. 1982. 75.55 (ISBN 0-86654-036-9). Inst Econ Finan.

--Successful Stock Selecting Methods in Wall Street. (The New Stock Market Reference Library). (Illus.). 118p. 1981. 139.45 (ISBN 0-918968-96-8). Inst Econ Finan.

Gannaway, Thomas W. & Sink, Jack M. Fundamentals of Vocational Evaluation. 1983. pap. text ed. price not set (ISBN 0-8391-1719-1, 13749). Univ Park.

Gannett, Henry. Origin of Certain Place Names in the United States. LC 68-23159. 1971. Repr. of 1902 ed. 27.00 o.p. (ISBN 0-8103-3382-1). Gale.

Gannett, Ruth. The Dragons of the Blueland. (gr. k-6). 1980. pap. 1.25 o.p. (ISBN 0-440-41044-4, YB). Dell.

Gannon, Martin J. Management: An Integrated Framework. 2nd ed. 1982. text ed. 22.95 (ISBN 0-316-30334-8); tchrs.' manual avail. (ISBN 0-316-30336-4); student guide 7.95 (ISBN 0-316-30338-0); TB avail. (ISBN 0-316-30335-6). Little.

--Management: An Organizational Perspective. 1977. 19.00 o.p. (ISBN 0-686-96747-X, CPCU 7). IIA.

--Organizational Behavior: A Managerial & Organizational Perspective. 1979. text ed. 20.95 (ISBN 0-316-30331-3); tchr's manual avail. (ISBN 0-316-30332-1). Little.

Gannon, Martin J., jt. auth. see Anderson, Carl R.

Gannon, Michael V. Cross in the Sand: The Early Catholic Church in Florida, 1513-1870. LC 65-27283. 1965. Repr. 9.00 o.p. (ISBN 0-8130-0084-X). U Presses Fla.

Gannon, Peter & Czerniewska, Pam. Using Linguistics: An Educational Focus. 224p. 1980. pap. text ed. 16.95 (ISBN 0-7131-6294-5). E Arnold.

Gannon, Robert. How to Raise & Train a Scottish Terrier. (Illus.). pap. 2.95 (ISBN 0-87666-383-8, DS1032). TFH Pubns.

--How to Raise & Train an English Cocker Spaniel. pap. 2.95 (ISBN 0-87666-291-2, DS1014). TFH Pubns.

--How to Raise & Train an Irish Setter. (Illus.). pap. 2.95 (ISBN 0-87666-319-6, DS1024). TFH Pubns.

--Start Right with Goldfish. (Orig.). pap. 2.95 (ISBN 0-87666-081-2, M504). TFH Pubns.

Ganoczy, Alexander. Becoming Christian: A Theology of Baptism As the Sacrament of Human History. Lynch, John G., tr. from Fr. LC 76-23530. 120p. 1976. pap. 2.95 o.p. (ISBN 0-8091-1980-3). Paulist Pr.

Ganong, James B. Mary, We Never Knew You. 246p. (Orig.). 1982. pap. 6.50 (ISBN 0-9608620-0-5). K Pillman.

Ganong, Joan, jt. auth. see Ganong, Warren.

Ganong, Joan M. & Ganong, Walter L. Help for the Licensed Practical Nurse. 2nd ed. (Help Series of Management Guides). 71p. 1981. pap. 9.85 (ISBN 0-933036-11-6). Ganong W L Co.

Ganong, Joan M. & Ganong, Warren L. Help for the Head Nurse: A Management Guide. 4th ed. LC 80-85412. (Help Series of Management Guides). (Illus.). 88p. (Orig.). 1981. pap. 9.95 (ISBN 0-933036-26-4). Ganong W L Co.

--Help for the Unit Secretary: The Service Coordinator Concept. (Help Series of Management Guides). 64p. 1980. pap. 8.25 (ISBN 0-933036-12-4). Ganong W L Co.

--Help with Annual Budgetary Planning & Control. (Help Series of Management Guides). 90p. 1976. pap. 13.95 (ISBN 0-933036-07-8). Ganong W L Co.

--Help with Career Ladders in Nursing. (Help Series of Management Guides). 142p. 1977. pap. 13.75 (ISBN 0-933036-06-X). Ganong W L Co.

--Help with Innovative Teaching Techniques. 2nd ed. (Help Series of Management Guides). 152p. 1976. pap. 13.95 (ISBN 0-933036-08-6). Ganong W L Co.

--Help with Managerial Leadership in Nursing: 101 Tremendous Trifles. (Help Series of Management Guides). 160p. 1980. pap. 13.95 (ISBN 0-933036-35-3). Ganong W L Co.

--Help with Performance Appraisal: A Results-Oriented Approach. (Help Series of Management Guides). 115p. 1981. pap. 11.50 (ISBN 0-933036-25-6). Ganong W L Co.

--Help with Primary Nursing: Accountability through the Nursing Process. 2nd ed. (Help Series of Management Guides). 90p. 1980. pap. 9.95 (ISBN 0-933036-13-2). Ganong W L Co.

--Help with Student Clinical Performance Evaluation. (Help Series of Management Guides). 90p. 1977. pap. 9.95 (ISBN 0-933036-14-0). Ganong W L Co.

--One Hundred One Exciting Exercise: HELP Worksheets for Nurse Managers & Educators. (Help Series of Management Guides). 109p. 1978. pap. 10.95 (ISBN 0-933036-16-7). Ganong W L Co.

Ganong, W. F. & Martini, L., eds. Frontiers in Neuroendocrinology, Vol. 7. (Frontiers in Neuroendocrinology Ser.). 400p. 1982. text ed. 49.50 (ISBN 0-89004-694-8). Raven.

Ganong, W. F., jt. ed. see Martini, L.

Ganong, Walter L., jt. auth. see Ganong, Joan M.

Ganong, Warren & Ganong, Joan. Cases in Nursing Management. LC 79-2572. 360p. 1979. text ed. 32.95 (ISBN 0-89443-152-8). Aspen Systems.

--Nursing Management. 2nd ed. LC 80-10865. 350p. 1980. text ed. 23.95 (ISBN 0-89443-278-8). Aspen Systems.

Ganong, Warren L., jt. auth. see Ganong, Joan M.

Ganong, William F., jt. auth. see Martini, Luciano.

Ganong, William F. & Martini, Luciano, eds. Frontiers in Neuroendocrinology, 1969. (Illus.). 1969. text ed. 29.50x o.p. (ISBN 0-19-501130-9). Oxford U Pr.

--Frontiers in Neuroendocrinology, 1973. (Illus.). 1973. text ed. 29.50x o.p. (ISBN 0-19-501672-6). Oxford U Pr.

Ganong, William F., jt. ed. see Martini, Luciano.

Gans, A. I., ed. see California State Library Sutro Branch San Francisco.

Gans, C. & Pough, F. H., eds. Biology of the Reptilia, Vol. 13. 360p. Date not set. 75.00 (ISBN 0-12-274613-9). Acad Pr.

Gans, Carl & Pough, Harvey. Biology of the Reptilia, Vol. 12. subscription price 82.50 96.50 (ISBN 0-12-274612-0). Acad Pr.

Gans, Carl & Parson, Thomas, eds. Biology of the Reptilia: Morphology, Vol. 3. 1970. by subscription 44.00 59.50 (ISBN 0-12-274603-1). Acad Pr.

Gans, Eric. The Origin of Language: A Formal Theory of Representation. LC 80-19653. 1981. 23.75x (ISBN 0-520-04202-6). U of Cal Pr.

Gans, Herbert J. Deciding What's News: A Study of CBS Evening News, NBC Nightly News, Newsweek & Time. LC 79-22849. 1980. pap. 6.95 (ISBN 0-394-74354-7, Vin). Random.

--The Levittowners: Ways of Life & Politics in a New Suburban Community. 512p. 1982. text ed. 30.00x (ISBN 0-231-05570-6, Pub. by MOrningside); pap. 10.95x (ISBN 0-231-05571-4). Columbia U Pr.

--Popular Culture & High Culture: An Analysis & Evaluation of Taste. LC 74-79287. 1975. pap. 5.95x o.p. (ISBN 0-465-09717-0, CN-5017). Basic.

--The Urban Villagers. (Illus.). 456p. 1982. pap. text ed. write for info. Free Pr.

Gans, Mozes Heiman. Memorbook: Pictorial History of Dutch Jewry from the Renaissance to 1940. (Illus.). 852p. 1983. 75.00 (ISBN 0-686-84728-8). Wayne St U Pr.

Gans, Roma. Birds at Night. LC 68-11062. (A Let's-Read-and-Find Out Science Bk). (Illus.). (ps-3). 1968. PLB 10.89 (ISBN 0-690-14444-X, TYC-J). Har-Row.

--Birds Eat & Eat & Eat. LC 63-9213. (A Let's-Read-&-Find-Out Science Bk). (Illus.). (gr. k-3). 1963. bds. 9.57i o.p. (ISBN 0-690-14514-4, TYC-J); PLB 6.89 o.p. (ISBN 0-690-14515-2). Har-Row.

--Birds Eat & Eat & Eat. LC 63-9213. (A Let's Read & Find Out Bk). (Illus.). 40p. (gr. k-3). 1975. pap. 1.45 o.p. (ISBN 0-690-00633-0, TYC-J). Har-Row.

--Caves. LC 76-4881. (Let's Read & Find Out Science Book Ser.). (Illus.). (gr. k-3). 1977. PLB 10.89 (ISBN 0-690-01070-2, TYC-J). Har-Row.

--Guiding Children's Reading Through Experience. LC 79-16407. 1979. pap. 7.95x (ISBN 0-8077-2569-2). Tchrs Coll.

--Hummingbirds in the Garden. LC 69-11083. (A Let's Read-&-Find-Out Science Bk). (Illus.). (gr. k-3). 1969. PLB 10.89 (ISBN 0-690-42562-7, TYC-J). Har-Row.

--Icebergs. LC 64-18163. (A Let's-Read-&-Find-Out Science Bk). (Illus.). (gr. k-3). 1964. PLB 10.89 (ISBN 0-690-42775-1, TYC-J). Har-Row.

--Oil: The Buried Treasure. LC 74-7375. (A Let's-Read-&-Find-Out Science Bk). (Illus.). (gr. k-3). 1975. PLB 10.89 (ISBN 0-690-00613-6, TYC-J). Har-Row.

--Water for Dinosaurs & You. LC 78-158691. (A Let's-Read-&-Find-Out Science Bk). (Illus.). (gr. k-3). 1972. PLB 10.89 (ISBN 0-690-87027-2, TYC-J); pap. 2.95 crocodile paperback ser. (ISBN 0-690-00202-5, TYC-J). Har-Row.

Gans, Stephen L. Pediatric Edoscopy. write for info (ISBN 0-8089-1547-9). Grune.

Gansert, Robert. Singing Energy in the Gan-Tone Method of Voice Production. Capano, Carmela, ed. LC 81-80960. 324p. 1981. 37.50 (ISBN 0-939458-00-4). Gan-Tone Pub.

Gansler, Jacques S. The Defense Industry. 432p. 1980. text ed. 19.95x (ISBN 0-262-07078-2); pap. text ed. 9.95 (ISBN 0-262-57059-9). MIT Pr.

Ganss, George E. Saint Ignatius' Idea of a Jesuit University. 2nd ed. (Illus.). 1956. pap. 16.95 (ISBN 0-87462-437-1). Marquette.

Ganss, George E., ed. Jesuit Religious Life Today: the Principal Features of its Spirit, in Excerpts... from Official Documents. LC 77-78816. (Jesuit Primary Sources in English Translation Ser.: No. 3). 190p. 1977. pap. 3.00 (ISBN 0-912422-27-0); pap. 4.00 smyth sewn (ISBN 0-912422-29-7). Inst Jesuit.

Ganss, George E., ed. see Fleming, David L.

Gansser, Augusto. Geology of the Himalayas. LC 64-8902. (De Sitter Regional Geology Ser). 289p. 1964. 109.50x o.p. (ISBN 0-470-29055-2, Pub. by Wiley-Interscience). Wiley.

Gant, George. Development Administration: Meaning & Application. LC 79-3966. 356p. 1979. 22.50 (ISBN 0-299-07980-5). U of Wis Pr.

Gant, R., tr. see Zola, Emile.

Gantert, Ann X., jt. auth. see Keenan, Edward P.

Gantmacher, Felix R. Theory of Matrices, 2 Vols. LC 59-11779. Vol. 1. 17.95 (ISBN 0-8284-0131-4); Vol. 2. 15.95 (ISBN 0-8284-0133-0). Chelsea Pub.

Ganton, Doris. Drive On. Date not set. pap. 7.00 (ISBN 0-87980-393-2). Wilshire.

Gantos, Jack & Rubel, Nicole. Greedy Greeny. LC 78-22630. (Illus.). 1979. 8.95a o.p. (ISBN 0-385-14685-X); PLB 8.95a (ISBN 0-385-14686-8). Doubleday.

Gantschev, Ivan. Journey of the Storks. LC 82-61835. (Picture Book Ser.). (Illus.). 32p. (gr. k-5). 1983. 9.95 (ISBN 0-907234-27-5). Neugebauer Pr.

Gantschev, Ivan, jt. auth. see Aoki, Hisako.

Gantt, Elisabeth, ed. Handbook of Phycological Methods. LC 78-67311. 1980. 37.50 (ISBN 0-521-22466-7). Cambridge U Pr.

Gantt, Michael D. & Gatza, James. Computers in Insurance. 1980. write for info. o.p. (CPCU 7). IIA.

--Computers in Insurance. LC 80-67525. 150p. 1981. pap. 7.00 (ISBN 0-89463-029-6). Am Inst Property.

Gantz, Charlotte O. A Naturalist in Southern Florida. LC 74-126195. (Illus.). 1971. 12.95 (ISBN 0-87024-172-9). U of Miami Pr.

Gantz, David. Captain Swifty & the Brook That Wouldn't Babble: A Book about Color. LC 82-45559. (Balloon Bks.). (Illus.). 48p. (gr. k-2). 1983. 5.95 (ISBN 0-385-17814-X). Doubleday.

--Captain Swifty Sails to the Shape Islands. LC 81-43623. (Balloon Bks.). (Illus.). 48p. (gr. k-2). 1983. 5.95 (ISBN 0-385-17813-1). Doubleday.

--Tungle Twisters. (Funnybones Ser.). (Illus.). 64p. (Orig.). 1982. pap. 1.95 (ISBN 0-671-44543-X). Wanderer Bks.

Gantz, Jeffrey, tr. The Mabinogion. (Classic Ser.). 1976. pap. 3.95 (ISBN 0-14-044322-3). Penguin.

Ganz, A. W. Berlioz in London. (Music Ser.). (Illus.). 222p. 1981. Repr. of 1950 ed. lib. bdg. 25.00 (ISBN 0-306-76092-4). Da Capo.

Ganz, Arthur, jt. auth. see Beckson, Karl.

Ganzel, Dewey. Fortune & Men's Eyes: The Career of John Payne Collier. (Illus.). 1982. 19.95 (ISBN 0-19-212231-2). Oxford U Pr.

Ganzhorn, Jack. I've Killed Men. (Illus.). 1959. 9.50 (ISBN 0-8159-5821-8). Devin.

Gao, E., ed. see Cao, Xueqin.

Gao E, jt. auth. see Cao Xuequin.

Gapinski, J. H. Macroeconomics Theory: Statics, Dynamics & Policy. 432p. 1982. 25.95x (ISBN 0-07-022765-9). McGraw.

Gapinski, James & Rockwood, Charles E., eds. Essays in Post-Keynesian Inflation. LC 79-22879. 336p. 1979. prof ref 27.50x (ISBN 0-88410-684-5). Ballinger Pub.

Gappert, Gary & Knight, Richard V. Cities of the Twenty First Century. (Urban Affairs Annual Reviews: Vol. 23). (Illus.). 320p. 1982. 25.00 (ISBN 0-8039-1910-7); pap. 12.50 (ISBN 0-8039-1911-5). Sage.

Gara, Otto G. & Naegeli, Bruce A. Technological Changes & the Law: A Reader. LC 79-92276. 925p. 1980. 30.00 (ISBN 0-89941-037-5). W S Hein.

Garabedian, Henry L. Analytic Criticality Studies Associated with Neutron Diffusion Theory. (Review Ser.: No. 26). (Illus.). 57p. 1962. pap. write for info. o.p. (STI/PUB/15/26, IAEA). Unipub.

Garabedian, Paul R. Partial Differential Equations. LC 64-11505. 672p. 1964. 39.95x (ISBN 0-471-29088-2). Wiley.

Garas, Klara, intro. by. Paintings in the Budapest Museum of Fine Arts. Halapy, Lili, tr. 292p. 1980. 15.95 (ISBN 0-89893-160-6). CDP.

Garattini, S., ed. Advances in Pharmacology & Chemotherapy, Vol. 19. 290p. 1982. 38.00 (ISBN 0-12-032919-0); lib ed 49.50 (ISBN 0-12-032988-3); microfiche 27.00 (ISBN 0-12-032989-1). Acad Pr.

Garattini, S. & Berendes, H. W., eds. Pharmacology of Steroid Contraceptive Drugs. LC 77-6100. (Monographs of the Mario Negri Institute for Pharmacological Research). 391p. 1977. 38.50 (ISBN 0-89004-187-3). Raven.

Garattini, S. & Franchi, G., eds. Chemotherapy of Cancer Dissemination & Metastasis. LC 72-96335. (Monographs of the Mario Negri Institute for Pharmacological Research). (Illus.). 400p. 1973. 38.00 (ISBN 0-911216-46-4). Raven.

Garattini, S. & Samanin, R., eds. Central Mechanisms of Anorectic Drugs. LC 77-17749. (Monographs of the Mario Negri Institute for Pharmacological Research). 501p. 1978. 44.00 (ISBN 0-89004-219-5). Raven.

Garattini, S. & Sigg, E., eds. Aggressive Behaviour. 1969. 41.00 (ISBN 90-219-2018-2, Excerpta Medica). Elsevier.

Garattini, S. & Sproston, E., eds. Antitumoral Effects of Vinca Rosea Alkaloids. (International Congress Ser.: No. 106). (Proceedings). 1966. pap. 22.50 (ISBN 90-219-0060-2, Excerpta Medica). Elsevier.

Garattini, S., et al, eds. Interactions Between Putative Neurotransmitters in the Brain. LC 77-83686. (Monographs of the Mario Negri Institute for Pharmacological Research). 431p. 1978. 38.00 (ISBN 0-89004-196-2). Raven.

Garattini, Silvio & Samanin, Rosario, eds. Anorectic Agents: Mechanisms of Action & Tolerance. (Monographs of the Mario Negri Institute for Pharmacological Research). 256p. 1981. text ed. 31.00 (ISBN 0-89004-640-9). Raven.

Garattini, Silvio, jt. ed. see De Gaetano, Giovanni.

Garaudy, Roger. Karl Marx, Evolution of His Thought. Apotheker, Nan, tr. from French. LC 76-43305. 1976. Repr. of 1967 ed. lib. bdg. 18.25x (ISBN 0-8371-9044-4, GAKM). Greenwood.

Garb, Forrest A. Waterflood Manual for Hewlett Packard Calculators. (Illus.). 94p. 1982. pap. 21.95x (ISBN 0-87201-895-4). Gulf Pub.

Garb, Gerald. Microeconomics: Theory Applications Innovations. 342p. 1981. text ed. 23.95 (ISBN 0-02-340400-0). Macmillan.

Garb, Solomon, jt. ed. see Gross, Stephen C.

Garbacz, Christopher. Economic Resources for the Elderly: Prospects for the Future. (Replica Edition Ser.). 235p. 1983. softcover 20.00x (ISBN 0-86531-947-2). Westview.

Garbade, K. Securities Markets. (Finance Ser.). 1982. 24.95x (ISBN 0-07-022780-2). McGraw.

Garbarino, James. Child Abuse: What Resources for Meeting the Problem? (Vital Issues, Vol. XXVIII 1978-79: No. 2). 0.60 (ISBN 0-686-81618-8). Ctr Info Am.

Garbarino, James & Asp, C. Elliott. Successful Schools & Competent Students. LC 81-47704. 176p. 1981. 22.95x (ISBN 0-669-04526-8). Lexington Bks.

Garbarino, James & Galambos, Nancy L. Vandalism: What Are its Whos, Whats, & Why? What Can be Done About It? (Vital Issues Ser.: Vol. XXXI, No. 2). 0.80 (ISBN 0-686-84135-2). Ctr Info Am.

Garbarino, James & Gilliam, Gwen. Understanding Abusive Families. LC 79-47983. 288p. 1980. 22.95 (ISBN 0-669-03621-8). Lexington Bks.

Garbarino, Merwyn, jt. auth. see World Book, Inc. Staff.

Garbassi, U., jt. auth. see McCracken, D. D.

Garbaty, Thomas J. Poetry & Prose of Medieval England. 960p. 1983. text ed. 24.95 (ISBN 0-686-78154-6). Heath.

Garbe, Detlef. Burgerbeteiligung. iv, 248p. (Ger.). 1982. write for info. (ISBN 3-8204-5840-9). P Lang Pubs.

Garbe, Richard. India & Christendom: The Historical Connections Between Their Religions. Robinson, Lydia J., tr. from Ger. xi, 321p. 1959. 21.00 (ISBN 0-87548-232-5). Open Court.

Garbee, Ed & Van Dyke, Henry. Dramas De Navidad. Prince, Soledad G. & Castellon, Guillermo, trs. 1981. pap. 1.35 (ISBN 0-311-08214-9). Casa Bautista.

Garber, B. J. Shards from the Heart: A Spiritual Odyssey in Twentieth Century America. LC 64-13358. (Freedeeds Books). 160p. 1965. 7.00 (ISBN 0-89345-004-9). Garber Comm.

Garber, Bernard J., ed. see Steiner, Rudolf.

Garber, Bernard J., ed. & intro. by see Steiner, Rudolf.

Garber, Eric & Paleo, Lyn. Uranian Worlds: A Reader's Guide to Alternative Sexuality in Science Fiction & Fantasy. 1983. lib. bdg. 28.50 (ISBN 0-8161-8573-5, Hall Reference). G K Hall.

Garber, Frederick, ed. see Radcliffe, Ann.

Garber, Janet S. The Mystery of Butch Cassidy & the Sundance Kid. LC 79-17622. (Unsolved Mysteries of the World Ser.). PLB 11.96 (ISBN 0-89547-075-6). Silver.

--Rasputin: The Mysterious Monk. LC 78-24348. (Unsolved Mysteries of the World). PLB 11.96 (ISBN 0-89547-072-1). Silver.

Garber, Lee O. & Hubbard, Ben C. Law, Finance, & the Teacher in Illinois. 1983. write for info. (ISBN 0-8134-2252-3). Interstate.

Garber, Lyman A. Of Men & Not of Law: The Courts are Usurping the Political Function. 1966. 6.50 (ISBN 0-8159-6400-5). Devin.

Garber, Max B. & Bond, P. S. A Modern Military Dictionary: Ten Thousand Technical & Slang Terms of Military Usage. 2nd ed. LC 74-31354. 1975. Repr. of 1942 ed. 34.00x (ISBN 0-8103-4208-1). Gale.

Garber, Robert A. The Only Tax Book You'll Ever Need. 1982. 14.95 (ISBN 0-517-54627-2, Harmony). Crown.

Garbett, Thomas. Corporate Advertising: The What, the Why, & the How. (Illus.). 224p. 1981. 27.95 (ISBN 0-07-022787-X, C). McGraw.

Garbicz, Adam & Klinowski, Jacek. Cinema, the Magic Vehicle: A Guide to It's Achievement. LC 82-10405. (Illus.). 560p. 1983. pap. 12.50 (ISBN 0-686-84572-2). Schocken.

Garbis, Marvin J. & Schwait, Allen L. Tax Court Practice. 1974. 56.00 (ISBN 0-88262-036-3). Warren.

Garbo, Norman. The Artist. 1978. 12.95 o.p. (ISBN 0-393-08790-5). Norton.

--Turner's Wife: A Novel. 1983. 16.50 (ISBN 0-393-01521-1). Norton.

Garbus, Terrie, et al. Living in Washington: A Moving Experience. (Illus.). 240p. pap. 3.50 o.p. (ISBN 0-517-51851-1). Crown.

Garbutt, Cameron W. Road to the Land of R. (Illus.). 1970. pap. text ed. 1.25x (ISBN 0-8134-1208-0, 1208). Interstate.

--Road to the Land of S. (Illus.). 1969. pap. text ed. 1.25x (ISBN 0-8134-1116-5, 1116). Interstate.

--Road to the Land of TH. (Illus.). 48p. 1971. pap. text ed. 1.25x (ISBN 0-8134-1324-9, 1324). Interstate.

Garbutt, J. W. & Bartlett, A. J. Experimental Biology with Micro-Organisms. 1972. pap. text ed. 4.95 o.p. (ISBN 0-408-70228-1); teachers' guide 12.95 o.p. (ISBN 0-408-70240-0). Butterworth.

Garcia. Diagnostic Neuropathology. 1983. write for info (ISBN 0-89352-013-6). Masson Pub.

Garcia, A. Dizionario Italiano-Spagnolo, Spagnolo-Italiano. 437p. (Span. & Ital.). 1980. leatherette 5.95 (ISBN 0-686-97347-X, S-31237). French & Eur.

Garcia, Anthony & Myers, Robert. Analogies: A Visual Approach to Writing. (Illus.). 256p. 1974. pap. text ed. 16.50 (ISBN 0-07-022825-6, C). McGraw.

Garcia, Bartnicki, jt. ed. see Erwin, D. C.

Garcia, C. B. & Zangwill, Willard I. Pathways to Solutions, Fixed Points, & Equilibria. (Computational Math Ser.). 336p. 1981. text ed. 29.95 (ISBN 0-13-653501-1). P-H.

Garcia, Celso-Ramon & Mastroianni, Luigi, Jr. Current Therapy of Infertility, 1982-1983. 256p. 1982. text ed. 32.00 (ISBN 0-941158-02-0, D1738-3). Mosby.

Garcia, Clarita. Clarita's Cocina: Great Traditional Recipes from a Spanish Kitchen. LC 74-113069. (Illus.). 1970. 13.95 (ISBN 0-385-04657-X). Doubleday.

Garcia, Connie & Medina, Arthur. Businessman's Guide to the Caribbean. 624p. 1983. text ed. 45.00 (ISBN 0-934642-05-2); pap. 35.00 (ISBN 0-934642-08-7). Puerto Rico Almanacs.

--Guia Turistica de Puerto Rico. Rivera, Evelyn, tr. from Sp. (Illus.). 192p. (Eng.). 1983. pap. 4.95 (ISBN 0-934642-04-4). Puerto Rico Almanacs.

--The Travel Guide to Puerto Rico: 1982-83. 2nd ed. (Illus.). 340p. 1983. pap. 9.95 (ISBN 0-934642-03-6). Puerto Rico Almanacs.

Garcia, David. Fairy Tales of Puerto Rico. (Children's Bks.: No. 166). (Illus.). 50p. (gr. 1-5). 1982. 9.95 (ISBN 0-934642-02-8). Puerto Rico Almanacs.

Garcia, E. The Role of Theory in Linguistic Analysis: The Spanish Pronoun System. (N-H Linguistic Ser.: Vol. 19). 522p. 1975. pap. 42.75 (ISBN 0-444-10940-4, North-Holland). Elsevier.

Garcia, Edward & Pellegrini, Nina. Homer the Homely Hound Dog. (Illus.). (gr. 2-6). pap. 3.95 (ISBN 0-686-36813-4). Inst Rat Liv.

Garcia, Edward J. & Blythe, Bruce T. Developing Emotional Muscle. pap. 7.95 (ISBN 0-686-36689-1). Inst Rat Liv.

Garcia, Frederick, ed. see Da Gama, Jose B.

Garcia, Joseph R. Wayside Poems. 96p. 1982. pap. 5.00 (ISBN 0-682-49908-0). Exposition.

Garcia, Juan R. Operation Wetback: The Mass Deportation of Mexican Undocumented Workers in 1954. LC 79-6189. (Contributions in Ethnic Studies: No. 2). (Illus.). xvii, 268p. 1980. lib. bdg. 29.95 (ISBN 0-313-21353-4, GOW/). Greenwood.

Garcia, Manuel, II. A Complete Treatise on the Art of Singing, Pt. 1. Paschke, Donald V., tr. from Fr. lxi, 221p. 1983. Repr. lib. bdg. 32.50 (ISBN 0-306-76212-9). Da Capo.

--A Complete Treatise on the Art of Singing, Pt. 2. Paschke, V., tr. from Span. & pref. by. LC 74-23382. xii, 261p. 1975. Repr. of 1972 ed. lib. bdg. 29.50 (ISBN 0-306-70660-1). Da Capo.

Garcia, Marcy. The Big E: Learning Package Two: Teacher's Program. (Illus.). 192p. (Orig.). (gr. 4-7). 1983. tchrs. ed. 9.95 (ISBN 0-88499-235-7); wkbk. 2.95 (ISBN 0-88499-236-5); Set Of 10. assessment tests 9.95 (ISBN 0-88499-237-3). Inst Mod Lang.

Garcia, Margot W., jt. ed. see KDaneke, Gregory A.

Garcia, Mariano. Spanish for Law Enforcement Officers, 2 vols. 1972. Vol. 1. pap. text ed. 6.95 (ISBN 0-88499-135-0); Vol. 2. pap. text ed. 6.95 (ISBN 0-88499-137-7); instructor's guide 3.95 (ISBN 0-88499-134-2); wkbk. 1 5.95 (ISBN 0-88499-136-9); wkbk. 2 5.95 (ISBN 0-88499-138-5). Inst Mod Lang.

Garcia, Mario R. Contemporary Newspaper Design: A Structural Approach. (Illus.). 240p. 1981. text ed. 29.95 (ISBN 0-13-170381-1); pap. text ed. 31.95 (ISBN 0-13-170373-0). P-H.

Garcia, Mary H. & Gonzalez-Mena, Janet. The Big E: Learning Package One. Ragan, Lise B., ed. LC 75-27579. (Prog. Bk.). (gr. 1-2). 1976. tchr's program 9.95 (ISBN 0-88499-228-4); student workbook 2.95 (ISBN 0-88499-230-6); pkg. of 10 tests 9.95 (ISBN 0-88499-229-2); program package 45.00 (ISBN 0-88499-231-4). Inst Mod Lang.

Garcia, Mary J., jt. auth. see Johnson, Barry L.

Garcia, Richard A., ed. The Chicanos in America, Fifteen Forty to Nineteen Seventy-Four: Chronology & Fact Book. LC 76-42300. (Ethnic Chronology Ser.: No. 26). 231p. 1977. 8.50 (ISBN 0-379-00516-6). Oceana.

Garcia, Robert, jt. auth. see Moore, Joan.

Garcia, Rolando V. Nature Pleads Not Guilty: An IFIAS Report. (Illus.). 330p. 1982. 60.00 (ISBN 0-08-025823-9). Pergamon.

Garcia, Rupert. Frida Kahlo. (Chicano Studies Library Publication: No. 7). (Orig.). 1983. pap. text ed. price not set (ISBN 0-918520-05-3). UC Chicano.

Garcia-Antezana, Jorge. Libro De Buen Amor: Concordancia Completa De los Codices De Salamanca, Toledo y Gayoso. 1100p. (Span.). 1981. microfiche 75.00x o.p. (ISBN 0-8020-2413-0). U of Toronto Pr.

Garcia-Diaz, Alberto, jt. auth. see Phillips, Don T.

Garcia Lorca, Federico. Five Plays: Comedies & Tragicomedies. O'Connell, Richard L. & Graham-Lujan, James, trs. from Span. LC 77-4654. 1977. Repr. of 1963 ed. lib. bdg. 20.00x (ISBN 0-8371-9583-7, LOFP). Greenwood.

--Three Tragedies: Blood Wedding, Yerma, Bernarda Alba. O'Connell, Richard L. & Graham-Lujan, James, trs. from Spanish. LC 77-3056. 1977. Repr. of 1955 ed. lib. bdg. 16.75x (ISBN 0-8371-9578-0, LOTT). Greenwood.

Garcia Lorca, Federico see Lorca, Federico Garcia.

Garcia Marquez, Gabriel. The Autumn of the Patriarch. Rabassa, Gregory, tr. from Span. LC 75-30349. 288p. 1976. 13.41i (ISBN 0-06-011419-3, HarpT). Har-Row.

--In Evil Hour. Rabassa, Gregory, tr. from Span. LC 74-15873. 10.53i (ISBN 0-06-011410-X, HarpT). Har-Row.

Garcia-Marquez, Gabriel. Innocent Erendira & Other Stories. Rabassa, Gregory, tr. from Span. LC 74-15873. 1979. pap. 4.50i (ISBN 0-06-090701-0, CN 701, CN). Har-Row.

Garcia Marquez, Gabriel. Innocent Erendira & Other Stories. Rabassa, Gregory, tr. from Spanish. LC 74-15873. 1978. 10.53i (ISBN 0-06-011416-9, HarpT). Har-Row.

Garcia-Marquez, Gabriel. Leaf Storm & Other Stories. Rabassa, Gregory, tr. from Span. LC 76-138784. 1979. pap. 4.50i (ISBN 0-06-090699-5, CN 699, CN). Har-Row.

--No One Writes to the Colonel & Other Stories. Bernstein, J. S., tr. from Span. LC 68-15977. 1979. pap. 4.95i (ISBN 0-06-090700-2, CN 700, CN). Har-Row.

Garcia-Moliner, F. & Flores, F. Introduction to the Theory of Solid Surfaces. LC 78-17617. (Cambridge Monographs on Physics). (Illus.). 1979. 79.50 (ISBN 0-521-22294-X). Cambridge U Pr.

Garcia-Prada, Carlos & Wilson, William E. Tres Cuentos. 2nd ed. LC 59-4973. (Span). 1959. pap. text ed. 9.50 (ISBN 0-395-04482-0). HM.

Garcilaso de la Vega. The Florida of the Inca. Varner, John & Varner, Jeannette, eds. Varner, Jeannette, tr. from Sp. 708p. 1951. 25.00x (ISBN 0-292-73238-4); pap. 12.95 (ISBN 0-292-72434-9). U of Tex Pr.

Garczynska, Marie J. Tales from Russia. LC 80-52512. (The World Folktale Library). PLB 12.68 (ISBN 0-382-06597-2). Silver.

Garczynski, W., ed. Gauge Field Theories: Theoretical Studies & Computer Stimulations. (Studies in High Energy Physics: Vol. 4). Date not set. price not set (ISBN 3-7186-0121-4). Harwood Academic.

Gard, Bertrand Du see Du Gard, Bertrand.

Gard, Robert E. This Is Wisconsin. LC 78-98074. (Illus.). 1969. 8.95 o.s.i. (ISBN 0-88361-006-X). Stanton & Lee.

Gard, Robert E. & Burley, Gertrude S. Community Theatre. LC 73-19113. 182p. 1975. Repr. of 1959 ed. lib. bdg. 18.75x (ISBN 0-8371-7304-3, GACT). Greenwood.

Gard, Wayne. The Chisholm Trail. (Illus., Orig.). 1954. 13.50 o.p. (ISBN 0-8061-0291-8); pap. 7.95 (ISBN 0-8061-1536-X). U of Okla Pr.

--Sam Bass. LC 36-17302. (Illus.). x, 262p. 1969. 17.50x o.p. (ISBN 0-8032-0868-5); pap. 3.65 o.p. (ISBN 0-8032-5068-1). U of Nebr Pr.

Gardam, Jane. The Hollow Lands. (Illus.). (gr. 5-9). 1982. 9.50 (ISBN 0-688-00873-9). Morrow.

--The Sidmouth Letters. LC 80-23940. 163p. 1980. 8.95 o.p. (ISBN 0-688-00134-3). Morrow.

Garde, Pauline, jt. auth. see Mayer, Henry.

Garde, R. J. & Raju, K. Ranga. Mechanics of Sediment Transportation & Alluvial Stream Problems. LC 77-13628. 483p. 1978. 32.95 o.p. (ISBN 0-470-99329-4). Halsted Pr.

Gardell, Bertil & Johansson, Gunn. Working Life: A Social Science Contribution to Work Reform. LC 80-40289. 347p. 1981. 45.00x (ISBN 0-471-27801-7, Pub. by Wiley-Interscience). Wiley.

Gardemal, Louis G., jt. auth. see Shroyer, Frederick B.

Garden Center of Greater Cleveland. Flowering Plant Index of Illustration & Information. 1979. lib. bdg. 200.00 (ISBN 0-8161-0301-1, Hall Library). G K Hall.

Garden, Edward. Balakirev: A Critical Study of His Life & Music. (Illus.). 1967. 12.50 o.p. (ISBN 0-312-06580-9, B04300). St Martin.

Garden, Nancy. Berlin: City Split in Two. LC 72-125385. (World Crisis Areas Ser.). (gr. 6-10). 1971. PLB 5.29 o.p. (ISBN 0-399-60054-X). Putnam Pub Group.

--Watersmeet. 192p. (gr. 5 up). 1983. 10.95 (ISBN 0-374-38244-1). FS&G.

--Werewolves. LC 72-13280. (gr. 7 up). 1973. 9.57i (ISBN 0-397-31463-9, JBL-J). Har-Row.

--Witches. LC 75-12621. (Weird & Horrible Library). (Illus.). 160p. (gr. 3-5). 1975. 9.57i (ISBN 0-397-31564-3, JBL-J, LSC-41). Har-Row.

Garden, R. J., ed. The Lum Hat & Other Stories: Last Tales of Violet Jacob. (Illus.). 172p. 1982. 19.50 (ISBN 0-08-028449-3); 10.50 (ISBN 0-08-028450-7). Pergamon.

Gardener, Lloyd C. Wilson & Revolutions: Nineteen Thirteen to Nineteen Twenty-One. LC 82-45089. 160p. (Orig.). 1982. pap. text ed. 9.25 (ISBN 0-8191-2416-8). U Pr of Amer.

Gardener, N. L., jt. auth. see Setchell, W. A.

Gardener's Catalog People. The Gardener's Catalog, No. 2. rev. ed. (Illus.). 320p. 1983. pap. 12.95 (ISBN 0-688-01238-8). Quill NY.

Gardezi, Hassan & Rashid, Jamil, eds. Pakistan: The Roots of Dictatorship. 448p. 1983. pap. 14.50 (ISBN 0-86232-046-1, Pub. by Zed Pr England). Lawrence Hill.

Gardi, Gavin L, jt. auth. see Cook, Richard J.

Gardin, J. C., et al. Archaeological Constructs. LC 78-54577. (Illus.). 1980. 37.50 (ISBN 0-521-22080-7). Cambridge U Pr.

Gardiner, Alan. Egyptian Grammar: An Introduction to the Study of Hieroglyphs. 1979. 55.00x (ISBN 0-686-97687-8, Pub. by Ashmolean Mus Oxford). State Mutual Bk.

Gardiner, Alan, jt. auth. see Cerny, Jaroslav.

Gardiner, C. F., jt. auth. see Firby, P. A.

Gardiner, C. Harvey. The Japanese & Peru, 1873-1973. LC 75-17371. 202p. 1975. 12.50x o.p. (ISBN 0-8263-0391-9). U of NM Pr.

Gardiner, C. W. Handbook of Stochastic Methods for Physics, Chemistry & the Natural Sciences. (Springer Series in Synergetics: Vol. 13). (Illus.). 450p. 1983. 42.00 (ISBN 0-387-11357-6). Springer-Verlag.

Gardiner, E. Norman. Athletics of the Ancient World. (Illus.). 1978. 22.00 (ISBN 0-89005-257-3); pap. 12.50 (ISBN 0-686-96662-7). Ares.

Gardiner, Eileen. The Video Register 1981 to 1982. LC 79-640381. 250p. 1981. 50.00x (ISBN 0-686-75633-9, Pub. by Knowledge Indus). Gale.

Gardiner, G. F. Greenhouse Gardening. 1968. 17.00 o.p. (ISBN 0-8206-0052-0). Chem Pub.

Gardiner, Harry N. Feeling & Emotion: A History of Theories. Repr. of 1937 ed. lib. bdg. 20.25x (ISBN 0-8371-3683-0, GAFE). Greenwood.

Gardiner, Harry W., jt. auth. see Gander, Mary J.

Gardiner, John & Mulkey, Michael, eds. Crime & Criminal Justice. 1974. pap. 6.00 (ISBN 0-918592-08-9). Policy Studies.

Gardiner, John A. The Politics of Corruption: Organized Crime in an American City. LC 79-107958. 130p. 1970. 7.50x (ISBN 0-87154-299-4). Russell Sage.

Gardiner, John A. & Lyman, Theodore R. Decision for Sale: Corruption & Reform in Local Land-Use & Building Regulation. LC 78-19758. 234p. 1978. 27.95 (ISBN 0-03-044691-0). Praeger.

Gardiner, John A. & Mulkey, Michael A., eds. Crime & Criminal Justice: Issues in Public Policy Analysis. 1977. pap. 8.95x o.p. (ISBN 0-669-01059-6). Heath.

Gardiner, John R. Going on Like This. LC 82-73016. 224p. 1983. 12.95 (ISBN 0-689-11347-1). Atheneum.

--Stone Fox. LC 79-7895. (A Trophy Bk.). (Illus.). 96p. (gr. 2-6). 1983. pap. 2.84i (ISBN 0-06-440132-4, Trophy). Har-Row.

Gardiner, Judy. Who Was Sylvia? 208p. 1983. 10.95 (ISBN 0-312-87030-2). St Martin.

Gardiner, Muriel. Code Name "Mary". An American Woman in the Australian Underground. LC 82-20213. (Illus.). 200p. 1983. 14.95 (ISBN 0-300-02940-3). Yale Univ. Pr.

Gardiner, Muriel, ed. The Wolf Man: With the Case of the Wolf Man by Sigmund Freud. LC 70-151227. 1971. pap. 5.95x o.s.i. (ISBN 0-465-09501-1, TB-5002). Basic.

Gardiner, P. A. Development of Vision, Vol. 4. 240p. 1981. 17.50 o.p. (ISBN 0-88416-379-2). Wright-PSG.

Gardiner, Stephen. Obedience in Church & State: Three Political Tracts. Janelle, Pierre, ed. LC 68-19272. 1968. Repr. of 1930 ed. lib. bdg. 15.50x (ISBN 0-8371-0081-X, GABW). Greenwood.

Gardiner, Ted. Broomstick Over Essex & East Anglia. 1981. 15.00x (ISBN 0-86025-851-3, Pub. by Ian Henry Pubns England). State Mutual Bk.

Gardiner, W. C. Rates & Mechanisms of Chemical Reactions. 1969. pap. 14.95 (ISBN 0-8053-3101-8). Benjamin-Cummings.

Gardiner, W. Lambert. The Psychology of Teaching. LC 78-32090. 1979. pap. text ed. 17.95 (ISBN 0-8185-0290-8). Brooks-Cole.

Gardiol, Rita M. Ramon Gomez de la Serna. (World Authors Ser.). 176p. 1974. lib. bdg. 15.95 (ISBN 0-8057-2379-X, Twayne). G K Hall.

Gardner. The Artist's Silkscreen Manual. (The Grosset Art Instruction Ser.). (Illus.). 48p. Date not set. pap. price not set (ISBN 0-448-11593-X, G&D). Putnam Pub Group.

--Master Creative Tape Recording. (Illus.). 1977. pap. 9.95 (ISBN 0-408-00244-1). Focal Pr.

Gardner, A. Ward. Good Housekeeping Dictionary of Symptoms. (Illus.). 1978. pap. 5.95 (ISBN 0-448-14731-9, G&D). Putnam Pub Group.

Gardner, A. Ward, ed. Current Approaches to Occupational Health, Vol. 2. (Illus.). 414p. 1982. text ed. 37.50 (ISBN 0-7236-0618-8). Wright-PSG.

Gardner, Albert T. Winslow Homer, American Artist: His World & Work. (Illus.). 266p. 1961. 25.00 o.p. (ISBN 0-517-03448-4). Crown.

Gardner, Albert T. & Feld, Stuart P. American Paintings: Vol. I, Painters Born by 1815. LC 65-16834. (Illus.). 1965. 6.95 (ISBN 0-87099-032-2); pap. 2.95 (ISBN 0-87099-033-0). Metro Mus Art.

Gardner, Alexander. Gardner's Photographic Sketch Book of the Civil War. (Illus.). 12.50 (ISBN 0-8446-0104-7). Peter Smith.

Gardner, Allen H. Primer on Planning an Estate. 1981. pap. 15.95 (ISBN 0-686-84884-5). Lerner Law.

Gardner, Alvin F., jt. auth. see McGregor, Ian P.

Gardner, Alvin F., ed. Dental Examination Review Book. Vol. 1, 5th Ed. 1977. spiral bdg. 20.50 (ISBN 0-87488-431-4); Vol. 2, 4th Ed. 1978. spiral bdg. 20.50 (ISBN 0-87488-432-2); Vol. 3, 3rd Ed. 1978. spiral bdg. 20.50 (ISBN 0-87488-433-0). Med Exam.

Gardner, Alvin F., ed. see Anbar, Michael.

Gardner, Alvin f., ed. see Joyce, Joan M.

Gardner, Alvin F., ed. see Kelsey, Charles A.

Gardner, Alvin F., ed. see Lauer, Gary.

Gardner, Alvin F., ed. see Robertson, Caroline E.

Gardner, Alvin F., ed. see Strum, Williamson B.

Gardner, Alvjn F., ed. see Lager, Eric & Zwerling, Isreal.

Gardner, Andrew B. The Artist's Silk Screen Manual. LC 73-22737. (Craft Books Ser.). (Illus.). 192p. 1976. pap. 5.95 (ISBN 0-448-11593-X, G&D). Putnam Pub Group.

Gardner, Annell. Family Reunion Profile. 1979. 4.50 o.p. (ISBN 0-8062-1366-3). Carlton.

Gardner, Bruce. Optimal Stockpiling of Grain. LC 78-24768. 192p. 1979. 23.95x (ISBN 0-669-02829-0). Lexington Bks.

Gardner, Carl, ed. Media, Politics, & Culture: A Socialist View. (Communications & Culture). 1979. text ed. 23.00x o.p. (ISBN 0-333-23588-6); pap. text ed. 10.50x o.p. (ISBN 0-333-23589-4). Humanities.

Gardner, David C. & Beatty, Grace J. Dissertation Proposal Guidebook: How to Prepare a Research Proposal & Get It Accepted. (Illus.). 112p. 1980. 9.50x (ISBN 0-398-04086-9); pap. 5.75x (ISBN 0-398-04087-7). C C Thomas.

Gardner, David M. & Winter, Frederick W., eds. Proceedings of the 11th Paul D. Converse Symposium. LC 81-22920. (Illus.). 123p. (Orig.). 1982. pap. text ed. 8.00 (ISBN 0-87757-155-4). Am Mktg.

Gardner, David P. The California Oath Controversy. LC 67-16840. 1967. 26.50x (ISBN 0-520-00455-8). U of Cal Pr.

Gardner, David P., jt. ed. see Furniss, W. Todd.

Gardner, Deborah, ed. New York Art Guide. (Art Guide Ser.). 118p. (Orig.). 1982. pap. 5.95 (ISBN 0-686-95015-1, Pub. by Art Guide England). Morgan.

Gardner, E. Clinton. Christocentrism in Christian Social Ethics: A Depth Study of Eight Modern Protestants. LC 82-21843. 264p. (Orig.). 1983. lib. bdg. 22.50 (ISBN 0-8191-2954-2); pap. text ed. 11.75 (ISBN 0-8191-2955-0). U Pr of Amer.

Gardner, Edmund G. Dante. 166p. 1982. Repr. of 1912 ed. lib. bdg. 20.00 (ISBN 0-8495-2132-7). Arden Lib.

--King of Court Poets: A Study of the Work, Life & Times of Lodovico Ariosto. Repr. of 1906 ed. lib. bdg. 17.50x (ISBN 0-8371-0440-8, GALA). Greenwood.

Gardner, Edward L. Fairies. LC 82-42707. (Illus.). 53p. 1983. pap. 5.75 (ISBN 0-8356-0569-8, Quest). Theos Pub Hse.

Gardner, Eldon J. Human Heredity. 460p. 1983. text ed. 20.95 (ISBN 0-471-08376-3). Wiley.

Gardner, Eldon J. & Snustad, D. Peter. Principles of Genetics. 6th ed. LC 80-12114. 688p. 1981. text ed. 27.95 (ISBN 0-471-04412-1). Wiley.

Gardner, Erle S. The Case of the Dubious Bridegroom. 224p. 1983. pap. 2.25 (ISBN 0-345-30881-6). Ballantine.

--The Case of the Glamorous Ghost. 240p. 1982. pap. 2.25 (ISBN 0-345-30781-X). Ballantine.

--The Case of the Lonely Heiress. 224p. 1983. pap. 2.25 (ISBN 0-345-31012-8). Ballantine.

--The Case of the Murderer's Bride. Queen, Ellery, intro. by. LC 77-81936. 1977. pap. 1.50 o.s.i. (ISBN 0-89559-003-4). Davis Pubns.

--Pay Dirt. Waugh, Charles G. & Greenberg, Martin H., eds. 324p. 1983. 15.95 (ISBN 0-688-01981-1). Morrow.

Gardner, Erle Stanley. Ellery Queen Presents. Bd. with The Amazing Adventures of Lester Leith. Gardner, Erle Stanley. 192p. 1981. 9.95 o.s.i. (ISBN 0-8037-1653-2). Davis Pubns.

Gardner, Floyd M. Phaselock Techniques. 2nd ed. LC 78-20777. 285p. 1979. 24.95x (ISBN 0-471-04294-3, Pub by Wiley-Interscience). Wiley.

Gardner, G. B. High Magic's Aid. LC 74-84852. 1975. pap. 3.95 o.p. (ISBN 0-87728-278-1). Weiser.

Gardner, G. H., jt. auth. see McDonald, John A.

Gardner, Geoffrey. The Key of Life. 1979. 6.95 o.p. (ISBN 0-533-04173-2). Vantage.

Gardner, Gerald. The I Hate Hollywood Joke Book. 128p. (Orig.). 1982. pap. 1.95 (ISBN 0-345-29630-3). Ballantine.

--New York, New York: Who's in Charge Here? 80p. (Orig.). 1981. pap. 3.95 o.p. (ISBN 0-425-05243-5). Berkley Pub.

--The Who's in Charge Here Yearbook 1981. (Illus.). 96p. 1982. pap. 3.95 (ISBN 0-399-50573-3, Perige). Putnam Pub Group.

Gardner, Gerald & Gardner, Harriet M. The Tara Treasury. (Illus.). 192p. 1980. 19.95 o.p. (ISBN 0-517-54819-4, Arlington Hse). Crown.

Gardner, Gerald B. Meaning of Witchcraft. (Illus.). 288p. 1982. pap. 9.95 (ISBN 0-939708-02-7). Magickal Childe.

Gardner, Gerard B. Witchcraft Today. (Illus.). 184p. pap. 9.95 (ISBN 0-939708-03-5). Magickal Childe.

Gardner, H. Stephen. Soviet Foreign Trade: The Decision Process. 1982. lib. bdg. 32.00 (ISBN 0-89838-111-8). Kluwer-Nijhoff.

Gardner, Harriet M., jt. auth. see Gardner, Gerald.

Gardner, Helen. The Composition of Four Quartets. 1978. 35.00x (ISBN 0-19-519989-8). Oxford U Pr.

--Reading of Paradise Lost. 1965. pap. 12.50x (ISBN 0-19-811662-4). Oxford U Pr.

Gardner, Helen, ed. The New Oxford Book of English Verse, 1250-1950. 1972. 25.00 (ISBN 0-19-812136-9); leather bdg. 85.00 (ISBN 0-19-196952-4). Oxford U Pr.

Gardner, Herb. A Thousand Clowns. 1983. pap. 4.95 (ISBN 0-14-048202-4). Penguin.

Gardner, Herman L. & Kaufman, Raymond H. Benign Diseases of the Vulva & Vagina. 2nd. ed. 1981. lib. bdg. 59.95 (ISBN 0-8161-2106-0, Hall Medical). G K Hall.

Gardner, Hershal. Handbook of Solid-State Troubleshooting. (Illus.). 320p. 1976. 19.95 (ISBN 0-87909-339-0). Reston.

--How to Troubleshoot & Repair Your Stereo System. (Illus.). 240p. 1976. 18.95 (ISBN 0-87909-349-8); pap. 8.95 (ISBN 0-8359-2976-0). Reston.

Gardner, Hope & Gunnell, Sally. Teach Me in My Way. 5.95 (ISBN 0-686-84351-7). Olympus Pub Co.

Gardner, Hope C. & Gunnell, Sally. Teach Me in My Way: A Collection for L.D.S. Children. LC 80-84147. 1980. soft cover 5.95 (ISBN 0-913420-85-9). Olympus Pub Co.

Gardner, Howard. Art, Mind, & Brain: A Cognitive Approach to Creativity. LC 82-70846. 1982. 20.00 (ISBN 0-465-00444-X). Basic.

--Artful Scribbles: The Significance of Children's Drawings. 1982. pap. 8.95 (ISBN 0-686-87008-5). Basic.

--The Arts & Human Development. LC 72-13404. (Illus.). 395p. 1973. 35.95x (ISBN 0-471-29145-5, Pub. by Wiley-Interscience). Wiley.

--Developmental Psychology: An Introduction. 2nd ed. 1982. text ed. 22.95 (ISBN 0-316-30380-1); tchrs'. manual avail. (ISBN 0-316-30386-0); students guide 7.95 (ISBN 0-316-30384-4); test bank avail. (ISBN 0-316-30385-2). Little.

--Developmental Psychology: An Introduction. 1978. text ed. 19.95 o.p. (ISBN 0-316-30373-9); study guide 7.95 o.p. (ISBN 0-316-30371-2); tchr's manual free o.p. (ISBN 0-316-30372-0); test bank avail. o.p. Little.

Gardner, J. D., ed. Highway Truck Collision Analysis. 1982. 20.00 (H00237). ASME.

Gardner, Jack I. Gambling: A Guide to Information Sources. LC 79-23797. (Sports, Games, & Pastimes Information Guide Ser.: Vol. 8). 1980. 42.00x (ISBN 0-8103-1229-8). Gale.

Gardner, James A. Legal Imperialism: American Lawyers & Foreign Aid in Latin America. 416p. 1981. 22.50 (ISBN 0-299-08130-3). U of Wis Pr.

Gardner, James B. & Adams, George R., eds. Ordinary People & Everyday Life: Perspectives on the New Social History. 1983. text ed. price not set (ISBN 0-910050-66-X). AASLH.

Gardner, James S. Physical Geography: An Introduction. (Illus.). 1977. text ed. 25.50 scp o.p. (ISBN 0-06-167411-7, HarpC); inst. manual free o.p. (ISBN 0-06-167414-1). Har-Row.

Gardner, John. Becoming a Novelist. LC 82-48662. (Becoming a... Ser.). 144p. 1983. 13.41i (ISBN 0-06-014956-6, HarpT). Har-Row.

--Best American Short Stories Nineteen Eighty-Two. 1982. 14.95 (ISBN 0-395-32207-3). HM.

--Chinese Politics & the Succession to Mao. (Illus.). 217p. 1982. text ed. 20.00x (ISBN 0-8419-0808-7); pap. text ed. 14.00x (ISBN 0-8419-0809-5). Holmes & Meier.

--Complete Works of the Gawain-Poet. LC 65-17291. (Illus.). 1965. 15.00x o.s.i. (ISBN 0-226-28329-1). U of Chicago Pr.

--For Special Services. 1982. 12.95 (ISBN 0-698-11163-X, Coward). Putnam Pub Group.

--For Special Services. (General Ser.). 355p. 1982. lib. bdg. 13.95 (ISBN 0-8161-3477-4, Large Print Bks). G K Hall.

--For Special Services. 304p. 1983. pap. 2.95 (ISBN 0-425-05860-3). Berkley Pub.

--Icebreaker. 304p. 1983. 10.95 (ISBN 0-686-43311-4). Putnam.

--The Last Trump. LC 80-16560. 256p. 1981. 11.95 o.p. (ISBN 0-07-022852-3, GB). McGraw.

--License Renewed. 256p. 1981. 9.95 (ISBN 0-399-90118-3, Marek). Putnam Pub Group.

--The Nostradamus Traitor. LC 78-60291. 1979. 8.95 o.p. (ISBN 0-385-13601-3). Doubleday.

Gardner, John, jt. auth. see White, Stephen.

Gardner, John C. The King's Indian. LC 73-22489. 1974. 12.50 o.s.i. (ISBN 0-394-49221-8). Knopf.

--On Moral Fiction. LC 77-20409. 1978. 10.95 o.s.i. (ISBN 0-465-05225-8); pap. 6.95 (ISBN 0-465-05226-6, CN-5048). Basic.

--Sir Gawain & the Green Knight Notes. (Orig.). 1967. pap. 2.75 (ISBN 0-8220-0515-8). Cliffs.

Gardner, John W. Excellence: Can We Be Equal & Excellent Too. 1971. pap. 1.95i o.p. (ISBN 0-06-080223-5, P223, PL). Har-Row.

--Self-Renewal: The Individual & the Innovative Society. 168p. 1983. pap. 4.50 (ISBN 0-393-30112-5). Norton.

Gardner, John W. & Reese, Francesca G., eds. Know or Listen to Those Who Know. 247p. 1975. 7.95 o.p. (ISBN 0-393-08735-2). Norton.

Gardner, Joseph L., ed. see Stewart, Desmond.

Gardner, Judith K. Readings in Developmental Psychology. 2nd ed. 1982. pap. text ed. 12.95 (ISBN 0-316-30382-8). Little.

Gardner, Katy, jt. auth. see Birke, Lynda.

Gardner, L. I. & Amacher, P., eds. Endocrine Aspects of Malnutrition: Marasmus, Kwashiorkor & Psychosocial Deprivation. LC 73-88110. 538p. 1973. 30.00 (ISBN 0-685-48386-X). Raven.

Gardner, Lewis, jt. auth. see Burger, John R.

Gardner, Linda. The Texas Supreme Court: An Index of Selected Sources on the Court & Its Members, 1836 to 1981. (Tarlton Law Library Legal Bibliography Ser.: No. 25). 142p. 1982. pap. 15.00 (ISBN 0-935630-08-2). U of Tex Tarlton Law Lib.

Gardner, Lloyd C. & LaFever, Walter F. Creation of the American Empire, 2 Vols. Incl. U.S. Diplomatic History to 1901. 2d ed. Vol. 1. pap. 15.50 (ISBN 0-395-30598-5); U.S. Diplomatic History Since 1893. 2d ed. Vol. 2. pap. 15.50 (ISBN 0395-30599-3). 1976. pap. HM.

Gardner, Lloyd C. & O'Neill, William L. Looking Backward: A Reintroduction to American History, 2 vols. (Illus.). 544p. 1974. Vol. 1. pap. o.p. (ISBN 0-07-022841-8, C); Vol. 2. pap. text ed. 18.95 (ISBN 0-07-022842-6). McGraw.

Gardner, Lynn, ed. see Wilson, Seth.

Gardner, M., ed. see Bombaugh, Charles C.

Gardner, Marjorie. Forbidden Reunion. (YA) 1980. 6.95 (ISBN 0-686-73926-4, Avalon). Bouregy.

Gardner, Marjorie H. A Question of Loving. 1982. pap. 6.95 (ISBN 0-686-84725-3, Avalon). Bouregy.

Gardner, Martin. Fads & Fallacies in the Name of Science. 2nd ed. Orig. Title: In the Name of Science. 1957. pap. 4.95 (ISBN 0-486-20394-8). Dover.

--Logic Machines & Diagrams. 2nd ed. LC 82-1157. xiv, 162p. 1983. lib. bdg. 16.00x (ISBN 0-226-28243-0); pap. 5.95 (ISBN 0-226-28244-9). U of Chicago Pr.

--Martin Gardner's New Mathematical Diversions from Scientific American. 1966. 9.95 o.s.i. (ISBN 0-671-45240-1). S&S.

--Mathematical Carnival: A New Round-up of Tantalizers & Puzzles from "Scientific American". 1977. 9.95 (ISBN 0-394-49406-7, Vin); pap. 4.95 (ISBN 0-394-72349-X). Random.

--New Mathematical Diversions from Scientific American. 1971. pap. 5.95 o.p. (ISBN 0-671-20913-2, Fireside). S&S.

--The Relativity Explosion: A Lucid Account of Why Quasars, Pulsars, Black Holes & the New Atomic Clocks Are Vindicating Einstein's Revolutionary Theory. LC 76-10588. 1976. pap. 4.95 (ISBN 0-394-72104-7, Vin). Random.

--Science Fiction Puzzle Tales. (Illus.). 128p. 1981. 10.95 (ISBN 0-517-54380-X, C N Potter Bks); pap. 4.95 (ISBN 0-517-54381-8, C N Potter Bks). Crown.

--Science: Good, Bad & Bogus. 432p. 1983. pap. 3.95 (ISBN 0-380-61754-4, Discus). Avon.

Gardner, N. L., jt. auth. see Setchell, W. A.

Gardner, Nord A. To Gather Stones. 1978. 5.95 o.p. (ISBN 0-533-03269-5). Vantage.

Gardner, P. Catalog of Greek Coins (in the British Museum) The Selected Kings of Syria. (Illus.). write for info. o.p. (ISBN 0-915262-86-X). S J Durst.

Gardner, Paul, jt. auth. see Woosnam, Phil.

Gardner, Percy. Samos & Samian Coins. 1983. Repr. of 1878 ed. lib. bdg. 20.00 (ISBN 0-915262-61-4). S J Durst.

Gardner, Philip. Kingsley Amis. (English Authors Ser.). 1981. lib. bdg. 12.95 (ISBN 0-8057-6809-2, Twayne). G K Hall.

--Norman Nicholson. (English Authors Ser.). 1973. lib. bdg. 14.95 (ISBN 0-8057-1418-9, Twayne). G K Hall.

Gardner, R. P. & Ely, R. L. Radioisotope Measurement Applications in Engineering. 496p. 1967. 21.50 o.p. (ISBN 0-442-35576-9, Pub. by Van Nos Reinhold). Krieger.

Gardner, Richard A. The Boys & Girls Book About One-Parent Families. LC 78-18388. 1978. 8.95 o.p. (ISBN 0-399-12181-1). Putnam Pub Group.

--Dr. Gardner's Stories About the Real World, Vol. II. (Illus.). 110p. (gr. k-6). 1983. write for info (ISBN 0-933812-05-1). Creative Therapeutics.

Gardner, Richard K. Library Collections: Their Origin, Selection, & Development. (Library Education Ser.). 384p. 1981. text ed. 24.00 (ISBN 0-07-022850-7, C). McGraw.

Gardner, Robert. This Is the Way It Works: A Collection of Machines. LC 79-7493. (Illus.). 1980. 9.95a o.p. (ISBN 0-385-14697-3); PLB 9.95a (ISBN 0-385-14698-1). Doubleday.

Gardner, Robert, jt. auth. see Flanagan, Henry E., Jr.

Gardner, Roberta A. Social Change. 1977. pap. 15.50 (ISBN 0-395-30599-3). HM.

Gardner, Robin P. & Ely, Ralph L., Jr. Radioisotope Measurement Applications in Engineering. LC 82-17126. 496p. 1983. Repr. of 1967 ed. lib. bdg. p.n.s. (ISBN 0-89874-558-6). Krieger.

Gardner, Sheldon & Stevens, Gwendolyn. The Care & Cultivation of Parents. LC 79-18566. 192p. (gr. 7 up). 1979. PLB 7.79 o.p. (ISBN 0-671-32955-3). Messner.

Gardner, Sheldon, jt. auth. see Stevens, Gwendolyn.

Gardner, Sylvana. When Sunday Comes. LC 82-10935. 46p. 1983. 14.50 (ISBN 0-7022-1822-7); pap. 7.50 (ISBN 0-7022-1832-4). U of Queensland Pr.

Gardner, Thomas J. Criminal Evidence: Principles, Cases & Readings. (Criminal Justice Ser.). (Illus.). 1978. text ed. 22.95 (ISBN 0-8299-0148-5); instrs.' maual avail. (ISBN 0-8299-0589-8). West Pub.

Gardner, Thomas J. & Manian, Victor. Criminal Law. 2nd ed. (Criminal Justice Ser.). (Illus.). 500p. 1980. text ed. 23.95 (ISBN 0-8299-0320-8). West Pub.

Gardner, Thomas J. & Victor, M. Principles & Cases of the Law of Arrest, Search, & Seizure. (Illus.). 552p. 1974. pap. text ed. 20.95 (ISBN 0-07-022837-X, G); instructor's manual 4.00 (ISBN 0-07-022838-8). McGraw.

Gardner, W. H., ed. see Hopkins, Gerard M.

Gardner, Wyland. Government Finance: National, State & Local. LC 77-3572. 1978. 23.95 (ISBN 0-13-360743-7). P-H.

Gardocki, Gloria J. Utilization of Outpatient Care Resources. Cox, Klaudia, ed. (Special Report Ser.). 60p. 1983. pap. text ed. 1.75 (ISBN 0-8406-0271-5). Natl Ctr Health Stats.

Gardon, Margarita. En Jaque El Jabonero. 80p. 1982. pap. 6.00 (ISBN 0-686-37369-3). Edit Asol.

Gardos, G., et al, eds. Biomembranes: Structures & Functions. (Proceedings). 1975. 32.75 (ISBN 0-444-10935-8). Elsevier.

Garduno, Joseph A. Memories of the Sangre De Cristo Mountains. LC 82-71884. (Illus.). 272p. (Orig.). 1982. pap. 15.95 (ISBN 0-9608806-0-7). Assoc Pubns.

Garee, Betty, ed. An Accent Guide: Going Places In Your Own Vehicle. (Illus.). 80p. (Orig.). 1982. pap. 6.50 (ISBN 0-915708-13-2). Cheever Pub.

Gareff, G. & Bassoli, F. Dizionario Italiano-Svedese, Svedese-Italiano. 442p. (Ital. & Swedish.). 1973. Leatherette 5.95 (ISBN 0-686-92541-6, M-9174). French & Eur.

Garel, Laurent, ed. see Moreau, Jean-Francois & Mazzara, Laure.

Garelick, Hemda, ed. see Feachem, Richard G. & Bradley, David J.

Gareth Jones, E. B. Recent Advances in Aquatic Mycology. LC 74-27179. 748p. 1976. 89.95 o.s.i. (ISBN 0-470-29176-1). Halsted Pr.

Garetz, Mark. Bits, Bytes & Buzzwords. 110p. (Orig.). 1983. pap. 7.95 (ISBN 0-88056-111-4). Dilithium Pr.

Garetz, Mark, jt. auth. see Libes, Sol.

Garey, John F., et al, eds. Condenser Biofouling Control. LC 79-56109. (Illus.). 526p. 1980. 49.95 (ISBN 0-250-40366-8). Ann Arbor Science.

Garff, Michael, jt. auth. see Fichtner, Hans.

Garfias, Robert. Gagaku: The Music & Dances of the Japanese Imperial Household. (Illus.). 1959. pap. 3.95 o.s.i. (ISBN 0-87830-540-8). Theatre Arts.

--Music of One Thousand Autumns: The Togaku Style of Japanese Courtly Music. LC 75-13865. 1976. 48.50x (ISBN 0-520-01977-6). U of Cal Pr.

Garfield, Brian. The Hit. 256p. 1982. pap. 2.50 o.p. (ISBN 0-505-51838-4). Tower Bks.

--The Paladin. (General Ser.). 1980. lib. bdg. 17.95 (ISBN 0-8161-3116-3, Large Print Bks). G K Hall.

--Thousand Mile War. 1975. pap. 1.95 (ISBN 0-345-24381-1). Ballantine.

--Valley of the Shadow. 176p. 1982. pap. 2.25 o.p. (ISBN 0-505-51855-4). Tower Bks.

Garfield, Brian & Hamilton, Peter. The Paladin. 1980. 12.95 o.p. (ISBN 0-671-24704-2). S&S.

Garfield, Brian, jt. auth. see Westlake, Donald E.

Garfield, Charles A. Psychosocial Care of the Dying Patient. (Illus.). 1978. text ed. 25.00 (ISBN 0-07-022860-4, HP). McGraw.

Garfield, Eugene. Citation Indexing: Its Theory & Application in Science, Technology & Humanities. LC 78-9713. (Information Science Ser.). 1979. 27.95 (ISBN 0-471-02559-3, Pub. by Wiley-Interscience). Wiley.

Garfield, Evelyn P. Julio Cortazar. LC 74-78440. (Literature and Life Ser.). 184p. 1975. 11.95 (ISBN 0-8044-2224-9). Ungar.

Garfield, James B. Follow My Leader. (Illus.). (gr. 4-7). 1957. PLB 10.95 (ISBN 0-670-32332-2). Viking Pr.

Garfield, Leon. The Confidence Man. LC 78-14770. (gr. 7 up). 1979. 10.00 o.p. (ISBN 0-670-23723-X). Viking Pr.

--The House of Cards. 304p. 1983. 12.95 (ISBN 0-312-39259-1). St Martin.

--Jack Holborn. (Windward Bks.). (gr. 7 up). 1965. 3.75 (ISBN 0-394-81323-5, BYR); PLB 5.99 (ISBN 0-394-91323-X). Random.

--King Nimrod's Tower. (Illus.). (ps-3). 1982. 10.50 (ISBN 0-688-01288-4). Morrow.

Garfield, Nancy J. & Nelson, Richard E. Career Exploration Groups: A Facilitators Guide. 48p. 1983. pap. write for info. (ISBN 0-89106-022-7, 7395). Consulting Psychol.

Garfield, Paul & Lovejoy, W. Public Utility Economics. (Illus.). 1963. text ed. 24.95 (ISBN 0-13-739367-9). P-H.

Garfield, Sol. L. Psychotherapy: An Eclectic Approach. LC 79-17724. (Personality Processes Ser.). 1980. 25.95x (ISBN 0-471-04490-3, Pub. by Wiley-Interscience). Wiley.

Garfield, Sol L. & Bergin, Allen E. Handbook of Psychotherapy & Behavior Change: An Empirical Analysis. 2nd ed. LC 78-8526. 1978. text ed. 60.95x (ISBN 0-471-29178-1). Wiley.

Garfield, Viola E., ed. Patterns of Land Utilization & Other Papers: Symposium. LC 62-6289. (American Ethnological Society Proceedings). 126p. 1961. pap. 10.00 (ISBN 0-295-73955-X). U of Wash Pr.

Garfink, Christine, jt. auth. see Pizer, Hank.

Garfinkel, Alan & Hamilton, Stanley. Designs for Foreign Language Teacher Education. LC 76-20755. (Innovations in Foreign Language Education Ser.). 1976. pap. text ed. 7.95 o.p. (ISBN 0-88377-062-8). Newbury Hse.

Garfinkel, Alan & Latorre, Guillermo. Trabajo Y Vida. 1982. pap. text ed. 7.95 (ISBN 0-88377-248-5, 184 PGS.); pap. text ed. 1.95 answer key (ISBN 0-88377-249-3, 24 PGS.); cassette 12.50 (ISBN 0-686-97271-6). Newbury Hse.

Garfinkel, Alan, et al. Modismos Al Momento. LC 76-51264. 1977. pap. text ed. 5.95 (ISBN 0-88377-070-9). Newbury Hse.

Garfinkel, Charles. Racquetball the Easy Way. LC 78-53835. (Illus., Orig.). 1978. pap. 6.95 (ISBN 0-689-70560-3). Atheneum.

Garfinkel, Harold. Studies in Ethnomethodology. 1967. text ed. 23.95 (ISBN 0-13-858381-1). P-H.

Garfinkel, Irwin. Income-Tested Transfer Programs: The Case for & Against. (Institute for Research on Proverty Monograph Ser.). 537p. 1982. 49.50 (ISBN 0-12-275880-3). Acad Pr.

Garfinkel, Robert & Nemhauser, George L. Integer Programming. LC 72-3881. (Decision & Control Ser.). 528p. 1972. 39.95x (ISBN 0-471-29195-1, Pub. by Wiley-Interscience). Wiley.

Garfinkel, Robin & Rubens, Yvonne A. The NLN Pre-Nursing & Guidance Examination: A Validation Study. 46p. 1979. 3.95 (ISBN 0-686-38305-2, 17-1788). Natl League Nurse.

Garfinkle, Adam M. Western Europe's Middle East Diplomacy & the United States. LC 82-21111. (Philadelphia Policy Papers). 116p. 1983. pap. 3.95 (ISBN 0-910191-05-0). For Policy Res.

Garforth, Francis W., ed. John Locke's of the Conduct of the Understanding. LC 66-20498. 1966. text ed. 9.00 o.p. (ISBN 0-8077-1401-1); pap. text ed. 4.50x (ISBN 0-8077-1398-8). Tchrs Coll.

--John Stuart Mill on Education. LC 75-115230. 1971. text ed. 10.00 (ISBN 0-8077-1403-8); pap. 5.50x (ISBN 0-8077-1402-X). Tchrs Coll.

Garfunkle, Stanley. Developing the Advertising Plan: A Practical Guide. 126p. 1980. pap. text ed. 4.95 o.p. (ISBN 0-394-32578-8). Random.

--Developing the Marketing Plan: A Practical Guide. 126p. 1980. pap. text ed. 4.95 o.p. (ISBN 0-394-32579-6). Random.

Garg, Ganga R. Encyclopedia of Indian Literature. 550p. 1982. text ed. 40.00x (ISBN 0-391-02779-4). Humanities.

Garg, H. P. Treatise on Solar Energy: Volume 1: Fundamentals of Solar Energy. LC 81-21951. 400p. 1982. 54.95x (ISBN 0-471-10180-X, Pub. by Wiley-Interscience). Wiley.

Gargan, John. Milking Your Business For All It's Worth: Tax Saving Opportunities for Small Business. (Illus.). 137p. 1982. 16.95 (ISBN 0-13-583005-2); pap. 7.95 (ISBN 0-13-582999-2). P-H.

Gargan, William & Sharma, Sue. Find that Tune: An Index to Rock, Folk-Rock, Disco & Soul in Collections. 400p. 1983. lib. bdg. 39.95 (ISBN 0-918212-70-7). Neal-Schuman.

Garganigo, John F. Javier de Viana. (World Authors Ser.). 15.95 (ISBN 0-8057-2952-6, Twayne). G K Hall.

Gargano, James W. Critical Essays on John William De Forest. (Critical Essays on American Literature). 1981. 25.00 (ISBN 0-8161-8441-0, Twayne). G K Hall.

Gargiulo, Albert F. & Carlucci, Rocco. The Questioned Stock Manual: A Guide to Determining the True Worth of Old & Collectible Securities. (Illus.). 1979. 21.50 (ISBN 0-07-022865-5). McGraw.

Garigue, Phillip. A Bibliographical Introduction to the Study of French Canada. LC 77-11621. 1977. Repr. of 1956 ed. lib. bdg. 16.00x (ISBN 0-8371-9807-0, GABI). Greenwood.

Garin, Eugenio. Astrology in the Renaissance. Jackson, Carolyn & Allen, June, trs. from Ital. 160p. 1983. 19.50 (ISBN 0-7100-9259-8). Routledge & Kegan.

--Italian Humanism: Philosophy & Civic Life in the Renaissance. Munz, Peter, tr. from It. LC 75-35025. 227p. 1976. Repr. of 1965 ed. lib. bdg. 19.25x (ISBN 0-8371-8578-5, GAIH). Greenwood.

Garioch, Robert. Collected Poems. (Carcanet New Poetry Ser.). 208p. (Orig.). 1981. pap. write for info. o.p. (ISBN 0-85635-316-7, Pub. by Carcanet New Pr England). Humanities.

Garioch, Robert, ed. Made in Scotland. (Essays, Prose, & Scottish Literature Ser.). 1979. 6.95 o.p. (ISBN 0-85635-083-4, Pub. by Carcanet New Pr England); pap. 4.95 o.p. (ISBN 0-85635-084-2). Humanities.

Garis, Howard. Uncle Wiggily Book. (Illus.). (gr. k-3). 1961. 4.95 o.p. (G&D). Putnam Pub Group.

--Uncle Wiggily Stories. (Illus.). (gr. 1-5). 1965. 1.50 o.s.i. (ISBN 0-448-00337-6, G&D). Putnam Pub Group.

--Uncle Wiggily's Storybook. (Illus.). 256p. (gr. 3-9). Date not set. price not set (ISBN 0-448-40090-1, G&D). Putnam Pub Group.

Garis, Howard R. Uncle Wiggily & His Friends. (Illus.). 98p. (ps-3). Date not set. price not set (G&D). Putnam Pub Group.

--The Uncle Wiggily Book. (Illus.). 108p. (gr. 1-7). Date not set. price not set (ISBN 0-448-02933-2, G&D). Putnam Pub Group.

Garite, Thomas, jt. auth. see Freeman, Roger.

Garitee, Jerome R. The Republic's Private Navy. 356p. 1977. 17.50 (ISBN 0-686-36493-7). Md Hist.

Garlan, Edwin N. Legal Realism & Justice. xii, 161p. 1981. Repr. of 1941 ed. lib. bdg. 20.00x (ISBN 0-8377-0614-9). Rothman.

Garlan, P. W. & Dunstan, M. Star Sight: Visions of the Future. 384p. 1977. pap. 12.95 (ISBN 0-13-840561-1). P-H.

Garlan, Patricia, jt. auth. see Dunstan, Mary J.

Garlan, Yvon. War in the Ancient World: A Social History. Finley, M. I., ed. Lloyd, Janet, tr. (Ancient Culture & Society Ser.). (Illus.). 200p. 1976. 7.95x (ISBN 0-393-05566-3). Norton.

Garland, Albert N. Infantry in Vietnam. (Vietnam Ser.: No. 1). (Illus.). 319p. 1982. Repr. of 1967 ed. 18.95x (ISBN 0-89839-065-6). Battery Pr.

Garland, D. David. Job: A Study Guide Commentary. 160p. 1971. pap. 3.95 (ISBN 0-310-24863-9). Zondervan.

Garland, Diana R. Couples Communication & Negotiation Skills. LC 77-26981. (Workshop Models for Family Life Education Ser.). 1978. plastic_comb 9.95 (ISBN 0-87304-158-5). Family Serv.

Garland, H. K. All About Prospecting: Panning, Detecting & Mining. rev. ed. (Illus.). 112p. 1981. pap. 8.00 (ISBN 0-589-50377-4, Pub. by Reed Books Australia). C E Tuttle.

Garland, Hamlin. Main-Travelled Roads. 1962. pap. 2.95 (ISBN 0-451-51734-2, CE1734, Sig Classics). NAL.

Garland, Harry. Introduction to Microprocessor System Design. (Illus.). 1979. 23.95 (ISBN 0-07-022871-X, C); pap. 16.95 (ISBN 0-07-022870-1). McGraw.

Garland, Henry B. Schiller. LC 76-39809. (Illus.). 1977. Repr. of 1949 ed. lib. bdg. 21.00x (ISBN 0-8371-9084-3, GASC). Greenwood.

Garland, Hugh. Life of John Randolph of Roanoke, 2 Vols. 11th ed. LC 68-24977. (American Biography Ser., No. 32). 1969. Repr. of 1856 ed. Set. lib. bdg. 79.95x (ISBN 0-8383-0159-2). Haskell.

Garland, Hugh A. Life of John Randolph of Roanoke. 11th ed. LC 68-57603. (Illus.). 1969. Repr. of 1856 ed. lib. bdg. 22.75x o.p. (ISBN 0-8371-1971-5, GAJR). Greenwood.

Garland, James A. The Private Stable. 50.00 o.p. (ISBN 0-88427-018-1). Green Hill.

Garland, Jim. Welcome the Traveler Home: Jim Garland's Story of the Kentucky Mountains. Ardery, Julia S., ed. LC 80-50564. 248p. 1983. 18.50 (ISBN 0-8131-1432-2). U Pr of Ky.

Garland, John S. Financing Foreign Trade in Eastern Europe: Problems of Bilateralism & Currency Inconvertibility. LC 76-24351. 1977. text ed. 27.95 o.p. (ISBN 0-275-23800-8). Praeger.

Garland, LaRetta & Bush, Carol. Coping Behavior. 1982. text ed. 13.95 (ISBN 0-87909-088-X); pap. text ed. 11.95 (ISBN 0-87909-089-8). Reston.

Garland, Martha M. Cambridge Before Darwin. LC 80-40327. 224p. 1980. 37.50 (ISBN 0-521-23319-4). Cambridge U Pr.

Garland, Nicholas. Buy Back the Dawn. 288p. 1980. 11.95 (ISBN 0-399-90087-X, Marek). Putnam Pub Group.

Garland, Paul G. American-Brazilian Private International Law. LC 59-8602. (Bilateral Studies in Private International Law: No. 9). 125p. 1959. 15.00 (ISBN 0-379-11409-7). Oceana.

Garland, Rosemary, ed. My Bedtime Book of Two-Minute Stories. LC 76-96773. (Illus.). 128p. (gr. k-2). 1976. 5.95 (ISBN 0-448-01873-X, G&D). Putnam Pub Group.

Garland, Sarah. Rose, the Bath & the Merboy. (Illus.). 32p. (ps-5). 6.95 o.p. (ISBN 0-571-09581-X). Faber & Faber.

Garland, William S. Earthquake New England: Learning to Live in a Seismic Zone. (Illus.). 64p. (Orig.). 1982. write for info. (ISBN 0-943440-00-9); pap. 6.95 (ISBN 0-686-99300-4). Home-Science.

Garlick, Kenneth, et al, eds. see Farington, Joseph.

Garlick, R. C., Jr. & Guidi, Angelo F. Italy & the Italians in Washington's Time. 132p. 1933. 6.50x o.p. (ISBN 0-913298-46-8). S F Vanni.

Garliner, Daniel. Myofunctional Therapy. LC 75-14781. (Illus.). 450p. 1976. text ed. 39.00 o.p. (ISBN 0-7216-4055-9). Saunders.

Garling, D. J. H., tr. see Koethe, G.

Garlock, Dorothy. A Love For All Time. (Loveswept Ser.: No. 6). 1983. pap. 1.95 (ISBN 0-686-43207-X). Bantam.

Garlow, James L. LITE Manual. 1982. pap. 6.95 o.p. (ISBN 0-686-38408-3); Leader's Guide 14.95 o.p. Beacon Hill.

Garman, Douglas, tr. see Flaubert, Gustave.

Garman, E. Thomas & Eckert, Sidney W. The Consumer's World: Economic Issues & Money Management. 2nd ed. (Illus.). 1979. pap. 20.00 (ISBN 0-07-022878-7); instructor's manual 7.85 (ISBN 0-07-022880-9); Practicum 8.95 (ISBN 0-07-022879-5). McGraw.

Garman, Michael, jt. ed. see Fletcher, Paul.

Garmey, Jane. Great British Cooking: A Well Kept Secret. LC 81-40247. (Illus.). 215p. 1981. 15.50 (ISBN 0-394-50876-9). Random.

Garmezy, Norman & Rutter, Michael, eds. Stress, Coping, & Development in Children. (Illus.). 384p. 1983. 24.95 (ISBN 0-07-022886-8, P&RB). McGraw.

Garmire, Bernard L., ed. Local Government Police Management. LC 77-3926. (Municipal Management Ser). (Illus.). 1977. text ed. 34.00 (ISBN 0-87326-016-3). Intl City Mgt.

Garmire, E., et al. Integrated Optics. LC 75-14482. (Topics in Applied Physics Ser.: Vol. 7). (Illus.). 330p. 1975. 41.60 o.p. (ISBN 0-387-07297-7). Springer-Verlag.

Garmon, Gerald R. John Reuben Thompson. (United States Authors Ser.: No. 346). 1979. lib. bdg. 13.95 o.p. (ISBN 0-8057-7284-7, Twayne). G K Hall.

Garmonsway. Anglo-Saxon Chronicle. Ingram, James, tr. 1978. 9.95x (ISBN 0-460-10624-4, Evman); pap. 3.50x (ISBN 0-460-11624-X, Evman). Biblio Dist.

Garms, Walter I., et al. School Finance: The Economics & Politics of Public Education. (Illus.). 1978. text ed. 24.95 (ISBN 0-13-793315-0). P-H.

Garn, Harvey A., et al. Evaluating Community Development Corporations. (An Institute Paper). 148p. 1976. pap. 4.50 o.p. (ISBN 0-685-99537-2, 13900). Urban Inst.

Garn, Paul, jt. auth. see Schwenker, Robert F., Jr.

Garn, Paul D., jt. ed. see Kambe, H.

Garn, Stanley M., ed. Culture & the Direction of Human Evolution. LC 64-16088. (Publications on Human Evolution Ser). 1964. 5.95x o.p. (ISBN 0-8143-1230-6). Wayne St U Pr.

Garnel, Donald. The Rise of Teamster Power in the West. 1971. 36.50x (ISBN 0-520-01733-1). U of Cal Pr.

Garner, Alan. The Aimer Gate. LC 78-20964. (Illus.). (gr. 4 up). 1979. 7.95 (ISBN 0-529-05506-6, Philomel). Putnam Pub Group.

--Alan Garner's Fairy Tales of Gold. LC 80-15240. (Illus.). 200p. (gr. 5 up). 1980. 15.95 (ISBN 0-399-20759-7, Philomel). Putnam Pub Group.

--Elidor. 160p. 1981. pap. 1.95 (ISBN 0-345-29042-9, Del Rey). Ballantine.

--Elidor. (gr. 5 up). 1979. 9.95 o.p. (ISBN 0-399-20809-7, Philomel). Putnam Pub Group.

--Granny Reardun. LC 78-8141. (Illus.). (gr. 4 up). 1978. 7.95 (ISBN 0-529-05505-8, Philomel). Putnam Pub Group.

--The Lad of the Gad. 128p. (gr. 5 up). 1981. 9.95 (ISBN 0-399-20784-8, Philomel). Putnam Pub Group.

--The Moon of Gomrath. LC 77-16425. (gr. 5 up). 1981. 9.95 o.p. (ISBN 0-399-20808-9, Philomel). Putnam Pub Group.

--The Owl Service. LC 79-10140. 1979. 9.95 o.p. (ISBN 0-399-20805-4, Philomel). Putnam Pub Group.

--The Stone Book. LC 78-7965. (Illus.). (gr. 4 up). 1978. 7.95 (ISBN 0-529-05503-1, Philomel). Putnam Pub Group.

--Tom Fobble's Day. (Illus.). (gr. 4 up). 1979. 7.95 (ISBN 0-529-05507-4, Philomel). Putnam Pub Group.

--The Weirdstone of Brisingamen. (Illus.). (gr. 5 up). 1979. 9.95 (ISBN 0-399-20806-2, Philomel). Putnam Pub Group.

Garner, Arthur E., et al. Curriculum for Better Schools. 368p. (Orig.). 1980. pap. 14.50 (ISBN 0-8403-2192-9). Kendall-Hunt.

Garner, Barry J., jt. auth. see Taaffe, Edward J.

Garner, Dwight L. Idea to Delivery: A Handbook of Oral Communication. 3rd ed. 1979. pap. 10.95x (ISBN 0-534-00599-3). Wadsworth Pub.

Garner, Edward. Sketchbook from Hell. LC 73-86778. 1974. 8.95 (ISBN 0-87716-051-1, Pub. by Moore Pub Co). F Apple.

Garner, Irene A., jt. auth. see Fearn, Leif.

Garner, J. F. Planning Law in Western Europe. LC 74-30920. 353p. 1975. 38.50 (ISBN 0-444-10833-5, North-Holland). Elsevier.

Garner, Jewell, jt. auth. see Scott, Louise B.

Garner, John. Modern Inshore Fishing Gear. 2nd ed. 15.25 (ISBN 0-686-70987-X, FN25, FNB). Unipub.

Garner, L. E. & Young, K. P. Report of Investigations No. Eighty-Six: Environmental Geology of the Austin Area-An Aid to Urban Planning, No. 86. (Illus.). 39p. 1976. 3.00 (ISBN 0-686-36607-7). Bur Econ Geology.

Garner, Philip. Philip Garner's Better Living Catalog. (Illus.). 96p. (Orig.). 1982. pap. 6.95 (ISBN 0-933328-39-7). Delilah Bks.

Garner, Richard L. & Henderson, Donald C. Columbus & Related Family Papers, 1451-1902: An Inventory of the Boal Collection. LC 74-12303. (Penn State Studies: No. 37). 96p. 1974. pap. 4.00x (ISBN 0-271-01174-2). Pa St U Pr.

Garner, Stanton, ed. see Frederic, Harold.

Garner, Stanton, et al, eds. The Correspondence of Harold Frederic, Vol. 1. LC 76-8562. (Harold Frederic Edition Ser.). 1977. text ed. 25.00x (ISBN 0-912646-15-2). Tex Christian.

Garner, Van H. The Broken Ring: The Destruction of the California Indians. LC 80-52892. (Illus.). 1982. 10.50 (ISBN 0-87026-057-X). Westernlore.

Garner, W. Textile Laboratory Manual, 6 vols. Incl. Vol. 1. Qualitative Methods. 1966 (ISBN 0-444-19933-0); Vol. 2. Resins & Finishes. 1966 (ISBN 0-444-19932-2); Vol. 3. Detergents. 1967 (ISBN 0-444-19931-4); Vol. 4. Dyestuffs. 1967 (ISBN 0-444-19930-6); Vol. 5. Wool & Hair Fibers. 1967 (ISBN 0-444-19929-2); Vol. 6. Additional Methods. 1967 (ISBN 0-444-19928-4). Set. 80.00 (ISBN 0-444-19927-6); 17.00 ea. Elsevier.

Garner, W. R. Uncertainty & Structure as Psychological Concepts. errata, new preface ed. LC 75-14000. 380p. 1975. Repr. of 1962 ed. 16.00 o.p. (ISBN 0-88275-318-5). Krieger.

Garner, William. A Big Enough Wreath. 256p. 1975. 7.95 o.p. (ISBN 0-399-11634-6). Putnam Pub Group.

--The Mobius Trip. LC 77-17939. 1978. 8.95 o.p. (ISBN 0-399-12114-5). Putnam Pub Group.

Garner, William E., jt. ed. see Howey, Kenneth R.

Garnero, R. S., jt. auth. see Manning, W. A.

Garnett, Constance, tr. see Dostoevsky, Fyodor.

Garnett, Constance, tr. see Dostoyevsky, Fedor.

Garnett, Constance, tr. see Dostoyevsky, Fyodor.

Garnett, Constance, tr. see Tolstoy, Leo.

Garnett, Constance, et al, trs. see Chekhov, Anton.

Garnett, David, ed. The White-Garnett Letters. LC 68-27294. 1968. 15.00 (ISBN 0-670-76257-1). Viking Pr.

Garnett, E. Turgenev. LC 75-25925. (Studies in Russian Literature & Life, No. 100). 1974. lib. bdg. 33.95x (ISBN 0-8383-2011-2). Haskell.

Garnett, Eugene R., jt. auth. see Rechenbach, Charles W.

Garnett, James L. Reorganizing State Government: The Executive Branch. (Westview Special Studies in Public Policy & Public Systems Management). (Illus.). 320p. 1980. lib. bdg. 32.00 (ISBN 0-89158-835-3). Westview.

Garnett, John C., ed. The Defense of Western Europe. LC 73-88028. 250p. 1974. 22.50 (ISBN 0-312-19110-3). St Martin.

--Theories of Peace & Security: A Reader in Contemporary Strategic Thought. 1970. 20.00 (ISBN 0-312-79695-1); pap. 9.95 o.p. (ISBN 0-312-79660-9). St Martin.

Garnett, R. William Blake: Painter & Poet. LC 77-115857. (Studies in Blake, No. 3). 1970. Repr. of 1895 ed. lib. bdg. 27.95x (ISBN 0-8383-1074-5). Haskell.

Garnett, William. The Extraordinary Landscape: Aerial Photographs of America. LC 82-60887. 183p. 1982. 60.00 (ISBN 0-8212-1507-8). NYGS.

Garnick, Marc B., jt. ed. see Rieselbach, Richard E.

Garnier. MG Sports Cars. Autocar Editors, ed. LC 78-65889. 1979. 14.95 (ISBN 0-312-50156-0). St Martin.

Garnsey, Gilbert. Holding Companies & Their Published Accounts Bound with Limitations of A Balance Sheet. LC 82-48364. (Accountancy in Transition Ser.). 232p. 1982. lib. bdg. 25.00 (ISBN 0-8240-5315-X). Garland Pub.

Garnsey, Henry E., tr. see Sachs, Julius Von.

Garnsey, P. D. & Whittaker, C. R., eds. Imperialism in the Ancient World. LC 77-85699. (Cambridge Classical Studies). (Illus.). 1979. 44.50 (ISBN 0-521-21882-9). Cambridge U Pr.

Garnsey, Peter & Hopkins, Keith, eds. Trade in the Ancient Economy. LC 81-13652. 250p. 1983. text ed. 32.00x (ISBN 0-520-04803-2). U of Cal Pr.

Garny, Patricia M. Alaskan Earthquake, Nineteen Sixty-Four. (Events of Our Times Ser.: No. 11). 32p. (Orig.). (gr. 7-12). 1973. lib. bdg. 2.95 incl. catalog cards (ISBN 0-87157-712-7); pap. 1.95 vinyl laminated covers (ISBN 0-87157-212-5). SamHar Pr.

Garofalo, Raffaele. Criminology. Millar, Robert W., tr. LC 68-55771. (Criminology, Law Enforcement, & Social Problems Ser.: No. 71). 1968. Repr. of 1914 ed. 24.00x (ISBN 0-87585-012-X). Patterson Smith.

Garon, Paul. Rana Mozelle. (Illus.). 16p. 1978. pap. 2.25 (ISBN 0-941194-05-1). Black Swan Pr.

Garon, Philip A., pref. by. Zoning Law Anthology, 1979-1980, Vol. II. LC 94-77644. (National Law Anthology Ser.). 1983. text ed. 59.95 (ISBN 0-914250-20-5). Intl Lib.

Garoogian, Andrew & Garoogian, Rhoda, eds. Child Care Issues for Parents & Society: A Guide to Information Sources. LC 77-82800. (Social Issues & Social Problems Information Guide Ser.: Vol. 2). 1977. 42.00x (ISBN 0-8103-1314-6). Gale.

Garoogian, Rhoda, jt. ed. see Garoogian, Andrew.

Garoutte, Sally, ed. Uncoverings Nineteen Eithty-Two. (Research Papers of American Quilt Study Group: Vol. 3). (Illus.). 1983. pap. write for info. (ISBN 0-9606590-2-1). Am Quilt.

GARP (Global Atmospheric Research Programme), Joint Organizing Committee, 7th Session. Report. pap. 9.00 (ISBN 0-686-93930-1, W336, WMO). Unipub.

GARP (Global Atmospheric Research Programme), Joint Organizing Committee, 6th Session. Report. pap. 5.00 (ISBN 0-686-93931-X, W337, WMO). Unipub.

GARP (Global Atmospheric Research Programme), Joint Organizing Committee, 5th Session. Report. pap. 5.00 (ISBN 0-686-93932-8, W338, WMO). Unipub.

GARP Meeting of Experts for the Development of a Data Management for the FGGE. Report. (GARP Special Reports Ser.: No. 16). pap. 15.00 (ISBN 0-686-93939-5, W313, WMO). Unipub.

GARP Planning Conference. Report. (GARP Special Reports Ser.: No. 1). pap. 5.00 (ISBN 0-686-93928-X, W328, WMO). Unipub.

GARP Planning Conference on the 1st GARP Global Experiment. Report. (GARP Special Reports Ser.: No. 8). pap. 8.00 (ISBN 0-686-93938-7, W321, WMO). Unipub.

GARP Planning Meeting for the Monsoon Experiment (MONEX), 5th. Report: Pt. 2, Summer MONEX. (GARP Special Reports Ser.: No. 37). pap. 15.00 (ISBN 0-686-93927-1, W437, WMO). Unipub.
GARP Tropical Experiment Board, 1st Session. Report. (GARP Special Reports Ser.: No. 4). pap. 8.00 (ISBN 0-686-93934-4, W325, WMO). Unipub.
GARP Tropical Experiment Board, 2nd Session. Report. (GARP Special Reports Ser.: No. 5). pap. 5.00 (ISBN 0-686-93935-2, W324, WMO). Unipub.
GARP Tropical Experiment Board, 8th Session. Report. (GARP Special Reports Ser.: No. 20). pap. 15.00 (ISBN 0-686-93940-9, W310, WMO). Unipub.
GARP Tropical Experiment Council, 1st Session. Report. (GARP Special Reports Ser.: No. 3). pap. 3.00 (ISBN 0-686-93933-6, W326, WMO). Unipub.
GARP Tropical Experiment in the Atlantic, Interim Planning Group. Report. (GARP Special Reports Ser.: No. 2). pap. 2.00 (ISBN 0-686-93929-8, W327, WMO). Unipub.
Garrard & Boyd. Practical Problems in Mathematics for Electricians. LC 79-56247. 1981. pap. text ed. 7.00 (ISBN 0-8273-1277-6); instructor's guide 3.75 (ISBN 0-8273-1278-4). Delmar.
Garrard, J., et al, eds. The Middle Class in Politics. 380p. 1978. text ed. 29.00x (ISBN 0-566-00225-6). Gower Pub Ltd.
Garrard, John. Mikhail Lermontov. (World Authors Ser.). 1982. lib. bdg. 15.95 (ISBN 0-8057-6514-X, Twayne). G K Hall.
Garrard, Lewis. Wah-To-Yah & the Taos Trail. (Classics of the Old West Ser.). 1982. lib. bdg. 17.28 (ISBN 0-8094-4011-3). Silver.
Garrard, Peter J. How To Paint with Oils. 64p. 1982. pap. 5.95 (ISBN 0-89586-160-7). H P Bks.
Garratt, Colin. The Last of Steam: Steam Locomotives Today. LC 82-75786. (Illus.). 128p. 1980. 24.95 (ISBN 0-8040-0754-3). Swallow.
Garratty, G., jt. auth. see Delaney, J. W.
Garraty, J. A. Perspectives on the American Past, 2 vols. 1970. combined ed. 18.95x (ISBN 0-02-340650-X); pap. 12.95x ea. Vol. 1 (ISBN 0-02-340670-4). Vol. 2 (ISBN 0-02-340680-1). Macmillan.
Garraty, John. New Commonwealth, 1877-1890. (New American Nations Ser). 1968. pap. 8.95xi (ISBN 0-06-131410-2, TB1410, Torch). Har-Row.
Garraty, John A. The American Nation: A History of the United States Since 1865, Vol. 2. 5th ed. 455p. 1983. pap. text ed. 18.50 scp (ISBN 0-06-042277-7, HarpC); instr's. manual avail. (ISBN 0-06-364687-0); scp stud rev. manual 8.50 (ISBN 0-06-044713-3). Har-Row.
--The American Nation: A History of the United States to 1877, Vol. 1. 5th ed. 455p. 1982. pap. text ed. 18.50 scp (ISBN 0-06-042274-2, HarpC); instr's manual avail. (ISBN 0-06-362367-6); scp stud rev. manual 8.50 (ISBN 0-06-044712-5). Har-Row.
--The American Nation: A History of the United States. 4th ed. LC 78-11617. 1979. text ed. 25.95 scp o.p. (ISBN 0-06-042269-6, HarpC); inst. manual avail. o.p. (ISBN 0-06-364694-3). Har-Row.
--Historical Viewpoints: Notable Articles from American Heritage, 2 Vols. 4th ed. 416p. 1983. Vol. 1, to 1877. pap. text ed. 11.50 scp (ISBN 0-06-042278-5, HarpC); Vol. 2, since 1865. pap. text ed. 11.50 scp (ISBN 0-06-042279-3). Har-Row.
--A Short History of the American Nation. 3rd ed. (Illus.). 577p. 1981. pap. text ed. 16.95 scp (ISBN 0-06-042271-8, HarpC); instructor's manual avail. (ISBN 0-06-362226-2). Har-Row.
--Theodore Roosevelt, the Strenuous Life. LC 67-17820. (American Heritage Junior Library). 154p. (YA) (gr. 7 up). 1967. 12.95 o.p. (ISBN 0-06-021931-9, HarpJ). Har-Row.
--Unemployment in History: Economic Thought & Public Policy. LC 76-26227. 1979. pap. 3.95i (ISBN 0-686-82910-7, CN 667, CN). Har-Row.
--Unemployment in History: Economic Thought & Public Policy. LC 76-26227. 1979. 18.50i (ISBN 0-06-011457-6, HarpT). Har-Row.
--Woodrow Wilson: A Great Life in Brief. LC 76-54860. 1977. Repr. of 1956 ed. lib. bdg. 19.00x (ISBN 0-8371-9371-0, GAWW). Greenwood.
Garrels, Robert M. & Christ, Charles L. Solutions, Minerals & Equilibria. LC 65-12674. Orig. Title: Mineral Equilibria. 1982. Repr. of 1965 ed. 24.00x (ISBN 0-87735-333-6). Freeman C.
Garrels, Robert M. & MacKenzie, Fred T. Principles of Global Biogeochemical Cycles: Assessing Human Influences. (Illus.). 222p. Date not set. 17.50 (ISBN 0-86576-024-1). W Kaufmann. Postponed.
Garret, Maxwell R. Science-Hobby Book of Boating. rev. ed. LC 68-28032. (Science-Hobby Books). (Illus.). (gr. 5-10). 1968. PLB 4.95g (ISBN 0-8225-0554-1). Lerner Pubns.
Garret-Jones, John. Tales & Teaching of the Buddha. 1979. 18.95 (ISBN 0-04-294104-0). Allen Unwin.
Garretson, Albert H., et al, eds. The Law of International Drainage Basins. LC 67-25904. 916p. 1968. 45.00 (ISBN 0-379-00320-1). Oceana.
Garretson, R. L. Music in Childhood Education. 2nd ed. (Illus.). 336p. 1976. ref. ed. 14.95x (ISBN 0-13-606988-6); pap. text ed. 15.95x (ISBN 0-13-606970-3). P-H.
Garrett & Hirtz. Drug Fate & Metabolism, Vol. 4. 408p. 1983. price not set (ISBN 0-8247-1849-6). Dekker.
Garrett, Albert. The History of British Wood Engraving. (Illus.). 1978. text ed. 120.00x o.p. (ISBN 0-391-00574-X). Humanities.
Garrett, Alfred B., et al. Semimicro Qualitative Analysis. 3rd ed. 1966. pap. 17.50 o.p. (ISBN 0-471-00192-9). Wiley.
Garrett, E. Business Ethics. 1966. pap. text ed. 13.95 (ISBN 0-13-095844-1). P-H.
Garrett, Elisabeth D. Antiques Book of American Interiors: The Colonial & Federal Styles. (Illus.). 160p. 1980. 17.95 o.p. (ISBN 0-517-54172-6). Crown.
Garrett, Florence. More Than the Quiet Pond. 1969. 4.00 o.p. (ISBN 0-8233-0140-0). Golden Quill.
Garrett, Garet. Where the Money Grows. 1966. Repr. of 1911 ed. flexible cover 3.00 (ISBN 0-87034-024-7). Fraser Pub Co.
Garrett, Henry E. Statistics in Psychology & Education. LC 82-15599. xii, 491p. 1982. Repr. of 1966 ed. lib. bdg. 45.00x (ISBN 0-313-23653-4, GAST). Greenwood.
Garrett, J. R., et al, eds. Histochemistry of Secretory Processes. 1977. 46.00x (ISBN 0-412-14870-6, Pub. by Chapman & Hall). Methuen Inc.
Garrett, James L., Jr. & Hinson, E. Glenn. Are Southern Baptists Evangelical. 208p. 1983. 14.95 (ISBN 0-86554-033-0). Mercer Univ Pr.
Garrett, Jane. The Triumphs of Providence. (Illus.). 250p. 1981. 24.95 (ISBN 0-521-23346-1). Cambridge U Pr.
Garrett, John, jt. auth. see Calder, Julian.
Garrett, Leonard J. & Silver, Milton. Production Management Analysis. 2nd ed. LC 73-7831. (Harbrace Business & Economics Ser.). 721p. 1973. text ed. 23.95 o.p. (ISBN 0-15-571991-2, HC); solutions manual avail. o.p. (ISBN 0-15-571992-0, HC). HarBraceJ.
Garrett, M. see Mehler, Jacques & Walker, Edward.
Garrett, Patrick. Analog I-O Design: Acquisition, Conversion, Recovery. (Illus.). 1981. text ed. 25.95 (ISBN 0-8359-0208-0); solutions manual o.p. avail. (ISBN 0-8359-0209-9). Reston.
Garrett, Patrick H. Analog Systems for Microprocessors & Minicomputers. (Illus.). 1978. 26.95 (ISBN 0-87909-035-9). Reston.
Garrett, Randall. Takeoff. Freas, Polly & Freas, Kelly, eds. LC 79-9140. (Illus.). 1980. pap. 5.95 (ISBN 0-915442-84-1, Starblaze). Donning Co.
--Too Many Magicians. 12.50 (ISBN 0-8398-2497-1, Gregg). G K Hall.
Garrett, Randall & Heydron, Vicki A. The Glass of Dyskornis. 144p. 1982. 2.50 (ISBN 0-553-20827-6). Bantam.
Garrett, Randall, jt. auth. see Silverberg, Robert.
Garrett, Richard. Famous Characters of the Wild West. LC 76-45855. 156p. 1977. 7.95 o.p. (ISBN 0-312-28157-9). St Martin.
--Royal Travel. (Illus.). 240p. 1983. 16.95 (ISBN 0-7137-1182-5, Pub. by Blandford Pr England). Sterling.
Garrett, S. D. Pathogenic Root-Infecting Fungi. LC 72-10024. (Illus.). 1970. 45.00 (ISBN 0-521-07786-9). Cambridge U Pr.
Garrett, Sean. The Suez Canal. Yapp, Malcolm, et al, eds. (World History Ser.). (Illus.). 32p. (gr. 10). 1980. Repr. of 1977 ed. lib. bdg. 6.95 (ISBN 0-686-59707-9); pap. text ed. 2.25 (ISBN 0-89908-205-X). Greenhaven.
Garrett, Stephen A. Ideals & Reality: An Analysis of the Debate Over Viet-Nam. LC 78-59852. 1978. pap. text ed. 11.25 (ISBN 0-8191-0555-4). U Pr of Amer.
Garrett, Thomas M. Cases in Business Ethics. 1968. pap. text ed. 14.95 (ISBN 0-13-118703-1). P-H.
Garrett, William. Charles Wentworth Dilke. (World Authors Ser.). 1982. lib. bdg. 17.95 (ISBN 0-8057-6792-4, Twayne). G K Hall.
Garrett, William R. The Early Political Caricature in America & the History of the United States. (Illus.). 1979. 51.45 (ISBN 0-89266-164-X). Am Classical Coll Pr.
Garrick, David. Journal of David Garrick Describing His Visit to France & Italy in 1763. Stone, G. W., Jr., ed. (MLA Rev. Fund Ser.: 10). 1939. pap. 10.00 (ISBN 0-527-32560-0). Kraus Repr.
Garrick, James G., jt. auth. see Foss, Merle L.
Garrigan, Timothy B. & Lopez, George A. Terrorism: A Problem of Political Violence. (CISE Learning Packages in International Studies). 40p. (Orig.). 1980. pap. text ed. 3.50x (ISBN 0-936876-36-0). Learn Res Intl Stud.
Garrigue, Jean, ed. Translations by American Poets. LC 76-86309. 371p. 1970. 15.00x (ISBN 0-8214-0062-2, 82-80687). Ohio U Pr.
Garrigue, Sheila. All the Children Were Sent Away. LC 75-33600. 192p. (gr. 3-6). 1976. 8.95 (ISBN 0-02-736630-8). Bradbury Pr.
--Between Friends. LC 77-90952. 176p. (gr. 4-7). 1978. 9.95 (ISBN 0-02-736620-0). Bradbury Pr.
Garrison, A. Joseph. Solar Projects: Working Solar Devices to Cut Out & Assemble. LC 81-5130. (Illus.). 128p. (Orig.). 1981. lib. bdg. 15.90 (ISBN 0-89471-129-6); pap. 8.95 (ISBN 0-89471-130-X). Running Pr.
Garrison, Cecil. One Thousand & One Media Ideas for the Teacher. 3rd ed. 1977. pap. text ed. 6.95x (ISBN 0-8211-0601-5). McCutchan.
Garrison, Charles E. On Being a Person in a World of Groups. LC 81-40113. 190p. (Orig.). 1981. pap. text ed. 9.50 (ISBN 0-8191-1693-9). U Pr of Amer.
Garrison, Christian. The Dream Eater. LC 78-55213. (Illus.). 32p. (ps-2). 1978. 10.95 (ISBN 0-02-736600-6). Bradbury Pr.
--Little Pieces of the West Wind. LC 75-887. (Illus.). 32p. (ps-3). 1975. 9.95 (ISBN 0-02-736610-3). Bradbury Pr.
--Paragon Man. 192p. (Orig.). 1981. pap. 2.25 o.p. (ISBN 0-380-78972-8, 78972). Avon.
--Snakedoctor. 1980. pap. 1.95 o.p. (ISBN 0-380-76232-3, 76232). Avon.
Garrison, Clay, ed. see Johnson, Paul R. & Eaves, Thomas F.
Garrison, David, tr. see Aleixandre, Vicente.
Garrison, Ernest R. The Art & Science of Breeding Dogs. 1979. 41.75 (ISBN 0-89266-163-1). Am Classical Coll Pr.
Garrison, Gene. Wedgewood. (Illus.). 48p. 1982. 24.00 (ISBN 0-88014-061-5). Mosaic Pr OH.
Garrison, George P. Westward Extension, Eighteen Forty One-Eighteen Fifty. Repr. of 1906 ed. lib. bdg. 15.00x o.p. (ISBN 0-8371-0997-3, GAWE). Greenwood.
Garrison, Guy, ed. Total Community Library Service. LC 73-4310. 1973. pap. 6.00 (ISBN 0-8389-0149-2). ALA.
Garrison, James. The Darkness of God: Theology After Hiroshima. 208p. 1983. pap. 6.95 (ISBN 0-8028-1956-7). Eerdmans.
Garrison, James D. Dryden & the Tradition of Panegyric. LC 73-91676. 1975. 23.50x (ISBN 0-520-02682-9). U of Cal Pr.
Garrison, Joe & Fletcher, David E. Management & Achievement Training for Oil & Gas Personnel. 1982. 35.00 (ISBN 0-89419-188-8). Inst Energy.
Garrison, John P. Applied Speech Communication. 1979. pap. text ed. 6.95 (ISBN 0-8403-2129-5). Kendall-Hunt.
Garrison, Julie. Democracy in the U. S. A. (Social Studies). 24p. (gr. 6-9). 1980. wkbk. 5.00 (ISBN 0-8209-0246-2, SS-13). ESP.
Garrison, Karl C. Psychology of Adolescence. 7th ed. 448p. 1975. 23.95 (ISBN 0-13-734996-3). P-H.
Garrison, Linda & Read, Ann K. Fitness for Every Body. LC 79-91831. (Illus.). 138p. 1980. pap. 4.95 (ISBN 0-87484-444-4). Mayfield Pub.
Garrison, Omar. Dicto Crats, Our Unelected Rulers. 1.25x o.p. (ISBN 0-686-29926-4). Cancer Control Soc.
--Tantra: The Yoga of Sex. 1983. 14.95 (ISBN 0-517-54947-6); pap. 7.95 (ISBN 0-517-54947-6). Crown.
Garrison, Paul. How the Air Traffic Control System Works. (Illus.). 1979. 8.95 (ISBN 0-8306-9798-5); pap. 5.95 o.p. (ISBN 0-8306-2262-4, 2262). TAB Bks.
--How to Select & Use Computers in Real Estate. (User-Friendly Computer Books). 159p. 1982. pap. 14.95 (ISBN 0-943628-01-6). East Palace.
--Investing in Oil in the Eighties. 176p. 1981. 32.95x (ISBN 0-87814-151-0). Pennwell Pub.
Garrison, Peter. Homebuilt Airplanes: Build One Yourself & Fly Away in It. LC 79-17448. (Illus., Orig.). 1979. pap. 8.95 (ISBN 0-87701-149-4, Prism Editions). Chronicle Bks.
Garrison, Robert. Nutrition Desk Reference Book. 1983. 25.00 (ISBN 0-87983-328-9). Keats.
Garrison, Robert, Jr. Lysine, Tryptophan & Other Amino Acids. Passwater, Richard A. & Mindell, Earl R., eds. (Good Health Guide Ser.). 32p. (Orig.). 1982. pap. 1.45 (ISBN 0-87983-268-1). Keats.
Garrison, V., jt. auth. see Crapanzano, V.
Garrison, Webb. Oglethorpe's Folly: The Birth of Georgia. (Illus.). 1982. 14.95 (ISBN 0-932298-30-3). Copple Hse.
--Strange Facts About the Bible. 1976. pap. 1.95 o.s.i. (ISBN 0-89129-174-1). Jove Pubns.
Garrison, William L., et al. Studies of Highway Development & Geographic Change. (Illus.). Repr. of 1959 ed. lib. bdg. 20.75x (ISBN 0-8371-2096-9, SHD). Greenwood.
Garrison, William N., jt. auth. see Henrichsen, Walter A.
Garrison, Winfred E. March of Faith: The Story of Religion in America Since 1865. LC 79-138112. 1971. Repr. of 1933 ed. lib. bdg. 17.00x (ISBN 0-8371-5688-2, GAMF). Greenwood.
Garritson, Mervin, jt. ed. see Caccamise, Frank.
Garrity, Devin A., ed. Forty-Four Irish Short Stories: An Anthology of Irish Short Fiction from Yeats to Frank O'Connor. 1980. 10.95 (ISBN 0-517-34295-2). Devin.
--New Irish Poets. (Illus.). 8.50 (ISBN 0-8159-6302-5). Devin.
Garrity, John. The George Brett Story. 256p. 1981. 12.95 (ISBN 0-698-11094-3, Coward). Putnam Pub Group.
Garrod, Claude, jt. auth. see Hurley, James P.
Garrod, D. J., ed. see Zoological Society of London - 29th Symposium.
Garrod, D. R. Cellular Development. 1973. pap. 6.50x (ISBN 0-412-11410-0, Pub. by Chapman Hall). Methuen Inc.
Garrod, D. R., ed. Specificity & Embryological Interactions. (Receptors & Recognition Series B.: Vol. 4). 1978. 49.95x (ISBN 0-412-14420-4, Pub. by Chapman & Hall). Methuen Inc.
Garrod, H. W., ed. see Horace.
Garrod, Heathcote W., ed. see Keats, John.
Garrod, J. W., ed. Testing for Toxicity. 365p. 1981. 90.00x (ISBN 0-85066-218-4, Pub. by Taylor & Francis). State Mutual Bk.
Garrod, R. P., jt. auth. see Barrett, W. H.
Garrod, S. C., jt. auth. see Sanford, A. J.
Garrone, Gabriel-Marie. Poor in Spirit: Awaiting All from God. 1978. pap. 2.50 (ISBN 0-914544-23-3). Living Flame Pr.
Garrow, David J. The FBI & Martin Luther King, Jr. 1983. pap. 5.95 (ISBN 0-14-006486-9). Penguin.
--Protest at Selma: Martin Luther King, Jr., & the Voting Rights Act of 1965. LC 78-5593. (Illus.). 1978. 25.00 (ISBN 0-300-02247-6); pap. 8.95x (ISBN 0-300-02498-3). Yale U Pr.
Garrow, Simon. The Amazing Adventures of Dan the Pawn. (Illus.). 1983. 7.25 (ISBN 0-671-46193-1). S&S.
Garside, Charles, Jr. Zwingli & the Arts. (Music Ser.). xiv, 190p. 1981. Repr. of 1966 ed. lib. bdg. 22.50 (ISBN 0-306-76018-5). Da Capo.
Garsoian, Nina & Mathews, Thomas, eds. East of Byzantium: Syria & Armenia in the Formative Period. LC 82-9665. (Dumbarton Oaks Symposium). (Illus.). 266p. 1982. 35.00x (ISBN 0-88402-104-1). Dumbarton Oaks.
Garsoian, Nina G., ed. see Faustos of Buzand.
Garson, jt. auth. see Stewart.
Garson, Arthur, Jr. The Electrocardiogram in Infants & Children: A Systematic Approach. (Illus.). 250p. 1983. text ed. price not set (ISBN 0-8121-0872-8). Lea & Febiger.
Garson, David. Power & Politics in the United States: A Political Economy Approach. 1977. pap. text ed. 8.95x (ISBN 0-669-92742-2). Heath.
Garson, Helen S. Truman Capote. LC 80-5336. (Literature and Life Ser.). (Illus.). 160p. 1980. 11.95 (ISBN 0-8044-2229-X); pap. 4.95 (ISBN 0-8044-6172-4). Ungar.
Garst, T. E. & Stephen, B. Change & Challenge. (Third Miracle Ser). 1972. 6.52 o.p. (ISBN 0-07-090691-2, W). McGraw.
Garst, Thomas E. Written Word. (The Third Miracle Ser). 1972. 4.48 o.p. (ISBN 0-07-090688-2, W). McGraw.
Garstang, B. M., jt. auth. see Bradshaw, M. E.
Garstein, Abe S. The How-to Handbook of Carpets. 400p. 1982. pap. text ed. 10.95 (ISBN 0-442-22998-4). Van Nos Reinhold.
Gart, Alan. The Insider's Guide to the Financial Services Revolution. (Illus.). 192p. 1983. 24.95 (ISBN 0-07-022891-4, P&RB). McGraw.
Gartenberg, Morris, jt. auth. see Gambino, Anthony J.
Gartenhaus, Jacob. Traitor? LC 80-20036. 298p. 1980. pap. 5.95 o.p. (ISBN 0-8407-5740-9). Nelson.
Garthoff, Raymond L. Soviet Strategy in the Nuclear Age. LC 74-10015. 283p. 1974. Repr. of 1958 ed. lib. bdg. 17.50x (ISBN 0-8371-7658-1, GASS). Greenwood.
Garthwiate, Elloyse M., jt. auth. see Bell, Laurel.
Gartland, John J. Fundamentals of Orthopaedics. 3rd ed. LC 74-4563. (Illus.). 487p. 1979. text ed. 27.50 (ISBN 0-7216-4046-X). Saunders.
Gartmann, H. DeLaval Engineering Handbook. 3rd ed. 1970. 32.95 (ISBN 0-07-022908-2, P&RB). McGraw.
Gartner, Alan & Riessman, Frank, eds. The Self-Help Revolution. (Community Psychology Ser.: Vol. 10). 204p. 1983. 29.95 (ISBN 0-89885-070-3). Human Sci Pr.
Gartner, Alan, et al, eds. What Reagan Is Doing to Us. LC 82-47559. 307p. (Orig.). 1982. pap. 3.37i (ISBN 0-06-080599-4, P-596, PL). Har-Row.
--A Full Employment program for the Nineteen Seventies. LC 75-36408. (Praeger Special Studies Ser.). 160p. 1976. 14.95 o.p. (ISBN 0-275-22810-X). Praeger.
Gartner, Carol B. Rachel Carson. LC 82-40285. (Literature & Life Ser.). 200p. 1983. 11.95 (ISBN 0-8044-5425-6); pap. 5.95 (ISBN 0-8044-6143-0). Ungar.
Gartner, Chloe. Still Falls the Rain. (Orig.). 1983. pap. 3.95 (ISBN 0-440-18329-4). Dell.
Gartner, Leslie P. Essentials of Oral Histology & Embryology. LC 82-90755. (Illus.). 120p. 1982. pap. text ed. 8.75 (ISBN 0-910841-00-4). Jen Hse Pub Co.
Gartner, Lloyd P., ed. Jewish Education in the United States. LC 73-112708. 1970. text ed. 10.00 (ISBN 0-8077-1404-6). Tchrs Coll.
Garton, George. Colt's SAA Post-War Models. 21.95 (ISBN 0-686-43083-2). Gun Room.
Garton-Springer, J., et al. Encounters. (Main Course English Ser.: Level 1). (Orig.). 1980. pap. text ed. 8.95x o.p. (ISBN 0-435-28477-0); tchrs. bk. 17.95x o.p. (ISBN 0-435-28476-2); tapes 144.00x o.p. (ISBN 0-435-28474-6); cassettes 128.00x o.p. (ISBN 0-435-28473-8). Heinemann Ed.

Gartside, I. Model Business Letters. 3rd ed. 528p. 1981. pap. 19.95x (ISBN 0-7121-1268-5, Pub. by Macdonald & Evans England). Intl Ideas.
Gartside, L. Commerce. 576p. 1977. 29.00x (ISBN 0-7121-0349-X, Pub. by Macdonald & Evans). State Mutual Bk.
--Der Englische Geschaftsbrief. 512p. 1977. 45.00x (ISBN 0-7121-0422-4, Pub. by Macdonald & Evans). State Mutual Bk.
--English for Business Studies. 416p. 1981. 30.00x (ISBN 0-7121-0582-4, Pub. by Macdonald & Evans). State Mutual Bk.
--Modern Business Correspondence. 480p. 1979. 30.00x (ISBN 0-7121-1392-4, Pub. by Macdonald & Evans). State Mutual Bk.
Garvan, Beatrice B. & Hummel, Charles F. The Pennsylvania Germans: A Celebration of Their Arts 1683-1850. LC 82-61416. (Illus.). 200p. 1982. pap. 18.95 (ISBN 0-87633-048-0). Phila Mus Art.
Garvan, Fran J. Farmers Market Cookbook. 176p. 1982. 14.95 (ISBN 0-916782-29-8); pap. 8.95 (ISBN 0-916782-30-1). Harvard Common Pr.
Garvan, Jurga. Best Restaurants Northern New England. (Best Restaurants Ser.). (Illus.). 200p. 1982. pap. 4.95 (ISBN 0-89286-213-0). One Hund One Prods.
Garve, Andrew. Counterstroke. LC 78-378. 1978. 11.49i (ISBN 0-690-01748-0, TYC-T). T Y Crowell.
Garver, John W. China's Decision for Rapprochement With the United States, 1968-1971. (Replica Edition). 250p. 1982. lib. bdg. 20.00 (ISBN 0-86531-915-4). Westview.
Garver, Will L. Brother of the Third Degree. LC 82-82475. 384p. 1982. Repr. of 1927 ed. 13.00 (ISBN 0-89345-404-4, Spirit Fiction). Garber Comm.
Garvey, Catherine, jt. auth. see Feagans, Lynne.
Garvey, John, jt. auth. see Morriss, Frank.
Garvey, Sr. M. Patricia, tr. see Augustine, Saint.
Garvey, Marcus. Philosophy & Opinions of Marcus Garvey. Jacques-Garvey, Amy, ed. LC 69-15523. (Studies in American Negro Life Ser). 1969. pap. text ed. 8.95x (ISBN 0-689-70079-2, NL14). Atheneum.
Garvey, Mona. Library Displays. LC 79-86918. 88p. 1969. 12.00 (ISBN 0-8242-0395-X). Wilson.
--Library Public Relations. 160p. 1980. 16.00 (ISBN 0-8242-0651-7). Wilson.
Garvey, Olive W. Produce or Starve: Bringing Up America. LC 76-21117. 240p. 1976. 8.95 o.p. (ISBN 0-916054-33-0, Caroline Hse Inc); pap. 4.95 o.p. (ISBN 0-916054-34-9). Green Hill.
Garvey, William D. Communication: The Essence of Science Facilitating Information Exchange Among Librarians, Scientists, Engineers, & Students. 1979. text ed. 53.00 (ISBN 0-08-022254-4); pap. text ed. 19.50 (ISBN 0-08-023344-9). Pergamon.
Garvin, Andrew & Bermont, Hubert. How to Win with Information or Lose Without It. (Bermont Bks.). 196p. 1980. 26.00 (ISBN 0-89696-110-9, An Everest House Book). Dodd.
Garvin, Charles, et al, eds. The Work Incentive Experience. LC 77-83926. 256p. 1978. text ed. 19.50x (ISBN 0-916672-99-9). Allanheld.
Garvin, Charles D. Contemporary Group Work. (P-H Ser. in Social Work Practice). (Illus.). 304p. 1981. text ed. 22.95 (ISBN 0-13-170233-5). P-H.
Garvin, Harry, ed. Science & Literature. LC 81-72026. 192p. 1983. 15.00 (ISBN 0-8387-5051-6). Bucknell U Pr.
Garvin, James. Historic Portsmouth. LC 73-76394. (Illus.). 144p. 1974. pap. 6.95 o.p. (ISBN 0-912274-32-8). NH Pub Co.
Garvy, George. Debits & Clearing Statistics & Their Use. LC 82-15572. ix, 144p. 1982. Repr. of 1959 ed. lib. bdg. 22.50x (ISBN 0-313-23660-7, GADE). Greenwood.
--Deposit Velocity & Its Significance. LC 78-14435. (Illus.). 1978. Repr. of 1959 ed. lib. bdg. 15.75x (ISBN 0-313-21022-5, GADV). Greenwood.
--Money, Financial Flows & Credit in the Soviet Union. LC 76-58491. (National Bureau of Economic Research. Studies in International Economic Relations: No. 7). 240p. 1977. prof ref 27.50x (ISBN 0-88410-475-3). Ballinger Pub.
Garvy, John W., Jr. Five Phase Facial Diagnosis. Liebermann, Jeremiah, ed. (Five Phase Energetics Ser.: No. 3). (Illus., Orig.). 1982. pap. 3.00 (ISBN 0-943450-02-0). Wellbeing Bks.
--The Five Phases of Food: How To Begin. 2nd ed. Liebermann, Jeremiah, ed. (Five Phase Energetics Ser.: No. 1). (Illus.). 1982. pap. 3.00 (ISBN 0-943450-03-9). Wellbeing Bks.
--Yin & Yang: Using the Traditional Chinese Approach. Liebermann, Jeremiah, ed. (Five Phase Energetics Ser.: No. 2). (Illus.). 1982. pap. 3.00 (ISBN 0-943450-01-2). Wellbeing Bks.
Garwood, Alfred N., ed. New Jersey Economic Almanac. 300p. Date not set. pap. 29.95 (ISBN 0-686-38088-6). NJ Assocs.
--The New Jersey Municipal Data Book. 3rd ed. 608p. 1983. pap. 59.95 (ISBN 0-686-38090-8). NJ Assocs.
Garwood, Darrell. American Shadow: The Real Case Against the CIA. 257p. (Orig.). 1980. 15.00 o.p. (ISBN 0-686-72685-5); pap. 5.00 o.p. (ISBN 0-686-72686-3). Dan River Pr.
Garwood, S. Gray. Educating Young Handicapped Children. 2nd ed. 1983. write for info. (ISBN 0-89443-929-4). Aspen Systems.
Garwood, S. Gray & Fewell, Rebecca R. Educating Handicapped Infants: Issues in Development & Intervention. LC 82-16274. 549p. 1982. 28.50 (ISBN 0-89443-836-0). Aspen Systems.
Garwood, S. Gray, jt. auth. see McDavid, John W.
Gary, Carey. Great Expectations Notes. (Orig.). 1979. pap. 3.95 (ISBN 0-8220-0551-4). Cliffs.
Gary, Charles L. & Landis, Beth. Comprehensive Music Program. 12p. (Orig.). pap. 1.00 (ISBN 0-940796-01-5). Music Ed.
Gary, Charles L., ed. see Music Education National Conference.
Gary, James H., ed. Proceedings of the Fifteenth Oil Shale Symposium: Proceedings of the Fifteenth Symposium. (Illus.). 606p. 1982. pap. 23.00 (ISBN 0-918062-50-0). Colo Sch Mines.
Gary, Joseph H., ed. Proceedings of the Thirteenth Oil Shale Symposium. (Oil Shale Ser.). (Illus.). 400p. (Orig.). 1980. pap. 16.00 (ISBN 0-918062-39-X). Colo Sch Mines.
Gary, Romain. The Dance of Genghis Cohn. Sykes, Camilla, tr. from Fr. LC 81-16531. 256p. 1982. pap. 6.95 (ISBN 0-8052-0693-0). Schocken.
--King Solomon. LC 82-48681. (Bessie Bks.). 256p. 1983. 16.00 (ISBN 0-06-039019-0, HarpT). Har-Row.
Gary, Skipper. America the Beautiful. (Social Studies). 24p. (gr. 4-5). 1979. wkbk. 5.00 (ISBN 0-8209-0238-1, SS-5). ESP.
--Basic Skills Colonies Workbook. (Basic Skills Workbooks). 32p. (gr. 4-7). 1983. 0.99 (ISBN 0-8209-0541-0, SSW-5). ESP.
--The Colonies. (Social Studies). 24p. (gr. 4-6). 1977. wkbk. 5.00 (ISBN 0-8209-0241-1, SS-8). ESP.
Garza, Hedda, compiled by. The Watergate Investigation Index: Senate Select Committee Hearings & Reports on Presidential Campaign Activities. LC 82-7353. 326p. 1982. lib. bdg. 95.00 (ISBN 0-8420-2175-2). Scholarly Res Inc.
Garza, J. Sanchez. Historical Notes on Coins of the Mexican Revolution 1913-1917. (Illus.). 1983. Repr. of 1932 ed. softcover 6.00 (ISBN 0-686-80810-X). S J Durst.
Garza-Swan, Gloria, jt. auth. see Mejias, Hugo.
Garzuel, Michel, jt. auth. see Van Ginneken, Wouter.
Gasaway, E. B. Grey Wolf, Grey Sea. (War Library). 256p. 1983. pap. 2.75 (ISBN 0-345-30859-X). Ballantine.
Gascar, Pierre. Women & the Sun. Lawrence, tr. LC 76-54791. 1977. Repr. of 1964 ed. lib. bdg. 17.75x (ISBN 0-8371-9360-5, GAWS). Greenwood.
Gascoigne, Christina. The Castles of Britain. (Illus.). 224p. 1975. 15.95 o.p. (ISBN 0-399-11676-1). Putnam Pub Group.
Gascoigne, Dinah. Yuma Dental Health Program. (Illus.). 23p. (Orig.). 1982. text ed. 9.95 o.p. (ISBN 0-9608146-5-5); pap. text ed. 6.25 o.p. (ISBN 0-9608146-3-9). Western Sun Pubns.
Gascoigne, George. The Green Knight: Selected Poetry & Prose. Pooley, Roger, ed. 160p. 1982. text ed. 12.50x (ISBN 0-85635-279-9, 60959, Pub. by Carcanet New Pr England). Humanities.
--Steeleglas, Fifteen Seventy-Five & the Complaynte of Philomene Fifteen Seventy-Six. Arber, EDward, ed. Date not set. pap. 12.50 (ISBN 0-87556-496-8). Saifer.
Gascoyne, David. Collected Poems. 1983. pap. 12.95 (ISBN 0-19-211801-3). Oxford U Pr.
--A Short Survey of Surrealism. (Illus.). 176p. 1982. 8.95cancelled (ISBN 0-87286-139-2); pap. 5.95 (ISBN 0-87286-137-6). City Lights.
Gash, Jonathan. The Grail Tree. LC 79-2647. 1980. 12.45i (ISBN 0-06-011462-2, HarpT). Har-Row.
--The Judas Pair. LC 77-6889. (Harper Novel of Suspense). 1977. 12.45i (ISBN 0-06-011464-9, HarpT). Har-Row.
--The Sleepers of Erin: A Lovejoy Novel of Suspense. 1983. 13.95 (ISBN 0-525-24163-9, 01355-400). Dutton.
--The Vatican Rip. 1983. pap. 2.95 (ISBN 0-14-006431-1). Penguin.
Gasiorowicz, Cathy, jt. auth. see Gasiorowicz, Nina.
Gasiorowicz, Nina & Gasiorowicz, Cathy. The Mime Alphabet Book. LC 72-13332. (General Juvenile Bks). (Illus.). 56p. (gr. 1-5). 1973. PLB 3.95g (ISBN 0-8225-0280-1). Lerner Pubns.
Gasiorowicz, Stephen. Elementary Particle Physics. LC 66-17637. 1966. 40.95 (ISBN 0-471-29287-7). Wiley.
Gasiorowicz, Stephen G. Quantum Physics. LC 73-22376. 528p. 1974. text ed. 35.95 (ISBN 0-471-29280-X). Wiley.
Gaskell, David R. Metallurgical Thermodynamics. 2nd ed. (Materials Engineering Ser.). 560p. 1981. text ed. 38.50 (ISBN 0-07-022946-5); solutions manual 11.95 (ISBN 0-07-022947-3). McGraw.
Gaskell, Elizabeth. Cranford. 1973. pap. 2.50x (ISBN 0-460-01083-2, Evman). Biblio Dist.
--Life of Charlotte Bronte. 300p. 1983. 12.95x o.p. (ISBN 0-460-00318-6, Evman); pap. 4.95 o.p. (ISBN 0-460-01318-1). Biblio Dist.
--Ruth. 1982. pap. 4.50x (ISBN 0-460-01673-3, Evman). Biblio Dist.
--Sylvia's Lovers. 300p. 1983. pap. text ed. 4.95x (ISBN 0-460-01524-9, Pub. by Evman England). Biblio Dist.
--Wives & Daughters. 1982. pap. 4.75x (ISBN 0-460-01110-3, Evman). Biblio Dist.
Gaskell, Elizabeth C. The Life of Charlotte Bronte. (World's Classics Ser: No. 214). 1975. 16.95 (ISBN 0-19-250214-X). Oxford U Pr.
--Mary Barton. 1958. pap. 5.95 (ISBN 0-393-00245-4, Norton Lib). Norton.
Gaskell, G. A. Dictionary of All Scriptures & Myths. 1960. 15.00 o.p. (ISBN 0-517-52763-4). Crown.
Gaskell, Jane. Atlan. 1978. 8.95 o.p. (ISBN 0-312-05940-X). St Martin.
Gaskell, Philip. From Writer to Reader: Studies in Editorial Method. (Illus.). 1978. text ed. 32.50x (ISBN 0-19-818171-X). Oxford U Pr.
--Morvern Transformed. (Illus.). 300p. 1968. 37.50 o.p. (ISBN 0-521-05060-X); pap. 16.95 (ISBN 0-521-29797-4). Cambridge U Pr.
--A New Introduction to Bibliography. 1972. text ed. 18.95x (ISBN 0-19-818150-7). Oxford U Pr.
Gaskell, Ronald. Drama & Reality: The European Theatre Since Ibsen. 1972. 14.95x (ISBN 0-7100-7145-0); pap. 6.95 (ISBN 0-7100-7146-9). Routledge & Kegan.
Gaskell, T. F., jt. auth. see Bates, C. C.
Gaskill, Jack D. Linear Systems, Fourier Transforms & Optics. LC 78-1118. (Pure & Applied Optics Ser.). 1978. 39.95x (ISBN 0-471-29288-5, Pub. by Wiley-Interscience). Wiley.
Gaskill, Pamela, jt. auth. see Carroll, Robert.
Gaskin, Catherine. Family Affairs. LC 79-8832. 528p. 1980. 14.95 o.p. (ISBN 0-385-13468-1). Doubleday.
Gaspar, E. & Oncoscl, M. Radioactive Tracers in Hydrology. (Developments in Hydrology Ser.: Vol. 1). 1972. 70.25 (ISBN 0-444-40986-6). Elsevier.
Gaspar, Max R. & Barker, Wiley F. Peripheral Arterial Disease. 3rd ed. (Illus.). 528p. 1981. text ed. 42.50 (ISBN 0-7216-4054-0). Saunders.
Gaspar, Sandor. The International Trade Union Movement. 382p. 1981. 45.00x (ISBN 0-569-08699-X, Pub. by Collets). State Mutual Bk.
Gasparin, A. De see De Gasparin, A.
Gasparin, Agenor De see De Gasparin, Agenor.
Gasparini, Francesco. The Practical Harmonist at the Harpsichord. Burrows, David L., ed. Stillings, Frank S., tr. from It. (Music Reprint Ser.: 1980). (Illus.). 1980. Repr. of 1963 ed. lib. bdg. 22.50 (ISBN 0-306-76017-7). Da Capo.
Gasparini, Paolo, jt. auth. see Bayon, Damian.
Gasquet, Francis A. Henry VIII & the English Monasteries, Vol. I. LC 74-39467. 478p. Repr. of 1887 ed. text ed. 32.00x (ISBN 0-8290-0466-1). Irvington.
Gass, I. G., ed. Volcanic Processes in Ore Genesis. 188p. (Orig.). 1980. pap. text ed. 46.00x (ISBN 0-900488-33-6). IMM North Am.
Gass, Saul I. Illustrated Guide to Linear Programming. 1970. 26.95 (ISBN 0-07-022960-0, P&RB). McGraw.
--Linear Programming. 4th ed. (Illus.). 480p. 1975. 37.95 (ISBN 0-07-022968-6, P&RB). McGraw.
Gass, William. Omensetter's Luck. pap. 5.95 (ISBN 0-452-25349-7, Z5349, Plume). NAL.
--On Being Blue: A Philosophical Inquiry. LC 75-43103. 1977. pap. 5.95 (ISBN 0-87923-237-4). Godine.
--The World Within the Word. LC 79-52634. 1979. pap. 7.95 (ISBN 0-87923-298-6, Nonpareil Bks.). Godine.
Gassen, Chris, jt. auth. see Mittre, Sid.
Gassen, Hans G. & Lang, Anne, eds. Chemical & Enzymatic Synthesis of Gene Fragments: A Laboratory Manual. (Illus.). 259p. 1982. 41.10x (ISBN 0-89573-068-5). Verlag-Chemie.
Gasser, J. K., ed. Modelling Nitrogen from Farm Wastes. (Illus.). 1979. 26.75 (ISBN 0-85334-869-3, Pub. by Applied Sci England). Elsevier.
Gasser, Michael, jt. auth. see Rossi, Lee D.
Gasser, Raymond. Atlas of Human Embryos. (Illus.). 1975. text ed. 45.00 (ISBN 0-06-140870-0, Harper Medical). Lippincott.
Gassert, Carole A., jt. auth. see Burrows, Susan G.
Gasset, jt. auth. see Ortega.
Gasset, Jose Ortega Y see Ortega Y Gasset, Jose.
Gassman, H. P. Information Computer & Communications Policies for the Eighties. 1982. prepub. 40.50 (ISBN 0-444-86327-3). Elsevier.
Gassmann, Robert H. Zur Syntax Von Einbettungsstrukturen Im Klassischen Chinesisch. 227p. (Ger.). 1982. write for info. (ISBN 3-261-05002-0). P Lang Pubs.
Gassner, John & Nicholas, Dudley. Best Film Plays Nineteen Forty-Five. Kupelnick, Bruce S., ed. LC 76-52103. (Classics of Film Literature Ser.). 1978. lib. bdg. 32.00 o.s.i. (ISBN 0-8240-2876-7). Garland Pub.
Gassner, John & Nichols, Dudley. Best Film Plays, Nineteen Forty-Three to Forty-Four. LC 76-52102. (Classics of Film Literature Ser.: Vol. 11). (Illus.). 1977. Repr. of 1945 ed. lib. bdg. 32.00 o.s.i. (ISBN 0-8240-2875-9). Garland Pub.
Gassner, John, intro. by. Best American Plays. (Third Series, 1945-1951). (Illus.). 736p. 15.95 (ISBN 0-517-50950-4). Crown.
Gassner, John, ed. A Treasury of the Theatre, 3 vols. Incl. Vol. 1. From Aeschylus to Ostrovsky. 1968. o.p. (ISBN 0-671-20137-9); Vol. 2. From Ibsen to Sartre (ISBN 0-671-75610-9); Vol. 3. From Wilde to Eugene Ionesco. 1951. 24.95 ea.; Set. 74.85 (ISBN 0-671-75630-3). S&S.
Gassner, John & Quinn, Edward, eds. Reader's Encyclopedia of World Drama. LC 69-11830. (Illus.). 1969. 17.26i (ISBN 0-690-67483-X). T Y Crowell.
Gassner, Julius S., tr. see La Perouse, Comte De.
Gasster, Michael. China's Struggle to Modernize. 1972. pap. 5.95 o.p. (ISBN 0-394-31504-9). Knopf.
Gast, Robert de see DeGast, Robert.
Gast, Ross H. & Conrad, Agnes C. Don Francisco De Paula Marin: A Biography with Letters & Journal. LC 77-188980. 300p. 1973. 12.95 (ISBN 0-8248-0220-9). UH Pr.
Gasten, Ruth S., jt. auth. see Carothers, James E.
Gaster, Adrian, ed. International Authors & Writers Who's Who. 9th ed. 400p. 1982. 95.00x (ISBN 0-8103-0428-7). Gale.
--International Who's Who in Music & Musician's Directory. 9th ed. LC 73-91185. 1000p. 1980. 75.00x (ISBN 0-8103-0427-9). Gale.
Gaster, Bertha, tr. see Vanbery, Armin.
Gaster, Theodor H. Festivals of the Jewish Year. 1962. 11.00 (ISBN 0-8446-2113-7). Peter Smith.
--The Holy & the Profane: "Evolution of Jewish Folkways". rev ed. LC 80-80325. 1980. pap. 4.95 o.p. (ISBN 0-688-06795-6, Quill). Morrow.
Gaster, Theodor H., ed. see Frazer, James G.
Gaster, Theodore, ed. see Frazer, James.
Gasteyger, Curt, et al. Energy, Inflation & International Economic Relations: Atlantic Institute Studies - Two. LC 75-19764. (Special Studies). (Illus.). 256p. 1975. 27.95 o.p. (ISBN 0-275-01250-6). Praeger.
Gastil, Raymond. Cultural Regions of the United States. LC 75-8933. (Illus.). 382p. 1976. pap. 9.95 (ISBN 0-295-95651-8); 21.00 (ISBN 0-295-95426-4). U of Wash Pr.
Gastil, Raymond D. Freedom in the World: Political Rights & Civil Liberties 1982. LC 80-66430. (Freedom House Annual Ser.). (Illus.). 416p. 1982. lib. bdg. 35.00 (ISBN 0-313-23178-8, FR82). Greenwood.
Gastil, Raymond D., ed. Freedom in the World: Political Rights & Civil Liberties. LC 80-50029. 331p. (Orig.). 1980. pap. 8.95 (ISBN 0-87855-852-7). Transaction Bks.
Gastmans, R., jt. ed. see Basdevant, J. L.
Gaston, Anne M. A Study of Siva in Dance, Myth & Iconography. (Illus.). 1981. 22.50c (ISBN 0-19-561354-6). Oxford U Pr.
Gaston, Blanche P. I Like Me, Vol. I. (Continuing Ser.). (Illus.). 24p. (Orig.). 1982. 6.95x (ISBN 0-9608516-0-7); pap. 4.95x (ISBN 0-9608516-1-5). I Like Me Pubs.
Gaston, E. Thayer. Music in Therapy. (Illus.). 1968. text ed. 21.95x (ISBN 0-02-340700-X, 34070). Macmillan.
Gaston, Edwin W., Jr. Conrad Richter. (U. S. Authors Ser.: No. 81). 1965. lib. bdg. 7.95 o.p. (ISBN 0-8057-0620-8, Twayne). G K Hall.
Gaston, Georg. Karel Reisz. (Filmmakers Ser.). 1980. lib. bdg. 13.95 (ISBN 0-8057-9277-5, Twayne). G K Hall.
Gaston, Georg M. Jack Clayton: A Guide to References & Resources. 1981. lib. bdg. 25.00 (ISBN 0-8161-8524-7, Hall Reference). G K Hall.
Gaston, Jerry. The Reward System in British & American Science. LC 77-17404. (Science, Culture & Society Ser.). 1978. 34.95 (ISBN 0-471-29293-1, Pub. by Wiley-Interscience). Wiley.
Gaston, P. J. Care, Handling & Disposal of Dangerous Chemicals. rev. & enl. ed. 1970. pap. 15.00 (ISBN 0-685-11997-1). Heinman.
Gaston, Pat. Love to be Loved. 464p. (Orig.). 1982. pap. 3.50 o.s.i. (ISBN 0-8439-1141-7, Leisure Bks). Dorchester Pub Co.
Gaston, Paul L. W. D. Snodgrass. (United States Authors Ser.). 1978. lib. bdg. 13.95 (ISBN 0-8057-7242-1, Twayne). G K Hall.
Gaston, Thomas, jt. auth. see Peacock, Frederick.
Gastonguay, Alberte. La Jeune Franco-Americaine. (Novels by Franco-Americans in New England 1850-1940 Ser.). 65p. (Fr.). (gr. 10 up). 1980. pap. 4.50x (ISBN 0-911409-18-1). Natl Mat Dev.
Gaswirth, Marc, et al. Teachers' Strikes in New Jersey. LC 81-23489. (Studies in Industrial Relations & Human Resources Ser.: No. 1). 179p. 1982. pap. 10.00 (ISBN 0-8108-1569-9). Scarecrow.
Gasztold, Carmen B. De see De Gasztold, Carmen B.
Gat, Dimitri. Nevsky's Demon. 304p. 1983. pap. 2.95 (ISBN 0-380-82248-2). Avon.
Gatch, Milton McC. & Berkhout, Carl T., eds. Anglo-Saxon Scholarship: The First Three Centuries. 1982. lib. bdg. 25.00 (ISBN 0-8161-8321-X, Hall Reference). G K Hall.
Gatchel, R. J., et al. Behavioral Medicine & Clinical Psychology. (Handbook of Psychology & Health Ser.: Vol. 1). (Illus.). 560p. 1982. text ed. 49.95 (ISBN 0-89859-183-X). L Erlbaum Assocs.
Gatchel, Robert J., jt. auth. see Mears, Frederick G.
Gate, John E. & Gates, John E. Dictionary of Idioms for the Deaf. rev. ed. Makkai, Adam, ed. LC 75-40451. 1983. text ed. 14.95 (ISBN 0-8120-5418-0); pap. text ed. 9.95 (ISBN 0-8120-2347-1). Barron. Postponed.
Gateley, Wilson Y., jt. auth. see Bitter, Gary G.
Gatell, Frank O., jt. ed. see Weinstein, Allen.

Gatell, Frank O., et al. The Growth of American Politics: A Modern Reader. Incl. Vol. 1. Through Reconstruction. avail.; pap. 9.95x (ISBN 0-19-501545-2); Vol. 2. Since the Civil War. avail.; pap. 9.95x (ISBN 0-19-501547-9). 1972. Oxford U Pr.

Gatell, Frank O., et al, eds. Readings in American Political History. 1972. pap. text ed. 7.95x o.p. (ISBN 0-19-501549-5). Oxford U Pr.

Gates, Alan F. Think China. LC 79-57246. (Illus., Orig.). 1980. pap. 6.95 o.p. (ISBN 0-87808-175-5). William Carey Lib.

Gates, Arthur I., et al. Gates-Peardon-LaClair Reading Exercises, 9 booklets. 2nd ed. Incl. Read & Remember - Book A. 64p. pap. text ed. 2.95 (ISBN 0-8077-5984-8); Read & Remember - Book B. 64p. pap. text ed. 2.95 (ISBN 0-8077-5985-6); Read & Remember - Book C. 64p. pap. text ed. 2.95 (ISBN 0-8077-5986-4); Read Beyond the Lines - Book A. 64p. pap. text ed. 2.95 (ISBN 0-8077-5987-2); Read Beyond the Lines - Book B. 64p. pap. text ed. 2.95 (ISBN 0-8077-5988-0); Read Beyond the Lines - Book C. 64p. pap. text ed. 2.95 (ISBN 0-8077-5989-9); Follow Directions - Book A. 64p. pap. text ed. 2.95 (ISBN 0-8077-5990-2); Follow Directions - Book B. 64p. pap. text ed. 2.95 (ISBN 0-8077-5991-0); Follow Directions - Book C. 64p. pap. text ed. 2.95x (ISBN 0-8077-5992-9); 2.50 (ISBN 0-686-82986-7). (gr. 2-7). 1982. pap. text ed. 2.95 (ISBN 0-8077-5993-7). Tchrs Coll.

Gates, Bruce C., et al. Chemistry of Catalytic Processes. (McGraw Hill Ser. in Chemical Engineering). (Illus.). 1978. text ed. 38.95 (ISBN 0-07-022987-2, C). McGraw.

Gates, Bryan. How to Represent Your Client Before the IRS. 256p. 1982. 24.95 (ISBN 0-07-022993-7, P&RB). McGraw.

Gates, Charles. From Cremation to Inhumation: Burial Practices at Ialysos & Kameiros During the Mid-Archaic Period, ca. 625-525 B.C. (Occasional Papers: No. 11). (Illus.). 1983. pap. text ed. 9.00 (ISBN 0-917956-39-7). UCLA Arch.

Gates, David A. Seasons of the Salt Marsh. LC 74-27956. 128p. 1975. 9.95 (ISBN 0-85699-121-X). Chatham Pr.

Gates, Don. I Thought I Heard a Baby Cry. 54p. 1983. pap. 4.25 (ISBN 0-940248-13-1). Guild Pr.

Gates, Doris. Lord of the Sky: Zeus. (Greek Myths Ser.). (Illus.). (gr. 3-7). 1982. pap. 2.95 (ISBN 0-14-031532-2, Puffin). Penguin.

--The Warrior Goddess: Athena. (Greek Myths Ser.). (Illus.). (gr. 3-7). 1982. pap. 2.95 (ISBN 0-14-031530-6, Puffin). Penguin.

Gates, Elgin. Gun Digest Book of Metallic Silhouette Shooting. (Illus.). 256p. 1979. pap. 8.95 (ISBN 0-695-81273-4). DBI.

--The Gun Digest of Metallic Silhouette Shooting. (Illus.). 1979. pap. 6.95 o.s.i. (ISBN 0-695-81273-4). Follett.

Gates, Frieda. North American Indian Masks. (Illus.). 64p. 1982. 8.95 (ISBN 0-8027-6462-2); lib. bdg. 9.85 (ISBN 0-8027-6463-0). Walker & Co.

Gates, George A. Current Therapy in Otolaryngology: Head & Neck Surgery 1982-1983. 391p. 1982. text ed. 44.00 (ISBN 0-941158-00-4, D1770-7). Mosby.

Gates, Gilman C. Saybrook at the Mouth of the Connecticut River: The First One Hundred Years. 1935. 49.50x (ISBN 0-685-89040-6). Elliots Bks.

Gates, Henry L., ed. see Wilson, H. E.

Gates, Hill, jt. ed. see Ahern, Emily M.

Gates, Jean K. Guide to the Use of Books & Libraries. 3rd ed. (McGraw-Hill Series in Library Science). (Illus.). 288p. 1973. text ed. 10.95 o.p. (ISBN 0-07-022984-8, C); pap. text ed. 6.95 o.p. (ISBN 0-07-022983-X). McGraw.

--Guide to the Use of Books & Libraries. 4th ed. (Illus.). 1979. text ed. 18.95 (ISBN 0-07-022986-4, C); pap. text ed. 12.95 (ISBN 0-07-022985-6). McGraw.

--Guide to the Use of Libraries & Information Sources. 5th ed. (Illus.). 288p. 1983. text ed. 19.95x (ISBN 0-07-022990-2, C); pap. text ed. 13.50x (ISBN 0-07-022989-9). McGraw.

--Introduction to Librarianship. 2nd ed. (Library Education Ser.). (Illus.). 1977. text ed. 24.50 (ISBN 0-07-022977-5, C). McGraw.

Gates, John E., jt. auth. see Boetner, Maxine.

Gates, John E., jt. auth. see Gate, John E.

Gates, John M. Schoolbooks & Krags: The United States Army in the Philippines, 1898-1902. LC 77-140917. (Contributions in Military History: No. 3). 320p. 1973. lib. bdg. 29.95 (ISBN 0-8371-5818-4, GSK/). Greenwood.

Gates, Paul W. The Farmer's Age: Agriculture 1815-1860. LC 76-48798. (The Economic History of the United States Ser.). 1977. pap. 11.95 o.p. (ISBN 0-87332-100-6). M E Sharpe.

Gates, Samuel K. Divorce in Pennsylvania: A People's Guide. LC 74-24433. (Illus.). 128p. 1975. pap. 1.95 o.p. (ISBN 0-87387-075-1). Shumway.

Gates, Wende D., jt. auth. see Fox, Michael W.

Gatewood, Charles. Great Pictures with Your Simple Camera. LC 81-43600. (Illus.). 1982. 14.95 (ISBN 0-385-18526-X). Doubleday.

--People in Focus. (Illus.). 1977. 14.95 o.p. (ISBN 0-8174-2429-6, Amphoto); pap. 8.95 o.p. (ISBN 0-8174-2107-6). Watson-Guptill.

Gatewood, Willard B., ed. Freeman of Color: The Autobiography of Willis Augustus Hodges. LC 82-2032. (Illus.). 168p. 1982. text ed. 11.95x (ISBN 0-87049-353-1). U of Tenn Pr.

Gatfield, George. Guide to Printed Books & Manuscripts Relating to English & Foreign Heraldry & Genealogy. 1966. Repr. of 1892 ed. 45.00x (ISBN 0-8103-3121-7). Gale.

Gath, Ann, jt. auth. see Stewart, Mark A.

Gath, Dennis, et al. Child Guidance & Delinquency in a London Borough. (Maudsley Monographs: No. 24). (Illus.). 1977. text ed. 15.75x o.p. (ISBN 0-19-712146-2). Oxford U Pr.

Gathje, Curtis. The Disco Kid. LC 78-24078. (Triumph Ser.). (Illus.). (gr. 5 up). 1979. PLB 8.90 s&l (ISBN 0-531-02895-X). Watts.

Gathorne-Hardy, Edward, ed. Adult's Garden of Bloomers. 1967. pap. 1.00 o.p. (ISBN 0-685-11945-9). Heineman.

Gathorne Hardy, G. Norway. LC 75-18358. 324p. 1975. Repr. of 1925 ed. lib. bdg. 18.25x (ISBN 0-8371-8325-1, GANO). Greenwood.

Gathorne-Hardy, John. Operation Peeg. LC 74-8908. (gr. 2-5). 1974. 10.53i (ISBN 0-397-31594-5, JBL-J). Har-Row.

Gathorne-Hardy, Jonathan. The Airship Ladyship Adventure. LC 7-54218. 1977. 10.53i (ISBN 0-397-31727-1, JBL-J). Har-Row.

Gathorne-Hardy, Robert. Amalfi: Aspects of the City & Her Ancient Territories. (Illus.). 1969. 10.00 o.p. (ISBN 0-571-08576-8). Transatlantic.

Gati, Charles. Caging the Bear: Containment & the Cold War. LC 73-19522. 1974. pap. text ed. 6.95 (ISBN 0-672-61351-4). Bobbs.

Gati, Charles, ed. The Politics of Modernization in Eastern Europe: Testing the Soviet Model. LC 73-15185. (Special Studies). (Illus.). 416p. 1974. text ed. 36.95 o.p. (ISBN 0-275-09440-5). Praeger.

Gatignon, Hubert, jt. auth. see Larreche, Jean-C.

Gatje, Helmut. The Qur'an & Its Exegesis: Selected Texts with Classical & Modern Muslim Interpretations. Welch, Alford T., ed. LC 74-82847. (Islamic World Ser). 1977. 42.50x (ISBN 0-520-02833-3). U of Cal Pr.

Gatland & Jeffries. Book of the Future. (World of the Future Ser.). (gr. 5-9). 1979. 10.95 (ISBN 0-86020-290-9, Usborne-Hayes). EDC.

--Future Cities. (World of the Future Ser.). (gr. 5-9). 1979. 6.95 (ISBN 0-86020-238-0, Usborne-Hayes); PLB 9.95 (ISBN 0-88110-004-8); pap. 3.95 (ISBN 0-86020-239-9). EDC.

Gatland, Kenneth. Rockets & Space Travel. LC 78-64659. (Fact Finders Ser.). (Illus.). 1979. PLB 8.00 (ISBN 0-686-51130-1). Silver.

--The Young Scientist Book of Spaceflight. LC 78-17504. (Young Scientist Ser.). (gr. 4-5). 1978. text ed. 7.95 (ISBN 0-88436-526-3). EMC.

Gatland, Kenneth, jt. auth. see Jefferis, David.

Gatley, Richard & Koulack, David. Single Father's Handbook. LC 78-1204. 1979. pap. 5.95 o.p. (ISBN 0-385-13653-6, Anch). Doubleday.

Gatlin, Carl. Petroleum Engineering: Drilling & Well Completion. 1960. ref. ed. 36.95 (ISBN 0-13-662155-4). P-H.

Gatner, Elliott S., jt. auth. see Cordasco, Francesco.

Gatrell, Simon, ed. see Hardy, Thomas.

Gatt, Giuseppe, ed. see Gainesborough, Thomas.

Gatt, Shimon, jt. ed. see Desnick, Robert J.

Gattegno, Caleb. Words in Color. Incl. Primer 1. pap. 0.40 (ISBN 0-87825-054-9); worksheets 1.65 (ISBN 0-685-64855-9); Primer 2. pap. 0.55 (ISBN 0-87825-055-7); worksheets 1.65 (ISBN 0-685-64856-7); Primer 3. pap. 0.70 (ISBN 0-87825-056-5); worksheets 1.65 (ISBN 0-685-64857-5). 1977. pap. Ed Solutions.

Gatterdam, Ronald W., jt. auth. see Fossum, Timothy V.

Gatti de Gamond, Zoe. Pauperisme et Association. (Conditions of the 19th Century French Working Class Ser.). 176p. (Fr.). 1974. Repr. of 1847 ed. lib. bdg. 52.00x o.p. (ISBN 0-8287-0366-3, 1058). Clearwater Pub.

Gattine, M. A. & Plaisance, D. De. Relation d'un Voyage au Congo Fait les Annees 1666 et 1667. (Bibliotheque Africaine Ser.). 300p. (Fr.). 1974. Repr. of 1680 ed. lib. bdg. 79.50x o.p. (ISBN 0-8287-0367-1, 72-2135). Clearwater Pub.

Gattinoni, C. T., jt. auth. see Jones, E. Stanley.

Gatto, Joseph A. Color & Value: Design Elements. LC 74-82682. (Concepts of Design Ser.). (Illus.). 80p. (gr. 7up). 1974. 9.95 (ISBN 0-87192-065-4). Davis Mass.

--Emphasis: A Design Principle. LC 75-21112. (Concepts of Design Ser.). (Illus.). 80p. (gr. 7-12). 1975. 9.95 (ISBN 0-87192-075-1). Davis Mass.

Gatto, R. R., jt. ed. see Costa, G.

Gatton, John S., et al. The W. Hugh Peal Collection at the University of Kentucky. (The Kentucky Review Ser.: Vol. IV, No. 1). 237p. 1982. pap. text ed. 3.50 (ISBN 0-910123-00-4). U KY Lib Assocs.

Gatty, Harold. How to Find Your Way on Land & Sea: Reading Nature's Maps. (Illus.). 272p. 1983. 8.95 (ISBN 0-8289-0502-9). Greene.

Gatty, Margaret. Parables from Nature. LC 75-32180. (Classics of Children's Literature, 1621-1932: Vol. 43). (Illus.). 1977. Repr. of 1880 ed. PLB 38.00 o.s.i. (ISBN 0-8240-2292-0). Garland Pub.

Gatty, Mrs.; see Avery, Gillian.

Gatza, James, jt. auth. see Gantt, Michael D.

Gatzke, Hans W., jt. auth. see Strayer, Joseph R.

Gau, George W., jt. ed. see Goldberg, Michael A.

Gauch, Patricia L. Aaron & the Green Mountain Boys. (Break of Day Bk). (Illus.). (gr. 1-4). 1972. PLB 6.99 (ISBN 0-698-30423-3, Coward). Putnam Pub Group.

--Christina Katerina & the Box. (Illus.). 48p. 1980. pap. 2.95 (ISBN 0-698-20524-3, Coward). Putnam Pub Group.

--Christina Katerina & the First Annual Grand Ballet. (Illus.). 48p. (gr. 1-4). 1974. PLB 5.59 o.p. (ISBN 0-698-30508-6, Coward). Putnam Pub Group.

--Fridays. LC 79-17047. (gr. 7-12). 1979. 9.95 (ISBN 0-399-20703-1). Putnam Pub Group.

--The Green of Me. LC 78-6606. (gr. 6-8). 1978. 7.95 (ISBN 0-399-20647-7). Putnam Pub Group.

--The Impossible Major Rogers. LC 76-51233. (gr. 3-5). 1977. 6.95 o.p. (ISBN 0-399-20593-4). Putnam Pub Group.

--Kate Alone. 112p. (YA) (gr. 5-12). 1980. 7.95 (ISBN 0-399-20738-4). Putnam Pub Group.

--Kate Alone. (gr. 4 up). Date not set. pap. 1.95 (ISBN 0-671-43870-0). Archway.

--The Little Friar Who Flew. (Illus., Orig.). (ps-4). 1980. 7.95 o.p. (ISBN 0-399-20714-7); pap. 3.95 o.p. (ISBN 0-399-20741-4). Putnam Pub Group.

--Morelli's Game. 160p. (gr. 6 up). 1981. 9.95 (ISBN 0-399-20825-9). Putnam Pub Group.

--On to Widecombe Fair. LC 76-48151. (Illus.). (gr. k-4). 1978. 7.95 o.p. (ISBN 0-399-20563-2). Putnam Pub Group.

--This Time, Tempe Wick? LC 74-79706. (Illus.). 48p. (gr. 2-6). 1974. 6.95 (ISBN 0-698-20300-3, Coward). Putnam Pub Group.

--Thunder at Gettysburg. LC 75-7561. (Illus.). 48p. 1975. 6.95 o.p. (ISBN 0-698-20329-1, Coward). Putnam Pub Group.

Gaudeloupe Confernce by L'Institut de la Vie, et al. Methods for Detection of Environmental Agents That Produce Congenital Defects: Proceedings. Shepard, T. H., et al, eds. 1976. 38.50 (ISBN 0-444-10997-8, North-Holland). Elsevier.

Gaudin, Anthony J., jt. auth. see Jones, Kenneth C.

Gaudin, C., ed. see Bachelard, Gaston.

Gaudon, J., ed. see Hugo, Victor.

Gaudreau, Carmen. Bernard et Bridget: a la cabane a sucre. (Illus.). 40p. (Fr.). (gr. k-1). 1979. pap. text ed. 1.50x (ISBN 0-911409-00-9); of 53 2x2 slides 13.25 set (ISBN 0-686-42727-0). Natl Mat Dev.

Gaudry, Eric & Spielberger, C. D. Anxiety & Educational Achievement. (Educational Achievement Ser.). 1971. pap. 8.95x o.p. (ISBN 0-471-29290-7, Pub. by Wiley-Interscience). Wiley.

Gaudy, Anthony & Gaudy, Elizabeth. Microbiology for Environment Science Engineers. (Water Resources & Environmental Engineering Ser.). (Illus.). 704p. 1980. 37.50 (ISBN 0-07-023035-8); solutions manual 22.50 (ISBN 0-07-023036-6). McGraw.

Gaudy, Elizabeth, jt. auth. see Gaudy, Anthony.

Gaugas, Joseph M., ed. Polyamines in Biomedical Research. LC 79-40651. 474p. 1980. 94.95 (ISBN 0-471-27629-4, Pub. by Wiley-Interscience). Wiley.

Gaugh, Harry. William de Kooning. (Modern Masters Ser.). (Illus.). 128p. 1983. 24.95 (ISBN 0-89659-332-0); pap. 16.95 (ISBN 0-89659-333-9). Abbeville Pr.

Gaughan, Edward D. College Algebra. 2nd ed. LC 79-22247. 1980. text ed. 20.95 o.p. (ISBN 0-8185-0351-3). Brooks-Cole.

--Introduction to Analysis. 2nd ed. LC 75-16601. (Contemporary Undergraduate Mathematics Ser.). 1975. text ed. 25.95 (ISBN 0-8185-0172-3); instructor's manual avail. (ISBN 0-685-55262-4). Brooks-Cole.

Gauhar, Altaf. Translation from the Quran. 8.50 (ISBN 0-686-18511-0). Kazi Pubns.

Gauld. An Intro to Differential Topology. (Texts & Monographs in Pure & Applied Mathematics). 312p. 1982. 29.75 (ISBN 0-8247-1709-0). Dekker.

Gauld, Alan. Mediumship & Survival: A Century of Investigations. 288p. 1982. 40.00x (ISBN 0-434-28320-7, Pub. by Heinemann England). State Mutual Bk.

Gaulke, Earle. You Can Have a Family Where Everybody Wins: Christian Perspectives on Parent Effectiveness Training. 1977. pap. 2.95 o.p. (ISBN 0-452-25164-8, Z5164, Plume). NAL.

Gaulle, Charles De see De Gaulle, Charles.

Gault, Jan, et al. Laboratory Investigations in Zoology. 176p. 1980. pap. 9.50 (ISBN 0-8403-2261-5). Kendall-Hunt.

Gault, John C. Public Utility Regulation of an Exhaustible Resource: The Case of Natural Gas. LC 78-75016. (Outstanding Dissertations in Economics). 1980. lib. bdg. 31.00 o.s.i. (ISBN 0-8240-4051-1). Garland Pub.

Gault, Lila. The Northwest Cookbook. (Illus.). 1978. pap. 6.95 (ISBN 0-8256-3089-4, Quick Fox). Putnam Pub Group.

Gault, Lila, jt. auth. see Weiss, Jeffrey.

Gault, William C. Super Bowl Bound. LC 80-1015. (gr. 7 up). 1980. 7.95 o.p. (ISBN 0-396-07889-3). Dodd.

Gaumnitz, Jack E., jt. auth. see Dougall, Herbert E.

Gaunilon see Anselm, St.

Gaunt, Joan, jt. auth. see Lancaster, Janet.

Gaunt, Larry D. & Williams, Numan A. Commercial Liability Underwriting. 1978. write for info. o.p. (UND 63). IIA.

--Commercial Liability Underwriting. 2nd ed. LC 82-82396. 672p. 1982. text ed. 18.00 (ISBN 0-89462-013-4). IIA.

Gaunt, Leonard. La Camera De 35mm. Alvarez, Ramon, tr. from Eng. (Focalguide Ser.). 245p. (Span.). 1976. pap. 8.95 o.p. (ISBN 0-240-51095-X, Pub. by Ediciones Spain). Focal Pr.

--Cameras. (Photographer's Library). (Illus.). 1983. pap. 12.95x (ISBN 0-240-51187-5). Focal Pr.

--Canon A Series Book. (Camera Bks.). 128p. 1983. pap. 9.95 (ISBN 0-240-51183-2). Focal Pr.

--The Canon SLR Book. (Camera Bks.). (Illus.). 1978. pap. 9.95 (ISBN 0-240-51121-2). Focal Pr.

--Electronic Flash Guide. 6th ed. 1977. pap. 3.95 (ISBN 0-240-44873-1). Focal Pr.

--Film & Paper Processing. (Photographer's Library). (Illus.). 168p. 1982. pap. 12.95 (ISBN 0-240-51110-7). Focal Pr.

--Focalguide to Camera Accessories. (Focalguide Ser.). (Illus.). 216p. 1979. pap. 7.95 (ISBN 0-240-51043-7). Focal Pr.

--Focalguide to the Darkroom. (Focalguide Ser.). 174p. 1978. pap. 7.95 (ISBN 0-240-51005-4). Focal Pr.

--Focalguide to 35 Millimeter. (Focalguide Ser.). (Illus.). 1975. pap. 7.95 (ISBN 0-240-50925-0). Focal Pr.

--Focalguide to 35 Millimeter: SLR. (Focalguide Ser.). (Illus.). 1973. pap. 7.95 (ISBN 0-240-50768-1). Focal Pr.

--Lens Guide. 5th ed. 1977. pap. 3.95 (ISBN 0-240-44859-6). Focal Pr.

--Los Objectivos Guia Aficionados. Larrea, Gabriel P., tr. from Eng. (Focalguide Ser.). 263p. (Span.). 1978. pap. 8.95 o.p. (ISBN 0-240-51096-8, Pub. by Ediciones Spain). Focal Pr.

--The Olympus Book. (Camera Book Ser.). 1977. 9.95 o.p. (ISBN 0-240-51105-0); pap. 7.95 (ISBN 0-240-50942-0). Focal Pr.

--The Photoguide to 35mm. LC 75-39554. (Photoguide Ser). (Illus.). 228p. 1976. pap. 9.95 o.p. (ISBN 0-8174-2623-X, Amphoto). Watson-Guptill.

--Practical Exposure in Photography. LC 80-40793. (Practical Photography Ser.). (Illus.). 192p. 1981. 19.95 (ISBN 0-240-51058-5). Focal Pr.

--Praktica Book. 2nd ed. (Camera Book Ser.). 120p. 1979. pap. 7.95 (ISBN 0-240-51052-6). Focal Pr.

Gaunt, Leonard & Petzold, Paul. Focal Encyclopedia of Photography. 1980. desk ed. 26.95 (ISBN 0-240-50680-4); 3210-240-50631-6 65.95. Focal Pr.

Gaunt, William. The Pre-Raphaelite Dream. LC 66-14869. (Illus.). 1966. pap. 3.95 (ISBN 0-8052-0119-X). Schocken.

--Renoir. (Phaidon Color Library). (Illus.). 84p. 1983. 27.50 (ISBN 0-686-38391-5, Pub. by Salem Hse Ltd); pap. 18.95 (ISBN 0-7148-2242-6). Merrimack Bk Serv.

--The Surrealists. (Illus.). 1972. 30.00 o.p. (ISBN 0-399-11001-1). Putnam Pub Group.

--Turner. (Phaidon Color Library). (Illus.). 84p. 1983. 25.00 (ISBN 0-7148-2159-4, Pub. by Salem Hse Ltd); pap. 17.95 (ISBN 0-7148-2131-4). Merrimack Bk Serv.

Gauquelin, Michel. The Cosmic Clocks. 1982. pap. 9.95 (ISBN 0-917086-42-2, Pub. by Astro Comp Serv). Para Res.

--How Atmospheric Conditions Affect Your Health. pap. 8.95 (ISBN 0-686-36349-3). Aurora Press.

Gaur, V. P. Mahatma Gandhi: A Study of His Message of Mpm-Violence. 145p. 1977. 12.95x (ISBN 0-940500-60-4, Pub. by Sterling India). Asia Bk Corp.

Gaura Purnima dasa, ed. see Das Goswami, Satsvarupa.

Gaury, Gerald De see De Gaury, Gerald.

Gaus, Andy, tr. see Rilke, Rainer M.

Gaus, John M. & Wolcott, Leon O. Public Administration & the Department of Agriculture. LC 75-8788. (FDR & the Era of the New Deal Ser.). 1975. Repr. of 1940 ed. lib. bdg. 65.00 (ISBN 0-306-70704-7). Da Capo.

Gause, G. F. Search for New Antibiotics: Problems & Perspectives. 1960. text ed. 29.50x (ISBN 0-686-83732-0). Elliots Bks.

Gause, Lynn. Matu & Matsue. LC 73-86775. (Illus.). (gr. 4-6). 1973. 6.95 (ISBN 0-87716-048-1, Pub. by Moore Pub Co). F Apple.

Gausewitz, Richard L. Patent Pending: Today's Inventors & Their Inventions. 240p. 1982. 14.95 (ISBN 0-936602-50-3). Harbor Pub CA.

Gausewitz, Rilchard L. Patent Pending. 1983. 14.95 (ISBN 0-8159-6522-2). Devin.

Gauss, Karl F. General Investigations of Curved Surfaces. Hiltebeitel & Moorehead, trs. LC 65-6415. 1965. 10.00 (ISBN 0-911216-02-2). Raven.

Gaustad, Edwin S. A Documentary History of Religion in America Since 1865. 640p. 1983. pap. 18.95 (ISBN 0-8028-1874-9). Eerdmans.

Gaustad, Edwin S., ed. see Bowden, Henry W.

Gaustad, John E., jt. auth. see Zeilik, Michael.

Gautam, M. R. Musical Heritage of India. 138p. 1981. text ed. 34.00x (ISBN 0-391-02237-7, Pub. by Abhinav India). Humanities.

Gaute, J. H. & Odell, Robin. The Murderer's Who's Who. LC 78-64828. (Illus.). 1979. 17.95 o.p. (ISBN 0-458-93900-5). Methuen Inc.

Gautherie, Michel & Albert, Ernest, eds. Biomedical Thermology. LC 82-21639. (Progress in Clinical & Biological Research Ser.: Vol. 107). 919p. 1982. 176.00 (ISBN 0-8451-0107-2). A R Liss.

Gauthier, Bernard & Edelman, Chester M. Nephrology & Urology for the Pediatrician. (Little, Brown Clinical Pediatrics Ser.). 1982. text ed. 28.50 (ISBN 0-316-30524-3). Little.

Gauthier, Howard L., jt. auth. see Taaffe, Edward.

Gauthier, Richard. Using the Unix System. 1981. text ed. 21.95 (ISBN 0-8359-8164-9); pap. 15.95 (ISBN 0-686-82961-1). Reston.

Gauthier, Serge, jt. auth. see Preaud, Tamara.

Gauthier-Lievre, L. Oedogoniacees Africaines. (Illus.). 1964. 32.00 (ISBN 3-7682-0216-X). Lubrecht & Cramer.

--Zygnemacees Africaines. 1965. 40.00 (ISBN 3-7682-5420-8). Lubrecht & Cramer.

Gauthier-Pilters, Hilde & Dagg, Anne I. The Camel: Its Evolution, Behavior, & Relationship to Man. LC 80-23822. (Illus.). xii, 240p. 1981. pap. 8.95 (ISBN 0-226-28454-9). U of Chicago Pr.

Gautier, Judith. Richard Wagner: Rienzi to Parsifal. (Music Reprint Ser.). (Illus.). 173p. (Fr.). 1982. Repr. of 1883 ed. lib. bdg. 22.50 (ISBN 0-306-76172-6). Da Capo.

Gautreau, Ronald & Savin, William. Schaum's Outline of Modern Physics. (Schaum's Outline Ser.). (Illus.). 1978. pap. 7.95 (ISBN 0-07-023062-5, SP). McGraw.

Gautschen, Ivan. Moon Lake. Gadsby, Oliver E., tr. from Ger. (Picture Book Studio Ser). Orig. Title: Der Mondsee. (Illus.). 29p. 1981. 9.95 (ISBN 0-907234-08-9). Neugebauer Pr.

Gautschi, Marcel. Tennis: Playing, Training & Winning. LC 78-17159. 1979. 8.95 o.p. (ISBN 0-668-04692-9); pap. 4.95 o.p. (ISBN 0-668-04700-3). Arco.

Gautschi, Theodore. Management Forum, Vol.1. 2nd ed. 1982. pap. 12.95 (ISBN 0-686-83908-0). Lord Pub.

--Management Forum, Vol. 2. pap. 12.95 (ISBN 0-686-83907-2). Lord Pub.

Gauvin, Marshall. Where is Hell? 32p. 1926. pap. 1.00 (ISBN 0-686-96417-9). Am Atheist.

Gauvin, Marshall, jt. auth. see Teller, Woolsey.

Gavalas, George R. Nonlinear Differential Equations of Chemically Reacting Systems. LC 68-31619. (Springer Tracts in Natural Philosophy: Vol. 17). 1968. 24.10 o.p. (ISBN 0-387-04345-4). Springer-Verlag.

Gaver, Mary V. Services of Secondary Schools Media Centers. LC 77-165675. pap. 7.00 (ISBN 0-8389-0095-X). ALA.

Gaviglio, Glen & Raye, David E. Society As It Is: A Reader. 3rd ed. (Illus.). 1980. pap. text ed. 14.95x (ISBN 0-02-341100-7). Macmillan.

Gaviria, Maria C. de see National Library of Peru.

Gavit, J. P; see Bernard, William S.

Gavriel, Salvendy & Smith, M. J., eds. Machine Pacing & Occupational Stress. (Illus.). 374p. 1981. 42.50x (ISBN 0-85066-225-7). Intl Pubns Serv.

Gavronsky, S., jt. auth. see Blanchard, J. M.

Gavronsky, Serge, tr. Francis Ponge: The Power of Language. LC 77-71060. 1979. 24.00x (ISBN 0-520-03441-4). U of Cal Pr.

Gavronsky, Serge, tr. see Ponge, Francis.

Gavurin, Lester L., jt. auth. see Forman, William.

Gaw, Walter A. Outline of Advertising. (Quality Paperback: No. 88). (Orig.). 1969. pap. 3.50 (ISBN 0-8226-0088-9). Littlefield.

Gawain, Elizabeth. The Dolphins' Gift. Clemens, Paul, ed. LC 81-3039. (Illus.). 256p. (Orig.). 1981. pap. 7.95 (ISBN 0-931432-10-3). Whatever Pub.

Gawain, Shakti. Creative Visualization. 144p. 1982. pap. 3.50 (ISBN 0-553-22689-4). Bantam.

--The Creative Visualization Workbook. 144p. (Orig.). 1982. pap. 9.95 (ISBN 0-931432-12-X). Whatever Pub.

Gawalt, Gerald W. The Promise of Power: The Emergence of the Legal Profession in Massachusetts, 1760-1840. LC 78-57765. (Contributions in Legal Studies: No. 6). 1979. lib. bdg. 29.95x (ISBN 0-313-20612-0, GPP/). Greenwood.

Gawalt, Gerard W., jt. ed. see Smith, Paul H.

Gawel, M., jt. auth. see Rose, Clifford F.

Gawne, Eleanor & Oerke. Dress. rev. ed. 672p. (gr. 9-12). 1975. 20.96 (ISBN 0-87002-069-2). Bennett IL.

Gawne, Eleanor J. Fabrics for Clothing. (gr. 10-12). 1973. pap. text ed. 8.64 (ISBN 0-87002-149-4). Bennett IL.

Gawron, Marlene. Ten Little Bunnies. (Flannel Board Ser.). (Illus.). (ps-1). 1981. 3.50 (ISBN 0-686-38113-0). Moonlight FL.

Gawron, Marlene E. Busy Bodies: Finger Plays & Action Rhymes. (Illus.). (ps-1). 1981. 4.50 (ISBN 0-686-38123-8). Moonlight FL.

Gawronski, Donald V. History: Meaning & Method. 3rd ed. 132p. 1975. pap. 6.95x (ISBN 0-673-07968-6). Scott F.

Gawthrop, Louis C. Administrative Politics & Social Change. LC 76-145413. (American Politics Ser). 1971. pap. text ed. 7.95 o.p. (ISBN 0-312-00455-9). St Martin.

Gay, Edwin F. Facts & Factors in Economic History. LC 67-27547. Repr. of 1932 ed. 37.50x (ISBN 0-678-00309-2). Kelley.

Gay, George A., jt. auth. see Dundon, Mary L.

Gay, James & Jacobs, Barbara S., eds. The Technolgy Explosion in Medical Science: Implications for the Health Care Industry & the Public (1981-2001) (Health Care Administration Monographs: Vol. 2). 128p. 1983. text ed. 14.95 (ISBN 0-89335-181-4). SP Med & Sci Bks.

Gay, Jeanne, ed. Travel & Tourism Audiovisual Guide. 2nd ed. 1982. pap. write for info. (ISBN 0-935638-05-9). Travel & Tourism Pr.

--Travel & Tourism Personnel Directory. 2nd ed. (Orig.). 1982. pap. cancelled (ISBN 0-935638-06-7). Travel & Tourism Pr.

Gay, John. Beggar's Opera. Roberts, Edgar V., ed. LC 68-21878. (Regents Restoration Drama Ser). xxx, 238p. 1969. 17.50x (ISBN 0-8032-0362-4); pap. 5.95x (ISBN 0-8032-5361-3, BB 269, Bison). U of Nebr Pr.

--John Gay's Book of Cats. LC 74-29039. (Illus.). 96p. 1975. 7.95 o.p. (ISBN 0-399-11522-6). Putnam Pub Group.

--Selected Poems. Walsh, Marcus, ed. (Fyfield Ser.). 96p. (Orig.). 1979. pap. text ed. 5.25x (ISBN 0-85635-280-2, Pub. by Carcanet New Pr England). Humanities.

Gay, John, jt. ed see Lloyd, Barbara.

Gay, John E., jt. auth. see Bruess, Clint E.

Gay, Kathleen. Eating What Grows Naturally. LC 80-70278. (Illus.). 120p. 1980. pap. 5.95 (ISBN 0-89708-031-9). And Bks.

Gay, Kathlyn. Be a Smart Shopper. LC 74-7593. (Illus.). 64p. (gr. 4-6). 1974. PLB 6.64 o.p. (ISBN 0-671-32696-1). Messner.

--Care & Share: Teenagers & Volunteerism. LC 76-56835. (Illus.). 160p. (gr. 7 up). 1977. PLB 7.29 o.p. (ISBN 0-671-32831-X). Messner.

--Junkyards. LC 82-11614. (Illus.). 48p. (gr. 3-5). 1982. PLB 8.95 (ISBN 0-89490-082-X). Enslow Pubs.

Gay, Kathlyn & Barnes, Ben. Your Fight Has Just Begun: The Sport of Boxing. LC 79-28242. (Illus.). 192p. (gr. 7 up). 1980. PLB 8.79 o.p. (ISBN 0-671-33005-5). Messner.

Gay, Kathlyn, jt. auth. see Barnes, Ben E.

Gay, Kathlyn, et al. Get Hooked on Vegetables. LC 77-29014. 160p. (gr. 7 up). 1978. PLB 7.29 o.p. (ISBN 0-671-32885-9). Messner.

Gay, L. R. Educational Evaluation & Measurement: Competencies for Analysis & Application. (Illus.). 576p. 1980. text ed. 21.95 (ISBN 0-675-08143-2). Additional supplements may be obtained from publisher. Merrill.

--Educational Research. 2nd ed. (Illus.). 464p. 1981. text ed. 21.95 (ISBN 0-675-08021-5); student guide 5.95 (ISBN 0-675-08020-7). Additional supplements may be obtained from publisher. Merrill.

Gay, Larry. Heating the Home Water Supply: Wood, Coal, Solar. Griffith, Roger, ed. (Illus.). 128p. 1983. pap. 7.95 (ISBN 0-88266-311-9). Garden Way Pub.

Gay, Peter. Age of Enlightenment. LC 66-18266. (Great Ages of Man). (Illus.). (gr. 6 up). 1966. PLB 19.96 (ISBN 0-8094-0368-4, Pub. by Time-Life). Silver.

--The Enlightenment: An Interpretation-the Rise of Modern Paganism, Vol. 1. 1977. pap. 8.95 (ISBN 0-393-00870-3, N870, Norton Lib). Norton.

--Freud, Jews & Other Germans: Masters & Victims in Modernist Culture. 1978. 19.95x (ISBN 0-19-502258-0). Oxford U Pr.

--A Loss of Mastery: Puritan Historians in Colonial America. LC 67-10969. (Jefferson Memorial Lectures). 1966. 21.50x (ISBN 0-520-00456-6). U of Cal Pr.

Gay, Peter, ed. The Enlightenment: A Comprehensive Anthology. 1974. 7.95 o.p. (ISBN 0-671-21915-4, Touchstone Bks). S&S.

--John Locke on Education. LC 64-14307. 1964. text ed. 10.00 (ISBN 0-8077-1419-4); pap. text ed. 5.00x (ISBN 0-8077-1416-X). Tchrs Coll.

Gay, Peter, ed. see Voltaire, F. M.

Gay, R., jt. auth. see Skillin, M.

Gay, Tim, ed. Cable Contacts Yearbook, 1983. 1982. deluxe ed. 170.00 (ISBN 0-935224-16-5). Larimi Comm.

Gay, Tim & Hurvitz, David, eds. Radio Contacts. 1982. deluxe ed. 136.00 (ISBN 0-935224-17-3). Larimi Comm.

--Television Contacts. 1982. deluxe ed. 127.00 (ISBN 0-935224-18-1). Larimi Comm.

Gay, Vernon, photos by. Discovering Pittsburgh's Sculpture. LC 82-50225. (Illus.). 462p. 1982. 21.95 (ISBN 0-8229-3467-1); pap. 12.95 (ISBN 0-8229-5348-X). U of Pittsburgh Pr.

Gaydon, A. G. The Shock Tube in High Temperature Chemical Physics. 400p. 1963. 22.00 (ISBN 0-442-15491-7, Pub. by Van Nos Reinhold). Krieger.

--The Spectroscopy of Flames. 2nd ed. 1974. 43.00x (ISBN 0-412-12870-5, Pub. by Chapman & Hall). Methuen Inc.

Gaydon, A. G. & Pearse, R. W. Identification of Molecular Spectra. 4th ed. 1976. 72.00x (ISBN 0-412-14350-X, Pub. by Chapman & Hall). Methuen Inc.

Gaydon, A. G. & Wolfhard, H. G. Flames: Their Structure, Radiation & Temperature. 4th ed. 1979. 57.00x (ISBN 0-412-15390-4, Pub. by Chapman & Hall). Methuen Inc.

Gaydos, Michael. Eyes to Behold. 1980. pap. 4.95 (ISBN 0-89221-069-9). New Leaf.

Gayeski, Diane M. Corporate & Instructional Video: Design & Production. (Illus.). 304p. 1983. 21.95 (ISBN 0-13-174243-4). P-H.

Gayford, M. L. Modern Relay Techniques. (Illus.). 149p. 1975. 15.00x o.s.i. (ISBN 0-408-06843-4). Transatlantic.

Gayle, Addison, Jr., ed. Bondage, Freedom & Beyond: The Prose of Black Americans. 1971. 4.95 (ISBN 0-385-08951-1). Doubleday.

Gayle, Margaret. Precious Interlude. (Superromances Ser.). 384p. 1983. pap. 2.50 (ISBN 0-373-70052-0, Pub. by Worldwide). Harlequin Bks.

Gayley, Charles M. Classic Myths in English Literature & in Art. rev. & enlarged ed. 1939. 20.95 o.p. (ISBN 0-471-00191-0). Scott F.

--The Classic Myths in English Literature & in Art. rev. & enl. ed. 1939. text ed. 25.50x (ISBN 0-673-15673-7). Scott F.

Gayley, Henry. How to Write for Development. 50p. 1981. 14.50 (ISBN 0-89964-186-5). CASE.

Gaylin, Willard. Caring. 1976. 9.95 o.s.i. (ISBN 0-394-49785-6). Knopf.

--Feelings: Our Vital Signs. (General Ser.). 1979. lib. bdg. 14.95 (ISBN 0-8161-6767-2, Large Print Bks). G K Hall.

--The Killing of Bonnie Garland: A Question of Justice. 1982. 15.95 (ISBN 0-671-44960-5). S&S.

Gaylor, Anne N. Abortion Is a Blessing. LC 75-24775. 140p. 1976. 4.95 (ISBN 0-88437-006-2). Psych Dimensions.

Gaylor, John. Military Badge Collecting. (Illus.). 176p. 1983. 31.50 (ISBN 0-436-37705-5, Pub. by Secker & Warburg). David & Charles.

Gaylord, C. N., jt. auth. see Gaylord, E. H., Jr.

Gaylord, Charles N., jt. auth. see Gaylord, Edwin H.

Gaylord, E. H., Jr. & Gaylord, C. N. Structural Engineering Handbook. 1979. 59.00 (ISBN 0-07-023123-0). McGraw.

Gaylord, E. W., jt. auth. see Hughes, G.

Gaylord, Edwin H. & Gaylord, Charles N. Design of Steel Structures. 2nd ed. (Civil Engineering Ser.). (Illus.). 640p. 1972. text ed. 35.00 (ISBN 0-07-023110-9, C). McGraw.

Gaylord, Louise, jt. auth. see Abercrombie, V. T.

Gaylord, Norman. High Polymers Series, Vol. 13, Pt. 3. LC 62-15824. 318p. 1962. 32.00 (ISBN 0-686-81269-7). Krieger.

Gaylord, Norman G. Reduction with Complex Metal Hydrides. LC 55-8227. (Illus.). 1062p. 1956. text ed. 38.00 (ISBN 0-470-29436-1, Pub. by Wiley). Krieger.

Gaylord, Sherwood. Sensible Speculating with Put & Call Options. LC 76-16547. 1976. 8.95 o.p. (ISBN 0-671-22322-4). S&S.

Gaynes, Martin J., jt. auth. see Zuckman, Harvey L.

Gaynor, Anne. Rebel Rapture. 1983. pap. 3.50 (ISBN 0-8217-1136-9). Zebra.

Gaynor, Frank, ed. New Military & Naval Dictionary. Repr. of 1951 ed. lib. bdg. 15.75x (ISBN 0-8371-2129-9, GAMN). Greenwood.

Gaynor, Frank, tr. see Friedrich, Johannes.

Gaynor, James K. Profile of the Law. 4th ed. 160p. 1978. 7.50 (ISBN 0-87179-284-2). BNA.

Gayral, P. Les Algues des Cotes Francaises: Manche et Atlantique. (Illus.). 632p. (Orig., Fr.). 1982. pap. text ed. 36.00x (ISBN 3-87429-204-5). Lubrecht & Cramer.

Gazda, George M. Basic Approaches to Group Psychotherapy & Group Counseling. 3rd ed. (Illus.). 608p. 1982. 27.50x (ISBN 0-398-04652-2). C C Thomas.

Gazda, George M. & Corsini, Raymond J. Theories of Learning: A Comparative Approach. LC 79-91101. 483p. 1980. text ed. 18.95 (ISBN 0-87581-253-8). Peacock Pubs.

Gazda, George M., ed. Basic Approaches to Group Psychotherapy & Group Counseling. 2nd ed. (Illus.). 560p. 1979. 21.50x o.p. (ISBN 0-398-03212-2). C C Thomas.

Gazdar, Gerald, et al. A Bibliography of Contemporary Linguistic Research. LC 77-83358. (Library of Humanities Reference Bks.: No. 119). lib. bdg. 42.00 o.s.i. (ISBN 0-8240-9852-8). Garland Pub.

Gazes. Clinical Cardiology. 1983. 34.95 (ISBN 0-8151-3319-7). Year Bk Med.

Gazet, J. C. Cancer of the Liver, Biliary Tract & Pancreas. (Management of Malignant Disease Ser.). 200p. 1983. text ed. price not set (ISBN 0-7131-4333-9). E Arnold.

Gazis, Denos C. Traffic Science. LC 73-21947. 304p. 1974. 43.50x o.p. (ISBN 0-471-29480-2, Pub. by Wiley-Interscience). Wiley.

Gazzaniga, Michael S. & Blakemore, Colin, eds. Handbook of Psychobiology. 1975. 57.00 o.p. (ISBN 0-12-278656-4). Acad Pr.

Gazzo, Michael see Strasberg, Lee.

Geach, P., ed. see Prior, Arthur N.

Geach, P. T. Logic Matters. LC 72-138286. 1972. 22.75x o.p. (ISBN 0-520-01851-6); pap. 6.95x (ISBN 0-520-03847-9, CAMPUS222). U of Cal Pr.

--Providence & Evil. LC 76-28005. 1977. 22.95 (ISBN 0-521-21477-7). Cambridge U Pr.

--The Virtues. LC 76-19627. 1977. 22.95 (ISBN 0-521-21350-9). Cambridge U Pr.

Geach, Peter. Mental Acts: Their Content & Their Objects. (Studies in Philosophical Psychology). 1971. pap. text ed. 6.00x (ISBN 0-391-00174-4); pap. text ed. 3.50x (ISBN 0-391-00174-4). Humanities.

Geanakoplos, Deno J. Western Medieval Civilization. 1979. text ed. 21.95 (ISBN 0-669-00868-0). Heath.

Gear, Bonnie. Seasons in Life. White, Mosazelle N., ed. 65p. (Orig.). pap. 6.95x (ISBN 0-936026-19-7). R&M Pub Co.

Gear, C. William. Computer Organization & Programming. 3rd ed. (Computer Systems Ser.). (Illus.). 1981. text ed. 31.95 (ISBN 0-07-023042-0); instructor's manual 11.00 (ISBN 0-07-023043-9). McGraw.

--Computer Organization & Programming. 2nd ed. (Computer Science Ser.). (Illus.). 448p. 1974. text ed. 31.95 (ISBN 0-07-023076-5, C); instructor's manual 5.50 (ISBN 0-07-023084-6). McGraw.

--Programming in PASCAL. 224p. 1983. text ed. write for info. (ISBN 0-574-21360-0, 13-4360). SRA.

Gear, Josephine. Masters or Servants? A Study of Selected English Painters & Their Patrons of the Late 18th & Early 19th Centuries. LC 76-23619. (Outstanding Dissertations in the Fine Arts Ser.-18th Century). (Illus.). 1977. Repr. lib. bdg. 56.00 o.s.i. (ISBN 0-8240-2690-X). Garland Pub.

Gear, Maria C. & Hill, Melvyn A. Working Through Narcissism: Treating Its Sado-Masochistic Structure. LC 81-65688. 512p. 1982. 30.00 (ISBN 0-87668-448-7). Aronson.

Gearheart, Bill. Learning Disabilities: Educational Strategies. 3rd ed. LC 80-39700. (Illus.). 302p. 1981. text ed. 20.95 (ISBN 0-8016-1768-5). Mosby.

Gearheart, Bill R. & Weishahn, Mel W. The Handicapped Student in the Regular Classroom. 2nd ed. LC 79-23706. 304p. 1980. text ed. 20.95 (ISBN 0-8016-1760-X). Mosby.

Gearing, Winifred. Salvation Patrol. (Illus.). 152p. (Orig.). 1981. pap. 4.95 (ISBN 0-86544-018-2). Salvation Army.

Gearson, jt. ed. see Kear.

Geary. The Complete Handbook of Home Exterior Repair & Maintenance. (Illus.). 352p. 1982. 16.95 (ISBN 0-8306-0066-3); pap. 9.95 (ISBN 0-8306-1382-X, 1382). TAB Bks.

--How to Design & Build Your Own Workspace-with Plans. 384p. 1981. 16.95 o.p. (ISBN 0-8306-9638-5); pap. 9.95 (ISBN 0-8306-1269-6, 1269). TAB Bks.

Geary, D. P., jt. auth. see Mayhall, P. D.

Geary, Patricia. Living in Ether. LC 81-47685. 228p. 1982. 13.41i (ISBN 0-06-014931-0, HarpT). Har-Row.

Geauque, Pierre. Kulani & the Shama Thrush. 1982. 5.00 (ISBN 0-87482-115-0). Wake-Brook.

--Paris, Jetaime. (Illus.). 1982. pap. 7.95 o.s.i. (ISBN 0-87482-116-9). Wake-Brook.

Gebauer, Emanuel L., jt. auth. see Cornberg, Sol.

Gebbers, J. O. & Burkhardt, A. Hair-Spray Induced Lung Lesion. (Illus.). 1982. 60.00 (ISBN 0-08-029788-9). Pergamon.

Gebbie, Donald A. Reproductive Anthropology: Descent Through Woman. LC 80-42013. 371p. 1981. 46.95x (ISBN 0-471-27985-4, Pub. by Wiley-Interscience). Wiley.

Gebbie, Kristine M. & Lavin, Mary A., eds. Classification of Nursing Diagnoses. LC 74-14869. 172p. 1975. pap. text ed. 9.50 o.p. (ISBN 0-8016-1769-3). Mosby.

Gebelein, Charles G., jt. ed. see Carraher, Charles E., Jr.

Gebert, Gordon, ed. Health-Care. 40p. 1981. pap. 16.50 (ISBN 0-08-028091-9). Pergamon.

Geberth. Practical Aspects of Homicide Investigation: Tactics, Procedures & Forensic Techniques. 488p. 1982. 24.95 (ISBN 0-444-00712-1). Elsevier.

Gebhard, David, ed. see Chase, John.

Gebhard, Ruth, jt. auth. see Davis, James A.

Gebhardt, Chuck. Inside Death Valley. LC 77-84819. (Illus.). 1977. pap. 5.95 o.p. (ISBN 0-9601410-0-6). C Gebhardt.

Gebhardt, Louis P. & Nicholes, Paul S. Microbiology. 5th ed. LC 74-10691. 1975. text ed. 16.95 o.p. (ISBN 0-8016-1784-7); lab manual 8.50 o.p. (ISBN 0-8016-1773-1). Mosby.

Gebhardt, Richard H., et al, eds. A Standard Guide to Cat Breeds. (Illus.). 1979. 24.95 o.p. (ISBN 0-07-023059-5, GB). McGraw.

Gebhart, B. Heat Transfer. 2nd ed. 1971. text ed. 26.00 (ISBN 0-07-023127-3, C); solutions manual 10.00 (ISBN 0-07-023132-X). McGraw.

Gecsei, Jan. Architecture of Videotex Systems. (Illus.). 320p. 1983. 29.95 (ISBN 0-13-044776-5). P H.

Geda, Carolyn L., et al. Archivists & Machine-Readable Records. 1980. pap. text ed. 11.00 (ISBN 0-931828-19-8). Soc Am Archivists.

Geddes, Ann E. Trends in Relief Expenditures, 1910-1935. LC 74-166327. (Research Monograph Ser.: Vol. 10). 1971. Repr. of 1937 ed. lib. bdg. 19.50 (ISBN 0-306-70342-4). Da Capo.

Geddes, Candida, jt. ed. see Edwards, Elwyn H.

Geddes, L. A. & Baker, L. E. Principles of Applied Biomedical Instrumentation. 2nd ed. LC 74-34390. (Biomedical Engineering & Health Systems Ser.). 616p. 1975. 42.50x (ISBN 0-471-29496-9, Pub. by Wiley-Interscience). Wiley.

Geddes, Marion & Strurtridge, Gill, eds. Video in the Language Classroom. (Practical Language Teaching Ser.: No. 7). (Illus.). 192p. (Orig.). 1982. pap. 9.00x (ISBN 0-435-28971-3). Heinemann Ed.

Geddes, Marion, ed. see Wallace, Michael.

Geddes, Paul. Hangman. 1978. lib. bdg. 10.95 o.p. (ISBN 0-8161-6556-4, Large Print Bks). G K Hall.

Geddes, William R. Migrants of the Mountains: The Cultural Ecology of the Blue Miao (Hmong Nyua) or Thailand. (Illus.). 1976. 35.00x (ISBN 0-19-823187-3). Oxford U Pr.

Gedney, J. Tumbling & Balancing: Basic Skills & Variations. 1977. 13.95 (ISBN 0-13-932798-3). P-H.

Gedney, William J., ed. see Anuman, Rajadhon Phraya.

Gedo, Andras. Crisis Consciousness in Contemporary Philosophy. Genin, Salomea, tr. from German. LC 81-8338. (Studies in Marxism: Vol. 11). 289p. 1982. 19.95x (ISBN 0-930656-21-0); pap. 9.95 (ISBN 0-930656-22-9). MEP Pubns.

Gedo, John E. & Pollock, George H., eds. Psychoanalysis: The Vital Issues. 1983. write for info (ISBN 0-8236-5385-4). Intl Univs Pr.

Gedo, Mary M. Picasso: Art As Autobiography. LC 80-11126. (Illus.). 288p. 1980. lib. bdg. 20.00 (ISBN 0-226-28482-4, PHOEN); pap. 10.95 (ISBN 0-226-28483-2). U of Chicago Pr.

Geduld, Carolyn. Bernard Wolfe. LC 78-187612. (United States Authors Ser.). lib. bdg. 13.95 (ISBN 0-8057-0832-4, Twayne). G K Hall.

Geduld, Harry M. Dr. Jekyll & Mr. Hyde: An Anthology of Commentary, Including the Text. LC 82-48271. 175p. 1983. lib. bdg. 25.00 (ISBN 0-8240-9469-7). Garland Pub.

Gedzelman, Stanley D. The Science & Wonders of the Atmosphere. LC 79-23835. 1980. text ed. 28.95x (ISBN 0-471-02972-6); Avail. Tchr's Manual (ISBN 0-471-08013-6). Wiley.

Gee, E. A. & Tyler, C. Managing Innovation. 267p. 1976. 40.50 o.p. (ISBN 0-471-29503-5, Pub. by Wiley-Interscience). Wiley.

Gee, E. Gordon, jt. auth. see Wood, Mary A.

Gee, Edwin A. & Tyler, Chaplin. Managing Innovation. LC 76-7056. 284p. Repr. of 1976 ed. text ed. 21.00 (ISBN 0-471-29503-5). Krieger.

Gee, John A. Life & Works of Thomas Lupset. 1928. 29.50x (ISBN 0-685-89763-X). Elliots Bks.

Gee, Maurice. The Half-Men of O. (Illus.). 204p. 1983. text ed. 11.95 (ISBN 0-19-558081-8, Pub. by Oxford U Pr Childrens). Merrimack Bk Serv.

Gee, O. Line Focus Sun Tracker Performance Assessment. (Progress in Solar Energy Supplements SERI Ser.). 1983. pap. text ed. 7.50x (ISBN 0-89553-094-5). Am Solar Energy.

Gee, Ralph D., jt. auth. see Townley, Helen M.

Gee, Renie. Who Said That? 64p. 1980. 7.50 o.p. (ISBN 0-7153-8085-0). David & Charles.

Gee, Sherman. Technology Transfer, Innovation, & International Competitiveness. LC 80-22786. 248p. 1981. 27.50x (ISBN 0-471-08468-9, Pub. by Wiley-Interscience). Wiley.

Geehr, jt. auth. see Auerbach.

Geehr, Richard S., ed. I Decide Who is a Jew! The Papers of Dr. Karl Lueger. LC 81-43702. (Illus.). 382p. (Orig.). 1982. PLB 26.50 (ISBN 0-8191-2493-1); pap. text ed. 14.50 (ISBN 0-8191-2494-X). U Pr of Amer.

Geelan, Agnes. The Minister's Daughters. 1982. 9.95 (ISBN 0-8062-1905-X). Carlton.

Geelhord. Problem Management in Endocrine Surgery: Problem Oriented Approach. 1982. 29.50 (ISBN 0-8151-3412-6). Year Bk Med.

Geen, Fox. Fitting Out a Moulded Hull. (Illus.). 176p. 1976. pap. 10.95 o.s.i. (ISBN 0-685-69131-4). Transatlantic.

--Improved Keelboat Performance. (Illus.). 224p. 1976. 11.95 o.s.i. (ISBN 0-370-10318-1); pap. 9.95 o.s.i. (ISBN 0-370-10342-4). Transatlantic.

Geen, Russell & Donnerstein, Edward, eds. Aggression: Theoretical & Methodologic Issues. LC 82-24348. Date not set. Vol. 1: Theoretical Issues. price not set (ISBN 0-12-278801-X); Vol. 2: Issues in Research. price not set (ISBN 0-12-278802-8). Acad Pr.

Geer, Richard. Star & Gate Diary of Discovery: A Record of Personal Insights. 80p. (Orig.). 1980. pap. 6.00 (ISBN 0-911167-00-5). Cloud Ent.

--Star & Gate Symbolic System. 1979. 12.00 (ISBN 0-911167-01-3). Cloud Ent.

--Star-Gate Circle Pattern. 1979. 6.00 (ISBN 0-911167-02-1). Cloud Ent.

Geerdes, Harold P. Planning & Equipping Educational Music Facilities. LC 75-15271. (Illus.). 96p. (Orig.). 1975. pap. 7.00x (ISBN 0-940796-13-9, 1036). Music Ed.

Geering, Lloyd. Religion of the Individual in the Modern World. LC 76-351596. (Illus.). 1975. pap. 2.50x o.p. (ISBN 0-7055-0549-9). Intl Pubns Serv.

Geering, R. G. Christina Stead. (World Authors Ser.: Australia: No. 95). lib. bdg. 12.50 o.p. (ISBN 0-8057-2858-9, Twayne). G K Hall.

Geerken, Michael & Grove, Walter. At Home & at Work: The Family's Allocation of Labor. (New Perspectives on Family Ser.). 200p. 1983. 22.00 (ISBN 0-8039-1940-9); pap. 10.95 (ISBN 0-8039-1941-7). Sage.

Geers, T. L., jt. ed. see Merchant, H. C.

Geertz, C., et al. Meaning & Order in Moroccan Society. LC 78-54327. (Illus.). 1979. 52.50 (ISBN 0-521-22175-7). Cambridge U Pr.

Geertz, Clifford. Agricultural Involution: The Processes of Ecological Change in Indonesia. LC 63-20356. 1963. 22.50x (ISBN 0-520-00458-2); pap. 6.50x (ISBN 0-520-00459-0, CAMPUS11). U of Cal Pr.

--Interpretation of Cultures. LC 73-81196. 1973. 17.95x o.s.i. (ISBN 0-465-03425-X); pap. 7.95x o.s.i. (ISBN 0-465-09719-7, CN-5019). Basic.

--The Social History of an Indonesian Town. LC 75-29282. (Illus.). 217p. 1975. Repr. of 1965 ed. lib. bdg. 19.75x (ISBN 0-8371-8431-2, GEIT). Greenwood.

Geertz, Clifford, ed. Myth, Symbol & Culture. (Daedalus Ser., 1973). 224p. 1974. 9.95x o.p. (ISBN 0-393-04254-5); pap. 6.95x o.p. (ISBN 0-393-09409-X). Norton.

Geery. Solar Greenhouses: Underground. (Illus.). 416p. 1982. 19.95 (ISBN 0-8306-0069-8); pap. 12.95 (ISBN 0-8306-1272-6, 1272). TAB Bks.

Geesink, R., et al. Thonner's Analytical Key to the Families of Flowering Plants. (Illus.). 253p. 1981. 37.00 (ISBN 0-686-93184-X, 0744-8, Pudoc); pap. 21.00 (ISBN 0-686-99008-0, 0730-8). Unipub.

Geest, Hans van der see Van Der Geest, Bans.

Geeting, Baxter & Geeting, Corinne. Confessions of a Tour Leader. LC 82-81127. 96p. (Orig.). 1982. pap. 4.95 (ISBN 0-88100-005-1). Natl Writers Club.

--How to Listen Assertively. 1983. 8.50 (ISBN 0-686-84062-3). Intl Gen Semantics.

Geeting, Corinne, jt. auth. see Geeting, Baxter.

Geevarghese, P. K. A Changing Small-Town in South India. LC 78-71371. (Illus.). 1979. pap. text ed. 12.25 o.p. (ISBN 0-8191-0666-6). U Pr of Amer.

Geffen, Roger J. Going Pro: The Athlete's Market Guide. (Illus.). 256p. (Orig.). 1983. pap. 9.95 (ISBN 0-8092-5562-6). Contemp Bks.

Geffner, Saul & Lauren, Paul. Experimental Chemistry & Workbook. 2nd ed. (gr. 10-12). 1968. pap. text ed. 7.17 (ISBN 0-87720-113-7); wkbk 8.00 (ISBN 0-87720-115-3). AMSCO Sch.

Geffre, Claude. The New Age in Theology. LC 74-12634. 128p. 1974. pap. 3.95 o.p. (ISBN 0-8091-1844-0). Paulist Pr.

Geffre, Claude & Jossua, Jean-Pierre. Indifference to Religion. (Concilium 1983: Vol. 165). 128p. (Orig.). 1983. pap. 6.95 (ISBN 0-8164-2445-4). Seabury.

Geffre, Claude & Jossua, Jean-pierre, eds. True & False Universality of Christianity. (Concilium Ser.: Vol. 135). 128p. (Orig.). 1980. pap. 5.95 (ISBN 0-8164-2277-X). Seabury.

Gefvert, Constance J., ed. Edward Taylor: An Annotated Bibliography, 1668-1970. LC 70-144811. (Serif Ser.: No. 19). 1971. 7.00x (ISBN 0-87338-113-0). Kent St U Pr.

Gega, Peter C. Science in Elementary Education. 4th ed. LC 81-16451. 600p. 1982. text ed. 23.95 (ISBN 0-471-09678-4); tchrs. manual avail. (ISBN 0-471-09894-9). Wiley.

Gegory, William K; see Gregory, William K.

Gehani, Narain. ADA: An Advanced Introduction. (Software Ser.). (Illus.). 336p. 1983. pap. text ed. 21.95 (ISBN 0-13-003962-4). P-H.

Geherin, David. Sons of Sam Spade: The Private Eye Novel in the Seventies. (Recognitions Ser.). 175p. 1983. pap. 6.95 (ISBN 0-8044-6170-8). Ungar.

--Sons of Sam Spade: The Private Eye Novel in the 70s. LC 79-4823. (Recognitions Ser.). 1980. 11.95 (ISBN 0-8044-2231-1). Ungar.

Gehl, Jurgen. Austria, Germany, & the Anschluss, Nineteen Thirty-One to Nineteen Thirty-Eight. LC 78-21293. (Illus.). 1979. Repr. of 1963 ed. lib. bdg. 20.75x (ISBN 0-313-20841-7, GEAG). Greenwood.

Gehlen, Sr. Raphaelis, jt. auth. see Wideman, Charles J.

Gehlmann, John & Eisman, Philip. Say What You Mean: The Sentence, Bk 1. LC 66-19065. 1967. 6.95 (ISBN 0-672-73232-7). Odyssey Pr.

Gehm, F. Commodity Market Money Management. 334p. 1983. 34.95x (ISBN 0-471-09908-2). Ronald Pr.

Gehm, Harry W. & Bregman, Jacob I. Handbook of Water Resources & Pollution Control. 2nd ed. LC 82-7323. 848p. 1982. Repr. of 1976 ed. 49.50 (ISBN 0-89874-494-6). Krieger.

Gehm, Katherine. Happiness Is Smiling. (Kindergarten Read-to Bks.). (Illus.). (gr. k-2). PLB 5.95 o.p. (ISBN 0-513-00344-4). Denison.

Gehman. Is Smoking Harmful? 1950. pap. 2.00 (ISBN 0-910140-27-8). Anthony.

Gehman, Henry S. The New Westminster Dictionary of the Bible. LC 69-10000. (Illus.). 1982. 21.95 (ISBN 0-664-21388-X). Westminster.

Gehman, Richard. Signet Book of Sausage. 1976. pap. 1.50 o.p. (ISBN 0-451-07066-6, W7066, Sig). NAL.

Gehmlich, D. K., jt. auth. see Hammond, Seymour B.

Gehrels, Tom, ed. Asteroids. 1979. text ed. 35.00x (ISBN 0-8165-0695-7). U of Ariz Pr.

Gehrig, Eleanor & Durso, Joe. My Luke & I. LC 75-44457. (Illus.). 224p. 1976. 11.49i (ISBN 0-690-01109-1). T Y Crowell.

Gehring, Robert E. Basic Behavioral Statistics. LC 77-78447. (Illus.). 1978. text ed. 26.50 (ISBN 0-395-24684-9); study guide 9.50 (ISBN 0-395-24683-0); instr's manual 1.00 (ISBN 0-395-25511-2). HM.

Gehringer, Edward F. Capability Architectures & Small Objects. Stone, Harold, ed. LC 82-6905. (Computer Science: Systems Programming Ser.: No. 10). 240p. 1982. 44.95 (ISBN 0-8357-1347-4, Pub. by UMI Res Pr). Univ Microfilms.

Gehrke, jt. ed. see Webb.

Gehrke, Dorothy. Genesis of Greed. 1983. 8.95 (ISBN 0-533-05408-7). Vantage.

Gehu, J. M. Documents Phytosociologiques. (Nouv. Ser.: No. 3). 1978. lib. bdg. 40.00 (ISBN 3-7682-1202-5). Lubrecht & Cramer.

Gehu, J. M., ed. Colloques Phytosociologiques VII: Lille 1978, le Vegetation des Sols Tourbeux. 556p. (Fr.). 1981. lib. bdg. 60.00x (ISBN 3-7682-1260-2). Lubrecht & Cramer.

--Documents Phytosociologiques. (Illus.). 521p. (Fr.). 1981. lib. bdg. 60.00x (ISBN 3-7682-1298-X). Lubrecht & Cramer.

--Documents Phytosociologiques, IV: Festschrift R. Tuexen", 2 vols. (Illus.). 1979. Set. lib. bdg. 80.00x (ISBN 3-7682-1233-5). Lubrecht & Cramer.

--La Vegetation Des Pelouses Seches a Therophytes. (Colloques Phytosociologiques Ser.: No. 6). 1979. lib. bdg. 48.00 (ISBN 3-7682-1207-6). Lubrecht & Cramer.

Gehweiler, John A., et al. The Radiology of Vertebral Trauma. LC 78-65376. (Monograph in Clinical Radiology: No. 16). (Illus.). 496p. 1980. text ed. 45.00 (ISBN 0-7216-4065-6). Saunders.

Geibel, James. The Blond Brother. LC 78-16330. (gr. 5-7). 1979. 7.95 o.p. (ISBN 0-399-20653-1). Putnam Pub Group.

Geiger, Adolph, jt. auth. see Jackson, Eugene.

Geiger, Dana F. Phaselock Loops for DC Motor Speed Control. LC 80-29578. 206p. 1981. 27.95 (ISBN 0-471-08548-0, Pub. by Wiley-Interscience). Wiley.

Geiger, Linda M. God Loves Me! 8 Lessons, Vol. 1. (Steps of Faith for Special Children Ser.). 1981. kit 19.95 (ISBN 0-86508-045-3); text ed. 4.95x (ISBN 0-86508-046-1). BCM Inc.

Geiger, Sister M. Daniel Carroll II: One Man & His Descendents, 1730-1978. (Illus.). 314p. 1979. pap. 20.00 (ISBN 0-686-36707-3). Md Hist.

Geijsbeek, John B. Ancient Double-Entry Bookkeeping. 1975. Repr. text ed. 20.00 (ISBN 0-914348-16-7). Scholars Bk.

Geikie, Roderick, et al. Dutch Barrier, 1705-1719. LC 69-10096. 1969. Repr. of 1930 ed. lib. bdg. 20.75x (ISBN 0-8371-0082-8, GEDB). Greenwood.

Geilhufe, Nancy L. Chicanos & the Police: A Study of the Politics of Ethnicity in San Jose, California, No. 13. 1979. pap. 9.00 (ISBN 0-686-36589-5). Am Anthro Assn.

Geipel, Robert. Disaster & Reconstruction. Wagner, Philip, tr. from Ger. (Illus.). 250p. 1983. text ed. 40.00 (ISBN 0-04-904006-5); pap. text ed. 19.95x (ISBN 0-04-904007-3). Allen Unwin.

Geiringer, Hilda, tr. see Mises, Richard Von.

Geiringer, Irene, jt. auth. see Geiringer, Karl.

Geiringer, Karl. The Bach Family: Seven Generations of Creative Genius. (Music Reprint 1980 Ser.). (Illus.). 1981. Repr. of 1954 ed. lib. bdg. 42.50 (ISBN 0-306-79596-5). Da Capo.

--Brahms: His Life & Work. 3rd ed. (Music Ser.). (Illus.). xvii, 383p. 1981. Repr. of 1948 ed. lib. bdg. 39.50 (ISBN 0-306-76093-2). Da Capo.

--Haydn: A Creative Life in Music. (Illus.). (YA) (gr. 9-12). 1968. 17.75x o.p. (ISBN 0-520-00460-4); pap. 8.95 (ISBN 0-520-00461-2, CAL143). U of Cal Pr.

--Instruments in the History of Western Music. 3rd ed. 1978. 25.00x (ISBN 0-19-520057-8). Oxford U Pr.

--Music of the Bach Family: An Anthology. (Music Reprint Ser.). (Illus.). viii, 248p. 1980. Repr. of 1955 ed. lib. bdg. 37.50 (ISBN 0-306-79597-3). Da Capo.

Geiringer, Karl & Geiringer, Irene. Haydn: A Creative Life in Music. rev., 3rd ed. (Illus.). 416p. 1983. pap. 8.95 (ISBN 0-520-04317-0, CAL 613). U of Cal Pr.

Geis, Darlene. Dinosaurs & Other Prehistoric Animals. (Illus.). (gr. 4-6). 1959. 4.95 (ISBN 0-448-02881-6, G&D). Putnam Pub Group.

Geis, Darlene, ed. Walt Disney's Treasury of Silly Symphonies. (Illus.). 224p. 1981. 28.50 (ISBN 0-8109-0813-1). Abrams.

Geis, F. L. Personality Research Manual. 227p. 1978. 13.95 (ISBN 0-471-29519-1); tchr's manual avail. (ISBN 0-471-05236-1). Wiley.

Geis, Gilbert. On White-Collar Crime. LC 81-47278. 240p. 1982. 25.95x (ISBN 0-669-04568-3). Lexington Bks.

Geis, I., jt. auth. see Dickerson, R. E.

Geis, Irving, jt. auth. see Dickerson, Richard E.

Geis, Irving, jt. auth. see Huff, Darrell.

Geis, Michael L. The Language of Television Advertising. (Perspectives in Neurolinguistics, Neuropsychology & Psycholinguistics Ser.). 257p. 1982. 26.50 (ISBN 0-12-278980-6). Acad Pr.

Geiser, Elizabeth & Dolin, Arnold, eds. The Business of Book Publishing. 360p. 1983. lib. bdg. 30.00x (ISBN 0-89158-998-8). Westview.

Geiser, Karl F. Redemptioners & Indentured Servants in the Colony & Commonwealth of Pennsylvania. 1901. 65.00x (ISBN 0-686-51298-7). Elliots Bks.

Geiser, Karl F., ed. see Sombart, Werner.

Geiser, Robert L. The Illusion of Caring: Children in Foster Care. LC 73-6246. (Illus.). 192p. 1973. 10.10 (ISBN 0-8070-2378-7); pap. 4.95 (ISBN 0-8070-2379-5, BP490). Beacon Pr.

Geisert, Paul & Futrell, Mynga. Getting Ready for the SAT. (Illus.). 224p. (Orig.). (gr. 7-12). 1983. pap. text ed. 9.95 (ISBN 0-941406-05-9). Betz Pub Co Inc.

Geisinger, Marion. The House of God. LC 79-51842. (Illus.). 1979. 25.00 o.s.i. (ISBN 0-89479-052-8). A & W Pubs.

Geiskopf, Susann & Toomay, Melinda. Fast & Natural Cuisine. 1983. pap. 6.95 (ISBN 0-930356-38-1). Quicksilver Prod.

Geisler, Charles & Popper, Frank. Land Reform, American Style. 256p. Date not set. text ed. 28.00x (ISBN 0-86598-016-0). Allanheld.

Geisler, Norman L. Is Man the Measure? An Evaluation of Contemporary. 160p. (Orig.). 1982. pap. 6.95 (ISBN 0-8010-3787-5). Baker Bk.

Geisler, Norman L. & Nix, William E. From God to Us. 302p. (Orig.). 1974. pap. 8.95 (ISBN 0-8024-2878-9). Moody.

--General Introduction to the Bible. LC 68-18890. 1968. 17.95 (ISBN 0-8024-2915-7). Moody.

Geisler, Norman L., ed. see Augustine, Aurelius.

Geisler, Rolf. Aquarium Fish Diseases. (Illus., Orig.). 1963. pap. 3.95 (ISBN 0-87666-008-1, M516). TFH Pubns.

Geismar, Joan H., ed. The Archaeology of Social Disintegration in Skunk Hollow: A Nineteenth-Century Rural Black Community. (Studies in Historical Archaeology). 230p. 1982. 24.50 (ISBN 0-12-279020-0). Acad Pr.

Geiss, Imanuel. German Foreign Policy, 1871-1914. (Orig.). 1976. 18.00 (ISBN 0-7100-8303-3). Routledge & Kegan.

--The Pan-African Movement: A History of Pan-Africanism in America, Europe & Africa. LC 74-78310. 546p. 1974. text ed. 45.50x (ISBN 0-8419-0161-9, Africana); pap. text ed. 15.95x (ISBN 0-8419-0215-1). Holmes & Meier.

Geiss, R. H., ed. Analytical Electron Microscopy: 1981. (Illus.). 1981. 25.00 (ISBN 0-911302-42-5). San Francisco Pr.

Geissbuehler, H., et al, eds. see International Congress of Pesticides Chemistry, 4th, Zurich, July 1978.

Geissler & Petzold. Psychophysical Judgement & the Process of Perception. Date not set. 64.00 (ISBN 0-444-86353-2). Elsevier.

Geissler, P., ed. see International Association of Briologists, Taxonomic Workshop, 1979.

Geissman, T. A. & Crout, D. H. Organic Chemistry of Secondary Plant Metabolism. LC 71-81384. 1969. pap. 12.75 (ISBN 0-87735-201-1). Freeman C.

Geissmar, Berta. Two Worlds of Music. LC 74-28326. Orig. Title: The Baton & the Jackboot. (Illus.). 327p. 1975. Repr. of 1946 ed. lib. bdg. 32.50 (ISBN 0-306-70664-4). Da Capo.

Geisst, Charles R. A Guide to the Financial Markets. 160p. 1981. 55.00x (ISBN 0-333-30919-7, Pub. by Macmillan England). State Mutual Bk.

Geist, Harold. Migraine: Psychological, Psychiatric & Physiological Aspects. LC 82-26856. 1983. text ed. 11.50 (ISBN 0-89874-601-9). Krieger.

Geist, Harry, jt. auth. see Pollack, Morris.

Geist, Kenneth. Pictures Will Talk: The Life & Films of Joseph L. Mankiewicz. (Quality Paperbacks Ser.). (Illus.). 458p. 1983. pap. 9.95 (ISBN 0-306-80188-4). Da Capo.

Geist, Valerius. Mountain Sheep: A Study in Behavior & Evolution. LC 77-149596. (Wildlife Behavior & Ecology Ser.). (Illus.). xvi, 384p. 1976. pap. 11.00x (ISBN 0-226-28573-1, P666, Phoen). U of Chicago Pr.

Geitner, F. K., jt. auth. see Bloch, H. P.

Geiwitz, James, jt. auth. see Schaie, K. Warner.

Geiwitz, P. James & Moursund, Janet. Approaches to Personality: An Introduction to People. LC 78-25934. (Psychology Ser.). (Illus.). 1979. text ed. 18.95 (ISBN 0-8185-0291-6). Brooks-Cole.

Gekas, Alexandra B. & Countryman, Kathleen M. Development & Implementation of a Patient's Bill of Rights for Hospitals. LC 80-11366. 24p. 1980. pap. 8.75 (ISBN 0-87258-306-6, AHA-157164). Am Hospital.

Gela, Darlene. Dinosaurs & Other Prehistoric Animals. (Illus.). 108p. (gr. 3-8). 1982. 6.95 (ISBN 0-448-02882-4, G&D). Putnam Pub Group.

Gelatt, Roland. Music Makers: Some Outstanding Musical Performers of Our Day. LC 72-2334. (Music Ser.). 1972. Repr. of 1953 ed. lib. bdg. 29.50 (ISBN 0-306-70519-2). Da Capo.

Gelb. Doris Day Scrapbook. 1977. 2.95 o.p. (ISBN 0-448-12868-3, G&D). Putnam Pub Group.

Gelb, Arthur, ed. see Analytical Sciences Corp-Technical Staff.

Gelb, Bernard & Pliskin, Jeffrey. Energy Use in Mining: Patterns & Prospects. LC 79-851. 240p. 1979. prof ref 30.00x (ISBN 0-88410-088-X). Ballinger Pub.

Gelb, Betsy & Gelb, Gabriel. Marketing Is Everybody's Business. 3rd ed. 1980. pap. text ed. 10.95x (ISBN 0-673-16112-9). Scott F.

Gelb, Betsy D., jt. ed. see Gelb, Gabriel M.

Gelb, Donald. Heart Attack: You Can Survive. 1979. pap. 2.95 o.p. (ISBN 0-89260-128-0). Hwong Pub.

Gelb, Donald M. Physician, Heal Thyself. (Orig.). 1980. pap. 2.95 o.p. (ISBN 0-89260-154-X). Hwong Pub.

Gelb, Gabriel, jt. auth. see Gelb, Betsy.

Gelb, Gabriel M. & Gelb, Betsy D., eds. Insights for Marketing Management. 2d ed. LC 76-53773. (Illus.). 1977. pap. 12.50x (ISBN 0-673-16106-4). Scott F.

Gelb, Leslie H. & Betts, Richard K. The Irony of Vietnam: The System Worked. 1979. 22.95 (ISBN 0-8157-3072-1); pap. 9.95 (ISBN 0-8157-3071-3). Brookings.

Gelb, Norman. The British: A Portrait of an Indomitable Island People. LC 81-22219. 256p. 1982. 13.95 (ISBN 0-89696-107-9, An Everest House Book). Dodd.

Gelbaum, Bernard R. & Olmsted, John M. Counterexamples in Analysis. LC 64-21715. 1964. pap. 15.95x (ISBN 0-8162-3214-8). Holden-Day.

Gelber, Harry G. Technology, Defense & External Relations in China, 1975-1978. 236p. 1979. lib. bdg. 26.00 o.p. (ISBN 0-89158-379-3). Westview.

Gelber, Leonard, jt. auth. see Martin, Michael.

Gelber, Lionel. Crisis in the West: American Leadership & the Global Balance. LC 75-857. 250p. 1975. 26.00 (ISBN 0-312-17395-4). St Martin.

Gelber, Lynne L. In Stability: The Shape & Space of Claudel's Art Criticism. Kuspit, Donald B., ed. LC 80-18445. (Studies in Fine Arts: Criticism: No. 4). 128p. 1980. 34.95 (ISBN 0-8357-1090-4, Pub. by UMI Res Pr). Univ Microfilms.

Gelber, S. M. Job Stands Up: Play with Music & Lyrics. (Orig.). 1975. pap. 5.00 o.p. (ISBN 0-8074-0189-7, 382660). UAHC.

Gelberg, Steven, ed. Hare Krishna Hare Krishna: Five Distinguished Scholars in Religion Discuss the Krishna Movement in the West. (Grove Press Eastern Philosophy & Literature Ser.). 224p. (Orig.). 1983. pap. 7.95 (ISBN 0-394-62454-8, Ever). Grove.

Geldard, Frank A. Fundamentals of Psychology. LC 62-8771. 437p. 1962. text ed. 16.50 (ISBN 0-471-29535-3, Pub. by Wiley). Krieger.

--Human Senses. 2nd ed. LC 72-37432. 1972. text ed. 39.95x (ISBN 0-471-29570-1). Wiley.

--Sensory Saltation: Metastability in the Perceptual World. LC 75-22269. 133p. 1975. 10.00 o.s.i. (ISBN 0-470-29571-6). Halsted Pr.

Geldart, L. P., jt. auth. see Sheriff, R. E.

Gelderman, Carol W. George Fitzmaurice. (English Authors Ser.). 1979. lib. bdg. 14.95 (ISBN 0-8057-6741-X, Twayne). G K Hall.

Geldzahler, Henry, intro. by. Francis Bacon: Recent Paintings, 1968-1974. LC 75-1250. (Illus.). 72p. 1975. pap. 5.95 o.s.i. (ISBN 0-87099-130-2). Metro Mus Art.

--Jean Arp at the Metropolitan Museum of Art. LC 72-77067. (Illus.). 1972. pap. 4.95 (ISBN 0-87099-117-5). Metro Mus Art.

--Joseph Albers at The Metropolitan Museum of Art. LC 73-175486. (Illus.). 1971. pap. 4.95 (ISBN 0-87099-114-0). Metro Mus Art.

Gelenbe, E., jt. ed. see Beilner, H.

Gelenberg, Alan J., jt. ed. see Bassuk, Ellen L.

Gelfand, Donald. Aging: The Ethnic Factor. (Orig.). 1982. text ed. 13.95 (ISBN 0-316-30713-0); pap. 7.95 (ISBN 0-316-30714-9). Little.

Gelfand, Donald E. & Olsen, Jody K. The Aging Network: Programs & Services, Vol.8. LC 80-12563. (Springer Ser. on Adulthood & Aging). 1980. text ed. 25.50 o.p. (ISBN 0-8261-3050-X); pap. text ed. 17.95 (ISBN 0-8261-3051-8). Springer Pub.

Gelfand, Donna M. & Hartmann, Donald P. Child Behavior Analysis & Therapy. 2nd ed. (General Psychology Ser.). 1983. 35.00 (ISBN 0-08-028054-4); pap. 14.95 (ISBN 0-08-028053-6). Pergamon.

Gelfand, Erwin W. & Dosch, Hans-Michael, eds. Biological Basis of Immunodeficiency. 334p. 1979. text ed. 40.00 (ISBN 0-89004-361-2). Raven.

Gelfand, I. M. Representation Theory: Selected Papers. LC 82-4440. (London Mathematical Society Lecture Notes Ser. 69). 330p. 1982. pap. 29.95 (ISBN 0-521-28981-5). Cambridge U Pr.

Gelfand, I. M., jt. auth. see Vasiliev, J. M.

Gelfand, I. M., ed. Method of Coordinates, Vol. 1. (Library of School Mathematics). 1967. text ed. 7.50x (ISBN 0-262-07028-6). MIT Pr.

Gelfand, I. M., et al, eds. Structural-Functional Organization of Biological Systems. 448p. 1971. 22.50x (ISBN 0-262-07042-1). MIT Pr.

Gelfand, Israel M., et al. Commutative Normed Rings. LC 61-15024. 1964. 14.95 (ISBN 0-8284-0170-5). Chelsea Pub.

Gelfand, Izrail M. & Fomin, S. V. Calculus of Variations. Silverman, R., tr. (Illus.). 1963. ref. ed. 29.95 (ISBN 0-13-112292-4). P-H.

Gelfand, Mark I. A Nation of Cities: The Federal Government & Urban America 1933-1965. (Urban Life in America Ser). 1975. 25.00 (ISBN 0-19-501941-5). Oxford U Pr.

Gelfand, Morris A. & Colby, Robert A. Access to Knowledge & Information in the Social Sciences & Humanities: Conference Proceedings. 1974. pap. 12.50 o.p. (ISBN 0-930146-06-9). Queens Coll Pr.

Gelfand, S. I., et al. Learn Limits Through Problems. (Pocket Mathematical Library Ser.). 78p. 1968. 19.00x (ISBN 0-677-20720-4). Gordon.

Geliabkova, N. Bulgarian Textiles. (Survey of World Textiles). (Illus.). 22.50x (ISBN 0-87245-321-9). Textile Bk.

Gelin, Jacques B. & Miller, David W. The Federal Law of Eminent Domain. (Federal Law Library). 605p. 1982. 40.00 (ISBN 0-87215-558-7). Michie-Bobbs.

Gelinas, Paul. Coping with Your Emotions. rev. ed. (gr. 7-12). 1982. PLB 7.97 (ISBN 0-8239-0492-X). Rosen Pr.

Gelineau, P. Experiences in Music. 1970. text ed. 13.95 o.p. (ISBN 0-07-023089-7, C). McGraw.

--Experiences in Music. 2nd ed. 1975. text ed. 27.50 (ISBN 0-07-023092-7, C). McGraw.

--Songs in Action. (Illus.). 320p. (Orig.). 1974. pap. text ed. 21.5003863955r (ISBN 0-07-023071-4, C). McGraw.

Gella, Aleksander. Humanism in Sociology: Its Historical Roots & Contemporary Problems. LC 78-61394. 1978. pap. text ed. 11.00 o.p. (ISBN 0-8191-0598-8). U Pr of Amer.

Gellatly, Peter, ed. The Management of Serials Automation: Current Technology & Strategies for Future Planning. LC 82-6166. (The Serials Librarian Monographic Supplement Ser.: Vol. 6). 301p. 1982. 45.00 (ISBN 0-917724-37-2, B37). Haworth Pr.

--Sex Magazines in the Library Collection: A Scholarly Study of Sex in Serials & Periodicals. LC 80-15011. (Serials Librarian Monographic Supplement Ser.: Vol. 4). 151p. 1981. text ed. 19.95 (ISBN 0-917724-16-X, B16). Haworth Pr.

Geller, Larry, jt. auth. see Stearn, Jess.

Geller, Leslie M. North Cape & Other Poems. LC 82-9082. 64p. (Orig.). 1982. 10.95 (ISBN 0-942190-04-1); pap. 4.95 (ISBN 0-686-98302-5). Pubn Arts.

Geller, Ruth. Pictures from the Past: And Other Stories. 203p. 1978. pap. 7.95 (ISBN 0-686-95889-6). Crossing Pr.

Geller, Stephen. Gad. LC 78-69620. 1979. 11.49i (ISBN 0-06-011493-2, HarpT). Har-Row.

Gellermann, William. Martin Dies. LC 77-151620. (Civil Liberties in American History Ser.). 1972. Repr. of 1944 ed. lib. bdg. 37.50 (ISBN 0-306-70200-2). Da Capo.

Gellert, Shepard D. Suffering Is Optional: How to Deal With Anger, Frustration, Guilt, Embarrassment, Anxiety, Insecurity, Rejection, Depression, Hostility, Jealousy, Sadness, Stress, & Other Feelings That Get You Down. 300p. (Orig.). 1982. pap. cancelled o.p. (ISBN 0-89505-093-5). Argus Comm.

Gelles, Richard J. & Cornell, Claire P. International Perspectives on Family Violence. LC 82-48524. 1983. write for info. (ISBN 0-669-06199-9); pap. write for info. (ISBN 0-669-06198-0). Lexington Bks.

Gelles, Richard J., jt. auth. see Bassis, Michael S.

Gelles, Richard J., jt. ed. see Finkelhor, David.

Gellhorn, Walter. Individual Freedom & Governmental Restraints. LC 68-54421. (Illus.). 1968. Repr. of 1956 ed. lib. bdg. 16.00x (ISBN 0-8371-0442-4, GEIF). Greenwood.

Gellhorn, Walter & Byse, Clark. Administrative Law Problems, 1983: For Use in Conjunction with Administrative Law, Cases & Comments, Seventh Edition. (University Casebook Ser.). 129p. 1982. pap. text ed. write for info. (ISBN 0-88277-113-2); write for info. tchr's manual (ISBN 0-88277-126-4). Foundation Pr.

Gellin, William. Hidden from View: & other Stories. LC 82-62517. 1983. 10.00 (ISBN 0-88400-092-3). Shengold.

Gellinek, Christian. Hugo Grotius. (World Authors Ser.: No. 680). 176p. 1983. lib. bdg. 19.95 (ISBN 0-8057-6525-5, Twayne). G K Hall.

Gellis, Roberta. Knight's Honor. LC 82-60687. 416p. 1983. pap. 3.50 (ISBN 0-86721-187-3). Playboy Pbks.

--Sybelle. 1983. pap. 3.50 (ISBN 0-515-07128-5). Jove Pubns.

Gellis, Sydney S. & Kagan, Benjamin M. Current Pediatric Therapy Nine. LC 64-10484. (Illus.). 793p. 1980. text ed. 40.00 o.p. (ISBN 0-7216-4078-8). Saunders.

Gellner, Ernest. Contemporary Thought & Politics. 1974. 21.95x (ISBN 0-7100-7743-2). Routledge & Kegan.

--Muslim Society. LC 80-41103. (Cambridge Studies in Social Anthropology: No. 32). 280p. 1981. 42.50 (ISBN 0-521-22160-9). Cambridge U Pr.

Gelly, David. The Facts About a Rock Group: Featuring Wings. (Illus.). 1977. 4.95 o.p. (ISBN 0-517-52983-1, Harmony). Crown.

Gelman, I. W. & Mazja, W. G. Abschatzung fur Differentialoperationen. 192p. (Ger.). 1981. text ed. 34.95x (ISBN 3-7643-1275-0). Birkhauser.

Gelman, Rita. Hey Kid. (Easy-Read Storybooks). (Illus.). (gr. k-3). 1977. PLB 3.95 s&l. Watts.

Gelman, Rita G. & Buxbaum, Susan K. Boats That Float. LC 81-711. (Easy-Read Activity Bks.). (Illus.). 32p. (gr. 1-3). 1981. PLB 8.90 (ISBN 0-531-04305-3). Watts.

Gelman, Steve, ed. see Jordan, Henry, et al.

Gelman, Woody, et al. Sam, the Ceiling Needs Painting. 1977. pap. 1.50 (ISBN 0-8431-0418-X). Price Stern.

Gelperin, Abraham & Gelperin, Eve A. Emergency Room Journal Articles. 2nd ed. 244p. 1977. pap. 15.00 (ISBN 0-87488-795-X). Med Exam.

Gelperin, Alan, jt. ed. see Jacobs, Barry L.

Gelperin, Eve A., jt. auth. see Gelperin, Abraham.

Gelpi, Barbara, jt. ed. see Rich, Adrienne.

Gelpke, R., ed. & tr. see Nizami.

Gelser, David, tr. see Stickelberger, E.

Gelsey, Rudi C. Imagine: A New Bible. 128p. 1982. 8.95 (ISBN 0-9608562-0-X); pap. 4.95 (ISBN 0-9608562-1-8). Good Hope Pub.

Gelso, Charles J. & Johnson, Deborah H. Explorations in Time-Limited Counseling & Therapy. (Guidance & Counseling Ser.). 300p. 1983. text ed. 25.95x (ISBN 0-8077-2726-1). Tchrs Coll.

Gelson, Hilary. Children About the House. LC 77-78533. (Design Centre Bks.). (Illus.). 1977. pap. 4.95 o.p. (ISBN 0-85072-024-9, 030076, Quick Fox). Putnam Pub Group.

Gelsthorpe, Annie L. Wings for Nurse Karen. (YA) 1978. 6.95 (ISBN 0-685-86417-0, Avalon). Bouregy.

Geltman, Eve. The Gift of Music: A New Tested Way to Progress Quickly from Rote to Reading. (Illus.). 200p. 1982. 7.95 (ISBN 0-686-81849-0). Diablo.

Geltner, Gerson, jt. auth. see Aspaklaria, Shelley.

Gelzer, Matthias. The Roman Nobility. Seager, R., tr. 180p. 1975. 15.00x o.p. (ISBN 0-631-11940-X, Pub. by Basil Blackwell England); pap. 5.95x o.p. (ISBN 0-631-11521-8, Pub. by Basil Blackwell England). Biblio Dist.

Geminiani, Francesco. Treatise on Good Taste in the Art of Musick. 2nd ed. LC 68-16233. (Music Reprint Ser). 1969. Repr. of 1749 ed. lib. bdg. 18.50 (ISBN 0-306-70985-6). Da Capo.

Gemme, Leila B. King on the Court: Billie Jean King. LC 75-42488. (Sports Profiles Ser.). (Illus.). 48p. (gr. 4-11). 1976. PLB 11.95 (ISBN 0-8172-0128-9). Raintree Pubs.

Gemme, Leila Boyle. True Book of the Mars Landing. LC 77-22106. (True Books). (Illus.). 48p. (gr. 2-5). 1977. PLB 9.25 (ISBN 0-516-01145-6). Childrens.

Gemmell, Alan R. Developmental Plant Anatomy. (Studies in Biology: No. 15). 64p. 1969. pap. text ed. 8.95 (ISBN 0-7131-2223-4). E Arnold.

Gemmell, Raymond P. Colonization of Industrial Wastelands. (Studies in Biology: No. 80). 80p. 1977. pap. text ed. 8.95 (ISBN 0-7131-2587-X). E Arnold.

Gemmett, Robert J. William Beckford. (English Authors Ser.). 1977. lib. bdg. 14.95 (ISBN 0-8057-6674-X, Twayne). G K Hall.

Gemmill, Helen. The Mercer Mile: The Story of Dr. Henry C. Mercer's Three Concrete Buildings. (Illus.). 28p. 1972. pap. 1.25 (ISBN 0-910302-06-5). Bucks Co Hist.

Gemming, Elizabeth. Blow Ye Winds Westerly: The Seaports & Sailing Ships of Old New England. LC 71-158692. (Illus.). (gr. 6-9). 1972. 9.95i o.p. (ISBN 0-690-14797-X, TYC-J). Har-Row.

--Born in a Barn: Farm Animals & Their Young. LC 73-94106. (Illus.). 48p. (gr. 1-4). 1974. 5.95 (ISBN 0-698-20293-7, Coward). Putnam Pub Group.

--Getting to Know the Connecticut River. LC 73-82990. (Illus.). 72p. (gr. 3-5). 1974. PLB 3.97 o.p. (ISBN 0-698-30507-8, Coward). Putnam Pub Group.

--Lost City in the Clouds: The Discovery of Machu Picchu. LC 78-31877. (Science Dicovery Ser.). (Illus.). (gr. 3-7). 1980. PLB 5.99 (ISBN 0-698-30698-8, Coward). Putnam Pub Group.

--Maple Harvest: The Story of Maple Sugaring. LC 75-45132. (Illus.). (gr. 3-5). 1976. 5.95 o.p. (ISBN 0-698-20360-7, Coward). Putnam Pub Group.

--Wool Gathering: Sheep Raising in Old New England. LC 78-24378. (Illus.). (gr. 3-5). 1979. 6.95 (ISBN 0-698-20482-4, Coward). Putnam Pub Group.

Genaway, David C. How to Make Big Money in the Stock Market: Good Times or Bad! LC 82-12841. (Illus.). 322p. (Orig.). 1982. pap. 19.95 (ISBN 0-943970-00-8, HG4527,G46). D C Genaway.

Genazzani, A. R., et al, eds. Adrenal Androgens. 390p. 1980. text ed. 47.50 (ISBN 0-89004-488-0). Raven.

Genazzani, E., et al, eds. Pharmacological Modulation of Steroid Action. 312p. 1980. text ed. 35.00 (ISBN 0-89004-373-6). Raven.

Genck, Frederic H. Improving School Performance: How New School Management Techniques Can Raise Learning, Confidence & Morale. 318p. 1983. 25.95 (ISBN 0-03-062477-0). Praeger.

Genck, Fredric H. & Klingenberg, Allen J. Effective Schools Through Effective Management. Seamon, Harold P., intro. by. (Illus.). 198p. (Orig.). 1978. pap. 8.00 (ISBN 0-686-36918-1). Inst Pub Mgmt.

Genders, Roy. Complete Book of Herbs & Herb Growing. LC 79-93206. (Illus.). 160p. 1980. 16.95 (ISBN 0-8069-3928-1); pap. 9.95 (ISBN 0-8069-3930-3). Sterling.

--Greyhounds. Foyle, Christina, ed. (Foyle's Handbks). 1973. 3.95 (ISBN 0-685-55807-X). Palmetto Pub.

--Home-Grown Food: A Guide for Town Gardeners. (Illus.). 1977. 11.50 o.p. (ISBN 0-7181-1473-6). Transatlantic.

Gendlin, Eugene T. Focusing. LC 78-57406. 1978. 7.95 (ISBN 0-89696-008-0, An Everest House Book). Dodd.

Gendrot, Marcel, ed. Make Way for Jesus Christ. pap. 4.95 (ISBN 0-910984-52-2). Montfort Pubns.

Gendzier, Irene L. Frantz Fanon: A Critical Study. 2nd ed. 312p. (Orig.). 1983. pap. 8.95 (ISBN 0-394-62453-X, Ever). Grove.

Genealogical Association of Southwestern Michigan. Cemetery Records of Bainbridge & Baroda Townships in Berrien County Michigan, 3 Vols. 30p. (Orig.). 1972. Genealog Assn SW.

--Cemetery Records of Bertrand Township in Berrien County, Michigan. 32p. (Orig.). 1978. pap. 4.00 (ISBN 0-686-37855-5). Genealog Assn SW.

--Cemetery Records of Chikaming Township in Berrien County, Michigan. 50p. (Orig.). 1982. pap. 8.00 (ISBN 0-686-37856-3). Genealog Assn SW.

--Cemetery Records of Coloma Township in Berrien County, Michigan. (Orig.). 1983. pap. 8.00 (ISBN 0-686-37858-X). Genealog Assn SW.

--Cemetery Records of New Buffalo Township in Berrien County, Michigan. 60p. (Orig.). 1978. pap. 6.00 (ISBN 0-686-37857-1). Genealog Assn SW.

General Agreement on Tariffs & Trade. The Activities of GATT, 4 vols. annual (Orig., English, French or Spanish editions available). 1960-1969. o.p. (ISBN 0-685-48317-7, G110, GATT); pap. 0.75, 1959-60 (ISBN 0-685-48318-5, G32, GATT); pap. 0.75, 1960-61 (ISBN 0-685-48319-3, G33, GATT); pap. 0.75, 1961-62 (ISBN 0-685-48320-7, G34, GATT); pap. 1.00, 1964-65 (ISBN 0-685-48321-5, G35, GATT); pap. 1.50, 1967-68 (ISBN 0-685-48322-3, GATT). Unipub.

--Basic Instruments & Selected Documents: 1st Through 19th Supplements. annual Incl. First. 1953. pap. 5.00 (ISBN 0-685-48339-8, G71); Second. 1954. pap. 5.00 (ISBN 0-685-48340-1, G72); Third. 1955. pap. 5.25 (ISBN 0-685-48341-X, G73); Fourth. 1956. pap. 5.00 (ISBN 0-685-48342-8, G74); Fifth. 1957. pap. 5.00 (ISBN 0-685-48343-6, G75); Sixth. 1958. pap. 5.00 (ISBN 0-685-48344-4, G76); Seventh. 1959. pap. 5.00 (ISBN 0-685-48345-2, G77); Eighth. 1960. pap. 8.50 (ISBN 0-685-48346-0, G78); Ninth. 1961. pap. 9.75 (ISBN 0-685-48347-9, G79); Tenth. 1962. pap. 9.75 (ISBN 0-685-48348-7, G80); Eleventh. 1963. pap. 8.50 (ISBN 0-685-48349-5, G81); Twelfth. 1964. pap. 8.50 (ISBN 0-685-48350-9, G82); Thirteenth. 1965. pap. 9.75 (ISBN 0-685-48351-7, G83); Fourteenth. 1966. pap. 9.75 (ISBN 0-685-48352-5, G84); Fifteenth. 1968. pap. 12.50 (ISBN 0-685-48353-3, G99); Sixteenth. 1969. pap. 12.50 (ISBN 0-685-48354-1, G85); Seventeenth. 1970. pap. 13.75 (ISBN 0-685-48355-X, G86); Eighteenth. 1972. pap. 15.75 (ISBN 0-685-48356-8, G87); Nineteenth. 1973. pap. 15.75 (ISBN 0-685-48357-6, G88). (Orig., English or French editions available, GATT). Unipub.

--Certification Relating to Rectifications & Modifications of Schedules. (Orig., English or French editions available). 1963. pap. 3.00 o.p. (ISBN 0-685-11719-7, GATT). Unipub.

General Agreement On Tariffs And Trade. Legal Instruments Embodying the Results of the 1964-1967 Trade Conference, 5 Vols. (Orig.). 1967. Set. pap. 130.00 (ISBN 0-685-11722-7, G22, GATT). Unipub.

General Conference. My Golden Key Prayer List. pap. 0.50 (ISBN 0-686-82634-5). Review & Herald.

General Conference Sabbath School Department. Sabbath School Manual. rev. ed. 1982. pap. 3.95 (ISBN 0-686-82635-3). Review & Herald.

General Conference Youth Department. Church Heritage: A Course in Church History. pap. 2.50 (ISBN 0-686-82636-1). Review & Herald.

General Drafting Co. Man's Domain: A Thematic Atlas of the World. 3rd ed. Thrower, Norman, ed. (Illus.). 80p. 1975. pap. text ed. 11.95 (ISBN 0-07-023083-8, C). McGraw.

General Electric Company. Modern Drafting Practices & Standards Manual. (Illus.). 940p. 1981. 140.00x (ISBN 0-931690-01-3). GE Tech Marketing.

General Federation of Jewish Labour in Israel Executive Committee. Documents & Essays on Jewish Labour Policy in Palestine. LC 76-97280. 239p. 1975. Repr. of 1930 ed. lib. bdg. 18.50x (ISBN 0-8371-2602-9, JELP). Greenwood.

General Fisheries Council for the Mediterranean. Establishment, Structure, Functions & Activities of International Fisheries Bodies V. 39p. 1968. pap. 7.50 (ISBN 0-686-92808-3, F1737, FAO). Unipub.

--Proceedings & Technical Papers, Vol. 7. 1964. pap. 27.50 o.p. (ISBN 0-685-36297-3, FAO). Unipub.

--Proceedings & Technical Papers, Vol. 8. 1967. pap. 49.50 o.p. (ISBN 0-685-36298-1, FAO). Unipub.

--Proceedings & Technical Papers, Vol. 10. (Orig.). 1970. pap. 9.25 o.p. (ISBN 0-685-04910-8, FAO). Unipub.

--Proceedings & Technical Papers, Vol. 11. 71p. (Orig.). 1973. pap. 7.25 o.p. (ISBN 0-685-32470-2, FAO). Unipub.

General Fisheries Council for the Mediterranean, 11th Session. Report. 71p. 1972. pap. 7.25 (ISBN 0-686-92911-X, F207, FAO). Unipub.

General Fisheries Council for the Mediterranean, 10th Session. Report. 80p. 1970. pap. 7.25 (ISBN 0-686-92914-4, F206, FAO). Unipub.

General Fisheries Council for the Mediterranean, 12th Session. Report. 53p. 1974. pap. 4.75 (ISBN 0-686-92917-9, F208, FAO). Unipub.

General Fisheries Council for the Mediterranean, 14th Session. Report. 42p. 1978. pap. 9.50 (ISBN 0-686-92920-9, F1617, FAO). Unipub.

General Fisheries Council for the Mediterranean, Committee on Resource Management, 2nd Session, Rome, 1978. Report. (FAO Fisheries Reports: No. 207). 42p. 1978. pap. 7.50 (ISBN 0-686-92925-X, F1498, FAO). Unipub.

General Fisheries Council for the Mediterranean. Report of the First Session of the Working Party on Acoustic Methods for Fish Detection & Abundance Estimation of the General Fisheries Council for the Mediterranean. (FAO Fisheries Report: No. 231). 27p. 1980. pap. 7.50 o.p. (ISBN 92-5-100928-7, F2039, FAO). Unipub.

General Mills. Betty Crocker's Microwave Cookbook. LC 81-40249. (Illus.). 288p. 1981. 13.50 (ISBN 0-394-51764-4). Random.

Generghty, John, jt. auth. see Estes, Bill.

Generowicz, Witold. The Train. LC 82-73216. (Illus.). 32p. (ps-3). 1983. 5.95 (ISBN 0-8037-8834-7, 0578-170). Dial Bks Young.

--The Train. (ps-3). Date not set. 5.95 (ISBN 0-8037-8834-7). Dial.

Genest, et al. Hypertension: Physiopathology & Treatment. 1st ed. (Illus.). 1977. 75.00 (ISBN 0-07-023060-9, HP). McGraw.

Genest, Jacques & Kuchel, Otto. Hypertension: Physiopathology & Treatment. 2nd ed. (Illus.). 1376p. 1983. 89.00 (ISBN 0-07-023061-7). McGraw.

Genet, see Flanner, Janet, pseud.

Genet, Jean. The Thief's Journal. Frechtman, Bernard, tr. from Fr. LC 64-24077. 1982. pap. 9.95 (ISBN 0-394-62437-8, E837, Ever). Grove.

Genet, Russell M., jt. auth. see Trueblood, Mark.

Genet, Russell M., jt. auth. see Wolpert, Robert C.

Genet, Russell M. & Wolpert, Robert C., eds. Microcomputers in Astronomy. LC 82-84769. 200p. (Orig.). 1983. pap. 18.95 (ISBN 0-911351-03-5). Fairborn Observ.

Genet, Russell M., jt. auth. see Hall, Douglas S.

Genetski, Robert J., jt. auth. see Sprinkel, Beryl W.

Genevie, Louis, ed. Collective Behavior & Social Movements. LC 77-83419. 1978. pap. text ed. 15.50 (ISBN 0-87581-228-7). Peacock Pubs.

Genfan, Herb & Taetzch, Lyn. Latigo Leather. (Illus.). 160p. 1976. pap. 7.95 (ISBN 0-8230-2651-5). Watson-Guptill.

Geniere, Renaud de la. Le Budget. (Cahiers Ser.: No. 201). (Fr.). 1977. 27.50 o.p. (ISBN 0-8287-1336-7, Pub by Presses de la Foundation Nationale des Sciences Politiques); pap. text ed. 19.50 o.p. (ISBN 2-7246-0336-2). Clearwater Pub.

Genin, Joseph, jt. auth. see Ginsberg, Jerry H.

Genin, Salomea, tr. see Gedo, Andras.

Genishi, Celia, jt. auth. see Almy, Millie.

Genn, Robert C., Jr. Digital Electronics: A Workbench Guide to Circuits, Experiments & Applications. 256p. 1982. 17.95 (ISBN 0-13-214163-9). P-H.

Gennadi, G. N. Les Ecrivains Franco-Russes. (Nineteenth Century Russia Ser.). 95p. (Fr.). 1974. Repr. of 1874 ed. lib. bdg. 34.50x o.p. (ISBN 0-8287-0368-X, R66). Clearwater Pub.

Gennaro, Alphonso R., ed. see Blakiston.

Gennaro, L. & Guzzon, F. Kirlian Photography: Research & Prospects. (Illus.). 152p. 1982. 14.95 (ISBN 0-85692-045-2, Pub. by Salem Hse Ltd.). Merrimack Bk Serv.

Genoud, C. & Inoue, T. Buddhist Wall-Painting of Ladakh. (Illus.). 116p. 1981. text ed. 67.95x (ISBN 2-88086-001-6, Pub. by Editions Olizane Switzerland). Humanities.

Genovese, Eugene D. Political Economy of Slavery: Studies in Economy & Society of the Slave South. 1967. pap. 4.95 (ISBN 0-394-70400-2, V400, Vin). Random.

--Roll, Jordan, Roll: The World the Slaves Made. 1976. pap. 9.95 (ISBN 0-394-71652-3, Vin). Random.

Genovese, Eugene D. & McDonald, Forrest. Debates on American History. 64p. (Orig.). 1982. pap. text ed. 4.95 (ISBN 0-686-98000-X). Revisionary.

Genovese, Eugene D., jt. auth. see Fox-Genovese, Elizabeth.

Genovese, Michael A. The Supreme Court, the Constitution, & Presidential Power. LC 80-5695. 345p. 1980. lib. bdg. 22.00 (ISBN 0-8191-1322-0); pap. text ed. 12.75 (ISBN 0-8191-1323-9). U Pr of Amer.

Genovese, Rosalie G. Families & Change: Social Needs & Public Policy. 320p. 1983. text ed. 27.95x (ISBN 0-89789-021-3); pap. 12.95. J F Bergin.

Gensch, D. Advertising Planning: Mathematical Models in Advertising Media Planning. 1973. 12.95 (ISBN 0-444-41074-0). Elsevier.

Gensemer, Robert & Behling, Mary. Beginning Softball. 1970. pap. 5.95x o.p. (ISBN 0-534-00643-4). Wadsworth Pub.

Gent, Thomas. Poetic Sketches; a Collection of Miscellaneous Poems, Repr. Of 1808 Ed. 2nd ed. Reiman, Donald H., ed. Bd. with Poems. Repr. of 1820 ed; Poems. Repr. of 1828 ed. LC 75-31205. (Romantic Context Ser.: Poetry 1789-1830). 1979. lib. bdg. 47.00 o.s.i. (ISBN 0-8240-2155-X). Garland Pub.

Genthner, Henry & Herbert, Joseph L., Jr. Automating Zero Base Budgeting. LC 77-16518. (Illus.). 1977. text ed. 22.95 (ISBN 0-89433-050-0). Petrocelli.

Gentilcore, R. Louis, ed. Ontario. (Studies in Canadian Geography). (Illus.). 1972. 15.00x (ISBN 0-8020-1919-6); pap. 6.00x (ISBN 0-8020-6160-5). U of Toronto Pr.

Gentile, Anne, jt. auth. see Gentile, Richard.

Gentile, Lance M. Using Sports for Reading & Writing Activities: Elementary & Middle Years. (A Fun with Reading Bk.). 248p. 1983. pap. text ed. 18.50 (ISBN 0-89774-023-8). Oryx Pr.

Gentile, Lance M. & Kamil, Michael L. Reading Research Revisited. 1983. text ed. 11.95 (ISBN 0-675-20028-8). Merrill.

Gentile, Richard & Gentile, Anne. Retailing Strategy: How to Do It! LC 78-65369. 1978. 20.95 (ISBN 0-86730-505-3). Lebhar Friedman.

Gentile, Richard J. Influence of Structural Movement on Sedimentation During the Pennsylvanian Period in Western Missouri. LC 74-4528. 108p. 1968. 7.50x (ISBN 0-8262-7619-9). U of Mo Pr.

--Retail Advertising: A Management Approach. new ed. LC 76-7296. (Illus.). 300p. 1976. 20.95 (ISBN 0-86730-509-6). Lebhar Friedman.

Gentilini, P., et al, eds. Intrahepatic Cholestasis. LC 75-10551. 199p. 1975. 27.00 (ISBN 0-89004-049-4). Raven.

Gentilli, J., ed. Climates of Australia & New Zealand. (World Survey of Climatology Ser.: Vol. 13). 1971. 125.75 (ISBN 0-444-40827-4). Elsevier.

Gentner, D. & Stevens, A. L. Mental Models. 352p. 1983. text ed. 29.95 (ISBN 0-89859-242-9). L Erlbaum Assocs.

Genton, Elisabeth. Goethe Zeit: La Vie et les Opinions de Heinrich Leopold Wagner (1747-1779) 516p. 1980. write for info. (ISBN 3-8204-6541-3). P Lang Pubs.

Gentry, Buck. The Scout, No. 1: Rowan's Raiders. 1981. pap. 2.50 (ISBN 0-89083-754-6). Zebra.

--The Scout, No. 2: Dakota Massacre. 1981. pap. 2.50 (ISBN 0-89083-794-5). Zebra.

--The Scout, No. 3. (Orig.). 1982. pap. 2.50 (ISBN 0-89083-853-4). Zebra.

--The Scout, No. 4: Cheyenne Vengeance. (Orig.). 1982. pap. 2.50 (ISBN 0-89083-969-7). Zebra.

--The Scout, No. 5: Sioux Slaughter. (Orig.). 1982. pap. 2.50 (ISBN 0-8217-1024-9). Zebra.

--The Scout, No. 7: Prairie Bush. 1982. pap. 2.50 (ISBN 0-8217-1110-5). Zebra.

Gentry, Christine. When Dogs Run Wild: The Sociology of Feral Animals & Wildlife. (Illus.). 220p. 1983. lib. bdg. 16.95X (ISBN 0-89950-062-5). McFarland & Co.

Gentry, Christine A., jt. auth. see Rourke, Margaret V.

Gentry, Curt & Horton, Tom. Dolphin Guide to San Francisco & the Bay Area. new rev. ed. LC 81-43252. (Illus.). 384p. 1982. pap. 6.95 (ISBN 0-385-17807-7, Dolp). Doubleday.

Gentry, Howard S. & Thomson, Paul H. Jojaba Handbook. 3rd ed. 168p. 1982. pap. 10.00x (ISBN 0-9602066-1-2). Bonsall Pub.

--Jojoba Handbook. Thomas, Paul H., ed. (Horticultural Handbooks Ser.). (Illus.). 156p. 1978. pap. 8.00 o.p. (ISBN 0-9602066-0-4). Bonsall Pub.

Gentry, J., jt. auth. see Johnson, G.

Gentry, John T. Introduction to Health Services & Community Health Systems. new ed. LC 77-78899. 1978. 22.95 (ISBN 0-8211-0612-0); text ed. 20.75 in ten or more copies (ISBN 0-685-48956-6). McCutchan.

Gentry, Sue. Relaxation. 1982. 1.50 o.p. (ISBN 0-89486-142-5). Hazelden.

--Relaxation: A Natural High. 1.95 (ISBN 0-89486-142-5, 1411B). Hazelden.

Gentry, W. Doyle. Applied Behavior Modification. LC 74-28290. (Illus.). 164p. 1975. pap. text ed. 9.50 o.p. (ISBN 0-8016-1803-7). Mosby.

Gentry, W. Doyle & Williams, Redford B. Psychological Aspects of Myocardial Infarction & Coronary Care. 2nd ed. LC 79-2554. (Illus.). 202p. 1979. pap. text ed. 13.95 o.p. (ISBN 0-8016-1796-0). Mosby.

Gentry, W. Doyle, ed. Geropsychology: A Model of Training & Clinical Service. LC 76-48949. 1977. prof ref 18.50x (ISBN 0-88410-503-2). Ballinger Pub.

Gentry, W. Doyle, jt. ed. see Williams, Redford B.

Gentz, Friedrich Von. The Origin & Principles of the American Revolution, Compared with the Origin & Principles of the French Revolution. Loss, Richard, ed. LC 77-16175. 1977. Repr. of 1800 ed. lib. bdg. 25.00x (ISBN 0-8201-1302-6). Schol Facsimiles.

Genua, Robert L. The Employer's Guide to Interviewing, Strategies & Tactics for Picking a Winner. (Illus.). 1979. 13.95 (ISBN 0-13-274696-4, Spec); pap. 5.95 (ISBN 0-13-274688-3, Spec). P-H.

Genyea, Julien, jt. auth. see Callewaert, Denis M.

Genzlinger, Anna L. The Jessup Dimension. 164p. 1981. pap. 9.95 (ISBN 0-911306-28-5). G Barker Bks.

Geo. Peabody College for Teachers. Free & Inexpensive Learning Materials. 21st biennial ed. Moore, Norman R., ed. LC 53-2471. 1983. pap. 4.95 (ISBN 0-933436-02-5, IP 00-9). Incentive Pubns.

Geodesic Services, Inc. The Dome Scrap Book. 176p. 1981. pap. text ed. 9.95 (ISBN 0-8403-2394-8). Kendall-Hunt.

Geoffrion, Charles A., ed. Africa: A Study Guide to Better Understanding. (African Humanities Ser.). (Orig.). 1970. pap. text ed. 2.00 (ISBN 0-941934-03-9). Ind U Afro-Amer Arts.

Geoffroy, Gregory & Elial, Ernest L. Topics in Inorganic & Organometallic Stereochemistry, Vol. 12. (Topics in Stereochemistry Ser.). 352p. 1981. 72.00 (ISBN 0-471-05292-2, Pub. by Wiley-Interscience). Wiley.

Geoffroy Saint-Hilaire, Etienne. Philosophie Anatomique Des Organes Respiratoires Sous le Rapport De la Determination et De L'identite De Leurs Pieces Osseuses. Repr. of 1818 ed. 154.00 o.p. (ISBN 0-8287-0370-1). Clearwater Pub.

Geoffroy Saint-Hilaire, Isidore. Vie, Travaux et Doctrine Scientifique D'etienne Geoffroy Sant-Hilaire. Repr. of 1847 ed. 132.00 o.p. (ISBN 0-8287-0371-X). Clearwater Pub.

Geoghegan, Sr. Barbara, et al. Developmental Psychology. 1963. 10.95 o.p. (ISBN 0-02-816970-0). Glencoe.

Georgacarakos, George N. & Smith, Robin. Elementary Formal Logic. 1978. text ed. 23.95 (ISBN 0-07-023051-X, C); instructor's manual 10.00 (ISBN 0-07-023052-8). McGraw.

Georgadze, M. U. S. S. R. Sixty Years of the Union. 391p. 1982. 9.95 (ISBN 0-8285-2423-8, Pub. by Progress PubS USSR). Imported Pubns.

Georgakas, Dan. The Methuselah Factors: Living Long & Living Well. 1981. 14.95 o.p. (ISBN 0-671-24064-1). S&S.

Georgakas, Dan & Rubenstein, Leonard, eds. The Cineaste Interviews: The Art & Politics of the Cinema. LC 82-83804. (A Cineaste Reader Ser.). (Illus.). 416p. 1982. 25.00 (ISBN 0-941702-02-2); pap. 11.95 (ISBN 0-941702-03-0). Lake View Pr.

Georgano, G. N., ed. The New Encyclopedia of Motorcars: 1885 to the Present. (Illus.). 704p. 1982. 39.95 (ISBN 0-525-93254-2). Dutton.

George. Modern Interstitial & Intracavitary Radiation Cancer Management. LC 80-28011. (Cancer Management Ser.: Vol. 6). 128p. 1981. 40.00x (ISBN 0-89352-118-3). Masson Pub.

George & Renwick. BIMR Clinical Pharmacology & Therapeutics: Vol. 1: Presystematic Drug Elimination. 1982. 49.95 (ISBN 0-407-02322-4). Butterworth.

George, A. G., ed. see Hawthorne, Nathaniel.

George, Alan & Liu, Joseph W. Computer Solution of Large Sparse Positive Definite. (Illus.). 256p. 1980. text ed. 29.95 (ISBN 0-13-165274-5). P-H.

George, Albert J. The Development of French Romanticism: The Impact of the Industrial Revolution on Literature. LC 77-10903. 1977. Repr. of 1955 ed. lib. bdg. 18.00x (ISBN 0-8371-9806-2, GEDF). Greenwood.

George, Alexander. Presidential Decisionmaking in Foreign Policy. (Westview Special Studies in International Relations). 1980. lib. bdg. 27.00 (ISBN 0-89158-380-7); pap. text ed. 11.00 (ISBN 0-89158-510-9). Westview.

George, Alexander L. Propaganda Analysis: A Study of Inferences Made from Nazi Propaganda in World War Two. LC 72-10717. (Illus.). 287p. 1973. Repr. of 1959 ed. lib. bdg. 20.00x (ISBN 0-8371-6630-6, GEPA). Greenwood.

George, Alexander L. & George, Juliette L. Woodrow Wilson & Colonel House: A Personality Study. 1956. pap. 5.00 (ISBN 0-486-21144-4). Dover.

George, Alexander L., ed. Managing U. S. Soviet Rivalry: Problems of Crisis Prevention. (Special Study in International Relations). 375p. 1983. lib. bdg. 30.00 (ISBN 0-86531-500-0); pap. text ed. 11.75 (ISBN 0-86531-501-9). Westview.

George, Barbara, jt. auth. see Doughty, Tom.

George, Catherine. Reluctant Paragon. (Harlequin Romances Ser.). 192p. 1983. pap. 1.75 (ISBN 0-373-02535-1). Harlequin Bks.

George, Charles H. Revolution: European Radicals from Hus to Lenin. 1971. pap. 7.95x (ISBN 0-673-05984-7). Scott F.

George, Charley. Amore. LC 75-30396. 1975. perfect bdg. 2.00 o.p. (ISBN 0-915214-08-9); signed ltd. ed. 15.00 o.p. (ISBN 0-685-70973-6). Litmus.

George, Claude. Supervision in Action. 3rd ed. 1982. text ed. 19.95 (ISBN 0-8359-7150-3); instrs' manual avail. (ISBN 0-8359-7151-1). Reston.

George, Claude S., Jr. Management for Business & Industry. Orig. Title: Management in Industry. 1970. text ed. 24.95 (ISBN 0-13-548578-9). P-H.

George, David L. Freddie Freightliner Goes to Hollywood. Murphy, Carol, ed. (Illus.). (gr. k-6). 1982. 5.95 (ISBN 0-89868-130-8); pap. 3.95 (ISBN 0-686-91784-7). ARO Pub.

George, David Lloyd see Lloyd George, David.

George, Denise. The Student Marriage. (Orig.). 1983. pap. 4.25 (ISBN 0-8054-6939-7). Broadman.

George, Don. Sweet Man: The Real Duke Ellington. (Illus.). 272p. 1981. 13.95 (ISBN 0-399-12660-0). Putnam Pub Group.

George, Emery, ed. An Anthology of Eastern European Poetry. 520p. 1983. 35.00 (ISBN 0-88233-747-5); pap. cancelled (ISBN 0-88233-748-3). Ardis Pubs.

George, Emily, ed. Martha W. Griffiths. LC 81-40922. 302p. (Orig.). 1982. lib. bdg. 24.00 (ISBN 0-8191-2347-1); pap. text ed. 11.75 (ISBN 0-8191-2348-X). U Pr of Amer.

George, F. H. The Science of Philosophy. 336p. 1981. 43.00 (ISBN 0-677-05550-1). Gordon.

George, F. H. & Humphries, J. D., eds. The Robots Are Coming. LC 74-80129. 190p. 1974. 27.50x (ISBN 0-85012-114-0). Intl Pubns Serv.

George, Gerald S. Biomechanics of Women's Gymnastics. 1980. text ed. 19.95 (ISBN 0-13-077461-8). P-H.

George, Henry. Progress & Poverty. 599p. 1983. pap. 5.00 (ISBN 0-911312-58-7). Schalkenbach.

George, Isaac. Heroes & Incidents of the Mexican War. LC 76-32051. 296p. 1982. lib. bdg. 22.95x (ISBN 0-89370-718-X). Borgo Pr.

--Heroes & Incidents of the Mexican War, Containing Doniphans' Expedition. (Illus.). 296p. 1971. Repr. of 1903 ed. 20.00x (ISBN 0-913330-00-0). Sun Dance Bks.

George, J. David & George, Jennifer. Marine Life: An Illustrated Encyclopedia of Invertebrates in the Sea. LC 79-10976. 1979. 58.95 (ISBN 0-471-05675-8, Pub. by Wiley-Interscience). Wiley.

George, Jean C. The Cry of the Crow. LC 79-2016. 160p. (gr. 5 up). 1980. o.p 7.95 (ISBN 0-06-021956-4, HarpJ); PLB 9.89 (ISBN 0-06-021957-2). Har-Row.

--The Grizzly Bear with the Golden Ears. LC 80-7908. (Illus.). 32p. (ps-3). 1982. 9.57i (ISBN 0-06-021965-3, HarpJ); PLB 9.89 (ISBN 0-06-021966-1). Har-Row.

--One Day in the Alpine Tundra. LC 82-45590. (Illus.). 48p. (gr. 5-7). 1983. 9.57i (ISBN 0-690-04325-2, TYC-J); PLB 9.89g (ISBN 0-690-04326-0). Har-Row.

George, Jennifer, jt. auth. see George, J. David.

George, John. Day in the Forest. 16p. (gr. 3-6). 1973. pap. text ed. 3.95 (ISBN 0-87487-629-X). Summy.

George, Jon. Day in the Jungle. 16p. (gr. 3-6). 1968. pap. text ed. 3.95 (ISBN 0-87487-630-3). Summy.

--Two at One Piano. Clark, Frances & Goss, Louise, eds. Incl. Book 1. 1969. pap. text ed. 3.75 (ISBN 0-87487-141-7); Book 2. 1972. pap. text ed. 3.50 (ISBN 0-87487-142-5); Book 3. 1976. pap. text ed. 3.95 (ISBN 0-87487-143-3). (Frances Clark Library for Piano Students Ser.). Summy.

George, Judith. Do You See What I See. 160p. 1982. 9.95 (ISBN 0-399-20912-3). Putnam Pub Group.

George, Judith St. see St. George, Judith.

George, Juliette L., jt. auth. see George, Alexander L.

George, K. D. & Joll, Caroline. Competition Policy in the UK & EEC. LC 75-9285. 1975. 39.50 (ISBN 0-521-20943-9). Cambridge U Pr.

George, Kenneth D., et al. Science Investigations for Elementary School Teachers. 1974. pap. text ed. 6.95x o.p. (ISBN 0-669-83154-9). Heath.

George, Levy, jt. auth. see Levy, Penny A.

George, Mary C., et al. Communication, Psychology, Nutrition, & Preventative Dentistry. 3rd ed. (Dental Assisting Manuals: No. 4). ix, 169p. 1980. pap. 8.00x (ISBN 0-8078-1378-8). U of NC Pr.

George, Nelson. Top of the Charts. (Illus.). 448p. (Orig.). 1983. pap. 14.95 (ISBN 0-8329-0260-8). New Century.

George, Peter. Dr. Strangelove. 1979. lib. bdg. 11.00 (ISBN 0-8398-2475-0, Gregg). G K Hall.

--The Emergence of Industrial America: Strategic Factors in American Economic Growth Since 1870. 232p. 1982. 33.50x (ISBN 0-87395-578-1); pap. 10.95x (ISBN 0-87395-579-X). State U NY Pr.

George, Phyllis & Adler, Bill. The I Love America Diet. (Illus.). 192p. 1983. 11.95 (ISBN 0-688-01621-9). Morrow.

George, R., jt. ed. see Zimmermann, E.

George, R., et al, eds. Annual Review of Pharmacology & Toxicology, Vol. 23. LC 61-5649. (Illus.). 1983. text ed. 27.00 (ISBN 0-8243-0423-3). Annual Reviews.

George, Rickey, jt. auth. see Dustin, Richard.

George, Rickey L. & Cristiani, Therese S. Theory, Methods, & Processes of Counseling & Psychotherapy. (Counseling & Human Development Ser.). (Illus.). 400p. 1981. 23.95 (ISBN 0-13-913905-2). P-H.

George, Robert F., photos by. Velo-News Cyclist's Training Diary. (Illus.). 176p. (Orig.). 1982. pap. 6.95 (ISBN 0-686-82523-3). Velo-News.

George, Rolf, ed. & tr. see Bolzano, Bernhard.

George, Rolf, tr. see Brentano, Franz.

George, S. C. Hidden Treasure. (Illus.). 73p. 1972. 2.95 o.p. (ISBN 0-7153-5540-6). David & Charles.

--The Vikings. 3.95 o.p. (ISBN 0-7153-6297-6). David & Charles.

George, Stefan. Poems, in German & English. LC 67-14958. 1967. pap. 2.45 o.p. (ISBN 0-8052-0147-5). Schocken.

George, Susan. How the Other Half Dies: The Real Reasons for World Hunger. LC 76-52614. 328p. 1977. text ed. 12.50x (ISBN 0-916672-07-7); pap. text ed. 6.95x (ISBN 0-916672-08-5). Allanheld.

George, Terry, ed. The On-Your-Own Guide to Asia. rev.& 6th ed. LC 77-90889. (Illus.). 416p. (Orig.). 1983. pap. 6.95 (ISBN 0-8048-1406-6, Co-Pub by Volunteers in Asia). C E Tuttle.

George, Timothy. Theology of the Reformers. 1984. 14.95 (ISBN 0-8054-6573-1). Broadman.

George, Uwe. In the Deserts of This Earth. Winston, Richard & Winston, Clara, trs. LC 78-23672. (Helen & Kurt Wolff Bks). (Illus.). 1979. 7.95 (ISBN 0-15-644435-6, Harv). HarBraceJ.

George, Victor. Social Security & Society. (Illus.). 164p. 1973. 21.95x (ISBN 0-7100-7642-8); pap. 7.95 (ISBN 0-7100-7643-6). Routledge & Kegan.

George, William E. Stability & Trim for the Ship's Officer. 3rd, rev. ed. LC 82-74137. (Illus.). 400p. 1983. text ed. 15.00 (ISBN 0-87033-297-X). Cornell Maritime.

George, William J., ed. see International Conference on Cyclic Nucleotide, 3rd, New Orleans, la., July 1977.

Georgel. Cat-Tales. (Illus.). 32p. (gr. 1-7). 1972. 2.50 (ISBN 0-912954-03-5). Edmond Pub Co.

Georges, J. M., ed. Microscopic Aspects of Adhesion & Lubrication. 1982. 138.50 (ISBN 0-444-42071-1). Elsevier.

Georges, Robert A. & Jones, Michael O. People Studying People: The Human Element in Fieldwork. LC 79-65767. 1980. 20.00x (ISBN 0-520-03989-0); pap. 5.95x (ISBN 0-520-04067-8, CAMPUS NO. 250). U of Cal Pr.

Georges, Robert A. & Stern, Stephen. American & Canadian Immigrant & Ethnic Folklore: An Annnotated Bibliography. LC 80-9019. (Folklore Bibliographies Ser.). 300p. 1982. lib. bdg. 35.00 (ISBN 0-8240-9307-0). Garland Pub.

Georges, Thomas M. Business & Technical Writing Cookbook: How to Write Coherently on the Job. (Illus.). 250p. 1983. pap. 9.95 (ISBN 0-910687-00-5). Syntax Pubns.

Georgescu, V., jt. ed. see Dita, P.

Georghiou, G. P. & Saito, Tetsuo, eds. Pest Resistance to Pesticides. 807p. 1983. 89.50x (ISBN 0-306-41246-2, Plenum Pr). Plenum Pub.

Georgia Bar Association. A Memorial of Logan Edwin Bleckley. LC 82-12459. 312p. 1982. 29.95x (ISBN 0-86554-039-X). Mercer Univ Pr.

Georgia Writers' Program. Drums & Shadows: Survival Studies Among the Georgia Coastal Negroes. LC 73-3018. (Illus.). 274p. 1973. Repr. of 1940 ed. lib. bdg. 18.50x (ISBN 0-8371-6832-5, WRDS). Greenwood.

Georgiade, Nicholas G. Aesthetic Breast Surgery. (Illus.). 378p. 1983. lib. bdg. price not set (ISBN 0-683-03450-2). Williams & Wilkins.

Georgiades, Thrasybulos. Greek Music, Verse & Dance. LC 73-4336. 156p. 1973. Repr. of 1955 ed. lib. bdg. 18.50 (ISBN 0-306-70561-3). Da Capo.

Georgiev, V. St. Aliphatic Derivatives. (Survey of Drug Research in Immunologic Disease: Vol. 1). (Illus.). x, 542p. 1983. 293.50 (ISBN 3-8055-3503-1). S Karger.

Georgii, H. & Pankrath, J. Deposition of Atmospheric Pollutants. 1982. 37.00 (ISBN 90-277-1438-X, Pub. by Reidel Holland). Kluwer Boston.

Georgii, H. W. & Jaeschke, W., eds. Chemistry of the Unpolluted & Polluted Troposphere. 1982. 63.00 (ISBN 90-277-1487-8, Pub. by Reidel Holland). Kluwer Boston.

Georgiou, Hara. The Late Minoan I Destruction of Crete: Metal Groups & Stratigraphic Considerations. (Monograph: IX). 66p. (Orig.). 1979. 7.00 (ISBN 0-917956-30-3). UCLA Arch.

Georgopoulos, Basil S. & Cook, Robert A. A Comparative Study of the Organization & Performance of Hospital Emergency Services. 512p. 1980. pap. 20.00x (ISBN 0-87944-253-0). Inst Soc Res.

Georgopoulos, Basil S., ed. Organization Research on Health Institutions. LC 72-619554. 429p. 1972. 20.00x (ISBN 0-87944-125-9). Inst Soc Res.

Georgopoulos, N., jt. ed. see Fischer, N.

Geothermal Resources Council, ed. Fractures in Geothermal Resevoirs: Presented August 27-28, Honolulu, Hawaii. (Special Report Ser.: No. 12). (Illus.). 174p. (Orig.). 1982. pap. 15.00 (ISBN 0-934412-12-X). Geothermal.

--Geothermal Potential of the Cascade Mountain Range: Exploration & Development. (Special Report Ser.: No. 10). (Illus.). 79p. (Orig.). 1981. pap. 12.00 (ISBN 0-934412-10-3). Geothermal.

Gephart, William J., jt. ed. see Cunningham, Luvern L.

Geraci, Philip C. Photojournalism: Making Pictures for Publication. 2nd ed. (Illus.). 1978. pap. text ed. 14.95 (ISBN 0-8403-1422-1). Kendall-Hunt.

Geraghty, Paul A. The History of Fijian Languages. LC 81-18523. (Oceanic Linguistics Special Publication Ser.: No. 19). (Illus.). 600p. 1983. pap. text ed. 18.50x (ISBN 0-8248-0802-9). UH Pr.

Geraghty, Richard P. The Object of Moral Philosophy According to St. Thomas Aquinas. LC 81-40713. 150p. (Orig.). 1982. lib. bdg. 19.75 (ISBN 0-8191-2161-4); pap. text ed. 8.25 (ISBN 0-8191-2162-2). U Pr of Amer.

Geraghty, Tony. This Is the SAS: A Pictorial History of the Special Air Service Regiment. LC 82-16264. (Illus.). 152p. 1983. 16.95 (ISBN 0-668-05725-4, 5725). Arco.

Gerald, Curtis F. Applied Numerical Analysis. 2nd ed. LC 77-79469. (Illus.). 1978. text ed. 25.95 (ISBN 0-201-02696-1). A-W.

Gerald, J. Edward. The British Press Under Government Economic Controls. LC 77-8442. 1977. Repr. of 1956 ed. lib. bdg. 20.00x (ISBN 0-8371-9690-6, GEBP). Greenwood.

Gerald, John B. Conventional Wisdom. 144p. 1972. 5.95 o.p. (ISBN 0-374-12892-8). FS&G.

Gerald, Mark & Eyman, William. Thinking Straight & Talking Sense: An Emotional Education Program. pap. 9.95 (ISBN 0-686-36676-X). Inst Rat Liv.

Gerald, Michael C. Pharmacology: An Introduction to Drugs. (Illus.). 720p. 1981. 24.95 (ISBN 0-13-662098-1). P-H.

Gerald Moore, 1899- Singer & Accompanist: The Performance of Fifty Songs. LC 73-11859. (Illus.). xi, 232p. 1973. Repr. of 1953 ed. lib. bdg. 21.00x (ISBN 0-8371-7090-7, MOSC). Greenwood.

Gerald of Wales. History & Topography of Ireland. O'Meara, John, tr. 1983. pap. 5.95 (ISBN 0-14-044423-8). Penguin.

Gerando, J. M. De la Bienfaisance Publique, 4 vols. (Conditions of the 19th Century French Working Class Ser.). (Fr.). 1974. Repr. of 1839 ed. lib. bdg. 950.00x set o.p. (ISBN 0-8287-0372-8). Vol. 1 (1188). Vol. 2 (1189). Vol. 3 (1190). Vol. 4 (1191). Clearwater Pub.

Gerando, J. M. de. Le Visiteur du Pauvre. (Conditions of the 19th Century French Working Class Ser.). 170p. (Fr.). 1974. Repr. of 1820 ed. lib. bdg. 51.00x o.p. (ISBN 0-8287-0373-6, 1017). Clearwater Pub.

Geranija & Muwanga. Dao la Mauti. (Swahili Literature). (Orig., Swahili.). 1978. pap. text ed. 3.50x o.p. (ISBN 0-686-74442-X, 00617). Heinemann Ed.

Gerard, A., jt. auth. see Bigwood, E. J.

Gerard, Albert S. Four African Literatures: Xhosa, Sotho, Zulu, Amharic. LC 74-126763. 1971. 40.00x (ISBN 0-520-01788-9). U of Cal Pr.

Gerard, Alexander. An Essay on Taste. LC 63-7081. Repr. of 1780 ed. 37.00x (ISBN 0-8201-1020-5). Schol Facsimiles.

Gerard, Alice. Please Breast-Feed Your Baby. LC 79-114559. 1970. pap. 1.75x (ISBN 0-451-11605-4, Pub. by NAL). Formur Intl.

--Please Breast Feed Your Baby. 1971. pap. 1.75 (ISBN 0-451-11605-4, AE1605, Sig). NAL.

Gerard, Jacqueline & Kamman, Madeleine. Larousse French Home Cooking. LC 80-14937. (Illus.). 320p. 1980. 15.95 o.p. (ISBN 0-07-023141-9). McGraw.

Gerardo, Machado. Memorias: Ocho Anos de Lucha. Gerardo, Morales & Gajate, Comandante, eds. LC 82-84134. (Historia y Biografias Ser.). (Illus.). 224p. (Orig., Spanish.). 1982. pap. 12.95 (ISBN 0-89729-328-2). Ediciones.

Gerardo, Morales, ed. see Gerardo, Machado.

Geras, Adele. Apricots at Midnight. LC 82-1728. (Illus.). 144p. (gr. 4-6). 1982. 9.95 (ISBN 0-689-30921-X). Atheneum.

--Voyage. LC 82-13760. 192p. (gr. 7 up). 1983. 10.95 (ISBN 0-689-30955-4). Atheneum.

Geras, Norman. The Legacy of Rosa Luxemburg. 1976. 11.00 (ISBN 0-8052-7034-5, Pub. by NLB). Schocken.

Gerassi, John & Browning, Frank. The American Way of Crime: From Salem to Watergate, a Stunning New Perspective on Crime in America. 1980. 15.00 (ISBN 0-399-11906-X). Putnam Pub Group.

Gerassimov, Todor, jt. auth. see Venedikov, Ivan.

Geraud, jt. auth. see Bes.

Gerbault, Alain. Firecrest Round the World. 1981. 12.50 o.p. (ISBN 0-679-51026-5). McKay.

Gerbeaux, Jacques, et al. Pediatric Respiratory Disease. 2nd ed. LC 81-10356. 939p. 1982. 95.00 (ISBN 0-471-03456-8, Pub. by Wiley-Med). Wiley.

Gerber & Storzer. French Conversation Through Idioms. 1984. pap. 6.95 (ISBN 0-8120-2107-X). Barron.

Gerber, Aaron. Biblical Attitudes on Human Sexuality. 176p. 1982. 15.95 (ISBN 0-89962-301-8). Todd & Honeywell.

Gerber, Adele. Goal: Carryover, an Articulation Manual & Program. LC 72-95886. (Illus.). 100p. 1973. 19.95 (ISBN 0-87722-021-2); 29 work sheets incl. (ISBN 0-685-26634-6). Temple U Pr.

Gerber, Barbara & Storzer, Gerald. French Idioms on the Way. (Illus.). 1984. pap. 4.95 (ISBN 0-8120-2108-8). Barron. Postponed.

Gerber, Barbara L. & Storzer, Gerald H. Dictionary of Modern French Idioms, 2 vols. LC 76-24743. (Reference Library of the Humanities Ser.: Vol. 63). 1977. Set. lib. bdg. 110.00 o.s.i. (ISBN 0-8240-9935-4). Garland Pub.

Gerber, Frederick H. Indigo & the Antiquity of Dyeing. LC 77-81540. 1977. pap. 4.75 (ISBN 0-685-53315-8). Arum Pr.

Gerber, Georg B. see Altman, Kurt I.

Gerber, John, jt. auth. see Blair, Walter.

Gerber, Leslie E. & McFadden, Margaret. Loren Eiseley. LC 82-40294. (Literature & Life). 200p. 1983. 11.95 (ISBN 0-8044-5424-8). Ungar.

Gerber, Linda L., jt. auth. see Haines, B. Joan.

Gerber, Margy & Cosentino, Christine, eds. Studies in GDR Culture & Society 2: Proceedings of the Seventh International Symposium on the German Democratic Republic. LC 81-43512. (Illus.). 298p. (Orig.). 1982. lib. bdg. 24.00 (ISBN 0-8191-2524-5); pap. text ed. 11.50 (ISBN 0-8191-2525-3). U Pr of Amer.

Gerber, Margy, et al, eds. see International Symposium on the German Democratic Republic, 6th.

Gerber, Merrill J. Name a Star for Me. 192p. (gr. 5-9). 1983. 12.50 (ISBN 0-670-50389-4). Viking Pr.

--Please Don't Kiss Me Now. 1982. pap. 1.95 (ISBN 0-451-11575-9, Sig Vista). NAL.

Gerber, Philip L. Robert Frost. rev. ed. (United States Authors Ser.). 1982. lib. bdg. 11.95 (ISBN 0-8057-7348-7, Twayne). G K Hall.

--Robert Frost. (U. S. Authors Ser.: No. 107). 1966. lib. bdg. 9.95 o.p. (ISBN 0-8057-0296-2, Twayne). G K Hall.

--Theodore Dreiser. (United States Authors Ser.). 1963. lib. bdg. 10.95 (ISBN 0-8057-0212-1, Twayne). G K Hall.

--Willa Cather. (United States Authors Ser.). 1975. lib. bdg. 10.95 (ISBN 0-8057-7155-7, Twayne). G K Hall.

Gerber, Philip L., ed. Critical Essays on Robert Frost. (Critical Essays on American Literature Ser.). 1982. lib. bdg. 28.50 (ISBN 0-8161-8442-9). G K Hall.

Gerber Products Co., ed. Five Hundred Questions New Parents Ask. (Norback Bks.). (Orig.). 1982. pap. 6.95 (ISBN 0-440-52609-4, Dell Trade Pbks). Dell.

Gerber, Rudolph J. & McAnany, Patrick D., eds. Contemporary Punishment: Views, Explanations, & Justifications. LC 72-185410. 275p. 1972. pap. 6.95x o.p. (ISBN 0-268-00487-0). U of Notre Dame Pr.

Gerber, William. American Liberalism. LC 74-32118. (World Leaders Ser.: No. 51). 1975. lib. bdg. 10.95 o.p. (ISBN 0-8057-3604-2, Twayne). G K Hall.

Gerberg, Mort. Your Official Guide to Reaganworld. 1982. 3.95 (ISBN 0-399-50658-6, Perige). Putnam Pub Group.

Gerbers, Teresa. The Laughing Willows. (YA) 1977. 6.95 (ISBN 0-685-71793-3, Avalon). Bouregy.

Gerbner, George, ed. Mass Media Policies in Changing Cultures. LC 77-2399. 1977. 34.95 (ISBN 0-471-01514-8, Pub. by Wiley-Interscience). Wiley.

Gerbracht, Carl & Babcock, Robert J. Elementary School Industrial Arts. 1969. 8.95 o.p. (ISBN 0-02-816990-5). Glencoe.

Gerbracht, Carl & Robinson, Frank E. Understanding America's Industries. (gr. 7-9). 1971. text ed. 18.64 (ISBN 0-87345-499-5). McKnight.

Gerbrandt, Gary L. An Idea Book: For Acting Out & Writing Language,K-8. LC 73-93836. 92p. (Orig.). 1974. pap. 7.00 (ISBN 0-8141-2221-3); pap. 5.00 members (ISBN 0-686-86421-2). NCTE.

Gerdel, Florence & Slocum, Marianna. Vocabulario Tzeltal de Bachajon. (Vocabularios Indigenas Ser.: No. 13). 215p. 1965. pap. 3.25x o.p. (ISBN 0-88312-667-2); 3.00 (ISBN 0-88312-589-7). Summer Inst Ling.

Gerdin, Ingela. The Unknown Balinese: Land, Labor & Inequality in Lombok. (Acta-Gothenburg Studies in Social Anthropology: No. 4). 246p. 1982. pap. text ed. 21.00x (ISBN 91-7346-108-3, Pub. by Acta-Universitas Sweden). Humanities.

Gerdts, William, jt. auth. see Merritt, Howard.

Gerdts, William H. & Stebbens, Theodore E., Jr. A Man of Genius: The Art of Washington Allston, 1779-1843. 2nd ed. LC 79-56222. (Illus.). 256p. 1979. pap. 19.95 (ISBN 0-87846-145-0, Dist. by U Pr of Va). Mus Fine Arts Boston.

Gere, J., jt. auth. see Timoshenko, Stephen P.

Gere, J. A. Taddeo Zuccaro: His Development Studied in His Drawings. LC 77-9471. 1970. 28.50 o.s.i. (ISBN 0-226-28821-8). U of Chicago Pr.

Gere, J. A. & Pouncey, Philip. Italian Drawings: Five Artists Working in Rome c.1550-c.1640. 176p. 1982. 395.00x (ISBN 0-7141-0783-2, Pub. by Brit Mus Pubns England). State Mutual Bk.

Gere, J. A. & Sparrow, John, eds. Geoffrey Madan's Notebook. 1981. 17.95x (ISBN 0-19-215870-8). Oxford U Pr.

Gere, James M. & Weaver, William, Jr. Matrix Algebra for Engineers. 2nd ed. LC 82-20631. (General Engineering Ser.). 175p. 1982. pap. text ed. 12.95 (ISBN 0-534-01274-4). Brooks-Cole.

Gerfin, Richard & Koch, Robert. Physical Geology: Student Handbook & Study Guide. 6th ed. 320p. 1982. pap. text ed. 10.95 (ISBN 0-13-669788-7). P-H.

Gergely, J., jt. auth. see Devenyi, T.

Gergely, J., et al, eds. Antibody Structure & Molecular Immunology. 1975p. (Proceedings). 17.75 (ISBN 0-444-10936-6). Elsevier.

Gergely, J., jt. ed. see Baum, H.

Gergely, T., jt. ed. see Domolki, B.

Gergely, Tibor. Animal Facts & Figures. LC 73-38956. (Illus.). 48p. (gr. 5 up). 1975. 7.95 (ISBN 0-07-023073-0, GB). McGraw.

--Busy Day, Busy People. (Illus.). (ps-1). 1973. pap. 1.50 (ISBN 0-394-82686-8). Random.

Gergen, Kenneth, ed. see Lynch, Mervin D., et al.

Gergen, Kenneth J. & Gergen, Mary M. Social Psychology. 570p. 1981. text ed. 22.95 (ISBN 0-15-581562-8, HC); 6.95 (ISBN 0-15-581564-4); 3.95 (ISBN 0-15-581563-6). HarBraceJ.

Gergen, Mary M., jt. auth. see Gergen, Kenneth J.

Gerhard, H. Harris, jt. auth. see Horvitz, Leslie.

Gerhardie, William. Futility. rev. ed. LC 73-92457. 205p. 1974. Repr. 7.95 o.p. (ISBN 0-312-31395-0). St Martin.

--Memoirs of a Polyglot. (Illus.). 1978. 10.00 o.p. (ISBN 0-312-52867-1). St Martin.

Gerhardt & King. Amputations: Immediate & Early Prosthetic Management. (Illus.). 305p. 1982. text ed. 99.00 (ISBN 3-456-80766-X, Pub by Hans Huber Switzerland). J K Burgess.

Gerhart, Gail M. Black Power in South Africa: The Evolution of an Ideology. LC 75-13149. (Perspectives on Southern Africa Ser.: Vol. 19). 1978. 22.50x o.p. (ISBN 0-520-03022-2); pap. 7.95 (ISBN 0-520-03933-5, CAL423). U of Cal Pr.

Gerhart, Genevra. The Russian's World: Life & Language. (Illus.). 257p. 1974. pap. text ed. 11.95 (ISBN 0-15-577983-4, HC). HarBraceJ.

Gericke, Helmuth. Lattice Theory. LC 66-26204. 10.50 (ISBN 0-8044-4266-5). Ungar.

Gerig, Reginald R. Famous Pianists & Their Technique. 3rd. ed. LC 73-18804. (Illus.). 576p. 1975. 19.95 (ISBN 0-88331-066-X). Luce.

Geriner, Laura. Seven True Bear Stories. 1979. 8.95 (ISBN 0-8038-6747-6). Hastings.

Geringer, Lauren R. Your Own Shortcut Shorthand. (Orig.). 1980. pap. 5.95 (ISBN 0-686-26260-3). Gehry Pr.

Gerischer, Heinz. Advances in Electrochemistry & Electrochemical Engineering, Vol. 12. Tobias, Charles W., ed. LC 61-15021. 361p. 1981. 44.50 (ISBN 0-471-87530-9, Pub. by Wiley-Interscience). Wiley.

Gerischer, Heinz & Tobias, Charles W., eds. Advances in Electrochemistry & Electrochemical Engineering. LC 61-15021. Vol. 10, 1977. 51.95x (ISBN 0-471-87527-9, Pub. by Wiley-Interscience); Vol. 11, 1978. 48.50x (ISBN 0-471-87528-7). Wiley.

Gerking, Shelby D. & Mutti, John H. Illegal Immigration: Economic Consequences for the United States. (A Westview Special Study Ser.). 130p. Date not set. lib. bdg. 14.00 (ISBN 0-89158-936-8). Westview.

Gerlach, Barbara. The Things That Make for Peace: Biblical Meditations. (Illus.). 64p. (Orig.). 1983. pap. 4.95 (ISBN 0-8298-0664-4). Pilgrim NY.

Gerlach, J., ed. see Kuhlenbeck, H.

Gerlach, Joel & Bolge, Richard. Preach the Gospel. 1982. 8.95 (ISBN 0-8100-0153-5, 15NO387). Northwest Pub.

Gerlach, John & Gerlach, Lana. The Critical Index: A Bibliography of Articles on Film in English, 1946-1973 - Arranged by Names & Topics. Milic, Louis T., ed. LC 74-1959. 1974. text ed. 20.00 o.p. (ISBN 0-8077-2442-4); pap. text ed. 11.95x (ISBN 0-8077-2438-6). Tchrs Coll.

Gerlach, Lana, jt. auth. see Gerlach, John.

Gerlach, Larry. The Men in Blue: Conversations with Major League Umpires. 320p. 1980. 12.95 o.p. (ISBN 0-670-46857-6). Viking Pr.

Gerlach, Larry R; see Weaver, Glenn.

Gerlach, Larry R., et al, eds. Legacies of the American Revolution. LC 78-5888. 242p. 1978. 11.95 (ISBN 0-87421-097-6); pap. 6.95 (ISBN 0-686-96915-4). Utah St U Pr.

Gerlach, Rex. The Complete Book of Casting. (Stoeger Bks). (Illus.). 224p. 1976. pap. 5.95 o.s.i. (ISBN 0-695-80662-9). Follett.

--Creative Fly Tying & Fly Fishing. (Illus.). 1978. pap. 6.95 o.s.i. (ISBN 0-695-80927-X). Follett.

--Creative Fly Tying & Fly Fishing. (Illus.). 244p. pap. 6.95 (ISBN 0-686-97180-9). Stoeger Pub Co.

Gerlach, Vernon S. A Systematic Approach to Basic. 326p. 1983. pap. text ed. 15.95 (ISBN 0-02-341500-2). Macmillan.

Gerlach, William G. Nostalgic Reminiscences of a Telegraph Operator. 1978. 4.95 o.p. (ISBN 0-533-03020-X). Vantage.

Gerler, Edwin, Jr. Counseling the Young Learner. (Illus.). 180p. 1982. 13.95 (ISBN 0-13-183228-X); pap. 6.95 (ISBN 0-13-183210-7). P-H.

Gerli, E. Michael. Alfonso Martinez de Toledo. (World Authors Ser). 1976. lib. bdg. 15.95 (ISBN 0-8057-6239-6, Twayne). G K Hall.

Gerli, E. Michael, ed. Triste deleytacion: An Anonymous Fifteenth Century Castilian Romance. LC 82-15742. 160p. (Orig., Span. & Eng.). 1983. lib. bdg. 14.95 (ISBN 0-87840-086-9). Georgetown U Pr.

Gerlinger, Lorena. Alvin, the Snowmobile. (Illus.). 11p. (ps). 1976. 2.25 (ISBN 0-9606712-4-2). L Gerlinger.

Gerloch, M. & Slade, R. C. Ligand-Field Parameters. LC 72-93139. (Illus.). 250p. 1973. 44.50 (ISBN 0-521-20137-3). Cambridge U Pr.

Gerloff, J., jt. auth. see Krieger, W.

Gerloff, J. & Cholnoky, B. J., eds. Friedrich-Hustedt-Gedenkband: Diatomaceae 2. 1970. 100.00 (ISBN 3-7682-5431-3). Lubrecht & Cramer.

Gerloff, J., jt. ed. see Hakansson, H.

Gerlovich, Jack A., jt. auth. see Downs, Gary E.

Germain, Bernard F., ed. Osteoarthritis & Musculoskeletal Pain Syndromes. (Contemporary Patient Management Ser.). 1982. 32.50 (ISBN 0-87488-873-5). Med Exam.

Germain, Walter M. Magic Power of Your Mind. pap. 5.00 (ISBN 0-87980-093-3). Wilshire.

German American Chamber of Commerce, Inc., ed. see Jander, Klaus H. & Mertin, Dietz.

German American Chamber of Commerce, ed. see Storette, Ronald F.

German American Chamber of Commerce, ed. American Susidiaries of German Firms: Tochtergesellschaften Deutscher Unternehmen in USA. 15th ed. 250p. (Ger.). 1983. Spiral Bdg. 55.00 (ISBN 0-86640-009-5). German Am Chamber.

German, Andrew W. Down on T Wharf: The Boston Fisheries as Seen Through The Photographs of Henry D. Fisher. (American Maritime Library: Vol. 10). (Illus.). 168p. 1982. 24.00 (ISBN 0-913372-26-9). Mystic Seaport.

German, Don & German, Joan. The Only Money Book for the Middle Class. LC 82-14236. (Illus.). 320p. 1983. 13.95 (ISBN 0-688-01567-0). Morrow.

German, Donald R. Bank Employee's Security Handbook. 233p. 1982. 29.50 (ISBN 0-88262-742-2). Warren.

German, Joan, jt. auth. see German, Don.

German, Joan W. The Money Book. (Illus.). 32p. (ps-2). 1981. 6.25 o.p. (ISBN 0-525-66726-1, 0607-180). Lodestar Bks.

--The Money Book. LC 80-25949. (Illus.). 32p. 1982. 5.95 (ISBN 0-525-66726-1). Dandelion Pr.

German Society for Documentation. International Symposium on Patent Information & Documentation, May 16-May 18, 1977, Munich. 479p. 1978. 65.00x (ISBN 0-89664-047-7, Pub. by K G Saur). Gale.

Germann, Donald R. & Fisher, James W. Practical Radiological Diagnosis. (Illus.). 352p. 1981. text ed. 21.95 (ISBN 0-8359-5590-7). Reston.

Germann, Richard & Arnold, Peter. Bernard Haldane Associates' Job & Career Building. LC 81-51898. 256p. 1982. pap. 6.95 (ISBN 0-89815-048-5). Ten Speed Pr.

--Bernard Haldane Associates Job & Career Building: A Step-by-Step Guide. LC 79-2620. (Illus.). 1980. 12.45i (ISBN 0-06-011486-X, HarpT). Har-Row.

Germany, Lucille, jt. auth. see Sumrall, Velma.

Gernet, Jacques. Les Aspects Economiques Du Bouddhisme Dans la Societe Chinoise Du V Au X Siecle. (Perspectives in Asian History Ser.: No. 15). (Illus.). 331p. Repr. of 1956 ed. lib. bdg. 27.50x (ISBN 0-87991-091-7). Porcupine Pr.

Gernsheim, Helmut. The Origins of Photography. (Illus.). 1983. slipcased 50.00 (ISBN 0-500-54080-2). Thames Hudson.

Gernyet, N. & Jagdfeld, G. Katya & the Crocodile. Corrin, Stephen, tr. (Illus.). (gr. 1-4). 1969. 4.00 o.p. (ISBN 0-900675-09-8). Transatlantic.

Gero, Gyozo. Turkish Monuments in Hungary. Horn, Zsuzsanna, tr. (Illus.). 92p. (Orig., Hungarian.). 1976. pap. 5.00x (ISBN 963-13-4704-4). Intl Pubns Serv.

Gerogiannis, Nicholas, ed. see Hemingway, Ernest.

Gerolde, Steven. Universal Conversion Factors. LC 71-164900. 288p. 1971. 23.95x (ISBN 0-87814-005-0). Pennwell Book Division.

Gerolde, Steven, jt. auth. see Langenkamp, Robert.

Gerould, Daniel, ed. American Melodrama: Plays & Documents. LC 82-62096. 1982. 21.95 (ISBN 0-933826-20-6); pap. 7.95 (ISBN 0-933826-21-4). Performing Arts.

--Gallant & Libertine: Divertissements & Parades from Eighteenth Century France. LC 82-62099. 1983. 18.95 (ISBN 0-933826-48-6); pap. 7.95 (ISBN 0-933826-49-4). Performing Arts.

Gerould, G. H., tr. Beowulf & Sir Gawain & the Green Knight. rev ed. 1935. 13.50 o.p. (ISBN 0-8260-3380-6). Wiley.

Gerould, Gordon H., tr. Beowulf & Sir Gawain & the Green Knight. rev. ed. 1935. text ed. 18.95x (ISBN 0-673-15674-5). Scott F.

Gerpen, Maurice Van see Van Gerpen, Maurice.

Gerrard, A. & Burch, J. Introduction to Matrix Methods in Optics. LC 72-21192. (Pure & Applied Optics Ser.). 1975. 68.95x (ISBN 0-471-29685-6, Pub. by Wiley-Interscience). Wiley.

Gerrard, Brian, et al. Interpersonal Skills for Health Professionals. (Illus.). 272p. 1980. text ed. 18.95 (ISBN 0-8359-3138-2); pap. text ed. 14.95 (ISBN 0-8359-3136-6). Reston.

Gerrard, Brian A., jt. auth. see Gray, William A.

Gerrard, John. Soils & Landforms. (Illus.). 256p. 1981. text ed. 35.00x (ISBN 0-04-551048-2); pap. text ed. 17.95x (ISBN 0-04-551049-0). Allen Unwin.

Gerrard, Michael B. The Economics of Pollution: A Bibliography, 4 pts. Incl. Pt. 1. Methods & Issues; Pt. 2. Role of Industries; Pt. 3. Effects of Pollution; Pt. 4. The Control of Pollution. (Public Administration Ser.). 1979. Pts. 1 & 2. pap. 9.50 (ISBN 0-88066-032-5, P-312, P-313); Pts. 3 & 4. pap. 9.00 (ISBN 0-88066-033-3). Vance Biblios.

Gerrard, Roy. The Favershams. (Illus.). 32p. (gr. 1 up). 1983. 10.95 (ISBN 0-374-32292-9). FS&G.

Gerrard, W., jt. auth. see Kertes.

Gerras, Charles, ed. see Albright, Nancy.

Gerras, Charles, ed. see Gorman, Marion.

Gerrath, Jean, et al. A Plant Biology Lab Manual for a One Semester Course Form & Function. 152p. 1982. pap. text ed. 7.95 (ISBN 0-8403-2814-1). Kendall-Hunt.

Gerraughty, Robert J., ed. Pharmacy Examination Review Book Vol. 1. 7th ed. 1979. pap. 12.75 (ISBN 0-87488-421-7). Med Exam.

Gerrick, David J. Mnemonics for Anatomy Students: A Guide to Memory Aids for the Students of Anatomy. 1975. pap. 3.45 (ISBN 0-916750-38-8). Dayton Labs.

Gerrish, B. A. The Old Protestantism & the New: Essays on the Reformation Heritage. LC 82-2730. 400p. 1983. lib. bdg. 35.00x (ISBN 0-226-28869-2). U of Chicago Pr.

Gerrish, H. & Dugger, W., Jr. Exploring Electricity & Electronics: Basic Fundamentals. rev. ed. LC 80-20830. (Illus.). 208p. 1981. text ed. 12.00 (ISBN 0-87006-308-1). Goodheart.

Gerrish, H. H. Electricity. 120p. 1983. 5.80 (ISBN 0-87006-412-6). Goodheart.

Gerrish, H. H. & Dugger, W. E., Jr. Transistor Electronics. LC 81-6740. 368p. 1981. 14.00 (ISBN 0-87006-394-4); wkbk. 5.28 (ISBN 0-87006-318-9). Goodheart.

Gerrish, Howard H. Electricity-Electronics Dictionary. LC 65-26090. (Illus.). 128p. 1970. 6.00 o.p. (ISBN 0-87006-118-6). Goodheart.

--Technical Dictionary. rev. ed. LC 81-20005. 368p. 1982. text ed. 10.00 (ISBN 0-87006-400-2). Goodheart.

Gerrish, Howard H. & Dugger, William E., Jr. Electricity & Electronics. LC 79-6345. (Illus.). 1980. text ed. 14.00 (ISBN 0-87006-284-0); lab manual 5.28 (ISBN 0-87006-310-3). Goodheart.

Gerrity, Bill, jt. auth. see Williams, Don.

Gerry, Chris, jt. ed. see Bromley, Ray.

Gerschenkron, Alexander. Europe in the Russian Mirror. LC 76-96090. 1970. 27.95 (ISBN 0-521-07721-4). Cambridge U Pr.

Gerschler, Malcolm C. The Clock & Watch Pronunciary. LC 82-91052. (Illus.). 256p. 1983. 16.95 (ISBN 0-9609628-1-6); pap. 11.95 (ISBN 0-9609628-2-4). Wag on Wall.

Gersh, Marvin J. How to Raise Children at Home in Your Spare Time. rev. ed. LC 82-42524. 324p. 1983. 14.95 (ISBN 0-8128-2888-7); pap. 3.95 (ISBN 0-8128-2501-2). Stein & Day.

Gershen, Helen. Four Seasons Cookbook. (Illus.). 120p. (Orig.). 1983. 14.95 (ISBN 0-915572-64-8); pap. 6.95 (ISBN 0-915572-63-X). Panjandrum.

Gershenfeld, jt. auth. see Napier.

Gershenfeld, Matti, jt. auth. see Napier, Rodney.

Gershon, R. Programmer's RPG. 1971. 7.75 (ISBN 0-07-023158-3, P&RB). McGraw.

Gershon, S., jt. auth. see Cooper, T. B.

Gershon, Samuel & Belmaker, Robert. Management of the Acute Psychotic Patient. Date not set. price not set (ISBN 0-89004-311-6, 378). Raven.

Gershwin, M. Eric & Robbins, Dick L., eds. Musculoskeletal Diseases of Children. Date not set. price not set (ISBN 0-8089-1528-2). Grune.

Gerside, Roger. Coming Alive: China After Mao. 1982. pap. 4.50 (ISBN 0-451-62087-9, ME2087, Ment). NAL.

Gerson, Joel & Madry, Bobbi R. Standard Textbook for Professional Estheticians. Rubinstein, Israel, ed. (Illus.). 1979. 20.50 (ISBN 0-87350-082-2); pap. 18.30 (ISBN 0-87350-090-3). Milady.

Gerson, Lennard D. The Secret Police in Lenin's Russia. LC 75-44707. 368p. 1976. 19.95 (ISBN 0-87722-085-9). Temple U Pr.

Gerson, Lloyd P., jt. auth. see Apostle, H. G.

Gerson, M. S., jt. auth. see Appleyard, Donald.

Gerson, Mary-Joan. Why the Sky Is Far Away. LC 73-17343. (gr. k-3). 1974. 8.95 (ISBN 0-15-296310-3, HJ). HarBraceJ.

Gerson, Menachem. Family, Women, & Socialization in the Kibbutz. LC 78-57188. (Illus.). 1978. 19.95x (ISBN 0-669-02371-X). Lexington Bks.

Gerson, Trina. Holiday Crafts. 80p. (ps-7). 1983. pap. text ed. write for info. (ISBN 0-9605878-1-0). Anirt Pr.

--Holiday Songs. 84p. (ps-7). 1984. pap. text ed. write for info. (ISBN 0-9605878-2-9). Anirt Pr.

Gersoni-Edelman, Diane. Work-Wise: Learning About the World of Work from Books--Critical Guide to Book Selection & Usage. LC 79-11920. (Selection Guide Ser.: No. 3). 258p. 1980. 16.50 o.s.i. (ISBN 0-87436-264-4, Co-Pub. by Neal-Schuman). ABC-Clio.

Gersovitz, Mark, jt. auth. see Eaton, Jonathan.

Gersovitz, Mark, ed. Selected Economic Writings of W. Arthur Lewis. (Selected Economic Writings Ser.). 832p. 1983. text ed. 65.00X (ISBN 0-686-82268-4). NYU Pr.

Gersovitz, Mark, et al, eds. The Theory & Experience of Economic Development: Essays in Honor of Sir W. Arthur Lewis. 416p. 1982. text ed. 37.50x (ISBN 0-04-330323-4). Allen Unwin.

Gerspach, M. Coptic Textile Designs. 1975. pap. 3.00 (ISBN 0-486-22849-5). Dover.

Gerstein, Dean R., jt. ed. see Levison, Peter K.

Gerstein, Marvin. Beat Me, Whip Me, Make Me Write Bad Checks. Johnston, William L., ed. 35p. 1982. pap. 3.00 (ISBN 0-932884-09-1). Red Herring.

Gerstein, Melvin see Heat Transfer & Fluid Mechanics Institute.

Gerstein, Mordicai. Arnold of the Ducks. LC 82-47735. (Illus.). 64p. (gr. k-3). 1983. 10.10i (ISBN 0-06-022002-3, HarpJ); PLB 10.89g (ISBN 0-06-022003-1). Har-Row.

Gerstein, Rosalyn see Edry, Carol F.

Gerstein, Rosalyn, jt. ed. see Edry, Carol F.

Gersten, Leon. How to Prepare for the Regents Competency Test In Writing. 224p. (gr. 9-12). 1983. pap. 4.95 (ISBN 0-8120-2381-1). Barron.

Gerstenberg, Walter see Roth, Ernst.

Gerstenberger, Donna. John Millington Synge. (English Authors Ser.: No. 12). 1964. lib. bdg. 14.95 o.p. (ISBN 0-8057-1532-0, Twayne). G K Hall.

Gerstenberger, Donna & Hendrick, George. Fourth Directory of Periodicals: Publishing Articles in English & American Literature & Language- LC 82-73732. 234p. 1974. 18.95x (ISBN 0-8040-0675-X); pap. 9.95x o.s.i. (ISBN 0-8040-0676-8). Swallow.

Gerstenblith, Patty. The Levant at the Beginning of the Middle Bronze Age. (American Schools of Oriental Research Dissertation Ser.: No. 5). 1983. pap. text ed. price not set (ISBN 0-89757-105-3, Pub. by Am Sch Orient Res). Eisenbrauns.

Gerstenfeld, Arthur. Innovation: A Study of Technological Policy. 1976. pap. text ed. 10.50 (ISBN 0-8191-0037-4). U Pr of Amer.

--Technological Innovation: Government-Industry Cooperation. LC 78-14800. 1979. 34.95x (ISBN 0-471-03647-1, Pub. by Wiley-Interscience). Wiley.

Gerstenfeld, Arthur, ed. Science Policy Perspectives U. S. A. The U. S. & Japan (Symposium) LC 82-18159. 1982. 29.00 (ISBN 0-12-281280-8). Acad Pr.

Gerstenzang, Adolph. Alphabet Shorthand in Fifteen Days. pap. 3.95 (ISBN 0-448-01501-3, G&D). Putnam Pub Group.

Gerster, Patrick & Cords, Nicholas. Myth in American History. 1977. pap. text ed. 11.95x (ISBN 0-02-473290-7). Macmillan.

Gerster, Patrick, jt. auth. see Cords, Nicholas.

Gersting, Judith L. & Kuczkowski. Yes-No, Stop-Go: Some Patterns in Mathematic Logic. LC 76-46376. (Young Math Ser.). (Illus.). (gr. k-3). 1977. PLB 10.89 (ISBN 0-690-01130-X, TYC-J). Har-Row.

Gerstinger, Heinz. Lope De Vega & Spanish Drama. Rosenbaum, Samuel, tr. from Ger. LC 72-90812. (Literature and Life Ser.). (Illus.). 1974. 11.95 (ISBN 0-8044-2227-3). Ungar.

--Pedro Calderon De la Barca. Peters, Diana, tr. (Literature and Life Ser.). (Illus.). 11.95 (ISBN 0-8044-2226-5). Ungar.

Gerstl, Joel & Jacobs, Glenn, eds. Professions for the People: The Politics of Skill. 1976. 13.95 (ISBN 0-87073-697-3); pap. 8.75 (ISBN 0-87073-698-1). Schenkman.

Gerstl, Joel E., jt. auth. see Perrucci, Robert.

Gerstle, Donna. Gentle People: Into the Heart of Vava'u, Kingdom of Tonga, 1781-1973. LC 73-88584. (Illus.). 65p. (Orig.). 1973. pap. 4.95 o.s.i. (ISBN 0-914488-00-7). Rand-Tofua.

Gerstle, K. H. Basic Structural Design. 1967. text ed. 38.50 (ISBN 0-07-023120-6, C). McGraw.

Gerstle, Kurt H. Basic Structural Analysis. (Civil Engineering & Engineering Mechanics Ser). (Illus.). 560p. 1974. ref. ed. 31.95 (ISBN 0-13-069393-6). P-H.

Gerstman, Daniel R. & Levene, John R. Optometry Examination Review Book: Clinical Optometry. 1975. spiral bdg. 16.00 o.p. (ISBN 0-87488-470-5). Med Exam.

Gerstner, John H. Teachings of Mormonism. pap. 1.75 (ISBN 0-8010-3719-0). Baker Bk.

Gerston, Larry N. Making Public Policy: From Conflict to Resolution. 1983. pap. text ed. 12.95x (ISBN 0-673-15644-3). Scott F.

Gerston, Rich. Just Open the Door: A Complete Guide to Experiencing Environmental Education. 2nd ed. (Illus.). 112p. 1983. pap. text ed. 5.95x (ISBN 0-8134-2249-3). Interstate.

Gerstung, Estella, ed. see Clark, Barbara R.

Gersuny, Carl. Work Hazards & Industrial Conflict. LC 80-51506. (Illus.). 176p. 1981. 15.00x (ISBN 0-87451-189-5). U Pr of New Eng.

Gerteis, Louis S. From Contraband to Freedman: Federal Policy Toward Southern Blacks, 1861-1865. LC 72-801. (Contributions in American History: No. 29). 255p. 1973. lib. bdg. 27.50 (ISBN 0-8371-6372-2, GFC/). Greenwood.

Gerth, Dawn M., ed. see Arnold, Lee E., Jr.

Gerth, Dawn M., ed. see McIntyre, Alice.

Gerth, Gayle, jt. auth. see Gerth, Teja.

Gerth, Hans H., tr. see Weber, Max.

Gerth, Teja & Gerth, Gayle. Photocollage Made Simple. (Illus.). 1977. pap. 6.95 o.p. (ISBN 0-8174-2112-2, Ampoto). Watson-Guptill.

Gertler, Edward. Maryland & Delaware Canoe Trails. (Illus.). 180p. (Orig.). 1979. pap. 7.95 o.s.i. (ISBN 0-9605908-0-3). Seneca Pr MD.

Gertman, Stuart A. And You Shall Teach Them Diligently: A Study of the Current State of Religious Education in the Reform Movement. 1977. pap. 5.00 o.p. (ISBN 0-8074-0052-1, 383760). UAHC.

Gertner, Richard, ed. Motion Picture Almanac, 1983, Vol. 54. 670p. 1981. 47.00 (ISBN 0-900610-28-X). Quigley Pub Co.

--Television Almanac, 1983, Vol. 28. 630p. 1981. 47.00 (ISBN 0-900610-29-8). Quigley Pub Co.

Gertsbakh, I. B. Models of Preventive Maintenance. (Studies in Mathematical & Managerial Economics: Vol. 23). 1977. text ed. 51.00 (ISBN 0-7204-0465-7, North-Holland). Elsevier.

Gertz, Elmer & Lewis, Felice F., eds. Henry Miller: Years of Trial & Triumph, 1962-1964: The Correspondence of Henry Miller & Elmer Gertz. LC 78-3547. (Illus.). 361p. 1978. 19.95 (ISBN 0-8093-0860-6). S Ill U Pr.

Gertz, Elmer, et al. A Guide to Estate Planning. LC 82-10790. 128p. (Orig.). 1983. pap. 9.95 (ISBN 0-8093-1103-8). S Ill U Pr.

Gervais, Marcel, ed. Journey: A Home & Group Bible Study Program. (Illus.). Set. 60.00 (ISBN 0-686-79559-8); Old Testament, Set 20 Bklts. 30.00 (ISBN 0-8091-9279-9); New Testament Set, 20 Bklts. 30.00 (ISBN 0-8091-9280-2); bklt. 1.50 ea. Paulist Pr.

Gervase, Charles J., jt. auth. see Dreher, Barbara B.

Gervasi, Tom. Arsenal of Democracy II: American Military Power in the 1980s & the Origins of the New Cold War. rev. ed. LC 80-993. (Illus.). 272p. (Orig.). 1981. pap. 12.95 (ISBN 0-394-17662-6, E760, Ever). Grove.

Gervassi, Frank. The Life & Times of Menahem Begin: Rebel to Statesman. LC 78-11555. (Illus.). 1979. 12.95 o.p. (ISBN 0-399-12299-0). Putnam Pub Group.

Gerver, Jane. Raggedy Ann & Andy & the Haunted Doll House. LC 81-18016. 1982. 4.95 (ISBN 0-672-52720-0). Bobbs.

Gerver, Jane, ed. see Hudson, Eleanor.

Gerwick, Ben C. Construction of Prestressed Concrete Structures. LC 71-140176. (Practical Construction Guides Ser). 1971. 36.95x (ISBN 0-471-29710-0, Pub. by Wiley-Interscience). Wiley.

Gerwick, Ben C. & Woolery, John C. Construction & Engineering Marketing for Major Project Services. (Practical Construction Guides Ser.). 416p. 1983. 45.95 (ISBN 0-471-09886-8, Pub. by Wiley-Interscience). Wiley.

Gerwig, Norma A., jt. auth. see King, Virginia G.

Gerwin, Donald. Budgeting Public Funds: The Decision Process in an Urban School District. LC 69-17326. 184p. 1969. 27.50 (ISBN 0-299-05270-2). U of Wis Pr.

--The Employment of Teachers. LC 73-20854. 1974. 24.75x (ISBN 0-8211-0610-4); text ed. 22.25x (ISBN 0-685-42632-7). McCutchan.

Gerwin, K. S. & Glorig, A. Detection of Hearing Loss & Ear Disease in Children. (Illus.). 208p. 1974. 16.75x (ISBN 0-398-03175-4). C C Thomas.

Gery, Jacques. Characoids of the World. (Illus.). 1978. 29.95 (ISBN 0-87666-458-3, H-961). TFH Pubns.

Gerzon, Mark F., jt. ed. see Hiatt, Thomas A.

Gesch, Roy. Lord of the Young Crowd. LC 72-162531. (Orig.). (gr. 7-10). 1971. pap. 3.50 (ISBN 0-570-03126-5, 12-2367). Concordia.

Gesch, Roy G. God's World Through Young Eyes. LC 69-13111. (Illus.). (gr. 4-8). 1969. 5.95 (ISBN 0-570-03020-X, 12-2727). Concordia.

--A Husband Prays. Bd. with A Wife Prays. LC 68-22574. 1968. 14.95 (ISBN 0-570-03066-8, 6-1126). Concordia.

Geschiere, Peter. Village Communities & the Authority of the State: Changing Relations in Maka Villages Since 1900. Rev., Abr. ed. (Monographs from the African Studies Centre). Orig. Title: Ger. 300p. 1983. Repr. of 1978 ed. 45.00 (ISBN 0-7103-0015-8, Kegan Paul). Routledge & Kegan.

Geschwender, J. A. Class, Race & Worker Insurgency. LC 76-62581. (American Sociological Association Rose Monograph Ser.). (Illus.). 1977. 27.95 (ISBN 0-521-21584-6); pap. 8.95 (ISBN 0-521-29191-7). Cambridge U Pr.

Gesell, Arnold. Atlas of Infant Behavior, Vol. 2. (Illus.). 1934. 125.00x o.p. (ISBN 0-685-69821-1). Elliots Bks.

Gesell, Arnold, et al. Youth: Years from Ten to Sixteen. 1956. 17.26i (ISBN 0-06-011510-6, HarpT). Har-Row.

Gesell, Arnold L. Infant Development: The Embryology of Early Human Behavior. LC 73-142858. (Illus.). 108p. 1972. Repr. of 1952 ed. lib. bdg. 20.75x (ISBN 0-8371-5957-1, GEID). Greenwood.

--Studies in Child Development. LC 76-138114. (Illus.). 224p. 1972. Repr. of 1948 ed. lib. bdg. 15.75x (ISBN 0-8371-5690-4, GECD). Greenwood.

Gesell, Thomas F., et al, eds. Natural Radiation Environment III: Proceedings, 2 vols. LC 80-607130. (DOE Symposium Ser.). 1789p. 1980. pap. 52.75 (ISBN 0-87079-129-X, CONF-780422); microfiche 4.50 (ISBN 0-87079-458-2, CONF-780422). DOE.

Geselowitz, David B., jt. auth. see Nelson, C. V.

Gesenius, William. Hebrew & Chaldee Lexicon, Tregelles Translation. 1949. 12.95 (ISBN 0-8028-8029-0). Eerdmans.

--Hebrew & English Lexicon to the Old Testament. 2nd ed. Brown, Francis, et al, eds. Robinson, Edward, tr. 1959. 34.95x (ISBN 0-19-864301-2). Oxford U Pr.

Gesick, Lorraine, et al, eds. The Classical States of Southeast Asia. Date not set. pap. price not set. Yale U SE Asia.

Gesner, Konrad. Beast & Animals in Decorative Woodcuts of the Renaissance. Grafton, Carol B., ed. (Illus.). 64p. (Orig.). 1983. pap. 3.95 (ISBN 0-486-24430-X). Dover.

Gess, Diane, ed. see Rothstein, Evelyn.

Gessa, G. L. & Corsini, G. U., eds. Apomorphine & Other Dopaminomimetics: Basic Pharmacology. 344p. 1981. text ed. 41.00 (ISBN 0-89004-667-0). Raven.

Gessa, G. L., jt. ed. see Costa, E.

Gessa, G. L., jt. ed. see Di Chiara, G.

Gessel, Van C., tr. see Endo, Shusaku.

Gessert, Kate R. Beautiful Food Garden. 1983. 24.95 (ISBN 0-442-23857-6). Van Nos Reinhold.

Gessford, John E. Modern Information Systems: Designed for Decision Support. LC 78-74684. 1980. text ed. 24.95 (ISBN 0-201-03099-3). A-W.

Gessler, U., jt. ed. see Seybold, D.

Gessner, Lynne. Navajo Slave. (RL 6). 1978. pap. 1.50 o.p. (ISBN 0-451-08128-5, W8128, Sig). NAL.

Gessner, Robert. Massacre: A Survey of Today's American Indian. LC 72-38831. (Civil Liberties in American History Ser). 418p. 1972. Repr. of 1931 ed. lib. bdg. 45.00 (ISBN 0-306-70445-5). Da Capo.

Gesswein, Armin R. With One Accord in One Place. 93p. (Orig.). 1978. pap. 1.75 (ISBN 0-87509-161-X). Chr Pubns.

Gest, John M. The Lawyer in Literature. LC 82-81089. xii, 249p. 1982. Repr. of 1913 ed. lib. bdg. 37.50 (ISBN 0-912004-21-5). W W Gaunt.

Geston, Mark S. Lords of the Starship. 10.95 (ISBN 0-8398-2447-5, Gregg). G K Hall.

Getchell, Bud. Physical Fitness: A Way of Life. 2nd ed. LC 78-13094. 1979. pap. text ed. 12.95 (ISBN 0-471-04037-1); avail tchr's manual (ISBN 0-471-04985-9). Wiley.

--Physical Fitness: A Way of Life. 3rd ed. LC 82-17654. 258p. 1983. text ed. 12.95 (ISBN 0-471-09635-0). Wiley.

Getches, David H., et al. Cases & Materials on Federal Indian Law. LC 79-3906. (American Casebook Ser.). 600p. 1979. text ed. 20.95 (ISBN 0-8299-2027-7); 1983 supplement avail. (ISBN 0-314-71765-X). West Pub.

Gethers, Judith & Lefft, Elizabeth. The World-Famous Ratner's Meatless Cookbook. 192p. 1983. pap. 2.95 (ISBN 0-345-30348-2). Ballantine.

Gething, Judith. Sex Discrimination & the Law in Hawaii: A Guide to Your Legal Rights. LC 78-10636. 1979. pap. 3.95 (ISBN 0-8248-0620-4). UH Pr.

Gethyn-Jones, Eric. George Thorpe & the Berkeley Company. 296p. 1982. text ed. 18.00x (ISBN 0-904387-83-6, Pub. by Sutton England). Humanities.

Getis, A. & Boots, B. Models of Spatial Processes. LC 75-17118. (Cambridge Geographical Studies Ser.: No.8). 1978. 37.50 (ISBN 0-521-20983-8). Cambridge U Pr.

Getis, Arthur, et al. Geography. 1981. text ed. 23.95x (ISBN 0-02-341550-9); student study guide 6.95 (ISBN 0-02-431580-X). Macmillan.

Getman, Julius, et al see Labor Law Group.

Getman, Julius G. & Blackburn, John D. Labor Relations: Law, Practice & Policy. 2nd ed. LC 82-21042. 749p. 1982. text ed. write for info. (ISBN 0-88277-102-7). Foundation Pr.

Getman, Julius G., et al. Union Representation Elections: Law & Reality. LC 78-13271. 218p. 1976. 9.95x (ISBN 0-87154-302-8). Russell Sage.

Gettel, Ronald. Twice Burned. 192p. (Orig.). 1983. 12.95 (ISBN 0-8027-5485-6). Walker & Co.

Gettel, Ronald E. Real Estate Guidelines & Rules of Thumb. new ed. (Illus.). 1976. 22.95 (ISBN 0-07-023173-7, P&RB). McGraw.

--You Can Get Your Real Estate Taxes Reduced. (Illus.). 1977. 4.95 (ISBN 0-07-023174-5, P&RB). McGraw.

Gettens, Rutherford J. & Stout, George L. Painting Materials: A Short Encyclopedia. (Illus.). 1965. pap. 5.00 (ISBN 0-486-21597-0). Dover.

Gettings, Fred. Ghosts in Photographs: The Extraordinary Story of Spirit Photography. 1978. 10.95 o.p. (ISBN 0-517-52930-0). Crown.

--The Salamander Tales. 1981. 10.95 (ISBN 0-903540-48-7, Pub. by Floris Books). St George Bk Serv.

Gettis, Alan. Zen & the Art of Self Help. 1982. 15.95 (ISBN 0-89002-199-6); pap. 9.95 (ISBN 0-89002-198-8). Northwoods Pr.

Gettleman, Marvin E. An Elusive Presence: The Discovery of John H. Finley & His America. (Illus.). 310p. 1983. Repr. of 1979 ed. lib. bdg. 22.25 (ISBN 0-8191-2714-0). U Pr of Amer.

Gettlemen, Marvin, jt. ed. see Fried, Jonathan L.

Getty, Mary A. & Karris, Robert J. First Corinthians, Second Corinthians, No. 7. (Collegeville Bible Commentary Ser.). 128p. 1983. pap. 2.50 (ISBN 0-8146-1307-1). Liturgical Pr.

Gettys, Joseph M. How to Study Acts. 219p. 1976. pap. 3.75x (ISBN 0-87921-028-1). Attic Pr.

--How to Study Ephesians. rev. ed. 64p. 1976. pap. 3.50x (ISBN 0-87921-056-7). Attic Pr.

--How to Study I Corinthians. 128p. 1968. pap. 3.75x (ISBN 0-8042-3532-5). Attic Pr.

--How to Study John. 153p. 1960. pap. 3.75x (ISBN 0-8042-3568-6). Attic Pr.

--How to Study Luke. rev. ed. 153p. 1975. pap. 3.75x (ISBN 0-87921-027-3). Attic Pr.

--How to Study Philippians, Colossians, & Philemon. 87p. 1964. pap. text ed. 3.75x (ISBN 0-8042-3472-8). Attic Pr.

--How to Study the Revelation. rev. ed. 117p. 1973. pap. 3.50x (ISBN 0-87921-029-X). Attic Pr.

--Surveying the Historical Books. 164p. 1963. pap. 3.00x (ISBN 0-8042-3664-X). Attic Pr.

--Surveying the Pentateuch. 147p. 1962. pap. 3.25x (ISBN 0-8042-3676-3). Attic Pr.

Getz, D. & Hakala, William T., eds. American-Swedish Handbook. 9th rev. ed. 140p. 1982. pap. 9.45 (ISBN 0-686-36451-1). Swedish Council.

Getz, Donald J. & McGraw, Lora. Vision Training for Better Learning. 1981. spiral bound 15.95 (ISBN 0-87804-430-2). Mafex.

Getz, Gene. Dimensiones Del Matrimonio. Carrodeguas, Andy, et al, eds. Lievano, Francisco, tr. from Eng. Orig. Title: The Measure Of A Marriage. 156p. (Span.). 1982. pap. 2.00 (ISBN 0-8297-1159-7). Life Pubs Intl.

--Loving One Another. 1979. pap. 4.50 (ISBN 0-88207-786-4). Victor Bks.

--Praying for One Another. 132p. 1982. pap. 4.50 (ISBN 0-88207-351-6). Victor Bks.

--A Profile for a Christian Life Style: Titus. pap. 2.95 o.p. (ISBN 0-310-25092-7). Zondervan.

Getz, Gene A. Audiovisual Media in Christian Education. rev. ed. LC 73-181587. (Illus.). 250p. 1972. 9.95 o.p. (ISBN 0-8024-0365-4). Moody.

--Les Dimension du Mariage. Cosson, Annie, ed. Cousin, Elvire, tr. from Eng. Orig. Title: The Measure of a Marriage. 128p. (Fr.). 1982. pap. 1.75 (ISBN 0-8297-1246-1). Life Pubs Intl.

--Dimensions de la Famille, Les. Cosson, Annie, ed. Audfray, Annie, tr. from Eng. Orig. Title: The Measure of a Family. 190p. (Fr.). 1982. pap. 2.25 (ISBN 0-8297-1053-1). Life Pubs Intl.

--Encouraging One Another. 1981. pap. 4.50 (ISBN 0-88207-256-0). Victor Bks.

--Joseph: From Prison to Palace. LC 82-18571. 1983. pap. 4.95 (ISBN 0-8307-0870-7, 5417907). Regal.

--The Measure of a Christian: A Study in James. (The Measure of...Ser.). 160p. 1983. pap. 4.95 (ISBN 0-8307-0881-2). Regal.

--The Measure of a Christian: A Study in Philippians. (The Measure of...Ser.). 200p. 1983. pap. 4.95 (ISBN 0-8307-0883-9). Regal.

--The Measure of a Christian: A Study in Titus. (A Measure of...Ser.). 200p. 1983. pap. 4.95 (ISBN 0-8307-0882-0). Regal.

--Moses: Moments of Glory, Feet of Clay. LC 75-23519. 160p. (Orig.). 1976. pap. 3.25 o.p. (ISBN 0-8307-0400-0, 54-032-00); study guide 1.39 o.p. (ISBN 0-8307-0514-7, 5403200). Regal.

--Sharpening the Focus of the Church. 350p. 1976. pap. 7.95 (ISBN 0-8024-7902-2). Moody.

Getz, M. E. & Thomas, L. C. Paper & Thin-Layer Chromatographic Analysis of Environmental Toxicants. 200p. 1979. 29.95 (ISBN 0-471-25723-0, Wiley Heyden). Wiley.

Getz, Malcolm, jt. auth. see Watson, Donald S.

Getz, Mike. Baseball's Three Thousand-Hit Men. 1982. 7.95 (ISBN 0-9608076-0-8). Gemmeg Pr.

Getz, William I. Patrolman. 1977. 5.95 o.p. (ISBN 0-533-02986-4). Vantage.

Getz, William L. & Allen, David B. Brief Counseling with Suicidal Persons. LC 80-8375. 288p. 1982. 23.95x (ISBN 0-669-04090-8). Lexington Bks.

Getzel, George S. & Mellor, M. Joanna, eds. Gerontological Social Work Practice in Long-Term Care. LC 82-21371. (Journal of Gerontological Social Work Ser.: Vol. 5, Nos. 1-2). 1983. text ed. 20.00 (ISBN 0-86656-146-3, B146). Haworth Pr.

Getzels, Jacob W. & Csikszentmihalyi, Mihaly. The Creative Vision: A Longitudinal Study of Problem Finding in Art. LC 76-16862. 304p. 1976. 31.95x (ISBN 0-471-01486-9, Pub. by Wiley-Interscience). Wiley.

Getzels, Judith, et al, eds. Rural & Small Town Planning. LC 79-93345. (Illus.). 326p. (Orig.). 1980. pap. 14.95 (ISBN 0-918286-19-0). Planners Pr.

Getzler, Israel. Kronstadt Nineteen Seventeen-Nineteen Twenty-One: The Fate of a Soviet Democracy. LC 82-9575. (Soviet & East European Studies). 296p. 1983. 44.50 (ISBN 0-521-24479-X). Cambridge U Pr.

--Martov: Political Biography of a Russian Social Democrat. 1967. 44.50 (ISBN 0-521-05073-1). Cambridge U Pr.

Geursen, R. G., jt. ed. see Seiler, F. R.

Geus, J. W., ed. see Symposium on Surface Physics, 3rd, June 26-28,1974.

Geuseau, Frans Alting von see Alting von Geuseau, Frans A.

Geuss, R. The Idea of a Critical Theory: Habermas & the Frankfurt School. LC 80-422474. (Modern European Philosophy Ser.). 140p. 1981. 21.95 (ISBN 0-521-24072-7); pap. 7.50 (ISBN 0-521-28422-8). Cambridge U Pr.

Geuther, Maria, tr. see Swedish Academy of Engineering.

Gevarter, William B., ed. Artificial Intelligence: An Overview. (Technology Update Ser.: Vol. 4). 165p. 1983. price not set (ISBN 0-89934-183-7, BT-904, Pub. by B-T Bks); pap. 34.50 (ISBN 0-89934-182-9, BT-004). Solar Energy Info.

--Computer Vision: An Overview. (Technology Update Ser.: Vol. 3). 175p. 1983. price not set (ISBN 0-89934-181-0, BT-903, Pub. by B-T Bks); pap. 29.50 (ISBN 0-89934-180-2, BT-003). Solar Energy Info.

--Expert Systems: An Overview. (Technology Update Ser.: Vol. 2). 70p. 1983. write for info. (ISBN 0-89934-179-9, BT-902, Pub. by B-T Bks); pap. 19.50x (ISBN 0-89934-178-0, BT-002). Solar Energy Info.

--Robotics: An Overview. (Technology Update Ser.: Vol. 1). 110p. 1983. write for info. (ISBN 0-89934-177-2, BT-901, Pub. by B-T Bks); pap. 24.50x (ISBN 0-89934-176-4, BT-001). Solar Energy Info.

--Technology Update Series: Vol. 1, Robotics; Vol. 2, Expert Systems; Vol. 3, Computer Vision; Vol. 4, Artificial Intelligence, 4 Vols. 530p. 1983. Repr. of 1982 ed. 85.00 (ISBN 0-89934-184-5, Pub. by B-T Bks). Solar Energy Info.

Gever, G., jt. ed. see Rawlins, M. D.

Gevitz, Norman. The D. O.'s Osteopathic Medicine in America. LC 82-47978. 168p. 1982. text ed. 18.50x (ISBN 0-8018-2777-9). Johns Hopkins.

Gewecke, Cliff. Day-by-Day in Dodgers History. LC 82-83940. (Illus.). 300p. (Orig.). 1983. pap. 9.95 (ISBN 0-88011-108-9). Leisure Pr.

Gewertz, Deborah B. Sepik River Societies: A Historical of the Chambri & Their Neighbors. LC 82-48902. 256p. 1983. text ed. 25.50x (ISBN 0-300-02872-5). Yale U Pr.

Gewirth, Alan. Human Rights: Essays on Justification & Applications. LC 81-21933. 384p. 1983. lib. bdg. 35.00x (ISBN 0-226-28877-3); pap. 9.95 (ISBN 0-226-28878-1). U of Chicago Pr.

--Political Philosophy. 1965. 11.95x (ISBN 0-02-341670-X, 34167). Macmillan.

Gewirtz, Allan & Quintas, Louis V., eds. Second International Conference on Combinatorial Mathematics. (Annals of the New York Academy of Sciences: Vol. 319). 602p. (Orig.). 1979. pap. 112.00x (ISBN 0-89766-010-2). NY Acad Sci.

Gewirtz, Herman. Barron's How to Prepare for the College Board Achievement Tests - Physics. rev. ed. LC 79-9283. (gr. 11-12). 1980. pap. 6.95 (ISBN 0-8120-2065-0). Barron.

Gewirtz, Herman, ed. Barron's Regents Exams & Answers Physics. rev. ed. LC 56-39359. 250p. (gr. 10-12). 1982. pap. text ed. 4.50 (ISBN 0-8120-3167-9). Barron.

Gewitz, Arthur. Restoration Adaptations of Early 17th Century Comedies. LC 82-15937. 214p. 1983. lib. bdg. 23.00 (ISBN 0-8191-2722-1); pap. text ed. 10.75 (ISBN 0-8191-2723-X). U Pr of Amer.

Geyer, Georgie A. Buying the Night Flight: The Autobiography of a Woman Foreign Correspondent. (Radcliffe Biography Ser.). 320p. 1983. 16.95 (ISBN 0-440-00725-9, Sey Lawr). Delacorte.

Geyer, R. A. Marine Environmental Pollution, Vol. 1: Hydrocarbons. (Oceanography Ser.: Vol. 27A). 1981. 102.25 (ISBN 0-444-41847-4). Elsevier.

--Submersibles & Their Use in Oceanography & Ocean Engineering. (Elsevier Oceanography Ser.: Vol. 17). 1977. 70.25 (ISBN 0-444-41545-9). Elsevier.

Geyer, R. F. & Zouwen, J. van der, eds. Dependence & Inequality: A Systems Approach to the Problems of Mexico & Other Developing Countries. (Systems Science & World Order Library: Innovations in Systems Science). (Illus.). 336p. 1982. 35.00 (ISBN 0-08-027952-X). Pergamon.

Geyer, R. Z., ed. Marine Environmental Pollution, Vol. 2: Dumping & Mining. (Oceanography Ser.: Vol. 27B). 1981. 102.25 (ISBN 0-444-41855-5). Elsevier.

Geyl, Pieter. Use & Abuse of History. 1955. text ed. 14.50x (ISBN 0-686-83843-2). Elliots Bks.

Geyser, O. & Coetzer, P. W. Bibliographies on South African Political History: General Sources on South African Political History Since 1902, Vol. 2. 1979. lib. bdg. 65.00 (ISBN 0-8161-8245-0, Hall Reference). G K Hall.

Geysson, Bernard. Soulages. (QLP Ser.). (Illus.). 96p. 1980. 7.95 (ISBN 0-517-54105-X). Crown.

Gezi, Kal, jt. auth. see Bradford, Ann.

Ghadar, Fariborz & Stobaugh, Robert. The Petroleum Industry in Oil-Importing Developing Countries. LC 81-48556. 240p. 1982. 26.95x (ISBN 0-669-05419-4). Lexington Bks.

Ghadially, Feroze N. Ultrastructural Pathology of the Cell. new ed. 530p. 1975. 149.00 o.p. (ISBN 0-407-00011-9). Butterworth.

Ghai, Dharam, jt. auth. see Khan, Azizur R.

Ghai, Dharam & Radwan, Samir, eds. Agrarian Policies & Rural Poverty in Africa. (World Employment Programme Study Ser.). ix, 311p. (Orig.). 1983. 21.40 (ISBN 92-2-103109-8); pap. 15.70 (ISBN 92-2-103100-4). Intl Labour Office.

Ghai, Gail. Surfaces of the Map. 1983. pap. 2.95 (ISBN 0-939736-36-5). Wings ME.

Ghai, Y., ed. Studies of Law in Social Change & Development: Law in the Political Economy of Public Enterprise-African Perspectives. 15.00 (ISBN 0-686-35892-9); pap. 10.00 (ISBN 0-686-37198-4). Intl Ctr Law.

Ghai, Y. & Luckham, R., eds. The Political Economy of Law: A Third World Reader. Date not set. price not set. Intl Ctr Law.

Ghai, Yash, ed. Studies of Law in Social Change & Development: Law in the Political Economy of Public Enterprise. 15.00 (ISBN 0-686-35905-4); pap. 10.00 (ISBN 0-686-37208-5). Intl Ctr Law.

Ghali, A. Circular Storage Tanks & Silos. LC 79-12406. 210p. 1979. 35.00x (ISBN 0-419-11500-5, Pub. by E & FN Spon England). Methuen Inc.

Ghali, A. & Neville, A. M. Structural Analysis: A Unified Classical & Matrix Approach. 2nd ed. 1978. pap. 27.95x (ISBN 0-412-14990-7, Pub. by Chapman & Hall). Methuen Inc.

Ghalioungui, Paul. The House of Life: Magic & Medical Science in Ancient Egypt. rev. ed. (Illus.). 198p. 1974. 22.50 o.p. (ISBN 0-8390-0144-4). Allanheld & Schram.

Ghandhi, Sorab K. Semiconductor Power Devices: Physics of Operation & Fabrication Technology. LC 77-8019. 1977. 37.96x (ISBN 0-471-02999-8, Pub by Wiley-Interscience). Wiley.

--VLSI Fabrication Principles: Silicon & Gallium Arsenide. LC 82-10842. 672p. 1982. 47.50 (ISBN 0-471-86833-7, Pub. by Wiley-Interscience). Wiley.

Ghandour, Mounir. Learn Arabic Reading & Writing I. pap. 5.00x (ISBN 0-86685-040-6); book & 2 cassettes 30.00 (ISBN 0-686-96752-6). Intl Bk Ctr.

Ghani, Noordin & Farrell, Edward. Microprocessor System Debugging. LC 80-40950. (Computer Engineering Ser.). 143p. 1981. 49.95 (ISBN 0-471-27860-2, Research Studies Press). Wiley.

Ghanoonparvar, Mohammad R. Persian Cuisine: Book One, Traditional Foods. LC 82-61281. (Illus.). 248p. (Orig.). 1982. write for info. (ISBN 0-939214-11-3); pap. 12.95 (ISBN 0-939214-10-5). Mazda Pubs.

Ghanoonparvar, Mohammad R., tr. see Azaad, Meyer.

Ghatak, Subrata. Monetary Economics in Developing Countries. 1981. 26.00 (ISBN 0-312-54418-9). St Martin.

--Technology Transfer to Developing Countries, Vol. 27. Altman, Edward I. & Walter, Ingo, eds. LC 80-82478. (Contemporary Studies in Economic & Financial Analysis). 200p. 1981. 34.50 (ISBN 0-89232-160-1). Jai Pr.

Ghauri, M. S. The Morphology & Taxonomy of Male Scale Insects (Homoptera: Coccoidea) (Illus.). vii, 221p. 1962. 24.50x (ISBN 0-565-00580-4, Pub. by British Mus Nat Hist England). Sabbot-Natural Hist Bks.

Ghausi, M. & Laker, K. Modern Filter Design: Active RC & Switched Capacitor. 1981. 37.00 (ISBN 0-13-594663-8). P-H.

Ghazali. Book of Counsel for Kings. I, Jalal Huma & Isaacs, H. D., eds. Bagley, F. R., tr. 1964. 24.95x o.p. (ISBN 0-19-713129-8). Oxford U Pr.

Ghazanfar, S. M. Idaho Statistical Abstract, 1980. 3rd ed. 1980. 30.00x (ISBN 0-940982-01-3). Ctr Bus Devel.

Ghazi, A. Mercy for the Mankind, Vol. I. 1981. 3.00 (ISBN 0-686-97847-1). Kazi Pubns.

--Mercy for the Mankind, Vol. II. 1981. 4.00 (ISBN 0-686-97848-X). Kazi Pubns.

--Messenger of Allah, Vol. I. 1981. 3.50 (ISBN 0-686-97850-1). Kazi Pubns.

--Messenger of Allah, Vol. II. 1981. 4.50 (ISBN 0-686-97851-X). Kazi Pubns.

--Our Prophet, Vol. II. 1981. 2.50 (ISBN 0-686-97846-3). Kazi Pubns.

Ghazi, Algosaibi, tr. see Ghazi, Algosaibi A.

Ghazi, Algosaibi A., ed. Lyrics of Arabia. Ghazi, Algosaibi, tr. from Arabic. 125p. 1983. 12.00x (ISBN 0-89410-379-2); pap. 5.00x (ISBN 0-89410-380-6). Three Continents.

Ghazi, R. World of Islam: Coloring Book. pap. 2.50 (ISBN 0-686-83562-X). Kazi Pubns.

Ghebali, Victor-Yves, ed. see Carnegie Endowment for International Peace.

Ghedini, Silvano. Software for Photometric Astronomy. LC 82-8574. (Illus.). 1982. pap. text ed. 26.95 (ISBN 0-943396-00-X). Willman-Bell.

Ghee, Lim T. Peasants & Their Agricultural Economy in Colonial Malaya, 1874-1941. (East Asian Historical Monographs). (Illus.). 1978. 27.50x o.p. (ISBN 0-19-580338-8). Oxford U Pr.

Gheerbrant, Philip A. Cases in Banking Law. 144p. 1980. 29.00x (ISBN 0-7121-0383-X, Pub. by Macdonald & Evans). State Mutual Bk.

Ghelis, Charis & Yon, Jeannine. Protein Folding. (Molecular Biology Ser.). 556p. 1982. 74.50 (ISBN 0-12-281520-3). Acad Pr.

Ghent, Dorothy Van see Van Ghent, Dorothy.

Gheorghiu, A. & Dragomir, V., eds. Geometry of Structural Forms. (Illus.). 1978. 47.25x (ISBN 0-85334-683-6, Pub. by Applied Sci England). Elsevier.

Gheorghiu, C. Virgil. The Death of Kyralessa. Mihalyi, Marika, tr. from Romanian. LC 75-3992. 268p. 1976. Repr. of 1968 ed. lib. bdg. 20.50x (ISBN 0-8371-7991-2, GHDK). Greenwood.

Ghering, W. L., ed. Reference Data for Acoustic Noise Control. LC 78-62291. (Illus.). 1978. 39.95 (ISBN 0-250-40257-2). Ann Arbor Science.

Ghersini, G., jt. ed. see Braun, T.

Ghezzi, Bert & Kinzer, Mark. Emotions as Resources: A Biblical & Pastorial Approach. 156p. 1983. pap. 3.95 (ISBN 0-89283-158-8). Servant.

Ghezzi, Carlo. Programming Language Concepts. LC 81-16032. 327p. 1982. text ed. 24.95 (ISBN 0-471-08755-6). Wiley.

Ghidalia, Vic, jt. ed. see Elwood, Roger.

Ghilchik, Margaret, jt. auth. see Price, Leonard.

Ghirardelli, B. & Holme, T. Viaggio a Roma. (Illus.). 1975. pap. text ed. 4.25x (ISBN 0-582-36209-1). Longman.

Ghiselin, Brewster, ed. Creative Process. pap. 3.50 (ISBN 0-451-62157-3, ME2157, Ment). NAL.

Ghiselin, Michael T. The Economy of Nature & the Evolution of Sex. LC 73-78554. 1974. 32.50x (ISBN 0-520-02474-5). U of Cal Pr.

Ghista, D. N. Osteoarthromechanics. 1982. 55.00 (ISBN 0-07-023168-0). McGraw.

Ghista, D. N. & Yang, W. J., eds. Cardiovascular Engineering. (Advances in Cardiovascular Physics: Pt. I-IV). (Illus.). xxxxviii, 960p. 1983. 260.00 (ISBN 3-8055-3613-5). S Karger.

--Cardiovascular Engineering, Part I: Modelling. (Advances in Cardiovascular Physics: Vol. 5). (Illus.). xiv, 230p. 1983. 85.75 (ISBN 3-8055-3609-7). S Karger.

--Cardiovascular Engineering, Part II: Monitoring. (Advances in Cardiovascular Physics: Vol. 5). (Illus.). viii, 280p. 1983. 85.75 (ISBN 3-8055-3610-0). S Karger.

--Cardiovascular Engineering, Part III: Diagnosis. (Advances in Cardiovascular Physics: Vol. 5). (Illus.). x, 158p. 1983. 68.50 (ISBN 3-8055-3611-9). S Karger.
--Cardiovascular Engineering: Protheses, Assist & Artificial Organs, Pt. IV. (Advances in Cardiovascular Physics: Vol. 5). (Illus.). viii, 292p. 1983. 85.75 (ISBN 3-8055-3611-9). S Karger.
Ghista, D. N., et al, eds. Perspective in Biomechanics, Vol. I. (Perspectives in Biomechanics Ser.). 891p. 1980. 214.50 o.p. (ISBN 3-7186-0006-4). Harwood Academic.
Ghista, Dhanjoo N., ed. Human Body Dynamics: Impact, Occupational & Athletic Aspects. (Oxford Medical Engineering Ser.). (Illus.). 1982. 69.00x (ISBN 0-19-857548-3). Oxford U Pr.
Ghose, Sankar. Changing India. 1978. 15.00x o.p. (ISBN 0-8364-0241-3). South Asia Bks.
Ghose, Sisirkumar. The Later Poems of Tagore. LC 74-27426. 304p. 1975. Repr. of 1961 ed. lib. bdg. 19.25x (ISBN 0-8371-7902-5, GHPT). Greenwood.
Ghose, Zulfikar. Hamlet, Prufrock & Language. 1978. 13.95x (ISBN 0-312-35723-0). St Martin.
--Hulme's Investigations into the Bogart Script. 1981. 9.95 (ISBN 0-931604-03-6); pap. 4.95 (ISBN 0-686-96698-8). Curbstone Pub NY TX.
Ghosh, Arabinda. OPEC, The Petroleum Industry, & United States Energy Policy. LC 82-13245. (Illus.). 296p. 1983. lib. bdg. 35.00 (ISBN 0-89930-010-3, HD9566, Quorum). Greenwood.
Ghosh, O. K. The Changing Indian Civilization, Vol. 1, 2. LC 76-52201. 1976. 17.00x ea. o.p.; Vol. 1. (ISBN 0-88386-502-5); Vol. 2. (ISBN 0-88386-805-9). South Asia Bks.
Ghosh, P. K. Introduction to Photoelectron Spectroscopy. (Chemical Analysis: A Series of Monographs on Analytical Chemisty & Its Applications). 352p. 1983. 40.00 (ISBN 0-471-06427-0, Pub. by Wiley-Interscience). Wiley.
Ghosh, Rabindra N. Agriculture in Economic Development, India. 1977. 10.00 o.p. (ISBN 0-8364-0086-0). South Asia Bks.
Ghosh, S. N., ed. Advances in Cement Technology: Critical Reviews & Case Studies on Manufacturing, Quality Control, Optimization & Use. (Illus.). 775p. 1982. 100.00 (ISBN 0-08-028670-4). Pergamon.
Ghosh, Sakti P., ed. see National Computer Conference, 1978.
Ghurye, G. S. The Scheduled Tribes of India. LC 79-66430. (Social Science Classics Ser.). 399p. 1980. text ed. 29.95 (ISBN 0-87855-308-8); pap. 7.95 (ISBN 0-87855-692-3). Transaction Bks.
Giacconi & Ruffini, R. Physics & Astrophysics of Neutron Stars & Black Holes: Proceedings. (Enrico Fermi Summer School: Vol. 65). 1979. pap. 57.50 (ISBN 0-444-85446-0, North-Holland). Elsevier.
Giacconi, Mirella, jt. auth. see Caglioti, Luciano.
Giacobini, Ezio, et al, eds. The Aging Brain: Cellular & Molecular Mechanism of Aging in the Nervous System. (Aging Ser.: Vol. 20). 304p. 1982. text ed. 37.00 (ISBN 0-89004-802-9). Raven.
--Tissue Culture in Neurobiology. 536p. 1980. text ed. 57.00 (ISBN 0-89004-461-9). Raven.
Giacobini, S., jt. ed. see Costa, E.
Giacoletto, L. J. Electronics Designer's Handbook. 2nd ed. 1977. 76.50 (ISBN 0-07-023149-4). McGraw.
Giacomo, Giuseppe & Illica, Luigi, eds. La Boheme. (Metropolitan Opera Classics Library). 224p. 1983. 17.45i (ISBN 0-316-56838-4); deluxe ed. 75.00 (ISBN 0-316-56840-6); pap. 9.70i (ISBN 0-316-56839-2). Little.
Giacomo, P., jt. auth. see Ferro Milone, A.
Giaconni, Mirella, tr. see Bellone, Enrico.
Giaconni, Ricardo, tr. see Bellone, Enrico.
Giaever, John. White Desert: The Official Account of the Norwegian-British-Swedish Antarctic Expedition. Huggard, E. M., tr. LC 69-10097. (Illus.). 1969. Repr. of 1954 ed. lib. bdg. 16.00x (ISBN 0-8371-1318-0, GIWD). Greenwood.
Giallombardo, Rose. Juvenile Delinquency: A Book of Readings. 4th ed. LC 81-6927. 591p. 1982. pap. text ed. 15.95 (ISBN 0-471-08344-5). Wiley.
--Society of Women: A Study of a Women's Prison. LC 66-14132. 1966. pap. text ed. 13.95x (ISBN 0-471-29729-1). Wiley.
Giallombardo, Rose, ed. Juvenile Delinquency: A Book of Readings. 3rd ed. LC 75-35887. 1976. pap. text ed. 17.95x (ISBN 0-471-29726-7). Wiley.
Giamatti, A. Bartlett. Western Literature, 3 vols. Incl. Vol. 1. The Ancient World. Von Staden, Heinrich, ed. 550p. pap. (ISBN 0-15-595276-5); Vol. 2. The Middle Ages, Renaissance, Enlightenment. Hollander, Robert, ed. 550p. pap. (ISBN 0-15-595277-3); Vol. 3. The Modern World. Brooks, Peter, ed. 552p. pap. (ISBN 0-15-595278-1). 1971. pap. text ed. 11.95 ea. (HC); instructor's manual avail. (ISBN 0-15-595279-X, HC). HarBraceJ.
Giammati, A. Bartlett, ed. Dante in America: The First Two Centuries. 1983. 20.00 (ISBN 0-86698-059-8). Medieval Renaissance.
Giammatteo, M. C. & Mattox, Phil. Paths of Life. 1977. pap. 5.00 (ISBN 0-918428-10-6). Sylvan Inst.
Giammatti, Victor M. Raising Small Meat Animals. LC 75-21050. 1976. 16.50 (ISBN 0-8134-1741-4); text ed. 12.50x. Interstate.
Gianakaris, C. J. Plutarch. (World Authors Ser.: Greece: No. 111). lib. bdg. 9.95 o.p. (ISBN 0-8057-2706-X, Twayne). G K Hall.
Gian-Carlo Rota, jt. auth. see Birkhoff, Garrett.
Giancoli, Douglas. The Ideas of Physics. 2nd ed. (Illus.). 528p. 1978. text ed. 21.95 (ISBN 0-15-540559-4, HC); instructor's manual avail. (ISBN 0-15-540560-8); supplement 4.95 (ISBN 0-15-540561-6). HarBraceJ.
Giancoli, Douglas C. Physics: Principle with Applications. 1980. text ed. 28.95 (ISBN 0-13-672600-3); solutions manual avail. P-H.
Giangreco, Marianne R. Waubonsie Encounter: Poems of Southwest Iowa. 75p. 1983. cancelled (ISBN 0-935054-07-3). Webb-Newcomb.
Giannessi, F. see Cottle, R. W., et al.
Giannestras, Nicholas J., ed. Foot Disorders: Medical & Surgical Management. 2nd ed. LC 72-13759. (Illus.). 699p. 1973. text ed. 37.50 o.p. (ISBN 0-8121-0407-2). Lea & Febiger.
Giannetti, Louis. Masters of the American Cinema. 255p. 1981. text ed. 17.95 (ISBN 0-13-560110-X); pap. text ed. 15.95 (ISBN 0-13-560102-9). P-H.
--Understanding Movies. 3rd ed. (Illus.). 512p. 1982. pap. 14.95 (ISBN 0-13-936310-6). P-H.
Giannini, A. James. Psychiatric, Psychogenic, & Somatopsychic Disorders Handbook. 1978. pap. 16.95 (ISBN 0-87488-596-5). Med Exam.
Giannini, A. James & Slaby, Andrew E. Emergency Guide to Overdose & Detoxification. 1983. pap. text ed. price not set (ISBN 0-87488-182-X). Med Exam.
Giannotti, John B. & Smith, Richard W. Treasury Management Practioners' Handbook: A Practical Approach to Treasury Management in the Multinational Corporation. LC 8-1523. 536p. 1981. 45.95x (ISBN 0-471-08062-4, Pub. by Wiley Interscience). Wiley.
Giantvalley, Scott. Walt Whitman, Eighteen Thirty-Eight to Nineteen Thirty-Nine: A Reference Guide. 1981. lib. bdg. 50.00 (ISBN 0-8161-7856-9, Hall Reference). G K Hall.
Gianutsos, Rosamond, jt. ed. see Ebihara, May.
Giap, Vo Nguyen. Military Art of People's War: Selected Writings. Stetler, Russell, ed. LC 75-105317. (Illus.). 1970. 8.50 o.p. (ISBN 0-85345-129-X, CL-129X); pap. 5.95 o.p. (ISBN 0-85345-193-1, PB-1931). Monthly Rev.
Giardinelli, Mempo. Vidas ejemplares. (Span.). 1982. pap. 7.00 (ISBN 0-910061-11-4). Ediciones Norte.
Giardini, Fabio. Loving Awareness of God's Presence in Prayer. LC 78-9654. 1978. 4.50 o.p. (ISBN 0-8189-0370-8). Alba.
Giaretto, Henry. Intergrated Treatment of Child Sexual Abuse. LC 81-86712. 25.00 (ISBN 0-8314-0061-7). Sci & Behavior.
Giarrantani, Frank, jt. auth. see Miernyk, William H.
Giarratano, Joseph. Foundations of Computer Technology. Date not set. pap. 22.95 (ISBN 0-672-21814-3). Sams.
--Modern Computer Concepts. Date not set. pap. 22.95 (ISBN 0-672-21815-1). Sams.
Giarratano, Joseph C. Timex-Sinclair One Thousand Pocket Dictionary. 1983. pap. 4.95 (ISBN 0-88022-028-7). Que Corp.
--Timex-Sinclair One Thousand User's Guide, Vol. II. 1983. pap. 12.95 (ISBN 0-88022-029-5). Que Corp.
Gibaldi, Joseph, ed. see Barricelli, Jean-Pierre, et al.
Gibaldi, M., jt. ed. see Prescott, L. F.
Gibaldi, Milo & Perrier, Donald. Pharmacokinetics. (Drugs & Pharmaceutical Sciences Ser.: Vol. 1). 352p. 1975. 27.25 o.p. (ISBN 0-8247-6264-9). Dekker.
Gibat, jt. auth. see Howard.
Gibb, A. Glasgow: The Making of a City. 224p. 1983. text ed. 25.25 (ISBN 0-7099-0161-5, Pub. by Croom Helm Ltd England). Biblio Dist.
Gibb, Allan & Webb, Terry. Policy Issues in Small Business Research. 1979. text ed. 27.00x (ISBN 0-566-00312-0). Gower Pub Ltd.
Gibb, C. C. More Than Enough. 83p. pap. 3.95 (ISBN 0-88172-071-2). Believers Bkshelf.
Gibb, George, ed. see Lam, Roger.
Gibb, Hamilton A. Mohammedanism: An Historical Survey. 2nd ed. 1953. pap. 4.95x (ISBN 0-19-500245-8, 90). Oxford U Pr.
Gibb, James. The Book of Sherborne. 1981. 39.50x o.p. (ISBN 0-86023-081-3, Pub. by Barracuda England). State Mutual Bk.
Gibb, Robin, et al. Bee Gees: The Biography. Leaf, David, ed. LC 78-74097. (Illus.). 1979. 6.95 (ISBN 0-440-04072-8). Delilah Bks.
Gibb, T. C., jt. auth. see Greenwood, N. N.
Gibb, Terence C. Principles of Mossbauer Spectroscopy. 254p. 1976. 39.95x (ISBN 0-412-13960-X, Pub. by Chapman & Hall England); pap. 18.95x (ISBN 0-412-23060-7, Pub. by Chapman & Hall England). Methuen Inc.
Gibbard, Mark. Guides to Hidden Springs: A History of Christian Spirituality Through the Lives of Some of Its Witnesses. (Student Christian Movement Press). (Orig.). 1970. pap. 6.95 o.p. (ISBN 0-19-520318-6). Oxford U Pr.
Gibbens, T. C., et al. Medical Remands in the Criminal Court. (Maudaley Monographs). 1977. text ed. 32.50x o.p. (ISBN 0-19-712147-0). Oxford U Pr.
Gibbins, Robert J., et al, eds. Research Advances in Alcohol & Drug Problems, 3 vols. LC 73-18088. 384p. 1974-76. Vol. 1. 60.95x o.p. (ISBN 0-471-29737-2); 47.95 o.p. (ISBN 0-686-76997-X); Vol. 3. 68.95x o.p. (ISBN 0-471-29736-4, Pub. by Wiley-Medical). Wiley.
Gibbon. Kittens. Date not set. 2.98 o.p. (ISBN 0-517-27548-1). Crown.
Gibbon, David. Holland: A Picture Book to Remember Her by. (Illus.). 3.98 o.p. (ISBN 0-517-28857-5). Crown.
Gibbon, Edward. Autobiography. (World's Classics, No. 139). 16.95 (ISBN 0-19-250139-9). Oxford U Pr.
--Gibbon's Autobiography. Reese, M. M., ed. (Routledge English Texts). 1970. 9.95x (ISBN 0-7100-6923-5); pap. 4.95 (ISBN 0-7100-6925-1). Routledge & Kegan.
Gibbon, Monk, ed. see Hyde, Douglas.
Gibbon, P., jt. auth. see Bew, P.
Gibbons, jt. auth. see Myant.
Gibbons, Alice. The People Time Forgot. LC 81-9466. 324p. 1981. pap. 5.95 (ISBN 0-8024-8692-4). Moody.
Gibbons, Barbara. The Slim Gourmet Cookbook. LC 75-23883. 416p. 1976. 16.30i (ISBN 0-06-011517-3, HarpT). Har-Row.
--Slim Gourmet Sweets & Treats. LC 82-47737. 320p. 1982. 14.37i (ISBN 0-06-015057-2, HarpT). Har-Row.
Gibbons, Don C. Delinquent Behavior. 3rd ed. (Illus.). 1981. text ed. 22.95 (ISBN 0-13-197962-0). P-H.
--Society, Crime, & Criminal Behavior. 4th ed. (Illus.). 576p. 1982. text ed. 24.95 (ISBN 0-13-820118-8). P-H.
Gibbons, Don C. & Jones, John F. The Study of Deviance: Perspectives & Problems. (Illus.). 192p. 1975. pap. text ed. 15.95 (ISBN 0-13-858936-4). P-H.
Gibbons, Euell & Tucker, Gordon. Euell Gibbons' Handbook of Edible Wild Plants. LC 79-14420. (Illus.). 1979. 9.95 (ISBN 0-915442-82-5, Unilaw); pap. 4.95 o.p. (ISBN 0-915442-78-7). Donning Co.
Gibbons, Francis M. Lorenzo Snow: Spiritual Giant, Prophet of God. (Illus.). 247p. 1982. 8.95 (ISBN 0-87747-936-4). Deseret Bk.
Gibbons, Gail. Boat Book. LC 82-15851. (Illus.). 32p. (ps-3). 1983. reinforced binding 11.95 (ISBN 0-8234-0478-1). Holiday.
--Christmas Time. LC 82-1038. (Illus.). 32p. (ps-3). 1982. Reinforced bdg. 10.95 (ISBN 0-8234-0453-6). Holiday.
--The Magnificent Morris Mouse Clubhouse. (Easy-Read Story Bks.). (Illus.). 32p. (gr. k-3). 1981. 3.95 (ISBN 0-531-03540-9); lib. bdg. 8.60 (ISBN 0-531-04302-9). Watts.
--Paper, Paper Everywhere. LC 82-3109. (Illus.). 32p. (gr. 6-10). 10.95 (ISBN 0-15-259488-4, HJ). HarBraceJ.
--The Too Great Bread Bake Book. LC 80-11743. (Illus.). 48p. (gr. k-3). 1980. 8.95 o.p. (ISBN 0-7232-6182-2). Warne.
Gibbons, J. Whitfield & Sharitz, Rebecca R., eds. Thermal Ecology: Proceedings. LC 74-600136. (AEC Symposium Ser.). 687p. 1974. pap. 25.25 (CONF-730505); microfiche 4.50 (ISBN 0-87079-225-3, CONF-730505). DOE.
Gibbons, J. Whitfield, jt. ed. see Thorp, James H.
Gibbons, James. Semiconductor Electronics. 1966. text ed. 38.00 (ISBN 0-07-023162-1, C). McGraw.
Gibbons, Jean D., et al. Selecting & Ordering Populations: A New Statistical Methodology. LC 77-3700. (Probability & Mathematical Statistics). 1977. 51.50x (ISBN 0-471-02670-0, Pub. by Wiley-Interscience). Wiley.
Gibbons, John, jt. auth. see Fraser, Edward.
Gibbons, John T., jt. auth. see Smith, Douglass.
Gibbons, Reginald, ed. The Poet's Work: Twenty-Nine Masters of Twentieth Century Poetry on the Origins & Practice of Their Art. 1979. 12.50 o.s.i. (ISBN 0-395-27616-0); pap. 5.95 (ISBN 0-395-28057-5). HM.
Gibbons, Reginald, tr. see Cernuda, Luis.
Gibbons, Robert & Ashford, Bob. The KIngdoms of the Himalayas: Nepal, Sikkim, & Bhutan. (Illus.). 250p. 1983. 17.50 (ISBN 0-88254-802-6). Hippocrene Bks.
Gibbons, Robert C. Woldman's Engineering Alloys. 6th ed. 1979. 81.00 (ISBN 0-87170-086-7). ASM.
Gibbons, Robert J., ed. Principles of Premium Auditing, 2 vols. LC 81-80773. 668p. 1981. Vol. 1. pap. 13.00 o.p. (ISBN 0-89462-008-8, PA 91); Vol. 2. pap. 13.00 o.p. (ISBN 0-89462-010-X). IIA.
Gibbons, Robert J., et al. Premium Auditing Applications, 2 vols. LC 81-80774. 681p. 1981. Vol. 1. pap. 13.00 (ISBN 0-89462-009-6); Vol. 2. pap. 13.00 (ISBN 0-686-83192-6). IIA.
Gibbons, William, jt. auth. see Hibbard, Lester T.
Gibbs, A. M., ed. see Davenant, William.
Gibbs, A. P. Christian Baptism. 1982. pap. 4.50 (ISBN 0-937396-62-1). Walteick Pubs.
--The Preacher & His Preaching. 13.00 (ISBN 0-937396-31-1); pap. 8.95 (ISBN 0-937396-30-3). Walterick Pubs.
--Scriptural Principles of Gathering. pap. 1.50 (ISBN 0-937396-37-0). Walterick Pubs.
--Through the Scriptures. pap. 5.95 (ISBN 0-937396-45-1). Walterick Pubs.
--Worship, the Christian's Highest Occupation: The Christian's Highest Occupation. pap. 5.00 (ISBN 0-937396-57-5). Walterick Pubs.
--Your Quiet Time. 16p. 1981. pap. 1.25 (ISBN 0-89107-244-6). Good News.
Gibbs, Barbara. Green Pharmacy. 384p. 1981. 40.00x o.p. (ISBN 0-906908-64-7, Pub. by A Hilger). State Mutual Bk.
Gibbs, Benjamin. Freedom & Liberation. LC 76-12234. 1976. 15.95 o.p. (ISBN 0-312-30415-3). St Martin.
Gibbs, C. E., jt. auth. see Gibbs, R. S.
Gibbs, Eddie. I Believe in Church Growth. 1982. pap. 8.95 (ISBN 0-8028-1921-4). Eerdmans.
Gibbs, George W. New Zealand Butterflies. (Illus.). 208p. 1983. 45.00 (ISBN 0-00-216955-X, Pub. by W Collins Australia). Intl Schol Bk Serv.
Gibbs, H. G. & Richards, T. H., eds. Stress, Vibration & Noise Analysis in Vehicles. LC 75-14389. 485p. 1975. 74.95 o.p. (ISBN 0-470-29742-5). Halsted Pr.
Gibbs, Jack P., ed. Social Control: Views from the Social Sciences. (Sage Focus Editions: Vol. 51). (Illus.). 288p. 1982. 20.00 (ISBN 0-8039-0615-3); pap. 9.95 (ISBN 0-8039-0616-1). Sage.
Gibbs, James A. Oregon's Salty Coast. LC 78-11899. (Illus.). 1978. 10.95 (ISBN 0-87564-222-5). Superior Pub.
Gibbs, Jim. Shipwrecks in Paradise. LC 76-16070. (Illus.). 1976. 13.95 o.s.i. (ISBN 0-87564-218-7). Superior Pub.
Gibbs, John W. & Paige, Robert. Financial Decision-Making in Business: Planning & Control Techniques to Increase Your Profits. (Illus.). 288p. 1980. text ed. 13.95 o.p. (ISBN 0-13-315994-9, Spec); pap. text ed. 6.95 o.p. (ISBN 0-13-315986-8). P-H.
Gibbs, Lois M. Love Canal: My Story. LC 82-47996. 192p. 1982. pap. 6.95 (ISBN 0-394-17994-3, E830, Ever). Grove.
Gibbs, Lois Marie. Love Canal: My Story. LC 81-14508. 174p. 1982. 12.95 (ISBN 0-87395-587-0); pap. 8.95x 321 0-87395-588-9. State U NY Pr.
Gibbs, Margaret C. How to Be a Useful Trustee. 1977. pap. 3.50 (ISBN 0-685-81997-3). Creative Pr.
Gibbs, Martin, jt. ed. see Ting, Irwin P.
Gibbs, P. E. The British Sipunculans: Keys & Notes for the Identification of the Species. (Synopses of the British Fauna Ser.). 1977. pap. 9.00 o.s.i. (ISBN 0-12-282050-9). Acad Pr.
Gibbs, R. S. & Gibbs, C. E. Ambulatory Obstetrics: A Clinical Guide. LC 79-18554. 1979. pap. text ed. 15.95x (ISBN 0-471-05227-2, Pub. by Wiley Medical). Wiley.
Gibbs, Richard. Women Prime Ministers. LC 81-86273. (In Profile Ser.). PLB 12.68 (ISBN 0-382-06638-3). Silver.
Gibbs, Richard C., jt. auth. see Costello, Maurice J.
Gibbs, Ronald S. Antibiotic Therapy in Obstetrics & Gynecology. LC 80-23095. 215p. 1981. 21.95 (ISBN 0-471-06003-8, Pub. by Wiley Med). Wiley.
Gibbs, Stephen, jt. auth. see Miles, Edward.
Gibbs, T. E., jt. auth. see Meredith, Jack R.
Gibbs, Tony. Advanced Sailing. new ed. LC 74-83575. (Illus.). 1975. 5.95 (ISBN 0-312-00630-6). St Martin.
--Pilot's Log Book. 1979. pap. 4.00 o.s.i. (ISBN 0-915160-04-8). Seven Seas.
Gibbs, Tony, ed. Pilot's Work Book. 1979. pap. 4.00 o.s.i. (ISBN 0-915160-03-X). Seven Seas.
Gibert, E. G. Observations sur les Ecrits De M. De Voltaire. Repr. of 1788 ed. 225.00 o.p. (ISBN 0-8287-0375-2). Clearwater Pub.
Gibilisco, Joseph A., jt. ed. see Laney, William R.
Giblin, James C. Fireworks, Pinics, & Flags: The Story of the Fourth of July Symbols. (Illus.). 96p. (gr. 3-6). 1983. 10.50 (ISBN 0-89919-146-0, Clarion); pap. 3.95 (ISBN 0-89919-174-6). HM.
Giblin, P. J. Graphs, Surfaces & Homology: An Introduction to Algebraic Topology. 2nd ed. 1981. pap. 15.95x (ISBN 0-412-23900-0, Pub. by Chapman & Hall). Methuen Inc.
Giblon, Shirley T., jt. auth. see Narrol, Harvey G.
Gibney, Frank. Japan: The Fragile Superpower. rev. ed. 1980. pap. 7.95 (ISBN 0-452-00593-0, F593, Mer). NAL.
--Japan: The Fragile Superpower. 1975. 10.95x o.p. (ISBN 0-393-05530-2). Norton.
--Japan: The Fragile Superpower. rev. ed. 1979. 12.95 o.p. (ISBN 0-393-05704-6). Norton.
--Miracle by Design: The Real Reasons Behind Japan's Economic Success. 256p. 1982. 16.82 (ISBN 0-8129-1024-9). Times Bks.
--The Operators. LC 75-32546. 284p. 1976. Repr. of 1960 ed. lib. bdg. 18.00x (ISBN 0-8371-8492-4, GIOP). Greenwood.
Gibney, Josephine. Joe McGarrigle's Daughter. 1980. 12.00x o.p. (ISBN 0-900093-62-5, Pub. by Roundwood). State Mutual Bk.
Gibney, Michael J., jt. ed. see Kritchevsky, David.
Gibran, Kahlil. Forerunner. (Illus.). 1920. 9.95 (ISBN 0-394-40350-9). Knopf.
--Madman. (Illus.). 1918. 8.95 (ISBN 0-394-40382-7). Knopf.
--Mirrors of the Soul. LC 70-136015. 1971. pap. 2.95 o.p. (ISBN 0-685-77486-4). Philos Lib.
--Prophet. (Illus.). (YA) 1923. 7.95 (ISBN 0-394-40428-9); deluxe ed. 13.95 (ISBN 0-394-40426-2); pocket ed. 7.95 (ISBN 0-394-40427-0). Knopf.

--Tear & a Smile. (Illus.). 1950. 9.95 (ISBN 0-394-44804-9). Knopf.

Gibson, jt. auth. see Golembiewski.

Gibson, A. H. & Newton, W. E., eds. Current Perspective in Nitrogen Fixation. 1981. 90.00 (ISBN 0-444-80291-6). Elsevier.

Gibson, Arrell. The American Indian: Prehistory to the Present. 618p. 1980. pap. text ed. 13.95 (ISBN 0-669-04493-8). Heath.

--West in the Life of the Nation. 1976. 20.95x (ISBN 0-669-61515-3). Heath.

Gibson, Arrell M. The Santa Fe & Taos Colonies: Age of the Muses, Nineteen Hundred to Nineteen Forty-Two. LC 82-40452. (Illus.). 328p. 1983. 24.95 (ISBN 0-8061-1835-0). U of Okla Pr.

Gibson, Arrell M., ed. see Kipling, Rudyard.

Gibson, Arthur. Biblical Semantic Logic. 1981. 30.00 (ISBN 0-312-07796-3). St Martin.

Gibson, Arthur C., jt. auth. see Brown, James H.

Gibson, Barbara G. Personal Computers in Business: An Introduction & Buyers Guide. (Illus., Orig.). 1982. pap. 2.95 (ISBN 0-9609780-0-3). Apple Comp.

Gibson, C. G. Singular Points of Smooth Mappings. (Research Notes in Mathematics Ser.: No. 25). 239p. 1979. pap. text ed. 21.95 (ISBN 0-273-08410-0). Pitman Pub MA.

Gibson, Charles. Inca Concept of Sovereignty & the Spanish Administration in Peru. LC 69-19004. Repr. of 1948 ed. lib. bdg. 15.75x (ISBN 0-8371-1021-1, TLGI). Greenwood.

--Spain in America. (New American Nation Ser.). 1968. pap. 4.95xi (ISBN 0-06-133077-9, TB3077, Torch). Har-Row.

--Spain in America. LC 66-21705. (New American Nation Ser.). (Illus.). 1966. 16.30xi (ISBN 0-06-011520-3, HarpT). Har-Row.

Gibson, Charles D. Boca Grande: A Series of Historical Essays. LC 82-90197. (Illus.). 250p. (Orig.). 1982. pap. text ed. 12.95 (ISBN 0-9608996-0-X). C D Gibson.

--Gibson Girl & Her America. Gillon, Edmund V., ed. LC 68-28065. (Illus., Orig.). 1969. pap. 5.00 (ISBN 0-486-21986-0). Dover.

Gibson, Charles H. & Frishkoff, Patricia A. Financial Statement Analysis. 2nd ed. 544p. 1982. text ed. 24.95x (ISBN 0-534-01344-9). Kent Pub Co.

Gibson, Colin, ed. see Massinger, Philip.

Gibson, Cyrusf., jt. auth. see Lucas, Henry.

Gibson, D. M. First Aid Homoeopathy in Accidents & Ailments. 1982. pap. 5.95 (ISBN 0-685-76564-4, Pub. by British Homoeopathy Assoc.). Formur Intl.

Gibson, Dennis L. Live, Grow & Be Free: A Guide to Self-Parenting. 136p. 1982. pap. 4.95 (ISBN 0-89840-031-7). Here's Life.

Gibson, Donald, ed. A Parson in the Vale of White Horse: George Woodward's Letters from East Hendred, 1753-61. 192p. 1982. pap. text ed. 8.25x (ISBN 0-86299-025-4, Pub. by Sutton England). Humanities.

Gibson, Duncan. Energy Graphics. (Illus.). 144p. 1983. 19.95 (ISBN 0-13-277624-3). P-H.

Gibson, Duncan L. America Today in Maps, Graphs & Tables. (Illus.). 160p. 1983. pap. text ed. 15.95 (ISBN 0-9608014-1-3). World Eagle.

Gibson, E. Principles of Perceptual Learning & Development. 1969. 27.95 (ISBN 0-13-709618-6). P-H.

Gibson, E. J., ed. Developments in Building Maintenance, Vol. 1. (Illus.). 1979. 35.00x (ISBN 0-85334-801-4, Pub. by Applied Sci England). Elsevier.

Gibson, Eleanor J. & Levin, Harry. The Psychology of Reading. 1975. 27.50x (ISBN 0-262-07063-4); pap. 9.95x (ISBN 0-262-57052-1). MIT Pr.

Gibson, Elizabeth, compiled by. Get Well Wishes & Sunny Thoughts to Cheer You. 1977. pap. 5.50 (ISBN 0-8378-5009-6). Gibson.

Gibson, Frank, jt. auth. see Golembiewski, Robert T.

Gibson, G. G. & Loannides, C., eds. Safety Evaluation of Nitrosatable Drugs & Chemicals. 275p. 1981. 90.00x (ISBN 0-85066-212-5, Pub. by Taylor & Francis). State Mutual Bk.

Gibson, G. L., ed. see Cooke, E. M.

Gibson, George H. Public Broadcasting: The Role of the Federal Government, 1912-76. LC 77-24422. (Praeger Special Studies). 1977. 27.95 o.p. (ISBN 0-03-022831-X). Praeger.

Gibson, Gerald D., jt. auth. see Gray, Michael H.

Gibson, Glenn A. & Liu, Yu-Cheng. Microcomputers for Engineers & Scientists. (Illus.). 1980. text ed. 32.95 (ISBN 0-13-580886-3). P-H.

Gibson, Grace E. Home in Time. Bayes, Ronald H., ed. 100p. (Orig.). 1977. pap. 3.00 (ISBN 0-932662-22-6). St Andrews NC.

Gibson, Grace L. & Bayes, Ronald H. Drakes Branch. Linehan, James, ed. LC 82-62745. 64p. 1982. pap. 6.95 (ISBN 0-932662-43-9). St Andrews NC.

Gibson, Graeme. Five Legs & Communion. 333p. (Orig.). 1979. pap. 5.95 o.p. (ISBN 0-88784-073-6, Pub. by Hse Anansi Pr Canada). U of Toronto Pr.

Gibson, Guadalupe, ed. Our Kingdom Stands on Brittle Glass. 1983. pap. text ed. 11.95x (ISBN 0-87101-119-0, CBF-103-C). Natl Assn Soc Wkrs.

Gibson, H. Lou. Photography by Infrared: Its Principles & Applications. 3rd ed. LC 77-26919. (Photographic Science & Technology & Graphic Arts Ser.). 1978. 54.50x (ISBN 0-471-15895-X, Pub. by Wiley-Interscience). Wiley.

Gibson, Henrik. Ibsen: The Complete Major Prose Plays. Fjelde, Rolf, tr. (Orig.). 1978. pap. 10.50 (ISBN 0-452-25300-4, Z5300, Plume). NAL.

Gibson, Ian. Assassination of Frederico Garcia Lorca. 1983. pap. 5.95 (ISBN 0-14-006473-7). Penguin.

Gibson, J., jt. auth. see Grainger, L.

Gibson, J. E. Computing in Structural Engineering. (Illus.). xv, 290p. 1975. 53.50 (ISBN 0-85334-614-3, Pub. by Applied Sci England). Elsevier.

--Designing the New City: A Systematic Approach. LC 76-44899. (Systems Engineering & Analysis Ser.). 288p. 1977. 39.95x (ISBN 0-471-29752-6, Pub. by Wiley-Interscience). Wiley.

Gibson, J. E., jt. auth. see LaConte, P.

Gibson, J. S., compiled by. Bishops Transcripts & Marriage Licences, Bonds & Allegations: A Guide to Their Location & Indexes. 2nd ed. 52p. 1982. pap. 5.00x (ISBN 0-906428-11-4). Intl Pubns Serv.

Gibson, James E. The Medical Background of the American Revolution: The Career of Dr. Bodo Otto, Senior Surgeon of the Continental Army. (Perspectives in American History Ser.: No. 42). (Illus.). ix, 345p. Repr. of 1937 ed. lib. bdg. 25.00x o.p. (ISBN 0-87991-366-5). Porcupine Pr.

Gibson, James E., ed. Formaldehyde Toxicity. LC 82-6189. (Chemical Industry Institute of Toxicology Ser.). (Illus.). 400p. 1983. text ed. 49.95 (ISBN 0-89116-275-5). Hemisphere Pub.

Gibson, James J. The Ecological Approach to Visual Perception. LC 78-69585. (Illus.). 1979. text ed. 35.95 (ISBN 0-395-27049-9). HM.

--The Senses Considered As Perceptual Systems. LC 66-7132. 1966. text ed. 34.50 o.p. (ISBN 0-395-04494-4). HM.

Gibson, James R. Imperial Russia in Frontier America: The Changing Geography of Supply of Russian America, 1784-1867. (The Andrew H. Clark Series in the Historical Geography of North America). (Illus.). 1976. text ed. 14.95x (ISBN 0-19-501876-1); pap. text ed. 9.95x (ISBN 0-19-501875-3). Oxford U Pr.

Gibson, James W. & Cornwell, Clifton. Creative Speech Communication. 1978. pap. text ed. 9.95x (ISBN 0-02-341720-X). Macmillan.

Gibson, Janice. Psychology for the Classroom. 2nd ed. (Illus.). 640p. 1981. pap. text ed. 23.95 (ISBN 0-13-733352-8); student study guide 11.95 (ISBN 0-13-733386-2). P-H.

Gibson, Janice T. Discipline Is Not a Dirty Word. 176p. 1983. 12.95 (ISBN 0-86616-027-2); pap. 7.95 (ISBN 0-86616-023-X). Lewis Pub Co.

--Discipline Is Not a Dirty Word. 1983. 12.95 (ISBN 0-86616-027-2); pap. 7.95 (ISBN 0-686-42867-6). Greene.

Gibson, Jean. Advanced Christian Training. (Believer's Bible Lessons Ser.). (Orig.). Date not set. pap. price not set (ISBN 0-937396-04-4). Walterick Pubs. Postponed.

Gibson, Jerry, ed. Meeting Student Aid Needs in a Period of Retrenchment. LC 81-48571. 1982. 7.95x (ISBN 0-87589-897-1, HE-39). Jossey-Bass.

Gibson, John. Fifty Hikes in Maine: Day Hikes & Backpacking Trips from the Coast to Katahdin. 2nd, rev. ed. LC 82-25276. (Fifty Hikes Ser.). (Illus.). 192p. (Orig.). 1983. pap. 8.95 (ISBN 0-942440-13-7). Backcountry Pubns.

--Go Light. LC 80-12051. (Illus.). 128p. (Orig.). 1980. pap. 4.95 o.p. (ISBN 0-89621-057-X). Thorndike Pr.

Gibson, John & French, Thomas. Nursing the Mentally Retarded. 4th ed. 184p. 1978. 11.95 o.p. (ISBN 0-571-04959-1); pap. 5.95 o.p. (ISBN 0-571-04941-9). Faber & Faber.

Gibson, John C. Genesis, Vol. 2. LC 81-7477. (Daily Study Bible Ser.). 1982. 12.95 (ISBN 0-664-21804-0); pap. 6.95 (ISBN 0-664-24571-4). Westminster.

Gibson, John C., ed. see Ellison, H. L.

Gibson, John C., ed. see Riggans, Walter.

Gibson, John C. L. Genesis, Vol. 1. LC 81-7477. (Daily Study Bible Ser.). 1981. 10.95 (ISBN 0-664-21801-6); pap. 5.95 (ISBN 0-664-24568-4). Westminster.

Gibson, John E. How to Size up People. LC 77-78111. 1977. 7.95 (ISBN 0-89310-015-3); pap. 4.50 o.p. (ISBN 0-89310-016-1). Carillon Bks.

--Managing Research & Development. LC 81-2033. 367p. 1981. 39.95x (ISBN 0-471-08799-8, Pub. by Wiley-Interscience). Wiley.

Gibson, John M. Soldier in White: The Life of General George Miller Sternberg. LC 58-9388. 1958. 16.25 o.p. (ISBN 0-8223-0065-6). Duke.

Gibson, John M., jt. auth. see Green, Richard L.

Gibson, John T. Financing Education. LC 80-1364. 498p. 1981. lib. bdg. 25.50 o.p. (ISBN 0-8191-1665-3); pap. text ed. 15.00 o.p. (ISBN 0-8191-1666-1). U Pr of Amer.

Gibson, Karon W., et al. On Our Own. Catterson, Joy S. & Skalka, Patricia, eds. 256p. 1981. 9.95 (ISBN 0-312-58455-5). St Martin.

Gibson, Katherine. The Tall Book of Bible Stories. LC 57-10952. (Tall Bks.). (Illus.). 128p. (gr. k-3). 1980. 5.95 (ISBN 0-06-021935-1, HarpJ); PLB 7.89 (ISBN 0-06-021936-X). Har-Row.

Gibson, Katherine W., et al. On Our Own. 224p. 1982. pap. 2.50 (ISBN 0-686-83053-9, 380-60269-5). Avon.

Gibson, L., jt. auth. see Alexander, John W.

Gibson, Margaret, jt. auth. see David, William.

Gibson, Margaret, ed. Boethius: His Life, Writings & Influence. (Illus.). 432p. 1982. text ed. 48.00x (ISBN 0-631-11141-7, Pub. by Basil Blackwell England). Biblio Dist.

Gibson, Margaret I. The Roots of Russian Through Chekhov: A Study in Word-Formation. LC 81-43705. 236p. (Orig.). 1982. lib. bdg. 22.50 (ISBN 0-8191-2681-0); pap. text ed. 10.75 (ISBN 0-8191-2682-9). U Pr of Amer.

Gibson, Margaret W. Emma Smith: Elect Lady. LC 54-7910. 1954. pap. 8.00 (ISBN 0-8309-0256-2). Herald Hse.

Gibson, Mary J. & Heath, Angela, eds. International Survey of Periodicals in Gerontology. 2nd ed. 53p. (Orig.). 1982. pap. text ed. 10.00 (ISBN 0-910473-02-1). Intl Fed Ageing.

Gibson, Michael & Box, Sue. Discovering Ancient Mysteries. (Full Color Fact Books). (Illus.). 32p. (gr. 4-12). 1982. PLB 7.95 (ISBN 0-8219-0015-3). EMC.

Gibson, Michael & Pike, Trisha. All About Knights. (Full Color Fact Books). (Illus.). 32p. (gr. 4-12). 1982. PLB 7.95 (ISBN 0-8219-0016-1, 35547). EMC.

Gibson, Michael & Strongman, Harry. The Vikings. LC 77-86712. (Peoples of the Past Ser.). (Illus.). 1977. PLB 12.68 (ISBN 0-8094-2332-4). Silver.

Gibson, Miles E. AG Pilot Employment Guide: Crop Dusting. 55p. (Orig.). 1978. pap. 6.95 o.s.i. (ISBN 0-942306-03-1). Diversified Pub Co.

Gibson, Morgan. Kenneth Rexroth. (U. S. Authors Ser.: No. 208). lib. bdg. 7.95 o.p. (ISBN 0-8057-0612-7, Twayne). G K Hall.

Gibson, Morris. One Man's Medicine. 218p. 1983. 12.95 (ISBN 0-686-84498-X). Beaufort Bks NY.

Gibson, Price. Quality Circles: One Approach to Productivity Improvement. (Work in America Institute Studies in Productivity). 1982. 35.00 (ISBN 0-08-029507-X). Pergamon.

Gibson, R. & Higgins, Robert. Techniques of Guidance: An Approach to Pupil Analysis. 1966. text ed. 12.95 o.s.i. (ISBN 0-574-50102-9, 5-0102). SRA.

Gibson, Ralph. Days at Sea. LC 74-13171. 72p. 1974. pap. 12.95 (ISBN 0-912810-15-7). Lustrum Pr.

--Deja-Vu: Second in the Black Trilogy. LC 72-96851. 52p. 1972. 12.95 (ISBN 0-912810-06-8). Lustrum Pr.

--The Somnambulist. 2nd ed. LC 73-88292. (Illus.). 48p. 1973. 12.95 (ISBN 0-912810-09-2). Lustrum Pr.

--Syntax. LC 82-83708. (Illus.). 80p. 1983. 24.95 (ISBN 0-912810-39-4). Lustrum Pr.

Gibson, Ralph, et al, eds. Contact: Theory. LC 80-7809. (Illus.). 176p. 1982. 35.00 (ISBN 0-912810-30-0); pap. 17.95 (ISBN 0-912810-31-9). Lustrum Pr.

Gibson, Ray. British Nemerteans. LC 81-18193. (Synopses of the British Fauna Ser.: No. 24). 200p. 1982. 32.50 (ISBN 0-521-24619-9). Cambridge U Pr.

--Nemerteans. (Illus.). 1972. text ed. 10.50x o.p. (ISBN 0-09-111990-1, Hutchinson U Lib); pap. text ed. 5.50x o.p. (ISBN 0-09-111991-X, Hutchinson U Lib). Humanities.

Gibson, Richard. African Liberation Movements: Contemporary Struggles Against White Minority Rule. (Illus.). 1972. pap. 4.95 (ISBN 0-19-501617-3, GB). Oxford U Pr.

Gibson, Robert. The Land Without a Name: Alain-Fournier & His World. LC 75-4392. (Illus.). 320p. 1975. text ed. 27.50 o.p. (ISBN 0-312-46515-7). St Martin.

Gibson, Robert L. & Mitchell, Marianne. An Introduction to Guidance. (Illus.). 1981. text ed. 20.95x (ISBN 0-02-341730-7). Macmillan.

Gibson, Robert W., ed. The Special Library Role in Networks: Proceedings of a Conference. pap. 10.50 (ISBN 0-87111-279-5). SLA.

Gibson, Ronald. The Family Doctor: His Life & History. 232p. 1982. text ed. 25.00x o.p. (ISBN 0-04-610017-2). Allen Unwin.

--Jefferson Davis & the Confederacy: Chronology-Documents-Bibliographical Aids. LC 77-10189. (Presidential Chronology Ser.). 205p. 1977. 15.00 (ISBN 0-379-12095-X). Oceana.

--Name & Subject Index to the Presidential Chronology Series: From George Washington to Gerald Ford. LC 77-21512. (Presidential Chronology Ser.). 141p. 1977. 15.00 (ISBN 0-379-12094-1). Oceana.

Gibson, Sam. Expressions: The Real Truths. 1982. 4.95 (ISBN 0-8062-1787-1). Carlton.

Gibson, Sonny, jt. auth. see Mazzola, Reparata.

Gibson, Stephen E., jt. auth. see Cohen, Kalman J.

Gibson, Stephen G., jt. auth. see Cohen, Kalman J.

Gibson, Stephen W. Amateur Radio License Guide. 1981. 19.95 (ISBN 0-8359-0214-5); pap. 12.95 (ISBN 0-8359-0213-7). Reston.

Gibson, Thomas. The Facts About Speculation. 1965. Repr. of 1923 ed. flexible cover 5.00 (ISBN 0-87034-014-X). Fraser Pub Co.

Gibson, W. M. & Pollard, B. R. Symmetry Principles in Elementary Particle Physics. LC 74-31796. (Cambridge Monographs on Physics). (Illus.). 395p. 1980. 72.50 (ISBN 0-521-20787-8); pap. 24.95 (ISBN 0-521-29964-0). Cambridge U Pr.

Gibson, Walker. Persona: A Style Study for Readers & Writers. 1969. pap. text ed. 5.50 (ISBN 0-394-30198-6). Random.

--Tough, Sweet & Stuffy: An Essay on Modern American Prose Styles. LC 66-22449. (Midland Bks.: No. 137). 192p. 1966. 8.50x o.p. (ISBN 0-253-18890-3); pap. 3.95x o.p. (ISBN 0-253-20137-3). Ind U Pr.

Gibson, Walter. Backgammon, the Ways to Play & Win. 144p. pap. 1.95 o.p. (ISBN 0-06-465004-9, BN). B&N NY.

--Black Americans: Biological Facts & Fancies. 1983. 7.95 (ISBN 0-533-05522-9). Vantage.

--How to Win at Backgammon. (Illus.). 166p. Date not set. pap. price not set (ISBN 0-448-14682-7, G&D). Putnam Pub Group.

--The Shadow: A Quarter of Eight & the Freak Show Murders. LC 77-82757. 1978. 10.95 (ISBN 0-385-13413-4). Doubleday.

--The Shadow: Jade Dragon & House of Ghosts. LC 81-43260. 205p. 1981. Repr. of 1943 ed. limited ed. 45.00 (ISBN 0-89296-056-6). Mysterious Pr.

--The Shadow Scrapbook. LC 78-22277. (Orig.). 1979. pap. 8.95 o.p. (ISBN 0-15-681475-7, Harv). HarBraceJ.

Gibson, Walter, ed. Mr. X. 210p. 1983. pap. 9.95 (ISBN 0-89650-800-5). Gamblers.

Gibson, Walter. Houdini's Book of Magic Tricks, Puzzles & Stunts. 1976. pap. 1.50 o.p. (ISBN 0-523-23970-X). Pinnacle Bks.

Gibson, Walter B. Complete Illustrated Book of Card Magic: The Principles & Techniques Fully Revealed in Text & Photographs. LC 69-10988. 1969. 19.95 (ISBN 0-385-06314-8). Doubleday.

--Houdini's Escapes & Magic. LC 75-30523. (Funk & W Bk.). (Illus.). 656p. 1976. 12.50i (ISBN 0-308-10220-7, TYC-T); pap. 6.95i o.p. (ISBN 0-308-10235-5, TYC-T). T Y Crowell.

--How to Play Winning Solitaire. LC 63-7724. 160p. 1976. 4.95 o.p. (ISBN 0-8119-0268-4); pap. 4.95 (ISBN 0-8119-0382-6). Fell.

--Magic with Science. (Illus.). 128p. (gr. 3-7). 1975. pap. 2.95 (ISBN 0-448-11564-6, G&D). Putnam Pub Group.

--Professional Magic for Amateurs. (Illus.). 225p. 1974. pap. 5.50 (ISBN 0-486-23012-0). Dover.

Gibson, William. Butterfingers Angel. 8.95 o.p. (ISBN 0-8091-0198-X); pap. 4.95 o.p. (ISBN 0-8091-1890-4). Paulist Pr.

--Family Life & Morality: Studies in Black & White. LC 79-57076. 116p. 1980. pap. text ed. 8.25 (ISBN 0-8191-0969-X). U Pr of Amer.

--Shakespeare's Game. LC 77-15912. 1978. cloth o.p. 10.95 (ISBN 0-689-10877-X); pap. 5.95 (ISBN 0-689-70573-5, 241). Atheneum.

Gibson, William C., jt. auth. see Craigie, E. Horne.

Gibson, William M. The Art of Mark Twain. LC 75-25455. 1976. 19.95x (ISBN 0-19-501993-8). Oxford U Pr.

Gibson, William M., ed. see Twain, Mark.

Gicovate, Bernard. Garcilaso de la Vega. LC 74-28304. (World Authors Ser.: Spain: No. 349). 1975. lib. bdg. 15.95 (ISBN 0-8057-2342-0, Twayne). G K Hall.

--San Juan de la Cruz. (World Authors Ser.). lib. bdg. 15.95 (ISBN 0-8057-2255-6, Twayne). G K Hall.

Gidbeau, Kenneth W., jt. auth. see Miller, George H.

Giddan, Norman S. & Austin, Michael J. Peer Counseling & Self-Help Groups on Campus. (Illus.). 184p. 1982. 16.75x (ISBN 0-398-04724-3). C C Thomas.

Giddens, A. Sociology: A Short Introduction. 1982. 55.00x (ISBN 0-333-30928-6, Pub. by Macmillan England). State Mutual Bk.

Giddens, A. & Held, D. Class, Conflict, & Power. 1982. 55.00x (ISBN 0-333-32289-4, Pub. by Macmillan England). State Mutual Bk.

Giddens, A., jt. ed. see Stanworth, P.

Giddens, Anthony. Capitalism & Modern Social Theory: An Analysis of the Writings of Marx, Durkheim & Max Weber. LC 70-161291. 1971. 37.50 (ISBN 0-521-08293-5); pap. 10.95x (ISBN 0-521-09785-1). Cambridge U Pr.

--Profiles & Critiques in Social Theory. 230p. 1983. 24.50x (ISBN 0-520-04933-0); pap. 10.95x (ISBN 0-520-04964-0). U of Cal Pr.

--Sociology: A Brief but Critical Introduction. 182p. 1982. pap. text ed. 6.95 (ISBN 0-15-505554-2, HC). HarBraceJ.

--Sociology: A Brief Critical Introduction. 160p. (Orig.). pap. text ed. 6.95 (ISBN 0-15-505554-2). HarBraceJ.

Giddens, Anthony & Held, David, eds. Classes, Power & Conflict: Classical & Contemporary Debates. LC 81-43382. 640p. 1982. 42.50x (ISBN 0-520-04489-4); pap. 14.95x (ISBN 0-520-04627-7, CAMPUS 290). U of Cal Pr.

Giddens, Anthony & Mackenzie, Gavin, eds. Social Class & the Divison of Labour. LC 82-4275. (Illus.). 374p. 1982. 34.50 (ISBN 0-521-24597-4); pap. 11.95 (ISBN 0-521-28809-6). Cambridge U Pr.

Giddens, Craig, jt. auth. see Babbel, Ulrich.

Giddings. Advances in Chromatography, Vol. 21. 368p. 1983. write for info. (ISBN 0-8247-1679-5). Dekker.

Giddings, John A., jt. ed. see Greenspan, Kalman.

Giddins, Gary. Riding on a Blue Note: Jazz & American Pop. 1982. pap. 9.95 (ISBN 0-19-503213-6, GB). Oxford U Pr.

Giddy, Ian H., jt. auth. see Dufey, Gunter.

Gide, Andre. Corydon. Howard, Richard, tr. from French. 1982. 15.50 (ISBN 0-374-13012-4); pap. 8.25 (ISBN 0-374-51777-0). FS&G.

--Counterfeiters. 1951. 4.95 o.s.i. (ISBN 0-394-60327-3, M327). Modern Lib.

--Immoraliste. Marks, Elaine & Tedeschi, Richard, eds. 1963. text ed. 8.95x (ISBN 0-02-342210-6). Macmillan.

--Notes on Chopin. Frechtman, Bernard, tr. from Fr. LC 78-3640. 1978. Repr. of 1949 ed. lib. bdg. 18.50x (ISBN 0-313-20371-7, GINC). Greenwood.

--Symphonie Pastorale. O'Brien, Justin & Shackleton, M., eds. 1954. pap. text ed. 5.95 (ISBN 0-669-27383-X). Heath.

Gide, Andre & Barrault, Jean-Louis. The Trial: A Dramatization Based on Kafka's Novel. LC 63-18574. (Illus.). (YA) (gr. 9 up). 1963. 3.50 o.p. (ISBN 0-8052-3266-4); pap. 3.95 (ISBN 0-8052-0053-3). Schocken.

Gide, Andre & Gosse, Edmund. The Correspondence of Andre Gide & Edmund Gosse: 1904-1928. Brugmans, Linette F., ed. LC 77-22619. (New York University. Studies in Romance Languages & Literature: No. 2). 1977. Repr. of 1959 ed. lib. bdg. 19.25x (ISBN 0-8371-9736-8, GICO). Greenwood.

Gide, Andre P. Dostoevsky. LC 78-14443. 1979. Repr. of 1961 ed. lib. bdg. 17.00x (ISBN 0-313-21178-7, GIDO). Greenwood.

Gide, Charles, ed. see Fourier, Charles.

Gideon, Virtus E. Luke: A Study Guide Commentary. (Orig.). 1967. pap. 3.95 (ISBN 0-310-24973-2). Zondervan.

Gidley, M. With One Sky above Us: Life on an Indian Reservation at the Turn of the Century. LC 79-63443. 1979. 14.95 (ISBN 0-399-12420-9). Putnam Pub Group.

Gidley, Richard, jt. auth. see Seymour, Dale.

Gidlow, Elsa. Sapphic Songs Eighteen to Eighty. (Illus.). 1982. 5.95 (ISBN 0-9606568-4-7). Druid Heights.

--Shattering the Mirror. (Illus.). 1977. 1.25 o.s.i. (ISBN 0-9606568-3-9). Druid Heights.

Gidmark, Jill B. Melville Sea Dictionary: A Glossed Concordance & Analysis of the Sea Language in Melville's Nautical Novels. LC 82-6122. 554p. 1982. lib. bdg. 45.00 (ISBN 0-313-23330-6, GMD/). Greenwood.

Gidwani, N. W., jt. auth. see Roy, Ashim K.

Gidwitz, Betsy. Politics of International Air Transport. LC 79-2706. 272p. 1980. 25.95 (ISBN 0-669-03234-4). Lexington Bks.

Giebelhaus, August W. Business & Government in the Oil Industry: A Case Study of Sun Oil, 1876 to 1945, Vol. 5. Porter, Glenn, ed. LC 77-7795. (Industrial Development & the Social Fabric Monographs). 425p. (Orig.). 1980. lib. bdg. 40.00 (ISBN 0-89232-089-3). Jai Pr.

Gieber, Robert L. An English-French Glossary of Educational Terminology. LC 80-5652. 212p. 1980. lib. bdg. 20.25 (ISBN 0-8191-1344-1); pap. text ed. 10.25 (ISBN 0-8191-1345-X). U Pr of Amer.

Giebink, Gerald A. & Hurst, Leonard L. Computer Projects in Health Care. LC 75-11023. 211p. 1975. pap. text ed. 25.00x o.p. (ISBN 0-914904-08-6). Health Admin Pr.

Giebisch, Gerhard H., jt. ed. see Hoffman, Joseph F.

Gieck, Kurt. Engineering Formulas. 4th ed. 260p. 1983. 16.95 (ISBN 0-07-023219-9, P&RB). McGraw.

Giedion, Siegfried. Mechanization Takes Command. 1969. pap. 12.95 (ISBN 0-393-00489-9, Norton Lib.). Norton.

Giedt, Warren H. see Heat Transfer & Fluid Mechanics Institute.

Giefer, Gerald J. & Todd, David K., eds. Water Publications of State Agencies - First Supplement. LC 72-75672. 1976. 28.00 (ISBN 0-912394-17-X). Water Info.

Giegel, Joseph L., jt. auth. see Henry, John B.

Giegling, John. Black Lightning: Three Years in the Life of a Fisher. (Illus.). 128p. (gr. 3-7). 1975. 6.95 o.p. (ISBN 0-698-20333-X, Coward). Putnam Pub Group.

Giegold, William C. Practical Management Skills for Engineers & Scientists. (Engineering Ser.). (Illus.). 430p. 1981. 31.50 (ISBN 0-686-86277-5). Lifetime Learn.

Giehl, Dudley. Vegetarianism: A Way of Life. LC 76-5126. (Illus.). 1979. 12.45i (ISBN 0-06-011504-1, HarpT). Har-Row.

Giehl, Franz J. The F-Four Phantom Two & the U. S. Sixth Fleet in the Mediterranean. 7.50 o.p. (ISBN 0-533-01981-8). Vantage.

Giele, Janet Z. Women in the Middle Years: Current Knowledge & Directions for Research & Policy. (Wiley Series on Personality Processes). 344p. 1981. 29.95x (ISBN 0-471-09611-3, Pub. by Wiley-Interscience). Wiley.

Gielen, M., jt. auth. see Brocas, J.

Gielgud, John. Gielgud: An Actor & His Time, a Memoir. (Illus.). 256p. 1980. 14.95 (ISBN 0-517-54179-3, C N Potter Bks). Crown.

--Stage Directions. LC 78-23580. 1979. Repr. of 1963 ed. lib. bdg. 18.25x (ISBN 0-313-21035-7, GISD). Greenwood.

Gier, Nicholas F. Wittgenstein & Phenomenology. LC 80-26980. (Ser. in Philosphy). 260p. 1981. 39.50x (ISBN 0-87395-518-8); pap. 10.95x (ISBN 0-87395-519-6). State U NY Pr.

Gierman, James, ed. see Kubota, Takayuki.

Gierz, G. Bundles of Topological Vector Spaces & Their Duality. (Lecture Notes in Mathematics: Vol. 955). 296p. 1983. pap. 13.50 (ISBN 0-387-11610-9). Springer-Verlag.

Gies, David T. Nicholas Fernandez de Moratin. (World Authors Ser.). 1979. lib. bdg. 15.95 (ISBN 0-8057-6400-3, Twayne). G K Hall.

Gies, Frances, jt. auth. see Gies, Joseph.

Gies, Joseph & Gies, Frances. Life in a Medieval Castle. LC 74-13058. (Illus.). 1979. pap. 4.95i (ISBN 0-06-090674-X, CN 674, CN). Har-Row.

--Women in the Middle Ages. 264p. 1980. pap. 4.50 (ISBN 0-06-464037-X, BN 4037, BN). B&N NY.

Gies, Joseph, jt. auth. see Kranzberg, Melvin.

Gies, Thomas G. & Sichel, Werner, eds. Deregulation: Appraisal Before The Fact. (Michigan Business Studies: Vol. 2, No. 4). (Illus.). 189p. 1982. 10.00 (ISBN 0-87712-222-9). U Mich Busn Div Res.

Giesbrecht, Martin G. Using Economics. LC 75-19127. (Illus.). 144p. 1976. pap. text ed. 4.95x o.p. (ISBN 0-913232-10-6). W Kaufmann.

Giese, A. C., ed. Photophysiology. Incl. Vol. 1. General Principles - Action of Light on Plants. 1964. 53.50 (ISBN 0-12-282601-9); Vol. 2. Action of Light on Animals & Microorganisms, Photobiochemical Mechanisms, Bioluminescence. 1964. 53.50 (ISBN 0-12-282602-7); Vols. 3 & 4. Current Topics. 1968. Vol. 3. 53.50 (ISBN 0-12-282603-5); Vol. 4. 53.50 o.p. (ISBN 0-12-282604-3); Vols. 5-7. Current Topics in Photobiology & Photochemistry. 1970-72. Vol. 5. 53.50 (ISBN 0-12-282605-1); Vol. 6. 53.50 (ISBN 0-12-282606-X); Vol. 7. 53.50 (ISBN 0-12-282607-8); Vol. 8. 1973. 53.50 (ISBN 0-686-77187-7). Acad Pr.

Giese, Arthur C. & Pearse, John S., eds. Reproduction of Marine Invertebrates: Acoelomate & Psuedocoelomate Metazoans, Vol. 1. 1974. 65.00 (ISBN 0-12-282501-2); 65.00 o.p. (ISBN 0-12-282607-8). Acad Pr.

Giese, Frank S. & Wilder, Warren F. French Lyric Poetry: An Anthology. LC 64-7849. 1965. pap. 6.50 (ISBN 0-672-63038-9). Odyssey Pr.

Giese, Lester J. Budget Builder I for Community Associations. LC 82-90784. 63p. 1982. 21.95 (ISBN 0-910049-01-7). Condo Mgmt.

--Condominium Reserve Builder. 1983. pap. text ed. 32.50 (ISBN 0-910049-02-5). Condo Mgmt.

Giese, William F. Sainte-Beuve: A Literary Portrait. LC 76-137054. (University of Wisconsin Studies, Language & Literature: No. 31). 368p. 1974. Repr. of 1931 ed. lib. bdg. 19.75x (ISBN 0-8371-5515-0, GISB). Greenwood.

Giesea, Roberta, jt. auth. see Coletti, Mina S.

Giesecke, F. H., et al. Technical Drawing Problems. 6th ed. (Series I). 1981. pap. text ed. 13.95x (ISBN 0-02-342740-X). Macmillan.

Giesecke, Frederick E., et al. Engineering Graphics. 3rd ed. (Illus.). 928p. 1981. text ed. 30.95x (ISBN 0-02-342620-9, 34272). Macmillan.

--Technical Drawing. 7th ed. (Illus.). 1980. text ed. 28.95 (ISBN 0-02-342610-1). Macmillan.

Giesecke, William B., jt. auth. see Speegle, Roger.

Gieseking, Hal. Protecting Your Pets. LC 78-65330. 1979. pap. 3.95 o.p. (ISBN 0-912944-53-6). Berkshire Traveller.

Gieseking, Walter & Leimer, Karl. Piano Technique. (Illus.). 140p. Repr. of 1932 ed. pap. 2.95 (ISBN 0-486-22867-3). Dover.

Gieselman, Robert D., ed. Readings in Business Communication. 1982. pap. 8.80x (ISBN 0-87563-223-8). Stipes.

Giesen, Rosemary, jt. auth. see Thompson, Brenda.

Giesey, R., ed. see Hotman, Francis.

Giessen, Bill C., jt. ed. see Grant, Nicholas J.

Giesser, Barbara, jt. auth. see Scheinberg, Labe C.

Giesy, J. U. Jason, Son of Jason. (YA) 6.95 (ISBN 0-685-07439-0, Avalon). Bouregy.

Giesy, John P., ed. Microcosms in Ecological Research: Proceedings. LC 80-23472. (DOE Symposium Ser.). 1140p. 1980. pap. 36.50 (CONF-781101); microfiche 4.50 (ISBN 0-87079-454-X, CONF-781101). DOE.

Giff, Patricia. Today Was a Terrible Day. LC 79-12420. (gr. k-3). 1980. 9.95 (ISBN 0-670-71830-0). Viking Pr.

Giff, Patricia R. The Fourth Grade Celebrity. (gr. k-6). 1981. pap. 1.95 (ISBN 0-440-42676-6, YB). Dell.

--The Gift of the Pirate Queen. (gr. k-6). 1983. pap. 2.25 (ISBN 0-440-43046-1, YB). Dell.

--The Girl Who Knew It All. (gr. k-6). 1981. pap. 1.95 (ISBN 0-440-42855-6, YB). Dell.

--Suspect. (Illus.). 80p. (gr. 7 up). 1982. 8.95 (ISBN 0-525-45108-0, 0869-260, Skinny Bk). Dutton.

--The Winter Worm Business. (Illus.). (gr. 4-7). 1983. pap. 1.95 (ISBN 0-440-49259-9, YB). Dell.

Giffin, James M., jt. auth. see Carlson, Delbert G.

Giffin, Kim & Barnes, Richard. Trust of Self & Others. (Interpersonal Communication Ser.). (Illus.). 96p. 1976. pap. text ed. 6.95 (ISBN 0-675-08647-7). Merrill.

Giffin, Mary & Felsenthal, Carol. A Cry for Help. LC 82-45395. 336p. 1983. 16.95 (ISBN 0-385-15599-9). Doubleday.

Gifford, Barry. The Neighborhood of Baseball: A Personal History of Chicago & the Cubs. 1981. 12.50 o.p. (ISBN 0-525-16457-X, 01214-360). Dutton.

--Port Tropique. LC 80-15440. (Black Lizard Fiction Ser.). 200p. 1980. 9.95 o.p. (ISBN 0-916870-32-4). Creative Arts Bk.

Gifford, Barry & Lee, Lawrence. Jack's Book: An Oral Biography of Jack Kerouac. LC 77-15824. (Illus.). 1978. 10.95 o.p. (ISBN 0-312-43942-3). St Martin.

Gifford, Courtney D., ed. Directory of U.S. Labor Organizations: 1982-83 Edition. 139p. 1982. pap. text ed. 15.00 (ISBN 0-686-84387-8). BNA.

Gifford, Denis. The British Comic Catalogue, 1874-1974. LC 75-35486. 210p. 1976. lib. bdg. 35.00 (ISBN 0-8371-8649-8, GCC/). Greenwood.

--The Illustrated Who's Who in British Films. (Illus.). 1980. 32.00 o.p. (ISBN 0-7134-1434-0). David & Charles.

Gifford, Douglas & Hoggarth, Pauline. Carnival & Coca-Leaf: Some Traditions of the Quechua Ayllu. LC 76-1302. 200p. 1976. 18.95 o.p. (ISBN 0-312-12215-2). St Martin.

Gifford, E. H., jt. auth. see Andrews, Samuel J.

Gifford, Ernest M., jt. ed. see Rost, Thomas L.

Gifford, F. Tape: a Radio News Handbook. (Communication Arts Bks.). 1977. 13.50 (ISBN 0-8038-7161-9); pap. text ed. 7.95 o.p. (ISBN 0-686-82917-4). Hastings.

Gifford, G. E., Jr. Cecil County, Maryland, Sixteen Hundred-Eight to Eighteen Fifty. (Illus.). 241p. 1974. 6.95 (ISBN 0-686-36643-3). Md Hist.

Gifford, George E., ed. Dear Jeffie: Being the Letters from Jeffries Wyman to His Son Jeffries Wyman, Jr. LC 78-58830. (gr. 6 up). 1978. 15.00 (ISBN 0-87365-796-9). Peabody Harvard.

Gifford, Henry. Pasternak: A Critical Study. LC 76-9735. (Major European Authors Ser.). (Illus.). 1977. 39.50 (ISBN 0-521-21288-X). Cambridge U Pr.

Gifford, Prosser, ed. The National Interests of the United States in Foreign Policy: Seven Discussions at the Wilson Center December 1980 - February 1981. LC 81-40792. 204p. (Orig.). 1981. lib. bdg. 13.75 (ISBN 0-8191-1786-2); pap. text ed. 7.25 (ISBN 0-8191-1787-0). U Pr of Amer.

Gifford, Prosser & Louis, William R., eds. The Transfer of Power in Africa: Decolonization 1940-1960. LC 81-1931. 704p. 1982. text ed. 35.00 (ISBN 0-300-02568-8). Yale U Pr.

Gifford, Thomas. The Cavanaugh Quest. LC 75-37083. 1976. 8.95 o.p. (ISBN 0-399-11631-1). Putnam Pub Group.

--The Glendower Legacy. LC 78-9818. 1978. 10.00 o.p. (ISBN 0-399-12183-8). Putnam Pub Group.

--Hollywood Gothic. LC 79-15618. 1979. 10.95 o.p. (ISBN 0-399-12411-X). Putnam Pub Group.

--Wind Chill Factor. LC 74-16598. 350p. 1975. 8.95 o.p. (ISBN 0-399-11439-4). Putnam Pub Group.

Gifford, William C. & Owens, Elisabeth A. International Aspects of U. S. Income Taxation: Cases & Materials, Vol. II, Pt. 3. LC 80-18605. 760p. (Orig.). 1982. pap. text ed. 25.00x (ISBN 0-915506-26-2). Harvard Law Intl Tax.

Gifford, William, Jr., tr. see Juvenal.

Gifford, Zelda. Apple Two DiskGuide. (DiskGuides Ser.). 32p. (Orig.). pap. 7.95 (ISBN 0-931988-96-9). Osborne-McGraw.

Gifis, Steven H. Dictionary of Legal Terms. 1983. pap. 3.95 (ISBN 0-8120-2013-8). Barron.

--Law Dictionary. rev. ed. LC 74-18126. 240p. 1975. pap. 4.95 (ISBN 0-8120-0543-0). Barron.

Gigase, P. L. & Van Marck, E. E., eds. From Parasitic Infection to Parasitic Disease. (Contributions to Microbiology & Immunology: Vol. 7). (Illus.). x, 270p. 1982. 108.00 (ISBN 3-8055-3543-0). S Karger.

Giggins, L. W. & Shoebridge, D. J. Tense Drills. (English As a Second Language Bk.). 163p. 1970. pap. text ed. 6.25x (ISBN 0-582-52173-4). Longman.

Gigliesi, Primerose & Friend, Robert, trs. from Chinese. The Effendi & the Pregnant Pot. (Illus.). 88p. (Orig.). 1982. pap. 2.25 (ISBN 0-8351-1027-3). China Bks.

Giglio, James M. H. M. Daugherty & the Politics of Expediency. LC 78-17106. 1978. 16.00x (ISBN 0-87338-215-3). Kent St U Pr.

Giglio, Richard. Ambulatory Care Systems, Vol. 2: Location, Layout, & Information Systems for Efficient Operations. LC 76-55865. 1977. 22.95x (ISBN 0-669-01324-2). Lexington Bks.

Giguette, Ray. How to Win at Video Games. (Game Book Strategies Ser.). (Illus.). 56p. (Orig.). 1981. pap. 2.50 (ISBN 0-941018-02-4). Martin Pr.

--How to Win! Video Games. 40p. 1981. pap. 2.50 (ISBN 0-686-78304-2). Martin Pr.

Gijsen, Marnix. Lament for Agnes. James-Gerth, W., tr. from Flemish. (International Studies & Transaltions Ser.). 1975. lib. bdg. 8.95 o.p. (ISBN 0-8057-8150-1, Twayne). G K Hall.

Gil, Carlos A., ed. Age of Porfirio Diaz: Selected Readings. LC 76-57535. (Illus.). 191p. 1977. 5.95x o.p. (ISBN 0-8263-0443-5). U of NM Pr.

Gil, Carlos B. Life in Provincial Mexico: National & Regional History as Seen from Mascota, Jalisco, 1867-1972. LC 82-620031. (Latin American Studies: Vol. 53). 1983. text ed. write for info. (ISBN 0-87903-053-4). UCLA Lat Am Ctr.

Gil, David G. Beyond the Jungle: Essays on Human Possibilities, Social Alternatives, & Radical Practice. 1979. lib. bdg. 14.00 (ISBN 0-8161-9004-6, Pub.by Univ Bks). G K Hall.

Gilb, Corinne L. Hidden Hierarchies: The Professions & Government. LC 76-22. 307p. 1976. Repr. of 1966 ed. lib. bdg. 20.00x (ISBN 0-8371-8751-6, GIHH). Greenwood.

Gilbar, Steven. The Book Book. 224p. 1981. 10.95 o.p. (ISBN 0-312-08803-5). St Martin.

--Good Books: A Book Lover's Companion. LC 82-5554. 464p. 1982. 20.00 (ISBN 0-89919-127-4); pap. 9.95 (ISBN 0-89919-132-0). Ticknor & Fields.

Gilbarg, D. & Trudinger, N. S. Elliptic Partial Differential Equations of Second Order, Vol. 224. (Grundlehren der Mathematischen Wissenschaften). 1977. 45.70 o.p. (ISBN 0-387-08007-4). Springer-Verlag.

Gilbart, Helen. Pathways: A Guide to Reading & Study Skills. LC 81-81701. (Illus.). 400p. 1982. pap. text ed. 9.50 (ISBN 0-395-31717-7); instr's. manual 1.00 (ISBN 0-395-31718-5). HM.

Gilbart, Helen & Howland, Joseph. Getting Ready for the College Level Academic Skills Test. Hackworth, Robert, ed. (Illus.). 160p. 1982. pap. text ed. 10.95 (ISBN 0-943202-06-X). H & H Pub.

Gilberstadt, Harold & Duker, Jan. A Handbook for Clinical & Actuarial MMPI Interpretation. LC 81-40902. 144p. 1982. pap. text ed. 8.25 (ISBN 0-8191-2257-2). U Pr of Amer.

Gilbert, Alan & Gugler, Josef. Cities, Poverty & Development: Urbanization in the Third World. (Illus.). 272p. 1982. 34.50 (ISBN 0-19-874083-2); pap. 12.95 (ISBN 0-19-874084-0). Oxford U Pr.

Gilbert, Alan, ed. Development Planning & Spatial Structure. LC 75-30804. 207p. 1976. 34.50x (ISBN 0-471-29904-9, Pub. by Wiley-Interscience). Wiley.

Gilbert, Allan H., ed. Literary Criticism: Plato to Dryden. LC 61-12266. (Waynebooks Ser: No. 1). 1962. pap. 8.95 (ISBN 0-8143-1160-1). Wayne St U Pr.

Gilbert, Anna. A Family Likeness. LC 77-22725. 1978. 8.95 o.p. (ISBN 0-312-28144-7). St Martin.

--Miss Bede is Staying. 320p. 1983. 12.95 (ISBN 0-312-53471-X). St Martin.

Gilbert, Anne. How to Be an Antiques Detective. LC 77-72621. (Illus.). 1978. pap. 7.95 o.p. (ISBN 0-448-14277-5, G&D). Putnam Pub Group.

--Investing in the Antiques Market. (Illus.). 224p. Date not set. pap. price not set (ISBN 0-448-16552-X, G&D). Putnam Pub Group.

Gilbert, Annie. All My Afternoons: The Heart & Soul of the TV Soap Opera. LC 78-70321. (Illus.). 192p. 1979. 14.95 o.s.i. (ISBN 0-89104-099-4); pap. 7.95 o.s.i. (ISBN 0-89104-098-6). A & W Pubs.

Gilbert, Arthur. Your Neighbor Worships. 31p. Date not set. 1.50 (ISBN 0-686-74968-5). ADL.

Gilbert, B. The Trailblazers. LC 73-76268. (Old West Ser). (Illus.). 1973. 17.28 (ISBN 0-8094-1459-7, Pub. by Time-Life). Silver.

Gilbert, Bentley B. Britain Since Nineteen Eighteen. 2nd ed. 1980. 22.50 (ISBN 0-312-09876-6). St Martin.

Gilbert, Bil. Westering Man: The Life of Joseph Walker. LC 82-69128. 352p. 1983. 14.95 (ISBN 0-689-11241-6). Atheneum.

Gilbert, Bob & Theroux, Gary. The Top Ten: Nineteen Fifty-Six to Present. LC 82-10478. (Illus.). 302p. pap. 12.95 (ISBN 0-671-43215-X, Fireside). S&S.

Gilbert, Byron. The Lord's Oysters. rev. ed. 330p. 1957. pap. 4.95 (ISBN 0-686-36630-1). Md Hist.

Gilbert, C. Italian Art: Fourteen Hundred to Fifteen Hundred. 1980. pap. 13.95 (ISBN 0-13-507947-0). P-H.

Gilbert, C. M. & Christensen, M. N. Physical Geology Laboratory Course. 2nd ed. 1967. 16.95 (ISBN 0-07-023206-7, C); instructor's manual 4.95 (ISBN 0-07-023209-1). McGraw.

Gilbert, Carolyn A. Communicative Performance of Literature. (Illus.). 1977. pap. 13.95 (ISBN 0-02-342900-3). Macmillan.

Gilbert, Celia. Bonfire. 72p. 1982. 12.95 (ISBN 0-914086-45-6); pap. 4.96 (ISBN 0-914086-44-8). Alicejamesbooks.

Gilbert, Charles. American Financing of World War One. LC 73-79060. (Contributions in Economics & Economic History: No. 1). (Illus.). 1970. lib. bdg. 29.95 (ISBN 0-8371-1496-9, GIA/). Greenwood.

Gilbert, Charles, jt. auth. see Krooss, Herman E.

Gilbert, Dave. Walkers Guide to Harpers Ferry. (Illus.). 80p. 1983. 4.95 (ISBN 0-933126-28-X). Pictorial Hist.

Gilbert, Doris W. Breaking the Reading Barrier. 1959. text ed. 11.95 (ISBN 0-13-081471-7). P-H.

--Breaking the Word Barrier. LC 77-173596. (Illus.). 240p. 1972. pap. text ed. 12.50 (ISBN 0-13-081661-2). P-H.

--Power & Speed in Reading. 1956. text ed. 12.95 (ISBN 0-13-685040-5). P-H.

--Study in Depth. (Orig.). 1966. pap. text ed. 15.95 (ISBN 0-13-858902-X). P-H.

--Turning Point in Reading. (Illus.). 1969. pap. text ed. 11.95 (ISBN 0-13-933085-2). P-H.

Gilbert, Doug. The Miracle Machine. LC 79-13603. (Illus.). 1980. 10.95 (ISBN 0-698-10952-X, Coward). Putnam Pub Group.

Gilbert, Edith. The Complete Wedding Planner. LC 82-83770. 256p. 1983. 14.95 (ISBN 0-8119-0485-7). Fell.

Gilbert, Edith W. All About Parties. LC 68-8522. (Illus.). 1968. 6.95 (ISBN 0-8208-0200-X). Hearthside.

Gilbert, Elizabeth R. Fairs & Festivals: A Smithsonian Guide to Celebrations in Maryland, Virginia, & Washington, D.C. LC 82-600152. (Illus.). 160p. 1982. pap. 4.50 (ISBN 0-87474-473-3). Smithsonian.

Gilbert, Elliot L. The Good Kipling. LC 73-122098. x, 216p. 1970. 13.50x (ISBN 0-8214-0085-1, 82-80893). Ohio U Pr.

Gilbert, G. G., ed. Pidgin & Creole Languages. LC 79-15866. 320p. 1980. 34.50 (ISBN 0-521-22789-5). Cambridge U Pr.

Gilbert, G. Nigel. Modelling Society: An Introduction to Loglinear Analysis for Social Researchers. (Contemporary Social Research Ser.). 1981. text ed. 28.50x (ISBN 0-04-312009-1); pap. text ed. 12.50x (ISBN 0-04-312010-5). Allen Unwin.

Gilbert, Gail, tr. see Briusov, Valery.

Gilbert, Geoffrey M., et al. Accounting & Auditing for Employee Benefit Plans. 1978. 54.00 (ISBN 0-88262-217-X, 78-56016). Warren.

Gilbert, George. Captain Cook's Final Voyage: The Journal of Midshipman George Gilbert. Holmes, Christine, ed. (Illus.). 166p. 1982. text ed. 20.00x (ISBN 0-8248-0787-1). UH Pr.

--Photography: The Early Years, a Historical Guide for Collectors. LC 78-20163. (Illus.). 181p. 1980. 21.10i (ISBN 0-06-011497-5, HarpT). Har-Row.

--The Sixty Dramatic Illustrations in Full Colours of the Cathedral Cities of England. (A Promotion of the Arts Library Bks.). (Illus.). 99p. 1983. 297.85 (ISBN 0-86650-046-4). Gloucester Art.

Gilbert, Harvey, jt. auth. see Weiss, Leonard.

Gilbert, Harvey A. & Kagan, Robert A. Radiation Damage to the Nervous System: A Delayed Therapeutic Hazard. (Illus.). 225p. 1980. text ed. 30.00 (ISBN 0-89004-418-X). Raven.

Gilbert, Harvey A., jt. auth. see Weiss, Leonard.

Gilbert, Harvey A., jt. ed. see Weiss, Leonard.

Gilbert, Herbert, ed. see Payne, Cril.

Gilbert, Isabel. The No Smoking Book: How to Quit Permanently. LC 79-27610. (Illus.). 1980. pap. 5.95 o.p. (ISBN 0-89141-101-1). Presidio Pr.

Gilbert, Jack. Advanced Applications for Pocket Calculators. LC 74-33620. (Illus.). 304p. 1975. 8.95 o.p. (ISBN 0-8306-5824-6); pap. 5.95 (ISBN 0-8306-4824-0, 824). TAB Bks.

Gilbert, Jack G. Edmund Waller. (English Authors Ser.: No. 266). 1979. lib. bdg. 14.95 (ISBN 0-8057-6763-0, Twayne). G K Hall.

Gilbert, Jacqueline. A House Called Bellevigne. (Harlequin Presents). 192p. 1983. pap. 1.95 (ISBN 0-373-10600-9). Harlequin Bks.

Gilbert, James. Another Chance: Postwar America, 1945-1968. Wilson, R. Jackson, frwd. by. LC 81-8916. 307p. 1981. 22.95 (ISBN 0-87722-224-X). Temple U Pr.

--Great Planes. LC 70-117510. 1970. Repr. 9.95 o.p. (ISBN 0-448-02229-X, G&D). Putnam Pub Group.

Gilbert, James, ed. Skywriting. LC 77-99126. 1978. 10.00 o.p. (ISBN 0-312-72787-9). St Martin.

Gilbert, James N. Criminal Investigation. (Public Service Technology Ser.). 496p. 1980. text ed. 20.95 (ISBN 0-675-08186-6). Additional supplements may be obtained from publisher. Merrill.

Gilbert, Janet P., jt. auth. see Beal, Mary R.

Gilbert, Jeanne G. & Sullivan, Catherine M. The Mental Health Aide. LC 76-14843. 1976. pap. text ed. 5.75 o.p. (ISBN 0-8261-2180-2). Springer Pub.

Gilbert, Jim, ed. see Bingham, Bruce.

Gilbert, Jimmie, et al. College Algebra. (Illus.). 496p. 1981. text ed. 21.95 (ISBN 0-13-141804-1). P-H.

Gilbert, John. NHL Shooters. (Illus.). 96p. 1982. pap. 9.95 (ISBN 0-943392-03-9). Tribeca Comm.

Gilbert, John, tr. see Taglianti, Augusto V.

Gilbert, John T. A Jacobite Narrative of the War in Ireland, 1688-1691. 358p. 1969. Repr. of 1892 ed. text ed. 25.00x (ISBN 0-7165-0050-7, Pub. by Irish Academic Pr. Ireland). Biblio Dist.

Gilbert, John T. E., ed. Environmental Planning Guidelines for Offshore Oil & Gas Development. (Illus.). 64p. 1982. pap. text ed. 6.00x (ISBN 0-8248-0792-8, Eastwest Ctr). UH Pr.

Gilbert, Kenneth, ed. Mountain Trace. (Illus.). 337p. 1980. 12.00 (ISBN 0-686-96759-3). Jalamap.

Gilbert, Kent S., jt. auth. see Watabe, Masakazu.

Gilbert, Kitty S., compiled by. Treasures from the Great Bronze Age of China: An Exhibition from the People's Republic of China. (Illus.). 192p. 1980. pap. 9.95 o.s.i. (ISBN 0-87099-230-9). Metro Mus Art.

Gilbert, Leopold & Daniel, Sol, eds. Medical State Board Examination Review Book, 2 pts. 6th ed. Incl. Vol. 1. Basic Sciences. 287p; Vol. 2. Clinical Sciences. 239p. 1976. spiral bdg. 12.00 ea. o.p. Med Exam.

Gilbert, Lucy & Webster, Paula. Bound by Love: The Sweet Trap of Daughterhood. LC 81-65760. 204p. 1982. 12.98 (ISBN 0-8070-3250-6). Beacon Pr.

Gilbert, Lynn & Moore, Gaylen. Particular Passions: Talks with Women Who Have Shaped Our Times. (Illus.). 352p. 1981. 19.95 (ISBN 0-517-54371-0, C N Potter Bks); pap. 10.95 (ISBN 0-517-54594-2). Crown.

Gilbert, M. Lloyd George. 1968. 8.95 (ISBN 0-13-353961-X, Spec); pap. 1.95. P-H.

Gilbert, M. T., jt. auth. see Pryde, A.

Gilbert, Marilyn B. Clear Writing. LC 70-38627. (Self-Teaching Guides Ser.). 336p. (Orig., Prog. Bk.). 1972. pap. 7.95 (ISBN 0-471-29896-4). Wiley.

--Communicating by Letter. LC 72-11879. (Self-Teaching Guides Ser.). 256p. 1973. 6.95 o.p. (ISBN 0-471-29897-2). Wiley.

Gilbert, Marilyn B., jt. auth. see Gilbert, Thomas F.

Gilbert, Martin. The Macmillan Atlas of the Holocaust. (Illus.). 255p. 1982. 19.75 (ISBN 0-02-543380-6). Macmillan.

--Winston Churchill: The Wilderness Years. LC 82-9279. (Illus.). 1982. 16.95 (ISBN 0-395-31869-6). HM.

Gilbert, Marvin. God, Me, & Thee. (Discovery Bk.). 1981. 1.35 (ISBN 0-88243-841-7, 02-0841). Gospel Pub.

Gilbert, Michael. The Danger Within. 1978. pap. 1.95i o.p. (ISBN 0-06-080448-3, P 448, PL). Har-Row.

--Mr. Calder & Mr. Behrens. 1983. pap. 2.95 (ISBN 0-14-006637-3). Penguin.

Gilbert, Michael A. How to Win an Argument. 1979. pap. 4.95 (ISBN 0-07-023215-6, SP). McGraw.

Gilbert, Milton. Quest for World Monetary System: Gold-Dollar System & It's Aftermath. LC 80-17865. 255p. 1980. 26.95x (ISBN 0-471-07998-7, Pub. by Wiley-Interscience). Wiley.

Gilbert, Miriam. Karen Gets a Fever. LC 61-13576. (Medical Bks for Children). (Illus.). (gr. k-7). 1961. PLB 3.95g (ISBN 0-8225-0011-6). Lerner Pubns.

--Rosie: The Oldest Horse in St. Augustine. LC 67-30409. (Illus., Eng., Fr. & Spain.). (gr. k-6). 1974. 4.95 o.p. (ISBN 0-87208-105-2); pap. 4.95 (ISBN 0-87208-007-2). Island Pr.

--Science-Hobby Book of Aquariums. rev. ed. LC 67-17406. (Science Hobby Bks). (Illus.). (gr. 5-10). 1968. PLB 4.95g (ISBN 0-8225-0551-7). Lerner Pubns.

--Science-Hobby Book of Shell Collecting. rev. ed. LC 67-17404. (Science Hobby Bks). (gr. 5-10). 1968. PLB 4.95g (ISBN 0-8225-0557-6). Lerner Pubns.

--Science-Hobby Book of Terrariums. rev. ed. LC 67-17405. (Science Hobby Bks). (Illus.). (gr. 5-10). 1968. PLB 4.95g (ISBN 0-8225-0558-4). Lerner Pubns.

Gilbert, Miriam, jt. auth. see Carlsen, G. R.

Gilbert, Miriam A., jt. tr. see Klaus, Carl H.

Gilbert, Mitchell. An Owner's Manual for the Human Being. 1980. pap. 4.95 (ISBN 0-87728-496-2). Weiser.

Gilbert, Neil & Specht, Harry. Dimensions of Social Welfare Policy. (Illus.). 208p. 1974. 19.95 (ISBN 0-13-214486-7). P-H.

--Dynamics of Community Planning. LC 77-22182. 216p. 1977. prof ref 20.00x (ISBN 0-88410-362-5). Ballinger Pub.

--Handbook of the Social Services. (Illus.). 704p. 1981. text ed. 45.00 (ISBN 0-13-381806-3). P-H.

Gilbert, Neil, ed. see Jaffe, Eliezer F.

Gilbert, Neil, et al. An Introduction to Social Work Practice. (P-H Ser. in Social Work Practice). (Illus.). 1980. text ed. 21.95 (ISBN 0-13-479105-3). P-H.

Gilbert, Pamela. Compendium of the Biographical Literature on Deceased Entomologists. (Illus.). 1977. 75.00x (ISBN 0-565-00786-6, Pub. by Brit Mus Nat Hist). Sabbot-Natural Hist Bks.

Gilbert, Philip. Software Design & Development. 608p. 1983. text ed. write for info. (ISBN 0-574-21430-5, 13-4430); write for info. instr's. guide (ISBN 0-574-21431-3, 13-4431). SRA.

Gilbert, R. & Weinacht, R. Function Theoretic Methods in Differential Equations. (Research Notes in Mathematics Ser.: No. 8). (Orig.). 1976. pap. text ed. 26.50 (ISBN 0-273-00306-2). Pitman Pub MA.

Gilbert, Rita K., jt. auth. see Kurzman, Robert G.

Gilbert, Robert E. Television & Presidential Politics. LC 76-189366. 240p. 1972. 9.75 o.p. (ISBN 0-8158-0281-1). Chris Mass.

Gilbert, Robert P. & Buchanan, James. First Order Elliptic Systems: A Functional Theoretic Approach. 1982. 45.00 (ISBN 0-12-283280-9). Acad Pr.

Gilbert, Robert P. & Newton, Roger G. Analytic Methods in Mathematical Physics. 590p. 1970. 97.00 (ISBN 0-677-13560-2). Gordon.

Gilbert, Rose B. & McMillan, Patricia H. Decorating Country-Style: The Look & How to Have It. LC 78-68324. (Illus.). 1980. 17.95 (ISBN 0-385-14086-X). Doubleday.

Gilbert, Russell W. Bilder und Gedanke: Poems, Vol. IX. LC 74-26228. 1975. 12.50 (ISBN 0-911122-31-1). Penn German Soc.

Gilbert, Sandra. In the Fourth World: Poems. LC 78-11144. 80p. 1979. 7.75 o.p. (ISBN 0-8173-8528-2); pap. 4.50 o.s.i. (ISBN 0-8173-8527-4). U of Ala Pr.

Gilbert, Sandra M. The Summer Kitchen. (Illus.). 48p. (Orig.). 1983. pap. 15.00 (ISBN 0-940592-14-2). Heyeck Pr.

Gilbert, Sara. How to Live with a Single Parent. (gr. 7 up). 1982. PLB 8.63 (ISBN 0-688-00633-7); pap. 6.00 (ISBN 0-688-00587-X). Morrow.

Gilbert, Stephen G. Atlas of General Zoology. LC 65-25236. 1965. pap. text ed. 10.95x (ISBN 0-8087-0709-4). Burgess.

Gilbert, Steven E., jt. auth. see Forte, Allen.

Gilbert, Stuart. James Joyce's Ulysses. 1955. pap. 4.95 (ISBN 0-394-70013-9, V13, Vin). Random.

Gilbert, Stuart, tr. see Camus, Albert.

Gilbert, Stuart, tr. see Malraux, Andre.

Gilbert, Stuart, tr. see Saint-Exupery, Antoine De.

Gilbert, Thomas F. Human Competence: Engineering Worthy Performance. 1978. 27.50 (ISBN 0-07-023217-2, P&RB). McGraw.

Gilbert, Thomas F. & Gilbert, Marilyn B. Thinking Metric. 2nd ed. LC 77-20190. (Self-Teaching Guide Ser.). 141p. 1978. pap. text ed. 6.95 (ISBN 0-471-03427-4). Wiley.

Gilbert, Victor F., compiled by. Labour & Social History Theses. 200p. 1982. 24.00 (ISBN 0-7201-1647-3, Mansell Pub.). Wilson.

Gilbert, W. S. Bab Ballads. Ellis, James, ed. LC 77-102668. 1970. 18.00x (ISBN 0-674-05800-3, Belknap Pr); pap. 9.95 (ISBN 0-674-05801-1). Harvard U Pr.

Gilbert, W. S. & Sullivan, Arthur. The Complete Plays of Gilbert & Sullivan. (Illus.). 640p. 1976. pap. 10.95 (ISBN 0-393-00828-2, Norton Lib). Norton.

Gilbert, William J. Modern Algebra with Applications. LC 76-22756. 348p. 1976. 32.95x (ISBN 0-471-29891-3, Pub by Wiley-Interscience). Wiley.

Gilbertie, Sal. Herb Gardening at Its Best. LC 77-23678. 1978. 12.95 (ISBN 0-689-10863-X); pap. 7.95, 1980. (ISBN 0-689-70595-6, 255). Atheneum.

Gilbertson, Catherine. Harriet Beecher Stowe. 330p. 1982. Repr. of 1937 ed. lib. bdg. 40.00 (ISBN 0-89987-316-2). Darby Bks.

Gilbertson, Irvy. Puppet Plays for Missionettes. LC 82-82483. 64p. (Orig.). 1982. pap. 2.95 saddlestitched (ISBN 0-88243-736-4, 02-0736). Gospel Pub.

Gilbertson, M. P., jt. auth. see Scrutton, D. R.

Gilbertson, Merrill T. Uncovering Bible Times. LC 68-25799. 1968. pap. 2.50 o.p. (ISBN 0-8066-0830-7, 15-7007). Augsburg.

Gilbertson, R. L., jt. auth. see Lindsey, J. P.

Gilbreath, Alice. Beginning Crafts for Beginning Readers. LC 71-184461. (Picture Bk). (Illus.). 32p. (gr. 1-4). 1972. 2.95 o.s.i. (ISBN 0-695-80317-4); PLB 5.97 o.s.i. (ISBN 0-695-40317-6). Follett.

--Making Toys That Swim & Float. LC 78-3225. (Illus.). (gr. k up). Date not set. lib. bdg. 5.97 o.s.i. (ISBN 0-695-40962-X); pap. 2.95 o.s.i. (ISBN 0-695-30962-5). Follett.

--More Beginners Crafts for Beginning Readers. (Illus.). 32p. (gr. k-3). 1976. 4.95 o.s.i. (ISBN 0-695-80635-1); lib. ed. 4.98 o.s.i. (ISBN 0-695-40635-3). Follett.

--Simple Decoupage: Having Fun with Cutouts. LC 77-22088. (Illus.). (gr. 3-7). 1978. 8.25 (ISBN 0-688-22134-3); PLB 7.92 (ISBN 0-688-32134-8). Morrow.

--Slab, Coil, & Pinch: A Beginners Pottery Book. (Illus.). (gr. 3-7). 1977. 8.50 (ISBN 0-688-22105-X); PLB 8.16 (ISBN 0-688-32105-4). Morrow.

--Spouts, Lids, Cans, Fun with Familiar Metal Objects. (Illus.). 48p. (gr. 3-7). 1973. PLB 7.63 (ISBN 0-688-30064-2). Morrow.

Gilbreath, Alice T. Beginning-To-Read Riddles & Jokes. (Beginning-to-Read Ser.). (Illus.). (gr. 2-4). 1967. lib. ed. o.s.i. 2.97 (ISBN 0-695-47740-4); pap. 1.95 (ISBN 0-695-37740-X). Follett.

Gilbreth, Frank B. Primer of Scientific Management. 2nd ed. LC 72-9513. (Management History Ser.: No. 12). 116p. 1973. Repr. of 1914 ed. 10.00 o.s.i. (ISBN 0-87960-024-1). Hive Pub.

Gilbreth, Frank B. & Carey, Ernestine G. Cheaper by the Dozen. rev. ed. LC 63-20411. (Illus.). 1963. 14.37i (ISBN 0-690-18632-0). T y Crowell.

Gilby, Thomas, ed. see Thomas Aquinas, St.

Gilchrist, Agnes A. William Strickland-Architect & Engineer 1788-1854. enl. ed. LC 69-13714. (Architecture & Decorative Art Ser). (Illus.). 1969. Repr. of 1950 ed. lib. bdg. 32.50 (ISBN 0-306-71235-0). Da Capo.

Gilchrist, Alexander. The Life of William Blake. Todd, Ruthven, ed. (Illus.). 300p. 1983. pap. text ed. 8.95x (ISBN 0-460-01971-6, Pub. by Evman England). Biblio Dist.

Gilchrist, Bruce & Wessel, Milton R. Government Regulation of the Computer Industry. LC 72-83726. ix, 247p. 1972. 14.50 (ISBN 0-88283-028-7). AFIPS Pr.

Gilchrist, Bruce, jt. ed. see Leininger, Joseph E.

Gilchrist, Ellen. The Annunciation. 1983. 13.45i (ISBN 0-316-31302-5). Little.

--The Land Surveyor's Daughter. LC 78-17908. (Lost Roads Poetry Ser: No. 14). 1979. pap. 4.00 o.p. (ISBN 0-918786-15-0). Lost Roads.

Gilchrist, Francis G. Survey of Embryology. 1968. text ed. 39.95 (ISBN 0-07-023208-3, C). McGraw.

Gilchrist, J. D. Extraction Metallurgy. 2nd ed. 1979. 54.00 (ISBN 0-08-021711-7); pap. 17.00 (ISBN 0-08-021712-5). Pergamon.

--Fuels & Refractories. 1969. 9.90 o.p. (ISBN 0-08-009780-4); pap. 4.95 o.p. (ISBN 0-08-009779-0). Pergamon.

Gilchrist, John. Church & Economic Activity in the Middle Ages. LC 69-1365. 1969. 17.95 o.p. (ISBN 0-312-13475-4). St Martin.

Gilchrist, LeWayne D., jt. auth. see Schinke, Steven P.

Gilchrist, R., ed. GLIM 82: Proceedings of the International Conference on Generalized Linear Models, 1982. (Lecture Notes in Statistics: Vol. 14). (Illus.). 188p. 1983. pap. 12.50 (ISBN 0-387-90777-7). Springer-Verlag.

Gilchrist, Rupert. Guns of Dragonard. 1982. pap. 2.95 (ISBN 0-553-22612-6). Bantam.

Gilchrist, T. L. & Storr, R. C. Organic Reactions & Orbital Symmetry. 2nd ed. LC 78-54578. (Cambridge Texts in Chemistry & Biochemistry Ser.). (Illus.). 1979. 65.00 (ISBN 0-521-22014-9); pap. 22.95 (ISBN 0-521-29336-7). Cambridge U Pr.

Gilchrist, Warren. Statistical Forecasting. LC 76-13504. 3058p. 1976. 51.95x (ISBN 0-471-99402-2, Pub. by Wiley-Interscience); pap. 22.95x (ISBN 0-471-99403-0). Wiley.

Gild, David C. Mayor of Casterbridge Notes. (Orig.). 1966. pap. 2.75 (ISBN 0-8220-0816-5). Cliffs.

Gildart, R. C. & Wassink, Jan. Montana Wildlife. (Montana Geographic Ser.: No. 3). (Illus.). 128p. 1982. pap. 12.95 (ISBN 0-938314-04-1). MT Mag.

Gildenberg, P. L., jt. ed. see Grossman, R. G.

Gilder, Cornelia B. Preservation for Profit: Ten Case Studies in Commercial Rehabilitation. (Illus.). 27p. (Orig.). 1980. pap. 3.00 (ISBN 0-942000-02-1). Pres League NY.

Gilder, George. Wealth & Poverty. LC 80-50556. 1981. 19.95 (ISBN 0-465-09105-9). Basic.

Gilder, Jules. More Telephone Accessories You Can Build. 129p. 1981. 6.50 (ISBN 0-686-98104-9). Telecom Lib.

Gilder, Jules H. Telephone Accessories You Can Build. 84p. 1976. 7.25 (ISBN 0-686-98103-0). Telecom Lib.

Gilderbloom, John I., et al, eds. Rent Control: A Source Book. 1st ed. LC 80-70624. 320p. 1981. 11.95 (ISBN 0-938806-01-7). Foun Natl Prog.

Gilderman, Martin S. Juan Rodriguez de la Camara. (World Authors Ser.). 1977. lib. bdg. 15.95 (ISBN 0-8057-6195-0, Twayne). G K Hall.

Gildersleeve, Thomas. Successful Data Processing System Analysis. (Illus.). 1978. ref. 23.95 (ISBN 0-13-860510-6). P-H.

Gildin, Hilail. Rousseau's Social Contract: The Design of the Argument. LC 82-20148. 240p. 1983. lib. bdg. 22.50x (ISBN 0-226-29368-8). U of Chicago Pr.

Gildon, Charles. The Golden Spy. LC 77-170519. (Foundations of the Novel Ser.: Vol. 14). lib. bdg. 50.00 o.s.i. (ISBN 0-8240-0526-0). Garland Pub.

Gildon, Charles see Collier, Jeremy.

Gildrie, Richard P. Salem, Massachusetts, Sixteen Twenty-Six to Sixteen Eighty-Three: A Covenant Community. LC 74-20841. (Illus.). 187p. 1975. 13.95x (ISBN 0-8139-0532-X). U Pr of Va.

Gile, Joanne, jt. auth. see Wilson, Eunice.

Gileadi, E., et al. Interfacial Chemistry: An Experimental Approach. 1975. text ed. 35.50 (ISBN 0-201-02398-9, Adv Bk Prog); pap. text ed. 24.50 (ISBN 0-201-02399-7). A-W.

Giles County Historical Society. Giles County Virginia History Families. (Illus.). 404p. 1982. 32.50 (ISBN 0-686-43043-3, Pub. by Walsworth). Aviation.

Giles, Eugene & Friedlaender, Jonathan S., eds. The Measures of Man: Methodologies in Biological Anthropology. LC 76-28638. (Peabody Museum Press Ser.). (Illus.). 1976. cloth 40.00x (ISBN 0-87365-800-0); pap. 25.00x (ISBN 0-87365-782-9). Peabody Harvard.

Giles, F. A. Herbaceous Perennials. (Illus.). 1980. text ed. 19.95 (ISBN 0-8359-2822-5). Reston.

Giles, Floyd, jt. auth. see Turgeon, A. J.

Giles, Frank. Toughen-Up. (Illus.). (gr. 6-8). 1963. PLB 5.49 o.p. (ISBN 0-399-60641-6). Putnam Pub Group.

Giles, G. D. Marketing. 256p. 1981. 19.00x (ISBN 0-7121-1290-1, Pub. by Macdonald & Evans). State Mutual Bk.

Giles, Gordon, et al. Killer Plants & Other Stories. Elwood, Roger, ed. LC 73-21479. (Science Fiction Bks). (Illus.). 48p. (gr. 4-8). 1974. PLB 3.95g (ISBN 0-8225-0953-9). Lerner Pubns.

Giles, Howard, jt. auth. see Ryan, Ellen B.

Giles, Howard, jt. ed. see St. Clair, Robert N.

Giles, Howard, jt. ed. see Scherer, Klaus R.

Giles, J. R. Convex Analysis with Application in the Differentiation of Convex Functions. (Research Notes in Mathematics Ser.: No. 58). 170p. (Orig.). 1982. pap. text ed. 21.95 (ISBN 0-273-08537-9). Pitman Pub MA.

Giles, James E. Esto Creemos los Bautistas. 1981. pap. 2.50 (ISBN 0-311-09091-5). Casa Bautista.

--Medical Ethics: A Patient-Centered Approach. 256p. 1983. 18.95 (ISBN 0-87073-314-1); pap. 9.95 (ISBN 0-87073-315-X). Schenkman.

--La Psicologia y el Ministerio Cristiano. 1982. Repr. of 1978 ed. 3.20 (ISBN 0-311-42059-1). Casa Bautista.

Giles, James R. Claude McKay. LC 76-10154. (U.S. Authors Ser.: No. 271). 1976. lib. bdg. 11.95 o.p. (ISBN 0-8057-7171-9, Twayne). G K Hall.

--Irwin Shaw. (United States Authors Ser.). 220p. 1983. lib. bdg. 13.95 (ISBN 0-8057-7382-7, Twayne). G K Hall.

--James Jones. (United States Authors Ser.). 1981. lib. bdg. 10.95 (ISBN 0-8057-7293-6, Twayne). G K Hall.

Giles, James V., jt. auth. see Smith, A. Robert.

Giles, Janice H. Janice Holt Giles Frontier Set, 4 bks. Incl. The Believers; Hannah Fowler; Johnny Osage; The Kentuckians. (Reader's Request Ser.). 1980. Set. lib. bdg. 58.00 (ISBN 0-686-62740-7, Large Print Bks). G K Hall.

--The Land Beyond the Mountains. new ed. LC 58-9062. 1974. 13.95 (ISBN 0-910220-62-X). Berg.

Giles, Janice Holt. The Land Beyond the Mountains. 1976. pap. 1.75 o.p. (ISBN 0-380-00593-X, 28787). Avon.

Giles, Kenneth L. & Sen, S. K., eds. Plant Cell Culture in Crop Improvement. (Basic Life Sciences Ser.: Vol. 22). 514p. 1983. 65.00x (ISBN 0-306-41160-1, Plenum Pr). Plenum Pub.

Giles, Lionel, jt. tr. see Johnstone, Charles.

Giles, Llewellyn I. Songs from My Father's Pockets. (Illus.). 64p. 1982. pap. 4.95 perf. bound (ISBN 0-937724-01-7). Shadow Pr.

Giles, Marian T., jt. auth. see Bush, Wilma J.

Giles, Peter. The Counter Tenor. 250p. 1982. 39.00x o.p. (ISBN 0-584-10474-X, Pub. by Muller Ltd). State Mutual Bk.

Giles, Raymond. Hellcat of Sabrehill. 384p. (Orig.). 1983. pap. 3.50 (ISBN 0-449-12382-0, GM). Fawcett.

Giles, Ronald V. Fluid Mechanics & Hydraulics. (Schaum's Outline Ser). (Orig.). 1962. pap. 7.95 (ISBN 0-07-023234-2, SP). McGraw.

Giles, Tony & Stansfield, Malcolm. The Farmer As Manager. (Illus., Orig.). 1980. text ed. 25.00x (ISBN 0-04-658228-2); pap. text ed. 10.50x (ISBN 0-04-658229-0). Allen Unwin.

Giles, William E. A Cruise in a Queensland Labour Vessel to the South Seas. Scarr, Deryck, ed. (Pacific History Ser.: No. 1). (Illus.). 1968. 7.50x (ISBN 0-87022-295-3). UH Pr.

Giles Of Rome. Giles of Rome: Errores Philosophorum. Riedl, John C., tr. 1944. 7.95 (ISBN 0-87462-429-0). Marquette.

--Giles of Rome: Theorems on Existence & Essence. Murray, Michael V., tr. (Medieval Philosophical Texts in Translation: No. 7). 1953. pap. 7.95 (ISBN 0-87462-207-7). Marquette.

Giles-Sims, Jean. Wife Battering: Perspectives on Marriage & the Family. 197p. 1983. 17.50x (ISBN 0-89862-075-9). Guilford Pr.

Gilfond, Henry. Black Hand at Sarajevo: Prologue to a World War. LC 74-17690. 176p. (gr. 7 up). 1975. 6.95 o.p. (ISBN 0-672-52070-2). Bobbs.

--Countries of the Sahara. LC 80-2269. (First Bks.). (Illus.). (gr. 4 up). 1981. PLB 8.90 (ISBN 0-531-04271-5). Watts.

--Disastrous Earthquakes. LC 81-4625. (First Bks.). (Illus.). 72p. (gr. 4 up). 1981. lib. bdg. 8.90 (ISBN 0-531-04324-X). Watts.

--Executive Branch. LC 80-25729. (First Books About Washington Ser.). (gr. 4 up). 1981. PLB 8.90 (ISBN 0-531-04251-0). Watts.

--Gambia Ghana Libia. LC 80-23043. (First Bks.). (gr. 4 up). 1981. PLB 8.90 (ISBN 0-531-04274-X). Watts.

--The New Ice Age. (Impact Bks). (Illus.). (gr. 7 up). 1978. PLB 8.90 s&l (ISBN 0-531-01458-4). Watts.

Gilford, James, jt. ed. see Shelsby, Earl.

Gilgoff, Alice. Home Birth. LC 77-14230. (Illus.). 1978. 8.95 o.p. (ISBN 0-698-10832-9, Coward). Putnam Pub Group.

Gilgun, John. Everything That Has Been Shall Be Again. (Illus.). 1981. 125.00 (ISBN 0-931460-11-5); pap. 7.95 (ISBN 0-931460-13-1). Bieler.

Gilhooly, K. J. Thinking: Directed, Undirected & Creative. 19.50 (ISBN 0-12-283480-1); pap. 9.50 (ISBN 0-12-283482-8). Acad Pr.

Gili. Demon Daisy's Dreadful Week. LC 80-80539. (ps-k). 1980. PLB 6.90 (ISBN 0-531-04179-4). Watts.

Gilinsky, Victor, jt. auth. see Wohlstetter, Albert.

Gilkerson, Seth W. Wait For Me & Other Stories. LC 82-82216. 144p. 1982. pap. write for info (ISBN 0-88100-014-0). Natl Writ Pr.

Gilkes, Michael. The West Indian Novel. (World Authors Ser.). 1981. lib. bdg. 13.95 (ISBN 0-8057-6434-8, Twayne). G K Hall.

Gilkes, Patrick. The Dying Lion: Feudalism & Modernization in Ethiopia. LC 75-9388. (Illus.). 356p. 1975. text ed. 22.50 (ISBN 0-312-22295-5). St Martin.

Gilkey, Langdon. Message & Existence: An Introduction to Christian Theology. 272p. 1980. 10.95 (ISBN 0-8164-0450-X); pap. 5.95 (ISBN 0-8164-2023-8). Seabury.

--Reaping the Whirlwind: A Christian Interpretation of History. 1977. 17.50 (ISBN 0-8164-0308-2); pap. 9.95 (ISBN 0-8164-2317-2). Seabury.

--Shantung Compound. LC 75-9312. 272p. 1975. pap. 7.64xi (ISBN 0-06-063112-0, RD101, HarpR). Har-Row.

Gilkey, Robert, ed. & intro. by. The Chinese Unicorn & Other Conceits from a Chinese Dictionary. 1973. pap. 3.95 (ISBN 0-686-02625-X). Noname Pr.

Gilkison, Jean, jt. auth. see Cardenas, Anthony.

Gill & Jackson. Adoption & Race. LC 82-42714. 160p. 1983. 22.50x (ISBN 0-686-84407-6). St Martin.

Gill, Adrian. Atmosphere-Ocean Dynamics. (International Geophysics Ser.). 1982. 60.00 (ISBN 0-12-283520-4); pap. 20.00 (ISBN 0-12-283522-0). Acad Pr.

Gill, Ann E. Beadwork: The Technique of Stringing, Threading & Weaving. (Illus.). 1977. 15.95 o.p. (ISBN 0-8230-0480-5). Watson-Guptill.

Gill, Arthur. Applied Algebra for the Computer Sciences. (Illus.). 416p. 1976. 30.95 (ISBN 0-13-039222-7). P-H.

--Introduction to the Theory of Finite-State Machines. (Electronic Systems Ser.). 1962. text ed. 32.50 o.p. (ISBN 0-07-023243-1, P&RB). McGraw.

--Machine & Assembly Language Programming of the PDP-Eleven. LC 78-9690. (Illus.). 1978. 25.95 (ISBN 0-13-541870-4). P-H.

Gill, Bob. Forget All the Rules You Ever Learned about Graphic Design. 168p. 1981. 40.00x (ISBN 0-686-97109-4, Pub. by Pitman Bks England). State Mutual Bk.

Gill, Brendan & Witney, Dudley. Summer Places. 35.00 o.p. (ISBN 0-458-93430-5). Methuen Inc.

Gill, Brendan, frwd. by see Schermerhorn, Gene.

Gill, C. B. Non-Ferrous Extractive Metallurgy. LC 79-28696. 346p. 1980. 49.95x (ISBN 0-471-05980-3, Pub. by Wiley-Interscience). Wiley.

Gill, Chris & Fatrell, Jon. The Illustrated Encyclopedia of Black Music. 208p. 1982. 19.95 (ISBN 0-517-54779-1, Harmony); pap. 12.95 (ISBN 0-517-54780-5). Crown.

Gill, Colin, et al. Industrial Relations in the Chemical Industry. 1978. text ed. 35.00x (ISBN 0-566-00215-9). Gower Pub Ltd.

Gill, Conrad. Merchants & Mariners of the Eighteenth Century. LC 78-5810. (Illus.). 1978. Repr. of 1961 ed. lib. bdg. 17.50x (ISBN 0-313-20386-5, GIMM). Greenwood.

Gill, Corrington. Wasted Manpower: The Challenge of Unemployment. LC 72-2371. (FDR & the Era of the New Deal Ser). 316p. 1973. Repr. of 1939 ed. lib. bdg. 39.50 (ISBN 0-306-70467-6). Da Capo.

Gill, Deemster, et al. The Manx National Songbook, Vol. 1. 1979. text ed. 14.50x o.p. (ISBN 0-904980-30-8). Humanities.

Gill, Derek. Quest: The Life of Elisabeth Kubler-Ross. LC 78-19823. (Illus.). 1980. 14.37i (ISBN 0-06-011543-2, HarpT). Har-Row.

Gill, Derek, jt. auth. see Graham, Robin L.

Gill, Derek, jt. auth. see Sullivan, Tom.

Gill, Derek L. Tom Sullivan's Adventures in Darkness. Date not set. pap. 1.95 o.p. (ISBN 0-451-09376-3, J9376, Sig). NAL.

Gill, Elaine, ed. Mountain Moving Day: An Anthology of Woman's Poetry. LC 73-77320. (Crossing Press Ser. of Contemporary Anthologies). 100p. (Orig.). 1973. 14.95 (ISBN 0-912278-37-4); pap. 4.95 (ISBN 0-912278-36-6). Crossing Pr.

Gill, F. W. & Bates, G. L. Airline Competition: A Study of the Effects of Competition on the Quality & Price of Airline Service & the Self-Sufficiency of the United States Domestic Airlines. 1949. 55.00 (ISBN 0-08-018738-2). Pergamon.

Gill, Frances M. & Abbe, Kathryn M. Twins on Twins. 1980. 17.95 (ISBN 0-517-54149-1, C N Potter Bks). Crown.

Gill, Frank B. Intra-island Variation in the Mascarene White-eye Zosterops Borbonica. 66p. 1973. 3.50 (ISBN 0-943610-12-5). Am Ornithologists.

Gill, G. B. & Willis, M. R. Pericyclic Reactions. 1974. pap. 15.50x (ISBN 0-412-12490-4, Pub. by Chapman & Hall). Methuen Inc.

Gill, Gordon N., ed. Pharmacology of Adrenal Cortical Hormones. LC 78-40135. 1979. text ed. 59.00 (ISBN 0-08-019619-5). Pergamon.

Gill, Harold B., Jr. Gunsmith in Colonial Virginia. (Williamsburg Research Studies Ser). (Illus.). 139p. 1974. 4.95x (ISBN 0-8139-0334-3); pap. 4.95x (ISBN 0-87935-009-1). U Pr of Va.

Gill, Harold, Jr. The Gunsmith in Colonial Virgina. LC 73-78366. (Williamsburg Research Studies Ser). 1974. pap. 4.50 o.p. (ISBN 0-87935-008-3, Pub. by Williamsburg). U Pr of Va.

Gill, Jack C. & Blitzer, Robert. Competency in College Mathematics. 400p. 1982. pap. text ed. 17.95 (ISBN 0-943202-02-7). H & H Pub.

--Competency in College Mathematics. 2nd ed. Hackworth, Robert D., intro. by. 488p. 1982. write for info. (ISBN 0-943202-07-8). H & H Pub.

Gill, Jack C., jt. auth. see Blitzer, Robert.

Gill, Jean. Images of My Self: Meditation & Self-Exploration Through the Imagery of the Gospels. 128p. 1982. pap. 3.95 (ISBN 0-8091-2463-7). Paulist Pr.

Gill, Jerry H. Metaphilosophy: An Introduction. LC 82-40230. (Orig.). 1982. pap. text ed. 6.75 (ISBN 0-8191-2650-0). U Pr of Amer.

--Toward Theology. LC 82-45009. 130p. (Orig.). 1982. PLB 18.75 (ISBN 0-8191-2429-X); pap. text ed. 8.00 (ISBN 0-8191-2430-3). U Pr of Amer.

--Wittgenstein & Metaphor. LC 80-5690. 246p. 1981. lib. bdg. 19.75 (ISBN 0-8191-1600-9); pap. text ed. 10.75 (ISBN 0-8191-1601-7). U Pr of Amer.

Gill, Joan. Golden Retrievers. LC 76-11000. (Illus.). 1976. bds. 2.25 o.p. (ISBN 0-668-03988-4). Arco.

--Golden Retrievers. Foyle, Christina, ed. (Foyles Handbks.). 1973. 3.95 (ISBN 0-685-55801-0). Palmetto Pub.

Gill, John. Country Pleasures. LC 75-28398. (Selected Poets Ser.). 80p. (Orig.). 1975. 13.95 (ISBN 0-912278-60-9); pap. 5.95 (ISBN 0-912278-61-7). Crossing Pr.

Gill, Joseph B. The Great Pyramid Speaks to You. 1983. 13.95 (ISBN 0-8022-2405-9). Philos Lib.

Gill, Joseph L. Personalized Stress Management: A Manual for Everyday Life & Work. LC 82-90115. (Illus.). 175p. 1983. 14.95 (ISBN 0-910819-00-9); pap. 9.95 (ISBN 0-910819-01-7). Counsel & Consult.

Gill, Kathleen D., ed. ERISA. 550p. 1983. pap. text ed. 20.00 (ISBN 0-87179-385-7). BNA.

Gill, Kay, jt. ed. see Kruzas, Anthony T.

Gill, Paul. Electrical Equipment Testing & Maintenance Handbook. 350p. 1981. text ed. 22.95 (ISBN 0-8359-1625-1). Reston.

Gill, Peter, jt. auth. see Ponton, Geoffrey.

Gill, Phillida. The Lost Ears. (Illus.). 32p. (ps-k). 1981. lib. bdg. 8.90 (ISBN 0-531-04065-8). Watts.

Gill, Richard. Economics: A Text with Readings. 3rd ed. LC 77-16814. (Illus.). 1977. text ed. 25.50x (ISBN 0-673-16166-8). Scott F.

--Economics & the Public Interest. 4th ed. 1980. 14.50x (ISBN 0-673-16160-9). Scott F.

Gill, Richard T. Economics & the Private Interest: An Introduction to Microeconomics. 2nd ed. LC 75-22754. 288p. 1976. pap. text ed. 14.50x (ISBN 0-673-16161-7); student guide 7.95x (ISBN 0-673-16159-5). Scott F.

Gill, Sam. Beyond the "Primitive". Religions of Nonliterate Peoples. (Illus.). 200p. 1982. pap. 9.95 (ISBN 0-13-076034-X). P-H.

Gill, Stephen, ed. see Dickens, Charles.

Gill, Stephen, ed. see Trollope, Anthony.

Gill, Susan, jt. auth. see Cate, Phillip D.

Gill, Suzanne L. File Management & Information Retrieval Systems: A Manual for Managers & Technicians. LC 80-22785. (Illus.). 193p. 1981. lib. bdg. 18.50 (ISBN 0-87287-229-7). Libs Unl.

Gill, T. P. The Doppler Effect: An Introduction to the Theory of the Effect. 1965. 28.50 o.p. (ISBN 0-12-283350-3). Acad Pr.

Gill, W. J. Captain John Smith & Virginia. Reeves, Marjorie, ed. (Then & There Ser.). (Illus.). 75p. (gr. 7-12). 1968. pap. text ed. 3.10 (ISBN 0-582-20413-5). Longman.

--The Pilgrim Fathers. Reeves, Marjorie, ed. (Then & There Ser.). (Illus.). 79p. (Orig.). (gr. 7-12). pap. text ed. 3.10 (ISBN 0-582-20395-3). Longman.

Gill, William J., jt. auth. see White, F. Clifton.

Gillam, Alan. The Principles & Practice of Selling. 160p. (Orig.). 1982. pap. 14.95 (Pub. by W Heinemann). David & Charles.

Gillam, W. S., ed. see Deming, H. G.

Gillan, Maria. Flowers from the Tree of Night. LC 81-18087. 64p. (Orig.). 1981. pap. 5.00 (ISBN 0-941608-00-X). Chantry Pr.

Gillard, Quentin, jt. auth. see Berry, Brian J.

Gillaspie, William R., ed. see Morison, James.

Gillbe, G. V., jt. ed. see Moore, J. R.

Gillean, James I., jt. auth. see Clark, Robert M.

Gilleland, Martha J. Basic Experiments for General, Organic, & Biological Chemistry. new ed. 226p. 1982. 11.95 (ISBN 0-314-63239-5). West Pub.

--Introduction to General, Organic & Biological Chemistry. (Illus.). 832p. 1982. text ed. 26.95 (ISBN 0-314-63173-9). West Pub.

Gillen, Bob, jt. auth. see Lund, Morten.

Gillen, Charles H. H. H. Munro (Saki) (English Authors Ser.: No. 102). lib. bdg. 9.95 o.p. (ISBN 0-8057-1408-1, Twayne). G K Hall.

Gillen, F. J., jt. auth. see Spencer, Baldwin.

Gillen, William J., jt. auth. see Cicchetti, Charles J.

Gillenwater, Jay Y. Year Book of Urology 1980. 1980. 30.95 (ISBN 0-8151-3470-3). Year Bk Med.

--Year Book of Urology 1983. 1983. 40.00 (ISBN 0-8151-3473-8). Year Bk Med.

Gillenwater, Jay Y., jt. auth. see Wyker, Arthur.

Gillenwater, Jay Y. & Howards, Stuart S., eds. Year Book of Urology, 1982. 1982. 37.00 (ISBN 0-8151-3472-X). Year Bk Med.

Gilleo, Alma. Amy Carter, Growing up in the White House. LC 78-7812. (Illus.). (gr. k-4). 1978. PLB 6.50 o.p. (ISBN 0-89565-028-2). Childs World.

Gillers, Stephen. Looking at Law School: A Student Guide from the Society of American Law Teachers. (Orig.). 1977. pap. 5.95 (ISBN 0-452-00555-8, F555, Mer). NAL.

Gilles, Floyd H., et al. Developing Human Brain: Growth & Epidemiologic Neuropathology. (Illus.). 320p. 1983. 49.50 (ISBN 0-7236-7017-X). Wright-PSG.

Gilles, G., jt. auth. see Romagnesi, H.

Gilles, Maria V. Byrons Dramen. 151p. (Ger.). 1982. write for info. (ISBN 3-8204-5818-2). P Lang Pubs.

Gilles, R. Mechanisms of Osmoregulation in Animals: Maintenance of Cell Volume. LC 78-4608. 667p. 1979. 114.75x (ISBN 0-471-99648-3, Pub. by Wiley-Interscience). Wiley.

Gillespie, A. R., jt. auth. see Siegal, B. S.

Gillespie, Angus K. Folklorist of the Coal Fields: George Korson's Life & Work. LC 79-25839. (Illus.). 1980. 18.95 (ISBN 0-271-00255-7). Pa St U Pr.

Gillespie, Cecil. Accounting Systems: Procedures & Methods. 3rd ed. (Illus.). 720p. 1971. ref. ed. 29.95x (ISBN 0-13-001933-X). P-H.

Gillespie, Charles A. Cone Four-Low Fire Pottery. 2nd. Ed ed. (Illus.). 72p. 1983. pap. 9.95 (ISBN 0-9609974-1-5). CA Gillespie.

Gillespie, David F. & Mileti, Dennis S. Technostructures & Inter-Organizational Relations. LC 78-19543. (Illus.). 176p. 1978. 21.95x (ISBN 0-669-02542-9). Lexington Bks.

Gillespie, James. Modern Livestock & Poultry Production. 2nd ed. (Illus.). 662p. 1983. text ed. 23.80 (ISBN 0-8273-2200-3); write for info. instr's guide (ISBN 0-8273-2201-1). Delmar.

Gillespie, Jane. Ladysmead. LC 82-16773. 176p. 1982. 9.95 (ISBN 0-312-46433-9). St Martin.

Gillespie, Joan. Algeria, Rebellion & Revolution. LC 75-25487. (Illus.). 208p. 1976. Repr. of 1960 ed. lib. bdg. 19.75x (ISBN 0-8371-8425-8, GIAL). Greenwood.

Gillespie, John, ed. Nineteenth-Century American Piano Music. LC 77-90383. 1978. pap. 10.95 (ISBN 0-486-23602-1). Dover.

Gillespie, John T. Model School District Media Program. LC 77-5022. 1977. pap. text ed. 12.00 (ISBN 0-8389-3192-8). ALA.

--Paperback Books for Young People: An Annotated Guide to Publishers & Distributors. 2nd ed. LC 77-21627. 1977. pap. 12.00 (ISBN 0-8389-0248-0). ALA.

Gillespie, John T. & Spirt, Diana L. Administering a School Media Program. 2nd ed. 256p. 1983. 27.50 (ISBN 0-8352-1514-8). Bowker.

Gillespie, John V., jt. ed. see Zinnes, Dina A.

Gillespie, Joseph E., jt. auth. see Fabreau, Donald F.

Gillespie, Judith A. & Zinnes, Dina A., eds. Missing Elements in Political Inquiry: Logic & Levels of Analysis. (Sage Focus Editions). 264p. 1982. 22.00 (ISBN 0-8039-1802-X); pap. 10.95 (ISBN 0-8039-1803-8). Sage.

Gillespie, K. & Hecht, J. C. Retail Business Management: Applications & Cases. 3rd ed. 160p. 1983. 7.95x (ISBN 0-07-023229-6). McGraw.

Gillespie, Karen & Hecht, Joseph. Retail Business Management. 2nd ed. (Illus.). 1977. text ed. 20.20 (ISBN 0-07-023232-6, G); instructor's manual 5.95 (ISBN 0-07-023233-4). McGraw.

Gillespie, Karen & Hecht, Joseph C. Retail Business Management. 3rd, rev. ed. LC 82-21700. (Illus.). 480p. 1983. text ed. 18.05x (ISBN 0-07-023228-8, G). McGraw.

Gillespie, Margaret C. & Connor, John W. Creative Growth Through Literature for Children & Adolescents. new ed. (Elementary Education Ser.). 416p. 1975. text ed. 20.95 (ISBN 0-675-08751-1). Merrill.

Gillespie, N. J. Mira Activities for Junior High Geometry. 1973. pap. 6.25 wkbk. (ISBN 0-88488-017-6). Creative Pubns.

Gillespie, Oscar. Herpes: What to Do When You Have It. LC 82-82318. 96p. (Orig.). 1982. pap. 4.95 (ISBN 0-448-12332-0, G&D). Putnam Pub Group.

Gillespie, Patricia. Teaching Reading to the Special Needs Child: An Ecological Approach. (Special Education Ser.). 1979. text ed. 23.95 (ISBN 0-675-08274-9). Merrill.

Gillespie, Patti P., jt. auth. see Cameron, Kenneth M.

Gillespie, Paul D. Problems of Document Delivery for the Euronet User: A Technical Report. Franklin Institute Gmbh, ed. 1979. 20.00 (ISBN 0-686-77578-3, Pub. by K G Saur). Shoe String.

Gillespie, R. D., jt. auth. see Henderson, David.

Gillespie, Richard. Soldiers of Peron: Argentina's Montoneros. 328p. 1982. 29.95 (ISBN 0-19-821131-7). Oxford U Pr.

Gillespie, Robert. The Man Chain. LC 79-12276. 75p. 1979. 4.00 (ISBN 0-87886-102-5). Ithaca Hse.

Gillespie, Robert B. Print-Out. 224p. 1983. 11.95 (ISBN 0-396-08100-2). Dodd.

Gillespie, Thomas, jt. auth. see Lang, Larry.

Gillespie, V. Bailey. Religious Conversion & Personal Identity. LC 79-15605. 264p. (Orig.). 1979. pap. 9.95 (ISBN 0-89135-018-7). Religious Educ.

Gillespie, W. Jay, jt. auth. see Cantu, Robert C.

Gillet. Quelques Reflexions sur l'Emploi des Enfants dans les Fabriques et sur les Moyens d'en Prevenir les Abus. (Conditions of the 19th Century French Working Class Ser.). 84p. (Fr.). 1974. Repr. of 1840 ed. lib. bdg. 31.50x o.p. (ISBN 0-8287-0377-9, 1150). Clearwater Pub.

Gilleto, Sebastian B. The Changing Tide. (Fictional Ser.). 246p. 1981. Leatherette cover 4.00 (ISBN 0-686-36143-1). Intl Print.

Gillett, B. E., jt. auth. see Carlile, R. E.

Gillett, Billy E. Methods of Operations Research. (Illus.). 1976. text ed. 33.95 (ISBN 0-07-023245-8, C); solutions manual o.p. 20.00 (ISBN 0-07-023246-6). McGraw.

Gillett, Dorothy. Comprehensive Musicianship Through Classroom Music: Zone 3, Book A. Burton, Leon & Thomson, William, eds. (University of Hawaii Music Project). (gr. 3). 1974. pap. text ed. 7.88 o.p. (ISBN 0-201-00858-0, Sch Div); tchr's ed. o.p. 12.52 o.p. (ISBN 0-201-00859-9). A-W.

Gillett, Margaret. We Walked Very Warily: A History of Women at McGill. (Illus.). 496p. 1981. 18.95 (ISBN 0-920792-08-1). Eden Pr.

Gillett, Philip. Calculus & Analytic Geometry. 928p. 1981. text ed. 33.95 (ISBN 0-669-00641-6); solutions guide, vol. 1 8.95 (ISBN 0-669-00642-4); solutions guide vol. 2 8.95 (ISBN 0-669-03212-3); solutions guide vol. 3 8.95 (ISBN 0-669-03213-1). Heath.

Gillett, Philip W. Introduction to Linear Algebra. 1975. text ed. 25.50 (ISBN 0-395-18574-2); solutions manual 3.25 (ISBN 0-395-18809-1). HM.

Gillette, Ethel M. Idaho Springs, Saratoga of the Rockies: A History of Idaho Springs, Colorado. 1978. 8.95 o.p. (ISBN 0-533-02974-0). Vantage.

Gillette, F. L., jt. auth. see Ziemann, Hugo.

Gillette, Howard, Jr., jt. ed. see Cutler, William W., 3rd.

Gillette, Paul. Buyers Guide to California Wines. (Wine Library Ser.: Vol. I). (Illus.). 1983. pap. 7.95 (ISBN 0-913290-42-4). Camaro Pub.

Gilley, Jeanne M., et al. Early Childhood: Development & Education. LC 78-73823. 1980. pap. 13.40 (ISBN 0-8273-1579-1); instructor's guide 4.25 (ISBN 0-8273-1580-5). Delmar.

Gillham, Anabel. Friends & Lovers for Life. 1982. pap. 5.95 (ISBN 0-8423-0931-4). Tyndale.

Gillham, Bill. The First Words Language Programme. 96p. 1980. pap. text ed. 12.95 (ISBN 0-04-371060-3). Univ Park.

--The First Words Picture Book. (Illus.). 32p. (gr. 1-5). 1982. 7.95 (ISBN 0-698-20560-X, Coward). Putnam Pub Group.

--Two Worlds Together: A First Sentences Language Programme. 64p. 1983. text ed. 19.50x (ISBN 0-04-371091-3); pap. text ed. 8.95x (ISBN 0-04-371092-1). Allen Unwin.

Gillham, D. G., ed. Keats: Poems of 1820. 224p. 1979. 15.00x (ISBN 0-7121-0141-1, Pub. by Macdonald & Evans). State Mutual Bk.

Gillham, Nicholas W. Organelle Heredity. LC 75-43195. 618p. 1978. 59.00 (ISBN 0-89004-102-4). Raven.

Gilli, Angelo C. Modern Organizations of Vocational Education. 1976. 20.00x (ISBN 0-271-01223-4, 76-1883). Pa St U Pr.

Gilli, Angelo C., Sr. Electrical Principles for Electronics. rev ed. LC 77-4676. (Illus.). 1977. text ed. 23.95 (ISBN 0-07-023293-8, G). McGraw.

Gilliam, A. The Principles & Practice of Selling. 256p. 1982. pap. 40.00 (ISBN 0-434-90661-1, Pub. by Heinemann England). State Mutual Bk.

Gilliam, Brenda, jt. auth. see Setliff, Gail.

Gilliam, Camp. Myths & Modern Education. LC 74-24849. viii, 108p. 1975. pap. text ed. 3.50x (ISBN 0-8134-1701-5, 1701). Interstate.

Gilliam, Dona & McCaskill, Mizzy. Tinwhistle for Beginners. (Illus.). 45p. (Orig.). (gr. 3-6). 1981. pap. 3.00 (ISBN 0-9604626-1-9). Twos Co Music.

Gilliam, Dorothy B. Paul Robeson: All American. LC 76-23233. (Illus.). 1976. 8.95 (ISBN 0-915220-15-6); pap. 3.95 o.si. (ISBN 0-915220-39-3). New Republic.

Gilliam, George H. Business Entities: A Virginia Law Practice System. 350p. 1982. 75.00 (ISBN 0-87215-509-9). Michie-Bobbs.

Gilliam, Gwen, jt. auth. see Garbarino, James.

Gilliam, Stan, jt. auth. see D'Ignazio, Fred.

Gilliam, Terry & Cowel, Lucinda. Animations of Mortality. LC 78-60982. (Illus.). 1978. pap. 9.95 (ISBN 0-413-39380-1). Methuen Inc.

Gilliant, M., ed. see Haws, Duncan.

Gilliard, Frank D., tr. see Bengtson, Hermann.

Gilliatt, Mary. Decorating on the Cheap. LC 82-40499. (Illus.). 192p. 1983. pap. 10.95 (ISBN 0-89480-353-0). Workman Pub.

Gilliatt, Penelope. The Cutting Edge. LC 78-13161. 1979. 8.95 o.p. (ISBN 0-698-10948-1, Coward). Putnam Pub Group.

--Jean Renoir: Essays, Conversations, Reviews. LC 75-6905. (McGraw-Hill Paperbacks). (Illus.). 136p. 1975. 5.95 o.p. (ISBN 0-07-023225-3, SP); pap. 2.95 (ISBN 0-07-023224-5). McGraw.

--Quotations From Other Lives. 160p. 1982. 12.95 (ISBN 0-698-11135-4, Coward). Putnam Pub Group.

--Splendid Lives. 1978. 7.95 o.p. (ISBN 0-698-10878-7, Coward). Putnam Pub Group.

--Three Quarter Face: Reports & Reflections. LC 79-20607. 1980. 12.95 (ISBN 0-698-11015-3, Coward). Putnam Pub Group.

Gillibrand, P. & Maddock, V., eds. The Manager & His Words: An Introduction to the Vocabulary of Business English Studies. (English for Specific Purposes Ser.). 96p. 1982. 8.95 (ISBN 0-686-98317-3). Pergamon.

Gillie, Angelo C. Principles of Post-Secondary Vocational Education. LC 73-87883. 1974. text ed. 19.95 (ISBN 0-675-08866-6). Merrill.

Gillie, C. Movements in English Literature, 1900-1940. LC 74-16993. 200p. 1975. 37.50 (ISBN 0-521-20655-3); pap. 9.95 (ISBN 0-521-09922-6). Cambridge U Pr.

Gillie, Christopher. Character in English Literature. 1965. text ed. 10.00x (ISBN 0-7011-0715-4). Humanities.

Gillie, Christopher, ed. Companion to British Literature. Orig. Title: Longman Companion to English Literature. (Illus.). 880p. 1980. Repr. of 1972 ed. 48.00x (ISBN 0-8103-2022-3). Gale.

Gillies, Dee A. Nursing Management: Systems Approach. (Illus.). 487p. 1982. 18.95 (ISBN 0-7216-4135-0). Saunders.

Gillies, Dee Ann & Alyn, Irene B. Saunders Tests for Self-Evaluation of Nursing Competence. 3rd ed. LC 77-77100. 1978. 11.95 o.p. (ISBN 0-7216-4132-6). Saunders.

Gillies, Eva, ed. see Evans-Pritchard, Edward E.

Gillies, George & Gillies, Harriet. Scriptural Outline of the Baptism of the Holy Spirit. 32p. 1972. pap. 1.00 (ISBN 0-88368-062-9). Whitaker Hse.

Gillies, Harriet, jt. auth. see Gillies, George.

Gillies, Jean. Patterns for Applique & Pieced Work & Ways to Use Them. LC 82-12020. (Illus.). 136p. 1982. 13.95 (ISBN 0-385-18135-3). Doubleday.

Gillies, Jerry. Friends: The Power & Potential of the Company You Keep. 224p. 1976. 8.95 o.p. (ISBN 0-698-10758-6, Coward). Putnam Pub Group.

--My Needs, Your Needs, Our Needs. pap. 1.75 o.p. (ISBN 0-451-08541-8, E8541, Sig). NAL.

--Psychological Immortality: Using Your Mind to Extend Your Life. 225p. 1981. 12.95 (ISBN 0-399-90103-5, Marek). Putnam Pub Group.

Gillies, John. The Martyrs of Guanabara. LC 76-14954. 1976. 7.95 (ISBN 0-8024-5187-X). Moody.

Gillies, R. F. Lecture Notes on Medical Microbiology. 2nd ed. (Illus.). 1978. softcover 13.00 (ISBN 0-632-00062-7, B1826-6, Blackwell). Mosby.

Gilligan & Nenno. Intermediate Algebra. LC 77-12374. 1977. pap. text ed. 21.95x (ISBN 0-673-16237-0); instructor's manual free (ISBN 0-87620-422-1); solutions manual 8.95 (ISBN 0-87620-421-3). Scott F.

Gilligan, Carol. In a Different Voice: Psychological Theory & Women's Development. 192p. 1983. pap. text ed. 5.95x (ISBN 0-674-44544-9). Harvard U Pr.

Gilligan, Gerald S. A Price Guide for Buying & Selling Rural Acreage. 2nd ed. LC 75-45444. 1976. pap. 11.00 o.p. (ISBN 0-07-023226-1, P&RB). McGraw.

Gilligan, Lawrence & Nenno, Bob. Finite Mathematics: An Elementary Approach. 2nd ed. 1979. text ed. 21.95x (ISBN 0-673-16235-4). Scott F.

Gilligan, Lawrence & Nenno, Robert. College Algebra. 1981. text ed. 23.50x (ISBN 0-673-16229-X). Scott F.

--College Algebra & Trigonometry: Precalculus Math. 1981. text ed. 23.50x (ISBN 0-673-16230-3). Scott F.

Gilliland, Alexis A. The Pirates of Rosinante. 224p. (Orig.). 1982. pap. 2.50 (ISBN 0-686-81743-5, Del Rey). Ballantine.

Gilliland, Dean S. Pauline Theology & Mission Practice. 304p. 1983. pap. 12.95 (ISBN 0-8010-3788-3). Baker Bk.

Gilliland, H. Readability Formula. 1980. 00.15 (ISBN 0-89992-508-1). MT Coun Indian.

Gilliland, Hap. Bill Red Coyote is a Nut. (Beginning Reading for All Ages Ser.). 1981. 1.95 (ISBN 0-89992-101-9). MT Coun Indian.

--How the Dogs Saved the Cheyennes. (Indian Culture Ser.). (gr. 1-4). 1972. 1.95 o.p. (ISBN 0-89992-017-9). MT Coun Indian.

--Materials for Remedial Reading & Their Use. 5th ed. 1976. 5.85 o.p. (ISBN 0-686-22258-X). MT Coun Indian.

--Practical Guide to Remedial Reading. 2nd ed. Heilman, Arthur, ed. (Elementary Education Ser.). 1978. text ed. 17.95 (ISBN 0-675-08359-1). Merrill.

--We Live on an Indian Reservation. (Beginning Reading for All Ages Ser.). 1981. 1.95 (ISBN 0-89992-100-0). MT Coun Indian.

Gilliland, Martha W., ed. Energy Analysis: A New Public Policy Tool. LC 77-15895. (AAAS Selected Symposium Ser.: No. 9). (Illus.). 1978. lib. bdg. 17.00x o.p. (ISBN 0-89158-437-4). Westview.

Gilliland, Mary. Gathering Fire. LC 82-13022. 65p. 1982. pap. 5.00 (ISBN 0-87886-119-X). Ithaca Hse.

Gillin, John L. Taming the Criminal: Adventures in Penology. LC 69-14927. (Criminology, Law Enforcement, & Social Problems Ser.: No. 71). (Illus.). 1969. Repr. of 1931 ed. 15.00x (ISBN 0-87585-071-5). Patterson Smith.

Gilling, Cynthia M., jt. auth. see Nash, D. F.

Gillingham, John. The Life & Times of Richard I. (Kings & Queens of England Ser.). (Illus.). 224p. 1973. text ed. 17.50x (ISBN 0-297-99572-3, Pub. by Weidenfeld & Nicolson England). Biblio Dist.

Gillingham, Peter N., jt. auth. see Schumacher, E. F.

Gillingwater, David, jt. auth. see Button, Kenneth.

Gillis, Everett A. Capsuled in Summer. 64p. 1983. 9.95 (ISBN 0-938328-03-4). Pisces Pr TX.

--Goldie. (Illus.). 64p. (Orig.). (gr. 3-7). 1982. pap. 8.00 (ISBN 0-938328-02-6). Pisces Pr TX.

Gillis, Frederick. Moonbeams for Ellen. 1983. 5.95 (ISBN 0-533-05439-7). Vantage.

Gillis, Jack. The Car Book. 1982. pap. 4.95 o.p. (ISBN 0-686-34583-5). Caroline Hse.

--The Car Book: 1983 Models. (Illus.). 104p. 1983. pap. 6.95 (ISBN 0-525-48049-8, 0675-200). Dutton.

Gillis, John. Social Influence in Psychotherapy. 59p. 1979. pap. 4.95 (ISBN 0-932930-08-5). Pilgrimage Inc.

Gillis, John R. The Development of European Society Seventeen Seventy to Eighteen Seventy. LC 82-20234. (Illus.). 316p. 1983. pap. text ed. 11.75 (ISBN 0-8191-2898-8). U Pr of Amer.

--The Development of European Society: 1770-1870. LC 76-10891. (Illus.). 1977. pap. text ed. 18.95 (ISBN 0-395-24482-X). HM.

Gillis, M. F., jt. ed. see Phillips, R. D.

Gillis, Malcolm, et al. Taxation & Mining: Nonfuel Minerals in Bolivia & Other Countries. LC 77-23806. 384p. 1978. prof ref 50.00x (ISBN 0-88410-458-3). Ballinger Pub.

--Economic Development. 650p. text ed. 21.95x (ISBN 0-393-95253-3). Norton.

Gillis, S. Malcolm, ed. Tax & Investment Policies for Hard Minerals: Public & Multinational Enterprise in Indonesia. Beals, Ralph E. 320p. 1980. prof ref 35.00x (ISBN 0-88410-488-5). Ballinger Pub.

Gillis-Lindsay. Orthoptics: A Discussion of Binocular Anomalies. (Illus.). 1972. 10.00 o.p. (ISBN 0-407-93408-1). Butterworth.

Gillison, A. N. & Anderson, D. J., eds. Vegetation Classification in Australia. 229p. 1983. text ed. 18.95 (ISBN 0-7081-1309-5, Pub. by CSIRO Australia). Intl Schol Bk Serv.

Gillispie, Charles C. The Montgolfier Brothers & the Invention of Aviation, 1783-1784: With a Word on the Importance of Ballooning for the Science of Heat & for the Art of Building Railroads. LC 82-61363. (Illus.). 272p. 1983. 35.00 (ISBN 0-691-08321-5). Princeton U Pr.

Gillispie, John V. & Zinnes, Dina A., eds. Mathematical Systems in International Relations Research. LC 75-23964. 1976. 47.95 o.p. (ISBN 0-275-55620-4). Praeger.

Gillman, L. & Jerison, M. Rings of Continuous Functions. LC 60-14787. xi, 300p. 1975. 23.00 (ISBN 0-387-90198-1). Springer-Verlag.

Gillman, Leonard & McDowell, Robert H. Calculus. 2nd ed. (Illus.). 1978. text ed. 34.95x (ISBN 0-393-09051-5); solutions manual 3.95x (ISBN 0-393-09054-X). Norton.

Gillman, Neil. Gabriel Marcel on Religious Knowledge. LC 80-5061. 315p. 1980. text ed. 22.25 (ISBN 0-8191-1034-5); pap. text ed. 12.50 (ISBN 0-8191-1035-3). U Pr of Amer.

Gillmer, Thomas & Johnson, Bruce. Introduction Naval Architecture. LC 81-85439. (Illus.). 400p. 1982. text ed. 23.95x (ISBN 0-87021-318-0). Naval Inst Pr.

Gillmoor, Desmond A., jt. auth. see Haughton, Joseph P.

Gillock, William L. Fanfare. 16p. (gr. 4-12). 1957. pap. text ed. 3.50 (ISBN 0-87487-632-X). Summy.

--Lyric Preludes. 32p. (gr. 4-12). 1958. pap. text ed. 5.05 (ISBN 0-87487-649-4). Summy.

Gillon, Adam. Conrad & Shakespeare & Other Essays. (English Authors Ser.). 1979. lib. bdg. 12.95 (ISBN 0-8057-9002-0, Twayne). G K Hall.

--Conrad & Shakespeare & Other Essays. LC 75-30140. 1976. 12.95 o.p. (ISBN 0-913994-27-8); pap. 8.95 o.p. (ISBN 0-686-67349-2). Hippocrene Bks.

--Joseph Conrad. (English Author Ser.). 1982. lib. bdg. 11.95 (ISBN 0-8057-6820-3, Twayne). G K Hall.

--Summer Morn... Winter Weather. LC 75-38484. 1976. pap. 4.00 o.p. (ISBN 0-913994-23-5). Hippocrene Bks.

Gillon, Adam & Krzyzanowski, Ludwik, eds. Introduction to Modern Polish Literature. rev. ed. 480p. Date not set. pap. 12.95 (ISBN 0-88254-516-7). Hippocrene Bks. Postponed.

--Introduction to Modern Polish Literature. (International Studies & Translations Ser.). 1963. lib. bdg. 15.95 (ISBN 0-8057-3133-4, Twayne). G K Hall.

Gillon, Edmond. Build Your Own Sawmill. (The Way Things Work Ser.). 40p. 1981. pap. 8.95 (ISBN 0-399-50560-1, Perige). Putnam Pub Group.

--Build Your Own Windmill. (The Way Things Work Ser.). 40p. 1981. pap. 8.95 (ISBN 0-399-50568-7, Perige). Putnam Pub Group.

Gillon, Edmund V., ed. see Gibson, Charles D.

Gillon, Edmund V., Jr. Build Your Own Catapult. (The Way Things Work Ser.). 40p. 1982. pap. 8.95 (ISBN 0-399-50636-5, Perige); pap. 107.40 12-copy counterpack (ISBN 0-399-50637-3). Putnam Pub Group.

--Build Your Own Guillotine. (The Way Things Work Ser.). 40p. 1982. pap. 8.95 (ISBN 0-399-50620-9, Perige); pap. 107.40 12-copy counterpack (ISBN 0-399-50629-2). Putnam Pub Group.

--Cartouches & Decorative Small Frames: 396 Examples from the Renaissance to Art Deco. LC 74-15173. (Pictorial Archive Ser). (Illus.). 128p. 1975. pap. 4.50 (ISBN 0-486-23122-4). Dover.

--Geometric Design & Ornament. abr. ed. Orig. Title: Ornament. (Illus.). 1970. pap. 3.95 (ISBN 0-486-22526-7). Dover.

--Victorian Stencils for Design & Decoration. LC 68-26054. (Illus., Orig.). 1968. pap. 4.50 (ISBN 0-486-21995-X). Dover.

Gillon, Werner. Collecting African Art. LC 79-89508. 216p. 45.00 o.p. (ISBN 0-8478-0262-0). Rizzoli Intl.

Gillquist, Peter E. Let's Quit Fighting About the Holy Spirit. 160p. 1974. pap. 4.95 (ISBN 0-310-25001-3). Zondervan.

Gillray, James. The Satirical Etchings of James Gillray. Hill, Draper, ed. (Illus.). 144p. (Orig.). 1976. pap. 5.00 o.s.i. (ISBN 0-486-23340-5). Dover.

Gillum, Gary P., jt. auth. see Dahlin, Therrin C.

Gillum, P. E. These Stones Speak. 1974. 3.50 o.s.i. (ISBN 0-934942-14-5). White Wing Pub.

Gilman, Albert, ed. see Shakespeare, William.

Gilman, Antonio. A Later Prehistory of Tangier, Morocco. LC 75-20595. (American School of Prehistoric Research Bulletins: No. 29). (Illus.). 1976. pap. 18.50x (ISBN 0-87365-531-1). Peabody Harvard.

Gilman, Dorothy. Amazing Mrs. Pollifax. LC 70-89067. 1970. 5.95 o.p. (ISBN 0-385-02907-1). Doubleday.

--The Elusive Mrs. Pollifax. (Nightingale Series Paperbacks). 1983. pap. 8.95 (ISBN 0-8161-3370-0, Large Print Bks). G K Hall.

--Maze in the Heart of the Castle. LC 82-45198. 192p. (gr. 7). 1983. 11.95 (ISBN 0-385-17817-4). Doubleday.

--Mrs. Pollifax on Safari. LC 76-18346. 1977. 7.95 o.p. (ISBN 0-385-07506-5). Doubleday.

--A New Kind of Country. 1979. lib. bdg. 9.50 o.p. (ISBN 0-8161-6694-3, Large Print Bks). G K Hall.

--A Palm for Mrs. Pollifax. (Nightingale Series Paperbacks). 1983. pap. 10.95 (ISBN 0-8161-3369-7, Large Print Bks). G K Hall.

--The Tightrope Walker. (General Ser.). 1980. lib. bdg. 12.95 (ISBN 0-8161-3026-4, Large Print Bks). G K Hall.

Gilman, George C. Crossfire. (Steele Ser.: No. 7). 1977. pap. 1.50 o.p. (ISBN 0-523-40575-8). Pinnacle Bks.

--Nightmare at Noon. (Steele Ser.: No. 16). 160p. 1980. pap. 1.50 o.p. (ISBN 0-523-40526-X). Pinnacle Bks.

--River of Death. (Steele Ser.: No. 15). (Orig.). 1980. pap. 1.50 o.p. (ISBN 0-523-40525-1). Pinnacle Bks.

Gilman, George G. Apache Death. (Edge Ser. No. 3). 1972. pap. 1.95 (ISBN 0-523-41769-1). Pinnacle Bks.

--Ashes & Dust. (Edge Ser: No. 19). (Orig.). 1976. pap. 1.75 (ISBN 0-523-41297-5). Pinnacle Bks.

--Black Vengeance. (Edge Ser.: No. 10). 1974. pap. 1.95 (ISBN 0-523-41771-3). Pinnacle Bks.

--Bloody Summer. (Edge Ser.: No. 9). 192p. 1974. pap. 1.75 (ISBN 0-523-41287-8). Pinnacle Bks.

--The Bounty Hunter. (Steele Ser.: No. 2). 160p. (Orig.). 1975. pap. 1.50 o.p. (ISBN 0-523-40545-6). Pinnacle Bks.

--California Kill. (Edge Ser., No. 7). 1974. pap. 1.75 (ISBN 0-523-41285-1). Pinnacle Bks.

--Comanche Carnage. (Steele Ser.: No. 8). 1977. pap. 1.50 o.p. (ISBN 0-523-40576-6). Pinnacle Bks.

--Death Deal. (Edge Ser.: No. 35). 160p. 1980. pap. 1.95 (ISBN 0-523-41776-4). Pinnacle Bks.

--Echoes of War. (The Edge Ser.: No. 23). 1977. pap. 1.50 o.p. (ISBN 0-523-40485-9). Pinnacle Bks.

--Edge. (Edge Ser., No. 5). 160p. 1973. pap. 1.95 (ISBN 0-523-41836-1). Pinnacle Bks.

--Edge Meets Steele: Matching Pair. 208p. (Orig.). 1982. pap. 2.25 (ISBN 0-523-41894-9). Pinnacle Bks.

--Edge, No. 40: Montana Melodrama. (Edge Ser.). 192p. (Orig.). 1982. pap. 2.25 (ISBN 0-523-41451-X). Pinnacle Bks.

--Edge, Number Thirty-Six: Town on Trial. 160p. 1981. pap. 1.95 (ISBN 0-523-41799-3). Pinnacle Bks.

--The Final Shot. (Edge Ser.: No. 16). 160p. (Orig.). 1975. pap. 1.75 (ISBN 0-523-41294-0). Pinnacle Bks.

--Fort Despair. (Steele Ser.: No. 23). 192p. 1983. pap. 1.95 (ISBN 0-523-41914-7). Pinnacle Bks.

--The Guilty Ones. (Edge Ser.: No. 31). 1979. pap. 1.95 (ISBN 0-523-42037-4). Pinnacle Bks.

--Gun Run. (Steele Ser.: No. 5). 160p. 1976. pap. 1.50 o.p. (ISBN 0-523-40548-0). Pinnacle Bks.

--Hell's Junction. (Steele Ser.: No. 3). 160p. (Orig.). 1976. pap. 1.50 o.p. (ISBN 0-523-40546-4). Pinnacle Bks.

--Hell's Seven. (Edge Ser.: No. 8). 160p. 1973. pap. 1.75 (ISBN 0-523-41286-X). Pinnacle Bks.

--Killer's Breed. (Edge Ser., No. 4). 192p. 1972. pap. 1.95 (ISBN 0-523-42032-3). Pinnacle Bks.

--The Killing Art. (Adam Steele Ser: No. 6). 1976. pap. 1.50 o.p. (ISBN 0-523-40549-9). Pinnacle Bks.

--The Living, the Dying & the Dead. (Edge Ser.: No. 29). 1979. pap. 1.95 (ISBN 0-523-41775-6). Pinnacle Bks.

--Massacre Mission. (Edge Ser.: No. 38). 160p. 1982. pap. 1.95 (ISBN 0-523-41449-8). Pinnacle Bks.

--Paradise Loses. (Edge Ser.: No. 15). 160p. 1975. pap. 1.75 (ISBN 0-523-41293-2). Pinnacle Bks.

--Rebels-Assassins Die Hard. (Steele Ser., No. 1). 160p. 1974. pap. 1.50 o.p. (ISBN 0-523-40544-8). Pinnacle Bks.

--Red Fury. (Edge Ser.: No. 33). 160p. 1980. pap. 1.95 (ISBN 0-523-42033-1). Pinnacle Bks.

--Red River. (Edge Ser.: No. 6). 192p. 1973. pap. 1.95 (ISBN 0-523-41770-5). Pinnacle Bks.

--Rhapsody in Red. (Edge Ser.: No. 21). 1977. pap. 1.50 o.p. (ISBN 0-523-40585-5). Pinnacle Bks.

--A Ride in the Sun. (Edge Ser.: No. 34). 160p. 1980. pap. 1.95 (ISBN 0-523-41987-2). Pinnacle Bks.

--Savage Dawn. (Edge Ser.: No. 26). 1978. pap. 1.95 (ISBN 0-523-41837-X). Pinnacle Bks.

--Slaughter Road. (Edge Ser.: No. 22). 160p. 1977. pap. 1.95 (ISBN 0-523-42029-3). Pinnacle Bks.

--Slaughterday. (Edge Ser: No. 24). 1977. pap. 1.75 (ISBN 0-523-41302-5). Pinnacle Bks.

--Steele: Valley of Blood. (Steele Ser.: No. 4). 160p. 1976. pap. 1.50 o.p. (ISBN 0-523-40547-2). Pinnacle Bks.

--Sullivan's Law. (Edge Ser.: No. 20). 1976. pap. 1.95 (ISBN 0-523-41774-8). Pinnacle Bks.

--Ten Grand. (Edge Ser.: No. 2). 160p. 1982. pap. 1.95 (ISBN 0-523-41868-X). Pinnacle Bks.

--Ten Tombstones. (Edge Ser.: No. 18). 192p. 1976. pap. 1.95 (ISBN 0-523-41773-X). Pinnacle Bks.
--Tiger's Gold. (Edge Ser.: No. 14). 192p. 1975. pap. 1.95 (ISBN 0-523-41772-1). Pinnacle Bks.
--Two of a Kind. 160p. 1980. pap. 2.25 (ISBN 0-523-42031-5). Pinnacle Bks.
--Vengeance Valley. (Edge Ser.: No. 17). 160p. (Orig.). 1976. pap. 1.95 (ISBN 0-523-41838-8). Pinnacle Bks.
--Violence Trail. (The Edge Ser.: No. 25). 1978. pap. 1.95 (ISBN 0-523-41802-7). Pinnacle Bks.
Gilman, H. Organic Syntheses Collective Volumes: Vols. 1-9, Vol. 1. 580p. 1941. 39.95 (ISBN 0-471-30030-6, Pub. by Wiley-Interscience). Wiley.
Gilman, J. J., ed. Metallic Glasses. Leamy, H. J. (TN 693.m4m37). 1978. 70.00 (ISBN 0-87170-051-4). ASM.
Gilman, John & Heide, Robert. Cowboy Collectibles. LC 82-47552. (Illus.). 224p. (Orig.). 1982. pap. 9.57i (ISBN 0-06-090985-4, CN985, CN). Har-Row.
Gilman, John, jt. auth. see Heide, Robert.
Gilman, John J. Art & Science of Growing Crystals. LC 63-11432. (Science & Technology of Materials Ser.). 493p. 1963. 63.50x (ISBN 0-471-30177-9, Pub. by Wiley-Interscience). Wiley.
Gilman, Kenneth & Public Management Institute Staff. Computer Resource Guide for Nonprofits. 175.00 (ISBN 0-686-82256-0, 68A). Public Management.
--Computers for Nonprofits. 47.50 (ISBN 0-686-82255-2, 58A). Public Management.
Gilman, Lawrence. Edward MacDowell: A Study. 2nd ed. LC 67-27455. (Music Ser). 1969. Repr. of 1908 ed. lib. bdg. 19.50 (ISBN 0-306-70979-1). Da Capo.
Gilman, Leonard & Rose, Allen J. APL: An Interactive Approach. 2nd rev. ed. LC 76-22478. 378p. 1976. pap. text ed. 21.95 (ISBN 0-471-30022-5). Wiley.
Gilman, Martin G. The Financing of Foreign Direct Investment. 200p. 1981. 26.00 (ISBN 0-312-28982-0). St Martin.
Gilman, Richard. Common & Uncommon Masks: Writings on Theatre 1960-1970. LC 72-117681. 1971. 1.95 (ISBN 0-394-71763-5). Random.
Gilman, Samuel. Memoirs of a New England Village Choir. (Music Reprint Ser.). 150p. 1983. Repr. of 1829 ed. lib. bdg. 22.50 (ISBN 0-306-76175-0). Da Capo.
Gilman, Sander. On Blackness without Blacks: Essays on the Image of the Black in Germany. 200p. 1982. lib. bdg. 24.95 (ISBN 0-8161-9026-7, Univ Bks). G K Hall.
Gilman, Sander L., ed. Introducing Psychoanalytic Theory. LC 82-9477. 280p. 1982. pap. 16.95 (ISBN 0-87630-312-2). Brunner-Mazel.
Gilman, Stephen. Accounting Concepts of Profit. LC 82-48365. (Accountancy in Transition Ser.). 656p. 1982. lib. bdg. 65.00 (ISBN 0-8240-5316-8). Garland Pub.
Gilman, W. H. see Emerson, Ralph W.
Gilman, W. H., et al see Emerson, Ralph W.
Gilman, William H. see Emerson, Ralph W.
Gilman, William H., ed. see Emerson, Ralph W.
Gilmartin, Jean. The Bromeliaceae of Ecuador. (Monographiae Phanerogamarum Ser.: No. 5). (Illus.). 1972. 48.00 (ISBN 3-7682-0725-0). Lubrecht & Cramer.
Gilmartin, Joe, jt. auth. see Brock, Jim.
Gilmartin, Kevin J., jt. auth. see Rossi, Robert J.
Gilmer, Ann. Love in the Sun. (YA) 1978. 6.95 (ISBN 0-685-53390-5, Avalon). Bouregy.
--Nurse at Breakwater Hotel. 1982. pap. 6.95 (ISBN 0-686-84730-X, Avalon). Bouregy.
Gilmer, B. V. Applied Psychology: Adjustments in Living & Work. 2nd ed. (Illus.). 464p. 1974. text ed. 24.50 (ISBN 0-07-023210-5, C); instructors' manual 15.00 (ISBN 0-07-023211-3). McGraw.
--Psychology. 2nd ed. 1973. pap. text ed. 21.50 scp o.p. (ISBN 0-06-042327-7, HarpC). Har-Row.
Gilmer, B. V & Deci, Edward L. Industrial & Organizational Psychology. 4th ed. (M-H Series in Psychology). (Illus.). 1976. text ed. 25.95 (ISBN 0-07-023289-X, C); instructor's manual 15.00 (ISBN 0-07-023290-3). McGraw.
Gilmore, Al-Tony, ed. Revisiting Blassingame's "The Slave Community". The Scholar's Respond. LC 77-84765. (Contributions in Afro-American & African Studies: No. 37). 1978. lib. bdg. 25.00 (ISBN 0-8371-9879-8, GJB/). Greenwood.
Gilmore, Anne, jt. ed. see Taylor, Rex.
Gilmore, Cecile. Hold Me Fast. (YA) 1972. 6.95 (ISBN 0-685-28627-4, Avalon). Bouregy.
--The Lesser Love. (YA) 1971. 6.95 (ISBN 0-685-23396-0, Avalon). Bouregy.
--Web of Honey. (YA) 1970. 6.95 (ISBN 0-685-07463-3, Avalon). Bouregy.
--Wedding Is Destiny. 256p. (YA) 1973. 6.95 (ISBN 0-685-30371-3, Avalon). Bouregy.
Gilmore, Charles M. Instruments & Measurements. Schuler, Charles A., ed. (Basic Skills in Electricity & Electronics Ser.). (Illus.). 192p. (gr. 11-12). 1980. pap. text ed. 14.96 (ISBN 0-07-023297-0, G). McGraw.
--Introduction to Microprocessors. LC 80-26115. (Basic Skills in Electricity & Electronics). 320p. 1981. 17.96 (ISBN 0-07-023304-7); pap. 14.96 (ISBN 0-07-023301-2); 4.00 (ISBN 0-07-023302-0); lab manual 10.96 (ISBN 0-07-023303-9). McGraw.
Gilmore, Christopher C. The Bad Room. 256p. 1983. pap. 2.95 (ISBN 0-380-82669-0). Avon.
Gilmore, Clarence P. Exercising for Fitness. LC 80-25815. (Library of Health). PLB 18.60 (ISBN 0-8094-3755-4). Silver.
Gilmore, D. E., ed. see Crouse, William H. & Anglin, Donald L.
Gilmore, D. E., ed. see Feirer, John L.
Gilmore, D. E., ed. see Schulz, Erich J.
Gilmore, Desmond. Environmental Factors in Mammal Reproduction. 340p. 1981. text ed. 49.95 (ISBN 0-8391-1656-X). Univ Park.
Gilmore, Eddy. Me & My Russian Wife. LC 69-10098. (Illus.). 1968. Repr. of 1954 ed. lib. bdg. 18.00x (ISBN 0-8371-0085-2, GIRW). Greenwood.
Gilmore, G. Don. No Matter How Dark, the Valley: The Power of Faith in Times of Need. LC 81-48208. 141p. 1982. pap. 7.64i (ISBN 0-06-063121-X, HarpR). Har-Row.
Gilmore, Gene. Modern Newspaper Editing. 3rd ed. 400p. 1982. text ed. 16.95x (ISBN 0-87835-127-2). Boyd & Fraser.
Gilmore, Gene & Root, Robert. Modern Newspaper Editing. 2nd ed. 1976. cancelled (ISBN 0-87835-054-3). Boyd & Fraser.
Gilmore, Grant. Ages of American Law. 1977. 15.00x (ISBN 0-300-01951-3); pap. 5.95x (ISBN 0-300-02352-9). Yale U Pr.
--Security Interests in Personal Property, 2 Vols. 1508p. 1965. 90.00 (ISBN 0-316-31374-2). Little.
Gilmore, Grant, jt. auth. see Kessler, Friedrich.
Gilmore, John S. & Duff, Mary K. Boom Town Growth Management: A Case Study of Rock Springs, Green River, Wyoming. LC 75-25905. 200p. 1975. 26.50 o.p. (ISBN 0-89158-010-7). Westview.
Gilmore, Joseph. Blue Flame. LC 82-5163. 1982. 13.95 (ISBN 0-396-08087-1). Dodd.
--Rattlers. 1979. pap. 1.95 o.p. (ISBN 0-451-08464-0, J8464, Sig). NAL.
Gilmore, Joseph P. Renal Physiology. LC 72-77317. 132p. 1972. pap. 12.00 (ISBN 0-683-03622-X). Krieger.
Gilmore, Lee. Folk Instruments. LC 62-18816. (Musical Books for Young People Ser). (gr. 5-11). 1962. PLB 3.95g (ISBN 0-8225-0051-5). Lerner Pubns.
Gilmore, M., ed. Twentieth Century Interpretations of Moby Dick. 1977. 9.95 o.p. (ISBN 0-13-586057-1, Spec); pap. 2.45 o.p. (ISBN 0-13-586032-6, Spec). P-H.
Gilmore, Myron P. Argument from Roman Law in Political Thought, 1200-1600. LC 66-27081. 1967. Repr. of 1941 ed. 7.00x o.p. (ISBN 0-8462-0930-6). Russell.
--World of Humanism, 1453-1517. (Rise of Modern Europe Ser). pap. 5.95xi o.p. (ISBN 0-06-133003-5, TB 3003, Torch). Har-Row.
Gilmore, Pauline. History of Turkey Community. 1977. 8.95 o.p. (ISBN 0-89015-205-5). Eakin Pubns.
Gilmore, Perry & Glatthorn, Allan A. Children in & Out of School. (Language & Ethnography Ser.: No. 2). 300p. 1982. 23.95x (ISBN 0-87281-167-0); pap. 12.95x (ISBN 0-686-96696-1). Ctr Appl Ling.
Gilmore, Robert. Lie Groups, Lie Algebras & Some of Their Applications. LC 73-10030. 587p. 1974. 52.95x (ISBN 0-471-30179-5, Pub. by Wiley-Interscience). Wiley.
Gilmore, Robert C., ed. New Hampshire Literature: A Sampler. LC 81-51608. (Illus.). 352p. 1981. text ed. 25.00x (ISBN 0-87451-210-7); pap. 9.95 (ISBN 0-87451-211-5). U Pr of New Eng.
Gilmore, Susan K. The Counselor-in-Training. (Illus.). 1973. 18.95x (ISBN 0-13-183293-X). P-H.
Gilmore, Susan K. & Fraleigh, Patrick W. Communication at Work. LC 80-69467. (Illus.). 150p. (Orig.). 1980. 6.95 (ISBN 0-938070-00-2). Friendly Oregon.
Gilmore, Theopolis L. & Kwasa, Shadrack O. Swahili Phrase Book. LC 63-12918. 8.75 (ISBN 0-8044-0172-1); pap. 3.95 (ISBN 0-8044-6176-7). Ungar.
Gilmore, Thomas B., ed. Early Eighteenth-Century Essays on Taste. LC 78-161932. 370p. 1972. 42.00x (ISBN 0-8201-1092-2). Schol Facsimiles.
Gilmore, William J. Elementary Literacy on the Eve of the Industrial Revolution: Trends in Rural New England. (Illus.). 91p. 1982. pap. 5.95 (ISBN 0-912296-57-7, Dist. by U Pr of VA). Am Antiquarian.
Gilmore-House, Gloria, jt. auth. see Husband, Timothy.
Gilmour, H. B. All That Jazz. (Orig.). pap. 2.25 o.s.i. (ISBN 0-515-05374-0). Jove Pubns.
--So Long, Daddy. 373p. 1983. 14.95 (ISBN 0-937858-13-7). Newmarket.
Gilmour, Ian. Voyages of Discovery. (Exploring History Ser.). (Illus., Orig.). (gr. 9-12). 1978. pap. text ed. 3.15 wkbk. (ISBN 0-05-003048-5); pap. text ed. 12.50 duplicating masters (ISBN 0-05-003180-5). Longman.
Gilmour, R. Business Systems Handbook: Analysis, Designs & Documentation Standards. 1979. 29.95 (ISBN 0-13-107755-4). P-H.
Giloi, Wolfgang K. Interactive Computer Graphics: Data Structures, Algorithms, Languages. (Illus.). 1978. ref. ed. 27.95 (ISBN 0-13-469189-X). P-H.
Gilpatric, Guy. Glencannon-Great Stories from the Saturday Evening Post. LC 77-23723. 320p. 1977. 5.95 (ISBN 0-89387-017-X, Co-Pub by Sat Eve Post). Curtis Pub Co.
Gilpatrick, Gil. Building a Strip Canoe: Easy Step-by-Step Instructions & Patterns for 5 Canoe Models. (Illus.). 96p. (Orig.). 1979. pap. 9.95 (ISBN 0-89933-000-2). DeLorme Pub.
Gilpin, R. Biblical Demonology: A Treatise on Satan's Temptations. 1982. lib. bdg. 20.00 (ISBN 0-86524-093-0, 9805). Klock & Klock.
Gilpin, Robert. War & Change in World Politics. LC 81-2885. (Illus.). 192p. 1981. 22.95 (ISBN 0-521-24018-2). Cambridge U Pr.
--War & Change in World Politics. LC 81-2885. (Illus.). 288p. Date not set. pap. price not set (ISBN 0-521-27376-5). Cambridge U Pr.
Gilpin, William. Mission of the North American People. 2nd ed. LC 68-16234. (American Scene Ser.). (Illus.). 218p. 1974. Repr. of 1874 ed. lib. bdg. 32.50 (ISBN 0-306-71013-7). Da Capo.
Gilreath, Charles L. Computer Literature Searching: Research Strategies & Databases. 108p. 1983. lib. bdg. 18.50x (ISBN 0-86531-526-4). Westview.
Gilreath, Esmarch S. Experimental Procedures in Elementary Qualitative Analysis. 1968. text ed. 14.95 (ISBN 0-07-023213-X, C). McGraw.
Gilroy, John & Meyer, John S. Medical Neurology. 3rd ed. (Illus.). 1979. text ed. 38.50x (ISBN 0-02-343640-9). Macmillan.
Gilsdorf, Gordon. Same Five Notes. 1967. 4.00 o.p. (ISBN 0-8233-0027-7). Golden Quill.
Gilsdorf, Helen M., ed. Modern Liturgy Index. 2nd ed. 1983. pap. 5.56 (ISBN 0-89390-040-0); pap. text ed. 6.95. Resource Pubns.
Gilsenan, Michael. Recognizing Islam: An Anthropologist's Introduction. 287p. 1983. 16.50 (ISBN 0-686-37688-9); pap. 7.95 (ISBN 0-686-37689-7). Pantheon.
Gilsinan, James F. Doing Justice: How the System Works - As Seen by the Participants. 251p. 1982. 13.95 (ISBN 0-13-217315-8); pap. 5.95 (ISBN 0-13-217307-7). P-H.
Gilson, Christopher & Berkman, Harold W. Advertising: Concepts & Strategies. 596p. 1980. text ed. 24.95 (ISBN 0-394-32265-7). Random.
Gilson, Christopher, jt. auth. see Berkman, Harold W.
Gilson, Christopher, et al. Consumer Revenge: How to Handle Greedy Landlords, Shoddy Sellers, Crooked Contractors & Other Consumer Frustrations. 300p. 1981. 13.95 (ISBN 0-399-12668-6). Putnam Pub Group.
Gilson, David, ed. A Bibliography of Jane Austen. (Soho Bibliographies Ser.). (Illus.). 900p. 1982. 110.00x (ISBN 0-19-818173-6). Oxford U Pr.
Gilson, Etienne. History of Philosophy & Philosophical Education. (Aquinas Lecture). 1947. 7.95 (ISBN 0-87462-112-7). Marquette.
--Wisdom & Love in Saint Thomas Aguinas. (Aquinas Lecture). 1951. 7.95 (ISBN 0-87462-116-X). Marquette.
Gilson, Jamie. Thirteen Ways to Sink a Tub. (Illus.). (gr. 3-7). 1982. 9.50 (ISBN 0-688-01304-X). Morrow.
Gilstrap, Robert, ed. see Dzama, Mary Ann.
Gilsvik, Bob. All Season Hunting. (A Guide to Early Season, Late Season, & Winter Hunting). 1977. pap. 5.95 o.s.i. (ISBN 0-695-80851-6). Follett.
Gilula, Norton B., ed. Membrane-Membrane Interactions. (Society of General Physiologists Ser.: Vol. 34). 230p. 1980. text ed. 32.00 (ISBN 0-89004-377-9). Raven.
Gilully, James. Volcanism, Tectonism, & Plutonism in the Western United States. LC 65-15799. (Special Paper: No. 80). (Illus., Orig.). 1965. pap. 4.00x (ISBN 0-8137-2080-X). Geol Soc.
GilYepes, Jose A. The Challenge of Venezuelan Democracy. 275p. 1981. 29.95 (ISBN 0-87855-401-7). Transaction Bks.
Gilzean, Elizabeth. Something to Do at Home. 14.50 (ISBN 0-392-12847-0, SpS). Sportshelf.
Gimblett, F. & Hood, K. Chemistry, Physics & Technology of Macromolecular Inorganic Compounds & Materials, Pt. 1. 1969. 13.00 o.p. (ISBN 0-686-92699-4). Elsevier.
--Chemistry, Physics & Technology of Macromolecular Inorganic Compounds & Materials, Pt. 2. Date not set. 13.00 (ISBN 0-686-92697-8). Elsevier.
Gimbutas, Marija, ed. Neolithic Macedonia. LC 76-18606. (Monumenta Archaeologica: No. 1). (Illus.). 470p. 1976. 28.00 o.p. (ISBN 0-917956-00-1). UCLA Arch.
Gimenez, P., ed. Muscular Exercise in Chronic Lung Disease: Proceedings of Meeting on Factors Limiting Exercise, Nancy, France, 13-15 Sept. 1978. LC 79-40806. (Special Issue of the Bulletin Europeen De Physiopathologie Respiratoire). (Illus.). 1980. 56.00 (ISBN 0-08-024930-2). Pergamon.
Gimlette, John D. Malay Poisons & Charm Cures. 3rd ed. (Oxford in Asia Paperbacks Ser.). 328p. 1982. pap. 13.95 (ISBN 0-19-638150-9). Oxford U Pr.
Gimmestad, Victor E. John Trumbull. (United States Authors Ser.: No. 240). lib. bdg. 12.95 (ISBN 0-8057-0746-8, Twayne). G K Hall.
Gimpel, James F. Algorithms in SNOBOL 4. LC 75-33850. 487p. 1976. 34.95 (ISBN 0-471-30213-9, Pub. by Wiley-Interscience). Wiley.
Gimson, A. G. Introduction to the Pronunciation of English. 2nd ed. 1970. 17.95 o.p. (ISBN 0-312-43260-7). St Martin.
Gin, Margaret. Ricecraft. LC 74-14290. (Illus.). 97p. 1975. pap. 5.95 (ISBN 0-394-73050-X, Dist. by Random). Taylor & Ng.
Gin, Margaret, jt. auth. see Allen, Jana.
Gin, Pierre C. Des Causes De Nos Maux, De Leurs Proges et Des Moyens D'y Remedier. (Rousseauism, 1788-1797). 1978. Repr. lib. bdg. 20.50x o.p. (ISBN 0-8287-0378-7). Clearwater Pub.
Gindick, Jon. The Natural Blues & Country Western Harmonica. 2nd ed. LC 77-83727. (Illus.). 1978. 5.95 (ISBN 0-930948-01-7). J Gindick.
--Rock N' Blurs Harmonica. 2nd ed. (Illus.). 1982. 7.95 (ISBN 0-930948-02-5). J Gindick.
Gindin, James, ed. see Hardy, Thomas.
Gine, Evarist, jt. auth. see Araujo, Aloisio.
Ginell, R. Association Theory: The Phases of Matter & Their Transformations. (Studies in Physical & Theoretical Chemistry: Vol. 1). 1979. 41.50 (ISBN 0-444-41753-2). Elsevier.
Giner, Salvador & Archer, Margaret S., eds. Contemporary Europe: Social Structures & Cultural Patterns. (International Library of Sociology). 1978. 28.95x (ISBN 0-7100-8790-X); pap. 15.95 (ISBN 0-7100-8926-0). Routledge & Kegan.
Gines, Deon J. Dietician's Handbook. (Allied Health Professions Monograph). 1983. write for info (ISBN 0-87527-268-1). Green.
Ginet, Carl & Shoemaker, Sydney, eds. Knowledge & Mind: Philosophical Essays. 272p. 1982. 29.50x (ISBN 0-19-503148-2). Oxford U Pr.
Ginever, C. A., tr. see Riedl, Frederick.
Gingell, Rika. Cooking on the Move. 160p. (Orig.). 1983. pap. 6.95 (ISBN 0-88427-052-1, Dist. by Everest Hse). North River.
Ginger, Ann, ed. The International Juridical Association Bulletin 1932-1942, 3 vols. (Franklin D. Roosevelt & the Era of the New Deal Ser.). 1232p. 1982. Repr. lib. bdg. 195.00 (ISBN 0-306-79176-5); lib. bdg. 70.00. Da Capo.
Ginger, Ann F., ed. Defunis Versus Odegaard & the University of Washington - the University Admissions Case, 3 vols. LC 74-13343. 1500p. 1974. Set. lib. bdg. 120.00 (ISBN 0-379-00442-9). Vol. 1 (ISBN 0-379-00442-9). Vol. 2 (ISBN 0-379-00443-7). Vol. 3 (ISBN 0-379-00444-5). Oceana.
--The Pentagon Papers Trial: Index-Catalog. LC 75-14531. 208p. 1975. pap. 17.50 (ISBN 0-379-00314-7). Oceana.
Ginger, Ray. Age of Excess: The United States from Eighteen Seventy-Seven to Nineteen Fourteen. 2nd ed. (Illus.). 416p. 1975. pap. text ed. 11.95x (ISBN 0-02-343700-6, 34370). Macmillan.
--Six Days or Forever? Tennessee Vs. John Thomas Scopes. 265p. 1974. pap. 7.95 (ISBN 0-19-519784-4, GB416, GB). Oxford U Pr.
Gingerich, Duane & F & S Press Book, eds. Medical Product Liability: A Comprehensive Guide & Sourcebook. 500p. 1981. prof ref. 74.50x (ISBN 0-86621-001-6). Ballinger Pub.
Gingerich, Martin E. W. H. Auden: A Reference Guide. 1977. lib. bdg. 19.00 (ISBN 0-8161-7889-5, Hall Reference). G K Hall.
Gingerich, Owen, ed. Theory & Observations of Normal Stellar Atmospheres: Proceedings of the Third Harvard-Smithsonian Conference on Stellar Atmosphere. 1970. 28.50x (ISBN 0-262-07035-9). MIT Pr.
Gingery, David J. The Dividing Head & Deluxe Accessories. LC 80-66142. (Build Your Own Metal Working Shop from Scrap Ser.: Bk. 6). (Illus.). 160p. (Orig.). 1982. pap. 8.95 (ISBN 0-9604330-5-8). D J Gingery.
Gingold, Alfred. Items from Our Catalog. 1982. pap. 4.95 (ISBN 0-686-83416-X, 380-81695-4). Avon.
Gingold, Kurt, tr. see Vol'pin, M. E.
Gingrich, Wilbur F. & Danker, Frederick W. Greek-English Lexicon of the New Testament. rev 2nd. ed. 1979. 37.50 (ISBN 0-310-20570-0). Zondervan.
Giniger, Ken S., compiled by. Compact Treasury of Inspiration. (Orig.). pap. write for info o.s.i. (ISBN 0-515-09715-2). Jove Pubns.
Ginn, Peter L. Introduction to Process Control & Digital Minicomputers. 280p. 1982. 29.95x (ISBN 0-87201-180-1). Gulf Pub.
Ginn, Robert J. The College Graduate's Career Guide. 256p. 1982. pap. 5.95 (ISBN 0-686-83719-3, ScribT). Scribner.
Ginn, Roman. Adventures in Spiritual Direction: A Prophetic Pattern. (Orig.). 1979. pap. 1.95 o.p. (ISBN 0-914544-27-6). Living Flame Pr.
--The Conversion of Samson. LC 82-24073. 1983. pap. 3.50 (ISBN 0-932506-21-6). St Bedes Pubns.
--Jonah: The Spirituality of a Reluctant Prophet. (Orig.). pap. 2.25 (ISBN 0-914544-21-7). Living Flame Pr.
Ginneken, Jaap Van see Van Ginneken, Jaap.
Ginneken, Wouter van see Van Ginneken, Wouter & Garzuel, Michel.
Ginnett, Elsie, jt. auth. see Storm, Margaret.
Gino, Carol. The Nurse's Story. 352p. 1982. 14.95 (ISBN 0-671-45390-4, Linden). S&S.
Ginott, Haim. Between Parent & Child. 1969. pap. 2.95 (ISBN 0-380-00821-1, 60616-X). Avon.

--Between Parent & Teenager. 1973. pap. 2.95 (ISBN 0-380-00820-3, 61283-6). Avon.

Ginott, Haim G. Group Psychotherapy with Children: The Theory & Practice of Play-Therapy. (Psychology & Human Development in Education). 1961. text ed. 24.00 o.p. (ISBN 0-07-023268-7, C). McGraw.

--Teacher & Child. Markel, Robert, ed. LC 70-182448. 323p. 1972. 14.95 (ISBN 0-02-543340-7). Macmillan.

Ginott, Hainor G. Teacher & Child. 1975. pap. 3.50 (ISBN 0-380-00323-6, 62570-9). Avon.

Ginsberg, Allen. Chicago Trial Testimony. LC 74-31252. (Illus.). 76p. (Orig.). 1975. pap. 2.50 o.p. (ISBN 0-87286-080-9). City Lights.

--Howl & Other Poems. LC 56-8587. (Pocket Poets Ser.: No. 4). (Orig.). 1956. pap. 2.50 (ISBN 0-87286-017-5, PP4). City Lights.

--Kaddish & Other Poems, Nineteen Fifty-Eight to Nineteen Sixty. LC 60-14775. (Pocket Poets Ser.: No. 14). (Orig.). pap. 2.95 (ISBN 0-87286-019-1). City Lights.

--Many Loves & Other Poems. 80p. 1983. pap. 4.95 (ISBN 0-912516-71-2). Grey Fox.

--Mostly Sitting Haiku. 2nd rev., exp. ed. (Xtras Ser.: No. 6). 36p. (Orig.). 1983. pap. 2.50 (ISBN 0-89120-014-2). From Here.

--Planet News. LC 68-25477. (Pocket Poet Ser.: No. 23). (Orig.). signed ed. 15.00 (ISBN 0-87286-020-5); pap. 3.50 (ISBN 0-685-08140-0, PP23). City Lights.

--Reality Sandwiches: 1953-1960. LC 63-12219. (Orig.). 1963. pap. 3.50 (ISBN 0-87286-021-3). City Lights.

Ginsberg, Elaine. Virginia Woolf: Centennial Papers. Gottlieb, Laura Moss, ed. LC 82-50826. 350p. 1983. 25.00x (ISBN 0-87875-242-0). Whitston Pub.

Ginsberg, Gerlad L. A User's Guide to Selecting Electronic Components. LC 80-25197. 249p. 1981. 33.50x (ISBN 0-471-08308-9, Pub. by Wiley-Interscience). Wiley.

Ginsberg, Jerry H. & Genin, Joseph. Dynamics. LC 76-40409. 1977. text ed. 22.95x (ISBN 0-471-29606-6). Wiley.

--Statics. LC 76-55753. 1977. text ed. 22.95x (ISBN 0-471-29607-4). Wiley.

--Statics & Dynamics Combined Edition. LC 76-30664. 1016p. 1977. text ed. 35.95x (ISBN 0-471-01795-7). Wiley.

Ginsberg, Leo. The Comprehensive Supplement to the Machzor. LC 72-85803. 1972. pap. 3.95 o.p. (ISBN 0-8197-0294-3). Bloch.

Ginsberg, Leon H. The Practice of Social Work in Public Welfare. LC 82-71888. 1983. 18.95 (ISBN 0-02-911760-7). Free Pr.

Ginsberg, Lev. Tartini: His Life & Times. Axelrod, Herbert, ed. Levin, I., tr. from Rus. (Illus.). 372p. 1981. 29.95 (ISBN 0-87666-590-3, Z-58). Paganiniana Pubns.

Ginsberg, Philip M., jt. auth. see Seidel, Andrew D.

Ginsberg, Ralph B., ed. see American Academy of Political & Social Science, Annual Meeting, 83rd.

Ginsberg, Ralph B., jt. ed. see Frey, James H.

Ginsberg, Ralph B., jt. ed. see Laurent, Pierre-Henri.

Ginsberg, Ralph B., jt. ed. see Rejda, George E.

Ginsberg, Ralph B., jt. ed. see Richardson, John, Jr.

Ginsberg, Ralph B., jt. ed. see Roof, Wade C.

Ginsberg, Robert. Welcome to Philosophy! A Handbook for Students. LC 76-29222. 1982. 6.95x (ISBN 0-87735-521-5); pap. 3.95x (ISBN 0-87735-522-3). Freeman C.

Ginsberg, Ruth. Crafts for the Jewish Child. (Illus.). (gr. 2-7). 1976. 5.00 o.p. (ISBN 0-914080-61-X). Shulsinger Sales.

Ginsberg, Stan. The Complete Handbook of Chinese Astrology. LC 78-67812. (Illus.). 1978. pap. 6.95 o.p. (ISBN 0-448-16361-6, G&D). Putnam Pub Group.

Ginsborg, Paul. Daniele Manin & the Venetian Revolution of 1848-49. LC 78-56180. (Illus.). 1979. 44.50 (ISBN 0-521-22077-7). Cambridge U Pr.

Ginsbourg, Sam. My First Sixty Years in China. (Illus.). 373p. 1982. pap. text ed. 5.95 (ISBN 0-8351-1109-1). China Bks.

Ginsburg, Christian D. The Essenes: Their History & Doctrines & The Kabbalah: Its Doctrines, Development & Literature. 246p. 1970. 15.00 (ISBN 0-7100-1449-X). Routledge & Kegan.

Ginsburg, Douglas H. & Abernathy, William J. Government, Technology & the Future of the Automobile. (Regulation of American Business & Industry Ser.). (Illus.). 1980. 46.95 (ISBN 0-07-023291-1). McGraw.

Ginsburg, G. P. Emerging Strategies in Social Psychological Research. LC 78-18506. 319p. 1979. 41.00x (ISBN 0-471-99690-4, Pub. by Wiley-Interscience). Wiley.

Ginsburg, Harvey, jt. auth. see McCoy, Ingeborg.

Ginsburg, Helen. Full Employment & Public Policy: The United States & Sweden. LC 76-55536. 256p. 1983. 24.95x (ISBN 0-669-01318-8). Lexington Bks.

Ginsburg, Helen, ed. Poverty, Economics, & Society. LC 80-6115. 361p. 1981. lib. bdg. 24.00 (ISBN 0-8191-1385-9); pap. text ed. 12.50 (ISBN 0-8191-1386-7). U Pr of Amer.

Ginsburg, Herbert. Children's Arithmetic: How They Learn It & How You Teach It. (Illus.). 208p. 1983. pap. text ed. 15.00 (ISBN 0-936104-29-5, 0377). Pro Ed.

--Myth of the Deprived Child: Poor Children's Intellect & Education. LC 76-166042. 1972. pap. text ed. 13.95 (ISBN 0-13-609149-0). P-H.

Ginsburg, Herbert, ed. The Development of Mathematical Thinking. (Developmental Psychology Ser.). 424p. 1982. 37.50 (ISBN 0-12-284780-6). Acad Pr.

Ginsburg, Lev. History of the Violoncello. Axelrod, Herbert R., ed. Tchistyakova, Tanya, tr. (Illus.). 1983. 30.00 (ISBN 0-87666-597-0). Paganiniana Pubns.

--Ysaye. Paradise, ed. (Illus.). 576p. 1980. text ed. 25.00 (ISBN 0-87666-620-9, Z-31). Paganiniana Pubns.

Ginsburg, M, jt. ed. see Lewis, G. P.

Ginsburg, Madeleine. Victorian Dress. (Illus.). 192p. 1983. text ed. 35.00 (ISBN 0-8419-0838-9). Holmes & Meier.

Ginsburg, Mirra. Across the Stream. (Illus.). (ps). 1982. 9.50 (ISBN 0-688-01204-3); PLB 8.59 (ISBN 0-688-01206-X). Morrow.

--The Strongest One of All. LC 76-44326. (Illus.). 1977. 8.95 o.p. (ISBN 0-688-80081-5); PLB 8.59 o.p. (ISBN 0-688-84081-7). Greenwillow.

Ginsburg, Mirra, ed. see Suteyev, V.

Ginsburg, Mirra, tr. Last Door to Aiya: A Selection of the Best New Science Fiction from the Soviet Union. LC 68-16347. (YA) 1968. 10.95 (ISBN 0-87599-135-1). S G Phillips.

Ginsburg, Mirra, tr. see Bulgakov, Mikhail.

Ginsburg, Mirra, tr. see Dostoyevsky, Fyodor.

Ginsburg, Mirra, tr. see Obukhova, Lydia.

Ginsburg, Norton & Fullard, Harold. World Patterns: The Aldine College Atlas. 1971. pap. 5.50x (ISBN 0-673-05995-2). Scott F.

Ginsburg, Norton, jt. auth. see Borgese, Elisabeth M.

Ginsburg, Norton, jt. ed. see Borgese, Elisabeth M.

Ginsburg, Norton, jt. ed. see Borgese, Elizabeth M.

Ginsburg, S. Algebraic & Automata-Theoretic Properties of Formal Languages. LC 73-86082. (Fundamental Studies in Computer Science: Vol. 2). 313p. 1975. text ed. 64.00 (ISBN 0-444-10586-7, North-Holland). Elsevier.

Ginsburg, S. G., jt. auth. see Karol, N. H.

Ginsburg, Victor. Biology of Carbohydrates, Vol. 1. LC 80-20758. 336p. 1981. 55.50 (ISBN 0-471-03905-5, Pub. by Wiley-Interscience). Wiley.

Ginsburgh, V. A. & Waelbroeck, J. L. Activity Analysis & General Equilibrium Modelling. (Contributions to Economic Analysis Ser.: Vol. 125). 1981. 57.50 (ISBN 0-444-86011-8). Elsevier.

Ginsburgs, George. Calendar of Diplomatic Affairs, Democratic People's Republic of Korea, 1945-1975. Kim, Roy U., ed. LC 77-71677. 257p. 1977. lib. bdg. 25.00 (ISBN 0-379-20354-5). Oceana.

--Soviet Foreign Policy Toward Western Europe. Rubinstein, Alvin Z, ed. LC 78-17925. (Praeger Special Studies). 1978. 27.95 o.p. (ISBN 0-03-044331-8). Praeger.

Ginter, Steven J. Douglas F3D Skyknight. (Naval Fighter Ser.: No. 4). (Illus.). 81p. (Orig.). 1982. pap. 9.95 (ISBN 0-942612-04-3). Naval Fighters.

Gintis, Herbert, jt. auth. see Bowles, Samuel.

Ginzberg. Decision Support Systems. 1982. 36.25 (ISBN 0-444-86472-5). Elsevier.

Ginzberg, Eli. Good Jobs, Bad Jobs, No Jobs. LC 79-10706. 1979. 16.50x (ISBN 0-674-35710-8). Harvard U Pr.

--Health Manpower & Health Policy. LC 78-62203. (Conservation of Human Resources Ser.: No. 10). 244p. 1978. text ed. 18.00x (ISBN 0-916672-19-0). Allanheld.

--The Human Economy. 1976. 21.95 (ISBN 0-07-023283-0). McGraw.

--Manpower Agenda for America. 1968. 9.50 (ISBN 0-07-023278-4, C). McGraw.

Ginzberg, Eli, ed. The Negro Challenge to the Business Community. 111p. pap. 1.65 o.p. (ISBN 0-686-74897-2). ADL.

Ginzberg, Eli, et al. The Negro Potential. LC 80-17250. (Illus.). xvi, 144p. 1980. Repr. of 1963 ed. lib. bdg. 19.25x (ISBN 0-313-22389-0, GINP). Greenwood.

Ginzburg, Natalia. No Way. 1976. pap. 1.75 (ISBN 0-380-00838-6, 310546, Bard). Avon.

--Ti Ho Sposato per Allegria. (Easy Readers, Ser. A). 48p. (Itol.). 1976. pap. text ed. 2.95 (ISBN 0-88436-228-0, 55252). EMC.

Ginzburg, Natalia & Pacifici, Sergio. La Voci Della Sera. 1971. pap. text ed. 3.50 (ISBN 0-685-55624-7, 31222). Phila Bk Co.

Ginzburg, V. L. Waynflete Lectures on Physics: Selected Topics in Contemporary Physics & Astrophysics. (International Series in Natural Philosophy: Vol. 106). (Illus.). 133p. 1983. 25.00 (ISBN 0-08-029147-3). Pergamon.

Gioello, Debbie A. Fairchild's Designer: Stylist Handbook, 2 vols. (Illus.). 1979. Vol. 1. (ISBN 0-87005-332-9); Vol. 2. (ISBN 0-87005-333-7); Set. 35.00 (ISBN 0-686-76815-9); tracing pad 7.95 (ISBN 0-87005-334-5). Fairchild.

Giolitti, Giovanni. Memoirs of My Life. LC 72-80619. 472p. 1973. Repr. of 1923 ed. 16.50 o.p. (ISBN 0-86527-127-5). Fertig.

Gioncu, Victor. Thin Reinforced Concrete Shells: Special Analysis Problems. LC 78-10338. 500p. 1980. 63.95x (ISBN 0-471-99735-8, Pub. by Wiley-Interscience). Wiley.

Giono, Jean. Blue Boy. Clarke, Katherine A., tr. from Fr. LC 81-4371. 256p. 1981. pap. 9.50 (ISBN 0-86547-037-5). N Point Pr.

--Ennemonde. 14.95 (ISBN 0-7206-2801-6). Dufour.

--Horseman on the Roof. Griffin, Jonathan, tr. from Fr. 426p. 1982. pap. 12.50 (ISBN 0-86547-060-X). N Point Pr.

--Joy of Man's Desiring. Clarke, Katherine A., tr. from Fr. LC 80-14932. 472p. 1980. pap. 12.50 (ISBN 0-86547-015-4). N Point Pr.

--The Song of the World. Fluchere, Henri & Myers, Geoffrey, trs. from Fr. LC 80-28523. 320p. 1981. pap. 11.00 (ISBN 0-86547-038-3). N Point Pr.

--The Straw Man. Johnson, Phyllis, tr. LC 82-73715. 472p. 1982. pap. 14.00 (ISBN 0-86547-071-5). N Point Pr.

Giordani, Igino. Diary of Fire. 127p. (Orig.). 1982. pap. 3.95 (ISBN 0-911782-41-9). New City.

Giordano, Al. Basic Business Machine Calculations: A Complete Course. 2nd ed. (Illus.). 1978. pap. 16.95x ref. ed. (ISBN 0-13-057315-9). P-H.

--Business Mathematics - Electronic Calculation. (Illus.). 304p. 1981. text ed. 20.95 (ISBN 0-13-105163-6); pap. text ed. 17.95 (ISBN 0-13-105155-5). P-H.

Giordano, Al & Maxwell, G. W. College Business Mathematics. (Illus.). 1977. pap. text ed. 17.95 (ISBN 0-13-142018-6). P-H.

Giorgi, A., ed. Journal of Phenomenological Psychology. (JPP Ser.: Vol. 13-1). 150p. 1982. pap. text ed. 7.50x. Humanities.

Giorgio Levi Della Vida Conference-2nd-los Angeles-1969. Proceedings: Theology & Law in Islam. Von Grunebaum, G. E., ed. 113p. 1971. 45.00x (ISBN 3-447-01273-0). Intl Pubns Serv.

Giovacchini, Peter. The Urge to Die. 1983. pap. 5.95 (ISBN 0-14-006314-5). Penguin.

Giovacchini, Peter & Boyer, L. Bryce, eds. Technical Factors in the Treatment of the Severely Disturbed Patient. LC 81-20587. 568p. 1982. 30.00 (ISBN 0-87668-429-0). Aronson.

Giovacchini, Peter L. A Clinician's Guide to Reading Freud. LC 82-14891. 251p. 1982. 25.00 (ISBN 0-87668-484-3). Aronson.

Giovannelli, G., et al, eds. Hypertension in Children & Adolescents. 364p. 1981. text ed. 43.00 (ISBN 0-89004-523-2). Raven.

Giovannetti, Alberto. Requiem for a Spy. LC 79-8926. 288p. 1983. 14.95 (ISBN 0-385-15612-X). Doubleday.

Giovanni, Di see Di Giovanni.

Giovanni, Nikki. Cotton Candy on a Rainy Day. LC 78-16897. 1978. pap. 4.50 (ISBN 0-688-08365-X). Morrow.

--Cotton Candy on a Rainy Day. LC 78-16897. 1980. pap. 4.50 (ISBN 0-688-08365-X). Quill NY.

--Ego Tripping & Other Poems for Young Readers. LC 73-81745. (Illus.). 48p. (gr. 2-7). 1974. 8.50 (ISBN 0-88208-020-2); pap. 5.95 (ISBN 0-88208-019-9). Lawrence Hill.

--Gemini: An Extended Autobiographical Statement on My First Twenty-Five Years of Being a Black Poet. 1976. pap. 3.95 (ISBN 0-14-004264-4). Penguin.

--Those Who Ride the Night Winds. 121p. 1983. 9.95 (ISBN 0-688-01906-4). Morrow.

Giovanni, Nikki & Walker, Margaret. A Poetic Equation: Conversations Between Nikki Giovanni & Margaret Walker. LC 73-85494. (Illus.). 160p. 1974. 7.95x (ISBN 0-88258-003-5). Howard U Pr.

Giovannoni, Jeanne M. & Becerra, Rosina. Defining Child Abuse. LC 79-7180. (Illus.). 1979. 19.95 (ISBN 0-02-911750-X). Free Pr.

Giovanoni, Richard & Warren, Roger G. Mosby's Fundamentals of Animal Health Technology: Principles of Pharmacology. (Illus.). 288p. 1983. pap. text ed. 17.95 (ISBN 0-8016-5402-5). Mosby.

Giovio, Paolo. The Worthy Tract of Paulus Iovius. Daniel, Samuel, tr. LC 76-13497. 300p. 1976. Repr. of 1585 ed. lib. bdg. 41.00x (ISBN 0-8201-1272-0). Schol Facsimiles.

Gipe, George. The Last Time When. 352p. 1982. pap. 8.95 (ISBN 0-911818-24-3). World Almanac.

Gipe, George & Winokur, Alice. Melvin & Howard. 224p. 1980. pap. 2.25 o.s.i. (ISBN 0-515-05442-9). Jove Pubns.

Gips, James, jt. auth. see Stiny, George.

Gipson, Fred. Curly & the Wild Boar. LC 77-25644. (Illus.). (gr. 5 up). 1979. 7.64i (ISBN 0-06-022014-7, HarpJ); PLB 8.89 (ISBN 0-06-022015-5). Har-Row.

--Little Arliss. LC 77-17643. (Illus.). 1978. 7.64i (ISBN 0-06-022008-2, HarpJ); PLB 8.89 (ISBN 0-06-022009-0). Har-Row.

--Old Yeller. 1964. pap. 2.95i (ISBN 0-06-080002-X, P2, PL). Har-Row.

--Savage Sam. LC 62-7948. (Illus.). 1962. o. p. 9.95i (ISBN 0-06-011560-2, HarpT); lib. bdg. 10.89i (ISBN 0-06-011561-0). Har-Row.

Gipson, Fred, jt. auth. see Langford, J. O.

Gipson, Leland F. How to Use the Tremendous Power of Creative Prayer. LC 80-85276. 114p. (Orig.). 1981. pap. 5.45 (ISBN 0-9605014-0-1). Levada.

Gipson, Morrell. Favorite Nursery Tales. LC 82-45304. (Illus.). 32p. 1983. 9.95a (ISBN 0-385-17960-X); PLB (ISBN 0-385-17961-8). Doubleday.

Gipson, R. McCandless. The Life of Emma Thursby. (Music Reprint Ser.). 1980. Repr. of 1940 ed. lib. bdg. 35.00 (ISBN 0-306-76016-9). Da Capo.

Giragosian, Paul A., jt. auth. see Lord, Norman W.

Giraldi, Lilio G. De Deis Gentium. LC 75-27850. (Renaissance & the Gods Ser.: Vol. 8). (Illus.). 1976. Repr. of 1548 ed. lib. bdg. 73.00 o.s.i. (ISBN 0-8240-2057-X). Garland Pub.

Giraldo, Z. I. Public Policy & the Family: Wives & Mothers in the Labor Force. LC 80-7692. 240p. 1980. 24.95x (ISBN 0-669-03762-1). Lexington Bks.

Giralt-Miracle, Daniel. New Interiors, No. 1. 246p. 1982. 9.95 (ISBN 84-7031-213-8, Pub. by Editorial Blume Spain). Intl Schol Bk Serv.

Girard, Augustin. Cultural Development: Experience & Policies. 145p. (Also avail. in Danish, Korean, Dutch, Serbo-Croation). 1972. pap. 7.00 (ISBN 92-3-100969-9, U742, UNESCO). Unipub.

Girard, Joe. How to Sell Yourself. 1980. 10.95 o.p. (ISBN 0-671-25038-8). S&S.

--How to Sell Yourself. 352p. 1981. pap. 7.95 (ISBN 0-446-37772-4). Warner Bks.

Girard, Joe & Brown, Stanley H. How to Sell Anything to Anybody. 1978. 8.95 o.p. (ISBN 0-671-22651-7). S&S.

--How to Sell Anything to Anybody. 240p. 1979. pap. 3.50 (ISBN 0-446-30540-5); pap. 5.95 (ISBN 0-446-37657-4). Warner Bks.

Girard, Kenneth. The Calling. 272p. (Orig.). 1980. pap. 2.50 o.p. (ISBN 0-523-41109-X). Pinnacle Bks.

Girard, Linda. You Were Born on Your Very First Birthday. Tucker, Kathy, ed. (Concept Bks). (Illus.). 32p. (ps-3). 1983. 8.25 (ISBN 0-8075-9455-5). A Whitman.

--You Were Born on Your Very First Birthday. (Concept Books). (gr. k-4). 8.25 (ISBN 0-686-36218-7). Whitman Pub.

Girard, Linda, ed. Teaching the Bible Inside Out. (Idea Bk.). 1978. pap. 1.50 o.p. (ISBN 0-89191-160-X). Cook.

Girard, Louis J. Advanced Techniques in Ophthalmic Microsurgery: Corneal Surgery, Vol. II. LC 78-31773. (Illus.). 305p. 1980. text ed. 94.50 (ISBN 0-8016-1835-5). Mosby.

Girard, Pat. Flying Machines. LC 79-28842. (Machine World Ser.). (Illus.). (gr. 2-4). 1980. PLB 13.85 (ISBN 0-8172-1333-3). Raintree Pubs.

Girard, Rene, ed. Proust: A Collection of Critical Essays. LC 77-9577. 1977. Repr. of 1962 ed. lib. bdg. 18.75x (ISBN 0-8371-9710-4, GIPR). Greenwood.

Girard, Robert C. Brethren, Hang Loose. 1972. pap. 5.95 (ISBN 0-310-25041-2). Zondervan.

--Brethren, Hang Together. 1980. pap. 7.95 (ISBN 0-310-39071-0). Zondervan.

Girard-Corkum, Jerria, jt. auth. see Corkum, Collin J.

Girardin, Emile de. L' Abolition de la Misere par l'Elevation des Salaires: Conditions of the 19th Century French Working Class. 160p. (Fr.). 1974. Repr. of 1850 ed. lib. bdg. 48.50 o.p. (ISBN 0-8287-0251-9, 1018). Clearwater Pub.

Giraroot, N. J. Myth & Meaning in Early Taoism: The Themes of Chaos (hun-tun) LC 81-21964. (Hermeneutics Ser.). (Illus.). 430p. 1983. 27.50x (ISBN 0-520-04330-8). U of Cal Pr.

Giraud. Mots dans le vent. 11.25 o.p. (ISBN 0-685-36202-7, 2727). Larousse.

Giraudoux, Jean. Giraudoux: Four Plays, Vol. 1. Incl. Ondine; The Enchanted; The Madwoman of Chaillot; The Apollo of Bellac. 255p. (Orig.). 1958. pap. 6.25 (ISBN 0-8090-0712-6, Mermaid). Hill & Wang.

--My Friend from Limousin. Willcox, L. C., tr. from Fr. LC 76-27657. 1977. Repr. of 1923 ed. 19.50x (ISBN 0-86527-279-4). Fertig.

Girault, C. & Reisig, W., eds. Application & Theory of Petri Nets-Strassbourg 1980 & Bad Honneff 1981: Proceedings. (Informatik-Fachberichte: Vol. 52). 337p. 1982. pap. 16.70 (ISBN 0-387-11189-1). Springer-Verlag.

Girdano, Daniel, jt. auth. see Everly, George.

Girdano, Daniel A. & Everly, George S., Jr. Controlling Stress & Tension: A Holistic Approach. (Illus.). 1979. 14.95 (ISBN 0-13-172114-3); pap. 6.95 (ISBN 0-13-172106-2). P-H.

Girdler, Allan. Customizing Your Van. LC 75-31459. (Illus.). 192p. 1975. 13.95 (ISBN 0-8306-5782-7); pap. 8.95 (ISBN 0-8306-4782-1, 782). TAB Bks.

Girdler, Jr. Crayon Techniques. (Pitman Art Ser.: No.63). pap. 2.95 (ISBN 0-448-00572-7, G&D). Putnam Pub Group.

Girdlestone, Robert B. Synonyms of the Old Testament: Numerically Coded to Strong's Exhaustive Concordance. White, Donald R., ed. 400p. 1983. pap. 13.95 (ISBN 0-8010-3789-1). Baker Bk.

Girdwood, R. Blood Disorders Due to Drugs & Other Agents. 1973. 35.25 (ISBN 0-444-15086-2). Elsevier.

Girgis, M. & Kiloh, L. G. Limbic Epilepsy & the Dyscontrol Syndrome. (Developments in Psychiatry Ser.: Vol. 4). 1980. 55.50 (ISBN 0-444-80251-7). Elsevier.

Girgis, M., jt. auth. see Blunt, Michael J.

Girgis, Maurice. Industrial Progress in Small Oil-Exporting Countries: The Prospect for Kuwait. 195p. 1983. lib. bdg. 30.00x (ISBN 0-86531-596-5). Westview.

Girgus, Sam B. The American Self: Myth, Ideology, & Popular Culture. 1982. pap. 8.95 (ISBN 0-8263-0646-2, A-41P). U of NM Pr.

Giri, V. V. Labour Problems in Indian Industry. 3rd rev. ed. 564p. 1973. pap. text ed. 12.50x o.p. (ISBN 0-210-33692-7). Asia.

Girifalco, Louis A. Statistical Physics of Materials. LC 73-2622. 1973. 34.50 o.p. (ISBN 0-471-30230-9, Pub. by Wiley-Interscience). Wiley.

Girion, Barbara. A Handful of Stars. (YA) (gr. 7-12). 1983. pap. 2.25 (ISBN 0-440-93642-X, LFL). Dell.

--In the Middle of a Rainbow. 192p. (gr. 7 up). 1983. 12.95 (ISBN 0-684-17885-0). Scribner.

Girl Scouts of the U. S. A. Brownies' Own Songbook. (gr. 1-3). 1968. pap. 2.00 (ISBN 0-88441-351-9, 23-130). GS.

--Mundos a Explorar: Manual Para las Brownie y las Junior Girl Scouts. 293p. (Orig., Span.). (gr. 1-6). 1981. pap. 3.25 (ISBN 0-88441-331-4, 20-708). GS.

Girl Scouts of the U.S. Daisy Low of the Girl Scouts: The Story of Juliette Gordon Low, Founder of the Girl Scouts of United States of America. rev. ed. 1975. pap. 0.25 (ISBN 0-88441-134-6, 19-991). GS.

Girl Scouts of the U.S.A. Careers to Explore for Brownie & Junior Girl Scouts. 80p. (Orig.). (gr. 6-12). 1979. 2.75 (ISBN 0-88441-324-1, 20-813). GS.

Girl Scouts of the USA. Exploring the Hand Arts: For Juniors, Cadettes, Seniors, & Leaders. (gr. 4-12). 1955. pap. 2.50 (ISBN 0-88441-140-0, 19-994). GS.

--Fun with Fundamentals. (gr. 4-12). 1969. pap. 0.35 (ISBN 0-88441-011-0, 19-930). GS.

Girl Scouts of the U.S.A. Girl Scout Pocket Songbook: For Juniors, Cadettes, Seniors, & Leaders. (gr. 5-12). 1956. pap. 0.50 (ISBN 0-88441-306-3, 20-192). GS.

Girl Scouts of the USA. The Great Cookie Caper or, How to Discover the World, Starting with a Cookie or Anything Else. (Illus., Minimum order 10). (gr. 1-3). 1973. 0.50 (ISBN 0-88441-138-9, 19-150). GS.

--Helping Leaders Help Girls Grow. 1972. 5.00 (ISBN 0-88441-252-0, 19-978). GS.

--Hiking-in Town or Country: For Juniors, Cadettes, Seniors & Leaders. (gr. 4-12). 1952. pap. 1.00 (ISBN 0-88441-419-1, 26-399). GS.

--Planning Trips with Girl Scouts. rev. ed. (gr. 1-8). 1980. pap. 1.25 (ISBN 0-88441-142-7, 19-998). GS.

--Safety-Wise: For Girls (Grade 7-12) & Adults Who Work Directly with Girls. new & rev. ed. 1982. pap. 1.00 (ISBN 0-88441-428-0, 26-203). GS.

--Skip to My Lou: For Brownies, Juniors, Cadettes, Seniors & Leaders. (gr. 1-8). 1958. pap. 0.95 (ISBN 0-88441-307-1, 20-199). GS.

Girodias, Maurice. The Frog Prince: An Autobiography. 384p. 1980. 14.95 o.p. (ISBN 0-517-54195-5). Crown.

Girodias, Maurice, ed. The Olympia Reader. LC 65-14205. (Illus.). 704p. 1980. pap. 3.95 (ISBN 0-394-17648-0, B437, BC). Grove.

Girolami, Anne-Marie, jt. auth. see Martineau, Richard.

Girolamo, Costanzo Di see Di Girolamo, Costanzo.

Giroud, J. P., jt. ed. see Willoughby, D. A.

Giroux, Henry A. Ideology, Culture & the Process of Schooling. 168p. 1981. 24.95 (ISBN 0-87722-228-2). Temple U Pr.

--Theory & Resistance in Education: A Pedagogy for the Opposition. Freire, Paulo, frwd. by. 256p. 1983. text ed. 24.95x; pap. text ed. 12.95. J F Bergin.

Giroux, Henry A., et al, eds. Curriculum & Instruction: Alternatives in Education. LC 80-84142. 1981. 23.50 (ISBN 0-8211-0615-5); text ed. 21.50 (ISBN 0-686-77729-8). McCutchan.

Giroux, James A. Drawing a Conclusion: Advanced Level. Spargo, Edward, ed. (Comprehension Skills Ser). (Illus.). 64p. (gr. 9-12). 1974. pap. text ed. 3.20x (ISBN 0-89061-015-0, CB-4A). Jamestown Pubs.

Giroux, James A. & Twining, James E. Making a Judgment: Advanced Level. Spargo, Edward, ed. (Comprehension Skills Ser.). (Illus.). 64p. (gr. 9-12). 1974. pap. text ed. 3.20x (ISBN 0-89061-013-4, CB-2A). Jamestown Pubs.

Giroux, James A. & Williston, Glenn R. Appreciation of Literary Forms: Advanced Level. Spargo, Edward, ed. (Comprehension Skills Ser). (Illus.). 64p. (gr. 9-12). 1974. pap. text ed. 3.20x (ISBN 0-89061-018-5, CB-7A). Jamestown Pubs.

--Isolating Details & Recalling Specific Facts. Spargo, Edward, ed. (Comprehension Skills Ser). (Illus.). 64p. 1976. Middle Level gr. 6-8. pap. text ed. 3.20x (ISBN 0-89061-072-X, CB-9M); Advanced Level gr. 9 up. pap. text ed. 2.40x (ISBN 0-89061-020-7, CB-9A). Jamestown Pubs.

--Recognizing Tone: Advanced Level. Spargo, Edward, ed. (Comprehension Skills Ser). (Illus.). 64p. (gr. 9-12). 1974. pap. text ed. 3.20x (ISBN 0-89061-017-7, CB-6A). Jamestown Pubs.

--Retaining Concepts & Organizing Facts: Advanced Level. Spargo, Edward, ed. (Comprehension Skills Ser). (Illus.). 64p. (gr. 9-12). 1974. pap. text ed. 3.20x (ISBN 0-89061-019-3, CB-8A). Jamestown Pubs.

--Understanding Characters: Advanced Level. Spargo, Edward, ed. (Comprehension Skills Ser). (Illus.). 64p. (gr. 9-12). 1974. pap. text ed. 3.20x (ISBN 0-89061-014-2, CB-3A). Jamestown Pubs.

--Understanding the Main Idea: Advanced Level. Spargo, Edward, ed. (Comprehension Skills Ser). (Illus.). 64p. (gr. 9-12). 1974. pap. text ed. 3.20x (ISBN 0-89061-012-6, CB-1). Jamestown Pubs.

Giroux, Roy F. & Biggs, Donald A., eds. College Student Development Revisited: Programs, Issues & Practices. rev. ed. 1979. 7.25 (ISBN 0-686-36444-9, 72104); nonmembers 9.75 (ISBN 0-686-37321-9). Am Personnel.

Girshin, Mark. Ubiystvo Emigranta. 145p. (Rus.). 1983. pap. 7.00 (ISBN 0-938920-29-4). Hermitage MI.

Girshov, Mark. Essential Judo. (Illus.). 224p. (Orig.). Date not set. pap. 9.95 (ISBN 0-88011-058-9). Leisure Pr. Postponed.

Girvan, Norman. Corporate Imperialism: Conflict & Expropriation. Transnational Corporations & Economic Nationalism in the Third World. LC 78-11411. 1978. pap. 5.95 (ISBN 0-85345-472-8, PB4728). Monthly Rev.

Girzone, Joseph F. Gloria. 53p. (gr. 7 up). 1982. 5.00 (ISBN 0-911519-01-7). Richelieu Court.

--Joshua. 320p. 1983. 11.95 (ISBN 0-911519-03-3). Richelieu Court.

--Who Will Teach Me? 61p. 1982. 5.00 (ISBN 0-911519-00-9). Richelieu Court.

Gisbert, M. Toro de see De Toro Gisbert, M.

Gisby, Jane. Making Posh Paws & His Prehistoric Friends. (Illus.). 96p. 1979. 9.50 o.p. (ISBN 0-263-06379-8). Transatlantic.

Gischler, Pearl. Lamplighters: Leaders in Learning, Vol. 2. (Illus.). 6.95 (ISBN 0-8323-0183-3, Pub. by Metro Pr). Binford.

Giscombe, C. S. Postcards. LC 77-13756. 57p. 1977. 3.50 (ISBN 0-87886-085-1). Ithaca Hse.

Gish, Arthur G. Beyond the Rat Race. LC 73-9336. 224p. (Orig.). 1973. pap. 1.45 o.p. (ISBN 0-87983-059-X). Keats.

Gish, Duane T. Dinosaurs: Those Terrible Lizards. LC 77-89152. (Illus.). 1977. 7.95 (ISBN 0-89051-039-3). CLP Pubs.

--Evolution? The Fossils Say No! 3rd ed. LC 79-52441. (Illus.). pap. 4.95 (ISBN 0-89051-057-1). CLP Pubs.

--Evolution? the Fossils Say No! Public School Edition. LC 78-52337. (Illus.). 1978. pap. 4.95 (ISBN 0-89051-046-6). CLP Pubs.

--Speculations & Experiments Related to the Origin of Life: A Critique. (ICR Technical Monograph: No. 1). (Illus.). 41p. 1972. pap. 5.95 (ISBN 0-89051-010-5). CLP Pubs.

--Up with Creation! Acts, Facts, Impacts, Vol. 3. LC 78-55612. (Illus.). 1978. pap. 6.95 (ISBN 0-89051-048-2). CLP Pubs.

Gish, Duane T. & Wilson, Clifford. Manipulating Life: Where Does It Stop? LC 81-64588. 1981. 9.95 (ISBN 0-89051-071-7, Pub. by Master Bks). CLP Pubs.

Gish, Duane T., jt. auth. see Morris, Henry M.

Gish, Duane T., ed. see Bliss, Richard.

Gish, Ira M. & Christman, H. K. Madison, God's Beautiful Farm. LC 78-70891. (Redwood Ser.). 1979. pap. 3.95 o.p. (ISBN 0-8163-0243-X). Pacific Pr Pub Assn.

Gish, Mark F. Pretty Things. 1983. 8.95 (ISBN 0-533-05150-9). Vantage.

Gish, Noel J. & Yockstick, Elizabeth. Long Island Studies Program: Activity Manual. (Illus.). 111p. (gr. 4). 1981. 49.00 (ISBN 0-943068-10-X). Graphic Learning.

Gish, Oscar. Guidelines for Health Planners-the Planning & Management of Health Services in Developing Countries. 96p. 1981. 15.00x o.p. (ISBN 0-905402-02-2, Pub. by Tri-Med England). State Mutual Bk.

Gisonny, Anne. Candlelight Ecstasies. Date not set. price not set. Dell.

Gispen, W. H. The Bible Student's Commentary: Exodus. (The Bible Student's Commentary). 352p. 1983. 15.95 (ISBN 0-310-43970-1). Zondervan.

--Brain Phosphoproteins: Characterization & Function: Proceedings of a Workshop at the State University of Utrecht, Sept. 1981. (Progress in Brain Research Ser.: Vol. 56). 454p. 1982. 97.50 (ISBN 0-444-80412-9). Elsevier.

Gispen, W. H. & Van Wimersma, Greidanus, eds. Hormones Homeostasis & the Brain. Bohus, B., tr. (Progress in Brain Research Ser.: Vol. 42). 400p. 1975. 101.50 (ISBN 0-444-41300-6, North Holland). Elsevier.

Gissel, Sven & Jutikkala, E. Desertion & Land Colonization in the Nordic Countries, 1300-1600. (Scandinavian Research Project on Deserted Farms & Villages Ser.: Vol. 11). 304p. 1982. text ed. 13.00x (ISBN 0-686-98022-0, Pub. by Almqvist & Wiksell Sweden). Humanities.

Gisser, David G., jt. auth. see Carlson, A. Bruce.

Gisser, Micha. Intermediate Price Theory: Analysis, Issues & Applications. (Illus.). 672p. 1981. text ed. 23.95 (ISBN 0-07-023312-8, C); instructor's manual 15.95 (ISBN 0-07-023313-6). McGraw.

Gissing, George. The Crown of Life. Ballard, M., ed. (Harvester Complete Critical Edition: No. 10). 1979. text ed. 18.75x o.p. (ISBN 0-85527-692-4). Humanities.

--George Gissing's Commonplace Book: A Manuscript in the Berg Collection of the New York Public Library. Korg, Jacob, ed. LC 62-12145. (Orig.). 1962. pap. 5.00 o.p. (ISBN 0-87104-085-9). NY Pub Lib.

--Letters of George Gissing to Gabrielle Fleury. Coustillas, Pierre, ed. LC 64-8185. 1965. 11.00 o.p. (ISBN 0-87104-106-5); pap. 8.50 o.p. (ISBN 0-87104-105-7). NY Pub Lib.

--The Nether World. 300p. 1983. pap. text ed. 6.95x (ISBN 0-460-01362-9, Pub. by Evman England). Biblio Dist.

--Sleeping Fires. (Society & the Victorians: No. 24). 1974. text ed. 17.00x o.p. (ISBN 0-85527-032-2). Humanities.

--Thyrza: A Tale. Korg, Jacob, ed. (Society & Victorians: No. 21). 1974. text ed. 19.50x o.p. (ISBN 0-901759-94-5). Humanities.

--Workers in the Dawn. Wolff, Robert L., ed. LC 75-1527. (Victorian Fiction Ser.). 1975. Repr. of 1880 ed. lib. bdg. 66.00 o.s.i. (ISBN 0-8240-1599-1). Garland Pub.

Gisslen, Wayne. Professional Cooking. LC 82-2610. 680p. 1983. 27.95 (ISBN 0-471-86758-6); text ed. 27.95 (ISBN 0-471-08248-1); tchr's. manual avail. (ISBN 0-471-89521-0). Wiley.

Gist, Noel P. & Wright, Roy D. Marginality & Identity. (Monographs & Studies in Sociology & Anthropology in Honour of Nels Anderson Ser: Vol. 3). (Illus.). 161p. 1973. text ed. 31.00x o.p. (ISBN 90-040-3638-5). Humanities.

Gist, Ronald R. Basic Retailing: Text & Cases. LC 73-165020. (Marketing Ser.). 1971. text ed. 15.50x o.p. (ISBN 0-471-30248-1, Pub. by Wiley Hamilton). Wiley.

Gitanjali. Poems of Gitanjali. 128p. 1982. 12.95 (ISBN 0-85362-195-0); pap. 8.95 (ISBN 0-85362-202-7). Routledge & Kegan.

Gitelson, Alan, jt. ed. see Dubnick, Mel.

Githens, Thomas S. Drug Plants of Africa. (African Handbooks Ser.: Vol. 8). 1949. 4.50x (ISBN 0-686-24086-3). Univ Mus of U.

Githens, Thomas S. & Wood, Carroll E. Food Resources of Africa. (African Handbooks Ser.: Vol. 3). (Illus.). 1943. 3.00x (ISBN 0-686-24087-1). Univ Mus of U PA.

Gitin, David. City Air. 52p. 1973. 4.95 (ISBN 0-87886-042-8); pap. 2.95 (ISBN 0-87886-041-X). Ithaca Hse.

--Guitar Against the Wall. 1972. 4.00 o.p. (ISBN 0-915572-08-7). Panjandrum.

Gitin, Maria. Little Movies. 59p. 1975. 3.50 (ISBN 0-87886-051-7). Ithaca Hse.

--The Melting Pot. LC 77-15580. (Illus.). 1977. 15.95 (ISBN 0-912278-94-3); pap. 6.95 (ISBN 0-912278-95-1). Crossing Pr.

Gitler, Ira. Jazz Masters of the Forties. (Roots of Jazz Ser.). 290p. 1982. Repr. of 1966 ed. lib. bdg. 25.00 (ISBN 0-306-76155-6). Da Capo.

Gitlin, Todd. Campfires of the Resistance: Poetry from the Movement. LC 72-123226. 1970. pap. 3.95 o.p. (ISBN 0-685-56649-8). Bobbs.

Gitman, L. J. & Robana, A. Portstrat: A Portfolio Strategy Simulation. 232p. 1982. pap. 16.95 (ISBN 0-471-08416-6). Wiley.

Gitman, Lawrence J. Principles of Managerial Finance. 3rd ed. 800p. 1982. text ed. 28.50 scp (ISBN 0-06-042334-X, HarpC); scp study guide 8.95 (ISBN 0-06-042333-1); instr's manual and test bank avail. (ISBN 0-06-362363-3); transparency master avail. Har-Row.

Gitman, Lawrence J. & Joehnk, Michael D. Fundamentals of Investing. 736p. 1981. text ed. 24.95 scp (ISBN 0-06-042338-2, HarpC); instructors manual & text bank avail. Har-Row.

Gitman, Lawrence J., ed. Business World. McDaniel, Carl. 600p. 1982. 23.95 (ISBN 0-471-08165-5); tchr's. manual avail. (ISBN 0-471-87095-1). Wiley.

Gitnick, G. L. Current Hepatology, Vol. 2. 1981. 55.00 (ISBN 0-471-09516-8, Pub. by Wiley Med). Wiley.

Gitnick, Gary L. Gastroenterology. (Internal Medicine Today: A Comprehensive Postgraduate Library). 424p. 1983. 35.00 (ISBN 0-471-09566-4, Pub. by Wiley Med). Wiley.

--Practical Diagnosis: Gastrointestinal & Liver Disease. 318p. 1979. pap. 25.00 (ISBN 0-471-09481-1, Pub. by Wiley Med). Wiley.

Gitnick, Gary L., ed. Current Gastroenterology & Hepatology. (Illus.). 510p. 1979. 55.00 (ISBN 0-471-09479-X, Pub. by Wiley Med). Wiley.

--Current Hepatology, Vol. 1. (Current Ser). (Illus.). 384p. 1980. 50.00 (ISBN 0-471-09518-4, Pub. by Wiley Med). Wiley.

Gitsch, E. & Reinold, E., eds. Jahrestagung der Oesterreichischen Gesellschaft fuer Gynaekologie und Geburtshilfe, Bad Ischl, Juni 1982. (Journal: Gynaekologische Rundschau: Vol. 22, Supplement 1). (Illus.). vi, 190p. 1982. pap. 30.00 (ISBN 3-8055-3625-9). S Karger.

Gittelman, Martin, ed. Strategic Intervention for Hyperactive Children. LC 81-14407. 224p. 1981. 25.00 (ISBN 0-87332-202-9). M E Sharpe.

Gittelsohn, Roland B. The Extra Dimension. 228p. 1983. pap. 7.95 (ISBN 0-8074-0170-6, 168500). UAHC.

Gittelson, Bernard. How to Make Your Own Luck. 256p. (Orig.). 1981. 13.95 (ISBN 0-446-51223-0); pap. 2.95 (ISBN 0-446-90883-5). Warner Bks.

Gittens, Diana. Fair Sex: Family Size & Structure in Britain, 1930-39. LC 81-21248. 256p. 1982. 27.50x (ISBN 0-312-27962-0). St Martin.

Gitter, A. George & Grunin, Robert, eds. Communication: A Guide to Information Sources. LC 79-54692. (Psychology Information Guide Ser.: Vol. 3). 1980. 42.00x (ISBN 0-8103-1443-6). Gale.

Gitter, Lena L. Montessori Approach to Art Education. LC 73-82978. (Illus.). 1973. pap. 3.50x o.p. (ISBN 0-87562-047-7). Spec Child.

--Montessori Approach to Special Education: An Equipment, Teaching & Feedback Manual. LC 75-171955. 1971. pap. 9.95 (ISBN 0-685-90520-9). Mafex.

--Montessori Way. LC 69-20317. (Illus., Orig.). 1970. pap. 9.00x o.p. (ISBN 0-87562-018-3). Spec Child.

Gitter, Samuel, ed. Symposium on Algebraic Topology in Honor of Jose Adem. LC 82-13812. (Contemporary Mathematics Ser.: Vol. 12). 23.00 (ISBN 0-8218-5010-5). Am Math.

Gittes, David L. A Practical Guide to Fund Accounting & Auditing. LC 81-20907. 270p. 1982. text ed. 89.50 (ISBN 0-87624-433-9). Inst Busn Plan.

Gittinger, J. Price. Economic Analysis of Agricultural Projects. 2nd ed. LC 82-15262. (World Bank Ser.). 512p. 1982. text ed. 37.50x (ISBN 0-8018-2912-7); pap. text ed. 13.50x (ISBN 0-8018-2913-5). Johns Hopkins.

Gittinger, Mattiebelle. Master Dyers to the World: Technique & Trade in Early Indian Dyed Cotton Textiles. McEuen, Caroline K., ed. (Illus.). 208p. 1982. pap. 20.00 (ISBN 0-87405-020-0). Textile Mus.

Gittings, John. Role of the Chinese Army. (Royal Institute of International Affairs Ser.). 1967. 17.95x (ISBN 0-19-500160-5). Oxford U Pr.

Gittings, Robert. American Journey: 25 Sonnets. 1972. pap. text ed. 3.00x o.p. (ISBN 0-435-14358-1). Heinemann Ed.

Gittins, H. Leigh. Pocatello Portrait: The Early Years, Eighteen Seventy-Eight to Nineteen Twenty-Eight. LC 82-50896. (Illus.). 1982. 19.95 (ISBN 0-89301-089-8). U Pr of Idaho.

Gittleman, Arthur. History of Mathematics. new ed. 304p. 1975. text ed. 21.95 (ISBN 0-675-08784-8). Merrill.

Gittleman, Sol. Frank Wedekind. LC 68-28489. 1980. Repr. 11.95 (ISBN 0-8044-2233-8). Ungar.

Gittler, Josephine. Standards Relating to Juvenile Probation Function: Intake & Predisposition Investigative Services. LC 77-3257. (IJA-ABA Juvenile Justice Standards Project Ser.). 208p. 1980. prof ref 20.00x (ISBN 0-88410-248-3); pap. 10.00x (ISBN 0-88410-828-7). Ballinger Pub.

Gittner, Louis. Words from the Source. Steiger, Brad, ed. 168p. 1975. 8.95 (ISBN 0-13-963348-0). Louis Found.

Gittus, Elizabeth. Flats, Families & the Under-Fives. (International Library of Social Policy). 1976. 21.95x (ISBN 0-7100-8284-3). Routledge & Kegan.

Gittus, J. Cavities & Cracks in Creep & Fatigue. (Applied Science Ser.). 1981. 61.50 o.s.i. (ISBN 0-85334-965-7). Elsevier.

--Irradiation Effects in Crystalline Solids. (Illus.). 1978. 82.00 (ISBN 0-85334-778-6, Pub. by Applied Sci England). Elsevier.

Gitzelmann, Richard, jt. ed. see Cockburn, Forrester.

Giuberti, F. Materials for a Study on Twelfth Century Scholasticism. (History of Logic Ser.: Vol. II). 158p. 1982. 34.95x (ISBN 0-686-42759-9, Pub. by Bibliopolis Italy); pap. text ed. 19.95x (ISBN 88-7088-056-7). Humanities.

Giuffey, George R. see Dryden, John.

Giuliani, George, jt. auth. see Minge, M. Ronald.

Giuliano, Vincent, et al. Into the Information Age: A Perspective for Federal Action on Information. 1979. pap. text ed. 9.00 (ISBN 0-8389-0283-9). ALA.

Giumarra, Nancy, ed. see Curran, June.

Giusti-Lanham, Hedy & Dodi, Andrea. The Cuisine of Venice. LC 78-8539. 1978. 17.95 (ISBN 0-8120-5138-6). Barron.

Given, H. Kyle, III. Corvette! Thirty Years of Great Advertising. Clark, William D., ed. LC 82-73577. (Collector Car Literature Ser.). (Illus.). 176p. 1983. 21.95 (ISBN 0-915038-38-2). Auto Quarterly.

Givens. Hormone Secreting Pituitary Tumors. 1982. 70.00 (ISBN 0-8151-3530-0). Year Bk Med.

Givens, Donald R. Processional Papers in Archiometric Dating. 66p. 1982. pap. 8.00 (ISBN 0-940604-02-7). Intl Inst Adv Stud.

Givens, Douglas R. An Analysis of Navajo Temporality. 1977. pap. text ed. 7.00 (ISBN 0-8191-0213-X). U Pr of Amer.

Givens, Ellen M., jt. auth. see Ehrlich, Ruth A.

Givens, Harold. Landscape It Yourself. LC 76-14436. (Illus.). 1977. pap. 12.95 o.p. (ISBN 0-15-147689-6, Harv). HarBraceJ.

Givens, J. R., jt. ed. see Flamigni, C.

Givens, R. A. Advocacy: The Art of Pleading a Case. 1980. 60.00 (ISBN 0-07-023355-1); pap. 20.00 (ISBN 0-07-023356-X); suppl. 20.00 (ISBN 0-686-42845-5). McGraw.

Givey, David W. The Social Thought of Thomas Merton. 1983. 10.00 (ISBN 0-8199-0859-2). Franciscan Herald.

Givner, Joan. Katherine Anne Porter: A Life. 1982. 19.95 (ISBN 0-671-43207-9). S&S.

Givone, D. D. Introduction to Switching Circuit Theory. 1970. 37.95 (ISBN 0-07-023310-1, C). McGraw.

Givone, Donald D. & Roesser, Robert P. Microprocessors - Microcomputers: An Introduction. (Illus.). 1979. text ed. 29.95 (ISBN 0-07-023326-8); solns. manual 7.95 (ISBN 0-07-023327-6). McGraw.

Giwojna, Peter. Marine Hermit Crabs. new ed. (Illus.). 1978. pap. 7.95 (ISBN 0-87666-471-0, PS-752). TFH Pubns.

Gizzi, Ippy. Letters to Pauline. (Illus.). 1975. pap. 3.00 (ISBN 0-930900-40-5). Burning Deck.

Gizzi, Michael. Species of Intoxication. (Burning Deck Poetry Ser.). 68p. 1983. 15.00 (ISBN 0-930901-10-X); pap. 4.00 (ISBN 0-930901-11-8). Burning Deck.

Gjelsvik, Atle. The Theory of Thin Walled Bars. LC 80-26501. 248p. 1981. 34.95x (ISBN 0-471-08594-4, Pub. by Wiley-Interscience). Wiley.

Gjerlov, P. & Helms, H., eds. APL Congress: Copenhagen 1973. 1974. 32.00 (ISBN 0-444-10559-X). Elsevier.

Gjessing, Dag T. Adaptive Radar in Remote Sensing. LC 81-68032. 150p. 1981. text ed. 27.50 (ISBN 0-250-40487-7). Ann Arbor Science.

--Remote Surveillance by Electromagnetic Waves for Air-Water-Land. LC 77-85089. (Illus.). 1978. 29.95 (ISBN 0-250-40203-3). Ann Arbor Science.

Gjessing, Egil, jt. ed. see Christman, Russell F.

Gjessing, Egil T. Physical & Chemical Characteristics of Aquatic Humus. LC 75-36278. (Illus.). 1976. 29.95 (ISBN 0-250-40115-0). Ann Arbor Science.

GJW Government Relations & Stephenson, Peter, eds. Handbook of World Development: The Guide to the Brandt Report. LC 81-48090. 187p. 1982. pap. 4.95x (ISBN 0-8419-0778-1). Holmes & Meier.

Glab, Edward, Jr., ed. Latin American Culture Studies: Information & Materials for Teaching about Latin America. 3rd ed. (Latin American Culture Studies Project Ser.). xi, 466p. 1981. pap. text ed. 9.95x (ISBN 0-86728-001-8). U TX Inst Lat Am Stud.

Glacken, Clarence J. The Great Loochoo: A Study of Okinawan Village Life. LC 73-6394. (Illus.). 324p. 1973. Repr. of 1955 ed. lib. bdg. 19.00x (ISBN 0-8371-6897-X, GLGL). Greenwood.

Glad, John, tr. see Ehrenburg, Ilya & Grossman, Vasily.

Glad, Paul W. Dissonance of Change, Nineteen Twenty-Nine to the Present. (Readings in American History Ser). (Orig.). 1970. pap. text ed. 3.95 (ISBN 0-685-19719-0). Phila Bk Co.

Gladden, L., jt. auth. see Couture, G. L.

Gladden, Lee & Gladden, Vivianne C. Heirs of the Gods: A Space Age Interpretation of the Bible. LC 78-53852. (Illus.). 324p. Repr. of 1979 ed. 15.95 (ISBN 0-686-37960-8). Bel-Air.

Gladden, Vivianne C., jt. auth. see Gladden, Lee.

Glade, William P., Jr. & Anderson, Charles W. Political Economy of Mexico: Two Studies. 256p. 1963. pap. 6.95 (ISBN 0-299-02894-1). U of Wis Pr.

Glades County Commissioners & Bass, Billy O. Glades County, Florida History. Wright, Betty, ed. LC 82-61321. (A Pioneer Heritage Presentation Ser.). 208p. 1983. pap. 10.00 (ISBN 0-935834-09-5). Rainbow Betty.

Gladfelter, Irl A. Dental Evidence: A Handbook for Police. (Illus.). 208p. 1975. photocopy ed. spiral 24.00x (ISBN 0-398-03323-4). C C Thomas.

Gladman, Donna. It's Sunday Night Again? Zapel, Arthur L., ed. LC 79-84726. (Illus.). 1979. pap. text ed. 3.95 (ISBN 0-916260-04-6). Meriwether Pub.

Gladstone, Bernard. Complete Book of Garden & Outdoor Lighting. LC 56-7386. (Illus.). 1956. 2.95 (ISBN 0-8208-0001-5). Hearthside.

Gladstone, Eugene A., jt. auth. see Weisz, Frank B.

Gladstone, Francis. The Politics of Planning. City Planning. LC 76-382545. 1976. pap. 7.50x (ISBN 0-85117-104-4). Intl Pubns Serv.

Gladstone, J. Mechanical Estimating Guidebook. 4th ed. 1970. 39.50 o.p. (ISBN 0-07-023318-7, P&RB). McGraw.

Gladstone, William. Test Your Own Mental Health. 1979. pap. 1.95 o.p. (ISBN 0-451-08757-7, J8757, Sig). NAL.

Gladstone, William E. The Gladstone Diaries: Vol. 7, January 1869-June 1871. Matthew, H. C., ed. (Illus.). 642p. 1982. 79.00x (ISBN 0-19-822445-1). Oxford U Pr.

--The Gladstone Diaries: Vol. 8, July 1871-December 1874. Matthew, H. C., ed. (Illus.). 620p. 1982. 79.00x (ISBN 0-19-822639-X). Oxford U Pr.

Gladwin, D. D. The Waterways of Britain: A Social Panorama. 1976. 22.50 (ISBN 0-7134-3159-8, Pub by Batsford, England). David & Charles.

Gladwin, John. God's People in God's World. LC 80-7726. 1980. pap. 5.95 o.p. (ISBN 0-87784-607-3). Inter-Varsity.

Gladwin, Thomas N. Environment, Planning & the Multinational Corporation. Altman, Edward I. & Walter, Ingo, eds. LC 76-10400. (Contemporary Studies in Economic & Financial Analysis: Vol. 8). 350p. 1977. lib. bdg. 36.50 (ISBN 0-89232-014-1). Jai Pr.

Gladwin, Thomas N. & Walter, Ingo. Multinationals Under Fire: Lessons in the Management of Conflict. LC 79-21741. 689p. 1980. 39.50x (ISBN 0-471-01969-0, Pub. by Wiley-Interscience). Wiley.

Glaeser, W. A., jt. ed. see Rigney, D. A.

Glaeser, Werner. What Am I Bid? LC 82-13862. 1983. 16.95 (ISBN 0-87949-217-1). Ashley Bks.

Glaesner, Kay M. Miracle of Christmas. (Orig.). 1982. pap. 1.95 (ISBN 0-937172-39-1). JLJ Pubs.

Glaessner, Verina. Kung Fu: Cinema of Vengeance. (Illus.). 1975. pap. 2.95 o.p. (ISBN 0-517-51832-5). Crown.

Glahe, F., ed. Adam Smith & the Wealth of Nations, 1776-1976: Bicentennial Essays. LC 77-91609. 1978. pap. 7.95x (ISBN 0-87081-082-0). Colo Assoc.

Glahe, F. R., jt. ed. see Dowling, M.

Glahe, Fred R. Macroeconomics: Theory & Policy. 2nd ed. (Illus.). 404p. 1977. text ed. 22.95 (ISBN 0-15-551266-8, HC). HarBraceJ.

Glahe, Fred R. & Lee, Dwight R. Microeconomics: Theory & Applications. 558p. 1981. text ed. 22.95 (ISBN 0-15-558623-8, HC); 8.95 (ISBN 0-15-558625-4); instructors manual 1.95, (ISBN 0-15-558624-6). HarBraceJ.

Glahe, Fred. R., ed. Collected Papers of Kenneth E. Boulding, Vol. 1. LC 77-135288. 1971. 15.95x (ISBN 0-87081-011-1). Colo Assoc.

Glahe, Fred R., ed. Collected Papers of Kenneth E. Boulding, Vol. 2. LC 77-135288. 1971. 15.95x (ISBN 0-87081-012-X). Colo Assoc.

Gland. Custodial Management Practices in Schools. (Research Bulletin Ser.: No.19). 1975. 2.00 o.p. (ISBN 0-685-57425-3). Assn Sch Busn.

Glanfield, P. Applied Cook-Freezing. 1980. 35.00 (ISBN 0-85334-888-X, Pub. by Applied Sci England). Elsevier.

Glang, R., jt. auth. see Maissel, L.

Glantz, Micheal H. & Thompson, J. Dana, eds. Resource Management & Environmental Uncertainty: Lessons from Coastal Upwelling Fisheries. LC 80-16645. (Advances in Environmental Science & Technology Ser.). 491p. 1980. 51.50x (ISBN 0-471-05984-6, Pub. by Wiley-Interscience). Wiley.

Glantz, Stanton A. Primer of Biostatistics. (Illus.). 384p. 1981. pap. text ed. 12.95 (ISBN 0-07-023370-5, HP). McGraw.

Glanvill, A. B. & Denton, E. N. Injection-Mould Design Fundamentals. (Illus.). 1965. 22.95 (ISBN 0-8311-1033-3). Indus Pr.

Glanvill, Joseph. Plus Ultra. LC 58-9452. 1978. Repr. of 1668 ed. 30.00x (ISBN 0-8201-1243-7). Schol Facsimiles.

--Saducismus Triumphatus: Or, Full & Plain Evidence Concerning Witches & Apparitions. LC 66-60009. 1966. Repr. of 1689 ed. 65.00x o.p. (ISBN 0-8201-1021-3). Schol Facsimiles.

Glanville, Brian. History of the World Cup. (Illus.). 255p. 1982. pap. 7.95 o.p. (ISBN 0-571-11919-0). Faber & Faber.

Glanville, Joseph. Two Choice & Useful Treatises. Wellek, Rene, ed. LC 75-11223. (British Philosophers & Theologians of the 17th & 18th Centuries Ser.). 1978. lib. bdg. 42.00 o.s.i. (ISBN 0-8240-1777-3). Garland Pub.

Glanz, Rudolf. Aspects of the Social, Political, & Economic History of the Jews in America, Vol. 1. 1983. 25.00x (ISBN 0-87068-463-9). Ktav.

Glare, P. G., ed. Oxford Latin Dictionary. 2150p. 1982. 145.00x (ISBN 0-19-864224-5). Oxford U Pr.

Glaros & Coleman, James C. Contemporary Psychology & Effective Behavior. 5th ed. 1983. text ed. 22.95x (ISBN 0-673-15640-0). Scott F.

Glasby, G. P., ed. Marine Manganese Deposits. LC 76-48895. (Elsevier Oceanography Ser.: Vol. 15). 1977. 78.75 (ISBN 0-444-41524-6). Elsevier.

Glasby, John S. Encyclopedia of Antibiotics. 2nd ed. LC 78-13356. 467p. 1979. 92.00x (ISBN 0-471-99722-6, Pub. by Wiley-Interscience). Wiley.

--Encyclopedia of the Alkaloids, Vol. 4. 370p. 1983. 65.00x (ISBN 0-306-41217-9, Plenum Pr). Plenum Pub.

--Encyclopedia of the Terpenoids. LC 81-19866. 1982. 335.00 (ISBN 0-471-27986-2, Pub by Wiley-Interscience). Wiley.

Glasco, Gordon. The Days of Eternity. 1983. 16.95 (ISBN 0-686-43295-9). Doubleday.

Glaser & Lompscher. Cognitive & Motivational Aspects of Instruction. Date not set. 47.00 (ISBN 0-444-86351-6). Elsevier.

Glaser, Arthur & Subak-Sharpe, Gerald E. Integrated Circuit Engineering: Fabrication, Design, Application. LC 77-73945. 1977. text ed. 34.95 (ISBN 0-201-07427-3); solution manual 3.00 (ISBN 0-201-07428-1). A-W.

Glaser, Daniel. Handbook of Criminology. 1974. 61.50 (ISBN 0-395-30603-5). HM.

Glaser, Diane. Diary of Trilby Frost. (YA) 1978. pap. 1.75 (ISBN 0-440-91893-6, LFL). Dell.

Glaser, G. H., et al, eds. Antiepileptic Drugs: Mechanisms of Action. Penry, J. Kiffin. (Advances In Neurology: Vol. 27). 750p. 1980. text ed. 82.00 (ISBN 0-89004-251-9). Raven.

Glaser, Joel S. Neuro-Ophthalmology. (Illus.). 1978. text ed. 49.00x o.p. (ISBN 0-06-140941-3, Harper Medical). Lippincott.

--Neuro Ophthalmology, Vol. 10. LC 64-18729. (Illus.). 242p. 1980. text ed. 46.00 o.p. (ISBN 0-8016-1876-2). Mosby.

Glaser, Joel S., ed. see Neuro-Opthamology Symposia of the University of Miami & the Bascom Palmer Eye Institute.

Glaser, Luis, jt. ed. see Frazier, William A.

Glaser, Michael. Does Anyone Know Where a Hermit Crab Goes? (Illus.). 32p. (Orig.). (ps-3). 1983. pap. 2.95 (ISBN 0-911635-00-9). Knickerbocker.

Glaser, Peter E., jt. ed. see Salisbury, John W.

Glaser, Rollin. Retail Personnel Management. LC 77-79342. 1977. 19.95 (ISBN 0-86730-506-1). Lebhar Friedman.

Glaser, William A. The Brain Drain: Emigration & Return-A UNITAR Study. LC 77-30576. 1978. 54.00 o.s.i. (ISBN 0-08-022419-9); pap. text ed. 24.00 (ISBN 0-08-022415-6). Pergamon.

--Health Insurance Bargaining: Foreign Lessons for Americans. 265p. 1978. 18.95 o.s.i. (ISBN 0-470-99398-7). Halsted Pr.

--Pretrial Discovery & the Adversary System. LC 68-54410. 300p. 1968. 10.00x (ISBN 0-87154-305-2). Russell Sage.

Glasgow, Ellen. Vein of Iron. LC 35-27270. (gr. 7-12). 1967. pap. 0.95 (ISBN 0-15-693476-0, Harv). HarBraceJ.

Glasgow, Winnette, jt. auth. see Seyling, Barbara.

Glasheen, Adaline. A Third Census of Finnegans Wake. LC 75-3770. 1977. 32.50x (ISBN 0-520-02980-1). U of Cal Pr.

Glashow & Goldstein, Mahler. Shoot the Works: How to Shoot It, How to Sell It. (Illus.). 96p. 14.95 (ISBN 0-87165-058-4, Amphoto); pap. 9.95 (ISBN 0-87165-059-2). Watson-Guptill.

Glaskov, I. B., jt. auth. see Estrin, Y. B.

Glasner, Lynne, jt. auth. see Thypin, Marilyn.

Glasner, Peter. The Sociology of Secularisation: A Critique of a Concept. (International Library of Sociology). 1977. 18.95x (ISBN 0-7100-8455-2). Routledge & Kegan.

Glasofer, Seymour. In Sickness & in Love. LC 80-21141. (Orig.). 1980. pap. 4.95 o.p. (ISBN 0-89865-086-0). Donning Co.

Glasofer, Seymour, jt. auth. see Loring, Murray.

Glass. Teaching Decoding As Separate from Reading. 2.95 o.p. (ISBN 0-88461-004-7). Adelphi Univ.

Glass, A. M. Ordered Permutation Groups. LC 81-16996. (London Mathematical Society Lecture Note Ser.: No. 55). (Illus.). 250p. 1982. pap. 26.00 (ISBN 0-521-24190-1). Cambridge U Pr.

Glass, Arnold L., et al. Cognition. LC 78-67941. 1979. text ed. 16.95 (ISBN 0-201-02449-7). A-W.

Glass, Billy P. Introduction to Planetary Geology. LC 81-17057. (Planetary Science Ser.: No. 2). (Illus.). 1982. 29.95 (ISBN 0-521-23579-0); pap. cancelled (ISBN 0-521-28052-4). Cambridge U Pr.

Glass, Carter M. Linear Systems with Applications & Discrete Analysis. LC 75-40282. (Illus.). 550p. 1976. text ed. 32.50 (ISBN 0-8299-0081-0). West Pub.

Glass, David C. Behavior Patterns, Stress, & Coronary Disease. LC 77-23788. (Complex Human Behavior Ser.). 217p. 1977. 14.95x o.p. (ISBN 0-470-99294-8). Halsted Pr.

Glass, David C., ed. Genetics. LC 68-24635. (Illus.). 1968. 13.00x (ISBN 0-87470-008-6). Rockefeller.

Glass, Dorothy F. Italian Romanesque Sculpture: An Annotated Bibliography. 1983. lib. bdg. 45.00 (ISBN 0-8161-8331-7, Hall Reference). G K Hall.

Glass, Elliot, et al. Everyday Spanish: A Basic Textbook. 1983. pap. text ed. 13.95 (ISBN 0-89529-155-X). Avery Pub.

Glass, Elliot S. El Politico Honesto. 157p. (Orig.). 1981. 8.50x (ISBN 0-916304-49-3). Campanile.

Glass, Gary E., ed. Bioassay Techniques & Environmental Chemistry. LC 72-96912. (Illus.). 1975. 27.50 o.p. (ISBN 0-250-40017-0). Ann Arbor Science.

Glass, Gene V. & Stanley, Julian C. Statistical Methods in Education & Psychology. (Educational Measurement, Research & Statistics Ser). 1970. text ed. 26.95x (ISBN 0-13-844928-7). P-H.

Glass, Gene V., jt. auth. see Hopkins, Kenneth D.

Glass, Gene V., et al. Design & Analysis of Time-Series Experiments. Willson, Victor L. & Gottman, John M., eds. LC 74-84779. (Illus.). 200p. 1975. text ed. 15.00x (ISBN 0-87081-063-4). Colo Assoc.

Glass, George. Your Book of Judo. (Your Book Of...Ser.). (Illus.). 80p. (gr. 3-6). 1977. 8.95 (ISBN 0-571-11054-1). Faber & Faber.

Glass, George B., ed. Gastrointestinal Hormones. (Comprehensive Endocrinology Ser.). 1028p. 1980. text ed. 98.00 (ISBN 0-89004-395-7). Raven.

Glass, H. Bentley, ed. The Roving Naturalists: Travel Letters of Theodosius Dobzhansky. LC 79-55229. (Memoirs Ser.: Vol. 139). 1980. pap. 10.00 (ISBN 0-87169-139-6). Am Philos.

Glass, J. Colin. Introduction to Mathematical Methods in Economics. 352p. 1980. text ed. 26.50 (ISBN 0-07-084116-0, C). McGraw.

Glass, Lillian & Liebmann-Smith, Richard. How to Deprogram Your Valley Girl. LC 82-21964. (Illus.). 64p. 1983. 2.95 (ISBN 0-89480-239-9). Workman Pub.

Glass, Marion & Atchison, Evelyn. Integrated Studies in Patient Care. LC 76-46127. 1978. pap. text ed. 13.00 (ISBN 0-8273-1608-9); instructor's guide 3.75 (ISBN 0-8273-1609-7). Delmar.

Glass, Robert. Office Gynecology. 2nd ed. (Illus.). 376p. 1981. lib. bdg. 32.00 (ISBN 0-683-03548-7). Williams & Wilkins.

Glass, Robert E. Gene Function: E. Coli & Its Heritable Elements. 450p. 1980. 60.00x o.p. (ISBN 0-686-69929-7, Pub. by Croom Helm England). State Mutual Bk.

Glass, Robert H. & Ericsson, Ronald J. Getting Pregnant in the Nineteen Eighties: New Advances in Infertility Treatment & Sex Preselection. (Illus.). 128p. 1982. 10.95 (ISBN 0-520-04828-8). U of Cal Pr.

Glass, Robert L. Computing Catastrophes. 1983. 11.00 (ISBN 0-686-35783-3). Computing Trends.

--The Power of Peonage. 1979. 9.00 (ISBN 0-686-23742-0). Computing Trends.

--The Second Coming: More Computing Projects Which Failed. 1980. 9.00 (ISBN 0-686-26939-X). Computing Trends.

--Software Reliability Guidebook. (Illus.). 1979. text ed. 25.00 (ISBN 0-13-821785-8). P-H.

--Software Soliloquies. 1981. 10.00 (ISBN 0-686-31797-1). Computing Trends.

--Tales of Computing Folk: Hot Dogs & Mixed Nuts. 1978. 9.00 (ISBN 0-686-23741-2). Computing Trends.

--The Universal Elixir & Other Computing Projects Which Failed. 1977. 9.00 (ISBN 0-686-23609-2). Computing Trends.

Glass, Robert L. & Noiseux, Ronald A. Software Maintenance Guidebook. (Illus.). 208p. 1981. text ed. 25.00 (ISBN 0-13-821728-9). P-H.

Glassbrook, D. W., jt. auth. see Arotsky, J.

Glassburner, Bruce, ed. Economy of Indonesia: Selected Readings. LC 77-127777. (Illus.). 448p. 1971. 34.95x (ISBN 0-8014-0600-5). Cornell U Pr.

Glassco, John. Memoirs of Montparnasse. 1970. 7.95x (ISBN 0-19-540202-2). Oxford U Pr.

Glasscock, Michael. The Real Estate Investing Profit Guide: How to Successfully Finance, Purchase, & Manage Income Property. (Illus.). 276p. 1982. 21.95 (ISBN 0-13-763136-7); pap. 11.95 (ISBN 0-13-763128-6). P-H.

Glasscock, Robin E., ed. The Lay Subsidy of 1334. (British Academy Records of Social & Economic History). 1975. 39.95x o.p. (ISBN 0-19-725933-2). Oxford U Pr.

Glasscote, R. M. Partial Hospitalization for the Mentally Ill: A Study of Programs & Problems. 187p. 1969. pap. 5.00 o.p. (ISBN 0-685-24873-9, P204-1). Am Psychiatric.

--The Psychiatric Emergency - a Study of Patterns of Service. 111p. 1966. pap. 3.50 o.p. (ISBN 0-685-24858-5, P179-0). Am Psychiatric.

Glasscote, R. M. & Fishman, M. E. Mental Health on the Campus: A Field Study. 216p. 1973. 8.50 o.p. (ISBN 0-685-77454-6, P202-0). Am Psychiatric.

Glasscote, R. M. & Gudeman, Jon E. The Staff of the Mental Health Center: A Field Study. 207p. 1969. 7.50- o.p. (ISBN 0-685-24872-0, P155-0). Am Psychiatric.

Glasscote, R. M. & Sussex, J. N. Community Mental Health Center-An Interim Appraisal, 1969. 156p. 1969. text ed. 8.00 o.p. (ISBN 0-685-31185-6, P206-0); pap. 5.00 o.p. (ISBN 0-685-31186-4, P206-1). Am Psychiatric.

Glasscote, R. M., et al. Halfway Houses for the Mentally Ill: A Study of Programs & Problems. LC 70-153492. 244p. 1971. casebound 7.50 (ISBN 0-89042-510-8). Am Psychiatric.

--Old Folks at Home: A Field Study of Nursing & Board-&-Care Facilities. LC 76-41660. 148p. 1976. casebound 8.00 (ISBN 0-89042-519-1, P222-0). Am Psychiatric.

--Preventing Mental Illness: Efforts & Attitudes. LC 80-65220. 138p. 1980. 10.00x (ISBN 0-89042-503-5). Am Psychiatric.

--Rehabilitating the Mentally Ill in the Community: A Study of Psychosocial Rehabilitation Centers. 214p. 1971. 7.50 o.p. (ISBN 0-685-24869-0, P-157-0). Am Psychiatric.

--Creative Mental Health Services for the Elderly. 189p. 1977. 10.00 o.p. (ISBN 0-685-86111-2). Am Psychiatric.

--Treatment of Drug Abuse: Programs, Problems, Prospects, 1972. 250p. 1972. pap. 8.00 o.p. (ISBN 0-686-57639-X, P197-0). Am Psychiatric.

Glasscote, Raymond M. & Fishman, M. E. Mental Health Programs for Preschool Children: A Field Study. 182p. 1974. pap. 8.50 o.p. (ISBN 0-685-65571-7, P208-0). Am Psychiatric.

Glasscote, Raymond M., et al. Alternate Services - Their Role in Mental Health: A Field Study of Free Clinics, Runaway Houses, Counseling Centers & the Like. 1975. pap. 10.00 o.p. (ISBN 0-685-63942-8, P209-0). Am Psychiatric.

--Children & Mental Health Centers: Programs, Problems, Prospects, 1972. 257p. 1972. pap. 7.50 o.p. (ISBN 0-686-76966-X, P172-0). Am Psychiatric.

--The Uses of Psychiatry in Smaller General Hospitals. LC 82-22719. 133p. 1983. pap. 12.00x (42-108-0). Am Psychiatric.

Glassenapp, C. F., jt. auth. see Ellis, William A.

Glasser, Ala. Synthetic Feelings & Popular Culture. LC 78-24017. 1979. 12.95 (ISBN 0-87949-132-9). Ashley Bks.

Glasser, Alan. Research & Development Management. (Illus.). 384p. 1982. 26.95 (ISBN 0-13-774091-3). P-H.

Glasser, Arthur F. & McGavran, Donald A. Contemporary Theologies of Mission. 320p. (Orig.). 1983. pap. 12.95 (ISBN 0-8010-3790-5). Baker Bk.

Glasser, Ellen. Looking into the Future: An Occupational Worktext. 1975. pap. 2.75x (ISBN 0-88323-118-2, 206). Richards Pub.

Glasser, Naomi, ed. What Are You Doing? LC 80-7586. 340p. 1982. pap. 6.68i (ISBN 0-06-090947-1, CN 947, CN). Har-Row.

Glasser, Paul H., et al, eds. Individual Change Through Small Groups. LC 73-14113. (Illus.). 1974. 18.00 (ISBN 0-02-911810-7); pap. text ed. 13.95 (ISBN 0-02-911800-X). Free Pr.

Glasser, Stephen P., ed. Noncardiac Surgery in the Cardiac Patient: Management & Assessment. LC 82-82381. (Illus.). 416p. 1983. 49.50 (ISBN 0-87993-183-3). Futura Pub.

Glasser, William. Identity Society. 320p. 1975. pap. 6.95i (ISBN 0-06-090446-1, CN446, CN). Har-Row.

--Identity Society. rev. ed. 1976. pap. 2.95i o.p. (ISBN 0-06-080359-2, P359, PL). Har-Row.

--Positive Addiction. LC 75-15305. (Illus.). 176p. 1976. 11.49i (ISBN 0-06-011558-0, HarpT). Har-Row.

--Positive Addiction. 10.95 o.p. (ISBN 0-686-92397-9, 6255). Hazelden.

--Reality Therapy. LC 65-14672. 1965. 11.49i (ISBN 0-06-002040-7, HarpT). Har-Row.

--Reality Therapy: A New Approach to Psychiatry. 1975. pap. 3.50i (ISBN 0-06-080348-7, P348, PL). Har-Row.

--Reality Therapy, A New Approach to Psychiatry. 9.95 o.p. (ISBN 0-686-92216-6, 6260); pap. 2.50 o.p. (ISBN 0-686-98494-3, 6605). Hazelden.

--Schools Without Failure. 320p. 1975. pap. 6.95i (ISBN 0-06-090421-6, CN421, CN). Har-Row.

Glasser, William & Powers, William T. Stations of the Mind: New Directions for Reality Therapy. LC 80-8205. (Illus.). 288p. 1981. 13.41i (ISBN 0-06-011478-9, HarpT). Har-Row.

Glassgold, A. E., ed. see Orion Nebula to Honor Henry Draper Symposium, Dec 4-5, 1981.

Glassgold, Peter, jt. ed. see Laughlin, J.

Glassheim, Eliot & Cargille, Charles, eds. Key Issues in Population & Food Policy: Capon Springs Public Policy Conference No. 2. LC 78-63063. (Illus.). 1978. pap. text ed. 15.75 o.p. (ISBN 0-8191-0613-5). U Pr of Amer.

Glassheim, Eliot, et al, eds. see Capon Springs Public Policy Conference, No. 1.

Glassie, Henry. Folk Housing in Middle Virginia: A Structural Analysis of Historic Artifacts. LC 75-11653. (Illus.). 1975. 18.50x (ISBN 0-87049-173-3); pap. 9.50x (ISBN 0-87049-268-3). U of Tenn Pr.

Glassman, Alan M. The Challenge of Management: A Behavioral Orientation. LC 77-16095. 304p. 1978. text ed. 14.95 (ISBN 0-471-02767-7); tchrs. manual o.p. avail. Wiley.

Glassman, Judith. The Sweater Book: 35 Original Sweater Patterns for Men, Women & Children. LC 76-8069. 1976. pap. 4.95 o.p. (ISBN 0-8256-3061-4, Quick Fox). Putnam Pub Group.

Glassman, Paul. Belize Guide. 128p. (Orig.). 1983. pap. 9.95 (ISBN 0-930016-03-3). Passport Pr.

Glassman, Sidney. A Guide to Residential Management. 2nd. ed. 260p. 1978. pap. 16.00 (ISBN 0-86718-053-6). Natl Assn Home Builders.

Glassmann, S. F. A Revision of B. E. Dahlgren's Index of American Palms. (Phaneroga Marum Mongraphiae: No. 6). 1972. 48.00 (ISBN 3-7682-0765-X). Lubrecht & Cramer.

Glassner, Martin I. & Deblij, Harm J. Systematic Political Geography. 3rd ed. LC 79-26750. 537p. 1980. text ed. 33.95 (ISBN 0-471-05228-0). Wiley.

Glassock, Richard J., jt. auth. see Massry, Shaul G.

Glasson, T. Francis. Moses in the Fourth Gospel. LC 63-5666. (Studies in Biblical Theology: No. 40). 1963. prebound o.p. 8.45x (ISBN 0-8401-4040-1); pap. 7.95x (ISBN 0-8401-3040-6). Allenson-Breckinridge.

Glasspool, Michael G. Problems in Ophthalmology. Fry, J. & Williams, K., eds. (Problems in Practice Ser.: Vol. 6). (Illus.). 141p. 1982. text ed. 16.50 (ISBN 0-8036-4158-3). Davis Co.

Glasstone, Samuel. Public Safety & Underground Nuclear Detonations. 276p. 1971. pap. 23.50 (ISBN 0-87079-315-2, TID-25708). DOE.

--Sourcebook on Atomic Energy. 3rd ed. LC 79-1206. 892p. 1979. Repr. of 1967 ed. lib. bdg. 47.50 (ISBN 0-88275-898-5). Krieger.

--Thermodynamics for Chemists. LC 72-189791. 528p. 1972. Repr. of 1947 ed. 26.50 (ISBN 0-88275-021-6). Krieger.

Glasunov, I. S. & Dowd, J. E. Kaunas Rotterdam intervention Study: Behavioural & Operational Components of Health Intervention Programmes. 1982. 58.75 (ISBN 0-444-80386-6). Elsevier.

Glatfelter, Charles H. Pastors & People: German & Lutheran Reformed Churches in the Pennsylvania Field, 1717-1793, Vol. II, The History. LC 80-83400. (Publications of the Pennsylvania German Society Ser.: Vol. 15). (Illus.). 25.00 (ISBN 0-911122-44-3). Penn German Soc.

--Pastors & People: German Lutheran & Reformed Churches in the Pennsylvania Field, 1717-1793, Vol. 1, Pastors & Congregations. LC 80-83400. (Publications of the Pennsylvania German Society: Vol. 13). (Illus.). 1979. 25.00 (ISBN 0-911122-40-0). Penn German Soc.

Glatstein, jt. auth. see Bleehan.

Glatt, M. M. & Marks, J., eds. The Dependence Phenomenon. 300p. 1982. 38.00 (ISBN 0-942068-03-3). Bogden & Son.

Glattbach, Jack. Media & the Developing World: Pluralism or Polarization? (Seven Springs Studies). 1982. pap. 3.00 (ISBN 0-943006-08-2). Seven Springs.

Glatthorn, Allan A. & Adams, Herbert R. Listening Your Way to Management Success. (Goals Ser.). 1983. pap. text ed. 7.95 (ISBN 0-673-15802-0). Scott F.

Glatthorn, Allan A., jt. auth. see Gilmore, Perry.

Glattke, Theodore J. Auditory Evoked Potentials. 1983. pap. 16.95 (ISBN 0-686-82638-8, 14710). Univ Park.

Glatzer, Nahum. The Judaic Tradition. 352p. 1982. pap. text ed. 9.95x (ISBN 0-87441-344-3). Behrman.

Glatzer, Nahum, ed. see Buber, Martin.

Glatzer, Nahum N. Franz Rosenzweig: His Life & Thought. 2nd ed. LC 53-656. 1962. pap. 8.95 (ISBN 0-8052-0021-5). Schocken.

Glatzer, Nahum N., ed. Hammer on the Rock: A Midrash Reader. LC 62-18155. 1962. pap. 4.95 (ISBN 0-8052-0032-0). Schocken.

--Language of Faith: A Selection from the Most Expressive Jewish Prayers. LC 65-14823. 1974. Eng. Language ed. 4.95 (ISBN 0-8052-3559-0); multilingual ed., o.p. 10.00 (ISBN 0-8052-3335-0). Schocken.

--Modern Jewish Thought: A Source Reader. LC 76-9139. 1976. 12.00x o.p. (ISBN 0-8052-3631-7); pap. 7.50 (ISBN 0-8052-0542-X). Schocken.

--Passover Haggadah: Including Readings on the Holocaust: With English Translation, Introduction & Commentary. 3rd ed. LC 69-10846. (Illus., Bilingual ed). 1979. pap. 3.95 (ISBN 0-8052-0624-8). Schocken.

Glatzer, Nahum N., ed. see Agnon, Y.

Glatzer, Nahum N., ed. see Buber, Martin.

Glatzer, Nahum N., ed. see Josephus, Flavius.

Glatzer, Nahum N., ed. see Kafka, Franz.

Glatzer, Nahum N., ed. see Schurer, Emil.

Glatzle, M. & Fiore, E. Muggable Mary. 1980. 9.95 o.p. (ISBN 0-13-604660-6). P-H.

Glauber, Helen M., ed. see Glauber, I. Peter.

Glauber, I. Peter. Stuttering: A Psychoanalytic Understanding. Glauber, Helen M., ed. LC 82-8125. 208p. 1983. 24.95 (ISBN 0-89885-154-8). Human Sci Pr.

Glaucia, Daria. Dios, Tu y Tu Vocacion. Baptista, W. S., tr. from Portuguese. Orig. Title: Deus, Voce E a Vocacao. Date not set. cancelled (ISBN 0-311-46201-4). Casa Bautista.

Glaudue, E. Ted, Jr. China's Perception of Global Politics. LC 82-13572. 258p. 1983. lib. bdg. 23.50 (ISBN 0-8191-2700-0); pap. text ed. 11.50 (ISBN 0-8191-2701-9). U Pr of Amer.

Glauert, A. M. Practical Methods in Electron Microscopy, Vols. 1-8. 1972-79. 87.25 (ISBN 0-444-10404-6, North-Holland); Vol. 2. 76.75 (ISBN 0-444-10644-8); Vol. 3. 76.75 (ISBN 0-444-10665-0); Vol. Vol. 4. 38.50 (ISBN 0-444-10807-6); Vol. 5. 103.00 (ISBN 0-7204-0605-6); Vol. 6. 91.50 (ISBN 0-7204-0636-6); Vol. 7. 70.25 (ISBN 0-7204-0665-X); Vol. 8. 70.25 (ISBN 0-444-80166-9). Elsevier.

Glauert, A. M., ed. Practical Methods in Electron Microscopy, Vol. 9: Experiments in the Electron Microscope. 1981. 83.00 (ISBN 0-444-80285-1, North Holland). Elsevier.

Glauert, M. B. Principles of Dynamics. (Library of Mathematics). 1969. pap. 5.00 o.p. (ISBN 0-7100-4348-1). Routledge & Kegan.

Glauert, Michael, jt. auth. see Kelsey, Hugh.

Glautier, M. W. & Underdown, B. Accounting Theory & Practice. 2nd ed. 688p. 1982. 50.00x (ISBN 0-273-01541-9, Pub. by Pitman Bks England). State Mutual Bk.

Glawischnig, Dieter, jt. auth. see Koerner, Friedrich.

Glawischnig, H., jt. auth. see Ryssel, H.

Glaze, Andre. The Trash Dragon of Shensi. (Illus.). 1978. pap. 4.50 (ISBN 0-686-82968-9, Pub. by Copper Beech). SBD.

Glaze, Jack A., tr. see Francisco, Clyde T.

Glazener, E. R., jt. auth. see Groneman, Chris H.

Glazer, A. N., et al, eds. Chemical Modification of Proteins. LC 74-84210. (Laboratory Techniques in Biochemistry & Molecular Biology: Vol. 4, Pt. 1). 205p. 1975. pap. 17.50 (ISBN 0-444-10811-4, North-Holland). Elsevier.

Glazer, Howard I., jt. ed. see Fensterheim, Herbert.

Glazer, Joan & Williams, Gurney, III. Introduction to Children's Literature. 2nd ed. (Illus.). 736p. 1979. 22.50 (ISBN 0-07-023380-2). McGraw.

Glazer, Joan I. Literature for Early Childhood. (Illus.). 240p. 1981. pap. text ed. 12.50 (ISBN 0-675-08039-8). Merrill.

Glazer, Lee. Cookie Becker Casts a Spell. (Illus.). 48p. (gr. 3-5). 1980. 6.95 o.p. (ISBN 0-316-31582-6). Little.

Glazer, Mark, jt. auth. see Bohannan, Paul.

Glazer, Myra, ed. Burning Air & a Clear Mind: Contemporary Israeli Women Poets. LC 80-22487. (Illus.). xxviii, 135p. 1981. 17.95x (ISBN 0-8214-0572-1, 82-83657); pap. 8.95 (ISBN 0-8214-0617-5, 82-83665). Ohio U Pr.

Glazer, Nathan. Affirmative Discrimination: Ethnic Inequality & Public Policy. LC 74-25924. 1976. pap. 6.95 (ISBN 0-465-09730-8). Basic.

--Mediating Structures & Welfare. 250p. cancelled o.s.i. (ISBN 0-88410-823-6). Ballinger Pub.

Glazer, Nathan & Moynihan, Daniel P. Beyond the Melting Pot: The Negroes, Puerto Ricans, Jews, Italians, & Irish of New York City. 2nd rev ed. 1970. 22.00x (ISBN 0-262-07039-1); pap. 5.95 (ISBN 0-262-57022-X). MIT Pr.

Glazer, Nathan & Ueda, Reed. How Ethnic Groups are Presented: A Study of Six American History Textbooks. 1982. pap. write for info. (ISBN 0-89633-064-8). Ethics & Public Policy.

Glazer, Nathan, et al. Twentieth Century Causes Celebres: Sacco-Vanzetti, Alger Hiss, the Rosenbergs. LC 81-85576. 335p. Date not set. 16.95 (ISBN 0-89526-663-6). Regnery-Gateway. Postponed.

Glazer, Nona Y. & Waehrer, Helen Y. Woman in a Man-Made World. 2nd ed. 1977. pap. 13.95 (ISBN 0-395-30604-3). HM.

Glazer, Robin K. Letting Go. (Illus.). 320p. 1983. 17.95 (ISBN 0-8065-0833-7); pap. 9.95 (ISBN 0-8065-0844-2). Citadel Pr.

Glazer, Sidney, ed. Manhaj as-Salik: Abu Hayyan's Commentary on the Alfiyya of Ibn Malik. (American Oriental Ser.: Vol. 31). 1947. 12.50x o.s.i. (ISBN 0-940490-31-5). Kraus Repr.

Glazer, Tom. Do Your Ears Hang Low? LC 78-20072. (Illus.). (gr. 1-3). 1980. 10.95a (ISBN 0-385-12602-6); PLB (ISBN 0-385-12603-4). Doubleday.

--Eye Winker, Tom Tinker, Chin Chopper. (Illus.). 1978. pap. 3.50 (ISBN 0-385-13344-8). Doubleday.

Glazer Malbin, Nona. Old Family-New Family. 1975. pap. text ed. 5.50x (ISBN 0-442-24976-4). Van Nos Reinhold.

Glazier, Richard. A Manual of Historic Ornament: Treating Upon the Evolution, Tradition & Development of Architecture & the Applied Arts. 5th ed. LC 70-163174. (Tower Bks). (Illus.). vi, 183p. 1972. Repr. of 1933 ed. 42.00x (ISBN 0-8103-3937-4). Gale.

Glazier, Stephen D., ed. Perspectives on Pentecostalism: Case Studies from the Caribbean & Latin America. LC 80-7815. 207p. 1980. lib. bdg. 20.00 (ISBN 0-8191-1071-X); pap. text ed. 10.50 (ISBN 0-8191-1072-8). U Pr of Amer.

Glazman, I. M., jt. auth. see Akheizer, N. I.

Gleadow, R. F. Chapter One - Engraved-Roller Printing. 75.00x (ISBN 0-686-98193-6, Pub. by Soc Dyers & Colour). State Mutual Bk.

Gleasner. Rock Climbing. 1981. 7.95 o.p. (ISBN 0-679-20925-5). McKay.

Gleasner, Bill & Gleasner, Diana. Sea Islands of the South. LC 79-24730. (Illus.). 176p. 1980. pap. 8.95 o.p. (ISBN 0-914788-21-3). East Woods.

Gleasner, Diana. The Movies. (Inventions That Changed Our Lives Ser.). (Illus.). (gr. 4-6). 1983. 7.95 (ISBN 0-8027-6482-7); lib. bdg. 8.85 (ISBN 0-8027-6483-5). Walker & Co.

Gleasner, Diana, jt. auth. see Gleasner, Bill.

Gleason & Cronquist. Manuel of Vascular Plants. 810p. 1963. text ed. write for info. Grant Pr.

Gleason, jt. auth. see Horn.

Gleason, Abbott. Young Russia: The/Genesis of Russian Radicalism in the 1860s. LC 82-23875. xiv, 438p. 1983. pap. 10.95 (ISBN 0-226-29961-9). U of Chicago Pr.

Gleason, Gayle, photos by. New York Restaurant Calendar 1983. (Illus.). 14p. 1982. 9.95 (ISBN 0-943998-00-X). Lake End.

Gleason, John J., Jr. Growing up to God: Eight Steps in Religious Development. LC 74-17093. 144p. 1975. pap. 3.50 o.p. (ISBN 0-687-15972-5). Abingdon.

Gleason, Judith. Leaf & Bone: African Praise Poems. LC 79-56265. 228p. 1980. 14.95 o.p. (ISBN 0-670-42178-2). Viking Pr.

Gleason, Ralph J. Celebrating the Duke. 1976. pap. 3.95 o.s.i. (ISBN 0-440-51154-2, Delta). Dell.

Gleason, Sarah. I'd Do It Again--50 Years a Colorado Teacher. 128p. (Orig.). 1982. pap. 6.00 o.p. (ISBN 0-937080-06-3). Century One.

Gleason, Walter. Essentials of Business Math. (Math Ser.). 496p. 1982. pap. text ed. write for info. (ISBN 0-87150-350-6, 2752). Prindle.

Gleason, Walter, tr. see Fonvizin, Dennis.

Gleaves, Edwin S. & Tucker, John M., eds. Reference Services & Library Education: Essays in Honor of Frances Neel Cheney. LC 81-48266. 320p. 1982. 29.95x (ISBN 0-669-05320-1). Lexington Bks.

Gleazer, Edmund J., Jr. Community Colleges: What Is Their Promise & Future Place in America? (Vital Issues, Vol. XXIX 1979-80: No. 1). 0.50 (ISBN 0-686-81606-4). Ctr Info Am.

Gleazer, Edmund J., Jr., ed. American Junior Colleges. 8th ed. 1971. 42.00 o.p. (ISBN 0-8268-1209-0). ACE.

Glebov, I. A. & Komarsky, E. G. Synchronous Generators in Electrophysical Installations. Skrebtsov, G. P., tr. from Rus. LC 81-48563. (Illus.). 208p. 1982. 27.95x (ISBN 0-669-05434-8). Lexington Bks.

Gleckner, Robert F. Blake's Prelude: Poetical Sketches. LC 82-47976. 208p. 1983. text ed. 15.00x (ISBN 0-8018-2850-3). Johns Hopkins.

Gledhill, Alan. Republic of India, Development of Its Laws & Constitution. LC 77-98761. Repr. of 1951 ed. lib. bdg. 15.75x (ISBN 0-8371-2813-7, GLRI). Greenwood.

Glees, Anthony. Exile Politics During the Second World: The German Social Democrats in Britain. (Oxford Historical Monographs). (Illus.). 284p. 1982. 39.95x (ISBN 0-19-821893-1). Oxford U Pr.

Gleeson, Denis & Whitty, Geoff. Developments in Social Studies Teaching. (Changing Classroom). 1976. text ed. 11.75x o.p. (ISBN 0-7291-0099-5); pap. text ed. 4.75x o.p. (ISBN 0-7291-0094-4). Humanities.

Gleeson, Patrick. First Reader of American Short Fiction. LC 74-158946. 1971. pap. text ed. 4.95 (ISBN 0-675-09826-2). Merrill.

Glegg, Gordon L. Design of Design. LC 69-12432. (Cambridge Engineering Pubns.). (Illus.). 1969. 18.95 (ISBN 0-521-07447-9). Cambridge U Pr.

--Making & Interpreting Mechanical Drawings. (Illus.). 1971. 7.95 (ISBN 0-521-09680-4). Cambridge U Pr.

--The Science of Design. (Illus.). 112p. 1973. 17.95 (ISBN 0-521-20327-9). Cambridge U Pr.

--The Selection of Design. LC 72-80591. (Illus.). 96p. 1972. 16.95 (ISBN 0-521-08686-8). Cambridge U Pr.

Glehn, M. E. Von see Hiller, Ferdinand.

Gleich, C. C. von. Die Bedeutung der Allgemeinen Musikalischen Zeitung: 1798-1848 & 1863-1882. 1969. wrappers 15.00 o.s.i. (ISBN 90-6027-072-X, Pub. by Frits Knuf Netherlands). Pendragon NY.

--Pianofortes uit de Lage Landen. (Haags Gemeentemuseum, Kijkboekjes Ser.: Vol. 4). (Illus.). 72p. (Dutch & Eng.). 1981. wrappers 15.00 o.s.i. (ISBN 0-686-30911-1, Pub. by Frits Knuf Netherlands). Pendragon NY.

Gleicher, Jules. The Accidental Revolutionary: Essays on the Political Teaching of Jean-Paul Sartre. LC 82-20067. 216p. (Orig.). 1983. lib. bdg. 18.75 (ISBN 0-8191-2835-X); pap. text ed. 7.75 (ISBN 0-8191-2836-8). U Pr of Amer.

Gleicher, Norbert, jt. ed. see Elkayam, Uri.

Gleim, Irvin M. & Delaney, Patrick R. CPA Examination Review: Problems & Solutions, Vol. 2. LC 81-4488. 1981. text ed. 23.95x o.p. (ISBN 0-471-08903-6); write for info. tchrs' ed. o.p. Wiley.

Gleim, Irvin N. & Delaney, Patrick R. CPA Examination Review: Outlines Study Guides, Vol. 1. 8th ed. LC 81-4488. 1981. text ed. 23.95x o.p. (ISBN 0-471-08905-2); write for info. tchrs' ed. o.p. (ISBN 0-471-09113-8). Wiley.

Gleim, Irwin N. & Delaney, Patrick R. CPA Examination Review, 2 vols. 8th ed. Incl. Vol. 1. Outlines & Study Guides. 1060p. text ed. 23.95x o.p. (ISBN 0-471-08905-2); Vol. 2. Problems & Solutions. 965p. text ed. 23.95x o.p. (ISBN 0-471-08903-6). 1980. Wiley.

Gleit, J., jt. auth. see Eckstein, J.

Gleitman, Henry. Basic Psychology. 500p. 1982. text ed. 21.95x (ISBN 0-393-95254-1); write for info. instr's manual; study guide 8.95x (ISBN 0-393-95261-4); write for info. test item file. Norton.

--Psychology. (Illus.). 1981. 22.95x (ISBN 0-393-95102-2); study guide 8.95x (ISBN 0-393-95110-3); instr's manual avail. (ISBN 0-393-95105-7); test item file avail. (ISBN 0-393-95114-6). Norton.

Gleitman, Lila R., jt. ed. see Wanner, Eric.

Glejser, H., ed. Quantitative Studies of International Economic Relations. 1976. 40.50 (ISBN 0-444-10902-1, North-Holland). Elsevier.

Glekel, Jeffrey. Business Crimes: A Guide For Corporate & Defense Counsel. 440p. 1982. text ed. 50.00 (ISBN 0-686-97902-8, C3-1172). PLI.

Glen, Duncan, ed. & intro. by see MacDiarmid, Hugh.

Glen, William. Continental Drift & Plate Tectonics. (Physics & Physical Science Ser.). 192p. 1975. pap. text ed. 10.95 (ISBN 0-675-08799-6). Merrill.

Glenbow Historical Library, Glenbow-Alberta Institute. Catalogue of the Glenbow Historical Library. 1973. Four Vols. lib. bdg. 385.00 (ISBN 0-8161-0994-X, Pub. by HallLibrary). G K Hall.

Glenday, Graham & Jenkins, Glenn P. Worker Adjustment to Liberalized Trade: Costs & Assistance Policies. (Working Paper: No. 426). i, 86p. 1980. 5.00 (ISBN 0-686-36212-8, WP-0426). World Bank.

Glendenning, G. William & Holtom, Robert B. Personal Lines Underwriting. 1979. write for info. o.p. (UND 62). IIA.

Glendenning, G. Williams & Holtom, Robert B. Personal Lines Underwriting. 2nd ed. LC 77-81989. 582p. 1982. text ed. 18.00 (ISBN 0-89462-003-7). IIA.

Glendenning, Norman R., ed. Direct Nuclear Reactions: Monograph. LC 82-24365. Date not set. price not set (ISBN 0-12-286320-8). Acad Pr.

Glendinning, Eric H. English in Mechanical Engineering. (English in Focus Ser). 1975. pap. text ed. 9.95x (ISBN 0-19-437512-9); tchr's ed. 12.00x (ISBN 0-19-437501-3). Oxford U Pr.

Glendinning, O. N., tr. see Baroja, Julio C.

Glendinning, Richard & Glendinning, Sally. Gargantua: The Mighty Gorilla. LC 73-21644. (Famous Animal Stories Ser.). (Illus.). 48p. (gr. 2-5). 1974. PLB 6.89 (ISBN 0-8116-4855-9). Garrard.

--Stubby: Brave Soldier Dog. LC 78-4575. (Famous Animal Stories). (Illus.). (gr. 2-5). 1978. PLB 6.89 (ISBN 0-8116-4864-8). Garrard.

Glendinning, Sally. Doll: Bottle-Nosed Dolphin. LC 80-13660. (Young Animal Adventures Ser.). 40p. (gr. 2). 1980. PLB 7.12 (ISBN 0-8116-7501-7). Garrard.

--Jimmy & Joe Find a Ghost. LC 79-82107. (Jimmy & Joe Ser.). (Illus.). (gr. k-3). 1969. PLB 7.12 (ISBN 0-8116-4701-3). Garrard.

--Jimmy & Joe Fly a Kite. LC 77-120461. (Jimmy & Joe Ser.). (Illus.). (gr. k-3). 1970. PLB 7.12 (ISBN 0-8116-4704-8). Garrard.

--Jimmy & Joe Get a Hens' Surprise. LC 74-97163. (Jimmy & Joe Ser.). (Illus.). (gr. k-3). 1970. PLB 7.12 (ISBN 0-8116-4702-1). Garrard.

--Jimmy & Joe Go to the Fair. LC 72-158356. (Jimmy & Joe Ser.). (Illus.). (gr. k-3). 1971. PLB 7.12 (ISBN 0-8116-4706-4). Garrard.

--Jimmy & Joe Have a Real Thanksgiving. LC 74-1184. (Jimmy & Joe Ser.). (Illus.). (gr. k-3). 1974. PLB 7.12 (ISBN 0-8116-4709-9). Garrard.

--Jimmy & Joe Look for a Bear. LC 71-102909. (Jimmy & Joe Ser.). (Illus.). (gr. k-3). 1970. PLB 7.12 (ISBN 0-8116-4703-X). Garrard.

--Jimmy & Joe Meet a Halloween Witch. LC 74-132036. (Jimmy & Joe Ser.). (Illus.). (gr. k-3). 1971. PLB 7.12 (ISBN 0-8116-4705-6). Garrard.

--Jimmy & Joe Save a Christmas Deer. LC 72-7835. (Jimmy & Joe Ser.). (Illus.). 40p. (gr. k-3). 1973. PLB 7.12 (ISBN 0-8116-4708-0). Garrard.

--Jimmy & Joe See a Monster. LC 74-190544. (Jimmy & Joe Ser.). (Illus.). 40p. (gr. k-3). 1972. PLB 7.12 (ISBN 0-8116-4707-2). Garrard.

--Little Blue & Rusty: Red Kangaroos. LC 80-13935. (Young Animal Adventures Ser.). 40p. (gr. 2). 1980. PLB 7.12 (ISBN 0-8116-7502-5). Garrard.

--Pen: Emperor Penguin. LC 80-13212. (Young Animal Adventures Ser.). 40p. (gr. 2). 1980. PLB 7.12 (ISBN 0-8116-7500-9). Garrard.

--Queen Victoria: English Empress. LC 71-116038. (Century Biographies Ser.). (Illus.). (gr. 6). 1971. PLB 3.98 (ISBN 0-8116-4750-1). Garrard.

Glendinning, Sally, jt. auth. see Glendinning, Richard.

Glendon, Mary A. State, Law & Family: Family Law in Transition in Germany, England, France & the United States. 1977. 26.25 (ISBN 0-7204-0574-2, North-Holland). Elsevier.

Glenmore Distilleries Company. Mr. Boston Spirited Dessert Guide. LC 82-2638. (Illus.). 160p. 1982. 13.50 (ISBN 0-446-51253-2). Warner Bks.

Glenn, Andrea. Kansas in Color: Photographs Selected by Kansas! Magazine. LC 82-60564. (Illus.). 128p. 1982. 14.95 (ISBN 0-7006-0229-1). Univ Pr KS.

Glenn, Barbara, jt. auth. see Green, Bruce.

Glenn, Barbara H., jt. ed. see Franta, Gregory E.

Glenn, Barbara H., ed. see International Solar Energy Society American Section Annual Meeting, Phoenix, 1980.

Glenn, Barbara H., ed. see International Solar Energy Society, American Section, Annual Meeting, Philadelphia, 1981.

Glenn, Constance W. Jim Dine Figure Drawings, Nineteen Seventy Five-Nineteen Seventy Nine. LC 79-3060. (Icon Edns.). (Illus.). 1980. pap. 12.95i o.p. (ISBN 0-06-430102-8, IN102, HarpT). Har-Row.

Glenn, Donna, jt. auth. see Becker, Sarah.

Glenn, Edmund S. Man & Mankind: Conflict & Communication Between Cultures. (Communication & Information Science Ser.). 300p. 1981. 34.00 (ISBN 0-89391-068-6). Ablex Pub.

Glenn, Elizabeth. What Love Endures. (Superromances Ser.). 384p. 1983. pap. 2.95 (ISBN 0-373-70067-9, Pub. by Worldwide). Harlequin Bks.

Glenn, Gary & Glenn, Peggy. Don't Get Burned: A Family Fire-Safety Guide. (Illus.). 210p. (Orig.). 1982. pap. 7.95 (ISBN 0-936930-81-0). Aames-Allen.

Glenn, Harold. Automechanics. rev. ed. (gr. 9-12). 1976. text ed. 18.00 (ISBN 0-87002-169-9); wkbk & ans. sheets 5.20 (ISBN 0-87002-180-X); tchr's. guide free. Bennett IL.

Glenn, Harold T. Glenn's Honda Two-Cylinder Repair & Tune-up Guide. 1971. 6.95 o.p. (ISBN 0-517-50790-0). Crown.

--Glenn's Outboard Motor Tune-up & Repair Ser, 6 bks. Incl. Johnson 1 & 2 Cylinder. pap. o.p. (ISBN 0-8092-8317-4); Johnson 3 & 4 Cylinder. pap. o.p. (ISBN 0-8092-8316-6); Evinrude 1 & 2 Cylinder. pap. o.p. (ISBN 0-8092-8315-8); Evinrude 3 & 4 Cylinder. pap. o.p. (ISBN 0-8092-8313-1); Chrysler 1 & 2 Cylinder. pap. o.p. (ISBN 0-8092-8312-3); Chrysler 3 & 4 Cylinder. pap. 7.75 o.p. (ISBN 0-8092-8311-5). (Illus.). 1974. pap. Contemp Bks.

--Glenn's Suzuki One Cylinder Repair & Tune-up Guide. (Illus.). 1972. pap. 7.50 o.p. (ISBN 0-517-50144-9). Crown.

Glenn, Harold T., jt. auth. see Coles, Clarence W.

Glenn, Howard J., ed. Biologic Applications of Radiotracers. 224p. 1982. 63.50 (ISBN 0-8493-6009-9). CRC Pr.

Glenn, James F., ed. Urologic Surgery. 3nd ed. (Illus.). 1168p. 1983. text ed. 125.00 (ISBN 0-06-140922-7, Harper Medical). Lippincott.

Glenn, Jerry. Paul Celan. (World Authors Ser.). 1973. lib. bdg. 15.95 (ISBN 0-8057-2205-X, Twayne). G K Hall.

Glenn, John. Children Learning Geometry. 1979. text ed. 15.50 (ISBN 0-06-318118-5, IntlDept); pap. text ed. 7.80 (ISBN 0-06-318119-3). Har-Row.

Glenn, Kathleen M. Azorin (Jose Martinez Ruiz) (World Authors Ser.). 1981. lib. bdg. 14.95 (ISBN 0-8057-6446-1, Twayne). G K Hall.

Glenn, Michael. Trouble on the Hill & Other Stories. LC 79-88413. 1979. pap. 3.95 (ISBN 0-930720-61-X). Liberator Pr.

Glenn, Morton B. But I Don't Eat That Much: The Medically Sound Method for "Once-and-for-All" Reducing. 1980. pap. 5.95 o.p. (ISBN 0-525-93106-6). Dutton.

Glenn, N. E., jt. auth. see Pierce, Anne E.

Glenn, Peggy, jt. auth. see Glenn, Gary.

Glenn, Peter & Seiffert, Dorothy. Everything You Wanted to Know About Modeling: But Didn't Know Whom or Where to Ask. 1976. pap. 2.50 o.p. (ISBN 0-87314-060-5); lib. bdg. 4.00 o.p. (ISBN 0-87314-061-3). Peter Glenn.

Glenn, Peter, et al, eds. National Radio Publicity Directory, 1981. 11th ed. 320p. 1981. 85.00 o.p. (ISBN 0-87314-047-8). Peter Glenn.

Glenn, Richard F. Juan de la Cueva. (World Authors Ser.). 1973. lib. bdg. 15.95 (ISBN 0-8057-2258-0, Twayne). G K Hall.

Glenn, William E., jt. auth. see Conrad, William R., Jr.

Glenner, G. G. Amyloid & Amyloidosis: Proceedings. (International Congress Ser.: No. 497). 1980. 119.25 (ISBN 0-444-90124-8). Elsevier.

Glennon, James. Making Friends with Opera. pap. 5.00x (ISBN 0-392-13769-0, ABC). Sportshelf.

--Making Friends with Orchestral Music. pap. 5.00x (ISBN 0-392-13741-0, ABC). Sportshelf.

--Making Friends with Piano Music. pap. 5.00x (ISBN 0-392-13738-0, ABC). Sportshelf.

--Making Friends with Symphony. pap. 5.00x (ISBN 0-392-13755-0, ABC). Sportshelf.

Glenny, Michael, tr. see Bulgakov, Mikhail.

Glenny, Michael, tr. see Kaminskaya, Dina.

Glenny, Michael, tr. see Lakshin, Vladimir.

Glenny, Michael, tr. see Trifonov, Yuri.

Glenora, Erb, jt. auth. see Kozier, Barbara.

Glerum, Richard Z. & Blake, Donna J. Vocational Decision Workbook. 1977. 3.50x (ISBN 0-910328-14-5); guide o.p. 2.50. Carroll Pr.

Gles, Margaret. Come Play Hide & Seek. LC 73-20376. (Easy Venture Ser). (Illus.). 32p. (gr. k-2). 1975. PLB 6.69 (ISBN 0-8116-6053-2). Garrard.

Gleser, Goldine C., et al. Prolonged Psychological Effects of a Disaster: A Study of Buffalo Creek. (Personality & Psychopathology Ser.). 1981. 19.50 (ISBN 0-12-286260-0). Acad Pr.

Gleser, Goldine G., jt. auth. see Ihilevich, David.

Glessing, Robert & White, William. Mass Media: The Invisible Environment Revisited. rev. ed. LC 75-44488. (Illus.). 352p. 1976. pap. text ed. 12.95 (ISBN 0-574-22700-8, 13-5700). SRA.

Glew, G. Advances in Catering Technology. 1980. 98.50 (ISBN 0-85334-844-8, Pub. by Applied Sci England). Elsevier.

--Catering Equipment & Systems Design. (Illus.). 1977. 71.75x (ISBN 0-85334-730-1, Pub. by Applied Sci England). Elsevier.

Glew, Geoffrey. Multiple Choice Questions in Psychiatry. 1978. pap. 10.95 (ISBN 0-407-00142-5). Butterworth.

Glezen, G. W., jt. auth. see Taylor, D. H.

Glezer, Leon. Tarriff Politics: Australian Policy-Making 1960-1980. 360p. 1982. 35.00 (ISBN 0-522-84190-2, Pub. by Melbourne U Pr). Intl Schol Bk Serv.

Glick, Carl. Shake Hands with the Dragon. LC 75-162513. 334p. 1971. Repr. of 1941 ed. 37.00x (ISBN 0-8103-3765-7). Gale.

Glick, Clarence E. Sojourners & Settlers: Chinese Migrants in Hawaii. LC 80-13799. 480p. 1980. text ed. 20.00x (ISBN 0-8248-0707-3). UH Pr.

Glick, D., ed. see Holmes, K. C. & Blow, D. M.

Glick, David. Methods of Biochemical Analysis, 23 vols. Incl. Vol. 1. 532p. 1954. o.p.; Vol. 2. 476p. 1955. o.p.; Vol. 3. 447p. 1955. 36.50x o.s.i. (ISBN 0-470-30492-8); Vol. 4. 372p. 1957. 31.50x o.p. (ISBN 0-470-30525-8); Vol. 5. 514p. 1957. 36.50x o.s.i. (ISBN 0-470-30558-4); Vol. 6. 368p. 1958. 33.00x o.s.i. (ISBN 0-470-30591-6); Vol. 7. 363p. 1959. o.p.; Vol. 8. 410p. 1960. 28.95 o.p. (ISBN 0-470-30657-2); Vol. 9. 462p. 1962. o.p.; Vol. 10. 399p. 1962. 33.50 o.p. (ISBN 0-686-76981-3). LC 54-7232. (Methods of Biochemical Analysis Ser.: Vols. 1-10, Pub. by Wiley-Interscience). Wiley.

--Methods of Biochemical Analysis, Vol. 28. LC 54-7232. 430p. 1982. 50.50 (ISBN 0-471-08370-4, Pub. by Wiley-Interscience). Wiley.

--Methods of Biochemical Analysis, Vol. 27. (Methods of Biochemical Analysis Ser.). 537p. 1981. 53.95 (ISBN 0-471-06503-X, Pub. by Wiley-Interscience). Wiley.

Glick, David, ed. Methods of Biochemical Analysis. LC 54-7273. 435p. Vol. 23, 1976. 40.50x o.p. (ISBN 0-471-01413-3, Pub. by Wiley Interscience); Vol. 25, 1979. 49.95 (ISBN 0-471-04397-4); Vol. 26, 1980. 46.50 (ISBN 0-471-04798-8); Vol. 24. 40.00 o.p. (ISBN 0-471-02764-2). Wiley.

--Methods of Biochemical Analysis: Analysis of Biogenic Amines & Their Related Enzymes. LC 54-7232. 358p. (Orig.). 1971. Supplemental Ed. 32.50 (ISBN 0-471-30420-4). Krieger.

Glick, David M. Biochemistry Review. 7th ed. LC 80-19927. (Basic Science Review Bks.). 1980. pap. 11.95 (ISBN 0-87488-202-8). Med Exam.

Glick, Ferne P. & Pellman, Donald R. Breaking Silence: A Family Grows with Deafness. LC 82-6067. 208p. (Orig.). 1982. 10.95 (ISBN 0-8361-1999-1); pap. 6.95 (ISBN 0-8361-3300-5). Herald Pr.

Glick, Henry R. Courts, Politics & Justice. (Illus.). 320p. 1982. pap. text ed. 11.95 (ISBN 0-07-023490-6, C). McGraw.

Glick, Ira, et al. Family Therapy & Research: An Annotated Bibliography. 2nd ed. 1982. 39.50 (ISBN 0-686-97202-3). Grune.

Glick, Ira D. & Haley, Jay. Family Therapy & Research: An Annotated Bibliography of Articles & Books, 1950-1970. LC 72-153577. 280p. 1971. 39.50 o.p. (ISBN 0-8089-0688-7). Grune.

Glick, Ira D. & Hargreaves, William A. Psychiatric Hospital Treatment for the Nineteen Eighties. LC 77-26995. 1979. 21.95x (ISBN 0-669-01502-4). Lexington Bks.

Glick, Ira O., et al. The First Year of Bereavement. LC 74-12499. 311p. 1974. 27.95 (ISBN 0-471-30421-2, Pub. by Wiley-Interscience). Wiley.

Glick, Leonard & Hebding, Daniel E. Introduction to Social Problems. LC 78-67953. (Sociology Ser.). 1980. pap. text ed. 15.95 (ISBN 0-201-02600-7); instrs' manual 2.50 (ISBN 0-201-02466-7). A-W.

Glick, Leslie A. Multilateral Trade Negotiations. 400p. Date not set. text ed. 48.50x (ISBN 0-86598-036-5). Allanheld.

Glick, Marianne, ed. see Basile, Frank M.

Glick, Wendell, ed. Great Short Stories of Henry David Thoreau. LC 82-47560. (Great Short Works Ser.). 352p. (Orig.). 1982. pap. 3.80i (ISBN 0-06-080598-6, P 598, PL). Har-Row.

Glickman, Frank, jt. auth. see Fritzhand, James.

Glickman, Harry. Promoter Ain't a Dirty Word. new ed. LC 78-5604. 1978. 9.95 (ISBN 0-917304-35-7); pap. 6.95 (ISBN 0-917304-54-3). Timber.

Glickman, Norman, jt. auth. see Adams, F. Gerard.

Glickman, Richard. Complete Guide to Accounting & Financial Methods & Controls for Service Businesses. (Illus.). 192p. 1979. 34.95 o.p. (ISBN 0-13-159962-3, Busn). P-H.

Glickman, S. Craig. Knowing Christ. 200p. 1980. pap. 5.95 (ISBN 0-8024-3502-5). Moody.

--A Song for Lovers. LC 75-21454. 204p. (Orig.). 1976. pap. 5.25 (ISBN 0-87784-768-1). Inter-Varsity.

Glicksberg, Charles I. Self in Modern Literature. LC 63-18887. 1963. 14.95x (ISBN 0-271-73101-X). Pa St U Pr.

Glickson, Jeannie L., ed. see Institute of Real Estate Management.

Glickson, Jeannie L., ed. see King, Carol S., et al.

Glickstein, Barbra. Bulletin Board Extravaganzas. (gr. k-8). 1981. 6.95 (ISBN 0-86653-002-9, GA229). Good Apple.

Glidden, Hope H. The Storyteller As Humanist: The Serees of Guillaume Bouchet. LC 80-70809. (French Forum Monographs: No. 25). 183p. (Orig.). 1981. pap. 12.50x (ISBN 0-917058-24-0). French Forum.

Glidden, Ralph. Exploring the Yellowstone High Country: A History of the Cooke City Area. 2nd & rev. ed. (Illus.). 120p. pap. 5.95 (ISBN 0-9608876-0-1). Cooke City.

Glidewell, John C. Choice Points: Essays on the Emotional Problems of Living with People. 1970. 11.00x o.p. (ISBN 0-262-07038-3); pap. 3.95x o.p. (ISBN 0-262-57026-2). MIT Pr.

Gliedman, John & Roth, William. The Unexpected Minority: Handicapped Children in America. LC 79-1823. 1979. 17.95 o.p. (ISBN 0-15-192845-2). HarBraceJ.

Gligoric, S. & Sokolov, V. The Sicilian Defence, Bk. I. 1972. pap. 10.95 (ISBN 0-08-017276-8). Pergamon.

Glimm, J., et al. Lectures in Modern Analysis & Applications - Two. Taam, C. T., ed. LC 76-94096. (Lecture Notes in Mathematics: Vol. 140). 1970. pap. 10.70 o.p. (ISBN 0-387-04929-0). Springer-Verlag.

Glimm, James Y. Flatlanders & Ridgerunners: Folktales from the Mountains of Northern Pennsylvania. LC 82-10895. (Illus.). 240p. 1983. 11.95 (ISBN 0-8229-3471-X); pap. 5.95 (ISBN 0-8229-5345-5). U of Pittsburgh Pr.

Glines, Carroll V. Jimmy Doolittle: Master of the Calculated Risk. 208p. 1980. pap. 4.95 o.p. (ISBN 0-442-23102-4). Van Nos Reinhold.

Glissant, Edouard. Monsieur Toussaint: A Play. Foster, Joseph G. & Franklin, Barbara A., trs. from Fr. LC 82-51665. (Illus.). 1982. 16.00x (ISBN 0-89410-128-5); pap. 8.00x (ISBN 0-89410-129-3). Three Continents.

Glisson, Jerry & Taylor, Jack R. The Church in a Storm. (Orig.). 1983. pap. 5.95. Broadman.

Glisson, O., jt. auth. see Tate, M.

Glisson, Oris, jt. auth. see Tate, Mildred T.

Glittenberg, Jody, jt. auth. see Deyoung, Carol.

Gloag, John. Enjoying Architecture. (Illus.). 1965. cased 7.95 o.p. (ISBN 0-85362-010-5, Oriel); pap. 2.95 o.p. (ISBN 0-85362-011-3). Routledge & Kegan.

Gloag, Paton J. A Critical & Exegetical Commentary on the Acts of the Apostles, 2 vols. 1979. 29.95 (ISBN 0-86524-006-X, 4402). Klock & Klock.

Glob, P. V. The Bog People: Iron-Age Man Preserved. Bruce-Mitford, R. L., tr. LC 69-20391. (Illus.). 200p. 1969. 22.50 (ISBN 0-8014-0492-4). Cornell U Pr.

Globe, Leah A., jt. auth. see Eisenberg, A.

Globus, Helen, jt. auth. see Globus, Leo.

Globus, Leo & Globus, Helen. The Wee Wisdom Record. 1983. 6.50 (ISBN 0-686-84074-7). Intl Gen Semantics.

Glock, Charles & Bellah, Robert N., eds. The New Religious Consciousness. 391p. 25.00 (ISBN 0-686-95181-6); pap. 6.95 (ISBN 0-686-99471-X). ADL.

Glock, Charles Y. & Stark, Rodney. Christian Beliefs & Anti-Semitism. (Patterns of American Prejudice Ser.). 266p. Repr. 4.00 (ISBN 0-686-95108-5). ADL.

Glock, Charles Y., jt. auth. see Quinley, Harold E.

Glock, Charles Y., jt. auth. see Stark, Rodney.

Glock, Charles Y., ed. Survey Research in the Social Sciences. LC 67-25911. 544p. 1967. 10.00x (ISBN 0-87154-331-1). Russell Sage.

Glock, Charles Y., jt. auth. see Apostle, Richard A.

Glock, Marvin D. & Bender, David. Probe. abridged ed. (Communication Skills Ser.). 1978. pap. text ed. 8.95x (ISBN 0-675-08373-7); suppl. material avail.; 1 set 80.00 (ISBN 0-675-08372-9). Merrill.

Glock, Marvin D. & Bender, David S. Probe: College Developmental Reading. 2nd ed. 1980. text ed. 11.95 (ISBN 0-675-08144-0, C57). Additional supplements may be obtained from publisher. Merrill.

Gloge, Detlef. Optical Fiber Technology. LC 75-23777. 1976. 31.95 (ISBN 0-87942-061-8). Inst Electrical.

Glogowski, Maryruth P., jt. ed. see Provan, Jill.

Gloor, P see International Symposium on Neurophysiology.

Glorfeld. The Short Story. 1967. pap. text ed. 5.95 (ISBN 0-675-09770-3). Merrill.

Glorig, A., jt. auth. see Gerwin, K. S.

Glorig, Aram, ed. Audiometry: Principles & Practices. LC 77-10869. 286p. 1977. lib. bdg. 18.00 (ISBN 0-88275-604-4). Krieger.

Glorioso, Robert M. & Hill, F. S., Jr. Introduction to Engineering. (Illus.). 448p. 1975. ref. ed. 27.95x (ISBN 0-13-482398-2). P-H.

Glossary of the Petroleum Industry. English-Spanish. 2nd ed. (Glossary of the Petroleum Industry Ser.). 378p. 21.95x (ISBN 0-87814-194-4). Pennwell Books Division.

Glossbrenner, Alfred. The Complete Handbook of Personal Computer Communications. 1983. pap. 14.95 (ISBN 0-312-15718-5). St Martin.

Glossop, Ronald J. Confronting War. LC 82-23950. 250p. 1983. lib. bdg. 19.95x (ISBN 0-89950-073-0). McFarland & Co.

Gloster, Jesse E. Minority Economic, Political & Social Development. LC 78-62738. 1978. pap. text ed. 19.00 (ISBN 0-8191-0593-7). U Pr of Amer.

Glotz, G. The Aegean Civilization. Dobie, M. R. & Riley, E. M., trs. (History of Civilization Ser.). (Illus.). 1968. Repr. of 1925 ed. 29.95x (ISBN 0-7100-6106-4). Routledge & Kegan.

Glotzer, Arline. Monarch's Complete Guide to Law Schools. 192p. 1982. pap. 6.95 o.p. (ISBN 0-671-09255-3). Messner.

Glotzer, Arline & Levy, Valerie. Lovejoy's Guide to Graduate Business Schools. (Orig.). 1983. pap. 6.95 (ISBN 0-671-44884-6). Monarch Pr.

Glotzhober, et al. Investigations Into Biology. 2.95 (ISBN 0-310-29511-4); students ed. 5.95 (ISBN 0-310-29521-1). Zondervan.

Glovach, L. Little Witch's Book of Games. 1979. pap. 1.95 o.p. (ISBN 0-13-537886-9). P-H.

Glovach, Linda. The Little Witch's Book of Yoga. LC 79-15556. (Illus.). (gr. 2-5). 1979. text ed. 7.95 o.p. (ISBN 0-13-538033-2). P-H.

--The Little Witch's Spring Holiday Book. (Illus.). 48p. (ps-4). 8.95 (ISBN 0-13-538108-8). P-H.

Glover, Albert. Next. 105p. (Orig.). 1982. 7.95x (ISBN 0-9607948-0-8). Burn Bks.

Glover, B. & Schuder, P. The Competitive Runner's Handbook. 1983. 15.75 (ISBN 0-670-23365-X). Viking Pr.

Glover, Bob & Schuder, Pete. The Competitive Runner's Handbook: The Complete Training Program for All Distance Running. 488p. 1983. pap. 7.95 (ISBN 0-14-046565-0). Penguin.

Glover, Bob & Shepherd, Jack. The Runner's Handbook Training Diary. (Handbooks Ser.). 1978. pap. 4.95 (ISBN 0-14-046373-9). Penguin.

Glover, D. M. Genetic Engineering. (Outline Studies in Biology). 1980. pap. 6.50x (ISBN 0-412-16170-2, Pub. by Chapman & Hall). Methuen Inc.

Glover, Dennis. Hot Water Sailor & Landlubber Ho. (Illus.). 248p. 1982. 15.95 (ISBN 0-00-216985-1, Pub. by W Collins Australia). Intl Schol Bk Serv.

Glover, Donald E. C. S. Lewis: The Art of Enchantment. LC 80-21421. xii, 235p. 1981. 16.95x (ISBN 0-8214-0566-7, 82-83582); pap. 7.95x (ISBN 0-8214-0609-4). Ohio U Pr.

Glover, Elizabeth. The Gold & Silver Wyre-Drawers. 1979. 65.00x (ISBN 0-686-97113-2, Pub. by Phillimore England). State Mutual Bk.

Glover, Harry. A Standard Guide to Pure Bred Dogs. (Illus.). 1978. 27.95 (ISBN 0-07-023501-5, GB). McGraw.

--Toy Dogs. 1977. 7.50 o.p. (ISBN 0-7153-7338-2). David & Charles.

Glover, J. C. B., ed. The Philosophy of Mind. (Oxford Readings in Philosophy). 1977. pap. text ed. 8.95x (ISBN 0-19-875038-2). Oxford U Pr.

Glover, J. D. The Attack on Big Business. 1954. 21.50 o.p. (ISBN 0-08-022304-4). Pergamon.

Glover, J. M., jt. auth. see Brookfield, Charles.

Glover, J. N. Laws of the Turks & Caicos Islands, 8 vols. rev. ed. 1970-80. 327.50 set (ISBN 0-379-12700-8); Vols. 1-3. o.p. Oceana.

Glover, Jane. Cavalli. LC 77-23638. (Illus.). 1978. 25.00 (ISBN 0-312-12546-1). St Martin.

Glover, John A. Becoming a More Creative Person. (Illus.). 256p. 1980. 10.95 o.p. (ISBN 0-13-072132-8, Spec); pap. 5.95 (ISBN 0-13-072124-7). P-H.

Glover, John D. & Simon, Gerald A., eds. The Chief Executives Handbook. LC 75-11387. (Illus.). 1129p. 1976. 45.50 (ISBN 0-87094-104-6). Dow Jones-Irwin.

Glover, John H., ed. see Muller, Herbert W.

Glover, Judith. The Place Names of Kent. 1976. 17.95 o.p. (ISBN 0-7134-3069-9, Pub. by Batsford England). David & Charles.

--The Stallion Man. 256p. 1983. 11.95 (ISBN 0-312-75542-2). St Martin.

Glover, Mary. From Horse & Buggy to the Space Age: Memoirs of a Peace Movement Leader. 100p. 1983. 10.95 (ISBN 0-931494-38-9). Brunswick Pub.

Glover, Michael. Gentleman Volunteer--Letters of George Hennell from the Peninsular War. 1979. 18.95 (ISBN 0-434-29561-2, Pub. by Heinemann). David & Charles.

--The Napoleonic Wars: An Illustrated History. 1979. 32.50 (ISBN 0-7134-1723-4, Pub. by Batsford England). David & Charles.

--The Napoleonic Wars: An Illustrated History 1792-1815. (Illus.). 240p. 1982. pap. 14.95 (ISBN 0-88254-710-0). Hippocrene Bks.

Glover, Robert W. Local Employment Policy in a High-Growth Economy: Matching Training & Jobs in Austin, Texas. (Policy Project Research Ser.: No. 49). 33p. 1982. 5.50 (ISBN 0-89940-652-1). LBJ Sch Public Affairs.

--Minority Enterprise in Construction. LC 77-10650. (Praeger Special Studies). 26.95 o.p. (ISBN 0-275-24070-3). Praeger.

Glover, Susanne & Grewe, Georgeann. Bone up on Book Reports. (gr. 3-8). 1981. 5.95 (ISBN 0-86653-001-0, GA228). Good Apple.

Glover, Warren. Sememic & Grammatical Structures in Gurung. (SIL Linguistics and Related Fields Ser: No. 49). 232p. 1974. 8.75x (ISBN 0-88312-059-3); microfiche 3.00x (ISBN 0-88312-459-9). Summer Inst Ling.

Glowinski & Lions, eds. Computing Methods in Applied Sciences & Engineering. 1980. 70.25 (ISBN 0-444-86008-8). Elsevier.

Glowinski, R. & Lions, J. L., eds. Computing Methods in Applied Sciences & Engineering V: Proceedings of the Fifth International Symposium, Versailles, France, December 14-18, 1981, Vol. 5. 626p. 1982. 102.25 (ISBN 0-444-86450-4). Elsevier.

Glowinski, R., et al. Numerical Analysis of Variational Inequations. (Studies in Mathematics & Its Applications: Vol. 8). 1981. 95.75 (ISBN 0-444-86199-8). Elsevier.

--Energy Methods in Finite Element Analysis. LC 78-13642. (Numerical Methods in Engineering Ser.). 361p. 1979. 67.00x (ISBN 0-471-99723-4, Pub. by Wiley-Interscience). Wiley.

Glubb, John. The Rise & Fall of Empires. 192p. 1983. 40.00x (ISBN 0-85683-056-9, Pub. by Shepheard-Walwyn England). State Mutual Bk.

Glubb, John B. The Story of the Arab Legion. LC 76-7060. (The Middle East in the 20th Century Ser.). 1976. Repr. of 1948 ed. lib. bdg. 42.50 (ISBN 0-306-70763-2). Da Capo.

Glubetich, Dave. Double Your Money in Real Estate Every Two Years. Moretz, Judy, ed. LC 80-142122. (Illus.). 232p. 1980. 13.95 (ISBN 0-9601530-4-7, Dist by Har-Row). Impact Pub.

--How to Grow a Moneytree. 2nd ed. Wigginton, Dave, ed. LC 81-80569. 137p. 1981. pap. 8.95 (ISBN 0-9601530-0-4, Dist. by Har-Row). Impact Pub.

--The Monopoly Game. 4th ed. Wigginton, Dave, ed. LC 75-20848. 1979. pap. 8.95 (ISBN 0-9601530-2-0, Dist. by Har-Row). Impact Pub.

Glubok, Shirley. Dolls, Dolls, Dolls. LC 73-93559. (Picture Bk). (Illus.). 64p. (gr. 2 up). 1975. 5.95 o.s.i. (ISBN 0-695-80483-9); lib. ed. 5.97 o.s.i. (ISBN 0-695-40483-0). Follett.

Glubok, Shirley, jt. auth. see Tamarin, Alfred.

Gluck, Cellin & Takeda, Yasushi, eds. You Mean to Say You Still Don't Know Who We Are? Seven Kabuki Plays. Unno, Mitsuko, tr. from Japanese. 260p. 1976. pap. 7.95 (ISBN 0-8048-1367-1, Pub. by Personally Oriental Ltd). C E Tuttle.

Gluck, Elsie. John Mitchell, Miner: Labor's Bargain with the Gilded Age. LC 69-13909. Repr. of 1929 ed. lib. bdg. 17.25x (ISBN 0-8371-2170-1, GLJM). Greenwood.

Gluck, Louise. Firstborn. LC 81-5454. (American Poetry Ser.). 53p. 1983. pap. 5.95 (ISBN 0-912946-93-8). Ecco Pr.

Gluck, Myke. Mechanics for Gymnastics Coaching: Tools for Skill Analysis. (Illus.). 176p. 1982. 29.75x (ISBN 0-398-04559-3). C C Thomas.

Gluck, Peter R. & Meister, Richard J. Cities in Transition: Social Changes & Institutional Responses in Urban Development. 1979. 12.95 o.p. (ISBN 0-531-05409-8); pap. 6.95 o.p. (ISBN 0-531-05623-6). Watts.

Gluck, Robert. Elements of a Coffee Service. LC 82-20143. 106p. (Orig.). 1983. pap. 5.95 (ISBN 0-87704-058-3). Four Seasons Foun.

Gluck, Robert & Boone, Bruce, trs. from Fr. La Fontaine. LC 81-90653. (Illus.). 72p. 1981. pap. 5.00 (ISBN 0-9607630-0-7). Black Star.

Gluckman, Janet. Rite of the Dragon. Stine, Hank, ed. LC 81-5094. 1981. text ed. 9.95 o.p. (ISBN 0-89865-101-8). Donning Co.

Gluckman, Max, ed. The Allocation of Responsibility. 321p. 1972. text ed. 19.50x o.p. (ISBN 0-7190-0491-8). Humanities.

Glucksman, Miriam. Structuralist Analysis in Contemporary Social Thought: A Comparison of the Theories of Claude Levi-Strauss & Louis Althusser. (International Library of Sociology). 1974. 20.00 (ISBN 0-7100-7773-4). Routledge & Kegan.

Glue, David, ed. The Garden Bird Book. 224p. 1982. 39.00x (ISBN 0-333-33151-6, Pub. by Macmillan England). State Mutual Bk.

Glueck, Eleanor, jt. auth. see Glueck, Sheldon.

Glueck, Nelson. The Other Side of the Jordan. 260p. 1970. pap. text ed. 10.00x (ISBN 0-89757-000-6, Am Sch Orient Res). Eisenbrauns.

Glueck, Sheldon & Glueck, Eleanor. Family Enviroment & Delinquency. (International Library of Sociology & Social Reconstruction Ser.). 328p. 1982. Repr. of 1962 ed. lib. bdg. 35.00x (ISBN 0-8377-0616-5). Rothman.

Glueck, William & Snyder, Neil. Readings in Business Policy & Strategy from Business Week. 2nd ed. (Management Ser.). (Illus.). 336p. 1982. 12.95x (ISBN 0-07-059540-2). McGraw.

Glueck, William F. Business Policy & Strategic Management. 3rd ed. (Management Ser.). (Illus.). 1980. text ed. 25.95x (ISBN 0-07-023519-8, C). McGraw.

--Readings in Business Policy from Business Week. (Management Ser.). (Illus.). 1978. pap. text ed. 13.95 (ISBN 0-07-023516-3, C). McGraw.

--Strategic Management & Business Policy. (Management Ser.). (Illus.). 288p. 1980. text ed. 14.95 (ISBN 0-07-023506-6, C). McGraw.

Glueck, William F., jt. auth. see Bedeian, Arthur G.

Glueck, William G. Management. 2nd ed. 640p. 1980. text ed. 21.95 o.p. (ISBN 0-03-050906-8). Dryden Pr.

Glueck, William G., et al. The Managerial Experience. 3rd ed. 704p. 1983. 10.95 (ISBN 0-03-050916-5). Dryden Pr.

Glusker, Irwin, ed. see Morris, Willie.

Glusker, Jenny P. & Trueblood, Kenneth N. Crystal Structure Analysis: A Primer. (Illus.). 1972. 19.95x (ISBN 0-19-501425-1); pap. 7.95x (ISBN 0-19-501426-X). Oxford U Pr.

Glusker, Jenny P., ed. Structural Crystallography in Chemistry & Biology. LC 80-13858. (Benchmark Papers in Physical Chemistry & Chemical Physics: Vol. 4). 421p. 1981. 50.00 (ISBN 0-87933-368-5). Hutchinson Ross.

Gluski, J. Proverbs: English, French, German, Italian, Spanish, Russian. 1971. 47.00 (ISBN 0-444-40904-1). Elsevier.

Glut, Donald F., jt. auth. see Czerkas, Sylvia M.

Gluyas, Constance. My Lady Benbrook. 1979. pap. 2.50 o.p. (ISBN 0-446-91124-0). Warner Bks.

--Savage Eden. 1976. pap. 2.50 (ISBN 0-451-09285-6, E9285, Sig). NAL.

Gluzman, Yakov, ed. Eukaryotic Viral Vectors. LC 82-4216. 221p. 35.00x (ISBN 0-87969-153-0). Cold Spring Harbor.

Glyn-Jones, Anne. Small Firms in a Country Town. 88p. 1982. 30.00x (ISBN 0-85989-138-0, Pub. by Exeter Univ England). State Mutual Bk.

Glyn-Jones, Kenneth, ed. see Barker, Edmund S.

Glynn, James A., jt. auth. see Stewart, Elbert W.

Glynn, Jeanne D. Answer Me, Answer Me. 1970. 4.95 o.p. (ISBN 0-685-07608-3, 80260). Glencoe.

Glynn, Joseph. The Eternal Mystic: St. Teresa of Avila, the First Woman Doctor of the Church. 271p. 1982. 7.95 (ISBN 0-533-05407-9). Vantage.

Glynn, L. E. & Steward, M. W. Immunochemistry: An Advanced Textbook. LC 77-1630. 628p. 1977. 121.00x (ISBN 0-471-99508-8, Pub. by Wiley-Interscience). Wiley.

--Structure & Function of Antibodies. 306p. 1981. 15.95 (ISBN 0-471-27917-X, Pub. by Wiley-Interscience). Wiley.

Glynn, L. E., ed. Tissue Repair & Regeneration. (Handbook of Inflammation: Vol. 3). 1981. 128.50 (ISBN 0-444-80278-9). Elsevier.

Glynn, L. E. & Steward, M. W., eds. Antibody Production. LC 80-41378. 231p. 1981. 14.95 (ISBN 0-471-27916-1, Pub. by Wiley-Interscience). Wiley.

Gmehling, et al, eds. Vapor-Liquid Equilibrium Data Collection Tables & Diagrams of Data for Binary & Multicomponent Mixtures up to Moderate Pressures; Constants of Correlation Equations for Computer Use: Part 2b: Organic Hydroxy Compounds: Alcohols & Phenols. LC 79-670289. (Dechema Chemistry Ser.: Vol. 1). 1978. text ed. 100.00x (ISBN 3-921567-12-2, Pub. by Dechema Germany). Scholium Intl.

Gmehling, J. & Inken, U. Vapor-Liquid Equilibrium Data Collection: Volume I, Part 1A - Supplement 1 to Aqueous Organic Systems. 1981. lib. bdg. 120.00x (ISBN 3-921-56733-5, Pub. by Dechema Germany). Scholium Intl.

Gmehling, J. & Onken, U. Vapor-Liquid Equilbrium Data Collection Part 2d, Organic Hydroxy Compounds: Alcohols & Phenols (Supplement 2) (Dechema Chemistry Data Ser.: Vol. I). (Illus.). 800p. 1982. 145.00 (ISBN 0-686-43226-6, Pub. by Dechema Germany). Scholium Intl.

--Vapor-Liquid Equilibrium Data Collection: Aqueous Organic Systems, Vol. I, Pt. I. rev. ed. Behrens, D. & Eckermann, R., eds. (Dechema Chemistry Data Ser.). 698p. 1981. text ed. 120.00x (ISBN 3-921567-01-7, Pub. by Dechema Germany). Scholium Intl.

--Vapor-Liquid Equilibrium Data Collection Part 5 Carboxylic Acids, Anhydrides, Esters. (Vol. I). (Illus.). 715p. 1982. 155.00x (ISBN 0-686-43231-2, Pub. by Dechema Germany). Scholium Intl.

--Vapor-Liquid Equilibrium Data Collection Tables & Diagrams of Data for Binary & Multicomponent Mixtures up to Moderate Pressures; Constants of Correlation Equations for Computer Use: Part 2a: Organic Hydroxy Compounds: Alcohols, No. 1. LC 79-670289. (Dechema Chemistry Data Ser.). 1978. text ed. 105.00x (ISBN 3-921567-09-2). Scholium Intl.

--Vapor-Liquid Equilibrium Data Collection Tables & Diagrams of Data for Binary & Multicomponent Mixtures up to Moderate Organic Hydroxy Compounds: Alcohols & Phenols, Vol. I, Pt. 2b. (Dechema Chemistry Data Ser.). 1979. text ed. 100.00x (ISBN 3-921567-01-7). Scholium Intl.

--Vapor-Liquid Equilibrium Data Collection: Volume I, Part 2C-Organic Hydroxy Compounds: Alcohols (Supplement 1) (Dechema Chemistry Data Ser.). (Illus.). 698p. 1982. lib. bdg. 110.00x (ISBN 3-921-56729-7). Scholium Intl.

Gmehling, J., et al. Aromatic Hydrocarbons: Vol. I, Pt. 7, Vapor-Liquid Equilibrium Data Collection. Behrens, D. & Eckermann, R., eds. (Dechema Chemistry Data Ser.). 564p. 1980. text ed. 112.00x (ISBN 3-9215-6723-8, Pub. by Dechema Germany). Scholium Intl.

--Vapor-Liquid Equilibrium Data Collection: Aldehydes, Ketones, Ethers, Vol. 1, Parts 3 & 4. Behrens, Dieter & Eckermann, Reiner, eds. LC 79-670289. (Dechema Chemistry Ser.). (Illus.). 1979. lib. bdg. 120.00x (ISBN 3-921-56714-9, Pub by Dechema Germany). Scholium Intl.

Gnagey, William J. Motivating Classroom Discipline. 148p. 1981. pap. text ed. 8.95 (ISBN 0-02-344140-2). Macmillan.

Gnaiger, E. & Forstner, H., eds. Polarographic Oxygen Sensors: Aquatic & Physiological Applications. (Illus.). 370p. 1983. 50.00 (ISBN 0-387-11654-0). Springer-Verlag.

Gnanadesikan, Ramanathan. Methods for Statistical Data Analysis of Multivariate Observations. LC 76-14994. (Probability & Mathematical Statics Ser.). 1977. 35.95x (ISBN 0-471-30845-5, Pub. by Wiley-Interscience). Wiley.

Gnecco, Donald. Success Manual: Perspectives & Processes for Elementary Education. LC 76-11925. (Illus.). 1976. pap. text ed. 4.75x (ISBN 0-685-70070-4). Leornian Educ & Res.

Gnedenko, B. V. & Kolmogorov, A. N. Limit Distributions for Sums of Independent Random Variables. rev. ed. 1968. 22.50 (ISBN 0-201-02420-9, Adv Bk Prog). A-W.

Gnielinski, Stefan Von see Von Gnielinski, Stefan.

Gnirk, P. F., jt. auth. see Lindblom, U. E.

Gnudi, Cesare, jt. ed. see Dupont, Jacques.

Gnugnoli, Guiliano, jt. auth. see Maisel, Herbert.

Goals, Guidelines & Standards Committee & Public Library Association. The Public Library Mission Statement & Its Imperatives for Service. 24p. 1979. pap. 2.50 (ISBN 0-8389-3233-9). ALA.

Goaman, Muriel. Fun with Travel. 1973. 8.75 o.p. (ISBN 0-7207-0452-9). Transatlantic.

Goanatilake, Susantha. Crippled Minds: An Exploration into Colonial Culture! 1982. 39.00x (ISBN 0-686-94059-8, Pub. by Garlandfold England). State Mutual Bk.

Goates, J. Rex, et al. General Chemistry: Theory & Description. 788p. 1981. text ed. 25.95 (ISBN 0-15-529535-7, HC); solutions manual avail. 3.95 (ISBN 0-15-529536-5). HarBraceJ.

Goaz, Paul W. & White, Stuart C. Oral Radiology: Principles & Interpretation. LC 81-18802. (Illus.). 695p. 1982. text ed. 34.95 (ISBN 0-8016-1886-X). Mosby.

Goaz, Paul W., jt. auth. see Wood, Norman K.

Gobbett, D. J. & Hutchinson, C. S. Geology of the Mulny Peninsula. 438p. 1973. 84.50x o.p. (ISBN 0-471-30850-1, Pub. by Wiley-Interscience). Wiley.

Go-Belmonte, Betty, ed. Philippines Yearbook 1979: Internationally Recognized Chronicler of Philippine Progress. LC 51-23935. Orig. Title: The Fookien Times Yearbook. (Illus.). 384p. (Orig.). 1979. pap. 20.00x o.p. (ISBN 0-8002-2447-7). Intl Pubns Serv.

Gobet, Nicolas. Les Anciens Mineralogietes Du Royaume De France. Repr. of 1779 ed. 259.00 o.p. (ISBN 0-8287-0379-5). Clearwater Pub.

Gobineau, Arthur De see De Gobineau, Arthur.

Goble, Alfred T. & Baker, D. K. Elements of Modern Physics. 2nd ed. (Illus.). 546p. 1971. 27.50x (ISBN 0-471-06755-5). Wiley.

Goble, Dorothy, jt. auth. see Goble, Paul.

Goble, E. A., et al. Rehabilitation of the Severely Disabled-1: Evaluation of a Disabled Living Unit. 268p. 1971. 15.95 o.p. (ISBN 0-407-38510-X). Butterworth.

Goble, Frank. Beyond Failure: How to Cure a Neurotic Society. LC 77-77328. 1977. 10.00 (ISBN 0-916054-48-9, Caroline Hse); pap. 4.95 (ISBN 0-916054-51-9, Caroline Hse). Green Hill.

--The Third Force: The Psychology of Abraham Maslow. 224p. pap. 2.95 o.s.i. (ISBN 0-671-42174-3). WSP.

Goble, Lou. The Kalevide. 1982. pap. 3.95 (ISBN 0-553-22531-6). Bantam.

Goble, Paul. The Gift of the Sacred Dog. LC 80-15843. (Illus.). 32p. (gr. k-4). 1980. 10.95 (ISBN 0-02-736560-3). Bradbury Pr.

--The Girl Who Loved Wild Horses. LC 77-20500. 32p. (gr. k-3). 1978. 10.95 (ISBN 0-02-736570-0). Bradbury Pr.

--Star Boy. (Illus.). 32p. (gr. k-3). 1983. 12.95 (ISBN 0-02-722660-3). Bradbury Pr.

Goble, Paul & Goble, Dorothy. Friendly Wolf. LC 74-77664. (Illus.). 32p. (gr. 1-3). 1975. 9.95 (ISBN 0-02-736540-9). Bradbury Pr.

--Lone Bull's Horse Raid. LC 73-76546. (Illus.). 64p. (gr. 4-6). 1973. 11.95 (ISBN 0-02-736580-8). Bradbury Pr.

Goble, Phillip. The Rabbi from Tarsus. 112p. 1981. pap. 4.95 (ISBN 0-8423-5124-8). Tyndale.

Gobran, Alfonse. Beginning Algebra. 3rd ed. (Math Ser.). 400p. 1982. text ed. write for info. (ISBN 0-87150-349-2, 2741). Prindle.

Goc, Michael. The Bud Norton Story. (Illus.). 168p. 1982. pap. 12.95 (ISBN 0-939398-02-8). Fox River.

Gochberg, Donald S. Classics of Western Thought: The Twentieth Century, Vol. IV. Greer, Thomas H., ed. 660p. 1980. pap. text ed. 10.95 (ISBN 0-15-507681-7, HC). HarBraceJ.

Gochros, Harvey L. & Gochros, Jean S., eds. The Sexually Oppressed. 14.95 o.s.i. (ISBN 0-695-81167-3). Follett.

Gochros, Harvey L. & Schultz, Leroy G., eds. Human Sexuality & Social Work. LC 71-129436. 1972. 9.95 o.s.i. (ISBN 0-8096-1808-7, Assn Pr). Follett.

Gochros, Jean S., jt. ed. see Gochros, Harvey L.

Gocke, B. W. & Payton, George T. Police Sergeants Manual. 5th ed. LC 71-122285. 1972. 16.00x (ISBN 0-910874-20-4). Legal Bk Co.

Gocke, David J., jt. auth. see Krugman, Saul.

Gockel, Herman W. Answer to Anxiety. 1965. pap. 4.95 (ISBN 0-570-03704-2, 12-2254). Concordia.

Gockel, Herman W. & Saleska, Edward J., eds. Child's Garden of Prayer. (Illus.). (gr. k-2). 1981. pap. 1.10 (ISBN 0-570-03412-4, 56-1016). Concordia.

Godaert, P. La Lettre D'Affaires. Le Courrier Quotidien. 161p. (Fr.). 1980. pap. 14.95 (ISBN 0-686-97424-7, M-9021). French & Eur.

Godard, Jean-Luc. Petit Soldat. (Film Scripts-Modern Ser.). 1970. pap. 1.95 o.p. (ISBN 0-671-20682-6, Touchstone Bks). S&S.

--Pierrot Le Fou. LC 75-92178. (Film Scripts Modern Ser). 1970. pap. 2.25 o.p. (ISBN 0-671-20448-3, Touchstone Bks). S&S.

Godber, Joyce. The Story of Bedford. 160p. 1982. 35.00x (ISBN 0-900804-24-6, Pub. by White Crescent England). State Mutual Bk.

Godbey, Geoffrey, et al. Triples: A New Tennis Game. (Illus.). 22p. (Orig.). 1980. pap. 2.98x (ISBN 0-910251-01-0). Venture Pub PA.

Godbillon, C. Dynamical Systems on Surfaces. (Univeritext Ser.). (Illus.). 201p. 1983. pap. 19.80 (ISBN 0-387-11645-1). Springer-Verlag.

Godbold, E. Stanley & Woody, Robert H. Christopher Gadsden & the American Revolution. LC 82-6915. (Illus.). 316p. 1983. text ed. 24.95x (ISBN 0-87049-362-0); pap. text ed. 12.95x (ISBN 0-87049-363-9). U of Tenn Pr.

Goddad, Don, ed. Watercolors & Drawings of the French Impressionists & Their Parisian Contemporaries. Korneitchouk, Ursula, tr. from Ger. LC 81-20558. 1982. pap. text ed. 60.00 (ISBN 0-8109-1103-5). Abrams.

Goddard, jt. auth. see Parish.

Goddard, A. J., ed. see International Seminar, Imperial College of Science & Technology, UK.

Goddard, Arthur, ed. Harry Elmer Barnes, Learned Crusader: The New History in Action. LC 68-57017. (Illus.). 1968. 19.50 (ISBN 0-87926-002-5). R Myles.

Goddard, Harold C. Studies in New England Transcendentalism. 1960. text ed. 15.00x (ISBN 0-391-00599-5). Humanities.

Goddard, John B. Office Location in Urban & Regional Development. (Theory & Practice in Geography Ser.). (Illus.). 1975. pap. text ed. 5.95x o.p. (ISBN 0-19-874033-6). Oxford U Pr.

Goddard, John L. California Landlord Tenant Law & Procedure. 6th ed. LC 76-53526. 1977. 24.00 (ISBN 0-910874-39-5). Legal Bk Co.

Goddard, K. Crime Scene Investigation. 1977. 19.95 (ISBN 0-87909-172-X); solns. manual avail. (ISBN 0-87909-165-7). Reston.

Godden, E. & Malnic, J. Rock Paintings of Aboriginal Australia. (Illus.). 1982. 50.00x (ISBN 0-589-50323-5, Pub by Reed Australia). Humanities.

Godden, Geoffrey. Godden's Guide to English Porcelain. (Illus.). 286p. 1980. text ed. 31.50x (ISBN 0-686-61566-2). Humanities.

Godden, Geoffrey A. British Porcelain: An Illustrated Guide. (Illus.). 456p. 1974. 15.00 o.p. (ISBN 0-517-51305-6, C N Potter Bks). Crown.

--British Pottery: An Illustrated Guide. (Illus.). 464p. 1975. 15.00 (ISBN 0-517-51868-6, C N Potter Bks). Crown.

--Encyclopedia of British Pottery & Porcelain Marks. 1970. 15.00 o.p. (ISBN 0-517-09729-X). Crown.

Godden, J., jt. ed. see Sink, L.

Godden, Malcolm, ed. see AElfric.

Godden, Rumer. Doll's House. (Puffin Story Books). 1976. pap. 2.95 o.p. (ISBN 0-14-030942-X, Puffin). Penguin.

Godden, Rumer, tr. see De Gasztold, Carmen B.

Gode, Alexander, tr. see Petersen, Carol.

Godefroy, Vincent. The Dramatic Genius of Verdi: Studies of Selected Operas, Vol. 1. LC 75-13981. 287p. 1976. 11.95 o.p. (ISBN 0-312-21945-8). St Martin.

Godelier, M. Perspectives in Marxist Anthropology. Brain, R., tr. LC 76-11081. (Studies in Social Anthropology: No. 18). (Illus.). 1977. 37.50 (ISBN 0-521-21311-8); pap. 10.95 (ISBN 0-521-29098-8). Cambridge U Pr.

Goden, D. Pest Slugs & Snails: Biology & Control. Gruber, S., tr. from Ger. (Illus.). 470p. 1983. 71.00 (ISBN 0-387-11894-2). Springer-Verlag.

Godey, John. The Snake. LC 78-1305. 1978. 8.95 o.p. (ISBN 0-399-12184-6). Putnam Pub Group.

--The Talisman. LC 75-44148. 1976. 8.95 o.p. (ISBN 0-399-11696-6). Putnam Pub Group.

Godey's Lady's Book & Peterson's Magazine. Victorian Needlepoint Designs. LC 74-24489. (Illus.). 48p. 1975. pap. 2.75 (ISBN 0-486-23163-1). Dover.

Godfraind. Cell Membrane in Function & Dysformation. 1981. 80.50 (ISBN 0-444-80316-5). Elsevier.

Godfraind, T. & Albertini, A., eds. Calcium Modulators: Proceedings of the International Symposium on Calcium Modulators, Venice, June 17-18, 1982. (Giovanni Lorenzini Foundation Ser.: Vol. 15). 380p. 1982. 68.00 (ISBN 0-444-80464-1, Biomedical Pr). Elsevier.

Godfrey & Chang. The Telidon Book. 1982. text ed. 39.95 (ISBN 0-8359-7548-7). Reston.

Godfrey Cave Associates. Identification Guide to Plants & Fish for Your Garden Pond. 1978. 6.95 (ISBN 0-906223-02-4). Palmetto Pub.

Godfrey, Dave & Parkhill, Douglas. Gutenberg Two: The New Electronics & Social Change. 2nd rev. ed. 224p. 1980. 10.95 (ISBN 0-686-98075-1). Telecom Lib.

Godfrey, James. Revolutionary Justice: A Study of the Organization, Personnel & Procedure of the Paris Tribunal 1793-1795. (Perspectives in Europen History Ser.: No. 42). vi, 166p. Repr. of 1951 ed. lib. bdg. 17.50x (ISBN 0-87991-640-0). Porcupine Pr.

Godfrey, Laurie R., ed. Scientists Confront Creationism. LC 82-12500. (Illus.). 288p. 1983. 19.00x (ISBN 0-393-01629-3). Norton.

Godfrey, Martin, jt. auth. see Bienefeld, Manfred.

Godfrey, Michael A. A Sierra Club Naturalist's Guide to the Piedmont of Eastern North America. LC 79-22328. (Naturalists Guide Ser.). (Illus.). 432p. 1980. 19.95 (ISBN 0-87156-268-5); pap. 9.95 (ISBN 0-87156-269-3). Sierra.

Godfrey, Robert. Outward Bound: Schools of the Possible. LC 77-82942. (Illus.). 1980. 16.95 o.p. (ISBN 0-385-12270-5, Anch). Doubleday.

Godfrey, Robert S. Appraisal Manual Nineteen Eighty. 320p. 1980. pap. 36.50 (ISBN 0-911950-27-3). Means.

--Appraisal Manual, 1981. 2nd ed. 320p. 1981. pap. 36.50 (ISBN 0-911950-35-4). Means.

--Building Construction Cost Data - 1978. 36th ed. LC 55-20084. 1978. pap. 30.50 (ISBN 0-911950-09-5). Means.

--Building Construction Cost Data 1980. 38th ed. LC 55-20084. 1980. pap. 30.50 (ISBN 0-911950-22-2). Means.

--Building Construction Cost Data, 1981. 39th ed. LC 55-20084. 1981. pap. 30.50 (ISBN 0-911950-29-X). Means.

--Building Construction Cost Data, 1982: Full Size Edition. 40th ed. LC 55-20084. 400p. 1982. pap. 30.50 (ISBN 0-911950-38-9). Means.

--Building Construction Cost Data, 1982: Pocket Edition. 40th ed. 350p. 1982. pap. 27.50 o.p. (ISBN 0-911950-45-1). Means.

--Building Construction Cost Data, 1983. 41st ed. LC 55-20084. 400p. 1983. pap. 30.50 (ISBN 0-911950-50-8). Means.

--Building Systems Cost Guide - 1978. 2nd ed. LC 76-17689. (Illus.). 1978. pap. 37.50 (ISBN 0-911950-10-9). Means.

--Building Systems Cost Guide: 1980. 3rd ed. LC 76-17689. (Illus.). 375p. 1980. pap. 37.50 (ISBN 0-911950-24-9). Means.

--Building Systems Cost Guide, 1982. 7th ed. LC 76-17689. 400p. 1982. pap. 37.50 (ISBN 0-911950-39-7). Means.

--Historical Cost Indexes, 1982. LC 81-642889. 24p. 1982. pap. 10.50 (ISBN 0-911950-44-3). Means.

--Historical Cost Indexes, 1983. 3rd ed. 24p. Date not set. pap. 12.25 (ISBN 0-911950-58-3). Means.

--Labor Rates for the Construction Industry 1980. 7th ed. LC 74-75990. 1980. pap. 31.25 (ISBN 0-911950-25-7). Means.

--Labor Rates for the Construction Industry - 1978. 5th ed. LC 74-75990. 1978. pap. 31.25 (ISBN 0-911950-11-7). Means.

--Labor Rates for the Construction Industry, 1981. 8th ed. LC 74-75990. 300p. 1981. pap. 31.25 (ISBN 0-911950-33-8). Means.

--Labor Rates for the Construction Industry, 1983. 10th ed. LC 74-75990. 300p. 1982. pap. 31.25 (ISBN 0-911950-57-5). Means.

--Means Historical Cost Indexes 1981. (Illus.). 20p. 1981. pap. 12.25 (ISBN 0-911950-37-0). Means.

--Means Site Work Cost Data, 1983. 2nd ed. 300p. 1983. pap. 34.75 (ISBN 0-911950-53-2). Means.

--Means Square Foot Costs, 1983. 4th ed. LC 82-643175. 350p. 1983. pap. 36.50 (ISBN 0-911950-54-0). Means.

--Means Systems Costs, 1983. 8th ed. LC 76-17689. 425p. 1983. pap. 37.50 (ISBN 0-911950-51-6). Means.

--Mechanical & Electrical Cost Data 1978. 1978. pap. 34.75 (ISBN 0-911950-12-5). Means.

--Mechanical & Electrical Cost Data, 1981. 4th ed. LC 79-643328. 400p. 1981. pap. 34.75 (ISBN 0-911950-31-1). Means.

--Mechanical & Electrical Cost Data, 1982. 5th ed. LC 79-643328. 425p. 1982. pap. 34.75 (ISBN 0-911950-41-9). Means.

--Mechanical & Electrical Cost Data, 1983. 6th ed. LC 79-643328. 475p. 1983. pap. 34.75 (ISBN 0-911950-56-7). Means.

--Mechanical & Electrical Cost Date 1979. 2nd ed. 1979. pap. 34.75 o.p. (ISBN 0-911950-16-8). Means.

--Repair & Remodeling Cost Data, 1981. 2nd ed. 325p. 1981. pap. 35.75 (ISBN 0-911950-34-6). Means.

--Repair & Remodeling Cost Data, 1982. 3rd ed. 350p. 1982. pap. 35.75 (ISBN 0-911950-42-7). Means.

--Repair & Remodeling Cost Data, 1983. 4th ed. LC 80-644930. 350p. 1983. pap. 35.75 (ISBN 0-911950-55-9). Means.

--Residential-Light Commercial Cost Data, 1983. 2nd ed. 275p. 1983. pap. 33.25 (ISBN 0-911950-52-4). Means.

Godfrey, Robert S., ed. Building Systems Cost Guide 1979. 4th ed. LC 76-17689. (Illus.). 1979. pap. 37.50 (ISBN 0-911950-17-6). Means.

--Labor Rates for the Construction Industry 1979. 6th ed. LC 74-75990. (Illus.). 1979. pap. 31.25 o.p. (ISBN 0-911950-18-4). Means.

Godfrey, S., jt. ed. see Clark, T. J.

Godfrey, Thomas, ed. Murder for Christmas. LC 82-60904. (Illus.). 480p. 1982. 19.95 (ISBN 0-89296-057-4); ltd. ed. 35.00 (ISBN 0-89296-058-2). Mysterious Pr.

Godin. The Analysis of Tides. 292p. 1982. 70.00x (ISBN 0-85323-441-8, Pub. by Liverpool Univ England). State Mutual Bk.

Godin, Andre. The Psychology of Religious Vocations: Problems of the Religious Life. Wauck, LeRoy A., ed. LC 82-24708. 136p. (Orig.). 1983. lib. bdg. 18.75 (ISBN 0-8191-3007-9); pap. text ed. 8.25 (ISBN 0-8191-3008-7). U Pr of Amer.

Godiwalla, Yezdi H. Strategic Management: Broadening Business Policy. 320p. 1983. 38.95 (ISBN 0-03-059388-3). Praeger.

Godley, Michael R. The Mandarin-Capitalists from Nanyang: Overseas Chinese Enterprise in the Modernisation of China 1893-1911. (Cambridge Studies in Chinese History, Literature & Institutions Ser.). (Illus.). 288p. 1981. 44.50 (ISBN 0-521-23626-6). Cambridge U Pr.

Godman, A. Illustrated Dictionary of Geology. (Illustrated Dictionaries Ser.). (Illus.). 192p. 1982. text ed. 7.95x (ISBN 0-582-55549-3). Longman.

Godman, A. & Payne, E. M. F. Longman Dictionary of Scientific Usage. (Illus.). 1979. pap. text ed. 15.50x (ISBN 0-582-52587-X). Longman.

Godman, Arthur. Barnes & Noble Thesaurus of Chemistry. (Illus.). 256p. (gr. 11-12). 1983. 13.41i (ISBN 0-06-015175-7); pap. 6.68i (ISBN 0-06-463578-3). B&N NY.

--Barnes & Noble Thesaurus of Science. (Illus.). 256p. (gr. 11-12). 1983. 13.41i (ISBN 0-06-015176-5, EH 580); pap. 6.68i (ISBN 0-06-463580-5). B&N NY.

--Illustrated Dictionary of Chemistry. (Illustrated Dictionaries Ser.). (Illus.). 256p. 1982. text ed. 7.95x (ISBN 0-582-55550-7). Longman.

Godman, F. Ducane, ed. see Maudslay, A. P.

Godman, Henry. Supreme Commander. Dudley, Cliff, ed. LC 80-80658. 160p. 1980. pap. 3.95 (ISBN 0-89221-076-1). New Leaf.

Godman, Peter, ed. Alcuin: The Bishops, Kings, & Saints of York. (Medieval Texts Ser.). 336p. 1983. 77.00x (ISBN 0-19-822262-9). Oxford U Pr.

Godman, Stanley, tr. see Blume, Friedrich.

Godnic, Joy, jt. auth. see Stevens, Ron.

Godolphin, F. R., ed. & intro. by. Great Classical Myths. LC 64-10293. 6.95 (ISBN 0-394-60417-2). Modern Lib.

Godow, Annette G. Human Sexuality. LC 81-14031. (Illus.). 669p. 1981. text ed. 18.95 (ISBN 0-8016-1861-4). Mosby.

Godschalk, David R. & Brower, David J. Constitutional Issues of Growth Management. LC 78-71241. 476p. 1979. pap. 20.95 (ISBN 0-918286-16-6). Planners Pr.

Godshalk, William, ed. see Jacobs, Henry.

Godson, Roy & Haseler, Stephen. Eurocommunism: Implications for East & West. LC 78-15475. 1979. 22.50x (ISBN 0-312-26720-7); pap. 8.95 (ISBN 0-312-26721-5). St Martin.

Godson, Roy, ed. Analysis & Estimates. (Intelligence Requirements for the 1980's: Vol. 2). 224p. 1980. pap. 7.50 (ISBN 0-87855-827-6). Transaction Bks.

--Clandestine Collection. (Intelligence Requirements for the Nineteen Eighties Ser.: Vol. 5). 225p. 1982. pap. 8.50 (ISBN 0-87855-831-4). Transaction Bks.

--Elements of Intelligence. (Intelligence Requirements for the 1980's: Vol. I). 124p. (Orig.). 1979. pap. 4.95 (ISBN 0-87855-826-8). Transaction Bks.

Godson, Susan H. Viking of Assault: Admiral John Lesslie Hall, Jr., & Amphibious Warfare. LC 81-43489. (Illus.). 250p. (Orig.). 1982. lib. bdg. 23.00 (ISBN 0-8191-2159-2); pap. text ed. 10.75 (ISBN 0-8191-2160-6). U Pr of Amer.

Godward, Maud B. Chromosomes of the Algae. (Illus.). 1969. 21.95 o.p. (ISBN 0-312-13440-1). St Martin.

Godwin, E. W. Art Furniture. Stansky, Peter & Shewan, Rodney, eds. Incl. Artistic Conservatories. Adams, Maurice. LC 76-18322. (Aesthetic Movement & the Arts & Crafts Movement Ser.: Vol. 14). 1978. Repr. of 1880 ed. lib. bdg. 44.00x o.s.i. (ISBN 0-8240-2463-X). Garland Pub.

Godwin, Gail. Dream Children. 256p. 1983. pap. 3.50 (ISBN 0-380-62406-0, Bard). Avon.

--Glass People. 224p. 1979. pap. 3.50 (ISBN 0-446-30568-5). Warner Bks.

--A Mother & Two Daughters. 608p. 1983. pap. 3.95 (ISBN 0-380-61598-3, 61598-3). Avon.

--The Odd Woman. 432p. 1983. pap. 3.95 o.p. (ISBN 0-446-30569-3, 305693). Warner Bks.

--The Perfectionists. 256p. 1983. pap. 3.50 o.p. (ISBN 0-446-30570-7). Warner Bks.

--Violet Clay. 368p. 1983. pap. 3.95 o.s.i. (ISBN 0-446-30567-7, 305677). Warner Bks.

Godwin, Harry. The Archives of the Peat Bogs. (Illus.). 1981. 55.00 (ISBN 0-521-23784-X). Cambridge U Pr.

--Fenland: Its Ancient Past & Uncertain Future. LC 77-8824. (Illus.). 1978. 34.50 (ISBN 0-521-21768-7). Cambridge U Pr.

Godwin, Parke. A Memory of Lions. 288p. (Orig.). 1983. pap. 2.95 (ISBN 0-425-05824-7). Berkley Pub.

Godwin, Parke, jt. auth. see Kaye, Marvin.

Godwin, Paul H. The Chinese Defense Establishment: Continuity & Change in the 1980s. (Special Studies on East Asia). 175p. 1983. lib. bdg. 17.50x (ISBN 0-86531-568-X). Westview.

Godwin, Terry & Rhys, Chris. The Guinness Book of Rugby Facts & Feats. (Illus.). 258p. 1982. pap. 12.95 (ISBN 0-85112-248-5). Sterling.

Godwin, William. De la Justice Politique. Pollin, Burton R., ed. Constant, Benjamin, tr. LC 72-6661. 1972. 44.50x (ISBN 0-87395-175-1). State U NY Pr.

--Fleetwood: or, The New Man of Feeling, 3 vols. Paulson, Ronald, ed. LC 78-60852. (Novel 1720-1805 Ser.: Vol. 14). 1979. Set. lib. bdg. 93.00 o.s.i. (ISBN 0-8240-3663-8). Garland Pub.

--Four Early Pamphlets, 1783-1784. LC 66-10082. 1966. 40.00x (ISBN 0-8201-1022-1). Schol Facsimiles.

--Imogen: A Pastoral Romance from the Ancient British, 1784. Marken, Jack W., et al, eds. LC 63-18142. (Orig.). 1963. pap. 5.00 o.p. (ISBN 0-87104-094-8). NY Pub Lib.

--Uncollected Writings 1785-1822. LC 68-24208. (Illus.). 1968. 60.00x (ISBN 0-8201-1023-X). Schol Facsimiles.

Goebel, Julius. The Struggle for the Falkland Islands: A Study in Legal & Diplomatic History. 512p. 1982. text ed. 35.00x (ISBN 0-300-02943-8); pap. text ed. 10.95x (ISBN 0-300-02945-4, Y-445). Yale U Pr.

Goebel, Julius & Naughton, T. Raymond. Law Enforcement in Colonial New York. LC 71-108239. (Criminology, Law Enforcement, & Social Problems Ser.: No. 122). 1970. Repr. of 1944 ed. 35.00x (ISBN 0-87585-122-3). Patterson Smith.

Goebel, K. Organopgraphy of Plants, Especially of the Archegoniatae & Spermatophyta, 2 Vols. Balfour, Issac B., tr. from Ger. (Illus.). 977p. 1969. Repr. of 1905 ed. lib. bdg. 35.00 (ISBN 0-02-845320-4). Lubrecht & Cramer.

Goebel, Patrice, ed. see Molnar, Paul J.

Goebel, Paul R. & Miller, Norman G. Handbook of Mortgage Mathematics & Financial Tables. (Illus.). 416p. 1981. 25.95 (ISBN 0-13-380410-0); pap. 11.95 (ISBN 0-686-71764-3). P-H.

Goebel, R., jt. auth. see Bock, Emil.

Goebell, H., ed. European Pancreatic Club: EPC XIV Meeting, Essen Sept.-Oct. 1982, Abstracts. (Journal: Digestion: Vol. 25, No. 1). 80p. 1982. pap. 34.75 (ISBN 3-8055-3633-X). S Karger.

Goebell, H., jt. ed. see Kasper, W.

Goedicke, Patricia. For the Four Corners. 60p. 1976. 3.50 (ISBN 0-87886-074-6). Ithaca Hse.

--The Trail That Turns on Itself. LC 78-7551. 81p. 1978. 3.50 (ISBN 0-87886-094-0). Ithaca Hse.

Goedken, James. I Will Search at Odd Angles. LC 77-71023. (Illus., Orig.). 1977. pap. 1.75 o.p. (ISBN 0-8189-1144-1, 144, Pub. by Alba Bks). Alba.

Goedsche, C. R. & Spann, Meno. Deutsch Fuer Amerikaner. 4th ed. (Illus., Ger.). 1979. text ed. 15.95 (ISBN 0-442-22058-8); tapes 95.00 (ISBN 0-442-22064-2); cassettes 59.95 (ISBN 0-442-22067-7); wkbk 3.50x (ISBN 0-442-22059-6). Van Nos Reinhold.

Goedsche, Curt R., jt. auth. see Spann, Meno.

Goehlert, Robert. Congress & Law-Making: Researching the Legislative Process. LC 79-11554. (Illus.). 168p. 1979. text ed. 19.25 o.p. (ISBN 0-87436-294-6); pap. text ed. 9.85 (ISBN 0-87436-335-7). ABC-Clio.

Goehlert, Robert & Martin, Fenton. The Parliament of Great Britain: A Bibliography. LC 82-47920. (Special Series in Libraries & Librarianship). 240p. 1982. 24.95x (ISBN 0-669-05700-2). Lexington Bks.

Goeke, K. & Reinhard, P. G. Time Dependent Hartree-Fock & Beyond, Bad Honnef, FRG, 1982 Proceedings, Vol. 171. (Lecture Notes in Physics). 426p. 1983. pap. 21.00 (ISBN 0-387-11950-7). Springer-Verlag.

Goel, M. L., jt. auth. see Milbrath, Lester W.

Goeldner, C. R. & Buchman, Tom. NSAA Economic Analysis of North American Ski Areas, 1981-82 Season. 136p. 1982. pap. text ed. 40.00 (ISBN 0-89478-073-5). U Co Busn Res Div.

Goeldner, C. R. & Frechtling, Douglas C. Tourism's Top Twenty. 90p. 1983. pap. text ed. 25.00 (ISBN 0-686-81949-7). U Co Busn Res Div.

Goeller, L. F., Jr. Design Background for Telephone Switching, Vol. IX. 1978. 10.75 (ISBN 0-686-98065-4). Telecom Lib.

Goeller, Lee & Goldstone, Gerald. The Business Communications Review Manual of PBXs. 2nd ed. 350p. 1982. 145.00 (ISBN 0-686-98056-5). Telecom Lib.

Goen, R. L., jt. auth. see Kinderman, E. M.

Goerge, Diana Hume & Nelson, Malcolm A. Epitaph & Icon: A Field Guide to the Old Burying Grounds of Cape Cod, Martha's Vineyard & Nantucket. (Illus.). 128p. (Orig.). 1983. 17.50 (ISBN 0-940160-21-8); pap. 12.50 (ISBN 0-940160-17-X). Parnassus Imprints.

Goergen, Don. The Sexual Celibate. 256p. 1975. 5.00 (ISBN 0-8164-0268-X). Seabury.

Goergen, Donald. The Sexual Celibate. 1979. pap. 4.95 o.p. (ISBN 0-385-14902-6, Im). Doubleday.

Goering, John M. The Best Eight Blocks in Harlem. 1977. pap. text ed. 10.25 (ISBN 0-8191-0261-X). U Pr of Amer.

Goering, T. James. Agricultural Land Settlement. (World Bank Issues Paper). 73p. 1978. pap. 5.00 (ISBN 0-686-36061-3, PP-7801). World Bank.

Goering, Theodore J. & D'Silva, Emmanuel H. Natural Rubber. (Illus.). 66p. (Orig.). 1982. pap. text ed. 5.00 (ISBN 0-8213-0045-8). World Bank.

Goerling, T. James. Tropical Root Crops & Rural Development. (Working Paper: No. 324). 85p. 1979. 5.00 (ISBN 0-686-36081-8, WP-0324). World Bank.

Goertz, Hans J. Profiles of Radical Reformers. 228p. 1982. pap. 9.95x (ISBN 0-8361-1250-4). Herald Pr.

Goertzel, Ted G. Political Society. 1976. pap. 15.50 (ISBN 0-395-30608-6). HM.

Goes. Das Brandopfer. (Easy Readers, C). pap. 3.95 (ISBN 0-88436-057-1, 45274). EMC.

Goessel, M. Nonlinear Time-Discrete Systems: A General Approach by Nonlinear Superposition. (Lecture Notes in Control & Information Science: Vol. 41). 112p. 1983. pap. 8.00 (ISBN 0-387-11914-0). Springer-Verlag.

Goethals, G., jt. auth. see Worchel, S.

Goethals, George W., jt. ed. see Bramson, Leon.

Goethe. Faust, Pt. 1. Prudhoe, J., tr. (Classics of Drama in English Translation Ser.). 1974. pap. 6.50 (ISBN 0-7190-0570-1). Manchester.

--Torquato Tasso. Prudhoe, J., tr. from Ger. (Classic of Drama in English Translation). 1979. pap. 6.50 (ISBN 0-7190-0720-8). Manchester.

Goethe, J. W. von see Von Goethe, J. W.

Goethe, J. W. Von see Von Goethe, J. W. & Steiner, Rudolf.

Goethe, Johann W. Elective Affinities. Mayer, Elizabeth & Bogan, Louise, trs. LC 63-18317. 305p. pap. 5.95 (ISBN 0-89526-956-2). Regnery-Gateway.

--Goethe's Faust. LC 61-5971. pap. 7.50 (ISBN 0-385-03114-9, Anch). Doubleday.

--Goethe's Faust. Fairley, Barker, tr. LC 74-151823. (Illus.). 1970. pap. 6.00 o.p. (ISBN 0-8020-6153-2). U of Toronto Pr.

--Theory of Colours. 1970. pap. 9.95 (ISBN 0-262-57021-1). MIT Pr.

Goethe, Johann W. Von. Faust. Hamlin, Cyrus, ed. Arndt, Walter, tr. from Ger. (Critical Edition Ser). 24p. 1976. pap. text ed. 9.95x (ISBN 0-393-09208-9). Norton.

Goethe, Johann W. Von see Von Goethe, Johann W.

Goethe, Johann W von see Von Goethe, Johann W.

Goethe, Johann W. Von see Von Goethe, Johann W.

Goethe, Johann W. von see Von Goethe, Johann W.

Goethert, Reinhard, jt. auth. see Caminos, Horacio.

Goetinck, Jean F. Essai sur le role des Allemands dans le "Dicctionnaire Historique et Critique". (Etudes Litteraires Francaises Ser.: No. 22). 121p. (Orig., Fr.). 1982. pap. 16.80 (ISBN 3-87808-960-0). Benjamins North Am.

Goetnick, Paul F., jt. ed. see Kelley, Robert O.

Goetsch, David L. Drafting for Structural Systems. 1982. 19.95 (ISBN 0-442-22996-8). Van Nos Reinhold.

--Introduction to Computer Aided Drafting. (Illus.). 272p. 1983. text ed. 20.95 (ISBN 0-13-479287-4). P-H.

Goetschalckx, J. & Rolling, L. Lexicography in the Electronic Age. Date not set. 38.50 (ISBN 0-444-86404-0). Elsevier.

Goetschius, Percy. Counterpoint Applied in the Invention, Fugue & Other Polyphonic Forms. LC 75-109734. (Illus.). 318p. 1975. Repr. of 1902 ed. lib. bdg. 18.50x (ISBN 0-8371-4224-5, GOCO). Greenwood.

--Lessons in Music Form. LC 79-109735. Repr. of 1904 ed. lib. bdg. 19.75x (ISBN 0-8371-4225-3, GOMF). Greenwood.

--Structure of Music. LC 72-109736. Repr. of 1934 ed. lib. bdg. 22.00x (ISBN 0-8371-4226-1, GOSM). Greenwood.

--The Theory & Practice of Tone-Relations. LC 72-109968. 187p. 1973. Repr. of 1931 ed. lib. bdg. 21.50x (ISBN 0-8371-6182-7, GOTR). Greenwood.

Goetz, Delia. Deserts. (Illus.). (gr. 3-7). 1956. PLB 8.16 (ISBN 0-688-31232-2). Morrow.

--Lakes. LC 72-7226. (Illus.). 64p. (gr. 3-7). 1973. 8.50 (ISBN 0-688-21866-0). Morrow.

--Rivers. (Illus.). (gr. 3-7). 1969. PLB 8.16 (ISBN 0-688-31480-5). Morrow.

--State Capital Cities. LC 70-155991. (Illus.). (gr. 5-9). 1971. PLB 9.55 (ISBN 0-688-31955-6). Morrow.

--Valleys. LC 75-26980. (Illus.). 64p. (gr. 3-7). 1976. 7.95 (ISBN 0-688-22059-2); PLB 7.63 (ISBN 0-688-32059-7). Morrow.

Goetz, Elizabeth M., jt. auth. see Allen, K. Eileen.

Goetz, Hermann. India. (Art of the World Library). (Illus.). 6.95 o.p. (ISBN 0-517-50844-3). Crown.

Goetz, Joan. El Amor y la Juventud. Montero, Lidia D., tr. from Eng. (Illus.). 96p. 1981. pap. 2.15 (ISBN 0-311-46058-5). Casa Bautista.

Goetze, Albrecht. Old Babylonian Omen Texts. 1947. text ed. 29.50x (ISBN 0-686-83651-0). Elliots Bks.

Goetze, Rolf. Building Neighborhood Confidence: A Humanistic Strategy for Urban Housing. LC 76-7469. 128p. 1976. prof ref 18.50x (ISBN 0-88410-442-7). Ballinger Pub.

--Rescuing the American Dream: Public & the Crisis in Housing. 128p. 1983. text ed. 22.50x (ISBN 0-8419-0855-9); pap. text ed. 10.50x (ISBN 0-8419-0862-1). Holmes & Meier.

--Understanding Neighborhood Change: The Role of Expectations in Urban Revitilization. LC 79-2539. 192p. 1979. prof ref 22.50x (ISBN 0-88410-493-1). Ballinger Pub.

Goetzman, William H. & Reese, Becky D. Texas Images & Visions. (Illus.). 1983. pap. text ed. 14.95 (ISBN 0-292-73832-3). U of Tex Pr.

Goetzmann, William H. When the Eagle Screamed: The Romantic Horizon in American Diplomacy, 1800-1860. (Illus.). 138p. (Orig.). 1966. pap. 10.95x (ISBN 0-471-31001-8). Wiley.

Goetzmann, William H., et al. The West As Romantic Horizon. LC 81-12424. 128p. (Orig.). 1981. 34.50 (ISBN 0-936364-04-1); pap. 17.95 (ISBN 0-936364-05-X). Joslyn Art.

Goff, Gerald K. & Berg, Milton E. Basic Mathematics. 1968. pap. 19.95 (ISBN 0-13-063438-7). P-H.

Goff, Paul E. Nature, Children & You. LC 81-18911. vi, 144p. 1982. 14.95 (ISBN 0-8214-0607-8, 82-83939); pap. 8.95 (ISBN 0-8214-0679-5, 82-84423). Ohio U Pr.

Goff, Richard & Moss, Walter. The Twentieth Century: A Brief Global History. 448p. 1983. pap. text ed. 13.95x (ISBN 0-471-09903-1); tchr's. manual avail. (ISBN 0-471-89490-7). Wiley.

Goff, Stanley, et al. Brothers: Black Soldiers in Nam. (Illus.). 224p. 1982. 14.95 (ISBN 0-89141-139-9). Presidio Pr.

Goffen, Rona & Soucek, Priscilla. The Calouste Gulbenkian Museum. LC 81-71000. (Museums Dicovered Ser.: Vol.7). (Illus.). 208p. 1982. 25.00 (ISBN 0-934516-45-6); pap. 18.00 (ISBN 0-934516-46-4). Shorewood Fine Art.

Goffer, Zvi. Archaeological Chemistry: A Sourcebook on the Applications of Chemistry to Archaeology, Vol. 55. LC 79-1425. (Chemical Analysis, Analytical Chemistry & Its Applications Ser.). 376p. 1980. 39.50x (ISBN 0-471-05156-X, Pub. by Wiley-Interscience). Wiley.

Goffin. Applications. (Mathematical Programming Studies: Vol. 20). 1982. 27.75 (ISBN 0-444-86478-4). Elsevier.

Goffin, J. L., jt. auth. see Buckley, A. G.

Goffin, R. J. The Testamentary Executor in England & Elsewhere. Helmholz, R. H. & Reams, Bernard D., Jr., eds. LC 80-84960. (Historical Writings in Law & Jurisprudence Ser.: No. 26, Bk. 40). 154p. 1981. Repr. of 1901 ed. lib. bdg. 30.00 (ISBN 0-89941-092-8). W S Hein.

Goffin, Robert. Horn of Plenty: The Story of Louis Armstrong. LC 77-8050. (Roots of Jazz). 1977. Repr. of 1947 ed. lib. bdg. 27.50 (ISBN 0-306-77430-5). Da Capo.

--Jazz: From the Congo to the Metropolitan. Schaap, Walter & Feather, Leonard G., trs. from Fr. LC 74-23384. (Roots of Jazz Ser). xii, 254p. 1975. Repr. of 1944 ed. lib. bdg. 25.00 (ISBN 0-306-70680-6). Da Capo.

Goffman, Casper & Pedrick, George. First Course in Functional Analysis. 2nd ed. LC 82-74164. 242p. 1983. text ed. 14.95 (ISBN 0-8284-0319-8). Chelsea Pub.

Goffman, Erving. Asylums: Essays on the Social Situation of Mental Patients & Other Inmates. LC 61-13812. pap. 6.95 (ISBN 0-385-00016-2, A277, Anch). Doubleday.

--Frame Analysis: An Essay on the Organization of Experience. 608p. (Orig.). 1974. pap. 7.95xi (ISBN 0-06-131961-9, TB1961, Torch). Har-Row.

Goffman, I. J., ed. Federal Taxation: As a Instrument of Social & Economic Policy: A Symposium. LC 72-5017. (Symposia on Law & Society Ser.). 104p. 1972. Repr. of 1968 ed. lib. bdg. 19.50 (ISBN 0-306-70501-X). Da Capo.

Gofman, John W. Radiation & Human Health. LC 80-26484. (Illus.). 928p. 1981. 29.95 (ISBN 0-87156-275-8). Sierra.

Gofman, John W. see Lawrence, John H. & Hamilton, J. G.

Goforth, Allene, ed. Energy & Agriculture: A Classified Title List to the Microfiche Collection. 116p. 1981. pap. text ed. 25.00 (ISBN 0-667-00666-4). Microfilming Corp.

Gogan, Brian. The Commom Corps of Christendom: Ecclesiological Themes in the Writing of Sir Thomas More. (Studies in the History of Christian Thought Ser.: Vol. 26). xii, 404p. 1982. write for info. (ISBN 90-04-06508-3). E J Brill.

Goggin, Jim. Turk Murphy: Just for the Record. LC 82-62235. (Illus.). 360p. 1983. 20.00 (ISBN 0-916870-57-X); pap. text ed. 12.95 (ISBN 0-916870-58-8). Creative Arts Bk.

Gogh, Vincent Van see Van Gogh, Vincent.

Gogniat, Raymond. Braque. (Quality-Low-Price Art Ser.). Date not set. 7.95 (ISBN 0-517-03300-3). Crown.

Gogol, Nicolai V. Dead Souls. Reavey, George, tr. from Rus. 1971. pap. 5.95 (ISBN 0-393-00600-X, Norton Lib). Norton.

Gogol, Nikolay. The Theater of Nikolay Gogol. Ehre, Milton & Gottschalk, Fruma, trs. LC 79-23745. xxvi, 206p. 1980. lib. bdg. 18.50x (ISBN 0-226-30064-1); pap. 5.95 (ISBN 0-226-30066-8). U of Chicago Pr.

Gogos, Costas G., jt. auth. see Tadmor, Zehev.

Gogou, Katerina. Three Clicks Left. Hirschman, Jack, tr. from Greek. 56p. 1983. pap. 4.50 (ISBN 0-941842-01-0). Night Horn Books.

Goguel, Catherine M. & Viatte, Francoise. Roman Drawings of the Sixteenth Century from the Musee Du Louvre, Paris. Carini, Anselmo & McCullagh, Suzanne Folds, trs. LC 79-90234. (Illus.). 166p. (Orig.). 1979. pap. 9.95 (ISBN 0-86559-036-2). Art Inst Chi.

Goh, B. S. Management & Analysis of Biological Populations. (Developments in Agricultural & Managed-Forest Ecology Ser.: Vol. 8). 1980. 70.25 (ISBN 0-444-41793-1). Elsevier.

Gohagan, John K. Quantitative Analysis for Public Policy. (Quantitative Methods for Management). (Illus.). 1980. text ed. 29.00x (ISBN 0-07-023570-8); instructor's manual 16.00 (ISBN 0-07-023571-6). McGraw.

Gohagan, John K., et al. Early Detection of Breast Cancer: Risk, Detection Protocols, & Therapeutic Implications. 224p. 1982. 24.95 (ISBN 0-03-059389-1). Praeger.

Gohberg, I., ed. see International Conference on Operator Theory, Timisoara & Herculane, Romania, June 2-12, 1980.

Gohdes, Clarence & Libman, Valentina A., eds. Russian Studies of American Literature: A Bibliography. Allen, Robert V., tr. (Comparative Literature Studies: No. 46). xiv, 218p. 1969. 16.00x (ISBN 0-8078-7046-3). U of NC Pr.

Gohier, Louis. La Mort De Cesar. 25.00 o.p. (ISBN 0-8287-0380-9). Clearwater Pub.

Gohler, Karl A. Die Messkataloge im Dienste der musikalischen Geschichtsforschung: Verzeichnis der in den Frankfurter und Leipziger Messkatalogen der Jahre 1564 bis 1759 angezeigten Musikalien, 2 vols. 1965. Repr. Set. wrappers 32.50 o.s.i. (ISBN 0-686-30880-8, Pub. by Frits Knuf Netherlands). Vol. 1 (ISBN 90-6027-013-4). Vol. 2 (ISBN 90-6027-014-2). Pendragon NY.

Gohlke, Annette, ed. Appealing Apple Recipes. LC 78-64516. 72p. 1978. pap. 2.95 (ISBN 0-89821-026-7). Reiman Assocs.

--Award Winning Recipes. 72p. 1978. pap. 2.95 (ISBN 0-89821-023-2). Reiman Assocs.

--Bar Cookie Bonanza. LC 82-60453. 68p. 1982. pap. 2.95 (ISBN 0-89821-044-5). Reiman Assocs.

--Cakes Aplenty. 72p. 1975. pap. 2.95 (ISBN 0-89821-008-9). Reiman Assocs.

--Cherry Delights. LC 82-50004. 68p. 1982. pap. 2.95 (ISBN 0-89821-041-0). Reiman Assocs.

--Chicken Country Style. LC 81-85696. 84p. 1982. pap. 2.95 (ISBN 0-89821-040-2). Reiman Assocs.

--Microwave Treats. LC 81-84087. 64p. 1981. pap. 2.95 (ISBN 0-89821-038-0). Reiman Assoc.

--Pasta, Please. LC 82-50005. 68p. 1982. pap. 2.95 (ISBN 0-89821-042-9). Reiman Assocs.

Gohlke, Madelon S. The Normal Heart. LC 81-8379. (Minnesota Voices Project Ser.: No. 4). (Illus.). 78p. 1981. pap. 3.00 (ISBN 0-89823-027-6). New Rivers Pr.

Gohlman, William E., tr. from see Sina, Ibn.

Goichberg, Renu. Spiked Flower. 2.00 (ISBN 0-686-10342-4). Cassandra Pubns.

Goicocchea, Ambrose, et al. Multiobjective Decision Analysis with Engineering & Business Applications. 528p. 1982. text ed. 34.95 o.s.i. (ISBN 0-471-06401-7). Wiley.

Goil, N. K., ed. Asian Social Science Bibliography with Annotations & Abstracts, 1966. 490p. 1971. 18.50 (ISBN 0-379-00303-1). Oceana.

Goin, Coleman J. & Goin, Olive B. Man & the Natural World: An Introduction to Life Science. 2nd ed. (Illus.). 672p. 1975. text ed. 19.95x (ISBN 0-02-344240-9, 34424). Macmillan.

Goin, Coleman J., jt. auth. see Cochran, Doris M.

Goin, John M. & Goin, Marcia K. Changing the Body: Psychological Effects of Plastic Surgery. 256p. 1981. soft cover 33.00 (ISBN 0-686-77737-9, 3630-0). Williams & Wilkins.

Goin, Kenneth L., jt. auth. see Pope, Alan.

Goin, Marcia K., jt. auth. see Goin, John M.

Goin, Olive B., jt. auth. see Goin, Coleman J.

Goines, David L. A Constructed Roman Alphabet. LC 80-83954. (Illus.). 1982. 50.00 (ISBN 0-87923-375-3); ltd. ed. 150.00 (ISBN 0-87923-376-1). Godine.

Goins, John E. Pocketknives-Markings, Manufacturers & Dealers. 2nd ed. LC 82-83511. (Illus.). 280p. (Orig.). 1982. pap. 8.95 (ISBN 0-940362-06-6). Knife World.

Goirand, Roger, jt. auth. see Cohen, Jean L.

Goirand, Roger, jt. auth. see Cohen, Jean P.

Goitein, S. D. Jews & Arabs: Their Contacts Through the Ages. 3rd ed. LC 74-9141. 271p. 1974. 10.00x o.p. (ISBN 0-8052-3567-1); pap. 5.95 (ISBN 0-8052-0464-4). Schocken.

--A Mediterranean Society: The Jewish Communities of the Arab World As Portrayed in the Documents of the Cairo Geniza. Bd. with Vol. I. Economic Foundations. 1968. 37.50x (ISBN 0-520-00484-1); Vol. 2. The Community. 1971. 42.50x (ISBN 0-520-01867-2); Vol. 3. The Family. 1978. 42.50x (ISBN 0-520-03265-9). LC 67-22430. (Near Eastern Center, UCLA). U of Cal Pr.

Gojmerac, Walter L. Bees, Beekeeping, Honey & Pollination. (Illus.). 1980. lib. bdg. 19.50 (ISBN 0-87055-342-9). AVI.

Gokel, George W., jt. auth. see Durst, H. Dupont.

Gokhale, B. G. Bharatavarsha: A Political & Cultural History of India. 360p. 1982. text ed. 21.50x (ISBN 0-391-02792-1, 41075, Pub. by Sterling India). Humanities.

Golab, Caroline. Immigrant Destinations. LC 77-81334. 256p. 1977. 29.95 (ISBN 0-87722-109-X). Temple U Pr.

Golab, Stanislaw, ed. Tensor Calculus. 371p. 1974. 85.00 (ISBN 0-444-41124-0). Elsevier.

Golan, Aviezer & Pinkas, Danny. Shula: Code Name the Pearl. 1980. 10.95 o.s.i. (ISBN 0-440-01516-2). Delacorte.

Golan, Galia. Czechoslovak Reform Movement. LC 76-163059. (Soviet & East European Studies). (Illus.). 1972. 52.50 (ISBN 0-521-08246-3). Cambridge U Pr.

--Reform Rule in Czechoslovakia: The Dubcek Era, 1968-1969. LC 72-83587. (Soviet & East European Studies). 336p. 1973. 37.50 (ISBN 0-521-08586-1). Cambridge U Pr.

--Yom Kippur & After. LC 76-2278. (Soviet & East European Studies). 1977. 47.50 (ISBN 0-521-21090-9). Cambridge U Pr.

Golan, Matti. Shimon Peres: A Biography. Friedman, Ina, tr. LC 82-7354. (Illus.). 275p. (Hebrew.). 1982. 22.50 (ISBN 0-312-71736-9). St Martin.

Golann, Čecil P. Mission on a Mountain: The Story of Abraham & Isaac. LC 73-7498. (Foreign Lands Ser.). (Illus.). 32p. (gr. k-5). 1975. PLB 5.95g (ISBN 0-8225-0363-8). Lerner Pubns.

Golann, S. & Fremouw, W. J., eds. The Right to Treatment for Mental Patients. LC 76-18917. 246p. 1976. 16.95 o.p. (ISBN 0-470-15172-2). Halsted Pr.

Golant, V. E., et al. Fundamentals of Plasma Physics. LC 79-19650. (Plasma Physics Ser.). 405p. 1980. 65.95x (ISBN 0-471-04593-4, Pub. by Wiley-Interscience). Wiley.

Golant, William. The Long Afternoon: British India 1601-1947. LC 74-15112. 282p. 1975. 22.50 (ISBN 0-312-49630-3). St Martin.

Golanty, Eric & Harris, Barbara. Marriage & the Family. LC 81-82013. (Illus.). 480p. 1982. text ed. 20.95 (ISBN 0-395-28721-9); instr's. manual 1.00 (ISBN 0-395-28722-7). HM.

Golany, Gideon. Earth-Sheltered Habitat: History, Architecture & Urban Design. 192p. 1982. text ed. 21.95 (ISBN 0-442-22992-5); pap. text ed. 14.95 (ISBN 0-442-22993-3). Van Nos Reinhold.

--Innovations for Future Cities. LC 75-36410. (Illus.). 1976. 29.95 o.p. (ISBN 0-275-22860-6). Praeger.

--International Urban Growth Policies: New-Town Contributions. LC 77-28274. 460p. 1978. 58.00x (ISBN 0-471-03748-6, Pub. by Wiley-Interscience). Wiley.

Golany, Gideon, ed. Desert Planning. 192p. 1983. 100.00 (ISBN 0-89397-119-7). Nichols Pub.

Golany, Gideon, adapted by. Urban Planning for Arid Zones: American Experiences & Directions. LC 77-10472. 245p. 1978. 42.50x (ISBN 0-471-02948-3, Pub. by Wiley-Interscience). Wiley.

Golany, Gideon S. Design for Arid Regions. 400p. 1982. text ed. 34.50 (ISBN 0-442-22924-0). Van Nos Reinhold.

Golay, Frank H. & Hauswedell, Marianne H. An Annotated Guide to Philippine Serials. (Data Papers: No. 101). 1976. pap. 5.00 (ISBN 0-87727-101-1, DP 101). Cornell SE Asia.

Golay, Keith J. Learning Patterns & Temperament Styles: A Systematic Guide to Maximizing Student Achievement. LC 82-62144. 109p. (Orig.). 1982. pap. text ed. 8.95 (ISBN 0-686-38240-4). Manas Sys.

Golbeck, Kay. Como Me Sacaras de Este Apuro, Senor? (Span.). pap. 2.25 (ISBN 0-8297-0561-9). Life Pubs Intl.

Golberg, Leon, ed. Structure Activity Correlation as a Predictive Tool in Toxicology: Fundamentals, Methods, & Applications. LC 82-3007. (Chemical Industry Institute of Toxicology Ser.). (Illus.). 450p. 1983. text ed. 49.50 (ISBN 0-89116-276-3). Hemisphere Pub.

Golberry, Silvain-Meinrad-Xavier de. Fragments d'Un Voyage En Afrique Fait Pendant les Annees 1785, 1786 et 1787 dans les Contrees Occidentales de ce Continent, Comprises Entre le Cap Blanc de Barbarie et le Cap des Palmes, 2 vols. (Bibliotheque Africaine Ser.). 1048p. (Fr.). 1974. Repr. of 1802 ed. lib. bdg. 257.50x o.p. (ISBN 0-8287-0381-7); Vol. 1. (ISBN 0-685-49519-1, 72-2128); Vol. 2. (ISBN 0-685-49520-5, 72-2129). Clearwater Pub.

Golbitz, Frances G., jt. auth. see Golos, Natalie.

Golbitz, Pat, ed. see Adams, Jane.

Golbitz, Pat, ed. see Blanchard, Kenneth & Johnson, Spencer.

Golbitz, Pat, ed. see Goodman, Eric K.

Golbitz, Pat, ed. see Meade, Marion.

Golbitz, Pat, ed. see Stewart, Fred M.

Golbitz, Pat, jt. auth. see Stern, Bert.

Gold, Anne & Briller, Sarah W. Diet Watchers Gourmet Cookbook. pap. 0.99 o.p. (ISBN 0-448-01814-4, G&D). Putnam Pub Group.

--Diet Watcher's Guide. (Illus., Orig.). 1968. pap. 2.50 o.p. (ISBN 0-685-11688-3, G&D). Putnam Pub Group.

Gold, Arthur & Fizdale, Robert. Misia: The Life of Misia Sert. LC 80-27340. (Illus.). 340p. 1981. Repr. pap. 8.95 (ISBN 0-688-00391-5). Quill NY.

Gold, Bela. Productivity, Technology, & Capital Economic Analysis, Managerial Strategies, & Government Policies. LC 79-4749. 352p. 1979. 28.95 (ISBN 0-669-02957-2). Lexington Bks.

Gold, Bela, ed. Research, Technological Change & Economic Analysis. LC 76-50496. (Illus.). 1977. 24.95x (ISBN 0-669-01286-6). Lexington Bks.

Gold, Bela, et al. Evaluating Technological Innovations: Methods, Expectations, & Findings. LC 79-4749. 384p. 1980. 33.95x (ISBN 0-669-03638-2). Lexington Bks.

Gold, Bernard & Rader, Charles M. Digital Processing of Signals. LC 82-14072. 282p. 1983. Repr. of 1969 ed. lib. bdg. p.n.s. (ISBN 0-89874-549-9). Krieger.

Gold, Bernard, jt. auth. see Rabiner, Lawrence R.

Gold, Carol S. Solid Gold Customer Relations: A Professional Resource Guide. 122p. 1983. 10.95 (ISBN 0-13-822338-6); pap. 5.95 (ISBN 0-13-822320-3). P-H.

Gold, Charlotte. Employer-Employee Committees & Worker Participation. (Key Issues Ser.: No. 20). 60p. 1976. pap. 3.00 (ISBN 0-87546-221-9). ILR Pr.

Gold, Charlotte H., jt. ed. see Powell, Mary Jo.

Gold, David T. Fire Brigade Training Manual: Emergency Forces Training for Work Environments. Carwile, Ruth, ed. LC 82-82125. (Illus.). 236p. 1982. pap. text ed. 17.00 (ISBN 0-87765-224-4, SPP-73); training manual 21.50 (SPP-73M). Natl Fire Prot.

Gold, Dick. Tennis, Anyone? 1976. pap. 1.75 (ISBN 0-451-09475-1, E9475, Sig). NAL.

Gold, Don. Bellevue. 1983. pap. price not set (ISBN 0-440-10473-4). Dell.

Gold, Edgar. Maritime Transport: The Evolution of International Marine Policy & Shipping Law. LC 80-8641. (Illus.). 448p. 1981. 36.95x (ISBN 0-669-04338-9). Lexington Bks.

Gold, Faye & Kushins, Milton. Modern Supermarket Operations. 3rd ed. (Illus.). 260p. 1981. text ed. 18.50 (ISBN 0-87005-263-2); instructor's guide 2.50 (ISBN 0-87005-366-3). Fairchild.

Gold, Fern R., jt. auth. see Conant, Melvin A.

Gold, Frances J. & Culbreth, M. The Instant Decorator. (Illus.). 1977. 27.50 o.p. (ISBN 0-685-82011-4, C N Potter Bks). Crown.

Gold, Gerald. Gandhi: A Pictorial Biography. (Illus.). 192p. 1983. 16.95 (ISBN 0-937858-27-7); pap. 9.95 (ISBN 0-937858-20-X). Newmarket.

Gold, Harry. The Sociology of Urban Life. (Illus.). 416p. 1982. 22.95 (ISBN 0-13-821371-2). P-H.

Gold, Harvey J. Mathematical Modeling of Biological Systems: An Introductory Guidebook. LC 77-8193. 357p. 1977. 34.95x (ISBN 0-471-02092-3, Pub. by Wiley-Interscience). Wiley.

Gold, Herbert. Family. 224p. 1983. pap. 2.75 (ISBN 0-523-41887-6). Pinnacle Bks.

Gold, Herbert & Stevenson, David L., eds. Stories of Modern America. 1969. pap. 11.95 (ISBN 0-312-76230-5). St Martin.

Gold, John. Valued Environments. Burgess, Jacquelin, ed. (Illus.). 1982. text ed. 35.00x (ISBN 0-04-710001-X). Allen Unwin.

Gold, John R. An Introduction to Behavioural Geography. 1980. 36.00x (ISBN 0-19-823233-0); pap. 12.95x (ISBN 0-19-823234-9). Oxford U Pr.

Gold, Joyce. From Windmills to the World Trade Center. (Illus.). 96p. (Orig.). 1983. pap. 1.95 (ISBN 0-686-38105-X). Old Warren.

Gold, Martin, jt. auth. see Douvan, Elizabeth.

Gold, Mary J. Crossroads Marseilles Nineteen Forty. LC 79-8551. (Illus.). 1980. 15.95 o.p. (ISBN 0-385-15618-9). Doubleday.

Gold, Michael. Jews Without Money. pap. 2.50 (ISBN 0-380-01309-6, 29520, Bard). Avon.

Gold, Michael E. Dialogue on Comparable Worth. (Orig.). 1983. pap. price not set (ISBN 0-87546-099-2). ILR Pr.

Gold, Phil, jt. auth. see Freedman, Samuel O.

Gold, Rahla, jt. auth. see Grand, Carole.

Gold, Richard H., jt. ed. see Bassett, Lawrence W.

Gold, Robert. Point of Departure. (gr. 7-12). 1981. pap. 2.25 (LE). Dell.

Gold, Robert, jt. auth. see Duncan, David.

Gold, Robert, ed. Stepping Stones. (Orig.). (YA) (gr. 7-12). 1981. pap. 2.25 (ISBN 0-440-98269-3, LE). Dell.

Gold, Robert S., ed. Point of Departure: Nineteen Stories of Youth & Discovery. (Orig.). 1961. pap. 2.25 (ISBN 0-440-96983-2, LFL). Dell.

Gold, Ruth, jt. auth. see Siegel, Ernest.

Gold, S. M. Recreation Planning & Design. 1980. 37.50 (ISBN 0-07-023644-5). McGraw.

Gold, Sharon. The Woman's Day Book of Beauty, Health & Fitness Hints. LC 80-12022. (Illus.). 166p. 1980. pap. 5.95 (ISBN 0-688-08611-X). Quill NY.

--Woman's Day One Thousand & One Beauty Aids & Fitness Hints. 1981. 10.95 (ISBN 0-688-03611-2). Morrow.

Gold, V. Advances in Physical Organic Chemistry, Vol. 19. (Serial Publication). Date not set. 69.50 (ISBN 0-12-033519-0). Acad Pr.

Gold, V., jt. ed. see Caldin, E. F.

Gold, Winifred A., jt. auth. see Bash, Deborah M.

Goldbach, John & Ross, Michael J. Politics, Parties & Power. LC 79-47991. 382p. 1980. 15.95x (ISBN 0-913530-21-2); pap. 10.95x (ISBN 0-686-64356-9). Palisades Pub.

Goldbarth, Albert. Faith. LC 81-82536. (Illus.). 108p. 1981. pap. 4.00 (ISBN 0-89823-030-6). New Rivers Pr.

--Keeping. 50p. 1975. 3.50 (ISBN 0-87886-053-3). Ithaca Hse.

--Original Light. 140p. 1983. 12.95 (ISBN 0-86538-031-7); pap. 7.95 (ISBN 0-86538-032-5). Ontario Rev NJ.

Goldbeck, David, jt. auth. see Goldbeck, Nikki.

Goldbeck, Janne, jt. auth. see Benzel, Kathryn N.

Goldbeck, Nikki. How to Cope with Menstrual Problems: A Wholistic Approach. Passwater, Richard A. & Mindell, Earl R., eds. (Good Health Guide Ser.). 32p. (Orig.). 1983. pap. 1.45 (ISBN 0-87983-300-9). Keats.

Goldbeck, Nikki & Goldbeck, David. The Dieter's Companion: A Guide to Nutritional Self-Sufficiency. LC 75-11585. 384p. 1976. 10.95 (ISBN 0-07-023654-2, GB). McGraw.

--The Dieter's Companion: A Guide to Nutritional Self-Sufficiency. 1977. pap. 2.95 (ISBN 0-451-11685-2, AE1685, Sig). NAL.

--The Good Breakfast Book: A Bringing-Back-Breakfast Cookbook. LC 74-21211. (Illus.). 224p. (Orig.). 1976. pap. 4.95 (ISBN 0-8256-3048-7, Quick Fox). Putnam Pub Group.

--Nikki & David Goldbeck's American Wholefoods Cuisine. (Illus.). 608p. 1983. 19.95 (ISBN 0-686-84824-1). NAL.

--The Supermarket Handbook. expanded ed. 1976. pap. 2.95 (ISBN 0-451-09635-5, E9635, Sig). NAL.

--The Supermarket Handbook: Access to Whole Foods. 1974. pap. 5.95 (ISBN 0-452-25151-6, Z5323, Plume). NAL.

Goldbeck, W. B. Mental Illness Programs for Employees. (Springer Ser. in Industry & Health Care: Vol. 9). 250p. 1980. pap. 12.00 o.p. (ISBN 0-387-90479-4). Springer-Verlag.

Goldbecker, William & Hart, Ernest H. This Is the German Shepherd. (Illus.). 296p. 12.95 (ISBN 0-87666-298-X, PS614). TFH Pubns.

Goldberg. Powtech Seventy-One. 1971. cased 83.00 (ISBN 0-471-25727-3). Wiley.

Goldberg, A. S., ed. Particle Technology Research Reviews, Vol. 1. 1973. 47.95 (ISBN 0-471-25734-6, Pub. by Wiley Heyden); pap. 42.95 (ISBN 0-471-25733-8). Wiley.

--Powtech '71 (Wiley Heyden). 83.00 (ISBN 0-471-25727-3). Wiley.

--Particulate Matter Powtech '73. 1973. 47.95 (ISBN 0-471-25729-X, Wiley Heyden); pap. 42.95 (ISBN 0-471-25728-1). Wiley.

--Powtech '75. 1976. 52.95 (ISBN 0-471-25732-X, Wiley Heyden). Wiley.

Goldberg, Adele & Robson, David. Smalltalk-Eighty: The Language & its Implementation. (Illus.). 544p. Date not set. text ed. price not set (ISBN 0-201-11371-6). A-W.

Goldberg, Alan J., ed. Hospital Departmental Profiles. LC 82-6250. 140p. (Orig.). 1982. pap. 25.00 (ISBN 0-87258-356-2, AHA-133120). Am Hospital.

Goldberg, Alan M. & Hanin, Israel, eds. Biology of Cholinergic Function. LC 74-14473. 730p. 1976. 53.00 (ISBN 0-911216-98-7). Raven.

Goldberg, Alan M., jt. ed. see Hanin, Israel.

Goldberg, Alvin & Larson, Carl. Group Communication: Discussion Processes & Application. LC 74-5295. (Speech Communication Ser.). (Illus.). 224p. 1975. ref. ed. 19.95x o.p. (ISBN 0-13-365221-1). P-H.

Goldberg, Arthur J., jt. auth. see Caradon.

Goldberg, Audrey G. Body Massage for the Beauty Therapist. (Illus.). 1972. pap. 11.50 (ISBN 0-686-84218-9, Pub. by W Heinemann). David & Charles.

--Care of the Skin. (Illus.). 1975. pap. 13.95 (ISBN 0-434-90672-7, Pub. by Heinemann). David & Charles.

Goldberg, Barry B. Abdominal Gray Scale Ultrasonography. LC 77-5889. (Diagnostic & Therapeutic Radiology Ser.). 372p. 1977. 55.00x (ISBN 0-471-01510-5, Pub. by Wiley Med). Wiley.

Goldberg, Ben Z. The Jewish Problem in the Soviet Union: Analysis & Solution. LC 82-15842. (Illus.). x, 374p. 1982. Repr. of 1961 ed. lib. bdg. 45.00x (ISBN 0-313-23692-5, GOJE). Greenwood.

Goldberg, Bernard, ed. Communication Channels: Characterization & Behavior. LC 75-23596. 1976. 18.95 (ISBN 0-87942-058-8). Inst Electrical.

Goldberg, David E., jt. auth. see Dillard, Clyde R.

Goldberg, David M. Clinical Biochemistry Reviews, Vol. 3. (Clinical Biochemistry Reviews Ser.). 477p. 1982. 40.00 (ISBN 0-471-09863-9, Pub. by Wiley Med). Wiley.

Goldberg, David M., ed. Annual Review of Clinical Biochemistry, Vol. 1. LC 80-15463. 379p. 1980. 31.95x (ISBN 0-471-04036-3, Pub. by Wiley Med); Vol. 2. 32.95 (ISBN 0-471-08297-X). Wiley.

Goldberg, David M. & Werner, Mario, eds. Progress in Clinical Enzymology. LC 80-80965. (Illus.). 304p. 1980. 52.00x (ISBN 0-89352-091-8). Masson Pub.

Goldberg, E. D., ed. Atmospheric Chemistry, Berlin, 1982. (Dahlem Workshop Reports, Physical & Chemical: Vol. 4). (Illus.). 400p. 1983. 20.00 (ISBN 0-387-11651-6). Springer-Verlag.

Goldberg, Edward D., ed. North Sea Science: Papers Presented at the NATO Science Committee Conference, November 1971. (Illus.). 420p. 1973. 30.00x (ISBN 0-262-07056-1). MIT Pr.

--Strategies for Marine Pollution Monitoring. LC 76-12490. 310p. 1976. 35.00x o.p. (ISBN 0-471-31070-0, Pub. by Wiley-Interscience). Wiley.

Goldberg, Edward D., et al, eds. The Sea: Marine Modeling. LC 62-18366. (Ideas & Observations on Progress in the Study on the Seas Ser.: Vol. 6). 992p. 1977. 87.95x (ISBN 0-471-31091-3, Pub. by Wiley-Interscience). Wiley.

Goldberg, Edward M., jt. auth. see Dial, O. E.

Goldberg, Enid A. How to Write an Essay. 1981. pap. text ed. 21.95x (ISBN 0-673-15181-6). Scott F.

Goldberg, Eugene P. Targeted Drugs. (Polymers in Biology & Medicine Ser.). 300p. 1983. 50.00 (ISBN 0-471-04884-4, Pub. by Wiley-Interscience). Wiley.

Goldberg, Gale, jt. auth. see Allen, Edward.

Goldberg, Gertrude S., jt. auth. see Johnson, Harriette C.

Goldberg, H. E. Cave Dwellers & Citrus Growers. LC 70-174260. (Illus.). 200p. 1972. pap. 29.95 (ISBN 0-521-08431-8). Cambridge U Pr.

Goldberg, Harold. Extending the Limits of Reliability Theory. LC 81-4534. 263p. 1981. 34.95 (ISBN 0-471-07799-2, Pub. by Wiley Interscience). Wiley.

Goldberg, Harriet L. Child Offenders: A Study in Diagnosis & Treatment. LC 69-14928. (Criminology, Law Enforcement, & Social Problems Ser.: No. 75). 1969. Repr. of 1948 ed. 15.00x (ISBN 0-87585-075-8). Patterson Smith.

Goldberg, Harry F., jt. auth. see Lynn, T. S.

Goldberg, Harry F., jt. auth. see Lynn, Theodore S.

Goldberg, Henry I. see Moss, Albert A.

Goldberg, Herb. The New Male-Female Relationship. 320p. 1983. 13.95 (ISBN 0-686-84632-X). Morrow.

Goldberg, Herb, jt. auth. see Bach, George.

Goldberg, Herman, et al. Dyslexia: Interdisciplinary Approaches to Reading Disabilities. Date not set. price not set (ISBN 0-8089-1484-7). Grune.

Goldberg, Herman K. & Schiffman, Gilbert B. Dyslexia: Problems of Reading Disabilities. LC 72-8139. 205p. 1972. 28.50 o.p. (ISBN 0-8089-0784-0). Grune.

--Learning Disabilities: An Interdisciplinary Approach. 1982. 19.50 (791628). Grune.

Goldberg, I. A. & Gordon, R. A. Introduction to Methods for Buying & Selling Stock. 110p. 1969. 21.00x (ISBN 0-685-11747-2). Gordon.

Goldberg, I. Ignacy. Selected Bibliography of Special Education. LC 67-19388. (Orig.). 1967. pap. 3.95x (ISBN 0-8077-1434-8). Tchrs Coll.

Goldberg, I. Ignacy, jt. auth. see Lippman, Leopold.

Goldberg, Isaac. Wonder of Words: An Introduction to Language for Every Man. LC 74-164294. 1971. Repr. of 1938 ed. 40.00x (ISBN 0-8103-3777-0). Gale.

Goldberg, Isaac, ed. see Andreyev, L. N.

Goldberg, Isaac, ed. see Artzibashev, Michael.

Goldberg, Isaac, ed. & tr. see Assis, Joaquim M.

Goldberg, Isaac, ed. see Babel, Isaac.

Goldberg, Isaac, ed. see Chekhov, Anton.

Goldberg, Isaac, ed. & tr. see Dolores, Carmen.

Goldberg, Isaac, ed. & tr. see Medeiros, E. Albuquerque.

Goldberg, Isaac, ed. & tr. see Netto, Coelho.

Goldberg, Isaac, ed. see Sologub, Feodor.

Goldberg, Isaac, tr. Modern Russian Classics. Incl. Silence. Andreyev, Leonid; White Dog. Sologub, Fyodor; Father. Chekhov, Anton; Her Lover. Gorki, Maxim; Letter. Babel, Isaac. pap. 3.00 (ISBN 0-8283-1450-0, IPL). Branden.

Goldberg, Issac, ed. Brazilian Tales. pap. 3.00 (ISBN 0-8283-1426-8, IPL). Branden.

Goldberg, J. H., ed. see McCalpin, James P.

Goldberg, J. H., ed. see Smith, Duane A.

Goldberg, Jeanne, jt. auth. see Mayer, Jean.

Goldberg, Joan R. You Can Afford a Beautiful Wedding. 160p. 1983. pap. 6.95 (ISBN 0-8092-5631-2). Contemp Bks.

Goldberg, Joe. Jazz Masters of the Fifties. (The Roots of Jazz Ser.). 246p. 1980. Repr. of 1965 ed. lib. bdg. 25.00 (ISBN 0-306-76031-2). Da Capo.

Goldberg, Joel. Fundamentals of Electricity. (Illus.). 352p. 1981. text ed. 19.95 (ISBN 0-13-337006-2). P-H.

--Fundamentals of Stereo Servicing. (Illus.). 304p. 1983. 21.95 (ISBN 0-686-81977-2, 382). P-H.

--Fundamentals of Television Servicing. (Illus.). 320p. 1982. 20.95 (ISBN 0-13-344598-4). P-H.

Goldberg, Judith. Laughter Through Tears: The Yiddish Cinema. LC 80-70900. (Illus.). 176p. 1982. 22.50 (ISBN 0-8386-3074-X). Fairleigh Dickinson.

Goldberg, Kenneth P. & Sherwood, Robert D. Microcomputers & Parents. (Education Ser.). 224p. 1983. pap. text ed. 8.50 (ISBN 0-471-87278-4). Wiley.

Goldberg, Kenneth P., jt. auth. see Weinberg, Sharon L.

Goldberg, Larry. Controlled Cheating: The Fats Goldberg Take It off, Keep It off Diet Program. LC 80-2838. (Illus.). 192p. 1981. 11.95 (ISBN 0-385-17379-2). Doubleday.

Goldberg, Lawrence G. & White, Lawrence J. The Deregulation of the Banking & Securities Industries. LC 78-19705. 368p. 1979. 25.95x (ISBN 0-669-02720-0). Lexington Bks.

Goldberg, Lea. Russian Literature in the Nineteenth Century. Halkin, Hillel, tr. from Hebrew. 205p. 1976. text ed. 17.25x o.p. (ISBN 0-686-74320-2, Pub. by Magnes Israel). Humanities.

Goldberg, Len. The Cure. 1982. pap. 2.50 (ISBN 0-451-11509-0, AE1509, Sig). NAL.

Goldberg, Leonard S. Transplant. (Orig.). 1980. pap. 1.95 o.p. (ISBN 0-451-09412-3, J9412, Sig). NAL.

Goldberg, Louis. Leviticus: A Study Guide Commentary. (A Study Guide Commentary Ser.). 128p. (Orig.). 1980. pap. 4.95 (ISBN 0-310-41813-5). Zondervan.

--Turbulence over the Middle East: Israel & the Nations in Confrontation & the Coming Kingdom of Peace on Earth. 320p. 1982. pap. 7.95 (ISBN 0-87213-240-4). Loizeaux.

Goldberg, Louis P. & Levenson, Eleanore. Lawless Judges. LC 73-138498. (Civil Liberties in American History Ser). 1970. Repr. of 1935 ed. lib. bdg. 37.50 (ISBN 0-306-70070-0). Da Capo.

Goldberg, Lucianne & Robinson, Sandra T. Friends in High Places. LC 78-26187. 1979. 11.95 (ISBN 0-399-90039-X, Marek). Putnam Pub Group.

Goldberg, Marcia B. Winning at the Occupational Safety & Health Review Commission: A Worker's Handbook on Enforcing Safety & Health Standards. 269p. 1982. 5.00 (ISBN 0-686-96339-3). Pub Citizen Health.

Goldberg, Mark. Graduate School Foreign Language Test: German. 3rd ed. (Orig.). 1968. pap. 3.95 o.p. (ISBN 0-668-01460-1). Arco.

Goldberg, Marshall. Nerve. 1981. 13.95 (ISBN 0-698-11101-X, Coward). Putnam Pub Group.

Goldberg, Marshall, jt. auth. see Kay, Kenneth.

Goldberg, Maxwell H. & Swinton, John, eds. Blindness Research: The Expanding Frontiers. LC 68-8179. 1969. 22.50x (ISBN 0-271-00073-2). Pa St U Pr.

Goldberg, Michael A. & Gau, George W., eds. North American Housing Markets into the 21st Century. 416p. 1983. prof ref 32.00x (ISBN 0-88410-880-5). Ballinger Pub.

Goldberg, Mitilda E. & Connelly, Naomi, eds. Evaluative Research in Social Care. (Policy Studies Institute). 320p. 1981. text ed. 30.00x (ISBN 0-435-83351-0). Heinemann Ed.

Goldberg, Morton E., ed. Pharmacological & Biochemical Properties of Drug Substances, Vol. I. LC 77-88184. 413p. 1979. 30.00 (ISBN 0-917330-17-X). Am Pharm Assn.

--Pharmacological & Biochemical Properties of Drug Substances, Vol. 2. 257p. 1977. 36.00 (ISBN 0-917330-25-0). Am Pharm Assn.

Goldberg, Morton F., jt. auth. see Paton, David.

Goldberg, Moses. Children's Theatre: A Philosophy & a Method. LC 73-12954. (P-H Series in Theatre & Drama). (Illus.). 256p. 1973. ref. ed. 18.95 (ISBN 0-13-132605-8). P-H.

Goldberg, Philip & Rubin, Richard. The Small Business Guide to Borrowing Money. (Illus.). 1980. 24.95 (ISBN 0-07-054198-1). McGraw.

Goldberg, Philip, jt. auth. see Hegarty, Christopher.

Goldberg, Phillip & Kaufman, Daniel. Natural Sleep: How to Get Your Share. LC 78-1745. (Illus.). 1979. pap. 7.95 o.p. (ISBN 0-87857-259-7). Rodale Pr Inc.

Goldberg, Phyllis Z. So What If You Can't Chew, Eat Hearty! Recipes & a Guide for the Healthy & Happy Eating of Soft & Pureed Foods. (Illus.). 152p. 1980. spiral 13.95x (ISBN 0-398-04065-6). C C Thomas.

Goldberg, Ray A. Agribusiness Coordination: A Systems Approach to the Wheat, Soybean & Florida Orange Economies. LC 68-118718. (Agribusinesss Management Ser.). 256p. 1965. prof ref 35.00x (ISBN 0-88410-270-X). Ballinger Pub.

--Agribusiness Management for Developing Countries - Latin America. LC 74-9525. (Agribusiness Management Ser). 432p. 1974. prof ref 35.00x (ISBN 0-88410-267-X). Ballinger Pub.

--Agribusiness Management for Developing Countries - Southeast Asian Corn Systems & American & Japanese Trends Affecting It. LC 78-31564. (Agribusiness Management Ser.). 672p. 1979. prof ref 42.50x (ISBN 0-88410-286-6). Ballinger Pub.

--Agribusiness Management: Text & Cases. (Agribusiness Management Ser). 592p. cancelled (ISBN 0-88410-285-8). Ballinger Pub.

--International Agribusiness Coordination. (Concepts in Agribusiness Management Ser). 184p. cancelled o.s.i. (ISBN 0-88410-284-X). Ballinger Pub.

--Research in Domestic & International Agribusiness Management, Vol. 1. 225p. 1981. 36.50 (ISBN 0-89232-172-5). Jai Pr.

Goldberg, Ray A., jt. auth. see Schrader, Lee F.

Goldberg, Rhoda, jt. auth. see Pakula, Marion B.

Goldberg, Rhoda O., jt. auth. see Pakula, Marion B.

Goldberg, Richard A., jt. auth. see Herman, John R.

Goldberg, Richard J. & Slaby, Andrew E. Diagnosing Disorders of Mood, Thought & Behavior. 1981. pap. text ed. 18.00 (ISBN 0-87488-574-4). Med Exam.

Goldberg, Richard R. Methods of Real Analysis. 2nd ed. LC 75-30615. 1976. text ed. 31.95x (ISBN 0-471-31065-4). Wiley.

Goldberg, Robert & Lorin, Harold. The Economics of Information Processing: Vol. 1, Management Perspectives. LC 81-11429. 238p. 1982. 29.95 (ISBN 0-471-09206-1, Pub. by Wiley Interscience). Wiley.

--Economics of Information Processing: Vol. 2, Operation Programming & Software Models. LC 81-11429. 185p. 1982. 26.50 (ISBN 0-471-09767-5, Pub. by Wiley Interscience). Wiley.

Goldberg, Robert & Lorin, Harold, eds. The Economics of Information Processing. 1982. Vol. I. 27.50 (ISBN 0-686-98049-2); Vol. II. 25.00 (ISBN 0-686-98050-6). Telecom Lib.

Goldberg, S. L. An Essay on King Lear. LC 73-84318. 212p. 1974. 34.50 (ISBN 0-521-20200-0); pap. 11.50 (ISBN 0-521-09831-9). Cambridge U Pr.

Goldberg, Samuel. Introduction to Difference Equations: With Illustrative Examples from Economics, Psychology & Sociology. LC 58-10223. (Illus.). 1958. pap. 18.50x (ISBN 0-471-31051-4). Wiley.

--Probability: An Introduction. (gr. 11 up). 1960. ref. ed. 23.95 (ISBN 0-13-711580-6); pap. 0.50 ans. bk. (ISBN 0-13-711572-5). P-H.

--Probability in Social Science. (Mathematical Modelling & Applications Ser.: Vol. 1). 186p. 1983. pap. text ed. write for info. (ISBN 3-7643-3089-9). Birkhauser.

Goldberg, Sheldon, et al, eds. Coronary Artery Spasm & Thrombosis: Clinical Aspects. (Cardiovascular Clinics Ser.: Vol. 14: No. 1). (Illus.). 255p. 1983. text ed. 40.00 (ISBN 0-8036-4161-3, 4161-3). Davis Co.

Goldberg, Steven S. Special Education Law: A Guide for Parents, Advocates, & Educators. (Critical Topics in Law & Society). 244p. 1982. 24.50x (ISBN 0-306-40848-1, Plenum Pr). Plenum Pub.

Goldberg, Stuart C. Private Placements & Restricted Securities, 2 vols. rev. ed. LC 70-163723. 1978. looseleaf with 1981 rev. pages 140.00 (ISBN 0-87632-078-7). Boardman.

Goldberg, Vicki. Photography in Print: Writings from Eighteen Sixteen to the Present. 1981. 22.50 o.p. (ISBN 0-671-25034-5, Touchstone Bks); pap. 9.95 o.p. (ISBN 0-671-25035-3). S&S.

Goldberg, Walter H. Mergers: Motives, Modes, Methods. 350p. 1983. 29.50 (ISBN 0-89397-155-3). Nichols Pub.

Goldberg, Walter H., ed. Governments & Multinationals: The Policy of Control vs. Autonomy. LC 82-3591. 300p. 1983. 30.00 (ISBN 0-89946-145-X). Oelgeschlager.

Goldberg, Yaffa G. A Gift of Challahs. Zakutinsky, R., ed. (Illus.). 32p. (Orig.). (gr. k-6). 1981. pap. 3.95 (ISBN 0-911643-00-1). Aura Pub.

Goldberger, A. S., jt. ed. see Aigner, D. J.

Goldberger, Arthur S. Econometric Theory. LC 64-10370. (Probability & Mathematical Statistics Ser.). (Illus.). 1964. 32.95x (ISBN 0-471-31101-4). Wiley.

Goldberger, Arthur S., jt. auth. see Klein, Lawrence R.

Goldberger, Ary L. & Goldberger, Emanuel. Clinical Electrocardiography: A Simplified Approach. 2nd ed. LC 80-27024. (Illus.). 305p. 1981. text ed. 19.95 (ISBN 0-8016-1865-7). Mosby.

Goldberger, Emanuel. Textbook of Clinical Cardiology. LC 81-38350. (Illus.). 1069p. 1982. text ed. 37.50 (ISBN 0-8016-1864-9). Mosby.

Goldberger, Emanuel & Wheat, Myron W., Jr. Treatment of Cardiac Emergencies. 3rd ed. LC 81-14155. (Illus.). 416p. 1982. pap. text ed. 29.95 (ISBN 0-8016-1857-6). Mosby.

Goldberger, Emanuel, jt. auth. see Goldberger, Ary L.

Goldberger, Leo & Breznitz, Shlomo. The Handbook of Stress. (Illus.). 832p. 1982. text ed. 49.95. Free Pr.

Goldberger, Leo & Breznitz, Shlomo, eds. Handbook of Stress: Theoretical & Clinical Aspects. 804p. 1983. 49.95 (ISBN 0-02-912030-6). Free Pr.

Goldberger, M. L. Collision Theory. rev ed. LC 75-15669. 930p. 1975. Repr. of 1964 ed. 52.50 (ISBN 0-88275-313-4). Krieger.

Goldberger, Paul. The Skyscraper. LC 81-47480. (Illus.). 224p. 1981. 25.00 o.p. (ISBN 0-394-50595-6); pap. 14.95 o.p. (ISBN 0-394-74964-2). Knopf.

Goldbeter, A., jt. ed. see Lefever, R.

Goldblatt, Burt. Burt Goldblatt's Jazz Gallery One. Schlamm, Rhoda, ed. LC 82-61418. (Illus.). 200p. 1982. pap. 18.95 (ISBN 0-910945-00-4). Newbold Pub.

Goldblatt, Burt, jt. auth. see Appel, Martin.

Goldblatt, Burt, jt. auth. see Messick, Hank.

Goldblatt, Howard. Hsiao Hung. (World Authors Ser.). 1976. lib. bdg. 12.50 (ISBN 0-8057-6228-0, Twayne). G K Hall.

Goldblatt, Howard, jt. auth. see Yaffe, Byron.

Goldblatt, Howard, tr. see Hwang, Chun-ming.

Goldblith, Samuel A. & Decareau, Robert V. An Annotated Bibliography on Microwaves: Their Properties, Production, & Application to Food Processing. 1973. 25.00x (ISBN 0-262-07049-9). MIT Pr.

Goldbratt, Howard, tr. see Hong, Xiao.

Golde, Roger A. Can You Be Sure of Your Experts. 1969. 5.95 o.s.i. (ISBN 0-02-544510-3). Macmillan.

Goldemberg, Isaac. La Vida a plazos de Don Jacobo Lerner. (Span.). 1980. pap. 8.50 (ISBN 0-910061-00-9). Ediciones Norte.

Goldemberg, Rose L. All About Jewelry: The One Indispensable Guide for Buyers, Wearers, Lovers, Investors. (Illus.). 1983. 15.95 (ISBN 0-87795-419-4, Pub. by Priam); pap. 6.95 (ISBN 0-87795-453-4). Arbor Hse.

--All About Jewelry: The One Indispensible Guide for Jewelry Buyers, Wearers, Lovers, & Investors. LC 82-72057. (Illus.). 165p. 1983. 15.95 (ISBN 0-686-84342-8); pap. 6.95. Arbor Hse.

Golden, Arthur see Whitman, Walt.

Golden, B. L. & Bodin, L. D. International Workshop on Current & Future Directions in the Routing & Scheduling of Vehicles & Crews: Proceedings. 139p. 1981. pap. 17.00 (ISBN 0-471-09897-3, Pub. by Wiley-Interscience). Wiley.

Golden, Charles, jt. ed. see Moses, James A., Jr.

Golden, Clinton S. & Ruttenberg, Harold J. The Dynamics of Industrial Democracy. LC 72-2372. (FDR & the Era of the New Deal Ser). 388p. 1973. Repr. of 1942 ed. lib. bdg. 42.50 (ISBN 0-306-70472-2). Da Capo.

Golden, Dale, jt. ed. see Anderson, Kenneth R.

Golden, Duke L. Statics & Strengths of Materials. LC 76-105328. 1970. text ed. 22.95 o.p. (ISBN 0-675-09366-X). Merrill.

Golden, Evelyn. Glimpses. (Living Poets' Library Ser.). 1983. pap. 3.50 (ISBN 0-686-84154-9). Dragons Teeth.

Golden, Frederic. The Trembling Earth: Probing & Predicting Quakes. (Illus.). 176p. 1983. 11.95 (ISBN 0-684-17884-2, ScribT). Scribner.

Golden, Gale, jt. auth. see Gotwald, William.

Golden, Harry. Only in America. LC 72-9917. 317p. 1973. Repr. of 1950 ed. lib. bdg. 29.50x (ISBN 0-8371-6607-1, PIOS). Greenwood.

Golden, Jack & Ouellette, Robert P. Environmental Impact Data Book. LC 77-92596. 1979. 59.95 (ISBN 0-250-40212-2). Ann Arbor Science.

Golden, James L., et al. The Rhetoric of Western Thought. 3rd ed. 1982. pap. text ed. 14.95 (ISBN 0-8403-2916-4, 40291601). Kendall Hunt.

Golden, James R. NATO Burden-Sharing. (Washington Papers: No. 96). 120p. 6.95 (ISBN 0-03-062769-9). Praeger.

Golden, Lawrence G. & Zimmerrian, Donald. Effective Retailing. 1980. 23.95 (ISBN 0-395-30609-4); Instr's. manual 1.65 (ISBN 0-395-30610-8). HM.

Golden, Leon, ed. Transformations in Literature & Film: Proceedings from the Florida State University Conference on Literature & Film. LC 82-20195. 114p. 1982. 8.00 (ISBN 0-8130-0744-5). U Presses Fla.

Golden, M. Patricia, ed. The Research Experience. LC 75-17321. 1976. pap. text ed. 13.95 (ISBN 0-87581-188-4, 188). Peacock Pubs.

Golden, Marita. Migrations of the Heart. LC 82-45248. 264p. 1983. 15.95 (ISBN 0-385-17519-1, Anchor Pr). Doubleday.

Golden, Renny & Collins, Shelia. Struggle Is a Name for Hope. (Worker Writer Ser.: No. 3). 48p. (Orig.). 1982. pap. 3.00 (ISBN 0-931122-24-4). West End.

Golden, Robert & Sullivan, Mary C. Flannery O'Connor & Caroline Gordon: A Reference Guide. 1977. lib. bdg. 27.00 (ISBN 0-8161-7845-3, Hall Reference). G K Hall.

Golden, Samuel A. Frederick Goodard Tuckerman. (United States Authors Ser.). 1966. lib. bdg. 13.95 (ISBN 0-8057-0748-4, Twayne). G K Hall.

--Jean Le Clerc. (World Authors Ser.). lib. bdg. 15.95 (ISBN 0-8057-2232-7, Twayne). G K Hall.

Goldenberg, Carl T. Read English, Bk. 4. (Speak English Ser.). (Illus.). 80p. (Orig.). 1983. pap. text ed. 4.95 (ISBN 0-88499-678-6). Inst Mod Lang.

Goldenberg, Herbert. Contemporary Clinical Psychology. 2nd ed. LC 82-12784. (Psychology Ser.). 480p. 1982. text ed. 23.95 (ISBN 0-534-01239-6). Brooks-Cole.

Goldenberg, Herbert, jt. auth. see Goldenberg, Irene.

Goldenberg, Irene & Goldenberg, Herbert. Family Therapy: An Overview. LC 79-9403. 1980. text ed. 18.95 (ISBN 0-8185-0361-0). Brooks-Cole.

Goldenberg, Susan. Men of Property: The Canadian Developers Who Are Buying America. (Illus.). 320p. 1981. 15.95 (ISBN 0-920510-46-9, Pub. by Personal Lib); pap. 10.95 (ISBN 0-920510-84-1). Dodd.

Goldensohn, Eli S. & Koehle, Ruth. EEG Interpretation: Problems of Over-Reading & Under-Reading. LC 75-7581. 200p. 1975. 30.00 o.p. (ISBN 0-87993-068-3). Futura Pub.

Goldenson, Robert M. Encyclopedia of Human Behavior. (Illus.). 1970. Set. Two-volume, slipcased edition 29.95 (ISBN 0-385-04074-1). Doubleday.

Goldenson, Robert M., et al. Disability & Rehabilitation Handbook. (Illus.). 1978. text ed. 35.95 (ISBN 0-07-023658-5, P&RB). McGraw.

Goldenthal, Allan B. The Teenage Employment Guide. Rev. ed. (Illus.). 208p. (Orig.). (gr. 9-12). 1983. pap. 8.95 (ISBN 0-671-43542-6). Monarch Pr.

Golder, F. A. Guide to Materials for American History in Russian Archives, 2 Vols. 1917-1937. Set. pap. 26.00 (ISBN 0-527-00694-7). Kraus Repr.

Goldern, Charles J., et al, eds. Clinical Neuropsychology: Interface with Neurological & Psychiatric Disorders. Date not set. price not set (ISBN 0-8089-1541-X). Grune.

Goldfarb, Alan S., et al. Organic Chemicals Manufacturing Hazards. LC 81-65889. 430p. 1981. text ed. 49.95 (ISBN 0-250-40409-5). Ann Arbor Science.

Goldfarb, Alvin, jt. auth. see Wilson, Edwin.

Goldfarb, I. William & Yates, Anthony P. Total Parenteral Nutrition: Concepts & Methods. 96p. pap. text ed. write for info. (ISBN 0-935170-07-3). Synapse Pubns.

Goldfarb, Jeffrey C. On Cultural Freedom: An Exploration of Public Life in Poland & America. LC 82-8325. (Chicago Original Paperbacks Ser.). 216p. 1983. lib. bdg. 25.00x (ISBN 0-226-30099-4); pap. text ed. 12.50x (ISBN 0-226-30100-1). U of Chicago Pr.

--The Persistence of Freedom: The Sociological Implications of Polish Student Theater. (Westview Replica Editions). 1979. lib. bdg. 20.00 (ISBN 0-89158-692-X). Westview.

Goldfarb, Mace. Fighters, Refugees, Immigrants: A Story of the Hmong. LC 82-4370. (Illus.). 48p. (gr. 4 up). 1982. lib. bdg. 9.95g (ISBN 0-87614-197-1). Carolrhoda Bks.

Goldfarb, Ronald & Raymond, James. Clear Understandings: A Guide to Legal Writing. 174p. 1983. pap. 8.95 (ISBN 0-394-70634-X). Random.

Goldfarb, Ronald L. & Singer, Linda R. After Conviction. LC 72-83076. 1973. 19.95 o.p. (ISBN 0-671-21206-0, Touchstone Bks); pap. 8.95 o.p. (ISBN 0-671-22785-8). S&S.

Goldfarb, Ronald L., jt. auth. see Friendly, Alfred.

Goldfarb, Sally F. Inside the Law Schools: A Guide by Students for Students, 1982 Edition. rev. ed. 320p. 1982. pap. 9.25 (ISBN 0-525-93243-7, 0898-270). Dutton.

Goldfarb, Warren D., jt. auth. see Dreben, Burton.

Goldfeld, L., ed. see Raedmacher, H.

Goldfeld, Stephen M. & Quandt, Richard E., eds. Studies in Nonlinear Estimation. LC 75-33779. 224p. 1976. prof ref 27.50x (ISBN 0-88410-281-5). Ballinger Pub.

Goldfield, David R. & Brownell, Blaine A. Urban America: From Downtown to No Town. LC 78-69562. (Illus.). 1979. pap. text ed. 14.50 (ISBN 0-395-27397-8). HM.

Goldfield, Randy J. The Word Processing Handbook. 1983. 25.00 (ISBN 0-02-912100-0). Free Pr.

Goldfrank, jt. auth. see Humez.

Goldfrank, Esther S. Notes on an Undirected Life: As an Anthropologist Tells It. (Queens College Publication in Anthropology: No. 3). 244p. (Orig.). 1979. pap. text ed. 10.00 o.p. (ISBN 0-930146-11-5). Queens Coll Pr.

--Social & Ceremonial Organization of Cochiti. LC 28-11444. 1927. pap. 15.00 (ISBN 0-527-00532-0). Kraus Repr.

Goldhaber, Gerald. Organizational Communication. 3rd ed. 450p. 1983. text ed. write for info. (ISBN 0-697-04219-7); instrs.' manual avail. (ISBN 0-697-04220-0). Wm C Brown.

Goldhaber, Gerald M. Organizational Communication. 2nd ed. 425p. 1979. text ed. write for info. o.p. (ISBN 0-697-04158-1); o.p. (ISBN 0-697-04210-3). Wm C Brown.

Goldhaber, Stanley, et al. Construction Management: Principles & Practices. LC 76-58397. (Construction Management & Engineering Ser.). 450p. 1977. 39.95x (ISBN 0-471-44270-4, Pub. by Wiley-Interscience). Wiley.

Goldhahn, W. E., jt. auth. see Merrem, G.

Goldhammer, Arthur, tr. see Badie, Bertrand & Birnbaum, Pierre.

Goldhammer, Arthur, tr. see Bourricaud, Francois.

Goldhammer, Arthur, tr. see Duby, Georges.

Goldhammer, Arthur, tr. see Schnapper, Dominique.

Goldhurst, Richard. The Midnight War. (Illus.). 1978. 14.95 o.p. (ISBN 0-07-023663-1, G). McGraw.

Goldie, W., jt. auth. see Reid, F. H.

Goldin, Amy. Manny Farber. LC 78-58402. 72p. (Orig.). 1978. pap. 7.00x (ISBN 0-934418-01-2). La Jolla Mus Contemp Art.

Goldin, Augusta. Bottom of the Sea. LC 66-10194. (A Let's-Read-&-Find-Out Science Bk). (Illus.). (ps-3). 1967. bds. 10.53i (ISBN 0-690-15863-7, TYC-J); PLB 7.89 o.p. (ISBN 0-690-15864-5). Har-Row.

--Ducks Don't Get Wet. LC 65-11647. (A Let's-Read-&-Find-Out Science Bk). (Illus.). (gr. k-3). PLB 10.89 (ISBN 0-690-24668-4, TYC-J). Har-Row.

--Let's Go to Build a Skyscraper. (Let's Go Ser.). (Illus.). 48p. (gr. 3-5). 1974. PLB 4.29 o.p. (ISBN 0-399-60857-5). Putnam Pub Group.

--Spider Silk. LC 64-18164. (A Let's-Read-&-Find-Out Science Bk). (Illus.). (gr. k-3). 1964. bds. 6.95 o.p. (ISBN 0-690-76074-5, TYC-J); PLB 10.89 (ISBN 0-690-76075-2). Har-Row.

--Straight Hair, Curly Hair. LC 66-12669. (A Let's-Read-&-Find-Out Science Bk). (Illus.). (gr. k-3). 1966. PLB 10.89 (ISBN 0-690-77921-6, TYC-J). Har-Row.

--Sunlit Sea. LC 68-17075. (A Let's-Read- & Find-Out Science Bk). (Illus.). (gr. k-3). 1968. bds. 10.53i (ISBN 0-690-79411-8, TYC-J); PLB 7.89 o.p. (ISBN 0-690-79412-6). Har-Row.

--Water: Too Much, Too Little, Too Polluted. LC 82-4760. (Illus.). 224p. (gr. 12 up). 12.95 (ISBN 0-15-294819-8, HJ). HarBraceJ.

Goldin, Bobbie. The Citizenship Handbook. 128p. (Orig.). 1982. pap. 6.95 (ISBN 0-671-45331-9). Monarch Pr.

Goldin, E. W. The Generation of Electricity by Wind Power. Rev. ed. 1976. 25.00x (ISBN 0-419-11070-4, Pub. by E & FN Spon). Methuen Inc.

Goldin, Edwin. Waves & Photons: An Introduction to Quantum Optics. (Pure & Applied Optics Ser.). 211p. 1982. 25.95x (ISBN 0-471-08592-8, Pub. by Wiley-Interscience). Wiley.

Goldin, Frederick, tr. The Song of Roland. 1978. 10.00x (ISBN 0-393-04523-4); pap. 4.95x (ISBN 0-393-09008-6). Norton.

Goldin, Judah. Living Talmud. pap. 2.75 (ISBN 0-451-62039-9, ME2039, Ment). NAL.

Goldin, Marshall D. Intensive Care of the Surgical Patient. 1981. 47.50 o.p. (ISBN 0-8151-3732-X). Year Bk Med.

Goldin, Stephen, jt. auth. see Smith, E. E.

Goldina, Miriam, tr. see Gorchakov, Nikolai M.

Golding, Douglas N. Tutorials in Clinical Rheumatology. 140p. 1981. 30.00x (ISBN 0-272-79611-5, Pub. by Pitman Bks England). State Mutual Bk.

Golding, Martin P. Philosophy of Law. (Foundation of Philosophy Ser.). 176p. 1975. text ed. 13.50 o.p. (ISBN 0-13-664136-9); pap. text ed. 9.95 (ISBN 0-13-664128-8). P-H.

Golding, Morton J. The Mystery of the Vikings in America. LC 73-4541. (Illus.). 160p. (gr. 7-10). 1973. 10.53i o.p. (ISBN 0-397-31247-4, JBL-J). Har-Row.

--A Short History of Puerto Rico. (Illus.). 160p. 1973. pap. 1.25 o.p. (ISBN 0-451-61214-0, MY1214, Ment). NAL.

Golding, P., ed. Alcoholism: A Modern Perspective. (Illus.). 539p. 1982. 44.00 (ISBN 0-942068-00-9). Bogden & Son.

Golding, William. Free Fall. LC 60-5431. (YA) (gr. 9-12). 1962. pap. 2.95 (ISBN 0-15-633468-2, Harv). HarBraceJ.

--Lord of the Flies. (gr. 9 up). 1978. 14.95 (ISBN 0-698-10219-3, Coward). Putnam Pub Group.

--Pincher Martin. LC 57-10059. Orig. Title: Two Deaths of Christopher Martin. 1968. pap. 2.95 (ISBN 0-15-671833-2, Harv). HarBraceJ.

--The Scorpion God. LC 70-174508. 178p. 1971. 5.95 o.p. (ISBN 0-15-136410-9). HarBraceJ.

Goldingay, John. Old Testament Commentary Survey. 2nd ed. Hubbard, Robert & Branson, Mark L., eds. 66p. 1981. pap. 2.95 (ISBN 0-8308-5499-1). Inter-Varsity.

Goldkamp, John S. Two Classes of Accused: A Study of Bail & Detention in America. LC 79-13042. (Illus.). 288p. 1979. prof ref 27.50x (ISBN 0-88410-802-3). Ballinger Pub.

Goldkuhl, G., jt. auth. see Sundburg, M.

Goldman & Cope. Radiographic Index. 6th ed. 104p. 1978. pap. 8.50 o.p. (ISBN 0-7236-0496-7). Wright-PSG.

Goldman, Alan. Public Communication: Perception, Criticism, Performance. LC 80-24016. 1983. lib. bdg. write for info. (ISBN 0-89874-244-7). Krieger.

--Unveiling the Self: Frontiers in Human Communication. 1979. pap. text ed. 16.95 (ISBN 0-8403-2072-8). Kendall-Hunt.

Goldman, Albert. Elvis. 736p. 1982. pap. 3.95 (ISBN 0-380-60350-0, 60350). Avon.

Goldman, Albert, ed. see Wagner, Richard.

Goldman, Alex J. Power of the Bible. 500p. 1983. Repr. of 1974 ed. 24.50x (ISBN 0-685-41733-6). Irvington.

Goldman, Alvin L., jt. auth. see Covington, Robert N.

Goldman, Alvin L. see Labor Law Group.

Goldman, Amy Beth & Dines, David M. Shoulder Arthrography. Goldman, Amy Beth, ed. (Little, Brown Library in Radiology). 1982. text ed. 42.50 (ISBN 0-316-31931-7). Little.

Goldman, Amy Beth, ed. see Goldman, Amy Beth & Dines, David M.

Goldman, Bert A., ed. Directory of Unpublished Experimental Mental Measures: Volume 4, 1975-1976. 1983. 39.95 (ISBN 0-89885-100-9). Human Sci Pr.

Goldman, Bert A. & Busch, John C., eds. Directory of Unpublished Experimental Mental Measures: Volume 3, 1973-74. LC 73-17342. 448p. 1982. 39.95 (ISBN 0-89885-095-9). Human Sci Pr.

Goldman, Charles & Horne, Alexander. Limnology. (Illus.). 633p. 1982. text ed. 30.95 (ISBN 0-07-023651-8, C). McGraw.

Goldman, Charles R., ed. Primary Productivity in Aquatic Environments. 1966. 32.50x (ISBN 0-520-01425-1). U of Cal Pr.

Goldman, Dave. Full-Time Restless. LC 79-20098. 1979. 12.95 (ISBN 0-399-90063-2, Marek). Putnam Pub Group.

Goldman, David. Presidential Losers. LC 75-103678. (Pull Ahead Books Ser.). (Illus.). (gr. 5-11). 1970. PLB 4.95g (ISBN 0-8225-0457-X). Lerner Pubns.

Goldman, Elizabeth, jt. auth. see Fearn, Leif.

Goldman, Emma. Living My Life, 2 Vols. LC 73-109546. (Civil Liberties in American History Ser.). 1976. Repr. of 1931 ed. Set. lib. bdg. 95.00 (ISBN 0-306-71900-2). Da Capo.

--Living My Life. abr. ed. Drinnon, Richard & Drinnon, Anna M., eds. 1977. pap. 9.95 (ISBN 0-452-00600-7, F600, Mer). NAL.

Goldman, Errol, jt. auth. see Billings, Rolland G.

Goldman, Ethel. I Like Fruit. LC 68-56699. (Nature Bks for Young Readers). (Illus.). (gr. k-5). 1969. PLB 4.95g (ISBN 0-8225-0270-4). Lerner Pubns.

Goldman, George D. & Stricker, George, eds. Practical Problems of a Private Psychotherapy Practice. LC 81-12684. 286p. 1982. 25.00 (ISBN 0-87668-483-5). Aronson.

Goldman, Henry M. & Cohen, D. Walter. Introduction to Periodontics. 5th ed. LC 77-22523. (Illus.). 580p. 1977. pap. text ed. 20.95 o.p. (ISBN 0-8016-1879-7). Mosby.

Goldman, Henry M., et al, eds. Current Therapy in Dentistry, Vols. 4-6. LC 64-23943. (Illus.). Vol. 4, 1970. 37.50 o.p. (ISBN 0-8016-1193-8); Vol. 5, 1974. 39.50 o.p. (ISBN 0-8016-1194-6); Vol. 6, 1977. 43.50 o.p. (ISBN 0-8016-1195-4). Mosby.

Goldman, Howard, jt. auth. see Tessler, Richard.

Goldman, I. & Krivchenkov, V. D. Problems in Quantum Mechanics. 1961. text ed. 26.00 o.p. (ISBN 0-08-009462-7). Pergamon.

Goldman, Irving. The Mouth of Heaven: An Introduction to Kwakiutl Religious Thought. LC 75-8742. 265p. 1975. 22.50 o.p. (ISBN 0-471-31140-5, Pub. by Wiley-Interscience). Wiley.

Goldman, James. The Lion in Winter. 1983. pap. 4.95 (ISBN 0-14-048174-5). Penguin.

Goldman, James & Sondheim, Stephen. Follies. 1971. 10.50 (ISBN 0-394-47362-0). Random.

Goldman, Jeanine, et al. Perspectives de France: Workbook. (Illus.). 224p. 1982. 8.95 (ISBN 0-13-660530-3). P-H.

Goldman, Jerome M., jt. auth. see Reinis, Stanislav.

Goldman, Katie. In the Wings. LC 82-70200. 176p. (gr. 6 up). 1982. 10.95 (ISBN 0-8037-3968-0). Dial.

Goldman, Larry. The Professional Photographer: Developing a Successful Career. LC 81-43582. (Illus.). 224p. 1983. pap. 12.95 (ISBN 0-385-15753-3, Dolp). Doubleday.

Goldman, Laurel. Sounding the Territory. LC 81-12409. 320p. 1982. 13.50 o.p. (ISBN 0-394-51935-3). Knopf.

--Sounding the Territory. (YA) (gr. 7-12). 1983. pap. 3.50 (ISBN 0-440-38176-2, LE). Dell.

Goldman, Lawrence S. New York Criminal Law Handbook. 500p. Date not set. 60.00x o.p. (ISBN 0-07-023669-0). Dist. by Shepard's Inc. McGraw.

Goldman, Leo, ed. Research Methods for Counselors: Practical Approaches in Field Settings. LC 77-10950. (Counseling & Human Development Ser.). 1978. text ed. 29.95x (ISBN 0-471-02339-6). Wiley.

Goldman, Leon. Applications of the Laser. LC 82-7834. 332p. 1982. Repr. of 1973 ed. lib. bdg. 49.95 (ISBN 0-89874-481-4). Krieger.

--Biomedical Aspects of the Laser. (Illus.). 1967. 39.80 (ISBN 0-387-90571-5). Springer-Verlag.

--Conference on the Lasar, Third, Vol. 267. (Annals of the New York Academy of Sciences). 481p. 1976. 57.00x (ISBN 0-89072-021-5). NY Acad Sci.

Goldman, Leon & Rockwell, James R., Jr. Lasers in Medicine. LC 77-163181. (Illus.). 394p. 1971. 80.00 (ISBN 0-677-02430-4). Gordon.

Goldman, Leon, et al. Laboratory Diagnosis in Dermatology. LC 70-176170. 300p. 1983. 37.50 (ISBN 0-87527-149-9). Green.

Goldman, Marion S. & Rabow, Jerome. Psychoanalytic Sociology: A Text & Reader. 1984. text ed. write for info. (ISBN 0-89874-608-6). Krieger.

Goldman, Marshall. Enigma of Soviet Petroleum: Half Empty or Half Full? (Illus.). 216p. (Orig.). 1980. text ed. 19.95x (ISBN 0-04-333015-0); pap. text ed. 8.95x (ISBN 0-04-333016-9). Allen Unwin.

Goldman, Marshall I. The Spoils of Progress: Environmental Pollution in the Soviet Union. 1972. 20.00x o.p. (ISBN 0-262-07053-7). MIT Pr.

--The U. S. S. R. in Crisis: The Failure of an Economic System. 1983. 15.00 (ISBN 0-393-01715-X); pap. 4.95x (ISBN 0-393-95336-X). Norton.

Goldman, Marvin & Bustad, Leo K., eds. Biomedical Implications of Radiostrontium Exposure: Proceedings. LC 72-600049. (AEC Symposium Ser.). 411p. 1972. pap. 18.25 (ISBN 0-87079-152-4, CONF-710201); microfiche 4.50 (ISBN 0-87079-153-2, CONF-710201). DOE.

Goldman, Mervin J. Principles of Clinical Electrocardiography. 11th ed. LC 62-13252. (Illus.). 438p. 1982. lexotone cover 15.00 (ISBN 0-87041-082-2). Lange.

Goldman, Myer & Cope, David. A Radiographic Index. 7th ed. (Illus.). 112p. 1982. pap. text ed. 10.00 (ISBN 0-7236-0660-9). Wright-PSG.

Goldman, Nahum. The Jewish Paradox. 1978. 4.95 o.p. (ISBN 0-448-15166-9, Fred Jordan Books). Putnam Pub Group.

Goldman, Norma & Szymanski, Ladislas. English Grammar for Students of Latin. Morton, Jacqueline, ed. 200p. 1983. pap. 5.00x (ISBN 0-934034-03-6). Olivia & Hill.

Goldman, Peter. Civil Rights: The Challenge of the Fourteenth Amendment. (Challenge Bk). (Illus.). (gr. 6-8). 1970. 4.00e o.p. (ISBN 0-698-20024-1, Coward). Putnam Pub Group.

--Report from Black America. LC 77-130194. 1970. 6.95 o.p. (ISBN 0-671-20609-5). S&S.

--Report from Black America. LC 77-130194. 1971. pap. 2.95 o.p. (ISBN 0-671-20899-3, Touchstone Bks). S&S.

Goldman, Peter & Fuller, Tony. Charlie Company: What Vietnam Did to Us. (Illus.). 384p. 1983. 15.95 (ISBN 0-688-01549-2). Morrow.

Goldman, Ralph F., jt. ed. see Hollies, Norman R.

Goldman, Ralph M. Arms Control & Peacekeeping. 301p. 1982. pap. text ed. 11.00 (ISBN 0-394-32886-8). Random.

--Search for Consensus: The Story of the Democratic Party. LC 79-1207. 417p. 1979. 32.95 (ISBN 0-87722-152-9). Temple U Pr.

Goldman, Richard, et al. Looking at Children: Field Experiences in Child Study. Peck, Johanne & Lehane, Stephen, eds. LC 76-15127. 1976. pap. text ed. 14.95 (ISBN 0-89334-001-4). Humanics Ltd.

Goldman, Robert P., tr. & annotations by. The Ramayana of Valmiki, Balakanda. LC 82-61364. (Princeton Library of Asian Translations: Vol. I). 450p. 1983. 37.50 (ISBN 0-691-06561-6). Princeton U Pr.

Goldman, Ronald. Readiness for Religion. 1970. pap. 4.95 (ISBN 0-8164-2060-2, SP70). Seabury.

--Religious Thinking from Childhood to Adolescence. 1968. pap. text ed. 6.95 (ISBN 0-8164-2061-0, SP53). Seabury.

Goldman, William. Adventures in the Screen Trade: A Personal View of Hollywood & Screenwriting. 416p. 1983. pap. 17.50 (ISBN 0-446-51273-7). Warner Bks.

--Control. 1983. pap. 3.95 (ISBN 0-440-11464-0). Dell.

--Marathon Man. 272p. 1975. pap. 2.75 (ISBN 0-440-15502-9). Dell.

--The Story of "A Bridge Too Far". (Orig.). 1977. pap. 1.75 o.p. (ISBN 0-440-18696-X). Dell.

Goldmann & Brown. Medical Care of the Surgical Patient: A Problem-Oriented Approach to Management. (Illus.). 897p. 1982. text ed. 38.50 (ISBN 0-397-50485-3, Lippincott Medical). Lippincott.

Goldmann, Lucien. Lukacs & Heidegger: Towards a New Philosophy. Boelhower, William Q., tr. 16.95x (ISBN 0-7100-8625-3); pap. 7.95 (ISBN 0-7100-8794-2). Routledge & Kegan.

Goldmann, Robert B., ed. Roundtable Justice: Case Studies in Conflict Resolution. (Westview Special Studies in Peace, Conflict, & Conflict Resolution). 231p. 1980. lib. bdg. 25.75x (ISBN 0-89158-962-7); pap. text ed. 10.00 (ISBN 0-86531-139-0). Westview.

Goldmark, Josephine C. Impatient Crusader: Florence Kelley's Life Story. LC 76-23383. 217p. 1976. Repr. of 1953 ed. lib. bdg. 18.00x (ISBN 0-8371-9011-8, GOIM). Greenwood.

Goldoni, Carolo. Il Capiello: A Venetian Comedy. Graham-Jones, Susanna, tr. from Ital. Bryden, Bill. (National Theatre Plays Ser.). viii, 64p. (Orig.). 1976. pap. text ed. 5.50x (ISBN 0-435-23359-9). Heinemann Ed.

Goldovsky, Boris & Schoep, Arthur. Bringing Soprano Arias to Life. 1973. pap. text ed. 11.95 (ISBN 0-02-870540-8). Schirmer Bks.

Goldreich, Gloria. Four Days. 352p. 1983. pap. 3.50 (ISBN 0-449-20091-4, Crest). Fawcett.

--This Burning Harvest. 1983. pap. 3.50 (ISBN 0-425-06078-0). Berkley Pub.

Goldring, Gvirol & Kalish, Rafael. Hyperfine Interactions of Excited Nuclei, 4 vols. LC 78-127883. (Illus.). 1378p. 1971. Set. 327.00x (ISBN 0-677-14600-0); 92.00x ea. Vol. 1, 386p (ISBN 0-677-15120-9). Vol. 2, 378p (ISBN 0-677-15130-6). Vol. 3 (ISBN 0-677-15140-3). Vol. 4, 392p (ISBN 0-677-15150-0). Gordon.

Goldring, Patrick. Britain by Train. 208p. 1983. pap. 5.95 (ISBN 0-600-20669-6, Pub. by Auto Assn-British Tourist Authority England). Merrimack Bk Serv.

Goldring, Sidney, jt. ed. see O'Leary, James L.

Goldrosen, John. Buddy Holly. 1979. pap. 7.95 (ISBN 0-8256-3936-0, Quick Fox). Putnam Pub Group.

Goldsborough, Jennifer F. Eighteenth & Nineteenth Century Maryland Silver in the Collection of the Baltimore Museum of Art. (Illus.). 204p. 1975. pap. 12.50 (ISBN 0-686-36474-0). Md Hist.

Goldsborough, June. My Telephone Book. (Illus.). 10p. (ps-3). 1981. 3.50 (ISBN 0-448-46826-3, G&D). Putnam Pub Group.

Goldsborough, June, jt. auth. see Foster, John.

Goldsborough, June, illus. The Dandelion Mother Goose. LC 78-72131. (Illus.). (gr. k-3). 1979. 6.75 (ISBN 0-89799-097-8); pap. 3.50 (ISBN 0-89799-052-8). Dandelion Pr.

--Look at Me. (Illus.). 14p. (ps). 1982. 2.95 (ISBN 0-448-12313-4, G&D). Putnam Pub Group.

Goldsby, Richard A. Biology. 2nd ed. (Illus.). 1979. text ed. 23.50 scp (ISBN 0-06-162409-8, HarpC); instr. manual avail. (ISBN 0-06-162413-6); 9.95 o.p. (ISBN 0-06-162412-8). Har-Row.

--Cells & Energy. 2nd ed. 1977. pap. text ed. 11.95x (ISBN 0-02-344300-6, 34430). Macmillan.

--Race & Races. 2nd ed. 1977. 12.95x (ISBN 0-02-344310-3, 34431). Macmillan.

Goldscheider, Calvin, jt. auth. see Kobrin, Frances E.

Goldscheider, Robert, jt. auth. see Finnegan, Marcus B.

Goldscheider, Robert, ed. Technology Management Handbook. 1982. softcover 27.50 (ISBN 0-87632-333-6). Boardman.

Goldschmid, H. J. Business Disclosure: Government's Need to Know. 1979. 39.95 (ISBN 0-07-023670-4). McGraw.

Goldschmid, Harvey J., et al, eds. Industrial Concentration: The New Learning. 1974. pap. 9.95 (ISBN 0-316-31941-4). Little.

Goldschmidt, Arthur, Jr. A Concise History of the Middle East. 2nd rev. ed. 450p. 1983. lib. bdg. 30.00x (ISBN 0-86531-598-1); pap. text ed. 11.50x (ISBN 0-86531-599-X). Westview.

Goldschmidt, W. R., ed. The Uses of Anthropology. 1979. pap. 7.50 (ISBN 0-686-36569-0). Am Anthro Assn.

Goldschmidt, Walter. Culture & Behavior of the Sebei: A Study in Continuity & Adaptation. LC 74-82848. 1976. 44.75x (ISBN 0-520-02828-7). U of Cal Pr.

--Kambuya's Cattle: The Legacy of an African Herdsman. LC 68-31589. 1968. 30.00x (ISBN 0-520-01472-3). U of Cal Pr.

Goldschmidt, Walter, ed. see Alkire, William.

Goldschmidt, Werner & Rodriguez-Novas, Jose. American-Argentine Private International Law. LC 66-17537. 117p. 1966. 15.00 (ISBN 0-379-11415-1). Oceana.

Goldschmidt, Y. & Admon, K. Profit Measurement During Inflation: Accounting, Economic & Financial Aspects. LC 77-4500. (Operations Managment Ser.). 1977. 39.95x (ISBN 0-471-01983-6, Pub. by Wiley-Interscience). Wiley.

Goldschmidt, Yaaqov, jt. auth. see Shashua, Leon.

Goldschmidt-Clermont, Luisella. Unpaid Work in the Household: A Review of Economic Evaluation Methods. (Women, Work & Development: No. 1). xi, 137p. 1982. 10.00 (ISBN 92-2-103085-7). Intl Labour Office.

Goldsmid, H. J., jt. auth. see Beeforth, T. H.

Goldsmid, Paula. Did You Ever. (Illus.). 30p. (ps-k). 1971. pap. 2.75 (ISBN 0-914996-01-0). Lollipop Power.

Goldsmith. Wise Fools in Shakespeare. 136p. 1982. 40.00x (ISBN 0-85323-263-6, Pub. by Liverpool Univ England). State Mutual Bk.

Goldsmith see Balderston, Katherine C.

Goldsmith, Alice, jt. auth. see Lansing, Adrienne.

Goldsmith, Arnold L. American Literary Criticism: Vol. III, 1905-1965. (United States Author Ser.). 1979. lib. bdg. 12.95 (ISBN 0-8057-7265-0, Twayne). G K Hall.

--The Golem Remembered 1909-1980: Variations of a Jewish Legend. (Illus.). 188p. 1981. 15.95 (ISBN 0-8143-1683-2). Wayne St U Pr.

Goldsmith, Arthur. The Camera & Its Images. LC 79-3937. (Illus.). 1979. 12.95 (ISBN 0-88225-272-0). Newsweek.

Goldsmith, Barbara. Little Gloria: Happy at Last. 1981. pap. 4.95 (ISBN 0-440-15120-1). Dell.

Goldsmith, D., jt. auth. see Wagoner, R.

Goldsmith, Donald. The Evolving Universe: An Introduction to Astronomy. 1981. 23.95 (ISBN 0-8053-3327-4); pap. 4.95 (ISBN 0-686-85713-5, 33328). Benjamin-Cummings.

Goldsmith, Donald & Levy, Donald. From the Black Hole to the Infinite Universe. LC 73-86412. (Illus.). 300p. 1974. pap. text ed. 12.50x (ISBN 0-8162-3323-3). Holden-Day.

Goldsmith, Donald, jt. auth. see Owen, Tobias.

Goldsmith, Elisabeth E. Ancient Pagan Symbols. LC 68-18025. (Illus.). xxxix, 220p. 1976. Repr. of 1929 ed. 30.00x (ISBN 0-8103-4140-9). Gale.

Goldsmith, Henry A., jt. ed. see Rosen, Milton J.

Goldsmith, Howard. Invasion Twenty-Two Hundred A. D. LC 78-22320. (Signal Bk.). 1979. 7.95 o.p. (ISBN 0-385-14247-1). Doubleday.

--What Makes a Grumble Smile? LC 76-25210. (Imagination). (Illus.). (gr. 1-5). 1977. lib. bdg. 6.69 (ISBN 0-8116-4403-0). Garrard.

Goldsmith, Howard R. How to Make a Fortune in Import-Export. 1981. text ed. 16.00 (ISBN 0-8359-2962-0, Reward Edn); pap. text ed. 10.00. Reston.

Goldsmith, Ilse. Anatomy for Children. LC 64-15111. (Illus.). (gr. 3-8). 1964. 8.95 (ISBN 0-8069-3000-4); PLB 10.99 (ISBN 0-8069-3001-2). Sterling.

--Human Anatomy for Children. (Illus.). (gr. 5-8). 1969. pap. 2.50 (ISBN 0-486-22355-8). Dover.

Goldsmith, Joe. How to Hand Rear Baby Birds. (Illus.). 48p. (Orig.). Date not set. pap. text ed. 3.95 (ISBN 0-910335-00-1). Avian Pubns.

Goldsmith, Joel S. Awakening Mystical Consciousness. Sinkler, Lorraine, ed. LC 79-3601. 176p. 1980. 9.95i (ISBN 0-06-063174-0). Har-Row.

--Infinite Way Letters. 1954. pap. 3.95 (ISBN 0-87516-137-5). De Vorss.

--Living the Infinite Way. rev. ed. LC 61-9646. 1961. 8.95i (ISBN 0-06-063190-2, HarpR). Har-Row.

--Parenthesis in Eternity. LC 64-10368. 1963. 14.90i (ISBN 0-06-063230-5, HarpR). Har-Row.

--Thunder of Silence. LC 61-7340. 1961. 9.57i (ISBN 0-06-063270-4, HarpR). Har-Row.

Goldsmith, John. Exodus Forty-Three. 1982. 13.95 (ISBN 0-698-11129-X, Coward). Putnam Pub Group.

Goldsmith, John & Briggs, Gordon. Bullion: A Novel of Financial Intrigue. 256p. 1983. 13.95 (ISBN 0-89479-122-2). A & W Pubs.

Goldsmith, Lee S., jt. ed. see Bertolet, Mary M.

Goldsmith, Lowell A., ed. Biochemistry & Physiology of the Skin, 2 vols. (Illus.). 1300p. 1983. Set. 150.00 (ISBN 0-19-261253-0). Oxford U Pr.

Goldsmith, M. & Shaw, Edwin. Europe's Giant Accelerator. 261p. 1977. 27.50x o.s.i. (ISBN 0-8448-1220-X). Crane-Russak Co.

Goldsmith, Martin. Islam & Christian Witness. 160p. 1983. pap. 4.95 (ISBN 0-87784-809-2). Inter-Varsity.

Goldsmith, Maurice. Young Scientists Companion. (Illus.). (gr. 9 up). 14.50x (ISBN 0-392-02027-0, SpS). Sportshelf.

Goldsmith, Oliver. Citizen of the World & the Bee. 1970. Repr. of 1934 ed. 7.95x (ISBN 0-460-00902-8, Pub. by Evman England). Biblio Dist.

--Poems & Plays. Davis, Tom, ed. (Rowman & Littlefield University Library). 258p. 1975. 17.50x o.p. (ISBN 0-87471-702-7). Rowman.

--She Stoops to Conquer. Balderston, Katherine G., ed. LC 51-6755. (Crofts Classics Ser.). 1951. pap. text ed. 3.25x (ISBN 0-88295-039-8). Harlan Davidson.

--She Stoops to Conquer. Shefter, Harry, ed. (Enriched Classics Edition Ser.). 176p. pap. 2.75 (ISBN 0-671-45535-4). WSP.

--Vicar of Wakefield. pap. 1.95 (ISBN 0-451-51723-7, CE1723, Sig Classics). NAL.

--The Vicar of Wakefield. Friedman, Arthur, ed. (World's Classics Ser.). 232p. 1982. pap. 4.95 (ISBN 0-686-95061-5). Oxford U Pr.

Goldsmith, Oliver see Morrell, Janet M.

Goldsmith, Raymond W. The Financial Development of India. LC 82-7094. 264p. 1983. text ed. 35.00x (ISBN 0-300-02030-9). Yale U Pr.

--The Financial Development of India, Japan, & the United States. LC 82-8541. 136p. 1983. text ed. 12.95x (ISBN 0-300-02934-9). Yale U Pr.

--The Financial Development of Japan. LC 82-8378. 256p. 1983. text ed. 30.00x (ISBN 0-300-02933-0). Yale U Pr.

--The National Balance of the United States, 1953 to 1980. LC 82-2746. (National Bureau of Economic Research Monograph). 1982. lib. bdg. 30.00x (ISBN 0-226-30152-4). U of Chicago Pr.

Goldsmith, Ruth M. Phoebe Takes Charge. LC 82-13955. 240p. (gr. 5-9). 1983. 11.95 (ISBN 0-689-50266-4, McElderry Bk). Atheneum.

Goldsmith, S. J. Twenty Twentieth Century Jews. LC 62-21948. (Illus.). 142p. 1962. 7.95 o.p. (ISBN 0-88400-021-4). Shengold.

Goldsmith, Ulrich K., ed. see Weigand, Hermann J.

Goldson, Rae L. New Trends in Flower Arrangement. (Illus.). 1966. 4.95 (ISBN 0-8208-0052-X). Hearthside.

Goldspink, D. F., ed. The Development & Specialisation of Skeletal Muscle. (Society for Experimental Biology Seminar Ser.: No. 7). (Illus.). 200p. 1981. 47.50 (ISBN 0-521-23317-8); pap. 21.95 (ISBN 0-521-29907-1). Cambridge U Pr.

Goldspink, G., ed. Differentiation & Growth of Cells in Vertebrate Tissues. 1977. 45.00x (ISBN 0-412-11390-2, Pub. by Chapman & Hall). Methuen Inc.

Goldspink, G., jt. ed. see Alexander, R. McNeill.

Goldstein. The Politics of Offshore Oil. 208p. 1982. 21.95 (ISBN 0-03-059813-3). Praeger.

Goldstein, et al. Contemporary Collection. 48p. (gr. 3-12). 1974. pap. text ed. 7.40 (ISBN 0-87487-627-3). Summy.

Goldstein, A. P., jt. auth. see Kanfer, F. H.

Goldstein, Abraham S. & Orland, Leonard. Criminal Procedure, Cases & Materials on the Administration of Criminal Law: 1978 Supplement. 1974. 26.50 o.p. (ISBN 0-316-31951-1); 6.95 o.p. (ISBN 0-686-96772-0). Little.

Goldstein, Aileen. Neurological Critical Care. (Series in Critical Care Nursing). (Illus.). 200p. (Orig.). Date not set. pap. text ed. 12.95. Wiley.

Goldstein, Alan. A Fistful of Sugar: The Sugar Ray Leonard Story. (Illus.). 1981. 13.95 (ISBN 0-698-11082-X, Coward). Putnam Pub Group.

Goldstein, Alan & Foa, Edna B. Handbook of Behavioral Interventions. LC 79-16950. (Personality Processes Ser.). 1980. 38.50x (ISBN 0-471-01789-2, Pub. by Wiley-Interscience). Wiley.

Goldstein, Alan J., jt. auth. see Chambless, Dianne L.

Goldstein, Allan, jt. ed. see Fefer, Alexander.

Goldstein, Allan L. & Chirigos, Michael A., eds. Lymphokines & Thymic Hormones: Their Potential Utilization in Cancer Therapeutics. (Progress in Cancer Research & Therapy Ser.: Vol. 20). 342p. 1981. text ed. 42.00 (ISBN 0-89004-697-2). Raven.

Goldstein, Alvin H. The Unquiet Death of Julius & Ethel Rosenberg. LC 75-8336. (Illus.). 96p. 1975. 8.95 (ISBN 0-88208-052-0); pap. 4.95 o.s.i. (ISBN 0-88208-053-9). Lawrence Hill.

Goldstein, Andrew & Wikler, Madeline. My Very Own Jewish Home. (Illus.). (ps-4). 1979. pap. 3.95 (ISBN 0-930494-08-3). Kar Ben.

Goldstein, Arnold P. & Sorcher, Melvin. Changing Supervisor Behavior. LC 73-10059. 1975. text ed. 13.75 o.p. (ISBN 0-08-017742-5); pap. text ed. 7.50 (ISBN 0-08-017769-7). Pergamon.

--Changing Supervisor Behavior. 160p. softcover 7.50 (ISBN 0-686-84791-1). Work in Amer.

Goldstein, Arnold P. & Stein, Norman. Prescriptive Psychotherapies. LC 75-5620. 1976. text ed. 34.00 (ISBN 0-08-019506-7, 75-5620); pap. text ed. 14.50 (ISBN 0-08-019505-9). Pergamon.

Goldstein, Arnold P. & Segall, Marshall H., eds. Aggression in Global Perspective. (Pergamon General Psychology Ser.: No. 115). (Illus.). 475p. 1983. 47.50 (ISBN 0-08-026346-1). Pergamon.

Goldstein, Arnold S. Complete Guide to Buying & Selling a Business. (Small Business Management Ser.). 310p. 1983. 23.95 (ISBN 0-471-87091-9). Ronald Pr.

--EMS & the Law: A Legal Handbook for EMS Personnel. (Illus.). 224p. 1983. 16.95 (ISBN 0-89303-423-1); pap. 9.95 (ISBN 0-89303-422-3). R J Brady.

--How to Save Your Business. 1983. 14.95 (ISBN 0-913864-74-9). Enterprise Del.

--The Small Business Legal Problem-Solver. 240p. 1983. 24.95 (ISBN 0-8436-0890-0); pap. 15.95 (ISBN 0-8436-0891-9). CBI Pub.

Goldstein, Avram, ed. The Opiate Narcotics: Neurochemical Mechanisms of Analgesia & Dependence. 270p. 1976. text ed. 26.50 (ISBN 0-08-019869-4). Pergamon.

Goldstein, Avram, et al. Principles of Drug Action: The Basis of Pharmacology. 2nd ed. LC 73-15871. 1974. 46.00x (ISBN 0-471-31260-6, Pub. by Wiley-Medical). Wiley.

Goldstein, B. Introduction to Human Sexuality. 1975. text ed. 17.50 o.p. (ISBN 0-07-023691-7, C); pap. text ed. 19.95 (ISBN 0-07-023690-9). McGraw.

Goldstein, Barbara, jt. auth. see McCoy, Esther.

Goldstein, Bernard & Goldstein, Estelle T. Toy Soldiers. (Illus.). 48p. 1982. 24.00 (ISBN 0-88014-047-X). Mosaic Pr OH.

Goldstein, Catherine, jt. auth. see Kohl, Sam.

Goldstein, D. M., ed. see Prange, G. W.

Goldstein, Darra, tr. see Teffi, Nadezhda.

Goldstein, David. The Jewish Poets of Spain. 1983. pap. 5.95 (ISBN 0-14-044250-2). Penguin.

Goldstein, David I. Dostoyevsky & the Jews. (University of Texas Press Slavic Ser.: No. 3). 256p. 1981. 20.00x (ISBN 0-292-71528-5). U of Tex Pr.

Goldstein, Donald P. Gestational Trophoblastic Disease. LC 74-12910. (Major Problems in Obstetrics & Gynecology Ser.: Vol. XII). (Illus.). 225p. 1979. text ed. write for info. o.p. (ISBN 0-7216-4147-4). Saunders.

Goldstein, Donald P., jt. auth. see Emans, S. J.

Goldstein, Donald P., jt. auth. see Emans, S. Jean.

Goldstein, Dora B. Pharmacology of Alcohol. (Illus.). 200p. 1983. text ed. 24.95x (ISBN 0-19-503111-3); pap. text ed. 16.95x (ISBN 0-19-503112-1). Oxford U Pr.

Goldstein, Doris M., ed. Bioethics: A Guide to Information Sources. (The Health Affairs Information Guide Ser.: Vol. 8). 375p. 1982. 42.00x (ISBN 0-8103-1502-5). Gale.

Goldstein, E. Bruce. Sensation & Perception. 512p. 1980. text ed. 26.95x (ISBN 0-534-00760-0). Wadsworth Pub.

Goldstein, Estelle T., jt. auth. see Goldstein, Bernard.

Goldstein, Gerald & Neuringer, Charles, eds. Empirical Studies of Alcoholism. LC 76-17285. 288p. 1976. prof ref 22.00x (ISBN 0-88410-127-4). Ballinger Pub.

Goldstein, Gersham & Bittker, Boris I. Index to Federal Tax Articles. 1982. 160.00 (ISBN 0-88262-018-5). Warren.

Goldstein, Harold M. & Horowitz, Morris A. Health Personnel: Meeting the Explosive Demand for Medical Care. LC 76-55042. 128p. 1977. 27.50 (ISBN 0-912862-36-X). Aspen Systems.

Goldstein, Harris A., jt. auth. see Starr, Bernard D.

Goldstein, Helen, jt. auth. see Goldstein, Shelly.

Goldstein, Herb, compiled by. Compendium of Land Trust Documents. pap. 3.00 (ISBN 0-686-84741-5). Comm Serv.

Goldstein, Herbert. Classical Mechanics. 2nd ed. LC 79-23456. (Illus.). 1980. text ed. 30.95 (ISBN 0-201-02918-9). A-W.

Goldstein, Herman. Policing a Free Society. LC 76-13589. 1977. 16.50 o.p. (ISBN 0-88410-216-5); pap. 9.95x prof ref (ISBN 0-88410-784-1). Ballinger Pub.

Goldstein, Imre, tr. see Biro, Yvette.

Goldstein, Jeffrey H. Aggression & Crimes of Violence. Lana, Robert & Rosnow, Ralph, eds. (Reconstruction of Society Ser). (Illus.). 1975. 15.95x (ISBN 0-19-501935-0); pap. 6.95x (ISBN 0-19-501936-9). Oxford U Pr.

Goldstein, Jonathan. Philadelphia & the China Trade, Sixteen Eighty-Two to Eighteen Forty-Six: Commercial, Cultural, & Attitudinal Effects. LC 77-1638. (Illus.). 1978. 13.95x (ISBN 0-271-00512-2). Pa St U Pr.

Goldstein, Jonathan A., tr. & intro. by. Maccabees One. LC 75-32719. (Anchor Bible Ser.: Vol. 41). (Illus.). 18.00 (ISBN 0-385-08533-8, Anchor Pr). Doubleday.

Goldstein, Joseph. The Experience of Insight: A Simple & Direct Guide to Buddhist Meditation. LC 82-42682. 185p. (Orig.). 1983. pap. 6.95 (ISBN 0-394-71430-X). Shambhala Pubns.

Goldstein, Joseph, et al. Beyond the Best Interests of the Child. LC 79-7630. 1980. 14.95 (ISBN 0-02-912200-7); pap. 4.95 (ISBN 0-02-912190-6). Free Pr.

Goldstein, Joseph, jt. auth. see Becker, Loftus E.

Goldstein, Joyce E. Feedback. LC 77-29263. 1978. 10.95 o.p. (ISBN 0-399-90002-0, Marek). Putnam Pub Group.

Goldstein, Kenneth M. & Blackman, Sheldon. Cognitive Style: Five Approaches & Relevant Research. LC 78-1378. 1978. 28.95 (ISBN 0-471-31275-4, Pub. by Wiley-Interscience). Wiley.

Goldstein, Kenneth S. A Guide for Field Workers in Folklore. LC 64-24801. xx, 199p. Repr. of 1964 ed. 30.00x (ISBN 0-8103-5000-9); pap. 16.00x (ISBN 0-8103-5041-6). Gale.

Goldstein, Kurt. Human Nature in the Light of Psychopathology. LC 63-20263. 1963. pap. 3.45 o.p. (ISBN 0-8052-0060-6). Schocken.

Goldstein, L., jt. auth. see Adams, W.

Goldstein, Larry. Finite Mathematics & Its Applications. (Illus.). 1980. text ed. 25.95 (ISBN 0-13-317263-5). P-H.

Goldstein, Larry, et al. Modern Mathematics & Its Applications. (Illus.). 816p. 1980. pap. text ed. 26.95 (ISBN 0-13-595173-9). P-H.

Goldstein, Larry J. Abstract Algebra: A First Course. LC 72-12790. (Illus.). 1973. 27.95x (ISBN 0-13-000851-6). P-H.

--The Graphics Generator: Business & Technical Graphics for the IBM Personal Computer. (Illus.). 155p. 1982. 60.00 (ISBN 0-89303-266-2). R J Brady.

Goldstein, Larry J. & Goldstein, Martin. Basic for the Apple II: Programming & Applications. (Illus.). 1982. lib. bdg. 19.95 (ISBN 0-89303-190-9); pap. 14.95 (ISBN 0-89303-189-5). R J Brady.

--The IBM Personal Computer: An Introduction to Programming & Applications. 350p. 1982. text ed. 19.95 (ISBN 0-89303-110-0); pap. 15.95 (ISBN 0-89303-111-9). R J Brady.

Goldstein, Larry J. & Lay, David. Calculus & Its Applications. 2nd ed. 1980. text ed. 26.95 (ISBN 0-13-111963-X). P-H.

Goldstein, Larry J., jt. auth. see Streitmatter, Gene.

Goldstein, Laurence. Ruins & Empire: The Evolution of a Theme in Augustan & Romantic Literature. LC 76-50889. (Illus.). 1977. 14.95x (ISBN 0-8229-3345-4). U of Pittsburgh Pr.

Goldstein, Leon J. Historical Knowing. LC 75-12037. 270p. 1976. 17.50x o.p. (ISBN 0-292-73002-0). U of Tex Pr.

Goldstein, M. & Dillon, W. R. Discrete Discriminant Analysis. 190p. 1978. 29.50x (ISBN 0-471-04167-X, Pub. by Wiley-Interscience). Wiley.

Goldstein, M. & Waldman, S., eds. The Creative Black Book: Europe 1983, Vol. 3. (Illus.). 205p. 1983. 40.00 (ISBN 0-916098-10-9). Friendly Pubns.

--The Creative Black Book North America 1983: Vol. I. (Illus.). 400p. 1983. 30.00 (ISBN 0-916098-08-7). Friendly Pubns.

--The Creative Black Book Photography: North America Vol. II. (Illus.). 565p. 1983. 40.00 (ISBN 0-916098-09-5). Friendly Pubns.

Goldstein, M., jt. ed. see Waldman, S.

Goldstein, Mahler, jt. auth. see Glashow.

Goldstein, Malcolm. George S. Kaufman: His Life, His Theater. (Illus.). 1979. 25.00x (ISBN 0-19-502623-3). Oxford U Pr.

Goldstein, Martin, jt. auth. see Goldstein, Larry J.

Goldstein, Martin & Simha, Robert, eds. The Glass Transition & the Nature of the Glassy State, Vol. 279. (Annals of the New York Academy of Sciences). 246p. 1976. 28.00x (ISBN 0-89072-025-8). NY Acad Sci.

Goldstein, Martin E. Nuclear Proliferation: International Politics in a Multinuclear World. LC 80-1367. 79p. 1980. pap. text ed. 6.75 (ISBN 0-8191-1243-7). U Pr of Amer.

Goldstein, Marty, jt. auth. see Waldman, Stu.

Goldstein, Marvin E. Aeroacoustics. 1976. text ed. 42.50x (ISBN 0-07-023685-2, C). McGraw.

Goldstein, Menek, et al. Ergot Compounds & Brain Function: Neuroendocrine & Neuropsychiatric Aspects. (Advances in Biochemical Psychopharmacology Ser.: Vol. 23). 441p. 1980. text ed. 49.50 (ISBN 0-89004-450-3). Raven.

Goldstein, Michael J., et al. Abnormal Psychology: Experiences, Origins, & Interventions. (Illus.). 622p. 1980. text ed. 21.95 (ISBN 0-316-31955-4); instuctor's manual avail. (ISBN 0-316-31956-2). Little.

--Pornography & Sexual Deviance. LC 72-97753. 1973. 26.50x (ISBN 0-520-02406-0); pap. 2.45 (ISBN 0-520-02619-5). U of Cal Pr.

Goldstein, Milton. The Magnificent West: Yosemite. LC 72-85054. 224p. 1976. 35.00 (ISBN 0-385-03296-X). Doubleday.

Goldstein, Murray, et al, eds. Cerebrovascular Disorders & Stroke. LC 78-62496. (Advances in Neurology Ser.: Vol. 25). 420p. 1979. text ed. 45.50 (ISBN 0-89004-294-2). Raven.

Goldstein, Nathan. The Art of Responsive Drawing. 2nd ed. LC 76-25001. (Illus.). 1977. 22.95 (ISBN 0-13-048629-9). P-H.

--Figure Drawing: The Structure, Anatomy, & Expressive Design of Human Form. (Illus.). 330p. 1981. text ed. 25.95 (ISBN 0-13-314518-2); pap. text ed. 21.95 (ISBN 0-13-314435-6). P-H.

--Painting: Visual & Technical Fundamentals. LC 78-15907. 1979. 21.95 (ISBN 0-13-647800-X). P-H.

Goldstein, Norm & Associated Press. Henry Fonda. LC 82-48627. (Illus.). 124p. 1982. pap. 7.70 (ISBN 0-03-063353-2, Owl Bks). HR&W.

Goldstein, Norman & Stone, Robert. The Skin You Live in. (Illus.). 208p. 1979. pap. 5.95 o.s.i. (ISBN 0-89104-249-0, A & W Visual Library). A & W Pubs.

Goldstein, Paul. Copyright, Patent, Trademark & Related State Doctrines: Cases & Materials on the Law of Intellectual Property. 2nd ed. (University Casebook Ser.). 183p. 1982. write for info. tchrs. manual (ISBN 0-88277-105-1). Foundation Pr.

Goldstein, Paul J. Prostitution & Drugs. LC 78-24766. 208p. 1979. 22.95x (ISBN 0-669-02833-9). Lexington Bks.

Goldstein, Phyllis J. How to Start a Successful, Money-Making "Business" while Attending College. (Illus.). 48p. (Orig.). 1982. pap. 6.95 (ISBN 0-910481-00-8). Money-Maker.

Goldstein, R., jt. ed. see Nordhaus, W. D.

Goldstein, R. J. Cichlids. 1970. 14.95 (ISBN 0-87666-020-0, H939). TFH Pubns.

--Diseases of Aquarium Fishes. (Illus.). pap. 7.95 (ISBN 0-87666-041-3, PS201). TFH Pubns.

--Introduction to Cichlids. 1970. pap. 9.95 (ISBN 0-87666-788-4, PS-662). TFH Pubns.

Goldstein, Richard & Sachs, Stephen, eds. Applied Poverty Research. (Orig.). 1982. pap. 6.00 (ISBN 0-918592-52-6). Policy Studies.

Goldstein, Richard J., ed. Fluid Mechanics Measurements. (Illus.). 740p. 1983. text ed. 37.50 (ISBN 0-89116-244-5). Hemisphere Pub.

Goldstein, Richard J., jt. ed. see Eckert, Ernest R.

Goldstein, Robert J. Anabantoids Gouramis & Related Species. (Illus.). 9.95 (ISBN 0-87666-750-7, PS672). TFH Pubns.

--Cichlids of the World. (Illus.). 382p. 1973. 29.95 (ISBN 0-87666-032-4, H-945). TFH Pubns.

--Political Repression in Modern America. 1978. lib. bdg. 24.00 (ISBN 0-8161-8253-1, Univ Bks). G K Hall.

Goldstein, Sam. A Printer's Limericks: Limericklets Ser. (No. 6). (Illus.). 1982. pap. 1.00 (ISBN 0-938338-18-8). Winds World Pr.

Goldstein, Sanford. Gaijin Aesthetics. (W.N.J Ser.: No. 17). 10.00; signed ed. 20.00; pap. 4.50. Juniper Pr WI.

Goldstein, Sanford, tr. see Takeda, Taijun.

Goldstein, Shelly & Goldstein, Helen. Coca Cola Collectibles, No. 4. (Illus.). soft cover 13.95 (ISBN 0-936118-03-2). Wallace-Homestead.

Goldstein, Sherry & D'Alessio, Barbara, eds. FINDex: The Directory of Market Research Reports, Studies & Surveys. 4th ed. 500p. 1982. pap. 139.00 (ISBN 0-931634-09-1, Dist. by Gale). Info Clearing House.

Goldstein, Stephen R. Law & Public Education, Cases & Materials. 2nd ed. Lee, Gordon, ed. (Contemporary Legal Education Ser). 25.00 (ISBN 0-672-84199-1, Bobbs-Merrill Law). Michie-Bobbs.

Goldstein, Stephen R., jt. auth. see Buss, William G.

Goldstein, Sue. The Underground Shopper: A Guide to Discount Mail-Order Shopping. 260p. 1983. pap. 5.95 (ISBN 0-8362-7915-8). Andrews & McMeel.

Goldstein, William. Supervision Made Simple. LC 82-60800. (Fastback Ser.: No. 180). 50p. 1982. pap. 0.75 (ISBN 0-87367-180-5). Phi Delta Kappa.

Goldstine, H. H. A History of the Calculus of Variations from the Seventeenth Through the Nineteenth Century. (Studies in the History of Mathematics & Physical Sciences Ser.: Vol. 5). (Illus.). 410p. 1981. 51.00 (ISBN 0-387-90521-9). Springer-Verlag.

Goldstine, Herman H. New & Full Moons One Thousand & One B. C. to A. D. Sixteen Fifty One. LC 72-89401. (Memoirs Ser.: Vol. 94). 1973. 10.00 (ISBN 0-87169-094-2). Am Philos.

Goldston, Angela, jt. auth. see Graham, Richard.

Goldston, Eli, et al. The American Business Corporations: New Perspectives on Profit & Purpose. 352p. 1972. 18.00x o.p. (ISBN 0-262-07052-9). MIT Pr.

Goldston, Robert. The American Nightmare. LC 73-1748. (gr. 7 up). 1973. pap. 7.95 o.p. (ISBN 0-672-52524-0). Bobbs.

--Life & Death of Nazi Germany. LC 66-29906. (gr. 7 up). 7.95 o.p. (ISBN 0-672-50354-9). Bobbs.

Goldstone, A. H., et al. Leukaemias, Lymphomas & Allied Disorders. LC 75-44603. (Illus.). 1976. text ed. 18.50 o.p. (ISBN 0-7216-4149-0). Saunders.

Goldstone, Gerald, jt. auth. see Goeller, Lee.

Goldstone, Harmon H. & Dalrymple, Martha. History Preserved: A Guide to New York City Landmarks & Historic Districts. LC 76-9142. (Illus.). 1976. pap. 9.95 (ISBN 0-8052-0544-6). Schocken.

Goldstone, Herbert. Coping with Vulnerability: The Achievement of John Osborne. 274p. (Orig.). 1982. lib. bdg. 22.50 (ISBN 0-8191-2617-9); pap. text ed. 11.50 (ISBN 0-8191-2618-7). U Pr of Amer.

Goldstone, Jerry. Decision Making in Vascular Surgery. 240p. 1983. text ed. 30.00 (ISBN 0-941158-14-4, D1889-4). Mosby.

Goldstone, Richard & Lass, A., eds. Mentor Book of Short Plays. pap. 3.95 (ISBN 0-451-62215-4, ME2215, Ment). NAL.

Goldstone, Richard A. Contexts of the Drama. LC 68-13092. (Illus.). 1968. text ed. 21.50 (ISBN 0-07-023662-3, C). McGraw.

Goldstrom, J. M. The Social Content of Education, 1808-1870: A Study of the Working-class School Reader in England & Ireland. 242p. 1972. text ed. 20.00x (ISBN 0-7165-1004-9, Pub. by Irish Academic Pr Ireland). Biblio dist.

Goldstrom, Robert, jt. auth. see Hollyn, Lynn.

Goldsworthy, Graeme. Gospel & Kingdom: A Chrisian's Guide to the Old Testament. 128p. 1983. pap. 6.95 (ISBN 0-86683-686-1). Winston Pr.

Goldsworthy, Maureen. Knowing Your Sewing. (gr. 10-12). 1973. 7.50 o.p. (ISBN 0-263-05148-X). Transatlantic.

Goldthorpe, J. E. An Introduction to Sociology. 2nd ed. LC 73-83107. (Illus.). 200p. 1974. text ed. 32.50 (ISBN 0-521-20338-4); pap. text ed. 10.95 (ISBN 0-521-09826-2). Cambridge U Pr.

--The Sociology of the Third World. LC 74-12979. (Illus.). 336p. 1975. 42.50 (ISBN 0-521-20521-2); pap. 11.95 (ISBN 0-521-09924-2). Cambridge U Pr.

Goldthorpe, John H., et al. Affluent Worker, in the Class Structure. (Studies in Sociology: No. 3). 1969. o. p. 32.50 (ISBN 0-521-07231-X); pap. 10.95x (ISBN 0-521-09533-6). Cambridge U Pr.

--Affluent Worker: Industrial Attitudes. LC 68-21192. (Cambridge Studies in Sociology: No. 1). 1968. 29.95 (ISBN 0-521-07109-7); pap. 10.95x (ISBN 0-521-09466-6). Cambridge U Pr.

--Affluent Worker: Political Attitudes. LC 68-21192. (Cambridge Studies in Sociology: No. 2). 1968. pap. 8.95 (ISBN 0-521-09526-3). Cambridge U Pr.

Goldwasser, Anita. Planning for Profits: The Retailers Guide to Success. 1981. 20.95 (ISBN 0-86730-531-2). Lebhar Friedman.

Goldwasser, Dan L. Sales & Resales of Restricted Securities: A Course Handbook. (Restricted Securities Library). 558p. 1979. pap. 20.00 o.p. (ISBN 0-686-80109-1, B4-6515). PLI.

Goldwater, John. The Best of Archie. Uslan, Michael & Mendel, Jeffrey, eds. (Illus.). 256p. 1980. 16.95 (ISBN 0-399-12562-0, Perige); pap. 7.95 (ISBN 0-399-50493-1). Putnam Pub Group.

Goldwater, Robert, intro. by. Art of Oceania, Africa, & the Americas from the Museum of Primitive Art. LC 73-77259. (Illus.). 1969. pap. 2.95 (ISBN 0-87099-044-6). Metro Mus Art.

Goldwert, Marvin. History As Neurosis: Paternalism and Machismo in Spanish America. LC 80-5640. 85p. 1980. lib. bdg. 14.75 (ISBN 0-8191-1226-7); pap. text ed. 7.00 (ISBN 0-8191-1227-5). U Pr of Amer.

--Psychic Conflict in Spanish America: Six Essays on the Psychohistory of the Region. LC 82-45059. 86p. (Orig.). 1982. lib. bdg. 18.00 (ISBN 0-8191-2413-3); pap. text ed. 7.00 (ISBN 0-8191-2414-1). U Pr of Amer.

--The Suicide & Rebirth of Western Civilization: A Collage of Psychohistorical Analogies. LC 81-40704. 76p. 1982. lib. bdg. 18.50 (ISBN 0-8191-1886-9); pap. text ed. 5.75 (ISBN 0-8191-1887-7). U Pr of Amer.

Goldwhite, Harold see Chang, Raymond.

Goldwin, Robert A. & Clor, Harry M., eds. Readings in American Foreign Policy. 2nd ed. 1971. pap. text ed. 9.95x (ISBN 0-19-501409-X). Oxford U Pr.

Goldwin, Robert A. & Schambra, William A., eds. How Capitalistic is the Constitution? 1982. 14.25 (ISBN 0-8447-3477-2); pap. 6.25 (ISBN 0-8447-3478-0). Am Enterprise.

Goldworthy, G. M. Why Nursery Schools? 1978. text ed. cancelled (ISBN 0-900675-57-8). Humanities.

Goldzband, Melvin G. Consulting in Child Custody: An Introduction to the Ugliest Litigation for Mental-Health Professionals. LC 81-48024. 208p. 1982. 25.95x (ISBN 0-669-05246-9). Lexington Bks.

Goldziher, Ignac. Muslim Studies, 2 vols. Stern, S. M., ed. & tr. Incl. Vol. 1. Muhammedanische Studien. LC 67-20745. 1967. 29.50x (ISBN 0-87395-234-0); Vol. 2. Hadith: The 'Traditions', Ascribed to Muhammed. LC 72-11731. 1972. 39.50x (ISBN 0-87395-235-9). State U NY Pr.

Goleman, Dan & Freedman, Johnathan. What Psychology Knows That Everyone Should. new paperback ed. (Illus.). 256p. 1983. pap. 8.95 (ISBN 0-86616-011-6). Lewis Pub Co.

Goleman, Daniel & Speeth, Kathleen. The Essential Psychothempies. 1982. pap. 3.95 (ISBN 0-451-62083-6, ME2083, Ment). NAL.

Goleman, Daniel, et al. Introductory Psychology. 2nd ed. 603p. 1982. text ed. 21.00 (ISBN 0-394-32090-5); wkbk. 8.95 (ISBN 0-394-32727-6). Random.

Golemba, Henry L. Frank R. Stockton. (United States Authors Ser.). 1981. lib. bdg. 12.95 (ISBN 0-8057-7288-X, Twayne). G K Hall.

--George Ripley. (United States Authors Ser.). 1977. lib. bdg. 13.95 (ISBN 0-8057-7181-6, Twayne). G K Hall.

Golembe, Carter H. & Holland, David S. The Federal Regulation of Banking. rev. ed. 200p. 1981. 19.50x (ISBN 0-686-34576-2). Golembe Assocs.

Golembiewski & Gibson. Readings in Public Administration: Institutions, Processes, Behavior, Policy. 4th ed. 1982. 17.95 (ISBN 0-686-84649-4). HM.

Golembiewski & Rabin. Public Budgeting & Finance. (Public Adminstration & Public Policy Ser.). 400p. 1983. price not set (ISBN 0-8247-1668-X). Dekker.

Golembiewski, Robert T. & Gibson, Frank. Public Administration: Readings in Institutions, Processes, Behavior Policy. 3rd ed. 1976. pap. 17.50 (ISBN 0-395-30805-4). HM.

--Readings in Public Administration: Institutions, Processes, Behavior, Policy. 4th ed. LC 82-81584. 544p. 1982. pap. text ed. 14.50 (ISBN 0-395-32765-2). HM.

Golembiewski, Robert T. & White, Michael. Cases in Public Management. 3rd ed. 1980. pap. 11.30 (ISBN 0-395-30807-0). HM.

--Cases in Public Management. 4th ed. LC 82-81583. 336p. 1982. pap. text ed. 11.50 (ISBN 0-395-32767-9). HM.

Golembiewski, Robert T. & Rabin, Jack, eds. Public Budgeting & Finance: Readings in Theory & Practice. 2nd ed. LC 73-85768. (Illus.). 515p. 1975. text ed. 23.95 (ISBN 0-87581-162-0). Peacock Pubs.

Golenbock, Peter. The Boss: George Steinbrenner's Story. Date not set. 10.95 o.p. (ISBN 0-686-80615-8). Crown. Postponed.

Golenbock, Peter, jt. auth. see Guidry, Ron.

Golenbock, Peter, jt. auth. see Lyle, Sparky.

Golenbock, Peter, jt. auth. see Martin, Billy.

Golf Digest Editors, jt. auth. see Davis, William H.

Golf Digest Editors, ed. The Best of Golf Digest. 224p. 1975. 10.00 o.p. (ISBN 0-671-22167-1). S&S.

Golf Magazine Editors, jt. ed. see Fishman, Lew.

Golf-Racht, T. Van see Van Golf-Racht, T.

Golgi Centennial Symposium, September 1973. Golgi Centennial Symposium: Perspectives in Neurobiology. Santini, Maurizo, ed. LC 74-21985. (Illus.). 686p. 1975. 75.00 o.p. (ISBN 0-911216-80-4). Raven.

Goliber, Paul F. Refrigeration Servicing. LC 75-6064. 91p. 1976. pap. 7.00 (ISBN 0-8273-1005-6). Delmar.

Golieb, D. E., jt. auth. see Ettinger, Richard P.

Goligher, J. C. Surgery of the Anus, Rectum & Colon. 4th ed. (Illus.). 1980. text ed. 125.00 (ISBN 0-02-857860-0, Pub. by Bailliere-Tindall). Saunders.

Golightly, Cecelia K. Help with Career Planning: A Workbook for Nurses. (Help Series of Management Guides). 95p. 1979. pap. 9.95 (ISBN 0-933036-17-5). Ganong W L Co.

Golightly, Jean. Circuit Hikes in Virginia, West Virginia, Maryland & Pennsylvania. 3rd ed. LC 78-54231. 1981. pap. text ed. 2.50 (ISBN 0-915746-09-3). Potomac Appalach.

Golinkoff, Roberta M., ed. The Transition from Prelinguistic to Linguistic Communication: Issues & Implications. 1983. text ed. price not set (ISBN 0-89859-257-7). L Erlbaum Assocs.

Golino, Carlo L., ed. Galileo Reappraised. LC 66-15485. (UCLA Center for Medieval & Renaissance Studies). 1966. 22.50x (ISBN 0-520-00490-6). U of Cal Pr.

Golisz-Benson, Ursula, jt. auth. see Fearn, Leif.

Goll, Yvan. Lackawanna Elegy. Kinnell, Galaway, tr. 1970. o. p. 7.50 (ISBN 0-912090-07-3); pap. 2.45 (ISBN 0-912090-06-5). Sumac Mich.

Golladay, Frederick. Health. (Sector Policy Paper). 90p. 1980. 5.00 (ISBN 0-686-36197-0, PP_8001). World Bank.

--Health Issues & Policies in the Developing Countries. (Working Paper: No. 412). ii, 53p. 1980. 5.00 (ISBN 0-686-36198-9, WP-0412). World Bank.

Golladay, Frederick L. Economics: Problems, Principles, Priorities. LC 76-19511. 1978. 26.95 (ISBN 0-8053-3302-9); instr's man. 4.95 (ISBN 0-8053-3304-5); study guide 9.95 (ISBN 0-8053-3303-7). Benjamin-Cummings.

--Macroeconomics: Problems, Principles, Priorities. LC 78-53018. 1978. 16.95 o.p. (ISBN 0-8053-3307-X). Benjamin-Cummings.

--Microeconomics: Problems, Principles & Priorities. LC 78-52927. 1978. 16.95 o.p. (ISBN 0-8053-3306-1). Benjamin-Cummings.

Gollak, B., ed. see Strogonov, B. P., et al.

Gollance, I., ed. A Petite Pallace of Pettie His Pleasure Containing Many Pretie Histories by Him Set Forth in Comely Colours & Most Delightfully Discoursed, 2 vols. 396p. 1982. Repr. Set. lib. bdg. 65.00 (ISBN 0-89760-022-3). Telegraph Bks.

Gollancz, Israel, ed. Medieval Library, 28 vols. Repr. of 1926 ed. write for info. o.p. Cooper Sq.

Gollasch, Frederick, ed. Language & Literacy: The Selected Writings of Kenneth S. Goodman: Reading, Language & the Classroom Teacher, Vol. II. 200p. 1982. 30.00 (ISBN 0-7100-9005-6). Routledge & Kegan.

Golledge, R. G., jt. ed. see Moore, Gary T.

Golledge, Reginald G., jt. auth. see Amedeo, Douglas.

Golledge, Reginald G., jt. ed. see Cox, Kevin R.

Gollek, B., ed. see Zaika, V. E.

Gollerbach, M. & Krasavina, L. K. Cumulative Index to the National Bibliography on Algae for 1737 to 1960. 1977. Repr. of 1971 ed. lib. bdg. 86.40x (ISBN 3-87429-118-9). Lubrecht & Cramer.

Gollery, F. B. & Lieth, H., eds. Tropical Rain Forest Ecosystems: Part A: Structure & Function. (Ecosystems of the World Ser.: Vol. 14A). 382p. 1982. 112.75 (ISBN 0-444-41986-1). Elsevier.

Golley, F. B., et al, eds. Small Mammals. LC 74-25658. (International Biological Programme Ser.: No. 5). (Illus.). 448p. 1975. 75.00 (ISBN 0-521-20601-4). Cambridge U Pr.

Golley, John. The Big Drop. (Illus.). 212p. 1982. 19.95 (ISBN 0-86720-635-7). Sci Bks Intl.

Gollin, Eugene S., ed. Developmental Plasticity: Behavioral & Biological Aspects of Variations in Development. LC 80-2331. (Developmental Psychology Ser.). 1981. 27.50 (ISBN 0-12-289620-3). Acad Pr.

Gollin, James. Eliza's Galiardo. 160p. 1983. 10.95 (ISBN 0-312-24244-1). St Martin.

--The Philomel Foundation. 1980. 10.00 o.p. (ISBN 0-312-60428-9). St Martin.

Gollin, Richard M., et al. Arthur Hugh Clough: A Descriptive Catalogue, Poetry, Prose, Biography & Criticism. LC 67-25798. (Illus.). 1968. 10.00 o.p. (ISBN 0-87104-016-6). NY Pub Lib.

Gollin, Rita. Nathaniel Hawthorne: An Iconography. 105p. 1983. 25.00 (ISBN 0-87580-087-4). N Ill U Pr.

Gollnick. Dynamic Structure of Household Expenditures in the Federal Republic of Germany. LC 74-84207. 1975. 30.00 (ISBN 0-444-10796-7, North-Holland). Elsevier.

Gollwitzer, Helmut. An Introduction to Protestant Theology. Cairns, David, tr. LC 82-4798. 240p. 1982. pap. 12.95 (ISBN 0-664-24415-7). Westminster.

--Unwilling Journey: A Diary from Russia. LC 74-7610. 316p. 1974. Repr. of 1965 ed. lib. bdg. 17.50x (ISBN 0-8371-7585-2, GOUJ). Greenwood.

Gollwitzer, P. M., jt. auth. see Wicklund, R. A.

Golomb, Louis. Brokers of Morality: Thai Ethnic Adaptation in a Rural Malaysian Setting. LC 78-4141. (Asian Studies at Hawaii: No. 23). 1979. pap. text ed. 10.75x (ISBN 0-8248-0629-8). UH Pr.

Golomb, Morris. Know Your Festivals & Enjoy Them. 3rd ed. LC 72-90771. (Illus.). 189p. (gr. 3-6). 1973. 10.00 (ISBN 0-88400-035-4). Shengold.

Golomb, Patricia C., ed. see Fox, Claire R.

Golombeck, Harry, tr. see Keres, Paul.

Golombek, Harry. Chess: A History. (Illus.). 1976. 16.95 o.p. (ISBN 0-399-11575-7). Putnam Pub Group.

Golon, Sergeanne. Angelique & the Ghosts. LC 77-20018. 1978. 8.95 o.p. (ISBN 0-399-11981-7). Putnam Pub Group.

Golos, Natalie & Golbitz, Frances G. If This Is Tuesday It Must Be Chicken or How to Rotate Your Food for Better Health. Martin, Joan, ed. LC 81-13509. 109p. (Orig.). 1981. pap. 6.95 (ISBN 0-941962-00-8). Human Eco Res.

Golos, Natalie, et al. Coping with Your Allergies. 1979. 17.25 (ISBN 0-671-24078-1). S&S.

Golovin, Pavel N. Civil & Savage Encounters: The Worldly Travel Letters of an Imperial Russian Navy Officer, 1860-61. Dmytryshyn, Basil & Crownhart-Vaughn, E. A., eds. (North Pacific Studies Ser.: No. 5). (Illus.). 224p. (Eng.). 1983. 21.95 (ISBN 0-295-95953-3, Pub by Oreg Hist Soc). U of Wash Pr.

--Civil & Savage Encounters: The Worldly Travel Letters of an Imperial Russian Navy Officer, 1860-61. Dmytryshyn, Basil & Crownhart-Vaughan, E. A., trs. from Rus. (North Pacific Studies Ser.). (Illus.). 208p. (Orig.). 1982. 21.95 (ISBN 0-87595-067-1, Western Imprints); pap. 14.95 (ISBN 0-87595-095-7, Western Imprints). Oreg Hist Soc.

Golovin, Pavel N. & Crownhart-Vaughan, E. A., eds. Civil & Savage Encounters: The Worldly Travel Letters of an Imperial Russian Navy Officer, 1860-61. (North Pacific Studies Ser. Five). (Illus.). 224p. 1982. 21.95 (ISBN 0-686-96433-0, Oregon Historical Soc.). U of Wash Pr.

Golovine, Ivan G. Autocratie Russe. (Nineteenth Century Russia Ser.). 144p. (Fr.). 1974. Repr. of 1860 ed. lib. bdg. 45.00 o.p. (ISBN 0-8287-0382-5, R10). Clearwater Pub.

Golovnin, V. N. Around the World on the "Kamchatka," 1817-1819. Wiswell, Ella L., tr. from Rus. LC 79-15230. (Illus.). 1979. text ed. 20.00x (ISBN 0-8248-0640-9). UH Pr.

Golson, G. Barry, ed. see Sheff, David.

Golt, Rick & Lagundimao, Clemente, Jr. Hawai'i Hawai'i. LC 81-50935. (Illus.). 128p. 1981. 19.95 (ISBN 0-8248-0772-3). UH Pr.

Golt, Sidney. World Trade Issues in the Mid-1980s. (British-North American Committee Ser.). 112p. 1982. pap. 7.00 (ISBN 0-902594-42-7, BN32-NPA198). Natl Planning.

Golterman, H. Methods for Chemical Analysis of Fresh Waters. 2nd ed. (Blackwell Scientific Pubns.: IBP Handbk. No. 8). (Illus.). 1978. pap. 17.50 (ISBN 0-8016-1888-6). Mosby.

Golub, Edward S. The Cellular Basis of the Immune Response. rev. & 2nd ed. LC 80-28080. (Illus.). 325p. 1981. pap. text ed. 15.95x (ISBN 0-87893-212-7). Sinauer Assoc.

Golub, Morton A. & Parker, John A., eds. Polymeric Materials for Unusual Service Conditions. 348p. 1973. pap. 22.50 o.p. (ISBN 0-471-31277-0). Krieger.

Golub, Sharon, ed. Menarche: The Physiological, Psychological, & Social Effects of the Onset of Menstruation. LC 82-48105. 352p. 1983. 29.95x (ISBN 0-669-05982-X). Lexington Bks.

Golubev, G. N. & Biswas, A. K., eds. Interregional Water Transfers: Projects & Problems: Proceedings of the Task Force Meeting, International Institute for Applied Systems Analysis, Laxenburg, Austria, Oct. 1977. 1979. text ed. 29.00 (ISBN 0-08-022430-X). Pergamon.

Golynets, Sergei. Ivan Bilibin. (Illus.). 227p. 1982. 28.50 o.p. (ISBN 0-8109-0699-6). Abrams.

Golzen, Godfrey. Introducing Vat: A Simplified Guide to Value Added Tax. LC 75-308993. 1973. pap. 5.00x o.p. (ISBN 0-85038-047-2). Intl Pubns Serv.

Golzen, Godfrey & Plumbley, Philip. Changing Your Job. 3rd ed. LC 72-193892. 1978. 11.25x (ISBN 0-85038-149-5); pap. 8.50x (ISBN 0-85038-152-5). Intl Pubns Serv.

Golzio, Vincent. Raphael: His Life, His Art, His Fortunes, 2 vols. (The Great Masters of the World Ser.). (Illus.). 765p. 1982. Repr. of 1968 ed. 237.45 (ISBN 0-89901-089-X). Found Class Reprints.

Gomara, Francisco Lopez De. The Conquest of the West India. Repr. of 1578 ed. 49.00x (ISBN 0-8201-1193-7). Schol Facsimiles.

Gomberg, et al, eds. Alcohol, Science, & Society Revisited. (Illus.). 432p. 1982. text ed. 20.00x (ISBN 0-472-10024-6); pap. text ed. 14.95x (ISBN 0-472-08028-8). U of Mich Pr.

Gomberg, Edith S. & Franks, Violet, eds. Gender & Disordered Behavior: Sex Differences in Psychopathology. LC 78-27390. 1979. 27.50 o.p. (ISBN 0-87630-188-X). Brunner Mazel.

Gombin, Richard. The Radical Tradition: A Study in Modern Revolutionary Thought. LC 78-31150. 1979. 20.00 (ISBN 0-312-66186-X). St Martin.

Gombos, Karoly. Armenia: Landscape & Architecture. LC 75-318270. (Illus.). 222p. 1974. 16.00x o.p. (ISBN 963-13-4605-6). Intl Pubns Serv.

--The Pearls of Uzbekistan: Bukhara, Samarkand, Khiva. Kemenes, I. & McRobbie, K., trs. from Hungarian. LC 80-451597. (Illus.). 206p. 1976. 25.00x (ISBN 963-13-4600-5). Intl Pubns Serv.

Gombosi, Otto, ed. see Capirola, Vincenzo.

Gombrich, E. H. In Search of Cultural History. 1969. pap. 5.95x o.p. (ISBN 0-19-817168-4). Oxford U Pr.

--The Story of Art. 13th ed. 506p. 1983. 25.00 (ISBN 0-686-84548-X); pap. text ed. 14.95 (ISBN 0-686-84549-8). P-H.

Gombrich, Richard, jt. ed. see Cone, Margaret.

Gombrich, Richard F. Precept & Practice: Traditional Buddhism in the Rural Highlands of Ceylon. 380p. 1971. 23.00x o.p. (ISBN 0-19-826525-5). Oxford U Pr.

Gombrowicz, Witold. A Kind of Testament. Hamilton, Alastair, tr. LC 72-89199. 158p. 1973. 14.95 (ISBN 0-87722-051-4). Temple U Pr.

Gomes, Leonard. International Economic Problems. 1979. 22.50x (ISBN 0-312-42158-3). St Martin.

Gomes Teixeira, Francisco. Traite des Courbes Speciales Remarquables Planes et Gauches, 3 vols. 2nd ed. LC 73-113153. 1337p. (Fr.). 1972. text ed. 65.00 set (ISBN 0-8284-0255-8). Chelsea Pub.

Gomez, Efrain A. For the Dead, for the Living. LC 81-81612. 1983. 8.95 (ISBN 0-87212-154-2). Libra.

Gomez, Ermilo A. Canek: History & Legend of a Maya Hero. 80p. 1983. pap. 2.50 (ISBN 0-380-61937-7, 61937, Bard). Avon.

Gomez, Joan. A Dictionary of Symptoms. rev. ed. LC 82-42525. (Illus.). 324p. 1983. 14.95 (ISBN 0-8128-2887-9); pap. 5.95 (ISBN 0-8128-1949-7). Stein & Day.

Gomez, Joan, jt. auth. see Dally, Peter.

Gomez, Joseph A. Peter Watkins. (Filmmakers Ser.). 1979. lib. bdg. 12.95 (ISBN 0-8057-9267-8, Twayne). G K Hall.

Gomez, Judith. Turning Point: A Workbook on Self Transformation. 144p. (Orig.). 1980. pap. text ed. 9.95 (ISBN 0-8403-2178-3). Kendall-Hunt.

Gomez, Manuel, ed. Radiation Hazards in Mining: Control, Measurement, & Medical Aspects. LC 81-70691. (Illus.). 1105p. 1982. 58.00x (ISBN 0-89520-290-5). Soc Mining Eng.

Gomez, Manuel R., ed. Tuberous Sclerosis. LC 78-94312. 264p. 1979. text ed. 28.50 (ISBN 0-89004-313-2). Raven.

Gomez, Miguel, jt. auth. see Nicholl, Larry.

Gomez, Rosendo A. Government & Politics in Latin America. rev. ed. 1963. pap. text ed. 3.10x (ISBN 0-685-19730-1). Phila Bk Co.

Gomez, Rudolph & Cottingham, Clement. The Social Reality of Ethnic America. 1974. pap. text ed. 11.95x (ISBN 0-669-84111-0). Heath.

Gomez de la Serna, Ramon. Greguerias: The Wit & Wisdom of Ramon Gomez de la Serna. Ward, Philip, tr. from Span. (Oleander Language & Literature Ser.: Vol. 12). (Illus.). iv, 220p. 1982. 29.95 (ISBN 0-900891-45-9); pap. 16.50 (ISBN 0-900891-49-1). Oleander Pr.

Gomez-Gil, Orlando & Stanislawczyk, Irene E., eds. Tierras, Costumbres y Tipos Hispanicos. LC 77-114675. (Span). (gr. 9-12). 1970. pap. 8.50 (ISBN 0-672-63126-1). Odyssey Pr.

Gomme, A. H. Dickens. (Literature in Perspective Ser.). (Illus.). 192p. 1971. 6.00x o.p. (ISBN 0-87471-246-7). Rowman.

Gomme, A. W., et al, eds. A Historical Commentary on Thucydides, Volume V: Book VIII. (Illus.). 1981. 74.00x (ISBN 0-19-814198-X). Oxford U Pr.

Gomme, Alice B. see Gomme, George L., et al.

Gomme, George L. Ethnology in Folklore. LC 79-75802. 1969. Repr. of 1892 ed. 30.00x (ISBN 0-8103-3832-7). Gale.

--Folklore As an Historical Science. LC 67-23898. (Illus.). 1968. Repr. of 1908 ed. 37.00x (ISBN 0-8103-3432-1). Gale.

--Primitive Folk-Moots: Or, Open-Air Assemblies in Britain. LC 67-23899. 1968. Repr. of 1880 ed. 34.00x (ISBN 0-8103-3433-X). Gale.

Gomme, George L., et al, eds. The Gentleman's Magazine Library: Being a Classified Collection of the Chief Contents of the Gentleman's Magazine from 1731-1868, 13 vols. Incl. Vol. 1. Manners & Customs. Repr. of 1886 ed (ISBN 0-8103-3434-8); Vol. 2. Dialect, Proverbs, & Word Lore. Repr. of 1886 ed (ISBN 0-8103-3435-6); Vol. 3. Popular Superstitions. Repr. of 1884 ed (ISBN 0-8103-3436-4); Vol. 4. English Traditional Lore. Repr. of 1885 ed (ISBN 0-8103-3437-2); Vols. 5 & 6. Archaeology. Repr. of 1886 ed (ISBN 0-8103-3438-0); Vols. 7 & 8. Romano-British Remains. Repr. of 1886 ed (ISBN 0-8103-3439-9); Vol. 9. Literary Curiosities & Notes. Gomme, Alice B., ed. Repr. of 1889 ed (ISBN 0-8103-3440-2); Vol. 10. Bibliographical Notes. Bickley, A. C., ed. Repr. of 1890 ed (ISBN 0-8103-3441-0); Vols. 11 & 12. Architectural Antiquities. Repr. of 1890 ed (ISBN 0-8103-3442-9); Vol. 13. Ecclesiology. Milne, F. A., ed. Repr. of 1886 ed (ISBN 0-8103-3443-7). LC 67-23900. Vols. 1-4, 9, 10, 13. 34.00x ea.; Vols. 5 & 6, 7 & **8, 11 & 12 (two Vol. Sets) 47.00x ea. Gale.**

Gomont, M. Monographie Des Oscillariees: 1892-93, 2 parts in 1 vol. (Illus.). 1962. 32.00 (ISBN 3-7682-0038-8). Lubrecht & Cramer.

Gomori, George. Cyprian Norwid. LC 73-17341. (World Author's Ser.: Poland: No. 305). 168p. 1974. lib. bdg. 10.95 o.p. (ISBN 0-8057-2656-X, Twayne). G K Hall.

Gomori, George & Atlas, James, eds. Attila Jozsef: Selected Poems & Texts. Batki, John, tr. from Hungarian. (Translation Ser.). 1979. 6.95 o.p. (ISBN 0-85635-062-1, Pub. by Carcanet New Pr England). Humanities.

Gomori, George, tr. see Radnoti, Miklos.

Gomoyunova, M. V., jt. auth. see Dobretsov, L. N.

Gompel, Claude. Atlas of Diagnostic Cytology. LC 77-27068. 1978. text ed. 80.00x (ISBN 0-471-02278-0, Pub. by Wiley Medical). Wiley.

Gompert, David C., et al. Nuclear Weapons & World Politics. LC 77-8695. (Nineteen Eighties Project-Council on Foreign Relations). 1977. text ed. 15.95 (ISBN 0-07-023713-1, P&RB); pap. 6.95 o.p. (ISBN 0-07-023714-X). McGraw.

Gomperz, Theodor. Greek Thinkers: A History of Ancient Philosophy, 4 vols. Incl. Vol. 1. text ed. o.p. (ISBN 0-687-01947-8); pap. text ed. (ISBN 0-7195-0498-8); Vol. 2. text ed. (ISBN 0-687-01948-6); pap. text ed. o. p. (ISBN 0-7195-0499-6); Vol. 3. text ed. (ISBN 0-7195-0500-3); pap. text ed. (ISBN 0-7195-0504-6); Vol. 4. text ed. (ISBN 0-7195-0501-1); pap. text ed. (ISBN 0-7195-0505-4). 1964. text ed. 17.50x ea.; pap. text ed. 13.75x ea. Humanities.

Goncourt, Edmond L. The Woman of the Eighteenth Century: Her Life, from Birth to Death, Her Love & Her Philosophy in the Worlds of Salon, Shop & Street. Le Clercq, Jacques & Roeder, Ralph, trs. from Fr. LC 79-2937. (Illus.). 347p. 1981. Repr. of 1927 ed. 27.25 (ISBN 0-8305-0103-7). Hyperion Conn.

Gondin, William R. & Mammen, Edward W. The Art of Speaking. rev. ed. LC 80-2671. (Made Simple Bk.). (Illus.). 192p. 1981. pap. 4.95 (ISBN 0-385-17485-3). Doubleday.

--Art of Speaking Made Simple. pap. 4.95 (ISBN 0-385-17485-3, Made). Doubleday.

Gondin, William R. & Sohmer, Bernard. Advanced Algebra & Calculus Made Simple. pap. 4.95 (ISBN 0-385-00438-9, Made). Doubleday.

--Intermediate Algebra & Analytic Geometry Made Simple. pap. 4.95 (ISBN 0-385-00437-0, Made). Doubleday.

Gonen, Jay Y. A Psychohistory of Zionism. 384p. 1976. pap. 3.95 o.p. (ISBN 0-452-00441-1, F441, Mer). NAL.

Gongora, M. Studies in the Colonial History of Spanish America. Southern, R., tr. from Span. LC 74-19524. (Latin American Studies: No. 20). 235p. 1975. 42.50 (ISBN 0-521-20686-3). Cambridge U Pr.

Gongora y Argote, Luis see De Gongora y Argote, Luis.

Gonick, Harvey C. Current Nephrology. (Current Nephrology Ser.: Vol. 6). 376p. 1983. 55.00 (ISBN 0-471-09559-1, Pub. by Wiley Med). Wiley.

Gonick, Harvey C., ed. Current Nephrology, Vol. 1. (Illus.). 1977. 55.00 (ISBN 0-471-09482-X, Pub. by Wiley Med). Wiley.

--Current Nephrology, Vol. 3. 1979. 55.00 (ISBN 0-471-09484-6, Pub. by Wiley Med). Wiley.

--Current Nephrology, Vol. 4. (Current Ser.). (Illus.). 500p. 1980. text ed. 55.00x (ISBN 0-471-09519-2, Pub. by Wiley Med). Wiley.

Gonick, Larry. The Cartoon History of the Universe, Book I. 1982. 6.50 (ISBN 0-688-01011-3). Morrow.

--The Cartoon History of the Universe, Book One: From the Big Bang to Babylon. (Illus.). 96p. (Orig.). 1980. pap. 6.95 (ISBN 0-89620-081-7). Rip Off.

Gonick, Larry & Hosler, Jay. Cartoon Guide to Computer Science. (Illus.). 224p. (Orig.). (gr. 11-12). 1983. pap. 4.76i (ISBN 0-06-460417-9, COS CO 417). B&N NY.

Gonick, Larry & Wheelis, Mark. Cartoon Guide to Genetics. (Illus.). 224p. (Orig.). 1983. pap. 4.76i (ISBN 0-06-460416-0, COS CO 416). B&N NY.

Gonis, Antonios & Panagoulias, Panagiotis. Mastering Skills in College Algebra & Trigonometry. (Illus.). 720p. Date not set. price not set. A-W.

Gonis, Antonios & Strnad, Wayne. Mastering Mathematical Skills. LC 80-19989. (Illus.). 432p. 1981. pap. text ed. 18.95 (ISBN 0-201-03062-4); instrs' manual 3.50 (ISBN 0-201-03063-2); study supplement 4.95 (ISBN 0-201-03064-0). A-W.

Gonnella, Gary, jt. auth. see Teja, Ed.

Gonnenweir, F., jt. ed. see Von Egidy, T.

Gonsalves, Carol. Sermon on the Mountain. (Arch Bk. Supplement Ser.). 1981. pap. 0.89 (ISBN 0-570-06149-0, 59-1304). Concordia.

Gonsalves, Milton. Fagothey's Right & Reason: Ethics in Theory & Practice. 7th ed. LC 80-39863. 574p. 1981. text ed. 21.95 (ISBN 0-8016-1541-0). Mosby.

Gonser, B. W. see Hausner, Henry.

Gonsiorek, John C., ed. Homosexuality & Psychotherapy: A Practitioner's Handbook of Affirmative Models. LC 82-3072. (Research on Homosexuality Ser.: No. 4). 216p. 1982. text ed. 25.00 (ISBN 0-917724-63-1, B63). Haworth Pr.

Gontarski, S. E., jt. ed. see Beja, Morris.

Gonzales, Carmen. The United States & the Moral Philosophy of the Gutter. (Illus.). 1977. 39.15 o.p. (ISBN 0-89266-055-4). Am Classical Coll Pr.

Gonzales, Laurence. El Vago. LC 82-71057. 320p. 1983. 14.95 (ISBN 0-689-11330-7). Atheneum.

--Jambeaux. LC 79-1824. 1979. 9.95 o.p. (ISBN 0-15-146038-8). HarBraceJ.

Gonzales, Manuel G. Andrea Costa & the Rise of Socialism in the Romagna. LC 79-6771. 419p. 1980. text ed. 24.25 (ISBN 0-8191-0952-5); pap. text ed. 15.00 (ISBN 0-8191-0953-3). U Pr of Amer.

Gonzales, N. V. The Bamboo Dancers. LC 82-70134. 276p. 1961. 8.95 (ISBN 0-8040-0018-2). Swallow.

Gonzalez. The Fallacy of Social Science Research: A Critical Examination & New Qualitative Model. (PPS on Social Policy Ser.). 75p. 1981. 15.00 (ISBN 0-08-027549-4). Pergamon.

Gonzalez, Ananias, ed. see Sisemore, J. T.

Gonzalez, Caleb. Strabismus & Ocular Motility. (Illus.). 298p. 1983. lib. bdg. price not set (ISBN 0-683-03629-7). Williams & Wilkins.

Gonzalez, Carlos F., et al. Computed Brain & Orbital Tomography: Technique & Interpretation. LC 76-28530. (Diagnostic & Therapeutic Radiology Ser.). 1976. 70.00x (ISBN 0-471-01692-6, Pub. by Wiley-Med). Wiley.

Gonzalez, Casanova P. Democracy in Mexico. 1972. pap. 7.95 (ISBN 0-19-501533-9, GB). Oxford U Pr.

Gonzalez, Catherine T. Cynthia Ann Parker: Indian Captive. (Stories for Young Americans Ser.). 1980. 5.95 (ISBN 0-89015-244-6). Eakin Pubns.

Gonzalez, D. Resumanes de Historia Universal. 1975. 2.20 o.p. (ISBN 0-07-090603-3, W). McGraw.

Gonzalez, Edward. Cuba Under Castro: The Limits of Charisma. 224p. 1974. pap. text ed. 13.95 (ISBN 0-395-14067-6). HM.

Gonzalez, Emilio, jt. auth. see Cioffari, Vincenzo.

Gonzalez, Emilio, et al. Spanish Cultural Reader. 1969. text ed. 12.95x o.p. (ISBN 0-669-49841-6). Heath.

Gonzalez, Gilbert G. Progressive Education: A Marxist Interpretation. LC 81-5787. (Studies in Marxism: Vol. 8). 197p. 1982. 17.95x (ISBN 0-930656-15-6); pap. 8.25 (ISBN 0-930656-16-4). MEP Pubns.

Gonzalez, Gloria. The Glad Man. (YA) 1979. pap. 1.50 o.p. (ISBN 0-440-92927-X, LFL). Dell.

--The Glad Man. LC 75-2541. 176p. (gr. 4 up). 1975. PLB 6.99 o.s.i. (ISBN 0-394-93065-7). Knopf.

Gonzalez, Gustavo. The Acquisition of Spanish Grammar by Native Spanish Speaking Children. LC 79-103428. 83p. (Orig.). 1978. pap. 6.75 (ISBN 0-89763-002-5). Natl Clearinghse Bilingual Ed.

Gonzalez, Harvey J. & Fein, Lois. Datatran: A Comprehensive & Practical System for Developing & Maintaining Data Processing Systems. (Illus.). 432p. 1983. text ed. 32.50 (ISBN 0-13-196493-3). P-H.

Gonzalez, J. A. & Gonzalez, Magda. Native American Tarot Deck. 108p. 1982. pap. 9.00 (ISBN 0-88079-009-1). US Games Syst.

Gonzalez, Jean. Complete Guide to Effective Dictation. 1980. pap. text ed. 13.95x (ISBN 0-534-00811-9). Kent Pub Co.

Gonzalez, Jean, jt. auth. see Bergerud, Marly.

Gonzalez, Jean, jt. auth. see Bergerud, Mary.

Gonzalez, Josue. Towards Quality in Bilingual Education: Bilingual Education in the Integrated School. 40p. 1979. pap. text ed. 5.25 (ISBN 0-89763-001-7). Natl Clearinghse Bilingual Ed.

Gonzalez, Justo L. La Era de los Dogmas y las Dudas. (Y hasta lo ultimo de la tierra Ser.: Tomo No. 8). (Illus.). 224p. (Orig.). 1983. pap. 4.95 (ISBN 0-89922-171-8). Edit Caribe.

Gonzalez, M., tr. see Abdel-Malek, Anouar.

Gonzalez, Magda, jt. auth. see Gonzalez, J. A.

Gonzalez, N. V. Children of the Ash-Covered Loam & Other Stories. 212p. 1979. pap. 5.00x o.p. (ISBN 0-686-27004-5, Pub. by Bookmark Philippines). Cellar.

--Mindoro & Beyond: Twenty-One Stories. 1979. 12.50x (ISBN 0-8248-0661-1); pap. 8.50x (ISBN 0-8248-0662-X). UH Pr.

Gonzalez, Nancie L., ed. Social & Technological Management in Dry Lands: Past & Present, Indigenous & Imposed. LC 77-93023. (AAAS Selected Symposium Ser.: No. 10). (Illus.). 1978. lib. bdg. 20.00 (ISBN 0-89158-438-2). Westview.

Gonzalez, Olimpia, tr. see Purcell, Julia Ann & Johnston, Barbara.

Gonzalez, R. C., jt. auth. see Tou, J. T.

Gonzalez, Rafael C. & Thomason, Michael G. Syntactic Pattern Recognition: An Introduction. (Applied Mathematics & Computation Ser.: No. 14). 1978. text ed. 35.95 (ISBN 0-201-02930-8, Adv Bk Prog); pap. text ed. 23.95 (ISBN 0-201-02931-6). A-W.

Gonzalez, Rafael C. & Wintz, Paul. Digital Image Processing & Recognition. LC 77-10317. (Applied Mathematics & Computation Ser.: No. 13). 1977. 35.95 (ISBN 0-201-03044-6, Adv Bk Prog); text ed. 25.95 (ISBN 0-201-03045-4). A-W.

Gonzalez, Richard F., jt. auth. see Harris, Roy D.

Gonzalez-Del Valle, Luis, jt. auth. see Shaw, Bradley.

Gonzalez Gordon, Manuel M. Sherry: The Noble Wine. LC 73-151683. (Illus.). 237p. 1972. 15.00x (ISBN 0-304-93472-0). Intl Pubns Serv.

Gonzalez-Mena, Janet. English Experiences. Incl. Teacher's Program for English Experiences. (Illus.), 142p. pap. 12.95 (ISBN 0-88499-225-X); My Book Workbook. (Illus.). 48p. pap. 3.95 (ISBN 0-88499-238-1). LC 75-5307. (ps). 1975. Program Package Set. 48.95 (ISBN 0-88499-244-6). Inst Mod Lang.

Gonzalez-Mena, Janet & Eyer, Dianne W. Infancy & Caregiving. LC 79-91838. (Illus.). 163p. 1980. pap. 8.95 (ISBN 0-87484-515-7). Mayfield Pub.

Gonzalez-Mena, Janet, jt. auth. see Garcia, Mary H.

Gonzalez-Ruiz, Jose M. Atheistic Humanism & the Biblical God. 1969. 7.95 o.p. (ISBN 0-685-01126-7, 80663). Glencoe.

Gonzalez-Wippler, Migene. Santeria: African Magic in Latin America. LC 73-82439. (Illus.). 192p. 1973. 6.50 o.p. (ISBN 0-517-52773-1). Crown.

Gooberman, Lawrence A. Operation Intercept. 1975. 25.00 (ISBN 0-08-017837-5); pap. 10.00 (ISBN 0-08-017836-7). Pergamon.

Gooch. Behavior of Joints in High Temperature Materials. Date not set. 53.30 (ISBN 0-85334-187-7). Elsevier.

Gooch, Bill & Carrier, Lois. Strategies for Success. 1983. pap. text ed. 15.95 (ISBN 0-534-01410-0, Breton Pubs). Wadsworth Pub.

Gooch, Brad. Daily News. (Orig.). 1977. pap. 5.00 (ISBN 0-915990-07-5). Z Pr.

Gooch, Bryan N. & Thatcher, David S. Musical Settings of Late Victorian & Modern British Literature. LC 75-24085. (Garland Ref. Lib. of Humanities). 1979. lib. bdg. 120.00 o.s.i. (ISBN 0-8240-9981-8). Garland Pub.

Gooch, John & Perlmutter, Amos, eds. Military Deception & Strategic Surprise. 200p. 1982. text ed. 30.00x (ISBN 0-7146-3202-3, F Cass Co). Biblio Dist.

Gooch, John, jt. ed. see Beckett, Ian.

Gooch, Ken & Caroline, John. Construction for Profit. (Illus.). 240p. 1980. text ed. 23.95 (ISBN 0-8359-0938-7). Reston.

Gooch, Stan. The Double Helix of the Mind. 1981. 40.00x o.p. (ISBN 0-7045-3037-6, Pub. by Wildwood House). State Mutual Bk.

--The Secret Life of Humans. 1982. cancelled (ISBN 0-460-04527-X, Pub. by J M Dent England). Biblio Dist.

Gooch, Steve, tr. see Wallraff, Gunter.

Goock, Roland. The World's One Hundred Best Recipes. Culinary Arts Institute, tr. from Ger. LC 73-9341. (Illus.). 1973. 14.95 (ISBN 0-8326-0542-5, 1650); pap. 8.95 (ISBN 0-686-67697-1, 2650). Delair.

Good, Carter. Dictionary of Education. 3rd ed. (Foundations in Education Ser.). 1973. 40.00 (ISBN 0-07-023720-4, C). McGraw.

Good, Charles M. Market Development in Traditionally Marketless Societies. LC 73-713883. (Papers in International Studies: Africa: No. 12). (Illus.). 1971. pap. 4.00x (ISBN 0-89680-045-8, Ohio U Ctr Intl). Ohio U Pr.

Good Cooking School, et al. The Garden to Table Cookbook. LC 76-3331. (Illus.). 400p. 1976. 15.00 o.p. (ISBN 0-07-023715-8, GB). McGraw.

Good, Donald W. & Minnick, Thomas L. Handbook. 1979. 14.95x (ISBN 0-02-344630-7); instrs'. manual avail. Macmillan.

Good, Edwin M. Giraffes, Black Dragons & Other Pianos: A Technological History from Christofori to the Modern Concert Grand. LC 81-50787. (Illus.). 328p. 1982. 29.50 (ISBN 0-8047-1120-8). Stanford U Pr.

Good Housekeeping Institute. Good Housekeeping's Children's Cook Book. (Illus.). 1972. 8.50x (ISBN 0-85223-069-9). Intl Pubns Serv.

Good, I. J. Good Thinking: The Foundations of Probability & its Applications. (Illus.). 320p. 1983. 35.00x (ISBN 0-8166-1141-6); pap. 14.95x (ISBN 0-8166-1142-4). U of Minn Pr.

Good, James. Sub Wars, No. 1: Target Delta V. (Orig.). 1982. pap. 2.50 (ISBN 0-8217-1046-X). Zebra.

--Sub Wars, No. 2: Target Sosus. 1982. pap. 2.50 (ISBN 0-8217-1092-3). Zebra.

Good, Judith, ed. Skillseekers 3: Decimal Computation Kit. (gr. 5-8). 1978. kit 227.55 (ISBN 0-201-23200-6, Sch Div). A-W.

Good, Mrs. Marvin. The Good Samaritan. 1978. pap. 2.30 (ISBN 0-686-24049-9). Rod & Staff.

--How God Made the World. 1978. pap. 2.30 (ISBN 0-686-24050-2). Rod & Staff.

--My Book About Bartemaeus. 1978. pap. 2.30 (ISBN 0-686-24052-9). Rod & Staff.

--A Shepherd Boy. 1978. pap. 2.30 (ISBN 0-686-24054-5). Rod & Staff.

Good, Merle. Happy As the Grass Was Green. LC 73-158174. 1971. 3.95 o.p. (ISBN 0-8361-1654-2); pap. 0.95 o.p. (ISBN 0-8361-1715-8). Herald Pr.

--Hazel's People. 1975. pap. 1.25 o.p. (ISBN 0-89129-008-7). Jove Pubns.

--These People Mine. LC 73-6196. 1973. pap. 1.25 o.p. (ISBN 0-8361-1718-2). Herald Pr.

Good, Phillip. Choosing a Word Processor. 1983. text ed. 18.95 (ISBN 0-8359-0761-9); pap. text ed. 12.95 (ISBN 0-8359-0760-0). Reston.

Good, Phyllis P. & Pellman, Rachel T., eds. Cakes: From Amish & Mennonite Kitchens. (Pennsylvania Dutch Cookbooks Ser.). (Illus., Orig.). 1983. pap. 1.95 (ISBN 0-934672-12-1). Good Bks PA.

--Candies, Beverages & Snacks: From Amish & Mennonite Kitchens. (Pennsylvania Dutch Cookbooks Ser.). (Illus., Orig.). 1983. pap. 1.95 (ISBN 0-934672-16-4). Good Bks PA.

--Casseroles: From Amish & Mennonite Kitchens. (Pennsylvania Dutch Cookbooks Ser.). (Illus., Orig.). 1983. pap. 1.95 (ISBN 0-934672-11-3). Good Bks PA.

--Desserts: From Amish & Mennonite Kitchens. (Pennsylvania Dutch Cookbooks Ser.). (Illus., Orig.). 1983. pap. 1.95 (ISBN 0-934672-13-X). Good Bks PA.

--Jams, Jellies & Relishes: From Amish & Mennonite Kitchens. (Pennsylvania Dutch Cookbooks Ser.). (Illus., Orig.). 1983. pap. 1.95 (ISBN 0-934672-14-8). Good Bks PA.

--Salads: From Amish & Mennonite Kitchens. (Pennsylvania Dutch Cookbooks Ser.). (Illus., Orig.). 1983. pap. 1.95 (ISBN 0-934672-10-5). Good Bks PA.

Good, Roger & Greensher, Arnold, eds. Guide to Ambulatory Surgery. (Monographs in Family Medicine Ser.). 1981. 29.50 (ISBN 0-8089-1418-9). Grune.

Good, Ronald G. How Children Learn Science: Conceptual Development & Implications for Teaching. (Illus.). 1977. text ed. 19.95x (ISBN 0-02-344640-4). Macmillan.

Good, Shirley R. & Rodgers, Susan S. Analysis for Action: Nursing Care of the Elderly. (Illus.). 1980. pap. text ed. 13.95 (ISBN 0-13-032623-2). P-H.

Good, Stephen M. How to Get a Job with the Post Office. LC 79-2240. 1980. pap. 5.95 (ISBN 0-06-463500-7, EH 500, EH). B&N NY.

Good, Thomas L. & Biddle, Bruce J. Teachers Make a Difference. 288p. 1982. pap. text ed. 11.50 (ISBN 0-8191-2157-6). U Pr of Amer.

Good, Thomas L., jt. ed. see Doyle, Walter.

Goodacre, J. Kenneth. Marine Insurance Claims. 1050p. 1981. 125.00 (ISBN 0-900886-53-6, Pub. By Witherby & Co England). State Mutual Bk.

Goodale, James C. Communications Law Nineteen Eighty Course Handbook, 2 vols. LC 80-83536. (Nineteen Eighty-Nineteen Eighty-One Patents, Copyrights, Trademarks, & Literary Property Course Handbook Ser. Subscription). 1402p. 1980. pap. text ed. 40.00 o.p. (ISBN 0-686-75084-5, G6-3680). PLI.

--Communications Law 1982: A Course Handbook, 2 Vols. 1402p. 1982. pap. 30.00 (G4-3714). PLI.

Goodale, Jerry, jt. auth. see Petersen, Dan.

Goodale, Katherine D. Pas de Trois: Fun with Ballet Words. Dreher, Denise, ed. (Illus.). 42p. (Orig.). (gr. k-5). 1982. pap. cancelled (ISBN 0-941082-01-6). Madhatter.

--Pas de Trois, Fun with Ballet Words. (Illus.). 25p. (Orig.). (gr. k-7). 1982. pap. 5.95 (ISBN 0-9609662-0-X). Goodale Pub.

Goodale, Thomas & Witt, Peter A., eds. Recreation & Leisure: Issues in an Era of Change. LC 79-92646. 394p. (Orig.). 1980. pap. text ed. 14.95x (ISBN 0-910251-00-2). Venture Pub PA.

Goodall, Bertha. Poems. 28p. (Orig.). 1982. pap. 3.00. Am Atheist.

Goodall, Blake. The Homilies of St. John Chrysostom on the Letters of St. Paul to Titus & Philemon. (Univ. of California Publications in Classical Studies: Vol. 20). 1979. 15.00x (ISBN 0-520-09596-0). U of Cal Pr.

Goodall, D. W. & Perry, R. A., eds. Arid Land Ecosystems, Vol. 1. LC 77-84810. (International Biological Programme Ser.: No. 16). (Illus.). 1979. 125.00 (ISBN 0-521-21842-X). Cambridge U Pr.

--Arid-Land Ecosystems: Structure, Functioning & Management, Vol. 2. LC 77-84810. (International Biological Programme Ser.: No. 17). 550p. 1981. 115.00 (ISBN 0-521-22988-X). Cambridge U Pr.

Goodall, Daphne M. Horses of the World. rev. ed. LC 73-7480. (Illus.). 272p. 1974. 14.95 o.p. (ISBN 0-02-544650-9). Macmillan.

Goodall, David W., jt. auth. see Frenkiel, Francois N.

Goodall, E. G., tr. see Von Cube, Hans L. & Staimle, Fritz.

Goodall, Geoffrey, ed. see Simenon, Georges.

Goodall, H. Lloyd, Jr. Human Communication: Creating Reality. 255p. 1983. pap. write for info. (ISBN 0-697-04216-2); instr's. manual avail. (ISBN 0-697-04224-3). Wm C Brown.

Goodall, H. Lloyd, Jr., jt. auth. see Phillips, Gerald M.

Goodall, Helen S. & Cooper, Ella G. Daily Lessons Received at 'Akka January 1908. rev. ed. LC 79-19806. 1979. pap. 3.00 (ISBN 0-87743-135-3, 332-041-10). Baha'i.

Goodall, John S. Above & Below Stairs. LC 82-48528. (Illus.). 34p. 1983. 9.95 (ISBN 0-689-50238-9, McElderry Bk). Atheneum.

--Lavinia's Cottage: A Pop-Up Story. LC 82-71160. (Illus.). 16p. 1983. 8.95 (ISBN 0-689-50257-5, McElderry Bk). Atheneum.

--Paddy Goes Traveling. LC 82-71159. (Illus.). 32p. 1982. 6.95 (ISBN 0-689-50239-7, McElderry Bk). Atheneum.

Goodall, Merrill, et al. California Water: A New Political Economy. LC 77-88255. 128p. 1978. text ed. 18.00x (ISBN 0-916672-86-7). Allanheld.

Goodard, T. & Schoen, S. Equipment Planning Guide for Vocational & Technical Training & Education Programmes: Carpentry & Joinery, No. 8. 134p. 1982. 22.80 (ISBN 92-2-102930-1). Intl Labour Office.

Goodavage, Joseph F. Write Your Own Horoscope. 3rd, rev. ed. 1979. pap. 2.95 (ISBN 0-451-11949-5, AE1949, Sig). NAL.

Gooday, G. W., et al, eds. The Eukaryotic Microbial Cell. LC 79-20741. (Society for General Microbiology Symposium: No. 30). (Illus.). 450p. 1980. 75.00 (ISBN 0-521-22974-X). Cambridge U Pr.

Goodban, W. T. & Hayslett, J. J. Architectural Drawing & Planning. 2nd ed. 1972. text ed. 21.05 (ISBN 0-07-023751-4, G). McGraw.

Goodban, William T., et al. Architectural Drawing & Planning. 3rd ed. (Illus.). 1979. pap. text ed. 23.95 (ISBN 0-07-023771-9, G). McGraw.

Goodbar, Joseph E. Managing the People's Money. 1935. 65.00x (ISBN 0-685-89765-6). Elliots Bks.

Goodbody, John. Judo: How to Become a Champ. (Illus.). 1976. pap. 7.50 o.p. (ISBN 0-86002-128-9). Transatlantic.

Goodbody, John, jt. ed. see Kirkley, George.

Goodburn, Roger. The Roman Inscriptions of Britain: Index. 96p. 1982. text ed. 15.75x (ISBN 0-86299-026-2, Pub. by Sutton England). Humanities.

Goodby, G. W., jt. auth. see Gray, G. W.

Goodchild, Jon. By Design. 1979. pap. 12.95 (ISBN 0-8256-3122-X, Quick Fox). Putnam Pub Group.

Goode. Eurocommunism. LC 79-26225. (gr. 7 up). PLB 8.90 (ISBN 0-531-02857-7, B02). Watts.

--The Nuclear Energy Controversy. (gr. 7 up). 1980. PLB 8.90 (ISBN 0-531-04165-4, G05). Watts.

Goode, Clement. Byron As Critic. LC 65-15893. (Studies in Byron, No., 5). 1969. Repr. of 1923 ed. lib. bdg. 49.95x (ISBN 0-8383-0696-9). Haskell.

Goode, Erich. Deviant Behavior: An Interactionist Approach. LC 77-20487. (P-H Ser. in Sociology). (Illus.). 1978. 22.95 (ISBN 0-13-208306-X). P-H.

--Drugs in American Society. 250p. 1972. pap. text ed. 9.50 (ISBN 0-394-31323-2). Knopf.

Goode, John W., Jr. & Barrows, Suzanne S., eds. Texas Guardianship Manual. LC 82-61569. 791p. 1982. law bk. binder 65.00 (ISBN 0-938160-31-1, 6335). State Bar TX.

Goode, Judith G., jt. auth. see Eames, Edwin.

Goode, Kenneth C. From Africa to the United States & Then: A Concise Afro-American History. 2nd ed. 1976. pap. 7.95x (ISBN 0-673-07969-4). Scott F.

Goode, Patrick, jt. ed. see Bottomore, Tom.

Goode, Richard. The Individual Income Tax. rev. ed. (Studies of Government Finance). 1976. 23.95 (ISBN 0-8157-3198-1); pap. 9.95 (ISBN 0-8157-3197-3). Brookings.

Goode, Ruth. Hands Up! LC 81-82018. (Illus.). 64p. (gr. 2-5). 1983. 8.95 (ISBN 0-02-736550-6). Macmillan.

Goode, Ruth, jt. auth. see Hurok, Solomon.

Goode, Stephan. The End of Detente? U. S. Soviet-Relations. LC 81-11370. (Impact Ser.). 96p. 1981. lib. bdg. 8.90 (ISBN 0-531-04334-7). Watts.

Goode, Stephen. The New Federalism. (Single Title Ser.). (Illus.). 160p. (gr. 7 up). 1983. PLB 9.90 (ISBN 0-531-04501-3). Watts.

--Reaganomics: Reagan's Economic Program. (Impact Bks). (Illus.). 96p. 1982. PLB 8.90 (ISBN 0-531-04422-X). Watts.

Goode, William J. The Celebration of Heroes: Prestige As a Social Control System. LC 77-20322. 1979. 29.50x (ISBN 0-520-03602-6); pap. 9.95x (ISBN 0-520-03811-8). U of Cal Pr.

--Principles of Sociology. 1st ed. 1977. text ed. 27.00 (ISBN 0-07-023758-1, C); instructor's manual 10.00 (ISBN 0-07-023759-X). McGraw.

--Religion Among the Primitives. 1951. pap. 3.50 (ISBN 0-02-912420-4). Free Pr.

Goode, William J. & Hatt, P. K. Methods in Social Research. (Sociology Ser.). 1952. text ed. 26.00 (ISBN 0-07-023755-7, C). McGraw.

Goode, William J., jt. auth. see Tavuchis, Nicholas.

Goodearl, K. R. Von Neumann Regular Rings. (Monographs & Studies: Vol. 4). 388p. 1979. text ed. 54.95 (ISBN 0-686-91967-X). Pitman Pub MA.

Goodefellowe, Robin, jt. auth. see Molin, Sven E.

Goodell, Gregory. Independent Feature Film Production: A Complete Guide from Concept Through Distribution. LC 82-5746. 352p. 1982. 17.95 (ISBN 0-312-41307-6). St Martin.

Goodell, Thomas D. Commemoration & Other Verses. 1921. text ed. 19.50x (ISBN 0-686-83507-7). Elliots Bks.

Gooden, George & Thomas, Frank. Sherlock Holmes, Bridge Detective. (Illus.). 288p. 1976. pap. 1.95 (ISBN 0-523-40038-1). Pinnacle Bks.

Goodenough, David J., jt. auth. see Reba, Richard.

Goodenough, Erwin R. Jurisprudence of the Jewish Courts in Egypt. 1929. text ed. 75.00x (ISBN 0-686-83604-9). Elliots Bks.

Goodenough, Erwin R. & Goodhart, H. L. Politics of Philo Judaeus. 1938. 65.00x (ISBN 0-685-69822-X). Elliots Bks.

Goodenough, Florence L. & Anderson, John E. Experimental Child Study. 546p. 1982. Repr. of 1931 ed. lib. bdg. 45.00 (ISBN 0-8495-2134-3). Arden Lib.

Goodenough, Simon. The Country Parson. (Illus.). 192p. 1983. 19.95 (ISBN 0-7153-8238-1). David & Charles.

--War Maps. (Illus.). 192p. 1983. 18.95 (ISBN 0-312-85584-2). St Martin.

--World Maps: World War II from September 1939-August 1945. (Illus.). 1983. 18.95 (ISBN 0-686-42933-8). St Martin.

Goodenough, Simon, ed. A Study in Scarlet: Based on the Story by Sir Arthur Conan Doyle. (Illus.). 120p. (Orig.). 1983. pap. 17.95 incl. facsimile documents & clues (ISBN 0-688-01951-X). Quill NY.

Goodenough, Ward. Language, Culture & Society. 2nd ed. 1981. pap. 8.95 (ISBN 0-8053-3341-X); pap. 5.95 o.p. (ISBN 0-686-69658-1). Benjamin-Cummings.

--Native Astronomy in the Central Carolines. (Museum Monographs). (Illus.). 46p. 1953. bound 1.50xsoft (ISBN 0-934718-02-4). Univ Mus of U PA.

Goodenough, Ward H. Cooperation in Change: An Anthropological Approach to Community Development. LC 63-20667. 544p. 1963. 11.95x (ISBN 0-87154-344-3). Russell Sage.

--Description & Comparison in Cultural Anthropology. LC 80-67925. (Lewis Henry Morgan Lectures). 192p. 1981. 27.95 (ISBN 0-521-23740-8); pap. 8.95 (ISBN 0-521-28196-2). Cambridge U Pr.

Goodenow, Earle, illus. Arabian Nights. (Illus.). (gr. 4-9). pap. 4.95 illus. jr. lib (ISBN 0-448-11006-7, G&D); deluxe ed. 8.95 (ISBN 0-448-06006-X); companion lib. ed. 2.95 (ISBN 0-448-05456-6). Putnam Pub Group.

Goodenow, Ronald K. & Ravitch, Diane, eds. Community Studies in Urban Educational History. 360p. 1983. text ed. 40.00x (ISBN 0-8419-0850-8). Holmes & Meier.

Goodenow, Ronald K. & White, Arthur O., eds. Education & the Rise of the New South. (University Bks). 1981. lib. bdg. 19.95 (ISBN 0-8161-9019-4, Univ Bks). G K Hall.

Gooder, Glenn G., jt. auth. see Grasham, John A.

Gooders, jt. auth. see Keith.

Gooders, John. Birds That Came Back. 1983. 25.00 (ISBN 0-88072-050-6). Longwood Pr.

--Collins British Birds. (Illus.). 384p. 1983. 39.95 (ISBN 0-00-219121-0, Collins Pub England). Greene.

Gooders, John, ed. The Illustrated Encyclopedia of Birds. (Illus.). 1320p. 1979. lib. bdg. 89.95x o.p. (ISBN 0-85685-251-1). M Cavendish Corp.

Goodfellow, Barbara. Make It Now--Bake It Later, 6 vols. Incl. Vol. 1. pap. (ISBN 0-448-16851-0); Vol. 2. pap. (ISBN 0-448-16852-9); Vol. 3. pap. (ISBN 0-448-16853-7); Vol. 4. pap. (ISBN 0-448-16854-5); Vol. 5. pap. (ISBN 0-448-16855-3); Vol. 6. pap. (ISBN 0-448-16856-1). 1979. pap. 2.50 ea. o.p. (G&D). Putnam Pub Group.

Goodfellow, Caroline. Understanding More About Dolls. 1983. write for info (ISBN 0-907462-19-7). Antique Collect.

Goodfellow, M., jt. auth. see Jones, D.

Goodfellow, Ron. Underwater Engineering. 160p. 1977. 33.95x (ISBN 0-87814-065-4). Pennwell Book Division.

Goodfield, June. An Imagined World: A Story of Scientific Discovery. LC 79-1664. (Illus.). 288p. 1981. 13.41i (ISBN 0-06-011641-2, HarpT). Har-Row.

Goodfriend, Lewis S., jt. auth. see Burris-Meyer, Harold.

Goodfriend, Ronnie S. Power in Perception for the Young Child: A Comprehensive Program for the Development of Pre-Reading Visual Perceptual Skills. LC 72-189232. 1972. pap. text ed. 7.95x (ISBN 0-8077-1430-5); pap. text ed. 6.95x suppl. (ISBN 0-8077-1429-1). Tchrs Coll.

Goodfriend, Theodore, ed. Hypertension Essentials: Concepts, Causes, Consequences & Control. Date not set. price not set (ISBN 0-8089-1534-7). Grune.

Goodger, E. M. Principles of Spaceflight Propulsion. LC 77-88306. 1970. inquire for price o.p. (ISBN 0-08-013884-5). Pergamon.

Goodgold, Ed, jt. auth. see Weiss, Ken.

Goodgold, Joseph. Electrodiagnosis of Neuromuscular Diseases. 3rd ed. 1983. 34.00 (ISBN 0-683-03686-6). Williams & Wilkins.

Goodgold, Joseph & Eberstein, Arthur. Electrodiagnosis of Neuromuscular Diseases. 3rd ed. (Illus.). 358p. 1983. lib. bdg. 34.00 (ISBN 0-683-03686-6). Williams & Wilkins.

Goodhart, Arthur L. Law of the Land. LC 66-16914. 68p. 1966. pap. 2.95 (ISBN 0-8139-0108-1). U Pr of Va.

Goodhart, H. L., jt. auth. see Goodenough, Erwin R.

Goodheart, Pat, tr. see Cardinal, Marie.

Goodhew, P. J. Speciman Preparation in Materials Science. (Practical Methods in Electron Microscopy: Vol. 1, Pt. 1). 17.00 (ISBN 0-444-10412-7, North-Holland). Elsevier.

Goodich, Michael. The Unmentionable Vice: Homosexuality in the Later Medieval Period. LC 78-13276. 164p. 1979. 16.50 o.p. (ISBN 0-87436-287-3). ABC-Clio.

Goodier, Alban. The Crown of Sorrow. 156p. 1982. 3.25 (ISBN 0-8198-1422-9, SP0093); pap. 2.25 (ISBN 0-8198-1423-7). Dghtrs St Paul.

--The Prince of Peace. 152p. 1982. 3.25 (ISBN 0-8198-5807-2, SP0585); pap. 2.25 (ISBN 0-8198-5808-0). Dghtrs St Paul.

Goodier, J. N., jt. auth. see Timoshenko, Stephen P.

Goodin, Robert E. Political Theory & Public Policy. LC 81-23120. 1982. lib. bdg. 27.50x (ISBN 0-226-30296-2). U of Chicago Pr.

--The Politics of Rational Man. LC 75-35616. 240p. 1976. 38.95x (ISBN 0-471-31360-2, Pub. by Wiley-Interscience). Wiley.

Gooding, Charles A., jt. ed. see Margulis, Alexander R.

Gooding, D. W. Relics of Ancient Exegesis. LC 74-19523. (Society for Old Testament Studies Monograph No. 4). 100p. 1976. 32.50 (ISBN 0-521-20700-2). Cambridge U Pr.

Gooding, D. W., ed. see Walters, Peter.

Gooding, Earl. The West Indies at the Crossroads. 256p. 1982. text ed. 16.95x (ISBN 0-87073-052-5); pap. text ed. 8.95x (ISBN 0-87073-053-3). Schenkman.

Goodjohn, Albert J. & Pomraning, Gerald C., eds. Reactor Physics in the Resonance & Thermal Regions, 2 vols. Incl. Vol. 1. Neutron Thermalization. 450p (ISBN 0-262-07023-5); Vol. 2. Resonance Absorbtion. 450p (ISBN 0-262-07024-3). 1966. text ed. 30.00x ea. o.s.i. MIT Pr.

Goodkin, Marie, jt. auth. see Billingham, Richard.

Goodkind, Howard. The Mysteries of the "Talking" Plants. LC 79-16901. (Unsolved Mysteries of the World Ser.). PLB 11.96 (ISBN 0-89547-081-0). Silver.

Goodkind, Richard J., jt. auth. see Baker, James L.

Goodlad. The Conventional & the Alternative in Education. new ed. LC 75-2780. 288p. 1975. 20.75x (ISBN 0-8211-0611-2); text ed. 18.60x (ISBN 0-685-53835-4). McCutchan.

Goodlad, John I. The Dynamics of Educational Change. (I-D-E-A Reports on Schooling). 288p. 1975. 14.95 o.p. (ISBN 0-07-023762-X, P&RB). McGraw.

Goodlad, John I., ed. see Culver, Carmen M. & Hoban, Gary J.

Goodlad, John I., jt. ed. see Fenstermacher, Gary D.

Goodlad, John I., et al. Early Schooling in the United States. (IDEA Reports on Schooling). 290p. 1973. 12.95 o.p. (ISBN 0-07-023763-8, P&RB). McGraw.

--Toward a Mankind School: An Adventure in Humanistic Education. 256p. 1974. 13.95 (ISBN 0-07-023624-0, P&RB). McGraw.

Goodland, R. J. & Irwin, H. S. Amazon Jungle: Green Hell to Red Desert. (Development in Landscape Management & Urban Planning Ser.: Vol. 1). 155p. 1975. 36.25 (ISBN 0-444-41318-9). Elsevier.

Goodland, Robert. Sobradinho Hydroelectic Project: Rio Sao Francisco, Brazil: Environmental Impact Reconnaissance. (Illus.). 1973. pap. 5.00 o.p. (ISBN 0-89327-206-X). NY Botanical.

Goodlin, Robert C. Care of the Fetus. LC 78-62542. (Illus.). 580p. 1979. 50.00x (ISBN 0-89352-021-7). Masson Pub.

Goodman. How to Troubleshoot & Repair Electronic Circuits. 378p. 1981. 16.95 (ISBN 0-8306-9656-3); pap. 10.95 (ISBN 0-8306-1218-1, 1218). TAB Bks.

Goodman, A. H. Music Education: Perspectives & Perceptions. 160p. 1982. pap. text ed. 8.95 (ISBN 0-8403-2689-0). Kendall-Hunt.

Goodman, A. W. Analytic Geometry & the Calculus. 4th ed. (Illus.). 1980. text ed. 35.95x (ISBN 0-02-344960-8). Macmillan.

--Analytic Geometry & the Calculus: Student Study Guide, 2 vols. 4th ed. (Illus.). 1980. pap. text ed. 10.95 ea. Vol. I (ISBN 0-02-344970-5). Vol. II (ISBN 0-02-344980-2). Macmillan.

--Univalent Functions, 2 vols. 47.50 ea. Vol. I (ISBN 0-936166-10-X). Vol. II (ISBN 0-936166-12-6). Mariner Pub.

Goodman, A. W. & Ratti, J. S. Finite Mathematics with Applications. 1979. text ed. 23.95x (ISBN 0-02-344760-5); instrs'. manual avail. Macmillan.

Goodman, A. W. & Saff, Edward. Calculus: Concepts & Calculations. 1981. text ed. 35.95x (ISBN 0-02-344740-0); Vol. 1. student study guide 6.95 (ISBN 0-02-344750-8); Vol. 2. student study guide o.p. 6.95 (ISBN 0-686-72521-2). Macmillan.

Goodman, A. W., et al. The Mainstream of Algebra & Trigonometry. 2nd ed. LC 79-90059. (Illus.). 1980. text ed. 23.95 (ISBN 0-395-26765-X); solutions manual 2.45 (ISBN 0-395-26761-7). HM.

Goodman, Allen C., jt. auth. see Begus, Sarah.

Goodman, Andrew. Gilbert & Sullivan at Law. LC 82-12175. (Illus.). 264p. 1982. 25.00 (ISBN 0-8386-3179-7). Fairleigh Dickinson.

Goodman, Ann, jt. auth. see Elting, Mary.

Goodman, Becky, ed. see Mindell, Arnold.

Goodman, Benjamin, intro. by. Malcolm X: The End of White World Supremacy. 160p. 1983. pap. 6.95 (ISBN 0-394-62469-6). Seaver Bks.

Goodman, Carlton. How to Be a Successful Bus Pastor or Bus Captain. 1976. pap. 3.95 o.p. (ISBN 0-8010-3661-5). Baker Bk.

Goodman, Charles D., et al, eds. PN Reaction & the Nucleon-Nucleon Force. 550p. 1980. 55.00x (ISBN 0-306-40351-X, Plenum Pr). Plenum Pub.

Goodman, David. Inner Power: Discovering Yourself & Manifesting Your Potentials. LC 81-23599. (Quality Paperback Ser.: No. 369). 172p. (Orig.). 1982. pap. text ed. 5.95 (ISBN 0-8226-0369-1). Littlefield.

Goodman, David, tr. see Domes, Jurgen.

Goodman, David M. Western Panorama: J. Ross Browne. (Illus.). 1965. 13.50 o.p. (ISBN 0-87062-017-7). A H Clark.

Goodman, Don. The Boy Who Made God Smile. LC 82-7532. (A Cory Story Ser.). (Illus.). 32p. (ps-4). 1982. pap. 2.95 (ISBN 0-8307-0859-6, 5608224). Regal.

--Cory Hears with His Heart. LC 82-12272. (A Cory Story Ser.). (ps-2). 1982. pap. 2.95 (ISBN 0-8307-0858-8, 5608318). Regal.

Goodman, Elaine, jt. auth. see Goodman, Walter.

Goodman, Ellen. At Large. 352p. 1983. pap. 3.50 (ISBN 0-449-20145-7, Crest). Fawcett.

--Close to Home. 1979. 9.95 o.p. (ISBN 0-671-24883-9). S&S.

--Turning Points. 320p. 1983. pap. 3.50 (ISBN 0-449-20103-1, Crest). Fawcett.

--Turning Points. Date not set. pap. 5.95 (ISBN 0-449-90015-0, Columbine). Fawcett.

Goodman, Eric K. The First Time I Saw Jenny Hall. Golbitz, Pat, ed. 224p. 1983. 13.95 (ISBN 0-688-01886-6). Morrow.

Goodman, Eugene B. All the Justice I Could Afford. 320p. 16.95 (ISBN 0-15-104778-2). HarBraceJ.

Goodman, F. D., et al. Trance, Healing, & Hallucination: Three Field Studies in Religious Experience. LC 80-20043. 414p. 1982. Repr. of 1974 ed. text ed. 20.95 (ISBN 0-89874-246-3). Krieger.

Goodman, Felicitas D. The Exorcism of Anneliese Michel. LC 80-910. 312p. 1981. 12.95 o.p. (ISBN 0-385-15789-4). Doubleday.

Goodman, Florence J. The A B C's of Feminine Happiness. 88p. 1980. 8.95x (ISBN 0-917232-10-0). Gee Tee Bee.

Goodman, Gary. Reach Out & Sell Someone: Phone Your Way to Success Through the Goodman System of Telemarketing. 156p. 1983. 12.95 (ISBN 0-13-753632-1); pap. 5.95 (ISBN 0-13-753624-0). P-H.

Goodman, Gerrie, et al. No Turning Back: Lesbian & Gay Liberation for the '80s. 1983. lib. bdg. 16.95 (ISBN 0-86571-019-8); pap. 7.95 (ISBN 0-86571-018-X). New Soc Pubs.

Goodman, Gerson. Cold Call Selling. 1979. text ed. 29.95 (ISBN 0-686-98285-1). Sales & Mktg.

Goodman, Grant K. American Occupation of Japan: A Retrospective View. LC 68-65352. (International Studies: East Asia Ser. No. 2). (Orig.). 1968. pap. 2.50x o.p. (ISBN 0-8188-0153-0). Paragon.

Goodman, Grant K. & Moos, Felix, eds. The United States & Japan in the Western Pacific. (Westview Replica Edition Ser.). (Illus.). 225p. 1981. lib. bdg. 24.00 (ISBN 0-89158-840-X). Westview.

Goodman, Herman, jt. auth. see Fredericks, Carlton.

Goodman, I., ed. Developments in Block Copolymers, Vol. 1. (Illus.). xiv, 355p. 1982. 82.00 (ISBN 0-85334-145-1, Pub. by Applied Sci England). Elsevier.

Goodman, Irving & Schein, Martin, eds. Birds: Brain & Behavior. 1974. 41.00 (ISBN 0-12-290350-1). Acad Pr.

Goodman, Jack, ed. While You Were Gone: A Report on Wartime Life in the United States. LC 73-19969. (FDR & the Era of the New Deal Ser). 625p. 1974. Repr. of 1946 ed. lib. bdg. 69.50 (ISBN 0-306-70605-9). Da Capo.

Goodman, James A., ed. Dynamics of Racism in Social Work Practice. LC 73-88446. 375p. 1973. pap. 12.00 (ISBN 0-87101-068-2, CBA-068-C). Natl Assn Soc Wkrs.

Goodman, Jane G. Aging Parents: Whose Responsibility? LC 80-149450. (Workshop Models for Family Life Education Ser.). 168p. 1980. plastic comb 11.95 (ISBN 0-87304-175-5). Family Serv.

Goodman, Jay S. The Dynamics of Urban Government & Politics. 2nd ed. (Illus.). 1980. pap. text ed. 14.95 (ISBN 0-02-344830-X). Macmillan.

Goodman, Jeffrey. Psychic Archeology: Time Machine to the Past. 1977. 8.95 o.p. (ISBN 0-399-11843-8, Pub. by Berkley). Putnam Pub Group.

Goodman, Jerome D. & Sours, John A. Child Mental Status Exam. LC 67-18208. 1967. text ed. 12.50x o.p. (ISBN 0-465-01010-5). Basic.

Goodman, Joan. Sport & Recreation in London. 1977. 7.50 o.p. (ISBN 0-7045-0095-7). State Mutual Bk.

Goodman, Joan E. Bear & His Book. Klimo, Kate, ed. (Illus.). 4p. 1982. 6.95 (ISBN 0-671-45156-1, Little Simon). S&S.

--Right's Animal Farm. LC 82-83069. (Little Golden Bk.). (Illus.). 24p. (ps-2). 1983. 0.89 (ISBN 0-307-02006-1, Golden Pr). Western Pr.

Goodman, Joel & Huggins, Kenneth. Let the Buyer Be Aware: Valuable Skills for Consumers, Parents & Teachers in the Eighties. 246p. 1981. pap. 9.95 (ISBN 0-940156-00-8). Wright Group.

Goodman, John C. Social Security in the United Kingdom. 1981. pap. 4.75 (ISBN 0-8447-3460-8). Am Enterprise.

Goodman, John C. & Dolan, Edwin G. Economics of Public Policy: The Micro View. 2nd ed. (Illus.). 225p. 1982. pap. text ed. 10.95 (ISBN 0-314-63240-9). West Pub.

Goodman, John, Jr. Regional Housing Assistance Allocations & Regional Housing Needs. 40p. 1979. pap. text ed. 4.00 (ISBN 0-87766-263-0). Urban Inst.

Goodman, John L., Jr. The Future Poor: Projecting the Population Eligible for Federal Housing Assistance. 15p. pap. text ed. 1.00 (ISBN 0-686-84410-6). Urban Inst.

Goodman, Jonathan. The Stabbing of George Harry Storrs. (Illus.). 200p. 1983. price not set (ISBN 0-8142-0349-3). Ohio St U Pr.

Goodman, Joseph W. Introduction to Fourier Optics. (Physical & Quantum Electronics Ser). 1968. text ed. 38.50 (ISBN 0-07-023776-X, C). McGraw.

Goodman, Julie, jt. auth. see Smith, Marjorie.

Goodman, Kenneth, et al. Reading in the Bilingual Classroom: Literacy and Biliteracy. 56p. 1979. pap. text ed. 5.25 (ISBN 0-89763-011-4). Natl Clearinghse Bilingual Ed.

Goodman, Kraines M. & Kan, Esther J. Jump into Jazz: A Primer for the Beginning Jazz Dance Student. (Illus.). 127p. 1983. pap. 6.59 (ISBN 0-87484-571-8). Mayfield Pub.

Goodman, Leni, jt. auth. see Goodman, Stuart.

Goodman, Lenn E. The Case of the Animals versus Man Before the King of the Jinn. (International Studies & Translations Program). 1980. 20.00 (ISBN 0-8057-8161-7, Twayne). G K Hall.

--Notes on Philosophy & Philosophers. 514p. 1982. pap. 25.95 (ISBN 0-917232-14-3). Gee Tee Bee.

--Philosophy & Philosophers. 603p. (Orig.). pap. text ed. 12.95x o.p. (ISBN 0-917232-10-0). Gee Tee Bee.

--RAMBAM: Readings in the Philosophy of Moses Maimonides. Patterson, David & Edelman, Lily, eds. LC 75-14476. 1978. text ed. 10.00 (ISBN 0-917232-07-0). Gee Tee Bee.

Goodman, Lenn E., jt. auth. see Goodman, Madeleine J.

Goodman, Lenn E., tr. see Tufayl, Ibn.

Goodman, Leonard H., compiled by. Current Career & Occupational Literature, 1982. 196p. 1982. 15.00 (ISBN 0-686-95208-1). Wilson.

Goodman, Leonard H., ed. Current Career & Occupational Literature, 1973-1977. 757p. 1978. 14.00 (ISBN 0-8242-0616-9). Wilson.

Goodman, Linda. Linda Goodman's Love Poems. LC 79-2731. 1980. 10.53i (ISBN 0-06-011643-9, HarpT). Har-Row.

Goodman, Lisl M. Death & the Creative Life. 1983. pap. 5.95 (ISBN 0-14-006275-0). Penguin.

Goodman, Louis W., jt. ed. see Apter, David E.

Goodman, M., jt. auth. see Falcaro, Joe.

Goodman, M. W., jt. auth. see Penzias, Walter.

Goodman, Madeleine J. & Goodman, Lenn E. Sex Differences in the Human Life Cycle. rev., 3rd ed. 393p. 1983. 27.95x (ISBN 0-917232-15-1). Gee Tee Bee.

--The Sexes in the Human Population. (Illus.). 203p. (Orig.). pap. text ed. 16.95 (ISBN 0-917232-12-7). Gee Tee Bee.

Goodman, Marguerite. Christmas Comes in Assorted Sizes. Ashton, Sylvia, ed. LC 77-80303. 1977. 12.95 (ISBN 0-87949-111-6). Ashley Bks.

Goodman, Martin. State & Society in Roman Galilee: A. D. 132-212. (Publications in the Oxford Centre for Postgraduate Hebrew Studies: Vol. 4). 220p. 1983. text ed. 30.00x (ISBN 0-86598-089-6). Allanheld.

Goodman, Mary E. Culture of Childhood: Child's-Eye Views of Society & Culture. LC 75-106992. 1970. pap. 7.95x (ISBN 0-8077-1444-5). Tchrs Coll.

Goodman, Mary Ellen. Race Awareness in Young Children. rev. ed. 352p. pap. 1.50 o.p. (ISBN 0-686-95013-5). ADL.

Goodman, Michael J. & Sparberg, Marshall. Ulcerative Colitis. LC 78-8686. (Clinical Gastroenterology Monographs). 1978. 39.95x (ISBN 0-471-48895-X, Pub. by Wiley Medical). Wiley.

Goodman, Miriam. Signal Noise. LC 82-71819. 61p. 1982. 12.95 (ISBN 0-914086-40-5); pap. 4.95 (ISBN 0-914086-39-1). Alicejamesbooks.

Goodman, Morris, ed. Macromolecular Sequences in Systematic & Evolutionary Biology. (Monographs in Evolutionary Biology). 432p. 1982. 45.00x (ISBN 0-306-41061-3, Plenum Pr). Plenum Pub.

Goodman, Morris C. Astrology & Sexual Analysis. LC 78-109373. (Illus.). 1972. 8.50 (ISBN 0-8303-0094-5). Fleet.

Goodman, Murray & Meienhofer, Johannes, eds. Peptides: Proceedings. American Peptide Symposium, Fifth. LC 77-88855. 612p. 1977. 49.95x o.p. (ISBN 0-470-99384-7). Halsted Pr.

Goodman, N., jt. auth. see Belkin, Gary S.

Goodman, Nelson. Fact, Fiction, & Forecast. 3rd ed. LC 73-11273. 1977. 17.50 o.p. (ISBN 0-672-51889-9); pap. text ed. 6.95x o.p. (ISBN 0-672-61347-6). Hackett Pub.

--Fact, Fiction & Forecast. 4th ed. 176p. 1983. text ed. 10.00x (ISBN 0-674-29070-4); pap. text ed. 4.95x (ISBN 0-674-29071-2). Harvard U Pr.

--Ways of Worldmaking. LC 78-56364. (Illus.). 1978. text ed. 13.50 (ISBN 0-915144-52-2); pap. 6.95 (ISBN 0-915144-51-4). Hackett Pub.

Goodman, Nelson, ed. see Lee, Sherman E.

Goodman, Norman & Marx, Gary. Society Today. 4th ed. 561p. 1982. text ed. 21.00 (ISBN 0-394-32550-8). Random.

Goodman, Paul S. Assessing Organizational Change: Rushton Quality of Work Experiment. LC 78-31857. (Organizational Behavior Assessment & Change Ser.). 1979. 32.50x (ISBN 0-471-04782-1, Pub. by Wiley-Interscience). Wiley.

Goodman, Paul S., et al. Change in Organizations: New Perspectives on Theory, Research, & Practice. LC 82-48069. (Social & Behavioral Science Ser.). 1982. text ed. 19.95x (ISBN 0-87589-547-6). Jossey Bass.

Goodman, Richard. Methods of Geological Engineering in Discontinuous Rocks. LC 75-42152. (Illus.). 1975. text ed. 35.00 (ISBN 0-8299-0066-7). West Pub.

Goodman, Richard E. Rock Mechanics. LC 80-13155. 478p. 1980. text ed. 39.95x (ISBN 0-471-04129-7). Wiley.

Goodman, Richard E. & Hueze, Francios E., eds. Issues in Rock Mechanics: Twenty-Third Symposium. LC 82-71989. (Illus.). 1133p. 1982. 45.00x (ISBN 0-89520-297-2). Soc Mining Eng.

Goodman, Richard M. & Gorlin, Robert J. Atlas of the Face in Genetic Disorders. 2nd ed. LC 76-40327. (Illus.). 586p. 1977. 69.50 o.p. (ISBN 0-8016-1895-9). Mosby.

--Malformations in Infants & Children: An Illustrated Guide. (Illus.). 450p. 1983. text ed. 35.00x (ISBN 0-19-503254-3); pap. text ed. 19.50x (ISBN 0-19-503255-1). Oxford U Pr.

Goodman, Richard M. & Motulsky, Arno G., eds. Genetic Diseases among Ashkenazi Jews. LC 77-90594. 454p. 1979. text ed. 43.00 (ISBN 0-89004-262-4). Raven.

Goodman, Robert. After the Planners. LC 74-154100. 1973. pap. 4.95 o.p. (ISBN 0-671-21530-2, Touchstone Bks). S&S.

--Troubleshooting with the Dual-Trace Scope. LC 75-41732. 224p. 1976. 8.95 o.p. (ISBN 0-8306-6772-5); pap. 5.95 o.p. (ISBN 0-8306-5772-X, 772). TAB Bks.

Goodman, Robert L. General Electric Color TV Service Manual, Vol. 1. LC 73-129048. (Orig.). 1970. pap. 8.95 o.p. (ISBN 0-8306-9536-2, 536). TAB Bks.

--How to Repair Video Games. (Illus.). 1978. vinyl 9.95 (ISBN 0-8306-9906-6, 1028); pap. 7.95 o.p. (ISBN 0-8306-1028-6, 1028). TAB Bks.

Goodman, Roger B. How to Prepare for the Graduate Record Examination - Verbal Section. 1979. pap. 5.95 o.p. (ISBN 0-07-023773-5, SP). McGraw.

Goodman, S. E. & Hedetniemi, S. T. Introduction to the Design & Analysis of Algorithms. (Computer Science Ser.). (Illus.). 1977. text ed. 33.95 (ISBN 0-07-023753-0, C); instructor's manual 12.00 (ISBN 0-07-023754-9). McGraw.

Goodman, Sam R. & Reece, James S. Controller's Handbook. LC 77-91319. 1978. 45.50 (ISBN 0-87094-157-7). Dow Jones-Irwin.

Goodman, Stanley, jt. auth. see Winters, Arthur A.

Goodman, Stanley J. How to Manage a Turnaround: A Senior Manager's Blueprint for Turning an Ailing Business into a Winner. LC 82-70077. 256p. 1982. 18.95 (ISBN 0-02-912480-8). Free Pr.

Goodman, Stuart & Goodman, Leni. Art from Shells. LC 72-84317. (Illus.). 224p. 1972. pap. 5.95 o.p. (ISBN 0-517-50025-6). Crown.

Goodman, W. Party System in America. 1980. pap. 12.95 (ISBN 0-13-652677-2). P-H.

Goodman, W. L., tr. see Prishvin, Mikhail.

Goodman, Walter & Goodman, Elaine. The Family: Yesterday, Today, Tomorrow. LC 74-32069. 128p. (gr. 7 up). 1975. 7.95 o.p. (ISBN 0-374-32260-0). FS&G.

Goodman, Wolf, tr. see Michelson, Frida.

Goodnow, J. & Burns, A. Children & Families in Australia: Contemporary Issues & Problems. (Studies in Society: No. 5). 1979. text ed. 22.50x (ISBN 0-86861-057-7); pap. text ed. 9.50x (ISBN 0-86861-065-8). Allen Unwin.

Goodpaster, Andrew J. For the Common Defense. LC 77-4562. 1977. 21.95x (ISBN 0-669-01620-9). Lexington Bks.

Goodpaster, Andrew J., jt. ed. see Elliott, Lloyd h.

Goodpoaster, Andrew J. & Elliott, Lloyd H. Toward a Consensus on Military Service. 70p. 1982. pap. 6.00x (ISBN 0-686-43306-8). Transaction Bks.

Goodrich, David L. Paint Me a Million. LC 77-16232. 1978. 7.95 o.p. (ISBN 0-399-12118-8). Putnam Pub Group.

Goodrich, Donna. How to Set Up & Run a Typing Service. (Small Business Ser.). 160p. 1983. pap. text ed. 8.95 (ISBN 0-471-86858-2). Wiley.

Goodrich, Gail & Levin, Rich. Winning Basketball. LC 76-11206. (Winning Ser.). (Illus.). 1976. 8.95 (ISBN 0-8092-8108-2); pap. 7.95 (ISBN 0-8092-8107-4). Contemp Bks.

Goodrich, L. Carrington. Short History of the Chinese People. (Illus.). pap. 6.50xi o.p. (ISBN 0-06-133015-9, TB3015, Torch). Har-Row.

Goodrich, Lawrence B. Ralph Earl: Recorder for an Era. LC 66-64728. (Illus.). 1967. 13.95x (ISBN 0-87395-020-8). State U NY Pr.

Goodrich, Leland M. Korea: A Study of U. S. Policy in the United Nations. LC 78-24120. 1979. Repr. of 1956 ed. lib. bdg. 20.75x (ISBN 0-313-20825-5, GOKO). Greenwood.

Goodrich, Lloyd. Thomas Eakins, 2 vols. (The Ailsa Mellon Bruce Studies in American Art). (Illus.). 1983. 90.00 (ISBN 0-674-88490-6); until 3/31/83 70.00 (ISBN 0-686-97507-3). Vol. I: 368p. Vol. II: 384p. Harvard U Pr.

Goodrich, Lois. Decentralized Camping. 1982. pap. 12.50 (ISBN 0-686-83992-7). Am Camping.

Goodrich, Nancy M. A Profile of the Competent Nursing Administrator. Kalisch, Philip & Kalisch, Beatrice, eds. LC 82-8479. (Studies in Nursing Management: No. 3). 180p. 1982. 39.95 (ISBN 0-8357-1360-1, Pub. by UMI Res Pr). Univ Microfilms.

Goodrich, Norma L. Ancient Myths. (RL 9). pap. 2.50 (ISBN 0-451-62133-6, ME2133, Ment). NAL.

--Medieval Myths. rev. ed. (RL 9). 1977. pap. 2.75 (ISBN 0-451-62117-4, ME2117, Ment). NAL.

Goodrich, Samuel G. Recollections of a Lifetime, or Men & Things I Have Seen. LC 67-23886. 1967. Repr. of 1857 ed. 37.00x (ISBN 0-8103-3041-5). Gale.

Goodrich, William, jt. auth. see Sissors, Jack.

Goodrick, A. T., tr. see Grimmelshausen, H. J. Von.

Goodrick, Edward W. & Kohlenberger, John R., III. The NIV Handy Concordance. 384p. (Orig.). 1982. pap. 4.95 (ISBN 0-310-43662-1). Zondervan.

Goodrick, Susan, jt. ed. see Donahue, Don.

Goodrum, Charles A. & Dalrymple, Helen W. The Library of Congress. 2nd ed. (Library of Federal Department, Agencies, & Systems Ser.). 300p. 1982. lib. bdg. 30.00 (ISBN 0-86531-303-2); pap. 11.95 (ISBN 0-86531-497-7). Westview.

Goodsell, Charles T. The Case for Bureaucracy: A Public Administration Polemic. 1983. pap. 8.95x (ISBN 0-934540-17-9). Chatham Hse Pubs.

Goodsell, Jane. Daniel Inouye. LC 77-1405. (Biography Ser.). (Illus.). (gr. 1-4). 1977. PLB 10.89 (ISBN 0-690-01358-2, TYC-J). Har-Row.

--Eleanor Roosevelt. LC 71-106573. (Biography Ser.). (Illus.). (gr. 2-5). 1970. PLB 10.89 (ISBN 0-690-25626-4, TYC-J). Har-Row.

Goodson, Carole E. & Miertschin, Susan. Technical Mathematics with Applications. 960p. 1983. 22.95x (ISBN 0-471-08244-9); tchr's. manual avail. (ISBN 0-471-89526-1); study guide avail. (ISBN 0-471-87578-3). Wiley.

Goodson, Gar. Many Splendored Fishes of the Atlantic Coast. LC 76-3231. 1976. pap. 4.95 o.s.i. (ISBN 0-916240-01-0). Marquest Colorguide.

Goodson, Ivor. School Subjects & Curriculum Change. (Curriculum Policy & Research Ser.). 222p. 1983. text ed. 32.00x (ISBN 0-7099-1104-1, Pub. by Croom Helm Ltd England). Biblio Dist.

Goodspeed, Donald J. The German Wars Nineteen Fourteen to Nineteen Forty-Five. LC 77-4967. 1977. 17.50 o.p. (ISBN 0-395-25713-1). HM.

Goodspeed, Edgar J. History of Early Christian Literature. rev. & enl. ed. Grant, Robert M., ed. LC 66-13871. 1966. pap. 1.95 (ISBN 0-226-30386-1). U of Chicago Pr.

--How Came the Bible. 1976. pap. 1.75 o.s.i. (ISBN 0-89129-125-3). Jove Pubns.

--Index Patristicus, sive clavis Patrum Apostolicorum operum. LC 60-52358. 1960. 12.50x (ISBN 0-8401-0863-X). Allenson-Breckinridge.

--A Life of Jesus. LC 78-21540. 1979. Repr. of 1950 ed. lib. bdg. 20.75x (ISBN 0-313-20728-3, GOLJ). Greenwood.

Goodspeed, Peter. A Rhinoceros Wakes Me up in the Morning. LC 81-21556. (Illus.). 32p. (ps-1). 1982. 10.95 (ISBN 0-02-736590-5). Bradbury Pr.

Goodspeed Publishing Company. History of Henderson, Chester, McNairy, Decatur & Hardin Counties. 1978. Repr. 17.50 (ISBN 0-89308-097-7). Southern Hist Pr.

Goodspeed, T. Harper. Plant Hunters in the Andes. 2nd rev. & enl. ed. LC 61-7533. 1961. 30.00x (ISBN 0-520-00495-7). U of Cal Pr.

Goodstadt, Leo. China's Watergate: Political & Economic Conflicts in China 1969-1977. LC 79-902871. 1979. text ed. 15.75x (ISBN 0-7069-0725-6). Humanities.

Goodstein, David L. States of Matter. 544p. 1975. 32.95 (ISBN 0-13-843557-X). P-H.

Goodstein, Leonard D. Consulting with Human Service Systems. LC 77-81194. (Topics in Clinical Psychology). (Illus.). 1978. pap. text ed. 8.95 (ISBN 0-201-02397-0). A-W.

Goodstein, Leonard D. & Calhoun, James F. Understanding Abnormal Behavior: Description, Explanation, Management. LC 81-17669. (Illus.). 560p. 1982. text ed. 23.95 (ISBN 0-201-04078-6). A-W.

Goodstein, Leonard D. & Lanyon, Richard I. Adjustment, Behavior, & Personality. 2nd ed. LC 78-62553. (Illus.). 1979. text ed. 20.95 (ISBN 0-201-02455-1); wkbk. 6.50 (ISBN 0-201-02456-X). A-W.

Goodstein, Leonard D., jt. auth. see Lanyon, Richard I.

Goodstein, Leonard D., jt. ed. see Burke, W. Warner.

Goodstein, Marvin, jt. ed. see Weintraub, Sidney.

Goodstein, R. L. Fundamental Concepts of Mathematics. 2nd ed. 1979. text ed. 48.00 (ISBN 0-08-021665-X); pap. text ed. 19.25 (ISBN 0-08-021666-8). Pergamon.

Goodwin & Mayall, eds. The New International Commodity Regime. 1980. 30.00 (ISBN 0-312-56812-6). St Martin.

Goodwin, Barbara. Using Political Ideas. LC 81-16009. 294p. 1982. 34.95 (ISBN 0-471-10115-X, Pub. by Wiley-Interscience); pap. 14.95x (ISBN 0-471-10116-8). Wiley.

Goodwin, Clive E. A Bird-Finding Guide to Ontario. (Illus.). 256p. 1982. pap. 12.50 (ISBN 0-8020-6494-9). U of Toronto Pr.

Goodwin, David. Delivering Educational Services. LC 76-54166. 1977. pap. text ed. 9.50x (ISBN 0-8077-2507-2). Tchrs Coll.

Goodwin, Donald W. & Guze, Samuel B. Psychiatric Diagnosis. 2nd ed. 1979. text ed. 18.95x (ISBN 0-19-502512-1); pap. text ed. 9.95x (ISBN 0-19-502513-X). Oxford U Pr.

Goodwin, George L. The Ontological Argument of Charles Hartshorne. LC 78-2821. 1978. pap. 9.95 (ISBN 0-89130-228-X, 01-01-20). Scholars Pr CA.

Goodwin, Grenville. Western Apache Raiding & Warfare. Basso, Keith H., ed. LC 73-142255. 1971. pap. 11.95 (ISBN 0-8165-0297-8). U of Ariz Pr.

Goodwin, Harold. Top Secret: Alligators. LC 74-81695. (Illus.). 112p. (gr. 3-5). 1975. 5.95 o.p. (ISBN 0-87888-102-6). Bradbury Pr.

Goodwin, J. W., et al. Perinatal Medicine. (Illus.). 642p. 1976. 63.00 o.p. (ISBN 0-683-03649-1). Williams & Wilkins.

Goodwin, Jill. A Dyer's Manual. (Illus.). 128p. 1983. 17.95 (ISBN 0-7207-1327-7, Pub by Michael Joseph). Merrimack Bk Serv.

Goodwin, John. High Points of Legal History: The Development of Business Law. LC 82-15127. 138p. (Orig.). 1982. pap. text ed. 9.95 (ISBN 0-942280-01-6). Pub Horizons.

Goodwin, John C. Insanity & the Criminal. (Historical Foundations of Forensic Psychiatry & Psychology Ser.). 308p. 1980. Repr. of 1924 ed. lib. bdg. 32.50 (ISBN 0-306-76061-4). Da Capo.

Goodwin, John F., jt. ed. see Krikler, Dennis M.

Goodwin, John F., jt. ed. see Yu, Paul N.

Goodwin, Ken. Understanding African Poetry: A Study of Ten Poets. 256p. 1982. text ed. 25.00x (ISBN 0-435-91325-5); pap. text ed. 12.50x (ISBN 0-435-91326-3). Heinemann Ed.

Goodwin, Lemuel R., Sr. & Goodwin, Mary J. Please Don't Cut the Ears Off. 1983. pap. 4.00 (ISBN 0-932632-07-6). MJG Co.

Goodwin, Leonard. Causes & Cures of Welfare: New Evidence on the Social Psychology of the Poor. LC 82-48634. 224p. 1983. 23.95x (ISBN 0-669-06370-3). Lexington Bks.

--Do the Poor Want to Work? A Social-Psychological Study of Work Orientations. 170p. 1972. 17.95 (ISBN 0-8157-3206-6); pap. 5.95 (ISBN 0-8157-3205-8). Brookings.

Goodwin, Mary J., jt. auth. see Goodwin, Lemuel R., Sr.

Goodwin, Maude W. Dutch & English on the Hudson. 1919. text ed. 8.50x (ISBN 0-686-83529-8). Elliots Bks.

Goodwin, R. M. Elementary Economics from the Higher Standpoints. LC 72-116842. 1970. 37.50 (ISBN 0-521-07923-3). Cambridge U Pr.

Goodwin, Reason A. Mind Your Q's & X's. 64p. (Orig.). 1983. pap. write for info. (ISBN 0-936368-04-7). Lexik Hse.

Goodwin, Robert P., tr. see Thomas Aquinas, St.

Goodwin, T. W. Biosynthesis of Vitamins & Related Compounds. 1964. 58.00 o.s.i. (ISBN 0-12-289858-3). Acad Pr.

Goodwin, Thomas H., tr. see Zander, Maximilian.

Goodwin, William L. & Driscoll, Laura A. Handbook for Measurement & Evaluation in Early Childhood Education: Issues, Measures, & Methods. LC 79-88768. (Social & Behavioral Science Ser.). 1980. text ed. 29.95x (ISBN 0-87589-440-2). Jossey-Bass.

Goodwin-Gill, Guy S. International Law & the Movement of Persons Between States. 1978. 57.00x (ISBN 0-19-825333-8). Oxford U Pr.

Goodwon, Katcha. Rate All the Contenders: Secrets of Longshot Handicapping. Date not set. pap. 12.95 o.s.i. (ISBN 0-932896-04-9). Westcliff Pubns.

--A Thinking Man's Guide to Handicapping. 1979. pap. text ed. 10.00 o.p. (ISBN 0-932896-01-4). Westcliff Pubns.

--Thinking Man's Guide to Handicapping. rev. enl. ed. 1980. pap. text ed. 11.00 o.p. (ISBN 0-932896-02-2). Westcliff Pubns.

Goodwyn, Lawrence. The Populist Moment: A Short History of the Agrarian Revolt in America. 1978. pap. 8.95 (ISBN 0-19-502417-6, GB 536, GB). Oxford U Pr.

Goody, Esther N. Contexts of Kinship: An Essay in the Family Sociology of the Gonja of Northern Ghana. LC 72-78892. (Cambridge Studies in Social Anthropology: No. 7). (Illus.). 300p. 1973. 34.50 (ISBN 0-521-08583-7). Cambridge U Pr.

--Questions & Politeness. LC 77-6577. (Cambridge Papers in Social Anthropology Ser.: No. 8). 1978. 32.50 o.p. (ISBN 0-521-21749-0); pap. 13.95 (ISBN 0-521-29250-6). Cambridge U Pr.

Goody, Esther N., ed. From Craft to Industry: The Ethnography of Proto-Industrial Cloth Production. LC 82-4205. (Cambridge Papers in Social Anthropology: No. 10). 304p. 1983. 39.50 (ISBN 0-521-24614-8). Cambridge U Pr.

Goody, Jack. Developmental Cycle in Domestic Groups. LC 78-160087. (Papers in Social Anthropology: No. 1). (Illus.). 1972. 27.95 (ISBN 0-521-05116-9); pap. 11.95 (ISBN 0-521-09660-X). Cambridge U Pr.

--Succession to High Office. LC 79-52487. (Cambridge Papers in Social Anthropology: No. 4). (Illus.). 1979. pap. 8.95x (ISBN 0-521-29732-X). Cambridge U Pr.

Goody, Jack & Tambiah, S. J. Bridewealth & Dowry. LC 72-95407. (Cambridge Papers in Social Anthropology Ser.: No. 7). (Illus.). 128p. 1973. 21.95 (ISBN 0-521-20169-1); pap. 8.95x (ISBN 0-521-09805-X). Cambridge U Pr.

Goody, Jack, ed. The Character of Kinship. LC 73-82448. (Illus.). 242p. 1973. 29.50 (ISBN 0-521-20290-6); pap. 11.95 (ISBN 0-521-29002-3). Cambridge U Pr.

--The Domestication of the Savage Mind. (Themes in the Social Sciences Ser.). (Illus.). 1977. 29.95 (ISBN 0-521-21726-1); pap. 9.95 (ISBN 0-521-29242-5). Cambridge U Pr.

--Production & Reproduction. LC 76-4238. (Cambridge Studies in Social Anthropology: No.17). (Illus.). 1977. 27.95 (ISBN 0-521-21294-4); pap. 8.95 (ISBN 0-521-29088-0). Cambridge U Pr.

--Technology, Tradition & the State in Africa. (Illus.). 88p. 1980. pap. 6.95x (ISBN 0-521-29892-X). Cambridge U Pr.

Goody, Jack, et al, eds. Family & Inheritance. LC 76-10402. (Past & Present Publications Ser.). (Illus.). 1976. 49.50 (ISBN 0-521-21246-4); pap. 15.95x (ISBN 0-521-29354-5). Cambridge U Pr.

Goody, Jack R., ed. Literacy in Traditional Societies. LC 69-10427. 1969. 29.95 o.p. (ISBN 0-521-07345-6); pap. 13.95 (ISBN 0-521-29005-8). Cambridge U Pr.

Goody, Richard & Walker, James C. Atmospheres. (Foundations of Earth Science Ser). (Illus.). 160p. 1972. ref. ed. o.p. 8.95 (ISBN 0-13-050096-8); pap. 11.95 ref. ed. (ISBN 0-13-050088-7). P-H.

Goody, Roy W. Microcomputer Fundamentals. 300p. 1979. pap. text ed. 15.95 (ISBN 0-574-21540-9, 13-4540); instr's. guide avail. (ISBN 0-574-21541-7, 13-4541). SRA.

Goodyear, Carmen. The Sheep Book. 26p. (ps-1). 1972. pap. 3.00 (ISBN 0-914996-02-9). Lollipop Power.

Goodyear, F. H. Archaeological Site Science. 1971. 23.95 o.p. (ISBN 0-444-19598-X). Elsevier.

Goodyear, Margaret & Klohr, M. C. Managing for Effective Living. 2nd ed. LC 65-10956. 290p. 1965. text ed. 13.00 (ISBN 0-471-31517-6, Pub. by Wiley). Krieger.

Googe, Barnabe. Eglogs, Epytaphes, & Sonettes, (1563) LC 68-24209. (Illus.). 1969. Repr. of 1563 ed. lib. bdg. 25.00x (ISBN 0-8201-1060-4). Schol Facsimiles.

--Eglogs, Epytaphes & Sonnettes: 1563. Arber, Edward, ed. 128p. Date not set. pap. 12.50 (ISBN 0-87556-103-9). Saifer.

--Selected Poems of Barnabe Googe. Stephens, Alan, ed. LC 80-29155. (Books of the Renaissance Ser.). 60p. 1981. Repr. of 1961 ed. lib. bdg. 19.25x (ISBN 0-313-22830-2, GOSEP). Greenwood.

Googe, Barnabe, tr. see Palingenius, Marcellus.

Goold-Adams, Richard. John Foster Dulles: A Reappraisal. LC 74-9272. 309p. 1974. Repr. of 1962 ed. lib. bdg. 17.50x (ISBN 0-8371-7638-7, GOJD). Greenwood.

Gooljar, Mahendranath. Sweet Remembrance of Silberkugel & Christmas Holidays in Summer. 1983. 7.95 (ISBN 0-686-84436-X). Vantage.

Goolrich, Robert, jt. auth. see Bach, Laurence.

Goolsby, Leroy. How Bitter Are The Sweets. 64p. 1983. 7.95 (ISBN 0-89962-321-2). Todd & Honeywell.

Gooneratne, Yasmine. Alexander Pope. LC 76-4758. (British Authors Ser). 160p. 1976. 29.95 (ISBN 0-521-21127-1); pap. 8.95 (ISBN 0-521-29051-1). Cambridge U Pr.

--Jane Austen. LC 75-123669. (British Authors Ser: Introductory Critical Studies). 1970. 29.95 (ISBN 0-521-07843-1); pap. 8.95 (ISBN 0-521-09630-8). Cambridge U Pr.

Gooneratne, Yasmine, ed. Poems from India, Sri Lanka, Malaysia & Singapore. (Writing in Asia Ser.). 1980. 4.50x (ISBN 0-686-66066-8, 00219). Heinemann Ed.

Goonetileke, H. A. Sri Lanka. (World Bibliographical Ser.: No. 20). 1983. write for info. (ISBN 0-903450-33-X). ABC Clio.

Goor, A. Y. & Barney, C. W. Forest Tree Planting in Arid Zones. 2nd ed. LC 76-22314. (Illus.). 1976. 31.00x o.p. (ISBN 0-471-06832-2, 39153, Pub. by Wiley-Interscience). Wiley.

Gooriah, B. D. & Williams, F. P. The Investigation of Air Pollution: National Survey of Smoke & Sulphur Dioxide--Annual Summary Statistics for the Period 1963-4 to 1977-8, 1979. 1981. 60.00x (ISBN 0-686-97088-8, Pub. by W Spring England). State Mutual Bk.

Goorney, Howard. The Theatre Workshop Story. 226p. 1982. 19.95x (ISBN 0-413-47610-3); pap. 11.95 (ISBN 0-413-48760-1). Methuen Inc.

Goosen, Kenneth R. Introduction to Managerial Accounting: A Business Game. 1976. pap. text ed. 16.50x (ISBN 0-673-15300-2). Scott F.

Goosens, Louis, jt. auth. see Driven, Rene.

Goot, Mary V. A Life Planning Guide for Women. 128p. 1982. pap. 9.95x (ISBN 0-88946-512-6). E Mellen.

Gootman. Perinatal Cardiovascular Function. 448p. 1983. 65.00 (ISBN 0-8247-1671-X). Dekker.

Goovaerts, A. Histoire et Bibliographie de la Typographie Musicale dans les Pays-Bas. 1963. Repr. of 1880 ed. 62.50 o.s.i. (ISBN 90-6027-002-9, Pub. by Frits Knuf Netherlands). Pendragon NY.

Gooze, M. The S-Sixty Eight Hundred Family: Hardware Fundamentals. LC 81-3673. 1982. pap. 18.95 (ISBN 0-201-03399-2). A-W.

Goozner, Calman. Arithmetic Skills Workbook. (gr. 7-12). 1973. text ed. 12.83 (ISBN 0-87720-238-9); pap. text ed. 6.83 (ISBN 0-87720-237-0); workbook 8.08, (ISBN 0-87720-236-2). AMSCO Sch.

--Business Math the Easy Way. 256p. 1983. pap. 6.95 (ISBN 0-8120-2513-X). Barron.

Gopal, jt. auth. see Sharma, Rama.

Gopal, Brij & Bhardwaj, N. Elements of Ecology. (Illus.). 200p. 1979. text ed. 15.00x (ISBN 0-7069-0754-X, Pub. by Vikas India). Advent NY.

Gopal, Kokila K., jt. auth. see Gopal, Rishane.

Gopal, M., jt. auth. see Nagrath, I. J.

Gopal, Rishane & Gopal, Kokila K. West Asia & North Africa: A Documentary Study of Major Crises, 1974-78. 434p. 1981. 37.50x (ISBN 0-86590-012-4). Apt Bks.

Gopal, S. The Mind of Jawaharlal Nehru. 50p. 1980. pap. text ed. 3.95x (ISBN 0-86131-205-8, Pub. by Orient Longman Ltd India). Apt Bks.

--Selected Works of Jawaharlal Nehru, Vol. 14. 1982. 36.00x (ISBN 0-8364-0904-3, Orient Longman). South Asia Bks.
Gopalakrishnan, Chennat. Natural Resources & Energy: Theory & Policy. LC 80-67657. (Illus.). 120p. 1980. 14.50 (ISBN 0-250-40385-4). Ann Arbor Science.
Gopalakrishnan, R. The Geography & Politics of Afghanistan. 275p. 1982. text ed. 19.50x (ISBN 0-391-02726-3, Pub. by Concept). Humanities.
Gopalan, S. Outlines of Jainism. LC 73-13196. 205p. 1973. pap. 10.95x o.p. (ISBN 0-470-31530-X). Halsted Pr.
Gopaleen, Myles na, pseud. The Best of Myles. O'Brien, Flann, ed. 400p. 1983. pap. 6.95 (ISBN 0-14-006366-8). Penguin.
Gopalkrishnan, S. & Salant, R. F., eds. Fluid Mechanics of Mechanical Seals. 1982. 14.00 (H00232). ASME.
Gopinath, Santha. Customer Satisfaction in the Postal Services. 105p. 1980. text ed. 10.75x (ISBN 0-391-02125-7). Humanities.
Gopiparanadhana dasa Adhikari, et al, eds. see Hridayananda dasa Goswami Acaryadeva.
Goplerud, C. Peter, III. Coal Development & Use: The Legal Constraints & Incentives. LC 80-8890. 320p. 1982. 27.95 (ISBN 0-669-04403-2). Lexington Bks.
Gopnik, Adam & Huberman, Jack. Voila Careme! The Gastronomic Adventures of History's Greatest Chef. 1980. pap. 4.95 o.p. (ISBN 0-312-85098-0). St Martin.
Goppelt, Leonard. Typos: The Typological Interpretation of the Old Testament in the New. 1982. 15.95 (ISBN 0-8028-3562-7). Eerdmans.
Goppelt, Leonhard. Theology of the New Testament: The Variety & Unity of the Apostolic Witness to Christ, Vol. II. 288p. 1983. 15.95 (ISBN 0-8028-2385-8). Eerdmans.
Gora. The New Female Criminal. 160p. 1982. 21.95 (ISBN 0-03-062007-4). Praeger.
Goralski, Robert. World War II Almanac, 1931-1945. 1982. 10.95 (ISBN 0-399-50673-X, Perige). Putnam Pub Group.
--World War Two Almanac: Nineteen Thirty-One to Nineteen Forty-Five A Political & Military Record. new ed. (Illus.). 484p. 1981. 17.95 (ISBN 0-399-12548-5). Putnam Pub Group.
Goran, Leslie. Covenant with Tomorrow. (Orig.). 1981. pap. 2.95 o.p. (ISBN 0-451-11202-4, AE 1202, Sig). NAL.
Goran, Lester. This New Land. (The Heritage Ser.: Pt. 1). (Orig.). 1980. pap. 2.75 o.p. (ISBN 0-451-09480-8, E9480, Sig). NAL.
Goransson, B., ed. Industrial Waste Water & Wastes II. 1977. text ed. 56.00 (ISBN 0-08-020954-8). Pergamon.
Gorbanevskaya, Natalia, tr. see Milosz, Czeslaw.
Gorbanevskaya, Natalya. Chuzhie Kamni. LC 82-61986. 70p. (Orig., Rus.). 1982. pap. 5.95 (ISBN 0-89830-068-1). Russica Pubs.
--Selected Poems. Weissbort, Daniel, ed. & tr. from Rus. (Translation Ser.). 1979. 5.95 o.p. (ISBN 0-85635-002-8, Pub. by Carcanet New Pr England). Humanities.
Gorbea. Tecnicas Mecanograficas Modernas. 3rd ed. 240p. 12.20 (ISBN 0-07-023791-3). McGraw.
Gorbea, J. Q., et al. Tecnicas Mecanograficas Modernas. 2nd ed. 1968. text ed. 12.70 (ISBN 0-07-023779-4, G). McGraw.
Gorbet, Larry P. A Grammar of Diegueno Nominals. LC 75-25116. (American Indian Linguistics Ser.). 1976. lib. bdg. 42.00 o.s.i. (ISBN 0-8240-1967-9). Garland Pub.
Gorbman, Aubrey, et al. Comparative Endocrinology. 592p. 1983. 40.00 (ISBN 0-471-06266-9, Pub. by Wiley-Interscience). Wiley.
Gorchakov, Nikolai M. Stanislavsky Directs. Goldina, Miriam, tr. LC 73-15243. 402p. 1974. Repr. of 1954 ed. lib. bdg. 29.75x (ISBN 0-8371-7164-4, GOSD). Greenwood.
Gordan, John D. Anniversary Exhibition: The Henry W. & Albert A. Berg Collection 1940-1965. 1965. pap. 3.00 o.p. (ISBN 0-87104-003-4). NY Pub Lib.
--Arnold Bennett, the Centenary of His Birth: An Exhibition in the Berg Collection. LC 68-21054. (Illus.). 1968. pap. 5.00 (ISBN 0-87104-015-8). NY Pub Lib.
--Bard & the Book: Editions of Shakespeare in the Seventeenth Century: An Exhibition. 1964. pap. 3.00 o.p. (ISBN 0-87104-019-0). NY Pub Lib.
--Doctors As Men of Letters: English & American Writers of Medical Background: An Exhibition in the Berg Collection. LC 64-8859. 1964. pap. 3.00 o.p. (ISBN 0-87104-064-6). NY Pub Lib.
--John Masefields 'Salt-Water Ballads' An Exhibition from the Berg Collection on the Fiftieth Anniversary of Its Publication. 1952. pap. 3.00 o.p. (ISBN 0-87104-102-2). NY Pub Lib.
--Joint Lives: Elizabeth Barrett & Robert Browning. (Illus.). 48p. 1975. pap. 6.00 o.p. (ISBN 0-87104-258-4). NY Pub Lib.
--Letters to an Editor: Georgian Poetry. 1967. pap. 3.00 o.p. (ISBN 0-87104-104-9). NY Pub Lib.
--Novels in Manuscript: An Exhibition from the Berg Collection. 1965. pap. 3.00 o.p. (ISBN 0-87104-134-0). NY Pub Lib.
--William Makepeace Thackeray: An Exhibition. 1947. pap. 3.00 o.p. (ISBN 0-87104-217-7). NY Pub Lib.
Gorden, Kurt V., jt. auth. see Metz, Gary.
Gorden, Morton, jt. auth. see Lerner, Daniel.
Gorden, Myron & Axelrod, Herbert P. Swordtails for the Advanced Hobbyist. pap. 6.95 (ISBN 0-87666-151-7, PS655). TFH Pubns.
Gorden, William I. & Miller, John R. Managing Your Communication: In & For the Organization. (Illus.). 280p. 1983. pap. 9.95x (ISBN 0-88133-007-8). Waveland Pr.
Gordh, Gordon & Trjapitzin, V. Taxonomic Studies of the Encyrtidae with the Desriptions of New Species & a New Genus: Hymenoptera: Chalcidoidea. (Publications in Entomology: Vol. 93). 1982. pap. 8.00 (ISBN 0-520-09629-0). U of Cal Pr.
Gordillo, Agustin. Participation in Latin America. 1983. 7.95 (ISBN 0-533-05291-2). Vantage.
Gordimer, Nadine. The Black Interpreters. 1973. 8.00 o.s.i. (ISBN 0-86975-026-7, Pub by Ravan Press). Three Continents.
--The Conservationist. LC 76-23435. (McGraw-Hill Paperbacks). 1976. pap. 3.50 o.p. (ISBN 0-07-023781-6, SP). McGraw.
--The Conservationist. 1983. pap. 4.95 (ISBN 0-14-004716-6). Penguin.
--Late Bourgeois World. 1983. pap. 3.95 (ISBN 0-14-005614-9). Penguin.
Gordis, Robert. Koheleth: The Man & His World: A Study of Ecclesiastes. rev. ed. LC 67-26988. 1968. pap. 10.95 (ISBN 0-8052-0166-1). Schocken.
--Leave a Little to God. LC 67-22706. 1967. 6.50x o.p. (ISBN 0-8197-0087-8). Bloch.
Gordon & Breach. Metallurgical Principles for Engineers. 5th ed. 1962. pap. 9.95 o.p. (ISBN 0-592-04707-5). Butterworth.
Gordon, jt. auth. see Fulton.
Gordon, A., jt. auth. see Fulton, O.
Gordon, Adele. Somebody's Mother. 48p. 1983. 6.95 (ISBN 0-89962-325-5). Todd & Honeywell.
Gordon, Adoniram J. Holy Spirit in Missions. pap. 2.75 (ISBN 0-87509-094-X). Chr Pubns.
--Ministry of Healing. 3.95 (ISBN 0-87509-106-7); pap. 3.25 (ISBN 0-87509-107-5). Chr Pubns.
Gordon, Adrian H. & Taylor, Ronald C. Computations of Surface Layer Air Trajectories, & Weather, in the Oceanic Tropics. LC 72-92065. (International Indian Ocean Expedition Meterological Monographs: No. 7). (Illus.). 128p. 1975. text ed. 17.50x (ISBN 0-8248-0253-5, Eastwest Ctr). UH Pr.
Gordon, Alan. Economics & Social Policy: An Introduction. (Illus.). 224p. 1982. text ed. 24.95x (ISBN 0-85520-527-X, Pub. by Martin Robertson England). Biblio Dist.
Gordon, Albert S., jt. ed. see LoBue, Joseph.
Gordon, Alice K. Games for Growth: Education Games in the Classroom. LC 72-120693. (Dimensions in Education Ser). (Illus.). 1970. pap. text ed. 8.95 (ISBN 0-574-17386-2, 13-0386). SRA.
Gordon, Andrew J., jt. ed. see Seiber, R. Timothy.
Gordon, Anna N. Nutritional Management of High-Risk Pregnancy: Reference Manual. 44p. (Orig.). 1981. pap. 5.00 (ISBN 0-686-32039-5); Leader's Guide. pap. 1.00 (ISBN 0-910869-09-X, 707-454). Soc Nutrition Ed.
Gordon, Arthur. Touch of Wonder. 256p. 1974. 10.95 (ISBN 0-8007-0695-1). Revell.
Gordon, Audrey & Klass, Dennis. They Need to Know: How to Teach Children About Death. (Illus.). 1979. 10.95 (ISBN 0-13-917104-5, Spec); pap. 5.95 (ISBN 0-13-917096-0, Spec). P-H.
Gordon, Barbara. Defects of the Heart. LC 82-48144. 352p. 1982. 14.37i (ISBN 0-06-015032-7, HarpT). Har-Row.
--I'm Dancing As Fast As I Can. LC 78-20165. 1979. 12.45i (ISBN 0-06-011499-1, HarpT). Har-Row.
Gordon, Barclay F. Olympic Architecture: Building for the Summer Games. 160p. 1983. 16.00 (ISBN 0-471-06069-0, Pub. by Wiley-Interscience). Wiley.
Gordon, Bernard K. & Rothwell, Kenneth J. The New Political Economy of the Pacific. LC 75-4717. 192p. 1975. prof ref 18.50x (ISBN 0-88410-279-3). Ballinger Pub.
Gordon, Bernard L., jt. auth. see Charlier, Roger H.
Gordon, Bernard L., ed. Energy from the Sea: Marine Resource Readings. LC 79-8826. (Illus.). 1980. pap. text ed. 15.00 (ISBN 0-8191-0887-1). U Pr of Amer.
Gordon, Beverly. Shaker Textile Arts. LC 78-69899. (Illus.). 343p. 1980. 25.00x (ISBN 0-87451-158-5); pap. 15.00 (ISBN 0-87451-242-5). U Pr of New Eng.
Gordon, Bonnie. The Anatomy of the Image Maps according to Merriam-Webster's Third International Dictionary of the English Language: Unabridged. LC 82-50789. (Artists' Book Ser.). 48p. (Orig.). 1983. pap. 10.00 (ISBN 0-89822-028-9). Visual Studies.
Gordon, Bonnie B. A Childhood in Reno. 32p. (Orig.). 1982. pap. text ed. 3.00 (ISBN 0-935252-33-9); cancelled (ISBN 0-686-97526-X). Street Pr.
Gordon, Burton L. Monterey Bay Area: Natural History & Cultural Imprints. 2nd ed. LC 74-13912. (Illus.). 192p. 1977. pap. text ed. 6.95 (ISBN 0-910286-37-X). Boxwood.
Gordon, Caroline. The Collected Stories of Caroline Gordon. 1981. 17.95 (ISBN 0-374-12630-5); pap. 9.95 (ISBN 0-374-51675-8). FS&G.
--None Shall Look Back. LC 72-164528. 1972. Repr. of 1937 ed. 22.50x o.p. (ISBN 0-8154-0397-6). Cooper Sq.
Gordon, Craig A. & Alexander, George L. Force & Statecraft: Diplomatic Problems of our Time. LC 81-22304. (Illus.). 1983. 19.95 (ISBN 0-19-503115-6); pap. 9.95 (ISBN 0-19-503116-4). Oxford U Pr.
Gordon, Cyrus H. Forgotten Scripts: Their Ongoing Discovery & Decipherment. rev. ed. 1982. 14.95 (ISBN 0-465-02484-X). Basic.
Gordon, David. Problems in the Law of Mass Communications: Programmed Instruction. 1982 ed. 183p. 1982. write for info. problems bk. (ISBN 0-88277-104-3); pap. text ed. write for info. Foundation Pr.
--Therapeutic Metaphors. LC 78-58574. 1978. 9.95x (ISBN 0-916990-04-4). Meta Pubns.
Gordon, David, tr. from Chinese. Equinox: A Gathering of T'ang Poets. LC 73-181682. xx, 88p. 1975. 9.95x (ISBN 0-8214-0162-9, 82-81628); pap. 3.50 o.s.i. (ISBN 0-8214-0173-4). Ohio U Pr.
Gordon, David, tr. Living in the Stream: Poems of Lu-Yu. 1977. 1.50 o.p. (ISBN 0-934834-06-7). White Pine.
Gordon, David B., ed. Hypertension: The Renal Basis. LC 79-6598. (Benchmark Papers in Human Physiology Ser.: Vol. 13). 448p. 1980. 51.50 (ISBN 0-87933-356-1). Hutchinson Ross.
Gordon, David C. The Republic of Lebanon: A Nation in Jeopardy. (Profiles-Nations of the Contemporary Middle East). 175p. 1983. price not set (ISBN 0-86531-450-0). Westview.
Gordon, David L. Employment & Development of Small Enterprises. (Sector Policy Paper). 93p. 1978. 5.00 (ISBN 0-686-36181-4, PP-7803). World Bank.
Gordon, David M. Problems in Political Economy: An Urban Perspective. 2nd ed. 1977. pap. text ed. 13.95x (ISBN 0-669-92841-0). Heath.
--Theories of Poverty & Underemployment. 1973. pap. text ed. 13.95x (ISBN 0-669-89268-8). Heath.
Gordon, David R. The Hidden Weapon: The Story of Economic Warfare. Dangerfield, Royden, ed. LC 76-5473. (World War II Ser.). 1976. Repr. of 1947 ed. 29.50 (ISBN 0-306-70769-1). Da Capo.
Gordon, Dellanna. The Boy King & the Witch. (Illus.). 124p. (Orig.). 1980. pap. 3.95 o.p. (ISBN 0-89260-180-9). Hwong Pub.
Gordon, Don E. Electronic Warfare: Element of Strategy & Multiplier of Combat Power. (Pergamon Policy Studies on Security Affairs). (Illus.). 200p. 1982. 16.00 (ISBN 0-08-027189-8). Pergamon.
Gordon, Donald I. see Thomas, David J.
Gordon, Donald J. W. B. Yeats: Images of a Poet. LC 79-9441. 1979. Repr. of 1961 ed. lib. bdg. 18.75x (ISBN 0-313-22069-7, GOWBY). Greenwood.
Gordon, Duncan. Rheumatoid Arthritis: Discussions in Patient Management. 1981. text ed. 22.00 (ISBN 0-87488-951-0). Med Exam.
Gordon, E., ed. A Basis & Practice of Neuroanaesthesia. 2nd ed. (Monographs in Anaesthesiology: Vol. 2). 1981. 82.75 (ISBN 0-444-80252-5). Elsevier.
--A Basis & Practice of Neuroanaesthesia. LC 74-21859. (Monographs in Anesthesiology: Vol. 2). 288p. 1975. 61.00 o.p. (ISBN 0-444-15157-5, Excerpta Medica). Elsevier.
Gordon, E. D., tr. see Bykhovskii, B. E.
Gordon, Edwin. Psychology of Music Teaching. (Contemporary Perspectives in Music Education Ser.). (Illus.). 1971. ref. ed. 13.95 (ISBN 0-13-736215-3). P-H.
--Tonal & Rhythm Patterns. LC 76-7947. 1976. 33.50x (ISBN 0-87395-354-1). State U NY Pr.
Gordon, Elinor. Collecting Chinese Porcelain. LC 77-70474. (Illus.). 1979. pap. 8.95 o.s.i. (ISBN 0-87663-995-3). Universe.
Gordon, Ethel. Freer's Cove. (Candlelight Romance Ser.). 1981. pap. 1.50 o.s.i. (ISBN 0-440-12704-1). Dell.
Gordon, Ethel E. The French Husband. LC 76-27349. 1977. 8.95i o.p. (ISBN 0-690-01207-1). T Y Crowell.
Gordon, Everett J. Practical Medico-Legal Guide for the Physician. (Illus.). 360p. 1973. 14.95x o.p. (ISBN 0-398-02688-2). C C Thomas.
Gordon, F. & Strober, M. Bringing Women into Management. 1975. text ed. 14.95 o.p. (ISBN 0-07-023806-5, C); pap. 14.95 o.p. (ISBN 0-07-023805-7). McGraw.
Gordon, Fee D., jt. ed. see Epp, Eldon J.
Gordon, Garry, jt. auth. see Walker, Morton.
Gordon, Geoffrey. The Application of GPSS Five to Discrete System Simulation. (Illus.). 336p. 1975. 27.95 (ISBN 0-13-039057-7). P-H.
--System Simulation. 2nd ed. LC 77-24579. (Illus.). 1978. ref. ed. 28.95 (ISBN 0-13-881797-9). P-H.
Gordon, George G. & Cummins, Walter. Managing Management Climate. (Illus.). 208p. 1979. 22.95x (ISBN 0-669-02545-3). Lexington Bks.
Gordon, George J. Public Administration in America. 2nd ed. LC 81-51847. 623p. 1982. text ed. 18.95 (ISBN 0-312-65388-3); Instr's. manual avail. St Martin.
Gordon, George K. & Stryker, Ruth. Creative Long-Term Care Administration. (Illus.). 414p. 1983. text ed. 34.50x (ISBN 0-398-04822-3). C C Thomas.
Gordon, Georgia Y. Between Two Georgia Rivers. 1981. 6.95 (ISBN 0-8062-1726-X). Carlton.
Gordon, Gerald & Fisher, G. Lawrence, eds. The Diffusion of Medical Technology: Policy & Research Planning Perspectives. LC 75-17638. 176p. 1975. prof ref 20.00x (ISBN 0-88410-129-0). Ballinger Pub.
Gordon, Gilbert & Pressman, Israel. Quantitative Decision-Making for Business. LC 77-25831. (Illus.). 1978. ref. ed. 26.95 (ISBN 0-13-746701-X). P-H.
Gordon, Giles, jt. auth. see Urquhart, Fred.
Gordon, Giles, ed. Shakespeare Stories. (Illus.). 224p. 1983. 16.95 (ISBN 0-241-10879-9, Pub. by Hamish Hamilton England). David & Charles.
Gordon, Glen, jt. auth. see Connolly, William H.
Gordon, Hampden. Lure of Antiques. pap. 2.45 o.p. (ISBN 0-7195-0516-X). Transatlantic.
Gordon, Harold J. & Gordon, Nancy M., eds. The Austrian Empire: Abortive Federation. (Problems in European Civilization Ser). 1974. pap. text ed. 5.50 (ISBN 0-669-90456-2). Heath.
Gordon, Harvey C. Grime & Punishment. (Orig.). 1981. pap. 1.95 (ISBN 0-446-90026-5). Warner Bks.
--Punishment: The Art of Punning or How to Lose Friends & Agonize People. 144p. 1983. pap. 1.95 (ISBN 0-446-90263-2). Warner Bks.
Gordon, Howard & Meador, Roy, eds. Perspectives on the Energy Crisis, Vol. 1. LC 77-74777. 1977. 37.50 o.p. (ISBN 0-250-40161-4). Ann Arbor Science.
--Perspectives on the Energy Crisis, Vol. 2. LC 77-74777. 1977. 37.50 o.p. (ISBN 0-250-40162-2). Ann Arbor Science.
Gordon, Huntly. The Minister's Wife. (Illus.). 1978. 16.95 (ISBN 0-7100-8846-9). Routledge & Kegan.
Gordon, I. Controlled Breeding in Farm Animals. 200p. 1983. 60.00 (ISBN 0-08-024410-6); pap. 30.00 (ISBN 0-08-024409-2). Pergamon.
Gordon, I. R. S. & Ross, F. G. M. Diagnostic Radiology in Pediatrics. (Postgraduate Pediatric Ser.). 1977. 119.95 (ISBN 0-407-00121-2). Butterworth.
Gordon, Ian A., ed. see Galt, John.
Gordon, J. L., ed. Platelets in Biology & Pathology. (Research Monographs in Cell & Tissue Physiology: Vol. 5). 1981. 92.00 (ISBN 0-444-80308-4). Elsevier.
Gordon, J. L., jt. ed. see Dingle, J. T.
Gordon, Joanne J., jt. auth. see Solmon, Lewis C.
Gordon, John E. How to Succeed in Organic Chemistry. LC 78-21496. (Self-Teaching Guide Ser.). 1979. pap. text ed. 9.95 (ISBN 0-471-03010-4). Wiley.
Gordon, John F. Miniature Schnauzers. Foyle, Christina, ed. (Foyle's Handbks). 1972. 3.95 (ISBN 0-685-55812-6). Palmetto Pub.
--Staffordshire Bull Terriers. LC 76-10635. (Illus.). 1976. bds. 2.25 o.p. (ISBN 0-668-03997-3). Arco.
--Staffordshire Bull Terriers. (Foyle's Handbks). (Illus.). 1973. 3.95 (ISBN 0-685-55791-X). Palmetto Pub.
Gordon, Karen E. The Well-Tempered Sentence: A Punctuation Handbook for the Innocent, the Eager, & the Doomed. LC 82-19704. (Illus.). 96p. 1983. 7.95 (ISBN 0-89919-170-3). Ticknor & Fields.
Gordon, Kent H. Phonology of Dhangar-Kurux. 153p. 1976. pap. 2.50x (ISBN 0-88312-853-5); microfiche 2.25 (ISBN 0-88312-488-2). Summer Inst Ling.
Gordon, Kristen A. Patterns of the Earth: A Design Manual of Earth People's Clothing. Gordon, Richard D., ed. LC 81-787939. (Illus.). 65p. (Orig.). 1981. pap. text ed. 10.00 (ISBN 0-9607002-0-X). K-Ten Pubns.
Gordon, L. Growth Policies & the International Order. 1979. pap. 6.95 (ISBN 0-07-023813-8). McGraw.
Gordon, L. I., ed. The Seafarer. LC 79-55530. (Old & Middle English Texts Ser.). 70p. 1979. pap. text ed. 6.75x (ISBN 0-06-492491-2). B&N Imports.
Gordon, L. L. British Battles & Medals. 1979. 42.00 (ISBN 0-685-51512-5, Pub by Spink & Son England). S J Durst.
Gordon, Laura B. Behavioral Intervention in Health Care. (Behavioral Sciences for Health Care Professionals Ser.). 128p. 1981. lib. bdg. 15.00 (ISBN 0-86531-018-1); pap. 7.00 (ISBN 0-86531-019-X). Westview.
Gordon, Laura K., jt. auth. see Davidson, Laurie.
Gordon, Lawrence A. & Cooper, Robert. The Pricing Decision. 52p. pap. 4.95 (ISBN 0-86641-001-5, 80123). Natl Assn Accts.
Gordon, Lawrence A., et al. Normative Models in Managerial Decision-Making. 121p. 12.95 (ISBN 0-686-11623-2, 7578). Natl Assn Accts.
Gordon, Leonard. Sociology & American Social Issues. LC 77-78577. (Illus.). 1978. pap. text ed. 24.95 (ISBN 0-395-25369-1); study guide 9.50 (ISBN 0-395-25371-3); instr's. manual 1.00 (ISBN 0-395-25370-5). HM.
Gordon, Leonard, jt. auth. see Mayer, Albert J.
Gordon, Lincoln. Growth Policies & the International Order. (Council on Foreign Relations 1980's Project). (Illus.). 1979. text ed. 16.95 (ISBN 0-07-023812-X, P&RB). McGraw.
Gordon, Lindsay. Rhyming Bible, 3 vols. 1.00 ea. o.p. Christ Nations.

Gordon, Lois. Donald Barthelme. (United States Author Ser.). 1981. lib. bdg. 13.95 (ISBN 0-8057-7347-9, Twayne). G K Hall.
--Robert Coover: The Universal Fictionmaking Process. (Crosscurrents-Modern Critques-New Issues Ser.). 208p. 1983. 15.95x (ISBN 0-8093-1092-9). S Ill U Pr.
Gordon, Louise. How to Draw the Human Head: Techniques & Anatomy. (Illus.). 1983. pap. 6.95 (ISBN 0-14-046560-X). Penguin.
Gordon, Lyndall. Eliot's Early Years. (Illus.). 1977. 14.95x (ISBN 0-19-812078-8). Oxford U Pr.
Gordon, M. Nursing Diagnosis: Process & Application. 400p. 1982. text ed. 18.95x (ISBN 0-07-023815-4). McGraw.
Gordon, M., jt. ed. see Meadows, A. J.
Gordon, Malcolm, et al. Animal Physiology. 4th ed. 1982. 26.95x (ISBN 0-02-345320-6). Macmillan.
Gordon, Marcy & Jenkins, Anita. Oil Industry U. S. A. 1981-82. 1981. 75.00 (ISBN 0-686-84377-0). Oil Daily.
Gordon, Margaret S. Employment Expansion & Population Growth: The California Experience. LC 76-5893. 192p. 1976. Repr. of 1954 ed. lib. bdg. 16.25x (ISBN 0-8371-8805-9, GOEE). Greenwood.
Gordon, Margaret T. Involving Paraprofessionals in the Helping Process: The Case of Federal Probation. LC 76-2438. 176p. 1976. prof ref 16.50x (ISBN 0-88410-138-X). Ballinger Pub.
Gordon, Marjory. Manual of Nursing Diagnosis. (Illus.). 240p. 1982. pap. text ed. 8.55x (ISBN 0-07-023816-2). McGraw.
Gordon, Marshall, jt. auth. see Simonsen, Clifford.
Gordon, Mary & Swinburne, Algernon C. The Children of the Chapel: A Tale. Lougy, Robert E., intro. by. LC 82-6436. 1185p. 1982. lib. bdg. 18.95x (ISBN 0-8214-0631-0, 82-84044). Ohio U Pr.
Gordon, Max. Live at the Village Vanguard. 192p. 1980. 12.95 o.p. (ISBN 0-312-48879-3). St Martin.
Gordon, Melvin, jt. auth. see Bromberg, Murray.
Gordon, Michael. The American Family: Past, Present, & Future. 1977. text ed. 20.00 (ISBN 0-394-31722-X). Random.
Gordon, Mildred, jt. auth. see Yates, Robert.
Gordon, Milton M. Assimilation in American Life: The Role of Race, Religion & National Origins. 1964. pap. 6.95x (ISBN 0-19-500896-0). Oxford U Pr.
Gordon, Milton M. & Lambert, Richard D., eds. America As a Multicultural Society. LC 80-70879. (Annals of the American Academy of Political & Social Science Ser.: No. 454). 250p. 1981. 7.50 o.p. (ISBN 0-87761-260-9); pap. text ed. 7.95 (ISBN 0-87761-261-7). Am Acad Pol Soc Sci.
Gordon, Myron. Making Meetings More Productive. LC 80-52335. (Illus.). 192p. 1980. 12.95 (ISBN 0-8069-0206-X); lib. bdg. 15.69 (ISBN 0-8069-0207-8). Sterling.
Gordon, Myron & Axelrod, Herbert R. Siamese Fighting Fish. pap. 2.50 o.p. (ISBN 0-87666-145-2, M536). TFH Pubns.
Gordon, Myron, jt. auth. see Whitern, Wilfred L.
Gordon, Nancy M., jt. ed. see Gordon, Harold J.
Gordon, Nancy M., tr. see Strieder, P.
Gordon, Neal J., jt. ed. see Farley, Frank.
Gordon, Noah. The Jerusalem Diamond. 1979. 9.95 o.p. (ISBN 0-394-50416-X). Random.
Gordon, O. Design, Analysis & Otimization of Solar Industrial Process Heat Plants Without Storage. (Progress in Solar Energy Supplements SERI Ser.). 1983. pap. text ed. 9.00x (ISBN 0-89553-092-9). Am Solar Energy.
Gordon, P. F. & Gregory, P. Organic Chemistry in Colour. (Illus.). 300p. 1983. 71.50 (ISBN 0-387-11748-2). Springer-Verlag.
Gordon, P. J. The Renaissance Imagination: Essays & Lectures. Orgel, Stephen, ed. LC 74-81432. 1976. 48.50x (ISBN 0-520-02817-1); pap. 8.95 (ISBN 0-520-04092-9). U of Cal Pr.
Gordon, Patricia. The Boy Jones. 1980. PLB 6.95 (ISBN 0-8398-2608-7, Gregg). G K Hall.
Gordon, Patrick. Passages from the Diary of General Patrick Gordon of Auchleuchries. (Russia Through European Eyes Ser). 1968. Repr. of 1859 ed. lib. bdg. 39.50 (ISBN 0-306-12210-3). Da Capo.
Gordon, Paul. Principles of Phase Diagrams in Materials Systems. LC 82-14073. 248p. 1983. Repr. of 1968 ed. 19.50 (ISBN 0-89874-408-3). Krieger.
Gordon, Paul L., ed. The Book of Film Care. (H-23 Ser.). (Illus.). 130p. (Orig.). Date not set. pap. text ed. price not set (ISBN 0-87985-321-2). Eastman Kodak.
Gordon, Pearl S. Simply Elegant: A Guide for Elegant but Simple Entertaining. rev. 8th ed. LC 77-13166. (Illus.). 208p. 1981. lib. bdg. 14.95 (ISBN 0-9600492-3-1). Simply Elegant.
Gordon, R. & Spaulding, M. L. Numerical Models for Tidal Rivers, Estuaries & Coastal Waters: Bibliography. (Technical Report Ser.: No. 32). 55p. 1974. 2.00 (ISBN 0-938412-31-0, P376). URI Mas.
Gordon, R. A., jt. auth. see Goldberg, I. A.
Gordon, R. L., ed. Myth, Religion & Society: Structuralist Essays by M. Detienne, L. Gernet, J. P. Vernant & P. Vidal-Naquet. (Illus.). 250p. 1982. text ed. 39.50 (ISBN 0-521-22780-1); pap. text ed. 12.95 (ISBN 0-521-29640-4). Cambridge U Pr.
Gordon, Raoul, ed. Puerto Rican & Caribbean Cookbook. (Puerto Rico Ser.). 1982. lib. bdg. 72.95 (ISBN 0-8490-3228-8). Gordon Pr.
Gordon, Rene, ed. see Bannister, Anthony & Johnson, Peter.
Gordon, Richard. Great Medical Disasters. 256p. 1983. 16.95 (ISBN 0-8128-2911-5). Stein & Day.
Gordon, Richard D., ed. see Gordon, Kristen A.
Gordon, Richard L. Coal in the U.S. Energy Market. LC 77-14625. (Illus.). 240p. 1978. 23.95x (ISBN 0-669-01987-9). Lexington Bks.
--An Economic Analysis of World Energy Problems. (Illus.). 320p. 1981. text ed. 32.50x (ISBN 0-262-07080-4). MIT Pr.
--Reforming the Regulation of Electric Utilities: Priorities for the 1980's. LC 81-48001. 336p. 1982. 33.95x (ISBN 0-669-05235-3). Lexington Bks.
Gordon, Richard S. Issues in Health Care Regulation. (Regulation of American Business & Industry Ser.). (Illus.). 400p. 1980. 39.75 (ISBN 0-07-023780-8, C). McGraw.
Gordon, Robert & Pelkmans, Jacques. Challenges to Interdependent Economies. (Illus.). 1979. text ed. 14.95 (ISBN 0-07-023810-3, P&RB); pap. 6.95 (ISBN 0-07-023811-1). McGraw.
Gordon, Robert A. Economic Instability & Growth: The American Record. (Illus.). 216p. 1974. pap. text ed. 13.95 scp o.p. (ISBN 0-06-042408-7, HarpC). Har-Row.
--Goal of Full Employment. LC 67-26636. 204p. 1967. 9.50 o.p. (ISBN 0-471-31605-9). Krieger.
Gordon, Robert D. Tax Planning Handbook. LC 81-14167. (Illus.). 512p. 1982. 29.95. NY Inst Finance.
Gordon, Robert J. & Schweitzer, Gemello. Macroeconomics. 2nd ed. 1981. text ed. 22.95 (ISBN 0-316-32125-7); wkbk. 7.95 (ISBN 0-316-32127-3); tchr's manual avail. (ISBN 0-316-32126-5). Little.
Gordon, Robert J., ed. see Friedman, Milton, et al.
Gordon, Roderick D. Doctoral Dissertations in Music & Music Education, 1972-1977. 296p. 1978. 3.00 (ISBN 0-686-37912-8). Music Ed.
Gordon, Ronni L. & Stillman, David M. Nuevos Rumbos: A Short Course for Elementary Spanish. 368p. 1982. text ed. 18.95 (ISBN 0-669-04094-0); wkbk. lab manual 8.95 (ISBN 0-669-04095-9); reels 45.00 (ISBN 0-669-04098-3). Heath.
Gordon, Ronni L., jt. auth. see Stillman, David M.
Gordon, Ruth. Ruth Gordon: An Open Book. LC 78-68335. 1980. 14.95 o.p. (ISBN 0-385-13480-0). Doubleday.
--Shady Lady. 1983. pap. 3.25 (ISBN 0-8217-1187-3). Zebra.
Gordon, S. D. Quiet Talks on Prayer. 1980. pap. 4.95 o.p. (ISBN 0-8007-5038-1, Power Bks). Revell.
Gordon, Sally. The Rider's Handbook. (Illus.). 224p. 1980. 19.95 (ISBN 0-399-12556-6). Putnam Pub Group.
Gordon, Samuel D. Quiet Talks on Power. 1960. 3.50 (ISBN 0-448-01656-7, G&D). Putnam Pub Group.
Gordon, Sanford D. & Dawson, George G. Introductory Economics. 4th ed. 1980. text ed. 19.95x (ISBN 0-669-02425-2); instr's manual with test item 1.95 (ISBN 0-669-02427-9); study guide 6.95 (ISBN 0-669-02426-0). Heath.
Gordon, Sharon. Trees. LC 82-20291. (Now I Know Ser.). (Illus.). 32p. (gr. k-2). 1982. lib. bdg. 8.89 (ISBN 0-89375-901-5). Troll Assocs.
Gordon, Sheila. A Monster in the Mailbox. (Illus.). (gr. 2-4). 1978. 8.25 (ISBN 0-525-35150-7, 0801-240). Dutton.
Gordon, Shirley. The Boy Who Wanted a Family. LC 79-2003. (Illus.). 96p. (gr. 1-4). 1980. 8.61i o.p. (ISBN 0-06-022051-1, HarpJ); PLB 8.89 (ISBN 0-06-022052-X). Har-Row.
--Crystal Is My Friend. LC 77-11853. (Illus.). 1978. 7.95 o.p. (ISBN 0-06-022112-7, HarpJ); PLB 8.89 (ISBN 0-06-022113-5). Har-Row.
--Happy Birthday, Crystal. LC 80-8941. (Illus.). 32p. (gr. k-4). 1981. 7.95 (ISBN 0-06-022006-6, HarpJ); PLB 8.89 (ISBN 0-06-022007-4). Har-Row.
Gordon, Shirley C., jt. ed. see Augier, F. R.
Gordon, Sol, jt. ed. see Albee, George.
Gordon, Stuart. Gordonstown, a New Design for America. (Illus.). 288p. 1980. pap. 5.95 (ISBN 0-9603942-0-6). Gordonstown.
--Smile on the Void. 264p. 1981. 12.95 (ISBN 0-399-12503-5). Putnam Pub Group.
Gordon, Susan. Your Career in Interior Design. (Arco's Career Guidance Ser.). (Illus.). 128p. 1983. lib. bdg. 7.95 (ISBN 0-668-05508-1); pap. 4.50 (ISBN 0-668-05516-2). Arco.
--Your Career in the Military. (Arco's Career Guidance Ser.). (Illus.). 128p. 1983. lib. bdg. 7.95 (ISBN 0-668-05502-2); pap. 4.50 (ISBN 0-668-05511-1). Arco.
Gordon, Suzanne. Lonely in America. 1977. pap. 5.95 o.p. (ISBN 0-671-22754-8, Touchstone). S&S.
--Off Balance: The Real World of Ballet. LC 82-18806. 256p. 1983. 14.95 (ISBN 0-686-38838-0). Pantheon.
Gordon, Victoria. Battle of Wills. (Harlequin Romances Ser.). 192p. 1983. pap. 1.75 (ISBN 0-373-02540-8). Harlequin Bks.
--Dinner at Wyatt's. (Harlequin Romances Ser.). 192p. 1983. pap. 1.50 (ISBN 0-373-02531-9). Harlequin Bks.
Gordon, Vivian V. The Self-Concept of Black Americans. 118p. 1977. pap. text ed. 7.50 (ISBN 0-8191-0151-6). U Pr of Amer.
Gordon, Vivian V., ed. Lectures: Black Scholars on Black Issues. LC 79-63259. 1979. pap. text ed. 12.50 (ISBN 0-8191-0709-3). U Pr of Amer.
Gordon, Walter K., ed. Literature in Critical Perspectives: An Anthology. LC 68-15855. 1968. text ed. 23.95 (ISBN 0-13-537613-0). P-H.
Gordon, Walter K., jt. ed. see Sanderson, James L.
Gordon, William A. The Reading Curriculum: A Reference Guide to Criterion-Based Skill Development in Grades K-8. 272p. 1982. 29.50 (ISBN 0-03-062128-3). Praeger.
--Writer & Critic: A Correspondence with Henry Miller. LC 68-15427. xxxvi, 88p. 1968. 8.95x o.p. (ISBN 0-8071-0513-9). La State U Pr.
Gordon, William C. Bible Word Search. (Quiz & Puzzle Bks.). 112p. 1983. 2.95 (ISBN 0-686-81737-0). Baker Bk.
Gordon, Yvonne. Escape to Ecstasy. (Aston Hall Romances Ser.: No. 102). 192p. (Orig.). 1980. pap. 1.50 o.p. (ISBN 0-523-41124-3). Pinnacle Bks.
Gordon-Bowe, Nicola. Harry Clarke: His Graphic Art. (Illus.). 112p. 1982. 40.00 (ISBN 0-943842-01-8); limited ed. 150.00 (ISBN 0-943842-00-X). H Keith Burns.
Gordon-Smith, W. Edinburgh. (Illus.). 128p. 1983. 22.95 (ISBN 0-686-42794-7, Collins Pub England). Greene.
Gordon-Watson, Mary. Handbook of Riding. LC 82-47795. 1982. 22.50 (ISBN 0-394-52110-2). Knopf.
Gordy, W. Techniques of Chemistry: Vol. 15 Theory & Application of Electron Spin Resonance. 625p. 1980. 69.95 (ISBN 0-471-93162-4). Wiley.
Gordy, W. & Cook, L., eds. Microwave Molecular Spectra. (Technique of Organic Chemistry Ser.: Vol.9, Pt.2). 747p. Repr. of 1970 ed. text ed. 67.50 (ISBN 0-471-93161-6). Krieger.
Gordy, Walter. Theory & Applications of Electron Spin Resonance. LC 79-12377. (Techniques of Chemistry Ser.: Vol. 15). 1980. 48.00 (ISBN 0-471-93162-4, Pub. by Wiley-Interscience). Wiley.
Gore, A. J., ed. Mires: Swamp, Fog, Fen & Moor. (Ecosystems of the World Ser.: Vol. 4). Date not set. Set. 161.75 (ISBN 0-444-42005-3); Pt. A: Analytical Studies. 161.75 (ISBN 0-444-42003-7); Pt. B: Descriptive Studies. 161.75 (ISBN 0-444-42004-5). Elsevier.
Gore, Alan, jt. auth. see Fleming, Laurence.
Gore, Art. Images of Yesterday. LC 75-6322. (Illus.). 104p. 1976. 12.95 o.p. (ISBN 0-517-52700-6). Crown.
Gore, Catherine. Dalmatians. Foyle, Christina, ed. (Foyle's Handbks). (Illus.). 1973. 3.95 (ISBN 0-685-55792-8). Palmetto Pub.
Gore, Daniel. To Know a Library: Essays & Annual Reports, 1970-1976. LC 77-84769. (New Directions in Librarianship: No. 1). 1978. lib. bdg. 35.00 (ISBN 0-8371-9881-X, GTK/). Greenwood.
Gore, Daniel, ed. Farewell to Alexandria: Solutions to Space, Growth & Performance Problems of Libraries. LC 75-35345. 224p. 1976. lib. bdg. 25.00 (ISBN 0-8371-8587-4, GGP/). Greenwood.
Gore, Daniel, ed. see Florida Atlantic University Conference.
Gore, Daniel, ed. see International Seminar on Approval & Gathering Plans in Large & Medium Size Academic Libraries, 3rd.
Gore, Daniel, et al, eds. Requiem for the Card Catalog: Management Issues in Automated Cataloging. LC 78-7129. (New Directions in Librarianship: No. 2). 1979. lib. bdg. 25.00 (ISBN 0-313-20608-2, GMI/). Greenwood.
Gore, Elizabeth. Child Psychiatry Observed. Nursten, Jean, ed. LC 75-6926. 264p. 1976. text ed. 28.00 (ISBN 0-08-017277-6); pap. text ed. 14.00 (ISBN 0-08-017278-4). Pergamon.
Gore, George J. & Wright, Robert G. The Academic-Consultant Connection. 1979. text ed. 21.95 (ISBN 0-8403-2079-5). Kendall-Hunt.
Gore, Marvin & Stubbe, John. Computers & Data Processing. (Illus.). 1979. pap. 22.95 (ISBN 0-07-023787-5, C); instructor's manual 25.00 (ISBN 0-07-023789-1); study guide 9.95 (ISBN 0-07-023788-3). McGraw.
--Elements of Systems Analysis. 3rd ed. 464p. 1983. text ed. write for info. (ISBN 0-697-08169-9); student wkbk avail. (ISBN 0-697-08131-1); instrs. resource manual avail. (ISBN 0-697-08178-8); alternate casebook avail. (ISBN 0-697-08147-8); avail. solutions manual to alternate casebook (ISBN 0-697-08148-6). Wm C Brown.
Gorecki, Henryk, et al. Analysis & Synthesis of Time Delay Systems. LC 79-40508. 1983. write for info. (ISBN 0-471-27622-7, Pub by Wiley-Interscience). Wiley.
Gorelick, Sherry. City College & the Jewish Poor: Education in New York 1880-1924. LC 80-22128. (Illus.). 288p. 1982. pap. 9.95 (ISBN 0-8052-0712-0). Schocken.
Gorelik, A. G., jt. ed. see Vinnichenko, N. K.
Goren, Arthur A. The American Jews. (Dimensions of Ethnicity Ser.). 128p. 1982. pap. text ed. 4.95x (ISBN 0-674-02516-4). Harvard U Pr.
Goren, Charles H. Goren's Bridge Complete. LC 73-75161. 736p. 1981. 16.95 (ISBN 0-385-17441-1). Doubleday.
Goren, Simon L., tr. from German. German Civil Code & the Introductory Act to the German Civil Code & the Marriage Law of the Federal Republic of Germany: 1981 Supplement. LC 75-7935. v, 73p. 1982. pap. text ed. 12.50x (ISBN 0-8377-0615-7). Rothman.
Gorer, Geoffrey. Exploring English Character. LC 55-11159. 18.95 (ISBN 0-87599-040-1). S G Phillips.
Gorer, Richard & Rochford, Thomas. Rochford's House-Plants for Everyone. (Illus.). 112p. (Orig.). 1978. 9.95; pap. 4.95 (ISBN 0-571-08827-9). Faber & Faber.
Gores, Joe. Gone, No Forwarding. 1978. 2.25 (ISBN 0-345-29208-1). Random.
Goreux, L. M. & Manne, A. S. Multi-Level Planning: Case Studies in Mexico. 1973. 47.00 (ISBN 0-444-10434-8, North-Holland); pap. 27.00 (ISBN 0-444-10531-X). Elsevier.
Gorey, Edward. Amphigorey. (Illus.). 1972. 14.95 (ISBN 0-399-11003-8). Putnam Pub Group.
--Amphigorey Too. (Illus.). 224p. 1975. 15.00 (ISBN 0-399-11565-X). Putnam Pub Group.
--The Audrey-Gore Legacy. (Illus.). 64p. 1982. pap. 4.95 (ISBN 0-312-92032-6). Congdon & Weed.
--Blue Aspic. (Illus.). 1969. 4.95 o.p. (ISBN 0-8015-0738-3, Hawthorn). Dutton.
--The Broken Spoke. (Illus.). 64p. 1982. pap. 6.95 (ISBN 0-312-92066-0). Congdon & Weed.
--The Curious Sofa. (Illus.). 64p. 1982. pap. 5.95 (ISBN 0-312-92112-8). Congdon & Weed.
--The Doubtful Guest. (Illus.). 64p. 1982. pap. 5.95 (ISBN 0-312-92145-4). Congdon & Weed.
--The Enraged Telephone. 64p. 1983. 6.95 (ISBN 0-312-92183-7). Congdon & Weed.
--The Epiplectic Bicycle. (Illus.). 64p. 1983. pap. 6.95 (ISBN 0-312-92185-3). Congdon & Weed.
--The Glorious Nosebleed. (Illus.). 64p. 1982. pap. 5.95 (ISBN 0-312-92252-3). Congdon & Weed.
--The Hapless Child. (Illus.). 64p. 1982. pap. 5.95 (ISBN 0-312-92282-5). Congdon & Weed.
--The Loathsome Couple. (Illus.). 64p. 1982. pap. 4.95 (ISBN 0-312-92453-4). Congdon & Weed.
--Sinking Spell. (Illus.). 1965. pap. 4.75 (ISBN 0-8392-1150-3). Astor-Honor.
--Utter Zoo Alphabet. (Illus.). 1967. 4.95 o.p. (ISBN 0-8015-8268-7, Hawthorn). Dutton.
--The Waterflowers. (Illus.). 64p. 1982. 6.95 (ISBN 0-312-92928-5). Congdon & Weed.
--The Willowdale Handcar. (Illus.). 64p. 1982. pap. 5.95 (ISBN 0-312-92946-3). Congdon & Weed.
Gorey, Edward & Neumeyer, Peter. Donald Has a Difficulty. (Illus.). 48p. 1982. pap. 4.95 (ISBN 0-88496-175-3). Capra Pr.
--Why We Have Day & Night. (Illus.). 42p. 1982. pap. 4.95 (ISBN 0-88496-174-5). Capra Pr.
Gorey, Edward, jt. auth. see Lamport, Felicia.
Gorey, Edward, jt. auth. see Moss, Howard.
Gorey, Edward, ed. see Eliot, T. S.
Gorge, Alice A. Creative Toymaking: Dolls, Animals, Puppets. (Illus.). 1981. pap. 7.25 (ISBN 0-903540-43-6, Pub. by Floris Books). St George Bk Serv.
Gorge, Peter, tr. see Schindler, Maria.
Gorges, Raymond. History of the Family of Gorges. 1944. 35.00 (ISBN 0-686-36478-3). Mass Hist Soc.
Gorham, Charles. Life Story of Robert Ingersoll. 56p. pap. 3.00 (ISBN 0-686-95278-2). Am Atheist.
Gorham, Charles T. Religion as a Bar to Progress. 31p. 1981. pap. 3.00 (ISBN 0-686-82051-7). Am Atheist.
Gorham, Deborah. The Victorian Girl & the Feminine Ideal. LC 82-47944. 240p. 1982. 20.00X (ISBN 0-253-36258-X). Ind U Pr.
Gorham, John P. Bookkeeping Simplified & Self-Taught. LC 82-11316. (Simplified & Self-Taught Ser.). 128p. 1983. pap. 4.95 (ISBN 0-668-05456-5, 5456). Arco.
Gori, Gio B. & Bock, Fred G., eds. Banbury Report 3: A Safe Cigarette? LC 79-47999. (Banbury Report Ser.: Vol. 3). (Illus.). 364p. 1980. 45.00x (ISBN 0-87969-202-2). Cold Spring Harbor.
Gorin, Edward, jt. auth. see Baron, Howard C.
Gorin, George. History of Opthalmology. LC 82-61325. xvi, 630p. 1982. text ed. 40.00 (ISBN 0-914098-25-X). Publish or Perish.
Goring, Charles. The English Convict: A Statistical Study to Which Is Added the Schedule of Measurements & General Anthropological Data. LC 71-129314. (Criminology, Law Enforcement, & Social Problems Ser.: No. 137). (Illus.). 530p. (With intro. essay added, Quarto). 1972. Repr. of 1913 ed. lib. bdg. 50.00x (ISBN 0-87585-137-1). Patterson Smith.
Goringe, Michael J., jt. auth. see Thomas, Gareth.
Gorio, A., jt. ed. see Weiss, D. G.
Gorio, Alfredo, jt. ed. see Rapport, Maurice M.
Gorio, Alfredo, et al, eds. Post Traumatic Peripheral Nerve Regeneration. 658p. 1981. text ed. 55.00 not set (ISBN 0-89004-754-5). Raven.
Goris, Michael L. & Briandet, Philippe A. A Clinical & Mathematical Introduction to Computer Processing of Scintigraphic Images. 1982. text ed. write for info. (ISBN 0-89004-766-9). Raven.
Gorki, Maxim see Goldberg, Isaac.
Gorky, Maxim. Foma Gordeyev. LC 74-10361. 264p. 1974. Repr. of 1956 ed. lib. bdg. 17.00x (ISBN 0-8371-7670-0, GOFG). Greenwood.
--Reminiscences of Tolstoy, Chekhov & Andreev. 1968. text ed. 4.50x o.p. (ISBN 0-7013-0313-1). Humanities.

Gorlich, P. Photoconductivity in Solids. (Solid-State Physics Ser.). 1967. pap. 3.75 o.p. (ISBN 0-7100-4387-2). Routledge & Kegan.

Gorlin, R. V., et al. Syndromes of the Head & Neck. 2nd ed. (Illus.). 1976. text ed. 75.00 o.p. (ISBN 0-07-023790-5, HP). McGraw.

Gorlin, Richard. Coronary Artery Disease. LC 76-14680. (Major Problems in Internal Medicine Ser.: Vol. XI). (Illus.). 1976. text ed. 17.50 o.p. (ISBN 0-7216-4165-2). Saunders.

Gorlin, Robert J., jt. auth. see Goodman, Richard M.

Gorlitz, Dietmar. Perspectives on Attribution Research & Theory: The Bielefeld Symposium. 1981. prof ref 25.00x (ISBN 0-88410-375-7). Ballinger Pub.

Gorlow, Leon, jt. auth. see Katkousky, Walter.

Gorman, Brian, compiled by. Finding Lost Alumni: Tracing Methods Used by 19 Institutions. 30p. 1981. 10.50 (ISBN 0-89964-181-4). CASE.

Gorman, Burton. Secondary Education: The High School America Needs. 1971. text ed. 7.95 (ISBN 0-685-55625-5, 31007). Phila Bk Co.

Gorman, D. J. Free Vibration Analysis of Beams & Shafts. LC 74-20504. 448p. 1975. 49.95x (ISBN 0-471-31770-5, Pub. by Wiley-Interscience). Wiley.

--Free Vibration Analysis of Rectangular Plates. 1981. 65.00 (ISBN 0-444-00601-X). Elsevier.

Gorman, G. E. The South African Novel in English Since 1950: An Information & Resource Guide. 1978. 35.00 (ISBN 0-8161-8178-0, Hall Reference). G K Hall.

Gorman, James. First Aid for Hypochondriacs. LC 82-60060. (Illus.). 160p. 1982. 4.95 (ISBN 0-89480-173-2). Workman Pub.

Gorman, John. To Build Jerusalem. 208p. 1980. 50.00x o.p. (ISBN 0-905906-26-8); pap. 26.00x o.p. (ISBN 0-905906-27-6). State Mutual Bk.

Gorman, John, tr. see Winter, Lorenz.

Gorman, John A. Western Horse. LC 66-12997. (Illus.). (gr. 9-12). 1967. 16.50 (ISBN 0-8134-0126-7); text ed. 12.50x. Interstate.

Gorman, Joseph B. Kefauver: A Political Biography. 1971. 19.95 (ISBN 0-19-501481-2). Oxford U Pr.

Gorman, Kenneth A., jt. auth. see Crowningshield, Gerald.

Gorman, M. L. Island Ecology. 1979. pap. 6.50x (ISBN 0-412-15540-0, Pub. by Chapman & Hall). Methuen Inc.

Gorman, Marion. Cooking with Fruit. Gerras, Charles, ed. (Illus.). 320p. 1983. 14.95 (ISBN 0-87857-414-X, 07-003-0). Rodale Pr Inc.

Gorman, Marvin, jt. ed. see Morin, Robert B.

Gorman, Michael. The Concise AACR2. LC 81-3496. 174p. 1981. pap. 8.00 (ISBN 0-8389-0325-8). ALA.

Gorman, Michael & Winkler, Paul, eds. Anglo-American Cataloguing Rules. 2nd ed. LC 78-13789. 1978. text ed. 22.50 (ISBN 0-8389-3210-X); pap. text ed. 17.50 (ISBN 0-8389-3211-8). ALA.

Gorman, Robert A. Neo-Marxism: The Meanings of Modern Radicalism. LC 81-13404. (Contributions in Political Science Ser.: No. 77). 320p. 1982. lib. bdg. 35.00 (ISBN 0-313-23264-4, GON/). Greenwood.

Gorman, Robert A., jt. auth. see Latman, Alan.

Gorman, Stephen M., jt. auth. see Maghroori, Ray.

Gormezano, C. & Leotta, G. G., eds. Heating in Toroidal Plasmas III: Proceedings of the 3rd Joint Varenna-Grenoble International Symposium, Grenoble, France, 22-26 March 1982, 3 vols. 1224p. 1982. pap. 150.00 set (ISBN 0-08-029984-9). Pergamon.

Gormley, Beatrice. Fifth Grade Magic. 144p. (gr. 3-6). 1982. 9.95 (ISBN 0-525-44007-0, 0966-290). Dutton.

Gormley, Chuck. Group Backpacking: A Leader's Manual. (Illus.). 160p. 1979. 7.95 o.p. (ISBN 0-916068-08-0). Groupwork Today.

Gormley, R. James. The Law of Accountants & Auditors: Rights, Duties & Liabilities. LC 80-53120. 1981. 58.00 (ISBN 0-88262-517-9). Warren.

Gormley, William T., Jr. The Politics of Public Utility Regulation. LC 82-42756. 288p. 1983. 22.95 (ISBN 0-8229-3479-5); pap. 8.95x (ISBN 0-8229-5351-X, 195). U of Pittsburgh Pr.

Gorn, Mordechai M. Journey to Fulfillment. LC 79-50790. (Illus.). 1979. 8.95 o.p. (ISBN 0-8197-0471-7). Bloch.

Gorner, P. A., tr. see Tugendhat, Ernst.

Gornick, Vivian. The Romance of American Communism. LC 77-75248. pap. 4.95 o.p. (ISBN 0-465-07111-2, CN-5039). Basic.

Gornitz, Vivien, ed. Geology of the Planet Mars. LC 78-13589. (Benchmark Papers in Geology Ser.: Vol. 48). 414p. 1979. 55.50 (ISBN 0-87933-339-1). Hutchinson Ross.

Gorny, Joseph. The British Labour Movement & Zionism 1917-1948. 200p. 1983. text ed. 32.00x (ISBN 0-7146-3162-0, F Cass Co). Biblio Dist.

Gorodetsky, Gabriel. The Precarious Truce. LC 76-2279. (Soviet & East European Studies). 1977. 44.50 (ISBN 0-521-21226-X). Cambridge U Pr.

Gorog, Judith. A Taste for Quiet: And Other Disquieting Tales. (Illus.). 124p. 1982. 9.95 (ISBN 0-399-20922-0, Philomel). Putnam Pub Group.

Gorog, S. & Szasz, G. Y. Analysis of Steroid Hormone Drugs. 1978. 64.00 (ISBN 0-444-99805-5). Elsevier.

Gorog, S., ed. Advances in Steroid Analysis: Proceedings of a Symposium in Egar, Hungary, May 1981. (Analytical Chemistry Symposia Ser.: Vol. 10). 1982. 95.75 (ISBN 0-444-99711-3). Elsevier.

Gorokhoff, Galina, ed. Anna Lea Merritt: Memoirs. (Illus.). 325p. Date not set. price not set (ISBN 0-87846-227-9). Mus Fine Arts Boston.

Gorostiza, C. Color De Nuestra Piel. Soto-Ruiz, Luis & Trifilo, S. Samuel, eds. (Orig.). 1966. pap. text ed. 8.95x (ISBN 0-02-345370-2). Macmillan.

Gorostiza, L. G., jt. ed. see Fleming, W. H.

Gorove, Stephen, ed. United States Space Law: National & International Regulation, Vols. I & II. LC 81-22465. 1982. loose-leaf 85.00 ea. (ISBN 0-379-20695-1); Set. 170.00. Oceana.

Gorovitz, Sam & Maklin, Ruth. Moral Problems in Medicine. 2nd ed. (Illus.). 640p. 1983. text ed. 23.95 (ISBN 0-13-600742-2). P-H.

Gorovitz, Samuel. Moral Problem in Medicine. 500p. 1976. 23.95 (ISBN 0-13-600817-8). P-H.

Gorovitz, Samuel, et al. Philosophical Analysis: An Introduction to Its Language & Techniques. 3rd ed. LC 78-5661. 1979. pap. text ed. 7.00x (ISBN 0-394-32284-3). Random.

Gorrell, Robert & Laird, Charlton. Modern English Handbook. 6th ed. 1976. text ed. 15.95 (ISBN 0-13-594283-7); tchr's man. free (ISBN 0-13-594275-6). P-H.

Gorrell, Robert M. & Laird, Charlton. Writing Modern English. (Illus.). 288p. 1973. pap. text ed. 10.95 (ISBN 0-13-970632-1). P-H.

Gorris, Greg. Bible for Bartenders. 243p. 1977. 6.50 o.p. (ISBN 0-682-48847-X). Exposition.

Gorrod, J. W., ed. Biological Oxidation of Nitrogen: Proceedings of the 2nd International Symposium on the Biological Oxidation of Nitrogen in Organic Molecules, Chelsea College, London, Sept. 1977. 1978. 94.00 (ISBN 0-444-80039-5, North-Holland). Elsevier.

Gorshkov, G. & Yakushova, A. Physical Geology. Gurevich, A., tr. (Russian Monographs Ser.). 1969. 109.00x (ISBN 0-677-20790-5). Gordon.

Gorski, Roger A. & Whalen, Richard E., eds. Brain & Behavior: Brain & Gonadal Function, Vol. 3. LC 65-27542. (UCLA Forum in Medical Sciences). 1966. 75.00x (ISBN 0-520-00506-6). U of Cal Pr.

Gorski-Popiel, J. Frequency Synthesis: Techniques & Applications. LC 74-82502. 1975. 19.95 (ISBN 0-87942-039-1). Inst Electrical.

Gorsky, Benjamin H. Pain: Origin & Treatment -- Discussions in Patient Management. LC 80-15857. 1981. 22.00 (ISBN 0-87488-448-9); pap. 13.00 (ISBN 0-87488-447-0). Med Exam.

Gorsky, Susan R. Virginia Woolf. (English Authors Ser.). 1978. 12.95 (ISBN 0-8057-6712-6, Twayne). G K Hall.

Gorsline, Douglas. What People Wore. (Illus.). 266p. 1974. pap. 5.95 o.p. (ISBN 0-517-14321-6). Crown.

Gorsline, Douglas, jt. auth. see Gorsline, Marie.

Gorsline, Douglas, illus. Nursery Rhymes. LC 76-24168. (Picturebacks Ser.). (Illus.). (ps-2). 1977. pap. 1.50 (ISBN 0-394-83550-6, BYR). Random.

Gorsline, G. Computer Orangization: Hardware-Software. 1980. 19.95 (ISBN 0-13-165290-7). P-H.

Gorsline, G. W. Computer Organization: Hardware-Software. (Illus.). 1980. text ed. 26.95 (ISBN 0-13-165290-7). P-H.

Gorsline, Marie & Gorsline, Douglas. Cowboys. LC 78-1131. (Picturebacks Ser.). (Illus.). 32p. (ps-2). 1980. PLB 4.99 (ISBN 0-394-93935-2, BYR); pap. 1.50 (ISBN 0-394-83935-8). Random.

--North American Indians. LC 77-79843. (Picturebacks Ser.). (ps-2). 1978. PLB 4.99 (ISBN 0-394-93702-3, BYR); pap. 1.50 (ISBN 0-394-83702-9). Random.

Gorst-Williams, J. Elizabeth the Winter Queen. 1977. 11.50 o.p. (ISBN 0-200-72472-X). Transatlantic.

Gorsuch, Richard L. Factor Analysis. 2nd ed. 375p. 1983. text ed. write for info. (ISBN 0-89859-202-X). L Erlbaum Assocs.

Gorter, Wytze. United States Shipping Policy. LC 77-6767. 1977. Repr. of 1956 ed. lib. bdg. 20.00x (ISBN 0-8371-9657-4, GOUS). Greenwood.

Gortner, Harold J. Administration in the Public Sector. 2nd ed. LC 80-19757. 413p. 1981. text ed. 19.95 (ISBN 0-471-06320-7). Wiley.

Gorton, Richard A. School Administration & Supervision: Leadership Challenges & Opportunities. 2nd ed. 440p. 1982. pap. text ed. write for info (ISBN 0-697-06246-5). Wm C Brown.

--School Administration: Challenge & Opportunity for Leadership. 1976. text ed. write for info. o.p. (ISBN 0-697-06244-9). Wm C Brown.

Gorton, Richard K. Practical Accounting: Ways to Increase Office Efficiency & Improve Career Skills. 85p. (Orig.). 1982. pap. 19.95 (ISBN 0-686-37985-3). Advance Pr.

--Underground Mine Accounting. 57p. (Orig.). 1982. pap. 19.95 (ISBN 0-686-37986-1). Advance Pr.

Gorwen, Leonard. How to Find & Land Your First Full-Time Job. LC 82-6742. 128p. 1983. lib. bdg. 9.95 (ISBN 0-668-05458-1); pap. 4.95 (ISBN 0-668-05463-8). Arco.

Gorz, Andre. Beyond the Proletariat. 250p. 1982. 20.00 (ISBN 0-89608-168-0); pap. 7.50 (ISBN 0-89608-167-2). South End Pr.

Gorzalka, Ann L. The Saddlemakers of Sheridan County, Wyoming. 1983. price not set (ISBN 0-87108-634-4). Pruett.

Gos, Michael W. Brackish Aquariums. (Illus.). 1979. 4.95 (ISBN 0-87666-519-9, KW-046). TFH Pubns.

--Doves. (Illus.). 96p. 1981. 4.95 (ISBN 0-87666-828-7, KW-123). TFH Pubns.

--Lories. (Illus.). 93p. 1981. 4.95 (ISBN 0-87666-832-5, KW-126). TFH Pubns.

--Waxbills. (Illus.). 93p. 1981. 4.95 (ISBN 0-87666-839-2, KW-136). TFH Pubns.

Goscilo, Helena, ed. & tr. see Lermontov, Mikhail.

Goscilo, Helena, tr. see Nagibin, Yuri.

Gosebrink, Jean E., ed. see Sweetland, James H.

Gosen, Patricia E. New York City Metropolitan Area, Studies Program, Work-A-Text. Irvin, J. L., ed. (Illus.). 76p. (Orig.). (gr. 4). 1981. wkbk. 3.50 (ISBN 0-943068-01-0). Graphic Learning.

Gosepath, J., jt. auth. see Reisner, K.

Gosfield, Alice. PSRO's: The Law & the Health Consumer. LC 75-13340. 288p. 1975. text ed. 18.50 o.p. (ISBN 0-88410-123-1). Ballinger Pub.

Goshen, Robert P. Tuna Chopper. write for info. Zoom.

Goshgarian, Gary. Atlantis Fire. 1981. pap. 2.75 o.p. (ISBN 0-380-56093-3, 56093, Flare). Avon.

Gosink, Barbara B. & Squire, Lucy F. Exercises in Diagnostic Radiology: Diagnostic Ultrasound, Vol. 8. LC 74-113034. (Illus.). 200p. 1976. pap. text ed. 11.95 o.p. (ISBN 0-7216-4176-8). Saunders.

--Exercises in Diagnostic Radiology: Vol. 8, Diagnostic Ultrasound. 2nd ed. (Illus.). 220p. 1981. text ed. 17.95 (ISBN 0-7216-4175-X). Saunders.

Gosler, John. Dinosaurs. LC 80-52532. (Starters Ser.). PLB 8.00 (ISBN 0-382-06485-2). Silver.

Goslin, David A. Handbook of Socialization Theory & Research. 1969. 52.95 (ISBN 0-395-30611-6). HM.

--The Search for Ability: Standardized Testing in Social Perspective. LC 63-12591. 204p. 1963. 7.95x (ISBN 0-87154-357-5). Russell Sage.

--Teachers & Testing. LC 67-25912. 202p. 1967. 8.95x (ISBN 0-87154-358-3). Russell Sage.

Goslin, Lewis N. & Rethans, Arno J. Basic Systems for Decision Making. 2nd ed. 208p. 1980. pap. text ed. 10.95 (ISBN 0-8403-2191-0). Kendall-Hunt.

Gosline, William A. Functional Morphology & Classification of Teleostean Fishes. LC 77-151454. (Illus.). 1971. pap. text ed. 8.00x (ISBN 0-87022-300-3). UH Pr.

Gosline, William A. & Brock, Vernon E. Handbook of Hawaiian Fishes. LC 58-11692. (Illus., Orig.). 1960. pap. text ed. 8.95x (ISBN 0-87022-302-X). UH Pr.

Gosling, C. T. Applied Air Conditioning & Refrigeration. 2nd ed. 1980. 45.00 (ISBN 0-85334-877-4, Pub. by Applied Sci England). Elsevier.

Gosling, J. A. & Dixon, J. S. Functional Anatomy of the Urinary Tract: An Integrated Text & Color Atlas. (Illus.). 132p. 1983. text ed. 127.50 (ISBN 0-8391-1772-8, 19518). Univ Park.

Gosling, Nigel. Nadar. 1977. 25.00 o.p. (ISBN 0-394-41106-4). Knopf.

Gosling, P. E. Continuing BASIC. 160p. 1980. pap. 9.95 (ISBN 0-333-26286-7). Robotics Pr.

Gosling, Paula. Fair Game. LC 78-5819. 1978. 8.95 o.p. (ISBN 0-698-10921-X, Coward). Putnam Pub Group.

--Solo Blues. 1981. 12.95 (ISBN 0-698-11107-9, Coward). Putnam Pub Group.

--Solo Blues. 256p. 1983. pap. 2.50 (ISBN 0-345-30643-0). Ballantine.

--The Zero Trap. LC 79-25758. 1980. 10.95 (ISBN 0-698-11020-X, Coward). Putnam Pub Group.

Gosling, William G. Life of Sir Humphrey Gilbert, England's First Empire Builder. LC 76-109737. Repr. of 1911 ed. lib. bdg. 17.00x (ISBN 0-8371-4227-X, GOHG). Greenwood.

Gosman, Martin L. Accounting Graffiti. LC 75-4144. (Illus.). 152p. 1975. pap. text ed. 8.95 (ISBN 0-8299-0058-6). West Pub.

Gosman, Martin L., jt. auth. see Backer, Morton.

Gosnell, Davina J. Help with the Nursing Process. LC 80-66120. (Help Series of Management Guides). 1980. pap. 11.95 (ISBN 0-933036-19-1). Ganong W L Co.

Gosnell, Harold F. Machine Politics: Chicago Model. LC 37-20974. (Illus.). 1969. Repr. of 1937 ed. lib. bdg. 15.50x (ISBN 0-8371-0451-3, GOMP). Greenwood.

Gosnell, Harold F. & Smolka, Richard G. American Parties & Elections. new ed. (Political Science Ser.). 288p. 1976. pap. text ed. 16.95 (ISBN 0-675-08620-5). Merrill.

Gosner, Kenneth. A Field Guide to the Atlantic Seashore. (Peterson Field Guide Ser.). (Illus.). 416p. 1982. 17.95 (ISBN 0-395-24379-3); pap. 9.95 (ISBN 0-395-31828-9). HM.

Gosner, Pamela. Caribbean Georgian: The Great Houses & Small of the Caribbean. LC 78-72966. (Illus.). 324p. (Orig.). 1982. 35.00x (ISBN 0-89410-011-4); pap. 15.00x (ISBN 0-89410-012-2). Three Continents.

--Historic Architecture of the U. S. Virgin Islands. LC 78-140952. (Illus.). 1979. pap. 5.50 (ISBN 0-87716-026-0, Pub. by Moore Pub Co). F Apple.

Gosney, Michael. We Are It. (Orig.). 1983. pap. 8.95 (ISBN 0-932238-19-X). Avant Bks.

Gospel Advocate. Commentaries on the New Testament. Incl. Matthew. Boles, H. Leo (ISBN 0-89225-001-1); Mark. Dorris, C. E (ISBN 0-89225-002-X); Luke. Boles, H. Leo (ISBN 0-89225-003-8); John. Dorris, C. E (ISBN 0-89225-004-6); Acts. Boles, H. Leo (ISBN 0-89225-005-4); Romans. Lipscomb, David & Shepherd, J. W. (ISBN 0-89225-006-2); Corinthians I. Lipscomb, David & Shepard, J. W. (ISBN 0-89225-007-0); Corinthians II - Galatians. Lipscomb, David & Shepherd, J. W. (ISBN 0-89225-008-9); Ephesians - Colossians. Shepherd, J. W (ISBN 0-89225-009-7); Thess. I, II; Tim. I, II; Titus; Philomen. Shepherd, J. W (ISBN 0-89225-010-0); Hebrews. Milligan, Robert (ISBN 0-89225-011-9); James. Woods, Guy N (ISBN 0-89225-012-7); Peter I, II; John I, II, III; Jude. Woods, Guy N (ISBN 0-89225-013-5); Revelation. Hinds, John T (ISBN 0-89225-014-3). Set. 125.00 (ISBN 0-89225-000-3); 9.95 ea. Gospel Advocate.

Goss, Ann, jt. ed. see Harris, Beatrice.

Goss, Blaine. Communication in Everyday Life. 320p. 1982. pap. text ed. 13.95x (ISBN 0-534-01215-9). Wadsworth Pub.

Goss, Clav see Harrison, Paul C.

Goss, Dinah B. & Schwartz, Marla S. The Bride Guide. LC 82-19777. (Illus.). 192p. (Orig.). 1983. pap. 12.95 (ISBN 0-934878-22-6). Dembner Bks.

Goss, Gordon J., ed. National Square Dance Directory: 1983 Edition. 4th ed. 208p. 1983. pap. 9.50 (ISBN 0-9605494-3-9). Natl Sq Dance.

Goss, Louise, jt. auth. see Clark, Frances.

Goss, Louise, jt. ed. see Clark, Frances.

Goss, Louise, ed. see George, Jon.

Goss, Louise, ed. see Kraehenbuehl, David.

Goss, R. O. Studies in Maritime Economics. LC 68-29328. (Illus.). 1968. 37.50 (ISBN 0-521-07329-4). Cambridge U Pr.

Goss, Richard J., ed. Deer Antlers: Regeneration, Function, & Evolution. LC 82-22795. (Monograph). Date not set. price not set (ISBN 0-12-293080-0). Acad Pr.

Gossage, Loyce C. Basic Mathematical Skills: A Text Workbook. 2nd ed. (Illus.). 320p. 1975. pap. text ed. 19.50 (ISBN 0-07-023852-9, C); instructor's manual 18.50 (ISBN 0-07-023853-7). McGraw.

Gossage, Richard C. & Gunton, Melvin. Bedmanship. (Illus.). 96p. (Orig.). 1983. pap. 3.95 (ISBN 0-8329-0259-4). New Century.

Gossard, E. E. Waves in the Atmosphere. LC 73-89155. (Developments in Atmospheric Science Ser: Vol. 2). 456p. 1975. 113.00 (ISBN 0-444-41196-8). Elsevier.

Gosse, Edmund. Father & Son. 1963. pap. 6.95 (ISBN 0-393-00195-4, Norton Lib). Norton.

--Father & Son. 1983. pap. 3.95 (ISBN 0-14-000700-8). Penguin.

Gosse, Edmund, jt. auth. see Gide, Andre.

Gosse, Philip. The History of Piracy. LC 75-16396. (Illus.). xvi, 349p. 1976. Repr. of 1934 ed. 40.00x (ISBN 0-8103-4156-5). Gale.

Gosse, Philip H. Letters from Alabama (U. S.) Chiefly Relating to Natural History. annotated facsimile ed. LC 82-61822. (Illus.). 352p. 1983. pap. 12.95 (ISBN 0-910773-00-9). Overbrook Hse.

Gosselin, Robert, et al. Clinical Toxicology of Commercial Products. 4th ed. 1810p. 1976. 75.00 (ISBN 0-683-03631-9). Williams & Wilkins.

Gosset, Melinda Lu. Doggerelimericks I. (Limericklets Ser.: No. 12). (Illus.). 1982. pap. 1.00 (ISBN 0-938338-23-4). Winds World Pr.

--Doggerelimericks II. (Limericklets Ser.: No. 13). (Illus.). 1982. pap. 1.00 (ISBN 0-938338-24-2). Winds World Pr.

--Doggerelimericks III. (Limericklets Ser.: No. 14). (Illus.). pap. 1.00 (ISBN 0-938338-25-0). Winds World Pr.

Gossett, Bruce. Boating. (Monarch Illustrated Guide Ser.). (Illus.). 1977. pap. 2.95 o.p. (ISBN 0-671-18765-1). Monarch Pr.

Gossett, Don. Confiado Como un Leon. Marosi, Esteban, et al, eds. Kjellgreen, Shily, tr. from Eng. 204p. (Span.). 1981. pap. 2.25 (ISBN 0-8297-1078-7). Life Pubs Intl.

Gossett, John T. & Lewis, Jerry M. To Find a Way: The Outcome of Hospital Treatment of Disturbed Adolescents. LC 82-17900. 200p. 1983. 20.00 (ISBN 0-87630-326-2). Brunner-Mazel.

Gossett, Thomas F. Race: The History of an Idea in America. rev. ed. LC 63-21187. (Sourcebooks in Negro History Ser.). (YA) (gr. 7 up). 1965. pap. 9.50 (ISBN 0-8052-0106-8). Schocken.

Gossling, Harry R., et al, eds. Complications in Fracture Management. (Illus.). 700p. 1983. text ed. price not set (ISBN 0-397-50584-1, Lippincott Medical). Lippincott.

Gossman, Lionel. The Empire Unpossess'd: An Essay on Gibbon's "Decline & Fall". LC 80-24008. (Illus.). 176p. 1981. 22.95 (ISBN 0-521-23453-0). Cambridge U Pr.

Gossman, N. J., jt. ed. see Baylen, J. O.

Gosson, Stephen. Schoole of Abuse Fifteen Seventy-Nine & A Short Apologie of the Schoole of Abuse Eighteen Sixty-Eight. 80p. pap. 12.50 (ISBN 0-87556-104-7). Saifer.

--The Schoole (Sic) of Abuse. Bd. with A Reply to Gosson's Schoole of Abuse. Lodge, Thomas. (The English Stage Ser.: Vol. 2). lib. bdg. 50.00 o.s.i. (ISBN 0-8240-0585-6). Garland Pub.

Gostelow, Mary. The Complete International Book of Embroidery. (Illus.). 9.98 o.p. (ISBN 0-517-31232-8). Crown.

Gostin, Larry O., jt. auth. see Weisstub, David N.

Goswami, Amit. The Concepts of Physics. 1979. text ed. 24.95 o.p. (ISBN 0-669-01897-X). Heath.

Goswami, Amit & Goswami, Maggie. The Cosmic Dancers: Exploring the Physics of Science Fiction. (Illus.). 288p. 1983. 17.95 (ISBN 0-06-015083-1, HarpT). Har-Row.

Goswami, Dixie, ed. see Emig, Janet.

Goswami, Maggie, jt. auth. see Goswami, Amit.

Goswami, Satsuarupa D. Opening a Temple in Los Angelos: A Visit to Boston. Dasa, Mandalesuaraba, et al, eds. (Prabhupada-Lila Ser.). 72p. 1981. pap. 2.25 (ISBN 0-911233-01-6). Gita Nagari.

Goswami, Satsvarupa D. A Handbook for Krishna Consciousness. LC 79-97. 1979. pap. 6.95 o.p. (ISBN 0-89647-008-3). Bala Bks.

Goswami, Satsvarupa das see Das Goswami, Satsvarupa.

Goswitz, Francis A., et al, eds. Clinical Uses of Radionuclides: Critical Comparison with Other Techniques, Proceedings. LC 72-660271. (AEC Symposium Ser.). 718p. 1972. pap. 26.00 (ISBN 0-87079-002-1, CONF-711101); microfiche 4.50 (ISBN 0-87079-164-8, CONF-711101). DOE.

Gotesky, Rubin & Laszlo, Ervin, eds. Evolution-Revolution. LC 74-160019. (Current Topics of Contemporary Thought Ser.). (Illus.). 364p. 1971. lib. bdg. 43.00x (ISBN 0-677-15090-3). Gordon.

Gothard, Bill. Men's Manual, Vol. 1. LC 79-88994. (Illus.). 160p. 1979. 25.00 (ISBN 0-916888-04-5). Inst Basic Youth.

--Men's Manual, Vol. 8. LC 79-88994. (Illus.). 270p. 1983. 20.00 (ISBN 0-916888-09-6). Inst Basic Youth.

Gothberg, Helen. Impact: Television-Video in Libraries & Schools. 1983. 22.50 (ISBN 0-208-01859-X, Lib Prof Pubns); pap. price not set (ISBN 0-208-01860-3, Lib Prof Pubns). Shoe String.

Gothie, Daniel L. A Selected Bibliography of Applied Ethics in the Professions, 1950-1970: A Working Sourcebook. LC 73-80627. 176p. 1973. 12.95x (ISBN 0-8139-0412-9). U Pr of Va.

Gothmann, William H. Digital Electronics. 2nd ed. (Illus.). 400p. 1982. 23.95 (ISBN 0-13-212159-X). P-H.

--Digital Electronics: An Introduction to Theory & Practice. LC 76-18258. (Illus.). 1977. 23.95 (ISBN 0-13-212217-0). P-H.

Gotleib, Phyllis. O Master Caliban. LC 76-5540. 244p. 1976. 12.50 (ISBN 0-06-011621-8). Ultramarine Pub.

Gotlieb, C. C. & Borodin, A. Social Issues in Computing. (Computer Science & Applied Mathematics Ser.). 1973. by subscription - 21.75 16.00 (ISBN 0-12-293750-3). Acad Pr.

Gotlieb, Phillis. Emperor, Swords, Pentacles. 304p. 1982. pap. 2.75 (ISBN 0-441-18067-1, Pub. by Ace Science Fiction). Ace Bks.

Gotlieb, Phyllis. Sunburst. 12.00 (ISBN 0-8398-2500-5, Gregg). G K Hall.

Gotlieb, Phyllis, et al. The Edge of Space: Three Original Novellas of Science Fiction. Silverberg, Robert, ed. LC 79-4406. (Science Fiction Ser.). 1979. 8.95 o.p. (ISBN 0-525-66625-7). Lodestar Bks.

Gotlieb, Sondra. A Woman of Consequence. 1983. 12.95 (ISBN 0-312-88643-8). St Martin.

Gotlieb, Yousef. Self-Determination in the Middle East. 190p. 1982. 22.95 (ISBN 0-03-062408-8). Praeger.

Gotlin, Stanley. Test Wise Tactics for Higher Scores in English. 128p. (gr. 9-12). 1984. pap. 3.95 (ISBN 0-8120-2578-4). Barron.

Gotlo, jt. auth. see DeBakey.

Goto, E., ed. RIMS Symposia on Software Science & Engineering: Proceedings, Kyoto, Japan, 1982. (Lecture Notes in Computer Science Ser.: Vol. 147). 232p. 1983. pap. 11.50 (ISBN 0-387-11980-9). Springer-Verlag.

Goto, H. E. Animal Toxonomy. (No. 143). 64p. 1982. pap. text ed. 8.95 (ISBN 0-7131-2847-X). E Arnold.

Goto, Y. & Horiuchi, A., eds. Diabetic Neuropathy: Proc. Internat. Symp. on Diabetic Neuropathy & its Treatment, Tokyo, September 18-19, 1981. (International Congress Ser.: Vol. 581). 390p. 1982. 90.75 (ISBN 0-444-90259-7). Elsevier.

Gotsch, Carl & Brown, Gilbert. Prices, Taxes & Subsidies in Pakistan Agriculture, 1960-1976. (Working Paper: No. 387). 108p. 1980. 5.00 (ISBN 0-686-36073-7, WP-0387). World Bank.

Gotshalk, Dilman W. Structure & Reality: A Study of First Principles. LC 68-19273. 1968. Repr. of 1937 ed. lib. bdg. 15.75x (ISBN 0-8371-0088-7, GOSR). Greenwood.

Gotshall, Daniel W. Marine Animals of Baja California. LC 82-50492. (Illus.). 112p. 1982. 30.00 o.p. (ISBN 0-930118-08-1); pap. 17.95 (ISBN 0-930030-24-9). Western Marine.

--Marine Animals of Baja California. LC 82-50492. (Illus.). 112p. 1982. ltd. ed. 29.95 (ISBN 0-930118-08-1, Dist. by Western Marine Enterprises); pap. 17.95 (ISBN 0-930030-24-9). Sea Chall.

--Pacific Coast Inshore Fishes. rev. ed. LC 80-53027. (Illus.). 96p. 1981. 22.95 (ISBN 0-930118-07-3, Western Marine Enterprises); pap. 12.95 (ISBN 0-930118-06-5). Sea Chall.

--Pacific Coast Inshore Fishes. LC 80-53027. (Illus.). 96p. 1981. pap. 12.95 (ISBN 0-930118-06-5). Western Marine Ent.

Gotshall, Daniel W. & Laurent, Laurence L. Pacific Coast Subtidal Marine Invertebrates, a Fishwatchers' Guide. LC 79-64128. 112p. 1979. 12.95 (ISBN 0-930118-02-2, Western Marine Enterprises); pap. 12.95 (ISBN 0-930118-03-0). Sea Chall.

Gottcent, John H. The Bible As Literature: A Selective Bibliography. 1979. lib. bdg. 25.00 (ISBN 0-8161-8121-7, Hall Reference). G K Hall.

Gottesman, R., ed. Focus on Orson Welles. 1976. 9.95 o.p. (ISBN 0-13-949214-3, Spec); pap. 4.95 o.p. (ISBN 0-13-949206-2). P-H.

Gottesman, Rita S. Arts & Crafts in New York, Eighteen Hundred to Eighteen-Four: Advertisements & News Items from New York City Newspapers. LC 38-18579. (Illus.). 11.25x o.p. (ISBN 0-685-73870-1, New York Historical Society). U Pr of Va.

--Arts & Crafts in New York, Seventeen Twenty-Six to Seventeen Seventy-Six. LC 70-127254. (Architecture & Decorative Art Ser.: Vol. 35). 1970. Repr. of 1938 ed. lib. bdg. 45.00 (ISBN 0-306-71129-X). Da Capo.

Gottesman, Ronald. Studies in Invisible Man. LC 75-149740. 1971. pap. text ed. 3.50 (ISBN 0-675-09210-8). Merrill.

Gottesman, Ronald, et al, eds. The Norton Anthology of American Literature. 1979. Vol I. text ed. 18.95x (ISBN 0-393-95026-3); Vol II. text ed. 18.95x (ISBN 0-393-95033-6); Vol. I. pap. text ed. 15.95x (ISBN 0-393-95030-1); Vol II. pap. text ed. 15.95x (ISBN 0-393-95035-2). Norton.

--The Norton Anthology of American Literature: Shorter Edition. 1980. text ed. 17.95x (ISBN 0-393-95119-7); pap. text ed. 15.95x (ISBN 0-393-95112-X). Norton.

Gottfredson, Don M., jt. auth. see Gottfredson, Michael R.

Gottfredson, Gary D. & Holland, John L. Dictionary of Holland Occupational Codes. 520p. (Orig.). 1982. pap. 17.75 (ISBN 0-89106-020-0, 7889). Consulting Psychol.

Gottfredson, Michael R. & Gottfredson, Don M. Decisionmaking in Criminal Justice: Toward the Rational Exercise of Discretion. 424p. 1980. prof ref 30.00x (ISBN 0-88410-234-3). Ballinger Pub.

Gottfried, Byron S. Introduction to Engineering Calculations. (Schaum's Outline Ser.). (Illus.). 1979. pap. 6.95 (ISBN 0-07-023837-5, SP). McGraw.

--Programming with BASIC. (Schaum Outline Ser.). (Illus.). 224p. 1975. pap. text ed. 6.95 (ISBN 0-07-023842-1, SP). McGraw.

Gottfried, Byron S. & Weisman, Joel. Introduction to Optimization Theory. (Illus.). 592p. 1973. ref. ed. 29.95 (ISBN 0-13-491472-4). P-H.

Gottfried, Nathan, jt. auth. see Seay, Bill M.

Gottfried, Robert S. The Black Death. LC 82-48745. 240p. 1983. 14.95 (ISBN 0-02-912630-4). Free Pr.

Gottheil, E. L., et al, eds. see Coatesville-Jefferson Conference on Addiction, 1st, October 1977.

Gottheil, Edward, et al. Etiologic Aspects of Alcohol & Drug Abuse. (Illus.). 362p. 1983. 39.75x (ISBN 0-398-04732-4). C C Thomas.

Gottheinerova, Till, tr. see Vana, Zdenek.

Gotthilf, Daniel L. Treasurer's & Controller's Desk Book. 512p. 1977. 45.00 (ISBN 0-686-92142-9). P-H.

Gottinger, W. Senile Retinoschisis: Morphological Relationship of the Formation of Spaces Within the Peripheral Retina to Senile Retinochisis & to Schisis Detachment. Bayo, J. W., tr. LC 77-93498. (Illus.). 66p. 1978. pap. 20.00 o.p. (ISBN 0-88416-243-5). Wright-PSG.

Gottleib, J. Educating Mentally Retarded Persons: Social & Behavioral Aspects. 304p. 1980. pap. text ed. 19.95 (ISBN 0-8391-1522-9). Univ Park.

Gottleib, Richard M., jt. auth. see Thompson, Waite.

Gottlieb & Ireland. Electro-Optical & Acoustic-Optical Scanning & Deflection. (Optical Engineering Ser.). 216p. 1983. price not set (ISBN 0-8247-1811-9). Dekker.

Gottlieb, Annie, jt. auth. see Sandulescu, Jacques.

Gottlieb, Beatrice, tr. see Febvre, Lucien.

Gottlieb, Bertram & Werner, Charles. Statutory Obligation of an Employer to Furnish Information to a Union. 1975. pap. text ed. 10.00 (ISBN 0-89806-019-2, 46); pap. text ed. 5.00 members. Inst Indus Eng.

Gottlieb, Bill, ed. see Morrison, Lester & Nugent, Nancy.

Gottlieb, Carla. The Art of Self-Portraiture. (Illus.). 480p. 1983. 26.50 (ISBN 0-525-93204-6, 02573-770); pap. 17.50 (ISBN 0-525-47672-5, 01699-510). Dutton.

--The Restoration of the "Nereid" Monument at Xanthos. LC 80-53356. (Illus.). xxii, 349p. 1980. lib. bdg. 60.00 (ISBN 0-9604420-0-6); pap. 40.00 (ISBN 0-9604420-3-0). Boian Bks.

--The Window as a Symbol in Western Painting: From Divinity to Doubt. LC 80-53355. (Illus.). 550p. 1983. 75.00 (ISBN 0-9604420-1-4); pap. 60.00 (ISBN 0-9604420-2-2). Boian Bks.

--The Window in Painting: A Study of It's Morphology as Basis for Motif Classification. LC 81-69473. (Illus.). 350p. 1983. 60.00 (ISBN 0-9604420-4-9); pap. 50.00 (ISBN 0-9604420-5-7). Boian Bks.

Gottlieb, Dale. Ontological Economy: Substitutional Quantification & Mathematics. (Clarendon Library of Logic & Philosophy Ser.). 1980. 28.00x (ISBN 0-19-824420-7). Oxford U Pr.

Gottlieb, David & Orszag, Steven A. Numerical Analysis of Spectral Methods: Theory & Applications. (CBMS-NSF Regional Conference Ser.: Vol. 26). (Illus.). v, 172p. (Orig.). 1977. pap. text ed. 16.00 (ISBN 0-89871-023-5). Soc Indus-Appl Math.

Gottlieb, Elaine, ed. see Hemley, Cecil.

Gottlieb, Gerald. Adventures of Ulysses. (World Landmark Ser.: No. 40). (Illus.). (gr. 5-9). 1959. 2.95 (ISBN 0-394-80540-2, BYR); PLB 4.39 o.p. (ISBN 0-394-90540-7). Random.

Gottlieb, Irving. Solid State High Frequency Power. 1981. text ed. 21.95 (ISBN 0-8359-7048-5). Reston.

Gottlieb, Jay & Strichart, Stephen S., eds. Developmental Theory & Research in Learning Disabilities. 352p. 1981. pap. text ed. 19.95 (ISBN 0-8391-1624-1). Univ Park.

Gottlieb, Laura Moss, ed. see Ginsberg, Elaine.

Gottlieb, Leon. The Best of Gottlieb's Food Service: A Practical Profit Guide for Today's Food Service Operator. LC 80-16535. 1980. 19.95 (ISBN 0-86730-229-1). Lebhar Friedman.

--Foodservice-Hospitality Advertising & Promotion. 363p. 1982. text ed. 18.50 (ISBN 0-672-97868-7); Tchr's Ed. 3.33 (ISBN 0-672-97869-5). Bobbs.

Gottlieb, Lois C. Rachel Crothers. (United States Authors Ser.). 1979. lib. bdg. 13.95 (ISBN 0-8057-7222-7, Twayne). G K Hall.

Gottlieb, Louise, jt. auth. see Bailey, David H.

Gottlieb, Manuel. The German Peace Settlement & the Berlin Crisis. 275p. 1960. 14.95 (ISBN 0-87855-033-X). Transaction Bks.

Gottlieb, Marvin. Oral Interpretation. (Illus.). 1980. text ed. 21.50x (ISBN 0-07-023838-3). McGraw.

Gottlieb, Marvin, jt. auth. see Cohn, Sidney A.

Gottlieb, Marvin I., jt. auth. see Cohn, Sidney A.

Gottlieb, Marvin I., et al. Basic Sciences. 6th ed. (Medical Examination Review Book Ser.: Vol. 3). 1974. spiral bdg. 8.50 o.p. (ISBN 0-87488-103-X). Med Exam.

Gottlieb, Marvin I., et al, eds. Pediatrics Specialty Board Review. 4th ed. 1974. spiral bdg. 20.50 o.p. (ISBN 0-87488-301-6). Med Exam.

Gottlieb, Marvine I., jt. auth. see Holmes, Marguerite C.

Gottlieb, Moshe R. American Anti-Nazi Resistance: An Historical Analysis. LC 81-8144. 1982. 35.00x (ISBN 0-87068-889-8). Ktav.

Gottlieb, Nora & Chapman, Raymond, eds. Letters to an Actress: The Story of Turgenev & Savina. LC 73-92898. 155p. 1973. 8.95 (ISBN 0-8214-0146-7, 82-81495). Ohio U Pr.

Gottlieb, Richard & Oddo, Sandra, eds. The Solar Energy Directory. 376p. 1983. 50.00 (ISBN 0-8242-0680-0). Wilson.

Gottlieb, Robert & Wolt, Irene. Thinking Big: The Story of the Los Angeles Times, Its Publishers & Their Influence on Southern California. LC 76-51847. (Illus.). 1977. 15.00 o.p. (ISBN 0-399-11766-0). Putnam Pub Group.

Gottlieb, Robert, jt. auth. see Wiley, Peter.

Gottlieb, Stephen E. Systematic Litigation Planning. LC 78-8522. 64p. 1978. 8.00 (ISBN 0-87179-282-6). BNA.

Gottlieb, Vera. Chekhov & the Vaudeville: A Study of Chekhov's One-Act Plays. LC 81-18142. 280p. 1982. 44.50 (ISBN 0-521-24170-7). Cambridge U Pr.

Gottlieb, William P. Science Facts You Won't Believe. (Single Titles Ser.). (Illus.). 128p. (gr. 6 up). 1983. PLB 9.90 (ISBN 0-531-02875-5). Watts.

Gottman, John, jt. ed. see Asher, Steven.

Gottman, John M., jt. auth. see Williams, Esther A.

Gottman, John M., ed. see Glass, Gene V., et al.

Gotto, A. M., et al. Brain Peptides: A New Endocrinology. 1979. 73.00 (ISBN 0-444-80138-3). Elsevier.

Gotto, Antonio & Panoletti, Rodolfo, eds. Atherosclerosis Reviews, Vol. 6. LC 75-14582. 181p. 1979. text ed. 31.00 (ISBN 0-89004-276-4). Raven.

Gotto, Antonio M., jt. ed. see Paoletti, Rodolfo.

Gotto, Antonio M., Jr., jt. ed. see Paoletti, Rodolfo.

Gottschalk, Alexander, et al. Diagnostic Nuclear Medicine. (Golden's Diagnostic Radiology Ser: Section 20). 610p. 1976. 60.00 (ISBN 0-683-03669-6). Williams & Wilkins.

Gottschalk, Fruma, tr. see Gogol, Nikolay.

Gottschalk, Louis. Lafayette Joins the American Army. LC 37-38848. (Midway Reprint Ser.). 400p. 1974. pap. 15.00x o.s.i. (ISBN 0-226-30542-2). U of Chicago Pr.

Gottschalk, Louis M. Notes of a Pianist. (Music Reprint Ser.). 1979. Repr. of 1964 ed. 39.50 (ISBN 0-306-79508-6). Da Capo.

Gottschalk, S. S. Communities & Alternatives: An Exploration of the Limits of Planning. LC 74-22269. 169p. 1975. pap. 6.95x o.s.i. (ISBN 0-470-31908-9). Halsted Pr.

Gottschalk, Stephen. The Emergence of Christian Science in American Religious Life. LC 72-85530. 1974. 16.95 (ISBN 0-520-02308-0); pap. 4.95 (ISBN 0-520-03718-9, CAL 398). U of Cal Pr.

Gottschalk, Edward M. Graphic Communication Eighties' (Illus.). 200p. 1981. 27.95 (ISBN 0-13-363382-9). P-H.

Gottsche, K. M., et al. Synopsis Hepaticarum. 1967. Repr. of 1844 ed. 64.00 (ISBN 3-7682-0516-9). Lubrecht & Cramer.

Gottschling, E. see Siegel, C. L.

Gottsdanker, Robert. Experimenting in Psychology. (P-H Ser. in Experimental Psychology). (Illus.). 1978. ref. ed. 23.95 (ISBN 0-13-295501-6). P-H.

Gottsegen, Abby J., jt. ed. see Gottsegen, Gloria B.

Gottsegen, Gloria B., ed. Group Behavior: A Guide to Information Sources. LC 79-63744. (Psychology Information Guide Ser.: Vol. 2). 1979. 42.00x (ISBN 0-8103-1439-8). Gale.

Gottsegen, Gloria B. & Gottsegen, Abby J., eds. Humanistic Psychology: A Guide to Information Sources. (Psychology Information Guide Ser.: Vol. 6). 175p. 1980. 42.00x (ISBN 0-8103-1462-2). Gale.

Gottsegen, Katherine. Cooking Is an Act of Love. (Illus.). 165p. (Orig.). 1983. 8.95 (ISBN 0-686-38740-6). Buckminster Pr.

Gottshall, F. H. How to Make Colonial Furniture. 1971. 8.95 o.p. (ISBN 0-685-01122-4, 80266). Glencoe.

Gottshall, Franklin H. Provincial Furniture, Design & Construction. (Illus.). 1983. 24.95 (ISBN 0-517-54930-1). Crown.

Gottwald, Norman K., ed. The Bible & Liberation: Politics & Social Hermeneutics. 624p. (Orig.). 1983. 35.00 (ISBN 0-88344-043-1); pap. 18.95 (ISBN 0-88344-044-X). Orbis Bks.

Gotwald, William & Golden, Gale. Human Sexuality: Biological & Behavioral Foundations. 1981. text ed. 21.95x (ISBN 0-02-344170-4). Macmillan.

Gotz, Ignacio L. No Schools. 198p. 1971. pap. text ed. 10.95x (ISBN 0-8422-0163-7). Irvington.

Goudar, Le Chevalier Ange. Testament Politique De Louis Mandrin. Repr. of 1755 ed. 21.00 o.p. (ISBN 0-8287-0385-X). Clearwater Pub.

Goudas, C. L. & Pande, G. C., eds. Computers: Applications in Industry & Management. 1980. 59.75 (ISBN 0-444-86053-3). Elsevier.

Goude, Jean-Paul & Hayes, Harold. Jungle Fever. (Illus.). 144p. 1982. 32.50 (ISBN 0-937950-01-7). Xavier-Moreau.

Goudge, Elizabeth. The Blue Hills. 288p. 1976. lib. bdg. 15.95x (ISBN 0-89966-100-9). Buccaneer Bks.

--A Book of Faith. LC 76-35977. 288p. 1976. 8.95 (ISBN 0-698-10705-5, Coward). Putnam Pub Group.

--A City of Bells. 1937. 6.95 (ISBN 0-698-10055-7, Coward). Putnam Pub Group.

--The Joy of the Snow. LC 73-93757. 330p. 1974. 8.95 o.p. (ISBN 0-698-10605-9, Coward). Putnam Pub Group.

--Linnets & Valerians. (gr. 7 up). 1978. pap. 1.75 o.p. (ISBN 0-380-01934-5, 37838). Avon.

--Linnets & Valerians. 1981. lib. bdg. 12.95 (ISBN 0-8398-2750-4, Gregg). G K Hall.

--Little White Horse. (YA) 1978. pap. 1.95 o.p. (ISBN 0-380-01875-6, 52050). Avon.

--The Little White Horse. 1980. PLB 9.95 (ISBN 0-8398-2607-9, Gregg). G K Hall.

--The Lost Angel. (Illus.). 1971. 7.95 o.p. (ISBN 0-698-10220-7, Coward). Putnam Pub Group.

--Pattern of People. LC 78-12123. 1979. 9.95 o.s.i. (ISBN 0-698-10965-1, Coward). Putnam Pub Group.

Goudie, A. & Wilkinson, J. The Warm Desert Environment. LC 76-9731. (Topics in Geography Ser). (Illus.). 1977. 15.95 (ISBN 0-521-21330-4); pap. 8.95 (ISBN 0-521-29105-4); slides 27.95x (ISBN 0-521-21912-4). Cambridge U Pr.

Goudie, A. S. & Pye, K., eds. Chemical Sediments & Geomorphology. Date not set. price not set (ISBN 0-12-293480-6). Acad Pr.

Goudinoff, Peter, jt. auth. see Tobias, Sheila.

Goudiss, Maria H. Wordstar in Everyday English. 1983. pap. 9.95 (ISBN 0-8159-7221-0). Devin.

Goudket, Michael. Audiovisual Primer. rev. ed. LC 72-93755. (Illus.). 77p. 1974. pap. text ed. 3.50x (ISBN 0-8077-2437-8). Tchrs Coll.

Goudriaan, J., jt. auth. see Kozai, T.

Goudsblom, Johan. Dutch Society. 1966. pap. text ed. 2.95 (ISBN 0-394-30771-2). Phila Bk Co.

Goudsmit, Samuel, jt. auth. see Claiborne, Robert.

Goudsmit, Samuel A. Alsos. (History of Modern Physics 1800-1950 Ser.: Vol. 1). (Illus.). 1983. Repr. of 1947 ed. write for info limited edition (ISBN 0-938228-09-9). Tomash Pubs.

Goudy, Frederic W. Typologia: Studies in Type Design & Type Making with Comments on the Invention of Typography, the First Types, Legibility & Fine Printing. 1978. 24.50x (ISBN 0-520-03308-6); pap. 3.95 (ISBN 0-520-03278-0, CAL 334). U of Cal Pr.

Goudzwaard, Maurice B., jt. ed. see Weston, J. Fred.

Gouge, William M. Curse of Paper-Money & Banking. LC 68-28633. 1968. Repr. of 1833 ed. lib. bdg. 18.50x (ISBN 0-8371-0452-1, GOCP). Greenwood.

Gough, Aidan. Standards Relating to Non-Criminal Misbehavior. LC 76-14394. (IJA-ABA Juvenile Justice Standards Project Ser.). 96p. 1982. prof ref 14.50x (ISBN 0-88410-232-7); pap. 7.50x (ISBN 0-88410-832-5). Ballinger Pub.

Gough, Aidan, jt. ed. see Teitelbaum, Lee E.

Gough, Irene. Golden Lamb. LC 68-20643. (Foreign Lands Bks.). (gr. 3-6). 1968. PLB 3.95g (ISBN 0-8225-0360-3). Lerner Pubns.

Gough, Kathleen. Ten Times More Beautiful: The Rebuilding of Vietnam. LC 78-14890. 1978. 12.50 (ISBN 0-85345-464-7, CL-4647). Monthly Rev.

Gough, Kathleen & Sharma, Hari P., eds. Imperialism & Revolution in South Asia. LC 78-14890. (Illus.). 480p. 1973. pap. 6.95 (ISBN 0-85345-305-5, PB-3055). Monthly Rev.

Gough, Richard. The History of Myddle. 1979. Repr. text ed. 25.00x (ISBN 0-686-58501-1). Humanities.

Gough, S. B., et al. Coal Fuel Cycle: Effects on Aquatic Resources. (Illus.). 180p. 1983. 22.50x (ISBN 0-937948-01-2). AATEC Pubns.

Gough, W. James, ed. see Seiden, Rudolph.

Gouies. Intro. to Calligraphy. 1980. pap. 10.00 (ISBN 0-686-84621-4, Nonpareil Bks). Godine.

Gouin, Jacques, tr. see Swettenham, John & Wood, Herbert.

Goulart, Frances S. Caffeine. 240p. (Orig.). 1983. pap. 2.95 (ISBN 0-446-30581-2). Warner Bks.

--The Official Eating to Win Cookbook: Super Foods for Super Athletic Performance. LC 81-40806. 224p. 1983. 16.95 (ISBN 0-8128-2832-1). Stein & Day.

--One Hundred & One Allergy-Free Desserts. 1983. pap. 7.95 (ISBN 0-671-45785-3, Wallaby). S&S.

Goulart, Ron. After Things Fell Apart. 1977. Repr. of 1970 ed. lib. bdg. 10.00 o.p. (ISBN 0-8398-2368-1, Gregg). G K Hall.

--Big Bang. 160p. 1982. pap. 2.25 (ISBN 0-87997-748-5, UE1748). DAW Bks.

--Hail Hibbler. (Science Fiction Ser.). 1980. pap. 1.75 o.p. (ISBN 0-87997-557-1, UE1557). Daw Bks.

Goulart, Ron, ed. The Great British Detective. 1982. pap. 3.95 (ISBN 0-451-62089-5, ME2089, Ment). NAL.

Gould. Reading into Writing: A Rhetoric-Reader-Handbook. pap. text ed. 15.95 (ISBN 0-686-84580-3, EN73); instr's. manual avail. (EN74). HM.

Gould & Fredericks. Official Price Guide to Music Collectibles. (Collector Ser.). (Illus.). 400p. 1980. pap. 9.95 (ISBN 0-87637-187-X, 010-05). Hse of Collectibles.

Gould, Ann, jt. auth. see Gould, Dick.

Gould, Bruce. Bruce Gould on Commodoties, Vol. 3. 213p. 1977. 14.00 (ISBN 0-686-84396-7). B Gould Pubns.

--Bruce Gould on Commodoties, Vol. 4. 213p. 1978. 14.00 (ISBN 0-686-84397-5). B Gould Pubns.

--Bruce Gould on Commodoties, Vol. 5. 213p. 1978. 14.00 (ISBN 0-686-84398-3). B Gould Pubns.

--Bruce Gould on Commodoties, Vol. 6. 213p. 1979. 14.00 (ISBN 0-686-84399-1). B Gould Pubns.

Gould, Bruce G. Bruce Gould on Commodities. 213p. 1983. Vol. 1, Pt. 1 & 2. pap. 12.95 ea. Vol. 1, Pt. 1 (ISBN 0-918706-05-X). Vol. 1, Pt. 2 (ISBN 0-918706-07-6). B Gould Pubns.

--Bruce Gould on Commodities. 1983. Vol. 3, Pt. 1, 231 pgs. pap. 12.95 (ISBN 0-918706-10-6); Vol. 3, Pt. 2, 244 pgs. pap. 12.95 (ISBN 0-918706-12-2). B Gould Pubns.

--Bruce Gould on Commodities. (Illus.). 218p. 1983. pap. 12.95 ea. Vol. 2, Pt. 1 (ISBN 0-918706-08-4). Vol. 2, Pt. 2 (ISBN 0-918706-06-8). B Gould Pubns.

--Bruce Gould On Commodoties, Vol. 2. 213p. 1977. 14.00 (ISBN 0-686-84395-9). B Gould Pubns.

--Commodity Trading Manual. 128p. 1983. pap. 65.00 (ISBN 0-918706-11-4). B Gould Pubns.

--The Dow Jones-Irwin Guide to Commodities Trading. rev. ed. LC 80-70272. 360p. 1981. 27.50 o.p. (ISBN 0-87094-193-3). Dow Jones-Irwin.

--How to Make Money in Commodities. 2nd ed. (Illus.). 186p. (Orig.). 1982. pap. 7.95x (ISBN 0-918706-09-2). B Gould Pubns.

--The Most Dangerous Money Book Ever Written. 444p. (Orig.). 1983. pap. 100.00 (ISBN 0-918706-13-0). B Gould Pubns.

Gould, Carol, ed. Beyond Domination: New Perspectives on Women & Philosophy. 220p. 1983. text ed. 21.50x (ISBN 0-8476-7202-6); pap. text ed. 9.95x (ISBN 0-8476-7236-0). Rowman.

Gould, Carol C. & Wartofsky, Marx W. Women & Philosophy: Toward a Theory of Liberation. LC 75-33604. 1976. 8.95 o.p. (ISBN 0-399-11652-4); pap. 4.95 (ISBN 0-399-50362-5). Putnam Pub Group.

Gould, Charles. Mythical Monsters. LC 74-75474. 1969. Repr. of 1886 ed. 34.00 o.p. (ISBN 0-8103-3834-3). Gale.

Gould, Charles E., Jr. The Toad at Harrow: P. G. Wodehouse in Perspective. (Wodehouse Monograph: No. 3). 10p. (Orig.). 1982. pap. 7.50 (ISBN 0-87008-102-0). Heineman.

Gould, D. W. The Top: Universal Toy, Enduring Pastime. 1973. 7.50 o.p. (ISBN 0-517-50416-2, C N Potter Bks). Crown.

Gould, David J. Law & the Administrative Process: Analytic Frameworks for Understanding Public Policy Making. LC 79-63850. 1979. pap. text ed. 12.25 (ISBN 0-8191-0746-8). U Pr of Amer.

Gould, Dick. Tennis, Anyone? 3rd ed. LC 78-51946. (Illus.). 101p. 1978. text ed. 13.95 o.p. (ISBN 0-87484-439-8); pap. text ed. 4.95 (ISBN 0-87484-438-X). Mayfield Pub.

Gould, Dick & Gould, Ann. Conditioning for Tennis: A Guide for Players & Coaches. LC 81-86513. (Illus.). 192p. Date not set. pap. 6.95 (ISBN 0-88011-030-9). Leisure Pr.

Gould Editorial Dept. FLorida Criminal Law. 1982. 12.00 (ISBN 0-87526-188-4); slide rule study guide 4.00 (ISBN 0-87526-274-0). Gould.

--Michigan Motor Vehicle Laws: Slide Rule. 1982. slide rule study guide 4.00 (ISBN 0-87526-286-4). Gould.

Gould Editorial Staff. California Penal Code. 600p. 1982. text ed. 10.95 looseleaf (ISBN 0-87526-268-6); slide rule 4.00 (ISBN 0-87526-291-0). Gould.

--Chicago Municipal Code Handbook. 350p. (Annual update). 1982. loose-leaf bdg. 10.95 (ISBN 0-87526-264-3). Gould.

--Criminal Laws of Massachusetts. 400p. (Supplemented annually). looseleaf 15.00 (ISBN 0-87526-135-3); slide rule study guide 4.00 (ISBN 0-87526-275-9). Gould.

--Florida Motor Vehicle Laws. 350p. (Updated annually). loose-leaf bdg. 12.50 (ISBN 0-87526-256-2); slide rule study guide 4.00 (ISBN 0-87526-280-5). Gould.

--Illinois Criminal Law & Procedure. (Annual). text ed. 10.95x (ISBN 0-87526-199-X); slide rule study guide 4.00 (ISBN 0-87526-270-8). Gould.

--Illinois Vehicle Code. 525p. (Updated annually). loose-leaf bdg. 9.95 (ISBN 0-87526-259-7); slide guide study guide 4.00. Gould.

--Massachusetts Motor Vehicle Laws. (Supplemented annually). looseleaf 12.50x (ISBN 0-87526-231-7); slide rule study guide 4.00 (ISBN 0-87526-281-3). Gould.

--New Jersey Criminal Justice Code. 150p. looseleaf 13.50 (ISBN 0-87526-024-1); abridged ed. 8.95 (ISBN 0-87526-271-6); slide rule study guide 4.00 (ISBN 0-87526-272-4). Gould.

--New Jersey Motor Vehicle & Traffic Laws. (Supplemented annually). looseleaf 13.50x (ISBN 0-87526-232-5); slide rule study guide 4.00 (ISBN 0-87526-284-8). Gould.

--New York City Housing Maintenance Code. 300p. 1982. text ed. 15.00 looseleaf (ISBN 0-87526-278-3). Gould.

--New York Family Court Act. 450p. (Supplemented annually). looseleaf 11.00 (ISBN 0-87526-143-4); abridged ed. 6.95 (ISBN 0-87526-277-5). Gould.

--New York Law Digest. 330p. (Supplemented annually). looseleaf 7.50 (ISBN 0-87526-252-X). Gould.

--New York Multiple Dwelling Law. 300p. (Supplemented annually). 1982. 15.00x (ISBN 0-87526-285-6). Gould.

--New York Vehicle & Traffic Law. 400p. (Supplemented annually). looseleaf 10.00 (ISBN 0-87526-130-2). Gould.

--New York Vehicle & Traffic Law: Slide Rule. 1982. slide rule study guide 4.00 (ISBN 0-87526-288-0). Gould.

Gould Editorial Staff, ed. Michigan Motor Vehicle Laws: With Uniform Traffic Code. 450p. text ed. 12.50 (ISBN 0-87526-253-8); slide rule study guide 4.00 (ISBN 0-87526-282-1). Gould.

--Michigan Penal Code. 2nd ed. 400p. text ed. 11.50 (ISBN 0-87526-200-7); slide rule study guide 4.00 (ISBN 0-87526-286-4). Gould.

--New York Environmental Conservation Law, 2 vols. 1008p. (Supplemented annually). Set. text ed. 18.50 (ISBN 0-87526-255-4). Gould.

Gould, Elaine & Gould, Loren. Arts & Crafts for Physically & Mentally Disabled: The How, What & Why of It. (Illus.). 368p. 1978. spiral 38.00x (ISBN 0-398-03783-3). C C Thomas.

Gould, Eric. Reading into Writing: A Rhetoric, Reader, & Handbook. 1982. pap. text ed. 16.95 (ISBN 0-395-32607-9). HM.

Gould, F. J. Life Story of Auguste Comte. 54p. 1948. pap. 3.00 (ISBN 0-686-96421-7). Am Atheist.

Gould, F. J., jt. auth. see Eppen, Gary D.

Gould, F. R. Specialty Papers. LC 76-24144. (Chemical Technology Review: No. 78). (Illus.). 1977. 32.00 o.p. (ISBN 0-8155-0639-2). Noyes.

Gould, Frank W. Grass Systematics. LC 68-25214. 1968. text ed. 24.00 o.p. (ISBN 0-07-023848-0, C). McGraw.

Gould, Frank W. & Shaw, Robert B. Grass Systematics. 2nd ed. LC 82-45894. (Illus.). 416p. 1983. pap. text ed. 15.00 (ISBN 0-89096-153-0). Tex A&M Univ Pr.

Gould, Frederick J. The Agnostic Island: A Tale. Wolff, Robert L., ed. Bd. with The Individualist. Mallock, W. H. Repr. of 1899 ed. LC 75-1536. (Victorian Fiction Ser.). 1975. lib. bdg. 66.00 o.s.i. (ISBN 0-8240-1608-4). Garland Pub.

Gould, G., jt. auth. see Chilver, P.

Gould, Gerald. Journey, Odes & Sonnets. 1921. text ed. 19.50x (ISBN 0-686-83603-0). Elliots Bks.

Gould, Geraldine & Wolfe, Ithmer. How to Organize & Maintain the Library Picture - Pamphlet File. LC 68-27154. (Illus.). 1968. 7.00 o.p. (ISBN 0-379-00357-0). Oceana.

Gould, H. & Matthews, H. R. Separation Methods for Nucleic Acids & Oligonucleotides. (Laboratory Techniques in Biochemistry & Molecular Biology: Vol. 4, Pt. 2). 1976. 23.50 (ISBN 0-444-10868-8, North-Holland). Elsevier.

Gould, Heywood. Complete Book of Camping. (RL 7). pap. 1.25 o.p. (ISBN 0-451-07009-7, 7009, Sig). NAL.

Gould, Howard E., ed. see Livy.

Gould, J. Sutherland. How to Publicize Yourself, Your Family, & Your Organization. (Illus.). 176p. 1983. 15.95 (ISBN 0-13-430645-7); pap. 7.95 (ISBN 0-13-430637-6). P-H.

Gould, James. Marketing Anthology. (Illus.). 1979. pap. text ed. 12.50 (ISBN 0-8299-0255-4). West Pub.

Gould, James A. Classic Philosophical Questions. 4th ed. 704p. 1982. pap. text ed. 17.95 (ISBN 0-675-09910-2). Additional Supplements May Be Obtained From Publisher. Merrill.

Gould, James A. & Truitt, Willis H. Political Ideologies. 576p. 1973. pap. text ed. 15.95x (ISBN 0-02-345470-9, 34547). Macmillan.

Gould, James A., jt. auth. see Bierman, Arthur K.

Gould, James A., jt. auth. see Copi, Irving M.

Gould, James A., jt. auth. see Dewey, Robert E.

Gould, Jay M. Input-Output Databases. 1978. lib. bdg. 32.50 o.s.i. (ISBN 0-8240-7058-5). Garland Pub.

Gould, Jean & Lorena, Hickok. Walter Reuther: Labor's Rugged Individualist. LC 71-39225. 1972. 8.95 o.p. (ISBN 0-396-06409-4). Dodd.

Gould, Joan. Otherborn. 160p. (gr. 6-8). 1980. 8.95 o.p. (ISBN 0-698-20497-2, Coward). Putnam Pub Group.

Gould, John. Greek Tragedy. pap. cancelled o.s.i. (ISBN 0-14-022100-X, Pelican). Penguin.

--John Gould's Birds. (Illus.). 240p. 1981. write for info. (ISBN 0-89479-088-9). A & W Pubs.

Gould, John & Kolb, Annette. Colourful Birdlife. LC 75-84770. (World in Color Ser.). (Illus.). 50p. 1976. 3.95 o.p. (ISBN 0-88254-391-1). Hippocrene Bks.

Gould, Joseph E. Chautauqua Movement. LC 61-8734. (Illus.). 1961. 29.50x (ISBN 0-87395-003-8); pap. 10.95x (ISBN 0-87395-004-6). State U NY Pr.

Gould, Judith. Sins. 1982. pap. 3.95 (ISBN 0-451-11859-6, AE1859, Sig). NAL.

Gould, Julius & Kolb, W. J. UNESCO Dictionary of the Social Sciences. LC 64-20307. 1964. 40.00 (ISBN 0-02-917490-2). Free Pr.

Gould, Karen L. Claude Simon's Mythic Muse. 16.00. French Lit.

Gould, Lawrence, ed. Drug Treatment of Cardiac Arrhythmias. LC 82-83705. 448p. 1983. monograph 49.50 (ISBN 0-87993-190-6). Futura Pub.

Gould, Leroy C., jt. ed. see Walker, Charles A.

Gould, Lewis L. Reform & Regulations: American Politics, 1900-1916. LC 77-21058. (Critical Episodes in American Policy Ser.). 1978. pap. text ed. 10.95 (ISBN 0-471-31914-7). Wiley.

--The Spanish-American War & President McKinley. LC 82-13672. (Illus.). x, 166p. 1982. pap. text ed. 4.95x (ISBN 0-7006-0227-5). Univ Pr KS.

Gould, Lois. A Sea-Change. 1977. pap. 1.95 o.p. (ISBN 0-380-01695-8, 33704). Avon.

--A Sea-Change. LC 76-13579. 1976. 6.95 o.p. (ISBN 0-671-22326-7). S&S.

Gould, Loren, jt. auth. see Gould, Elaine.

Gould, Marjorie, jt. auth. see Larson, Carroll B.

Gould, Murray, jt. auth. see Hill, George R.

Gould, P. & Olsson, G., eds. A Search for Common Ground. 1982. 25.00x (ISBN 0-85086-093-8, Pub by Pion England). Methuen Inc.

Gould, Peter. The Complete Taupo Fishing Guide. (Illus.). 248p. 1982. 19.95 (ISBN 0-00-216969-X, Pub. by W Collins Australia). Intl Schol Bk Serv.

Gould, Phillip L. Static Analysis of Shell Structure. LC 76-47142. (Illus.). 432p. 1977. 47.95x (ISBN 0-669-00966-0). Lexington Bks.

Gould, R. A. Living Archaeology. LC 79-20788. (New Studies in Archaeology). (Illus.). 1980. 32.50 (ISBN 0-521-23093-4); pap. 10.95 (ISBN 0-521-29959-4). Cambridge U Pr.

Gould, R. G. & Lum, L. F., eds. Communication Satellite Systems: An Overview of the Technology. LC 75-39327. 1976. 21.95 (ISBN 0-87942-065-0). Inst Electrical.

Gould, Roger. Transformations. 1978. 9.95 o.p. (ISBN 0-671-22521-9). S&S.

Gould, Roger L. Transformations. 1979. 6.75 (ISBN 0-671-25066-3, Touchstone Bks). S&S.

Gould, Rupert T. The Case for the Sea Serpent. LC 72-75791. 1969. Repr. of 1930 ed. 30.00x (ISBN 0-8103-3833-5). Gale.

Gould, S. H., tr. see Behnke, H., et al.

Gould, Shirley. The Challenge of Achievement: Helping Your Child Succeed. LC 78-53400. 1983. pap. 4.95 (ISBN 0-8015-3386-4, Hawthorn). Dutton.

Gould, Shirley G. Teenagers: The Continuing Challenge. 1977. 7.95 (ISBN 0-8015-5800-X, Hawthorn); pap. 5.95 (ISBN 0-8015-5801-8, 0577-180, Hawthorn). Dutton.

Gould Staff Editors. New York Estates, Powers & Trusts Law. 150p. (Supplemented annually). looseleaf 7.50 (ISBN 0-87526-140-X). Gould.

Gould, Stephen J. Ever Since Darwin: Reflections in Natural History. 1979. pap. 4.95 (ISBN 0-393-00917-3). Norton.

--Hen's Teeth & Horse's Toes: Further Reflections in Natural History. (Illus.). 1983. 15.50 (ISBN 0-393-01716-8). Norton.

--The Mismeasure of Man. (Illus.). 1981. 14.95 (ISBN 0-393-01489-4). Norton.

--The Mismeasure of Man. 352p. 1983. pap. 5.95 (ISBN 0-393-30056-0). Norton.

Gould, T. & Herington, J., eds. Greek Tragedy. LC 76-8156. (Yale Classical Studies: No. 25). 1977. 42.50 (ISBN 0-521-21112-3). Cambridge U Pr.

Gould, W. T. Planning the Location of Schools: Ankole District, Uganda. (Illus.). 88p. (Orig.). 1973. pap. 10.50 o.p. (ISBN 92-803-1057-7, U463, UNESCO). Unipub.

Gould, Wilbur A. Tomato Production, Processing & Quality Evaluation. 2nd ed. (Illus.). 1983. text ed. 49.00 (ISBN 0-87055-426-3). AVI.

Goulden, Clyde E. Systematics & Evolution of the Moinidae. LC 68-54558. (Transactions Ser.: Vol. 58, Pt. 6). (Illus.). 1968. pap. 1.50 o.p. (ISBN 0-87169-586-3). Am Philos.

Goulden, J. C. Korea: The Untold Story of the War. 736p. 1983. pap. 12.95 (ISBN 0-07-023580-5, GB). McGraw.

Goulden, Joseph, jt. auth. see Dickson, Paul.

Goulden, Joseph C. The Million Dollar Lawyer's. 336p. 1981. pap. 2.95 o.p. (ISBN 0-425-05149-8). Berkley Pub.

--The Million Dollar Lawyers. LC 78-4680. 1978. 10.95 o.p. (ISBN 0-399-12239-7). Putnam Pub Group.

Goulden, P. D. Environmental Pollution Analysis. 248p. 1980. 42.95 (ISBN 0-471-25736-2, Pub. by Wiley Heyden). Wiley.

Goulden, Shirley. Royal Book of Ballet. LC 64-16319. (Illus.). (gr. 5 up). 1964. 7.95 (ISBN 0-695-90040-4, Dist. by Caroline Hse). Follett.

Gouldman, W. Clyde & Hess, Amy M. Virginia Forms. 1978. 65.00 (ISBN 0-87215-205-7). Michie-Bobbs.

Gould-Marks, Beryl. Preserves & How to Make Them. 1972. 12.50 o.p. (ISBN 0-571-09837-1). Transatlantic.

Gouldner, Alvin W. The Coming Crisis of Western Sociology. LC 77-75252. 528p. 1980. pap. 8.95 (ISBN 0-465-01279-5, TB-5066). Basic.

--For Sociology: Renewal & Critique in Sociology Today. LC 73-82891. 480p. 1974. text ed. 12.95x o.s.i. (ISBN 0-465-02495-5). Basic.

--Patterns of Industrial Bureaucracy: A Case Study of Modern Factory Administration. 1954. 14.95 (ISBN 0-02-912730-0); pap. text ed. 7.95 (ISBN 0-02-912740-8). Free Pr.

Gouldner, Helen. Teacher's Pets, Troublemakers, & Nobodies: Black Children in Elementary School. LC 78-53660. (Contributions in Afro-American & African Studies: No. 41). (Illus.). 1978. lib. bdg. 25.00 (ISBN 0-313-20417-9, GOE/). Greenwood.

Goulet, Denis. Mexico: Development Strategies for the Future. LC 82-40379. 208p. 1983. text ed. 16.95 (ISBN 0-268-01355-1); pap. text ed. 8.95 (ISBN 0-268-01356-X). U of Notre Dame Pr.

Goulet, Rosalina M., jt. auth. see Ramos, Teresita.

Gounod, Charles. Autobiographical Reminiscences: With Family Letters & Notes on Music. LC 68-16235. (Music Ser.). 1970. Repr. of 1896 ed. lib. bdg. 27.50 (ISBN 0-306-71081-1). Da Capo.

Gounod, Charles F. Mozart's Don Giovanni: A Commentary. LC 78-125050. (Music Ser). 1970. Repr. of 1895 ed. lib. bdg. 19.50 (ISBN 0-306-70015-8). Da Capo.

Gouran, Dennis S. Making Decisions in Groups. 1982. pap. text ed. 10.95x (ISBN 0-673-15386-X). Scott F.

Gourd, L. M. An Introduction to Engineering Materials. 1982. pap. text ed. write for info. E Arnold.

Gourdin, M. Formalisme Langrangien et Lois de Symetrie. (Cour & Documents de Mathematiques & de Physique Ser.). 108p. (Fr). 1967. 32.00x (ISBN 0-677-50070-X). Gordon.

--Langrangian Formalism & Symmetry Laws. (Documents on Modern Physics Ser). 108p. 1969. 24.00x (ISBN 0-677-30070-0). Gordon.

Goure, Leon, et al. The Emerging Strategic Environment: Implications for Ballistic Missile Defense. LC 79-53108. 75p. 1979. 6.50 (ISBN 0-89549-008-0). Inst Foreign Policy Anal.

Gourevitch, D. & Stadler, E. M. Premiers Textes Litteraires. 2nd ed. LC 74-83346. 242p. 1975. text ed. 11.50x (ISBN 0-471-00811-7). Wiley.

Gourevitch, Peter A. Paris & the Provinces: The Politics of Local Government Reform in France. LC 79-64666. 256p. 1981. 23.75x (ISBN 0-520-03971-8). U of Cal Pr.

Gourfinkel, Nina. Gorky. Feshbach, Ann, tr. LC 75-11423. (Illus.). 192p. 1975. Repr. of 1960 ed. lib. bdg. 17.75x (ISBN 0-8371-8190-9, GOGO). Greenwood.

--Lenin. Thornton, Maurice, tr. LC 75-11424. (Illus.). 189p. 1975. Repr. of 1961 ed. lib. bdg. 19.00x (ISBN 0-8371-8191-7, GOLE). Greenwood.

Gourgues, Harold W., Jr. Financial Planning Handbook. 416p. 1983. 34.95 (ISBN 0-13-316398-9). NY Inst Finance.

Gourieres, D. le see Le Gourieres, D.

Gourlay, A. R. & Watson, G. A. Computational Methods for Matrix Eigenproblems. LC 73-2783. 1979. pap. text ed. 14.95x (ISBN 0-471-27586-7, Pub. by Wiley-Interscience). Wiley.

Gourlay, Alastair & Walsh, James. Fifty 1K-2K Games for the Timex-Sinclair 1000 & ZX81. 1983. text ed. 16.95 (ISBN 0-8359-1979-X); pap. text ed. 10.95 (ISBN 0-8359-1978-1). Reston.

Gourlay, Carol. Computers & Mathemtics. LC 82-50387. (Visual Science Ser.). PLB 13.00 (ISBN 0-382-06662-6). Silver.

Gourley, R., jt. auth. see Yeager, D.

Gourman, Jack. The Gourman Report: A Rating of Graduate & Professional Programs in American & International Universities. 2nd ed. LC 82-73149. 163p. (Orig.). 1983. pap. 24.95 (ISBN 0-918192-03-X). Natl Ed Stand.

--The Gourman Report: A Rating of Undergraduate Programs in American & International Universities. 4th ed. LC 82-73150. 165p. 1983. pap. 24.95 (ISBN 0-918192-04-8). Natl Ed Stand.

Gourvish, T. R. Railways in the British Economy: 1830-1914. (Studies in Economic & Social History). 64p. 1980. pap. text ed. 5.50x (ISBN 0-333-28365-1, Pub. by Macmillan England). Humanities.

Gouwenius, Peder. Power to the People: South Africa in Struggle, a Pictorial History, Pt. 1. (Illus.). 96p. (Orig.). 1981. write for info. (ISBN 0-905762-72-X, Pub. by Zed Pr England); pap. 8.95 (ISBN 0-905762-66-5, Pub. by Zed Pr England). Lawrence Hill.

Gouy, Louis P. De see De Gouy, Louis P.

Govan, Christine, jt. auth. see West, Emmy.

Govan, Christine N. Rachel Jackson: Tennessee Girl. (Childhood of Famous Americans Ser). (Illus.). (gr. 3-7). 1955. 3.95 o.p. (ISBN 0-672-50152-X). Bobbs.

Gove, Samuel, ed. Higher Education Policy. (Orig.). 1981. pap. 6.00 (ISBN 0-918592-48-8). Policy Studies.

Gove, Samuel & Wirt, Frederick, eds. Critical Issues in Educational Policy. 1976. pap. 6.00 (ISBN 0-918592-15-1). Policy Studies.

Gove, Samuel K. & Wirt, Frederick M., eds. Political Science & School Politics: The Princes & Pundits. (A Policy Studies Organization Bk). 1976. 17.95x (ISBN 0-669-00739-0, Dist. by Transaction Bks). Lexington Bks.

Gove, Walter, jt. ed. see Langland, Elizabeth.

Gove, Walter R. & Carpenter, G. Russell. The Fundamental Connection Between Nature & Nurture: A Review of the Evidence. LC 80-8961. 320p. 1981. 28.95x (ISBN 0-669-04483-0). Lexington Bks.

Government Consultation on an International Convention for the Control of the Spread of Major Communicable Fish Diseases, Scotland, 1974. Control of the Spread of Major Communicable Fish Diseases: Report. (FAO Fisheries Reports: No. 149). 20p. 1974. pap. 7.50 (ISBN 0-686-93214-5, F792, FAO). Unipub.

Government Consultation on Codes of Practice for Fish & Fishery Products, Rome, 1974. Report. (FAO Fisheries Report: No. 155). 5p. 1976. pap. 10.50 (ISBN 0-685-68965-4, F796, FAO). Unipub.

Government Documents Round Table, ed. Directory of Government Document Collections & Librarians. LC 78-5459. 1981. pap. text ed. 32.50 o.p. (ISBN 0-912380-49-7). Cong Info.

Government Printing Office. Prospector, Cowhand & Sodbuster. 1967. 2.00 (ISBN 0-686-95758-X). Jefferson Natl.

Govers, T. R. & De Heer, F. J. The Physics of Electronic & Atomic Collisions. 1972. 60.50 (ISBN 0-444-10361-9, North-Holland). Elsevier.

Govett, G. J. Rock Geochemistry in Mineral Exploration. (Handbook of Mineral Exploration Geology Ser.: Vol. 3). 462p. 1982. 100.00 (ISBN 0-444-42021-5). Elsevier.

Govett, G. J. & Govett, M. H. World Mineral Supplies. (Developments in Economic Geology: Vol. 3). 1976. 66.00 (ISBN 0-444-41366-9). Elsevier.

Govett, M. H., jt. auth. see Govett, G. J.

Govier, George W. & Aziz, Khalid. The Flow of Complex Mixture in Pipes. LC 77-2591. 842p. 1977. Repr. of 1972 ed. 50.50 (ISBN 0-88275-547-1). Krieger.

Govier, Katherine. Going Through the Motions. 256p. 1983. 13.95 (ISBN 0-312-33135-5). St Martin.

Govinda, L. Anagarika. Foundations of Tibetan Mysticism. (Illus.). 1970. pap. 5.95 (ISBN 0-87728-064-9). Weiser.

Govinda, Lama A. The Way of the White Clouds. (Clear Light Ser). (Illus.). 1970. pap. 9.95 (ISBN 0-394-73005-4). Shambhala Pubns.

Govindarajulu, Zakkula. The Sequential Statistical Analysis of Hypothesis Testing, Point & Interval Estimation, & Decision Theory. LC 80-68287. (The American Sciences Press Ser. in Mathematical & Management Sciences: Vol. 5). 1982. text ed. 48.50 (ISBN 0-935950-02-8). Am Sciences Pr.

Govindjee, ed. Photosynthesis: Vol. 1: Energy Conversion by Plants & Bacteria. (Cell Biology: A Series of Monographs). 690p. 1982. 79.00 (ISBN 0-12-294301-5). Acad Pr.

--Photosynthesis: Vol. 2, Carbon Metabolism and Plant Productivity. (Cell Biology: Monographs). 1983. 59.00 (ISBN 0-12-294302-3). Acad Pr.

Govindjee, G., jt. auth. see Rabinowitch, Eugene.

Govoni, Norman A. & Deneault, Henry N. Cases in Marketing. 2nd ed. LC 82-6076. (Grid Series in Marketing). 274p. 1982. text ed. 10.95 (ISBN 0-88244-252-X). Grid Pub.

Govoni, Norman A., jt. ed. see Joyce, George.

Gow, A. S., tr. see Theocritus.

Gow, Andrew S. & Page, D. L. Greek Anthology: Hellenistic Epigrams, 2 Vols. 1965. Set. 150.00 set (ISBN 0-521-05124-X). Cambridge U Pr.

Gow, Andrew S., ed. see Horace.

Gow, David D., jt. ed. see Morss, Elliott R.

Gow, James. Short History of Greek Mathematics. LC 68-21639. 1968. 14.95 (ISBN 0-8284-0218-3). Chelsea Pub.

Gow, Kathleen. Yes, Virginia, There Is Right & Wrong. (Illus.). 256p. 1982. 13.95 o.p. (ISBN 0-920510-68-X, Pub. by Personal Lib). Dodd.

Gowa, Joanne & Wessell, Nils H. Ground Rules: Soviet & American Involvement in Regional Conflicts. (Philadelphia Policy Papers). 1982. pap. 3.95 (ISBN 0-910191-05-0). For Policy Res.

Gowan, John C. & Bruch, Catherine B. Academically Talented Student & Guidance. (Guidance Monograph). 1970. pap. 2.60 o.p. (ISBN 0-395-10850-0, 9-78853). HM.

Gowan, John C., et al. Educating the Ablest. 2nd ed. LC 78-61876. 1979. pap. text ed. 15.50 (ISBN 0-87581-235-X). Peacock Pubs.

Gowar, Antonia. Cashing In. 1983. pap. 3.50 (ISBN 0-441-09231-4, Pub. by Charter Bks). Ace Bks.

Gowar, R. G., ed. Developments in Fire Protection of Offshore Platforms, Vol. 1. (Illus.). 1978. text ed. 47.25 (ISBN 0-85334-792-1, Pub. by Applied Sci England). Elsevier.

Gowda, H. H., jt. auth. see Wells, Henry.

Gowdy, Spenser O., jt. auth. see Costello, John J.

Gowen, James A. English Review Manual. 2nd ed. 1970. text ed. 10.95 o.p. (ISBN 0-07-023881-2, C); pap. text ed. 10.95 o.p. (ISBN 0-07-023880-4). McGraw.

--English Review Manual: A Program for Self-Instruction. 3rd rev. ed. Talkington, William A., ed. 1980. pap. text ed. 14.95 (ISBN 0-07-023895-2); tchr's. manual & key 10.95 (ISBN 0-07-023897-9). McGraw.

--Progress in Writing: A Learning Program. 230p. 1973. pap. text ed. 13.95 (ISBN 0-07-023859-6, C); instructor's guide 16.00 (ISBN 0-07-023861-8); tests 7.95 (ISBN 0-07-023870-7). McGraw.

Gower, A. M. Water Quality in Catchment Ecosystems. LC 79-42907. (Institution of Environmental Sciences Ser.). 335p. 1980. 54.95x (ISBN 0-471-27692-8, Pub. by Wiley-Interscience). Wiley.

Gower, Charlotte D. Northern & Southern Affiliations of Antillean Culture. LC 28-7691. 1927. pap. 8.00 (ISBN 0-527-00534-7). Kraus Repr.

Gower, John. Selected Poetry. Weinberg, Carole, ed. 192p. 1982. pap. text ed. 8.50x (ISBN 0-85635-415-5, 80679, Pub. by Carcanet New Pr England). Humanities.

Gower Publications, ed. Guide to Commercial Property Development. 550p. 1974. 26.95x o.p. (ISBN 0-8464-0459-1). Beekman Pubs.

Gowers, Ernest, ed. see Fowler, H. W.

Gowers, Ernest, ed. see Fowler, Henry W.

Gowin, D., jt. auth. see Millman, Jason.

Gowin, Emmet. Photographs. 1976. 17.50 o.p. (ISBN 0-394-40195-6); pap. 8.95 o.p. (ISBN 0-394-73249-9). Knopf.

Gowing, Lawrence, ed. The Encyclopedia of Visual Arts, 2 vols. 1983. 100.00 set (ISBN 0-13-276543-8). P-H.

Gowing, Margaret. Independence & Deterrence-Britain & Atomic Energy 1945-52, Vol. 1: Policy Making. LC 74-81481. 500p. 1975. 36.00 (ISBN 0-312-41230-4). St Martin.

--Independence & Deterrence-Britain & Atomic Energy, 1945-52, Vol. 2: Policy Execution. LC 74-81481. 560p. 1975. 36.00 (ISBN 0-312-41265-7). St Martin.

Gowing, Margaret & Arnold, Lorna. The Atomic Bomb. (Science in a Social Context Ser.). 1979. pap. text ed. 3.95 o.p. (ISBN 0-408-71311-9). Butterworth.

Gowing, Mary. Virginia Beyond the Blue Ridge. LC 74-84705. 183p. 1974. 12.95 o.p. (ISBN 0-89227-020-9). Commonwealth Pr.

Gowing, Roland. Roger Cotes: Natural Philosopher. LC 82-1154. (Illus.). 200p. Date not set. 29.50 (ISBN 0-521-23741-6). Cambridge U Pr.

Gowland, D. A. Methodist Secessions. 192p. 1979. 24.00 (ISBN 0-7190-1335-6). Manchester.

Gowland, D. H. Modern Economic Analysis. new ed. 224p. (Orig.). 1982. text ed. write for info.; pap. write for info. (ISBN 0-408-10772-3). Butterworth.

Gowland, David H., ed. Modern Economic Analysis. (Illus.). 1979. 12.50 (ISBN 0-408-10632-8). Butterworth.

Gowland, Peter. Electronic Flash Simplified. (Illus.). 96p. 1975. pap. 4.95 o.p. (ISBN 0-8174-0185-7, Amphoto); Spanish Ed. pap. 6.95 o.p. (ISBN 0-8174-0324-8). Watson-Guptill.

--Gowland's Guide to Glamour Photography. (Illus.). 160p. 1972. 9.95 (ISBN 0-517-50189-9). Crown.

Goy, Robert W. & McEwen, Bruce S., eds. Sexual Differentiation of the Brain. (Illus.). 1980. text ed. 22.00x (ISBN 0-262-07077-4). MIT Pr.

Goya, Francisco. Disasters of War. (Illus., Bilingual). (YA) (gr. 7-12). 1968. pap. 4.50 (ISBN 0-486-21872-4). Dover.

Goyal, B. R. Educating Harijans. 1982. 11.50x (ISBN 0-8364-0863-2, Pub by Academic India). South Asia Bks.

Goyal, Bhagwat S. The Strategy of Survival. 244p. 1975. text ed. 13.00x (ISBN 0-391-02714-X, Pub. by UBS India). Humanities.

Goyder, D. G., jt. auth. see Neale, Alan D.

Goyder, Jane, jt. auth. see Lowe, Philip.

Goyen, William. A Book of Jesus. 1974. pap. 1.25 o.p. (ISBN 0-451-06217-5, Y6217, Sig). NAL.

--The House of Breath. LC 74-23987. 1975. pap. 4.95 (ISBN 0-394-73053-4). Random.

Goyer, Doreen S. & Domschke, Eliane. The Handbook of National Population Censuses: Latin America & the Caribbean, North America & Oceania. LC 82-9390. (Illus.). 736p. 1983. lib. bdg. 75.00 (ISBN 0-313-21352-6, GHP/). Greenwood.

Goyette, Richert E. Digestive & Hepatobiliary Pathology & Pathophysiology Case Studies. 1977. spiral bdg. 12.00 o.p. (ISBN 0-87488-078-5). Med Exam.

Goytortua, Jesus. Lluvia Roja. Walsh, Donald D., ed. (Orig., Span.). 1962. pap. text ed. 10.95 (ISBN 0-13-538876-7). P-H.

Goyvaerts, D. L. Present Day Historical & Comparative Linguistics, No. 2. 1980. pap. text ed. write for info. o.p. (ISBN 0-391-01599-0). Humanities.

Goyvaerts, Didier & Pullum, Geoffrey, eds. Essays on the Sound Pattern of English. (Illus.). 1975. text ed. 94.00x (ISBN 0-686-86088-8). Humanities.

Gozna, Eric R. & Harrington, Ian J. Biomechanics of Musculoskeletal Injury. (Illus.). 242p. 1982. text ed. 33.00 (ISBN 0-683-03728-5). Williams & Wilkins.

Graa, Albert, ed. Vocabularium Pharmaceuticum. 2nd ed. 125p. 1964. text ed. 13.50x (ISBN 0-8002-3024-8). Intl Pubns Serv.

Graaf, Frank de see De Graaf, Frank.

Graaf, G. A. de. Literatuur over het orgel -- Literature on the Organ - Literatur uber die Orgel. (Bibliotheca Organologica Ser.: Vol. 51). (Dutch, Eng., Ger.). 1957. wrappers 15.00 o.s.i. (ISBN 90-6027-229-3, Pub. by Frits Knuf Netherlands). Pendragon NY.

Graaskamp, James A. Fundamentals of Real Estate Development. LC 81-51563. (Development Component Ser.). (Illus.). 31p. 1980. pap. 10.00 (ISBN 0-87420-601-4, D16). Urban Land.

Grabar, Andre, jt. auth. see Muraro, Michelangelo.

Grabar, Oleg. The Formation of Islamic Art. LC 72-75193. (Illus.). 352p. 1973. 27.50x o.p. (ISBN 0-300-01505-4); pap. 14.95x (ISBN 0-300-02187-9). Yale U Pr.

Grabar, Oleg, ed. Muqarnas: An Annual on Islamic Art & Architecture, Volume I. (Illus.). 246p. 1983. 27.50x (ISBN 0-300-02837-7). Yale U Pr.

Grabar, Pierre & Miescher, Peter A., eds. Immunopathology of Malignacy: Fourth International Symposium on Immunopathology. (Illus.). 468p. 1966. 89.50 o.p. (ISBN 0-8089-0626-7). Grune.

--Mechanisms of Inflammation Induced by Immune Reactions: Fifth International Symposium of Immunopathology. (Illus.). 425p. 1968. 89.50 o.p. (ISBN 0-8089-0627-5). Grune.

Grabb, William C. & Myers, M. Bert, eds. Skin Flaps. LC 74-20219. 440p. 1975. 75.00 (ISBN 0-316-32267-9). Little.

Grabb, William X. & Smith, James W., eds. Plastic Surgery. 3rd ed. 1980. text ed. 38.50 (ISBN 0-316-32269-5); pap. text ed. 32.50 (ISBN 0-316-32268-7). Little.

Grabendorff, Wolf & Krumwiede, Heinrich. Change in Central America: Internal & External Dimensions. (Special Studies in Latin America & the Caribbean). 175p. 1983. lib. bdg. 16.50x (ISBN 0-86531-609-0). Westview.

Graber, Alan L., et al. Diabetes & Pregnancy: A Guide for the Prospective Mother with Diabetes. Pearson, Patricia C., ed. LC 73-6653. (Illus.). 80p. 1973. pap. 2.95x (ISBN 0-8265-1192-9). Vanderbilt U Pr.

Graber, Ana M., jt. auth. see Rosenbusch, Maria H.

Graber, B., ed. Circumvaginal Musculature & Sexual Function. (Illus.). x, 126p. 1982. 29.50 (ISBN 3-8055-3017-X). S Karger.

Graber, Benjamin, jt. auth. see Kline-Graber, Georgia.

Graber, C. D. Rapid Diagnostic Methods in Medical Microbiology. LC 77-113627. 343p. 1970. 18.00 (ISBN 0-683-03741-2). Krieger.

Graber, Doris A., ed. The President & the Public. LC 82-3032. 324p. 1982. text ed. 17.50 (ISBN 0-89727-038-X); pap. text ed. 7.95 (ISBN 0-89727-042-8). Inst Study Human.

Graber, Edith E., jt. auth. see Colton, David L.

Graber, Edward A., jt. auth. see Barber, Hugh R.

Graber, T. M. Orthodontics: Principles & Practice. 3rd ed. LC 73-186950. (Illus.). 953p. 1972. text ed. 39.50 (ISBN 0-7216-4182-2). Saunders.

Graber, T. M. & Swain, Brainerd F., eds. Current Orthodontic Concepts & Techniques, 2 vols. 2nd ed. LC 74-11686. (Illus.). 1137p. 1975. Vol. 1. text ed. 49.50 o.p. (ISBN 0-7216-4187-3); Vol. 2. text ed. 49.50 o.p. (ISBN 0-7216-4188-1); Set. text ed. 99.00 o.p. (ISBN 0-7216-4189-X). Saunders.

Grabert, H. Projection Operator Techniques in Nonequilibrium Statistical Mechanics. (Springer Tratcs in Modern physics Ser.: Vol. 95). (Illus.). 220p. 1982. 31.00 (ISBN 0-387-11635-4). Springer-Verlag.

Grabes, Herbert. The Mutable Glass: Mirror Imagery in Titles & Texts of the Middle Ages & the English Renaissance. Collier, Gordon, tr. LC 82-4263. (Illus.). 532p. 79.00 (ISBN 0-521-22203-6). Cambridge U Pr.

Grabill, Paul. Youth's a Stuff Will Not Endure. 1978. pap. 1.75 o.p. (ISBN 0-380-01938-8, 37879). Avon.

Grable, Ron, jt. auth. see Olney, Ross R.

Grabmuller, H. Singular Perturbation Techniques Applied to Integro-Differential Equations. (Research Notes in Mathematics: No. 20). 148p. (Orig.). 1978. pap. text ed. 20.95 (ISBN 0-273-08409-7). Pitman Pub MA.

Grabner, Doris A. Mass Media & American Politics. LC 80-10836. 320p. 1980. pap. 8.95 (ISBN 0-87187-181-5). Congr Quarterly.

Grabo, Norman S. Edward Taylor. (United States Authors Ser.). lib. bdg. 13.95 (ISBN 0-8057-0720-4, Twayne). G K Hall.

Grabowicz, Paul, jt. auth. see Kotkin, Joel.

Grabowski, John, jt. ed. see Thompson, Travis.

Grace, Clive & Wilkinson, Philip. Sociological Inquiry & Legal Phenomena. LC 78-55401. 1978. 20.00x (ISBN 0-312-73972-9). St Martin.

Grace, Eugene V. RX for America. 258p. 1971. 12.00 (ISBN 0-87716-034-1, Pub. by Moore Pub Co). F Apple.

Grace, Eugene V., jt. auth. see Pritikin, Roland I.

Grace, Evelyn. Introduction to Fashion Merchandising. LC 78-1318. (Illus.). 1978. ref. ed. 19.95 (ISBN 0-13-483206-X). P-H.

Grace, Fran. Branigan's Dog. LC 81-6188. 224p. (gr. 7 up). 1981. 10.95 (ISBN 0-02-736660-X). Bradbury Pr.

Grace, Gerald R. Role Conflict & the Teacher. (International Library of Sociology). 1972. 16.95x (ISBN 0-7100-7353-4). Routledge & Kegan.

Grace, John A. & Young, Alfred. The Algebra of Invariants. LC 65-11860. 1965. 15.95 (ISBN 0-686-70735-4). Chelsea Pub.

Grace, Miriam S., et al. Your Self. 784p. 1976. 15.00 o.s.i. (ISBN 0-89104-255-5, A & W Visual Library); pap. 10.95 (ISBN 0-89104-190-7). A & W Pubs.

Grace, Robert A. Marine Outfall Systems: Planning, Design, & Construction. LC 77-20980. (P-H Environmental Engineering Ser.). 1978. ref. ed. 48.00 (ISBN 0-13-556951-6). P-H.

Grace, Ron, jt. auth. see Wilkins, Tony.

Grace, William J., Jr. The ABC'S of IRA'S: The Complete Guide to Individual Retirement Accounts. 1982. pap. 3.95 (ISBN 0-440-50398-1, Dell Trade Pbks). Dell.

Gracey, H. L., jt. auth. see Wrong, Dennis H.

Gracey, J. E. Thornton's Meat Hygiene. 7th ed. (Illus.). 436p. 1981. text ed. 61.00 o.p. (ISBN 0-8121-0825-6). Lea & Febiger.

Gracey, William. Measurement of Aircraft Speed & Altitude. LC 80-23503. 262p. 1981. 34.95x (ISBN 0-471-08511-1, Pub. by Wiley-Interscience). Wiley.

Gracy, David B. An Introduction to Archives & Manuscripts. LC 81-5677. (Professional Development Ser.: No. 2). 1981. pap. 7.25 (ISBN 0-87111-288-4). SLA.

Gracza, Margaret. Looking Forward to a Career: Art. 2nd ed. LC 76-4925. (Looking Forward to a Career Ser.). (Illus.). (gr. 6 up). 1976. PLB 6.95 o.p. (ISBN 0-87518-130-9). Dillon.

Gracza, Margaret Y. Bird in Art. LC 65-29035. (Fine Art Books). (Illus.). (gr. 5-11). 1966. PLB 4.95g (ISBN 0-8225-0158-9). Lerner Pubns.

--Ship & Sea in Art. LC 64-8203. (Fine Art Books). (Illus.). (gr. 5-11). 1965. PLB 4.95g (ISBN 0-8225-0153-8). Lerner Pubns.

Grad, A. Dizionario Moderno Slovene-Italian-Slovene. 445p. (Ital. & Slovene.). 1979. leatherette 14.95 (ISBN 0-686-97353-4, M9704). French & Eur.

Grad, A., et al. English-Slovene Dictionary. 1120p. (Eng. & Slovene.). 1979. 49.95 (ISBN 0-686-97378-X, M-9695). French & Eur.

Grad, Eli & Roth, Bette. Congregation Shaarey Zedek: 5622-5742 1861-1981. 198p. 1982. 25.00 (ISBN 0-8143-1713-8). Wayne St U Pr.

Grad, Frank, ed. Public Health Law Manual. LC 74-120960. 234p. 1973. 6.50x (ISBN 0-87553-058-3, 060). Am Pub Health.

Grad, Laurie B. Dining In--Los Angeles. (Dining In--Ser.). (Illus.). 190p. 1982. pap. 8.95 (ISBN 0-89716-121-1). Peanut Butter.

Graddock, Johnnie. Wine for Today. (Illus.). 1976. pap. 9.75 o.p. (ISBN 0-584-10344-1). Transatlantic.

Graddy, Duane B. The Bank Holding Company Performance Controversy. LC 78-65842. 1979. pap. text ed. 27.00 (ISBN 0-8191-0678-X). U Pr of Amer.

Gradinger, Gilbert P., jt. auth. see Kaye, Bernard L.

Gradl, M. J., ed. Authentic Art Nouveau Stained Glass Designs in Full Color. (Crafts Ser.). (Illus.). 32p. 1982. pap. 4.50 (ISBN 0-486-24362-1). Dover.

Gradner, Alvin F., ed. see Mathis, James L.

Gradon, Pamela. Form & Style in Early English Literature. 1974. pap. 10.95x o.p. (ISBN 0-416-81300-3). Methuen Inc.

Gradwell, D. J., ed. Database: The Second Generation. (Computer State of the Art Report, Series 10: No. 7). (Illus.). 662p. 1982. 445.00 (ISBN 0-08-028570-8). Pergamon.

Grady, Denice. Basic Skills Creative Writing Workbook. (Basic Skills Workbooks). 32p. (gr. 5-9). 1983. 0.99 (ISBN 0-8209-0549-6, EW-3). ESP.

--Creative Writing. (Language Arts Ser.). 24p. (gr. 3-5). 1977. wkbk. 5.00 (ISBN 0-8209-0326-4, LA-12). ESP.

Grady, James. Catch the Wind. 432p. 1980. 12.95 (ISBN 0-698-11043-9, Coward). Putnam Pub Group.

Grady, John L. Abortion: Yes or No? 32p. 1968. pap. 1.00 (ISBN 0-686-81634-X). TAN Bks Pubs.

Grady, Kathleen, jt. ed. see Ganikos, Mary.

Grae, Ida. Nature's Colors: Dyes from Plants. (Illus.). 1979. pap. 10.95 (ISBN 0-02-012390-6, Collier). Macmillan.

Graebner, Alan. Uncertain Saints. LC 75-1573. (Contributions in American History: No. 42). 320p. 1975. lib. bdg. 29.95 (ISBN 0-8371-7963-7, GUS/). Greenwood.

Graebner, Norman. The Cold War. 2nd ed. (Problems in European Civilization). 1976. pap. text ed. 5.50 (ISBN 0-669-81984-0). Heath.

--Nationalism & Communism in Asia: The American Response. (Problems in American Civilization Ser.). 1976. pap. text ed. 5.95 (ISBN 0-669-00683-1). Heath.

Graebner, Norman A. The Age of Global Power: The United States Since Nineteen Thirty-Nine. LC 78-12294. (American Republic Ser.). 1979. pap. text ed. 12.95 (ISBN 0-471-32082-X). Wiley.

--Empire On the Pacific. c, 280p. (gr. 12). 1983. lib. bdg. 22.50 (ISBN 0-87436-033-1). ABC Clio.

Graebner, Norman A., jt. auth. see Fite, Gilbert C.

Graebner, Norman A., ed. Freedom in America: A 200-Year Perspective. LC 76-43022. 1977. 18.50x (ISBN 0-271-01234-X). Pa St U Pr.

Graebner, Norman A., compiled by. American Diplomatic History Before 1900. LC 77-85991. (Goldentree Bibliographies in American History). 1978. text ed. 22.50x (ISBN 0-88295-573-X); pap. text ed. 13.95x (ISBN 0-88295-543-8). Harlan Davidson.

Graebner, Norman A., et al. A History of the American People, 2 vols. 2nd ed. LC 74-26670. (Illus.). 1975. text ed. 18.50 1 vol. ed. o.p. (ISBN 0-07-023887-1, C); Vol. 1. pap. text ed. 22.50 (ISBN 0-07-023885-5); Vol. 2. pap. text ed. 22.50 (ISBN 0-07-023886-3); instructor's manual 2.95 (ISBN 0-07-055642-3). McGraw.

Graedon, Joe. The People's Pharmacy. 5.95 o.p. (ISBN 0-686-92234-4, 4295). Hazelden.

Graef, Hilda. Mystics of Our Time. pap. 2.95 o.p. (ISBN 0-8091-1641-3). Paulist Pr.

Graef, Judy & Strom, J. Concepts in Clothing. 1976. 18.32 (ISBN 0-07-023889-8, W). McGraw.

Graeff, Burt & Eckhouse, Morris. Day by Day in Cleveland Indians History. (Day by Day in Baseball History Ser.). (Illus.). 288p. (Orig.). 1983. pap. 9.95 (ISBN 0-940056-02-X, Pub. by Leisure Pr). Chapter & Cask.

Graeff, H. & Kuhn, W. Coagulation Disorders in Obstetrics: Pathobiochemistry-Pathophysiology-Diagnosis-Treatment. Davis, A., tr. from Ger. LC 79-48020. (Major Problems in Obstetrics & Gynecology Ser.: No. 13). 1980. 10.00 (ISBN 0-7216-4192-X). Saunders.

Graeff, H., jt. ed. see Henschen, A.

Graeme, Jerald G. Application of Operational Amplifiers: Third Generation Techniques. (Illus.). 1973. 37.00 (ISBN 0-07-023890-1, P&RB). McGraw.

--Designing with Operational Amplifiers: Applications, Alternatives. (Illus.). 1977. 36.00 (ISBN 0-07-023891-X, P&RB). McGraw.

Graendorf, Werner, ed. Introduction to Biblical Christian Education. LC 81-1608. 1981. text ed. 13.95 (ISBN 0-8024-4128-9). Moody.

Graendorf, Werner & Mattson, Lloyd, eds. An Introduction to Christian Camping. 1979. 6.95 o.p. (ISBN 0-8024-4131-9). Moody.

Graeser, Kathi, jt. ed. see Ring, Jeanne.

Graetzer, G. Universal Algebra. LC 68-55539. xvi, 368p. 1975. 34.95 (ISBN 0-387-90355-0). Springer-Verlag.

Graf, Edward R., jt. auth. see Irwin, J. David.

Graf, Herbert. Opera for the People. LC 68-23811. (Music Reprint Ser.). 1973. Repr. of 1951 ed. lib. bdg. 32.50 (ISBN 0-306-70984-8). Da Capo.

Graf, LeRoy P. & Haskins, Ralph W., eds. The Papers of Andrew Johnson, Vol. 6: 1862-1864. LC 67-25733. (Illus.). 1000p. 1983. text ed. 27.50 (ISBN 0-87049-346-9). U of Tenn Pr.

Graf, Max. From Beethoven to Shostakovich: The Psychology of the Composing Process. LC 73-94607. Repr. of 1947 ed. lib. bdg. 19.00x (ISBN 0-8371-2452-2, GRBS). Greenwood.

--Legend of a Musical City. LC 71-90515. Repr. of 1945 ed. lib. bdg. 15.75x (ISBN 0-8371-2128-0, GRLM). Greenwood.

Graf, Nanette. Beowulf Notes. (Orig.). 1966. pap. 2.95 (ISBN 0-8220-0228-0). Cliffs.

Graf, R. & Whalen, G. Home Wiring. 1982. 16.95 (ISBN 0-13-392977-9). P-H.

Graf, T. & Jaenisch, R., eds. Tumorviruses, Neoplastic Transformation & Differentiation. (Current Topics in Microbiology & Immunology Ser.: Vol. 101). (Illus.). 198p. 1983. 40.00 (ISBN 0-387-11665-6). Springer-Verlag.

Graf, W. H. Hydraulics of Sediment Transport. 1971. 43.50 (ISBN 0-07-023900-2, C). McGraw.

Graf, W. H. & Mortimer, C. H., eds. Hydrodynamics of Lakes: Proceeding of the Symposium, Switzerland, Oct. 1978. LC 79-17492. (Developments in Water Science Ser.: Vol. 11). 360p. 1979. 66.00 (ISBN 0-444-41827-X). Elsevier.

Grafe, Louis. Get Rich in Spite of Yourself. 1962. pap. 2.00 (ISBN 0-910140-22-7). Anthony.

Graff, Harvey J. & Monaco, Paul, eds. Quantification & Psychology: Toward a "New" History. LC 79-3854. 526p. 1980. pap. text ed. 17.00 (ISBN 0-8191-0942-8). U Pr of Amer.

Graff, Sr. Laurine. Handbook of Routine Urinalysis. (Illus.). 304p. 1983. pap. text ed. 24.95 (ISBN 0-686-83099-7, Lippincott Medical). Lippincott.

Graff, Michelle & Reese, Loretta. Thirty-Four Craft Stick Projects. LC 82-61453. (Illus.). 48p. 1983. pap. 3.50 (ISBN 0-87239-622-3, 2104). Standard Pub.

Graff, Polly A., jt. auth. see Graff, Stewart.

Graff, Robert. Communications for National Development: Roles, Methods, Values (Published for the Salzburg Seminar) 196p. 1983. text ed. 22.50 (ISBN 0-89946-161-1). Oelgeschlager.

Graff, Stewart. George Washington. (Illus.). (gr. 2-6). 1966. pap. 1.25 o.p. (ISBN 0-440-42858-0, YB). Dell.

--George Washington: Father of Freedom. LC 64-10212. (Discovery Books Ser.). (Illus.). (gr. 2-5). 1964. PLB 6.09 o.p. (ISBN 0-8116-6280-2). Garrard.

--The Story of World War II. (Illus.). (gr. 3-6). 1978. 9.25 (ISBN 0-525-40355-8, 0898-270). Dutton.

Graff, Stewart & Graff, Polly A. Helen Keller: Toward the Light. LC 65-14550. (Discovery Bks). (gr. 2-5). 1965. PLB 6.69 (ISBN 0-8116-6288-8). Garrard.

--Squanto: Indian Adventurer. LC 65-10158. (Indians Ser.). (Illus.). (gr. 2-5). 1965. PLB 6.69 (ISBN 0-8116-6601-8). Garrard.

Graffi, D. Nonlinear Partial Differential Equations in Physical Problems. (Research Notes in Mathematics Ser.: No. 42). 105p. (Orig.). 1980. pap. text ed. 19.95 (ISBN 0-273-08474-7). Pitman Pub MA.

Grafftey-Smith, Sir Laurence. Hands to Play. 1975. 14.00 (ISBN 0-7100-8063-8). Routledge & Kegan.

Grafton, C. W. The Rat Began to Gnaw the Rope. LC 82-48243. 256p. 1983. pap. 2.84i (ISBN 0-06-080639-7, P 639, PL). Har-Row.

Grafton, Carol. Historic Alphabets & Initials. (Dover Pictorial Archive Ser.). (Illus.). 1977. pap. 6.00 (ISBN 0-486-23480-0). Dover.

Grafton, Carol B. Banners, Ribbons & Scrolls: An Archive For Artists & Designers, Five Hundred & Three Copyright Free Designs. (Illus.). 96p. (Orig.). 1983. pap. 4.00 (ISBN 0-486-24443-1). Dover.

--Geometric Patchwork Patterns: Full-Size Cut-Outs & Instructions for 12 Quilts. LC 74-31894. (Illus.). 64p. (Orig.). 1975. pap. 3.25 (ISBN 0-486-23183-6). Dover.

--Optical Designs in Motion with Moire Overlays. (Illus.). 32p. (Orig.). 1976. pap. 5.95 (ISBN 0-486-23284-0). Dover.

--Shapes & Colors: Cutouts for Creative Geometric Designs. (Illus.). 32p. (Orig.). 1976. pap. 3.00 (ISBN 0-486-23290-5). Dover.

--Victorian Color Vignettes & Illustrations for Artists & Craftsmen: 344 Antique Chromolithographs. (Illus.). 48p. (Orig.). 1983. pap. 4.95 (ISBN 0-486-24477-6). Dover.

Grafton, Carol B., ed. Authentic Victorian Stencil Designs. (Illus.). 64p. (Orig.). 1982. pap. 3.50 (ISBN 0-486-24337-0). Dover.

--Three Hundred Art Nouveau Designs & Motifs in Full Color. (Illus.). 48p. pap. 6.00 (ISBN 0-486-24354-0). Dover.

--Treasury of Japanese Designs & Motifs for Artists & Craftsmen. (Illus.). 96p. (Orig.). 1982. pap. 4.00 (ISBN 0-486-24435-0). Dover.

Grafton, Carol B., ed. see Gesner, Konrad.

Grafton, John. New York in the Nineteenth Century: Engravings from Harper's Weekly & Other Contemporary Sources. LC 77-73339. (Illus.). 1977. pap. 8.95 (ISBN 0-486-23516-5). Dover.

Gragert, Steven K., ed. He Chews to Run: Will Rogers Life Magazine Articles, 1928. LC 82-801415. (The Writings of Will Rogers Ser.: Ser. V, Vol. 1). (Illus.). 133p. 1982. 9.95 (ISBN 0-914956-20-5). Okla State Univ Pr.

Gragert, Steven K., ed. see Rogers, Will.

Gragg, Gerald R., ed. see Wesley, John.

Gragoe, Elizabeth. The Untidy Gardener. 192p. 1982. 22.50 (ISBN 0-241-10759-8, Pub. by Hamish Hamilton England). David & Charles.

Graham. Cannabis Now. 11.95 (ISBN 0-471-25737-0, Pub. by Wiley Heyden). Wiley.

Graham, et al, eds. Glasgow Story of a Missouri Rivertown. (Illus.). 237p. 1979. 8.00 (ISBN 0-930552-03-2). Tech Ed Serv.

Graham, A. Floristics & Paleofloristics of Asia & Eastern North America. 1972. 74.50 o.p. (ISBN 0-444-40958-0). Elsevier.

--Vegetation & Vegetational History of Northern Latin America. LC 72-87955. 416p. 1973. 86.00 (ISBN 0-444-41056-2). Elsevier.

Graham, A., jt. auth. see Martelli, L.

Graham, A. Richard. An Introduction to Engineering Measurements. (Illus.). 224p. 1975. ref. ed 24.95 (ISBN 0-13-482406-7). P-H.

Graham, Ada & Graham, Frank. Bears in the Wild. (Illus.). 176p. (gr. 4-8). 1983. pap. 2.25 (ISBN 0-440-40897-0, YB). Dell.

--Birds of the Northern Seas. (Illus.). 96p. 1981. 8.95a o.p. (ISBN 0-385-12565-8); PLB (ISBN 0-385-12566-6). Doubleday.

--Bug Hunters. LC 77-20532. (Audubon Readers: No. 2). (gr. 5 up). 1978. 7.95 o.s.i. (ISBN 0-440-00909-X); PLB 7.89 o.s.i. (ISBN 0-440-00910-3). Delacorte.

--Busy Bugs. LC 82-22085. (Illus.). 64p. (gr. 5 up). 1983. PLB 9.95 (ISBN 0-396-08126-6). Dodd.

--Coyote Song. LC 78-50436. (Audubon Readers Ser.: No. 4). (gr. 5 up). 1978. 6.95 o.s.i. (ISBN 0-440-01544-8); PLB 6.46 o.s.i. (ISBN 0-440-01545-6). Delacorte.

--Falcon Flight. LC 78-50442. (Audubon Readers Ser.: No. 3). (gr. 5 up). 1978. 7.95 o.s.i. (ISBN 0-440-02485-4); PLB 7.89 o.s.i. (ISBN 0-440-02486-2). Delacorte.

--Jacob & Owl. (Illus.). (gr. 3-7). 1981. 9.95 (ISBN 0-698-20516-2, Coward). Putnam Pub Group.

--Whale Watch: An Audubon Reader. (Illus.). 128p. (gr. 4-8). 1983. pap. 2.25 (ISBN 0-440-49250-5, YB). Dell.

Graham, Ada & Graham, Frank, Jr. The Milkweed & Its World of Animals. LC 74-18801. 96p. (gr. 3-5). 1976. 7.95 o.p. (ISBN 0-385-09933-9). Doubleday.

Graham, Alan K., jt. auth. see Alfeld, Louis.

Graham, Allison. Lindsay Anderson. (Filmmakers Ser.). 1981. lib. bdg. 15.95 (ISBN 0-8057-9283-X, Twayne). G K Hall.

Graham, Alma, jt. auth. see Martelli, Len.

Graham & Trotman Ltd., ed. Nigeria: Its Petroleum Geology, Resources & Potential, Vol. 1. 176p. 1982. 110.00x (ISBN 0-86010-264-5, Pub. by Graham & Trotman England). State Mutual Bk.

Graham, Benjamin & McGolrick, Charles. The Interpretation of Financial Statements. 3rd rev. ed. LC 74-15829. 128p. 1975. 12.45i (ISBN 0-06-011566-1, HarpT). Har-Row.

Graham, Benjamin, et al. Security Analysis. 4th ed. 1962. text ed. 33.95 (ISBN 0-07-023957-6, C). McGraw.

Graham, Billy. Billy Graham Talks to Teenagers. (Zondervan Teen Paperback). (gr. 8 up). pap. 2.25 o.p. (ISBN 0-310-25052-8). Zondervan.

--El Espiritu Santo. Sipowicz, A. Edwin, tr. from Eng. Orig. Title: The Holy Spirit. 252p. (Span.). 1981. pap. 6.25 (ISBN 0-311-09096-6). Casa Bautista.

--The Holy Spirit. (General Ser.). 1979. lib. bdg. 13.95 (ISBN 0-8161-6779-6, Large Print Bks). G K Hall.

--Holy Spirit. 336p. 1980. pap. 3.95 (ISBN 0-446-30733-5). Warner Bks.

--El Mundo en Llamas. Orig. Title: World Aflame. 272p. (Span.). 1982. pap. 5.25 (ISBN 0-311-46091-7). Casa Bautista.

--My Answer. LC 60-15942. 1960. 3.95 (ISBN 0-385-01027-3). Doubleday.

--Paz Con Dios. Muntz, Carrie, tr. from Eng. Orig. Title: Peace with God. 272p. 1981. pap. 3.75 (ISBN 0-311-43037-6). Casa Bautista.

--El Secreto de la Felicidad. Orig. Title: The Secret of Happiness. 192p. (Span.). 1981. pap. 2.75 (ISBN 0-311-04352-6). Casa Bautista.

Graham, Mrs. Billy. Our Christmas Story. LC 73-84958. (Illus.). 96p. 1973. Repr. of 1959 ed. 5.95 o.p. (ISBN 0-89066-004-2). World Wide Pubs.

Graham, Carolyn. The Electric Elephant & Other Stories. (Illus.). 128p. (Orig.). 1982. pap. text ed. 4.95x (ISBN 0-19-503229-2). Oxford U Pr.

--Jazz Chants. 1978. pap. text ed. 6.95x (ISBN 0-19-502407-9); cassette 10.95x (ISBN 0-19-502410-9); text & cassette 13.95x (ISBN 0-19-502429-X). Oxford U Pr.

--Jazz Chants for Children. (Illus.). 1979. pap. text ed. 7.50x (ISBN 0-19-502496-6); tchrs ed. 10.95x (ISBN 0-19-502497-4); cassette 12.00x (ISBN 0-19-502575-X). Oxford U Pr.

Graham, Clarence H., et al, eds. Vision & Visual Perception. LC 65-12711. 1965. 69.95x (ISBN 0-471-32170-2). Wiley.

Graham, Clive. Hyperion, Classic Race Horse Sire. (Illus.). 25.00x o.p. (ISBN 0-87556-107-1). Saifer.

Graham, Colin, jt. auth. see Lane, Billy.

Graham, Daniel O. The Non-Nuclear Defense of Cities: The High Frontier Space-Based Defense Against ICBM Attack. 1983. Repr. of 1982 ed. text ed. 25.00 (ISBN 0-89011-586-9). Abt Bks.

--Shall America Be Defended? Salt II & Beyond. 1979. 10.95 o.p. (ISBN 0-87000-458-1, Arlington Hse). Crown.

Graham, David. Down to a Sunless Sea. 1981. 13.95 o.p. (ISBN 0-671-41217-5). S&S.

Graham, David C. The Tribal Songs & Tales of the Ch'uan-Miao. (Asian Folklore & Social Life Monographs: Vol. 102). 1980. 20.50 (ISBN 0-89986-333-7). Oriental Bk Store.

Graham, Don. Critical Essays on Frank Norris. 1980. lib. bdg. 25.00 (ISBN 0-8161-8307-4, Twayne). G K Hall.

Graham, Donald. Composing Pictures: Still & Moving. 1982. pap. 19.95 (ISBN 0-442-22854-6). Van Nos Reinhold.

Graham, Dougal. Collected Writings of Dougal Graham, Skellat Bellman of Glasgow, 2 Vols. LC 69-16478. 1968. Repr. of 1883 ed. Set. 34.00x (ISBN 0-8103-3535-2). Gale.

Graham, Douglas. Moral Learning & Development. 1974. pap. 16.95 o.p. (ISBN 0-7134-2842-2, Pub. by Batsford England). David & Charles.

Graham, Edward H. Natural Principles of Land Use. Repr. of 1944 ed. lib. bdg. 17.00x (ISBN 0-8371-2394-1, GRLU). Greenwood.

Graham, Elizabeth. Vision of Love. (Harlequin Presents Ser.). 192p. 1983. pap. 1.95 (ISBN 0-373-10583-5). Harlequin Bks.

Graham, Frank. Power Plant Engineers Guide. 2nd ed. LC 74-78686. (Illus.). 816p. 1974. 15.95 o.p. (ISBN 0-672-23220-0). Audel.

Graham, Frank & Buffington. Power Plant Engineers Guide. new ed. (Audel Ser.). 1983. 16.95 (ISBN 0-672-23329-0). Bobbs.

Graham, Frank, jt. auth. see Graham, Ada.

Graham, Frank, Jr. Great No Hit Games of the Major Leagues. (Major League Baseball Library: No. 9). (Illus.). (gr. 1-6). 1968. 2.50 (ISBN 0-394-80189-X, BYR); PLB 3.69 (ISBN 0-394-90189-4). Random.

Graham, Frank, Jr., jt. auth. see Graham, Ada.

Graham, Franklinn & Lockerbie, Jeanette. Bob Pierce: This One Thing I Do. 1983. 9.95 (ISBN 0-8499-0097-2). Word Bks.

Graham, G., ed. Historical Explanation Reconsidered. (Scots Philosophical Monographs: No. 4). 96p. 1983. pap. 12.00 (ISBN 0-08-028478-7). Pergamon.

Graham, George, et al. Children Moving: A Reflective Approach to Teaching Physical Education. LC 79-91832. (Illus.). 497p. 1980. text ed. 18.95 (ISBN 0-87484-467-3); pap. 6.95 study guide (ISBN 0-87484-562-9). Mayfield Pub.

Graham, George G., jt. auth. see MacLean, William C., Jr.

Graham, George P., jt. auth. see Easton, Richard J.

Graham, Gerald H. Business: The Process of Enterprise. LC 76-45808. 580p. 1977. text ed. 17.95 (ISBN 0-574-19300-6, 13-2300); instr's guide avail. (ISBN 0-574-19301-4, 13-2301); study guide 6.95 (ISBN 0-574-19302-2, 13-2302); lecture resource & trans. masters 7.95 (ISBN 0-574-19303-0, 13-2304); filmstrip-tape 35.00 (ISBN 0-685-93534-5, 13-2306); test bank 5.75 (ISBN 0-574-19311-1, 13-2305). SRA.

Graham, Gerald S. Sea Power & British North America, 1783-1820: A Study in British Colonial Policy. LC 69-10101. 1969. Repr. of 1941 ed. lib. bdg. 19.00x (ISBN 0-8371-0453-X, GRBP). Greenwood.

Graham, Gwethalyn & Rolland, Solange C. Dear Enemies: A Dialogue on French & English Canada. 1965. 6.50 (ISBN 0-8159-5300-3). Devin.

Graham, H. T. Human Resources Management. 288p. 1981. 29.00X (ISBN 0-7121-0817-3, Pub. by Macdonald & Evans). State Mutual Bk.

Graham, Heather. A Season For Love. (Candlelight Ecstasy Ser.: No. 154). (Orig.). 1983. pap. 1.95 (ISBN 0-440-18041-4). Dell.

--Tempestuous Eden. (Candlelight Ecstasy Supreme Ser.: No. 1). (Orig.). 1983. pap. 2.95 (ISBN 0-440-18646-3). Dell.

--Tender Taming. (Candlelight Ecstasy Ser.: No. 125). (Orig.). 1983. pap. 1.95 (ISBN 0-440-18803-2). Dell.

--When Next We Love. (Candlelight Ecstasy Ser.: No. 117). (Orig.). 1983. pap. 1.95 (ISBN 0-440-19588-8). Dell.

Graham, Horace D. Safety of Foods. 2nd ed. (Illus.). 1980. lib. bdg. 57.00 (ISBN 0-87055-337-2). AVI.

Graham, Horace D., jt. auth. see Telek, Lehel.

Graham, Hugh F., ed. & tr. The Moscovia of Antonio Possevino, S. J. LC 77-12648. (Ser. in Russian & East European Studies: No. 1). (Illus.). 1977. 20.00 (ISBN 0-8229-4202-X). U of Pittsburgh Pr.

Graham, Hugh F., ed. see Skrynnikov, R. G.

Graham, Ian. Corpus of Maya Hieroglyphic Inscriptions: Xultun, la Honradex, Vol. 5, No. 2. 1981. 12.00 o.s.i. (ISBN 0-87365-793-4). Peabody Harvard.

Graham, J. D. An Introduction to Human Pharmacology. (Illus.). 1979. pap. text ed. 18.95x o.p. (ISBN 0-19-263333-3). Oxford U Pr.

Graham, John. Ancient Mesoamerica: Selected Readings. rev. ed. (Illus.). 334p. 1982. text ed. cancelled (ISBN 0-917962-77-X); pap. text ed. 12.95 (ISBN 0-917962-70-2). Peek Pubns.

--I Love You, Mouse. LC 78-6214. (Illus.). (ps-3). 1978. pap. 1.75 (ISBN 0-15-644106-3, VoyB). HarBraceJ.

--Merrill Studies in Second Skin. LC 71-160518. 1971. pap. text ed. 3.50 (ISBN 0-675-09496-8). Merrill.

--Mold Me & Shape Me. 144p. 1983. 9.95 (ISBN 0-310-60170-3). Chosen Bks Pub.

Graham, John, jt. auth. see Brown, Skip.

Graham, John, ed. & intro. by see Sinclair, Upton.

Graham, John, jt. ed. see Wyand, Roy.

Graham, John R. & Arthur, Charles S. Keeping What's Yours. 201p. 1977. 11.95 o.p. (ISBN 0-686-36320-5); pap. 8.95 o.p. (ISBN 0-686-37288-3). R L DeBruyen.

Graham, Jorie. Erosion. LC 82-61365. (Princeton Series of Contemporary Poets). 92p. 1983. 12.50x (ISBN 0-691-06570-5); pap. 6.95 (ISBN 0-691-01405-1). Princeton U Pr.

Graham, Judy. Bird's Eye. pap. 8.95 (ISBN 0-914676-62-8). Green Tiger Pr.

Graham, Julia B. & Wiedeman, Varley E. Biology of Populations. 136p. 1982. pap. text ed. 8.95 (ISBN 0-8403-2784-6). Kendall-Hunt.

Graham, Kenneth see Swan, D. K.

Graham, Kenneth R. Psychological Research: Controlled Interpersonal Interaction. LC 77-5065. 1977. text ed. 10.95 o.p. (ISBN 0-8185-0229-0). Brooks-Cole.

Graham, Lawrence. Jobs in the Real World: The Student Job-Search Handbook. LC 81-85476. 160p. 1982. pap. 6.95 (ISBN 0-448-12268-5, G&D). Putnam Pub Group.

--Ten-Point College Plan. 144p. 1982. pap. 6.95 (ISBN 0-399-50678-0, Perige). Putnam Pub Group.

--Ten-Point Plan for College Acceptance. (Illus.). 144p. 1981. pap. 6.95 (ISBN 0-8256-3226-9, Quick Fox). Putnam Pub Group.

Graham, Lawrence S. & Wheeler, Douglas L., eds. In Search of Modern Portugal: The Revolution & its Consequences. 402p. 1983. text ed. 30.00 (ISBN 0-299-08990-8). U of Wis Pr.

Graham, Lillian S., jt. auth. see Wackerbarth, Marjorie.

Graham, Lorenz. Return to South Town. LC 75-33712. (gr. 7 up). 1976. 10.53i (ISBN 0-690-01081-8, TYC-J). Har-Row.

--South Town. (RL 6). 1966. pap. 1.75 (ISBN 0-451-11483-3, AE1483, Sig). NAL.

Graham, Lou & Bibb, John. Mastering Golf. LC 77-91155. 1978. o. p. 9.95 (ISBN 0-8092-7763-8); pap. 7.95 (ISBN 0-8092-7761-1). Contemp Bks.

Graham, Lyle J. Your IBM PC: A Guide to the IBM Personal Computer. 384p. (Orig.). 1983. pap. text ed. 16.95 (ISBN 0-931988-85-3). Osborne-McGraw.

Graham, M., jt. ed. see Davy, B.

Graham, M. F. Inner Energy: How to Overcome Fatigue. LC 78-7089. 1978. 9.95 o.p. (ISBN 0-8069-8440-6); PLB 8.29 o.p. (ISBN 0-8069-8441-4). Sterling.

Graham, Malcolm. Modern Elementary Mathematics. 3rd ed. 470p. 1979. text ed. 19.95 (ISBN 0-15-561041-4, HC); instructor's manual avail. (ISBN 0-15-561042-2). HarBraceJ.

Graham, Malcolm & House, William F., eds. Disorders of the Facial Nerve: Anatomy, Diagnosis & Management. (House Ear Institute Ser.). 576p. 1982. text ed. 69.50 (ISBN 0-89004-624-7). Raven.

Graham, Margaret B. Be Nice to Spiders. LC 67-17101. (gr. k-3). 1967. 10.53i (ISBN 0-06-022072-4, HarpJ); PLB 10.89 (ISBN 0-06-022073-2). Har-Row.

--Benjy & the Barking Bird. LC 79-129856. (Illus.). (ps-3). 1971. PLB 10.89 (ISBN 0-06-022080-5, HarpJ). Har-Row.

--Benjy's Dog House. LC 72-9854. (Illus.). 32p. (ps-3). 1973. 10.53i (ISBN 0-06-022083-X, HarpJ); PLB 10.89 (ISBN 0-06-022084-8). Har-Row.

Graham, Michael, jt. auth. see Cleary, Edward.

Graham, Michael H. Tightening the Reins of Justice in America: A Comparative Analysis of the Criminal Jury Trail in England & the United States. LC 82-12029. (Contributions in Legal Studies: No. 26). (Illus.). 376p. 1983. lib. bdg. 35.00 (ISBN 0-313-23598-8, GJA/). Greenwood.

Graham, Michael H., jt. auth. see Cleary, Edward W.

Graham, Munir & De la Torre Bueno, Laura, eds. Index to the Sayings of Hazrat Inayat Khan. (The Collected Works of Hazrat Inayat Khan). 144p. (Orig.). Date not set. pap. 3.95 cancelled o.s.i. (ISBN 0-930872-23-1, 1009P). Omega Pr NM. Postponed.

Graham, Neil. Introduction to PASCAL. 272p. 1980. pap. text ed. 14.95 (ISBN 0-8299-0334-8). West Pub.

--Microprocessor Programming for Computer Hobbyists. (Illus.). 1977. 12.95x (ISBN 0-8306-7952-9); pap. 8.95x o.p. (ISBN 0-8306-6952-3, 952). TAB Bks.

Graham, Neill. Artificial Intelligence. (Illus.). 1979. 12.95 o.p. (ISBN 0-8306-9835-3); pap. 7.95 (ISBN 0-8306-1076-6, 1076). TAB Bks.

--Computing & Computers: An Introduction Through BASIC. (Illus.). 525p. 1982. text ed. 18.95 (ISBN 0-8299-0382-8). West Pub.

--Introduction to Computer Science: A Structure Approach. 2nd ed. (Illus.). 568p. 1982. text ed. 24.95 (ISBN 0-314-63243-3). West Pub.

--The Mind Tool: Computers & Their Impact on Society. LC 76-3545. (Illus.). 239p. 1976. pap. text ed. 10.95 o.s.i. (ISBN 0-8299-0091-8). West Pub.

--The Mind Tool: Computers & Their Impact on Society. 2nd ed. (Illus.). 1980. pap. 15.95 (ISBN 0-8299-0272-4); instrs.' manual avail. (ISBN 0-8299-0483-2); study guide 6.95 (ISBN 0-8299-0350-X). West Pub.

--The Mind Tool: Computers & Their Impact on Society. 3rd ed. (Illus.). 410p. 1983. pap. text ed. 13.95 (ISBN 0-314-69650-4); study manual avail. (ISBN 0-314-71093-0); instrs.' manual avail. (ISBN 0-314-71094-9). West Pub.

Graham, Otis, jt. auth. see Borden, Morton.

Graham, Otis L. Toward a Planned Society: From Franklin D. Roosevelt to Richard Nixon. 1976. 19.95x (ISBN 0-19-501985-7). Oxford U Pr.

Graham, Otis L., jt. auth. see Borden, Morton.

Graham, Otis L., Jr. Encore for Reform: The Old Progressives & the New Deal. 1967. 16.95x (ISBN 0-19-500558-9). Oxford U Pr.

--Illegal Immigration & the New Reform Movement. 1980. pap. text ed. 2.50 (ISBN 0-935776-01-X). F A I R.

--Toward a Planned Society: From Roosevelt to Nixon. LC 75-10189. 1977. pap. 7.95 (ISBN 0-19-502181-9, 486, GB). Oxford U Pr.

Graham, Patricia A. Community & Class in American Education: 1865 to 1918. LC 84-562. 268p. Repr. of 1974 ed. text ed. 11.50 (ISBN 0-471-32091-9). Krieger.

--Progressive Education: From Arcady to Academe: A History of the Progressive Education Association: 1919-1955. LC 67-26480. 1967. text ed. 10.95x (ISBN 0-8077-1452-6). Tchrs Coll.

Graham, Patricia A., jt. ed. see Furniss, W. Todd.

Graham, R. Britain & the Onset of Modernization in Brazil, 1850-1914. LC 68-21393. (Latin American Studies: No. 4). (Illus.). 1972. 47.50 (ISBN 0-521-07078-3); pap. 13.95 (ISBN 0-521-09681-2). Cambridge U Pr.

Graham, R. B. Pedro De Valdivia, Conqueror of Chile. LC 74-3619. (Illus.). 227p. 1974. Repr. of 1926 ed. lib. bdg. 15.75x (ISBN 0-8371-7454-6, GRPV). Greenwood.

Graham, R. Cunninghame. Conquest of the River Plate. LC 68-23293. (Illus.). 1969. Repr. of 1924 ed. lib. bdg. 19.00x (ISBN 0-8371-0454-8, GRRP). Greenwood.

--Reincarnation: The Best Short Stories of Cunninghame Graham. LC 79-28208. 160p. 1980. 8.95 (ISBN 0-89919-004-9). Ticknor & Fields.

Graham, Richard. Cuisine for Cats. 1980. 15.00 (ISBN 0-686-96956-1, Pub. by J Landesman England). State Mutual Bk.

Graham, Richard & Goldston, Angela. Social Studies: History. (Latin American Curriculum Units for Junior & Community Colleges Ser.). v, 46p. 1981. pap. text ed. 3.95 (ISBN 0-86728-008-5). U TX Inst Lat Am Stud.

Graham, Richard, jt. auth. see Beer, Alice S.

Graham, Richard B., jt. auth. see Devol, Terry B.

Graham, Robert. Iran: The Illusion of Power. LC 78-65258. (Illus.). 272p. 1980. 17.95x o.p. (ISBN 0-312-43587-8); pap. 6.95 (ISBN 0-312-43589-4). St Martin.

Graham, Robert E., Jr., ed. see U. S. Office Of Business Economics.

Graham, Robert M. Principles of Systems Programming. LC 74-19390. 368p. 1975. text ed. 30.95 (ISBN 0-471-32100-1). Wiley.

Graham, Robert W., jt. auth. see Hsu, Y.

Graham, Robert W., ed. Rechargeable Batteries: Advances Since 1977. LC 80-13152. (Energy Technology Review Ser. No. 55; Chemical Technology Review Ser. No.160). 452p. 1980. 54.00 (ISBN 0-8155-0802-6). Noyes.

Graham, Robin & Roy, Ronald. Slipper Orchids: The Art of Digby Graham. (Illus.). 128p. 1982. 39.95 (ISBN 0-589-01387-4, Pub. by Reed Pub). David & Charles.

Graham, Robin L. & Gill, Derek. Home is the Sailor. LC 82-48835. (Illus.). 192p. 1983. 12.45i (ISBN 0-06-015154-4, HarpT). Har-Row.

Graham, Ronald. The Aluminum Industry & the Third World. 288p. 1983. pap. 10.50 (ISBN 0-86232-057-7, Pub. by Zed Pr England). Lawrence Hill.

Graham, Ronald, et al. Ramsey Theory. LC 80-14110. (Interscience in Discrete Mathematics Ser.). 174p. 1980. 26.95x (ISBN 0-471-05997-8, Pub. by Wiley Interscience). Wiley.

Graham, S. Graham on Bread. 1983. pap. 3.95x (ISBN 0-686-76735-7). Regent House.

Graham, Samuel. Fleetwood Mac: The Authorized History. (Illus.). 1978. pap. 1.95 o.p. (ISBN 0-446-89984-4). Warner Bks.

Graham, Scroggie W. Studies in Philemon. LC 77-79186. 1982. pap. 3.95 (ISBN 0-686-98143-X). Kregel.

Graham, Sharon K. One Thousand & One Tips for Successful Gardening: Easy Ways to Grow the Best Vegetables, Fruits, Herbs, Flowers & Houseplants. 160p. 1983. 6.95 (ISBN 0-525-93278-X, 0675-200). Dutton.

Graham, Sheila Y. Sentencecraft. (Illus.). 128p. 1976. pap. text ed. 9.95 (ISBN 0-13-806224-2). P-H.

--Writingcraft: The Paragraphs & the Essays. (Illus.). 192p. 1976. pap. text ed. 9.95x (ISBN 0-13-970152-4). P-H.

Graham, Shelia Y. Harbrace College Workbook: Form 8B. 1978. pap. text ed. 7.95 o.p. (ISBN 0-15-531831-4, HC); instructor's key avail. o.p. (ISBN 0-15-531832-2). HarBraceJ.

Graham, Stephen. Peter the Great: A Life of Peter I of Russia. LC 75-138241. (Illus.). 1971. Repr. of 1950 ed. lib. bdg. 18.50x (ISBN 0-8371-5598-3, GRPG). Greenwood.

Graham, Susan. Quick Simple Meals. (Leisure Plan Bks). 1971. pap. 2.95 o.p. (ISBN 0-600-01354-5). Transatlantic.

Graham, Terry. Let Loose on Mother Goose. LC 81-80248. (Illus.). 96p. (gr. k-1). 1982. pap. text ed. 6.95 (ISBN 0-86530-030-5, IP 30-5). Incentive Pubns.

Graham, Tether. Fudge Dream Supreme. LC 73-16815. (ps-2). 1975. 4.99 (ISBN 0-87955-109-7); PLB 3.99 (ISBN 0-686-57941-0). O'Hara.

Graham, Tom M. Biology Laboratory Manual for the Nonscience Major I. 2nd ed. 1978. pap. text ed. 10.95 (ISBN 0-8403-1137-0). Kendall-Hunt.

Graham, W. Fred. Constructive Revolutionary: John Calvin & His Socio-Economic Impact. LC 72-107321. 1971. 5.95 (ISBN 0-8042-0880-8). John Knox.

--The Constructive Revolutionary: John Calvin & His Socio-Economic Impact. LC 72-107321. 1978. pap. 5.95 (ISBN 0-8042-0881-6). John Knox.

Graham, Winifred. The Vegetarian Treasure Chest. Fraser, Lisa, ed. Orig. Title: The Vegetable, Fruit & Nut Cookbook. 224p. 1983. pap. 6.95 (ISBN 0-930356-33-0). Quicksilver Prod.

Graham, Winston. The Angry Tide. (Reader's RRequest Ser.). 1979. lib. bdg. 19.95 (ISBN 0-8161-6682-X, Large Print Bks). G K Hall.

--The Four Swans. (Reader's Request Ser.). 1979. lib. bdg. 19.95 (ISBN 0-8161-6681-1, Large Print Bks). G K Hall.

--Merciless Ladies. (General Ser.). 1980. lib. bdg. 14.95 (ISBN 0-8161-3119-8, Large Print Bks). G K Hall.

--Miller's Dance: A Novel of Cornwell 1812-1813. LC 82-45596. 408p. 1983. 15.95 (ISBN 0-385-18405-0). Doubleday.

Graham-Cameron, M. The Farmer. (Cambridge Dinosaur Information Ser.). (Illus.). 26p. (gr. 7-10). 1983. pap. 1.50 (ISBN 0-521-27162-2). Cambridge U Pr.

Grahame. Wind in the Willows. (Illus.). jr. lib. 5.95 (ISBN 0-448-05828-6, G&D); deluxe ed. 7.95 (ISBN 0-448-06028-0); Companion lib. ed. 2.95 (ISBN 0-448-05481-7). Putnam Pub Group.

Grahame, A., jt. ed. see Shoham, S. G.

Grahame, Anthony see Shoham, S. Giora.

Grahame, Kenneth. Wind in the Willows. (Illus., Orig.). (RL 4). 1969. pap. 1.95 (ISBN 0-451-51733-4, CJ1733, Sig Classics). NAL.

--Wind in the Willows. LC 66-14847. (Illus.). (gr. 5 up). 1966. 12.95 o.p. (ISBN 0-529-00119-5, Philomel). Putnam Pub Group.

--The Wind in the Willows. (Bantam Classics Ser.). (Illus.). 256p. (gr. 4-12). 1982. pap. 1.75 (ISBN 0-553-21074-2). Bantam.

--The Wind in the Willows. (Illus.). 240p. 1983. 15.75 (ISBN 0-670-77120-1). Viking Pr.

--The Wind in the Willows. Green, Peter, ed. (The World's Classics Ser.). 224p. 1983. pap. 3.95 (ISBN 0-19-281640-3, GB). Oxford U Pr.

--The Wind in the Willows Coloring Book. 64p. 1976. pap. 2.00 (ISBN 0-486-23292-1). Dover.

Grahame, R. Low Back Pain, Vol. 1. Horrobin, D. F., ed. (Annual Research Reviews Ser.). 1980. 18.00 (ISBN 0-88831-068-4). Eden Pr.

Grahame, R. & Anderson, J. A. Low Back Pain, Vol. 2. (Annual Research Reviews). 83p. 1981. 14.00 (ISBN 0-88831-095-1). Eden Pr.

Grahame-Smith, D. G. & Hippius, H., eds. Psychopharmacology, Vol. 1. 935p. 1982. Part 1: Basic Preclinical Neuropharmacology. 80.75 (ISBN 0-686-84508-0, Excerpta Medica); Part 2: Clinical Psychopharmacology. 85.00 (ISBN 0-686-84509-9); Set. 153.25 (ISBN 0-444-90294-5). Elsevier.

Graham-Jones, Susanna, tr. see Goldoni, Carolo.

Graham-Lujan, James, tr. see Garcia Lorca, Federico.

Graham-Lujan, James, tr. see Lorca, Federico Garcia.

Graham-Pole, John, ed. Non-Hodgkin's Lymphomas in Children. LC 80-81990. (Masson Monographs in Pediatric Hematology - Oncology: Vol. 2). (Illus.). 192p. 1980. 30.75x (ISBN 0-89352-068-3). Masson Pub.

Grahan, Frank. Hattie. (Illus.). 80p. Date not set. 7.95 (ISBN 0-89962-269-0). Todd & Honeywell. Postponed.

Grahm, Leroy. Baltimore: The Nineteenth Century Black Capital. 346p. (Orig.). 1982. lib. bdg. 24.00 (ISBN 0-8191-2624-1); pap. text ed. 12.75 (ISBN 0-8191-2625-X). U Pr of Amer.

Grahm, Milton, et al. Legal Typewriting. 1968. text ed. 13.00 (ISBN 0-07-024045-0, G). McGraw.

Grahm, Winston. Forgotten Story. LC 82-45109. 240p. 1982. cancelled (ISBN 0-385-18181-7). Doubleday.

Grahman, Lorenz. Song of the Boat. LC 74-5183. (Illus.). (gr. 2-5). 1975. 9.57i o.p. (ISBN 0-690-75231-8, TYC-J); PLB 7.89 o.p. (ISBN 0-690-75232-6). Har-Row.

Grahn, Judy. Another Mother Tongue: Stories from the Ancient Gay Tradition. (Orig.). 1983. pap. price not set (ISBN 0-930436-13-X). Persephone.

--The Queen of Wands. 64p. 1982. 13.95 (ISBN 0-89594-095-7); pap. 5.95 (ISBN 0-89594-094-9). Crossing Pr.

--The Work of a Common Woman. 1980. 8.95 o.p. (ISBN 0-312-88947-X). St Martin.

Graig, Marjorie G., tr. see De Forges, Maria T.

Grail Simplified Documents. Church in the World. 1967. pap. 1.00 o.p. (ISBN 0-02-644150-0, 64415). Glencoe.

--This Is Ecumenism. 1967. pap. 0.80 o.p. (ISBN 0-02-644170-5, 64417). Glencoe.

--This Is the Church. 1967. pap. 0.80 o.p. (ISBN 0-02-644190-X, 64419). Glencoe.

--This Is the Lay Apostolate. 1967. pap. 0.80 o.p. (ISBN 0-02-644210-8, 64421). Glencoe.

--This Is the Liturgy. (Orig.). 1967. pap. 0.80 o.p. (ISBN 0-02-644230-2, 64423). Glencoe.

Grainger, L. & Gibson, J. Coal Utilisation: Technology, Economics & Policy. LC 81-7249. 503p. 1982. 49.95x (ISBN 0-470-27272-4). Halsted Pr.

Grainger, Margaret, ed. The Natural History Prose Writings of John Clare. (Illus.). 472p. 1982. 69.00 (ISBN 0-19-818517-0). Oxford U Pr.

Grainger, Ronald G., jt. ed. see Veiga-Pires, J. A.

Grais, Wafik. Aggregate Demand & Macroeconomic Imbalances in Thailand: Simulations with the SIAM 1 Model. (Working Paper: No. 448). 70p. 1981. 5.00 (ISBN 0-686-36163-6, WP-0448). World Bank.

Grais, Wafik, jt. auth. see Drud, Arne.

Graivier, Pauline, jt. auth. see Hoffman, Gloria.

Grala, Maria. Say It in Polish: An Intensive Course for Beginners. 110p. (gr. 6 up). pap. 4.95 (ISBN 83-01-03922-1, Ars Polana Poland). Hippocrene Bks.

Gralnick, Alexander, jt. ed. see Greenhill, Maurice.

Gram, Moltke S., ed. Interpreting Kant. LC 82-13627. 200p. 1982. text ed. 15.00x (ISBN 0-87745-118-4). U of Iowa Pr.

Gramatky, Hardie. Happy's Christmas. (Illus.). (gr. k-3). 1970. 6.95 o.p. (ISBN 0-399-20085-1). Putnam Pub Group.

--Hercules. (Illus.). (gr. k-3). 1940. PLB 5.99 (ISBN 0-399-60240-2); pap. 3.95 (ISBN 0-399-20728-7, Peppercorn). Putnam Pub Group.

--Little Toot. (Illus.). (gr. k-3). 1939. 8.95 (ISBN 0-399-20144-0); PLB 8.99 (ISBN 0-399-60422-7). Putnam Pub Group.

--Little Toot. LC 78-4801. (Illus.). (gr. k-2). 1978. pap. 4.95 (ISBN 0-399-20649-3). Putnam Pub Group.

--Little Toot on the Mississippi. (Illus.). 96p. (gr. k-3). 1973. 8.95 (ISBN 0-399-20364-8). Putnam Pub Group.

--Little Toot Through the Golden Gate. LC 75-10450. (Illus.). 92p. (gr. k-2). 1975. 6.95 o.p. (ISBN 0-399-20483-0). Putnam Pub Group.

--Loopy. (Illus.). (gr. k-3). 1941. PLB 5.99 (ISBN 0-399-60428-6). Putnam Pub Group.

--Nikos & the Sea God. (Illus.). (gr. 1-3). 1963. PLB 4.76 o.p. (ISBN 0-399-60492-8). Putnam Pub Group.

Grambert, Joseph. La Voltairiade, Ou Aventures De Voltaire Dans L'autre Monde, Occasionees Par un Evenement Arrive Dans Celui-Ci. Repr. of 1815 ed. 36.00 o.p. (ISBN 0-8287-0387-6). Clearwater Pub.

Grambs, Jean D., ed. Teaching About Women in the Social Studies: Concepts, Methods & Materials. LC 75-43431. 1976. pap. 6.95 (ISBN 0-87986-005-7, 498-15254). Coun Soc Studies.

Gramelsbach, Helen. Seventy-One Creative Bible Story Projects: Patterns for Crafts, Visuals, & Learning Centers. (Illus.). 64p. 1983. pap. 3.95 (ISBN 0-87239-607-X, 2103). Standard Pub.

Gramlich, Edward M. Benefit-Cost Analysis of Government Programs. (Illus.). 304p. 1981. text ed. 21.00 (ISBN 0-13-074757-2). P-H.

Gramlich, Edward M. & Koshel, Patrica P. Educational Performance Contracting: An Evaluation of an Experiment. (Studies in Social Experimentation). 76p. 1975. pap. 4.95 (ISBN 0-8157-3239-2). Brookings.

Gramm, Phil. The Role of Government in a Free Society: A Collection of Speeches & Articles. 150p. 1982. text ed. 11.95 (ISBN 0-933028-19-9); pap. text ed. 7.95 (ISBN 0-933028-20-2). Fisher Inst.

Grammentine, Ray, ed. see Thompson, David W.

Gramont, Sanche De see De Gramont, Sanche.

Grams, Betty J. Femmes De Grace. Cosson, Annie, ed. Orig. Title: Women Of Grace. (FR.). 1982. pap. 2.00 (ISBN 0-8297-1199-6). Life Pubs Intl.

--Ministrando Com Musica. (Portugese Bks.). (Port.). 1979. 1.70 (ISBN 0-8297-0732-8). Life Pubs Intl.

Gramsci, Antonio. Modern Prince & Other Writings. LC 67-25646. 1959. 5.95 o.p. (ISBN 0-7178-0134-9); pap. 2.95 (ISBN 0-7178-0133-0). Intl Pub Co.

Gran, Claurene du see Du Gran, Claurene.

Grana, Cesar. Fact & Symbol: Essays in the Sociology of Art & Literature. 1971. 16.95x (ISBN 0-19-501285-2). Oxford U Pr.

Granath, Olle, jt. auth. see Hulten, Pontus.

Granatstein, J. L. Broken Promises: A History of Conscription in Canada. 1977. pap. 8.50x o.p. (ISBN 0-19-540258-8). Oxford U Pr.

--Canada's War: The Politics of the Mackenzie King Government 1939-1945. (Illus.). 1975. 25.00x o.p. (ISBN 0-19-540228-6). Oxford U Pr.

Granatstein, J. L. & Stevens, Paul, eds. Canada Since Eighteen Sixty-Seven: A Critical Bibliography. 2nd ed. 173p. 1977. 9.95 o.p. (ISBN 0-88866-583-0); pap. 4.95 o.p. (ISBN 0-88866-584-9). Samuel Stevens.

Granbeck, Marilyn. Celia. 1977. pap. 1.95 o.s.i. (ISBN 0-515-03951-9). Jove Pubns.

--Elena. (Orig.). pap. 2.25 o.s.i. (ISBN 0-515-04420-2). Jove Pubns.

--Finding Your Job Skillbook. LC 66-40358. (Illus.). (gr. 7 up). 1980. write for info. (ISBN 0-912486-08-2); wkbk 2.25 (ISBN 0-912486-39-2). Finney Co.

--Maura. (Orig.). 1979. pap. 2.50 o.s.i. (ISBN 0-515-04626-4). Jove Pubns.

Grand, Carole & Gold, Rahla. Guiding the Learning Process: A Manual for Teachers of Young Children. 190p. Repr. 10.00 o.p. (ISBN 0-686-95035-6). ADL.

Grande, Frank & Nathan, Simon. Leicaflex System of Photography. (Illus.). 1972. 10.95 o.p. (ISBN 0-8174-0539-9, Amphoto). Watson-Guptill.

Grande, J. J. Del see Del Grande, J. J. & Duff, G. F.

Grandin, Nicole. Le Soudan Nilotique et L'Administration Britannique (1898-1956) Elements D'Interpretation Sociohistorique d'une Experience Coloniale. (Social, Economic, & Political Studies of the Middle East: Vol. 29). (Illus.). xiv, 348p. 1982. pap. write for info. (ISBN 90-04-06404-4). E J Brill.

Grandis, Sue L. Instrumentation for Coronary Care. (Techniques of Measurement in Medicine Ser.: No. 5). (Illus.). 150p. 1981. 37.50 (ISBN 0-521-23548-0); pap. 13.95 (ISBN 0-521-28024-9). Cambridge U Pr.

Grandjean, Etienne. Fitting the Task to the Man: An Ergonomic Approach. 3rd ed. LC 77-447838. 379p. 1980. 35.00 (ISBN 0-85066-191-9); pap. 22.50 (ISBN 0-8002-2225-3). Intl Pubns Serv.

Grandjean, Etienne, ed. Sitting Posture. LC 70-23595. (Illus.). 253p. 1976. 32.50x (ISBN 0-85066-029-7). Intl Pubns Serv.

Grandower, Elissa. Blackbourne Hall. LC 78-22771. (Romantic Suspense Ser.). 1979. 9.95 o.p. (ISBN 0-385-14472-5). Doubleday.

--Rivergate House. large print ed. LC 80-29028. 1981. Repr. of 1980 ed. 11.95x o.p. (ISBN 0-89621-268-8). Thorndike Pr.

Grandpre, Louis De. Voyage a la Cote Occidentale d'Afrique dans les Annees 1786 et 1787, 2 vols. (Bibliotheque Africaine Ser.). 628p. (Fr.). 1974. Repr. of 1801 ed. lib. bdg. 165.00x o.p. (ISBN 0-8287-0391-4). Clearwater Pub.

Grandy, Richard E., ed. Theories & Observation in Science. vii, 184p. 1980. lib. bdg. 24.00 (ISBN 0-917930-39-8); pap. 7.50x (ISBN 0-917930-19-3). Ridgeview.

Graneau, Peter. Underground Power Transmission: The Science, Technology, & Economics of High Voltage Cables. LC 79-15746. 1979. 47.50x (ISBN 0-471-05757-6, Pub. by Wiley-Interscience). Wiley.

Granet, Irving. Fluid Mechanics for Engineering Technology. 2nd ed. (Illus.). 416p. 1981. text ed. 21.95 (ISBN 0-13-322610-7). P-H.

Granet, Marcel. The Religion of the Chinese People. Freedman, Maurice, tr. from Fr. 1977. pap. 5.95xi (ISBN 0-06-131905-8, TB 1905, Torch). Har-Row.

Granfield, Michael L. An Econometric Model of Residential Location. LC 75-2246. 150p. 1975. prof ref 17.50 (ISBN 0-88410-410-9). Ballinger Pub.

Grange, J. M. Mycobacterial Diseases. (Current Topics in Infection Ser.: Vol. 1). 1981. 32.50 (ISBN 0-444-00625-7). Elsevier.

Grange, McQuilkin de see De Grange, McQuilkin.

Grange, W. J. & Woodbury, T. C. Manual of Real Estate Law, Procedures, & Forms. 2nd ed. 470p. 1968. 29.50 o.p. (ISBN 0-471-06614-1, Pub. by Wiley-Interscience). Wiley.

Grange, W. J., et al. Manual for Corporation Officers: The Law, Procedures & Forms. 840p. 1967. 33.95 o.p. (ISBN 0-471-06613-3, Pub. by Wiley-Interscience). Wiley.

Granger, Bill. Public Murders. 288p. (Orig.). 1980. pap. 1.95 o.s.i. (ISBN 0-515-05130-6). Jove Pubns.

--Schism. 1982. pap. 3.50 (ISBN 0-671-45274-6). PB.

Granger Book Co. Editorial Board. Index to Poetry in Periodicals: American Poetic Renaissance, 1915 to 1919. LC 81-80120. 228p. 1981. lib. bdg. 39.99x (ISBN 0-89609-212-7). Granger Bk.

--Survey of American Poetry: Vol. I-Colonial Period, 1607-1765. LC 81-83526. (The Granger Anthology, Series II). 220p. 1982. 34.95x (ISBN 0-89609-213-5). Granger Bk.

Granger Book Company, Inc, ed. Index to Poetry in Periodicals: 1920 to 1924. LC 81-80120. 230p. 1983. 39.99x (ISBN 0-89609-224-0). Granger Bk.

Granger Book Company, Inc., ed. Index to Poetry in Periodicals: 1925 to 1929. LC 81-80120. 230p. 1983. 39.99x (ISBN 0-89609-235-6). Granger Bk.

Granger, Bruce I., tr. see Irving, Washington.

Granger, Carol. Jailer Who Changed His Mind: Paul & Silas. (Arch Bks: Set 8). (Illus., Orig.). (ps-4). 1971. pap. 0.89 (ISBN 0-570-06058-3, 591175). Concordia.

Granger, Clive W., jt. auth. see Labys, Walter.

Granger, Colin & Hicks, Tony. Contact English, Bk. 1. 1977. 5.95x (ISBN 0-435-28371-5); tchr's manual 14.95x (ISBN 0-435-28370-7); 3 tapes 90.00 (ISBN 0-435-28372-3); 3 cassettes 70.00x (ISBN 0-435-28373-1); wallcharts o. p. 40.00x (ISBN 0-435-28374-X). Heinemann Ed.

Granger, Harris J., ed. see Bishop, Vernon S.

Granger, Katherine. A Man's Persuasion. (Second Chance at Love Ser.: No. 89). 1982. pap. 1.75 (ISBN 0-515-06851-9). Jove Pubns.

Granger, Mary, tr. see Landry, Monica & Olivier, Julien.

Granger, P., jt. auth. see Brevard, C.

Granger, Stewart. Sparks Fly Upward. (Illus.). 416p. 1981. 14.95 (ISBN 0-399-12674-0). Putnam Pub Group.

Granick, David. Management of the Industrial Firm in the USSR. LC 74-6752. 346p. 1974. Repr. of 1954 ed. lib. bdg. 20.50x (ISBN 0-8371-7555-0, GRIF). Greenwood.

Granier, Camille. Essai de Bibliographie Charitable. (Conditions of the 19th Century French Working Class Ser.). 458p. (Fr.). 1974. Repr. of 1891 ed. lib. bdg. 115.00 o.p. (ISBN 0-8287-0392-2, 1090). Clearwater Pub.

Granier, Jacqueline P., jt. ed. see Kavaas, Igor I.

Granit, R., ed. see IBRO Symposium, Italy, September 1978.

Granit, Ragnar. The Purposive Brain. 1977. text ed. 18.50x (ISBN 0-262-07069-3); pap. 5.95x (ISBN 0-262-57054-8). MIT Pr.

Granito, Anthony R. Fire Instructor's Training Guide. (Illus.). 1972. 12.00 (ISBN 0-686-12261-5). Fire Eng.

Granits. Mechanisms Regulating the Discharge of Motoneurons. 92p. 1982. 50.00x (ISBN 0-85323-340-3, Pub. by Liverpool Univ England). State Mutual Bk.

Grannis, Gary E., jt. auth. see Groneman, Chris H.

Grannis, Valleria B. Dramatic Parody in Eighteenth Century France. (Studies in Comparative Literature: No. 5). 428p. Repr. of 1931 ed. lib. bdg. 27.50x (ISBN 0-87991-504-8). Porcupine Pr.

Granof, Michael H. Accounting for Managers & Investors. 768p. 1983. 27.95 (ISBN 0-13-002725-1). P-H.

Granof, Michael H. & Evans, Thomas G. Financial Accounting: Principles & Issues. 2nd ed. (Illus.). 352p. 1980. text ed. 25.95 (ISBN 0-13-314153-5); student guide 11.95 (ISBN 0-13-314179-9). P-H.

--Financial Accounting: Principles & Issues. 2nd ed. 352p. 1980. student guide 11.95 (ISBN 0-13-314179-9). P-H.

Granom, Lewis. Plain & Easy Instructions for Playing the German-Flute. (The Flute Library: Vol. 11). 1981. Repr. of 1770 ed. write for info. o.s.i. (ISBN 90-6027-230-7, Pub. by Frits Knuf Netherlands). Pendragon NY.

Granrose, John T., jt. auth. see Frankena, William K.

Gransden, K. W., ed. Tudor Verse Satire. (Athlone Renaissance Library). 1970. pap. text ed. 11.75x (ISBN 0-485-13601-5, Athlone Pr); pap. text ed. 4.75x o. p. (ISBN 0-485-12601-X, Athlone Pr). Humanities.

Gransden, K. W., ed. see Virgil.

Granstrand, Ove. Technology, Management & Marketing. LC 82-16804. 300p. 1982. 25.00x (ISBN 0-312-79007-4). St Martin.

Granstrom, B., jt. ed. see Carlson, R.

Grant, jt. auth. see Anderson.

Grant, Aline. Susan Ferrier of Edinburgh: A Biography. 174p. 1957. 4.95 o.p. (ISBN 0-8040-0286-X). Swallow.

Grant, Barbara M. & Hennings, Dorothy G. The Teacher Moves: An Analysis of Non-Verbal Activity. LC 71-148592. 1971. pap. text ed. 6.50x (ISBN 0-8077-1456-9). Tchrs Coll.

Grant, Blanche. When Old Trails Were New: The Story of Taos. LC 63-21230. 348p. 1983. Repr. of 1963 ed. softcover 12.00 (ISBN 0-87380-140-7). Rio Grande.

Grant, Brian W. From Sin to Wholeness. LC 81-16122. 1982. pap. write for info (ISBN 0-664-24399-1). Westminster.

Grant, C. D., jt. ed. see Johnston, Gary.

Grant, C. H. The Making of Modern Belize. LC 75-36022. (Cambridge Commonwealth Ser.). (Illus.). 400p. 1976. 54.50 (ISBN 0-521-20731-2). Cambridge U Pr.

Grant, Carolyn, jt. auth. see Wakeman, Frederic.

Grant, Charles F. Introductory Accounting: An Audio-Tutorial Approach. (Business Ser.). 1977. pap. text ed. 17.95 (ISBN 0-675-08502-0); audio cassettes 140.00 (ISBN 0-675-08501-2). Additional supplements may be obtained from publisher. Merrill.

Grant, Charles L. The Dodd, Mead Gallery of Horror. 1983. 15.95 (ISBN 0-396-08160-6). Dodd.

--The Soft Whisper of the Dead. (Illus.). 208p. 1983. 15.00 (ISBN 0-937986-55-0); Signed & Slipcased ed. 40.00x (ISBN 0-937986-56-9). D M Grant.

Grant, Charles L., ed. Fears. 288p. (Orig.). 1983. pap. 2.95 (ISBN 0-425-06066-7). Berkley Pub.

Grant, Cynthia D. Joshua Fortune. LC 80-11983. 156p. (gr. 6-9). 1980. 9.95 (ISBN 0-689-30777-2). Atheneum.

Grant, D., ed. see Baker, Robert F.

Grant, Damian. Realism. (Critical Idiom Ser.). 1970. pap. 4.95x (ISBN 0-416-17820-0). Methuen Inc.

Grant, Daniel A., et al. Periodontics in the Tradition of Orban & Gottlieb. 5th ed. LC 79-10615. (Illus.). 974p. 1979. text ed. 46.95 (ISBN 0-8016-1961-0). Mosby.

Grant, Dave. The Ultimate Power. 192p. 1983. 9.95 (ISBN 0-8007-1337-0). Revell.

Grant, Don. Purrplexities: A Book that Gives Us Paws. 64p. 1982. 3.95 (ISBN 0-399-50649-7, Perige). Putnam Pub Group.

Grant, Donald P. Design by Objectives: Multiple Objective Design Analysis & Evaluation in Architectural, Environmental & Product Design. LC 82-73290. 50p. (Orig.). 1982. pap. text ed. 4.00 (ISBN 0-910821-00-3). Design Meth.

Grant, Douglas, ed. see Churchill, Charles.

Grant, Douglas, ed. see James, Henry.

Grant, E. Physical Science in the Middle Ages. LC 77-8393. (History of Science Ser.). (Illus.). 1978. 19.95 o.p. (ISBN 0-521-21862-4); pap. 8.95 (ISBN 0-521-29294-8). Cambridge U Pr.

Grant, Edward. Much Ado About Nothing: Theories of Space & Vacuum from the Middle Ages to the Scientific Revolution. LC 80-13876. (Illus.). 545p. 1981. 65.00 (ISBN 0-521-22983-9). Cambridge U Pr.

Grant, Edward, ed. Nicole Oresme & the Kinematics of Circular Motion: Tractatus De Commensurabilitate Vel Incommensurabilitate Motuum Celi. Grant, Edward, tr. LC 79-133238. (Medieval Science Ser). (Illus.). 438p. 1971. 50.00 (ISBN 0-299-05830-1). U of Wis Pr.

Grant, Edward, tr. see Oresme, Nicole.

Grant, Elliott M. Emile Zola. (World Authors Ser.). 1966. lib. bdg. 13.95 (ISBN 0-8057-2996-8, Twayne). G K Hall.

Grant, Ellsworth S. The Colt Legacy. LC 81-85196. (Illus.). 234p. 1982. 30.00 (ISBN 0-686-91789-8); pap. 17.00 (ISBN 0-686-98228-2). MowBray Co.

Grant, Eugene, jt. ed. see Ireson, W. Grant.

Grant, Eugene L. Statistical Quality Control. 4th ed. (Illus.). 650p. 1972. text ed. 22.95 o.p. (ISBN 0-07-024097-3, C); solutions manual 5.95 o.p. (ISBN 0-07-024098-1). McGraw.

Grant, Eugene L. & Bell, L. F. Basic Accounting & Cost Accounting. 2nd ed. 1964. text ed. 29.65 (ISBN 0-07-024094-9, C); tchrs' manual 2.50 (ISBN 0-07-024091-4); problem-solution forms 18.95 (ISBN 0-07-024090-6). McGraw.

Grant, Eugene L. & Leavenworth, Richard. Statistical Quality Control. 5th ed. (Industrial Engineering & Management Science Ser.). (Illus.). 1979. text ed. 32.50x o.p. (ISBN 0-07-024114-7); solutions manual 13.50 o.p. (ISBN 0-07-024115-5). McGraw.

Grant, Eugene L., et al. Principles of Engineering Economy. 6th ed. LC 76-9559. 1976. 24.95 o.p. (ISBN 0-8260-3516-7). Wiley.

Grant, Eugene L., et al, eds. Principles of Engineering Economy. 7th ed. LC 81-10399. 687p. 1982. text ed. 28.95 (ISBN 0-471-06436-X); Avail Tchr's Manual (ISBN 0-471-08439-5). Wiley.

Grant, Eva. A Cow for Jaya. (Break-of-Day Bk.). (Illus.). 64p. (gr. 1-3). 1973. PLB 4.69 o.p. (ISBN 0-698-30484-5, Coward). Putnam Pub Group.

Grant, F. S. & West, G. F. Interpretation Theory in Applied Geophysics. (Illus.). 1965. text ed. 55.00 (ISBN 0-07-024100-7, C). McGraw.

Grant, F. W. The Crowned Christ. 5.00 (ISBN 0-88172-072-0); pap. 3.25 (ISBN 0-88172-073-9). Believers Bkshelf.

--Genesis in the Light of the New Testament. 5.50 (ISBN 0-88172-076-3); pap. 3.95 (ISBN 0-88172-077-1). Believers Bkshelf.

--Lessons from Exodus. 5.25 (ISBN 0-88172-074-7); pap. 3.50 (ISBN 0-88172-075-5). Believers Bkshelf.

Grant, F. W., ed. The Divine Movement. pap. 2.95 (ISBN 0-88172-138-7). Believers Bkshelf.

--Nicolaitanism, the Rise & Growth of the Clergy. pap. 2.25 (ISBN 0-88172-139-5). Believers Bkshelf.

Grant, Francis J. The Manual of Heraldry. LC 75-23365. (Illus.). 1976. Repr. of 1929 ed. 30.00x (ISBN 0-8103-4252-9). Gale.

Grant, Frederick C. Ancient Judaism & the New Testament. LC 77-18848. 1978. Repr. of 1959 ed. lib. bdg. 19.75x (ISBN 0-313-20204-4, GRAJ). Greenwood.

Grant, Gi-Gi. Thirty-Three Prayers. 1983. 6.95 (ISBN 0-533-05468-0). Vantage.

Grant, Gilbert S. Avian Incubation: Egg Temperature, Nest Humidity, & Behavioral Thermoregulation in a Hot Environment. 75p. 1982. 9.00 (ISBN 0-943610-30-3). Am Ornithologists.

Grant, Glen, jt. auth. see Ogawa, Dennis M.

Grant, H. Vehicle Rescue. (Illus.). 1975. pap. 18.95 (ISBN 0-87618-137-X); instr's guide o.p. 7.95 (ISBN 0-87618-611-8); systems chart 7.95 (ISBN 0-87618-610-X). R J Brady.

Grant, H. & Murray, R., Jr. Emergency Care. 2nd ed. LC 78-17756. (Illus.). 1978. 13.95 o.p. (ISBN 0-87618-886-2). R J Brady.

Grant, H. Roger. Self-Help in the 1890's Depression. 160p. 1982. text ed. 11.95x (ISBN 0-8138-1634-3). Iowa St U Pr.

Grant, Harvey & Murray, Robert. Course Planning Guide for Emergency Care. 2nd ed. (Illus.). 336p. 1978. pap. text ed. 17.95 o.p. (ISBN 0-87618-961-3). R J Brady.

--Vehicle Rescue. 2nd ed. (Illus.). 320p. Date not set. pap. text ed. 18.95 (ISBN 0-89303-118-6). R J Brady.

Grant, Harvey D. & Murray, Robert H. Emergency Care. 3rd ed. (Illus.). 512p. 1982. pap. text ed. 14.95 (ISBN 0-89303-116-X). R J Brady.

Grant, Hiram E. Engineering Drawing with Creative Design. 2nd ed. 1968. text ed. 18.50 o.p. (ISBN 0-07-024104-X, C); instructor's solutions book 2.95 o.p. (ISBN 0-07-024101-5). McGraw.

Grant, I. F. Along a Highland Road. 208p. 1982. 16.00 (ISBN 0-85683-048-8, Pub by Shepheard-Walwyn England). Flatiron Book.

--Everyday Life on an Old Highland Farm 1769-1782. 320p. 1982. 20.00 (ISBN 0-85683-058-5, Pub by Shepheard-Walwyn England). Flatiron Book.

--Highland Folk Ways. (Illus.). 1961. 25.00 (ISBN 0-7100-1466-X); pap. 11.95 (ISBN 0-7100-8064-6). Routledge & Kegan.

Grant, I. S. & Phillips, W. R. Electromagnetism. LC 73-17668. (Manchester Physics Ser). 1975. 54.50x o.p. (ISBN 0-471-32245-8); pap. 23.00x (ISBN 0-471-32246-6, Pub. by Wiley-Interscience). Wiley.

Grant, J. Douglas, jt. auth. see Toch, Hans.

Grant, James. The Mysteries of All Nations. LC 79-150243. 1971. Repr. of 1880 ed. 61.00x (ISBN 0-8103-3391-0). Gale.

Grant, Jan. Our New Baby. LC 79-22048. (Social Values Ser.). (Illus.). 32p. (gr. k-3). 1980. PLB 9.25 (ISBN 0-516-01480-3); pap. 2.95 (ISBN 0-516-41480-1). Childrens.

Grant, Jeanne. Man From Tennessee. (Second Chance at Love Ser.: No. 119). 1983. pap. 1.75 (ISBN 0-515-07207-9). Jove Pubns.

Grant, Jim. A Thief in the Night. 128p. 1974. pap. 2.95 (ISBN 0-8024-8688-6). Moody.

Grant, Joan. Lord of the Horizon. 1976. pap. 1.95 o.p. (ISBN 0-380-00731-2, 300494). Avon.

Grant, Joanne, jt. auth. see Berke, Melvyn.

Grant, John P., jt. ed. see Cusine, Douglas J.

Grant, Joy. Harold Monro & the Poetry Bookshop. LC 66-11437. 1967. 26.50x (ISBN 0-520-00512-0). U of Cal Pr.

Grant, Julius. Hackh's Chemical Dictionary. 4th ed. 1968. 63.25 (ISBN 0-07-024064-7, P&RB). McGraw.

Grant, Kenneth. Cults of the Shadow. 1976. 12.50 o.p. (ISBN 0-87728-310-9). Weiser.

Grant, Kenneth, ed. see Crowley, Aleister.

Grant, Kenneth, jt. ed. see Symonds, John.

Grant, Kerry S. Dr. Charles Burney as Critic & Historian of Music. Beulow, George, ed. (Studies in Musicology: No. 62). 1983. 59.95 (ISBN 0-8357-1375-X). Univ Microfilms.

Grant, L. Comments on the Book of Romans. pap. 2.95 (ISBN 0-88172-078-X). Believers Bkshelf.

Grant, L., jt. ed. see Schneider, T.

Grant, L. M. First & Second Thessalonians. 46p. pap. 2.25 (ISBN 0-88172-079-8). Believers Bkshelf.

Grant, Lawrence V., jt. auth. see Jaros, Dean.

Grant, Lewis, jt. ed. see Davis, Ray J.

Grant, M. From Imperium to Auctoritas. (Illus.). 1983. Repr. of 1946 ed. lib. bdg. 50.00 (ISBN 0-942666-20-8). S J Durst.

Grant, M. D., jt. auth. see Davies, R.

Grant, Malcolm A., et al. Geothermal Reservoir Engineering. LC 82-4105. (Energy Science & Technology Ser.). Date not set. 45.00 (ISBN 0-12-295620-6). Acad Pr.

Grant, Marcia L., et al. Case Studies in Clinical Pharmacology. LC 77-519. 169p. 1977. pap. text ed. 8.95x (ISBN 0-8036-4280-6). Davis Co.

Grant, Marcus. Alcoholism in Perspective. 173p. 1979. text ed. 22.95 o.p. (ISBN 0-8391-1332-3). Univ Park.

Grant, Marcus, jt. ed. see Edwards, Griffith.

Grant, Matthew G. Robert E. Lee. LC 73-18078. 1974. PLB 6.95 (ISBN 0-87191-302-X). Creative Ed.

Grant, Maxwell. Inherit the Sun. 1981. 13.95 (ISBN 0-698-11074-9, Coward). Putnam Pub Group.

Grant, Michael. The Decline & Fall of the Roman Empire: A Reappraisal. (Illus.). 320p. 1976. 14.95 o.p. (ISBN 0-685-58362-7, C N Potter Bks). Crown.

--Fall of the Roman Empire, The: A Reappraisal of Our Own Times. 1976. 14.95 o.p. (ISBN 0-517-52448-1). Crown.

--Myths of the Greeks & Romans. (Illus.). 1964. pap. 3.95 (ISBN 0-451-62118-2, ME2118, Ment). NAL.

Grant, Mildred B., compiled by. Indexes to "The Competitor". LC 77-15303. 1978. lib. bdg. 25.00x (ISBN 0-313-20032-7, GIC/). Greenwood.

Grant, Murray. Scaffold Falsework Design. (Viewpoint Publication Ser.). (Illus.). 1982. pap. text ed. 16.50x (ISBN 0-86310-005-8). Scholium Intl.

Grant, Myrna. Ivan & the Daring Escape. (Ivan Ser.). (gr. 3-8). 1976. pap. 2.95 (ISBN 0-8423-1847-X). Tyndale.

--Ivan and the Hidden Bible. (Ivan Ser.). (gr. 3-8). 1975. pap. 2.50 (ISBN 0-8423-1848-8). Tyndale.

--Ivan & the Informer. (Ivan Ser.). 1977. pap. 2.25 (ISBN 0-8423-1846-1). Tyndale.

--Ivan & the Moscow Circus. (gr. 4-8). 1980. pap. 2.95 (ISBN 0-8423-1843-7). Tyndale.

--Ivan & the Secret in the Suitcase. (Ivan Ser.). (gr. 3-8). 1975. pap. 2.95 (ISBN 0-8423-1849-6). Tyndale.

--Ivan & the Star of David. (Ivan Ser.). 1977. pap. 2.95 (ISBN 0-8423-1845-3). Tyndale.

--Ivan y el Delator. 112p. Date not set. 1.95 (ISBN 0-88113-154-7). Edit Betania.

--Ivan y el Secreto en la Valija. 160p. Date not set. 2.25 (ISBN 0-88113-152-0). Edit Betania.

--Ivan y la Biblia Escondida. 128p. Date not set. 1.95 (ISBN 0-88113-150-4). Edit Betania.

--Ivan y la Estrella de David. 144p. Date not set. 2.25 (ISBN 0-88113-155-5). Edit Betania.

--Ivan y la Fuga Audaz. 176p. Date not set. 2.50 (ISBN 0-88113-151-2). Edit Betania.

--La Jornada. 208p. Date not set. 2.95 (ISBN 0-88113-200-4). Edit Betania.

--Mision Secreta de Alexis. 144p. Date not set. 2.25 (ISBN 0-88113-202-0). Edit Betania.

--Tanya y el Guarda Fronterizo. 96p. Date not set. 1.75 (ISBN 0-88113-321-3). Edit Betania.

--Vanya. LC 73-89729. 1974. pap. 5.95 (ISBN 0-88419-009-9). Creation Hse.
--Vanya. 208p. Date not set. 2.75 (ISBN 0-88113-310-8). Edit Betania.
Grant, Neil. Explorers. LC 82-50399. (History Eye Witness Ser.). PLB 15.96 (ISBN 0-382-06665-0). Silver.
Grant, Neil & Jones, Jo. Discovering the World. (Full Color Fact Books). (Illus.). 32p. (gr. 4-12). 1982. PLB 7.95 (ISBN 0-8219-0011-0, 35548). EMC.
Grant, Neil, rev. by see Albert, Burton, Jr.
Grant, Neville see Allen, W. S.
Grant, Nicholas J. & Giessen, Bill C., eds. Rapidly Quenched Metals. 1976. text ed. 35.00x (ISBN 0-262-07066-9). MIT Pr.
Grant, Nigel, jt. auth. see Bell, Robert.
Grant, Peter, jt. auth. see Harrison, Jeffery.
Grant, R. A. Applied Protein Chemistry. 1980. 53.50 (ISBN 0-85334-865-0, Pub. by Applied Sci England). Elsevier.
Grant, Raymond J. S. Cambridge, Corpus Christi College Forty One: The Loricas & the Missal. (Costerus New Ser.: No. XVII). 1979. pap. 17.25x o.p. (ISBN 90-6203-762-3). Humanities.
Grant, Richard B. The Goncourt Brothers. (World Authors Ser.: France: No. 183). lib. bdg. 15.95 (ISBN 0-8057-2384-6, Twayne). G K Hall.
--Theophile Gautier. (World Authors Ser.). 1975. lib. bdg. 14.95 (ISBN 0-8057-6213-2, Twayne). G K Hall.
Grant, Rita, jt. auth. see O'Conner, Melvin C.
Grant, Robert. A Historical Introduction to the New Testament. 1972. pap. 4.95 o.p. (ISBN 0-671-21406-3, Touchstone Bks). S&S.
Grant, Robert M., ed. see Goodspeed, Edgar J.
Grant, Roger H. Insurance Reform: Consumer Action in the Progressive Era. (Illus.). 1979. text ed. o.p. (ISBN 0-8138-0935-5); pap. text ed. 9.50x (ISBN 0-8138-1210-0). Iowa St U Pr.
Grant, Rose. Fast & Delicious Cookbook. LC 81-81484. (Illus.). 183p. (Orig.). 1981. pap. 5.95 (ISBN 0-911954-62-7). Nitty Gritty.
Grant, Ruthie. Scattered Moments. Richard, L. E. & Lorenzo, Thomas, eds. LC 82-74055. (Illus.). 96p. 1983. pap. 5.95 (ISBN 0-911657-00-2). Creative Gen.
Grant, Sister Marie, jt. auth. see Ashlock, Patrick.
Grant, Steven A., jt. auth. see Brown, John H.
Grant, Steven C. A Management Guide to Automatic Call Distributors. 240p. 1981. 125.00 (ISBN 0-686-98043-3). Telecom Lib.
Grant, U. S. Personal Memoirs of U. S. Grant. (Quality Paperbacks Ser.). 608p. 1982. pap. 10.95 (ISBN 0-306-80172-8). Da Capo.
Grant, Ulysses S. The Papers of Ulysses S. Grant, Vol. 10: January 1 - May 31, 1864. Simon, John Y., ed. LC 67-10725. (Illus.). 648p. 1982. 40.00x (ISBN 0-8093-0980-7). S Ill U Pr.
--The Papers of Ulysses S. Grant, Vol. 9: July 7-December 31, 1863. Simon, John Y., ed. LC 67-10725. (Illus.). 672p. 1982. 40.00x (ISBN 0-8093-0979-3). S Ill U Pr.
Grant, W. A. & Balfour, D., eds. Vacuum '82: Proceedings of the Biennial Conference of the Vacuum Group of the Institute of Physics, Chester, 29-31 March 1982. 112p. 1982. pap. 28.00 (ISBN 0-08-029999-7). Pergamon.
Grant, W. E., tr. see Zlotin, R. I. & Khodashova, K. S.
Grant, W. Harold, jt. auth. see Stefflre, Buford.
Grant, Wilson W. The Caring Father. LC 82-72990. (Orig.). 1983. pap. 5.95 (ISBN 0-8054-5654-6). Broadman.
--De Padres a Hijos Acerca Del Sexo. La Valle, Maria T., et al, trs. from Eng. (Sexo en la Vida Christiana Ser.). (Illus.). 192p. (Span.). 1980. pap. 3.75 (ISBN 0-311-46255-3). Casa Bautista.
Grantham, Dewey W. United States Since Nineteen Forty-Five: The Ordeal of Power. (Modern America Ser.). 1975. 14.95 (ISBN 0-07-024116-3, C). McGraw.
Grantham, Donald, jt. auth. see Kennan, Kent.
Grantham, Donald J. Antennas, Transmission Lines, & Microwaves. LC 77-25369. (The Grantham Electronics-with-Mathematics Ser.: Vol. 6). (Illus.). 1977. pap. text ed. 18.95x (ISBN 0-915668-06-8). G S E Pubns.
--Basic Electronic Devices & Circuits. LC 77-22488. (The Grantham Electronics-with-Mathematics Ser.: Vol. 4). (Illus.). 1977. pap. text ed. 18.95x (ISBN 0-915668-04-1). G S E Pubns.
--Basic Radio & Television Systems. LC 79-11773. (Grantham Electronics-with-Mathematics Ser.: Vol. 5). (Illus.). 1979. pap. 17.95x (ISBN 0-915668-05-X). G S E Pubns.
--Fundamental Properties of AC Circuits. LC 75-18398. (Grantham Electronics-with-Mathematics Ser.: Vol. 2). (Illus.). 1976. pap. text ed. 15.95x (ISBN 0-915668-02-5). G S E Pubns.
--Geometry for Science & Technology. LC 76-40924. 121p. 1976. pap. text ed. 8.95x (ISBN 0-915668-28-9). G S E Pubns.
--Grantham's FCC License Study Guide. LC 75-18397. (Illus.). 440p. 1975. pap. text ed. 15.95x o.p. (ISBN 0-915668-25-4). G S E Pubns.
--Introductory Electricity with Mathematics. LC 75-2797. (Grantham Electronics-with-Mathematics Ser.: Vol. 1). (Illus.). 288p. 1975. pap. text ed. 16.95x (ISBN 0-915668-01-7). G S E Pubns.
--Mathematics for Basic Circuit Analysis. LC 76-40449. (Grantham Electronics-with-Mathematics Ser: Vol. 3). 1976. pap. text ed. 18.95x (ISBN 0-915668-03-3). G S E Pubns.
Grantham, Walter J., jt. auth. see Vincent, Thomas L.
Granville, W. A., et al. Elements of the Differential & Integral Calculus. new & rev. ed. 1962. text ed. 31.95 (ISBN 0-471-00206-2). Wiley.
Granville-Baker, Harley. Preface to Shakespeare: Volume 1, Hamlet. 1977. pap. 9.95 (ISBN 0-7134-2050-2, Pub. by Batsford England). David & Charles.
Granville-Barker, Harley. Prefaces to Shakespeare: Vol. 2, King Lear, Antony & Cleopatra. 176p. 1978. pap. 9.95 (ISBN 0-7134-2064-2, Pub. by Batsford England). David & Charles.
--Prefaces to Shakespeare: Vol. 3, Julius Caesar, Cymbeline, the Merchant of Venice. 192p. 1971. pap. 9.95 (ISBN 0-7134-2065-0, Pub. by Batsford England). David & Charles.
--Prefaces to Shakespeare: Vol. 6, a Winter's Tale, Twelfth Night, Midsummer Night's Dream, Macbeth, from Henry V to Hamlet. 176p. 1974. pap. 9.95 (ISBN 0-7134-2791-4, Pub. by Batsford England). David & Charles.
Granzig, William, jt. auth. see Peck, Ellen.
Graper, Elmer D. American Police Administration: A Handbook on Police Organization & Methods of Administration in American Cities. LC 69-14929. (Criminology, Law Enforcement, & Social Problems Ser.: No. 37). (With intro. added). 1969. Repr. of 1921 ed. 17.00x (ISBN 0-87585-037-5). Patterson Smith.
Graphic Arts Trade Journals Int'l. Inc. Export Graficas U. S. A. 1983-84. Miura, Lydia, ed. (Illus.). 115p. (Span.). 1983. pap. 15.00 (ISBN 0-910762-11-2). Graphic Arts Trade.
--Export Graficas USA, 1982-83. Humphrey, G. A. & Miura, Lydia, eds. (Illus.). 132p. (Orig., Span.). 1982. pap. 15.00 (ISBN 0-910762-09-0). Graph Arts Tra.
Graphic Committee Centre Ltd. The Best of British Illustrators Fifth Annual (1981) 224p. 1981. 95.00x (ISBN 0-686-97067-5, Pub. by Graphic Comm England). State Mutual Bk.
Graphics Arts Trade Journals International Inc. Export Grafics USA, 1982-83. Humphrey, G. A. & Miura, Lydia, eds. (Illus.). 106p. (Orig.). 1982. pap. 6.00 (ISBN 0-910762-10-4). Graph Arts Trade.
Grappa, Carol di see Di Grappa, Carol.
Grappa, Carol di see Di Grappa, Carol, et al.
Grappel, Robert D. & Hemenway, Jack E. Link Sixty-Eight: An M6800 Linking Loader. LC 78-17819. 1979. pap. 8.00 (ISBN 0-07-024120-1, BYTE Bks). McGraw.
--Tracer: A 6800 Debugging Program. LC 78-7326. 1978. pap. 6.00 (ISBN 0-07-024121-X, BYTE Bks). McGraw.
Gras, Norman S. Business & Capitalism: An Introduction to Business History. LC 68-55720. (Illus.). Repr. of 1939 ed. 27.50x (ISBN 0-678-00747-0). Kelley.
Grasbeck, Ralph & Alstrom, Torgny, eds. Reference Values in Laboratory Medicine: The Current State of the Art. LC 80-42312. 413p. 1982. 44.95x (ISBN 0-471-28025-9, Pub. by Wiley-Interscience). Wiley.
Graselli, Rose N. & Hegner, Priscilla A. Playful Parenting. LC 80-39665. (Illus.). 317p. 1981. 14.95 (ISBN 0-399-90117-5, Marek). Putnam Pub Group.
Grasha, Anthony F. Practical Applications of Psychology. 2nd ed. 1982. pap. text ed. 14.95 (ISBN 0-316-32408-6); tchrs' manual avail. (ISBN 0-316-32409-4); students' guide 7.95 (ISBN 0-316-32411-6). Little.
Grasha, Anthony F. & Kirchenbaum, Daniel S. Psychology of Adjustment & Competence: An Applied Approach. (Orig.). 1980. text ed. 17.95 (ISBN 0-316-32412-4); tchr's manual free (ISBN 0-316-32421-3); study guide 7.95 (ISBN 0-316-32413-2). Little.
Grasham, John A. & Gooder, Glenn G. Improving Your Speech. (Illus.). 326p. (Orig.). 1960. pap. text ed. 12.95 o.p. (ISBN 0-15-541260-4, HC). HarBraceJ.
Grass, Gunter. Cat & Mouse. pap. 1.95 (ISBN 0-451-09855-2, J9855, Sig). NAL.
--Davor: Ein Stuck in Thirteen Szenen. Lange, Victor & Lange, Frances, eds. 182p. (Ger.). 1975. pap. text ed. 4.95 o.p. (ISBN 0-686-97843-9). HarBraceJ.
--Four Plays. Manheim, Ralph & Willson, A. Leslie, trs. Incl. Flood; Mister, Mister; Only Ten Minutes to Buffalo; The Wicked Cooks. LC 67-11968. 289p. 1968. pap. 3.25 o.p. (ISBN 0-15-633150-0, HB138, Harv). HarBraceJ.
--Headbirths; or, The Germans Are Dying Out. 160p. 1983. pap. 2.95 (ISBN 0-449-20057-4, Crest). Fawcett.
--Katz und Maus. Brookes, H. F. & Fraenkel, C. E., eds. 272p. (Orig.). 1971. pap. text ed. 9.00 (ISBN 0-686-83757-6). Heinemann Ed.
--Kinderlied. (Illus.). 60p. 1983. 50.00 (ISBN 0-935716-18-1). Lord John.
--Local Anaesthetic. Manheim, Ralph, tr. LC 78-100501. (Helen & Kurt Wolff Bk). 1970. 6.95 o.p. (ISBN 0-15-152957-4). HarBraceJ.
--Tin Drum. Manheim, Ralph, tr. 1971. 10.95 (ISBN 0-394-44902-9, V-300, Vin); pap. 3.95 (ISBN 0-394-74560-4). Random.
Grasselli, Jeanette G., et al. Chemical Applications of Raman Spectroscopy. LC 81-1326. 198p. 1981. 33.95 (ISBN 0-471-08541-3, Pub. by Wiley-Interscience). Wiley.
Grasselli, Margaret M., tr. see Brayer, Yves & Faxon, Alicia.
Grasselli, Margaret M., tr. see Guibert, Herve.
Grasser, E., ed. CEB-FIP Manual on Bending & Compression. (Euro-International Committee for Concrete Ser.). (Illus.). 128p. 1982. text ed. 35.00x (ISBN 0-86095-701-2). Longman.
Grasshoff, Klaus, ed. Methods of Seawater Analysis. 2nd ed. write for info. (ISBN 0-89573-070-7). Verlag-Chemie.
Grassi, Ernesto. Heidegger & the Question of Renaissance Humanism: Four Studies, Vol. 24. Krois, John M., tr. 110p. 1983. 11.00 (ISBN 0-86698-062-8). Medieval & Renaissance NY.
Grassi, G. & Palz, W., eds. Energy from Biomass. 1982. 39.50 (ISBN 90-277-1482-7, Pub. by Reidel Holland). Kluwer Boston.
Grassi, G., jt. ed. see Bloss, W. H.
Grassi, G. G. & Sabath, L. J., eds. New Trends in Antibiotics. (Research & Theraphy Symposia of the Giovanni Lorenzini Foundation: Vol. 10). 1981. 73.00 (ISBN 0-444-80326-2). Elsevier.
Grassi, Giacomo Di see Jackson, James L.
Grassi, Joseph A. Jesus As Teacher: A New Testament Guide to Learning the Way. LC 78-62676. 1978. pap. 4.95 o.p. (ISBN 0-88489-106-2). St Mary's.
--Teaching the Way: Jesus, The Early Church & Today. LC 82-7054. 176p. 1982. lib. bdg. 21.25 (ISBN 0-8191-2501-6); pap. text ed. 10.00 (ISBN 0-8191-2502-4). U Pr of Amer.
Grassian, Victor. Moral Reasoning: Ethical Theory & Some Contemporary Moral Problems. 400p. 1981. pap. text ed. 14.95 (ISBN 0-13-600759-7). P-H.
Grassie, A. D. The Superconducting State. 40.00x (ISBN 0-686-97024-1, Pub. by Scottish Academic Pr Scotland). State Mutual Bk.
Grassie, N., ed. Developments in Polymer Degradation, Vol. 4. (Illus.). x, 296p. 1982. 71.75 (ISBN 0-85334-132-X, Pub. by Applied Sci England). Elsevier.
--Developments in Polymer Degradation - 3. (Developments Ser.). (Illus.). 319p. 1981. 74.00 (ISBN 0-85334-942-8, Pub. by Applied Sci England). Elsevier.
Grassl, Wolfgang, ed. Lectures in the Philosophy of Mathematics. Waismann, Friedrich. (Studien Zur Oesterreichischen Philosophie). 125p. 1981. pap. text ed. 17.00x (ISBN 90-6203-613-9, Pub. by Rodopi Holland). Humanities.
Grassmann, Hermann G. Ausdehungslehre Von 1878. 4th ed. LC 68-53944. (Ger). 1969. 27.50 (ISBN 0-8284-0222-1). Chelsea Pub.
Grassmuck, George & Salibi, Kamal. Reformed Administration in Lebanon. LC 66-3550. 1964. pap. text ed. 1.00x o.p. (ISBN 0-932098-00-2). Ctr for NE & North African Stud.
Grassner, Nathan. Transformers for Electronic Circuits. 2nd ed. (Illus.). 400p. 1983. 42.50 (ISBN 0-07-024979-2, P&RB). McGraw.
Grasso, Joseph E., jt. auth. see Miller, Ernest L.
Grasso, Mary E. & Maney, Margaret. You Can Write. 1975. pap. text ed. 10.95 (ISBN 0-316-32422-1); tchr's manual free (ISBN 0-316-32419-1). Little.
Gratch, Alan S. Board Members Are Child Advocates. (Orig.). 1980. pap. text ed. 4.95 (ISBN 0-87868-198-1, AM-31). Child Welfare.
Gratch, Bonnie, compiled by. Sports & Physical Education: A Guide to Reference Resources. LC 82-24159. 224p. 1983. lib. bdg. 29.95 (ISBN 0-313-23433-7, GED/). Greenwood.
Grater, Michael. Cut & Color Toys & Decorations. (Illus.). 40p. (Orig.). (gr. 1-6). 1974. pap. 2.00 (ISBN 0-486-23013-9). Dover.
--Cut & Fold Extraterrestrial Invaders That Fly: Twenty-Two Full-Color Spaceships. (Illus.). 36p. (Orig.). 1983. pap. 4.95 (ISBN 0-486-24473-3). Dover.
--Make It in Paper: Creative Three-Dimensional Paper Projects. (Illus.). 96p. (gr. 5 up). 1983. pap. 2.50 (ISBN 0-486-24468-7). Dover.
--Paper Things. (Make & Play Ser.). (Illus.). 48p. (gr. k-6). 1976. pap. 1.50 o.p. (ISBN 0-263-05899-9). Transatlantic.
Gratry, A. Logic. Singer, Helen & Singer, Milton, trs. from Fr. xii, 640p. 1944. 30.00 (ISBN 0-87548-035-7). Open Court.
Grattan, Kevin. Go Away, Billy Wind! (Irish Play Ser.). pap. 2.95x (ISBN 0-912262-66-4). Proscenium.
Grattan-Guinness, I., ed. From the Calculus to Set Theory, 1630-1910: An Introductory History. 306p. 1980. 49.50x o.p. (ISBN 0-7156-1295-6, Pub. by Duckworth England). Biblio Dist.
Gratton, Carolyn. Trusting: Theory & Practice. 240p. 1982. 17.50 (ISBN 0-8245-0496-8). Crossroad NY.
--Trusting: Theory & Practice. 256p. 1983. pap. 9.95 (ISBN 0-8245-0548-4). Crossroad NY.
Gratwick, Reginald T. Dampness in Buildings, Vol. 1: Basement & Ground Floor Conditions. 1967. 6.50 o.p. (ISBN 0-258-96757-9). Transatlantic.
Gratz, David B. Fire Department Management: Scope & Method. (Fire Science Ser.). 1972. text ed. 21.95x (ISBN 0-02-474620-7, 47462). Macmillan.
Gratz, Ron. The Football Coaches Guide to Developing a Multi-Set Offense. LC 81-86511. (Illus.). 160p. 1982. pap. 7.95 (ISBN 0-88011-038-4). Leisure Pr.
Gratzner, H. G., jt. ed. see Schultz, J.
Grau, Joseph J. Criminal & Civil Investigation Handbook. (Illus.). 1088p. 1982. 52.50 (ISBN 0-07-024130-9). McGraw.
Grau, Robert. The Business Man in the Amusement World: A Volume of Progress in the Field of the Theatre. LC 73-160233. (Moving Pictures Ser). xiv, 362p. 1971. Repr. of 1910 ed. lib. bdg. 23.95x (ISBN 0-89198-034-2). Ozer.
Grau, T., et al. African Urban Development: Four Political Approaches. Koll, Michael, ed. 230p. 1972. pap. 15.00x o.p. (ISBN 3-571-09139-6). Intl Pubns Serv.
Graubard, Stephen R. Kissinger: Portrait of a Mind. 288p. 1973. text ed. 9.95 o.p. (ISBN 0-393-05481-0); pap. text ed. 3.45x (ISBN 0-393-09278-X). Norton.
Grauer, R. Cobol: A Vehicle for Information Systems. 1981. 22.95 (ISBN 0-13-139709-5). P-H.
Grauer, Robert G. & Crawford, Marshall A. Cobol: A Pragmatic Approach. (Illus.). 1978. pap. 19.95 ref. (ISBN 0-13-139097-X). P-H.
Grauer, Robert T. A Cobol Book of Practice & Reference. (P-H Software Ser.). (Illus.). 352p. 1981. text ed. 20.95 (ISBN 0-13-139725-7); pap. text ed. 15.95 (ISBN 0-13-139717-6). P-H.
Graulich, David J. Your Career in the Drug Industry & in Pharmacy. LC 81-12832. (Arco's Career Guidance Ser.). (Illus.). 144p. 1982. lib. bdg. 7.95 (ISBN 0-668-05227-9); pap. 4.50 (ISBN 0-668-05231-7). Arco.
Graupe, Daniel. Time Series Analysis & Adaptive Filtering. LC 81-20738. (Orig.). 1983. price not set (ISBN 0-88275-713-X). Krieger.
Graupe, Heinz M. The Rise of Modern Judaism: An Intellectual History of German Jewry 1650-1942. LC 77-9059. 344p. 1979. lib. bdg. 19.50 (ISBN 0-88275-395-9); pap. text ed. 9.50 (ISBN 0-89874-562-4). Krieger.
Grausz, Ilse, tr. see Horowitz, Inge & Windmueller, Ida.
Gravanis, Michael B. & Johnson, Lewis D. Specialty Board Review: Anatomic Pathology. LC 76-23577. (Arco Medical Ser.). 1976. pap. 14.00x (ISBN 0-668-03858-6). Arco.
Grave, Gilman. Thyroid Hormones & Brain Development. LC 76-52899. 392p. 1977. 39.50 (ISBN 0-89004-146-6). Raven.
Grave, Gilman, ed. Early Detection of Potential Diabetes: The Problems & the Promise. 277p. 1979. 31.00 (ISBN 0-89004-301-9). Raven.
Grave, S. A. The Scottish Philosophy of Common Sense. LC 72-7859. 262p. 1973. Repr. of 1960 ed. lib. bdg. 17.25x (ISBN 0-8371-6539-3, GRSC). Greenwood.
Gravel-Kellogg, Orlentha, ed. Bloom on the Land: A Prairie Pioneer Experience. LC 81-90537. (Illus.). 608p. 1982. 25.00x (ISBN 0-9608684-0-2). Gravel-Kellogg.
Gravelle, I. H., jt. auth. see Evans, K. T.
Gravelle, Susan, jt. auth. see Soltow, Martha J.
Gravelles, William D. De see DeGravelles, William D. & Kelley, John H.
Gravenstein, J. S. & Paulus, David A. Clinical Monitoring Practice in Anesthesia. (Illus.). 288p. 1982. text ed. 35.00 (ISBN 0-397-50494-2, Lippincott Medical). Lippincott.
Graver, Fred, ed. see Issacs, Susan.
Graver, Jane. Just As I Am. 80p. (gr. 5-8). 1975. 5.95 (ISBN 0-570-03034-X, 6-1160); pap. 2.75 (ISBN 0-570-03035-8, 6-1161). Concordia.
--Puppets. (A Nice Place to Live Ser.). 1978. pap. 2.25 o.p. (ISBN 0-570-07757-5, 12-2716). Concordia.
--Single But Not Alone. 1983. pap. 2.25 (ISBN 0-570-03880-4). Concordia.
Graver, Lawrence. Conrad's Short Fiction. LC 69-14302. 1968. 24.50x (ISBN 0-520-00513-9). U of Cal Pr.
Graver, Thomas H. Paul Brach & Miriam Shapiro Paintings & Graphic Works. (Illus.). 31p. 1969. 5.00x (ISBN 0-686-99833-2). La Jolla Mus Contemp Art.
Graves, C. B., et al. Catalogue of the Flowering Plants & Ferns of Connecticut Growing Without Cultivation. (Illus.). 1974. 24.00 (ISBN 3-7682-0952-0). Lubrecht & Cramer.
Graves, Carson. The Zone System for 35mm Photographers: A Basic Guide to Exposure Control. (Illus.). 112p. 1982. pap. 13.95 (ISBN 0-930764-39-0). Curtin & London.
--The Zone System for 35mm Photographers: A Basic Guide to Exposure Control. 128p. 1982. pap. 13.95 (ISBN 0-930764-39-0). Van Nos Reinhold.
Graves, Charles P. Benjamin Franklin. (Illus.). (gr. 2-6). pap. 0.95 o.p. (ISBN 0-440-40499-1, YB). Dell.
--Eleanor Roosevelt. LC 66-10019. (Illus.). (gr. 2-8). 1968. pap. 0.95 o.p. (ISBN 0-440-42238-8, YB). Dell.
--Eleanor Roosevelt: First Lady of the World. LC 66-10019. (Discovery Books Ser). (Illus.). (gr. 2-5). 1966. PLB 6.09 o.p. (ISBN 0-8116-6293-4). Garrard.

--Fourth of July. LC 63-13625. (Holiday Bks.). (Illus.). (gr. 2-5). 1963. PLB 7.56 (ISBN 0-8116-6550-X). Garrard.
--Frederick Douglass. (See & Read Biographies). (Illus.). (gr. k-4). 1970. PLB 4.49 o.p. (ISBN 0-399-60187-2). Putnam Pub Group.
--Grandma Moses. LC 69-14830. (Americans All Ser.). (Illus.). 96p. (gr. 4). 1969. PLB 6.48 o.p. (ISBN 0-8116-4553-3). Garrard.
--Matthew Henson. (See & Read Biographies). (Illus.). (gr. 2-4). 1971. PLB 4.49 o.p. (ISBN 0-399-60456-1). Putnam Pub Group.
--Robert F. Kennedy: Man Who Dared to Dream. LC 76-101302. (Americans All Ser). (Illus.). (gr. 3-6). 1970. PLB 7.12 (ISBN 0-8116-4557-6). Garrard.
--The Wright Brothers. new ed. (See & Read Biographies). (Illus.). 64p. (gr. 2-4). 1973. PLB 4.49 o.p. (ISBN 0-399-60790-0). Putnam Pub Group.
Graves, Clay. Hurry up, Christmas! LC 75-11504. (Easy Venture Ser.). (Illus.). 32p. (gr. k-2). 1976. PLB 6.69 (ISBN 0-8116-6068-0). Garrard.
Graves, Donald. Writing: Teachers & Children at Work. 312p. (Orig.). 1982. pap. text ed. 10.00x (ISBN 0-435-08203-5). Heinemann Ed.
Graves, Douglas R. Drawing Portraits. 160p. (Orig.). 1983. pap. 14.95 (ISBN 0-8230-2151-3). Watson-Guptill.
Graves, Edgar B., ed. Bibliography of British History to Fourteen Eighty-Five. 1080p. 1975. 129.00x (ISBN 0-19-822391-9). Oxford U Pr.
Graves, Edward S., jt. auth. see Boyd, T. Munford.
Graves, Elizabeth, tr. see Simatupang, T. B.
Graves, Harold F. & Hoffman, L. Report Writing. 4th ed. 1965. text ed. 15.95 (ISBN 0-13-773671-1). P-H.
Graves, Harvey W. Nuclear Fuel Management. LC 78-19119. 1979. text ed. 37.95x (ISBN 0-471-03136-4). Wiley.
Graves, Henry S. & Guise, C. H. Forest Education. 1932. 49.50x (ISBN 0-686-51388-6). Elliots Bks.
Graves, Herbert S., jt. auth. see Ficker, Victor B.
Graves, John. Goodbye to a River. LC 77-7198. (Illus.). x, 306p. 1977. pap. 7.50 (ISBN 0-8032-5876-3, BB 642, Bison). U of Nebr Pr.
--Hard Scrabble. 1974. 13.50 (ISBN 0-394-48386-3). Knopf.
Graves, John, jt. auth. see Bones, Jim, Jr.
Graves, John C. Conceptual Foundations of Contemporary Relativity Theory. 1971. pap. text ed. 7.95x (ISBN 0-262-57049-1). MIT Pr.
Graves, Joseph J. Managing Investor Relations: Strategies & Techniques. LC 82-71348. 430p. 1982. 27.50 (ISBN 0-87094-346-4). Dow Jones-Irwin.
Graves, Joy D. Early Interventions in Child Abuse: The Role of the Police Officer. LC 81-85982. 125p. 1983. pap. 14.95 (ISBN 0-88247-697-1). R & E Res Assoc.
Graves, Judy, ed. Directory of Pathology Training Programs, 1984-85. (Illus.). 500p. (Orig.). 1983. pap. 30.00 (ISBN 0-686-42864-1). Intersoc Comm Path Info.
Graves, Judy, ed. see Intersociety Committee on Pathology Information, Inc.
Graves, Maitland E. Art of Color & Design. 2nd ed. (Illus.). 1951. text ed. 37.50 (ISBN 0-07-024119-8, C). McGraw.
Graves, Peter. The Seventh Gate. 1978. pap. 9.75 o.p. (ISBN 0-85117-078-1). Transatlantic.
Graves, Philip E., jt. ed. see Tolley, George S.
Graves, Richard, ed. Rhetoric & Composition: A Sourcebook for Teachers & Writers. 2nd, rev. ed. 384p. 1983. pap. text ed. 11.50x (ISBN 0-86709-029-4). Boynton Cook Pubs.
Graves, Richard L. Rhetoric & Composition: A Sourcebook for Teachers. LC 76-13016. 1976. pap. text ed. 9.25x (ISBN 0-8104-5984-1). Boynton Cook Pubs.
Graves, Richard P. The Brothers Powys. (Illus.). 384p. 1983. 25.00 (ISBN 0-684-17880-X, ScribT). Scribner.
Graves, Robert. Apuleius' The Golden Ass. 293p. 1951. pap. 6.25 (ISBN 0-374-50532-2). FS&G.
--Claudius the God. 592p. 8.95 (ISBN 0-394-60812-7). Modern Lib.
--Hercules, My Shipmate. 464p. 1945. pap. 8.95 (ISBN 0-374-51677-4). FS&G.
--Homer's Daughter. 283p. 1982. 14.95 (ISBN 0-89733-058-7); pap. 6.95 (ISBN 0-89733-059-5). Academy Chi Ltd.
--I, Claudius. 448p. 8.95 (ISBN 0-394-60811-9). Modern Lib.
Graves, Robert & Patai, Raphael. Hebrew Myths. 1966. pap. 5.95 (ISBN 0-07-024125-2, SP). McGraw.
Graves, Will. Raising Your Own Meat for Pennies a Day. Stetson, Fred, ed. (Illus.). 160p. (Orig.). 1983. pap. 6.95 (ISBN 0-88266-330-5). Garden Way Pub.
Graves, William W. The Church Teaching & Training. 2nd ed. Viertel, Weldon & Viertel, Joyce, eds. (Religious Education Ser.). 152p. 1982. Repr. of 1975 ed. 7.50 (ISBN 0-311-72681-X, Carib Pubns). Casa Bautista.
Graves-Morris, P. R., jt. auth. see Baker, G. A., Jr.
Graveson, R. H. Comparative Conflict of Laws, Vol. 1: Selected Essays. new ed. (European Studies in Law). 1977. 44.75 (ISBN 0-7204-0486-X, North-Holland). Elsevier.
--One Law: On Jurisprudence & the Unification of Law - Selected Essays, Vol. 2. 1977. 42.75 (ISBN 0-7204-0487-8, North-Holland). Elsevier.
Graveson, R. H., ed. Law: An Outline for the Intending Student. (Outlines Ser). 1967. cased 17.95x (ISBN 0-7100-2999-3); pap. 9.95 (ISBN 0-7100-6028-9). Routledge & Kegan.
Grawe, Paul H. Comedy in Space, Time, & the Imagination. LC 82-10603. 368p. 1983. text ed. 27.95 (ISBN 0-88229-631-0). Nelson-Hall.
Grawe, Roger. Ability in Pre-Schoolers, Earnings, & Home Enviroment. (Working Paper: No. 322). 92p. 1979. 5.00 (ISBN 0-686-36052-4, WP-0322). World Bank.
Grawoig, Dennis E. & Hubbard, Charles L. Strategic Financial Planning with Simulation. (Illus.). 1982. 35.00 (ISBN 0-89433-115-9). Petrocelli.
Grawoig, Dennis E., jt. auth. see Hughes, Ann J.
Grawoig, Dennis E., et al. Mathematics: A Foundation for Decisions. LC 75-12097. (Illus.). 542p. 1976. text ed. 25.95 (ISBN 0-201-02598-1); instr's guide 4.50 (ISBN 0-201-02595-7). A-W.
Gray. The Ecology of Soil Bacteria. 698p. 1982. 70.00x (ISBN 0-85323-161-3, Pub. by Liverpool Univ England). State Mutual Bk.
--Quality Control in Diagnostic Imaging. 320p. 1982. text ed. 34.95 (ISBN 0-8391-1681-0). Univ Park.
Gray, A. see Wilkes, Charles.
Gray, A. H., jt. auth. see Markel, J. E.
Gray, A. P. Mammalian Hybrids: A Check-List with Bibliography. 256p. 1971. 40.00X (ISBN 0-85198-170-4, CAB Bks). State Mutual Bk.
Gray, Asa. Darwiniana: Essays & Reviews Pertaining to Darwinism. Dupree, A. Hunter, ed. LC 63-19136. (The John Harvard Library). 1963. 18.50x o.p. (ISBN 0-674-19300-8). Harvard U Pr.
Gray, Barry. Barry Gray: My Night People. LC 75-14039. 192p. 1975. 7.95 o.p. (ISBN 0-671-22090-X). S&S.
Gray, Betty, jt. auth. see Gray, William B.
Gray, Bettyanne. Manya's Story. LC 77-92305. (Adult & Young Adult Books). (Illus.). (gr. 5-9). 1978. PLB 7.95g (ISBN 0-8225-0762-5). Lerner Pubns.
Gray, Bonnie, et al. Every Woman Works: A Complete Manual for Women Re-Entering the Job Market or Changing Jobs. (Career Development Ser.). (Illus.). 315p. 1981. 19.95 (ISBN 0-534-97981-5); pap. 11.95 (ISBN 0-534-97928-9); leader's guide 5.95 (ISBN 0-534-97927-0). Lifetime Learn.
Gray, C. H. & Howarth, P. J. Clinical Chemical Pathology. 288p. 1979. pap. text ed. 16.50 (ISBN 0-7131-4352-5). E Arnold.
Gray, C. H. & James, V. H., eds. Hormones in Blood, Vol. 4. 3rd ed. Date not set. price not set (ISBN 0-12-296204-4). price not set (ISBN 0-12-296205-2). Acad Pr.
Gray, Catherine D. & Gray, James. Tammy & the Gigantic Fish. LC 82-47732. (Illus.). 32p. (ps-1). 1983. 8.61i (ISBN 0-06-022138-0, HarpJ); PLB 8.89g (ISBN 0-06-022139-9). Har-Row.
Gray, Cecil. Forty-Eight Preludes & Fugues of J. S. Bach. (Music Reprint Ser.). 1979. Repr. of 1938 ed. 19.50 (ISBN 0-306-79559-0). Da Capo.
Gray, Charles, ed. see Juba, Robert D.
Gray, Charles E., jt. auth. see Pierce, Walter D.
Gray, Christopher. Sculpture & Ceramics of Paul Gauguin. LC 79-91819. (Illus.). 330p. 1980. Repr. of 1963 ed. lib. bdg. 75.00 (ISBN 0-87817-263-7). Hacker.
Gray, Colin S. The Geopolitics of the Nuclear Era: Heartland, Rimlands, & the Technological Revolution. LC 77-83666. 70p. 1977. 9.95x (ISBN 0-8448-1257-9); pap. 4.95x (ISBN 0-8448-1258-7). Crane-Russak Co.
--U. S. Military Space Policy to the Year 2000. 1983. text ed. 28.00 (ISBN 0-89011-591-5). Abt Bks.
Gray, Collen. Peru. (World Education Ser.). (Illus., Orig.). 1983. pap. text ed. write for info. (ISBN 0-910054-77-0). Am Assn Coll Registrars.
Gray, D. Pereira. Training for General Practice. 352p. 1981. 49.00x (ISBN 0-7121-2004-1, Pub. by Macdonald & Evans). State Mutual Bk.
Gray, D. R. Non-Private Foundations. 1978. 40.00 (ISBN 0-07-024230-5); forms suppl. avail. McGraw.
Gray, Daniel S. Troy State University Writings & Research, Vol. III. 32p. 1974. pap. 1.95 (ISBN 0-686-97227-9). TSU Pr.
Gray, Douglas, ed. A Selection of Religious Lyrics. (Clarendon Medieval & Tudor Ser). 198p. 1975. 19.95x o.p. (ISBN 0-19-871085-2). Oxford U Pr.
Gray, Douglas M., jt. auth. see Forrester, James.
Gray, E. G., jt. ed. see Bellairs, R.
Gray, Eden. Mastering the Tarot. 1971. 5.95 o.p. (ISBN 0-517-50014-0). Crown.
--Mastering the Tarot: Basic Lessons in an Ancient Mystic Art. 208p. 1973. pap. 3.50 (ISBN 0-451-12320-4, AE2320, Sig). NAL.
--Tarot Revealed: A Modern Guide to Reading the Tarot Cards. 1971. pap. 3.50 (ISBN 0-451-11965-7, AE1965, Sig). NAL.
Gray, Edwyn. Action Atlantic. (Orig.). 1976. pap. 1.25 o.p. (ISBN 0-523-22898-8). Pinnacle Bks.
Gray, Francine, frwd. by see Badinter, Elisabeth.
Gray, Francis C. Prison Discipline in America. LC 77-172599. (Criminology, Law Enforcement, & Social Problems Ser.: No. 189). (With intro. & index added). 1973. Repr. of 1847 ed. 15.00x (ISBN 0-87585-189-4). Patterson Smith.
Gray, G. & Hoel, L. Public Transportation: Planning, Operations & Management. 1979. 38.00 (ISBN 0-13-739169-2). P-H.
Gray, G. W. & Goodby, G. W. Liquid Crystals: Identification, Classification & Structure. (Illus.). 250p. 1983. 87.01 (ISBN 0-08-025299-0). Pergamon.
Gray, Genevieve. Alaska Woman. LC 77-7040. (Time of Danger, Time for Courage Ser.). (Illus.). (gr. 3-9). 1977. PLB 6.95 (ISBN 0-88436-386-4); pap. 3.95 (ISBN 0-88436-387-2). EMC.
--Break-In. LC 73-4505. (Girl Stuff Ser.). (Illus.). (gr. 4-8). 1973. PLB 6.95 (ISBN 0-912022-64-7); pap. 3.95 (ISBN 0-912022-65-5). EMC.
--The Dark Side of Nowhere. LC 77-7110. (Time of Danger, Time for Courage Ser.). (Illus.). (gr. 3-9). 1977. PLB 6.95 (ISBN 0-88436-390-2); pap. 3.95 (ISBN 0-88436-391-0). EMC.
--Has Anyone Seen Buddy Bascom? LC 77-7926. (Time of Danger, Time for Courage Ser.). (Illus.). 40p. (gr. 3-9). 1977. PLB 6.95 (ISBN 0-88436-384-8); pap. 3.95 (ISBN 0-88436-385-6). EMC.
--Hot Shot. LC 73-4585. (Girl Stuff Ser). (Illus.). 32p. (gr. 4-8). 1973. 5.95 o.p. (ISBN 0-912022-62-0); pap. 3.95 (ISBN 0-912022-63-9). EMC.
--I Know a Bus Driver. (Community Helper Bks.). (Illus.). 48p. (gr. 1-3). 1972. PLB 4.29 o.p. (ISBN 0-399-60703-X). Putnam Pub Group.
--The Magic Bears. LC 75-29316. (Blessingway: Tales of a Navajo Family). (Illus.). 40p. (gr. 4-9). 1975. PLB 6.95 (ISBN 0-88436-223-X); pap. 3.95 (ISBN 0-88436-224-8). EMC.
--The Secret of the Mask. LC 75-30708. (Blessingway: Tales of a Navajo Family). (Illus.). 40p. (gr. 4-9). 1975. PLB 6.95 (ISBN 0-88436-221-3); pap. 3.95 (ISBN 0-88436-222-1). EMC.
--Send Wendell. LC 73-17414. (Illus.). 40p. (ps-4). 1974. 7.95 o.p. (ISBN 0-07-024195-3, GB). McGraw.
--The Spiderweb Stone. LC 75-30529. (Blessingway: Tales of a Navajo Family). (Illus.). 40p. (gr. 4-9). 1975. PLB 6.95 (ISBN 0-88436-219-1); pap. 3.95 (ISBN 0-88436-220-5). EMC.
--Stand-off. LC 73-4722. (Girl Stuff Ser.). (gr. 4-8). 1973. PLB 6.95 (ISBN 0-912022-68-X); pap. 3.95 (ISBN 0-912022-69-8). EMC.
--Stray. LC 73-4587. (Girl Stuff Ser). (Illus.). 40p. (Orig.). (gr. 4-8). 1973. PLB 6.95 (ISBN 0-912022-66-3); pap. 3.95 (ISBN 0-912022-67-1). EMC.
--The Tall Singer. LC 75-30531. (Blessingway: Tales of a Navajo Family). (Illus.). 40p. (gr. 4-9). 1975. PLB 6.95 (ISBN 0-88436-217-5); pap. 3.95 (ISBN 0-88436-218-3). EMC.
--Two Tickets to Memphis. LC 77-23394. (Time of Danger, Time for Courage Ser.). (Illus.). 40p. (gr. 3-9). 1977. PLB 6.95 (ISBN 0-88436-388-0); pap. 3.95 (ISBN 0-88436-389-9). EMC.
Gray, George & Darley, H. C. Composition & Properties of Oil Well Driling Fluids. 4th ed. 59.95x (ISBN 0-87201-129-1). Gulf Pub.
Gray, George W. Education on an International Scale: A History of the International Education Board, 1923-1938. LC 78-800. (Illus.). 1978. Repr. of 1941 ed. lib. bdg. 17.00x (ISBN 0-313-20268-0, GREI). Greenwood.
Gray, H. B., jt. ed. see Lever, A. B.
Gray, H. Peter. International Trade, Investment & Payments. LC 78-69573. (Illus.). 1979. text ed. 25.95 (ISBN 0-395-26659-9). HM.
Gray, Harold. Little Orphan Annie. (Illus.). 64p. (gr. 2 up). 1982. pap. 1.95 (ISBN 0-486-24420-2). Dover.
--Little Orphan Annie & Little Orphan Annie in Cosmic City. (Illus.). 1974. pap. 2.75 o.p. (ISBN 0-486-23107-0). Dover.
--Little Orphan Annie in Cosmic City. (Illus.). 64p. (gr. 2 up). 1982. pap. 1.95 (ISBN 0-486-24421-0). Dover.
--Little Orphan Annie in the Great Depression. (Illus.). 64p. (gr. 2 up). 1982. pap. 1.95 (ISBN 0-486-23737-0). Dover.
Gray, Harry B., jt. auth. see DeKock, Roger L.
Gray, Henry. Gray's Anatomy. LC 76-52804. 1977. 10.00 (ISBN 0-517-22365-1, Pub. by Bounty). Formur Intl.
Gray, Howard L. English Field Systems. 1980. Repr. of 1915 ed. lib. bdg. 25.00x (ISBN 0-678-08069-0). Kelley.
Gray, Hugh, tr. see Bazin, Andre.
Gray, I. Engineer in Transition to Management. LC 78-61533. (IEEE Reprint Ser.). 1979. 22.95x (ISBN 0-471-05212-4); pap. 14.95x (ISBN 0-471-05213-2, Pub. by Wiley-Interscience). Wiley.
Gray, Irvine. Antiquaries of Gloucestershire & Bristol. 208p. 1981. text ed. 18.00x (ISBN 0-900197-14-5, Pub. by Sutton England). Humanities.
Gray, Irwin. The Engineer in Transition to Management. LC 78-61533. 1979. 22.95 (ISBN 0-87942-111-8). Inst Electrical.
Gray, J. & Ricketts, D. E. Cost & Managerial Accounting. 800p. 1982. 29.95x (ISBN 0-07-024220-8); study guide 10.95x (ISBN 0-07-024221-6). McGraw.
Gray, J., jt. auth. see Leeson, J.
Gray, J., jt. auth. see McPherson, A.
Gray, J. A., jt. auth. see Wilcock, G. K.
Gray, J. E. Indian Tales & Legends. (Myths & Legends Ser.). (gr. 6-12). 1979. Repr. 12.95 (ISBN 0-19-274113-6). Oxford U Pr.
Gray, Jack C. & Johnston, Kenneth S. Accounting & Management Action. 2nd ed. (Illus.). 1977. text ed. 25.95 (ISBN 0-07-024216-X, C). solutions manual 10.95 (ISBN 0-07-024217-8). McGraw.
Gray, James, jt. auth. see Gray, Catherine D.
Gray, James, jt. ed. see Myers, Miles.
Gray, James M. Commentary on the Whole Bible. pap. 2.95 o.p. (ISBN 0-8007-8374-3, Spire Bks). Revell.
Gray, James R. Modern Process Thought: A Brief Ideological History. LC 81-43672. 272p. 1982. lib. bdg. 24.00 (ISBN 0-8191-2310-2); pap. text ed. 11.50 (ISBN 0-8191-2311-0). U Pr of Amer.
Gray, Jeffrey, ed. see Pavlov, I. P.
Gray, Jerry. The Third Strike. 5.95 (ISBN 0-89486-163-8). Hazelden.
Gray, Jerry L. & Starke, Frederick A. Organizational Behavior. 2nd ed. (Marketing & Management Ser.). 464p. 1980. text ed. 23.95 (ISBN 0-675-08141-6). Additional supplements may be obtained from publisher. Merrill.
Gray, John. First & Second Kings: A Commentary. rev. ed. 2nd ed. LC 73-134271. (Old Testament Library). 1978. 22.50 (ISBN 0-664-20898-3). Westminster.
Gray, John E. Energy Policy: Industry Perspectives. LC 74-22454. (Ford Foundation Energy Policy Project Ser.). 1975. prof ref 16.50 (ISBN 0-88410-314-5); pap. text ed. 7.95 (ISBN 0-88410-315-3). Ballinger Pub.
Gray, John E., ed. see Atlantic Council Working Group on Nuclear Fuels Policy.
Gray, John M. History of Zanzibar, from the Middle Ages to 1856. LC 75-3732. (Illus.). 314p. 1975. Repr. of 1962 ed. lib. bdg. 18.25x (ISBN 0-8371-8057-0, GRHZ). Greenwood.
Gray, John N. Mill on Liberty: A Defence. (International Library of Philosophy). 120p. 1983. 17.95 (ISBN 0-7100-9270-9). Routledge & Kegan.
Gray, John S. Centennial Campaign: The Sioux War of 1876. LC 76-47160. (Source Custeriana Ser.: Vol. 8). (Illus.). 1983. pap. 10.95 (ISBN 0-686-43313-0). Old Army.
Gray, John W. & Rea, Richard. Parliamentary Procedure: A Programmed Introduction. rev. ed. 1974. pap. 7.95x (ISBN 0-673-07671-7). Scott F.
Gray, Joseph B., jt. ed. see Uhl, Vincent.
Gray, Kenneth L. Energy Crisis: Fact or Fiction. 1979. pap. 2.95 o.p. (ISBN 0-89036-119-3). Hawkes Pub Inc.
Gray, Kevin, jt. auth. see Pearl, David.
Gray, Lawrence V. Simian Horizons. 1983. 10.95 (ISBN 0-533-05546-6). Vantage.
Gray, Lee L. Better & Faster Reading. pap. text ed. 6.33 (ISBN 0-8428-0006-9); key 0.93 (ISBN 0-8428-0034-4). Cambridge Bk.
Gray, Lois S. & Beamesderfer, Alice O. Apprenticeship Training: Where Does It Stand Today? (Vital Issues, Vol. XXIX 1979-80: No. 5). 0.60 (ISBN 0-686-81610-2). Ctr Info Am.
Gray, Lynton & Waitt, Ian, eds. Perspectives on Academic Gaming & Simulation Seven: Simulation in Management & Business Education. 160p. 1982. 34.00 (ISBN 0-89397-139-1). Nichols Pub.
Gray, Madeline. Changing Years: The Menopause Without Fear. 1970. pap. 3.50 (ISBN 0-451-11777-8, AE1777, Sig). NAL.
--Margaret Sanger: A Biography of the Champion of Birth Control. LC 78-13000. (Illus.). 1979. 15.00 o.p. (ISBN 0-399-90019-5, Marek). Putnam Pub Group.
Gray, Marlowe & Gray, Urna. The Lovers Guide to Sensuous Astrology. 1974. pap. 2.95 (ISBN 0-451-12364-6, AE2364, Sig). NAL.
Gray, Martin. The Force of Life. (Orig.). 1978. pap. 1.95 o.p. (ISBN 0-451-08123-4, J8123, Sig). NAL.
Gray, Mary A. The Truth About Fathers. LC 81-21571. 192p. (gr. 7 up). 1982. 9.95 (ISBN 0-02-736700-2). Bradbury Pr.
Gray, Mary A., jt. auth. see Simpson, Elizabeth.
Gray, Mary L., jt. auth. see Bach, Ira J.
Gray, Michael & James, Francis. Marlborough in Old Photographs. 128p. 1982. pap. text ed. 8.25x (ISBN 0-86299-018-1, Pub. by Sutton England). Humanities.
Gray, Michael H. & Gibson, Gerald D. Bibliography of Discographies: Vol. 3: Popular Music. 200p. 1983. 37.50 (ISBN 0-8352-1683-7). Bowker.
Gray, Mike & Rosen, Ira. The Warning: Accident at Three Mile Island. 288p. 1983. pap. 7.95 (ISBN 0-8092-5547-2). Contemp Bks.
Gray, N. Rossetti, Dante & Ourselves. LC 74-6406. (Studies in Italian Literature, No. 46). 1974. lib. bdg. 47.95x (ISBN 0-8383-1917-3). Haskell.
Gray, Nicolete. Nineteenth-Century Ornamented Type Faces. LC 75-17294. 1977. 60.00 (ISBN 0-520-03074-5). U of Cal Pr.
Gray, Nigel. It'll All Come Out in the Wash. LC 78-22482. (Illus.). (ps-2). 1979. 9.57i (ISBN 0-06-022067-8, HarpJ); PLB 9.89 (ISBN 0-06-022074-0). Har-Row.
Gray, P. A Student Guide to IFPS. 384p. 1983. 12.95x (ISBN 0-07-024322-0, C). McGraw.
Gray, P. R., et al, eds. Analog MOS Integrated Circuits. LC 80-22116. 1980. 33.95 (ISBN 0-87942-141-X). Inst Electrical.

Gray, Parke H., et al. Whole Birth Book. 1979. 10.95 o.p. (ISBN 0-671-24000-5). S&S.

Gray, Paul. Analog MOS Integrated Circuits. LC 80-22116. 405p. 1980. 33.95x (ISBN 0-471-08966-4, Pub. by Wiley-Interscience); pap. 22.00x (ISBN 0-471-08964-8). Wiley.

Gray, Paul, jt. auth. see Chinese, U. S. Symposium on Systems Analysis.

Gray, Paul E. & Searle, Campbell L. Electronic Principles: Physics, Models & Circuits. LC 78-107884. 1969. text ed. 44.95 (ISBN 0-471-32398-5). Wiley.

Gray, Paul R. & Meyer, Robert G. Analysis & Design of Analog Integrated Circuits. LC 77-7211. 1977. text ed. 33.95 (ISBN 0-471-01367-6); solutions manual avail. (ISBN 0-471-03047-3). Wiley.

Gray, Paula G. Dramatics for the Elderly: A Guide for Directors of Dramatics Groups in Senior Centers & Residential Care Settings. LC 74-3185. 1974. pap. text ed. 3.95x (ISBN 0-8077-2400-9). Tchrs Coll.

Gray, Peter. Encyclopedia of the Biological Sciences. LC 80-28590. 1056p. 1981. Repr. lib. bdg. 52.50 (ISBN 0-89874-326-5). Krieger.

--Handbook of Basic Microtechnique. 3rd ed. 1964. text ed. 32.50 (ISBN 0-07-024206-2, C). McGraw.

--The Microtomists Formulary & Guide. LC 74-23818. 808p. 1975. Repr. of 1954 ed. 44.50 (ISBN 0-88275-247-2). Krieger.

--Use of the Microscope. (Illus.). 1967. text ed. 7.95 o.p. (ISBN 0-07-024208-9, C). McGraw.

Gray, Phillip M., intro. by. Extraction Metallurgy '81. 441p. (Orig.). 1981. pap. text ed. 115.00x (ISBN 0-900488-59-X). IMM North Am.

Gray, Ralph D., ed. The Hoosier State: Readings in Indiana History. Incl. Vol. 1. Indian Prehistory to 1880. 406p. pap. 6.95x (ISBN 0-8028-1842-0); Vol. 2. The Modern Era. 504p. pap. 6.95x (ISBN 0-8028-1843-9). LC 80-12496. (Orig.). 1982. pap. Ind U Pr.

Gray, Richard. The Two Nations. LC 73-21175. (Illus.). 373p. 1974. Repr. of 1960 ed. lib. bdg. 20.00x (ISBN 0-8371-6069-3, GRTN). Greenwood.

Gray, Richard, ed. American Verse of the Nineteenth Century. (Rowman & Littlefield University Library). 234p. 1973. 12.50x (ISBN 0-87471-404-4); pap. 4.95x (ISBN 0-87471-397-8). Rowman.

Gray, Richard L., jt. auth. see Parham, Russell A.

Gray, Roland P., ed. Songs & Ballads of the Maine Lumberjacks. LC 73-75944. 1969. Repr. of 1924 ed. 30.00x (ISBN 0-8103-3835-1). Gale.

Gray, Ronald. Christopher Wren & St. Paul's Cathedral. LC 81-13696. (Cambridge Topic Bks.). (Illus.). 52p. (gr. 6 up). 1982. PLB 6.95g (ISBN 0-8225-1222-X). Lerner Pubns.

Gray, Simon. Otherwise Engaged & Other Plays. (Penguin Plays). 1976. pap. 2.50 o.p. (ISBN 0-14-048136-2). Penguin.

Gray, Stephen, ed. Lifetime Furniture. (Mission Furniture Catalogues Ser.: No. 2). 112p. 1981. pap. 8.95 (ISBN 0-940326-02-7). Turn of Cent.

--Quaint Furniture. (Mission Furniture Catalogues Ser.: No. 1). 80p. 1981. pap. 5.95 (ISBN 0-940326-01-9). Turn of Cent.

--Roycroft Furniture. (Mission Furniture Cataloges: No. 3). 52p. 1981. pap. 4.95 (ISBN 0-940326-03-5). Turn of Cent.

Gray, Stephen E. Community Health Today. (Illus.). 1978. 21.95x (ISBN 0-02-346160-8). Macmillan.

Gray, Stephen E. & Matson, Hollis N. Health Now. (Illus.). 352p. 1976. pap. text ed. 12.95x (ISBN 0-02-346140-3, 34614). Macmillan.

Gray, Stephen W. & Skandalakis, John E. Embryology for Surgeons. LC 72-126453. (Illus.). 1972. 44.00 o.p. (ISBN 0-7216-4220-9). Saunders.

Gray, Stephen W., jt. auth. see Skandalakis, John E.

Gray, Steven & Steffy, Wilbert. Hospital Cost Containment through Productivity Management. 256p. 1982. text ed. 19.95 (ISBN 0-442-22921-6). Van Nos Reinhold.

Gray, Susan, jt. auth. see Morse, Dean.

Gray, Susan W., et al. Before First Grade: Training Project for Culturally Disadvantaged Children. LC 66-24872. (Orig.). 1966. pap. text ed. 6.35x (ISBN 0-8077-1464-X). Tchrs Coll.

--From Three to Twenty: The Early Training Project. 360p. 1981. text ed. 19.95 (ISBN 0-8391-1685-3). Univ Park.

Gray, Thomas. Selected Poems. Heath-Stubbs, John, ed. (Fyfield Ser.). 128p. (Orig.). 1981. pap. text ed. 5.25x (ISBN 0-85635-317-5, Pub. by Carcanet New Pr England). Humanities.

Gray, Tony. The Orange Order. 292p. 1974. 12.00 o.p. (ISBN 0-370-10371-8). Transatlantic.

Gray, Tony, jt. auth. see Villa, Leo.

Gray, Urna, jt. auth. see Gray, Marlowe.

Gray, Vanessa. The Duke's Messenger. 1982. pap. 2.25 (ISBN 0-451-11868-5, AE1868, Sig). NAL.

--The Innocent Deceiver. 1980. pap. 1.75 o.p. (ISBN 0-451-09463-8, E9463, Sig). NAL.

--The Lonely Earl. 1978. pap. 1.75 o.p. (ISBN 0-451-07922-1, E7922, Sig). NAL.

--The Reckless Orphan. (Orig.). 1981. pap. write for info. o.p. (ISBN 0-451-11208-3, AE 1208, Sig). NAL.

--The Wayward Governess. 1979. pap. 1.75 o.p. (ISBN 0-451-08696-1, E8696, Sig). NAL.

--The Wicked Guardian. 1978. pap. 1.75 (ISBN 0-451-08390-3, E8390, Sig). NAL.

Gray, Virginia & Dye, Thomas. Determinants of Public Policy: Cities, States, Nations. new ed. 1979. pap. 6.00 (ISBN 0-918592-32-1). Policy Studies.

Gray, Virginia & Williams, Bruce. The Organizational Politics of Criminal Justice: Policy in Context. LC 77-18590. 1980. 19.95x (ISBN 0-669-02108-3). Lexington Bks.

Gray, W. & Rizzo, N. D., eds. Unity Through Diversity: Festschrift in Honor of Ludwig, 2 vols. (Current Topics of Contemporary Thought Ser.). 1973. Set. 107.00x (ISBN 0-677-14860-7); 60.00x ea. Vol. 1, 596p (ISBN 0-677-14840-2). Vol. 2, 572p (ISBN 0-677-14850-X). Gordon.

Gray, Wanda. I Live Here Too. LC 77-82740. 1978. pap. 8.95 (ISBN 0-89334-013-8). Humanics Ltd.

Gray, Willaim & Jay, W. General Systems Theory & the Psychological Sciences, Vols. 1 & 2. (Systems Inquiry Ser.). 550p. 1982. pap. 21.95 set (ISBN 0-686-37577-7). Intersystems Pubns.

Gray, William. Venezuela, Uncle Sam & OPEC: A Story for All Americans. 189p. (Orig.). 1982. pap. 7.50 (ISBN 0-686-94960-9, Pub by O. E. G. Foundation). Exposition.

Gray, William A. & Gerrard, Brian A. Understanding Yourself & Others: A Workbook of Psychological Activities & Experiments. 179p. 1981. pap. text ed. 10.50scp (ISBN 0-06-042471-0, HarpC); instr's. manual avail. (ISBN 0-06-362480-X). Har-Row.

Gray, William B. & Gray, Betty. Episcopal Church Welcomes You: An Introduction to Its History, Worship & Mission. rev. ed. LC 73-17898. 168p. 1974. 6.95 o.p. (ISBN 0-8164-0253-1); pap. 3.95 (ISBN 0-8164-2087-4). Seabury.

Gray, William G. Concepts of Qabalah. (The Sangreal Sodality Ser.: Vol.3). Date not set. pap. price not set (ISBN 0-87728-561-6). Weiser.

--Inner Traditions of Magic. 1978. pap. 5.95 (ISBN 0-87728-447-4). Weiser.

--The Sangreal Sacrament, Vol. 2. (The Sangreal Sodality Ser.). 170p. Date not set. pap. price not set (ISBN 0-87728-562-4). Weiser.

--A Self Made by Magic. 1982. pap. 5.95 (ISBN 0-87728-577-2). Weiser.

--The Tree of Evil. Date not set. pap. 7.95 (ISBN 0-87728-539-X). Weiser.

--Western Inner Workings. (The Sangreal Sodality Ser.: Vol. 1). 188p. Date not set. pap. price not set (ISBN 0-87728-560-8). Weiser.

Gray, William S. On Their Own in Reading: How to Give Children Independence in Analyzing New Words. rev. ed. 1960. text ed. 10.95x (ISBN 0-673-05510-8). Scott F.

Gray, Wilson, tr. see Marvan, Jiri.

Gray, Wood, et al. Historian's Handbook: A Key to the Study & Writing of History. 2nd ed. (Orig.). 1964. pap. text ed. 6.50 (ISBN 0-395-04537-1). HM.

Graybill, F. A., jt. auth. see Krumbein, William C.

Graybill, Franklin A. Introduction to Linear Statistical Models, Vol. 1. 1961. text ed. 39.95 o.p. (ISBN 0-07-024331-X, C). McGraw.

--Matrices with Applications in Statistics. 2nd ed. LC 82-8485. (Wadsworth Statistics-Probability Ser.). 461p. 1983. 31.95 (ISBN 0-534-98038-4). Wadsworth Pub.

Graydon, Nell S. South Carolina Ghost Tales. 10.95 (ISBN 0-910206-06-6). Beaufort Bk Co.

Grayeff, F. Kant's Theoretical Philosophy. 240p. 1970. pap. 7.50 (ISBN 0-7190-0441-1). Manchester.

Graymont, Barbara. Iroquois in the American Revolution. LC 73-170096. (New York State Studies). (Illus.). 1972. 17.95x (ISBN 0-8156-0083-6); pap. 9.95 (ISBN 0-8156-0116-6). Syracuse U Pr.

Graymont, Barbara, ed. Fighting Tuscarora: The Autobiography of Chief Clinton Rickard. LC 73-8208. (Illus.). 224p. 1973. 12.95 (ISBN 0-8156-0092-5). Syracuse U Pr.

Grayser, Stephen A., jt. auth. see Bursk, Edward C.

Grayson, A. K. Babylonian Historical-Literary Texts. LC 74-80888. (Illus.). 1975. 27.50x o.p. (ISBN 0-8020-5315-7). U of Toronto Pr.

Grayson, Benson L. Saudi-American Relations. LC 82-40075. 178p. (Orig.). 1982. lib. bdg. 21.50 (ISBN 0-8191-2528-8); pap. text ed. 9.75 (ISBN 0-8191-2529-6). U Pr of Amer.

--United States-Iranian Relations. LC 81-40305. 194p. (Orig.). 1981. lib. bdg. 20.75 (ISBN 0-8191-1796-X); pap. text ed. 10.00 (ISBN 0-8191-1797-8). U Pr of Amer.

--The Unknown President: The Administration of President Millard Fillmore. LC 80-5962. 179p. 1981. lib. bdg. 20.00 (ISBN 0-8191-1456-1); pap. text ed. 9.50 (ISBN 0-8191-1457-X). U Pr of Amer.

Grayson, Cary T., Jr., ed. see Shosteck, Robert.

Grayson, Don, et al. Component Testers. Cole, Sandy, ed. (Seventy-Three Test Equipment Library: Vol. 1). 104p. 1976. pap. text ed. 4.95 o.p. (ISBN 0-88006-010-7, LB 7359). Green Pub Inc.

Grayson, Donald K., ed. The Establishment of Human Antiquity (Monograph) LC 82-11571. 280p. 1983. 27.50 (ISBN 0-12-297250-3). Acad Pr.

Grayson, Donald K., jt. ed. see Sheets, Payson D.

Grayson, Ellis S. The Elements of Short-Term Group Counseling. rev. ed. (Illus.). 112p. (Orig.). 1978. pap. 5.00 (ISBN 0-942974-10-7). Am Correctional.

Grayson, Fred N. The Office Handbook for Civil Service Employers. LC 82-18480. 288p. 1983. pap. 8.00 (ISBN 0-668-05605-3). Arco.

--Oysters. LC 76-16023. (Illus.). 64p. (gr. 4 up). 1976. 6.64 o.p. (ISBN 0-671-32797-6). Messner.

Grayson, Henry & Loew, Clemens, eds. Changing Approaches to the Psychotherapies. LC 77-24270. 335p. 1978. 25.00X o.s.i. (ISBN 0-470-99177-1). Halsted Pr.

Grayson, Joan. The Repair & Restoration of Pottery & Porcelain. (Illus.). 152p. 1982. 14.95 (ISBN 0-8069-5466-3); lib. bdg. 11.69 o.p. (ISBN 0-8069-5467-1). Sterling.

Grayson, L. Library & Information Services to Local Government. 1978. pap. 15.75x (ISBN 0-85365-810-2, Pub. by Lib Assn England). Oryx Pr.

Grayson, L. E. European National Oil Companies. 256p. 1981. 47.95 (ISBN 0-471-27861-0, Wiley-Interscience). Wiley.

Grayson, Marion. Let's Do Fingerplays. LC 62-10217. (Illus.). (ps-3). 1962. 9.95 (ISBN 0-88331-003-1). Luce.

Grayson, Martin. Encyclopedia of Composite Materials & Components, Vol. 2. 1200p. 1983. 49.50 (ISBN 0-471-87357-8, Pub. by Wiley-Interscience). Wiley.

--Information Retrieval in Chemistry & Chemical Patent Law. (Encylopedia Reprint Ser.). 125p. 1983. 17.95 (ISBN 0-471-89057-X, Pub. by Wiley-Interscience). Wiley.

Grayson, Martin & Griffith, E. J. Topics in Phosphorus Chemistry, Vol. 2. 352p. 1983. 80.00 (ISBN 0-471-89628-4, Pub. by Wiley-Interscience). Wiley.

Grayson, Martin & Griffith, Edward J. Topics in Phosphorus Chemistry, Vol. 10. 1980. 89.50 (ISBN 0-471-05890-4, Pub. by Wiley-Interscience). Wiley.

Grayson, Merrill. Diseases of the Cornea. (Illus.). 640p. 1983. text ed. 89.50 (ISBN 0-686-43076-X). Mosby.

Grayson, Richard. Death of Abbe Didier. 180p. 1981. 9.95 o.p. (ISBN 0-312-18648-7). St Martin.

--I Brake for Delmore Schwartz. 96p. 1983. 7.95 (ISBN 0-939010-04-6); pap. 4.95 (ISBN 0-939010-03-8). Zephyr Pr.

Grayson, Stan. Old Marine Engines: The World of the One Longer. LC 82-80402. (Illus.). 224p. 1982. 22.50 (ISBN 0-87742-155-2). Intl Marine.

Grayzel, Solomon. A History of the Jews. 768p. 1975. pap. 4.95 (ISBN 0-451-62061-5, ME2061, Ment). NAL.

Graz, Liesl. The Omanis: Sentinels of the Gulf. (Illus.). 216p. 1982. text ed. 25.00x (ISBN 0-582-78348-8). Longman.

Grazda, Edward E., et al. Handbook of Applied Mathematics. 4th ed. LC 77-10309. 1128p. 1977. Repr. of 1966 ed. 56.00 (ISBN 0-88275-615-X). Krieger.

Grazia, Bob Di see Palone, Joe & Di Grazia, Bob.

Graziano, Anthony M. Child Without Tomorrow. LC 73-3394. 1974. 25.00 o.s.i. (ISBN 0-08-017085-4). Pergamon.

Graziano, Frank, ed. see Trakl, Georg.

Graziano, Frank, jt. ed. see Wild, Peter.

Greacen, E. L. Soil Water Assessment by the Neutron Method. 1982. 60.00x (ISBN 0-686-97898-6, Pub. by CSIRO Australia). State Mutual Bk.

Grealey, S., jt. ed. see Jones, G. B.

Greaney, Vincent, ed. The Rights of Children. 250p. 1983. text ed. 19.95x (ISBN 0-8290-1297-4). Irvington.

Greanias, George C. The Board of Directors: Selection, Responsibility & Performance. 500p. Date not set. cancelled (ISBN 0-87094-245-X). Dow Jones-Irwin. Postponed.

--The Foreign Corrupt Practices Act: Anatomy of a Statute. LC 81-48265. (Illus.). 208p. 1982. 23.95x (ISBN 0-669-05254-X). Lexington Bks.

Greasybear, Charley J. Songs. Trusky, Tom & Crews, Judson, eds. LC 78-58484. (Modern & Contemporary Poets of the West). (Orig.). 1979. pap. 3.00 (ISBN 0-916272-10-9). Ahsahta Pr.

Great Britain. Parliament. Proceedings & Debates of the British Parliaments Respecting North America, 5 vols. Stock, Leo F., ed. LC 24-7105. 1976. Set. 290.00 (ISBN 0-527-35720-0). Kraus Repr.

Great Britain. Parliament. House of Commons. Fifth Report from the Select Committee of the House of Commons on the Affairs of the East India Company, 3 Vols. Firminger, Walter K., ed. LC 67-30063. Repr. of 1918 ed. lib. bdg. 125.00x (ISBN 0-678-00520-6). Kelley.

Greater London Council. Survey of London, Vol. 39: The Grosvenor Estate in Mayfair, Part. 1, General History. (Survey of London Ser.). 1977. text ed. 78.00x o.p. (ISBN 0-485-48239-8, Athlone Pr). Humanities.

Greater Portland Landmarks, Inc. Staff. Walking Through History. 100p. (Orig.). 1982. pap. 5.95 (ISBN 0-686-97646-0). G Gannett.

Greathead, D. J. A Review of Biological Control in the Ethipian Region. 162p. 1971. 42.00X (ISBN 0-85198-022-8, CAB Bks). State Mutual Bk.

--A Review of Biological Control in Western & Southern Europe. 182p. 1976. 45.00X (ISBN 0-85198-369-3, CAB Bks). State Mutual Bk.

Greathouse, M., ed. see Martin, T. E.

Greathouse, Willam M. Beacon Bible Expositions: Vol. 6, Romans. Taylor, Willard H., ed. (Beacon Bible Exposition Ser.). 1975. 6.95 (ISBN 0-8341-0317-6). Beacon Hill.

Greathouse, William & Dunning, H. Ray. An Introduction to Wesleyan Theology. 1982. 4.95 (ISBN 0-8341-0762-7). Beacon Hill.

Greathouse, William M. From the Apostles to Wesley. 124p. 1979. pap. 3.50 (ISBN 0-8341-0588-8). Beacon Hill.

Greathouse, William M., jt. auth. see Sanner, A. Elwood.

Greathouse, William M., ed. see Airhart, Arnold E.

Greathouse, William M, ed. see Martin, Sydney.

Greathouse, William M., ed. see Purkiser, W. T.

Greathouse, William M., ed. see Welch, Reuben.

Greathouse, William M., ed. see Young, Samuel.

Greatorex, Wilfred. Three Potato, Four. 1977. 8.95 o.p. (ISBN 0-698-10764-0, Coward). Putnam Pub Group.

Greaves, A. A. Maurice Barres. (World Authors Ser.). 1978. lib. bdg. 15.95 (ISBN 0-8057-6291-4, Twayne). G K Hall.

Greaves, C. Desmond. The Easter Rising in Song & Ballad. 88p. 1980. 10.00 (ISBN 0-900707-51-8, Pub. by Stanmore Pr England); pap. 4.95 (ISBN 0-686-36894-0). Facsimile Bk.

--The Irish Crisis. new ed. LC 70-188753. 1974. pap. 1.95 o.p. (ISBN 0-7178-0405-4). Intl Pub Co.

--The Irish Transport & General Workers' Union: The Formative Years. 1982. 60.00x (ISBN 0-7171-1199-7, Pub. by Gill & Macmillan Ireland). State Mutual Bk.

--Life & Times of James Connolly. (Orig.). 1972. pap. 2.25 (ISBN 0-7178-0330-9). Intl Pub Co.

Greaves, M. F. Cellular Recognition. 1975. pap. 6.50x (ISBN 0-412-13110-2, Pub. by Chapman & Hall). Methuen Inc.

Greaves, M. F., jt. ed. see Cuatrecasas, P.

Greaves, Margaret. Cat's Magic. LC 80-8451. 192p. (gr. 5 up). 1981. 9.57i (ISBN 0-06-022122-4, HarpJ); PLB 9.89 (ISBN 0-06-022123-2). Har-Row.

Greaves, R. & Zaller, R., eds. Biographical Dictionary of British Radicals in the Seventeenth Century, Vol. 1 A-F. 308p. 1982. text ed. 75.00x (ISBN 0-85527-133-7, Pub. by Harvester England). Humanities.

Greaves, Richard & Zaller, Robert, eds. Biographical Dictionary of British Radicals in the Seventeenth Century, Vol. 2. 352p. 1982. text ed. 75.00x (ISBN 0-7108-0430-X, Pub. by Harvester England). Humanities.

Greaves, Richard L. Elizabeth First, Queen of England. (Problems in European Civilization Ser). 1974. pap. text ed. 5.50 (ISBN 0-669-86371-8). Heath.

Greaves, Richard L., jt. auth. see Forrest, James F.

Greaves, Richard L., compiled by. An Annotated Bibliography of John Bunyan Studies. LC 72-177693. 1972. 7.00 (ISBN 0-931222-04-4). Pitts Theolog.

Greaves, Richard L., ed. see Bunyan, John.

Greaves, Roger, tr. see Eisner, Lotte.

Grebe, Paul, et al, eds. Deutscher Wortschatz-deutsch erklart. (Illus.). 444p. 1971. 7.50x (ISBN 3-468-96100-6). Intl Film.

Grebene, A. B. Analog Integrated Circuits. (IEEE Reprint Ser.). 439p. 1978. 34.95x (ISBN 0-471-05211-6, Pub. by Wiley-Interscience); pap. 22.95x (ISBN 0-471-05210-8). Wiley.

Grebene, A. B., ed. Analog Integrated Circuits. LC 78-59636. 1978. 34.95 (ISBN 0-87942-113-4). Inst Electrical.

Grebene, Alan B. Analog Integrated Circuit Design. LC 78-15389. 416p. 1978. Repr. of 1972 ed. lib. bdg. 24.50 (ISBN 0-88275-710-5). Krieger.

Grebenik, E., tr. see Pressat, Roland.

Grebenshchikov, O. S. Geobotanic Dictionary: Russian-English-German-French. 1979. lib. bdg. 36.00x (ISBN 3-87429-164-2). Lubrecht & Cramer.

Grebler, L., jt. auth. see Burns, L. S.

Grebler, Leo & Mittelbach, Frank G. The Inflation of House Prices: Its Extent, Causes & Consequences. LC 78-20272. (Special Series in Real Estate & Urban Land Economics). 1979. 27.95x (ISBN 0-669-02708-1). Lexington Bks.

Grebstein, Sheldon. Studies in For Whom the Bell Tolls. LC 77-146318. 1971. pap. text ed. 3.50 (ISBN 0-675-09221-3). Merrill.

Grebstein, Sheldon N. Hemingway's Craft. LC 70-183304. (Crosscurrents-Modern Critiques Ser.). 1973. 12.95 (ISBN 0-8093-0611-5). S Ill U Pr.

--Sinclair Lewis. (United States Authors Ser.). lib. bdg. 11.95 (ISBN 0-8057-0448-5, Twayne). G K Hall.

Greck, K. Engineering Formulas. 3rd ed. 1979. 15.95 (ISBN 0-07-023216-4). McGraw.

Greco, Ben. How to Get the Job That's Right for You: A Career Guide for the 80's. rev. ed. LC 79-56085. 210p. (Orig.). 1981. 11.95 o.p. (ISBN 0-87094-219-0); pap. 6.95 (ISBN 0-87094-194-1). Dow Jones-Irwin.

Greco, Leonard, jt. auth. see Chang, Diana.

Gree & Camps. La Pandilla En la Carretera. 1980. 9.95 (ISBN 0-686-69157-1). Larousse.

Gree, Alain. Pandilla Elige un Oficio. (Illus.). (gr. 3). 1981. 9.95 (ISBN 0-686-73727-X). Larousse.

--Pandilla En la Orilla Del Mar. (Illus.). (gr. 3). 1981. 9.95 (ISBN 0-686-73331-2, 23980). Larousse.

--Sailing: A Basic Guide. (Illus.). 1980. 14.95 (ISBN 0-670-61523-4, The Vendome Pr.). Viking Pr.

Gree, Alain & Camps, Luis. Farfeluches autour du Monde. (Illus.). 1982. 8.95 (ISBN 2-203-12316-8, 2787). Larousse.

--Les Farfeluches Prennent le Train. (Illus.). 1973. 8.95 o.p. (ISBN 0-88332-242-0, 2918). Larousse.

--Les Farfeluches sur la route. (Illus.). 1973. 8.95 o.p. (ISBN 0-88332-243-9, 2917). Larousse.

--La Pandilla Va a las Tiendas. (Illus., Span.). (gr. 2). 1979. 9.95 (ISBN 0-88332-111-4). Larousse.

Greebaum, Edward I. Radiology of the Emergency Patient: An Atlas Approach. LC 81-16282. 831p. 1982. 72.95 o.s.i. (ISBN 0-471-08562-6, Pub. by Wiley Med). Wiley.

Greeley, Andrew. No Bigger Than Necessary: An Alternative to Capitalism, Socialism, & Anarchism. (Orig.). 1977. pap. 3.95 o.p. (ISBN 0-452-00471-3, F471, Mer). NAL.

--Nora, Maeve & Sebi: A Story by Andrew Greeley. LC 76-18047. (Fantasy Tales Ser.). 64p. 1976. 5.95 o.p. (ISBN 0-8091-0214-5); pap. 3.95 o.p. (ISBN 0-8091-1974-9). Paulist Pr.

--Unsecular Man: The Persistence of Religion. LC 72-79446. 289p. 1972. 7.95x (ISBN 0-8052-3463-2). Schocken.

--Young Catholic Family. (Illus.). 1980. pap. 14.95 o.p. (ISBN 0-88347-122-1). Thomas More.

Greeley, Andrew H., ed. Ethnic Drinking Subcultures. 138p. 1980. 19.95x (ISBN 0-686-92320-0). J F Bergin.

Greeley, Andrew M. Ascent Into Hell. 368p. 1983. 16.50 (ISBN 0-446-51254-0). Warner Bks.

--The Cardinal Sins. (Orig.). 1982. 12.95 (ISBN 0-446-51236-2); pap. 3.95 (ISBN 0-446-90913-0). Warner Bks.

--The Communal Catholic: A Personal Manifesto. 220p. 1976. 2.00 (ISBN 0-8164-0299-X). Seabury.

--The Denominational Society: A Sociological Approach to Religion in America. 1973. pap. 8.95x o.p. (ISBN 0-673-07920-1). Scott F.

--Ethnicity in the United States: A Preliminary Reconnaissance. LC 74-11483. (Urban Research Ser). 347p. 1974. 27.50x (ISBN 0-471-32465-5, Pub. by Wiley-Interscience). Wiley.

--Friendship Game. LC 79-117979. 1971. pap. 3.50 o.p. (ISBN 0-385-04230-2, Im). Doubleday.

--The Great Mysteries: An Essential Catechism. (Orig.). 1976. 8.95x (ISBN 0-8164-0309-0); pap. 5.95x (ISBN 0-8164-2128-5). Seabury.

--The Irish Americans: The Rise to Money & Power. LC 81-47353. 215p. 1981. 14.37i (ISBN 0-06-038001-2). Har-Row.

--Life for a Wanderer: A New Look at Christian Spirituality. LC 70-78701. 1971. pap. 3.50 (ISBN 0-385-02961-6, Im). Doubleday.

--Love & Play. LC 77-5798. (Orig.). 1977. pap. 2.00 (ISBN 0-8164-1222-7). Seabury.

--The Mary Myth: On the Femininity of God. 1977. 5.00 (ISBN 0-8164-0333-3). Seabury.

--A Piece of My Mind... On Just about Everything. LC 82-45966. 240p. 1983. 13.95 (ISBN 0-385-18461-1). Doubleday.

--Religious Imagination. 14.95 (ISBN 0-8215-9876-7). Sadlier.

--The Sinai Myth. LC 72-79390. 200p. 1975. pap. 3.50 o.p. (ISBN 0-385-08824-8, Im). Doubleday.

--Unsecular Man. 1974. pap. 2.95 o.s.i. (ISBN 0-440-58832-4, Delta). Dell.

--Young Catholics in U. S. & Canada. 14.95 (ISBN 0-8215-9875-9). Sadlier.

Greeley, Horace, ed. The Great Industries of the United States: Being an Historical Summary of the Origin, Growth, & Perfection of the Chief Industrial Arts of This Country, 2 vols. (The Neglected American Economists Ser.). 1974. Set. lib. bdg. 76.00 o.s.i. (ISBN 0-8240-1007-8); lib. bdg. 50.00 ea. o.s.i. Garland Pub.

Greeley, Richard S., et al. Solar Heating & Cooling of Buildings. LC 80-68828. 1981. 47.50 (ISBN 0-250-40353-6). Ann Arbor Science.

Greeley, Roger, ed. The Best of Robert Ingersoll. Rev. ed. LC 77-90495. 1982. pap. 8.95 (ISBN 0-87975-209-2). Prometheus Bks.

Greely, Deborah W., jt. ed. see Campbell, Mary M.

Greely, Roger & Nicholas, Constantine. Don't Touch Your Toes! The Right Way to Total Fitness. (Illus.). 112p. 1982. pap. 6.95 (ISBN 0-528-88057-8). Rand.

Green & Morphet. Research & Technology As Economic Activities. (Sicon Bks.). 1977. 3.95 o.p. (ISBN 0-408-71300-3). Butterworth.

Green & Nessen. Problems, Cases & Materials on Evidence. 1983. text ed. price not set (ISBN 0-316-32646-1). Little.

Green, jt. auth. see Donovan.

Green, A. E. & Bourne, A. J. Reliability Technology. LC 73-161691. 636p. 1972. 99.95 (ISBN 0-471-32480-9, Pub. by Wiley-Interscience). Wiley.

Green, A. Richard & Costain, David W. Pharmacology & Biochemistry of Psychiatric Disorders. 232p. 1981. 33.50x (ISBN 0-471-09998-8, Pub. by Wiley-Interscience); pap. 15.50 (ISBN 0-471-10000-5, Pub. by Wiley-Interscience). Wiley.

Green, A. Wigfall. Inns of Court & Early English Drama. 1931. text ed. 39.50x (ISBN 0-686-83590-5). Elliots Bks.

--Sir Francis Bacon. (English Authors Ser.: No. 40). 1966. lib. bdg. 11.95 o.p. (ISBN 0-8057-1016-7). G K Hall.

Green, A. Wigfall, jt. ed. see Webb, James W.

Green, Adam B. D-Base II User's Guide with Applications. 192p. 1983. pap. 29.00 (ISBN 0-13-196519-0). P-H.

Green, Adele, jt. auth. see Nitsche, Richard A.

Green, Alan, jt. auth. see Green, Barry.

Green, Alex, pseud. Money Magic: Incredible Low-Risk Way to Build your Fortune. LC 82-82535. (Illus.). 112p. (Orig.). 1983. pap. 5.95 (ISBN 0-910067-00-7). G K Pr.

Green, Allen V. Jumbo Book of Crossword Puzzles. (Activity Bks.). (gr. 4 up). 1981. pap. 3.95 o.p. (ISBN 0-385-15786-X). Doubleday.

Green, Alyce, jt. auth. see Green, Elmer.

Green, Andrew, ed. Emerging High Performance Structural Plastic Technology. LC 82-70767. 92p. 1982. pap. text ed. 16.00 (ISBN 0-87262-305-X). Am Soc Civil Eng.

Green, Anthony, jt. auth. see Sharp, Rachel.

Green, Arnold W. Social Problems: Arena of Conflict. (Sociology Ser.). 384p. 1975. text ed. 21.00 (ISBN 0-07-024310-7, C). McGraw.

Green, B. S. & Ashani, Y. Chemical Approaches to Understanding Enzyme Catalysis: Biomimentic Chemistry & Transition State Analogs. (Studies in Organic Chemistry: Vol. 10). 1982. 91.50 (ISBN 0-444-42063-0). Elsevier.

Green, B. S. & Johns, E. A. An Introduction to Sociology. 1967. 12.00 (ISBN 0-08-012155-1); pap. 6.25 (ISBN 0-08-012154-3). Pergamon.

Green, Barry & Green, Alan. The Directory of Athletic Scholarships: Where They Are & How to Get Them. 312p. 1981. 14.95 (ISBN 0-399-12620-1, Perige); pap. 6.95 (ISBN 0-399-50533-4). Putnam Pub Group.

Green, Barth, et al, eds. Intensive Care for Neurological Trauma & Disease. LC 82-8903. 390p. 1982. 32.50 (ISBN 0-12-788284-7). Acad Pr.

Green, Ben K. Horse Tradin' (Illus.). (YA) 1967. 13.95 (ISBN 0-394-42929-X). Knopf.

--Village Horse Doctor, West of the Pecos. LC 79-118716. (YA) 1971. 13.50 (ISBN 0-394-42922-2). Knopf.

--Wild Cow Tales. (Illus.). (YA) 1969. 11.95 (ISBN 0-394-45188-0). Knopf.

Green, Bill. Alcoholism. Rahmas, Sigurd C., ed. (Topics of Our Times Ser.: No. 19). 32p. (Orig.). 1982. 2.95x (ISBN 0-87157-520-7); pap. text ed. 1.95 (ISBN 0-87157-320-2). SamHar Pr.

--J. R. R. Tolkien, Master of Fantasy. Rahmas, Sigurd C., ed. (Outstanding Personalities Ser.: No. 91). 32p. (gr. 9-12). 1982. 2.95 (ISBN 0-87157-591-4); pap. text ed. 1.95 (ISBN 0-87157-091-2). SamHar Pr.

--Jack Dempsey, Champion Heavyweight Boxer. new ed. LC 74-14588. (Outstanding Personalities Ser.). 32p. 1974. lib. bdg. 2.95 incl. catalog cards (ISBN 0-87157-576-0); pap. 1.95 vinyl laminated covers (ISBN 0-87157-076-9). SamHar Pr.

Green, Bruce & Glenn, Barbara. Community Planner's Guidebook to Renewable Technologies. 250p. 1983. pap. 17.95x (ISBN 0-89553-071-6). Am Solar Energy.

Green, Bruce M., jt. auth. see Baughman, Kenneth L.

Green, Bryan S. Knowing the Poor: A Case Study in Teaxtual Reality Construction. (International Library of Phenomology & Moral Sciences). 224p. 1983. 25.95 (ISBN 0-7100-9282-2). Routledge & Kegan.

Green, C. Tale of Theodore Bear. LC 68-56812. (Illus.). (gr. 1-2). 1968. PLB 6.75x (ISBN 0-87783-038-X). Oddo.

Green, C. & Bourgue, R. Theory & Servicing of AM, FM & FM Stereo Receivers. 1980. 27.95 (ISBN 0-13-913590-1). P-H.

Green, Candide L., jt. auth. see Evans, Tony.

Green, Carl R., jt. auth. see Sanford, William R.

Green, Carol H., jt. ed. see Mason, Mary G.

Green, Carolyna. Vagabond Healer. LC 82-90766. 232p. 1983. pap. text ed. 6.95 (ISBN 0-936958-02-2). Emerald Hse.

Green, Catherine J., jt. ed. see Millon, Theodore.

Green, Clifford J. Bonhoeffer: The Sociality of Christ & Humanity. 6.95 (ISBN 0-686-96182-X, 01 01 06). Scholars Pr CA.

Green, Constance M. Eli Whitney & the Birth of American Technology. (The Library of American Biography). 1965. pap. 5.95 (ISBN 0-316-32621-6, 1965). Little.

Green, D. H. The Art of Recognition in Wolfram's "Parzifal". LC 82-1283. 400p. 1982. 67.50 (ISBN 0-521-24500-1). Cambridge U Pr.

Green, Dallas W. Chief Joseph's Alps. 1972. 5.95x (ISBN 0-87315-003-1). Golden Bell.

Green, David. The Irish Language: Great Languages. Date not set. text ed. price not set (ISBN 0-391-01135-9). Humanities.

--Marble Mountain Wilderness. Winnett, Thomas, ed. LC 79-57598. (Trail Guide Ser.). (Illus.). 168p. (Orig.). 1980. pap. 9.95 (ISBN 0-911824-93-6). Wilderness.

Green, David & Ashburner, Jenni. Dyes from the Kitchen. 1979. 17.95 o.p. (ISBN 0-7134-1565-7, Pub. by Batsford England). David & Charles.

Green, David E., tr. see Schweizer, Eduard.

Green, Dennis H. Millstatter Exodus: A Crusading Epic. 1966. 80.00 (ISBN 0-521-05139-8). Cambridge U Pr.

Green, Earl L. Genetics & Probability. (Illus.). 1981. text ed. 45.00x (ISBN 0-19-520159-0). Oxford U Pr.

Green, Edith P. Sneaks. 1982. pap. 2.25 o.p. (ISBN 0-425-05040-8). Berkley Pub.

--Sneaks. 1979. 9.95 o.p. (ISBN 0-525-20632-9). Dutton.

Green, Edward T., jt. auth. see O'Reilly, Robert C.

Green, Edwin & Moss, Michael. Business of National Importance. 1983. 29.95x (ISBN 0-416-32220-4). Methuen Inc.

Green, Elizabeth A. The Modern Conductor. 3rd ed. (Illus.). 288p. 1981. text ed. 22.95 (ISBN 0-13-590216-9); wkbk. 16.95 (ISBN 0-13-590224-X). P-H.

Green, Elmer & Green, Alyce. Beyond Biofeedback. 1977. 10.95 o.s.i. (ISBN 0-440-00583-3, Sey Lawr). Delacorte.

Green, Ernest J. Marriage & Family. LC 76-30848. (McGraw-Hill Basic Self-Instructional Guide Ser.). 1977. pap. text ed. 14.95 (ISBN 0-07-024261-5, C); instructor's guide 7.95 (ISBN 0-07-024262-3). McGraw.

--Personal Relationships: An Approach to Marriage & Family. (Illus.). 1978. text ed. 26.00 (ISBN 0-07-024270-4, C); instructor's manual with test bank 3.95 (ISBN 0-07-024271-2). McGraw.

Green, Eugene & Sachse, William L. Names of the Land. LC 82-82167. (Illus.). 192p. (Orig.). 1983. pap. 8.95 (ISBN 0-87106-974-1). Globe Pequot.

Green, Fitzhugh. The U. S. Information Agency. (WV Library of Federal Department Agencies & Systems Ser.). 285p. 1983. lib. bdg. 25.00 cancelled (ISBN 0-86531-228-1). Westview.

Green, Fletcher. Constitutional Development in the South Atlantic States, 1776-1860. LC 71-158485. (Civil Liberties in American History Ser.). 1971. Repr. of 1930 ed. lib. bdg. 42.50 (ISBN 0-306-70189-8). Da Capo.

Green, Fred, et al. Strategies for Improving Reading in Social Studies. 1979. pap. text ed. 9.95 (ISBN 0-8403-2098-1). Kendall-Hunt.

Green, G. D., tr. see Fichte, J. G.

Green, Geoffrey. Literary Criticism & the Structures of History: Erich Auerbach & Leo Spitzer. LC 82-2654. x, 186p. 1982. 17.95x (ISBN 0-8032-2108-8). U of Nebr Pr.

Green, George. Mathematical Papers. LC 70-92316. 19.95 (ISBN 0-8284-0229-9). Chelsea Pub.

Green, George F. Elementary School Mathematics: Activities & Materials. 1974. text ed. 18.95x o.p. (ISBN 0-669-84582-5). Heath.

Green, George N. Liberal View of Texas Politics Since the 1930s. Rosenbaum, Robert J., ed. (Texas History Ser.). (Illus.). 52p. 1982. pap. text ed. 1.95x (ISBN 0-89641-088-9). American Pr.

--Liberal View of Texas Politics, 1890-1930s. Rosenbaum, Robert J., ed. (Texas History Ser.). (Illus.). 45p. 1982. pap. text ed. 1.95x (ISBN 0-89641-087-0). American Pr.

Green, Geral. Karpov's Brain. 1983. 15.95 (ISBN 0-688-01889-0). Morrow.

Green, Gerald. Cactus Pie: Ten Stories. 1979. 9.95 o.p. (ISBN 0-395-27761-2). HM.

Green, H. & Spencer. Drugs with Possible Ocular Side-Effects. 1969. 15.95 o.p. (ISBN 0-407-93263-1). Butterworth.

Green, Hannah. The Dead of the House. LC 70-172559. 1972. 8.95 (ISBN 0-385-02557-2). Doubleday.

Green, Harriet & Martin, Sue. Sprouts. (gr. 3-8). 1981. 9.95 (ISBN 0-86653-028-2, GA256). Good Apple.

Green, Helen H. & Morton, Margaret A. Transcription & Skill Building, Bk. 11. (Hedman Stenotype System Ser.). 354p. 1978. text ed. 17.00x (ISBN 0-939056-01-1). Hedman Steno.

Green, Helen H., et al. The Secretary: An Integrated Secretarial Block Program; Integrated Skill Builders. (Illus.). (gr. 12). 1978. pap. text ed. 9.50 o.p. (ISBN 0-07-024296-8, G). McGraw.

--The Secretary: An Integrated Secretarial Block Program; Training Handbooks, Pts. 1-4. (Illus.). (gr. 12). 1977. pap. text ed. 18.88 (ISBN 0-07-024295-X, G); prog. mgmt. guide 7.85 (ISBN 0-07-024297-6). McGraw.

Green, Henry. Blindness. (General Ser.). 1979. lib. bdg. 12.95 (ISBN 0-8161-6743-5, Large Print Bks). G K Hall.

Green, Howard. The Cockpit of Europe. LC 75-29813. (Illus.). 144p. 1976. 10.00 o.p. (ISBN 0-88254-367-9). Hippocrene Bks.

Green, I. Conservation from A to Z. LC 66-11443. (Illus.). (gr. 4 up). PLB 6.75x (ISBN 0-87783-009-6); pap. 2.95x deluxe ed. (ISBN 0-87783-088-6). Oddo.

--Where Is Duckling Three? LC 68-16402. (Illus.). (gr. 1-2). 1967. PLB 6.75x (ISBN 0-87783-048-7). Oddo.

Green, Ivah. Splash & Trickle. LC 68-56818. (Illus.). (gr. 2-3). 1968. PLB 6.75x (ISBN 0-87783-037-1); pap. 2.95x deluxe ed. (ISBN 0-87783-109-2); cassette 5.95x (ISBN 0-87783-226-9). Oddo.

Green, Ivah J. Loon. LC 65-22310. (Illus.). (gr. 4 up). 1968. PLB 6.75x (ISBN 0-87783-025-8). Oddo.

Green, J. see Barnes, R. S.

Green, J. H. Basic Clinical Physiology. 3rd ed. (Illus.). 1979. pap. text ed. 16.95x (ISBN 0-19-263331-7). Oxford U Pr.

Green, J. H. & Silver, P. H. An Introduction to Human Anatomy. (Illus.). 1981. pap. text ed. 29.95x (ISBN 0-19-261196-8). Oxford U Pr.

Green, J. Keith & Perkins, Philip H. Concrete Liquid Retaining Structures. (Illus.). 1979. 53.50x (ISBN 0-85334-856-1, Pub. by Applied Sci England). Elsevier.

Green, J. R. & Margerison, D. Statistical Treatment of Experimental Data. rev. ed. (Physical Sciences Data: Vol. 2). 1978. 41.75 (ISBN 0-444-41725-7). Elsevier.

Green, J. R., ed. Some Aspects of the Foundations of General Equilibrium Theory: The Posthumous Papers of Peter J. Kalman. LC 78-14520. (Lecture Notes in Economics & Mathematical Systems: Vol. 159). 1978. pap. 12.00 (ISBN 0-387-08918-7). Springer-Verlag.

Green, J. R., jt. ed. see Thompson, Richard A.

Green, Jack P., jt. ed. see Weinstein, Harel.

Green, James & Lewis, David. The Hidden Language of Your Handwriting: The Remarkable New Science of Graphonomy & What It Reveals about Personality & Health & Emotions. 256p. 1983. pap. 5.95 (ISBN 0-89104-330-6, A & W Visual Library). A & W Pubs.

Green, James R., ed. Workers' Struggles, Past & Present: A "Radical America" Reader. 1983. write for info. (ISBN 0-87722-293-2). Temple U Pr.

Green, Jane, jt. auth. see Choate, Judith.

Green, Jay, tr. Interlinear Bible, 4 vols. 79.95 o.p. (ISBN 0-8010-3763-8); 44.95 o.p. (ISBN 0-8010-3766-2). Baker Bk.

Green, Jeffrey P. Edmund Thorton Jenkins: The Life & Times of an American Black Composer, 1894-1926. LC 81-23721. (Contributions to the Study of Music & Dance Ser.: No. 2). (Illus.). 200p. 1982. lib. bdg. 25.00 (ISBN 0-313-23253-9, GRJ). Greenwood.

Green, Jerald. Direction: Tacuba: An Introductory Conversational Reader. pap. 9.75 o.p. (ISBN 0-395-30981-6). HM.

Green, Jerald R. Direction: Moncloa: An Intermediate Cultural Reader. 1977. pap. 13.95 (ISBN 0-395-30980-8). HM.

Green, Jerold. Revolution in Iran. 218p. 1982. 24.95 (ISBN 0-03-062409-6). Praeger.

Green, John. Dakota Days: The Untold Story of John Lennon's Final Years. 1983. 15.95 (ISBN 0-312-18176-0). St Martin.

Green, John, tr. see Ahmad, Jalal Al-e.

Green, John C., Jr. Ritchie's First Steps in Latin. 3rd ed. 1978. text ed. 6.85x (ISBN 0-582-28085-0). Longman.

--Ritchie's Second Steps in Latin. 3rd ed. 1924. text ed. 6.85x (ISBN 0-582-28086-9). Longman.

Green, John H. An Introduction to Human Physiology. 4th ed. (Illus.). 1976. pap. text ed. 25.00x (ISBN 0-19-263328-7). Oxford U Pr.

--Speak to Me. LC 62-14943. (Orig.). 1962. pap. 4.95 (ISBN 0-672-63116-4). Odyssey Pr.

Green, John R., jt. ed. see Thompson, Richard A.

Green, Johnnie. Bentley Fifty Years of the Marque. 296p. 1981. 75.00x (ISBN 0-686-97071-3, Pub. by D Watson England). State Mutual Bk.

Green, Jonathan. Morrow's International Dictionary of Contemporary Quotations. LC 82-12633. 1982. 14.95 (ISBN 0-688-01537-9). Morrow.

Green, Jonathan H. Gambling Exposed, a Full Exposition of the Various Arts, Mysteries, Miseries of Gambling. LC 78-172603. (Criminology, Law Enforcement, & Social Problems Ser.: No. 193). (Illus., With intro. & index added). 1973. Repr. of 1857 ed. 15.00x (ISBN 0-87585-193-2). Patterson Smith.

Green, Jonathon, compiled by. Famous Last Words. 1979. pap. 4.95 (ISBN 0-8256-3930-1, Quick Fox). Putnam Pub Group.

Green, Judith. Review of Maternal Child Nursing. 1978. pap. text ed. 12.95 (ISBN 0-07-024302-6, HP). McGraw.

Green, Judith & Wallat, Cynthia, eds. Ethnography & Language in Educational Settings. (Advances in Discourse Processes Ser.: Vol. 5). 368p. 1981. text ed. 32.50 (ISBN 0-89391-035-X); pap. 16.50 (ISBN 0-89391-078-3). Ablex Pub.

Green, Judith, ed. see Tannen, Deborah.

Green, Judith A. A City for Ransom. (Adult Basic Learner Ser.). (Illus.). 225p. (Orig.). (gr. 9-12). 1980. pap. text ed. 4.00x (ISBN 0-89061-216-1, 205). Jamestown Pubs.

--Dr. Valdez. (Adult Learner Ser.). (Illus.). 215p. (Orig.). (gr. 9-12). 1980. pap. text ed. 4.00x (ISBN 0-89061-211-0, 203). Jamestown Pubs.

--The Man Who Stopped Time. (Adult Learner Ser.). (Illus.). 189p. (Orig.). 1979. pap. text ed. 4.00x (ISBN 0-89061-173-4, 201). Jamestown Pubs.

--The Man with the Scar. (Adult Learner Ser.). (Illus.). 203p. (Orig.). 1979. pap. text ed. 4.00x (ISBN 0-89061-153-X, 202). Jamestown Pubs.

--Murder by Radio. (Adult Learner Ser.). (Illus.). 191p. (Orig.). 1979. pap. text ed. 4.00x (ISBN 0-89061-152-1, 200). Jamestown Pubs.

--The Secret of Room 401. (Adult Learner Ser.). (Illus.). 223p. (Orig.). (gr. 9-12). 1980. pap. text ed. 4.00x (ISBN 0-89061-210-2, 204). Jamestown Pubs.

Green, Julien. The Dark Journey. Holland, Vyvyan, tr. from Fr. LC 76-152597. 376p. Repr. of 1929 ed. lib. bdg. 18.50x (ISBN 0-8371-6031-6, GRDJ). Greenwood.

--Memories of Evil Days. Piriou, Jean-Pierre J., ed. LC 75-44037. 200p. 1976. 14.95 (ISBN 0-8139-0553-2). U Pr of Va.

Green, Justin J., jt. ed. see Chipp, Sylvia A.

Green, K. & Coombs, Rod. The Effects of Microelectronic Technologies on Employment Prospects. 209p. 1980. text ed. 36.75x (ISBN 0-566-00418-6). Gower Pub Ltd.

Green, Karen. Japanese Cooking for the American Table. (Illus.). 174p. 1982. 14.95 (ISBN 0-686-84175-1). J P Tarcher.

Green, Kenneth. Better Grades in College with Less Effort. (gr. 10-12). 1983. pap. text ed. 3.25 (ISBN 0-8120-2268-8). Barron.

Green, Kenneth A., et al. Better Grades in College with Less Effort. LC 70-134238. 176p. (Orig.). 1971. pap. 3.95 (ISBN 0-8120-0415-9). Barron.

Green, Lawrence & Kansler, Connie, eds. Professional & Scientific Literature on Patient Education: A Guide to Information Sources. (Health Affairs Information Guide Ser.: Vol. 5). 330p. 1980. 42.00x (ISBN 0-8103-1422-3). Gale.

Green, Lee & Dengerink, Don. Five Hundred One Ways to Use the Overhead Projector. 200p. pap. text ed. 18.50 (ISBN 0-87287-339-0). Libs Unl.

Green, Leon. The Litigation Process in Tort Law. 2nd ed. 1977. pap. text ed. 12.50x (ISBN 0-672-82836-7, Bobbs-Merrill Law). Michie-Bobbs.

Green, Leslie C. International Law Through the Cases. 4th ed. LC 78-1420. (Illus.). 836p. 1978. lib. bdg. 50.00 (ISBN 0-379-20404-5); pap. text ed. 29.50 (ISBN 0-379-20405-3). Oceana.

Green, Lila. Tales from Africa. LC 78-54623. (The World Folktale Library). (Illus.). 1979. PLB 12.68 (ISBN 0-382-03350-7). Silver.

--Tales from Hispanic Lands. LC 78-54624. (The World Folktale Library). (Illus.). 1979. PLB 12.68 (ISBN 0-382-03349-3). Silver.

Green, Louis. Chronicle into History: An Essay on the Interpretation of History in Florentine Fourteenth Century Cronicles. LC 71-186249. (Cambridge Studies in Early Modern History). 180p. 1972. 29.95 (ISBN 0-521-08517-9). Cambridge U Pr.

Green, M. B. Pesticides: Boon or Bane? LC 76-5881. (Westview Environmental Studies Ser.: Vol. 1). 1976. 18.00 (ISBN 0-89158-610-5). Westview.

Green, M. C. The Voice & its Disorders. 494p. 1979. 179.00x (ISBN 0-686-98001-8, Pub. by Pitman Bks England). State Mutual Bk.

Green, Margaret L. The Voice & Its Disorders. 4th ed. (Illus.). 446p. 1980. text ed. 50.00 o.p. (ISBN 0-686-97928-1, Lippincott Medical). Lippincott.

Green, Marilyn L. & Harry, Joann. Nutrition in Contemporary Nursing Practice. LC 80-22426. 864p. 1981. 25.95 (ISBN 0-471-03892-X, Pub. by Wiley Med). Wiley.

Green, Mark. The Other Government. 318p. 1975. 12.50 (ISBN 0-686-36548-8). Ctr Responsive Law.

Green, Mark, jt. auth. see Nader, Ralph.

Green, Mark, ed. The Closed Enterprise System. 288p. 1972. pap. 1.95 (ISBN 0-686-36547-X). Ctr Responsive Law.

Green, Mark R. & Serbein, Oscar N. Risk Management: Text & Cases. (Illus.). 1978. text ed. 19.95 (ISBN 0-87909-730-2); instrs'. manual avail. (ISBN 0-87909-737-X). Reston.

Green, Martin. The Home Pet Vet Guide for Cats. pap. 7.95 o.p. (ISBN 0-380-43406-7, 43406). Avon.

--The Home Pet Vet Guide for Dogs. pap. 7.95 o.p. (ISBN 0-380-43414-8, 43414). Avon.

--Tolstoy & Gandhi, Men of Peace (A Biography) 500p. 1983. 23.50 (ISBN 0-465-08631-4). Basic.

Green, Martin A. Solar Cells: Operation Principles Technology & Systems Applications. (Illus.). 256p. 1982. 29.95 (ISBN 0-13-822270-3). P-H.

Green, Martin B. Science & the Shabby Curate of Poetry: Essays About the Two Cultures. LC 77-27419. 1978. Repr. of 1964 ed. lib. bdg. 17.00x (ISBN 0-313-20191-9, GRSS). Greenwood.

Green, Martyn, ed. Martyn Green's Treasury of Gilbert & Sullivan. 1961. 19.95 o.p. (ISBN 0-671-45250-9). S&S.

Green, Mary J. Louis Guilloux: An Artisan of Language. 17.00 (ISBN 0-917786-15-7). French Lit.

Green, Mary J., jt. auth. see Ansberger, Carolyn.

Green, Mary J., jt. auth. see Ausberger, Carloyn.

Green, Mary J., jt. auth. see Ausberger, Carolyn.

Green, Maureen. Life Without Fathering. LC 75-26874. 1976. 7.95 o.p. (ISBN 0-07-024290-9, GB). McGraw.

Green, Maurice B. Eating Oil: Energy Use in Food Production. 1978. lib. bdg. 25.00 o.p. (ISBN 0-89158-244-4). Westview.

Green, Maurice R., ed. Violence & the Family. (AAAS Selected Symposium: No. 47). 200p. 1980. lib. bdg. 17.50 (ISBN 0-89158-841-8); pap. text ed. 8.00 (ISBN 0-86531-141-2). Westview.

Green, Michael. Evangelism: Now & Then. 150p. 1982. pap. 3.50 (ISBN 0-87784-394-5). Inter-Varsity.

--Tonight Josephine: And Other Undiscovered Letters. 1982. 14.95 (ISBN 0-395-32112-3). HM.

Green, Michael, ed. The Daily Telegraph Peterborough Book. LC 80-69341. 64p. 1981. 7.50 (ISBN 0-7153-8082-6). David & Charles.

Green, Michael, annotations by. & illus. Unicornis: On the History & Truth of the Unicorn. (Illus.). 64p. (Orig.). 1983. 14.95 (ISBN 0-89471-216-0); lib. bdg. 15.90 (ISBN 0-89471-207-1). Running Pr.

Green, Michael, tr. from Rus. The Russian Symbolist Theatre: An Anthology of Plays & Critical Texts. 350p. 1983. 37.50 (ISBN 0-686-82225-0); pap. 10.00 (ISBN 0-88233-798-X). Ardis Pubs.

Green, Michael E. & Turk, Amos. Laboratory Safety. (Illus.). 1978. pap. text ed. 11.95x (ISBN 0-02-346420-8). Macmillan.

Green, Mildred D. Black Women Composers: A Genesis. (Music Ser.). 174p. 1983. lib. bdg. 18.95 (ISBN 0-8057-9450-6, Twayne). G K Hall.

Green, Mimi & Naab, Maxine. Lamaze is for Chickens: A Manual for Prepared Childbirth. 2nd ed. (Avery's Childbirth Education Ser.). (Illus.). 128p. 1983. pap. 6.95 (ISBN 0-89529-181-9). Avery Pub.

Green, Miranda. Roman Technology & Crafts. Hodge, Peter, ed. (Aspects of Roman Life Ser.). 48p. (Orig.). (gr. 7-12). 1979. pap. text ed. 3.50 (ISBN 0-582-20162-4). Longman.

Green, Morris & Haggerty, Robert J., eds. Ambulatory Pediatrics Two: Personal Health Care of Children in the Office. LC 76-55067. 1977. text ed. 26.00 (ISBN 0-7216-4236-5). Saunders.

Green, N. Maryan. International Law: Law of Peace. 2nd ed. 336p. 1982. text ed. 26.50x (ISBN 0-7121-0956-0). Sheridan.

Green, Nan, tr. see Carrillo, Santiago.

Green, Nancy R., jt. auth. see Kinder, Faye.

Green Note Music Publications Staff. Country Rock Guitar, Vol. 2. (Guitar Transcription Ser.). 1980. pap. 7.95 (ISBN 0-912910-10-0). Green Note Music.

--Improvising Blues Guitar, Vol. 2. (Guitar Transcription Ser.). 1980. pap. 7.95 (ISBN 0-912910-11-9). Green Note Music.

--Improvising Blues Guitar, Vol. 3. (Guitar Transcription Ser.). 1982. pap. 7.95 (ISBN 0-912910-12-7). Green Note Music.

--Improvising Rock Guitar, Vol. 2. (Guitar Transcription Ser.). 1980. pap. 7.95 (ISBN 0-912910-08-9). Green Note Music.

--Improvising Rock Guitar, Vol. 3. (Guitar Transcription Ser.). 1980. pap. 7.95 (ISBN 0-912910-09-7). Green Note Music.

--Improvising Rock Guitar, Vol. 4. (Guitar Transcription Ser.). 1982. pap. 7.95 (ISBN 0-912910-13-5). Green Note Music.

Green, Otis H. Spain & the Western Tradition: The Castilian Mind in Literature from "El Cid" to Calderon, Vols. 1-4. 1963. pap. 7.95 ea.; Vol. 1. (ISBN 0-299-02954-9); Vol. 2. (ISBN 0-299-03294-9); Vol. 3. (ISBN 0-299-03794-0); Vol. 4. (ISBN 0-299-04084-4). U of Wis Pr.

Green, P. E. & Lucky, R. W., eds. Computer Communications. LC 74-82501. 1975. 31.95 (ISBN 0-87942-041-3). Inst Electrical.

Green, P. V. The Need for Long Term Lagoons: A Literature Survey, 1980. 1981. 69.00x (ISBN 0-686-97125-6, Pub. by W Spring England). State Mutual Bk.

Green, Paul. The Common Glory. LC 72-11622. (Illus.). 273p. 1973. Repr. of 1948 ed. lib. bdg. 17.00x (ISBN 0-8371-7080-X, GRCH). Greenwood.

--The Outdoor Leadership Handbook. 42p. 1982. pap. write for info. (ISBN 0-913724-32-7). Survival Ed Assoc.

Green, Percy B. History of Nursery Rhymes. LC 68-31082. 1968. Repr. of 1899 ed. 34.00x (ISBN 0-8103-3481-X). Gale.

Green, Peter. The Shadow of the Parthenon: Studies in Ancient History & Literature. LC 72-87205. 1973. 29.75x (ISBN 0-520-02322-6). U of Cal Pr.

Green, Peter, ed. see Grahame, Kenneth.

Green, Peter, tr. see Ovid.

Green, Philip. Deadly Logic: The Theory of Nuclear Deterrence. LC 68-23258. 1969. pap. 3.45 o.p. (ISBN 0-8052-0190-4). Schocken.

Green, Phyllis. Eating Ice Cream with a Werewolf. LC 82-47727. (Illus.). 128p. (gr. 3-7). 1983. 9.57i (ISBN 0-06-022140-2, HarpJ); PLB 9.89g (ISBN 0-06-022141-0). Har-Row.

Green, R., jt. ed. see Pavoni, N.

Green, R. F. Chess. rev. ed. (Illus.). 113p. 1974. 7.50 o.p. (ISBN 0-7135-0506-0). Transatlantic.

Green, R. L. The Tale of Thebes. LC 76-22979. (Illus.). 1977. 14.95 (ISBN 0-521-21410-6); pap. 5.95 (ISBN 0-521-21411-4). Cambridge U Pr.

Green, Rayna. Native American Women: A Contextual Bibliography. LC 82-48571. 160p. 1983. 19.50x (ISBN 0-253-33976-6). Ind U Pr.

Green, Richard L. & Gibson, John M. A Bibliography of A. Conan Doyle. (Soho Bibliographies Ser.). (Illus.). 1982. 49.00x (ISBN 0-19-818190-6). Oxford U Pr.

Green, Robert. Seditious Mandibles. (Illus.). 24p. 1981. pap. 3.00 (ISBN 0-941194-13-2). Black Swan Pr.

Green, Robert L. Robert L. Green's Live with Style. LC 78-9457. 1978. 10.95 o.s.i. (ISBN 0-698-10920-1, Coward). Putnam Pub Group.

--The Urban Challenge: Poverty & Race. 1978. pap. 12.95 (ISBN 0-695-80853-2, T0853); pap. 9.95 (ISBN 0-695-81145-2, T1145). Follett.

Green, Robert T. & Lutz, James. The United States & World Trade: Changing Patterns & Dimensions. LC 78-19762. 336p. 1978. 34.95 o.p. (ISBN 0-03-045351-8). Praeger.

Green, Robert W., jt. auth. see Bernstein, Paul.

Green, Robert W., ed. Protestantism & Capitalism & Social Science: The Webster Thesis Controversy. 2nd ed. (Problems in American Civilization Ser). 1973. pap. text ed. 5.50 o.p. (ISBN 0-669-81737-6). Heath.

Green, Roberta. Joshua: Promises to Keep. (Young Fisherman Bible Studyguides). (Illus.). 80p. (gr. 7-12). 1982. saddle-stitched tchr's ed. 3.95 (ISBN 0-87788-434-X); student ed. 2.95 (ISBN 0-87788-433-1). Shaw Pubs.

Green, Roger, jt. auth. see Tunnadine, David.

Green, Roger, compiled by. The Train. (Small Oxford Books). (Illus.). 1982. 9.95 (ISBN 0-19-214127-9). Oxford U Pr.

Green, Roger L., ed. Strange Adventures in Time. (Childrens Illustrated Classics Ser). (Illus.). 192p. 1974. 9.00x o.p. (ISBN 0-460-05097-4, Pub. by J. M. Dent England). Biblio Dist.

--Ten Tales of Adventure. (Childrens Illustrated Classics Ser). (Illus.). 204p. 1972. 9.00x o.p. (ISBN 0-460-05093-1, Pub. by J. M. Dent England). Biblio Dist.

--Ten Tales of Detection. (Childrens Illustrated Classics Ser). (Illus.). 220p. 1968. Repr. of 1967 ed. 9.00x o.p. (ISBN 0-460-05072-9, Pub. by J. M. Dent England). Biblio Dist.

--Thirteen Uncanny Tales. (Childrens Illustrated Classics Ser). (Illus.). 218p. 1970. 9.00x o.p. (ISBN 0-460-05085-0, Pub. by J. M. Dent England). Biblio Dist.

Green, Roger L., ed. see Carroll, Lewis.

Green, Roland, jt. auth. see Dickson, Gordon R.

Green, Roland, jt. auth. see Pournelle, Jerry.

Green, Ronald M. Religious Reason: The Rational & Moral Basis of Religious Belief. 1978. text ed. 16.95x (ISBN 0-19-502388-9); pap. text ed. 6.95x (ISBN 0-19-502389-7). Oxford U Pr.

Green, S. International Disaster Relief: Toward a Responsive System. 1977. 14.95 (ISBN 0-07-024287-9); pap. 3.95 (ISBN 0-07-024288-7). McGraw.

Green, Samuel & Long, John V. Modern Family Law, 3 vols. 1800p. Date not set. Set. 180.00 o.p. (ISBN 0-07-024275-5). McGraw.

Green, Samuel, ed. see Trager, Philip, et al.

Green, Sharon. The Crystals of Mida. 352p. 1982. pap. 2.95 (ISBN 0-87997-735-3, UE1735). DAW Bks.

--The Warrior Enchained. 352p. 1983. pap. 2.95. NAL.

Green, Stuart A. Complications of External Skeletal Fixation: Causes, Prevention & Treatment. (Illus.). 208p. 1981. 32.75x (ISBN 0-398-04482-1). C C Thomas.

Green, Susan. Gentle Gorilla: The Story of Patty Cake. LC 77-19009. (Illus.). 1978. 10.00 o.p. (ISBN 0-399-90004-7, Marek). Putnam Pub Group.

Green, T., jt. auth. see Smith, H. T.

Green, T. F. Activities of Teaching. 1971. 25.00 (ISBN 0-07-024336-0, C). McGraw.

Green, Thomas & Payne, Stephen J., eds. The Psychology of Computer Use. (Computer & People Ser.). Date not set. price not set (ISBN 0-12-297420-4). Acad Pr.

Green, Thomas H. Opening to God: A Guide to Prayer. LC 77-83197. 144p. 1977. pap. 2.95 (ISBN 0-87793-136-4). Ave Maria.

Green, Thomas H., ed. see Hume, David.

Green Tiger Press, ed. Books & Readers. (Illus.). 12p. 1982. pap. 2.50 (ISBN 0-914676-99-7, Pub. by Envelope Bks). Green Tiger Pr.

--Bubbles & Bubble Blowers. (Illus.). 12p. 1982. pap. 2.50 (ISBN 0-88138-000-8, Pub. by Envelope Bks). Green Tiger Pr.

--Flying Horse. 12p. (Orig.). 1982. pap. 2.50 (ISBN 0-88138-005-9, Pub. by Envelope Bks). Green Tiger Pr.

--Mermaids. (Illus.). 12p. (Orig.). 1982. pap. 2.50 (ISBN 0-88138-001-6, Pub. by Envelope Bks). Green Tiger Pr.

Green Tiger Staff. The Green Tiger's Caravan. (Illus.). 96p. 1982. pap. 10.00 (ISBN 0-914676-58-X, Star Eleph Bks). Green Tiger Pr.

Green, Walter L., jt. auth. see Speckhart, Frank H.

Green, Wayne, et al. Hobby Computers Are Here! 96p. 1976. pap. 4.95 o.p. (ISBN 0-88006-020-4, BK 7322). Green Pub Inc.

Green, William & Swanborough, Gordon. The Observer's Directory of Military Aircraft. LC 82-71835. (Illus.). 256p. 1983. 16.95 (ISBN 0-668-05649-5, 5649). Arco.

Green, William, ed. see Brown, Eric.

Green, William B. Digital Image Processing: A Systems Approach. (Van Nostrand Reinhold Electrical-Computer Science & Engineering Ser.). 203p. 1982. text ed. 34.50 (ISBN 0-442-28801-8). Van Nos Reinhold.

Green, William H. The Argument of the Book of Job Unfolded. 13.50 (ISBN 0-86524-101-5, 1802). Klock & Klock.

Green, William M. The Man Who Called Himself Devlin. LC 78-55653. 1978. 8.95 o.p. (ISBN 0-685-53363-8). Bobbs.

Green, William S. Approaches to Ancient Judaism II. LC 76-57656. (Brown Judaic Studies). 1980. 15.00 (ISBN 0-89130-447-9, 14-00-09); pap. 10.50 (ISBN 0-686-96880-8). Scholars Pr CA.

--Approaches to Ancient Judaism: Theory & Practice. LC 76-57656. 1978. pap. 16.50 (ISBN 0-89130-130-5, 14-00-01). Scholars Pr CA.

Greenacre, C. T. Templeman on Marine Insurance. 600p. 1981. 70.00x (ISBN 0-7121-1395-9, Pub. by Macdonald & Evans). State Mutual Bk.

Greenaway, D. S. & Warman, E. A., eds. Eurographics Eighty-Two: Proceedings of the International Conference & Exhibition, U.M.I.S.T., Manchester, U.K., 1982. 396p. 1982. 55.75 (ISBN 0-444-86480-6, North Holland). Elsevier.

Greenaway, David. Trade Policy & the New Protectionism. LC 82-10621. 232p. 1982. 25.00x (ISBN 0-312-81213-2). St Martin.

Greenaway, Kate. Kate Greenaway's Birthday Coloring Book. (Illus.). 96p. (ps-2). 1974. pap. 2.75 (ISBN 0-486-23050-3). Dover.

--Marigold Garden. (Illus.). (gr. k-3). 1885. 7.95 o.s.i. (ISBN 0-7232-1800-5). Warne.

--Under the Window. (Illus.). (gr. 1-4). 1879. 7.95 o.s.i. (ISBN 0-7232-1799-8). Warne.

Greenaway, Peter Van see Van Greenaway, Peter.

Greenbank, Anthony. A Handbook for Emergencies: Coming Out Alive. LC 74-25104. 192p. (gr. 7 up). 1976. 8.95 (ISBN 0-385-09842-1); pap. 4.95 o.p. (ISBN 0-385-09822-7). Doubleday.

Greenbaum, Fred. Robert Marion La Follette. LC 74-26675. (World Leaders Ser: No. 44). 1975. lib. bdg. 12.50 o.p. (ISBN 0-8057-3057-5, Twayne). G K Hall.

Greenbaum, Joan M. In the Name of Efficiency: Management Theory & Shopfloor Practice in Data Processing Work. 210p. 1979. 24.95 (ISBN 0-87722-151-0). Temple U Pr.

Greenbaum, Sidney, jt. auth. see Quirk, Randolph.

Greenbaum, Walter W. The Gemstone Identifier. LC 82-4074. (Illus.). 128p. 1982. 13.95 (ISBN 0-668-05387-9); pap. 7.95 (ISBN 0-668-05391-7). Arco.

Greenberg, jt. auth. see Asimov, Isaac.

Greenberg, Alan, tr. see Herzog, Werner.

Greenberg, Alvin. Dark Lands. 68p. 1973. 2.95 (ISBN 0-87886-024-X). Ithaca Hse.

--Delta q: Stories. LC 82-20075. (AWP Ser.: No.5). 208p. (Orig.). 1983. pap. 8.95 (ISBN 0-8262-0397-3). U of Mo Pr.

Greenberg, Alvin, et al. X-One: Experimental Fiction Project. Smith, Harry, ed. LC 76-20256. (Illus.). 1976. pap. 5.00 (ISBN 0-912292-41-5). The Smith.

Greenberg, Arnold, jt. auth. see Greenberg, Harriet.

Greenberg, Arnold, et al, eds. Standard Methods for the Examination of Water & Wastewater. 15th ed. LC 55-1979. 1134p. 1981. 50.00x (ISBN 0-87553-091-5, 035). Am Pub Health.

Greenberg, Bernice, jt. auth. see Lipson, Greta.

Greenberg, Bette, ed. How to Find Out in Psychiatry: A Guide to Sources of Mental Health Information. LC 78-16005. 1979. text ed. 15.75 (ISBN 0-08-021860-1). Pergamon.

Greenberg, Blu. How to Run a Traditional Jewish Household. 1983. 17.50 (ISBN 0-671-41700-2). S&S.

Greenberg, Bradley S. Life on Television: Content Analysis of U.S. TV Drama. LC 80-14478. (Communication & Information Science Ser.). 224p. 1980. text ed. 23.50 (ISBN 0-89391-039-2); pap. text ed. 13.95 (ISBN 0-89391-062-7). Ablex Pub.

Greenberg, Bradley S., et al. Mexican Americans & the Mass Media. (Communication & Information Science Ser.). 304p. 1983. text ed. 35.00 (ISBN 0-89391-126-7). Ablex Pub.

Greenberg, Bruce. Greenberg's Price Guide to Lionel Trains: 0 & 0-27 Trains, 1945-1978. (Illus.). 1978. 13.95 o.p. (ISBN 0-517-53795-8). Crown.

Greenberg, Bruce C. Greenberg's Guide to American Flyer: Prewar 0 & Standard. (Orig.). 1983. pap. 29.95 (ISBN 0-89778-014-0). Greenberg Pub Co.

--Greenberg's Price Guide to Lionel Trains: 1901-1942. 2nd ed. Greenberg, Linda, ed. (Illus.). 1979. 19.95 o.p. (ISBN 0-89778-088-4); pap. 12.95 O.P. o.p. (ISBN 0-89778-072-8). Greenberg Pub Co.

--Greenberg's Price Guide to Lionel Trains: Prewar-1901-1942. 160p. (Orig.). 1983. pap. 24.95 (ISBN 0-89778-502-9). Greenberg Pub.

Greenberg, Bruce C., jt. ed. see Klein, Maury D.

Greenberg, D. M., ed. Metabolic Pathways. 3rd ed. Incl. Vol. 1. 1967. 68.00, by subscription 68.00 (ISBN 0-12-299251-2); Vol. 2. 1968. 59.50, by subscription 59.50 (ISBN 0-12-299252-0); Vol. 3. 1969. 79.00, by subscription 79.00 (ISBN 0-12-299253-9); Vol. 4. 1970. 68.00, by subscription 68.00 (ISBN 0-12-299254-7); Vol. 5. Vogel, Henry J., ed. 1971. 73.00, by subscription 73.00 (ISBN 0-12-299255-5); Vol. 6. Hokin, L. E., ed. 1972. by subscription - 79.00 79.00 (ISBN 0-12-299256-3). Acad Pr.

Greenberg, David. Slugs. (Illus.). 32p. (gr. k-5). 1983. 13.45i (ISBN 0-316-32658-5, Pub. by Atlantic Monthly Pr); pap. 5.70i (ISBN 0-316-32659-3, Pub. by Atlantic Monthly Pr); 8-copy counter display 45.60 (ISBN 0-686-42954-0). Little.

Greenberg, Edward & Webster, Charles E. Advanced Econometrics: A Bridge to the Current Literature. (Probability & Mathematical Statistics Ser.). 352p. 1983. text ed. 34.95 (ISBN 0-471-09077-8). Wiley.

Greenberg, Edward, et al. Regulation, Market Prices, & Process Innovation: The Case of the Ammonia Industry. (Westview Replica Edition). 1979. lib. bdg. 28.00 o.p. (ISBN 0-89158-381-5). Westview.
Greenberg, Edward S. The American Political System: A Radical Approach. 2nd ed. 1980. text ed. 13.95 (ISBN 0-316-32662-3); tchr's manual free (ISBN 0-316-32663-1). Little.
--Understanding Modern Government: The Rise & Decline of the American Political Economy. LC 78-10104. 197p. 1979. pap. text ed. 11.95 (ISBN 0-471-02913-0). Wiley.
Greenberg, Eliezer, jt. ed. see Howe, Irving.
Greenberg, Eliezer, ed. see Peretz, I. L.
Greenberg, Eric R. The Celebrant. LC 82-9236. 272p. 1983. 14.95 (ISBN 0-89696-171-0, An Everest House Book). Dodd.
Greenberg, H. J. & Murphy, F. H. Advanced Techniques in the Practice of Operations Research. (Publications in Operations Research Ser.: Vol. 4). 470p. 1982. 47.50 (ISBN 0-444-00750-4, North Holland). Elsevier.
Greenberg, Harriet. U. S. Virgin Islands Alive. 1983. pap. 5.95 (ISBN 0-935572-11-2). Alive Pubns.
--U. S. Virgin Islands Alive. (Alive Publication Travel Guides). (Illus.). 200p. (Orig.). 1983. pap. 4.95 (ISBN 0-935572-11-2, Alive Pubns). Hippocrene Bks.
Greenberg, Harriet & Greenberg, Arnold. Panama Alive. 1974. pap. 2.00 o.p. (ISBN 0-686-23070-1). Alive Pubns.
Greenberg, Harvey. Hanging In: What You Need to Know About Psychotherapy. 1982. 12.95 (ISBN 0-686-38403-2). Four Winds Pr.
Greenberg, Hazel, ed. see Equal Rights Amendment Project.
Greenberg, Henry F., et al. Child Care Manual. 6th ed. St. Geme, Joseph W., Jr., ed. LC 75-21904. (Illus., Orig.). 1982. pap. text ed. 9.50 (ISBN 0-89119-000-7). Sutherland Learn Assocs.
Greenberg, Herbert. Quest for the Necessary: W. H. Auden & the Dilemma of Divided Consciousness. LC 68-54019. 1968. 12.50x o.p. (ISBN 0-674-74265-6). Harvard U Pr.
Greenberg, Howard. The Standard Periodical Directory: 1979-80. 6th ed. LC 64-7598. 1978. lib. bdg. 90.00 o.p. (ISBN 0-917460-03-0). Oxbridge Comm.
Greenberg, Howard, ed. Oxbridge Directory of Newsletters - 1979. 1979. pap. 35.00 o.p. (ISBN 0-917460-04-9). Oxbridge Comm.
Greenberg, Idaz. Hawaiian Fishwatcher's Field Guide. (Illus.). 1983. plastic card 3.95x (ISBN 0-913008-13-3). Seahawk Pr.
Greenberg, J., jt. ed. see Maquet, J.
Greenberg, Jack & Lambert, Richard D., eds. Blacks & the Law. new ed. LC 72-93252. (Annals of the American Academy of Political & Social Science: No. 407). 250p. 1973. 15.00 (ISBN 0-87761-163-7); pap. 7.95 (ISBN 0-87761-162-9). Am Acad Pol Soc Sci.
Greenberg, Jan. Theater Careers. (Illus.). 216p. (gr. 7 up). 1983. 13.95 (ISBN 0-03-061568-2). HR&W.
Greenberg, Janelle R., jt. auth. see Weston, Corinne.
Greenberg, Jay N., jt. ed. see Choi, Thomas.
Greenberg, Jerrold S. Comprehensive Stress Management. 350p. 1983. pap. text ed. write for info. (ISBN 0-697-07199-5). Wm C Brown.
Greenberg, Jerrold S., jt. auth. see Dintiman, George B.
Greenberg, Joanne. In This Sign. 288p. 1972. pap. 2.50 (ISBN 0-380-00941-2, 52712). Avon.
Greenberg, Joanne C., et al. The Language Arts Handbook: A Total Communication Approach. 1982. text ed. 19.95x (ISBN 0-673-15808-X). Scott F.
Greenberg, Kathy, jt. auth. see Kyte, Barbara.
Greenberg, Leon. A Practical Guide to Productivity Measurement. LC 73-75981. 78p. 1973. pap. 10.00 (ISBN 0-87179-190-0). BNA.
Greenberg, Linda, ed. see Greenberg, Bruce C.
Greenberg, Margaret & Olds, Nancy J. The Sanibel Shell Guide. LC 82-71090. (Illus.). 117p. (Orig.). 1982. pap. 4.95 (ISBN 0-89305-041-5). Anna Pub.
Greenberg, Marilyn. Rabbi's Life Contract. LC 82-45834. 312p. 1983. 15.95 (ISBN 0-385-19003-4). Doubleday.
Greenberg, Mark. The Hague. Bayrd, Edwin, ed. (Wonders of Man Ser.). (Illus.). 176p. 1982. 19.95 (ISBN 0-88225-310-7). Newsweek.
Greenberg, Mark D., ed. see Slatkes, Leonard J.
Greenberg, Marshall G., jt. auth. see Frank, Ronald E.
Greenberg, Martin, tr. see Kafka, Franz.
Greenberg, Martin H., jt. auth. see Waugh, Charles G.
Greenberg, Martin H. & Olander, Joseph D., eds. Philip K. Dick. LC 77-76723. (Writers of the Twenty-First Century Ser.). 1983. 12.95 (ISBN 0-8008-6292-9); pap. 5.95 (ISBN 0-8008-6291-0). Taplinger.
--Run to Starlight: Sports Through Science Fiction. LC 75-8005. 288p. (gr. 7 up). 1975. 9.95 o.s.i. (ISBN 0-440-07401-0). Delacorte.
Greenberg, Martin H. & Waugh, Charles G., eds. The Arbor House Celebrity Book of the Greatest Stories Ever Told. 1983. 15.95 (ISBN 0-87795-448-8). Arbor Hse.
Greenberg, Martin H., jt. ed. see Asimov, Isaac.
Greenberg, Martin H., ed. see Asimov, Isaac.
Greenberg, Martin H., jt. ed. see Asimov, Isaac.
Greenberg, Martin H., ed. see Gardner, Erle S.
Greenberg, Martin H., jt. ed. see Silverberg, Robert.
Greenberg, Martin H., jt. auth. see Asimov, Isaac.
Greenberg, Martin H., jt. ed. see Asimov, Isaac.
Greenberg, Martin J., jt. auth. see Cooper-Hill, James.
Greenberg, Martin S. & Ruback, R. Barry. Social Psychology of the Criminal Justice System. LC 81-18084. (Psychology Ser.). 497p. 1982. text ed. 20.95 (ISBN 0-8185-0508-7). Brooks-Cole.
Greenberg, Michael, et al. Solid Waste Planning in Metropolitan Areas. 1976. pap. 10.00 o.p. (ISBN 0-88285-031-8). Ctr Urban Pol Res.
--A Primer on Industrial Environmental Impact. LC 78-11642. 1979. text ed. 17.95 o.p. (ISBN 0-88285-050-4). Ctr Urban Pol Res.
Greenberg, Michael D. Foundations of Applied Mathematics. LC 77-11125. (Illus.). 1978. ref. ed. 35.95 (ISBN 0-13-329623-7). P-H.
Greenberg, Michael R. Urbanization & Cancer Mortality: The United States Experience, 1950-1975. (Monographs in Epidemiology & Biostatistics). (Illus.). 276p. 1983. 45.00x (ISBN 0-19-503173-3). Oxford U Pr.
Greenberg, Moshe. Ezekiel, 1-20: A New Translation with Introduction & Commentary. LC 77-12855. (Anchor Bible Ser.: Vol. 22). (Illus.). 384p. 1983. 16.00 (ISBN 0-385-00954-2, Anchor Pr). Doubleday.
--Introduction to Hebrew. 1964. text ed. 18.95 (ISBN 0-13-484469-6). P-H.
Greenberg, Naomi S. A Genealogical History of an Extended Family. (Illus.). 160p. 1981. 19.95 (ISBN 0-9607262-0-9). Everlast Pr.
--Occupational Therapy Assistant's Handbook. (Allied Health Professions Monograph). (Illus.). 186p. 1983. 11.50 (ISBN 0-87527-270-3). Green.
Greenberg, Noah, ed. see Auden, W. H. & Kallman, Chester.
Greenberg, P., ed. see Dukhin, S. S. & Shilov, V. N.
Greenberg, P., ed. see Sedunov, Yu. S.
Greenberg, Pearl, tr. see Buhler, Charlotte.
Greenberg, Polly. I Know I'm Myself Because... LC 80-25358. 32p. 1981. 9.95x (ISBN 0-89885-045-2). Human Sci Pr.
Greenberg, Robert, ed. see Swift, Jonathan.
Greenberg, Robert A., jt. auth. see Miller, Ruth.
Greenberg, Roger, jt. ed. see Fisher, Seymour.
Greenberg, Roger P., jt. auth. see Fisher, Seymour.
Greenberg, Samuel. Neurosis Is a Painful Style of Living. rev. ed. 1978. pap. 1.75 (ISBN 0-451-09417-4, E9417, Sig). NAL.
Greenberg, Selma. Right from the Start: A Guide to Nonsexist Child Rearing. LC 77-20000. 1978. 8.95 o.s.i. (ISBN 0-395-25714-X). HM.
Greenberg, Sidney & Levine, Jonathan. Likrat Shabbat. LC 72-97593. 8.95 (ISBN 0-685-40686-5). Prayer Bk.
Greenberg, Sidney & Silverman, Morris. Siddurenu. (gr. 3-7). 6.95 (ISBN 0-685-23437-1). Prayer Bk.
Greenberg, Sidney & Sugarman, Allan S. Junior Contemporary Prayer Book for the High Holidays. (gr. 3-8). pap. 4.95 (ISBN 0-87677-054-5). Prayer Bk.
Greenberg, Sidney, ed. New Model Seder. pap. 1.65 (ISBN 0-87677-058-8). Prayer Bk.
Greenberger, Martin. Caught Unawares: The Energy Decade in Retrospect. 400p. 1983. prof ref. 24.50 (ISBN 0-88410-916-X). Ballinger Pub.
Greenberger, Martin, et al. Models in the Policy Process: Public Decision Making in the Computer Era. LC 76-1815. 376p. 1976. 16.00x (ISBN 0-87154-369-9). Russell Sage.
Greenberger, Martin, et al, eds. Networks for Research & Education: Sharing of Computer & Information Resources Nationwide. 1974. 17.50x (ISBN 0-262-07057-X). MIT Pr.
Greenberger, Monroe E. & Siegel, Mary-Ellen. What Every Man Should Know About His Prostate. (Illus.). Date not set. 12.95 (ISBN 0-8027-0725-4). Walker & Co.
Greenbie, B. B. Design for Diversity. (Developments in Landscape Management & Urban Planning: Vol. 2). 1976. 49.00 (ISBN 0-444-41329-4). Elsevier.
Greenbie, Barrie B. Spaces: Dimensions of the Human Landscape. LC 81-50435. (Illus.). 448p. 1981. text ed. 47.50x (ISBN 0-300-02549-1); pap. 15.95x (ISBN 0-300-02560-2). Yale U Pr.
Greenbie, Marjorie L. American Saga: The History & Literature of the American Dream of a Better Life. Repr. of 1939 ed. lib. bdg. 25.75x o.p. (ISBN 0-8371-4228-8, GRAM). Greenwood.
Greenblat, Cathy & Cottle, Thomas J. Getting Married. LC 80-16369. 276p. 1980. 11.95 o.p. (ISBN 0-07-024330-1). McGraw.
Greenblat, Cathy S., jt. auth. see Gagnon, John H.
Greenblat, Cathy S., et al. The Marital Game: Personal Growth & Fulfillment. 2nd ed. 1977. pap. text ed. 7.95x o.p. (ISBN 0-394-31136-1). Random.
Greenblat, Sidney L. Social Interaction in Chinese Society. Wilson, Richard & Wilson, Amy A., eds. 272p. 1982. 29.95 (ISBN 0-03-058021-8). Praeger.
Greenblatt, Augusta & Greenblatt, I. J. Your Genes & Your Destiny. LC 78-55655. 1978. 8.95 o.p. (ISBN 0-672-52302-7). Bobbs.
Greenblatt, David J., jt. ed. see Miller, Russell R.
Greenblatt, I. J., jt. auth. see Greenblatt, Augusta.
Greenblatt, M., et al, eds. Poverty & Mental Health: PRR 21. 275p. 1967. pap. 5.00 o.p. (ISBN 0-685-24868-2, P021-0). Am Psychiatric.
Greenblatt, Milton, et al. Dynamics of Institutional Change: The Hospital in Transition. LC 79-139597. (Contemporary Community Health Ser). 1971. 12.95 o.p. (ISBN 0-8229-3222-9). U of Pittsburgh Pr.
Greenblatt, Robert B. Geriatric Endocrinology. LC 75-43196. (Aging Ser.: Vol. 5). 256p. 1978. 27.00 (ISBN 0-89004-112-1). Raven.
Greenblatt, Robert B., jt. auth. see Semm, Kurt.
Greenblatt, Sidney L., ed. People of Taihang: An Anthology of Family Histories. LC 74-15389. (The China Book Project Ser.). 1976. 25.00 o.p. (ISBN 0-87332-059-X). M E Sharpe.
Greenbow, Desna. Devon Mill: The Restoration of a Corn Mill. 49p. 1982. 25.00x (ISBN 0-284-98624-0, Pub. by C Skilton Scotland). State Mutual Bk.
Greenburg, Dan. How to Be a Jewish Mother. (Illus.). 1965. pap. 2.95 (ISBN 0-8431-0030-3). Price Stern.
Greenburg, Dan & Jacobs, Marcia. How to Make Yourself Miserable. pap. 3.95 (ISBN 0-686-36757-X). Inst Rat Liv.
Greendyke, Robert M. & Banzhaf, Jane C. Blood Bank Policies & Procedures. 1976. spiral bdg. 12.00 o.p. (ISBN 0-87488-652-X). Med Exam.
Greene & Dicker. Sign Language. 1981. 8.90 (ISBN 0-686-94639-1). Watts.
Greene, Audrey. Audreys Add No Salt Cookery. Orig. Title: Audrey's Add No Salt Cookery. (Illus.). 1982. write for info (ISBN 0-9608892-0-5). Greene Pubns.
Greene, Barbara, jt. auth. see Greene, Eva.
Greene, Bert. Bert Greene's Kitchen Bouquets. LC 79-50976. (Illus.). 1979. 17.95 o.p. (ISBN 0-8092-7710-7). Contemp Bks.
Greene, Bette. Get on Out of Here, Philip Hall. (gr. k-6). 1983. pap. 2.50 (ISBN 0-440-43038-0, YB). Dell.
--Philip Hall Likes Me, I Reckon, Maybe. 144p. 1975. pap. 1.95 (ISBN 0-440-45755-6, YB). Dell.
--Them That Glitter & Them That Don't. LC 92-13020. 224p. 1983. 10.95 (ISBN 0-394-84692-3); lib. bdg. 10.99 (ISBN 0-394-94692-8). Knopf.
Greene, Bill. Think Like a Tycoon. Date not set. pap. 5.95 (ISBN 0-449-90068-1, Columbine). Fawcett.
Greene, Bill, jt. auth. see Leonard, Cliff R.
Greene, Bob. Twenty Five Quick-N-Easy Electronics Projects. 96p. (Orig.). 1982. pap. 4.95 (ISBN 0-86668-023-3). ARCsoft.
Greene, Bruce M. & Robertson, David, eds. Problems in Internal Medicine. 368p. (Orig.). 1980. pap. text ed. 17.95 (ISBN 0-8391-1594-6). Univ Park.
Greene, Carla. Trip to the Aquarium. (Illus.). (gr. 1-5). 1967. PLB 6.19 o.p. (ISBN 0-8313-0066-3). Lantern.
Greene, Carol. England, Enchantment of the World. LC 82-4471. (Illus.). (gr. 5-9). 1982. PLB 13.25g (ISBN 0-516-02763-8). Childrens.
--Holidays. LC 82-9734. (New True Books). (Illus.). (gr. k-4). 1982. PLB 9.25g (ISBN 0-516-01624-5). Childrens.
--Kiri & the First Easter. (Arch Bks: Set 9). (Illus.). 32p. (ps-4). 1972. pap. 0.89 (ISBN 0-570-06064-8, 59-1182). Concordia.
--No More Than a Mustard Seed. 1980. pap. 0.89 (ISBN 0-570-06134-2, 59-1252, Arch Bk). Concordia.
--Please, Wind? LC 82-4548. (Rookie Readers Ser.). (Illus.). (ps-2). 1982. PLB 8.65g (ISBN 0-516-02033-1); pap. 1.95 (ISBN 0-516-42033-X). Childrens.
--Proverbs-Important Things to Know. 1980. pap. 0.89 (ISBN 0-570-06140-7, 59-1303, Arch Bk). Concordia.
--Rain! Rain! LC 82-9509. (Rookie Readers Ser.). (Illus.). (ps-2). 1982. PLB 8.65g (ISBN 0-516-02034-X); pap. 1.95 (ISBN 0-516-42034-8). Childrens.
--Snow Joe. LC 82-9403. (Rookie Readers Ser.). (Illus.). (ps-2). 1982. PLB 8.65g (ISBN 0-516-02035-8); pap. 1.95 (ISBN 0-516-42035-6). Childrens.
Greene, Constance C. Al(Exandra) the Great. LC 81-16058. 144p. (gr. 5-9). 1982. 9.95 (ISBN 0-670-11197-X). Viking Pr.
--Al(exandra) the Great. (gr. k-6). 1983. pap. 2.25 (ISBN 0-440-40350-2, YB). Dell.
--Ask Anybody. 156p. (gr. 5-9). 1983. 10.95 (ISBN 0-670-13813-4). Viking Pr.
--Dotty's Suitcase. (gr. 3-7). 1982. pap. 2.25 (ISBN 0-440-42108-X, YB). Dell.
--Double-Dare O'Toole. 176p. (gr. 4-7). 1983. pap. 2.25 (ISBN 0-440-41982-4, YB). Dell.
--A Girl Called Al. 1977. pap. 1.75 (ISBN 0-440-42810-6, YB). Dell.
--I & Sproggy. (Illus.). 144p. (gr. 5 up). pap. 1.95 (ISBN 0-440-43986-8, YB). Dell.
--I Know You Al. 1977. pap. 1.95 (ISBN 0-440-44123-4, YB). Dell.
--Isabelle the Itch. 128p. (gr. 2-4). 1974. pap. 1.95 (ISBN 0-440-44345-8, YB). Dell.
--Your Old Pal, Al. 160p. (gr. k-6). 1981. pap. 1.95 (ISBN 0-440-49862-7, YB). Dell.
Greene, D. & Knuth, D., eds. Mathematics for the Analysis of Algorithms. 2nd ed. (Progress in Computer Science: Vol. 1). 123p. text ed. 10.00x (ISBN 3-7643-3102-X). Birkhauser.
Greene, Daniel E. Pastel: A Comprehensive Guide to Pastel Painting. Singer, Joe, ed. LC 74-13740. (Illus.). 160p. 1974. 19.95 (ISBN 0-8230-3899-8). Watson-Guptill.
Greene, David, ed. see Sophocles.
Greene, David H., jt. ed. see Mercier, Vivian.
Greene, Diane S. Sunrise, a Whole Grain, Natural Food Breakfast Cook Book. LC 80-20749. 240p. 1980. 15.95 (ISBN 0-89594-041-8); pap. 6.95 (ISBN 0-89594-040-X). Crossing Pr.
Greene, Donald. The Age of Exuberance: Backgrounds to Eighteenth Century Literature, 1660-1785. (Language & Literature Studies). (Orig.). 1967. pap. text ed. 5.00 (ISBN 0-394-30638-4, RanC). Random.
--Samuel Johnson. (English Authors Ser.: No. 95). lib. bdg. 10.95 o.p. (ISBN 0-8057-1296-8, Twayne). G K Hall.
Greene, Donald J., ed. see Johnson, Samuel.
Greene, Edward J. T. S. Eliot, et la France. 248p. 1982. Repr. lib. bdg. 75.00 (ISBN 0-89760-252-8). Telegraph Bks.
Greene, Edward L. Landmarks of Botanical History, 2 vols. Egerton, Frank N., ed. LC 79-66057. (Illus.). 1248p. 1983. Set. text ed. 100.00 (ISBN 0-8047-1075-9). Stanford U Pr.
Greene, Ellin, jt. auth. see Baker, Augusta.
Greene, Ellin & Schoenfeld, Madalynne, eds. A Multimedia Approach to Children's Literature: A Selective List of Films, Filmstrips & Recordings Based on Children's Books. 2nd ed. LC 77-10802. 1977. pap. 8.00 (ISBN 0-8389-0249-9). ALA.
Greene, Ethel J., jt. auth. see Robinson, Kitty K.
Greene, Eva & Greene, Barbara. Chance of a Lifetime: An Anthology for the Ageless. LC 67-16829. (Illus.). 1968. 6.95 (ISBN 0-87027-095-8). Cumberland Pr.
Greene, Felix. Let There Be a World: A Call for an End to the Arms Race. (Illus.). 65p. 1982. pap. 4.95 (ISBN 0-575-03136-0, Pub. by Gollancz England). David & Charles.
Greene, Fred. Stresses in U. S.-Japanese Security Relations. (Studies in Defense Policy). 120p. 1975. pap. 4.95 (ISBN 0-8157-3271-6). Brookings.
Greene, Gardiner C. How to Start & Manage Your Own Small Business. 243p. 1975. 19.95 (ISBN 0-07-024350-6, P&RB). McGraw.
Greene, Gardiner G. How to Start & Manage Your Own Business. (Executive Library Ser.). 256p. 1975. pap. 3.95 (ISBN 0-451-62146-8, ME2146, Ment). NAL.
Greene, Gerald. The Healers. LC 78-24534. 1979. 10.95 o.p. (ISBN 0-399-12119-6). Putnam Pub Group.
Greene, Graham. A Burnt-Out Case. 1977. pap. 3.50 (ISBN 0-14-001894-8). Penguin.
--The Collected Essays. 1983. 18.75 (ISBN 0-670-22740-4). Viking Pr.
--Collected Stories. 1973. 16.95 (ISBN 0-670-22911-3). Viking Pr.
--The Comedians. 1976. pap. 3.95 (ISBN 0-14-002766-1). Penguin.
--The Confidential Agent. 256p. 17.95 (ISBN 0-670-23725-6). Viking Pr.
--The End of the Affair. 1977. pap. 3.95 (ISBN 0-14-004696-8). Penguin.
--The End of the Affair. 1982. 16.95 (ISBN 0-670-29457-8). Viking Pr.
--Graham Greene: Journey Without Maps. (Uniform Edition). 336p. 1983. 18.75 (ISBN 0-670-40974-X). Viking Pr.
--The Heart of the Matter. 1978. pap. 3.50 (ISBN 0-14-001789-5). Penguin.
--The Honorary Consul. 1983. 18.75 (ISBN 0-670-37872-0). Viking Pr.
--The Human Factor. 1978. 10.95 o.p. (ISBN 0-671-24085-4). S&S.
--The Human Factor. 1983. 18.75 (ISBN 0-670-38625-1). Viking Pr.
--It's a Battlefield. 224p. 1982. 17.95 (ISBN 0-670-40431-4). Viking Pr.
--J'accuse: Nice, the Dark Side. 48p. (Eng. & Fr.). 1982. pap. 3.95 (ISBN 0-370-30930-8, Pub. by Chatto-Bodley-Jonathan). Merrimack Bk Serv.
--The Man Within. 1982. pap. 3.95 (ISBN 0-14-003283-5). Penguin.
--The Ministry of Fear. 272p. 1982. 17.95 (ISBN 0-670-47682-X). Viking Pr.
--Our Man in Havana. 1979. pap. 3.50 (ISBN 0-14-001790-9). Penguin.
--The Quiet American. 1977. pap. 3.95 (ISBN 0-14-001792-5). Penguin.
--Shades of Greene. 1977. pap. 3.50 (ISBN 0-14-004023-4). Penguin.
--Stamboul Train. 1983. pap. 3.95 (ISBN 0-14-001898-0). Penguin.
--The Third Man & The Fallen Idol. 1981. pap. 3.95 (ISBN 0-14-003278-9). Penguin.
--The Third Man, Loser Takes All. 208p. 1983. 18.75 (ISBN 0-670-70084-3). Viking Pr.
--Twenty-One Stories. 200p. 1981. pap. 3.50 (ISBN 0-14-003093-X). Penguin.
--Ways of Escape. 288p. 1982. pap. 3.95 (ISBN 0-671-43820-4). WSP.
Greene, H. L., jt. ed. see Winters, R. W.
Greene, Harry P. Interpretation in Song. LC 79-4135. (Music Reprint Ser.). 307p. 1979. Repr. of 1912 ed. 32.50 (ISBN 0-306-79509-4). Da Capo.

Greene, Herb & Greene, Nanine H. Building to Last. (Illus.). 168p. 1981. 26.95 (ISBN 0-8038-0028-2). Hastings.

Greene, J. H. Production & Inventory Control Handbook. 1970. 59.50 (ISBN 0-07-024332-8, P&RB). McGraw.

Greene, J. R. The Creation of Quabbin Reservoir: Death of the Swift River Valley. 2nd. Ed ed. (Illus.). 123p. 1982. pap. 9.95 (ISBN 0-9609404-0-5). J R Greene.

--Death of Disco & Other Poems. 40p. (Orig.). 1982. pap. 3.25 (ISBN 0-9609404-1-3). J R Greene.

Greene, Jack P., compiled by. American Colonies in the Eighteenth Century, 1689-1763. LC 73-79166. (Goldentree Bibliographies in American History Ser). (Orig.). 1969. pap. 13.95x (ISBN 0-88295-514-4). Harlan Davidson.

Greene, Jack P., ed. Colonies to Nation, 1763-1789: A Documentary History of the American Revolution. 608p. 1975. pap. 11.95x (ISBN 0-393-09229-1). Norton.

Greene, Jane B., tr. see Rilke, Rainer M.

Greene, Jerome A. Slim Buttes, Eighteen Seventy-Six: An Episode of the Great Sioux War. LC 81-40291. (Illus.). 224p. 1982. 14.95 (ISBN 0-8061-1712-5). U of Okla Pr.

Greene, John, jt. auth. see Curtis, John.

Greene, John C. American Science in the Age of Jefferson. (Illus.). 1983. write for info (ISBN 0-8138-0101-X). Iowa St U Pr.

Greene, Joseph N., Jr. & Klutznick, Philip M. The Path to Peace: Arab-Israeli Peace & the United States. 50p. 1981. pap. 3.00 (ISBN 0-943006-13-9). Seven Springs.

Greene, Joshua. The King Who Swept the Road. LC 78-16369. (The Pastimes of Shri Chaitanya Maharbhu Ser.). (Illus.). (gr. 6-9). 1978. pap. 2.95 o.p. (ISBN 0-89647-002-4). Bala Bks.

--Readings in Vedic Literature for Children. LC 77-17485. (gr. 5-8). 1977. 4.95 o.p. (ISBN 0-89647-001-6). Bala Bks.

--El Rey Qui Barrio el Camino. LC 78-15235. 1978. 2.95 o.p. (ISBN 0-89647-003-2). Bala Bks.

Greene, Judith. Psycholinguistics. (Education Ser.). 1973. pap. 2.95 o.p. (ISBN 0-14-080704-7). Penguin.

Greene, Kenyon De see De Greene, Kenyon.

Greene, Kevin. Archaeology: An Introduction. (Illus.). 168p. 1983. text ed. 25.00x (ISBN 0-389-20362-9). B&N Imports.

Greene, L. L. Sleeping Beauty. (Orig.). 1982. pap. 2.50 (ISBN 0-451-11548-1, AE1548, Sig). NAL.

Greene, Larry J. Kid Who Hate School. 250p. (Orig.). 1982. pap. 12.95 (ISBN 0-89334-035-9). Humanics Ltd.

Greene, Lee. The Johnny Unitas Story. (Putnam Sports Shelf). (Illus.). (gr. 5-8). 1962. PLB 4.97 o.p. (ISBN 0-399-60325-5). Putnam Pub Group.

Greene, Leonard M. Free Enterprise Without Poverty. 192p. 1983. pap. 4.50 (ISBN 0-393-30083-8). Norton.

Greene, Liz. The Outer Planets & Their Cycles: The Astrology of the Collective. LC 82-45633. (Lectures on Modern Astrology Ser.: Vol. II). 200p. 1982. pap. 7.95 (ISBN 0-916360-17-2). CRCS Pubns NV.

--Star Signs for Lovers. LC 80-5890. 400p. 1980. 7.95 (ISBN 0-916360-08-3). CRCS Pubns NV.

Greene, Liz, jt. auth. see Arroyo, Stephen.

Greene, Lorenzo P., et al. Missouri's Black Heritage. LC 79-54887. (Orig.). 1980. pap. text ed. 11.95x (ISBN 0-88273-115-7). Forum Pr IL.

Greene, Lorne. The Lorne Greene Book of Remarkable Animals. 1980. 10.95 o.p. (ISBN 0-671-24012-9). S&S.

Greene, M., ed. see Zoschenko, Mikhail.

Greene, M. Louise. Development of Religious Liberty in Connecticut. LC 74-99858. (Civil Liberties in American History Ser). 1970. Repr. of 1905 ed. lib. bdg. 59.50 (ISBN 0-306-71861-8). Da Capo.

Greene, Margaret. The Voice & Its Disorders. 4th ed. 446p. 1980. 50.00 (ISBN 0-397-50300-8, Lippincott Medical). Lippincott.

Greene, Maxine. Existential Encounters for Teachers. 1967. pap. text ed. 3.25x (ISBN 0-394-30646-5). Phila Bk Co.

--Landscapes of Learning. LC 78-6571. 1978. pap. text ed. 12.50x (ISBN 0-8077-2534-X). Tchrs Coll.

Greene, Mott. Geology in the Nineteenth Century: Changing Views of a Changing World. LC 82-7456. (Illus.). 320p. 1982. 29.50x (ISBN 0-8014-1467-9). Cornell U Pr.

Greene, Myles. Adventures in Philosophical Poetry & Literature. 48p. 1983. 1.95 (ISBN 0-9606994-2-2). Greenview Pubns.

--CIRCA Nineteen Sixty-Eight. 24p. 1982. pap. text ed. 2.95 (ISBN 0-9606994-0-6). Greenview Pubns.

Greene, Nanine H., jt. auth. see Greene, Herb.

Greene, Nathanael. From Versailles to Vichy: The Third French Republic 1919-1940. LC 75-101945. (Europe Since 1500 Ser.). 1970. pap. 7.95x (ISBN 0-88295-737-6). Harlan Davidson.

--The Papers of General Nathanael Greene, 1766-1786: 1 January 1777 to 16 October 1778. Showman, Richard K., et al, eds. xxxix, 606p. 1980. 22.00x (ISBN 0-8078-1384-2). U of NC Pr.

Greene, Nathanael, ed. Fascism: An Anthology. LC 67-30582. (Orig.). 1968. pap. 10.95x (ISBN 0-88295-736-8). Harlan Davidson.

Greene, Nicholas M. Key Words in Anesthesiology. 2nd ed. 80p. 1980. pap. 8.95 o.p. (ISBN 0-683-03768-4). Williams & Wilkins.

--Physiology of Spinal Anesthesia. 3rd ed. 289p. 1981. 34.00 (ISBN 0-686-77758-1, 3554-1). Williams & Wilkins.

Greene, Norbert D., jt. auth. see Fontana, Mars G.

Greene, Orville & Durr, Frank. The Practical Inventor's Handbook. LC 78-26666. (Illus.). 1979. 29.95 (ISBN 0-07-024320-4, P&RB). McGraw.

Greene, Owne & Rubin, Barry. London After the Bomb: What a Nuclear Attack Really Means. (Ser. K). (Illus.). 152p. 1983. pap. 4.95 (ISBN 0-19-285123-3). Oxford U Pr.

Greene, Ralph C. Medical Overkill. (Illus.). 320p. 1983. 14.50. G F Stickley.

Greene, Raymond, ed. Current Concepts in Migraine Research. LC 77-83690. 181p. 1978. 25.00 (ISBN 0-89004-199-7). Raven.

Greene, Richard. Assuring Quality in Medical Care: The State of the Art. LC 75-37567. 320p. 1976. prof ref 25.00x (ISBN 0-88410-116-9). Ballinger Pub.

Greene, Richard C. The King of Instruments. LC 82-4282. (Illus.). 32p. (gr. 1-5). 1982. lib. bdg. 7.95g (ISBN 0-87614-186-6). Carolrhoda Bks.

Greene, Richard L., ed. The Early English Carols. 2nd ed. 1977. 94.00x (ISBN 0-19-812715-4). Oxford U Pr.

Greene, Robert F. Tennis Tactics. LC 77-26216. (Illus.). 1978. 12.95 o.p. (ISBN 0-399-12120-X). Putnam Pub Group.

Greene, Robert W. The Sting Man: The Inside Story of Abscam. (Illus.). 256p. 1981. 13.50 o.p. (ISBN 0-525-20985-9, 01311-390). Dutton.

Greene, S. W., ed. see International Association of Briologists, Taxonomic Workshop, 1979.

Greene, Samuel S. An Analysis of the English Language. LC 82-10272. (American Linguistics Ser.). 1983. Repr. of 1874 ed. 40.00 (ISBN 0-8201-1384-0). Schol Facsimiles.

--First Lessons in Grammar. LC 81-16559. (Amer. Linguistics Ser.). 1982. Repr. of 1848 ed. 30.00x (ISBN 0-8201-1349-2). Schol Facsimiles.

Greene, Sheldon. Lost & Found. 1980. 9.95 o.p. (ISBN 0-394-51250-2). Random.

Greene, Suzanne E. Baltimore: An Illustrated History. (Illus.). 325p. 1980. 19.50 (ISBN 0-686-36494-5). Md Hist.

Greene, Tom, ed. see Barham, Martha.

Greene, Vaughn M. Astronauts of Ancient Japan. LC 78-78289. (Illus.). 200p. (Orig.). 1978. 8.95 (ISBN 0-8048-1311-6, Dist. by C E Tuttle). Merlin Engine Wks.

--The Six Thousand Year-Old Spacesuit. (Illus.). 104p. (Orig.). 1982. pap. 9.95 (ISBN 0-8048-1311-6). Merlin Engine Wks.

Greene, W. T. Parrots in Captivity. (Illus.). 1979. 29.95 (ISBN 0-87666-979-8, H-1018). TFH Pubns.

Greene, Wade. Disarmament: The Challenge of Civilization. (Challenge Bk). (gr. 6-8). 1966. 4.00e o.p. (ISBN 0-698-20033-0, Coward). Putnam Pub Group.

Greene, Walter H., jt. auth. see Jenne, Frank H.

Greene, Walter H., jt. auth. see Read, Donald A.

Greenes, Carole, jt. auth. see Seymour, Dale.

Greenes, Carole, et al. The Mathworks. (gr. k-8). 1978. pap. 21.50 (ISBN 0-88488-117-2). Creative Pubns.

--Successful Problem Solving Techniques. (gr. 6-12). 1977. tchrs. ed. 9.50 (ISBN 0-88488-086-9). Creative Pubns.

Greenes, Carole E., et al. Problem-Mathics. (gr. 7-12). 1977. tchrs. ed. 8.50 (ISBN 0-88488-085-0). Creative Pubns.

Greenewalt, C. H., Jr. Ritual Dinners in Early Historic Sardis. (Publications in Classical Studies: Vol. 17). 1978. pap. 15.50x (ISBN 0-520-09563-4). U of Cal Pr.

Greenfeld, Howard. Caruso. LC 82-13301. 304p. 1983. 17.95 (ISBN 0-399-12736-4). Putnam Pub Group.

--Puccini. 320p. 1981. 16.95 (ISBN 0-399-12551-5). Putnam Pub Group.

--Purim. LC 82-11676. (Illus.). 32p. (gr. 3-7). 1983. 9.70 (ISBN 0-03-061478-3). HR&W.

Greenfeld, Howard, tr. see Memmi, Albert.

Greenfield, Darby. Indonesia: A Traveler's Guide. Incl. Vol. 1o. p. Java & Sumatra (ISBN 0-902675-46-X); Vol. 2. Bali & East Indonesia. 1976. 9.95 (ISBN 0-902675-48-6). (Illus.). 1975. 9.95 (ISBN 0-686-77077-3). Oleander Pr.

Greenfield, Edward, et al. The New Penguin Stereo Record & Cassette Guide. 832p. (Orig.). 1983. pap. 12.95 (ISBN 0-14-046500-6). Penguin.

--Penguin Cassette Guide. (Handbooks Ser.). 1980. pap. 12.50 o.p. (ISBN 0-14-046372-0). Penguin.

Greenfield, Eloise. Africa Dream. LC 77-5080. (Illus.). (gr. k-4). 1977. 10.53i (ISBN 0-381-90061-4, JD-J). Har-Row.

--Darlene. (Illus.). 32p. (ps). 1980. 8.95 (ISBN 0-416-30701-9). Methuen Inc.

--Good News. LC 76-54900. (Illus.). 32p. (gr. k-3). 1977. 5.95 o.p. (ISBN 0-698-20406-9, Coward). Putnam Pub Group.

--Grandmama's Joy. LC 79-11403. (Illus.). 32p. (gr. 2-5). 1980. 8.95 (ISBN 0-529-05536-8, Philomel); PLB 8.99 (ISBN 0-529-05537-6). Putnam Pub Group.

--Mary McLeod Bethune. LC 76-11522. (Biography Ser.). (Illus.). (gr. 2-5). 1977. PLB 10.89 (ISBN 0-690-01129-6, TYC-J). Har-Row.

--Me & Neesie. LC 74-23078. (Illus.). 40p. (gr. 1-4). 1975. PLB 10.89 (ISBN 0-690-00715-9, TYC-J). Har-Row.

--Paul Robeson. LC 74-13663. (Biography Ser.). (Illus.). (gr. 1-5). 1975. PLB 10.89 (ISBN 0-690-00660-8, TYC-J). Har-Row.

--Rosa Parks. LC 72-83782. (Biography Ser.). (Illus.). (gr. 1-5). 1973. 7.95 o.p. (ISBN 0-690-71210-3, TYC-J); PLB 10.89 (ISBN 0-690-71211-1). Har-Row.

Greenfield, Eloise & Little, Lessie J. Childtimes: A Three-Generation Memoir. LC 77-26581. (Illus.). (gr. 5 up). 1979. 9.57i (ISBN 0-690-03874-7, TYC-J); PLB 8.79 o.p. (ISBN 0-690-03875-5). Har-Row.

Greenfield, Eloise & Revis, Alesia. Alesia. (Illus.). 80p. (gr. 5 up). 1981. 9.95 (ISBN 0-399-20831-3, Philomel). Putnam Pub Group.

Greenfield, Eric V., jt. auth. see D'Eca, Raul.

Greenfield, Harry, ed. Theory for Economic Efficiency: Essays in Honor of Abba P. Lerner. 1979. text ed. 30.00x (ISBN 0-262-07074-X). MIT Pr.

Greenfield, Howard. Gertrude Stein: A Biography. 1973. 5.95 o.p. (ISBN 0-517-50260-7). Crown.

Greenfield, Jeff. Television: The First Fifty Years. (Illus.). 1977. 50.00 (ISBN 0-8109-1651-7). Abrams.

Greenfield, Joel I., jt. auth. see Blonien, Rodney.

Greenfield, Joseph D. Using Microprocessors & Microcomputers: The 6800 Family. LC 80-18090. (Electronic Technology Ser.). 512p. 1981. text ed. 27.95 (ISBN 0-471-02727-8); Avail Student Manual. Wiley.

Greenfield, Kent R. American Strategy in World War II: A Reconsideration. LC 78-12870. 1979. Repr. of 1963 ed. lib. bdg. 18.75x (ISBN 0-313-21175-2, GRAW). Greenwood.

--American Strategy in World War II: A Reconsideration. LC 82-14881. 158p. 1982. pap. 7.50 (ISBN 0-89874-557-8). Krieger.

--The Museum, Its First Half Century: Annual I. (Illus.). 1968. pap. 7.50 (ISBN 0-912298-25-1). Baltimore Mus.

Greenfield, Larry D. & Uszler, J. Michael, eds. Nuclear Medicine in Clinical Practice: Selective Correlation with Ultrasound & Computerized Tomography. LC 81-23155. (Illus.). 427p. 1982. 47.50x (ISBN 0-89573-110-X). Verlag Chemie.

Greenfield, Margaret. Medicare & Medicaid: The 1965 & 1967 Social Security Amendments. LC 82-25157. x, 143p. 1983. Repr. of 1968 ed. lib. bdg. 25.00x (ISBN 0-313-23841-3, GRME). Greenwood.

Greenfield, Michael, ed. see Thackery, William M.

Greenfield, Michael M. Consumer Transactions. (University Casebook Ser.). 729p. 1983. text ed. write for info. (ISBN 0-88277-110-8). Foundation Pr.

--Statutory Supplement to Consumer Transactions. (University Casebook Ser.). 576p. 1983. pap. text ed. write for info. (ISBN 0-88277-114-0). Foundation Pr.

Greenfield, Natalee S. First Do No Harm... A Dying Woman's Battle Against the Physicians & Drug Companies Who Misled Her About the Hazards of the Pill. 1976. 7.95 o.p. (ISBN 0-8467-0198-7, Pub. by Two Continents). Hippocrene Bks.

Greenfield, Norman S., ed. see Interdisciplinary Research Conference - 1961.

Greenfield, Pete. The First Ferro Boat Book. Desoutter, Denny, ed. (Practical Handbooks for the Yachtsman Ser.). (Illus.). 1979. 15.00 o.p. (ISBN 0-370-30066-1); pap. 10.50 o.p. (ISBN 0-370-30090-4). Transatlantic.

Greenfield, Richard. The Wretched of the Horn: Forgotten Refugees in Black Africa. LC 80-13204. (Illus.). 144p. (Orig.). 1983. pap. 11.95x (ISBN 0-936508-01-9). Barber Pr.

Greenfield, Robert. Temple. 480p. 1983. 15.95 (ISBN 0-671-44735-1). Summit Bks.

Greenfield, Stanley B. & Robinson, Fred C. Bibliography of Publications on Old English Literature to the End of Nineteen Seventy-Two. LC 78-4989. 1980. 85.00x o.p. (ISBN 0-8020-2292-8); pap. 30.00 (ISBN 0-8020-6505-8). U of Toronto Pr.

Greenfield, Stanley B. & Weatherhead, A. Kingsley, eds. Poem: An Anthology. 2nd ed. LC 68-15582. (Orig.). 1972. pap. text ed. 14.95 (ISBN 0-13-684431-6). P-H.

Greenfield, Stanley B., tr. A Readable "Beowulf". The Old English Epic Newly Translated. LC 81-16933. (Illus.). 173p. 1982. 18.95x o.p. (ISBN 0-8093-1059-7); pap. 8.95x (ISBN 0-8093-1060-0). S Ill U Pr.

Greenfield, Thomas A. Work & the Work Ethic in American Drama, 1920-1970. LC 82-4909. 200p. 1982. 20.00 (ISBN 0-8262-0374-4). U of Mo Pr.

Greenfield Tool Company. Eighteen Fifty-Four Price List of Joiners' Bench Planes & Moulding Tools. Roberts, Kenneth D., ed. 32p. 1981. 12.50 o.p. (ISBN 0-686-86234-1); pap. 2.50 (ISBN 0-913602-43-4). K Roberts.

Greenfingers, G. & Bicknell, Andrew. Dr. Greenfingers' Rx for Healthy, Vigorous Houseplants. (Illus.). 160p. 1980. 12.95 (ISBN 0-517-53821-0, Michelman Bks); pap. 6.95 o.p. (ISBN 0-517-53822-9). Crown.

Greengard, P. & Costa, E., eds. Role of Cyclic AMP in Cell Function. LC 73-84113. (Advances in Biochemical Psychopharmacology Ser.: Vol. 3). 386p. 1970. 27.00 (ISBN 0-911216-15-4). Raven.

Greengard, P. & Robison, G. A., eds. Advances in Cyclic Nucleotide Research, Vol. 6. LC 71-181305. 368p. 1975. 38.00 (ISBN 0-89004-042-7). Raven.

Greengard, P., jt. ed. see Costa, E.

Greengard, Paul. Cyclic Nucleotides, Phosphorylated Proteins, & Neuronal Function. LC 78-66349. (Distinguished Lecture Series of the Society of General Physiologists: Vol. 1). 134p. 1978. 16.50 (ISBN 0-89004-281-0). Raven.

Greengard, Paul & Robison, Alan, eds. Advances in Cyclic Nucleotide Research, Vol. 13. 352p. 1980. text ed. 42.00 (ISBN 0-89004-471-6). Raven.

Greengard, Paul & Robison, G. Alan, eds. Advances In Cyclic Nucleotide Research, Vol. 3. 416p. 1973. text ed. 38.00 (ISBN 0-911216-38-3). Raven.

--Advances in Cyclic Nucleotide Research, Vol. 4. LC 71-181305. 498p. 1974. 43.00 (ISBN 0-911216-76-6). Raven.

--Advances in Cyclic Nucleotide Research, Vol. 7. LC 71-181305. 302p. 1976. 38.00 (ISBN 0-89004-107-5). Raven.

--Advances in Cyclic Nucleotide Research, Vol. 8. LC 71-181305. 302p. 1977. 48.00 (ISBN 0-89004-169-5). Raven.

--Advances in Cyclic Nucleotide Research, Vol. 11. LC 71-181305. 397p. 1979. text ed. 43.00 (ISBN 0-89004-363-9). Raven.

Greengard, Paul, jt. ed. see Costa, E.

Greengard, Paul, et al, eds. New Assay Methods for Cyclic Nucleotides. (Advances in Cyclic Nucleotide Research Ser.: Vol. 2). 145p. 1972. text ed. 21.00 (ISBN 0-911216-21-9). Raven.

Greengerg, Allen M. Standards Relating to Architecture of Facilities. (IJA-ABA Juvenile Justice Standards Project Ser.). 96p. 1980. prof ref 14.00x (ISBN 0-88410-249-1); pap. 7.00x prof ref (ISBN 0-88410-773-6). Ballinger Pub.

Greenhalgh, Michael. The Classical Tradition in Art. LC 81-48063. (Icon Editions Ser.). (Illus.). 271p. 1982. 9.95i (ISBN 0-06-430118-4, IN-118). Har-Row.

--Donatello & His Sources. (Illus.). 200p. 1982. text ed. 54.50x (ISBN 0-8419-0827-3). Holmes & Meier.

Greenhalgh, Michael & Megaw, Vincent, eds. Art in Society: Studies in Style, Culture & Aesthetics. LC 78-69954. 1978. 32.50 (ISBN 0-312-05267-7). St Martin.

Greenhalgh, P. A. Early Greek Warfare. LC 72-87437. 228p. 1973. 35.00 (ISBN 0-521-20056-3). Cambridge U Pr.

Greenhall, Ken. Childgrave. 304p. (Orig.). 1982. pap. 2.95 (ISBN 0-671-42161-1). PB.

Greenhaw, Wayne. Elephants in the Cottonfields: Ronald Reagan & the New Republican South. 320p. 1982. 15.75 (ISBN 0-02-545500-1). Macmillan.

Greenhill, Basil, ed. The National Maritime Museum. (Illus.). 144p. 1982. 19.95 o.p. (ISBN 0-85667-133-9, Pub. by Sotheby Pubns England); pap. 12.50 (ISBN 0-686-37759-1, Pub. by Sotheby Pubns England). Biblio Dist.

Greenhill, Frank. Incised Effigial Slabs, 2 vols. 432p. 1976. Set. 75.00; Vol. 1. (ISBN 0-571-10741-9); Vol. 2. (ISBN 0-571-10880-6). Faber & Faber.

Greenhill, George. Gyroscopic Theory. LC 66-30616. 22.50 (ISBN 0-8284-0205-1). Chelsea Pub.

Greenhill, J. P. Miracle of Life: The Story of a Baby from Conception to Birth & a Bit Beyond. (Illus.). 1971. pap. 6.25 o.p. (ISBN 0-8151-3947-0). Year Bk Med.

Greenhill, J. P. & Friedman, Emanuel A. Biological Principles & Modern Practice of Obstetrics. LC 73-77938. (Illus.). 837p. 1974. text ed. 30.00 o.p. (ISBN 0-7216-4257-8). Saunders.

Greenhill, Lawrence & Shopsin, Baron, eds. Biological Influences of Child Psychiatry. 288p. 1983. text ed. 35.00 (ISBN 0-89335-192-X). SP Med & Sci Bks.

Greenhill, Maurice & Gralnick, Alexander, eds. Psychopharmacology & Psychotherapy. 1982. text ed. write for info. (ISBN 0-02-912780-7). Free Pr.

Greenhouse, Herbert K. Book of Psychic Knowledge. 1975. pap. 1.75 o.p. (ISBN 0-451-08035-1, E8035, Sig). NAL.

Greenhut, Frederic A., II. The Tibetan Frontiers Question: From Curzon to the Colombo Conference. (Illus.). 178p. 1982. 24.95x (ISBN 0-940500-71-X, Pub by S Chand India). Asia Bk Corp.

Greening. Construction Drawing. 1982. text ed. 19.95 (ISBN 0-408-00672-2); pap. text ed. 9.95 (ISBN 0-408-00646-3). Butterworth.

Greening, J. R., ed. Medical Physics: Proceedings of the International School of Physics Course, LXXCI, Varenna, Italy, June 25 - July 7, 1979. (Enrico Fermi International Summer School of Physics: Vol. 76). 526p. 1981. 95.75 (ISBN 0-444-85457-6). Elsevier.

Greenkorn. Flow Phenomena. (Energy, Power & Environment Ser.). 520p. 1983. 75.00 (ISBN 0-8247-1861-5). Dekker.

GreenKorn, R. A. & Kessler, D. P. Transfer Operations. LC 70-168450. (Illus.). 576p. 1972. text ed. 37.50 (ISBN 0-07-024351-4, C); solutions manual 2.95 (ISBN 0-07-024353-0). McGraw.

Greenland, D. J. & Hayes, M. H. The Chemistry of Soil Constituents. 508p. 1978. 110.00 (ISBN 0-471-99619-X, Pub. by Wiley-Interscience). Wiley.

--The Chemistry of Soil Processes. LC 79-42908. 714p. 1981. 110.00 (ISBN 0-471-27693-6, Pub. by Wiley-Interscience). Wiley.

Greenland, D. J. & Lal, R., eds. Soil Conservation & Management in the Humid Tropics. LC 76-8908. 283p. 1977. 74.95 (ISBN 0-471-99473-1, Pub. by Wiley-Interscience). Wiley.

Greenland, D. J., jt. ed. see Lal, R.

Greenland, David. Guidelines for Modern Resource Management. 224p. 1983. pap. text ed. 11.95 (ISBN 0-675-20004-0). Merrill.

Greenland, David E. & Deblij, Harm J. The Earth in Profile: A Physical Geography. 1977. text ed. 22.50 scp o.p. (ISBN 0-06-383615-7, HarpC); tchrs manual avail. o.p. (ISBN 0-06-371810-3). Har-Row.

Greenlaw, Barry A. New England Furniture at Williamsburg. LC 73-90536. 1975. 10.00x o.p. (ISBN 0-87935-020-2, Williamsburg Decorative Arts Ser.). U Pr of Va.

Greenlaw, Jean-Pierre. The Coral Buildings of Suakin. (Illus.). 1976. 35.00 o.p. (ISBN 0-85362-158-6, Oriel). Routledge & Kegan.

Greenlaw, Ralph W. The Social Origins of the French Revolution. pap. 5.95 (ISBN 0-669-91116-X). Heath.

Greenleaf, Barbara Kaye. Children Through the Ages. LC 77-78758. (Illus.). 1978. 9.95 o.p. (ISBN 0-07-024355-7, GB). McGraw.

Greenleaf, E. Pricky, a Pet Porcupine. LC 65-22311. (Illus.). (gr. 2-5). 1968. PLB 6.75x (ISBN 0-87783-031-2); pap. 2.95x deluxe ed. (ISBN 0-87783-158-0). Oddo.

--Who Wants to Nap? LC 68-56820. (Illus.). (gr. 2-3). PLB 6.75x (ISBN 0-87783-050-9). Oddo.

Greenleaf, Elisabeth, ed. Ballads & Sea Songs of Newfoundland. LC 68-20767. (Illus.). xix, 395p. 1968. Repr. of 1933 ed. 30.00x (ISBN 0-8103-5013-0). Gale.

Greenleaf, Nancy P., ed. The Politics of Self-Esteem. LC 78-55202. 84p. 1978. pap. text ed. 12.95 (ISBN 0-913654-48-5). Aspen Systems.

Greenleaf, Robert K. The Servant: A Series of Essays-The Servant as Leader; The Institution as Servant; Trustees as Servants; Servant, Retrospect & Prospect; Seminary as Servant. pap. 1.50 ea. 10-24 copies; pap. 1.20 ea. 24-99 copies; pap. 1.00 ea. over 100 copies. Windy Row.

Greenleaf, Stephen. State's Evidence. 288p. 1983. pap. 2.95 (ISBN 0-345-30869-7). Ballantine.

Greenleaf, William. The Tartarus Incident. 1983. pap. 2.50 (ISBN 0-441-79846-2, Pub. by Ace Science Fiction). Ace Bks.

Greenlee, Carolyn W. & Greenlee, Dennis L. Applied Electro-Acupoint Therapy Workshop Manual. rev. ed. (Illus.). 152p. 1977. 40.00 (ISBN 0-9607836-0-1). See Do Pr.

Greenlee, Dennis L., jt. auth. see Greenlee, Carolyn W.

Greenlee, J. Harold. Concise Exegetical Grammar of New Testament Greek. (Orig.). 1963. pap. 3.95 (ISBN 0-8028-1092-6). Eerdmans.

Greenler, Robert. Rainbows, Halos & Glories. LC 80-143722. (Illus.). 304p. 1980. 29.95 (ISBN 0-521-23605-3). Cambridge U Pr.

Greenley, Michael. The Communist Millionaire. 1983. 8.95 (ISBN 0-533-05626-8). Vantage.

Greenman, D., jt. ed. see Streater, R. A.

Greenman, Frederick P. Wire-Tapping: Its Relation to Civil Liberties. 1938. ltd. ed. 49.50x (ISBN 0-686-51326-6). Elliots Bks.

Greenman, Robert. Words in Action. 1983. 16.95 (ISBN 0-8129-1025-7). Times Bks.

Greenman, Russell L. & Schmertz, Eric J. Personnel Administration & the Law. 2nd ed. 486p. 1979. 22.00 (ISBN 0-87179-234-6). BNA.

Greenough, Chester N. Bibliography of the Theophrastan Character in English. Repr. of 1947 ed. lib. bdg. cancelled o.p. (ISBN 0-8371-3542-7, GRTC). Greenwood.

Greenough, Frances, ed. Letters of Horatio Greenough. LC 70-96437. (Library of American Art Ser.). 1970. Repr. of 1887 ed. lib. bdg. 32.50 (ISBN 0-306-71828-6). Da Capo.

Greenough, Horatio. The Miscellaneous Writings of Horatio Greenough. LC 75-1118. 1975. lib. bdg. 25.00x (ISBN 0-8201-1152-X). Schol Facsimiles.

Greenough, Paul R. Prosperity & Misery in Modern Bengal: The Famine of 1943-1944. (Illus.). 362p. 1982. 37.00x (ISBN 0-19-503082-6). Oxford U Pr.

Greenough, Sarah & Hamilton, Juan, eds. Alfred Stieglitz: Photographs & Writings. LC 82-7925. (Illus.). 248p. 75.00 (ISBN 0-935112-09-X); pap. write for info. (ISBN 0-89468-027-7). Callaway Edns.

Greenow, Linda. Credit & Socioeconomic Change in Colonial Mexico: Loans & Mortgages in Guadalajara, 1720-1820. (Dellplain Latin American Studies: No. 12). 200p. 1982. softcover 16.50x (ISBN 0-86531-467-5). Westview.

Greensher, Arnold, jt. ed. see Good, Roger.

Greenshields, Bruce L., jt. ed. see Bellamy, Margot A.

Greenshields, Roderick, jt. auth. see Rothman, Harry.

Greenslet, Ferris. James Russell Lowell: His Life & Work. LC 77-77162. 1969. Repr. of 1905 ed. 34.00x (ISBN 0-8103-3893-9). Gale.

Greensmith, J. T. Petrology of the Sedimentary Rocks. 6th ed. (Textbook of Petrology Ser.). (Illus.). 1978. text ed. 30.00x (ISBN 0-04-552011-9); pap. text ed. 14.95x (ISBN 0-04-552012-7). Allen Unwin.

Greenspan, Bud. Numero Uno. 1982. pap. 2.75 (ISBN 0-451-11760-3, AE1760, Sig). NAL.

--We Wuz Robbed. LC 74-27946. (Illus.). 192p. 1976. pap. 6.95 o.p. (ISBN 0-448-12456-4, G&D). Putnam Pub Group.

Greenspan, Donald. Discrete Models. LC 73-7957. (Applied Mathematics & Computation Ser: No. 3). (Illus.). xvi, 165p. 1973. text ed. 16.00 (ISBN 0-201-02612-0, Adv Bk Prog); pap. text ed. 19.50 (ISBN 0-201-02613-9, Adv Bk Prog). A-W.

Greenspan, E., ed. Clinical Cancer Chemotherapy. LC 75-14575. 432p. 1975. 28.50 (ISBN 0-89004-069-9). Raven.

Greenspan, Emily. Little Winners: The World of the Child Sports Superstar. (Illus.). 320p. 1983. 14.45i (ISBN 0-316-32667-4). Little.

Greenspan, Ezra. Clinical Interpretation & Practice of Cancer Chemotherapy. 679p. 1982. text ed. 64.00 (ISBN 0-89004-566-6). Raven.

Greenspan, H. P. Theory of Rotating Fluids. LC 68-12058. (Cambridge Monographs on Mechanics & Applied Mathematics). (Illus.). 1968. text ed. 49.50 (ISBN 0-521-05147-9). Cambridge U Pr.

--The Theory of Rotating Fluids. (Cambridge Monographs on Mechanics & Applied Mathematics). (Illus.). 328p. 1980. pap. 19.95 (ISBN 0-521-29956-X). Cambridge U Pr.

Greenspan, Harvey P. & Benney, David. Calculus: An Introduction to Applied Mathematics. (Illus.). 736p. 1973. text ed. 32.50 (ISBN 0-07-024342-5, C); solutions manual 5.50 (ISBN 0-07-024343-3). McGraw.

Greenspan, Jack. Accountability & Quality Assurance. LC 80-11308. (Illus.). 288p. 1980. text ed. 34.95 o.p. (ISBN 0-89303-007-4). Charles.

Greenspan, Kalman & Fischer, John, eds. Cardiovascular Diseases. (Medical Examination Review Ser.: No. 28). 1973. pap. 23.00 spiral bdg. (ISBN 0-87488-138-2). Med Exam.

Greenspan, Kalman & Giddings, John A., eds. Physiology Review. 6th ed. 1981. pap. 11.95 (ISBN 0-87488-206-0). Med Exam.

Greenspan, M. A New Approach to Women & Therapy. 384p. 1983. 19.95 (ISBN 0-07-024349-2, GB). McGraw.

Greenspan, Ralph J., jt. auth. see Hall, Jeffrey C.

Greenspan, Stanley I. The Clinical Interview of the Child: Theory & Practice. 224p. 1981. 19.95 (ISBN 0-07-024340-9). McGraw.

Greensted, C. S. & Jardine, A. K. Essentials of Statistics in Marketing. 1978. pap. 13.95 (ISBN 0-686-84209-X, Pub. by W Heinemann). David & Charles.

Greenstein, F. I. & Polsby, N. W. The Handbook of Political Science, 8 vols. Incl. Vol. 1. Political Science: Scope & Theory. 21.95 (ISBN 0-201-02601-5); Vol. 2. Micropolitical Theory. 19.95 (ISBN 0-201-02602-3); Vol. 3. Macropolitical Theory. 26.95 (ISBN 0-201-02603-1); Vol. 4. Nongovernmental Politics. 20.95 (ISBN 0-201-02604-X); Vol. 5. Governmental Institutions & Processes. 26.95 (ISBN 0-201-02605-8); Vol. 6. Politics & Policymaking. 24.95 (ISBN 0-201-02606-6); Vol. 7. Strategies of Inquiry. 19.95 (ISBN 0-201-02607-4); Vol. 8. International Politics. 24.95 (ISBN 0-201-02608-2). 1975. Set With Index. boxed 160.00 (ISBN 0-201-02611-2). A-W.

Greenstein, Fred I. The Hidden-Hand Presidency: Eisenhower as Leader. LC 82-70849. 1982. 16.95 (ISBN 0-465-02948-5). Basic.

Greenstein, Fred L. American Party System & the American People. 2nd ed. LC 73-110080. (Foundations of Modern Political Science Ser). 1970. pap. 9.95 ref. ed. (ISBN 0-13-028415-7). P-H.

Greenstein, Howard R. Judaism: An Eternal Covenant. LC 82-17601. 208p. 1983. pap. 9.95 (ISBN 0-8006-1690-1, 1-1690). Fortress.

Greenstein, Jesse P. & Haddow, Alexander, eds. Advances in Cancer Research, Vol. 38. (Serial Publication). Date not set. price not set (ISBN 0-12-006638-6). Acad Pr.

Greenstein, Jesus P. & Winitz, M. Chemistry of the Amino Acids, 3 Vols. LC 61-6474. 2872p. 1961. Set. 295.00x o.p. (ISBN 0-471-32637-2, Pub. by Wiley-Interscience). Wiley.

Greenston, Peter & Hagan, Michael. Insuring the Disabled: A Study of the Impact of Changes to the Social Security Disability Insurance Program. LC 81-50055. (Illus.). 69p. (Orig.). 1981. pap. text ed. 5.75 (ISBN 0-87766-292-4, URI 31700). Urban Inst.

Greenstone, Arthur W. & Harris, Sydney P. Concepts in Chemistry. 3rd ed. 644p. (gr. 10-12). 1975. text ed. 9.45 (ISBN 0-15-362426-4, HC); tchrs manual 3.75 (ISBN 0-15-362427-2); lab manual 3.90 (ISBN 0-15-362429-9); tests 1.95 (ISBN 0-15-362428-0). HarBraceJ.

Greenstone, J. David & Peterson, Paul E. Race & Authority in Urban Politics: Community Participation & the War on Poverty. LC 73-76763. 326p. 1973. 12.50x (ISBN 0-87154-373-7). Russell Sage.

Greenstone, James L. & Levton, Sharon C. Crisis Intervention: A Handbook for Interveners. 224p. 1982. pap. text ed. 19.95 (ISBN 0-8403-2739-0). Kendall-Hunt.

Greenstone, Julius H. The Messiah Idea in Jewish History. LC 70-97284. 347p. 1972. Repr. of 1906 ed. lib. bdg. 21.00x (ISBN 0-8371-2606-1, GRMI). Greenwood.

Greenup, Leonard, jt. auth. see Greenup, Ruth.

Greenup, Ruth & Greenup, Leonard. Revolution Before Breakfast. LC 73-20877. (Illus.). 266p. 1974. Repr. of 1947 ed. lib. bdg. 15.50x (ISBN 0-8371-5854-0, GRRB). Greenwood.

Greenwald & Associates. The McGraw-Hill Dictionary of Modern Economics: A Handbook of Terms & Organizations. 2nd ed. (Illus.). 800p. 1973. 49.95 (ISBN 0-07-024369-7, P&RB). McGraw.

Greenwald, Anthony G., jt. ed. see Suls, Jerry.

Greenwald, Anthony G., et al. Psychological Foundations of Attitudes. (Social Psychology Ser.). 1968. text ed. 16.00 (ISBN 0-12-300750-X). Acad Pr.

Greenwald, Carol. Conservation of Our Natural Resources. (Science Ser.). 24p. (gr. 5 up). 1979. wkbk. 5.00 (ISBN 0-8209-0149-0, S-11). ESP.

--Crime & Punishment. (Social Studies). 24p. (gr. 7 up). 1977. wkbk. 5.00 (ISBN 0-8209-0252-7, SS-19). ESP.

--Women in Management, Vol. 12. LC 80-20757. (Work in America Institute Studies in Productivity). (Orig.). 1982. pap. 35.00 (ISBN 0-08-029493-6). Pergamon.

Greenwald, Douglas. Encyclopedia of Economics. (Illus.). 1056p. 1982. 54.95 (ISBN 0-07-024367-0). McGraw.

Greenwald, Douglas, et al. The McGraw-Hill Dictionary of Modern Economics. 3rd ed. (Illus.). 656p. 1983. 49.95 (ISBN 0-07-024376-X, P&RB). McGraw.

Greenwald, Edith D. & Greenwald, Edward S. Cancer Epidemiology for Health Professionals. 1983. pap. text ed. price not set (ISBN 0-87488-334-2). Med Exam.

Greenwald, Edward S. Cancer Chemotherapy. 2nd ed. (Medical Outline Ser.). 1973. spiral bdg. 13.50 o.p. (ISBN 0-87488-631-7). Med Exam.

Greenwald, Edward S., jt. auth. see Greenwald, Edith D.

Greenwald, Edward S., et al. Cancer Chemotherapy: Supplement. 2nd. ed. 1974. pap. 4.00 o.p. (ISBN 0-87488-630-9). Med Exam.

Greenwald, G. Dale & Superka, Douglas P. Evaluating Social Studies Programs: Focus on Law-Related Education. 240p. (Orig.). 1982. pap. 14.95 (ISBN 0-89994-277-6). Soc Sci Ed.

Greenwald, H., jt. auth. see Shaffer, H.

Greenwald, Howard P. Social Problems in Cancer Control. LC 79-15385. 320p. 1979. prof ref 27.00x (ISBN 0-88410-708-6). Ballinger Pub.

Greenwald, Judy, ed. The Spa Book. 1983. 8.95 o.p. (ISBN 0-517-54910-7). Crown.

Greenwald, Maurine W. Women, War, & Work: The Impact of World War I on Women Workers in the United States. LC 80-540. (Contributions in Women's Studies: No. 12). (Illus.). xxvii, 309p. 1980. lib. bdg. 29.95 (ISBN 0-313-21355-0, GWW/). Greenwood.

Greenwald, Michael R. The Cruising Chef. LC 76-45064. (Illus.). 1977. 12.95 (ISBN 0-8306-7864-6); pap. 8.95 o.p. (ISBN 0-8306-6864-0, 864). TAB Bks.

Greenwald, Nancy. Ladycat. 256p. 1980. 8.95 o.p. (ISBN 0-517-54102-5). Crown.

--Ladycat. 1981. pap. 2.75 o.p. (ISBN 0-451-09762-9, E9762, Sig). NAL.

Greenwald, Sheila. Blissful Joy: A Multiple Test Romance. 128p. (gr. 7). 1982. 9.95 (ISBN 0-316-32673-9, Pub. by Atlantic Monthly Pr). Little.

--Blissful Joy & the SATs. (YA) (gr. 7-12). 1983. pap. 2.25 (ISBN 0-440-90481-1, LFL). Dell.

--Give Us a Great Big Smile, Rosy Cole. (Illus.). 80p. (gr. 3 up). 1981. 9.70i (ISBN 0-316-32672-0, Pub. by Atlantic). Little.

--Will the Real Gertrude Hollings Please Stand Up? 168p. (gr. 3-7). 1983. 10.45i (ISBN 0-316-32707-7, Pub. by Atlantic Monthly Pr). Little.

Greenwalt, Emmett A. California Utopia, Point Loma, Eighteen Ninety-Seven to Nineteen Forty-Two. 2nd rev. ed. Small, W. Emmett & Todd, Helen, eds. (Illus.). 1978. 9.95 (ISBN 0-913004-30-8); pap. 5.95 (ISBN 0-913004-31-6). Point Loma Pub.

Greenway, John. Literature Among the Primitives. LC 64-13289. xviii, 346p. 1964. Repr. of 1964 ed. 40.00x (ISBN 0-8103-5001-7). Gale.

--The Primitive Reader: An Anthology of Myths, Tales, Songs, Riddles, & Proverbs of Aboriginal Peoples Around the World. LC 65-21986. viii, 211p. Repr. of 1965 ed. 30.00x (ISBN 0-8103-5014-9). Gale.

--Tales from the British Isles. LC 78-56058. (The World Folktale Library). (Illus.). 1979. lib. bdg. 12.68 (ISBN 0-382-03353-1). Silver.

--Tales from the United States. LC 78-54626. (The World Folktale Library). (Illus.). 1979. PLB 12.68 (ISBN 0-686-51166-2). Silver.

Greenway, Rogelio S. Una Estrategia Urbana Para Evangelizar: A la America Latina. Kratzig, Guillermo, tr. (Illus.). 1977. pap. 6.50 (ISBN 0-311-13825-X). Casa Bautista.

Greenway, William. Pressure under Grace. LC 82-1284. 45p. 1982. pap. 5.95 (ISBN 0-932576-10-9); limited, signed 50.00 (ISBN 0-932576-11-7). Breitenbush Pubns.

Greenwich, Lorenzo K., jt. auth. see Jones, Charles K.

Greenwood & Ross. Index of Vibrational Spectra of Inorganic & Organometallic Compounds, Vol. I. 1976. 89.95 o.p. (ISBN 0-408-70351-2). Butterworth.

Greenwood, Allan. Electrical Transients in Power Systems. LC 70-127664. 544p. 1971. 54.95 (ISBN 0-471-32650-X, Pub. by Wiley-Interscience). Wiley.

Greenwood, C. T., jt. auth. see MacGregor, A.

Greenwood, Colin. Firearms Control: A Study of Armed Crime & Firearms Control in England & Wales. (Illus.). 272p. 1972. 27.50x (ISBN 0-7100-7435-2). Routledge & Kegan.

Greenwood, D. Classical Dynamics. 1977. 33.95 (ISBN 0-13-136036-1). P-H.

Greenwood, D. J. Unrewarding Wealth. LC 75-25429. (Illus.). 310p. 1976. 32.50 (ISBN 0-521-21021-6). Cambridge U Pr.

Greenwood, David. Antibiotics of the Beta-Lactam Group. (Antimicrobial Chemotherapy Research Studies). 84p. 1982. 19.95 (ISBN 0-471-10473-6, Pub by Res Stud Pr). Wiley.

Greenwood, Davydd J. & Stini, William A. Nature, Culture, & Human History: A Bio-Cultural Introduction to Anthropology. (Illus.). 1977. text ed. 23.50 scp o.p. (ISBN 0-06-042505-9, HarpC). Har-Row.

Greenwood, Donald T. & Fung, Y., eds. Principles of Dynamics. 1965. text ed. 34.95 (ISBN 0-13-708974-0). P-H.

Greenwood, Douglas C. Product Engineering Design Manual. LC 80-23595. (Illus.). 342p. 1982. Repr. text ed. 29.50 (ISBN 0-89874-273-0). Krieger.

Greenwood, E. B. Tolstoy: The Comprehensive Vision. LC 74-23030. 192p. 1975. 22.50 (ISBN 0-312-80850-X). St Martin.

Greenwood, Ernest, jt. auth. see Mayer, K.

Greenwood, Frank. Profitable Small Business Computing. 1982. text ed. 18.95 o.p. (ISBN 0-316-32711-5); pap. 9.95 (ISBN 0-316-32712-3). Little.

Greenwood, James. The Seven Curses of London. LC 82-195528. xxvi, 293p. 1982. Repr. of 1869 ed. 27.50x (ISBN 0-686-84020-8, Pub. by B Blackwell England). Porcupine Pr.

Greenwood, James W., III & Greenwood, James W., Jr. Managing Executive Stress: A Systems Approach. LC 79-4100. 1979. 27.95x (ISBN 0-471-04084-3, Pub. by Wiley-Interscience). Wiley.

Greenwood, K. Weaving: Control of Fabric Structure. 1975. 18.00x (ISBN 0-87245-557-2). Textile Bk.

Greenwood, Kathryn M. & Murphy, Mary F. Fashion Innovation & Marketing. (Illus.). 1978. 22.95x (ISBN 0-02-346950-1). Macmillan.

Greenwood, Larry, jt. auth. see Timberlake, Charles.

Greenwood, Marjorie. Roads & Canals in the Eighteenth Century. Reeves, Marjorie, ed. (Then & There Ser.). (Illus.). 92p. (Orig.). (gr. 7-12). 1977. pap. text ed. 3.10 (ISBN 0-582-20383-X). Longman.

Greenwood, Michael & Tollar, Jerry R., eds. Evaluation Guidebook to Computer-Aided Transcription. 1975. pap. 3.84 (ISBN 0-89656-001-5, R0019). Natl Ctr St Courts.

Greenwood, N. N. & Gibb, T. C. Mossbauer Spectroscopy. 1971. 75.00x (ISBN 0-412-10710-4, Pub. by Chapman & Hall). Methuen Inc.

Greenwood, P. H. The Cichlid Fishes of Lake Victoria, East Africa: Biology & Evolution of a Species Flock. (Bulletin of the British Museum Natural History Zool. Ser.: No. 6). (Illus.). 1974. text ed. 24.00x (ISBN 0-565-00761-0, Pub. by Brit Mus Nat Hist); pap. text ed. 17.50x (ISBN 0-8277-4357-2). Sabbot-Natural Hist Bks.

Greenwood, Peter W., et al. The Criminal Investigation Process. 1977. pap. 8.95x o.p. (ISBN 0-669-01067-7). Heath.

Greenwood, Ronald G. Managerial Decentralization: A Study of the General Electric Philosophy. rev. 2nd. ed. (Hive Management History Ser.: No. 89). (Illus.). 225p. 1982. lib. bdg. 18.50 (ISBN 0-87960-123-X); pap. text ed. 9.00 (ISBN 0-87960-124-8). Hive Pub.

Greenwood, Royston, et al. Patterns of Management in Local Government. (Government & Administration Ser.). 192p. 1983. 27.50x (ISBN 0-85520-244-0, Pub. by Martin Robertson England). Biblio Dist.

Greenwood, Ted. Making the Mirv: A Study of Defense Decision-Making. LC 75-11635. 256p. 1975. prof ref 19.50x (ISBN 0-88410-033-2). Ballinger Pub.

Greenwood, Ted, et al. Nuclear Proliferation: Motivation, Capabilities, & Strategies for Control. (Nineteen Eighties Project (Council on Foreign Relations)). 1977. 9.95 o.p. (ISBN 0-07-024344-1, P&RB); pap. 4.95 o.p. (ISBN 0-07-024345-X). McGraw.

Greenya, John, jt. auth. see Bailey, F. Lee.

Greep, Roy O., jt. auth. see Weiss, Leon.

Greep, Roy O., ed. Recent Progress in Hormone Research, Vol. 35. 1979. 52.50 (ISBN 0-12-571135-2). Acad Pr.

--Reproductive Physiology IV. (International Review of Physiology Ser.: Vol. 27). 1983. text ed. 49.50 (ISBN 0-8391-1555-5, 14206). Univ Park.

Greep, Roy O. & Koblinsky, Majorie A., eds. Frontiers in Reproduction & Fertility Control. 1977. 40.00x (ISBN 0-262-07068-5). MIT Pr.

Greep, Roy O., ed. see American Physiological Society.

Greep, Roy O. see Laurentian Hormone Conferences.

Greep, Roy O., et al. Reproduction & Human Welfare: A Challenge to Research-A Review of the Reproductive Sciences & Contraceptive Development. 1976. text ed. 25.00x (ISBN 0-262-07067-7). MIT Pr.

Greer, Colin. The Divided Society: The Ethnic Experience in America. LC 73-88029. 1974. 12.50x o.p. (ISBN 0-465-01679-0); pap. text ed. 6.95x o.s.i. (ISBN 0-465-01680-4). Basic.

Greer, Colin, jt. ed. see Shields, James J.

Greer, Don, jt. auth. see Davis, Larry.

Greer, Douglas. Design for Music Learning. LC 79-21117. 1980. pap. text ed. 13.95x (ISBN 0-8077-2573-0). Tchrs Coll.

Greer, Douglas F. Business, Government, & Society. 640p. 1983. text ed. 24.95 (ISBN 0-02-347050-X). Macmillan.

--Cases in Marketing: Orientation, Analysis, & Problems. 3rd ed. 1983. pap. text ed. 11.95x (ISBN 0-02-347100-X); instrs'. manual avail. Macmillan.

--Industrial Organization & Public Policy. (Illus.). 1979. text ed. 26.95x (ISBN 0-02-347020-8). Macmillan.

Greer, Francesca. Bright Dawn. 400p. 1983. pap. 3.50 (ISBN 0-446-90942-4). Warner Bks.

Greer, G. E. The Real Estate Investor & the Federal Income Tax. 2nd ed. 267p. 1982. text ed. 29.95x (ISBN 0-471-09738-1). Ronald Pr.

Greer, Gaylon E. The Real-Estate Investment Decision. LC 77-81792. (Special Ser. in Real Estate & Urban Land Economics). (Illus.). 352p. 1979. 25.95x (ISBN 0-669-01951-8). Lexington Bks.

--The Real Estate Investor & the Federal Income Tax. LC 78-569. (Real Estate for Professional Practitioners Ser.). 278p. 1978. 33.95x o.p. (ISBN 0-471-01882-1, Pub. by Wiley-Interscience). Wiley.

Greer, Gaylon E. & Farrell, Michael. Contemporary Real Estate: Theory & Practice. 480p. 1983. text ed. 26.95 (ISBN 0-03-056682-7). Dryden Pr.

Greer, Germaine, jt. auth. see Hardison, O. B., Jr.

Greer, Gery & Ruddick, Bob. Max & Me & the Time Machine. LC 82-48762. 140p. (gr. 9-12). 11.95 (ISBN 0-15-253134-3, HJ). HarBraceJ.

Greer, Harold E. Greer's Guidebook to Available Rhododendrons, Species & Hybrids. LC 82-90128. (Illus.). 152p. 1982. pap. 12.95 (ISBN 0-910013-00-4). Offshoot Pub.

Greer, Harold E., Jr., jt. auth. see Ward, Harry M.

Greer, John G. & Anderson, Robert M. Strategies for Helping Severely & Multiply Handicapped Citizens. (Illus.). 448p. 1982. text ed. 18.95 (ISBN 0-8391-1692-6, 16918). Univ Park.

Greer, John G., jt. ed. see Anderson, Robert M.

Greer, John G., et al. Motivating Learners with Instructional Games. LC 77-75525. 1977. pap. text ed. 7.50 (ISBN 0-8403-1738-7). Kendall-Hunt.

Greer, Louise. Browning & America. LC 72-7819. (Illus.). 355p. 1973. Repr. of 1952 ed. lib. bdg. 19.00x (ISBN 0-8371-6525-3, GRBA). Greenwood.

Greer, Rebecca. How to Live Rich When You're Not: The Smart Women's Guide to Getting More for Your Money. LC 75-4369. 224p. 1975. 2.95 o.p. (ISBN 0-448-11886-6, G&D). Putnam Pub Group.

Greer, Scott A. Governing the Metropolis. LC 81-4211. xi, 153p. 1981. Repr. of 1966 ed. lib. bdg. 20.50x (ISBN 0-313-23038-2, GRGM). Greenwood.

Greer, Thomas H., ed. Classics of Western Thought, 4 Vols. 3rd ed. Incl. Vol. 1. The Ancient World. 421p. 1980. pap. text ed. 10.95 (ISBN 0-15-507678-7); Vol. II. Middle Ages, Renaissance, & Reformation. 575p. 1980. pap. text ed. 10.95 (ISBN 0-15-507679-5); Vol. III. The Modern World. 666p. 1980. pap. text ed. 10.95 (ISBN 0-15-507680-9); Vol. IV. The Twentieth Century. 660p. 1980. pap. text ed. 10.95 (ISBN 0-15-507681-7). 1980. pap. HarBraceJ.

Greer, Thomas H., ed. see Gochberg, Donald S.

Greer, Thomas J., Jr. Writing & Understanding U.S. Patent Claims. 125p. 1979. pap. 17.50 (ISBN 0-87215-238-3). Michie-Bobbs.

Greerhalgh, L., jt. auth. see Wasmuth, W.

Greet, Anne Hyde, tr. & annotations by see Apollinaire, Guillaume.

Greeve, Alec. Build Your Boat with Me. 17.50x (ISBN 0-392-07728-0, SpS). Sportshelf.

Greever, Jack. Marcos: Estudios Para un Joven En Busca De Identidad. Orig. Title: Mark: an Inductive Bible Study. 64p. (Span.). 1982. pap. 2.50 (ISBN 0-311-12325-2, Edit Mundo). Casa Bautista.

Greevy, Doug, jt. ed. see Weinberger, Marvin I.

Greg, W. Variants in the First Quarto of King Lear. LC 68-1839. (Studies in Shakespeare, No. 24). 1969. Repr. of 1940 ed. lib. bdg. 49.95x (ISBN 0-8383-0559-8). Haskell.

Greg, Walter. List of English Plays Written Before 1643 & Printed Before 1700. LC 68-25311. (Studies in Drama, No. 39). 1969. Repr. of 1900 ed. lib. bdg. 32.95x (ISBN 0-8383-0950-X). Haskell.

--List of Masques, Pageants, Etc. Supplementary to a List of English Plays. LC 68-25312. (Studies in Drama, No. 39). 1969. Repr. of 1902 ed. lib. bdg. 32.95x (ISBN 0-8383-0942-9). Haskell.

Greger, Debora. Cartography. 1980. signed 50.00x (ISBN 0-686-28114-4). Penumbra Press.

Gregerson, Kenneth. Predicate & Argument of Rengao Grammar. (Sil Publications in Linguistics Ser.: No. 61). 141p. (Orig.). 1979. pap. text ed. 6.50x (ISBN 0-88312-075-5); microfiche 2.25x (ISBN 0-88312-485-8). Summer Inst Ling.

Gregerson, Kenneth & Thomas, David, eds. Mon-Khmer Studies V. 313p. 1979. pap. 11.00 (ISBN 0-88312-788-1); microfiche 3.75 (ISBN 0-88312-358-4). Summer Inst Ling.

Gregerson, Linda. Fire in the Conservatory. 65p. 1982. 13.00 (ISBN 0-937872-06-7); pap. 6.00 (ISBN 0-937872-07-5). Dragon Gate.

Gregerson, Marilyn & Thomas, Dorothy, eds. Notes from Indochina: On Ethnic Minority Culture. LC 78-65445. (Museum of Anthropology: No. 6). 254p. (Orig.). 1980. pap. 9.45x (ISBN 0-88312-155-7); microfiche 2.20x (ISBN 0-88312-244-8); 3.00 (ISBN 0-88312-335-5). Summer Inst Ling.

Gregg, Alan. Furtherance of Medical Research. 1941. 22.50x (ISBN 0-685-89754-0). Elliots Bks.

Gregg, Charles T. A Virus of Love & other Tales of Medical Detection. 336p. 1983. 15.95 (ISBN 0-684-17766-8, ScribT). Scribners.

Gregg, David L. The Diaries of David Lawrence Gregg, 1853-1858: An American Diplomat in Hawaii. King, Pauline, ed. LC 82-80764. (Illus.). 605p. 1982. 25.00x (ISBN 0-8248-0861-4). UH Pr.

Gregg, Edith E., ed. The Letters of Ellen Tucker Emerson, 2 Vols. LC 82-10069. (Illus.). 1982. Set. 75.00x (ISBN 0-87338-274-9); Vol. 1, 700p. (ISBN 0-87338-275-7); Vol. 2, 700p. (ISBN 0-87338-276-5). Kent St U Pr.

Gregg, Elizabeth & Knotts, Judith. Growing Wisdom, Growing Wonder: Helping Your Child Learn from Birth Through Five Years. (Illus.). 1980. 13.95 o.p. (ISBN 0-02-545580-X). Macmillan.

Gregg, Frank. Federal Land Transfers: The Case for a Westwide Program Based on the Federal Land Policy & Management Act. LC 82-8126. 34p. (Orig.). 1982. pap. 5.00 (ISBN 0-89164-071-1). Conservation Foun.

Gregg International, ed. The Harmonicon, 11 vols. 5527p. 1982. Repr. of 1823 ed. Set. 650.00x (ISBN 0-576-28500-5, Gregg Intl). State Mutual Bk.

Gregg, Irwin. The Divine Science Way. 1975. 5.95 (ISBN 0-686-24352-8); pap. 3.95 (ISBN 0-686-24353-6). Divine Sci Fed.

Gregg, James R. Your Future in Optometry. LC 72-114107. (Career Guidance Ser). 1971. pap. 4.50 (ISBN 0-668-02259-0). Arco.

Gregg, Joan. Communication & Culture: A Reading-Writing Text. (Orig.). 1980. pap. text ed. 8.95 (ISBN 0-442-23895-9); instr's. manual 2.95 (ISBN 0-686-77565-1). Van Nos Reinhold.

Gregg, Joan Y. & Russel, Joan. Past, Present, & Future: A Reading-Writing Text. 384p. 1982. pap. text ed. 12.95x (ISBN 0-534-01218-3). Wadsworth Pub.

Gregg, John R. Frases y Palabras de Uso Mas Frecuente en Taguigrafi: A Gregg Edicio. (Span) 1971. 7.80 (ISBN 0-07-024598-3, G). McGraw.

--Gregg Shorthand Dictionary. anniversary ed. 1930. 13.64 o.p. (ISBN 0-07-024464-2, G). McGraw.

--Gregg Shorthand Manual. anniversary ed. 1929. 13.72 (ISBN 0-07-024501-0, G); tchr's key 6.25 (ISBN 0-07-024503-7). McGraw.

--Taquigrafia Gregg, Primer Curso. 1974. 13.35 o.p. (ISBN 0-07-024620-3, G). clave 8.50 o.p. (ISBN 0-07-024619-X). McGraw.

--Taquigrafia Gregg, Segundo Curso: Edicion Diamante. (Span.). 1970. text ed. 14.60 o.p. (ISBN 0-07-024621-1, G); tchr's manual 8.10 o.p. (ISBN 0-07-024401-4); clave 8.35 o.p. (ISBN 0-07-024622-X). McGraw.

Gregg, John R., et al. Gregg Shorthand. (Diamond Jubilee Ser). 1963. text ed. 13.96 (ISBN 0-07-024591-6, G); student transcript 4.76 (ISBN 0-07-024525-8); wkbk. 6.12 (ISBN 0-07-037308-6). McGraw.

--Gregg Shorthand Dictionary. 2nd ed. (Diamond Jubilee Ser). 1974. 13.08 (ISBN 0-07-024632-7, G). McGraw.

--Gregg Shorthand Dictionary Simplified. 1949. 8.95 (ISBN 0-07-024545-2, G); text ed. 13.72 (ISBN 0-07-024547-9). McGraw.

--Gregg Shorthand Manual, Simplified. 2nd ed. 1955. 8.95 (ISBN 0-07-024548-7, G); text ed. 13.96 (ISBN 0-07-024549-5); student's transcript 4.76 (ISBN 0-07-024551-7). McGraw.

--Gregg Speed Building. 2nd ed. (Diamond Jubilee Ser.). 1972. text ed. 14.16 (ISBN 0-07-024635-1, G); instructor's handbk. 5.75 (ISBN 0-07-024636-X); wkbk. 6.32 (ISBN 0-07-024638-6); key to wkbk. 5.65 (ISBN 0-07-024639-4); student's transcript 5.64 (ISBN 0-07-024637-8); tapes 625.00 (ISBN 0-07-087630-4). McGraw.

--Gregg Speed Building for Colleges. diamond jubilee ed. 1966. text ed. 14.70 o.p. (ISBN 0-07-024610-6, G); instructor's handbk. 5.65 o.p. (ISBN 0-07-024613-0); wkbk. 6.40 o.p. (ISBN 0-07-024611-4); student's transcript 5.40 o.p. (ISBN 0-07-024612-2). McGraw.

--Taquigrafia Gregg Simplificada. 1953. 11.60 o.p. (ISBN 0-07-024582-7, G). McGraw.

--Gregg Shorthand. 2nd ed. (Diamond Jubilee Ser). 1972. 13.96 (ISBN 0-07-024625-4, G). instructor's handbk. 5.60 (ISBN 0-07-024626-2); students transcript 4.76 (ISBN 0-07-024627-0); wkbk 6.12 (ISBN 0-07-037250-0); key to wkbk. 3.90 (ISBN 0-07-037251-9). McGraw.

--Most Used Words & Phases. 1963. 5.88 (ISBN 0-07-024592-4, G). McGraw.

--Gregg Shorthand Dictionary. 2nd ed. (Diamond Jubilee Ser.). 416p. (gr. 7 up). 1974. minature ed. 11.84 (ISBN 0-07-024633-5, G). McGraw.

Gregg, Lee W., ed. Knowledge & Cognition. LC 74-16105. (Carnegie Mellon U. Cognition Ser.). 320p. 1974. 16.50x o.s.i. (ISBN 0-470-32657-3). Halsted Pr.

Gregg, Leslie. Four Golden Everything Workbooks: Featuring Marvel Superheroes. 48p. (ps). 1980. 3.95 (ISBN 0-307-13624-8, Golden Pr). Western Pub.

Gregg, O. W, jt. ed. see Freeman, T. M.

Gregg, Pauline. King Charles I. (Illus.). 508p. 1982. text ed. 24.95x (ISBN 0-460-04437-0, Pub. by J. M. Dent England). Biblio Dist.

--Social & Economic History of Britain, 1760-1980. 8th ed. (Illus.). 636p. (Orig.). 1982. 22.50x (ISBN 0-245-53938-7). Intl Pubns Serv.

Gregg, Phillip, ed. Current Problems in Policy Theory. 1975. pap. 6.00 (ISBN 0-918592-10-0). Policy Studies.

Gregg, Richard B. The Power of Nonviolence. rev. ed. LC 66-24905. 1966. 6.00 o.p. (ISBN 0-8052-3206-0); pap. 1.95 o.p. (ISBN 0-8052-0136-X). Schocken.

Gregg, Robert E. The Ants of Colorado: Their Ecology, Taxonomy & Geographic Distribution. LC 62-63446. (Illus.). 1963. 22.50x (ISBN 0-87081-027-8). Colo Assoc.

Gregg, Robert S. Influence of Border Troubles on Relations Between the United States & Mexico, 1876-1910. LC 72-98181. (American Scene Ser). 1970. Repr. of 1937 ed. lib. bdg. 32.50 (ISBN 0-306-71833-2). Da Capo.

Gregg, Thomas G., jt. auth. see Mettler, Lawrence E.

Gregg, W. David. Analog & Digital Communications: Concepts, Systems & Applications, & Services in Electrical Dissemination of Aural, Visual & Data Information. LC 76-58417. 603p. 1977. text ed. 38.95x (ISBN 0-471-32661-5); Avail Tchr's Manual (ISBN 0-471-03046-5). Wiley.

Grego, Joseph. A History of Parliamentary Elections & Electioneering: From the Stuarts to Queen Victoria. LC 73-141755. (Illus.). 403p. 1974. Repr. of 1892 ed. 61.00x (ISBN 0-8103-4030-5). Gale.

Grego, M., jt. auth. see Lennie, Delia.

Gregoir, Edouard G. Bibliographie musicale: Histoire de l'Orgue. 2nd ed. (Bibliotheca Organologica Ser.: Vol. 15). 1972. Repr. of 1865 ed. 47.50 o.s.i. (ISBN 90-6027-231-5, Pub. by Frits Knuf Netherlands). Pendragon NY.

Gregoire, Abbe. De la Traite et de l'Esclavage des Noirs et des Blancs, par un Ami des Hommes de Toutes les Couleurs. (Slave Trade in France Ser., 1744-1848). 84p. (Fr.). 1974. Repr. of 1815 ed. lib. bdg. 31.50x o.p. (ISBN 0-8287-0397-3, TN146). Clearwater Pub.

--Oeuvres, 1788-1832. Repr. 483.00 o.p. (ISBN 0-8287-0398-1). Clearwater Pub.

Gregoire, Abbe H. De la Litterature des Negres, ou Recherches sur Leurs Facultes Intellectuelles, Leurs Qualites Morals et Leur Litterature. (Slave Trade in France, 1744-1848, Ser.). 302p. (Fr.). 1974. Repr. of 1808 ed. lib. bdg. 80.00x o.p. (ISBN 0-8287-0399-X, TN121). Clearwater Pub.

Gregoire, Abbe Henri de see De Gregoire, Abbe Henri.

Gregoire, R. The University Teaching of Social Sciences: Business Management. 1966. pap. 4.00 (ISBN 92-3-100583-9, U706, UNESCO). Unipub.

Gregold, W. C. MBO: A Self Instructional Approach. 1978. 32.50 (ISBN 0-07-079291-7); supplementary materials avail. McGraw.

Gregonis, Linda M. Hohokam Indians of the Tucson Bascu. 1979. pap. 3.50 (ISBN 0-8165-0700-7). U of Ariz Pr.

Gregor, A. James. Ideology & Development: Sun Yat-Sen & the Economic History of Taiwan. (China Research Monographs: No. 23). 1982. 8.00x (ISBN 0-686-86115-9). IEAS.

--Young Mussolini & the Intellectual Origins of Fascism. LC 78-64470. 1979. 26.50x (ISBN 0-520-03799-5). U of Cal Pr.

Gregor, Arthur. Embodiment & Other Poems. LC 82-3268. 110p. 1982. 14.95 (ISBN 0-935296-28-X); pap. 7.95 (ISBN 0-935296-29-8). Sheep Meadow.

Gregor, Carol. Working Out Together: A Complete Fitness Program for Partners. (Illus.). 224p. (Orig.). 1983. pap. 9.95 (ISBN 0-425-05878-6). Berkley Pub.

Gregor, D. B. Romagnol: Language & Literature. (Oleander Language & Literature Ser.). (Illus.). 1972. 25.00 (ISBN 0-902675-12-5). Oleander Pr.

Gregor, Douglas B. Romontsch: Language & Literature: Sursilvan Riveto Romance of Switzerland. (Oleander Language & Literature Ser.: Vol. 11). viii, 388p. 1982. pap. 29.95 (ISBN 0-900891-39-4). Oleander Pr.

Gregor, Hugh. Armor. LC 78-64662. (Fact Finders Ser.). (Illus.). 1979. PLB 8.00 (ISBN 0-382-06238-8). Silver.

--Warships. LC 78-64660. (Fact Finders Ser.). (Illus.). 1979. PLB 8.00 (ISBN 0-686-51132-8). Silver.

Gregorakis, Karen & Lotskar, Elaine. Dining In--Seattle, Vol. III. (Dining In--Ser.). 210p. 1982. pap. 8.95 (ISBN 0-89716-112-2). Peanut Butter.

Gregor-Dellin, Martin. Richard Wagner: His Life, His Work, His Century. Brownjohn, J. Maxwell, tr. (Helen & Kurt Wolff Bks.). 554p. 1983. 25.00 (ISBN 0-686-82640-X). HarBraceJ.

Gregoriadis, G. & Allison, A. C. Liposomes in Biological Systems. LC 79-40507. 1980. 81.95 (ISBN 0-471-27608-1, Pub. by Wiley-Interscience). Wiley.

Gregorian, Joyce B. The Broken Citadel. 1983. pap. 3.95 (ISBN 0-441-08099-5, Pub. by Ace Science Fiction). Ace Bks.

--Castledown: A Haunting Tale of Magic & Nature. 1983. pap. 2.95 (ISBN 0-441-09240-3, Pub. by Ace Science Fiction). Ace Bks.

Gregorio, M. Pauline, ed. Medical Record Library Science Examination Review Book, Vol. 1. 3rd ed. 1976. spiral bdg. 14.00 (ISBN 0-87488-496-9). Med Exam.

Gregorowski, Christopher. Why a Donkey Was Chosen. LC 75-24951. (gr. 1-3). 1978. 6.95 o.p. (ISBN 0-385-11569-5); PLB (ISBN 0-385-14447-4). Doubleday.

Gregory, Alexis K., ed. see Massie, Robert & Sweezey, Marilyn P.

Gregory, Andre, jt. auth. see Shawn, Wallace.

Gregory, C. A. Gifts & Commodities. (Studies in Political Economy: Vol. 2). 37.00 (ISBN 0-12-301460-3); pap. 16.00 (ISBN 0-12-301462-X). Acad Pr.

Gregory, C. E. Explosives for Australasian Engineers. 3rd ed. (Illus.). 1977. 25.00x (ISBN 0-7022-1391-8). U of Queensland Pr.

Gregory, Charles, et al. Cases & Materials on Torts: 1981 Supplement. 1982. pap. 6.95 (ISBN 0-316-32782-4). Little.

Gregory, Charles O. & Kalven, Harry, Jr. Cases & Materials on Torts. 3rd ed. 1351p. 1977. 28.00 o.p. (ISBN 0-316-32775-1); pap. supplement, 1974 3.75 o.p. (ISBN 0-316-32774-3). Little.

Gregory, Derek. Ideology, Science & Human Geography. 1979. 20.00x (ISBN 0-312-40477-8). St Martin.

--Regional Transformation & Industrial Revolutions: A Geography of the Yorkshire Woollen Industry. (Illus.). 1982. 39.50x (ISBN 0-8166-1139-4); pap. 15.95x (ISBN 0-8166-1140-8). U of Minn Pr.

Gregory, Diana. Dairy Goats. LC 76-235. 1976. o. p. 7.95 o.p. (ISBN 0-668-03938-8); pap. 3.95 o.p. (ISBN 0-668-03941-8). Arco.

Gregory, Dick. Dick Gregory's Natural Diet for Folks Who Eat: Cookin' with Mother Nature. McGraw, James R. & Fulton, Alvenia M., eds. 192p. 1974. pap. 2.95i (ISBN 0-06-080315-0, P315, PL). Har-Row.

Gregory, Donald R., et al, eds. The Questions Behind the Answers: A Sampler in the Philosophy. LC 80-1373. 164p. 1983. lib. bdg. 20.75 (ISBN 0-8191-2703-5); pap. text ed. 9.25 (ISBN 0-8191-2704-3). U Pr Of Amer.

Gregory, Fitzgerald. Hunting the Yahoos. LC 81-69451. (Illus.). 58p. (Orig.). 1982. pap. 5.00 (ISBN 0-934996-14-8). Am Stud Pr.

Gregory, G. I. Recent Advances in the Chemistry of B-Lactam Antibiotics. 388p. 1982. 69.00x (ISBN 0-85186-815-0, Pub. by Royal Soc Chem England). State Mutual Bk.

Gregory, G. Robinson. Forest Resource Economics. 548p. 1972. 28.95 (ISBN 0-471-06833-0, 40503). Wiley.

Gregory, Grace C. Sagebrush, Gunnysacks & Bailing Wire. Guthridge, Sharyn G., ed. 1982. 22.50 (ISBN 0-936204-36-2). Jelm Mtn.

Gregory, H. Controversies about Stuttering Therapy. 336p. 1978. text ed. 19.95 (ISBN 0-8391-1257-2). Univ Park.

Gregory, Hamilton, ed. The Religious Case for Abortion. LC 82-61786. 96p. (Orig.). 1983. pap. 9.95 (ISBN 0-910915-00-8). Madison Polk.

Gregory, Herbert E. Military Geology & Topography. 1918. text ed. 39.50x (ISBN 0-686-83626-X). Elliots Bks.

Gregory, Horace, ed. see Longfellow, Henry W.

Gregory, Horace, tr. see Ovid.

Gregory, Howard. Parachuting's Unforgettable Jumps. LC 73-75365. (Illus.). 1974. 12.00 o.p. (ISBN 0-686-08989-8). H Gregory.

--Southern California's Seacoast: Then & Now. 1982. 19.95 (ISBN 0-9607086-1-8); pap. 10.95 (ISBN 0-9607086-0-X). H Gregory.

Gregory, Isabella A. A Book of Saints & Wonders: Put Down Here by Lady Gregory According to the Old Writings & Memory of the People of Ireland. (CECWLG Ser.). (Illus.). 1971. 13.95x o.p. (ISBN 0-19-519685-6). Oxford U Pr.

--Collected Plays, 4 vols. Saddlemyer, Ann, ed. Incl. Vol. 1. The Comedies. 17.95x (ISBN 0-19-519473-X); Vol. 2. The Tragedies & Tragic-Comedies. 19.95x (ISBN 0-19-519474-8); Vol. 3. Wonder & Supernatural. 29.95x (ISBN 0-19-519475-6); Vol. 4. Translations, Adaptions & Collaborations. 19.95x (ISBN 0-19-519476-4). 1971. Oxford U Pr.

Gregory, J. S., jt. ed. see Clarke, Prescott.

Gregory, James, ed. The Patent Book. LC 78-68388. (Illus.). 128p. 1979. 12.95 o.s.i. (ISBN 0-89479-037-4). A & W Pubs.

Gregory, Janet. Inherit the Sea. 1980. pap. 2.75 o.p. (ISBN 0-451-09113-2, E9113, Sig). NAL.

Gregory, John, ed. see Thornton, Carol A.

Gregory, John, ed. see Thornton, Carol A. & Noxon, Cathy.

Gregory, John M. Seven Laws of Teaching. 1954. 6.95 (ISBN 0-8010-3652-6). Baker Bk.

Gregory, Julia, jt. auth. see Bartlett, Hazel.

Gregory, K. J., ed. River Channel Changes. LC 77-4342. 448p. 1978. 99.95 (ISBN 0-471-99524-X, Pub. by Wiley-Interscience). Wiley.

Gregory, Lady. Cuchulain of Muirthemhe: The Story of the Men of the Red Branch of Ulster. 5th ed. (Coole Edition of the Collected Works of Lady Gregory Ser.). 1970. 21.95x (ISBN 0-19-519477-2). Oxford U Pr.

Gregory, Lee. Colorado Scenic Guide: Northern Region. (Illus.). 240p. (Orig.). 1983. pap. price not set (ISBN 0-933472-73-0). Johnson Bks.

Gregory, Lisa. Bonds of Love. (Orig.). 1978. pap. text ed. 1.95 o.s.i. (ISBN 0-515-04646-9). Jove Pubns.

--The Rainbow Season. (Orig.). 1979. pap. 2.25 (ISBN 0-515-05350-3). Jove Pubns.

Gregory, Michael. The Valley Floor. (Orig.). 1978. 10.00x (ISBN 0-934600-07-4); pap. 3.50x o.p. (ISBN 0-934600-00-7). Mother Duck Pr.

Gregory, Michael & Carroll, Susanne. Language & Situation: Language Varieties & Their Social Contexts. (Language & Sociaty Ser). 1978. 14.95x (ISBN 0-7100-8756-X); pap. 7.95 (ISBN 0-7100-8773-X). Routledge & Kegan.

Gregory, Norma, jt. auth. see Watling, Roy.

Gregory, P., jt. auth. see Gordon, P. F.

Gregory, Paul & Stuart, Robert. Comparative Economic Systems. LC 79-87859. 1980. text ed. 22.95 (ISBN 0-395-28183-0); instr's. manual 1.00 (ISBN 0-395-28184-9). HM.

Gregory, Paul, jt. auth. see Ruffin, Roy J.

Gregory, Paul R. Russian National Income, Eighteen Eighty-Five to Nineteen Thirteen. (Illus.). 350p. Date not set. Repr. price not set (ISBN 0-521-24382-3). Cambridge U Pr.

Gregory, Peter. Industrial Wages in Chile. LC 67-63229. (International Report Ser.: No. 8). 128p. 1967. 5.50 (ISBN 0-87546-012-7); pap. 3.00 (ISBN 0-87546-042-9). ILR Pr.

Gregory, Robert & Karney, David L. A Collection of Matrices for Testing Computational Algorithms. LC 77-19262. 164p. 1978. Repr. of 1969 ed. lib. bdg. 15.00 (ISBN 0-88275-649-4). Krieger.

Gregory, Robert T. Error-Free Computation: Why It Is Needed & Methods for Doing It. LC 80-23923. 152p. (Orig.). 1980. pap. 7.50 (ISBN 0-89874-240-4). Krieger.

Gregory, Ruth & Stoffel, Lester. Public Libraries in Cooperative Systems. LC 78-172295. 324p. 1971. 12.00 o.p. (ISBN 0-8389-0110-7). ALA.

Gregory, Ruth W. Anniversaries & Holidays. 3rd ed. LC 75-23163. 260p. 1975. text ed. 15.00 o.p. (ISBN 0-8389-0200-6). ALA.

--Anniversaries & Holidays. 4th ed. 1983. pap. text ed. price not set (ISBN 0-8389-0389-4). ALA.

Gregory, Stephen, jt. auth. see Sakano, Theodore.

Gregory, Theodore E., ed. Select Statutes, Documents & Reports Relating to British Banking, 1832-1928, 2 Vols. LC 67-93658. Repr. of 1929 ed. 57.50x (ISBN 0-678-05169-0). Kelley.

Gregory, Thomas B., jt. auth. see Harmin, Merrill.

Gregory, W., ed. American Newspapers, Eighteen Twenty-One to Eighteen Thirty-Six: A Union List of Files Available in the United States & Canada. LC 37-12783. 1937. 130.00 (ISBN 0-527-02250-0). Kraus Repr.

Gregory, William K. Studies on the Evolution of the Primates. Bd. with The Dentition of Dryopithecus & the Origin of Man. Gegory, William K. LC 78-72720. 67.50 (ISBN 0-404-18295-X). AMS Pr.

Gregson, Robert A. Time Series in Psychology. 560p. 1983. text ed. write for info. (ISBN 0-89859-250-X). L Erlbaum Assocs.

Greif, Martin. The Gay Book of Days. 224p. 1982. 17.95 (ISBN 0-8184-0332-2). Lyle Stuart.

--The Holiday Book. LC 77-91924. (Illus.). 1979. 14.95x o.p. (ISBN 0-87663-309-2, Main St); pap. 7.95 o.p. (ISBN 0-87663-985-6). Universe.

Greifer, Elisha, ed. see De Maistre, Joseph.

Greiff, Barrie S. & Munter, Preston K. Tradeoffs: Executive, Family & Organizational Life. 224p. 1980. 10.00 o.p. (ISBN 0-453-00374-5, H374). NAL.

Greig, C., jt. auth. see Johnston, T. H.

Greig, J. C., tr. see Wrede, William.

Greil, Arthur L. Georges Sorel & the Sociology of Virtue. LC 80-69046. 262p. (Orig.). 1982. lib. bdg. 22.25 (ISBN 0-8191-1988-1); pap. text ed. 11.00 (ISBN 0-8191-1989-X). U Pr of Amer.

Greimas, A. J. & Courtes, J. Semiotics & Language: An Analytical Dictionary. Crist, Larry, et al, trs. LC 81-47828. (Advances in Semiotics Ser.). (Illus.). 512p. 1983. 45.00x (ISBN 0-253-35169-3). Ind U Pr.

Greinacher, Norbert, jt. ed. see Elizondo, Virgil.

Greiner, Donald J. Comic Terror: The Novels of John Hawkes. rev. ed. LC 78-16886. 1978. pap. 6.95x o.p. (ISBN 0-87870-044-7). Memphis St Univ.

--Comic Terror: The Novels of John Hawkes. LC 73-81555. 1973. 11.95x o.p. (ISBN 0-87870-017-X). Memphis St Univ.

Greiner, Donald J., ed. American Poets Since World War II, 2 vols. (Dictionary of Literary Biography Ser.: Vol. 5). (Illus.). 1980. 148.00x set (ISBN 0-8103-0924-6, Broccoli Clark). Gale.

Greiner, James. The Red Snow: Story of the Alaska Gray Wolf. LC 77-82943. 240p. 1980. 10.95 o.p. (ISBN 0-385-13169-0). Doubleday.

Greiner, N. Gretchen, ed. A Batch of the Best. (gr. 3 up). 1979. pap. 1.50 (ISBN 0-307-21623-3, Golden Pr); PLB 6.08 (ISBN 0-307-61623-1, Golden Pr). Western Pub.

Greiner, W., jt. auth. see Eisenberg, J. M.

Greiner, Walter, jt. auth. see Eisenberg, Judah.

Greisman, Joan & Wittels, Harriet. How to Spell It. LC 77-85636. (gr. 3 up). 1978. pap. 6.95 (ISBN 0-448-14614-2, G&D). Putnam Pub Group.

Greisman, Joan, jt. auth. see Wittels, Harriet.

Greisman, Joan, jt. auth. see Wittles, Harriet.

Greist. Greist Anti-Depressant Treatment: The Essentials. 1979. pap. 11.95 o.p. (ISBN 0-683-03591-6). Williams & Wilkins.

Greist, John H. & Jefferson, James W., eds. Treatment of Mental Disorders. 1982. text ed. 35.00x (ISBN 0-19-503101-6); pap. text ed. 26.95x (ISBN 0-19-503107-5). Oxford U Pr.

Greist, John H., jt. auth. see Jefferson, James W.

Grekov, A. A., jt. ed. see Fridkin, V. M.

Grele, Ronald, ed. see Terkel, Studs, et al.

Gremy, F., ed. see IFIP TC Four Working Conference.

Grenander, M. E. Ambrose Bierce. (U. S. Authors Ser.: No. 180). lib. bdg. 8.50 o.p. (ISBN 0-8057-0056-0, Twayne). G K Hall.

Grenander, U., jt. auth. see Freiberger, W.

Grenander, Ulf. Mathematical Experiments on the Computer. (Pure & Applied Mathematics Ser.). 1982. 39.50 (ISBN 0-12-301750-5). Acad Pr.

Grenard. Advanced Study in Respiratory Therapy Carousel Slide Tray Set. 1978. 134.95 o.p. (ISBN 0-8151-3983-7). Year Bk Med.

Grenard, S. Introduction to Respiratory Therapy Complete Learning Package. 1978. 230.00 o.p. (ISBN 0-8151-3985-3). Year Bk Med.

Grender, Iris. Playing with Shapes & Sizes. (Pinwheel Preschool Activity Books). (Illus.). Date not set. pap. 1.25 o.p. (ISBN 0-515-09347-5). Knopf.

Grene, David see Sophocles.

Grene, David, ed. see Euripides.

Grene, Marjorie. Philosophy in & Out of Europe & Other Essays. LC 75-27924. 1976. 17.50x (ISBN 0-520-03121-0). U of Cal Pr.

Grene, Nicholas, ed. see Synge, J. M.

Grenell, Robert & Gabay, Sabit, eds. Biological Foundations of Psychiatry, 2 vols. LC 74-15664. 1976. 48.00 ea.; Vol. 1, 613pgs. (ISBN 0-911216-96-0); Vol. 2, 477 Pgs. (ISBN 0-89004-126-1). Raven.

Grenfell, Cynthia. Stone Run: Tidings. Hausman, Gerald, ed. 96p. (Orig.). 1983. pap. 11.95 (ISBN 0-86534-023-4). Sunstone Pr.

Grenfell, Newell. Switch on: Switch off: The Mass Media Audiences of Malaysia. (Illus.). 1979. 34.00x o.p. (ISBN 0-19-580407-4). Oxford U Pr.

Grenier, Albert, jt. auth. see Amiel-Tison, Claudine.

Grenier, Fernand, ed. Quebec. (Studies in Canadian Geography). (Illus., Fr.). 1972. 15.00x (ISBN 0-8020-1918-8); pap. 6.00x (ISBN 0-8020-6159-1). U of Toronto Pr.

Grenier, M. Special Day Prayers for the Very Young Child. (gr. 1-4). 1983. 7.95 (ISBN 0-570-04076-0). Concordia.

Grenier, Richard. The Marrakesh One-Two. LC 82-15818. 350p. 1983. 14.95 (ISBN 0-395-33099-8). HM.

Grenier, Robert, ed. see Eigner, Larry.

Grenlee, Geraldine, et al. Kinesiology. Kneer, Marian, ed. (Basic Stuff Ser.: No. 1, 2 of 6). (Illus.). 90p. (Orig.). 1981. pap. text ed. 6.25 (ISBN 0-88314-025-X). AAHPERD.

Grennell, Dean A. ABC's of Reloading. 1974. pap. 6.95 o.s.i. (ISBN 0-695-80467-7). Follett.

--Pistol & Revolver Digest. (DBI Bks). (Illus., Orig.). 1976. pap. 7.95 o.s.i. (ISBN 0-695-80687-4). Follett.

Grennell, Dean A., ed. Law Enforcement Handgun Digest. 2nd. rev. ed. (DBI Bks). 1976. pap. 6.95 o.s.i. (ISBN 0-695-80646-7). Follett.

--Pistol & Revolver Digest. 2nd ed. (Illus.). 1979. pap. 7.95 o.s.i. (ISBN 0-695-81274-2). Follett.

Grennes, Thomas, et al. Economics of World Grain Trade. LC 77-13715. (Praeger Special Studies). 1978. 26.95 o.p. (ISBN 0-03-022836-0). Praeger.

Grenon, Michele, jt. auth. see Hollomon, J. Herbert.

Grenville, Peter. Kurt Tucholsky: The Ironic Sentimentalist. (German Literature & Society Ser.: Vol. 1). 1980. pap. text ed. 10.75 (ISBN 0-85496-074-0). Humanities.

Grenzke, Janet M. Influence, Change, & the Legislative Process. LC 82-9383. (Contributions in Political Science Ser.: No. 89). (Illus.). 216p. 1983. lib. bdg. 35.00 (ISBN 0-313-23385-3, GRI/). Greenwood.

Greppin, John A. Classical & Middle Armenian Bird Names. LC 77-25361. 1978. 35.00x (ISBN 0-88206-017-1). Caravan Bks.

Gresh, Sean. Becoming a Father: A Handbook for Expectant Fathers. 192p. 1982. pap. 2.95 (ISBN 0-553-22744-0). Bantam.

Gresham, Charles R. What the Bible Says about Resurrection. (What the Bible Says Ser.). 350p. 1983. 13.50 (ISBN 0-89900-090-8). College Pr Pub.

Gresham, Grits. Complete Wildflower. (Stoeger Bks). 1975. pap. 5.95 o.s.i. (ISBN 0-695-80562-2). Follett.

--The Complete Wildflower. (Illus.). 304p. pap. 5.95 o.p. (ISBN 0-88317-024-8). Stoeger Pub Co.

Gress, James R. & Purpel, David E., eds. Curriculum: An Introduction to the Field. LC 77-23651. (National Society for the Study of Education Series on Contemporary Educ. Issues). 1978. 21.25 (ISBN 0-8211-0613-9); text ed. 19.25 ten copies (ISBN 0-686-52368-7). McCutchan.

Gressel, Jonathan, jt. auth. see Lebaron, Homer M.

Gresser, I., ed. Interferon 3, 1981. LC 79-4142. 164p. 1982. 19.00 (ISBN 0-12-302252-5). Acad Pr.

Gresser, Ion, ed. Interferon Eighty-Two. (Serial Publication). Date not set. 18.50 (ISBN 0-12-302253-3). Acad Pr.

Gresser, Julian, et al. Environmental Law in Japan. (Illus.). 520p. 1981. text ed. 65.00x (ISBN 0-262-07076-6). MIT Pr.

Gresser, Sy. Fragments & Others. LC 82-73260. (Illus.). 50p. (Orig.). 1982. pap. 5.00 (ISBN 0-934996-18-0). Am Stud Pr.

Gressitt, J. L., ed. Entomology of Antarctica. LC 67-62159. (Antarctic Research Ser.: Vol. 10). 1967. 22.00 (ISBN 0-87590-110-7). Am Geophysical.

Gressman, Eugene, jt. auth. see Stern, Robert L.

Gresson, Aaron D., III. The Dialectics of Betrayal. (Modern Sociology Ser.). 160p. 1982. text ed. 19.95 (ISBN 0-89391-101-1); pap. text ed. 11.95. Ablex Pub.

Gresswell, Fred. Bright Boots: An Autobiography. (Illus.). 232p. 1982. 22.50 (ISBN 0-7153-8400-7). David & Charles.

Grethe, G. Isoquinolines, Vol. 38. (Pt. 1). 561p. 1981. 175.95 (ISBN 0-471-37481-4, Pub. by Wiley-Interscience). Wiley.

Grether, Donald, ed. see Birdahl, Paul, et al.

Gretler, Kathryn & Roberts, Wayne. Elementary Linear Algebra: Student's Solution Manual. 1982. pap. 5.95 (ISBN 0-8053-8302-6). Benjamin-Cummings.

Gretry, Andre. Memoires, Ou Essais Sur la Musique, 3 Vols. LC 73-160852. (Music Ser). (Fr., Fr). 1971. Repr. of 1789 ed. Set. lib. bdg. 110.00 (ISBN 0-306-70194-4). Da Capo.

Gretton, John & Harrison, Anthony, eds. How Much are Public Servants Worth? 44p. 1983. pap. text ed. 12.00x (ISBN 0-631-13251-1, Pub. by Basil Blackwell England). Biblio Dist.

Gretz, Marit, illus. Green Acres School's Going Places with Children in Washington. rev., 10th ed. Tippet, Katherine S. & Parsons, E. Susan, eds. LC 81-84373. (Illus.). 227p. (Orig.). 1982. pap. 4.95 (ISBN 0-686-37129-1). Green Acres Schl.

Gretz, Susanna. Teddy Bears Go Shopping. (Illus.). (gr. k-3). 1982. 9.95 (ISBN 0-590-07861-5, Four Winds). Schol Bk Serv.

Greub, Werner, et al. Connections, Curvature, & Cohomology, 3 vols. Incl. Vol. 1. De Rham Cohomology of Manifold & Vector Bundles. 1972. 55.50 o.s.i. (ISBN 0-12-302701-2); Vol. 2. Lie Groups, Principal Bundles & Characteristic Classes. 1973. 63.00 (ISBN 0-12-302702-0); Vol. 3. Cohomology of Principle Bundles & Homogeneous Spaces. 1976. 78.00 (ISBN 0-12-302703-9). (Pure & Applied Mathematics Ser.). Acad Pr.

Greulach, Victor A. & Adams, J. Edison. Plants: An Introduction to Modern Botany. 3rd ed. LC 75-16134. 586p. 1976. text ed. 27.95x o.p. (ISBN 0-471-32769-7); Avail Tchr's Manual o.p. (ISBN 0-471-29223-0). Wiley.

Greulach, Victor A. & Chiappetta, Vincent J. Biology: The Science of Life. 1977. text ed. 24.50x (ISBN 0-673-15301-0); study guide 7.95x (ISBN 0-673-15302-9). Scott F.

Greutzfeldt, W. Cimetidine. (International Congress Ser.: No. 443). 1978. 71.00 (ISBN 0-444-90048-9). Elsevier.

Greve, Alice W. Shadow on the Plains. 1944. 5.95 (ISBN 0-8323-0113-2). Binford.

Grevel, H., ed. see Bouchot, Henri.

Grevich, J. D. Testing Procedures for Automotive AC & DC Charging Systems. 1972. text ed. 19.95 (ISBN 0-07-024673-4, G). McGraw.

Greville, Fulke. Selected Writings of Fulke Greville. Rees, ed. (Athlone Renaissance Library). 1973. text ed. 23.50x (ISBN 0-485-12603-6, Athlone Pr); pap. text ed. 13.00x (ISBN 0-686-66967-3). Humanities.

Greville, R. K. Descriptions of New & Rare Diatoms. (Trans. Microscop. Soc. Ser.). (Illus.). 1968. 32.00 (ISBN 3-7682-0570-3). Lubrecht & Cramer.

Greville, Thomas N., jt. auth. see Ben-Israel, Adi.

Grevisse, M. Le Bon Usage. (Fr). 49.95 (ISBN 0-685-20226-7). Schoenhof.

Grevlich, Richard C., jt. ed. see Slavkin, Harold C.

Grew, Eva & Grew, Sydney. Bach. (Illus.). 256p. 1972. pap. 2.95 o.p. (ISBN 0-07-024678-5, SP). McGraw.

Grew, James H. & Olivier, Daniel D. One Thousand & One Pitfalls in French. rev. ed. LC 73-7323. (gr. 9up). 1974. pap. text ed. 4.50 (ISBN 0-8120-0471-X). Barron.

Grew, N. Experiments Inconsort of the Luctation Arising From the Affusion of Several Menstrums Upon All Sorts of Bodies: 1678. 120p. Date not set. pap. 12.50 (ISBN 0-87556-114-4). Saifer.

Grew, Sydney, jt. auth. see Grew, Eva.

Grewe, Georgeann, jt. auth. see Glover, Susanne.

Grewe, Horst-Eberhard & Kremer, Karl. Atlas of Surgery, Vol 1. 2nd ed. Hirsch, H. J., tr. from Ger. LC 77-84671. 1981. 69.50 (ISBN 0-7216-4273-X). Saunders.

Grey, Anthony. The Chinese Assassin. 272p. 1982. pap. 2.95 (ISBN 0-441-10438-X, Pub. by Charter Bks). Ace Bks.

--Saigon. 825p. 1982. 17.95 (ISBN 0-316-32822-7). Little.

Grey, Arthur, jt. auth. see Elliott, John E.

Grey, J. Turtle Who Wanted to Run. LC 68-56813. (Illus.). (gr. 1-3). 1968. PLB 6.75x (ISBN 0-87783-045-2). Oddo.

Grey, Jerry. Beachheads in Space: A Blueprint for the Future. (Illus.). 288p. 1983. 14.95 (ISBN 0-02-545590-7). Macmillan.

--Enterprise. LC 79-10544. (Illus.). 1979. 10.95 o.p. (ISBN 0-688-03462-4). Morrow.

Grey, L. Discipline Without Fear. 1974. pap. 5.25 (ISBN 0-8015-2132-7, Hawthron). Dutton.

Grey, Loren. Discipline Without Fear. 192p. 1982. pap. 6.00 (ISBN 0-939654-02-4). Social Interest.

--Discipline Without Tyranny. 192p. 1982. pap. 6.00 (ISBN 0-939654-03-2). Social Interest.

Grey, Loren, jt. auth. see Dreikurs, Rudolf.

Grey, M. Cameron, ed. Angels & Awakenings: Stories of the Miraculous by Great Modern Writers. (Illus.). 432p. 1980. 15.95 o.p. (ISBN 0-385-15311-2). Doubleday.

Grey, Naidra. The Foxglove Summer. LC 76-26086. 1976. 7.95 o.p. (ISBN 0-399-11765-2). Putnam Pub Group.

Grey, Robert W., jt. ed. see Stone, Nancy.

Grey, Rodney. United States Trade Policy Legislation: A Canadian View. 130p. (Orig.). 1982. pap. text ed. 7.95x (ISBN 0-920380-86-7, Pub. by Inst Res Pub Canada). Renouf.

Grey, Rowland, jt. auth. see Dark, Sidney.

Grey, Seymour. Beyond the Veil: The Adventures of an American Doctor in Saudi Arabia. (Bessie Bks.). 320p. 1983. 17.26i (ISBN 0-06-039014-X, HarpT). Har-Row.

Grey, Vivian. The Chemist Who Lost His Head: The Story of Antoine Lavoisier. (Illus.). 112p. 1982. 9.95 (ISBN 0-698-20559-6, Coward). Putnam Pub Group.

Grey, Zane. The Call of the Canyon. large type ed. LC 82-10448. 355p. 1982. Repr. of 1921 ed. 11.95 (ISBN 0-89621-386-2). Thorndike Pr.

--Forlorn River. 1977. lib. bdg. 11.95 o.p. (ISBN 0-8161-6526-2, Large Print Bks). G K Hall.

--Majesty's Rancho. Large Print ed. LC 82-709. 501p. 1982. Repr. of 1937 ed. 11.95x (ISBN 0-89621-347-1). Thorndike Pr.

--The U. P. Trail. Large Print ed. LC 82-711. 608p. 1982. Repr. of 1981 ed. 11.95x (ISBN 0-89621-348-X). Thorndike Pr.

--The Westerner. (General Ser.). 1980. lib. bdg. 10.95 (ISBN 0-8161-3125-2, Large Print Bks). G K Hall.

Greydanus, Rose. Changing Seasons. LC 82-19959. (Now I Know Ser.). (Illus.). 32p. (gr. k-2). 1982. PLB 8.89 (ISBN 0-89375-902-3). Troll Assocs.

--Horses. LC 82-20296. (Now I Know Ser.). (Illus.). 32p. (gr. k-2). 1982. lib. bdg. 8.89 (ISBN 0-89375-900-7). Troll Assocs.

Grey Owl & Little Pigeon. Cry of the Ancients. 1974. pap. 9.00 (ISBN 0-8309-0108-6). Herald Hse.

Greyser, Stephen A. Cases in Advertising & Communications Management. 2nd ed. 300p. 1981. text ed. 25.95 (ISBN 0-13-118513-6). P-H.

Greyser, Stephen A., jt. auth. see Young, Robert F.

Greyset, Stephen A., jt. ed. see Bursk, Edward C.

Grey-Wilson & Blamey. The Alpine Flowers of Britain & Europe. pap. 19.95 (ISBN 0-686-42736-X, Collins Pub England). Greene.

Grey-Wilson, Christopher & Mathew, Brian. Bulbs: The Bulbous Plants of Europe & Their Allies. (Illus.). 1983. 32.95 (ISBN 0-686-42797-1, Collins Pub England). Greene.

Gribbin, J., ed. Climatic Change. LC 76-52185. 1978. 69.50 (ISBN 0-521-21594-3); pap. 21.95x (ISBN 0-521-29205-0). Cambridge U Pr.

Gribbin, John. The Death of the Sun. 1980. 9.95 o.s.i. (ISBN 0-440-01924-9, E Friede). Delacorte.

--Death of the Sun. 1981. pap. 4.95 o.s.i. (ISBN 0-440-51854-7, Delta). Dell.

--Genesis. 240p. 1982. cancelled (ISBN 0-460-04505-9, Pub. by J. M. Dent England). Biblio Dist.

--Genesis: The Origins of Man & the Universe. (Illus.). 384p. 1981. 13.95 o.s.i. (ISBN 0-440-02832-9). Delacorte.

--This Shaking Earth. LC 78-52980. (Illus.). 1978. 17.95 o.p. (ISBN 0-399-12185-4). Putnam Pub Group.

--Timewarps. 1979. 8.95 o.s.i. (ISBN 0-440-08509-8, E Friede). Delacorte.

--Weather Force: Climate & Its Impact on Our World. LC 79-51033. (Illus.). 1979. 20.00 o.p. (ISBN 0-399-12400-4). Putnam Pub Group.

--White Holes: Cosmic Gushers in the Universe. 1977. 8.95 o.s.i. (ISBN 0-440-09529-8, E Friede). Delacorte.

Gribbin, John, jt. auth. see Orgill, Douglas.

Gribble, C. J., jt. ed. see Atherton, M. P.

Gribble, Charles E. Short Dictionary of Eighteenth Century Russian. 1976. soft cover 8.95 (ISBN 0-89357-039-7). Slavica.

Gribble, Francis. Rousseau & the Women He Loved. 443p. 1983. Repr. of 1908 ed. lib. bdg. 40.00 (ISBN 0-89760-368-0). Telegraph Bks.

Gribble, Leonard. Famous Mysteries of Modern Times. 1977. 9.50 o.p. (ISBN 0-584-10240-2). Transatlantic.

--Stories of Famous Spies. 14.50 (ISBN 0-392-16333-0, SpS). Sportshelf.

Gribble, McPhee. Bicycles: All About Them. (Practical Puffins Ser.). 32p. (gr. 5 up). 1976. pap. 2.95 (ISBN 0-14-049145-7, Puffin). Penguin.

--Body Tricks: To Teach Yourself. (Practical Puffins Ser.). 32p. (gr. 5 up). 1982. pap. 2.25 (ISBN 0-14-049138-4, Puffin). Penguin.

Gribkovskii, V. P., jt. auth. see Stepanov, B. I.

Gribnau, T. C., et al, eds. Affinity Chromatography & Related Techniques: Theoretical Aspects. (Analytical Chemistry Symposia Ser.: Vol. 9). 1981. 83.00 (ISBN 0-444-42031-2). Elsevier.

Grice, Julia. Emerald Fire. 1978. pap. 3.50 (ISBN 0-380-38596-1, 82347-0). Avon.

Grice, William A. Badminton. 3rd ed. (Illus.). 91p. 1981. pap. text ed. 3.95x (ISBN 0-89641-068-4). American Pr.

Grice, William A., jt. auth. see Barton, Joel R., III.

Grider, Edgar M. Can I Make It One More Year? Overcoming the Hazards of the Ministry. LC 79-87755. 1980. pap. 3.49 (ISBN 0-8042-1568-5). John Knox.

Grider, J. Kenneth. Born Again & Growing. 118p. 1982. pap. 3.50 (ISBN 0-8341-0758-9). Beacon Hill.

Gridgeman, N. T. Biological Sciences at the National Research Council of Canada: The Early Years to 1952. 153p. 1979. text ed. 11.25x (ISBN 0-88920-082-3, Pub. by Wilfrid Laurier U Pr Canada). Humanities.

Gridley, Marion E. Pontiac. (See & Read Biographies). (Illus.). (gr. 1-3). 1970. PLB 4.49 o.p. (ISBN 0-399-60516-9). Putnam Pub Group.

--Story of the Navajo. Country Beautiful Editors, ed. (Indian Nations Ser.). (Illus.). (gr. 4-7). 1971. PLB 5.97 o.p. (ISBN 0-399-60611-4). Putnam Pub Group.

--The Story of the Seminole. new ed. Country Beautiful Editors, ed. (Indian Nations Ser.). (Illus.). 64p. (gr. 4-7). 1973. PLB 5.97 o.p. (ISBN 0-399-60806-0). Putnam Pub Group.

Gridley, Mark C. Jazz Styles. (Illus.). 352p. 1978. text ed. 15.95 (ISBN 0-13-509885-8); pap. text ed. 16.95 (ISBN 0-13-509877-7). P-H.

Gridley, Roy E. Browning. (Routledge Author Guides). 1972. 18.95x (ISBN 0-7100-7368-2); pap. 7.95 (ISBN 0-7100-7369-0). Routledge & Kegan.

--The Brownings & France: A Chronicle with Commentary. 320p. 1982. text ed. 38.00x (ISBN 0-485-11231-0, Althlone Pr). Humanities.

Grieb, Kenneth J. The Latin American Policy of Warren G. Harding. LC 74-26229. (Series on the American Presidency: Vol. 1). (Illus.). 1978. text ed. 12.50x (ISBN 0-912646-46-2). Tex Christian.

Grieco, Victor A. Management of Small Business. new ed. (Business Ser). 1975. text ed. 19.95 o.p. (ISBN 0-675-08731-7). Additional supplements may be obtained from publisher. Merrill.

Grieder, Josephine, jt. auth. see Grieder, Theodore.

Grieder, Theodore. Acquisitions: Where, What, & How - a Guide to Orientation & Procedures for Students in Librarianship, Librarians, & Academic Faculty. LC 77-84762. (Contributions in Librarianship & Information Science: No. 22). 1978. lib. bdg. 29.95x (ISBN 0-8371-9890-9, GAL/). Greenwood.

Grieder, Theodore & Grieder, Josephine. A Student's First Aid to Writing. LC 72-81176. (Quality Paperback: No. 254). (Orig.). 1979. pap. 4.95 (ISBN 0-8226-0254-7). Littlefield.

Grieg, Russell & Ellis, Albert, eds. Handbook of Rational-Emotive Therapy. 22.50 (ISBN 0-686-36744-8); pap. 16.95 (ISBN 0-686-37352-9). Inst Rat Liv.

Grieger, Ingrid, jt. ed. see Grieger, Russell.

Grieger, Ingrid Z., jt. ed. see Grieger, Russell.

Grieger, Russell & Boyd, John. Rational-Emotive Therapy: A Skills-Based Appproach. 15.95 (ISBN 0-686-36792-8). Inst Rat Liv.

Grieger, Russell & Grieger, Ingrid, eds. Cognition & Emotional Disturbance. 26.95 (ISBN 0-686-36681-6). Inst Rat Liv.

Grieger, Russell & Grieger, Ingrid Z., eds. Cognition & Emotional Disturbance. LC 81-6461. 232p. 1982. 26.95x (ISBN 0-89885-022-3). Human Sci Pr.

Grier, James W. Biology of Animal Behavior. 550p. 1983. pap. text ed. 21.95 (ISBN 0-8016-1971-8). Mosby.

Grierson, Edward. King of Two Worlds: Philip II of Spain. LC 74-78401. (Illus.). 224p. 1974. 12.95 o.p. (ISBN 0-399-11384-3). Putnam Pub Group.

Grierson, Herbert J. & Wason, Sandy, eds. The Personal Note: Or First & Last Words from Prefaces, Introductions, Dedications, Epilogues. LC 77-27022. 1978. Repr. of 1946 ed. lib. bdg. 18.25x (ISBN 0-313-20063-7, GRPN). Greenwood.

Grierson, Mary. Donald Francis Tovey: A Biography Based on Letters. LC 70-104237. (Illus.). xi, 337p. Repr. of 1952 ed. lib. bdg. 17.00x (ISBN 0-8371-3935-X, GRDT). Greenwood.

Grierson, Philip. Byzantine Coinage, No. 4. (Byzantine Collection Publications Ser.). (Illus.). 32p. 1982. pap. 4.50x (ISBN 0-88402-112-2). Dumbarton Oaks.

--Byzantine Coins. LC 82-50853. (The Library of Numismatics). (Illus.). 479p. 1983. 75.00 o.p. (ISBN 0-520-04897-0). U of Cal Pr.

--Catalogue of the Byzantine Coins in the Dumbarton Oaks Collection & in the Whittemore Collection Vol. III: Leo III to Nicephorus III, 717-1081. LC 67-9186. (Illus.). 887p. 1973. 90.00x o.p. (ISBN 0-88402-045-2, Ctr Byzantine). Dumbarton Oaks.

Griesbach, Heinz. Deutsch X 3. Incl. Gespraechsbuch I mit Uebungen, "Unterwegs". (Illus.). 1975. pap. text ed. 4.30x (ISBN 3-468-49556-0); Glossary I, German-English. 1974. pap. text ed. 2.10x (ISBN 3-468-49511-0); Glossary II, German-English. 1976. pap. text ed. 2.65x (ISBN 3-468-49611-7); Lehrerheft I. (Illus.). 1974. pap. text ed. 2.10x (ISBN 3-468-49506-4); Lehrerheft II. 1976. pap. text ed. 2.10x (ISBN 3-468-49606-0); Lernbuch I. Horn, Herbert, illus. 1974. pap. text ed. 4.85x (ISBN 3-468-49501-3); Lernbuch II. Horn, Herbert, illus. 1975. pap. text ed. 4.85x (ISBN 3-468-49601-X); Lernbuch III. (Illus.). 1977. pap. text ed. 4.85x (ISBN 3-468-49701-6); Leseheft I mit Uebungen, "Aktuell und interessant". (Illus.). 1975. pap. text ed. 3.75x (ISBN 3-468-49561-7); Leseheft II mit Uebungen, "Aktuell und interessant". Die Laender der Bundesrepublik Deutschland. (Illus.). 1977. pap. text ed. 3.75x (ISBN 3-468-49661-3); Loesungsheft I. 1974. pap. text ed. 2.10x (ISBN 3-468-49541-2); Loesungsheft **II. 1976. pap. text ed. 2.65x (ISBN 3-468-49641-9); Sprachlabor-Cassetten, Saemtliche Sprechuebungen, Doppelspur Mitnachsprechpausen, 10 Casetten. 1974. pap. text ed. 136.80x (ISBN 3-468-84722-X); Sprachlabor-Tonbaender saemtliche Sprechuebungen, Vollspur mit Nachsprechpausen, 10 Tonbaender. 1974. pap. text ed. 239.40x (ISBN 3-468-84726-2); Sprechuebungem I - Textheft. 1974. pap. text ed. 3.75x (ISBN 3-468-49546-3).** M S Rosenberg.

Griesbach, Heinz, jt. auth. see Schulz, Dora.

Griesbach, Marc F. & Carmichael, John P., eds. The ACPA in Today's Intellectual World: Proceedings, 1983, Vol. 57. LC 82-73233. 250p. 1984. pap. 8.00 (ISBN 0-918090-17-2). Am Cath Philo.

Griese, Arnold. The Way of Our People. LC 74-23086. (Illus.). 90p. (gr. 2-5). 1975. 6.95 o.p. (ISBN 0-690-00706-X, TYC-J); PLB 10.89 (ISBN 0-690-00707-8). Har-Row.

Griese, Arnold A. Do You Read Me? Practical Approaches to Teaching Reading Comprehension. LC 76-9913. (Illus.). 1977. pap. 11.95x (ISBN 0-673-16354-7); text ed. 12.95x (ISBN 0-673-16353-9). Scott F.

Grieser, E. H., jt. auth. see Sturm, Mary M.

Grieshaber, Erich & Grieshaber, Jean. Expose of Jehovah's Witnesses. 128p. 1983. pap. text ed. 2.95 (ISBN 0-936728-08-6). Word for Today.

Grieshaber, Jean, jt. auth. see Grieshaber, Erich.

Griesinger, F. K. How to Cut Costs & Improve Service of Your Telephone, Telex, TWX & Other Telecommunications. LC 73-21616. (Illus.). 320p. 1974. 32.50 o.p. (ISBN 0-07-024760-9, P&RB). McGraw.

Grieson, Ronald E., ed. Public & Urban Economics. LC 74-31877. 432p. 1976. 29.95x (ISBN 0-669-98400-0). Lexington Bks.

--The Urban Economy & Housing. LC 81-48269. 256p. 1982. 27.95X (ISBN 0-669-05331-7). Lexington Bks.

Griesser, G. Data Protection in Health Information Systems: Considerations & Guidelines. 1980. 38.50 (ISBN 0-444-86052-5). Elsevier.

Griesser, G, ed. see IFIPtC4 Working Conference, Germany, 1976.

Griest, W. H., et al, eds. Health Effects Investigation of Oil Shale Development. LC 80-70323. 1981. text ed. 39.95 (ISBN 0-250-40169-X). Ann Arbor Science.

Grieve, M. A Modern Herbal. Leyel, Mrs. C. F., ed. LC 72-169784. (Illus.). 1971. pap. 7.50 ea.; Vol. 1. pap. (ISBN 0-486-22798-7); Vol. 2. pap. (ISBN 0-486-22799-5). Dover.

Grieve, M. J., jt. auth. see Donelan, M. D.

Grieve, Michael, ed. see MacDiarmid, Hugh.

Grieve, Norma & Grimshaw, Patricia, eds. Australian Women: Feminist Perspectives. (Illus.). 256p. 1981. 34.00x (ISBN 0-19-554314-9). Oxford U Pr.

Grieves, Forest L. Conflict & Order: An Introduction to International Relations. LC 76-10901. (Illus.). 1977. pap. text ed. 20.95 (ISBN 0-395-24332-7); inst. manual 1.65 (ISBN 0-395-24335-1). HM.

Griffee, Dale. Listen & Act: Scenes for Language Learning. Rost, Michael, ed. (Illus.). 96p. 1982. pap. text ed. 5.50 (ISBN 0-940264-18-8); of two 20.00 set (ISBN 0-940264-21-8); of 20 cards 4.00 set (ISBN 0-940264-20-X). Lingual Hse Pub.

Griffen, Dana T., jt. auth. see Phillips, W. Revell.

Griffen, Jeff. How to Raise & Train Your Puppy. pap. 3.00 (ISBN 0-87980-330-4). Wilshire.

Griffen, M. R., ed. see Pliny.

Griffen, Ward O., Jr., jt. auth. see Maull, Kimball I.

Griffen, William L. & Marciano, John. Teaching the Vietnam War: A Critical Examination of School Texts & Interpretive Conparative History Utilizing the Penragon Papers & other Documents. LC 78-73553. 204p. 1980. text ed. 14.50x (ISBN 0-916672-23-9); pap. text ed. 6.50x (ISBN 0-916672-27-1). Allanheld.

Griffes, Ernest J., ed. Employee Benefits Programs: Management, Planning & Control. 250p. 1983. 30.00 (ISBN 0-686-83835-1). Dow Jones-Irwin.

Griffeth, Robert & Thomas, Carol G., eds. The City-State in Five Cultures. LC 81-7897. 237p. 1981. text ed. 22.50 (ISBN 0-87436-316-0). ABC-Clio.

Griffin & Beale. World of Electronics, 4 Bks. (Electronic World Ser.). (gr. 5-9). Date not set. 10.95 (ISBN 0-86020-643-2, 21131, Usborne-Hayes). Spanish ed. French ed (ISBN 0-86020-267-4). German ed. EDC.

Griffin & D'Arcy. Drug Induced Emergencies. 398p. 1980. pap. 24.50 (ISBN 0-7236-0522-X). Wright-PSG.

--Manual of Adverse Drug Interactions. 2nd ed. 416p. 1979. pap. 21.50 (ISBN 0-7236-0508-4). Wright-PSG.

Griffin & Duax. Molecular Structure & Biological Activity. 1982. 65.00 (ISBN 0-444-00751-2). Elsevier.

Griffin, jt. auth. see American Institute of Architects.

Griffin, et al. Welding Processes. 2nd ed. LC 76-28745. (gr. 9-12). 1978. 19.60 (ISBN 0-8273-1257-1); instr.'s guide 3.75 (ISBN 0-8273-1259-8). Delmar.

Griffin, A. Clark, ed. see Annual Symposium on Fundamental Cancer Research, No. 31.

Griffin, Appleton P. Bibliography of American Historical Societies. 2nd ed. rev. ed. LC 67-480. 1966. Repr. of 1907 ed. 68.00x (ISBN 0-8103-3080-6). Gale.

Griffin, Betty F. Family to Family. 78p. 1980. pap. text ed. 6.75 (ISBN 0-88200-140-X, 16008). Alexander Graham.

Griffin, Bryan F. Panic Among the Philistines. LC 82-60663. 1983. 12.95 (ISBN 0-89526-633-4). Regnery-Gateway.

Griffin, C. S. Ferment of Reform, Eighteen Thirty to Eighteen Sixty. LC 67-13380. (AHM American History Ser.). (Orig.). 1968. pap. 5.95x (ISBN 0-88295-738-4). Harlan Davidson.

Griffin, Clarence W. History of Old Tryon & Rutherford Counties, North Carolina,1730-1936. LC 77-24691. (Illus.). 1977. Repr. of 1937 ed. 35.00 (ISBN 0-87152-252-7). Reprint.

Griffin, D. M. Ecology of Soil Fungi. LC 72-247. (Illus.). 208p. 1972. text ed. 19.95x (ISBN 0-8156-5035-3). Syracuse U Pr.

Griffin, D. S., jt. ed. see Udoguchi, T.

Griffin, David H. Fungal Physiology. LC 81-3344. 383p. 1981. 32.50x (ISBN 0-471-05748-7, Pub. by Wiley-Interscience). Wiley.

Griffin, David R. God, Power, & Evil: A Process Theodicy. LC 76-21631. 1976. 17.50 o.s.i. (ISBN 0-664-20753-7). Westminster.

Griffin, David R. & Altizer, Thomas J., eds. John Cobb's Theology in Process. LC 77-23135. 1977. 17.50 (ISBN 0-664-21292-1). Westminster.

Griffin, David R. & Cobb, John B., Jr., eds. Mind in Nature: Essays on the Interface of Science & Philosophy. 1977. pap. text ed. 9.25 (ISBN 0-8191-0157-5). U Pr of Amer.

Griffin, Dick, jt. ed. see Warden, Rob.

Griffin, Dustin H. Satires Against Man: The Poems of Rochester. LC 72-95304. 1974. 26.50x (ISBN 0-520-02394-3). U of Cal Pr.

Griffin, E. P. Financial Development in Latin America. 280p. 1971. 25.00 (ISBN 0-312-28945-6). St Martin.

Griffin, Em. The Mind Changers. 1976. pap. 6.95 (ISBN 0-8423-4290-7). Tyndale.

Griffin, Ernest G. John Middleton Murray. (English Authors Ser.). 14.95 (ISBN 0-8057-1412-X, Twayne). G K Hall.

Griffin, Frank. Industrial Gases. (Illus.). (gr. 7 up). 12.75x (ISBN 0-392-03372-0, SpS). Sportshelf.

Griffin, Frank M., Jr., jt. auth. see Cobbs, C. Glenn.

Griffin, G. Edward. Fearful Master: A Second Look at the United Nations. LC 64-22761. (Illus.). 1964. 5.00 (ISBN 0-88279-204-0); pap. 4.95 (ISBN 0-88279-102-8). Western Islands.

Griffin, Gary A., ed. Staff Development, Pt. II. LC 82-62382. (The National Society for the Study of Education 82nd Yearbook). 275p. 1983. lib. bdg. 16.00x (ISBN 0-226-60136-6). U of Chicago Pr.

Griffin, Gerald & Burks, David R. Appraising Administrative Operations: A Guide for Universities & Colleges. 1976. 3.50 o.p. (ISBN 0-8268-1203-1). ACE.

Griffin, Graeme M. & Tobin, Des. In the Midst of Life: The Australian Response to Death. (Illus.). 191p. 1983. pap. 9.95 (ISBN 0-522-84248-8, Pub. by Melbourne U Pr). Intl Schol Bk Serv.

Griffin, I. H., et al. Basic Tig & Mig Welding. 2nd ed. LC 76-14085. 1977. pap. text ed. 7.00 (ISBN 0-8273-1260-1); instructor's guide 2.00 (ISBN 0-8273-1262-8). Delmar.

--Pipe Welding Techniques. 2nd ed. LC 76-51121. 1978. pap. text ed. 8.80 (ISBN 0-8273-1256-3). Delmar.

Griffin, Ivan H., et al. Basic Arc Welding. LC 76-4309. 1977. pap. text ed. 7.00 (ISBN 0-8273-1250-4); instructor's guide 2.00 (ISBN 0-8273-1251-2). Delmar.

--Basic Oxyacetylene Welding. LC 76-4307. 1977. pap. 7.00 (ISBN 0-8273-1252-0); instr's. guide 2.50 (ISBN 0-8273-1253-9). Delmar.

Griffin, J. Morgodor, jt. auth. see Jeavons, John.

Griffin, J. P., jt. auth. see D'Arcy, P. F.

Griffin, James. Manual of Clinical Endocrinology & Metabolism. (PreTest Manuals of Clinical Medicine Ser.). 317p. (Orig.). 1982. manual 14.95 (ISBN 0-07-024776-5, HP). McGraw.

Griffin, James A., jt. auth. see Quinn, A. James.

Griffin, James B., jt. auth. see Hamilton, Henry W.

Griffin, James M. Energy Conservation in the OECD: 1980 to 2000. LC 78-24109. 320p. 1979. prof ref 27.50x (ISBN 0-88410-087-1). Ballinger Pub.

Griffin, James M. & Steele, Henry B. Energy Economics & Policy. 1980. text ed. 18.50 (ISBN 0-12-303950-9). Acad Pr.

Griffin, James M. & Teece, David J., eds. OPEC Behavior & World Oil Prices. 256p. 1982. text ed. 28.50 (ISBN 0-04-338102-2); pap. 9.95x (ISBN 0-04-338103-0). Allen Unwin.

Griffin, James S. How to Make Money in Commercial Land: A Guide for Investors & Residential Salespersons. (Illus.). 1982. 7.95 (ISBN 0-916682-37-4). Outdoor Empire.

Griffin, Jasper. Homer. Thomas, Keith, ed. (Pastmasters Ser.). 1981. 7.95 (ISBN 0-8090-5523-6); pap. 2.95 (ISBN 0-8090-1413-0). Hill & Wang.

Griffin, Jasper, compiled by. Snobs. (Small Oxford Books). (Illus.). 100p. 1982. 9.95 (ISBN 0-19-214128-7). Oxford U Pr.

Griffin, Jeff W. Study Guide for the Airline Transport Pilot's Written Exam. (Modern Aviation Ser.). (Illus.). 1979. 8.95 (ISBN 0-8306-9764-0); pap. 4.95 (ISBN 0-8306-2276-4, 2276). TAB Bks.

Griffin, Jocelyn. Battle With Desire. (Superromances). 384p. 1983. pap. 2.95 (ISBN 0-373-70069-5, Pub. by Worldwide). Harlequin Bks.

Griffin, John, jt. auth. see Kostenuk, Samuel.

Griffin, John H. Black Like Me. (RL 8). pap. 2.25 (ISBN 0-451-09703-3, E9703, Sig). NAL.

--The Hermitage Journals. LC 82-45833. (Illus.). 240p. 1983. pap. 6.95 (ISBN 0-385-18470-0, Im). Doubleday.

--A Hidden Wholeness: The Visual World of Thomas Merton. LC 72-120827. (Illus.). 1977. 14.95 (ISBN 0-910220-90-5). Berg.

Griffin, John R. Binocular Anomalies: Procedures foe Vision Therapy. 2nd ed. LC 82-61252. 1982. 48.00 (ISBN 0-686-43308-4). Prof Press.

--The Oxford Movement: A Revision. 104p. 1980. pap. 2.50 o.p. (ISBN 0-686-74211-7). Christendom Pubns.

Griffin, Jonathan, tr. see De Sena, Jorge.

Griffin, Jonathan, tr. see Giono, Jean.

Griffin, Judith B. The Magic Mirrors. (Illus.). (gr. 2-6). 1971. PLB 3.99 o.p. (ISBN 0-698-30225-7, Coward). Putnam Pub Group.

--Nat Turner. (Illus.). (gr. 7 up). 1970. PLB 3.99 o.p. (ISBN 0-698-30249-4, Coward). Putnam Pub Group.

--Phoebe & the General. (Illus.). (gr. 2-6). 1977. 7.95 o.p. (ISBN 0-698-20377-1, Coward). Putnam Pub Group.

Griffin, Keith & Kahn, Azizur R., eds. Growth & Inequality in Pakistan. LC 70-190776. 278p. 1972. 25.00 (ISBN 0-312-35175-5). St Martin.

Griffin, Keith, jt. ed. see Robinson, E. A.

Griffin, Marvin A., et al. Computer Science Using BASIC. 1978. pap. text ed. 12.95 (ISBN 0-8403-1965-7, 40196502). Kendall-Hunt.

Griffin, Merv & Barsocchini, Peter. Merv. 1980. 11.95 o.p. (ISBN 0-671-22764-5). S&S.

Griffin, Michael M. Motorcycles: From the Inside Out (& How to Keep Them Right Side up) (Illus.). 1978. ref. ed. 16.95 (ISBN 0-13-604041-1); pap. text ed. 9.95 (ISBN 0-13-604033-0). P-H.

Griffin, N. B., ed. see Dummer, Geoffrey W.

Griffin, P. Bion, jt. ed. see Tuggle, H. David.

Griffin, Rick. Rick Griffin. (Paper Tiger Ser.). (Illus.). 96p. 1980. pap. 6.98 (ISBN 0-399-50496-6, Perige). Putnam Pub Group.

Griffin, Ricky W. Task Design: An Integrative Approach. (The Scott, Foresman Series in Management & Organizations). 1982. pap. text ed. 12.50x (ISBN 0-673-16544-2). Scott F.

Griffin, Robert. Clement Marot & the Inflections of Poetic Voice. LC 73-84394. 1976. 32.50x (ISBN 0-520-02586-5). U of Cal Pr.

--Ludovico Ariosto. (World Authors Ser.). 1974. lib. bdg. 15.95 o.p. (ISBN 0-8057-2063-4, Twayne). G K Hall.

Griffin, Sue, jt. auth. see Shoden, Rebecca.

Griffin, Susan. Made from This Earth. 288p. 1983. write for info. (ISBN 0-06-015118-8, HarpT). Har-Row.

--Made from This Earth: An Anthology of Writings. LC 82-48229. 288p. 1983. pap. 6.68i (ISBN 0-06-090995-1, CN 995, CN). Har-Row.

--Pornography & Silence: Culture's Revolt Against Nature. LC 80-8206. 320p. 1982. 13.41i (ISBN 0-06-011647-1, CN-915, HarpT); pap. 5.72i (ISBN 0-06-090915-3). Har-Row.

--Woman & Nature: The Roaring Inside Her. LC 77-11812. 1979. pap. 5.95i (ISBN 0-06-090744-4, CN 744, CN). Har-Row.

Griffin, Suzanne. Follow Me to San Francisco. (Illus.). 128p. (Orig.). (gr. 9-12). 1981. pap. text ed. 5.25 (ISBN 0-582-79794-2); tchr's manual 3.25x (ISBN 0-582-79795-0); video cassette-Betamax 395.00x (ISBN 0-582-79792-6); video cassette-Sony u-matic 410.00 (ISBN 0-582-79793-4); video cassette-VHS 395.00 (ISBN 0-582-79791-8). Longman.

Griffin, Suzanne M. & Dennis, John. Reflections: A Reader for Intermediate Level ESL Students. LC 78-26469. 1979. pap. text ed. 7.95 (ISBN 0-88377-129-2). Newbury Hse.

Griffin, Ted. Namu: Quest for the Killer Whale. 1982. 14.95 (ISBN 0-943482-00-3). Gryphon West Pubs.

Griffin, Thomas. A Practical Guide for Beginning Painters. (Art & Design Ser.). (Illus.). 184p. 1981. 19.95 (ISBN 0-13-689513-1, Spec); pap. 11.95 (ISBN 0-13-689505-0). P-H.

Griffin, W. E. The Majors. (Brotherhood of War Ser.: No. 3). 384p. 1983. pap. 3.50 (ISBN 0-515-05645-6). Jove Pubns.

Griffin, William, ed. Teaching Effective Writing in All Disciplines. LC 81-48585. 1982. 7.95x (ISBN 0-87589-926-9, TL-12). Jossey-Bass.

Griffin, William D. A Portrait of the Irish in America. (Illus.). 272p. 1982. pap. 14.95 (ISBN 0-686-83722-3, ScribT). Scribner.

Griffin, William D., ed. & compiled by. Ireland 6000 B.C.-1972: A Chronology & Fact Book. LC 73-12694. (World Chronology Ser.). 154p. 1973. lib. bdg. 8.50x (ISBN 0-379-16302-0). Oceana.

--The Irish in America 550-1972: Chronology & Factbook. LC 73-3405. (Ethnic Chronology Ser.: No. 10). 154p. 1973. 8.50 (ISBN 0-379-00501-8). Oceana.

Griffin, William R. Instructors Guide to Comprehensive Custodial Training Programs. 1977. tchr's. ed 65.00 (ISBN 0-9601054-2-5). Cleaning Consul.

--Supervisors' Guide to Successful Training. (Illus.). 1977. pap. text ed. 24.00 (ISBN 0-9601054-3-3). Cleaning Consul.

Griffith. Forward Into Battle: Fighting Tactics from Waterloo to Vietnam. 1982. 20.00 (ISBN 0-907319-01-7). Hippocrene Bks.

Griffith, Albert R., ed. Black Career Development. 1980. 2.50 (ISBN 0-686-36382-5); nonmembers 3.00 (ISBN 0-686-37298-0). Am Personnel.

Griffith, Beatrice. American Me. LC 72-14087. (Illus.). 341p. 1973. Repr. of 1948 ed. lib. bdg. 21.00x (ISBN 0-8371-6756-6, GRAN). Greenwood.

Griffith, Belver C., ed. Key Papers in Information Science. LC 79-24288. 439p. 1980. 25.00 (ISBN 0-914236-50-4, ASIS). Knowledge Indus.

Griffith, Bill. Time For Frankie Coolin. 1982. 13.50 (ISBN 0-394-52123-4). Random.

--Zippy: Nation of Pinheads. (Illus.). 96p. (Orig.). 1982. pap. 4.95 (ISBN 0-915904-71-3). And-or Pr.

Griffith, Carol F., ed. Christianity & Politics: Catholic & Protestant Perspectives. LC 81-19412. 124p. 1981. pap. 5.00 (ISBN 0-89633-050-8). Ethics & Public Policy.

Griffith, E. J., jt. auth. see Grayson, Martin.

Griffith, Edward J., jt. auth. see Grayson, Martin.

Griffith, Edward J., et al, eds. Environmental Phosphorus Handbook. LC 72-11574. 718p. 1973. 42.50 (ISBN 0-471-32779-4, Pub. by Wiley). Krieger.

Griffith, Ernest S. The American System of Government. 3rd ed. 1976. 29.95x (ISBN 0-416-70400-X); pap. 13.95x (ISBN 0-416-70410-7). Methuen Inc.

--History of American City Government. LC 72-3615. (Law, Politics & History Ser.). 1972. Repr. of 1938 ed. lib. bdg. 55.00 (ISBN 0-306-70526-5). Da Capo.

--A History of American City Government: The Conspicuous Failure, 1870-1900. LC 82-23872. 320p. 1983. lib. bdg. 26.50 (ISBN 0-8191-3001-X, Co-pub. by Natl Municipal League); pap. text ed. 14.50 (ISBN 0-8191-3002-8). U Pr of Amer.

--A History of American City Government: The Progressive Years & Their Aftermath, 1900-1920. 364p. 1983. lib. bdg. 27.50 (ISBN 0-8191-3003-6, Co-pub. by Natl Municipal League); pap. text ed. 15.50 (ISBN 0-8191-3004-4). U Pr of Amer.

Griffith, Ernest S. & Adrian, Charles R. A History of American City Government: The Formation of Traditions, 1775-1870. LC 82-23877. 240p. 1983. lib. bdg. 24.75 (ISBN 0-8191-2999-2, Co-pub. by Natl Municipal League); pap. text ed. 13.50 (ISBN 0-8191-3000-1). U Pr of Amer.

Griffith, F. L. & Thompson, Herbert, eds. The Leyden Papyrus: An Egyptian Magical Book. LC 73-90639. 224p. 1974. pap. 4.00 (ISBN 0-486-22994-7). Dover.

Griffith, Francis, jt. auth. see Mersand, Joseph.

Griffith, H. Winter. Drug Information for Patients. LC 76-58602. 1978. 39.00 o.p. (ISBN 0-7216-4275-6). Saunders.

--Instructions for Patients. LC 74-6684. (Illus.). 360p. 1975. pap. text ed. 44.00 o.p. (ISBN 0-7216-4281-0). Saunders.

Griffith, Helen V. Alex Remembers. LC 82-11913. (Illus.). 32p. (gr. k-3). 1983. 10.00 (ISBN 0-688-01800-9); PLB 9.55 (ISBN 0-688-01801-7). Greenwillow.

--Mine Will, Said John. LC 79-27886. (Illus.). 32p. (ps). 1980. 9.75 (ISBN 0-688-80267-2); PLB 9.36 (ISBN 0-688-84267-4). Greenwillow.

Griffith, J. D. Electron Microscopy in Biology, Vol. 2. 349p. 1982. text ed. 85.00x (ISBN 0-471-05526-3, Pub. by Wiley-Interscience). Wiley.

Griffith, J. Neal. Linton Park: American Primitive. 125p. (Orig.). 1982. pap. 5.00 (ISBN 0-935648-11-9). Halldin Pub.

Griffith, Jack D. Electron Microscopy in Biology, Vol. 1. (Electron Microscopy in Biology Ser.). 296p. 1981. 48.95x (ISBN 0-471-05525-5, Pub. by Wiley-Interscience). Wiley.

Griffith, Janet W. & Christensen, Paula J. Nursing Process: Application of Theories, Frameworks & Models. LC 81-14191. (Illus.). 301p. 1982. pap. text ed. 12.95 (ISBN 0-8016-1984-X). Mosby.

Griffith, Jerry & Miner, Lynn E. Phonetic Context Drill Book. 1979. pap. 15.95 (ISBN 0-13-665398-7). P-H.

Griffith, John L. & Weston, Edward G. Programmed Newswriting. (Basic Skills in Journalism Ser.). (Illus.). 1978. pap. text ed. 8.95 (ISBN 0-13-730630-X). P-H.

Griffith, John R. Measuring Hospital Performance. LC 78-793. xiii, 87p. (Orig.). 1978. pap. text ed. 10.00 (ISBN 0-914818-03-1, Inquiry Bk). Blue Cross Shield.

Griffith, John R., jt. auth. see Warner, D. Michael.

Griffith, John R., jt. ed. see Weeks, Lewis E.

Griffith, John R., et al. Cost Control in Hospitals. 450p. 1976. 17.50 (ISBN 0-686-68582-2, 14916). Healthcare Fin Man Assn.

Griffith, John S. Theory of Transition-Metal Ions. 1961. 89.50 (ISBN 0-521-05150-9). Cambridge U Pr.

Griffith, John W. & Frey, Charles H. Classics of Children's Literature. 1981. 17.95x (ISBN 0-02-347190-5). Macmillan.

Griffith, Kate, tr. see Camus, Albert.

Griffith, Kelly, Jr. Writing Essays about Literature: A Guide & Style Sheet. 195p. 1982. pap. text ed. 6.95 (ISBN 0-15-597860-8, HC). HarBraceJ.

Griffith, Liddon R. Mugging: You Can Protect Yourself. LC 78-4265. (Illus.). 1978. 11.95 (ISBN 0-13-604876-5, Spec); pap. 4.95 (ISBN 0-13-604868-4). P-H.

Griffith, Lucille, ed. see Royall, Anne N.

Griffith, Malcolm A., jt. auth. see Kartiganer, Donald M.

Griffith, Marlene, jt. auth. see Muscatine, Charles.

Griffith, Mary. Three Hundred Years Hence. (Science Fiction Ser). 144p. 1975. Repr. of 1950 ed. lib. bdg. 9.95 o.p. (ISBN 0-8398-2303-7, Gregg). G K Hall.

Griffith, Nancy S. & Person, Laura. Albert Schweitzer: An International Bibliography. 1981. lib. bdg. 45.00 (ISBN 0-8161-8531-X, Hall Reference). G K Hall.

Griffith, O. Hayes, jt. auth. see Jost, Patricia C.

Griffith, Paddy. A Book of Sandhurst Wargames. 64p. 1982. 22.95 (ISBN 0-698-11198-2, Coward). Putnam Pub Group.

Griffith, Richard. The World of Robert Flaherty. LC 72-166104. 1972. Repr. of 1953 ed. lib. bdg. 27.50 (ISBN 0-306-70296-7). Da Capo.

--World of Robert Flaherty. Repr. of 1953 ed. lib. bdg. 18.00x (ISBN 0-8371-3400-5, GRRF). Greenwood.

Griffith, Roger, jt. auth. see Rogers, Marc.

Griffith, Roger, ed. see Campbell, Stu.

Griffith, Roger, ed. see Gay, Larry.

Griffith, S. K., et al. Foreign Application & Export Potential for Wind Energy Systems. (Progress in Solar Energy Ser.: Suppl.). 250p. 1983. pap. 19.00 (ISBN 0-89553-130-5). Am Solar Energy.

Griffith, Samuel B. Chinese People's Liberation Army. (Illus.). 1967. 10.95 o.p. (ISBN 0-07-024794-3, P&RB). McGraw.

Griffith, Samuel B., tr. & intro. by see Sun Tzu.

Griffith, Samuel B., II. The Battle for Guadalcanal. LC 79-90112. (Great War Stories Ser.). (Illus.). 282p. 1979. Repr. of 1963 ed. 17.95 (ISBN 0-933852-04-5). Nautical & Aviation.

Griffith, Susan. Traveller's Survival Kit to the East: Turkey, Iraq, Iran, Afghanistan, India, Nepal, Sri Lanka, Burma. 2nd ed. 176p. 1982. pap. 9.95 (ISBN 0-907638-03-1, Pub. by Vacation Wk). Bradt Ent.

Griffith, Susan, ed. Summer Jobs in Britain, Nineteen Eighty-Three. 167p. (Orig.). 1983. pap. 7.95 (ISBN 0-907638-13-9, Pub. by Vacation-Work England). Writers Digest.

Griffith, William E. The Ostpolitik of the Federal Republic of Germany. (MIT Studies in Communism, Revisionism, & Revolution Ser.). 1978. 25.00x (ISBN 0-262-07072-3). MIT Pr.

--Sino-Soviet Relations, 1964-1965. 16.00x o.p. (ISBN 0-262-07027-8); pap. 5.95 o.s.i. (ISBN 0-262-57012-2). MIT Pr.

--The Superpowers & Regional Tensions: Russia, America, & Europe. LC 81-47649. 144p. 1981. 19.95x (ISBN 0-669-04702-3). Lexington Bks.

Griffith, William E., ed. Communism in Europe: Continuity, Change & the Sino-Soviet Dispute, 1 vol. Incl. Vol. 2. East Germany, Czechoslovakia, Sweden, Norway, Finland. pap. 5.95x o.p. (ISBN 0-262-57009-2). 1967. MIT Pr.

--The European Left: Italy, France, & Spain. LC 79-7711. 272p. 1979. 27.95x (ISBN 0-669-03199-2). Lexington Bks.

--The World & the Great-Power Triangles. LC 74-31219. 695p. 1975. text ed. 30.00x (ISBN 0-262-07064-2). MIT Pr.

Griffith, William E., ed. see Commission on Critical Choices.

Griffith, William E., ed. see Johnson, A. Ross.

Griffith, Wyn, tr. see Roberts, Kate.

Griffiths, A. Philips, ed. Knowledge & Belief. 1967. pap. 8.95x (ISBN 0-19-500328-4). Oxford U Pr.

Griffiths, Adrian, et al. An Annotated Bibliography of Health Economics: Western European Sources. 1980. 40.00 (ISBN 0-312-03874-7). St Martin.

Griffiths, Anna H. Latin. (Blue Book Ser). pap. 1.25 o.p. (ISBN 0-671-18122-X). Monarch Pr.

Griffiths, Antony. Prints & Printmaking: An Introduction to the History & Techniques. 152p. 1981. text ed. 16.00 (ISBN 0-394-32673-3). Knopf.

Griffiths, Bede. The Cosmic Revelation. 128p. 1983. pap. 6.95 (ISBN 0-87243-119-3). Templegate.

Griffiths, Brian, ed. Monetary Targets. Wood, Geoffrey E. write for info (ISBN 0-312-54421-9). St Martin.

Griffiths, D. Introduction to Electro-Dynamics. 1981. 29.95 (ISBN 0-13-481374-X). P-H.

Griffiths, D. F., jt. auth. see Mitchell, A. R.

Griffiths, David. Psychology & Medicine. (Psychology for Professional Groups Ser.). 320p. 1981. text ed. 25.00x (ISBN 0-333-31862-5, Pub. by Macmillan England); pap. text ed. 10.95x (ISBN 0-333-31877-3). Humanities.

Griffiths, G. C. Flies of the Nearctic Region Vol. VIII: Cyclorrhapha II (Schizophora. Calyptratae, Pt. 2 Anthomyiidae, No. 1. (Illus.). 160p. (Orig.). 1982. pap. text ed. 53.76 (ISBN 3-510-70004-X). Lubrecht & Cramer.

Griffiths, G. D. Abandoned. LC 74-18131. 96p. (gr. 4 up). 1975. 4.95 o.s.i. (ISBN 0-695-80537-1); lib. ed. 4.98 o.s.i. (ISBN 0-695-40537-3). Follett.

Griffiths, H. B. Surfaces. 2nd ed. 131p. 1981. 32.50 (ISBN 0-521-23570-7); pap. 12.95 (ISBN 0-521-29977-2). Cambridge U Pr.

Griffiths, H. B. & Howson, A. G. Mathematics: Society & Curricula. (Illus.). 400p. 1974. 49.50 o.p. (ISBN 0-521-20287-6); pap. 19.95x (ISBN 0-521-09892-0). Cambridge U Pr.

Griffiths, Helen. The Dancing Horses. LC 81-6762. (gr. 7 up). 1982. 9.95 (ISBN 0-8234-0437-4). Holiday.

--Grip, a Dog Story. LC 78-6819. (Illus.). 160p. (gr. 5-9). 1978. 9.95 (ISBN 0-8234-0335-1). Holiday.

--The Mysterious Appearance of Agnes. LC 74-21793. (Illus.). 160p. (gr. 7 up). 1975. 9.95 (ISBN 0-8234-0267-3). Holiday.

Griffiths, J. F. Climates of Africa. (World Survey of Climatology: Vol. 10). 1972. 149.00 (ISBN 0-444-40893-2). Elsevier.

Griffiths, J. N. The Golden Years of Bridge. (Master Bridge Ser.). (Illus.). 128p. (Orig.). 1981. pap. 9.50 (ISBN 0-575-02906-4, Pub. by Gollanz England). David & Charles.

Griffiths, John C. Afghanistan: Key to a Continent. 200p. 1981. 21.50 (ISBN 0-86531-080-7). Westview.

--Clinical Enzymology. LC 79-84461. (Illus.). 222p. 1979. 26.00x (ISBN 0-89352-030-6). Masson Pub.

Griffiths, John F. Climate & the Environment: The Atmospheric Impact on Man. LC 76-5801. (Westview Environmental Studies Ser.: Vol. 2). 1976. pap. text ed. 11.00 (ISBN 0-236-40022-3). Westview.

Griffiths, John F. & Driscoll, Dennis M. Survey of Climatology. 368p. 1982. text ed. 26.95 (ISBN 0-675-09994-3). Additional supplements may be obtained from publisher. Merrill.

Griffiths, Mary. Introduction to Human Physiology. 2nd ed. 1981. text ed. 26.95x (ISBN 0-02-347230-8). Macmillan.

Griffiths, Michael. Don't Soft Pedal God's Call. 1968. pap. 0.60 o.p. (ISBN 0-85363-063-1). OMF Bks.

--Get Your Church Involved in Missions. 1980. pap. 0.90 o.p. (ISBN 0-686-27991-3). OMF Bks.

--Get Your Church Involved in Missions. 1972. pap. 1.25 (ISBN 0-85363-084-4). OMF Bks.

Griffiths, P. Exterior Differential Systems & the Calculus of Variations. (Progress in Mathematics Ser.: Vol. 25). 349p. 1982. text ed. 30.00 (ISBN 3-7643-3103-8). Birkhauser.

Griffiths, P. J. & Thomas, J. D. Calculations in Advanced Physical Chemistry. 280p. 1983. pap. text ed. price not set (ISBN 0-7131-3483-6). E Arnold.

Griffiths, P. R. Transform Techniques in Chemistry. 412p. 1978. 99.95 (ISBN 0-471-25742-7, Pub. by Wiley Heyden). Wiley.

Griffiths, Patricia B. Tennessee Blue. 192p. 1981. 10.95 o.p. (ISBN 0-517-54187-4, C N Potter Bks); pap. 5.95 (ISBN 0-517-54430-X). Crown.

Griffiths, Paul. Cage. (Oxford Studies of Composers). (Illus.). 56p. (Orig.). 1981. pap. 9.95 (ISBN 0-19-315450-1). Oxford U Pr.

Griffiths, Paul, ed. Igor Stravinsky: The Rake's Progress. LC 81-17071. (Cambridge Opera Handbooks Ser.). (Illus.). 120p. 1982. 19.95 (ISBN 0-521-23746-7); pap. 7.95 (ISBN 0-521-28199-7). Cambridge U Pr.

Griffiths, Peter. Better Chess for Club Players. (Illus.). 117p. (Orig.). 1983. pap. 7.95 (ISBN 0-7158-0788-9, Pub. by EP Publishing England). Sterling.

Griffiths, R. F., jt. auth. see Britter, R. E.

Griffiths, Richard F. Dealing with Risk. 144p. 1982. pap. 13.95X (ISBN 0-470-27341-0). Halsted Pr.

--Dealing with Risk the Planning Management & Acceptability of Technological Risk. 144p. 1981. 19.95 o.p. (ISBN 0-470-27136-1). Halsted Pr.

Griffiths, Thomas M. San Juan Country. (Illus.). 1983. price not set (ISBN 0-87108-505-4). Pruett.

Griffiths, Trevor. Oil for England. 48p. 1982. pap. 4.95 (ISBN 0-571-11977-8). Faber & Faber.

Grifith, Helen V. Alex & the Cat. (gr. 1-5). 1982. 6.50 (ISBN 0-688-00420-2); PLB 5.71 (ISBN 0-688-00421-0). Greenwillow.

Grifone, J., jt. ed. see Crumeyrolle, A.

Grigarick, A. A. & Stange, L. A. The Pollen-Collecting Bees of the Anthidiini of California (Hymenoptera: Megachilidae) (Bulletin of the California Insect Survey: Vol. 9). 1968. pap. 10.50x (ISBN 0-520-09034-9). U of Cal Pr.

Grigg, A. E. Town of Trains: Bletchley & the Oxbridge Line. 1981. 39.50x o.p. (ISBN 0-86023-115-1, Pub. by Barracuda England). State Mutual Bk.

Grigg, Carolyn D., compiled by. Music Translation Dictionary: An English, Czech, Danish, Dutch, French, German, Hungarian, Italian, Polish, Portuguese, Russian, Spanish, Swedish Vocabulary of Music. LC 78-60526. 1978. lib. bdg. 35.00 (ISBN 0-313-20559-0, GMT/). Greenwood.

Grigg, D. B. Population Growth & Agrarian Change. LC 79-4237. (Cambridge Geographical Studies: No. 13). 368p. 1981. 52.50 (ISBN 0-521-22760-7); pap. 18.95 (ISBN 0-521-29635-8). Cambridge U Pr.

Grigg, David. Harsh Lands: A Study in Agricultural Development. LC 73-98070. (Focal Problems in Geography Ser.). 300p. 1970. pap. 12.95 o.p. (ISBN 0-312-36365-6). St Martin.

Grigg, John. Lloyd George: The People's Champion, 1902-1911. LC 77-91762. 1979. 37.50x (ISBN 0-520-03634-4). U of Cal Pr.

Griggs, Donald L. Twenty New Ways of Teaching the Bible. (Griggs Educational Resources Ser.). 1979. pap. 5.95 (ISBN 0-687-42740-1). Abingdon.

Griggs, Earl L., ed. see Christophe, Henri.

Griggs, M. J., ed. Selections from the Ars Amatoria. LC 74-139865. 1971. text ed. 8.95 (ISBN 0-312-04970-6). St Martin.

Grigorenko. The Grigorenko Papers: Writings by General P. G. Grigorenko & Documents on His Case. LC 76-5912. (Illus.). 194p. 1976. 25.00 o.p. (ISBN 0-89158-603-2). Westview.

Grigorenko, Petro. Memoirs. (Illus.). 1983. 19.95 (ISBN 0-393-01570-X). Norton.

Grigorieff, W. W., ed. Abundant Nuclear Energy: Proceedings. LC 71-600642. (AEC Symposium Ser.). 352p. 1969. pap. 16.75 (ISBN 0-87079-130-3, CONF-680810); microfiche 4.50 (ISBN 0-87079-131-1, CONF-680810). DOE.

Grigsby, Hugh B. History of the Virginia Convention of 1788, 2 Vols. LC 70-75319. (American History, Politics & Law Ser). 1969. Repr. of 1890 ed. Set. lib. bdg. 85.00 (ISBN 0-306-71280-6). Da Capo.

--Virginia Convention of 1776. LC 75-75320. (American History, Politics & Law Ser). 1969. Repr. of 1855 ed. lib. bdg. 29.50 (ISBN 0-306-71281-4). Da Capo.

--Virginia Convention of 1829-1830. LC 79-75321. (American History, Politics & Law Ser). 1969. Repr. of 1854 ed. lib. bdg. 25.00 (ISBN 0-306-71282-2). Da Capo.

Grigson. Art of Charcuterie. 17.95x o.p. (ISBN 0-911202-00-5). Radio City.

--The Gambit Book of Love Poems. 1983. 10.95 (ISBN 0-87645-088-5); pap. 6.95 (ISBN 0-87645-115-6). Gambit.

--The Gambit Book of Popular Verse. 1971. 10.95 o.s.i. (ISBN 0-87645-052-4); pap. 6.95 (ISBN 0-87645-114-8). Gambit.

Grigson, Geoffrey. Blessings, Kicks & Curses. 256p. 1983. 17.00 (ISBN 0-8052-8120-7, Pub. by Allison & Busby England). Schocken.

--Collected Poems, 1963-1980. 256p. 1983. 17.00 (ISBN 0-8052-8121-5, Pub. by Allison & Busby England). Schocken.

--The Private Art: A Poetry Notebook. 256p. 1983. 9.95 (ISBN 0-8052-8125-8, Pub. by Allison & Busby England). Schocken.

--Rainbows, Fleas, & Flowers: A Nature Anthology. 280p. 1983. 12.95 (ISBN 0-8149-0754-7). Vanguard.

Grigson, Geoffrey, ed. Country Poems. (Pocket Poet Ser.). 1959. pap. 1.25 (ISBN 0-8023-9046-3). Dufour.

--The Faber Book of Poems & Places. 387p. 1983. pap. 7.95 (ISBN 0-571-13008-9). Faber & Faber.

Grigson, Jane. Mushroom Feast. 1983. pap. 5.95 (ISBN 0-14-046273-2). Penguin.

Grigull, H., ed. Properties of Water & Steam in SI-Units. 3rd, rev. ed. (Illus.). 194p. 1982. 32.50 (ISBN 0-387-09601-9). Springer-Verlag.

Grigull, U., ed. see Seventh International Heat Transfer Conference, Munich, 1982.

Grijalva, Josue, tr. see Sisemore, J. T.

Grile, George, Jr. Surgery. 1980. pap. 4.95 o.s.i. (ISBN 0-440-57835-3, Delta). Dell.

Griliches, A. & Intriligator, M. D., eds. Handbook of Econometrics, 3 Vols. 1200p. 1983. Set. 198.00 (ISBN 0-444-86188-2, North Holland); 65.00 ea. Vol. 1 (ISBN 0-444-86185-8). Vol. 2 (ISBN 0-444-86186-6). Vol. 3 (ISBN 0-444-86187-4). Elsevier.

Griliches, Zvi, ed. see Schmookler, Jacob.

Griliches, Zvi, et al, eds. Income Distribution & Economic Inequality. 335p. 1978. 49.95 o.p. (ISBN 0-470-26331-8). Halsted Pr.

Grill & Brown. ASBO, the First 50 Years: The Building of the School Business Management Profession. (Research Bulletin: No. 20). pap. 0.69 (ISBN 0-685-57188-2). Assn Sch Busn.

Grill, Johnpeter H. The Nazi Movement in Baden, 1920-1945. LC 82-13383. xvii, 720p. 1983. 32.00x (ISBN 0-8078-1472-5). U of NC Pr.

Grill, Tom & Scanlon, Mark. The Art of Scenic Photography: Technical & Asthetic Guidelines for the Creative Photographer. (Illus.). 144p. 1982. 19.95 (ISBN 0-8174-3538-7, Amphoto). Watson-Guptill.

--The Essential Darkroom Book: A Complete Guide to Black & White Processing. (Illus.). 176p. 1983. pap. 14.95 (ISBN 0-8174-3838-6, Amphoto). Watson-Guptill.

--Photographic Composition: Guidelines for Total Image Control Through Effective Design. 144p. 1983. 22.50 (ISBN 0-8174-5419-5, Amphoto). Watson-Guptill.

--Photography: Turning Pro. (Illus.). 176p. 1982. 17.95 (ISBN 0-8174-5517-5, Amphoto). Watson-Guptill.

--Twenty-Five Projects to Improve Your Photography. (Illus.). 168p. 1981. 19.95 (ISBN 0-8174-6298-8, Amphoto); pap. 12.95 (ISBN 0-8174-6299-6). Watson-Guptill.

Grill, Tom, jt. auth. see Scanlon, Mark.

Grilley, Kate, jt. ed. see Vanderheiden, Gregg C.

Grilliot. Introduction to Law & the Legal System. 3d ed. 1983. text ed. 23.95 (ISBN 0-686-84528-5, BS13); instr's manual avail.; study guide 7.95 (ISBN 0-686-84529-3, BS15). HM.

Grilliot, Harold J. Introduction to Law & the Legal System. 2nd ed. LC 78-69579. (Illus.). 1979. text ed. 23.50 (ISBN 0-395-26866-4); instr's. manual 1.00 (ISBN 0-395-26865-6). HM.

--Introduction to Law & the Legal System. 3rd ed. 672p. 1983. text ed. 24.95 (ISBN 0-395-32701-6); write for info. supplementary materials. HM.

Grillo, Jean, jt. auth. see Picon, Molly.

Grillo, John P. & Robertson, J. D. Color Computer Applications. 256p. 1983. pap. text ed. 10.95 (ISBN 0-471-86922-8). Wiley.

--Data & File Management for the IBM Personal Computer. (Microcomputer Power Ser.). 240p. 1983. pap. write for info. (ISBN 0-697-09987-3); diskette avail. (ISBN 0-697-09988-1). Wm C Brown.

--Introduction to Graphics for the IBM Personal Computer. (Microcomputer Power Ser.). 165p. 1983. pap. write for info. (ISBN 0-697-09989-X); diskette avail. (ISBN 0-697-09990-3). Wm C Brown.

--More Subroutine Sandwich. 224p. 1983. pap. text ed. 12.95 (ISBN 0-471-86921-X). Wiley.

--Subroutine Sandwich. 224p. 1983. pap. text ed. 12.95 (ISBN 0-471-86920-1). Wiley.

--Users Guide with Applications for the IBM Personal Computer. (Microcomputer Power Ser.). 330p. 1983. pap. write for info. (ISBN 0-697-09985-7); diskette avail. (ISBN 0-697-09986-5). Wm C Brown.

Grillo, R. D. African Railwaymen. LC 73-79302. (African Studies: No. 10). (Illus.). 228p. 1973. 27.95 (ISBN 0-521-20276-0). Cambridge U Pr.

Grillo, Salvatore. The Gospel According to Barabbas. Cavoto, Nino, tr. from Italian. Orig. Title: Vangelo Secondo Barabba. 294p. (Orig.). 1982. pap. 4.95 (ISBN 0-89944-041-X, P 041-X). D Bosco Multimedia.

Grillo, Virgil. Charles Dickens' Sketches by Boz: End in the Beginning. LC 73-89257. (Illus.). 1974. 13.95x (ISBN 0-87081-054-5). Colo Assoc.

Grillos, Steve J. Ferns & Fern Allies of California. (California Natural History Guides: No. 16). (Illus., Rita Whittmore). 1966. 14.95x o.p. (ISBN 0-520-03091-5); pap. 2.65 (ISBN 0-520-00519-8). U of Cal Pr.

Grillot De Givry, Emile. Illustrated Anthology of Sorcery, Magic & Alchemy. 1973. Repr. 34.00 o.p. (ISBN 0-685-70658-3). Gale.

Grillparzer, F. Traum Ein Leben. Yates, W. E., ed. 1968. text ed. 7.95x (ISBN 0-521-05154-1). Cambridge U Pr.

Grills, Norma J. & Bosscher, Marcia V. Manual of Nutrition & Diet Therapy. 10th ed. 1981. pap. text ed. 21.95x (ISBN 0-02-347280-4). Macmillan.

Grim, Patrick. Philosophy of Science & the Occult. LC 81-13552. 320p. 1982. 30.50x (ISBN 0-87395-572-2); pap. 9.95x (ISBN 0-87395-573-0). State U NY Pr.

Grim, Ralph E. Clay Mineralogy. 2nd ed. LC 67-24951. (International Earth & Planetary Sciences Ser). (Illus.). 1968. text ed. 55.00 (ISBN 0-07-024836-2, C). McGraw.

Grim, Ronald E., ed. Historical Geography of the United States & Canada: A Guide to Information Sources. (Geography & Travel Information Guide Ser.: Vol. 5). 350p. 1982. 42.00x (ISBN 0-8103-1471-1). Gale.

Grimal, Pierre. Roman Cities: 'Les villes romaines". Woloch, G. Michael, ed. (Illus.). 320p. 1983. text ed. 30.00 (ISBN 0-299-08930-4); pap. 12.50 (ISBN 0-299-08934-7). U of Wis Pr.

Grimaldi, Alfonsina A. The Universal Humanity of Giambattista Vico. 1958. 12.50x (ISBN 0-913298-62-X). S F Vanni.

Grimaldi, Paul L. Medicaid Reimbursement of Nursing-Home Care. 1982. 15.95 (ISBN 0-8447-3456-X); pap. 7.95 (ISBN 0-8447-3457-8). Am Enterprise.

Grime, Philip N., jt. ed. see Lipke, William C.

Grimes, Alan P. Democracy & the Amendments to the Constitution. LC 78-4342. (Illus.). 1978. 22.95x (ISBN 0-669-02344-2). Lexington Bks.

Grimes, Barbara F. Ethnologue. 416p. 1978. pap. 9.60x (ISBN 0-88312-909-4); microfiche 4.50x (ISBN 0-88312-597-8). Summer Inst Ling.

Grimes, David, jt. auth. see Withington, Amelia.

Grimes, Dennis & Kelly, Brian. The Personal Computer Buyers Guide. 350p. (Orig.). 1983. 14.95 (ISBN 0-88410-917-8). Ballinger Pub.

Grimes, John S. Thompson on Real Property, 24 vols. Set. 400.00 (ISBN 0-672-83972-5, Bobbs-Merrill Law); 1981 cum. suppl. 100.00 (ISBN 0-672-84139-8). Michie-Bobbs.

Grimes, Joseph, jt. auth. see Liccardi, Millicent.

Grimes, Joseph E. Network Grammars. (SIL Linguistic & Related Fields Ser: No. 45). 198p. 1975. 8.50x (ISBN 0-88312-055-0); microfiche 3.00x (ISBN 0-88312-455-6). Summer Inst Ling.

--Papers on Discourse. (Publications in Linguistics & Related Fields Ser: No. 51). 1978. pap. 13.80x (ISBN 0-88312-061-5); microfiche 4.50x (ISBN 0-88312-461-0). Summer Inst Ling.

--Phonological Analysis. 187p. 1969. pap. 3.00 o.p. (ISBN 0-88312-903-5); microfiche 2.25 (ISBN 0-88312-360-6). Summer Inst Ling.

Grimes, Judith A. & Rushforth, S. R. Diatoms of Recent Bottom Sediments of Utah Lake, Utah, USA. (Bibliotheca Phycologica Ser.: No. 55). (Illus.). 180p. 1982. text ed. 24.00x (ISBN 3-7682-1310-2). Lubrecht & Cramer.

Grimes, Larry M. El Tabu Linguistico en Mexico: El Lenguaje erotico de los mexicanos. LC 78-52419. 1978. lib. bdg. 10.95x (ISBN 0-916950-10-7); pap. 7.95x (ISBN 0-916950-09-3). Bilingual Pr.

Grimes, Martha. The Anodyne Necklace. 252p. 1983. 13.45i (ISBN 0-316-32882-0). Little.

Grimes, Ronald L. Beginnings in Ritual Studies. LC 81-40521. 312p. (Orig.). 1982. lib. bdg. 25.25 (ISBN 0-8191-2210-6); pap. text ed. 13.25 (ISBN 0-8191-2211-4). U Pr of Amer.

Grimke, Archibald H. William Lloyd Garrison, the Abolitionist. LC 75-92746. Repr. of 1891 ed. 15.00x o.p. (ISBN 0-8371-2190-6). Greenwood.

Grimke, Thomas S. Address on the Truth, Dignity, Power & Beauty of the Principles of Peace, & on the Unchristian Character & Influence of War & the Warrior. LC 72-137542. (Peace Movement in America Ser). 56p. 1972. Repr. of 1832 ed. lib. bdg. 9.75x (ISBN 0-89198-070-9). Ozer.

Grimm Brothers. Animal Band. (gr. 2-4). 1967. 4.50 o.p. (ISBN 0-685-20560-6). Transatlantic.

--The Best of Grimm's Fairy Tales. LC 79-63439. (Illus.). (gr. k-3). 1980. PLB 10.95 (ISBN 0-88332-122-X). Larousse.

--German Folk Tales. Magoun, Francis P., Jr. & Krappe, Alexander H., trs. LC 59-5095. (Arcturus Books Paperbacks). 682p. (gr. 5 up). 1969. pap. 13.95 (ISBN 0-8093-0356-6). S Ill U Pr.

--Grimms' Fairy Tales. (Nancy Drew's Favorite Classics). (Illus.). (gr. 6-9). 1978. 2.95 (ISBN 0-448-14942-7, G&D). Putnam Pub Group.

--Grimms' Fairy Tales. (Illus.). (gr. 4-9). pap. 4.95 (ISBN 0-448-11009-1, G&D); companion lib. ed. 2.95 (ISBN 0-448-05460-4); deluxe ed. 8.95 (ISBN 0-448-06009-4). Putnam Pub Group.

--Grimms' Fairy Tales. Morel, Eve, ed. (Grow-up Books Ser.). (Illus.). (gr. k-3). 1962. 1.95 (ISBN 0-448-02251-6, G&D). Putnam Pub Group.

--Hansel & Gretel. Crawford, Elizabeth D., tr. from Ger. LC 79-989. (Illus.). 25p. (gr. k-3). 1980. 9.75 (ISBN 0-688-22198-X); PLB 9.36 (ISBN 0-688-32198-4). Morrow.

Grimm, Brothers. Hansel & Gretel. 1982. 9.90 (ISBN 0-531-04062-3). Watts.

Grimm Brothers. Poor Woodcutter & the Dove. LC 79-125037. (Illus.). (ps-3). 1970. 5.95 o.s.i. (ISBN 0-440-06991-2, Sey Lawr); PLB 5.47 o.s.i. (ISBN 0-440-06992-0, Sey Lawr). Delacorte.

--The Table, the Donkey & the Stick. (Illus.). (ps-3). 1976. 7.95 (ISBN 0-07-022700-4, GB); PLB 8.95 (ISBN 0-07-022701-2). McGraw.

Grimm Brothers & Pincus, Harriet. Little Red Riding Hood. LC 68-11505. (Illus.). 32p. (ps-3). 1973. pap. 1.25 (ISBN 0-15-652850-9, AVB75, VoyB). HarBraceJ.

Grimm, Brothers see Brothers Grimm.

Grimm Brothers, ed. King Thrushbeard. LC 74-123890. (Illus.). (gr. k-3). 1970. 5.95 (ISBN 0-15-242940-9, HJ). HarBraceJ.

--Seven Ravens. LC 63-2506. (Illus.). (gr. k-3). 1963. 6.95 (ISBN 0-15-272920-8, HJ). HarBraceJ.

Grimm Brothers & Ayer, Jacqueline, eds. Rumpelstiltskin. LC 67-20165. (gr. k-3). 7.50 (ISBN 0-15-269525-7, HJ). HarBraceJ.

Grimm, George. Buddhist Wisdom: The Mystery of the Self. 2nd, rev. ed. Keller-Grimm, M., ed. Aikins, Carrol, tr. from Ger. 1982. 11.50 (ISBN 0-89684-041-7, Pub. by Motilal Banarsidass India). Orient Bk Dist.

Grimm, Harold J. The Reformation Era: 1500-1650. 2nd ed. (Illus.). 700p. 1973. text ed. 25.95x (ISBN 0-02-347270-7, 34727). Macmillan.

Grimm, Jacob & Grimm, Wilhelm. Grimm: Selected Tales. Luke, David, tr. 1983. pap. 3.95 (ISBN 0-14-044401-7). Penguin.

--The Juniper Tree & Other Tales from Grimm, 2 vols. Lore, Segal & Jarrell, Randall, trs. LC 73-82698. 332p. (gr. 4 up). 1973. boxed set 20.00 (ISBN 0-374-18057-1); pap. 10.95 (ISBN 0-374-51358-9). FS&G.

Grimm, Jakob L. Grimm's Household Tales, 2 Vols. Hunt, Margaret, tr. LC 68-31090. 1968. Repr. of 1884 ed. 58.00 o.p. (ISBN 0-8103-3463-1). Gale.

Grimm, Michele, jt. auth. see Grimm, Tom.

Grimm, Reinhold, ed. The Birth of Tragedy & Related Writings, Friedrich Nietzsche. (The German Library: Vol. 44). 320p. 1982. 17.50 (ISBN 0-8264-0278-X); pap. 8.95 (ISBN 0-8264-0279-8). Continuum.

Grimm, Reinhold, et al, eds. From Kafka & Dada to Brecht & Beyond. 96p. 1982. text ed. 17.00 (ISBN 0-299-97014-0). U of Wis Pr.

Grimm, Susan J. How to Write Computer Manuals for Users. (Computer Technology Ser.). (Illus.). 192p. 1982. 18.95 (ISBN 0-534-97941-6). Lifetime Learn.

Grimm, Tom & Grimm, Michele. All About Thirty-Five mm Photography. (Illus.). 1979. pap. 8.95 (ISBN 0-02-012380-9, Collier). Macmillan.

--The Good Guide for Bad Photographers: How to Avoid Mistakes & Take Better Pictures. (Illus.). 1982. pap. 7.95 (ISBN 0-452-25327-6, Z5327, Plume). NAL.

Grimm, Tona. Basic Book of Photography. rev. ed. (RL 9). 1979. pap. 7.95 (ISBN 0-452-25216-4, Z5216, Plume). NAL.

Grimm, Werner, tr. see Althoff, Karl F.

Grimm, Wilhelm, jt. auth. see Grimm, Jacob.

Grimm, William. Indian Harvests. (Illus.). 128p. (gr. 5 up). 1977. PLB 7.95 (ISBN 0-07-024840-0, GB). McGraw.

Grimm Brothers. Bremen Town Musicians. (Illus.). (gr. k-3). 1968. PLB 8.95 o.p. (ISBN 0-07-022705-5, GB). McGraw.

--King Grisly-Beard: A Tale from the Brothers Grimm. Taylor, Edgar, tr. LC 73-77911. (Illus.). (ps-3). 1973. 6.95 (ISBN 0-374-34134-6). FS&G.

--Rapunzel. LC 75-8847. 32p. (ps-3). 1975. 8.95i o.p. (ISBN 0-690-00979-8, TYC-J); PLB 9.89 (ISBN 0-690-00980-1). Har-Row.

--Rapunzel. Rogasky, Barbara, retold by. LC 81-6419. (Illus.). 32p. (ps-3). 1982. Reinforced bdg. 12.95 (ISBN 0-8234-0454-4). Holiday.

--The Sleeping Beauty. LC 78-64772. (Illus.). 32p. (gr. 1-9). 1979. 9.95 (ISBN 0-689-50131-5, McElderry Bk). Atheneum.

--Thorn Rose. LC 75-16835. (Illus.). 32p. (ps-3). 1977. 8.95 (ISBN 0-02-737270-7). Bradbury Pr.

Grimmelshausen, H. J. Von. Adventurous Simplicissimus. Goodrick, A. T., tr. LC 62-8406. (Illus.). xxxiv, 398p. 1962. pap. 7.95x (ISBN 0-8032-5077-0, BB 134, Bison). U of Nebr Pr.

Grimmett, Geoffrey & Stirzaker, David. Probability & Random Processes. (Illus.). 1982. 45.00x (ISBN 0-19-853184-2); pap. 19.95x (ISBN 0-19-853185-0). Oxford U Pr.

Grimmett, Jennifer, jt. auth. see Thomis, Malcolm.

Grimmond, Jo. The Common Welfare. 1979. 22.00 o.s.i. (ISBN 0-85117-159-1). Transatlantic.

Grimond, Jo. Memoirs. 316p. 1980. 27.50x (ISBN 0-686-81251-4). Holmes & Meier.

Grimond, Joseph. The Liberal Challenge. LC 75-2696. 317p. 1975. Repr. of 1963 ed. lib. bdg. 18.25x (ISBN 0-8371-8025-2, GRLC). Greenwood.

Grimshaw. Union Rule in the Schools: Big-City Politics in Transformation. LC 78-24631. (Politics of Education Ser.). (Illus.). 176p. 1979. 21.95x (ISBN 0-669-02769-3). Lexington Bks.

Grimshaw, Allen D., jt. auth. see Armer, Michael.

Grimshaw, Anne. The Horse: A Bibliography of British Books 1851-1976. (Illus.). 480p. 1982. write for info. (ISBN 0-85365-533-2, Pub. by Lib Assn England). Oryx Pr.

Grimshaw, James A., Jr., ed. Robert Penn Warren's Brother to Dragons: A Discussion. (Southern Literary Studies). 344p. 1983. text ed. 27.50X (ISBN 0-8071-1065-5). La State U Pr.

Grimshaw, Nigel see Allen, W. S.

Grimshaw, Patricia, jt. ed. see Grieve, Norma.

Grimsley, Bob. Management Accounting Systems & Records. 117p. 1982. text ed. 42.00x (ISBN 0-686-87211-8). Gower Pub Ltd.

Grimsley, Ronald. Jean-Jacques Rousseau. LC 82-24409. 192p. 1983. text ed. 27.50x (ISBN 0-389-20378-5). B&N Imports.

Grimstad, Kirsten, jt. ed. see Rennie, Susan.

Grimstad, William. Antizion: The Jewish & Zionist Question Through the Ages. 1982. lib. bdg. 69.95 (ISBN 0-686-97529-4). Revisionist Pr.

Grimstad, William, jt. auth. see Committee for Truth in History.

Grimsted, Patricia K. The Foreign Ministers of Alexander First: Political Attitudes & the Conduct of Russian Diplomacy, 1801-1825. LC 69-11615. (Illus.). 1969. 32.50x (ISBN 0-520-01387-5). U of Cal Pr.

Grimstone, A. V. Electron Microscope in Biology. 2nd ed. (Studies in Biology: No. 9). 72p. 1978. pap. text ed. 8.95 (ISBN 0-7131-2611-6). E Arnold.

Grimstone, A. V. & Skaer, R. J. A Guidebook to Microscopical Methods. LC 70-182027. (Illus.). 150p. 1972. 29.95 (ISBN 0-521-08445-8); pap. 9.95x (ISBN 0-521-09700-2). Cambridge U Pr.

Grimvall, G. The Electro-Phonon Interaction in Metals. (Selected Topics in Solid State Physics: Vol. 16). 1981. 58.50 (ISBN 0-444-86105-X). Elsevier.

Grimwade, Arthur G. London Goldsmiths Sixteen Ninety-Seven to Eighteen ThirtySeven: Their Marks & Lives from the Original Registers at Goldsmiths's Hall. rev. ed. (Illus.). 740p. 1983. 89.95 (ISBN 0-571-18065-5). Faber & Faber.

Grimwood-Jones, Diana, ed. Middle East & Islam: A Bibliographical Introduction. 2nd rev. & enl. ed. LC 72-85349. 429p. 1979. 57.50x o.p. (ISBN 3-85750-032-8). Intl Pubns Serv.

Grindal, Bruce T. & Warren, Dennis M. Essays in Humanistic Anthropology: Festschrift in Honor of Davis Bidney. LC 78-66121. (Orig.). 1979. pap. text ed. 15.25 (ISBN 0-8191-0682-8). U Pr of Amer.

Grindal, Richard. Death Stalk. 192p. 1983. 10.95 (ISBN 0-312-18805-6). St Martin.

Grinder, Robert E. Studies in Adolescence: A Book of Readings in Adolescent Development. 3rd ed. (Illus.). 576p. 1975. pap. text ed. 15.95x (ISBN 0-02-347300-2, 34730). Macmillan.

Grindlays Bank Economics Dept. see Blauvelt, Evan, et al.

Grindle, Juliet, ed. see Hardy, Thomas.

Grindle, Merilee S. Bureaucrats, Politicians, & Peasants in Mexico: A Case Study in Public Policy. LC 76-7759. 1977. 26.50x (ISBN 0-520-03238-1). U of Cal Pr.

Grindley, J. H. Principles of Electrical Transmission Lines in Power & Communication. 1967. 27.00 o.p. (ISBN 0-08-012111-X); pap. 13.25 o.p. (ISBN 0-08-012112-8). Pergamon.

Griner, Lynn A. Pathology of Zoo Animals: A Revised of Necropsies Conducted Over A Fourteen Year Period At The San Diego Zoo. LC 82-62698. (Illus.). 1983. 25.00 (ISBN 0-911461-11-6). Zoological Soc.

Gringhuis, Dirk, et al. Mackinac History, Vol. 2. (Illus.). 76p. (Orig.). 1982. pap. 5.00 (ISBN 0-911872-34-5). Mackinac Island.

Grinich, Victor. Introduction to Integrated Circuits. (Illus.). 672p. 1975. text ed. 37.50 (ISBN 0-07-024875-3, C); instructors' manual 25.00 (ISBN 0-07-024876-1). McGraw.

Grinims, Mark & Fischman, Walter. M.R.T. Music Response Test. LC 78-15488. (Illus.). 1979. 9.95 o.p. (ISBN 0-399-90011-X, Marek). Putnam Pub Group.

Grinnell, Alan & Barber, Albert A. Laboratory Experiments in Physiology. 9th ed. (Illus.). 200p. 1976. pap. 8.95 o.p. (ISBN 0-8016-2978-0). Mosby.

Grinnell, George B. The Fighting Cheyennes. LC 56-10392. (The Civilization of the American Indian Ser.: Vol. 44). (Illus.). 450p. 1983. pap. 14.95 (ISBN 0-8061-1839-3). U of Okla Pr.

--Two Great Scouts & Their Pawnee Battalion. LC 29-2718. (Illus.). vi, 299p. 1973. pap. 5.25 (ISBN 0-8032-5775-9, BB 564, Bison). U of Nebr Pr.

Grinnell, Joseph. Gold Hunting in Alaska. facsimile ed. (Shorey Historical Ser.). (Illus.). 96p. Repr. of 1901 ed. pap. 6.95 (ISBN 0-8466-0023-4, SJS23). Shorey.

Grinnell, Richard M., Jr. Social Work Research & Evaluation. LC 80-52448. 736p. 1981. text ed. 24.50 (ISBN 0-87581-261-9). Peacock Pubs.

Grinsell, L. V. The Ancient Burial-Mounds of England. LC 73-13037. (Illus.). 278p. 1975. Repr. of 1953 ed. lib. bdg. 20.00x (ISBN 0-8371-7101-6, GRAB). Greenwood.

Grinsell, Leslie & Rantz, Phillip. The Preparation of Archaeological Reports. 2nd ed. LC 74-82135. 1974. 26.00 (ISBN 0-312-63945-7). St Martin.

Grinsell, Leslie V. Folklore of Prehistoric Sites in Britain. LC 76-8624. (Illus.). 304p. 1976. 12.00 o.p. (ISBN 0-7153-7241-6). David & Charles.

Grinspoon, Lester & Bakalar, James B. Psychedelic Drugs Reconsidered. 1981. pap. 9.50 (ISBN 0-465-06451-5). Basic.

Grinspoon, Lester, ed. & intro. by. Psychiatry Update: The American Psychiatric Association Annual Review, Vol. II. (Illus.). 544p. 1983. text ed. 45.00x (ISBN 0-88048-007-6). Am Psychiatric.

Grinspoon, Lester & Bakalar, James B., eds. Psychedelic Reflections. 256p. 1983. 26.95 (ISBN 0-89885-129-7). Human Sci Pr.

Grinspoon, Lester, et al. Schizophrenia: Pharmacotherapy & Psychotherapy. LC 77-11667. 312p. 1977. lib. bdg. 17.50 (ISBN 0-88275-603-6). Krieger.

Grinstead, Wayne. Two Prayers: One Mile, One Miracle. (Home Mission Graded Ser.). (Illus.). 40p. (gr. 4-7). Date not set. pap. 2.00 (ISBN 0-937170-23-2). Home Mission.

Grinstein, Alexander. Freud's Rules of Dream Interpretation. 1983. write for info (ISBN 0-8236-2035-2). Intl Univs Pr.

Grioll, G. Mathematical Theory of Elastic Equilibrum. (Ergebnisse der Angewandten Mathematik: Vol. 7). 1962. pap. 34.00 (ISBN 0-387-03408-0). Springer-Verlag.

Gripe, Herald, tr. see Gripe, Maria.

Gripe, Maria. Elvis & His Secret. La Farge, Sheila, tr. from Swedish. LC 75-8000. (Illus.). 208p. 1976. 6.95 o.s.i. (ISBN 0-440-02282-7, Sey Lawr); PLB 6.46 o.s.i. (ISBN 0-440-02283-5). Delacorte.

--The Green Coat. La Farge, Sheila, tr. from Swedish. LC 76-47235. (gr. 7 up). 1977. 6.95 o.s.i. (ISBN 0-440-03232-6, Sey Lawr). Delacorte.

--In the Time of the Bells. La Farge, Sheila & Gripe, Herald, trs. from Swedish. LC 76-5594. (Illus.). (gr. 7 up). 1976. 6.95 o.s.i. (ISBN 0-440-04012-4, Sey Lawr); PLB 6.46 o.s.i. (ISBN 0-440-04014-0). Delacorte.

Grippando, Gloria M. Nursing Perspectives & Issues. 2nd ed. LC 82-71087. 512p. 1983. pap. text ed. 14.00 (ISBN 0-8273-2078-7). Delmar.

Griqull, U., ed. Selected Publications of Wilhelm Nusselt & Ernst Schmidt. LC 82-9199. 272p. 1982. pap. text ed. 10.00 (ISBN 0-89116-329-8). Hemisphere Pub.

Grisbrooke, W. Jardine. The Spiritual Counsels of Father John of Kronstadt. 228p. (Orig.). 1982. pap. 7.95 (ISBN 0-913836-92-3). St Vladimirs.

Grisby, Robert F. R. F. Grigsby's Sierra Madre Journal: 1864: An American Prospector's Adventures. Boudreau, Eugene H., ed. LC 76-43601. 1976. pap. 8.00 (ISBN 0-686-16316-8). Pleasant Hill.

Griscom, Hilda, jt. auth. see Rosenzweig, Norman.

Grise, Jeannette. Robert Benjamin & the Great Blue Dog Joke. LC 78-17006. (Illus.). (gr. 3-6). 1978. pap. over bds. 8.95 (ISBN 0-664-32637-4). Westminster.

Grisebach, A. H. Flora of the British West Indian Islands. 1963. Repr. of 1864 ed. 80.00 (ISBN 3-7682-7054-8). Lubrecht & Cramer.

Grisez, Germain. Christian Moral Principles. 1983. 15.00 (ISBN 0-8199-0861-4). Franciscan Herald.

Grisez, Germain & Shaw, Russell. Beyond the New Morality: The Responsibilities of Freedom. LC 73-17772. 240p. 1974. 3.25 (ISBN 0-268-00533-8); pap. 3.25x o.p. (ISBN 0-268-00534-6). U of Notre Dame Pr.

--A Grisez Reader for Beyond the New Morality. Casey, Joseph H., ed. LC 81-43481. 218p. (Orig.). 1982. lib. bdg. 23.00 (ISBN 0-8191-2243-2); pap. text ed. 10.75 (ISBN 0-8191-2244-0). U Pr of Amer.

Grisham, Roy A., Jr., ed. Encyclopedia of U. S. Government Benefits. 1024p. 1981. 14.95 (ISBN 0-89696-127-3, An Everest House Book). Dodd.

Grishman, Ralph. Assembly Language Programming for Control Data 6000 & Cyber Ser. (Illus.). 248p. 1981. 15.00x (ISBN 0-917448-04-9). Algorithmics.

--Assembly Language Programming for the Control Data Six Thousand Series & the Cyber Seventy Ser. (Illus.). 212p. 1974. pap. text ed. 9.50x o.p. (ISBN 0-917448-00-6). Algorithmics.

Grismer, Karl H. The Story of Fort Myers: The History of the Land of the Caloosahatchee & Southwest Florida. LC 82-80620. (Illus.). 360p. 1982. pap. 15.00 (ISBN 0-87208-226-1). Island Pr.

Grismer, Raymond L., compiled by. Bibliography of Lope De Vega, 2 vols. in 1. LC 65-90686. Repr. of 1965 ed. 18.00 o.p. (ISBN 0-527-36195-X). Kraus Repr.

Grissim, John. Pure Stoke. LC 82-47551. (Illus.). 176p. (Orig.). 1983. pap. 9.57i (ISBN 0-06-090972-2, CN 972, CN). Har-Row.

Grissom, Ken. Buckskind & Black Powder. (Illus.). 224p. 1983. 14.95 (ISBN 0-8329-0285-3, Pub. by Winchester Pr.). New Century.

Griswold, A. Whitney. Liberal Education & the Democratic Ideal & Other Essays. LC 76-43025. 1976. Repr. of 1962 ed. lib. bdg. 18.00x (ISBN 0-8371-8977-2, GRLE). Greenwood.

Griswold, Deirdre, jt. auth. see Marcy, Sam.

Griswold, Madge T., jt. auth. see Griswold, Ralph E.

Griswold, P. R., jt. auth. see Newell, John C.

Griswold, Ralph E. & Griswold, Madge T. The ICON Programming Language. (Illus.). 336p. 1983. pap. text ed. 18.95 (ISBN 0-13-449777-5). P-H.

--A Snobol Four Primer. (Illus.). 128p. 1973. pap. 14.95 (ISBN 0-13-815381-7). P-H.

Griswold, Ralph E., et al. Snobol Four Programming Language. 2nd ed. (Automatic Computation Ser). 1971. pap. 17.95 (ISBN 0-13-815373-6). P-H.

Griswold, Robert L. Family & Divorce in California, 1850-1890: Victorian Illusions & Everyday Realities. (American Social History Ser.). 320p. 1982. 34.50x (ISBN 0-87395-633-8); pap. 9.95x (ISBN 0-87395-634-6). State U NY Pr.

Griswold, Whit. Berkshire Trails for Walking & Ski Touring. LC 79-4901. (Illus.). 224p. 1978. pap. 7.95 (ISBN 0-914788-13-2). East Woods.

Grivart, De see Crawford, Williame & Kerstrat, Francoise.

Grivet, P. Electron Optics, 2 pts. 2nd ed. Incl. Pt. 1. Optics. pap. 14.50 o.p. (ISBN 0-08-016226-6); Pt. 2. Instruments. pap. 16.00 o.p. (ISBN 0-08-016228-2). 1972. Set. 67.00 o.s.i. (ISBN 0-08-016086-7). Pergamon.

Grizzard, Lewis. They Tore out My Heart & Stomped That Sucker Flat. LC 82-18119. 140p. 1982. 9.95 (ISBN 0-931948-38-X). Peachtree Pubs.

Groah, Linda. Operating Room Nursing. 1982. text ed. 20.95 (ISBN 0-8359-5248-7); instrs'. manual o.p. avail. (ISBN 0-8359-5249-5). Reston.

Groat, Dick & Dascenzo, Frank. Groat: I Hit & Ran. LC 78-65167. (Illus.). 1978. 8.95 (ISBN 0-87716-094-5, Pub. by Moore Pub Co). F Apple.

Grob, Bernard. Basic Electronics. 4th ed. (Illus.). (gr. 11-12). 1977. text ed. 24.95 (ISBN 0-07-024923-7, G); solutions manual 3.00 (ISBN 0-07-024926-1); Math Outline Review Problems 8.95 (ISBN 0-07-024924-5). McGraw.

--Basic Television. 4th ed. 1975. text ed. 26.95 (ISBN 0-07-024927-X, G). McGraw.

--Electronic Circuits & Applications. LC 81-14298. (Illus.). 576p. 1982. text ed. 24.95 (ISBN 0-07-024931-8). McGraw.

Grob, Bernard & Kiver, M. S. Applications of Electronics. 2nd ed. 1966. text ed. 26.95 (ISBN 0-07-024930-X, G). McGraw.

Grob, David, ed. Myasthenia Gravis, Vol. 274. (Annals of the New York Academy of Sciences). 682p. 1976. 43.00x (ISBN 0-89072-053-3). NY Acad Sci.

Grob, Fritz. Relativity of War & Peace. 1949. 42.50x o.p. (ISBN 0-685-69824-6). Elliots Bks.

Grob, Gerald N. & Billias, George A. Historical Interpretations, 3 vols. Incl. Vol. 1. From Puritanism to the First Party System. pap. text ed. 5.95 (ISBN 0-02-912900-1); Vol. 2. From Jacksonian Democracy to the Gilded Age. pap. text ed. 4.95 o.p. (ISBN 0-02-912910-9, 91291); Vol. 3. From Progressivism to the Cold War. pap. text ed. 5.95 (ISBN 0-02-912920-6, 91292). LC 67-12834. 1972. pap. text ed. 5.95 ea. Free Pr.

Grob, Paul & Brown, Nina W., eds. Readings in Education & Psychology. 333p. 1969. pap. text ed. 12.95x (ISBN 0-686-84056-9). Irvington.

Grob, R. L. & Kaiser, M. A. Environmental Problem Solving Using Gas & Liquid Chromatography. (Journal of Chromatography Lib.: Vol. 21). 1982. 54.00 (ISBN 0-444-42065-7). Elsevier.

Grob, Robert L., ed. Modern Practice of Gas Chromatography. LC 77-779. 654p. 1977. text ed. 51.00 (ISBN 0-471-01564-4, Pub. by Wiley-Interscience). Wiley.

Grobani, Anton, ed. Guide to Baseball Literature. LC 74-17223. 363p. 1975. 36.00x (ISBN 0-8103-0962-9). Gale.

--Guide to Football Literature. LC 75-1478. xvi, 319p. 1975. 32.00x (ISBN 0-8103-0964-5). Gale.

Grobler, N. J. Textbook of Clinical Anatomy, Vol. 1. 1977. 125.25 (ISBN 0-444-41581-5, North Holland); pap. 62.25 (ISBN 0-685-82198-6). Elsevier.

Grobman, Alex & Landes, Daniel, eds. Genocide: Critical Issues of the Holocaust. (Illus.). 450p. 1983. 19.95 (ISBN 0-940646-04-8, Co-Pub by Simon Wiesenthal). Rossel Bks.

Grobman, Hulda. Developmental Curriculum Projects: Decision Points & Processes. LC 70-132165. 1970. text ed. 12.00 (ISBN 0-87581-069-1). Peacock Pubs.

Grobstein, C. From Chance to Purpose: An Appraisal of External Human Fertilization. 1981. pap. 18.50 (ISBN 0-201-04585-0). A-W.

Groddeck, Marie. The Seven Training Sketches for the Painter by Rudolf Steiner. Fletcher, John, ed. Martin, Inge, tr. from Ger. 23p. 1982. pap. 1.95 (ISBN 0-88010-059-1, Pub. by Steinerbooks). Anthroposophic.

Grode, Susan A., ed. see Beverly Hills Bar Association & Barristers Committee for the Arts.

Grodecki, Louis. Gothic Architecture. (History of World Architecture Ser.). (Illus.). 220p. 1983. pap. 17.50 (ISBN 0-8478-0473-9). Rizzoli Intl.

Groden, Michael. James Joyce's Manuscripts: An Index. LC 78-64575. (Garland Reference Library of the Humanities). 190p. 1980. 25.00 o.s.i. (ISBN 0-8240-9540-5). Garland Pub.

Groden, Michael, ed. see Joyce, James.

Grodin, Joseph & Grodin, Sharon. High Sierra Hiking Guide to Silver Lake. 3rd ed. Winnett, Thomas, ed. (High Sierra Hiking Guide Ser.: No. 17). (Illus.). 96p. 1983. pap. 4.95 (ISBN 0-89997-027-3). Wilderness Pr.

Grodin, Joseph R., jt. ed. see Stern, James L.

Grodin, Joseph R., et al, eds. Collective Bargaining in Public Employment: Labor Relations & Social Problems: a Course Book, Unit 4. 3rd ed. Alleyne, Reginald H., Jr. 430p. 1979. text ed. 15.00 (ISBN 0-87179-310-5). BNA.

Grodin, Joseph R., et al see Labor Law Group.

Grodin, Sharon, jt. auth. see Grodin, Joseph.

Grodins, Fred S. & Yamashiro, Stanley M. Respiratory Function of the Lung & Its Control. (Illus.). 176p. 1978. text ed. 18.95 (ISBN 0-02-348190-0); pap. text ed. 14.95 (ISBN 0-686-71603-5). Macmillan.

Grodzins, Morton. The American System: A New View of Government in the United States. Elazar, Daniel J., ed. (Political Theory Ser.). 404p. 1983. 19.95 (ISBN 0-87855-916-7). Transaction Bks.

Grodzinsky, Stephen, jt. auth. see Kirwin, Gerald J.

Groebbels, F. Der Vogel Atmungs-und Nahrungswelt, Gesehlecht und Fortoflanzung. 1969. 88.00 (ISBN 3-7682-0241-0). Lubrecht & Cramer.

Groebner, David & Shannon, Patrick. Business Statistics: A Decision-Making Approach. (Illus.). 800p. 1981. text ed. 24.95 (ISBN 0-675-08083-5); student guide 7.95x (ISBN 0-675-08084-3). Additional supplements may be obtained from publisher. Merrill.

Groebner, David E., jt. auth. see Merz, C. Mike.

Groeg, Otto J., ed. Who's Who in Germany, 1980, 2 vols. 7th ed. LC 56-3621. 1500p. 1980. Set. 175.00x (ISBN 3-921220-28-9). Intl Pubns Serv.

Groeneveld, Judith, jt. auth. see Shain, Martin.

Groenewegen Frankfort, Mrs. H. & Ashmole, Bernard. Art of the Ancient World. (Janson Art History Ser). (Illus.). 512p. 1972. text ed. 27.95x (ISBN 0-13-047001-5). P-H.

Groenfeldt, John S. We Gather Together: The Church Worships God. (Orig.). 1971. pap. 1.65 o.p. (ISBN 0-8042-9060-1). John Knox.

Groening, W. A. The Modern Corporate Manager: Responsibility & Regulation. 1981. 25.95 (ISBN 0-07-024940-7). McGraw.

Groer, Maureen W. & Shekleton, Maureen E. Basic Pathophysiology: A Conceptual Approach. 2nd ed. (Illus.). 630p. 1982. pap. text ed. 19.95 (ISBN 0-8016-2023-6). Mosby.

Groeschel, Benedict J. Spiritual Passages. 176p. 1983. 12.95 (ISBN 0-8245-0497-6). Crossroad NY.

Groetsch, Charles W. Elements of Applicable Functional Analysis. (Pure & Applied Mathematics: Monographs & Textbooks: Vol. 55). (Illus.). 320p. 1980. 28.75 (ISBN 0-8247-6986-4). Dekker.

Grofman, Bernard, et al. Reapportionment Policy. (Orig.). 1981. pap. 6.00 (ISBN 0-918592-45-3). Policy Studies.

--Representation & Redistricting Issues. LC 81-47783. (A Policy Studies Organization Bk.). 304p. 1982. 28.95x (ISBN 0-669-04718-X). Lexington Bks.

Grogan, Kaye. The Teacher's Pet. 1982. 6.75 (ISBN 0-8062-1966-1). Carlton.

Grogan, Raymond G., et al, eds. Annual Review of Phytopathology, Vol. 20. LC 63-8847. (Illus.). 1982. text ed. 22.00 (ISBN 0-8243-1320-8). Annual Reviews.

Groger, Molly. Eating Awareness Training. 224p. 1983. 14.95 (ISBN 0-671-46887-1). Summit Bks.

Grogono, Peter. Mouse: A Language for Microcomputers. (Illus.). 200p. 1983. text ed. 17.50 (ISBN 0-89433-201-5). Petrocelli.

--Programming in Pascal. rev. ed. LC 79-24640. 384p. 1980. pap. text ed. 18.95 (ISBN 0-201-02775-5). A W.

Groh, John E. Nineteenth Century German Protestantism: The Church As Social Model. LC 80-6286. 636p. (Orig.). 1982. lib. bdg. 33.00 (ISBN 0-8191-2077-4); pap. text ed. 21.75 (ISBN 0-8191-2078-2). U Pr of Amer.

Groh, Lynn. New Year's Day. LC 64-11363. (Holiday Books Ser). (Illus.). (gr. 2-5). 1964. PLB 7.56 (ISBN 0-8116-6554-2). Garrard.

Groia, Philip. They All Sang on the Corner. (Illus.). 1973. pap. 4.95 (ISBN 0-912954-08-6). Edmond Pub Co.

Groisser, Philip L. The United States & the Middle East. Lachman, Seymour P., ed. LC 81-8967. 300p. 1982. lib. bdg. 29.50x (ISBN 0-87395-547-1); pap. 7.95x (ISBN 0-87395-548-X). State U NY Pr.

Grolich, E., ed. Functional Analysis & Approximation. (ISNM Ser.: 60). 500p. 1981. text ed. 51.65x (ISBN 3-7643-1212-2). Birkhauser.

Grolier Club. Catalogue of Original & Early Editions of Some of the Poetical & Prose Works of English Writers, 4 vols. Incl. Vol. 1. From Langland to Wither. (Illus.); Vols. 2-4. From Wither to Prior. (Illus.). LC 63-20468. 1964. Repr. of 1905 ed. Set. 55.00x o.p. (ISBN 0-8154-0091-8). Cooper Sq.

--Grolier Seventy-Five, a Bibliographical Retrospective to Celebrate the 75th Anniversary of The Grolier Club. LC 59-15011. 44p. 1959. 4.00 (ISBN 0-8139-0449-8, Dist. by U Pr of Va). Grolier Club.

Groll, Sarah I. Egyptological Studies. (Scripta Hierosolymitana Ser.: No. XXVIII). (Illus.). 537p. 1983. text ed. 53.50x (ISBN 0-85668-911-4, Pub. by Aris & Phillips England). Humanities.

Grollenberg, Lucas. Rediscovering the Bible. (Student Christian Movement Press Ser.). (Orig.). 1978. pap. 9.95x (ISBN 0-19-520319-4). Oxford U Pr.

Grollman, Earl A. Talking About Divorce & Separation: A Dialogue Between Parent & Child. LC 75-5289. (Illus.). (YA) (gr. k-4). 7.69 (ISBN 0-8070-2374-4); pap. 5.50 (ISBN 0-8070-2375-2, BP524). Beacon Pr.

Grollman, Earl A., ed. Concerning Death: A Practical Guide for the Living. LC 73-17117. 384p. 1974. pap. 6.97 (ISBN 0-8070-2765-0, BP484). Beacon Pr.

--Explaining Death to Children. LC 67-4891. 1969. pap. 6.97 (ISBN 0-8070-2385-X, BP317). Beacon Pr.

--What Helped Me: When My Loved One Died. LC 80-68166. 160p. 1981. 10.10 o.p. (ISBN 0-8070-3228-X). Beacon Pr.

Grollman, Sigmund. A Laboratory Manual of Mammalian Anatomy & Physiology. 4th ed. (Illus.). 266p. 1978. pap. text ed. 13.95x (ISBN 0-02-348090-4, 34809). Macmillan.

Gromacki, Robert G. Stand True to the Charge: An Exposition of I Timothy. 200p. 1982. pap. 7.95 (ISBN 0-8010-3786-7). Baker Bk.

--Stand United in Joy. pap. 5.95 o.p. (ISBN 0-8010-3760-3). Baker Bk.

Groman, George L., ed. The City Today. 1978. pap. text ed. 11.50 scp (ISBN 0-06-160420-8, HarpC). Har-Row.

Gromisch, Donald S., jt. auth. see Wasserman, Edward.

Gromyko, A. A. & Ponomarev, B. N., eds. Soviet Foreign Policy, Nineteen Forty-Five to Nineteen Eighty. 728p. 1981. 14.00 (ISBN 0-8285-2294-4, Pub. by Progress Pubs USSR). Imported Pubns.

--Soviet Foreign Policy, 1917-1945. 501p. 1981. 11.00 (ISBN 0-8285-2293-6, Pub. by Progress Pubs. USSR). Imported Pubns.

Gronbech, Bo. Hans Christian Andersen. (World Authors Ser.). 1980. lib. bdg. 12.95 (ISBN 0-8057-6454-2, Twayne). G K Hall.

Gronbech, Kaare & Krueger, John R., eds. An Introduction to Classical (Literary) Mongolian. 2nd, Rev. ed. 91p. (Orig.). 1976. pap. 22.50x (ISBN 3-447-01661-2). Intl Pubns Serv.

Gronbeck, Bruce E. The Articulate Person: A Guide to Everyday Public Speaking. 1979. pap. 12.50x (ISBN 0-673-15113-1). Scott F.

--The Articulate Person: A Guide to Everyday Public Speaking. 2nd ed. 1983. pap. text ed. 12.95x (ISBN 0-673-15628-1). Scott F.

Groneman, Chris. Leathercraft. (gr. 9-12). 1963. pap. 13.20 (ISBN 0-87002-204-0). Bennett IL.

Groneman, Chris H. General Woodworking. 4th ed. 1971. text ed. 18.00 (ISBN 0-07-024952-0, W). McGraw.

--General Woodworking. 5th ed. 1975. text ed. 18.00 (ISBN 0-07-024985-7, W); study guide 6.88 (ISBN 0-07-024986-5); tchr's. resource guide 2.64 (ISBN 0-07-024988-1). McGraw.

--General Woodworking. 6th, rev. ed. Lindquist, Hal, ed. (Publications in Industrial Education). (Illus.). 344p. (gr. 9-10). 1981. text ed. 18.00 (ISBN 0-07-025003-0, W); tchrs. guide 2.64 (ISBN 0-07-025005-7); activity bk. 6.88 (ISBN 0-07-025004-9). McGraw.

--Leather Tooling & Carving. LC 74-75258. (Illus.). 128p. 1974. pap. 4.00 (ISBN 0-486-23061-9). Dover.

--Leather Tooling & Carving. (Illus.). 8.50 (ISBN 0-8446-5042-0). Peter Smith.

Groneman, Chris H. & Feirer, John L. General Industrial Education. 5th ed. LC 73-9827. Orig. Title: General Shop. (Illus.). 584p. (gr. 7-9). 1973. text ed. 19.20 (ISBN 0-07-024965-2, W); tchr's. resource guide 2.64 (ISBN 0-07-024976-8); study guide 6.40 (ISBN 0-07-024968-7). McGraw.

--General Industrial Education. 6th ed. (M-H Publications in Industrial Education). (gr. 7-9). 1979. text ed. 19.20 (ISBN 0-07-024991-1, W); study guide 6.40 (ISBN 0-07-024992-X); tchr's. guide 2.64 (ISBN 0-07-024993-8). McGraw.

--Getting Started in Drawing & Planning. (M-H Publications in Industrial Ed.). (Illus.). 1979. pap. 6.40 (ISBN 0-07-024996-2, W). McGraw.

--Getting Started in Electricity & Electronics. (M-H Publications in Industrial Ed.). (Illus.). (gr. 7-9). 1979. pap. text ed. 6.40 (ISBN 0-07-024999-7, W). McGraw.

--Getting Started in Metalworking. (M-H Publications in Industrial Ed.). (Illus.). 1979. pap. 6.40 (ISBN 0-07-024998-9, W). McGraw.

--Getting Started in Woodworking. (M-H Publications in Industrial Ed.). (Illus.). (gr. 7-9). 1979. pap. text ed. 6.40 (ISBN 0-07-024997-0, W). McGraw.

Groneman, Chris H. & Glazener, E. R. Technical Woodworking. 2nd ed. 1975. 22.1503894320q (ISBN 0-07-024964-4, W). McGraw.

Groneman, Chris H. & Grannis, Gary E. Exploring the Industries. LC 79-55313. 1981. pap. text ed. 17.80 (ISBN 0-8273-1757-3); instr's. guide 2.75 (ISBN 0-8273-1758-1). Delmar.

Groneman, Nancy J. Business Mathematics Using Electronic Calculators. (Illus.). 240p. 1982. 15.95 (ISBN 0-13-105205-5). P-H.

Groner & Fraisse. Cognition & Eye Movements. Date not set. 55.50 (ISBN 0-444-86354-0). Elsevier.

Groner, Alfred M. The Monopoly Players. LC 81-22798. 1982. 16.50 (ISBN 0-87949-207-4). Ashley Bks.

Groner, Marina, jt. ed. see Groner, Rudolph.

Groner, Rudolph & Groner, Marina, eds. Methods of Heuristics. 488p. 1983. text ed. write for info. (ISBN 0-89859-251-8). L Erlbaum Assocs.

Groner, Samuel. Modern Business Law. 1982. text ed. 23.95 (ISBN 0-8359-4555-3); wkbk. 7.95 (ISBN 0-8359-4557-X); instrs'. manual avail. (ISBN 0-8359-4556-1). Reston.

Gronicka, Andre Von see Von Gronicka, Andre.

Gronicka, Andre Von see Von Gronicka, Andre & Bates-Yakobson, Helen.

Gronlund, Norman E. Preparing Criterion-Referenced Tests for Classroom Instruction. 55p. 1973. pap. text ed. 3.95 (ISBN 0-02-348270-2). Macmillan.

Gronner, Alfred D. Transistor Circuit Analysis. (Monarch Technical Outlines). 1970. pap. 4.25 o.p. (ISBN 0-671-18906-9). Monarch Pr.

Gronner, Georgina. Viennese Desserts Made Easy. (Illus.). 128p. (Orig.). 1983. pap. 7.95 (ISBN 0-8092-5621-5). Contemp Bks.

Gronvik, Ottar. The Words of "Heir", "Inheritance", & "Funeral Feasts" in Early Germanic. 28p. (Orig.). 1982. pap. 11.00 (ISBN 82-00-05896-4). Universitet.

Grood, E. S. & Smith, C. R., eds. Advances in Bioengineering, 1977. 1977. pap. text ed. 16.00 o.p. (ISBN 0-685-86869-9, H00103). ASME.

Groom, Winston. As Summers Die. 336p. 1982. pap. 3.25 o.p. (ISBN 0-425-05632-5). Berkley Pub.

--Better Times Than These. LC 78-4182. 1978. 10.95 o.p. (ISBN 0-671-40007-X). Summit Bks.

Grooms, Clarence. Out of the Night. 1979. 5.95 o.p. (ISBN 0-533-03025-0). Vantage.

Grooms, Kathe, ed. see Audette, Vicki.

Grooms, Kathe, ed. see Masters, M.

Grooms, Kathe, ed. see Olson, Craig.

Grooms, Kathe, ed. see Sehnert, Keith W.

Groot, Irene de see Niemeijer, J. W. & De Groot, Irene.

Groot, Roy A. de see De Groot, Roy A.

Groot, Roy A. De see De Groot, Roy A.

Groot, Roy De see De Groot, Roy A.

Groot, S. R. de see De Groot, S. R. & Vanleeuwen, W. A.

Groover, Mikell P. Automation, Production Systems & Computer-Aided Manufacturing. 1980. text ed. 29.95 (ISBN 0-13-054668-2). P-H.

Gropius, et al. Four Great Makers of Modern Architecture: Gropius, Le Corbusier, Mies Van der Rohe, Wright. LC 78-130312. (Architecture & Decorative Art Ser.: Vol. 37). 1970. Repr. of 1963 ed. lib. bdg. 32.50 (ISBN 0-306-70065-4). Da Capo.

Gropius, Walter, et al. Town Plan for the Development of Selb. 1970. 15.00 o.p. (ISBN 0-262-07029-4). MIT Pr.

Gropman, Donald, jt. auth. see Schachter-Shalomi, Zalman.

Groppel, Jack L. & Shay, Arthur. Optimal Tennis: The Freeze-Frame Photographic Approach to a Better Game. (Illus.). 128p. (Orig.). 1983. pap. 8.95 (ISBN 0-8092-5602-9). Contemp Bks.

Grosberg, P. Introduction to Textile Mechanics. 1968. 15.95x (ISBN 0-87245-124-0). Textile Bk.

Grose, Mary L. The Care & Feeding of Infant Orphaned Wild Birds. 1981. 1.95 (ISBN 0-915096-11-0). Palmetto Pub.

Grose, Peter. The Next Steps Toward Peace Between Israel & Its Neighbors. (Seven Springs Reports). 45p. 1980. pap. 2.00 (ISBN 0-943006-09-0). Seven Springs.

--The United States, NATO & Israeli-Arab Peace. (Seven Springs Reports). 1980. pap. 2.00 (ISBN 0-943006-11-2). Seven Springs.

Grose, Thomas H., ed. see Hume, David.

Groseclose, Elgin. America's Money Machine: The Story of the Federal Reserve. 320p. 1980. 14.95 o.p. (ISBN 0-87000-477-8, Arlington Hse). Crown.

Groseclose, Kel. Three-Speed Dad in a Ten-Speed World. 160p. (Orig.). 1983. pap. 4.95 (ISBN 0-87123-585-4). Bethany Hse.

Grose-Hodge, Humfrey, ed. see Cicero.

Grosicki. Watsons Advanced Textile Design. 4th ed. Watson, ed. 1977. 49.95 (ISBN 0-408-00250-6). Butterworth.

Grosicki, Z. J., ed. see Watson, William.

Grosjean, Daniel, ed. Nitrogenous Air Pollutants: Chemical & Biological Implications. LC 79-84379. 1979. 37.50 o.p. (ISBN 0-250-40294-7). Ann Arbor Science.

Grosjean, Francois. Life with Two Languages: An Introduction to Bilingualism. (Illus.). 1982. text ed. 20.00x (ISBN 0-674-53091-8). Harvard U Pr.

Grosjean, J., tr. see Thureau, P. & Lecler, D.

Grosjean, Paul, ed. The Best of SYNC. 170p. 1983. pap. 9.95 (ISBN 0-916688-43-7). Creative Comp.

Grosjean-Maupin, E., et al. Plena Vortaro De Esperanto Kun Suplemento. 9th ed. (Esperanto.). 1980. 10.95x (ISBN 0-685-71605-8, 1070). Esperanto League North Am.

Groslier, Bernard P. Indochina. (Art of the World Library). (Illus.). 6.95 o.p. (ISBN 0-517-50845-1). Crown.

Grosmann, M., et al, eds. see European Congress on Molecular Spectroscopy, 12th, Strasbourg, 1975, et al.

Gross & Peterson. Business Forecasting. 2d ed. 1983. text ed. 27.95 (ISBN 0-686-84530-7, BS17); answer bk. avail. (BS18). HM.

Gross, jt. auth. see Morehouse.

Gross, Alan. I Don't Want to go to School. LC 81-17034. (Illus.). (ps-3). 1982. PLB 9.25g (ISBN 0-516-03496-0). Childrens.

Gross, B. Charge Storage in Charged Dielectrics ESL, 1964. 1966. 14.75 (ISBN 0-444-40262-4). Elsevier.

Gross, Barbara & Shuman, Bernard. Essentials of Parenting in the First Years of Life. LC 79-23739. (Orig.). 1980. pap. text ed. 4.95 (ISBN 0-87868-184-1, CD-16). Child Welfare.

Gross, Beatrice, jt. auth. see Gross, Ronald.

Gross, Beatrice, jt. ed. see Gross, Ronald.

Gross, Bertram. Friendly Fascism: The New Face of Power in America. 350p. 1982. pap. 8.00 (ISBN 0-89608-149-4). South End Pr.

Gross, Bertram M. & Lambert, Richard D., eds. Political Intelligence for America's Future. LC 78-112787. (Annals of the American Academy of Political & Social Science: No. 388). 1970. 15.00 (ISBN 0-87761-126-2); pap. 7.95 (ISBN 0-87761-125-4). Am Acad Pol Soc Sci.

Gross, Bertram M. & Moses, Stanley, eds. Planning for Full Employment. new ed. LC 74-84801. (Annals Ser: No. 418). 1975. pap. 7.95 (ISBN 0-87761-187-4). Am Acad Pol Soc Sci.

Gross, C. A. Power System Analysis. 478p. 1979. 31.50 (ISBN 0-471-01899-6); Avail Tchr's Manual (ISBN 0-471-03682-X). Wiley.

Gross, Charles & Peterson, Robin. Business Forecasting. 2nd ed. 384p. 1982. text ed. 25.00 (ISBN 0-395-31762-2); instrs.' manual avail. HM.

Gross, Charles W. & Peterson, Robin T. Business Forecasting. LC 75-31029. (Illus.). 320p. 1976. text ed. 26.95 (ISBN 0-395-19505-5). HM.

Gross, Charles W., jt. auth. see Verma, Harish L.

Gross, David C., ed. Love Poems from the Hebrew. 1976. 5.95 o.p. (ISBN 0-385-11136-3). Doubleday.

Gross, Erhard & Meiehnhofer, Hohannes, eds. The Peptides: Analysis, Synthesis, Biology, Vol. 5. (Special Methods in Peptide Synthesis Ser.: Part B). Date not set. price not set (ISBN 0-12-304205-4). Acad Pr.

Gross, Erhard & Meienhofer, Johannes, eds. The Peptides: Analysis, Synthesis, Biology: Vol. I, Pt. a, Major Methods of Peptide Bond Formation. LC 78-31958. 1979. 49.50, by subscription 42.00 (ISBN 0-12-304201-1). Acad Pr.

--The Peptides: Analysis, Synthesis, Biology: Vol. 4, Modern Techniques of Peptide & Amino Acid Anaysis. 1981. 51.50 (ISBN 0-686-85538-8); subscripton price 44.00 (ISBN 0-12-304204-6). Acad Pr.

Gross, Erhard & Meinhoper, Johannes, eds. The Peptides: Analysis, Synthesis, Biology, Vol. 2: Special Methods in Peptide Synthesis, Pt. A. LC 78-31958. 1980. by subscription - 50.00 59.50 (ISBN 0-12-304202-X). Acad Pr.

Gross, Feliks. Ethnics in a Borderland: An Inquiry into the Nature of Ethnicity & Reduction of Ethnic Tensions in a One-Time Genocide Area. LC 77-94741. (Contributions in Sociology: No. 32). 1978. lib. bdg. 25.00 (ISBN 0-313-20310-5, GET/). Greenwood.

Gross, Fletcher, jt. ed. see Scott, William R.

Gross, Franz, et al, eds. Enzymatic Release of Vasoactive Peptides: Eighth Workshop Conference HOECHST. (Illus.). 430p. 1980. text ed. 45.00 (ISBN 0-89004-458-9). Raven.

Gross, Gerald, ed. Responsibility of the Press. 1969. pap. 2.95 o.p. (ISBN 0-671-20245-6, Touchstone Bks). S&S.

Gross, Grant M. Ocean World. new ed. (Physical Science Ser.). (Orig.). 1976. pap. text ed. 7.95 (ISBN 0-675-08576-4); cassettes & filmstrips 135.00 (ISBN 0-675-08575-6). Merrill.

Gross, H. Privacy, Its Legal Protection. rev. ed. LC 76-43110. (Legal Almanac Ser.: No. 54). 108p. 1976. 5.95 (ISBN 0-379-11099-7). Oceana.

Gross, Hans. Criminal Psychology: A Manual for Judges, Practioniers & Student. Kallen, Horace M., tr. LC 68-55772. (Criminology, Law Enforcement, & Social Problems Ser.: No. 13). 1968. Repr. of 1911 ed. 24.00x (ISBN 0-87585-013-8). Patterson Smith.

Gross, Harriet & Sussman, Marvin B., eds. Alternatives to Traditional Family Living: An Update. LC 82-9250. (Marriage & Family Review: Vol. 5, No. 2). 134p. 1982. text ed. 20.00 (ISBN 0-917724-59-3, B59); pap. text ed. 9.95 (ISBN 0-917724-82-8, B82). Haworth Pr.

Gross, Harvey. Contrived Corridor: History & Fatality in Modern Literature. LC 74-163621. 1972. 7.95 o.p. (ISBN 0-472-39390-1). U of Mich Pr.

Gross, Herbert F. Algebra by Example: An Elementary Course. 1978. pap. text ed. 18.95x (ISBN 0-669-00473-1); instr's manual avail. (ISBN 0-669-00474-X); solutions manual 9.95x (ISBN 0-669-01014-6); cassettes 150.00 (ISBN 0-669-01154-1); avail. tapescript. Heath.

Gross, Hyman. A Theory of Criminal Justice. 1979. 25.00x (ISBN 0-19-502349-8); pap. 9.95x (ISBN 0-19-502350-1). Oxford U Pr.

Gross, Irene, jt. auth. see Friedland, Joyce.

Gross, Irman H., et al. Management for Modern Families. 4th ed. (Illus.). 1980. text ed. 21.95 (ISBN 0-13-549477-X). P-H.

Gross, James A. The Reshaping of the National Labor Relations Board: National Labor Policy in Transition, 1937-1947. LC 74-5284. 400p. 1981. 49.00x (ISBN 0-87395-516-1); pap. 18.95x (ISBN 0-87395-517-X). State U NY Pr.

Gross, Jan T., ed. see Staniszkis, Jadwiga.

Gross, Jim, et al. April Fourth, Nineteen Eighty-One: Pivotal Day in a Critical Year. (Illus.). 1980. pap. 4.00 (ISBN 0-933646-12-7). Aries Pr.

Gross, John, compiled by. The Oxford Book of Aphorisms. 320p. 1983. 15.95 (ISBN 0-19-214111-2). Oxford U Pr.

Gross, John A. & Flicek, Barbara D. Electromyographic Technologists Handbook. (Allied Health Professions Monograph). 1983. write for info. (ISBN 0-87527-271-1). Green.

Gross, John J. John P. Marquand. (United States Authors Ser.: No. 33). 1962. lib. bdg. 12.95 o.p. (ISBN 0-8057-0476-0, Twayne). G K Hall.

Gross, Jonathan L. & Brainerd, Walter S. Fundamental Programming Concepts. Perlis, Alan J., ed. (Information Sciences Ser). (Illus.). 1972. text ed. 23.50 scp o.p. (ISBN 0-06-042531-8, HarpC); instructor's manual avail. o.p. (ISBN 0-06-362534-2). Har-Row.

Gross, Joseph F., ed. Mathematics of Microcirculation Phenomena. 186p. 1980. text ed. 26.50 (ISBN 0-89004-449-X). Raven.

Gross, Joy & Freifeld, Karen. The Vegetarian Child. 224p. 1983. 12.00 (ISBN 0-8184-0342-X). Lyle Stuart.

Gross, Le Roy. Art of Selling Intangibles: How to Make a Million Investing Other People's Money. LC 81-11349. (Illus.). 302p. 1982. 24.95 (ISBN 0-13-048777-5). NY Inst Finance.

Gross, Leo, ed. The Future of the International Court of Justice, 2 vols. LC 76-2646. 1976. Set. text ed. 76.00 (ISBN 0-686-96818-2); Vol 1. text ed. 38.00 (ISBN 0-379-00298-1); Vol 2. text ed. 38.00 (ISBN 0-379-00299-X). Oceana.

Gross, Ludwik. Oncogenic Viruses. 3rd ed. 1200p. 1983. 200.00 (ISBN 0-08-026830-7). Pergamon.

Gross, Lynne S. The New Television Technologies. 190p. 1983. pap. text ed. write for info. (ISBN 0-697-04362-2). Wm C Brown.

--See-Hear: Introduction to Broadcasting. 450p. 1979. text ed. write for info. o.p. (ISBN 0-697-04331-2); o.p. Wm C Brown.

--Telecommunications: An Introduction to Radio, Television & the Developing Media. 380p. 1983. pap. text ed. write for info. (ISBN 0-697-04359-2); instrs.' manual avail. (ISBN 0-697-04361-4). Wm C Brown.

Gross, M. G., jt. ed. see Palmer, H. D.

Gross, M. Grant. Oceanography. 4th ed. (Physics & Physical Science Ser.). 152p. 1980. pap. text ed. 9.95 (ISBN 0-675-08110-6). Merrill.

--Oceanography: A View of the Earth. 3rd ed. (Illus.). 544p. 1982. 26.95 (ISBN 0-13-629683-1). P-H.

--Oceanography: A View of the Earth. 2nd ed. (Illus.). 1977. 25.95 o.p. (ISBN 0-13-629675-0). P-H.

Gross, M. J. & Warshauer, W. Financial & Accounting Guide for Nonprofit Organizations. 3rd ed. 568p. 1979. 44.95x (ISBN 0-471-04974-3, Pub. by Wiley-Interscience); tchr's manual avail. (ISBN 0-471-05949-8). Wiley.

Gross, Malvern J. & Warshauer, William. Financial & Accounting Guide for Nonprofit Organizations. 3rd ed. 568p. 1983. price not set (ISBN 0-471-87113-3). Ronald Pr.

Gross, Martin. The Nostalgia Quiz Book, No. 2. 1975. pap. 1.25 o.p. (ISBN 0-451-06554-9, Y6554, Sig). NAL.

--The Psychological Society. 1979. 4.95 o.p. (ISBN 0-671-24995-9, Touchstone Bks). S&S.

Gross, Martin A. Nostalgia Quiz Book No. 3. 1976. pap. 1.50 o.p. (ISBN 0-451-08412-8, W8412, Sig). NAL.

--The Official Movie Trivia Quiz Book No. 2. 1978. pap. 1.50 o.p. (ISBN 0-451-07898-5, W7898, Sig). NAL.

Gross, Michael see Holmes, Helen B., et al.

Gross, Milt. Hearts of Gold. (Illus.). 1983. pap. 7.95 (ISBN 0-89659-367-3). Abbeville Pr.

Gross, Miriam, ed. The World of Raymond Chandler. LC 77-85348. (Illus.). 224p. 1978. 9.95 o.s.i. (ISBN 0-89479-016-1). A & W Pubs.

Gross, Neal & Trask, Anne E. The Sex Factor & the Management of Schools. LC 75-34337. 279p. 1976. 32.95x o.p. (ISBN 0-471-32800-6, Pub. by Wiley-Interscience). Wiley.

Gross, Neal, jt. ed. see Herriott, Robert E.

Gross, Neal, et al. Implementing Organizational Innovations: A Sociological Analysis of Planned Change in Schools. LC 76-147016. (Illus.). 1971. text ed. 12.50x o.p. (ISBN 0-465-03213-3). Basic.

Gross, P. L. Ninety-Nine Pages to Promotion. LC 78-68899. 1979. 6.95 o.p. (ISBN 0-533-04186-4). Vantage.

Gross, R. W. & Bott, J. F. Handbook of Chemical Lasers. LC 76-6865. 864p. 1976. 79.50 (ISBN 0-471-32804-9, Pub. by Wiley-Interscience). Wiley.

Gross, Richard. American Citizenship. (gr. 8). 1979. text ed. 17.60 (ISBN 0-201-42008-2, Sch Div); tchr's ed. 20.36 (ISBN 0-201-42009-0); inst. manual 32.00 (ISBN 0-201-42010-4). A-W.

Gross, Richard, jt. auth. see Kammerer, William.

Gross, Richard E., ed. British Secondary Education: Overview & Appraisal. (Orig.). 1965. pap. 8.95x o.p. (ISBN 0-19-919035-6). Oxford U Pr.

Gross, Robert. The Coming of the Andromedans. 1978. 4.95 o.p. (ISBN 0-533-03803-0). Vantage.

Gross, Robert E. Atlas of Children's Surgery. LC 70-108366. (Illus.). 1970. 12.00 (ISBN 0-7216-4287-X). Saunders.

Gross, Ronald & Gross, Beatrice. Teaching Under Pressure. LC 78-13238. 1979. pap. text ed. 11.95x (ISBN 0-673-16451-9). Scott F.

--Will It Grow in a Classroom. 1974. pap. 3.25 o.s.i. (ISBN 0-440-58725-5, Delta). Dell.

Gross, Ronald & Murphy, Judith. The Revolution in the Schools. LC 64-24558. (Orig.). 1964. pap. 2.95 (ISBN 0-15-677086-5, Harv). HarBraceJ.

Gross, Ronald & Osterman, Paul. High School. LC 71-139623. 1971. 8.95 o.p. (ISBN 0-671-20838-1). S&S.

--High School. 1972. pap. 3.45 o.p. (ISBN 0-671-21237-0, Touchstone Bks). S&S.

Gross, Ronald, ed. Open Poetry: Four Anthologies of Expanded Poems. 1973. 17.50 o.p. (ISBN 0-671-21139-0). S&S.

Gross, Ronald & Gross, Beatrice, eds. Radical School Reform. LC 72-92188. 1970. pap. 4.95 o.p. (ISBN 0-671-20915-9, Touchstone Bks). S&S.

Gross, Ronald, et al, eds. The New Old: Struggling for Decent Aging. LC 77-12857. 1978. pap. 6.95 o.p. (ISBN 0-385-12763-4, Anch). Doubleday.

Gross, Ruth B. Dangerous Adventure! Lindbergh's Famous Flight. LC 77-79269. (Illus.). (gr. 2-6). 1977. 5.95 o.s.i. (ISBN 0-8027-6309-X); reinf. 5.85 o.s.i. (ISBN 0-8027-6310-3). Walker & Co.

Gross, S. More Gross: Cartoons. LC 82-73194. (Illus.). 128p. 1982. 10.95. Congdon & Weed.

Gross, Sam. More Gross. 128p. 1982. 9.95 (ISBN 0-312-92540-9). Congdon & Weed.

Gross, Seymour L, jt. ed. see Stern, Milton R.

Gross, Sidney & Gross, Sue. Recipes from a Brooklyn Childhood. pap. write for info. cancelled o.p. (ISBN 0-917234-14-6). Kitchen Harvest.

Gross, Sidney A., jt. auth. see Gross, Sue A.

Gross, Sri D. Consciousness: The Key to Life. LC 82-81647. (Orig.). 1982. pap. 5.95 (ISBN 0-914766-82-1, 0114). IWP Pub.

Gross, Stephen C. & Garb, Solomon, eds. Humanism & Science in Cancer Research & Therapy. 1982. cancelled 25.00 (ISBN 0-86531-126-9). Westview.

Gross, Sue, jt. auth. see Gross, Sidney.

Gross, Sue A. Pizza to Your Taste. 1978. pap. 2.95 o.p. (ISBN 0-917234-11-1). Kitchen Harvest.

Gross, Sue A. & Gross, Sidney A. The Early Spring Garden Book. 1975. pap. 2.50 o.p. (ISBN 0-917234-05-7). Kitchen Harvest.

Gross, Theodore & Kelvin, Norman. Introduction to Literature: Fiction. 1967. pap. text ed. 4.50 (ISBN 0-685-19691-7). Phila Bk Co.

Gross, Theodore L. Albion W. Tourgee. (United States Authors Ser.). 14.95 (ISBN 0-8057-0744-1, Twayne). G K Hall.

Gross, Theodore L. & Levin, David. America in Literature, Vol. I. 1978. pap. text ed. 20.95x (ISBN 0-673-15676-1). Scott F.

Gross, Theodore L. & Trachtenberg, Alan. America in Literature, Vol. II. 1978. pap. text ed. 20.95x (ISBN 0-673-15677-X). Scott F.

Gross, W. F. Applications Manual for Paint & Protective Coatings: A Guide to Types of Coatings, Methods of Surface Preparation & Hand Application Techniques. 1970. 32.50 o.p. (ISBN 0-07-024970-9, P&RB). McGraw.

Gross, William & Matsch, Lee A. Fluid Film Lubrication. Vohr, John H. & Wildman, Manfred, eds. LC 80-36889. 773p. 1980. 42.50x (ISBN 0-471-08357-7, Pub. by Wiley-Interscience). Wiley.

Grossbach, Robert. Neil Simon's Chapter Two. (Orig.). 1980. pap. 2.25 o.p. (ISBN 0-446-92279-X). Warner Bks.

--Never Say Die: An Autonecrographical Novel. LC 78-69502. 1979. 10.53i (ISBN 0-06-011629-3, HarpT). Har-Row.

Grossbard, Hyman. Cottage Parents-What They Have to Be, Know & Do. LC 60-53475. 1960. pap. 2.25 (ISBN 0-87868-064-0, I-22). Child Welfare.

Grossbart, Francine B. Big City. LC 66-5842. (Illus.). (ps-2). 1966. PLB 10.89 o.p. (ISBN 0-06-022124-0, HarpJ). Har-Row.

Grossbart, June, et al. An Introductory Textile Manual. LC 81-40721. (Illus.). 110p. (Orig.). 1982. pap. text ed. 9.00 (ISBN 0-8191-1897-4). U Pr of Amer.

Grosse, Arthur E., jt. auth. see Butler, Ian S.

Grosse, John, ed. Age of Kipling. 1972. 12.95 o.p. (ISBN 0-671-21405-5). S&S.

Grosse, Lloyd T. & Lyster, Alan F. Fifteen Hundred Literary References Everyone Should Know. LC 82-18444. 256p. (Orig.). 1983. pap. 3.95 (ISBN 0-668-05596-0, 5596). Arco.

Grosseck, Joyce. Great Explorers. rev. ed. LC 80-69168. (American History & Culture Ser.). (Illus.). (gr. 4 up). 1981. text ed. 9.95 ea. 1-4 copies (ISBN 0-88296-031-8); text ed. 7.96 5 or more copies (ISBN 0-686-98160-X). Fideler.

Grosser, Alfred. French Foreign Policy under de Gaulle. LC 77-21747. 1977. Repr. of 1967 ed. lib. bdg. 20.00x (ISBN 0-8371-9795-3, GRFR). Greenwood.

Grosser, Arthus E. The Cookbook Decoder. 304p. 1983. pap. 3.50 (ISBN 0-446-30605-3). Warner Bks.

Grosser, Paul E. & Halperin, Edwin G. The Causes & Effects of Anti-Semitism. 1983. 15.00 (ISBN 0-8022-2418-0). Philos Lib.

Grosshandler, William L. see Heat Transfer & Fluid Mechanics Institute.

Grosshans, Henry. Hitler & the Artists. (Illus.). 180p. 1983. text ed. 24.00x (ISBN 0-8419-0746-3). Holmes & Meier.

Grossinger, Jennie. Art of Jewish Cooking. 1958. 13.50 (ISBN 0-394-40106-9). Random.

Grossinger, Richard. The Night Sky: The Science & Anthropology of the Stars & Planets. LC 81-5293. 544p. 1981. 16.95 (ISBN 0-87156-288-X). Sierra.

--Planet Medicine: From Stone Age Shamanism to Post-Industrial Healing. LC 79-7073. 1980. pap. 5.95 o.s.i. (ISBN 0-385-14053-3, Anch). Doubleday.

--Planet Medicine: From Stone Age Shamanism to Post-Industrial Healing. Rev. ed. LC 82-50278. 432p. 1982. pap. 9.95 (ISBN 0-394-71238-2). Shambhala Pubns.

Grossinger, Richard, jt. auth. see Kerrane, Kevin.

Grossinger, Tania & Neiderman, Andrew. Weekend. 352p. 1980. 12.95 o.p. (ISBN 0-312-86006-4). St Martin.

Grosskopf, Susan A. Fabric Frames From Stretch Bars. (Illus.). 40p. 1983. pap. 5.00 (ISBN 0-943574-19-6). That Patchwork.

Grossman, Bob, jt. auth. see Grossman, Ruth.

Grossman, Carol. Better English Simplified & Self-Taught. LC 82-3944. 128p. (Orig.). 1982. pap. 5.95 (ISBN 0-668-05392-5, 5392). Arco.

Grossman, Edith. The Antipoetry of Nicanor Parra. LC 74-21609. 201p. 1975. pap. 11.50x (ISBN 0-8147-2969-X); pap. 9.00x (ISBN 0-686-82948-4). NYU Pr.

Grossman, Eli A. Life Reinsurance. 79p. (Orig.). 1980. pap. text ed. 4.50 o.p. (ISBN 0-915322-38-2). Loma.

Grossman, Ellie. Dilys. 220p. 1982. 13.50 (ISBN 0-02-545840-X). Macmillan.

Grossman, Florence. Getting from Here to There: Writing & Reading Poetry. LC 82-4319. 176p. (YA) (gr. 10-12). 1982. pap. 7.25x (ISBN 0-86709-033-2, Pub. by Writers & Readers). Boynton Cook Pub.

Grossman, George S., ed. Omnibus Copyright Revision: Legislative History, 1960-76, Vols. 1-17. LC 76-54492. 1976. Repr. Set. lib. bdg. 495.00 (ISBN 0-930342-36-4). W S Hein.

Grossman, Gregory. Economic Systems. 2nd ed. (Foundations of Modern Economics Ser). (Illus.). 192p. 1974. ref. ed o.p. 13.95 (ISBN 0-13-233486-0); pap. text ed. 10.95 (ISBN 0-13-233478-X). P-H.

Grossman, H. I., jt. auth. see Barro, R. J.

Grossman, Harold J. Grossman's Guide to Wines, Beers, & Liquors. Rev., 7th ed. (Illus.). 640p. 29.95 (ISBN 0-684-17772-2, ScribT). Scribner.

Grossman, Irwin & Wolanin, Ron. Twenty-Five Ski Tours in Eastern Massachusetts: Cross Country Trails from the Quabbin Resevoir to Cape Cod. LC 82-4019. (Twenty-Five Ski Tours Ser.). (Illus.). 144p. 1982. pap. 6.95 (ISBN 0-942440-03-X). Backcountry Pubns.

Grossman, J. B., et al. Social Science Approaches to the Judicial Process. LC 74-153371. (Symposia on Law & Society Ser). 1971. Repr. of 1966 ed. lib. bdg. 19.50 (ISBN 0-306-70135-9). Da Capo.

Grossman, Jack H. The Promise of Love. 1977. pap. 1.45 o.p. (ISBN 0-87029-133-5, 20159-0). Abbey.

Grossman, Jeffrey E., jt. auth. see Kravitt, Gregory I.

Grossman, Joan D., ed. The Diary of Valery Bryusov (1893-1905) With Reminiscences by V. F. Khodasevich & Marina Tsvetaeva. LC 78-66013. (Documentary Studies in Modern Russian Poetry). 200p. 1980. 19.50x (ISBN 0-520-03858-4). U of Cal Pr.

Grossman, Joel B. & Tanenhaus, Joseph. Frontiers of Judicial Research. LC 68-55334. 492p. 1969. text ed. 21.00 (ISBN 0-686-86252-X, Pub. by Wiley). Krieger.

Grossman, Joel B. & Wells, Richard S. Constitutional Law & Judicial Policy-Making. 2nd ed. LC 79-20206. 1980. text ed. 34.50 (ISBN 0-471-32849-9). Wiley.

--Supplement Cases for Constitutionnal Law & Judicial Policy Making. 1981. pap. 10.95 (ISBN 0-471-09793-4). Wiley.

Grossman, Karl. The Poison Conspiracy. 281p. 1983. 15.95 (ISBN 0-932966-26-8). Permanent Pr.

Grossman, Lee. Executive Survival in a World of Change. rev. ed. LC 81-18664. 176p. 1982. Repr. of 1974 ed. 12.50 (ISBN 0-89874-458-X). Krieger.

Grossman, Louis I., ed. Mechanism & Control of Pain. LC 79-84476. (Masson Monographs in Dentistry: Vol. 1). 256p. 1979. 30.00x (ISBN 0-89352-048-9). Masson Pub.

Grossman, Mary L. & Hamlet, John N. Our Vanishing Wilderness. 1969. 10.95 (ISBN 0-448-01208-1, G&D). Putnam Pub Group.

Grossman, N. J., jt. auth. see Baylen, J. O.

Grossman, Paul, jt. auth. see Schlei, Barbara L.

Grossman, R., jt. ed. see Slaby, R. J.

Grossman, R. G. & Gildenberg, P. L., eds. Head Injury: Basic & Clinical Aspects. (Seminars in Neurological Surgery Ser.). 300p. 1982. text ed. 52.00 (ISBN 0-89004-615-8). Raven.

Grossman, Reinhardt. The Categorial Structure of the World. LC 81-48615. 448p. 1983. 25.00x (ISBN 0-253-31324-4). Ind U Pr.

Grossman, Richard. The Animals. LC 81-50385. 516p. 1983. fine cloth with slipcase 30.00 (ISBN 0-939358-00-X). Zygote Pr.

Grossman, Richard & Daneker, Gail. Energy, Jobs & the Economy. 128p. 1979. 3.45 (ISBN 0-932870-00-7). Alyson Pubns.

Grossman, Robert G., jt. auth. see Willis, William D.

Grossman, Ruth & Grossman, Bob. The New Kosher-Cookbook Trilogy. Rev. ed. (Illus.). 304p. 1983. pap. 9.95 (ISBN 0-8397-6310-7). Eriksson.

Grossman, Siegfried. Stewards of God's Grace. 192p. (Orig.). Date not set. pap. text ed. 8.95 (ISBN 0-85364-287-7). Attic Pr.

Grossman, Stanley. Calculus: Pt. 1: The Calculus of One Variable. 816p. 1981. 19.25 (ISBN 0-12-304301-8). Acad Pr.

Grossman, Stanley I. Calculus. 2nd ed. 1176p. 1981. 27.25 (ISBN 0-12-304360-3); solns. manual 9.00 (ISBN 0-12-304355-7). Acad Pr.

Grossman, Stanley I., jt. auth. see Derrick, William R.

Grossman, Steven D., jt. auth. see Crumbley, D. Larry.

Grossman, Steven D., jt. auth. see Lindhe, Richard.

Grossman, Stewart, jt. auth. see Vye, George.

Grossman, Vasily, jt. ed. see Ehrenburg, Ilya.

Grossman, Vigdor. Employing Handicapped Persons: Meeting EEO Obligations. 154p. 1980. pap. 19.50 (ISBN 0-87179-319-9). BNA.

Grossman, W. & Pflug, G., eds. Probability & Statistical Inference. 1982. lib. bdg. 49.50 (ISBN 90-277-1427-4, Pub. by Reidel Holland). Kluwer Boston.

Grossman, William & Farrell, Jack. The Heart of Jazz. LC 76-75730. (Roots of Jazz Ser.). 1976. Repr. of 1956 ed. lib. bdg. 29.50 (ISBN 0-306-70811-6). Da Capo.

Grossman, William L., ed. Modern Brazilian Short Stories. LC 67-13379. 1974. 29.00x (ISBN 0-520-00523-6); pap. 2.25 (ISBN 0-520-02766-3). U of Cal Pr.

Grossmark, D. R., ed. Leica Collectors Guide. 1976. pap. 12.95 (ISBN 0-85242-458-2). Hove Camera.

Grossner, N. R. Transformers for Electronic Circuits. 1967. 32.50 o.p. (ISBN 0-07-024978-4, P&RB). McGraw.

Grosso, Sonny & Rosenberg, Philip. Point Blank. 1978. 10.00 o.p. (ISBN 0-448-14547-2, G&D). Putnam Pub Group.

Grossvogel, David I. The Blasphemers: The Theater of Brecht, Ionesco, Beckett, Genet. 227p. 1965. pap. 3.95x (ISBN 0-8014-9006-5). Cornell U Pr.

--Four Playwrights & a Postscript: Brecht, Ionesco, Beckett, Genet. LC 75-27654. 209p. 1976. Repr. of 1962 ed. lib. bdg. 15.75x (ISBN 0-8371-8438-X, GRFP). Greenwood.

--Twentieth Century French Drama. LC 68-16434. 1966. Repr. of 1961 ed. 10.00x (ISBN 0-87752-048-8). Gordian.

Grosswald, Emil, ed. see Rademacher, Hans.

Grosswirth, Marvin. Beginners Guide to Home Computers. LC 77-16918. 1978. pap. 5.95 o.p. (ISBN 0-385-13572-6, Dolp). Doubleday.

--Beginner's Guide to Small Computers. updated ed. Amyx, Richard, rev. by. LC 82-45324. (Illus.). 144p. 1983. pap. 7.95 (ISBN 0-385-17931-6, Dolp). Doubleday.

--The Heraldry Book: A Guide to Designing Your Own Coat of Arms. LC 78-22321. (Illus.). 240p. 1981. 11.95 o.p. (ISBN 0-385-14157-2). Doubleday.

Grosu, A. Approaches to Island Phenomena. (North-Holland Linguistic Ser.: Vol. 45). 1981. 47.00 (ISBN 0-444-86278-1). Elsevier.

Grote, David. The End of Comedy: Sit-Com & the Comedic Tradition. 208p. 1983. 19.50 (ISBN 0-208-01991-X, Archon Bks). Shoe String.

Grote, R. Positive Discipline. 1979. leader's guide 125.00 (ISBN 0-07-025007-3, T&D); 3-ring binder 45.00 (ISBN 0-07-025006-5). McGraw.

Groth, Alexander J. Major Ideologies: An Interpretative of Democracy, Socialism & Nationalism. LC 82-18755. 256p. 1983. Repr. of 1971 ed. text ed. write for info. (ISBN 0-89874-579-9). Krieger.

Groth, J. L. Prayer: Learning How To Talk To God. (Concept Bks.: Ser. 4). 1983. pap. 3.50 ea.; Set. pap. 12.95. Concordia.

Groth, Jeanette. Thank You for My Spouse. 1983. pap. 2.25 (ISBN 0-570-03885-5). Concordia.

Grotius Society. Grotius Society Transactions, 45 vols. incl. index. LC 16-15222. 1915-59. Set. 550.00 o.s.i. (ISBN 0-379-20500-9); 20.00 ea. o.s.i. Oceana.

Grotowski, Jerzy. Towards a Poor Theatre. 1970. pap. 4.95 o.p. (ISBN 0-671-20414-9, Touchstone Bks). S&S.

Grotty, Robert B., jt. auth. see Hunt, Arnold D.

Grotz, George. From Gunk to Glow: The Gentle Art of Refinishing Antiques & Other Furniture. 1983. pap. 4.95 (ISBN 0-440-53053-9, Delta). Dell.

--The Fun of Refinishing Furniture. LC 78-22809. 1979. pap. 9.95 (ISBN 0-385-14916-6, Dolp). Doubleday.

--Furniture Doctor. LC 62-7640. 1962. 7.95 (ISBN 0-385-01444-9). Doubleday.

--Grotz's Decorative Collectibles Price Guide. LC 82-45288. (Illus.). 256p. 1983. pap. 14.95 (ISBN 0-385-17870-0, Dolp). Doubleday.

Grouchy, Jean De see De Grouchy, Jean & Turleau, Catherine.

Groucutt, jt. auth. see Arnell.

Groundwater Seminar. Proceedings. 293p. 1973. pap. 16.00 o.p. (ISBN 0-686-92961-6, F987, FAO). Unipub.

Group for Environmental Education, Inc. Our Man-Made Environment, Book 7. 1973. pap. 5.95x (ISBN 0-262-07050-2); Fr. ed. 5.95x (ISBN 0-262-57037-8). MIT Pr.

Group for the Advancement of Psychiatry Committee on Child Psychiatry. The Process of Child Therapy. LC 82-45469. 224p. 1982. 17.50 (ISBN 0-87630-310-6). Brunner-Mazel.

Grouse, Phil, jt. auth. see Brookes, Cyril.

Grousset, Rene. The Empire of the Steppes. LC 77-108759. 1970. 47.50x o.p. (ISBN 0-8135-0627-1). Rutgers U Pr.

Grout, Donald J. Alessandro Scarlatti: An Introduction to His Operas. LC 78-54796. 1979. 20.00x (ISBN 0-520-03682-4). U of Cal Pr.

Grout, Donald J. & Calisca, Claude. A History of Western Music. 3rd, shorter ed. (Illus.). 1980. pap. cancelled (ISBN 0-393-01411-8); 18.95x (ISBN 0-393-95142-1). Norton.

Grout, Jarrell C. Fundamental Computer Programming Using FORTRAN 77. (Software Ser.). (Illus.). 432p. 1983. pap. text ed. 17.95 (ISBN 0-13-335141-6). P-H.

Grove & Creswell. City Landscape. 1982. text ed. 65.00 (ISBN 0-408-01165-3). Butterworth.

Grove, A. T. Africa. (Illus.). 1978. pap. text ed. 19.95x (ISBN 0-19-913244-5). Oxford U Pr.

Grove, A. T. & Klein, F. Rural Africa. LC 77-82496. (Topics in Geography Ser.). (Illus.). 1979. 24.95 (ISBN 0-521-21825-X); pap. 8.95 (ISBN 0-521-29282-4). Cambridge U Pr.

Grove, Andrew S. Physics & Technology of Semiconductor Devices. LC 67-17340. 366p. 1967. 33.95 (ISBN 0-471-32998-3). Wiley.

Grove, Edward A. & Ladas, Gerasimbs E. Introduction to Complex Variables. 1974. 25.95 (ISBN 0-395-17087-7). HM.

Grove, Fred. Phantom Warrior. large print ed. LC 82-713. 324p. 1982. Repr. of 1981 ed. 10.95x (ISBN 0-89621-349-8). Thorndike Pr.

--The Running Horses. LC 79-7625. (Double D Western Ser.). 264p. 1980. 11.95 o.p. (ISBN 0-385-14741-4). Doubleday.

Grove, George. Beethoven & His Nine Symphonies. 3rd ed. 9.50 (ISBN 0-8446-2171-4). Peter Smith.

Grove, Hugh D., jt. auth. see Mock, Theodore J.

Grove, Lilly. Dancing: A Handbook of the Terpsichorean Arts in Diverse Places & Times, Savage & Civilized. LC 76-76138. (Illus.). xviii, 454p. 1969. Repr. of 1895 ed. 34.00x (ISBN 0-8103-3469-0). Gale.

Grove, Pat. Sweet & Sour: Humorous Cartoons. 7.50 (ISBN 0-392-08426-0, SpS). Sportshelf.

Grove, Pearce S., ed. Nonprint Media in Academic Libraries. LC 74-23972. (ACRL Publications in Librarianship: No. 34). 239p. 1975. pap. 11.00 (ISBN 0-8389-0153-0). ALA.

Grove, Pierce & Clement, Evelyn, eds. Bibliographic Control of Nonprint Media. LC 70-183706. 1972. 15.00 o.p. (ISBN 0-8389-0109-3). ALA.

Grove, Roger. Light Blue. 16p. (gr. 3-12). 1973. pap. text ed. 3.95 (ISBN 0-87487-648-6). Summy.

Grove, Tami. A Collective History of the Early Years of Settlement in Surprise Valley. (ANCRR Research Paper: No. 4). 1977. 7.50 (ISBN 0-686-38933-6). Assn NC Records.

Grove, Theodore S. Experiences in Interpersonal Communication. (Illus.). 224p. 1976. pap. 14.95 o.p. (ISBN 0-13-294975-X). P-H.

Grove, W. B. British Stem-&-Leaf-Fungi: Coelomysycetes, 2 vols. (Illus.). 1967. Set. pap. 40.00 (ISBN 3-7682-0500-2). Lubrecht & Cramer.

Grove, Walter, jt. auth. see Geerken, Michael.

Grove, Wendell E. Brief Numerical Methods. 1966. text ed. 23.95x (ISBN 0-13-082917-5). P-H.

Grover, E. B. & Hamby, D. S. Handbook of Textile Testing & Quality Control. 1960. 64.95x (ISBN 0-87245-125-9). Textile Bk.

--Handbook of Textile Testing & Quality Control. (Illus.). 622p. 1960. 64.95 (ISBN 0-470-32901-7, Pub. by Wiley-Interscience). Wiley.

Grover, Eulalie O. Robert Louis Stevenson, a Teller of Tales. LC 71-164308. x, 265p. (YA) 1975. Repr. of 1940 ed. 34.00x (ISBN 0-8103-4080-1). Gale.

Grover, Linda, jt. auth. see Cho, Emily.

Grover, Margaret, jt. auth. see Alperin, Kenneth.

Grover, Ray. New Zealand. (World Bibliographical Ser.: No. 18). 254p. 1980. 36.25 (ISBN 0-903450-31-3). ABC-Clio.

Grover, Sonja C. The Analysis of Human Behavior: A Psychological Laboratory Manual. 130p. 1982. pap. text ed. 12.95x (ISBN 0-8290-1256-7). Irvington.

--Toward a Psychology of the Scientist: Implications of Psychological Research for Contemporary Philosophy of Science. LC 80-6092. 102p. (Orig.). lib. bdg. 17.00 (ISBN 0-8191-1574-6); pap. text ed. 8.00 (ISBN 0-8191-1575-4). U Pr of Amer.

Groves, David, jt. auth. see Poirot, James.

Groves, David L., ed. Behavior: Recreation & Leisure Programming. 1983. pap. 11.00 (ISBN 0-940414-04-X). Appalach Assoc.

Groves, Donald G. & Hunt, Lee M. The Ocean World Encyclopedia. LC 79-21093. (Illus.). 1980. 39.95 (ISBN 0-07-025010-3). McGraw.

Groves, Harold M. Tax Philosophers: Two Hundred Years of Thought in Great Britain & the United States. Curran, Donald J., ed. LC 74-5901. 168p. 1974. 27.50 (ISBN 0-299-06660-6). U of Wis Pr.

Groves, Harry E. Comparative Constitutional Law. LC 63-8501. 1963. 22.50 o.p. (ISBN 0-379-00154-3). Oceana.

Groves, Ivor D., Jr., ed. Acoustic Transducers. LC 81-4113. (Benchmark Papers in Acoustics Ser.: Vol. 14). 391p. 1981. 51.00 (ISBN 0-87933-387-1). Hutchinson Ross.

Groves, L., ed. Physical Education for Special Needs. LC 78-68389. 1979. 21.95 (ISBN 0-521-22391-1); pap. 10.95 (ISBN 0-521-29471-1). Cambridge U Pr.

Groves, Leslie M. Now It Can Be Told: The Story of the Manhattan Project. (Quality Paperbacks Ser.). (Illus.). 464p. 1983. pap. 9.95 (ISBN 0-306-80189-2). Da Capo.

Groves, Martha, jt. ed. see Warden, Rob.

Groves, Norris A. Christian Devotedness. pap. 1.50 o.p. (ISBN 0-937396-63-X). Walterick Pubs.

Groves, R. H., ed. Australian Vegetation. LC 80-40421. (Illus.). 350p. 1981. 69.50 (ISBN 0-521-23436-0). Cambridge U Pr.

Grow, James R., jt. auth. see Blumberg, Richard E.

Grow, Lawrence, compiled by. Old House Plans: Two Centuries of Domestic Architecture. LC 77-91927. (Illus.). 1978. pap. 5.95 o.s.i. (ISBN 0-87663-981-3, Main St). Universe.

Grow, Lawrence, jt. ed. see Lancaster, Clay.

Grow, Lucille. Early Childrearing by Young Mothers: A Research Study. LC 79-53504. 1979. pap. text ed. 9.95 (ISBN 0-87868-138-8, YF-1). Child Welfare.

Grow, Lucille J. & Shapiro, Deborah. Black Children-White Parents: A Study of Transracial Adoption. LC 74-29169. (Orig.). 1974. pap. 7.95 (ISBN 0-87868-152-3, A-37). Child Welfare.

--Transracial Adoption Today: Views of Adoptive Parents & Social Workers. LC 75-7553. 1975. pap. 4.75 (ISBN 0-87868-153-1, A-38). Child Welfare.

Grow, Thomas A. Construction: A Guide for the Profession. (Illus.). 224p. 1975. ref. ed. 16.95 (ISBN 0-13-169326-3). P-H.

Growther, Jonathan. Advanced Crosswords, for Learners of English as a Foreign Language. 58p. (Orig.). 1981. pap. 3.25x (ISBN 0-19-581752-4). Oxford U Pr.

Grozdanic, S., jt. ed. see Pasic, N.

Grubb & Ellis Commercial Brokerage Co., jt. auth. see Real Estate Education Co.

Grubb, Davis. The Siege of Three Eighteen: Thirteen Mystical Stories. LC 78-61067. 180p. 1978. 9.00 (ISBN 0-686-37046-5). Back Fork Bks.

Grubb, Frederick, ed. see Roberts, Michael.

Grubb, John D., ed. see King, C. D.

Grubb, Mary L, ed. see King, C. D.

Grubb, Nancy, ed. see Hoy, Anne.

Grubb, Norman. Key to Everything. 1975. pap. 3.50 o.p. (ISBN 0-8024-4545-4). Moody.

--Yes I Am. 1982. pap. text ed. 4.95 (ISBN 0-87508-206-8). Chr Lit.

Grubb, Norman P. C. T. Studd. 1972. pap. 4.95 (ISBN 0-87508-202-5). Chr Lit.

--Rees Howells: Intercessor. 1964-1967. 4.95 o.p. (ISBN 0-87508-220-3); pap. 4.50 (ISBN 0-87508-219-X). Chr Lit.

Grubb, Norton. Funds, Force, Friction: Intergovernmental Relations in Programs for Children & Youth in Texas. (Policy Research Project Ser.: No. 48). 96p. 1982. 7.50 (ISBN 0-89940-651-3). LBJ Sch Public Affairs.

Grubb, Norton & Heilburn, Patricia G. Far, Far to Go: Public Spending on Children & Youth in Texas. LC 82-50321. (Special Project Report Ser.). 1982. 5.50 (ISBN 0-89940-805-2). LBJ Sch Public Affairs.

Grubb, Reba. God's Beautiful World. Sparks, Judith, ed. (A Happy Day Book). (Illus.). 24p. (gr. k-2). 1980. 1.29 (ISBN 0-87239-402-6, 3634). Standard Pub.

Grubb, Reba D. & Ondov, Geraldine. Planning Ambulatory Surgery Facilities. LC 79-10123. (Illus.). 198p. 1979. 19.95 o.p. (ISBN 0-8016-1986-6). Mosby.

Grubb, Thomas. Singing in French: A Manual of French Diction & French Vocal Repertoire. LC 77-18473. 1979. pap. text ed. 12.95 (ISBN 0-02-870790-7). Schirmer Bks.

Grubb, W. Norton, jt. auth. see Lazerson, Marvin.

Grubb, W. Norton, jt. ed. see Lazerson, Marvin.

Grubbs, H. A. & Kneller, J. W. Introduction a la Poesie Francaise. 275p. 1962. 18.50x o.p. (ISBN 0-471-00217-8). Wiley.

Grubbs, R. & Weaver, D. H. Typing Improvement Practice for Electric Typists. write for info. o.p. (ISBN 0-07-025066-9, G). McGraw.

--Typing Improvement Practice for Manual Typists. write for info. o.p. (ISBN 0-07-025065-0, G). McGraw.

Grubbs, Robert & White. Sustained Time Writings. 3rd ed. 1971. 6.80 o.p. (ISBN 0-07-025062-6, G). McGraw.

Grubbs, Robert L. & Ober, B. Scot. Gregg Shorthand for Colleges, Speed Building. Lemaster, A. James, ed. LC 79-11915. (Series 90). (Illus.). 448p. 1981. text ed. 20.00 (ISBN 0-07-025055-3, G); instr's. handbook 5.20 (ISBN 0-07-025059-6); wkbk. 6.60 (ISBN 0-07-025057-X); key to wkbk. 4.15 (ISBN 0-07-025058-8); student's transcript 7.15 (ISBN 0-07-025056-1). McGraw.

Grubbs, Robert L. & White, James L. Sustained Timed Writings. 4th ed. 96p. 1982. pap. 6.80 (ISBN 0-07-025063-4). McGraw.

Grubbs, Robert L., et al. Exploratory Business. 6th ed. (Illus.). (gr. 9-10). 1978. text ed. 7.80 (ISBN 0-07-025050-2, G); teachers manual & key 7.40 (ISBN 0-07-025051-0). McGraw.

Grubbs, Sylvia. Friends, a Guest Book. 1982. gift, padded cover 7.95 (ISBN 0-87162-261-0). Warner Pr.

Grube, G. M., tr. see Aristotle.

Grube, G. M., tr. see Plato.

Grube, G. M., tr. & intro. by see Plato.

Gruber, Alain. Silverware. LC 82-50422. (Illus.). 306p. 1982. 75.00 (ISBN 0-8478-0440-2). Rizzoli Intl.

Gruber, Arnold, jt. auth. see Spiegel, Herbert J.

Gruber, Barbara. Barbara Jean's Household Money Tips: Hundreds of Ideas for Saving Money on Food, Clothing, Decorating. 256p. 1983. pap. 7.95 (ISBN 0-525-93294-1, 0772-230). Dutton.

Gruber, Edward & Gruber, Gary R. Graduate Record Examination. rev. ed. 1978. pap. 7.95 (ISBN 0-671-18993-X). Monarch Pr.

Gruber, Edward C. Graduate Management Admissions Test. (Exam Preparation Ser.). 1975. pap. 7.95 (ISBN 0-671-18995-6). S&S.

--Miller Analogies Test. 1976. pap. 5.95 (ISBN 0-671-18981-6). Monarch Pr.

Gruber, Edward C. & Gruber, Gary R. Graduate Management Admission Test (GMAT) 1976. pap. 7.95 (ISBN 0-671-18995-6). Monarch Pr.

Gruber, Edward C. & Wildorf, Barry L. Law School Admission Test. (Exam Prep. Ser.). pap. 7.95 (ISBN 0-671-45883-3). Monarch Pr.

Gruber, F. A., jt. auth. see Segalowitz, S. J.

Gruber, Frank. Broken Lance. 1982. pap. 1.95 (ISBN 0-451-11353-5, AJ1353, Sig). NAL.

--Bugles West. large print ed. 1981. 18.00x o.p. (ISBN 0-89340-075-0, Pub. by Curley Assoc England). State Mutual Bk.

--Fighting Man. (Westerns Ser.). lib. bdg. cancelled (ISBN 0-8398-2660-5, Gregg). G K Hall.

--Fighting Man. Bd. with The Marshal. 1980. pap. 2.50 (ISBN 0-451-11601-1, AE1601, Sig). NAL.

Gruber, Gary. American College Test. new ed. (Exam Preparation Ser.). 528p. (Orig.). (gr. 11-12). 1978. pap. 7.75 (ISBN 0-671-18996-4). S&S.

--Physics. (College Outline Ser.). pap. 4.95 o.p. (ISBN 0-671-08049-0). Monarch Pr.

--SAT-Standard Written English Test. (Exam Preparation Ser.). 180p. (Orig.). (gr. 11-12). 1977. pap. 6.75 (ISBN 0-671-18994-8). S&S.

Gruber, Gary R. College Level Examination Program (CLEP) (Exam Prep. Ser.). pap. 6.95 (ISBN 0-671-47248-8). Monarch Pr.

--Inside Strategies for the SAT. 144p. 1982. pap. 5.95 (ISBN 0-87694-185-4). Ed Design Inc.

--Standard Written English Test (SWET) pap. 6.95 (ISBN 0-671-18994-8). Monarch Pr.

Gruber, Gary R., jt. auth. see Gruber, Edward.

Gruber, Gary R., jt. auth. see Gruber, Edward C.

Gruber, Helmut. The Temptation of Adam. LC 78-65530. 1979. 9.95 o.p. (ISBN 0-89696-036-6, An Everest House Book). Dodd.

Gruber, Howard E. & Voneche, J. Jacques, eds. The Essential Piaget. 1982. pap. 18.50 (ISBN 0-465-02058-5). Basic.

Gruber, J., ed. Econometric Decision Models: Proceedings, Hagen, FRG, 1981. (Lecture Notes in Economics & Mathematical Systems Ser.: Vol. 208). (Illus.). 364p. 1983. pap. 24.50 (ISBN 0-387-11554-4). Springer-Verlag.

Gruber, Jeffrey S. Lexical Structures in Syntax & Semantics. new ed. (North Holland Linguistics Ser.: Vol. 25). 1976. 39.00 (ISBN 0-7204-0410-X, North-Holland). Elsevier.

Gruber, M. J., jt. auth. see Elton, E. J.

Gruber, Martin J., jt. auth. see Elton, Edwain J.

Gruber, Martin J., jt. auth. see Elton, Edwin J.

Gruber, Michael, ed. see Leo, Miriam & Forlini, Gary.

Gruber, Murray L., ed. Management Systems in the Human Services. 378p. 1981. 29.95 (ISBN 0-87722-207-X); pap. 12.95 (ISBN 0-87722-214-2). Temple U Pr.

Gruber, Ruth. Raquela: A Woman of Israel. LC 78-107. (Illus.). 1978. 11.95 (ISBN 0-698-10895-7, Coward). Putnam Pub Group.

Gruber, Ruth, jt. auth. see Margolies, Marjorie.

Gruber, S., tr. see Goden, D.

Gruber, Terry. Fat Cats. LC 81-47086. (Illus.). 192p. (Orig.). 1981. pap. 8.61i (ISBN 0-06-090897-1, CN 897, CN). Har-Row.

Gruber, William H. & Niles, John S. The New Management: Line Executive & Staff Professional in the Future Firm. 1976. 4.75 (ISBN 0-07-025073-1, P&RB). McGraw.

Gruber, William H., jt. auth. see Synott, William R.

Gruberg, Edward & Raymond, Stephen. Beyond Cholesterol. 208p. 1983. pap. 4.95 (ISBN 0-686-42893-5). St Martin.

Gruchcow, Jack. The Visicalc Applications Book. 1982. text ed. 21.95 (ISBN 0-8359-8390-0); pap. 16.95. Reston.

Gruchy, Allan G. Comparative Economic Systems: Competing Ways to Stability, Growth & Welfare. 2nd ed. LC 76-10899. (Illus.). 1977. 25.95 (ISBN 0-395-18606-4). HM.

Grudem, Wayne A. The Gift of Prophecy in One Corinthians. LC 81-40583. 358p. (Orig.). 1982. lib. bdg. 25.25 (ISBN 0-8191-2083-9); pap. text ed. 14.00 (ISBN 0-8191-2084-7). U Pr of Amer.

Grudin, L. Mister Eliot Among the Nightingales. LC 78-174691. (Studies in T. S. Eliot, No. 11). 1972. Repr. of 1932 ed. lib. bdg. 24.95x (ISBN 0-8383-1346-9). Haskell.

Grudin, Robert. Mighty Opposites: Shakespeare & Renaissance Contrariety. LC 78-51753. 1979. 21.75x (ISBN 0-520-03666-2). U of Cal Pr.

Grudzinskas, J. B. & Seppala, M., eds. Pregnancy Proteins: Biology, Chemistry & Clinical Application (Australia) 474p. 1982. 47.00 (ISBN 0-12-304850-8). Acad Pr.

Gruebel-Lee, David, ed. Disorders of the Hip. (Illus.). 300p. 1983. text ed. price not set (ISBN 0-397-50465-9, Lippincott Medical). Lippincott.

Gruelle, Johnny. Raggedy Ann & the Nice Fat Policeman. (ps-3). 1979. pap. 1.95 o.p. (ISBN 0-440-47451-5, YB). Dell.

Gruen, Al. Contact Sheet: The Secret of Creative Photography. (Illus.). 192p. (Orig.). 1982. 19.95 (ISBN 0-8174-3705-3, Amphoto). Watson-Guptill.

Gruen, Claude, jt. auth. see Gruen, Nina.

Gruen, Erich S. The Last Generation of the Roman Republic. LC 72-89244. 1974. 45.00x (ISBN 0-520-02238-6). U of Cal Pr.

Gruen, F. H., ed. Surveys of Australian Economics, Vol. III. 272p. 1983. text ed. 35.00x (ISBN 0-86861-396-7). Allen Unwin.

Gruen, Gerd. The Development of the Vertebrate Retina: A Comparative Survey. (Advances in Anatomy, Embryology, & Cell Biology Ser.: Vol. 78). (Illus.). 130p. 1982. pap. 24.00 (ISBN 0-387-11770-9). Springer-Verlag.

Gruen, Nina & Gruen, Claude. Demographic Changes & Their Effects on Real Estate Markets in the '80s. LC 82-60314. (Development Component Ser.). (Illus.). 27p. 1982. pap. 10.00 (ISBN 0-87420-609-X, D22). Urban Land.

Gruenberger, F. J. & Jaffray, G. Problems for Computer Solution. LC 65-24303. 1965. pap. 22.95 (ISBN 0-471-32908-8). Wiley.

Gruenberger, Fred J. & McCracken, Daniel D. Introduction to Electronic Computers: Problem Solving with the IBM 1620. 178p. 1963. 7.50 o.p. (ISBN 0-686-81273-5). Krieger.

Gruendemann, Barbara J. & Meeker, Margaret H. Alexander's Care of the Patient in Surgery. 7th ed. (Illus.). 882p. 1983. text ed. 35.95 (ISBN 0-8016-4147-0). Mosby.

Gruendemann, Barbara J., et al. The Surgical Patient: Behavioral Concepts for the Operating Room Nurse. 2nd ed. LC 76-51725. (Illus.). 190p. 1977. pap. text ed. 10.50 o.p. (ISBN 0-8016-1981-5). Mosby.

Gruenfeld, Elaine F. Performance Appraisal: Promise & Peril. LC 81-3920. (Key Issues Ser.: No. 25). 72p. 1981. pap. 4.00 (ISBN 0-87546-088-7). ILR Pr.

--Promotion: Practices, Policies, & Affirmative Action. (Key Issues Ser.: No. 17). 64p. 1975. pap. 3.00 (ISBN 0-87546-222-7). ILR Pr.

Gruenler, Royce G. New Approaches to Jesus & the Gospels: A Phenomenological & Exegetical Study of Jesus & the Gospels. 208p. (Orig.). 1982. pap. 13.95 (ISBN 0-8010-3782-4). Baker Bk.

Gruenwald, Oskar. The Yugoslav Search for Man: Marxist Humanism in Contemporary Yugoslavia. 448p. 1983. 29.95x (ISBN 0-89789-005-1). J F Bergin.

Gruerio, Anthony. Painting with a Palette Knife. (Pitman Art Ser.: Vol. 81). pap. 1.95 o.p. (ISBN 0-448-00592-1, G&D). Putnam Pub Group.

--Portraits in Pencil. (Pitman Art Ser.: Vol. 70). pap. 2.95 (ISBN 0-448-00583-2, G&D). Putnam Pub Group.

Gruetzner & Johnson. Dictionary of British Artists 1880-1940. 45.00 o.s.i. (ISBN 0-912728-30-2). Newbury Bks.

Grugel, Lee E. Society & Religion During the Age of Industrialization: Christianity in Victorian England. LC 78-65844. (Illus.). 1979. pap. text ed. 8.25 (ISBN 0-8191-0671-2). U Pr of Amer.

Grugeon, E., jt. ed. see Cashdan, A.

Gruhl, Jim, ed. see Kirsner, Gary.

Gruhn, Isebill V. Regionalism Reconsidered: The Economic Commission for Africa. LC 79-5060. (Special Studies on Africa). 1979. lib. bdg. 20.00 (ISBN 0-89158-576-1). Westview.

Gruijter, Dato N. De see De Gruijter, Dato N. & Van Der Kamp, Leo. J.

Gruijter, J. J. De see De Gruijter, J. J.

Gruizelier, J. H. & Flor-Henry, P. Hemisphere Asymetries of Function in Psychopathology. (Developments in Psychiatry Ser.: Vol. 3). 1980. 75.75 (ISBN 0-444-80189-8). Elsevier.

Grujic, B. Serbocroatian-English, English-Serbocroatian Dictionary. Rev. & enl. ed. 1980. 25.00 (ISBN 0-685-65374-9). Heinman.

--Serbocroatian-English-Serbocroatian Dictionary: Short Grammar. 33rd ed. 624p. 1982. text ed. 18.00x (ISBN 0-89918-647-5, Y-647). Vanous.

Gruliou, Leo. Moscow. (The Great Cities Ser.). (Illus.). (gr. 6 up). 1977. PLB 11.97 o.p. (ISBN 0-8094-2275-1, Pub. by Time-Life). Silver.

Grum, Fran & Bartleson, James, eds. Optical Radiation Measurements, Vol. 4. Date not set. price not set (ISBN 0-12-304904-0). Acad Pr.

Grum, Franc & Becherer, Richard, eds. Optical Radiation Measurements, Vol. 3. 314p. 1982. 47.00 (ISBN 0-12-304903-2). Acad Pr.

Grumann, V. Biographisch-bibliographisches Handbuch der Lichenologie. Nach dem Tode des Verfassers ed. by O. Klement. 1979. lib. bdg. 100.00x (ISBN 3-7682-0907-5). Lubrecht & Cramer.

Grumbach, Doris. The Missing Person. 256p. 1981. 11.95 o.p. (ISBN 0-399-12587-6). Putnam Pub Group.

Grumbach, Jane & Emerson, Robert, eds. Monologues: Men, Vol. 2. 56p. (Orig.). 1983. pap. 3.95x (ISBN 0-89676-065-0). Drama Bk.

--Monologues: Women, Vol. 2. LC 76-1975. 56p. (Orig.). 1981. pap. 3.95x (ISBN 0-89676-066-9). Drama Bk.

Grumbach, Jane, jt. ed. see Emerson, Robert.

Grumelli, Antonio, jt. ed. see Caporale, Rocco.

Grumet, Robert S. Native Americans of the Northwest Coast: A Critical Bibliography. LC 79-2165. (Newberry Library Center for the History of the American Indian Bibliographical Ser.). 128p. 1980. pap. 5.95x (ISBN 0-253-30385-0). Ind U Pr.

Grumm, John & Wasby, Stephen, eds. The Analysis of Policy Impact. 1980. pap. 6.00 (ISBN 0-918592-39-9). Policy Studies.

Grumm, John G. & Wasby, Stephen L., eds. The Analysis of Policy Impact. (A Policy Studies Orgnization Bk.). 224p. 1981. 25.95x (ISBN 0-669-03951-9). Lexington Bks.

Grumman, Joan, jt. auth. see Webber, Jeanette.

Grun, jt. auth. see Kissel, Irwin R.

Grun, Bernard. The Timetables of History. 1979. 29.95 o.p. (ISBN 0-671-24987-8). S&S.

--The Timetables of History. rev. ed. 1982. pap. 13.95 (ISBN 0-671-24988-6). S&S.

Grun, M., jt. ed. see Liehr, H.

Grun, Max von der see Von der Grun, Max.

Grunbaum, Dorien, jt. auth. see Markstein, Linda.

Grunberg, Emanuel, jt. auth. see Schnitzer, Robert J.

Grunberg, Leon. Failed Multinational Ventures. LC 80-8364. (Illus.). 192p. 1981. 25.95x (ISBN 0-669-04032-0). Lexington Bks.

Grunberger, Richard. Red Rising in Bavaria. LC 73-76430. 168p. 1973. 17.95 o.p. (ISBN 0-312-66675-6). St Martin.

Grunberg-Manago & Safer. Interaction of Translation & Transcriptual Controls in the Regulation of Gene Expression. (Developments in Biochemistry Ser.: Vol. 24). 1982. 75.00 (ISBN 0-444-00760-1). Elsevier.

Grund. Benezit Dictionary of Artists, 10 Vols. Date not set. 500.00 (ISBN 0-686-43137-5). Apollo.

Grund, D. W. & Harrison, K. A. Nova Scotian Boletes. (Bibliotheca Mycologica Ser.: No. 47). 1976. text ed. 24.00 (ISBN 3-7682-1062-6). Lubrecht & Cramer.

Grundberg, Sibyl, jt. ed. see Dowrick, Stephanie.

Grunder, Garel A. & Livezey, William E. The Philippines & the United States. LC 72-12327. (Illus.). 315p. 1973. Repr. of 1951 ed. lib. bdg. 20.00x (ISBN 0-8371-6731-0, GRTP). Greenwood.

Grundon, M. A. & Henbest, H. B. Organic Chemistry: An Introduction. 2nd ed. 1968. 17.95 (ISBN 0-444-19921-7). Elsevier.

Grundtvig, Svendt. Danish Fairy Tales. Cramer, J. Grant, tr. from Danish. (Illus.). 136p. (gr. k-5). 1972. pap. 4.50 (ISBN 0-486-22891-6). Dover.

Grundy, Julia M. Ten Days in the Light of 'Akka. rev. ed. LC 79-12177. 1979. pap. 3.00 (ISBN 0-87743-131-0, 332-040-10). Baha'i.

Grundy, Kenneth W. Confrontation & Accomodation in Southern Africa. LC 72-78950. (Perspectives on Southern Africa Ser., No. 10). 1973. 32.50x (ISBN 0-520-02271-8). U of Cal Pr.

--Defense Legislation & Communal Politics. LC 77-620051. (Papers in International Studies: Southeast Africa: No. 33). 1977. pap. 5.00 (ISBN 0-89680-065-2, Ohio U Ctr Intl). Ohio U Pr.

Grundy, Kenneth W. & Weinstein, Michael A. Ideologies of Violence. LC 73-91055. 1974. pap. 7.95x (ISBN 0-675-08835-6). Merrill.

Grundy, P. J. & Jones, G. A. Electron Microscopy in the Study of Materials. (Structure & Properties of Solids Ser.). 186p. 1976. pap. text ed. 16.95 (ISBN 0-7131-2522-5). E Arnold.

Grundy, Richard D., jt. ed. see Epstein, Samuel S.

Grundy, Stuart, jt. auth. see Tobler, John.

Gruneau, Richard S. Class, Sports, & Social Development. LC 82-21896. 192p. 1983. lib. bdg. 18.50 (ISBN 0-87023-387-4). U of Mass Pr.

Grunebaum, G. E. Von see Giorgio Levi Della Vida Conference-2nd-los Angeles-1969.

Grunebaum, Henry & Weiss, Justin L. Mentally Ill Mothers & Their Children. 2nd ed. LC 82-10911. xvii, 378p. 1982. lib. bdg. 30.00x (ISBN 0-226-31029-9); pap. 9.95 (ISBN 0-226-31022-1). U of Chicago Pr.

Grunebaum, Henry, et al. Mentally Ill Mothers & Their Children. LC 74-5740. xxii, 346p. 1975. 15.50x o.s.i. (ISBN 0-226-31021-3). U of Chicago Pr.

Gruneberg, Michael M. & Oborne, David J. Industrial Productivity: A Psychological Perspective. 232p. 1982. 60.00 (ISBN 0-333-28160-8, Pub. by Macmillan England). State Mutual Bk.

Gruneberg, Michael M., ed. Job Satisfaction. LC 75-43852. 254p. 1976. 36.95x o.s.i. (ISBN 0-470-32911-4). Halsted Pr.

Grunes, Barbara. Dining In: Chicago, Vol. 2. (Dining In Ser.). 200p. (Orig.). 1982. pap. 8.95 (ISBN 0-89716-108-4). Peanut Butter.

Grunewald, Alan E., jt. auth. see Nemmers, Erwin E.

Grunewald, Donald, jt. auth. see Flink, Salomon J.

Grunfeld, Emil N. The Blessed Yoke. 304p. (Orig.). 1982. pap. 5.95 (ISBN 0-686-42885-4). Makor Pub.

Grunfeld, Frederick V. Berlin. (The Great Cities Ser.). (Illus.). (gr. 6 up). 1977. 13.00 (ISBN 0-8094-2283-2, Pub by Time-Life). Silver.

Grunhut, Max. Juvenile Offenders Before the Courts. LC 77-27073. (Illus.). 1978. Repr. of 1956 ed. lib. bdg. 15.50x (ISBN 0-313-20194-3, GRJU). Greenwood.

--Penal Reform: A Comparative Study. LC 71-172568. (Criminology, Law Enforcement, & Social Problems Ser.: No. 149). 502p. 1972. Repr. of 1948 ed. 22.00x (ISBN 0-87585-149-5). Patterson Smith.

Grunin, Robert, jt. ed. see Gitter, A. George.

Grunmann-Gaudet, Minnette & Jones, Robin F., eds. The Nature of Medieval Narrative. LC 80-66330. (French Forum Monographs: No. 22). 218p. (Orig.). 1980. pap. 12.50x (ISBN 0-917058-21-6). French Forum.

Grunow, A., jt. auth. see Cleve, P. T.

Grunow, Oskar, tr. see Jaspers, Karl.

Grunwald, Stefan. Voices, Voices. LC 80-20881. (Orig.). 1980. pap. 5.95 o.p. (ISBN 0-89865-040-2). Donning Co.

Grupenhoff, John T., ed. Directory of Federal Health-Medicine Grants & Contracts Programs 1980. 340p. text ed. 35.00 (ISBN 0-89443-351-2). Aspen Systems.

--National Health Directory, 1983. 600p. 1983. price not set (ISBN 0-89443-811-5). Aspen Systems.

Grupp, Stanley. Marijuana. LC 72-157698. 1971. pap. text ed. 6.95 (ISBN 0-675-09834-3). Merrill.

Gruppe, M. The Frigates. LC 79-10643. (The Seafarers Ser.). (Illus.). 1979. lib. bdg. 19.92 (ISBN 0-8094-2716-8); 17.28 (ISBN 0-8094-2717-6). Silver.

Grusa, Jiri. Kafka from Prague. (Illus.). 128p. (Orig.). pap. 12.50. Schocken.

Grushcow, Jack & Smith, Courtney. Profits Through Seasonal Trading. 184p. 1980. 47.95 (ISBN 0-471-06158-1, Ronald). Ronald Pr.

Grushkin, Paul, et al. Grateful Dead: The Official Book of the Deadheads. (Illus.). 224p. 1983. pap. 12.95 (ISBN 0-688-01520-4); deluxe ed. 25.00 (ISBN 0-688-01917-X). Quill NY.

Gruss, Jane F. Counseling Stutterers. (Publications on Stuttering: No. 18). 80p. 1982. pap. 1.00 (ISBN 0-933388-18-7). Speech Found Am.

Gruver, Rebecca B. An American History. 3rd ed. LC 75-14794. 1981. text ed. 22.95 (ISBN 0-201-05051-X); Vol. 1. pap. text ed. 15.95 (ISBN 0-201-05052-8); Vol. 2. pap. text ed. 15.95 (ISBN 0-201-05053-6); write for info. mstr's manual (ISBN 0-201-05054-4); Vol. 1. write for info. study guide (ISBN 0-201-05055-2); Vol. 2. write for info. study guide (ISBN 0-201-05056-0). A-W.

Gruver, W. A. & Sachs, E. Algorithmic Methods in Optimal Control. (Research Notes in Mathematics Ser.: No. 47). 256p. 1981. pap. text ed. 25.00 (ISBN 0-273-08473-9). Pitman Pub MA.

Gruzalski, Bart, jt. ed. see Nelson, Carl.

Gryboski, Joyce. Gastrointestinal Problems in the Infant. LC 74-21012. (Mpcp Ser.: Vol. 13). (Illus.). 811p. 1975. text ed. 32.00 o.p. (ISBN 0-7216-4323-X). Saunders.

Gryna, Frank M., Jr., jt. auth. see Juran, Joseph M.

Gryson, R. Le Receuil Arien de Verone. 1983. pap. text ed. 46.00 (ISBN 90-247-2705-7, Pub. by Martinus Nijhoff Netherlands). Kluwer Boston.

Grzybowski, Kazimierz. Soviet Legal Institutions: Doctrines & Social Functions. LC 62-12163. (Michigan Legal Studies). xiv, 285p. 1982. Repr. of 1962 ed. lib. bdg. 30.00 (ISBN 0-89941-172-X). W S Hein.

Grzybowski, Kazimierz, ed. East-West Trade. LC 73-22437. (Library of Law & Contemporary Problems Ser.). 307p. 1973. lib. bdg. 20.00 (ISBN 0-379-11519-0). Oceana.

Grzybowski, Stefan. Tuberculosis & Its Prevention. (Illus.). 224p. 1983. 23.50 (ISBN 0-87527-210-X). Green.

Gschneider, K. A., Jr. & Eyring, L., eds. Handbook on the Physics & Chemistry of Rare Earths, Vol. 5. Date not set. 149.00 (ISBN 0-444-86375-3). Elsevier.

Gschneidner, K. A. & Eyring, L., eds. Handbook of the Physics & Chemistry of Rare Earths, Vol. 5: Rare Earth Handbook. 700p. 1983. 149.00 (ISBN 0-444-86375-3, North Holland). Elsevier.

Gschossman, Elke. German Grammar. (Schaum Outline Ser.). 256p. 1975. pap. text ed. 4.95 (ISBN 0-07-025090-1, SP). McGraw.

Gschossmann-Hendershot, E. Schaum's Outline of German Grammar. 2nd ed. 272p. 1982. pap. text ed. 5.95x (ISBN 0-07-025097-9). McGraw.

Gschwend, N. Surgical Management of Rheumatoid Arthritis. (SMCO). (Illus.). 260p. 1981. text ed. 60.00 o.p. (ISBN 0-7216-4332-9). Saunders.

--Surgical Treatment of Rheumatoid Arthritis. LC 79-3795. (Illus.). 248p. 1981. text ed. 35.00 (ISBN 0-7216-4332-9). Saunders.

Gsovski, Vladimir, ed. see Mid-European Law Project.

Guacho, Juan N. & Burns, Donald H. Bosquejo Gramatical del Quichua de Chimborazo. 203p. (Orig., Span.). 1975. pap. 8.00 (ISBN 0-88312-741-5); microfiche (3) 3.00 (ISBN 0-88312-373-8). Summer Inst Ling.

Guadarrama, Argelia A. Steps to English Kindergarten Teacher's Manual. 128p. 1983. pap. text ed. 7.68 (ISBN 0-07-033110-3, W); kit 266.64 (ISBN 0-07-033100-6). McGraw.

Gualt, J. W. & Pimmel, R. L. Introduction to Microcomputer-Based Digital Systems. (McGraw-Hill Ser. in Electronics). 1981. 32.50 (ISBN 0-07-023047-1); solutions manual 12.50 (ISBN 0-07-023048-X). McGraw.

Gualtieri, F., et al, eds. Recent Advances in Receptor Chemistry. 1979. 62.25 (ISBN 0-444-80094-8, Biomedical Pr). Elsevier.

Guandolo, John. Transportation Law. 4th ed. 800p. 1983. text ed. write for info. (ISBN 0-697-08516-3). Wm C Brown.

Guandolo, John, jt. auth. see Fair, Marvin L.

Guangtian, Li. A Pitiful Plaything & Other Essays. Yang, Gladys, tr. (Panda Ser.). 154p. (Orig.). 1982. pap. 2.95 (ISBN 0-8351-1024-9). China Bks.

Guarasci, Richard. The Theory & Practice of American Marxism, Nineteen Fifty-Seven to Nineteen Seventy. LC 80-1376. 170p. 1980. lib. bdg. 20.75 (ISBN 0-8191-1148-1); pap. text ed. 11.00 (ISBN 0-8191-1149-X). U Pr of Amer.

Guard, Charles. The Manx National Songbook, Vol. 2. 1980. text ed. 22.25x o.p. (ISBN 0-904980-32-4). Humanities.

Guardini, Romano. Freedom, Grace, & Destiny. Murray, John, tr. from Ger. LC 75-8786. 384p. 1975. Repr. of 1961 ed. lib. bdg. 14.50x o.p. (ISBN 0-8371-8111-9, GUFG). Greenwood.

Guardo, Carol J. The Adolescent As Individual: Issues & Insights. 352p. 1975. pap. text ed. 13.50 scp o.p. (ISBN 0-06-042228-9, HarpC). Har-Row.

Guare, John. Three Exposures. LC 82-47922. 256p. 1982. 16.95 (ISBN 0-15-190178-3). HarBraceJ.

Guareschi. Don Camillo. (Easy Reader, B). 1972. pap. 3.95 (ISBN 0-88436-121-7, 55255). EMC.

Guarini, Battista. Il Pastor Fido (The Faithful Shepherd) Whitfield, J. H., ed. Fanshawe, Richard, tr. from It. LC 76-11575. (Edinburgh Bilingual Library: No. 11). 423p. 1976. text ed. 20.00x (ISBN 0-292-76431-6). U of Tex Pr.

Guarnieri, M. & Guarnieri, O. Dizionario Tecnico Tedesco-Italiano, Italiano-Tedesco Garzanti. 2032p. (Ger. & Ital.). 1979. 75.00 (ISBN 0-686-97355-0, M9184). French & eur.

Guarnieri, O., jt. auth. see Guarnieri, M.

Gubbay, Sasson S. The Clumsy Child. LC 75-12487. (MPN: Vol. 5). (Illus.). 275p. 1975. text ed. 9.00 (ISBN 0-7216-4340-X). Saunders.

Gubbins, K. E., jt. auth. see Reed, T. M.

Gubelin, Edward. Internal World of Gemstones. (Illus.). 1979. text ed. 150.00 o.p. (ISBN 0-408-00436-3). Butterworth.

Gubellini, C. E., jt. auth. see Keith, L. A.

Guberlet, Muriel L. Animals of the Seashore. LC 62-142921. (Illus.). 1981. 12.50 o.p. (ISBN 0-8323-0121-3). Binford.

Gubernatis, Angelo De. Zoological Mythology, 2 Vols. LC 68-58904. 1968. Repr. of 1872 ed. Set. 56.00x (ISBN 0-8103-3527-1). Gale.

Gubert, Robert P., ed. Plane Ellipticity & Related Problems. LC 82-11562. (Contemporary Mathematics Ser.: Vol. 2). 19.00 (ISBN 0-8218-5012-1, CONTM/11). Am Math.

Gubitosi, Camillo & Izzo, Alberto. Marcel Breuer. LC 80-54884. (Illus.). 200p. 1981. pap. cancelled (ISBN 0-8478-0374-0). Rizzoli Intl.

Gubitz, Myron, tr. see Guggenbuhl-Craig, Adolf.

Gubser, Elsie. Bobbin Lace. (Illus.). 6.00 (ISBN 0-686-09828-5). Robin & Russ.

Gubser, Peter. Politics & Change in Al-Karak, Jordan: A Study of a Small Arab Town & Its District. (Middle Eastern Monographs: No. 11). (Illus.). 1973. 14.50x o.p. (ISBN 0-19-215805-8). Oxford U Pr.

Gucker, Philip. Essential English Grammar. (Orig.). 1966. pap. 2.75 (ISBN 0-486-21649-7). Dover.

Guclu, Meral. Turkey. (World Bibliographical Ser.: No. 27). 331p. 1981. text ed. 49.00 (ISBN 0-903450-39-9). ABC-Clio.

Gudder, Stanley. A Mathematical Journey. 1976. text ed. 23.00 (ISBN 0-07-025105-3, C); instructor's manual 4.95 (ISBN 0-07-025106-1). McGraw.

Gudehus, G. Finite Elements in Geomechanics. LC 77-792. (Wiley Series in Numerical Methods of Engineering). 464p. 1977. 91.95 (ISBN 0-471-99446-4, Pub. by Wiley-Interscience). Wiley.

Gudel, Paul J., jt. ed. see Philipson, Morris.

Gudeman, Howard E., jt. auth. see Craine, James F.

Gudeman, Jon E., jt. auth. see Glasscote, R. M.

Gudeman, Stephen. The Demise of a Rural Economy: From Subsistence to Capitalism in a Latin American Village. (International Library of Anthropology). 1978. 21.00x (ISBN 0-7100-8835-3); pap. 8.95x (ISBN 0-7100-8836-1). Routledge & Kegan.

Guder, Darrell L., tr. see Jungel, Eberhard.

Guder, Darrell L., tr. see Weber, Otto.

Gudgin, G. Industrial Location Processes & Employment Growth. 352p. 1978. text ed. 35.75x (ISBN 0-566-00144-6). Gower Pub Ltd.

Gudjin, Graham & Taylor, Peter J. Seats, Votes & the Spatial Organization of Elections. 240p. 1979. 25.50x (ISBN 0-85086-073-3, Pub. by Pion England). Methuen Inc.

Gudnason, C. H. & Corlett, E. N., eds. Development of Production Systems. 920p. 1974. write for info (ISBN 0-85066-078-5, Pub. by Taylor & Francis). Intl Pubns Serv.

Gudorf, Christine E. Catholic Social Teaching on Liberation Themes. LC 80-5382. 394p. 1980. lib. bdg. 23.00 (ISBN 0-8191-1080-9); pap. text ed. 13.75 (ISBN 0-8191-1081-7). U Pr of Amer.

Gudschinsky, Sarah C. A Manual of Literacy for Preliterate Peoples. x, 180p. 1973. pap. 4.00x (ISBN 0-7263-0054-3); microfiche 2.25x (ISBN 0-88312-354-1). Summer Inst Ling.

Gudschinsky, Sarah C., et al. Estudos sobre Linguas e Culturas Indigenas. 212p. (Eng. & Port.). 1971. pap. 5.00 o.p. (ISBN 0-88312-760-1); microfiche 3.00x (ISBN 0-88312-346-0). Summer Inst Ling.

Guecioueur, Adda, ed. The Problems of Arab Economic Development & Integration. (Special Studies on the Middle East). 275p. 1983. price not set (ISBN 0-86531-595-7). Westview.

Guedalla, Philip. Argentine Tango. 254p. 1982. Repr. of 1933 ed. lib. bdg. 30.00 (ISBN 0-89987-313-8). Darby Bks.

--Gladstone & Palmerston: Being the Correspondence of Lord Palmerston with Mr. Gladstone, 1851-1865. 367p. 1982. Repr. of 1928 ed. lib. bdg. 40.00 (ISBN 0-89987-314-6). Darby Bks.

--The Hundredth Year. 312p. 1982. Repr. of 1939 ed. lib. bdg. 35.00 (ISBN 0-89987-315-4). Darby Bks.

Guedes, M. Morphology of Seed Plants. (Plant Science Ser.: No. 2). (Illus.). 1979. lib. bdg. 19.20x (ISBN 3-7682-1195-9). Lubrecht & Cramer.

Guedeville, Nicolas. Critique Generale des Aventures de Telemarque. (Utopias in the Enlightenment Ser.). 87p. (Fr.). 1974. Repr. of 1700 ed. 25.00x o.p. (ISBN 0-8287-0401-5, 037). Clearwater Pub.

Guedj, R. A., ed. Methodology of Interaction: SEILLAC II. 1980. 42.75 (ISBN 0-444-85479-7). Elsevier.

Guedj, R. A., ed. see IFIP Workshop on Methodology in Computer Graphics, France, May 1976.

Guelff, Richard, jt. ed. see Roberts, Adam.

Guelke, Leonard T. Historical Understanding in Geography: An Idealistic Approach. LC 82-4356. (Cambridge Studies in Historical Geography: No. 3). 112p. 1982. 24.95 (ISBN 0-521-24678-4). Cambridge U Pr.

Guelloz, Ezzedine. Pilgrimage to Mecca. (Illus.). 208p. 1982. 60.00 (ISBN 0-85692-059-2, Pub. By Salem Hse Ltd.). Merrimack Bk Serv.

Guelph. Biophysics Handbook II. 208p. 1982. pap. text ed. 7.95 (ISBN 0-8403-2816-8). Kendall-Hunt.

Guenter, Clarence A. & Welch, Martin H., eds. Pulmonary Medicine. 2nd ed. (Illus.). 896p. 1982. text ed. 75.00 (ISBN 0-397-50444-6, Lippincott Medical). Lippincott.

Guentert, Kenneth. What's Ahead for Childless Couples? 1977. 0.25 o.p. (ISBN 0-89570-110-3). Claretian Pubns.

Guenther, A. Andrew Garrett's Fische der Suedsee, 3 vols. in 1. (Illus.). 1966. 144.00 (ISBN 3-7682-0351-4). Lubrecht & Cramer.

Guenther, Anthony L. Criminal Behavior & Social Systems. 2nd ed. 1976. 15.95 (ISBN 0-395-30612-4). HM.

Guenther, C., jt. ed. see Mueller, U.

Guenther, Ernest, et al. The Essential Oils: Individual Essential Oils of the Plant Families, 6 vols. Vol. 1, 444p. 25.25 (ISBN 0-88275-073-9); Vol. 2, 866p. 43.50 (ISBN 0-88275-338-X); Vol. 3, 794p. 39.75 (ISBN 0-88275-163-8); Vol. 4, 766p. 42.50 (ISBN 0-88275-074-7); Vol. 5, 526p. 28.50 (ISBN 0-88275-354-1); Vol. 6, 498p. 32.50 (ISBN 0-88275-092-5); 184.50 set (ISBN 0-88275-953-1). Krieger.

Guenther, Gloria M. Crisis. (Contemporary Problems Reading Ser). (Illus.). (gr. 7-12). 1972. pap. 3.50 with tchrs'. guide (ISBN 0-685-64476-6). Activity Rec.

--Drunk. (Contemporary Problems Reading Ser.). (Illus.). (gr. 7-12). 1972. pap. 3.50 with tchrs'. guide (ISBN 0-914296-07-8). Activity Rec.

--Help. (Contemporary Problems Reading Ser.). (Illus.). (gr. 7-12). 1972. pap. 3.50 with tchrs' guide (ISBN 0-914296-06-X). Activity Rec.

--Secret. Harris, Norma, ed. (Contemporary Problems Reading Ser). (Illus.). 86p. (gr. 7-12). 1974. pap. 3.50 (ISBN 0-914296-20-5); tchr's guide avail. (ISBN 0-685-58279-5). Activity Rec.

Guenther, H. V. Philosophy & Psychology in the Abhidharma. 2nd rev. ed. 1974. 13.95 (ISBN 0-87773-048-2). Orient Bk Dist.

Guenther, Herbert V. Buddhist Philosophy in Theory & Practice. LC 76-14203. (Illus.). 240p. 1976. pap. 2.95 o.p. (ISBN 0-394-73271-5). Shambhala Pubns.

--Matrix of Mystery: Scientific & Humanistic Aspects of Rdzogs-chen Thought. (Illus.). 320p. 1983. pap. 15.00 (ISBN 0-87773-766-5). Great Eastern.

Guenther, John. Fun with the Funnies: Fifty Motivating Activities for Language Arts, Writing, & Social Studies, Grades 4-6. 1983. pap. text ed. 7.95 (ISBN 0-673-15637-0). Scott F.

Guenther, Nancy A. United States Supreme Court Decisions: An Index to Excerpts, Reprints & Discussions. 2nd ed. LC 82-10518. (Illus.). 864p. 1983. 52.50 (ISBN 0-8108-1578-8). Scarecrow.

Guenther, Ruth. Nutritional Guide for the Problem Drinker. (Good Health Guide Ser.). 32p. (Orig.). 1983. pap. 1.45 (ISBN 0-87983-295-9). Keats.

Guenther, William C. Concepts of Statistical Inference. 2nd ed. (Illus.). 512p. 1973. text ed. 16.95 o.p. (ISBN 0-07-025098-7, C); instructors' manual 1.50 o.p. (ISBN 0-07-025099-5). McGraw.

Guenthner & Rohrer. Studies in Formal Semantics: Intensionality, Temporality, Negation, Vol. 35. (North Holland Linguistics Ser.). 1978. 42.75 (ISBN 0-7204-0508-4, LIS, 35, North-Holland). Elsevier.

Guepin, Ange. Nantes au Dix-Neuvieme Siecle. Statistique Topographique, Industrielle et Morale: Hygenie Physique et Morale. (Conditions of the 19th Century French Working Class Ser.). 203p. (Fr.). 1974. Repr. of 1835 ed. lib. bdg. 58.00x o.p. (ISBN 0-8287-0402-3, 1187). Clearwater Pub.

Guerard, Albert. France: A Modern History. rev. & enl. ed. LC 69-19782. (Illus.). 632p. 1969. 15.00 (ISBN 0-472-08390-2). U of Mich Pr.

Guerard, Albert, tr. see Michelet, Jules.

Guerard, Albert J. The Triumph of the Novel: Dickens, Dostoevsky & Faulkner. LC 75-46357. 1976. 22.50x (ISBN 0-19-502066-9). Oxford U Pr.

Guerard, Albert L. Napolean Third: A Great Life in Brief. LC 78-13974. 1979. Repr. of 1966 ed. lib. bdg. 18.75x (ISBN 0-313-21062-4, GUNA). Greenwood.

Guerber, Helene A. Myths & Legends of the Middle Ages: Their Origin & Influence on Literature & Art. LC 72-2464. (Illus.). xvi, 405p. 1974. Repr. of 1909 ed. 31.00 o.p. (ISBN 0-8103-3873-4). Gale.

--Myths of Northern Lands: Narrated with Special Reference to Literature & Art. 1970. Repr. 34.00 o.p. (ISBN 0-8103-3862-9). Gale.

Guercio, E., et al. General Mathematical Ability: Preparation & Review for the Mathematics Part of the High School Equivalency Diploma Test. LC 74-19738. (GED Preparation Ser.). 160p. (Orig.). 1975. lib. bdg. 7.00 o.p. (ISBN 0-668-03841-1); pap. 6.00 (ISBN 0-668-03689-3). Arco.

--Reading Interpretation in Social Sciences, Natural Sciences & Literature: Preparation & Review for the Reading Parts of the High School Equivalency Diploma Test. LC 74-19739. (GED Preparation Ser.). 224p. (Orig.). 1975. lib. bdg. 7.00 o.p. (ISBN 0-668-03843-8); pap. 5.00 (ISBN 0-668-03690-7). Arco.

Gueriguian, J. L., et al, eds. Insulins, Growth Hormone, & Recombinant DNA Technology. 248p. 1981. 32.50 (ISBN 0-89004-544-5). Raven.

Guerin, Gilbert & Maier, Arlee. Informal Assessment in Education. 418p. 1982. pap. text ed. 11.95 (ISBN 0-87484-533-5). Mayfield Pub.

Guerin, Polly. Fashion Writing. 1972. pap. text ed. 15.10 o.p. (ISBN 0-672-96033-8); tchr's manual 6.67 o.p. (ISBN 0-672-96034-6). Bobbs.

Guerin, Wilfred L., et al. Mandala: Literature for Critical Analysis. LC 72-103917. (Orig.). 1970. pap. text ed. 15.50 scp o.p. (ISBN 0-06-043825-8, HarpC); instructor's manual avail. o.p. (ISBN 0-06-363828-2). Har-Row.

Gueritz, Caroline, tr. see Broger, Achim.

Guerke, W. R. A Monograph of the Genus Jubula Dumortier. (Bryophytorum Bibliotheca: No. 17). (Illus.). 1979. pap. 16.00 (ISBN 3-7682-1213-0). Lubrecht & Cramer.

Guerney, Louise, jt. auth. see Keat, Donald B.

Guerney, Louise F. Parenting: A Skills Training Manual. (Illus.). 151p. 1980. pap. 4.95 (ISBN 0-932990-00-2). Ideals PA.

Guernsey, JoAnn B. Five Summers. 192p. (gr. 6 up). 1983. write for info. (ISBN 0-89919-147-9, Clarion). HM.

Guernsey, Otis L. Best Plays 1981-1982. LC 20-21432. (The Burns Mantle Yearbook of the Theatre Ser.). 1983. 24.95 (ISBN 0-396-08124-X). Dodd.

Guerrant, Edward O. Modern American Diplomacy. LC 54-7823. 1954. 6.00 (ISBN 0-8263-0186-X). U of NM Pr.

Guerry, Andre-Michel. Essai sur la Statistique Morale de la France. (Conditions of the 19th Century French Working Class Ser.). 90p. (Fr.). 1974. Repr. of 1833 ed. lib. bdg. 33.00x o.p. (ISBN 0-8287-0403-1, 1152). Clearwater Pub.

Guerry, Herbert, ed. A Bibliography of Philosophical Bibliographies. LC 77-71862. 1977. lib. bdg. 35.00x (ISBN 0-8371-9542-X, GUC/). Greenwood.

Guers, K., jt. auth. see Beck, R.

Guertler, John T., ed. The Records of Baltimore's Private Organizations: A Guide to Archival Resources. 1981. lib. bdg. 40.00 o.s.i. (ISBN 0-8240-9360-7). Garland Pub.

Guertner, Beryl. Gregory's Two Hundred Home Plan Ideas. pap. 7.50x o.p. (ISBN 0-392-05865-0, ABC). Sportshelf.

Guesry, P., jt. ed. see Maupas, P.

Guess, jt. auth. see Sailor.

Guess, Doug, jt. auth. see Sailor, Wayne.

Guess, Vincent C. Manufacturing Control System User's Guide. (Illus.). 32p. (Orig.). 1982. pap. 10.00 (ISBN 0-940964-03-1). PSE.

Guest, Arthur. Advanced Practical Geography. 5th ed. 1977. text ed. 14.95x o.p. (ISBN 0-435-35356-X). Heinemann Ed.

--Man & Landscape. 2nd ed. 1978. text ed. 10.50x o.p. (ISBN 0-435-35355-1). Heinemann Ed.

Guest, Barbara. Biography. (Burning Deck Poetry Ser.). 24p. (Orig.). 1980. pap. 3.00 (ISBN 0-930900-93-6); pap. 20.00 signed, special ed. (ISBN 0-930900-94-4). Burning Deck.

Guest, C. Z. First Garden. LC 75-34655. (Illus.). 1976. 8.95 o.p. (ISBN 0-399-11712-1). Putnam Pub Group.

Guest, Charlotte. Mabinogion. (Illus.). 1978. 22.50 o.p. (ISBN 0-902375-34-2); pap. 9.95 (ISBN 0-89733-000-5). Academy Chi Ltd.

Guest, David & Knight, Kenneth. Putting Participation into Practice. 1979. text ed. 37.25x (ISBN 0-566-02086-6). Gower Pub Ltd.

Guest, Diana, jt. auth. see Harrison, Jim.

Guest, Edgar H. Collected Verse. 17.95 (ISBN 0-8092-8828-1). Contemp Bks.

Guest, Judith. Ordinary People. new ed. LC 76-2368. 288p. (YA) 1976. 12.95 (ISBN 0-670-52831-5). Viking Pr.

Guest, Lynn. The Sword of Hachiman. 1982. pap. 3.50 (ISBN 0-8217-1104-0). Zebra.

Guest, R., et al. Organizational Change Through Effective Leadership. 1977. 14.95 o.p. (ISBN 0-13-641316-1); pap. text ed. 14.95 (ISBN 0-13-641308-0). P-H.

Gue Trapier, E. Du see Du Gue Trapier, E.

Gueudeville, Nicolas, tr. see More, Thomas.

Guffey, Mary E. Business English. 356p. 1983. pap. text ed. 19.95x (ISBN 0-534-01396-1). Kent Pub Co.

Guffroy, Armand B. Le Tocsin, Sur le Permanence De la Garde Nationale, Sur L'organisation Des Muncipalites, et Des Assemblees Provinciales, Sur L'emploi Des Biens D'eglise a L'acquit Des Dettes De la Nation. (Rousseauism, 1788-1797). 1978. Repr. lib. bdg. 41.00x o.p. (ISBN 0-8287-0405-8). Clearwater Pub.

Gugan, Keith. Unconfined Vapor Cloud Explosions. 250p. 1979. 32.50x (ISBN 0-87201-887-3). Gulf Pub.

Guggenberger, L. J., et al, eds. The Structural Aspects of Homogeneous, Heterogeneous & Biological Catalysis. pap. 7.50 (ISBN 0-686-60384-2). Polycrystal Bk Serv.

Guggenbuehl-Craig, A. Macht als Gefahr beim Helfer. 4th ed. (Psychologische Praxis: Vol. 45). vi, 106p. 1982. pap. 11.50 (ISBN 3-8055-3664-X). S Karger.

Guggenbuhl-Craig, A. Marriage - Dead or Alive? Stein, Murray, tr. 126p. 1977. pap. 7.00 (ISBN 0-88214-309-3). Spring Pubns.

Guggenbuhl-Craig, Adolf. Power in the Helping Professions. Gubitz, Myron, tr. from Ger. 155p. 1971. text ed. 7.00 (ISBN 0-88214-304-2). Spring Pubns.

Guggenheim. Major Psychiatric Disorders. 1982. 19.95 (ISBN 0-444-00663-X). Elsevier.

Guggenheim, Alan, ed. see Guggenheim, Gus N.

Guggenheim, Gus N. Protocol for Productivity. Guggenheim, Alan, ed. (Textile Industry Management Ser.: No. 1). 132p. 1982. 17.95x (ISBN 0-910377-03-0); pap. 13.95x (ISBN 0-910377-00-6). Guggenheim.

Guggenheim, Hans. Dogon Art: Children's Brochure. (Illus.). 1973. pap. 1.00 o.p. (ISBN 0-88397-021-X, Pub. by Intl Exhibit Foun). C E Tuttle.

Guggenheim, Harry F. United States & Cuba: A Study in International Relations. Repr. of 1934 ed. lib. bdg. 15.00x o.p. (ISBN 0-8371-4230-X, GUUS). Greenwood.

Guggenheim, Peggy. Out of This Century: Confessions of an Art Addict. LC 80-722. (Illus.). 360p. (Orig.). 1980. pap. 8.95 o.p. (ISBN 0-385-17109-9, Anch). Doubleday.

Guggenheim, Scott E., jt. ed. see Weller, Robert P.

Guggenheimer, Heinrich W. Mathematics for Engineering & Science. LC 76-28336. (Applied Math Ser.). 290p. 1976. pap. 14.50 (ISBN 0-88275-462-9). Krieger.

Gughemetti, Joseph M. & Wheeler, Eugene D. The Taking. Rev. ed. (Illus.). 197p. 1982. lib. bdg. cancelled (ISBN 0-9608474-1-3); pap. 6.95 (ISBN 0-9608474-0-5). Terra View.

Gugler, J. & Flanagan, W. Urbanization & Social Changes in West Africa. LC 76-9175. (Urbanisation in Developing Countries Ser.). (Illus.). 1978. 29.95 (ISBN 0-521-21348-7); pap. 9.95 (ISBN 0-521-29118-6). Cambridge U Pr.

Gugler, Josef, jt. auth. see Gilbert, Alan.

Guha, Ranajit. A Rule of Property for Benga: An Essay on the Idea of Permanent Settlement. 2nd ed. 22p. 1982. text ed. 17.95x (ISBN 0-86131-289-9, Pub. by orient Longman Ltd India). Apt Bks.

Guha, Ranajit, ed. Subaltern Studies One: Writings on South Asian History & Society. (Illus.). 1982. 17.95x (ISBN 0-19-561355-4). Oxford U Pr.

Guiasu, Silviu. Information Theory with New Applications. (Illus.). 1977. text ed. 55.00 (ISBN 0-07-025109-6, C). McGraw.

Guibert, Herve. Bonjour Monsieur Lartigue. Walker, Janet M., ed. Grasselli, Margaret M., tr. LC 82-83899. (Illus.). 68p. (Orig.). 1982. pap. 11.25 (ISBN 0-88397-044-9). Intl Exhibit Foun.
Guibert, Joseph De see De Guibert, Joseph.
Guiberteau, Milton J., jt. ed. see Mettler, Fred A.
Guichard, Ami, ed. Automobile Year: No. 24, 1976-1977. 1977. 39.95 o.p. (ISBN 0-87799-066-2). Aztex.
--Automobile Year: No. 25, 1977-78. 1978. 39.95 (ISBN 0-87799-072-7). Aztex Pub.
Guicharnaud, June, tr. see Delay, Jean.
Guidano, V. F. & Liotti, G. Cognitive Processes of Emotional Disorders. LC 83-13188. (Psychology & Psychotherapy Ser.). 347p. 1983. text ed. 24.50x (ISBN 0-89862-006-6). Guilford Pr.
Guidelines Subcommittee, SLA Networking Committee. Getting into Networking: Guidelines for Special Libraries. LC 76-58875. (State-of-the-Art Review: No. 5). 1977. pap. 6.00 (ISBN 0-685-85830-8). SLA.
Guideposts Associates. The Guideposts Christmas Treasury. LC 79-6597. (Illus.). 320p. 1980. 14.95 (ISBN 0-385-14977-8). Doubleday.
Guidi, Angelo F., jt. auth. see Garlick, R. C., Jr.
Guido, Dennis, ed. see Martin, Philip R.
Guidoni, Enrico & Magni, Roberto. The Andes. Mondadori, tr. from Ital. LC 74-3643. (Monuments of Civilization Ser.). Orig. Title: Civilta Andine Grandi Monumenti. (Illus.). 1977. 25.00 (ISBN 0-448-02025-4, G&D). Putnam Pub Group.
Guidos, Barbara & Hamilton, Betty. MASA: Medical Acronyms, Symbols, & Abbreviations. 300p. 1983. lib. bdg. 49.95 (ISBN 0-918212-72-3). Neal-Schuman.
Guidotti, C., jt. ed. see Rahman, N. K.
Guidry, Ron & Golenbock, Peter. Guidry. LC 80-13732. 1980. 8.95 o.p. (ISBN 0-13-371609-0). P-H.
Guignard, M. Optimality & Stability in Mathematical Programming. (Mathematical Programming Studies: Vol. 19). 1982. 27.75 (ISBN 0-444-86441-5). Elsevier.
Guignon, Charles B. Heidegger & the Problem of Knowledge. 380p. 1983. text ed. 30.00 (ISBN 0-915145-21-9). Hackett Pub.
Guigoile, E. Nobody Listens to Andrew. (gr. 4-6). pap. 1.95 (ISBN 0-695-36345-X, Dist. by Caroline Hse). Follett.
Guild, Nelson & Palmer, Kenneth. Introduction to Politics: Essays & Readings. LC 67-29016. 341p. 1968. 13.50 (ISBN 0-471-33034-5, Pub. by Wiley). Krieger.
Guild, Nicholas. Chain Reaction. 384p. 1983. 13.95 (ISBN 0-312-12785-5). St Martin.
--The Favor. 320p. 1981. 12.95 o.p. (ISBN 0-312-28512-4). St Martin.
--Old Acquaintance. (Orig.). pap. 2.50 o.s.i. (ISBN 0-515-05229-9). Jove Pubns.
Guild, Reuben A. The Librarian's Manual: A Treatise on Bibliography, Comprising a Select & Descriptive List of Bibliographical Works; to Which Are Added, Sketches of Public Libraries. LC 70-174942. (Illus.). x, 304p. 1972. Repr. of 1858 ed. 40.00x (ISBN 0-8103-3811-4). Gale.
Guilfoile, Elizabeth. Have You Seen My Brother. (gr. 1-3). 1962. 2.50 o.s.i. (ISBN 0-695-83685-4); PLB 2.97 o.s.i. (ISBN 0-685-78823-7). Follett.
--Nobody Listens to Andrew. (Beginning-to-Read Bks). (Illus.). (gr. 1-3). 1957. PLB 3.39 o.s.i. (ISBN 0-695-46345-4, Dist. by Caroline Hse); pap. 1.95 (ISBN 0-685-10944-5). Follett.
--Valentine's Day. LC 65-10086. (Holiday Books Ser). (Illus.). (gr. 2-5). 1965. PLB 7.56 (ISBN 0-8116-6556-9). Garrard.
Guilford, J. P. Way Beyond the IQ: Guide to Improving Intelligence & Creativity. LC 77-80536. 1977. pap. 9.50 (ISBN 0-930222-01-6). Creat Educ Found.
Guilford, Joy P. Psychometric Methods. 2nd ed. (Psychology Ser.). 1964. text ed. 37.00 o.p. (ISBN 0-07-025129-0, C). McGraw.
Guilford, Joy P. & Fruchter, Benjamin. Fundamental Statistics in Psychology & Education. 6th ed. LC 77-5768. (McGraw-Hill Series in Psychology). (Illus.). 1977. text ed. 28.00 (ISBN 0-07-025150-9, C); instructor's manual 15.00 (ISBN 0-07-025151-7). McGraw.
Guilford, Joy P. & Hoepfner, R. Analysis of Intelligence. (Psychology Ser.). 1971. 32.00 o.p. (ISBN 0-07-025137-1, C). McGraw.
Guilfoyle, Ann. Amiable Little Beasts: Investigating the Lives of Young Animals. (Illus.). 171p. 1980. 24.95 o.p. (ISBN 0-02-546560-0). Macmillan.
Guilfoyle, Ann & Rayfield, Susan. Wildlife Photography. (Illus.). 176p. 1982. 24.95 (ISBN 0-8174-6417-4, Amphoto). Watson-Guptill.
Guiliani, jt. auth. see Nasser.
Guiliano, Edward. Lewis Carroll: A Celebration. 224p. 1982. 17.95 (ISBN 0-517-54557-8, C N Potter Bks). Crown.
Guiliano, Edward & Dodgson, Charles L., eds. Lewis Carroll Observed: A Collection of Unpublished Photographs, Drawings, Poetry & New Essays. (Illus.). 1976. 12.95 o.p. (ISBN 0-517-52497-X, C N Potter Bks). Crown.
Guiliano, Francis A., ed. Introduction to Oil & Gas Technology. 2nd ed. (Short Course Handbooks). (Illus.). 194p. 1981. text ed. 29.00 (ISBN 0-934634-48-3); pap. text ed. 21.00. Intl Human Res.
Guilland, Antoine. Modern Germany & Her Historians. Repr. of 1915 ed. lib. bdg. 17.00x (ISBN 0-8371-4506-6, GUMG). Greenwood.
Guillano, Edward. Lewis Carroll: An Annotated International Bibliography, 1960-1977. LC 80-13975. 253p. 1980. 15.00x (ISBN 0-8139-0862-0). U Pr of Va.
Guillaume, A., intro. by see Ishaq, I.
Guillaumin, Emile. The Life of a Simple Man. rev. ed. Weber, Eugen & Weber, Eugen, trs. from Fr. LC 82-40339. 264p. 1982. text ed. 16.00 (ISBN 0-87451-247-6); pap. 7.95 (ISBN 0-87451-246-8). U Pr of New Eng.
Guillebaud, John. The Pill. (Illus.). 1980. 19.95x (ISBN 0-19-217675-7); pap. 9.95x (ISBN 0-19-286002-X). Oxford U Pr.
Guillemin, Anne. The Kennedys Abroad: Ann & Peter in Brittany. 10.50 (ISBN 0-392-15943-0, SpS). Sportshelf.
Guillemin, Ernest A. Synthesis of Passive Networks: Theory & Methods Appropriate to the Realization & Approximation Problems. LC 76-50044. 760p. 1977. Repr. of 1957 ed. 36.50 (ISBN 0-88275-481-5). Krieger.
Guillemin, Victor & Pollack, Alan. Differential Topology. (Math. Ser). (Illus.). 324p. 1974. 27.95x (ISBN 0-13-212605-2). P-H.
Guillemin, Victor, ed. Studies in Applied Mathematics: Volume Dedicated to Irving Segal. (Advances in Mathematics: Supplementary Studies: Vol. 8). Date not set. 36.00 (ISBN 0-12-305480-X). Acad Pr.
Guilleminault, Christian, jt. auth. see Korobkin, Rowena.
Guilleminault, Christian, jt. ed. see Czeisler, Charles A.
Guillen, Nicolas. Man-Making Words: Selected Poems of Nicolas Guillen. Marquez, Robert & McMurray, David, eds. LC 78-181363. 248p. (Span. & Eng.). 1972. pap. 5.95x (ISBN 0-87023-102-2). U of Mass Pr.
Guillermaz, Jacques. Chinese Communist Party in Power, Nineteen Forty-Nine to Nineteen Seventy-Eight. LC 76-7593. 1976. 33.75 (ISBN 0-89158-041-7); softcover 16.00 (ISBN 0-89158-348-3). Westview.
Guillet, Alain & La Fauci, Nunzio, eds. Actes du ler Colloque Europeen sur la Grammaire et le Lexique Compares des Langues Romanes, 23-26 Septembre 1981. (Linguisticae Investigationes Supplementa Ser.: No. 9). 230p. (Fr.). 1983. 26.00 (ISBN 90-272-3119-2). Benjamins North Am.
Guillet, Edwin C. The Great Migration: The Atlantic Crossing by Sailing-Ship Since 1770. LC 73-145482. (The American Immigration Library). xii, 316p. 1971. Repr. of 1937 ed. lib. bdg. 17.95x (ISBN 0-89198-013-X). Ozer.
--Pioneer Settlements in Upper Canada. (Illus.). 1970. pap. 5.95 o.p. (ISBN 0-8020-6110-9). U of Toronto Pr.
Guillet, Ernest B. Un Theatre Francophone dans un milieu Franco-Americain. (Illus.). 52p. (Fr.). 1981. pap. text ed. 1.50x (ISBN 0-911409-37-8). Natl Mat Dev.
Guillet, J. Religious Experience of Jesus & His Disciples. Richards, M. Innocentia, tr. LC 75-210. (Religious Experience Ser: Vol. 9). 1975. pap. 2.95 (ISBN 0-87029-044-4, 20132-7). Abbey.
Guillet, Jacques. A God Who Speaks. LC 78-65898. 108p. 1979. pap. 4.95 o.p. (ISBN 0-8091-2195-6). Paulist Pr.
Guillet-Rydell, Mireille, jt. auth. see Bull, Vivien.
Guillory, John. Poetic Authority: Spenser, Milton, & Literary History. 224p. 1983. text ed. 25.00x (ISBN 0-231-05540-4); pap. 12.50x (ISBN 0-231-05541-2). Columbia U Pr.
Guillot, Genevieve & Prudhommeau, Germaine. The Book of Ballet. (Reference Shelf Ser.). (Illus.). 384p. 1980. pap. 3.95 (ISBN 0-13-079764-2, Spec). P-H.
Guillot, Genevieve, jt. auth. see Prudhommeau, Germaine.
Guillot, Rene. Prince of the Jungle. LC 59-60132. (Illus.). (gr. 7-9). 1959. 10.95 (ISBN 0-87599-045-2). S G Phillips.
--Sirga. LC 59-12198. (Illus.). (gr. 6-9). 1959. 10.95 (ISBN 0-87599-046-0). S G Phillips.
--Three Hundred Ninety-Seventh White Elephant. LC 57-6246. (Illus.). (gr. 4-6). 1957. 10.95 (ISBN 0-87599-043-6). S G Phillips.
--Wind of Chance. Dale, Norman, tr. (Illus.). (gr. 6-9). 1958. 10.95 (ISBN 0-87599-048-7). S G Phillips.
Guillou. Beginners Guide to Electric Wiring. 3rd ed. 1982. text ed. 9.95 (ISBN 0-408-01130-0). Butterworth.
Guilmartin, J. F., Jr. Gunpowder & Galleys. LC 73-83109. (Early Modern History Studies). (Illus.). 380p. 1975. 49.50 (ISBN 0-521-20272-8). Cambridge U Pr.
Guilpin, Everard. Skialethia Or a Shadowe of Truth, in Certaine Epigrams & Satyres. Carroll, D. Allen, ed. LC 73-14841. vii, 248p. 1974. 20.00x (ISBN 0-8078-1220-X). U of NC Pr.
Guiltinan, J. P. & Paul, G. W. Marketing Management. (Marketing Ser.). 1982. 23.95x (ISBN 0-07-048920-3); instr's. manual 20.00 (ISBN 0-07-048921-1). McGraw.
Guin, Ursula K. Le see Le Guin, Ursula K.
Guin, Ursula K. Le see LeGuin, Ursula K.
Guin, Ursula K. Le see Le Guin, Ursula K.
Guinagh, Kevin, ed. & tr. Dictionary of Foreign Phrases & Abbreviations. 2nd ed. 352p. 1972. 12.00 o.p. (ISBN 0-8242-0460-3). Wilson.
Guinagh, Kevin, jt. ed. see Lyle, Guy R.
Guinagh, Kevin, tr. & compiled by. Dictionary of Foreign Phrases & Abbreviations. 3rd ed. 288p. 1982. 28.00 (ISBN 0-8242-0675-4). Wilson.
Guinan, Edward, ed. Peace & Non-Violence: Basic Writings. LC 73-75741. 192p. (Orig.). 1973. pap. 4.95 o.p. (ISBN 0-8091-1770-3). Paulist Pr.
Guinan, John, jt. auth. see Fitzmaurice, George.
Guindey, Guillaume. The International Monetary Tangle: Myths & Realities. Hoffman, Michael L., tr. LC 77-77797. (Fr.). 1977. 22.50 (ISBN 0-87332-108-1). M E Sharpe.
Guindon, Kathleen M., ed. see Dawley, Gloria & Sorger, James.
Guindon, Richard. Cartoons by Guindon. (Illus.). 1980. pap. 6.95 (ISBN 0-8256-3180-7, Quick Fox). Putnam Pub Group.
Guinee, Kathleen K. Teaching & Learning in Nursing. (Illus.). 1978. pap. text ed. 10.95 (ISBN 0-02-348360-1). Macmillan.
Guiney, Louise, tr. see Bree, Germine.
Guiney, Louise, tr. see Follain, Jean.
Guiney, Louise I. Happy Ending: The Collected Lyrics of Louise I. Guiney. LC 78-11678. 1979. Repr. of 1927 ed. lib. bdg. 18.00x (ISBN 0-313-20702-X, GUHE). Greenwood.
Guinguene, Pierre-Louis. Lettres Sur les Confessions De J. J. Rousseau. (Rousseauism, 1788-1797). 1978. Repr. lib. bdg. 44.50x o.p. (ISBN 0-8287-0410-4). Clearwater Pub.
Guinness, Desmond & Ryan, William. The White House: An Architectural History. (Illus.). 1980. 29.95 (ISBN 0-07-054352-6). McGraw.
Guinness Editors, ed. Guinness Book of College Records & Facts. LC 81-85043. (Illus.). 192p. 1982. 7.95 (ISBN 0-8069-0230-2); lib. bdg. 9.99 (ISBN 0-8069-0231-0). Sterling.
Guinness, F. E., jt. auth. see Clutton-Brock, T. H.
Guinness, H. The Man They Crucified. pap. 0.50 (ISBN 0-87784-112-8). Inter-Varsity.
Guinness, Howard. Sacrifice. 6th ed. LC 75-21451. 96p. (Orig.). 1975. pap. 1.95 o.p. (ISBN 0-87784-307-4). Inter-Varsity.
Guinness, Os. The Dust of Death. LC 72-94670. 430p. 1973. pap. 9.95 (ISBN 0-87784-911-0). Inter-Varsity.
Guinot, B., jt. auth. see Debarbat, S.
Guinther, John. Philadelphia: Dream for the Keeping. Silvey, Kitty & Mason, Sharon, eds. LC 81-86566. (American Portrait Ser.). (Illus.). 240p. 1982. 29.95 (ISBN 0-932986-23-4). Continent Herit.
Guion, Robert M. Personnel Testing. (Psychology Ser.). (Illus.). 1965. text ed. 44.00 (ISBN 0-07-025170-3, C). McGraw.
Guiry, M. D. A Consensus & Bibliography of Irish Seaweeds. (Bibliotheca Phycologica Ser.: No. 44). 1979. pap. text ed. 16.00x (ISBN 3-7682-1209-2). Lubrecht & Cramer.
Guise, C. H., jt. auth. see Graves, Henry S.
Guisewite, Cathy. Cathy's Valentine Day Survival Kit. 24p. 1983. pap. 2.95 (ISBN 0-8362-1204-5). Andrews & McMeel.
--Eat Your Way to a Better Relationship. LC 82-72420. 60p. (Orig.). 1983. pap. 2.95 (ISBN 0-8362-1987-2). Andrews & McMeel.
--How to Get Rich, Fall in Love, Lose Weight, & Solve All Your Problems by Saying "No". LC 82-72412. (Illus.). 60p. (Orig.). 1983. pap. 2.95 (ISBN 0-8362-1986-4). Andrews & McMeel.
Guitar Player Magazine Editors, ed. Rock Guitarists, Vol II. LC 77-87210. (Illus.). 222p. 1977. 7.95 (ISBN 0-8256-9506-6). Guitar Player.
Guiterrez, Alfredo. Uruguay: Economic Memorandum. viii, 201p. 1979. pap. 15.00 (ISBN 0-686-36124-5, RC-7902). World Bank.
Guither, Harold D. The Food Lobbyists: Behind the Scenes of Food & Agri-Politics. LC 79-6734. 352p. 1980. 29.95x (ISBN 0-669-03539-4). Lexington Bks.
Guithues, Henry J., jt. auth. see Kim, Suk H.
Guitton, H., jt. ed. see Margolis, J.
Gujarati, Damodar N. Basic Econometrics. 1978. text ed. 25.95 (ISBN 0-07-025182-7, C); instructor's manual 15.95 (ISBN 0-07-025183-5). McGraw.
Gula, Robert J. Precision: A Reference Handbook for Writers. (Orig.). 1980. pap. text ed. 9.95 (ISBN 0-316-33140-6). Little.
Gulati, Bodh R. & Bass, Helen. Algebra & Trigonometry. 676p. 1982. text ed. 22.95 (ISBN 0-205-07686-6, 567686X); tchr's ed. free (ISBN 0-205-07687-4); study guide avail. (ISBN 0-205-07688-2). Allyn.
Gulati, I. S. International Monetary Development & the Third World: A Proposal to Readress the Balance. (R. C. Dutt Lectures on Political Economy Ser.: 1978). 48p. 1980. pap. text ed. 2.95x (ISBN 0-686-42711-4, Pub. by Orient Longman Ltd India). Apt Bks.
Gulati, R. D. & Parma, S. Studies on Lake Vechten & Tjeukemeer: The Netherlands. 1982. 87.00 (ISBN 90-6193-762-0, Pub. by Junk Pubs Netherlands). Kluwer Boston.
Gulcher, Conrad. Racing Techniques Explained. rev. ed. (Illus.). 1972. 7.50 o.p. (ISBN 0-8286-0062-7). De Graff.
Guldmann, Jean-Michel & Shefer, Daniel. Industrial Location & Air Quality Control: A Planning Approach. LC 80-15380. (Environmental Science & Technology Monograph). 237p. 1980. 47.95 (ISBN 0-471-05377-5, Pub. by Wiley-Interscience). Wiley.
Gulezian, Ronald & Tingey, Henry. Business Mathematics for College Students. LC 82-10986. 463p. 1983. text ed. 20.95 (ISBN 0-471-08121-3); tchr's ed. (ISBN 0-471-87479-5). Wiley.
Gulhati, Ravi & Sekhar, Uday. Industrial Strategy for Late Starters: The Experience of Kenya, Tanzania & Zambia. (Working Paper: No. 457). 63p. 1981. 3.00 (ISBN 0-686-36175-X, WP-0457). World Bank.
Gulick, Bill. They Came to a Valley. (Western Fiction Ser.). 1981. lib. bdg. cancelled o.s.i. (ISBN 0-8398-2683-4, Gregg). G K Hall.
--Treasure in Hell's Canyon. LC 78-20235. 1979. 10.95 o.p. (ISBN 0-385-09848-0). Doubleday.
Gulick, Denny, jt. auth. see Ellis, Robert.
Gulick, Edward V. Europe's Classical Balance of Power. (Illus.). 1967. pap. 7.95 (ISBN 0-393-00413-9, Norton Lib). Norton.
Gulick, Sidney L. The American Japanese Problem: A Study of the Racial Relations of the East & the West. LC 77-145483. (The American Immigration Library). x, 372p. 1971. Repr. of 1914 ed. lib. bdg. 19.95x (ISBN 0-89198-014-8). Ozer.
Gulik, Robert Van see Van Gulik, Robert.
Gulkin, Sydney, jt. auth. see Notkin, Jerome J.
Gulla, Kell, tr. see Malum, Amadu.
Gullahorn, Jeanne E., jt. ed. see Donelson, Elaine.
Gullan, Marjorie. Poetry Speaking for Children, Pt. 2. (gr. 4-8). 1973. text ed. 2.25 o.p. (ISBN 0-686-09418-2). Expression.
Gulland, John A., ed. Fish Population Dynamics. LC 75-45094. 1977. 64.95 (ISBN 0-471-01575-X, Pub by Wiley-Interscience). Wiley.
Gullans, Charles. Diatribe to Dr. Steele. 18p. 1982. pap. 16.50 (ISBN 0-936576-09-X). Symposium Pr.
Gullason, Thomas A., ed. see Crane, Stephen.
Gullath, Brigitte. Untersuchungen Zur Geschichte Boiotiens In Der Zeit Alexanders Und Der Diadochen. 249p. 1982. write for info (ISBN 3-8204-7026-3). P Lang Pubs.
Gullberg, Elsa & Astrom, Paul. The Thread of Ariadne: A Study of Ancient Greek Dress. (Studies in Mediterranean Archaeology Ser.: No. XXI). (Illus.). 1970. pap. text ed. 15.00x (ISBN 91-85058-34-3). Humanities.
Gullett, C. Ray, jt. auth. see Hicks, Herbert G.
Gullette, Margaret M. The Lost Bellybutton. LC 76-26377. (Illus.). 31p. (ps-2). 1976. pap. 2.75 (ISBN 0-914996-11-8). Lollipop Power.
Gulley, Bill & Reese, Mary Ellen. Breaking Cover. 1980. 11.95 o.p. (ISBN 0-671-24548-1). S&S.
Gullick, J. M. Malaysia & Its Neighbours. (World Studies). 1967. 9.75x o.p. (ISBN 0-7100-4141-1). Routledge & Kegan.
Gulliford, Ronald. Special Educational Needs. 1971. cased 18.95x (ISBN 0-7100-7011-X); pap. 7.95 (ISBN 0-7100-7012-8). Routledge & Kegan.
Gullino, Pietro M., jt. ed. see Jain, Rakesh K.
Gulliver, P. H. Neighbours & Networks: The Idiom of Kinship Among the Ndendeuli of Tanzania. LC 71-115491. 1971. 32.00x (ISBN 0-520-01722-6). U of Cal Pr.
Gulliver, P. H., ed. Tradition & Transition in East Africa: Studies of the Tribal Factor in the Modern Era. LC 78-84787. 1969. 34.00x (ISBN 0-520-01402-2). U of Cal Pr.
Gullotta, Thomas, jt. auth. see Adams, Gerald R.
Gullvag, Ingemund & Wetlesen, Jon, eds. In Skeptical Wonder: Inquiries into the Philosophy of Arne Naess on the Occasion of His 70th Birthday. 328p. 1982. 46.00 (ISBN 82-00-05867-0). Universitet.
Gulvin, Harold E., jt. auth. see Stone, Archie A.
Gulyas, Gyula, tr. see Kallai, Gyula.
Gumerman, G. J., jt. ed. see Schiffer, M. B.
Guminsky, C., jt. auth. see Kertes.
Gummere. Choosing a College Major: Humanities. 1980. 11.95 o.p. (ISBN 0-679-50952-6); pap. 6.95 o.p. (ISBN 0-679-50953-4). McKay.
Gummerman, G. S., jt. ed. see Evler, R. C.
Gummett, Philip, jt. ed. see Johnston, Ron.
Gump, Margaret. Adalbert Stifter. (World Authors Ser.). 1974. lib. bdg. 15.95 (ISBN 0-8057-2864-3, Twayne). G K Hall.
Gump, Richard. Jade: Stone of Heaven. LC 62-12100. (Illus.). 1962. 14.95 (ISBN 0-385-01705-7). Doubleday.
Gumpert, Gary & Cathcart, Robert, eds. Inter-Media: Interpersonal Communication in a Media World. LC 78-12227. 1979. 10.95x o.p. (ISBN 0-19-502505-9). Oxford U Pr.
--Inter-Media: Interpersonal Communication in a Media World. 2nd ed. (Illus.). 600p. 1982. pap. text ed. 14.95x (ISBN 0-19-503078-8). Oxford U Pr.
Gumpertz, Robert, jt. auth. see Thayer, Philip.

Gumperz, John J. Discourse Strategies. LC 81-20627. (Studies in Interactional Sociolinguistics 1). 200p. 1982. 29.95 (ISBN 0-521-24691-1); pap. 9.95 (ISBN 0-521-28896-7). Cambridge U Pr.

Gumperz, John J., ed. Language & Social Identity. 2nd ed. LC 82-4331. (Studies in Interactional Sociolinguistics 2). 250p. 1983. 34.50 (ISBN 0-521-24692-X); pap. 12.95 (ISBN 0-521-28897-5). Cambridge U Pr.

Gumplowicz, Ludwig. Outlines of Sociology. LC 78-62687. (Social Science Classics Ser.). 336p. 1980. 29.95 (ISBN 0-87855-309-6); pap. text ed. 6.95 (ISBN 0-87855-693-1). Transaction Bks.

Gunatilleke, Godfrey & Tiruchelvan, Nellan, eds. Ethical Dilemmas of Development in Asia. LC 81-47964. 1983. write for info. (ISBN 0-669-05147-0). Lexington Bks.

Gunby, R. A. Sport Parachuting Manual. 5th ed. Jeppesen Sanderson, ed. (Illus.). 162p. 1974. pap. text ed. 4.35 (ISBN 0-88487-008-1, RE314751). Jeppesen Sanderson.

Gundel, Karoly. Hungarian Cookery. (Illus.). 11.00x (ISBN 0-392-03341-0, LTB). Sportshelf.

--Hungarian Cookery Book: 140 Hungarian Specialties. 6th ed. 5.00 o.s.i. (ISBN 0-8283-1550-7). Branden.

Gunden, Heidi Von see Von Gunden, Heidi.

Gundersheimer, Karen. Happy Winter. LC 81-48650. (Illus.). 40p. (gr. k-3). 1982. 9.57i (ISBN 0-06-022172-0, HarpJ); PLB 9.89g (ISBN 0-06-022173-9). Har-Row.

Gunderson, Andy. City Pauses. 18p. (Orig.). 1980. pap. 1.50 o.p. (ISBN 0-938566-02-4). Adastra Pr.

Gunderson, Carl. Quick Reference to Clinical Neurology. (Illus.). 448p. 1982. pap. text ed. 24.00 (ISBN 0-397-50498-5, Lippincott Medical). Lippincott.

Gunderson, E. K., ed. Human Adaptability to Antarctic Conditions. LC 74-18498. (Antarctic Research Ser.: Vol. 22). (Illus.). 1974. 17.00 (ISBN 0-87590-122-0). Am Geophysical.

Gunderson, Gerald. A New Economic History of America. 1976. text ed. 24.95 (ISBN 0-07-025180-0, C). McGraw.

Gunderson, Harvey L. Mammalogy. 1976. text ed. 37.50 (ISBN 0-07-025190-8, C). McGraw.

Gunderson, John G. Principles & Practices of Milieu Therapy. LC 80-70244. 224p. 1982. 25.00 (ISBN 0-87668-439-8). Aronson.

Gunderson, Keith. A Continual Interest in the Sun & Sea & Inland Missing the Sea. (Illus.). 154p. 1977. pap. 3.95 (ISBN 0-686-83870-X). Nodin Pr.

--To See a Thing. (Poetry Ser). (Illus.). 1975. pap. 3.50 (ISBN 0-685-79526-8). Nodin Pr.

Gunderson, Loren. The Gold Book: The Businessman's Guide to the State of Montana's Procedures for the Procurement of Goods & Services. (Illus.). 150p. 1983. pap. 30.00 (ISBN 0-934318-12-3). Falcon Pr MT.

Gunderson, Morley, ed. Collective Bargaining in the Essential & Public Service Sectors. LC 75-3167. 1975. 20.00x o.p. (ISBN 0-8020-2222-7); pap. 7.50x (ISBN 0-8020-6283-0). U of Toronto Pr.

Gunderson, Richard U. The Power of Positive Shrinking: Appetite - Weight Control by Hypnosis & Behavior Modification. 54p. (Orig.). 1981. 12.95 (ISBN 0-686-36697-2). Gunderson.

Gunderson, Robert G. The Log-Cabin Campaign. LC 76-49604. (Illus.). 1977. Repr. of 1957 ed. lib. bdg. 20.50x (ISBN 0-8371-9395-8, GULC). Greenwood.

--Old Gentlemen's Convention: The Washington Peace Conference of 1861. LC 80-24747. (Illus.). xiii, 168p. 1981. Repr. of 1961 ed. lib. bdg. 19.25x (ISBN 0-313-22584-2, GUOG). Greenwood.

Gunderson, Vivian. Gospel of Mark. (Illus.). 1982. pap. 1.25 (ISBN 0-8323-0412-3). Binford.

Gundlach, H., ed. see Rose, A. W.

Gundry, Paricia. Heirs Together. 192p. 1982. pap. 5.95 (ISBN 0-310-25371-3). Zondervan.

Gundry, R. Soma, in Biblical Theology, with Emphasis on Pauline Anthropology. LC 75-22927. (Society for New Testament Studies: No. 29). 300p. 1976. 47.50 (ISBN 0-521-20788-6). Cambridge U Pr.

Gundry, Stanley, jt. auth. see Thomas, Robert.

Gundry, Stanley N. Love Them In: The Proclamation Theology of D. L. Moody. 252p. 1982. pap. 6.95 (ISBN 0-8010-3783-2). Baker Bk.

Gundry, Stanley N. & Johnson, Alan F., eds. Tensions in Contemporary Theology. LC 76-7629. 384p. 1979. 12.95 (ISBN 0-8024-8586-3). Moody.

Gundy, Elizabeth. Bliss. 1978. pap. 1.95 o.s.i. (ISBN 0-515-04706-6). Jove Pubns.

Gundy, John H. Assessment of the Child in Primary Health Care. (Illus.). 208p. 1981. pap. text ed. 12.95 (ISBN 0-07-025197-5). McGraw.

Gundy, Samuel C., jt. auth. see Quirk, Thomas C., Jr.

Gun Hoy Siu, Ralph. Ch'i: A Neo-Taoist Approach to Life. LC 74-1139. (Illus.). 435p. 1974. 14.00x (ISBN 0-262-19123-7); pap. 8.95 (ISBN 0-262-69054-3). MIT Pr.

Gunn. Manual of Document Photomicrography. 1983. 91.95x (ISBN 0-240-51146-8). Focal Pr.

Gunn, A. D., jt. auth. see Lodewick, L.

Gunn, Betty R. Nurse Whitney's Paradise. (YA) 1981. 6.95 (ISBN 0-686-85731-3, Avalon). Bouregy.

Gunn, D. M. The Story of King David: Genre & Interpretation. (JSOT Supplement Ser.: No. 6). 164p. 1978. text ed. 29.95x o.p. (ISBN 0-905774-11-6, Pub. by JSOT Pr England); pap. text ed. 16.95x (ISBN 0-905774-05-1, Pub. by JSOT Pr England). Eisenbrauns.

Gunn, D. M., jt. auth. see Clines, D. J.

Gunn, Donald L. & Stevens, John G. R. Pesticides & Human Welfare. (Illus.). 1977. text ed. 19.95x o.p. (ISBN 0-19-854522-3); pap. text ed. 9.95x (ISBN 0-19-854526-6). Oxford U Pr.

Gunn, Drewey W. Tennessee Williams: A Bibliography. LC 80-12714. (Scarecrow Author Bibliographies: No. 48). 270p. 1980. 14.50 o.p. (ISBN 0-8108-1310-6). Scarecrow.

Gunn, Edward M., ed. Twentieth Century Chinese Drama: An Anthology. (Midland Bks.). (Illus.). 560p. (Orig.). 1983. 22.50x (ISBN 0-253-36109-5); pap. 15.00x (ISBN 0-253-20310-4). Ind U Pr.

Gunn, Fenja. The Artificial Face: A History of Cosmetics. (Illus.). 220p. (gr. 6 up). 1983. pap. 9.95 (ISBN 0-88254-795-X). Hippocrene Bks.

Gunn, George S. Indispensable Christ: Sermons. 266p. 1962. 8.95 (ISBN 0-227-67661-0). Attic Pr.

Gunn, Giles. The Interpretation of Otherness: Literature Religion & the American Imagination. 1979. 17.95x (ISBN 0-19-502453-2). Oxford U Pr.

Gunn, Giles, ed. New World Metaphysics: Readings on the Religious Meaning of the American Experience. 1981. text ed. 19.95x (ISBN 0-19-502873-2); pap. text ed. 9.95x (ISBN 0-19-502874-0). Oxford U Pr.

Gunn, Harry & Gunn, Violet C. The Test for Success Book. 100p. pap. 7.95 (ISBN 0-914091-22-0). Chicago Review.

Gunn, J. A. Beyond Liberty & Property: The Process of Self-Recognition in Eighteenth-Century Political Thought. (McGill-Queen's Studies in the History of Ideas). 336p. 1983. 35.00x (ISBN 0-7735-1006-0). McGill-Queens U Pr.

Gunn, James. Christ: The Fullness of the Godhead, a Study in New Testament Christology. 256p. 1983. pap. 5.50 (ISBN 0-87213-283-8). Loizeaux.

--Isaac Asimov: The Foundations of Science Fiction. (Science-Fiction Writers Ser.). 1982. 18.95x (ISBN 0-19-503059-1); pap. 6.95 (ISBN 0-19-503060-5, GB). Oxford U Pr.

--Road to Science Fiction, No. 4. 1982. pap. 4.95 (ISBN 0-451-62136-0, ME2136, Ment). NAL.

Gunn, James, ed. From Here to Forever. (The Road to Science Fiction: No. 4). 1982. pap. 4.95 (ISBN 0-451-62136-0, Ment). NAL.

--The Road to Science Fiction, No. 2. (Orig.). (RL 10). 1979. pap. 2.75 (ISBN 0-451-61859-9, ME1859, Ment). NAL.

--The Road to Science-Fiction: From Gilgamesh to Wells. (Orig.). (RL 9). 1977. pap. 2.75 (ISBN 0-451-61850-5, ME1850, Ment). NAL.

Gunn, James W. A Time & Times & Half a Time. pap. 1.25 o.p. (ISBN 0-8042-9371-6). John Knox.

Gunn, John & Farrington, David P. Abnormal Offenders, Delinquency & the Criminal Justice System. LC 81-14657. (Wiley Series on Current Research in Forensic Psychiatry & Psychology). 384p. 1982. 47.95x (ISBN 0-471-28047-X, Pub. by Wiley-Interscience). Wiley.

Gunn, Peter, jt. auth. see Beny, Roloff.

Gunn, Peter, ed. see Byron.

Gunn, Scout & Peterson, Carol A. Therapeutic Recreation Program Design: Principles & Procedures. 1978. ref. ed. 20.95 (ISBN 0-13-914804-3). P-H.

Gunn, Thom. To the Air. Schreiber, Jan, ed. LC 73-89045. (Chapbook Series One). 1974. 5.00 (ISBN 0-87923-086-X). Godine.

Gunn, Violet C., jt. auth. see Gunn, Harry.

Gunn, Virginia S. The Wayward Season. LC 79-7686. 1980. 10.95 o.p. (ISBN 0-385-15391-0). Doubleday.

Gunnel, John, ed. The Standard Catalog of American Cars, 1946-1975. (Illus.). 704p. 1982. pap. 19.95 (ISBN 0-87341-027-0). Krause Pubns.

Gunnell, John G. Political Theory: Tradition & Interpretation. (Orig.). 1979. pap. text ed. 8.95 (ISBN 0-316-33150-3). Little.

Gunnell, Robert. This Changing World. 14.50x (ISBN 0-392-04974-0, SpS). Sportshelf.

Gunnell, Sally, jt. auth. see Gardner, Hope.

Gunnell, Sally, jt. auth. see Gardner, Hope C.

Gunner, Jean. Simple Repair & Preservation Techniques for Collection Curators, Librarians & Archivists. (Illus.). 14p. (Orig.). 1980. pap. 2.00x o.p. (ISBN 0-913196-32-0). Hunt Inst Botanical.

Gunneweg, A. H. Understanding the Old Testament. Bowden, John, tr. LC 78-6696. (Old Testament Library). 1978. 15.95 (ISBN 0-664-21371-5). Westminster.

Gunning, Monica, tr. see Fry, Edward B.

Gunning, Monica, tr. see Mountain, Lee.

Gunning, Robert. Technique of Clear Writing. rev. ed. 1968. 14.95 (ISBN 0-07-025206-8, GB). McGraw.

Gunning, Stella, et al. Topic Teaching in the Primary School: Teaching about Society Through Topic Work. 220p. 1981. 23.00x (ISBN 0-7099-0437-1, Pub. by Croom Helm Ltd England). Biblio Dist.

Gunning, Thomas G. Unexplained Mysteries. LC 82-19950. (High Interest, Low Vocabulary Ser.). (Illus.). 128p. (gr. 4 up). 1983. 8.95 (ISBN 0-396-08122-3). Dodd.

Gunsaulus, H. C. Japanese Sword-Mounts. (Illus.). 1923. pap. 26.00 (ISBN 0-527-01876-7). Kraus Repr.

Gunsburg, Jeffrey A. Divided & Conquered: The French High Command & the Defeat of the West, Nineteen Forty. LC 78-22725. (Contributions in Military History Ser.: No. 18). (Illus.). 1979. lib. bdg. 29.95 (ISBN 0-313-21092-6, GDC/). Greenwood.

Gunson, Niel. Messengers of Grace: Evangelical Missionaries in the South Seas 1797-1860. (Illus.). 1978. 44.00x (ISBN 0-19-550517-4). Oxford U Pr.

Gunson, Niel, ed. Changing Pacific: Essays in Honour of H. E. Maude. (Illus.). 1978. text ed. 39.50x o.p. (ISBN 0-19-550518-2). Oxford U Pr.

Gunsteren, Herman Van see Van Gunsteren, Herman R.

Gunston, Bill. An Illustrated Guide to the Bombers of World War II. LC 80-67628. (Illustrated Guide Ser.). 1981. 8.95 (ISBN 0-668-05094-2). Arco.

--An Illustrated Guide to the Israeli Air Force. LC 81-71938. (Illustrated Military Guides Ser.). (Illus.). 160p. 1983. 9.95 (ISBN 0-668-05506-5, 5506). Arco.

--Jane's Aerospace Dictionary. 492p. 1980. 34.95 (ISBN 0-86720-573-3). Sci Bks Intl.

--Water. LC 82-50389. (Visual Science Ser.). PLB 13.00 (ISBN 0-382-06659-6). Silver.

Gunston, David. Finding Out About the Japanese. 11.75x o.p. (ISBN 0-392-09284-0, SpS). Sportshelf.

Gunstone, Anthony, ed. Sylloge of Coins of the British Isles, Lincolnshire Collection: Coins in the Lincolnshire Collection. (Illus.). 1980. 79.00x (ISBN 0-19-725993-6). Oxford U Pr.

Gunstone, F. D. Aliphatic & Related Natural Product Chemistry, Vol. 2. 278p. 1982. 110.00x (ISBN 0-85186-652-2, Pub. by Royal Soc Chem England). State Mutual Bk.

--Topics in Lipid Chemistry, Vol. 2. 313p. 1971. 39.95x o.s.i. (ISBN 0-471-33350-6). Halsted Pr.

Gunstone, F. D. & Norris, F. D. Lipids in Foods: Chemistry, Biochemistry & Application Technology. 175p. 1983. 40.01 (ISBN 0-08-025499-3); pap. 18.01 (ISBN 0-08-025498-5). Pergamon.

Gunstream, Stanley E., jt. auth. see Benson, Harold J.

Gunter, Hans. Transnational Industrial Relations. 1972. 36.00 (ISBN 0-312-81480-1). St Martin.

Gunter, Jonathan F. NFE-TV: Television for Nonformal Education. 286p. (Orig.). 1975. pap. 6.00 (ISBN 0-932288-32-4). Ctr Intl Ed U of MA.

Gunter, Laurie M. & Ryan, Joanne E. Self-Assessment of Current Knowledge in Geriatric Nursing. 1976. spiral bdg. 12.00 o.p. (ISBN 0-87488-295-8). Med Exam.

Gunter, Pete A., jt. ed. see Sibley, Jack R.

Gunter, Richard. Reading Poems. 1975. pap. text ed. 1.95 (ISBN 0-917496-06-X). Hornbeam Pr.

Guntermann, Karl L., jt. auth. see Cooper, James R.

Gunther, Bernard. Energy Ecstasy & Your Seven Vital Shakras. 200p. (Orig.). 1983. pap. 9.95 (ISBN 0-87877-066-6). Newcastle Pub.

--Energy Ecstasy & Your Seven Vital Shakras. 200p. 1983. lib. bdg. 17.95x (ISBN 0-89370-666-3). Borgo Pr.

Gunther, D., et al. Writing: A Sourcebook of Exercises. (gr. 10-12). 1978. pap. text ed. 10.00 (ISBN 0-201-02632-5, Sch Div); dupl. masters 4.60 (ISBN 0-201-02716-X). A-W.

Gunther, Erna, tr. see Jacobsen, Johan A.

Gunther, Erna, tr. see Jacobsen, Johann A.

Gunther, F. A., ed. Residue Reviews, Vols. 1-11. Incl. Vol. 1. (Illus.). iv, 162p. 1962. 27.20 (ISBN 0-387-02899-4); Vol. 2. (Illus.). iv, 156p. 1963. 27.20 (ISBN 0-387-03047-6); Vol. 3. (Illus.). iv, 170p. 1963. 27.20 (ISBN 0-387-03048-4); Vol. 4. (Illus.). iv, 175p. 1963. 27.20 (ISBN 0-387-03049-2); Vol. 5. Instrumentation for the Detection & Determination of Pesticides & Their Residues in Foods. (Illus.). viii, 176p. 1964. 27.20 (ISBN 0-387-03201-0); Vol. 6. (Illus.). iv, 165p. 1964. 27.20 (ISBN 0-387-03202-9); Vol. 7. vi, 161p. 1964. 20.90 (ISBN 0-387-03203-7); Vol. 8. (Illus.). viii, 183p. 1965. 23.00 (ISBN 0-387-03390-4); Vol. 9. (Illus.). viii, 175p. 1965. o.p. (ISBN 0-387-03391-2); Vol. 10. With Comprehensive Cumulative Contents, Subjectmatter, & Author Indexes of Volume 1-10. (Illus.). viii, 159p. 1965. 20.90 (ISBN 0-387-03392-0); Vol. 11. (Illus.). viii, 164p. 1965. 23.00 (ISBN 0-387-03393-9). LC 62-18595. (Eng, Fr, Ger.). Springer-Verlag.

--Residue Reviews, Vol. 85. (Illus.). 307p. 1983. 39.80 (ISBN 0-387-90751-3). Springer-Verlag.

--Residue Reviews, Vol. 86. (Illus.). 133p. 1983. 24.80 (ISBN 0-387-90778-5). Springer-Verlag.

--Residue Reviews, Vol. 87. (Illus.). 152p. 1983. 21.50 (ISBN 0-387-90781-5). Springer-Verlag.

Gunther, Gerald. Cases & Materials Constitutional Law, 10th Ed., & Cases & Materials on Individual Rights in Constitutional Law 3rd Ed. 1982 Supplement. (University Casebook Ser.). 370p. 1982. pap. text ed. write for info. (ISBN 0-88277-100-0). Foundation Pr.

Gunther, H. NMR Spectroscopy: An Introduction. LC 78-31736. 1980. 74.95x (ISBN 0-471-27580-8, Pub. by Wiley-Interscience); pap. 28.95x (ISBN 0-471-27579-4, Pub. by Wiley-Interscience) Wiley

Gunther, John. Death Be Not Proud. LC 53-5344. 1953. 5.95 (ISBN 0-394-60469-5). Modern Lib.

--The Riddle of MacArthur: Japan, Korea, & the Far East. LC 74-11880. 240p. 1974. Repr. of 1951 ed. lib. bdg. 19.75x (ISBN 0-8371-7701-4, GURM). Greenwood.

Gunther, Lenworth, ed. Black Image: European Eyewitness Accounts of Afro-American Life. (National University Publications Ser. in American Studies). 1977. 15.95 o.p. (ISBN 0-8046-9188-6). Kennikat.

Gunther, Louise. Anna's Snow Day. LC 78-22050. (For Real Ser.). (Illus.). (gr. k-6). 1979. PLB 6.69 (ISBN 0-8116-4310-7). Garrard.

--A Tooth for the Tooth Fairy. LC 77-16422. (For Real Ser.). (Illus.). (gr. k-6). 1978. PLB 6.69 (ISBN 0-8116-4308-5). Garrard.

--Where Is Maria? LC 79-11733. (For Real Ser.). (Illus.). (gr. 1-5). 1979. PLB 6.69 (ISBN 0-8116-4311-5). Garrard.

Gunther, Peter F., ed. Sermon Classics by Great Preachers. LC 81-16899. 1982. pap. 5.95 (ISBN 0-8024-3328-6). Moody.

Gunther, R. T. Robert T. Gunther 1869-1940: A Pioneer in the History of Science. 160p. 1981. 50.00x (ISBN 0-686-97622-3, Pub. by Dawson). State Mutual Bk.

Gunther, Wolfgang H., jt. auth. see Klayman, Daniel L.

Gunton, Melvin, jt. auth. see Gossage, Richard C.

Gunton, Sharon, ed. Contemporary Literary Criticism. (Contemporary Literary Criticism Ser.: Vol. 23). 600p. 1982. 74.00x (ISBN 0-8103-0113-X). Gale.

--Contemporary Literary Criticism: Excerpts from the Criticism of the Works of Today's Novelists, Poets, Playwrights & Other Creative Writers, 22 vols. Incl. Vol. 1. 1973. (ISBN 0-8103-0100-8); Vol. 2. 1974. (ISBN 0-8103-0102-4); Vol. 3. 1975. (ISBN 0-8103-0104-0); Vol. 4. 1975. (ISBN 0-8103-0106-7); Vol. 5. 1976. (ISBN 0-8103-0108-3); Vol. 6. 1976. (ISBN 0-8103-0110-5); Vol. 7. 1977. (ISBN 0-8103-0112-1); Vol. 8. 1978. (ISBN 0-8103-0114-8); Vol. 9. 1978. (ISBN 0-685-92122-0); Vol. 10. 1979. (ISBN 0-8103-0118-0); Vol. 11. 1979 (ISBN 0-8103-0120-2); Vol. 12. 1979 (ISBN 0-8103-0122-9); Vol. 13. 1979 (ISBN 0-8103-0124-5); Vol. 14. 1980 (ISBN 0-8103-0101-6); Vol. 15. 1980 (ISBN 0-8103-0103-2); Vol. 16. 1981 (ISBN 0-8103-0105-9); Vol. 17. 1981 (ISBN 0-8103-0107-5); Vol. 18. 1981 (ISBN 0-8103-0123-7); Vol. 19. 1981 (ISBN 0-8103-0120-2); Vol. 20. 1982 (ISBN 0-8103-0119-9); Vol. 21. 1982 (ISBN 0-8103-0117-2); Vol. 22. 1982 (ISBN 0-8103-0115-6). LC 76-38938. (Contemporary Literary Criticism Ser.). 74.00x ea. Gale.

Guntrip, Harry. Psychoanalytic Theory, Therapy & the Self. LC 79-135563. 1973. pap. 6.95x (ISBN 0-465-09715-9, TB-5012). Basic.

Gunz, F. W. & Henderson, Edward S., eds. Leukemia. 4th ed. 1982. 95.00 (ISBN 0-8089-1513-4). Grune.

Gunz, Frederick W. & Baikie, A. G., eds. Leukemia. rev. 3rd ed. LC 74-13366. 864p. 1974. 89.50 o.p. (ISBN 0-8089-0843-X). Grune.

Gunzburg, H. C. Experiments in the Rehabilitation of the Mentally Handicapped. 21.95 o.p. (ISBN 0-407-17080-4). Butterworth.

Gunzel, David, ed. see Lien, David A.

Gup, Benton. Guide to Strategic Planning. (McGraw-Hill Series in Finance). (Illus.). 1980. text ed. 19.95 (ISBN 0-07-025210-6); pap. text ed. 14.95 (ISBN 0-07-025211-4). McGraw.

Gup, Benton E. The Basics of Investing. LC 78-17521. (Ser. in Finance). 1979. text ed. 29.95 (ISBN 0-471-33620-3); tchrs.' manual 6.00 (ISBN 0-471-04813-5); tests 3.00 (ISBN 0-471-05663-4); study guide 9.95 (ISBN 0-471-05573-5). Wiley.

--Financial Intermediaries: An Introduction. 2nd ed. LC 79-87858. 1980. text ed. 24.95 (ISBN 0-395-28138-5); instr's. manual 1.65 (ISBN 0-395-28157-1). HM.

Gupta, A. K. Das see Das Gupta, A. K.

Gupta, A. P. Insect Hemocytes. LC 78-10477. 1979. 115.00 (ISBN 0-521-22364-4). Cambridge U Pr.

--Neurohemal Organs of Arthropods: Their Development, Evolution, Structures, & Functions. (Illus.). 642p. 1983. 74.50x (ISBN 0-398-04728-6). C C Thomas.

Gupta, Anandswarup. The Police in British India, Eighteen Sixty-One to Nineteen Forty-Seven. 1980. text ed. 23.00x (ISBN 0-391-01843-4). Humanities.

Gupta, Ashin Das see Das Gupta, Ashin.

Gupta, B. K., jt. auth. see Agnihotri, O. P.

Gupta, B. P. Calculus for Engineering Students. 1968. pap. 4.00x o.p. (ISBN 0-210-22679-X). Asia.

Gupta, D. B. Consumption Patterns in Industry. 1974. 4.95 o.p. (ISBN 0-07-096430-0, P&RB). McGraw.

Gupta, Dharmendra K. Recent Studies in Sanskirt & Indology. 1982. 28.00x (ISBN 0-8364-0913-2, Pub. by Ajanta). South Asia Bks.

Gupta, G. R. Marriage, Religion, & Society: Tradition & Change in an Indian Village. LC 73-5903. 180p. 1974. 16.95x o.p. (ISBN 0-470-33648-X). Halsted Pr.

Gupta, Giri R., ed. Family & Social Change in Modern India. LC 76-9126. (Main Currents in Indian Sociology Ser.: Vol. 2). 1977. 13.95 (ISBN 0-89089-060-9). Carolina Acad Pr.

Gupta, H. & Rastogi, B. Dams & Earthquakes. (Developments in Geotechnical Engineering Ser.: Vol. 11). 1976. 64.00 (ISBN 0-444-41330-8). Elsevier.

Gupta, H. K. Geothermal Resources: An Energy Alternative. (Developments in Economic Geology Ser.: Vol. 12). 1981. 59.75 (ISBN 0-444-41865-2). Elsevier.

Gupta, Hari R. Panjab on the Eve of First Sikh War. 2nd rev. ed. LC 75-903634. 1975. 12.50x o.p. (ISBN 0-88386-653-6). South Asia Bks.

Gupta, J. S. Textbook of Algae. 348p. 1981. 60.00x (ISBN 0-686-84468-8, Pub. by Oxford & I B H India). State Mutual Bk.

--Textbook of Fungi. 305p. 1981. 60.00x (ISBN 0-686-84469-6, Pub. by Oxford & I B H India). State Mutual Bk.

Gupta, Jyotirindra Das see Das Gupta, Jyotirindra.

Gupta, Kanhaya L. & Islam, M Anisul. Foreign Capital, Savings & Growth. 1983. lib. bdg. 34.50 (ISBN 90-277-1449-5, Pub. by Reidel Holland). Kluwer Boston.

Gupta, Karunakar. The Hidden History of the Sino-Indian Frontier. LC 74-903923. 200p. 1974. 9.50x o.p. (ISBN 0-88386-438-X). South Asia Bks.

Gupta, M. M. & Sanchez, E., eds. Approximate Reasoning in Decision Analysis. 480p. 1982. 68.50 (ISBN 0-444-86492-X, North Holland). Elsevier.

--Fuzzy Information & Decision Processes. 480p. 1982. 74.50 (ISBN 0-686-83998-6, North Holland). Elsevier.

Gupta, M. M., et al, eds. Advances in Fuzzy Set Theory & Applications. 753p. 1979. 95.75 (ISBN 0-444-85372-3, North Holland). Elsevier.

Gupta, Madhu S. Electrical Noise: Fundamentals & Sources. LC 76-57816. (IEEE Press Selected Reprint Ser.). 1977. 40.00 (ISBN 0-471-03116-X); pap. 26.00 (ISBN 0-471-03117-8, Pub. by Wiley-Interscience). Wiley.

Gupta, Madhu S., ed. Electrical Noise: Fundamentals & Sources. LC 76-57816. 1977. 19.95 (ISBN 0-87942-086-3). Inst Electrical.

Gupta, O. P. Commitment to work. 260p. 1982. text ed. 13.00x (ISBN 0-391-02723-9, Pub. by Concept India). Humanities.

Gupta, P. Geography in Ancient Indian Inscriptions, up to 650 A. D. (Illus.). 350p. 1973. text ed. 17.75x (ISBN 0-391-00498-0). Humanities.

Gupta, Partha S. Imperialism & the British Labour Movement 1914-1964. LC 74-28203. 438p. 1975. text ed. 45.00x (ISBN 0-8419-0191-0). Holmes & Meier.

Gupta, R., ed. Applied Statistics. (Proceedings). 1975. 53.25 (ISBN 0-444-10772-X). Elsevier.

Gupta, R. P., ed. Multivariate Statistical Analysis. 1980. 59.75 (ISBN 0-444-86019-3). Elsevier.

Gupta, Ramesh, jt. ed. see Cheremisinoff, Nicholas P.

Gupta, S. C. Transform & State Variable Methods in Linear Systems. LC 66-17635. 444p. 1971. Repr. of 1966 ed. text ed. 22.00 (ISBN 0-88275-022-4). Krieger.

Gupta, S. P. Archaeology of Central Asia & the Indian Border Lands, 2 vols. 1979. text ed. 60.00x ea. Vol. 1 (ISBN 0-391-01855-8). Vol. 2 (ISBN 0-391-02092-7). Humanities.

Gupta, S. P., jt. auth. see Majupuria, Trilok C.

Gupta, S. P., jt. auth. see Pandit, G. S.

Gupta, S. P., ed. Mahabharata: Myth & Reality. LC 76-902982. 1976. 17.50x o.p. (ISBN 0-88386-856-3). South Asia Bks.

Gupta, S. R. Textbook of Chemistry for Polytechnic Students. pap. 5.50x o.p. (ISBN 0-210-27197-3). Asia.

Gupta, Satyadev. The World Zinc Industry. LC 81-47075. (Illus.). 224p. 1981. 24.95x (ISBN 0-669-04587-X). Lexington Bks.

Gupta, Shanti S. & Berger, James O., eds. Statistical Decision Theory & Related Topics III, Vol. II. 534p. 1982. 36.00 (ISBN 0-12-307502-5). Acad Pr.

--Statistical Decision Theory & Related Topics III, Vol. I. LC 82-11528. 526p. 1982. 36.00 (ISBN 0-12-307501-7). Acad Pr.

Gupta, Shiv K. & Hamman, Ray T. Starting a Small Business: A Simulation Game. (Illus.). 64p. 1974. pap. text ed. 15.95 (ISBN 0-13-842963-4). P-H.

Gupta, Sisir. Kashmir: A Study of India-Pakistan Relations. 1967. 17.50x (ISBN 0-210-22625-0). Asia.

Gupta, Someshwar C. & Hasdorff, Lawrence. Fundamentals of Automatic Control. 1970. 41.50x o.p. (ISBN 0-471-33645-9). Wiley.

--Fundamentals of Automatic Control. LC 82-20338. 602p. 1983. Repr. of 1970 ed. lib. bdg. write for info. (ISBN 0-89874-578-0). Krieger.

Gupta, Tarun, tr. see Tagore, Rabindranath.

Gupta, Vinod. Natural Cooling of Buildings. 31p. 1981. pap. 4.75x (ISBN 0-910661-00-6). Innovative Inform.

Gupta, Yogi. Yoga & Long Life. 5th ed. LC 58-9502. (Illus.). 1983. 14.00 (ISBN 0-911664-01-7). Yogi Gupta.

--Yoga & Yogic Powers. LC 63-14948. (Illus.). 1963. 15.00 (ISBN 0-911664-02-5). Yogi Gupta.

Guptill, A. Sketching as a Hobby. 1982. pap. 7.25 (ISBN 0-442-22988-7). Van Nos Reinhold.

Gupton, Oscar W. & Swope, Fred C. Wildflowers of Tidewater Virginia. LC 81-16247. (Illus.). 207p. 1982. 10.95 (ISBN 0-8139-0922-8). U Pr of Va.

Gur, Arieh. From Kiev to Tel Aviv: Escape from Russia. 1982. 16.00 (ISBN 0-931556-02-3). Translation Pr.

Gura, Philip F. & Myerson, Joel, eds. Critical Essays on American Transcendentalism. (Critical Essays on American Literature). 1982. lib. bdg. 60.00 (ISBN 0-8161-8466-6). G K Hall.

Gura, Timothy, jt. auth. see Lee, Charlotte I.

Guralnick. Early Intervention & the Integration of Handicapped & Nonhandicapped Children. (Illus.). 320p. 1977. text ed. 16.95 (ISBN 0-8391-1165-7). Univ Park.

Guralnick, jt. auth. see Levitt.

Guralnick, Michael J. Pediatric Education & the Needs of Exceptional Children. 240p. 1979. text ed. 24.95 (ISBN 0-8391-1500-8). Univ Park.

Guralnik, David. Webster's New World Dictionary of the American Language. 704p. 1982. pap. 2.95 (ISBN 0-446-31051-4). Warner Bks.

Gurau, Peter K. & Lieberthal, E. A. Fingermath, Bk. 1. (Fingermath Ser.). 1979. pap. 5.72 pupil's ed. (ISBN 0-07-025221-1, W); tchr's. ed 11.36 (ISBN 0-07-025231-9). McGraw.

Gurau, Peter K. & Lieberthal, Edwin M. Fingermath, Bk. 2. Gafney, Leo, ed. (Fingermath Ser.). (Illus.). (gr. 2-6). 1980. pap. text ed. 5.72 (ISBN 0-07-025222-X, W); tchr's ed. 11.36 (ISBN 0-07-025232-7). McGraw.

--Fingermath Book. Gafney, Leo, ed. (Fingermath Ser.: Bk. 3). 192p. (gr. 3-8). 1980. pap. text ed. 5.72 (ISBN 0-07-025223-8, W); tchrs. ed. 11.36 (ISBN 0-07-025233-5). McGraw.

Gurdjian, E. Stephen & Thomas, L. Murray. Operative Neurosurgery. 3rd ed. LC 74-11097. 632p. 1975. Repr. of 1970 ed. 30.00 (ISBN 0-88275-191-3). Krieger.

Gurdjieff, G. I. Beelzebub's Tales to His Grandson, 3 vols. 1973. Set. pap. 19.75 (ISBN 0-525-47351-3, 01917-580). Dutton.

--Life Is Real Only Then, When "I Am". 177p. 1981. 13.50 (ISBN 0-525-14547-8, 01311-390). Dutton.

--Meetings with Remarkable Men. Orage, Alfred R., tr. 1969. pap. 5.25 (ISBN 0-525-47242-8, 0510-150). Dutton.

--Views from the Real World: Early Talks, 1918-1934. 1975. pap. 8.50 (ISBN 0-525-47408-0, 0825-250). Dutton.

Gurdon, J. B. Control of Gene Expression in Animal Development. LC 74-76589. 1974. text ed. 6.50x o.p. (ISBN 0-674-16975-1); pap. 5.95x o.p. (ISBN 0-674-16977-8). Harvard U Pr.

Gurdus, Luba K. The Death Train. LC 78-54657. (Illus.). 1979. 10.00 (ISBN 0-8052-5005-0, Pub. by Holocaust Library). Schocken.

--The Death Train. (Illus.). 164p. Repr. 10.00 (ISBN 0-686-95062-3). ADL.

Gurel, Lois M. & Beeson, Marianne S. Dimensions of Dress & Adornment: A Book of Readings. 3rd ed. LC 74-20103. 1979. pap. text ed. 12.95 (ISBN 0-8403-2038-8). Kendall-Hunt.

Gurel, Lois M., jt. auth. see Horn, Marilyn J.

Gurel, Okan, ed. Bifurcation Theory & Applications in Scientific Disciplines, Vol. 316. Rossler, Otto E. (Annals of the New York Academy of Sciences). 708p. (Orig.). 1979. pap. 87.00x (ISBN 0-89766-000-5). NY Acad Sci.

Gurevich, A., tr. see Gorshkov, G. & Yakushova, A.

Gurevich, I. I. & Tarasov, L. V., eds. Low-Energy Neutron Physics. 1968. 63.50 (ISBN 0-444-10210-8, North-Holland). Elsevier.

Gurevich, Ilya. The Fountains of Petrodvorets Near Leningrad. 124p. 1980. 60.00x (ISBN 0-686-97671-1, Pub. by Collet's). State Mutual Bk.

Gurevitch, Michael, et al, eds. Culture, Society & the Media. (Illus.). 1982. 29.95x (ISBN 0-416-73500-2); pap. 12.95x (ISBN 0-416-73510-X). Methuen Inc.

Gurewitsch, Bonnie. Bibliography. (Bibliography Ser.). 27p. (Orig.). Date not set. pap. 3.00 (ISBN 0-9609970-0-8). Ctr For Holo.

Gurewitsch, Brana, jt. auth. see Eliach, Yaffa.

Gurfinkel, German, jt. auth. see Khachaturian, Narbey.

Gurian, Anita & Formanek, Ruth. The Socially Competent Child: A Parent's Guide to Social Development from Infancy to Early Adolescence. 206p. 1983. 12.95 (ISBN 0-395-32205-7). HM.

Gurin, Arnold, jt. auth. see Perlman, Robert.

Gurin, Gerald. National Attitude Study of Trainees in MDTA Institutional Programs. 258p. 1970. pap. 5.50x (ISBN 0-87944-086-4). Inst Soc Res.

Gurin, Patricia & Epps, Edgar G. Black Consciousness, Identity & Achievement: A Study of Students in Historically Black Colleges. LC 75-5847. 545p. 1975. text ed. 34.95 (ISBN 0-471-33670-X). Wiley.

Gurion, David Ben see Ben Gurion, David & Pearlman, Moshe.

Gurko, Miriam. The Ladies of Seneca Falls: The Birth of the Woman's Rights Movement. LC 76-9144. (Studies in the Life of Women). (Illus.). 1976. pap. 8.95 (ISBN 0-8052-0545-4). Schocken.

Gurland, Barry see Aronson, Miriam K. & Bennett, Ruth.

Gurland, Barry J. & Copeland, John. The Mind & Mood of Aging: Mental Health Problems of the Community Elderly in New York & London. (Illus.). 150p. 1983. text ed. 29.95 (ISBN 0-917724-28-3, B28). Haworth Pr.

Gurland, H. J., et al, eds. Therapeutic Plasma Exchange. (Illus.). 250p. 1981. pap. 22.90 o.p. (ISBN 0-387-10590-5). Springer-Verlag.

Gurley, John G. & Shaw, Edward S. Money in a Theory of Finance. 1960. 22.95 (ISBN 0-8157-3322-4). Brookings.

Gurley, LaVerne T. & Callaway, William J. Introduction to Radiologic Technology. LC 81-82005. (Illus.). 300p. (Orig.). 1982. pap. 14.95x (ISBN 0-940122-02-2). Multi Media CO.

Gurman, Alan S., ed. Questions & Answers in the Practice of Family Therapy, Vol. 2. LC 80-22460. 320p. 1982. 27.50 (ISBN 0-87630-308-4). Brunner-Mazel.

Gurney, Edmund. Phantasms of the Living, 2 Vols. LC 71-119868. (Hist. of Psych. Ser.). 1970. Repr. of 1886 ed. Set. 130.00x set (ISBN 0-8201-1075-2). Schol Facsimiles.

Gurney, Eric. The Calculating Cat Returns. LC 78-61782. (Illus.). 1978. 5.95 o.p. (ISBN 0-13-110213-3); pap. 2.95 o.p. (ISBN 0-13-110205-2). P-H.

--How to Live with a Headstrong Horse. (Illus.). 192p. 1982. 6.95 (ISBN 0-13-415406-1). P-H.

Gurney, Eric, jt. auth. see Gurney, Nancy.

Gurney, Gene. Five Down & Glory. (War Library). 288p. 1983. pap. 2.95 (ISBN 0-345-30799-2). Ballantine.

--Flying Aces of World War One. (gr. 5-9). 1965. 2.95 (ISBN 0-394-80560-7, BYR); PLB 5.99 (ISBN 0-394-90560-1). Random.

--Space Technology Spinoffs. (Impact Ser.). (Illus.). (gr. 7 up). 1979. PLB 8.90 s&l (ISBN 0-531-02290-0). Watts.

--The War in the Air. (Illus.). 1967. 7.50 o.p. (ISBN 0-517-09948-9). Crown.

Gurney, Gene & Wise, Harold. The Official Washington D.C. Directory. 1977. 10.00 o.p. (ISBN 0-517-53029-5); pap. 5.95 o.p. (ISBN 0-517-53030-9). Crown.

Gurney, Gene, jt. auth. see Willinger, Kurt.

Gurney, Ivor. Collected Poems of Ivor Gurney. Kavanagh, P. J., ed. 320p. 1983. 24.95 (ISBN 0-19-200940-0). Oxford U Pr.

--The War Letters. Thornton, R. K., ed. 224p. 1982. text ed. 14.75 (ISBN 0-85635-408-2, 80753, Pub. by Carcanet Pr England). Humanities.

Gurney, Joseph J. Journey in North America. LC 71-159795. (The American Scene Ser.). 422p. 1973. Repr. of 1841 ed. lib. bdg. 49.50 (ISBN 0-306-70572-9). Da Capo.

Gurney, Nancy & Gurney, Eric. The King, the Mice & the Cheese in English & Spanish. Rivera, Carlos, tr. (Spanish Beginner Bks.). (gr. k-3). 1967. PLB 5.99 o.p. (ISBN 0-394-91600-X). Random.

Gurney, R. Bibliography of the Larvae of Dacapod Crustaces & Larvae of Decapod Crustacea, 2 vols. in 1. 1960. 30.40 (ISBN 3-7682-0029-9). Lubrecht & Cramer.

Gurney, R., jt. auth. see Harris, A.

Gurney, T. R. Fatigue of Welded Structures. 2nd ed. LC 78-21885. (British Welding Research Association Ser.). (Illus.). 1980. 72.50 (ISBN 0-521-22558-2). Cambridge U Pr.

Gurney, W. S., jt. auth. see Nisbet, R. M.

Guro, Elena. The Little Camels of the Sky. O'Brien, Kevin, tr. from Rus. 1983. 16.00 (ISBN 0-88233-437-9). Ardis Pubs.

Guroff, Gregory & Carstensen, Fred V. Entrepreneurship in Imperial Russia & the Soviet Union. LC 82-15056. 384p. 1983. 40.00x (ISBN 0-691-05376-6); pap. 12.95 (ISBN 0-691-10141-8). Princeton U Pr.

Gurpide, Erlio, ed. Biochemical Actions of Progesterone & Progestins, Vol. 286. (Annals of the New York Academy of Sciences). 449p. 1977. 43.00x (ISBN 0-89072-032-0). NY Acad Sci.

Gurr, Andrew. Hamlet & the Distracted Globe. (Text & Context). 1978. text ed. 9.25x (ISBN 0-85621-069-2). Humanities.

--Hamlet & the Distracted Globe. 26.00x (ISBN 0-686-97004-7, Pub. by Scottish Academic Pr Scotland). State Mutual Bk.

--The Shakespearean Stage, 1574-1642. 2nd ed. LC 80-40085. (Illus.). 220p. 1981. 49.50 (ISBN 0-521-23029-2); pap. 13.50 (ISBN 0-521-29772-9). Cambridge U Pr.

Gurr, David. Troika. 1981. pap. 2.75 o.p. (ISBN 0-425-04662-1). Berkley Pub.

--Troika. LC 79-10534. 1979. 9.95 o.p. (ISBN 0-416-00001-0). Methuen Inc.

Gurr, John E. Principle of Sufficient Reason in Some Scholastic Systems, 1750-1900. 1959. 12.95 (ISBN 0-87462-411-8). Marquette.

Gurr, M. I. & James, A. T. Lipid Biochemistry: An Introduction. 3rd ed. 1980. 34.00x (ISBN 0-412-22620-0, Pub. by Chapman & Hall); pap. 18.95x (ISBN 0-412-22630-8). Methuen Inc.

Gurr, Ted R., jt. auth. see Eckstein, Harry.

Gurry, R. W., jt. auth. see Darken, Lawrence S.

Gurung, Deu B., et al. Gurung-Nepali-English Glossary. 223p. 1976. pap. 3.00x (ISBN 0-88312-854-3); 3.00 (ISBN 0-88312-391-6). Summer Inst Ling.

Gurvich, L. V., ed. Thermodynamic Properties of Individual Substances, 2 vols, Pt. I. 3rd rev. & enl. ed. (Illus.). 830p. 1983. 150.00 set (ISBN 0-08-027585-0); prepub. 120.00 (ISBN 0-08-029998-9). Pergamon.

Gurvitch, Georges. Sociology of Law. (International Library of Sociology). 264p. 1973. 18.00x o.p. (ISBN 0-7100-7519-7). Routledge & Kegan.

Gurwitsch, Aron. Field of Consciousness. LC 63-13565. (Psychological Ser.: No. 2). 1976. pap. text ed. 14.50x (ISBN 0-8207-0043-6). Duquesne.

Gurwitz, Aaron S., ed. The Economics of Public School Finance. (Rand Education Policy Ser.). 232p. 1982. prof ref 20.00x (ISBN 0-88410-859-7). Ballinger Pub.

Gusberg, S. B. & Frick, H. C., II. Corscaden's Gynecologic Cancer. 5th ed. (Illus.). 494p. 1978. 54.00 (ISBN 0-683-03854-0). Williams & Wilkins.

Gusfield, Joseph R. Symbolic Crusade: Status Politics & the American Temperance Movement. LC 80-13342. viii, 198p. 1980. Repr. of 1963 ed. lib. bdg. 20.00x (ISBN 0-313-22423-4, GUSC). Greenwood.

Gush, George. Renaissance Armies 1480-1650. (Illus.). 1982. Repr. 22.50 (ISBN 0-85059-604-1). Aztex.

Gusky, Jeff, et al. Medical Student Ward Survival Manual. LC 82-60882. (Illus.). 22p. (Orig.). 1982. pap. text ed. 13.95 (ISBN 0-910015-00-7). Med Student Pubs.

Guss, David, ed. see De Civrieux, Marc.

Guss, David, jt. ed. see Koran, Dennis.

Guss, David, ed. see Rothenberg, et al.

Gussmann, Edmund. Studies in Abstract Phonology. (Linguistic Inquiry Monographs). 176p. (Orig.). 1980. 25.00x (ISBN 0-262-07081-2); pap. text ed. 13.50x (ISBN 0-262-57057-2). MIT Pr.

Gussow, Don. Chaia Sonia: A Family's Odyssey - Russian Style. 258p. 1980. 10.95 o.s.i. (ISBN 0-440-02459-5). Delacorte.

Gussow, Joan D., jt. auth. see Birch, Herbert G.

Gustafson, Anita. Some Feet Have Noses. LC 81-15573. (Illus.). (gr. 4 up). 10.00 (ISBN 0-688-00925-5); PLB 9.55 (ISBN 0-688-00926-3). Lothrop.

Gustafson, Anita & Kriney, Marilyn. Monster Rolling Skull & Other Native American Tales. LC 79-7890. (Illus.). (gr. 4-6). 1980. 7.95i o.p. (ISBN 0-690-04019-9, TYC-J); PLB 7.89 (ISBN 0-690-04020-2). Har-Row.

Gustafson, Clair, jt. auth. see Becker, Leonard, Jr.

Gustafson, Daniel R. Physics: Health & the Human Body. 528p. 1979. text ed. 22.95x (ISBN 0-534-00756-2). Wadsworth Pub.

Gustafson, James M. Can Ethics Be Christian? LC 74-11622. xii, 192p. 1975. 8.95x o.s.i. (ISBN 0-226-31103-1). U of Chicago Pr.

--The Contributions of Theology to Medical Ethics. (Pere Marquette Theology Lectures). 1975. 7.95 (ISBN 0-87462-507-6). Marquette.

Gustafson, Jim. Shameless. 1979. pap. 4.00 o.p. (ISBN 0-939180-07-3). Tombouctou.

Gustafson, Milton O., ed. The National Archives & Foreign Relations Research. LC 74-82494. (National Archives Conferences Ser.: Vol. 4). xvii, 292p. 1974. 17.50x (ISBN 0-8214-0163-7, 82-81644). Ohio U Pr.

Gustafson, R. D. & Frisk, Peter D. College Algebra. 2nd ed. LC 82-4389. (Mathematics Ser.). 475p. 1982. text ed. 22.95 (ISBN 0-534-01202-7). Brooks-Cole.

--College Algebra & Trigonometry. LC 82-4388. (Mathematics Ser.). 600p. 1982. text ed. 23.95 (ISBN 0-534-01204-3). Brooks-Cole.

Gustafson, R. David & Frisk, Peter D. Plane Trigonometry. LC 81-10232. (Mathematics Ser.). 518p. 1982. text ed. 20.95 (ISBN 0-8185-0483-8). Brooks-Cole.

Gustafson, Ray L. Buying, Selling, Starting a Business. LC 82-90702. 152p. 1982. pap. 19.95 (ISBN 0-9609046-0-3, DEPT. OR-1). Gustafson Horse.

Gustafson, Richard F. The Imagination of Spring: The Poetry of Afanasy Fet. LC 76-15198. 1976. Repr. lib. bdg. 20.50x (ISBN 0-8371-8146-1, GUIS). Greenwood.

Gustafson, Robert, jt. auth. see Schmalleger, Frank.

Gustafson, Thane. Reform in Soviet Politics: The Lessons of Recent Policies on Land & Water. LC 80-24286. (Illus.). 224p. 1981. 29.95 (ISBN 0-521-23377-1). Cambridge U Pr.

Gustafson, William F., jt. auth. see Bosco, James S.

Gustafsson, Bo, ed. Post-Industrial Society. LC 78-18793. 1979. 22.50x o.p. (ISBN 0-312-63226-6). St Martin.

Gustafsson, J. A. Biochemistry, Biophysics & Regulation of Cytochrome P-450: Proceedings. (Developments in Biochemistry Ser.: Vol. 13). 1981. 92.00 (ISBN 0-444-80282-7). Elsevier.

Gustafsson, Lars. The Tennis Players. Sandstroem, Yvonne L., tr. 96p. (Swedish.). 1983. 13.00 (ISBN 0-8112-0861-3); pap. 6.25 (ISBN 0-8112-0862-1, NDP551). New Directions.

Gustafsson, Uwe. Kotia Oriya Phonemic Summary. 43p. 1974. pap. 1.80x (ISBN 0-88312-779-2); microfiche 1.50 (ISBN 0-88312-398-3). Summer Inst Ling.

Gustason, jt. auth. see Wojcio.

Gustason, Gerilee, ed. Using Signing Exact English in Total Communication: A Collection of Articles. LC 80-84549. (Illus.). 68p. (Orig.). 1980. pap. 5.00x (ISBN 0-916708-04-7). Modern Signs.

Gustason, Gerilee, et al. Signing Exact English. 1980 ed. LC 80-80571. (Illus.). 460p. (gr. k-12). 1980. text ed. 24.00x (ISBN 0-916708-02-0); pap. text ed. 18.00x (ISBN 0-916708-03-9). Modern Signs.

Gustav, Bergmann. Philosophy of Science. LC 77-5439. 181p. lib. bdg. 65.00x (ISBN 0-8371-9623-X, BEPH). Greenwood.

Gustave, Maurice, jt. auth. see Tallon, Eugene.

Gustavson, Carl G. The Institutional Drive: A Study in Pluralistic Democracy. LC 66-14029. xviii, 199p. 1966. 15.00x (ISBN 0-8214-0019-3, 82-80216). Ohio U Pr.
--Preface to History. (YA) (gr. 9-12). 1955. pap. 4.95 (ISBN 0-07-025279-3, SP). McGraw.
Gustavson, Frances & Sackson, Marian. Problem Solving in Basic: A Modular Approach. LC 78-21904. 1979. pap. text ed. 12.95 (ISBN 0-574-21240-X, 13-4240); instr's guide avail. (ISBN 0-574-21241-8, 13-4241). SRA.
Gustavson, Frances G. The Automatic Revision of Storage Structures. Stone, Harold, ed. LC 82-6974. (Computer Science: Systems Programming Ser.: No. 11). 154p. 1982. 34.95 (ISBN 0-8357-1345-8, Pub. by UMI Res Pr). Univ Microfilms.
Gustavson, T. C. & Bassett, R. L. Geology & Geohydrology of the Palo Duro Basin, Texas Panhandle, A Report on the Progress of Nuclear Waste Isolation Feasibility Studies: Geological Circular 81-3. (Illus.). 173p. 1981. 4.50 (ISBN 0-686-36581-X). Bur Econ Geology.
Gustavson, T. C., jt. auth. see Finley, R. J.
Gustavus, Susan O., jt. auth. see Nam, Charles B.
Gustkey, Earl. Roman Gabriel: Outstanding Pro. new ed. (Putnam Sports Shelf). 192p. (gr. 5 up). 1974. PLB 4.97 o.p. (ISBN 0-399-60878-8). Putnam Pub Group.
Gutcheon, Beth. Still Missing. 336p. 1981. 11.95 (ISBN 0-399-12578-7). Putnam Pub Group.
--Without a Trace. 384p. 1983. pap. 3.95 (ISBN 0-440-19496-2). Dell.
Gutcheon, Elizabeth. The New Girls. LC 79-12245. 1979. 11.95 o.p. (ISBN 0-399-12362-8). Putnam Pub Group.
Gutcho, M. H. Microcapsules & Other Capsules: Advances Since 1975. LC 79-15917. (Chemical Technology Review Ser.: No. 135). (Illus.). 346p. 1980. 40.00 (ISBN 0-8155-0776-3). Noyes.
Gutcho, Marcia, ed. Adhesives Technology: Developments Since 1979. LC 82-19096. (Chemical Technology Review: No. 215). (Illus.). 452p. 1983. 48.00 (ISBN 0-8155-0921-9). Noyes.
Gutcho, S. J. Waste Treatment with Polyelectrolytes & Other Flocculants. LC 76-2124. (Pollution Technology Review Ser.: No. 31). (Illus.). 1977. 39.00 o.p. (ISBN 0-8155-0648-1). Noyes.
Gutek, Gerald L. A History of the Western Educational Experience. 448p. 1972. text ed. 15.95x o.p. (ISBN 0-394-31355-0, RanC). Random.
--Pestalozzi & Education. (Orig.). 1968. pap. text ed. 3.10 (ISBN 0-685-19698-4). Phila Bk Co.
--Philosophical Alternatives in Education. LC 73-76802. 1974. pap. 14.95 04020261x o.p. (ISBN 0-675-08926-3). Merrill.
Guterman, Norbert, ed. see Schelling, Friedrich.
Gutfinger, Chaim, ed. Topics in Transport Phenomena: Bioprocesses, Mathematical Treatment, Mechanisms. LC 75-15867. 622p. 1975. 39.50x o.p. (ISBN 0-470-33712-5). Halsted Pr.
Gutfreund, H. Enzymes: Physical Principles. rev. ed. LC 75-39068. 268p. 1972. 19.95 (ISBN 0-471-33716-1, Pub. by Wiley-Interscience). Wiley.
Guth, Delloyd J. & McKenna, John W. Tudor Rule & Revolution. LC 82-4266. 400p. p.n.s. (ISBN 0-521-24841-8). Cambridge U Pr.
Guth, DeLloyd J. & Wrone, David R.compiled By. The Assassination of John F. Kennedy: A Comprehensive Historical & Legal Bibliography, 1963-1979. LC 79-6184. (Illus.). lvi, 442p. 1980. lib. bdg. 45.00 (ISBN 0-313-21274-0, GJK/). Greenwood.
Guth, H. P. Advanced Composition. (American English Today Ser.). 1980. text ed. 7.36 (ISBN 0-07-025013-8). McGraw.
--Basic Composition Two. (American English Today Ser.). 1980. text ed. 7.36 (ISBN 0-07-025012-X). McGraw.
Guth, Hans P. Advanced Composition: The Writer at Work. 1971. text ed. 6.00 o.p. (ISBN 0-07-025256-4, W). McGraw.
--American English Today, Bk. 10, The Structure Of English. (Illus.). (gr. 10). 1970. text ed. 15.16 (ISBN 0-07-025288-2, W); tchr's. manual & key 12.36 (ISBN 0-07-025273-4, 25282). McGraw.
--American English Today: Our Challenging Language. 3rd ed. (Illus.). (gr. 12). 1980. text ed. 14.76 (ISBN 0-07-025022-7); tchr's manual 13.16 (ISBN 0-07-025032-4). McGraw.
--American English Today: The World of English. 3rd ed. (American English Today Ser.). (Illus.). (gr. 10). 1980. text ed. 14.64 (ISBN 0-07-025020-0); tchrs. ed. 13.16 (ISBN 0-07-025030-8). McGraw.
--Basic Composition: How We Write. 1971. text ed. 7.72 (ISBN 0-07-025254-8, W). McGraw.
--Intermediate Composition: The Writer's Purpose. 1971. text ed. 7.72 (ISBN 0-07-025255-6, W). McGraw.
--Language One: How English Works. (gr. 10). 1970. text ed. 7.72 (ISBN 0-07-025251-3, W). McGraw.
--Language Three: Your Language & Its History. 1971. text ed. 7.72 (ISBN 0-07-025253-X, W). McGraw.
--Language Two: American English in Action. 1970. text ed. 7.72 (ISBN 0-07-025252-1, W). McGraw.
--Today: A Text-Workbook for English Language & Composition, Level C. (Illus.). 160p. (gr. 9). 1971. pap. text ed. 5.36 (ISBN 0-07-025263-7, W); tchr's ed. 3.80 (ISBN 0-07-025246-7). McGraw.
--Today: A Text-Workbook for English Language & Composition, Level B. (Illus.). 128p. (gr. 8). 1972. pap. text ed. 5.36 (ISBN 0-07-025262-9, W); tchr's ed. 3.80 (ISBN 0-07-025245-9). McGraw.
--Today: A Text-Workbook for English Language & Composition, Level C. Wilson, Paul H., ed. (Illus.). 160p. (gr. 9). 1979. pap. 5.20 (ISBN 0-07-025039-1, W); ans. key 1.44 (ISBN 0-07-025045-6). McGraw.
--Today: A Text-Workbook for English Language & Composition, Level D. Wilson, Paul H., ed. (Illus.). 176p. (gr. 10). 1979. pap. text ed. 5.20 (ISBN 0-07-025040-5, W); ans. key 1.44 (ISBN 0-07-025046-4). McGraw.
--Today Workbooks & Answer Keys A-F. 2nd ed. Incl. A. wkbk. (ISBN 0-07-025361-7); ans. key (ISBN 0-07-025371-4); B. wkbk. (ISBN 0-07-025362-5); ans. key (ISBN 0-07-025372-2); C. wkbk. (ISBN 0-07-025363-3); ans. key (ISBN 0-07-025373-0); D. wkbk. (ISBN 0-07-025364-1); ans. key (ISBN 0-07-025374-9); E. wkbk. (ISBN 0-07-025365-X); ans. key (ISBN 0-07-025375-7); F. wkbk. (ISBN 0-07-025366-8); ans. key (ISBN 0-07-025376-5). (Today Ser.). (YA) (gr. 7-12). 1976. wkbks. 5.36 ea. (W); ans. key 1.52 ea. McGraw.
--The Uses of Language. 3rd ed. (American English Today Ser.). (gr. 11). 1980. text ed. 14.76 (ISBN 0-07-025021-9); tchrs'. manual 13.16 (ISBN 0-07-025031-6). McGraw.
--Words & Ideas. 5th ed. 528p. 1980. text ed. 13.95x (ISBN 0-534-00815-1). Wadsworth Pub.
Guth, Hans P. & McLaughlin, B. K. Today: A Text-Workbook for English Language & Composition, Level D. (Illus.). 176p. (gr. 10). 1971. pap. text ed. 5.36 (ISBN 0-07-025264-5, W); tchr's ed. 3.80 (ISBN 0-07-025247-5). McGraw.
Guth, Hans P. & Schuster, E. H. American English Today, Bk. 10: The World of English. 2nd ed. (gr. 10). 1977. text ed. 15.16 (ISBN 0-07-025336-6, W); tchr's. manual 9.60 (ISBN 0-07-025330-7); tchr's. manual with key 15.76 (ISBN 0-07-025340-4). McGraw.
--American English Today, Bk. 11: The Uses of Language. 2nd ed. (gr. 11). 1975. text ed. 15.16 (ISBN 0-07-025289-0); tchr's ed. 9.60 (ISBN 0-07-025331-5). McGraw.
--American English Today, Bk. 11: The Uses of Language. 2nd rev. ed. LC 75-4772. (gr. 11). 1977. text ed. 15.28 (ISBN 0-07-025337-4). McGraw.
--American English Today, Bk. 12: The Growth of English. 2nd ed. (gr. 12). 1975. text ed. 15.16 (ISBN 0-07-025290-4); tchr's. manual & key 9.60 (ISBN 0-07-025332-3). McGraw.
--American English Today, Bk. 12: The Growth of English. 2nd rev. ed. LC 75-4948. (Illus.). 1977. text ed. 15.28 (ISBN 0-07-025338-2). McGraw.
--Today: A Text-Workbook for English Language & Composition, Level E. (Illus.). 160p. (gr. 11). 1972. text ed. 5.36 (ISBN 0-07-025265-3, W); tchrs' ed. 3.80 (ISBN 0-07-025248-3). McGraw.
--Today: A Text-Workbook for Language & Composition, Level F. 5.36 (ISBN 0-07-025266-1, W); tchrs' ed. 3.44 (ISBN 0-07-025249-1). McGraw.
Guth, Hans P. & Schuster, Edgar H. American English Today: The Tools of English. 3rd ed. LC 79-4066. (American English Today Ser.). 1980. text ed. 14.24 (ISBN 0-07-025019-7); 13.16 (ISBN 0-07-025029-4). McGraw.
--Our Common Language. 3rd ed. (American English Today Ser.). (Illus.). 480p. (gr. 8). 1980. text ed. 14.24 (ISBN 0-07-025018-9, W); tchrs. manual 13.16 (ISBN 0-07-025028-6). McGraw.
--Today: A Text-Workbook for English Language & Composition, Level E. (Illus.). 160p. (gr. 11). 1980. pap. text ed. 5.20 (ISBN 0-07-025041-3, W); ans. key 1.44 (ISBN 0-07-025047-2). McGraw.
--Today: A Text-Workbook for English Language & Composition, Level F. Wilson, Paul H., ed. (Illus.). 160p. (gr. 12). 1980. pap. text ed. 5.20 (ISBN 0-07-025042-1, W); ans. key 1.44 (ISBN 0-07-025048-0). McGraw.
Guth, Hans P., et al. American English Today, Bk. 7, Exploring English. (gr. 7). 1970. text ed. 12.52 o.p. (ISBN 0-07-025285-8, W). McGraw.
--American English Today, Bk. 8, Our Common Language. (gr. 8). 1970. text ed. 12.84 o.p. (ISBN 0-07-025286-6, W). McGraw.
Guth, Lloyd, tr. see Ramon y Cajal, Santiago.
Guth, Paul. Le Naif Aux Quarante Enfants. (Easy Readers, C). 1977. pap. 3.95 (ISBN 0-88436-294-9). EMC.
Guth de Lloyd, J. Late-Medieval England, 1377-1485. LC 75-23845. (Conference on British Studies Bibliographical Handbooks Ser.). 164p. 1976. 19.95 (ISBN 0-521-20877-7). Cambridge U Pr.
Guthe, Carl E. Management of Small History Museums. 2nd ed. 1964. pap. 4.50 (ISBN 0-910050-04-X). AASLH.
Gutheil, Emil. Music & Your Emotions. new ed. LC 75-131283. 1970. pap. 5.95 (ISBN 0-87140-232-7). Liveright.
Gutheim, Frederick, ed. In the Cause of Architecture. (Illus.). 246p. 1975. 27.50 (ISBN 0-07-025350-1, P&RB). McGraw.
Guthke, Karl S. Modern Tragicomedy: An Investigation into the Nature of the Genre. 1966. pap. text ed. 3.95 (ISBN 0-685-19746-8). Phila Bk Co.
Guthkelch, A. C., ed. see Swift, Jonathan.
Guthorn, Peter J. The Sea Bright Skiff & Other Shore Boats. rev. ed. (Illus.). 256p. 1983. pap. 13.95 (ISBN 0-916838-73-0). Schiffer.
Guthridge, G. L. Revenge Rides High. 208p. 1982. pap. 2.25 o.s.i. (ISBN 0-8439-1159-X, Leisure Bks). Nordon Pubns.
Guthridge, Sharyn G., ed. see Gregory, Grace C.
Guthridge, Sue. Thomas A. Edison. new ed. (Childhood of Famous Americans). (Illus.). 204p. (Orig.). (gr. 2 up). 1983. pap. 3.95 (ISBN 0-672-52751-0). Bobbs.
Guthrie, et al. Nuevo Comentario Biblico. Orig. Title: The New Bible Commentary Revised. 136p. 1981. pap. 43.75 (ISBN 0-311-03001-7). Casa Bautista.
Guthrie, A. B. Arfive. 1982. pap. 2.95 (ISBN 0-553-22756-4). Bantam.
Guthrie, A. B., Jr. The Big It & Other Stories. 1980. lib. bdg. 9.95 (ISBN 0-8398-2680-X, Gregg). G K Hall.
--No Second Wind. 1980. 9.95 o.s.i. (ISBN 0-395-29069-4). HM.
--These Thousand Hills. 1979. lib. bdg. 9.95 (ISBN 0-8398-2584-6, Gregg). G K Hall.
--These Thousand Hills. 288p. 1982. pap. 3.25 (ISBN 0-553-20928-0). Bantam.
Guthrie, Anne. Madame Ambassador: The Life of Vijaya Lakshima Pandit. LC 62-9478. (Illus.). (gr. 9 up). 1962. 4.95 (ISBN 0-15-250165-7, HJ); pap. 0.60 (ISBN 0-15-655104-7, VoyB). HarBraceJ.
Guthrie, D. M. & Tindall, A. R. Biology of the Cockroach. LC 68-26564. (Illus.). 1968. 19.95 o.p. (ISBN 0-312-07980-X). St Martin.
Guthrie, David L. & Riley, Robert A., eds. A Solar Energy Bibliography. 1977. softcover 15.00 o.p. (ISBN 0-686-26011-2). Info Transfer.
Guthrie, Diana W. & Guthrie, Richard A. Nursing Management of Diabetes Mellitus. 2nd ed. LC 81-14062. (Illus.). 389p. 1982. pap. text ed. 15.95 (ISBN 0-8016-1996-3). Mosby.
Guthrie, Donald. The Apostles. 432p. 1981. pap. 10.95 (ISBN 0-310-25421-3). Zondervan.
--The Epistle to the Hebrews: An Introduction & Commentary. (Tyndale New Testament Commentaries: Vol. 15). 1983. pap. 4.95 (ISBN 0-8028-1427-1). Eerdmans.
--Jesus the Messiah. 400p. 1981. pap. 12.95 (ISBN 0-310-25431-0). Zondervan.
Guthrie, Edwin R. The Psychology of Human Conflict: The Clash of Motives Within the Individual. LC 70-138115. 408p. 1938. Repr. lib. bdg. 21.00x (ISBN 0-8371-5691-2, GUPH). Greenwood.
Guthrie, Helen. Introductory Nutrition. 4th ed. LC 78-16649. (Illus.). 694p. 1979. text ed. 22.95 o.p. (ISBN 0-8016-2001-5). Mosby.
--Introductory Nutrition. 5th ed. 692p. 1983. pap. text ed. 23.95 (ISBN 0-8016-1997-1). Mosby.
Guthrie, James W. School Finance Policies & Practices: The Nineteen-Eighties: Decade of Conflict. (American Education Finance Association). 312p. 1981. 24.50x (ISBN 0-88410-195-9); pap. 12.95x (ISBN 0-88410-396-X). Ballinger Pub.
Guthrie, Lady, tr. see Vecchio, Giorgio del.
Guthrie, Mearl, et al. Business Mathematics for the Consumer. 2nd ed. (gr. 9-12). 1975. pap. 10.00 (ISBN 0-8224-3034-7); ed. 10.00tchrs'. (ISBN 0-8224-3035-5). Pitman Learning.
Guthrie, Ramon. Maximum Security Ward & Selected Poems. Gall, Sally M., ed. (Persea Lamplighter Ser.). 216p. 1983. 20.00 (ISBN 0-89255-079-1); pap. 9.95 (ISBN 0-89255-080-5). Persea Bks.
Guthrie, Ramon, tr. see Rousset, David.
Guthrie, Richard A., jt. auth. see Guthrie, Diana W.
Guthrie, Thomas. Seed-Time and Harvest of Ragged Schools: Three Pleas for Ragged Schools. LC 75-172569. (Criminology, Law Enforcement, & Social Problems Ser.: No. 150). 250p. (With a new chapter & index added). 1973. Repr. of 1860 ed. lib. bdg. 10.00x (ISBN 0-87585-150-9). Patterson Smith.
Guthrie, Tyrone. In Various Directions: A View of the Theatre. LC 78-9989. 1979. Repr. of 1965 ed. lib. bdg. 20.00x (ISBN 0-313-21224-4, GUVD). Greenwood.
Guthrie, Virgil B. Petroleum Products Handbook. 1960. 47.50 o.p. (ISBN 0-07-025295-5, P&RB). McGraw.
Guthrie, Virgil B., ed. Petroleum Products Handbook. LC 81-14261. 864p. 1983. Repr. of 1960 ed. lib. bdg. write for info. (ISBN 0-89874-382-6). Krieger.
Guthrie, W. D. Lectures on the Fourteenth Article of Amendment to the Constitution of the United States. LC 74-118030. (American Constitutional & Legal History Ser). 1970. Repr. of 1898 ed. lib. bdg. 35.00 (ISBN 0-306-71941-X). Da Capo.
Guthrie, W. K. A History of Greek Philosophy, 2 vols. LC 62-52735. 1979. pap. 19.95 ea. Vol. 1 (ISBN 0-521-29420-7). Vol. 2 (ISBN 0-521-29421-5). Cambridge U Pr.
--A History of Greek Philosophy, 6 vols. LC 62-52735. 1975. Vols. 1-5. 69.50 ea. Vol. 1 (ISBN 0-521-05159-2). Vol. 2 (ISBN 0-521-05160-6). Vol. 3 (ISBN 0-521-07566-1). Vol. 4 (ISBN 0-521-20002-4). Vol. 5 (ISBN 0-521-20003-2). Vol. 6. 65.00 (ISBN 0-521-23573-1). Cambridge U Pr.
Guthrie, W. K., tr. see Plato.
Guthrie, William, tr. see Von Savigny, Friedrich Carl.
Guthrie, William K. Socrates. 1971. pap. 11.95 (ISBN 0-521-09667-7). Cambridge U Pr.
--Sophists. 1971. pap. 13.95 (ISBN 0-521-09666-9). Cambridge U Pr.
Guthrie, William K., ed. see Cornford, Francis M.
Guthrie, Woody. Bound for Glory. (RL 10). 1976. pap. 1.95 o.p. (ISBN 0-451-07119-0, J7119, Sig). NAL.
Gutierrez, Alfredo. Paraguay: Regional Development in Eastern Paraguay. vii, 50p. 1978. pap. 10.00 (ISBN 0-686-36114-8, RC-7802). World Bank.
Gutierrez, Edna L., tr. see Mandeville, Sylvia.
Gutierrez, Edna L., tr. see Mandeville, Sylvia & Pierson, Lance.
Gutierrez, Gustavo. Power of the Poor in History. Barr, Robert R., tr. from Span. LC 82-22252. Orig. Title: La fuerza historica de los pobres. 272p. (Orig.). 1983. pap. 10.95 (ISBN 0-88344-388-0). Orbis Bks.
Gutierrez, Gustavo & Shaull, Richard. Liberation & Change. LC 76-44970. 1977. pap. 2.75 (ISBN 0-8042-0661-9). John Knox.
Gutierrez, Luis T. & Fey, Willard R. Ecosystem Succession: A General Hypothesis & a Test Model of a Grassland. (Illus.). 1980. text ed. 27.50x (ISBN 0-262-07075-8). MIT Pr.
Gutierrez, Ralph J., jt. auth. see Leopold, A. Starker.
Gutierrez, Rolando. El Mensaje De los Salmos En Nuestro Contexto, Tomo II. 160p. 1980. pap. 5.50 (ISBN 0-311-04025-X). Casa Bautista.
Gutierrez, Rolando C. El Mensaje de los Salmos en Nuestro Contexto Tomo I. 160p. 1979. 5.95 (ISBN 0-311-04023-3). Casa Bautista.
Gutin, Brenard & Kessler, Gail. The High-Energy Factor. 1983. 14.95 (ISBN 0-686-43194-4). Random.
Gutjahr, H. Chapter Five - Direct Print Coloration. 75.00x (ISBN 0-686-98200-2, Pub. by Soc Dyers & Colour); pap. 50.00x (ISBN 0-686-98201-0). State Mutual Bk.
Gutjahr, Rainer. Sailboard Racing. (Illus.). 119p. 1982. 14.95 (ISBN 0-914814-38-9). Sail Bks.
Gutkind, Erwin A. International History of City Development, 8 vols. Incl. Vol. 1. Urban Development in Central Europe. 1964. 50.00 o.p. (ISBN 0-02-913250-9); Vol. 2. Urban Development in Alpine & Scandinavian Countries. 1965. 50.00 (ISBN 0-02-913260-6); Vol. 3. Urban Development in Southern Europe; Spain & Portugal. 1967. 50.00 (ISBN 0-02-913270-3); Vol. 4. Urban Development in Southern Europe; Italy & Greece. 1969. 50.00 (ISBN 0-02-913280-0); Vol. 5. Urban Development in Western Europe; France & Belgium. 1970. 50.00 (ISBN 0-02-913300-9); Vol. 6. Urban Development in Western Europe: The Netherlands & Great Britain. 1971. 50.00 (ISBN 0-02-913310-6); Vol. 7. Urban Development in East-Central Europe: Poland, Czechoslavia, & Hungary. 1972. 45.00 (ISBN 0-02-913320-3); Vol. 8. Urban Development in Eastern Europe: Bulgaria, Romania, & U.S.S.R. 1972. 50.00 (ISBN 0-02-913330-0). LC 64-13231. Free Pr.
Gutkind, Lee. God's Helicopter. (Slow Loris Press Fiction Ser.). (Illus.). 180p. 1982. write for info. (ISBN 0-918366-25-9); pap. write for info. (ISBN 0-918366-26-7). Slow Loris.
Gutkind, Pete C. W. & Waterman, Peter, eds. African Social Studies: A Radical Reader. LC 75-43575. 1978. pap. 6.95 (ISBN 0-85345-460-4, PB-4604). Monthly Rev.
Gutkind, Peter C., jt. ed. see Morrison, Minion K.
Gutkind, Peter C. W. & Waterman, Peter, eds. African Social Studies: A Radical Reader. LC 75-43575. 481p. 1977. 17.50 (ISBN 0-85345-381-0, CL3810). Monthly Rev.
Gutman, Bill. Baseball Stars of Tomorrow: An Inside Look at the Minor Leagues. 192p. 1982. pap. 2.50 (ISBN 0-448-16937-1, Pub. by Tempo). Ace Bks.
--Football Superstars of the '70s. LC 75-12751. (Messner Sports Bks). (Illus.). 192p. (gr. 7 up). 1975. PLB 7.29 o.p. (ISBN 0-671-32751-8). Messner.
--Gamebreakers of the NFL. (NFL Punt, Pass & Kick Library: No. 18). (Illus.). (gr. 5 up). 1973. 2.50 o.p. (ISBN 0-394-82501-2, BYR); PLB 3.69 (ISBN 0-394-92501-7). Random.
--Great Baseball Stories Today & Yesterday. LC 78-480. (Messner Sports Book). (Illus.). 192p. (gr. 7 up). 1978. PLB 7.79 o.p. (ISBN 0-671-32881-6). Messner.
--The Harlem Globetrotters: Basketball's Funniest Team. LC 76-44411. (Sports Library). (Illus.). (gr. 4). 1977. lib. bdg. 7.12 (ISBN 0-8116-6680-8). Garrard.
--My Father, the Coach & Other Sports Stories. LC 75-42217. 192p. (gr. 7 up). 1976. PLB 5.79 o.p. (ISBN 0-671-32787-9). Messner.
--Pro Sports Champions. LC 80-28131. (Illus.). 192p. (gr. 7 up). 1981. PLB 9.79 o.p. (ISBN 0-671-34028-X). Messner.
--Superstars of the Sports World. LC 77-28762. (Illus.). 96p. (gr. 3 up). 1978. PLB 7.29 o.p. (ISBN 0-671-32827-1). Messner.
Gutman, David. Prokofiev: His Life & Times. (Illus.). 150p. (gr. 7 up). 1983. 16.95 (ISBN 0-88254-730-5, Pub. by Midas Bks England). Hippocrene Bks.
Gutman, Herbert G. Work Culture & Society in Industrializing America: Essays in America's Working Class & Social History. 1977. pap. 6.95 (ISBN 0-394-72251-5, Vin). Random.

Gutman, Judith M. Through Indian Eyes. (Illus.). 1982. 16.50 (ISBN 0-19-503135-0); pap. 16.50 (ISBN 0-19-503136-9). Oxford U Pr.

Gutmann, Amy. Liberal Equality. LC 79-27258. 320p. 1980. 39.50 (ISBN 0-521-22828-X); pap. 14.95 (ISBN 0-521-29665-X). Cambridge U Pr.

Gutmann, Felix & Lyons, Lawrence. Organic Semiconductors, Pt. A. LC 78-25782. 876p. 1981. Repr. of 1967 ed. text ed. 48.50 (ISBN 0-88275-823-3); Pt. B. write for info. (ISBN 0-89874-316-8). Krieger.

Gutmann, Fredrick T. Metric Guide to Mechanical Design & Drafting. LC 78-8632. (Illus.). 76p. 1978. 12.00 o.p. (ISBN 0-8311-1122-4). Indus Pr.

Gutmann, James, tr. see Schelling, Friedrich W.

Gutmann, Joseph, ed. The Image & the Word: Confrontations in Judaism, Christianity & Islam. LC 77-23470. (American Academy of Religion & Society of Biblical Literature. Religion & the Arts Ser.: Vol. 4). 1977. 9.00 (ISBN 0-89130-143-7, 09-01-03); pap. write for info. Scholars Pr Ca.

Gutnov, Alexei, et al. The Ideal Communist City. 1978. text ed. 12.50x (ISBN 0-262-07073-1); pap. 4.95x (ISBN 0-262-57053-X). MIT Pr.

Gutowski, Michael & Feild, Tracey. The Graying of Suburbia. (Illus.). 107p. (Orig.). 1979. pap. text ed. 5.50 (ISBN 0-87766-255-X). Urban Inst.

Gutrick, Martin J. Science of Classification: Finding Order Among Living & Nonliving Objects. (gr. 4 up). 1980. PLB 8.90 (ISBN 0-531-04160-3). Watts.

Gutsche, C. David & Pasto, Daniel G. Fundamentals of Organic Chemistry. (Illus.). 1248p. 1975. 34.95 (ISBN 0-13-333443-0); solutions manual 9.95 (ISBN 0-13-333435-X). P-H.

Gutsche, George J. & Leighton, Lauren G., eds. New Perspectives on Nineteenth Century Russian Prose. 146p. (Orig.). 1982. pap. 9.95 (ISBN 0-89357-094-X). Slavica.

Gutta, Margit. Cold Platters-Cold Buffets. (Illus.). 64p. 1983. cancelled (ISBN 0-8120-5400-8). Barron.

Guttchen, Robert S. Felix Adler. (World Leaders Ser.). 1974. lib. bdg. 13.95 (ISBN 0-8057-3650-6, Twayne). G K Hall.

Guttentag, Marcia & Bray, Helen. Undoing Sex Stereotypes: Research & Resources for Educators. 1976. pap. 9.95 (ISBN 0-07-025381-1, P&RB). McGraw.

Guttentag, Marcia & Secord, Paul F. Too Many Women? The Sex Ratio Question. 336p. 1983. 27.50 (ISBN 0-8039-1918-2); pap. 12.95 (ISBN 0-8039-1919-0). Sage.

Guttentag, Marcia, jt. ed. see Struening, Elmer L.

Gutteridge, W. E. & Coombs, G. H. The Biochemistry of Parasitic Protozoa: An Introductory Text. (Illus.). 184p. 1977. pap. text ed. 19.95 (ISBN 0-8391-0886-9). Univ Park.

Gutteridge, W. F. Military Regimes in Africa. LC 74-31587. (Studies in African History). 195p. 1975. 15.95x (ISBN 0-416-78230-2); pap. 9.95x (ISBN 0-416-78240-X). Methuen Inc.

Gutterman, Sy. Business Management for the Professional Photographer. (Illus.). 1980. text ed. 14.95 (ISBN 0-8174-3568-9, Amphoto). Watson-Guptill.

Guttetag, Marcia. The Evaluation of Training in Mental Health. LC 74-8506. 131p. 1975. 19.95 (ISBN 0-87705-161-5). Human Sci Pr.

Gutting, Gary. Religious Belief & Religious Skepticism. LC 82-50287. 160p. 1982. text ed. 15.95 (ISBN 0-268-01613-5). U of Notre Dame Pr.

--Religious Belief & Religious Skepticism. LC 82-50287. xi, 192p. 1983. pap. text ed. 9.95x (ISBN 0-268-01618-6, 85-16189). U of Notre Dame Pr.

Guttmacher, A. see Sanger, Margaret.

Guttmacher, Alan. Pregnancy, Birth & Family Planning. (Reference Ser.). 352p. 1973. pap. 3.50 (ISBN 0-451-11906-1, AE1906, Sig). NAL.

Guttman, Anthony J. Programming & Algorithms. 1977. text ed. 14.00x o.p. (ISBN 0-435-77541-3). Heinemann Ed.

Guttman, Irwin, et al. Introductory Engineering Statistics. 2nd ed. LC 72-160214. (Ser. in Probability & Mathematical Statistics: Applied Probability & Statistics). (Illus.). 1971. 31.95x o.p. (ISBN 0-471-33770-6). Wiley.

--Introductory Engineering Statistics. 3rd ed. 580p. 1982. text ed. 33.95 (ISBN 0-471-07859-X); solutions manual avail. (ISBN 0-471-08659-2). Wiley.

Guttman, Samuel & Jones, Randall L., eds. The Concordance to the Standard Edition of the Complete Psychological Works of Sigmund Freud. 1980. lib. bdg. 550.00 (ISBN 0-8161-8383-X, Hall Reference). G K Hall.

Guttman, V., ed. Phase Stability in High Temperature Alloys. (Illus.). vii, 155p. 1981. 43.00 (ISBN 0-85334-946-0, Pub. by Applied Sci England). Elsevier.

--Phase Stability in High Temperature Alloys. (Illus.). 154p. 1981. 43.00 (ISBN 0-85334-946-0, Pub. by Applied Sci England). Elsevier.

Guttman, V. & Merz, M., eds. Corrosion & Mechanical Stress at High Temperatures. (Illus.). 477p. 1981. 53.50 (ISBN 0-85334-956-8, Pub. by Applied Sci England). Elsevier.

Guttmann. Textbook of Sport for the Disabled. 33.95 (ISBN 0-471-25751-6, Wiley Heyden). Wiley.

Guttmann, Allen. Freedom & Authority in Puritan New England. Brown, Richard H. & Halsey, Van R., eds. (Amherst Project Units in American History). (gr. 11-12). 1970. pap. text ed. 5.16 (ISBN 0-201-02666-X, Sch Div); tchr's manual o.p. 1.92 (ISBN 0-201-02668-6). A-W.

Guttmann, Allen & Sappenfield, James, eds. Complete Works of Washington Irving: Life of George Washington, 5 vols. (Critical Editions Program). 1981. 80.00 (ISBN 0-8057-8511-6, Twayne). G K Hall.

Guttmann, H. Peter. The International Consultant. (Engineering News Record Ser.). 1976. 21.50 o.p. (ISBN 0-07-025306-4, P&RB). McGraw.

Guttschuss, Heather. Growing More Like Jesus. 128p. (ps). Date not set. pap. 5.95 (ISBN 0-8163-0486-6). Pacific Pr Pub Assn.

Gutwein, Kenneth C. Third Palestine: A Regional Study in Byzantine Urbanization. LC 81-40340. 430p. 1982. lib. bdg. 25.50 (ISBN 0-8191-1907-5); pap. text ed. 16.25 (ISBN 0-8191-1908-3). U Pr of Amer.

Gutwinski, Waldemar, ed. see Linguistic Association of Canada & the U. S.

Gutwirth, Madelyn, et al, eds. Sources et Reflets De l'Histoire De France. (Illus., Fr). 1972. pap. text ed. 10.95x (ISBN 0-19-501465-0). Oxford U Pr.

Gutwirth, Marcel. Stendhal. (World Authors Ser.: France: No. 174). lib. bdg. 12.50 o.p. (ISBN 0-8057-2862-7, Twayne). G K Hall.

Guty, Stephen G., ed. see McGilton, Henry & McGilton, Rachel.

Gutzke, Manford G. Plain Talk on Deuteronomy. 1980. pap. 4.95 (ISBN 0-310-25691-7). Zondervan.

--Plain Talk on Exodus. new ed. 224p. (Orig.). 1974. pap. 6.95 (ISBN 0-310-25521-X). Zondervan.

--Plain Talk on Luke. 1966. pap. 5.95 (ISBN 0-310-25581-3). Zondervan.

--Plain Talk on Mark. 295p. 1975. pap. 5.95 (ISBN 0-310-25591-0). Zondervan.

--Plain Talk on Matthew. pap. 6.95 (ISBN 0-310-25601-1). Zondervan.

--Plain Talk on the Minor Prophets. (Plain Talk Series of Bible Study Bks.). 160p. (Orig.). 1980. pap. 4.95 (ISBN 0-310-41941-7, 9868P). Zondervan.

--Plain Talk on Timothy, Titus, & Philemon. (Plain Talk Ser.). 1978. pap. 6.95 (ISBN 0-310-25661-5). Zondervan.

Guy, A. G. Essentials of Materials Science. 1976. text ed. 32.50 (ISBN 0-07-025351-X, C); solutions manual 12.50 (ISBN 0-07-025352-8). McGraw.

Guy, Clifford M. Retail Location & Retail Planning in Britain. 208p. 1980. text ed. 30.00x (ISBN 0-566-00270-1). Gower Pub Ltd.

Guy, Dan M. Statistical Sampling in Auditing. LC 80-17279. (Wiley Series in Accounting & Info. Systems). 229p. 1981. text ed. 26.95 (ISBN 0-471-04232-3); 6.75 (ISBN 0-471-09092-1). Wiley.

Guy, David. Football Dreams. 1982. pap. 2.25 (ISBN 0-451-11086-2, Sig). NAL.

Guy, Edward T. & Merrigan, John J. Forms for Safety & Security Management. 448p. 1980. text ed. 29.95 (ISBN 0-409-95089-0). Butterworth.

Guy, P. K., jt. auth. see Armstrong, L.

Guy, Rosa. The Disappearance. LC 79-50672. (gr. 7 up). 1979. 9.95 o.s.i. (ISBN 0-440-01189-2). Delacorte.

--A Measure of Time. LC 82-15461. 384p. 1983. 16.95 (ISBN 0-03-057653-9). HR&W.

--New Guys Around the Block. LC 82-72818. 192p. (YA) (gr. 8 up). 1983. 11.95 (ISBN 0-440-06005-2). Delacorte.

Guy, William A. The Factors of the Unsound Mind. (Historical Foundations of Forensic Psychiatry & Psychology Ser.). xx, 232p. 1983. Repr. of 1881 ed. lib. bdg. 25.00 (ISBN 0-306-76186-6). Da Capo.

Guyatt, John. The American Revolution. Yapp, Malcolm, et al, eds. (World History Ser.). (Illus.). 32p. (gr. 10). 1980. Repr. of 1977 ed. lib. bdg. 6.95 (ISBN 0-89908-135-5); pap. text ed. 2.25 (ISBN 0-89908-110-X). Greenhaven.

--Ancient America. Killingray, Margaret, et al, eds. (World History Ser.). (Illus.). 32p. (gr. 10). 1980. Repr. of 1977 ed. lib. bdg. 6.95 (ISBN 0-89908-033-2); pap. text ed. 2.25 (ISBN 0-89908-008-1). Greenhaven.

--Bolivar. Yapp, Malcolm, et al, eds. (World History Ser.). (Illus.). 32p. (gr. 10). 1980. lib. bdg. 6.95 (ISBN 0-89908-045-6); pap. text ed. 2.25 (ISBN 0-89908-020-0). Greenhaven.

Guyau, M. The Non-Religion of the Future: A Sociological Study. LC 62-19393. 1962. pap. 2.95 o.p. (ISBN 0-8052-0039-8). Schocken.

Guyer, Kenneth E., jt. auth. see Seibel, Hugo.

Guyette, Dale & Guyette, Gary. Decoys of Maritime Canada. (Illus.). 204p. 1983. text ed. 35.00 (ISBN 0-916838-76-5). Schiffer.

Guyette, Gary, jt. auth. see Guyette, Dale.

Guyler, Vivan V. Design in Nature. LC 76-93119. (gr. 9-12). 1970. 12.95 o.p. (ISBN 0-87192-031-X). Davis Mass.

Guynn, J., jt. auth. see Bailey, William J.

Guynn, Stephen J., jt. auth. see Bailey, William J.

Guyol, N. B. The World Electric Power Industry. LC 68-54567. 1969. 75.00x (ISBN 0-520-01484-7). U of Cal Pr.

Guyon, Jean. Spiritual Writings of Madame Guyon. 640p. (Orig.). 1982. pap. 19.80 (ISBN 0-940232-07-3). Christian Bks.

Guyon, Y. Limit-State Design of Prestressed Concrete, Vol. 2: The Design of the Member. Turner, F. H., tr. from Fr. LC 72-2655. 469p. 1974. 64.95 o.s.i. (ISBN 0-470-33791-5). Halsted Pr.

Guyot, Jacqueline & Raynal, Francois. Angela & Elton at Play. (Woofits Ser.). (Illus.). 24p. 1982. 3.95 (ISBN 0-8431-0980-7). Price Stern.

--Flowers for Angela's Mother. (Woofits Ser.). (Illus.). 24p. 1982. 3.95 (ISBN 0-8431-0981-5). Price Stern.

Guyton, Arthur C. Basic Human Neurophysiology. 3rd ed. (Illus.). 345p. 1981. 22.00 (ISBN 0-7216-4367-1). Saunders.

--Basic Human Physiology: Normal Function & Mechanisms of Disease. 2nd ed. LC 76-4248. (Illus.). 1977. text ed. 22.50 o.p. (ISBN 0-7216-4383-3). Saunders.

--Human Physiology & Mechanisms of Disease. 3rd. ed. (Illus.). 720p. 1982. 26.50 (ISBN 0-7216-4384-1). Saunders.

--Textbook of Medical Physiology. 5th ed. LC 75-8178. (Illus.). 1200p. 1976. 29.00 o.p. (ISBN 0-7216-4393-0, 4393-0). Saunders.

--Textbook of Medical Physiology. 6th ed. (Illus.). 1237p. 1981. text ed. 42.00 (ISBN 0-7216-4394-9). Saunders.

Guyton, Arthur C., et al. Circulatory Physiology I: Cardiac Output & Its Regulation. 2nd ed. LC 72-90721. (Illus.). 556p. 1973. 27.50 o.p. (ISBN 0-7216-4360-4). Saunders.

Guyton, Emma J. W. The Wife's Trials; or, Lilian Grey. Repr. Of 1858 Ed. Wolff, Robert L., ed. Bd. with Married Life. Repr. of 1863 ed; Husbands & Wives. Repr. of 1873 ed. LC 75-492. (Victorian Fiction Ser.). 1975. lib. bdg. 66.00 o.s.i. (ISBN 0-8240-1568-1). Garland Pub.

Guze, Samuel B. Criminality & Psychiatric Disorders. 1976. text ed. 18.95x (ISBN 0-19-501973-3). Oxford U Pr.

Guze, Samuel B., jt. auth. see Goodwin, Donald W.

Guzie, Tad W. For Adult Catholics Only. LC 69-17920. (Orig.). 1969. pap. 1.75 o.p. (ISBN 0-685-07632-6, 80287). Glencoe.

Guzman, Betty, jt. auth. see Romero, Jose.

Guzman, Gaston. The Genus Psilocybe: Revision of the Known Species (Hallucinogenic Species) (Beiheft to Nova Hedwigia Ser.). (Illus.). 650p. 1983. lib. bdg. 80.00 (ISBN 3-7682-1319-6). Lubrecht & Cramer.

Guzman, Juan P., tr. see Taylor, Jack R.

Guzman, Maria O. Tagalog-English - English-Tagalog Dictionary. rev. ed. pap. 22.50 (ISBN 0-686-68939-9). Heinman.

Guzman, Martin L. The Eagle & the Serpent. De Onis, Harriet, tr. 7.50 (ISBN 0-8446-0668-5). Peter Smith.

--Memoirs of Pancho Villa. Taylor, Virginia, tr. LC 65-11146. (Texas Pan American Ser.). (Illus.). 528p. 1965. 25.00x (ISBN 0-292-73301-1); pap. 0.00 o.p. U of Tex Pr.

Guzman, Videa De see Ramos, Teresita V. & De Guzman, Videa.

Guzzo, Richard A. & Bondy, Jeffrey S. A Guide to Worker Productivity Experiments in the U. S., 1976-81. (Pergamon Press-Work in America Institute Ser.). 125p. 1983. 17.50 (ISBN 0-08-029548-7). Pergamon.

--A Guide to Worker Productivity Experiments in the U. S., 1976-1981. 125p. 14.50 (ISBN 0-686-84782-2). Work in Amer.

Guzzon, F., jt. auth. see Gennaro, L.

Gvishiani, J. M., ed. Systems Research: Methodological Problems. 380p. 1983. 75.00 (ISBN 0-08-030000-6). Pergamon.

Gwilt, Joseph. The Encyclopedia of Architecture: Historical, Theoretical & Practical. (Illus.). 1392p. 1982. pap. 10.95 (ISBN 0-517-54729-5). Crown.

Gwin, Catherine, jt. auth. see Camps, Miriam.

Gwin, Lucy. Going Overboard: The Onliest Little Woman in the Offshore Oilfields. LC 81-16408. 288p. 1982. 15.95 (ISBN 0-670-34360-9). Viking Pr.

Gwin, Paul, jt. auth. see Lionberger, Herbert F.

Gwin, Yolande. Yolande's Atlanta. 1983. 9.95 (ISBN 0-931948-44-4). Peachtree Pubs.

Gwinner, Robert F., et al. Marketing: An Environmental Perspective. (Illus.). 1977. text ed. 22.95 (ISBN 0-8299-0119-1); instrs.' manual avail. (ISBN 0-8299-0484-0). West Pub.

Gwon, Pu G. Dynamic Art of Breaking. 1977. 6.95x o.s.i. Wehman.

Gwynn, Frederick L. & Blotner, Joseph L., eds. Faulkner in the University: Class Conferences at the University of Virginia, 1957-1958. LC 59-13713. (Illus.). 294p. 1977. Repr. of 1959 ed. 14.95x (ISBN 0-8139-0843-4). U Pr of Va.

Gwynn, R. S. The Narcissiad: A Long Satirical Poem. (Cedar Rock Poetry Ser.). (Illus.). 40p. 1981. pap. 4.50 (ISBN 0-930024-16-8). Cedar Rock.

Gwynn, S. Life of Horace Walpole. LC 76-160467. (English Biography Ser., No. 31). 1971. Repr. of 1932 ed. lib. bdg. 54.95x (ISBN 0-8383-1302-7). Haskell.

--Oliver Goldsmith. LC 74-30338. (English Literature Ser., No. 33). 1974. lib. bdg. 41.95x (ISBN 0-8383-1843-6). Haskell.

--Tennyson. LC 74-16313. (Studies in Tennyson, No. 27). 1974. lib. bdg. 33.95x (ISBN 0-8383-1796-0). Haskell.

Gwynne, G. V., ed. see Miller, E. J.

Gwynne, Michael. Sequence Dancing. 22.50x (ISBN 0-392-06935-0, LTB). Sportshelf.

Gwynne, Peter, jt. auth. see Hooper, Henry O.

Gwynne, Walker. The Christian Year; Its Purpose & Its History. LC 74-89269. xiv, 143p. 1972. Repr. of 1917 ed. 37.00x (ISBN 0-8103-3814-9). Gale.

Gy, P. M. Sampling of Particulate Materials. 2nd ed. LC 79-16075. (Developments in Geomathematics Ser.: Vol. 4). 432p. 1982. 59.75 (ISBN 0-444-42079-7). Elsevier.

Gyarmathi, Samuel. Grammatical Proof of the Affinity of the Hungarian Language with Languages of Fennic Origin: (Gottingen Dietrich, 1799) Hanzeli, Victor E., tr. from Ger. (Amsterdam Classics in Linguistics (ACIL): No. 15). 350p. 1983. 37.00x (ISBN 90-272-0976-6). Benjamins North Am.

--Grammatical Proof of the Affinity of the Hungarian Language with Languages of Fennic Origin. 350p. 1982. 37.00 o.p. (ISBN 90-272-0976-6). Benjamins North Am.

Gyarmathy, S. Affinitas Linguae Hungaricae cum Linguis Fennicae Originis Grammatice Demonstrata. (Linguistics 13th-18th Centuries). 406p. (Fr.). 1974. Repr. of 1799 ed. lib. bdg. 103.00 o.p. (ISBN 0-8287-0412-0, 71-5043). Clearwater Pub.

Gyatso, Kalzang. Songs of Spiritual Change. Mullin, Glenn H., ed. LC 82-81034. 205p. 1982. 16.00 (ISBN 0-937938-07-6, Pub. by Snow Lion); lib. bdg. 16.00 (ISBN 0-686-97715-7); pap. 9.95 (ISBN 0-937938-08-4). Gabriel Pr.

Gyatso, Sonam & Gyatso, Tenzin. Essence of Refined Gold. Mullin, Glen, ed. LC 80-85453. 1982. 16.00 (ISBN 0-937938-10-6, Pub. by Snow Lion); pap. 9.95 (ISBN 0-937938-09-2). Gabriel Pr.

Gyatso, Tenzin, jt. auth. see Gyatso, Sonam.

Gyekye, Kwame, ed. & tr. Arabic Logic: Ibn Al-Tayyib on Porphyry's "Eisagoge". LC 76-4071. 1979. 49.50x (ISBN 0-87395-308-8). State U NY Pr.

Gyenes, I. Titration in Non-Aqueous Media. 474p. 1968. 19.50 (ISBN 0-442-32925-3, Pub. by Van Nos Reinhold). Krieger.

Gyftopoulos, Elias P., ed. see Dyer, D., et al.

Gyftopoulos, Elias P., ed. see Stephanopoulos, G.

Gygax, E. Gary & Irons, Greg. Advance Dungeons & Dragons. (Illus.). 32p. 1979. pap. 3.95 (ISBN 0-89844-009-2). Troubador Pr.

Gyi, M. The Crossed Swords. 44p. (Orig.). 1982. pap. write for info. Am Bando Assn.

Gyires, B. Analytic Function Methods in Probability Theory. (Colloquia Mathematics Societatis Janos Bolyoi Ser.: Vol. 21). 379p. 1979. 72.50 (ISBN 0-444-85333-2, North Holland). Elsevier.

Gyllenskold, Karin. Breast Cancer: The Psychological Effects of the Disease & Its Treatment. Crampton, Patricia, tr. 1982. 26.00x (ISBN 0-422-76820-0, Pub. by Tavistock); pap. 12.95x (ISBN 0-422-76830-8). Methuen Inc.

Gylys, Barbara A. & Wedding, Mary E. Medical Terminology: A Systems Approach. LC 82-12927. (Illus.). 430p. 1983. pap. text ed. 14.95 (ISBN 0-8036-4492-2). Davis Co.

Gymer, Roger G. Chemistry in the Natural World. 1976. text ed. 22.95 o.p. (ISBN 0-669-00343-3); instructor's manual free o.p. (ISBN 0-669-00352-2). Heath.

Gyorgy, Paul see Sebrell, W. H., Jr. & Harris, Robert S.

Gyorgyey, Clara. Ferenc Molnar. (World Authors Ser.). 1980. lib. bdg. 15.95 (ISBN 0-8057-6416-X, Twayne). G K Hall.

Gyory, Richard A. The Emergence of Being: Through Indian & Greek Thought. LC 78-70692. 1978. pap. text ed. 10.00 (ISBN 0-8191-0646-1). U Pr of Amer.

Gypsy Boots. Bare Feet & Good Things to Eat. 1965. 2.00x (ISBN 0-686-36336-1). Cancer Control Soc.

Gysi, Lydia. Platonism & Cartesianism in the Philosophy of Ralph Cudworth. 163p. 1962. write for info. (ISBN 3-261-00648-X). P Lang Pubs.

Gysin, Brion. Brion Gysin Let the Mice In. Herman, Jan, ed. LC 72-96737. (Illus.). 74p. 1973. 15.00 (ISBN 0-87110-105-X). Ultramarine Pub.

Gysin, H. P. Studien zum Vokabular der Musiktheorie Im Mittelalter: Eine linguistische Analyse. 1972. Repr. of 1959 ed. wrappers 22.50 o.s.i. (ISBN 90-6027-250-1, Pub. by Frits Knuf Netherlands). Pendragon NY.

Gyula, Illyes. People of the Puszta. 2nd ed. LC 68-2212. 308p. 1979. 12.50x (ISBN 963-13-0594-5). Intl Pubns Serv.

Gyulay, Jo-Eileen. The Dying Child. 1977. pap. text ed. 14.95 (ISBN 0-07-025360-9, HP). McGraw.

Gzowski, Peter. The Sacrament. 1981. pap. 2.50 o.p. (ISBN 0-451-11116-8, AE1116, Sig). NAL.

H

H & R Block. H & R Block Income Tax Workbook. 1982. 5.95 (ISBN 0-02-079200-X). Macmillan.

H. F. M. A. Staff. Patient Account Management Techniques. 1976. 8.50 (ISBN 0-930228-01-4, 1443). Healthcare Fin Man Assn.

--Review Procedures for the Medicare Hospital Statement of Reimbursable Cost. 2nd ed. 249p. 1977. pap. 2.00x (ISBN 0-930228-04-9). Healthcare Fin Man Assn.

H. F. M. A. Staff, jt. auth. see Record Controls, Inc.

H, Francis & Wise, Joyce M. Dr. Wise Arithmetic Series, Vol. II. (Illus.). 105p. 1980. pap. text ed. 7.50 (ISBN 0-915766-56-6). Wise Pub.

H P Books, ed. Basic Guide to Black & White Darkroom Techniques. 96p. 1982. pap. 5.95 (ISBN 0-89586-196-8). H P Bks.

--Basic Guide to Creative Darkroom Techniques. 96p. 1982. pap. 5.95 (ISBN 0-89586-197-6). H P Bks.

--How to Photograph Women. LC 81-82135. 1981. 5.95 (ISBN 0-89586-117-8). H P Bks.

--How to Take Pictures Like a Pro. 96p. 1982. pap. 5.95 (ISBN 0-89586-198-4). H P Bks.

--SLR Tips & Techniques. 96p. 1982. pap. 5.95 (ISBN 0-89586-187-9). H P Bks.

Ha, Ta. Al-Dhabh. 2.50 (ISBN 0-686-83897-1). Kazi Pubns.

Ha, Tri T. see Tri T. Ha.

Haab, Armin, et al. Lettera, 4 vols. 1960. pap. 25.00 ea. Vol. 1 (ISBN 0-8038-4233-3). Vol. 2 (ISBN 0-8038-4232-5). Vol. 3 (ISBN 0-8038-4231-7). Vol. 4 (ISBN 0-8038-4331-3). Set. pap. 82.50 (ISBN 0-686-82916-6). Hastings.

Haac, Oscar A. Jules Michelet. (World Authors Ser.). 1982. 15.95 (ISBN 0-8057-6482-8, Twayne). G K Hall.

--Marivaux. (World Authors Ser.). 1974. lib. bdg. 14.95 (ISBN 0-8057-2593-8, Twayne). G K Hall.

Haac, Oscar A. & Bieler, Arthur. Actualite et Avenir: A Guide to France & to French Conversation. LC 74-30489. (Illus.). 256p. 1975. pap. text ed. 12.95 (ISBN 0-13-003855-5). P-H.

Haack, Susan. Deviant Logic. LC 74-76949. 208p. 1975. 27.95 (ISBN 0-521-20500-X). Cambridge U Pr.

--Philosophy of Logics. LC 77-17071. (Illus.). 1978. 42.00 (ISBN 0-521-21988-4); pap. 12.95x (ISBN 0-521-29329-4). Cambridge U Pr.

Haag, Diana B., jt. auth. see Wrasman, Marilyn W.

Haag, Herbert. Sport Pedagogy. LC 77-25144. (International Series on Sport Sciences: Vol. 4). 286p. 1977. text ed. 29.95 o.p. (ISBN 0-8391-1201-7). Univ Park.

Haag, Kimberley & Kasper, Keith. Common Solutions for the Uncommon Child K-8. (Illus.). 128p. 1982. pap. text ed. 7.50x (ISBN 0-8134-2239-6). Interstate.

Haag, Michael, jt. auth. see Leon, Vicki.

Haag, Michael Von see Von Haag, Michael.

Haagense, Cusman D., et al. Breast Carcinoma: Risk & Detection. LC 80-53370. 542p. 1981. 65.00 (ISBN 0-7216-4438-4). Saunders.

Haagensen, Cushman D. Diseases of the Breast. rev. 2nd ed. LC 79-118590. (Illus.). 820p. 1974. text ed. 46.00 o.p. (ISBN 0-7216-4441-4). Saunders.

Haakonssen, Knud. The Science of a Legislator: The Natural Jurisprudence of David Hume & Adam Smith. LC 80-42001. (Illus.). 256p. 1981. 37.50 (ISBN 0-521-23891-9). Cambridge U Pr.

Haan, Maria N., jt. auth. see Hammerstrom, Richard.

Haan, Marina N. & Hammerstrom, Richard B. Readers' Favorite Graffiti. (Illus.). 160p. (Orig.). 1983. pap. 4.95 (ISBN 0-9604534-2-3). Brown Hse Gall.

Haan, Martin R. De see De Haan, Martin R.

Haar, Charles. Property & the Law: 1982 Supplement. 1982. pap. text ed. 7.95 (ISBN 0-316-33678-5). Little.

Haar, Charles M. Between the Idea & the Reality: A Study in the Origin, Fate, & Legacy of the Model Cities Program. 310p. 1975. 20.00 o.p. (ISBN 0-316-33675-0). Little.

--The End of Innocence: A Suburban Reader. 224p. 1972. pap. 5.95x o.p. (ISBN 0-673-07760-8). Scott F.

--Land-Use Planning: A Casebook on the Use, Misuse, & Re-Use of Urban Land. 3rd ed. 1976. 26.00 (ISBN 0-316-33676-9); suppl. 5.95 (ISBN 0-316-33681-5). Little.

Haar, Charles M. & Liebman, Lance. Property & Law. 1977. text ed. 27.50 (ISBN 0-316-33679-3). Little.

Haar, D. Ter see Kapitza, P. L.

Haar, D. Ter see Ter Haar, D.

Haar, D. Ter see Ter Haar, D. & Scully, M. O.

Haar, Francis. Artists of Hawaii, Vol. 2. Turnbull, Murray, ed. LC 74-78861. (Illus.). 1977. 25.00 (ISBN 0-8248-0467-8). UH Pr.

Haar, Francis & Neogy, Prithwish. Artists of Hawaii: Nineteen Painters & Sculptors, Vol. 1. LC 74-7886. (Illus.). 168p. 1974. 25.00 (ISBN 0-8248-0338-8). UH Pr.

Haar, Lester & Gallagher, John S. NBS -NCR Steam Tables. (Illus.). 400p. 1983. text ed. 29.95 (ISBN 0-89116-354-9); pap. text ed. 16.95 (ISBN 0-89116-353-0). Hemisphere Pub.

Haard, Karen & Haard, Richard. Foraging for Edible Wild Mushrooms. rev. ed. (Illus.). 1978. lib. bdg. 11.95 o.p. (ISBN 0-88930-015-1, Pub. by Cloudburst Canada); pap. 5.95 o.p. (ISBN 0-88930-017-8). Madrona Pubs.

Haard, Richard, jt. auth. see Haard, Karen.

Haarhoff, T. J. The Stranger at the Gate. 2nd ed. LC 74-12322. 354p. 1974. Repr. of 1948 ed. lib. bdg. 19.75x (ISBN 0-8371-7669-7, HASAG). Greenwood.

Haarmann, Harald, jt. ed. see Niederehe, Hans Josef.

Haas, Albert, et al. Pulmonary Therapy & Rehabilitation: Principles & Practice. (Rehabilitation Medicine Library). (Illus.). 192p. 1979. 22.00 (ISBN 0-683-03886-9). Williams & Wilkins.

Haas, Alfred. Industrial Electronics: Principles & Practice. LC 78-178690. 10.95d o.p. (ISBN 0-8306-1583-0, 583). TAB Bks.

Haas, C., et al. Translator's Handbook on the Letters of John. (Helps for Translators Ser.). 1979. Repr. of 1972 ed. softcover 1.90x (ISBN 0-8267-0154-X, 08516). United Bible.

Haas, Edward F. DeLesseps S. Morrison & the Image of Reform: New Orleans Politics, 1946-1961. LC 73-90867. (Illus.). 432p. 1974. 27.50x o.p. (ISBN 0-8071-0073-0). La State U Pr.

Haas, Evelyn, jt. auth. see Cooper, Gwen.

Haas, Georg see Hass, Georg, et al.

Haas, Gerda S. These I Do Remember: Fragments from the Holocaust. LC 82-71674. 300p. 1983. 16.95 (ISBN 0-87027-203-9). Cumberland pr.

Haas, Harold I. El Cristiano Frente a los Problemas Mentales. De Molina, Sara Pais, tr. 1977. Repr. of 1975 ed. 2.60 (ISBN 0-311-42500-3). Casa Bautista.

Haas, Irene, jt. auth. see De Regniers, Beatrice S.

Haas, Irvin. Citadels, Ramparts, & Stockades: America's Historic Forts. LC 78-74583. (Illus.). 1979. 11.95 o.p. (ISBN 0-89696-038-2, An Everest House Book). Dodd.

Haas, J. Eugene & Drabek, Thomas E. Complex Organizations: A Sociological Perspective. (Illus.). 416p. 1973. text ed. 24.95x (ISBN 0-02-348550-7, 34855). Macmillan.

Haas, J. Eugene, jt. auth. see White, Gilbert F.

Haas, J. Eugene, et al. Reconstruction Following Disaster. LC 77-23176. (Mit Press Environmental Studies Ser). 1977. text ed. 25.00x (ISBN 0-262-08094-X). MIT Pr.

Haas, Jessie. Keeping Barney. (gr. 5-9). 1982. 9.50 (ISBN 0-688-00859-3). Greenwillow.

Haas, John, ed. see Johnson, Earl S.

Haas, John J. Corporate Social Responsibilities in a Changing Society. LC 73-78107. (Illus.). 65p. 1973. 4.00 o.p. (ISBN 0-685-32282-3). Gaus.

Haas, John J., et al. Beyond Management. new ed. LC 74-76951. 72p. 1974. 5.00 o.p. (ISBN 0-685-46413-X). Gaus.

Haas, Kenneth B. & Ernest, John. Principles of Creative Selling. 3rd ed. 1978. text ed. 22.95x (ISBN 0-02-474980-X). Macmillan.

Haas, Mark, ed. see Schultz, Lawrence.

Haas, Mark, ed. see Tischler, Morris.

Haas, Merle, tr. see De Brunhoff, Jean.

Haas, Michael. Basic Documents of Asian Regional Organizations, 8 vols. LC 74-2248. 1974. 47.50 ea. (ISBN 0-379-00177-2); Set. 380.00; Vols. 1-4. o.p. Oceana.

Haas, Peter J. & Neusner, Jacob. A History of the Mishnaic Law of Agriculture: Tractate Maaser Sheni. LC 80-25479. (Brown Judaic Studies). 1980. 15.00 (ISBN 0-89130-442-8, 14-00-18); pap. 10.50 (ISBN 0-89130-443-6). Scholars Pr CA.

Haas, Ralph & Hudson, W. Ronald. Pavement Management Systems. (Illus.). 1978. text ed. 26.00 o.p. (ISBN 0-07-025391-9, C). McGraw.

Haas, Robert B., ed. see Stein, Gertrude.

Haas, Ronald & Hamel, Lawrence, eds. Readings in Foundations of Education. 263p. 1971. pap. text ed. 9.95x (ISBN 0-8422-0159-9). Irvington.

Haas, W. Phono-Graphic Translation. 1970. 14.50 (ISBN 0-7190-0394-6). Manchester.

--Writing Without Letters. (Illus.). 216p. 1976. 16.50x (ISBN 0-87471-850-3). Rowman.

Haas, W., ed. Alphabets for English. 1969. 14.50 (ISBN 0-7190-0391-1). Manchester.

Haas, Werner & Mathieu, Gustave B. Deutsch Fur Alle: Beginning College German: a Comprehensive Approach. LC 79-21295. 1980. text ed. 21.95 (ISBN 0-471-02210-1); tchrs. manual 6.00 (ISBN 0-471-04192-0); wkbk. 9.50 (ISBN 0-471-02211-X); tapes o.p. avail. (ISBN 0-471-02211-X). Wiley.

Haas, Werner, jt. auth. see Babbitt, Diane H.

Haas, Willy. Bertolt Brecht. LC 68-31450. (Literature and Life Ser.). 1970. 11.95 (ISBN 0-8044-2323-7); pap. 4.95 (ISBN 0-8044-6237-2). Ungar.

Haase, John. Big Red. LC 79-2648. 1980. 12.45i (ISBN 0-06-011809-1, HarpT). Har-Row.

--San Francisco. 544p. 1983. pap. 3.50 (ISBN 0-523-41866-3). Pinnacle Bks.

Haase, W., ed. Recent Contributions to Fluid Mechanics. (Illus.). 338p. 1983. 23.00 (ISBN 0-387-11940-X). Springer-Verlag.

Haasen, Peter. Physical Metallurgy. Mordike, Janet, tr. LC 76-53517. (Illus.). 1978. 71.50 (ISBN 0-521-21548-X); pap. 19.95x (ISBN 0-521-29183-6). Cambridge U Pr.

Haast, William E. & Anderson, Robert. Complete Guide to Snakes of Florida. LC 81-80463. (Illus.). 139p. Date not set. pap. 8.95 (ISBN 0-686-84307-X). Banyan Bks.

Habakkuk, H. J. American & British Technology in the Nineteenth Century. 34.50 (ISBN 0-521-05162-2); pap. 10.95 (ISBN 0-521-09447-X). Cambridge U Pr.

Habashi, Fathi. Chalcopyrite: Its Chemistry & Metallurgy. (Illus.). 1978. text ed. 38.50x (ISBN 0-07-025383-8, C). McGraw.

Habe, Hans. Palazzo. LC 77-2261. 1977. 9.95 o.p. (ISBN 0-399-11983-3). Putnam Pub Group.

Habeeb, Virginia T. The Ladies Home Art Journal of Homemaking: Everything You Need to Know to Run Your Home with Ease & Style. LC 72-90393. 1973. 14.95 o.p. (ISBN 0-671-21487-X). S&S.

Habel, Norman C., ed. What Are We Going To Do With All These Rotting Fish? & Seven Other Short Plays for Church & Community. LC 79-119766. (Open Bks). (Illus.). 160p. (Orig.). 1970. pap. 3.25 o.p. (ISBN 0-8006-0147-5, 1-147). Fortress.

Habel, R. E., jt. auth. see Sack, W. O.

Habel, Robert E. Applied Veterinary Anatomy. 2nd ed. (Illus.). 1981. pap. text ed. 7.00x (ISBN 0-9600444-4-2). Habel.

--Guide to the Dissection of Domestic Ruminants. rev. 3rd ed. LC 64-63902. (Illus.). 165p. 1983. Repr. of 1975 ed. text ed. 4.00x (ISBN 0-9600444-1-8). Habel.

Habenstein, R. W., jt. ed. see Mindel, C.

Habenstein, Robert W., jt. ed. see Mindel, Charles H.

Habenstreit, Barbara. Changing America & the Supreme Court. rev. ed. LC 74-7598. 192p. (gr. 7 up). 1974. PLB 6.29 o.p. (ISBN 0-671-32682-1). Messner.

Haber, A., jt. auth. see Runyon, R.

Haber, Audrey & Runyon, Richard P. General Statistics. 3rd ed. LC 76-23985. 1977. text ed. 20.95 (ISBN 0-201-02729-1). A-W.

Haber, Barbara, ed. Women in America: A Guide to Books, 1963-1975. 1978. 19.50 (ISBN 0-8161-7877-1, Hall Reference). G K Hall.

--The Women's Annual: Nineteen Eighty-The Year in Review. 1981. 50.00 (ISBN 0-8161-8530-1, Hall Reference). G K Hall.

--The Women's Annual, 1981: The Year in Review. 1982. lib. bdg. 50.00 (ISBN 0-8161-8614-6, Hall Reference). G K Hall.

Haber, Carole. Beyond Sixty-Five: The Dilemma of Old Age in America's Past. LC 82-12786. 175p. Date not set. price not set (ISBN 0-521-25096-X). Cambridge U Pr.

Haber, D. F., jt. auth. see Dransfield, P.

Haber, E. S., jt. auth. see Mahlstede, John P.

Haber, Edgar & Krause, Richard M., eds. Antibodies in Human Diagnosis & Therapy. LC 75-32089. (Royal Society of Medicine Foundation Ser.). 431p. 1977. 38.00 (ISBN 0-89004-089-3). Raven.

Haber, Eitan, jt. auth. see Bar-Zohar, Michael.

Haber, J., jt. ed. see Dyrek, K.

Haber, Judith, et al. Comprehensive Psychiatric Nursing. (Illus.). 1977. text ed. 24.95 (ISBN 0-07-025384-6, HP). McGraw.

--Comprehensive Psychiatric Nursing. 2nd ed. (Illus.). 1216p. 1982. 29.95x (ISBN 0-07-025411-7). McGraw.

Haber, Michelle I. & Kantrowitz, Barbara. Ultimate Baby Catalog. LC 82-60064. (Illus.). 192p. 1982. 7.95 (ISBN 0-89480-174-0). Workman Pub.

Haber, Paul. Inside Handball. LC 72-126157. (Illus.). 1970. 7.95 o.p. (ISBN 0-8092-8868-0); pap. 5.95 o.p. (ISBN 0-8092-8867-2). Contemp Bks.

Haber, Stephen, jt. ed. see Wilkie, James W.

Haber, Tom B. A. E. Housman. (English Authors Ser.). 1967. lib. bdg. 11.95 (ISBN 0-8057-1272-0, Twayne). G K Hall.

Haberer, Joseph. Science & Technology Policy: Perspectives & Developments. LC 77-70081. (Policy Studies Organization Book Ser.). (Illus.). 240p. 1977. 22.95x (ISBN 0-669-01374-9, Dist. by Transaction Bks). Lexington Bks.

Haberer, Joseph, ed. Science & Technology Policy. 1976. pap. 6.00 (ISBN 0-918592-17-8). Policy Studies.

Haberkamp De Anton, G., jt. auth. see Haensch, G.

Haberlen, John. Mastering Conducting Techniques. LC 77-78469. (Illus.). 1977. pap. text ed. 11.95 wire bdg. (ISBN 0-916656-01-2). Mark Foster Mus.

Haberlen, John & Rosolack, Stephen. Elizabethan Madrigal Dinners: Scripts, with Music for Singers, Players, & Dancers. LC 78-70082. 1978. pap. 16.95 (ISBN 0-916656-09-8); wire bdg. 17.95 (ISBN 0-916656-12-8). Mark Foster Mus.

Haberly, David T. Three Sad Races: Racial Identity & National Consciousness in Brazilian Literature. LC 82-4467. (Illus.). 198p. p.n.s. (ISBN 0-521-24722-5). Cambridge U Pr.

Haberman, Fredric & Fortino, Denise. Your Skin: A Dermatologist's Guide to a Lifetime of Beauty & Health. LC 82-60711. 256p. 1983. pap. 3.50 (ISBN 0-86721-237-3). Playboy Pbks.

Haberman, Martin & Stinnett, T. M. Teacher Education & the New Profession of Teaching. LC 73-7238. 1973. 20.75x (ISBN 0-8211-0751-8); text ed. 18.60x (ISBN 0-685-42633-5). McCutchan.

Haberman, Paul W. & Baden, Michael M. Alcohol, Other Drugs & Violent Death. 1978. text ed. 18.95x (ISBN 0-19-502359-5). Oxford U Pr.

Haberman, R. Mathematical Models: Mechanical Vibrations, Population, Dynamics & Traffic Flow, An Introduction to Applied Mathematics. 1977. 31.95 (ISBN 0-13-561738-3). P-H.

Haberman, Richard. Elementary Applied Partial Differential Equations. (Illus.). 560p. 1983. text ed. 34.95 (ISBN 0-13-252833-9). P-H.

Haberman, Shelby. C-Tab: Analysis of Multidimensional Contingency Tables by Log-linear Models. pap. 2.75 (ISBN 0-89498-006-8). Natl Ed Res.

Haberman, W., jt. auth. see John, J.

Habermann, Gerhard. Maksim Gorki. Schlant, Ernestine, tr. LC 75-129114. (Literature and Life Ser.). 1971. 11.95 (ISBN 0-8044-2326-1); pap. 4.95 (ISBN 0-8044-6239-9). Ungar.

Habermann, Helen M., jt. auth. see Moment, Gairdner B.

Habermas, Gary B., jt. auth. see Stevenson, Kenneth.

Habermas, Jurgen. Theory & Practice. Viertel, John, tr. from Ger. LC 72-6227. 320p. 1973. pap. 4.95x (ISBN 0-8070-1527-X, BP489). Beacon Pr.

Habershon, Ada R. Hidden Pictures in the Old Testament. 304p. 1983. pap. 7.95 (ISBN 0-8254-2855-6). Kregel.

Habgood, jt. auth. see Taylor.

Habict, Werner, ed. English & American Studies in German: Summaries of Theses & Monographs, 1981. 168p. (Orig.). 1982. pap. 42.50x (ISBN 3-484-43081-8). Intl Pubns Serv.

Habif, Thomas P. Dermatology: A Color Atlas & Practical Manual. 1983. price not set (ISBN 0-8067-0841-7). Urban & S.

Habig, Inge. Sich ein Bild Machen. 140p. (Ger.). 1982. write for info. (ISBN 3-8204-5709-7). P Lang Pubs.

Habig, Marian A. The Alamo Mission. LC 77-6702. (Illus.). 1977. pap. 3.95 (ISBN 0-8199-0676-X). Franciscan Herald.

Habington, William. Castara: From the Third ed., 1635. Arber, Edward, tr. 144p. Date not set. pap. 15.00 (ISBN 0-87556-118-7). Saifer.

Hacche, Graham. The Theory of Economic Growth: An Introduction. LC 79-18078. 1979. 30.00x (ISBN 0-312-79775-3). St Martin.

Haccoun, D., jt. auth. see Bhargava, V. K.

Hachenberg, H. Industrial Gas Chromatographic Trace Analysis. 1973. 38.50 o.p. (ISBN 0-85501-079-7). Wiley.

Hachenberg, H. & Schmidt, A. P. Gas Chromatographic Head Space Analysis. 1977. 42.95 (ISBN 0-471-25753-2, Pub. by Wiley Heyden). Wiley.

Hachey, Thomas, ed. Anglo-Vatican Relations, 1914-1939: Confidential Annual Reports of the British Ministers to the Holy See. 1972. lib. bdg. 22.00 (ISBN 0-8161-0991-5, Hall Reference). G K Hall.

Hachiya, Michihiko. Hiroshima Diary. Wells, Warner, ed. & tr. xiii, 238p. 1969. pap. 6.95 o.p. (ISBN 0-8078-4044-0). U of NC Pr.

Hacht, E. Ducal Talers & Multiples of Bavaria Prior to 1800. 1983. Repr. of 1954 ed. softcover 12.00 (ISBN 0-915262-87-8). S J Durst.

Hachten, William A. Muffled Drums: The News Media in Africa. facsimile ed. (Illus.). 1971. pap. 12.50x o.p. (ISBN 0-8138-2475-3). Iowa St U Pr.

--Supreme Court on Freedom of the Press: Decisions & Dissents. facsimile ed. 1968. pap. text ed. 14.40x o.p. (ISBN 0-8138-2330-7). Iowa St U Pr.

Hachtman, T. Gertrude's Follies. 80p. 1981. pap. 5.95 o.p. (ISBN 0-312-32630-0). St Martin.

Hackbusch, W. & Trottenberg, U., eds. Multigrid Methods, Koeln-Porz, FRG, 1981: Proceedings. (Lecture Notes in Mathematics Ser.: Vol. 960). 652p. 1983. pap. 28.80 (ISBN 0-387-11955-8). Springer-Verlag.

Hackel, Emanuel & Mallory, Delores, eds. Theoretical Aspects of HLA. (Illus.). 141p. 1982. 21.00 (ISBN 0-914404-71-7); non-members 23.00 (ISBN 0-686-83049-0). Am Assn Blood.

Hackel, Sergei. The Byzantine Saint. 245p. 1982. lib. bdg. 22.95x (ISBN 0-89370-081-9); pap. text ed. 15.95x (ISBN 0-7044-0451-6). Borgo Pr.

--Pearl of Great Price: The Life of Mother Maria Skobtsova 1891-1945. rev. ed. LC 81-21356. 160p. 1982. pap. 5.95 (ISBN 0-913836-85-0). St Vladimirs.

Hackelman, Michael. Waterworks: An Owner-Builder Guide to Rural Water Systems. LC 82-45289. (Illus.). 1983. pap. 14.95 (ISBN 0-385-17559-0, Dolp). Doubleday.

Hacken, Sara. Games & Puzzles for Mormon Youth. 64p. 1982. 4.95 (ISBN 0-87747-932-1). Deseret Bk.

Hackenberg, Robert & Magalit, Henry. Demographic Responses to Development: Sources of Declining Fertility in the Philippines. (Replica Edition). 265p. 1982. pap. 20.00 (ISBN 0-86531-930-8). Westview.

Hackenbroch, M., ed. see Wilhelm, Friedrich & Schlegel, Karl F.

Hackenbroch, Yvonne. Catalogue of the Irwin Untermyer Collection, Vols. 2, 5, 6. Incl. Vol. 1. Meissen & Other Continental Porcelain, Faience & Enamel. (Illus.). 1956. write for info. o.s.i. (ISBN 0-87099-103-5); Vol. 2. Chelsea & Other English Porcelain, Pottery, & Enamel. (Illus.). 1957. 12.50 o.s.i. (ISBN 0-87099-102-7); Vol. 5. Bronzes, Other Metalwork & Sculpture. 2nd ed. (Illus.). 1962. 27.50 o.s.i. (ISBN 0-87099-101-9); English & Other Silver. 2nd ed. (Illus.). 1969. Vol. 6. write for info o.s.i. (ISBN 0-87099-104-3). Metro Mus Art.

Hackenbroch, Yvonne & Hawes, Vivian. The Markus Collection of European Ceramics & Enamels. (Illus.). 220p. 1983. write for info. Mus Fine Arts Boston.

Hacker & Volper. Cognitive & Motivational Aspects of Action. Date not set. 44.75 (ISBN 0-444-86348-6). Elsevier.

Hacker, Andrew. The Study of Politics. 2nd ed. LC 72-4851. (Foundations of American Government & Political Science). (Illus.). 144p. 1972. text ed. 13.95 (ISBN 0-07-025395-1); pap. text ed. 13.95 (ISBN 0-07-025394-3). McGraw.

--U. S. A Statistical Portrait. 1983. 25.00 (ISBN 0-670-73842-5). Viking Pr.

Hacker, Andrew & Millman, Lorrie, eds. U. S. A Statistical Portrait of the American People. 1983. pap. 8.95 (ISBN 0-14-006579-2). Penguin.

Hacker, Jeffrey H. Franklin D. Roosevelt. (Impact Biography Ser.). (Illus.). 128p. (gr. 7 up). 1983. PLB 8.90 (ISBN 0-531-04592-7). Watts.

--Government Subsidy to Industry. (Impact Ser.). (Illus.). 96p. (gr. 7 up). 1982. PLB 8.90 (ISBN 0-531-04487-4). Watts.

Hacker, Katherine F. & Turnbull, Krista J. Courtyard, Bazaar, Temple: Tradition of Textile Expression in India. LC 82-50077. (Illus.). 64p. (Orig.). 1982. pap. 10.00 (ISBN 0-295-95966-5, Pub. by S Asia Studies). U of Wash Pr.

Hacker, Louis. Alexander Hamilton in the American Tradition. LC 74-25994. 273p. 1975. Repr. of 1957 ed. lib. bdg. 17.25x (ISBN 0-8371-7878-9, HAAL). Greenwood.

Hacker, Marilyn. Separations. LC 75-36789. 109p. 1976. 8.00 (ISBN 0-394-40070-4). Ultramarine Pub.

Hackett, Brian. Planting Design. (Illus.). 1979. 27.50 (ISBN 0-07-025402-8, P&RB). McGraw.

Hackett, Brian & Smith, Rosemary. Landscape Development of Steep Slopes. (Illus.). 1972. 23.50 o.p. (ISBN 0-85362-061-X, Oriel). Routledge & Kegan.

Hackett, Earl. Blood. LC 72-88895. 1973. 9.95 o.p. (ISBN 0-8415-0215-3, Hawthorn). Dutton.

Hackett, Francis. Francis the First. LC 68-8334. (Illus.). 1968. Repr. of 1935 ed. lib. bdg. 20.25x (ISBN 0-8371-0093-3, HAFF). Greenwood.

Hackett, L. C. & Lawrence, C. C. Water Learning. 1975. pap. text ed. 5.95 o.p. (ISBN 0-917962-37-0). Peek Pubns.

Hackett, Neil, et al. The World of Europe to Seventeen Fifteen, Vol. I. rev. ed. LC 78-67276. pap. text ed. 10.50x (ISBN 0-88273-328-1). Forum Pr IL.

Hackett, Neil J. Ancient World to Eight Hundred. LC 78-67276. Date not set. pap. text ed. 2.95x (ISBN 0-88273-319-2). Forum Pr IL.

Hackett, Neil J., et al. World of Europe to Fifteen Hundred, Vol. 1. 1979. pap. text ed. 10.85x. Forum Pr IL.

Hackett, Patricia. Melody Book: Three-Hundred Selections from the World of Music for Autoharp, Guitar, Piano, Recorder & Voice. (Illus.). 320p. 1983. 14.95 (ISBN 0-13-574343-5). P-H.

Hackett, Patricia, et al. The Musical Classroom: Models, Skills, & Backgrounds for Elementary Teaching. 1979. pap. 19.95 ref. (ISBN 0-13-608356-0). P-H.

Hackett, Stuart C. Oriental Philosophy: A Westerner's Guide to Eastern Thought. LC 78-65010. 252p. 1979. 17.50 (ISBN 0-299-07790-X); pap. 8.95t (ISBN 0-299-07794-2). U of Wis Pr.

--The Resurrection of Theism: Prolegomena to Christian Apology. (Twin Brooks Ser.). 381p. 1982. pap. 11.95 (ISBN 0-8010-4263-1). Baker Bk.

Hackett, Thomas P. & Cassem, Ned H. Massachusetts Gen. Hosp. Handbook of General Hospital Psychiatry. LC 78-15146. (Illus.). 594p. 1978. pap. 25.95 (ISBN 0-8016-0931-3). Mosby.

Hackforth, R., ed. see Plato.

Hacking, Ian. Concise Introduction to Logic. (Orig.). 1971. pap. text ed. 12.00 (ISBN 0-394-31008-X). Random.

Hacking, Ian M. The Emergence of Probability. LC 74-82224. 216p. 1975. 32.50 (ISBN 0-521-20460-7). Cambridge U Pr.

--Logic of Statistical Inference. 1966. 39.50 (ISBN 0-521-05165-7); pap. 12.95x (ISBN 0-521-29059-7). Cambridge U Pr.

--Why Does Language Matter to Philosophy. LC 75-19432. 180p. 1975. 27.95 (ISBN 0-521-20923-4); pap. 8.95x (ISBN 0-521-09998-6). Cambridge U Pr.

Hackleman, Edwin C., jt. auth. see Boone, Louis E.

Hackleman, Wauneta, ed. The Study & Writing of Poetry: American Women Poets Discuss Their Craft. LC 82-50773. 420p. 1983. 27.50X (ISBN 0-87875-259-5); pap. 12.50X (ISBN 0-87875-266-8). Whitston Pub.

Hackler, James C. The Prevention of Youthful Crime: The Great Stumble Forward. 1979. pap. 12.00x (ISBN 0-416-60001-8). Methuen Inc.

Hackley, Mike, jt. auth. see Hackley, Sharon.

Hackley, Sharon & Hackley, Mike. Environmental Science: Activities with Plants of the Southwest. (Illus.). 64p. 1982. workbook 6.95 (ISBN 0-9607366-6-2, KP112). Kino Pubns.

Hackman, George G., ed. Temple Documents of the Third Dynasty of Ur From Umma. 1937. text ed. 27.50x (ISBN 0-686-83806-8). Elliots Bks.

Hackman, J. Richard & Suttle, J. Lloyd, eds. Improving Life at Work: Behavorial Science Approaches to Organizational Change. LC 76-7667. 600p. 1977. pap. 17.95x (ISBN 0-673-16087-4). Scott F.

Hackman, Martha. Komo the Shepherd Boy. (Illus.). 12p. (Orig.). 1982. pap. 2.50 (ISBN 0-88138-002-4, Pub. by Envelope Bks). Green Tiger Pr.

--The Lost Forest. (Illus.). 12p. 1982. pap. 2.50 (ISBN 0-914676-97-0, Pub. by Envelope Bks). Green Tiger Pr.

--The Old Woman of Trora. (Illus.). 12p. (Orig.). 1982. pap. 2.50 (ISBN 0-914676-70-9, Pub. by Envelope Bks). Green Tiger Pr.

Hackman, Porter L., et al. Perspectives on Behavior in Organizations. 1977. pap. text ed. 15.50 (ISBN 0-07-025413-3, C). McGraw.

Hackney, Harold, jt. auth. see Dye, H. Allan.

Hackney, Harold L. & Cormier, Sherilyn N. Counseling Strategies & Objectives. 2nd ed. (P-H Series in Counseling & Human Development). 1979. ref. o.p. 16.95 (ISBN 0-13-183319-7); pap. 14.95 (ISBN 0-13-183301-4). P-H.

Hackney, John W. Control & Management of Capital Projects. LC 65-26846. 1965. 46.50 (ISBN 0-471-33846-X, Pub. by Wiley-Interscience). Wiley.

Hackston, Michael G., tr. see Esser, Karl.

Hackwood, Frederick W. Christ Lore: Being the Legends, Traditions, Myths, Symbols, Customs, & Superstitions of the Christian Church. LC 69-16064. (Illus.). 1971. Repr. of 1902 ed. 34.00x (ISBN 0-8103-3528-X). Gale.

--Good Cheer: The Romance of Food & Feasting. LC 68-9571. 1968. Repr. of 1911 ed. 34.00x (ISBN 0-8103-3508-5). Gale.

Hackworth, Green H. Digest of International Law from 1906 to 1944, 8 vols. LC 70-147741. (Library of War & Peace; International Law). Set. lib. bdg. 400.00 o.s.i. (ISBN 0-8240-0489-2). Garland Pub.

Hackworth, Robert, ed. see Gilbart, Helen & Howland, Joseph.

Hackworth, Robert D. Math Anxiety Reduction: A Workbook. (Illus.). 210p. (Orig.). 1982. pap. text ed. 12.95x (ISBN 0-943202-04-3). H & H Pub.

Hackworth, Robert D. & Howland, Joseph W. College Algebra & Trigonometry As Socrates Might Have Taught Them. rev. ed. (Illus.). 295p. 1981. pap. text ed. 14.95x (ISBN 0-943202-01-9). H & H Pub.

--Programmed Arithmetic. (Illus.). 446p. (Orig.). 1979. pap. text ed. 13.95x (ISBN 0-943202-00-0). H & H Pub.

Hackworth, Robert D., jt. auth. see Alwin, Robert H.

Hackworth, Robert D., intro. by see Gill, Jack C. & Blitzer, Robert.

Hacsi, Jacqueline. Too Rich for Her Pride. (Candlelight Romance Ser.). (Orig.). 1981. pap. 1.50 o.s.i. (ISBN 0-440-18619-6). Dell.

Hadary & Cohen. Laboratory Science & Art for Blind, Deaf & Emotionally Disturbed Children: A Mainstreaming Approach. 400p. 1978. text ed. 27.95 (ISBN 0-8391-1230-0). Univ Park.

Hadary, Simone. Embraced by Destiny. 192p. 1982. pap. 1.75 (ISBN 0-515-06596-X). Jove Pubns.

--The Golden Touch. 192p. 1982. pap. 1.75 (ISBN 0-515-06411-4). Jove Pubns.

--Spring Fever. (Second Chance at Love Ser.: No. 108). pap. 1.75 (ISBN 0-515-06872-1). Jove Pubns.

Hadas, Moses. A History of Rome from Its Origins to Five Twenty-Nine A. D. 8.00 (ISBN 0-8446-2182-X). Peter Smith.

--Imperial Rome. LC 65-24363. (Great Ages of Man Ser.). 1965. lib. bdg. 11.97 o.p. (ISBN 0-8094-0364-1). Silver.

Hadas, Moses, ed. The Complete Plays of Sophocles. Jebb, Richard C., tr. from Greek. (Bantam Classics Ser.). 288p. 1982. pap. 2.95 (ISBN 0-553-21076-9). Bantam.

--Greek Drama. Incl. Agamemnon. Aeschylus; Antigone. Sophocles; Eumenides. Aeschylus; Frogs. Aristophanes; Hippolytus. Euripides; Medea. Euripides; Oedipus, the King. Sophocles; Philoctetes. Sophocles; Trojan Women. Euripides. (Bantam Classics Ser.). 337p. (Orig.). (gr. 9-12). 1982. pap. 2.95 (ISBN 0-553-21095-5). Bantam.

Hadas, Moses, intro. by. & t see Aristophanes.

Hadas, Moses, ed. see Cicero, Marcus T.

Hadas, Moses, ed. see Seneca.

Hadas, Moses & McLean, John, trs. from Greek. Euripides Ten Plays. (Bantam Classics Ser.). 384p. (gr. 9-12). 1981. pap. text ed. 2.50 (ISBN 0-553-21060-2). Bantam.

Hadas, Moses, tr. see Heliodorus Of Emesa.

Hadas, Moses, tr. see Seneca.

Hadas, Pamela W. Beside Herself: Pocahontas to Patty Hearst. LC 82-49003. 1983. 12.95 (ISBN 0-394-52993-6); pap. 7.95 (ISBN 0-394-71343-5). Knopf.

Hadaway, C. Kirk, jt. ed. see Rose, Larry L.

Hadawi, Sami. Bitter Harvest: Palestine Between 1914-1979. LC 79-16750. 1979. 35.00x (ISBN 0-88206-025-2). Caravan Bks.

Hadcock, R. Neville, jt. auth. see Knowles, David.

Haddad, Fuad I., tr. see Hashimi, Ali Ibn Sulayman al.

Haddad, Raymond. English Words of Arabic Origin. (Illus.). 140p. 500.00 (ISBN 0-9608594-0-3); abridged. 75.00. Genie Ent.

Haddad, Robert M. Syrian Christians in Muslim Society: An Interpretation. LC 81-6202. (Princeton Studies on the Near East). viii, 118p. 1981. Repr. of 1970 ed. lib. bdg. 20.50x (ISBN 0-313-23054-4, HASYC). Greenwood.

Haddad, W., jt. auth. see Avalos, B.

Haddad, Wadi D. Education. (Sector Policy Paper). 143p. 1980. 5.00 (ISBN 0-686-36053-2, PP-8002). World Bank.

Haddad, Yvonne Y., jt. auth. see Smith, Jane I.

Haddad, Yvonne Yazbeck. Contemporary Islam & the Challenge of History. LC 81-8732. 272p. 1982. 34.50x (ISBN 0-87395-543-9); pap. 10.95x (ISBN 0-87395-544-7). State U NY Pr.

Haddad-Garcia, George. The Films of Jane Fonda. (Illus.). 256p. 1983. 16.95 (ISBN 0-8065-0752-7); pap. 9.95 (ISBN 0-8065-0829-9). Citadel Pr.

Haddan, Eugene E., jt. ed. see Trow, W. Clark.

Haddard, Joyce, jt. auth. see Deming, Mary.

Hadden, Jeffrey K. & Long, Theodore E., eds. Religion & Religiosity in America. (Studies in Honor of Joseph H. Fichter). 192p. 1983. 15.95 (ISBN 0-8245-0555-7). Crossroad NY.

Hadden, Susan, ed. Public Policy Towards Risk. (Orig.). 1982. pap. 6.00 (ISBN 0-918592-53-4). Policy Studies.

Haddock, B. A. & Hamilton, W. A., eds. Microbial Energetics. LC 76-54367. (Society for General Microbiology: Symposium 27). (Illus.). 1977. 70.00 (ISBN 0-521-21494-7). Cambridge U Pr.

Haddock, Frank C. Power of Will. 10.95 (ISBN 0-912576-03-0). R Collier.

Haddon, A. C. & Start, L. E. Iban or Sea Dayak Fabrics & Their Patterns. pap. 14.95 (ISBN 0-903585-11-1). Robin & Russ.

Haddon, Cecilia. The Sensuous Lie: The Sexual Revolution & It's Aftermath. LC 82-40169. 226p. 1983. 14.95 (ISBN 0-8128-2883-6). Stein & Day.

Haddon, Celia. Be Beautiful the Country Way. LC 78-31775. (Country Way Bks.). 1979. op 4.95 (ISBN 0-671-40090-8). Summit Bks.

Haddon, Celita. The Limits of Sex. LC 82-40169. 226p. 1982. 14.95 o.p. (ISBN 0-8128-2883-6). Stein & Day.

Haddon, Hathleen. Cat's Cradle from Many Lands: String Figures. (Illus.). 95p. Date not set. pap. 12.50 (ISBN 0-87556-497-6). Saifer.

Haddow, Alexander, jt. ed. see Greenstein, Jesse P.

Haden, Douglas. Total Business Systems: Computers in Business. (Illus.). 1978. text ed. 23.95 (ISBN 0-8299-0092-6). West Pub.

Haden, Douglas H., jt. auth. see Adams, J. Mack.

Haden, James, tr. see Cassirer, Ernst.

Haden, James C., tr. from Ger. The Recorder Player's Handbook. 1974. pap. 22.00 (ISBN 0-930448-11-1, 7000060). Eur-Am Music.

Haden, Pat & Kaiser, Robert B. Pat Haden: My Rookie Season with the Los Angeles Rams. LC 77-9411. (Illus.). 1977. 8.95 o.p. (ISBN 0-688-03224-9). Morrow.

Haden, Peter. Elementary Knowledge: A Story of the Creation of the Hebrew Alaphabet. (Illus.). 68p. 1981. 25.00 (ISBN 0-87663-357-2). Universe.

Haden-Guest, Anthony. Bad Dreams. 480p. 1983. pap. 3.95 (ISBN 0-345-30720-8). Ballantine.

Hadfield, Alice M., jt. auth. see Hadfield, Charles.

Hadfield, Charles. Waterways Sights to See. LC 76-45513. (Illus.). 1977. 4.50 o.p. (ISBN 0-7153-7303-X). David & Charles.

Hadfield, Charles & Hadfield, Alice M. Introducing the Cotswolds. (Illus.). 192p. 1976. 5.50 o.p. (ISBN 0-7153-7169-X). David & Charles.

Hadfield, Debra. ABC'S of Grade Success. 3.95 (ISBN 0-686-84353-3). Olympus Pub Co.

Hadfield, J. & Hobsley, M., eds. Current Surgical Practice, Vol. 2. 390p. 1978. pap. text ed. 34.50 (ISBN 0-686-43103-0). E Arnold.

Hadfield, John, ed. The Saturday Book: Number Thirty-Four. (Illus.). 256p. 1975. PLB 15.95 o.p. (ISBN 0-517-52442-2, C N Potter Bks). Crown.

--Walter De La Mare. (Pocket Poet Ser.). 1962. pap. 1.25 (ISBN 0-8023-9044-7). Dufour.

Hadfield, John & Hobsley, Michael, eds. Current Surgical Practice, Vol. 3. (Current Surgical Practice Ser.). 320p. 1981. pap. text ed. 34.50 (ISBN 0-7131-4397-5). E Arnold.

Hadfield, Miles. A History of British Gardening. 3rd ed. (Illus.). 1979. text ed. 26.00x o.p. (ISBN 0-7195-3644-8). Humanities.

Hadgopoulos, Saralyn P. Imagination's Wine. LC 77-90954. 1977. 5.50 (ISBN 0-911838-51-1). Windy Row.

Hadidian, Allen. A Single Thought. LC 81-38347. 123p. 1981. pap. 5.95 (ISBN 0-8024-0878-8). Moody.

Hadingham, Evans. Secrets of the Ice Age: A Reappraisal of Prehistoric Man. 342p. 1981. pap. 9.95 (ISBN 0-8027-7192-0). Walker & Co.

Hadjimichalakis, Michael G. Monetary Policy & Modern Money Markets: Fixed versus Market-Determined Deposit Rates. LC 82-47638. 272p. 1982. 27.95 (ISBN 0-669-05550-6). Lexington Bks.

Hadjimichalakis, Michael G. Modern Macroeconomics: An Intermediate Text. (Illus.). 640p. 1982. text ed. 23.95 (ISBN 0-13-595074-0). P-H.

Hadjitarkhani, Naimeh, jt. auth. see Maubouche, Robert.

Hadlai, H. C., jt. auth. see Nie, Norman H.

Hadler, Norton M., jt. auth. see Bacon, Paul.

Hadley, Arthur T. Education & Government. 1934. 29.50x (ISBN 0-686-51376-2). Elliots Bks.

--Moral Basis of Democracy. 1920. 24.50x (ISBN 0-686-51418-1). Elliots Bks.

Hadley, E. C. The Song of Solomon. pap. 1.95 (ISBN 0-88172-080-1). Believers Bkshelf.

Hadley Editorial Staff. Payroll Recordkeeping. 7th ed. 1965. text ed. 8.40 (ISBN 0-07-025408-7, G); tchr's key 3.95 (ISBN 0-07-025409-5). McGraw.

Hadley, George. Linear Programming. (Illus.). 1962. 24.95 (ISBN 0-201-02660-0). A-W.

Hadley, George & Whitin, T. M. Analysis of Inventory Systems. (Illus.). 1963. ref. ed. 23.95 (ISBN 0-13-032953-3). P-H.

Hadley, Jack. More Medical Care, Better Health? An Economic Analysis of Mortality Rates. LC 82-70898. 235p. 1982. 20.00 (ISBN 0-87766-303-3, 32900). Urban Inst.

Hadley, James. Introduction to Roman Law. 1931. text ed. 39.50x (ISBN 0-686-83592-1). Elliots Bks.

Hadley, Jay, jt. auth. see Wilson, Justin.

Hadley, Lee A. Anatomico-Roentgenographic Studies of the Spine. (Illus.). 560p. 1981. 34.50x (ISBN 0-398-02818-4). C C Thomas.

Hadley, Morris. Arthur Twining Hadley. 1948. text ed. 39.50x (ISBN 0-686-83481-X). Elliots Bks.

Hadley, Norman H. Fingernail Biting Theory, Research & Treatment. 200p. 1983. text ed. 20.00 (ISBN 0-89335-183-0). Spec Med & Sci Bks.

Hadley, Richard, jt. auth. see Swit, David.

Hadley, Richard D., ed. see Food & Drug Administration.

Hadlock, Richard. Jazz Masters of the Twenties. 1974. 5.95 o.p. (ISBN 0-685-15381-9); pap. 2.95 o.p. (ISBN 0-02-060770-9). Macmillan.

Hadni, A. Essentials of Modern Physics Applied to the Study of the Infrared. 1967. 69.00 o.p. (ISBN 0-08-011902-6). Pergamon.

Hadow, Grace E., tr. see Litzmann, Berthold.

Hadrian, Henry. Wyckoff's Techniques for Stock Market Profits. (Illus.). 150p. 1972. 97.75 (ISBN 0-913314-11-0). Am Classical Coll Pr.

Hadway, L. Jane. Pearls of Thought. (Illus.). 24p. 1983. 5.95 (ISBN 0-533-05542-3). Vantage.

Hadwiger, Don, jt. ed. see Browne, William.

Hadwiger, Don, et al. New Politics of Food. LC 77-11574. (Policy Studies Organization Ser.). 288p. 1978. 23.95x (ISBN 0-669-01986-0). Lexington Bks.

Hadwiger, Don F. The Politics of Agricultural Research. LC 81-24077. x, 230p. 1982. 16.95x (ISBN 0-8032-2322-6). U of Nebr Pr.

Hadwiger, Don F., jt. ed. see Browne, William P.

Hady, Maureen B., jt. auth. see Danky, James P.

Hadziselimovic, F. Cryptorchidism: Management & Implications. (Illus.). 135p. 1983. 49.00 (ISBN 0-387-11881-0). Springer-Verlag.

Hadzsits, George D., ed. Our Debt to Greece & Rome, 44 Vols. Repr. of 1930 ed. buckram 7.50x ea. o.p. Cooper Sq.

Haeberle, Billi. Looking Forward to a Career: Radio & Television. 3rd ed. LC 78-11380. (Looking Forward to a Career Ser.). (Illus.). (gr. 6 up). 1979. PLB 6.95 o.p. (ISBN 0-87518-168-6). Dillon.

Haeberle, Erwin J. The Sex Atlas. rev. ed. (Illus.). 568p. 1983. pap. 14.95 (ISBN 0-8264-0233-X). Crossroad NY.

Haeberlin, Herman K. The Idea of Fertilization in the Culture of the Pueblo Indians. LC 16-25723. Repr. of 1916 ed. pap. 8.00 (ISBN 0-527-00512-6). Kraus Repr.

Haebler, K. Study of Incunibula. Osborne, Lucy E., tr. Repr. of 1933 ed. 30.00 o.s.i. (ISBN 0-527-37100-9). Kraus Repr.

Haegeman, J. Tuberous Begonias: Origin & Development. 1979. lib. bdg. 32.00x (ISBN 3-7682-1219-X). Lubrecht & Cramer.

Haeger, John D., et al. Bosses. rev. ed. 1979. pap. text ed. 4.95x (ISBN 0-88273-103-3). Forum Pr IL.

Haehling von Lanzenauer, Christoph. Cases in Operations Research. 1975. 13.50x (ISBN 0-8162-3546-5); instr's manual 6.00x (ISBN 0-8162-3556-2). Holden-Day.

Haelussler, Ernest F. & Paul, Richard S. Calculus: For the Managerial, Life & Social Sciences. (Illus.). 1980. text ed. 22.95 (ISBN 0-8359-0628-0); free solutions manual (ISBN 0-8359-0629-9); test bank o.p. avail. (ISBN 0-8359-0630-2). Reston.

Haenchen, Ernst. Acts of the Apostles, a Commentary. LC 78-161218. 1971. 27.50 (ISBN 0-664-20919-X). Westminster.

Haendel, Dan. The Process of Priority Formulation: U.S. Foreign Policy in the Indo-Pakistani War of 1971. LC 77-21372. 1978. lib. bdg. 36.00 o.p. (ISBN 0-89158-322-X). Westview.

Haensch, G. Dictionary of Agriculture in German, French, Spanish, & Russian. 4th ed. De Anton, Haberkamp G., ed. 1000p. 1976. 110.75 (ISBN 0-444-99849-7). Elsevier.

Haensch, G. & Haberkamp De Anton, G. Dictionary of Biology in English, French, German & Spanish. 2nd, rev. & enl. ed. 1981. 106.50 (ISBN 0-444-41968-3). Elsevier.

Haensel, Phyllis C. Certain Choices. Hoff, Marshall G. & Bock, Glenn H., eds. (Illus.). 32p. (Orig.). (gr. 7-9). Date not set. pap. text ed. price not set (ISBN 0-940210-01-0). U Minn Pediatric.

Haertig, Evelyn M. Antique Combs & Antique Purses: A Collector's Guide. LC 81-128. (Illus.). 304p. 1982. 69.00 (ISBN 0-943294-00-2); pap. 35.00 (ISBN 0-943294-01-0). Gallery Graphics.

Haese, Richard. Rebels & Precursors. 356p. 1982. 75.00x o.p. (ISBN 0-7139-1362-2, Pub. by Penguin Bks). State Mutual Bk.

Haeusler, Ernest F., Jr., jt. auth. see Paul, Richard S.

Hafeez-Uddin. Love Letters from a Fallen Woman. 1978. 4.95 o.p. (ISBN 0-533-03469-8). Vantage.

Hafele, Wolf & International Institute for Applied Syetem Analysis, eds. Energy in a Finite World: Vol. I: Paths to a Sustainable Future. 256p. 1981. prof ref 25.00x (ISBN 0-88410-641-1). Ballinger Pub.

Hafele, Wolf & International Institute for Applied Systems Analysis, eds. Energy in a Finite World: Vol. II: Global Systems Analysis. 880p. 1981. prof ref 50.00x (ISBN 0-88410-642-X). Ballinger Pub.

Hafellner, J. Karschia: Revision einer Sammelgattung an der Grenze von lichenisierten und nicht lichenisierten Ascomyceten. (Beihefte Nova Hedwigia: No. 62). (Illus., Ger.). 1979. lib. bdg. 48.00 (ISBN 3-7682-5462-3). Lubrecht & Cramer.

Hafen, Ann W., jt. auth. see Hafen, LeRoy.

Hafen, Ann W., jt. ed. see Hafen, LeRoy R.

Hafen, B., et al. How to Live Longer. 199p. 1981. 13.95 (ISBN 0-13-415265-4); pap. 4.95 (ISBN 0-13-415257-3). P-H.

Hafen, Brent Q. Alcohol: The Crutch That Cripples. LC 75-43736. (Illus.). 240p. 1977. pap. text ed. 11.95 (ISBN 0-8299-0083-7). West Pub.

--Faces of Death: Grief, Dying, Euthanasia, Suicide. 276p. 1983. pap. text ed. 10.00x (ISBN 0-89582-092-7). Morton Pub.

--First Aid for Health Emergencies. 2nd ed. 587p. 1980. pap. text ed. 13.95 o.s.i. (ISBN 0-8299-0302-X). West Pub.

--Medical Self Care & Assessment. (Illus.). 400p. 1983. pap. text ed. 11.95X (ISBN 0-89582-095-1). Morton Pub.

Hafen, Brent Q. & Brog, Molly J. Alcohol. 2nd ed. (Illus.). 250p. 1983. pap. text ed. 9.95 (ISBN 0-314-69652-0). West Pub.

--Emotional Survival. 114p. 1983. 11.95 (ISBN 0-13-274480-5); pap. 5.95 (ISBN 0-13-274472-4). P-H.

Hafen, Brent Q. & Frandsen, Kathryn J. Cocaine. 1.95 (ISBN 0-89486-141-7, 1195B). Hazelden.

--PCP, Phencyclidine, "Angel Dust". 1.25 (ISBN 0-89486-074-7, 1942B). Hazelden.

Hafen, Brent Q. & Karren, Kieth J. First Aid & Emergency Care Skills Manual. (Illus.). 224p. 1983. pap. text ed. 12.95x (ISBN 0-89582-079-X). Morton Pub.

Hafen, Brent Q. & Peterson, Brenda. First Aid for Health Emergencies. (Illus.). 1977. pap. text ed. 9.95 o.s.i. (ISBN 0-8299-0093-4). West Pub.

Hafen, LeRoy & Hafen, Ann W. Reports from Colorado, 1859-65. (Illus.). 1961. 15.00 o.p. (ISBN 0-87062-040-1). A H Clark.

Hafen, LeRoy R. & Hafen, Ann W., eds. The Utah Expedition, 1857-1858: A Documentary Account. LC 58-11786. (Far West & Rockies Ser.: Vol.VIII). (Illus.). 375p. 1983. Repr. of 1958 ed. 27.50 (ISBN 0-87062-035-5). A H Clark.

Hafen, LeRoy R., ed. see Ruxton, George F.

Hafen, Mary A. Recollections of a Handcart Pioneer of 1860: A Woman's Life on the Mormon Frontier. (Illus.). 117p. 1983. 10.95x (ISBN 0-8032-2325-0); pap. 4.50 (ISBN 0-8032-7219-7, BB 841, Bison). U of Nebr Pr.

Hafer, Charles R. Electronics Engineering for Professional Engineer's Examinations. (Illus.). 1980. 19.50 (ISBN 0-07-025430-3); pap. 24.75 (ISBN 0-07-025431-1). McGraw.

Hafer, W. Keith & White, Gordon E. Advertising Writing. 2nd ed. (Illus.). 1982. text ed. 24.50 (ISBN 0-314-63246-8). West Pub.

Hafernik, John E., Jr. Phenetics & Ecology of Hybridization in Buckeye Butterflies (Lepidoptera, Nymphalidae) (University of California Publications in Entomology: Vol. 96). 221p. 1982. 16.50x (ISBN 0-520-09649-5). U of Cal Pr.

Hafez, E. S. Carcinoma of the Cervix. 1982. 89.50 (ISBN 90-247-2574-7, Pub. by Martinus Nijhoff Netherlands). Kluwer Boston.

--Instrumental Insemination. 1982. 79.00 (ISBN 90-247-2530-5, Pub. by Martinus Nijhoff Netherlands). Kluwer Boston.

Hafez, E. S. & Kenemans, P. An Atlas of Human Reproduction: By Scanning Electron Microscopy. 300p. 1982. text ed. 60.00 (ISBN 0-85200-411-7, Pub. by MTP Pr England). Kluwer Boston.

Hafez, E. S. & Audebert, A. J., eds. IUD Technology. (Progress in Contraceptive Delivery Systems Ser.: Vol. 4). (Illus.). 1981. text ed. 45.00 (ISBN 0-85200-356-0, Pub. by MTP Pr England). Kluwer Boston.

Hafez, E. S. & Evans, T. N., eds. The Human Vagina. (Human Reproductive Medicine: Vol. 2). 1978. 126.50 (ISBN 0-7204-0648-X, North Holland). Elsevier.

Haffenden, John. The Life of John Berryman. 384p. 1982. 22.50 (ISBN 0-7100-9216-4). Routledge & Kegan.

Haffenden, John, selected by see Berryman, John.

Haffer, Jurgen. Avian Speciation in Tropical South America: With a Systematic Survey of the Toucans (Ramphastidae) & Jacamars (Galbulidae) (Illus.). 390p. 1974. 19.00 (ISBN 0-686-35803-1). Nuttall Ornithological.

Haffert, John M. World's Greatest Secret. 312p. 1968. pap. 4.50 (ISBN 0-911988-22-X). AMI Pr.

Haffner, Sebastian. The Meaning of Hitler. Osers, Ewald, tr. from Ger. 180p. 1983. pap. text ed. 5.95x (ISBN 0-674-55776-X). Harvard U Pr.

Haffner, Sylvia. Judaic Tokens & Medals. Sobel, Nathan, ed. LC 78-54682. (Illus.). 1978. 25.00 (ISBN 0-9601658-1-9). Am Israel Numismatic.

Haffner, Sylvia, ed. Israel's Money & Medals. 2nd ed. LC 75-46129. 1976. with supplement 25.00 (ISBN 0-685-92169-7). Am Israel Numismatic.

Hafiz, M. Virtues of Darood Sharif. pap. 1.50 o.p. (ISBN 0-686-18589-7). Kazi Pubns.

--Virtues of Islamic Tabligh. pap. 1.50 o.p. (ISBN 0-686-18453-X). Kazi Pubns.

--Virtues of the Holy Quran. pap. 5.95 (ISBN 0-686-18508-0). Kazi Pubns.

Hafner, Anne L., jt. auth. see Bailey, Robert L.

Hafner, Lawrence E. Developmental Reading in Middle & Secondary Schools. (Illus.). 1977. text ed. 20.95x (ISBN 0-02-348820-4). Macmillan.

--Improving Reading in the Secondary Schools. 2nd ed. 1974. pap. 13.95x (ISBN 0-02-348680-5, 34868). Macmillan.

Haft, Marilyn G., jt. auth. see Hermann, Michele G.

Haft, Richard A. Investing in Securities: A Handbook for Today's Market. (Orig.). 1975. pap. 5.95 op o.p. (ISBN 0-13-502708-X); pap. 5.95 o.p. (ISBN 0-13-502716-0). P-H.

Haft, Robert J. & Fass, Peter M. Tax Sheltered Investments. 3rd ed. LC 81-6179. 1981. 320.00 (ISBN 0-87632-093-0). Boardman.

--Tax Sheltered Investments Handbook. 1981. pap. 36.50 (ISBN 0-87632-305-0). Boardman.

Hagan, Chet. Country Music Legends in the Hall of Fame. 256p. (Orig.). 1982. pap. 8.95 (ISBN 0-8407-4104-9). Nelson.

Hagan, Frank E. Research Methods in Criminal Justice & Criminology. 1982. text ed. 23.95x (ISBN 0-02-477340-9). Macmillan.

Hagan, John, ed. Quantitative Criminology: Innovations & Applications. (Research Progress Series in Criminology: Vol. 24). 160p. 1982. 18.95 (ISBN 0-8039-0948-9); pap. 8.95 (ISBN 0-8039-0949-7). Sage.

Hagan, Kenneth J. American Gunboat Diplomacy & the Old Navy. LC 75-176288. (Contributions in Military History Ser.: No. 4). 262p. 1973. lib. bdg. 29.95 (ISBN 0-8371-6274-2, HCN/). Greenwood.

Hagan, Kenneth J., ed. In Peace & War: Interpretations of American Naval History, 1775-1978. LC 77-91108. (Contributions in Military History: No. 16). (Illus.). 1978. lib. bdg. 22.50 (ISBN 0-313-20039-4, HPW/). Greenwood.

Hagan, Michael, jt. auth. see Greenston, Peter.

Hagan, Patricia. Passion's Fury. 400p. 1981. pap. 2.95 (ISBN 0-380-77727-4, 81497-8). Avon.

--The Raging Hearts. 480p. 1982. pap. 3.50 (ISBN 0-380-46201-X, 80085). Avon.

--Souls Aflame. 416p. 1980. pap. 3.50 (ISBN 0-380-75507-6, 79988X). Avon.

Hagan, Ross E., jt. auth. see Wang, Jaw-Kai.

Hagan, William T. American Indians. rev. ed. LC 78-72176. (Chicago History of American Civilization Ser.). (Illus.). 1979. lib. bdg. 15.00x (ISBN 0-226-31234-8); pap. 5.95 (ISBN 0-226-31235-6, CHAC 8). U of Chicago Pr.

--Indian Police & Judges: Experiments in Acculturation & Control. LC 79-18496. xiv, 206p. 1980. 14.95x (ISBN 0-8032-2308-0); pap. 4.95 (ISBN 0-8032-7205-7, BB 722, Bison). U of Nebr Pr.

Hagberg, David. Heartland. 416p. (Orig.). 1983. pap. 3.50 (ISBN 0-523-48051-2). Pinnacle Bks.

Hagburg, Eugene C. & Levine, Marvin J. Labor Relations: An Integrated Perspective. 1978. text ed. 22.95 (ISBN 0-8299-0168-X). West Pub.

Hagburg, Eugene C., jt. auth. see Levine, Marvin J.

Hage, George & Dennis, Everette. New Strategies for Public Affairs Reporting: Investigation & Research. 2nd ed. (Illus.). 336p. 1983. text ed. 18.95 (ISBN 0-13-615740-8). P-H.

Hage, Jerald. Techniques & Problems of Theory Construction in Sociology. LC 72-6447. 272p. 1972. 31.50 o.s.i. (ISBN 0-471-33860-5, Pub. by Wiley-Interscience). Wiley.

Hage, R. E., jt. auth. see Perkins, Courtland D.

Hagebak, Beaumont R. Getting Local Agencies to Cooperate: A Grassroots Primer for Human Services. 144p. 1981. pap. text ed. 9.95 (ISBN 0-8391-1702-7). Univ Park.

Hagedoern, Peter. Non-Linear Oscillations. Stadler, Wolfram, tr. (Illus.). 1981. text ed. 55.00x o.p. (ISBN 0-19-856142-3). Oxford U Pr.

Hagedorn, Peter. Non-Linear Oscillations. (Engineering Science Ser.). (Illus.). 308p. 1982. pap. 19.95 (ISBN 0-19-856156-3). Oxford U Pr.

Hagedorn, Robert, ed. Sociology. 720p. 1983. text ed. write for info. (ISBN 0-697-07571-0); instr's. manual avail. (ISBN 0-697-07572-9); avail. study guide (ISBN 0-697-07573-7). Wm C Brown.

Hagedorn, Robert B., jt. auth. see Labovitz, Sanford I.

Hagel, John, jt. ed. see Barnett, Randy.

Hagel, John, III. Alternative Energy Strategies: Constraints & Opportunities. LC 75-23968. 1976. 32.95 o.p. (ISBN 0-275-56090-2). Praeger.

Hagel, William C., jt. ed. see Sims, Chester T.

Hagelman, Charles W., Jr., ed. see Wollstonecraft, Mary.

Hageman, Elizabeth H. Robert Herrick: A Reference Guide. 1983. lib. bdg. 34.00 (ISBN 0-8161-8012-1, Hall Reference). G K Hall.

Hageman, Jack. Contractors' Guide to the Building Code. 200p. (Orig.). 1983. pap. 16.25 (ISBN 0-910460-91-4). Craftsman.

Hagemann, E. R. A Comprehensive Index to Black Mask, 1920-1951. 236p. 1982. 15.95 (ISBN 0-87972-201-0); pap. 8.95 (ISBN 0-87972-202-9). Bowling Green Univ.

Hagemann, G. see Von Wiesner, J. & Von Regel, C.

Hagemeyer, Robert W., et al. Future Technical Needs & Trends in the Paper Industry-III. (TAPPI PRESS Reports). (Illus.). 102p. 1979. pap. 29.95 (ISBN 0-89852-378-8, 01-01-R078). TAPPI.

Hagen, E. P., jt. auth. see Thorndike, R. L.

Hagen, Ed, jt. auth. see Nissman, David M.

Hagen, Elizabeth. Identification of the Gifted. Tannenbaum, Abraham J., ed. (Perspectives on Gifted & Talented Education Ser.). (Orig.). 1980. pap. text ed. 5.95x (ISBN 0-8077-2588-9). Tchrs Coll.

Hagen, H. A. Bibliotheca Entomologica, 2 vols. in 1. 1960. 80.00 (ISBN 3-7682-0035-3). Lubrecht & Cramer.

Hagen, John. The Disreputable Pleasures: Crime & Deviance in Canada. (Ryerson Series Canadian Sociology). (Illus.). 260p. 1980. pap. text ed. 14.95 (ISBN 0-07-082447-9). McGraw.

Hagen, Lawrence S. The Crisis in Western Security. LC 81-14340. 1982. 27.50 (ISBN 0-312-17397-0). St Martin.

Hagen, Lorinda. Amy Jean. 256p. 1982. pap. 2.75 o.p. (ISBN 0-505-51848-1). Tower Bks.

--Amy Jean. 256p. 1983. pap. 2.95 (ISBN 0-8439-2001-7, Leisure Bks). Dorchester Pub Co.

Hagen, Piet J., ed. Blood: Gift or Merchandise-Towards an International Policy. LC 82-12742. 246p. 1982. 29.50 (ISBN 0-8451-0219-2). A R Liss.

Hagen, Uta. Sources: A Memoir. LC 82-62095. 1982. 19.95 (ISBN 0-933826-54-0); pap. 7.95 (ISBN 0-933826-55-9). Performing Arts.

Hagen, Uta & Frankel, Haskel. Respect for Acting. LC 72-2328. 227p. 1973. 12.95 (ISBN 0-02-547390-5). Macmillan.

Hagen, Victor W. Von see Prescott, William H.

Hagen, Willis W. & Johnson, Gordon H. Digest of Business Law. 2nd ed. 1979. pap. text ed. 10.95 (ISBN 0-8299-0261-9). West Pub.

Hagen-Ansert, Sandra L. Textbook of Diagnostic Ultrasonography. 2nd ed. 800p. 1983. text ed. 54.95 (ISBN 0-8016-2016-3). Mosby.

Hagendorf, Stanley. Tax Guide for Buying & Selling a Business. 5th ed. 1981. 34.95 (ISBN 0-13-885079-8, Busn). P-H.

Hagenmuller, P., jt. auth. see Bevan, D.

Hagens, James A., ed. Importance of Experimental Design & Biostatistics. Peltier, Hubert C. LC 74-14600. (Principles & Techniques of Human Research & Therapeutics Ser: Vol. 4). (Illus.). 96p. 1974. 8.50 o.p. (ISBN 0-87993-045-4). Futura Pub.

Hager, Jean. Captured by Love. (Orig.). 1981. pap. 1.50 o.s.i. (ISBN 0-440-11122-6). Dell.

--Captured By Love. Large Print ed. LC 82-10667. 299p. 1982. 10.95 (ISBN 0-89621-389-7). Thorndike Pr.

--Portrait of Love. (Orig.). 1981. pap. 1.50 o.s.i. (ISBN 0-440-17013-3). Dell.

Hager, Philip & Taylor, Desmond. The Novels of World War I: An Annotated Bibliography. LC 80-8496. 450p. 1981. lib. bdg. 40.00 o.s.i. (ISBN 0-8240-9491-3). Garland Pub.

Hager, W., jt. auth. see Kohnstamm, M.

Hager, Wolfgang. Europe's Economic Security. (The Atlantic Papers: No. 75/3). 78p. (Orig.). 1976. pap. text ed. 4.75x (ISBN 0-686-83635-9). Allanheld.

Hagerman, Paul S. It's an Odd World. LC 76-51184. (Illus.). (gr. 6 up). 1977. 5.95 o.p. (ISBN 0-8069-0112-8); lib. bdg. 5.89 o.p. (ISBN 0-8069-0113-6). Sterling.

--The Odd, Mad World of Paul Stirling Hagerman. 1981. pap. 2.50 o.p. (ISBN 0-451-11025-0, AE1025, Sig). NAL.

Hagerty, N., jt. auth. see Dick, W.

Hagg, Thomas. The Novel in Antiquity. LC 82-45906. (Illus.). 288p. 1983. text ed. 30.00x (ISBN 0-520-04923-3). U of Cal Pr.

Haggai, J. E. Victoria Sobre las Preocupaciones. Levy, Donald L., tr. from Eng. Orig. Title: How to Win Over Worry & Care. 96p. 1981. Repr. of 1980 ed. 2.15 (ISBN 0-311-46063-1, Edit Mundo). Casa Bautista.

Haggard, H. Rider see Swan, D. K.

Haggard, Howard W. The Doctor in History. 1934. 24.50x (ISBN 0-685-89747-8). Elliots Bks.

Haggard, Keith, jt. ed. see Harris, Jeffrey.

Haggard, Keith W., jt. ed. see Franta, Gregory E.

Haggard, M. P., jt. ed. see Lutman, M. E.

Haggard, Merle & Russell, Peggy. Sing Me Back Home. 1983. pap. 2.95 (ISBN 0-671-45275-4). PB.

Haggard, William. A Cool Day for Killing. 192p. Date not set. pap. 2.95 (ISBN 0-8027-3010-8). Walker & Co.

--Visa to Limbo. (Walker Mystery Ser.). 1979. 8.95 o.s.i. (ISBN 0-8027-5412-0). Walker & Co.

--Visa to Limbo. 202p. 1983. pap. 2.95 (ISBN 0-8027-3009-4). Walker & Co.

Haggarty & Rogge, eds. The Wisdom of Adam Smith. LC 76-43441. 1976. 7.95 (ISBN 0-913966-22-3, Liberty Press); pap. 1.95 (ISBN 0-686-96770-4). Liberty Fund.

Haggblade, Berle. Business Communication. (Illus.). 500p. 1982. text ed. 19.95 (ISBN 0-314-63247-6). West Pub.

Hagger, A. J., ed. Guide to Australian Economic & Social Statistics. (Guides to Australian Information Ser.). 120p. 1983. pap. 10.50 (ISBN 0-08-029833-8). Pergamon.

Hagger, Mark, jt. auth. see Herman, Valentine.

Haggerty, jt. auth. see Sebrell, Jr.

Haggerty, Arthur J. & Benjamin, Carol L. Dog Tricks. LC 77-16919. (Illus.). 160p. 1982. Repr. 9.95 (ISBN 0-87605-517-X). Howell Bk.

Haggerty, Brian A., jt. auth. see Alexander, Herbert E.

Haggerty, Brian A., jt. auth. see Champlin, Joseph M.

Haggerty, Charles E. Nuzum Family History. Rev. ed. (Illus.). 400p. 1983. lib. bdg. 30.00x (ISBN 0-686-43327-0). D G Nuzum.

Haggerty, Chas. P. Light Flashbacks to a Dark Time. (Illus.). 130p. 1981. pap. 6.95 (ISBN 0-9609936-0-6). Santiam Bks.

Haggerty, Nancy, ed. see Mock, Lonnie.

Haggerty, Robert J., jt. ed. see Green, Morris.

Haggett, P., jt. auth. see Chorley, R. J.

Haggett, Peter. Geography: A Modern Synthesis. 3rd ed. 1979. text ed. 26.95 scp (ISBN 0-06-042578-4, HarpC); scp study guide 8.95 o.p. (ISBN 0-06-042728-0); instructor's manual avail. o.p. (ISBN 0-06-362561-X). Har-Row.

--Geography: A Modern Synthesis. 3rd. rev. ed. 640p. 1983. text ed. 23.50 scp (ISBN 0-06-042579-2, HarpC); instr's. manual avail. (ISBN 0-06-362693-4); scp study guide 8.50 (ISBN 0-06-042729-9). Har-Row.

Haggett, Peter see Chorley, Richard J.

Haggett, Peter, jt. ed. see Chorley, Richard J.

Haggett, Peter, et al. Locational Analysis in Human Geography, 2 vols. 2nd ed. LC 77-8967. 1977. Set. 64.95 o.p. (ISBN 0-470-99207-7); Vol. 1, Locational Models. pap. 22.95 (ISBN 0-470-99208-5); Vol. 2, Locational Methods. pap. 24.95 o.p. (ISBN 0-470-99209-3). Halsted Pr.

Haggh, Raymond H., tr. see Turk, Daniel G.

Haggitt, T. W. Working with a Language. (Illus.). 12.50x (ISBN 0-392-01959-0, Sps). Sportshelf.

Hagihara, Yusuke. Celestial Mechanics Vol. 1: Dynamical Principles & Transformation Theory. 1970. 45.00x (ISBN 0-262-08037-0). MIT Pr.

--Celestial Mechanics, Vol. 2: Perturbation Theory, 2 pts. 1972. 50.00x ea. Pt. 1 (ISBN 0-262-08048-6). Pt. 2 (ISBN 0-262-08053-2). MIT Pr.

Hagin, F. G. A First Course in Differential Equations. (Illus.). 384p. 1975. text ed. 24.95 (ISBN 0-13-318394-7). P-H.

Hagin, Josef & Tucker, Billy. Fertilization of Dryland & Irrigated Soils. (Advanced Series in Agricultural Sciences: Vol. 12). (Illus.). 210p. 1982. 39.50 (ISBN 0-387-11121-2). Springer-Verlag.

Hagin, Keeneth, Jr. How to be a Success in Life. 1982. pap. 0.50 (ISBN 0-89276-713-8). Hagin Ministry.

Hagin, Kenneth E. The Art of Intercession. 1980. pap. 3.50 (ISBN 0-89276-503-8). Hagin Ministries.

--A Better Covenant. 1981. pap. 0.50 (ISBN 0-89276-251-9). Hagin Ministry.

--Bible Faith Study Course. 1974. pap. 5.00 (ISBN 0-89276-080-X). Hagin Ministry.

--The Bible Way to Receive the Holy Spirit. 1981. pap. 0.50 (ISBN 0-89276-255-1). Hagin Ministry.

--Casting Your Cares Upon the Lord. 1981. pap. 1.00 (ISBN 0-89276-023-0). Hagin Ministry.

--A Commonsense Guide to Fasting. 1981. pap. 1.50 (ISBN 0-89276-403-1). Hagin Ministry.

--Concerning Spiritual Gifts. 1974. pap. 2.50 (ISBN 0-89276-072-9). Hagin Ministry.

--Five Hindrances to Growth in Grace. 1981. pap. 0.50 (ISBN 0-89276-253-5). Hagin Ministry.

--Godliness Is Profitable. 1982. pap. 0.50 (ISBN 0-89276-256-X). Hagin Ministry.

--God's Medicine. 1977. mini bk. 0.50 (ISBN 0-89276-053-2). Hagin Ministries.

--Having Faith in Your Faith. 1981. pap. 0.50 (ISBN 0-89276-252-7). Hagin Ministry.

--The Holy Spirit & his Gifts. 1974. pap. 5.00 (ISBN 0-89276-082-6). Hagin Ministry.

--How to Keep Your Healing. 1980. pap. 0.50 (ISBN 0-89276-059-1). Hagin Ministry.

--How You Can Be Led by the Spirit of God. 1978. pap. text ed. 3.50 (ISBN 0-89276-500-3). Hagin Ministries.

--I Went to Hell. 1982. pap. 0.50 (ISBN 0-89276-257-8). Hagin Ministry.

--In Him. 1975. pap. 0.50 (ISBN 0-89276-052-4). Hagin Ministry.

--The Ministry Gifts Study Guide. 1981. pap. 10.00 spiral bdg. (ISBN 0-89276-092-3). Hagin Ministry.

--Must Christmas Suffer? 1982. pap. 1.50 (ISBN 0-89276-404-X). Hagin Ministry.

--The Name of Jesus. 1979. pap. 3.50 (ISBN 0-89276-502-X). Hagin Ministries.

--The New Birth. 1975. pap. 0.50 (ISBN 0-89276-050-8). Hagin Ministry.

--New Thresholds of Faith. 1972. pap. 2.50 (ISBN 0-89276-070-2). Hagin Ministry.

--Prevailing Prayer to Peace. 1973. pap. 2.50 (ISBN 0-89276-071-0). Hagin Ministry.

--Seven Steps for Judging Prophecy. 1982. pap. 1.00 (ISBN 0-89276-024-9). Hagin Ministry.

--Seven Things You Should Know About Divine Healing. 1979. pap. 2.50 (ISBN 0-89276-400-7). Hagin Ministries.

--El Shaddai. 1980. pap. 1.50 (ISBN 0-89276-401-5). Hagin Ministries.

--Turning Hopeless Situations Around. 1981. pap. 1.00 (ISBN 0-89276-022-2). Hagin Ministry.

--What to Do When Faith Seems Weak & Victory Lost. 1979. pap. 3.50 (ISBN 0-89276-501-1). Hagin Ministries.

--Why do People Fall under the Power? 1981. pap. 0.50 (ISBN 0-89276-254-3). Hagin Ministry.

--Why Tongues? 1975. pap. 0.50 (ISBN 0-89276-051-6). Hagin Ministry.

--ZOE: The God-Kind of Life. 1981. pap. 2.50 (ISBN 0-89276-402-3). Hagin Ministry.

Hagin, Kenneth, Jr. Blueprint for Building Strong Faith. 1980. pap. 0.50 mini bk. (ISBN 0-89276-704-9). Hagin Ministry.

--Faith Takes Back What the Devil's Stolen. 1982. pap. 0.50 (ISBN 0-89276-709-X). Hagin Ministry.

--Healing: A Forever-Settled Subject. 1981. pap. 0.50 (ISBN 0-89276-707-3). Hagin Ministry.

--How to Make the Dream God Gave You Come True. 1981. pap. 1.00 (ISBN 0-89276-708-1). Hagin Ministry.

--Itching Ears. 1982. pap. 0.50 (ISBN 0-89276-711-1). Hagin Ministry.

--Man's Impossibility, God's Possibility. 1978. pap. 2.50 (ISBN 0-89276-700-6). Hagin Ministries.

--The Past Tense of God's Word. 1980. pap. 0.50 mini bk. (ISBN 0-89276-706-5). Hagin Ministry.

--The Prison Door Is Open: What Are You Still Doing Inside? 1982. pap. 0.50 (ISBN 0-89276-710-3). Hagin Ministry.

--Seven Hindrances to Healing. 1980. pap. 0.50 mini bk. (ISBN 0-89276-705-7). Hagin Ministry.

--Where Do We Go from Here? 1982. pap. 0.50 (ISBN 0-89276-712-X). Hagin Ministry.

Hagin, Robert. The Dow Jones-Irwin Guide to Modern Portfolio Theory. LC 79-51785. 1980. 17.50 (ISBN 0-87094-181-X). Dow Jones-Irwin.

Hagin, Rosa. Write Right-or Left. (gr. k-3). 1981. Set of 6. cancelled (ISBN 0-8027-9140-9); cancelled (ISBN 0-8027-9120-4). Walker & Co.

Hagins, Kenneth E. Bible Prayer Study Course. 1974. pap. 5.00 (ISBN 0-89276-081-8). Hagin Ministry.

Hagiwara, M. Peter, jt. auth. see Lindell, Anne.

Hagiwara, Michio P., jt. auth. see Politzer, Robert L.

Hagiwara, Peter M., jt. auth. see Carduner, Sylvie.

Haglen, Ronald. Where's That Rule? A Cross Index of the Two Editions of the Anglo-American Cataloguing Rules. 1979. pap. 6.00 o.p. (ISBN 0-8389-3235-5). ALA.

Hagler, M. O. & Kristiansen, M. An Introduction to Controlled Thermonuclear Fusion. LC 74-33596. 208p. 1977. 23.95x (ISBN 0-669-99119-8). Lexington Bks.

Hagler, Ronald. Bibliographic Record & Information Technology. 1982. text ed. 25.00 (ISBN 0-8389-0367-3). ALA.

Haglund, Elaine & Harris, Marcia. On This Day: A Collection of Everyday Learning Events & Activities for the Media Center, Library, & Classroom. 500p. 1982. lib. bdg. 27.50 (ISBN 0-87287-345-5). Libs Unl.

Hagman, Donald G. Public Planning & Control of Urban & Land Development-Cases & Materials: 1982 Supplement to Teacher's Manual. 2nd ed. (American Casebook Ser.). 51p. 1982. pap. text ed. write for info. (ISBN 0-314-66383-5). West Pub.

Hagman, Donald G. & Misczynski, Dean J., eds. Windfalls for Wipeouts: Land Value Capture & Compensation. LC 77-82573. 660p. (Orig.). 1978. pap. 5.00 (ISBN 0-918286-11-5). Planners Pr.

Hagman, Harlan L. Bright Michigan Morning: The Years of Governor Tom Mason. LC 81-6682. (Illus.). xvi, 154p. (Orig.). 1981. 9.25 (ISBN 0-931600-02-2); pap. 5.50 (ISBN 0-931600-03-0). Green Oak Pr.

Hagner, Donald A. Hebrews: A Good News Commentary. LC 82-48410. (Good News Commentary Ser.). 288p. 1983. pap. 8.61 (ISBN 0-06-063555-X, HarpR). Har-Row.

Hagood, Margaret J. Mothers of the South: Portraiture of the White Tenant Farm Woman. (Illus.). 1977. pap. 5.95 (ISBN 0-393-00816-9, Norton Lib). Norton.

Hagood, Patricia, ed. Oxbridge Directory of Newsletters 1983-84. 3rd rev. ed. 400p. 1983. pap. 60.00 (ISBN 0-917460-11-1). Oxbridge Comm.

Hagopian, Viola L. Italian Ars Nova Music: A Bibliographic Guide to Modern Editions & Related Literature. 2nd, rev. ed. LC 70-187748. 1973. 27.50x (ISBN 0-520-02223-8). U of Cal Pr.

Hagstad, Harry V. & Hubbert, William T. Food Quality Control: A Syllabus for Veterinary Students. (Illus.). 152p. 1982. pap. text ed. 11.95x (ISBN 0-8138-0701-8). Iowa St U Pr.

Hagstrom, Dick. Getting along with Yourself & Others. 1982. pap. 6.95 (ISBN 0-8423-0998-5). Tyndale.

Hagstrom, Jerry, jt. auth. see Peirce, Neal R.

Hagstrom, Julie. Games Toddlers Play: Learning Fun & Activity Games for Baby's Second Year. (Games Babies Play Ser.). (Illus.). 128p. (Orig.). Date not set. pap. 5.95 (ISBN 0-89104-306-3, A & W Visual Library). A & W Pubs. Postponed.

Hagstrom, Julie & Morrill, Joan. Games Babies Play: A Handbook of Games to Play with Infants. LC 78-70684. (Games Babies Play Ser.). 96p. 1979. 9.95 (ISBN 0-89104-130-3, A & W Visual Library); pap. 4.95 (ISBN 0-89104-119-2, A & W Visual Library). A & W Pubs.

Hagstrum, Jean H. Sex & Sensibility: Ideal & Erotic Love from Milton to Mozart. LC 79-20657. (Illus.). 1980. text ed. 30.00x (ISBN 0-226-31289-5). U of Chicago Pr.

Hague, Clifford W. Printing Instruction Sheets: Letterpress Printing. (Illus., Orig.). 1961. pap. 2.24 o.p. (ISBN 0-02-818310-X). Glencoe.

Hague, Douglas C., ed. Price Formation in Various Economies. (International Economic Assn. Ser). 1967. 26.00 (ISBN 0-312-64260-1). St Martin.

Hague, Douglas C., jt. ed. see Harrod, Roy F.

Hague, Hawdon. The Organic Organization & How to Manage It. LC 78-23272. 1979. 35.95x o.s.i. (ISBN 0-470-26563-9). Halsted Pr.

Hague, John A. American Character & Culture in a Changing World: Some Twentieth-Century Perspectives. (Contributions in American Studies: No. 42). 1979. lib. bdg. 35.95 (ISBN 0-313-20735-6, HAM/). Greenwood.

Hague, Kathleen & Hague, Michael. The Man Who Kept House. LC 80-26258. (Illus.). 32p. (ps-3). 1981. 11.95 (ISBN 0-15-251698-0, VoyB). HarBraceJ.

Hague, Michael, jt. auth. see Hague, Kathleen.

Hague, Paul. Sea Battles in Miniature: A Guide to Naval Wargaming. (Illus.). 160p. 1981. 14.95 (ISBN 0-85059-414-6). Naval Inst Pr.

Hague, R. & Harrop, M. Comparative Government. 256p. 1982. text ed. 22.95x (ISBN 0-333-25636-0, 40592, Pub. by Macmillan England); pap. text ed. 9.95x (ISBN 0-333-25637-9, 40707). Humanities.

Hague, William. Remodel, Don't Move: Make Your Home Fit Your Lifestyle. LC 80-498. (Illus.). 256p. 1981. 11.95 o.p. (ISBN 0-385-15910-2). Doubleday.

Hahable, William S. Alaska's Copper River: The 18th & 19th Centuries. LC 82-71377. (Alaska Historical Commission Series in History: No. 21). (Illus.). 110p. (Orig.). 1982. pap. text ed. write for info. (ISBN 0-943712-10-6). Alaska Hist.

Hahn, Albert & Williams, Roger. Petrochemical Industry: Markets & Economics. LC 69-12408. 1970. 7.75 (ISBN 0-07-025503-2, P&RB). McGraw.

Hahn, Anne B., et al. Pharmacology in Nursing. 15th ed. LC 66-10935. (Illus.). 1078p. 1982. text ed. 32.50 (ISBN 0-8016-0633-0). Mosby.

Hahn, Beverly. Chekhov. 300p. 1977. 44.50 (ISBN 0-521-20951-X). Cambridge U Pr.

--Chekhov. LC 75-22557. (Major European Authors Ser.). 1979. pap. 12.95 (ISBN 0-521-29670-6). Cambridge U Pr.

Hahn, Celia A., jt. auth. see Fenhagen, James C.

Hahn, E. A., jt. auth. see Sturtevant, Edgar H.

Hahn, Eily. The Islands: America's Imperial Adventure in the Philippines. (Illus.). 384p. 1981. 14.95 (ISBN 0-698-11097-8, Coward). Putnam Pub Group.

Hahn, Emily. China to Me: A Partial Autobiography. LC 74-23432. (China in the 20th Century Ser). 429p. 1975. Repr. of 1944 ed. lib. bdg. 45.00 (ISBN 0-306-70695-4). Da Capo.

--Chinese Cooking. LC 68-56965. (Foods of the World Ser.). (Illus.). 200p. (gr. 6 up). 1968. lib. bdg. 17.28 (ISBN 0-8094-0062-6, Time-Life). Silver.

--Once Upon a Pedestal. (RL 9). 1975. pap. 2.25 o.p. (ISBN 0-451-61415-1, ME1415, Ment). NAL.

--Once Upon a Pedestal: An Informal History of Women's Lib. 224p. 1974. 10.53i (ISBN 0-690-00507-5). T Y Crowell.

--Soong Sisters. Repr. of 1941 ed. lib. bdg. 18.75x (ISBN 0-8371-4429-9, HASI). Greenwood.

Hahn, F. H., ed. Readings in the Theory of Growth. LC 70-140572. 1971. 25.00 (ISBN 0-312-66465-6). St Martin.

Hahn, F. H., ed. see International Economic Association.

Hahn, Ferdinand. Historical Investigation & New Testament Faith. Krentz, Edgar, ed. Maddox, Robert, tr. from Ger. LC 82-48547. 112p. 1983. pap. 6.95 (ISBN 0-8006-1691-X, 1-1691). Fortress.

Hahn, Frank. Money & Inflation. 136p. 1983. 12.50x (ISBN 0-262-08129-6). MIT Pr.

Hahn, Frank & Hollis, Martin, eds. Philosophy & Economic Theory. (Oxford Readings in Philosophy Ser.). 1979. pap. text ed. 7.95x (ISBN 0-19-875042-0). Oxford U Pr.

Hahn, George M. Hyperthermia & Cancer. 204p. 35.00x (ISBN 0-306-40958-5, Plenum Pr.). Plenum Pub.

Hahn, Gerald J. & Shapiro, S. S. Statistical Models in Engineering. LC 67-12562. (Wiley Series on Systems Engineering & Analysis). 1967. 35.95 (ISBN 0-471-33915-6, Pub. by Wiley-Interscience). Wiley.

Hahn, H. George & Behm, Carl. Towson. (Illus.). 208p. 1977. 15.95 (ISBN 0-686-36702-2). Md Hist.

--Towson: A Pictorial History of a Maryland Town. LC 77-20052. (Illus.). 1977. 15.95 o.p. (ISBN 0-915442-36-1). Donning Co.

Hahn, Hannelore. On the Way to Feed the Swans. LC 82-99824. 80p. 1982. pap. 15.00 (ISBN 0-9603310-3-4). Tenth Hse Ent.

Hahn, Harlan, jt. auth. see Feagin, Joe R.

Hahn, Harold M. The Colonial Schooner: 1763 to 1775. LC 80-84052. (Illus.). 126p. 1981. 19.95 (ISBN 0-87021-927-8). Naval Inst Pr.

Hahn, James & Hahn, Lynn. Ali! The Sports Career of Muhammad Ali. Schroeder, Howard, ed. LC 81-5378. (Sports Legends Ser.). (Illus.). 48p. (gr. 3 up). 1981. PLB 6.95 (ISBN 0-89686-130-9); pap. text ed. 3.95 (ISBN 0-89686-145-7). Crestwood Hse.

--Babe! The Sports Career of George Ruth. LC 81-5377. (Sports Legends Ser.). (Illus.). 48p. (gr. 3 up). 1981. PLB 6.95 (ISBN 0-89686-129-5); pap. text ed. 3.95 (ISBN 0-89686-144-9). Crestwood Hse.

--Bill Walton: Maverick Cager. LC 78-9447. (Champions & Challengers 1). (gr. 3-5). 1978. text ed. 6.95 (ISBN 0-88436-443-7). EMC.

--Bjorn Borg: The Coolest Ace. LC 78-13127. (Champions & Challengers II). (gr. 3-5). 1979. text ed. 6.95 (ISBN 0-88436-478-X); pap. text ed. 3.95 (ISBN 0-88436-479-8). EMC.

--Brown! The Sports Career of James Brown. Schroeder, Howard, ed. LC 81-9837. (Sports Legends Ser.). (Illus.). 48p. (gr. 3 up). 1981. PLB 6.95 (ISBN 0-89686-128-7); pap. text ed. 3.95 (ISBN 0-89686-143-0). Crestwood Hse.

--Casey! The Sports Career of Charles Stengel. Schroeder, Howard, ed. LC 80-28602. (Sports Legends Ser.). (Illus.). 48p. (Orig.). (gr. 3-5). 1981. PLB 6.95 (ISBN 0-89686-126-0); pap. text ed. 3.95 (ISBN 0-89686-141-4). Crestwood Hse.

--Chris! The Sports Career of Chris Evert Lloyd. Schroeder, Howard, ed. LC 81-9808. (Sports Legends Ser.). (Illus.). 48p. (gr. 3 up). 1981. PLB 6.95 (ISBN 0-89686-131-7); pap. text ed. 3.95 (ISBN 0-89686-146-5). Crestwood Hse.

--Franco Harris: The Quiet Ironman. LC 78-12841. (Champions & Challengers II). (gr. 3-5). 1979. text ed. 6.95 (ISBN 0-88436-447-X); pap. text ed. 3.95 (ISBN 0-88436-448-8). EMC.

--Franz Beckenbauer: Soccer Superstar. LC 78-18736. (Champions & Challengers 1). (gr. 3-5). 1978. text ed. 6.95 (ISBN 0-88436-445-3). EMC.

--Hamsters, Gerbils, Guinea Pigs, Pet Mice, & Pet Rats. LC 77-1389. (Illus.). (gr. 4 up). 1977. PLB 8.90 (ISBN 0-531-01287-5). Watts.

--Henry! The Sports Career of Henry Aaron. Schroeder, Howard, ed. LC 81-355. (Sports Legends Ser.). (Illus.). 48p. (gr. 3-5). 1981. PLB 6.95 (ISBN 0-89686-120-1); pap. text ed. 3.95 (ISBN 0-89686-135-X). Crestwood Hse.

--Janet Guthrie: Champion Racer. LC 78-12670. (Champions & Challengers II). (gr. 3-5). 1979. text ed. 6.95 (ISBN 0-88436-476-3); pap. text ed. 3.95 (ISBN 0-88436-477-1). EMC.

--Killy! The Sports Career of Jean-Claude Killy. Schroeder, Howard, ed. LC 81-5419. (Sports Legends Ser.). (Illus.). 48p. (gr. 3 up). 1981. PLB 6.95 (ISBN 0-89686-132-5); pap. text ed. 3.95 (ISBN 0-89686-147-3). Crestwood Hse.

--King! The Sports Career of Billie Jean King. Schroeder, Howard, ed. LC 81-9822. (Sports Legends Ser.). (Illus.). 48p. (gr. 3 up). 1981. PLB 6.95 (ISBN 0-89686-134-1); pap. text ed. 3.95 (ISBN 0-89686-149-X). Crestwood Hse.

--Nancy Lopez: Golfing Pioneer. LC 78-13162. (Champions & Challengers II). (gr. 3-5). 1979. text ed. 6.95 (ISBN 0-88436-480-1); pap. text ed. 3.95 (ISBN 0-88436-481-X). EMC.

--Patty! The Sports Career of Patricia Berg. Schroeder, Howard, ed. (Sports Legends Ser.). (Illus.). 48p. (Orig.). (gr. 3-5). PLB 6.95 (ISBN 0-89686-127-9); pap. text ed. 3.95 (ISBN 0-89686-142-2). Crestwood Hse.

--Pele'! The Sports Career of Edson do Naseimento. Schroeder, Howard, ed. (Sports Legends Ser.). (Illus.). 48p. (Orig.). (gr. 3-5). 1981. PLB 6.95 (ISBN 0-89686-125-2); pap. text ed. 3.95 (ISBN 0-89686-140-6). Crestwood Hse.

--Reggie Jackson: Slugger Supreme. LC 78-12937. (Champions & Challengers II). (gr. 3-5). 1979. text ed. 6.95 (ISBN 0-88436-449-6); pap. text ed. 3.95 (ISBN 0-88436-475-5). EMC.

--Rod Carew: A Promise & a Dream. LC 78-9721. (Champions & Challengers 1). (gr. 3-5). 1978. text ed. 6.95 (ISBN 0-88436-441-0). EMC.

--Sayers! The Sports Career of Gale Sayers. Schroeder, Howard, ed. LC 81-9836. (Sports Legends Ser.). (Illus.). 48p. (gr. 3 up). 1981. PLB 6.95 (ISBN 0-89686-133-3); pap. text ed. 3.95 (ISBN 0-89686-148-1). Crestwood Hse.

--Tark! The Sports Career of Francis Tarkenton. Schroeder, Howard, ed. (Sports Legends Ser.). (Illus.). 48p. (Orig.). (gr. 3-5). 1981. PLB 6.95 (ISBN 0-89686-121-X); pap. text ed. 3.95 (ISBN 0-89686-136-8). Crestwood Hse.

--Thorpe! James Thorpe. Schroeder, Howard, ed. (Sports Legends Ser.). (Illus.). 48p. (Orig.). (gr. 3-5). 1981. PLB 6.95 (ISBN 0-89686-123-6); pap. text ed. 3.95 (ISBN 0-89686-138-4). Crestwood Hse.

--Tracy Austin: Powerhouse in Pinafore. LC 78-18902. (Champions & Challengers Ser.: No. 1). (gr. 3-5). 1978. text ed. 6.95 (ISBN 0-88436-439-9). EMC.

--Wilt! The Sports Career of Wilton Chamberlain. Schroeder, Howard, ed. LC 80-28746. (Sports Legends Ser.). (Illus.). 48p. (Orig.). (gr. 3-5). 1981. PLB 6.95 (ISBN 0-89686-124-4); pap. text ed. 3.95 (ISBN 0-89686-139-2). Crestwood Hse.

--Zaharias: The Sports Career of Mildred Didrickson Zaharias. Schroeder, Howard, ed. LC 80-28383. (Sports Legends Ser.). (Illus.). 48p. (Orig.). (gr. 3-5). 1981. PLB 6.95 (ISBN 0-89686-122-8); pap. text ed. 3.95 (ISBN 0-89686-137-6). Crestwood Hse.

Hahn, Lynn, jt. auth. see Hahn, James.

Hahn, Lynne C., jt. auth. see McKoski, Martin M.

Hahn, Martin E., jt. ed. see Simmel, Edward C.

Hahn, Nan L. Medieval Mensuration: Quadrans Vetus & Pratica Geometrie, Pt. 8. LC 81-71030. (Transactions Ser.: Vol. 72). 1982. 15.00 (ISBN 0-87169-728-9). Am Philos.

Hahn, Roger. The Anatomy of a Scientific Institution: The Paris Academy of Sciences, 1666-1803. LC 70-130795. (Illus.). 1971. 38.50x (ISBN 0-520-01818-4). U of Cal Pr.

--Bibliography of Quantitative Studies on Science & Its History. LC 79-65637. (Berkeley Papers in History of Science: No. 3). (Orig.). 1980. pap. 5.00x (ISBN 0-918102-04-9). U Cal Hist Sci Tech.

Hahn, Roger, compiled by. Calendar of the Correspondence of Pierre Simon Laplace. LC 81-51031. (Berkeley Papers in History of Science: No. 8). 100p. (Orig.). 1982. pap. 5.00x (ISBN 0-918102-07-3). U Cal Hist Sci Tech.

Hahn, Thomas F. Chesapeake & Ohio Canal Old Picture Album. (Illus.). 104p. 1976. pap. 4.95 (ISBN 0-686-36753-7). Md Hist.

Hahne, E., ed. see Seventh International Heat Transfer Conference, Munich, 1982.

Hahnemann, Samuel. Organon of Medicine. Kunzli, Naude & Pendleton, trs. 1980. 7.95 (ISBN 0-87477-223-0, Pub. by Houghton Mifflin). Formur Intl.

Haich, Elisabeth. The Day with Yoga. pap. 2.50 (ISBN 0-686-36351-5). Aurora Press.

--Sexual Energy & Yoga. pap. 6.95 (ISBN 0-686-36352-3). Aurora Press.

--Wisdom of the Tarot. 1983. pap. 12.50. Aurora Press.

--Yoga & Destiny. 1983. pap. price not set (ISBN 0-943358-01-9). Aurora Press.

Haider, Muhiuddin. Village Level Integrated Population Education: A Case Study of Bangladesh. LC 81-43722. (Illus.). 184p. (Orig.). text ed. 22.50 (ISBN 0-8191-2489-3); pap. text ed. 10.25 (ISBN 0-8191-2490-7). U Pr of Amer.

Haidinger, Timothy P. & Richardson, Dana R. A Manager's Guide to Computer Timesharing. LC 74-18413. (Manager's Guide Ser.). 192p. 1975. 28.95 (ISBN 0-471-33925-3, Pub. by Wiley-Interscience). Wiley.

Haieh, Ching-yao, et al. A Short Introduction to Modern Growth Theory. LC 78-61916. 1978. pap. text ed. 9.75 (ISBN 0-8191-0628-3). U Pr of Amer.

Haifeez, Moonat. Reminiscent Singapore. 1978. 6.95 o.p. (ISBN 0-533-03477-9). Vantage.

Haig, H. H. Return to Mount Ararat. 1979. 5.95 o.p. (ISBN 0-533-04273-9). Vantage.

Haig, J. A. Headmaster. 1982. 4.95 (ISBN 0-941478-06-8). Paraclete Pr.

Haig-Brown, Roderick. Bright Waters, Bright Fish. (Illus.). 160p. 1980. 19.95 (ISBN 0-917304-59-4). Timber.

--A Primer of Fly Fishing. LC 82-50124. (Illus.). 192p. (Orig.). 1982. pap. 8.95 (ISBN 0-295-95932-0). U of Wash Pr.

--River Never Sleeps. (Sportsmen's Classics Ser.). 352p. 1974. 7.50 o.p. (ISBN 0-517-51601-2). Crown.

--Writings & Reflections: From the World of Roderick Haig-Brown. Haig-Brown, Valerie, ed. LC 82-10942. 222p. 1982. 16.95 (ISBN 0-295-95945-2). U of Wash Pr.

Haig-Brown, Valerie, ed. see Haig-Brown, Roderick.

Haigh, Basil, tr. see Shimanovskaya, K. & Shiman, Alexander.

Haigh, C. Last Days of the Lancashire: Monasteries & the Pilgrimage of Grace. 182p. 1969. 19.00 (ISBN 0-7190-1150-7). Manchester.

--Reformation & Resistance in Tudor Lancashire. LC 73-88308. (Illus.). 416p. 1974. 49.50 (ISBN 0-521-20367-8). Cambridge U Pr.

Haigh, D. Dyeing & Finishing Knitted Goods. 14.00 o.s.i. (ISBN 0-87245-496-7). Textile Bk.
Haigh, Frank, jt. auth. see Dillon, Mark.
Haigh, Gerald. Teaching Slow Learners. 1978. 15.95 o.p. (ISBN 0-85117-128-1); pap. 7.50 o.p. (ISBN 0-85117-131-1). Transatlantic.
Haigh, R. H. & Morris, D. S. War & Politics in Twentieth Century Europe: Essays in Military & Diplomatic History. 1982. Vol. 1. 32.00 (ISBN 0-686-96382-2); Vol. 2. 37.00 (ISBN 0-686-99777-8). MA-AH Pub.
Haigh, Robert, et al. Communications in the Twenty-First Century. LC 81-14797. 240p. 1981. 24.95 (ISBN 0-471-09910-4, Pub. by Wiley-Interscience). Wiley.
Haigh, Robert W., jt. auth. see McLean, John G.
Haigh, Roger & Radford, Loren. BASIC for Microcomputers. 300p. 1982. pap. text ed. write for info. (ISBN 0-87150-334-4, 8050). Prindle.
Haight, Elizabeth H. Apuleius & His Influence. 190p. 1983. Repr. of 1927 ed. lib. bdg. 12.50 (ISBN 0-89760-369-9). Telegraph Bks.
Haight, Fulton & Cotchett, Joseph W. California Courtroom Evidence. rev. 2nd ed. LC 72-79475. 429p. 1981. 45.00 (ISBN 0-911110-07-0); 1983 suppl. incl. (ISBN 0-685-26721-0). Parker & Son.
Haight, Gordon S. Mrs. Sigourney: The Sweet Singer of Hartford. 1930. 39.50x (ISBN 0-686-51419-X). Elliots Bks.
Haight, Grace W. Cathie Remembers. 0.75 o.p. (ISBN 0-87213-290-0). Loizeaux.
Haight, Sandy, jt. auth. see Elliot, Sharon A.
Haight, William. Retail Advertising: Management & Technique. 1976. text ed. 18.95x (ISBN 0-673-15299-5). Scott F.
Haigney-Timmis, Jessica. Readings in the Fine Arts. 1978. pap. text ed. 14.95 (ISBN 0-8403-1920-7). Kendall-Hunt.
Haikalis, Peter D. & Freeman, Jean K., eds. Real Estate: A Bibliography of the Monographic Literature. LC 82-23071. 323p. 1983. lib. bdg. 45.00 (ISBN 0-313-23680-1, HAK/). Greenwood.
Haile, Berard. Love-Magic & Butterfly People: The Slim Curly Version of the Ajiee & Mothway Myths. LC 78-59705. (Illus.). xii, 153p. 1978. pap. 13.95x (ISBN 0-89734-026-4). Mus Northern Ariz.
--Starlore among the Navaho. LC 76-53085. 1977. lib. bdg. 15.00x (ISBN 0-88307-532-6); pap. 6.95 (ISBN 0-88307-533-4). Gannon.
--Waterway: A Navajo Ceremonial Myth told by Black Moustache Circle. LC 79-66605. (Illus.). vi, 153p. 1977. pap. 12.95x (ISBN 0-89734-030-2). Mus Northern Ariz.
Hailes, W. & Hubbard, R. Small Business Management. 3rd ed. 240p. 1983. pap. text ed. 8.80 (ISBN 0-8273-2108-2); write for info. instr's guide (ISBN 0-8273-2109-0). Delmar.
Hailey, Arthur. Airport. LC 68-11755. 1968. 14.95 (ISBN 0-385-04139-X). Doubleday.
--Final Diagnosis. LC 59-12829. 1969. 12.95 (ISBN 0-385-03588-8). Doubleday.
--In High Places. LC 61-9513. 1961. 10.95 (ISBN 0-385-04159-4). Doubleday.
--The Moneychangers. LC 74-12689. 480p. 1975. 14.95 (ISBN 0-385-00896-1). Doubleday.
--Overload. LC 77-16920. 1979. 14.95 (ISBN 0-385-02104-6). Doubleday.
--Wheels. LC 77-152790. 1971. 12.95 (ISBN 0-385-02829-6). Doubleday.
Hailey, Elizabeth. A Woman of Independent Means. 1979. pap. 3.50 (ISBN 0-380-42390-1, 60491-4). Avon.
Hailey, Elizabeth F. Life Sentences. 288p. 1982. 14.95 (ISBN 0-440-04924-5). Delacorte.
--Life Sentences. (General Ser.). 1983. lib. bdg. 16.95 (ISBN 0-8161-3473-1, Large Print Bks). G K Hall.
--A Woman of Independent Means. 1978. 14.95 (ISBN 0-670-77795-1). Viking Pr.
Hailey, Homer. That You May Believe: Studies in the Gospel of John. (Illus.). 1982. 9.95 (ISBN 0-913814-51-2). Nevada Pubns.
Hailey, William M. The Republic of South Africa & the High Commission Territories. LC 82-11865. vii, 136p. 1982. Repr. of 1963 ed. lib. bdg. 25.00x (ISBN 0-313-23625-9, HARS). Greenwood.
Hailperin, T. Boole's Logic & Probability Theory. (Studies in Logic & the Foundations of Mathematics: Vol. 85). 1976. 51.00 (ISBN 0-7204-0374-X, North-Holland). Elsevier.
Hails, J. & Carr, A., eds. Nearshore Sediment Dynamics & Sedimentation. LC 75-6950. 316p. 1975. 69.95 (ISBN 0-471-33946-6, Pub. by Wiley-Interscience). Wiley.
Hails, Jack. Classic Moments of Boxing. 144p. 1982. 35.00x (ISBN 0-86190-054-5, Pub. by Moorland). State Mutual Bk.
Hails, John R., ed. Applied Geomorphology. 1977. pap. text ed. 51.00 (ISBN 0-444-41317-0). Elsevier.
Hailstones, Thomas J. & Rothwell, John C. Introduction to Managerial Economics. (Illus.). 1979. ref. 23.95 (ISBN 0-13-486290-2). P-H.
Haim, S. Persian-English, English-Persian Shorter Dictionary, 2 vols. rev., enl. ed. 1979. Set. 50.00 (ISBN 0-686-77974-6). Heinman.
Haim, Sylvia G., ed. Arab Nationalism: An Anthology. LC 62-11492. (California Library Reprint Ser.). 1974. 28.50x (ISBN 0-520-02645-4); pap. 7.95 (ISBN 0-520-03043-5). U of Cal Pr.
Haiman, John, ed. see Symposium on Switch Reference & Universal Grammar.
Haimann, Theo. Supervisory Management for Health Care Institutions. 3rd ed. 420p. Date not set. text ed. price not set (ISBN 0-87125-081-0). Cath Health.
Haimann, Theo, et al. Managing the Modern Organization. 4th ed. LC 81-82568. 1982. 23.95 (ISBN 0-395-31719-3); instr's manual 2.00 (ISBN 0-395-31720-7); study guide 9.95 (ISBN 0-395-31721-5); test bank A 1.50 (ISBN 0-395-32026-7); test bank B 1.50 (ISBN 0-395-32027-5). HM.
Haimes, jt. auth. see Chankong.
Haimes, Y. Y. Large Scale Systems. (Studies in Management Sciences & Systems: Vol. 7). Date not set. 42.75 (ISBN 0-444-86367-2). Elsevier.
Haimes, Yacov Y. Hierarchical Analyses of Water Resources Systems: Modeling & Optimization of Large-Scale Systems. (Illus.). 1977. text ed. 47.95x (ISBN 0-07-025507-5, C). McGraw.
--Scientific, Technological & Institutional Aspects of Water Resource Policy. (AAAS Selected Symposium: No. 49). 125p. 1980. lib. bdg. 15.50 (ISBN 0-89158-842-6). Westview.
Haimovici, Henry. Vascular Surgery. (Illus.). 1976. text ed. 90.00 (ISBN 0-07-025514-8, HP). McGraw.
Haimson, Leopold H. Russian Marxists & the Origins of Bolshevism. 1966. pap. 4.95x o.p. (ISBN 0-8070-5675-8, BP220). Beacon Pr.
Hain, Paul L., jt. auth. see Harris, Fred R.
Hainaux, Rene & Bonnat, Yves, eds. Stage Design Throughout the World Since 1960. 2nd ed. LC 72-87117. 1972. 39.95 o.s.i. (ISBN 0-87830-129-1). Theatre Arts.
Haine, Malou. Adolphe Sax: Sa vie, son oeuvre, ses instruments de musique. (Illus.). 283p. 1980. 37.50 o.s.i. (ISBN 90-6027-235-8, Pub. by Frits Knuf Netherlands); wrappers 25.00 o.s.i. (ISBN 90-6027-234-X, Pub. by Frits Knuf Netherlands). Pendragon NY.
Haine, Malou & Keyser, Ignace de. Catalogue des Instruments Sax au Musee Instrumental de Bruxelles: Suivi de la liste de 400 instruments Sax conserves dans des collections publiques et privees. (Illus.). vi, 280p. 1980. 40.00 o.s.i. (ISBN 90-6027-397-4, Pub. by Frits Knuf Netherlands). Pendragon NY.
Haines, Aubrey L. Historic Sites Along the Oregon Trail. 2nd ed. Franzwa, Gregory, ed. LC 81-9628. (Illus.). 453p. 1981. 24.95 (ISBN 0-935284-21-4). Patrice Pr.
Haines, Aubrey L., ed. see Russell, Osborne.
Haines, B. Joan & Gerber, Linda L. Leading Young Children to Music: A Resource Book for Teachers. (Early Childhood Education Ser.: No. C24). 288p. 1980. pap. text ed. 16.95 spiral bdg. (ISBN 0-675-08161-0). Merrill.
Haines, Charles G. The American Doctrine of Judicial Supremacy. LC 73-250. (American Constitutional & Legal History Ser.). 726p. 1973. Repr. of 1932 ed. lib. bdg. 85.00 (ISBN 0-306-70569-9). Da Capo.
--The Role of the Supreme Court in American Government & Politics 1835-1864. LC 73-604. (American Constitutional & Legal History Ser.). 544p. 1973. Repr. of 1957 ed. lib. bdg. 59.50 (ISBN 0-306-70566-4). Da Capo.
--The Role of the Supreme Court in American Government & Politics 1795-1835. LC 73-604. (American Constitutional & Legal History Ser.). 698p. 1973. Repr. of 1944 ed. lib. bdg. 79.50 (ISBN 0-306-70571-0). Da Capo.
Haines, Charles G. & Dimock, Marshall E., eds. Essays on the Law & Practice of Governmental Administration: A Volume in Honor of Frank Johnson Goodnow. Repr. of 1935 ed. lib. bdg. 17.00x (ISBN 0-8371-0459-9, HAGA). Greenwood.
Haines, Duane E. Neuroanatomy: An Atlas of Structures, Sections & Systems. (Illus.). 184p. 1983. text ed. write for info. (ISBN 0-8067-0851-4). Urban & S.
Haines, E. Early American Brides. 150p. 1982. pap. 12.95 (ISBN 0-87588-176-9). Hobby Hse.
Haines, F. The Plains Indians: Their Origins, Migrations, & Cultural Development. LC 75-23259. (Illus.). 224p. 1976. 12.45i (ISBN 0-690-01031-1, TYC-T). T Y Crowell.
Haines, Francis. Nez Perces: Tribesmen of the Columbia Plateau. LC 55-9626. (Civilization of American Indian Ser.: No. 42). (Illus.). 1955. 14.95 o.p. (ISBN 0-8061-0325-6); pap. 9.95 (ISBN 0-8061-0982-3). U of Okla Pr.
Haines, Gail K. Baking in a Box, Cooking on a Can. LC 80-26678. (Illus.). 128p. (gr. 4-6). 1981. PLB 7.63 (ISBN 0-688-00376-1); pap. 4.95 o.s.i. (ISBN 0-688-00373-7). Morrow.
--Brain Power: What Does It Mean to Be Smart? LC 78-1085. (Impact Ser.). (Illus.). (gr. 7 up). 1979. PLB 8.90 s&l (ISBN 0-531-02287-0). Watts.
--Cancer. LC 80-14870. (gr. 4 up). 1980. PLB 8.90 (ISBN 0-531-04159-X). Watts.
--Explosives. LC 75-26707. (Illus.). 32p. 1976. 7.95 (ISBN 0-688-22058-4); lib. bdg. 7.63 (ISBN 0-688-32058-9). Morrow.
--Fire. LC 74-13396. (Illus.). 32p. (gr. 1-5). 1975. PLB 8.16 (ISBN 0-688-32009-0). Morrow.
--Natural & Synthetic Poisons. (Illus.). (gr. 4-6). 1978. 6.95 o.s.i. (ISBN 0-688-22157-2); PLB 8.40 (ISBN 0-688-32157-7). Morrow.
--Test-Tube Mysteries. LC 82-45380. (Illus.). 192p. (gr. 7 up). 1982. PLB 11.95 (ISBN 0-396-08075-8). Dodd.
Haines, J. Harry. Committed Locally-Living Globally. (Into our Third Century Ser.). 96p. (Orig.). 1982. pap. 3.50 (ISBN 0-687-09149-7). Abingdon.
--Ten Hands for God. 80p. (Orig.). 1983. pap. 3.50 (ISBN 0-8358-0449-6). Upper Room.
Haines, Joey, jt. auth. see Johnson, Dewayne J.
Haines, John. Living off the Country: Essays on Poetry & Place. (Poets on Poetry Ser.). 176p. 1981. pap. 7.95 (ISBN 0-472-06333-2). U of Mich Pr.
--Other Days. (Illus.). 52p. 1981. 60.00x (ISBN 0-915308-29-0); pap. 5.00x (ISBN 0-915308-30-4). Graywolf.
Haines, John E. Automatic Control of Heating & Air Conditioning. 2nd ed. (Illus.). 1961. 49.00 (ISBN 0-07-025529-6, P&RB). McGraw.
Haines, Pamela. Kissing Gate. 1982. pap. 3.50 (ISBN 0-451-11449-3, AE1449, Sig). NAL.
Haines, R. M. The Church & Politics in Fourteenth Century England. LC 76-54062. (Studies in Medieval Life & Thought: No. 10). 1978. 47.50 (ISBN 0-521-21544-7). Cambridge U Pr.
Haines, Robert E. The Inner Eye of Alfred Stieglitz. LC 82-13641. (Illus.). 170p. (Orig.). 1983. lib. bdg. 22.00 (ISBN 0-8191-2717-5); pap. text ed. 10.00 (ISBN 0-8191-2718-3). U Pr of Amer.
Haines, Robert G. Math Principles for Food Service Occupations. LC 77-88118. 1979. pap. text ed. 10.60 (ISBN 0-8273-1680-1); instr.'s guide 4.75 (ISBN 0-685-91755-X). Delmar.
Haines, Roger. Control Systems for Heating, Ventilating & Airconditioning. 3rd ed. 1983. write for info (ISBN 0-442-23649-2). Van Nos Reinhold.
Haines, Walter W. Money, Prices & Policy. 2nd ed. 1966. text ed. 16.00 o.p. (ISBN 0-07-025525-3, C). McGraw.
Haines, Wesley N. see Reggie the Retiree, pseud.
Haines, Y. Y., jt. auth. see LaConte, P.
Haining, Peter. H. G. Wells Scrapbook. (Illus.). 1979. 10.00 o.p. (ISBN 0-517-53722-2, C N Potter Bks). Crown.
Haining, Peter, ed. The Edgar Allan Poe Scrapbook. LC 77-87863. (Illus.). 1978. 15.00 o.p. (ISBN 0-8052-3679-1); pap. 7.95 o.p. (ISBN 0-8052-0583-7). Schocken.
--The Hashish Club: An Anthology of Drug Literature. Incl. Vol. 1. Founding of the Modern Tradition: from Coleridge to Crowley. Aldiss, Brian W., pref. by. text ed. 11.75x o.p. (ISBN 0-7206-0303-X); Vol. 2. Psychedelic Era: from Huxley to Lennon. text ed. 8.50x o.p. (ISBN 0-7206-0014-6). 1975. Humanities.
Hainline, Patricia H, jt. auth. see Carey, Margaret S.
Hains, D. R. The Sydney Traders: Simeon Lord & His Comtemporaries 1788-1821. 264p. 1982. pap. 21.00 (ISBN 0-522-84217-8, Pub. by Melbourne U Pr). Intl Schol Bk Serv.
Hainsou, Ada. Lucy's Village. 5.95 (ISBN 0-85967-524-6). Green Tiger Pr.
Hainstock, Elizabeth. The Essential Montessori. (Orig.). 1978. pap. 2.50 (ISBN 0-451-62109-3, ME2109, Ment). NAL.
--Teaching Montessori in the Home: The School Years. 1978. pap. 4.95 (ISBN 0-452-25420-5, Z5420, Plume). NAL.
Hainstock, Elizabeth G. Teaching Montessori in the Home: The Pre-School Years. 1976. pap. 4.50 (ISBN 0-452-25418-3, Z5418, Plume). NAL.
Hainsworth, F. Reed. Animal Physiology: Adaptations in Function. (Life Sciences Ser.). (Illus.). 600p. 1981. text ed. 27.95 (ISBN 0-201-03401-8). A-W.
Hainsworth, P. H. Agriculture: The Only Right Approach. Bargyla & Rateaver, Gylver, eds. LC 74-33125. (Conservation Gardening & Farming Ser: Ser. C). 1976. pap. 13.00 (ISBN 0-9600698-5-2). Rateavers.
Hainworth, Henry. A Collector's Dictionary. (Illus.). 128p. 1981. 9.95 (ISBN 0-7100-0745-0). Routledge & Kegan.
Hair, Joseph F., et al. Multivariate Data Analysis. 353p. 1979. 24.95 (ISBN 0-87814-077-8). Pennwell Pub.
Hair, Michael, ed. Chemistry of Biosurfaces, Vol. 1. 1971. 55.00 o.p. (ISBN 0-8247-1283-8). Dekker.
--Chemistry of Biosurfaces, Vol. 2. 1972. 65.00 o.p. (ISBN 0-8247-1284-6). Dekker.
Hairston, jt. auth. see Trimmer.
Hairston, Florence. Nifty Nina, Ghetto Girl. 1979. 4.50 o.p. (ISBN 0-533-03561-9). Vantage.
Hairston, Maxine, jt. auth. see Trimmer, Joseph.
Hairston, Maxine C. A Contemporary Rhetoric. 3rd ed. LC 81-83233. 1982. 14.95 (ISBN 0-395-31494-1); instr's manual 1.00 (ISBN 0-395-31495-X). HM.
--Successful Writing: A Rhetoric for Advanced Composition. 284p. text ed. 14.95x (ISBN 0-393-95148-0); instructor's manual avail. (ISBN 0-393-95171-5). Norton.
Haisman, P. & Muller, B. R. Glossary of Clinical Chemistry Terms. 133p. 1974. 13.95 (ISBN 0-407-72700-0). Butterworth.
Haist, Grant. Modern Photographic Processing, 2 vols. LC 78-17559. (Photographic Science & Technology & Graphic Arts Ser.). 1979. Set. 117.50 (ISBN 0-471-04286-2); Vol. 1. 69.95 (ISBN 0-471-02228-4); Vol. 2. 67.50 (ISBN 0-471-04285-4, Pub. by Wiley-Interscience). Wiley.
Haitani, Kanji. The Japanese Economic System: An Institutional Overview. LC 76-11972. 208p. 1976. 21.95x (ISBN 0-669-00716-1). Lexington Bks.
Haitani, Kanji, jt. auth. see Batchelder, Alan.
Haith, Douglas A. Environmental Systems Optimization. LC 81-3050. 306p. 1982. text ed. 35.95 (ISBN 0-471-08287-2) (ISBN 0-471-86673-3). avail. solutions manual. Wiley.
Haith, Douglas A., ed. see Cornell University Agricultural Waste Management Conference, 10th, 1978.
Haith, Marshall M. Rules That Babies Look by: The Organization of Newborn Visual Activity. LC 80-10601. (Illus.). 146p. 1980. text ed. 19.95x (ISBN 0-89859-033-7). L Erlbaum Assocs.
Haiz, Danah. Jonah's Journey. LC 72-268. (Foreign Lands Bks.). Orig. Title: Jonah Learns a Lesson. (Illus.). 32p. (gr. k-5). 1973. PLB 5.95g (ISBN 0-8225-0362-X). Lerner Pubns.
Hajarnavis, C. R., jt. auth. see Chatters, A. W.
Hajdu, George, tr. see Pecsi, Kalman.
Hajdu, P., jt. ed. see Deszo, L.
Hajdu, P., jt. ed. see Dezso, L.
Hajek, V. Management of Engineering Projects. 2nd ed. 1977. 27.50 (ISBN 0-07-025534-2). McGraw.
Hajnal, A. & Bos, V. T., eds. Combinatorics, 2 Vols. (Proceedings). 1978. Set. 159.75 (ISBN 0-444-85095-3). Elsevier.
Hajnal, A., et al, eds. see International Colloquium, June 25-July 1, 1973.
Hajnal, Gabriella. The Prince & His Magic Horse. (Illus.). 110p. (gr. 3-7). Date not set. pap. write for info o.p. Newbury Bks.
Hajos, A. Complex Hydrides & Related Reducing Agents in Organic Synthesis. LC 78-14524. (Studies in Organic Chemistry: Vol. 1). 1979. 74.50 (ISBN 0-444-99791-1). Elsevier.
Hajtun, Jozsef, jt. auth. see Tal, Mikhail.
Hakak, Lev. The Foundlings. 1982. pap. write for info. (ISBN 0-86628-028-6). Ridgefield Pub.
Hakala, William T., jt. ed. see Getz, D.
Hakansson, H. International Marketing & Purchasing of Industrial Goods. LC 81-13070. 406p. 1982. 41.95x (ISBN 0-471-27987-0, Pub. by Wiley-Interscience). Wiley.
Hakansson, H. & Gerloff, J., eds. Diatomaceae III: Festschrift Niels Foged on the Occassion of his 75th Birthday. (Nova Hedwigia Beiheft: 73.). (Illus.). 386p. (Orig., Eng. & Ger.). 1982. lib. bdg. 67.50x (ISBN 3-7682-5473-9). Lubrecht & Cramer.
Hake, A. African Metropolis: Nairobi's Self-Help City. 40.00x (ISBN 0-686-96988-X, Pub. by Scottish Academic Pr Scotland). State Mutual Bk.
Hake, Andrew. African Metropolis. LC 75-4266. 1977. 26.00 (ISBN 0-312-00980-1). St Martin.
Hakel, Milton D. & Sorcher, Melvin. Making it Happen: Designing Research with Implementation in Mind. (Studying Organizations: Innovations in Methodology). (Illus.). 144p. 1982. 17.95 (ISBN 0-8039-1865-8); pap. 7.95 (ISBN 0-8039-1866-6). Sage.
Haken, H. Evolution of Order & Chaos in Physics, Chemistry, & Biology: Schloss Elmau, FRG, 1982 Proceedings. (Springer Series in Synergetics: Vol. 17). (Illus.). 287p. 1983. 32.00 (ISBN 0-387-11904-3). Springer-Verlag.
--Light, Vol. 1: Waves, Photons, Atoms. 1981. 34.00 (ISBN 0-444-86020-7). Elsevier.
Haken, H. P. Quantum Field Theory of Solids: An Elementary Introduction. 1977. 64.00 (ISBN 0-7204-0545-9, North-Holland). Elsevier.
Hakenewerth, Quentin. Mary in Modern Spirituality. 52p. (Orig.). 1966. pap. 1.25 (ISBN 0-9608124-2-3). Marianist Com Ctr.
Haker, Loren F. The Li'l Rascals: Tale of a Fish. (Illus.). 66p. (gr. 1-8). Date not set. 7.95 (ISBN 0-9609964-2-7); pap. 4.95 (ISBN 0-9609964-3-5). Haker Books.
--The Li'l Rascals: Timmy & the Bees. (Illus.). 56p. (gr. 1-8). 1983. 7.95 (ISBN 0-9609964-0-0); pap. 4.95 (ISBN 0-9609964-1-9). Haker Books.
Hakes, Adelaide R. Typewriting Speed Studies. 3rd ed. 1938. pap. 3.92 o.p. (ISBN 0-07-025512-1, G). McGraw.
Hakes, David T., jt. auth. see Foss, Donald J.
Hakim, K. A. Islam & Communism. pap. 8.50 (ISBN 0-686-18576-5). Kazi Pubns.
--The Prophet & His Message. 6.50 (ISBN 0-686-18422-X). Kazi Pubns.
Hakkert, A. S., et al, eds. Traffic, Transportation & Urban Planning, Vols. I & II. (International Forum Ser.). 1981. Set. 65.00 (ISBN 0-87933-041-4). Vol. I, 245pp (ISBN 0-87933-402-9). Vol. II, 260pp (ISBN 0-87933-403-7). Hutchinson Ross.
Haklisch, Carmela S., jt. ed. see Fusfeld, Herbert I.
Hakluyt, Richard. Voyages & Discoveries. Beeching, Jack, ed. (Penguin English Library). 1982. pap. 5.95 (ISBN 0-14-043073-3). Penguin.
Hakon, H. Concepts & Models of a Quantitative Sociology: The/Dynamics of Interacting Populations. (Ser. in Synergetics: Vol. 14). (Illus.). 217p. 1983. 31.50 (ISBN 0-387-11358-4). Springer-Verlag.

Hakutani, Yoshinobu. Critical Essays on Richard Wright. (Critical Essays on American Literature). 1982. 25.00 (ISBN 0-8161-8425-9, Twayne). G K Hall.

Halacsy, E. de see De Halacsy, E.

Halacy, D. S. Feast & Famine. (Nature of Man Ser). (Illus.). (gr. 7up). 1971. 6.25 (ISBN 0-8255-4031-3). Macrae.

Halacy, D. S., Jr. Century Twenty-One: Your Life in the Year 2001 & Beyond. LC 68-31148. (Illus.). (gr. 5-8). 1968. 5.95 (ISBN 0-8255-4028-3). Macrae.

--The Coming Age of Solar Energy. 1975. pap. 2.25 o.s.i. (ISBN 0-380-00233-7, 38034). Avon.

--The Coming Age of Solar Energy. rev. ed. LC 72-79670. (Illus.). 256p. (YA) 1973. 12.45i (ISBN 0-06-011714-1, HarpT). Har-Row.

--Earth, Water, Wind & Sun: The Energy Alternatives. LC 76-5128. (Illus.). 192p. (YA) 1977. 11.49i (ISBN 0-06-011777-X, HarpT). Har-Row.

--Government by the States. LC 72-88760. 1973. 6.95 o.p. (ISBN 0-672-51707-8). Bobbs.

--Habitat: Man's Universe & Ecology. LC 70-127428. (Nature of Man Ser). (gr. 7 up). 1970. 6.25 (ISBN 0-8255-4029-1). Macrae.

--Man Alive: Life & Man's Physical Nature. LC 70-112731. (Nature of Man Ser.). (Illus.). 192p. (gr. 7 up). 1970. 6.50 (ISBN 0-8255-4040-2). Macrae.

--On the Move: Man & Transportation. (Nature of Man Ser.: Bk. 5). (Illus.). 192p. (gr. 7 up). 1974. 6.25 (ISBN 0-8255-4042-9). Macrae.

--Social Man: The Relationships of Humankind. (Nature of Man Ser.: Bk. 4). 176p. (gr. 7up). 1973. 6.25 (ISBN 0-8255-4041-0). Macrae.

Halacy, Daniel S., Jr. X-Rays & Gamma Rays. (Illus.). 160p. (gr. 7 up). 1969. 6.95 o.p. (ISBN 0-8234-0154-5). Holiday.

Halamandaris, Val J., jt. auth. see Moss, Frank E.

Halapy, Lili, tr. see Garas, Klara.

Halapy, Lili, tr. see Mucsi, Andras.

Halapy, Lilli, tr. see Sebestyen, Tibor.

Halapy, Lily, tr. see Kisdegi-Kirimi, Iren.

Halasi-Kun, George J. Pollution & Water Resources: Water Quality, Plant Fertilization & Other Topics. (Columbia University Seminar Ser.: Vol. 15-1). (Illus.). 252p. 1983. 50.00 (ISBN 0-08-029400-6). Pergamon.

Halasz, Nicholas. Captain Dreyfus: The Story of Mass Hysteria. 1968. pap. 7.75 (ISBN 0-671-20029-1, Touchstone Bks). S&S.

Halasz, Zoltan. Hungarian Paprika Through the Ages. LC 67-1396. (Illus.). 1963. 4.50x o.p. (ISBN 0-8002-0829-3). Intl Pubns Serv.

--Hungary. (Illus.). 212p. 1982. 34.95 (ISBN 0-8044-5476-0). Ungar.

Halbach, Edward C. & Scoles, Eugene F. Cases & Materials on Future Interests. 1977. pap. text ed. 12.50 (ISBN 0-316-33840-0). Little.

Halbash, Mary F. The Fallible Plot. LC 81-85572. 144p. 1983. pap. 5.95. GWP.

Halberg, F., ed. see International Congress of Pharmacology.

Halberstam, David. The Breaks of the Game. 480p. 1983. pap. 3.95 (ISBN 0-345-29625-7). Ballantine.

--Unfinished Odyssey of Robert Kennedy. LC 69-14435. 1969. 4.95 (ISBN 0-394-45025-6). Random.

Halberstam, H. & Roth, K. Sequences. 293p. 1983. Repr. of 1966 ed. 28.00 (ISBN 0-387-90801-3). Springer-Verlag.

Halberstam, H., ed. see Hamilton, William R.

Halbert, H. S. & Ball, T. H. Creek War of 1813 & 1814. Owsley, Frank L., Jr., ed. LC 74-92656. (Southern Historical Ser: Vol. 15). 331p. 1969. Repr. of 1895 ed. 19.95 o.s.i. (ISBN 0-8173-5220-1). U of Ala Pr.

Halbfas, Hubert. Theory of Catechetics: Language & Experience in Religious Education. LC 74-114153. 1971. 1.00 (ISBN 0-8164-1130-1). Seabury.

Halbouty, Michel T. Salt Domes, Gulf Region, United States & Mexico. 2nd ed. 584p. 1979. 64.95 (ISBN 0-87201-803-2). Gulf Pub.

Halbur, Bernice T. Turnover Among Nursing Personnel in Nursing Homes. Kalisch, Philip & Kalisch, Beatrice, eds. LC 82-8353. (Studies in Nursing Management: No. 2). 116p. 1982. 34.95 (ISBN 0-8357-1354-7). Univ Microfilms.

Halbwachs, Maurice. The Collective Memory. Ditter, Francis J., Jr. & Ditter, Vida Y., trs. from Fr. LC 74-18576. 256p. (Orig.). 1980. pap. 5.95i o.p. (ISBN 0-06-090800-9, CN 800, CN). Har-Row.

Halcombe, Alvin. Find-a-Word Puzzles for Vo-Ag Students: Set 1. 1981. pap. 10.75x (ISBN 0-8134-2164-0, 2164). Interstate.

Halcroft, H. An Outline of Great Western Locomotive Practice Eighteen Thirty-Seven to Nineteen Forty-Seven. 18.50 (ISBN 0-392-08863-0, SpS). Sportshelf.

Halcrow, Harold G. Economics of Agriculture. (Illus.). 352p. 1980. text ed. 27.50x (ISBN 0-07-025556-3). McGraw.

--Food Policy for America. (TBD Ser.). (Illus.). 1977. text ed. 32.50 (ISBN 0-07-025550-4, C). McGraw.

Hald, Marie M. Jesus Jewels. 112p. 1983. 5.00 (ISBN 0-682-49963-3). Exposition.

Hald, Tage & Bradley, William E. The Urinary Bladder - Neurology & Dynamics. (Illus.). 339p. 1982. 50.00 (ISBN 0-683-03866-4). Williams & Wilkins.

Haldane, Bernard. How to Make a Habit of Success. 240p. 1977. pap. 3.50 o.p. (ISBN 0-446-30501-4). Warner Bks.

Haldane, Charlotte. Mozart. LC 75-3733. (Illus.). 1976. Repr. of 1960 ed. lib. bdg. 15.50x (ISBN 0-8371-8062-7, HAMOZ). Greenwood.

Haldane, Charlotte, tr. see Lange, Johannes.

Haldane, Duncan. Mamluk Painting. 107p. 1978. text ed. 48.00x (ISBN 0-686-86097-7, Pub. by Aris & Phillips England). Humanities.

Haldane, E. George Eliot & Her Times. LC 74-11022. (George Eliot Ser., No. 74). 1974. lib. bdg. 36.95x (ISBN 0-8383-1848-7). Haskell.

Haldane, E. S., ed. see Descartes, Rene.

Haldane, E. S., tr. see Hegel, Georg W.

Haldane, J. D. & Alexander, D. A., eds. Models for Psychotherapy: A Primer. 96p. 1982. pap. 9.00 (ISBN 0-08-028446-9). Pergamon.

Haldane, John S. Organisms & Enviorment as Illustrated by the Physiology of Breathing. 1917. text ed. 32.50x (ISBN 0-686-83659-6). Elliots Bks.

Haldane, R. A. The Hidden War. LC 77-12279. (Illus.). 1978. 8.95 o.p. (ISBN 0-312-37197-7). St Martin.

--The Hidden World. LC 76-23196. 1977. 8.95 o.p. (ISBN 0-312-37205-1). St Martin.

Halde, du see Du Halde.

Haldeman, Jack C., II. Vector Analysis. LC 78-16216. 1978. 8.95 o.p. (ISBN 0-399-12267-2, Pub. by Berkley). Putnam Pub Group.

Haldeman, Jack C., II, jt. auth. see Haldeman, Joe.

Haldeman, Joe & Haldeman, Jack C., II. There is No Darkness. Date not set. pap. price not set (Pub. by Ace Science Fiction). Ace Bks.

Haldeman, Joe, ed. Study War No More: A Selection of Alternatives. 1978. pap. 2.25 (ISBN 0-380-40519-9, 52205). Avon.

--Study War No More: A Selection of Alternatives. 1977. 8.95 o.p. (ISBN 0-312-77315-3). St Martin.

Haldeman-Julius, E. Iconoclastic Literary Reactions. 128p. pap. 4.00 (ISBN 0-686-95280-4). Am Atheist.

--What Can a Free Man Believe. 55p. pap. 3.00 (ISBN 0-686-95351-7). Am Atheist.

Halderman, John W. United Nations & the Rule of Law. LC 66-25578. 248p. 1966. 12.50 (ISBN 0-379-00287-6). Oceana.

Haldi, John F. Basic Mathematics: Skills & Structure. (Illus., LC 77-073943). 1978. pap. text ed. 19.95 (ISBN 0-395-25117-6); instr's manual 2.15 (ISBN 0-395-25114-1). HM.

Hale, Alan M. Patenting Manual. Rev. ed. (Illus.). 362p. 1982. pap. 58.50 (ISBN 0-943418-01-1). Self Patent.

--Self-Patenting Manual: How to Get a United States Patent. (Illus.). 360p. 1982. pap. 58.50 o.p. (ISBN 0-943418-00-3). Self Patent.

Hale, Annie R. These Cults. 1981. 7.95 (ISBN 0-686-76751-9). Regent House.

Hale, Arlene. In the Name of Love. (Candlelight Romance Ser.: No. 679). (Orig.). 1981. pap. 1.75 o.s.i. (ISBN 0-440-14724-7). Dell.

--In the Name of Love. LC 82-10666. 285p. 1982. 10.95 (ISBN 0-89621-388-9). Thorndike Pr.

--Love's Sweet Surrender. (Orig.). 1980. pap. 1.50 o.s.i. (ISBN 0-440-15105-8). Dell.

--Nurse in the Rockies. (YA) 1980. 6.95 (ISBN 0-686-76782-9, Avalon). Bouregy.

--The Other Side of the World. 1976. Repr. lib. bdg. 11.50 o.p. (ISBN 0-8161-6406-1, Large Print Bks). G K Hall.

--The Stormy Sea of Love. (Orig.). 1976. pap. 1.50 o.p. (ISBN 0-451-07938-8, W7938, Sig). NAL.

Hale, Austin. Worksheets for a First Course in Transformational Snytax. 84p. 1965. pap. 5.00 o.p. (ISBN 0-88312-670-2); 1.50 o.p. (ISBN 0-88312-725-3). Summer Inst Ling.

Hale, Austin, ed. Clause, Sentence & Discourse Patterns in Selected Languages of Nepal, 4 pts. Pt. 1, 462p. pap. 10.50x (ISBN 0-88312-043-7); Pt. 2, 248p. pap. 7.50x (ISBN 0-88312-044-5); Pt. 3, 434p. pap. 10.00x (ISBN 0-88312-045-3); Pt. 4, 314p. pap. 8.50x (ISBN 0-88312-046-1); Set. pap. 35.00x (ISBN 0-88312-042-9); microfiche pt. 1 4.50x, (0-88312-443-2), microfiche pt. 2 3.00x, (0-88312-444-0), microfiche pt. 3 4.50x, (0-88312-445-9), microfiche pt. 4 2.25x, (0-88312-446-7), set 14.25x (ISBN 0-88312-442-4). Summer Inst Ling.

Hale, Charles D. Police Patrol: Operations & Administration. LC 80-36814. 328p. 1981. text ed. 24.95 (ISBN 0-471-03291-3); Avail Tchr's Manual (ISBN 0-471-08901-X). Wiley.

Hale, Clarence B. Let's Study Greek. rev. ed. LC 82-3619. 1982. 12.95 (ISBN 0-8024-4666-3). Moody.

Hale, Clarence E. From a New England Town. LC 75-21355. (Illus.). 104p. 1975. pap. 3.95 o.p. (ISBN 0-914016-23-7). Phoenix Pub.

Hale, Creighton H. Official Little League Baseball Rules in Pictures. (Illus.). 80p. (gr. 3-7). 1981. pap. 3.95 (ISBN 0-686-79526-1, G&D). Putnam Pub Group.

Hale, Creighton J. Official Little League Baseball Rules in Pictures. (Illus.). 80p. (gr. 2-7). 1982. pap. 3.95 (ISBN 0-448-15465-X, G&D). Putnam Pub Group.

Hale, Dennis. The United States Congress. 360p. 1983. pap. 14.95 (ISBN 0-87855-939-6). Transaction Bks.

Hale, Donald, jt. auth. see Robicsek, Francis.

Hale, E. M., et al. Introduction to Applied Drawing. rev. ed. (gr. 7 up). 1962. pap. 5.28 (ISBN 0-87345-051-5). McKnight.

Hale, Ellen T. What If There's a Rainbow. LC 79-90649. (Illus.). 1979. 7.95 (ISBN 0-87716-112-7, Pub. by Moore Pub Co). F Apple.

Hale, Francis J. Introduction to Control System Analysis & Design. (Illus.). 400p. 1973. ref. ed. 29.95 (ISBN 0-13-479824-4). P-H.

Hale, Francis J., jt. auth. see Doolittle, Jesse S.

Hale, Frederick, jt. ed. see Sandeen, Ernest R.

Hale, Geoffrey & Roberts, Nesta. A Doctor in Practice. 1974. 10.25x o.p. (ISBN 0-7100-7745-9). Routledge & Kegan.

Hale, George, jt. auth. see Palley, Marion.

Hale, Guy A., jt. auth. see Plunkett, Lorne C.

Hale, Irina. Brown Bear in a Brown Chair. LC 82-16244. (Illus.). 32p. (ps-3). 1983. 9.95 (ISBN 0-689-50267-2, McElderry Bk). Atheneum.

Hale, J. R. Renaissance Europe: The Individual & Society, 1480-1520. LC 77-73495. (Library Reprint Ser.). 1978. 27.50x (ISBN 0-520-03470-8); pap. 7.95x (ISBN 0-520-03471-6). U of Cal Pr.

Hale, J R., ed. Concise Encyclopedia of the Italian Renaissance. (World of Art Ser.). (Illus.). 1981. pap. 9.95 (ISBN 0-19-520285-6). Oxford U Pr.

Hale, John. The Fundamentals of Radiological Science. (Illus.). 356p. 1974. 21.50x o.p. (ISBN 0-398-02805-2). C C Thomas.

Hale, John, jt. ed. see Highfield, Beryl S.

Hale, John R. Age of Exploration. LC 66-20552. (Great Ages of Man). (Illus.). (gr. 6 up). 1966. PLB 11.97 o.p. (ISBN 0-8094-0369-2, Pub. by Time-Life). Silver.

--Renaissance. LC 65-28051. (Great Ages of Man). (Illus., Fr.). (gr. 6 up). 1965. PLB 11.97 o.p. (ISBN 0-8094-0366-8, Pub. by Time-Life). Silver.

Hale, John R., ed. Renaissance Venice. LC 72-12940. (Illus.). 483p. 1973. 40.00x o.p. (ISBN 0-87471-166-5); pap. 14.50x o.p. (ISBN 0-87471-825-2). Rowman.

Hale, Judson. Inside New England. LC 82-47524. 224p. 1982. 12.45i (ISBN 0-06-015033-5, HarpT). Har-Row.

Hale, Julian. Black Summer. 296p. 1982. 16.95 (ISBN 0-241-10767-9, Pub. by Hamish Hamilton England). David & Charles.

--Radio Power: Propaganda & International Broadcasting. LC 75-18694. (International & Comparative Broadcasting Ser.). 216p. 1975. 19.95 (ISBN 0-87722-049-2). Temple U Pr.

Hale, Leon. A Smile from Katie Hattan & Other Natural Wonders. LC 82-60563. 288p. 1982. 13.95 (ISBN 0-940672-07-3). Shearer Pub.

Hale, Mabel. Emma Bailey Seeks Truth. 24p. 1982. pap. 0.25 (ISBN 0-686-36258-6); pap. 1.00 5 copies (ISBN 0-686-37283-2). Faith Pub Hse.

Hale, Mason E. The Biology of Lichens. 2nd ed. LC 74-12607. (Contempory Biology Ser.). 181p. 1980. 22.00 (ISBN 0-444-19531-9); pap. 9.00 (ISBN 0-444-19530-0). Univ Park.

--Biology of Lichens. 192p. 1974. pap. text ed. 14.95 (ISBN 0-7131-2457-1). E Arnold.

Hale, Matthew, Jr. Human Science & Social Order: Hugo Munsterberg & the Origins of Applied Psychology. 256p. 1980. 29.95 (ISBN 0-87722-154-5). Temple U Pr.

Hale, Merle L., ed. Year Book of Dentistry 1983. 1983. 40.00 (ISBN 0-8151-4093-2). Year Bk Med.

Hale, Merle L., et al, eds. Year Book of Dentistry, 1982. (Illus.). 520p. 1982. 39.00 (ISBN 0-8151-4098-3). Year Bk Med.

Hale, Nancy. The Night of the Hurricane. LC 77-15454. (gr. 6-10). 1978. 6.95 o.p. (ISBN 0-698-20437-9, Coward). Putnam Pub Group.

--The Realities of Fiction: A Book About Writing. LC 76-53839. 1977. Repr. of 1962 ed. lib. bdg. 18.75x (ISBN 0-8371-9351-6, HARE). Greenwood.

Hale, Nathan C. Welded Sculpture. (Illus.). 192p. 1968. 14.95 o.p. (ISBN 0-8230-5700-3). Watson-Guptill.

Hale, Nathan C., jt. auth. see Nygaard, Kaare.

Hale, Norman B., jt. auth. see Rugg, Donald D.

Hale, P., jt. auth. see McClelland, L.

Hale, Philip. Great Concert Music: Philip Hale's Boston Symphont Programme Notes. Burk, John N., ed. LC 75-109742. xix, 400p. Repr. of 1939 ed. lib. bdg. 19.00x (ISBN 0-8371-4232-6, HACM). Greenwood.

Hale, Ralph W. & Krieger, John A. Concise Textbook of Gynecology. (Concise Textbook Ser.). 1982. pap. text ed. 21.00 (ISBN 0-87488-585-X). Med Exam.

Hale, Robert B. & Coyle, Terence. Albinus on Anatomy. (Illus.). 1979. 19.95 (ISBN 0-8230-0221-7). Watson-Guptill.

Hale, Robert G. & Smith, Lotsee P. Readings in Instructional Media & Special Education. (Special Education Ser.). (Illus., Orig.). 1980. pap. text ed. 15.00 (ISBN 0-89568-191-9). Spec Learn Corp.

Hale, Sara A., tr. see Mullins, Edgar Y.

Hale, Sara A., tr. see Robertson, A. T.

Hale, William H. World of Rodin. LC 70-105511. (Library of Art Ser.). (Illus.). (gr. 6 up). 1969. 19.92 (ISBN 0-8094-0283-1, Pub. by Time-Life). Silver.

Halebsky, S. Mass Society & Political Conflict. LC 75-18118. (Illus.). 320p. 1976. 37.50 (ISBN 0-521-20541-7); pap. 11.95 (ISBN 0-521-09884-X). Cambridge U Pr.

Halecki, O. Borderlands of Western Civilization: A History of East Central Europe. 1952. 26.95 (ISBN 0-471-07048-3). Wiley.

Halecki, Oscar. A History of Poland. (Illus.). 384p. 1976. 9.95 o.p. (ISBN 0-679-50593-8); pap. 7.95 (ISBN 0-679-51087-7). McKay.

--The History of Poland. 1982. pap. 5.95 cancelled (ISBN 0-89526-865-5). Regnery-Gateway.

Halek, V. & Svec, J. Groundwater Hydraulics. (Development in Water Science: Vol. 7). 1979. 104.25 (ISBN 0-444-99820-9). Elsevier.

Hales. Contact Lenses: A Clinical Approach to Fitting. (Illus.). 261p. 1978. pap. 26.50 o.p. (ISBN 0-683-03850-8). Williams & Wilkins.

Hales, Ann. The Children of Skylard Ward. LC 77-80836. 1978. 14.95 (ISBN 0-521-21752-0). Cambridge U Pr.

Hales, Dianne & Creasy, Robert K. New Hope for Problem Pregnancies: Helping Babies Before They're Born. LC 81-47657. (Illus.). 288p. 1982. 14.37i (ISBN 0-06-014934-5, HarpT). Har-Row.

Hales, Dianne, jt. auth. see DeVries, Herbert A.

Hales, J. P., Jr., ed. Precipitation Chemistry, Vol. 2. 200p. 1982. 35.00 (ISBN 0-08-028782-4). Pergamon.

Hales, John W., et al, eds. see Percy, Bishop.

Hales, Peter B. Silver Cities: The Photography of American Urbanization. 1983. write for info. (ISBN 0-87722-299-1). Temple U Pr.

Hales, Robert. Contact Lenses: A Clinical Approach to Fitting. 2nd ed. 369p. 1982. text ed. 49.95 (ISBN 0-683-03851-6). Williams & Wilkins.

Hales, S. Vegetable Staticks. 1970. 8.95 (ISBN 0-444-19704-4). Elsevier.

Halevi, Z'Ev B. Kabbalah & Exodus. LC 80-50743. 234p. Date not set. pap. 7.95 o.p. (ISBN 0-394-73950-7). Random.

--The Way of the Kabbalah. 1982. pap. 5.00 (ISBN 0-87728-305-2). Weiser.

Haley, Alex. Roots. 1977. pap. 4.95 (ISBN 0-440-17464-3). Dell.

Haley, Charles W. & Schall, Larry. The Theory of Financial Decisions. 2nd ed. (Illus.). 1979. text ed. 28.95 (ISBN 0-07-025568-7, C). McGraw.

Haley, Charles W. & Schall, Lawrence D. Theory of Financial Decisions. (Finance Ser.). (Illus.). 1973. text ed. 19.00 o.p. (ISBN 0-07-025567-9, C). McGraw.

Haley, Charles W., jt. auth. see Schall, Lawrence D.

Haley, Gail E. Costumes for Plays & Playing. (Illus.). (gr. 3 up). 1978. 9.95 (ISBN 0-416-30581-4). Methuen Inc.

--Jack Jouett's Ride. (Viking Seafarer Ser.). (Illus.). (gr. 1-4). 1976. pap. 2.95 o.p. (ISBN 0-670-05102-0, Puffin). Penguin.

Haley, J., jt. auth. see Bachelor, A.

Haley, J. Evetts. Jeff Milton: A Good Man with a Gun. (Illus.). 432p. 1981. 25.00 (ISBN 0-8061-0182-2); pap. 11.95 (ISBN 0-8061-1756-7). U of Okla Pr.

Haley, Jay. Leaving Home: The Therapy of Disturbed Young People. 1980. 21.95 (ISBN 0-07-025570-9). McGraw.

--Problem Solving Therapy. 1978. pap. 5.72i (ISBN 0-06-090583-2, CN 583, CN). Har-Row.

--Uncommon Therapy: The Psychiatric Techniques of Milton H. Erickson, M. D. 1977. Repr. of 1973 ed. 10.00x o.p. (ISBN 0-393-01100-3, Norton Lib); pap. 4.95 (ISBN 0-393-00846-0). Norton.

Haley, Jay, jt. auth. see Glick, Ira D.

Haley, Jocelyn. La Nymph de Sioux Lake. (Harlequin Seduction Ser.). 332p. 1983. pap. 3.25 (ISBN 0-373-45016-8). Harlequin Bks.

--Serenade for a Lost Love. (Super Romances Ser.). 384p. 1983. pap. 2.95 (ISBN 0-373-70054-7, Pub. by Worldwide). Harlequin Bks.

Haley, K. B., jt. auth. see IFORS International Conference on Operational Research, 7th, Japan, 1975.

Haley, K. H. William of Orange & the English Opposition, 1672-4. LC 74-30846. 231p. 1975. Repr. of 1953 ed. lib. bdg. 15.50x (ISBN 0-8371-7934-3, HAWO). Greenwood.

Haley, K. H., ed. The Stuarts. LC 73-82822. 224p. 1973. 22.50 (ISBN 0-312-76930-X). St Martin.

Halfacre, Gordon & Barden, John A. Horticulture. (Illus.). 1979. text ed. 31.00 (ISBN 0-07-025573-3, C). McGraw.

Halfin, Ross & Makowski, Pete. Heavy Metal. (Illus., Orig.). 1982. pap. 8.95 (ISBN 0-933328-38-9). Delilah Bks.

Halfman, Marsha, jt. auth. see Hojnacki, Linda.

Halfpenny, Peter. Positivism & Sociology: Explaining Social Life. (Controversies in Sociology Ser.: Vol. 13). 130p. 1982. text ed. 22.50x (ISBN 0-04-300084-3); pap. text ed. 7.95x (ISBN 0-04-300085-1). Allen Unwin.

Haliburton, Gordon M. The Prophet Harris: A Study of an African Prophet & His Mass-Movement in the Ivory Coast & the Gold Coast, 1913-1915. (Illus.). 1973. pap. 3.95 o.p. (ISBN 0-19-501625-4). Oxford U Pr.

Haliczer, Stephen. The Comuneros of Castile: The Forging of a Revolution 1475-1521. LC 80-52294. 320p. 1981. 22.50x (ISBN 0-299-08500-7). U of Wis Pr.

Halifax, Joan. Shamanic Voices: A Survey of Visionary Narratives. 1979. pap. 9.95 (ISBN 0-525-47525-7, 0966-290). Dutton.

Halio, Jay, ed. British Novelists Since 1960, 2 vols. (Dictionary of Literary Biography Ser.: Vol. 14). (Illus.). 400p. 1983. 148.00x (ISBN 0-8103-0927-0). Gale.

Halioua, Jean-Pierre, et al. Aventures En Ville. LC 79-63579. (gr. 9-12). 1980. pap. text ed. 6.64 (ISBN 0-395-27833-3). HM.

Halkias, Christos, jt. auth. see Millman, Jacob.

Halkin, A. S., tr. see Ibn-Tahir, Abd-Al-Kahir.

Halkin, Francois. Etudes D'Epigraphie Grecque et D'Hagiographique Byzantine. 416p. 1973. 55.00x (ISBN 0-686-97603-7, Pub. by Variorum). State Mutual Bk.

Halkin, Hillel, tr. see Goldberg, Lea.

Hall. Dictionary of Energy. (Energy, Power & Environment Ser.). 360p. 1983. price not set (ISBN 0-8247-1793-7). Dekker.

--Language of Advertising & Merchandising in English. (English for Careers Ser.). (gr. 10 up). 1982. pap. text ed. 3.75 (ISBN 0-88345-353-3). Regents Pub.

Hall, jt. auth. see Barrows.

Hall, A. Drought & Irrigation in North-East Brazil. LC 77-82497. (Latin American Studies: No. 29). (Illus.). 1978. 29.95 (ISBN 0-521-21811-X). Cambridge U Pr.

--Scandal, Sensation & Social Democracy. LC 76-46856. 1977. 37.50 (ISBN 0-521-21531-5). Cambridge U Pr.

Hall, A. R. Philosophers at War. LC 79-15724. 1980. 34.50 (ISBN 0-521-22732-1). Cambridge U Pr.

Hall, A. S., et al. Machine Design. (Orig.). 1961. pap. 8.95 (ISBN 0-07-025595-4, SP). McGraw.

Hall, Adam. The Scorpion Signal. LC 79-8284. 1980. 10.00 o.p. (ISBN 0-385-12277-2). Doubleday.

Hall, Alla T., tr. see Rottgen, Steffi, et al.

Hall, Allan, jt. ed. see Kenward, Harry.

Hall, Amanda B. Frosty Harp. 1954. 2.50 o.p. (ISBN 0-8233-0037-4). Golden Quill.

--View from the Heart. 1964. 3.00 o.p. (ISBN 0-8233-0038-2). Golden Quill.

Hall, Anna H. & Ford, George A. Personal Planning Workbook. 3rd ed. 1979. 9.95 (ISBN 0-934698-12-0). New Comm Pr.

Hall, Archibald J. Standard Handbook of Textiles. 8th ed. 1970. 41.95x (ISBN 0-87245-596-3). Textile Bk.

Hall, Audley S., jt. auth. see Quinn, William A.

Hall, Avery & Korty, John. Twice Upon a Time. (Illus.). 48p. 1983. 6.95 (ISBN 0-671-27074-5, Little). S&S.

Hall, B. C., jt. auth. see Lancaster, Bob.

Hall, B. P. & Moreau, R. E. An Atlas of Speciation in African Passerine Birds. (Illus.). 422p. 1970. text ed. 102.50x (ISBN 0-565-00680-0, Pub. by Brit Mus Nat Hist). Sabbot-Natural Hist Bks.

Hall, B. P., ed. Birds of the Harold Hall Australian Expeditions: 1962-1970. (Illus.). 1974. text ed. 47.50x (ISBN 0-565-00745-9, Pub. by Brit Mus Nat Hist). Sabbot-Natural Hist Bks.

Hall, B. T. Auditing the Modern Hospital. 256p. 1977. 32.95 (ISBN 0-686-68587-3, 14920). Healthcare Fin Man Assn.

Hall, Barbara, jt. auth. see Hall, Claude.

Hall, Ben M. The Best Remaining Seats: The Story of the Golden Age of the Movie Palace. (Illus.). 278p. 1961. 15.00 (ISBN 0-517-02057-2, C N Potter Bks). Crown.

--The Golden Age of the Movie Palace: The Best Remaining Seats. (Illus.). 272p. 1975. pap. 4.95 o.p. (ISBN 0-517-52450-3, C N Potter Bks). Crown.

Hall, Benjamin H. Collection of College Words & Customs. LC 68-17995. 1968. Repr. of 1856 ed. 42.00x (ISBN 0-8103-3282-5). Gale.

Hall, Bill, ed. Bill Hall & the Killer Chicken. (Illus.). 102p. 1981. pap. 4.95 (ISBN 0-9607506-0-6). News Rev Pub.

Hall, Brandon, ed. OBM in Multiple Business Environments: New Applications for Organizational Behavior Management. LC 82-15417. (Journal of Organizational Behavior Management Ser.: Vol. 4, Nos. 1 & 2). 188p. 1983. text ed. 19.95 (ISBN 0-86656-189-7, B189). Haworth Pr.

Hall, Brenny, illus. Old MacDonald. (Cut & Paste Ser.). (Illus.). (ps-3). 1981. 3.50 (ISBN 0-686-38117-3). Moonlight FL.

Hall, Brian. The Wizard of Maldoone. LC 75-34844. 1976. 8.95 o.p. (ISBN 0-8091-0203-X); pap. 4.95 o.p. (ISBN 0-8091-1922-6). Paulist Pr.

Hall, Brian, et al. Readings in Value Development. 1982. pap. 11.95 (ISBN 0-8091-2448-3). Paulist Pr.

Hall, Brian K., ed. Cartilage: Biomedical Aspects, Vol. 3. LC 82-20566. Date not set. price not set (ISBN 0-12-319503-9). Acad Pr.

--Cartilage: Structure & Function & Biochemistry, Vol. 1. LC 82-11566. 420p. 1982. 55.00 (ISBN 0-12-319501-2). Acad Pr.

Hall, Bud L. & Kidd, Roby, eds. Adult Learning: A Design for Action: A Comprehensive International Survey. 1978. write for info. (ISBN 0-08-022245-5). Pergamon.

Hall, C. & Sayles, S. The Sewing Machine Craft Book. 1982. pap. 9.95 (ISBN 0-442-23654-9). Van Nos Reinhold.

Hall, Calvin S. Meaning of Dreams. 1966. pap. 5.95 (ISBN 0-07-025608-X, SP). McGraw.

--A Primer of Freudian Psychology. (25th Anniversary Ed.). 1979. pap. 1.95 (ISBN 0-451-62030-5, MJ2030, Ment). NAL.

Hall, Calvin S. & Lindzey, Gardner. Theories of Personality. 3rd ed. LC 77-26692. 1978. text ed. 28.95 (ISBN 0-471-34227-0); wkbk. 9.95 (ISBN 0-471-72926-4); test 3.00 (ISBN 0-471-03755-9). Wiley.

Hall, Calvin S. & Nordby, Vernon. The Individual & His Dream. 1972. pap. 1.95 o.p. (ISBN 0-451-61635-9, MJ1635, Ment). NAL.

Hall, Calvin S. & Nordby, Vernon J. A Primer of Jungian Psychology. 144p. 1973. pap. 1.95 (ISBN 0-451-62067-4, ME2067, Ment). NAL.

Hall, Carol, jt. auth. see Calloway, Northern J.

Hall, Caroline, jt. auth. see Breese, Burtis B.

Hall, Cecil E. Introduction to Electron Microscopy. LC 80-39788. 410p. 1983. Repr. of 1966 ed. lib. bdg. write for info. (ISBN 0-89874-302-8). Krieger.

--Introduction to Electron Microscopy. 2nd ed. (Illus.). 1966. text ed. 46.00 o.p. (ISBN 0-07-025606-3, P&RB). McGraw.

Hall, Charles A. & Day, John W., Jr., eds. Ecosystems Modeling in Theory & Practice: An Introduction with Case Histories. LC 76-57204. 1977. 54.95 (ISBN 0-471-34165-7, Pub. by Wiley-Interscience). Wiley.

Hall, Charlotte, ed. see Schuyler, Arlene A.

Hall, Claude & Hall, Barbara. This Business of Radio Programming. (Illus.). 1977. 16.50 (ISBN 0-8230-7760-8, Billboard Bks). Watson-Guptill.

Hall, Clayton C. Great Seal of Maryland. 52p. 1886. 5.50 (ISBN 0-686-36849-5). Md Hist.

Hall, Colby D. Texas Disciples. 1953. 10.00 (ISBN 0-912646-32-2). Tex Christian.

Hall, D. History of the Earth Sciences During the Scientific & Industrial Revolution with Special Emphasis on Physical Geosciences. 1976. 42.75 (ISBN 0-444-41440-1). Elsevier.

Hall, D. J. The Discharge of Fume Cupboard Effluents into the Atmosphere, 1979. 03/1981 ed. 30.00x (ISBN 0-686-97058-6, Pub. by W Spring England). State Mutual Bk.

--Further Experiments on a Model of an Escape of Heavy Gas, 1979. 1981. 45.00x (ISBN 0-686-97083-7, Pub. by W Spring England). State Mutual Bk.

Hall, D. J., et al. Windtunnel Model Experiments on a Buoyant Emission from a Building, 1980. 1981. 40.00x (ISBN 0-686-97134-5, Pub. by W Spring England). State Mutual Bk.

Hall, D. O. & Rao, K. K. Photosynthesis. 3rd ed. (Studies in Biology: No. 37). 80p. 1981. pap. text ed. 8.95 (ISBN 0-7131-2827-5). E Arnold.

Hall, D. O., et al. Biomass for Energy in the Developing Countries: Current Role-Potential-Problems-Prospects. (Illus.). 200p. 1982. 20.00 (ISBN 0-08-028689-5). Pergamon.

Hall, D. V. Microprocessors & Digital Systems. 1980. text ed. 24.50 (ISBN 0-07-025571-7); instr's. manual & key avail. McGraw.

Hall, Daniel G. History of South-East Asia. 3rd ed. LC 68-15302. (Illus.). 1968. 19.95 o.p. (ISBN 0-312-38640-0); pap. 10.95 o.p. (ISBN 0-312-38605-2). St Martin.

Hall, Daniel W., jt. ed. see Block, Richard A.

Hall, David. Eros & Irony: A Prelude to Philosophical Anarchism. LC 81-16579. 288p. 1982. 33.50x (ISBN 0-87395-585-4); 10.95x (ISBN 0-87395-586-2). State U NY Pr.

Hall, David see Bates, Martin & Dudley-Evans, Tony.

Hall, David D., jt. ed. see Joyce, William L.

Hall, David L. The Uncertain Phoenix: Adventures Toward a Post-Cultural Sensibility. LC 80-67033. xviii, 426p. 1982. 40.00 (ISBN 0-8232-1053-7); pap. 20.00 (ISBN 0-8232-1054-5). Fordham.

Hall, David M. Chemical Testing of Textiles. 1975. 26.50x (ISBN 0-87245-544-0). Textile Bk.

Hall, Deborah, jt. auth. see Wilson, Christopher.

Hall, Derek R. A Spatial Analysis of Urban Community Development Policy in India. LC 80-40952. (Geography & Public Policy Research Studies Ser.). 180p. 1980. 49.95 (ISBN 0-471-27862-9, Pub. by Res Stud Pr). Wiley.

Hall, Donald. Goatfoot Milktongue Twinbird. LC 77-3248. (Poets on Poetry Ser.). pap. 7.95 (ISBN 0-472-40000-2). U of Mich Pr.

--Ox-Cart Man. LC 79-14466. (Illus.). (gr. k-3). 1979. 12.95 (ISBN 0-670-53328-9). Viking Pr.

--The Weather for Poetry: Essays, Reviews & Notes on Poetry, 1977-1981. LC 82-8544. (Poets on Poetry Ser.). 304p. 1982. pap. 7.95 (ISBN 0-472-06340-5). U of Mich Pr.

Hall, Donald, ed. Claims for Poetry. 528p. 1982. pap. text ed. 8.95x (ISBN 0-472-06308-1). U of Mich Pr.

--The Pleasures of Poetry. 1971. pap. text ed. 13.50 scp (ISBN 0-06-042604-7, HarpC). Har-Row.

Hall, Donald, ed. see Kinnell, Galway.

Hall, Donald, ed. see Stafford, William.

Hall, Donald, ed. see Whitman, Walt.

Hall, Donald A. Elements of Astronomy & Physical Geography. 176p. (Orig.). 1963. pap. text ed. 8.40 (ISBN 0-686-37058-9). Trippensee Pub.

Hall, Douglas J. Has the Church a Future? LC 79-29647. 1980. pap. 8.95 (ISBN 0-664-24308-8). Westminster.

Hall, Douglas K., jt. auth. see Ferrigno, Lou.

Hall, Douglas K., jt. auth. see Schwarzenegger, Arnold.

Hall, Douglas S. & Genet, Russell M. Photoelectric Photometry of Variable Stars: A Practical Guide for the Smaller Observatory. (Illus.). 282p. (Orig.). 1982. pap. 17.95 (ISBN 0-911351-00-0). Fairborn Observ.

Hall, Douglas T. Careers in Organizations. Porter, Lyman W., ed. LC 75-13446. (Scott Foresman Series in Management & Organizations). 230p. 1976. pap. text ed. 12.50x (ISBN 0-673-16077-7). Scott F.

Hall, Douglas V. Microprocessors & Digital Systems. 2nd ed. (Illus.). 480p. 1983. 22.05 (ISBN 0-07-025552-0, G). McGraw.

Hall, Douglas V. & Hall, Marybelle B. Experiments in Microprocessors & Digital Systems. (Illus.). 176p. 1981. 10.95x (ISBN 0-07-025576-8, G). McGraw.

--Experiments in Microprocessors & Digital Systems. 2nd ed. (Illus.). 192p. 1983. 10.95x (ISBN 0-07-025553-9, Gregg). McGraw.

Hall, E. Carl, jt. auth. see Troelstrup, Archibald.

Hall, E. G. & Scott, K. J. Storage & Market Diseases of Fruit. 1982. 35.00x (ISBN 0-686-97896-X, Pub. by CSIRO Australia). State Mutual Bk.

Hall, E. J. & Rossi, H. H. Californium Two-Fifty-Two in Teaching & Research. (Technical Reports Ser.: No. 159). (Illus.). 141p. 1974. pap. 14.50 (ISBN 92-0-115174-8, IDC159, IAEA). Unipub.

Hall, E. Swann, ed. see Holz, R., et al.

Hall, Edward N. The Art of Destructive Management: What Hath Man Wrought. 1983. 8.95 (ISBN 0-533-05601-2). Vantage.

Hall, Edward T. Dance of Life: The Other Dimension of Time. LC 81-43650. 240p. 1983. 15.95 (ISBN 0-385-15964-1, Anchor Pr). Doubleday.

--Hidden Dimension. LC 66-11173. (Illus.). 1966. pap. 4.50 (ISBN 0-385-08476-5, A609, Anch). Doubleday.

Hall, Eleanor & Skinner, Nancy. Somewhere to Turn: Strategies for Parents of Gifted & Talented Children. Tannenbaum, Abraham J., ed. (Perspectives on Gifted & Talented Education Ser.). (Orig.). 1980. pap. text ed. 5.95x (ISBN 0-8077-2589-7). Tchrs Coll.

Hall, Elizabeth. Child Psychology Today. 608p. 1982. text ed. 21.00 (ISBN 0-394-32568-0). Random.

Hall, Elizabeth, jt. auth. see Hall, James B.

Hall, Elizabeth S., compiled by. Matching Gift Details 1982. 170p. 1981. 25.00 (ISBN 0-89964-197-0); nonmembers 60.00 (ISBN 0-686-82675-2). CASE.

Hall, Ellen & Hall, Emily. Halls of Ravenswood. Mills, A. R., ed. (Illus.). 1968. 6.95 o.p. (ISBN 0-685-20591-6). Transatlantic.

Hall, Elvajean. The Land & People of Norway. rev ed. LC 72-10777. (Portraits of the Nations Series). (Illus.). 1973. 10.53i (ISBN 0-397-31408-6, JBL-J). Har-Row.

Hall, Emily, jt. auth. see Hall, Ellen.

Hall, Eugene. Practical Conversation in English 1. (Practical Conversations in English Ser.). (gr. 9-12). 1981. pap. text ed. 3.95 o.p. (ISBN 0-88345-438-6, 20052). Regents Pub.

Hall, Eugene J. The Language of Mining & Metallurgy in English. (English for Careers Ser.). (gr. 10 up). 1978. pap. text ed. 3.75 (ISBN 0-88345-307-X). Regents Pub.

Hall, Eugene J., ed. The Food We Eat. rev. ed. (Adult ESL Skillbuilders). 64p. 1983. Repr. of 1969 ed. pap. text ed. 4.95 (ISBN 0-88499-812-6). Inst Mod Lang.

--Making Government Work for You. rev. ed. (Adult ESL Skillbuilders Ser.). 80p. (gr. 7-12). 1983. pap. 4.95 (ISBN 0-88499-815-0). Inst Mod Lang.

--The Signs of Life. rev. ed. (Adult ESL Skillbuilders Ser.). 64p. (gr. 7-12). 1983. pap. text ed. 4.95 (ISBN 0-88499-811-8). Inst Mod Lang.

--Sounds & Syllables. rev. ed. (Adult ESL Skillbuilders). 1983. pap. text ed. 4.95 (ISBN 0-88499-816-9). Inst Mod Lang.

Hall, F. M. Introduction to Abstract Algebra, Vol. 1. 2nd ed. (Illus.). 314p. 1980. pap. 14.95 (ISBN 0-521-29861-X). Cambridge U Pr.

--Introduction to Abstract Algebra, Vol. 2. LC 66-10040. (Illus.). 1969. text ed. 39.50x (ISBN 0-521-07055-4). Cambridge U Pr.

--Introduction to Abstract Algebra, Vol. 2. (Illus.). 400p. 1980. pap. 19.95 (ISBN 0-521-29862-8). Cambridge U Pr.

Hall, Fergus. Groundsel. (Illus.). 32p. (ps-4). 1983. 10.95 (ISBN 0-224-01938-4, Pub by Jonathan Cape). Merrimack Bk Serv.

Hall, Florence P., tr. see Jullien, Adolphe.

Hall, Francine & Albrecht, Maryann. The Management of Affirmative Action. new ed. LC 78-24516. (Illus.). 1979. text ed. 25.95x o.p. (ISBN 0-673-16108-0). Scott F.

Hall, Francis B., jt. auth. see Freer, Harold W.

Hall, G. & Jones, H. Competency-Based Education: Process for Improvement of Education. LC 75-17564. (Illus.). 384p. 1975. 24.95 (ISBN 0-13-154864-6). P-H.

Hall, G. K., ed. see Emerson, Ellen T.

Hall, G. Stanley & Mansfield, John M. Hints Toward a Select & Descriptive Bibliography of Education. LC 72-10907. xx, 332p. 1973. Repr. of 1886 ed. 42.00x (ISBN 0-8103-3176-4). Gale.

Hall, George & Burks, John. Working Fire: The San Francisco Fire Department. (Illus.). 1982. pap. 14.94 (ISBN 0-916290-14-X). SquareBooks.

Hall, Gerry. Offbeat Canada: One Hundred & One Unusual Vacation Adventures. (Orig.). 1981. pap. 2.50 o.p. (ISBN 0-451-09842-0, E9842, Sig). NAL.

Hall, Gimone. Fury's Sun, Passion's Moon. 1979. pap. 2.50 o.p. (ISBN 0-451-08748-8, E8748, Sig). NAL.

--Jasmine Veil. 1982. pap. 2.95 (ISBN 0-451-11451-5, AE1451, Sig). NAL.

--Rapture's Mistress. (Orig.). 1978. pap. 2.25 o.p. (ISBN 0-451-08422-5, E8422, Sig). NAL.

Hall, Gus. Ecology: Can We Survive Under Capitalism? LC 72-184673. (Illus.). 96p. (Orig.). 1972. pap. 1.50 o.p. (ISBN 0-7178-0347-3). Intl Pub Co.

--Steel & Metal Workers-It Takes a Fight to Win! 2nd ed. (Illus.). 64p. 1972. pap. 0.25 (ISBN 0-87898-094-6). New Outlook.

Hall, H. Gaston & Brooks, Richard A., eds. A Critical Bibliography of French Literature: Vol. III-A, the Seventeenth Century, Supplement. 464p. 1983. text ed. 65.00x (ISBN 0-8156-2275-9). Syracuse U Pr.

Hall, H. Gaston, ed. see Simone, Franco.

Hall, H. U. The Sherbro of Sierra Leone. (Illus.). 15p. 1938. 4.00x (ISBN 0-686-17762-2). Univ Mus of U PA.

Hall, H. W., ed. Science Fiction & Fantasy Research Index, Vol. 2. 72p. (Orig.). 1982. pap. 7.50x (ISBN 0-935064-12-5). H W Hall.

--Science Fiction Book Review Index, 1923-1973. LC 74-29085. 1975. 110.00x (ISBN 0-8103-1054-6). Gale.

--Science Fiction Book Review Index, 1974 to 1979. 300p. 1981. 110.00x (ISBN 0-8103-1107-0). Gale.

Hall, Hal W., ed. Science-Fiction Collections: Fantasy, Supernatural & Weird Tales. LC 82-21355. (Special Collection Ser.: Vol. 2, Nos. 1 & 2). 1983. 29.95 (ISBN 0-917724-49-6, B49). Haworth Pr.

Hall, Homer L. Junior High Journalism. LC 68-25400. (gr. 7-9). 1981. PLB 7.97 (ISBN 0-8239-0370-2); teacher's wkbk. 5.97 (ISBN 0-685-19889-8); student's wkbk 1.50 (ISBN 0-8239-0277-3). Rosen Pr.

Hall, Howard & Farley, Lauren. Howard Hall's Guide to Successful Underwater Photography. (Illus.). 192p. (Orig.). 1982. pap. text ed. 15.95 (ISBN 0-932248-03-9). Marcor Pub.

Hall, Isaac. The Growth & the Essence of Buddhism. (Illus.). 148p. 1982. Repr. of 1883 ed. 79.75 (ISBN 0-89901-060-1). Found Class Reprints.

Hall, J. B. Realm of Fiction: Sixty Five Short Stories. 2nd ed. 1970. pap. 7.50 o.p. (ISBN 0-07-025592-X, C). McGraw.

Hall, J. L. & Flowers, T. J. Plant Cell Structure & Metabolism. 2nd ed. (Illus.). 480p. (Orig.). 1982. pap. 22.00x (ISBN 0-582-44408-X). Longman.

Hall, J. L. & Brown, M. J., eds. On-Line Bibliographic Data Bases: An International Directory. 2nd ed. 213p. 1981. 84.00x (ISBN 0-8103-0528-3, Pub. by Aslib England). Gale.

Hall, J. Tillman. Total Fitness for Men. 1980. pap. text ed. 7.95x (ISBN 0-673-16206-0). Scott F.

Hall, J. Tillman, et al. Until the Whistle Blows: A Collection of Games, Dances & Activities for Four to Eight Year Olds. LC 76-41737. (Illus.). 1977. pap. text ed. 15.50x (ISBN 0-673-16208-7). Scott F.

--Until the Whistle Blows: A Collection of Games, Dances & Activities for Eight to Twelve Year Olds. LC 76-55311. (Illus.). 1977. text ed. 15.50x (ISBN 0-673-16210-9); pap. text ed. 14.50x (ISBN 0-673-16211-7). Scott F.

Hall, J. W., jt. auth. see Kulp, C. A.

Hall, Jack & Lessard, Victoria C. The Vocational-Technical Core Collection: Vol. II, Media. 275p. Date not set. 35.00 (ISBN 0-918212-47-2). Neal-Schuman.

Hall, Jack C. A Review of the North & Central American Species of Paravilla Painter (Diptera--Bombyliidae) (U. C. Publications in Entomology Ser.: Vol. 92). 192p. 1981. 12.00x (ISBN 0-520-09625-8). U of Cal Pr.

Hall, Jacqueline & Hall, Jo E. Italian-Swiss Settlement of Plumas County, 1860-1920. (ANCRR Occasional Paper: No. 1). 55p. 1973. 4.00 (ISBN 0-686-38934-4). Assn NC Records.

Hall, James. Dictionary of Subjects & Symbols in Art. 2nd, rev. ed. LC 74-6578. (Icon Editions). (Illus.). 1979. o. p. 15.95i (ISBN 0-06-433316-7, HarpT); pap. 8.95i (ISBN 0-06-430100-1, IN-100, HarpT). Har-Row.

--Knowledge, Belief, & Trancedence: Philosophical Problems in Religion. LC 82-21757. 254p. 1983. pap. text ed. 10.75 (ISBN 0-8191-2912-7). U Pr of Amer.

--Letters from the West. LC 67-10123. 1967. Repr. of 1828 ed. 45.00x (ISBN 0-8201-1024-8). Schol Facsimiles.

--The Tragic Comedians: Seven Modern British Novelists. LC 77-18009. 1978. lib. bdg. 18.25x (ISBN 0-313-20106-4, HATC). Greenwood.

Hall, James, jt. ed. see Brady, John.

Hall, James B. Music from a Broken Piano. 1983. 11.95 (ISBN 0-914590-78-2); pap. 5.95 (ISBN 0-914590-79-0). Fiction Coll.

Hall, James B. & Hall, Elizabeth. The Realm of Fiction: 74 Short Stories. 3rd ed. 1977. pap. text ed. 17.50 (ISBN 0-07-025594-6, C); instructor's manual 13.95 (ISBN 0-07-025604-7). McGraw.

Hall, James B. & Ulanov, Barry. Modern Culture & the Arts. 2nd ed. LC 79-177373. (Illus.). 592p. 1972. 19.00 o.p. (ISBN 0-07-025588-1, C); pap. text ed. 21.95 (ISBN 0-07-025587-3); instructor's manual 12.00 (ISBN 0-07-025589-X). McGraw.

Hall, James B., et al. Women: Portraits. (Patterns in Literary Art Ser). 1976. pap. text ed. 9.16 (ISBN 0-07-025575-X, W). McGraw.

Hall, James J. & Bunton, John. Wines. 5.50x (ISBN 0-392-06157-0, LTB). Sportshelf.

Hall, James N. My Island Home, an Autobiography. LC 78-109306. (Illus.). 374p. Repr. of 1952 ed. lib. bdg. 17.75x (ISBN 0-8371-3581-8, HAIH). Greenwood.

Hall, James N., jt. auth. see Nordhoff, Charles.

Hall, James W. Forging the American Character. LC 79-28117. (American Problem Studies). 128p. 1980. Repr. of 1971 ed. pap. 5.50 (ISBN 0-89874-091-6). Krieger.

Hall, Jay. Ponderables. LC 82-83907. 93p. 1982. pap. text ed. 9.95 (ISBN 0-937932-02-7). Teleometrics.

Hall, Jeffrey C. & Greenspan, Ralph J. Genetic Neurobiology. 1982. 29.95 (ISBN 0-262-08111-3). MIT Pr.

Hall, Jerome. Comparative Law & Social Theory. LC 63-20406. (Edward Douglass White Lectures). viii, 168p. 1963. 12.50x o.p. (ISBN 0-8071-0518-X). La State U Pr.

--Readings in Jurisprudence. 1938. 18.00 (ISBN 0-672-81013-1, Bobbs-Merrill Law). Michie-Bobbs.

Hall, Jerry & Watts, Charles. Learning to Work with Integrated Circuits. LC 77-77774. 49p. pap. 2.00 o.p. (ISBN 0-87259-331-2). Am Radio.

Hall, Jim. The Lady from the Dark Green Hills. LC 76-56966. (Three Rivers Poetry Selection Ser.). 1977. 2.95 o.p. (ISBN 0-915606-00-3). Carnegie-Mellon.

Hall, Jo E., jt. auth. see Hall, Jacqueline.

Hall, Joan, tr. see Boitani, Piero.

Hall, John. Maze Craze Three. (Illus.). 40p. (gr. 1-12). 1974. pap. 2.95 (ISBN 0-912300-43-4). Troubador Pr.

--Maze Craze Two. (Illus.). 40p. (gr. 1-12). 1972. pap. 2.95 (ISBN 0-912300-30-2). Troubador Pr.

--Psychology for Nurses & Health Visitors. Chapman, Antony & Gale, Anthony, eds. (Psychology for Professional Groups Ser.). 320p. 1982. 49.00x (ISBN 0-333-31863-3, Pub. by Macmillan England). State Mutual Bk.

--Psychology for Nurses & Health Visitors. (Psychology for Professional Groups Ser.). 320p. 1982. text ed. 25.00x (ISBN 0-333-31863-3, Pub. by Macmillan England); pap. text ed. 10.95x (ISBN 0-333-31876-5). Humanities.

Hall, John & Beardsley, R. K. Twelve Doors to Japan. 1965. text ed. 22.00 o.p. (ISBN 0-07-025610-1, C). McGraw.

Hall, John C. Cross-Country to Danger. (Voyager Ser.). 80p. (Orig.). 1983. pap. 2.95 (ISBN 0-8010-4269-0). Baker Bk.

Hall, John I. & Moore, Anthony L., eds. Isolation of Membranes & Organelles from Plants Cells. (Biological Techniques Ser.). Date not set. price not set (ISBN 0-12-318820-2). Acad Pr.

Hall, John R. & Meritt, Herbert D. Concise Anglo-Saxon Dictionary. 4th ed. 1961. 59.95 (ISBN 0-521-05179-7). Cambridge U Pr.

Hall, John W. Japan. 1971. pap. 9.95 (ISBN 0-440-54189-1, Delta). Dell.

Hall, John W. & Toyoda, Takeshi, eds. Japan in the Muromachi Age. LC 74-22963. 1977. 34.50x (ISBN 0-520-02888-0); pap. 9.95x (ISBN 0-520-03214-4). U of Cal Pr.

Hall, Katy. Nothing but Soup. (Picture Bk). (Illus.). 32p. (gr. 1 up). 1976. 5.95 o.s.i. (ISBN 0-695-80670-X); lib. ed. 5.97 o.s.i. (ISBN 0-695-40670-1). Follett.

Hall, Kenneth. The Origins of the English-Speaking People. 1978. 7.50 o.p. (ISBN 0-533-03592-9). Vantage.

Hall, Kenneth R. & Whitmore, John K., eds. Explorations in Early Southeast Asian History: The Origins of Southeast Asian Statecraft. LC 76-6836. (Michigan Papers on South & Southeast Asia: No. 11). (Illus.). xiv, 358p. (Orig.). 1976. pap. 9.50x (ISBN 0-89148-011-0). Ctr S&SE Asian.

Hall, Kermit L. A Comprehensive Bibliography of American Constitutional & Legal History, 1896-1979, 2 vols. (Orig.). 1983. Set. lib. bdg. 320.00 (ISBN 0-527-37408-3). Kraus Intl.

Hall, L. M., jt. ed. see Sattelle, D. B.

Hall, L. W. Wright's Veterinary Anaesthesia & Analgesia. 8th ed. (Illus.). 515p. 1982. text ed. write for info o.p. (ISBN 0-8121-0742-X). Lea & Febiger.

Hall, Laurence S. How Thinking Is Written, an Analytic Approach to Writing. LC 73-21176. (Illus.). 312p. 1975. Repr. of 1963 ed. lib. bdg. 19.00x (ISBN 0-8371-6059-6, HATW). Greenwood.

Hall, Lenwood W., et al. Power Plant Chlorination: A Biological & Chemical Assessment. LC 80-69427. 237p. 1981. text ed. 49.95 (ISBN 0-250-40396-X). Ann Arbor Science.

Hall, Leonard. A Journal of the Seasons on an Ozark Farm. LC 80-17831. (Illus.). 242p. 1980. 11.95 (ISBN 0-8262-0326-4); pap. 6.95 (ISBN 0-8262-0317-5). U of Mo Pr.

Hall, Leslie, jt. auth. see Farman, J. V.

Hall, Linda, jt. auth. see Whiddon, N.

Hall, Louis B. The Perilous Vision of John Wyclif. LC 82-18890. 288p. 1983. lib. bdg. 23.95X (ISBN 0-8304-1006-6). Nelson-Hall.

Hall, Lynn. Barry: The Bravest Saint Bernard. LC 73-7557. (Famous Animal Stories Ser.). (Illus.). 48p. (gr. 2-5). 1973. PLB 6.89 (ISBN 0-8116-4852-4). Garrard.

--Bob: Watchdog of the River. LC 73-13573. (Famous Animal Stories). (Illus.). 48p. (gr. 2-5). 1974. PLB 6.89 (ISBN 0-8116-4853-2). Garrard.

--Captain: Canada's Flying Pony. LC 75-6765. (Famous Animal Stories Ser). (Illus.). 64p. (gr. 2-5). 1976. PLB 6.89 (ISBN 0-8116-4857-5). Garrard.

--Careers for Dog Lovers. LC 77-88638. (Illus.). (gr. 5). 1978. PLB 7.98 o.s.i. (ISBN 0-695-40877-1); pap. 3.95 o.s.i. (ISBN 0-695-30877-7). Follett.

--The Disappearing Grandad. 64p. 1980. lib. bdg. 5.39 (ISBN 0-695-41467-4, Dist. by Caroline Hse). Follett.

--Dog of the Bondi Castle. (gr. 2-5). 3.48 (ISBN 0-695-81255-6, Dist. by Caroline Hse); PLB 4.65 (ISBN 0-695-41255-8). Follett.

--Dragon Defiant. (gr. 5-9). 1977. trade ed. 4.95 (ISBN 0-695-80697-1, Dist. by Caroline Hse); lib. ed. 5.97 (ISBN 0-695-40697-3). Follett.

--Dragon's Delight. (Dragon Ser.). 112p. 1980. lib. bdg. 5.97 (ISBN 0-695-41366-X, Dist. by Caroline Hse). Follett.

--Flash, Dog of Old Egypt. LC 73-6577. (Famous Animal Stories Ser.). (Illus.). 48p. (gr. 2-5). 1973. PLB 6.89 (ISBN 0-8116-4851-6). Garrard.

--Flowers of Anger. LC 76-2235. (Illus.). 128p. (gr. 10 up). 1976. trade ed. 5.95 (ISBN 0-695-80669-6); lib. ed. 3.96 (ISBN 0-695-40669-8). Follett.

--The Haunting of the Green Bird. 64p. 1980. lib. bdg. 5.39 (ISBN 0-695-41466-6, Dist. by Caroline Hse). Follett.

--Horse Called Dragon. LC 71-121411. (Illus.). (gr. 5 up). 1971. trade ed. 5.95 (ISBN 0-695-80134-1, Dist. by Caroline Hse); PLB 4.98 lib. ed. (ISBN 0-695-40134-3). Follett.

--Kids & Dog Shows. LC 73-93558. 160p. (gr. 4-7). 1974. 5.95 o.s.i. (ISBN 0-695-80482-0); lib. bdg. 5.97 o.s.i. (ISBN 0-695-40482-2). Follett.

--Megan's Mare. 64p. (gr. 4-6). 1983. 10.95 (ISBN 0-684-17874-5). Scribner.

--The Mysterious Moortown Bridge. 64p. 1980. PLB 5.39 (ISBN 0-695-41468-2). Follett.

--The Mystery of Plum Park Pony. LC 79-28125. (Mystery Ser.). 64p. (gr. 3). 1980. PLB 6.89 (ISBN 0-8116-6414-7). Garrard.

--The Mystery of Pony Hollow. LC 78-8137. (Mystery Ser.). (Illus.). (gr. 3-6). 1978. PLB 6.89 (ISBN 0-8116-6404-X). Garrard.

--The Mystery of Pony Hollow Panda. LC 81-6389. (Mystery Ser.). (Illus.). 64p. (gr. 1-4). 1983. PLB write for info. (ISBN 0-8116-6416-3). Garrard.

--The Mystery of the Lost & Found Hound. LC 78-27502. (Mystery Ser.). (Illus.). (gr. 3-6). 1979. PLB 6.89 (ISBN 0-8116-6408-2). Garrard.

--The Mystery of the Schoolhouse Dog. LC 78-12181. (Illus.). (gr. 3-6). 1979. PLB 6.89 (ISBN 0-8116-6406-6). Garrard.

--The Mystery of the Stubborn Old Man. LC 79-28287. (Mystery Ser.). 64p. (gr. 3). 1980. PLB 6.89 (ISBN 0-8116-6413-9). Garrard.

--A New Day for Dragons. (Illus.). 1976. pap. 1.25 o.p. (ISBN 0-380-00763-0, 30528, Camelot). Avon.

--Owney: The Traveling Dog. LC 76-46292. (Famous Animal Stories). (Illus.). (gr. 2-5). 1977. PLB 6.89 (ISBN 0-8116-4860-5). Garrard.

--Riff Remember. LC 73-81998. (Illus.). 112p. (gr. 4-7). 1973. trade ed. 2.47 (ISBN 0-695-80413-8); lib. ed. 3.96 (ISBN 0-695-40413-X). Follett.

--Shadows. LC 76-50324. (gr. 3-8). 1977. 4.95 o.s.i. (ISBN 0-695-80741-2); lib. bdg. 4.98 o.s.i. (ISBN 0-695-40741-4). Follett.

--The Shy Ones. (YA) (gr. 9-12). 1977. pap. 1.95 (ISBN 0-380-01723-7, 63263-2, Camelot). Avon.

--The Siege of Silent Henry. (YA) (gr. 7 up). 1977. pap. 1.50 o.p. (ISBN 0-380-01744-X, 49445). Avon.

--The Siege of Silent Henry. LC 72-2789. 160p. (gr. 7 up). 1972. 4.95 o.s.i. (ISBN 0-695-80041-8). Follett.

--Sticks & Stones. (gr. 7 up). 1977. trade ed. 3.00 (ISBN 0-695-80237-2); lib. ed. o.s.i. 5.97 (ISBN 0-695-40237-4). Follett.

--Stray. (gr. 2-4). 1975. pap. 1.95 o.p. (ISBN 0-380-00202-7, 53116, Camelot). Avon.

--Stray. (Illus.). (gr. 5 up). 1974. 3.00 (ISBN 0-695-80442-1); PLB 3.96 (ISBN 0-695-40442-3). Follett.

--To Catch a Tartar. LC 72-85582. 96p. (gr. 4-6). 1973. 4.95 o.s.i. (ISBN 0-695-80370-0, T0370); PLB 5.97 o.s.i. (ISBN 0-695-40370-2, L0370). Follett.

--Troublemaker. LC 74-78455. (Illus.). 96p. (gr. 3-6). 1974. 4.95 o.s.i. (ISBN 0-695-80479-0); lib. bdg. 4.98 o.s.i. (ISBN 0-695-40479-2). Follett.

Hall, Malcolm. Caricatures. LC 77-16631. (Break-of-Day Bk.). (Illus.). (gr. 1-3). 1978. PLB 6.99 (ISBN 0-698-30685-6, Coward). Putnam Pub Group.

--Deadlines. (Break of Day Ser.). (Illus.). (gr. 6-9). 1982. pap. 6.99 (ISBN 0-698-30739-9, Coward). Putnam Pub Group.

--Derek Koogar Was a Star. (Break of Day Ser.). (Illus.). 64p. (gr. 1-4). 1975. PLB 6.59 o.p. (ISBN 0-698-30581-7, Coward). Putnam Pub Group.

--Edward, Benjamin & Butter. (Illus.). 48p. (gr. 6-9). 1981. PLB 6.99 (ISBN 0-698-30731-3, Coward). Putnam Pub Group.

--The Electric Book. LC 75-10454. (Illus.). 128p. (gr. 5-11). 1975. 6.99 o.p. (ISBN 0-698-20339-9, Coward). Putnam Pub Group.

--Forecast. LC 77-1265. (Break-of-Day Bk.). (Illus.). (gr. k-4). 1977. PLB 6.99 (ISBN 0-698-30666-X, Coward). Putnam Pub Group.

--The Friends of Charlie Ant Bear. (A Break-of-Day Bk.). (Illus.). 64p. (gr. 3-5). 1980. PLB 6.99 (ISBN 0-698-30711-9, Coward). Putnam Pub Group.

--Headlines. (Break-of-Day Bk.). (Illus.). 64p. (gr. 1-3). 1973. PLB 6.99 (ISBN 0-698-30482-9, Coward). Putnam Pub Group.

Hall, Malcolm H., jt. auth. see Wilson, David H.

Hall, Manly. Meditation Disciplines. pap. 3.50 (ISBN 0-89314-800-8). Philos Res.

Hall, Manly P. Adventures in Understanding. pap. 6.50 (ISBN 0-89314-809-1). Philos Res.

--Blessed Angels. pap. 2.95 (ISBN 0-89314-807-5). Philos Res.

--Collected Writings, No. 3. pap. 10.00 (ISBN 0-89314-507-6). Philos Res.

--Drugs of Vision. pap. 0.25 o.p. (ISBN 0-89314-313-8). Philos Res.

--Freemasonry of the Ancient Egyptians. 7.50 (ISBN 0-89314-803-2). Philos Res.

--How Belief in Rebirth Enriches Life. pap. 2.00 (ISBN 0-89314-318-9). Philos Res.

--Impressions of Modern Japan. pap. 2.50 (ISBN 0-89314-319-7). Philos Res.

--Lady of Dreams. pap. 2.00 o.p. (ISBN 0-89314-327-8). Philos Res.

--Lectures on Ancient Philosophy. 12.50 (ISBN 0-89314-512-2). Philos Res.

--Lost Keys of Freemasonry. 8.95 (ISBN 0-89314-500-9). Philos Res.

--Man, the Grand Symbol of the Mysteries. 12.95 (ISBN 0-89314-513-0); pap. 8.95 (ISBN 0-89314-389-8). Philos Res.

--Orders of Universal Reformation - Utopias. 5.95 (ISBN 0-89314-535-1); pap. 3.95 (ISBN 0-89314-380-4). Philos Res.

--Psychoanalyzing the Twelve Zodiacal Types. pap. 2.95 (ISBN 0-89314-813-X). Philos Res.

--Questions & Answers on Problems of Life. pap. 6.95 (ISBN 0-89314-801-6). Philos Res.

--Quiet Way. pap. 2.00 (ISBN 0-89314-348-0). Philos Res.

--Right Thinking. pap. 2.50 (ISBN 0-89314-812-1). Philos Res.

--Sermon on the Mount. pap. 2.00 (ISBN 0-89314-353-7). Philos Res.

--The Space-Born. pap. 3.95 (ISBN 0-89314-399-5). Philos Res.

--The Story of Astrology. 6.75 (ISBN 0-89314-525-4). Philos Res.

--Survey Course in Philosophy. 4.00 o.p. (ISBN 0-89314-359-6). Philos Res.

--Therapeutic Value of Music. pap. 2.95 (ISBN 0-89314-815-6). Philos Res.

--Twelve World Teachers. pap. 6.50 (ISBN 0-89314-816-4). Philos Res.

--What Ancient Wisdom Expects of Its Disciples. pap. 2.50 (ISBN 0-89314-370-7). Philos Res.

--Words to the Wise. pap. 4.95 (ISBN 0-89314-814-8). Philos Res.

Hall, Manly P., frwd. by. Music of the Comte De St. Germain. 10.00 (ISBN 0-686-98020-4). Philos Res.

Hall, Margaret E., ed. Alexander Hamilton Reader. LC 57-6014. (Docket Ser.: No. 9). 257p. (Orig.). 1957. 15.00 (ISBN 0-379-11309-0); pap. 2.50 (ISBN 0-686-96811-5). Oceana.

Hall, Marshall, Jr. The Theory of Groups. 2nd ed. LC 75-42306. xiii, 434p. text ed. 14.95 (ISBN 0-8284-0288-4). Chelsea Pub.

Hall, Martha L. Call It Living. 1982. pap. 5.00 (ISBN 0-912960-13-2). Nightowl.

Hall, Mary. The Impossible Dream: The Spirituality of Dom Helder Camara. LC 79-26888. 96p. (Orig.). 1980. pap. 4.95 (ISBN 0-88344-212-4). Orbis Bks.

Hall, Mary A. Teaching Reading As a Language Experience. 3rd ed. (Illus.). 160p. 1981. pap. text ed. 8.95 (ISBN 0-675-08080-0). Merrill.

Hall, Mary A. & Ramig, Christopher J. Linguistic Foundations for Reading. 1978. pap. text ed. 9.95 (ISBN 0-675-08448-2). Merrill.

Hall, Marybelle B., jt. auth. see Hall, Douglas V.

Hall, Maureen & Reilly, Cari. The Gut Course in College Cookery. LC 82-61570. (Illus.). 250p. 1982. 9.95 (ISBN 0-910963-00-2). Mercury Bks.

Hall, N. John. Trollope & His Illustrators. LC 79-476. (Illus.). 1979. 26.00x (ISBN 0-312-81888-2). St Martin.

Hall, N. John, ed. The Letters of Anthony Trollope, 2 vols. LC 79-64213. (Illus.). 1100p. 1983. Set. 87.50x (ISBN 0-8047-1076-7). Vol. 1, 1835-1870. Vol. 2, 1871-1882. Stanford U Pr.

Hall, Nancy C. Macmillan Fairy Tale Alphabet Book. LC 82-20905. (Illus.). 64p. 1983. 9.95 (ISBN 0-02-741960-6). Macmillan.

Hall, Nancy C., ed. Platt & Munk Treasury of Stories for Children. LC 79-56868. (Illus.). 128p. (ps-3). 1981. 9.95 (ISBN 0-448-47722-X, G&D). Putnam Pub Group.

Hall, Nor. The Moon & the Virgin: Reflections on the Archetypal Feminine. LC 78-2138. (Illus.). 1981. pap. 6.25i (ISBN 0-06-090793-2, CN 793, CN). Har-Row.

--The Moon & the Virgin: Reflections on the Archetypal Feminine. LC 78-2138. (Illus.). 1980. 12.45i (ISBN 0-06-011703-6, HarpT). Har-Row.

Hall, Olive, jt. auth. see Compton, Norma.

Hall, Olive A. & Paolucci, Beatrice. Teaching Home Economics. 2nd ed. LC 73-109432. 1970. text ed. 26.95x o.p. (ISBN 0-471-34288-2). Wiley.

Hall, Olive A., jt. auth. see Ruud, Josephine B.

Hall, Pam. On the Edge of the Eastern Ocean. LC 82-945714. (gr. 5 up). 13.00 (ISBN 0-88874-055-7). Silver.

Hall, Patricia, jt. auth. see Hillery, Mable.

Hall, Peter. Rates of Convergence in the Central Limit Theorem. (Research Notes in Mathematics: No. 62). 230p. 1982. pap. text ed. 24.00 (ISBN 0-273-08565-4). Pitman Pub MA.

Hall, Peter & Hay, Dennis. Growth Centres in the European Urban System. 1980. 33.00x (ISBN 0-520-04198-4). U of Cal Pr.

Hall, Peter, ed. The Inner City in Context. 175p. (Orig.). 1981. pap. text ed. 11.00x (ISBN 0-435-35718-2). Heinemann Ed.

Hall, Phoebe. Part-Time Social Work. 1980. text ed. 25.00x (ISBN 0-435-82401-5). Heinemann Ed.

--Reforming the Welfare: The Politics of Change in the Personal Social Services. LC 77-363531. 1976. text ed. 15.00x (ISBN 0-435-82400-7). Heinemann Ed.

Hall, Phoebe, et al. Change, Choice & Conflict in Social Policy. 1975. text ed. 15.00x (ISBN 0-435-82670-0); pap. text ed. 11.00x (ISBN 0-435-82671-9). Heinemann Ed.

Hall, R. Proto-Romance Phonology. 1976. 33.95 (ISBN 0-444-00183-2, North Holland). Elsevier.

Hall, R. J. The History of Ideas & Images in Italian Art. LC 82-48154. (Icon Editions). (Illus.). 320p. 1983. 24.01i (ISBN 0-06-433317-5, HarpT). Har-Row.

Hall, R. Vance & Houten, Ron V. Managing Behavior: The Measurement of Behavior, Pt. 1. 1983. 4.50 (ISBN 0-89079-072-8). H & H Ent.

Hall, Raymond E., ed. see Fitch, Henry S.

Hall, Renee, et al, eds. see Sandifer, Kevin W.

Hall, Richard. Three Plays for a Gay Theater. LC 82-12099. 188p. (Orig.). 1983. pap. 6.95 (ISBN 0-912516-73-9). Grey Fox.

Hall, Richard C., ed. Psychiatry in Crisis. LC 80-22379. 156p. 1982. text ed. 18.00 (ISBN 0-89335-133-4). Spectrum Pub.

Hall, Richard C., jt. ed. see Levenson, Alvin J.

Hall, Richard H. Occupations & the Social Structure. 2nd ed. LC 74-23243. (Illus.). 384p. 1975. text ed. 22.95 (ISBN 0-13-629345-X). P-H.

Hall, Robert & Davis, John. Moral Education in Theory & Practice. LC 75-21078. 189p. 1975. 12.95 (ISBN 0-87975-052-9). Prometheus Bks.

Hall, Robert A. Descriptive Italian Grammar. LC 74-1556. (Cornell Romance Studies: Vol. 2). 228p. 1974. Repr. of 1948 ed. text ed. 18.75x (ISBN 0-8371-7396-5, HAIG). Greenwood.

Hall, Robert A., Jr. Antonio Fogazzaro. (World Authors Ser.). 1978. lib. bdg. 15.95 (ISBN 0-8057-6311-2, Twayne). G K Hall.

Hall, Robert B. Anyone Can Prophesy. LC 77-8267. 1977. pap. 1.00 (ISBN 0-8164-2158-7). Seabury.

--Area Studies: With Special Reference to Their Implications for Research in the Social Sciences. LC 47-5403. 1947. pap. 4.00 (ISBN 0-527-03295-6). Kraus Repr.

--Church Growth for Episcopalians. 1982. pap. 3.95 (ISBN 0-686-37069-4). Episcopal Ctr.

--Pastoring the Renewed. 1982. pap. 3.95 (ISBN 0-686-37068-6). Episcopal Ctr.

Hall, Robert E. Nine Months Reading: A Medical Guide for Pregnant Women. rev. ed. LC 81-43143. (Illus.). 192p. 1983. 13.95 (ISBN 0-385-17726-7). Doubleday.

Hall, Robert E., ed. Inflation: Causes & Effects. LC 82-10932. (National Bureau of Economic Research-Project Reports Ser.). (Illus.). 1983. lib. bdg. 27.00x (ISBN 0-226-31323-9). U of Chicago Pr.

Hall, Robert F. & Rabushka, Alvin. Low Tax, Simple Tax, Flat Tax. 91st ed. LC 82-21655. 144p. 1983. 18.95 (ISBN 0-07-025670-5, GB); pap. 9.95 (ISBN 0-07-025669-1). McGraw.

Hall, Robert L. & Stack, Carol B., eds. Holding on to the Land & the Lord: Kinship, Ritual, Land Tenure & Social Policy in the Rural South. (Southern Anthropological Society Proceedings Ser.: No.15). 176p. 1982. text ed. 12.00x (ISBN 0-8203-0584-7); pap. text ed. 5.95x (ISBN 0-8203-0596-0). U of Ga Pr.

Hall, Robert W. Real Estate Investment Analysis: How to Spot the Top Performers for High Return Real Estate Investing. LC 82-9239. 232p. text ed. 89.50 (ISBN 0-87624-487-8). Inst Busn Plan.

Hall, Robert Wo. Kawasaki U.S.A. Transferring Japanese Production Methods to the United States: a Case Study. LC 81-71742. 22p. 1982. pap. text ed. 7.50 (ISBN 0-935406-07-7). Am Prod & Inventory.

Hall, Rodney. Just Relations. 516p. 1983. 16.75 (ISBN 0-670-41114-0). Viking Pr.

Hall, Roger. You're Stepping on My: Cloak & Dagger. 1957. 5.50 o.p. (ISBN 0-393-08458-2). Norton.

Hall, Roger L., ed. The Happy Journey: Thirty-Five Shaker Spirituals Compiled by Miss Clara Endicott Sears. LC 81-69875. (Illus.). 60p. (Orig.). 1982. 8.00 (ISBN 0-941632-00-8). Fruitlands Mus.

Hall, Ruth & James, Selma. Rapist Who Pays the Rent. 64p. (Orig.). 1982. pap. 3.95 (ISBN 0-905046-21-8). Falling Wall.

Hall, Ruth K. A Place of Her Own: The Story of Elizabeth Garrett. (Illus.). 1976. pap. 5.95 (ISBN 0-913270-68-7). Sunstone Pr.

Hall, S. & Jacques, M. The Politics of Thatcherism. 265p. 1983. text ed. 23.00x (ISBN 0-85315-553-4, Pub. by Lawrence & Wishart Ltd England). Humanities.

Hall, Sandra P. & Hirsch, Felice L. Fingertip Reference for Dental Materials. LC 79-54689. (Dental Assisting Ser.). 161p. 1981. pap. text ed. 10.20 (ISBN 0-8273-1863-4). Delmar.

Hall, Sharon K. & Mendelson, Phyllis C., eds. Twentieth-Century Literary Criticism Series, 7 vols. Incl. Vol. 1. 1978 (ISBN 0-8103-0179-2); Vol. 2. O.P.; Vol. 3. 600p. 1980 (ISBN 0-8103-0177-6); Vol. 4. 650p. 1981 (ISBN 0-8103-0178-4); Vol. 5. 700p. 1981 (ISBN 0-8103-0179-2); Vol. 6. 600p. 1982 (ISBN 0-8103-0180-6); Vol. 7. 600p. 1982 (ISBN 0-8103-0181-4). LC 76-46132. 74.00x. Gale.

Hall, Steve. Itasca: Source of America's Greatest River. LC 82-12598. (Minnesota Historic Sites Pamphlet Ser.: No. 19). 32p. 1982. pap. 4.95 (ISBN 0-87351-157-3). Minn Hist.

Hall, T. William, ed. Introduction to the Study of Religion. LC 78-4427. (Orig.). 1978. pap. text ed. 9.95xi (ISBN 0-06-063572-X, RD 281, HarpR). Har-Row.

Hall, Terry. Bible Panorama. 1983. text ed. 9.95 (ISBN 0-88207-273-0). Victor Bks.

Hall, Theodore P. & Farmer, Silas. Grosse Pointe on Lake Sainte Claire. LC 73-17472. 114p. 1974. Repr. of 1886 ed. 10.00x (ISBN 0-8103-3879-3). Gale.

Hall, Thor. The State of the Arts in North America: Systematic Theology Today. LC 78-70520. 1978. pap. text ed. 10.00 (ISBN 0-8191-0645-3). U Pr of Amer.

Hall, Timothy. HMAS Melbourne. (Illus.). 224p. 1982. 19.95 (ISBN 0-86861-284-7). Allen Unwin.

Hall, Tom. Perceptual-Motor Whole Numbers: A Perceptual-Motor Academic Program of Whole Number Math & Time Telling Activities for Elementary Grades. Alexander, Frank, ed. 99p. 1982. pap. 5.95 (ISBN 0-915256-11-8). Front Row.

Hall, Tom T. The Storyteller's Nashville. LC 78-22632. (Illus.). 1979. 12.95 o.p. (ISBN 0-385-14690-6). Doubleday.

Hall, Trevor. Born to be King: Prince William of Wales. (Illus.). 128p. 1983. 25.00 (ISBN 0-517-39675-0). Crown.

Hall, Trevor H. Sherlock Holmes. (Griffin Paperbacks Ser.). (Illus.). 157p. 1975. pap. 3.95 o.p. (ISBN 0-312-71715-6). St Martin.

Hall, Virginia, jt. auth. see Lowman, Robert.

Hall, Virginius C., Jr. Portraits in the Collection of the Virginia Historical Society: A Catalogue. LC 80-14079. 283p. 1981. 50.00x (ISBN 0-8139-0813-2). U Pr of Va.

Hall, Vivian A. Be My Guest. LC 79-22028. 1979. 7.95 (ISBN 0-8024-0480-4). Moody.

Hall, Vivian S. & Spencer, Margaret R. Bibliography of Evaporites, Brines & Salt. 1983. write for info. (ISBN 0-89774-042-4). Oryx Pr.

Hall, Viviana C. Miedos: Poemas del Cielo y de la Tierra, 2 bks. Anastasio, William T., ed. (Illus.). 55p. (Orig., Span.). 1982. pap. text ed. 6.95 (ISBN 0-686-43162-6). Visual Art.

Hall, W. A. & Dracup, J. A. Water Resources Systems Engineering. 1970. 37.95 (ISBN 0-07-025590-3, C). McGraw.

Hall, W. Dallas, jt. ed. see Wollam, Gary L.

Hall, W. P., et al. History of England & the Empire Commonwealth. 5th ed. 1971. text ed. 35.95 (ISBN 0-471-00225-9). Wiley.

Hall, W. S. & Freedle, R. O. Culture & Language: The Black American Experience. LC 75-12534. 191p. 1975. 10.95x o.p. (ISBN 0-470-34156-4). Halsted Pr.

Hall, Wally, jt. auth. see Holtz, Lou.

Hall, Walter. Barnacle Parp's Chain Saw Guide. LC 77-10328. 1977. 12.95 o.p. (ISBN 0-87857-197-3); pap. 9.95 o.p. (ISBN 0-87857-190-6). Rodale Pr Inc.

--Barnacle Parp's Guide to Garden & Yard Power Tools: Selection, Maintenance & Repair. Wallace, Dan, ed. (Illus.). 200p. 1983. 18.95 (ISBN 0-87857-446-8, 14-012-0); pap. 11.95 (ISBN 0-87857-472-7, 14-012-1). Rodale Pr Inc.

Hall, Willis, tr. see De Filippo, Eduardo.

Hall, Z. W., jt. ed. see Otsuka, Masanori.

Halla, Chris. Best Wisconsin Rivers: A Canoeist's Journal & Guide. (Illus.). 80p. (Orig.). 1983. pap. 8.95 (ISBN 0-942802-02-0). Northword.

Hallahan, D. & Kauffman, J. Introduction to Learning Disabilities: The Psycho-Behavioral Approach. 1976. 23.95 (ISBN 0-13-485524-8). P-H.

Hallahan, Daniel P. & Kauffman, James M. Exceptional Children: Introduction to Special Education. 2nd ed. (Illus.). 480p. 1982. 23.95 (ISBN 0-13-293969-X). P-H.

--Exceptional Children: Introduction to Special Education. (Special Education Ser.). 1978. ref. ed. 23.95 (ISBN 0-13-293944-4). P-H.

Hallahan, William H. The Dead of Winter. pap. 1.75 (ISBN 0-380-01692-3, 24216). Avon.

--The Monk. LC 82-18782. 256p. 1983. 12.50 (ISBN 0-688-01112-8). Morrow.

--The Trade. 320p. 1983. pap. 3.50 (ISBN 0-380-57737-2, 57737). Avon.

Hallak, J., et al. The Financial Aspects of First-Level Education in Iran. LC 72-93794. (Financing Educational Systems Ser.). (Illus.). 59p. (Orig.). 1973. pap. 4.50 o.p. (ISBN 92-803-1051-8, U272, UNESCO). Unipub.

Hallak, Jacques & McCabe, James. Planning the Location of Schools: County Sligo, Ireland. (Illus.). 109p. (Orig.). 1973. pap. 10.50 o.p. (ISBN 92-803-1056-9, U461, UNESCO). Unipub.

Hallam, A. Atlas of Palaeobiogeography: 1972. 1973. 98.00 (ISBN 0-444-40975-0). Elsevier.

--Jurassic Environments. LC 74-80359. (Earth Science Ser.). (Illus.). 260p. 1975. 49.95 (ISBN 0-521-20555-7). Cambridge U Pr.

--A Revolution in the Earth Sciences: From Continental Drift to Plate Tectonics. (Illus.). 1975. pap. text ed. 6.95x (ISBN 0-19-858145-9). Oxford U Pr.

Hallam, A., ed. Patterns of Evolution: As Illustrated by the Fossil Record. (Developments in Paleontology & Stratigraphy: Vol. 5). 1977. 85.00 (ISBN 0-444-41495-9). Elsevier.

Hallam, Arthur F. William Lloyd's Life of Pythagoras, with a New Thesis On the Origin of the New Testament. 84p. (Orig.). 1982. pap. 8.50 (ISBN 0-938770-01-2). Capitalist Pr OH.

Hallam, Jack. Ghosts' Who's Who. 1977. 7.95 o.p. (ISBN 0-7153-7452-4). David & Charles.

Hallas, et al. Care & Training of the Mentally Handicapped. 6th ed. 302p. 1978. 19.95 o.p. (ISBN 0-7236-0486-X). Wright-PSG.

Hallas, Charles H. & Fraser, William I. The Care & Training of the Mentally Handicapped: A Manual for the Caring Professionals. 7th ed. (Illus.). 424p. 1982. pap. text ed. 15.00 (ISBN 0-7236-0624-2). Wright-PSG.

Hallas, Richard. You Play the Black & the Red Comes Up. 1980. lib. bdg. 11.95 (ISBN 0-8398-2653-2, Gregg). G K Hall.

Hallberg, Edmond C. The Gray Itch: The Male Metapause Syndrome. 1980. pap. 3.95 (ISBN 0-446-30833-1). Warner Bks.

Hallberg, Kurt, jt. ed. see Sawyer, John W.

Hallberg, Peter. Halldor Laxness. (World Authors Ser.: No. 89). 12.50 o.p. (ISBN 0-8057-2516-4, Twayne). G K Hall.

--Old Icelandic Poetry: Eddic Lay & Skaldic Verse. Schach, Paul & Lindgrenson, Sonja, trs. LC 74-27186. (Illus.). xii, 219p. 1975. 15.95x (ISBN 0-8032-0855-3). U of Nebr Pr.

Halldin, S. Comparison of Forest Water & Energy Exchange Models. (Developments in Agriculture & Managed-Forest Ecology Ser.: Vol. 9). 1980. 59.75 (ISBN 0-444-41844-X). Elsevier.

Halle, Antoinette & Mundt, Barbara. Porcelain of the Nineteenth Century. LC 82-50108. (Illus.). 296p. 1983. 85.00 (ISBN 0-8478-0437-2). Rizzoli Intl.

Halle, Louis J. Civilization & Foreign Policy. LC 74-31364. 277p. 1975. Repr. of 1955 ed. lib. bdg. 17.00x o.p. (ISBN 0-8371-7930-0, HACI). Greenwood.

--Dream & Reality: Aspects of American Foreign Policy. 327p. 1973. Repr. of 1959 ed. lib. bdg. 17.50x (ISBN 0-8371-6646-2, HADR). Greenwood.

--The Search for an Eternal Norm: As Represented by Three Classics. LC 80-5793. 220p. 1981. lib. bdg. 21.25 (ISBN 0-8191-1444-8); pap. text ed. 10.25 (ISBN 0-8191-1445-6). U Pr of Amer.

--The Society of Man. LC 78-31208. 1979. Repr. of 1965 ed. lib. bdg. 18.50x (ISBN 0-313-20942-1, HASM). Greenwood.

Halle, Louis J. & Thompson, Kenneth W., eds. Foreign Policy & the Democratic Process: The Geneva Papers. LC 78-64523. 1978. pap. text ed. 6.25 (ISBN 0-8191-0633-X). U Pr of Amer.

Halle, Morris, et al, eds. Linguistic Theory & Psychological Reality. LC 77-29054. (MIT Bicentennial Studies Ser.: NO. 4). 1978. 25.00x (ISBN 0-262-08095-8); pap. 7.95 (ISBN 0-262-58043-8). MIT Pr.

Halleck, Fitz-Greene. Poetical Writings of Fitz-Greene Halleck. Wilson, James G., ed. 1969. Repr. of 1869 ed. lib. bdg. 16.25x (ISBN 0-8371-0460-2). Greenwood.

Halleck, Reuben P. Halleck's New English Literature. 647p. 1982. Repr. of 1913 ed. lib. bdg. 30.00 (ISBN 0-8495-2434-2). Arden Lib.

Hallenbeck, Cleve. Legends of the Spanish Southwest. LC 71-164316. 1971. Repr. of 1938 ed. 37.00x (ISBN 0-8103-3799-1). Gale.

Haller, A. Von. Lettres De Feu M. De Haller Contre M. De Voltaire. Repr. of 1780 ed. 166.00 o.p. (ISBN 0-685-89934-9). Clearwater Pub.

Haller, Bill. Gunfight at Commanche Creek. 160p. (Orig.). 1980. pap. 1.50 o.p. (ISBN 0-523-40463-8). Pinnacle Bks.

Haller, C. E., jt. auth. see Rubin, Murry.

Haller, David. Swimming. (Pelham Pictorial Sports Instruction Ser.). (Illus.). 1979. 9.95 o.p. (ISBN 0-7207-0954-7). Transatlantic.

Haller, Dorcas W., jt. auth. see Jensen, Virginia A.

Haller, Mark H., jt. ed. see Davis, Allen F.

Haller, Mike. TV Self-Defense Kit. 1982. 10 copy prepak 49.50 (ISBN 0-686-84818-7); 4.95 (ISBN 0-686-84819-5). HM.

Haller, R. Grazer Philosophische Studien, Vol. 10. 210p. 1980. pap. text ed. 20.75x (Pub. by Rodopi England). Humanities.

--Grazer Philosophische Studien, Vol. 11. 199p. 1980. pap. text ed. 20.75x (Pub. by Rodopi England). Humanities.

--Grazer Philosophische Studien, Vol. 14. 221p. 1981. pap. text ed. 20.75x (Pub. by Rodopi England). Humanities.

--Grazer Philosphische Studien, Vol. 9. 211p. 1979. pap. text ed. 20.75x (Pub. by Rodopi England). Humanities.

Haller, Terry. Danger: Marketing Researcher at Work. LC 82-13261. (Illus.). 312p. 1983. lib. bdg. 35.00 (ISBN 0-89930-026-X, HMK/, Quorum). Greenwood.

Hallert, Bertil. X-Ray Photogrammetry: 1970. 1970. 34.00 (ISBN 0-444-40805-3). Elsevier.

Hallett, Christine & Stevenson, Olive. Child Abuse. (Studies in the Personal Social Services: No. 2). 1980. text ed. 19.95x (ISBN 0-04-362027-2); pap. text ed. 7.95x (ISBN 0-04-362028-0). Allen Unwin.

Hallett, Garth. Wittgenstein's Definition of Meaning As Use. LC 66-23620. (Orestes Brownson Ser: No. 6). 1967. 22.50 (ISBN 0-8232-0750-1). Fordham.

Hallett, Garth L. Christian Moral Reasoning: An Analytic Guide. LC 82-13436. 272p. 1982. text ed. 20.00 (ISBN 0-268-00740-3); pap. text ed. 8.95 (ISBN 0-268-00741-1). U of Notre Dame Pr.

Hallett, Graham. Housing & Land Policies in West Germany & Britain: A Record of Success & Failure. 1978. text ed. 23.50x o.s.i. (ISBN 0-8419-5037-7). Holmes & Meier.

--The Social Economy of West Germany. LC 73-85268. 160p. 1974. 22.50 (ISBN 0-312-73255-4). St Martin.

Hallett, John W., Jr. & Brewster, David C. Manual of Patient Care in Vascular Surgery. (Spiral Manual Ser.). 262p. 1982. spiralbound 15.95 (ISBN 0-316-34050-2). Little.

Hallett, Kathryn. A Guide for Single Parents: Transactional Analysis for People in Crisis. LC 73-92524. (Illus.). 96p. 1974. 7.95 o.p. (ISBN 0-912310-64-2); pap. 4.95 o.p. (ISBN 0-912310-55-3). Celestial Arts.

Hallett, R. People & Progress in West Africa. 1966. 6.05 o.p. (ISBN 0-08-011326-5); pap. 5.25 o.p. (ISBN 0-08-011325-7). Pergamon.

Hallett, R. W. Isaac Babel. LC 72-79939. (Literature and Life Ser.). 1973. 11.95 (ISBN 0-8044-2337-7). Ungar.

Hallewell, L. Books in Brazil: A History of the Publishing Trade. LC 82-10826. 537p. 1982. 27.50 (ISBN 0-8108-1591-5). Scarecrow.

Halley. Agricultural Note. 17th ed. 1982. text ed. 39.95 (ISBN 0-408-10701-4). Butterworth.

--Manual Biblique de Halley. Cosson, Annie, ed. Wiles, M. A., tr. from Eng. Orig. Title: Halley's Bible Handbook. 974p. (Fr.). 1982. pap. 14.00 (ISBN 0-8297-0900-2). Life Pubs Intl.

Halley, Henry H. Compendio Manual de la Biblia. Denyer, C. P., tr. (Illus., Span.). 1981. Repr. of 1977 ed. 15.95 (ISBN 0-311-03666-X). Casa Bautista.

--Compendio Manual De La Biblia Halley's Bible Hand Book. (Span). 13.95 (ISBN 0-8024-1230-0). Moody.

Halley, Richard. Poems in the Romantic Style. 1978. 5.95 o.p. (ISBN 0-533-02868-X). Vantage.

Hallgarten, F. L. Wines & Wine Gardens of Austria. (Illus.). 1979. 17.50x o.p. (ISBN 0-85242-643-7). Intl Pubns Serv.

Hallgarten, Peter A. Spirits & Liqueurs. 2nd ed. (Books on Wine). 192p. 1983. pap. 7.95 (ISBN 0-571-13057-7). Faber & Faber.

Hallgarten, S. F. German Wines. 399p. 1981. 12.50 (ISBN 0-686-43334-3). Intl Pubns Serv.

Halliburton, John H., Jr. Clarksville Architecture. Smith, Barbara A., ed. (Illus.). 1978. 15.95 (ISBN 0-686-26142-9). J Halliburton.

Halliburton, R., Jr. Red Over Black: Black Slavery Among the Cherokee Indians. LC 76-15329. (Illus.). 1977. lib. bdg. 25.00 (ISBN 0-8371-9034-7, HAR/). Greenwood.

Halliburton, Warren. The Fighting Redtails: America's First Black Airmen. LC 78-13173. (Famous Firsts Ser.). (Illus.). 1978. PLB 10.76 (ISBN 0-89547-061-6). Silver.

Hallick, R. B., jt. ed. see Edelman, M.

Halliday, David & Resnick, Robert. Fundamentals of Physics: Extended Version. LC 80-23013. 985p. 1981. text ed. 34.50 (ISBN 0-471-08005-5); sol. 3.00 (ISBN 0-471-06463-7). Wiley.

--Physics, Pt 2. 3rd ed. LC 77-1295. (Arabic Translation Available). 1978. text ed. 27.50 (ISBN 0-471-34529-6); solutions manual o.p. 4.00 (ISBN 0-471-03559-9). Wiley.

Halliday, David, jt. auth. see Resnick, Robert.

Halliday, F. E., ed. see Carew, Richard.

Halliday, Fred. Ambler. 240p. 1983. 13.95 (ISBN 0-671-41184-5). S&S.

--Murder in the Kitchen. 1979. pap. 2.50 o.p. (ISBN 0-523-40665-7). Pinnacle Bks.

--The Origins of the Second Cold War. 176p. 1983. 18.50 (ISBN 0-8052-7132-5, Pub. by NLB England); pap. 6.25 (ISBN 0-8052-7133-3). Nichols Pub.

Halliday, Henry L., et al. Handbook of Neonatal Intensive Care. 1981. pap. text ed. 19.95x o.p. (ISBN 0-02-858100-8, Bailliere-Tindall). Saunders.

Halliday, James. Wines & Wineries of Western Australia. (Illus.). 119p. 1983. text ed. 12.50x (ISBN 0-7022-1673-9). U of Queensland Pr.

Halliday, Jon. A Political History of Japanese Capitalism. LC 78-18882. 1978. pap. 8.95 (ISBN 0-85345-471-X, PB471X). Monthly Rev.

Halliday, M. A. Language As Social Semiotic. 256p. 1978. text ed. 26.95 (ISBN 0-8391-1183-5). Univ Park.

Halliday, M. A. K. Halliday: System & Function in Language: Selected Papers. Kress, Gunther, ed. (Language & Language Learning Ser.). 1976. pap. text ed. 11.00x o.p. (ISBN 0-19-437062-3). Oxford U Pr.

Halliday, Michael A. Learning How to Mean: Explorations in the Development of Language. new ed. LC 76-51756. 1977. 9.95 o.p. (ISBN 0-444-00200-6, North Holland). Elsevier.

Halliday, N. A. & Martin, J. R., eds. Readings in Systemic Linguistics. 320p. 1981. 40.00 o.p. (ISBN 0-7134-3677-8, Pub. by Batsford England); pap. 22.50 (ISBN 0-7134-3678-6). David & Charles.

Halliday, Robert & Resnick, David. Physics, Pts. 1 & 2. 3rd combined ed. 1978. text ed. 42.95 (ISBN 0-471-34530-X); avail tchr's manual (ISBN 0-471-09712-8). Wiley.

Halliday, Tim. Sexual Strategy. LC 82-2607. (Phoenix). (Illus.). 160p. 1982. pap. 10.95 (ISBN 0-226-31387-5). U of Chicago Pr.

Halliday, W. J. Glossary of Immunological Terms. 102p. 1971. 13.95 (ISBN 0-407-72740-X). Butterworth.

Halliday, W. R. Folklore Studies, Ancient & Modern. LC 76-78175. 1971. Repr. of 1924 ed. 27.00 o.p. (ISBN 0-8103-3676-6). Gale.

Halliday, William H. American Caves & Caving. rev. ed. (Illus.). 368p. 1982. pap. 8.61i (ISBN 0-06-463556-2, EH556, EH). B&N NY.

Halline, Allan G., ed. & intro. by. Six Great American Plays. 7.95 (ISBN 0-394-60457-1). Modern Lib.

Halling, Roy E. The Genus Collybia (Agaricales) in the Northeastern U. S. & Adjacent Canada. (Mycologia Memoirs 8). (Illus.). 150p. 1983. 27.00 (ISBN 3-7682-1345-5). Lubrecht & Cramer.

Hallissey, Robert C. The Rajput Rebellion Against Aurangzeb: A Study of the Mughal Empire in Seventeenth-Century India. LC 77-268. (Illus.). 136p. 1977. 13.00x (ISBN 0-8262-0222-5). U of Mo Pr.

Halliwell, Leslie. Halliwell's Film Guide. (Illus.). 1018p. 1979. 36.00x o.p. (ISBN 0-8464-1259-4). Beekman Pubs.

--Halliwell's Hundred: A Nostalgic Choice of Films from the Golden Age. LC 81-84272. 403p. 1982. 25.00 (ISBN 0-684-17447-2). Scribner.

Halliwell-Phillipps, James O. Dictionary of Archaic & Provincial Words, Obsolete Phrases, Proverbs, & Ancient Customs, from the Fourteenth Century, 2 vols. LC 66-27837. 1968. Repr. of 1847 ed. Set. 86.00x (ISBN 0-8103-3283-3). Gale.

--Nursery Rhymes of England. LC 67-23936. 1969. Repr. of 1843 ed. 34.00x (ISBN 0-8103-3482-8). Gale.

--Popular Rhymes & Nursery Tales. LC 68-23470. 1968. Repr. of 1849 ed. 34.00x (ISBN 0-8103-3484-4). Gale.

Hallman, E. S. Broadcasting in Canada. (Case Studies on Broadcasting Systems). (Orig.). 1977. pap. 14.00 o.p. (ISBN 0-7100-8528-1). Routledge & Kegan.

Hallman, G. V. & Rosenbloom, J. S. Personal Financial Planning: How to Plan for Your Financial Freedom. 2nd ed. (McGraw-Hill Paperback Ser.). 1981. pap. 5.95 o.p. (ISBN 0-07-025644-6). McGraw.

Hallman, G. Victor & Rosenbloom, Jerry. Personal Financial Planning. 2nd ed. (Illus.). 1978. 22.95 o.p. (ISBN 0-07-025641-1, P&RB). McGraw.

Hallman, G. Victor, jt. auth. see Rosenbloom, Jerry.

Hallman, Howard W. The Organization & Operation of Neighborhood Councils: A Practical Guide. LC 77-1872. (Special Studies). 1977. 25.95 o.p. (ISBN 0-03-022716-X). Praeger.

Hallman, Ruth. Breakaway. (YA) (gr. 7-12). 1983. pap. 1.75 (ISBN 0-440-90864-7, LFL). Dell.

--Gimme Something, Mister! LC 78-16721. (A Hiway Bk). (gr. 3). 1978. 8.95 (ISBN 0-664-32638-2). Westminster.

--Rescue Chopper. (gr. 7-12). 1981. pap. 1.75 (ISBN 0-440-97398-8, LE). Dell.

--Secrets of a Silent Stranger. LC 76-13598. (A Hiway Bk.). 1976. 6.95 o.s.i. (ISBN 0-664-32598-X). Westminster.

Hallmark, Clayton. Auto Electronics Simplified. LC 74-25566. (Illus.). 256p. 1975. pap. 5.95 o.p. (ISBN 0-8306-3749-4, 749). TAB Bks.

--Computerist's Handy Manual. (Illus.). 1979. pap. 3.95 (ISBN 0-8306-1107-X, 1107). TAB Bks.

--How to Install Everything Electronic in Cars, Boats, Planes, Trucks & RVs. (Illus.). 1978. 10.95 (ISBN 0-8306-9902-3); pap. 7.95 o.p. (ISBN 0-8306-1056-1, 1056). TAB Bks.

--Lasers, the Light Fantastic. (Illus.). 1979. 14.95 (ISBN 0-8306-9857-4); pap. 8.95 (ISBN 0-8306-1108-8, 1108). TAB Bks.

Hallmark, Clayton L. The Master IC Cookbook. (Illus.). 476p. (Orig.). 1980. 17.95 (ISBN 0-8306-9964-3); pap. 11.95 (ISBN 0-8306-1199-1, 1199). TAB Bks.

Hallo, W. W., et al, eds. Scripture in Context II: More Essays on the Comparative Method. 1983. text ed. 15.00x (ISBN 0-931464-14-5). Eisenbrauns.

Halloran, J. Supervision: The Art of Management. 1981. 21.95 (ISBN 0-13-876276-7); pap. 8.95 study guide (ISBN 0-13-876292-9). P-H.

Halloran, Jack. Activity Giude for Applied Human Relations. 2nd ed. (Illus.). 192p. 1983. Workbook 8.95 (ISBN 0-686-38835-6). P H.

--Applied Human Relations: An Organizational Approach. (Illus.). 1978. ref. ed. 20.95 (ISBN 0-13-040857-3); activity guide 7.95 (ISBN 0-13-040824-7). P-H.

--Applied Human Relations: An Organizational Approach. 2nd ed. (Illus.). 496p. 1983. 22.95 (ISBN 0-13-040808-5). P-H.

Halloran, James D. Attitude Formation & Change. LC 75-41501. (Television Research Committee Working Paper Ser.: No. 2). 167p. 1976. Repr. of 1967 ed. lib. bdg. 25.00x (ISBN 0-8371-8700-1, HAFC). Greenwood.

Halloran, Joe. Understanding Homosexual Persons: Straight Answers from Gays. 1979. 6.00 o.p. (ISBN 0-682-49468-2). Exposition.

Hallowell, John H., ed. see Voegelin, Eric.

Hallows, Ian, jt. ed. see Bird, Anthony.

Halls, Geraldine. The Last Inheritor. 224p. 1980. 9.95 o.p. (ISBN 0-312-47087-8). St Martin.

Halls, W. D. International Equivalences in Access to Higher Education. (Studies on International Equivalences of Degrees). 137p. 1972. pap. 7.00 o.p. (ISBN 92-3-100909-5, U327, UNESCO). Unipub.

--Maurice Maeterlinck: A Study of His Life & Thought. LC 78-16379. 1978. Repr. of 1960 ed. lib. bdg. 19.25x (ISBN 0-313-20574-4, HAMM). Greenwood.

Halls, W. D., tr. see Durkheim, Emile.

Halls, W. D., tr. see Hubert, Henri & Mauss, Marcel.

Hallstead, William F. Ghost Plane of Blackwater. LC 74-17071. 156p. (gr. 7 up). 1975. pap. 1.75 (ISBN 0-15-634730-X, AVB95, VoyB). HarBraceJ.

--The Launching of Linda Bell. 160p. 1983. pap. 1.95 (ISBN 0-449-70053-4, Juniper). Fawcett.

Hallstein, Walter. European Community: A New Path to Peaceful Union. 1964. 6.25x o.p. (ISBN 0-210-31238-6). Asia.

Hallwas, John, ed. The Poetry of H: Lost Poet of Lincoln's Illinois. 240p. 1982. 22.95 (ISBN 0-933180-38-1). Ellis Pr.

Hallwood, C. Paul & Sinclair, Stuart W. Oil Debt & Development: OPEC in the Third World. 208p. 1981. pap. text ed. 10.95x (ISBN 0-04-382027-1). Allen Unwin.

Hallwood, Paul. Stabilization of International Commodity Markets. Altman, Edward I. & Walter, Ingo, eds. LC 77-7793. (Contemporary Studies in Economic & Financial Analysis: Vol. 18). 200p. 1979. 36.00 (ISBN 0-89232-086-9). Jai Pr.

Halm, John Van see Van Halm, John.

Halman, Talat S. Modern Turkish Drama: An Anthology. LC 73-79204. (Studies in Middle Eastern Literatures: No. 5). 1976. 25.00x o.p. (ISBN 0-88297-007-0). Bibliotheca.

Halme, A., ed. see IFAC.

Halmi, Robert. Photographing Women Simplified. (Illus.). 96p. 1976. pap. 4.95 o.p. (ISBN 0-8174-0189-X, Amphoto); Spanish Ed. pap. 6.95 o.p. (ISBN 0-8174-0323-X). Watson-Guptill.

Halmos, P. R. A Hilbert Space Problem Book. LC 74-10673. (Graduate Texts in Mathematics Ser.: Vol. 19). 385p. 1974. 22.00 o.p. (ISBN 0-387-90090-X). Springer-Verlag.

--A Hilbert Space Problem Book. rev., enl. ed. (Graduate Texts in Mathematics Ser.: Vol. 19). 369p. 1982. 28.00 (ISBN 0-387-90685-1). Springer-Verlag.

--Measure Theory. LC 74-10690. (Graduate Texts in Mathematics Ser.: Vol. 18). 305p. 1974. 21.00 o.p. (ISBN 0-387-90088-8). Springer-Verlag.

--Naive Set Theory. LC 74-10687. (Undergraduate Texts in Mathematics Ser.). 110p. 1974. pap. 13.00 o.p. (ISBN 0-387-90092-6). Springer-Verlag.

--Selecta Volume One: Research Contributions. (Illus.). 458p. 1983. 32.00 (ISBN 0-387-90755-6). Springer-Verlag.

--Selecta Volume Two: Expository Writing. (Illus.). 256p. 1983. 19.80 (ISBN 0-387-90756-4). Springer-Verlag.

Halmos, P. R., ed. see Conway, J. B.

Halmos, Paul R. Algebraic Logic. LC 61-17955. 1962. 12.95 (ISBN 0-8284-0154-3). Chelsea Pub.

--Introduction to Hilbert Space. 2nd ed. LC 57-12834. 9.95 (ISBN 0-8284-0082-2). Chelsea Pub.

--Lectures on Ergodic Theory. LC 60-8964. 8.95 (ISBN 0-8284-0142-X). Chelsea Pub.

Halmshaw, R. Industrial Radiology: Theory & Practice. (Illus.). xii, 329p. 1982. 65.75 (ISBN 0-85334-105-2, Pub. by Applied Sci England). Elsevier.

Halpenny, Frances see Halpenny, Francess.

Halpenny, Francess, ed. Dictionary of Canadian Biography. Incl. Vol. I. 1000-1700. Brown, G. W. & Trudel, Marcel, eds. xxiii, 755p. 1966. 35.00 (ISBN 0-8020-3142-0); laurentian ed. 100.00 (ISBN 0-8020-3139-0); Vol. II. 1701-1740. Hayne, David & Vachon, Andre, eds. xli, 759p. 1969. 35.00 (ISBN 0-8020-3240-0); Laurentian ed. 100.00 (ISBN 0-8020-3249-4); Vol. III. 1741-1770. La Terreur, Marc, ed. 1974. 35.00 (ISBN 0-8020-3314-8); laurentian ed. 100.00 (ISBN 0-8020-3315-6); Vol. IV. 1771-1800. Halpenny, Frances, ed. 1979. 35.00 (ISBN 0-8020-3351-2); laurentian ed. 100.00 (ISBN 0-8020-3352-0); Vol. IX. 1861-1870. Hamelin, Jean, ed. 1976. 35.00 (ISBN 0-8020-3319-9); laurentian ed. 100.00 (ISBN 0-8020-3320-2); Vol. X. 1871-1880. La Terreur, Marc, ed. 1972. 35.00 (ISBN 0-8020-3287-7); laurentian ed. 100.00 (ISBN 0-8020-3288-5); Vol. XI. 1881-1890. Halpenny, Francess G., ed. 1100p. 1982. 35.00 (ISBN 0-8020-3367-9); laurentian ed. 125.00 (ISBN 0-8020-3368-7). LC 66-31909. U of Toronto Pr.

Halpenny, Francess G. see Halpenny, Francess.

Halper, H. Robert & Foster, Hope S. Laboratory Regulation Manual. LC 76-56666. 1977. 325.00 (ISBN 0-912862-29-7). Aspen Systems.

Halper, Thomas. Power, Politics, & American Democracy. 1981. pap. text ed. 16.50x (ISBN 0-673-16273-7). Scott F.

Halperin. Religion, Sect & Cult. 416p. 1983. pap. text ed. write for info. (ISBN 0-7236-7029-3). Wright PSG.

Halperin, David M. Before Pastoral: Theocritus & the Ancient Tradition of Bucolic Poetry. LC 82-10879. 296p. 1983. text ed. 26.00x (ISBN 0-300-02582-3). Yale U Pr.

Halperin, Ed, et al. Symbol Simons Too. (Orig.). (gr. 3-7). 1981. pap. 2.95 o.p. (ISBN 0-671-42537-4). Wanderer Bks.

Halperin, Edwin, et al. Symbol Simons: A New Type of Word Game & Puzzle. (Illus., Orig.). (gr. 5 up). 1979. pap. 1.95 o.p. (ISBN 0-671-33060-8). Wanderer Bks.

Halperin, Edwin G., jt. auth. see Grosser, Paul E.

Halperin, J., ed. Jane Austen: Bicentenary Essays. 368p. 1975. 37.50 (ISBN 0-521-20709-6); pap. 12.95 (ISBN 0-521-09929-3). Cambridge U Pr.

Halperin, John. Gissing: A Life in Books. (Illus.). 1982. 29.95x (ISBN 0-19-812677-8). Oxford U Pr.

Halperin, Mark. A Place Made Fast. 80p. (Orig.). 1982. pap. 6.00 (ISBN 0-914742-62-0). Copper Canyon.

--The White Coverlet. 1979. 2.50 o.p. (ISBN 0-918116-14-7). Jawbone Pr.

Halperin, Morton H. Defense Strategies for the Seventies. LC 82-45020. 164p. 1983. pap. text ed. 9.25 (ISBN 0-8191-2710-8). U Pr of Amer.

--Limited War in the Nuclear Age. LC 77-18193. 1978. Repr. of 1963 ed. lib. bdg. 19.25x (ISBN 0-313-20116-1, HALW). Greenwood.

Halperin, Morton H. & Hoffman, Daniel N. Top Secret: National Security & the Right to Know. LC 77-5349. 1977. 8.95 (ISBN 0-915220-27-X); pap. 3.95 (ISBN 0-915220-28-8). New Republic.

Halperin, Morton H., jt. ed. see Adler, Allan.

Halperin, Morton H., et al. Bureaucratic Politics & Foreign Policy. LC 73-22384. 340p. 1974. 22.95 (ISBN 0-8157-3408-5); pap. 8.95 (ISBN 0-8157-3407-7). Brookings.

Halperin, Stephen. Convention. (Orig.). 1983. pap. 3.50 (ISBN 0-440-11573-6). Dell.

Halpern, Andrew S. Contemporary Assessment for Mentally Retarded Adolescents & Adults. LC 82-2636. 112p. 1982. pap. text ed. 12.95 (ISBN 0-8391-1737-X, 18139). Univ Park.

Halpern, Ben. The American Jew: A Zionistic Analysis. LC 82-16875. 192p. 1983. pap. 6.95 (ISBN 0-8052-0742-2). Schocken.

Halpern, Daniel. Seasonal Rights. 1982. pap. 6.95 (ISBN 0-14-042304-4). Penguin.

Halpern, Daniel, ed. The American Poetry Anthology. 1975. pap. 7.95 o.s.i. (ISBN 0-380-00399-6, 52126). Avon.

--Antaeus, No. 47. 1982. pap. 4.00 (ISBN 0-88001-019-3). Ecco Pr.

--Antaeus, No. 48/9. 1982. pap. 5.00 (ISBN 0-88001-020-7). Ecco Pr.

--Antaeus, No. 49. 1983. pap. 5.00 (ISBN 0-88001-026-6). Ecco Pr.

Halpern, Florence. Survival: Black & White. 225p. 1973. text ed. 25.00 o.p. (ISBN 0-08-016994-5); pap. text ed. 10.00 (ISBN 0-08-017193-1). Pergamon.

Halpern, Frances. Writer's Guide to West Coast Publishing. 1980. 9.95 o.p. (ISBN 0-89260-160-4). Hwong Pub.

Halpern, Howard M. No Strings Attached. 1980. 9.95 o.p. (ISBN 0-671-24047-1). S&S.

Halpern, Ilsa, jt. auth. see Halpern, James.

Halpern, Irving W. Decade of Probation, a Study & Report. LC 69-14930. (Criminology, Law Enforcement, & Social Problems Ser.: No. 66). (With an intro. added). 1969. Repr. of 1939 ed. 12.00x (ISBN 0-87585-066-9). Patterson Smith.

Halpern, James & Halpern, Ilsa. Projections: Our World of Imaginary Relationships. 192p. 1983. 13.95 (ISBN 0-399-31017-7). Seaview Bks.

Halpern, Joseph, et al, eds. The Myths of Deinstitutionalization: Policies for the Mentally Disabled. (Westview Special Studies in Health Care & Medical Science). 152p. 1980. lib. bdg. 17.50 (ISBN 0-89158-843-4). Westview.

Halpern, M. G., ed. Polishing & Waxing Compositions: Recent Developments. LC 82-7691. (Chemical Technology Rev. 213). (Illus.). 301p. 1983. 36.00 (ISBN 0-8155-0916-2). Noyes.

Halpern, Moyshe-Leyb. In New York: A Selection. Hellerstein, Kathryn, tr. from Yiddish. (The Jewish Poetry Ser.). 192p. 1982. 14.95 (ISBN 0-8276-0209-X); pap. 9.95 (ISBN 0-8276-0210-3). Jewish Pubn.

Halpern, S. The Assurance Sciences: An Introduction to Quality Control & Reliability. 1978. 23.95 (ISBN 0-13-049601-4). P-H.

Halpert, Herbert & Story, G. M., eds. Christmas Mumming in Newfoundland: Essays in Anthropology, Folklore & History. LC 71-391290. 1969. 27.50x o.p. (ISBN 0-8020-7065-5). U of Toronto Pr.

Halpert, Herbert, ed. see Hudson, A. P.

Halpert, Inge, jt. auth. see Madrigal, Margarita.

Halphen, L. Charlemagne & the Carolingian Empire. (Europe in the Middle Ages Ser.: Vol. 3). 1978. 61.75 (ISBN 0-444-11078-X, North-Holland). Elsevier.

Halpin, Anne, ed. Gourmet Gardening. (Illus.). 256p. 1981. pap. 9.95 o.p. (ISBN 0-87857-349-6). Rodale Pr Inc.

Halpin, Anne, ed. see Ball, Jeff.

Halpin, Anne, ed. see Carr, Anna.

Halpin, Anne, ed. see Keisling, Bill.

Halpin, Anne, ed. see Proulx, E. Annie.

Halpin, Anne, ed. see Rodale Press Editors.

Halpin, Anne, ed. see Simonds, Calvin.

Halpin, Anne M., ed. Unusual Vegetables: Something New for This Year's Garden. LC 78-528. 1978. 14.95 o.p. (ISBN 0-87857-214-7). Rodale Pr Inc.

Halpin, D. W. & Woodhead, R. W. Construction Management. 483p. 1980. 34.50 (ISBN 0-471-34566-0). Wiley.

Halpin, Daniel W. & Woodhead, Ronald W. Design of Construction & Process Operations. LC 76-9784. 424p. 1976. 41.95 (ISBN 0-471-34565-2). Wiley.

Halpin, Marjorie M. Totem Poles: An Illustrated Guide. (Illus.). 64p. (Orig.). 1983. pap. 8.95 (ISBN 0-295-96026-4). U of Wash Pr.

Halpin, Marlene. Imagine That! 144p. 1982. pap. 4.50 (ISBN 0-697-01812-1); videotapes avail. Wm C Brown.

Halporn, James W., et al. The Meters of Greek & Latin Poetry. LC 77-25945. (The Library of Liberal Arts). 1978. Repr. of 1963 ed. lib. bdg. 15.50x (ISBN 0-313-20090-4, HAGL). Greenwood.

Halprin, jt. auth. see Tijssen.

Halprin, Lawrence, et al. Taking Part: A Workshop Approach for Collective Creativity. 1975. 25.00x (ISBN 0-262-08079-6); pap. 9.95 o.p. (ISBN 0-262-58028-4). MIT Pr.

Halsall, E. The Comprehensive School: Guidelines for the Reorganization of Secondary Education. rev ed. LC 72-10107. 248p. 1974. pap. text ed. 17.50 (ISBN 0-08-018231-3). Pergamon.

Halsbard, Robert, ed. see Montagu, Mary W.

Halse, Albert O. Architectural Rendering: The Technique of Contemporary Presentation. 2nd ed. (Illus.). 323p. 1972. 49.50 (ISBN 0-07-025628-4, P&RB). McGraw.

--The Use of Color in Interiors. 2nd ed. (Illus.). 1978. 39.50 (ISBN 0-07-025624-1, P&RB). McGraw.

Halsell, Grace. Getting to Know Guatemala & the Two Honduras. (Getting to Know Ser.). (Illus.). (gr. 3-5). 1964. PLB 3.97 o.p. (ISBN 0-698-30121-8, Coward). Putnam Pub Group.

Halsey, A. H., ed. Heredity & Environment. LC 77-2530. 1977. 13.95 (ISBN 0-02-913670-9). Free Pr.

Halsey, A. H., jt. ed. see Karabel, Jerome.

Halsey, Albert H. & Heath, Anthony F. Origins & Destinations: Family, Class & Education in Modern Britain. (Illus.). 1980. text ed. 29.50x (ISBN 0-19-827224-3); pap. 15.95x (ISBN 0-19-827249-9). Oxford U Pr.

Halsey, Martha T. Antonio Buero Vallejo. (World Authors Ser.: Spain: No. 260). 1971. lib. bdg. 10.95 o.p. (ISBN 0-8057-2925-9, Twayne). G K Hall.

Halsey, Rosalie V. Forgotten Books of the American Nursery. LC 68-31084. 1969. Repr. of 1911 ed. 30.00x (ISBN 0-8103-3483-6). Gale.

Halsey, S. H., jt. auth. see Mound, L. A.

Halsey, Van R., ed. see Bennett, P.

Halsey, Van R., ed. see Casey, Dayle A.

Halsey, Van R., ed. see Guttmann, Allen.

Halsey, Van R., ed. see Harris, Jonathan.

Halsey, William & Bryan, J. Admiral Halsey's Story. (Politics & Strategy of World War II Ser.). 1976. Repr. of 1917 ed. lib. bdg. 37.50 (ISBN 0-306-70770-5). Da Capo.

Halsman, Phillippe. Halsman: Sight & Insight. (Illus.). 1972. 25.00 (ISBN 0-8174-0313-2, Amphoto). Watson-Guptill.

Halstead, Beverly. A Closer Look at Prehistoric Reptiles. LC 78-23770. (Closer Look at Ser.). (Illus.). (gr. 4-8). 1978. PLB 9.40 (ISBN 0-531-01477-0, Gloucester Pr); pap. 1.95 o.p. (ISBN 0-531-02487-3). Watts.

Halstead, Caroline. Richard the Third as Duke of Gloucester & King of England, 2 Vols. 1027p. 1980. text ed. 67.50x set (ISBN 0-904387-14-3, Pub. by Sutton England); pap. text ed. 36.00x_set (ISBN 0-904387-41-0). Humanities.

Halstead, Charles L., et al. Physical Evaluation of the Dental Patient. LC 81-18676. (Illus.). 422p. 1982. text ed. 29.95 (ISBN 0-8016-0887-2). Mosby.

Halstead, George B., tr. see Poincare, H.

Halstead, George B., tr. see Saccheri, Girolamo.

Halstead, L. B. Search for the Past. LC 82-45203. 208p. 1983. 19.95 (ISBN 0-385-18212-0). Doubleday.

Halstead, L. B., jt. auth. see Lambert, David.

Halstead, L. B. & Ajayi, S. S., eds. Wildlife Management in Savannah Woodland. 237p. 1978. write for info. (ISBN 0-85066-175-7, Pub. by Taylor & Francis). Intl Pubns Serv.

Halstead, Lauro S. & Claus-Walker, Jacqueline. Neuroactive Drugs of Choice in Spinal Cord Injury: A Guide for Using Neurologically Active Medications in Spinal Injured Patients. 96p. 1981. pap. text ed. 7.50 (ISBN 0-89004-750-2). Raven.

Halstead, William P. Shakespeare As Spoken: a Collation of Five Thousand Acting Editions & Promptbooks of Shakespeare: Vol. 8: Richard III, Henry VIII, Troilus & Cressida. LC 77-84909. 1978. 39.75 o.p. (ISBN 0-8357-0335-5, SS-00062). Univ Microfilms.

Halstead, William P. Statistical History of Acting Editions of Shakespeare: Supplement to Shakespeare as Spoken, Vol. 13. LC 82-20232. 628p. 1983. lib. bdg. 35.25 (ISBN 0-8191-2854-6). U Pr of Amer.

--Statistical History of Acting Editions of Shakespeare: Supplement to Shakespeare as Spoken, Vol. 14. LC 82-20232. 654p. 1983. lib. bdg. 32.25 (ISBN 0-8191-2855-4). U Pr of Amer.

Halsted, Charles H. & Halsted, James A. The Laboratory in Clinical Medicine. (Illus.). 1083p. 1981. text ed. 72.00 (ISBN 0-7216-4479-1). Saunders.

Halsted, James A., jt. auth. see Halsted, Charles H.

Halsted, James A., ed. The Laboratory in Clinical Medicine: Interpretation & Application. LC 74-12912. (Illus.). 1976. text ed. 45.00 o.p. (ISBN 0-7216-4478-3). Saunders.

Halston, Carole. Undercover Girl. (Nightingale Ser.). 1982. pap. 8.95 (ISBN 0-8161-3461-8, Large Print Bks). G K Hall.

Haltenorth & Diller. A Field Guide to the Mammals of Africa. 34.95 (ISBN 0-686-42780-7, Collins Pub England). Greene.

Halter, F., ed. Antacids in the Eighties. (Illus.). 160p. 1982. text ed. 22.50 (ISBN 0-8067-0831-X). Urban & S.

Halter, Jon C. Bill Bradley: One to Remember. new ed. LC 74-80655. (Putnam Sports Shelf). 160p. (gr. 5-8). 1974. PLB 6.29 o.p. (ISBN 0-399-60916-4). Putnam Pub Group.

--Reggie Jackson: All-Star in Right. (Putnam Sports Shelf). 1975. PLB 5.49 o.p. (ISBN 0-399-60962-8). Putnam Pub Group.

--Their Backs to the Wall: Famous Last Stands. LC 80-10683. (Illus.). 224p. (gr. 7 up). 1980. PLB 8.29 o.p. (ISBN 0-671-32957-X). Messner.

--Top Secret Projects of World War II. LC 77-18779. (Illus.). 192p. (gr. 7 up). 1978. PLB 7.79 o.p. (ISBN 0-671-32857-3). Messner.

Halterman, Jean C., jt. auth. see Frey, Albert W.

Haltiner, G. J. & Martin, F. L. Dynamical & Physical Meteorology. 1957. text ed. 41.95 o.p. (ISBN 0-07-025640-3, C). McGraw.

Halton, B., jt. auth. see Coxon, J. M.

Halton, Frances, jt. auth. see Millard, Anne.

Halton, Thomas P. & O'Leary, Catherine S. Classical Scholarship: An Annotated Bibliography. LC 82-48984. 1983. lib. bdg. price not set (ISBN 0-527-37436-9). Kraus Intl.

Halttunen, Karen. Confidence Men & Painted Women: A Study of Middle-Class Culture in America, 1830-1870. LC 82-8336. (Yale Historical Publications Misc.: No. 129). (Illus.). 280p. 1983. text ed. 19.95x (ISBN 0-300-02835-0). Yale U Pr.

Halverhout, H. Dutch Cooking. 1975. pap. 20.00 o.s.i. (ISBN 0-911268-20-0). Rogers Bk.

Halverson, Richard C. The Timelessness of Jesus Christ. LC 82-8008. Orig. Title: Relevance. 1982. Repr. of 1968 ed. 7.95 (ISBN 0-8307-0838-3, 5109902). Regal.

Halverson, Sandy. Book of Mormon Activity Book. (Illus.). 80p. (gr. 3-8). 1982. pap. 2.50 (ISBN 0-88290-188-5, 4521). Horizon Utah.

Halverson, William H. A Concise Introduction to Philosophy. 4th ed. 493p. 1981. text ed. 18.00 (ISBN 0-394-32533-8). Random.

Halverstadt, Robert. God's Word for Your Healing. 1982. pap. 1.75 (ISBN 0-88144-003-5, CPS-003). Christian Pub.

--God's Word for Your Prosperity. 1982. pap. 1.75 (ISBN 0-88144-002-7, CPS-002). Christian Pub.

--Your New Birth. 1982. pap. 0.75 (ISBN 0-88144-001-9, CPS-001). Christian Pub.

Halvorsen, Robert & Ruby, Michael G. Benefit-Cost Analysis of Air-Pollution Control. LC 78-19587. (Illus.). 288p. 1981. 28.95x (ISBN 0-669-02647-6). Lexington Bks.

Halvorson, E. W., jt. auth. see Ball, V. A.

Ham. Geriatrics. 464p. 1983. text ed. price not set (ISBN 0-7236-7052-8). Wright-PSG.

Ham, Arthur W., et al. Blood Cell Formation & the Cellular Basis of Immune Responses. (Illus.). 1979. pap. text ed. 12.00 flexible bdg. (ISBN 0-397-50461-6, Lippincott Medical). Lippincott.

Ham, C. Health Policy in Britain: The Politics & Organization of the NHS. 208p. 1982. text ed. 23.25x (ISBN 0-333-30737-2, Pub. by Macmillan England). Humanities.

Ham, C. W., et al. Mechanics of Machinery. 4th ed. (Mechanical Engineering Ser.). 1958. text ed. 36.00 (ISBN 0-07-025688-8, C). McGraw.

Ham, Inyong & Bhattacharyya, Amitabha. Design of Cutting Tools: Use of Metal Cutting Theory. LC 68-29237. (Manufacturing Data Ser). (Illus.). 1969. 11.00 (ISBN 0-87263-014-5). SME.

Ham, N. D., jt. auth. see Noll, R. B.

Ham, Randall E. The Country & the Kingdom: Sir Herbert Croft & the Elizabethan State. 316p. 1977. pap. text ed. 11.75 (ISBN 0-8191-0260-1). U Pr of Amer.

Ham, Roswell G. Otway & Lee: Biography from a Baroque Age. LC 31-4706. (Illus.). 1969. Repr. of 1931 ed. lib. bdg. 16.00x (ISBN 0-8371-0462-9, HAOL). Greenwood.

Hamabe, Mototsugu, jt. ed. see FAO Fisheries Technology Service.

Hamacher, V. C., et al. Computer Organization. Feigenbaum, E., ed. (Computer Science). (Illus.). 1978. text ed. 32.95 (ISBN 0-07-025681-0, C); solutions manual 3.50 (ISBN 0-07-025682-9). McGraw.

Hamada, Hiroshi. Spirit of Karate-Doh. 112p. 1982. pap. text ed. 13.95 (ISBN 0-8403-2693-9). Kendall-Hunt.

Hamaguchi, Koza, ed. Aspects of Cellular & Molecular Physiology. 1973. 25.00x (ISBN 0-86008-078-1, Pub. by Japan Sci Soc). Intl Schol Bk Serv.

Hamaker-Zondag, Karen. Interpretation: Jungian Symbolism & Astrology, Pt. 1. 192p. Date not set. write for info. (ISBN 0-87728-523-3). Weiser.

Hamalainen, Marilyn. What's Wrong with Melissa? LC 82-82670. 96p. (Orig.). (YA) (gr. 9-12). 1983. pap. 1.95 (ISBN 0-88243-641-4, 02-0641). Gospel Pub.

Hamalian, Leo. D. H. Lawrence in Italy. LC 81-502261. 224p. 1982. 12.95 (ISBN 0-8008-4572-2). Taplinger.

Hamalian, Leo & Karl, Frederick R. The Shape of Fiction: British & American Short Stories. 2nd ed. LC 77-5839. 1978. pap. text ed. 16.00x (ISBN 0-07-025699-3, C). McGraw.

Hamalian, Leo, ed. In Search of Eden. (Orig.). 1981. pap. 3.50 o.p. (ISBN 0-451-61912-9, ME1912, Ment). NAL.

Hamalian, Leo & Karl, Frederick R., eds. Short Fiction of the Masters. rev. ed. 1973. pap. 4.95 (ISBN 0-399-30023-6). Putnam Pub Group.

Hamalian, Leo & Volpe, Edmond, eds. Grammar in Context. rev. ed. Krishna, Valerie. LC 75-34840. 1976. pap. text ed. 6.95c o.p. (ISBN 0-399-30027-9). Putnam Pub Group.

Hamalian, Leo & Volpe, Edmond L., eds. Eleven Modern Short Novels. 1971. pap. 7.95 (ISBN 0-399-30004-X). Putnam Pub Group.

Hamamura, John & Hamamura, Susan. Woven Works. Vandenburgh, Jane, ed. LC 78-17810. 1978. 14.95 o.p. (ISBN 0-87701-118-4, Prism Editions); pap. 6.95 o.p. (ISBN 0-87701-117-6, Prism Editions). Chronicle Bks.

Hamamura, Susan, jt. auth. see Hamamura, John.

Hamann, Donald L. Introduction to the Classical Guitar: An Ensemble Approach for the Classroom. LC 82-16100. (Illus.). 148p. (Orig.). 1983. lib. bdg. 19.75 (ISBN 0-8191-2758-2); pap. text ed. 8.25 (ISBN 0-8191-2759-0). U Pr of Amer.

Hamann, H. P. A Popular Guide to New Testament Criticism. 1977. pap. 3.95 (ISBN 0-570-03760-3, 12-2671). Concordia.

Hamata, V., jt. auth. see Heller, B.

Hamaya, Hiroshi, photos by. Landscapes. (Illus.). 178p. 1982. 125.00 (ISBN 0-8109-1278-3). Abrams.

Hamberger, John. The Birth of a Pond. (Illus.). 32p. (gr. 3-7). 1976. 5.95 o.p. (ISBN 0-698-20337-2, Coward). Putnam Pub Group.

Hambidge, Jay. The Greek Vase: Dynamic Symmetry. (Promotion of the Arts Library). (Illus.). 131p. Date not set. Repr. of 1917 ed. 97.45 (ISBN 0-89901-030-X). Found Class Reprints.

Hamblen, John W. & Landis, Carolyn R., eds. Fourth Inventory of Computers in Higher Education. (EDUCOM Oser. in Computing & Telecommunications in Higher Education: No. 4). 1970. lib. bdg. 35.00 (ISBN 0-89158-568-0). Westview.

Hambley, Edmund C. Bridge Deck Behavior. 1976. 39.95x (ISBN 0-412-13190-0, Pub. by Chapman & Hall). Methuen Inc.

Hamblin, Douglas, ed. Problems & Practice of Pastoral Care. (Illus.). 314p. 1981. 29.50x o.p. (ISBN 0-631-12921-9, Pub. by Basil Blackwell); pap. 10.95x o.p. (ISBN 0-631-12931-6). Biblio Dist.

Hamblin, Douglas H. The Teacher & Counselling. 346p. 1974. 29.00x o.p. (ISBN 0-631-15230-X, Pub. by Basil Blackwell); pap. 11.25x o.p. (ISBN 0-631-19140-2). Biblio Dist.

--The Teacher & Pastoral Care. 287p. 1978. 29.00x o.p. (ISBN 0-631-18670-0, Pub. by Basil Blackwell England); pap. 11.25x o.p. (ISBN 0-631-18680-8). Biblio Dist.

Hamblin, Kenneth W. The Earth's Dynamic Systems: A Textbook of Physical Geology. 3rd ed. LC 80-68323. (Illus.). 544p. 1982. text ed. 22.95x (ISBN 0-8087-3172-6). Burgess.

Hamblin, Robert L. & Miller, Jerry L. Introduction to Mathematical Patterns of Cultural Diffusion. (CISE Learning Package Ser.: No. 20). (Illus.). 39p. (Orig.). 1976. pap. text ed. 3.00x (ISBN 0-936876-32-8). Learn Res Intl Stud.

Hamblin, Robert L. & Kunkel, John, eds. Behavioral Theory in Sociology: Essays in Honor of George C. Homans. LC 76-1776. 546p. 1976. 29.95 (ISBN 0-87855-149-2). Transaction Bks.

Hamblin, Robert W. & Brodsky, Louis D. Selections from the William Faulkner Collection of Louis Daniel Brodsky: A Descriptive Catalogue. LC 79-375. 171p. 1979. 17.50x (ISBN 0-8139-0830-2). U Pr of Va.

Hamblin, T. J. Plasmapheresis & Plasma Exchange, Vol. 1. Horrobin, D. F., ed. (Annual Research Reviews). 1979. 18.00 (ISBN 0-88831-065-X, Dist. by Pergamon). Eden Pr.

Hambly, Barbara. The Quirnal Hill Affair. 320p. 1983. 15.95 (ISBN 0-312-66123-1). St Martin.

--The Walls of Air. 320p. (Orig.). 1983. pap. 2.95 (ISBN 0-345-29670-2, Del Rey). Ballantine.

Hambly, Wilfrid D. The History of Tattooing & Its Significance, with Some Account of Other Forms of Corporal Marking. LC 73-174052. (Illus.). 346p. 1975. Repr. of 1925 ed. 45.00x (ISBN 0-8103-4024-0). Gale.

Hambourg, Maria M., jt. auth. see Szarkowski, John.

Hambrick, Ralph S., Jr. & Snyder, William P. The Analysis of Policy Arguments. (Learning Packages in the Policy Sciences Ser.: No. 13). 72p. 1979. pap. text ed. 3.00x (ISBN 0-936826-02-9). Pol Stud Assocs.

Hamburg, David A. & McGown, Elizabeth R. The Great Apes. 1979. text ed. 29.95 (ISBN 0-8053-3669-9). Benjamin-Cummings.

Hamburg, David A., et al, eds. Perception & Its Disorders. (ARNMD Research Publications Ser: Vol. 48). 446p. 1970. 24.50 o.p. (ISBN 0-683-00241-4). Raven.

Hamburg, H. R. & Morgans, W. M., eds. Hess's Paint Film Defects: Their Causes & Cure. 3rd ed. 1979. 73.00x (ISBN 0-412-13880-8, Pub. by Chapman & Hall). Methuen Inc.

Hamburg, Joseph, ed. Review of Allied Health Education, No. 1. LC 74-7876. (Illus.). 244p. 1974. 13.00x (ISBN 0-8131-1322-9). U Pr of Ky.

--Review of Allied Health Education, No. 3. LC 74-7876. 168p. 1979. 13.00x (ISBN 0-8131-1367-9). U Pr of Ky.

Hamburg, Marian & Hopp, Joyce, eds. Cross-Cultural Aspects of School Health: Journal of School Health. 1983. pap. 4.50 (ISBN 0-917160-18-5). Am Sch Health.

Hamburg, Morris. Statistical Analysis for Decision Making. 2nd ed. (Illus.). 801p. 1977. text ed. 25.95 (ISBN 0-15-583747-8, HC); solutions manual avail. (ISBN 0-15-583748-6). HarBraceJ.

Hamburger. Advances in Nephrology, Vol. 12. 1983. 55.00 (ISBN 0-8151-4135-1). Year Bk Med.

Hamburger, Estelle. The Fashion Business: It's All Yours. 1976. text ed. 15.95 scp o.p. (ISBN 0-06-453503-7, HarpC); pap. text ed. 13.50 scp o.p. (ISBN 0-06-453502-9). Har-Row.

Hamburger, J., et al. Nephrology. 1193p. 1979. 135.00 (ISBN 0-471-01762-0, Pub. by Wiley Med). Wiley.

Hamburger, Jean. Advances in Nephrology, Vol. 7. 1978. 55.00 (ISBN 0-8151-4116-5). Year Bk Med.

--Advances in Nephrology, Vol. 8. 1979. 55.00 (ISBN 0-8151-4117-3). Year Bk Med.

--Advances in Nephrology, Vol. 9. 1980. 55.00 (ISBN 0-8151-4118-1). Year Bk Med.

--Advances in Nephrology, Vol. 10. 1981. 55.00 (ISBN 0-8151-4119-X). Year Bk Med.

--Discovering the Individual. 1978. 7.95 o.p. (ISBN 0-393-06433-6). Norton.

Hamburger, Jean, et al. Renal Transplantation: Theory & Practice. 2nd ed. (Illus.). 395p. 1981. 47.00 (ISBN 0-686-77747-6, 3872-9). Williams & Wilkins.

--Structure & Function of the Kidney. LC 72-151678. (Organ Physiology Ser.). (Illus.). 1971. 7.00 o.p. (ISBN 0-7216-4490-2). Saunders.

Hamburger, M., tr. see Holderlin, F.

Hamburger, M., tr. see Muschg, Adolf.

Hamburger, Michael. German Literature from Nietzsche to the Present Day, Vol. 1. 320p. 1983. text ed. 21.00x (ISBN 0-85635-467-8, Pub. by Carcanet New Pr England). Humanities.

--A Mug's Game: Intermittent Memoirs. (Essays, Prose, & Scottish Literature). 1979. 10.00 o.p. (ISBN 0-85635-047-8, Pub. by Carcanet New Pr England). Humanities.

--Ownerless Earth: New & Selected Poems. (Poetry Ser.). 160p. 1973. text ed. 10.50x (ISBN 0-85635-038-9, Pub. by Carcanet New Pr England); pap. text ed. 7.50x (ISBN 0-85635-039-7). Humanities.

--Real Estate. (Poetry Ser.). 1979. 7.95 o.p. (ISBN 0-85635-216-0, Pub. by Carcanet New Pr England); pap. 5.95 o.p. (ISBN 0-85635-234-9). Humanities.

--The Truth of Poetry: Tensions in Modern Poetry from Baudelaire to the 1960's. 352p. 1982. text ed. 21.00x (ISBN 0-85635-438-4, 51378, Pub. by Carcanet New Pr England). Humanities.

--Variations. (Literary Ser.). 110p. 1982. 17.50x (ISBN 0-933806-14-0). Black Swan CT.

Hamburger, Michael, ed. East German Poetry: An Anthology. Levenson, Christopher, et al, trs. from Ger. (Translation Ser.). 1979. 12.95 o.p. (ISBN 0-85635-034-6, Pub. by Carcanet New Pr England). Humanities.

--German Poetry Nineteen Ten to Nineteen Seventy-Five: An Anthology in German & English. 533p. 1977. text ed. 22.50x (ISBN 0-85635-161-X, Pub. by Carcanet New Pr England). Humanities.

Hamburger, Michael, tr. see Huchel, Peter.

Hamburger, Michael, tr. see Sorescu, Marin.

Hamburger, Robert. All the Lonely People: Life in a Single Room Occupancy Hotel. LC 82-19128. 352p. 1983. 15.95 (ISBN 0-89919-159-2). Ticknor & Fields.

Hamburger, Robert & Stern, Susan. The Thirties. Weiss, Jeffrey, ed. LC 75-16985. (Illus.). 144p. 1975. pap. 4.95 (ISBN 0-8256-4194-2, Quick Fox). Putnam Pub Group.

Hamburgh, Max. Theories of Differentiation. 200p. 1971. pap. text ed. 14.95 (ISBN 0-686-43105-7). E Arnold.

Hamby, Alonzo L., ed. Harry S. Truman & the New Deal. (Problems in American Civilization Ser). 1974. pap. text ed. 5.95 (ISBN 0-669-87080-3). Heath.

Hamby, D. S. American Cotton Handbook, 2 Vols. 1965. Vol. 1. 61.95x (ISBN 0-87245-007-4); Vol. 2. 76.95 (ISBN 0-87245-008-2). Textile Bk.

Hamby, D. S., jt. auth. see Grover, E. B.

Hamby, R., jt. ed. see Hoffman, I.

Hamdani, jt. auth. see Barker, Muhammad.

Hamdun, Said, tr. see Battuta, Ibn.

Hameedullah. Introduction to Islam. pap. 7.95 (ISBN 0-686-18488-2). Kazi Pubns.

Hameka, H. Advanced Quantum Chemistry. 1965. 15.50 o.p. (ISBN 0-201-02778-X, Adv Bk Prog). A-W.

Hameka, Hendrik F. Quantum Mechanics. LC 81-3430. 387p. 1981. 32.50x (ISBN 0-471-09223-1, Pub. by Wiley-Interscience). Wiley.

Hamel, Daniel A., jt. auth. see Krumboltz, John D.

Hamel, Esther V. Encyclopedia of Judging & Exhibiting Floriculture & Flora-Artistry. rev. 5th ed. 560p. 1982. 13.95 (ISBN 0-913162-01-9). Ponderosa.

--Gestalt & Floral Design, Judging. 2nd ed. 1975. pap. 2.00 o.p. (ISBN 0-913162-03-5). Ponderosa.

Hamel, Fred. Die Psalmenkompositionen Johann Rosenmullers. (Sammlung MW. Abh. 11-1933 Ser.). 128p. 25.00 o.s.i. (ISBN 90-6027-236-6, Pub. by Frits Knuf Netherlands). Pendragon NY.

Hamel, J. England & Russia Comprising the Voyages of John Tradescant the Elder, Sir Hugh Willoughby, Richard Chancellor, Nelson and Others, to the White Sea. (Russia Through European Eyes Ser). 1968. Repr. of 1854 ed. lib. bdg. 55.00 (ISBN 0-306-77026-1). Da Capo.

Hamel, Lawrence, jt. ed. see Haas, Ronald.

Hamelin, Jean see Halpenny, Francess.

Hamelink, Cees J. Finance & Information: A Study of Converging Interests. Voigt, Melvin J., ed. (Communication & Information Science Ser.). 192p. 1982. text ed. 29.50 (ISBN 0-89391-091-0). Ablex Pub.

Hamelsdorf, Ora & Adelsberg, Sandra, eds. Jewish Women & Jewish Law Bibliography. 60p. 1981. pap. 3.50 o.p. (ISBN 0-686-82245-5). Biblio NY.

Hamer, Frank & Hamer, Janet. Clays: A Ceramic Skillbook. (Illus.). 1977. 8.95 o.p. (ISBN 0-8230-0589-5). Watson-Guptill.

Hamer, H. Den see Den Hamer, H. E.

Hamer, Janet, jt. auth. see Hamer, Frank.

Hamer, John & Steinbring, Jack, eds. Alcohol & Native Peoples of the North. LC 80-8301. 323p. lib. bdg. 21.50 (ISBN 0-8191-1197-X); pap. text ed. 12.50 (ISBN 0-8191-1198-8). U Pr of Amer.

Hamer, Martin. Sniper. (City Limits Ser). 1970. text ed. 2.20 o.p. (ISBN 0-07-025708-6, W). McGraw.

Hamer, Martyn. Cats. (Easy-Read Fact Bks.). (Illus.). 32p. (gr. 2-4). 1983. PLB 8.60 (ISBN 0-531-04510-2). Watts.

--Trees. (Easy Read Fact Bk.). (Illus.). 32p. (gr. 2-4). 1983. PLB 8.60 (ISBN 0-531-04513-7). Watts.

Hamer, P. M. Secession Movement in South Carolina, 1847-1852. LC 75-124883. (American Scene Ser). 1971. Repr. of 1918 ed. lib. bdg. 22.50 (ISBN 0-306-71036-6). Da Capo.

Hamerlynck, L. A. Behavioral Systems for the Developmentally Disabled: Institutional, Clinic & Community Environments, Vol. 2. LC 78-21562. 1979. 20.00 (ISBN 0-87630-187-1). Brunner-Mazel.

Hamermesh, Morton, tr. see Novikov, S. P.

Hamernik, Roger P., et al, eds. New Perspectives on Noise-Induced Hearing Loss. 550p. 1982. text ed. 69.50 (ISBN 0-89004-601-8). Raven.

Hamerow, Theodore S., ed. Otto Von Bismarck: A Historical Assessment. 2nd, new ed. (Problems in European Civilization Ser.). (Orig.). 1972. pap. text ed. 5.50 (ISBN 0-669-82008-3). Heath.

Hamerstrom, Frances. Walk When the Moon Is Full. LC 75-33878. (Illus.). 64p. (gr. 3-8). 1975. 9.95 (ISBN 0-912278-69-2); pap. 3.95 (ISBN 0-912278-84-6). Crossing Pr.

Hamerton-Kelly, R. G. Pre-Existence, Wisdom & the Son of Man: A Study of the Idea of Pre-Existence in the New Testament. LC 72-78890. (New Testament Studies Monographs: No. 21). 340p. 1973. 47.50 (ISBN 0-521-08629-9). Cambridge U Pr.

Hamerton-Kelly, Robert G. Sprung Time: Seasons of the Christian Year. LC 79-56162. 144p. (Orig.). 1980. pap. 4.50 (ISBN 0-8358-0397-X). Upper Room.

Hames, B., jt. ed. see Rickwood, D.

Hames, Raymond B. & Vickers, William T., eds. Adaptive Response of Native Amazonians: Studies in Anthropology Ser. LC 82-18399. Date not set. price not set (ISBN 0-12-321250-2). Acad Pr.

Hamet, Pavel & Sands, Howard, eds. Pathophysiological Aspects of Cyclic Nucleotides, Vol. 12. (Advances in Cyclic Nucleotide Research). 470p. 1980. text ed. 53.50 (ISBN 0-89004-454-6). Raven.

Hamey, J. A., jt. auth. see Hamey, L. A.

Hamey, L. A. & Hamey, J. A. The Roman Engineers. LC 81-13746. (Cambridge Topics Bks.). (Illus.). 52p. (gr. 6 up). 1982. PLB 6.95g (ISBN 0-8225-1227-0). Lerner Pubns.

Hamidullah, D. M. Holy Quran, 2 vols. (Arabic, Fr.). 1981. Set. french & arabic 55.00 (ISBN 0-686-77430-2). Kazi Pubns.

Hamill, Dennis. Stomping Ground. 1980. 9.95 o.s.i. (ISBN 0-440-07741-9). Delacorte.

Hamill, Desmond. Bitter Orange. LC 80-14024. 288p. 1980. Repr. 10.95 o.p. (ISBN 0-688-03711-9). Morrow.

Hamill, Ethel. Honeymoon in Honolulu. (YA) 1970. 6.95 (ISBN 0-685-03335-X, Avalon). Bouregy.

Hamill, Paul, ed. Church Music Handbook 1982-1983. (Annual Ser.). (Illus.). 79p. (Orig.). 1982. 5.95 (ISBN 0-686-95001-1, Gemini Music). Pilgrim NY.

--The Church Music Handbook 1983-4: Annual Planning Guide for the Music of the Church. 80p. (Orig.). 1983. pap. 5.95 (ISBN 0-8298-0672-5). Pilgrim NY.

--Introits & Responses for Contemporary Worship. 32p. (Orig.). 1983. pap. 2.95 (ISBN 0-8298-0649-0). Pilgrim NY.

Hamill, Sam. At Home in the World: Views & Reviews. 191p. 1981. 17.00 (ISBN 0-918116-23-6); pap. 6.00 (ISBN 0-918116-22-8). Jawbone Pr.

--Living Light. 1977. 3.00 (ISBN 0-918116-12-0). Jawbone Pr.

Hamilton. Getting in Shape to Ski. new ed. (Orig.). 1979. pap. 3.95 o.p. (ISBN 0-8015-2957-3, Hawthorn). Dutton.

--Mythology. 4.95 (ISBN 0-448-00093-8, G&D). Putnam Pub Group.

Hamilton, jt. auth. see Simon.

Hamilton, A. Sources of the Religious Element in Flaubert's Salammbo. (Elliott Monographs: Vol. 4). 1917. pap. 12.00 (ISBN 0-527-02608-5). Kraus Repr.

Hamilton, A., tr. see Artaud, Antonin.

Hamilton, A. G. Logic for Mathematicians. LC 77-84802. (Illus.). 1978. 57.50 (ISBN 0-521-21838-1); pap. 15.95x (ISBN 0-521-29291-3). Cambridge U Pr.

Hamilton, Alan. Essential Edinburgh. (Illus.). 1978. pap. 7.95 o.s.i. (ISBN 0-233-96984-5). Transatlantic.

--Paul McCartney. (Profiles Ser.). (Illus.). 64p. (gr. 4-6). 1983. 7.95 (ISBN 0-241-10930-2, Pub. by Hamish Hamilton England). David & Charles.

Hamilton, Alastair. The Family of Love. 185p. text ed. 29.95 (ISBN 0-227-67845-1). Attic Pr.

Hamilton, Alastair, tr. see Gombrowicz, Witold.

Hamilton, Alastair, tr. see Simenon, Georges.

Hamilton, Alexander. Gentleman's Progress: The Itinerarium of Dr. Alexander Hamilton, 1744. Bridenbaugh, Carl, ed. & intro. by. (Illus.). 267p. 1973. Repr. of 1948 ed. lib. bdg. 20.50x (ISBN 0-8371-6637-3, HAGP). Greenwood.

Hamilton, Alexander, et al. Federalist. Wright, Benjamin F., ed. LC 61-6355. (The John Harvard Library). 1961. 20.00x o.p. (ISBN 0-674-29800-4). Harvard U Pr.

Hamilton, Alfred S. Poems of Alfred Starr Hamilton. LC 77-76735. 1969. 10.00 (ISBN 0-912330-14-7, Dist. by Inland Bk); pap. 6.00 (ISBN 0-912330-15-5). Jargon Soc.

Hamilton, Andrew. Enquiry into the Principles of Taxation. LC 74-12040. Repr. of 1790 ed. lib. bdg. 37.50x (ISBN 0-678-01105-2). Kelley.

Hamilton, Anne. Seven Principles of Poetry. 8.95 o.p. (ISBN 0-87116-029-3). Writer.

Hamilton, Bernard. Monastic Reform, Catharism & the Crusades (900 - 1300) 376p. 1979. 60.00x (ISBN 0-686-97625-8, Pub. by Variorum). State Mutual Bk.

Hamilton, Betty, jt. auth. see Guidos, Barbara.

Hamilton, Betty, ed. Medical Diagnostic Imaging Systems: Technology & Applications. (F & S Press Bk.). 232p. 1982. prof. ref. 34.95x (ISBN 0-686-97886-2). Ballinger Pub.

Hamilton, Bruce. Too Much of Water. LC 82-48242. 288p. 1983. pap. 2.84i o.p. (ISBN 0-06-080635-4, P 635, HarpR). Har-Row.

Hamilton, Carl. Effects of Non-Tariff Barriers to Trade on Prices, Employment, & Imports: The Case of the Swedish Textile & Clothing Industry. (Working Paper: No. 429). ii, 61p. 1980. 3.00 (ISBN 0-686-36206-3, WP-0429). World Bank.

--In No Time at All. 1974. 7.95 (ISBN 0-8138-0825-1). Iowa St U Pr.

Hamilton, Charles. American Autographs: Signers of the Declaration of Independence, Revolutionary War Leaders, Presidents. LC 81-2505. (Illus.). 643p. 1983. 150.00x (ISBN 0-8061-1658-7). U of Okla Pr.

--Auction Madness: An Uncensored Look Behind the Velvet Drapes of the Great Auction Houses. LC 81-12504. 224p. 1982. 13.95 (ISBN 0-89696-123-0, An Everest House Books). Dodd.

--The Book of Autographs. 1979. 10.00 o.p. (ISBN 0-671-24258-X). S&S.

--Great Forgers & Famous Fakes: The Manuscript Forgers of America & How They Duped the Experts. (Illus.). 288p. 1980. 12.95 o.p. (ISBN 0-517-54076-2, Michelman Bks). Crown.

Hamilton, Charles see Todd, Peter, pseud.

Hamilton, Charles V. American Government. 1981. text ed. 24.50x (ISBN 0-673-15220-0). Scott F.

--The Bench & the Ballot: Southern Federal Judges & Black Votes. 1974. pap. 5.95x o.p. (ISBN 0-19-501719-6). Oxford U Pr.

Hamilton, Charles V. & Hill, Herbert. Black Experience in American Politics. (New Perspective on Black America). (Illus.). 384p. 1973. 7.95 o.p. (ISBN 0-399-10916-1). Putnam Pub Group.

Hamilton, Cicely M. Marriage As a Trade. LC 71-149782. 1971. Repr. of 1909 ed. 30.00x (ISBN 0-8103-3394-5). Gale.

Hamilton, Darlene S., jt. auth. see Flemming, Bonnie M.

Hamilton, David. Bilitis. LC 82-50003. (Illus.). 112p. (Orig.). 1982. pap. 12.95 (ISBN 0-688-01522-0). Quill NY.

--Dreams of a Young Girl. (Illus.). 1977. pap. 12.45 (ISBN 0-688-06482-5). Morrow.

--A Primer on the Economics of Poverty. 1968. pap. text ed. 2.50x (ISBN 0-685-55614-X, 30726). Phila Bk Co.

--A Summer in Saint-Tropez. LC 82-61576. (Illus.). 122p. 1983. 19.95 (ISBN 0-688-01966-8). Morrow.

--The Thames & Hudson Manual of Stoneware & Porcelain. (Thames & Hudson Manuals Ser.). (Illus., Orig.). 1982. pap. 12.95 (ISBN 0-500-68024-8). Thames Hudson.

Hamilton, David, photos by. The Best of David Hamilton. LC 80-83280. (Illus.). 144p. 1980. pap. 10.95 (ISBN 0-688-00403-2). Quill NY.

--David Hamilton's Private Collection. LC 80-83281. (Illus.). 128p. 1980. pap. 10.95 (ISBN 0-688-00402-4). Quill NY.

Hamilton, David, et al, eds. Beyond the Numbers Game: A Reader in Educational Evaluation. (Education Ser.). 1977. 21.25 (ISBN 0-8211-0416-0); text ed. 19.25x (ISBN 0-685-04966-3). McCutchan.

Hamilton, Donna M. After Fifty Cookbook: A Treasury of Creative Recipes for 1 or 2, Retired People, or Those on Special Diets. LC 82-73658. 377p. 1974. 13.50 (ISBN 0-8040-0667-9). Swallow.

Hamilton, Dorothy. Christmas at Metamora. (Illus.). 104p. (Orig.). (gr. 3-5). 1978. pap. 3.95 (ISBN 0-935306-04-8). Barnwood Pr.

--Daniel Forbes: A Pioneer Boy. (Illus., Orig.). (gr. 3-5). 1980. pap. 3.95 (ISBN 0-686-32860-4). Barnwood Pr.

--Jim Musco. LC 71-189563. (Illus.). 104p. (YA) (gr. 4-9). 1972. pap. 3.25 (ISBN 0-8361-1668-2). Herald Pr.

--Ken's Bright Room. (Illus.). 88p. (Orig.). 1982. 6.95 (ISBN 0-8361-3327-7); pap. 3.50 (ISBN 0-8361-3328-5). Herald Pr.

Hamilton, Douglas & Howard, William. Basic Integrated Circuits. (Illus.). 608p. 1975. text ed. 38.95 (ISBN 0-07-025763-9, C); solutions manual 10.50 (ISBN 0-07-025764-7). McGraw.

Hamilton, Douglas M. & Robb, William. Mechanical Engineering for Public Cleansing. (Illus.). 1969. 16.50 (ISBN 0-85334-121-4, Pub. by Applied Sci England). Elsevier.

Hamilton, E. H. China Diary. write for info (ISBN 0-89989-019-9). Cross Roads.

Hamilton, Earl J. Money, Prices, & Wages in Valencia, Aragon & Navarre 1351-1500. LC 75-25653. (Perspectives in European Hist. Ser.: No. 6). (Illus.). xxviii, 310p. Repr. of 1936 ed. lib. bdg. 22.50x (ISBN 0-87991-613-3). Porcupine Pr.

Hamilton, Edith. Mythology. (RL 7). 1971. pap. 2.75 (ISBN 0-451-62189-1, ME2189, Ment). NAL.

Hamilton, Edith, tr. Three Greek Plays: The Trojan Women of Euripedes & Prometheus Bound & Aggamemnon of Aeschylus. 1958. pap. 5.95 (ISBN 0-393-00203-9, Norton Lib). Norton.

Hamilton, Edmond. The Horror on the Asteroid & Other Tales of Planetary Horror. (Science Fiction Ser). 272p. 1975. Repr. of 1936 ed. lib. bdg. 12.50 o.p. (ISBN 0-8398-2304-5, Gregg). G K Hall.

--Starwolf. 1982. pap. 3.50 (ISBN 0-441-78422-4, Pub. by Ace Science Fiction). Ace Bks.

Hamilton, Edward W. Diary of Sir Edward Walter Hamilton, Eighteen-Eighty to Eighteen-Eighty Five, 2 vols. Bahlman, Dudley W., ed. 1972. 54.00x o.p. (ISBN 0-19-822324-2). Oxford U Pr.

Hamilton, Elizabeth. I Stay in the Church. 183p. 1973. 5.95 o.p. (ISBN 0-85478-053-X). Attic Pr.

--Memoirs of Modern Philosophers: A Novel, 3 vols. Luria, Gina, ed. (The Feminist Controversy in England, 1788-1810). 1974. lib. bdg. 50.00 ea. o.s.i. (ISBN 0-8240-0866-9). Garland Pub.

Hamilton, Elizabeth V. Storm Center. (Illus.). 200p. 1982. write for info. (ISBN 0-937684-16-3). Tradd St Pr.

Hamilton, Emelou M. Little Rock Photograph Album of the 1890's: The Mary E. Parker Collection. (Illus.). 1981. write for info. (ISBN 0-939130-01-7); pap. 10.95 (ISBN 0-939130-02-5). J W Bell.

Hamilton, Eva M. & Whitney, Eleanor N. Nutrition. 2nd ed. (Illus.). 650p. 1982. 21.95 (ISBN 0-314-66862-4). West Pub.

Hamilton, Eva M., jt. auth. see Whitney, Eleanor N.

Hamilton, F. E. Regional Economic Analysis in Great Britain & the Commonwealth: A Bibliographic Guide. LC 79-97254. 1970. 12.50x o.p. (ISBN 0-8052-3346-6). Schocken.

Hamilton, F. E. & Linge, G. J. Spatial Analysis, Industry & the Industrial Environment: Progress in Research. LC 80-41418. (International Industrial Systems Ser.: Vol. 2). 672p. 1981. 67.95 (ISBN 0-471-27918-8, Pub. by Wiley-Interscience). Wiley.

Hamilton, F. E., ed. Spatial Perspectives on Industrial Organization & Decision-Making. LC 73-14379. 533p. 1974. 72.95 (ISBN 0-471-34715-9, Pub. by Wiley-Interscience). Wiley.

Hamilton, F. E. & Linge, G. J., eds. Spatial Analysis, Industry & the Industrial Environment-Progress in Research & Applications: Industrial Systems, Vol. 1. LC 78-10298. 1979. 59.95 (ISBN 0-471-99738-2, Pub. by Wiley-Interscience). Wiley.

Hamilton, F. Ian, jt. auth. see French, R. A.

Hamilton, Gavin, tr. see Ambrosi, Hans.

Hamilton, Gene. Home Appliance Repair Guide. (Successful Ser.). (Illus.). 96p. 1982. pap. 3.95 (ISBN 0-8249-6125-0). Ideals.

Hamilton, George H. Art & Architecture of Russia. 1983. pap. 16.95 (ISBN 0-14-056106-4, Pelican). Penguin.

Hamilton, H., ed. Future Directions in Studies of Nuclei Far From Stability. 1980. 79.75 (ISBN 0-444-85448-7). Elsevier.

Hamilton, Harley, jt. auth. see Kelly-Jones, Nancy.

Hamilton, Helen K., ed. Procedures. LC 82-15643. (Nurse's Reference Library). (Illus.). 1000p. 1982. text ed. 23.95 (ISBN 0-916730-40-9). Intermed Comm.

Hamilton, Henry W. & Griffin, James B. The Spiro Mound, Vol. 14. Chapman, Carl H., ed. (The Missouri Archaeologist). (Illus.). 276p. 1981. pap. 10.00 (ISBN 0-943414-06-7). MO Arch Soc.

Hamilton, Holman. Prologue to Conflict: The Crisis & Compromise of 1850. 1966. pap. 3.95 o.p. (ISBN 0-393-00345-0, Norton Lib). Norton.

--Prologue to Conflict: The Crisis & Compromise of 1850. LC 64-13999. 248p. 1964. 15.00x o.p. (ISBN 0-8131-1090-4). U Pr of Ky.

Hamilton, Ian. Robert Lowell: A Biography. LC 82-40121. 480p. 1982. 19.95 (ISBN 0-394-50965-X). Random.

Hamilton, J. G., jt. ed. see Lawrence, John H.

Hamilton, James. Directions. 1976. pap. 2.00 (ISBN 0-8341-0396-6). Beacon Hill.

Hamilton, James F. Rousseau's Theory of Literature: The Poetics of Art & Nature. 18.00. French Lit.

Hamilton, James R., et al. Readings for an Introduction to Philosophy. 544p. 1976. text ed. 21.95x (ISBN 0-02-349550-2). Macmillan.

Hamilton, James W. PWO Karen at the Edge of Mountain & Plain. (American Ethnological Society Ser.). (Illus.). 300p. 1976. text ed. 23.95 (ISBN 0-8299-0075-6). West Pub.

Hamilton, Jean. Introduction to Wallpaper. (The Victoria & Albert Museum Introductions to the Decorative Arts). (Illus.). 1983. 9.95 (ISBN 0-88045-020-7). Stemmer Hse.

Hamilton, Joseph H. & Manthuruthil, Jose, eds. Radioactivity in Nuclear Spectroscopy, 2 vols. 1972. Vol. 1, 592p. 109.00 (ISBN 0-677-12410-4); Vol. 2. 152.00 (ISBN 0-677-12420-1); Set. 236.00 (ISBN 0-677-14220-X). Gordon.

Hamilton, Juan, jt. ed. see Greenough, Sarah.

Hamilton, Kenneth G. The Two Harmonies: Poetry & Prose in the Seventeenth Century. LC 77-18929. 1978. Repr. of 1963 ed. lib. bdg. 20.25x (ISBN 0-313-20180-3, HATH). Greenwood.

Hamilton, L. F., et al. Calculations of Analytical Chemistry. 7th ed. LC 68-24345. (Illus.). 1968. text ed. 28.50 (ISBN 0-07-025733-7, C). McGraw.

Hamilton, Lawrence S., ed. Forest & Watershed Development & Conservation in Asia & the Pacific. (Special Studies in Natural Resources & Energy Management). 650p. 1982. lib. bdg. 25.00 (ISBN 0-86531-534-5). Westview.

Hamilton, Leicester F. & Simpson, Stephen G. Calculations of Analytical Chemistry. 7th ed. LC 82-8993. 526p. 1983. Repr. of 1969 ed. lib. bdg. write for info cancelled o.p. (ISBN 0-89874-485-7). Krieger.

Hamilton, Louis J., jt. auth. see Duderstadt, James J.

Hamilton, M. N. Music in Eighteenth Century Spain. LC 74-162868. (Music Ser). 1971. Repr. of 1937 ed. lib. bdg. 29.50 (ISBN 0-306-70279-7). Da Capo.

Hamilton, Madison. Federalist: Selections. Commager, Henry S., ed. LC 49-11364. (Crofts Classics Ser.). 1949. pap. text ed. 3.50x (ISBN 0-88295-041-X). Harlan Davidson.

Hamilton, Marian W., tr. see Jaspers, Karl.

Hamilton, Mark. My Brother's Image. 160p. 1983. pap. 2.50 (ISBN 0-380-82230-X, 82230-X). Avon.

--Poker Answers. 1978. pap. 2.00 (ISBN 0-911752-25-0). I & O Pub.

Hamilton, Mary A., tr. see Kurlbaum-Siebert, Margarete.

Hamilton, Michael. God's Plan for the Church-Growth! LC 81-82021. (Radiant Life Ser.). 128p. (Orig.). 1981. 2.50 (ISBN 0-88243-885-9, 02-0885); teacher's ed. 3.95 (ISBN 0-88243-194-3, 32-0194). Gospel Pub.

Hamilton, Morse. How Do You Do, Mr. Birdsteps? 32p. pap. 2.25 (ISBN 0-380-82875-8, Camelot). Avon.

--Who's Afraid of the Dark? 32p. pap. 2.25 (ISBN 0-380-82883-9, Camelot). Avon.

Hamilton, Neil W. & Hamilton, Peter R. Governance of Public Enterprise: A Case Study of Urban Mass Transit. LC 80-5349. 176p. 1981. 21.95x (ISBN 0-669-03867-9). Lexington Bks.

Hamilton, Patricia A. Health Care Consumerism. LC 81-14009. 172p. 1981. pap. text ed. 11.95 (ISBN 0-8016-2024-4). Mosby.

Hamilton, Peter. Knowledge & Social Structure: An Introduction to the Classical Argument in the Sociology of Knowledge. (International Library of Sociology). 174p. 1974. 19.95x (ISBN 0-7100-7746-7); pap. 7.95 (ISBN 0-7100-7786-6). Routledge & Kegan.

Hamilton, Peter, jt. auth. see Garfield, Brian.

Hamilton, Peter R., jt. auth. see Hamilton, Neil W.

Hamilton, R. J. & Sewell, P. A. Introduction to High Performance Liquid Chromatography. 2nd ed. 1982. 28.00x (ISBN 0-686-92746-X, Pub. by Chapman & Hall). Methuen Inc.

Hamilton, R. J. & Bhati, A., eds. Fats & Oils: Chemistry & Technology. (Illus.). 263p. 1981. 53.50 (ISBN 0-85334-915-0, Pub. by Applied Sci England). Elsevier.

Hamilton, Raphael. Marquette's Explorations: The Narratives Reexamined. (Illus.). 292p. 1970. 27.50 (ISBN 0-299-05570-1). U of Wis Pr.

Hamilton, Richard. Collected Words Nineteen Fifty-Three to Eighty-One. (Illus.). 1983. 24.95 (ISBN 0-500-01293-8). Thames Hudson.

Hamilton, Rita, tr. see Michael, Ian.

Hamilton, Robert. An Introduction to Merchandise, Parts IV & V: Italian Bookkeeping & Practical Bookkeeping, with a Note by B. S. Yamey. LC 82-48366. (Accountancy in Transition Ser.). 247p. 1982. lib. bdg. 25.00 (ISBN 0-8240-5317-6). Garland Pub.

Hamilton, Robert B. Comparative Behavior of the American Avocet & the Black-Necked Stilt (Recurvirostridae) 98p. 1975. 7.50 (ISBN 0-943610-17-6). Am Ornithologists.

Hamilton, Robert W. Cases & Materials on Corporations: Including Partnerships & Limited Partnerships. 2nd ed. LC 81-4507. (American Casebook Ser.). 1108p. 1981. text ed. 23.95 (ISBN 0-314-58808-6); avail. tchrs. manual (ISBN 0-314-66032-1); Statutory Suppl. 1981 avail. West Pub.

--Corporations. LC 82-1893. (Black Letter Ser.). 415p. 1982. pap. text ed. 10.95 (ISBN 0-314-65091-1). West Pub.

Hamilton, Roberta. The Liberation of Women: A Study of Patriarchy & Capitalism. (Controversies in Sociology Ser.). 1978. text ed. 19.95x (ISBN 0-04-301085-7); pap. text ed. 7.95x (ISBN 0-04-301086-5). Allen Unwin.

Hamilton, Roger. The Life of Prehistoric Animals. LC 77-88446. (Easy Reading Edition of Introduction to Nature Ser.). (Illus.). 1978. PLB 12.68 (ISBN 0-382-06130-6). Silver.

Hamilton, S. S. Accounting Applications for the Microcomputer. Date not set. 6.95 (ISBN 0-07-025736-1). McGraw.

Hamilton, S. S., et al. Microcomputer Accounting Applications. 128p. 1982. text ed. 5.56 (ISBN 0-07-025818-X). McGraw.

Hamilton, Stanley, jt. auth. see Garfinkel, Alan.

Hamilton, T. H., et al, eds. Ontogeny of Receptors & Reproductive Hormone Action. LC 77-92523. 471p. 1979. text ed. 47.00 (ISBN 0-89004-254-3). Raven.

Hamilton, Tamsin. The Gypsy from Cadiz. LC 77-7619. 1977. 8.95 o.p. (ISBN 0-698-10785-3, Coward). Putnam Pub Group.

Hamilton, Vernon. The Cognitive Structures & Processes of Human Motivation & Personality. 575p. 1983. price not set (ISBN 0-471-10526-0, Pub. by Wiley Interscience). Wiley.

Hamilton, Vernon & Warburton, David M. Human Stress & Cognition: An Information Processing Approach. LC 78-31691. 1979. 82.95 (ISBN 0-471-27572-7, Pub. by Wiley-Interscience). Wiley.

Hamilton, Virginia. Dustland. LC 79-19003. 192p. (gr. 7 up). 1980. 10.72 (ISBN 0-688-80228-1); PLB 10.32 (ISBN 0-688-84228-3). Greenwillow.

--Hugo Black: The Alabama Years. LC 75-181566. (Illus.). 352p. 1982. pap. text ed. 12.50 (ISBN 0-8173-0128-3). U of Ala Pr.

--The Magical Adventures of Pretty Pearl. LC 82-48629. 320p. (gr. 6 up). 1983. 11.06i (ISBN 0-06-022186-0, HarpJ); PLB 11.89g (ISBN 0-06-022187-9). Har-Row.

--Paul Robeson: The Life & Times of a Free Black Man. (YA) 1979. pap. 1.50 o.p. (ISBN 0-440-96806-2, LFL). Dell.

--Sweet Whispers, Brother Rush. 224p. (gr. 7 up). 1982. 10.95 (ISBN 0-399-20894-1, Philomel). Putnam Pub Group.

Hamilton, W. Clinical Pediatric Endocrinology. Apley, John, ed. (Postgraduate Pediatric Ser.). (Illus.). 1972. 21.95 o.p. (ISBN 0-407-13710-6). Butterworth.

Hamilton, W. A., jt. ed. see Haddock, B. A.

Hamilton, W. D. Charles Sangster. (World Authors Ser.). 15.95 (ISBN 0-8057-2786-8, Twayne). G K Hall.

Hamilton, W. H. & Adair, D. The Power to Govern. LC 77-37759. (American Constitutional & Legal History Ser). 252p. 1972. Repr. of 1937 ed. lib. bdg. 32.50 (ISBN 0-306-70433-1). Da Capo.

Hamilton, W. R. The Life of Animals with Hooves. LC 78-56566. (Easy Reading Edition of Introduction to Nature Ser.). (Illus.). 1979. PLB 12.68 (ISBN 0-382-06191-8). Silver.

Hamilton, Wallace. Coming Out. (Orig.). 1977. pap. 2.50 (ISBN 0-451-09972-9, E9972, Sig). NAL.

--Kevin. 1981. pap. 2.50 (ISBN 0-451-12199-6, AE2199, Sig). NAL.

Hamilton, Walter. Poets Laureate of England. LC 68-30621. 1968. Repr. of 1879 ed. 32.00x (ISBN 0-8103-3150-0). Gale.

Hamilton, Walton & Till, Irene. Antitrust in Action. LC 78-166328. (FDR & the Era of the New Deal Ser.). 146p. 1974. Repr. of 1940 ed. lib. bdg. 22.50 (ISBN 0-306-70379-3). Da Capo.

Hamilton, William. Money Should Be Fun. 1980. 9.95 o.s.i. (ISBN 0-395-28218-7); pap. 5.95 (ISBN 0-686-65605-9). HM.

--My Sixty Years on the Plains Trapping, Trading & Indian Fighting. LC 82-17547. (Classics of the Old West). lib. bdg. 17.28 (ISBN 0-8094-4030-X). Silver.

--Terribly Nice People. 192p. 1975. 6.95 o.p. (ISBN 0-399-11677-X). Putnam Pub Group.

Hamilton, William F. Electric Automobiles: Energy, Environmental & Economic Prospects for the Future. (Illus.). 1979. 38.50 (ISBN 0-07-025735-3). McGraw.

Hamilton, William J., 3rd. Life's Color Code. (Series in Population Biology). (Illus.). 288p. 1972. text ed. 16.95 (ISBN 0-07-025741-8, C). McGraw.

Hamilton, William P. & Lavin, Mary A. Decision Making in the Coronary Care Unit. 2nd ed. LC 75-30994. (Illus.). 158p. 1976. pap. text ed. 9.50 o.p. (ISBN 0-8016-2026-0). Mosby.

Hamilton, William R. Elements of Quaternions, 2 Vols. 3rd ed. Joly, Charles J., ed. LC 68-54711. 1969. Repr. of 1901 ed. Set. 65.00 (ISBN 0-8284-0219-1). Chelsea Pub.

--Mathematical Papers of Sir William Rowan Hamilton, Vol. 3. Halberstam, H. & Ingram, R. E., eds. 1967. 133.00 (ISBN 0-521-05183-5). Cambridge U Pr.

Hamilton, William S. Introduction to Russian Phonology & Word Structure. (Illus.). 187p. (Orig.). 1980. pap. 9.95 (ISBN 0-89357-063-X). Slavica.

Hamilton-Edwards, G. In Search of Scottish Ancestry. 1972. 30.00x (ISBN 0-686-97131-0, Pub. by Phillimore England). State Mutual Bk.

Hamilton-Head, Ian. Leatherwork. 134p. 1983. pap. 7.50 (ISBN 0-7137-1342-9, Pub. by Blandford Pr England). Sterling.

Hamilton-Merritt, Jane. Our New Baby. (New Feelings Bks.). (Illus.). 32p. (ps-k). 1982. 4.95 (ISBN 0-671-44416-6, Little Simon). S&S.

Hamilton-Paterson, James. Hostage! LC 79-25114. 192p. (gr. 7-12). 1980. 8.95 (ISBN 0-529-05596-1, Philomel). Putnam Pub Group.

--House in the Waves. LC 76-103043. (gr. 8 up). 1970. 10.95 (ISBN 0-87599-171-8). S G Phillips.

Hamish, Keith, jt. auth. see Brown, Gordon H.

Hamlet, John N., jt. auth. see Grossman, Mary L.

Hamley, Dennis. Pageants of Despair. LC 74-10841. 180p. (gr. 7-10). 1974. 10.95 (ISBN 0-87599-205-6). S G Phillips.

Hamlin, Cyrus, ed. see Goethe, Johann W. Von.

Hamlin, Marie C. Legends of Le Detroit. LC 68-26179. (Illus.). 1977. Repr. of 1884 ed. 31.00 o.p. (ISBN 0-8103-3330-9). Gale.

Hamlin, Marjorie, jt. auth. see Polette, Nancy.

Hamlin, Paul L. Legal Education in Colonial New York. LC 70-129082. (American Constitutional and Legal History Ser.). (Illus.). 1970. Repr. of 1939 ed. lib. bdg. 32.50 (ISBN 0-306-70062-X). Da Capo.

Hamlin, Robert W., jt. auth. see Brodsky, Louis D.

Hamlin, Roger, ed. Guide to Graduate Education in Urban & Regional Planning. 3rd ed. LC 78-71242. 401p. 1978. pap. 5.00 (ISBN 0-918286-15-8). Planners Pr.

Hamlin, Talbot. Architecture: An Art for All Men. LC 75-3798. (Illus.). 279p. 1975. Repr. of 1947 ed. lib. bdg. 21.00x (ISBN 0-8371-8079-1, HAAR). Greenwood.

--Architecture Through the Ages. (Illus.). 1953. 27.50 (ISBN 0-399-30001-5). Putnam Pub Group.

Hamlin, Talbot F. American Spirit in Architecture. 1926. text ed. 22.50x (ISBN 0-686-83465-8). Elliots Bks.

Hamlin, Vincent T. Alley Oop. 256p. (Orig.). 1983. pap. 2.50 (ISBN 0-523-49026-7). Pinnacle Bks.

Hamlyn, D. W. Experience & the Growth of Understanding. (International Library of the Philosophy of Education Ser.). 1978. 17.50x o.p. (ISBN 0-7100-8735-7). Routledge & Kegan.

--Psychology of Perception: A Philosophical Examination of Gestalt Theory & Derivative Theories of Perception. (Studies in Philosophical Psychology). 1961. pap. text ed. 7.50x (ISBN 0-391-01104-9). Humanities.

Hamlyn, E., ed. see Hannemann.

Hamm, Charles. Music in the New World. (Illus.). 1983. 25.00x (ISBN 0-393-95193-6). Norton.

--Yesterdays: Popular Song in America. (Illus.). 1979. 11.95x (ISBN 0-393-01257-3). Norton.

--Yesterdays: Popular Song in America. (Illus.). 560p. 1983. pap. 10.50 (ISBN 0-393-30062-5). Norton.

Hamm, Jack. Cartooning the Head & Figure. (Illus., Orig.). (gr. 9 up). 1967. pap. 4.95 (ISBN 0-448-01541-2, G&D). Putnam Pub Group.

--Drawing Head & Figures. pap. 4.95 o.p. (ISBN 0-448-01587-0, G&D). Putnam Pub Group.

--Drawing Scenery: Landscapes & Seacapes. (Illus.). 120p. Date not set. pap. price not set (ISBN 0-448-01508-0, G&D). Putnam Pub Group.

--Drawing the Head & Figure. (Illus.). 120p. Date not set. pap. price not set (G&D). Putnam Pub Group.

--How to Draw Animals. (gr. 7 up). 1969. pap. 4.95 (ISBN 0-448-01908-6, G&D). Putnam Pub Group.

--Still Life Drawing & Painting. (Illus.). 120p. Date not set. pap. price not set (ISBN 0-448-11526-3, G&D). Putnam Pub Group.

Hamm, Margherita A. Eminent Actors in Their Homes. 336p. 1982. Repr. of 1902 ed. lib. bdg. 40.00 (ISBN 0-89984-915-6). Century Bookbindery.

Hamm, Russell L. Philosophy & Education: Alternatives in Theory & Practice. 2nd ed. xviii, 330p. 1981. pap. text ed. 8.95x (ISBN 0-8134-2203-5, 2203). Interstate.

Hamm, Victor M. Language, Truth & Poetry. (Aquinas Lecture). 1960. 7.95 (ISBN 0-87462-125-9). Marquette.

--Taste & the Audio-Visual Arts. 1960. pap. 1.95 o.p. (ISBN 0-87462-414-2). Marquette.

Hammacher, A. M. Phantoms of the Imagination: Fantasy in Art & Literature from Blake to Dali. Langham, Tony & Peters, Plym, trs. (Illus.). 320p. 1981. 45.00 o.p. (ISBN 0-8109-1468-9). Abrams.

Hammacher, A. M. & Hammacher, Renilde. Van Gogh: A Documentary Biography. 240p. 1982. 36.50 (ISBN 0-02-547710-2). Macmillan.

Hammacher, Arno, jt. auth. see Tagliaferri, Aldo.

Hammacher, Renilde, jt. auth. see Hammacher, A. M.

Hammack, David C. Power & Society: Greater New York at the Turn of the Century. LC 81-66977. (Illus.). 450p. 1982. 29.95x (ISBN 0-87154-348-6). Russell Sage.

Hammack, Edie, ed. see Mann, Wayne M.

Hammack, Susan M., ed. see Mann, Wayne M.

Hamman, Ray T., jt. auth. see Gupta, Shiv K.

Hammann, Hermann, jt. auth. see Ort, Walter.

Hammann, Louis J. The Puzzle of Religion: The Parts & the Whole. 1977. 9.50 (ISBN 0-8191-0309-8). U Pr of Amer.

Hammar, Willie. Occupational Safety Management & Engineering. 2nd ed. (Illus.). 608p. 1981. text ed. 21.95 (ISBN 0-13-629410-3). P-H.

Hammarskjold, Dag. Markings. (Epiphany Bks.). 1983. pap. 2.95 (ISBN 0-345-30699-6). Ballantine.

Hammarstrom, David L. Circus Rings Around Russia. 1983. lib. bdg. 22.50 (ISBN 0-208-01965-0, Archon). Shoe String.

Hammel, Bob, ed. The Champs 1981: Indiana Basketball. LC 81-47625. (Illus.). 128p. 1981. pap. 6.95x (ISBN 0-253-22700-3). Ind U Pr.

Hammelmann, H. A. Hugo von Hofmannsthal. 1957. text ed. 29.50x (ISBN 0-686-83571-9). Elliots Bks.

Hammelmann, Hanns, tr. see Strauss, Richard & Von Hofmannsthal, Hugo.

Hammer, A. G. Elementary Matrix Algebra for Psychologists & Social Scientists. LC 72-117464. 212p. 1971. 18.00 (ISBN 0-08-017502-3). Pergamon.

Hammer, Carl, ed. Studies in German Literature. LC 82-15862. (Louisiana State University Studies: Humanities Ser.: No. 13). xviii, 172p. 1982. Repr. of 1963 ed. lib. bdg. 35.00x (ISBN 0-313-23735-2, HASGL). Greenwood.

Hammer, Carl, Jr., ed. Studies in German Literature. LC 63-9645. (University Studies, Humanities Ser.: Vol. 13). 1963. pap. 9.95x o.p. (ISBN 0-8071-0520-1). La State U Pr.

Hammer, D. A. German Grammar & Usage. 456p. 1977. pap. text ed. 13.95 (ISBN 0-7131-5699-6). E Arnold.

Hammer, David L. The Game Is Afoot: A Travel Guide to the England of Sherlock Holmes. LC 81-82194. (Illus.). 200p. 1983. 22.50 (ISBN 0-934468-11-7). Gaslight.

Hammer, Howard. Paddleball--How to Play the Game. (Illus.). 96p. 1972. pap. 2.95 o.p. (ISBN 0-448-01496-3, G&D). Putnam Pub Group.

Hammer, Hy. Electrician-Electrician's Helper. LC 82-11405. 256p. 1982. pap. 8.00 (ISBN 0-668-05492-1, 5492). Arco.

--Practice for Clerical, Typing & Stenographic Tests. 6th ed. LC 82-13912. 208p. (Orig.). 1983. pap. 8.00 (ISBN 0-668-05616-9, 5616). Arco.

--Principal Clerk-Principal Stenographer. rev. ed. LC 82-11446. 224p. 1982. pap. 8.00 (ISBN 0-668-05536-7, 5536). Arco.

--Senior Clerical Series. LC 82-11412. 256p. 1982. pap. 8.00 (ISBN 0-668-05523-5, 5523). Arco.

Hammer, Hy, ed. Bookkeeper-Account Clerk. 6th ed. LC 82-11427. 224p. (Orig.). 1983. pap. text ed. 8.00 (ISBN 0-668-05398-4, 5398). Arco.

--Bus Operator-Conductor. Rev. ed. 224p. (Orig.). 1983. pap. 8.00 (ISBN 0-668-05489-1, 5489). Arco.

--Correction Officer. LC 81-7892. 224p. (Orig.). 1983. pap. 8.00 (ISBN 0-668-05322-4, 5322). Arco.

--Federal Office Assistant GS 2-4. LC 82-11413. 240p. (Orig.). 1983. pap. 8.00 (ISBN 0-668-05490-5, 5490). Arco.

--Home Study Course for Civil Service Jobs. 6th ed. LC 82-3944. 288p. (Orig.). 1983. pap. 8.00 (ISBN 0-668-05413-1, 5413). Arco.

--Home Study Course for Scoring High on Law Enforcement Tests. LC 81-17649. 272p. (Orig.). 1983. pap. 9.00 (ISBN 0-668-05410-7, 5410). Arco.

--Special Officer-Senior Special Officer-Bridge & Tunnel Officer. 3rd ed. (Illus.). 192p. (Orig.). 1983. pap. 8.00 (ISBN 0-668-05614-2, 5614). Arco.

--Stenographer - Typist Practical Preparation. LC 82-11429. 208p. (Orig.). 1982. pap. 8.00 (ISBN 0-668-05535-9, 5535). Arco.

--Stenographer-Typist: U.S. Government Positions GS2 & GS7. 8th ed. LC 81-17675. (Illus.). 224p. (Orig.). 1983. pap. 8.00 (ISBN 0-668-05412-3). Arco.

Hammer, Joseph. Unsolved Problems Concerning Lattice Points. LC 72-95013. (Research Notes in Mathematics Ser.: No. 15). 1978. pap. text ed. 15.50 (ISBN 0-8224-1717-0, 1717). Pitman Pub MA.

Hammer, Kathryne. Nerve Conduction Studies. (Illus.). 166p. 1982. pap. 21.75x spiral (ISBN 0-398-04519-4). C C Thomas.

Hammer, Kenneth. The Springfield Carbine on the Western Frontier. (Illus.). 1970. pap. 2.50 (ISBN 0-88342-214-X). Old Army.

Hammer, Kenneth M. The Glory March. (Custer Monograph Ser.: No. 7). 1980. pap. 2.50x (ISBN 0-940696-03-7). Monroe County Lib.

Hammer, Mark J. Water & Waste Water Technology. LC 75-2000. 502p. 1975. text ed. 29.95x (ISBN 0-471-34726-4); solutions manual avail. (ISBN 0-471-03819-9); tchr's manual avail. (ISBN 0-471-34727-2). Wiley.

Hammer, Mark J. & Mackichan, Kenneth A. Hydrology & Quality of Water Resources. LC 80-209. 486p. 1981. text ed. 26.95 (ISBN 0-471-02681-6); solutions manual avail. (ISBN 0-471-08573-1); problem papers avail. Wiley.

Hammer, P. L., ed. see Institute of Operations Research, Sponsored by IBM, University of Bonn, Germany, Sept. 8-12, 1975.

Hammer, Richard. The Vatican Connection: The Astonishing Account of a Billion-Dollar Counterfeit Stock Deal Between the Mafia & the Church. LC 82-1044. 1982. 14.45 (ISBN 0-03-060146-0). HR&W.

Hammer, Signe. Passionate Attachments: Fathers & Daughters in America Today. 1982. 13.95 (ISBN 0-89256-182-3). Rawson Wade.

Hammer, Tove H. & Bacharach, Samuel B., eds. Reward Systems & Power Distribution: Searching for Solutions. (Pierce Ser.: No. 5). 124p. 1977. pap. 4.75 (ISBN 0-87546-223-5); pap. 7.75 special bdg. (ISBN 0-87546-290-1). ILR Pr.

Hammer, Tove H., jt. auth. see Whyte, William F.

Hammer, W. Product Safety Management & Engineering. 1980. 26.95 (ISBN 0-686-51706-7). P-H.

Hammer, Willie. Handbook of System & Product Safety. LC 72-2683. (Illus.). 368p. 1972. ref. ed. 42.95 (ISBN 0-13-382226-5). P-H.

Hammergren, Linn. Development & the Politics of Administrative Reform: Lessons from Latin America. (Replica Edition Ser.). 220p. 1983. softcover 19.00x (ISBN 0-86531-956-1). Westview.

Hammerlin, G., ed. Numerical Integration. (International Series of Numerical Mathematics: Vol. 57). 275p. text ed. 29.95x (ISBN 3-7643-1254-8). Birkhauser.

Hammerling, G. L., et al, eds. Monoclonal Antibodies & T-Cell Hybridomas: Perspectives & Technical Notes. (Research Monographs in Immunology: Vol. 3). 1982. 107.75 (ISBN 0-444-80351-3). Elsevier.

Hammerman, Susan & Maikowski, Stephen, eds. The Economics of Disability: International Perspectives. LC 81-4397. (Illus.). 238p. (Orig.). 1981. pap. 15.00 (ISBN 0-9605554-0-4). UNIPUB.

Hammermeister, Karl E. Coronary Bypass Surgery. 464p. 1983. 43.50 (ISBN 0-03-059588-6). Praeger.

Hammerschlag, Wilhelm. The Kondratieff Theory & the Discovery of the Exact Date for the Explosion of the Third World War. (Illus.). 117p. 1983. 87.95 (ISBN 0-86722-031-7). Inst Econ Pol.

Hammerslag, Julius G. Simple Solution Series. 72p. Date not set. 6.95 (ISBN 0-686-82049-5). Dorrance.

Hammersley, J. M. & Handscomb, D. C. Monte Carlo Methods. (Monographs on Statistics & Applied Probability). 1964. 17.50x (ISBN 0-412-15870-1, Pub. by Chapman & Hall). Methuen Inc.

Hammersley, Martyn, jt. ed. see Woods, Peter.

Hammersley, P., jt. ed. see Deen, S. M.

Hammersley, Peter, ed. New Approaches to Systems Analysis & Design. 1980. 19.00 (ISBN 0-471-25755-9, Wiley Heyden). Wiley.

Hammerstein & Lachnit-Fixson. Androgenization in Women. (International Congress Ser.: No. 493). 1980. 63.50 (ISBN 0-444-90142-6). Elsevier.

Hammerstein, Oscar, jt. auth. see Rodgers, Richard.

Hammerstorm, Richard B. Make Your Home Party a Success. (Illus.). 128p. (Orig.). 1982. pap. 2.25 (ISBN 0-9604534-1-5). Brown Hse Gall.

Hammerstrom, Gary. Energy Consumption & Conservation. (Learning Packages in Policy Issues Ser.: No. 2). (Illus.). 58p. (Orig.). 1977. pap. text ed. 1.50x (ISBN 0-936826-11-8). Pol Stud Assocs.

--The Hazards of Nuclear Energy: A Policy & Planning Approach. (Learning Packages in Policy Issues Ser.: No. 3). (Illus.). 86p. (Orig.). 1977. pap. text ed. 2.00x (ISBN 0-936826-12-6). Pol Stud Assocs.

Hammerstrom, Richard & Haan, Maria N. Graffiti in the Ivy League, the Seven Sisters, & Thereabouts. 1981. pap. 4.95 (ISBN 0-446-37602-7). Warner Bks.

--Graffiti in the Pac 10. 1981. pap. 4.95 (ISBN 0-446-37603-5). Warner Bks.

--Graffiti in the Southwest Conference. 1981. pap. 4.95 (ISBN 0-446-37604-3). Warner Bks.

Hammerstrom, Richard B., jt. auth. see Haan, Marina N.

Hammes, Carol A. & Anderson, Ronald T. Agency Operations & Sales Management. LC 82-82395. 653p. 1982. pap. text ed. 17.00 (ISBN 0-89462-037-1). IIA.

Hammes, G. G. Techniques of Chemistry: Investigation of Rates & Mechanisms of Reactions, Vol. 6. 3rd ed. 665p. 1974. 83.50 (ISBN 0-471-93127-6, Pub. by Wiley-Interscience). Wiley.

Hammett, Dashiell. The Continental Op. LC 74-9050. 1974. 2.95 (ISBN 0-394-72013-X). Random.

--The Dain Curse. 1972. pap. 2.95 (ISBN 0-394-71827-5, Vin). Random.

Hammett, Dashiell & Raymond, Alex. Dashiell Hammett's Secret Agent X-9. Sparafucile, Tony, ed. (Illus., Orig.). 1983. pap. 9.95 (ISBN 0-930330-05-6). Intl Polygonics.

Hammett, Jenny. Woman's Transformation: A Psychological Theology. (Symposium Ser.). 112p. 1982. pap. 11.95 (ISBN 0-88946-918-0). E Mellen.

Hammett, K. R. Soil Care. (Illus.). 1978. 6.65 (ISBN 0-589-01034-4, Pub. by Reed Books Australia). C E Tuttle.

Hammett, Louis P. Physical Organic Chemistry: Reaction Rates, Equilibria & Mechanisms. 2nd ed. LC 73-91680. 1970. text ed. 26.00 o.p. (ISBN 0-07-025905-4, C). McGraw.

Hammett, Ralph W. Architecture in the United States: A Survey of Architectural Styles Since 1776. LC 76-4917. 1976. 39.50 (ISBN 0-471-34721-3, Pub. by Wiley-Interscience). Wiley.

Hammick, Georgina, et al. A Poetry Quintet. (Gollancz Poets Ser.). 1977. pap. 7.50 o.p. (ISBN 0-575-02156-X). Transatlantic.

Hammil, Carrie E. The Celestial Journey & the Harmony of the Spheres. 1980. 13.50 o.p. (ISBN 0-912646-53-5). Tex Christian.

Hammill, Carrie E. Celestial Journey & the Harmony of the Spheres. LC 79-28416. 183p. 1980. pap. 13.50 o.p. (ISBN 0-686-77617-8). Carrollton Pr.

Hammill, Donald D., jt. auth. see Myers, Patricia L.

Hammill, Donald D., jt. auth. see Wiederholt, J. Lee.

Hamming, ed. see Kohavi, Zvi.

Hamming, Richard W. Coding & Information Theory. (Illus.). 1980. text ed. 30.00 (ISBN 0-13-139139-9). P-H.

--Introduction to Applied Numerical Analysis. 1970. text ed. 29.95 o.p. (ISBN 0-07-025889-9, C). McGraw.

--Numerical Methods for Scientists & Engineers. rev. ed. (Illus.). 612p. 1973. text ed. 34.00 (ISBN 0-07-025887-2, C). McGraw.

Hammitt, Frederick G. Cavitation & Multiphase Flow Phenomena. 448p. 1980. text ed. 70.00 (ISBN 0-07-025907-0). McGraw.

Hammock, Allan S., jt. auth. see DiClerico, Roberts.

Hammock, M. Kathryn & Milhorat, Thomas H. Cranial Computed Tomography in Infancy & Childhood. (Illus.). 360p. 1981. lib. bdg. 85.00 (ISBN 0-683-03906-7). Williams & Wilkins.

Hammon, Paul Y. & Louscher, David J. The Reluctant Supplier: U. S. Decision-Making for Arms Sales. 336p. 1983. 25.00 (ISBN 0-89946-149-2). Oelgeschlager.

Hammond. A George Orwell Companion. LC 82-875. 304p. 1982. 28.50x (ISBN 0-312-32452-9). St Martin.

Hammond, Antony, ed. see Shakespeare, William.

Hammond, Bernice. Hokus-Pokus the Goodwill Pixie. Davis, Audrey, ed. (Illus.). 110p. 1981. text ed. 10.50 (ISBN 0-9609398-0-6). Assn Preserv.

Hammond, Bill. How to Make Money in Advertising Photography. (Illus.). 160p. 1975. 17.95 o.p. (ISBN 0-8174-0581-X, Amphoto). Watson-Guptill.

Hammond, Debbie, ed. see Beavers, Dorothy J.

Hammond, Debbie, ed. see Friend, Paul D.

Hammond, Debbie, ed. see Smolen, Maxine.

Hammond, Diana. Let's Go to a Harbor. (Let's Go Ser.). (Illus.). (gr. 2-4). 1959. PLB 4.29 o.p. (ISBN 0-399-60373-5). Putnam Pub Group.

Hammond, Dorothea E. Beggar in the Street. 700p. (Orig.). Date not set. pap. 14.95 (ISBN 0-942874-02-1). Hammond Records. Postponed.

--Date with the Dead. 250p. 1983. pap. 6.95 (ISBN 0-942874-00-5). Hammond Records.

Hammond, Dorothy. Pictorial Price Guide to American Antiques. 5th ed. (Illus.). 224p. 1982. pap. 12.95 (ISBN 0-525-47706-3, 01258-370). Dutton.

Hammond, E. Teaching Writing. 168p. 1983. 10.95x (ISBN 0-07-025893-7). McGraw.

Hammond, E. Cuyler & Selikoff, Irving J. Public Control of Environmental Health Hazards, Vol. 329. (Annals of the New York Academy of Sciences). 405p. 1979. 74.00x (ISBN 0-89766-031-5). NY Acad Sci.

Hammond, E. Cuyler, jt. ed. see Selikoff, Irving J.

Hammond, Ed. To Embrace the Moon: An Illustrated Biography of Mao Zedong. 196p. 1980. 9.95 (ISBN 0-89581-455-2); pap. 4.95 (ISBN 0-89581-502-8). Lancaster-Miller.

Hammond, Edward H. & Shaffer, Robert H. The Legal Foundations of Student Personnel Services in Higher Education. 174p. 1978. 10.00 (ISBN 0-686-36426-0, 72167). Am Personnel.

Hammond, Gerald. The Game. 176p. 1982. 10.95 (ISBN 0-312-31590-2). St Martin.

--The Making of the English Bible. 256p. 1983. 20.00 (ISBN 0-8022-2419-9). Philos Lib.

Hammond, Gerald, ed. see Skelton, John.

Hammond Inc. Favorite Recipes from My Kitchen. (Illus.). 1979. pap. 6.95 (ISBN 0-8437-3419-1). Hammond Inc.

Hammond Incorporated. The Whole Earth Atlas. new ed. (Illus.). 256p. (Orig.). 1983. pap. 8.95 o.p. (ISBN 0-8437-2500-1). Hammond Inc.

Hammond Incorporated Editors. History Atlas of Our Country. text ed. 3.33x (ISBN 0-8437-7435-5). Hammond Inc.

--Intermediate World Atlas. LC 76-23502. (gr. 5-9). text ed. 3.99x (ISBN 0-8437-7466-5). Hammond Inc.

--World Atlas for Students. (gr. 8-12). 1980. pap. text ed. 3.33x (ISBN 0-8437-7820-2). Hammond Inc.

Hammond, J., Jr. & Robinson, T. Hammond's Farm Animals. 350p. 1982. pap. text ed. 35.00 (ISBN 0-686-38087-8). E Arnold.

Hammond, J. R. An Edgar Allan Poe Companion: A Guide to the Short Stories, Romances & Essays. LC 81-167695. (Companion Ser.). (Illus.). 218p. 1981. 27.50x (ISBN 0-389-20172-3). B&N Imports.

Hammond, James J., et al. Woodworking Technology. rev. ed. (Illus.). (gr. 10-12). 1980. text ed. 19.96 (ISBN 0-87345-893-1); study guide 6.00 (ISBN 0-87345-894-X); ans. key avail. (ISBN 0-87345-895-8). McKnight.

Hammond, Jerome W., jt. auth. see Dahl, Dale C.

Hammond, John H. The Camera Obscura. 182p. 1981. 33.50 (ISBN 0-9960023-0-8, Pub. by A Hilger England). Heyden.

--Jerome A. Moore: A Man of TCU. LC 74-75867. (Illus.). 86p. 1974. 5.00 (ISBN 0-912646-41-1). Tex Christian.

Hammond, Jonathan. China. LC 75-44869. (Macdonald Countries). (Illus.). (gr. 6 up). 1976. PLB 12.68 (ISBN 0-382-06101-2, Pub. by Macdonald Ed). Silver.

Hammond, Lucille. When Dog Was Little. LC 82-82649. (First Little Golden Book). (Illus.). 24p. (ps). 1983. price not set (ISBN 0-307-10145-2, Golden Pr). Western Pub.

Hammond, Mac. Cold Turkey. LC 82-70290. 61p. 1969. 7.50 (ISBN 0-8040-0044-1). Swallow.

Hammond, Mildred. Square Dancing Is For Me. LC 82-17134. (Sports For Me Bks.). (Illus.). 48p. (gr. 2-5). 1983. PLB 6.95g (ISBN 0-8225-1138-X). Lerner Pubns.

Hammond, N. G. & Scullard, H. H., eds. Oxford Classical Dictionary. 2nd ed. 1970. 45.00 (ISBN 0-19-869117-3). Oxford U Pr.

Hammond, Nicholas G. Alexander the Great: King, Commander, & Statesman. LC 80-18573. (Illus.). 358p. 1981. 24.00 o.p. (ISBN 0-8155-5058-8, NP). Noyes.

--History of Greece to 322 B. C. 2nd ed. (Illus.). 1967. 22.50x (ISBN 0-19-873019-5). Oxford U Pr.

Hammond, Norman, ed. Social Process in Maya Prehistory: Studies in Honor of Sir Eric Thompson. 1978. 95.50 (ISBN 0-12-322050-5). Acad Pr.

Hammond, P., et al. The Structure of Human Society. 736p. 1975. text ed. 19.95x o.p. (ISBN 0-669-81315-X); instructor's manual 1.95 o.p. (ISBN 0-669-90266-7). Heath.

Hammond, Paul, jt. auth. see Allen, John.

Hammond, Peter. Offenbach: His Life & Times. (Life & Times Ser.). (Illus.). 192p. (YA) 1981. Repr. of 1980 ed. 12.95 (ISBN 0-87666-583-0, Z-52). Paganiniana Pubns.

Hammond, Peter, jt. ed. see Sutton, Anne.

Hammond, Peter B. An Introduction to Cultural & Social Anthropology. 1978. text ed. 22.95x (ISBN 0-02-349790-4, 34979). Macmillan.

Hammond, Philip. American Mosaic: Social Patterns of Religion in the United States. 1970. pap. text ed. 6.25x (ISBN 0-394-31009-8). Phila Bk Co.

--The Excavation of the Main Theater at Petra, Nineteen Sixty-One to Nineteen Sixty-Two: Final Report. (Colt Archaeological Institute Ser.). 90p. 1965. text ed. 22.00x (ISBN 0-85668-070-2, Pub. by Aris & Phillips England). Humanities.

Hammond, Philip C. The Nabataeans--Their History, Culture & Archaeology. (Studies in Mediterranean Archaeology Ser.: No. XXXVII). 1973. pap. text ed. 30.00x (ISBN 91-85058-57-2). Humanities.

Hammond, R. Air Survey in Economic Development. 1967. 10.00 (ISBN 0-444-19916-0). Elsevier.

Hammond, R. & McCullagh, P. S. Quantitative Techniques in Geography. 2nd ed. 1978. 14.95x (ISBN 0-19-874066-2); pap. 13.95x (ISBN 0-19-874067-0). Oxford U Pr.

Hammond, Robert & Rogers, William. Introduction to FORTRAN IV. rev. ed. (Illus.). 358p. 1982. text ed. 12.95x (ISBN 0-07-025908-9, C); solutions manuel 10.00 (ISBN 0-07-025909-7). McGraw.

Hammond, Robert, et al. Introduction to FORTRAN IV. 2nd ed. (Illus.). 1978. text ed. 9.95 o.p. (ISBN 0-07-025897-X, C); solutions manual 10.95 o.p. (ISBN 0-07-025898-8). McGraw.

Hammond, Robert H., et al. Engineering Graphics: Design-Analysis-Communication. 2nd ed. LC 79-12166. 654p. 1971. Repr. of 1964 ed. lib. bdg. 26.50 (ISBN 0-88275-979-5). Krieger.

Hammond, Seymour B. & Gehmlich, D. K. Electrical Engineering. 2nd ed. 1971. text ed. 40.00 (ISBN 0-07-025901-1, C). McGraw.

Hammond Staff, ed. Hammond Road Atlas & Vacation Guide 1983. (Illus.). 48p. 1983. pap. 2.50 (ISBN 0-8437-2625-3). Hammond Inc.

--Road Atlas America 1983. rev. ed. (Illus.). 72p. 1983. pap. 3.95 (ISBN 0-8437-2631-8). Hammond Inc.

Hammond, Thomas T. & Farrell, Robert, eds. The Anatomy of Communist Takeovers. LC 74-79975. 600p. 1975. 45.00x (ISBN 0-300-01727-8); pap. 10.95x o.p. (ISBN 0-300-01799-5). Yale U Pr.

Hammond, V. J., jt. auth. see Birchall, D. W.

Hammond, William, jt. auth. see Bucknill, John C.

Hammond, Winifred G. Corn: From Farm to Market. LC 72-76707. (From Farm to Market Ser.). (Illus.). 96p. (gr. 3-7). 1972. PLB 4.59 o.p. (ISBN 0-698-30439-X, Coward). Putnam Pub Group.

--Cotton: From Farm to Market. LC 68-31741. (From Farm to Market Ser). (Illus.). (gr. 3-6). 1968. PLB 4.59 o.p. (ISBN 0-698-30055-6, Coward). Putnam Pub Group.

--The Riddle of Teeth. (Illus.). (gr. 3-5). 1971. PLB 4.99 (ISBN 0-698-30294-X, Coward). Putnam Pub Group.

--The Story of Your Eye. (Illus.). 64p. (gr. 3-7). 1975. PLB 6.99 (ISBN 0-698-30577-9, Coward). Putnam Pub Group.

Hammonds, Michael. Incident on the Way to a Killing. 176p. 1980. pap. 1.75 o.s.i. (ISBN 0-515-04681-7). Jove Pubns.

Hammons, Anna S., ed. Methods for Ecological Toxicology: A Critical Review of Laboratory Multispecies Tests. LC 81-67259. 310p. 1981. text ed. 39.95 (ISBN 0-250-40480-X). Ann Arbor Science.

Hammons, Jim, ed. Organization Development & Management. LC 81-48473. 1982. 7.95x (ISBN 0-87589-883-1, CC-37). Jossey-Bass.

Hammontree, Marie. Will & Charlie Mayo: Boy Doctors. (Childhood of Famous Americans Ser). (Illus.). (gr. 3-7). 3.95 o.p. (ISBN 0-672-50185-6). Bobbs.

Hamner, Robert D. Derek Walcott. (World Authors Ser.). 1981. lib. bdg. 14.95 (ISBN 0-8057-6442-9, Twayne). G K Hall.

--V. S. Naipaul. (World Authors Ser.). 1973. lib. bdg. 13.95 (ISBN 0-8057-2647-0, Twayne). G K Hall.

Hamner, W. Clay. Organizational Shock. LC 80-11910. (St. Clair Series in Management & Organizational Behavior). 1980. pap. text ed. 19.95 (ISBN 0-471-06251-0). Wiley.

Hamner, W. Clay & Schmidt, Frank L., eds. Contemporary Problems in Personnel. rev. ed. (Illus.). 1977. 21.95 (ISBN 0-471-06238-3). Wiley.

Hamner, W. Clay, jt. ed. see Tosi, Henry L.

Hamnett, Brian R. Politics & Trade in Southern Mexico, 1750-1821. LC 70-116839. (Latin American Studies: No. 12). (Illus.). 1971. 27.95 (ISBN 0-521-07860-1). Cambridge U Pr.

Hamnett, Ian. Chieftainship & Legitimacy. (International Library of Anthropology). 1975. 16.95x (ISBN 0-7100-8177-4). Routledge & Kegan.

Hamnett, Michael P., ed. Research in Culture Learning: Language & Conceptual Studies. Brislin, Richard W. LC 80-21761. 195p. 1980. pap. 10.00x (ISBN 0-8248-0738-3). UH Pr.

Hamon, Henry. New York Stock Exchange Manual. Repr. of 1865 ed. lib. bdg. 20.75x (ISBN 0-8371-4580-5, HANM). Greenwood.

Hamori, Laszlo. Dangerous Journey. MacMillan, Annabelle, tr. LC 62-8742. (Illus.). (gr. 4-6). 1966. pap. 1.75 (ISBN 0-15-623821-7, VoyB). HarBraceJ.

Hamparian, Donna, et al. The Violent Few. LC 77-9128. (The Dangerous Offender Project). 240p. 1978. 21.95 (ISBN 0-669-01779-5). Lexington Bks.

Hampden-Turner, Charles. Maps of the Mind. LC 80-21886. (Illus.). 224p. 1981. pap. 8.95 (ISBN 0-02-547710-2). Macmillan.

--Sane Asylum. LC 76-53595. 1977. pap. 4.50 o.p. (ISBN 0-688-08182-7). Morrow.

Hampe, Roland & Simon, Erika. The Birth of Greek Art: From the Mycenaean to the Archaic Period. (Illus.). 1981. 65.00x (ISBN 0-19-520226-0). Oxford U Pr.

Hampel, Clifford A., ed. Encyclopedia of Electrochemistry. LC 64-22288. 1224p. 1972. Repr. of 1964 ed. 52.50 (ISBN 0-88275-023-2). Krieger.

--Rare Metal Handbook. 2nd ed. LC 61-10449. 732p. 1971. Repr. of 1961 ed. 42.00 (ISBN 0-88275-024-0). Krieger.

Hamphill, B. J. Evaluative Process in Psychiatric Occupational Therapy. 1981. pap. 24.50 (ISBN 0-913590-80-0). Slack Inc.

Hample, Naomi C., jt. auth. see Marshall, Eric.

Hample, Stoo. Stoo Hample's Silly Joke Book. LC 78-50431. (Illus.). (gr. 1-6). 1978. PLB 5.47 o.s.i. (ISBN 0-440-08160-2); pap. 2.50 o.s.i. (ISBN 0-440-08154-8). Delacorte.

--Yet Another Big Fat Funny Silly Book. LC 80-66202. (Illus.). 96p. (gr. 1-4). 1980. 4.95 o.s.i. (ISBN 0-440-09796-7); PLB 6.46 o.s.i. (ISBN 0-440-09797-5). Delacorte.

Hampshire, S. Public & Private Morality. LC 78-2839. 1978. 20.95 (ISBN 0-521-22084-X); pap. 7.95 (ISBN 0-521-29352-9). Cambridge U Pr.

Hampshire, Stuart, ed. Age of Reason: The Seventeenth Century Philosophers. (Orig.). pap. 1.95 (ISBN 0-451-61872-6, MJ1872, Ment). NAL.

Hampshire, Susan. Susan's Story: An Autobiographical Account of My Struggle with Words. (Illus.). 168p. 1982. 11.95 (ISBN 0-312-77966-6). St Martin.

Hampson, Anne. The Dawn Steals Softly. 192p. (Orig.). 1980. pap. 1.50 (ISBN 0-671-57027-7, Pub. by Silhouette Bks). S&S.

--Man of the Outback. 192p. (Orig.). 1980. pap. 1.50 (ISBN 0-671-57028-5, Pub. by Silhouette Bks). S&S.

--Man Without a Heart. 192p. 1981. pap. 1.50 (ISBN 0-671-57052-8, Pub. by Silhouette Bks). S&S.

--Payment in Full. 192p. (Orig.). 1980. pap. 1.50 (ISBN 0-671-57001-3, Pub. by Silhouette Bks). S&S.

--Second Tomorrow. 192p. (Orig.). 1980. pap. 1.50 (ISBN 0-671-57016-1, Pub. by Silhouete Bks). S&S.

--Seule Sans Lui. (Harlequin Romantique Ser.). 192p. pap. 1.95 (ISBN 0-373-41178-2). Harlequin Bks.

--Shadow of Apollo. 192p. 1981. pap. 1.50 (ISBN 0-671-57064-1, Pub. by Silhouette Bks). S&S.

--Stormy Masquerade. 192p. (Orig.). 1980. pap. 1.50 (ISBN 0-671-57004-8, Pub. by Silhouette Bks). S&S.

--Where Eagles Nest. 192p. (Orig.). 1980. pap. 1.50 (ISBN 0-671-57040-4, Pub. by Silhouette Bks). S&S.

Hampson, David, jt. auth. see Schaffarcick, Jon.

Hampson, Norman. Will & Circumstance: Montesquieu, Rousseau, & the French Revolution. LC 82-40455. 208p. 1983. 17.50x (ISBN 0-8061-1843-1). U of Okla Pr.

Hampton, C. W. & Clifford, E. Planecraft. LC 79-57129. (Illus.). 1982. pap. 6.00 (ISBN 0-918036-00-3). Woodcraft Supply.

Hampton, Christopher. Philanthropist: A Bourgeois Comedy. 78p. 1970. pap. 3.95 (ISBN 0-571-09527-5). Faber & Faber.

--Savages. 86p. 1974. pap. 5.95 (ISBN 0-571-10348-0). Faber & Faber.

--Tales from Hollywood. 96p. (Orig.). 1983. pap. 7.95 (ISBN 0-571-11883-6). Faber & Faber.

Hampton, Christopher, tr. see Von Horvath, Odon.

Hampton, David R. Contemporary Management. 2nd ed. (Management Ser.). (Illus.). 528p. 1981. text ed. 24.95x (ISBN 0-07-025935-6); instructor's manual 18.95 (ISBN 0-07-025936-4); write for info study guide 8.95 (ISBN 0-07-025937-2); test file 18.50 (ISBN 0-07-025938-0). McGraw.

Hampton, David R. & Summer, Charles E. Organizational Behavior & the Practice of Management. 4th ed. Webber, Ross A., ed. 1982. text ed. 25.50x (ISBN 0-673-15580-3). Scott F.

Hampton, David R., jt. auth. see Belasco, James A.

Hampton, J. Handbook for Financial Decision Makers. 1978. 31.95 (ISBN 0-87909-353-6). Reston.

Hampton, James C., ed. The Cell Cycle in Malignancy & Immunity: Proceedings. LC 74-600181. (ERDA Symposium Ser.). 614p. 1975. pap. 23.25 (CONF-731005); microfiche 4.50 (ISBN 0-87079-158-3, CONF-731005). DOE.

Hampton, John J. Financial Decision Making: Concepts, Problems, & Cases. 2nd ed. (Illus.). 1979. text ed. 22.95 (ISBN 0-8359-2008-9); instrs' manual avail. (ISBN 0-8359-2010-0). Reston.

Hampton, R. E. & Zabin, J. B. College Salesmanship. 1970. text ed. 22.45 (ISBN 0-07-025921-6, G). McGraw.

Hampton, Veita J. & Kuykendall, Bill. The Best of Photojournalism, No. 7. (Illus.). 256p. 1982. pap. write for info. (ISBN 0-930552-06-7). Tech Ed Serv.

Hampton, Veita J., ed. see National Press Photographers Association & University of Missouri School of Journalism.

Hampton, William J. Fifty Ways to Take Better Pictures. (Illus.). 144p. (Orig.). 1982. pap. 11.95 (ISBN 0-8174-5519-1, Amphoto). Watson-Guptill.

Hamric, Ann B. & Sprose, Judith. The Clinical Nurse Specialist in Theory & Practice. Date not set. price not set (ISBN 0-8089-1519-3). Grune.

Hamrick, Becky & Wiesenfeld, S. L. The Egg-Free, Milk-Free, Wheat-Free Cookbook. LC 81-48036. (Illus.). 224p. 1982. 15.86i (ISBN 0-06-014978-7, HarpT). Har-Row.

Hamrock, Bernard J. & Dowson, Duncan. Ball Bearing Lubrication: The Elastohydrodynamics of Elliptical Contacts. LC 81-3006. 386p. 1981. 52.50x (ISBN 0-471-03553-X, Pub. by Wiley-Interscience). Wiley.

Hamsa, Bobbie. Your Pet Gorilla. LC 81-2532. (Far-Fetched Pets Ser.). (Illus.). 32p. (ps-3). 1981. PLB 9.25 (ISBN 0-516-03365-4); pap. 2.95 (ISBN 0-516-43365-2). Childrens.

--Your Pet Lion. LC 81-4597. (Far-Fetched Pets Ser.). (Illus.). 32p. (ps-3). 1981. PLB 9.25 (ISBN 0-516-03366-2); pap. 2.95 (ISBN 0-516-43366-0). Childrens.

Hamsher, jt. auth. see Chesebro.

Hamsher, Donald H., ed. Communications System Engineering Handbook. 1967. 74.50 (ISBN 0-07-025960-7, P&RB). McGraw.

Hamsun, Knul. Hunger. 1975. pap. 2.25 o.p. (ISBN 0-380-00556-5, 42028, Bard). Avon.

Hamsun, Knut. Hunger. Bly, Robert, tr. from Nor. 256p. 1967. pap. 6.95 (ISBN 0-374-50520-9, N302). FS&G.

--Pan: From Lieutenant Thomas Glahn's Papers. McFarlane, James W., tr. from Nor. 192p. (Orig.). 1956. pap. 6.25 (ISBN 0-374-50016-9, N104). FS&G.

Han, Bong Soo. Hapkido Korean Art of Self-Defense. Cocoran, John, ed. LC 74-15500. (Ser. 116). (Illus.). 1974. pap. text ed. 6.95 (ISBN 0-89750-011-3). Ohara Pubns.

Han, Henry H., ed. World in Transition: Challenges to Human Rights, Development & World Order. LC 79-66422. 1979. pap. text ed. 19.00 (ISBN 0-8191-0824-3). U Pr of Amer.

Han, Seong S. Cell Biology. (Illus.). 1978. pap. text ed. 25.00 (ISBN 0-07-025965-8, HP). McGraw.

--Human Microscopic Anatomy. (Illus.). 1981. text ed. 31.95x (ISBN 0-07-025961-5). McGraw.

Han, Woo-Keun. The History of Korea. Mintz, Grafton K., ed. Lee, Kyung-Shik, tr. from Korean. (Illus.). 568p. 1971. 15.00 o.p. (ISBN 0-8248-0106-7, Eastwest Ctr); pap. text ed. 8.95x (ISBN 0-8248-0334-5). UH Pr.

Han, Wu. Hai Jui Dismissed from Office. Huang, C. C., tr. from Chinese. (Asian Studies at Hawaii Ser.: No. 7). 120p. 1972. pap. text ed. 6.00x (ISBN 0-8248-0215-2). UH Pr.

Hana, W. J. English Lantern Clocks. (Illus.). 1979. 14.95 o.p. (ISBN 0-7137-1011-X, Pub by Blandford Pr England). Sterling.

Hanaburgh, David H. Your Future in Forestry. LC 75-114121. (Career Guidance Ser). 1971. pap. 4.50 (ISBN 0-668-02245-0). Arco.

Hanafee, William N., jt. ed. see Wilson, Gabriel H.

Hanagan, Micahel P. The Logic of Solidarity: Artisans & Industrial Workers in Three French Towns, Eighteen Seventy-One to Nineteen-Fourteen. LC 79-13181. (The Working Class in European History Ser.). 280p. 1982. pap. 7.50 (ISBN 0-252-01007-8). U of Ill Pr.

Hanai, Tetsuro. Studies on Japanese Ostracoda. (Illus.). 320p. 1982. text ed. 60.00 (ISBN 0-86008-314-4, Pub. by U of Tokyo Japan). Columbia U Pr.

Hanak, H., ed. Soviet Foreign Policy Since the Death of Stalin. (World Studies Ser). 1972. 27.50x (ISBN 0-7100-7215-5). Routledge & Kegan.

Hanak, Marcia & Scott, Ann. Spinal Cord Injury: An Illustrated Guide to Patient Care. 1983. text ed. 15.95 (ISBN 0-8261-4171-4). Springer Pub.

Hanak, Mirko, illus. Animals We Love, Bks. 1 & 2. LC 72-89571. (Illus.). 32p. (gr. k-4). 1973. 6.50 ea. Bk. 1 (ISBN 0-87592-005-5). Bk. 2 (ISBN 0-87592-006-3). Scroll Pr.

Hanan, Mack. Accelerated Growth Planning: Profit Improvement Strategies for Consumer, Industrial, & Service Business Game Plans. LC 77-13201. (Illus.). 1978. 24.95 (ISBN 0-07-025971-2, P&RB). McGraw.

--Key Account Selling: New Strategies for Maximizing Profit & Penetration. 192p. 1983. 15.95 (ISBN 0-8144-5751-7). Am Mgmt.

--Organizing for Profitable Selling. 1976. pap. text ed. 6.95 (ISBN 0-686-98294-0). Sales & Mktg.

--Suprise! You're Really A Manager. Date not set. pap. text ed. 6.95 (ISBN 0-686-98282-7). Sales & Mktg.

--Venture Management: A Game Plan for Corporate Growth & Diversification. new ed. (Illus.). 1976. 27.50 (ISBN 0-07-025970-4, P&RB). McGraw.

Hanau, Laia. The Study Game. 4th ed. 1979. pap. 4.50 (ISBN 0-06-463489-2, EH 489, EH). B&N NY.

Hanauer, Elsie V. The Horse Owner's Concise Guide. LC 69-14880. (Illus.). 1978. pap. 2.95 (ISBN 0-668-04661-9, 4661). Arco.

Hanawalt, jt. auth. see Friedberg.

Hanayama, Shoyu. Buddhist Handbook for Shinshu Followers. 1969. 5.95 o.p. (ISBN 0-89346-057-5, Pub. by Hokuseido Pr). Heian Intl.

Hanbery, jt. auth. see Visse.

Hanbury-Tenison, R. Aborigines of the Amazon Rain Forest. (Peoples of the Wild Ser.). 1983. 15.96 (ISBN 0-7054-0707-1, Pub. by Time-Life). Silver.

Hanby, V., jt. auth. see Jackson, M. P.

Hanby, Victor J., jt. auth. see Jackson, Michael P.

Hancer, Kevin. Paperback Price Guide. 2nd ed. (Illus.). 440p. 1982. pap. 9.95. Overstreet.

Hancer, Kevin B. & Reginald, R. The Paperback Price Guide. 430p. (Orig.). 1982. lib. bdg. 14.95x (ISBN 0-89370-049-5). Borgo Pr.

Hanchett, E. S. Community Health Assessment: A Conceptual Tool Kit. LC 78-13648. 1979. pap. 13.95 (ISBN 0-471-34776-0, Pub. by Wiley Medical). Wiley.

Hanck, Paul A. How To Do What You Want To Do. pap. 5.95 (ISBN 0-686-36754-5). Inst Rat Liv.

Hancock, B. W. Assessment of Tumor Response. 1983. 49.50 (ISBN 90-247-2712-X, Pub. by Martinus Nijhoff Netherlands). Kluwer Boston.

Hancock, C. V. Rod in Hand. 10.50x (ISBN 0-392-06434-0, SpS). Sportshelf.

Hancock, E. G., ed. Toluene, the Xylenes & Their Industrial Derivatives. (Chemical Engineering Monographs: Vol. 15). 552p. 1982. 125.75 (ISBN 0-444-42058-4). Elsevier.

Hancock, Harris. Development of the Minkowski Geometry of Numbers, 2 vols. pap. text ed. 3.50 ea. o.p. Vol. 1 (ISBN 0-486-61203-1). Vol. 2 (ISBN 0-486-61204-X). Dover.

Hancock, Harry L., jt. auth. see Crooks, Thomas C.

Hancock, Keith, ed. History of the Second World War: United Kingdom Civil Series. (Orig.). 1975. write for info. Kraus Intl.

Hancock, L. & Krieger, M. The C Primer. 256p. 1983. pap. 14.95 (ISBN 0-07-025981-X, P&RB). McGraw.

Hancock, Lyn. Gypsy in the Classroom. LC 79-92182. (Illus.). 1980. 9.95x o.p. (ISBN 0-89696-085-4, An Everest House Book). Dodd.

Hancock, M. A. Menace on the Mountain. LC 68-31142. (Illus.). 192p. (gr. 6 up). 1968. 6.25 (ISBN 0-8255-4090-9). Macrae.

--Thundering Prairie. LC 79-87990. (Illus.). (gr. 4 up). 1969. 6.25 (ISBN 0-8255-4100-X); PLB 6.47 (ISBN 0-8255-4101-8). Macrae.

Hancock, Maxine. Crianca Em Formacao, A. (Port.). 1980. pap. 1.60 (ISBN 0-8297-0570-8). Life Pubs Intl.

--The Forever Principle. 160p. 1980. 6.95 o.p. (ISBN 0-8007-1110-6). Revell.

--Living on Less & Liking It More. LC 76-40220. 1977. 6.95 (ISBN 0-8024-4912-3). Moody.

--Love, Honor & Be Free. 1976. pap. 7.95 study ed. (ISBN 0-8024-5015-6). Moody.

--Love, Honor & Be Free: Leader's Guide. 1979. pap. 4.95 o.p. (ISBN 0-8024-5016-4). Moody.

Hancock, Moffatt. Torts in the Conflict of Laws. (Michigan Legal Studies). viii, 288p. 1982. Repr. of 1942 ed. lib. bdg. 30.00x cancelled (ISBN 0-8377-0643-2). Rothman.

Hancock, Niel. Circle of Light, No. 1: Greyfax Grimwald. 1982. pap. 2.95 (ISBN 0-446-31093-X). Warner Bks.

--Circle of Light, No. 2: Faragon Fairingay. 1982. pap. 2.95 (ISBN 0-446-31095-6). Warner Bks.

--Circle of Light, No. 3: Calix Stay. 1982. pap. 2.95 (ISBN 0-446-31097-2). Warner Bks.

--Circle of Light, No. 4: Squaring the Circle. 1982. pap. 2.95 (ISBN 0-446-31099-9). Warner Bks.

Hancock, Richard. Hancock's Diary. 644p. 1981. 35.00 (ISBN 0-686-97668-1). Pr of Morningside.

Hancock, Richard R. Hancock's Diary. 644p. 1982. Repr. of 1887 ed. 35.00 (ISBN 0-686-43277-0). Pr of Morningside.

Hancock, Rose, tr. see Carretto, Carlo.

Hancock, Rose M., tr. see Carretto, Carlo.

Hancock, Sibyl. Bill Pickett: First Black Rodeo Star. LC 76-41741. (Let Me Read Ser). (Illus.). (gr. k-3). 1977. pap. 1.95 (ISBN 0-15-207393-0, VoyB). HarBraceJ.

--The Blazing Hills. (See & Read Storybooks). (Illus.). 1975. PLB 5.49 o.p. (ISBN 0-399-60913-X). Putnam Pub Group.

--Famous Firsts of Black Americans. (gr. 3-9). 1983. 9.95 (ISBN 0-88289-240-1). Pelican.

--Old Blue. (See & Read Book). (Illus.). 48p. (gr. 1-4). 1980. PLB 6.99 (ISBN 0-399-61141-X). Putnam Pub Group.

--Spindletop. (Stories for Young Americans Ser.). (Illus.). 1981. 5.95 (ISBN 0-89015-265-9). Eakin Pubns.

--Theodore Roosevelt. LC 77-22614. (Beginning Biographies Ser.). (Illus.). (gr. k-3). 1978. PLB 5.99 o.p. (ISBN 0-399-61107-X). Putnam Pub Group.

Hancock, Sibyl & Cauley, Lorinda. Bill Pickett: First Black Rodeo Star. LC 76-41741. (Let-Me-Read Ser). (Illus.). (gr. 1-5). 1977. 4.95 (ISBN 0-15-207392-2, HJ). HarBraceJ.

Hancock, Virgil & Spanbauer, Larry. The Standard Catalog of United States Altered & Counterfeit Coins. (Illus.). 1979. deluxe ed. 37.50 (ISBN 0-685-91296-5); lib. bdg. 30.00 (ISBN 0-915262-26-6). S J Durst.

Hancock, William A. Executive's Guide to Business Law. 1979. 43.95 (ISBN 0-07-025978-X). McGraw.

--Saving Money Through Ten-Year Trusts. (Illus.). 1979. 19.95 (ISBN 0-07-025983-6, P&RB). McGraw.

--The Small Business Legal Advisor. 288p. 1982. 24.95 (ISBN 0-07-025979-8). McGraw.

Hancock, William K. Discovering Monaro: A Study of Man's Impact on His Environment. LC 78-178280. (Illus.). 256p. 1972. 34.50 (ISBN 0-521-08439-3). Cambridge U Pr.

--Smuts, 2 vols. Incl. Vol. 1. The Sanguine Years, 1870-1919. (ISBN 0-521-05187-8); Vol. 2. The Fields of Force, 1919-1950. (ISBN 0-521-05188-6). 1962. 57.50 ea. Cambridge U Pr.

Hancock, William K., ed. see Smuts, J. C.

Hancox, N. M. Biology of Bone. LC 73-169578. (Biological Structure & Function Ser). (Illus.). 1972. 60.00 (ISBN 0-521-08342-7). Cambridge U Pr.

Hand, A. J. Home Energy How to. LC 75-29777. (Popular Science Bk.). Orig. Title: How to Use Natural Energy in Your Home. (Illus.). 1977. 12.45i (ISBN 0-06-011774-5, HarpT). Har-Row.

Hand, Bruce A., et al. Traffic Investigation & Control. 2nd ed. (Public Service Technology Ser.). 272p. 1980. text ed. 18.95 (ISBN 0-675-08112-2). Merrill.

Hand, D. J. Discrimination & Classification. LC 81-13045. (Wiley Ser. in Probability & Mathematical Statistics). 224p. 1981. 38.95x (ISBN 0-471-28048-8, Pub. by Wiley Interscience). Wiley.

--Kernel Discriminant Analysis. (Pattern Recognition & Image Processing Research Studies). 1982. 37.95 (ISBN 0-471-10211-3, Pub. by Res Stud Pr). Wiley.

Hand, D. J., jt. auth. see Everitt, B. S.

Hand, Jackson. Home Guide to Solar Heating & Cooling. LC 77-26481. (Popular Science Skill Bks.). 1978. pap. 3.95i o.p. (ISBN 0-06-090650-2, CN 650, CN). Har-Row.

Hand, Katharine. Rhymes of Blithe Spirit. 1977. pap. 1.75 (ISBN 0-685-82001-7). Creative Pr.

Hand, Katherine. Lessons from the Little Old Schoolhouse. 1977. pap. 1.75 (ISBN 0-685-81998-1). Creative Pr.

Hand, Katherine, jt. auth. see Shrader, Elizabeth H.

Hand, Learned. Bill of Rights. LC 58-8248. 1964. pap. text ed. 3.95x (ISBN 0-689-70085-7, 53). Atheneum.

--Bill of Rights. LC 58-8248. (Oliver Wendell Holmes Lectures Ser: 1958). 1958. 6.95x o.p. (ISBN 0-674-07300-2). Harvard U Pr.

Hand, Lee. Nursing Supervision. (Illus.). 368p. 1980. text ed. 19.95 (ISBN 0-8359-5044-1); pap. 15.95 (ISBN 0-8359-5043-3). Reston.

Hand, Phyllis. The Name of the Game Is... Learning. (gr. 2-6). 1982. 9.95 (ISBN 0-86653-096-7, GA 436). Good Apple.

Hand, Robert. Essays on Astrology. 1982. pap. 9.95 (ISBN 0-914918-42-7). Para Res.

Hand, Samuel B. Counsel & Advise: A Political Biography of Samuel I. Rosenman. Freidel, Frank, ed. LC 78-62383. (Modern American History Ser.: Vol. 8). 225p. 1979. lib. bdg. 30.00 o.s.i. (ISBN 0-8240-3632-8). Garland Pub.

Hand, Samuel D. see Muller, H. Nicholas, III.

Hand, Wayland D., ed. American Folk Legend: A Symposium. (Library Reprint Ser.: No. 98). 1979. Repr. of 1971 ed. 27.50x (ISBN 0-520-03836-3). U of Cal Pr.

Hand, William P. & Williams, Gerald. Basic Electronics: Components, Devices, & Circuits. Vorndran, Richard A., ed. LC 79-93245. 336p. 1980. text ed. 12.76 (ISBN 0-02-818260-X); instrs'. manual 4.40 (ISBN 0-686-61258-2). Glencoe.

Handa, Shizuo, jt. ed. see Makita, Akira.

Handal, Joan S., jt. auth. see Frisch, Vern A.

Handberg, Ejner. Measure & Drawings of 18th-Century American Furniture. LC 82-72163. (Illus.). 74p. 1982. pap. 5.95 (ISBN 0-912944-72-2). Berkshire Traveller.

Handbuck, Ein, jt. auth. see Meder, J.

Handel, George. Handel's Messiah: The Original Manuscripts in Facsimile. Chrysander, F. Melius, ed. LC 71-86581. (Music Reprint Ser). 1969. Repr. of 1892 ed. lib. bdg. 95.00 (ISBN 0-306-71815-4). Da Capo.

Handel, George F. Keyboard Works for Solo Instruments. (Music Ser.). 169p. 1982. pap. 7.50 (ISBN 0-486-24338-9). Dover.

Handel, Gerald & Elkin, Frederick. Social Welfare in Western Society. 357p. 1982. text ed. 22.00 (ISBN 0-394-32213-4). Random.

Handel, J. S., jt. auth. see Frisch, Vern A.

Handel, J. Van Den see Van Den Handel, J.

Handel, Judith. Introductory Statistics for Sociology. Smelser, Neil J. & Castner, Herbert, eds. LC 77-20158. (Prentice-Hall Methods & Theories in the Social Sciences Ser.). 387p. 1978. 22.95 (ISBN 0-13-503060-9). P-H.

Handel, Warren. Ethnomethodology: How People Make Sense. 176p. (Orig.). 1982. pap. 12.95 reference (ISBN 0-13-291708-4). P-H.

Handel, Warren H., jt. auth. see Lauer, Robert H.

Handelman, Ira, jt. auth. see Thompson, Gene E.

Handelman, Susan A. The Slayers of Moses: The Emergence of Rabbinic Interpretation in Modern Literary Theory. LC 81-16522. (Modern Jewish Literature & Culture Ser.). 284p. 1982. 39.00x (ISBN 0-87395-576-5); pap. 12.95x (ISBN 0-87395-577-3). State U NY Pr.

Handford, C. Robertson, et al. Regional Cross Sections of the Texas Panhandle: Precambrian to Mid-Permian. (Illus.). 1982. 3.00 (ISBN 0-686-36995-5). U of Tex Econ Geology.

Handford, Elizabeth R. The Mystery of the Smudged Postmark. (Preteen Ser.). 128p. (gr. 4-7). 1974. pap. 2.95 o.p. (ISBN 0-8024-3540-8). Moody.

--Woman in Despair: A Christian Guide to Self-Repair. 132p. 1983. 9.95 (ISBN 0-13-961797-3); pap. 4.95 (ISBN 0-13-961789-2). P-H.

Handford, J. Professional Pattern Making for Designers of Women's Wear. 1974. 21.95x (ISBN 0-87245-545-9). Textile Bk.

Handford, S. A., tr. see Aesop.

Handford, S. A., tr. see Caesar, Julius.

Handler, Edward & Mulkern, John R. Business in Politics: Campaign Strategies of Corporate Political Action Committees. LC 81-48560. 144p. 1982. 18.95x (ISBN 0-669-05428-3). Lexington Bks.

Handler, Gabriel Y. & Mirchandani, Pitu. Location on Networks: Theory & Algorithms. (Illus.). 1979. text ed. 32.50x (ISBN 0-262-08090-7). MIT Pr.

Handler, Herb. Year by Year in the Rock Era. LC 82-11722. (Illus.). 380p. 1983. lib. bdg. 29.95 (ISBN 0-313-23456-6, HRE/). Greenwood.

HAndler, Janet R., jt. auth. see Bellon, Jerry.

Handler, Joel F., ed. see Ten Broek, Jacobus.

Handler, M., et al. Federal Trade Commission: A Fiftieth Anniversary Symposium. LC 78-152229. (Symposia on Law & Society Ser). 1971. Repr. of 1964 ed. lib. bdg. 27.50 (ISBN 0-306-70119-7). Da Capo.

Handler, Stuart. How to Be a Superstar Selling Commercial & Investment Real Estate. 1983. text ed. 17.95 (ISBN 0-8359-2910-8). Reston.

Handley, Cathy. Encyclopedia of Women's Wit, Anecdotes & Stories. 347p. 1982. 24.50 (ISBN 0-13-276584-5, Busn). P-H.

Handley, Max. Meanwhile. 1979. pap. 5.95 o.p. (ISBN 0-446-87643-7). Warner Bks.

Handlin, Lilian, jt. auth. see Handlin, Oscar.

Handlin, Mary, jt. auth. see Handlin, Oscar.

Handlin, Mary F., jt. ed. see Handlin, Oscar.

Handlin, Oscar. Al Smith & His America. (Library of American Biography). 1958. pap. 5.95 (ISBN 0-316-34305-6). Little.

--Chance or Destiny: Turning Points in American History. LC 76-54255. 1977. Repr. of 1955 ed. lib. bdg. 19.00x (ISBN 0-8371-9334-6, HACD). Greenwood.

Handlin, Oscar & Handlin, Lilian. Abraham Lincoln & the Union. (Library of American Biography). 224p. (Orig.). 1980. 10.95 (ISBN 0-316-34315-3); pap. 5.95 (ISBN 0-316-34314-5). Little.

Handlin, Oscar & Handlin, Mary. Danger in Discord. 32p. 0.50 o.p. (ISBN 0-686-74956-1). ADL.

--The Wealth of a Nation. LC 75-6962. 276p. 1975. 10.00 o.p. (ISBN 0-07-025985-2, GB). McGraw.

Handlin, Oscar, ed. Readings in American History from Reconstruction to the Present. 2nd ed. 6.50 (ISBN 0-685-39880-3). Phila Bk Co.

--Readings in American History from Settlement to Reconstruction. 2nd ed. 6.50 (ISBN 0-685-39881-1). Phila Bk Co.

Handlin, Oscar & Burchard, John, eds. The Historian & the City. 320p. 1966. pap. 5.95x (ISBN 0-262-58006-3). MIT Pr.

Handlin, Oscar & Handlin, Mary F., eds. Popular Sources of Political Authority: Documents on the Massachusetts Constitution of 1780. LC 66-18247. (Center for the Study of the History of Liberty in America Ser.). 1966. 40.00x (ISBN 0-674-69000-1, Belknap Pr). Harvard U Pr.

Handlin, Oscar, ed. see Perkins, Dexter.

Handlin, Oscar, ed. see Tolles, Frederick B.

Handloser, J. S., jt. auth. see Willis, C. A.

Handman, Heidi & Brennan, Peter. The Sex Handbook: Information & Help for Minors. LC 73-87191. 224p. 1974. 6.95 o.p. (ISBN 0-399-11258-8). Putnam Pub Group.

Hands, A. W. Italo-Greek Coins. (Illus.). 1983. Repr. of 1912 ed. lib. bdg. 30.00 (ISBN 0-942666-12-7). S J Durst.

Handschin, Jacques. In memoriam...Moskou - Eighteen Sixty-Six to Basel - Nineteen Fifty-Five. 1962. 47.50 o.s.i. (ISBN) 90-6027-241-2, Pub. by Frits Knuf Netherlands); wrappers 35.00 o.s.i. (ISBN 90-6027-237-4, Pub by Frits Knuf Netherlands). Pendragon NY.

Handscomb, D. C., jt. auth. see Hammersley, J. M.

Handtschutter, J., jt. ed. see L'Hermite, P.

Handwriting Institute. Better Handwriting for You. rev. ed. (gr. 1-8). 1982. Bks. 1-8. text ed. 2.58 ea.; Bks. 1-3. pap. text ed. 2.58 ea.; Bks. 1-8. tchr's. eds. 4.20 ea.; Bks. 2-3. pap. text ed. 2.28 ea. transition eds.; tchr's. eds. 4.20 ea. Bowmar-Noble.

Handy, E. G., jt. auth. see Handy, E. S.

Handy, E. S. & Handy, E. G. Native Planters of Old Hawaii: Their Life, Lore & Environment. LC 78-119560. (Bulletin Ser.: No. 223). (Illus.). 641p. 1972. pap. 22.00 (ISBN 0-910240-11-6). Bishop Mus.

Handy, Jim. How to Uncover Hidden Business Opportunities that Make Money. LC 82-12574. 216p. 1983. 14.95 (ISBN 0-13-436071-0, Parker); pap. 4.95 (ISBN 0-13-436063-X). P-H.

Handy, L. J. Wages Policy in the British Coalmining Industry: A Study of National Wage Bargaining. LC 80-40229. (Department of Applied Economics Monograph: No. 27). 312p. 1981. 49.50 (ISBN 0-521-23535-9). Cambridge U Pr.

Handy, Ralph S. & Cronk, Louise H. Handbook for Transcribers & Style Manual for Business Writers. Rev. ed. (Illus.). 104p. 1977. pap. text ed. 4.20 (ISBN 0-686-38129-7). Morrison Pub Co.

Handy, Robert T. American Religious Depression 1925-1935. Wolf, Richard C., ed. LC 68-31338. (Facet Bks.). (Orig.). 1968. pap. 0.50 o.p. (ISBN 0-8006-3048-3, 1-3048). Fortress.

--Christian America: Protestant Hopes & Historical Realities. LC 78-161888. 1974. pap. 5.95x (ISBN 0-19-501784-6). Oxford U Pr.

--A History of the Churches in the United States & Canada. 1979. pap. 8.95 (ISBN 0-19-502531-8, GB577, GB). Oxford U Pr.

--Protestant Quest for a Christian America, 1830-1930. Wolf, Richard C., ed. LC 67-22986. (Facet Bks.). 1967. pap. 0.50 o.p. (ISBN 0-8006-3041-6, 1-3041). Fortress.

Handy, William J. & Westbrook, Max. Twentieth Century Criticism: The Major Statements. LC 73-3898. (Illus.). 1974. text ed. 14.95 (ISBN 0-02-913710-1). Free Pr.

Handy, Willowdean C. Thunder from the Sea. 356p. 1973. 12.00 (ISBN 0-8248-0284-5). UH Pr.

Hane, Mikiso, tr. from Japanese. Emperor Hirohito & His Chief Aide de Camp: The Honjo Diary, 1933-36. 250p. 1982. text ed. 22.50 (ISBN 0-686-82128-9, Pub. by U of Tokyo Japan). Columbia U Pr.

Hanes, D. A. & Madore, B. F., eds. Globular Clusters. LC 79-41472. (Cambridge Astrophysics Ser.: No. 2). (Illus.). 288p. 1980. 64.50 (ISBN 0-521-22861-1). Cambridge U Pr.

Hanes, Mari. The Child Within. 1983. pap. 2.50 (ISBN 0-8423-0219-0). Tyndale.

--Wild Child. 1982. pap. 2.95 (ISBN 0-686-82561-6). Tyndale.

Hanes, Mari & Rearick, Ron. Iceman: The Story of Ron Rearick. LC 82-90708. 85p. (Orig.). 1982. pap. write for info. (ISBN 0-9609206-0-9). Rearick.

Hanes, Steven, jt. auth. see Drisdale, Tommy.

Hanes, Ted, jt. auth. see MacQueen, Jean.

Haney, Alan W. Plants & Life. (Illus.). 1978. text ed. 24.95x (ISBN 0-02-349950-8). Macmillan.

Haney, C. Michele & Boenisch, Edmond W., Jr. Stressmap. LC 82-15391. (Orig.). 1982. pap. 5.95 (ISBN 0-915166-19-4). Impact Pubs Cal.

Haney, David. El Ministerio de Todo Creyente. Martinez, Jose Luis, ed. Kratzig, Guillermo, tr. Orig. Title: The Idea of Laity. 200p. Date not set. pap. price not set (ISBN 0-311-09099-0). Casa Bautista.

--Renueva Mi Iglesia. Martinez, Jose Luis, ed. Kratzig, Guillermo, tr. Orig. Title: Renew My Church. 104p. (Span.). Date not set. pap. price not set (ISBN 0-311-17025-0). Casa Bautista.

--El Senor y Sus Laicos. Martinez, Jose Luis, ed. Orig. Title: The Lord & His Laity. 84p. (Span.). Date not set. pap. price not set (ISBN 0-311-09095-8). Casa Bautista.

Haney, Lynn. Chris Evert: The Young Champion. LC 76-26716. (Women in Sports Ser.). (Illus.). (gr. 4-8). 1977. 7.95 o.p. (ISBN 0-399-20548-9). Putnam Pub Group.

--I Am a Dancer. (Illus.). 64p. (gr. 10 up). 1981. 8.95 (ISBN 0-399-20724-4); pap. 4.95 (ISBN 0-399-20792-9). Putnam Pub Group.

--Perfect Balance: The Story of an Elite Gymnast. LC 78-11634. (Illus.). (gr. 5-12). 1979. 9.95 (ISBN 0-399-20661-2). Putnam Pub Group.

--Ride 'em Cowgirl! LC 75-21085. (Women in Sports Ser.). (Illus.). (gr. 6-8). 1975. 6.95 o.p. (ISBN 0-399-20484-9). Putnam Pub Group.

--Show Rider. (Illus.). 96p. 1982. 11.95 (ISBN 0-399-20908-5); pap. 5.95 (ISBN 0-399-20909-3). Putnam Pub Group.

Haney, Lynn, adapted by. The Flash Gordon Book. (Illus.). 64p. 1980. 5.95 (ISBN 0-399-20782-1). Putnam Pub Group.

Haney, Margaret, jt. auth. see Alpaugh, Patricia.

Haney, Robert W. Comstockery in America: Patterns of Censorship & Control. LC 74-1241. (Civil Liberties Ser.). 199p. 1974. Repr. of 1960 ed. lib. bdg. 29.50 (ISBN 0-306-70654-7). Da Capo.

Hanf, C. H. & Schiefer, G. W. Planning & Decision in Agribusiness-Principles & Experiences: A Case Study Approach to the Use of Models in Decision Making. (Developments in Agricultural Economics Ser.: No. 1). 374p. 1982. 83.00 (ISBN 0-444-42134-3). Elsevier.

Hanff, Helene. Movers & Shakers: Young Activists of the Sixties. LC 77-110432. (Illus.). 1970. 12.95 (ISBN 0-87599-166-1). S G Phillips.

Hanfmann, Eugenia, tr. see Vygotsky, Lev S.

Hanfmann, George M. From Croesus to Constantine: The Cities of Western Asia Minor & Their Arts in Greek & Roman Times. LC 73-80574. (Jerome Lecture Ser: No. 10). (Illus.). 1974. text ed. 20.00x (ISBN 0-472-08420-8). U of Mich Pr.

--Roman Art: A Modern Survey of the Art of Ancient Rome. (Illus.). 250p. 1975. pap. text ed. 9.95x (ISBN 0-393-09222-4). Norton.

Hanfmann, George M. & Mierse, William E. Sardis from Prehistoric to Roman Times: Results of the Archaeological Exploration of Sardis, 1958-1975. (Illus.). 528p. 1983. text ed. 35.00x (ISBN 0-674-78925-3). Harvard U Pr.

Hanford, James H. & McQueen, William A. Milton. 2nd ed. LC 76-4625. (Goldentree Bibliographies in Language & Literature). 1979. text ed. 22.50x (ISBN 0-88295-571-3); pap. text ed. 13.95x (ISBN 0-88295-561-6). Harlan Davidson.

Hanford, Lloyd D., Sr. Analysis & Management of Investment Property. 3rd ed. 178p. 1970. pap. text ed. 13.95 (ISBN 0-912104-06-6). Inst Real Estate.

Hanford, Robert T. Complete Book of Puppets & Puppeteering. LC 74-22590. (Illus.). 160p. 1981. 13.95 (ISBN 0-8069-7032-4); lib. bdg. 11.69 o.p. (ISBN 0-8069-7033-2); pap. 8.95 (ISBN 0-8069-8970-X). Sterling.

Hanft, Ethel W. Outstanding Iowa Women: Past & Present, Vol. 2. 1983. price not set. River Bend.

Hanft, Ethel W. & Manley, Paula J. Outstanding Iowa Women: Past & Present. LC 80-53730. (Illus.). 135p. 1980. pap. 6.50 (ISBN 0-9605162-0-4). River Bend.

Hanham, Alison. Richard Third & His Early Historians 1483-1535. 1975. 39.00x (ISBN 0-19-822434-6). Oxford U Pr.

Hanham, H. J., ed. Bibliography of British History Eighteen Fifty-One to Nineteen Fourteen. 1976. 145.00x (ISBN 0-19-822389-7). Oxford U Pr.

--Nineteenth Century Constitution, Eighteen Fifteen to Nineteen Fourteen. LC 69-11148. 1969. 49.50 (ISBN 0-521-07351-0); pap. 19.95 (ISBN 0-521-09560-3, 560). Cambridge U Pr.

Hanham, Robert Q., jt. auth. see Smith, Christopher J.

Hanif, M., jt. auth. see Brewer, K. R.

Hanifhen, Frank C. & Engelbrecht, Helmuth C. Merchants of Death: A Study of the International Armaments Industry. LC 79-147546. (Library of War & Peace; Control & Limitation of Arms). lib. bdg. 38.00 o.s.i. (ISBN 0-8240-0327-6). Garland Pub.

Hanifi, M. Jamil. Annotated Bibliography of Afghanistan. 4th ed. LC 82-82467. (Bibliography Ser.). 561p. 1982. pap. text ed. 45.00 (ISBN 0-87536-230-3). HRAFP.

Hanig, Martin. Catheter Center. 141p. (Orig.). 1973. pap. 2.95 o.p. (ISBN 0-910286-32-9). Boxwood.

Hanin, Israel, ed. Choline & Acetylcholine: Handbook of Chemical Assay Methods. LC 73-79289. 246p. 1974. 27.00 (ISBN 0-911216-51-0). Raven.

Hanin, Israel & Goldberg, Alan M., eds. Progress in Cholinergic Biology: Model Cholinergic Synapses. 420p. 1982. text ed. 46.00 (ISBN 0-89004-758-8). Raven.

Hanin, Israel & Koslow, Stephen, eds. Physico-Chemical Methodologies in Psychiatric Research. 277p. 1980. text ed. 45.00 (ISBN 0-89004-411-2). Raven.

Hanin, Israel, jt. ed. see Goldberg, Alan M.

Hankamer, Jorge, ed. see Aissen, Judith.

Hankamer, Jorge, ed. see Akmajian, Adrian.

Hankamer, Jorge, ed. see Fodor, Janet D.

Hankamer, Jorge, ed. see Higgins, F. R.

Hankamer, Jorge, ed. see Partee, Barbara H.

Hanke, Jean J., jt. auth. see Harlow, Dorothy N.

Hankel, Wilhelm. Prosperity Amidst Crisis: Austria's Economic Policy & the Energy Crunch. Steinberg, Jean, tr. 234p. 1981. lib. bdg. 23.50 (ISBN 0-86531-101-3). Westview.

Hankey, John, ed. see John, Timothy.

Hankin, C. A. Katherine Mansfield & Her Confessional Stories. LC 81-21340. 320p. 1982. 22.50x (ISBN 0-312-45095-8). St Martin.

Hankins, Frank W., jt. auth. see Barefoot, A. C.

Hankins, Norman E. Psychology for Contemporary Education. LC 72-91246. 1973. text ed. 16.95 (ISBN 0-675-09019-9); study guide O.S.I. 3.95x (ISBN 0-686-86341-0); suppl. material O.S.I. avail. Merrill.

Hankinson, Ken. Fiberglass Boat Building for Amateurs. LC 82-80253. (Illus.). 1982. text ed. 19.95 (ISBN 0-686-37096-1). Glen-L Marine.

Hankla, Cathryn. Pheonmena: Poems. LC 82-11013. (Breakthrough Bks.: No. 40). 80p. (Orig.). 1983. pap. 5.95 (ISBN 0-8262-0386-8). U of Mo Pr.

Hanks, Geoffrey. Children of Naples. 1974. 1.55 (ISBN 0-08-017619-4). Pergamon.

--Helen: The Story of Helen Keller. 1977. pap. 1.55 (ISBN 0-08-021235-2). Pergamon.

Hanks, John, jt. ed. see Mahaffey, Maryann.

Hanks, John W., ed. see Fifth Symposium, Nov. 19-22, 1977.

Hanks, Joyce M. Ronsard & Biblical Tradition. (Etudes litteraires francaises: 17). 176p. (Orig.). 1982. pap. 17.50 (ISBN 3-87808-896-5). Benjamins North Am.

Hanks, Kurt, jt. auth. see Belliston, Larry.

Hanks, Lucien M. Rice & Man: Agricultural Ecology in Southeast Asia. LC 78-169512. (Worlds of Man Ser). 1972. text ed. 12.95x (ISBN 0-88295-606-X); pap. text ed. 6.95x (ISBN 0-88295-607-8). Harlan Davidson.

Hanks, Robert, jt. auth. see Dobbs, David.

Hanks, Robert J. The Cape Route: Imperiled Western Lifeline. LC 81-80472. (Special Report Ser.). 80p. 1981. 6.50 (ISBN 0-89549-028-5). Inst Foreign Policy Anal.

--The U. S. Military Presence in the Middle East: Problems & Prospects. LC 82-84308. (Foreign Policy Reports Ser.). 88p. 1982. 7.50 (ISBN 0-89549-047-1). Inst Foreign Policy Anal.

Hanks, Robert J., jt. auth. see Record, Jeffrey.

Hanlan, James P. The Working Population of Manchester, New Hampshire, 1840-1886. Berkhofer, Robert, ed. LC 81-3355. (Studies in American History & Culture: No. 29). 260p. 1981. 39.95 (ISBN 0-8357-1193-5, Pub. by UMI Res Pr). Univ Microfilms.

Hanle, Zack, as told to see Blanchard, Leslie.

Hanley, Boniface. No Greater Love: Maximilian Kolbe. LC 82-72656. (Illus.). 80p. (Orig.). (gr. 9-12). 1982. pap. 3.95 (ISBN 0-87793-257-3). Ave Maria.

Hanley, Christina. Pig Out. 1983. pap. 5.95 (ISBN 0-8065-0843-4). Citadel Pr.

Hanley, D. E. Guidance & the Needs of the Special Child. (Guidance Monograph). 1975. pap. 2.40 o.p. (ISBN 0-395-20059-8). HM.

Hanley, Elizabeth. The Flame & the Fire. 272p. 1982. pap. write for info o.p. (ISBN 0-505-51858-9). Tower Bks.

Hanley, Evelyn A. The Subjective Vision: Six Victorian Women Poets. 1978. 8.00 o.p. (ISBN 0-913994-32-4, Pub. by Astra Bks.); pap. 4.50 o.p. (ISBN 0-913994-33-2, Pub. by Astra Bks.). Hippocrene Bks.

Hanley, Gerald. Noble Descents. 352p. 1983. 12.95 (ISBN 0-312-57618-8). St Martin.

Hanley, Julian R., et al. Legal Aspects of Criminal Evidence. 2nd ed. LC 76-28825. 1977. 24.50 (ISBN 0-8211-0758-5); text ed. 19.50x 10 or more copies (ISBN 0-685-78479-7). McCutchan.

Hanley, Keith, ed. see Landor, Walter S.

Hanley, Reid, jt. auth. see Jarman, Tom.

Hanley, Sarah. The Lit De Justice of the Kings of Francs: Constitutional Ideology in Legend, Ritual, & Discourse. LC 82-61374. (Illus.). 440p. 1983. 45.00x (ISBN 0-691-05382-0). Princeton U Pr.

Hanley, W. S. & Cooper, M. J. Man & the Australian Environment. 362p. 1981. 22.00x (ISBN 0-07-072952-2). McGraw.

Hanlin, R. T. Index to Genera & Authors in Grevillea. (Bibliotheca Mycologica Ser.: No. 64). 1978. pap. text ed. 16.00x (ISBN 3-7682-1205-X). Lubrecht & Cramer.

Hanlon, Emily. Circle Home. LC 81-6171. 224p. (gr. 6-9). 1981. 9.95 (ISBN 0-02-742640-8). Bradbury Pr.

--It's Too Late for Sorry. LC 78-4422. 224p. (gr. 6-8). 1978. 9.95 (ISBN 0-02-742590-8). Bradbury Pr.

--Love Is No Excuse. LC 82-9580. 256p. (gr. 7 up). 1982. 10.95 (ISBN 0-02-742520-7). Bradbury Pr.

--The Swing. LC 78-26400. 224p. (gr. 5-7). 1979. 9.95 (ISBN 0-02-742580-0). Bradbury Pr.

--What If a Lion Eats Me & I Fall into a Hippopotamus' Mud Hole. LC 75-8007. 32p. (ps-3). 1975. 5.95 o.s.i. (ISBN 0-440-05950-X); PLB 5.47 o.s.i. (ISBN 0-440-05951-8). Delacorte.

--The Wing & the Flame. LC 80-15082. 160p. (YA) (gr. 7 up). 1980. 9.95 (ISBN 0-02-742540-1). Bradbury Pr.

Hanlon, J. R. Handbook of Package Engineering. 1971. 43.50 (ISBN 0-07-025993-3, P&RB). McGraw.

Hanlon, John J. & Pickett, George E. Public Health: Administration & Practice. 7th ed. LC 79-16132. (Illus.). 788p. 1979. text ed. 35.50 (ISBN 0-8016-2046-5). Mosby.

Hanlon, Joseph, ed. Packaging Marketplace: The Practical Guide to Packaging Sources. LC 78-53442. 1978. 85.00x (ISBN 0-8103-0989-0, Norback Bk). Gale.

Hanlon, Joseph F. Handbook of Package Engineering. 2nd ed. 576p. 1983. 63.00 (ISBN 0-07-025994-1, P&RB). McGraw.

Hanlon, LaVonne R. The Marriage of Catherine & David. (Illus.). 68p. (Orig.). 1982. pap. text ed. 7.00 (ISBN 0-9609326-0-7). Fay-West Her.

Hanlon, R. Brendan. A Guide to Taxes & Record Keeping for Performers, Designers & Directors. rev. ed. LC 79-25783. (Illus.). 96p. 1980. pap. text ed. 4.95x o.p. (ISBN 0-89676-032-4). Drama Bk.

Hanly, David. In Guilt & in Glory. LC 78-12474. 1979. 10.95 o.p. (ISBN 0-688-03421-7). Morrow.

Hann, C. M. Tazlar, A Village in Hungary. LC 79-14810. (Changing Cultures Ser.). (Illus.). 280p. 1980. 37.50 (ISBN 0-521-22591-4); pap. 10.95 (ISBN 0-521-29571-8). Cambridge U Pr.

Hann, Ian M., ed. Colour Atlas of Pediatric Haematology. (Illus.). 1982. text ed. 59.50x (ISBN 0-19-261227-1). Oxford U Pr.

Hann, Robert R. The Bible. 160p. 1983. pap. 5.95 (ISBN 0-8091-2503-X). Paulist Pr.

Hanna, Alfred & Hanna, Kathryn. Lake Okeechobee. new ed. LC 48-5872. (Lakes of America Ser). (Illus.). 400p. 1973. 14.95 (ISBN 0-910220-44-1). Berg.

Hanna, Alfred J. & Hanna, Kathryn A. Napoleon III & Mexico: American Triumph Over Monarchy. LC 72-156761. (Illus.). xxii, 350p. 1971. 24.00x (ISBN 0-8078-1171-8). U of NC Pr.

Hanna, Archibald, ed. see Streater, Thomas.

Hanna, Barbara & Hoover, Janet. Teaching Preschoolers. 3.95 (ISBN 0-89137-608-9). Quality Pubns.

Hanna, David. Opera House Murders. 256p. (Orig.). Date not set. pap. cancelled o.s.i. (ISBN 0-8439-1027-5, Leisure Bks). Nordon Pubns.

Hanna, Donald G., jt. auth. see Cizankas, Victor I.

Hanna, Evelyn. A Woman Against the World. 480p. (Orig.). 1983. pap. 3.50 (ISBN 0-345-28931-5). Ballantine.

Hanna, G. Dallas. Species-Index to Schmidt-Hustedt: Atlas Zur Diatomaceen Kunde. (Illus.). 1969. pap. 16.00 (ISBN 3-7682-0611-4). Lubrecht & Cramer.

Hanna, J., jt. auth. see Melish, J. S.

Hanna, J. Gordon, jt. auth. see Siggia, Sidney.

Hanna, J. Marshall, jt. auth. see Weaver, David H.

Hanna, J. Ray. Fourier Series & Integrals of Boundary Value Problems. LC 81-16063. (Pure & Applied Mathematics: A Wiley Interscience Series of Texts, Monographs, & Tracts). 271p. 1982. 31.95x (ISBN 0-471-08129-9, Pub. by Wiley-Interscience). Wiley.

Hanna, James. Ambulance & EMS Driving. 1981. text ed. 14.95 (ISBN 0-8359-0205-6). Reston.

Hanna, John P. Complete Layman's Guide to the Law. 1980. 18.95 (ISBN 0-13-161232-8, Spec). P-H.

--Complete Layman's Guide to the Law. (Illus.). 544p. pap. 8.95 o.p. (ISBN 0-13-161224-7, Spec). P-H.

Hanna, Kathryn, jt. auth. see Hanna, Alfred.

Hanna, Kathryn A., jt. auth. see Hanna, Alfred J.

Hanna, M. G., Jr., et al, eds. Inhalation Carcinogenesis: Proceedings. LC 76-605835. (AEC Symposium Ser.). 524p. 1970. pap. 21.00 (ISBN 0-87079-246-6, CONF-691001); microfiche 4.50 (ISBN 0-87079-247-4, CONF-691001). DOE.

Hanna, Melvin W. Quantum Mechanics in Chemistry. 3rd ed. 1981. text ed. 20.95 (ISBN 0-8053-3708-3); pap. text ed. 12.95 (ISBN 0-8053-3705-9, 33705); student solutions manual 5.95 (ISBN 0-8053-3707-5). Benjamin-Cummings.

Hanna, Paul R. & Hodges, Richard E. Spelling: Structure & Strategies. LC 82-40222. (Illus.). 304p. 1982. pap. text ed. 11.25 (ISBN 0-8191-2460-5). U Pr of Amer.

Hanna, Sherman D., jt. auth. see Lindamood, Suzanne.

Hanna, Steven R. & Pell, Jerry. Cooling Tower Environment 1974: Proceedings. LC 75-600010. (ERDA Symposium Ser.). 648p. 1975. pap. 24.25 (CONF-740302); microfiche 4.00 (ISBN 0-87079-171-0, CONF-740302). DOE.

Hanna, Steven R., et al, eds. Handbook on Atmospheric Diffusion. Hosker, Rayford P., Jr. LC 81-15149. (DOE Technical Information Center Ser.). 110p. 1981. pap. 10.75 (ISBN 0-87079-127-3, DOE/TIC-11223); microfiche 4.50 (ISBN 0-87079-464-7, DOE/TIC-11223). DOE.

Hanna, Thomas H. Foundations in Tension: Ground Anchors. (Illus.). 700p. 1983. 54.95 (ISBN 0-07-026017-6). McGraw.

Hanna, William J., ed. University Students & African Politics. LC 73-89778. 400p. 1975. text ed. 35.00x (ISBN 0-8419-0145-7, Africana). Holmes & Meier.

Hannaford, Peter. The Reagans: A Personal Portrait. (Illus.). 1983. 14.95 (ISBN 0-698-11083-8, Coward). Putnam Pub Group.

Hannaford, William, jt. auth. see Blocker, Gene.

Hannah, Barry. Airships. 1979. pap. 4.95 o.s.i. (ISBN 0-440-50155-5, Delta). Dell.

--Geronimo Rex. (Contemporary American Fiction Ser.). 1983. pap. 5.95 (ISBN 0-14-006472-9). Penguin.

--The Tennis Handsome. LC 82-48752. 175p. 1982. 11.95 (ISBN 0-394-52876-X). Knopf.

Hannah, Clayton L. A Collection: My Innermost Thoughts. 1982. 5.95 (ISBN 0-533-04703-X). Vantage.

Hannah, Donald, jt. ed. see Rutherford, Anna.

Hannah, Jean, jt. auth. see Trudgill, Peter.

Hannah, Perrin K. A Compendium of Burlington Lines Employee Timetables. (Railway History Monograph). 1982. lib. bdg. write for info. (ISBN 0-916170-20-9). J-B Pubs.

Hannam, Charles L., tr. see Wolffheim, Nelly.

Hannan, Michael T. Problems of Aggregation & Disaggregation in Sociological Research. (Working Papers in Methodology: No. 4). 207p. 1970. pap. text ed. 4.00 o.p. (ISBN 0-89143-028-8). U NC Inst Res Soc Sci.

Hannan, William. Peanut Power, a World of Tiny Flying Models. (Building & Flying Model Airplanes Ser.). (Illus.). 80p. 1980. pap. 8.95 (ISBN 0-686-82919-0). Hist Aviation.

Hannant, D. J. Fibre Cements & Fibre Concretes. 219p. 1978. 53.95 (ISBN 0-471-99620-3, Pub. by Wiley-Interscience). Wiley.

Hannawell, Peggy & Sorenson, Marge. Wordstar Training Manual. (Illus.). 100p. 1982. pap. 9.00 (ISBN 0-942728-09-2). Custom Pub Co.

Hannay, Allen. Love & Other Natural Disasters. 224p. (gr. 9). 1982. 12.95 (ISBN 0-316-34362-5, Pub. by Atlantic Monthly Pr). Little.

Hannay, Alstair. Kierkegaard. (Arguments of the Philosophers Ser.). 262p. 1982. 29.95 (ISBN 0-7100-9190-7). Routledge & Kegan.

Hannay, Margaret P. C. S. Lewis. LC 80-53700. (Literature and Life Ser.). 350p. 1981. 14.50 (ISBN 0-8044-2341-5); pap. 6.95 (ISBN 0-8044-6242-9). Ungar.

Hanne, John A. Prayer or Pretense? 96p. (Orig.). 1974. pap. 1.50 o.p. (ISBN 0-310-25882-0). Zondervan.

Hanneman, Gerhard J. see Voigt, Melvin J.

Hanneman, L. J. Modern Cake Decoration. 2nd ed. (Illus.). 1978. 33.00 (ISBN 0-85334-785-9, Pub. by Applied Sci England). Elsevier.

--Patisserie. (Illus.). 360p. 1971. 22.50x (ISBN 0-434-90707-3). Intl Pubns Serv.

Hanneman, L. J. & Marshall, G. I. Cake Design & Decoration. 4th ed. (Illus.). 1979. text ed. 30.00x (ISBN 0-85334-793-X, Pub. by Applied Sci England). Burgess-Intl Ideas.

Hannemann. Healing Art of Homeopathy. Hamlyn, E., ed. 1979. 4.95x (ISBN 0-87983-228-2). Cancer Control Soc.

Hannenbaum, L. Landscape Design: A Practical Approach. 1981. text ed. 20.95 (ISBN 0-8359-3934-0); instr's. manual free (ISBN 0-8359-3936-7). Reston.

Hannerz, Ulf. Exploring the City: Inquiries Toward an Urban Anthropology. 378p. 1983. pap. 12.00 (ISBN 0-231-08376-9). Columbia U Pr.

Hannesdottir, Sigrun K., ed. Education of School Librarian for Central America & Panama. (IFLA Publications: No. 22). 120p. 1983. 20.00 (ISBN 3-598-20384-5, Pub. by K G Saur). Shoe String.

Hannibal, A. J., jt. ed. see Berman, A.

Hannibal, Edward. Chocolate Days, Popsicle Weeks. 1971. pap. 1.75 o.p. (ISBN 0-451-07051-8, E7051, Sig). NAL.

--Liberty Square Station. LC 77-21868. 1977. 9.95 o.p. (ISBN 0-399-12058-0). Putnam Pub Group.

Hannigan, Jane A. & Estes, Glenn E., eds. Media Center Facilities Design. LC 78-9336. 1978. pap. 13.00 (ISBN 0-8389-3212-6). ALA.

Hannigan, Jane Anne, ed. see Antczak, Janice.

Hanning, Robert W. & Rosand, David. Castiglione: The Ideal & the Real in Renaissance Culture. LC 82-6944. (Illus.). 240p. 1983. text ed. 22.50x (ISBN 0-300-02649-8). Yale U Pr.

Hannon, Leslie F. The Second Chance: The Life & Work of the Pioneer of Rejuvenation-Dr. Paul Niehans. 1973. 8.95 o.p. (ISBN 0-491-00469-9). Transatlantic.

Hannon, Ralph H. Mathematics for Technical Careers. new ed. (Mathematics Ser.). 304p. 1976. text ed. 19.95 (ISBN 0-675-08656-6). Additional supplements may be obtained from publisher. Merrill.

Hannon, Ruth. Children's Bible Stories from the Old Testament. (Illus.). 1978. 4.95 (ISBN 0-307-13740-6, 13740, Golden Pr); PLB 9.15 (ISBN 0-307-63740-9). Western Pub.

Hannsgen, Kenneth B. & Herdman, Terry L., eds. Volterra & Functional Differential Equations. (Lecture Notes in Pure & Applied Mathematics: Vol. 81). (Illus.). 352p. 1982. 45.00 (ISBN 0-8247-1721-X). Dekker.

Hannula, Reino. Computers & Programming: A System Three Sixty-Three Seventy Assembler Language Approach. LC 73-9192. 1983. pap. 21.00 (ISBN 0-9605044-1-9). Quality Hill.

Hannum, H. G., jt. auth. see Lohner, Edgar.

Hannum, Hildegarde, tr. see Miller, Alice.

Hannum, Hunter, tr. see Miller, Alice.

Hano, Arnold. Kareem! Basketball Great. (Putnam Sports Shelf). 160p. (gr. 5 up). 1974. PLB 6.29 o.p. (ISBN 0-399-60917-2). Putnam Pub Group.

--Muhammad Ali: The Champion. LC 76-50101. (Putnam Sports Shelf). (Illus.). (gr. 6-8). 1977. PLB 6.99 o.p. (ISBN 0-399-61091-X). Putnam Pub Group.

--Roberto Clemente: Batting King. rev. ed. (Putnam Sports Shelf). 192p. (gr. 5 up). 1973. PLB 5.29 o.p. (ISBN 0-399-60865-6). Putnam Pub Group.

--Sandy Koufax: Strikeout King. (Putnam Sports Shelf). (Illus.). (gr. 5-8). 1964. PLB 5.29 o.p. (ISBN 0-399-60555-X). Putnam Pub Group.

Hanoteau, Jean, ed. see Caulaincourt, Armand.

Hanover, Nathan. The Abyss of Despair. Mesch, Abraham J., tr. from Hebrew. 210p. 1983. Repr. pap. 14.95 (ISBN 0-87855-927-2). Transaction Bks.

Hanrahan, Barbara. Dove: A Novel. LC 81-10952. 203p. 1982. 14.95 (ISBN 0-7022-1880-4); pap. 7.95 (ISBN 0-7022-1890-1). U of Queensland Pr.

Hanrahan, Jack, ed. see Bent, Allen H.

Hanrahan, John. Government by Contract. 1983. 17.00 (ISBN 0-393-01717-6). Norton.

Hanrahan, Kathleen, jt. auth. see Von Hirsch, Andrew.

Hanrath, P. Cardiovascular Diagnosis by Ultrasound. 1982. 39.50 (ISBN 90-247-2692-1, Pub. by Martinus Nijhoff Netherlands). Kluwer Boston.

--Evaluation of Left Ventricular Function by Ultrasound. 1982. 39.50 (ISBN 0-686-38401-6, Pub. by Martinus Nijhoff Netherlands). Kluwer Boston.

Hanreider, Wolfram F. Economic Issues & the Atlantic Community. 192p. 1982. 22.95 (ISBN 0-03-060584-9). Praeger.

Hanrieder, Wolfram & Auton, Graeme P. Foreign Policies of West Germany, France, & Britian. 1980. pap. text ed. 14.95 (ISBN 0-13-326397-5). P-H.

Hanrieder, Wolfram F., ed. Arms Control & Security: Current Issues. 1979. lib. bdg. 32.00 o.p. (ISBN 0-89158-382-3); pap. text ed. 16.50 (ISBN 0-89158-385-8). Westview.

--West Germany's Foreign Policy: Nineteen Forty-Nine to Nineteen Seventy-Nine. (Special Study in West European Politics & Society). 1979. lib. bdg. 27.50 (ISBN 0-89158-579-6). Westview.

Hanrieder, Wolfram F. & Buel, Larry V., eds. Words & Arms: A Dictionary of Security & Defense Terms with Supplementary Data. 1979. lib. bdg. 32.50 (ISBN 0-89158-383-1). Westview.

Hanriot, Hugo. Johnny Ortiz, Presidente de USA. SLUSA, ed. 100p. (Orig., Sp.). 1982. lib. bdg. 12.00 (ISBN 0-9606758-3-3); pap. 6.00 (ISBN 0-686-37649-8). SLUSA.

Hans-Albrecht, Koch, ed. International Bibliography of German Studies, 1980, Vol. 1. 854p. 1981. 120.00x (ISBN 3-598-10405-7, Pub. by K G Saur). Gale.

--International Bibliography of German Studies, 1981, Vol. 2. 800p. 1983. 120.00x (ISBN 0-686-82085-1, Pub. by K G Saur). Gale.

Hansard-Winkler, Glenda A., jt. auth. see Feingold, S. Norman.

Hansberry, Lorraine. The Movement. pap. 2.95 o.p. (ISBN 0-671-49411-2, Touchstone Bks). S&S.

--Raisin in the Sun. Bd. with The Sign in Sidney Brustein's Window. pap. 3.50 (ISBN 0-451-11303-9, AE1303, Sig). NAL.

--Raisin in the Sun. (gr. 4 up). 1969. 11.50 (ISBN 0-394-40688-5). Random.

Hansch, August C. Controlling Tomorrow. LC 79-49831. 1979. 14.95 (ISBN 0-87863-202-6). Farnswth Pub.

Hanscombe, Gillian E. The Art of Life: Dorothy Richardson & the Development of Feminist Consciousness. 200p. 1983. text ed. 20.95x (ISBN 0-8214-0739-2, 82-85082); pap. 10.95 (ISBN 0-8214-0740-6, 82-85090). Ohio U Pr.

Hansen. Geometric Theory of Diffraction. 376p. 1981. 40.95x (ISBN 0-471-09842-6, Pub. by Wiley-Interscience); pap. 26.95x (ISBN 0-471-09841-8, Pub. by Wiley-Interscience). Wiley.

Hansen, Alvin. Monetary Theory & Fiscal Policy. LC 82-20924. ix, 236p. 1983. Repr. of 1949 ed. lib. bdg. 29.75x (ISBN 0-313-23736-0, HAMT). Greenwood.

Hansen, Alvin H. The American Economy. LC 77-10028. (Economics Handbook Ser.). 1977. Repr. of 1957 ed. lib. bdg. 17.50x (ISBN 0-8371-9717-1, HAAEC). Greenwood.

Hansen, B. E. & Skaff, L. B. Progressive Typewriting Speed Practice. 4th ed. 1976. text ed. 8.44 (ISBN 0-07-026061-3, G). McGraw.

Hansen, Bent. Study in the Theory of Inflation. LC 68-4112. Repr. of 1951 ed. 19.50x (ISBN 0-678-06019-3). Kelley.

Hansen, Bertrand. Quality Control: Theory & Applications. (Illus.). 1963. 29.95 (ISBN 0-13-745208-X). P-H.

Hansen, Carl L., jt. auth. see Butzer, Karl W.

Hansen, Chad. Language & Logic in Ancient China. (Michigan Studies on China Ser.). 224p. 1982. text ed. 25.00x (ISBN 0-472-10020-3). U of Mich Pr.

Hansen, E. C. Rural Catalonia under the Franco Regime. LC 76-9177. 1977. 24.95 (ISBN 0-521-21457-2). Cambridge U Pr.

Hansen, Edward C., jt. auth. see Wolf, Eric R.

Hansen, Eldon R. Table of Series & Products. 544p. 1975. ref. ed. 82.00 (ISBN 0-13-881938-6). P-H.

Hansen, Elo H., jt. auth. see Ruzicka, Jaromir.

Hansen, Eric C. Disaffection & Decadence: A Crisis in French Intellectual Thought 1848-1898. LC 82-17326. 304p. (Orig.). 1983. lib. bdg. 22.50 (ISBN 0-8191-2821-X); pap. text ed. 12.25 (ISBN 0-8191-2822-8). U Pr of Amer.

Hansen, F. Adjustment of Precision Mechanisms. 9.00 o.p. (ISBN 0-592-04223-5). Transatlantic.

Hansen, Gary E., ed. Agricultural & Rural Development in Indonesia. (Special Studies in Social, Political, & Economic Development). 312p. 1981. softcover 21.50 (ISBN 0-86531-124-2). Westview.

Hansen, Gerald. Arizona: Its Constitution & Government. LC 78-65846. (Illus.). 1979. text ed. 8.25 (ISBN 0-8191-0673-9). U Pr of Amer.

Hansen, H. Morris. The Wealth Transfer of Inflation: How to Compute It, Account for It, & Profit from It. LC 81-6250. 250p. 1981. 49.50 o.p. (ISBN 0-87624-014-7). Inst Busn Plan.

Hansen, Harold A. The Witch's Garden. LC 78-5469. 128p. 1983. pap. write for info. (ISBN 0-87728-551-9). Weiser.

Hansen, Harry. Longfellow's New England. (Illus.). 192p. 1972. 8.75 o.p. (ISBN 0-8038-4279-1). Hastings.

Hansen, Harry, ed. see Henry, O.

Hansen, James & L'Abate, Lucinano. Approaches to Family Therapy. 1982. text ed. 22.95x (ISBN 0-02-350010-7). Macmillan.

Hansen, James & Cramer, Stanley, eds. Group Guidance & Counseling in the Schools: Selected Readings. 1971. pap. text ed. 18.95 o.p. (ISBN 0-13-365304-8). P-H.

Hansen, James C. Counseling Process & Procedures. (Illus.). 1978. pap. 17.95x (ISBN 0-02-350030-1). Macmillan.

Hansen, James C. & Stevic, Richart R. Appalachian Students & Guidance. (Guidance Monograph). 1971. pap. 2.40 o.p. (ISBN 0-395-12437-9, 9-78861). HM.

Hansen, James C. & Warner, Richard W. Group Counseling. 2nd ed. 1980. 23.50 (ISBN 0-395-30809-7). HM.

Hansen, James C., jt. auth. see Peters, Herman J.

Hansen, James C., ed. Family Therapy Collection: Collection I, Values, Ethics, Legalities, & the Family Therapist (Luciano L'Abate, issue editor) LC 81-20577. 134p. 1982. 18.00 (ISBN 0-89443-600-7). Aspen Systems.

Hansen, James C. & Barnhill, Laurence, eds. Family Therapy Collections: Collection III: Clinical Approaches to Family Violence. LC 82-11444. 157p. 1982. 18.00 (ISBN 0-89443-804-2). Aspen Systems.

Hansen, James C. & Keeney, Bradford P., eds. Family Therapy Collections: Collection IV: Diagnosis & Assessment in Family Therapy. LC 82-6799. 184p. 1982. 18.00 (ISBN 0-89443-603-1). Aspen Systems.

Hansen, James C., jt. ed. see Messinger, Lillian.

Hansen, James C., et al, eds. Family Therapy Collections, Collection V: Sexual Issues in Family Therapy. 200p. 1983. price not set (ISBN 0-89443-605-8). Aspen Systems.

Hansen, John R. Guatemala: Economic & Social Position & Prospects. 181p. 1978. pap. 20.00 (ISBN 0-686-36107-5, RC-7801). World Bank.

Hansen, L. Sunny, jt. auth. see Tennyson, W. Wesley.

Hansen, Laurence. What It Was Like Flying for Ike. pap. 5.95 (ISBN 0-912522-73-9). Aero Medical.

Hansen, Mary L. Your Career As a Writer. (Arco Career Guidance Ser.). lib. bdg. 7.95 (ISBN 0-668-04500-0); pap. 4.50 (ISBN 0-668-04503-5). Arco.

Hansen, Max. Constitution of Binary Alloys. 2nd ed. (Metallurgy & Metallurgical Engineering Ser.). 1958. 75.00 o.p. (ISBN 0-07-026050-8, P&RB). McGraw.

Hansen, Niles M. Improving Access to Economic Opportunity: Non-metropolitan Labor Markets in an Urban Society. LC 75-38800. 208p. 1976. prof ref 18.50x (ISBN 0-88410-289-0). Ballinger Pub.

Hansen, Niles M., ed. Human Settlement Systems: International Perspectives on Structure, Change & Public Policy. LC 77-9964. 328p. 1977. prof ref 20.00x (ISBN 0-88410-176-2). Ballinger Pub.

Hansen, Paul E. Business Flying: The Profitable Use of Personal Aircraft. (Illus.). 288p. 1982. 22.50 (ISBN 0-07-026071-0). McGraw.

Hansen, Per B. Operating System Principles. (Illus.). 496p. 1973. ref. ed. 28.95 (ISBN 0-13-637843-9). P-H.

--Programming a Personal Computer. (Illus.). 400p. 1983. text ed. 18.95 (ISBN 0-13-730267-3). P-H.

Hansen, Philip L. Alcoholism: The Afflicted & the Affected. 2.95 o.p. (ISBN 0-686-92086-4). Hazelden.

--Sick & Tired of Being Sick & Tired. 2.95 o.p. (ISBN 0-686-92066-X). Hazelden.

Hansen, R. C., ed. Microwave Scanning Antennas, 3 vols. Incl. Vol. 1. Apertures. 1964. 64.00 o.p. (ISBN 0-12-323901-X); Vol. 2. Array Theory. 1966. o.p. (ISBN 0-12-323902-8); Vol. 3. Array Systems. 1966. o.p. (ISBN 0-12-323903-6). Acad Pr.

Hansen, R. G., jt. auth. see Beitz, Donald.

Hansen, Robin. Fox & Geese & Fences: A Collection of Maine Traditional Mittens. (Illus.). 64p. 1983. pap. 4.95t (ISBN 0-89272-162-6). Down East.

Hansen, Roger D. Beyond the North-South Stalemate. (Council on Foreign Relations, 1980's Project). (Illus.). 1979. 16.95 (ISBN 0-07-026048-6, P&RB). McGraw.

Hansen, Rosanna. The Fairytale Book of Ballet. (Illus.). 80p. (gr. 1-7). 7.95 (ISBN 0-448-11499-2, G&D). Putnam Pub Group.

--Wolves & Coyotes. LC 80-84447. (Illus.). 48p. (gr. 1-9). 1981. 6.95 (ISBN 0-448-47489-1, G&D). Putnam PubGroup.

Hansen, Rosanna, jt. auth. see Engel.

Hansen, T. L. & Wilkins, E. J. Espanol A lo Vivo. 5th ed. 528p. 1982. 20.95 (ISBN 0-471-06297-9). Wiley.

--Espanol a lo Vivo: Level Two. 2nd ed. 313p. 1972. 20.95 o.p. (ISBN 0-471-00725-0); wkbk. 10.95 (ISBN 0-471-00727-7). Wiley.

Hansen, Ted. Twentieth Century Harmonic & Melodic Aural Perception. LC 82-8385. (Illus.). 74p. (Orig.). 1982. pap. text ed. 8.25 (ISBN 0-8191-2517-2). U Pr of Amer.

Hansen, Terrence L. & Wilkins, Ernest J. Espanol a lo vivo: Level 1. 4th ed. LC 77-27041. 1978. text ed. 19.95x o.p. (ISBN 0-471-01807-4); Avail Tchr's Manual o.p. (ISBN 0-471-04151-3). Wiley.

Hansen, Terrence L., et al. Beginning German: A Practical Approach. LC 73-180137. (Ger). 1972. text ed. 25.50 (ISBN 0-471-00671-8); tchr's manual 6.50 (ISBN 0-471-00766-8); wkbk. 10.95 (ISBN 0-471-00672-6). Wiley.

--Le Francais Vivant. 2nd ed. Kaplow, Julian, ed. LC 77-27029. 1978. text ed. 22.50 (ISBN 0-471-01782-5); wkbk. 10.50 (ISBN 0-471-03539-4); tchrs.' manual 8.00 (ISBN 0-471-04150-5). Wiley.

Hansen, V. E. & Israelsen, O. W. Irrigation Principles & Practices. 4th ed. 417p. 1980. 38.95 (ISBN 0-471-03058-9). Wiley.

Hansen, Vee, et al. Macoy's Short Addresses & Ceremonies for Matron's Use. 24p. 1975. Repr. pap. 1.50 (ISBN 0-88053-330-7, S-84). Macoy Pub.

Hansen, Wilfred J., jt. auth. see Reingold, Edward.

Hansen, William F. Saxo Grammaticus & the Life of Hamlet: A Translation, History, & Commentary. LC 82-2671. xvi, 206p. 1982. 17.95x (ISBN 0-8032-2318-8). U of Nebr Pr.

Hanser, Richard. A Noble Treason: The Revolt of the Munich Students Against Hitler. LC 78-20832. (Illus.). 1979. 12.50 o.p. (ISBN 0-399-12041-6). Putnam Pub Group.

Hansford, Kier, et al. Index of Nigerian Languages. (Language Data-African Ser.: No. 13). (Illus.). 204p. (Orig.). 1978. pap. 3.75 (ISBN 0-88312-613-3); microfiche 3.00 (ISBN 0-88312-713-X). Summer Inst Ling.

Hansgirg, A. Prodromus der Algenflora von Boehmen. (From: Archiv F. Naturw. Landesdurchf.. (Boehmens)). (Ger.). 1979. Repr. of 1892 ed. lib. bdg. 80.00x (ISBN 3-7682-0922-9). Lubrecht & Cramer.

Hansjurgen Press & Littlewood, Barbara. The Adventures of the Black Hand Gang. (Illus.). 128p. (gr. 3-7). 1983. pap. 4.95 (ISBN 0-13-014035-X). P-H.

Hanslick, Eduard. The Beautiful in Music: A Contribution to the Revisal of Musical Aesthetics. rev. ed. Cohen, Gustav, tr. LC 74-1362. (Music Ser.). 174p. 1974. Repr. of 1891 ed. lib. bdg. 22.50 (ISBN 0-306-70649-0). Da Capo.

Hanslowe, Kurt L. Procedures & Policies of the New York State Labor Relations Board. LC 63-63909. (Cornell Studies Ser.: No. 12). 224p. 1964. 4.00 o.s.i. (ISBN 0-87546-005-4). ILR Pr.

Hanslowe, Kurt L., et al. Union Security in Public Employment: Of Free Riding & Free Association. LC 78-620002. (Institute of Public Employment Monograph: No.8). 54p. 1978. pap. 3.25 (ISBN 0-87546-065-8). ILR Pr.

Hanslowe, Kurt L., jt. auth. see Oberer, Walter E.

Hansma, Paul K., ed. Tunneling Spectroscopy: Capabilities, Applications & New Techniques. 485p. 1982. 65.00x (ISBN 0-306-41070-2, Plenum Pr). Plenum Pub.

Hansman, Henning, et al. Curative Education: The Course at the Camphill Rudolf Steiner Schools, Aberdeen. 38p. 1982. pap. 2.40 (ISBN 0-08-028440-X). Pergamon.

Hansman, Robert J. & Larrabee, John W. Deferred Compensation: The New Methodology for Executive Reward. LC 82-48596. 1983. write for info. (ISBN 0-669-06329-0). Lexington Bks.

Hansmann, Klaus, jt. auth. see Bachman, Manfred.

Hanson, Agnes O., ed. Executive & Management Development for Business & Government: A Guide to Information Sources. LC 76-8337. (Management Information Guide Ser.: No. 31). 490p. 1976. 42.00x (ISBN 0-8103-0831-2). Gale.

Hanson, Anne C. Manet & the Modern Tradition. LC 75-43319. 1977. 40.00x (ISBN 0-300-01954-8); pap. 15.95x (ISBN 0-300-02492-4). Yale U Pr.

Hanson, Anthony. Burgundy. (Wine Bks.). 354p. (Orig.). 1982. 24.95 (ISBN 0-571-11797-X); pap. 10.95 (ISBN 0-571-11798-8). Faber & Faber.

Hanson, C. Recent Advances in Liquid - Liquid Extraction. 1971. inquire for price o.p. (ISBN 0-08-015682-7). Pergamon.

Hanson, Calvin, jt. auth. see Perry, Lloyd.

Hanson, D. & Herrington, M. From College to Classroom: The Probationary Year. (Student's Library of Education Ser). 1976. 14.95x (ISBN 0-7100-8335-1); pap. 6.95 (ISBN 0-7100-8336-X). Routledge & Kegan.

Hanson, Dian. How to Pick Up a Man. 192p. 1982. 9.95 (ISBN 0-399-12719-4). Putnam Pub Group.

Hanson, Dirk. The New Alchemists: Silicon Valley & the Microelectronics Revolution. 1982. 15.95 (ISBN 0-316-34342-0). Little.

Hanson, Earl D. Animal Diversity. 3rd ed. (Foundations of Modern Biology Ser). (Illus.). 192p. 1972. pap. 12.95 ref. ed. (ISBN 0-13-037150-5). P-H.

--Understanding Evolution. (Illus.). 576p. 1981. text ed. 24.95x (ISBN 0-19-502784-1). Oxford U Pr.

Hanson, Elizabeth, jt. ed. see Tanaka, Yukiko.

Hanson, F. Allan. Meaning in Culture. 1975. 16.50x o.p. (ISBN 0-7100-8132-4). Routledge & Kegan.

Hanson, Gary R., ed. Measuring Student Development. LC 81-48582. 1982. 7.95x (ISBN 0-87589-922-6, SS-20). Jossey-Bass.

Hanson, Gilbert N., jt. ed. see Morey, G. B.

Hanson, Gote. Social Clauses & International Trade. LC 82-42563. 1982. 22.50x (ISBN 0-312-73162-0). St Martin.

Hanson, Haldore & Borlaug, Norman. Wheat in the Third World. (IADS Development Oriented Literature Ser.). 192p. 1982. lib. bdg. 18.00 (ISBN 0-86531-357-1). Westview.

Hanson, Harold P., jt. ed. see Bradley, W. F.

Hanson, J. A., ed. see Seventh Technical Conference of the BPMA in Conjunction with BHRA.

Hanson, J. L. A Dictionary of Economics & Commerce. 480p. 1977. 29.00x (ISBN 0-7121-0424-0, Pub. by Macdonald & Evans). State Mutual Bk.

Hanson, J. R. Terpenoids & Steroids, Vol. 10. 295p. 1982. 150.00x (ISBN 0-85186-336-1, Pub. by Royal Soc Chem England). State Mutual Bk.

Hanson, James A., jt. ed. see Behrman, Jere R.

Hanson, Jeanne K. Game Plans for Children: Raising a Brighter Child in Ten Minutes a Day. (Illus.). 216p. 1982. 12.95 (ISBN 0-399-12670-8, Perige); pap. 6.95 (ISBN 0-399-50597-0). Putnam Pub Group.

Hanson, Joan. Alfred Snood. (Illus.). 1972. 5.50 o.p. (ISBN 0-399-20253-6). Putnam Pub Group.

--Antonyms: Hot & Cold & Other Words That Are Different As Day & Night. LC 72-1119. (Joan Hanson Word Bks). (Illus.). 32p. (gr. k-3). 1972. PLB 4.95g (ISBN 0-8225-0276-3). Lerner Pubns.

--British-American Synonyms. LC 72-3971. (Joan Hanson Word Bks.). (Illus.). 32p. (gr. k-3). 1972. PLB 4.95g (ISBN 0-8225-0279-8). Lerner Pubns.

--Homographic Homophones: Fly & Fly & Other Words That Look & Sound the Same but Are As Different in Meaning As Bat & Bat. LC 73-11973. (Joan Hanson Word Bks). (Illus.). 32p. (gr. k-3). 1973. PLB 4.95g (ISBN 0-8225-0288-7). Lerner Pubns.

--Homographs: Bow & Bow & Other Words That Look the Same but Sound As Different As Sow & Sow. LC 72-1122. (Joan Hanson Word Bks). (Illus.). 32p. (gr. k-3). 1972. PLB 4.95g (ISBN 0-8225-0278-X). Lerner Pubns.

--Homonyms: Hair & Hare & Other Words That Sound the Same but Look As Different As Bear & Bare. LC 72-1121. (Joan Hanson Word Bks). (Illus.). 32p. (gr. k-3). 1972. PLB 4.95g (ISBN 0-8225-0277-1). Lerner Pubns.

Hanson, Joanna K. The Civilian Population & the Warsaw Uprising of 1944. LC 81-15545. (Illus.). 375p. 1982. 34.50 (ISBN 0-521-23421-2). Cambridge U Pr.

Hanson, Judith. Re-Enter Laughing. (Illus.). 36p. (Orig.). 1977. pap. 4.00 (ISBN 0-940592-00-2). Heyeck Pr.

Hanson, Judy B. Spirit of the Winding Water: A Novel of the Epic 1877 Wilderness Plight of the Nez Perce Indians. 1979. 7.50 o.p. (ISBN 0-682-49345-7, Lochinvar). Exposition.

Hanson, Julie. CLEP Subject Examinations: College Composition & Freshman English. LC 78-11550. 1979. pap. text ed. 5.95 (ISBN 0-668-03798-9, 3798). Arco.

Hanson, Karen. Spine. 69p. 1971. 2.95 (ISBN 0-87886-009-6). Ithaca Hse.

Hanson, Kenneth O. Lighting the Night Sky. 1983. 14.95 (ISBN 0-932576-16-8); pap. 6.95 (ISBN 0-932576-15-X). Breitenbush Pubns.

Hanson, Kitty. Disco Fever. (Orig.). 1978. pap. 1.95 o.p. (ISBN 0-451-08452-7, J8452, Sig). NAL.

Hanson, L. A. & Kallos, P., eds. Host Parasite Relationship in Gram-Negative Infections. (Progress in Allergy: Vol. 33). (Illus.). viii, 344p. 1982. 118.75 (ISBN 3-8055-3584-8). S Karger.

Hanson, Lars A., jt. ed. see Blombach, Birger.

Hanson, Louise G. Beekeeping for Fun & Profit. (Illus.). 1980. 8.95 o.p. (ISBN 0-679-20529-2). McKay.

Hanson, Marci J., ed. Atypical Infant Development. (Illus.). 1983. pap. text ed. price not set (ISBN 0-8391-1788-4, 18414). Univ Park.

Hanson, Marilyn & Segura, Robert. To Baby with Love: Your Pre-Natal Nutrition Diary. (Illus.). 300p. (Orig.). 1982. pap. 9.95 (ISBN 0-915950-55-3). Bull Pub.

Hanson, Martha G., jt. auth. see Hanson, Robert P.

Hanson, Marvin L., jt. auth. see Barrett.

Hanson, Mary. Wicklow Castle. (Orig.). 1980. pap. 1.50 o.s.i. (ISBN 0-440-19597-7). Dell.

Hanson, Michael L. Pocket Handbook for Hi-Tensile Fencing. (Illus.). 58p. (Orig.). 1982. write for info. Agri-Fence.

Hanson, Nancy E., jt. auth. see Christenson, Boyd.

Hanson, Norwood R. Patterns of Discovery: An Enquiry into the Conceptual Foundations of Science. 1958-1965. 42.50 (ISBN 0-521-05197-5); pap. 11.95 (ISBN 0-521-09261-2). Cambridge U Pr.

Hanson, Owen. Design of Computer Data Flies. 1982. 24.95 (ISBN 0-914894-17-X). Computer Sci.

Hanson, Paul D. Dynamic Transcendence: The Correlation of Confessional Heritage & Contemporary Experience in a Biblical Model of Divine Activity. LC 78-54552. 112p. 1978. pap. 4.95 o.p. (ISBN 0-8006-1338-4, 1-1338). Fortress.

Hanson, Paul D., ed. see Wolff, Hans W.

Hanson, Peggy. Keypunching. 3rd ed. (Illus.). 1977. pap. text ed. 16.95 (ISBN 0-13-514935-5). P-H.

Hanson, R. Galen. A New Day Still Dawning: A Sequel to Surgery in Personal Experience & a Reaffirmation of the Joy of Living. 70p. 1983. 5.50 (ISBN 0-682-49937-4). Exposition.

Hanson, R. Galen, jt. auth. see Martindale, Don.

Hanson, R. N. & Rigby, D. S. Gregg Keyboarding for Information Processing: Apple Version. 1982. write for info. (ISBN 0-07-026109-1). McGraw.

Hanson, R. N., jt. auth. see Rigby, D. S.

Hanson, R. P. The Life & Writings of the Historical St. Patrick. 144p. 1983. 11.95 (ISBN 0-8164-0523-9). Seabury.

Hanson, Ranae, ed. Institutional Abuse of Children & Youth. LC 81-7194. (Child & Youth Services Ser.: Vol. 4, Nos. 1 & 2). 164p. 1982. text ed. 22.95 (ISBN 0-917724-97-6, B97). Haworth Pr.

Hanson, Richard & Reynolds, Rebecca. Child Development: Concepts, Issues, & Readings. 550p. 1980. text ed. 21.95 (ISBN 0-8299-0336-4); instrs.' manual avail. (ISBN 0-8299-0486-7); study guide 7.50 (ISBN 0-8299-0312-7). West Pub.

Hanson, Richard E. The Manager's Guide to Copying & Duplicating. (Illus.). 1980. 18.95 (ISBN 0-07-026080-X). McGraw.

Hanson, Richard J., jt. auth. see Lawson, Charles L.

Hanson, Richard S. Tyrian Influence in the Upper Galilee. LC 79-11775. (Meiron Excavation Project Ser.: Vol. 2). (Illus.). 89p. 1980. text ed. 12.00x (ISBN 0-89757-504-0, Am Sch Orient Res); pap. text ed. 8.00x (ISBN 0-89757-505-9). Eisenbrauns.

Hanson, Richard W., ed. see Symposium Held at the University of Nebraska Medical School, Omaha, Nebr., May, 1972.

Hanson, Robert L., ed. Staffing for Nurse Managers. (Nursing Management Anthology Ser.). 225p. 1983. price not set (ISBN 0-89443-843-3). Aspen Systems.

Hanson, Robert N. & Rigby, D. Sue. Keyboarding: For Information Processing. (Illus.). 96p. 1981. pap. text ed. 7.95 (ISBN 0-07-026105-9, G). McGraw.

Hanson, Robert P. & Hanson, Martha G. Animal Disease Control: Regional Programs. (Illus.). 200p. 1983. pap. text ed. 15.00 (ISBN 0-8138-0121-4). Iowa St U Pr.

Hanson, Roger. From Frequently Frivolous & Flippant to Fairly Fancy, Fervent & Fatherly Free Verse. 43p. 1978. 4.50 o.p. (ISBN 0-533-03193-1). Vantage.

Hanson, Simon G. Utopia in Uruguay: Chapters in the Economic History of Uruguay. LC 79-1579. 1981. Repr. of 1938 ed. 20.75 (ISBN 0-88355-885-8). Hyperion Conn.

Hanson, Wayne C., ed. Transuranic Elements in the Environment: A Summary of Environmental Research on Transuranium Radionuclides Funded by the U. S. Department of Energy Through Calendar Year 1979. LC 80-607069. (DOE Technical Information Center Ser.). 746p. 1980. hardbound 26.75 (ISBN 0-87079-119-2, DOE/TIC-22800); microfiche 4.50 (ISBN 0-87079-331-4, DOE/TIC-22800). DOE.

Hanson, William, jt. auth. see Maxwell, Gordon.

Hanson, William L. World War I: I Was There. Franzwa, Gregory M., ed. LC 82-8228. (Illus.). 126p. 1982. 11.95 (ISBN 0-935284-24-9). Patrice Pr.

Hansot, Elisabeth. Perfection & Progress: Two Modes of Utopian Thought. LC 74-7106. 219p. 1974. 23.00x o.p. (ISBN 0-262-08077-X). MIT Pr.

--Perfection & Progress: Two Modes of Utopian Thought. 240p. 1974. pap. 6.95x (ISBN 0-262-58054-3). MIT Pr.

Hansotte, Louis B. Legal Aspects of California Real Estate. LC 81-19676. (California Real Estate Ser.). 363p. 1982. text ed. 25.95 (ISBN 0-471-07698-8); tchrs. manual avail. (ISBN 0-471-86616-4). Wiley.

Hansson, Lennart, jt. ed. see Magnani, Bruno.

Hansteen, H. Electricians Vest Pocket Reference Book. 190p. 1983. pap. 6.95 (ISBN 0-13-247973-7). P-H.

Hansteen, Henry B. The Electrician's Vest Pocket Reference Book. rev. ed. LC 72-12321. 144p. 1973. 6.95 (ISBN 0-13-247973-7). P-H.

Hanten, Edward W., jt. ed. see Ma, Laurence J.

Hantrais, L. Contemporary French Society. 1982. 50.00x (ISBN 0-333-28062-8, Pub. by Macmillan England). State Mutual Bk.

Hantske, Madeline H. The Song of the Cotton Picker. (Illus.). 1977. 5.95 o.p. (ISBN 0-533-03208-3). Vantage.

Hantula, Richard, ed. History of Russia: Vol. 35: The Rules of Empress Anna. 1982. 21.50 (ISBN 0-87569-047-5). Academic Intl.

Hanus, Jerome J., ed. The Nationalization of State Government. LC 80-8635. (Illus.). 192p. 1981. 22.95x (ISBN 0-669-04334-6). Lexington Bks.

Hanzak, J. The Pictorial Encyclopedia of Birds. Campbell, Bruce, ed. 1965. 10.00 o.p. (ISBN 0-517-00549-2). Crown.

Hanzak, Jan & Veselovsky, Zdenek. Encyclopedia of Animals. Stephen, David & McCormack, Tom, eds. LC 78-24833. (Illus.). 1979. 15.95 o.p. (ISBN 0-312-24571-8). St Martin.

Hanzek, Donald, jt. auth. see Kakonis, Tom E.

Hanzeli, Victor E., tr. see Gyarmathi, Samuel.

Hanzen, Judith F. Sociocultural Perspectives on Human Learning: An Introduction to Educational Anthropology. 1979. pap. 14.95 (ISBN 0-13-821041-1). P-H.

Hanzlicek, C. G. Calling the Dead. LC 82-70743. 1982. 12.95 (ISBN 0-915604-70-1); pap. 4.95 (ISBN 0-915604-71-X). Carnegie-Mellon.

Hanzowat, M. & Tournier, T. H. System for the Collection of Ships' Weather Reports. (World Weather Watch Planning Report Ser.: No. 25). 1968. pap. 12.00 (ISBN 0-685-22344-2, W237, WMO). Unipub.

Hapgood, David. The Screwing of the Average Man. 288p. 1975. pap. 2.50 (ISBN 0-686-82863-1, 12913-9). Bantam.

--The Tax to End All Taxes. (Illus.). 8p. 1978. pap. 0.00 free (ISBN 0-911312-42-0). Schalkenbach.

Hapgood, Fred. Why Males Exist: An Inquiry into the Evolution of Sex. 1980. pap. 2.95 (ISBN 0-451-61908-0, ME1908, Ment). NAL.

Hapgood, Hutchins. The Spirit of the Ghetto. Rischin, Moses, ed. (Illus.). 360p. 1983. pap. 7.95x (ISBN 0-674-83266-3, Belknap Pr). Harvard U Pr.

--The Spirit of the Ghetto: Studies of the Jewish Quarter of New York. rev. ed. LC 76-21184. (Illus.). 1976. pap. 5.50 (ISBN 0-8052-0553-5). Schocken.

Hapgood, Isabel F. Epic Songs of Russia. Repr. of 1886 ed. lib. bdg. 17.50x (ISBN 0-8371-4507-4, HASR). Greenwood.

Hapgood, Isabel F., tr. see Leskov, Nikolai S.

Hapgood, Ruth. First Horse: Basic Horse Care Illustrated. LC 72-76929. (Illus.). 160p. 1972. 6.95 o.p. (ISBN 0-87701-015-3). Chronicle Bks.

Hapkemeyer, Andreas. Die Sprachthematik In der Prosa Ingeborg Bachmanns. 131p. (Ger.). 1982. write for info. (ISBN 3-8204-5771-2). P Lang Pubs.

Happe, Bernard. Your Film & the Lab. (Media Manual Ser.). (Illus.). 1974. pap. 10.95 o.s.i. (ISBN 0-240-50855-6). Focal Pr.

--Your Film & the Lab. (Media Manuals Ser.). 1975. pap. 8.95 o.s.i. (ISBN 0-8038-8595-4). Hastings.

Happel, Edward, ed. Fountain of Youth. (The Best of U.S. College Magazines Ser.). (Illus.). 100p. (Orig.). 1982. pap. 4.95 (ISBN 0-910127-00-X). Student Ed Assoc.

Happel, John R., jt. ed. see Moser, William R.

Happey, F., ed. Contemporary: Textile Engineering. write for info. (ISBN 0-12-323750-5). Acad Pr.

Haq, Ehsanul. Education & Political Culture in India. 176p. 1981. 22.50x (ISBN 0-940500-54-X, Pub. by Sterling India). Asia Bk Corp.

Haque, R., ed. Dynamics, Exposure & Hazard Assessment of Toxic Chemicals. LC 79-55141. (Illus.). 1980. 49.95 (ISBN 0-250-40301-3). Ann Arbor Science.

Hara, H. & Williams, L. H. Enumeration of the Flowering Plants of Nepal: Vol. 2, Dicotyledons. 1979. pap. 60.00x (ISBN 0-565-00810-2, Pub. by Brit Mus Nat Hist). Sabbot-Natural Hist Bks.

Hara, H., et al. Enumeration of the Flowering Plants of Nepal: Vol. 1, Monocotyledons. (Illus.). 1978. pap. 60.00x (ISBN 0-565-00777-7, Pub. by Brit Mus Nat Hist). Sabbot-Natural Hist Bks.

Hara, Hiroshi. Enumeratio Spermatophytum Japonicarum. 1972. 104.00 (ISBN 3-87429-040-9). Lubrecht & Cramer.

Hara, T. J. Chemoreception in Fishes. (Developments in Agriculture & Fisheries Science Ser.: Vol. 8). 1982. 91.50 (ISBN 0-444-42040-1). Elsevier.

Harada, Nobuyuki, jt. auth. see Nakanishi, Koji.

Haraguchi, Torao, et al, trs. from Jap. The Status System & Social Organization of Satsuma. LC 75-15936. 271p. 1975. text ed. 17.50x (ISBN 0-8248-0390-6). UH Pr.

Harahap, Marwali. Skin Surgery. (Illus.). 900p. 1983. price not set (ISBN 0-87527-317-3). Green.

Harak, Charles. The Utility Companies & You: Your Rights & How to Preserve Them. Spriggs, Marshall T., ed. (Orig.). 1983. pap. write for info (ISBN 0-910001-03-0). MA Poverty Law.

Harakas, Emily. Daily Lenten Meditations for Orthodox Christians. 1983. pap. 2.95 (ISBN 0-937032-27-1). Light&Life Pub Co MN.

Harakas, S. S. Contemporary Moral Issues Facing the Orthodox Christian. 1982. pap. 4.95 (ISBN 0-937032-24-7). Light&Life Pub Co MN.

--Toward Transfigured Life. 1983. pap. 9.95 (ISBN 0-937032-28-X). Light&Life Pub Co MN.

Haralick, Robert M., jt. auth. see Creese, Thomas M.

Harari, Herbert & Kaplan, Robert M. Social Psychology: Basic & Applied. LC 81-15468. (Psychology Ser.). 592p. 1982. text ed. 21.95 (ISBN 0-8185-0481-1). Brooks-Cole.

Harary, Frank, et al, eds. Topics in Graph Theory. (Annals of the New York Academy of Sciences: Vol. 328). 206p. (Orig.). 1979. pap. 42.00x (ISBN 0-89766-028-5). NY Acad Sci.

Haraszty, Eszter. The Embroiderer's Portfolio of Flower Designs. (Illus.). 1982. spiral bound 29.95 (ISBN 0-87140-643-8, A Liveright Bk). Norton.

Harbage, Alfred, ed. see Shakespeare, William.

Harbage, Alfred B., ed. Shakespeare's Songs. LC 73-127429. (Illus.). 1970. 6.25 (ISBN 0-8255-4110-7). Macrae.

Harbaugh, Frederick W. Think It Clearly, Make It Tell with Information Impact. 1978. 6.95 o.p. (ISBN 0-8158-0361-3). Chris Mass.

Harbaugh, John W. Field Guide: Northern California. LC 73-88485. (Geology Field Guide Ser.). (Illus.). 1975. perfect bdg. 5.95 (ISBN 0-8403-1273-3). Kendall-Hunt.

Harbaugh, John W., et al. Probability Methods in Oil Exploration. LC 76-50631. 1977. 36.95 (ISBN 0-471-35129-6, Pub. by Wiley-Interscience). Wiley.

Harbaugh, William H. The Life & Times of Theodore Roosevelt. new rev. ed. Orig. Title: Power & Responsibility. 1975. pap. 12.95 (ISBN 0-19-519822-0, 447, GB). Oxford U Pr.

Harben, Frank. Hunting Wild Turkeys in the Everglades. LC 82-90090. (Illus.). 340p. 1982. pap. 8.95 (ISBN 0-9608158-0-5). Harben Pub.

Harben, Perter. The Earth. LC 80-50334. (World of Knowledge Ser.). 16.72 (ISBN 0-382-06406-2). Silver.

Harben, William N. The Land of the Changing Sun. 256p. 1975. Repr. of 1894 ed. lib. bdg. 11.50 o.p. (ISBN 0-8398-2305-3, Gregg). G K Hall.

Harber, Leonard C. & Bickers, David. Clinical Photobiology of Skin. (Illus.). 372p. 1981. text ed. 55.00 o.p. (ISBN 0-7216-4505-4). Saunders.

Harber, Leonard C. & Bickers, David R. Photosensitivity Diseases. (Illus.). 372p. 1981. text ed. 60.00 (ISBN 0-7216-4505-4). Saunders.

Harbert, Anita S. Federal Grants-in-Aid: Maximizing Benefits to the States. LC 76-12854. 1976. text ed. 28.95 o.p. (ISBN 0-275-23370-7). Praeger.

Harbert, David L. Existence, Knowing, & Philosophical Systems. LC 82-17565. 226p. (Orig.). 1983. lib. bdg. 21.75 (ISBN 0-8191-2804-X); pap. text ed. 10.25 (ISBN 0-8191-2805-8). U Pr of Amer.

Harbert, Earl N. Critical Essays on Henry Adams. (Critical Essays on American Literature). 1981. 25.00 (ISBN 0-8161-8280-9, Twayne). G K Hall.

Harbert, Joseph R., jt. ed. see Finger, Seymour M.

Harbert, Lloyd & Scandizzo, Pasquale L. Food Distribution & Nutrition Intervention: The Case of Chile. LC 82-8370. (World Bank Staff Working Papers: No. 512). (Orig.). 1982. pap. text ed. 5.00 (ISBN 0-8213-0001-6). World Bank.

Harbin, Robert. New Adventures in Origami. (Funk & W Bk). (Illus.). 192p. 1972. pap. 4.76i (ISBN 0-06-463555-4, EH-555). T Y Crowell.

Harbin, Vernon, ed. see Jewell, Richard B.

Harbinson, W. A. The Illustrated Elvis. (Illus.). 160p. 1982. pap. 7.95 (ISBN 0-448-12461-0, G&D). Putnam Pub Group.

--Revelation. (Orig.). 1983. pap. 3.95 (ISBN 0-440-17216-0). Dell.

Harbison, Anne, jt. auth. see Olsson, Axel A.

Harbison, Craig. The Last Judgment in Sixteenth Century Northern Europe: a Study of the Relation Between Art & the Reformation. LC 75-23793. (Outstanding Dissertations in the Fine Arts - 16th Century). (Illus.). 1976. lib. bdg. 45.00 o.s.i. (ISBN 0-8240-1988-1). Garland Pub.

Harbison, Samuel A., jt. auth. see Martin, Alan.

Harbison, Winfred A., jt. auth. see Kelly, Alfred H.

Harborne, J. B. Introduction to Ecological Biochemistry. 1977. 20.00 o.s.i. (ISBN 0-12-324670-9). Acad Pr.

Harbottle, Thomas B. Dictionary of Battles. LC 66-22672. 1966. Repr. of 1905 ed. 33.00x (ISBN 0-8103-3004-0). Gale.

--Dictionary of Historical Allusions. LC 68-23163. 1968. Repr. of 1904 ed. 34.00x (ISBN 0-8103-3088-1). Gale.

Harbou, Thea Von. Metropolis. (Science Fiction Ser). 264p. 1975. Repr. of 1929 ed. lib. bdg. 12.50 o.p. (ISBN 0-8398-2317-7, Gregg). G K Hall.

--The Rocket to the Moon. 1977. Repr. of 1930 ed. lib. bdg. 12.00 (ISBN 0-8398-2378-9, Gregg). G K Hall.

Harbou, Thea Von see Harbou, Thea Von.

Harbour, Brian L. Famous Singles of the Bible. LC 79-56309. 1980. pap. 3.95 (ISBN 0-8054-5640-6). Broadman.

--From Cover to Cover. LC 81-67197. 1982. pap. 5.95 (ISBN 0-8054-2241-2). Broadman.

Harbour, Dave. Advanced Wild Turkey Hunting & World Records. (Illus.). 264p. 1983. 19.95 (ISBN 0-8329-0286-1, Pub. by Winchester Pr.). New Century.

--Hunting the American Wild Turkey. LC 74-31449. (Illus.). 258p. 1974. 14.95 (ISBN 0-8117-0863-2). Stackpole.

Harbron, John D. Communist Ships & Shipping. (Illus.). 264p. 1962. 11.25 (ISBN 0-8002-0498-0). Intl Pubns Serv.

Harburg, E. Y. At This Point in Rhyme. (gr. 9 up). 1976. 5.95 o.p. (ISBN 0-517-52727-8). Crown.

Harbury, C. D., ed. Workbook in Introductory Economics. 3rd ed. (Illus.). 176p. 1982. 7.00 (ISBN 0-08-027442-0). Pergamon.

Harby, Mary L., jt. auth. see McCall, William A.

Harcharik, Kathleen & Armijo, Moses A. Business Computations. (Illus.). 320p. 1982. pap. 16.95 (ISBN 0-13-093104-7). P-H.

Harcourt, G., tr. see Tsushima, Yuko.

Harcourt, G. C. Some Cambridge Controversies in the Theory of Capital. LC 71-161294. (Illus.). 1972. 39.50 (ISBN 0-521-08294-3); pap. 14.95x o. p. (ISBN 0-521-09672-3). Cambridge U Pr.

Harcourt, G. C., jt. ed. see Parker, R. H.

Hard, Walter, ed. see Candy, Robert.

Hardach, Gerd, et al. A Short History of Socialist Economic Thought. LC 78-21053. 1979. 15.95x (ISBN 0-312-72146-3); pap. 6.95 (ISBN 0-312-72147-1). St Martin.

Hardanek, Anita. Critical Reading Improvement. 2nd ed. 1977. pap. text ed. 11.95 (ISBN 0-07-044412-9). McGraw.

Hardaway, Francine. Creative Rhetoric. 304p. 1976. pap. text ed. 12.95 (ISBN 0-13-191072-8). P-H.

Hardaway, Francine, jt. auth. see Hardaway, John M.

Hardaway, John M. & Hardaway, Francine. Thinking into Writing: The Basis & Beyond. (Orig.). 1978. pap. text ed. 10.95 (ISBN 0-316-34594-6); tchr's ed. avail. (ISBN 0-316-34595-4). Little.

--Writing Through Reading. (Orig.). 1977. pap. text ed. 8.95 o.p. (ISBN 0-316-34593-8). Little.

Hardberger, Phillip D. Texas Courtroom Evidence. LC 77-90279. 1978. incl. 1983 suppl 48.50 (ISBN 0-911110-26-7). Parker & Son.

Hardcastle, Lena L. Parliamentary Law Rules & Procedures for Conducting Conventions. LC 81-85392. 272p. 1982. 17.95 (ISBN 0-9608716-0-8). Stuart Bks.

Hardeman, N. B. Hardeman Tabernacle Sermons, 5 vols. 8.00 ea.; Set. 37.50 (ISBN 0-89225-195-6). Vol. 1 (ISBN 0-89225-196-4). Vol. 2 (ISBN 0-89225-197-2). Vol. 3 (ISBN 0-89225-198-0). Vol. 4 (ISBN 0-89225-199-9). Vol. 5 (ISBN 0-89225-203-0). Gospel Advocate.

Harden, Evelyn, tr. see Dostoevsky, F. M.

Harden, Gerald, jt. auth. see Harden, Linda B.

Harden, John. The Devil's Tramping Ground & Other North Carolina Mystery Stories. xiii, 178p. 1980. 9.95 (ISBN 0-8078-0561-0); pap. 4.95 (ISBN 0-8078-4070-X). U of NC Pr.

--Tar Heel Ghosts. xiv, 178p. 1980. 9.95 (ISBN 0-8078-0660-9); pap. 4.95 (ISBN 0-8078-4069-6). U of NC Pr.

Harden, Linda B. & Harden, Gerald. The LTR Money Book: The Personal Finance Guide for Every Kind of Living Together Relationship. 1978. 9.95 o.p. (ISBN 0-89696-011-0, An Everest House Book). Dodd.

Harden, M. L., jt. auth. see Lamb, M. W.

Harden, William. History of Savannah & South Georgia, Vol. I. LC 72-97929. (Illus.). 1981. Repr. of 1913 ed. Vol. I, 543p. bds. 25.00 (ISBN 0-87797-008-4); Vol. II, 554p. bds. 25.00 (ISBN 0-87797-058-0); Set. bds. 45.00. Cherokee.

Hardenbrook, Harry. The Insulator's Estimating Handbook. (Illus.). 128p. 1982. pap. 11.95 (ScribT). Scribner.

--Walker's Insulation Techniques & Estimating Handbook. 2nd, rev. ed. Cook, Gary D., ed. (Illus.). 131p. 1983. pap. text ed. 8.95 (ISBN 0-911592-51-2). F R Walker.

Hardendorff, Jeanne B. Libraries & How to Use Them. LC 78-12992. (First Bks.). (Illus.). (gr. 4 up). 1979. PLB 8.90 s&l (ISBN 0-531-02259-5). Watts.

Harder, Edwin L. Fundamentals of Energy Production. LC 81-16257. (Wiley Alternate Energy Ser.). 368p. 1982. 44.50x (ISBN 0-471-08356-9, Pub. by Wiley-Interscience). Wiley.

Harder, Marvin A., jt. auth. see Palumbo, Dennis J.

Harder, Wilhelm. Anatomy of Fishes, 2 vols. 2nd rev. ed. (Illus.). 1976. Set. text ed. 104.75 (ISBN 3-510-65067-0). Lubrecht & Cramer.

Hardesty, D. L. Ecological Anthropology. 1977. 25.95 (ISBN 0-471-35144-X). Wiley.

Hardesty, Jim, tr. see Shan, Han.

Hardesty, Margaret A. That Momentary Peace: The Poem. LC 81-40934. 178p. (Orig.). 1982. lib. bdg. 23.00 (ISBN 0-8191-2248-3); pap. text ed. 10.00 (ISBN 0-8191-2249-1). U Pr of Amer.

Hardesty, Von. Red Phoenix: The Rise of Soviet Air Power 1941-1945. (Illus.). 288p. 1982. 22.50 (ISBN 0-87474-510-1). Smithsonian.

Hardgrave, Robert L., Jr. The Nadars of Tamilnad: The Political Culture of a Community in Change. LC 69-13726. (Center for South & Southeast Asia Studies, UC Berkeley). (Illus.). 1969. 30.00x (ISBN 0-520-01471-5). U of Cal Pr.

Hardgrove, Carol, jt. auth. see Azarnoff, Pat.

Hardie, Colin, tr. see Dante Alighieri.

Hardie, Glenn M. Construction Contracts & Specifications. (Illus.). 1981. text ed. 26.95 (ISBN 0-8359-0923-9). Reston.

Hardiman, G. & Zernich, T. Art Activities for Children. 1981. 20.95 (ISBN 0-13-046631-X). P-H.

Hardiman, Jim, jt. auth. see Robinson, Jay.

Hardiman, Margaret & Midgley, James. The Social Dimensions of Development: Social Policy & Planning in the Third World. LC 81-22006. (Social Development in Third World Ser.). 317p. 1982. 41.95x (ISBN 0-471-10184-2, Pub. by Wiley-Interscience). Wiley.

Hardiman, N. J. Exploring University Mathematics, 3 Vols. Vol. 1. 1967. text ed. 16.25 (ISBN 0-08-011990-5); Vol. 2. 1968. text ed. 17.75 (ISBN 0-08-012567-0); Vol. 3. 1969. text ed. 16.25 (ISBN 0-08-012903-X); Vol. 1. pap. 7.00 (ISBN 0-08-011991-3); Vol. 2 1968. pap. 7.75 (ISBN 0-08-012566-2); Vol. 3 1969. pap. 7.00 (ISBN 0-08-012902-1). Pergamon.

Hardin, Garrett. Exploring New Ethics for Survival: The Voyage of the Spaceship Beagle. 320p. 1972. 10.95 o.p. (ISBN 0-670-30268-6). Viking Pr.

--Nature & Man's Fate. pap. 1.25 o.p. (ISBN 0-451-61170-5, MY1170, Ment). NAL.

Hardin, Garrett J. Naked Emperors: Essays of a Taboo-Stalker. LC 82-7209. (Illus.). 287p. 1982. 15.00x (ISBN 0-86576-033-0); pap. 8.95 (ISBN 0-86576-032-2). W Kaufmann.

Hardin, H., tr. see Gambaryan, P. R.

Hardin, J. D. Apache Gold. 224p. (Orig.). 1983. pap. 2.25 (ISBN 0-425-06152-3). Berkley Pub.

--Bibles, Bullets & Brides. LC 82-60685. (J. D. Hardin Western Ser.). 224p. 1983. pap. 2.25 (ISBN 0-86721-241-1). Playboy Pbks.

--Bibles, Bullets & Brides. 224p. 1983. pap. 2.25 (ISBN 0-425-06001-2). Berkley Pub.

--Hellfire Hideaway. 192p. (Orig.). 1983. pap. 2.25 (ISBN 0-686-42863-3). Berkley Pub.

Hardin, James. John Beer. (World Authors Ser.). 128p. 1983. lib. bdg. 18.95 (ISBN 0-8057-6536-0, Twayne). G K Hall.

Hardin, John A., jt. auth. see Hayslett, John P.

Hardin, Mark, ed. Foster Children in the Courts. 912p. (Orig.). 1983. text ed. write for info (ISBN 0-88063-000-0). Butterworth Legal Pubs.

Hardin, Russell. Collective Action. LC 81-48247. 264p. 1982. text ed. 24.00x (ISBN 0-8018-2818-X); pap. text ed. 9.00x (ISBN 0-8018-2819-8). Johns Hopkins.

Hardin, Terri. Nimue & Other Poems. 50p. (Orig.). 1983. pap. 3.50 (ISBN 0-941062-10-4); pap. 30.00 ltd. ed. (ISBN 0-941062-11-2). Guignol Bks.

Harding, jt. auth. see Walraven.

Harding, A. F., jt. auth. see Coles, J. M.

Harding, A. J. Coleridge & the Idea of Love. 1975. 42.50 (ISBN 0-521-20639-1). Cambridge U Pr.

Harding, Anthony. Guinness Book of Car Facts & Feats. (Illus.). 288p. 1983. 19.95 (ISBN 0-85112-207-8, Pub. by Guinness Superlatives England). Sterling.

Harding, Anthony, ed. Car Facts & Feats. LC 76-51170. (Guinness Family Ser.). (Illus.). 1977. 19.95 (ISBN 0-8069-0108-X); lib. bdg. 23.59 (ISBN 0-8069-0109-8). Sterling.

Harding, Brian. American Literature in Context, Two: 1830-1865. 1982. 22.00x (ISBN 0-416-73900-8); pap. 8.95x (ISBN 0-416-73910-5). Methuen Inc.

Harding, Chester A. Sketch of Chester A. Harding, Artist. White, Margaret E., ed. LC 70-87681. (Library of American Art Ser.). (Illus.). 1970. Repr. of 1929 ed. lib. bdg. 29.50 (ISBN 0-306-71711-5). Da Capo.

Harding, Claudius H. The Innermost Nature of the World Crisis & Its Catastrophic Potential for the Future of Humanity. (The Great Currents of History Library Book). (Illus.). 128p. 1983. 83.55 (ISBN 0-86722-019-8). Inst Econ Pol.

Harding, Colin & Roper, Christopher, eds. Latin America Review of Books One. LC 73-17942. (Latin America Review Ser.). 220p. 1974. pap. 3.95 (ISBN 0-87867-048-3); 12.00 (ISBN 0-87867-047-5). Ramparts.

Harding, D. W. Words into Rhythm. LC 76-7805. 1976. 29.95 (ISBN 0-521-21267-7). Cambridge U Pr.

Harding, David J., jt. auth. see Packham, John R.

Harding, Diana & Manzolillo, Deborah. Baboon Orphan. (Illus.). 48p. (gr. 3-5). 1981. 9.95 (ISBN 0-525-40747-2, 0966-290). Dutton.

Harding, Gordon, ed. see Rosenberg, Isaac.

Harding, J. M., tr. see Descombes, Vincent.

Harding, Jim & International Project for Soft Energy Paths. Tools for the Soft Path. 1982. pap. 11.95 (ISBN 0-913890-53-7); 25.00 (ISBN 0-913890-52-9). Friends Earth.

Harding, John. Victims & Offenders: Needs & Responsibilities. 54p. 1982. pap. 7.25 (ISBN 0-7199-1083-8, Pub. by Bedford England). Renouf.

Harding, John J. & Harding, Justin J. Birding the Delaware Valley Region: A Comprehensive Guide to Birdwatching in Southeastern Pennsylvania, Central & Southern New Jersey, & Northcentral Delaware. 233p. 1980. 15.95x (ISBN 0-87722-179-0); pap. 8.95 (ISBN 0-87722-182-0). Temple U Pr.

Harding, Justin J., jt. auth. see Harding, John J.

Harding, Lee. The Fallen Spaceman. LC 79-2006. (Illus.). 96p. (gr. 3-7). 1980. 7.95 o.p. (ISBN 0-06-022212-3, HarpJ); PLB 10.89 (ISBN 0-06-022213-1). Har-Row.

--Misplaced Persons. (gr. 12). Date not set. pap. 2.25. Bantam.

Harding, Lee, ed. see Le Guin, Ursula K.

Harding, M. Esther. The Way of All Women. 288p. 1975. pap. 5.72i (ISBN 0-06-090399-6, CN399, CN). Har-Row.

--Woman's Mysteries. 1976. pap. 5.95i (ISBN 0-06-090525-5, CN525, CN). Har-Row.

Harding, Neil. Lenin's Political Thought, Vols. 1 & 2. 550p. 1982. pap. text ed. 19.95x (ISBN 0-391-02698-4). Humanities.

--Lenin's Political Thought, Vol. 2. LC 78-423. 1981. 32.50 (ISBN 0-312-47959-X). St Martin.

--Lenin's Political Thought: Theory & Practice in the Democratic Revolution, Vol. 1. LC 78-423. (Illus.). 1979. 32.50x (ISBN 0-312-47958-1). St Martin.

Harding, R. Brewster. Roadside New England, 1900-1955. 80p. pap. 9.95 (ISBN 0-89272-158-8). Down East.

Harding, Robert T. & Holmes, A. L. Jacqueline Kennedy: A Woman for the World. (Illus.). 11.95 (ISBN 0-8149-0115-8). Vanguard.

Harding, Rosamund E. Piano-Forte. LC 69-15634. (Music Ser.). 1973. Repr. of 1933 ed. lib. bdg. 35.00 (ISBN 0-306-71084-6). Da Capo.

Harding, Sandra, jt. ed. see Hintikka, Merrill.

Harding, Steven. Grey Ghost: RMS Queen Mary at War. (Illus.). 92p. 1982. 8.95 (ISBN 0-933126-26-3). Pictorial Hist.

Harding, T. & Wallace, B. Cultures of the Pacific. LC 70-91883. 1970. 19.95 (ISBN 0-02-913810-8); pap. text ed. 10.95 (ISBN 0-02-913800-0). Free Pr.

Harding, T. D. Better Chess for Average Chess-Players. (Illus.). 1977. pap. 9.95 o.p. (ISBN 0-19-217550-5). Oxford U Pr.

--French: MacCutcheon & Advance Lines. (Illus.). 130p. 1980. pap. 13.95 (ISBN 0-7134-2026-X, Pub. by Batsford England). David & Charles.

Harding, Vincent. There Is a River: The Black Struggle for Freedom in American. LC 82-40024. 480p. 1983. pap. 6.95 (ISBN 0-394-71148-3, Vin). Random.

Harding, Walter. The Days of Henry Thoreau: A Biography. (Illus.). 544p. pap. 8.95 (ISBN 0-486-24263-3). Dover.
Harding, Walter, ed. Thoreau Centennial. LC 65-19729. 1964. 15.95x (ISBN 0-87395-015-1). State U NY Pr.
Harding, Walter, ed. see Thoreau, Henry D.
Harding, William E. Between Jobs. 152p. 1976. pap. 5.95 (ISBN 0-686-16828-3). Executive Ent.
Harding, William H. Young Hart. LC 82-15493. 372p. 1983. 16.95 (ISBN 0-03-062754-0). HR&W
Hardinge, George & Stevens, George. Chalmeriana & Mr. Ireland's Vindication of His Conduct, Respecting the Publication of the Supposed Shakespeare Manuscripts. 162p. 1971. Repr. of 1800 ed. 27.50x (ISBN 0-7146-2527-2, F Cass Co). Biblio Dist.
Hardison, David. From Ideology to Incrementalism: The Concept of Urban Enterprise Zones in Great Britain & the United States. LC 81-85641. 41p. (Orig.). 1982. pap. 5.00 (ISBN 0-938882-02-3, Dist. by Transaction Bks). PURRC.
Hardison, O. B., jt. ed. see Preminger, Alex, Jr.
Hardison, O. B., Jr. The Enduring Moment. LC 73-3023. 240p. 1973. Repr. of 1962 ed. lib. bdg. 17.50x (ISBN 0-8371-6821-X, HATE). Greenwood.
--Entering the Maze: Identity & Change in Modern Culture. 1981. 22.50x (ISBN 0-19-502953-4). Oxford U Pr.
Hardison, O. B., Jr. & Greer, Germaine. Politics, Power, & Shakespeare. Leonard, Frances M., ed. LC 81-70219. (Illus., Orig.). pap. write for info. (ISBN 0-942484-00-2). U TX Arl TX Hum.
Hardison, O. B., Jr., ed. Medieval & Renaissance Studies: Proceedings. 1971. 11.50x o.p. (ISBN 0-8078-1172-6). U of NC Pr.
--Modern Continental Literary Criticism. (Orig.). 1962. pap. text ed. 6.95 o.p. (ISBN 0-13-590802-7). P-H.
Hardison, O. B., Jr., jt. ed. see Preminger, Alex.
Hardison, Thomas B. Fluid Mechanics for Technicians. (Illus.). 272p. 1977. ref. ed. 19.95 o.p. (ISBN 0-87909-297-1); solns. manual avail. o.p. (ISBN 0-87909-301-3). Reston.
--Introduction to Kinematics. (Illus.). 1979. text ed. 22.95 (ISBN 0-8359-3228-1); solutions manual avail. (ISBN 0-8359-3229-X). Reston.
Hardisty, M. W. Biology of the Cyclostomes. LC 79-40803. 350p. 1979. 59.95x (ISBN 0-412-14120-5, Pub. by Chapman & Hall England). Methuen Inc.
Hardisty, M. W. & Potter, I. G., eds. Biology of Lampreys. Vol. 4A. write for info.; Vol. 4B. write for info. (ISBN 0-12-324824-8). Acad Pr.
Hardley, Dennis, jt. auth. see Carter, Jenny.
Hardman, Keith J. The Spiritual Awakeners. 240p. (Orig.). 1983. pap. 6.95 (ISBN 0-8024-0177-5). Moody.
Hardman, Michael. Beer Naturally. (Illus., Orig.). 1978. pap. 4.50 o.p. (ISBN 0-8467-0430-7, Pub. by Two Continents). Hippocrene Bks.
Hardman, Michael L., jt. auth. see Drew, Clifford J.
Hardman, William E. How To Read Shop Prints & Drawings With Blueprints. 236p. 1982. pap. text ed. 19.95 (ISBN 0-910399-01-8). Natl Tool & Mach.
Hardon, John. Spiritual Life in the Modern World. 1982. 3.50 (ISBN 0-8198-6839-6, SP0708); pap. 2.50 (ISBN 0-8198-6840-X). Dghtrs St Paul.
Hardon, John A. The Catholic Catechism. LC 73-81433. 1973. pap. 9.95 (ISBN 0-385-08045-X). Doubleday.
--Modern Catholic Dictionary. LC 77-82945. 1980. 19.95 (ISBN 0-385-12162-8). Doubleday.
Hardouin-Fugier, E. Simon Saint-Jean 1808-1860: A Lyonnais Flower Painter. (Illus.). 1980. text ed. 37.00x (ISBN 0-85317-064-9, Pub. by A & C Black England). Humanities.
Hardoy, Jorge E. & Satterthwaite, David. Shelter Need & Response: Housing, Land & Settlement Policies in Seventeen Third World Nations. LC 80-41417. 1981. 53.95 (ISBN 0-471-27919-6, Pub. by Wiley-Interscience). Wiley.
Hardre, Jacques, ed. see Camus, Albert.
Hardre, Jacques, ed. see Sartre, Jean-Paul.
Hardt, D. E., ed. Measurement & Control for Batch Manufacturing. 1982. 40.00 (H00244). ASME.
Hardt, Ulrich H., ed. Mary Wollstonecraft's a Vindication of the Rights of Women with Structures on Political & Moral Subjects: A Critical Edition. LC 81-50048. 573p. 1982. 45.00x (ISBN 0-87875-212-9). Whitston Pub.
Hardwick, Ann B., jt. auth. see Wiess, Christine.
Hardwick, Elizabeth. Seduction & Betrayal: Women & Literature. 1974. 6.95 o.p. (ISBN 0-394-49069-X); pap. 3.95 (ISBN 0-394-71407-5). Random.
Hardwick, Elizabeth, ed. see James, Williams.
Hardwick, Homer. Winemaking at Home. rev. ed. LC 68-13032. (Funk & W Bk.). (Illus.). 1970. 12.45i (ISBN 0-308-70206-9). T Y Crowell.
Hardwick, Michael. A Guide to Jane Austen. 228p. 1982. pap. 6.95 (ISBN 0-684-17652-1, ScribT). Scribner.
--Literary Atlas & Gazetteer of the British Isles. LC 73-7185. (Illus.). 208p. 1973. 43.00x (ISBN 0-8103-2004-5). Gale.
--Regency Royal. LC 78-5554. 1978. 9.95 o.p. (ISBN 0-698-10874-4, Coward). Putnam Pub Group.
Hardwick, Michael & Hardwick, Mollie. The Bernard Shaw Companion. LC 73-86599. 193p. 1974. 6.50 o.p. (ISBN 0-312-07665-7). St Martin.
Hardwick, Michael, ed. see Trollope, Anthony.
Hardwick, Mollie. Beauty's Daughter. LC 76-28761. 1977. 8.95 o.p. (ISBN 0-698-10805-1, Coward). Putnam Pub Group.
--Charlie Is My Darling. LC 77-22839. 1977. 8.95 o.p. (ISBN 0-698-10867-1, Coward). Putnam Pub Group.
--I Remember Love. 352p. 1983. 11.95 (ISBN 0-312-40265-1). St Martin.
--Thomas & Sarah. 288p. (Orig.). 1981. pap. 2.50 o.s.i. (ISBN 0-515-06003-8). Jove Pubns.
--Willowood. 322p. 1980. 10.95 o.p. (ISBN 0-312-88207-6). St Martin.
Hardwick, Mollie, jt. auth. see Hardwick, Michael.
Hardwicke, Cedric. A Victorian in Orbit. LC 72-7504. 311p. 1973. Repr. of 1961 ed. lib. bdg. 17.50x (ISBN 0-8371-6516-4, HAVO). Greenwood.
Hardy, Albert V. The British Isles. 2nd ed. (Geography of the British Isles Ser.). (Illus.). 160p. 1981. pap. 8.95 (ISBN 0-521-22258-3). Cambridge U Pr.
Hardy, Anne. Where to Eat in Canada. rev. ed. 1982. pap. 9.95 (ISBN 0-88750-435-3, Pub. by Oberon Pr Canada). Berkshire Traveller.
Hardy, Arthur C., ed. Handbook of Colorimetry. (Illus.). 1936. 45.00x (ISBN 0-262-08001-X). MIT Pr.
Hardy, Arthur E. Beginner's Guide to Coarse (Bait) Fishing. (Illus.). 128p. 1973. 10.00 o.p. (ISBN 0-7207-0585-1). Transatlantic.
Hardy, Barbara. Particularities: Readings in George Eliot. 204p. 1983. text ed. 20.95x (ISBN 0-8214-0741-4, 82-85108); pap. 10.95 (ISBN 0-8214-0742-2, 82-85116). Ohio U Pr.
--Tellers & Listeners: The Narrative Imagination. 279p. 1976. text ed. 36.75x (ISBN 0-485-11153-5, Athlone Pr). Humanities.
Hardy, Barbara, ed. Critical Essays on George Eliot. 282p. 1979. Repr. 22.00 (ISBN 0-7100-6758-5). Routledge & Kegan.
Hardy, C. Colburn. Dun & Bradstreet's Guide to Your Investments: 1983. 28th ed. LC 73-18050. (Illus.). 224p. 1983. write for info. (ISBN 0-06-015098-X, HarpT); pap. 9.57 (ISBN 0-06-091037-2, CN-1037). Har-Row.
--The Investor's Guide to Technical Analysis. (Illus.). 1978. 23.95 o.p. (ISBN 0-07-026365-5, P&RB). McGraw.
--You're Financially Secure Retirement. LC 82-47525. (Illus.). 288p. 1983. 14.37i (ISBN 0-06-015034-3, HarpT). Har-Row.
Hardy, D. Elmo. Insects of Hawaii: Diptera: Cyclorrhapha IV, Vol. 14. LC 48-45482. (Illus.). 500p. (Orig.). 1981. pap. 35.00x (ISBN 0-8248-0647-6). UH Pr.
Hardy, D. Elmo & Delfinado, Mercedes D. Insects of Hawaii, Vol. 13. LC 48-45482. (Illus.). 1980. text ed. 30.00x (ISBN 0-8248-0341-8). UH Pr.
Hardy, D. Elmo, jt. auth. see Delfinado, Mercedes D.
Hardy, D. Elmo, jt. auth. see Zimmerman, Elwood C.
Hardy, Edward R., ed. Christology of the Later Fathers. LC 54-9949. (Library of Christian Classics). 1977. pap. 8.95 (ISBN 0-664-24152-2). Westminster.
Hardy, Evelyn. The Conjured Spirit: Swift. LC 70-136933. (Illus.). 266p. 1973. Repr. of 1949 ed. lib. bdg. 16.00x (ISBN 0-8371-5405-7, HACJ). Greenwood.
Hardy, Frank. Power Without Glory. pap. 3.95x o.p. (ISBN 0-8464-0740-X). Beekman Pubs.
Hardy, G. Gathorne see Gathorne Hardy, G.
Hardy, Gene B. Tolkien's the Lord of the Rings & the Hobbit Notes. (Orig.). 1977. pap. text ed. 2.95 (ISBN 0-8220-1286-3). Cliffs.
Hardy, George. Advance Oil & Gas Taxation. 1982. 48.00 (ISBN 0-89419-242-6). Inst Energy.
--Advanced Louisiana Petroleum Land Operations. 1980. cancelled 58.00 (ISBN 0-89419-088-1). Inst Energy.
--Basic Oil & Gas Taxation. 1982. 50.00 (ISBN 0-89419-240-X). Inst Energy.
--Pooling & Unitization: Rockey Mountain. 1982. 39.00 (ISBN 0-89419-250-7). Inst Energy.
--Regulation of Oil & Gas Profits. 1981. 30.00 (ISBN 0-89419-137-3). Inst Energy.
--Royalties & Division Orders. 1982. 50.00 (ISBN 0-89419-201-9). Inst Energy.
Hardy, George, ed. Pooling & Unitization in Louisiana. 1982. 39.00 (ISBN 0-89419-229-9). Inst Energy.
--Pooling & Utilization in Texas. 1982. 39.00 (ISBN 0-89419-226-4). Inst Energy.
Hardy, George W., ed. Basic Louisiana Mineral Law. 1978. 28.50 o.p. (ISBN 0-685-41834-0); 48.00 o.p. (ISBN 0-89419-186-1). Inst Energy.
Hardy, Gerry & Hardy, Sue. Fifty Hikes in Connecticut: A Guide to Short Walks & Day Hikes Around the Nutmeg State. LC 77-94006. (Fifty Hikes Ser.). (Illus.). 152p. 1982. pap. 8.95 (ISBN 0-942440-05-6). Backcountry Pubns.
Hardy, Godfrey H. The Collected Papers of G. H. Hardy: Theory of Series, Vol. 6. London Mathematical Society Committee, ed. 1974. 82.00x (ISBN 0-19-853340-3). Oxford U Pr.
--Divergent Series. 1949. 55.00x o.p. (ISBN 0-19-853309-8). Oxford U Pr.
--Mathematician's Apology. rev. ed. LC 67-21958. 1969. 19.95 (ISBN 0-521-05207-6); pap. 6.95 (ISBN 0-521-09577-8). Cambridge U Pr.
--Pure Mathematics. 1959. text ed. 65.50 (ISBN 0-521-05203-3); pap. text ed. 19.95 (ISBN 0-521-09227-2). Cambridge U Pr.
--Ramanujan. 3rd ed. LC 59-10268. 1978. 11.95 (ISBN 0-8284-0136-5). Chelsea Pub.
Hardy, Godfrey H., et al. Inequalities. 2nd ed. 1952. 46.00 (ISBN 0-521-05206-8). Cambridge U Pr.
Hardy, Helen H. & Martinez, Raymond J. Louisiana's Fabulous Foods. (Illus.). 80p. 1982. pap. 3.25 (ISBN 0-911116-82-6). Pelican.
Hardy, Henry, ed. see Berlin, Isaiah.
Hardy, Henry R. Mackenzie King of Canada: A Biography. LC 77-135245. (Illus.). xii, 390p. Repr. of 1949 ed. lib. bdg. 19.75x (ISBN 0-8371-5164-3, HAMK). Greenwood.
Hardy, J. P. The Political Writings of Doctor Johnson. 1968. text ed. 7.50x o.p. (ISBN 0-391-02026-9). Humanities.
--Reinterpretations: Essays on Poems by Milton, Pope & Johnson. 1971. 12.50x o.p. (ISBN 0-7100-7103-5). Routledge & Kegan.
Hardy, James. Electronic Communication. 1981. text ed. 18.95 (ISBN 0-8359-1604-9); solutions manual free (ISBN 0-8359-1605-7). Reston.
Hardy, James C. Cerebral Palsy. (Illus.). 288p. 1983. 20.95 (ISBN 0-13-122820-X). P-H.
Hardy, James D. Complications in Surgery & Their Management. 4th ed. (Illus.). 919p. 1981. text ed. 65.00 (ISBN 0-7216-4509-7). Saunders.
Hardy, James D., ed. Critical Surgical Illness. LC 74-108367. (Illus.). 1971. 32.00 o.p. (ISBN 0-7216-4510-0). Saunders.
Hardy, James D., et al. Hardy's Textbook of Surgery. (Illus.). 1400p. 1983. text ed. 49.50 (ISBN 0-397-52108-1, Lippincott Medical); flex. binding 37.50 (ISBN 0-397-50614-7). Lippincott.
Hardy, Jim. High Frequency Circuit Design. (Illus.). 1979. ref. 23.95 (ISBN 0-8359-2824-1). Reston.
Hardy, John E. Katherine Anne Porter. LC 72-79929. (Literature and Life Ser.). 1973. 11.95 (ISBN 0-8044-2351-2). Ungar.
Hardy, Karen. Not Just Another Pretty Face: An Intimate Look at America's Top Male Models. 1984. 11.95 (ISBN 0-452-25395-0, Plume). NAL.
Hardy, Larry, et al. Objective Behavioral Assessment of the Severely & Moderately Mentally Handicapped: The OBA. 136p. 1981. spiral 14.75x (ISBN 0-398-04636-0). C C Thomas.
Hardy, Max. Five Card Majors, Western Style. rev. ed. LC 80-123372. 96p. 1975. pap. 4.95 o.p. (ISBN 0-939460-01-7). M Hardy.
--Five Card Majors: Western Style. 1974. pap. 4.95 o.p. (ISBN 0-686-32134-0). M Hardy.
Hardy, Merrill, jt. auth. see Walsh, Eleanor.
Hardy, Owen B., jt. auth. see Lifton, James.
Hardy, P. Muslims of British India. LC 77-184772. (South Asian Studies: No. 13). (Illus.). 300p. 1973. 44.50 (ISBN 0-521-08488-1); pap. 13.95 (ISBN 0-521-09783-5). Cambridge U Pr.
Hardy, R. Allen. The Jewelry Repair Manual. 2nd ed. 272p. 1982. pap. 6.95 (ISBN 0-442-23680-8). Van Nos Reinhold.
Hardy, R. Allen & Bowman, John J. Jewelry Repair Manual. 2nd ed. (Illus.). 1967. 9.95 o.p. (ISBN 0-442-03130-0). Van Nos Reinhold.
Hardy, R. H. Accidents & Emergencies: A Practical Handbook for Personal Use. 3rd ed. (Illus.). 1981. text ed. 16.95x (ISBN 0-19-261321-9). Oxford U Pr.
Hardy, R. W. A Treatise on Dinitrogen Fixation: Agronomy & Ecology, Sect. 4. 527p. 1977. 59.95x (ISBN 0-471-02343-4, Pub. by Wiley-Interscience). Wiley.
Hardy, R. W. F., et al. A Treatise on Dinitrogen Fixation Sections I & II: Inorganic & Physical Chemistry & Biochemistry. LC 76-15278. 1979. 72.50x (ISBN 0-471-35134-2, Pub. by Wiley-Interscience); Sect. IV. 59.95x (ISBN 0-471-02343-4); Sect III. 69.50 (ISBN 0-471-35138-5). Wiley.
Hardy, Randall W. China's Oil Future: A Case of Modest Expectations. LC 77-27555. (Westview Special Studies on China & East Asia Ser.). 1978. lib. bdg. 24.75x o.p. (ISBN 0-89158-156-1). Westview.
Hardy, Robin. The Education of Don Juan. 1981. pap. 3.50 o.p. (ISBN 0-451-09764-5, E9764, Sig). NAL.
Hardy, Ronald. Rivers of Darkness. LC 78-11788. 1979. 10.95 (ISBN 0-399-12266-4). Putnam Pub Group.
Hardy, Russell W., Jr., ed. Lumbar Disc Disease. (Seminars in Neurological Surgery Ser.). 344p. 1982. text ed. 42.00 (ISBN 0-89004-616-6). Raven.
Hardy, Sally M., illus. The Three Bears. (Cut & Paste Puppet Ser.). 1982. 3.50 (ISBN 0-686-38118-1). Moonlight FL.
Hardy, Shirley. Adventures of Arnold. (gr. k). 1983. 4.95 (ISBN 0-8062-2142-9). Carlton.
Hardy, Sue, jt. auth. see Hardy, Gerry.
Hardy, Thomas. The Bedside Thomas Hardy. Leeson, Edward, ed. 1979. 15.00 o.p. (ISBN 0-312-07131-0). St Martin.
--The Complete Poetical Works of Thomas Hardy, Vol. I: Wessex Poems, Poems of the Past & Present, Time's Laughingstocks. Hynes, Samuel, ed. (English Texts Ser.). (Illus.). 1982. 39.50x (ISBN 0-19-812708-1). Oxford U Pr.
--Far from the Madding Crowd. 1895. 12.45i (ISBN 0-06-011755-9, HarpT). Har-Row.
--Far from the Madding Crowd. pap. 2.75 (ISBN 0-451-51660-5, CE1660, Sig Classics). NAL.
--Jude the Obscure. Southerington, F. R., ed. LC 76-140800. (Library of Literature Ser: No. 35). 1972. pap. 9.95 (ISBN 0-672-61022-1, LL35). Bobbs.
--Jude the Obscure. Slack, Robert C., ed. LC 67-18704. 1927. 6.95 (ISBN 0-394-60462-8). Modern Lib.
--Jude the Obscure. pap. 2.95 (ISBN 0-451-51783-0, CE1783, Sig Classics). NAL.
--A Laodicean. LC 77-81876. (Hardy New Wessex Editions Ser.). 1978. pap. 3.95 (ISBN 0-312-46936-5). St Martin.
--Letters. Weber, Carl J., ed. Repr. of 1954 ed. 10.00 o.s.i. (ISBN 0-527-37850-X). Kraus Repr.
--The Mayor of Casterbridge. (Bantam Classics Ser.). 326p. (gr. 9-12). 1981. pap. 1.95 (ISBN 0-553-21024-6). Bantam.
--Mayor of Casterbridge. LC 77-70264. (The Hardy New Wessex Editions). 1977. pap. 2.95 (ISBN 0-312-52326-2). St Martin.
--The Portable Thomas Hardy. Moynahan, Julian, ed. (Viking Portable Library). 1977. pap. 6.95 (ISBN 0-14-015082-X). Penguin.
--The Return of the Native. (Bantam Classics Ser.). 371p. (gr. 9-12). 1981. pap. 1.95 (ISBN 0-686-82862-3). Bantam.
--The Return of the Native. 414p. 1973. pap. 1.95 (ISBN 0-451-51796-2, CJ1796, Sig Classics). NAL.
--Return of the Native. Gindin, James, ed. (Critical Ed. Ser). 1969. 7.00 o.s.i. (ISBN 0-393-04300-2); pap. 7.95x (ISBN 0-393-09791-9). Norton.
--The Return of the Native. (English Library Ser). 1978. pap. 2.95 o.p. (ISBN 0-14-043122-5). Penguin.
--Return of the Native. (Enriched Classic Ser.). 528p. (gr. 9 up). pap. 1.75 o.s.i. (ISBN 0-671-48917-8). WSP.
--Tess of the D'Urbervilles. (Bantam Classics Ser.). 414p. (gr. 9-12). 1981. pap. 2.75 (ISBN 0-553-21061-0). Bantam.
--Tess of the D'Urbervilles. (Movie tie-in ed.). 1981. pap. 2.50 (ISBN 0-451-51686-9, CE1686, Sig Classics). NAL.
--Tess of the D'Urbervilles. Grindle, Juliet & Gatrell, Simon, eds. 1982. 89.00x (ISBN 0-19-812495-3). Oxford U Pr.
--Tess of the D'Urbervilles. 6.95 (ISBN 0-686-38448-2). Modern Lib.
--Two on a Tower. LC 77-70263. (The Hardy New Wessex Editions). 1977. pap. 3.95 (ISBN 0-312-82742-3). St Martin.
--Two Wessex Tales. Incl. Withered Arm; Three Strangers. Aiken, Conrad, frwd. by.. pap. 2.50 (ISBN 0-8283-1461-6, IPL). Branden.
Hardy, Thomas see Eyre, A. G.
Hardy, Tom. Closet Shots. 256p. 1983. 12.95 (ISBN 0-89696-164-8, An Everest House Book). Dodd.
Hardy, W. Carey, jt. auth. see Merklein, Helmut A.
Hardy, W. G. The Greek & Roman World. rev. ed. (Illus.). 128p. 1970. pap. 6.95 (ISBN 0-87073-111-4). Schenkman.
Hardy, Willene S. Mary McCarthy. LC 81-40462. (Literature and Life Ser.). 223p. 1981. 14.50 (ISBN 0-8044-2350-4). Ungar.
Hare, jt. auth. see Kut.
Hare, A. Paul, jt. auth. see Blumberg, Herbert H.
Hare, Cyril. An English Murder. 1978. pap. 2.50i (ISBN 0-06-080455-6, P 455, PL). Har-Row.
--Suicide Expected. LC 82-48244. 256p. 1983. pap. 2.84i (ISBN 0-06-080636-2, P 636, PL). Har-Row.
Hare, David. Fanshen. 86p. 1976. pap. 6.95 (ISBN 0-571-11019-3). Faber & Faber.
--A Map of the World. 84p. 1983. pap. 7.95 (ISBN 0-571-11996-4). Faber & Faber.
Hare, F., jt. ed. see Bryson, R. A.
Hare, F. K. & Thomas, M. K. Climate Canada. 2nd ed. 296p. 1980. 24.50 (ISBN 0-471-08326-7). Wiley.
Hare, F. Kenneth. The Experiments of Life: Science & Religion. 192p. 1983. 25.00x (ISBN 0-8020-2486-6); pap. 7.95 (ISBN 0-8020-6506-6). U of Toronto Pr.
Hare, Francis H., Jr. & Ricci, Edward M., eds. The Anatomy of a Personal Injury Lawsuit. 2nd ed. LC 81-70743. (Illus.). 508p. 1981. pap. 35.00 (ISBN 0-941916-00-6). Assn Trial Ed.
Hare, Lorraine. Who Needs Her? LC 82-13899. (Illus.). 32p. (gr. 2-5). 1983. 9.95 (ISBN 0-689-50268-0, McElderry Bk). Atheneum.
Hare, Norma Q. Mystery at Mouse House. LC 79-28254. (Mystery Ser.). 48p. (gr. k-3). 1980. PLB 6.79 (ISBN 0-8116-6412-0). Garrard.
--Who Is Root Beer? LC 76-16015. (Imagination Ser.). (Illus.). (gr. 1). 1977. lib. bdg. 6.69 (ISBN 0-8116-4400-6). Garrard.
--Wish upon a Birthday. LC 79-14596. (Imagination Ser.). (Illus.). (gr. 1-5). 1979. PLB 6.69 (ISBN 0-8116-4418-9). Garrard.
Hare, P. E., et al. Biogeochemistry of Amino Acids. LC 79-25824. 1980. 84.50 (ISBN 0-471-05493-3, Pub. by Wiley-Interscience). Wiley.
Hare, Paul, jt. auth. see Cave, Martin.
Hare, R. M. Applications of Moral Philosophy. LC 74-187323. (New Studies in Practical Philosophy). 130p. 1972. 13.95x (ISBN 0-520-02232-7). U of Cal Pr.

--Essays on the Moral Concepts. LC 70-187322. (New Studies in Practical Philosophy). 150p. 1972. 15.95x (ISBN 0-520-02231-9). U of Cal Pr.
--Plato. (Past Masters Ser.). 96p. 1982. 13.95 (ISBN 0-19-287586-8). Oxford U Pr.
--Plato. Thomas, Keith, ed. (Past Masters Ser.). 96p. 1983. pap. 3.95 (ISBN 0-19-287585-X, GB). Oxford U Pr.
Hare, Robert D. Psychopathy: Theory & Research. LC 79-120704. (Foundations of Abnormal Psychology Ser). 1970. pap. text ed. 16.30 (ISBN 0-471-35147-4). Wiley.
Hare, William. Open-Mindedness & Education. 1979. pap. 14.95 (ISBN 0-7735-0411-7). McGill-Queens U Pr.
Hare, William S., jt. auth. see Minns, Johnny.
Harel, ed. At Risk Infant: Proceedings of the International Workshop on the At Risk Infant, Tel Aviv, July 1979. (International Conference Ser.: No. 492). 1980. 87.25 (ISBN 0-444-90120-5). Elsevier.
Harel, M. M. Voltaire. Repr. of 1781 ed. 49.00 o.p. (ISBN 0-8287-0414-7). Clearwater Pub.
Har-El, Menashe & Zeevy, Rechavam. This Is Jerusalem. 2nd ed. (The Har-El Ser.). (Illus.). 1982. text ed. 16.00 (ISBN 0-86628-041-3). Ridgefield Pub.
Harell, Moshe, jt. auth. see Rahamimoff, P.
Hare-Mustin, Rachel, jt. ed. see Brodsky, Annette M.
Harer, Katharine. In These Bodies. 40p. (Orig.). 1982. pap. write for info. (ISBN 0-939952-00-9). Moving Parts.
Haresign, ed. Sheep Breeding. 2nd ed. LC 78-41188. (Studies in the Agricultural & Food Sciences Ser.). 1979. text ed. 89.95 (ISBN 0-408-10633-6). Butterworth.
Haresign, W., ed. Recent Advances in Animal Nutrition - 1980. LC 80-41606. (Studies in the Agricultural & Food Sciences). (Illus.). 256p. 1981. text ed. 44.95 (ISBN 0-408-71013-6). Butterworth.
Hareven, Tamara. Eleanor Roosevelt: An American Conscience. LC 74-26539. (FDR & the Era of the New Deal Ser). (Illus.). xx, 326p. 1975. Repr. of 1968 ed. lib. bdg. 39.50 (ISBN 0-306-70705-5). Da Capo.
Hareven, Tamara K. & Adams, Kathleen J., eds. Aging & Life Course Transitions: An Interdisciplinary Perspective. LC 82-989. (Adult Development & Aging Ser.). 281p. 1982. text ed. 24.50 (ISBN 0-89862-125-9). Guilford Pr.
Harfax. The Harfax Directory of Industry Data Sources: The United States of America & Canada, 3 vols. 2nd ed. 2256p. 1982. Set. ref 225.00x (ISBN 0-88410-883-X). Ballinger Pub.
--Harfax Directory of Industry Data Sources: Western Europe. 400p. 1983. ref 125.00x (ISBN 0-88410-918-6). Ballinger Pub.
--Harfax Guide to the Energy Industry. 360p. 1983. ref 45.00x (ISBN 0-88410-919-4). Ballinger Pub.
--Harfax Guide to the High Tech Industries. 344p. 1983. ref 65.00x (ISBN 0-88410-619-5). Ballinger Pub.
Harfield, H. Bank Credits & Acceptances. 5th ed. (Illus.). 363p. 1974. 32.95 (ISBN 0-471-06564-1, Pub. by Wiley-Interscience). Wiley.
Harford, John S. The Life of Michael Angelo Buonarroti: With Tranlations of Many of His Poems & Letters, also Memoirs of Savonarola, Raphael, & Vittoria Colonna, 2 vols. 415p. 1982. Repr. of 1858 ed. lib. bdg. 200.00 set (ISBN 0-89984-702-1). Century Bookbindery.
Hargeaves, Roger. Mr. Greedy. (Mr. Books). 1980. 1.00 (ISBN 0-8431-0817-7). Price Stern.
Hargens, Alan R. Tissue Fluid Pressure & Composition. (Illus.). 282p. 1981. lib. bdg. 37.00 o.p. (ISBN 0-683-03891-5). Williams & Wilkins.
Hargittai, I. & Orville-Thomas, W. F. Diffraction Studies in Non-Crystalline Substances. (Studies in Physical & Theoretical Chemistry: Vol. 13). 1982. 106.50 (ISBN 0-444-99752-0). Elsevier.
Hargittai, I., jt. auth. see Hargittai, M.
Hargittai, M. & Hargittai, I. The Molecular Geometries of Coordination Compounds in the Vapour Phase. 1977. 49.00 (ISBN 0-444-99832-2). Elsevier.
Hargrave, Basil. Origins & Meanings of Popular Phrases & Names. LC 68-23164. 1968. Repr. of 1925 ed. 40.00x (ISBN 0-8103-3089-X). Gale.
Hargrave, Madelyn. Nutritional Care of the Physically Disabled. 50p. 1979. 18.00 (ISBN 0-686-95727-X, 719). Sis Kenny Inst.
Hargreaves, David H., et al. Deviance in Classrooms. 280p. 1975. 22.50x (ISBN 0-7100-8275-4); pap. 8.95 (ISBN 0-7100-8490-0). Routledge & Kegan.
Hargreaves, J. Aberdenshire to Africa: Northeast Scots & British Overseas Expansion. (Illus.). 1982. 17.00 (ISBN 0-08-025764-X); pap. 9.00 (ISBN 0-08-028459-0). Pergamon.
--Good Communications: What Every Good Manager Should Know. LC 76-40317. 116p. 1977. 21.95x o.s.i. (ISBN 0-470-98958-0). Halsted Pr.
Hargreaves, J. D. Prelude to the Partition of West Africa. (International Economics Assn. Ser). (Illus.). 1963. 19.95 o.p. (ISBN 0-312-63910-4). St Martin.
Hargreaves, Jennifer, ed. Sport, Culture & Ideology. 200p. (Orig.). 1983. pap. 15.95 (ISBN 0-7100-9242-3). Routledge & Kegan.
Hargreaves, John. A Guide to St Mark's Gospel. 1978. pap. 6.95 o.p. (ISBN 0-8170-0765-2). Judson.
Hargreaves, Joyce. Techniques of Hand Print-Making. LC 82-74212. (Illus.). 128p. 1983. 12.95 (ISBN 0-8008-7555-9, Pentalic). Taplinger.
Hargreaves, Mary W., ed. see Clay, Henry, II.
Hargreaves, P. H., ed. see Quinlan, P. M. & Compton, W. V.
Hargreaves, Pat. The Antarctic. LC 80-52510. (Seas & Oceans Ser.). 13.00 (ISBN 0-382-06467-4). Silver.
--The Arctic. LC 81-50488. (Seas & Oceans Ser.). 13.00 (ISBN 0-382-06583-2). Silver.
--The Atlantic. LC 80-52511. (Seas & Oceans Ser.). 13.00 (ISBN 0-382-06466-6). Silver.
--The Caribbean & the Gulf of Mexico. LC 80-52508. (Seas & Oceans Ser.). 13.00 (ISBN 0-382-06469-0). Silver.
--The Indian Ocean. LC 81-50490. (Seas & Oceans Ser.). 13.00 (ISBN 0-382-06582-4). Silver.
--The Mediterranean. LC 80-52509. (Seas & Oceans Ser.). 13.00 (ISBN 0-382-06468-2). Silver.
--The Pacific. LC 81-50489. (Seas & Oceans Ser.). 13.00 (ISBN 0-382-06581-6). Silver.
--The Red Sea & the Persian Gulf. LC 81-50491. (Seas & Oceans Ser.). 13.00 (ISBN 0-382-06584-0). Silver.
Hargreaves, Reginald, jt. auth. see Melville, Lewis.
Hargreaves, Reginald, jt. ed. see Melville, Lewis.
Hargreaves, Roger. Albert the Alphabetical Elephant. LC 81-84548. (Illus.). 32p. (ps-1). 1982. 3.95 (ISBN 0-448-12319-3, G&D). Putnam Pub Group.
--Count Worm. LC 81-84547. (Illus.). 32p. (ps-1). 1982. 3.95 (ISBN 0-448-12318-5, G&D). Putnam Pub Group.
--Grandfather Clock. LC 81-84549. (Illus.). 32p. (ps-1). 1982. 3.95 (ISBN 0-448-12320-7, G&D). Putnam Pub Group.
--Hippo Leaves Home. LC 81-84546. (Illus.). 32p. (ps-1). 1982. 3.95 (ISBN 0-448-12317-7, G&D). Putnam Pub Group.
--Hippo, Potto & Mouse. LC 81-84544. (Illus.). 32p. (ps-1). 1982. 3.95 (ISBN 0-448-12315-0, G&D). Putnam Pub Group.
--Mr. Bounce. (Mr. Books). 1980. 1.00 (ISBN 0-8431-0809-6). Price Stern.
--Mr. Bump. (Mr. Books). 1980. 1.00 (ISBN 0-8431-0814-2). Price Stern.
--Mr. Chatterbox. (Mr. Books). 1980. 1.00 (ISBN 0-8431-0808-8). Price Stern.
--Mr. Forgetful. (Mr. Books). 1980. 1.00 (ISBN 0-8431-0805-3). Price Stern.
--Mr. Fussy. (Mr. Books). 1980. 1.00 (ISBN 0-8431-0807-X). Price Stern.
--Mr. Grumpy. (Mr. Books). 1980. 1.00 (ISBN 0-8431-0804-5). Price Stern.
--Mr. Happy. (Mr. Books). 1980. 1.00 (ISBN 0-8431-0813-4). Price Stern.
--Mr. Lazy. (Mr. Books). 1980. 1.00 (ISBN 0-8431-0806-1). Price Stern.
--Mr. Men Picture Dictionary. (Mr. Men Bks.). (Illus.). 256p. (ps-1). Date not set. pap. 7.95 (ISBN 0-8431-1300-6). Price Stern. Postponed.
--Mr. Messy. (Mr. Books). 1980. 1.00 (ISBN 0-8431-0812-6). Price Stern.
--Mr. Mischief. (Mr. Books). 1980. 1.00 (ISBN 0-8431-0802-9). Price Stern.
--Mr. Noisey. (Mr. Books). 1980. 1.00 (ISBN 0-8431-0810-X). Price Stern.
--Mr. Nosey. (Mr. Books). 1980. 1.00 (ISBN 0-8431-0816-9). Price Stern.
--Mr. Quiet. (Mr. Books). 1980. 1.00 (ISBN 0-8431-0803-7). Price Stern.
--Mr. Silly. (Mr. Books). 1980. 1.00 (ISBN 0-8431-0811-8). Price Stern.
--Mr. Worry. (Mr. Books). 1980. 1.00 (ISBN 0-8431-0800-2). Price Stern.
--Mouse Gets Caught. LC 81-84545. (Illus.). 32p. (ps-1). 1982. 3.95 (ISBN 0-448-12316-9, G&D). Putnam Pub Group.
Hargreaves, William A., jt. auth. see Glick, Ira D.
Hargrove, Barbara J., jt. auth. see Carroll, Jackson W.
Hargrove, Erwin C. The Power of the Modern Presidency. 365p. 1975. 24.95 (ISBN 0-87722-039-5). Temple U Pr.
--Presidential Leadership: Personality & Political Style. (Orig.). 1966. pap. text ed. 7.95x (ISBN 0-02-350190-1, 35019). Macmillan.
Hargrove, Jim. Mountain Climbing. LC 82-21690. (Superwheels & Thrill Sports Bks.). (Illus.). (gr. 4 up). 1983. PLB 7.95g (ISBN 0-8225-0505-3). Lerner Pubns.
Hargrove, Penny & Liebrenz, Noelle. Backpackers' Sourcebook. Winnett, Thomas, ed. LC 82-50739. 128p. 1983. pap. 2.95 (ISBN 0-89997-025-7). Wilderness Pr.
Hargrove, Richard J. General John Burgoyne. LC 80-54788. (Illus.). 296p. 1982. 28.50 (ISBN 0-87413-200-2). U Delaware Pr.
Harhszti-Takacs, M. The Masters of Mannerism. 15.00 (ISBN 0-912728-99-X). Newbury Bks.
Hari, Anna M. An Investigation of the Tones of Lhasa Tibetan. (Language Data Asia-Pacific Ser.: No. 13). 232p. (Orig.). pap. 7.50 (ISBN 0-88312-213-8); micro fiche 3.00 (ISBN 0-88312-313-4). Summer Inst Ling.
Hari, Anna M., ed. Conversational Nepali. 1971. 10.00 o.p. (ISBN 0-88312-743-1); pap. 8.00 o.p. (ISBN 0-685-48683-4); microfiche 6.00x (ISBN 0-88312-573-0). Summer Inst Ling.
Harian. Bargain Paradises of the World. 4.95 (ISBN 0-448-06955-5, G&D). Putnam Pub Group.
--Investing for a Sound Six Percent & More. 3.50 o.p. (ISBN 0-448-06962-8, G&D). Putnam Pub Group.
Hari Dass, Baba. A Child's Garden of Yoga. Ault, Karuna, ed. LC 80-80299. (Illus.). 108p. (ps-7). 1980. pap. 6.95 (ISBN 0-918100-02-X). Sri Rama.
Haried, Andrew A., et al. Advanced Accounting. 2nd ed. 912p. 1982. text ed. 29.95 (ISBN 0-471-08717-3); cancelled tests (ISBN 0-471-05874-2); study guide avail. (ISBN 0-471-09235-5); tchrs. manual avail. (ISBN 0-471-86340-8); wkg. papers avail. (ISBN 0-471-86339-4); checklist avail. (ISBN 0-471-86553-2). Wiley.
Hariharan, H., jt. auth. see Kuppuswamy, Gowri.
Hariman, Jusuf. The Therapeutic Efficacy of the Major Psychotherapeutic Techniques. (Illus.). 344p. 1983. 29.50x (ISBN 0-398-04771-5). C C Thomas.
Haring, Clarence H. The Spanish Empire in America. LC 47-1142. 1963. pap. 4.95 (ISBN 0-15-684701-9, Harv). HarBraceJ.
Haring, Donald R. Sequential-Circuit Synthesis: State Assignment Aspects. (Press Research Monographs: No. 31). 1966. 21.00x o.s.i. (ISBN 0-262-08024-9). MIT Pr.
Haring, Elda. Begonias for Beginners. 1977. 7.95 o.p. (ISBN 0-916302-17-2); pap. 4.95 o.p. (ISBN 0-916302-08-3). Bookworm NY.
Haring, J. Vreeland. Hand of Hauptmann: The Handwriting Expert Tells the Story of the Lindbergh Case. (Illus.). 1937. 10.00x (ISBN 0-87585-702-7). Patterson Smith.
Haring, Joseph E. & Humphrey, Joseph F., eds. Utility Regulation During Inflation. LC 77-22837. 1971. pap. 3.85x o.p. (ISBN 0-686-02420-6). Econ Res Ctr.
Haring, Lloyd & Lounsbury, John F. Introduction to Scientific Geographic Research. 2nd ed. 144p. 1975. pap. text ed. write for info. o.p. (ISBN 0-697-05255-9). Wm C Brown.
Haring, Norris & Bateman, Barbara. Teaching the Learning Disabled Child. LC 76-15965. (P-H Series in Education). (Illus.). 1977. 24.95 (ISBN 0-13-893503-3). P-H.
Haring, Norris G. Exceptional Children & Youth. 3rd ed. 480p. 1982. pap. text ed. 22.95 (ISBN 0-675-09889-0). Additional Supplements May Be Obtained From Publisher. Merrill.
Haring, Norris G. & Phillips, E. L. Teaching Special Children. (Special Education Ser). 1976. text ed. 26.00 (ISBN 0-07-026430-9, C). McGraw.
Haring, Norris G., jt. auth. see White, Owen R.
Haring, Norris G., ed. Behavior of Exceptional Children: An Introduction to Special Education. 2nd ed. 1978. text ed. 20.95 (ISBN 0-675-08398-2). Additional supplements may be obtained from publisher. Merrill.
Haring, Norris G. & Brown, Louis J., eds. Teaching the Severely Handicapped, 2 vols. LC 76-25992. (Illus.). Vol. 1, 1976 320pps. 29.50 (ISBN 0-8089-0945-2); Vol. 2, 1977 224pps. 33.50 (ISBN 0-8089-0980-0); Set. 58.00 o.p. (ISBN 0-686-86006-3). Grune.
Haring, Norris G. & Hayden, Alice H., eds. Improvement of Instruction. LC 75-170091. (Orig.). 1972. pap. 9.00x o.p. (ISBN 0-87562-032-9). Spec Child.
Haring, Norris G., et al. The Fourth R: Research in the Classroom. 1978. 18.95 (ISBN 0-675-08387-7). Merrill.
Harish, Yvonne. Patient Care Guides: Practical Information for Public Health Nurses. (League Exchange Ser.: No. 111). 354p. 1976. 12.95 (ISBN 0-686-38189-0, 21-1610). Natl League Nurse.
Harjunpaa, T. Christians of Vision & Venture. 1971. pap. 3.50 o.p. (ISBN 0-02-802880-5). Glencoe.
Hark, Ina R. Edward Lear. (English Authors Ser.). 1982. lib. bdg. 12.95 (ISBN 0-8057-6822-X, Twayne). G K Hall.
Harkabi, Yehoshafat. The Bar Kokhba Syndrome: Risk & Realism in International Relations. Ticktin, Max, tr. from Hebrew. (Incl. additions & enandations to the original Hebrew). 1982. 15.95 (ISBN 0-940646-01-3). Rossel Bks.
Harkavey, Robert & Kolodziej, Edward, eds. American Security Policy & Policy-Making. LC 77-14868. (A Policy Studies Organization Book). (Illus.). 288p. 1980. 27.95x (ISBN 0-669-01998-4). Lexington Bks.
Harkavy, Robert & Kolodziej, Edward. Security Policy: Dilemmas of Using & Controlling Military Power. 1979. pap. 6.00 (ISBN 0-918592-34-8). Policy Studies.
Harkavy, Robert E. Great Power Competition for Overseas Bases. (Pergamon Policy Studies On Security Affairs Ser.). 360p. 1982. 34.50 (ISBN 0-08-025089-0, T130). Pergamon.
Harker, A. Metamorphism: A Study of the Transformation of Rock Masses. LC 74-11728. (Illus.). 362p. 1974. 20.00x (ISBN 0-412-12940-X, Pub. by Chapman & Hall England). Methuen Inc.
Harker, Herbert. Goldenrod. pap. 1.95 o.p. (ISBN 0-451-08557-4, J8557, Sig). NAL.
--Goldenrod. 1972. 6.95 o.s.i. (ISBN 0-394-47890-8). Random.
Harker, J. H., jt. auth. see Backhurst, J. R.
Harker, Laurence A., jt. auth. see Thompson, Arthur R.
Harker, Ralph J. Generalized Methods of Vibration Analysis. 480p. 1983. 44.95 (ISBN 0-471-86735-7, Pub. by Wiley Interscience). Wiley.
Harkess, Shirley, jt. ed. see Stromberg, Ann H.
Harkins, C. & Plung, D. L., eds. A Guide to Writing Better Technical Papers. LC 81-20042. 1981. 22.95 (ISBN 0-87942-157-6). Inst Electrical.
Harkins, Conrad L., ed. Franciscan Studies. (Annual review). 14.00 (ISBN 0-686-12038-8). Franciscan Inst.
Harkins, Craig & Plung, Daniel L. A Guide for Writing Better Technical Papers. LC 8-20042. 219p. 1982. 22.95x (ISBN 0-471-86865-5, Pub. by Wiley-Interscience); pap. 15.00x (ISBN 0-471-86866-3). Wiley.
Harkins, Dorothy, jt. auth. see Wakefield, Frances.
Harkins, Harry L. Basketball's Pro-Set Playbook: The Complete Offensive Arsenal. LC 82-3487. 188p. 1982. 14.95 (ISBN 0-13-056366-8, Parker). P-H.
Harkins, Philip. The Day of the Drag Race. (gr. 7 up). 1960. 8.95 (ISBN 0-688-21223-9). Morrow.
Harkness, David J. & McMurtry, R. Gerald. Lincoln's Favorite Poets. LC 59-9718. 1959. 8.50x (ISBN 0-87049-026-5). U of Tenn Pr.
Harkness, E. L. & Mehta, M. L. Solar Radiation Control in Buildings. (Illus.). 1978. text ed. 63.75x (ISBN 0-85334-764-6, Pub. by Applied Sci England). Elsevier.
Harkness, Georgia E. The Modern Rival of Christian Faith: An Analysis of Secularism. LC 77-27000. 1978. Repr. of 1952 ed. lib. bdg. 20.25x (ISBN 0-313-20174-9, HAMR). Greenwood.
Harkness, James, tr. see Foucault, Michel.
Harkness, John E. & Wagner, Joseph E. The Biology & Medicine of Rabbits & Rodents. 2nd ed. LC 82-13050. (Illus.). 250p. 1983. pap. write for info (ISBN 0-8121-0849-3). Lea & Febiger.
Harkness, Judith. Lady Charlotte's Rune. 1982. pap. 2.25 (ISBN 0-451-11738-7, AE1738, Sig). NAL.
Harkness, Kenneth, jt. auth. see Chernev, Irving.
Harkness, Marjory G., ed. see Lubbock, Percy.
Harkness, R. OTC Handbook: What to Recommend & Why. 2nd ed. 1983. 12.95 (ISBN 0-87489-303-8). Med Economics.
Harkness, S. D., jt. ed. see Peterson, N. L.
Harkonen, Helen B. Circuses & Fairs in Art. LC 64-8205. (Fine Art Books). (Illus.). (gr. 5-11). 1965. PLB 4.95g (ISBN 0-8225-0156-2). Lerner Pubns.
--Farms & Farmers in Art. LC 64-8204. (Fine Art Books). (Illus.). (gr. 5-11). 1965. PLB 4.95g (ISBN 0-8225-0152-X). Lerner Pubns.
Harlan. Science Experiences for the Early Childhood Years. 2nd ed. (Early Childhood Education Ser.: No. C24). 256p. 1980. pap. text ed. 13.95 (ISBN 0-675-08155-6). Merrill.
Harlan, Calvin. Vision & Invention: A Course in Art Fundamentals. 1969. ref. ed. 22.95 (ISBN 0-13-942243-9). P-H.
Harlan, Elizabeth. Footfalls. LC 86-6727. 144p. 1982. 9.95 (ISBN 0-689-50255-9, McElderry Bk). Atheneum.
Harlan, James K. Starting With Synfuels: Benefits, Costs & Program Design Assessments. 376p. 1982. prof ref 35.00x (ISBN 0-88410-869-4). Ballinger Pub.
Harlan, Jean D. Science Experiences for the Early Childhood Years. new ed. (Elementary Education Ser.). 240p. 1976. pap. text ed. 12.95x (ISBN 0-675-08649-3). Merrill.
Harlan, John C. Zwingo in the Twenty-Third Century. (Illus.). 64p. 1983. 5.95 (ISBN 0-89962-296-8). Todd & Honeywell.
Harlan, John M. The Evolution of a Judicial Philosophy: Selected Opinions & Papers of Justice John M. Harlan. Shapiro, David L., ed. 331p. 1969. text ed. 15.00x (ISBN 0-674-27125-4). Harvard U Pr.
Harlan, Louis R. Booker T. Washington: The Making of a Black Leader, 1856-1901. 1972. 22.50x (ISBN 0-19-501596-7). Oxford U Pr.
--Booker T. Washington: The Making of a Black Leader, 1856-1901. LC 72-77499. (Illus.). 1975. pap. 7.95 (ISBN 0-19-501915-6, GB428, GB). Oxford U Pr.
--Booker T. Washington: The Wizard of Tuskegee, 1901-1915. (Illus.). 540p. 1983. 24.95 (ISBN 0-19-503202-0). Oxford U Pr.
Harlan, N. E. Management Control in Airframe Subcontracting. 1956. 21.00 (ISBN 0-08-018741-2). Pergamon.
Harland, Marion. Romantic Colonial Homesteads & Their Stories of Strange Intrigue. (An American Culture Library Bk.). (Illus.). 128p. 1983. Repr. of 1897 ed. 78.45 (ISBN 0-89901-096-2). Found Class Reprints.
Harland, O. H. Some Implications of Social Psychology. 104p. 1982. Repr. of 1928 ed. lib. bdg. 30.00 (ISBN 0-89987-392-8). Darby Bks.
Harle, J. C., jt. auth. see Digby, S.
Harle, Vilho, ed. Political Economy of Food. 346p. 1978. text ed. 35.00x (ISBN 0-566-00206-X). Gower Pub Ltd.
Harlen, Wynne, jt. auth. see Ennever, Len.
Harless, Dan. Discoveries. 1982. pap. 4.95 (ISBN 0-89225-207-3). Gospel Advocate.
Harless, Marjorie, ed. see Forrest, Lewis C., Jr.

Harley. Artists Pigments. 2nd ed. 1982. text ed. 49.95 (ISBN 0-408-70945-6). Butterworth.

Harley, J. L. & Smith, S. E., eds. Mycorrhizal Symbiosis. write for info. (ISBN 0-12-325560-0). Acad Pr.

Harley, John B., et al, eds. Hematology Case Studies. 1973. pap. 17.00 (ISBN 0-87488-020-3). Med Exam.

Harley, John E. World-Wide Influences of the Cinema: A Study of Official Censorship & the International Cultural Aspects of Motion Pictures. LC 77-160234. (Moving Pictures Ser). xvi, 320p. 1971. Repr. of 1940 ed. lib. bdg. 19.95x (ISBN 0-89198-035-0). Ozer.

Harley, R. Artist's Pigments Circa, Sixteen Hundred to Eighteen Thirty-Five. 1970. 12.50 (ISBN 0-444-19652-8). Elsevier.

Harley, R. G., jt. auth. see Adkins, B.

Harloe, Michael. Swindon: A Town in Transition, a Study in Urban Development & Overspill Policy. 1975. text ed. 27.50x o.p. (ISBN 0-435-85300-7). Heinemann Ed.

Harloe, Michael, ed. New Perspectives in Urban Change & Conflict. vi, 265p. 1982. text ed. 30.00x (ISBN 0-435-82404-X). Heinemann Ed.

Harlow, Barbara, tr. see Derrida, Jacques.

Harlow, Clarissa & Bedford, Mary A. The Princess Diana Paper Doll Book of Fashion. (Illus.). 40p. 1982. pap. 4.95 (ISBN 0-399-50645-4, Perige); pap. 59.40 12-copy counterpack (ISBN 0-399-50646-2). Putnam Pub Group.

Harlow, Dorothy N. & Hanke, Jean J. Situational Administration. LC 81-40339. Orig. Title: Behavior in Organizations. (Illus.). 674p. 1981. lib. bdg. 36.50 (ISBN 0-8191-1837-0); pap. text ed. 24.25 (ISBN 0-8191-1838-9). U Pr of Amer.

Harlow, Enid. Crashing. 1980. 9.95 o.p. (ISBN 0-312-17099-8). St Martin.

Harlow, Jay, jt. auth. see Cronin, Isaac.

Harlow, Joan. The Shadow Bear. LC 80-7507. (Illus.). 32p. (gr. 3). 1981. 7.95a o.p. (ISBN 0-385-15066-0); PLB 7.95a (ISBN 0-385-15067-9). Doubleday.

Harlow, Neal. California Conquered: War & Peace on the Pacific, 1846-1850. LC 81-7588. (Illus.). 544p. 1982. 25.00 (ISBN 0-520-04430-4). U of Cal Pr.

Harlow, Nora, jt. ed. see Montilla, M. Robert.

Harlow, Nora, jt. ed. see Wenk, Ernst.

Harlow, Richard R., jt. auth. see Beasley, Maurine H.

Harlow, William M. Textbook of Dendrology. 6th ed. (Illus.). 1979. text ed. 33.00 (ISBN 0-07-026570-4, C). McGraw.

Harlowe, Justine. Memory & Desire. 432p. 1982. pap. 15.50 (ISBN 0-446-51246-X). Warner Bks.

Harm, Walter. Biological Effects of Ultraviolet Radiation. LC 77-88677. (IUPAB Biophysics Ser.: No. 1). (Illus.). 1980. 39.50 (ISBN 0-521-22121-8); pap. 13.95 (ISBN 0-521-29362-6). Cambridge U Pr.

Harman, Alec. Medieval & Early Renaissance Music. LC 70-75742. (Man & His Music Ser.: Vol. 1). 1969. pap. 4.95 (ISBN 0-8052-0261-7). Schocken.

Harman, Alec, ed. Popular Italian Madrigals of the Sixteenth Century. 1977. pap. 11.95x (ISBN 0-19-343646-9). Oxford U Pr.

Harman, Bob & Monroe, Keith. Use Your Head in Tennis. rev. 2nd ed. LC 74-10715. 256p. 1975. 12.45i (ISBN 0-690-00584-9). T Y Crowell.

Harman, Claire, ed. see Warner, Sylvia T.

Harman, D. D. Natives in Exile & Other Stories. (Illus.). 160p. (Orig.). Date not set. pap. 0.00 cancelled (ISBN 0-88496-156-7). Capra Pr.

Harman, Donna. Back to Basics. (gr. k-6). 1981. 9.95 (ISBN 0-86653-000-2, GA277). Good Apple.

Harman, Elizabeth J. & Head, Brian W., eds. State Capital & Resources in the North & West of Australia. (Illus.). 388p. 1982. pap. text ed. 18.00 (ISBN 0-686-83952-8, Pub. by U of W Austral Pr). Intl Schol Bk Serv.

Harman, Gilbert. The Nature of Morality: An Introduction to Ethics. 1977. text ed. 9.95x o.p. (ISBN 0-19-502142-8); pap. text ed. 7.95x (ISBN 0-19-502143-6). Oxford U Pr.

Harman, Ian & Vriends, Matthew M. All About Finches. (Illus.). 1978. 14.95 (ISBN 0-87666-965-8, PS-765). TFH Pubns.

Harman, John D., ed. Volunteerism in the Eighties: Fundamental Issues in Voluntary Action. LC 81-40622. (Illus.). 292p. (Orig.). 1982. lib. bdg. 24.00 (ISBN 0-8191-2398-6); pap. text ed. 11.50 (ISBN 0-8191-2399-4). U Pr of Amer.

Harman, Nicholas. Dunkirk. 1980. 12.95 o.p. (ISBN 0-671-25389-1). S&S.

Harman, R. Joyce, jt. ed. see Overhage, Carl F.

Harman, Susan E. & House, H. Descriptive English Grammar. 2nd ed. 1950. text ed. 18.95 (ISBN 0-13-199083-7). P-H.

Harman, Thomas L. & Allen, Charles E. Guide to the National Electrical Code. 1979. 19.95 o.p. (ISBN 0-13-370510-2). P-H.

Harman, Willis W., jt. auth. see Armstrong, Joe E.

Harmar, Hilary. Dogs & How to Breed Them. new ed. 1975. 29.95 (ISBN 0-87666-289-0, H937). TFH Pubns.

--Dogs: How to Train & Show Them. (Illus.). 192p. 1983. 22.50 (ISBN 0-7153-8323-X). David & Charles.

--The Pomeranian. Foyle, Christina, ed. (Foyle's Handbks). (Illus.). 1973. 3.95 (ISBN 0-685-55796-0). Palmetto Pub.

Harmatz. Abnormal Psychology. 1978. 26.95 (ISBN 0-13-000885-0); study guide & wkbk. o.p. 4.95 (ISBN 0-13-000901-6). P-H.

Harmatz, Morton G. & Novak, Melina A. Human Sexuality. 608p. 1983. text ed. 22.50 scp (ISBN 0-06-042632-2, HarpC); Instr's. Manual Avail. (ISBN 0-06-362573-3). Har-Row.

Harmeling, Jean. The Incredible Will of H. R. Heartman. 128p. (gr. 5-9). 1983. pap. 2.95 (ISBN 0-89107-279-9, Crossway Bks). Good News.

Harmelink, Herman. Ecumenism & the Reformed Church. 1969. pap. 3.95 (ISBN 0-8028-1281-3). Eerdmans.

Harmer, Hilary. Showing & Judging Dogs. LC 75-795. 1976. 29.95 o.p. (ISBN 0-668-03793-8). Arco.

Harmer, J see Allen, W. S.

Harmer, Jeremy, jt. auth. see Arnold, John.

Harmer, Mabel. Circus. LC 81-7709. (The New True Bks.). (Illus.). 48p. (gr. k-4). 1981. PLB 9.25 (ISBN 0-516-01610-5). Childrens.

Harmetz, Aljean. Rolling Breaks: And other Movie Business. LC 82-49191. 1983. 13.95 (ISBN 0-394-52886-7). Knopf.

Harmin, Merrill & Gregory, Thomas B. Teaching Is... LC 73-91283. (Illus.). 272p. 1974. pap. text ed. 13.95 (ISBN 0-574-19112-7, 13-2112). SRA.

Harmon. Care of the Trauma Patient. Date not set. write for info. Wiley.

Harmon, A. J. Remodeling for Security. (Illus.). 1979. 14.95 o.p. (ISBN 0-07-026627-1, C). McGraw.

Harmon, Alvin B. The Answers to Wall Street's Trade Secrets. 1983. 14.95 (ISBN 0-533-05341-2). Vantage.

Harmon, Glynn. Human Memory & Knowledge: A Systems Approach. LC 72-809. (Contributions in Librarianship & Information Science: No. 6). (Illus.). 159p. 1973. lib. bdg. 25.00 (ISBN 0-8371-6379-X, HAH/). Greenwood.

Harmon, Ian. Birdkeeping in Australia. (Illus.). 176p. 1980. 12.95 (ISBN 0-207-13422-7). Avian Pubns.

Harmon, Lily. Freehand: The Life & Art of a Lady Who Made Her Own Rules. 1981. 15.95 o.s.i. (ISBN 0-671-41452-6). S&S.

Harmon, Margaret, ed. Careers for Writers: Working with Words. (Everyday Handbook Ser.). pap. 2.95 o.p. (ISBN 0-06-463469-8, EH 469, EH). B&N NY.

--Working with Words: Careers for Writers. LC 76-57192. (gr. 7 up). 1977. 7.95 (ISBN 0-664-32610-2). Westminster.

Harmon, Mont J. Political Thought: From Plato to the Present. (Political Science Ser.). 1964. text ed. 31.00 (ISBN 0-07-026625-5, C). McGraw.

Harmon, N. Paul, jt. auth. see Margolis, Neal.

Harmon, Nolan B. Understanding the United Methodist Church, 1977 Edition. LC 73-20001. 1982. pap. 5.95 (ISBN 0-687-43005-4). Abingdon.

Harmon, Paul. Small Business Management. LC 78-62923. 362p. 1979. text ed. 19.95x (ISBN 0-442-20970-3). Kent Pub Co.

--Successful Management. 224p. 1982. pap. text ed. 14.95 (ISBN 0-8403-2833-8). Kendall-Hunt.

Harmon, Robert B. Government & Politics in Illinois: An Information Source Survey. 32p. 1978. pap. 3.00 (ISBN 0-686-37407-X). Vance Biblios.

Harmon, Susan M., ed. Readings in Income Taxation. (Huebner School Ser.). (Orig.). 1982. pap. text ed. 12.00 (ISBN 0-943590-04-3). Amer College.

Harmon, Thomas. The Registration of J. S. Bach's Organ Works. (Bibliotheca Organologica Ser.: Vol. 70). 65.00 o.s.i. (ISBN 90-6027-245-5, Pub. by Frits Knuf Netherlands); wrappers 50.00 o.s.i. (ISBN 90-6027-243-9, Pub. by Frits Knuf Netherlands). Pendragon NY.

Harmon, William. One Long Poem: Poems. 72p. 1982. 12.95x (ISBN 0-8071-1026-4); pap. 5.95 (ISBN 0-8071-1027-2). La State U Pr.

Harmon, William, ed. Oxford Book of America Light Verse. 1979. 17.95 (ISBN 0-19-502509-1). Oxford U Pr.

Harmonay, Maureen & Action for Children's Television, Inc., eds. Promise & Performance: ACT's Guide to TV Programming for Children, 2 vols. Incl. Vol. I. Children with Special Needs. LC 77-8903. 1977. prof ref 17.00x (ISBN 0-88410-180-0); pap. 7.95x (ISBN 0-88410-177-0); Vol. II. The Arts. LC 79-17020. 240p. 18.50x (ISBN 0-88410-174-6); pap. 8.95x (ISBN 0-686-60776-7); Vol. III. Role Models. cancelled (ISBN 0-88410-173-8); Vol. IV. Sciences. cancelled (ISBN 0-88410-172-X); Vol. V. Consumer Education. cancelled (ISBN 0-88410-175-4). (Action for Children's Television Ser.). Ballinger Pub.

Harms, A. A. & Heindler, M. Nuclear Energy Synergetics: An Introduction to Conceptual Models of Integrated Nuclear Energy Systems. 252p. 1982. 35.00x (ISBN 0-306-40951-8, Plenum Pr). Plenum Pub.

Harms, Alvin. Jose-Maria de Heredia. LC 74-22312. (World Authors Ser.). 1975. lib. bdg. 15.95 (ISBN 0-8057-2421-4, Twayne). G K Hall.

Harms, David, jt. auth. see Marshak, Samuil.

Harms, Edward & Zabinski, Michael P. Introduction to APL & Computer Programming. LC 76-20587. 1977. pap. text ed. 21.95 (ISBN 0-471-35201-2). Wiley.

Harms, Ernest, jt. ed. see Jenkins, Richard L.

Harms, H., jt. auth. see Von Dalla Torre, K. W.

Harms, L. S. & Richstad, Jim, eds. Evolving Perspectives on the Right to Communicate. 1977. pap. text ed. 7.50x o.p. (ISBN 0-8248-0576-3, Eastwest Ctr). UH Pr.

Harms, L. S., et al, eds. Right to Communicate: Collected Papers. LC 77-71944. 1977. pap. text ed. 6.00x (ISBN 0-8248-0567-4). UH Pr.

Harms, Paul. Power from the Pulpit. (Preacher's Workshop Ser.). 48p. 1977. pap. 2.50 (ISBN 0-570-07406-1, 12-2678). Concordia.

Harms, Robert T. Finnish Structural Sketch. LC 64-64593. (Uralic & Altaic Ser: Vol. 42). (Orig.). 1964. pap. text ed. 3.00x o.p. (ISBN 0-87750-011-8). Res Ctr Lang Semiotic.

Harms, T., jt. auth. see Veitch, B.

Harms, Thelma & Clifford, Richard M. Early Childhood Environment Rating Scale. (Orig.). 1980. pap. 5.50x (ISBN 0-8077-2632-X); 30 scoring sheets 4.95 (ISBN 0-8077-2635-4). Tchrs Coll.

Harms, William C. Who Are We & Where Are We Going: A Parish Planning Guide. 96p. (Orig.). 1981. pap. 5.95 (ISBN 0-8215-9872-4). Sadlier.

Harms, Wolfgang & Schilling, Michael, eds. Deutsche Illustrierte Flugblatter des sixteen & seventeen Jahrhunderts, Vol. II. (Illus.). 1980. lib. bdg. 220.00 (ISBN 3-601-00049-0). Kraus Intl.

Harmsen, K. Behavior of Heavy Metals in Soil. (Agricultural Research Reports Ser.: No. 866). (Illus.). 1977. pap. 13.25 (ISBN 90-220-0635-2, PDC17, Pub. by PUDOC). Unipub.

Harmston, Floyd K. Community as an Economic System. 1983. pap. write for info (ISBN 0-8138-0327-6). Iowa St U Pr.

Harmuth, H. F., jt. ed. see Marton, C.

Harmuth, Henning F. see Marton, L.

Harn, Alan D., jt. auth. see Munson, Patrick J.

Harnack, R. Victor, et al. Group Discussion: Theory & Technique. 2nd ed. (Illus.). 1977. text ed. 21.95 (ISBN 0-13-365247-5). P-H.

Harnad, Stevan, ed. Peer Commentary on Peer Review: A Case Study in Scientific Quality Control. LC 82-19860. 80p. Date not set. pap. 12.95 (ISBN 0-521-27306-4). Cambridge U Pr.

Harnad, Stevan, et al, eds. Origins & Evolution of Language & Speech, Vol. 280. (Annals of the New York Academy of Sciences). 914p. 1976. 61.00x (ISBN 0-89072-026-6). NY Acad Sci.

Harnden, D. G., jt. auth. see Bridges, B. A.

Harned, David B. Images for Self-Recognition: The Christian As Player, Sufferer, Vandal. 1977. 2.00 (ISBN 0-8164-0334-1). Seabury.

Harned, Joseph W., ed. see Atlantic Council Working Group on Nuclear Fuels Policy.

Harner, James L. Samuel Daniel & Michael Drayton: A Reference Guide. 1980. lib. bdg. 35.00 (ISBN 0-8161-8322-8, Hall Reference). G K Hall.

Harner, Michael. The Way of the Shaman: A Guide to Power & Healing. LC 79-2995. 192p. 1980. 8.95i o.p. (ISBN 0-06-063710-2, HarpR). Har-Row.

Harner, Philip B. I Am of the Fourth Gospel: A Study in Johannine Usage & Thought. Reumann, John, ed. LC 72-123506. (Facet Bks.). 72p. (Orig.). 1970. pap. 1.00 o.p. (ISBN 0-8006-3060-2, 1-3060). Fortress.

--An Inductive Approach to Biblical Study. LC 82-40213. 132p. (Orig.). 1982. lib. bdg. 18.75 (ISBN 0-8191-2608-X); pap. text ed. 7.00 (ISBN 0-8191-2609-8). U Pr of Amer.

Harness, Alta M., jt. auth. see McQuigg, James D.

Harnett, Cynthia. The Writing on the Hearth. (Illus.). 320p. (gr. 7 up). 1973. PLB 9.95 o.p. (ISBN 0-670-79119-9). Viking Pr.

Harnett, D. L. Statistical Methods. 3rd ed. 147p. 1982. pap. text ed. 21.00 (ISBN 0-201-03914-1). A-W.

Harnett, D. L. & Cummings, L. L. Bargaining Behavior: An International Study. LC 79-67421. (Illus.). 307p. 1980. text ed. 28.95x (ISBN 0-931920-14-0). Dame Pubns.

Harnett, D. L. & Murphy, J. L. Introductory Statistical Analysis. 2nd ed. 1980. 25.95 (ISBN 0-201-02758-5); student's wkbk. 5.95 (ISBN 0-201-02859-X); instructor's manual 2.95 (ISBN 0-201-02759-3). A-W.

Harnett, Donald L. Introduction to Statistical Methods. 2nd ed. LC 74-10353. (Illus.). 500p. 1975. text ed. 25.95 (ISBN 0-201-02752-6). A-W.

Harney. Oil from Shale. (Special Report Ser.). 289p. 1983. price not set (ISBN 0-8247-1777-5). Dekker.

Harnick, Frances S. Games Babies Play. (Illus.). 1978. pap. text ed. 5.95 (ISBN 0-8403-1911-8). Kendall-Hunt.

Harnish, Robert M., jt. auth. see Bach, Kent.

Harnishfeger, Lloyd. Prisoner of the Mound Builders. LC 72-7655. (Adult & Young Adult Bks.). (Illus.). (gr. 9 up). 1973. PLB 5.95g (ISBN 0-8225-0754-4). Lerner Pubns.

Harnishfeger, Lloyd C. A Collector's Guide to American Indian Artifacts. LC 74-33525. (Bks for Adults & Young Adults). (Illus.). 96p. (gr. 5 up). 1976. PLB 6.95 o.p. (ISBN 0-8225-0759-5). Lerner Pubns.

--Hunters of the Black Swamp. LC 70-128803. (Real Life Bks). (gr. 5-11). 1971. PLB 4.95g (ISBN 0-8225-0701-3). Lerner Pubns.

Harnwell, G. P. & Livingood, J. J. Experimental Atomic Physics. LC 77-10147. 486p. 1979. Repr. of 1933 ed. lib. bdg. 27.50 (ISBN 0-88275-600-1). Krieger.

Haro, Michael S., et al. Explorations in Personal Health. LC 76-10900. (Illus.). 1977. text ed. 20.95 (ISBN 0-395-24478-1); instr's. manual 1.35 (ISBN 0-395-24479-X). HM.

Harold 011w Publishers, ed. The Personal Promise Pocketbook: A Pocketpac Book. LC 80-52398. 128p. 1980. pap. 1.95 (ISBN 0-87788-673-3). Shaw Pubs.

Haroldsen, Edwin O., jt. auth. see Blake, Reed H.

Harootunian, H. D. Toward Restoration: The Growth of Political Consciousness in Tokugawa Japan. LC 79-94993. (Center for Japanese & Korean Studies, UC Berkeley). 1970. 34.50x (ISBN 0-520-01566-5). U of Cal Pr.

Harpaz, Itzhak. Job Satisfaction: Theories, Models & Longitudinal Analysis. LC 81-84847. 1983. 8.95 (ISBN 0-87212-155-0). Libra.

Harper. Early Painters & Engravers in Canada. 1981. 75.00 (ISBN 0-686-43128-6). Apollo.

--The Peripheral Blood Film. 2nd ed. (Illus.). 1974. 18.95 o.p. (ISBN 0-407-76001-6). Butterworth.

Harper, A. Patricia, ed. Ultrasound Mammography. (Illus.). 1983. price not set (ISBN 0-8391-1807-4, 18090). Univ Park.

Harper, Alan D. The Politics of Loyalty. LC 73-95509. (Contributions in American History: No. 2). (Illus.). 1969. lib. bdg. 29.95 (ISBN 0-8371-2343-7, HAL/). Greenwood.

Harper, Alfred F. Acts One-Twelve: The Spirit-Filled Church. (Beacon Small-Group Bible Studies). 96p. 1982. pap. 2.25 (ISBN 0-8341-0800-3). Beacon Hill.

Harper, Ann & Lewis, Glenn. The Big Beauty Book: Glamour for the Fuller-Figure Woman. (Illus.). 256p. 1983. 17.50 (ISBN 0-03-060561-X). HR&W.

Harper, Charles A. Handbook of Components for Electronics. 1977. 55.00 (ISBN 0-07-026682-4, P&RB). McGraw.

--Handbook of Electronic Packaging. 1968. 51.25 (ISBN 0-07-026671-9, P&RB). McGraw.

--Handbook of Electronic Systems Design. new ed. (Handbook Ser.). (Illus.). 832p. 1979. 52.25 (ISBN 0-07-026683-2, P&RB). McGraw.

--Handbook of Materials & Processes for Electronics. 1970. 46.75 (ISBN 0-07-026673-5, P&RB). McGraw.

--Handbook of Plastics & Elastomers. 950p. 1975. 62.25 (ISBN 0-07-026681-6, P&RB). McGraw.

--Handbook of Thick Film Hybrid Microelectronics: A Practical Sourcebook for Designers, Fabricators & Users. 1024p. 1974. 55.00 (ISBN 0-07-026680-8, P&RB). McGraw.

--Handbook of Wiring, Cabling, & Interconnecting for Electronics. LC 72-4069. 1152p. 1972. 44.00 (ISBN 0-07-026674-3, P&RB). McGraw.

Harper, Charles G. Haunted Houses: Tales of the Supernatural with Some Account of Hereditary Curses & Family Legends. LC 79-164326. (Illus.). xvi, 283p. 1971. Repr. of 1907 ed. 39.00 o.p. (ISBN 0-8103-3928-5). Gale.

Harper, Charles L., et al. Financial Systems for Community Health Organizations: A Manager's Guide. 1981. text ed. 22.95 (ISBN 0-534-97976-9). Lifetime Learn.

Harper, Charlie. Introduction to Mathematical Physics. (Physics Ser.). 352p. 1976. ref. ed. 26.95 o.p. (ISBN 0-13-487538-9). P-H.

Harper, Dennis, jt. auth. see Fonda, Peter.

Harper, Donald V. Transportation in America: Users, Carriers, Government. 2nd ed. (Illus.). 624p. 1982. text ed. 26.95 (ISBN 0-13-930297-2). P-H.

--Transportation in America: Users, Carriers, Government. (Illus.). 1978. ref. ed. 26.95 (ISBN 0-13-930214-X). P-H.

Harper, E. J. & Henry, Donald L. Banker's Complete Letter Book. 1978. 32.00 (ISBN 0-13-055582-7, Busn). P-H.

Harper, F. A. Towards Liberty, 2 vols. (Humane Studies). 914p. 1980. Set. text ed. 20.00x o.p. (ISBN 0-391-02090-0). Humanities.

Harper, Fowler V. Justice Rutledge & the Bright Constellation. 1965. 10.00 o.p. (ISBN 0-672-80053-5, Bobbs-Merrill Law). Michie-Bobbs.

Harper, Fowler V. & James, Fleming, Jr. The Law of Torts, 3 Vols. 1956. Set. 140.00 (ISBN 0-316-34703-5); pap supplement to volume two 1968 25.00 (ISBN 0-316-34701-9). Little.

Harper, Francis, ed. see Bartram, John.

Harper, Frederick D. & Bruce, Gail C. Counseling Techniques: An Outline & Overview. 270p. 1983. pap. text ed. price not set (ISBN 0-935392-04-1). Douglas Pubs.

Harper, G. Neil. Computer Applications in Architecture & Engineering. 1968. text ed. 27.50 o.p. (ISBN 0-07-026672-7, P&RB). McGraw.

Harper, Glynn C. Clap Your Hands. LC 81-3643. 1983. 16.95 (ISBN 0-87949-205-8). Ashley Bks.

Harper, Harold W. & Culbert, Michael L. How You Can Beat the Killer Diseases. LC 77-10782. 1978. 9.95 o.p. (ISBN 0-87000-387-9, Arlington Hse). Crown.

Harper, J., jt. auth. see Percival, D.

Harper, J. A. Right Way. 1965. pap. 1.95 o.p. (ISBN 0-87508-233-5). Chr Lit.

Harper, J. C., jt. auth. see Crimes, T. P.

Harper, J. D. Small Scale Foundries for Developing Countries: A Guide to Process Selection. (Illus.). 66p. (Orig.). 1981. pap. 9.50x (ISBN 0-903031-78-7, Pub. by Intermediate Tech England). Intermediate Tech.

Harper, J. J., jt. auth. see Pope, Alan.

Harper, J. Russell. Krieghoff. LC 79-94272. (Illus.). 1979. 40.00 (ISBN 0-8020-2348-7). U of Toronto Pr.

--Painting in Canada: A History. 2nd ed. (Illus.). 1977. 35.00 (ISBN 0-8020-2271-5); pap. 14.75 (ISBN 0-8020-6307-1). U of Toronto Pr.

Harper, John, jt. auth. see Ambrose, Peter.

Harper, Karen. Passion's Reign. 1983. pap. 3.95 (ISBN 0-8217-1177-6). Zebra.

Harper, Lawrence V., jt. auth. see Bell, Richard Q.

Harper, Marilynn O. Shaw's Plays: Pygmalion Notes & Arms & the Man Notes. (Orig.). 1981. pap. 2.50 (ISBN 0-8220-1103-4). Cliffs.

Harper, Michael. Poder para Vencer. Date not set. 2.50 (ISBN 0-88113-245-4). Edit Betania.

Harper, Michael J. Birth Control Technologies: Prospects by the Year 2000. (Illus.). 288p. 1983. text ed. 27.50x (ISBN 0-292-70739-8). U of Tex Pr.

Harper, Michael S., selected by see Brown, Sterling A.

Harper, Mike. Through France to the Med. 216p. 1982. 40.00x (ISBN 0-85614-034-1, Pub. by Gentry England). State Mutual Bk.

Harper, Peter S. Practical Genetic Counseling. 296p. 1981. text ed. 35.00 (ISBN 0-8391-1669-1). Univ Park.

Harper, Richard. The Kill Factor. 208p. (Orig.). 1983. pap. 2.50 (ISBN 0-449-12383-9, GM). Fawcett.

Harper, Richard C. The Course of the Melting Pot Idea to 1910. Cordasco, Francesco, ed. LC 80-862. (American Ethnic Groups Ser.). 1981. lib. bdg. 39.00x (ISBN 0-405-13425-8). Ayer Co.

Harper, Robert A. & Schmudde, Theodore H. Between Two Worlds: An Introduction to Geography. 2nd ed. LC 77-76418. (Illus.). 1978. text ed. 27.95 (ISBN 0-395-25164-8); instr's. manual 1.00 (ISBN 0-395-25165-6); 20 35mm slides 15.95 (ISBN 0-395-25167-2). HM.

Harper, Robert A., jt. auth. see Ellis, Albert.

Harper, Rosalind W. A Guide to Respiratory Care: Physiology & Clinical Applications. (Illus.). 361p. 1982. pap. text ed. 21.00 (ISBN 0-397-54243-7, Lippincott Nursing). Lippincott.

Harper, Susan, ed. see Stokell, Marjorie.

Harper, T. A. Laboratory Guide to Disordered Hemostasis. 1970. 14.95 o.p. (ISBN 0-407-74250-6). Butterworth.

Harper, Victor L. Handbook of Investment Products & Services. rev. ed. LC 75-26986. (Illus.). 429p. 1977. 17.95 (ISBN 0-13-378737-0). NY Inst Finance.

Harper, W. M. Cost Accounting. (Cost & Management Accounting Ser.: Vol. 1). 250p. 1982. pap. text ed. 13.95 (ISBN 0-7121-0468-2). Intl Ideas.

--Management Accounting (Cost & Management Accounting, Vol. 2. 250p. 1982. pap. text ed. 13.95x (ISBN 0-7121-0469-0). Intl Ideas.

Harper, W. M. & Lim, H. C. Operational Research. (Illus.). 310p. 1982. pap. text ed. 13.50x (ISBN 0-7121-1539-0). Intl Ideas.

Harper, W. M. & Stafford, L. W. Basic Mathematics. 176p. 1981. 29.00x (ISBN 0-7121-0287-6, Pub. by Macdonald & Evans). State Mutual Bk.

Harper, William A. & Malloch, Theodore R., eds. Where Are We Now? The State of Christian Political Reflection. LC 81-40061. 390p. (Orig.). 1981. lib. bdg. 25.25 (ISBN 0-8191-1739-0); pap. text ed. 14.75 (ISBN 0-8191-1740-4). U Pr of Amer.

Harper, William L. Data Processing Documentation: Standards, Procedures & Applications. 2nd. ed. 288p. 1980. 39.50 (ISBN 0-686-92178-X). P-H.

Harpole, Patricia C. & Nagle, Mary D., eds. Minnesota Territorial Census, 1850. LC 70-188492. 115p. 1972. pap. 5.50 (ISBN 0-87351-065-8). Minn Hist.

Harpwood, Diane. Tea & Tranquillisers. 164p. 1983. pap. 5.95 (ISBN 0-86068-124-6, Virago Pr). Merrimack Bk Serv.

Harr, Barbara. Mortgaged Wife. LC 82-71488. (New Poetry Ser,No.41). 85p. 1970. 5.00 o.p. (ISBN 0-8040-0215-0); pap. 3.50 (ISBN 0-8040-0216-9). Swallow.

Harr, Herbert L. Essays on Bentham: Jurisprudence & Political Theory. (Illus.). 250p. 1982. text ed. 29.95x (ISBN 0-19-825348-6); pap. text ed. 12.95x (ISBN 0-19-825468-7). Oxford U Pr.

Harr, Milton E. Mechanics of Particulate Media: A Probabilistic Approach. (Illus.). 1977. text ed. 39.50x (ISBN 0-07-026695-6, C); solutions manual 10.00 (ISBN 0-07-026696-4). McGraw.

Harragan, Betty L. Games Mother Never Taught You: Corporate Gamesmanship for Women. 400p. 1978. pap. 3.95 (ISBN 0-446-30654-1); pap. 6.95 (ISBN 0-446-97726-8). Warner Bks.

Harrah, Michael. First Offender. LC 79-21821. 192p. (gr. 7-12). 1980. 8.95 (ISBN 0-529-05540-6, Philomel). Putnam Pub Group.

Harrap, Elizabeth. The Dachshund. 1977. pap. 3.50 (ISBN 0-7028-1025-8). Palmetto Pub.

Harrap, K. R., jt. ed. see Davis, W.

Harre, E. A., jt. auth. see Harris, G. T.

Harre, R. Matter & Method. 1979. Repr. of 1964 ed. lib. bdg. 22.00 (ISBN 0-917930-28-2); pap. text ed. 6.00x (ISBN 0-917930-08-8). Ridgeview.

Harre, R., ed. Scientific Thought Nineteen Hundred to Nineteen Sixty: A Selective Survey. 1969. 24.95x o.p. (ISBN 0-19-858125-4); pap. 14.95x (ISBN 0-19-858126-2). Oxford U Pr.

Harre, R., ed. see Waismann, Friedrich.

Harre, Rom. Life Sentences: Aspects of the Social Role of Language. LC 75-40021. 1976. text ed. 34.95 (ISBN 0-471-35245-4); pap. 15.95x (ISBN 0-471-35244-6, Pub. by Wiley-Interscience). Wiley.

Harre, Rom see Von Cranach, Mario.

Harre, Ron. Great Scientific Experiments: Twenty Experiments That Changed Our View of the World. (Illus.). 224p. 1983. pap. 8.95 (ISBN 0-19-286036-4, GB 733, GB). Oxford U Pr.

Harrel, Monette R. & Harrel, Robert W., Jr. The Ham Book. (Illus.). 224p. 1977. pap. 4.95 (ISBN 0-686-36731-6). Md Hist.

Harrel, Robert W., Jr., jt. auth. see Harrel, Monette R.

Harrell, et al. A Basic Course in Moroccan Arabic. 395p. 1980. in cl. 16 audiocassettes 175.00x (ISBN 0-88432-052-9). J Norton Pubs.

Harrell, Costen J. Stewardship & the Tithe. (Orig.). 1953. pap. 0.75 o.p. (ISBN 0-687-39353-1). Abingdon.

Harrell, Irene, jt. auth. see Hill, Harold.

Harrell, Irene B. The General's Lady. 160p. 1981. pap. 4.95 (ISBN 0-8423-0997-7). Tyndale.

Harrell, Irene B., jt. auth. see Hill, Harold.

Harrell, John. Basic Media in Education. LC 73-81823. (Illus.). 80p. (Orig.). 1974. 3.50 o.p. (ISBN 0-88489-057-0). St Marys.

Harrell, Monette R. & Harrell, Robert W., Jr. The Ham Book: A Comprehensive Guide to Ham Cookery. LC 77-1233. (Illus.). 1977. pap. 6.95 (ISBN 0-915442-14-0). Donning Co.

Harrell, Pauline C. & Chase, Charlotte. Arrowhead Farm: 300 Years of New England Husbandry & Cooking. (Illus.). 240p. 1983. 16.95 (ISBN 0-914378-98-8); pap. 10.95. Countryman.

Harrell, Rhett D. Developing a Financial Management Information System for Local Govcernments: The Key Systems. LC 80-84383. (Illus.). 42p. 1980. pap. 8.00 Nonmember (ISBN 0-686-84364-9); pap. 7.00 Member (ISBN 0-686-84365-7). Municipal.

Harrell, Rhett D. & Cole, Lisa A. Banking Relations: A Guide for Local Governments. (Illus.). 100p. 1982. pap. 14.00 Nonmember (ISBN 0-686-84372-X); pap. 12.00 Member (ISBN 0-686-84373-8). Municipal.

Harrell, Richard S. A Basic Course in Moroccan Arabic. (Richard Slade Harrell Arabic Ser). 395p. 1965. pap. 9.50 (ISBN 0-87840-005-2); cassettes 80.00 (ISBN 0-87840-014-1); 5 inch reels 140.00 (ISBN 0-686-82908-5). Georgetown U Pr.

Harrell, Robert A. & Firestein, Gary S. The Effective Scoutboy. LC 82-11483. (Illus.). 176p. 1983. pap. text ed. 7.50 (ISBN 0-668-05627-4, 5627). Arco.

Harrell, Robert W., Jr., jt. auth. see Harrell, Monette R.

Harrell, Stevan. Ploughshare Village: Culture & Context in Taiwan. LC 82-8333. (Publications of the School of International Studies on Asia: No. 35). (Illus.). 248p. 1982. 20.00 (ISBN 0-295-95946-0). U of Wash Pr.

Harrell, Stevan, jt. ed. see Amoss, Pamela T.

Harrell, Virginia C. Vicksburg & the River. LC 82-4947. (Illus.). 112p. (Orig.). 1982. pap. 12.50 (ISBN 0-87805-161-9). U Pr of Miss.

Harrell, W. R., jt. auth. see Jacobs, C. O.

Harrer, G. A., jt. auth. see Howe, George.

Harrer, Heinrich. Ladakh: Gods & Mortals Behind the Himalayas. Rickett, Richard, tr. from Ger. (Illus.). 170p. 1980. 27.50x (ISBN 3-524-76002-3). Intl Pubns Serv.

Harrer, Joseph M. & Beckerley, James G., eds. Nuclear Power Reactor Instrumentation Systems Handbook, 2 vols. LC 72-600355. (AEC Technical Information Center Ser.). 313p. 1973. Vol. 1, 313 pg., 1973. pap. 16.00 (ISBN 0-87079-005-6, TID-25952-P1); microfiche 4.50 (ISBN 0-87079-299-7, TID-25952-P1); Vol. 2, 282 pg., 1974. pap. 15.00 (ISBN 0-87079-144-3, TID-25952-P2); microfiche 4.50 (ISBN 0-87079-300-4, TID-25952-P2). DOE.

Harrex, S. C., jt. ed. see Amirthanayagam, G.

Harri-Augstein, Sheila, et al. Reading to Learn. 1982. pap. 6.95 (ISBN 0-416-72660-7). Methuen Inc.

Harrickman, Ray E. Business Failures: Causes Remedies & Cures. LC 79-84672. 1979. pap. text ed. 17.75 o.p. (ISBN 0-8191-0742-5). U Pr of Amer.

Harrier, Richard A., jt. auth. see Martin, Michael R.

Harries, Elizabeth W., et al. Writing Papers: A Handbook for Students at Smith College. 2nd ed. 52p. (Orig.). 1980. pap. 1.00 (ISBN 0-87391-018-4). Smith Coll.

Harries, Joan. They Triumphed Over Their Handicaps. LC 80-25016. (Triumph Bks.). (YA) (gr. 7 up). 1981. PLB 8.90 (ISBN 0-531-04267-7). Watts.

Harries, Karsten. The Bavarian Rococo Church: Between Faith & Aestheticism. LC 82-1116. (Illus.). 304p. 1983. text ed. 37.00x (ISBN 0-300-02720-6). Yale U Pr.

Harries, Keith D. & Brunn, Stanley D. The Geography of Laws & Justice: Spatial Perspectives on the Criminal Justice System. LC 77-25460. (Praeger Special Studies). 1978. 27.95 o.p. (ISBN 0-03-022331-8). Praeger.

Harries, Lyndon, ed. see Ahmed, Said B.

Harries-Jenkins, Gwyn. Armed Forces & the Welfare Societies: Challenges in the 1980's. LC 82-10500. 256p. 1982. 27.50x (ISBN 0-312-04926-9). St Martin.

Harries-Jones, Peter. Freedom & Labour: Mobilization & Political Control on the Zambian Copperbelt. LC 75-592. (Illus.). 250p. 1975. 25.00 o.p. (ISBN 0-312-30380-7). St Martin.

Harrigan, John J. Politics & Policy in States & Communities. (Illus.). 475p. 1980. text ed. 17.95 (ISBN 0-316-34742-6); instructor's manual avail. (ISBN 0-316-34743-4). Little.

Harrigan, Patrick J. Mobility, Elites, & Education in French Society of the Second Empire. 203p. 1980. text ed. 11.00x (ISBN 0-88920-087-4, Pub. by Wilfrid Laurier U Pr Canada). Humanities.

Harrigan, W. F. & McCance, M. E., eds. Laboratory Methods in Food & Dairy Microbiology. 1977. 59.50 o.s.i. (ISBN 0-12-326040-X). Acad Pr.

Harriman. Leroy the Lobster & Crabby Crab. (gr. 1-3). 1967. pap. 4.50 (ISBN 0-89272-000-X). Down East.

Harriman, A. & West, M. A., eds. Photogeneration of Hydrogen. Date not set. price not set (ISBN 0-12-326380-8). Acad Pr.

Harriman, Ann. The Work-Leisure Trade Off: Reduced Work Time for Managers & Professionals. 200p. 1982. 21.95 (ISBN 0-03-058966-5). Praeger.

Harriman, Sarah. Book of Ginseng. (Health Ser.). (Orig.). 1973. pap. 1.75 o.s.i. (ISBN 0-515-05438-0, A2988). Jove Pubns.

Harring, H. K. & Myers, F. J. The Rotifer Fauna of Wisconsin. (Illus.). 1973. Repr. of 1927 ed. 64.00 (ISBN 3-7682-0820-6). Lubrecht & Cramer.

Harrington, A. P. Defend Yourself with Kung Fu. LC 75-40969. 1976. 8.95 (ISBN 0-87523-189-6). Emerson.

Harrington, Alan. Psychopaths... 1973. pap. 3.95 o.p. (ISBN 0-671-21640-6, Touchstone Bks). S&S.

Harrington, Anthony. Tersery Versery: World's First Individual Collection of Double Dactyls. (Illus.). 120p. (Orig.). 1982. pap. 5.95 (ISBN 0-943764-00-9). Hendricks Pub.

Harrington, Anthony P. Every Boy's Judo. (Illus.). (gr. 7 up). 8.95 (ISBN 0-87523-125-X). Emerson.

--Every Girl's Judo. (Illus.). (gr. 7 up). 8.95 (ISBN 0-87523-127-6). Emerson.

Harrington, Avery R. & Zimmerman, Stephen W. Renal Pathophysiology. LC 81-7454. (Wiley Series in Pathophysiology). 258p. 1982. 19.50 (ISBN 0-471-07815-8, Pub. by Wiley Med). Wiley.

Harrington, Charles D. Uranium Production Technology. LC 59-13493. 584p. 1959. 30.00 (ISBN 0-442-03154-8, Pub. by Van Nos Reinhold). Krieger.

Harrington, Daniel J. Access Guide for Scripture Study: Luke. Date not set. 2.95 (ISBN 0-8215-5929-X); 3.95 (ISBN 0-8215-5934-6). Sadlier.

--Access Guide for Scripture Study: Mark. Date not set. 2.95 (ISBN 0-8215-5928-1); 3.95 (ISBN 0-8215-5933-8). Sadlier.

--The Gospel According to Matthew, No. 1. Karris, Robert J., ed. LC 82-20333. (Collegeville Bible Commentary Ser.). (Illus.). 128p. 1983. pap. 2.50 (ISBN 0-8146-1301-2). Liturgical Pr.

Harrington, David O. The Visual Fields: A Textbook & Atlas of Clinical Perimetry. 5th ed. LC 81-2558. (Illus.). 437p. 1981. text ed. 39.50 (ISBN 0-8016-2059-7). Mosby.

Harrington, Diana R. Modern Portfolio Theory & the Capital Asset Pricing Model: A User's Guide. (Illus.). 160p. 1983. pap. 13.95 (ISBN 0-13-597245-0). P-H.

Harrington, Dick, jt. auth. see Russell, Dale.

Harrington, Fred H. Fighting Politician, Major N. P. Banks. Repr. of 1948 ed. lib. bdg. 15.00 o.p. (ISBN 0-8371-3007-7, HAFP). Greenwood.

Harrington, Geri. Cash Crops for the Thrifty Gardener. LC 82-82305. 192p. (Orig.). 1982. pap. 7.95 (ISBN 0-448-07354-4, G&D). Putnam Pub Group.

--Grow Your Own Chinese Vegetables. 1978. 14.95 o.p. (ISBN 0-02-548430-3). Macmillan.

--The New College Cookbook. LC 82-82317. 264p. (Orig.). 1982. pap. 6.95 (ISBN 0-448-16606-2, G&D). Putnam Pub Group.

Harrington, H. D. How to Identify Grasses & Grasslike Plants. LC 82-74144. (Illus.). 142p. 1977. pap. 6.95x (ISBN 0-8040-0746-2). Swallow.

Harrington, H. D. & Durrell, L. W. How to Identify Plants. LC 82-70928. (Illus.). 203p. 1957. pap. 6.95x (ISBN 0-8040-0149-9). Swallow.

Harrington, Ian J., jt. auth. see Gozna, Eric R.

Harrington, J. B. Cereal Breeding Procedures. (FAO Agricultural Development Paper, No. 28, FAO Plant Production & Protection Ser.: No. 14). 122p. 1952. pap. 5.50 (ISBN 0-686-93144-0, F88, FAO). Unipub.

Harrington, J. C. Archeology & the Historical Society. (Illus.). 1965. pap. 3.50 (ISBN 0-910050-01-5). AASLH.

Harrington, Joan & Brener, Etta R. Patient Care in Renal Failure. LC 73-76185. (Monographs in Clinical Nursing: No. 5). (Illus.). 305p. 1973. text ed. 13.95 o.p. (ISBN 0-7216-4528-3). Saunders.

Harrington, John. Film &-as Literature. (Illus.). 1977. pap. text ed. 14.50 (ISBN 0-13-315945-0). P-H.

Harrington, John W. Discovering Science. LC 80-80721. (Illus.). 144p. 1981. pap. text ed. 9.50 (ISBN 0-395-25527-9). HM.

Harrington, John W. & Gallagher, Janice. Dance of the Continents: Adventures with Rocks & Time. (Illus.). 224p. 1983. 13.95 (ISBN 0-87477-168-4); pap. 9.50 (ISBN 0-87477-247-8). J P Tarcher.

Harrington, Joyce. Family Reunion. 320p. pap. 2.95 (ISBN 0-380-63099-0). Avon.

--No One Knows My Name. 256p. 1980. 10.95 o.p. (ISBN 0-312-57568-8). St Martin.

Harrington, Lyn. The Polar Regions: Earth's Frontiers. LC 73-10191. (World Neighbors Ser.). (Illus.). (gr. 5 up). 1973. 7.95 o.p. (ISBN 0-525-66338-X). Lodestar Bks.

Harrington, M. R. Sacred Bundles of the Sac & Fox Indians. (Anthropological Publications Ser.: Vol. 4-2). (Illus.). 1914. 7.00x (ISBN 0-686-24093-6). Univ Mus of U.

Harrington, Michael. Decade of Decision. 1980. 11.95 o.p. (ISBN 0-671-24112-5, 24112). S&S.

--Decade of Decision. 1981. pap. 7.50 (ISBN 0-671-42808-X, Touchstone). S&S.

--Fragments of the Century. LC 76-53796. 1977. pap. 3.95 o.p. (ISBN 0-671-22653-3, Touchstone Bks). S&S.

--Twilight of Capitalism. 1977. pap. 7.95 (ISBN 0-671-22759-9, Touchstone Bks). S&S.

--The Vast Majority. 1978. pap. 5.95 (ISBN 0-671-24407-8, Touchstone Bks). S&S.

Harrington, Michael, jt. auth. see Lindsay, T. F.

Harrington, Michael, jt. auth. see Rodgers, Harrell R.

Harrington, Mildred P. & Thomas, Josephine H., eds. Our Holidays in Poetry. 479p. 1929. 14.00 (ISBN 0-8242-0039-X). Wilson.

Harrington, Norman. Shaping of Religion in America. (Illus.). 137p. 1980. 29.95 (ISBN 0-686-36658-1). Md Hist.

Harrington, R. E. Death of a Patriot. LC 78-27809. 1979. 8.95 o.p. (ISBN 0-399-12187-0). Putnam Pub Group.

--Proud Man. 400p. 1983. pap. 3.50 (ISBN 0-345-30032-7). Ballantine.

--Proud Man. 416p. 1983. 17.95 (ISBN 0-436-19113-X, Pub. by Secker & Warburg). David & Charles.

--Quintain. LC 77-4598. 1977. 7.95 o.p. (ISBN 0-399-11908-6). Putnam Pub Group.

Harrington, Richard, jt. auth. see Morgan, E. Victor.

Harrington, Roger F. Time-Harmonic Electromagnetic Fields. (Electronic & Electrical Engineering Ser.). 1961. text ed. 46.50 (ISBN 0-07-026745-6, C). McGraw.

Harrington, Thomas F. Handbook of Career Planning for Special Needs Students. LC 82-11419. 358p. 1982. 28.95 (ISBN 0-89443-661-9). Aspen Systems.

Harrington, Wilfrid J. Key to the Parables. LC 64-24516. 164p. (Orig.). 1964. pap. 2.45 o.p. (ISBN 0-8091-1612-X, Deus). Paulist Pr.

Harriot, Thomas. A Briefe & True Report of the New Found Land of Virginia. (Illus.). 91p. 1972. pap. 6.00 (ISBN 0-486-21092-8). Dover.

Harriott, Peter. Process Control. LC 81-18558. 392p. 1983. Repr. of 1964 ed. text ed. write for info. (ISBN 0-89874-399-0). Krieger.

Harris. The Copper King. 212p. 1982. 49.00x (ISBN 0-85323-111-7, Pub. by Liverpool Univ England). State Mutual Bk.

--A Field Guide to the Birds of the Galapagos. 25.95 (ISBN 0-686-42757-2, Collins Pub England). Greene.

--The Use of Computers in Perinatal Medicine. 416p. 1982. 41.95 (ISBN 0-03-061513-5). Praeger.

Harris, A. & Gurney, R. Argument. 1968. 3.95x (ISBN 0-521-05216-5). Cambridge U Pr.

Harris, Abram L. Economics & Social Reform. 357p. 1973. Repr. of 1958 ed. lib. bdg. 18.75x (ISBN 0-8371-6629-2, HAEC). Greenwood.

Harris, Alan. Teaching Morality & Religion. (Classroom Close-Ups Ser.). 1975. text ed. 10.95x o.p. (ISBN 0-04-371029-8); pap. text ed. 6.50x o.p. (ISBN 0-04-371030-1). Allen Unwin.

Harris, Alan, et al. Physiological & Clinical Aspects of Cardiac Ausculation. 1976. 60.00 (ISBN 0-397-57104-6). Lippincott.

Harris, Alfred. Baroni. LC 75-24851. 1975. 7.95 o.p. (ISBN 0-399-11626-5). Putnam Pub Group.

Harris, Alice C. Georgian Syntax: A Study in Relational Grammar. (Cambridge Studies in Linguistics: No. 33). (Illus.). 300p. 1981. 74.50 (ISBN 0-521-23584-7). Cambridge U Pr.

Harris, Alice K., ed. see Yezierska, Anzia.

Harris, Anastas. Journal of Holsitic Health: Vol. VI. (Illus.). 144p. 1981. pap. 12.00 (ISBN 0-939410-07-9). Mandala Holistic.

Harris, Ann S., ed. see Marrow, Deborah.

Harris, Ann S., ed. see Saward, Susan.

Harris, Ann S., ed. see Schloss, Christine S.

Harris, Ann S., ed. see Steadman, David W.

Harris, Anthony. Human Measurement. LC 79-670125. 1978. pap. text ed. 14.50x o.p. (ISBN 0-435-60360-4). Heinemann Ed.

Harris, Audrey. Why Did He Die? LC 65-22217. (Medical Bks for Children). (Illus.). (gr. k-5). 1965. PLB 3.95g (ISBN 0-8225-0256-9). Lerner Pubns.

Harris, Barbara, jt. auth. see Golanty, Eric.

Harris, Barbara J. Beyond Her Sphere: Women & the Professions in American History. LC 78-4017. (Contributions in Women's Studies: No. 4). 1978. lib. bdg. 25.00x (ISBN 0-313-20415-2, HBS/). Greenwood.

Harris, Barbara J., jt. auth. see McNamara, Jo A.

Harris, Beatrice, ed. Electronic Industry Telephone Directory, 1982-83. 552p. (Annual). 1982. 35.95 (ISBN 0-916512-08-8). Harris Pub.

--Harris Indiana Marketers Industrial Directory, 1982. Harsey, Paula. (Illus.). 696p. 1982. 42.50 o.p. (ISBN 0-916512-28-2). Harris Pub.

Harris, Beatrice & Edmonds, Peggy, eds. Harris Michigan Marketers Industrial Directory, 1982-83. (Illus.). 956p. 1982. 79.50 (ISBN 0-916512-18-5). Harris Pub.

Harris, Beatrice & Goss, Ann, eds. Harris Illinois Marketers Industrial Directory, 1982. (Illus.). 1064p. 1982. 76.00 (ISBN 0-916512-38-X). Harris Pub.

Harris, Beatrice & Lace, Vivian, eds. Harris Ohio Marketers Industrial Directory, 1982. (Illus.). 1112p. 1981. 72.50 o.p. (ISBN 0-916512-57-6). Harris Pub.

Harris, Beatrice & Lange, Debbie, eds. Harris Indian Marketers Industrial Directory, 1983. (Illus.). 700p. 1982. 52.50 (ISBN 0-916512-29-0). Harris Pub.

Harris, Ben C., ed. The Compleat Herbal. LC 77-185615. 243p. (Orig.). 1972. pap. 2.95 (ISBN 0-915962-15-2). Larchmont Bks.

Harris, Ben M. Supervisory Behavior in Education. 2nd ed. LC 74-13100. (Illus.). 480p. 1975. ref. ed. 23.95 (ISBN 0-13-877118-9). P-H.

Harris, Benjamin. The Protestant Tutor. Lurie, Alison & Schiller, Justin G., eds. Incl. The New-England Primer, Enlarged. LC 75-32135. (Classics of Children's Literature 1621-1932 Ser.). PLB 38.00 o.s.i. (ISBN 0-8240-2252-1). Garland Pub.

Harris, Bernard, ed. Essays & Studies-1971. (Essays & Studies: Vol. 24). 122p. 1971. text ed. 12.50 (ISBN 0-7195-2325-7, Pub. by Murray England). Humanities.

Harris, Bernard, jt. ed. see Brown, John R.

Harris, Bill. Washington, D.C. (Illus.). 224p. 1982. 50.00 (ISBN 0-8109-1787-4). Abrams.

Harris, Bruce. Hampshire County Cricket. 13.50x (ISBN 0-392-07079-0, SpS). Sportshelf.

Harris, Bruce & Harris, Seena, eds. Honore Daumier: Selected Works. (Illus.). 1969. 4.98 o.p. (ISBN 0-517-09527-0, Bounty). Crown.

Harris, C. C. Readings in Kinship in Urban Society. 1970. 25.00 o.s.i. (ISBN 0-08-016039-5); pap. 12.75 (ISBN 0-08-016038-7). Pergamon.

--The Sociological Enterprise: A Discussion of Fundamental Concepts. LC 79-21637. 1980. 26.00x (ISBN 0-312-73968-0). St Martin.

Harris, C. C., jt. auth. see Rosser, Colin.

Harris, C. J. & Billings, S. A. Self Tuning & Adaptive Control: Theory & Applications. (IEE Control Engineering Ser.: No. 15). 352p. 1981. casebound 44.00 (ISBN 0-906048-62-1). Inst Elect Eng.

Harris, C. Leon, ed. Evolution: Genesis & Revelations: Readings from Empedocles to Wilson. LC 81-2555. 400p. 1981. lib. bdg. 34.50x (ISBN 0-87395-486-6); pap. text ed. 9.95x (ISBN 0-87395-487-4). State U NY Pr.

Harris, Cecelia C. A Primer of Cardiac Arrhythmias: A Self Instructional Program. LC 78-27022. 112p. 1979. pap. text ed. 11.95 (ISBN 0-8016-2070-8). Mosby.

Harris, Charles. Islington. LC 75-20479. (Illus.). 222p. 1976. 15.00 o.p. (ISBN 0-312-43750-1). St Martin.

--What's Ahead? LC 80-84173. (Radiant Life Ser.). 128p. (Orig.). 1982. pap. 2.50 (ISBN 0-88243-897-2, 02-0897); teacher's ed. 3.95 (ISBN 0-88243-195-1, 32-0195). Gospel Pub.

Harris, Charles O. Statics & Strength of Materials. 552p. 1982. text ed. 24.95 (ISBN 0-471-08293-7); tchr's ed. 30.00 (ISBN 0-471-86318-1). Wiley.

Harris, Curtis C. & Cerutti, Peter A., eds. Mechanisms of Chemical Carcinogenesis. LC 82-6556. (UCLA Symposia on Molecular & Cellular Biology Ser.: Vol. 2). 606p. 1982. 98.00 (ISBN 0-8451-2601-6). A R Liss.

Harris, Cyril M. Dictionary of Architecture & Construction. 1975. 42.50 (ISBN 0-07-026756-1, P&RB). McGraw.

--Handbook of Noise Control. 2nd ed. (Illus.). 1979. 52.25 (ISBN 0-07-026814-2, P&RB). McGraw.

--Historic Architecture Sourcebook. new ed. (Illus.). 320p. 1977. 34.95 (ISBN 0-07-026755-3, P&RB). McGraw.

Harris, Cyril M. & Crede, Charles E. Shock & Vibration Control Handbook. rev. ed. 1976. 52.25 (ISBN 0-07-026799-5, P&RB). McGraw.

Harris, D. J. & Robson, P. D. Vacuum & Solid State Electronics. 1963. 23.00 o.p. (ISBN 0-08-009960-2); pap. 11.25 o.p. (ISBN 0-08-009959-9). Pergamon.

Harris, D. V. The Geologic Story of the National Parks & Monuments. 3rd ed. 344p. 1980. pap. 22.95 (ISBN 0-471-09764-0, Pub. by Wiley Med). Wiley.

Harris, Daniel. The Fence. 288p. 1982. 12.00 (ISBN 0-682-49893-9). Exposition.

Harris, Daniel C. & Bertolucci, Michael D. Symmetry & Spectroscopy: An Introduction to Vibrational & Electronic Spectroscopy. (Illus.). 1978. pap. 18.95x (ISBN 0-19-855152-5). Oxford U Pr.

Harris, David. I Shoulda Been Home Yesterday. 1976. 7.95 o.s.i. (ISBN 0-440-04156-2, Sey Lawr). Delacorte.

--The Last Scam. 1981. 13.95 o.s.i. (ISBN 0-440-04674-2, Sey Lawr). Delacorte.

Harris, David see Stuart-Harris, Charles.

Harris, David F. Saint Cecilia's Hall in the Niddry Wynd. (Music Ser.). (Illus.). 303p. 1983. Repr. of 1911 ed. lib. bdg. 25.00 (ISBN 0-306-76142-4). Da Capo.

Harris, David P. Reading Improvement: Exercises for Students of English As a Second Language. (Orig.). 1966. pap. text ed. 10.95 (ISBN 0-13-755058-8). P-H.

Harris, Derek, jt. ed. see Edkins, Anthony.

Harris, Diana & Collison, Beth, eds. Proceedings of NECC 2. (Illus., Orig.). 1980. pap. 15.00 (ISBN 0-937114-00-6). Weeg Comp.

Harris, Diana & Nelson-Heern, Laurie, eds. Proceedings of NECC 1981. (Illus., Orig.). 1981. pap. 15.00 (ISBN 0-937114-01-4). Weeg Comp.

Harris, Diana K. & Cole, William E. Sociology of Aging. LC 79-89741. (Illus.). 1980. text ed. 20.95 (ISBN 0-395-28528-3); instr's. manual 1.00 (ISBN 0-395-28529-1). HM.

Harris, Diane. Woman's Day Book of Baking. (Illus.). 1978. 9.95 o.p. (ISBN 0-671-22506-5). S&S.

Harris, Diane F., ed. see Albert, Linda.

Harris, Diane F., ed. see Mayer, Jean & Goldberg, Jeanne.

Harris, Dorothy, jt. auth. see Peterson, James A.

Harris, Dorothy D. Born to Dance. 1971. 5.00 o.p. (ISBN 0-8233-0169-9). Golden Quill.

--Plateau Pauses. 1970. 5.00 o.p. (ISBN 0-8233-0149-4). Golden Quill.

Harris, Dorothy J. The House Mouse. LC 72-89476. (Illus.). 48p. (gr. k-3). 1973. PLB 6.95 o.p. (ISBN 0-7232-6096-6). Warne.

Harris, Dudley. Hydroponics: Growing Without Soil. rev. ed. (Illus.). 160p. 1975. 23.95 (ISBN 0-7153-6397-2). David & Charles.

Harris, E. Ebanisteria y Carpinteria De la Construccion. 1974. text ed. 14.05 (ISBN 0-07-091585-7, G). McGraw.

Harris, E. Edward. Marketing Research. 2nd ed. Dorr, Eugene L., ed. (Occupational Manuals & Projects in Marketing Ser.). (Illus.). (gr. 7-12). 1978. pap. text ed. 7.32 (ISBN 0-07-026837-1, G); instructor's manual & key 4.50 (ISBN 0-07-026838-X). McGraw.

Harris, Edward P. & Schade, Richard, eds. Lessing Yearbook XII, 1980. 336p. 1982. 25.00 (ISBN 0-8143-1681-6). Wayne St U Pr.

Harris, Edward P. & Wucherpfennig, Wolf, eds. Lessing Yearbook XIV 1982. 308p. 1983. 25.00 (ISBN 0-8143-1733-2). Wayne St U Pr.

Harris, Edwin S. Made in U. S. A. LC 82-62374. (Illus.). 160p. (Orig.). 1982. pap. 6.95 (ISBN 0-686-43326-2). RBA Pr.

Harris, Ellen T. Handel & The Pastoral Tradition. (Illus.). 1980. 42.00x (ISBN 0-19-315236-3). Oxford U Pr.

Harris, Enriqueta. Velazquez. LC 82-70748. (Illus.). 240p. 1982. 48.50x (ISBN 0-8014-1526-8). Cornell U Pr.

Harris, Ernest E., ed. Music Education: A Guide to Information Sources. LC 74-11560. (Education Information Guide Ser.: Vol. 1). 1978. 42.00x (ISBN 0-8103-1309-X). Gale.

Harris, Errol E. & Litt, D. The Problem of Evil. LC 77-72325. (Aquinas Lecture Ser.). 1977. 7.95 (ISBN 0-87462-142-9). Marquette.

Harris, Errol E., ed. see Joachim, Harold H.

Harris, F. C., jt. auth. see Jessop, H. T.

Harris, Forest K. Electrical Measurements. LC 74-32236. 798p. 1975. Repr. of 1952 ed. 29.50 (ISBN 0-88275-261-8). Krieger.

Harris, Frank. Oscar Wilde: His Life & Confessions. 1974. 10.00 (ISBN 0-8180-0225-5); pap. 12.95 (ISBN 0-8180-1137-8). Horizon.

Harris, Frank W. Games. rev. ed. (Illus.). 89p. 1983. pap. 6.95 (ISBN 0-686-42928-1). F Harris.

Harris, Fred R. America's Democracy: The Ideal & the Reality. 1980. text ed. 23.50x (ISBN 0-673-15162-X); pap. 6.95x study guide (ISBN 0-673-15163-8). Scott F.

--America's Democracy: The Ideal & the Reality. 2nd ed. 1983. text ed. 22.95x (ISBN 0-673-15819-5). Scott F.

Harris, Fred R. & Hain, Paul L. America's Legislative Process. 1983. 21.95x (ISBN 0-673-15357-6). Scott F.

Harris, Frederick. Encounters With Darkness: French & German Writers on World War II. 320p. 1983. 17.95 (ISBN 0-19-503246-2). Oxford U Pr.

Harris, G. T. & Harre, E. A. World Fertilizer Situation & Outlook 1978-85. (Technical Bulletin Ser.: T-13). (Illus.). 31p. (Orig.). 1979. pap. 4.00 (ISBN 0-88090-012-1). Intl Fertilizer.

Harris, George A. Broken Ears, Wounded Hearts. (Illus.). xiv, 174p. 1983. 10.95 (ISBN 0-913580-83-X). Gallaudet Coll.

Harris, George S. The Origins of Communism in Turkey. LC 67-26980. (Publications Ser.: No. 63). 1967. 9.95x o.p. (ISBN 0-8179-1631-8). Hoover Inst Pr.

Harris, Geraldine. Prince of the Godborn. LC 82-11999. (Seven Citadels Ser.: Pt. 1). 196p. 1983. 9.00 (ISBN 0-688-01792-4). Greenwillow.

Harris, Gertrude. Foods of the Frontier. LC 72-77565. (Illus.). 192p. 1972. pap. 4.95 o.s.i. (ISBN 0-912238-25-9). One Hund One Prods.

Harris, Grace G. Casting Out Anger. LC 77-80837. (Studies in Anthropology: No. 21). (Illus.). 1978. 27.95 (ISBN 0-521-21729-6). Cambridge U Pr.

Harris, Grace M. West to the Sunrise. (Illus.). 1980. 6.95 (ISBN 0-8138-0895-2). Iowa St U Pr.

Harris, H. & Hopkinson, D. A. Handbook of Enzyme Electrophoresis in Human Genetics: 1977 Supplement. 1978. 87.25 (ISBN 0-444-11203-0, North-Holland). Elsevier.

Harris, H., ed. Principles of Human Biochemical Genetics. 3rd ed. LC 75-108280. (Frontiers of Biology Ser.: Vol. 19). 477p. 1981. 71.00 (ISBN 0-444-80264-9, North-Holland); pap. 25.00 (ISBN 0-444-80256-8). Elsevier.

Harris, H. G. Collecting & Identifying Old Clocks. (Illus.). 12.95 (ISBN 0-87523-187-X). Wallace-Homestead.

--Collecting & Identifying Old Watches. (Illus.). 13.95 (ISBN 0-87523-190-X). Wallace-Homestead.

--Handbook of Watch & Clock Repair. (Illus.). 8.95 (ISBN 0-87523-141-1). Wallace-Homestead.

Harris, H. S. Hegel's Development: Night Thoughts (Jena 1801-1806) (Illus.). 1982. 94.00x (ISBN 0-19-824654-4). Oxford U Pr.

--Hegel's Development: Toward the Sunlight, 1770-1801. 1972. text ed. 64.00x (ISBN 0-19-824358-8). Oxford U Pr.

Harris, Harold A. Greek Athletes & Athletics. LC 78-10139. (Illus.). 1979. Repr. of 1966 ed. lib. bdg. 31.25x (ISBN 0-313-20754-2, HAGR). Greenwood.

Harris, Harry. Prenatal Diagnosis & Selective Abortion. 110p. 1974. 20.00x (ISBN 0-686-96984-7, Pub. by Nuffield England). State Mutual Bk.

Harris, Harry G., ed. Dynamic Modeling of Concrete Structures. LC 82-70083. (SP-73). 248p. (Orig.). 1982. pap. 30.95 (ISBN 0-686-95252-9). ACI.

Harris, Helen & Chauhan, Ela. So You Want to Buy a Word Processor? 147p. (Orig.). 1982. pap. text ed. 24.90x (ISBN 0-09-150351-5, Pub. by Busn Bks England). Renouf.

Harris, Henry. The Alma (1854) (Knight's Battles for Wargamers Ser.). (Illus.). 102p. 1973. 3.95 o.p. (ISBN 0-88254-211-7). Hippocrene Bks.

--Nucleus & Cytoplasm. 3rd ed. (Illus.). 1974. text ed. 18.95x o.p. (ISBN 0-19-854124-4); pap. text ed. 7.95x o.p. (ISBN 0-19-854125-2). Oxford U Pr.

Harris, Herbert. American Labor. 1938. text ed. 39.50x (ISBN 0-686-83463-1). Elliots Bks.

Harris, Herbert, ed. John Creasey's Crime Collection 1982. 192p. 1982. 12.95 (ISBN 0-312-44296-3). St Martin.

Harris, Herbert I., jt. auth. see Gallagher, J. Roswell.

Harris, Ian. The Price Guide to Victorian Silver. (Price Guide Ser.). (Illus.). 276p. 1977. 25.50 o.p. (ISBN 0-902028-09-X). Antique Collect.

Harris, Irving. The Breeze of the Spirit: Sam Shoemaker & the Story of Faith-at-Work. (Illus.). 1978. 8.95 o.p. (ISBN 0-8164-0399-6). Seabury.

Harris, Iverson L. Mme. Blavatsky Defended. 174p. (Orig.). 1971. pap. 3.00 (ISBN 0-913004-01-4). Point Loma Pub.

--Theosophy Under Fire: A Miniature Key to Theosophy As Recorded in a Legal Deposition. 88p. (Orig.). 1970. pap. 3.00 (ISBN 0-913004-03-0, 913004-03). Point Loma Pub.

--The Wisdom of Confucius. 45p. 1957. pap. 0.75 (ISBN 0-913004-09-X). Point Loma Pub.

--The Wisdom of Laotse. 36p. 1972. pap. 0.75 (ISBN 0-913004-05-7). Point Loma Pub.

Harris, J. D., jt. auth. see Croke, B. F.

Harris, J. Milton & Wamser, Carl C. Fundamentals of Organic Reaction Mechanisms. LC 75-40275. 1976. 33.95 (ISBN 0-471-35400-7). Wiley.

Harris, J. N. Mechanical Working of Metals: Theory & Practice. (International Series on Materials Science & Technology: Vol. 36). (Illus.). 275p. 1983. 40.00 (ISBN 0-08-025464-0); pap. 17.50 (ISBN 0-08-025463-2). Pergamon.

Harris, J. R., ed. Electron Microscopy of Protein, Vol. 3. 1982. 57.00 (ISBN 0-12-327603-9). Acad Pr.

Harris, J. W. Law & Legal Science: An Inquiry into the Concepts Legal Rule & Legal System. 1979. 29.95x (ISBN 0-19-825353-2). Oxford U Pr.

Harris, Jacqueline. Martin Luther King, Jr. (Impact Biography Ser.). (Illus.). 128p. (gr. 7 up). 1983. PLB 8.90 (ISBN 0-531-04588-9). Watts.

Harris, James. Hermes: Or, a Philosophical Inquiry Concerning Universal Grammar. (Linguistics, 13th-18th Centuries Ser.). 464p. (Fr.). 1974. Repr. of 1801 ed. lib. bdg. 115.50 o.p. (ISBN 0-8287-0415-5, 5044). Clearwater Pub.

--High Ideals? LC 77-13737. 1978. 8.95 o.p. (ISBN 0-15-140221-3, Harv); pap. 3.95 (ISBN 0-15-640195-9). HarBraceJ.

--The Peregrine Falcon in Greenland: Observing an Endangered Species. LC 78-67404. (Illus.). 256p. (Orig.). 1981. 19.00x (ISBN 0-8262-0267-5); pap. 8.95 (ISBN 0-8262-0343-4). U of Mo Pr.

--Philological Inquiries. (Linguistics 13th-18th Centuries Ser.). 338p. (Fr.). 1974. Repr. of 1801 ed. lib. bdg. 88.00x o.p. (ISBN 0-8287-0416-3, 5045). Clearwater Pub.

--Spanish Phonology. 1969. 22.50x (ISBN 0-262-08032-X). MIT Pr.

Harris, James B., tr. see Rampo, Edogawa.

Harris, James W. Syllable Structure & Stress in Spanish: A Nonlinear Analysis. (Linguistic Inquiry Monographs). 176p. 1983. 25.00x (ISBN 0-262-08124-5); pap. 15.00x (ISBN 0-262-58060-8). MIT Pr.

Harris, Janet. Crisis in Corrections: The Prison Problem. LC 73-8017. 160p. (gr. 9-12). 1973. 5.95 o.p. (ISBN 0-07-026780-4, GB). McGraw.

Harris, Janet C. & Park, Roberta J., eds. Play, Games, & Sports in Cultural Contexts. LC 82-83148. 500p. 1983. text ed. 24.95x (ISBN 0-931250-36-6). Human Kinetics.

Harris, Jay & Harris, Jean. The Roots of Artifice: On the Origin & Development of Literary Creativity. LC 80-23061. 320p. 1981. 29.95 (ISBN 0-89885-004-5). Human Sci Pr.

Harris, Jay, ed. see Harris, Jean.

Harris, Jay, et al. TV Guide: The First 25 Years. 1978. 14.95 o.p. (ISBN 0-671-23065-4). S&S.

Harris, Jay S. TV Guide: The First Twenty-Five Years. 1980. pap. 9.95 (ISBN 0-452-25348-9, Z5348, Plume). NAL.

Harris, Jean. The One-Eyed Doctor: Sigismund Freud. Harris, Jay, ed. LC 81-65787. 256p. 1983. write for info (ISBN 0-87668-453-3). Aronson.

Harris, Jean, jt. auth. see Harris, Jay.

Harris, Jed. A Dance on the High Wire. 1979. 10.00 o.p. (ISBN 0-517-53921-7). Crown.

Harris, Jeffrey & Haggard, Keith, eds. What Works? Documenting the Results of Energy Conservation in Buildings. (Progress in Solar Energy Ser.). 1983. text ed. 50.00 Selected Papers (ISBN 0-89553-111-9); text ed. 15.00 (ISBN 0-89553-110-0). Am Solar Energy.

Harris, Jeffrey P. & Hollander, Jack M., eds. Improving Energy Systems in Buildings: Progress & Problems: Supplement. (Progress in Solar Energy Ser.). 650p. 1983. pap. text ed. 43.50 (ISBN 0-89553-122-4). Am Solar Energy.

Harris, Jessica, tr. see Senghor, Leopold S.

Harris, Jessica L., ed. Cumulative Index to the Annual Review of Information Science & Technology, Vol. 1-10. LC 66-25096. 250p. 1976. lexhide 27.50 (ISBN 0-685-56510-6). Am Soc Info Sci.

Harris, Joanna C. Let's Go to a Sanitation Department. (Let's Go Ser.). (Illus.). 48p. (gr. 3-6). 1972. PLB 4.29 o.p. (ISBN 0-399-60705-6). Putnam Pub Group.

Harris, Joel C. Brer Rabbit & Brer Fox. (gr. 3 up). 1969. 5.95 o.p. (ISBN 0-00-138188-1, Philomel). Putnam Pub Group.

--Nights with Uncle Remus: Myths & Legends of the Old Plantation. LC 70-164329. 1971. Repr. of 1883 ed. 42.00x (ISBN 0-8103-3866-1). Gale.

--Stories of Georgia. LC 73-174943. 1975. Repr. of 1896 ed. 34.00x (ISBN 0-8103-4082-8). Gale.

--Uncle Remus. LC 65-14828. (Illus.). (gr. 3 up). 1966. 8.95x (ISBN 0-8052-3273-7); pap. 3.95 (ISBN 0-8052-0101-7). Schocken.

--Uncle Remus: His Songs & His Sayings. Hemenway, Robert, intro. by. 256p. 1982. pap. 4.95 (ISBN 0-14-039014-6). Penguin.

--Uncle Remus: His Songs & Sayings. LC 74-1958. (Thrushwood Bks). (Illus.). 288p. (gr. 3-9). 1974. Repr. 3.95 (ISBN 0-448-02382-2, G&D). Putnam Pub Group.

--Uncle Remus Stories. (Illus.). (gr. 3up). 1960. 5.95 o.p. (ISBN 0-00-138187-3, Philomel). Putnam Pub Group.

Harris, John. The Artist & the Country House. 1981. 100.00x o.p. (ISBN 0-686-78788-9, Pub. by RHS Ent England). State Mutual Bk.

--English Decorative Ironworks from Contemporary Source Books. pap. 20.00 o.s.i. (ISBN 0-85458-608-3). Transatlantic.

--Hot Men: An Erotic Coloring Book. (Illus.). 32p. 1982. pap. 7.95 (ISBN 0-312-39240-0). St Martin.

--Sir William Chambers. LC 70-113198. (Illus.). 1971. 50.00x (ISBN 0-271-00133-X). Pa St U Pr.

Harris, John & Pahl, Aleta. Endangered Predators. LC 75-34051. 96p. (gr. 4-7). 1976. PLB 7.95 o.p. (ISBN 0-385-08012-3). Doubleday.

Harris, John B., ed. Muscular Dystrophy & Other Inherited Diseases of Skeletal Muscle in Animals, Vol. 317. LC 78-27609. (Annals of the New York Academy of Science Ser.). 716p. 1979. pap. 82.00x (ISBN 0-89766-005-6). NY Acad Sci.

Harris, John H., Jr. & Harris, William H. The Radiology of Emergency Medicine. 2nd ed. (Illus.). 720p. 1981. 68.95 (ISBN 0-683-03883-4, 3883-4). Williams & Wilkins.

Harris, John W. & Kellermeyer, Robert. Red Cell: Production, Metabolism, Destruction, Normal & Abnormal. rev. ed. (Commonwealth Fund Publications Ser). 1970. 32.50x o.p. (ISBN 0-674-75101-9); pap. 12.50x (ISBN 0-674-75102-7). Harvard U Pr.

Harris, Jonathan. Hiroshima: A Study in the Science, Politics, & the Ethics of War. Brown, Richard H. & Halsey, Van R., eds. (Amherst Ser). (gr. 10-12). 1970. pap. text ed. 5.16 (ISBN 0-201-02687-2, Sch Div). A-W.

--Terrorism: The New Politics. (Illus.). 160p. (gr. 9-12). 1983. PLB 9.29 (ISBN 0-671-45807-8). Messner.

Harris, Joseph E., ed. Global Dimensions of the African Diaspora. 1983. 19.95 (ISBN 0-88258-022-1). Howard U Pr.
Harris, Joseph P. Congress & the Legislative Process. 2nd ed. (Illus.). 208p. 1972. pap. text ed. 13.95 (ISBN 0-07-026822-3, C). McGraw.
Harris, Joseph P., jt. auth. see Corson, John J.
Harris, Kaasa, tr. see Molland, Einar.
Harris, Karen, jt. auth. see Baskin, Barbara.
Harris, Karl N. Model Stationary & Marine Steam Engines. 1964. 10.00x (ISBN 0-85344-072-7). Intl Pubns Serv.
Harris, Karyn J. Costume Display Techniques. LC 77-5404. 1977. pap. 6.50 (ISBN 0-910050-27-9). AASLH.
Harris, Kathryn G. Robert Frost: Studies of the Poetry. 1980. lib. bdg. 21.00 (ISBN 0-8161-8397-X, Hall Reference). G K Hall.
Harris, Keith, jt. auth. see Norris, Robert E.
Harris, Ken. World Diesel Locomotives. (Illus.). 160p. 1982. 19.95 (ISBN 0-86720-625-X). Sci Bks Intl.
--World Electric Locomotives. (Illus.). 160p. 1981. 17.95 (ISBN 0-86720-569-5). Sci Bks Intl.
Harris, Kenn. The Ultimate Opera Quiz Book. (Illus.). 256p. 1982. pap. 7.95 (ISBN 0-14-005884-2). Penguin.
Harris, L. Monetary Theory. 1980. 26.95 (ISBN 0-07-026840-1). McGraw.
Harris, L. C. & Feinstein, Ellen. Understanding EOGs in Infants & Children. 1979. 12.50 o.p. (ISBN 0-316-34826-0); 16.95 o.p. (ISBN 0-316-34826-0). Little.
Harris, L. James & Patent, Trademark & Copyright Institute of the George Washington University, eds. Nurturing New Ideas: Legal Rights & Economic Roles. LC 76-83776. 660p. 1969. 23.50 (ISBN 0-87179-081-5). BNA.
Harris, L. M. Design for Reliability in Deepwater Floating Drilling Operations. 266p. 1980. 44.95x (ISBN 0-87814-082-4). Pennwell Books Division.
--An Introduction to Deepwater Floating Drilling Operations. LC 72-76603. 272p. 1972. 29.95x (ISBN 0-87814-011-5). Pennwell Pub.
Harris, Latif, jt. auth. see McHugh, Joseph.
Harris, Laurie L. Nineteenth-Century Literature Criticism: Excerpts from Criticism of the Works of Nineteenth-Century Novelists, Poets, Playwrights, Short-Story Writers, & Other Creative Writers, Vol. 1. 68.00x (ISBN 0-8103-5801-8). Gale.
--Nineteenth-Century Literature Criticism, Vol. 2. LC 81-6943. 600p. 1982. 68.00x (ISBN 0-8103-5802-6). Gale.
--Shakespearean Criticism, Vol. 1. 600p. 1982. 55.00 (ISBN 0-8103-6125-6). Gale.
Harris, Laurie L., ed. Nineteenth-Century Literature Criticism, Vol. 3. 600p. 1982. 70.00x (ISBN 0-8103-5803-4). Gale.
Harris, Lloyd J. The Book of Garlic. 3rd rev. ed. LC 79-20972. (Illus.). 286p. 1980. pap. 9.95 (ISBN 0-943186-00-5). Aris Bks.
Harris, Lorle. Biography of a River Otter. LC 78-3606. (Nature Biography Bks.). (Illus.). (gr. 3-6). 1979. PLB 5.49 o.p. (ISBN 0-399-61127-4). Putnam Pub Group.
--Biography of a Whooping Crane. LC 76-23240. (Nature Biography Ser.). (Illus.). (gr. 3-5). 1977. PLB 6.99 (ISBN 0-399-61063-4). Putnam Pub Group.
Harris, Lorle K. Biography of a Mountain Gorilla. (Nature Biography Bk.). (Illus.). 64p. (gr. 3-6). 1981. lib. bdg. 6.99 (ISBN 0-399-61144-4). Putnam Pub Group.
Harris, Louis, jt. auth. see Brink, William.
Harris, Loyd J. The Book of Garlic. Rev.,2nd ed. LC 75-5452. 1976. pap. 9.95 (ISBN 0-915572-30-3). Panjandrum.
Harris, Lucy. Harris College of Nursing: Five Decades of Struggle for a Cause. new ed. LC 73-78068. 1973. 6.00 o.p. (ISBN 0-912646-43-8). Tex Christian.
Harris, M. The Heart of Boswell: Six Journals in One Volume. 1981. 17.95 (ISBN 0-07-026775-8); pap. 7.95 (ISBN 0-07-026778-2). McGraw.
Harris, M. J., jt. auth. see Kelly, Anthony.
Harris, Madalene, jt. auth. see Irwin, Mary.
Harris, Marcia, jt. auth. see Haglund, Elaine.
Harris, Marilyn. The Diviner. LC 82-13216. 448p. 1983. 15.95 (ISBN 0-399-12739-9). Putnam Pub Group.
--The Eden Passion. LC 78-21602. 1979. 12.95 o.p. (ISBN 0-399-12269-9). Putnam Pub Group.
--Eden Rising. 400p. 1982. 15.95 (ISBN 0-399-12687-2). Putnam Pub Group.
--Hatter Fox. 256p. 1983. pap. 2.75 (ISBN 0-345-30026-2). Ballantine.
--The Last Great Love. 324p. 1981. 14.95 (ISBN 0-399-12649-X). Putnam Pub Group.
--The Last Great Love. 1982. pap. 3.50 (ISBN 0-8217-1088-5). Zebra.
--The Portent. 324p. 1980. 11.95 (ISBN 0-399-12506-X). Putnam Pub Group.
--The Portent. 432p. 1982. pap. 3.50 (ISBN 0-515-06882-9). Jove Pubns.
--Prince of Eden. LC 77-25420. 1978. 12.50 o.p. (ISBN 0-399-12059-9). Putnam Pub Group.
--The Runaway's Diary. (gr. 7-9). 1974. pap. 1.75 o.p. (ISBN 0-671-41304-X). Archway.
--This Other Eden. 1978. pap. 3.50 (ISBN 0-380-01840-3, 58784). Avon.
--This Other Eden. LC 76-25236. 1977. 9.95 o.p. (ISBN 0-399-11844-6). Putnam Pub Group.
--The Women of Eden. LC 79-19757. 1980. 12.95 o.p. (ISBN 0-399-12478-0). Putnam Pub Group.
Harris, Mark & Wright, R. Glenn. Index to Birthplaces of United Kingdom Authors. 1979. lib. bdg. 15.00 (ISBN 0-8161-8273-6, Hall Reference). G K Hall.
Harris, Marshall D. Origin of the Land Tenure System in the United States. Repr. of 1953 ed. lib. bdg. 20.25x (ISBN 0-8371-3731-4, HATS). Greenwood.
Harris, Martin, jt. ed. see Vincent, Nigel.
Harris, Marvin. America Now. 1982. pap. 4.80 (ISBN 0-671-45701-2, Touchstone Bks). S&S.
--America Now: The Anthropology of a Changing Culture. 1981. 12.95 o.s.i. (ISBN 0-671-43148-X). S&S.
--Cannibals & Kings: The Origins of Cultures. 1977. 3.95 (ISBN 0-394-72700-2). Random.
--Cultural Anthropology. 448p. 1983. pap. text ed. 17.50 scp (ISBN 0-06-042668-3, HarpC); Instr's. Manual Avail. (ISBN 0-06-362666-7). Har-Row.
--Patterns of Race in the Americas. LC 80-11594. (Illus.). v, 154p. 1980. Repr. of 1964 ed. lib. bdg. 18.50x (ISBN 0-313-22359-9, HAPS). Greenwood.
Harris, Max. Angry Eye: A Comment on Life & Letters. 1974. text ed. 23.00 (ISBN 0-08-017373-X). Pergamon.
Harris, Melinda. Embrace the Wind. (Second Chance at Love Ser.: No. 98). 192p. 1983. pap. 1.75 (ISBN 0-515-06862-4). Jove Pubns.
Harris, Michael. Gresley's Coaches: Coaches Built for GNR, ECJS & LNER 1905-53. (Illus.). 1973. 16.95 o.p. (ISBN 0-7153-5935-5). David & Charles.
Harris, Michael G. Light Engineering Production Draughting. (Illus.). (gr. 10 up). 1968. text ed. 7.25x o.p. (ISBN 0-85429-070-2). Transatlantic.
Harris, Michael H., ed. Advances in Librarianship, Vol. 9. LC 79-88675. 1979. 27.50 (ISBN 0-12-785009-0); lib. ed. 35.50 (ISBN 0-12-785021-X); microfiche 23.00 (ISBN 0-12-785022-8). Acad Pr.
Harris, Michael H., jt. ed. see Cutler, Wayne.
Harris, Michael J. & Voight, Melvin J., eds. Advances in Librarianship, 8 vols. Incl. Vol. 1. 294p. 1970. 43.00 (ISBN 0-12-785001-5); Vol. 2. 388p. 1971. 43.00 (ISBN 0-12-785002-3); Vol. 3. 275p. 1972. 43.00 (ISBN 0-12-785003-1); Vol. 4. 1974. 43.00 (ISBN 0-12-785004-X); Vol. 5. 1975. 43.00 (ISBN 0-12-785005-8); lib ed. 55.00 (ISBN 0-12-785012-0); microfiche 31.50 (ISBN 0-12-785013-9); Vol. 6. 1976. 34.50 (ISBN 0-12-785006-6); lib ed. 42.50 (ISBN 0-12-785014-7); microfiche 26.00 (ISBN 0-12-785015-5); Vol. 7. 1977. lib ed. 53.50 (ISBN 0-12-785016-3); 43.00 (ISBN 0-12-785007-4); microfiche 32.50 (ISBN 0-12-785017-1); Vol. 8. 32.00 (ISBN 0-12-785008-2); lib. ed. 40.00 (ISBN 0-12-785018-X); microfiche 25.00 (ISBN 0-12-785019-8). LC 79-88675. Acad Pr.
Harris, Middleton, et al. The Black Book. 1973. pap. 11.95 (ISBN 0-394-70622-6). Random.
Harris, Milton. Ship of Love & Other Poems. 1980. 4.00 o.p. (ISBN 0-8062-1277-2). Carlton.
Harris, Mollie. From Acre End: Portrait of a Village. (Illus.). 154p. 1983. 14.95 (ISBN 0-7011-2630-2, Pub. by Chatto & Windus). Merrimack Bk Serv.
Harris, Muriel S. Tutoring Writing: Sourcebook for Writing Labs. 1981. pap. text ed. 12.50x (ISBN 0-673-15526-9). Scott F.
Harris, N. & Hemmerling, E. M. Experiments in Applied Physics. 3rd ed. 1980. text ed. 12.95 (ISBN 0-07-026818-5). McGraw.
Harris, N., jt. auth. see Conde, D. F.
Harris, Norma, ed. see Guenther, Gloria M.
Harris, Norman & Hemmerling, Edwin M. Introductory Applied Physics. 4th ed. (Illus.). 1980. text ed. 24.10x (ISBN 0-07-026816-9, G); instructor's manual 6.95 (ISBN 0-07-026817-7). McGraw.
Harris, Norman, jt. auth. see Player, Gary.
Harris, Norman C. & Conde, D. F. Modern Air Conditioning Practice. 2nd ed. 25.95 (ISBN 0-07-026811-8, G); answer bk problem solutions manual 3.50 (ISBN 0-07-026812-6). McGraw.
Harris, Norman C. & Hemmerling, E. M. Experiments in Applied Physics. 2nd ed. 1972. pap. text ed. 11.05 (ISBN 0-07-026806-1, G). McGraw.
Harris, O. Jeff. How to Manage People at Work: A Short Course for Professionals. LC 76-45821. (Wiley Professional Development Programs Ser.). 300p. 1977. 55.95 (ISBN 0-471-01930-5). Wiley.
Harris, O. Jeff, Jr. Managing People at Work: Concepts & Cases in Interpersonal Behavior. LC 75-19272. 608p. 1976. text ed. 30.95 (ISBN 0-471-35410-4). Wiley.
Harris, Ollie K. & Slover, Elizabeth. So Let It Be. Ericson, Carolyn, ed. LC 82-84481. 99p. (Orig.). 1982. pap. 12.50 (ISBN 0-911317-03-1). Ericson Bks.
Harris, P. J. Manufacturing Technology Two. (Illus.). 1979. pap. text ed. 11.95 (ISBN 0-408-00410-X). Butterworth.
Harris, P. M., ed. The Potato Crop: The Scientific Basis for Improvement. 1978. 79.95x (ISBN 0-412-12830-6, Pub. by Chapman & Hall). Methuen Inc.
Harris, Paula. Pisces. (Sun Signs Ser.). (Illus.). (gr. 4-12). 1978. PLB 6.95 (ISBN 0-87191-652-5); pap. 3.25 (ISBN 0-89812-082-9). Creative Ed.
--Scorpio. (Sun Signs). (Illus.). (gr. 4-12). 1978. PLB 6.95 (ISBN 0-87191-648-7); pap. 3.25 (ISBN 0-89812-078-0). Creative Ed.
Harris, Peggy, jt. auth. see Hubbard, W. P.
Harris, Philip R. New World, New Ways, New Management. 320p. 1983. 22.95 (ISBN 0-8144-5755-X). Am Mgmt.
Harris, Philip R. & Moran, Robert T. Managing Cultural Differences, Vol. 1. (International Management Productivity Ser.). 432p. 1979. 21.95 (ISBN 0-87201-160-7). Gulf Pub.
Harris, R. Baine, ed. Neoplatonism & Indian Thought. (Ancient & Modern Ser.). 353p. 1981. lib. bdg. 44.50x (ISBN 0-87395-545-5); pap. 14.95x (ISBN 0-87395-546-3). State U NY Pr.
--The Significance of Neoplatonism. LC 76-21254. 1976. 34.50x (ISBN 0-87395-800-4). State U NY Pr.
--The Structure of Being: A Neoplatonic Interpretation. LC 81-5627. (Neoplatonism: Ancient & Modern Ser.). 320p. 1981. 44.50x (ISBN 0-87395-532-3); pap. 14.95x (ISBN 0-87395-533-1). State U NY Pr.
Harris, R. Cole & Warkentin, John. Canada Before Confederation: A Study in Historical Geography. (Historical Geography of North America Ser). (Illus.). 1974. pap. text ed. 9.95x (ISBN 0-19-501791-9). Oxford U Pr.
Harris, R. Laird. Inspiration & Canonicity of the Bible. (Contemporary Evangelical Perspectives Ser). kivar 7.95 (ISBN 0-310-25891-X). Zondervan.
Harris, R. Laird, et al, eds. Theological Wordbook of the Old Testament. LC 80-28047. 1800p. 1980. text ed. 39.95 (ISBN 0-8024-8631-2). Moody.
Harris, Radie. Radie's World. LC 75-29667. (Illus.). 1975. 8.95 o.p. (ISBN 0-399-11667-2). Putnam Pub Group.
Harris, Ralph. Et Maintenant?--L'Evan Juan. Cosson, Annie, et al, eds. Cosson, Annie, tr. from Eng. Orig. Title: And Now What? 80p. (FR.). 1981. pap. 0.70 (ISBN 0-8297-1077-9). Life Pubs Intl.
Harris, Raymond. Best-Selling Chapters. (Illus.). 496p. (gr. 9 up). 1978. pap. text ed. 10.00x (ISBN 0-89061-151-3, 791); 14.00. Jamestown Pubs.
--Best-Selling Chapters, Middle Level. (Illus.). 450p. (Orig.). (gr. 6-8). 1982. pap. text ed. 8.00x (ISBN 0-89061-248-X, 790); 14.00. Jamestown Pubs.
--Best Short Stories. (Illus.). 560p. (Orig.). (gr. 9 up). 1980. pap. text ed. 8.00x (ISBN 0-89061-234-X, 792); 14.00. Jamestown Pubs.
Harris, Raymond, jt. auth. see Spargo, Edward.
Harris, Raymond, ed. see Conan Doyle, Arthur.
Harris, Raymond, ed. see Harte, Bret.
Harris, Raymond, ed. see Henry, O.
Harris, Raymond, ed. see London, Jack.
Harris, Raymond, ed. see Poe, Edgar Allan.
Harris, Raymond, ed. see Stevenson, Robert Louis.
Harris, Richard. Death of a Friend. 288p. 1982. cancelled o.s.i. (ISBN 0-399-90121-3, Marek). Putnam Pub Group.
--Enemies. LC 78-27831. 1979. 9.95 (ISBN 0-399-90040-3, Marek). Putnam Pub Group.
Harris, Richard C. Seigneurial System in Early Canada: A Geographical Study. (Illus.). 264p. 1966. 20.00x o.p. (ISBN 0-299-03980-3). U of Wis Pr.
--William Sidney Porter (O. Henry): A Reference Guide. 1980. lib. bdg. 21.00 (ISBN 0-8161-8006-7, Hall Reference). G K Hall.
Harris, Richard H., ed. Modern Drama in America & England, Nineteen Fifty to Nineteen Seventy: A Guide to Information Sources. (American Literature, English Literature & World Literatures in English Ser.: Vol. 34). 400p. 1982. 42.00x (ISBN 0-8103-1493-2). Gale.
Harris, Richard J., ed. Information Processing Research in Advertising. 1983. text ed. write for info. (ISBN 0-89859-204-6). L Erlbaum Assocs.
Harris, Robert. Gotcha! The Media, the Government & the Falklands Crisis. 176p. (Orig.). 1983. pap. 5.95 (ISBN 0-571-13052-6). Faber & Faber.
Harris, Robert, jt. auth. see Paxton, Jeremy.
Harris, Robert B. Precedence & Arrow Networking Techniques for Construction. LC 78-5786. 1978. text ed. 37.95 (ISBN 0-471-04123-8). Wiley.
Harris, Robert D. Necker: Reform Statesman of the Ancien Regime. LC 77-93464. 1979. 28.50x (ISBN 0-520-03647-6). U of Cal Pr.
Harris, Robert J. The Quest for Equality: The Constitution, Congress & the Supreme Court. LC 77-1851. 1977. Repr. of 1960 ed. lib. bdg. 18.75x (ISBN 0-8371-9524-1, HAQE). Greenwood.
Harris, Robert P. Nevada Postal History. (Illus.). 1973. 35.00 o.p. (ISBN 0-913814-04-0). Nevada Pubns.
Harris, Robert S., ed. Feeding & Nutrition of Nonhuman Primates. 1970. 41.50 (ISBN 0-12-327360-9). Acad Pr.
Harris, Robert S., jt. ed. see Sebrell, W. H., Jr.
Harris, Robert S., et al, eds. Vitamins & Hormones: Advances in Research & Applications. Incl. Vols. 1-8. 1943-50. 53.00 ea. Vol. 1 (ISBN 0-12-709801-1). Vol. 2 (ISBN 0-12-709802-X). Vol. 3 (ISBN 0-12-709803-8). Vol. 4 (ISBN 0-12-709804-6). Vol. 5 (ISBN 0-12-709805-4). Vol. 6 (ISBN 0-12-709806-2). Vol. 7 (ISBN 0-12-709807-0). Vol. 8 (ISBN 0-12-709808-9); Vol. 9. 1951. 53.00 (ISBN 0-12-709809-7); Vol. 10. 1952. 48.00 (ISBN 0-12-709810-0); Vols. 11-16. 1953-58. Vols. 11-12. 48.00 ea.; Vol. 11. (ISBN 0-12-709811-9); Vol. 12. (ISBN 0-12-709812-7); Vols. 13-16. 48.00 ea.; Vol. 13. (ISBN 0-12-709813-5); Vol. 14. (ISBN 0-12-709814-3); Vol. 15. (ISBN 0-12-709815-1); Vol. 16. (ISBN 0-12-709816-X); Vol. 17. Harris, Robert S., ed. 1959. 48.00 ea. (ISBN 0-12-709817-8); Vol. 18. 1960. 48.00 (ISBN 0-12-709818-6); Vol. 19. 1961. 48.00 (ISBN 0-12-709819-4); Vol. 20. Incl. International Symposium on Vitamin E & Metabolism. Wool, I. G. 1962. 48.00 (ISBN 0-12-709820-8); Vol. 21. 1963. 53.00 (ISBN 0-12-709821-6); Vol. 22. **Incl. International Symposium on Vitamin B6. 1964. 53.00 (ISBN 0-12-709822-4); Vol. 23. 1965. 53.00 (ISBN 0-12-709823-2); Vol. 24. 1966. 48.00 (ISBN 0-12-709824-0); Vol. 25. 1967. 53.00 (ISBN 0-12-709825-9); Vol. 26. 1968. 53.00 (ISBN 0-12-709826-7); Vol. 27. 1970. 53.00 (ISBN 0-12-709827-5); Vol. 28. Munson, Paul L., ed. 1971. 53.00 (ISBN 0-12-709828-3); Vol. 29. 1971. 53.00 (ISBN 0-12-709829-1); Vol. 30. 1972. 54.00 (ISBN 0-12-709830-5); Vol. 35. Munson, Paul L., et al, eds. 1978. 48.00 (ISBN 0-12-709835-6); Vol. 36. Munson, Paul L., et al, eds. 1979. 59.50 (ISBN 0-12-709836-4). Acad Pr.**
Harris, Rodney E., et al. Palabres: Contes et Poemes De L'afrique Noire et Des Antilles. 1973. pap. 7.95x o.p. (ISBN 0-673-07585-0). Scott F.
Harris, Rosemary. Child in the Bamboo Grove. LC 72-4064. (Illus.). (gr. 1-3). 1972. 10.95 (ISBN 0-87599-194-7). S G Phillips.
Harris, Rosemary, retold by. Beauty & the Beast. LC 79-7482. (Illus.). (gr. 1-3). 1980. PLB 8.95a (ISBN 0-385-15483-6). Doubleday.
Harris, Roy D. & Gonzalez, Richard F. The Operations Manager. (Illus.). 490p. 1981. text ed. 25.95 (ISBN 0-8299-0332-1). West Pub.
Harris, Roy D., et al. Computer Models in Operations Research: A Computer Augmented Approach. 1974. pap. text ed. 17.50 scp (ISBN 0-06-042662-4, HarpC); inst. manual avail. (ISBN 0-06-362578-4); scp sourcedeck 30.00 (ISBN 0-06-042661-6). Har-Row.
Harris, Ruth. Decades. 1975. pap. 2.25 o.p. (ISBN 0-451-08545-0, E8545, Sig). NAL.
--Kinesiology: Workbook & Laboratory Manual. (Illus.). 1977. 14.95 (ISBN 0-395-20668-5). HM.
Harris, Sandra L. Families of the Developmentally Disabled: A Guide to Behavioral Interventions. (General Psychology Ser.: No. 119). 170p. 1983. 16.50 (ISBN 0-08-030125-8). Pergamon.
Harris, Sandra L., jt. auth. see Nathan, Peter E.
Harris, Seena, jt. ed. see Harris, Bruce.
Harris, Seymour. Inflation & the American Economy. LC 76-10838. 659p. 1976. Repr. of 1945 ed. lib. bdg. 69.50 (ISBN 0-306-70827-2). Da Capo.
--Price & Related Controls in the United States. LC 76-10831. 393p. 1976. Repr. of 1945 ed. lib. bdg. 49.50 (ISBN 0-306-70828-0). Da Capo.
Harris, Seymour E. Economics of Harvard. 1970. 20.50 o.p. (ISBN 0-07-026832-0, C). McGraw.
--Economics of Mobilization & Inflation. LC 68-28586. (Illus.). 1968. Repr. of 1951 ed. lib. bdg. 16.00x (ISBN 0-8371-0097-6, HAEM). Greenwood.
Harris, Sheldon. Blues Who's Who. (Quality Paperbacks Ser.). (Illus.). 775p. 1981. pap. 18.95 (ISBN 0-306-80155-8). Da Capo.
Harris, Sherry S., ed. Accredited Institutions of Post-Secondary Education & Programs: 1982-83. 1981. 13.50 o.p. (ISBN 0-8268-1112-4). ACE.
Harris, Sidney. What's So Funny about Computers? LC 82-21227. (Illus.). 128p. 1983. pap. 6.95 (ISBN 0-86576-049-7). W Kaufmann.
Harris, Spencer P., compiled by. The Legal Connection. 1982. 87.00 (ISBN 0-685-90845-3). Data Financial.
--Who Audits America. (Corporations & Accountants Ser.). 1982. 62.00 (ISBN 0-933088-03-5); pap. 54.00 (ISBN 0-685-90844-5). Data Financial.
Harris, Stacy. Comedians of Country Music. LC 77-90150. (Country Music Bks). (gr. 5 up). 1978. PLB 5.95g (ISBN 0-8225-1409-5). Lerner Pubns.
Harris, Stacy & Krishef, Robert K. The Carter Family. LC 77-90154. (Country Music Bks.). (Illus.). (gr. 5 up). 1978. PLB 5.95g (ISBN 0-8225-1403-6). Lerner Pubns.
Harris, Stephen. Fire & Ice: The Cascade Volcanoes. rev. ed. LC 80-16095. (Illus.). 1980. pap. 7.95 o.p. (ISBN 0-89886-009-1). Mountaineers.
Harris, Styron. Charles Kingsley: A Reference Book. 1981. 26.00 (ISBN 0-8161-8166-7, Hall Reference). G K Hall.
Harris, Susan. Boats & Ships. (Easy-Read Fact Bks.). (Illus.). (gr. 2-4). 1979. PLB 8.60 s&l (ISBN 0-531-02270-6). Watts.
--Crocodiles & Alligators. LC 79-13103. (gr. 2-4). 1980. PLB 8.60 (ISBN 0-531-00443-0). Watts.
--Gems & Minerals. (gr. 2-4). 1980. PLB 8.60 (ISBN 0-531-03241-8). Watts.

--Helicopters. (Easy-Read Fact Bks.). (Illus.). (gr. 2-4). 1979. s&l 8.60 (ISBN 0-531-02850-X). Watts.
--Space. (Easy-Read Fact Bks.). (Illus.). (gr. 2-4). 1979. PLB 8.60 s&l (ISBN 0-531-02852-6). Watts.
--Upside Down Creatures. (Easy-Read Wildlife Books Ser.). (Illus.). (gr. 2-4). 1978. PLB 8.60 s&l (ISBN 0-531-02918-2). Watts.
--Volcanoes. (Easy-Read Fact Bks.). (Illus.). (gr. 2-4). 1979. PLB 8.60 s&l (ISBN 0-531-02277-3). Watts.
--Whales. (gr. 2-4). PLB 8.60 (ISBN 0-531-00444-9). Watts.
--The World Beneath the Sea. LC 78-10880. (Easy-Read Fact Bks.). (Illus.). (gr. 2-4). 1979. PLB 8.60 s&l o.p. (ISBN 0-531-02854-2). Watts.
Harris, Susan K. Mark Twain's Escape from Time: A Study of Patterns & Images. LC 82-1981. 186p. 1982. 16.00 (ISBN 0-8262-0369-8). U of Mo Pr.
Harris, Sydney P., jt. auth. see Greenstone, Arthur W.
Harris, Tedric A. Rolling Bearing Analysis. LC 66-25221. 1966. 69.95x (ISBN 0-471-35265-9, Pub. by Wiley-Interscience). Wiley.
Harris, Teresa & Epps, Louvella. God! Please Stop Drugs. 1982. 5.95 (ISBN 0-533-04435-9). Vantage.
Harris, Thomas. Black Sunday. LC 74-16601. 320p. 1975. 7.95 (ISBN 0-399-11443-2). Putnam Pub Group.
--I'm OK-You're OK. 1973. pap. 3.50 (ISBN 0-380-00772-X, 58909-5). Avon.
--Red Dragon. 352p. 1981. 13.95 (ISBN 0-399-12442-X). Putnam Pub Group.
--Red Dragon. 1982. pap. 3.95 (ISBN 0-553-22746-7). Bantam.
Harris, Thomas A. I'm OK-You're OK. pap. 2.75 o.p. (ISBN 0-686-92370-7, 6477). Hazelden.
--I'm Ok-You're Ok: A Practical Guide to Transactional Analysis. LC 69-13495. (Illus.). 1969. 11.49i (ISBN 0-06-002385-6, HarpT). Harper-Row.
Harris, Thomas M. Yorkshire Jurassic Flora: Vol. II, Caytoniales, Cycadales, & Pteridisperms. (Illus.). 1964. 34.00x (ISBN 0-565-00622-3, Pub. by Brit Mus Nat Hist). Sabbot-Natural Hist Bks.
--Yorkshire Jurassic Flora: Vol. III, Bennettitales. (Illus.). 1969. 35.00x (ISBN 0-565-00675-4, Pub. by Brit Mus Nat Hist). Sabbot-Natural Hist Bks.
Harris, Thomas Maxwell. Yorkshire Jurassic Flora: Vol. I, Thallophyta-Pteridophyta. (Illus.). 1961. 30.00x (ISBN 0-565-00148-5, Pub. by Brit Mus Nat Hist). Sabbot-Natural Hist Bks.
Harris, Tim. Practical English One, Bk. 1. 227p. 1981. pap. text ed. 5.95 (ISBN 0-15-570900-3, HC); instructor's manual avail. 3.81 (ISBN 0-15-570901-1); cassette tapes avail. 35.00 (ISBN 0-15-570909-7); writing practical English 1 2.50 (ISBN 0-15-570904-6). HarBraceJ.
--Practical English Three, Bk. 3. 292p. 1981. pap. text ed. 6.48 (ISBN 0-15-570906-2, HC); instructors manual 3.81, (ISBN 0-15-570907-0); tapes 3.81 (ISBN 0-15-570911-9). HarBraceJ.
--Practical English Two, Bk. 2. 240p. 1980. pap. text ed. 5.95 (ISBN 0-15-570902-X, HC); instrs. manual avail. 3.81 (ISBN 0-15-570903-8); cassettes avail. 35.00 (ISBN 0-15-570910-0); writing practical English 2 2.50 (ISBN 0-15-570905-4). HarBraceJ.
Harris, Timothy. Goodnight & Goodbye. 1979. 8.95 o.s.i. (ISBN 0-440-03234-2). Delacorte.
Harris, Tomas. Goya: Lithographs & Engravings, 2 vols. (Illus.). 1983. Repr. of 1964 ed. Vol. 1: 472 p. 175.00 set (ISBN 0-915346-72-9). Vol. 2: 248 p. A Wofsy Fine Arts.
Harris, Trudier. From Mammies to Militants: Domestics in Black American Literature. LC 82-10567. 379p. 1982. text ed. 22.95 (ISBN 0-87722-279-7). Temple U Pr.
Harris, Victor, jt. auth. see Smith, Lawrence.
Harris, Victor, tr. see Musashi, Miyamoto.
Harris, Vivian. A Worthy Charade. (Orig.). 1980. pap. 1.50 o.s.i. (ISBN 0-440-14378-0). Dell.
Harris, Vivian J. Lesions of the Jawbone: Radiographic Features. (Illus.). 280p. 1983. 32.50 (ISBN 0-87527-212-6). Green.
Harris, W. E. Jogging: A Complete Physical Fitness Program for All Ages. (Illus., Orig.). 1967. pap. 2.50 (ISBN 0-448-01191-3, G&D). Putnam Pub Group.
--Programmed Temperature Gas Chromatography. LC 66-17633. 305p. 1966. 18.00 (ISBN 0-471-35270-5, Pub. by Wiley). Krieger.
Harris, W. T. The Mythology of Plato & Dante & the Future Life. (The Essential Library of the Great Philosophers). (Illus.). 107p. 1983. Repr. of 1896 ed. 71.85 (ISBN 0-89901-091-1). Found Class Reprints.
Harris, Walt. The Chequamegon Country Sixteen Fifty-Nine to Nineteen Seventy-Six. LC 76-3114. (Illus.). 1976. 20.00 (ISBN 0-9608156-0-0). W J Harris.
Harris, Walter D., Jr. The Growth of Latin American Cities. LC 76-141378. (Illus.). xvii, 314p. 1971. 20.00x (ISBN 0-8214-0086-X, 82-80901). Ohio U Pr.
Harris, Walter E., jt. auth. see Laitinen, Herbert A.
Harris, Wendell V. Arthur Hugh Clough. (English Authors Ser.). 14.95 (ISBN 0-8057-1096-5, Twayne). G K Hall.
Harris, William. The Harder We Run: Black Workers Since the Civil War. LC 80-27897. (Illus.). 1981. 17.95 o.p. (ISBN 0-19-502940-2); pap. text ed. 4.95x (ISBN 0-19-502941-0). Oxford U Pr.
Harris, William see Allen, W. S.
Harris, William H., jt. auth. see Harris, John H., Jr.
Harris, William J. Hey Fella Would You Mind Holding This Piano a Moment? 42p. 1974. 4.95 (ISBN 0-87886-044-4); pap. 2.95 (ISBN 0-87886-043-6). Ithaca Hse.
--In My Own Dark Way. LC 77-11726. 38p. 1977. 3.50 (ISBN 0-87886-088-6). Ithaca Hse.
Harris, William M. A Design for Desegregation Evaluation. 1976. pap. text ed. 6.25 (ISBN 0-8191-0006-4). U Pr of Amer.
Harris, William W. Taking Root: Israeli Settlement in the West Bank, the Golan & Gaza-Sinai, 1967-1980. LC 80-40953. (Geographical Research Studies). 223p. 1980. 54.95 (ISBN 0-471-27863-7, Pub. by Res Stud Pr). Wiley.
Harris, Wilson. The Angel at the Gate. 128p. 1983. 12.95 (ISBN 0-571-11929-8). Faber & Faber.
--Da Silva's Cultivated Wilderness & Genesis of the Clowns. 160p. 1978. 9.95 (ISBN 0-571-10819-9). Faber & Faber.
Harris, Zellig. A Grammar of English on Mathematical Principles. LC 81-13003. 429p. 1982. 43.50x (ISBN 0-471-02958-0, Pub. by Wiley-Interscience). Wiley.
Harris, Zellig S. Development of the Canaanite Dialects: An Investigation in Linguistic History. 1939. pap. 12.00 (ISBN 0-527-02690-5). Kraus Repr.
--A Grammar of the Phoenician Language. (American Oriental Ser.: Vol. 8). 1936. 11.00 (ISBN 0-940490-08-0). Am Orient Soc.
Harrison. Asia & World Textiles. 1975. 25.50x (ISBN 0-87245-546-7). Textile Bk.
--A Field Guide to Nests, Eggs, & Nestlings of North American Birds. 24.95 (ISBN 0-686-42754-8, Collins Pub England). Greene.
--A Field Guide to Nests, Eggs, Nestlings of British & European Birds. 29.95 (ISBN 0-686-42753-X, Collins Pub England). Greene.
--Hydrocarbons in Biotechnology. 1980. 42.95 (ISBN 0-471-25756-7, Pub. by Wiley Heyden). Wiley.
--New Ways to Produce Textiles. 12.95 o.s.i. (ISBN 0-87245-604-8). Textile Bk.
Harrison & Musial. Other Ways, Other Means: Altered Awareness Activities for Receptive Learning. LC 77-14045. (Illus.). 1978. text ed. 13.95x (ISBN 0-673-16409-8); pap. text ed. 11.95x (ISBN 0-673-16410-1). Scott F.
Harrison, jt. auth. see Frascina.
Harrison, A. J. Economics & Land Use Planning. LC 76-62533. 1977. 27.50x (ISBN 0-312-23432-5). St Martin.
Harrison, A. J., jt. auth. see Atkinson, A. B.
Harrison, Alec. With Cartier up the St. Lawrence. (Illus.). (gr. 7 up). 12.75x (ISBN 0-392-01864-0, LTB). Sportshelf.
Harrison, Alferdteen. Piney Woods School: An Oral History. (Illus.). 220p. 1982. 17.95x (ISBN 0-87805-167-8). U Pr of Miss.
Harrison, Alice W. & Collister, Edward A. The Conservation of Archival & Library Materials: A Resource Guide to Audiovisual Aids. LC 82-652. 202p. 1982. 13.50 (ISBN 0-8108-1523-0). Scarecrow.
Harrison, Allan J. Preparing & Presenting Your Arbitration Case. 82p. 1979. pap. 6.00 (ISBN 0-87179-303-2). BNA.
Harrison, Anthony, jt. ed. see Gretton, John.
Harrison, B. Henry Fielding's "Tom Jones". The Novelist as Moral Philosopher. 20.00x (ISBN 0-686-97005-5, Pub. by Scottish Academic Pr Scotland). State Mutual Bk.
Harrison, Barbara G. Visions of Glory. 1978. 12.95 o.p. (ISBN 0-671-22530-8). S&S.
Harrison, Bennett, jt. auth. see Blueston, Barry.
Harrison, Bernard. An Introduction to the Philosophy of Language. LC 79-28463. 340p. 1980. 27.50 (ISBN 0-312-43109-0). St Martin.
Harrison, Bette K. The Garage Sale Handbook. rev. ed. (Illus.). 1979. pap. 2.50 o.p. (ISBN 0-448-15578-8, G&D). Putnam Pub Group.
Harrison, Brian. The Danger Light & Other Stories. (Readers Ser.: Stage 4). 1978. pap. text ed. 6.95 (ISBN 0-88377-090-3). Newbury Hse.
--Peaceable Kingdom: Stability & Change in Modern Britain. 400p. 1982. 39.95x (ISBN 0-19-822603-9). Oxford U Pr.
Harrison, Brian, jt. auth. see Ford, Colin.
Harrison, Bruce M. Dissection of the Cat & Comparisons with Man: A Laboratory Manual on Felis Domestica. 7th ed. (Illus.). 168p. 1976. pap. text ed. 7.50 o.p. (ISBN 0-8016-2075-9). Mosby.
Harrison, Buddy. Understanding Authority-For Effective Leadership. 119p. 1982. pap. 4.95 (ISBN 0-89274-218-6, HH218). Harrison Hse.
Harrison, C. J., jt. auth. see Warren, Rachel L.
Harrison, C. J., jt. auth. see Warren, Rachel M.
Harrison, C. R., jt. auth. see Harrison, R. E.
Harrison, C. William. Here Is Your Career: Auto Mechanic. (Here Is Your Career Ser.). (Illus.). (gr. 6-8). 1977. PLB 5.89 o.p. (ISBN 0-399-61054-5). Putnam Pub Group.
--Here Is Your Career: The Building Trades. LC 78-31385. (Here Is Your Career Ser.). (Illus.). (gr. 6-12). 1979. 7.95 (ISBN 0-399-20674-4). Putnam Pub Group.
Harrison, Charles, jt. auth. see Frascina, Francis.
Harrison, Charles R. Ornamental Conifers. (Illus.). 224p. 1982. Repr. of 1975 ed. pap. text ed. 37.50 (ISBN 0-7153-6848-6). David & Charles.
Harrison, Cynthia E., ed. Women in American History: A Bibliography. LC 78-26194. (Clio Bibliography Ser.: No. 5). 374p. (LC f8-26194). 1979. text ed. 58.00 (ISBN 0-87436-260-1). ABC-Clio.
Harrison, D., jt. auth. see Benson, F. A.
Harrison, D. A., jt. auth. see Hayward, P. L.
Harrison, D. L. Book of Giant Stories. 1972. 7.95 (ISBN 0-07-026857-6, GB); PLB 6.95 o.p. (ISBN 0-07-026858-4). McGraw.
Harrison, David, Jr. Who Pays for Clean Air: The Cost & Benefit Distribution of Federal Automobile Emission Standards. LC 75-22060. 192p. 1975. prof ref 20.00x (ISBN 0-88410-451-6). Ballinger Pub.
Harrison, Dennis R. Win at the Casino. LC 82-71742. 128p. 1982. 12.95 (ISBN 0-8119-0450-4); pap. 7.95 (ISBN 0-8119-0451-2). Fell.
Harrison, Doniel P. Social Forecasting Methodology: Suggestions for Research. LC 75-41511. (Social Science Frontiers Ser.). 97p. 1976. pap. 3.00x (ISBN 0-87154-376-1). Russell Sage.
Harrison, E. Frank. Management & Organizations. LC 77-75476. (Illus.). 1978. text ed. 24.95 (ISBN 0-395-25481-7); instr's manual 1.00 (ISBN 0-395-25482-5). HM.
Harrison, E. J. The Fighting Spirit of Japan. LC 81-83227. (Illus.). 272p. 1982. 15.95 (ISBN 0-87951-142-7). Overlook Pr.
Harrison, E. J., tr. see Kawaishi, M.
Harrison, Edward R. Cosmology: The Science of the Universe. LC 80-18703. (Illus.). 480p. 1981. 27.95 (ISBN 0-521-22981-2). Cambridge U Pr.
Harrison, Evalee, jt. auth. see Solomon, Neil.
Harrison, Evelyn B. Archaic & Archaistic Sculpture. (Athenian Agora Ser: Vol. 11). (Illus.). 1965. 20.00x o.p. (ISBN 0-87661-211-7). Am Sch Athens.
Harrison, Everett. Colossians. (Everyman's Bible Commentary Ser). 128p. (Orig.). 1971. pap. 4.50 (ISBN 0-8024-2051-6). Moody.
Harrison, Everett F. Acts: The Expanding Church. 450p. 1976. 12.95 o.p. (ISBN 0-8024-0035-3). Moody.
Harrison, Everett F., ed. Baker's Dictionary of Theology. 17.95 (ISBN 0-8010-4042-6). Baker Bk.
Harrison, Frank. The Managerial Decision-Making Process. 2nd ed. LC 80-82459. (Illus.). 496p. 1981. text ed. 25.95 (ISBN 0-395-30073-8); instr's manual 1.00 (ISBN 0-395-30074-6). HM.
Harrison, Frank, ed. Time, Place & Music: An Anthology of Ethnomusicological Observation C.1550 to 1800. (Music Import, 1978 Ser.). (Illus.). 1978. pap. text ed. 22.50 (ISBN 0-306-77592-1). Da Capo.
Harrison, Frank L. Music in Medieval Britain. 4th ed. (Illus.). xx, 491p. 1980. 45.00 o.s.i. (ISBN 90-6027-252-8, Pub. by Frits Knuf Netherlands); wrappers 35.00 o.s.i. (ISBN 90-6027-251-X). Pendragon NY.
--Time, Place & Music: An Anthology of Ethnomusicological Observation ca. 1550-ca. 1800. (Source Materials & Studies in Ethnomusicology Ser.: Vol. 1). 1973. 42.50 o.s.i. (ISBN 90-6027-247-1, Pub. by Frits Knuf Netherlands); wrappers 30.00 o.s.i. (ISBN 90-6027-246-3, Pub. by Frits Knuf Netherlands). Pendragon NY.
Harrison, Fraser. Strange Land: The Countryside-Myth & Reality. 133p. 1982. pap. 10.95 (ISBN 0-283-98861-4, Pub. by Sidgwick & Jackson). Merrimack Bk Serv.
Harrison, Frederic. John Ruskin. LC 72-78229. 1971. Repr. of 1902 ed. 30.00x (ISBN 0-8103-3719-3). Gale.
Harrison, Frederick W. & Cowden, Ronald R., eds. Developmental Biology or Freshwater Invertebrates. LC 82-14964. 588p. 1982. 72.00 (ISBN 0-8451-0222-2). A R Liss.
Harrison, G. A., ed. Population Structure & Human Variation. LC 76-22987. (International Biological Programme Ser.: No. 11). (Illus.). 1977. 80.00 (ISBN 0-521-21399-1). Cambridge U Pr.
Harrison, G. A. & Boyce, A. J., eds. The Structure of Human Populations. (Illus.). 1972. 24.00x o.p. (ISBN 0-19-857117-8); pap. 17.95x o.p. (ISBN 0-19-857120-8). Oxford U Pr.
Harrison, G. A., et al. Human Biology: An Introduction to Human Evolution, Variation, Growth, & Ecology. 2nd ed. (Illus.). 1977. text ed. 36.50x o.p. (ISBN 0-19-857164-X); pap. text ed. 18.95x (ISBN 0-19-857165-8). Oxford U Pr.
Harrison, G. B., ed. Bible for Students of Literature & Art. LC 64-13820. 1964. pap. 8.50 (ISBN 0-385-04475-5, A394, Anch). Doubleday.
Harrison, G. T. Mormonism, Now & Then. 357p. 1961. 16.00 o.p. (ISBN 0-686-96149-8). Am Atheist.
--That Mormon Book. 161p. 1981. pap. 5.00 (ISBN 0-686-96163-3). Am Atheist.
Harrison, George B., ed. see Shakespeare, William.
Harrison, George R., ed. MIT Wavelength Tables. 2nd ed. 1970. 60.00x (ISBN 0-262-08002-8). MIT Pr.
Harrison, Graham, tr. see Von Speyr, Adrienne.
Harrison, Gregory, jt. auth. see Scannel, Vernon.
Harrison, H. B. Structural Analysis & Design: Some Minicomputer Applications, 2 pts. (Illus.). 1980. Set. 85.00 (ISBN 0-08-023239-6); pap. text ed. 30.00 (ISBN 0-08-023240-X). Pergamon.
Harrison, H. R. & Nettleton, T. Principles of Engineering Mechanics. 264p. 1978. pap. text ed. 18.95 (ISBN 0-7131-3378-3). E Arnold.
Harrison, Harry. Bill, the Galactic Hero. 1979. pap. 1.75 (ISBN 0-380-00395-3, 47183). Avon.
--Great Balls of Fire. Shaw, Grace, ed. (Illus.). 1977. 14.95 o.p. (ISBN 0-448-14377-1, G&D); pap. 6.95 o.p. (ISBN 0-448-14378-X, Today Press). Putnam Pub Group.
--Invasion Earth. 1983. pap. 2.75 (ISBN 0-441-37154-X, Pub. by Ace Science Fiction). Ace Bks.
--Make Room! Make Room! 1979. lib. bdg. 12.00 (ISBN 0-8398-2565-X, Gregg). G K Hall.
--Mechanismo: An Illustrated Manual of Science Fiction Hardware. LC 78-50948. (Illus.). 1978. 15.95 (ISBN 0-89169-505-2); pap. 8.95 (ISBN 0-89169-504-4). Reed Bks.
--Planet of No Return. 256p. 1982. pap. 2.75 (ISBN 0-523-48557-3). Pinnacle Bks.
--Planet of the Damned. 256p. 1981. pap. 2.95 (ISBN 0-523-48565-4). Pinnacle Bks.
--Planet Story. LC 78-65675. (Illus.). 120p. 1979. 19.95 o.s.i. (ISBN 0-89104-136-2, A & W Visual Library); pap. 10.95 o.s.i. (ISBN 0-89104-135-4). A & W Pubs.
--A Rebel in Time. 320p. 1983. pap. 3.50 (ISBN 0-523-48554-9). Pinnacle Bks.
--Skyfall. LC 76-23433. 1977. 8.95 o.p. (ISBN 0-689-10764-1). Atheneum.
--The Stainless Steel Rat for President. 192p. 1982. pap. 2.50 (ISBN 0-686-82107-6). Bantam.
--The Technicolor Time Machine. 256p. 1981. pap. 2.50 o.p. (ISBN 0-523-48506-9). Pinnacle Bks.
Harrison, Harry, jt. auth. see Aldiss, Brian W.
Harrison, Helen P. Picture Librarianship. 372p. 1981. lib. bdg. 37.50x (ISBN 0-89774-011-4); pap. text ed. 27.50 (ISBN 0-89774-013-0). Oryx Pr.
Harrison, Howard. How to Play the Flute. (Illus.). 112p. 1983. 17.50 (ISBN 0-241-10875-6, Pub. by Hamish Hamilton England); pap. 9.95 (ISBN 0-241-10876-4). David & Charles.
Harrison, J. The Library of Isaac Newton. LC 77-83994. (Illus.). 1978. 80.00 (ISBN 0-521-21868-3). Cambridge U Pr.
Harrison, J. A. Do-It-Yourself Guide to Natural Stonework. (Illus.). 1979. 18.95 (ISBN 0-7153-7840-6). David & Charles.
Harrison, J. A., jt. auth. see Thirsk, H. R.
Harrison, J. Hartwell, et al, eds. Campbells Urology. 4th ed. LC 75-44604. (Illus.). 1978. Vol. I. 75.00 (ISBN 0-7216-4540-2). Saunders.
--Campbell's Urology, Vol. II. 4th ed. LC 75-44604. (Illus.). 1001p. 1979. 75.00 (ISBN 0-7216-4541-0). Saunders.
--Campbell's Urology, Vol. III. 4th ed. LC 75-44604. (Illus.). 687p. 1979. 75.00 (ISBN 0-7216-4542-9). Saunders.
Harrison, J. S., jt. ed. see Rose, A. H.
Harrison, James. Rudyard Kipling. (English Authors Ser.). 1982. lib. bdg. 12.50 (ISBN 0-8057-6825-4, Twayne). G K Hall.
Harrison, James P. Communists & Chinese Peasant Rebellions: A Study in the Rewriting of Chinese History. LC 68-16867. 1971. pap. text ed. 3.45x (ISBN 0-689-70269-8, 176). Atheneum.
--The Endless War: Fifty Years of Struggle in Vietnam. (Illus.). 320p. 1982. text ed. 17.95 (ISBN 0-686-76562-1, 914040). Free Pr.
Harrison, James Q., jt. auth. see Benor, Daniel.
Harrison, Jane. Prolegomena to the Study of Greek Religion. 682p. 1981. text ed. 26.00x (ISBN 0-85036-262-8, Pub. by Merlin, England); pap. 13.25x (ISBN 0-686-69802-9). Humanities.
Harrison, Jane E. Ancient Art & Ritual. Repr. of 1951 ed. lib. bdg. 18.75x (ISBN 0-8371-1981-2, HAAA). Greenwood.
Harrison, Jane E., tr. see Paris, Pierre.
Harrison, Jeffery & Grant, Peter. The Thames Transformed: London's River & Its Waterflow. (Illus.). 1977. 15.00 o.s.i. (ISBN 0-233-96840-7). Transatlantic.
Harrison, Jim. Farmer. 1980. pap. 6.95 (ISBN 0-440-52113-0, Delta). Dell.
--Legends of the Fall. 1979. 10.95 o.s.i. (ISBN 0-440-05461-3, Sey Lawr); Three Vol. Boxed Set. 20.00 o.s.i. (ISBN 0-440-05462-1); Limited Signed Edition. 50.00 o.s.i. (ISBN 0-440-05465-6). Delacorte.
--Legends of the Fall. 1980. pap. 6.95 (ISBN 0-440-55093-9, Delta). Dell.
--Natural World. (Illus.). 48p. 1982. 100.00 (ISBN 0-940170-08-6). Open Bk Pubns.
--Selected & New Poems: 1961-1981. (Illus.). 1982. 14.95 (ISBN 0-440-07994-2, Sey Lawr). Delacorte.
--Warlock. 1981. 13.95 o.s.i. (ISBN 0-440-09462-3, Sey Lawr). Delacorte.
--Wolf: A False Memoir. 1981. pap. 5.95 (ISBN 0-440-59598-3, Delta). Dell.
Harrison, Jim & Guest, Diana. Natural World. (Illus.). 48p. 1983. limited ed. 100.00 (ISBN 0-940170-08-6). Station Hill Pr.
Harrison, Joann. A Manual for Teachers of English. 1977. tchrs ed 8.95 o.p. (ISBN 0-87397-124-8). Strode.

Harrison, John, jt. auth. see Harrison, Shirley.
Harrison, John, et al. Akbar & the Mughal Empire. Yapp, Malcolm & Killingray, Margaret, eds. (Greenhaven World History Ser.). (Illus.). 32p. (gr. 10). lib. bdg. 6.95 (ISBN 0-89908-031-6); pap. text ed. 2.25 (ISBN 0-89908-006-5). Greenhaven.
Harrison, John A. China Since Eighteen Hundred. LC 66-28625. (Illus., Orig.). 1967. pap. 3.45 (ISBN 0-15-616880-4, Harv). HarBraceJ.
--The Chinese Empire. LC 73-178591. (Illus.). 364p. 1972. pap. 5.95 (ISBN 0-15-617093-0, Harv). HarBraceJ.
--The Founding of the Russian Empire in Asia & America. LC 73-121685. (Illus.). 156p. 1971. 10.95x (ISBN 0-87024-160-5). U of Miami Pr.
--Story of the Ionosphere. (Illus.). 1963. 5.25 o.p. (ISBN 0-7175-0112-4). Dufour.
Harrison, John F., ed. Utopianism & Education: Robert Owen & the Owenites. LC 68-54675. (Orig.). 1969. pap. text ed. 6.00x (ISBN 0-8077-1498-4). Tchrs Coll.
Harrison, John M. & Stein, Harry H., eds. Muckraking: Past, Present, & Future. LC 73-6876. 200p. 1973. 16.50x (ISBN 0-271-01118-1). Pa St U Pr.
Harrison, John S. Platonism in English Poetry of the Sixteenth & Seventeenth Centuries. LC 80-11587. (Columbia University Studies in Comparative Literature). xi, 235p. 1980. Repr. of 1903 ed. lib. bdg. 20.75x (ISBN 0-313-22374-2, HAPL). Greenwood.
Harrison, Joyce M. Instructional Strategies for Physical Education. 510p. 1983. text ed. write for info. (ISBN 0-697-07205-3). Wm C Brown.
Harrison, Julius. Brahms & His Four Symphonies. LC 76-127285. (Music Ser). (Illus.). 1971. Repr. of 1939 ed. lib. bdg. 27.50 (ISBN 0-306-70033-6). Da Capo.
Harrison, K. The Framework of Anglo-Saxon History to A. D. 900. LC 75-13450. 176p. 1976. 37.50 (ISBN 0-521-20935-8). Cambridge U Pr.
Harrison, K. A., jt. auth. see Grund, D. W.
Harrison, K. C. First Steps in Librarianship: A Students' Guide. 192p. 1980. 17.00 (ISBN 0-233-97235-8, 05790-8, Pub. by Gower Pub Co England). Lexington Bks.
--Libraries in Scandinavia. (Grafton Books in Library Science). 1977. lib. bdg. 12.00 o.p. (ISBN 0-233-95968-8). Westview.
--Libraries in Scandinavia. 288p. 1969. 17.00 (ISBN 0-233-95968-8, 05791-6, Pub. by Gower Pub Co England). Lexington Bks.
--The Library & the Community. 128p. 1977. 12.50 (ISBN 0-233-96875-X, 05792-4, Pub. by Gower Pub Co England). Lexington Bks.
Harrison, K. C., ed. Prospects for British Librarianship. 1978. pap. 12.50 o.p. (ISBN 0-85365-009-8, 6505). Gaylord Prof Pubns.
Harrison, Keith. The Basho Poems. 66p. 1981. pap. 4.50 (ISBN 0-931714-09-5). Nodin Pr.
Harrison, Lewis, jt. auth. see Lawrence, D. Baloti.
Harrison, Lionel. Laboratory Course in Chemistry. 1963. text ed. 4.50 o.p. (ISBN 0-07-094512-8, C). McGraw.
Harrison, Lowell H., jt. auth. see Bennett, James D.
Harrison, M. John. The Floating Gods. 1983. pap. 2.50 (ISBN 0-686-43182-0, Timescape). PB.
--A Storm of Wings. LC 79-7198. (Double D Science Fiction Ser.). 1980. 10.95 o.p. (ISBN 0-385-14765-1). Doubleday.
Harrison, Malcolm C. Data Structures & Programing. 1973. text ed. 21.95x (ISBN 0-673-05964-2). Scott F.
Harrison, Mark. Byteing Deeper in Your Timex Sinclair 1000. LC 82-61778. 160p. 1982. pap. text ed. 12.95 (ISBN 0-471-89888-0). Wiley.
Harrison, Mary. Life of Connie. 1980. 4.75 o.p. (ISBN 0-8062-1395-7). Carlton.
Harrison, Michael. Fire from Heaven. 1978. 11.95 (ISBN 0-458-93400-3). Methuen Inc.
--A Study in Surmise: The Making of Sherlock Holmes. LC 81-82193. (Illus.). 200p. 1983. 14.95 (ISBN 0-934468-10-9). Gaslight.
Harrison, Michael A. Electronic Banking: The Revolution in Financial Services. (Illus.). 200p. 1983. 32.95 (ISBN 0-86729-060-9). Knowledge Indus.
Harrison, Michelle. A Woman in Residence. 1983. pap. 5.95 (ISBN 0-14-006723-X). Penguin.
--A Woman in Residence: A Physician's Account of Her Training in Obstetrics & Gynecology. 1982. 13.95 (ISBN 0-394-51885-3). Random.
Harrison, Molly. The English Home. (Local Search). (Illus.). 1969. 3.75 o.p. (ISBN 0-7100-6606-6). Routledge & Kegan.
--Museums & Galleries. (Local Search Ser). (Illus.). 1973. 8.95 (ISBN 0-7100-7588-X). Routledge & Kegan.
Harrison, P. G. Military Helicopters. (Battlefields Weapons Systems & Technology Ser.: Vol. XI). 200p. 1983. 26.00 (ISBN 0-08-029958-X); pap. 13.00 (ISBN 0-08-029959-8). Pergamon.
Harrison, P. M. & Hoare, R. J. Metals in Biochemistry. LC 79-41813. 80p. 1980. pap. 6.50x (ISBN 0-412-13160-9, Pub. by Chapman & Hall England). Methuen Inc.
Harrison, Paul. Third World Tomorrow: A Report from the Battlefront on the War Against Poverty. LC 82-19095. 416p. (Orig.). 1983. pap. 7.95 (ISBN 0-8298-0646-6). Pilgrim NY.
Harrison, Paul C., ed. Kundu Drama. Incl. A Beast Story. Kennedy, Adrienne; Devil's Mask. Brown, Lennox; Great Goodness of Life. Amiri, Imanu; The Great MacDaddy. Harrison, Paul C; Kabnis. Toomer, Jean; Mars. Goss, Clav; The Owl Answers. Kennedy, Adrienne; A Season in the Congo. Cesaire, Aime. 12.50 (ISBN 0-394-17806-8, E615). Grove.
Harrison, Peter D., jt. ed. see Turner, B. L., II.
Harrison, R. E. & Harrison, C. R. Know Your Garden Series: Trees & Shrubs. 199p. 1982. 22.50 (ISBN 0-589-00163-9, Pub. by Timmins S Africa). Intl Schol Bk Serv.
Harrison, R. J. & Holmes, R. L., eds. Progress in Anatomy, Vol. 1. (Illus.). 250p. 1981. 67.50 (ISBN 0-521-23603-7). Cambridge U Pr.
Harrison, R. M. & Laxen, D. P. Lead Pollution: Causes & Control. 1981. 23.00x (ISBN 0-412-16360-8, Pub. by Chapman & Hall). Methuen Inc.
Harrison, Randall P. Beyond Words: An Introduction to Nonverbal Communication. LC 73-17202. (Speech Communication Ser). (Illus.). 208p. 1974. ref. ed. 19.95 (ISBN 0-13-076141-9); pap. 14.95 (ISBN 0-13-076133-8). P-H.
Harrison, Randall P., jt. ed. see Wiemann, John M.
Harrison, Richard J., jt. ed. see Felts, William J.
Harrison, Richmond E. Know Your Lilies. (Illus.). 84p. 1982. 12.50 (ISBN 0-589-00430-1, Pub. by H Timmins S Africa). Intl Schol Bk Serv.
Harrison, Rick K. Progressive Anagrams. 96p. (Orig.). 1978. pap. 2.95 o.s.i. (ISBN 0-89104-246-6, A & W Visual Library). A & W Pubs.
Harrison, Robert. Gallic Salt: Eighteen Fabliaux Translated from the Old French. LC 72-97748. 1974. 34.50x (ISBN 0-520-02418-4). U of Cal Pr.
Harrison, Robert, tr. Song of Roland. 1970. pap. 2.50 (ISBN 0-451-61973-0, ME1973, Ment). NAL.
Harrison, Robyn. The Great Christmas Strike. 1983. pap. 2.50 (ISBN 0-686-38756-2). Eldridge Pub.
Harrison, Royden, ed. Independent Colliers: The Coal Miner As Proletarian Reconsidered. LC 78-3119. 1979. 25.00x (ISBN 0-312-41290-8). St Martin.
Harrison, S. G., et al. Oxford Book of Food Plants. (Illus.). 1969. 27.95x (ISBN 0-19-910006-3). Oxford U Pr.
Harrison, Sam. The Krone Chronicles: A True Story. LC 80-23505. (Orig.). 1981. pap. 5.95 o.p. (ISBN 0-89865-030-5). Donning Co.
--Okra. pap. 3.00 (ISBN 0-686-81807-5). Anhinga Pr.
Harrison, Samuel A. Memoir of John Leeds Bozman: The First Historian of Maryland. 69p. 1888. 5.00 (ISBN 0-686-36850-9). Md Hist.
--Wenlock Christison & Early Friends in Talbot County, Maryland. 76p. 1878. 3.00 (ISBN 0-686-36842-8). Md Hist.
Harrison, Sarah. The Flowers of the Field. 1980. 11.95 (ISBN 0-698-11008-0, Coward). Putnam Pub Group.
Harrison, Sheldon P. Mokilese Reference Grammar. LC 76-2687. (Pali Language Texts: Micronesia). 1976. pap. text ed. 14.50x (ISBN 0-8248-0412-0). UH Pr.
Harrison, Sheldon P. & Albert, Salich. Mokilese-English Dictionary. LC 76-41796. (PALI Language Tests Ser.: Micronesia). (Orig.). 1976. pap. text ed. 7.50x (ISBN 0-8248-0512-7). UH Pr.
Harrison, Shirley & Harrison, John. Austria & Switzerland. LC 82-61195. (Pocket Guide Ser.). (Illus.). 1983. pap. 4.95 (ISBN 0-528-84892-5). Rand.
Harrison, Shirley, jt. auth. see Franklin, Lynn.
Harrison, Sidney. The Young Person's Guide to Playing the Piano. (Illus.). 104p. (Orig.). 1982. pap. 5.95 (ISBN 0-571-11864-X). Faber & Faber.
Harrison, Stanley. Poor Men's Guardians: Survey of the Radical & Working-Class Press in England. (Illus.). 246p. 1973. 17.50x o.p. (ISBN 0-8464-0734-5); pap. 9.95 o.p. (ISBN 0-686-77083-8). Beekman Pubs.
Harrison, Stanley R. Edgar Fawcett. (United States Authors Ser.). lib. bdg. 13.95 (ISBN 0-8057-0248-2, Twayne). G K Hall.
Harrison, Thomas, tr. see Ballerini, Luigi.
Harrison, Tony, tr. Aeschylus: The Oresteia. 126p. 1982. pap. text ed. 6.95x (ISBN 0-8476-4766-8). Rowman.
Harrison, W., ed. Poetry, Prose & Public Opinion of Russian 1850-1950. 1981. 70.00x o.p. (ISBN 0-86127-209-9, Pub. by Avebury Pub England). State Mutual Bk.
Harrison, William. Burton & Speke. 1982. 17.95 (ISBN 0-312-10873-7, Pub. by Marek). St Martin.
--Savannah Blue. 288p. 1981. 12.95 (ISBN 0-399-90081-0, Marek). Putnam Pub Group.
--Savannah Blue. 1982. pap. 2.75 (ISBN 0-451-11455-8, AE1455, Sig). NAL.
Harrison, William & Mullen, J. Passive Voice & Agreement of the Verb Predicate with a Collective Subject. (Studies in the Modern Russian Language Ser: Nos. 4 & 5). (Rus). 15.95 (ISBN 0-521-05218-1). Cambridge U Pr.
Harrison, William, et al. Colloquial Russian. (Trubners Colloquial Manuals). 1973. 17.00 (ISBN 0-7100-7021-7); pap. 9.95 (ISBN 0-7100-8965-1). Routledge & Kegan.
Harriss, C. L., ed. Government Spending & Land Values. LC 72-9988. 262p. 1973. 27.50 (ISBN 0-299-06320-8). U of Wis Pr.
Harriss, E. G. & Williams, N. G. Mixtures of Insecticides for Tsetse Fly Control: Potentiation Between a-Endosulfan & Deltalmethrin Applied to Glossina Austeni Newst. 1981. 35.00x (ISBN 0-85135-122-0, Pub. by Centre Overseas Research). State Mutual Bk.
Harriss, Ernest C. Johann Mattheson's Der vollkommene Capellmeister: A Revised Translation with Critical Commentary. Buelow, George, ed. LC 80-29132. (Studies in Musicology: No. 21). 932p. 1981. 79.95 (ISBN 0-8357-1134-X, Pub. by UMI Res Pr). Univ Microfilms.
Harriss, John. Capitalism & Peasant Farming: Agrarian Structure & Ideology in Northern Tamil Nadu. (Illus.). 1982. 27.50x (ISBN 0-19-561340-6). Oxford U Pr.
Harriss, Joseph. The Tallest Tower: Eiffel & the Belle Epoque. LC 74-31279. 256p. 1975. 10.00 o.p. (ISBN 0-395-20435-6). HM.
Harriss, Julian & Leiter, Kelly. The Complete Reporter. 4th ed. 499p. 1981. pap. text ed. 16.95 (ISBN 0-02-350600-8). Macmillan.
Harriss, Will. Bay Psalm Book Murder. 192p. 1983. 12.95 (ISBN 0-8027-5494-5). Walker & Co.
Harris-Salomon, Julian. Indians of the Lower Hudson Region: The Munsee. (Illus.). 95p. 1982. 18.95 (ISBN 0-686-38723-6); pap. 14.95 (ISBN 0-89062-134-9). Hist Soc Rockland.
Harrod, Frederick S. Manning the New Navy: The Development of a Modern Naval Enlisted Force, 1899-1940. (Contributions in American History: No. 68). 1978. lib. bdg. 29.95 (ISBN 0-8371-9759-7, HEM/). Greenwood.
Harrod, L. M. The Librarians' Glossary & Reference Book: Of Terms Used in Librarianship Documentation & the Book Trade. (Grafton Library Ser.). 904p. 1982. Repr. of 1977 ed. 49.95x (ISBN 0-233-96744-3). Lexington Bks.
--Library Work with Children. 216p. 1969. 17.00 (ISBN 0-233-95994-7, 05796-7, Pub. by Gower Pub Co England). Lexington Bks.
Harrod, Roy. International Economics. (Cambridge Economic Handbook Ser). 1957. pap. 11.95x (ISBN 0-521-08780-5). Cambridge U Pr.
--Sociology: Morals & Mystery. LC 71-143998. 1971. 17.95 o.p. (ISBN 0-312-74060-3). St Martin.
Harrod, Roy F. Economic Dynamics. LC 72-88004. 192p. 1973. 22.50 (ISBN 0-312-23205-5). St Martin.
--Towards a Dynamic Economics: Some Recent Developments of Economic Theory & Their Application to Policy. LC 79-20398. 1980. Repr. of 1948 ed. lib. bdg. 18.25x (ISBN 0-313-22089-1, HATD). Greenwood.
Harrod, Roy F. & Hague, Douglas C., eds. International Trade Theory in a Developing World: Proceedings. (International Economic Assn. Ser). 1969. 32.50 (ISBN 0-312-42385-3). St Martin.
Harrod-Eagles, Cynthia. The Black Pearl. (Morland Dynasty Ser.: No. 5). (Orig.). 1983. pap. 3.95 (ISBN 0-440-10728-8). Dell.
--The Crystal Crown. (Morland Dynasty Ser.: No. 4). (Orig.). 1983. pap. 3.50 (ISBN 0-440-11568-X). Dell.
Harrold, Robert, jt. auth. see Wingrave, Helen.
Harrold, William E. The Variance & the Unity: A Study of the Complementary Poems of Robert Browning. LC 72-85542. x, 245p. 1973. 12.00x (ISBN 0-8214-0129-7, 82-81321). Ohio U Pr.
Harron, Frank & Burnside, John. Health & Human Values: A Guide to Making Your Own Decisions. LC 82-13394. 212p. 1983. text ed. 24.95x (ISBN 0-300-02898-9); pap. 6.95 (ISBN 0-300-03026-6). Yale U Pr.
--Health & Human Values: A Guide to Making Your Own Decisions. 24.95 (ISBN 0-686-42812-9); pap. 6.95 (ISBN 0-686-42813-7, Y-448). Yale U Pr.
Harron, Frank & United Ministries in Education Health & Human Values Program. Biomedical Ethical Issues: A Digest of Law & Policy Development. LC 82-13394. 112p. 1983. pap. text ed. 4.95x (ISBN 0-300-02974-8). Yale U Pr.
--Human Values in Medicine & Health Care: Audio-Visual Resources. LC 82-13394. 96p. 1983. pap. text ed. 3.95x (ISBN 0-300-02975-6). Yale U Pr.
--Leader's Manual. LC 82-13394. 48p. 1983. pap. text ed. 2.95x (ISBN 0-300-02972-1). Yale U Pr.
Harron, Frank, et al. Health & Human Values: Making Your Own Decisions. 185p. 1983. 24.95 (ISBN 0-686-83922-6); pap. 6.95 (ISBN 0-686-83923-4). Yale U Pr.
Harrop, David. Paychecks: Who Makes What. LC 79-6817. 1980. pap. 5.95i o.p. (ISBN 0-06-090790-8, CN 790, CN). Har-Row.
Harrop, John, jt. auth. see Cohen, Robert.
Harrop, M., jt. auth. see Hague, R.
Harrop, Martin, jt. ed. see Worcester, Robert M.
Harrop, P. J. Dielectrics. 1972. 12.95 o.p. (ISBN 0-408-70387-3); pap. 7.95 o.p. (ISBN 0-408-70388-1). Butterworth.
Harroun, Catherine, jt. auth. see Teiser, Ruth.
Harrowe, Fiona. Passion's Child. 480p. (Orig.). 1983. pap. 3.50 (ISBN 0-449-12392-8, GM). Fawcett.
Harrower, Molly, ed. see Block, Jack.
Harrower, Molly R., et al. Creative Variation in the Projective Techniques. (Illus.). 160p. 1960. photocopy ed. spiral 16.75x (ISBN 0-398-00790-X). C C Thomas.
Harry, Hahnewald, jt. ed. see Roald, Albert.
Harry, Joann, jt. auth. see Green, Marilyn L.
Harry, Joseph & Devall, William B. The Social Organization of Gay Males. LC 78-8381. (Praeger Special Studies). 1978. 27.95 o.p. (ISBN 0-03-044696-1). Praeger.
Harry, Keith, jt. ed. see Rumble, Greville.
Harry, P., tr. see Lozina-Lozinskii, L. K.
Harsanyi, Dr. Andrew, jt. ed. see Unterkoefler, Ernest L.
Harsanyi, J. C. Bargaining Equilibrium in Games & Social Situations. LC 75-39370. (Illus.). 352p. 1977. 59.50 (ISBN 0-521-20886-6). Cambridge U Pr.
Harsanyi, Zsolt & Hutton, Richard. Genetic Prophecy: Beyond the Double Helix. 288p. 1982. pap. 3.95 (ISBN 0-553-22601-0). Bantam.
Harsey, Paula see Harris, Beatrice.
Harshaw, Lou. Asheville: Places of Discovery. 1981. pap. 10.95 (ISBN 0-932298-09-5). Copple Hse.
--Trains, Trestles, & Tunnels. 1981. pap. 8.95 (ISBN 0-932298-10-9). Copple Hse.
Harshbarger, Gretchen F. McCall's Garden Book. 1968. 12.95 o.p. (ISBN 0-671-45887-6). S&S.
Harshbarger, Karl. Sophocle's Oedipus. LC 79-66476. 1979. text ed. 17.75 (ISBN 0-8191-0834-0); pap. text ed. 8.25 (ISBN 0-8191-0835-9). U Pr of Amer.
Harshbarger, Ronald J. Introductory Algebra. 294p. 1976. text ed. 21.50 scp (ISBN 0-06-042682-9, HarpC); scp study guide o.p. 9.95 (ISBN 0-06-042673-X); instructor's manual avail. (ISBN 0-06-362662-4). Har-Row.
Harshbarger, Ronald J. & Reynoldds, James J. Mathematical Applications for Management, Life & Social Studies. 604p. 1981. text ed. 24.95 (ISBN 0-669-03209-3); student solotions guide 3.95 (ISBN 0-669-03211-5). Heath.
Harshberger, J. W. Phytogeographic Survey of North America: A Consideration of the Phytogeography of the North American Continent, Including Mexico, Central America & the West Indies, Together with the Evolution of North American Plant Distribution. (Illus.). 1958. Repr. of 1911 ed. 40.00 (ISBN 3-7682-0003-5). Lubrecht & Cramer.
Har-Shefi, Yoella. Beyond the Gunsights: One Arab Family in the Promised Land. 1980. 9.95 o.p. (ISBN 0-395-27614-4). HM.
Harssel, Jan van see Van Harssel, Jan.
Harssuape, Brian. Railway Design Since Eighteen Thirty: 1914-1969, Vol. 2. 25.00 (ISBN 0-7110-0072-7, SpS). Sportshelf.
Hart. Organic Chemistry: A Short Course. 6th ed. 1983. text ed. 28.95 (ISBN 0-686-84540-4, CH26); write for info. supplementary materials. HM.
--Speedy French: To Get You There & Back. (Speedy Language Ser.). 24p. (Orig., Fr.). 1976. pap. 1.75 (ISBN 0-9602838-1-1). Baja Bks.
--Speedy Russian: To Get You There & Back. 24p. (Orig., Russian.). 1979. pap. 1.75 (ISBN 0-9602838-5-4). Baja Bks.
--Speedy Spanish: To Get You There & Back. (Speedy Language Ser.). 24p. (Orig., Spanish.). 1975. pap. 1.75 (ISBN 0-9602838-0-3). Baja Bks.
Hart, A. Dog Owner's Encyclopedia of Veterinary Medicine. 1970. 12.95 (ISBN 0-87666-287-4, H-934). TFH Pubns.
Hart, A. W. & Hart, A. W. Industrial Hygiene. (Illus.). 400p. 1976. 22.95 (ISBN 0-13-461202-7). P-H.
Hart, Albert B. Foundations of American Foreign Policy. LC 74-109549. (Law, Politics & History Ser). 1970. Repr. of 1901 ed. lib. bdg. 39.50 (ISBN 0-306-71903-7). Da Capo.
--Southern South. LC 74-96438. (American Scene Ser). 1969. Repr. of 1969 ed. lib. bdg. 55.00 (ISBN 0-306-71826-X). Da Capo.
Hart, Albert B. & Chapman, Annie B. How Our Grandfathers Lived. LC 78-164331. 1971. Repr. of 1921 ed. 37.00x (ISBN 0-8103-3795-9). Gale.
Hart, Angela. Dogs. LC 82-50064. (Easy-Read Fact Bks.). (Illus.). (gr. 2-4). 1982. PLB 8.60 (ISBN 0-531-04446-7). Watts.
--Prehistoric Man. (Easy-Read Fact Bk.). (Illus.). 32p. (gr. 2-4). 1983. PLB 8.60 (ISBN 0-531-04511-0). Watts.
Hart, Anita, jt. auth. see King, Ruth.
Hart, Babe. Speedy German: To Get You There & Back. Hart, Babe, ed. & tr. (Speedy Language Ser.). (Illus.). 24p. (Ital.). 1977. pap. 1.75 (ISBN 0-9602838-3-8). Baja Bks.
--Speedy Greek. Hart, Babe, ed. & illus. (Speedy Language Ser.). (Illus.). 24p. (Orig.). 1983. pap. 1.75 (ISBN 0-9602838-8-9). Baja Bks.
--Speedy Ingles. (Speedy Language Ser.). 24p. (Orig.). 1982. pap. 1.75 (ISBN 0-9602838-7-0). Baja Bks.
--Speedy Italian: To Get You There & Back. Hart, Babe, ed. & tr. (Speedy Language Ser.). (Illus.). 24p. 1977. pap. 1.75 (ISBN 0-686-84388-6). Baja Bks.
--Speedy Japanese: To Get You There & Back. (Speedy Language Ser.). (Illus.). 24p. (Orig., Japanese.). 1979. pap. 1.75 (ISBN 0-9602838-4-6). Baja Bks.
Hart, Babe, ed. see Hart, T. L.
Hart, Babe, tr. see Hart, T. L.
Hart, Basil H. Liddell see Liddell Hart, Basil H.
Hart, Basil L., et al. Great Battles of the 20th Century. LC 77-78750. (Illus.). Repr. of 1977 ed. 9.95 o.p. (ISBN 0-448-14458-1, G&D). Putnam Pub Group.

Hart, Bertha S. The Official History of Laurens County, Georgia, 1807-1941. LC 78-58066. 546p. 1978. bds. 25.00 (ISBN 0-87797-042-4). Cherokee.

Hart, C. R. The Early Charters of Northern England & the North Midlands. (Studies in Early English History Ser: No. 6). 424p. 1975. text ed. 36.50x o.p. (ISBN 0-7185-1131-X, Leicester). Humanities.

Hart, Carole. Delilah. LC 73-5483. (Illus.). 64p. (gr. 2-6). 1973. PLB 9.89 (ISBN 0-06-022236-0, HarpJ). Har-Row.

--Delilah. 64p. (gr. 2-5). 1983. pap. 1.95 (ISBN 0-380-62729-9, Camelot). Avon.

Hart, Carole, ed. Free to be...You & Me. 6.95 (ISBN 0-686-95936-1). Alternatives.

Hart, Clive, ed. see Power, Arthur.

Hart, David. Nuclear Power in India: A Comparative Analysis. 192p. 1983. text ed. 24.00x (ISBN 0-04-338101-4). Allen Unwin.

Hart, Donn V., ed. Philippine Studies: Political Science, Economics, & Linguistics, No. 8. (NIU Center for SEAsian Studies, Occasional Papers). 294p. 1981. pap. 14.00x (ISBN 0-686-35858-9). North Ill U Ctr SE Asian.

Hart, Donn V., tr. see Echau, Robustiano.

Hart, Douglas C., jt. auth. see Pohle, Robert W., Jr.

Hart, Dudley. The Treatment of Chronic Pain. (Illus.). 191p. 1974. text ed. 18.50x o.p. (ISBN 0-8036-4600-3). Davis Co.

Hart, E. Encyclopedia of Dog Breeds. (Illus.). 782p. 14.95 (ISBN 0-87666-285-8, H927). TFH Pubns.

--This Is the Bassett Hound. (Illus.). 224p. 1974. text ed. 12.95 (ISBN 0-87666-241-6, PS-701). TFH Pubns.

Hart, Edward. Heavy Horses Past & Present. LC 75-31325. (Illus.). 112p. 1976. 16.95 o.p. (ISBN 0-7153-7146-0). David & Charles.

--Working Dogs. (Illus.). 64p. 1983. pap. 4.95 (ISBN 0-7134-3731-6, Pub. by Batsford England). David & Charles.

Hart, Ernest. Budgerigar Handbook. 14.95 (ISBN 0-87666-414-1, H901). TFH Pubns.

--Your German Shepherd Puppy. text ed. 6.95 (ISBN 0-87666-300-5, PS643). TFH Pubns.

--Your Poodle Puppy. 7.95 (ISBN 0-87666-360-9, PS646). TFH Pubns.

Hart, Ernest H. Cocker Spaniel Handbook. text ed. 12.95 (ISBN 0-87666-270-X, H923). TFH Pubns.

--Dog Breeding. (Illus.). text ed. 12.95 (ISBN 0-87666-654-3, H-958). TFH Pubns.

--How to Train Your Dog. 9.95 (ISBN 0-87666-284-X, PS644). TFH Pubns.

--Poodle Handbook. 12.95 (ISBN 0-87666-359-5, H924). TFH Pubns.

--This Is the Weimaraner. 1965. 12.95 (ISBN 0-87666-406-0, PS638). TFH Pubns.

Hart, Ernest H., jt. auth. see Goldbecker, William.

Hart, F. Dudley. Drug Treatment of the Rheumatic Diseases. 216p. 1979. text ed. 24.95 (ISBN 0-8391-1306-4). Univ Park.

Hart, Frank D. Overcoming Arthritis. LC 80-22466. (Positive Health Guides Ser.). (Illus.). 112p. 1981. 11.95 (ISBN 0-668-04679-1); pap. 5.95 (ISBN 0-668-04686-4). Arco.

Hart, Frederick. Art: History of Painting, Sculpture, & Architecture, 2 vols. Incl. Vol. 1. Prehistory to the Renaissance; Vol. 2. The Renaissance to Contemporary Trends. (Illus.). 996p. 1976. Set 55.00 o.p. (ISBN 0-8109-0264-8). Abrams.

Hart, Gary, jt. auth. see Englekirk, Robert.

Hart, Gary C. Uncertainty Analysis Loads & Safety in Structural Engineering. (Illus.). 240p. 1982. 28.95 (ISBN 0-13-935619-3). P-H.

Hart, George L., III. The Poems of Ancient Tamil: Their Milieu & Their Sanskrit Counterparts. LC 73-91667. 300p. 1975. 32.50x (ISBN 0-520-02672-1). U of Cal Pr.

Hart, Gordon M., Jr. The Process of Clinical Supervision. (Illus.). 288p. 1982. pap. text ed. 25.95 (ISBN 0-8391-1700-0, 14257). Univ Park.

Hart, Gwen. A History of Cheltenham. 2nd ed. 349p. 1981. text ed. 26.50x (ISBN 0-904387-87-9, Pub. by Sutton England). Humanities.

Hart, Harold. Organic Chemistry: A Short Course. 6th ed. LC 82-84391. 448p. 1983. text ed. 24.95 (ISBN 0-395-32611-7); write for info. supplementary materials. HM.

Hart, Harold & Schuetz, Robert D. Organic Chemistry: A Short Course. 5th ed. LC 77-75880. (Illus.). 1978. text ed. 22.95 (ISBN 0-395-25161-3); lab manual 11.95 (ISBN 0-395-25163-X); study guide & solutions bk. 10.50 (ISBN 0-395-25162-1). HM.

Hart, Harold H. The Mammoth Book of the Incredible. (Illus.). 512p. (Orig.). Date not set. pap. 8.95 (ISBN 0-89104-284-9, A & W Visual Library). A & W Pubs. Postponed.

Hart, Harold H., ed. Chairs Through the Ages: A Pictorial Archive of Woodcuts & Engraving. (Pictorial Archives Ser.). (Illus.). 144p. 1982. pap. 6.50 (ISBN 0-486-24348-6). Dover.

Hart, Harold H., compiled by. Encyclopedia of Design. (Illus.). 432p. 1982. cancelled (ISBN 0-89479-114-1). A & W Pubs.

--Grab a Pencil, No. 2. (Illus.). 384p. 1981. pap. 5.95 (ISBN 0-89104-272-5, A & W Visual Library). A & W Pubs.

Hart, Henry C., ed. Indira Ghandi's India: The Political System Reappraised. LC 76-5433. (Special Studies on South & Southeast Asia Ser). 1976. lib. bdg. 30.00 o.p. (ISBN 0-89158-042-5); pap. text ed. 10.95 o.p. (ISBN 0-89158-109-X). Westview.

Hart, Henry H. Conceptual Index to Psychoanalytic Technique & Training. LC 72-77268. xxi, 1584p. 1972. lib. bdg. 295.00x (ISBN 0-88427-001-7). Vol. 1 (ISBN 0-88427-021-1). Vol. 2 (ISBN 0-88427-022-X). Vol.3 (ISBN 0-88427-023-8). Vol. 4 (ISBN 0-88427-024-6). Vol. 5 (ISBN 0-88427-025-4). North River.

--Sea Road to the Indies: An Account of the Voyages & Exploits of the Portuguese Navigators, Together with the Life & Times of Dom Vasco De Gama, Capitao-Mor, Viceroy of India & Count of Vidigueira. LC 70-135246. (Illus.). 1971. Repr. of 1950 ed. lib. bdg. 15.50x (ISBN 0-8371-5165-1, HARO). Greenwood.

Hart, Henry H., ed. Poems of the Hundred Names: A Short Introduction to Chinese Poetry, Together with 208 Original Translations. 3rd ed. LC 68-23295. (Illus.). 1968. Repr. of 1954 ed. lib. bdg. 16.25x (ISBN 0-8371-0098-4, HACP). Greenwood.

Hart, Herbert L. Punishment & Responsibility: Essays in the Philosophy of Law. (Orig.). 1968. 17.95x (ISBN 0-19-500162-1); pap. 9.95x (ISBN 0-19-825181-5). Oxford U Pr.

Hart, Jack & Mahan, Don. Cross Reference Utility: A Programming Aid for the IBM Personal Computer. (Illus.). 192p. 1983. pap. 29.95 (ISBN 0-13-194746-X). P-H.

Hart, Jack R. The Information Empire: The Rise of the Los Angeles Times & the Times Mirror Corporation. LC 80-69048. 420p. (Orig.). 1981. lib. bdg. 24.50 (ISBN 0-8191-1580-0); pap. text ed. 14.75 (ISBN 0-8191-1581-9). U Pr of Amer.

Hart, James. Ordinance Making Powers of the President of the United States. LC 78-87482. (Law, Politics & History Ser.). 1970. Repr. of 1925 ed. lib. bdg. 39.50 (ISBN 0-306-71487-6). Da Capo.

Hart, James, jt. auth. see Clar, Lawrence.

Hart, James A., jt. auth. see Clar, Lawrence M.

Hart, James D., ed. see Norris, Frank.

Hart, Jane. Singing Bee! A Collection of Favorite Children's Songs. (Illus.). 1982. 16.50 (ISBN 0-688-41975-5). Morrow.

Hart, Jean. Kate Daniels, TV Star. (YA) 1979. 6.95 (ISBN 0-686-52551-5, Avalon). Bouregy.

Hart, Jerrems C. & Stone, William T. A Cruising Guide to the Caribbean & the Bahamas: Including the North Coast of South America, Central America & Yucatan, 1982. rev. ed. (Illus.). 600p. 1982. 29.95 (ISBN 0-396-08023-5). Dodd.

--A Cruising Guide to the Caribbean & the Bahamas. LC 75-43577. (Illus.). 1979. 20.00 o.p. (ISBN 0-396-07774-9). Dodd.

Hart, Joan, ed. see Campion, Thomas.

Hart, Joanne. In These Hills: A Collection of Poems & Drawings of Grand Portage, Minnesota. (Illus.). 24p. (Orig.). 1982. pap. 2.50 (ISBN 0-910259-00-3). Womens Times.

Hart, John. Fifty Portrait Lighting Techniques for Pictures That Sell: Demonstrations of Techniques That Can Put You in Business as a Portrait Photographer. 144p. 1983. 22.50 (ISBN 0-8174-3861-0, Amphoto). Watson-Guptill.

--Hiking the Great Basin: The High Desert Country of California, Oregon, Nevada, & Utah. LC 80-23105. (Totebooks Ser.). (Illus.). 320p. (Orig.). 1981. pap. 9.95 (ISBN 0-87156-245-6). Sierra.

--Modern Small Boat Sailing. (Illus.). 228p. 1974. 19.50 o.s.i. (ISBN 0-7135-1754-9). Transatlantic.

--Regard the Lilies, Regard the Blood: Poems to the Blessed Virgin. 80p. 1983. 6.00 (ISBN 0-682-49941-2). Exposition.

Hart, John E. Albert Halper. (United States Authors Ser.). 1980. lib. bdg. 12.95 (ISBN 0-8057-7291-X, Twayne). G K Hall.

--Floyd Dell. (United States Authors Ser.). 13.95 (ISBN 0-8057-0196-6, Twayne). G K Hall.

Hart, John F. The Look of the Land. LC 74-20995. (Foundations of Cultural Geography Ser.). (Illus.). 224p. 1975. text ed. 17.95 ref. ed. o.p. (ISBN 0-13-540534-3); pap. text ed. 11.95 (ISBN 0-13-540526-2). P-H.

Hart, John F., ed. Regions of the United States. 1972. pap. text ed. 12.50 scp o.p. (ISBN 0-06-042676-4, HarpC). Har-Row.

Hart, Johnny. Star Light, Star Bright, First... (Orig.). 1982. pap. 1.95 (ISBN 0-449-12365-0, GM). Fawcett.

Hart, Kitty. Return to Auschwitz. LC 81-69155. 200p. 1983. pap. 7.95 (ISBN 0-689-70637-5, 283). Atheneum.

Hart, Leon A. Anybody Can Do It-Acupressure. Mark, Lynn, ed. LC 76-16924. (Illus.). 1977. pap. 2.25 (ISBN 0-918322-01-4). L Mark Lib.

Hart, Leslie. Classroom Disaster. LC 69-18133. 1969. text ed. 10.95 (ISBN 0-8077•1496-8). Tchrs Coll.

Hart, Leslie A. Human Brain & Human Learning. 256p. 1983. text ed. 22.50x (ISBN 0-686-37692-7); pap. text ed. 12.50x (ISBN 0-582-28379-5). Longman.

Hart, Lois B. & Dalke, J. David. The Sexes at Work. 192p. 1983. 12.95 (ISBN 0-13-807321-X); pap. 5.95 (ISBN 0-13-807313-9). P-H.

Hart, Martin. Rats. 1980. 18.00x o.p. (ISBN 0-85031-297-3, Pub. by Allison & Busby England). State Mutual Bk.

--Rats. 192p. 1983. 14.95 (ISBN 0-8052-8133-9, Pub. by Allison & Busby England). Schocken.

Hart, Maxine. A Nest of Dragons. LC 78-59350. 1978. 15.00 (ISBN 0-89002-106-6); pap. 5.00 (ISBN 0-89002-105-8). Northwoods Pr.

--Piping Down the Valleys Wild. LC 80-81363. 1980. 15.00 (ISBN 0-89002-146-5); pap. 5.00 (ISBN 0-89002-145-7). Northwoods Pr.

Hart, Monte M., jt. auth. see Schulman, Benson R.

Hart, Newell. The Bear River Massacre. (Illus.). 300p. 1982. 30.00 (ISBN 0-941462-01-3). Cache Valley.

--Hometown Album. 550p. 1973. pap. 25.00 o.p. (ISBN 0-941462-03-X). Cache Valley.

Hart, Newell, ed. The Trail Blazer: History of S.E. Idaho, Daughters of Pioneers. Rev., 1930 ed. 1976. 11.00 (ISBN 0-941462-02-1). Cache Valley.

Hart, Nicky. When Marriage Ends: A Study in Status Passage. 277p. 1976. pap. 11.95 (ISBN 0-422-74690-8, Pub. by Tavistock England). Methuen Inc.

Hart, Norman, jt. auth. see Doyle, Peter.

Hart, Norman A. Industrial Advertising & Publicity. 300p. 1978. 29.95x o.p. (ISBN 0-470-99375-8). Halsted Pr.

Hart, P. E., et al. Mergers & Concentration in British Industry. (National Institute of Economic & Social Research, Occasional Papers: No. 26). (Illus.). 176p. 1973. 24.95 (ISBN 0-521-20238-8). Cambridge U Pr.

Hart, P. J., ed. The Earth's Crust & Upper Mantle. LC 75-600572. (Geophysical Monograph Ser.: Vol. 13). 1969. pap. 10.00 (ISBN 0-87590-000-3). Am Geophysical.

Hart, Pamela. An Unbroken Heart. Date not set. pap. cancelled (ISBN 0-89293-070-5). Beta Bk.

Hart, Parker T. America & the Middle East. new ed. Lambert, Richard D., ed. LC 72-78294. (Annals Ser.: 401). 300p. 1972. pap. 7.95 (ISBN 0-87761-148-3). Am Acad Pol Soc Sci.

Hart, Paul & Pitcher, Tony. Fisheries Ecology. 224p. 1980. 35.00x o.p. (ISBN 0-85664-894-9, Pub. by Croom Helm England). State Mutual Bk.

Hart, Peter E., jt. auth. see Duda, Richard O.

Hart, Pierre, tr. see Briusov, Valery.

Hart, R. W. Witchcraft. (Putnam Documentary History Ser.). (Illus.). 1972. 6.95 o.p. (ISBN 0-399-10868-8). Putnam Pub Group.

Hart, Ray L. Unfinished Man & the Imagination: Toward an Ontology & a Rhetoric of Revelation. 1979. pap. 9.95 (ISBN 0-8164-2009-2). Seabury.

Hart, Robert. These From the Land of Sinim: Essays on the Chinese Question. LC 79-2826. 302p. 1983. Repr. of 1903 ed. 22.50 (ISBN 0-8305-0022-7). Hyperion Conn.

Hart, Roderick, jt. auth. see Applbaum, Ronald.

Hart, Roderick, jt. ed. see Applbaum, Ronald.

Hart, Roderick, ed. see Baird.

Hart, Roderick, ed. see Campbell, John A.

Hart, Roderick, ed. see Chesebro & Hamsher.

Hart, Roderick, ed. see Colburn, William & Weinberg, Sanford.

Hart, Roderick, ed. see Doolittle.

Hart, Roderick, ed. see Eadie & Kline.

Hart, Roderick, ed. see Felsenthal, Norman.

Hart, Roderick, ed. see Frandsen & Benson.

Hart, Roderick, ed. see Leathers.

Hart, Roderick, ed. see Measell.

Hart, Roderick, ed. see Motley.

Hart, Roderick, ed. see Osborn.

Hart, Roderick, ed. see Robb.

Hart, Roderick, ed. see Smith.

Hart, Roderick, ed. see Swanson, Delia.

Hart, Roderick P. Public Communication. 2nd ed. 368p. 1983. text ed. 13.50 scp (ISBN 0-06-042687-X, HarpC); instr's. manual avail. (ISBN 0-06-362667-5). Har-Row.

Hart, Roderick P., et al. Public Communication. (Auer Ser.). 291p. 1975. text ed. 21.50 scp o.p. (ISBN 0-06-042685-3, HarpC); instructor's manual avail. o.p. (ISBN 0-06-362610-1). Har-Row.

Hart, Ronald & Massoud, Aly, eds. Technology Transfer to Third World Nations: Social-Biomedical Impact. Scherr, George H. 400p. 1982. text ed. 43.00 (ISBN 0-930376-14-5). Chem-Orbital.

Hart, S. R., jt. ed. see Allegre, C. J.

Hart, Shirley. Caught in the Rain. (Candlelight Ecstasy Ser.: No. 116). (Orig.). 1983. pap. 1.95 (ISBN 0-440-10999-X). Dell.

--A Dangerous Haven. (Candlelight Ecstasy Ser.: No. 161). (Orig.). 1983. pap. 1.95 (ISBN 0-440-12032-2). Dell.

--Surrender to the Night. (Candlelight Ecstasy Ser.: No. 144). (Orig.). 1983. pap. 1.95 (ISBN 0-440-18473-8). Dell.

--Wild Rhapsody. (Candlelight Ecstasy Ser.: No. 123). (Orig.). 1983. pap. 1.95 (ISBN 0-440-19545-4). Dell.

Hart, Stephanie. Is There Any Way Out of Sixth Grade? LC 78-17388. (gr. 3-5). 1978. 6.95 o.p. (ISBN 0-698-20445-X, Coward). Putnam Pub Group.

Hart, Stephen H., ed. see Pike, Zebulon M.

Hart, Stuart L. & Enk, Gordon A. Green Goals & Greenbacks: State-Level Environmental Review Programs & Their Associated Costs. LC 79-5229. (A Westview Replica Edition Ser.). (Illus.). 364p. 1979. lib. bdg. 32.00 o.p. (ISBN 0-89158-752-7). Westview.

Hart, T. L. Speedy Spanish for Medical Personnel. Hart, T. L. & Hart, Babe, eds. Hart, Babe, tr. (Speedy Language Ser.). (Illus.). 24p. (Orig., Span.). 1980. pap. 1.95 (ISBN 0-9602838-6-2). Baja Bks.

Hart, Terril H. Tender Loving Care for Your New Baby. (Illus.). 112p. (Orig.). 1983. pap. 4.95 (ISBN 0-915658-03-8). Meadowbrook Pr.

Hart, Terril H., ed. see Meadowbrook Medical Reference Group.

Hart, Thomas L., ed. Instruction in School Media Center Use. LC 78-9717. 1978. pap. 10.00 o.p. (ISBN 0-8389-0255-3). ALA.

Hart, Tony. Fun with Historial Projects. new ed. (Learning with Fun Ser.). (Illus.). 64p. (gr. 5 up). 1976. 13.50x o.p. (ISBN 0-7182-0074-8, SpS). Sportshelf.

--Fun with Map Making. (Learning with Fun Ser.). 13.50x o.p. (ISBN 0-7182-0062-4, SpS). Sportshelf.

Hart, V. E. Lloyd see LLoyd Hart, V. E.

Hart, Virginia L. So Wild a Rose. 288p. (Orig.). 1980. pap. 2.25 o.p. (ISBN 0-523-40543-X). Pinnacle Bks.

Hart, Vivien. Distrust & Democracy. LC 77-84803. (Illus.). 1978. 29.95 (ISBN 0-521-21857-8). Cambridge U Pr.

Hart, William L. & Waits, Bert K. College Algebra. 6th ed. 1978. text ed. 20.95 (ISBN 0-669-01025-1); instr's manual 1.95 (ISBN 0-669-01026-X). Heath.

--College Algebra & Trigonometry. 2nd ed. 1978. text ed. 20.95 (ISBN 0-669-01460-5); instr's. manual 1.95 (ISBN 0-669-01462-1). Heath.

Hartbarger, Janie C. & Hartbarger, Neil J. Eating for the Eighties: A Complete Guide to Vegetarian Nutrition. 352p. 1983. pap. 3.50 (ISBN 0-425-05827-1). Berkley Pub.

Hartbarger, Neil. Your Career in Banking. (Arco's Career Guidance Ser.). (Illus.). 1980. lib. bdg. 7.95 (ISBN 0-668-04797-6, 4797-6); pap. 4.50 (ISBN 0-668-04802-6, 4802-6). Arco.

--Your Career in Teaching. LC 79-14287. (Arco's Career Guidence Ser.). 1979. lib. bdg. 7.95 (ISBN 0-668-04741-0, 4741); pap. 4.50 (ISBN 0-668-04752-6, 4752). Arco.

Hartbarger, Neil J., jt. auth. see Hartbarger, Janie C.

Hart-Davis, Phyllida. Grace: The Story of a Princess. (Illus.). 144p. 1982. pap. 9.95 (ISBN 0-312-34209-8). St Martin.

Hart-Davis, Rupert, ed. see Sassoon, Seigfried.

Hart-Davis, Rupert, ed. see Sassoon, Siegfried.

Hart-Davis, Rupert, ed. see Wilde, Oscar.

Harte, Bret. The Girl from Pike County. Pauk, Walter & Harris, Raymond, eds. (Jamestown Classics Ser.). (Illus.). 43p. (gr. 5). 1976. pap. text ed. 2.00x (ISBN 0-89061-050-9, 521); tchrs. ed. 3.00 (ISBN 0-89061-053-3, 523). Jamestown Pubs.

--The Luck of Roaring Camp. Pauk, Walter & Harris, Raymond, eds. (Jamestown Classics Ser.). (Illus.). 35p. (gr. 6-12). 1976. pap. text ed. 2.00x (ISBN 0-89061-054-1, 529); tchrs. ed. 3.00 (ISBN 0-89061-055-X, 531). Jamestown Pubs.

--Mliss. Pauk, Walter & Harris, Raymond, eds. (Jamestown Classics Ser.). 47p. (gr. 6-12). 1976. pap. text ed. 2.00x (ISBN 0-89061-048-7, 517); tchrs. ed. 3.00 (ISBN 0-89061-049-5, 519). Jamestown Pubs.

--The Outcasts of Poker Flat. (Creative's Classics Ser.). (Illus.). 48p. (gr. 4-9). 1980. PLB 7.95 (ISBN 0-87191-768-8). Creative Ed.

--The Outcasts of Poker Flat. Pauk, Walter & Harris, Raymond, eds. (Jamestown Classics Ser.). (Illus.). 37p. (gr. 6-12). 1976. pap. text ed. 2.00x (ISBN 0-89061-052-5, 525); tchrs. ed. 3.00 (ISBN 0-89061-053-3, 527). Jamestown Pubs.

--Outcasts of Poker Flat. (RL 8). pap. 2.50 (ISBN 0-451-51594-3, CE1594, Sig Classics). NAL.

--Outcasts of Poker Flat & Luck of Roaring Camp. rev. ed. Dixson, Robert J., ed. (American Classics Ser.: Bk. 5). (gr. 9 up). 1973. pap. text ed. 3.25 (ISBN 0-88345-201-4, 18124); cassettes 40.00 (ISBN 0-685-38996-0); 40.00 o.p. tapes (ISBN 0-685-38997-9). Regents Pub.

Harte, N. B. & Pointing, K. G. Cloth & Clothing in Medieval Europe: Essays in Memory of Professor E. M. Carus-Wilson. 448p. 1982. 90.00x (ISBN 0-435-32382-2, Pub. by Heinemann England). State Mutual Bk.

Harte, N. B. & Ponting, K. G., eds. Textile History & Economic History: Essays in Honour of Miss Julia de Lacy Mann. (Illus.). 396p. 1973. 23.50x o.p. (ISBN 0-87471-455-9). Rowman.

Harte, Samantha. The Snows of Craggmoor. (YA) 1978. 6.95 (ISBN 0-685-87350-1, Avalon). Bouregy.

Harteis, Richard. Morocco Journal. LC 81-69798. 1981. pap. 4.95 (ISBN 0-915604-63-9). Carnegie-Mellon.

Hartel, Herbert & Yaldiz, Marianne. Along the Ancient Silk Routes: Central Asian Art from the West Berlin State Museums. Laing, M. E. D., ed. (Illus.). 200p. 1982. 45.00 (ISBN 0-8109-1800-5); pap. 19.95 (ISBN 0-87099-300-3). Metro Mus Art.

Hartel, Herbert, intro. by. Along the Ancient Silk Routes: Central Asian Art from the West Berlin State Museums. (Illus.). 224p. 1982. 45.00 (ISBN 0-8109-1800-5). Abrams.

Harten, A. Van see Eckhaus, W. & Van Harten, A.

Hartenberg, Richard S. & Denavit, Jacques. Kinematic Synthesis of Linkages. (Mechanical Engineering Ser.). 1964. text ed. 39.50 o.p. (ISBN 0-07-026910-6, C). McGraw.

Hartenstein, R., jt. ed. see Breuer, M.

Hartenstein, R., jt. ed. see Wilmanns, W.

Harter, H. Leon. The Chronological Annotated Bibliography of Order Statistics: Vol. I: Pre-1950. rev. ed. LC 81-66077. (The American Sciences Press Series in Mathematical & Management Sciences: Vol. 7). 1983. 89.55 (ISBN 0-935950-04-4). Am Sciences Pr.

--The Chronological Annotated Bibliography of Order Statistics: Vol. II, 1950-1959. LC 81-66077. (The American Sciences Press Series in Mathematical & Management Sciences: Vol. 8). 1983. 149.50 (ISBN 0-935950-05-2). Am Sciences Pr.

Harter, Hugh A. Gertrudis Gomez De Avellaneda. (World Authors Ser.: No. 599). 1981. lib. bdg. 15.95 (ISBN 0-8057-6441-0, Twayne). G K Hall.

Harter, James & Beitzel, Wallace. Mathematics Applied to Electronics. (Illus.). 1980. text ed. 21.95 (ISBN 0-8359-4288-0); solutions manual avail. Reston.

Harter, Jim. Men: A Pictorial Archive from Nineteenth-Century Sources. (Pictorial Archive Ser.). (Illus., Orig.). 1980. pap. 5.00 (ISBN 0-486-23952-7). Dover.

Harter, Jim & Lin, Paul. Essentials of Electric Circuits. 1982. text ed. 24.95 (ISBN 0-8359-1767-3); instrs.' manual free. Reston.

Harter, JIm, ed. Transportation: A Pictorial Archive From 19th Century Sources with 400 Copyright-Free Illustrations for Artists & Designs. (Illus.). 160p. (Orig.). 1983. pap. 6.95 (ISBN 0-486-24499-7). Dover.

--Women: A Pictorial Archive from 19th Century Sources. (Pictorial Achive Ser.). 1978. pap. 4.95 (ISBN 0-486-23703-6). Dover.

Harter, Lafayette G., Jr. Economic Responses to a Changing World. 1972. text ed. 16.50x (ISBN 0-673-05187-0). Scott F.

Harter, Lafayette G., Jr. & Moghaddam, Reza. Working with Introductory Economics: Study Guide to Accompany Economic Responses to a Changing World. 1972. pap. 5.50x (ISBN 0-673-07845-0). Scott F.

Harter, Penny. White Flowers in the Snow. LC 81-80549. (Illus.). 95p. 1981. pap. 3.00 (ISBN 0-89823-024-1). New Rivers Pr.

Harter, Walter. Birds: In Fact & Legend. LC 79-65065. (Illus.). 1979. 6.95 o.p. (ISBN 0-8069-3740-8); lib. bdg. 6.69 o.p. (ISBN 0-8069-3741-6). Sterling.

--The Phantom Hand. (Illus.). 128p. (gr. 4 up). 1976. pap. 5.96 (ISBN 0-13-661843-X, Pub. by Treehouse). P-H.

Harter, Walter L. How to Shoot & Make Money Selling Pictures. (Illus.). 1972. 6.95 o.p. (ISBN 0-8174-0460-0, Amphoto). Watson-Guptill.

Hartert, E. Die Voegel der Palaearkischen Fauna. 1970. 240.00 (ISBN 3-7682-0604-1). Lubrecht & Cramer.

Hartfeld, Hermann. Irina's Story. 320p. 1983. pap. 4.95 (ISBN 0-87123-261-8, 210261). Bethany Hse.

Harth, Erich. Windows on the Mind: Reflections on the Physical Basis of Consciousness. LC 81-11158. (Illus.). 272p. 1983. Repr. pap. 7.95 (ISBN 0-688-01596-4). Quill NY.

Harthan, John. Illuminated Manuscripts: The Victoria & Albert Museum Introductions to the Decorative Arts. (Illus.). 48p. 9.95 (ISBN 0-88045-019-3). Stemmer Hse.

Harthan, John, ed. see Klingender, Francis D.

Harthoorn, A. M. The Chemical Capture of Animals: A Guide to the Chemical Restraint of Wild & Captive Animals. (Illus.). 1976. 35.00 o.s.i. (ISBN 0-7020-0558-4). R Curtis Bks.

Hartigan, J. A. Clustering Algorithms. LC 74-14573. (Wiley Series in Probability & Mathematical Statistics). 368p. 1975. 38.50 (ISBN 0-471-35645-X, Pub. by Wiley-Interscience). Wiley.

Hartigan, Joe. To Own a Racehorse. pap. 7.50x (ISBN 0-87556-601-4). Saifer.

Hartigan, Karelisa V. All the World... Drama Past & Present. LC 82-40207. 148p. 1983. lib. bdg. 20.00 (ISBN 0-8191-2711-6); pap. text ed. 8.25 (ISBN 0-8191-2712-4). U Pr of Amer.

Hartigan, Karelisa V., ed. To Hold a Mirror to Nature: Dramatic Images & Reflections. LC 81-40310. (The University of Florida Department of Classics Comparative Drama Conference Papers: Vol. 1). 176p. (Orig.). 1982. lib. bdg. 21.25 (ISBN 0-8191-2275-0); pap. text ed. 10.00 (ISBN 0-8191-2276-9). U Pr of Amer.

Hartigan, Richard S. The Forgotten Victim: A History of the Civilian. (Illus.). 1982. 14.95 (ISBN 0-913750-19-0). Precedent Pub.

Hartigan, Richard S., ed. see Lieber, Francis.

Hartill, J. Edwin. Principles of Biblical Hermeneutics. 11.95 (ISBN 0-310-25900-2). Zondervan.

Harting, E. & Read, F. H. Electrostatic Lenses. 1976. 72.50 (ISBN 0-444-41319-7). Elsevier.

Harting, James. The Ornithology of Shakespeare. (Illus.). 321p. 1978. 15.00x (ISBN 0-905418-26-3). Intl Pubns Serv.

Hartje, Robert G. Bicentennial USA: Pathways to Celebration. LC 73-83813. (Illus.). 334p. 1973. pap. 5.50 o.p. (ISBN 0-910050-09-0). AASLH.

Hartjen, Clayton, jt. auth. see Duberman, Lucile.

Hart-Johns, Martha & Johns, Bruce. Give Your Child a Chance. 1982. text ed. 15.95 (ISBN 0-8359-2553-6); pap. text ed. 9.95 (ISBN 0-8359-2552-8). Reston.

Hartl, Daniel L. A Primer of Population Genetics. LC 80-23009. (Illus.). 175p. (Orig.). 1981. pap. text ed. 9.95x (ISBN 0-87893-271-2). Sinauer Assoc.

--Principles of Population Genetics. LC 79-28384. (Illus.). 225p. 1980. text ed. 21.00x (ISBN 0-87893-272-0). Sinauer Assoc.

Hartl, Emil, et al. Physique & Delinquent Behavior: A Thirty Year Followup of W. H. Sheldon's Varieties of Delinquent Youth. (Personality & Psychopathology Ser.). 582p. 1982. 49.50 (ISBN 0-12-328480-5). Acad Pr.

Hartland, Edwin S. Matrilineal Kinship & the Question of Its Priority. LC 18-15715. 1917. pap. 12.00 (ISBN 0-527-00516-9). Kraus Repr.

--Science of Fairy Tales: An Inquiry into Fairy Mythology. LC 68-31149. 1968. Repr. of 1891 ed. 40.00x (ISBN 0-8103-3464-X). Gale.

Hartland, Edwin S., ed. English Fairy & Other Folktales. LC 68-21772. 1968. Repr. of 1890 ed. 34.00x (ISBN 0-8103-3465-8). Gale.

Hartland, J. Medical & Dental Hypnosis & Its Clinical Application. 2nd ed. 1971. 25.00 o.s.i. (ISBN 0-02-858000-1, Pub. by Bailliere-Tindall); pap. text ed. 28.95 (ISBN 0-02-858010-9). Saunders.

Hartland, Michael. Down Among the Dead Men. (Illus.). 320p. 1983. 13.95 (ISBN 0-02-548520-2). Macmillan.

Hartland, Robert. Design of Precast Concrete: An Introduction to Practical Design. LC 75-23528. 148p. 1976. 22.95x o.p. (ISBN 0-470-35654-5). Halsted Pr.

Hartland, S. & Hartley, R. W. Axisymmetric Fluid-Liquid Interfaces. 1976. 117.00 (ISBN 0-444-41396-0). Elsevier.

Hartland, S., jt. auth. see Mecklenburgh, J. C.

Hartland-Thunberg, Penelope. Botswana: An African Growth Economy. LC 78-3477. (Westview Special Studies on Africa). (Illus.). 1978. lib. bdg. 22.50 o.p. (ISBN 0-89158-171-5). Westview.

--Trading Blocs, U. S. Exports, & World Trade. (Westview Special Studies in International Economics & Business). 197p. 1980. lib. bdg. 25.00 (ISBN 0-89158-967-8). Westview.

Hartley. Linguistics for Language Learners. 1982. 50.00x (ISBN 0-333-26683-8, Pub. by Macmillan England). State Mutual Bk.

Hartley, Alan, jt. auth. see Zeoli, Billy.

Hartley, Allan. Adam & Eve. (Illus.). 1975. pap. 0.79 (ISBN 0-8007-8517-7, Spire Comics). Revell.

--Alpha & Omega. (Illus.). 1978. pap. 0.69 o.p. (ISBN 0-8007-8534-7, Spire Comics). Revell.

--Archie Gets a Job. (Illus.). (gr. 1 up). 1977. 0.69 o.p. (ISBN 0-8007-8531-2, Spire Comics). Revell.

--Archie's Clean Slate. (Illus.). 1974. pap. 0.79 (ISBN 0-8007-8507-X, Spire Comics). Revell.

--Archie's Family Album. (Illus.). (gr. 1 up). 1978. pap. 0.49 o.p. (ISBN 0-8007-8532-0, Spire Comics). Revell.

--Archie's Love Scene. (Illus.). (gr. 1 up). 1973. 0.79 (ISBN 0-8007-8505-3, Spire Comics). Revell.

--Archie's World. (gr. 1 up). 1975. 0.79 (ISBN 0-8007-8524-X, Spire Comics). Revell.

--Born Again. (Illus.). 1978. pap. 0.79 (ISBN 0-8007-8535-5, Spire Comics). Revell.

--The Cross & the Switchblade. (Illus.). pap. 0.79 (ISBN 0-8007-8500-2, Spire Comics). Revell.

--Crossfire. (Illus.). (YA) 1975. pap. 0.49 o.p. (ISBN 0-8007-8525-8, Spire Comics). Revell.

--Flying Colors. (ps-3). 1981. pap. 0.99 o.p. (ISBN 0-8007-8605-X). Revell.

--Fun in the Car. (ps-3). 1980. pap. 0.99 o.p. (ISBN 0-8007-8603-3). Revell.

--Fun with Friends. (ps-3). 1981. pap. 0.99 o.p. (ISBN 0-8007-8604-1). Revell.

--God Is... (Illus.). (gr. 1-4). 1975. pap. 0.69 o.p. (ISBN 0-8007-8600-9, Spire Comics). Revell.

--In His Steps. 1977. pap. 0.79 (ISBN 0-8007-8530-4, Spire Comics). Revell.

--Jesus. (Illus.). 1979. pap. 0.79 (ISBN 0-8007-8538-X, Spire Comics). Revell.

--Noah's Ark. 1976. pap. 0.79 (ISBN 0-8007-8522-3, Spire Comics). Revell.

--Paul. (gr. 3up). 1979. pap. 0.79 (ISBN 0-8007-8533-9, Spire Comics). Revell.

--There's a New World Coming. 1974. pap. 0.69 o.p. (ISBN 0-8007-8516-9, Spire Comics). Revell.

Hartley, David. Observations on Man, His Frame, His Duty & His Expectations, 2 vols. LC 66-11026. (Hist. of Psych. Ser.). 1966. Repr. of 1749 ed. 95.00x (ISBN 0-8201-1025-6). Schol Facsimiles.

Hartley, Fred. One Hundred Percent. 160p. (Orig.). 1983. pap. 5.95 (ISBN 0-8007-5112-4, Power Bks). Revell.

Hartley, Joe, jt. auth. see Healy, Bill.

Hartley, Joel. First Aid Without Panic. (Illus.). 400p. 1982. 9.95 (ISBN 0-448-12333-9, G&D). Putnam Pub Group.

Hartley, John. Understanding News. (Studies in Communication). 1982. 19.95x (ISBN 0-416-74540-7); pap. 7.95x (ISBN 0-416-74550-4). Methuen Inc.

Hartley, John, jt. auth. see Fiske, John.

Hartley, John E. & Shelton, R. L., eds. An Inquiry Into Soteriology, Vol. I. 14.95 (ISBN 0-87162-240-8, WP#4850). Warner Pr.

Hartley, Keith. NATO Arms Co-Operation: A Study in Economics & Politics. 240p. 1983. text ed. 35.00x (ISBN 0-04-341022-7). Allen Unwin.

Hartley, Keith & Tisdell, Clem. Micro Economic Policy. LC 80-42311. 410p. 1981. 46.95 (ISBN 0-471-28026-7, Pub. by Wiley-Interscience); pap. 16.95x (ISBN 0-471-28027-5, Pub. by Wiley-Interscience). Wiley.

Hartley, L. P see Allen, W. S.

Hartley, L. P., et al see Allen, W. S.

Hartley, Lodwick C. William Cowper, Humanitarian. ix, 277p. Repr. of 1938 ed. lib. bdg. 22.50x (ISBN 0-87991-099-2). Porcupine Pr.

Hartley, M. G. & Buckley, A., eds. Challenge of Microprocessors. 208p. 1979. 18.50 (ISBN 0-7190-0757-7). Manchester.

Hartley, Michael G. & Buckley, Anne, eds. Microelectronics & Microcomputer Applications. 200p. 1983. 15.00 (ISBN 0-7190-0905-7). Manchester.

Hartley, Norman. ShadowPlay. LC 81-69237. 288p. 1982. 12.95 (ISBN 0-689-11249-1). Atheneum.

Hartley, R. W., jt. auth. see Hartland, S.

Hartley, Robert. Big Jim Thompson of Illinois. LC 79-19262. (Illus.). 1979. 9.95 o.p. (ISBN 0-528-81824-4). Rand.

Hartley, Robert F. Management Mistakes. LC 82-12102. (Grid Series in Management). 220p. 1983. text ed. 11.95 (ISBN 0-88244-256-2). Grid Pub.

--Marketing Fundamentals. 704p. 1983. text ed. 24.50 scp (ISBN 0-06-042675-6, HarpC); instr's manual avail. (ISBN 0-06-362671-3); scp study guide 7.00 (ISBN 0-06-042679-9); transparency avail. Har-Row.

--Retailing: Challenge & Opportunity. 2nd ed. LC 79-88102. 1980. text ed. 23.95 (ISBN 0-395-28185-7); instr's. manual 2.50 (ISBN 0-395-28186-5). HM.

--Sales Management. LC 78-69614. (Illus.). 1979. text ed. 24.50 (ISBN 0-395-26511-8); instr's. manual 1.50 (ISBN 0-395-26512-6); test bank 1.50 (ISBN 0-395-29301-4). HM.

Hartley, Shirley F. Illegitimacy. LC 73-83057. 1975. 23.75x (ISBN 0-520-02533-4). U of Cal Pr.

Hartley, T. C. The Foundations of European Community Law: An Introduction to the Constitutional & Administrative Law of the European Community. (Clarendon Law Ser.). (Illus.). 1981. 52.00x (ISBN 0-19-876081-7); pap. 36.50 (ISBN 0-19-876082-5). Oxford U Pr.

Hartley, T. C. & O'Bryant, D. C. Problems in Engineering. (Graphics Ser.: No. 31). 1975. pap. 7.20 (ISBN 0-87563-109-6). Stipes.

Hartley-O'Brien, Sandra J. Coaching the Female Gymnast. (Illus.). 440p. 1983. pap. 29.50x spiral (ISBN 0-398-04687-5). C C Thomas.

Hartline, Jane & Budrow, Nancy. Cross Country Ski Lodges: Montana, Wyoming, Utah. LC 82-51030. (Illus.). 200p. (Orig.). 1982. pap. 9.95 (ISBN 0-9606752-2-1). Sauvie Island.

Hartline, Jane & Budrow, Nancy S. Cross Country Ski Lodges: Washington, Oregon, Idaho. LC 81-52225. (Illus.). 162p. (Orig.). 1981. pap. 8.95 (ISBN 0-9606752-0-5). Sauvie Island.

Hartline, Jessie, jt. ed. see Dutta, M.

Hartline, Jo E. Me!? Resources for Enhancing the Self-Esteem of Students, K-8. (Illus.). 76p. 1982. write for info. Hartline Pub.

Hartling, John. Structured Approach to Problem Solving & Computer Programming. 450p. 1983. 24.00 (ISBN 0-932376-21-5). Digital Pr.

Hartman, A. Carol, jt. auth. see Stephens, Thomas M.

Hartman, Bernard. Fundamentals of Television: Theory & Service. new ed. (Technology Ser). (Illus.). 272p. 1975. text ed. 19.95 (ISBN 0-675-08745-7). Merrill.

Hartman, Betty G., jt. auth. see Sanborn, Marion A.

Hartman, Charles O. The Pigfoot Rebellion. LC 80-83946. (Poetry Chapbook, Fourth Ser.). 42p. 1981. 8.95 (ISBN 0-87923-364-8). Godine.

Hartman, Chester. Housing & Social Policy. (Ser. in Social Policy). 176p. 1975. ref. ed. 14.95 (ISBN 0-13-394999-0). P-H.

--Yerba Buena: Land Grab & Community Resistance in San Francisco. LC 74-6049. (Illus.). 224p. 1974. 8.95 o.p. (ISBN 0-912078-36-7); pap. 4.95 o.p. (ISBN 0-912078-37-5). Volcano Pr.

Hartman, Dane. Dirty Harry, No. 10: Blood of the Strangers. (Men of Action Ser.). 208p. 1982. pap. 1.95 (ISBN 0-446-30053-5). Warner Bks.

--Dirty Harry, No. 11: Death in the Air. (Men of Action Ser.). 192p. (Orig.). 1983. pap. 1.95 (ISBN 0-446-90853-3). Warner Bks.

--Dirty Harry, No. 12: Dealer of Death. (Men of Action Ser.). 224p. 1983. pap. 1.95 (ISBN 0-446-30054-3). Warner Bks.

--Dirty Harry, No. 8: Hatchet Men. (Men of Action Ser.). 176p. 1982. pap. 1.95 (ISBN 0-446-30049-7). Warner Bks.

--Dirty Harry, No. 9: The Killing Connection. (Men of Action Ser.). 192p. (Orig.). 1983. pap. 1.95 (ISBN 0-446-30050-0). Warner Bks.

Hartman, David. Joy & Responsibility: Israel, Modernity & the Renewal of Judaism. 286p. 12.50 (ISBN 0-686-95138-7). ADL.

Hartman, Don. How to Enter & Profit from American Oil & Gas Lotteries. (Illus.). 192p. 1982. pap. 8.95 (ISBN 0-9609470-0-0). Baja Enter.

Hartman, Doug & Sutherland, Doug. Guidebook to Discipleship. 2nd ed. LC 76-20398. (Illus.). 176p. 1983. pap. 4.95 (ISBN 0-89081-062-1). Harvest Hse.

Hartman, Gary V., tr. see Ziegler, Alfred J.

Hartman, Geoffrey. Akiba's Children. 64p. (Orig.). 1978. pap. 12.50 (ISBN 0-931182-00-X). Iron Mtn Pr.

Hartman, Geoffrey, intro. by. Selected Poetry & Prose of William Wordsworth. (Orig.). 1970. pap. 2.25 o.p. (ISBN 0-451-51049-6, CE1049, Sig Classics). NAL.

Hartman, Geoffrey H. The Fate of Reading & Other Essays. LC 74-11624. xiv, 352p. 1975. 9.00x (ISBN 0-226-31844-3). U of Chicago Pr.

Hartman, Howard L. Mine Ventilation & Air Conditioning. (Illus.). 1961. 39.95x o.p. (ISBN 0-8260-3860-3, Pub. by Wiley-Interscience). Wiley.

Hartman, Howard L., ed. Proceedings, First Mine Ventilation Symposium. LC 82-71996. (Illus.). 312p. 1982. 22.00x (ISBN 0-89520-298-0). Soc Mining Eng.

Hartman, Howard L., et al. Mine Ventilation & Air Conditioning. 2nd ed. Mutmansky, Jan M. & Wang, Y. J., eds. LC 81-19662. 791p. 1982. 47.50x (ISBN 0-471-05690-1, Pub. by Wiley-Interscience). Wiley.

Hartman, Joan E., jt. ed. see Messer-Davidow, Ellen.

Hartman, John J. & Hedblom, Jack H. Methods for the Social Sciences: A Handbook for Students & Non-Specialists. LC 78-72796. (Contributions in Sociology: No. 37). (Illus.). 1979. lib. bdg. 35.00 (ISBN 0-313-20894-8, HMS/). Greenwood.

Hartman, Louis F. & Oppenheim, A. Leo. Beer & Brewing Techniques in Ancient Mesopotamia According to the XXIIIrd Tablet of the Series HAR. Ra-Hubullu. 1950. 1.00 o.s.i. (ISBN 0-686-00046-3). Am Orient Soc.

Hartman, Michael. Days of Thunder. 224p. 1980. 9.95 o.p. (ISBN 0-312-18485-9). St Martin.

Hartman, O., ed. Polychaeta Errantia of Antarctica. LC 64-60091. (Antarctic Research Ser.: Vol. 3). 1964. 12.00 (ISBN 0-87590-103-4). Am Geophysical.

--Polychaeta Myzostomidae & Sedentaria of Antarctica. LC 66-61601. (Antarctic Research Ser.: Vol. 7). 1966. 13.00 (ISBN 0-87590-107-7). Am Geophysical.

Hartman, P. Ordinary Differential Equations. 2nd ed. 1982. text ed. 29.95 (ISBN 3-7643-3068-6). Birkhauser.

Hartman, Paul J. Federal Limitations on State & Local Taxation. LC 81-80818. 1981. 62.50 (ISBN 0-686-35940-2). Lawyers Co-Op.

Hartman, Philip, ed. see Stahl, Franklin W.

Hartman, Robert. The Remainder Biscuit. 6.75 o.p. (ISBN 0-685-44123-7). Transatlantic.

Hartman, Robert W. Pay & Pensions for Federal Employees. 150p. 1983. 18.95 (ISBN 0-8157-3496-4); pap. 7.95 (ISBN 0-8157-3495-6). Brookings.

Hartman, Robert W. & Weber, Arnold R., eds. The Rewards of Public Service: Compensating Top Federal Officials. 1980. 18.95 (ISBN 0-8157-3494-8); pap. 7.95 (ISBN 0-8157-3493-X). Brookings.

Hartman, Rose. Birds of Paradise. (Orig.). 1980. pap. 9.95 o.s.i. (ISBN 0-440-50894-0, Delta). Dell.

Hartman, Von Aue. Erec. Thomas, J. W., tr. from Ger. LC 81-7471. viii, 146p. 1982. 11.95x (ISBN 0-8032-4408-8). U of Nebr Pr.

Hartman, W. & Williams, F. Pipe Drafting. 1981. 13.95 (ISBN 0-07-026945-9). McGraw.

Hartman, William T., jt. ed. see Chambers, Jay G.

Hartmanis, Juris. Feasible Computations & Provable Complexity Properties. (CBMS-NSF Regional Conference Ser.: Vol. 30). iii, 62p. (Orig.). 1978. pap. text ed. 10.50 (ISBN 0-89871-027-8). Soc Indus-Appl Math.

Hartmann, A. & Brock, M., eds. Treatment of Cerebral Edema. (Illus.). 176p. 1983. pap. 26.00 (ISBN 0-387-11751-2). Springer-Verlag.

Hartmann, Donald P., jt. auth. see Gelfand, Donna M.

Hartmann, Eduard Von see Von Hartmann, Eduard.

Hartmann, Franz. Jacob Boehme: Life & Doctrine. 2nd ed. LC 76-53631. (Spiritual Science Library). 352p. 1982. lib. bdg. 15.00 (ISBN 0-89345-016-2, Steinerbks); pap. 9.00 (ISBN 0-89345-017-0). Garber Comm.

Hartmann, Frederick H. Relations of Nations. 5th ed. Carroll, James, ed. (Illus.). 700p. 1978. text ed. 23.95x o.p. (ISBN 0-02-351270-9, 35127). Macmillan.

--World in Crisis. 4th ed. Carroll, James J., ed. 519p. 1973. pap. text ed. 13.95x (ISBN 0-02-351380-2). Macmillan.

Hartmann, Frederick N. The Relations of Nations. 6th ed. 736p. 1983. text ed. 23.95 (ISBN 0-02-351350-0). Macmillan.

Hartmann, H. & Wanczek, K. P. Ion Cyclotron Resonance Spectrometry, Vol. II. (Lecture Notes in Chemistry Ser.: Vol. 31). 538p. 1983. pap. 32.80 (ISBN 0-387-11957-4). Springer-Verlag.

Hartmann, Hudson T. & Kester, Dale E. Plant Propagation: Principles & Practices. 4th ed. (Illus.). 704p. 1983. text ed. 29.95 (ISBN 0-13-681007-1). P-H.

Hartmann, Jerry. Palace Politics: An Inside Account of the Ford Years. 320p. 1980. 14.95 o.p. (ISBN 0-07-026951-3). McGraw.

Hartmann, John F., ed. Mechanism & Control of Animal Fertilization. (Cell Biology Ser.). Date not set. price not set (ISBN 0-12-328520-8). Acad Pr.

Hartmann, Michael. The Hunted. 1982. pap. 2.95 o.p. (ISBN 0-425-05170-6). Berkley Pub.

Hartmann, Nicolai. Ethics, 3 vols. Coit, Stanton, tr. Incl. Vol. 1. Moral Phenomena. 1958. text ed. 17.50x o.p. (ISBN 0-04-170006-6); Vol. 2. Moral Values. 1963. text ed. 17.50x o.p. (ISBN 0-04-170007-4); Vol. 3. Moral Freedom. 1951. text ed. 17.50x o.p. (ISBN 0-04-170007-4). (Muirhead Library of Philosophy). Humanities.

Hartmann, R. R. & Stork, F. C., eds. Dictionary of Language & Linguistics. LC 72-6251. 302p. 1976. 39.95x o.p. (ISBN 0-470-35667-7); pap. 29.95 (ISBN 0-470-15200-1). Halsted Pr.

Hartmann, R. T. Palace Politics: An Inside Account of the Ford Years. 1980. 15.95 (ISBN 0-07-026951-3). McGraw.

Hartmann, S. Jacob Extra. 1983. pap. cancelled (ISBN 0-8120-2397-8); pap. cancelled (ISBN 0-8120-2396-X). Barron.

Hartmann, S. & Hartner, T. Jacob Three: The Dog on the Roof. 80p. 1982. pap. cancelled (ISBN 0-8120-2394-3). Barron.

Hartmann, Susan M. The Home Front & Beyond: American Women in the 1940s. 1982. lib. bdg. 15.00 (ISBN 0-8057-9901-X, Twayne). G K Hall.

Hartmann, Sven & Hartner, Thoman. Jacob Two: Me & My Human. Bernard, Jack, ed. Macri, Angelika, tr. 80p. (gr. k-6). 1981. pap. 4.95 (ISBN 0-8120-2391-9). Barron.

Hartmann, William H., et al. Endocrine Pathology. LC 78-11793. (Anatomic Pathology Slide Seminar Proceedings Ser.). (Illus.). 1979. pap. text ed. 15.00 o.p. (ISBN 0-89189-054-8, 50-1-043-00); slides 84.00 o.p. (ISBN 0-686-67346-8, 01-0-077-01). Am Soc Clinical.

Hartmann, William K. Astronomy: The Cosmic Journey. 1978. text ed. 24.95x o.p. (ISBN 0-534-00546-2); study guide 1979 8.95x o.p. (ISBN 0-534-00711-2). Wadsworth Pub.

--Moon & Planets. 1972. 24.95x o.p. (ISBN 0-534-00321-4). Wadsworth Pub.

Hartmann Von Aue. Iwein. Thomas, J. W., tr. LC 79-1139. x, 149p. 1979. 11.95x (ISBN 0-8032-4404-5). U of Nebr Pr.

Hartnell, Tim. Forty-Nine Explosive Games for the ZX-81. 1982. 17.95 (ISBN 0-8359-2087-9); pap. text ed. 10.95 (ISBN 0-8359-2086-0). Reston.

--Getting Acquainted with Your ZX-81. 3rd ed. 120p. 1981. pap. 9.95 (ISBN 0-916688-33-X). Creative Comp.

--The Timex Sinclair Two Thousand Explored. 218p. 1983. text ed. 14.95 (ISBN 0-471-89099-5). Wiley.

Hartnell, Tim & Ramshaw, Mark. Zap! Pow! Boom! Arcade Games for the VIC-20. 1983. text ed. 17.95 (ISBN 0-8359-9539-9); pap. text ed. 12.95 (ISBN 0-8359-9538-0). Reston.

Hartner, Elizabeth P. An Introduction to Automated Literature Searching. (Bks in Library & Information Science: Vol. 36). (Illus.). 168p. 1981. 23.50 (ISBN 0-8247-1293-5). Dekker.

Hartner, T., jt. auth. see Hartmann, S.

Hartner, Thoman, jt. auth. see Hartmann, Sven.

Hartnett, Donald L., jt. auth. see Cabot, A. Victor.

Hartnett, J. P., jt. auth. see Rohsenow, Warren.

Hartnett, J. P., jt. ed. see Irvine, T. F.

Hartnett, J. P., et al. Studies in Heat Transfer: A Festschrift for E.R.G. Eckert. LC 79-15633. (Illus.). 1979. text ed. 48.50 (ISBN 0-07-026962-9). McGraw.

Hartnett, Rodney T., jt. ed. see Katz, Joseph.

Hartnoll, Phyllis, ed. Oxford Companion to the Theatre. 4th ed. 1983. 49.95 (ISBN 0-19-211546-4). Oxford U Pr.

Harto, Joy. She Had Some Horses. 73p. (Orig.). 1983. text ed. 13.95 (ISBN 0-938410-07-5); pap. 6.95 (ISBN 0-938410-06-7). Thunder's Mouth.

Hartocollis, Peter. Time & Timelessness. 1982. 40.00 (ISBN 0-686-96332-6). Intl Univs Pr.

Hartog, Jacob P. Den see Den Hartog, Jacob P.

Hartog, Jan de see De Hartog, Jan.

Harton, Merle, jt. auth. see Cruise, Boyd.

Hartong, Bernard D. Elsevier's Dictionary of Barley, Malting, & Brewing. (Eng., Ger., Fr., Danish, Ital., & Span., Polyglot). 1961. 76.75 (ISBN 0-444-40270-5). Elsevier.

Hartrich, Edwin. The American Opportunity. (Illus.). 320p. 1983. 17.95 (ISBN 0-02-548510-5). Macmillan.

Hartshorn, Leon. Memorable Christmas Stories. LC 74-15999. 245p. 1974. 6.95 o.p. (ISBN 0-87747-536-9). Deseret Bk.

Hartshorn, Leon R. Inspirational Missionary Stories. 1976. 7.95 o.p. (ISBN 0-87747-588-1). Deseret Bk.

Hartshorn, S. R. Aliphatic Nucleophilic Substitution. LC 72-96675. (Chemistry Texts Ser.). (Illus.). 150p. 1973. 34.50 (ISBN 0-521-20177-2); pap. 13.95x (ISBN 0-521-09801-7). Cambridge U Pr.

Hartshorn, Truman A. Metropolis in Georgia: Atlanta's Rise As a Major Transaction Center. LC 76-47530. (Contemporary Metropolitan Analysis Ser.). 1976. pap. 8.95x prof ref (ISBN 0-88410-468-0). Ballinger Pub.

Hartshorne, Charles. Anselm's Discovery: A Re-Examination of the Ontological Proof for God's Existence. LC 65-20278. 349p. 1965. 21.00 (ISBN 0-87548-216-3); pap. 8.50 (ISBN 0-87548-217-1). Open Court.

--Aquinas to Whitehead: Seven Centuries of Metaphysics of Religion. LC 76-5156. (Aquinas Lectures Ser.). 1976. 7.95 (ISBN 0-87462-141-0). Marquette.

--Creative Synthesis & Philosophic Method. LC 82-23780. 358p. 1983. pap. text ed. 13.50 (ISBN 0-8191-2979-8, Co-pub. by Ctr Process Studies). U Pr of Amer.

--The Divine Relativity: A Social Conception of God. LC 48-7802. (The Terry Lectures Ser.). 184p. 1982. pap. 4.95x (ISBN 0-300-02880-6, Y-430). Yale U Pr.

--The Logic of Perfection & Other Essays in Neoclassical Metaphysics. LC 61-11286. 351p. 1972. pap. 8.50 (ISBN 0-87548-037-3). Open Court.

--A Natural Theology for Our Time. LC 66-14722. 158p. 1967. 16.00 (ISBN 0-87548-238-4); pap. 5.00 (ISBN 0-87548-239-2). Open Court.

Hartshorne, Charles, ed. see Peirce, Charles S.

Hartshorne, Hugh & Miller, J. Q. Community Organization in Religious Education. 1932. 42.50x (ISBN 0-686-51356-8). Elliots Bks.

Hartsuch, Paul J. Think Metric Now! A Step-by-Step Guide to Understanding & Applying the Metric System. 1975. pap. 1.50 o.p. (ISBN 0-14-004010-2). Penguin.

Hartt, Frederick. History of Italian Renaissance Art. 2nd ed. (Illus.). 1980. text ed. 27.95 (ISBN 0-13-392043-7). P-H.

--History of Italian Renaissance Art: Painting, Sculpture, Architecture. 2nd ed. (Illus.). 1980. 45.00 (ISBN 0-8109-1067-5). Abrams.

Hartung, Rolf. Clay. 1972. 15.95 o.p. (ISBN 0-7134-2383-8, Pub. by Batsford England). David & Charles.

--Plywood. 1971. 15.50 o.p. (ISBN 0-7134-2380-3, Pub. by Batsford England). David & Charles.

Hartunian, Nelson S., et al. The Incidence & Economic Costs of Major Health Impairments: A Comparative Analysis of Cancer,Motor-Vehicle Injuries, Coronary Heart Disease, & Stroke. LC 80-8189. 448p. 1981. 36.95x (ISBN 0-669-03975-6). Lexington Bks.

Hartup, Willard W., ed. Review of Child Development Research, Vol. 6. LC 64-20472. (Review of Child Development Research Ser.). 780p. 1982. lib. bdg. 40.00x (ISBN 0-226-31873-7). U of Chicago Pr.

Hartup, Willard W., jt. ed. see Higgins, E. Tory.

Hartwell, David G., ed. Destination Moon. 1979. lib. bdg. 15.00 (ISBN 0-8398-2501-3, Gregg). G K Hall.

Hartwell, David G. & Currey, L. W., eds. The Battle of the Monsters & Other Stories: An Anthology of American Science Fiction 1878-1908. (Science Fiction Ser.). 240p. 1976. lib. bdg. 12.00 o.p. (ISBN 0-8398-2347-9, Gregg). G K Hall.

Hartwell, David G., ed. see Curry, Lloyd W.

Hartwell, Jonathan L. Plants Used Against Cancer. (Bioactive Plants Ser.: Vol. 2). 754p. Date not set. Repr. lib. bdg. 60.00x (ISBN 0-88000-130-5). Quarterman. Postponed.

Hartwig, G. W. & O'Barr, W. M. The Student Africanist's Handbook: A Guide to Resources. 152p. 1974. text ed. 6.50x o.s.i. (ISBN 0-470-35773-8). Halsted Pr.

Hartwig, Gerald. The Art of Survival in East Africa: The Kerebe & Long-Distance Trade, 1800-1895. LC 74-84653. 250p. 1976. text ed. 35.00x (ISBN 0-8419-0182-1, Africana). Holmes & Meier.

Hartwig, Marie D. & Meyers, Bettye B. Camping Leadership: Counseling & Programming. LC 75-33168. (Illus.). 156p. 1976. pap. 9.95 o.p. (ISBN 0-8016-2081-3). Mosby.

Hartwiger, Sidney M., ed. see Boelt, Martha M.

Harty, Annelle, jt. auth. see Harty, Robert.

Harty, F. J. Endodontics in Clinical Practice. 2nd ed. (Illus.). 296p. 1982. pap. text ed. 19.95 (ISBN 0-7236-0643-9). Wright-PSG.

Harty, Robert & Harty, Annelle. Creados Para Crecer. De Plou, Dafne C., tr. (Sexo en la Vida Cristiana Ser.). (Illus.). 1981. pap. 1.35 (ISBN 0-311-46251-0). Casa Bautista.

Hartz, Louis, et al. The Founding of New Societies: Studies in the History of the United States, Latin America, South Africa, Canada, & Australia. LC 64-11535. 1969. pap. 3.25 (ISBN 0-15-632728-7, Harv). HarBraceJ.

Hartzel, John, jt. auth. see Francis, Linda.

Hartzler, F. E. The Retail Salesperson: A Programmed Text. 2nd ed. (Illus.). 1978. pap. text ed. 8.92 (ISBN 0-07-026967-X, G); instr's. manual & key 4.50 (ISBN 0-07-026968-8). McGraw.

Hartzler, Jonas S. Mennonites in the World War; or, Nonresistance Under Test. LC 76-137543. (Peace Movement in America Ser). 246p. 1972. Repr. of 1922 ed. lib. bdg. 16.95x (ISBN 0-89198-071-7). Ozer.

Hartzog, Martha, tr. see Irving, Washington.

Hartzschel, Walter. Treatise on Invertebrate Paleontology, Pt. W., Suppl. 1: Miscellanea, (Trace Fossils & Problematica) 2nd. rev. & enl. ed. LC 53-12913. (Illus.). 1975. 20.00x (ISBN 0-8137-3027-9). Geol Soc.

Harvald, Svend A. Resistance & Propulsion of Ships. (Ocean Engineering Ser.). 608p. 1983. 42.95 (ISBN 0-471-06353-3, Pub. by Wiley-Interscience). Wiley.

Harvard Business Review. Catching Up with the Computer Revolution. (Harvard Business Review Executive Bk. Ser.). 500p. 1983. 22.95 (ISBN 0-471-87594-5, Pub. by Wiley Interscience). Wiley.

--Financial Management. (Harvard Business Review Executive Bk. Ser.). 550p. 1983. 22.95 (ISBN 0-471-87598-8, Pub. by Wiley Interscience). Wiley.

--Harvard Business Review: Executive Success Managing Your Way to the Top. (Harvard Business Review Book Ser.). 500p. 1983. 22.95 (ISBN 0-471-87595-3, Pub. by Wiley-Interscience). Wiley.

--Managing Effectively in the World Market Place. (Harvard Business Review Executive Book Program). 600p. 1982. 22.95 (ISBN 0-471-87683-6, Pub. by Wiley-Interscience). Wiley.

--Survival Strategies for American Industry. LC 82-13408. 500p. 1983. 22.95 (ISBN 0-471-87632-1, Pub. by Wiley-Interscience). Wiley.

Harvard Business Review Editors. Harvard Business Reviews on Human Relations. LC 78-20166. (Illus.). 1979. 18.22i (ISBN 0-06-011789-3, HarpT). Har-Row.

Harvard Business Review Editors, ed. Harvard Business Review - on Management. LC 75-6339. (Illus.). 448p. 1976. 21.10i (ISBN 0-06-011769-9, HarpT). Har-Row.

Harvard Child Health Project. Harvard Child Health Project Report: Developing a Better Health Care System for Children. LC 77-3367. (Harvard Child Health Project Ser.: Vol. III). 296p. 1977. prof ref 19.00x (ISBN 0-88410-509-1). Ballinger Pub.

Harvard Educational Review, ed. Education, Participation, & Power: Essays in Theory & Practice. LC 76-433. (Reprint Ser.). (Illus.). 168p. (Orig.). pap. 4.95 (ISBN 0-916690-01-6). Harvard Educ Rev.

Harvard Educational Review Editorial Board, ed. see Pettigrew, Thomas F., et al.

Harvard Educational Review Editorial Board. Stage Theories of Cognitive & Moral Development: Criticisms & Application. (HER Reprint Ser.). 1978. pap. 6.50 (ISBN 0-916690-16-4). Harvard Educ Rev.

Harvard, J. Bilingual Guide to Business & Professional Correspondence, English-German, German-English. 1973. 16.25 (ISBN 0-08-017654-2); pap. 7.95 (ISBN 0-08-017655-0). Pergamon.

--Bilingual Guide to Business & Professional Correspondence: Spanish-English, English-Spanish. 1970. 25.00 o.s.i. (ISBN 0-08-015793-9); pap. 7.75 (ISBN 0-08-015792-0). Pergamon.

Harvard Lampoon, et al. Bored of the Rings or Tolkien Revisited. 1971. pap. 1.75 (ISBN 0-451-09441-7, E9441, Sig). NAL.

Harvard Lampoon, Inc. The Harvard Lampoon: Big Book of College Life. LC 77-15165. 1978. pap. 9.95 o.p. (ISBN 0-385-13446-0, Dolp). Doubleday.

Harvard Law School Library. Index to Multilateral Treaties: A Chronological List of Multiparty International Agreements from the 16th Century through 1963 with Citations to Text. Mostecky, Vaclav, ed. 301p. 1965. 22.50 (ISBN 0-379-00384-8). Oceana.

Harvard Medical Library & Boston Medical Library. Author-Title Catalog of the Francis A. Countway Library of Medicine for Imprints Through 1959, 10 vols. 8104p. 1973. Set. lib. bdg. 1530.00 (ISBN 0-8161-1024-7, Hall Library). G K Hall.

Harvard Student Agencies. Let's Go Britain & Ireland. (The Let's Go Ser.). (Illus.). 450p. 1983. pap. 7.95 (ISBN 0-312-48210-8). St Martin.

--Let's Go Europe. (Let's Go Ser.). (Illus.). 825p. 1983. pap. 8.95 (ISBN 0-312-48211-6). St Martin.

--Let's Go France. (Let's Go Ser.). (Illus.). 380p. 1983. pap. 7.95 (ISBN 0-312-48212-4). St Martin.

--Let's Go Greece, Israel, & Egypt. (The Let's Go Ser.). (Illus.). 474p. 1983. pap. 7.95 (ISBN 0-312-48213-2). St Martin.

--Let's Go Italy. (The Let's Go Ser.). (Illus.). 416p. 1983. pap. 7.95 (ISBN 0-312-48214-0). St Martin.

--Let's Go U. S. A. (The Let's Go Ser.). (Illus.). 605p. 1983. pap. 7.95 (ISBN 0-312-48215-9). St Martin.

Harvard University. Catalog of the Farlow Reference Library of Cryptogamic Botany. 1979. lib. bdg. 660.00 (ISBN 0-8161-0279-1, Hall Library). G K Hall.

--Catalog of the Harvard University Fine Arts Library, 15 vols. Fogg Art Museum, ed. 1971. Set. lib. bdg. 1680.00 (ISBN 0-8161-0919-2, Hall Library); Catalogue of Auction Sales Catalogues 100.00 (ISBN 0-8161-0105-1). G K Hall.

--Catalogue of the Library of the Graduate School of Design: Third Supplement. (Library Catalogs). 1979. lib. bdg. 425.00 (ISBN 0-8161-0284-8, Hall Library). G K Hall.

Harvard University Center for Italian Renaissance Studies at Villa I Tatti (Florence, Italy) Catalogues of the Berenson Library, 4 vols. 1973. lib. bdg. 415.00 (ISBN 0-8161-0973-7, Hall Library). G K Hall.

Harvard University Dumbarton Oaks Research Library. Dictionary Catalogue of the Byzantine Collection of the Dumbarton Oaks Research Library, 12 vols. 1975. Set. lib. bdg. 1335.00 (ISBN 0-8161-1150-2, Hall Library). G K Hall.

Harvard University, Fogg Art Museum. Catalogue of the Harvard University Fine Arts Library, First Supplement, 3 vols. 1976. Set. lib. bdg. 380.00 (ISBN 0-8161-1224-X, Hall Library). G K Hall.

Harvard University, Graduate School of Business Administration. Author-Title Catalog of the Baker Library, 22 vols. 1971. Set. 2380.00 (ISBN 0-8161-0893-5, Hall Library). G K Hall.

--Author-Title Catalog of the Baker Library, First Supplement, 2 vols. 1974. Set. lib. bdg. 230.00 (ISBN 0-8161-1158-8, Hall Library). G K Hall.

Harvard University, Graduate School of Design. Catalog of the Library of the Graduate School of Design, Second Supplement, 5 vols. 1974. Set. lib. bdg. 575.00 (ISBN 0-8161-1173-1, Hall Library). G K Hall.

Harvard University - Graduate School Of Design. Catalogue of the Library of the Graduate School of Design, 44 Vols. 1968. Set. 3580.00 (ISBN 0-8161-0812-9, Hall Library). G K Hall.

--Catalogue of the Library of the Graduate School of Design, First Supplement, 2 vols. 1970. Set. 230.00 (ISBN 0-8161-0831-5, Hall Library). G K Hall.

Harvard University, Graduate School of Business Administration. Subject Catalog of the Baker Library, 10 vols. 1971. Set. 1020.00 (ISBN 0-8161-0186-8, Hall Library). G K Hall.

--Subject Catalog of the Baker Library: First Supplement. 1974. 115.00 (ISBN 0-8161-1180-4, Hall Library). G K Hall.

Harvard University, Gray Herbarium. Gray Herbarium Index, 10 Vols. 1968. Set. lib. bdg. 825.00 (ISBN 0-8161-0754-8, Hall Library). G K Hall.

Harvard University Library. Catalogue of English & American Chap-Books & Broadside Ballads in Harvard College Library. LC 67-23932. 1968. Repr. of 1905 ed. 30.00x (ISBN 0-8103-3420-8). Gale.

Harvard University Museum of Comparative Zoology. Catalogue of the Library of the Museum of Comparative Zoology, 8 Vols. 1967. 760.00 (ISBN 0-8161-0767-X, Hall Library). G K Hall.

--Catalogue of the Library of the Museum of Comparative Zoology, First Supplement. 1976. lib. bdg. 120.00 (ISBN 0-8161-0811-0, Hall Library). G K Hall.

Harvard University, Peabody Museum of Archaeology & Ethnology. Author & Subject Catalogues of the Library of the Peabody Museum of Archaeology & Ethnology, Second Supplement, 6 vols. 1971. Set. 800.00 (ISBN 0-8161-0960-5, Hall Library). G K Hall.

--Author & Subject Catalogues of the Library of the Peabody Museum of Archaeology & Ethnology, First Supplement, 12 vols. 1970. Set. 900.00 (ISBN 0-8161-0861-7, Hall Library). G K Hall.

--Author & Subject Catalogues of the Library of the Peabody Museum of Archaeology & Ethnology, 54 vols. 1963. Set. lib. bdg. 5600.00 (ISBN 0-8161-0647-9, Hall Library). G K Hall.

--Author & Subject Catalogues of the Library of the Peabody Museum of Archaeology & Ethnology: Index to Subject Headings. lib. bdg. 48.00 (ISBN 0-8161-0187-6, Hall Library). G K Hall.

Harvard University Peabody Museum of Archaeology & Ethnology. Author & Subject Catalogues of the Library of the Peabody Museum of Archaeology & Ethnology, Third Supplement, 7 vols. 1975. Set. lib. bdg. 925.00 (ISBN 0-8161-1168-5, Hall Library). G K Hall.

Harven, Emile De see De Harven, Emile.

Harvester, Simon. Assassin's Road. 189p. 1983. pap. 2.95 (ISBN 0-8027-3014-0). Walker & Co.

--Moscow Road. 209p. 1983. pap. 2.95 (ISBN 0-8027-3012-4). Walker & Co.

--Yesterday's Enemy. 204p. 1983. pap. 2.95 (ISBN 0-8027-3011-6). Walker & Co.

--Zion Road. 208p. 1983. pap. 2.95 (ISBN 0-8027-3013-2). Walker & Co.

Harvey, A. E. New English Bible Companion to the New Testament. 1979. 59.50 (ISBN 0-521-07705-2); pap. 21.95 (ISBN 0-521-50539-9). Cambridge U Pr.

--The New English Bible Companion to the New Testament. rev. ed. (Illus.). 1980. pap. 22.50x (ISBN 0-19-213229-6). Oxford U Pr.

--The New English Bible Companion to the New Testament: The Gospels. 1972. pap. 12.95x (ISBN 0-19-826168-3). Oxford U Pr.

Harvey, Anne. Jewels. (Leprechaun Library). (Illus.). 64p. 1981. 4.95 (ISBN 0-399-12663-5). Putnam Pub Group.

Harvey, Anthony, jt. auth. see Diment, Judith.

Harvey, Anthony, jt. auth. see Steel, Rodney.

Harvey, Arnold. English Poetry in a Changing Society, Seventeen Eighty to Eighteen Twenty-Five. 1980. 26.00 (ISBN 0-312-25502-0). St Martin.

--English Poetry in a Changing Society Seventeen Eighty to Eighteen Twenty-Five. 1980. 24.00x o.p. (ISBN 0-85031-365-1, Pub. by Allison & Busby England). State Mutual Bk.

Harvey, Arthur. The Apple Picker's Manual. 2nd ed. 27p. 1981. pap. 1.50 (ISBN 0-934676-05-4). Greenlf Bks.

--Theory & Practice of Civil Disobedience. 27p. 1961. pap. 1.25 (ISBN 0-934676-04-6). Greenlf Bks.

Harvey, B. J. & Hoar, W. S. La Reproduction Provoquee chez les Poissons: Theorie et Pratique. 48p. 1980. pap. 3.00 o.p. (ISBN 0-88936-254-8, IDRC-TS21F, IDRC). Unipub.

--Teoria y Practica de la Reproduccion Inducida en los Peces. 48p. 1980. pap. 3.00 o.p. (ISBN 0-88936-253-X, IDRC-TS21S, IDRC). Unipub.

Harvey, Barbara. Westminster Abbey & Its Estates in the Middle Ages. (Illus.). 1977. text ed. 55.00x (ISBN 0-19-822449-4). Oxford U Pr.

Harvey, Barbara F., jt. ed. see Hector, L. C.

Harvey, Bill. Mind Magic. 4th ed. Bertisch, Jan & Bragg, Yana, eds. (Illus.). 1982. write for info. (ISBN 0-918538-08-4). Ourobourus.

Harvey, Carol D. & Bahr, Howard M. The Sunshine Widows: Adapting to Sudden Bereavement. LC 79-8317. 176p. 1980. 21.95x (ISBN 0-669-03375-8). Lexington Bks.

Harvey, Catherine, tr. see Chetin, Helen.

Harvey, Chris. Healey: The Handsome Brute. LC 78-458. (Illus.). 1978. 29.95 (ISBN 0-312-36518-7). St Martin.

--MG the A, B & C. 232p. 1982. 29.95 (ISBN 0-902280-69-4). Haynes Pubns.

--The Porsche 911. 224p. 1982. 29.95 (ISBN 0-902280-78-3). Haynes Pubns.

--Super Profile: Porsche 911 Carrera. 56p. Date not set. 9.95 (ISBN 0-85429-311-6). Haynes Pubns.

Harvey Comics. Casper Ghost Stories. (Illus.). (gr. 3-6). 1979. pap. 0.95 o.s.i. (ISBN 0-448-16489-2, G&D). Putnam Pub Group.

Harvey, D. & Brown, Donald R. An Experiential Approach to Organization Development. (Illus.). 336p. 1976. pap. text ed. 15.95 (ISBN 0-13-294983-0). P-H.

Harvey, D. T. Exploring Science. 1975. pap. text ed. 4.50x o.p. (ISBN 0-435-80608-4). Heinemann Ed.

Harvey, David. Explanation in Geography. 1970. 17.95 o.p. (ISBN 0-312-27755-5). St Martin.

--Limits to Capital. LC 82-40322. 452p. 1982. lib. bdg. 30.00x (ISBN 0-226-31952-0). U of Chicago Pr.

Harvey, David C. Harvey's Law of Real Property & Title Closings, 3 vols. rev. ed. Biskind, Elliot L., ed. LC 66-23512. 1966. looseleaf with 1980 suppl. 165.00 (ISBN 0-87632-058-2). Boardman.

Harvey, Don. Business Policy & Strategic Management. 640p. 1982. text ed. 20.95 (ISBN 0-686-84128-X). Additional supplements may be obtained from publisher. Merrill.

--Strategic Management. 736p. 1983. text ed. 24.95 (ISBN 0-675-20052-0); Additional supplements may be obtained from publisher. casebk. 10.95 (ISBN 0-675-20024-5). Merrill.

Harvey, Donald F. & Brown, Donald R. An Experimental Approach to Organization Development. 2nd ed. (Illus.). 592p. 1982. 22.95 (ISBN 0-13-295360-9). P-H.

Harvey, E. R., jt. auth. see Ashley, John P.

Harvey, Earle & Harvey, Jim. Funny Laws. 1982. pap. 1.75 (ISBN 0-451-11651-8, AE1651, Sig). NAL.

Harvey Famous Cartoons. Casper the Friendly Ghost & Wendy the Good Little Witch Storybook. LC 77-94036. (Illus.). (ps-2). 1978. 4.95 (ISBN 0-448-14743-2, G&D). Putnam Pub Group.

Harvey Famous Name Comics. Casper's Dental Hygiene Activity Book. Duenewald, Doris, ed. (Elephant Bks.). (Illus.). (gr. k-7). 1978. pap. 1.50 (ISBN 0-448-16167-2, G&D). Putnam Pub Group.

Harvey, Geoffrey. The Art of Anthony Trollope. LC 80-5088. x, 177p. 1980. 25.00 (ISBN 0-312-04998-6). St Martin.

Harvey, H. La Iglesia: Su Forma De Gobierno y Sus Ordenanzas. 284p. 1981. pap. 4.50 (ISBN 0-311-09022-2). Casa Bautista.

--El Pastor. Trevino, Alejandro, tr. Orig. Title: The Pastor. 232p. (Span.). 1982. pap. 3.75 (ISBN 0-311-42025-7). Casa Bautista.

Harvey, Harriet. Stories Parents Seldom Hear: College Students Write about Their Lives & Families. 1983. pap. 10.95 (ISBN 0-440-58262-8, Delta). Dell.

Harvey, Harriet, compiled by. Stories Parents Seldom Hear: College Students Write about Their Lives & Families. 320p. 1983. 18.95 (ISBN 0-440-07661-7, Sey Lawr). Delacorte.

Harvey, Heather J. Consultation & Co-Operation in the Commonwealth. LC 70-141273. xii, 411p. 1972. Repr. of 1952 ed. lib. bdg. 19.00x (ISBN 0-8371-5883-4, HACA). Greenwood.

Harvey, Hildebrande W. Chemistry & Fertility of Sea Waters. 2nd ed. 1957. 45.00 (ISBN 0-521-05225-4). Cambridge U Pr.

Harvey, James. Librarians Censorship, & Intellectual Freedom. LC 72-7737. pap. 3.00 o.p. (ISBN 0-8389-3139-1). ALA.

Harvey, Jim, jt. auth. see Harvey, Earle.

Harvey, Joan M. Statistics America: Sources for Social, Economic, & Marketing Research. 2nd ed. 300p. 1980. 175.00x (ISBN 0-900246-16-2). Gale.

Harvey, Joan M., ed. Statistics, Africa: Sources for Social, Economic, & Market Research. 2nd ed. 1978. 120.00x (ISBN 0-900246-26-X, Pub. by CBD Research Ltd.). Gale.

Harvey, John. Cathedrals of England & Wales. 1974. 38.00 o.p. (ISBN 0-7134-0616-X, Pub by Batsford, England). David & Charles.

--Mediaeval Craftsmen. 1975. 25.00 o.p. (ISBN 0-7134-2934-8, Pub. by Batsford England). David & Charles.

Harvey, John & Parks, Marge, eds. Psychotherapy Research & Behavior Change. (Masters Lecture Ser.). 176p. (Orig.). 1982. 13.00x (ISBN 0-912704-62-4). Am Psychol.

Harvey, John A. Behavioral Analysis of Drug Action: Research & Commentary. 1971. pap. 8.95x (ISBN 0-673-05444-6). Scott F.

Harvey, John B. Hart One: Cherokee Outlet. 1982. pap. 10.00x (ISBN 0-686-98216-9, Pub. by Pan Bks). State Mutual Bk.

Harvey, John C. Geology for Geotechnical Engineers. (Illus.). 136p. 1983. 24.95 (ISBN 0-521-24629-6); pap. 9.95 (ISBN 0-521-28862-2). Cambridge U Pr.

Harvey, John C., tr. see Matthes, Georg.

Harvey, John F. & Dickinson, Elizabeth M., eds. Librarians' Affirmative Action Handbook. LC 82-10644. 316p. 1983. 18.50 (ISBN 0-8108-1581-8). Scarecrow.

Harvey, John H., jt. auth. see Lindgren, Henry C.

Harvey, Jonathan. The Music of Stockhausen: An Introduction. (Illus.). 1975. 27.50x o.p. (ISBN 0-520-02311-0). U of Cal Pr.

Harvey, Karen G. St. Augustine & St. Johns County: A Pictoral History. LC 79-19039. (Illus.). 1980. pap. 13.95 (ISBN 0-89865-011-9). Donning Co.

Harvey, Linda & Roper, Ann. Dots Math. (Illus.). (gr. k-4). 1978. 6.25 (ISBN 0-88488-104-0). Creative Pubns.

--Pattern Blocks Problems for Primary People. (ps-3). 1979. 5.95 (ISBN 0-88488-123-7). Creative Pubns.

Harvey, Linda, jt. auth. see Roper, Ann.

Harvey, M., ed. Current Accounting Literature. 1971. 26.00 o.p. (ISBN 0-7201-0295-2, Pub. by Mansell England); pap. 19.00 o.p. (ISBN 0-7201-0292-8). Wilson.

Harvey, Miranda. Piranesi. (Illus.). 1979. pap. 12.95 (ISBN 0-517-53826-1, Harmony). Crown.

Harvey, P. D., jt. auth. see Skelton, R. A.

Harvey, Paul, ed. Oxford Companion to Classical Literature. 2nd ed. (Illus.). (YA) (gr. 9 up). 1937. 25.00 (ISBN 0-19-866103-7). Oxford U Pr.

Harvey, Paul & Eagle, Dorothy, eds. Oxford Companion to English Literature. 4th ed. (YA) (gr. 9 up). 1967. 35.00 (ISBN 0-19-500163-X). Oxford U Pr.

Harvey, Paul & Heseltine, Janet E., eds. Oxford Companion to French Literature. (YA) (gr. 9 up). 1959. 49.50x (ISBN 0-19-866104-5). Oxford U Pr.

Harvey, R., jt. ed. see Sobrero, A.

Harvey, R. J. Kidneys & the Internal Environment. 1974. 10.95x (ISBN 0-412-12260-X, Pub. by Chapman & Hall England). Methuen Inc.

Harvey, Richard. Genealogy for Librarians. 200p. 1983. 19.50 (Pub. by Bingley England). Shoe String.

Harvey, Robert. Portugal: Birth of a Democracy. LC 78-4507. 1978. 24.00x (ISBN 0-312-63184-7). St Martin.

Harvey, Robert O., jt. auth. see Wurtzebach, Charles H.

Harvey, Samantha. Boy with Kite. (Harlequin Romances Ser.). 192p. 1983. pap. 1.75 (ISBN 0-373-02541-6). Harlequin Bks.

Harvey, Virginia I. & Tidball, Harriet. Weft Twining. LC 76-24017. (Shuttle Craft Guild Monograph: No. 28). (Illus.). 39p. 1969. pap. 7.45 (ISBN 0-916658-28-7). HTH Pubs.

Harvey, Virginia I., ed. Multiple Tabby Weaves, Based on Dr. William G. Bateman's Manuscript. LC 81-80587. (Shuttle Craft Guild Monograph: No. 35). (Illus.). 90p. 1981. pap. 10.95 (ISBN 0-916658-37-6). HTH Pubs.

Harvey, W. H. Nereis Australis, or Algae of the Southern Ocean: 1847-49. (Illus.). 1965. 64.00 (ISBN 3-7682-0261-5). Lubrecht & Cramer.

--Nereis Boreali-Americana: 1852-1858, 3 parts in 1. (Illus.). 1976. 100.00 (ISBN 3-7682-1063-4). Lubrecht & Cramer.

Harvey, W. J., ed. Discrete Groups & Automorphic Functions. 1978. 64.50 (ISBN 0-12-329950-0). Acad Pr.

Harvey, William. La Circulation Du Sang: Des Mouvements Du Coeur Chez L'homme et Chez les Animaux, Deux Reponses a Riolan. Repr. of 1879 ed. 87.00 o.p. (ISBN 0-8287-0417-1). Clearwater Pub.

--Lectures on the Whole of Anatomy. O'Malley, C. D., et al, trs. LC 61-16879. 1961. 25.00x o.p. (ISBN 0-520-00540-6). U of Cal Pr.

Harvey, William F., tr. see Nyrop, Christopher.

Harvey, William H. & Sonder, Otto W. Flora Capensis, 7 vols. bd. in 11. 240.00 (ISBN 3-7682-0637-8). Lubrecht & Cramer.

Harvey, Youngsook K. Six Korean Women: The Socialization of Shamans. (American Ethnological Society Ser). (Illus.). 1979. text ed. 23.95 (ISBN 0-8299-0243-0). West Pub.

Harvill, L. R., jt. auth. see Pipes, L. A.

Harville, Charles. Sports in North Carolina: A Photographic History. LC 77-17890. (Illus.). 1977. pap. 9.95 o.p. (ISBN 0-915442-42-6). Donning Co.

Harward, Donald W., ed. Power: Its Nature, Its Use, & Its Limits. 1979. lib. bdg. 18.00 (ISBN 0-8161-9011-9, Univ Bks). G K Hall.

Harwell, Delores T., jt. auth. see Harwell, Henry O.

Harwell, Edward M. Personnel Management & Training. LC 74-80815. (Illus.). 1969. 20.95 (ISBN 0-86730-308-5). Lebhar Friedman.

Harwell, Edward M. & Kinslow, William E. New Horizons in Checkout Management. LC 78-61790. 1978. 21.95 (ISBN 0-86730-301-8). Lebhar Friedman.

Harwell, Edward M., et al. Meat Management & Operations. LC 74-21115. (Illus.). 285p. 1974. 20.95 (ISBN 0-86730-306-9). Lebhar Friedman.

Harwell, Henry O. & Harwell, Delores T. The Creek Verb. 57p. 1981. 8.00x (ISBN 0-940392-03-8). Indian U Pr.

Harwell, Richard. GWTW: The Screenplay by Sidney Howard. 1980. 19.95 o.p. (ISBN 0-02-548660-8). Macmillan.

Harwell, Richard, ed. Gone With the Wind as Book & Film. (Illus.). 300p. 1983. 19.95 (ISBN 0-686-82616-7). U. of SC Pr.

Harwell, Richard, intro. by see Myrick, Susan.

Harwell, Richard B. The Mint Julep. LC 75-18114. 54p. 1977. 5.00x (ISBN 0-8139-0736-5); pap. 2.95 (ISBN 0-8139-0737-3). U Pr of Va.

Harwin, Judith, jt. ed. see Orford, Jim.

Harwit, Martin. Astrophysical Concepts. 576p. 1982. Repr. of 1973 ed. lib. bdg. cancelled o.p. (ISBN 0-89874-544-6). Krieger.

--Astrophysical Concepts. LC 73-3135. (Illus.). xiv, 561p. 1982. Repr. of 1973 ed. pap. text ed. 17.95 (ISBN 0-910533-00-8). Concepts.

Harwood & Jacobus. Texas Real Estate. 3rd ed. 1983. text ed. 21.95 (ISBN 0-8359-7554-1). Reston.

Harwood & Thompson. Florida Real Estate. (Illus.). 672p. 1980. ref. ed. 19.95 (ISBN 0-8359-2067-4). Reston.

Harwood, jt. auth. see Jacobus.

Harwood, A. C. The Way of a Child. 144p. pap. 9.95 (ISBN 0-85440-352-3). Anthroposophic.

Harwood, A. C., tr. & intro. by see Schoer, Karl J.

Harwood, Alan. Rx: Spiritist As Needed; a Study of a Puerto Rican Community Mental Health Resource. LC 76-54841. (Contemporary Religious Movements). 1977. 38.95 (ISBN 0-471-35828-2, Pub. by Wiley-Interscience). Wiley.

Harwood, Ann L. Cardiopulmonary Resuscitation. (Illus.). 196p. 1982. lib. bdg. 24.95 (ISBN 0-683-03895-8). Williams & Wilkins.

Harwood, Bruce & Synek, Elmer. Ohio Real Estate. (Illus.). 640p. 1980. ref. ed 19.95 (ISBN 0-8359-5189-8); pap. 18.95 o.p. (ISBN 0-686-96869-7). Reston.

Harwood, Bruce, jt. auth. see Jones, Richard O.

Harwood, Bruce, jt. auth. see New York Assn. of Realtors.

Harwood, Cecil, jt. auth. see Raffe, Marjorie.

Harwood, Corbin C. Using Land to Save Energy. LC 77-739. (Environmental Law Institute State & Local Energy Conservation Project Ser.). 352p. 1977. prof ref 22.50x (ISBN 0-88410-061-8). Ballinger Pub.

Harwood, Herbert. Blue Ridge Trolly: The Hagerstown & Frederick Railway. LC 73-97231. 17.95 o.p. (ISBN 0-87095-034-7). Golden West.

Harwood, Michael. Games to Play in the Car. (Illus.). 96p. 1983. pap. 6.95 (ISBN 0-312-92239-6). Congdon & Weed.

Harwood, Michael, jt. auth. see Porter, Eliot.

Harwood, Pearl A. Carnival with Mr. & Mrs. Bumba. LC 76-156360. (Easy-Readers Ser). (gr. k-3). 1971. PLB 3.95g (ISBN 0-8225-0128-7). Lerner Pubns.

--Climbing a Mountain with Mr. & Mrs. Bumba. LC 70-156353. (Easy-Readers Ser). (gr. k-3). 1971. PLB 3.95g (ISBN 0-8225-0129-5). Lerner Pubns.

--Long Vacation for Mr. & Mrs. Bumba. LC 71-156359. (Easy-Readers Ser). (Illus.). (gr. k-3). 1971. PLB 3.95g (ISBN 0-8225-0121-X). Lerner Pubns.

--Make-It Room of Mr. & Mrs. Bumba. LC 74-156357. (Easy-Readers Ser). (gr. k-3). 1971. PLB 3.95g (ISBN 0-8225-0124-4). Lerner Pubns.

--Mr. Bumba & the Orange Grove. LC 64-19773. (Mr. Bumba Bks). (gr. k-3). 1964. PLB 3.95g (ISBN 0-8225-0104-X). Lerner Pubns.

--Mr. Bumba Has a Party. LC 64-19775. (Mr. Bumba Bks). (gr. k-3). 1964. PLB 3.95g (ISBN 0-8225-0106-6). Lerner Pubns.

--Mr. Bumba Keeps House. LC 64-19772. (Mr. Bumba Bks). (gr. k-3). 1964. PLB 3.95g (ISBN 0-8225-0103-1). Lerner Pubns.

--Mr. Bumba Plants a Garden. LC 64-19771. (Mr. Bumba Bks). (gr. k-3). 1964. PLB 3.95g (ISBN 0-8225-0102-3). Lerner Pubns.

--Mr. Bumba Rides a Bicycle. LC 65-27997. (Mr. Bumba Bks). (gr. k-3). 1966. PLB 3.95g (ISBN 0-8225-0109-0). Lerner Pubns.

--Mr. Bumba's Four-Legged Company. LC 65-27996. (Mr. Bumba Bks). (gr. k-3). 1966. PLB 3.95g (ISBN 0-8225-0108-2). Lerner Pubns.

--Mr. Bumba's New Home. LC 64-19775. (Mr. Bumba Bks). (gr. k-3). 1964. PLB 3.95g (ISBN 0-8225-0101-5). Lerner Pubns.

--Mr. Bumba's New Job. LC 64-19774. (Mr. Bumba Bks.). (gr. k-3). 1964. PLB 3.95g (ISBN 0-8225-0105-8). Lerner Pubns.

--Mr. Bumba's Tuesday Club. LC 65-27998. (Mr. Bumba Bks). (gr. k-3). 1966. PLB 3.95g (ISBN 0-8225-0110-4). Lerner Pubns.

--Mrs. Moon & Her Friends. LC 67-15688. (Mrs. Moon Bks). (gr. k-3). 1967. PLB 3.95g (ISBN 0-8225-0112-0). Lerner Pubns.

--Mrs. Moon & the Dark Stairs. LC 67-15693. (Mrs. Moon Bks). (gr. k-3). 1967. PLB 3.95g (ISBN 0-8225-0117-1). Lerner Pubns.

--Mrs. Moon Goes Shopping. LC 67-15691. (Mrs. Moon Bks). (gr. k-3). 1967. PLB 3.95g (ISBN 0-8225-0115-5). Lerner Pubns.

--Mrs. Moon Takes a Drive. LC 67-15695. (Mrs. Moon Bks). (gr. k-3). 1967. PLB 3.95g (ISBN 0-8225-0119-8). Lerner Pubns.

--Mrs. Moon's Cement Hat. LC 67-15696. (Mrs. Moon Bks). (gr. k-3). 1967. PLB 3.95g (ISBN 0-8225-0120-1). Lerner Pubns.

--Mrs. Moon's Harbor Trip. LC 67-15692. (Mrs. Moon Bks). (gr. k-3). 1967. PLB 3.95g (ISBN 0-8225-0116-3). Lerner Pubns.

--Mrs. Moon's Picnic. LC 67-15690. (Mrs. Moon Bks). (gr. k-3). 1967. PLB 3.95g (ISBN 0-8225-0114-7). Lerner Pubns.

--Mrs. Moon's Polliwogs. LC 67-15689. (Mrs. Moon Bks). (gr. k-3). 1967. PLB 3.95x (ISBN 0-8225-0113-9). Lerner Pubns.

--Mrs. Moon's Rescue. LC 67-15694. (Mrs. Moon Bk). (gr. k-3). 1967. PLB 3.95g (ISBN 0-8225-0118-X). Lerner Pubns.

--Mrs. Moon's Story Hour. LC 67-15687. (Mrs. Moon Bks.). (gr. k-3). 1967. PLB 3.95g (ISBN 0-8225-0111-2). Lerner Pubns.

--New Year's Day with Mr. & Mrs. Bumba. LC 77-156355. (Easy-Readers Ser). (Illus.). (gr. k-3). 1971. PLB 3.95g (ISBN 0-8225-0127-9). Lerner Pubns.

--Rummage Sale & Mr. & Mrs. Bumba. LC 70-156361. (Easy-Readers Ser). (gr. k-3). 1971. PLB 3.95g (ISBN 0-8225-0122-8). Lerner Pubns.

--Special Guest for Mr. & Mrs. Bumba. LC 78-156358. (Easy-Readers Ser). (Illus.). (gr. k-3). 1971. PLB 3.95g (ISBN 0-8225-0123-6). Lerner Pubns.

--Thief Visits Mr. & Mrs. Bumba. LC 70-156356. (Easy-Readers Ser). (Illus.). (gr. k-3). 1971. PLB 3.95g (ISBN 0-8225-0125-2). Lerner Pubns.

--Very Big Problem of Mr. & Mrs. Bumba. LC 73-156354. (Easy-Readers Ser). (Illus.). (gr. k-3). 1971. PLB 3.95g (ISBN 0-8225-0130-9). Lerner Pubns.

--Widdles. LC 66-14896. (General Juvenile Bks). (Illus.). (gr. k-5). 1966. PLB 3.95g (ISBN 0-8225-0257-7). Lerner Pubns.

Harwood, Richard K., jt. auth. see Bachhuber, Thomas D.

Harwood, William. Writing & Editing School News: A Basic Project Text in Scholastic Journalism. 1977. lib. bdg. 8.40 (ISBN 0-931054-04-4). Clark Pub.

Harwood, William N. Writing & Editing School News. 2nd & rev. ed. (Illus.). 364p. (gr. 10-12). 1983. pap. 8.40 (ISBN 0-931054-11-7). Clark Pub.

Harzem, P. & Miles, T. R. Conceptual Issues in Operant Psychology. LC 77-21280. 1978. 37.95 (ISBN 0-471-99603-3, Pub. by Wiley-Interscience). Wiley.

Harzem, Peter, jt. auth. see Zeiler, Michael D.

Harzem, Peter & Zeiler, Michael D., eds. Predictability, Correlation & Contiguity. LC 80-40843. (Wiley Series on Advances in Analysis of Behavior). 432p. 1981. 54.95 (ISBN 0-471-27847-5, Pub. by Wiley-Interscience). Wiley.

Hasan, Khalid, ed. Versions of Truth: Urdu Short Stories from Pakistan. 1983. text ed. write for info. (ISBN 0-7069-2128-3, Pub. by Vikas India). Advent NY.

Hasan, Noorul. Thomas Hardy: The Sociological Imagination. 200p. 1982. text ed. 21.00x (ISBN 0-333-32628-8, Pub. by Macmillan England). Humanities.

Hascall, Leonard B. The Revelation: A Multi-Dimensional Autobiography. 1976. 4.95 (ISBN 0-686-21680-6). Law of One.

Haschemeyer, Audrey H., jt. auth. see Haschemeyer, Rudolph.

Haschemeyer, Rudolph & Haschemeyer, Audrey H. Proteins: A Guide to Study by Physical & Chemical Methods. LC 72-13134. 528p. 1973. 43.95x (ISBN 0-471-35850-9, Pub. by Wiley-Interscience). Wiley.

Haschen, R. J., et al, eds. Multiple Forms of Enzymes. (Advances in Clinical Enzymology: Vol. 2). 250p. 1982. 83.25 (ISBN 3-8055-2921-X). S Karger.

Hasci, Jacqueline. East to Paradise. (Orig.). 1980. pap. 1.50 o.s.i. (ISBN 0-440-12243-0). Dell.

--Paradise Isle. (Orig.). 1981. pap. 1.50 o.s.i. (ISBN 0-440-16966-6). Dell.

Hasdorff, Lawrence. Gradient Optimization & Nonlinear Control. LC 75-40187. 1976. text ed. 37.50 o.p. (ISBN 0-471-35870-3, Pub. by Wiley-Interscience). Wiley.

Hasdorff, Lawrence, jt. auth. see Gupta, Someshwar C.

Hasebroek, Johannes. Trade & Politics in Ancient Greece. LC 65-15245. 1933. 15.00x (ISBN 0-8196-0150-0). Biblo.

Hasegawa, Akira & Uberoi, Chanchal. The Alfven Wave. LC 81-607894. (DOE Critical Review Advances in Fusion Science & Engineering Ser.). 138p. 1981. pap. 11.50 (ISBN 0-87079-125-7, DOE/TIC-11197); microfiche 4.50 (ISBN 0-87079-236-9, DOE/TIC-11197). DOE.

Hasegawa, Hideo. Ice Carving. Athey, Jackie, ed. LC 77-83288. (Illus.). 1978. text ed. 45.00 (ISBN 0-916096-11-4). Continental CA.

Hasegawa, T., ed. see IFAC-IFIP Workshop, Kyoto, Japan, August 31 - Sept. 2, 1981.

Hasek, Jaroslav. Good Soldier Schweik. (Orig.). pap. 3.95 (ISBN 0-451-51687-7, CE1687, Sig Classics). NAL.

Haseler, Stephen. The Tragedy of Labour. (Mainstream Ser.). 249p. 1980. pap. 7.95x (ISBN 0-631-12836-0, Pub. by Basil Blackwell England). Biblio Dist.

Haseler, Stephen, jt. auth. see Godson, Roy.

Haseley, Dennis. The Pirate Who Tried to Capture the Moon. LC 82-47734. (Illus.). 48p. (gr. k-4). 1983. 8.61i (ISBN 0-06-022226-3, HarpJ); PLB 8.89g (ISBN 0-06-022227-1). Har-Row.

Haselkorn, Anne M. Prostitution in Elizabethan & Jacobean Comedy. 1983. 15.00 (ISBN 0-87875-247-1). Whitston Pub.

Haseloff, C. H. Marauder. 176p. 1982. pap. 2.25 (ISBN 0-553-20400-9). Bantam.

Haseloff, H. P. Veraenderungen Im 002.-Gaswechsel bel Laubmoosen nach Experimentellen Be-Lastungen mit Schwermetallverbingungen. (Bryohpytorum Bibliotheca 19). (Illus.). 1979. pap. text ed. 12.00x (ISBN 3-7682-1234-3). Lubrecht & Cramer.

Hasenfeld, Yeheskel & English, Richard A., eds. Human Service Organizations: A Book of Readings. 1974. pap. text ed. 10.95x (ISBN 0-472-08986-2). U of Mich Pr.

Hasenfratz, Hans-Peter. Die Toten Lebenden: Eine Religions Phanomenologische Studie zum Sozialen Tod in Archaischen Gasellschaften. Zugleichj ein Kritischer Beitrag zur Sogenannten Strafopfertheorie. (Zeitschrift fur Religions-und Geistesgeschichte, Beiheft: Vol. 24). xii, 167p. 1982. pap. write for info. (ISBN 90-04-06595-4). E J Brill.

Hasenohrl, Fritz, ed. see Boltzmann, Ludwig.

Hasenpflug, H., jt. auth. see Sauvant, K.

Hashagen, August. Let Us Have Love. rev. ed. 1967. pap. 2.00 (ISBN 0-910140-06-5). Anthony.

Hashian, Jack. Mamigon. 320p. 1982. 16.95 (ISBN 0-698-11186-9, Coward). Putnam Pub Group.

Hashim. Arabic Made Easy. pap. 7.50 (ISBN 0-686-18331-2). Kazi Pubns.

Hashim, A. S. How to Be Your Child's Doctor (Sometimes) LC 82-82302. (Illus.). 368p. (Orig.). 1983. pap. 13.95 (ISBN 0-448-11897-1, G&D). Putnam Pub Group.

Hashimi, Ali Ibn Sulayman al. The Book of the Reasons Behind Astronomical Tables (Kitab Fi 'ilal Al-Zijat) Kennedy, E. S. & Pingree, David, eds. Haddad, Fuad I., tr. from Arabic. LC 77-14160. 408p. 1981. 55.00x (ISBN 0-8201-1298-4). Schol Facsimiles.

Hashimoto, K., et al, eds. Methodology in Human Fatigue Assessment. 232p. 1975. 40.00x o.p. (ISBN 0-85066-049-1, Pub. by Taylor & Francis). State Mutual Bk.

Hashimoto, Yasuko & Edades, Jean. Tales of a Japanese Grandmother, 5 Vols. (Illus., Orig.). (gr. k-3). 1982. Set. pap. 16.00 (ISBN 0-686-37564-5, Pub. by New Day Philippines). Cellar.

Hashisaki, J., jt. auth. see Peterson, J. A.

Hashisaki, Joseph. Theory & Applications of Mathematics for Elementary School Teachers. 450p. 1984. text ed. 23.95 (ISBN 0-471-09637-7); tchr's. manual avail. (ISBN 0-471-87234-2). Wiley.

Hashmi, M. H. Assay of Vitamins in Pharmaceutical Preparation. LC 72-2640. 592p. 1973. 102.00x (ISBN 0-471-35880-0, Pub. by Wiley-Interscience). Wiley.

Hasiguti, Ryukiti R., ed. Lattice Defects & Their Interactions. 1152p. 1967. 188.00x (ISBN 0-677-11230-0). Gordon.

Hasinbiller, Dolly, ed. see Emmer, Rae.

Haskell, Arnold & Nouvel, Walter W. Diaghileff: His Artistic & Private Life. LC 78-9314. (Series in Dance). 1977. Repr. of 1935 ed. lib. bdg. 29.50 (ISBN 0-306-70869-8); pap. 6.95 (ISBN 0-306-80085-3). Da Capo.

Haskell, Arnold, tr. see Kschessinska, Mathilde.

Haskell, Barbara. Milton Avery. LC 82-47547. (Icon Edtiions). 224p. 1982. 28.80 (ISBN 0-06-433320-5, IN-121, HarpT); pap. write for info (ISBN 0-06-430121-4). Har-Row.

Haskell, Daniel C. A Tentative Check-List of Early European Railway Literature, 1831-1848. LC 75-20977. 1977. Repr. of 1955 ed. lib. bdg. 20.25x (ISBN 0-8371-8349-9, HATCL). Greenwood.

Haskell, Daniel C., jt. auth. see Stokes, I. N.

Haskell, Daniel C., jt. ed. see Brown, Karl.

Haskell, Francis, tr. see Venturi, Franco.

Haskell, Francis, et al, eds. The Artist & the Writer in France: Essays in Honour of Jean Seznec. (Illus.). 1974. 36.00x o.p. (ISBN 0-19-817187-0). Oxford U Pr.

Haskell, H. S., jt. auth. see McDougall, W. B.

Haskell, John, jt. ed. see Haskell, John D., Jr.

Haskell, John D., Jr., ed. Maine: A Bibliography of Its History. (Reference Publications Ser.). 1977. lib. bdg. 28.50 o.p. (ISBN 0-8161-8010-5). G K Hall.

Haskell, John D., Jr. & Haskell, John, eds. Massachusetts: A Bibliography of Its History. 1976. lib. bdg. 32.00 (ISBN 0-8161-1212-6, Hall Reference). G K Hall.

Haskell, Martin R. & Yablonsky, Lewis. Crime & Delinquency. 3rd ed. 1978. 22.95 (ISBN 0-395-30616-7). HM.

--Criminology. 2nd ed. pap. 16.95 (ISBN 0-395-30620-5). HM.

--Criminology: Crime & Criminality. 3rd ed. LC 82-81586. 560p. 1983. pap. text ed. 19.50 (ISBN 0-395-32574-9); instrs.' manual avail. (ISBN 0-395-32575-7). HM.

--Juvenile Delinquency. 2nd ed. 1978. pap. 14.95 o.p. (ISBN 0-395-30618-3); Instr's. manual 0.55 o.p. (ISBN 0-395-30619-1). HM.

--Juvenile Delinquency. 3rd ed. LC 81-82668. 1982. 19.95 (ISBN 0-395-31724-X); instr's man. pap. 1.00 (ISBN 0-395-31725-8); test items 1.00. HM.

Haskell, Patricia & Marquis, Vivienne. The Cheese Book. (Illus.). 1965. 10.95 o.p. (ISBN 0-671-13330-6). S&S.

Haskell, Richard. Apple II: Six-Five-Zero-Two Assembly Language Tutor. (Illus.). 240p. 1983. 34.95 (ISBN 0-13-039230-8). P-H.

--Atari BASIC. (Illus.). 224p. 1983. 19.95 (ISBN 0-13-049809-2); pap. 13.95 (ISBN 0-13-049791-6). P-H.

--TRS-Eighty Extended Color BASIC. (Illus.). 192p. 1983. 19.95 (ISBN 0-13-931253-6); pap. 12.95 (ISBN 0-13-931246-3). P-H.

Haskell, Richard A. Sell Your House Through Creative Financing Without a Broker! 1982. 17.95 (ISBN 0-671-44524-3); pap. 7.95 (ISBN 0-671-45077-8). S&S.

Haskell, Richard E. FORTRAN Programming Using Structured Flowcharts. LC 77-23931. 320p. 1978. pap. text ed. 15.95 (ISBN 0-574-21135-7, 13-4135). SRA.

Haskett, M. R., ed. see Haskett, William P.

Haskett, Meredith R. Patches of Life: Volume I-Special, Philosophical in Nature. (Illus.). 36p. (Orig.). 1982. pap. 8.00 chrome coated (ISBN 0-9609724-1-2). Haskett Spec.

Haskett, William P. Grandpa Haskett Presents: Original New Christmas Stories for the Young & Young-at-Heart. Haskett, M. R., ed. (Illus.). 20p. (Orig.). 1982. pap. 3.00g (ISBN 0-9609724-0-4). Haskett Spec.

Haskew, Laurence D. & McLendon, Jonathon C. This Is Teaching: Foundations of American Education. 3rd ed. 1968. text ed. 15.50x (ISBN 0-673-05822-0). Scott F.

Haskin, Frederic J. Ten Thousand Answers to Questions. LC 79-99074. 1970. Repr. of 1937 ed. 35.00 o.p. (ISBN 0-8103-3861-0). Gale.

Haskin, Marvin E., jt. auth. see Teplick, J. G.

Haskin, Marvin E., jt. auth. see Teplick, J. George.

Haskin, Steve, jt. auth. see Fingerhut, Bruce M.

Haskins & Sells Government Services Group. Implementing Effective Cash Management in Local Government: A Practical Guide. LC 76-52520. 1977. looseleaf with vinyl binder 10.00 o.p. (ISBN 0-89125-004-2). Municipal.

Haskins, Caryl P., ed. Search for Understanding. 1970. 20.00x (ISBN 0-262-08042-7). MIT Pr.

--The Search for Understanding: Selected Writings of Scientists of the Carnegie Institution. (Illus.). 330p. 1967. 5.00 (ISBN 0-87279-954-9). Carnegie Inst.

Haskins, Earl R., Jr., ed. see U. S. National Committee on Rock Mechanics, 15th, South Dakota School of Mines & Technology, Sept. 1973 & American Society of Civil Engineers.

Haskins, James. The Guardian Angels. LC 82-11615. (Illus.). 64p. (gr. 5-12). 1983. PLB 8.95 (ISBN 0-89490-081-1). Enslow Pubs.

--Katherine Dunham. (Illus.). 176p. 1982. 10.95 (ISBN 0-698-20549-9, Coward). Putnam Pub Group.

--Leaders of the Middle East. (Illus.). 192p. (gr. 5-12). 1983. 10.95 (ISBN 0-89490-086-2). Enslow Pubs.

--Magic: A Biography of Earvin Johnson. LC 80-27691. (Illus.). 160p. (gr. 5-12). 1982. PLB 9.95 (ISBN 0-89490-044-7). Enslow Pubs.

--The New Americans: Cuban Boat People. LC 82-8906. (Illus.). 64p. (gr. 5-12). 1982. PLB 8.95 (ISBN 0-89490-059-5). Enslow Pubs.

--The Story of Stevie Wonder. (YA) 1979. pap. 1.25 o.p. (ISBN 0-440-98259-6, LFL). Dell.

--Sugar Ray Leonard. LC 82-15227. (Illus.). 160p. (gr. 4 up). 1982. 9.50 (ISBN 0-688-01436-4). Lothrop.

Haskins, James, jt. auth. see Bricktop.

Haskins, James S. Pele: A Biography. LC 75-39123. (Signal Bks.). (Illus.). 144p. (gr. 7-9). 1976. 6.95 (ISBN 0-385-11565-2). Doubleday.

Haskins, Jim. Gambling: Who Really Wins? (First Bks.). (Illus.). (gr. 4 up). 1979. PLB 8.90 (ISBN 0-531-02942-5). Watts.

--Real Estate Careers. (Career Concise Guides Ser.). (Illus.). (gr. 7 up). 1978. PLB 8.90 s&l (ISBN 0-531-01423-1). Watts.

Haskins, Jim & Stifle, J. M. Donna Summer: An Unauthorized Biography. (Illus.). 144p. (gr. 7 up). 1983. 10.45i (ISBN 0-316-35003-6, Pub. by Atlantic Monthly Pr). Little.

Haskins, Jim, ed. Black Manifesto for Education. 1973. 7.95 o.p. (ISBN 0-688-00029-0); pap. 2.95 o.p. (ISBN 0-688-05029-8). Morrow.

Haskins, Lola. Planting the Children. LC 82-1958. (University of Central Florida Contemporary Poetry Ser.). 96p. Date not set. pap. 8.95 (ISBN 0-8130-0727-5). U Presses Fla.

Haskins, Ralph W., jt. ed. see Graf, LeRoy P.

Haskins, Ron & Gallagher, James J. Models for Analysis of Social Policy. (Child & Family Policy Ser.: Vol. 1). 265p. 1981. text ed. 24.50 (ISBN 0-89391-084-8). Ablex Pub.

Haskins, Ron & Gallagher, James J., eds. Care & Education of Young Children in America: Policy, Politics & Social Science. LC 80-11788. (Illus.). 224p. 1980. text ed. 22.50x (ISBN 0-89391-040-6). Ablex Pub.

--Child Health Policy in an Age of Fiscal Austerity: Critiques of the Select Panel Report. (Child & Family Policy Ser.: Vol. 12). 1983. 24.50 (ISBN 0-89391-118-6). Ablex Pub.

Haskins, Sam. Photographics. (Illus.). 1981. 30.00 (ISBN 2-88046-016-6, Pub. by Roto-Vision Switzerland). Norton.

Haslam, E. The Shikimate Pathway. LC 73-18377. 316p. 1974. 54.95x o.p. (ISBN 0-470-35882-3). Halsted Pr.

Haslam, J., et al. Identification & Analysis of Plastics. 756p. 1979. 66.95 (ISBN 0-471-25757-5, Pub. by Wiley Heyden). Wiley.

Haslam, M. T. Psychiatric Illness in Adolescence. 1975. 21.95 o.p. (ISBN 0-407-00019-4). Butterworth.

Haslam, Robert H. & Valetutti, Peter J., eds. Medical Problems in the Classroom: The Teacher's Role in Diagnosis & Management. (Illus.). 344p. 1976. text ed. 18.95 (ISBN 0-8391-0823-0). Univ Park.

Haslam, S. M. River Plants. LC 76-46857. (Illus.). 1978. 90.00 (ISBN 0-521-21493-9); pap. 24.95x (ISBN 0-521-29172-0). Cambridge U Pr.

Hasler, August B. How the Pope Became Infallible: Pius IX & the Politics of Persuasion. Heinegg, Peter, tr. LC 79-6851. (Illus.). 400p. 1981. 14.95 o.p. (ISBN 0-385-15851-3). Doubleday.

Hasler, Doris. Practical Nurse & Today's Family. 2nd ed. 1972. pap. text ed. 11.95x (ISBN 0-02-351700-X). Macmillan.

Hasler, Doris & Hasler, Norman B. Personal, Home & Community Health. (Orig.). 1967. pap. text ed. 10.95x (ISBN 0-02-351650-X). Macmillan.

Hasler, John, jt. ed. see Pendleton, David.

Hasler, Norman B., jt. auth. see Hasler, Doris.

Hasler, Richard A. Journal of Prayer. 144p. 1982. 12.95 (ISBN 0-8170-0965-5). Judson.

Haslett, John W. Business Systems Handbook: Strategies for Administrative Control. (Illus.). 1979. 28.95 (ISBN 0-07-026980-7, P&RB). McGraw.

Haslewood, G. A. The Biological Importance of Bile Salts. LC 78-14494. (Frontiers of Biology Ser.: Vol. 47). 1978. 78.50 (ISBN 0-7204-0662-5, Biomedical Pr). Elsevier.

Hasling. The Audience, the Message, the Speaker. 2nd ed. 1975. 13.95 (ISBN 0-07-026990-4, C); instructor's manual 15.95 (ISBN 0-07-026991-2). McGraw.

Hasling, Jack. The Message, the Speaker, the Audience. 3rd ed. (Illus.). 144p. 1982. pap. 12.95x (ISBN 0-07-026995-5); instr's manual 8.95 (ISBN 0-07-026996-3). McGraw.

Hasling, John. The Professional Radio Broadcaster. (Illus.). 1980. pap. text ed. 16.50x (ISBN 0-07-026992-0). McGraw.

Haslip, Joan. Catherine the Great: A Biography. LC 76-20630. (Illus.). 1977. 12.95 o.p. (ISBN 0-399-11666-4). Putnam Pub Group.

Hasluck, Paul N. Telescope Making Nineteen Hundred-Five. (Illus.). 160p. Date not set. pap. 12.50 (ISBN 0-87556-498-4). Saifer.

Haslund-Christensen, Henning & Cmshevner, Ernst. Music of the Mongols: Eastern Mongolia. LC 79-125045. (Music Ser). 1971. Repr. of 1943 ed. lib. bdg. 27.50 (ISBN 0-306-70009-3). Da Capo.

Haspels, A. A. Psychosomatics in PeriMenopause. 124p. 1979. text ed. 14.95 o.p. (ISBN 0-8391-1379-X). Univ Park.

Hass, E. A. Come Quick, I'm Sick! LC 82-6771. (Aladdin Ser.). (Illus.). 48p. (Orig.). (gr. k-3). 1982. pap. 2.95 (ISBN 0-689-70757-6, A-134, Aladdin). Atheneum.

Hass, Georg, ed. Physics of Thin Films, Vol. 12. 1982. 49.50 (ISBN 0-12-533012-X); lib. ed. 64.50 (ISBN 0-12-533082-0); microfiche 35.00 (ISBN 0-12-533083-9). Acad Pr.

Hass, Georg & Francombe, Maurice H., eds. Physics of Thin Films: Advances in Research & Development, Vol. 11. (Serial Publication Ser.). 1980. 46.00 (ISBN 0-12-533011-1); lib. ed 52.50 (ISBN 0-12-533080-4); microfiche 39.50 (ISBN 0-12-533081-2). Acad Pr.

Hass, Georg, et al, eds. Physics of Thin Films: Advances in Research & Development. Incl. Vol. 1. Haas, Georg, ed. 1963. 68.50 (ISBN 0-12-533001-4); Vol. 2. Haas, Georg & Thun, R. E., eds. 1964. 68.50 (ISBN 0-12-533002-2); Vol. 3. 1966. 68.50 (ISBN 0-12-533003-0); Vol. 4. 1967. 68.50 (ISBN 0-12-533004-9); Vol. 5. 1969. 68.50 (ISBN 0-12-533005-7); Vol. 6. Francombe, Maurice H. & Hoffman, Richard W., eds. 1971. 68.50 (ISBN 0-12-533006-5); Vol. 7. 1974. 68.50 (ISBN 0-12-533007-3); Vol. 10. 1977. 57.00 (ISBN 0-12-533010-3); lib ed. 72.50 (ISBN 0-12-533078-2); microfiche 41.50 (ISBN 0-12-533079-0). Acad Pr.

Hass, Patricia, jt. auth. see Queen, Richard.

Hass, Robert, et al. Five American Poets: An Anthology. Mathias, John, ed. 160p. (Orig.). 1981. pap. 7.95 o.p. (ISBN 0-85635-259-4, Pub. by Carcanet New Pr England). Humanities.

Hassal, K. A. & Dobinson, M. A. Essential Chemistry, 2 Vols. (gr. 10-12). text ed. 5.00 ea. o.p.; Vol. 1. text ed. (ISBN 0-592-01202-6). Transatlantic.

Hassall, Kenneth A. The Chemistry of Pesticides: Their Metabolism, Mode of Action & Uses in Crop Protection. (Illus.). 372p. (Orig.). 1982. 79.50x (ISBN 0-89573-054-5). Verlag Chemie.

Hassall, Mark. The Romans. (Young Archaeologist Ser.). (gr. 5-9). 1972. PLB 4.49 o.p. (ISBN 0-399-60743-9). Putnam Pub Group.

Hassam, Abdul S. The Learning Process: How to Pass Examinations. 1978. 5.50 o.p. (ISBN 0-682-49117-9, University). Exposition.

Hassan, Bernard. The American Catholic Catalog. LC 79-1758. (Illus.). 1980. pap. 9.95i o.p. (ISBN 0-06-063735-8, RD 287, HarpR). Har-Row.

Hassan, E. Major Insect & Mite Pest of Australian Crops. Swarbrick, J. T., ed. (Illus.). 238p. 25.00 (ISBN 0-686-97011-X, Pub by Ento Pr Australia). Intl Schol Bk Serv.

Hassan, Farooq. The Concept of State & Law in Islam. LC 80-69038. 321p. (Orig.). 1981. lib. bdg. 23.25 (ISBN 0-8191-1426-X); pap. text ed. 12.25 (ISBN 0-8191-1427-8). U Pr of Amer.

Hassan, Ihab. Literature of Silence: Henry Miller & Samuel Beckett. 1967. pap. text ed. 3.95x (ISBN 0-685-39884-6). Phila Bk Co.

Hassan, M. Zia, jt. auth. see Pantumsinchai, Pricha.

Hassan, Mulhim A. Prevention & Control of Cancer. 240p. 1983. 11.50 (ISBN 0-682-49957-9). Exposition.

Hassan, Zahair A., jt. auth. see Johnson, Stanley R.

Hassard, D. B., et al. Theory of Applications of Hopf Bifurcation. (London Mathematical Society Lecture Notes Ser.: No. 41). (Illus.). 300p. (Orig.). 1981. 37.50 (ISBN 0-521-23158-2). Cambridge U Pr.

Hassard, Jack, jt. auth. see Abruscato, Joe.

Hassay, Karen A., jt. auth. see Lee, Steven J.

Hasse, Adelaide R. Index of Economic Material in Documents of the States of the United States, 13 vols. 1907-1922. Set. 675.00 (ISBN 0-527-00708-0). Kraus Repr.

--Index to United States Documents Relating to Foreign Affairs, 1828-1861, 3 Vols. 1914-1921. Set. 261.00 (ISBN 0-527-38700-2). Kraus Repr.

Hasse, Ann F., jt. auth. see Fingarette, Herbert.

Hasse, R. L., jt. auth. see Hoffman, B.

Hassel, David J. Radical Prayer. 160p. 1983. 6.95 (ISBN 0-8091-0340-0). Paulist Pr.

Hassell, Thomas, et al, eds. Phenytoin-Induced Teratology & Gingival Pathology. 252p. 1980. text ed. 30.00 (ISBN 0-89004-412-0). Raven.

Hasselmeyer, Eileen G., jt. auth. see Kretchmer, Norman.

Hasselriis, Floyd. Refuse-Derived Feul Processing. LC 82-46061. (Design & Management for Resource Recovery Ser.). 400p. 1983. 29.95 (ISBN 0-250-40314-5). Ann Arbor Science.

Hasselstrom, Linda M., ed. A Bird Begins to Sing: Northwest Poetry & Prose. 1979. pap. 2.25x o.p. (ISBN 0-917624-12-2). Lame Johnny.

Hasselt, Carlos Van see Schatborn, Peter & Van Hasselt, Carlos.

Hassenzahl, W. V., ed. Electrochemical, Electrical & Magnetic Storage of Energy. LC 81-6476. (Benchmark Papers on Energy: Vol. 8). 368p. 1981. 50.00 (ISBN 0-87933-376-6); 90.00 set (ISBN 0-87933-093-7). Hutchinson Ross.

--Mechanical, Thermal & Chemical Storage of Energy. LC 81-6485. (Benchmark Papers on Energy Ser.: Vol. 9). 379p. 1981. 50.00 (ISBN 0-87933-392-8); 90.00 (ISBN 0-87933-093-7). Hutchinson Ross.

Hassett, jt. auth. see Chapin.

Hassett, Constance W. The Elusive Self in the Poetry of Robert Browning. LC 81-22575. 186p. 1982. text ed. 19.95 (ISBN 0-8214-0629-9, 82-84028). Ohio U Pr.

Hassett, Matthew, jt. auth. see Weiss, Neil.

Hassinger, E., ed. see North Central Regional Center for Rural Development.

Hassinger, Edward W. Rural Health Organization: Social Networks & Regionalization. 192p. 1982. pap. text ed. 11.50x (ISBN 0-8138-1589-4). Iowa St U Pr.

Hassler, Donald M. Erasmus Darwin. (English Authors Ser.). 1974. 13.95 (ISBN 0-8057-1138-4, Twayne). G K Hall.

--Hal Clement. (Starmont Reader's Guide Ser.: No. 11). 64p. 1982. Repr. lib. bdg. 10.95x (ISBN 0-89370-042-8). Borgo Pr.

--Reader's Guide to Hal Clement. Schlobin, Roger C., ed. (Reader's Guides to Contemporary Science Fiction & Fantasy Authors Ser.: Vol. 11). (Illus., Orig.). 1982. 10.95x (ISBN 0-916732-30-4); pap. text ed. 4.95x (ISBN 0-916732-27-4). Starmont Hse.

Hassler, Donald M., ed. Patterns of the Fantastic: Academic Programming at Chicon IV. (Illus.). 1983. 11.95x (ISBN 0-916732-63-0); pap. 5.95x text ed. (ISBN 0-916732-62-2). Starmont Hse.

Hassler, Jon. Love Hunter. 1982. pap. 3.50 (ISBN 0-553-22945-1). Bantam.

--Simon's Night. LC 79-10900. 1979. 9.95 o.p. (ISBN 0-689-10981-4). Atheneum.

--Staggerford. LC 76-57757. 1977. 8.95 o.p. (ISBN 0-689-10793-5). Atheneum.

Hassler, Kenneth. Mark Twain, Dean of American Humorists. new ed. (Outstanding Personalities Ser.). 32p. 1975. lib. bdg. 2.95 incl. catalog cards (ISBN 0-686-11227-X); pap. 1.95 vinyl laminated covers (ISBN 0-686-11228-8). SamHar Pr.

Hassler, Warren W., Jr. With Shield & Sword: American Military Affairs, Colonial Times to the Present. (Illus.). 446p. 1982. text ed. 29.50x (ISBN 0-8138-1627-0). Iowa St U Pr.

Hassler, William T., jt. auth. see Ackerman, Bruce A.

Hassner, Alfred. Small Ring Heterocycles, Pt. 1. (The Chemistry of Heterocyclic Compounds, A Series of Monographs). 680p. 1983. 175.00x (ISBN 0-471-05626-X, Pub. by Wiley-Interscience). Wiley.

Hasso, Anton N., jt. auth. see Thompson, Joseph R.

Hassrick, Peter H., jt. auth. see Trenton, Patricia.

Hastenrath, Stefan & Lamb, Peter J. Climatic Atlas of the Tropical Atlantic & Eastern Pacific Oceans. 114p. 1977. pap. 50.00 (ISBN 0-299-07234-7). U of Wis Pr.

Hastie, John W. High Temperature Vapors: Science & Technology. (Materials Science & Technology Ser.). 1975. 63.50 (ISBN 0-12-331950-1). Acad Pr.

Hastie, W., tr. see Kant, Immanuel.

Hastin, Bud. Avon Bottle Encyclopedia. 9th ed. (Illus.). 600p. 1982. 19.95. Avon Res.

--Bud Hastin's Collector's Price Guide: Avon Bottle Encyclopedia. 9th ed. (Illus.). 1982. 19.95 (ISBN 0-89145-152-8). Avons Res.

Hastin, Bud & Hastin, Vickie. Bud Hastin's Avon Bottle Encyclopedia: 1982-83. (Illus.). 19.95 (ISBN 0-89145-200-1). Wallace-Homestead.

Hastin, Vickie, jt. auth. see Hastin, Bud.

Hastings. Rufus & Christopher & the Box of Laughter. LC 77-190270. (Rufus & Christopher Ser.). (Illus.). (gr. 2-4). 1972. PLB 6.75x (ISBN 0-87783-060-6); pap. 2.95x deluxe ed. (ISBN 0-87783-106-8); cassette 5.95 (ISBN 0-87783-196-3). Oddo.

--Rufus & Christopher & the Magic Bubble. LC 73-87799. (Rufus & Christopher Ser.). (Illus.). (gr. k-2). 1974. 6.75x (ISBN 0-87783-127-0); pap. 2.95x deluxe ed. (ISBN 0-87783-128-9); cassette 5.95 (ISBN 0-87783-197-1). Oddo.

--Rufus & Christopher in the Land of Lies. LC 70-190271. (Rufus & Christopher Ser.). (Illus.). (gr. 2-4). 1972. PLB 6.75x (ISBN 0-87783-061-4); pap. 2.95x deluxe ed. (ISBN 0-87783-107-6); cassette 5.95 (ISBN 0-87783-198-X). Oddo.

Hastings, et al. Health for the Whole Person. Date not set. cancelled o.p. (ISBN 0-89158-884-1). Cancer Control Soc.

Hastings, A. A History of African Christianity: 1950-1975. LC 78-16599. (Illus.). 1979. 44.50 (ISBN 0-521-22212-5); pap. 14.95 (ISBN 0-521-29397-9). Cambridge U Pr.

Hastings, Arthur C., et al, eds. Health for the Whole Person: A Comprehensive Guide to Holistic Medicine. 608p. 1980. 31.25 o.p. (ISBN 0-89158-883-3); pap. 5.95 o.p. (ISBN 0-89158-884-1). Westview.

Hastings, Ashley, jt. ed. see Eckman, Fred R.

Hastings, Brooke. Rough Diamond. (Nightingale Series Paperbacks). 1983. pap. 10.95 (ISBN 0-8161-3523-1, Large Print Bks). G K Hall.

Hastings, De Cronin. The Alternative Society: Software for the Nineteen-Eighties. 160p. 1980. 17.95 o.p. (ISBN 0-7153-7880-5). David & Charles.

Hastings, Elizabeth H. & Hastings, Philip K., eds. Index to International Public Opinion, 1981-1982. LC 80-643917. xviii, 682p. 1983. lib. bdg. 85.00 (ISBN 0-313-23362-4, IN82). Greenwood.

Hastings, Evelyn. Big New School. (Beginning-to-Read Bks). (Illus.). (gr. 1-3). 2.50 o.s.i. (ISBN 0-695-80781-1); lib. ed. 2.97 o.s.i. (ISBN 0-695-40781-3); pap. 1.50 o.s.i. (ISBN 0-695-30781-9). Follett.

Hastings, Lansford W. Emigrant's Guide to Oregon & California. 2nd ed. LC 68-8691. (American Scene Ser). 1969. Repr. of 1845 ed. lib. bdg. 24.50 (ISBN 0-306-71172-9). Da Capo.

Hastings, Margaret. Medieval European Society, One Thousand to Fourteen Fifty. LC 81-40772. 250p. 1981. pap. text ed. 8.75 (ISBN 0-8191-1810-9). U Pr of Amer.

Hastings, Michael. Sir Richard Burton. LC 78-5486. (Illus.). 1978. 10.95 o.p. (ISBN 0-698-10936-8, Coward). Putnam Pub Group.

Hastings, N. A. & Mello, J. M. Decision Networks. 196p. 1978. 53.95 (ISBN 0-471-99531-2, Pub. by Wiley-Interscience). Wiley.

Hastings, Paul G. Introduction to Business. 2nd ed. (Illus.). 640p. 1974. pap. text ed. 26.95 (ISBN 0-07-027020-1, C); instructors' manual 5.95 (ISBN 0-07-027021-X). McGraw.

Hastings, Paul G. & Mietus, Norbert J. Personal Finance. 2nd ed. (Finance Ser.). 1977. text ed. 20.00 o.p. (ISBN 0-07-027013-9, C); instructor's manual 9.00 o.p. (ISBN 0-07-027014-7). McGraw.

Hastings, Philip K., jt. ed. see Hastings, Elizabeth H.

Hastings, R. Nature & Reason in the Decameron. 1975. 22.50 (ISBN 0-7190-1281-3). Manchester.

Hastings, Thomas. Dissertation on Musical Taste. LC 68-16237. (Music Ser.). 228p. 1974. Repr. of 1822 ed. lib. bdg. 27.50 (ISBN 0-306-71085-4). Da Capo.

Hastorf & Isen. Cognitive Social Psychology. 1981. 39.00 (ISBN 0-444-00617-6). Elsevier.

Hasty, Ronald W. Retailing. 3rd ed. 640p. 1982. text ed. 24.50 scp (ISBN 0-06-042689-6, HarpC); instr's. manual & test bank avail. (ISBN 0-06-362680-2). Har-Row.

Hasty, Ronald W., jt. auth. see Will, R. Ted.

Haswell. Civil Engineering: Contracts. 1982. text ed. 29.95 (ISBN 0-408-00526-2). Butterworth.

Haswell, Harold A., jt. auth. see Eells, Walter C.

Haswell, Margaret. The Nature of Poverty: A Case History of the First Quarter-Century After World War Two. LC 75-21705. 1975. 18.95x o.p. (ISBN 0-312-56245-4). St Martin.

Haszonics, Joseph J. Front Office Operation. LC 77-146929. 1971. text ed. 16.50 (ISBN 0-672-96074-5); tchr's manual 8.50 (ISBN 0-672-96076-1); wkbk. 8.50 (ISBN 0-672-96075-3). Bobbs.

Haszpra, Otto. Modelling Hydroelastic Vibrations. (Water Resources Engineering Ser.). 136p. 1979. text ed. 27.50x (ISBN 0-273-08441-0). Pitman Pub MA.

Hatab, Lawrence J. Nietzsche & Eternal Recurrence: The Redemption of Time & Becoming. LC 78-62266. 1978. pap. text ed. 8.50 (ISBN 0-8191-0564-3). U Pr of Amer.

Hatano, Sadashi. Cell Motility. 708p. 1979. text ed. 64.50 o.p. (ISBN 0-8391-1474-5). Univ Park.

Hatano, Sumi. Cooking from Mainland China: One Hundred Fifty-Eight Authentic Recipes from the People's Republic of China. Fessler, Stella L., tr. from Chinese. LC 79-54702. (Illus.). 1979. 10.95 (ISBN 0-8120-5375-3). Barron.

Hatch, Alden. Buckminster Fuller. 288p. 1976. pap. 3.25 o.s.i. (ISBN 0-440-54408-4, Delta). Dell.

Hatch, Charles E., Jr. The First Seventeen Years: Virginia, 1607-1624. (Jamestown 350th Anniversary Historical Booklets). 118p. 1980. pap. 2.95x (ISBN 0-8139-0130-8). U Pr of Va.

Hatch, Denison. Cedarhurst Alley. LC 76-13243. 256p. Date not set. pap. 9.95 cancelled o.p. (ISBN 0-8397-1326-6). Eriksson. Postponed.

Hatch, Edwin & Redpath, Henry A. A Concordance to the Septuagint & Other Greek Versions of the Old Testament (Including the Apocryphal Books, 3 vols. in 2. 1088p. 1983. Repr. of 1906 ed. Set. 75.00 (ISBN 0-8010-4270-4). Baker Bk.

Hatch, Eric. What Goes on in Horses' Heads. LC 77-113513. (Illus.). (gr. 6 up). 1970. 4.95 o.p. (ISBN 0-399-20229-3). Putnam Pub Group.

Hatch, Evelyn. Second Language Acquisition: A Book of Readings. 1978. pap. 17.95 (ISBN 0-88377-086-5). Newbury Hse.

Hatch, Evelyn & Farhady, Hossein. Research Design & Statistics for Applied Linguistics. 272p. 1982. pap. text ed. 16.95 (ISBN 0-88377-202-7). Newbury Hse.

Hatch, Evelyn M. Psycholinguistics: A Second Language Perspective. 1983. pap. text ed. 15.95 (ISBN 0-88377-250-7). Newbury Hse.

Hatch, Frederick see Shore, Bernard.

Hatch, James V. & Shine, Ted, eds. Black Theater, U. S. A. Forty-Five Plays by Black Americans, 1847-1974. LC 75-169234. 1974. 29.95 (ISBN 0-02-914160-5). Free Pr.

Hatch, Jan, ed. Public Employees Conference, 1975, Hollywood, Fla. Proceedings. (Civil Service Pensions). 145p. 1976. spiral bdg 3.75 (ISBN 0-89154-044-X). Intl Found Employ.

Hatch, Jane M., ed. American Book of Days. 1212p. 1978. 60.00 (ISBN 0-8242-0593-6). Wilson.

Hatch, John, jt. auth. see Redwood, John.

Hatch, Louis C., ed. Maine: A History. new ed. LC 73-86844. (Illus.). 1000p. 1974. Repr. of 1920 ed. 25.00 o.p. (ISBN 0-912274-36-0). NH Pub Co.

Hatch, M. D., jt. ed. see Stumpf, P. K.

Hatch, Melville H., et al. Beetles of the Pacific Northwest, 5 pts. Incl. Pt. 1. Introduction & Adephaga. 348p. 1953. o.p. (ISBN 0-295-73715-8); Pt. 2. Staphyliniformia. 384p. 1957. o.p. (ISBN 0-295-73716-6); Pt. 3. Pselaphidae & Diversicornia 1. 503p. 1962. 25.00 o.p. (ISBN 0-295-73717-4); Pt. 4. Macrodactyles, Palpicornes, & Heteromera. 268p. 1965. o.p. (ISBN 0-295-73718-2); Pt. 5. Rhipiceroidea, Sternoxi, Phytophaga, Rhynchophora, & Lamellicornia. 650p. 1971. 25.00 o.p. (ISBN 0-295-73719-0). LC 53-9444. (Publications in Biology Ser.: No. 16). (Illus.). U of Wash Pr.

Hatch, Pamela, jt. auth. see Phillips, Phoebe.

Hatch, Richard. Communicating in Business. LC 76-39844. 336p. 1977. text ed. 17.95 (ISBN 0-574-20015-0, 13-3015); instr's guide 2.50 (ISBN 0-574-20016-9, 13-3016). SRA.

Hatch, Richard A. Business Communication. 608p. 1983. text ed. write for info. (ISBN 0-574-20660-4, 13-3660); write for info. instr's. guide (ISBN 0-574-20661-2, 13-3661). SRA.

--Business Writing. 528p. 1983. pap. text ed. write for info. (ISBN 0-574-20665-5, 13-3665); write for info. instr's. guide (ISBN 0-574-20666-3, 13-3666). SRA.

Hatch, Robert. The Collection Boulliau. LC 82-72157. 1982. 25.00 (ISBN 0-87169-984-2). Am Philos.

Hatch, Shirley C. Wind Is to Feel. (Illus.). 32p. (ps-2). 1973. PLB 5.29 o.p. (ISBN 0-698-30494-2, Coward). Putnam Pub Group.

Hatcher, Anna, ed. see Spitzer, Leo.

Hatcher, Evelyn. Visual Methaphors: A Formal Analysis of Navajo Art. LC 74-20691. (AES Ser). 1975. text ed. 23.95 (ISBN 0-8299-0026-8). West Pub.

Hatcher, Harlan H. Lake Erie. (Illus.). Repr. of 1945 ed. lib. bdg. 18.50x o.p. (ISBN 0-8371-5790-0, HALA). Greenwood.

Hatcher, Orie L. Book for Shakespeare Plays & Pageants. Repr. of 1916 ed. lib. bdg. 21.00x (ISBN 0-8371-3105-7, HAPP). Greenwood.

Hatcher, Richard, et al. It's Your Choice: A Personal Guide to Birth Control Methods for Women... & Men, Too! Stoner, Carol, ed. (Illus.). 144p. (Orig.). 1983. pap. 7.95 (ISBN 0-87857-471-9, 05-172-1). Rodale Pr Inc.

Hatcher, Robert A. & Josephs, Nancy. It's Your Choice: A Personal Guide to Birth Control Methods for Women... & Men Too! (Illus.). 140p. 1983. text ed. 16.95x. Irvington.

Hatchett, David. Country House Garden. (Illus.). 192p. 1983. 23.95 (ISBN 0-7153-8250-0). David & Charles.

Hatchtt, Shirley, jt. auth. see Schuman, Howard.

Hatem, Mary B., jt. auth. see Bryer, Jackson.

Hater, Robert J. The Ministry Explosion. 96p. (Orig.). 1979. pap. 3.25 (ISBN 0-697-01709-5). Wm C Brown.

Hatfield, Edwin F. Poets of the Church: A Series of Biographical Sketches of Hymn-Writers, with Notes on Their Hymns. 1979. Repr. of 1884 ed. 99.00x (ISBN 0-8103-4291-X). Gale.

Hatfield, Frederick C. Weight Training for the Young Athelete. LC 79-55614. (Illus.). 128p. 1982. 9.95 (ISBN 0-689-11041-3); pap. 6.95 (ISBN 0-689-70632-4, 285). Atheneum.

Hatfield, Henry. From "The Magic Mountain". Mann's Later Masterpieces. LC 78-74213. (Illus.). 1979. 19.50 (ISBN 0-8014-1204-8). Cornell U Pr.

Hatfield, Henry R. Accounting: Its Principles & Problems. LC 78-12596. 1971. Repr. of 1927 ed. text ed. 20.00 (ISBN 0-914348-02-7). Scholars Bk.

Hatfield, Mark, et al. Confessing Christ & Doing Politics. Skillen, James, ed. LC 80-71233. 100p. (Orig.). 1982. pap. 3.95 (ISBN 0-936456-02-7). Assn Public Justice.

Hatfield, Mark O., jt. auth. see Stockdale, James B.

Hatfield, Tom. Sandstone Experience. Date not set. pap. 2.50 o.p. (ISBN 0-686-73800-4, E9731, Sig). NAL.

Hathaway, Baxter. Marvels & Commonplaces: Renaissance Literary Criticism. 1968. pap. text ed. 3.95 (ISBN 0-685-19695-X). Phila Bk Co.

--The Petulant Children. LC 78-14869. 36p. 1978. 3.50 (ISBN 0-87886-099-1). Ithaca Hse.

Hathaway, Flora. Old Man Coyote. (Indian Culture Ser.). (gr. 2-9). 1970. 1.95 o.p. (ISBN 0-89992-008-X). MT Coun Indian.

Hathaway, J. M. Ordinary Level Physics Workbook. 1974. pap. 4.50x o.p. (ISBN 0-435-67392-0). Heinemann Ed.

Hathaway, James. Foraging. LC 78-3518. 41p. 1978. 3.50 (ISBN 0-87886-097-5). Ithaca Hse.

Hathaway, Nancy. The Unicorn. LC 80-5364. (Illus.). 192p. 1980. 30.00 (ISBN 0-670-74075-6, Studio). Viking Pr.

Hathaway, Richard B., jt. auth. see Ellinger, Herbert E.

Hathaway, Richard D. Sylvester Judd's New England. LC 81-17854. (Illus.). 362p. 1982. 18.50x (ISBN 0-271-00307-3). Pa St U Pr.

Hathaway, William. True Confessions & False Romances. 64p. 1972. 2.95 (ISBN 0-87886-013-4). Ithaca Hse.

--A Wilderness of Monkeys. 70p. 1975. 3.50 (ISBN 0-87886-072-X). Ithaca Hse.

Hathaway-Bates, John. How to Organize your Marketing. 162p. (Orig.). 1981. pap. 9.25 (ISBN 0-910333-01-7). Asigan Ltd.

--How to Promote your Business. 162p. (Orig.). 1981. pap. 9.25 (ISBN 0-910333-00-9). Asigan Ltd.

Hathcock, John, ed. Nutritional Toxicology, Vol. 1. LC 82-4036. (Nutrition: Basic & Applied Science Ser.). 1982. 57.00 (ISBN 0-12-332601-X). Acad Pr.

Hathorn, Raban, et al, eds. Marriage: An Interfaith Guide for All Couples. Date not set. 5.95 o.s.i. (ISBN 0-8096-1760-9). Follett.

Hathorne, B. C., jt. auth. see Resnik, H. L.

Hathrill, Robert. The Bell Ringer. 1983. 8.95 (ISBN 0-533-05631-4). Vantage.

Hatle, Liv & Angelsen, Bjorn. Doppler Ultrasound in Cardiology Physical Principles & Clinical Applications. LC 82-9974. (Illus.). 1982. text ed. 27.00 (ISBN 0-8121-0852-3). Lea & Febiger.

Hatlen, Burton, ed. George Oppen: Man & Poet. (Illus.). 514p. (Orig.). 1981. 28.50 (ISBN 0-915032-53-8); pap. 15.95 (ISBN 0-686-96804-2). Natl Poet Foun.

Hatlen, Theodore W. Orientation to the Theatre. 3rd ed. (Speech & Theatre Ser.). (Illus.). 512p. 1981. text ed. 17.95 (ISBN 0-13-642108-3). P-H.

Haton, Jean-Paul, ed. Automatic Analysis & Recognition of Speech. 1982. lib. bdg. 48.00 (ISBN 90-277-1443-6, Pub. by Reidel Holland). Kluwer Boston.

--Automatic Speech Analysis & Recognition. 1982. lib. bdg. 48.00 (ISBN 90-277-1443-6, Pub. by Reidel Holland). Kluwer Boston.

Hatry, Harry, jt. auth. see Schainblatt, Al.

Hatry, Harry, et al. Efficiency Measurement for Local Government Services: Some Initial Suggestions. 204p. pap. text ed. 6.50 (ISBN 0-87766-266-5). Urban Inst.

Hatry, Harry P., et al. Practical Program Evaluation for State & Local Governments. 2nd ed. LC 81-51346. 124p. 1981. pap. text ed. 7.50 (ISBN 0-87766-296-7, URI 32100). Urban Inst.

Hatsley, Nivessa R. Growing Down With Mama. 1983. 6.95 (ISBN 0-686-84440-8). Vantage.

Hatsukami, Dorothy & Pickens, Roy. Depression & Alcoholism. 1.50 (ISBN 0-89486-081-X, 1934B). Hazelden.

Hatt, Carolyn. The Maya: Based on the Edgar Cayce Readings. 67p. 1972. pap. 2.95 o.p. (ISBN 0-87604-059-8). ARE Pr.

Hatt, Gudmund. Moccasins & Their Relation to Arctic Footwear. LC 18-6197. 1916. pap. 12.00 (ISBN 0-527-00514-2). Kraus Repr.

--Notes on Reindeer Nomadism. LC 20-5783. 1919. pap. 8.00 (ISBN 0-527-00525-8). Kraus Repr.

Hatt, P. K., jt. auth. see Goode, William J.

Hattaway, Herman & Jones, Archer. How the North Won: A Military History of the Civil War. LC 81-16332. (Illus.). 780p. 1983. 24.95 (ISBN 0-252-00918-5). U of Ill Pr.

Hattaway, Michael. Elizabethan Popular Theatre: Plays in Performance. (Theatre Production Ser.). (Illus.). 220p. 1982. 27.95 (ISBN 0-7100-9052-8). Routledge & Kegan.

Hatten, John T., jt. auth. see Emerick, Lon L.

Hatten, Mary L. Macroeconomics for Management. (Illus.). 384p. 1981. text ed. 22.95 (ISBN 0-13-542498-4). P-H.

Hattery, Lowell H. Executive Control & Data Processing. 1959. 6.95 (ISBN 0-910136-03-3). Anderson Kramer.

Hattich, William. Tombstone. LC 80-5947. (Illus.). 64p. 1981. 12.95 (ISBN 0-8061-1753-2). U of Okla Pr.

Hattinga-Vershure. Changes in Caring for Health. 11.95 (ISBN 0-471-25758-3, Pub. by Wiley Heyden). Wiley.

Hatto, A. T., jt. auth. see Norman, F.

Hatton, E. M. The Tent Book. 1979. 18.95 o.p. (ISBN 0-395-27613-6); pap. 9.95 o.p. (ISBN 0-395-28264-0). HM.

Hatton, Edward. The Merchants Magazine or Trades-Man's Treasury. LC 82-48367. (Accountancy in Transition Ser.). 200p. 1982. lib. bdg. 22.00 (ISBN 0-8240-5318-4). Garland Pub.

Hatton, H. William III & Luis XIV. 342p. 1982. 49.00x (ISBN 0-85323-253-9, Pub. by Liverpool Univ England). State Mutual Bk.

Hatton, Hap, jt. auth. see Torbet, Laura.

Hatton, Joseph, ed. see Streeter, Edwin W.

Hatton, Richard G. Handbook of Plant & Floral Ornament from Early Herbals. 11.00 (ISBN 0-8446-2219-2). Peter Smith.

Hatton, Thomas J. Playwriting for Amateurs. Zapel, Arthur L., ed. LC 81-82438. (Illus.). 80p. (Orig.). 1981. pap. text ed. 6.95 (ISBN 0-916260-13-5). Meriwether Pub.

Hatton, Timothy. Three Tales of Imminent Dreams. 1978. 5.95 o.p. (ISBN 0-533-03420-5). Vantage.

Hatts, Leigh. Country Walks Around London. (Illus.). 160p. 1983. 18.95 (ISBN 0-7153-8439-2). David & Charles.

Hattum, Rolland J. Van see Van Hattum, Rolland J.

Hatvary, George E. Horace Binney Wallace. (United States Authors Ser.). 1977. lib. bdg. 12.95 (ISBN 0-8057-7190-5, Twayne). G K Hall.

--The Suitor. 192p. 1981. pap. 2.25 o.p. (ISBN 0-380-78188-3, 78188). Avon.

Hatzios, Kriton K. & Penner, Donald. Metabolism of Organic Herbicides in Higher Plants. LC 81-68903. 142p. (Orig.). 1982. text ed. 29.95x (ISBN 0-8087-2987-X). Burgess.

Hauberg, Clifford A. Puerto Rico & the Puerto Ricans. (Immigrant Heritage of America Ser). 1974. lib. bdg. 12.95 o.p. (ISBN 0-8057-3259-4, Twayne). G K Hall.

Haubrich, Vernon F. & Apple, Michael W., eds. Schooling & the Rights of Children. LC 74-24477. 200p. 1975. 19.95x (ISBN 0-8211-0755-0); text ed. 17.95x (ISBN 0-685-51464-1). McCutchan.

Hauck, Alice, et al. American Silver, 1670-1830: The Cornelius C. Moore Collection at Providence College. (Illus.). 156p. 1980. write for info. (ISBN 0-917012-18-6, Co-Pub. by Providence Coll). RI Pubns Soc.

Hauck, John W. The C, L & N: The Narrow Gauge in Ohio. (Illus.). 1983. price not set (ISBN 0-87108-629-8). Pruett.

Hauck, Paul. Brief Counseling with RET. pap. 11.95 (ISBN 0-686-36683-2). Inst Rat Liv.

Hauck, Paul A. How to Do What You Want to Do: The Art of Self Discipline. LC 76-15248. 1976. pap. 6.95 (ISBN 0-664-24122-0). Westminster.

--How to Stand up for Yourself. LC 78-15066. 1979. pap. 5.95 (ISBN 0-664-24223-5). Westminster.

--How to Stand Up for Yourself. 4.95 o.p. (ISBN 0-686-92354-5, 6449). Hazelden.

--Marriage Is a Loving Business. LC 77-2202. 1977. pap. 4.95 (ISBN 0-664-24137-9). Westminster.

--Marriage is a Loving Business. pap. 4.95 (ISBN 0-686-36807-X). Inst Rat Liv.

--Overcoming Depression. 4.25 o.p. (ISBN 0-686-92386-3, 6585). Hazelden.

--Overcoming Frustration & Anger. 4.95 o.p. (ISBN 0-686-92392-8, 6587). Hazelden.

--Overcoming Frustration & Anger. pap. 4.95 (ISBN 0-686-36775-8). Inst Rat Liv.

--Overcoming Jealousy & Possessiveness. LC 81-3040. 1981. pap. 5.95 (ISBN 0-664-24374-6). Westminster.

--Overcoming Jealousy & Possessiveness. pap. 6.95 (ISBN 0-686-36679-4). Inst Rat Liv.

--Overcoming Worry & Fear. 4.95 o.p. (ISBN 0-686-92394-4, 6589). Hazelden.

--Overcoming Worry & Fear. pap. 4.95 (ISBN 0-686-36777-4). Inst Rat Liv.

--The Rational Management of Children. 7.95 (ISBN 0-686-36823-1). Inst Rat Liv.

Hauck, Roland D. & Bystrom, Marcia. Fifteen N: A Selected Bibliography for Agricultural Scientists. 1970. 7.95x (ISBN 0-8138-0575-9). Iowa St U Pr.

Hauck, William, jt. auth. see Reigh, Mildred.

Hauenstein & Bachmeyer. Introduction to Communications Careers. (gr. 9-10). 1975. pap. text ed. 7.33 activity ed. (ISBN 0-87345-183-X). McKnight.

Hauer, et al. Autotransfusion. 1981. 38.00 (ISBN 0-444-00599-4). Elsevier.

Hauer, Christian E., Jr. Crisis & Conscience in the Middle East. 159p. 5.95 (ISBN 0-686-95156-5); pap. 2.45 (ISBN 0-686-99469-8). ADL.

Hauer, E. & Hurdle, V. F., eds. Transportation & Traffic Theory Eighth International Symposium. 744p. 1983. 35.00x (ISBN 0-8020-2461-0). U of Toronto Pr.

Hauer, Gerhard. Longing for Tenderness. 160p. (Orig.). 1983. pap. 4.95 (ISBN 0-87784-835-1). Inter-Varsity.

Hauer, Mary, et al. Books, Libraries, & Research. 1978. pap. text ed. 7.95 (ISBN 0-8403-1953-3, 40195303). Kendall-Hunt.

Hauerwas, Stanley. Responsibility for Devalued Persons: Ethical Interaction Between Society, the Family, & the Retarded. 122p. 1982. 14.75x (ISBN 0-398-04705-7). C C Thomas.

Hauerwas, Stanley & MacIntyre, Alasdair, eds. Revisions: Changing Perspectives in Moral Philosophy. (Revisions Ser.). 320p. 1983. text ed. 19.95 (ISBN 0-268-01614-3); pap. text ed. 9.95 (ISBN 0-268-01617-8). U of Notre Dame Pr.

Hauf, H. D., jt. auth. see Parker, Harry.

Hauf, Harold D. Building Contracts for Design & Construction. 2nd ed. LC 76-2701. 304p. 1976. 37.95 (ISBN 0-471-36003-1, Pub. by Wiley-Interscience). Wiley.

Hauf, Harold D., jt. auth. see Parker, Harry.

Haug, E. J. & Cea, J. Optimization of Distributed Parameter Structures, Vol. 1. 1981. 93.50 (ISBN 0-686-36957-2, Pub. by Martinus Nijhoff Netherlands). Kluwer Boston.

Haug, Edward J. & Arora, Jasbir S. Applied Optimal Design: Mechanical & Structural Systems. LC 79-11437. 1979. 44.95x (ISBN 0-471-04170-X, Pub. by Wiley-Interscience). Wiley.

Haug, F. M. Sulphide Silver Pattern & Cytoarchitectonics of Parahippocampal Areas in the Rat. (Advances in Anatomy, Embryology & Cell Biology: Vol. 52, Pt. 4). (Illus.). 1976. soft cover 21.30 o.p. (ISBN 0-387-07850-9). Springer-Verlag.

Haug, Marie, jt. auth. see Breslau, Lawrence.

Haug, Roger T. Compost Engineering Principles & Practice. LC 79-56119. (Illus.). 655p. 1980. 49.95 (ISBN 0-250-40347-1). Ann Arbor Science.

Haugan, Randolf E., ed. Christmas: An American Annual of Christmas Literature & Art, Vol. 45. LC 32-30914. (Illus.). 68p. (Orig.). 1975. 11.50 (ISBN 0-8066-8946-3, 17-0110); pap. 5.75 (ISBN 0-8066-8945-5, 17-0109). Augsburg.

Haugan, Randolph, ed. Christmas, Vol. 47. LC 32-30914. 1977. 11.50 (ISBN 0-8066-8951-X, 17-0115); pap. 5.75 (ISBN 0-8066-8950-1, 17-0114). Augsburg.

Haugan, Randolph E., ed. Christmas, an American Annual of Christmas Literature & Art, Vol. 50. LC 32-30914. (Illus.). 64p. 1980. 11.50 (ISBN 0-8066-8957-9); pap. 5.75 (ISBN 0-8066-8956-0). Augsburg.

--Christmas: An American Annual of Christmas & Art, Vol. 48. LC 32-30914. (Illus.). 1978. 11.50 (ISBN 0-8066-8953-6, 17-0117); pap. 5.75 (ISBN 0-8066-8952-8, 17-0116). Augsburg.

Hauge, Alfred. Cleng Peerson. (International Studies & Translations Ser.). 25.00 (ISBN 0-8057-8153-6, Twayne). G K Hall.

Hauge, Ragnar, jt. auth. see Brunn, Kettil.

Haugeland, John C., ed. Mind Design: Philosophy, Psychology & Artifical Intelligence. LC 81-24275. (Illus.). 368p. 1981. 24.50x (ISBN 0-262-08110-5, Pub. by Bradford); pap. text ed. 10.00 (ISBN 0-262-58052-7). MIT Pr.

Haugen, E. Beginning Norwegian: A Grammar & Reader. 3rd ed. 1957. text ed. 16.95 (ISBN 0-13-073239-7). P-H.

Haugen, Einar, jt. auth. see Haugen, Eva Lund.

Haugen, Einar, ed. & tr. see Dumezil, Georges.

Haugen, Eva Lund & Haugen, Einar. A Bibliography of Scandinavian Dictionaries. LC 82-48985. 300p. (Orig.). 1983. lib. bdg. write for info. (ISBN 0-527-38842-4). Kraus Intl.

Haugh, James B. Power & Influence in a Southern City: Compared with the Classic Community Power Studies of the Lynds, Hunter, Vidich & Bensman & Dahl. LC 80-5231. (Illus.). 160p. 1980. lib. bdg. 19.75 (ISBN 0-8191-1060-4); pap. text ed. 9.25 (ISBN 0-8191-1061-2). U Pr of Amer.

Haugh, Oscar M., jt. auth. see Anderson, Kenneth E.

Haugh, Robert F. Nadine Gordimer. (World Authors Ser.: South Africa: No. 315). 1974. lib. bdg. 13.95 o.p. (ISBN 0-8057-2387-0, Twayne). G K Hall.

Haughey, Betty E. William Penn: American Pioneer. (American Hero Biographies). (Illus.). (gr. 3-5). 1968. PLB 3.97 o.p. (ISBN 0-399-60671-8). Putnam Pub Group.

Haughey, John C. Conspiracy of God: The Holy Spirit in Men. LC 73-80730. 120p. 1976. pap. 2.95 (ISBN 0-385-11558-X, Im). Doubleday.

--Should Anyone Say Forever on Making, Keeping & Breaking Commitments. LC 74-12690. 1977. pap. 3.50 (ISBN 0-385-13261-1, Im). Doubleday.

Haught, J. J. Has Dr. Max Gerson a True Cancer Cure. 1.75x (ISBN 0-89041-272-3). Cancer Control Soc.

Haught, Jean. Ecstasy's Treasure. (Orig.). 1982. pap. 3.50 (ISBN 0-7217-1053-0). Zebra.

Haught, John F. Nature & Purpose. LC 80-5738. 131p. 1980. lib. bdg. 18.25 (ISBN 0-8191-1257-7); pap. text ed. 8.25 (ISBN 0-8191-1258-5). U Pr of Amer.

--Religion & Self-Acceptance: A Study of the Relationship Between Belief in God & the Desire to Know. LC 80-5872. 195p. 1980. lib. bdg. 19.50 (ISBN 0-8191-1296-8); pap. text ed. 9.50 (ISBN 0-8191-1297-6). U Pr of Amer.

Haughton, Joseph P. & Gillmoor, Desmond A. The Geography of Ireland. (Aspects of Ireland Ser.: Vol. 5). (Illus.). 59p. 1979. pap. 5.95 (ISBN 0-906404-05-3, Pub. by Dept Foreign Ireland). Irish Bks Media.

Haughton, Rosemary. The Catholic Thing. 1980. pap. 8.95 (ISBN 0-87243-116-9). Templegate.

--The Drama of Salvation. 154p. 1975. 2.50 (ISBN 0-8164-1201-4). Seabury.

--The Mystery of Sexuality. LC 72-82768. 84p. (Orig.). 1972. pap. 2.45 o.p. (ISBN 0-8091-1736-3, Deus). Paulist Pr.

Haughton, Victor M. & Williams, Alan L. Computed Tomography of the Spine. LC 81-18695. (Illus.). 288p. 1982. text ed. 49.50 o.p. (ISBN 0-8016-2118-6). Mosby.

Haugland, Vern. The Eagles' War: The Saga of the Eagle Squadron Pilots 1900-1945. LC 82-1766. 240p. 1982. 18.50 (ISBN 0-87668-495-9). Aronson.

Haugse, Vera L., jt. auth. see Lauerhass, Ludwig, Jr.

Haulice. Index of Artistic Biography, 2 Vols. 1973. 50.00 (ISBN 0-686-43143-X). Apollo.

--Index to Artistic Biography. Suppl. ed. Date not set. 60.00 (ISBN 0-686-43141-3). Apollo.

Haun, Connie M. Faraway Places. 1977. 6.95 o.p. (ISBN 0-533-02689-X). Vantage.

Haun, Donna H., jt. auth. see Fairweather, Brenda C.

Haun, Harry. The Movie Quote Book. LC 82-48799. (Illus.). 432p. (Orig.). 1983. pap. 8.61i (ISBN 0-06-091045-3, CN 1045, CN). Har-Row.

Hauner, Milan. Hitler: A Chronology of His Life & Time. LC 82-16718. 250p. 1982. 25.00x (ISBN 0-312-38816-0). St Martin.

Haupt, Georges, ed. see Medvedev, Roy A.

Haupt, R., et al. Introductory Physiology & Anatomy: A Laboratory Guide. 4th ed. 1977. pap. text ed. 13.95x (ISBN 0-02-351710-7). Macmillan.

Hauptly, Denis J. The Journey From the Past: A History of the Western World. LC 82-13740. (Illus.). 240p. (gr. 5-9). 1983. 12.95 (ISBN 0-689-30973-2). Atheneum.

Hauptman, jt. auth. see Fornes.

Hauptman, Herbert & Karle, Jerome. Solution of the Phase Problem, Pt. 1: The Centrosymmetric Crystal. pap. 3.00 (ISBN 0-686-60369-9). Polycrystal Bk Serv.

Hauptman, Terry. Rattle. 52p. saddle-stitched 4.00 (ISBN 0-943594-04-9). Cardinal Pr.

Hauptmann, Gerhart see Dent, Anthony.

Hauret, Charles. Beginnings: Genesis & Modern Science. McDonnell, John F., tr. 240p. 1978. pap. 6.95 o.p. (ISBN 0-87061-055-4). Chr Classics.

Haurwitz, B. Tidal Phenomena in the Upper Atmosphere. (Technical Note Ser.). 1964. pap. 6.00 (ISBN 0-685-22345-0, W27, WMO). Unipub.

Haury, Samuel S. Letters Concerning the Spread of the Gospel. (Missionary Studies: No. 8). 50p. 1982. pap. 3.95x (ISBN 0-8361-1252-0). Herald Pr.

Hausauer, Nancy. Nordic Heritage Northwest. Veirs, Christina, et al, eds. (Illus.). 160p. 1982. 24.95 (ISBN 0-686-83070-9); pap. 12.95 (ISBN 0-686-83071-7). Writing.

Hausbrandt, Andrzej. Tomaszewski's Mime Theatre. (Theatre, Film & Literature Ser.). (Illus.). 176p. 1977. 15.00 (ISBN 0-306-77436-4). Da Capo.

Hauschild, Jana. Danish Cross-Stitched Zodiac Samplers: Charted Designs for the Astrological Year. (Illus.). 1980. pap. 2.25 saddlewire (ISBN 0-486-24032-0). Dover.

Hausdorff, Felix. Set Theory. 2nd ed. LC 57-8493. 16.95 (ISBN 0-8284-0119-5). Chelsea Pub.

Hausen, Helmuth. Heat Transfer: In Counterflow, Parallel Flow & Cross Flow. 2nd ed. Wilmott, A. J. & Sayer, M. S., trs. from Ger. (Illus.). 544p. 1982. 59.50 (ISBN 0-07-027215-8, P&RB). McGraw.

Hauser, Gayelord. The Gayelord Hauser Cookbook. 320p. 1980. pap. 5.95 o.s.i. (ISBN 0-399-50475-3, Perige). Putnam Pub Group.

Hauser, Joan, ed. Manhattan Epicure. (Epicure Ser.). 160p. 1983. pap. 8.95 (ISBN 0-89716-123-8). Peanut Butter.

Hauser, John R., jt. auth. see Urban, Glen.

Hauser, Leopold, III. Five Steps to Success. (Orig.). 1983. pap. 3.75x (ISBN 0-935538-04-6). Pathway Bks.

Hauser, Nao, jt. auth. see Spitler, Sue.

Hauser, Philip M. Population Perspectives. LC 80-13915. (Illus.). 183p. 1980. Repr. of 1960 ed. lib. bdg. 19.00x (ISBN 0-313-22455-2, HAPU). Greenwood.

--Social Statistics in Use. LC 74-24747. 400p. 1975. 13.50x (ISBN 0-87154-375-3). Russell Sage.

Hauser, Philip M., et al. Population & the Urban Future. 174p. 1982. 39.50x (ISBN 0-87395-591-9); pap. 14.95x (ISBN 0-87395-592-7). State U NY Pr.

Hauser, Robert M., jt. auth. see Sewell, William H.

Hauser, Robert M, jt. ed. see Sewell, William H.

Hauser, Ronald. Georg Buchner. (World Authors Ser.). 1974. lib. bdg. 13.95 (ISBN 0-8057-2183-5, Twayne). G K Hall.

Hauser, Stuart T. & Kasendorf, E. Black & White Identity Formation. rev. ed. LC 82-16221. 1983. write for info. (ISBN 0-89874-055-X). Krieger.

Hauser, Thomas. The Trail of Patrolman Thomas Shea. 288p. pap. 3.50 (ISBN 0-380-62778-7, Discus). Avon.

Hauser, W. B. Economic Institutional Change in Tokugawa Japan: Osaka & the Kinai Cotton Trade. LC 73-80478. (Illus.). 320p. 1974. 37.50 (ISBN 0-521-20302-3). Cambridge U Pr.

Hauser, William E. Feedback Loop: A Real Estate Workbook. (Illus.). 35p. (Orig.). 1982. pap. 9.95x (ISBN 0-686-37158-5). Mission Pubns.

Hauser-Cram, Penny & Carrozza-Martin, Fay, eds. Essays on Educational Research: Methodology, Testing & Application. LC 82-84690. (Reprint Ser.: No. 16). 1983. 16.95 (ISBN 0-916690-19-9). Harvard Educ Rev.

Hauserman, Genevieve W. Loves from the Kitchen. 1978. 6.95 o.p. (ISBN 0-533-03254-7). Vantage.

Hausknecht, Richard & Heilman, Joan R. Having a Cesarean Baby: The Mother's Complete Guide for a Safe & Happy Cesarean Childbirth Experience. rev. ed. (Illus.). 208p. 1983. pap. 6.95 (ISBN 0-525-93266-6, 0704-210). Dutton.

Hausle, Vivian. Porcelain Porcelain Porcelain. (Illus.). 94p. 1981. 5.00 (ISBN 0-686-36027-3); pap. text ed. o.p. (ISBN 0-686-37272-7). Scott Pubns MI.

Hausman, Gerald, ed. see Barker, Elliott S.

Hausman, Gerald, ed. see Chavez, Fray A.

Hausman, Gerald, ed. see Grenfell, Cynthia.

Hausman, Gerald, ed. see Henderson, Eva P.

Hausman, Gerald, ed. see Irving, Blanche M.

Hausman, Gerald, ed. see Kloss, Phillips.

Hausman, Gerald, ed. see Lovato, Charles.

Hausman, Gerald, ed. see Ortiz y Pino, Jose, III.

Hausman, Gerald, ed. see Overhage, Carl.

Hausman, Gerald, ed. see Pomonis, Carolyn.

Hausman, Gerald, ed. see Price, Bren.

Hausman, Gerald, ed. see Thompson, Waite & Gottleib, Richard M.

Hausman, Jerome J. Arts & the Schools. (IDEA Study of Schooling in the United States Ser.). (Illus.). 332p. 1980. text ed. 17.95 (ISBN 0-07-027225-5). McGraw.

Hausman, Leon A. Beginner's Guide to Freshwater Life. (Putnam Beginner's Guide to Nature Ser.). (Illus.). 1950. 3.50 o.p. (ISBN 0-399-10078-4). Putnam Pub Group.

--Field Book of Eastern Birds. (Putnam Nature Field Bks.). (Illus.). 1946. 5.95 o.p. (ISBN 0-399-10287-6). Putnam Pub Group.

Hausman, Louis. Atlases of the Spinal Cord & Brainstem & the Forebrain: Atlas I. (Illus.). 68p. 1969. photocopy ed. spiral 9.50x (ISBN 0-398-00798-5). C C Thomas.

--Clinical Neuroanatomy, Neurophysiology & Neurology: With a Method of Brain Reconstruction. (Illus.). 484p. 1971. photocopy ed. spiral 48.50x (ISBN 0-398-00803-5). C C Thomas.

Hausman, Patricia. Jack Sprat's Legacy: The Science & Politics of Fat & Cholesterol. 320p. 1981. 12.95 (ISBN 0-399-90111-6, Marek). Putnam Pub Group.

--Jack Sprat's Legacy: The Science & Politics of Fat & Cholesterol. 288p. 1982. 6.95 (ISBN 0-686-95501-3). Ctr Sci Public.

Hausman, W. H., jt. auth. see Searle, S. R.

Hausner, Gideon. Justice in Jerusalem. LC 68-16363. 1978. pap. 6.95 (ISBN 0-8052-5003-4, Pub by Holocaust Library). Schocken.

--Justice in Jerusalem. (Illus.). 560p. pap. 6.95 (ISBN 0-686-95074-7). ADL.

Hausner, H. H. & Mal, M. K. Handbook of Powder Metallurgy. 2nd ed. (Illus.). 1982. 85.00 (ISBN 0-8206-0301-5). Chem Pub.

Hausner, Henry, ed. Modern Materials: Advances in Development & Applications. Incl. Vol. 1. 1958. o.p. (ISBN 0-12-462201-1); Vol. 2. 1960. 64.00 (ISBN 0-12-462202-X); Vol. 3. 1963. 64.00 (ISBN 0-12-462203-8); Vol. 4. Gonser, B. W. & Hausner, Henry H., eds. 1964. 64.00 (ISBN 0-12-462204-6); Vol. 5. Gonser, B. W., ed. 1965. o.p. (ISBN 0-12-462205-4); Vol. 6. 1968. 56.50 o.p. (ISBN 0-12-462206-2); Vol. 7. 1970. 64.00 (ISBN 0-12-462207-0). Acad Pr.

Hausner, Henry H. see Hausner, Henry.

Hausner, John H. Sebastian, the Essence of My Soul. (Illus.). 1982. 5.95 (ISBN 0-533-05510-5). Vantage.

Hausrath, A. H. Venture Simulation in War, Business & Politics. 1971. 34.95 o.p. (ISBN 0-07-027230-1, P&RB). McGraw.

Hauss, Charles. The New Left in France: The Unified Socialist Party. LC 77-94753. (Contributions in Political Science: No. 9). (Illus.). 1978. lib. bdg. 29.95 (ISBN 0-313-20113-7, HNL/). Greenwood.

Hausser, Doris L., et al. Survey-Guided Development II: A Manual for Consultants. rev. ed. LC 77-75523. 161p. 1977. pap. 11.50 (ISBN 0-88390-138-2). Univ Assocs.

Hauswedell, Marianne H., jt. auth. see Golay, Frank H.

Haut, Irwin H. The Talmud as Law or Literature: An Analysis of David W. Halivni's Mekorot Umasorot. x, 83p. pap. 6.95 (ISBN 0-87203-107-1). Hermon.

Hautala, Rick. Moonbog. 1982. pap. 2.95 (ISBN 0-8217-1087-7). Zebra.

Havard, William C. Henry Sidgwick & Later Utilitarian Political Philosophy. LC 59-15744. 1959. 7.50 o.p. (ISBN 0-8130-0106-4). U Presses Fla.

Havard, William C. & Bernd, Joseph L., eds. Two Hundred Years of the Republic in Retrospect. LC 76-45777. 348p. 1976. Repr. 13.95x (ISBN 0-8139-0690-3). U Pr of Va.

Havekamp, Katharina. The Empty Face. LC 78-12154. 1979. 8.95 o.p. (ISBN 0-399-90031-4, Marek). Putnam Pub Group.

Havelick, Franklin J., ed. Collective Bargaining: New Dimensions in Labor Relations. (Westview Special Study). 1979. lib. bdg. 27.50 (ISBN 0-89158-386-6). Westview.

Havelick, Joseph, Jr., jt. ed. see Tolley, George S.

Havelock, Mary C., jt. auth. see Havelock, Ronald G.

Havelock, Ronald G. & Havelock, Mary C. Training for Change Agents: A Guide to the Design of Training Programs in Education & Other Fields. LC 72-86337. 262p. 1973. 18.00x (ISBN 0-87944-126-7). Inst Soc Res.

Havelock, Ronald G., et al. Bibliography on Knowledge Utilization & Dissemination. rev. ed. LC 75-184872. 217p. 1972. pap. 6.00 o.s.i. (ISBN 0-87944-061-9). Inst Soc Res.

--Planning for Innovation Through Dissemination & Utilization of Knowledge. LC 78-634679. 538p. 1969. 24.00x (ISBN 0-87944-075-9). Inst Soc Res.

Haveman, Robert & Margolis, Julius. Public Expenditure & Policy Analysis. 3rd ed. LC 82-81354. 608p. pap. text ed. 18.95 (ISBN 0-686-82250-1). HM.

Haveman, Robert, jt. auth. see Burkhauser, Richard V.

Haveman, Robert H. The Economics of the Public Sector. 2nd ed. LC 76-186. (Introduction to Economics Ser). 224p. 1976. text ed. 9.95 (ISBN 0-471-36182-8, Pub. by Wiley-Hamilton). Wiley.

Havemann, Ernest, jt. auth. see Kagan, Jerome.

Havemen, Robert H. The Market System: An Introduction to Microeconomics. 4th ed. LC 80-21972. (Introduction to Economics Ser.). 280p. 1981. text ed. 16.50 (ISBN 0-471-08530-8); avail tchr's manual (ISBN 0-471-08531-6). Wiley.

Haven, Diana. Menus for Romance. (Candlelight Romance Cookbook Ser.). (Orig.). pap. 1.50 o.s.i. (ISBN 0-440-16169-X). Dell.

Haven, Josephine, jt. auth. see Haven, Richard.

Haven, Richard & Haven, Josephine. Samuel Taylor Coleridge: An Annotated Bibliography of Criticism & Scholarship, 1793-1899. 1976. lib. bdg. 31.00 (ISBN 0-8161-7829-1, Hall Reference). G K Hall.

Havener, Ivan & Karris, Robert J. First Thessalonians, Philippians, Philemon, Second Thessalonians, Colossians, Ephesians, No. 8. (Collegeville Bible Commentary Ser.). (Illus.). 112p. 1983. pap. 2.50 (ISBN 0-8146-1308-X). Liturgical Pr.

Havener, Ivan, et al, trs. Early Monastic Rules: The Rules of the Fathers & the Regula Orientalis. LC 82-51. 88p. (Orig.). 1982. pap. 5.95 (ISBN 0-8146-1251-2). Liturgical Pr.

Havenon, Andre de see De Havenon, Andre.

Havens, George. Abbe Prevost & English Literature. LC 65-15884. (Studies in Comparative Literature, No. 35). 1969. Repr. of 1921 ed. lib. bdg. 48.95x (ISBN 0-8383-0568-7). Haskell.

--Voltaire's Marginalia on the Pages of Rousseau: A Comparative Study of Ideas. LC 68-762. (Studies in French Literature, No. 45). 1969. Repr. of 1933 ed. lib. bdg. 49.95x (ISBN 0-8383-0695-0). Haskell.

Havens, George R. Abbe Prevost & English Literature. (Elliott Monographs: Vol. 9). 1921. pap. 15.00 (ISBN 0-527-02613-1). Kraus Repr.

--Jean-Jacques Rousseau. (World Authors Ser.: France: No. 471). 1978. lib. bdg. 10.95 o.p. (ISBN 0-8057-6312-0, Twayne). G K Hall.

Havens, Murray C. The Challenges to Democracy: Consensus & Extremism in American Politics. 119p. 3.75 o.p. (ISBN 0-686-95042-9); pap. 1.95 o.p. (ISBN 0-686-99453-1). ADL.

Havens, Robert I, jt. auth. see Morrison, Kenneth.

Haver, Jurgen F. Personalized Guide to Marketing Strategy. Snyder, Thomas L. & Felmeister, Charles J., eds. (Dental Practice Management Ser.). (Illus.). 118p. 1983. pap. text ed. 12.95 (ISBN 0-8016-4725-8). Mosby.

Haverkamp, J., jt. auth. see Meuzelaar, H. L.

Haverkate, H. Impositive Sentences in Spanish: Theory & Description in Linguistic Pragmatics. (Linguistic Ser.: Vol. 42). 1979. 38.50 (ISBN 0-444-85317-0, North Holland). Elsevier.

Havers, J. & Stubbs, F. Handbook of Heavy Construction. 2nd ed. 1971. 85.00 (ISBN 0-07-027278-6, P&RB). McGraw.

Haverson, M., jt. auth. see Beazley, E.

Haverson, Wayne W. & Haynes, Judith L. ESL-Literacy for Adult Learners. (Language in Education Ser.: No. 49). 72p. (Orig.). 1982. pap. 6.00x (ISBN 0-686-97844-7). Ctr Appl Ling.

Haviaris, Stratis. When the Tree Sings. 1979. 9.95 o.p. (ISBN 0-671-24754-9). S&S.

Havighurst, A. F. Modern England: 1901-1970. LC 75-23844. (Conference on British Studies Bibliographical Handbooks Ser.). 118p. 1976. 17.95 (ISBN 0-521-20941-2). Cambridge U Pr.

Havighurst, Alfred F. The Pirenne Thesis. 4th ed. (Problems in European Civilization Ser.). 236p. 1976. pap. text ed. 5.50 (ISBN 0-669-94680-X). Heath.

Havighurst, Clark. Deregulating the Health Care Industry: Planning for Competition. 520p. 1982. prof ref 37.50x (ISBN 0-88410-736-1). Ballinger Pub.

Havighurst, Robert J. & Moreira, J. Roberto. Society & Education in Brazil. LC 65-14298. (Pitt Latin American Ser). 1965. pap. 5.95x o.p. (ISBN 0-8229-5207-6). U of Pittsburgh Pr.

Havighurst, Robert J. & Morgan, Hugh G. Social History of a War-Boom Community. Repr. of 1951 ed. lib. bdg. 18.75x (ISBN 0-8371-0468-8, HAWC). Greenwood.

Havighurst, Robert J., jt. ed. see Levine, Daniel V.

Havighurst, Walter. Alexander Spotswood. LC 67-14348. (Williamsburg in America Ser.: Vol. 5). 1967. 3.95 o.p. (ISBN 0-910412-48-0). Williamsburg.

Havighurst, Walter, ed. Midwest & Great Plains. rev. ed. LC 78-54255. (United States Ser). (Illus.). (gr. 5 up). 1979. text ed. 9.93 1-4 copies (ISBN 0-88296-070-9); 5 or more 7.94 (ISBN 0-686-96718-6); tchrs'. annotated ed. 13.68 (ISBN 0-88296-347-3). Fideler.

Haviland, David. Managing Architectural Projects: Case Studies - Hansen, Lind, Meyer. 36p. 1981. pap. 8.50x (ISBN 0-913962-40-6). Am Inst Arch.

--Managing Architectural Projects: Case Studies - Moreland, Unruh, Smith. 36p. 1981. pap. 8.50x (ISBN 0-913962-39-2). Am Inst Arch.

--Managing Architectural Projects: Case Studies - Naramore, Bain, Brady, Johanson: The NBBJ Group. 36p. 1981. pap. 8.50x (ISBN 0-913962-41-4). Am Inst Arch.

--Managing Architectural Projects: The Effective Project Manager. 42p. 1981. pap. 12.50x (ISBN 0-686-81353-7). Am Inst Arch.

--Managing Architectural Projects: The Process. (Illus.). 112p. 1981. pap. 22.50x (ISBN 0-913962-31-7). Am Inst Arch.

Haviland, David S. Life Cycle Cost Analysis 2: Using It in Practice. LC 78-70466. (Illus.). 1978. pap. 20.00x (ISBN 0-913962-07-4). Am Inst Arch.

Haviland, David S., ed. Life Cycle Cost Analysis: A Guide for Architects. 1977. pap. 15.00x (ISBN 0-913962-21-X). Am Inst Arch.

Haviland, Diana. Proud Surrender. 384p. (Orig.). 1983. pap. 3.50 (ISBN 0-449-12406-1, GM). Fawcett.

Haviland, Jeannette & Scarborough, Hollis. Adolescent Development in Contemporary Society. 1980. text ed. 16.95 (ISBN 0-442-25862-3). Van Nos Reinhold.

Haviland, R. P. Build-It Book of Digital Electronic Timepieces. LC 77-79350. (Illus.). 1977. 9.95 o.p. (ISBN 0-8306-7905-7); pap. 6.95 (ISBN 0-8306-6905-1, 905). TAB Bks.

Haviland, Robert. Build-It Book of Miniature Test & Measurement Instruments. LC 75-41720. (Illus.). 238p. 1976. 7.95 o.p. (ISBN 0-8306-6792-X); pap. 4.95 o.p. (ISBN 0-8306-5792-4, 792). TAB Bks.

Haviland, Virginia. The Fairy Tale Treasury. (Illus.). 192p. 1980. 12.95 (ISBN 0-698-20184-1, Coward). Putnam Pub Group.

--The Fairy Tale Treasury. (Illus.). 192p. (gr. k-4). 1972. PLB 8.49 o.p. (ISBN 0-698-30438-1, Coward). Putnam Pub Group.

--Favorite Fairy Tales Told in France. (Illus.). (gr. 2-6). 1959. 6.95g o.p. (ISBN 0-316-35054-0); 6.95 o.p. (ISBN 0-316-35054-0). Little.

--Favorite Fairy Tales Told in India. LC 71-117019. (Illus.). 96p. (gr. k-3). 1973. 7.95g (ISBN 0-316-35055-9). Little.

--Favorite Fairy Tales Told in Spain. (Illus.). (gr. 3 up). 1963. 6.95 o.p. (ISBN 0-316-35047-8). Little.

--Favorite Fairy Tales Told in Sweden. (Illus.). (gr. 2-6). 1966. 6.95g o.p. (ISBN 0-316-35052-4). Little.

Haviland, Virginia, ed. North American Legends. (gr. 4 up). 1979. 9.95 o.p. (ISBN 0-399-20810-0, Philomel). Putnam Pub Group.

--The Openhearted Audience: Ten Authors Talk about Writing for Children. LC 79-15085. (Illus.). viii, 198p. 1980. 13.00 (ISBN 0-8444-0288-5). Lib Congress.

Haviland, William & Power, Morgory W. THe Original Vermonters: Native Inhabitants, Past & Present. LC 80-54465. (Illus.). 346p. 1981. 20.00 (ISBN 0-87451-196-8). U Pr of New Eng.

Haviland, William A. Excavations in Small Residential Groups of Tikal: Group 4F-1 & 4F-2. (Tikal Reports Ser.: No. 19). 1983. price not set. Univ Mus of U PA.

Haviland, William A. & Power, Marjory W. The Original Vermonters: Native Inhabitants, Past & Present. LC 80-54465. (Illus.). 346p. 1983. text ed. 12.95 (ISBN 0-87451-253-0). U Pr of New Eng.

Haviland, William A., jt. auth. see Coe, William R.

Haviland, William A., jt. auth. see Hewitt, Karen.

Havill, Steven. The Killer. LC 80-1987. (Double D Western Ser.). 192p. 1981. 10.95 o.p. (ISBN 0-385-17287-7). Doubleday.

Havingha, Gerhardus. Oorspronk en Voortgang der Orgelen met de Voortreffelijkheit van Alkmaars groote Orgel. (Bibliotheca Organologica Ser.: Vol. 13). 1981. Repr. of 1727 ed. wrappers 35.00 o.s.i. (ISBN 90-6027-253-6, Pub. by Frits Knuf Netherlands). Pendragon NY.

Havlice, Patricia P. World Painting Index: First Supplement 1973-1980, 2 vols. Incl. Vol. I. Bibliography, Paintings by Unknown Artists, Painters & Their Works; Vol. II. Titles of Works & Their Painters. LC 82-3355. 1233p. 1982. 62.50 (ISBN 0-8108-1531-1). Scarecrow.

Havner, Vance. Hope Thou in God. 128p. 1978. 8.95 (ISBN 0-8007-0902-0). Revell.

--In Times Like These. 128p. 1969. 8.95 (ISBN 0-8007-0160-7). Revell.

--Jesus Only. rev. ed. 128p. 6.95 o.p. (ISBN 0-8007-0165-8). Revell.

--Pleasant Paths. (Direction Bks.). 96p. 1983. pap. 2.95 (ISBN 0-8010-4268-2). Baker Bk.

--Secret of Christian Joy. 128p. 1938. 8.95 (ISBN 0-8007-0284-0). Revell.

--Though I Walk Through the Valley. 128p. 1974. 7.95 (ISBN 0-8007-0654-4). Revell.

--Vance Havner: Just a Preacher. 160p. 1981. pap. 4.95 (ISBN 0-8024-9142-1); 7.95 (ISBN 0-8024-9143-X). Moody.

Havoc, June. More Havoc. LC 79-2732. (Illus.). 1980. 13.41i (ISBN 0-06-011811-3, HarpT). Har-Row.

Havrella, Raymond. Heating, Ventilating & Air Conditioning Fundamentals. LC 80-17155. (Contemporary Construction Ser.). (Illus.). 288p. (gr. 10-12). 1981. text ed. 19.96x (ISBN 0-07-027281-6, G); wkbk. 11.96 (ISBN 0-07-027283-2). McGraw.

Havrilesky, Thomas M. & Boorman, John T. Monetary Macroeconomics. LC 77-85996. (Illus.). 1978. pap. text ed. 18.95x (ISBN 0-88295-401-6). Harlan Davidson.

Havrilesky, Thomas M., jt. auth. see Boorman, John T.

Havrilesky, Thomas M. & Schweitzer, Robert, eds. Contemporary Developments in Financial Institutions & Markets. LC 82-19901. (Illus.). 450p. 1983. pap. 18.95 (ISBN 0-88295-409-1). Harlan Davidson.

Havrylyshyn, Oil & Wolf, Martin. Trade Among Developing Countries: Theory, Policy Issues, & Principal Trends. (Working Paper: No. 479). iv, 112p. 1981. 5.00 (ISBN 0-686-36202-0, WP-0479). World Bank.

Hawa, Jean. Beirut! Beirut! 1983. 5.95 (ISBN 0-533-05424-9). Vantage.

Haward, Anne, ed. see Virgil.

Haward, R. N., ed. Developments in Polymerisation, Vols. 1 & 2. 1979. Vol. 1. 57.50 (ISBN 0-85334-822-7, Pub. by Applied Sci England); Vol. 2. 69.75 (ISBN 0-85334-821-9). Elsevier.

--Physics of Glassy Polymers. (Illus.). 620p. 1973. 88.25 (ISBN 0-85334-565-1, Pub. by Applied Sci England). Elsevier.

Hawarth, R. J., ed. Statistics & Data Analysis in Geochemical Prospecting. (Handbook of Exploration Geochemistry Ser.: Vol. 2). 438p. 1982. 100.00 (ISBN 0-444-42038-X). Elsevier.

Hawawini, Gabriel A., ed. Bond Duration & Immunization: Early Developments & Recent Contributions. LC 82-82490. (Accountancy in Transition Ser.). 322p. 1982. lib. bdg. 42.00 (ISBN 0-8240-5338-9). Garland Pub.

Hawbolt, E. B. & Mitchell, A. Materials to Supply the Energy Demand. 1981. 75.00 (ISBN 0-87170-114-6). ASM.

Haweis, E. The Art of Decoration. LC 76-17761. (Aesthetic Movement Ser.: Vol. 17). 1977. Repr. of 1889 ed. lib. bdg. 44.00x o.s.i. (ISBN 0-8240-2466-4). Garland Pub.

Hawes, Carolyn & Johnson, Margaret. Your Career in Art & Design. LC 76-41912. 1977. pap. 4.50 (ISBN 0-668-04141-2). Arco.

Hawes, Clair E. Couples Growing Together: A Leader's Guide for Couple Enrichment Study Groups. 2nd ed. 84p. 1982. pap. 7.00x (ISBN 0-939654-01-6). Social Interest.

Hawes, Elizabeth, jt. auth. see Stewart, Martha.

Hawes, Gene & Novalis, Peter. The New American Guide to Colleges. rev. ed. 1977. pap. 2.50 o.p. (ISBN 0-451-07298-7, E7298, Sig). NAL.

Hawes, Gene R. Careers Tomorrow. (Orig.). 1979. pap. 5.95 (ISBN 0-452-25318-7, Z5318, Plume). NAL.

Hawes, Gene R. & Hawes, Lynne Salop. Hawes Guide to Successful Study Skills: How to Earn High Marks in Your Courses & Tests. Date not set. pap. 5.95 (ISBN 0-452-25415-9, Z5415, Plume). NAL.

Hawes, Jon M. Retailing Strategies for Generic Brand Grocery Products. Farmer, Richard, ed. LC 82-17631. (Research for Business Decisions Ser.: No. 54). 190p. 1982. 39.95 (ISBN 0-8357-1376-8). Univ Microfilms.

Hawes, Joseph M. Children in Urban Society: Juvenile Delinquency in Nineteenth-Century America. (Urban Life in America Ser). 1971. 17.95x (ISBN 0-19-501410-3). Oxford U Pr.

Hawes, Judy. Bees & Beelines. LC 64-10864. (A Let's-Read-&-Find-Out Science Bk). (Illus.). (gr. k-3). 1964. bds. 6.95 o.p. (ISBN 0-690-12739-1, TYC-J); PLB 10.89 (ISBN 0-690-12740-5). Har-Row.

--Ladybug, Ladybug, Fly Away Home. LC 67-15399. (A Let's-Read-&-Find-Out Science Bk). (Illus.). (gr. k-3). 1967. bds. 6.95 o.p. (ISBN 0-690-48383-X, TYC-J); PLB 10.89 (ISBN 0-690-48384-8). Har-Row.

--My Daddy Longlegs. LC 74-175107. (A Let's-Read-&-Find-Out Science Bk). (Illus.). (gr. k-3). 1972. 10.53i (ISBN 0-690-56655-7, TYC-J); PLB 9.89 (ISBN 0-690-56656-5). Har-Row.

--Spring Peepers. LC 74-2038. (A Let's-Read-&-Find-Out Science Bk). (Illus.). (ps-3). 1975. 10.53i (ISBN 0-690-00522-9, TYC-J); PLB 10.89 (ISBN 0-690-00523-7). Har-Row.

--What I Like About Toads. LC 76-78262. (A Let's Read & Find Out Science Bk). (Illus.). (gr. k-3). 1969. PLB 10.89 (ISBN 0-690-87577-0, TYC-J). Har-Row.

Hawes, Louis. Presences of Nature: British Landscape 1780-1830. LC 82-50608. (Center for British Art Publication Ser.). (Illus.). 224p. 1982. text ed. 45.00x (ISBN 0-300-02930-6); pap. 17.95x (ISBN 0-300-02931-4). Yale U Pr.

Hawes, Lynne Salop, jt. auth. see Hawes, Gene R.

Hawes, Maurice A. Source Book on Gear Design, Technology & Performance. 1979. 46.00 (ISBN 0-87170-092-1). ASM.

Hawes, Stephen. The Works of Stephen Hawes. LC 75-14304. 400p. 1975. Repr. lib. bdg. 45.00x (ISBN 0-8201-1148-1). Schol Facsimiles.

Hawes, Vivian, jt. auth. see Hackenbroch, Yvonne.

Hawgood, J., ed. Evolutionary Information Systems: The Proceedings of IFIP TC Working Conference on Evolutionary Information Systems, 8, Budapest, Hungary, September 1-3, 1981. 256p. 1982. 32.00 (ISBN 0-444-86359-1). Elsevier.

Hawisher, Margaret, jt. auth. see Calhoun, Mary L.

Hawisher, Margaret F. & Calhoun, Mary L. The Resource Room: An Educational Asset for Children with Special Needs. (Special Education Ser.). 1978. pap. text ed. 12.95 (ISBN 0-675-08354-0). Additional supplements may be obtained from publisher. Merrill.

Hawk, Barry E. United States Antitrust Laws & Multinational Business. (Seven Springs Studies). 1982. pap. 3.00 (ISBN 0-943006-06-6). Seven Springs.

Hawk, Curtis E., jt. auth. see Tees, David W.

Hawk, Harold W., ed. Animal Reproduction. LC 78-65535. (Beltsville Symposia in Agricultural Research Ser.: No. 3). (Illus.). 446p. 1979. text ed. 27.50x o.p. (ISBN 0-686-85576-0). Allanheld.

Hawk, M. C. Descriptive Geometry. (Orig.). 1962. pap. 5.95 (ISBN 0-07-027290-5, SP). McGraw.

Hawke, D. M, tr. see Pellat, Charles.

Hawke, David F., ed. see Smith, John.

Hawken, Paul. The Nest Economy. (Illus.). 252p. 1983. 12.95 (ISBN 0-686-84860-8). HR&W.

--The Next Economy. (Illus.). 252p. Date not set. 12.95 (ISBN 0-03-062631-5). HR&W.

Hawken, William R. Close-Up Photography. (Illus.). 132p. (Orig.). 1982. pap. 10.95 (ISBN 0-930764-33-1). Curtin & London.

--You & Your Camera. (Illus.). 160p. 1977. pap. 6.95 (ISBN 0-8174-0560-7, Amphoto); Spanish Ed. pap. 9.95 o.p. (ISBN 0-686-66808-1). Watson-Guptill.

--You & Your Lenses. (Illus.). 144p. 1975. pap. 6.95 o.p. (ISBN 0-8174-0592-5, Amphoto). Watson-Guptill.

--You & Your Prints. (Illus.). 1978. 9.95 o.p. (ISBN 0-8174-2452-0, Amphoto); pap. 6.95 (ISBN 0-8174-2114-9). Watson-Guptill.

Hawker, Geoffrey. Who's Master, Who's Servant: Reforming Bureaucracy. 160p. 1981. 22.50x (ISBN 0-86861-075-5); pap. text ed. 12.50x (ISBN 0-686-85579-5). Allen Unwin.

Hawker, J. P., ed. Electronics Pocketbook. (gr. 11-12). text ed. 6.50x o.p. (ISBN 0-408-00047-3). Transatlantic.

Hawker, Lilian A. & Linton, Alan H., eds. Micro-Organisms. 2nd ed. 400p. 1979. pap. text ed. 24.95 o.p. (ISBN 0-8391-1308-0). Univ Park.

Hawker, Lilian E. Physiology of Fungi. (Illus.). 1968. Repr. of 1950 ed. 32.00 (ISBN 3-7682-0530-4). Lubrecht & Cramer.

Hawker, Peter. The Sportsman's Pocket Companion. 1982. pap. 125.00x (ISBN 0-686-94024-5, Pub. by A Atha Pub). State Mutual Bk.

Hawkes, Ann. Rose Kennedy. LC 74-83015. (See & Read Biographies). (Illus.). 64p. (gr. k-4). 1975. PLB 4.49 o.p. (ISBN 0-399-60921-0). Putnam Pub Group.

Hawkes, David, tr. see Cao, Xueqin.

Hawkes, David, tr. see Cao Xuequin.

Hawkes, Ellen & Manso, Peter. The Shadow of the Moth: A Novel of Espionage with Virginia Woolf. 272p. 1983. 12.95 (ISBN 0-312-71414-9). St Martin.

Hawkes, Glenn R., jt. auth. see Frost, Joe L.

Hawkes, J. Atlas of Ancient Archaeology. 1974. 32.95 (ISBN 0-07-027293-X, P&RB). McGraw.

Hawkes, J. G. The Diversity of Crop Plants. (Illus.). 208p. 1983. text ed. 20.00x (ISBN 0-674-21286-X). Harvard U Pr.

Hawkes, J. G., jt. ed. see Frankel, O. H.

Hawkes, J. G., et al, eds. Computer Mapped Flora: A Study of the County of Warwickshire. 1972. 69.00 o.p. (ISBN 0-12-333360-1). Acad Pr.

Hawkes, Jacquetta. Adventure in Archaeology: The Biography of Sir Mortimer Wheeler. (Illus.). 416p. 1982. 19.95 (ISBN 0-312-00658-6). St Martin.

--World of the Past, 2 vols. 1975. Vol. 1. pap. 5.95 o.p. (ISBN 0-671-22033-0, Touchstone Bks); Vol. 2. pap. 5.95 o.p. (ISBN 0-671-22034-9). S&S.

Hawkes, James, tr. see Wohmann, Gabriele.

Hawkes, Jean, tr. The London Journal of Flora Tristan 1842: The Aristocracy & the Working Class of England. 310p. 1983. pap. 7.95 (ISBN 0-86068-214-5, Virago Pr). Merrimack Bk Serv.

Hawkes, John. The Passion Artist. LC 79-1707. 1979. 11.49i (ISBN 0-06-011808-3, HarpT). Har-Row.

--Second Skin. LC 64-10674. 1964. pap. 4.95 (ISBN 0-8112-0067-1, NDP146). New Directions.

Hawkes, Nigel. Space Shuttle. (Inside Story Ser.). (Illus.). 40p. (gr. 4 up). 1983. PLB 9.90 (ISBN 0-531-04583-8). Watts.

Hawkes, P. W. Electron Optics & Electron Microscopy. 264p. 1972. write for info. (ISBN 0-85066-056-4, Pub. by Taylor & Francis). Intl Pubns Serv.

Hawkes, P. W. see Marton, L.

Hawkes, Susan & Wang, John L., eds. Extracellular Matrix: Symposium. LC 82-22631. 1982. 34.00 (ISBN 0-12-333320-2). Acad Pr.

Hawkes, Terence. Metaphor. (Critical Idiom Ser.). 1972. pap. 4.95x (ISBN 0-416-09030-3). Methuen Inc.

--Structuralism & Semiotics. LC 76-55560. 1977. 18.95x (ISBN 0-520-03398-1); pap. 5.95x (ISBN 0-520-03422-8). U of Cal Pr.

Hawkesworth, Eric. Puppet Shows to Make. 1972. 4.95 o.p. (ISBN 0-571-09836-3). Faber & Faber.

Hawkesworth, Jenny. The Lonely Skyscraper. LC 79-6703. (Illus.). 32p. (gr. 1-3). 1980. 9.95 o.p. (ISBN 0-385-15947-1); PLB 9.95 (ISBN 0-385-15948-X). Doubleday.

Hawkey, Nancy J., jt. auth. see Salerno, Nicolas A.

Hawkey, R. B. Newer Angles on Squash. 143p. 1973. 7.50 o.p. (ISBN 0-571-10259-X). Transatlantic.

Hawkey, Richard. Beginner's Guide to Squash. 141p. 1973. 14.50 o.p. (ISBN 0-7207-0682-3). Transatlantic.

Hawking, Stephen & Israel, W., eds. General Relativity: An Einstein Centenary Survey. LC 78-62112. (Illus.). 900p. 1980. pap. 32.50 (ISBN 0-521-29928-4). Cambridge U Pr.

Hawking, Stephen & Rocek, Martin, eds. Superspace & Supergravity. (Illus.). 500p. 1981. 54.50 (ISBN 0-521-23908-7). Cambridge U Pr.

Hawking, Steven & Ellis, G. F. The Large Scale Structure of Space-Time. LC 72-93671. (Illus.). 376p. 1973. 67.50 (ISBN 0-521-20016-4); pap. 27.95 (ISBN 0-521-09906-4). Cambridge U Pr.

Hawkins. Audio & Radio. (Electronic World Ser.). 32p. (gr. 5-9). 1982. 6.95 (ISBN 0-86020-642-4, Usborne-Hayes); PLB 9.95 (ISBN 0-88110-001-3); pap. 3.95 (ISBN 0-86020-641-6). EDC.

Hawkins & Higgins. Maternity & Gynecological Nursing: Women's Health Care. text ed. 19.00 (ISBN 0-686-97970-2, Lippincott Nursing). Lippincott.

Hawkins & Preston. Managerial Communication. 1981. text ed. 21.95x (ISBN 0-673-16543-4). Scott F.

Hawkins, A. D., jt. ed. see Schuijf, A.

Hawkins, Andrew, jt. auth. see Avon, Dennis.

Hawkins, Arthur. The Architectural Cookbook. LC 75-5090. (Illus.). 144p. 1975. pap. 6.00 o.p. (ISBN 0-915404-00-1, Architectural Rec Bks). McGraw.

Hawkins, Bobbie L. Almost Everything. (Illus.). 176p. 1982. 15.00 (ISBN 0-942986-00-8); pap. 7.00 (ISBN 0-942986-01-6). Longriver Bks.

Hawkins, Colin. Adding Animals. (Illus.). 12p. 1982. 9.95 (ISBN 0-399-20940-9). Putnam Pub Group.

Hawkins, D. F. Gynecological Therapeutics. 2nd ed. 1981. text ed. 37.50 (ISBN 0-02-858040-0, Bailliere-Tindall). Saunders.

--Obstetric Therapeutics: Clinical Pharmacology & Therapeutics in Obstetric Practice. (Illus.). 1974. text ed. 38.50 o.p. (ISBN 0-02-858030-3, Pub. by Bailliere-Tindall). Saunders.

Hawkins, D. F., jt. auth. see Elder, M. G.

Hawkins, D. M. Identification of Outliers. 200p. 1980. 27.50x (ISBN 0-412-21900-X, Pub. by Chapman & Hall England). Methuen Inc.

Hawkins, David, et al. Project Y: The Los Alamos Story. (History of Modern Physics 1800-1950 Ser.: Vol. 2). 1983. write for info limited edition (ISBN 0-938228-08-0). Tomash Pubs.

Hawkins, Del I., jt. auth. see Tull, Donald S.

Hawkins, Denis J. The Essentials of Theism. LC 72-9373. 151p. 1973. Repr. of 1949 ed. lib. bdg. 18.50x (ISBN 0-8371-6579-2, HAET). Greenwood.

Hawkins, Desmond. Avalon & Sedgemoor. 192p. 1982. pap. text ed. 9.50x (ISBN 0-86299-016-5, 10011, Pub. by Sutton England). Humanities.

--Concerning Agnes-Thomas Hardy's "Good Little Pupil". (Illus.). 160p. 1982. text ed. 16.75x (ISBN 0-904387-97-6, Pub. by Sutton England). Humanities.

Hawkins, Edward K. The Philippines: Aspects of the Financial Sector. ix, 99p. 1980. pap. 10.00 (ISBN 0-686-36115-6, RC-8006). World Bank.

--The Solomon Islands: An Introductory Economic Report. vii, 134p. 1980. pap. 10.00 (ISBN 0-686-36120-2, RC-8004). World Bank.

Hawkins, Elza M. From Now to Pentecost: A Mirrored View of Development in Christianity. 260p. (Orig.). 1982. pap. 11.00 (ISBN 971-10-0038-5, Pub. by New Day Philippines). Cellar.

Hawkins, Emily A. Pedagogical Grammar of Hawaiian: Recurrent Problems. 205p. 1982. pap. text ed. 6.00x (ISBN 0-8248-0812-6). UH Pr.

Hawkins, Eric. Modern Languages in the Curriculum. (Illus.). 200p. 1981. 32.50 (ISBN 0-521-23211-2). Cambridge U Pr.

Hawkins, Frank N., Jr. Ritter's Gold. (Orig.). 1980. pap. 1.95 o.p. (ISBN 0-451-09067-5, J9067, Sig). NAL.

Hawkins, G. A., jt. auth. see Jakob, Max.

Hawkins, George A., jt. auth. see Jones, James B.

Hawkins, George J. Military Madness. (Orig.). 1982. pap. 5.95 (ISBN 0-9609860-0-6). Hawkline Bks.

Hawkins, Gerald S., jt. auth. see Morrison, Tony.

Hawkins, Gordon, jt. auth. see Sherman, Michael.

Hawkins, Harry. Residential Wiring: Concepts & Practices. 1983. text ed. 16.95 (ISBN 0-534-01356-2). Breton Pubs.

Hawkins, Hugh. The Abolitionists: Means, Ends, & Motivations. 2nd ed. (Problems in American Civilization Ser). 1972. pap. text ed. 5.95 (ISBN 0-669-81992-1). Heath.

--Booker T. Washington & His Critics. 2nd ed. (Problems in American Civilization Ser.). 1974. pap. text ed. 5.95 (ISBN 0-669-87049-8). Heath.

Hawkins, J. W., jt. auth. see Thibodeau, J. A.

Hawkins, Jim, jt. auth. see Le Flore, Ron.

Hawkins, Jim W. Baton Twirling Is for Me. LC 82-245. (Sports for Me Bks.). (Illus.). 48p. (gr. 2-5). 1982. PLB 6.95g (ISBN 0-8225-1134-7). Lerner Pubns.

--Cheerleading is for Me. LC 81-3719. (Sports for Me Bks.). (Illus.). (gr. 2-5). 1981. PLB 6.95g (ISBN 0-8225-1127-4, AACRZ). Lerner Pubns.

Hawkins, John. Definiteness & Indefiniteness: A Study in Reference & Grammaticality Prediction. (Croom Helm Linguistics Ser.). 1978. text ed. 26.00x (ISBN 0-391-00880-3). Humanities.

Hawkins, John, jt. ed. see Kendall, Carl.

Hawkins, Judith, jt. auth. see Rogers, Maggie.

Hawkins, Laurence F. Notescript. (Orig.). 1964. pap. 2.95 o.p. (ISBN 0-06-463232-6, EH 232, EH). B&N NY.

Hawkins, Leslie V. Art Metal & Enameling. 234p. (gr. 9-12). 1974. text ed. 15.72 (ISBN 0-87002-157-5). Bennett IL.

Hawkins, M. D. Technician Safety & Laboratory Practice. 256p. 1980. 30.00x (ISBN 0-304-30550-2, Pub. by Cassell England). State Mutual Bk.

Hawkins, M. F., jt. auth. see Craft, Benjamin C.

Hawkins, Martin, jt. auth. see Escott, Colin.

Hawkins, Mary E., ed. see De Mente, Boye.

Hawkins, O. S. Clues to a Successful Life. LC 82-71561. (Orig.). 1982. pap. 5.95 (ISBN 0-8054-5515-9). Broadman.

Hawkins, P. Social Class: The Nominal Group & Verbal Strategies. (Primary Socialization, Language & Education Ser.). 1977. 24.50x (ISBN 0-7100-8375-0). Routledge & Kegan.

Hawkins, Peter. Guide to Antique Guns & Pistols. (Illus.). 32.50 o.s.i. (ISBN 0-912729-09-0). Newbury Bks.

Hawkins, Peter S. The Language of Grace. LC 82-72130. (Orig.). 1983. pap. 6.95 (ISBN 0-936384-07-7). Cowley Pubns.

Hawkins, Richard & Tiedman, Gary. The Creation of Deviance: Interpersonal & Organizational Determinants. new ed. (Sociology Ser). 320p. 1975. text ed. 17.95x o.p. (ISBN 0-675-08693-0). Merrill.

Hawkins, Richard, jt. auth. see Akers, Ronald L.

Hawkins, Robert A. Bible Songs for Children. 0.75 o.p. (ISBN 0-686-12693-9). Providential Pr.

Hawkins, Robert B., Jr., ed. American Federalism: A New Partnership for the Republic. LC 82-80329. 280p. 1982. pap. text ed. 7.95 (ISBN 0-917616-50-2). ICS Pr.

Hawkins, Robert G., ed. The Economic Effects of Multinational Corporations, Vol. 1. (Research in International Business & Finance Ser). 1979. lib. bdg. 42.50 (ISBN 0-89232-031-1). Jai Pr.

--Research in International Business & Finance, Vol. 1. 330p. 1979. 42.50 (ISBN 0-89232-031-1). Jai Pr.

--Research in International Business & Finance, Vol. 2. 350p. 1981. 42.50 (ISBN 0-89232-140-7). Jai Pr.

Hawkins, Robert O., Jr., jt. auth. see Moses, A. Elfin.

Hawkins, Robert P. & McGinnis, Lyn D. The School & Home Enrichment Program for Severely Handicapped Children. 350p. 1983. price not set (ISBN 0-87822-297-9). Res Press.

Hawkins, Susan, jt. auth. see Bleything, Dennis.

Hawkins, Thomas. Lebesgue's Theory of Integration: Its Origins & Development. 3rd ed. LC 74-8402. xv, 227p. 1975. text ed. 13.95 (ISBN 0-8284-0282-5). Chelsea Pub.

Hawkins, Tomas. Homiletica Practica. 1989. Repr. of 1978 ed. 1.75 (ISBN 0-311-42041-9). Casa Bautista.

Hawkins, W. Lincoln, ed. Polymer Stabilization. LC 70-154324. 1971. 68.95 (ISBN 0-471-36300-6, Pub. by Wiley-Interscience). Wiley.

Hawkinson, John. Old Stump. LC 65-23883. (Self Starter Bks.). (Illus.). (ps-2). 1965. 7.75 (ISBN 0-8075-5969-5). A Whitman.

Hawks, David, tr. see Cao Xuequin.

Hawks, Francis L., tr. see Rivero, Mariano E. & Von-Tschudi, John J.

Hawks, Linda, jt. auth. see Baudhuin, John.

Hawksworth. British Poultry: Standards. 4th ed. 1982. text ed. 49.95 (ISBN 0-408-70952-9). Butterworth.

Hawkweed Group. The Hawkweed Passive Solar House Book. (Illus.). 192p. 1980. 14.95 o.p. (ISBN 0-528-81107-X); pap. 8.95 (ISBN 0-528-88034-9). Rand.

Hawkyard, C. J. Chapter Two - Screen Printing. 75.00x (ISBN 0-686-98194-4, Pub. by Soc Dyers & Colour); pap. 50.00x (ISBN 0-686-98195-2). State Mutual Bk.

Hawley, Amos H. Urban Society: An Ecological Approach. 2nd ed. LC 80-17925. 383p. 1981. 19.95 (ISBN 0-471-05753-3). Wiley.

Hawley, G. G. Spanish-English, English-Spanish Dictionary of Chemisty & Chemical Products. 2nd, Rev. ed. 75.00 (ISBN 84-282-0418-7). Heinman.

Hawley, Gloria H. Frankly Feminine: God's Idea of Womanhood. LC 81-50348. 128p. (Orig.). 1981. pap. 3.50 (ISBN 0-87239-455-7, 2969). Standard Pub.

--Laura's Legacy. pap. 5.95 (ISBN 0-310-70251-8). Zondervan.

Hawley, Isabel L., jt. auth. see Hawley, Robert C.

Hawley, John S. Krishna, the Butter Thief. LC 82-61366. 400p. 1983. 40.00 (ISBN 0-691-06551-9). Princeton U Pr.

Hawley, Mones E., ed. Coal: Scientific & Technical Aspects. (Benchmark Papers on Energy: Vol. 4, Pt. 2). 1977. 60.50 (ISBN 0-12-786642-6). Acad Pr.

Hawley, Monroe E. Searching for a Better Way. 1980. pap. 5.35 (ISBN 0-89137-525-2). Quality Pubns.

Hawley, R., jt. auth. see Zaky, A. A.

Hawley, Robert C. Ten Steps for Motivating Reluctant Learners. 42p. (Orig.). pap. 3.95 (ISBN 0-913636-14-2). Educ Res MA.

--Value Exploration Through Role Playing. 124p. (Orig.). 1974. pap. 5.95 (ISBN 0-913636-03-7). Educ Res MA.

Hawley, Robert C. & Hawley, Isabel L. Human Values in the Classroom. 320p. 1975. 12.50 o.s.i. (ISBN 0-89104-237-7, A & W Visual Library); pap. 6.95 o.s.i. (ISBN 0-89104-236-9). A & W Pubs.

Hawley, Walter A. Oriental Rugs Antique & Modern. (Illus.). 1970. pap. 7.95 (ISBN 0-486-22366-3). Dover.

Hawley, Willis D., ed. Strategies for Effective Desegration: Lessons from Research. LC 82-47968. 224p. 1982. 23.95x (ISBN 0-669-05722-3); pap. 13.95 (ISBN 0-669-06376-2). Lexington Bks.

Hawley, Willis D. & Svara, James H., eds. The Study of Community Power: A Bibliographic Review. LC 72-83287. 123p. 1972. text ed. 17.50 o.p. (ISBN 0-87436-088-9); pap. text ed. 9.50 o.p. (ISBN 0-87436-089-7). ABC-Clio.

Haworth, Charles, jt. auth. see Rassmussen, David.

Haworth, J. T. & Smith, M. A., eds. Work and Leisure: An Inter-Disciplinary Study in Theory, Education, and Planning. 216p. 1983. Repr. of 1975 ed. pap. 9.95 (ISBN 0-86019-009-9, Pub. by Kimpton); 15.00. Princeton Bk Co.

Haworth-Booth, Mark, jt. ed. see Brandt, Bill.

Hawrylyshyn, Oli. The Economic Value of Household Services: An International Comparison of Empirical Estimates. 1980. cancelled o.p. (ISBN 0-03-023211-2). Praeger.

Hawrylyshyn, Oli, et al. Planning for Economic Development: The Construction & Use of a Multisectoral Model for Tunisia. LC 76-12857. 1976. 25.95 o.p. (ISBN 0-275-02300-1). Praeger.

Haws, Duncan. Merchant Fleets in Profile, Four: The Ships of the Hamburg-American, Adler & Carr Lines. 248p. 1980. 22.50 o.p. (ISBN 0-85059-397-2). Aztex.

--Merchant Fleets in Profile: The Ships of the Cunard, White Star Dominion, Alantic Transport, Leyland, Red Star & Inman Lines. (No. 2). (Illus.). 1979. 22.50 o.p. (ISBN 0-85059-324-7). Aztex.

--Merchant Fleets in Profile: The Ships of the P & O, Orient & Blue Anchor Lines. Gilliant, M., ed. (No. 1). (Illus.). 1979. 17.95 o.p. (ISBN 0-85059-319-0). Aztex.

Haws, E. S., et al. Interpretation of Proton Magnetic Resonance Spectra. 192p. 1979. 29.95 (ISBN 0-471-25762-1). Wiley.

Haws, Frank. InterAct: French & English in Canada. Renwick, George W., ed. LC 80-84804. (Country Orientation Ser.). 80p. (Orig.). Date not set. pap. text ed. 10.00x (ISBN 0-933662-20-3). Intercult Pr.

Hawsby & Chisholm. Cameras & Photography. (Beginner's Guides Ser.). (gr. 4-9). 1979. 5.95 (ISBN 0-86020-308-5, Usborne-Hayes); PLB 8.95 (ISBN 0-88110-033-1); pap. 2.95 (ISBN 0-86020-307-7). EDC.

Hawse, Alberta. Vinegar Boy. 1970. pap. 3.95 (ISBN 0-8024-9171-5). Moody.

Hawthorn, G. Enlightenment & Despair. LC 76-7803. 1976. 34.50 (ISBN 0-521-21308-8); pap. 10.95x (ISBN 0-521-29093-7). Cambridge U Pr.

Hawthorn, H. D. Maori: A Study in Acculturation. LC 44-47267. (American Anthropological Association Memoirs). Repr. of 1944 ed. pap. 13.00 (ISBN 0-527-00563-0). Kraus Repr.

Hawthorn, J. Virginia Woolf's "Mrs. Dalloway". A Study in Alienation. 20.00x (ISBN 0-686-97031-4, Pub. by Scottish Academic Pr Scotland). State Mutual Bk.

Hawthorn, J., jt. auth. see Corner, J.

Hawthorne, Charles W. Hawthorne on Painting. 1938. pap. 2.25 (ISBN 0-486-20653-X). Dover.

Hawthorne, Clive. Poems & Translations. LC 79-51457. (Illus.). 1983. pap. 8.00 (ISBN 0-912908-07-6). Tamal Land.

Hawthorne, D. G., jt. auth. see Solomon, D. H.

Hawthorne, Lesleyanne. Refugee: The Vietnamese Experience. 288p. 1982. 49.00x (ISBN 0-19-554338-6). Oxford U Pr.

Hawthorne, Minnie. Here We Go Again Lord. 1982. 4.50 (ISBN 0-8062-1659-X). Carlton.

Hawthorne, Nathaniel. Blithedale Romance. 1958. pap. 2.45 (ISBN 0-393-00164-4, N164, Norton Lib). Norton.

--Celestial Railroad & Other Stories. pap. 2.50 (ISBN 0-451-51641-9, CE1641, Sig Classics). NAL.

--The Complete Novels & Selected Tales of Nathaniel Hawthorne. Pearson, Norman H., ed. & intro. by. 10.95 (ISBN 0-394-60404-0). Modern Lib.

--Great Short Works of Nathaniel Hawthorne. Crews, Frederick C., ed. pap. 3.50i (ISBN 0-06-083074-3, P3074, PL). Har-Row.

--Hawthorne's Lost Notebook, Eighteen Thirty-Five to Eighteen Forty-One. Waggoner, Hyatt H. & Mouffe, Barbara S., eds. LC 78-50772. 1978. 15.95x (ISBN 0-271-00549-1). Pa St U Pr.

--House of the Seven Gables. (Bantam Classics Ser.). 245p. (gr. 7-12). 1981. pap. 1.50 (ISBN 0-553-21010-6). Bantam.

--House of the Seven Gables. rev. ed. Dixson, Robert J., ed. (American Classics Ser.: Bk. 1). 113p. (gr. 9 up). 1973. pap. 3.25 (ISBN 0-88345-197-2, 18120); cassettes 40.00 (ISBN 0-685-38988-X); 40.00 o.p. tapes (ISBN 0-685-38989-8). Regents Pub.

--Marble Faun. (Classics Ser). (gr. 11 up). pap. 1.95 (ISBN 0-8049-0104-X, CL-104). Airmont.

--Marble Faun. pap. 2.95 (ISBN 0-451-51771-7, CE1771, Sig Classics). NAL.

--Mosses from an Old Manse. Charvat, William, et al, eds. LC 73-5364. (Centenary Edition of the Works of Nathaniel Hawthorne: Vol. 10). 1974. 30.00 (ISBN 0-8142-0203-9). Ohio St U Pr.

--Novels. Bell, Millicent, ed. LC 82-18031. 1272p. 1983. 25.00 (ISBN 0-940450-08-9). Literary Classics.

--Our Old Home. Charvat, William, et al, eds. LC 75-92336. (Centenary Edition of the Works of Nathaniel Hawthorne: Vol. 5). (Illus.). 1970. 22.50 (ISBN 0-8142-0002-8). Ohio St U Pr.

--Pandora's Box. (Illus.). (gr. 2-6). 1967. PLB 5.72 o.p. (ISBN 0-07-027318-9, GB). McGraw.

--The Portable Hawthorne. rev. ed. Cowley, Malcolm, ed. (Portable Library: No. 38). 1969. 18.75 (ISBN 0-670-36404-5). Viking Pr.

--The Scarlet Letter. Rajan, B. & George, A. G., eds. Bd. with The Life of Hawthorne. James, Henry. 7.95x o.p. (ISBN 0-210-26920-0). Asia.

--The Scarlet Letter. Spector, Robert D., ed. (Bantam Classics Ser.). 245p. (Orig., Incl. analysis & background material). (gr. 8-12,RL 8). 1981. pap. 1.50 (ISBN 0-553-21009-2, 13104-4). Bantam.

--Scarlet Letter. Levin, H., ed. (Riverside Library). 5.95 o.s.i. (ISBN 0-395-08128-9). HM.

--Scarlet Letter. New ed. 1981. pap. 4.95 (ISBN 0-394-30921-9, T21, Mod LibC). Modern Lib.

--Scarlet Letter. (RL 10). pap. 1.50 (ISBN 0-451-51652-4, CW1652, Sig Classics). NAL.

--The Scarlet Letter. Charvat, William, et al, eds. (Centenary Edition of the Works of Nathaniel Hawthorne: Vol. 1). (Illus.). 1963. 20.00 (ISBN 0-8142-0059-1). Ohio St U Pr.

--The Scarlet Letter. 1983. pap. 2.50 (ISBN 0-14-039019-7). Penguin.

--The Scarlet Letter & Selected Tales. Connolly, Thomas E., ed. (English Library Ser). 1978. pap. 2.25 (ISBN 0-14-043052-0). Penguin.

--Tanglewood Tales. (Companion Lib.). (Illus.). (gr. 4-9). 1967. 2.95 (ISBN 0-448-05486-8, G&D). Putnam Pub Group.

--Twice-Told Tales. Charvat, William, et al, eds. LC 73-5363. (Centenary Edition of the Works of Nathaniel Hawthorne: Vol. 9). 1974. 30.00 (ISBN 0-8142-0202-0). Ohio St U Pr.

--Wonder Book & Tanglewood Tales. Charvat, William, et al, eds. LC 77-150221. (Centenary Edition of the Works of Nathaniel Hawthorne: Vol. 7). (Illus.). (gr. 5 up). 1972. 25.00 (ISBN 0-8142-0158-X). Ohio St U Pr.

Hawthorne, Steven C., jt. ed. see Winter, Ralph D.

Hawton, Hector. Why Be Moral? 23p. 1947. pap. 3.00 (ISBN 0-686-96424-1). Am Atheist.

Hawton, Keith & Catalan, Jose. Attempted Suicide: A Practical Guide to its Nature & Management. (Illus.). 150p. 1982. 14.95 (ISBN 0-19-261289-1). Oxford U Pr.

Hawtrey, Ralph. Commentary on Plato's Euthydemos. (Memoirs Ser.: Vol. 147). 1982. pap. 10.00 (ISBN 0-686-73984-1). Am Philos.

Hawtrey, Ralph G. Art of Central Banking. 2nd ed. 484p. 1962. 35.00x (ISBN 0-7146-1227-8, F Cass Co). Biblio Dist.

--Century of Bank Rate. 2nd ed. 328p. 1962. 35.00x (ISBN 0-7146-1228-6, F Cass Co). Biblio Dist.

Hax, A. Studies in Operations Management. (Studies in Management Science & Systems Ser.: Vol. 6). 1979. 81.50 (ISBN 0-444-85161-5, North Holland). Elsevier.

Haxthausen, August Von. Etudes sur la Situation Interieure, la Vie Nationale et les Institutions de la Russie, 3 vols. (Nineteenth Century Russia Ser.). (French.). 1974. Repr. of 1847 ed. Set. lib. bdg. 436.50x o.p. (ISBN 0-8287-0419-8). Clearwater Pub.

Hay, Alastair. The Chemical Scythe: The Lessons of 2, 4, 5-T & Dioxin. LC 82-12249. (Disaster Research in Practice Ser.). 250p. 1982. 27.50x (ISBN 0-306-40973-9, Plenum Pr). Plenum Pub.

Hay, Camillus. The Eucharist in the Churches. 1976. pap. 2.50 o.p. (ISBN 0-685-77521-6). Franciscan Herald.

Hay, Carla H. James Burgh, Spokesman for Reform in Hanoverian England. LC 79-89204. 1979. pap. text ed. 9.75 (ISBN 0-8191-0800-6). U Pr of Amer.

Hay, D. The Medieval Centuries. 1964. pap. 7.95x (ISBN 0-416-68270-7). Methuen Inc.

Hay, David E. & Howell, James F. Contact with Drama. LC 73-88146. (Illus.). 576p. 1974. pap. text ed. 12.95 (ISBN 0-574-19020-1, 13-2020). SRA.

Hay, Deborah. Moving Through the Universe in Bare Feet: Ten Circle Dances for Everybody. 2nd ed. LC 82-73799. (Illus.). 234p. 1975. pap. 6.95 (ISBN 0-8040-0686-5). Swallow.

Hay, Dennis, jt. auth. see Hall, Peter.

Hay, Denys. The Church in Italy in the Fifteenth Century. LC 76-47409. (Birkbeck Lectures: 1971). 1977. 34.50 (ISBN 0-521-21532-3). Cambridge U Pr.

--Italian Renaissance in Its Historical Background. 2nd ed. (Illus.). 1977. 39.50 (ISBN 0-521-21321-5); pap. 9.95 (ISBN 0-521-29104-6). Cambridge U Pr.

Hay, Donald A. & Morris, Derek J. Industrial Economics: Theory & Evidence. (Illus.). 1979. text ed. 45.00x (ISBN 0-19-877112-6); pap. text ed. 16.95x (ISBN 0-19-877113-4). Oxford U Pr.

Hay, Edward A., jt. auth. see McAlester, A. Lee.

Hay, Eloise K. T. S. Eliot's Negative Way. 224p. 1982. text ed. 17.50x (ISBN 0-674-24675-6). Harvard U Pr.

Hay, George. Architecture of Scotland. (Oriel Guides). (Illus.). 11.50 o.p. (ISBN 0-85362-038-5, Oriel). Routledge & Kegan.

--Two Essays on the Liberty of the Press. LC 75-112703. (Civil Liberties in American History Ser). 1970. Repr. of 1803 ed. lib. bdg. 19.50 (ISBN 0-306-71918-5). Da Capo.

Hay, Gilbert. Golden Harvest. LC 76-56297. (Illus.). 1979. 10.95 (ISBN 0-385-12747-2). Doubleday.

Hay, Harold, jt. auth. see Chandra, Subrato.

Hay, Henry. The Amateur Magician's Handbook. 4th, rev. ed. LC 72-78265. (Illus.). 400p. 1982. 16.30i (ISBN 0-06-014865-9). T Y Crowell.

--Learn Magic. LC 74-80337. (Illus.). 320p. 1975. Repr. of 1947 ed. 4.50 (ISBN 0-486-21238-6). Dover.

--Learn Magic. LC 74-80337. 1975. lib. bdg. 11.50x (ISBN 0-88307-542-3). Gannon.

Hay, J. Biomechanics of Sports Techniques. 2nd ed. 1978. 23.95 (ISBN 0-13-077164-3). P-H.

Hay, J. R. The Development of the British Welfare State, 1880-1975. LC 77-28671. 1978. 25.00 (ISBN 0-312-19749-7). St Martin.

Hay, J. Thomas. Five Hundred & Thirty-Four Ways to Raise Money. 256p. 1983. 15.95 (ISBN 0-671-47167-8); pap. 7.95 (ISBN 0-671-47286-0). S&S.

Hay, James G. & Reid, J. Gavin. The Anatomical & Mechanical Bases of Human Motion. (Illus.). 432p. 1982. text ed. 21.95 (ISBN 0-13-035139-3). P-H.

Hay, John. Oedipus Tyrannus: Lame Knowledge & the Homosporic Womb. LC 78-57075. 1978. pap. text ed. 9.50 (ISBN 0-8191-0518-X). U Pr of Amer.

--The Run. (General Ser.). 1980. lib. bdg. 9.95 (ISBN 0-8161-3019-1, Large Print Bks). G K Hall.

Hay, Keith A. Canadian Perspectives on Economic Relations with Japan. 381p. 1980. pap. text ed. 18.95x (ISBN 0-920380-72-7, Inst Res Pub Canada). Renouf.

Hay, Kenneth, ed. see Madders, Jane.

Hay, Malcolm. The Roots of Christian Anti-Semitism. 356p. 10.00 (ISBN 0-686-95112-3). ADL.

Hay, Malcolm & Roberts, Philip. Bond: A Study of His Plays. 320p. 1981. 24.95x o.p. (ISBN 0-413-38290-7); pap. 10.95 (ISBN 0-413-47060-1). Methuen Inc.

Hay, P. An Introduction to United States Law. 1976. text ed. 47.00 (ISBN 0-444-11059-3, North-Holland); pap. text ed. 20.00 o.p. (ISBN 0-444-11091-7). Elsevier.

Hay, Peter & Rotunda, Ronald D. The United States Federal System: Legal Integration in the American Federal Experience. (Studies in Comparative Law: No. 22). Date not set. lib. bdg. 35.00 (ISBN 0-379-20800-8). Oceana.

Hay, Peter, jt. auth. see Scoles, Eugene F.

Hay, Richard, jt. ed. see Abu-Lughod, Janet.

Hay, Richard L. Geology of the Olduvai Gorge: A Study of Sedimentation in a Semiarid Basin. LC 74-29804. 1976. 47.50x (ISBN 0-520-02963-1). U of Cal Pr.

Hay, Robert D., jt. auth. see Broyles, J. Frank.

Hay, Robert K. Chemistry for Agriculture & Ecology. (Illus.). 240p. 1981. pap. text ed. 13.95 (ISBN 0-632-00699-4, B 2114-3). Mosby.

Hay, Roy & Synge, Patrick M. The Color Dictionary of Flowers & Plants for Home & Garden. (Illus.). 373p. 1969. 15.00 o.p. (ISBN 0-517-50670-X); pap. 14.95 o.p. (ISBN 0-517-52458-9). Crown.

Hay, Sara H. Story Hour. LC 84-4898. 48p. 1982. 10.95 (ISBN 0-938626-08-6); pap. 6.95 (ISBN 0-938626-11-6). U of Ark Pr.

Hay, Suzanne. Savage Destiny. 1979. pap. 2.25 o.s.i. (ISBN 0-515-04891-7). Jove Pubns.

Hay, William H. Railroad Engineering, Vol. 1. 2nd ed. LC 81-23117. 784p. 1982. 47.50x (ISBN 0-471-36400-2, Pub. by Wiley-Interscience). Wiley.

Hay, William H. & Nathan, Peter E., eds. Clinical Case Studies in the Behavioral Treatment of Alcoholism. 324p. 1982. 27.50x (ISBN 0-306-40940-2, Plenum Pr). Plenum Pub.

Hay, William W. An Introduction to Transportation Engineering. 2nd ed. LC 77-9293. 1977. text ed. 40.95x (ISBN 0-471-36433-9). Wiley.

Hayaischi, O. & Ishimura, Y., eds. Biochemical & Medical Aspects of Tryptophan Metabolism. (Development in Biochemistry Ser.: Vol. 16). 1981. 67.25 (ISBN 0-444-80297-5). Elsevier.

Hayaishi, O., jt. auth. see Suda, M.

Hayaishi, Osamu, ed. Enzyme Mechanisms. (Selected Papers in Biochemistry: Vol. 11). (Illus.). 1973. 29.50 o.p. (ISBN 0-8391-0621-1). Univ Park.

Hayaishi, Osamu & Ueda, Kunihiro, eds. ADP-Ribosylation Reactions: Biology & Medicine. (Molecular Biology Ser.). 674p. 1982. 67.50 (ISBN 0-12-333660-0). Acad Pr.

Hayakawa, S. Cosmic Ray Physics: Nuclear & Astrophysical Aspects. LC 69-19930. (Monographs & Texts in Physics & Astronomy Ser: Vol. 22). 774p. 1969. text ed. 44.50 o.p. (ISBN 0-471-36320-0, Pub. by Wiley). Krieger.

Hayakawa, T., jt. auth. see Siotani, Minoru.

Hayami, Yujiro, et al, eds. Agricultural Growth in Japan, Taiwan, Korea & the Philippines. LC 77-26817. 1979. text ed. 15.00x (ISBN 0-8248-0391-4, Eastwest Ctr); pap. text ed. 10.00x (ISBN 0-8248-0613-1, Eastwest Ctr). UH Pr.

Hayashi, Hiroko, jt. auth. see Cook, Alice H.

Hayashi, Tetsumaro. William Faulkner: Research Opportunities & Dissertation Abstracts. LC 82-15236. 336p. 1982. lib. bdg. 29.95x (ISBN 0-89950-048-X). McFarland & Co.

Hayashi, Tetsuro. The Theory of English Lexicography 1530-1791. (Studies in the History of Linguistics Ser.). xii, 168p. 1978. 21.00 (ISBN 90-272-0959-6, 18). Benjamins North Am.

Hayashida, Nelson O. Stormy Road for This Pilgrim. 1978. 4.95 o.p. (ISBN 0-533-03031-5). Vantage.

Hayasi, Shoji & Murao, Satoru, eds. Cardiology: Proceedings of the 8th Congress in Tokyo, Sept. 1978. (International Congress Ser.: No. 470). 1980. 208.00 (ISBN 0-444-90071-3). Elsevier.

Hayat, M. A. Introduction to Biological Scanning Electron Microscopy. LC 77-17783. 320p. 1977. pap. 24.95 o.p. (ISBN 0-8391-1173-8). Univ Park.

--X-Ray Micro-Analysis in Biology. 496p. 1980. text ed. 49.50 (ISBN 0-8391-1511-3). Univ Park.

Haycock, G. Sibley. The Teaching of Speech. 1933. pap. text ed. 9.95 (ISBN 0-88200-087-X, A1886). Alexander Graham.

Haycock, Ken & Isberg, Lynne, eds. Sears List of Subject Headings: Canadian Companion. 50p. 1978. 5.50 o.p. (ISBN 0-8242-0629-0). Wilson.

Haycox, Ernest. Action by Night. 1978. pap. 1.50 o.p. (ISBN 0-451-08297-4, W8297, Sig). NAL.

--The Border Trumpet. 1978. lib. bdg. 8.95 (ISBN 0-8398-2474-2, Gregg). G K Hall.

--Bugles in the Afternoon. 1978. lib. bdg. 9.95 (ISBN 0-8398-2473-4, Gregg). G K Hall.

--Bugles in the Afternoon. 1982. pap. 2.25 (ISBN 0-451-11467-1, AE1467, Sig). NAL.

--Canyon Passage. 1979. lib. bdg. 9.95 (ISBN 0-8398-2575-7, Gregg). G K Hall.

--Canyon Passage. 1982. pap. 2.25 (ISBN 0-451-11782-4, AE1782, Sig). NAL.

--Chaffee of Roaring Horse. 1982. pap. 1.95 (ISBN 0-451-11424-8, AJ1424, Sig). NAL.

--Deep West. 1982. pap. 2.25 (ISBN 0-451-11883-9, AE1883, Sig). NAL.

--The Earthbreakers. 1979. lib. bdg. 9.95 (ISBN 0-8398-2576-5, Gregg). G K Hall.

--Free Grass. 1982. pap. 2.25 (ISBN 0-451-11838-3, AE1838, Sig). NAL.

--Head of the Mountain. 1977. lib. bdg. 10.50 o.p. (ISBN 0-8161-6534-3, Large Print Bks). G K Hall.

--Return of a Fighter. 1980. pap. 1.75 (ISBN 0-451-09419-0, E9419, Sig). NAL.

--A Rider of the High Mesa. 1979. pap. 1.50 o.p. (ISBN 0-451-08962-6, W8962, Sig). NAL.

--Stagecoach & Other Stories. (Westerns Ser.). 1981. lib. bdg. cancelled o.s.i. (ISBN 0-8398-2677-X, Gregg). G K Hall.

--Sundown Jim. (General Ser.). 1982. lib. bdg. 13.95 (ISBN 0-8161-3357-3, Large Print Bks). G K Hall.

--Trail Smoke. 1982. pap. 1.95 (ISBN 0-451-11282-2, AJ1282, Sig). NAL.

--The Wild Brunch. (General Ser.). 1983. lib. bdg. 14.95 (ISBN 0-8161-3443-X, Large Print Bks). G K Hall.

Haycraft, B. The Teaching of Pronunciation. (Longman Handbooks for Language Teachers). 1975. pap. text ed. 8.75x (ISBN 0-582-52434-2). Longman.

Haycraft, Brita & Lee, W. R. It Depends on How You Say It: Dialogues in Everyday Social English. LC 80-41174. (Illus.). 128p. 1982. 14.00 (ISBN 0-08-025315-6); pap. 4.95 (ISBN 0-08-025314-8). Pergamon.

Haycraft, Howard, ed. Boys' Second Book of Great Detective Stories. LC 40-7099. (gr. 7 up). 1940. 12.45i (ISBN 0-06-022255-7, HarpJ); PLB 12.89 (ISBN 0-06-022256-5). Har-Row.

Haycraft, Howard, jt. ed. see Kunitz, Stanley J.

Haycroft, W. C. Book of Panther H-WT. pap. 5.00x (ISBN 0-392-02335-0, SpS). Sportshelf.

--Book of the A. J. S. pap. 5.00x (ISBN 0-392-13562-0, SpS). Sportshelf.

--Book of the Royal Enfield. pap. 5.00x (ISBN 0-392-02349-0, SpS). Sportshelf.

Hayden, Alice H., jt. ed. see Haring, Norris G.

Hayden, Arthur. Chats on Old Silver. (Chats Ser: Practical Handbooks for Collectors). (Illus.). 1970. pap. 4.00 o.s.i. (ISBN 0-486-22086-9). Dover.

Hayden, B. Palaeolithic Reflections: Lithic Technology & Ethnographic Excavation Among Australian Aborigines. (AIAS New Ser.: 5). 1979. text ed. 17.00x (ISBN 0-391-00945-1). Humanities.

Hayden, Bob, ed. Model Railroader Cyclopedia, Vol. III: Freight Equipment. (Illus.). 224p. (Orig.). 1984. pap. 30.00 (ISBN 0-89024-038-8). Kalmbach.

Hayden, Bob, ed. see Armstrong, John H.

Hayden, Bob, ed. see Dolzall, Gary & Dolzall, Stephen.

Hayden, Bob, ed. see Drury, George.

Hayden, Bob, ed. see Olson, John.

Hayden, Bob, ed. see Paine, Shep & Stewart, Lane.

Hayden, Bob, ed. see Snell, Wilma S.

Hayden, Bob, ed. see Sperandeo, Andy.

Hayden, Dolores. The Grand Domestic Revolution: A History of Feminist Designs for American Homes, Neighborhoods, & Cities. (Illus.). 366p. 1981. 19.95x (ISBN 0-262-08108-3); pap. 9.95 (ISBN 0-262-58055-1). MIT Pr.

--Seven American Utopias: The Architecture of Communitarian Socialism, 1790-1975. LC 75-23148. 352p. 1976. 27.50x (ISBN 0-262-08082-6); pap. 12.50 (ISBN 0-262-58037-3). MIT Pr.

Hayden, Eric W. Technology Transfer to East Europe: U.S. Corporate Experience. LC 76-12855. (Illus.). 1976. 24.95 o.p. (ISBN 0-275-23240-9). Praeger.

Hayden, H. W., et al see Wulff, J.

Hayden, Harrold H. Selling Successfully By Telephone. 1977. cassette/spiral wkbk. prog. 99.50 (ISBN 0-686-98290-8). Sales & Mktg.

Hayden, John L. How to Incorporate in Tax Free Nevada for Only 50 Dollars. LC 80-85433. 88p. (Orig.). pap. 8.97 (ISBN 0-940008-00-9). Entrepreneurs.

Hayden, John O. Inside Poetry Out: An Introduction to Poetry. 224p. 1983. text ed. 18.95x (ISBN 0-8304-1011-2); pap. text ed. 9.95x (ISBN 0-88229-805-4). Nelson-Hall.

Hayden, John P., Jr., ed. see Olian, JoAnne.

Hayden, Naura. Astro-Logical Love. 288p. 1982. 12.95 (ISBN 0-942104-00-5, 01258-370, Pub. by Bibli O'Phile Publishing Co.). Dutton.

Hayden, R. E., et al. Mastering American English: A Handbook-Workbook of Essentials. 1956. pap. text ed. 11.95 (ISBN 0-13-560045-6). P-H.

Hayden, Ralston. Senate & Treaties, 1789-1817. LC 73-127295. (Law, Politics, & History Ser). 1970. Repr. of 1920 ed. lib. bdg. 32.50 (ISBN 0-306-71164-8). Da Capo.

Hayden, Rebecca, jt. auth. see Danielson, Dorothy.

Hayden, Robert, et al. Afro-American Literature: An Introduction. 1971. pap. text ed. 10.95 (ISBN 0-15-502075-7, HC). HarBraceJ.

Hayden, Sandy, et al. Women in Motion: The Basic Stuff to Get You Started & Keep You Going to Total Fitness. LC 82-70572. (Illus.). 248p. 1982. 13.41 (ISBN 0-8070-2156-3). Beacon Pr.

Hayden, Seymour & Mineka, John. Algebra & Geometry: An Introduction with Applications. LC 74-23358. 400p. 1976. 12.50 o.p. (ISBN 0-683-03913-X). Krieger.

Hayden, Shelby M., jt. auth. see Zitner, Rosalind.

Hayden, Sterling. Voyage: A Novel of 1896. 1976. 12.95 (ISBN 0-399-11665-6). Putnam Pub Group.

--Wanderer: A Reissue with a New Introduction & Illustrations. (Illus.). 1977. 10.95 o.p. (ISBN 0-686-86524-3). Norton.

Hayden, Torey L. Murphy's Boy. 288p. 1983. 13.95 (ISBN 0-399-12748-8). Putnam Pub Group.

--One Child. LC 79-20265. 1980. 9.95 o.p. (ISBN 0-399-12467-5). Putnam Pub Group.

--Somebody Else's Kids. 384p. 1981. 11.95 (ISBN 0-399-12602-3). Putnam Pub Group.

--Someone Else's Kids. 1982. pap. 2.95 (ISBN 0-686-95533-1, 380-59949-X). Avon.

Hayden, Trudy & Novik, Jack. Your Rights to Privacy. (ACLU Handbook Ser.). 1980. pap. 2.50 (ISBN 0-380-75895-4, 75895). Avon.

Haydn, Hiram, ed. The Portable Elizabethan Reader. 1980. pap. 6.95 (ISBN 0-14-015027-7). Penguin.

--A World of Great Stories. Cournos, John. 1977. pap. 2.98 o.p. (ISBN 0-517-53034-1, Bounty Books). Crown.

Haydn, Hiram C. The Counter-Renaissance. LC 50-3937. 1967. pap. 3.95 (ISBN 0-15-622680-4, Harv). HarBraceJ.

Haydn, Joseph. Twelve String Quartets: Opus 55, 64 & 71 Complete. 288p. 1980. pap. 7.95 (ISBN 0-486-23933-0). Dover.

Haydock, Bob, jt. auth. see Haydock, Yukiko.

Haydock, Roger & Herr, David. Discovery Practice. LC 81-81902. 704p. 1982. 55.00 (ISBN 0-316-35160-1). Little.

Haydock, Yukiko & Haydock, Bob. More Japanese Garnishes. LC 82-15563. (Illus.). 128p. 1983. 15.95 (ISBN 0-03-063611-6). HR&W.

Haydon, D. A., jt. auth. see Aveyard, R.

Haydon, G., tr. see Jeppesen, Knud.

Haydon, Glen. Evolution of the Six-Four Chord: A Chapter in the History of Dissonant Treatment. LC 75-125052. (Music Ser). 1971. Repr. of 1933 ed. lib. bdg. 21.50 (ISBN 0-306-70017-4). Da Capo.

Hayduk, W. & Kertes, eds. Ethane. (Solubility Data Ser.: Vol. 9). 286p. 1982. 100.00 (ISBN 0-08-026230-9). Pergamon.

Hayduke, George. Getting Even II. (Illus.). 160p. 1983. pap. 9.95 (ISBN 0-8184-0337-3). Lyle Stuart.

Haye, Beverly La see La Haye, Beverly.

Haye, Kh A. Stories of Great Muslims. LC 82-72578. 85p. (Orig.). 1982. write for info o.p. (ISBN 0-89259-020-3); pap. 2.50 o.p. (ISBN 0-686-92028-7). Contemp Bks.

Hayek, Ann & Sherwin, Dee. Your Name Is Your Fortune. Date not set. cancelled. Amber Crest.

Hayek, F. A. Individualism & Economic Order. 1977. Repr. of 1958 ed. 19.95x o.p. (ISBN 0-7100-8521-4). Routledge & Kegan.

Hayes, Alfred, tr. see Pushkin, Alexander.

Hayes, Ann. The Living & the Dead. LC 75-4385. (Poetry Ser.). pap. 2.95 o.p. (ISBN 0-915604-01-9). Carnegie-Mellon.

Hayes, Arlene S., jt. auth. see Anderson, Mary Jo.

Hayes, Bartlett. Tradition Becomes Innovation: Modern Religious Architecture in America. LC 82-18581. (Illus.). 176p. 1982. 27.50 (ISBN 0-8298-0635-0); pap. 12.95 (ISBN 0-8298-0624-5). Pilgrim NY.

Hayes, Carlton. Wartime Mission in Spain. LC 76-18191. (Politics & Strategy of World War II Ser.). 1976. Repr. of 1945 ed. lib. bdg. 37.50 (ISBN 0-306-70771-3). Da Capo.

Hayes, Carlton J. Generation of Materialism, 1871-1900. (Rise of Modern Europe Ser). pap. 6.75xi o.p. (ISBN 0-06-133039-6, TB3039, Torch). Har-Row.

--United States & Spain: An Interpretation. Repr. of 1951 ed. lib. bdg. 15.00 o.p. (ISBN 0-8371-2805-6, HAAS). Greenwood.

Hayes, Catherine. Skirmishes. 61p. 1983. pap. 5.95 (ISBN 0-571-11979-4). Faber & Faber.

Hayes, Charles R., jt. auth. see Mayer, Harold M.

Hayes, Curtis & Kessler, Carolyn, eds. Linguistics for the Second-Foreign Language Teacher. (Teacher Idea Ser.). 80p. (Orig.). 1983. pap. text ed. 7.95 (ISBN 0-88499-627-1). Inst Mod Lang.

Hayes, Curtis, ed. see Streiff, Virginia.

Hayes, D. S., jt. ed. see Philip, A. G.

Hayes, Dale G. Lost Horizon Notes. (Orig.). 1980. pap. 2.50 (ISBN 0-8220-0771-1). Cliffs.

Hayes, David. Sorry! No Hard Feelings? (Irish Play Ser.). pap. 2.50x (ISBN 0-912262-44-3). Proscenium.

Hayes, Debbie. Prized Possession. 192p. (Orig.). Date not set. pap. cancelled o.p. (ISBN 0-505-51828-7). Tower Bks.

Hayes, Dennis E., ed. Antarctic Oceanology Two: The Australian-New Zealand Sector. LC 78-151300. (Antarctic Research Ser.: Vol. 19). (Illus.). 364p. 1972. 41.00 (ISBN 0-87590-119-0). Am Geophysical.

Hayes, Douglas A. & Bauman, W. Scott. Investments: Analysis & Management. 3rd ed. (Illus.). 1976. text ed. 25.95x (ISBN 0-02-352710-2). Macmillan.

Hayes, E. Kent & Lazzarino, Alex A. Broken Promise. LC 78-4832. 1978. 8.95 o.p. (ISBN 0-399-12188-9). Putnam Pub Group.

Hayes, Elizabeth R. An Introduction to the Teaching of Dance. LC 80-15371. 354p. 1980. Repr. of 1964 ed. lib. bdg. 16.00 (ISBN 0-89874-227-7). Krieger.

Hayes, Ernest H., ed. Fifty Favorite Bible Stories. 1963. pap. 4.55 (ISBN 0-08-006196-6, Religious Educ Pr). Pergamon.

Hayes, Francis C. Lope de Vega. (World Authors Ser.: No. 28). 1968. lib. bdg. 8.95 o.p. (ISBN 0-8057-2932-1, Twayne). G K Hall.

Hayes, Frederick O., et al. Linkages: Improving Financial Management in Local Government. LC 82-60180. 184p. (Orig.). 1982. pap. text ed. 12.00 (ISBN 0-87766-313-0, 33700). Urban Inst.

Hayes, Gail B. Solar Access Law: Protecting Access to Sunlight for Solar Energy Systems. LC 79-9392. (An Environmental Law Institute Bk.). 328p. (4#320). 1979. prof ref 26.00x (ISBN 0-88410-091-X). Ballinger Pub.

Hayes, Geoffrey. Elroy & the Witch's Child. LC 81-48645. (Illus.). 32p. (gr. 1-4). 1982. PLB 8.89g (ISBN 0-06-022259-X, HarpJ); pap. 4.76i (ISBN 0-06-022258-1). Har-Row.

--The Secret Inside. LC 79-8519. (Illus.). (gr. 1-4). 1980. 8.61i (ISBN 0-06-022273-5, HarpJ); PLB 8.89 (ISBN 0-06-022274-3). Har-Row.

Hayes, Gerald R. King's Music: An Anthology. LC 78-66906. (Encore Music Editions Ser.). (Illus.). 1981. Repr. of 1937 ed. write for info. o.p. (ISBN 0-88355-746-0). Hyperion Conn.

Hayes, Glenn E. & Romig, Harry G. Modern Quality Control. 1982. text ed. 37.50 (ISBN 0-02-802910-0). Glencoe.

Hayes, Harold. Three Levels of Time. LC 80-22963. 1981. 13.50 o.p. (ISBN 0-525-21853-X, 01311-390). Dutton.

Hayes, Harold, jt. auth. see Goude, Jean-Paul.

Hayes, Harold P. Realism in EEO. LC 79-2295. 1980. 39.5006739519x (ISBN 0-471-05796-7, Pub. by Wiley-Interscience). Wiley.

Hayes, Harold T. The Last Place on Earth. LC 76-15562. (Illus.). 288p. Date not set. pap. 8.95 (ISBN 0-8128-6087-X). Stein & Day.

Hayes, Heidi, ed. see Educational Challenges, Inc.

Hayes, Irene. What's Cooking in Kentucky. rev. ed. 400p. 1982. laminated cover 12.95 (ISBN 0-938402-01-3). T I Hayes.

Hayes, Irene E. The Airdale Terrier. Foyle, Christina, ed. (Foyle's Handbks). 1973. 3.95 (ISBN 0-685-55814-2). Palmetto Pub.

Hayes, J., jt. auth. see Hopson, B.

Hayes, J. A., jt. ed. see Homburger, F.

Hayes, J. L. Nepal Trail Guide Series. Incl. No. 1: Everest & Solu-Khumbu. 75p; No. 2: North of Pokhara. 75p; No. 3: North of Kathmandu. 75p. (Illus.). price 9.95 set (ISBN 0-686-43407-2). Bradt Ent.

Hayes, J. P. Digital System Design Using Microprocessors. 656p. 1982. 24.95x (ISBN 0-07-027367-7). McGraw.

Hayes, Janice E., jt. auth. see Hoexter, Joan C.

Hayes, John. Computer Architecture & Organization. (Illus.). 1978. text ed. 36.95 (ISBN 0-07-027363-4, C); instructor's manual 11.50 (ISBN 0-07-027364-2). McGraw.

--Gainsborough's Landscape Paintings: With a Catalogue Raisonne, 2 vols. (Illus.). 550p. 1983. Set. slipcase 180.00x (ISBN 0-85667-114-2, Pub. by Sotheby Pubns England). Biblio Dist.

--The Landscape Paintings of Thomas Gainsborough: A Critical Text & Catalogue Raisonne, 2 Vols. LC 82-70753. (Illus.). 550p. 1983. 150.00x (ISBN 0-8014-1528-4). Cornell U Pr.

--Sutherland. (Illus.). 192p. 1980. 55.00 (ISBN 0-933516-18-5). Alpine Bk Co.

Hayes, John & Nutman, Peter. Understanding the Unemployed: The Psychological Effects of Unemployment. 192p. 1981. 16.95x o.p. (ISBN 0-422-77820-6, Pub by Tavistock England); pap. 7.95x (ISBN 0-422-77830-3). Methuen Inc.

Hayes, John, ed. First & Second Corinthians. Baird, William. (Knox Preaching Guides Ser.). pap. 4.95 (ISBN 0-8042-3239-3). John Knox.

--Progress in Passive Solar Energy Systems: Vol. 7, The World Turns to Solar. 1983. prepub. 100.00x (ISBN 0-89553-035-X); pap. text ed. 145.00x (ISBN 0-686-86926-5). Am Solar Energy.

Hayes, John, ed. see National Passive Solar Conference, 5th, Amherst, 1980.

Hayes, John H. & Holladay, Carl. Biblical Exegesis. LC 82-17999. 1982. pap. 6.95 (ISBN 0-8042-0030-0). John Knox.

Hayes, John H. & Miller, J. Maxwell, eds. Israelite & Judaean History. LC 76-41913. (Old Testament Library). 1977. 27.50 (ISBN 0-664-21291-3). Westminster.

Hayes, John H., ed. see Craddock, Fred B.

Hayes, John P. Philadelphia in Color. (Illus., Orig.). 1983. 7.95 (ISBN 0-8038-5898-1). Hastings.

Hayes, John P., jt. auth. see Brill, Peter L.

Hayes, John R. The Complete Problem Solver. LC 81-3295. 1981. 19.50 (ISBN 0-89168-028-4). Franklin Inst Pr.
--The Genius of Arab Civilization: Source of Renaissance. LC 78-1001. (Illus.). 1978. arabic 50.00 o.p. (ISBN 0-262-08098-2); pap. 15.00 english o.p. (ISBN 0-262-58035-7). MIT Pr.
Hayes, John T; see Weaver, Glenn.
Hayes, Joseph. The Desperate Hours. 1977. pap. 1.95 o.p. (ISBN 0-451-07689-3, J7689, Sig). NAL.
--Winner's Circle. 1980. 10.95 o.s.i. (ISBN 0-440-09538-7). Delacorte.
Hayes, Louis, jt. auth. see Woodin, J. C.
Hayes, M. H., jt. auth. see Greenland, D. J.
Hayes, Margaret D. Latin America & the U. S. National Interest: A Basis for U. S. Foreign Policy. (Special Studies on Latin America & the Caribbean). 240p. 1983. lib. bdg. 23.50x (ISBN 0-86531-462-4); pap. text ed. 10.95x (ISBN 0-86531-547-7). Westview.
Hayes, Marilyn. Alphabet & Words. (Early Education Ser.). 24p. (gr. 1). 1982. wkbk. 5.00 (ISBN 0-8209-0214-4, K-16). ESP.
--Basic Skills Alphabet Workbook. (Basic Skills Workbooks). 32p. (gr. k-1). 1983. 0.99 (ISBN 0-8209-0551-8, EEW-2). ESP.
--Basic Skills Health Workbook: Grade 3. (Basic Skills Workbooks). 32p. 1982. tchrs' ed. 0.99 (ISBN 0-686-38397-4, HW-D). ESP.
--Basic Skills Health Workbook: Grade 4. (Basic Skills Workbooks). 32p. 1982. tchrs' ed. 0.99 (ISBN 0-8209-0414-7, HW-E). ESP.
--Basic Skills Health Workbook: Grade 5. (Basic Skills Workbooks). 32p. 1982. tchrs' ed. 0.99 (ISBN 0-8209-0415-5, HW-F). ESP.
--Basic Skills Nutrition Workbook: Grade 5. (Basic Skills Workbooks). 32p. (gr. 5). tchrs' ed. 0.99 (ISBN 0-8209-0411-2, NW-F). ESP.
--Basic Skills Seeing Differences Workbook. (Basic Skills Workbooks). 32p. (gr. k-1). 1983. 0.99 (ISBN 0-8209-0588-7, EEW-11). ESP.
--Basic Skills Social Studies Workbook: Grade 5. (Basic Skills Workbooks). 32p. (gr. 5). 1982. wkbk. 0.99 (ISBN 0-8209-0400-7, SSW-F). ESP.
--Basic Skills Words We Use Workbook. (Basic Skills Workbooks). 32p. (gr. k-1). 1983. 0.99 (ISBN 0-8209-0577-1, EEW-7). ESP.
--Jumbo Health Yearbook: Grade 3. (Jumbo Health Ser.). 96p. (gr. 3). 1978. 14.00 (ISBN 0-8209-0063-X, JHY 3). ESP.
--Jumbo Health Yearbook: Grade 4. (Jumbo Health Ser.). 96p. (gr. 4). 1979. 14.00 (ISBN 0-8209-0064-8, JHY 4). ESP.
--Jumbo Nutrition Yearbook: Grade 4. (Jumbo Nutrition Ser.). 96p. (gr. 4). 1981. 14.00 (ISBN 0-8209-0043-5, JNY 4). ESP.
--Jumbo Nutrition Yearbook: Grade 5. (Jumbo Nutrition Ser.). 96p. (gr. 5). 1981. 14.00 (ISBN 0-8209-0044-3, JNY 5). ESP.
--Jumbo Social Studies Yearbook: Grade 5. (Jumbo Social Studies). 96p. (gr. 5). 1981. 14.00 (ISBN 0-8209-0077-X, JSSY 4). ESP.
--Learning Opposite Words. (Early Education Ser.). 24p. (gr. 1). 1982. wkbk. 5.00 (ISBN 0-686-42827-7, K-13). ESP.
--Lower-Case, Upper-Case Words. (Early Education Ser.). 24p. (gr. 1). 1980. wkbk. 5.00 (ISBN 0-8209-0217-9, K-19). ESP.
--My Picture & Word Book. (Early Education Ser.). 24p. (gr. 1). 1981. wkbk. 5.00 (ISBN 0-8209-0215-2, K-17). ESP.
--Seeing Differences. (Early Education Ser.). 24p. (gr. k). 1982. wkbk. 5.00 (ISBN 0-8209-0210-1, K-12). ESP.
--Social Studies Reading. (Reading Ser.). 24p. (gr. 2). 1980. wkbk. 5.00 (ISBN 0-8209-0195-4, RSS-2). ESP.
--Words We Use. (Early Education Ser.). 24p. (gr. 1). 5.00 (ISBN 0-8209-0218-7, K-20). ESP.
Hayes, Marnell. Tuned-in, Turned-on Book About Learning Problems. LC 74-80091. 1974. pap. 2.50x (ISBN 0-87879-090-X); optional 90-minute cassette tape 7.95 (ISBN 0-686-96646-5). Acad Therapy.
Hayes, Marshall, ed. The Thirties: An American Decade. (Illus.). 150p. 1983. 10.95 (ISBN 0-8180-0827-X). Horizon.
Hayes, Norvel. God's Boot Camp. 32p. 1983. pap. 1.75 (ISBN 0-686-83913-7). Harrison Hse.
--God's Medicine of Faith: The Word. 96p. 1983. pap. 2.25 (ISBN 0-89274-278-X). Harrison Hse.
--God's Power Through the Laying On of Hands. 45p. 1982. pap. 1.95 (ISBN 0-89274-280-1). Harrison Hse.
--How to Protect Your Faith. 80p. 1983. pap. 2.95 (ISBN 0-89274-279-8). Harrison Hse.
--Jesus Taught Me to Cast out Devils. 89p. 1982. pap. 2.50 (ISBN 0-89274-272-0). Harrison Hse.
--The Seven Ways Jesus Heals. 142p. 1982. pap. 4.95 (ISBN 0-89274-235-6, HH-235). Harrison Hse.
--The Unopened Gift. cancelled (ISBN 0-89841-002-9). Zoe Pubns.
--Your Faith Can Heal You. 78p. 1982. pap. 2.50 (ISBN 0-89274-273-9). Harrison Hse.
Hayes, Paul. The Twentieth Century, Eighteen Eighty to Nineteen Thirty-Nine. LC 77-93695. (Modern British Foreign Policy). 1978. 22.50x (ISBN 0-312-82409-2). St Martin.
Hayes, Paul M. The Nineteenth Century: Eighteen-Fourteen to Eighteen-Eighty. LC 75-10760. (Modern British Foreign Policy Ser.). 300p. 1975. 15.00 (ISBN 0-312-57470-3). St Martin.
Hayes, Paul W. & Worton, Scott M. Essentials of Photography. (Illus.). 288p. (Orig.). 1983. pap. text ed. 14.95 (ISBN 0-672-97492-4); instr's. guide 3.33 (ISBN 0-672-97494-0); wkbk. 4.80 (ISBN 0-672-97493-2). Bobbs.
Hayes, Phyllis. Food Fun. LC 81-979. (Easy-Read Activity Bks.). (Illus.). 32p. (gr. 1-3). 1981. lib. bdg. 8.90 (ISBN 0-531-04308-8). Watts.
Hayes, R. S. & Baker, C. R. Simplified Accounting for Non-Accountants. 291p. 1980. 18.95 (ISBN 0-471-04977-8). Ronald Pr.
--Simplified Accounting for the Computer Industry. 191p. 1981. 29.95x (ISBN 0-471-05703-7). Ronald Pr.
Hayes, R. S., jt. auth. see Baker, C. R.
Hayes, Ralph. Savage Dawn. (Orig.). 1979. write for info. (ISBN 0-515-05075-X). Jove Pubns.
--The Scorpio Cipher. 320p. (Orig.). 1983. pap. 3.25 (ISBN 0-8439-1060-7, Leisure Bks). Dorchester Pub Co.
Hayes, Raymond L., et al, eds. Radioisotopes in Medicine - In Vitro Studies: Proceedings. LC 68-60071. (AEC Symposium Ser.). 753p. 1968. pap. 26.75 (ISBN 0-87079-327-6, CONF-671111); microfiche 4.50 (ISBN 0-87079-328-4, CONF-671111). DOE.
Hayes, Richard E., jt. auth. see Evans, Gary T.
Hayes, Rick S. & Howell, John C. How to Finance Your Small Business with Government Money: SBA & Other Loans. 2nd ed. LC 82-16060. (Small Business Management Ser.). 258p. 1983. pap. 17.95 (ISBN 0-471-86563-X). Ronald Pr.
Hayes, Rick S., jt. auth. see Baker, Richard.
Hayes, Robert, jt. ed. see Keith, Henry.
Hayes, Robert M. & Becker, Joseph. Handbook of Data Processing for Libraries. 2nd ed. LC 74-9690. (Information Sciences Ser). 712p. 1974. 49.95x (ISBN 0-471-36483-5, Pub. by Wiley-Interscience). Wiley.
Hayes, Robert M., jt. auth. see Becker, Joseph.
Hayes, Samuel L., III & Spence, A. Michael. Competition in the Investment Banking Industry. (Illus.). 176p. 1983. text ed. 20.00x (ISBN 0-674-15415-0). Harvard U Pr.
Hayes, Sheila. Me & My Mona Lisa Smile. 128p. (gr. 7 up). 1981. 9.95 (ISBN 0-525-66731-8, 0966-290). Lodestar Bks.
--Speaking of Snapdragons. 160p. (gr. 5-9). 1982. 10.95 (ISBN 0-525-66785-7, 01063-320). Lodestar Bks.
Hayes, Stephanie & Ladzik, Kathleen. Conestoga Language Interaction Program: A Parent Training Guide. 1982. 3-ring binder 15.95 (ISBN 0-88450-823-4, 2073-B). Communication Skill.
Hayes, Steve. The Osprey Dilemma. (Orig.). 1983. pap. 3.95 (ISBN 0-440-16159-2). Dell.
Hayes, Steven C., jt. auth. see Cone, John D.
Hayes, Steven C., jt. auth. see Barlow, David H.
Hayes, W. The Genetics of Bacteria & Their Viruses: Studies in Basic Genetics & Molecular Biology. 2nd ed. LC 69-16199. 925p. 1976. pap. text ed. 34.95x o.s.i. (ISBN 0-470-36474-2). Halsted Pr.
Hayes, Walter M. & Killeen, Veronica A. Introductory French Program, 2 Bks. (Prog. Bk.). (gr. 9-12). 1970. Set. pap. 13.00 o.p. (ISBN 0-8294-0197-0); 15 tapes s.p. 85.00 o.p. (ISBN 0-686-86294-5). Loyola.
Hayes, Wanda. Bible Stories Make Me Happy. (A Happy Day Book). (Illus.). 24p. (gr. k-3). 1979. 1.29 (ISBN 0-87239-352-6, 3622). Standard Pub.
--A Child's First Book of Bible Stories. Gambill, Henrietta, ed. (Illus.). 128p. (ps). 1983. text ed. 6.95 (ISBN 0-87239-659-2, 2949). Standard Pub.
--Jesus Makes Me Happy. (A Happy Day Book). (Illus.). 24p. (gr. k-3). 1979. 1.29 (3620). Standard Pub.
--My Friends Make Me Happy. (A Happy Day Book). (Illus.). 24p. (gr. k-3). 1979. 1.29 (ISBN 0-87239-351-8, 3621). Standard Pub.
--Saying Thank You Makes Me Happy. (A Happy Day Book). (Illus.). 24p. (gr. k-3). 1979. 1.29 (ISBN 0-87239-353-4, 3623). Standard Pub.
Hayes, Wayland J. Pesticides Studied in Man. (Illus.). 685p. 1982. text ed. 49.95 (ISBN 0-683-03896-6). Williams & Wilkins.
Hayes, William & Loudon, Rodney. Scattering of Light by Crystals. LC 78-9008. 1978. 52.95 (ISBN 0-471-03191-7, Pub. by Wiley-Interscience). Wiley.
Hayes-McCoy, G. A. A History of Irish Flags from Earliest Times. 1980. lib. bdg. 45.00 (ISBN 0-8161-8400-3, Hall Reference). G K Hall.
Hayes-Roth, Rick, jt. ed. see Waterman, Don.
Hayes-Steinert, Jan. Your Face After Thirty: The Total Guide to Skin Care & Makeup for the Realistic Woman. LC 77-87151. (Illus.). 254p. 1978. 9.95 o.s.i. (ISBN 0-89479-015-3). A & W Pubs.
Hayford, Harrision, ed. see Melville, Herman.
Hayford, Harrison see Emerson, Ralph W.
Hayford, Jack. The Church on the Way. 200p. 1983. 9.95 (ISBN 0-310-60370-6). Chosen Bks Pub.
--Prayer Is Invading the Impossible. 1977. pap. 4.95 (ISBN 0-88270-218-1, Pub. by Logos). Bridge Pub.
Hayhoe, F. G. & Flemans, R. J. A Colour Atlas of Haematological Cytology. 2d ed. LC 81-71285. 240p. 1982. 75.00 (ISBN 0-471-86868-X, Pub. by Res Stud Pr). Wiley.
Hayhoe, F. G., jt. auth. see Cawley, J. C.
Hayhurst, Emma L. I Will. 2nd ed. 1982. pap. 4.95 (ISBN 0-938736-09-4). Life Enrich.
Hayim, Gila J. The Existential Sociology of Jean-Paul Sartre. LC 80-10131. 176p. 1982. pap. text ed. 7.00 (ISBN 0-87023-381-5). U of Mass Pr.
Haykin, S., ed. Array Processing. LC 79-11772. (Benchmark Papers in Electrical Engineering & Computer Science: Vol. 22). 362p. 1979. 56.50 (ISBN 0-87933-351-0). Hutchinson Ross.
Haykin, S. S. Active Network Theory. 1970. 31.95 (ISBN 0-201-02680-5). A-W.
Haykin, Simon. Communication Systems. LC 77-26752. 1978. text ed. 34.95 (ISBN 0-471-02977-7). Wiley.
--Communication Systems. 2nd ed. 625p. 1983. 33.95 (ISBN 0-471-09691-1); tchrs.' avail. (ISBN 0-471-87155-9). Wiley.
Hayley, Barbara. Carleton's 'Traits & Stories' & the 19th Century Anglo-Irish Tradition. LC 82-6847. (Irish Literary Studies: No. 12). 200p. 1983. text ed. 26.50x (ISBN 0-389-20308-4). B&N Imports.
Hayley, William. Essay on Epic Poetry. LC 68-17013. 1968. Repr. of 1782 ed. 36.00x (ISBN 0-8201-1026-4). Schol Facsimiles.
--An Essay on Sculpture, in a Series of Epistles to John Flaxman...with Notes...(Plates Engraved by Blake) Reiman, Donald H., ed. LC 75-31210. (Romantic Context Ser.: Poetry 1789-1830: Vol. 61). 1979. Repr. of 1800 ed. lib. bdg. 47.00 o.s.i. (ISBN 0-8240-2160-6). Garland Pub.
--The Eulogies of Howard, a Vision, Repr. Of 1791. Reiman, Donald H., ed. Bd. with Ballads, Founded on Anecdotes Relating to Animals, with Prints...by William Blake. Repr. of 1805 ed; Poems on Serious & Sacred Subjects, Printed Only As Private Tokens of Regard, for the Particular Friends of the Author. Repr. of 1818 ed. LC 75-31209. (Romantic Context Ser.: Poetry 1789-1830: Vol. 60). 1979. lib. bdg. 47.00 o.s.i. (ISBN 0-8240-2159-2). Garland Pub.
--Life of Milton. LC 78-122485. 1970. Repr. of 1796 ed. 42.00x (ISBN 0-8201-1081-7). Schol Facsimiles.
--A Poetical Epistle to an Eminent Painter, Repr. Of 1778. Reiman, Donald H., ed. Bd. with An Elegy, on the Ancient Greek Model. Addressed to the Right Reverend Robert Lowth. Repr. of 1779 ed; Epistle to Admiral Keppel. Repr. of 1779 ed; Epistle to a Friend, on the Death of John Thornton Esq. 2nd, corrected ed. Repr. of 1780 ed; An Essay on History; in Three Epistles to Edward Gibbon, Esq. with Notes. Repr. of 1780 ed. LC 75-31206. (Romantic Context Ser.: Poetry 1789-1830: Vol. 57). 1979. lib. bdg. 47.00 o.s.i. (ISBN 0-8240-2156-8). Garland Pub.
--Two Dialogues: Containing a Comparative View of the Lives, Characters, & Writings of Philip, the Late Earl of Chesterfield, & Dr. Samuel Johnson. LC 71-122486. 1970. Repr. of 1787 ed. 33.00x (ISBN 0-8201-1080-9). Schol Facsimiles.
Hayman, jt. auth. see Brooten.
Hayman, David. Ulysses: The Mechanics of Meaning. 2nd ed. LC 81-70007. 174p. 1982. 17.50 (ISBN 0-299-09020-5); pap. 6.95 (ISBN 0-299-09024-8). U of Wis Pr.
Hayman, David & Rabkin, Eric S. Form in Fiction. 400p. (Orig.). 1974. pap. text ed. 12.95 (ISBN 0-312-29925-7). St Martin.
Hayman, David & Anderson, Elliott, eds. In the Wake of the "Wake". 216p. 1978. 6.95 (ISBN 0-299-07600-8). U of Wis Pr.
Hayman, H. G. Statistical Thermodynamics. 1967. 23.50 (ISBN 0-444-40272-1). Elsevier.
Hayman, John, ed. see Ruskin, John.
Hayman, Leroy. Up, up, & Away: All About Balloons, Blimps, & Dirigibles. LC 79-27824. (Illus.). 192p. (gr. 7-12). 1980. PLB 8.29 o.p. (ISBN 0-671-33001-2). Messner.
Hayman, Peter. The Birds of Paradise. (Illus.). 1979. 22.50 o.p. (ISBN 0-399-12412-8). Putnam Pub Group.
Hayman, Rex. Filters. (Photographer's Library). (Illus.). 1983. pap. 12.95x (ISBN 0-240-51114-X). Focal Pr.
Hayman, Ronald. Arnold Wesker. LC 78-15320. (Literature and Life Ser.). (Illus.). 1973. 11.95 (ISBN 0-8044-2387-3). Ungar.
--Artaud & After. (Illus.). 1977. 12.50x (ISBN 0-19-211744-0). Oxford U Pr.
--Arthur Miller. LC 75-153122. (Literature & Life Ser.). (Illus.). 11.95 (ISBN 0-8044-2374-1). Ungar.
--Edward Albee. LC 71-153121. (Literature and Life Ser.). (Illus.). 11.95 (ISBN 0-8044-2385-7). Ungar.
--Eugene Ionesco. LC 75-10103. (Literature and Life Ser.). (Illus.). 150p. 1976. 11.95 (ISBN 0-8044-2388-1). Ungar.
--Harold Pinter. LC 72-79936. (Literature & Life Ser.). (Illus.). 1973. 11.95 (ISBN 0-8044-2371-7). Ungar.
--How to Read a Play. LC 77-2455. 1977. pap. 4.95 (ISBN 0-394-17022-9, E695, Ever). Grove.
--John Osborne. LC 79-153123. (Literature and Life Ser.). (Illus.). 11.95 (ISBN 0-8044-2386-5). Ungar.
--Kafka: A Biography. (Illus.). 1982. 19.95 (ISBN 0-19-520279-1). Oxford U Pr.
--Kafka: A Biography. 380p. 1983. pap. 8.95 (ISBN 0-19-520411-5, GB 722, GB). Oxford U Pr.
--Nietzsche: A Critical Life. 1982. pap. 6.95 (ISBN 0-14-006274-2). Penguin.
--Playback. 192p. 1974. 6.95 (ISBN 0-8180-0622-6). Horizon.
--Samuel Beckett. LC 72-79935. (Literature and Life Ser.). (Illus.). 1974. 11.95 (ISBN 0-8044-2373-3). Ungar.
Hayman, W. K., jt. ed. see Clunie, J. G.
Haymon, S. T. Ritual Murder. LC 82-5781. 224p. 1982. 10.95 (ISBN 0-312-68478-9). St Martin.
Hayna, Lois B., jt. auth. see Peckinpaugh, Angela.
Hayne, Arlene & Warren Bailey, Zeila. Nursing Administration of Critical Care. LC 81-20677. 292p. 1982. text ed. 28.95 (ISBN 0-89443-397-0). Aspen Systems.
Hayne, David see Halpenny, Francess.
Haynes, Betsy. The Power. (Twilight Ser.). (Orig.). (gr. 5 up). 1982. pap. 1.95 (ISBN 0-440-97164-0, LFL). Dell.
Haynes, Brian, jt. auth. see Keene, Tom.
Haynes, James. Voices in the Dark. (Twilight Ser.). (Orig.). (gr. 5 up). 1982. pap. 1.95 (ISBN 0-440-99317-2, LFL). Dell.
Haynes, John E. Pseudonyms of Authors. LC 68-30620. 1969. Repr. of 1882 ed. 31.00x (ISBN 0-8103-3142-X). Gale.
Haynes, Judith L., jt. auth. see Haverson, Wayne W.
Haynes, Judy L. Organizing a Speech: A Programmed Guide. 2nd ed. (Speech Communication Ser.). (Illus.). 192p. 1981. pap. text ed. 12.95 (ISBN 0-13-641530-X). P-H.
Haynes, Ken F., jt. auth. see Birch, Martin C.
Haynes, Marilyn. Basic Skills Nutrition Workbook: Grade 4. (Basic Skills Workbooks). 32p. (gr. 4). tchrs' ed. 0.99 (ISBN 0-8209-0410-4, NW-E). ESP.
Haynes, Mary. Pot Belly Tales. (gr. 3-7). 1982. 9.50 (ISBN 0-688-00892-5); PLB 8.59 (ISBN 0-688-00893-3). Lothrop.
Haynes, Michael D. Haynes on Air Brush Taxidermy. LC 78-13541. (Illus.). 1979. 12.95 (ISBN 0-668-04569-8, 4634). Arco.
Haynes, R., ed. Environmental Science Methods. (Illus.). 1982. 39.95x (ISBN 0-412-23280-4, Pub. by Chapman & Hall England); pap. 19.95x (ISBN 0-412-23290-1). Methuen Inc.
Haynes, R. H., jt. auth. see Plants, H.
Haynes, R. M. & Bentham, C. G. Community Hospital & Rural Accessibility. 1979. text ed. 29.00x (ISBN 0-566-00271-X). Gower Pub Ltd.
Haynes, Stephen N. Principles of Behavioral Assessment. LC 77-19134. 530p. 1978. 24.95 o.p. (ISBN 0-470-26292-3). Halsted Pr.
Haynes, Una H. Holistic Health Care for Young Children with Developmental Disabilities. 240p. 1982. pap. text ed. 19.95 (ISBN 0-8391-1699-3). Univ Park.
Haynes, William W. Nationalization in Practice: The British Coal Industry. Repr. of 1953 ed. 27.50 o.p. (ISBN 0-08-022305-2). Pergamon.
Haynes-Klassen, Joanne. Learning to Live, Learning to Love: A Book About You, A Book About Everyone. (Illus.). 150p. 1983. pap. 7.95 (ISBN 0-915190-38-9). Jalmar Pr.
Haynie, Miriam. The Stronghold: A Story of Historic Northern Neck of Virginia & Its People. 1959. 7.50 (ISBN 0-685-47900-5). Dietz.
Haynie, Paul J. Cabinetmaking. (Illus.). 272p. 1976. 18.95 (ISBN 0-13-110239-7). P-H.
Hays, Anne M. & Hazelton, Harriet R. Chesapeake Kaleidoscope. (Illus.). 148p. 1975. pap. 5.00 (ISBN 0-686-36755-3). Md Hist.
Hays, Arthur G. Trial by Prejudice. LC 79-109550. (Civil Liberties in American History Ser). 1970. Repr. of 1933 ed. lib. bdg. 45.00 (ISBN 0-306-71904-5). Da Capo.
Hays, Arthur Garfield. Let Freedom Ring. LC 71-166329. (Civil Liberties in American History Ser). (Illus.). 1972. Repr. of 1937 ed. lib. bdg. 57.50 (ISBN 0-306-70227-4). Da Capo.
Hays, Edward. Sundancer. LC 82-83135. (Illus.). 64p. (Orig.). 1982. pap. 5.95 (ISBN 0-939516-04-7). Forest Peace.
--Twelve & One-Half Keys. Turkle, Thomas, ed. LC 81-50505. (Illus.). 152p. (Orig.). 1981. pap. 5.95 (ISBN 0-939516-00-4). Forest Peace.
Hays, H. R. Children of the Raven: The Seven Indian Nations of the Northwest Coast. LC 75-6668. (Illus.). 352p. 1975. 12.95 o.p. (ISBN 0-07-027372-3, GB). McGraw.
Hays, James D. Our Changing Climate. LC 77-5055. (Illus.). (gr. 5 up). 1977. 6.95 o.p. (ISBN 0-689-30586-9). Atheneum.
Hays, Joyce S. & Larson, Kenneth H. Interacting with Patients. 1963. text ed. 14.95x (ISBN 0-02-352810-9). Macmillan.
Hays, Mary. Memoirs of Emma Courtney, 2 vols. (The Feminist Controversy in England, 1788-1810 Ser.). 1974. Set. lib. bdg. 76.00 o.s.i. (ISBN 0-8240-0870-7); lib. bdg. 50.00 ea. o.s.i. Garland Pub.
Hays, R., et al. International Business: An Introduction to the World of the Multinational Firm. 1972. ref. ed. 22.95 (ISBN 0-13-472472-0). P-H.
Hays, Richard C. Brother Freddy: Posthumously. 1983. 7.50 (ISBN 0-8062-1967-X). Carlton.

Hays, Samuel. Chemicals & Allied Industries. (Studies in British Economy Ser.). 1973. pap. text ed. 5.50x o.p. (ISBN 0-435-84557-8). Heinemann Ed.

--The Engineering Industries. (Studies in the British Economy). 1972. pap. text ed. 5.50x o.p. (ISBN 0-435-84552-7). Heinemann Ed.

Hays, Samuel P. American Political History As Social Analysis: Essays by Samuel P. Hays. LC 79-17567. (Twentieth-Century America Ser.). 560p. 1980. 27.50x (ISBN 0-87049-276-4). U of Tenn Pr.

Hays, Wilma P. Abe Lincoln's Birthday. (Illus.). (gr. 3-5). 1961. PLB 5.99 (ISBN 0-698-30001-7, Coward). Putnam Pub Group.

--Christmas on the Mayflower. (Illus.). (gr. 2-4). 1956. PLB 5.99 (ISBN 0-698-30043-2, Coward). Putnam Pub Group.

--Easter Fires. (Illus.). (gr. 3-5). 1960. PLB 5.29 o.p. (ISBN 0-698-30067-X, Coward). Putnam Pub Group.

--For Ma & Pa: On the Oregon Trail 1844. (Illus.). 64p. (gr. 3-6). 1972. 5.29 o.p. (ISBN 0-698-30425-X, Coward). Putnam Pub Group.

--Little Yellow Fur: Homesteading in 1913. (Break-of-Day Bk.). (Illus.). 64p. (gr. 1-3). 1973. PLB 6.99 o.p. (ISBN 0-698-30503-5, Coward). Putnam Pub Group.

--Noko, Captive of Columbus. (Illus.). (gr. 3-7). 1967. PLB 4.49 o.p. (ISBN 0-698-30259-1, Coward). Putnam Pub Group.

--Pilgrim Thanksgiving. (Illus.). (gr. 2-4). 1955. PLB 4.99 o.p. (ISBN 0-698-30281-8, Coward). Putnam Pub Group.

--Siege: The Story of St. Augustine in 1702. LC 75-22276. (Illus.). 96p. (gr. 3-6). 1976. 6.95 o.p. (ISBN 0-698-20357-7, Coward). Putnam Pub Group.

--The Story of Valentine. (Illus.). (gr. 2-4). 1956. PLB 5.99 (ISBN 0-698-30340-7, Coward). Putnam Pub Group.

--Yellow Fur & Little Hawk. (Break-of-Day Bk.). (Illus.). (gr. 1-3). 1979. PLB 6.99 (ISBN 0-698-30687-2, Coward). Putnam Pub Group.

Hayslett, J. J., jt. auth. see Goodban, W. T.

Hayslett, John P. & Hardin, John A. Advances in Systematic Lupus Erythematosis. Repr. write for info (ISBN 0-8089-1560-6). Grune.

Hayt, William & Hughes, George W. Introduction to Electrical Engineering. LC 81-19334. 458p. 1983. Repr. of 1968 ed. write for info. (ISBN 0-89874-440-7). Krieger.

Hayt, William & Kemmerly, Jack. Engineering Circuit Analysis. 3rd ed. (Illus.). 1978. text ed. 34.50 (ISBN 0-07-027393-6, C); solns. manual 12.50 (ISBN 0-07-027394-4). McGraw.

Hayt, William H. & Nevdeck, Gerold W. Electronic Circuit Analysis & Design. LC 75-31032. (Illus.). 384p. 1976. text ed. 33.95 (ISBN 0-395-21919-1). solutions manual 6.95 (ISBN 0-395-21923-X). HM.

Hayt, William H., Jr. Engineering Electromagnetics. 3rd ed. (Electrical Engineering Ser). (Illus.). 140p. 1974. text ed. 25.50 o.p. (ISBN 0-07-027390-1, C); solutions manual 3.50 o.p. (ISBN 0-07-027391-X). McGraw.

--Engineering Electromagnetics. 4th ed. (Electrical Engineering Ser.). (Illus.). 512p. 1981. text ed. 35.95 (ISBN 0-07-027395-2, C); solns. manual 12.50 (ISBN 0-07-027396-0). McGraw.

Hayt, William H., Jr. & Hughes, George W. Introduction to Electrical Engineering. LC 68-27506. (Illus.). 1968. text ed. 33.00 (ISBN 0-07-027384-7, C). McGraw.

Hayter, Alethea, ed. see De Quincy, Thomas.

Haythornthwaite, Philip, jt. auth. see Kemp, Anthony.

Hayward. Computers for Film Makers. (Illus.). 1983. 31.95 (ISBN 0-240-51049-6). Focal Pr.

Hayward, Arthur H. Colonial Lighting. 3rd enl. ed. (Illus.). 9.25 (ISBN 0-8446-2224-9). Peter Smith.

Hayward, Charles & Lento, Robert. The Woodworkers Pocket Book. 1982. 12.95 o.p. (ISBN 0-686-97519-7). P-H.

Hayward, Charles H. Cabinet Making for Beginners. rev. ed. LC 78-24432. (Illus.). 1980. pap. 6.95 (ISBN 0-8069-8186-5); lib. bdg. 6.39 o.p. (ISBN 0-8069-8187-3). Sterling.

--Making Toys in Wood. rev. ed. LC 80-52501. (Illus.). 168p. 1980. pap. 6.95 (ISBN 0-8069-8496-1). Sterling.

--Period Furniture Designs. LC 82-50557. (Illus.). 112p. (Orig.). 1982. pap. 7.95 (ISBN 0-8069-7664-0). Sterling.

--Practical Veneering. LC 79-65083. (Illus.). 1979. pap. 6.95 (ISBN 0-8069-8876-2). Sterling.

--Staining & Wood Polishing. (Illus.). 214p. 1980. pap. 6.95 (ISBN 0-8069-8684-0). Sterling.

--Woodwork Joints: Kinds of Joints., How They Are Cut, & Where Used. LC 75-16454. (Illus.). 176p. 1974. pap. 6.95 (ISBN 0-8069-8806-1). Sterling.

Hayward, Charles H., jt. auth. see Wheeler, William.

Hayward, Christopher. Handel: His Life & Times. (Midas Composer's Life & Times Ser.). (Illus.). 150p. (gr. 7 up). 1983. 16.95 (ISBN 0-88254-807-7). Hippocrene Bks.

Hayward, E., jt. ed. see Fuller, E. G.

Hayward, Frank H. The Educational Ideas of Pestalozzi & Frobel. LC 79-14250. (Illus.). 1979. Repr. of 1905 ed. lib. bdg. 16.25x (ISBN 0-8371-3940-6, HAEI). Greenwood.

Hayward, Herman E. The Structure of Economic Plants. (Illus.). 1967. Repr. of 1938 ed. 28.00 (ISBN 3-7682-0503-7). Lubrecht & Cramer.

Hayward, J. & Narkiewicz, O. Planning in Europe. LC 77-25975. 1978. 22.50x (ISBN 0-312-61406-3). St Martin.

Hayward, J. & Watson, M., eds. Planning, Politics & Public Policy. LC 74-82587. 496p. 1975. 59.50 (ISBN 0-521-20570-0). Cambridge U Pr.

Hayward, Jack & Berki, R. N., eds. State & Society in Contemporary Europe. LC 78-26049. 1979. 26.00x (ISBN 0-312-75604-6). St Martin.

Hayward, John, ed. Oxford Book of Nineteenth-Century English Verse. 1964. 39.95x (ISBN 0-19-812130-X). Oxford U Pr.

Hayward, Keith. Government & British Civil Aerospace: A Case Study in Post-War Technology Policy. 224p. 1983. write for info. (ISBN 0-7190-0877-8). Manchester.

Hayward, Mary & Clark, Connie. Medical Science for Medical Assistants. 1982. text ed. 19.95x (ISBN 0-02-352850-8). Macmillan.

Hayward, Max. Writers in Russia. Blake, Patricia, ed. Schapiro, Leonard. LC 82-47671. (A Helen & Kurt Wolff Bk.). 352p. 1983. 19.95 (ISBN 0-15-183278-1). HarBraceJ.

Hayward, Max & Labedz, Leopold, eds. Literature & Revolution in Soviet Russia, 1917-1962. LC 75-38382. 235p. 1976. Repr. of 1963 ed. lib. bdg. 17.50x (ISBN 0-8371-8651-X, HALR). Greenwood.

Hayward, Max, tr. see Babel, Isaac.

Hayward, Max, tr. see Tertz, Abram & Sinyavsky, Andrei.

Hayward, P. J., jt. auth. see Ryland, J. S.

Hayward, P. L. & Harrison, D. A. Batch Lead Refining: A Casestudy for Process Modelling, 1979. 1981. 70.00x (ISBN 0-686-97039-X, Pub. by W Spring England). State Mutual Bk.

Hayward, R. J. & Ryland, J. British Ascophoran Bryozoans: Keys & Notes for the Identification of the Species. (Synopses of the British Fauna Ser.). 1979. pap. 16.50 o.s.i. (ISBN 0-12-335050-6). Acad Pr.

Hayward, Stan. Scriptwriting for Animation. (Media Manual Ser.). (Illus.). 1977. pap. 10.95 o.s.i. (ISBN 0-240-50967-6). Focal Pr.

Hayward, W. H. Introduction to Radio Frequency Design. (Illus.). 384p. 1982. 28.95 (ISBN 0-13-494021-0). P-H.

Haywood, Carolyn. Away Went the Balloons. (Illus.). (gr. 3-7). 1973. 6.95 o.s.i. (ISBN 0-688-20095-8); PLB 9.55 (ISBN 0-688-30095-2). Morrow.

--B Is for Betsy. LC 39-6264. (Illus.). (gr. 1-5). 1968. pap. 2.50 (ISBN 0-15-611695-2, VoyB). HarBraceJ.

--Back to School with Betsy. LC 43-51225. (Illus.). 176p. (gr. 1-5). 1973. pap. 3.95 (ISBN 0-15-610200-5, VoyB). HarBraceJ.

--Betsy & Billy. LC 41-51926. (Illus.). (gr. 1-5). 1941. 7.95 (ISBN 0-15-206765-5, HJ). HarBraceJ.

--Betsy & Billy. LC 79-10634. (Illus.). (gr. 3-6). 1979. pap. 2.50 (ISBN 0-15-611868-8, VoyB). HarBraceJ.

--Betsy & Mr. Kilpatrick. (Illus.). (gr. 3-7). 1967. 7.25 o.s.i. (ISBN 0-688-21085-6); PLB 9.55 (ISBN 0-688-31085-0). Morrow.

--Betsy & the Boys. LC 77-17266. (Illus.). (gr. 3-7). 1978. pap. 2.95 (ISBN 0-15-611688-X, VoyB). HarBraceJ.

--Betsy & the Circus. (Illus.). (gr. 4-6). 1954. PLB 9.55 (ISBN 0-688-31086-9). Morrow.

--Betsy's Busy Summer. (Illus.). (gr. 3-7). 1956. PLB 10.08 (ISBN 0-688-31087-7). Morrow.

--Betsy's Little Star. (Illus.). (gr. k-3). 1950. PLB 9.55 (ISBN 0-688-31088-5). Morrow.

--Betsy's Play School. LC 77-1615. (Illus.). (gr. 4-6). 1977. 8.95 o.s.i. (ISBN 0-688-22115-7); PLB 9.55 (ISBN 0-688-32115-1). Morrow.

--Betsy's Winterhouse. (Illus.). (gr. 3-7). 1958. PLB 9.55 (ISBN 0-688-31090-7). Morrow.

--A Christmas Fantasy. LC 71-184244. (Illus.). 32p. (gr. k-3). 1972. lib. bdg. 8.25 o.p. (ISBN 0-688-20094-X); PLB 9.55 (ISBN 0-688-30094-4). Morrow.

--Eddie & Gardenia. (Illus.). (gr. 3-7). 1951. PLB 9.55 (ISBN 0-688-31255-1). Morrow.

--Eddie & His Big Deals. (Illus.). (gr. 3-7). 1955. PLB 9.55 (ISBN 0-688-31251-9). Morrow.

--Eddie & Louella. (Illus.). (gr. 3-7). 1959. PLB 9.55 (ISBN 0-688-31254-3). Morrow.

--Eddie & the Fire Engine. (Illus.). (gr. 1-5). 1949. PLB 9.55 (ISBN 0-688-31252-7). Morrow.

--Eddie Makes Music. (Illus.). (gr. 3-7). 1957. PLB 10.08 (ISBN 0-688-31256-X). Morrow.

--Eddie the Dog Holder. (Illus.). (gr. 3-7). 1966. PLB 9.55 (ISBN 0-688-31253-5). Morrow.

--Eddie's Green Thumb. (Illus.). (gr. 3-5). 1980. pap. 1.75 o.p. (ISBN 0-671-56051-4). Archway.

--Eddie's Green Thumb. (Illus.). (gr. 3-7). 1964. PLB 9.55 (ISBN 0-688-31257-8). Morrow.

--Eddie's Happenings. (Illus.). (gr. 3-7). 1971. PLB 9.55 (ISBN 0-688-31258-6). Morrow.

--Eddie's Menagerie. (Illus.). (gr. 4-6). 1978. 10.75 (ISBN 0-688-22158-0); PLB 10.32 (ISBN 0-688-32158-5). Morrow.

--Eddie's Pay Dirt. (Illus.). (gr. 3-7). 1953. PLB 9.55 (ISBN 0-688-31259-4). Morrow.

--Eddie's Valuable Property. LC 74-17499. (Illus.). 192p. (gr. 3-7). 1975. 9.95 (ISBN 0-688-22014-2); PLB 9.55 (ISBN 0-688-32014-7). Morrow.

--Halloween Treats. LC 81-3959. (Illus.). 176p. (gr. 4-6). 1981. 9.95 o.s.i. (ISBN 0-688-00708-2); 9.95 (ISBN 0-688-00708-2). Morrow.

--Here Comes the Bus. (Illus.). (gr. 1-5). 1963. PLB 9.55 (ISBN 0-688-31843-6). Morrow.

--Here's a Penny. LC 44-7329. (Illus.). 150p. (gr. 1-5). 1965. pap. 1.75 (ISBN 0-15-640062-6, VoyB). HarBraceJ.

--The King's Monster. LC 79-18134. (Illus.). 32p. (gr. k-3). 1980. 9.75 (ISBN 0-688-22214-5); PLB 9.36 (ISBN 0-688-32214-X). Morrow.

--Little Eddie. (Illus.). (gr. 1-5). 1947. PLB 9.55 (ISBN 0-688-31682-4). Morrow.

--Penny & Peter. LC 46-21128. (Illus.). (gr. k-3). 1946. 7.95 (ISBN 0-15-260465-0, HJ). HarBraceJ.

--A Valentine Fantasy. LC 75-23083. (Illus.). 32p. (gr. k-3). 1976. 8.95 (ISBN 0-688-22055-X); PLB 8.59 (ISBN 0-688-32055-4). Morrow.

Haywood, Eliza. The Fortunate Foundlings, Seventeen Forty-Four. (The Flowering of the Novel, 1740-1775 Ser: Vol. 10). 1974. lib. bdg. 50.00 o.s.i. (ISBN 0-8240-1109-0). Garland Pub.

--Four Novels of Eliza Haywood. LC 81-24000. 1983. Repr. of 1728 ed. 45.00x (ISBN 0-8201-1376-X). Schol Facsimiles.

--The History of Jemmy & Jenny Jessamy, 1753, 3 vols. (The Flowering of the Novel, 1740-1775 Ser.: Vol. 39). 1974. lib. bdg. 50.00 o.s.i. (ISBN 0-8240-1138-4). Garland Pub.

--The History of Miss Betsy Thoughtless, 4 vols. Paulson, Ronald, ed. LC 78-60837. (Novel 1720-1805 Ser.: Vol. 4). 1979. Set. lib. bdg. 124.00 o.s.i. (ISBN 0-8240-3653-0). Garland Pub.

--Memoirs of a Certain Island Adjacent to the Kingdom of Utopia, Vol. 45. LC 75-170564. (Novel in England, 1700-1775 Ser). lib. bdg. 50.00 o.s.i. (ISBN 0-8240-0557-0). Garland Pub.

--The Secret History of the Present Intrigues of the Court of Caramania. LC 71-170571. (Foundations of the Novel Ser.: Vol. 50). lib. bdg. 50.00 o.s.i. (ISBN 0-8240-0562-7). Garland Pub.

Haywood, Eliza see Walker, Charles.

Haywood, Elizabeth. Adventures of Eovaai, Princess of Ijaveo. LC 70-170595. (Foundations of the Novel Ser.: Vol. 65). lib. bdg. 50.00 o.s.i. (ISBN 0-8240-0577-5). Garland Pub.

Haywood, H. Care & Newbrough, J. R., eds. Living Environments for Developmentally Retarded Persons. 360p. 1981. pap. text ed. 18.95 (ISBN 0-8391-1663-2). Univ Park.

Haywood, H. Carl, jt. ed. see Begab, Michael J.

Haywood, Harry. For a Revolutionary Position on the Negro Question. 46p. (Orig.). 1975. pap. 3.95 (ISBN 0-686-94097-0). Lake View Pr.

--Negro Liberation. 1978. pap. 5.95 (ISBN 0-930720-50-4). Liberator Pr.

--Negro Liberation. 2nd ed. 252p. 1978. pap. text ed. 6.95x (ISBN 0-686-94096-2). Lake View Pr.

Haywood, Kathleen, et al. Motor Development. Kneer, Marian, ed. (Basic Stuff Ser.: No. I, 6 of 6). (Illus.). 55p. (gr. k up). 1981. pap. text ed. 6.25 (ISBN 0-88314-029-2). AAHPERD.

Haywood, R. W. Equilibrium Thermodynamics for Engineers & Scientists. LC 79-40650. 1980. 66.95x (ISBN 0-471-27631-6, Pub. by Wiley-Interscience); pap. o.p. (ISBN 0-471-27630-8). Wiley.

--Thermodynamics Tables in SI Units. 2nd ed. 1972. 8.95 (ISBN 0-521-09714-2). Cambridge U Pr.

Haywood, Richard M. The Myth of Rome's Fall. LC 78-12128. 1979. Repr. of 1958 ed. lib. bdg. 17.25x (ISBN 0-313-21108-6, HAMY). Greenwood.

Haywood, William D. Bill Haywood's Book: The Autobiography of William D. Haywood. LC 82-25134. 368p. 1983. Repr. of 1929 ed. lib. bdg. 35.00x (ISBN 0-313-23842-1, HABI). Greenwood.

Hazan, Baruch A. Olympic Sports & Propaganda Games: Moscow 1980. LC 81-7447. 250p. 1982. text ed. 19.95 (ISBN 0-87855-436-X); pap. 8.95 o.p. (ISBN 0-87855-881-0). Transaction Bks.

Hazan, Marcella. The Classic Italian Cook Book. 1976. 16.50 (ISBN 0-394-40510-2). Knopf.

--More Classic Italian Cooking. LC 78-54923. (Illus.). 1978. 16.95 (ISBN 0-394-49855-0). Knopf.

Hazan, Victor. Italian Wine. LC 82-47831. 1982. 17.95 (ISBN 0-394-50266-3). Knopf.

Hazard, Barbara. The Disobedient Daughter. 1982. pap. 2.25 (ISBN 0-451-11557-0, AE1557, Sig). NAL.

Hazard, C. & Mitton, S., eds. Active Galactic Nuclei. LC 78-67426. 1979. 42.50 (ISBN 0-521-22494-2). Cambridge U Pr.

Hazard, Charles. Baltimore Coloring Book. (Illus.). 32p. (Orig.). 1983. pap. 3.25 (ISBN 0-88045-025-8). Stemmer Hse.

Hazard, Geoffrey, jt. auth. see James, Fleming, Jr.

Hazard, Geoffrey C. Pleading & Procedure; State & Federal Cases & Materials: 1982 Supplement. 4th ed. 78p. 1982. pap. text ed. write for info. (ISBN 0-88277-073-X). Foundation Pr.

Hazard, Geoffrey C., Jr., jt. auth. see Ehrlich, Thomas.

Hazard, Geoffrey C., Jr., ed. Law in a Changing America. LC 68-27498. 1968. 4.95 (ISBN 0-936904-02-X); pap. 2.45 (ISBN 0-936904-27-5). Am Assembly.

Hazard, Harry W. & Setton, Kenneth M., eds. A History of the Crusades, Vol. 4: The Art & Architecture of the Crusader States. LC 68-9837. (Illus.). 444p. 1977. 40.00x (ISBN 0-299-06820-X). U of Wis Pr.

Hazard, J. N. Soviet Legal System. 3rd ed. LC 77-24349. 621p. 1977. 20.00. Oceana.

Hazard, James E., jt. auth. see Carr, Robert F.

Hazard, John N. Soviet System of Government. 4th ed. LC 68-24557. 1968. 11.50x o.s.i. (ISBN 0-226-32191-6); pap. text ed. 3.50x o.s.i. (ISBN 0-226-32192-4). U of Chicago Pr.

Hazard, Paul. Books, Children & Men. 1960. 9.00 o.p. (ISBN 0-87675-050-1); pap. 6.50 o.p. (ISBN 0-87675-051-X). Horn Bk.

--European Mind, Sixteen Eighty to Seventeen Fifteen. pap. 4.95 o.p. (ISBN 0-452-00410-1, F410, Mer). NAL.

Hazard, William R. Tort Liability & the Music Educator. 32p. 1979. 2.00 (ISBN 0-686-37919-5). Music Ed.

Hazari, Bharat, et al. Non-Traded & Intermediate Goods & the Pure Theory of International Trade. 1981. 32.50 (ISBN 0-312-57728-1). St Martin.

Hazari, Bharat R. The Pure Theory of International Trade & Distortions. LC 78-9092. 206p. 1978. 34.95x o.s.i. (ISBN 0-470-26430-6). Halsted Pr.

Hazarika, Niru. Public Service Commissions. 1979. text ed. 9.50x (ISBN 0-391-01847-7). Humanities.

Hazaz, Haim. Gates of Bronze. Levi, S. Gershon, tr. from Heb. LC 74-15463. 1975. 7.95 o.p. (ISBN 0-8276-0059-3, 359). Jewish Pubn.

Hazel, Jon, ed. Ovid-The Roman World: Selections from the Poems. (Illus.). 122p. 1971. pap. text ed. 4.50x (ISBN 0-04-871001-6). Bolchazy-Carducci.

Hazel, Joseph, jt. ed. see Kaufman, Erle.

Hazelbauer, G., ed. Taxis & Behavior. (Receptors & Recognition Series B: Vol. 5). 1978. 47.95x (ISBN 0-412-14880-3, Dist. by Chapman & Hall). Methuen Inc.

Hazelden. Stadus Guide & Survey Book. 1979. pap. 3.50 (ISBN 0-89486-066-6). Hazelden.

--Stadus Survey Book. 1979. pap. 1.50 (ISBN 0-89486-067-4). Hazelden.

Hazelip, Harold, jt. auth. see Baxter, Batsell B.

Hazelkorn, Ellen. Marx & Engels: On Ireland - an Annotated Checklist. (Bibliographical Ser.: No. 15). 1981. 2.00 o.p. (ISBN 0-89977-031-2). Am Inst Marxist.

Hazeltine, Barrett. Introduction to Electronic Circuits & Applications: Preliminary Edition. 384p. (Orig.). 1980. pap. text ed. 13.95 (ISBN 0-8403-2182-1). Kendall-Hunt.

Hazelton, Charles J. Pocket Concordance of the New Testament. 1979. leatherflex 4.95 o.p. (ISBN 0-8407-5691-7). Nelson.

Hazelton, Harriet R., jt. auth. see Hays, Anne M.

Hazelton, Jared & Hazleton, Jared. Gold Rush Economics: Development Planning in the Persian-Arabian Gulf. (Working Paper Ser.: No. 4). 40p. 1976. 2.50 (ISBN 0-686-10608-3). LBJ Sch Public Affairs.

Hazelton, John H. Declaration of Independence: Its History. LC 79-124892. (American Constitutional & Legal History Ser). (Illus.). 1970. Repr. of 1906 ed. lib. bdg. 55.00 (ISBN 0-306-71987-8). Da Capo.

Hazelton, Lesley. Israeli Women. 1979. pap. 3.95 o.p. (ISBN 0-671-24408-6, Touchstone Bks). S&S.

Hazelton, Nika. The Regional Italian Kitchen. (Illus.). 370p. 1983. pap. 7.95 (ISBN 0-87131-413-4). M Evans.

Hazelton, Nika, jt. auth. see Stewart-Gordon, Faith.

Hazelwood, Arthur. Economic Integration: The East African Experience. LC 75-19687. (Illus.). 192p. 1976. 22.50 (ISBN 0-312-23415-5). St Martin.

Hazen, Barbara S. Even If I Did Something Awful? LC 81-1907. (Illus.). 32p. (ps-2). 1981. 8.95 o.p. (ISBN 0-689-30843-4). Atheneum.

--It's a Shame About the Rain: The Bright Side of Disappointment. LC 81-13163. (Illus.). 32p. 1982. 9.95 (ISBN 0-89885-050-9). Human Sci Pr.

--Very Shy. LC 81-6809. (Illus.). 32p. 1982. 9.95 (ISBN 0-89885-067-3). Human Sci Pr.

Hazen, Barbara S., compiled by. Happy Fiftieth Anniversary. (Illus.). 1979. boxed 5.50 (ISBN 0-8378-1702-1). Gibson.

--Happy Twenty-Fifth Anniversary. (Illus.). 1979. boxed 5.50 (ISBN 0-8378-1701-3). Gibson.

--You're One in a Millon, Grandpa! 1979. pap. 5.50 boxed (ISBN 0-8378-5022-3). Gibson.

Hazen, Charles D. Contemporary American Opinion of the French Revolution. 1964. 8.50 o.p. (ISBN 0-8446-1228-6). Peter Smith.

--The French Revolution & Napoleon. 385p. 1982. Repr. of 1917 ed. lib. bdg. 50.00 (ISBN 0-89987-390-1). Darby Bks.

Hazen, Helen. Endless Rapture: Rape, Romance, & the Female Imagination. 192p. 1983. 11.95 (ISBN 0-686-83854-8, ScribT). Scribner.

Hazen, M. Hindle, jt. ed. see Hazen, R. M.

Hazen, Nancy. Grownups Cry Too: Los Adultos Tambien Lloran. 2nd ed. Cotera, Martha P., tr. LC 78-71542. (Illus.). 25p. (ps-1). 1978. pap. 2.95 (ISBN 0-914996-19-3). Lollipop Power.

Hazen, R. M., ed. North American Geology: Early Writings. LC 79-708. (Benchmark Papers in Geology: Vol. 51). 356p. 1979. 46.50 (ISBN 0-87933-345-6). Hutchinson Ross.

Hazen, R. M. & Hazen, M. Hindle, eds. American Geological Literature 1669-1850. LC 79-25898. 448p. 1980. 36.50 (ISBN 0-87933-371-5). Hutchinson Ross.

Hazen, Rachel. Words Ready for Music -- Poems of a Young Teenager. (gr. 6-12). 1983. pap. 4.95 case bound (ISBN 0-8283-1853-0). Branden.

Hazen, Robert M. & Finger, Larry W. Comparative Crystal Chemistry: Temperature, Pressure, Composition & the Variation of Crystal Structure. LC 82-2834. 229p. 1982. 43.95 (ISBN 0-471-10268-7, Pub. by Wiley-Interscience). Wiley.

Hazewindus, Nico & Phillips, N. V. The U. S. Microelectronics Industry: Technical Change, Industry Growth, & Social Impact. LC 82-12191. (The Technology & Economic Growth Ser.). (Illus.). 165p. 1982. 25.00 (ISBN 0-08-029376-X). Pergamon.

Hazlehurst, F. Hamilton. Gardens of Illusion: The Genius of Andre Le Nostre. (Illus.). 448p. 1981. 47.50 (ISBN 0-8265-1209-7). Vanderbilt U Pr.

Hazleman, Brian L., jt. auth. see Watson, Peter G.

Hazleton, J. E. & Bell, F. W. Recent Developments & Research in Fisheries Economics: Papers. LC 66-27364. 233p. 1967. 15.00 (ISBN 0-379-00317-1). Oceana.

Hazleton, Jared, jt. auth. see Hazelton, Jared.

Hazlett, Thomas W. see Theberge, Leonard J.

Hazlewood, A. & Livingstone, I. Irrigation Economics in Poor Countries: Illustrated by the Usango Plains of Tanzania. 150p. 1982. 25.00 (ISBN 0-08-027451-X). Pergamon.

Hazlitt, Henry. Economics in One Lesson. 1979. 8.95 o.p. (ISBN 0-87000-427-1, Arlington Hse). Crown.

--Economics in One Lesson. 218p. 1981. pap. 5.95 (ISBN 0-517-54823-2, Arlington Hse). Crown.

--The Failure of the 'New Economics' An Analysis of the Keynesian Fallacies. 1974. Repr. of 1959 ed. 11.95 o.p. (ISBN 0-87000-266-X, Arlington Hse). Crown.

Hazlitt, W., tr. see De Vigny, Alfred.

Hazlitt, William. Essay on the Principles of Human Action, 1805. LC 70-75943. (Hist. of Psych. Ser.). 1969. 33.00x (ISBN 0-8201-1053-1). Schol Facsimiles.

--William Hazlitt: Selected Writings. Blythe, William, ed. 1982. pap. 5.95 (ISBN 0-14-043050-4). Penguin.

Hazlitt, William C. English Proverbs & Proverbial Phrases. LC 67-23914. 1969. Repr. of 1907 ed. 42.00x (ISBN 0-8103-3199-3). Gale.

--Gleanings in Old Garden Literature. LC 68-21773. 1968. Repr. of 1887 ed. 30.00x (ISBN 0-8103-3509-3). Gale.

--Old Cookery Books & Ancient Cuisine. LC 68-30612. 1968. Repr. of 1886 ed. 30.00x (ISBN 0-8103-3306-6). Gale.

--Studies in Jocular Literature. LC 67-24352. 1969. Repr. of 1890 ed. 30.00x (ISBN 0-8103-3529-8). Gale.

Hazm, Imam Ibn. Al Muhalla. Quinlan, Hamid, ed. Ayad, Foaud, tr. LC 82-70454. (Illus.). 125p. 1983. pap. 4.50 (ISBN 0-89259-037-8). Am Trust Pubns.

Hazo, Samuel. Blood Rights. LC 68-21627. (Pitt Poetry Ser.). 1968. 9.95 o.p. (ISBN 0-8229-3147-8); pap. 4.50 (ISBN 0-8229-5157-6). U of Pittsburgh Pr.

--Inscripts. LC 75-14553. xiv, 140p. 1975. 10.00x (ISBN 0-8214-0199-8, 82-82048); pap. 6.00 (ISBN 0-8214-0205-6, 82-82055). Ohio U Pr.

--Smithereened Apart: A Critique of Hart Crane. LC 62-22179. (Illus.). x, 146p. 1977. 10.00x (ISBN 0-8214-0373-7, 82-82675); pap. 4.95x (ISBN 0-8214-0383-4, 82-82683). Ohio U Pr.

--Thank a Bored Angel: Selected Poems. 128p. 1983. 14.00 (ISBN 0-8112-0869-9); pap. 6.25 (ISBN 0-8112-0868-0). New Directions.

Hazo, Samuel, tr. see De Rougemont, Denis.

Hazo, Samuel, tr. see Said, Ali A.

Hazon, M. Dizionario Garzanti: Italiano-Inglese, Inglese-Italiano. 1024p. (Eng. & Ital.). 1980. 19.95 (ISBN 0-686-97642-8, M-9187). French & Eur.

--Grande Dizionario Hazon Garzanti Inglese-Italiano, Italiano-Inglese. 2112p. (Eng. & Ital.). 1980. 49.95 (ISBN 0-686-97429-8, M-9186). French & Eur.

Hazrat Inayat Khan. Aphorisms. (The Collected Works of Hazrat Inayat Khan). 128p. (Orig.). Date not set. pap. 4.95 cancelled o.s.i. (ISBN 0-930872-22-3, 1008P). Omega Pr NM.

--The Awakening of the Human Spirit. LC 82-80091. (The Collected Works of Hazyat Inayat Khan Ser.). 224p. (Orig.). 1982. pap. 8.95 (ISBN 0-930872-27-4, 1014P). Omega Pr NM.

--The Bowl of Saki. LC 80-54276. (The Collected Works of Hazrat Inayat Khan). 144p. (Orig.). 1981. pap. 4.95 (ISBN 0-930872-20-7, 1007P). Omega Pr NM.

Hazzard, Gene. Yesterday's Memories, Today's Smiles. 1979. 4.95 o.p. (ISBN 0-533-03895-2). Vantage.

Hazzard, Mary. Sheltered Lives. LC 79-25492. 256p. 1980. 11.95 (ISBN 0-914842-43-9). Madrona Pubs.

Hazzard, Mary E. Critical Care Nursing. (Nursing Outline Ser.). 1978. spiral bdg. 12.75 (ISBN 0-87488-384-9). Med Exam.

Hazzlewood, John W. House Journals. LC 67-874. (Facts of Print Ser). 1967. Repr. of 1963 ed. 8.95 o.p. (ISBN 0-289-27810-4). Dufour.

H. D., pseud. Trilogy. Incl. The Walls Do Not Fall; Tribute to the Angels; The Flowering of the Rod. LC 73-78848. 128p. 1973. 5.95 (ISBN 0-8112-0490-1); pap. 3.95 o.s.i. (ISBN 0-8112-0491-X, NDP362). New Directions.

HDD Resource Consultants, Ltd. Marketing Guide for Gold. LC 82-61849. (A World Mining Report). 206p. 1982. pap. 247.50 (ISBN 0-87930-139-2, 624). Miller Freeman.

H'Doubler, Margaret N. Dance: A Creative Art Experience. 2nd ed. (Illus.). 200p. 1957. 17.50 (ISBN 0-299-01520-3); pap. 6.95 (ISBN 0-299-01524-6). U of Wis Pr.

He, Li. Goddesses, Ghosts, & Demons: The Collected Poems of Li He (790-816) Rev. ed. Frodsham, J. D., tr. from Chinese. LC 82-81477. Orig. Title: The Poems of Li Ho. 384p. (Orig.). 1983. pap. 21.00 (ISBN 0-86547-084-7). N Point Pr.

Heacham, R. H. Pay Systems. 120p. 1979. 25.00x (ISBN 0-686-92009-0, Pub. by Heinemann England). State Mutual Bk.

Heacock, John, ed. The Earth's Crust. LC 77-83153. (Geophysical Monograph Ser.: Vol. 20). 1977. text ed. 45.00 (ISBN 0-87590-020-8). Am Geophysical.

Heacock, John G., ed. The Structure & Physical Properties of the Earth's Crust. LC 75-182370. (Geophysical Monograph Ser.: Vol. 14). (Illus.). 1971. 19.00 o.p. (ISBN 0-87590-014-3). Am Geophysical.

Heacock, William. Encyclopedia of Victorian Colored Pattern Glass Book IV: Custard Glass from A to Z. (Illus.). pap. 12.95 (ISBN 0-915410-08-7); price guide 1.00 (ISBN 0-686-50067-9). Wallace-Homestead.

--Encyclopedia of Victorian Colored Pattern Glass, Book II: Opalescent Glass from A to Z. (Illus.). 12.95 (ISBN 0-915410-03-6); price guide 1.00 (ISBN 0-686-50063-6). Wallace-Homestead.

--Encyclopedia of Victorian Colored Pattern Glass, Book III: Syrups, Sugar Shakers & Cruets. (Illus.). 12.95 (ISBN 0-915410-05-2); price guide 1.00 (ISBN 0-686-50065-2). Wallace-Homestead.

--Encyclopedia of Victorian Colored Pattern Glass, Book I: Toothpick Holders from A to Z. (Illus.). 9.95 (ISBN 0-915410-01-X); price guide 1.00 (ISBN 0-686-50061-X). Wallace-Homestead.

--Encyclopedia of Victorian Colored Pattern Glass, Book V: The History of the United States Glass Company. (Illus.). pap. 14.95 (ISBN 0-915410-11-7); price guide 1.00 (ISBN 0-686-50069-5). Wallace-Homestead.

--Fenton Art Glass Co. The First Twenty-Five Years. (Illus.). pap. 14.95 (ISBN 0-686-51489-0, 99024); price guide 1.00 (ISBN 0-686-51490-4). Wallace-Homestead.

--One Thousand Toothpick Holders. (Illus.). softcover 10.95 (ISBN 0-915410-10-9); price guide 1.00 (ISBN 0-686-51588-9). Wallace-Homestead.

Heacox, Cecil E. & Heacox, Dorothy. The Gallant Grouse: All about the Hunting & Natural History of Old Ruff. (Illus.). 1980. 14.95 o.p. (ISBN 0-679-51052-4). McKay.

Heacox, Dorothy, jt. auth. see Heacox, Cecil E.

Head, jt. auth. see Williams.

Head, Ann. Always in August. 1974. pap. 1.25 o.p. (ISBN 0-451-06023-7, Y6023, Sig). NAL.

--Everybody Adored Cara. (Orig.). 1975. pap. 1.25 o.p. (ISBN 0-451-06356-2, Y6356, Sig). NAL.

--Fair with Rain. 128p. 1973. pap. 0.95 o.p. (ISBN 0-451-05526-8, Q5526, Sig). NAL.

--Mr. & Mrs. Bo Jo Jones. 192p. (YA) (RL 9). 1973. pap. 1.95 (ISBN 0-451-12375-1, AE2375, Sig). NAL.

--Mr. & Mrs. Bo Jo Jones. 1967. 9.95 (ISBN 0-399-10562-X). Putnam Pub Group.

Head, B. V. Historia Numorum. (Illus.). 1983. Repr. of 1911 ed. lib. bdg. 60.00 (ISBN 0-942666-17-8). S J Durst.

Head, Barclay V. Historia Numorum. 1977. 55.00 o.p. (ISBN 0-685-51525-7, Pub by Spink & Son England). S J Durst.

Head, Barkley. Coinage of Lydia & Persia. LC 80-70068. 1983. Repr. of 1876 ed. lib. bdg. 30.00 (ISBN 0-915262-44-4). S J Durst.

Head, Barry & Sequin, Jim. Who Am I? (I Am, I Can, I Will Ser.). 36p. (Orig.). 1975. pap. 3.95 (ISBN 0-8331-0035-1). Hubbard Sci.

Head, Barry, jt. auth. see Paylor, Neil.

Head, Barry, jt. auth. see Rogers, Fred.

Head, Bessie. When the Rain Clouds Gather. LC 69-12089. 1969. 5.95 o.p. (ISBN 0-671-20176-X). S&S.

Head, Brian. State & Economy in Australia. 248p. 1982. 18.50x (ISBN 0-19-554261-4). Oxford U Pr.

Head, Brian, jt. auth. see Patience, Allan.

Head, Brian W., jt. ed. see Harman, Elizabeth J.

Head, Constance. Emperor Julian. LC 75-15724. (World Leaders Ser.: No. 53). 1976. lib. bdg. 12.50 o.p. (ISBN 0-8057-7650-8, Twayne). G K Hall.

--Imperial Byzantine Portraits. (Illus.). 280p. 1982. lib. bdg. 50.00 (ISBN 0-686-94736-3). Caratzas Bros.

--Justinian Two of Byzantium. (Illus.). 196p. 1972. 19.50x o.p. (ISBN 0-299-06030-6). U of Wis Pr.

--The Man Who Carried the Cross for Jesus. (Arch Bk.: No. 16). (Illus.). 1979. 0.89 (ISBN 0-570-06124-5, 59-1242). Concordia.

--The Story of Deborah. (Arch Bk Ser.: No. 15). (Illus.). (gr. k-3). 1978. 0.89 (ISBN 0-570-06116-4, 59-1234). Concordia.

Head, Derek. Marinas: Harbor Design, Vol. 2. (Viewpoint Marina Ser.). (Illus.). 1976. pap. 11.75x (ISBN 0-7210-1022-9). Scholium Intl.

--Marinas: Water Recreation, Vol. 1. (Viewpoint Marina Ser.). (Illus.). 1974. pap. 12.50x (ISBN 0-685-82987-1). Scholium Intl.

--Residential Marinas & Yachting Amenities. (Marinas Ser.: No. 3). (Illus.). 84p. (Orig.). 1980. pap. text ed. 18.50x (ISBN 0-7210-1135-7, Pub. by C & CA London). Scholium Intl.

Head, E. D., ed. see Scarborough, Lee R.

Head, George L., jt. auth. see Williams, C. Arthur, Jr.

Head, J. J., ed. see Ayala, F. J.

Head, J. J., ed. see Bonner, James.

Head, J. J., ed. see Colbert, Edwin H.

Head, J. J., ed. see Fincham, J. R.

Head, J. J., ed. see John, Bernard & Lewis, Kenneth.

Head, J. J., ed. see Jordan, E. G.

Head, J. J., ed. see Nachmias, Vivianne T.

Head, J. J., ed. see Nicholls, Peter.

Head, J. J., ed. see Pardee, Arthur B. & Veer Reddy, G. P.

Head, J. J., ed. see Pringle, W. S.

Head, J. J., ed. see Randle, P. J. & Denton, R. M.

Head, J. J., ed. see Rhodes, Philip.

Head, J. J., ed. see Richard, Alison F.

Head, J. J., ed. see Sanders, F. Kingsley.

Head, J. J., ed. see Satir, Peter.

Head, J. J., ed. see Tata, J. R.

Head, J. J., ed. see Wigglesworth, V. B.

Head, John, jt. ed. see Beatts, Anne.

Head, K. Maynard. Brogans, Clothespins & a Twist of Tobacco. (Illus.). 160p. (Orig.). 1983. 8.95 (ISBN 0-89769-077-X); pap. 4.95 (ISBN 0-89769-050-8). Pine Mntn.

Head, Lee. The Crystal Clear Case. LC 77-8431. 1977. 7.95 o.p. (ISBN 0-399-11984-1). Putnam Pub Group.

--The First of January. 250p. 1974. 6.95 o.p. (ISBN 0-399-11221-9). Putnam Pub Group.

--Horizon. 312p. 1981. 15.95 (ISBN 0-399-12638-4). Putnam Pub Group.

Head, R. E. Lace & Embroidery Collector. LC 74-2031. 1971. Repr. of 1922 ed. 37.00x (ISBN 0-8103-3663-4). Gale.

Head, Sidney W., jt. auth. see Eastman, Susan T.

Head, Sydney W., ed. & pref. by. Broadcasting in Africa: A Continental Survey of Radio & Television. LC 73-79478. (International & Comparative Broadcasting Ser.). 469p. 1974. 34.95 (ISBN 0-87722-027-1). Temple U Pr.

Head, Sydney W., et al. Broadcasting in America. 4th ed. LC 81-83274. 1982. 21.95 (ISBN 0-395-28657-3); instr's manual 1.25 (ISBN 0-395-28658-1); study guide 7.50 (ISBN 0-395-29624-2). HM.

Head, William C. Pharmaceutical Quality Control. 144p. 1983. 8.00 (ISBN 0-682-49983-8). Exposition.

Headey, Bruce. Housing Policy in the Developed Economy: UK, USA, & Sweden. LC 78-9404. (Illus.). 1978. 30.00x (ISBN 0-312-39353-9). St Martin.

Heading, J. Mathematical Methods in Science & Engineering. 1970. 26.95 (ISBN 0-444-19680-3). Elsevier.

--Mathematical Methods in Science & Engineering. 688p. 1970. pap. text ed. 19.95 (ISBN 0-7131-3219-1). E Arnold.

Heading, John. From Now to Eternity (Revelation) 1980. pap. 3.95 o.p. (ISBN 0-937396-15-X, Everyday Pub). Walterick Pubs.

Headings, Philip R. T. S. Eliot. (U. S. Authors Ser.: No. 57). 1964. lib. bdg. 10.95 o.p. (ISBN 0-8057-0236-9, Twayne). G K Hall.

--T. S. Eliot. Rev. ed. (United States Authors Ser.). 1982. lib. bdg. 13.95 (ISBN 0-8057-7357-6, Twayne). G K Hall.

Headington, Bonnie J. Communication in the Counseling Relationship. LC 78-9026. 1979. 15.50x (ISBN 0-910328-24-2); pap. 10.00x (ISBN 0-910328-23-4). Carroll Pr.

Headington, Christopher. Britten. Lade, John, ed. (The Composer as Contemporary Ser.: No. 1). (Illus.). 166p. 1982. text ed. 14.50 (ISBN 0-8419-0802-8); pap. text ed. 9.50 (ISBN 0-8419-0803-6). Holmes & Meier.

--The History of Western Music. LC 76-20883. 1977. 15.50 (ISBN 0-02-871090-8); pap. text ed. 8.95 (ISBN 0-02-871080-0). Schirmer Bks.

--Illustrated Dictionary of Musical Terms. LC 79-48042. (Illus.). 160p. 1980. 12.95i o.p. (ISBN 0-06-011819-9, HarpT). Har-Row.

--The Performing World of the Musician. LC 81-50299. (The Performing World Ser.). 15.20 (ISBN 0-382-06592-1). Silver.

Headland, Isaac T. Home Life in China. LC 79-177278. (Illus.). xii, 319p. 1971. Repr. of 1914 ed. 45.00x (ISBN 0-8103-3822-X). Gale.

Headley, Elizabeth see Cavanna, Betty, pseud.

Headley, Joel T. The Adirondack, or, Life in the Woods: Facsim of 1849 ed., with added chapters. LC 82-15610. (Illus.). 512p. 24.95 (ISBN 0-916346-47-1). Harbor Hill Bks.

Headley, John M. The Emperor & His Chancellor: A Study of the Imperial Chancellery of Gattinara. LC 82-4525. (Cambridge Studies in Early Modern History). 208p. Date not set. 42.50 (ISBN 0-521-24444-7). Cambridge U Pr.

--Luther's View of Church History. 1963. 47.50x (ISBN 0-686-51413-0). Elliots Bks.

Headon, Deidre. Mythical Beasts. (Leprechaun Library). (Illus.). 64p. 1981. 4.95 (ISBN 0-399-12664-3). Putnam Pub Group.

Headrick, Daniel R. The Tools of Empire: Technology & European Imperialism in the Nineteenth Century. 1981. text ed. 17.95x (ISBN 0-19-502831-7); pap. text ed. 7.95x (ISBN 0-19-502832-5). Oxford U Pr.

Headstrom, Richard. Adventures with Freshwater Animals. (Illus.). 217p. (gr. 5 up). 1983. pap. 5.00 (ISBN 0-486-24453-9). Dover.

--Identifying Animal Tracks: Mammals, Birds & Other Animals of the Eastern United States. (Illus.). 128p. 1983. pap. 2.50 (ISBN 0-486-24442-3). Dover.

Heady, E. B., jt. auth. see Heady, H. F.

Heady, Earl O., jt. auth. see Agrawal, R. C.

Heady, Earl O., jt. auth. see Hopkins, John A.

Heady, Earl O., ed. Economic Models & Quantitative Methods for Decisions & Planning in Agriculture. 1971. 12.50x (ISBN 0-8138-0540-6). Iowa St U Pr.

Heady, Earl O. & Whiting, Larry, eds. Externalities in the Transformation of Agriculture: Distribution of Benefits & Costs from Development. (Illus.). 352p. 1975. text ed. 13.50x (ISBN 0-8138-0045-5). Iowa St U Pr.

Heady, Earl O., et al. Roots of the Farm Problem. (Illus.). 1965. 4.50x o.p. (ISBN 0-8138-1365-4). Iowa St U Pr.

Heady, Eleanor. Tales of the Nimipoo: From the Land of the Nez Perce' Indians. LC 74-18129. (Illus.). 128p. (gr. 3 up). 1975. lib. ed. 4.98 o.s.i. (ISBN 0-695-40535-7). Follett.

Heady, Eleanor B. Safiri the Singer: East African Tales. LC 76-161551. (Illus.). 96p. (gr. 2-4). 1972. 5.95 o.s.i. (ISBN 0-695-80244-5); PLB 5.97 o.s.i. (ISBN 0-695-40244-7). Follett.

--Sage Smoke: Tales of the Shoshoni-Bannock Indians. LC 73-81997. (Illus.). 96p. (gr. 2-5). 1973. trade ed. 4.95 (ISBN 0-695-80408-1). Follett.

Heady, F. Public Administration: A Comparative Perspective. (Public Administration & Public Policy Ser.; a Comprehensive Publication Program: Vol. 6). 1979. 26.50 (ISBN 0-8247-6802-7). Dekker.

Heady, H. F. & Heady, E. B. Range & Wildlife Management in the Tropics. LC 81-23604. (Illus.). 192p. (Orig.). 1982. pap. text ed. 6.95 (ISBN 0-582-60896-1). Longman.

Heady, Harold F. Rangeland Management. (American Forestry Ser.). (Illus.). 500p. 1975. text ed. 22.00 o.p. (ISBN 0-07-027693-5, C). McGraw.

Heafford, Philip. The Math Entertainer. LC 82-40420. (Illus.). 176p. 1983. pap. 3.95 (ISBN 0-394-71374-5, Vin). Random.

Heal, Ambrose. The London Furniture Makers, 1660-1840. LC 72-87434. (Illus.). 320p. 1973. pap. 6.00 o.p. (ISBN 0-486-22903-3). Dover.

Heal, Felicity. Of Prelates & Princes: A Study of the Economic & Social Position of the Tudor Episcopate. LC 79-41791. (Illus.). 368p. 1980. 52.50 (ISBN 0-521-22950-2). Cambridge U Pr.

Heal, Felicity, jt. ed. see O'Day, Rosemary.

Heal, G. M., jt. auth. see Dasgupta, P. S.

Heal, G. M., jt. auth. see Hughes, G. A.

Heald, Dorothy, ed. Reading for Young People: The Southeast. 176p. 1980. pap. text ed. 11.00 (ISBN 0-8389-0300-2). ALA.

Heald, M. A. & Wharton, C. B. Plasma Diagnostics with Microwaves. LC 77-13781. 470p. 1978. Repr. of 1965 ed. 27.00 (ISBN 0-88275-626-5). Krieger.

Heald, M. A., jt. auth. see Elmore, W. C.

Heald, Mark A., jt. auth. see Marion, Jerry.

Heald, Morrell & Kaplan, Lawrence S. Culture & Diplomacy: The American Experience. LC 77-71863. (Contributions in American History: No. 63). 1977. lib. bdg. 29.95 (ISBN 0-8371-9541-1, HEA/). Greenwood.

Healey, Alan, ed. Language Learner's Field Guide. 500p. 1975. pap. 9.50x (ISBN 0-7263-0356-9); microfiche 6.00 (ISBN 0-88312-323-1). Summer Inst Ling.

Healey, Deryck. Living with Color: The Workbook for Managing the Colors in Your Home. LC 82-80278. (Illus.). 160p. 1982. 29.95 (ISBN 0-528-81549-0). Rand.

Healey, Edna. Lady Unknown: The Life of Angela Burdett-Coutts. LC 78-5470. (Illus.). 1978. 12.50 o.p. (ISBN 0-698-10939-2, Coward). Putnam Pub Group.

Healey, F. G. Foreign Language Teaching in the Universities. 1967. 23.50 (ISBN 0-7190-0291-5). Manchester.

Healey, J. A., jt. auth. see Allsop, R. T.

Healey, Larry. Angry Mountain. LC 82-45998. 192p. (gr. 6 up). 1983. PLB 9.95 (ISBN 0-396-08129-0). Dodd.

--The Claw of the Bear. LC 77-17299. (gr. 6 up). 1978. PLB 8.90 s&l (ISBN 0-531-01469-X). Watts.

--The Hoard of the Himalayas. 160p. (gr. 7 up). 1981. PLB 7.95 (ISBN 0-396-07978-4). Dodd.

--The Town Is on Fire. (gr. 6 up). 1979. PLB 8.90 s&l (ISBN 0-531-02898-4). Watts.

Healey, M. Advances in Small Computer Technolog. 35p. 1981. pap. 28.60x (ISBN 0-686-97774-2). Renouf.

Healey, Martin. Principles of Automatic Control. 333p. 1968. 14.00 (ISBN 0-442-33279-3, Pub. by Van Nos Reinhold). Krieger.

Healey, P. & McDougall, G., eds. Planning Theory-Prospects for the Nineteen Eighties: Selected Papers from a Conference Held in Oxford, UK, 2-4 April 1981. (Urban & Regional Planning Ser.). 330p. 1982. 40.00 (ISBN 0-08-027449-8). Pergamon.

Healey, Richard. Reduction, Time & Reality: Studies in the Philosophy of the Natural Sciences. 208p. 1981. 29.95 (ISBN 0-521-23708-4). Cambridge U Pr.

Healey, Tim. Disasters. LC 79-64165. (Timespan Ser.). PLB 12.68 (ISBN 0-382-06301-5). Silver.

--Escapes. LC 79-66102. (Timespan Ser.). PLB 12.68 (ISBN 0-382-06334-1). Silver.

--Explorers. LC 80-52505. (Timespan Ser.). PLB 12.68 (ISBN 0-382-06413-5). Silver.

--Mysteries. LC 79-93058. (Timespan Ser.). PLB 12.68 (ISBN 0-382-06357-0). Silver.

--Spies. LC 79-64164. (Timespan Ser.). PLB 12.68 (ISBN 0-382-06300-7). Silver.

Health, Cyril. Yesterday's Town: Hertford. 1981. 39.50x o.p. (ISBN 0-86023-086-4, Pub. by Barracuda England). State Mutual Bk.

Health Law Center. Hospital Law Manual: Administrator's & Attorney's Set, 6 vols. LC 74-80713. 495.00; Administrator's Set, 3 Vols. 350.00 (ISBN 0-912862-06-8); Attorney's Set 3 Vols. 425.00 (ISBN 0-912862-05-X). Aspen Systems.

Healy, ed. Famous Science-Fiction Stories. 1957. 5.95 o.s.i. (ISBN 0-394-60731-7, G31). Modern Lib.

Healy, Bill & Hartley, Joe. Ten Great Basketball Offenses. (Illus.). 1971. 14.95 (ISBN 0-13-903294-0, Parker). P-H.

Healy, Bruce & Bugat, Paul. The Art & Science of French Pastry. 284p. 1983. 19.95 (ISBN 0-8120-5456-3). Barron.

Healy, C., jt. auth. see Winn, Charles S.

Healy, Charles C. Career Counseling for Teachers & Counselors. (Guidance Monograph). 1975. pap. 2.40 o.p. (ISBN 0-395-20043-1). HM.

Healy, David. U. S. Expansionism: The Imperialist Urge in the 1890's. LC 71-121769. (Illus.). 326p. 1970. 25.00 (ISBN 0-299-05851-4); pap. text ed. 9.95 (ISBN 0-299-05854-9). U of Wis Pr.

Healy, Dermot. Banished Misfortune. 128p. 1982. 13.95 (ISBN 0-8052-8130-4, Pub. by Allison & Busby England). Schocken.

Healy, Eloise K. A Packet Beating Like A Heart. 65p. 1981. pap. 6.00 (ISBN 0-686-95885-3). Crossing Pr.

Healy, F. G., jt. auth. see Judge, Anne.

Healy, G. P. A. Reminiscences of a Portrait Painter. LC 78-96439. (Library of American Art Ser). (Illus.). 1970. Repr. of 1894 ed. lib. bdg. 32.50 (ISBN 0-306-71829-4). Da Capo.

Healy, J. W. Plutonium, Health Implications for Man: Proceedings of the 2nd Los Alamos Life Sciences Symposium. 1976. 30.00 (ISBN 0-08-019751-5). Pergamon.

Healy, John D. The Language Tutor's Legacy. LC 80-12976. 1983. 15.95 (ISBN 0-87949-188-4). Ashley Bks.

Healy, John E. How to Match Properties, Financing & Prospects for Quick Profitable Real Estate Sales. 1982. 89.50 (ISBN 0-13-423822-2). Exec Reports.

Healy, Juanita see Summerlin, Lee R.

Healy, Kathleen, jt. auth. see Van Kamm, Adrian.

Healy, M. Tables of Laplace, Heaviside, Fourier & Z Transforms. 78p. 1972. 6.50 (ISBN 0-470-36663-X). Krieger.

Healy, Mary T., jt. auth. see Healy, William.

Healy, P. A., jt. auth. see Bleeker, P.

Healy, Paul F. Archaeology of the Rivas Region, Nicragua. 382p. 1980. text ed. 19.50x (ISBN 0-88920-094-7, Pub. by Wilfrid Laurier U Pr Canada). Humanities.

Healy, R. E., jt. auth. see McCarthy, G. D.

Healy, R. J. Design for Security. LC 61-21179. 1968. 36.95x (ISBN 0-471-36664-1, Pub. by Wiley-Interscience). Wiley.

Healy, Rett, jt. auth. see Raphael, Levine.

Healy, Richard J. Design for Security. 2nd ed. 300p. 1983. 39.95 (ISBN 0-471-06429-7, Pub. by Wiley Interscience). Wiley.

Healy, Robert G. America's Industrial Future: An Environment Perspective. LC 82-19941. 49p. (Orig.). 1982. pap. 5.00 (ISBN 0-89164-073-8). Conservation Foun.

Healy, Tim. Secret Armies. LC 81-59556. (Armies of the Past Ser.). PLB 12.68 (ISBN 0-382-06587-5). Silver.

Healy, Timothy. Basic Manx, Irish & Scottish Gaelic. 1977. pap. text ed. 9.25x o.p. (ISBN 90-6296-021-9). Humanities.

Healy, Timothy & Houle, Paul. Energy & Society. 2nd ed. 480p. 1983. pap. text ed. 14.95x (ISBN 0-87835-132-9). Boyd & Fraser.

Healy, W. P. Non-Relativistic Quantum Electrodynamics. 38.00 (ISBN 0-12-335720-9). Acad Pr.

Healy, William. Individual Delinquent, A Text-Book of Diagnosis & Prognosis for All Concerned in Understanding Offenders. LC 69-16238. (Criminology, Law Enforcement, & Social Problems Ser.: No. 85). (Illus.). 1969. Repr. of 1915 ed. 30.00x (ISBN 0-87585-085-5). Patterson Smith.

--Mental Conflicts & Misconduct. LC 69-16237. (Criminology, Law Enforcement, & Social Problems Ser.: No. 88). 1969. Repr. of 1917 ed. 12.50x (ISBN 0-87585-088-X). Patterson Smith.

Healy, William & Bronner, Augusta F. Delinquents & Criminals. (Historical Foundations of Forensic Psychiatry & Psychology Ser.). x, 317p. 1983. Repr. of 1928 ed. lib. bdg. 32.50 (ISBN 0-306-76187-4). Da Capo.

--Delinquents & Criminals, Their Making & Unmaking, Studies in Two American Cities. LC 69-14931. (Criminology, Law Enforcement, & Social Problems Ser.: No. 69). (With an intro added). 1969. Repr. of 1926 ed. 12.00x (ISBN 0-87585-069-3). Patterson Smith.

Healy, William & Healy, Mary T. Pathological Lying, Accusation & Swindling, a Study in Forensic Psychology. LC 69-14932. (Criminology, Law Enforcement, & Social Problems Ser.: No. 63). 1969. Repr. of 1915 ed. 12.50x (ISBN 0-87585-063-4). Patterson Smith.

Healy, William, jt. auth. see Alexander, Franz.

Heaney, Howell J., jt. ed. see Weiser, Frederick S.

Heaney, Seamus. Poems: Nineteen Sixty-Five to Nineteen Seventy-Five. 228p. 1980. text ed. 12.95 (ISBN 0-374-23496-5); pap. 7.25 (ISBN 0-374-51652-9). FS&G.

--Preoccupations: Selected Prose Nineteen Sixty-Eight to Nineteen Seventy-Eight. 224p. 1980. text ed. 15.00 (ISBN 0-374-23703-4); pap. 7.95 (ISBN 0-374-51650-2). FS&G.

Heanue, James E., Jr., ed. see Meinong, Alexius.

Heap, Ken. Process & Action in Work with Groups: The Preconditions for Treatment & Growth. 1979. text ed. 32.00 (ISBN 0-08-023023-7); pap. text ed. 11.25 (ISBN 0-08-023022-9). Pergamon.

Heaphy, James J., jt. ed. see Baaklini, Abdo I.

Heaps, Ian & Mitchell, Colin. Ian Heaps on Fishing. 128p. 1982. 25.00x (ISBN 0-907675-02-6, Pub. by Muller Ltd). State Mutual Bk.

Heard, Alexander. The Costs of Democracy. (Illus.). xxv, 493p. 1967. 24.00x (ISBN 0-8078-0781-8); pap. 6.00x (ISBN 0-8078-4001-7). U of NC Pr.

Heard, Alexander, ed. State Legislatures in American Politics. LC 66-23439. 1966. 3.95 o.p. (ISBN 0-936904-03-8). Am Assembly.

Heard, Franklin F. Oddities of the Law. 192p. 1983. Repr. of 1885 ed. lib. bdg. 20.00x (ISBN 0-8377-0648-3). Rothman.

Heard, Gerald. Five Ages of Man. LC 63-22142. 1960. 8.50 o.p. (ISBN 0-517-52775-8). Crown.

Heard, H. C., et al, eds. Flow & Fracture of Rocks. LC 72-91609. (Geophysical Monograph Ser.: Vol. 16). (Illus.). 1972. 23.00 (ISBN 0-87590-016-X). Am Geophysical.

Heard, J. Norman. White into Red: A Study of the Assimilation of White Persons Captured by Indians. LC 72-13133. (Illus.). 1973. 11.00 o.p. (ISBN 0-8108-0581-2). Scarecrow.

Heard, John, tr. see Rochefoucauld, La Duc De.

Heard Museum. Fred Harvey Fine Arts Collection. LC 81-171446. (Heard Museum Ser.). (Illus.). 138p. (Orig.). 1981. pap. 10.00 (ISBN 0-295-95860-X, Heard Museum). U of Wash Pr.

Heard, Nathan. The House of Slammers: A Novel. 256p. 1983. 9.95 o.p. (ISBN 0-686-68675-6). Macmillan.

Heard, Nathan C. Howard Street. 256p. 1973. pap. 2.50 (ISBN 0-451-09542-1, E9542, Sig). NAL.

--To Reach a Dream. 160p. 1973. pap. 1.25 o.p. (ISBN 0-451-05490-3, Y5490, Sig). NAL.

Hearder, H. & Waley, Daniel P. Short History of Italy. (Illus.). 1963. pap. 11.95 (ISBN 0-521-09394-5). Cambridge U Pr.

Hearl, Trevor, ed. see Barnes, William.

Hearn, C. V. A Duty to the Public: Assessment of Police Force. 16.50x (ISBN 0-392-13531-0, SpS). Sportshelf.

Hearn, Charles R. The American Dream in the Great Depression. LC 76-56623. (Contributions in American Studies Ser: No. 28). 1977. lib. bdg. 27.50 (ISBN 0-8371-9478-4, HAD/). Greenwood.

Hearn, D. Donald & Baker, M. Pauline. Microcomputer Graphics: Techniques & Applications. (Illus.). 272p. 1983. text ed. 24.95 (ISBN 0-13-580670-4); pap. text ed. 18.95 (ISBN 0-13-580662-3). P-H.

Hearn, Edward R., jt. auth. see Erickson, J. Gunnar.

Hearn, Emily. Around Another Corner. LC 71-161026. (Venture Ser). (Illus.). (gr. 1). 1971. PLB 6.69 (ISBN 0-8116-6718-9). Garrard.

--Ring Around Duffy. LC 74-8102. (Venture Ser). (Illus.). 64p. (gr. 2). 1974. PLB 6.89 (ISBN 0-8116-6976-9). Garrard.

--Stop It's a Birthday. LC 72-1926. (Venture Ser). (Illus.). 64p. (gr. 2). 1972. PLB 6.89 (ISBN 0-8116-6968-8). Garrard.

--TV Kangaroo. LC 75-9919. (Easy Venture Ser.). (Illus.). 32p. (gr. k-2). 1975. PLB 6.69 (ISBN 0-8116-6069-9). Garrard.

Hearn, Francis. Domination, Legitimation, & Resistance: The Incorporation of the Nineteenth-Century English Working Class. LC 77-84753. (Contributions in Labor History: No. 3). 1978. lib. bdg. 29.95 (ISBN 0-8371-9847-X, HDL/). Greenwood.

Hearn, Lafcadio. The Buddhist Writings of Lafcadio Hearn. 304p. 1982. 30.00x (ISBN 0-7045-0421-9, Pub. by Wildwood House). State Mutual Bk.

--Exotics & Retrospectives. LC 72-138069. (Illus.). 1971. pap. 6.95 (ISBN 0-8048-0962-3). C E Tuttle.

--Japanese Miscellany. 1954. pap. 5.75 (ISBN 0-8048-0307-2). C E Tuttle.

--Kokoro: Hints & Echoes of Japanese Inner Life. Repr. of 1896 ed. lib. bdg. 18.75x (ISBN 0-8371-1633-3, HEKO). Greenwood.

--Kwaidan. (Illus.). 1968. pap. 2.75 (ISBN 0-486-21901-1). Dover.

--On Poetry. rev. ed. 1941. 25.00 o.p. (ISBN 0-89346-078-8, Pub. by Hokuseido Pr). Heian Intl.

--On Poets. rev. ed. 1941. 25.00 o.p. (ISBN 0-89346-079-6, Pub. by Hokuseido Pr). Heian Intl.

Hearn, Michael P. The Annotated Christmas Carol. (Illus.). 1976. 15.00 (ISBN 0-517-52741-3, C N Potter Bks). Crown.

--The Annotated Wizard of Oz. (Illus.). 384p. 1973. 20.00 (ISBN 0-517-50086-8, C N Potter Bks). Crown.

Hearn, Michael P., ed. Annotated Huckleberry Finn: Adventures of Huckleberry Finn. (Illus.). 352p. 1982. 25.00 (ISBN 0-517-53031-7, C N Potter Bks). Crown.

Hearn, Patrick. The Business of Industrial Licensing: A Practical Guide to Patents, Know-How Trademarks & Industrial Designs. 272p. 1981. text ed. 45.00x (ISBN 0-566-02212-5). Gower Pub Ltd.

Hearnden, Arthur. Education in the Two Germanies. LC 75-46557. 1974. 24.50 o.p. (ISBN 0-89158-539-7). Westview.

Hearne, Mary see Barker, Jane.

Hearon, Shelby. Afternoon of a Faun. LC 82-16301. 224p. 1983. 12.95 (ISBN 0-689-11350-1). Atheneum.

Hearon, Shelly. Armadillo in the Grass. 150p. 1983. price not set (ISBN 0-939722-18-6). Pressworks.

Hearse, David J., et al. Protection of the Ischemic Myocardium: Cardioplegia. 432p. 1981. text ed. 46.00 (ISBN 0-89004-423-6, 479). Raven.

--Enzymes in Cardiology Diagnosis & Research. LC 78-13633. 1979. 115.95 (ISBN 0-471-99724-2, Pub. by Wiley-Interscience). Wiley.

Heartman, C. F. & Canny, J. R. A Bibliography of the First Printings of the Writings of Edgar Allan Poe. Repr. of 1943 ed. 18.00 o.s.i. (ISBN 0-527-39200-6). Kraus Repr.

Heartz, Daniel. Pierre Attaingnant, Royal Printer of Music: A Historical Study & Bibliographical Catalogue. LC 68-13959. 1970. 66.00x (ISBN 0-520-01563-0). U of Cal Pr.

Heasler, Richard. Whispers on the Wind. 84p. 1979. pap. 4.50 (ISBN 0-686-38083-5). Jelm Mtn.

Heasley, Bernice E. Auditory Processing Disorders & Remediation. 2nd ed. (Illus.). 168p. 1980. spiral 16.50x (ISBN 0-398-04047-8). C C Thomas.

Heasley, Jerry. The Ford Mustang Nineteen Sixty Four to Nineteen Seventy Three. (Illus.). 1979. 9.95 (ISBN 0-8306-9856-6); pap. 7.95 (ISBN 0-8306-2048-6, 2048). TAB Bks.

Heasley, Victor L. & Christensen, Val J. Chemistry & Life in the Laboratory: Experiments in General, Organic & Biological Chemistry. 2nd ed. 264p. 1982. pap. text ed. 10.95x (ISBN 0-8087-4716-9). Burgess.

Heasley Cox, Martha & Chatterton, Wayne. Nelson Algren. (U. S. Authors Ser.: No. 249). 192p. 1975. lib. bdg. 10.95 o.p. (ISBN 0-8057-0014-5, Twayne). G K Hall.

Heat Transfer & Fluid Mechanics Institute. Proceedings. Incl. 1958 Sessions. viii, 264p. pap. 12.50x (ISBN 0-8047-0422-8); 1959 Sessions. x, 242p. pap. 12.50x (ISBN 0-8047-0423-6); 1960 Sessions. Mason, David M, et al, eds. x, 260p. 12.50x (ISBN 0-8047-0424-4); 1961 Sessions. Binder, Raymond C., et al, eds. xi, 236p. 12.50x (ISBN 0-8047-0425-2); 1962 Sessions. Ehlers, F. Edward, et al, eds. x, 294p. 12.50x (ISBN 0-8047-0426-0); 1963 Sessions. Roshko, Anatol, et al, eds. xii, 280p. 12.50x (ISBN 0-8047-0427-9); 1964 Sessions. Giedt, Warren H. & Levy, Salomon, eds. x, 275p. 12.50x (ISBN 0-8047-0428-7); 1965 Sessions. Charwat, Andrew F., et al, eds. xii, 372p. 16.50x (ISBN 0-8047-0429-5); 1966 Sessions. Saad, Michel A. & Miller, James A., eds. xii, 444p. 17.50x (ISBN 0-8047-0430-9); 1967 Sessions. Libby, Paul A., et al, eds. x, 468p. 17.50x (ISBN 0-8047-0431-7); 1968 Sessions. Emery, Ashley F. & Depew, Creighton A., eds. ix, 272p. 12.50x (ISBN 0-8047-0438-4); 1970 Sessions. Sarpkaya, Turgut, ed. xii, 370p. 15.00x (ISBN **0-8047-0744-8); 1974 Sessions. Davis, Lorin R. & Wilson, Robert E., eds. xiv, 364p. 17.50x (ISBN 0-8047-0865-7); 1976 Sessions. McKillop, Allan A., et al, eds. xvi, 526p. 29.50x (ISBN 0-8047-0917-3); 1978 Sessions. Crowe, Clayton T. & Grosshandler, William L., eds. 344p. 28.50x (ISBN 0-8047-1002-3); 1980 Sessions. Gerstein, Melvin & Choudhury, P. Roy, eds. 22.50x (ISBN 0-8047-1087-2). Stanford U Pr.**

Heater, D., jt. auth. see Crick, B.

Heater, Derek & Owen, Gwyneth. Health & Wealth. Yapp, Malcolm & Killingray, Margaret, eds. (World History Ser.). (Illus.). (gr. 10). 1980. Repr. of 1977 ed. lib. bdg. 6.95 (ISBN 0-89908-142-8); pap. text ed. 2.25 (ISBN 0-89908-117-7). Greenhaven.

Heath & Marx. Calcium Disorders vs Clinical Endocrine Health. 1982. text ed. 59.95 (ISBN 0-407-02273-2). Butterworth.

Heath, A. Rational Choice & Social Exchange. LC 75-39391. (Themes in the Social Sciences Ser.). (Illus.). 200p. 1976. 27.95 (ISBN 0-521-21132-8); pap. 7.95x o.p. (ISBN 0-521-29053-8). Cambridge U Pr.

Heath, Ambrose. Good Sandwiches & Picnic Dishes. 1949. 4.00 o.p. (ISBN 0-693-11415-0). Transatlantic.

--Personal Choice. 1972. 7.50 o.p. (ISBN 0-233-96251-4). Transatlantic.

Heath, Angela, jt. ed. see Gibson, Mary J.

Heath, Anthony F., jt. auth. see Halsey, Albert H.

Heath, C., ed. Medical Work: Realities & Routines. Atkinson, P. 187p. 1981. text ed. 41.00x (ISBN 0-566-00319-8). Gower Pub Ltd.

Heath, Charles D. Your Future As a Legal Assistant. (Careers in Depth Ser.). (gr. 7-12). 1982. PLB 7.97 o.p. (ISBN 0-8239-0477-6). Rosen Pr.

Heath, Cyril. The Book of Hertford. 1977. 20.00x o.p. (ISBN 0-86023-005-8). State Mutual Bk.

Heath, Douglas H. The Peculiar Mission of a Friends School. LC 79-84919. 1979. pap. 1.50 o.p. (ISBN 0-87574-225-4). Pendle Hill.

Heath, E. G. Archery: The Modern Approach. rev. 2nd ed. LC 78-316213. (Illus.). 160p. 1978. 12.95 o.p. (ISBN 0-571-04957-5); pap. 6.50 o.p. (ISBN 0-571-11168-8). Faber & Faber.

Heath, Earl J. Mentally Retarded Student & Guidance. (Guidance Monograph). 1970. pap. 2.40 o.p. (ISBN 0-395-09946-3, 9-78846). HM.

Heath, I. B., ed. Nuclear Division in the Fungi. 1978. 28.50 (ISBN 0-12-335950-3). Acad Pr.

Heath, Jeffrey M. The Picturesque Prison: Evelyn Waugh & His Writing. 352p. 1982. 35.00x (ISBN 0-7735-0377-3); pap. 14.95 (ISBN 0-7735-0407-9). McGill Queens U Pr.

Heath, L., jt. auth. see Winn, Charles S.

Heath, Lou. Daniel: Faithful Captive. (Biblearn Ser.). (Illus.). (gr. 1-6). 1977. bds. 5.95 (ISBN 0-8054-4231-6). Broadman.

Heath, Mary E. Benjamin & Jon. LC 79-84794. (Orig.). 1979. pap. 2.95 (ISBN 0-89877-008-4). Jeremy Bks.

Heath, Mary L. How to Use Conjunctions, Prepositions & Interjections. King, Denise S. & Lawrence, Leslie, eds. (What I Really Meant to Say Ser.). (Illus.). 16p. (gr. 4-8). 1982. pap. 4.00 (ISBN 0-88049-016-0). Milton Bradley.

Heath, Michael, jt. ed. see Tydeman, William.

Heath, Monica. Chateau of Shadows. Incl. Legeng of Crown Point. 1977. pap. 2.50 (ISBN 0-451-11692-5, AE1692, Sig). NAL.

--Clerycastle & Return to Clerycastle. 1978. pap. 2.50 (ISBN 0-451-11693-3, AE1693, Sig). NAL.

--Duncraig. 192p. 1974. pap. 1.50 o.p. (ISBN 0-451-07935-3, W7935, Sig). NAL.

--Woman in Black. 176p. 1974. pap. 0.95 o.p. (ISBN 0-451-06073-3, Q6073, Sig). NAL.

Heath, O. V. Investigation by Experiements. (Studies in Biology: No. 23). 80p. 1970. pap. text ed. 8.95 (ISBN 0-7131-2290-0). E Arnold.

Heath, Peter, ed. see Fichte, J. G.

Heath, Peter, tr. see Fichte, J. G.

Heath, Phillip A., jt. ed. see Kristo, Janice V.

Heath, Robert W., jt. auth. see Downie, N. M.

Heath, Roy A. From the Heat of the Day. 160p. 1980. 9.95 (ISBN 0-8052-8003-0, Pub. by Allison & Busby England); pap. 5.95 (ISBN 0-8052-8071-5). Schocken.

--The Murderer. 190p. 1981. pap. 5.95 (ISBN 0-8052-8072-3, Pub. by Allison & Busby England); 9.95 (ISBN 0-8052-8002-2). Schocken.

Heath, Royal V. Mathemagic: Magic, Puzzles & Games with Numbers. 1953. pap. 2.50 (ISBN 0-486-20110-4). Dover.

Heath, Royton. Collectors Alpines. (Illus.). 144p. 1982. 39.95 (ISBN 0-600-36784-3). Timber.

Heath, Royton E. Rock Plants for Small Gardens. (Illus.). 144p. 1982. 17.95 (ISBN 0-600-36811-4). Timber.

Heath, Sandra. The Courting of Jenny Bright. (Orig.). 1980. pap. 1.95 o.p. (ISBN 0-451-09248-1, J9248, Sig). NAL.

--Fashion's Lady. 1982. pap. 2.25 (ISBN 0-451-11829-4, AE1829, Sig). NAL.

--The Sherborne Sapphires. 1982. pap. 2.25 (ISBN 0-451-11513-9, AE1513, Sig). NAL.

Heath, Shirley B. Telling Tongues: Language Policy in Mexico, Colony to Nation. LC 72-408. (Illus.). 1972. text ed. 12.95x o.p. (ISBN 0-8077-1508-5); pap. text ed. 9.95x (ISBN 0-8077-1507-7). Tchrs Coll.

Heath, Sidney. The Romance of Symbolism & It's Relation to Church Ornament & Architecture. LC 70-174054. (Illus.). 1976. Repr. of 1909 ed. 34.00x (ISBN 0-8103-4302-9). Gale.

Heath, Spencer. Citadel, Market & Altar: Emerging Society. LC 57-14589. 1957. 17.95 (ISBN 0-9600300-1-8). Heather Foun.

Heath, Stephen. The Nouveau Roman: A Study in the Practice of Writing. LC 72-83512. 252p. 1972. 14.95 (ISBN 0-87722-050-6). Temple U Pr.

Heath, Stephen, jt. ed. see DeLaurentis, Teresa.

Heath, Thomas. Mathematics in Aristotle. LC 78-66593. (Ancient Philosophy Ser.). 305p. 1980. lib. bdg. 30.00 o.s.i. (ISBN 0-8240-9595-2). Garland Pub.

Heath, Thomas L., ed. see Euclid.

Heath, Veronica. Beginner's Guide to Riding. 1971. 8.50 o.p. (ISBN 0-7207-0440-5). Transatlantic.

Heath, Wendy Y., ed. Book Auction Records: August 1980-July 1981, Vol. 78. LC 5-18641. 547p. 1981. 130.00x (ISBN 0-7129-1018-2). Intl Pubns Serv.

Heath, William W. Major British Poets of the Romantic Period. 1140p. 1973. text ed. 29.95x (ISBN 0-02-352900-8). Macmillan.

Heathcock, jt. auth. see Streitwiesser.

Heathcote, Anthony. Vicente Espinel. (World Authors Ser.). 1977. lib. bdg. 15.95 (ISBN 0-8057-6169-1). G K Hall.

Heathcote, J. G. & Hibbert, J. R. Aflatoxins: Chemical & Biological Aspects. (Developments in Food Science Ser.: Vol. 1). 1978. 51.00 (ISBN 0-444-41686-2). Elsevier.

Heathcote, Nina, jt. auth. see Burns, Arthur L.

Heathe, Roy A. One Generation. 176p. 1981. 13.95 (ISBN 0-8052-8074-X, Pub. by Allison & Busby England); pap. 5.95 (ISBN 0-8052-8073-1). Schocken.

Heather, Basil. Bitch. 1979. pap. 1.75 o.p. (ISBN 0-451-08659-7, E8659, Sig). NAL.

Heather, Nick & Robertson, Ian. Controlled Drinking. 350p. 1981. 33.00x (ISBN 0-416-71970-8). Methuen Inc.

Heatherington, Madelon E. Outside-In. 1971. pap. 7.95x (ISBN 0-673-07677-6). Scott F.

Heathers, Anne. Four Puppies. (ps-2). 1960. PLB 5.77 (ISBN 0-307-61405-0, Golden Pr). Western Pub.

Heathfield, David, ed. see Southampton Conf. on Short-Run Econometric Models of UK Economy.

Heathkit-Zenith Educational Systems. AC Electronics. (Spectrum Fundamentals of Electronics Ser.). (Illus.). 288p. 1983. 19.95 (ISBN 0-13-002121-0); pap. 12.95 (ISBN 0-13-002113-X). P-H.

--DC Electronics. (Spectrum Fundamentals of Electronics Ser.). 288p. 1983. 19.95 (ISBN 0-13-198192-7); pap. 12.95 (ISBN 0-13-198184-6). P-H.

--Digital Techniques. 480p. 1983. 21.95 (ISBN 0-13-214049-7); pap. 14.95 (ISBN 0-13-214031-4). P-H.

--Electronic Communications. (Spectrum Fundamentals of Electronics Ser.). (Illus.). 300p. 1983. 19.95 (ISBN 0-13-250423-5); pap. 12.95 (ISBN 0-13-250415-4). P-H.

--Electronic Test Equipment. 512p. 1983. 21.95 (ISBN 0-13-252205-5); pap. 14.95 (ISBN 0-13-252197-0). P-H.

--Electronics Circuits. 352p. 1983. 19.95 (ISBN 0-13-250183-X); pap. 12.95 (ISBN 0-13-250175-9). P-H.

--Microprocessors. 407p. 1983. 21.95 (ISBN 0-13-581074-4); pap. 14.95 (ISBN 0-13-581082-5). P-H.

--Semiconductor Devices. (Spectrum Fundamentals of Electronics Ser.). (Illus.). 288p. 1983. 19.95 (ISBN 0-13-806174-2); pap. 12.95 (ISBN 0-13-806166-1). P-H.

Heath-Stubbs, John. Naming the Beasts. 64p. 1982. pap. text ed. 8.95x (ISBN 0-85635-432-5, 80241, Pub. by Carcanet New Pr England). Humanities.

--The Watchman's Flute. (Poetry Ser.). 1978. pap. 6.25x (ISBN 0-85635-245-4, Pub. by Carcanet New Pr England). Humanities.

Heath-Stubbs, John, ed. see Gray, Thomas.

Heathwood Hall Parents Guild. Palmetto Pantry. (Illus.). 242p. 1983. pap. 9.50 (ISBN 0-686-82273-0). Wimmer Bks.

Heatley, Rachel. Poverty & Power: The Case for a Political Approach to Development. 96p. (Orig.). 1981. pap. 6.00 (ISBN 0-905762-52-5, Pub. by Zed Pr). Lawrence Hill.

Heaton, jt. ed. see Ho, C.

Heaton, Cherrill P., jt. auth. see Ford, Robert C.

Heaton, E. W. Solomon's New Men. LC 74-13412. (Illus.). 216p. 1975. 15.00x (ISBN 0-87663-714-4, Pica Pr). Universe.

Heaton, Eric W. Hebrew Kingdoms. (New Clarendon Bible Ser.). 1968. 10.95x (ISBN 0-19-836922-0). Oxford U Pr.

Heaton, Herbert. Productivity in Service Organizations: Organizing for People. (Illus.). 1977. 24.95 (ISBN 0-07-027705-2, P&RB). McGraw.

Heaton, Israel C. & Thorstenson, Clark T. Planning for Social Recreation. LC 77-85148. (Illus.). 1978. pap. text ed. 15.50 (ISBN 0-395-25052-8). HM.

Heaton, J. B. Beginning Composition through Pictures. (English As a Second Language Bk.). (Illus.). 1975. pap. text ed. 3.95x (ISBN 0-582-55519-1). Longman.

--Composition Through Pictures. (English As a Second Language Bk.). 1975. pap. 3.95x (ISBN 0-582-52125-4). Longman.

--Practice Through Pictures. (English As a Second Language Bk.). 1975. pap. text ed. 2.95x (ISBN 0-582-52135-1); teacher's bk. 2.75x (ISBN 0-582-52136-X). Longman.

--Prepositions & Adverbial Particles. (English As a Second Language Bk.). 160p. 1965. pap. text ed. 6.95 (ISBN 0-582-52121-1). Longman.

--Using Prepositions & Particles. (English As a Second Language Bk.). 1965. wkbk. 1 2.75x (ISBN 0-582-52122-X); wkbk. 2 2.75x (ISBN 0-582-52123-8); wkbk. 3 2.75x (ISBN 0-582-52124-6); key 2.75x (ISBN 0-582-52120-3). Longman.

--Writing English Language Tests. (Longman Handbooks for Language Teachers). 1975. 9.95x (ISBN 0-582-55080-7). Longman.

Heaton, J. B see Allen, W. S.

Heaton, Jane. Journey of Struggle, Journey in Hope. (Orig.). 1983. pap. write for info. (ISBN 0-377-00126-0). Friend Pr.

Heaton, Leroy, jt. auth. see Ewan, Dale.

Heaton, Mary M. K. The Life of Albrecht Durer of Nuremberg. (Illus.). 373p. 1983. pap. 8.75 (ISBN 0-686-38398-2). Tanager Bks.

Heaton, William P., jt. auth. see Endicott, John E.

Heaton, William R. Mongolia. 1983. 16.50 (ISBN 0-89158-911-2). Westview.

Heaton-Ward, W. A. Left Behind: A Study of Mental Handicap. 256p. 1977. 29.00x (ISBN 0-7121-1236-7, Pub. by Macdonald & Evans). State Mutual Bk.

Heatter, Basil. Devlin's Triangle. (Orig.). 1980. pap. 1.75 o.p. (ISBN 0-523-40856-0). Pinnacle Bks.

Heatter, Justin W. The Small Investor's Guide to Large Profits in the Stock Market. 192p. 1983. 14.95 (ISBN 0-686-83838-6, ScribT). Scribner.

Heatter, Maida. Maida Heatter's Book of Great Cookies. (Illus.). 1977. 15.00 (ISBN 0-394-41021-1). Knopf.

--Maida Heatter's Book of Great Desserts. LC 73-20764. 1974. 16.50 (ISBN 0-394-49111-4). Knopf.

Heaven, Constance. The Astrov Legacy. 224p. 1973. 5.95 o.p. (ISBN 0-698-10519-2, Coward). Putnam Pub Group.

--The Fires of Glenlochy. LC 75-44091. 240p. 1976. 8.95 o.p. (ISBN 0-698-10726-8, Coward). Putnam Pub Group.

--The Fires of Glenlochy. 1977. pap. 1.75 o.p. (ISBN 0-451-07452-1, E7452, Sig). NAL.

--Heir to Kuragin. LC 78-14442. 1979. 8.95 (ISBN 0-698-10943-0, Coward). Putnam Pub Group.

--Heir to Kuragin. 1980. pap. 1.95 o.p. (ISBN 0-451-09015-2, J9015, Sig). NAL.

--Lord of Ravensley. LC 77-11966. 1978. 9.95 o.p. (ISBN 0-698-10856-6, Coward). Putnam Pub Group.

--Lord of Ravensley. 1979. pap. 2.25 o.p. (ISBN 0-451-08460-8, E8460, Sig). NAL.

--The Place of Stones. LC 74-30595. 208p. 1975. 6.95 o.p. (ISBN 0-698-10659-8, Coward). Putnam Pub Group.

--The Queen & the Gypsy. 1977. 8.95 o.p. (ISBN 0-698-10794-2, Coward). Putnam Pub Group.

--The Ravensley Touch. 336p. 1982. 13.95 (ISBN 0-698-11109-5, Coward). Putnam Pub Group.

Heavey, Susan, jt. auth. see Heavey, Thomas.

Heavey, Thomas & Heavey, Susan. Twenty Bicycle Tours in New Hampshire. LC 78-71716. (Twenty Bicycle Tours Ser.). (Illus.). 1979. pap. 5.95 (ISBN 0-89725-001-X). Backcountry Pubns.

Heaviside, Oliver. Electrical Papers, 2 Vols. 2nd ed. LC 78-118634. 1970. text ed. 59.50 set (ISBN 0-8284-0235-3). Chelsea Pub.

--Electromagnetic Theory: Including an Account of Heaviside's Unpublished Notes, 3 Vols. 3rd ed. LC 74-118633. 1971. Set. text ed. 79.50 (ISBN 0-8284-0237-X). Chelsea Pub.

Heavrin, Charles A. Baskets, Boxes & Boards: A History of Anderson-Tully Company. (Illus.). 144p. 1982. 17.50 o.p. (ISBN 0-87870-206-7). Memphis St Univ.

Hebant, C. The Conducting Tissues of Bryophytes. 1977. 40.00 (ISBN 3-7682-1110-X). Lubrecht & Cramer.

Hebard, Edna L., jt. auth. see Clurman, David.

Hebblethwaite, B. L. The Problems of Theology. LC 79-41812. 176p. 1980. 24.95 (ISBN 0-521-23104-3); pap. 7.95 (ISBN 0-521-29811-3). Cambridge U Pr.

Hebblethwaite, Brian. Evil, Suffering & Reflection. 132p. 1976. pap. 2.00 (ISBN 0-8164-1237-5). Seabury.

Hebblethwaite, P. & Kaufmann, L. Juan Pablo II: Una Biografia Ilustrada. 1980. pap. 7.95 (ISBN 0-07-033422-6). McGraw.

Hebblethwaite, Peter & Kaufmann, Ludwig. John Paul II: A Pictorial Biography. LC 79-53120. (Illus.). 1979. 14.95x o.p. (ISBN 0-07-033327-0); pap. 7.95x (ISBN 0-07-033328-9). McGraw.

Hebblethwaite, Peter, jt. auth. see Whale, John.

Hebden, Mark. Death Set to Music. 192p. 1983. 12.95 (ISBN 0-8027-5487-2). Walker & Co.

--Pel & the Faceless Corpse. 1979. 17.95 o.p. (ISBN 0-241-10085-2, Pub. by Hamish Hamilton England). David & Charles.

Hebden, Norman & Smith, W. S. State-City Relationships in Highway Affairs. 1950. text ed. 42.50x (ISBN 0-686-83784-3). Elliots Bks.

Hebdige, Dick. Subculture: The Meaning of Style. 1979. 16.50x (ISBN 0-416-70850-1); pap. 6.95x (ISBN 0-416-70860-9). Methuen Inc.

Hebding, Daniel E., jt. auth. see Glick, Leonard.

Hebel, Doris. Chart Interpretation. pap. 5.00 (ISBN 0-686-36350-7). Aurora Press.

Hebel, Rudolph & Stromberg, Melvin W. Anatomy of the Laboratory Rat. 1976. 26.50 o.p. (ISBN 0-683-03950-4). Williams & Wilkins.

Heber, Reginald. Poems & Translations, Repr. Of 1812 Ed. Reiman, Donald H., ed. Bd. with Hymns, Written & Adapted to the Weekly Church Service of the Year. Repr. of 1827 ed. LC 75-31212. (Romantic Context Ser.: Poetry 1789-1830). 1979. lib. bdg. 47.00 o.s.i. (ISBN 0-8240-2162-2). Garland Pub.

Hebert, Malcolm. Wine Lovers Cookbook. 128p. 1983. pap. 6.95 (ISBN 0-932664-29-6). Wine Appreciation.

Hebert, R. H., jt. auth. see Ekelund, R. B.

Hebhard, David. Herbert Bayer: Paintings, Architecture, Graphics. (Illus.). 8p. 1962. 0.75x (ISBN 0-686-99843-X). La Jolla Mus Contemp Art.

Hecaen, Henri & Albert, Martin L. Human Neuropsychology. LC 77-14158. 1978. 38.50x (ISBN 0-471-36735-4, Pub. by Wiley-Interscience). Wiley.

Hechinger, Fred & Hechinger, Grace. Growing Up in America. LC 75-2083. 468p. 1975. 15.00 o.p. (ISBN 0-07-027715-X, GB). McGraw.

Hechinger, Fred M., jt. auth. see Hechinger, Grace.

Hechinger, Grace & Hechinger, Fred M. Restoring Confidence in Public Education. (Seven Springs Studies). 1982. pap. 3.00 (ISBN 0-943006-01-5). Seven Springs.

Hechinger, Grace, jt. auth. see Hechinger, Fred.

Hechler, Ken. Working with Truman: A Personal Memoir of the White House Years. (Illus.). 320p. 1982. 16.95 (ISBN 0-399-12762-3). Putnam Pub Group.

Hecht, Anthony. A Love for Four Voices: Homage to Franz Joseph Haydn. (Chapbook Ser.: No. 1). (Illus.). 32p. 1983. 75.00 (ISBN 0-915778-48-3); pap. 10.00 (ISBN 0-915778-46-7); pap. 35.00 signed (ISBN 0-686-82484-9). Penmaen Pr.

Hecht, Arthur & Stevens, Byron. The Business Beastiary. LC 82-42730. 96p. 1983. 14.95 (ISBN 0-8128-2908-5); pap. 7.95 (ISBN 0-8128-6176-0). Stein & Day.

Hecht, Caroline, jt. auth. see Hecht, Miriam.

Hecht, E. & Zajac, A. Optics. 1974. 30.95 (ISBN 0-201-02835-2). A-W.

Hecht, Eugene. Optics. 256p. 1975. pap. text ed. 8.95 (ISBN 0-07-027730-3, SP). McGraw.

--Physics in Perspective. LC 79-73369. (Physics Ser.). (Illus.). 1980. text ed. 22.95 (ISBN 0-201-02830-1); instr's manual 2.50 (ISBN 0-686-85487-X). A-W.

Hecht, Helen. Cuisine for All Seasons. LC 82-73033. 320p. 1983. 12.95 (ISBN 0-689-11351-X). Atheneum.

Hecht, Herbert T. Timely Tales. (Illus.). 47p. 1983. 5.95 (ISBN 0-533-05574-1). Vantage.

Hecht, J. C., jt. auth. see Gillespie, K.

Hecht, Joseph, jt. auth. see Gillespie, Karen.

Hecht, Joseph C., jt. auth. see Gillespie, Karen.

Hecht, Max K. & Wallace, Bruce, eds. Evolutionary Biology. (Vol.15). 440p. 49.50x (ISBN 0-306-41042-7, Plenum Pr). Plenum Pub.

Hecht, Miriam. Dropping Back In: How to Complete Your College Education Quickly & Economically. 224p. 1982. 14.95 (ISBN 0-525-93229-1, 01451-440); pap. 8.95 (ISBN 0-525-93228-3, 0869-260). Dutton.

Hecht, Miriam & Hecht, Caroline. Modumath: Arithmetic. LC 77-75447. 1978. pap. text ed. 20.95 (ISBN 0-395-24424-2); instr's. manual 0.75 (ISBN 0-395-24421-8). HM.

Hecht, Norman L. Design Principles. LC 82-46060. (Design & Management for Resource Recovery Ser.: Vol. 5). (Illus.). 120p. 1983. 29.95 (ISBN 0-250-40315-3). Ann Arbor Science.

Hecht, Richard, jt. ed. see Smart, Ninian.

Hecht, Robert A. Continents in Collision: Documents. LC 82-45064. 152p. (Orig.). 1982. lib. bdg. 19.75 (ISBN 0-8191-2374-9); pap. text ed. 8.75 (ISBN 0-8191-2375-7). U Pr of Amer.

--Continents in Collision: The Impact of Europe on the North American Indian Societies. LC 80-1381. 337p. 1980. lib. bdg. 22.25 (ISBN 0-8191-1199-6); pap. text ed. 12.50 (ISBN 0-8191-1200-3). U Pr of Amer.

--Joseph Brant, Iroquois Ally of the British. Rahmas, D. Steve, ed. (Outstanding Personalities Ser.). 32p. 1975. lib. bdg. 2.95 incl. catalog cards (ISBN 0-87157-583-3); pap. 1.95 vinyl laminated covers (ISBN 0-87157-083-1). SamHar Pr.

--Occupation of Wounded Knee. Rahmas, Sigurd C., ed. (Events of Our Times Ser.: No. 22). 32p. (Orig.). 1982. 2.95x (ISBN 0-87157-723-2); pap. text ed. 1.95 (ISBN 0-87157-223-0). SamHar Pr.

Hecht, Roger. Signposts. LC 82-71942. 56p. 1973. 7.95 (ISBN 0-8040-0277-0); pap. 4.25 (ISBN 0-8040-0639-3). Swallow.

--Twenty Seven Poems. LC 82-72148. 64p. 1966. 5.95 (ISBN 0-8040-0300-9). Swallow.

Hechter, Michael. Internal Colonialism: The Celtic Fringe in British National Development. LC 73-84392. 1975. 30.00x (ISBN 0-520-02559-8); pap. 8.50x (ISBN 0-520-03512-7). U. of Cal Pr.

Hechter, Michael, ed. The Microfounations of Macrosociology. 1983. write for info. (ISBN 0-87722-298-3). Temple U Pr.

Hechtle, Ranier, ed. see Reay, Lee.

Hechtlinger, Adelaide. The Seasonal Hearth: The Woman at Home in Early America. LC 75-27290. (Illus.). 256p. 1977. 19.95 (ISBN 0-87951-052-8). Overlook Pr.

--Simple Soupbook. LC 69-18890. 1969. pap. 2.50 o.p. (ISBN 0-8283-1031-9). Branden.

Heck, Glenn & Shelly, Marshall. How Children Learn. (Idea Bk.). 1979. pap. 1.50 o.p. (ISBN 0-89191-161-8). Cook.

Heck, Joseph. Dinosaur Riddles. Barish, Wendy, ed. (Illus.). 128p. (gr. 3-7). 1982. pap. 3.95 (ISBN 0-671-45547-8). Wanderer Bks.

Heck, Shirley & Cobes, Jon P. All the Classroom Is a Stage: The Creative Classroom Environment. LC 78-7600. (Illus.). 1979. 19.50 (ISBN 0-08-022248-X); pap. 9.95 (ISBN 0-08-022247-1). Pergamon.

Hecke, Erich. Algebraische Zahlen. 2nd ed. LC 50-3732. (Ger). 1970. 12.95 (ISBN 0-8284-0046-6). Chelsea Pub.

Hecke, G. Van see Van Hecke, G.

Hecke, Karl-Heinz. Die Alttestamentlichen Perikopen der Reihen III-VI. 203p. (Ger.). 1982. write for info. (ISBN 3-8204-5759-3). P Lang Pubs.

Hecke, Roswitha. Love Life. (Illus.). 144p. 1982. 17.95 (ISBN 0-394-52894-8, CP860, BC); pap. 9.95 (ISBN 0-394-62425-4, E832). Grove.

Heckel, Frederick C., ed. see Steiner, Rudolf.

Heckendorf, Robyn, jt. auth. see Krenzel, Kathleen.

Heckens, Gertrude & Friedman, Lynne. Lunching in Chicago. (Illus.). 1983. pap. 7.95 (ISBN 0-89651-426-9). Icarus.

Hecker, Erich, ed. Cocarcinogenesis & Biological Effects of Tumor Promoters. (Carcinogenesis: A Comprehensive Survey Ser.: Vol. 7). 692p. 1982. text ed. 76.00 (ISBN 0-89004-618-2). Raven.

Hecker, R. F. Introduction to Paleoecology. 1965. 21.95 (ISBN 0-444-00006-2, North Holland). Elsevier.

Heckhausen, Heinz. Anatomy of Achievement Motivation. (Personality & Psychopathology Ser.: Vol. 1). 1967. 36.50 (ISBN 0-12-336350-0). Acad Pr.

Hecklinger, Fred J. & Curtin, Bernadette M. Training for Life: A Practical Guide to Career & Life Planning. 256p. 1982. pap. text ed. 13.95 (ISBN 0-8403-2839-7). Kendall-Hunt.

Heckmann, Wolf. Rommel's War in Africa. LC 78-68330. (Illus.). 384p. 1981. 14.95 o.p. (ISBN 0-385-14420-2). Doubleday.

Heckner, Fritz. Practical Microscopic Hematology. 2nd ed. Lehmann, Peter & Yuan Kao, eds. Lehmann, H. L., tr. from Ger. LC 82-4738. 140p. 1982. pap. text ed. 19.50 (ISBN 0-8067-0812-3). Urban & S.

Heckrotte, Warren, ed. see Livermore Arms Control Conference.

Heckscher, Eli F. The Continental Systems. 1964. 10.00 o.p. (ISBN 0-8446-1230-8). Peter Smith.

Hecksel, Arlene, jt. auth. see Conrow, Robert.

Heclo, Hugh. A Government of Strangers: Executive Politics in Washington. LC 76-51882. 1977. 22.95 (ISBN 0-8157-3536-7); pap. 8.95 (ISBN 0-8157-3535-9). Brookings.

Heclo, Hugh & Wildavsky, Aaron. The Private Government of Public Money: Community & Policy in British Political Administration. LC 73-79474. 1974. 37.50x (ISBN 0-520-02497-4). U of Cal Pr.

Hector, L. C & Harvey, Barbara F., eds. The Westminster Chronicle Thirteen Eighty-One to Thirteen Ninety-Four. (Illus.). 1981. 115.00x (ISBN 0-19-822255-6). Oxford U Pr.

Hector, Winifred. Modern Nursing. 7th ed. (Illus.). 596p. 1982. pap. text ed. 32.50x (ISBN 0-433-14218-9). Intl Ideas.

Hedberg, G. & Vander Mrck, J. Charles Biederman: Retrospective. LC 76-43512. (Illus.). 1976. 9.00 (ISBN 0-912964-04-9). Minneapolis Inst Arts.

Hedblom, Jack H., jt. auth. see Hartman, John J.

Hedde, Wilhelmina G. Pioneer Saga. 1978. 8.95 o.p. (ISBN 0-533-03708-5). Vantage.

Heddens, James. Today's Mathematics. 4th ed. 1980. pap. text ed. 17.95 (ISBN 0-574-23095-5, 13-6095); instr. guide 1.95 (ISBN 0-574-23096-3, 13-6096). SRA.

Heddesheimer, Janet & Erpenback, William J. Government Liaison Worker Handbook. 1979. 7.50 (ISBN 0-686-36432-5, 72127); nonmembers 8.50 (ISBN 0-686-37317-0). Am Personnel.

Heddesheimer, Janet C. Managing Elementary School Guidance Problems. 1975. pap. 2.40 o.p. (ISBN 0-395-20052-0). HM.

Heddle, John A., ed. Mutagenicity: New Horizons in Genetic Toxicology. LC 81-22940. (Cell Biology Ser.). 1982. 55.00 (ISBN 0-12-336180-X). Acad Pr.

Hedemann, Ed, ed. War Resisters League Organizer's Manual. (Illus.). 222p. 1981. pap. 8.00 (ISBN 0-940862-00-X). War Resisters NY.

Heden, Karl. Directory of Shipwrecks of the Great Lakes. 11.00 (ISBN 0-8283-1390-3). Branden.

Hedetniemi, S. T., jt. auth. see Goodman, S. E.

Hedgecoe, John. The Art of Color Photography. (Illus.). 1978. 33.95 (ISBN 0-671-24274-1). S&S.

--The Art of Color Photography. 1983. pap. 14.95 (ISBN 0-671-46096-X). S&S.

--John Hedgecoe's Advanced Photography. LC 82-717. (Illus.). 304p. 1982. 35.95 (ISBN 0-671-42624-9). S&S.

Hedgecoe, John, ed. John Hedgecoe's Complete Course in Photographing Children. 1980. 14.95 o.p. (ISBN 0-671-41220-5). S&S.

Hedgecoe, John, illus. Possessions. (Illus.). 128p. 1978. 25.00 o.s.i. (ISBN 0-89479-023-4). A & W Pubs.

Hedgeman, Anna A. The Gift of Chaos. LC 76-9242. 1977. 14.95x (ISBN 0-19-502196-7). Oxford U Pr.

Hedges, Alan, jt. auth. see Selwood, Neville.

Hedges, Charles S. Industrial Fluid Power, Vol. 1. 2nd ed. LC 66-28254. (Illus.). 240p. 1972. pap. 11.95 cancelled. Womack Educ Pubns.

--Industrial Fluid Power, Vol. 2. 3rd ed. LC 66-28254. (Illus.). 248p. 1982. pap. 11.95 cancelled. Womack Educ Pubns.

--Industrial Fluid Power, Vol. 3. 2nd ed. LC 66-28254. (Illus.). 224p. 1978. pap. cancelled. Womack Educ Pubns.

--Practical Fluid Power Control: Electrical & Fluidic. LC 77-156757. (Illus.). 208p. 1971. pap. 11.95. Womack Educ Pubns.

Hedges, Charles S. & Womack, R. C. Fluid Power in Plant & Field. LC 68-22573. (Illus.). 176p. 1968. pap. 11.95 (ISBN 0-9605644-3-8). Womack Educ Pubns.

Hedges, Inez. Languages of Revolt: Dada & Surrealist Literature & Film. (Illus.). 220p. 1983. text ed. 20.00 (ISBN 0-8223-0493-7). Duke.

Hedges, Sid. Games for Children While Traveling. 80p. (gr. 1 up). 1975. pap. 1.25 (ISBN 0-448-11919-6, G&D). Putnam Pub Group.

--Popular Party Games. 80p. (gr. 1 up). 1975. pap. 1.25 (ISBN 0-448-11918-8, G&D). Putnam Pub Group.

Hedgpeth, J. W. Animal Diversity: Organisms. (Biocore Ser: Unit 14). 1974. 17.50 o.p. (ISBN 0-07-005345-6, C). McGraw.

Hedin, Diane, jt. ed. see Conrad, Dan.

Hedin, Sven. Chiang Kai-Shek: Marshal of China. Norbelle, Bernard, tr. from Swedish. LC 74-31277. (China in the 20th Century Ser). (Illus.). xiv, 290p. 1975. Repr. of 1940 ed. lib. bdg. 32.50 (ISBN 0-306-70690-3). Da Capo.

Hedin, Thomas. The Sculputure of Gaspard & Balthazard Marsy: Art & Patronage in the Early Reign of Louis XIV. LC 82-17415. (Illus.). 288p. 1983. text ed. 49.00x (ISBN 0-8262-0395-7). U of Mo Pr.

Hedinsson, Elias. TV, Family & Society: The Social Origins & Effects of Adolescents' TV Use. 216p. 1981. text ed. 28.75x (ISBN 91-22-00461-0, Pub. by Almquist & Wiksell Sweden). Humanities.

Hedley, Arthur, ed. see Chopin, Fryderyk.

Hedley, Eugene. Boating For the Handicapped: Guidelines for the Physically Handicapped. LC 79-91181. (Illus.). 124p. 1979. 5.65 (ISBN 0-686-38820-8). Human Res Ctr.

Hedley, George P. The Superstitions of the Irreligious. LC 78-10274. 1979. Repr. of 1951 ed. lib. bdg. 15.50x (ISBN 0-313-20755-0, HESU). Greenwood.

Hedley, Patricia. Overcoming Handicap. pap. 4.50 o.p. (ISBN 0-263-05062-9). Transatlantic.

Hedlund, Roger E., ed. World Christianity: South Asia. 320p. 1980. 12.50 (ISBN 0-912552-33-6). MARC.

Hedman, Richard. Stop Me Before I Plan Again. LC 77-73251. (Illus.). 112p. (Orig.). 1977. pap. 9.95 (ISBN 0-918286-10-7). Planners Pr.

Hedren, Paul L. First Scalp for Custer: The Skirmish at Warbonnet Creek, Nebraska, July 17, 1876. LC 80-68844. (Hidden Springs of Custeriana Ser.: No. V). (Illus.). 106p. 1981. 38.00 o.p. (ISBN 0-87062-137-8). A H Clark.

Hedrick. Sturtevant's Edible Plants of the World. 686p. 1972. pap. 10.95 (ISBN 0-486-20459-6). Dover.

--Sturtevant's Edible Plants of the World. 10.50 (ISBN 0-8446-4552-4). Peter Smith.

Hedrick, Addie M. Cup of Stars. LC 69-19405. 1969. 4.00 o.p. (ISBN 0-8233-0128-1). Golden Quill.

Hedrick, Henry B., jt. auth. see Brown, Ernest.

Hedrick, Marshall, ed. see Poling, Carol.

Hedrick, Philip W. Genetics of Populations. 600p. 1983. text ed. 29.50 (ISBN 0-86720-011-1). Sci Bks Intl.

Hedwig, J. Species Muscorum Frondosorum. (Illus.). 1960. Repr. of 1801 ed. 37.80 o.p. (ISBN 3-7682-7055-6). Lubrecht & Cramer.

Hedy, Maureen E. & Danky, James P., eds. Women's Periodicals & Newspapers from the Eighteenth Century to 1981: A Union List of the Holdings of Madison, Wisconsin Libraries. LC 82-11903. (Reference Publications in Women's Studies). (Illus.). 376p. 1982. 38.00 (ISBN 0-8161-8107-1). G K Hall.

Heelan, Patrick A. Space-Perception & the Philosophy of Science. LC 82-4842. (Illus.). 300p. 1982. 27.50x (ISBN 0-520-04611-0). U of Cal Pr.

Heer, Friedrick. Medieval World: Europe Eleven Hundred to Thirteen Fifty. 1964. pap. 4.95 (ISBN 0-451-62165-4, ME2165, Ment). NAL.

Heer, Nancy W. History & Politics in the Soviet Union. 1971. 17.50x (ISBN 0-262-08045-1); pap. 4.95 (ISBN 0-262-58022-5). MIT Pr.

Heer, Nicholas L., tr. see Abd al-Rahman al Jami.

Heeren, Vern E., jt. auth. see Miller, Charles D.

Heers, J., ed. Parties & Political Life in the Medieval West. (Europe in the Middle Ages Selected Studies: Vol. 7). 1978. 61.75 (ISBN 0-7204-0539-4, North-Holland). Elsevier.

Heersoma, Kathleen, ed. see Read, Jenny.

Heertje, Arnold, et al. Economics. 480p. 1983. pap. text ed. 18.95 (ISBN 0-03-059336-0). Dryden Pr.

Heery, Joseph M., ed. Harris Postage Stamp Catalog: Summer 1983. (Illus.). 416p. (Orig.). 1982. pap. 2.95 (ISBN 0-937458-33-3). Harris & Co.

Heery, Joseph M. & Musial, James, eds. U. S. Liberty Album. (Illus.). 416p. (gr. 6 up). 1982. text ed. 14.95 (ISBN 0-937458-29-5). Harris & Co.

Heese, Viktor. Zur Permanenten "Uberinvestition" In Sozialistischen Wirtschaftssystemen. 338p. (Ger.). 1982. write for info. (ISBN 3-8204-7241-X). P Lang Pubs.

Heezen, B. C. Influence of Abyssal Circulation on Sedimentary Accumulations in Space & Time. (Developments in Sedimentology: Vol. 23). 1977. 47.00 (ISBN 0-444-41569-6). Elsevier.

Heffer, Linda, jt. auth. see Bidwell, Bruce.

Hefferling, Jonathan. Making Inflation Pay. (Illus.). 224p. 1980. 9.95 (ISBN 0-937554-00-6). Regency Pubs CA.

Hefferman, Terry, jt. auth. see Johnson, Brian.

Hefferman, William A. & Degnan, James P. Language & Literature Reader. 1968. 7.95x o.p. (ISBN 0-02-474240-6, 47424). Glencoe.

Heffern, Richard. The Herb Buyers Guide. (Orig.). pap. 1.50 o.s.i. (ISBN 0-515-04635-3). Jove Pubns.

Heffernan, Charles W. Choral Music: Technique & Artistry. (Illus.). 224p. 1982. 18.95 (ISBN 0-13-133330-5). P-H.

Heffernan, H., jt. auth. see Todd, V. E.

Heffernan, Ildiko & Schnee, Sandra. Art, the Elderly, & a Museum. (Illus.). 32p. 1980. pap. 2.50 (ISBN 0-87273-079-4). Bklyn Mus.

Heffernan, James A. & Lincoln, John E. Writing-A College Workbook: Ancillary for Writing a College Handbook. 300p. 1982. pap. 6.95x (ISBN 0-393-95177-4); instr's manual avail. (ISBN 0-393-95181-2); write for info. diagnostic tests; write for info answer pamphlet (ISBN 0-393-95229-0). Norton.

Heffernan, James A. W. & Lincoln, John R. Writing: A College Workbook. 1982. pap. text ed. 6.95x (ISBN 0-393-95177-4); instr's. manual avail.; diagnostic tests avail. Norton.

Heffernan, James M. Educational & Career Services for Adults. LC 79-3279. 1981. 28.95x (ISBN 0-669-03440-1). Lexington Bks.

Heffernan, Joseph. Introduction to Social Welfare Policy. LC 78-61882. 1979. text ed. 15.95 (ISBN 0-87581-241-4). Peacock Pubs.

Heffernan, Patrick, et al. Environmental Impact Assessment. LC 75-17326. (Illus.). 1975. pap. text ed. 12.95x (ISBN 0-87735-061-2). Freeman C.

Heffernan, Thomas. The Liam Poems. LC 81-67497. (Living Poets' Library Ser.: Vol. 27). 1981. pap. 6.00 (ISBN 0-934218-22-6). Dragons Teeth.

Heffernan, Virginia M. Bible for Everyone. 1968. 4.95 o.p. (ISBN 0-685-07611-3, 80290). Glencoe.

Heffernan, Wwilliam. Broderick. 320p. 1980. 11.95 o.p. (ISBN 0-517-53732-X). Crown.

Hefferren, John J. & Moller, Mary L., eds. Patterns & Effects of Diet & Disease Today. (AAAS Selected Symposium: No. 59). 225p. 1981. lib. bdg. 18.75 o.p. (ISBN 0-89158-844-2). Westview.

Heffner, Elaine. Mothering: The Emotional Experience of Motherhood After Freud & Feminism. LC 79-7799. 1980. pap. 4.95 o.p. (ISBN 0-385-15551-4, Anch). Doubleday.

Heffner, G., jt. auth. see Energy Development International.

Heffner, Hubert C., et al. Modern Theatre Practice: A Handbook of Play Production. 5th ed. LC 72-89404. (Illus.). 656p. 1973. 26.95 (ISBN 0-13-598805-5). P-H.

Heffner, Richard D. Documentary History of the United States. (RL 7). pap. 2.95 (ISBN 0-451-62073-9, ME2073, Ment). NAL.

Heffner, Richard D., ed. see De Tocqueville, Alexis.

Heffner, Roe-Merrill S., ed. Word-Index to the Texts of Steinmeyer: "Die kleineren althochdeutschen Sprachdenkmaler". 184p. 1961. 17.50 (ISBN 0-299-02393-1). U of Wis Pr.

Heffner, Roe-Merrill S. & Lehmann, W. P., eds. Word-Index to the Poems of Walther von der Vogelweide. 2nd ed. 82p. 1950. pap. 11.50x (ISBN 0-299-00663-8). U of Wis Pr.

Heffner, Roe-Merrill S., et al, eds. Goethe's "Faust" Incl. Vol. I. Introduction, Pts. I & II. 582p. pap. text ed. 12.50 (ISBN 0-299-06874-9, 687); Vol. II. Vocabulary & Notes. 414p. pap. text ed. 10.00 (ISBN 0-299-06884-6, 688). LC 75-12216. 1975. pap. U of Wis Pr.

Hefley, Beryl F., jt. auth. see Swihart, Stanley J.

Hefley, James & Hefley, Marti. The Church That Takes on Trouble. LC 76-6579. 256p. 1976. 6.95 o.p. (ISBN 0-912692-95-2). Cook.

--God's Tribesman, the Rochunga Pudaite Story. LC 74-3346. (Illus.). 152p. 1974. 5.95 o.p. (ISBN 0-87981-031-9). Holman.

--No Time for Tombstones. LC 74-80772. 1974. 3.95 (ISBN 0-87509-111-3). Chr Pubns.

Hefley, James C. God's Free-Lancers. 1978. pap. 3.95 (ISBN 0-8423-1076-2). Tyndale.

Hefley, James C., jt. auth. see Lester, Lane P.

Hefley, Jim. Life in the Balance. 1980. pap. 4.50 (ISBN 0-88207-797-X). Victor Bks.

Hefley, Marti. In His Steps Today. LC 75-42375. 192p. 1978. 1.50 (ISBN 0-8024-4058-4); pap. 2.95 (ISBN 0-8024-4058-4). Moody.

Hefley, Marti, jt. auth. see Dean, Dave.

Hefley, Marti, jt. auth. see Hefley, James.

Hefley, Marti, jt. auth. see Moore, Barry.

Hefner, Philip, jt. auth. see Benne, Robert.

Hefner, Robert L. & Seifert, Edward H., eds. Studies in Administrative Theory. 466p. 1980. pap. text ed. 15.95x (ISBN 0-89641-046-3). American Pr.

Hefter. One Bear, Two Bears: The Strawberry Number Book. 118p. 1980. 4.95 o.p. (ISBN 0-07-027825-3). McGraw.

--The Strawberry Look Book. 120p. 1980. 4.95 o.p. (ISBN 0-07-027824-5). McGraw.

Hefter, G. T., jt. ed. see Bond, A. M.

Hefter, R. Yes & No: A Book of Opposites. 1980. 4.50 (ISBN 0-07-027809-1). McGraw.

Hefter, Richard. Animal Alphabet. (Strawberry Books Ser.). (Illus.). (ps-4). 1977. pap. 1.25 o.s.i. (ISBN 0-448-14401-8, G&D). Putnam Pub Group.

--Formas. (Paperback Ser.). (gr. 6-12). pap. 5.95 (ISBN 0-686-94088-1). Larousse.

--Noses & Toes. (Strawberry Books Ser.). (Illus.). (ps-4). 1977. pap. 1.25 (ISBN 0-448-14403-4, G&D). Putnam Pub Group.

--One White Crocodile. (Strawberry Books Ser.). (Illus.). 1977. pap. 1.25 (ISBN 0-448-14404-2, G&D). Putnam Pub Group.

--Si & No. (Paperback Ser.). (gr. 6-12). pap. 5.95 (ISBN 0-686-94089-X). Larousse.

--Strawberry Word Book. (Strawberry Book Ser.). (ps-4). 1977. pap. 1.25 o.p. (ISBN 0-448-14402-6, G&D). Putnam Pub Group.

Hefter, Richard & Moskof, Martin S. The Great Big Alphabet Book with Lots of Words. (Illus.). 32p. Date not set. pap. price not set (ISBN 0-448-11811-4, G&D). Putnam Pub Group.

Hefter, Richard, illus. Cabezas & Pies. (gr. 6-12). pap. 5.95 (ISBN 0-686-94013-X). Larousse.

--El Libro de los Numeros: Paperback Ser. (gr. 6-12). pap. 5.95 (ISBN 0-686-94014-8). Larousse.

--Libros de la Fresa, 4. (Paperback Ser.). (gr. 6-12). pap. 5.95ea. (ISBN 0-686-94011-3). Larousse.

Heftmann, E. Chromatography, 2 Pts. (Journal of Chromatography Library: Vol. 22). Date not set. Set. price not set (ISBN 0-444-42045-2); Pt. A: Fundamentals & Techniques. 83.00 (ISBN 0-444-42043-6); Pt. B: Applications. 138.50 (ISBN 0-444-42044-4). Elsevier.

--Chromatography of Steroids. (Journal of Chromatography Library: Vol. 8). 1976. 42.75 (ISBN 0-444-41441-X). Elsevier.

Hegar, E. Die Anfange der neueren Musikgeschichtsschreibung um 1770 bei Gerbert, Burney und Hawkins. (Sammlung MW Abh. 7-1933 Ser.). vi, 90p. 25.00 o.s.i. (ISBN 90-6027-254-4, Pub. by Frits Knuf Netherlands). Pendragon NY.

Hegar, Rebecca L., et al see Pardeck, John T.

Hegarty, Christopher & Goldberg, Philip. How to Manage Your Boss. rev. ed. 320p. Date not set. pap. cancelled (ISBN 0-89581-043-3). Lancaster-Miller.

--How to Manage Your Boss. 312p. 1982. pap. 9.95 (ISBN 0-931432-15-4). Whatever Pub.

Hegarty, E. Making What-You Say Pay Off. 14.95 o.p. (ISBN 0-13-547901-0, Parker). P-H.

Hegarty, Edward J. How to Succeed in Company Politics. 2nd ed. 1976. 17.95 o.p. (ISBN 0-07-027847-4, P&RB). McGraw.

Hegarty, Walter. An Age for Fortunes. LC 78-25674. 1979. 10.95 o.p. (ISBN 0-698-10845-0, Coward). Putnam Pub Group.

Hegedus, Andras. Socialism & Bureaucracy. LC 76-41634. (Motive Ser). 1977. 26.00x (ISBN 0-312-73640-1). St Martin.

--Structure of Socialist Society. LC 74-17724. 1977. 17.95x (ISBN 0-312-76825-7). St Martin.

Hegedus, Andras, et al. The Humanization of Socialism: Writings of the Budapest School. LC 76-41636. (Motive Ser.). 1977. 20.00 (ISBN 0-312-39970-7). St Martin.

Hegedus, Frank, jt. auth. see Florence, D.

Hegedus, L. Louis, jt. ed. see Bell, Alexis T.

Hegedus, Louis S. & Wade, Leroy. Compendium of Organic Synthetic Methods, Vol. 3. LC 71-162800. 1977. 28.50x (ISBN 0-471-36752-4, Pub by Wiley-Interscience). Wiley.

Hegedus, Louis S., jt. auth. see Collman, James P.

Hegel, G. W. Aesthetics: Lectures on Fine Art, Vol. 1 & 2. Knox, T. M., tr. (Illus.). 1975. Set. 125.00x (ISBN 0-19-824371-5). Oxford U Pr.

--The Difference Between the Fichtean & Schellingian Systems of Philosophy. Surber, Jere P., tr. from Ger. 1978. pap. text ed. 6.50x (ISBN 0-917930-12-6); lib. bdg. 23.00 (ISBN 0-917930-32-0). Ridgeview.

--The Essential Writings. Weiss, Frederick G., ed. 1974. pap. 8.50xi (ISBN 0-06-131831-0, TB1831, Torch). Har-Row.

--Hegel's Phenomenology of Spirit. Miller, A. V., tr. from Ger. 1979. pap. 11.95 (ISBN 0-19-824597-1, GB569, GB). Oxford U Pr.

--Hegel's Philosophy of Nature, 3 Vols. Petry, Michael J., tr. (Muirhead Library of Philosophy). 1974. Repr. of 1970 ed. Set. text ed. 55.00x. Vol. 1 (ISBN 0-04-100021-8). Vol. 2 (ISBN 0-04-100022-6). Vol. 3 (ISBN 0-04-100023-4). Humanities.

Hegel, Georg W. George Wilhelm Friedrich Hegel: Lectures on the Philosophy of World History. Nisbet, H. B. & Forbes, D., eds. LC 74-79137. (Studies in the History & Theory of Politics). 280p. 1975. 29.95 o.p. (ISBN 0-521-20520-4). Cambridge U Pr.

--Lectures on the History of Philosophy, 3 Vols. Haldane, E. S. & Simson, F. H., trs. 1974. Repr. of 1896 ed. Set. text ed. 55.00x (ISBN 0-7100-1514-3). Vol. 1 (ISBN 0-7100-1514-3). Vol. 2 (ISBN 0-7100-1515-1). Vol. 3 (ISBN 0-7100-1516-X). Humanities.

--Lectures on the Philosophy of World History: Reason in History. Forbes, D. & Nisbet, H. B., eds. (Cambridge Studies in the History & Theory of Politics). 290p. (Ger.). 1981. pap. 13.95 (ISBN 0-521-28145-8). Cambridge U Pr.

Hegeler, Inge & Hegeler, Sten. An ABZ of Love. 384p. 11.50x o.p. (ISBN 0-85435-333-X, Pub. by Spearman England). State Mutual Bk.

Hegeler, Sten, jt. auth. see Hegeler, Inge.

Hegener, Karen C., jt. auth. see Zuker, R. Fred.

Heger, Joel. Cardiology for the House Officer. (House Officer Ser.). (Illus.). 296p. 1982. softcover 10.95 (ISBN 0-683-03946-6). Williams & Wilkins.

Hegg. Selling Co-Op & Condo Apartments. Date not set. price not set (ISBN 0-442-23682-4). Van Nos Reinhold.

Hegge, Kirk. Remedial Reading Drills with Directions. 1953. 5.00x (ISBN 0-685-21801-5). Wahr.

Heggelund, Per O., jt. auth. see Sullivan, Jeremiah J.

Heggestad, Arnold A., ed. Public Regulation of Financial Services: Costs & Benefits to Consumers-A Bibliography. LC 77-88804. 1977. lib. bdg. 30.00 o.p. (ISBN 0-89158-406-4). Westview.

Heggie, Donald C., ed. Archaeoastronomy in the Old World. LC 82-4233. 1982. 37.50 (ISBN 0-521-24734-9). Cambridge U PR.

Heggie, Douglas C. Megalithic Science: Ancient Mathematics & Astronomy in Northwest Europe. (Illus.). 256p. 1982. 27.50 (ISBN 0-500-05036-8). Thames Hudson.

Heggie, I. G., jt. auth. see Rothenberg, J.

Heggie, I. G., jt. ed. see Rothenberg, J. G.

Heggie, Ian G. Model Choice & the Value of Travel Time. (Illus.). 1976. 36.00x o.p. (ISBN 0-19-828404-7). Oxford U Pr.

Heggoy, Alf A. & Cooke, James J., eds. Proceedings of the Fourth Meeting of the French Colonial Historical Society. LC 79-63751. 1979. pap. text ed. 10.75 (ISBN 0-8191-0738-7). U Pr of Amer.

Heggoy, Alf A., et al, eds. Through Foreign Eyes: Western Attitudes Toward North Africa. LC 81-43474. 200p. (Orig.). 1982. lib. bdg. 21.25 (ISBN 0-8191-2181-9); pap. text ed. 10.25 (ISBN 0-8191-2182-7). U Pr of Amer.

Hegmann, J. P., jt. auth. see Dingle, H.

Hegner, jt. auth. see Caldwell.

Hegner, Barbara, jt. auth. see Caldwell, Esther.

Hegner, Barbara R., jt. auth. see Caldwell, Esther.

Hegner, Priscilla A., jt. auth. see Graselli, Rose N.

Hegner, Robert W., jt. auth. see Engemann, Joseph G.

Hegre, T. A. La Fe Creative. 128p. Date not set. 1.95 (ISBN 0-88113-086-9). Edit Betania.

--Libre Para Vivir. 96p. Date not set. 1.75. Edit Betania.

--La Vida Que Nace de la Muerte. 272p. Date not set. 2.50 (ISBN 0-88113-311-6). Edit Betania.

Hegyeli, Ruth J., ed. Measurement & Control of Cardiovascular Risk Factors. (Atherosclerosis Reviews Ser.: Vol. 7). 352p. 1980. 40.00 (ISBN 0-89004-396-5). Raven.

--Nutrition & Cardiovascular Disease. (Progress in Biochemical Pharmacology: Vol. 19). (Illus.). x, 316p. 1982. 138.50 (ISBN 3-8055-3571-6). S Karger.

--Prostaglandins & Cardiovascular Disease. (Atherosclerosis Reviews: Vol. 8). 218p. 1981. text ed. 27.50 (ISBN 0-89004-516-X). Raven.

Hegyvary, Sue T. The Change to Primary Nursing: A Cross-Cultural View of Professional Nursing Practice. LC 81-16987. (Illus.). 190p. 1982. pap. text ed. 14.95 (ISBN 0-8016-2127-5). Mosby.

Heiber, Helmut. Goebbels: A Biography. Dickinson, John K., tr. from Ger. (Quality Paperbacks Ser.). (Illus.). 393p. 1983. pap. 9.95 (ISBN 0-306-80187-6). Da Capo.

Heiberg, Milton. Yashica FR, FR-I & FR-II: Amphoto Pocket Companion. (Illus.). 128p. 1981. pap. 4.95 (ISBN 0-8174-5534-5, Amphoto). Watson-Guptill.

--The Yashica Guide. (Modern Camera Guide Ser.). (Illus.). 1979. 11.95 (ISBN 0-8174-2479-2, Amphoto); pap. 6.95 o.p. (ISBN 0-8174-2151-3). Watson-Guptill.

Heiberg, Milton J. The Olympus Guide. (Modern Camera Guide Ser.). (Illus.). 1978. 11.95 o.p. (ISBN 0-8174-2449-0, Amphoto); pap. 6.95 o.p. (ISBN 0-8174-2104-1). Watson-Guptill.

--Olympus OM-Ten, OM-One & OM-Two. (Amphoto Pocket Companion Ser.). (Illus.). 1980. pap. 4.95 (ISBN 0-8174-2188-2, Amphoto). Watson-Guptill.

Heichelheim, Fritz M. & Yeo, C. A. History of the Roman People. 1962. text ed. 24.95 (ISBN 0-13-392126-3). P-H.

Heid, Jim, ed. see Ewing, George M.

Heide, F. P. Jesus Says I Am. (gr. 2-5). 1983. 6.95 (ISBN 0-570-04077-9). Concordia.

Heide, Florence P. The Adventures of Treehorn. (gr. k-6). 1983. pap. 1.95 (ISBN 0-440-40045-7, YB). Dell.

--Banana Blitz. LC 82-48753. (Illus.). 128p. (gr. 3-7). 1983. 9.95 (ISBN 0-8234-0480-3). Holiday.

--Banana Twist. 112p. 1982. pap. 1.95 (ISBN 0-553-15159-2). Bantam.
--The Problem with Pulcifer. LC 81-48606. (Illus.). 64p. (gr. 3-6). 8.61i (ISBN 0-397-32001-9, JBL-J); PLB 8.89g (ISBN 0-397-32002-7). Har-Row.
--The Shrinking of Treehorn. LC 78-151753. (Illus.). 64p. (gr. 3-6). 1971. PLB 8.95 (ISBN 0-8234-0189-8). Holiday.
--Treehorn's Treasure. LC 81-4043. (Illus.). 64p. (gr. 3-7). 1981. PLB 8.95 (ISBN 0-8234-0425-0). Holiday.
Heide, Florence P. & Heide, Roxanne. A Monster Is Coming! A Monster Is Coming! (gr. k-3). 1980. PLB 8.60 (ISBN 0-531-04136-0); PLB 7.90. Watts.
--Mystery of the Midnight Message, No. 3. (Spotlight Club Mystery Ser.). (Illus.). (gr. 3-6). 1982. pap. 1.95 (ISBN 0-671-43980-4). Archway.
--Mystery of the Vanishing Visitor. (A Spotlight Club Mystery: No. 2). (Illus.). (gr. 3-7). 1982. pap. 1.95 (ISBN 0-671-43977-4). Archway.
--Mystery on Danger Road. Fay, Ann, ed. (High-Low Mysteries (Spotlight Club) Ser.). (Illus.). 128p. (gr. 3-8). 1983. PLB 7.50 (ISBN 0-8075-5396-4). A Whitman.
Heide, Florence P. & Van Clief, Sylvia. Hidden Box Mystery. LC 72-13351. (Pilot Bks. - Spotlight Club Mysteries Ser.). (Illus.). 128p. (gr. 3-6). 1973. 7.50g o.p. (ISBN 0-8075-3270-3). A Whitman.
Heide, Robert & Gilman, John. Dime Store Dream Parade: Popular Culture 1925-1955. 1979. 25.00 o.p. (ISBN 0-525-18150-4); pap. 14.95 o.p. (ISBN 0-525-47473-0). Dutton.
Heide, Robert, jt. auth. see Gilman, John.
Heide, Roxanne, jt. auth. see Heide, Florence P.
Heidegger, Martin. Being & Time. LC 72-78334. 1962. 22.06xi (ISBN 0-06-063850-8, HarpR). Har-Row.
--Early Greek Thinking. Krell, David & Capuzzi, Frank, trs. LC 74-6767. 160p. 1975. 12.95xi (ISBN 0-06-063858-3, HarpR). Har-Row.
--Existence & Being. 372p. 1949. pap. 5.95 (ISBN 0-89526-935-X). Regnery-Gateway.
--Nietzsche: Vol. IV, Nihilism. Capuzzi, Frank, tr. from Ger. LC 78-19509. 352p. 1982. 17.07i (ISBN 0-06-063857-5, HarpR). Har-Row.
--Poetry, Language, Thought. Hofstadter, Albert, tr. from Ger. 1975. pap. 5.72i (ISBN 0-06-090430-5, CN430, CN). Har-Row.
--The Question Concerning Technology & Other Essays. Lovitt, William, tr. (Orig.). 1977. pap. 5.95xi (ISBN 0-06-131969-4, TB 1969, Torch). Har-Row.
Heidel, Werner, ed. see American Physiological Society.
Heidemann, R. Export Marketing (German) 1978. pap. text ed. 8.75x (ISBN 0-582-35158-8); cassettes 30.00x (ISBN 0-582-37374-3). Longman.
Heidenheimer, Arnold J. & Elvander, Nile, eds. The Shaping of the Swedish Health System. LC 80-12410. 256p. 1980. 27.50 (ISBN 0-312-71627-3). St Martin.
Heidenheimer, Arnold J., jt. ed. see Flora, Peter.
Heidenheimer, Arnold J., et al. Comparative Public Policy: Policies of Social Choice in Europe & America. LC 75-10557. 256p. 1975. text ed. 15.95 o.p. (ISBN 0-312-15365-1); pap. text ed. 10.95 (ISBN 0-312-15400-3). St Martin.
Heidenreich, Alfred. Growing Point. (Illus.). 18.95 (ISBN 0-903540-17-7, Pub. by Floris Books). St George Bk Serv.
Heidenreich, Alfred, ed. see Bock, Emil & Goebel, R.
Heidenreich, Manfred, jt. auth. see Bielfeld, Horst.
Heidensohn, Klaus, ed. The Book of Money. (Illus.). 1979. 24.95 o.p. (ISBN 0-07-027862-8, GB). McGraw.
Heidenstam, Oscar. The New Muscle Building for Beginners. (Illus.). 96p. 1983. pap. 3.95 (ISBN 0-668-05731-9, 5731). Arco.
Heidenstam, Verner Von see Von Heidenstam, Verner.
Heider, Fritz. The Life of a Psychologist: An Autobiography. LC 82-21803. (Illus.). xii, 196p. 1983. text ed. 12.95x (ISBN 0-7006-0232-1). Univ Pr KS.
--The Psychology of Interpersonal Relations. reprint ed. Krauss, Robert M., intro. by. 336p. 1982. Repr. of 1958 ed. write for info. (ISBN 0-89859-282-8). L Erlbaum Assocs.
Heider, W. M. Von see Von Heider, W. M.
Heiderbrecht, Paul & Rohrbach, Jerry. Fathering a Son. LC 78-21871. 1979. pap. 5.95 (ISBN 0-8024-3356-1). Moody.
Heiderich, Manfred W. The German Novel of Eighteen Hundred: A Study of Popular Prose Fiction. 347p. 1982. write for info. (ISBN 3-261-04803-4). P Lang Pubs.
Heidish, Marcy. The Secret Annie Oakley. (Illus.). 205p. 1983. 14.95 (ISBN 0-453-00437-7). NAL.
Heidrick, T. R., ed. Measurement in Polyphase Flows-Nineteen Eighty-Two. 129p. 30.00 (G00209). ASME.
Heifetz, Josefa. From Bach to Verse: Comic Mnemonics for Famous Musical Themes. (Orig.). 1983. pap. 4.95 (ISBN 0-14-006691-8). Penguin.
Heijkoop, H. J. Holy Spirit Is a Divine Person. 5.50 (ISBN 0-88172-084-4); pap. 3.95 (ISBN 0-88172-085-2). Believers Bkshelf.
Heijkoop, H. L. Beginning with Christ. 5.25 (ISBN 0-88172-081-X); pap. 3.95 (ISBN 0-88172-082-8). Believers Bkshelf.
--The Book of Ruth. 5.50 (ISBN 0-88172-086-0). Believers Bkshelf.
--Faith Healing & Speaking in Tongues. 40p. pap. 2.00 (ISBN 0-88172-083-6). Believers Bkshelf.
--Unto Christ. 47p. pap. 0.60 (ISBN 0-88172-087-9). Believers Bkshelf.
Heikkenen, Herman J., jt. auth. see Knight, Fred B.
Heikoff, Joseph M. Coastal Resources Management. LC 76-50986. 1977. 22.50 o.p. (ISBN 0-250-40157-6). Ann Arbor Science.
--Management of Industrial Particulates: Corporate, Government, Citizen Action. LC 74-83855. (Illus.). 1975. 20.00 o.p. (ISBN 0-250-40069-3). Ann Arbor Science.
--Politics of Shore Erosion: Westhampton Beach. LC 76-1727. (Illus.). 1976. 22.50 o.p. (ISBN 0-250-40130-4). Ann Arbor Science.
Heil, John. Logic & Language: An Introduction to Elementary Logic & the Theory of Linguistic Descriptions. 1978. pap. text ed. 16.75 o.p. (ISBN 0-8191-0396-9). U Pr of Amer.
Heil, Ruth. My Child Within: A Young Woman's Reflections on Becoming Pregnant, Being Pregnant & Giving Birth. 128p. 1983. pap. 5.95 (ISBN 0-89107-268-3). Good News.
Heilborn, John & Talbott, Ran. VIC-Twenty User Guide. 250p. (Orig.). 1983. pap. 14.95 (ISBN 0-931988-86-1). Osborne-McGraw.
Heilbron, J. L., jt. auth. see Shumaker, Wayne.
Heilbron, J. L., jt. ed. see Wheaton, Bruce R.
Heilbron, John L. H. G. J. Moseley: The Life & Letters of an English Physicist, 1887-1915. LC 72-93519. 1974. 37.50x (ISBN 0-520-02375-7). U of Cal Pr.
Heilbroner & Thurow. The Economic Problem. 2nd ed. 1981. 20.00 o.p. (ISBN 0-686-95950-7). IIA.
Heilbroner, R. & Thorou, L. Understanding Microeconomics. 5th ed. 1981. pap. 15.95 (ISBN 0-13-936567-2); pap. 10.95 study guide (ISBN 0-13-233296-5). P-H.
Heilbroner, R. & Thurow, L. Economic Problem. 6th ed. 1981. 25.95 (ISBN 0-13-233304-X). P-H.
Heilbroner, R. L. & London, P. Corporate Social Policy: Selections from Business & Society Review. 1975. pap. 15.95 (ISBN 0-201-04360-2). A-W.
Heilbroner, Robert. The Worldly Philosophers. 5th ed. 1980. 13.95 o.p. (ISBN 0-671-25595-9, 21325, Touchstone Bks); pap. 6.95 (ISBN 0-671-25596-7, 21326, Touchstone Bks). S&S.
Heilbroner, Robert & Thurow, Lester. Economics Explained. LC 81-20975. 256p. 1982. 12.95 (ISBN 0-13-229708-6); pap. 6.95 (ISBN 0-13-229690-X). P-H.
Heilbroner, Robert L. Future As History. 1968. pap. 4.95xi o.p. (ISBN 0-06-131386-6, TB1386, Torch). Har-Row.
Heilbroner, Robert L. & Thurow, Lester C. The Economic Problem. 1978. write for info. o.p. (CPCU 9). IIA.
--The Economic Problem: (Second CPCU Edition) 6th ed. LC 80-16631. 670p. 1981. Repr. of 1981 ed. text ed. 22.00 (ISBN 0-89463-032-6). Am Inst Property.
Heilbroner, Robert L., jt. auth. see Bernstein, Peter L.
Heilbroner, Robert L. & Ford, Arthur M., eds. Economic Relevance: A Second Look. LC 75-35004. 300p. 1976. pap. 13.50x (ISBN 0-673-16164-1). Scott F.
Heilbronner, E. & Bock, H. The HMO Model & Its Application, 3 vols. Incl. Vol. 1. Basis & Manipulation. 469p. 46.50x (ISBN 3-527-25654-7); Vol. 2. Problems with Solutions. 457p. 41.20x (ISBN 3-527-25655-5); Vol. 3. Tables of Huckel Molecular Orbitals. 197p. 25.90x (ISBN 3-527-25656-3). 1976. Verlag Chemie.
Heilbronner, E. & Straub, P. A. HMO-Hueckel Molecular Orbitals. 1966. looseleaf bdg 58.00 o.p. (ISBN 0-387-03566-4). Springer-Verlag.
Heilburn, Patricia G., jt. auth. see Grubb, Norton.
Heilbut, Anthony. Exiled in Paradise: German Refugee Artists & Intellectuals in America, from the 1930's to the Present. 480p. 1983. 23.50 (ISBN 0-670-51661-9). Viking Pr.
Heilig, Bruno. Why the German Republic Fell. 40p. (Eng. & Ger.). pap. 0.25 (ISBN 0-911312-43-9). Schalkenbach.
Heiliger, Wilhelm S. Soviet & Chinese Personalities. LC 80-1383. 221p. 1980. lib. bdg. 20.00 (ISBN 0-8191-1213-5); pap. text ed. 10.50 (ISBN 0-8191-1214-3). U Pr of Amer.
Heilling, Roma J. Adolescent Suicidal Behavior: A Family Systems Model. Nathan, Peter E., ed. (Research in Clinical Psychology Ser.: No. 7). 1983. 39.95 (ISBN 0-8357-1390-3). Univ Microfilms.
Heilman, Arthur, ed. see Gilliland, Hap.
Heilman, Arthur, et al. Principles & Practices of Teaching Reading. 5th ed. (Illus.). 544p. 1981. text ed. 19.95 (ISBN 0-675-08150-5). Additional supplements may be obtained from publisher. Merrill.
Heilman, Arthur W. Improve Your Reading Ability. 4th ed. 176p. 1983. pap. text ed. 11.95 (ISBN 0-675-20040-7). Merrill.
Heilman, Arthur W. & Holmes, Eliazbeth A. Smuggling Language into the Teaching of Reading. 2nd ed. (Elementary Education Ser.). 1978. pap. text ed. 10.95 (ISBN 0-675-08360-5). Merrill.
Heilman, Arthur W., ed. see Mangrum, Charles T. & Forgan, Harry W.
Heilman, Arthur W., ed. see Pflaum-Connor, Susanna.
Heilman, Grace E., ed. see Poinsett, Joel R.
Heilman, Joan, jt. auth. see Eden, Alvin N.
Heilman, Joan, jt. auth. see Nachtigall, Lila.
Heilman, Joan R., jt. auth. see Hausknecht, Richard.
Heilman, Joan R., jt. auth. see Mirsky, Stanley.
Heilman, Madeline E. & Hornstein, Harvey. Managing Human Forces in Organizations. LC 81-71159. 270p. 1982. 17.50 (ISBN 0-87094-283-2). Dow Jones-Irwin.
Heilman, Robert, ed. see Shakespeare, William.
Heilman, Samuel C. The People of the Book: Drama, Fellowship, & Religion. LC 82-13369. 264p. 1983. lib. bdg. 22.50x (ISBN 0-226-32492-3). U of Chicago Pr.
Heilmeyer, L., ed. see Begemann, H. & Rastetter, J.
Heilpern, John. Conference of the Birds. LC 78-55648. (Illus.). 1978. 10.95 o.p. (ISBN 0-672-52489-9). Bobbs.
Heilveil, Ira. Video in Mental Health Practice: An Activities Handbook. 1983. pap. text ed. price not set (ISBN 0-8261-4331-8). Springer Pub.
Heilweil, M., jt. auth. see Hoernes, G.
Heim, Alice. Thicker Than Water? Adoption. 208p. 1983. 21.50 (ISBN 0-436-19155-5, Pub. by Secker & Warburg); pap. 12.50 (ISBN 0-436-19156-3, Pub. by Secker & Warburg). David & Charles.
Heim, David. Basic Carpentry for Apartments. LC 75-7705. (Illus.). 128p. 1975. 10.00 o.p. (ISBN 0-312-06720-8); pap. 4.50 o.p. (ISBN 0-312-06755-0). St Martin.
Heim, David, jt. auth. see Carlinsky, Dan.
Heim, Kathleen M., ed. The Status of Women in Librarianship: Historical, Sociological, & Economic Issues. 350p. 1983. 29.95 (ISBN 0-918212-62-6). Neal-Schuman.
Heim, Michael, jt. auth. see Matich, Olga.
Heim, Michael H., tr. see Kundera, Milan.
Heim, Ralph D. Reader's Companion to the Bible. LC 74-26329. 144p. 1975. pap. 0.50 o.p. (ISBN 0-8006-1090-3, 1-1090). Fortress.
Heim, U., et al. Small Fragment Set Manual: Technique Recommended by the ASIF-Group (Swiss Association for the Study of Internal Fixation) Kirschaum, R. & Batten, R. L., trs. from Ger. LC 74-13966. (Illus.). xii, 300p. 1975. 75.10 o.p. (ISBN 0-387-06904-6). Springer-Verlag.
Heiman, J., et al. Becoming Orgasmic: A Sexual Growth Program for Women. 1976. text ed. 11.95 (ISBN 0-13-072652-4, Spec); pap. text ed. 6.95 (ISBN 0-13-072645-1). P-H.
Heimburger, Donald J., ed. see Norwood, John B.
Heimburger, Marilyn M., ed. see Norwood, John B.
Heimendahl, Manfred Von see Von Heimendahl, Manfred & Wolff, U.
Heimerdinger, Mark C., jt. auth. see Fontenilles, Alfred.
Heimler, Eugene. Night of the Mist. LC 77-28508. 1978. Repr. of 1960 ed. lib. bdg. 19.00x (ISBN 0-313-20229-X, HENM). Greenwood.
Heimlich, Milton, jt. auth. see Jawin, Ann.
Heimlich, Richard A., jt. auth. see Feldmann, Rodney M.
Heims, Pam. Home Sweet Battleground. 1981. pap. 3.50 (ISBN 0-88207-586-1). Victor Bks.
Heims, Peter. Countering Industrial Espionage. (Illus.). 290p. 1982. text ed. 29.50 (ISBN 0-905961-03-X). Sheridan.
Heims, Steve J. John Von Neumann & Norbert Wiener: From Mathematics to the Technologies of Life & Death. 546p. 1980. 19.95x (ISBN 0-262-08105-9); pap. 10.95 (ISBN 0-262-58056-X). MIT Pr.
Heimsath, Clovis & Heimsath, MaryAnn. Pioneer Texas Buildings: A Geometry Lesson. LC 68-25947. (Illus.). 169p. 1968. 19.95 (ISBN 0-292-73699-1). U of Tex Pr.
Heimsath, MaryAnn, jt. auth. see Heimsath, Clovis.
Heimstra, Norman & McFarling, Leslie H. Environmental Psychology: Second Edition. Walker, Edward L., ed. LC 78-913. (Core Books in Psychology). (Illus.). 1978. text ed. 19.95 (ISBN 0-8185-0266-5). Brooks-Cole.
Hein, Eleanor C. & Nicholson, M. Jean. Contemporary Leadership Behavior: Selected Readings. 1982. pap. 14.95 (ISBN 0-316-35447-3). Little.
Hein, J. R., jt. ed. see Iijima, A.
Hein, Lucille E. I Can Make My Own Prayers. LC 72-154026. (Illus.). (gr. k-4). 1971. 3.95 (ISBN 0-8170-0528-5). Judson.
--My Very Special Friend. (Illus.). 32p. 1974. pap. 3.95 o.p. (ISBN 0-8170-0618-4). Judson.
Hein, Morris. Foundations of College Chemistry. 5th ed. (Chemistry Ser.). 600p. 1982. text ed. 24.95 (ISBN 0-8185-0476-5). Brooks-Cole.
--Foundations of College Chemistry. 4th ed. 1977. text ed. 22.95x o.p. (ISBN 0-8221-0181-5). Dickenson.
--Foundations of College Chemistry: The Alternate Edition. LC 80-259. 1980. text ed. 16.95 (ISBN 0-8185-0402-1). Brooks-Cole.
Hein, Morris & Best, Leo. College Chemistry: An Introduction to Inorganic, Organic & Biochemistry. 2nd ed. LC 80-257. 1980. text ed. 25.95 (ISBN 0-8185-0349-1). Brooks-Cole.
Hein, Morris, et al. Foundations of Chemistry in the Laboratory. 4th ed. (Orig.). 1977. pap. 13.95x o.p. (ISBN 0-8221-0206-4). Dickenson.
Hein, Rolland. The Harmony Within: The Spiritual Vision of George MacDonald. 1982. pap. 6.95 (ISBN 0-8028-1912-5). Eerdmans.
Hein, Ruth, tr. see Bruckner, Christine.
Hein, Ruth, tr. see Kruger, Horst.
Hein, Ruth, tr. see Nossack, Hans E.
Hein, Ruth, tr. see Paretti, Sandra.
Hein, Ruth, tr. see Tau, Max.
Heinberg, et al. Housing Allowances in Kansas City & Wilmington: An Appraisal. (Illus.). 41p. (Orig.). 1976. pap. text ed. 4.00 (ISBN 0-87766-143-X). Urban Inst.
Heindel, Ned D., et al, eds. The Chemistry of Radiopharmaceuticals. LC 77-94827. (Cancer Management Ser.: Vol. 3). (Illus.). 304p. 1978. 43.50x (ISBN 0-89352-019-5). Masson Pub.
Heindler, M., jt. auth. see Harms, A. A.
Heine, Alice. Fireside Tales. 1978. 5.95 o.p. (ISBN 0-533-03637-2). Vantage.
Heine, Carl. Micronesia at the Crossroads: A Reappraisal of the Micronesian Political Dilemma. LC 73-78977. 256p. 1974. 12.00x (ISBN 0-8248-0273-X, Eastwest Ctr); pap. 2.95 (ISBN 0-8248-0278-0). UH Pr.
Heine, Heinrich. The Lazarus Poems. Eliot, Alistair, tr. from Ger. (Translations Ser.). 79p. 1980. 11.95 o.p. (ISBN 0-85635-287-X, Pub. by Carcanet New Pr England). Humanities.
--The North Sea. Jones, Howard M., tr. LC 73-83869. 12.00 (ISBN 0-87548-266-X); pap. 5.00 (ISBN 0-87548-272-4). Open Court.
Heine, Helen. Friends. LC 82-45313. (Illus.). 32p. (ps-3). 1982. 10.95 (ISBN 0-689-50256-7, McElderry Bk). Atheneum.
Heine, Ronald E., tr. see Origen.
Heine, William C. Historic Ships of the World. LC 76-57879. (Illus.). 1977. 12.95 o.p. (ISBN 0-399-11957-4). Putnam Pub Group.
Heinegg, Peter, jt. auth. see Holl, Adolf.
Heinegg, Peter, tr. see Hasler, August B.
Heineke, J. Microeconomics for Business Decisions: Theory & Application. 1976. text ed. 21.00 (ISBN 0-13-581389-1). P-H.
Heineke, J. M., ed. Economic Models of Criminal Behavior. (Contributions to Economic Analysis Ser.: Vol. 118). 1979. 64.00 (ISBN 0-444-85261-1, North Holland). Elsevier.
Heineman, E. Richard. Plane Trigonometry. 5th ed. (Illus.). 1980. text ed. 23.50 (ISBN 0-07-027932-2); instr's manual 15.00 (ISBN 0-07-027933-0). McGraw.
--Plane Trigonometry with Tables. 4th ed. (Illus.). 352p. 1974. text ed. 18.95 (ISBN 0-07-027931-4, C); instr's manual 15.00 (ISBN 0-07-028054-1). McGraw.
Heineman, Helen. Mrs. Trollope: The Triumphant Feminine in the Nineteenth Century. LC 78-9940. (Illus.). 316p. 1979. 18.00 (ISBN 0-8214-0354-0, 82-82477). Ohio U Pr.
--Mrs. Trollope: The Triumphant Feminine in the Ninteenth Century. LC 78-9940. xii, 316p. 1982. pap. 9.00 (ISBN 0-8214-0698-1, 82-84671). Ohio U Pr.
--Restless Angels: The Friendship of Six Victorian Women-Frances Wright, Camilla Wright, Harriet Garnett, Frances Garnett, Julia Garnet Pertz, Frances Trollope. LC 82-12421. (Illus.). 230p. 1983. text ed. 23.95x (ISBN 0-8214-0673-6, 82-84416); pap. 12.95 (ISBN 0-8214-0674-4, 82-84424). Ohio U Pr.
Heineman, James H. & Bensen, Donald R., eds. P. G. Wodehouse: A Centenary Celebration (1881-1981) (Illus.). 1982. 65.00x (ISBN 0-19-520357-7). Oxford U Pr.
--P. G. Wodehouse: A Centennary Celebration 1881-1981. 1981. pap. 25.00 o.p. (ISBN 0-87598-073-2). Pierpont Morgan.
Heineman, John L. Hitler's First Foreign Minister: Constantin Freiherr von Neurath. LC 77-71061. 1980. 40.00x (ISBN 0-520-03442-2). U of Cal Pr.
--Readings in European History: A Collection of Primary Sources, 1789 to the Present. 1979. pap. text ed. 14.95 (ISBN 0-8403-1984-3, 40198402). Kendall-Hunt.
Heinemann & Petuchowski. Literature of the Synagogue. LC 75-25536. 15.95x o.p. (ISBN 0-87441-217-X). Behrman.
Heinemann, E. Richard. College Algebra. (Illus.). 1973. text ed. 21.00 (ISBN 0-07-027936-5, C); 1.95 o.p. instructor's manual (ISBN 0-07-027937-3). McGraw.
Heinemann Educational Bk. Ltd., ed. The Catalogue of the Alpine Club Library. 750p. 1982. 195.00x (ISBN 0-686-82314-1, Pub. by Heinemann England). State Mutual Bk.
Heinemann, Frederick H. Existentialism & the Modern Predicament. LC 78-14042. 1979. Repr. of 1958 ed. lib. bdg. 20.00x (ISBN 0-313-21103-5, HEEX). Greenwood.
Heinemann, Gisella. Skirts: Sew Your Own. (Illus.). 1978. pap. 7.95 o.p. (ISBN 0-07-027940-3, SP). McGraw.
Heinemann, M. Edith, jt. auth. see Estes, Nada J.

Heinemann, Margot. Puritanism & Theatre: Thomas Middleton & Opposition Drama Under the Early Stuarts. LC 79-14991. (Past & Present Publications Ser.). 309p. 1982. 29.50 (ISBN 0-521-22602-3); pap. 11.95 (ISBN 0-521-27052-9). Cambridge U Pr.
Heinemann, Ronald L. Depression & New Deal in Virginia: The Enduring Dominion. LC 82-13487. 1983. write for info. (ISBN 0-8139-0946-5). U Pr of Va.
Heiner, Carol W. & Hendrix, Wayne R. People Create Technology. LC 79-53802. (Technology Series). (Illus.). 256p. (gr. 5-9). 1980. text ed. 13.95 (ISBN 0-87192-109-X, 000-2); tchr's guide 11.95 (ISBN 0-87192-111-1); activity manual 5.95 (ISBN 0-87192-110-3). Davis Mass.
Heinerman, John. Complete Book of Spices: Their Medical, Nutritional & Cooking Uses. LC 82-80700. 1983. pap. 11.95 (ISBN 0-87983-281-9). Keats.
--First Aid with Herbs. Passwater, Richard A. & Mindell, Earl, eds. (Good Health Guide Ser.). 32p. 1983. pap. 1.45 (ISBN 0-87983-304-1). Keats.
Heinesen, William. The Lost Musicians. Friis, Erick J., tr. from Danish. 364p. 1972. pap. 3.95x o.p. (ISBN 0-88254-002-5). Hippocrene Bks.
Heiney, Donald. America in Modern Italian Literature. 278p. 1965. 20.00 (ISBN 0-8135-0471-6). Rutgers U Pr.
Heinhold. Power Cables & Their Applications. 1980. 64.95 (ISBN 0-471-26129-7, Wiley Heyden). Wiley.
Heinich, R. & Molenda, M. Instructional Media: The New Technologies of Instruction. 375p. 1982. 23.95 (ISBN 0-471-36893-8). Wiley.
Heinich, Robert. Technology & the Management of Instruction. 193p. pap. 9.95 (ISBN 0-89240-023-4, 304). Assn Ed Comm Tech.
Heinig, Ruth & Stillwell, Lyda. Creative Drama for the Classroom Teacher. 2nd ed. (Illus.). 352p. 1981. text ed. 17.95 (ISBN 0-13-189415-3). P-H.
Heiniger, E. A. Grand Canyon. Osers, Edward, tr. from Ger. (Illus.). 1975. 30.00 o.p. (ISBN 0-88331-074-0). Luce.
Heiniger, Margot C. & Randolph, Shirley L. Neurophysiological Concepts in Human Behavior: The Tree of Learning. LC 80-25454. (Illus.). 350p. 1981. text ed. 27.95 (ISBN 0-8016-2203-4). Mosby.
Heinl, Tina. The Baby Massage Book: Using Touch for Better Bonding & Happier Babies. (Illus.). 144p. 1983. 15.95 (ISBN 0-13-056226-2); pap. 7.95 (ISBN 0-13-056218-1). P-H.
Heinlein, Robert. A Double Star. 1978. lib. bdg. 10.00 (ISBN 0-8398-2446-7, Gregg). G K Hall.
Heinlein, Robert A. Beyond This Horizon. 1981. PLB 14.95 (ISBN 0-8398-2672-9, Gregg). G K Hall.
--Beyond This Horizon. (RL 7). 1974. pap. 1.95 (ISBN 0-451-09833-1, E9833, Sig). NAL.
--Day After Tomorrow. (RL 7). pap. 1.95 (ISBN 0-451-12139-2, AJ2139, Sig). NAL.
--The Door into Summer. (Science Fiction Ser.). 1979. lib. bdg. 12.50 o.p. (ISBN 0-8398-2506-4, Gregg). G K Hall.
--Door into Summer. (RL 7). pap. 2.50 (ISBN 0-451-12363-8, AE2363, Sig). NAL.
--Farnham's Freehold. pap. 2.75 (ISBN 0-425-04856-X, Dist. by Putnam). Berkley Pub.
--Glory Road. (Science Fiction Ser.). 1979. lib. bdg. 12.50 o.p. (ISBN 0-8398-2448-3, Gregg). G K Hall.
--The Green Hills of Earth. 176p. (RL 7). 1973. pap. 2.50 (ISBN 0-451-12371-9, AE2371, Sig). NAL.
--I Will Fear No Evil. (Science Fiction Ser.). 15.00 o.p. (ISBN 0-8398-2449-1, Gregg). G K Hall.
--The Man Who Sold the Moon. (RL 7). 1973. pap. 2.50 (ISBN 0-451-11587-2, AE1587, Sig). NAL.
--Menace from Earth. (RL 7). 1970. pap. 2.50 (ISBN 0-451-11948-7, AE1948, Sig). NAL.
--The Moon Is a Harsh Mistress. 1966. 9.95 (ISBN 0-399-10556-5). Putnam Pub Group.
--The Notebooks of Lazarus Long. LC 78-8050. (Illus.). 1978. pap. 6.95 (ISBN 0-399-12242-7). Putnam Pub Group.
--Orphans of the Sky. 1964. 6.95 (ISBN 0-399-10613-8). Putnam Pub Group.
--The Past Through Tomorrow: Future History Stories. 1967. 9.95 (ISBN 0-399-10620-0). Putnam Pub Group.
--Podkayne of Mars. 1963. 7.95 (ISBN 0-399-10642-1). Putnam Pub Group.
--The Puppet Masters. (Science Fiction Ser.). 1979. lib. bdg. 11.00 o.p. (ISBN 0-8398-2508-0, Gregg). G K Hall.
--Puppet Masters. pap. 2.50 (ISBN 0-451-11964-9, AE1964, Sig). NAL.
--Starship Troopers. 1960. 9.95 o.p. (ISBN 0-399-20209-9). Putnam Pub Group.
--Stranger in a Strange Land. 1961. 11.95 (ISBN 0-399-10772-X). Putnam Pub Group.
--Stranger in a Strange Land: The Great Science Fiction of Robert A. Heinlein, 5 bks. Incl. Stranger in a Strange Land; I Will Fear No Evil. pap. 3.25 (ISBN 0-425-06171-X); The Moon Is a Harsh Mistress. pap. 2.95 (ISBN 0-425-06262-7); Starship Troopers. pap. 2.75 (ISBN 0-425-05773-9); The Past Through Tomorrow. pap. 3.75 (ISBN 0-425-06056-X). 1982. Boxed Set. pap. 14.40 (ISBN 0-425-05838-7). Berkley Pub.
--Time Enough for Love: The Lives of Lazarus Long. 1973. 7.95 (ISBN 0-399-11151-4). Putnam Pub Group.
--Waldo & Magic, Inc. (Science Fiction Ser.). 1979. lib. bdg. 12.50 o.p. (ISBN 0-8398-2507-2, Gregg). G K Hall.
--Waldo & Magic, Inc. (RL 7). pap. 2.50 (ISBN 0-451-12365-4, AE2365, Sig). NAL.
Heinlein, W. E. & Holmes, W. H. Active Filters for Integrated Circuits. 65.50 o.p. (ISBN 0-387-91070-0). Springer Verlag.
Heinowitz, Jack. Pregnant Fathers: How Fathers Can Enjoy & Share the Experiences of Pregnancy & Childbirth. LC 81-21147. (Transformation Ser.). 126p. 1982. 11.95 (ISBN 0-13-694935-5, Spec); pap. 5.95 (ISBN 0-13-694927-4, Spec). P-H.
Heinrich, Adel. Bach's Die Kunst Der Fuge: A Living Compendium of Fugal Procedures with a Motivic Analysis of All the Fugues. LC 82-20095. (Illus.). 370p. (Orig.). 1983. text ed. 24.75 (ISBN 0-8191-2866-X); pap. text ed. 13.75 (ISBN 0-8191-2867-8). U Pr of Amer.
Heinrich, Amy V. Fragments of Rainbows: The Life & Poetry of Saito Mokichi, 1882-1953. LC 82-12989. (Studies of the East Asian Institute). (Illus.). 224p. 1983. text ed. 22.50x (ISBN 0-231-05428-9). Columbia U Pr.
Heinrich, Anthony P. The Dawning of Music in Kentucky. LC 79-39732. (Earlier American Music Ser: Vol. 10). 297p. 1973. Repr. of 1820 ed. lib. bdg. 32.50 (ISBN 0-306-77310-4). Da Capo.
Heinrich, Bernd. Insect Thermoregulation. LC 80-19452. 328p. 1981. 44.50 (ISBN 0-471-05144-6, Pub. by Wiley-Interscience). Wiley.
Heinrich, E. Wm. The Geology of Carbonatites. LC 78-27358. 652p. 1980. Repr. of 1966 ed. 34.50 (ISBN 0-88275-847-0). Krieger.
Heinrich, Eberhardt W. Microscopic Identification of Minerals. 1965. text ed. 37.50 (ISBN 0-07-028055-X, C). McGraw.
Heinrich, Herbert W. Industrial Accident Prevention. 4th ed. 1959. text ed. 27.50 (ISBN 0-07-028058-4, C). McGraw.
Heinrich, Herbert W., et al. Industrial Accident Prevention: A Safety Management Approach. 5th rev. ed. (Illus.). 1980. text ed. 29.95 (ISBN 0-07-028061-4); instructor's manual 20.00 (ISBN 0-07-028062-2). McGraw.
Heinrich, June S. & Heinrich, June S. Educating Older People: Another View of Mainstreaming. LC 82-60801. (Fastback Ser.: No. 181). 50p. 1982. pap. 0.75 (ISBN 0-87367-181-3). Phi Delta Kappa.
Heinrichs, Kurt, jt. auth. see Arman, Mike.
Heinritz, Fred J., jt. auth. see Dougherty, Richard M.
Heinritz, Stuart F. & Farrell, Paul V. Purchasing: Principles & Applications. 6th ed. (Illus.). 448p. 1981. text ed. 27.95 (ISBN 0-13-742163-X). P-H.
Heins, C. P. & Firmage, D. A. Design of Modern Steel Highway Bridges. 463p. 1979. 45.95x (ISBN 0-471-04263-3, Pub. by Wiley-Interscience). Wiley.
Heins, Conrad, jt. auth. see Derucher, Kenneth.
Heins, Paul, tr. see Brothers Grimm.
Heins, Richard M., jt. auth. see Williams, C. Arthur, Jr.
Heinsdijk, D. Forest Assessment. 359p. 1975. 33.25 (ISBN 90-220-0550-X, PDC36, Pub. by PUDOC). Unipub.
Heintz, W., jt. ed. see Jaschek, C.
Heintzelman, Donald S. A Guide to Eastern Hawk Watching. LC 76-2002. (Keystone Bks.). (Illus.). 1976. 10.00x o.s.i. (ISBN 0-271-01222-6); pap. 5.95 o.s.i. (ISBN 0-271-01246-3). Pa St U Pr.
--A Guide to Hawk Watching in North America. LC 78-21003. (Keystone Bks.). (Illus.). 1979. 12.95x (ISBN 0-271-00212-3); pap. 7.95 (ISBN 0-271-00217-4). Pa St U Pr.
Heintzelman, Oliver K. & Highsmith, R. M., Jr. World Regional Geography. 4th ed. (Illus.). 1973. text ed. 27.95 (ISBN 0-13-969006-9). P-H.
Heintzen, Paul H. & Bursch, J. H., eds. Roentgen-Video-Techniques. LC 77-99147. (Illus.). 354p. 1978. 33.00 o.p. (ISBN 0-88416-237-0). Wright-PSG.
Heiny, Mary, jt. auth. see Monkerud, Donald.
Heinz, Cecilia & Straw Dog. Improvising Blues Guitar: A Programmed Manual of Instruction. LC 70-143775. (Contemporary Guitar Styles Ser.). (Illus.). 84p. (Prog. Bk.). 1970. pap. 6.95 o.p. (ISBN 0-912910-01-1). Green Note Music.
Heinz, Grete, tr. see Kehr, Eckart.
Heinz, John P. & Laumann, Edward O. Chicago Lawyers: The Social Structure of the Bar. LC 82-50355. 550p. 1983. 27.50x (ISBN 0-87154-378-8). Russell Sage.
Heinz, John P., jt. auth. see Laumann, Edward O.
Heinz, W. C. American Mirror: A Distinguished Writer Writes on Valor. LC 80-723. (Illus.). 272p. 1982. 19.95 (ISBN 0-385-12672-7). Doubleday.
Heinz, W. C., jt. auth. see Lombardi, Vince.
Heinze, Evelyn B., jt. auth. see Macdonald, Eleanor J.
Heinze, R. M. The Proclamations of Tudor Kings. LC 27-22983. 320p. 1976. 54.50 (ISBN 0-521-20938-2). Cambridge U Pr.
Heinzel & Fitter. The Birds of Britian & Europe with North Africa & the Middle East. pap. 14.95 (ISBN 0-686-42723-8, Collins Pub England). Greene.
Heinzel, jt. auth. see Woodcock.
Heinzen. Digital Radiography. 1983. write for info. (ISBN 0-86577-093-X). Thieme-Stratton.
Heinzl, Brigitte, ed. see Durer, Albrecht.
Heir, Malcolm. Epic of Industry. 1926. text ed. 22.50x (ISBN 0-686-83536-0). Elliots Bks.
Heirtzler, J. R., ed. Indian Ocean Geology & Biostratigraphy. LC 77-88320. (Special Publication Ser.). 1978. 25.00 (ISBN 0-87590-208-1, SP0019). Am Geophysical.
Heise, David R. Causal Analysis. LC 75-20465. 301p. 1975. 33.95 (ISBN 0-471-36898-9, Pub. by Wiley-Interscience). Wiley.
--Understanding Events. LC 78-2417. (American Sociological Association Rose Monograph Ser.). (Illus.). 1979. 24.95 (ISBN 0-521-22539-6); pap. 8.95 (ISBN 0-521-29544-0). Cambridge U Pr.
Heise, Eorge W., jt. auth. see Cahoon, N. Corey.
Heise, Jon O., ed. Travel Guidebooks in Review. 1978. pap. 9.95 o.p. (ISBN 0-915794-25-X, 9335/78). Gaylord Prof Pubns.
Heisel, D. Biofeedback Guide. 282p. 1977. 20.00 (ISBN 0-677-00020-0). Gordon.
Heisel, Dorelle. Biofeedback Strategies for Interpersonal Relationships. 204p. 1981. 20.00 (ISBN 0-677-05649-4). Gordon.
Heisenberg, Werner. Philosophical Problems of Quantum Physics. LC 79-89842. Orig. Title: Philosophic Problems of Nuclear Science. 1979. 16.00 (ISBN 0-918024-14-5); pap. text ed. 10.00 (ISBN 0-918024-15-3). Ox Bow.
--Physics & Philosophy: The Revolution in Modern Science. (World Perspectives Ser.). pap. 4.95xi (ISBN 0-06-130549-5, TB549, Torch). Har-Row.
Heiser, Dick. Personal Computers for Managers. 1983. pap. 14.95 (ISBN 0-88022-031-7). Que Corp.
Heiser, Edward J. & Allswede, Jerry L., eds. Blade Coating Defect Terminology. (Illus.). 53p. 1982. pap. 24.95 (ISBN 0-686-43234-7, 01 01 R094). TAPPI.
Heiser, F. A., jt. auth. see Colangelo, Vito J.
Heiserman. How to Design & Build Your Own Custom Robot. 462p. 1981. 18.95 (ISBN 0-8306-9629-6); pap. 12.95 (ISBN 0-686-71471-7, 1341). TAB Bks.
Heiserman, D. Handbook of Digital IC Applications. 1980. 25.95 (ISBN 0-13-372698-3). P-H.
--Programming in BASIC for Personal Computers. 1981. 20.95 (ISBN 0-13-730747-0); pap. 9.95 (ISBN 0-13-730739-X). P-H.
Heiserman, D. L. Handbook of Major Appliance Trouble-Shooting & Repair. LC 76-10684. (Illus.). 1977. 21.95 (ISBN 0-13-380295-7). P-H.
Heiserman, David L. How to Build Your Own Self-Programming Robot. (Illus.). 1979. 15.95 (ISBN 0-8306-9760-8); pap. 9.95 (ISBN 0-8306-1241-6, 1241). TAB Bks.
--How to Design & Build Your Own Custom TV Games. (Illus.). 1979. 15.95 o.p. (ISBN 0-8306-9859-0); pap. 13.95 (ISBN 0-8306-9815-9, 1101). TAB Bks.
--Miniprocessors: From Calculators to Computers. 1978. 9.95 o.p. (ISBN 0-8306-7971-5); pap. 8.95 o.p. (ISBN 0-8306-6971-X, 971). TAB Bks.
--Pascal. (Illus.). 350p. (Orig.). 1980. 16.95 (ISBN 0-8306-9934-1); pap. 10.95 (ISBN 0-8306-1205-X, 1205). Tab Bks.
--Projects in Machine Intelligence for Your Home Computer. (Illus.). 103p. 1982. 17.95 (ISBN 0-8306-0057-4); pap. 10.95 (ISBN 0-8306-1391-9, 1391). TAB Bks.
--Radio Astronomy for the Amateur. LC 74-33624. (Illus.). 252p. 1975. 8.95 (ISBN 0-8306-5714-2); pap. 5.95 o.p. (ISBN 0-8306-4714-7, 714). TAB Bks.
--Robot Intelligence...with Experiments. (Illus.). 308p. 1981. 16.95 (ISBN 0-8306-9685-7, 1191); pap. 10.95 (ISBN 0-8306-1191-6). TAB Bks.
Heiserman, Russell L. Electrical & Electronic Measuring Instruments. 208p. 1983. pap. text ed. 16.95 (ISBN 0-471-86178-2). Wiley.
--Electronic Equipment Wiring & Assembly. LC 82-13678. 98p. 1983. pap. text ed. 14.95 (ISBN 0-471-86176-6). Wiley.
Heisey, Marion J. Clinical Case Studies in Psychodrama. LC 81-40109. 212p. (Orig.). 1982. lib. bdg. 22.25 (ISBN 0-8191-2531-8); pap. text ed. 10.75 (ISBN 0-8191-2532-6). U Pr of Amer.
Heiskanen, Piltti, ed. see Tuominen, Arvo P.
Heisler, Helmuth. Urbanization & the Government of Migration. LC 73-88673. 160p. 1974. 26.00 (ISBN 0-312-83510-8). St Martin.
Heisler, Martin O. & Lambert, Richard D., eds. Ethnic Conflict in the World Today. LC 77-81968. (Annals of the American Academy of Political & Social Science: No. 433). 1977. pap. 7.95 (ISBN 0-87761-219-6). Am Acad Pol Soc Sci.
Heisler, Martin O., jt. ed. see Lawrence, Robert M.
Heisler, Roland C. Federal Incorporation: Constitutional Questions Involved. LC 13-8920. (University of Pennsylvania Law School Ser.: No. 3). viii, 231p. 1982. Repr. of 1913 ed. lib. bdg. 28.50 (ISBN 0-89941-179-7). W S Hein.
Heiss, Jerold. The Social Psychology of Interaction. (Ser. in Biology). 400p. 1981. text ed. 19.95 (ISBN 0-13-817718-X). P-H.
Heiss, Marie L., jt. auth. see Wallace, Roberta.
Heiss, Robert. Hegel, Kierkegaard, Marx. 448p. 1975. pap. 3.95 o.s.i. (ISBN 0-440-53529-8, Delta). Dell.
Heiss, U. Askania-Nova: Animal Paradise in Russia. 8.75 o.p. (ISBN 0-370-01338-7). Transatlantic.
Heiss, W. D. & Phelps, M. F., eds. Positron Emission Tomography of the Brain. (Illus.). 300p. 1983. 51.50 (ISBN 0-387-12130-7). Springer-Verlag.
Heissig, Walther. The Religions of Mongolia. Samuel, Geoffrey, tr. from Ger. 1980. 24.75x (ISBN 0-520-03857-6). U of Cal Pr.
Heistad & Marcus. Cerebral Blood Flow: Effects of Nerves & Neurotransmitters. (Developments in Neuroscience Ser.: Vol. 14). 1982. 95.00 (ISBN 0-444-00689-3). Elsevier.
Heitger, Lester E. & Matulich, Serge. Managerial Accounting. 1980. text ed. 24.95 (ISBN 0-07-027941-1); study guide 9.95 (ISBN 0-07-027942-X); job costing packet 8.50 (ISBN 0-07-027943-8); profit planning packet 8.50 (ISBN 0-07-027946-2); solutions manual 31.50 (ISBN 0-07-027944-6); examination questions 19.95 (ISBN 0-07-027945-4); overhead transparencies 350.00 (ISBN 0-07-074792-X). McGraw.
Heitger, Lester E., jt. auth. see Matulich, Serge.
Heitlinger, E. I. von see Von Heitlinger, E. I. & Ursus, Thomas O.
Heitman, H. & Kneer, N. Physical Education Instructional Techniques: An Individualized, Humanistic Approach. 1976. text ed. 19.95 (ISBN 0-13-668251-0). P-H.
Heitner, Jack. The Search for the Real Self: Humanistic Psychology & Literature. LC 78-62174. 1978. pap. text ed. 9.50 (ISBN 0-8191-0474-4). U Pr of Amer.
Heitz, True. Mommy Moon & the Rainbow Children. (Illus.). 13p. (Orig.). (ps-2). 1982. pap. 3.00 (ISBN 0-686-37664-1). True Heitz.
Heitzman, Charles. Lofts for Racing Pigeons. (Illus.). 1963. 2.50 o.p. (ISBN 0-911466-20-7). Swanson.
Heitzman, E. Robert. The Lung: Radiologic - Pathologic Correlations. LC 73-6926. (Illus.). 381p. 1973. 46.50 o.p. (ISBN 0-8016-2134-8). Mosby.
Heizer, Robert F. & Almquist, Alan J. The Other Californians: Prejudice & Discrimination Under Spain, Mexico, & the United States to 1920. LC 76-121186. 1971. 27.50x (ISBN 0-520-01735-8); pap. 3.95 (ISBN 0-520-03415-5). U of Cal Pr.
Heizer, Robert F. & Baumhoff, Martin A. Prehistoric Rock Art of Nevada & California. LC 62-13074. (California Library Reprint). (Illus.). 430p. 1976. Repr. 55.00x (ISBN 0-520-02911-9). U of Cal Pr.
Heizer, Robert F. & Elsasser, Albert B. The Natural World of the California Indians. LC 79-65092. (Illus.). 1980. 14.95 o.s.i. (ISBN 0-520-03895-9); pap. 7.95 (ISBN 0-520-03896-7). U of Cal Pr.
Heizer, Robert F. & Whipple, M. A., eds. The California Indians: A Source Book. 2nd rev. & enl. ed. LC 72-122951. (Illus.). 1971. 30.00x (ISBN 0-520-01770-6); pap. 11.95 (ISBN 0-520-02031-6, CAL231). U of Cal Pr.
Hekelman, Francine & Ostendarp, Carol. Nephrology Nursing. (Illus.). 1979. text ed. 23.50 (ISBN 0-07-027948-9, HP). McGraw.
Hekinian, R. Petrology of the Ocean Floor. (Oceanography Ser.: Vol. 33). Date not set. 85.00 (ISBN 0-444-41967-5). Elsevier.
Hektoen, Faith H. & Rinehart, Jeanne B., eds. Toys to Go. 1976. pap. text ed. 4.00 (ISBN 0-8389-3186-3). ALA.
Hela, Ilmo & Laevastu, Taivo. Fisheries Oceanography. (Illus.). 254p. 22.00 o.p. (ISBN 0-85238-009-7, FNB). Unipub.
Helal, Basil, jt. auth. see Benjamin, Alexander.
Heland, Victoria. The Artful Cousin. (Regency Romance Ser.). 192p. (Orig.). 1982. pap. 2.50 (ISBN 0-515-05707-X). Jove Pubns.
Helander, Brock. The Rock Who's Who: A Biographical Dictionary & a Critical Discography. LC 82-80804. 684p. 1982. 25.00 (ISBN 0-02-871250-1); pap. 14.95 (ISBN 0-686-83123-3). Schirmer Bks.
Helander, Joel E. Noose & Collar: The Story of the Rockland Murder, Madison, Connecticut. LC 79-91416. (Illus.). 90p. (Orig.). 1979. pap. 4.75 (ISBN 0-935600-07-8). Helander.
Helander, Martin. Human Factors-Ergonomics for Building & Construction. LC 80-26717. (Construction Management & Engineering Ser.). 361p. 1981. 39.95x (ISBN 0-471-05075-X, Pub. by Wiley-Interscience). Wiley.
Helberg, Kristen & Lewis, Daniel. The Victorian House Coloring Book. (Pictorial Archive Ser.). (Illus.). 1980. pap. 2.25 (ISBN 0-486-23908-X). Dover.
Helberg, Kristin, jt. auth. see Fleischman, Charles.
Helbling, Robert E., ed. see Durrenmatt, Friedrich.
Held, Bruce, jt. auth. see Ruch, Walter E.
Held, D., jt. auth. see Giddens, A.
Held, David, jt. ed. see Giddens, Anthony.
Held, Gilbert. Apple II BASIC: A Quick Reference Guide. 1982. of 10 29.50 set (ISBN 0-471-87043-9). Wiley.
--Data Communications Procurement Manual. LC 79-18075. (Illus.). 1979. text ed. 24.50 o.p. (ISBN 0-07-606534-0). McGraw.
--Data Communications Procurement Manual. (Electronics Magazine Book Ser.). (Illus.). 164p. 1980. 32.50 (ISBN 0-07-027952-7, P&RB). McGraw.
--IBM PC Basic: Quick Reference Guide. (Illus.). 1982. pap. text ed. 2.95 (ISBN 0-471-87042-0). Wiley.

Held, Heinz. Laughing Camera I. Reich, Hanns, ed. (Illus.). 1983. pap. 4.95 (ISBN 0-8090-1506-4, Terra Magica). Hill & Wang.

Held, Julius & Posner, Donald. Seventeenth & Eighteenth Century Art: Baroque Painting, Sculpture & Architecture. Janson, H., ed. (Illus.). 492p. 1972. text ed. 26.95 (ISBN 0-13-807339-2). P-H.

Held, McDonald W., jt. auth. see Moulton, Eugene R.

Held, Michael & Naylor, Colin. Contemporary Photographers. 1024p. 1982. 70.00x (ISBN 0-312-16791-1). St Martin.

Held, Virginia, et al, eds. Philosophy & Political Action. 1972. pap. text ed. 4.95x o.p. (ISBN 0-19-501503-7). Oxford U Pr.

Held, Warner & Nauroth, Holger. The Defense of the Reich: Hitler's Nightfighter Planes & Pilots. (Illus.). 232p. 1982. 19.95 (ISBN 0-668-05393-3). Arco.

Heldman, Gladys. The Harmonetics Investigation. 1979. 10.95 o.p. (ISBN 0-517-53926-8). Crown.

Heldman, Gladys, jt. auth. see Segura, Pancho.

Heldmann, Carl. Recycling Living Spaces: Manage Your Own Renovation Project & Save 30 per cent of the Cost (Without Lifting a Finger) LC 82-82301. 192p. (Orig.). 1983. pap. 7.95 (ISBN 0-448-16610-0, G&D). Putnam Pub Group.

Helena, M., tr. see Simma, Maria.

Helf, Sally A. Lhasa Apso Primer. (Illus.). 232p. 1983. write for info. (ISBN 0-931866-12-X). Alpine Pubns.

Helfand, Arthur E. Clinical Podogeriatrics. (Illus.). 245p. 1981. 33.00 (ISBN 0-683-03951-2, 3951-2). Williams & Wilkins.

Helfand, Gary, jt. auth. see Davis, Glenn.

Helfer, Ray E., jt. auth. see Kempe, C. Henry.

Helfer, Ray E. & Kempe, C. Henry, eds. Child Abuse & Neglect: The Family & the Community. LC 76-8891. 1976. pap. 11.50x (ISBN 0-88410-240-8). Ballinger Pub.

Helfgot, Joseph H. Professional Reforming: Mobilization for Youth & the Failure of Social Science. 240p. 1981. 25.95x (ISBN 0-669-04100-9). Lexington Bks.

Helfgott, R. Labor Economics. 1974. text ed. 21.00 (ISBN 0-394-32325-4, RanC). Random.

Helfman, Harry. Making Pictures Without Paint. LC 72-4234. (Illus.). 48p. (gr. 3-7). 1973. 5.75 o.s.i. (ISBN 0-688-20068-0); PLB 7.63 (ISBN 0-688-30068-5). Morrow.

--Making Your Own Sculpture. LC 73-155992. (Illus.). (gr. 3-7). 1971. 7.95 (ISBN 0-688-21878-4); PLB 7.63 (ISBN 0-688-31878-9). Morrow.

Helfrich, jt. auth. see Collier.

Helfrich, G. W. & O'Neil, Gladys, eds. Lost Bar Harbor. LC 82-71103. (Illus.). 136p. 1982. pap. 7.95 (ISBN 0-89272-142-1, PIC493). Down East.

Helfrick, Albert D. Amateur Radio Equipment Fundamentals. (Illus.). 336p. 1982. 20.95 (ISBN 0-13-023655-1). P-H.

Helgerson, Richard. The Elizabethan Prodigals. LC 76-14305. 1977. 20.00x (ISBN 0-520-03264-0). U of Cal Pr.

--Self-Crowned Laureates: Spenser, Jonson, Milton, & the Literary System. LC 82-8496. 330p. 1983. text ed. 22.00x (ISBN 0-520-04808-3). U of Cal Pr.

Helgesen, Sally. Wildcatters. LC 79-7867. 216p. 1981. 11.95 o.p. (ISBN 0-385-14637-X). Doubleday.

Helick, R. Martin. Little Boxes. 1982. spiral 17.50 (ISBN 0-912710-10-1). Regent Graphic Serv.

--Varieties of Human Habitation. LC 73-19343. 1970. spiral 17.50x (ISBN 0-912710-02-0). Regent Graphic Serv.

Heline, Corinne. The Blessed Virgin Mary: Her Life & Mission. pap. 6.95 (ISBN 0-87613-074-0). New Age.

--Color & Music in the New Age. 1964. pap. 3.95 o.p. (ISBN 0-87613-004-X). New Age.

Heline, Theodore. Capital Punishment: Trends Toward Abolition. 1965. pap. 1.00 o.p. (ISBN 0-87613-033-3). New Age.

--Romeo & Juliet: An Esoteric Interpretation. pap. 1.00 o.p. (ISBN 0-87613-042-2). New Age.

Heliodorus Of Emesa. An Ethiopian Romance. Hadas, Moses, tr. LC 76-28171. 1976. Repr. of 1957 ed. lib. bdg. 20.50x (ISBN 0-8371-9085-1, HEER). Greenwood.

Hell, J. The Arab Civilization. 8.25 (ISBN 0-686-18337-1). Kazi Pubns.

Hellborn, Heinrich K. von see Von Hellborn, Heinrich K.

Hellebust, J. A. & Craigie, J. S. Handbook of Phycological Methods. LC 73-79496. (Illus.). 1978. 49.50 (ISBN 0-521-21855-1). Cambridge U Pr.

Helleiner, G. K., ed. A World Divided. LC 75-16606. (Perspectives on Development Ser.: No. 5). 1976. 49.50 (ISBN 0-521-20948-X); pap. 16.95x (ISBN 0-521-29006-6). Cambridge U Pr.

Helleiner, Gerald K. Intra - Firm Trade & the Developing Countries. 1981. 26.00 (ISBN 0-312-42538-4). St Martin.

Helleiner, Gerald K., ed. For Good or Evil: Economic Theory & North-South Negotiations. 200p. 1982. 27.50x (ISBN 0-8020-2465-3); pap. 10.00 (ISBN 0-8020-6482-5). U of Toronto Pr.

Helleman, Robert H., ed. see New York Academy of Sciences, Dec. 17-21, 1979.

Heller, Agnes. The Theory of Need in Marx. LC 76-19162. 1976. 18.95x (ISBN 0-312-79800-8). St Martin.

Heller, Al, jt. auth. see Fontanetta, John.

Heller Associates. The Heller Report: The National Plan for Science Abstracting & Indexing Services. 1963. 15.00 (ISBN 0-942308-01-8). NFAIS.

Heller, B. & Hamata, V. Harmonic Field Effects in Induction Machines. 1977. 68.00 (ISBN 0-444-99856-X). Elsevier.

Heller, Celia, ed. Structured Social Inequality: A Reader in Social Stratification. (Illus.). 1969. text ed. 21.95x (ISBN 0-02-353490-7). Macmillan.

Heller, Celia S. Mexican American Youth: Forgotten Youth at the Crossroads. 1966. pap. text ed. 3.40x (ISBN 0-394-30380-6). Phila Bk Co.

Heller, Elaine. Half & Half Design & Color, Book 1. 22p. (gr. 1-3). 1981. wkbk 3.50. Ann Arbor Pubs.

--Half & Half Design & Color, Bk 2. 43p. (gr. 4-6). 1981. wkbk 3.50 (ISBN 0-686-99800-6). Ann Arbor Pubs.

Heller, Erich. Thomas Mann: The Ironic German. LC 79-63046. 314p. 1979. pap. 6.95 (ISBN 0-89526-906-6). Regnery-Gateway.

Heller, Erich, ed. see Kafka, Franz.

Heller, Erich, tr. see Mann, Thomas.

Heller, Frank A. Competence & Power in Management Decision-Making. Wilpert, Bernhard, ed. LC 80-49978. 242p. 1981. 44.95 (ISBN 0-471-27837-8, Pub. by Wiley-Interscience). Wiley.

Heller, H. Robert. International Monetary Economics. (Illus.). 256p. 1974. ref. ed. 21.00 (ISBN 0-13-473140-9). P-H.

Heller, Jack. Typing for Individual Achievement. Rubin, Audrey, ed. LC 80-26244. (Illus.). 192p. 1981. text ed. 15.96 (ISBN 0-07-027921-7, G); tchrs. sourcebk. 50.00 (ISBN 0-07-027922-5); instructional recordings 350.00 (ISBN 0-07-087945-1). McGraw.

--Typing for the Physically Handicapped: Methods & Keyboard Presentation Charts. (gr. 10-12). 1978. text ed. 140.00 (ISBN 0-07-028079-7, G). McGraw.

Heller, James E. Our Share of Morning. LC 73-5262. 360p. 1974. Repr. of 1961 ed. lib. bdg. 18.50x (ISBN 0-8371-6874-0, BUOS). Greenwood.

Heller, Janet R., ed. see Miller, Leslie A., et al.

Heller, Joseph. British Policy Towards the Ottoman Empire Nineteen Hundred Eight to Nineteen Fourteen. 1983. 30.00x (ISBN 0-7146-3127-2, F Cass Co). Biblio Dist.

--Catch-Twenty-Two. 1966. pap. 3.95 o.p. (ISBN 0-394-60375-3, M375). Modern Lib.

--Good As Gold. 1979. 12.95 o.p. (ISBN 0-671-22923-0). S&S.

Heller, Lois J. & Mohrman, David E. Cardiovascular Physiology. Mixter, Richard W., ed. (Illus.). 176p. 1980. pap. text ed. 12.95 (ISBN 0-07-027973-X). McGraw.

Heller, Marjorie K. Legal P's & Q's in the Doctor's Office. (Orig.). 1981. pap. cancelled o.p. (ISBN 0-686-59766-4). Monarch Pr.

Heller, Mark. Ski. 1970. 9.50 o.p. (ISBN 0-571-09106-7). Transatlantic.

--The World Ski Atlas. LC 78-58333. (Illus.). 256p. 1978. 25.00 o.s.i. (ISBN 0-89479-027-7). A & W Pubs.

Heller, Mark A. A Palestinian State. 192p. 1983. text ed. 16.00x (ISBN 0-674-65221-5). Harvard U Pr.

Heller, Otto, ed. see Nagel, Charles.

Heller, Peter & Ehrlich, Edith. Dichter, Denker und Erzahler. 1982. text ed. 14.95x (ISBN 0-02-353420-6). Macmillan.

Heller, R. International Trade: Theory & Empirical Evidence. 2nd ed. 1973. 21.00 (ISBN 0-13-473918-3). P-H.

Heller, R. K. Deprogramming for Do-it-Yourselfers: A Cure for the Common Cult! 5.95 (ISBN 0-686-36890-8). Gentle Pr.

Heller, Rachelle & Martin, C. D. Bits 'n Bytes About Computing: A Computer Literacy Primer. 1982. text ed. 17.95x (ISBN 0-914894-26-9). Computer Sci.

Heller, Rachelle & Martin, Dianne. Bits 'n Bytes About Computing for Everyone. write for info. (ISBN 0-914894-92-7). Computer Sci.

--Bits 'n Bytes Gazette. write for info. (ISBN 0-914894-88-9). Computer Sci.

Heller, Rebecca, ed. My Little Book of Poems. (First Little Golden Bk.). (Illus.). 24p. (ps). 1983. 0.69 (ISBN 0-307-10142-8, Golden Press); PLB price not set (ISBN 0-307-68142-4). Western Pub.

Heller, Richard M. see Squire, Lucy F., et al.

Heller, Robert. Super Self: The Art & Science of Self-Management: A Practical Guide to Getting the Most Out of Your Life. LC 78-20365. 1979. 9.95 o.p. (ISBN 0-689-10971-7, Atheneum SMI). Atheneum.

Heller, Robert, jt. auth. see Salvadori, Mario G.

Heller, Robert, et al. Earth Science. 2nd ed. (Challenges to Science). (Illus.). 1978. text ed. 18.96 (ISBN 0-07-028037-1, W); tchr's. ed 23.20 (ISBN 0-07-028038-X); activity bk. 6.36 (ISBN 0-07-068311-5); tests 46.64 (ISBN 0-07-051865-3). McGraw.

Heller, Robert, et al, eds. Challenges to Science: Earth Science. (Challenges to Science Ser.). (Illus.). 480p. (gr. 8). 1973. text ed. 19.64 (ISBN 0-07-028045-2, W); tchr's. ed. 24.00 (ISBN 0-07-028046-0); tests 48.20 (ISBN 0-07-028047-9); work-study guide 5.12 (ISBN 0-07-032007-1). McGraw.

Heller, Ruth. Animals Born Alive & Well. LC 82-80872. (Illus.). 48p. (gr. k-2). 1982. 5.95 (ISBN 0-448-01822-5, G&D). Putnam Pub Group.

--Chicken's Aren't the Only Ones. LC 80-85257. (Illus.). 48p. (ps-1). 1981. 5.95 (ISBN 0-448-01872-1, G&D). Putnam Pub Group.

--Creative Coloring-Geometric Designs. (Creative Coloring Pandabacks Ser.). (Illus.). 32p. 1982. pap. 1.50 (ISBN 0-448-49632-1, G&D). Putnam Pub Group.

--Creative Coloring-Seashells. (Creative Coloring Pandabacks Ser.). 32p. 1982. pap. 1.50 (ISBN 0-448-49629-1, G&D). Putnam Pub Group.

--Creative Coloring-Simple Designs. (Creative Coloring Pandabacks Ser.). 32p. 1982. pap. 1.50 (ISBN 0-448-49630-5, G&D). Putnam Pub Group.

--Creative Coloring-Super Designs. (Creative Coloring Pandabacks Ser.). (Illus.). 32p. 1982. pap. 1.50 (ISBN 0-448-49631-3, G&D). Putnam Pub Group.

--Deluxe Designs for Coloring Transfers. Incl. Bk. 1. (Illus.). 48p. pap. 2.95 (ISBN 0-448-14759-9); Bk. 2. (Illus.). 48p. pap. 2.95 (ISBN 0-448-14760-2). 1981 (G&D). Putnam Pub Group.

--The Endangered Species Coloring Book. (Illus.). 48p. (Orig.). (gr. 3-6). 1973. pap. 1.95 o.s.i. (ISBN 0-8431-0219-5). Price Stern.

--Maze Craze. (Illus.). 40p. (gr. 1-12). 1971. pap. 2.95 (ISBN 0-912300-18-3). Troubador Pr.

--Tropical Fish Coloring Book. 1972. pap. 1.95 o.s.i. (ISBN 0-8431-0145-8). Price Stern.

Heller, Samuel. Direct Current Motors & Generators: Repairing, Rewinding & Redesigning. LC 82-72814. (Illus.). 1660p. (Orig.). 1982. Set. pap. 140.00 (ISBN 0-911740-09-0). Datarule.

Heller, Steve, ed. see Feiffer, Jules.

Heller, Steven & Schwartz, Steven. The Book of Waters. 1979. 12.95 o.s.i. (ISBN 0-89104-140-0, A & W Visual Library); pap. 5.95 o.s.i. (ISBN 0-89104-139-7, A & W Visual Library). A & W Pubs.

Heller, Steven, compiled by. The Ultimate Stocking Stuffer. (Illus.). 96p. Date not set. 6.95 (ISBN 0-89479-118-4). A & W Pubs. Postponed.

Heller, Steven, ed. War Heads: Cartoonists Draw the Line. 1983. pap. 4.95 (ISBN 0-14-006620-9). Penguin.

Heller, Steven, et al. The Empire State Building Book. (Illus.). 96p. 1980. 14.95 o.p. (ISBN 0-312-24456-8); pap. 7.95 (ISBN 0-686-96892-1). St Martin.

Heller, Walter W. The Economy: Old Myths & New Realities. 1976. 8.95 o.p. (ISBN 0-393-05595-7); pap. 4.95x o.p. (ISBN 0-393-09151-1). Norton.

--New Dimensions of Political Economy. LC 66-23467. (Godkin Lectures Ser.: 1966). 1966. 12.50x (ISBN 0-674-61100-4). Harvard U Pr.

Heller, Wilfried. Light Scattering Functions of Flow: Oriented Spheroids. 1124p. 1974. 50.00 (ISBN 0-686-92644-7). Wayne St U Pr.

Hellerman, Herbert. Digital Computer System Principles. 2nd ed. (Computer Science Ser). (Illus.). 480p. 1973. text ed. 36.95 (ISBN 0-07-028073-8, C). McGraw.

Hellerman, Herbert & Conroy, F. F. Computer System Performance. 1975. text ed. 33.95 (ISBN 0-07-027953-5, C). McGraw.

Hellerman, Herbert & Smith, I. APL Three-Sixty Programming & Applications. 1977. 21.95 (ISBN 0-07-027950-0, C); solns. manual 2.95 (ISBN 0-07-027951-9). McGraw.

Hellerstein, H. K., jt. auth. see Wenger, Nanette K.

Hellerstein, Kathryn, tr. see Halpern, Moyshe-Leyb.

Hellige. Cerebral Hemisphere Asymmetry. 425p. 1983. 29.95 (ISBN 0-03-058638-0). Praeger.

Hellinger, Ernst & Toeplitz, Otto. Integralgleichungen. LC 54-2866. (Ger). 16.95 (ISBN 0-8284-0089-X). Chelsea Pub.

Hellman, Aviva. Double Standards. 1983. pap. 3.95 (ISBN 0-671-45048-4). PB.

--In Place of Love. LC 77-10098. 1978. 8.95 o.p. (ISBN 0-399-12029-7). Putnam Pub Group.

Hellman, Caroline J. C. & Hellman, Richard. The Competitive Economics of Nuclear & Coal Power. LC 82-47500. 208p. 1982. 23.95x (ISBN 0-669-05533-6). Lexington Bks.

Hellman, Charles S. & Tiritilli, Robert A. Olympix: A Spoof on the Games. (Illus.). 1980. 4.95x (ISBN 0-935938-01-X). Hit Ent.

Hellman, Donald C., jt. auth. see Commission on Critical Choices.

Hellman, Hal. Computer Basics. (Illus.). 48p. (gr. 3-7). 1983. pap. 8.95 (ISBN 0-13-164574-9). P-H.

Hellman, Hugo E & Staudacher, Joseph H. Fundamentals of Speech. 1969. pap. text ed. 4.95x (ISBN 0-685-69591-3). Phila Bk Co.

Hellman, Joan R. Bluebird Rescue. (gr. 3-7). 1982. 9.50 (ISBN 0-688-00894-1); PLB 8.59 (ISBN 0-688-00895-X). Lothrop.

Hellman, John. Simone Weil: An Introduction to Her Thought. 170p. 1982. text ed. 11.00x (ISBN 0-88920-121-8, 40905, Pub. by Laurier U Pr). Humanities.

Hellman, Lillian. Maybe: A Story. 1982. pap. 4.95 (ISBN 0-316-35509-7). Little.

--Pentimento. pap. 4.95 o.p. (ISBN 0-452-25107-9, Z5107, Plume). NAL.

--Pentimento (Julia) movie ed. (Illus.). (RL 10). 1977. pap. 2.95 (ISBN 0-451-11543-0, AE1543, Sig). NAL.

--Scoundrel Time. 1977. lib. bdg. 8.95 o.p. (ISBN 0-8161-6446-0, Large Print Bks). G K Hall.

Hellman, Lillian see Strasberg, Lee.

Hellman, Peter & Meier, Lilly. The Auschwitz Album: A Book Based Upon an Album Discovered by a Concentration Camp Survivor, Lilly Meier. LC 80-53907. 180p. 1982. 23.50 (ISBN 0-394-51932-9). Random.

Hellman, R. G. & Rosenbaum, H. J. Latin America: The Search for a New International Role. LC 75-692. (Latin American International Affairs Ser: Vol. 1). 297p. 1975. 17.50 o.s.i. (ISBN 0-470-36917-5). Halsted Pr.

Hellman, Rainer. Gold Dollars, & the European Currency System: The Seven Year Monetary War. (Praeger Special Studies). 1979. 27.95 o.p. (ISBN 0-03-041611-6). Praeger.

--Transnational Control of Multinational Corporations. LC 77-7342. (Praeger Special Studies). 1977. text ed. 24.95 o.p. (ISBN 0-03-021941-8). Praeger.

Hellman, Renee. Food & Wine in Europe. 128p. 1972. pap. 1.95 o.p. (ISBN 0-452-00376-8, FM376, Mer). NAL.

Hellman, Richard, jt. auth. see Hellman, Caroline J. C.

Hellman, Robert & O'Gorman, Richard, trs. from Fr. Fabliaux: Ribald Tales from the Old French. LC 75-3993. (Illus.). 196p. 1976. Repr. of 1965 ed. lib. bdg. 16.25x (ISBN 0-8371-7414-7, HEFA). Greenwood.

Hellman, Samuel, jt. auth. see DeVita, Vincent T., Jr.

Hellmann, Ellen & Lever, Henry, eds. Race Relations in South Africa, Nineteen Twenty-Nine to Nineteen Seventy-Nine. LC 80-7473. 278p. 1980. 26.00 (ISBN 0-312-66142-8). St Martin.

Hellmich, Nanci, ed. see Kornberg, Patti.

Hellmuth, Jerome, ed. Educational Therapy, Vol. 1. LC 67-8807. (Illus.). 1966. pap. 9.00 o.p. (ISBN 0-87562-001-9). Spec Child.

--Educational Therapy, Vol. 2. LC 67-8807. 1968. text ed. 10.50 o.p. (ISBN 0-87562-011-6); pap. 9.00 o.p. (ISBN 0-87562-020-5). Spec Child.

--Learning Disorders, Vol. 1. LC 68-85. (Illus.). 1965. text ed. 10.50 o.p. (ISBN 0-87562-002-7); pap. 9.00 o.p. (ISBN 0-87562-003-5). Spec Child.

--Learning Disorders, Vol. 2. LC 68-85. (Illus.). 1966. text ed. 16.40 o.p. (ISBN 0-87562-004-3); pap. 8.25 o.p. (ISBN 0-87562-005-1). Spec Child.

--Learning Disorders, Vol. 3. LC 68-85. 1968. text ed. 10.50x o.p. (ISBN 0-87562-006-X); pap. 9.00 o.p. (ISBN 0-87562-021-3). Spec Child.

--Special Child in Century 21. LC 64-55973. 1964. 16.00x o.p. (ISBN 0-87562-008-6). Spec Child.

Hellot, Jean. L'art De la Teinture Des Laines et Des Etoffes De Laine. Repr. of 1750 ed. 175.00 o.p. (ISBN 0-8287-0420-1). Clearwater Pub.

Hellriegel, Don & Slocum, John. Organizational Behavior. 2nd ed. (Management Ser.). (Illus.). 1979. text ed. 24.50 (ISBN 0-8299-0195-7); instrs. manual avail. (ISBN 0-8299-0487-5). West Pub.

--Organizational Behavior. 3rd ed. (Management Ser.). (Illus.). 700p. 1983. 19.95 (ISBN 0-314-69653-9); tchrs.' manual avail. (ISBN 0-314-71096-5); study guide avail. (ISBN 0-314-71097-3). West Pub.

Hellriegel, Don & Slocum, John W., Jr. Management. LC 81-3641. (Business Ser.). (Illus.). 736p. 1982. text ed. 25.95 (ISBN 0-201-04070-0); Instructor's Resource Guide 25.95 (ISBN 0-201-04071-9); write for info. study guide & exercises (ISBN 0-201-04989-9). A-W.

--Management: Contingency Approaches. 2nd ed. LC 77-76177. 1978. text ed. 25.95 (ISBN 0-201-02854-9). A-W.

Hellstedt, Leone M. Women Physicians of the World: Autobiographies of Medical Pioneers. (Illus.). 1978. text ed. 35.00 (ISBN 0-07-027954-3, HP). McGraw.

Hellstrom, Sten-Gunnar, et al. Rendez-Vous en France. 1972. pap. text ed. 5.95 (ISBN 0-912022-28-0); exercise bk 5.25 (ISBN 0-912022-29-9). EMC.

Hellweg, Susan A. & Samovar, Larry A. Organizational Communication. (Comm Comp Ser.). (Illus.). 60p. 1981. pap. text ed. 2.95 (ISBN 0-89787-310-6). Gorsuch Scarisbrick.

Hellwege, A. M., ed. see Hellwege, K. H.

Hellwege, K. H. Elastic, Piezoelectric, Pyroelectric, Piezooptic Electrooptic Constants & Nonlinear Dielectric Susceptibilities of Crystals. Hellwege, A. M., ed. LC 62-53136. (Landolt-Boernstein New Ser. Group III: Vol. 11). (Illus.). 1979. 483.80 o.p. (ISBN 0-387-08506-8). Springer-Verlag.

Hellwege, K. H., ed. Magnetic & Other Properties of Xides & Related Compounds: Hexagonal Ferrites. Special Lanthanide & Actinide Compounds. (Landolt-Boernstein Ser.: Group III, Vol. 12, Pt. C). (Illus.). 650p. 1983. 408.00 (ISBN 0-387-10137-3). Springer-Verlag.

--Metals: Phonon States, Electron States, & Fermi States, Subvolume B: Phonon States of Alloys; Electron States & Fermi Surfaces of Strained Elements. (Landolt-Boernstein--Numerical Data & Functional Relationships in Science & Technology, New Ser.: Group III, Vol. 13). (Illus.). 410p. 1983. 289.00 (ISBN 0-387-10661-8). Springer-Verlag.

--Molecular Constants. (Landolt-Boerstein Ser.: Group II, Vol. 14, Subvol. A). 790p. 1983. 542.00 (ISBN 0-387-11365-7). Springer-Verlag.

--Physical Properties of Rocks. (Landolt-Boernstein Ser.: Group V, Vol. 1, Subvol. b). (Illus.). 610p. 1982. 389.00 (ISBN 0-387-11070-4). Springer-Verlag.

--Semiconductors, Subvolume B: Physics of II-VI & I-VII Compounds, Semimagnetic Conductors. (Landolt-Berstein, Numerical Data & Functional Relationships in Science & Technology, New Series: Group III, Vol. 17, Subvolume b). (Illus.). 540p. 1982. 354.00 (ISBN 0-387-11308-8). Springer-Verlag.

Hellyer & Sinclair. Questions & Answers: Radio & TV. 4th ed. (Illus.). 1976. pap. 4.95 (ISBN 0-408-00249-2). Focal Pr.

Hellyer, Arthur. Dobics Book of Greenhouses. (Illus.). 1981. pap. 12.50 (ISBN 0-434-32626-7, Pub. by Heinemann). David & Charles.

--Garden Shrubs. 256p. 1982. 39.00x (ISBN 0-686-97608-8, Pub. by Dent Australia). State Mutual Bk.

--Your Lawn. (Leisure Plan Books in Color). pap. 2.95 o.p. (ISBN 0-600-44325-6). Transatlantic.

Hellyer, Henry W. Practical Wireless Service Manual. 5.95x o.p. (ISBN 0-600-41228-8). Transatlantic.

Helm, Alice K., et al, eds. The Family Legal Advisor. (Illus.). 480p. 1974. 12.95 o.p. (ISBN 0-517-51547-4). Crown.

Helm, Eugene & Luper, Albert T. Words & Music: Form & Procedure in Theses. Dissertations, Research Papers, Book Reports, Programs, & Theses in Composition. 1971. pap. 7.50 (ISBN 0-913574-00-7). Eur-Am Music.

Helm, Eugene E., jt. ed. see Gallagher, Charles C.

Helm, Harvey E. Making Wood Banks. (Illus.). 128p. (Orig.). 1983. pap. 6.95 (ISBN 0-8069-7714-0). Sterling.

Helm, June. The Indians of the Subarctic: A Critical Bibliography. LC 76-12373. (Newberry Library Center for the History of the American Indian Bibliographical Ser.). 104p. 1976. pap. 6.95x (ISBN 0-253-33004-1). Ind U Pr.

Helm, Mackinley. John Marin. LC 75-87484. (Library of American Art Ser.). (Illus.). 1970. Repr. of 1948 ed. lib. bdg. 32.50 (ISBN 0-306-71489-2). Da Capo.

Helm, Mike. Ghosts, Monsters, & Wild Men: Legends of the Oregon Country. (Illus.). 1983. write for info. (ISBN 0-931742-03-X). Rainy Day Oreg.

--Oregon Country Indian Legends. LC 81-51426. (Oregon Country Library: Vol. 5). 300p. (Orig.). 1983. pap. 8.95 (ISBN 0-931742-07-2). Rainy Day Oreg.

Helm, Mike, ed. & intro. by see Lockley, Fred.

Helm, Robert M., jt. auth. see Angell, J. William.

Helm, Sanford M. Catalog of Chamber Music for Wind Instruments. rev. ed. LC 70-86597. (Music Reprint Ser). 1969. Repr. of 1952 ed. lib. bdg. 16.50 (ISBN 0-306-71490-6). Da Capo.

Helman, Edith F., tr. see Salinas, Pedro.

Helmberg, Gilbert M. Introduction to Spectral Theory in Hilbert Space. (Applied Mathematics & Mechanics Ser: Vol. 6). 1969. 64.00 (ISBN 0-444-10211-6, North-Holland). Elsevier.

Helmbold, F. Wilbur. Tracing Your Ancestry: A Step-by-Step Guide to Researching Your Family History. LC 76-14109. (Illus.). 1976. 9.95 o.p. (ISBN 0-8487-0415-0); logbook o.p. 3.95 o.p. (ISBN 0-8487-0414-2). Oxmoor Hse.

Helmcke, J. G. & Krieger, W. Diatomeenschalen Im Elektronenmikroskopischen Bild. Incl. Part 6. 1966 (ISBN 3-7682-0174-0); Part 7. Marine Diatoms. Okumo, H., ed. 1969 (ISBN 3-7682-0175-9). (Illus.). 60.00 ea. Lubrecht & Cramer.

Helmcke, J. G., ed. see Krammer, Kurt.

Helmer, Karl. Weltordnung und Bildung. 254p. (Ger.). 1982. write for info. (ISBN 3-8204-5839-5). P Lang Pubs.

Helmers, Dow. Historic Alpine Tunnel. (Illus.). 208p. 1978. 15.00 (ISBN 0-937080-02-0); pap. 12.50 (ISBN 0-937080-03-9). Century One.

Helmes, Winifred G. Notable Maryland Women. 418p. 1977. pap. 8.00 (ISBN 0-686-36709-X). Md Hist.

Helmholz, R. H., ed. see Ault, Warren O.

Helmholz, R. H., ed. see Burge, William.

Helmholz, R. H., ed. see Goffin, R. J.

Helmholz, R. H., ed. see Hughes, David.

Helmholz, R. H., ed. see Plucknett, Theodore F.

Helmholz, R. H., ed. see Street, Thomas A.

Helmkamp, John G. & Imdieke, Leroy F. Principles of Accounting. LC 82-20124. 1150p. 1983. text ed. 26.95 instrs. manual (ISBN 0-471-08510-3). Wiley.

Helmken, Charles M. Creative Newsletter Graphics. 3rd ed. 280p. 1981. 40.00 (ISBN 0-89964-195-4). CASE.

Helmlinger, Trudy. After You've Said Goodbye: How to Recover After Ending a Relationship. 1977. 8.95 o.p. (ISBN 0-8467-0214-2, Pub. by Two Continents). Hippocrene Bks.

--After You've Said Goodbye: Learning How to Stand Alone. Weine, Ruth, ed. LC 82-9472. 288p. 1982. 14.95 (ISBN 0-932370-35-7); pap. 7.95 (ISBN 0-932370-36-5). Brooks Pub Co.

Helmrath, M. O. & Bartlett, J. L. Bobby Bear & the Bees. LC 68-56806. (Bobby Bear Ser.). (Illus.). (ps-1). 1970. PLB 7.99x prebound (ISBN 0-87783-003-7); pap. 2.75x deluxe ed. o.p. (ISBN 0-87783-080-0); cassette 5.95x (ISBN 0-87783-177-7). Oddo.

--Bobby Bear Finds Maple Sugar. LC 68-56805. (Bobby Bear Ser.). (Illus.). (ps-1). 1970. PLB 7.99x prebound (ISBN 0-87783-005-3); pap. 2.75x deluxe ed. o.p. (ISBN 0-87783-081-9); cassette 5.95x (ISBN 0-87783-178-5). Oddo.

--Bobby Bear Goes Fishing. LC 68-56807. (Bobby Bear Ser.). (Illus.). (ps-1). 1970. PLB 7.99x prebound (ISBN 0-87783-006-1); pap. 2.75x deluxe ed. o.p. (ISBN 0-87783-082-7); cassette 5.95x (ISBN 0-87783-179-3). Oddo.

--Bobby Bear in the Spring. LC 68-56810. (Bobby Bear Ser.). (Illus.). (ps-1). 1970. PLB 7.99x prebound (ISBN 0-87783-007-X); pap. 2.75x deluxe ed. o.p. (ISBN 0-87783-083-5); cassette 5.95x (ISBN 0-87783-180-7). Oddo.

--Bobby Bear Series, 13 bks. (Illus., Five titles by marilue, two titles by Kay D. Oana). (ps-1). Set. PLB 93.95x set (ISBN 0-87783-163-7). (10) cassettes 59.50x (ISBN 0-87783-181-5). Oddo.

--Bobby Bear's Halloween. LC 68-56808. (Bobby Bear Ser.). (Illus.). (ps-1). 1970. PLB 6.75x (ISBN 0-87783-004-5); pap. 2.75x deluxe ed. o.p. (ISBN 0-87783-084-3); cassette 5.95x (ISBN 0-87783-183-1). Oddo.

--Bobby Bear's Rocket Ride. LC 68-56809. (Bobby Bear Ser.). (Illus.). (ps-1). 1970. PLB 7.99x prebound (ISBN 0-87783-008-8); pap. 2.75x deluxe ed. o.p. (ISBN 0-87783-087-8); cassettes 5.95x (ISBN 0-87783-186-6). Oddo.

Helmreich, Robert, jt. auth. see Aronson, Elliot.

Helmreich, William B. The Things They Say Behind Your Back. LC 81-43854. 288p. 1982. 14.95 (ISBN 0-385-15606-5). Doubleday.

Helmreich, William B., compiled by. Afro-Americans & Africa: Black Nationalism at the Crossroads. LC 76-56621. (Special Bibliographic Series, New Series: No. 3). 1977. lib. bdg. 22.50 (ISBN 0-8371-9439-3, HAA/). Greenwood.

Helms, Clyde A. Don't Touch Lessons. 1983. write for info. (ISBN 0-87527-273-8). Green.

Helms, Cynthia. Favourite Sories from Persia. (Favourite Stories Ser.). (Illus.). ix, 61p. (Orig.). 1982. pap. text ed. 2.00x (ISBN 9971-64-041-4). Heinemann Ed.

Helms, H., jt. ed. see Gjerlov, P.

Helms, H. L. The McGraw-Hill Computer Handbook. 1200p. 1983. 79.50 (ISBN 0-07-027972-1, P&RB). McGraw.

Helms, Hal M., ed. see Bunyan, John.

Helms, Hal M., ed. see Fenelon, Archbishop.

Helms, Harry. The BASIC Book: A Cross-Reference Guide to the BASIC Language. (Illus.). 96p. 1983. pap. 6.95 (ISBN 0-07-027959-4, P&RB). McGraw.

Helms, Harry L., ed. see Mims, Forrest.

Helms, Howard D., et al, eds. Literature in Digital Signal Processing: Authors & Permitted Title Index. rev & expanded ed. LC 75-61351. 1975. 11.45 (ISBN 0-87942-052-9). Inst Electrical.

Helms, Janet E. A Practitioner's Guide to the Edwards Personal Preference Schedule. (Illus.). 240p. 1983. 22.50x (ISBN 0-398-04740-5). C C Thomas.

Helms, John, jt. auth. see Daniel, Theodore W.

Helms, L. C., ed. A Modern Mason Examines His Craft: Fact Versus Fiction. (Illus.). 86p. 1981. pap. 5.00 (ISBN 0-88053-065-0). Macoy Pub.

Helms, Lloyd A. The Contributions of Lord Overstone to the Theory of Currency & Banking. 142p. Repr. of 1939 ed. lib. bdg. 17.50x (ISBN 0-87991-088-7). Porcupine Pr.

Helms, Mary W. Ancient Panama: Chiefs in Search of Power. (Texas Pan American Ser.). (Illus.). 244p. 1979. text ed. 20.00x o.p. (ISBN 0-292-73817-X). U of Tex Pr.

--Middle America: A Culture History of Heartland & Frontiers. LC 81-40008. (Illus.). 384p. 1982. lib. bdg. 25.50 (ISBN 0-8191-2229-7); pap. text ed. 14.00 (ISBN 0-8191-2230-0). U Pr of Amer.

Helms, Tom. Against All Odds. LC 78-3302. 1978. 12.45i (ISBN 0-690-01763-4). T Y Crowell.

Helmsen, R. J., ed. Immunology of the Eye II: Autoimmune Phenomena & Ocular Disorders. 322p. 1981. pap. 25.00 (ISBN 0-917000-07-2). IRL Pr.

Helmstrom, C. W. Statistical Theory of Signal Detection. 2nd ed. 1968. 28.00 o.p. (ISBN 0-08-013265-0). Pergamon.

Heloise. Help! From Heloise. 1982. pap. 3.50 (ISBN 0-380-61226-7, 61226). Avon.

Helpern, Milton & Knight, Bernard. Autopsy: The Memoirs of a Medical Detective. LC 77-66639. 1977. 10.00 o.p. (ISBN 0-312-06211-7). St Martin.

--Autopsy: The Memoirs of Milton Helpern-the World's Greatest Medical Detective. 1979. pap. 2.95 (ISBN 0-451-11026-9, AE1026, Sig). NAL.

Helpman, Elhanan, ed. Social Policy Evaluation: An Economic Perspective. LC 82-22681. (Symposium). Date not set. price not set (ISBN 0-12-339660-3). Acad Pr.

Helprin, Mark. Refiner's Fire. 1981. pap. 6.95 o.s.i. (ISBN 0-440-57486-2, Delta). Dell.

--Refiner's Fire. 1977. 12.50 o.s.i. (ISBN 0-394-41273-7). Knopf.

Helps, Arthur. Life & Labours of Mister Brassey, 1805-1870. LC 69-17620. (Illus.). Repr. of 1872 ed. 27.50x (ISBN 0-678-07500-X). Kelley.

Helsdon, Harry. Mechanical Engineering Science. 1968. text ed. 6.50x (ISBN 0-442-03313-3). Van Nos Reinhold.

Helsel, J., jt. auth. see Jensen, C.

Helsel, James L. Modern Real Estate Practice in Pennsylvania. 3rd ed. Bellairs, Herbert J. & Caldwell, Thomas D., eds. 496p. 1982. pap. 27.95 (ISBN 0-88462-298-3); pap. text ed. 20.95 (ISBN 0-686-96934-0). Real Estate Ed Co.

Helsel, Jay. Reading Engineering Drawings Through Conceptual Sketching. (Illus.). 1979. pap. text ed. 15.95 (ISBN 0-07-028031-2, G); tchr's. manual 6.30 (ISBN 0-07-028032-0). McGraw.

Helsel, Jay & Urbanick, Byron. Mechanical Drawing. 9th ed. Lindquist, Hal, ed. (Illus.). 1980. text ed. 23.28 (ISBN 0-07-022313-0). McGraw.

Helsel, Jay, jt. auth. see Jensen, Cecil.

Helsinger, Elizabeth & Sheets, Robin. The Woman Question: Society & Literature in Britain & America, 1837-1883, 3 Vols. Incl. Vol. 1. Defining Voices (ISBN 0-8240-9301-1); Vol. 2. Social Issues (ISBN 0-8240-9232-5); Vol. 3. Literary Issues (ISBN 0-8240-9233-3). LC 80-9040. 1982. lib. bdg. 30.00 each (ISBN 0-686-82015-0). Garland Pub.

Helstrom, Jo & Metz, Mary. Le Francais a Decouvrir: Learning French the Modern Way, Level 1. 3rd ed. (Illus.). 432p. (gr. 9). 1972. text ed. 16.80 o.p. (ISBN 0-07-027960-8); tchr's. ed. 20.24 o.p. (ISBN 0-07-027961-6); wkbk. 4.80 o.p. (ISBN 0-07-027962-4); filmstrips, tapes, tests & dupl. masters avail. o.p. McGraw.

Helstrom, Jo & Metz, Mary S. Le Francais a Decouvrir. 4th ed. LC 77-12172. (Illus.). 1978. text ed. 17.24 (ISBN 0-07-027966-7, W); tchr's. ed. 18.64 (ISBN 0-07-027967-5); wkbk. 5.00 (ISBN 0-07-027968-3); tests 103.48 (ISBN 0-07-027969-1); filmstrips 152.32 (ISBN 0-07-097690-2); tapes, cassettes & dupl. masters avail. McGraw.

Helstrom, Jo, jt. auth. see Metz, Mary.

Helstrom, Jo, jt. auth. see Metz, Mary S.

Helszajn, J. Nonreciprocal Microwave Junctions & Circulators. LC 75-5588. 368p. 1975. 34.95 o.p. (ISBN 0-471-36935-7, Pub. by Wiley-Interscience). Wiley.

--Nonreciprocal Microwave Junctions & Circulators. LC 75-5588. 370p. Repr. of 1975 ed. text ed. 34.95 (ISBN 0-471-36935-7). Krieger.

--Passive & Active Microwave Circuits. LC 78-5787. 1978. 42.50x (ISBN 0-471-04292-7, Pub. by Wiley-Interscience). Wiley.

Helterman, Jeffrey, ed. American Novelists Since World War Two. LC 77-82804. (Dictionary of Literary Biography: Vol. 2). (Illus.). 1978. 74.00x (ISBN 0-8103-0914-9, Bruccoli Clark Book). Gale.

Helton, Floyd F. & Lial, Margaret L. Precalculus Mathematics: A Functions Approach. 1983. text ed. 23.95x (ISBN 0-673-15507-2). Scott F.

Helton, George, et al. Psychoeducational Assessment: Contexts, Concepts & Measures. Date not set. price not set (ISBN 0-8089-1482-0). Grune.

Helvetius, Claude-Adrien. Les Progres de la Raison, dans la Recherche du Vrai. (Holbach & His Friends Ser). 203p. (Fr.). 1974. Repr. of 1775 ed. lib. bdg. 58.00x o.p. (ISBN 0-8287-0421-X, 1534). Clearwater Pub.

--Le Vrai sens du Systeme de la Nature. (Holbach & His Friends Ser). 86p. (Fr.). 1974. Repr. of 1774 ed. lib. bdg. 32.50x o.p. (ISBN 0-8287-0422-8, 1523). Clearwater Pub.

Helvie. Community Health Nursing, Theory & Process. pap. text ed. 18.50 (ISBN 0-686-97979-6, Lippincott Nursing). Lippincott.

Helweg, Marianne, tr. see Lilius, Irmelin S.

Helwig, David. It Is Always Summer: A Novel. LC 82-4256. 208p. 1982. 12.95 (ISBN 0-8253-0097-5). Beaufort Bks NY.

Helwig, Elson B. & Mostofi, F. K., eds. The Skin. LC 79-28744. (I.A.P. Ser.). 640p. 1980. Repr. lib. bdg. 34.50 (ISBN 0-89874-123-8). Krieger.

Hemans, Felicia D. The Domestic Affections, & Other Poems. 1812. Reiman, Donald H., ed. LC 75-31214. (Romantic Context Ser.: Poetry 1789-1830). 1978. lib. bdg. 47.00 o.s.i. (ISBN 0-8240-2164-9). Garland Pub.

--The Siege of Valencia...the Last Constantine & Other Poems. 1823. Reiman, Donald H., ed. LC 75-31216. (Romantic Context Ser.: Poetry 1789-1830). 1978. lib. bdg. 47.00 o.s.i. (ISBN 0-8240-2165-7). Garland Pub.

--Tales & Historic Scenes, in Verse. 1819. Reiman, Donald H., ed. LC 75-31215. (Romantic Context Ser.: Poetry 1789-1830). 1978. lib. bdg. 47.00 o.s.i. (ISBN 0-8240-2165-7). Garland Pub.

--The Vespers of Palermo, 1823; The Forest Sanctuary; & Other Poems, 1825. Reiman, Donald H., ed. LC 75-31217. (Romantic Context Ser.: Poetry 1789-1930). 1978. lib. bdg. 47.00 o.s.i. (ISBN 0-8240-2167-3). Garland Pub.

Hembree, Ron. Good Morning, Lord: Devotions for Everday Living. (Good Morning Lord Ser.). 1971. 3.95 o.p. (ISBN 0-8010-4020-5). Baker Bk.

--Good Morning, Lord: Devotions for New Christians. (Good Morning, Lord Ser.). 96p. 1983. 4.95 (ISBN 0-8010-4271-2). Baker Bk.

Hemdal, John. Cogeneration: A Practical Guide to Energy Efficiency. (Illus.). 200p. 1983. 22.50x (ISBN 0-937948-03-9). Aatec Pubns.

Hemdal, John F. The Energy Center: New Alternative for Effective Energy Use. LC 78-65334. 1979. 37.50 o.p. (ISBN 0-250-40283-1). Ann Arbor Science.

Hemelt, M. & MacKert, M. Dynamics of Law in Nursing & Health Care. 2nd ed. 1978. 18.95 (ISBN 0-8359-1499-2). Reston.

Hemenway, David. Industrywide Voluntary Product Standards. LC 74-28269. 160p. 1975. prof ref 17.50x (ISBN 0-88410-275-0). Ballinger Pub.

--Prices & Choices: Microeconomic Vignettes. LC 77-2733. 1977. 15.00 o.p. (ISBN 0-88410-663-2); pap. 10.95x prof ref (ISBN 0-88410-660-8). Ballinger Pub.

Hemenway, Jack E. RA Sixty Eight Hundred ML: An M6800 Relocatable Macro Assembler. LC 78-22084. (Illus.). 1979. pap. 25.00 o.p. (ISBN 0-07-582022-6, BYTE Bks). McGraw.

Hemenway, Jack E., jt. auth. see Grappel, Robert D.

Hemenway, Robert, intro. by see Harris, Joel C.

Hemery, Eric. Historic Dart. (Illus.). 304p. 1982. 32.50 (ISBN 0-7153-8142-3). David & Charles.

--Walking the Dartmoor Railroads. (Illus.). 152p. (Orig.). 1983. 14.95 (ISBN 0-7153-8348-5). David & Charles.

Hemigway, Ernest. For Whom the Bell Tolls. 482p. 1983. pap. 14.95 (ISBN 0-686-83800-9, ScribT). Scribner.

Hemingway, Amanda. Pzyche. 250p. 1983. 13.95 (ISBN 0-87795-479-8). Arbor Hse.

Hemingway, Ernest. Complete Poems. Gerogiannis, Nicholas, ed. LC 82-16082. (Illus.). xxvii, 162p. 1983. pap. 5.95 (ISBN 0-8032-7217-0, BB 830, Bison). U of Nebr Pr.

--A Farewell to Arms. 336p. 1983. 13.95 (ISBN 0-686-83803-3, ScribT). Scribner.

--For Whom the Bell Tolls. 480p. 1982. pap. 4.95 (ISBN 0-684-17660-2, ScribT). Scribner.

--The Old Man & the Sea. 128p. 1983. pap. 10.95 (ISBN 0-686-83799-1, ScribT). Scribner.

--The Sun Also Rises. 256p. 1983. pap. 12.95 (ISBN 0-686-83801-7, ScribT). Scribner.

Hemingway, P. D. The Well-Dressed Woman. 1979. pap. 3.50 (ISBN 0-451-11959-2, AE1959, Sig). NAL.

Hemingway, Richard W. Handbook of the Law of Oil & Gas. (Hornbook Ser.). 507p. 1983. text ed. price not set (ISBN 0-314-71558-4). West Pub.

Hemingway, Thomas K. Electronic Designer's Handbook. 3rd ed. (Illus.). 1979. 14.95 o.p. (ISBN 0-8306-9808-6); pap. 9.95 o.p. (ISBN 0-8306-1038-3, 1038). TAB Bks.

Hemker, A. H., ed. see FEBS Meeting, Eighth.

Hemley, Cecil. Dimensions of Midnight: Poetry & Prose. Gottlieb, Elaine, ed. LC 66-25957. xv, 233p. 1966. 12.00 (ISBN 0-8214-0023-1, 82-80257). Ohio U Pr.

Hemlow, Joyce, et al. Catalogue of the Burney Family Correspondence 1749-1878. LC 67-31117. 1971. 25.00 o.p. (ISBN 0-87104-037-9). NY Pub Lib.

Hemmant, Lynette, jt. auth. see Austen, Jane.

Hemmant, Lynette, jt. auth. see Fitzgerald, Edward.

Hemmer, William J. Arithmetic by Example. (Basic Math Ser.). 1979. text ed. 18.95x (ISBN 0-669-01068-5); instr's resource manual 1.95 (ISBN 0-669-01069-3); student solutions manual 9.95x (ISBN 0-669-01070-7); cassettes 150.00 (ISBN 0-669-01704-3); avail. transcript (ISBN 0-669-01702-7); demonstration tape avail. (ISBN 0-669-01703-5). Heath.

Hemmerling, E. M., jt. auth. see Harris, N.

Hemmerling, E. M., jt. auth. see Harris, Norman C.

Hemmerling, Edwin M. Elementary Mathematics for the Technician. 1974. text ed. 23.50 (ISBN 0-07-028074-6, G); answers to even-numbered problems 3.00 (ISBN 0-07-028075-4). McGraw.

--Fundamentals of College Geometry. 2nd ed. (Illus.). 1970. text ed. 26.50x (ISBN 0-471-37034-7). Wiley.

Hemmerling, Edwin M., jt. auth. see Harris, Norman.

Hemmerling, Joachim, jt. auth. see Kabisch, Klaus.

Hemmi, Kenzo, jt. ed. see Castle, Emery N.

Hemming, jt. auth. see Modigliani.

Hemming, C. F. & Symmons, P. M. The Germination & Growth of Schouwia Purpurea (Forskal) Schweinf & Its Role as a Habitat of the Desert Locust. 1969. 35.00x (ISBN 0-85135-054-2, Pub. by Centre Overseas Research). State Mutual Bk.

Hemming, C. F. & Taylor, T. H., eds. Proceedings of the International Study Conference on the Current & Future Problems of Acridology, London, 1970. 1972. 50.00x (ISBN 0-686-82422-9, Pub. by Centre Overseas Research). State Mutual BK.

Hemming, John. Monuments of the Incas. 224p. 1982. 45.00 (ISBN 0-8212-1521-3). NYGS.

Hemminger, Wolfgang. Thermal Analysis. Vol. 2: Organic Chemistry, Melallurgy, Earth Sciences, Organic Chemistry, Polymers, Biological Sciences, Medicine, Pharmacy. 606p. 1980. 95.00 (ISBN 3-7643-1086-3). Birkhauser.

Hemmings, F. W. Baudelaire the Damned. (Illus.). 256p. 1982. text ed. 17.95 (ISBN 0-684-17774-9, ScribT). Scribner.

Hemmings, Gwynneth. Biological Aspects of Schizophrenia & Addiction. 296p. 1982. 43.95 (ISBN 0-471-10117-6, Pub. by Wiley-Interscience). Wiley.

--Biological Basis of Schizophrenia. 288p. 1979. text ed. 39.50 o.p. (ISBN 0-8391-1329-3). Univ Park.

Hemmings, Gwynneth, ed. Biochemistry of Schizophrenia & Addiction. 360p. 1980. text ed. 39.50 (ISBN 0-8391-4135-1). Univ Park.

Hemmings, Muriel. Through a Needle's Eye. (Arch Bk.: No. 16). (Illus.). 1979. 0.89 (ISBN 0-570-06125-3, 59-1243). Concordia.

Hemmings, Ray. Children's Freedom: A. S. Neill & the Evolution of the Summerhill Idea. LC 72-94295. (Illus.). 240p. 1972. pap. 3.45 o.p. (ISBN 0-8052-0455-5). Schocken.

Hemmings, W. A., ed. Materno Foetal Transmission of Immunoglobulins. LC 75-2721. (Clinical & Experimental Immunoreproduction: No. 2). (Illus.). 400p. 1975. 67.50 (ISBN 0-521-20747-9). Cambridge U Pr.

Hemmingsen, Ib, jt. auth. see Klausen, Klaus.

Hemminki, Kari & Sorsa, Marja, eds. Occupational Hazards & Reproduction. (Illus.). 495p. Date not set. text ed. 49.50 (ISBN 0-89116-281-X). Hemisphere Pub.

Hemp, William H. New York Enclaves. (Illus.). 64p. 1975. 6.95 o.p. (ISBN 0-517-51999-2, C N Potter Bks). Crown.

Hempel, Carl. Philosophy of Natural Science. (Orig.). 1966. pap. 8.95x ref. ed. (ISBN 0-13-663823-6). P-H.

Hempel, Goerge, jt. auth. see Crosse, Howard.

Hempen, Carl L. The Greatest of These Is Love. 1978. 7.50 o.p. (ISBN 0-533-03576-7). Vantage.

Hempfling, W. P., ed. Microbial Respiration. LC 78-22097. (Benchmark Papers in Microbiology: Vol. 13). 337p. 1979. 43.00 (ISBN 0-87933-344-8). Hutchinson Ross.

Hemphill, C., Jr. Modern Security Methods. 1979. 20.95 (ISBN 0-13-597625-1). P-H.

Hemphill, Charles. Business Communications with Writing Improvement Exercises. 256p. 1981. pap. text ed. 16.95 (ISBN 0-13-093880-7). P-H.

Hemphill, Charles F. Criminal Procedure: The Administration of Justice. LC 77-21985. (Illus.). 1978. text ed. 21.95x o.p. (ISBN 0-673-16301-6). Scott F.

Hemphill, Charles F., jt. auth. see Hemphill, Phyllis D.

Hemphill, Charles F., Jr. Famous Phrases from History. 225p. 1982. pap. 16.95x (ISBN 0-89950-052-8). McFarland & Co.

Hemphill, Charles F., Jr., jt. auth. see Gammage, Allen Z.

Hemphill, Gary B. Blasting Operations. (Illus.). 1980. 27.50 (ISBN 0-07-028093-2). McGraw.

Hemphill, J., jt. auth. see Kuriloff, A.

Hemphill, John, Jr., jt. auth. see Kuriloff, Arthur.

Hemphill, John M., jt. auth. see Kuriloff, Arthur H.

Hemphill, Phyllis D. & Hemphill, Charles F. A Practical Guide to Real Estate Law. (Illus.). 272p. 1980. text ed. 14.95 o.p. (ISBN 0-13-691022-X, Spec); pap. text ed. 7.95 o.p. (ISBN 0-13-691014-9). P-H.

Hempleman, H. V. & Lockwood, A. P. Physiology of Diving in Man & Other Animals. (Studies in Biology: No. 99). 64p. 1978. pap. text ed. 8.95 (ISBN 0-686-43110-3). E Arnold.

Hemplemann. The Physiology of Diving in Man & Other Animals. (Studies in Biology: No. 99). 1978. 5.95 o.p. (ISBN 0-7131-2692-2). Univ Park.

Hempstead, Walter E., Jr. Y.O.L. (Your Own Law) A Complete Guide for the Layman. 240p. Date not set. 9.95 (ISBN 0-686-37904-7). Hempstead House.

Hems, D. A. Biologically Active Substances: Exploration & Exploitation. 309p. 1978. 59.00x (ISBN 0-471-99489-8, Pub. by Wiley-Interscience). Wiley.

Hems, Jack. Goldfishes. (South Group Colorguide Ser.). 1982. pap. 2.25 (ISBN 0-940842-07-6). South Group.

Hems, Jack, jt. auth. see Hervey, George F.

Hemsley, J. Soviet Troop Control: The Role of Command Technology in the Soviet Military System. (Illus.). 300p. 1982. 52.50 (ISBN 0-08-027008-5, T120); firm 25.00 (ISBN 0-686-97499-9). Pergamon.

Hemsoth, et al. Becoming a Parent. Zak, Therese A., ed. LC 79-18187. (Lifeworks Ser.). 1980. pap. text ed. 5.28 (ISBN 0-07-060911-X). McGraw.

Henaghan, Jim. Azor! 1978. pap. 1.75 o.p. (ISBN 0-451-07967-1, E7967, Sig). NAL.

Henahan, John F. The Ascent of Man: Sources & Interpretations. (Orig.). 1975. pap. text ed. 10.95 (ISBN 0-316-35620-4); Student's Guide 9.95 (ISBN 0-316-56940-2); Student's Guide 9.95 (ISBN 0-316-88730-7). Little.

Henault, Marie. Stanley Kunitz. (United States Authors Ser.). 1980. lib. bdg. 11.95 (ISBN 0-8057-7224-3, Twayne). G K Hall.

Henbest, H. B., jt. auth. see Grundon, M. A.

Henbest, Nigel, jt. auth. see Jay, Michael.

Henbest, Nigel, jt. auth. see Couper, Heather.

Hench, L. L. & Ethridge, E. C. Biomaterials: An Interfacial Approach. (Biophysics & Bioengineering Ser.). 335p. 1982. 42.00 (ISBN 0-12-340280-8). Acad Pr.

Hench, Larry L., jt. ed. see Onoda, George Y., Jr.

Henchy, Thomas, jt. ed. see Bickman, Leonard.

Henck, Karl N. How to Start Your Own Microcomputer Based Mail Order Business. LC 81-65513. (Illus., Orig.). 1982. pap. 15.00 (ISBN 0-939258-00-5). Bork Res.

Hencken, Hugh. The Earliest European Helmets: Bronze Age or Early Iron Age. LC 78-152525. (American School of Prehistoric Researh Bulletins: No. 28). 1971. pap. text ed. 18.50x (ISBN 0-87365-530-3). Peabody Harvard.

Hendee, W. R. Radioactive Isotopes in Biological Research. LC 73-8966. 48.50 (ISBN 0-471-37043-6, Pub. by Wiley-Interscience). Wiley.

Hendel, Samuel & Bishop, Hillman. Basic Issues of American Democracy. 8th ed. 1975. pap. 13.95 (ISBN 0-13-062521-3). P-H.

Hendel, Samuel, ed. The Soviet Crucible. 5th ed. LC 80-14249. 483p. 1980. write for info. (ISBN 0-87872-256-4). Duxbury Pr.

Hendersen, Robert, ed. Learning in Animals. LC 81-2247. (Benchmark Papers in Behavior Ser.: Vol. 14). 1982. 46.00 (ISBN 0-87933-348-0). Hutchinson Ross.

Hendershot, Carl H. Programmed Learning & Individually Paced Instruction Bibliography: Inc. Suppl. 1-6, 2 Vols. 5th ed. 1983. Set. 130.00 (ISBN 0-911832-16-5). Hendershot.

Hendershot, Gerry E. Predicting Fertility. Placek, Paul J., ed. LC 79-9686. 352p. 1981. 25.95x (ISBN 0-669-03618-8). Lexington Bks.

Hendershot, Kathy. Obedience: The Road to Reality. 176p. (Orig.). 1982. pap. 3.00 (ISBN 0-911567-00-3). Christian Mini.

Henderson & Bracker. Performance Workbook to Compensation Management. 2nd ed. 224p. (Orig.). pap. 9.95 (ISBN 0-8359-0909-3). Reston.

Henderson & Kelly. Questions & Answers on General Surgery. 278p. 1979. pap. 13.95 (ISBN 0-7236-0523-8). Wright-PSG.

Henderson, et al. Real Estate Examination Guide. (Business Ser.). 1977. pap. text ed. 18.95 (ISBN 0-675-08506-3). Merrill.

Henderson, A. Corbin. Brothers of Light: The Penitentes of the Southwest. LC 77-88835. 1977. Repr. of 1937 ed. lib. bdg. 15.00x (ISBN 0-88307-534-2). Gannon.

Henderson, Alexander, tr. see Bauer, Arnold.

Henderson, Algo D. & Henderson, Jean G. Higher Education in America: Problems, Priorities & Prospects. LC 73-21071. (Higher Education Ser.). 1974. 17.95x (ISBN 0-87589-227-2). Jossey-Bass.

Henderson, Andrew. Scottish Proverbs. LC 70-75962. 1969. Repr. of 1881 ed. 34.00x (ISBN 0-8103-3894-7). Gale.

Henderson, Anthony, ed. see Congreve, William.

Henderson, Archibald. George Bernard Shaw, 2 vols. LC 79-87485. (Illus.). 1078p. 1972. Repr. of 1956 ed. Set. lib. bdg. 65.00 (ISBN 0-306-71491-4). Da Capo.

Henderson, B. & Wertz, J. E. Defects in the Alkaline Earth Oxides: With Applications to Radiation Damage & Catalysis. LC 77-23366. 159p. 1977. 34.95 o.s.i. (ISBN 0-470-99205-0). Halsted Pr.

Henderson, Bill. His Son: A Child of the Fifties. 1982. pap. 6.50 (ISBN 0-688-00983-2). Morrow.

Henderson, Bill, ed. Pushcart Prize, VII: The Best of the Samll Presses. 576p. 1983. pap. 8.95 (ISBN 0-380-62851-1). Avon.

--Pushcart Prize VIII: Best of the Small Presses, 1983-84 Edition. 500p. 1983. 24.00 (ISBN 0-916366-18-9). Pushcart Pr.

Henderson, Bruce. Oakland Organic. (Illus.). 216p. (Orig.). 1982. pap. 8.95 (ISBN 0-9608064-0-7). Caboose Pr.

Henderson, Bruce D. Henderson on Corporate Strategy. 1982. pap. 3.50 (ISBN 0-451-62127-1, ME2127, Ment). NAL.

Henderson, C. Awakening: Ways to Psycho-Spiritual Growth. 1975. 10.95 o.p. (ISBN 0-13-055467-7, Spec); pap. 3.95 o.p. (ISBN 0-13-055459-6, Spec). P-H.

Henderson, D. see Eyring, H., et al.

Henderson, Daniel M. Hidden Coasts: A Biography of Admiral Charles Wilkes. LC 78-138589. (Illus.). 1971. Repr. of 1953 ed. lib. bdg. 16.00x o.p. (ISBN 0-8371-5789-7, HEHI). Greenwood.

Henderson, David & Gillespie, R. D. Textbook of Psychiatry for Students & Practitioners. 10th ed. Batchelor, Ivor R., ed. 1969. 18.95x o.p. (ISBN 0-19-264412-2); pap. 21.95x (ISBN 0-19-264413-0). Oxford U Pr.

Henderson, Davis & Steffel, Victor L. McCracken's Removable Partial Prosthodontics. 6th ed. LC 80-28701. (Illus.). 477p. 1981. text ed. 37.95 (ISBN 0-8016-2146-1). Mosby.

Henderson, Dion. Algonquin. (gr. 3 up). 1979. pap. 1.50 (ISBN 0-307-21618-7, Golden Pr). Western Pub.

Henderson, Donald, et al, eds. Effects of Noise on Hearing. LC 75-14576. 580p. 1976. 48.00 (ISBN 0-89004-012-5). Raven.

Henderson, Donald C., jt. auth. see Garner, Richard L.

Henderson, Douglas, jt. ed. see Eyring, Henry.

Henderson, Edward S., jt. ed. see Gunz, F. W.

Henderson, Elizabeth, tr. see Bauer, Arnold.

Henderson, Elizabeth, tr. see Ropke, Wilhelm T.

Henderson, Ernest F., ed. Select Historical Documents of the Middle Ages. LC 65-15247. 1892. 10.00x (ISBN 0-8196-0149-7). Biblo.

Henderson, Euan S., jt. auth. see Ashton, Patricia M.

Henderson, Eva P. Wild Horses, Turn of the Century Prairie Girlhood. Hausman, Gerald, ed. LC 82-10631. (Illus.). 96p. (Orig.). 1983. pap. 8.95 (ISBN 0-86534-013-7). Sunstone Pr.

Henderson, Faye & Rosenau, Fred S., eds. Information Sources, 1983-1984. 1982. 37.50 (ISBN 0-686-34582-7). Info Indus.

Henderson, Francis M. Open Channel Flow. 1966. 29.95x (ISBN 0-02-353510-5). Macmillan.

Henderson, G. E. Planning for an Individual Water System. 8.65 o.p. (ISBN 0-914452-45-2). Green Hill.

Henderson, G. L. & Voiles, P. R. Business English Essentials. 6th ed. 1980. 10.85 (ISBN 0-07-027984-5); tchr's ed. avail. McGraw.

Henderson, G. M., et al, eds. The International Encyclopedia of Cats. Coffey, D. J. LC 72-10958. (Illus.). 256p. 1973. 24.95 (ISBN 0-07-028163-7, GB). McGraw.

Henderson, G. P. E. P. Papanoutsos. (World Authors Ser.). 184p. 1983. lib. bdg. 24.95 (ISBN 0-8057-6526-3, Twayne). G K Hall.

Henderson, G. P., ed. European Companies: A Guide to Sources of Information. 3rd ed. LC 73-151246. (Illus.). 250p. 1972. 42.00x (ISBN 0-685-28245-7, Pub. by CBD Research Ltd.). Gale.

Henderson, George. The Farming Ladder. LC 79-670246. 192p. 1979. pap. 6.95 (ISBN 0-571-11059-2). Faber & Faber.

--The Human Rights of Professional Helpers. 214p. 1983. text ed. price not set (ISBN 0-398-04820-7). C C Thomas.

Henderson, Gordon. American Democracy: People, Politics, & Policies. (Orig.). 1979. pap. text ed. 13.95 (ISBN 0-316-35607-7); tchr's ed. avail. (ISBN 0-316-35608-5); study guide 7.95 (ISBN 0-316-35609-3). Little.

Henderson, Hamish M. Oil & Gas: The North Sea Exploitation. LC 79-13457. 1980. looseleaf 45.00; Set. 100.00 (ISBN 0-379-10250-1). Oceana.

Henderson, Harold. Queen of Spades. LC 82-83127. 208p. 1983. 12.95 (ISBN 0-932966-27-6). Permanent Pr.

--Seizing the Day: How to Take the Day Off & Change Your Life. 172p. 1983. pap. 7.95 (ISBN 0-87243-120-7). Templegate.

Henderson, Harold G. Introduction to Haiku. LC 58-11314. (Illus.). 1958. pap. 2.50 o.p. (ISBN 0-385-09376-4, A150, Anch). Doubleday.

Henderson, Harold G., tr. An Introduction to Haiku: An Anthology of Poems & Poets from Basho to Shiki. (Anchor Literary Library). 1983. pap. 4.95 (ISBN 0-686-42703-3, Anch). Doubleday.

Henderson, Herbert D. Cotton Control Board. (Economic & Social History of the World War Ser.). 1922. text ed. 39.50x (ISBN 0-686-83513-1). Elliots Bks.

Henderson, Hubert. Supply & Demand. (Cambridge Economic Handbook Ser). 1958. pap. 9.95x (ISBN 0-521-08760-0). Cambridge U Pr.

Henderson, Ian. Pictorial Souvenirs of Britain. 1979. 15.00x o.p. (ISBN 0-7153-6660-2, Pub. by Milestone Pub Ltd.). State Mutual Bk.

Henderson, Ingeborg. Strickers Daniel Von Dem Bluehenden Tal: Werkstruktur und Interpretation. (German Language & Literature Monographs). viii, 206p. 1979. 21.00 (ISBN 90-272-0961-8, 1). Benjamins North Am.

Henderson, J. Foreign Investment Laws & Agriculture. (FAO Legislative Ser.: No. 9), (Orig.). 1970. pap. 14.25 o.p. (ISBN 0-685-02924-7, F194, FAO). Unipub.

Henderson, J., ed. Aristophanes: Essays in Interpretation. LC 80-40042. (Yale Classical Studies: No. 26). 248p. 1981. 37.50 (ISBN 0-521-23120-5). Cambridge U Pr.

Henderson, J. L. Education for World Understanding. 1969. 13.25 o.s.i. (ISBN 0-08-013217-0); pap. 5.75 (ISBN 0-08-013216-2). Pergamon.

Henderson, J. Vernon, ed. Research in Urban Economics, Vol. 1. 300p. 1981. 42.50 (ISBN 0-89232-070-2). Jai Pr.

--Research in Urban Economics, Vol.2. 400p. 1981. 47.50 (ISBN 0-89232-212-8). Jai Pr.

Henderson, J. Youngblood, jt. auth. see Barsh, Russel L.

Henderson, Jacqueline. The Woman's Day Book of Designer Crochet. LC 80-693. (Illus.). 192p. 1980. 17.95 o.p. (ISBN 0-672-52580-1). Bobbs.

Henderson, James & Quandt, Richard E. Microeconomic Theory. 3rd ed. (Illus.). 1980. 26.95 (ISBN 0-07-028101-7); solns. manual 16.95 (ISBN 0-07-028102-5). McGraw.

Henderson, Jay, jt. ed. see Montaperto, Ronald N.

Henderson, Jean G., jt. auth. see Henderson, Algo D.

Henderson, Jeff, jt. auth. see Forrest, Ray.

Henderson, Joe. Running A to Z. 1983. pap. 8.95 (ISBN 0-8289-0504-5). Greene.

Henderson, John. Emergency Medical Guide. 4th ed. (McGraw Hill Paperbacks). 1978. 23.95 (ISBN 0-07-028168-8, SP); pap. 5.95 (ISBN 0-07-028169-6). McGraw.

Henderson, Katherine U. Joan Didion. LC 80-53705. (Literature & Life Ser.). 1981. 11.95 (ISBN 0-8044-2370-9); pap. 5.95 (ISBN 0-8044-6265-8). Ungar.

Henderson, Kathryn L., jt. ed. see Henderson, William T.

Henderson, Laurance G., jt. ed. see Rains, Albert.

Henderson, Laurence. Major Enquiry. LC 76-1481. 1976. 7.95 o.p. (ISBN 0-312-50470-5). St Martin.

Henderson, Linda D. The Fourth Dimension & Non-Euclidean Geometry in Modern Art. LC 82-15076. (Illus.). 496p. 1983. 55.00x (ISBN 0-686-43212-6); pap. 16.50 (ISBN 0-691-10142-6). Princeton U Pr.

Henderson, Lois. A Candle in the Dark. (Orig.). (gr. 5-9). 1983. pap. 2.95 (ISBN 0-89191-504-4, 55046). Cook.

Henderson, Lois T. Abigail. LC 80-65429. 256p. 1980. 8.95 (ISBN 0-915684-62-4, HarpR). Har-Row.

--Another Way of Seeing. rev. ed. LC 81-68642. 256p. 1982. pap. 6.95 (ISBN 0-915684-99-3, HarpR). Har-Row.

--Ruth: A Novel. LC 81-65722. 256p. 1981. 8.95 (ISBN 0-915684-91-8, HarpR). Har-Row.

Henderson, M. R. Common Malayan Wildflowers. (Malayan Nature Handbooks). (Illus.). 1961. 7.50x o.p. (ISBN 0-582-69448-5). Intl Pubns Serv.

Henderson, Madeline B., ed. Interactive Bibliographic Systems: Proceedings. LC 73-600098. (AEC Symposium Ser.). 211p. 1973. pap. 13.25 (ISBN 0-87079-003-X, CONF-711010); microfiche 4.50 (ISBN 0-87079-248-2, CONF-711010). DOE.

Henderson, Mae G., jt. auth. see Blassingame, John W.

Henderson, Martha & Paladin Press, eds. Great Survival Resource Book. (Illus.). 188p. 1981. 19.95 (ISBN 0-87364-199-X). Paladin Pr.

Henderson, Maureen M., jt. auth. see White, Kerr L.

Henderson, Nancy. Celebrate America: A Baker's Dozen of Plays. LC 78-15169. (Illus.). 128p. (gr. 4 up). 1978. PLB 7.79 o.p. (ISBN 0-671-32907-3). Messner.

--Walk Together: Five Plays on Human Rights. LC 72-1423. (Illus.). 128p. (gr. 4 up). 1972. PLB 6.64 o.p. (ISBN 0-671-32538-8). Messner.

Henderson, Nicholas. The Birth of NATO. 135p. 1983. lib. bdg. 17.50 (ISBN 0-86531-466-7). Westview.

Henderson, P. And Morning in His Eyes. LC 75-39861. (English Literature Ser., No. 33). 1972. Repr. of 1937 ed. lib. bdg. 42.95x (ISBN 0-8383-1406-6). Haskell.

Henderson, Paul. Inorganic Chemistry. (Illus.). 372p. 1982. 42.00 (ISBN 0-08-020448-1); pap. 18.50 (ISBN 0-08-020447-3). Pergamon.

Henderson, Peter. Disability in Childhood & Youth. 1974. pap. text ed. 6.95x o.p. (ISBN 0-19-264168-9). Oxford U Pr.

--Functional Programming. (Ser. in Computer Science). (Illus.). 1980. text ed. 36.95 (ISBN 0-13-331579-7). P-H.

Henderson, Philip. Christopher Marlowe. Dobree, Bonamy, et al, eds. Bd. with Ben Jonson. Bamborough, J. B; John Webster. Scott-Kilvert, Ian; John Ford. Leech, Clifford. LC 63-63096. (British Writers & Their Work Ser: Vol. 11). vi, 182p. 1966. pap. 3.25x (ISBN 0-8032-5661-2, BB 460, Bison). U of Nebr Pr.

--Richard Coeur De Lion: A Biography. (Illus.). 256p. (LC 76-00004). 1976. Repr. of 1959 ed. lib. bdg. 18.00x (ISBN 0-8371-8724-9, HERI). Greenwood.

Henderson, R. G. Case Studies in Systems Design. 208p. 1980. 25.00x (ISBN 0-7121-0387-2, Pub. by Macdonald & Evans). State Mutual Bk.

Henderson, Richard. Compensation Management. 3rd ed. 1982. text ed. 25.95 (ISBN 0-8359-0913-1); instrs'. manual avail. (ISBN 0-8359-0914-X); 10.95 (ISBN 0-8359-0915-8). Reston.

--Compensation Management: Rewarding Performance in the Modern Organization. 2nd ed. 1979. 21.95 o.p. (ISBN 0-8359-0907-7); wkbk 8.95 o.p. (ISBN 0-8359-0908-5). Reston.

--Hand, Reef & Steer: A Practical Handbook on Sailing. LC 77-91229. 1978. pap. 7.95 (ISBN 0-8092-7527-9). Contemp Bks.

--A Practical Guide to Performance Appraisal. 2nd ed. 1983. text ed. 15.00 (ISBN 0-8359-5576-1). Reston.

--Singlehanded Sailing: The Experiences & Techniques of the Lone Voyagers. LC 75-37369. (Illus.). 320p. 1976. 22.50 (ISBN 0-87742-062-9). Intl Marine.

Henderson, Richard, jt. auth. see Carrick, Robert.

Henderson, Richard I. Performance Appraisal: Theory to Practice. (Illus.). 1980. text ed. 18.95 (ISBN 0-8359-5498-6). Reston.

Henderson, Richard I., jt. auth. see Suojanen, Waino.

Henderson, Robbin, jt. auth. see Faulkner, Janette.

Henderson, Robert T. Joy to the World: An Introduction to Kingdom Evangelism. LC 80-14597. 207p. (Orig.). 1980. pap. 3.49 (ISBN 0-8042-2096-4). John Knox.

Henderson, Robert T., jt. auth. see Paulston, Christina B.

Henderson, Robert W. Ball, Bat & Bishop: The Origin of Ball Games. LC 73-10389. (Illus.). 221p. 1974. Repr. of 1947 ed. 24.00 o.p. (ISBN 0-8103-3877-7). Gale.

Henderson, Ronald W. & Bergan, John R. The Cultural Context of Childhood. new ed. 1976. text ed. 20.95 (ISBN 0-675-08599-3). Additional supplements may be obtained from publisher. Merrill.

Henderson, S. D., tr. see Carqou, J. M.

Henderson, S. T. Daylight & Its Spectrum. 2nd ed. LC 77-88254. 349p. 1978. 49.95 o.s.i. (ISBN 0-470-99328-6). Halsted Pr.

Henderson, Sara C., jt. auth. see Trager, Edith C.

Henderson, Stephen E., jt. auth. see Cook, Mercer.
Henderson, T. F., ed. see Scott, Walter.
Henderson, Thomas. The Osborne Portable Computer. Cardona, Elizabeth & Noble, David, eds. LC 82-42766. 1983. pap. 12.95 (ISBN 0-88022-015-5). Que Corp.
Henderson, Thomas A. & Foster, John L. Urban Policy Game: A Simulation of Urban Politics. LC 78-17118. 1978. pap. text ed. 14.95 (ISBN 0-471-03398-7); Avail Tchr's Manual (ISBN 0-471-04219-6). Wiley.
Henderson, Thomas E., jt. auth. see Moore, Ballard J.
Henderson, Thomas F. Scottish Vernacular Literature: A Succinct History. 3rd. ed. LC 70-75473. 1969. Repr. of 1910 ed. 40.00x (ISBN 0-8103-3884-X). Gale.
Henderson, Virginia & Nite, Gladys. The Principles & Practice of Nursing. 6th ed. (Illus.). 1978. text ed. 9.95 (ISBN 0-02-353580-6). Macmillan.
Henderson, W. J. The Art of Singing. LC 78-4953. (Music Reprint 1978 Ser.). 1978. Repr. of 1938 ed. lib. bdg. 39.50 (ISBN 0-306-77593-X). Da Capo.
Henderson, W. O. The Life of Friedrich List. 200p. 1983. text ed. 30.00x (ISBN 0-7146-3161-2, F Cass Co). Biblio Dist.
--The Rise of German Industrial Power, 1834-1914. LC 75-17293. 1976. 32.00x (ISBN 0-520-03073-7); pap. 7.95x (ISBN 0-520-03120-2). U of Cal Pr.
Henderson, W. O., ed. The Natural System of Political Economy of Friedrich List. 200p. 1983. text ed. 30.00x (ISBN 0-7146-3206-6, F Cass Co). Biblio Dist.
Henderson, William C. & Cameron, Helen. The Public Economy: An Introduction to Government Finance. 1969. text ed. 9.95 (ISBN 0-685-41968-1). Phila Bk Co.
Henderson, William D. Gilded Age City: Politics, Life, & Labor in Petersburg, Virginia, 1874-1889. LC 80-1385. (Illus.). 603p. 1980. lib. bdg. 28.25 (ISBN 0-8191-1294-1); pap. text ed. 18.00 o.p. (ISBN 0-8191-1295-X). U Pr of Amer.
--Why the Vietcong Fought: A Study of Motivation & Control in a Modern Army in Combat. LC 79-7062. (Contributions in Political Science: No. 31). 1979. lib. bdg. 25.00 (ISBN 0-313-20708-9, HVC/). Greenwood.
Henderson, William T. & Henderson, Kathryn L., eds. Conserving & Preserving Library Materials. (Allerton Park Institutes Ser.: No. 27). 1983. write for info. (ISBN 0-87845-067-X). U of Ill Lib Info Sci.
Henderson, Yandell. Incomes & Living Costs of a University Faculty. 1928. 29.50x (ISBN 0-685-89757-5). Elliots Bks.
Henderson, Zenna. Holding Wonder. 304p. 1972. pap. 1.75 o.p. (ISBN 0-380-01251-0, 44081). Avon.
--Pilgrimage: The Book of the People. (Science Fiction Ser.). 12.50 o.p. (ISBN 0-8398-2498-X, Gregg). G K Hall.
Hendessen, J. Frank, jt. auth. see Bridger, William A.
Hendey, N. I. Introductory Account of the Smaller Algae of British Coastal Waters: Bacillariophyceae, Pt. V. (Illus.). 317p. 1976. Repr. of 1964 ed. lib. bdg. 72.00x (ISBN 3-87429-103-0). Lubrecht & Cramer.
Hendin, David & Marks, Joan. Genetic Connection. 1979. pap. 1.95 o.p. (ISBN 0-451-08558-2, J8558, Sig). NAL.
Hendin, Josephine. Vulnerable People: A View of American Fiction Since 1945. 1979. pap. 6.95 (ISBN 0-19-502620-9, GB 583, GB). Oxford U Pr.
--The World of Flannery O'Connor. LC 76-108208. (Midland Bks.: No. 150). 192p. 1970. pap. 2.50x o.p. (ISBN 0-253-20150-0). Ind U Pr.
Hendler, Muncie. Infinite Design Coloring Book. (Illus.). pap. 2.25 (ISBN 0-486-23285-9). Dover.
--Ready-to-Use Art Nouveau Dollhouse Wallpaper. (Illus.). 48p. (Orig.). 1983. pap. 3.95 (ISBN 0-486-24446-6). Dover.
--Ready-to-Use Dollhouse Floor Coverings: Eight Full-Color Patterns to Decorate 8 Rooms. (Illus.). 1978. pap. 3.50 (ISBN 0-486-23666-8). Dover.
--Ready-to-Use Early American Dollhouse Wallpaper. (Illus.). 48p. (Orig.). 1980. pap. 3.95 (ISBN 0-486-23937-3). Dover.
Hendler, Nelson, ed. Diagnosis & Nonsurgical Management of Chronic Pain. LC 78-51277. 262p. 1981. 31.50 (ISBN 0-89004-289-6). Raven.
Hendler, Nelson H., ed. Diagnosis & Treatment of Chronic Pain. Wise, Thomas N. LC 82-4733. (Illus.). 272p. 1982. 22.50 (ISBN 0-7236-7011-0). Wright-PSG.
Hendon, Rufus S. Six Indonesian Short Stories. LC 68-56638. (Translation Ser.: No. 7). viii, 123p. 1968. 5.50x (ISBN 0-686-30906-5). Yale U SE Asia.
Hendon, William S. Evaluating Urban Parks & Recreation. 288p. 1981. 29.95 (ISBN 0-03-059422-7). Praeger.
Hendra, Judith, ed. The Illustrated Treasury of Humor for Children. (Illus.). 256p. 1980. 10.95 (ISBN 0-448-16429-9, G&D); PLB 15.20 (ISBN 0-686-64626-6). Putnam Pub Group.
Hendra, Tony & Kelly, Sean. Not the Bible. 96p. (Orig.). 1983. pap. 4.95 (ISBN 0-345-30249-4). Ballantine.
Hendrick, Burton J. Age of Big Business. 1919. text ed. 8.50x (ISBN 0-686-37860-1). Elliots Bks.
--The Training of an American: The Early Life & Letters of Walter H. Page, 1855-1913. LC 28-11821. 1970. 16.95 (ISBN 0-910220-12-3). Berg.
Hendrick, Clyde & Hendrick, Susan. Liking, Loving & Relating. LC 82-14561. (Psychology Ser.). 300p. 1982. pap. text ed. 10.95 (ISBN 0-534-01263-9). Brooks-Cole.
Hendrick, Eddie. I Write for You. 48p. 1983. 5.95 (ISBN 0-686-82586-1). Todd & Honeywell.
Hendrick, George. Katherine Anne Porter. (United States Authors Ser.). 1965. lib. bdg. 10.95 (ISBN 0-8057-0592-9, Twayne). G K Hall.
--Mazo de la Roche. (World Authors Ser.). lib. bdg. 13.95 (ISBN 0-8057-2766-3, Twayne). G K Hall.
Hendrick, George, jt. auth. see Gerstenberger, Donna.
Hendrick, George, ed. & see Jones, Samuel A.
Hendrick, Irving G. California Education: A Brief History. Hundley, Norris, Jr. & Schutz, John A., eds. LC 80-80027. (Golden State Ser.). (Illus.). 80p. 1980. pap. text ed. 5.95x (ISBN 0-87835-097-7). Boyd & Fraser.
Hendrick, Joanne. Total Learning for the Whole Child: Holistic Curiculum for Children Ages Two to Five. LC 79-20624. 406p. 1980. 19.95 (ISBN 0-8016-2150-X). Mosby.
--The Whole Child: New Trends in Early Education. 2nd ed. LC 79-9135. 1980. 20.95 (ISBN 0-8016-2145-3). Mosby.
Hendrick, John R. Opening the Door of Faith: The Why, When & Where of Evangelism. LC 76-12404. 1977. pap. 4.75 o.p. (ISBN 0-8042-0675-9). John Knox.
Hendrick, Susan, jt. auth. see Hendrick, Clyde.
Hendricks, C. & Leavenworth, C. Living: The Adult Centering Book. 1978. 8.95 o.p. (ISBN 0-13-538512-1); pap. 3.95 o.p. (ISBN 0-13-538504-0). P-H.
Hendricks, C. Davis, jt. auth. see Hendricks, Jon.
Hendricks, C. G. & Wills, Russell. The Centering Book: Awareness Activities for Children, Parents & Teachers. (Transpersonal Bks.). (Illus.). 192p. 1975. 12.95 (ISBN 0-13-122192-2, Spec); pap. 5.95 (ISBN 0-13-122184-1, Spec). P-H.
Hendricks, Evan. Former Secrets: Government Records Made Public Through the Freedom of Information Act. Shaker, Peggy, ed. 204p. 1982. pap. 15.00 (ISBN 0-910175-01-2). Campaign Political.
Hendricks, G. & Roberts, T. The Second Centering Book: More Awareness Activites for Children, Parents, & Teachers. 1977. 11.95 o.p. (ISBN 0-13-797332-2, Spec); pap. 5.95 (ISBN 0-13-797324-1, Spec). P-H.
Hendricks, Gary, jt. auth. see Storey, James R.
Hendricks, Gary, et al. Consumer Durables & Installment Debt: A Study of American Households. LC 72-619719. 231p. 1973. pap. 6.00x (ISBN 0-87944-117-8). Inst Soc Res.
Hendricks, Gay. The Centered Teacher: Awareness Activities for Teachers & Their Students. (Transformation Ser.). 192p. 1981. 11.95 (ISBN 0-13-122234-1, Spec); pap. 5.95 (ISBN 0-13-122226-0). P-H.
Hendricks, Gay & Carlson, Jon. The Centered Athlete: A Conditioning Program for Your Mind. 160p. 1981. 11.95 (ISBN 0-13-122218-X); pap. 5.95 (ISBN 0-13-122200-7). P-H.
Hendricks, Geoffrey. A Sheep's Skeleton & Rocks. (Illus.). 1977. pap. 3.50 (ISBN 0-914162-21-7, Dist. by Writers & Books). Printed Edns.
Hendricks, Glenn. The Dominican Diaspora: From the Dominican Republic to New York City, Villagers in Transition. LC 74-4203. 1974. text ed. 13.95x (ISBN 0-8077-2426-2); pap. text ed. 9.95x (ISBN 0-8077-2459-9). Tchrs Coll.
Hendricks, Howard. Las Familias Conviven Mejor con Amor. 48p. Date not set. 1.35 (ISBN 0-88113-095-8). Edit Betania.
Hendricks, Howard G. Heaven Help the Home! LC 73-78689. 1974. pap. 4.50 (ISBN 0-88207-240-4). Victor Bks.
--Say It with Love. 143p. 1972. pap. 4.50 (ISBN 0-88207-050-9). Victor Bks.
Hendricks, Jon & Hendricks, C. Davis. Aging in Mass Society: Myths & Realities. 2nd. ed. 1981. text ed. 17.95 (ISBN 0-316-35623-9); tchr's ed. free (ISBN 0-316-35624-7). Little.
--Dimensions of Aging: Readings. (Orig.). 1979. pap. text ed. 12.95 (ISBN 0-316-35627-1). Little.
Hendricks, Jon, ed. Perspectives on Aging & Human Development Series, 3 vols. Incl. Vol. 1. Being & Becoming Old. 160p (ISBN 0-89503-014-4); Vol. 2. In the Country of the Old. 160p (ISBN 0-89503-015-2); Vol. 3. Institutionalization & Alternative Futures. 160p (ISBN 0-89503-016-0). 1979. Set. pap. 17.95 (ISBN 0-89503-024-1). Baywood Pub.
Hendricks, Marjorie E., jt. auth. see Enk, Mary J.
Hendricks, N. S., ed. Michigan Manufacturers Directory. 1983. 118.36 (ISBN 0-936526-01-7). Pick Pub MI.
Hendricks, N. S. & Pickell, M. R., eds. Michigan Purchasing Directory. 1983. pap. 15.00 (ISBN 0-936526-02-5). Pick Pub MI.
Hendricks, W. Grammars of Style & Styles of Grammar. (Studies in Theoretical Poetics: Vol. 3). 1976. pap. 42.75 (ISBN 0-444-11095-X, North-Holland). Elsevier.
Hendricks, William. Bible Alphabet Word Puzzles. 1980. pap. 2.50 (ISBN 0-310-37202-X). Zondervan.
--Bible Jumble Word Puzzles. 1978. pap. 2.50 o.p. (ISBN 0-310-37192-9). Zondervan.
Hendrickson, Gordon, jt. auth. see Willems, Arnold.
Hendrickson, Marilyn & Hendrickson, Robert. Two Thousand & One Free Things for the Garden. 256p. 1983. 16.95 (ISBN 0-312-82746-6); pap. 7.95 (ISBN 0-312-82747-4). St Martin.
Hendrickson, Michael R. & Kempson, Richard L. Surgical Pathology of the Uterine Corpus. LC 79-3920. (Major Problems in Pathology Ser.: Vol. XII). (Illus.). 589p. 1980. text ed. 55.00 o.p. (ISBN 0-7216-4644-1). Saunders.
Hendrickson, Paul. The Seminary: A Search. 320p. 1983. 14.95 (ISBN 0-671-42030-5). Summit Bks.
Hendrickson, Robert. Animal Crackers. 1983. pap. 6.95 (ISBN 0-14-006487-7). Penguin.
--Literary Life & Other Curiosities. 1982. pap. 9.95 (ISBN 0-14-006318-8). Penguin.
--More Cunning Than Man: A Social History Of Rats & Men. LC 82-48512. 288p. 1983. 17.95 (ISBN 0-8128-2894-1). Stein & Day.
Hendrickson, Robert, jt. auth. see Hendrickson, Marilyn.
Hendrickson, Walter B., Jr. Manned Spacecraft to Mars & Venus: How They Work. LC 74-16627. (How It Works Ser.). (Illus.). (gr. 5-8). 1975. PLB 4.79 o.p. (ISBN 0-399-60928-8). Putnam Pub Group.
--Who Really Invented the Rocket? new ed. LC 73-189238. (Who Really Invented Ser.). (Illus.). 96p. (gr. 5-9). 1974. PLB 4.29 o.p. (ISBN 0-399-60852-4). Putnam Pub Group.
--Winging into Space. LC 65-21404. (Illus.). (gr. 4-8). 1965. 3.95 o.p. (ISBN 0-672-50588-6). Bobbs.
Hendrickson, William see Summerlin, Lee R.
Hendriksen, William. Galatians & Ephesians. (New Testament Commentary). 290p. 1979. 18.95 (ISBN 0-8010-4211-9). Baker Bk.
--Mark. (New Testament Commentary Ser). 708p. 1975. 21.95 (ISBN 0-8010-4114-7). Baker Bk.
--More Than Conquerors. Commerative ed. 9.95 (ISBN 0-8010-4026-4). Baker Bk.
Hendrix, John D. To Thessalonians with Love. LC 81-70974. (Orig.). 1983. pap. 6.50 (ISBN 0-8054-1312-X). Broadman.
Hendrix, T. G. & LaFevor, C. S. Mathematics for Auto Mechanics. LC 77-72431. 1978. pap. text ed. 13.00 (ISBN 0-8273-1630-5); instr.'s guide 4.75 (ISBN 0-8273-1631-3). Delmar.
Hendrix, Wayne R., jt. auth. see Heiner, Carol W.
Hendrix, William & William, Meiden. Beginning French: A Cultural Approach. 5th ed. LC 77-93107. (Illus.). 1978. pap. text ed. 20.50 (ISBN 0-395-25739-5); wkbk. 8.50 (ISBN 0-395-25740-9); tapes 280.00 (ISBN 0-395-25741-7). HM.
Hendry, Allan A. The UFO Handbook-A Guide to Investigating, Evaluating & Reporting UFO Sightings. (Illus.). 1979. pap. 8.95 o.p. (ISBN 0-385-14348-6, Dolp). Doubleday.
Hendry, Fay L. Outdoor Sculpture in Lansing. LC 80-7502. (Illus.). 153p. (Orig.). pap. 3.50 (ISBN 0-936412-02-X). Iota Pr.
Hendry, George S. The Westminister Confession for Today. LC 60-6283. 1980. pap. 3.13 (ISBN 0-8042-0756-9). John Knox.
Hendry, J. F. The Sacred Threshold: The Life of Rainer Maria Rilke - Citizen of Europe. 280p. 1982. text ed. 21.00x (ISBN 0-85635-369-8, 30143, Pub. by Carcanet New Pr England). Humanities.
Hendry, L., ed. Growing Up & Going Out. 176p. 1983. 18.00 (ISBN 0-08-025768-2); pap. 9.50 (ISBN 0-08-025769-0). Pergamon.
Hendry, Norman J., jt. auth. see Johns, Trevor W.
Henefin, Mary S., jt. auth. see Hubbard, Ruth.
Heneghan, Donald A. A Concordance to the Poems & Fragments of Wilfred Owen. 1979. lib. bdg. 32.50 (ISBN 0-8161-8371-6, Hall Reference). G K Hall.
Heneghan, James B., ed. Germfree Research: Biological Effects of Gnotobiotic Environments. 1973. 58.50 o.s.i. (ISBN 0-12-340650-1). Acad Pr.
Heneman, Harlow J. The Growth of Executive Power in Germany. LC 74-11935. 256p. 1975. Repr. of 1934 ed. lib. bdg. 17.50x (ISBN 0-8371-7721-9, HEEP). Greenwood.
Heneman, Herbert G., jt. ed. see Yoder, Dale.
Heneman, Herbert G., III, et al. Managing Personnel & Human Resources: Strategies & Programs. LC 80-69960. 420p. 1981. 21.95 (ISBN 0-87094-234-4). Dow Jones-Irwin.
Heneman, Herbert G., Jr., jt. auth. see Yoder, Dale.
Heneman, Herbert G., Jr., jt. ed. see Yoder, Dale.
Heneman, Herbert G., Jr., jt. ed. see Yoder, Dale, Jr.
Henessy, Josselyn, jt. auth. see Paish, F. W.
Henfrey, J., tr. see Leal, V. N.
Heng, Liang & Shapiro, Judith. Son of the Revolution. LC 82-18704. 364p. 1983. 15.00 (ISBN 0-394-52568-X). Knopf.
Heng Chau, jt. auth. see Sure, Heng.
Heng Ch'ih, Bhikshuni, tr. see Master Hua, Ch'an.
Heng Ch'ih, Bhikshuni, et al, trs. see Master Hua, Ch'an.
Hengel, Jean V. Everything You Need to Teach a Child to Read. (Illus.). 79p. (Orig.). 1982. pap. 22.50 (ISBN 0-686-36169-5). Van Dean.
Hengel, Martin. Christ & Power. Kalin, Everett R., tr. from Ger. LC 76-62608. 96p. (Orig.). 1977. pap. 1.50 o.p. (ISBN 0-8006-1256-6, 1-1256). Fortress.
--Crucifixion: In the Ancient World & the Folly of the Message of the Cross. Bowden, John, tr. from Ger. LC 77-78629. 118p. 1977. pap. 4.95 (ISBN 0-8006-1268-X, 1-1268). Fortress.
--Judaism & Hellenism: Studies in Their Encounter in Palestine During the Early Hellenistic Period. Bowden, John, tr. from Ger. 672p. 1981. Set. 19.95 o.p. (ISBN 0-8006-1495-X, 1-1495). Fortress.
Hengeveld, H. Role of Water in Urban Ecology. (Developments in Landscape Management & Urban Planning Ser.: Vol. 5). 1982. 78.75 (ISBN 0-444-42078-9). Elsevier.
Henggeler, Scott W., ed. Delinquency & Adolescent Psychopathology. LC 81-22027. 272p. 1982. text ed. 25.00 (ISBN 0-7236-7041-2). Wright-PSG.
Heng Hsien, Bhikshuni, et al, trs. see Master Ch'ing Liang.
Hengst, Herbert R., jt. auth. see Monahan, William G.
Hengstenberg, E. W. Commentary on the Gospel of John, 2 vols. 1980. Set. 34.95 (ISBN 0-86524-047-7, 4302). Klock & Klock.
Heng Tao, Bhikshuni, et al, trs. see Master Hua, Ch'an.
Heng Yin, Bhikshuni, tr. see Ch'an Master Hua.
Heng Yin, Bhikshuni, tr. see Master Hua, Ch'an.
Henifin, Mary S., jt. auth. see Hubbard, Ruth.
Henig, Gerald S. Henry Winter Davis. 1973. lib. bdg. 9.95 (ISBN 0-8057-5383-4, Twayne). G K Hall.
Henig, Martin. Handbook of Roman Art. (Illus.). 320p. 1982. 39.50 (ISBN 0-8014-1539-X); pap. 19.95 (ISBN 0-8014-9242-4). Cornell U Pr.
Henige, David. Oral Historiography. LC 82-168. 208p. 1982. text ed. 28.00x (ISBN 0-582-64364-3); pap. text ed. 9.95x (ISBN 0-582-64363-5). Longman.
Henige, David P., ed. Colonial Governors from the Fifteenth Century to the Present. LC 73-81320. 482p. 1970. 50.00x (ISBN 0-299-05440-3). U of Wis Pr.
Henin, Claude G. & Ryan, Peter J. Options: Theory & Practice. LC 77-2687. 208p. 1977. 23.95x (ISBN 0-669-01623-3). Lexington Bks.
Heninger, S. K. Hand Book of Renaissance Meteorology. LC 69-10106. 1969. Repr. of 1960 ed. lib. bdg. 15.75x (ISBN 0-8371-0472-6, HERM). Greenwood.
Heninger, S. K., Jr., ed. English Prose, Prose Fiction, & Criticism to 1660: A Guide to Information Sources. LC 73-16980. (American Literature, English Literature, & World Literatures in English Information Guide Ser.: Vol. 2). 350p. 1975. 42.00x (ISBN 0-8103-1233-6). Gale.
Henisch, Bridget Ann. Fast and Feast: Food in Medieval Society. LC 76-15677. (Illus.). 1977. 17.95x (ISBN 0-271-01230-7). Pa St U Pr.
Henisch, H. K. & Roy, R. Silicon Carbide-1968. 1974. 30.00 (ISBN 0-08-006768-9). Pergamon.
Henisch, Heinz K. Crystal Growth in Gels. LC 77-86379. (Illus.). 1970. text ed. 10.95 (ISBN 0-271-00104-6). Pa St U Pr.
Henissart, Paul. The Winter Spy. 1977. 8.95 o.p. (ISBN 0-671-22375-5). S&S.
Henke, Dan. California Law Guide. LC 76-19950. 757p. 1976. 50.00 (ISBN 0-911110-21-6); 1983 suppl. incl. Parker & Son.
Henke, Emerson O. Accounting for Non-Profit Organizations. 2nd ed. pap. 9.95x (ISBN 0-534-00543-8). Kent Pub Co.
--Accounting for Nonprofit Organizations. 3rd ed. 228p. 1983. pap. text ed. 11.95x (ISBN 0-534-01429-1). Kent Pub Co.
--Introduction to Nonprofit Organization Accounting. (Business Ser.). 500p. 1980. text ed. 24.95x (ISBN 0-534-00742-2). Kent Pub Co.
Henke, Emerson O., jt. auth. see Thomas, C. William.
Henke, Shirley & Mann, Stephanie. Alternative to Fear: A Citizen's Manual for Crime Prevention Through Neighborhood Involvement. (Illus.). 1975. pap. 4.95 (ISBN 0-912558-03-2). Lex-Cal-Tex Pr.
Henkel, D. J., jt. auth. see Bishop, A. W.
Henkel, James G., jt. auth. see Abdel-Monem, Mahmoud M.
Henkel, Stephen C. Bikes. LC 73-172354. 1975. pap. 5.95 (ISBN 0-85699-033-7). Chatham Pr.
Henkels, Stan V., ed. see Bradford, Thomas L.
Henken, Louis, ed. Arms Control: Issues for the Public. LC 61-14148. 1961. 3.50 (ISBN 0-936904-00-3); pap. 1.95 (ISBN 0-936904-25-9). Am Assembly.
Henker, Barbara, jt. ed. see Whalen, Carol K.
Henkes, Kevin. All Alone. LC 81-105. (Illus.). 32p. (gr. k-3). 1981. 8.95 (ISBN 0-688-00604-3); PLB 8.59 (ISBN 0-688-00605-1). Greenwillow.
--Clean Enough. (Illus.). (ps). 1982. 8.00 (ISBN 0-688-00427-X); PLB 7.63 (ISBN 0-688-00428-8). Greenwillow.
Henkin, Bill. The Rocky Horror Picture Show Book. LC 79-63619. (Illus., Orig.). 1979. pap. 10.95 (ISBN 0-8015-6436-0, Hawthorn). Dutton.
Henkin, Harmon. Complete Fisherman's Catalog: A Source Book of Information About Tackle & Accessories. LC 76-56200. 1977. 14.95 o.s.i. (ISBN 0-397-01186-5); pap. 8.95i (ISBN 0-397-01205-5, LP-116). Har-Row.
--Crisscross. LC 76-2505. 1976. 7.95 o.p. (ISBN 0-399-11747-4). Putnam Pub Group.

Henkin, Louis. Arms Control & Inspection in American Law. LC 74-5783. 289p. 1974. Repr. of 1958 ed. lib. bdg. 18.75x (ISBN 0-8371-7501-1, HEAC). Greenwood.

--Foreign Affairs & the Constitution. 576p. 1975. pap. 8.95x (ISBN 0-393-00768-5, Norton Lib). Norton.

--The Rights of Man Today. LC 78-6722. 1978. lib. bdg. 18.00 (ISBN 0-89158-174-X). Westview.

Henkind, Paul, ed. Classics in Opthalmology Series, 5 vols. 1979. leather 295.00 (ISBN 0-88275-934-5); cloth 169.50 (ISBN 0-88275-933-7). Krieger.

Henle, James M. & Kleinberg, Eugene M. Infinitesimal Calculus. 1979. text ed. 13.75x (ISBN 0-262-08097-4). MIT Pr.

Henle, Robert J. Method in Metaphysics. (Aquinas Lecture). 1950. 7.95 (ISBN 0-87462-115-1). Marquette.

Henley, Arthur, jt. auth. see Brooks, Dennis L.

Henley, Beth. Crimes of the Heart. LC 81-24026. 112p. 1982. 12.95 (ISBN 0-670-24781-2). Viking Pr.

Henley, Clark. The Butch Manual. LC 82-62117. 120p. (Orig.). 1982. pap. 6.95 (ISBN 0-933322-11-9). Sea Horse.

Henley, E. Reliability Engineering & Risk Assessment. 1980. 42.00 (ISBN 0-13-772251-6). P-H.

Henley, Ernest J. & Seader, J. D. Equilibrium-Stage Separation Operations in Chemical Engineering. LC 80-13293. 742p. 1981. text ed. 48.95 (ISBN 0-471-37108-4, Pub by Wiley-Interscience). Wiley.

Henley, Ernest M., jt. auth. see Frauenfelder, Hans.

Henley, Gail. Where the Cherries End up. 1979. 9.95 (ISBN 0-686-86287-2). Little.

Henley, Karyn. Hatch! LC 79-91306. (Carolrhoda on My Own Bks.). (Illus.). (gr. 1-2). 1980. PLB 6.95g (ISBN 0-87614-122-X). Carolrhoda Bks.

Henley, Nancy, ed. see Thorne, Barrie.

Henley, Paul. Amazon Indians. LC 80-52874. (Surviving Peoples Ser.). PLB 12.68 (ISBN 0-382-06419-4). Silver.

--The Panare: Tradition & Change on the Amazonian Frontier. LC 81-40432. (Illus.). 320p. 1982. text ed. 30.00x (ISBN 0-300-02504-1). Yale U Pr.

Henley, S., jt. ed. see Cubitt, J. M.

Henley, Wallace. White House Mystique. 1977. pap. 1.50 o.p. (ISBN 0-89129-253-5). Jove Pubns.

Henly, Elton F. Words for Reading: Reading for Words. 1980. pap. text ed. 11.95 (ISBN 0-13-964171-8). P-H.

Henman, T. J. World Index of Polyolefin Stabilizers. 1983. text ed. 135.00 (ISBN 0-87201-920-9). Gulf Pub.

Henn, Harry G. Handbook of the Laws of Corporations & Other Business Enterprises. 3rd ed. LC 82-23695. (Hornbook Ser.). 1167p. 1983. text ed. write for info. (ISBN 0-314-69870-1). West Pub.

--Handbook on the Laws of Corporations & Other Business Enterprises. 3rd ed. (Handbook Ser.). 1267p. 1983. text ed. write for info. (ISBN 0-314-74292-1). West Pub.

Henn, R., jt. ed. see Eichorn, W.

Hennart, Jean-Francois. A Theory of Multinational Enterprise. 208p. text ed. 16.50x (ISBN 0-472-10017-3). U of Mich Pr.

Henneberg, N. C. & Cherryh, C. J. The Green Gods. (Science Fiction Ser.). 1980. pap. 1.75 o.p. (ISBN 0-87997-538-5). DAW Bks.

Henneberry, Mrs. Janet, jt. auth. see McCarty, Diane.

Hennen, Brian, jt. auth. see Shires, David B.

Hennequin, Amedee. De l'Organisation de la Statistique du Travail et du Placement des Ouvriers. (Conditions of the 19th Century French Working Class Ser.). 44p. (Fr.). 1974. Repr. of 1848 ed. lib. bdg. 23.50 o.p. (ISBN 0-8287-0423-6, 1019). Clearwater Pub.

Hennes, James D., jt. auth. see Stahl, Sidney M.

Hennes, Robert G. & Ekse, Martin. Fundamentals of Transportation Engineering. 2nd ed. LC 68-27507. (Transportation Ser). (Illus.). 1969. text ed. 39.95 (ISBN 0-07-028171-8, C). McGraw.

Hennesey, James. American Catholics: A History of the Roman Catholic Community in the United States. 414p. 1983. pap. 8.95 (ISBN 0-19-503268-3, GB 724). Oxford U Pr.

Hennessee, Leona. Liberty or Bondage? 1982. pap. 4.95 (ISBN 0-88270-531-8). Bridge Pub.

Hennessen, W., ed. Immunization of Adult Birds with Inactive Oil Adjuvant Vaccines. (Developments in Biological Standardization Ser.: Vol. 51). (Illus.). 400p. 1982. pap. 60.00 (ISBN 3-8055-3473-6). S Karger.

Hennessen, W., jt. ed. see Bonneau, M.

Hennessey, J., ed. see Woollcott, Alexander.

Hennessey, James. Catholics in the Promised Land of the Saints. LC 81-80935. (Pere Marquette Lecture Ser.). 100p. 1981. 7.95 (ISBN 0-87462-536-X). Marquette.

Hennessey, Paul. Managing Non-Profit Agencies For Results. 42.00 (ISBN 0-686-38900-X). Public Serv Materials.

Hennessy, Alistair. The Frontier in Latin American History. LC 78-58816. (Histories of the American Frontier Ser). 1978. pap. 8.95x (ISBN 0-8263-0467-2). U of NM Pr.

Hennessy, Bernard C. Public Opinion. 4th ed. LC 80-27733. 350p. (Orig.). 1981. pap. text ed. 14.95 (ISBN 0-8185-0449-8). Brooks-Cole.

Hennessy, John H. Ripping off Welfare. LC 81-80166. 192p. 1983. 10.95 (ISBN 0-86666-026-7). GWP.

Hennessy, Max. The Bright Blue Sky. LC 82-73019. 250p. 1983. 10.95 (ISBN 0-689-11352-8). Atheneum.

--The Lion at Sea. LC 77-20779. 1978. 8.95 o.p. (ISBN 0-689-10845-1). Atheneum.

Hennessy, Thomas, ed. Value Moral Education. LC 78-70814. 1979. pap. 9.95 o.p. (ISBN 0-8091-2150-6). Paulist Pr.

Hennessy, Thomas C., ed. Values & the Counselor. 1980. members 2.00 (ISBN 0-686-36375-2); non-members 2.75 (ISBN 0-686-37295-6). Am Personnel.

Hennesy. Fra Angelico. pap. 12.50 (ISBN 0-935748-23-7). ScalaBooks.

Hennesy, Peter, jt. auth. see Jeffery, Keith.

Hennig, John, et al. New Foundations: The Polish Strike Wave of 1980-81. (Illus.). 85p. (Orig.). pap. 5.00 (ISBN 0-933522-08-8). Kent Popular.

Hennig, Margaret & Jardim, Anne. The Managerial Woman. LC 73-9161. 1977. 11.95 o.p. (ISBN 0-385-02287-5, Anchor Pr). Doubleday.

Hennig, Willi. Insect Phylogeny. LC 80-40853. 514p. 1981. 82.95 (ISBN 0-471-27848-3, Pub. by Wiley-Interscience). Wiley.

Hennigan, Patrick J., jt. ed. see Mertins, Herman.

Henning, Basil D., ed. see Dering, Edward.

Henning, Charles N., et al. Financial Markets & the Economy. 3rd ed. (Illus.). 608p. 1981. text ed. 23.95 (ISBN 0-13-316067-X). P-H.

--International Financial Management. (Illus.). 1978. text ed. 24.95x (ISBN 0-07-028175-0, C); instructor's manual 7.95 (ISBN 0-07-028176-9). McGraw.

Henning, Fritz. Concept & Composition: The Basis of Successful Art. 208p. 1983. 22.50 (ISBN 0-89134-059-9); pap. 11.95 (ISBN 0-89134-060-2). North Light Pub.

Henning, Joel. Holistic Running: Beyond the Threshold of Fitness. LC 78-3191. 1978. 7.95 o.p. (ISBN 0-689-10924-5). Atheneum.

--Holistic Running: Beyond the Threshold of Fitness. (Orig.). (RL 8). 1978. pap. 1.75 o.p. (ISBN 0-451-08257-5, E8257, Sig). NAL.

Hennings, Dorothy G. Communication in Action. 1978. pap. 18.50 o.p. (ISBN 0-395-30624-8); Instr's. manual 1.00 o.p. (ISBN 0-686-97262-7). HM.

--Communication in Action: Teaching the Language Arts. 2nd ed. 1982. 19.95 (ISBN 0-395-31702-9); instr's manual 1.00 (ISBN 0-395-31703-7). HM.

Hennings, Dorothy G. & Hennings, George. Today's Elementary Social Studies. 1980. pap. 22.50 (ISBN 0-395-30626-4); instr's. manual 1.25 (ISBN 0-395-30627-2). HM.

Hennings, Dorothy G., jt. auth. see Grant, Barbara M.

Hennings, George, jt. auth. see Hennings, Dorothy G.

Henningsen, B., et al, eds. Endocrine Treatment of Breast Cancer: A New Approach. (Recent Results in Cancer Research: Vol. 71). (Illus.). 260p. 1980. 47.00 o.p. (ISBN 0-387-09781-3). Springer-Verlag.

Henningsen, C. F. Revelations sur la Russie, 3 vols. (Nineteenth Century Russia Ser.). (Fr.). 1974. Repr. of 1845 ed. Set. lib. bdg. 309.00x o.p. (ISBN 0-8287-0424-4). Clearwater Pub.

Henningsen, Rodney J. Probation & Parole. (Criminal Justice Ser.). 144p. 1981. pap. text ed. 8.95 (ISBN 0-15-571980-7, HC). HarBraceJ.

Henrey, Mrs. Robert. The Golden Visit. 232p. 1979. 10.00x o.p. (ISBN 0-460-04433-8, Pub. by J. M. Dent England). Biblio Dist.

Henri, Florette, jt. auth. see Barbeau, Arthur E.

Henri, Raymond. Dispatches from the Fields. LC 81-67496. (Living Poets' Library Ser.: Vol. 26). 1981. pap. 4.50 (ISBN 0-686-81660-9). Dragons Teeth.

Henri, Robert. Art Spirit. Ryerson, Margery A., ed. LC 39-4273. (Illus.). 1960. pap. 5.95i (ISBN 0-397-00121-5, LP-077, Key). Har-Row.

Henrichsen, Lynn, jt. auth. see Pack, Alice C.

Henrichsen, Lynn E., jt. auth. see Pack, Alice C.

Henrichsen, Walter A. Disciples Are Made-Not Born. LC 74-79162. 160p. 1974. pap. 4.50 (ISBN 0-88207-706-6). Victor Bks.

--Un Hogar para Cristo. Carrodeguas, Andy & Marosi, Esteban, eds. Marosi, Antonio, tr. 176p. (Span.). 1982. pap. 2.00 (ISBN 0-8297-1313-1). Life Pubs Intl.

Henrichsen, Walter A. & Garrison, William N. Layman, Look Up! God Has a Place for You. 128p. 1983. pap. 4.95 (ISBN 0-310-37721-8). Zondervan.

Henrici, Henry. Applied & Computational Complex Analysis: Power Series, Integration-Conformal Mapping-Location of Zeroes. LC 73-19723. (Pure & Applied Mathematics Ser.: Vol. 1). 704p. 1974. 51.95x (ISBN 0-471-37244-7, Pub. by Wiley-Interscience). Wiley.

Henrici, Peter. Applied & Computational Complex Analysis: Special Functions-Integral Transforms-Asymptotics-Continued Fractions, Vol. 2. LC 73-19723. 1977. 59.95x (ISBN 0-471-01525-3, Pub. by Wiley-Interscience). Wiley.

--Computational Analysis with the Hp 25 Pocket Calculator. LC 77-1182. 1977. 22.50x (ISBN 0-471-02938-6, Pub. by Wiley-Interscience). Wiley.

--Discrete Variable Methods in Ordinary Differential Equations. LC 61-17359. 1962. 37.50x (ISBN 0-471-37224-2, Pub. by Wiley-Interscience). Wiley.

--The Essentials of Numerical Analysis with Pocket Calculator Demonstrations. LC 81-10468. 409p. 1982. text ed. 28.95 (ISBN 0-471-05904-8); avail. solns. manual (ISBN 0-471-09704-7). Wiley.

Henrici, Peter K. Elements of Numerical Analysis. LC 64-23840. 1964. 34.95 (ISBN 0-471-37241-2). Wiley.

Henrici-Olive, G. & Olive, S. Coordination & Catalysis. LC 77-460277. (Monographs in Modern Chemistry: Vol. 9). (Illus.). 1977. 90.00x (ISBN 3-527-25686-5). Intl Pubns Serv.

Henricks, Robert C., tr. Philosophy & Argumentation in Third-Century China: The Essays of Hsi K'ang. LC 82-61367. (Princeton Library of Asian Translations). 224p. 1983. 30.00 (ISBN 0-691-05378-2). Princeton U Pr.

Henrickson, Charles & Byrd, Larry. Chemistry for the Health Professions. (Illus.). 798p. 1980. text ed. 21.95 (ISBN 0-442-23258-6); instr's. manual 3.50 (ISBN 0-442-26252-3); Student Self Study Guide by John R. Wilson 7.95 (ISBN 0-686-77564-3). Van Nos Reinhold.

Henrickson, Robert L. Meat, Poultry & Seafood Technology. LC 77-25350. (Illus.). 1978. ref. ed. 21.95 (ISBN 0-13-568600-8). P-H.

Henrie. Cats. (gr. 2-5). 1980. PLB 7.90 (ISBN 0-531-04119-0, E18). Watts.

--Gerbils. (gr. 2-5). 1980. PLB 7.90 (ISBN 0-531-04121-2, E40). Watts.

--Hamsters. 1981. 7.90 (ISBN 0-531-04186-7). Watts.

Henrie, Fiona. Fish. LC 80-50481. (Junior Petkeeper's Library). (gr. 2-5). 1981. PLB 7.90 (ISBN 0-531-04184-0). Watts.

--Guinea Pigs. LC 80-50482. (Junior Petkeeper's Library). (gr. 2-5). 1981. PLB 7.90 (ISBN 0-531-04185-9). Watts.

--Mice & Rats. LC 80-50484. (Junior Petkeeper's Library). (gr. 2-5). 1981. PLB 7.90 (ISBN 0-531-04187-5). Watts.

--Rabbits. (gr. 2-5). 1980. PLB 7.90 (ISBN 0-531-04122-0, G10). Watts.

Henrie, Fiora. Dogs. LC 79-57274. (gr. 2-5). 1980. PLB 7.40 (ISBN 0-531-04120-4, E30). Watts.

Henried, Doris E. Le Francais Intensif. 1976. pap. 8.95x (ISBN 0-442-23260-8); tapes 95.00 (ISBN 0-442-23261-6); cassettes 59.95 (ISBN 0-442-23262-4). Van Nos Reinhold.

Henriksen, Soren, et al, eds. The Use of Artificial Satellites for Geodesy. LC 72-88669. (Geophysical Monographs: Vol. 15). (Illus.). 298p. 1972. 35.00 (ISBN 0-87590-015-1). Am Geophysical.

Henriksen, Vera. Christmas in Norway: Past & Present. LC 75-584137. (Norwegian Guide Ser). (Illus., Orig.). 1970. pap. 9.00 (ISBN 0-8002-0714-9). Intl Pubns Serv.

Henriod, Lorraine. Ancestor Hunting. LC 79-10767. (Illus.). 64p. (gr. 3-5). 1979. PLB 7.29 o.p. (ISBN 0-671-32998-7). Messner.

--Grandma's Wheelchair. Tucker, Cathy, ed. LC 81-12918. (Illus.). 32p. (ps-1). 1982. 8.25 (ISBN 0-8075-3035-2). A Whitman.

--I Know a Grocer. (Community Helper Bks.). (Illus.). (gr. 1-3). 1970. PLB 4.29 o.p. (ISBN 0-399-60282-8). Putnam Pub Group.

--I Know a Zoo Keeper. (Community Helper Bks.). (Illus.). (gr. 1-3). 1969. PLB 4.29 o.p. (ISBN 0-399-60295-X). Putnam Pub Group.

Henrion, F. H. Top Graphic Design. (Illus.). 180p. 1983. 67.50 (ISBN 0-8038-7227-5). Hastings.

Henripin, Jacques, jt. auth. see Lachapelle, Rejean.

Henriques, E. Frank. The Signet Encyclopedia of Wine. (Orig.). 1975. pap. 2.75 (ISBN 0-451-09511-1, E9511, Sig). NAL.

Henriques, Zelma W. Imprisoned Mothers & Their Children: A Descriptive & Analytical Study. LC 81-43513. 226p. (Orig.). 1982. lib. bdg. 23.00 (ISBN 0-8191-2225-4); pap. text ed. 10.75 (ISBN 0-8191-2226-2). U Pr of Amer.

Henroid, Lorraine. Special Olympics & Paralympics. (First Bks.). (Illus.). (gr. 4 up). 1979. PLB 8.90 s&l (ISBN 0-531-02263-3). Watts.

Henry. Current Clinical Neurophysiology: Update on EEG & Evoked Potentials. 1981. 75.00 (ISBN 0-444-00639-7). Elsevier.

Henry, Allan. Nuclear Reactor Analysis. LC 74-19477. 1975. 42.50x (ISBN 0-262-08081-8). MIT Pr.

Henry, Bamman A., ed. see Belden, Bernard R.

Henry, Bill, et al. Bill Henry: An Approved History of the Olympic Games, 1981 Edition. (Illus.). 504p. 1981. 17.50 (ISBN 0-9606628-0-4). S CA Committee.

Henry, Carl F. Christian Personal Ethics. (Twin Brooks Ser). 1977. pap. 12.95 (ISBN 0-8010-4165-1). Baker Bk.

--God, Revelation & Authority, Vol. 6, Part 2. (The God Who Stands & Stays Ser.). 1983. 19.95 (ISBN 0-8499-0333-5). Word Pub.

Henry, Carl F., ed. The Biblical Expositor. LC 73-599. 1982. Repr. of 1960 ed. 9.95 o.p. (ISBN 0-8054-1146-1). Broadman.

Henry, Carl F., ed. see Holmes, Arthur F.

Henry, Charles, jt. auth. see Morris, Lorenzo.

Henry, Charlier H. & Justus, John R. Handbook of Ocean Energy. (Illus.). 1983. 34.95 (ISBN 0-8311-1133-X). Indus Pr.

Henry, Christopher D., jt. auth. see Galloway, William E.

Henry, Dennis C., et al. Experiments in Light, Electricity, & Modern Physics, Laboratory Manual. 1978. pap. text ed. 7.95 (ISBN 0-8403-1889-8). Kendall-Hunt.

Henry, Desmond P. Philosophy in the Middle Ages: Teaching & Study Companion. LC 77-5556. 42p. (Orig.). 1977. pap. text ed. 1.60 (ISBN 0-915144-32-8). Hackett Pub.

Henry, Donald L., jt. auth. see Harper, E. J.

Henry Ford Museum Staff. Greenfield Village & the Henry Ford Museum. (Illus.). 1972. 8.95 (ISBN 0-517-50121-X); pap. 3.95 o.p. (ISBN 0-517-50678-5). Crown.

--The Henry Ford Museum. (Illus.). 128p. 1972. pap. 4.95 o.p. (ISBN 0-517-50679-3). Crown.

Henry, Frances L., jt. auth. see Sawyers, Phyllis.

Henry, Glenn E. The Christmas Owl. 48p. 1983. 5.00 (ISBN 0-682-49928-5). Exposition.

Henry, Joanne L. Robert Fulton: Steamboat Builder. LC 74-18326. (Discovery Ser). (Illus.). 80p. (gr. 2-5). 1975. PLB 6.69 (ISBN 0-8116-6317-5). Garrard.

Henry, John B. & Giegel, Joseph L. Quality Control in Laboratory Medicine. LC 77-78559. (Illus.). 250p. 1977. 40.50 (ISBN 0-89352-008-X). Masson Pub.

Henry, Jules. Culture Against Man. 1965. pap. 6.95 (ISBN 0-394-70283-2, Vin). Random.

Henry, Kenneth. Social Problems: Institutional & Interpersonal Perspectives. 1978. pap. 10.95x o.p. (ISBN 0-673-15101-8). Scott F.

Henry, Lawrence. ABC's. Klimo, Kate, ed. (Learn with E.T. Ser.). (Illus.). 24p. 1982. pap. 1.75 (ISBN 0-671-46439-6, Little). S&S.

--E.T. Counting. Klimo, Kate, ed. (Learn with E.T. Ser.). (Illus.). 24p. 1982. pap. 1.75 (ISBN 0-671-46440-X, Little). S&S.

--What Is This For. Klimo, Kate, ed. (Learn with E.T. Ser.). (Illus.). 24p. 1982. pap. 1.75 (ISBN 0-671-46444-2, Little). S&S.

Henry, Leigh. Doctor John Bull 1562-1628. LC 68-15589. (Music Ser). (Illus.). 1968. Repr. of 1937 ed. lib. bdg. 32.50 (ISBN 0-306-70982-1). Da Capo.

Henry, Leslie R. Model T Ford Restoration Handbook. Clymer Publications, ed. pap. 6.00 o.p. (ISBN 0-89287-256-X, H506). Clymer Pubns.

Henry, M. Daniel, jt. auth. see Morell, R. W.

Henry, Mabel W., ed. Creative Experiences in Oral Language. 1967. pap. 5.00 o.p. (ISBN 0-8141-0902-0); pap. 3.50 members o.p. (ISBN 0-686-86398-4). NCTE.

Henry, Marguerite. All About Horses. (Allabout Ser.: No. 43). (Illus.). (gr. 5-9). 1962. 6.95 (ISBN 0-394-80243-8, BYR); PLB 5.39 o.p. (ISBN 0-394-90243-2). Random.

--Benjamin West & His Cat Grimalkin. (gr. 3-7). 1947. 7.95 (ISBN 0-672-50220-8). Bobbs.

--Marguerite Henry's All About Horses. (gr. 4-8). 1967. deluxe ed. 6.95 (ISBN 0-394-81699-4, BYR); PLB 6.99 o.p. (ISBN 0-394-91699-9). Random.

--Marguerite Henry's Misty Treasury. (Illus.). 570p. (gr. 3-6). 1982. 14.95 (ISBN 0-528-82423-6). Rand.

--One Man's Horse. LC 77-10080. (Illus.). (gr. 3-6). 1977. 4.95 o.p. (ISBN 0-528-82092-3); PLB 4.97 o.p. (ISBN 0-528-80057-4). Rand.

Henry, Marilyn & DeSourdis, Ron. The Films of Alan Ladd. (Illus.). 256p. 1981. 16.95 (ISBN 0-8065-0736-5); pap. 9.95 (ISBN 0-8065-0835-3). Citadel Pr.

Henry, Matthew. Matthew-John. (A Commentary on the Whole Bible Ser.: Vol. 5). 1240p. 15.95 (ISBN 0-8007-0201-8). Revell.

Henry, Matthew & Scott, Thomas. Matthew Henry..Concise Commentary on the Whole Bible. 22.95 (ISBN 0-8024-5190-X). Moody.

Henry, N. Public Administration & Public Affairs. 2nd ed. 1980. 22.95 (ISBN 0-13-737296-5). P-H.

Henry, Nicholas J. Governing at the Grassroots: State & Local Politics. (Illus.). 1980. text ed. 22.95 (ISBN 0-13-360602-3). P-H.

Henry, O. Alias Jimmy Valentine. Pauk, Walter & Harris, Raymond, eds. (Jamestown Classics Ser.). (Illus.). 37p. (gr. 5). 1979. pap. text ed. 2.00x (ISBN 0-89061-192-0, 409); tchrs. ed. 3.00 (ISBN 0-89061-194-7, 411). Jamestown Pubs.

--The Best of O. Henry. LC 78-14841. 1978. lib. bdg. 12.90 (ISBN 0-89471-047-8); pap. 4.95 (ISBN 0-89471-046-X). Running Pr.

--The Best Short Stories of O. Henry. Cerf & Cartmell, eds. 6.95 (ISBN 0-394-60423-7). Modern Lib.

--Best Stories of O. Henry. 1965. 10.95 (ISBN 0-385-00020-0). Doubleday.

--Complete Works of O. Henry. LC 53-6098. 1953. 19.95 (ISBN 0-385-00961-5). Doubleday.

--Four Million & Other Stories. (Classics Ser.). (gr. 8 up). 1964. pap. 1.25 (ISBN 0-8049-0025-6, CL-25). Airmont.

--The Gentle Grafter. (Literature of Mystery & Detection). (Illus.). 1976. Repr. of 1908 ed. 14.00x (ISBN 0-405-07889-7). Ayer Co.

--The Gift of the Magi. LC 78-55660. (Illus.). 1978. Repr. 7.95 (ISBN 0-672-52296-9). Bobbs.

--The Gift of the Magi. (Creative's Classics Ser.). 32p. (gr. 4-9). 1980. PLB 6.95 (ISBN 0-87191-775-0). Creative Ed.

--The Gift of the Magi. Pauk, Walter & Harris, Raymond, eds. (Classics Ser.). (Illus.). 35p. (gr. 5). 1979. pap. text ed. 2.00x (ISBN 0-89061-186-6, 401); tchrs. ed. 3.00x (ISBN 0-89061-188-2, 403). Jamestown Pubs.

--The Gift of the Magi. (Picture Book Studio Ser.). (Illus.). 32p. 1982. 11.95 (ISBN 0-907234-17-8). Neugebauer Pr.

--The Last Leaf. (Creative's Classics Ser.). (Illus.). 32p. (gr. 4-9). 1980. PLB 7.95 (ISBN 0-87191-774-2). Creative Ed.

--The Last Leaf. Pauk, Walter & Harris, Raymond, eds. (Jamestown Classics Ser.). (Illus.). 35p. (Orig.). (gr. 6-12). 1979. pap. text ed. 2.00x (ISBN 0-89061-195-5, 413); tchrs. ed. 3.00 (ISBN 0-89061-197-1, 415). Jamestown Pubs.

Henry, O., pseud. O. Henry Stories. (Great Writers Collection). (gr. 7 up). 5.95 o.p. (ISBN 0-448-41105-9). Platt.

Henry, O. The Pocket Book of O. Henry Stories. Hansen, Harry, ed. 256p. pap. 2.95 (ISBN 0-671-45360-2). WSP.

--Pocket Book of O. Henry's Stories. pap. 1.95 o.p. (ISBN 0-671-80385-9). PB.

--The Ransom of Red Chief. (Creative's Classics Ser.). (Illus.). 40p. (gr. 4-9). 1980. PLB 7.95 (ISBN 0-87191-776-9). Creative Ed.

--The Ransom of Red Chief. Pauk, Walter & Harris, Raymond, eds. (Jamestown Classics Ser.). (Illus.). 40p. (Orig.). (gr. 6-12). 1979. pap. text ed. 2.00x (ISBN 0-89061-189-0, 405); tchrs. ed. 3.00 (ISBN 0-89061-191-2, 407). Jamestown Pubs.

--Surprises: Twenty Stories by O. Henry. Corbin, Richard & Hoopes, Ned E., eds. (Orig.). 1966. pap. 0.95 o.p. (ISBN 0-440-98390-8, LFL). Dell.

Henry, O., et al. The Gifts & Other Stories. (Progressive English Readers Ser.). (Illus.). (gr. 3up). 1974. pap. text ed. 3.50x (ISBN 0-19-580574-7). Oxford U Pr.

--Inspiration Three, Vol. 5: Three Famous Classics in One Book. LC 73-80032. (Pivot Family Reader Ser.). 1973. pap. 1.25 (ISBN 0-87983-045-X). Keats.

Henry, Orville & Bailey, Jim. The Razorbacks: A Story of Arkansas Football. LC 73-87000. (College Sports Ser.). 1980. 10.95 (ISBN 0-87397-024-1). Strode.

Henry, Paget & Stone, Carl, eds. Newer Caribbean: Decolonization, Democracy, & Development. LC 82-11817. (Inter-American Politics Ser.: Vol. 4). 350p. 1983. text ed. 30.00x (ISBN 0-89727-039-8). Inst Study Human.

Henry, Patrick & Stransky, Thomas F. God on Our Minds. LC 81-70593. 176p. 1982. pap. 6.95 (ISBN 0-8146-1249-0). Liturgical Pr.

Henry, Porter J., jt. auth. see Barry, John W.

Henry, R. M. The Psychodynamic Foundations of Morality. (Contributions to Human Development Ser.: Vol. 7). (Illus.). 160p. 1983. pap. 62.50 (ISBN 3-8055-3603-8). S Karger.

Henry, Rene A., Jr. How to Profitably Buy & Sell Land. LC 76-22522. (Real Estate for Professional Practitioners: a Wiley Ser.). 1977. 25.95 (ISBN 0-471-37291-9, Pub by Wiley-Interscience). Wiley.

Henry, Sondra & Taitz, Emily. Written Out of History: Our Jewish Foremothers. 2nd, rev. ed. (Illus.). 1983. pap. 8.50x (ISBN 0-9602036-8-0). Biblio NY.

Henry, Stuart C., ed. Miscellany of American Christianity: Essays in Honor of H. Shelton Smith. LC 63-14288. 1963. 16.25 o.p. (ISBN 0-8223-0085-0). Duke.

Henry, Sue. Group Skills in Social Work: A Four Dimensional Approach. LC 80-83378. 385p. 1981. text ed. 16.50 (ISBN 0-87581-268-6). Peacock Pubs.

Henry, Thomas. Monstruo y Milagro. 1946. pap. 0.75 (ISBN 0-87535-060-7). Hispanic Soc.

Henry, Vernon J., jt. ed. see Rezak, Richard.

Henry, Will. Chiricahua. LC 78-38941. (YA) 1972. 10.53i (ISBN 0-397-00887-2). Har-Row.

--Chiricuhua. 256p. 1982. pap. 2.50 (ISBN 0-553-20718-0). Bantam.

--From Where the Sun Now Stands. (Western Fiction Ser.). 1978. lib. bdg. 9.95 (ISBN 0-8398-2461-0, Gregg). G K Hall.

--The Gates of the Mountains. 1980. lib. bdg. 13.95 (ISBN 0-8398-2689-3, Gregg). G K Hall.

--One More River to Cross. 1979. lib. bdg. 9.95 (ISBN 0-8398-2585-4, Gregg). G K Hall.

--The Summer of the Gun. 1978. 11.49i (ISBN 0-397-01309-4). Har-Row.

Henry, William & Yeomans, Patricia Henry. An Approved History of the Olympic Games. LC 76-20304. 1976. 12.50 o.p. (ISBN 0-399-11818-7). Putnam Pub Group.

Henrych, J. The Dynamics of Arches & Frames. (Developments in Civil Engineering Ser.: Vol. 2). 1981. 95.75 (ISBN 0-444-99792-X). Elsevier.

--The Dynamics of Explosion & Its Use. LC 76-29648. (Developments in Civil Engineering: Vol. 1). 1979. 108.50 (ISBN 0-444-99819-5). Elsevier.

Henryson, Robert. Selected Poems. Barron, W. R., ed. (Fyfield Ser.). 125p. (Orig.). 1981. pap. text ed. 5.25x (ISBN 0-85635-301-9, Pub. by Carcanet New Pr England). Humanities.

Henrysson, Harald, jt. auth. see Porter, Jack W.

Henry Tall Bull & Weist, Tom. Mista. (Indian Culture Ser.). (gr. 2-12). 1971. 1.95 o.p. (ISBN 0-89992-011-X). MT Coun Indian.

Henschel, Georgie. Basic Riding Explained. LC 80-253. (Horseman's Handbooks Ser.). (Illus.). 96p. 1980. 8.95 o.p. (ISBN 0-668-04950-2); pap. 4.95 (ISBN 0-668-04961-8). Arco.

Henschel, Stan. How to Raise & Train a Chesapeake Bay Retriever. (Orig.). 1965. pap. 2.50 o.p. (ISBN 0-87666-265-3, DS1069). TFH Pubns.

--How to Raise & Train a Coonhound. (Orig.). pap. 2.95 (ISBN 0-87666-274-2, DS1057). TFH Pubns.

--How to Raise & Train a Labrador Retriever. (Illus.). pap. 2.95 (ISBN 0-87666-330-7, DS1095). TFH Pubns.

Henschen, A. & Graeff, H., eds. Fibrinogen. (Illus.). x, 400p. 1982. 67.50x (ISBN 3-11-008543-7). De Gruyter.

Hensel, Carol. Carol Hensel's Aerobic Dance & Exercise Book. (Illus.). 128p. (Orig.). 1983. pap. 7.95 (ISBN 0-8092-5538-3). Contemp Bks.

Hensel, Evelyn & Deveillette, Peter. Purchasing Library Materials in Public & School Libraries: A Study of Purchasing Procedures & the Relationship Between Libraries, Purchasing Agencies & Dealers. Hickey, Doralyn J., ed. LC 70-88860. 1969. pap. 4.00 o.p. (ISBN 0-8389-3103-0). ALA.

Hensel, Fanny. Trio in D Minor for Piano, Violin & Cello. (Women Composer Ser.: No. 6). (Illus.). 58p. 1980. Repr. of 1850 ed. lib. bdg. 18.95 (ISBN 0-306-76052-5). Da Capo.

Hensel, Herbert. Thermal Sensations & Thermoreceptors in Man. (Illus.). 208p. 1982. 21.75x (ISBN 0-398-04698-0). C C Thomas.

Hensel, Kurt & Landsberg, G. Algebraische Funktionen. LC 65-11624. (Ger). 1965. 35.00 (ISBN 0-8284-0179-9). Chelsea Pub.

Hensel, Mary D., jt. auth. see Lipson, Stephen H.

Henshall, Don, jt. auth. see Mumford, Enid.

Henshaw, D. E. Self-Twist Yarns. 1971. 15.00 o.s.i. (ISBN 0-87245-415-0). Textile Bk.

Henshaw, Richard. The Encyclopedia of World Soccer. LC 78-26570. (Illus.). 1979. 25.00 (ISBN 0-915220-34-2). New Republic.

Hensher, D. A., ed. Urban Transport Economics. LC 76-11061. (Illus.). 1977. 49.50 (ISBN 0-521-21128-X); pap. 16.95 (ISBN 0-521-29140-2). Cambridge U Pr.

Hensher, David & Dalvi, Quasia. Determinants of Travel Choice. LC 78-58818. 1978. 41.95 o.p. (ISBN 0-03-046236-3). Praeger.

Henshu-sha, Century, tr. see Asano, Osamu & Ishiwata, Mutsuko.

Henshu-sha, Century E., tr. see Asano, Osamu & Ishiwata, Mutsuko.

Henshu-sha, Century Eibun, tr. see Asano, Osamu & Ishiwata, Mutsuko.

Hensinger, Robert N., jt. auth. see Fraser, Beverly A.

Hensley, Dana & Prentice, Diana. Mastering Competitive Debate. 1977. lib. bdg. 6.75 o.p. (ISBN 0-931054-05-2). Clark Pub.

--Mastering Competitive Debate. rev. ed. 190p. 1982. pap. text ed. 7.03 (ISBN 0-931054-08-7). Clark Pub.

Hensley, E. S. Basic Concepts of World Nutrition. 302p. 1981. pap. 21.75x (ISBN 0-398-04544-5). C C Thomas.

Hensley, Jeffrey. The Zero People. 310p. 1983. pap. 7.95 (ISBN 0-89283-126-X). Servant.

Hensley, Joe L. Outcasts. LC 80-705. (Crime Club Ser.). 192p. 1981. 10.95 o.p. (ISBN 0-385-15820-3). Doubleday.

Hensley, Thomas R. The Kent State Incident: Impact of Judicial Process on Public Attitudes. LC 80-1712. (Contributions in Political Science Ser.: No. 56). 264p. 1981. lib. bdg. 29.95 (ISBN 0-313-21220-1, HKS/). Greenwood.

Hensley, Thomas R. & Lewis, Jerry M. Kent State & May 4th: A Social Science Perspective. 1978. pap. text ed. 9.95 (ISBN 0-8403-1856-1). Kendall-Hunt.

Henslin, James M. & Light, Donald, Jr. Social Problems. (Illus.). 656p. 1983. text ed. 23.95 (ISBN 0-07-037836-3, C); study guide 8.95 (ISBN 0-07-037839-8). McGraw.

Henslin, James M. & Sagarin, Edward, eds. Sociology of Sex: An Introductory Reader. 1978. 16.95x o.p. (ISBN 0-8052-3680-5); pap. 6.95 (ISBN 0-8052-0584-5). Schocken.

Henson, Curtis, jt. auth. see Culbertson, Jack A.

Henson, H. H. The Liberty of Prophesying: With Its Just Limits & Temper Considered with Reference to the Circumstances of the Modern Church. 1910. 37.50x (ISBN 0-686-51411-4). Elliots Bks.

Henson, Kenneth T. Secondary Teaching Methods. 384p. 1981. text ed. 18.95 (ISBN 0-669-03316-2). Heath.

Henson, Kenneth T. & Higgins, James E. Personalizing Teaching in the Elementary School. 1978. text ed. 17.95 (ISBN 0-675-08427-X). Merrill.

Henson, Kenneth T., jt. auth. see Stinnett, T. M.

Henson, Margaret S. Anglo American Women in Texas, 1820-1950. Rosenbaum, Robert J., ed. (Texas History Ser.). 30p. 1982. pap. text ed. 1.95x (ISBN 0-89641-104-4). American Pr.

--Juan Davis Bradburn: A Reappraisal of the Mexican Commander of Anahuac. LC 82-40312. (Essays on the American West Ser.: No. 6). 96p. (YA) 1982. 9.50 (ISBN 0-89096-135-2). Tex A&M Univ Pr.

Henson, Michael P. A Guide to Treasure in Kentucky. (Illus.). 104p. (Orig.). 1983. pap. 6.95 (ISBN 0-941620-29-8). H G Carson Ent.

Henstell, Bruce. Los Angeles: The Only City Ever. LC 79-51791. (Illus.). 1980. cancelled (ISBN 0-89169-525-7). Reed Bks.

Henstock. Disposal & Recovers of Municipal Solid Waste. 1983. text ed. write for info. (ISBN 0-408-01174-2). Butterworth.

Henstock, M. E. & Biddulph, M. W., eds. Solid Waste As a Resource. LC 77-24726. 1978. text ed. 28.50 (ISBN 0-08-021571-8). Pergamon.

Henstra, Friso. Mighty Mizzling Mouse. LC 82-48459. (Illus.). 24p. (ps-2). 1983. 10.53i (ISBN 0-397-32003-5, JBL-J); PLB 10.89g (ISBN 0-397-32004-3). Har-Row.

Henszey, Benjamin & Friedman, Ronald. Real Estate Law. LC 78-24808. 383p. 1979. pap. text ed. 17.95 o.p. (ISBN 0-88262-310-9). Warren.

Henszey, Benjamin, jt. auth. see Friedman, Ronald.

Henszey, Benjamin N. & Friedman, Ronald M. Real Estate Law. LC 78-24808. 383p. 1982. text ed. 24.95 (ISBN 0-471-87753-0); write for info. (ISBN 0-471-89517-2). Wiley.

Hentig, Hans Von. The Criminal & His Victim: Studies in the Sociobiology of Crime. LC 78-25998. 1979. pap. 8.95 o.p. (ISBN 0-8052-0614-0). Schocken.

Hentig, Hans Von see Von Hentig, Hans.

Hentoff, Nat. Blues for Charlie Darwin. LC 82-3484. 228p. 1982. 11.50 (ISBN 0-688-01260-4). Morrow.

--Does This School Have Capital Punishment? (YA) (gr. 7-12). 1983. pap. 2.25 (ISBN 0-440-92070-1, LFL). Dell.

--I'm Really Dragged but Nothing Gets Me Down. LC 68-29762. (gr. 7 up). 1968. PLB 5.79 o.p. (ISBN 0-671-65045-9). S&S.

--Jazz Is. 1978. pap. 2.25 o.p. (ISBN 0-380-01858-6, 36558, Discus). Avon.

--The Jazz Life. LC 74-23383. (The Roots of Jazz Ser.). 1975. lib. bdg. 25.00 (ISBN 0-306-70681-4); pap. 6.95 (ISBN 0-306-80088-8). Da Capo.

--Jazz: New Perspectives on the History of Jazz by Twelve of the World's Foremost Jazz Critics & Scholars. McCarthy, Albert J., ed. LC 74-20882. (Roots of Jazz Ser.). xiv, 399p. 1975. pap. 7.95 (ISBN 0-306-80002-0). Da Capo.

Hentoff, Nat & McCarthy, Albert. Jazz: New Perspectives on the History of Jazz. (Roots of Jazz Ser.). 1974. Repr. of 1959 ed. lib. bdg. 29.50 (ISBN 0-306-70592-3). Da Capo.

Hentoff, Nat, ed. see Muste, A. J.

Hentschke, Guilbert C. Management Operations in Education. LC 75-9168. (Illus.). 280p. 1976. 22.50x (ISBN 0-8211-0757-7); text ed. 20.50x (ISBN 0-685-61057-8). McCutchan.

Hentzberg, Robert. The Home Owner Handbook of Electrical Repairs. (The Home Owner Handbooks Ser.). (Illus.). 124p. 1974. 1.98 o.p. (ISBN 0-517-51440-0). Crown.

Henwood, George. Cornwall's Mines & Miners. 240p. 1981. 35.00x (ISBN 0-686-97149-3, Pub. by D B Barton England). State Mutual Bk.

Henwood, Kay, jt. auth. see Stringer, Michael.

Heny, Frank W., jt. auth. see Akmajian, Adrian.

Heny, Frank W. & Schnelle, Helmut, eds. Syntax & Semantics Vol. 10: Selections from the Third Groningen Round Table. (Syntax & Semantics Ser.). 1979. 45.00 (ISBN 0-12-613510-X). Acad Pr.

Henze, Donald F., jt. auth. see Saunders, John T.

Henze, Hans W. Music & Politics: Collected Writings, 1953-81. Labanyi, Peter, tr. LC 82-71806. (Illus.). 296p. 1982. 24.95X (ISBN 0-8014-1545-4). Cornell U Pr.

Henzel, D. S., et al. Handbook for Flue Gas Desulfurization Scrubbing with Limestone. LC 82-7926. (Pollution Technology Rev. 94). (Illus.). 424p. 1983. 44.00 (ISBN 0-8155-0912-X). Noyes.

Henzel, S. Sylvia. Old Costume Jewelry: A Collector's Dream, with Prices. (Illus.). 1978. 7.95 o.p. (ISBN 0-87069-228-3). Wallace-Homestead.

Henzke, Lucile. Art Pottery of America. LC 82-60328. (Illus.). 480p. 1982. 45.00 (ISBN 0-916838-69-2). Schiffer.

Hepburn. Nationalism & Socialism in Twentieth-Century Ireland. 268p. 1982. 55.00x (ISBN 0-85323-343-8, Pub. by Liverpool Univ England). State Mutual Bk.

Hepburn, A. C. Minorities in History. 1979. 35.00 (ISBN 0-312-53423-X). St Martin.

Hepburn, A. C., ed. Conflict of Nationality in Modern Ireland. 1980. 22.50 (ISBN 0-312-16231-6). St Martin.

Hepburn, Andrew H. Great Houses of American History. 1972. 25.00 o.p. (ISBN 0-517-50374-3, C N Potter Bks). Crown.

Hepburn, C. Polyurethane Elastomers. (Illus.). ix, 400p. 1982. 82.00 (ISBN 0-85334-127-3, Pub. by Applied Sci England). Elsevier.

Hepburn, C. & Reynolds, J. W. Elastomers: Criteria for Engineering Design. (Illus.). 1979. 57.50x (ISBN 0-85334-809-X, Pub. by Applied Sci England). Elsevier.

Hepburn, Daisy. Lead, Follow or Get Out of the Way! (Orig.). 1982. pap. 4.95 (ISBN 0-8307-0822-7); write for info. resource manual (ISBN 0-8307-0797-2). Regal.

--Lead, Follow or Get Out of the Way. 1983. resource manual 2.95 (ISBN 0-8307-0872-3). Regal.

--Why Doesn't Somebody Do Something? 204p. 1980. pap. 5.95 (ISBN 0-88207-606-X). Victor Bks.

Hepburn, H. R. & Mitchell, G. Milk & Honey. 1981. 23.00 (ISBN 0-444-80272-X). Elsevier.

Hepburn, H. R., ed. The Insect Integument. 1976. 149.50 (ISBN 0-444-41436-3). Elsevier.

Hepburn, John R., jt. auth. see Thomas, Charles W.

Hepburn, Lawrence R. The Georgia History Book. 212p. (gr. 8-9). 1982. text ed. 11.95 (ISBN 0-89854-080-1). U of GA Inst Govt.

Hepburne, Melissa. Passion's Blazing Triumph. 272p. (Orig.). 1980. pap. 2.50 o.p. (ISBN 0-523-40654-1). Pinnacle Bks.

--Passion's Proud Captive. (Orig.). 1978. pap. 2.25 o.p. (ISBN 0-523-40329-1). Pinnacle Bks.

--Passion's Sweet Sacrifice. 1979. pap. 2.50 o.p. (ISBN 0-523-40471-9). Pinnacle Bks.

Hepher, Dalfour & Pruginin, Yoel. Commercial Fish Farming: With Special Reference to Fish Culture in Israel. LC 80-28593. 261p. 1981. 36.50x (ISBN 0-471-06264-2, Pub. by Wiley-Interscience). Wiley.

Hephner, Thomas, jt. auth. see Koeninger, Jimmy.

Hepler, D. E., et al. Interior Design Fundamentals. 1982. 19.95 (ISBN 0-07-028296-X); 6.95 (ISBN 0-07-028297-8). McGraw.

Hepler, Don, jt. auth. see Wallach, Paul.

Hepler, Donald & Wallach, Paul. Architecture: Drafting & Design. 3rd ed. (YA) (gr. 9-12). 1976. text ed. 22.76 (ISBN 0-07-028291-9, W). McGraw.

Hepler, Donald, et al. Architecture: Drafting & Design. 4th ed. (Illus.). 608p. (gr. 10-12). 1981. 23.28 (ISBN 0-07-028301-X, W); drawings set 73.60 (ISBN 0-07-028304-4); tchr's manual 6.64 (ISBN 0-07-028302-8); 9.24 (ISBN 0-07-028303-6). McGraw.

Hepler, Donald E., jt. auth. see Wallach, Paul I.

Hepner, Harry W. Psychology Applied to Life & Work. 6th ed. LC 78-11923. (Illus.). 1979. text ed. 23.95 (ISBN 0-13-732461-8). P-H.

Hepp, Maylon H., jt. auth. see Titus, Harold H.

Heppenheimer, T. A. The Real Future: Tomorrow's Technology Today. LC 82-45291. (Illus.). 400p. 1983. 17.95 (ISBN 0-385-17688-0). Doubleday.

Heppenstall, Rayner. The Pier. 192p. 1982. 13.95 (ISBN 0-8052-8131-2, Pub. by Allison & Busby England); pap. 5.95 (ISBN 0-8052-8132-0, Pub. by Allison & Busby England). Schocken.

--Woodshed. 1968. pap. 6.95 (ISBN 0-214-15817-9). Dufour.

Hepper, F. Nigel, ed. Kew: The Royal Botanic Gardens: Gardens for Science & Pleasure. (Illus.). 210p. 1982. 24.95 (ISBN 0-88045-010-X). Stemmer Hse.

Hepple, P. & Institute of Petroleum. Application of Computer Techniques in Chemical Research. 1972. 45.00 (ISBN 0-85334-488-4). Elsevier.

Hepple, P., ed. Lead in the Environment. 1972. 20.50 (ISBN 0-85334-485-X, Pub. by Applied Sci England). Elsevier.

Hepple, Peter, ed. Outlook for Natural Gas: A Quality Fuel. LC 73-661. 268p. 1973. 44.95x o.s.i. (ISBN 0-470-37303-2). Halsted Pr.

Heptinstall, William. Gourmet Recipes from a Highland Hotel. 8.95 o.p. (ISBN 0-685-20589-4). Transatlantic.

Hepworth, Andrew & Osbaldeston, Michael. The Way We Work. 1979. text ed. 31.50x (ISBN 0-566-00212-4). Gower Pub Ltd.

Hepworth, Brian. Robert Lowth. (English Authors Ser.). 1978. lib. bdg. 14.95 (ISBN 0-8057-6695-2, Twayne). G K Hall.

Hepworth, Brian, ed. The Rise of Romanticism. 363p. 1978. text ed. 21.00x (ISBN 0-85635-112-1, Pub. by Carcanet New Pr England). Humanities.

Hepworth, Brian, ed. see Young, Edward.

Hepworth, J. B. & Rahde, H. F. Heiteres und Ernstes. 2nd ed. 1967. pap. text ed. 10.95 (ISBN 0-02-353700-0). Macmillan.

Hepworth, Mike. Blackmail: Publicity & Secrecy in Everyday Life. 192p. 1975. 14.95x o.p. (ISBN 0-7100-8235-5); pap. 6.95 (ISBN 0-7100-8236-3). Routledge & Kegan.

Hepworth, Mike, jt. auth. see Turner, Bryan S.

Her Britannic Majesty's Stationery Office. The Sales Catalogues of British Government Publications, 1837-1921, 4 vols. LC 75-6964. 1977. lib. bdg. 85.00 ea (ISBN 0-379-00550-6). Oceana.

Her Majesty's Stationery Office. The Catalogue of the Translator's Library in the Department of Trade & Industry, London, 3 vols. LC 74-31406. 1600p. 1975. Set. lib. bdg. 90.00 ea. Oceana.

Heraclitus. Cosmic Fragments. Kirk, G. S., ed. 1954. 69.50 (ISBN 0-521-05245-9). Cambridge U Pr.

Herak, M. & Stringfield, V. T., eds. Important Karst Regions of the Northern Hemisphere. LC 74-151736. (Illus.). 565p. 1972. 106.50 (ISBN 0-444-40849-5). Elsevier.

Herander, Mark G., jt. auth. see Hodgson, John S.

Heraud, Brian. Training for Uncertainty: A Sociological Approach to Social Work Education. (Library of Social Work). 138p. 1981. 20.00x (ISBN 0-7100-0889-9). Routledge & Kegan.

Herault, G. L' Aizi: Esquisse Phonologique et Enquete Lexicale. (Black Africa Ser.). 126p. (Fr.). 1974. Repr. of 1971 ed. lib. bdg. 41.00x (ISBN 0-8287-0425-2, 71-2008). Clearwater Pub.

--Etude Phonetique et Syntaxique du Francais d'Eleves de Cours Preparatoire de la Region d'Abidjan, 2 vols. (Black Africa Ser.). 250p. (Fr.). 1974. Repr. lib. bdg. 69.00x o.p. (ISBN 0-8287-0426-0, 71-2024). Clearwater Pub.

Herb Society of America, ed. Herbs for Use & for Delight: An Anthology from The Herbarist. LC 74-80287. (Illus.). 352p. 1974. pap. 5.00 (ISBN 0-486-23104-6). Dover.

Herber, Harold L. Teaching Reading in Content Areas. 2nd ed. (Illus.). 1978. ref. ed. 22.95 (ISBN 0-13-894170-X). P-H.

Herber, Reginald. Palestine, a Prize Poem, Recited in the Theatre, Oxford, June 15, 1803, Repr. Of 1803. Bd. with Europe: Lines on the Present War. Repr. of 1809 ed; Palestine...to Which Is Added, the Passage of the Red Sea, a Fragment. Repr. of 1809 ed. LC 75-31211. (Romantic Context Ser.: Poetry 1789-1830: Vol. 62). 1978. lib. bdg. 47.00 o.s.i. (ISBN 0-8240-2161-4). Garland Pub.

Herberg, Will, ed. Four Existentialist Theologians. LC 75-17472. 346p. 1975. Repr. of 1958 ed. lib. bdg. 29.75x (ISBN 0-8371-8303-0, HEFE). Greenwood.

Herberg, Will, ed. see Buber, Martin.

Herberhold, M. Metal Pi Complexes, 2 Pts, Vol. 2. LC 65-13231. 1972-74. Pt. 1: General Survey. 127.75 (ISBN 0-444-40899-1); Vol. 2: Specific Aspects. 127.75 (ISBN 0-444-41061-9). Elsevier.

Herberman, R. B., ed. Compendium of Assays for Immunodiagnosis of Human Cancer. (Developments in Cancer Research: Vol. 1). 1979. 70.00 (ISBN 0-444-00313-4, Biomedical Pr); pap. 32.95 (ISBN 0-444-00336-3). Elsevier.

Herberman, Ronald B., ed. NK Cells & Other Natural Effector Cells. LC 82-11406. 1566p. 1982. 74.50 (ISBN 0-12-341360-5). Acad Pr.

Herbert, A. J. The Structure of Technical English. (English As a Second Language Bk.). 208p. 1965. pap. text ed. 6.25x (ISBN 0-582-52523-3). Longman.

Herbert, A. J., jt. auth. see Needham, R. M.

Herbert, A. P. More Uncommon Law. 1982. pap. write for info. o.p. (ISBN 0-413-38540-X). Methuen Inc.

Herbert, A. S. Genesis Twelve-Fifty. (Student Christian Movement Press-Torch Bible Ser.). (Orig.). 1962. pap. 7.95x (ISBN 0-19-520297-X). Oxford U Pr.

Herbert, Anthony B. The Complete Security Handbook. (Illus.). 384p. 1983. 14.95 (ISBN 0-02-551140-8); pap. 6.95 (ISBN 0-02-080030-4). Macmillan.

--A Military Manual of Self Defense: A Complete Guide to Hand-to-Hand Combat. (Illus.). 280p. 1983. 19.95 (ISBN 0-88254-708-9). Hippocrene Bks.

Herbert, Barry. German Expressionism: Die Brucke & Der Blaue Reiter. (Illus.). 256p. 1982. cancelled (ISBN 0-8317-3828-6). Smith Pubs.

Herbert, Cindy & Russell, Susan. Everychild's Everyday: The Learning About Learning Educational Foundation Series 2. LC 79-7074. (Illus.). 1980. pap. 7.95 o.p. (ISBN 0-385-04155-1, Anch). Doubleday.

Herbert, D. T. & Johnston, R. J. Geography & the Urban Environment: Progress in Research & Applications, 3 vols. LC 77-13555. 1979. Vol. 1. 59.95 (ISBN 0-471-99575-4, Pub. by Wiley-Interscience); Vol. 2. 53.95x (ISBN 0-471-99725-0); Vol. 3. 64.95 (ISBN 0-471-27632-4). Wiley.

--Georaphy & the Urban Environment: Progress in Research & Applications, Vol. 4. LC 77-13555. (Geography & the Urban Environment Ser.). 354p. 1982. 48.95 (ISBN 0-471-28051-8, Pub. by Wiley-Interscience). Wiley.

--Social Areas in Cities, 2 vols. Incl. Vol. 1. Spatial Processes & Forms. 49.95 (ISBN 0-471-99417-0); Vol. 2. Spatial Perspectives on Problems & Policies. 56.95 (ISBN 0-471-37305-2). 1976. Wiley.

Herbert, D. T. & Johnston, R. T. Social Areas in Cities: Processes, Patterns & Problems (Selected Chapters of Vols. 1&2. 311p. 1978. 26.95 (ISBN 0-471-99691-2, Pub. by Wiley-Interscience). Wiley.

Herbert, David, ed. Comic Verse. (Pocket Poet Ser.). 1962. pap. 1.25 (ISBN 0-8023-9047-1). Dufour.

--Everyman's Book of Evergreen Verse. 396p. 1983. pap. text ed. 7.95x (ISBN 0-460-01246-0, Pub. by Evman England). Biblio Dist.

Herbert, David T. & Thomas, Colin J. Urban Geography: A First Approach. LC 81-16041. 508p. 1982. 46.95 (ISBN 0-471-10137-0, Pub. by Wiley-Interscience); pap. 21.95 (ISBN 0-471-10138-9, Pub. by Wiley-Interscience). Wiley.

Herbert, Don. Mister Wizard's Experiments for Young Scientists. LC 59-7907. (gr. 5 up). 1959. 9.95 o.p. (ISBN 0-385-07798-X); PLB (ISBN 0-385-04540-9). Doubleday.

--Mr. Wizard's Supermarket Science. LC 79-27217. (Illus.). 96p. (gr. 4-7). 1980. PLB 6.99 (ISBN 0-394-93800-3); pap. 5.95 (ISBN 0-394-83800-9). Random.

Herbert, Edward H. Autobiography of Edward, Lord Herbert of Cherbury. 2nd ed. Lee, Sidney, ed. Repr. of 1906 ed. lib. bdg. 19.75x (ISBN 0-8371-4235-0, HEAU). Greenwood.

Herbert, Eugenia W., jt. auth. see Lopez, Claude-Anne.

Herbert, Frank. Destination: Void. (Science Fiction Ser.). 1981. lib. bdg. cancelled o.s.i. (ISBN 0-8398-2550-1, Gregg). G K Hall.

--The Dosadi Experiment. LC 77-3653. (YA) 1977. 2.95 (ISBN 0-425-06236-8, Dist. by Putnam). Berkley Pub.

--The Dragon in the Sea. 1980. lib. bdg. 13.95 (ISBN 0-8398-2646-X, Gregg). G K Hall.

--Dune Messiah. 1976. 14.95 (ISBN 0-399-10226-4). Putnam Pub Group.

--God Emperor of Dune. 432p. 1981. 12.95 (ISBN 0-399-12593-0). Putnam Pub Group.

--God Emperor of Dune. 1982. pap. 7.95 trade (ISBN 0-425-06128-0). Berkley Pub.

--God Emperor of Dune. 432p. 1983. pap. 3.95 mass (ISBN 0-425-06233-3). Berkley Pub.

--The Green Brain. 1981. PLB 13.95 (ISBN 0-8398-2667-2, Gregg). G K Hall.

--Whipping Star. 1980. pap. 13.95 (ISBN 0-8398-2648-6, Gregg). G K Hall.

--The White Plague. 400p. 1982. 14.95 (ISBN 0-399-12721-6); ltd. ed 50.00 (ISBN 0-399-12722-4). Putnam Pub Group.

--The Worlds of Frank Herbert. 1980. lib. bdg. 13.50 (ISBN 0-8398-2649-4, Gregg). G K Hall.

Herbert, Frank & Barnard, Max. Without Me You're Nothing: The Essential Guide to Home Computers. 1981. 14.95 o.p. (ISBN 0-671-41287-6). S&S.

Herbert, Frank, ed. Nebula Winners Fifteen. LC 78-645226. 256p. 1981. 13.41i (ISBN 0-06-014830-6, HarpT). Har-Row.

Herbert, George. Bodleian Manuscript of George Herbert's Poems. LC 81-18454. 1983. write for info (ISBN 0-8201-1373-5). Schol Facsimiles.

--Poems of George Herbert. 2nd ed. (World's Classics Ser: No. 109). 1961. 14.95 (ISBN 0-19-250109-7). Oxford U Pr.

--The Williams Manuscript of George Herbert's Poems. Charles, Amy, ed. LC 76-54153. 1977. 40.00x (ISBN 0-8201-1286-0). Schol Facsimilies.

--Works. Hutchinson, F. E., ed. (Oxford English Texts Ser.). 1941. 44.00x (ISBN 0-19-811812-0). Oxford U Pr.

Herbert, George, ed. The Latin Poetry of George Herbert: A Bilingual Edition. Murphy, Paul R. & McCloskey, Mark, trs. from Latin & Eng. LC 64-22888. vii, 181p. 1965. 10.95x o.p. (ISBN 0-8214-0007-X). Ohio U Pr.

Herbert, Ian, ed. Who's Who in the Theatre, 2 vols. 17th ed. 1500p. 1981. Set. 160.00x (ISBN 0-8103-0234-9). Gale.

--Who's Who in the Theatre: Biographies, Vol. 1. 17th ed. 1981. 96.00x (ISBN 0-8103-0235-7). Gale.

--Who's Who in the Theatre: Playbills, Vol. 2. 17th ed. 1981. 64.00x (ISBN 0-8103-0236-5). Gale.

Herbert, J. Conference Terminology in English, Spanish, Russian, Italian, German & Hungarian. 1976. 25.00 (ISBN 0-444-41354-5). Elsevier.

Herbert, James. The Dark. 1980. pap. 2.95 (ISBN 0-451-09403-4, E9403, Sig). NAL.

--The Survivor. 1977. pap. 2.50 (ISBN 0-451-11395-0, AE1395, Sig). NAL.

Herbert, Janice S. Oriental Rugs. Rev., Enl. ed. (Illus.). 176p. 1982. 20.75 (ISBN 0-02-551130-0). Macmillan.

Herbert, John, ed. Christie's Review of the Season, 1980. 1981. 45.00 (ISBN 0-8478-0354-6). Rizzoli Intl.

--Christie's Review of the Season 1982. (Illus.). 520p. 1982. 50.00 (ISBN 0-89659-320-7). Abbeville Pr.

Herbert, Joseph L., Jr., jt. auth. see Genthner, Henry.

Herbert, Kevin & Symeonoglou, Sarantis, eds. Ancient Collections in Washington University. LC 73-92729. (Illus.). 52p. 1973. pap. 2.00 (ISBN 0-686-84007-0). Wash U Gallery.

Herbert, Leo. Auditing the Performance of Management. LC 79-4551. 1979. 30.95 (ISBN 0-534-97998-X); ans. bk. 5.95 (ISBN 0-534-97997-1). Lifetime Learn.

Herbert, Marie. Winter of the White Seal. large type ed. LC 82-10339. 458p. 1982. Repr. of 1982 ed. 12.95 (ISBN 0-89621-378-1). Thorndike Pr.

Herbert, Martin. Conduct Disorders of Childhood & Adolescence: A Behavioral Approach to Assessment & Treatment. LC 77-9633. 1978. 44.00 o.p. (ISBN 0-471-99509-6, Pub. by Wiley-Interscience). Wiley.

--Psychology for Social Workers. (Psychology for Professional Groups Ser.). 350p. 1981. text ed. 25.00x (ISBN 0-333-31866-8, Pub. by Macmillan England); pap. text ed. 10.95x (ISBN 0-333-31878-1). Humanities.

Herbert, Miranda, jt. auth. see McNeil, Barbara.

Herbert, Miranda, jt. ed. see McNeil, Barbara.

Herbert, Miranda C. & McNeil, Barbara, eds. Biography & Genealogy Master Index: Supplement to the Second Edition, 3 Vols. rev. 2nd ed. 1982. 235.00x (ISBN 0-8103-1095-3). Gale.

--Biography & Geneology Master Index, 8 vols. 2nd ed. (Gale Biographical Index Ser.: No. 1). 1980. Set. 725.00x (ISBN 0-8103-1094-5). Gale.

Herbert, Miranda C., jt. ed. see McNeil, Barbara.

Herbert, Paul D. The Sincerest Form of Flattery: An Historical Survey of Parodies, Pastiches & Other Imitative Writings of Sherlock Holmes. LC 80-67699. (Sherlock Holmes Reference Ser.). 120p. 1983. 14.95 (ISBN 0-934468-04-4). Gaslight.

Herbert, Peter & Schiffer, Nancy. Chinese Export Porcelain. (Illus.). 27.50 (ISBN 0-916838-01-3). Wallace-Homestead.

Herbert, R. B. Biosynthesis of Secondary Metabolites. 1981. 32.00x (ISBN 0-412-16370-5, Pub. by Chapman & Hall England); pap. 14.95x (ISBN 0-412-16380-2). Methuen Inc.

Herbert, R. T. Paradox & Identity in Theology. LC 78-20784. 1979. 19.50x (ISBN 0-8014-1222-6). Cornell U Pr.

Herbert, Robert E., jt. auth. see Ekelund, Robert B.

Herbert, Theodore T. Dimensions of Organizational Behavior. 2nd ed. 513p. 1981. text ed. 24.95 (ISBN 0-02-353670-5). Macmillan.

Herbert, Theodore T. & Lorenzi, Peter. Experiential Organizational Behavior. 241p. 1981. pap. text ed. 9.95 (ISBN 0-02-353620-9). Macmillan.

Herbert, Theodore T. & Yost, Edward. Management Education & Development: An Annotated Resource Book. LC 77-91110. 1978. lib. bdg. 27.50 (ISBN 0-313-20040-8, HME/). Greenwood.

Herbert, Theodore T., jt. auth. see Fulmer, Robert M.

Herbert, Theodore T., ed. Organizational Behavior Reading & Cases. 2nd ed. 403p. 1981. pap. text ed. 13.95 (ISBN 0-02-353610-1). Macmillan.

Herbert, W. L. & Jarvis, F. J. Marriage Counselling in the Community. 1970. 8.75 o.p. (ISBN 0-08-006911-8); pap. 6.25 o.p. (ISBN 0-08-006910-X). Pergamon.

Herbert, Wally. Hunters of the Polar North: The Eskimos. (Peoples of the Wild Ser.). 1981. 15.96 (ISBN 0-7054-0701-2, Pub. by Time-Life). Silver.

Herbert, William. Amaryllidacea..&...a Treatise on Cross-Bred Vegetables. (Illus.). 1970. 64.00 (ISBN 3-7682-0672-6). Lubrecht & Cramer.

Herbert, Xavier. Poor Fellow My Country. 1466p. 1980. 17.95 o.p. (ISBN 0-312-63015-8). St Martin.

Herbic, Herbert J., jt. auth. see Cahill, Robert B.

Herbich, John B. Coastal & Deep Ocean Dredging. 622p. 1975. 39.95x (ISBN 0-87201-194-1). Gulf Pub.

Herbig, George H., ed. Spectroscopic Astrophysics: An Assessment of the Contributions of Otto Struve. LC 69-15939. 1970. 47.50x (ISBN 0-520-01410-3). U of Cal Pr.

Herbin, Robert & Rethacker, J. P. Soccer the Way the Pros Play. LC 77-79514. (Illus.). 256p. 1980. pap. 7.95 (ISBN 0-8069-8894-0). Sterling.

--Soccer the Way the Pros Play. LC 77-79514. (Illus.). 1978. 12.95 (ISBN 0-8069-4122-7); lib. bdg. 15.69 (ISBN 0-8069-4123-5). Sterling.

Herbold, Nancie, jt. auth. see Howard, Rosanne B.

Herbold, Nancy H., ed. see Howard, Rosanne B.

Herbst, John. Farm Management: Principles, Plan. Budgets. 1983. pap. text ed. 11.00x (ISBN 0-87563-229-7). Stipes.

Herbst, Judith. Sky Above & Worlds Beyond. LC 82-13749. (Illus.). 224p. (gr. 5 up). 1983. 13.95 (ISBN 0-689-30974-0). Atheneum.

Herbst, L. J. Discrete & Integrated Semiconductor Circuitry. 197p. 1969. 8.95x (ISBN 0-412-09360-X, Pub. by Chapman & Hall). Methuen Inc.

Herbst, P. G. Socio-Technical Design: Strategies in Multidisciplinary Research. 1974. 23.95x o.p. (ISBN 0-422-73980-4, Pub. by Tavistock England). Methuen Inc.

Herbst, Robert & Readett, Alan G. The Herbst Dictionaries of Commercial, Financial & Legal Terms, Vol. 3. (The Three-Language Ser.). 980p. 1982. text ed. 98.95x (ISBN 0-686-98023-9). Birkhauser.

Herbst, Robert & Readett, Alan G., eds. Herbst Dictionay of Commercial, Financial & Legal Terms. (Two-Language Ser.: Vol. A). 688p. (Eng. Ger.). 1975. text ed. 69.95 (ISBN 0-686-97268-6). Birkhauser.

Hercules, Costas. Selfishians, Otherishites & Fairishers: A Guide to Harmonious Relationships. (Illus.). 96p. 1982. 10.00 (ISBN 0-943900-01-8); pap. 5.95 (ISBN 0-943900-00-X). Fairisher Pr.

Hercus, L. A. Indological & Buddhist Studies. LC 81-71413. 692p. (Orig.). 1982. pap. text ed. 39.95 (ISBN 0-686-37605-6, 1187, Pub. by ANUP Australia). Bks Australia.

Herd, E. D., Jr. The South Carolina Upcountry, Fifteen Forty to Nineteen Eighty: Historical & Biographical Sketches, Vol. II. 308p. (Orig.). Date not set. pap. 9.95 (ISBN 0-686-92002-3). Attic Pr.

Herd, Shirley. Easy Spanish for the Yachtsman, RV'er, Motorist, Fisherman, Aviator, Traveler. (Illus.). 264p. (Orig., Span. & Eng. phonetic.). 1982. pap. text ed. 8.95 (ISBN 0-930006-01-1). S Deal Assoc.

Herda, D. J. Christmas. (First Bks.). (Illus.). 72p. (gr. 4 up). 1983. PLB 8.90 (ISBN 0-531-04524-2). Watts.

--Dirt Bike Racing. Anderson, Madelyn K., ed. (Illus.). 96p. (gr. 4-6). 1982. lib. bdg. 8.79 o.p. (ISBN 0-671-44249-X). Messner.

--Halloween. (First Bks.). (Illus.). 72p. (gr. 4 up). 1983. PLB 8.90 (ISBN 0-531-04527-7). Watts.

--Making a Native Plant Terrarium. LC 77-10583. (Illus.). 96p. (gr. 3 up). 1977. PLB 7.29 o.p. (ISBN 0-671-32880-8). Messner.

--Model Boats & Ships. (First Bks.). (Illus.). 72p. (gr. 4 up). 1982. PLB 8.90 (ISBN 0-531-04463-7). Watts.

--Model Cars & Trucks. LC 82-6887. (First Bks.). (Illus.). 72p. (gr. 4 up). 1982. PLB 8.90 (ISBN 0-531-04464-5). Watts.

--Model Railroads. (First Bks.). (Illus.). 72p. (gr. 4 up). 1982. PLB 8.90 (ISBN 0-531-04466-1). Watts.

--Roller Skating. (First Bks.). (Illus.). (gr. 4 up). 1979. PLB 8.90 s&l (ISBN 0-531-02262-5). Watts.

--Vegetables in a Pot. LC 78-23936. (Illus.). 96p. (gr. 3 up). 1979. PLB 8.29 o.p. (ISBN 0-671-32929-4). Messner.

Herdeck, Donald E., ed. African Authors: A Companion to Black African Writing 1300-1973, Vol. 1. LC 73-172338. (Illus.). 605p. 1973. 58.00x (ISBN 0-685-53608-4, Pub. by Black Orpheus Press). Gale.

Herdeg, Walter. Photographis Eighty-Three. (Illus.). 264p. 1983. 59.50 (ISBN 0-8038-5897-3). Hastings.

Herder, J. G. Abhandlung uber den Ursprung der Sprache. (Linguistics 13th-18th Centuries). 154p. (Fr.). 1974. Repr. of 1789 ed. lib. bdg. 47.00 o.p. (ISBN 0-8287-0001-X, 5046). Clearwater Pub.

Herder, Johann G. Outlines of a Philosophy of the History of Man. Churchill, T., tr. Repr. of 1800 ed. text ed. 27.50x o.p. (ISBN 0-391-02020-X). Humanities.

Herdman, John. Voice Without Restraint - Bob Dylan: A Study of the Lyrics & Their Background. LC 81-69870. 160p. (Orig.). 1982. pap. 8.95 (ISBN 0-933328-18-4). Delilah Bks.

Herdman, Margaret & Osborn, Jeanne. Classification. 3rd ed. LC 78-11079. 1978. pap. text ed. 5.00 (ISBN 0-8389-0277-4). ALA.

Herdman, Terry L., jt. ed. see Hannsgen, Kenneth B.

Herdog, Walter. Graphis Annual 1982-83: International Annual of Advertising & Editorial Graphics. (Illus.). 247p. (Eng., Fr. & Ger.). 1982. 59.50 (ISBN 0-686-97799-8). Hastings.

Herdt, Gilbert H. Guardians of the Flutes: Idioms of Masculinity. (Illus.). 1980. 19.95 (ISBN 0-07-028315-X). McGraw.

Herdt, Gilbert H., ed. Rituals of Manhood: Male Initiation in Papua New Guinea. 392p. 1982. 32.50x (ISBN 0-520-04448-7); pap. 10.95 (ISBN 0-520-04454-1). U of Cal Pr.

Herfindal, Eric T. & Hirschman, Joseph L. Clinical Pharmacy & Therapeutics. 2nd ed. (Illus.). 772p. 1979. 32.95 o.p. (ISBN 0-683-03961-X). Williams & Wilkins.

Herford, C. H., et al, eds. see Jonson, Ben.

Herford, Julius, jt. ed. see Decker, Harold A.

Herford, R. Travers, ed. The Ethics of the Talmud: Sayings of the Fathers. LC 62-13138. 1962. pap. 5.95 (ISBN 0-8052-0023-1). Schocken.

Herge. Land of Black Gold. (Adventures of Tintin). (Illus., Eng.). 1975. pap. 3.95 (ISBN 0-316-35844-4, Pub. by Atlantic Monthly Pr). Little.

Hergenhahn, B. R. An Introduction to the Theories of Personality. (Illus.). 1980. 23.95 (ISBN 0-13-498766-7). P-H.

--An Introduction to Theories of Learning. 2nd ed. 512p. 1982. 23.95 (ISBN 0-13-498725-X). P-H.

Hergert, Douglas. Mastering VisiCalc. 224p. 1982. pap. text ed. 11.95 (ISBN 0-89588-090-3). Sybex.

--Your Timex Sinclair 1000 & ZX81. 176p. 1982. pap. 6.95 (ISBN 0-89588-099-7). Sybex.

Hergert, Douglas, jt. auth. see Hergert, Richard.

Hergert, Richard & Hergert, Douglas. Doing Business with Pascal. 380p. 1982. pap. text ed. 16.95 (ISBN 0-89588-091-1). Sybex.

Herget, C., jt. auth. see Michel, A.

Heriman, Anderson. Package of Love for Young & Old. 1980. 3.50 (ISBN 0-934860-12-2). Adventure Pubns.

Herington, J., jt. ed. see Gould, T.

Herington, Sharon. Activities for Rainy Days & Sundays. 1982. pap. 3.50 (ISBN 0-8341-0786-4). Beacon Hill.

Heriot, Angus. The Castrati in Opera. LC 74-1332. (Music Ser.). 243p. 1974. Repr. of 1956 ed. lib. bdg. 25.00 (ISBN 0-306-70650-4). Da Capo.

--The Castrati in Opera. LC 74-22310. (Music Reprint Ser). (Illus.). 243p. 1975. pap. 5.75 (ISBN 0-306-80003-9). Da Capo.

Heritage Home Plans, Inc. Luxury Home Plans. LC 79-2769. (Illus.). 1980. pap. 7.95 o.p. (ISBN 0-15-654309-5, Harv). HarBraceJ.

Heriteau, Jacqueline. Best of Electric Crockery Cooking. (Illus.). 256p. 1976. 4.95 (ISBN 0-448-12156-5, G&D). Putnam Pub Group.

--Oriental Cooking the Fast Wok Way. 1977. pap. 2.50 (ISBN 0-451-12052-3, AE2052, Sig). NAL.

Heritte-Viardot, Louise. Memories & Adventures. LC 77-22220. (Music Reprint Ser.). (Illus.). 1978. Repr. of 1913 ed. lib. bdg. 29.50 (ISBN 0-306-77515-8). Da Capo.

Herken, Gregg. Accidental Nuclear War: On the Brink of a Holocaust? (Vital Issues Ser.: Vol. XXXI, No. 8). 0.80 (ISBN 0-686-84147-6). Ctr Info Am.

Herkimer, Allen B., Jr. Patient Account Management. LC 82-16318. 293p. 1982. 28.50 (ISBN 0-89443-835-2). Aspen Systems.

Herkless, John L., ed. see Rein, G. A.

Herlevich, F. Ann, jt. auth. see Waddington, D.

Herlick, Stanford D. California Workers' Compensation Law Handbook, 2 vols. 2nd ed. 1064p. 1981. Set. incl. 1983 suppl. 92.00 (ISBN 0-911110-25-9). Parker & Son.

Herlihy, David, ed. Medieval Culture & Society. (Documentary History of Western Civilization). (Orig.). 1968. pap. 7.95xi (ISBN 0-06-131340-8, TB1340, Torch). Har-Row.

Herlin, Hans. Solo Run. LC 82-45145. 288p. 1983. 15.95 (ISBN 0-385-17621-X). Doubleday.

Herling, Gustaw. A World Apart. Marek, Joseph, tr. LC 74-7538. (Illus.). 262p. 1974. Repr. of 1951 ed. lib. bdg. 16.25x (ISBN 0-8371-7581-X, HEWA). Greenwood.

Herlinger. Clinical Radiology of the Liver, Pts. A & B. (Diagnostic Radiology Ser.: Vol. 1). 1983. 295.00 set (ISBN 0-8247-1069-X). Vol. A. 542 p. Vol. B 656 p. Dekker.

Hermalin, Jared & Morrell, Jonathan A., eds. Evaluation & Prevention in Human Services. LC 81-7001. (Prevention in Human Services Ser.: Vol. 1, Nos. 1 & 2). 128p. 1982. text ed. 20.00 (ISBN 0-917724-61-5, B61). Haworth Pr.

Hermalin, Jared, jt. ed. see Hess, Robert.

Hermalyn, Gary, ed. see Mead, Edna.

Herman, A. L. & Blackwood, R. T., eds. Problems in Philosophy: West & East. 544p. 1975. 22.95 (ISBN 0-13-719708-X). P-H.

Herman, Arnold, et al, eds. Cardiovascular Pharmacology of the Prostaglandins. (Vol. 7). 472p. 1982. text ed. 60.50 (ISBN 0-89004-629-8). Raven.

Herman, Daniel J. The Philosophy of Henri Bergson. LC 80-5044. 117p. 1979. text ed. 19.00 o.p. (ISBN 0-8191-1029-9); pap. text ed. 8.25 o.p. (ISBN 0-8191-1030-2). U Pr of Amer.

Herman, E. Edward. Collective Bargaining & Labor Relations. (Illus.). 576p. 1981. text ed. 23.95 (ISBN 0-13-140558-6). P-H.

Herman, E. Edward & Skinner, Gordon S. Labor Law: Cases, Text, & Legislation. LC 81-40786. 368p. 1981. pap. text ed. 13.50 (ISBN 0-8191-1821-4). U Pr of Amer.

Herman, Edward S. Corporate Control, Corporate Power: A Twentieth Century Fund Study. LC 80-29447. (Illus.). 336p. 1982. 24.95 (ISBN 0-521-23996-6); pap. 9.95 (ISBN 0-521-28907-6). Cambridge U Pr.

Herman, Esther, jt. ed. see Wasserman, Paul.

Herman, G. T. & Rozenberg, G. Developmental Systems & Languages. LC 74-80114. 363p. 1975. 59.75 (ISBN 0-444-10650-2, North-Holland). Elsevier.

Herman, Gary. Burt Reynolds: Flesh & Blood Fantasy. (Illus.). 144p. (Orig.). 1983. pap. 9.95 (ISBN 0-933328-64-8). Delilah Bks.

--Rock 'N' Roll Babylon. (Illus.). 192p. 1982. 19.95 (ISBN 0-698-11168-0, Coward). Putnam Pub Group.

--Rock 'n' Roll Babylon. LC 82-80094. (Illus.). 192p. 1982. 9.95 (ISBN 0-399-50641-1, Perige). Putnam Pub Group.

Herman, Gary, jt. auth. see Dowing, David.

Herman, H. & Tu, K. N., eds. Treatise on Materials Science & Technology, Vol. 24. 306p. 1982. 48.00 (ISBN 0-12-341824-0). Acad Pr.

Herman, Herbert, ed. Treatise on Materials Science & Technology: Embrittlement of Engineering Alloys, Vol. 25. (Serial Publication). Date not set. price not set (ISBN 0-12-341825-9). Acad Pr.

Herman, Herbert & Tomozawa, Minoru, eds. Treatise on Materials Science & Technology: Vol. 22, Glass III. LC 77-378180. 1982. 48.00 (ISBN 0-12-341822-4). Acad Pr.

Herman, Jan, ed. see Gysin, Brion.

Herman, Jerry. And Death Won't Come: Three Short Stories. 1976. pap. 1.50 (ISBN 0-916692-07-8). Black River.

--A Time in Their Lives. 384p. 1973. pap. text ed. 12.50 scp o.p. (ISBN 0-06-383630-0, HarpC). Har-Row.

Herman, Jill, jt. auth. see Rossant, Colette.

Herman, John R. Handbook of Urology. (Illus.). 350p. 1982. pap. text ed. 19.50 (Harper Medical). Lippincott.

Herman, John R. & Goldberg, Richard A. Sun, Weather, & Climate. LC 79-22363. (Illus.). 1980. Repr. of 1978 ed. 40.00x (ISBN 0-8103-1018-X). Gale.

Herman, Judith. Father-Daughter Incest. LC 81-2534. (Illus.). 285p. 1981. 15.95 (ISBN 0-674-29505-6); pap. 7.95 (ISBN 0-674-29506-4). Harvard U Pr.

Herman, Lloyd. American Porcelain. (Illus.). 150p. 1980. pap. 14.95 (ISBN 0-917304-60-8). Timber.

Herman, Magaretha G., jt. auth. see Donovan, Dennis G.

Herman, Marian A., jt. ed. see Merman, Marian A.

Herman, Masako. The Japanese in America, 1843-1973: A Chronology & Factbook. LC 74-13106. (Ethnic Chronology Ser.: No. 15). 152p. (gr. 9-12). 1974. text ed. 8.50 (ISBN 0-379-00512-3). Oceana.

Herman, P. G., ed. Iatrogenic Thoracic Complications. (Radiology of Iatrogenic Disorders Ser.). (Illus.). 243p. 1983. 54.90 (ISBN 0-387-90729-7). Springer-Verlag.

Herman, Peter, jt. auth. see Polivy, Janet.

Herman, Stephen A., et al. Natural Gas Users' Handbook. LC 76-27247. 122p. 1976. 12.50 o.p. (ISBN 0-87179-236-2). BNA.

Herman, V. & Van Schendelen, M. P. The European Parliament & the National Parliaments. 1978. text ed. 31.50x (ISBN 0-566-00251-5). Gower Pub Ltd.

Herman, Valentine & Hagger, Mark. The Legislation of Direct Elections to the European Parliament. 1979. text ed. 36.00 (ISBN 0-566-00247-7). Gower Pub Ltd.

Herman, Valentine & Lodge, Juliet. The European Parliament & the European Community. 1978. 25.00x (ISBN 0-312-27074-7). St Martin.

Herman, Valentine & Alt, James E., eds. Cabinet Studies: A Reader. LC 75-2952. 320p. 1975. 22.50 o.p. (ISBN 0-312-11305-6). St Martin.

Herman, Victor. Coming Out of the Ice: An Unexpected Life. LC 78-14075. (Illus.). 1979. 14.95 (ISBN 0-15-143288-0). HarBraceJ.

Herman, William P. A Look into BASIC Using CP-6. 64p. 1982. pap. text ed. 3.95 (ISBN 0-8403-2761-7). Kendall-Hunt.

Hermann, A. H. Conflicts of National Laws with International Business Activity: Issues of Extraterritoriality. (British-North America Committee Ser.). 104p. 1982. pap. 6.00 (ISBN 0-902594-41-9, BN30-NPA195). Natl Planning.

Hermann, Henry. Social Insects, Vol. 3. 459p. 1982. 58.00 (ISBN 0-12-342203-5). Acad Pr.

Hermann, Henry R. Social Insects, Vol. 4. 385p. 1982. 52.00 (ISBN 0-12-342204-3). Acad Pr.

Hermann, Janet S. The Pursuit of a Dream. LC 82-40416. 290p. 1983. pap. 5.95 (Vin). Random.

Hermann, Michele G. & Haft, Marilyn G. Prisoners' Rights Sourcebook: Theory-Litigation-Practice, Vol. 1. LC 73-82906. 1973. 50.00 (ISBN 0-87632-100-7). Boardman.

Hermann, Michele G., ed. Federal Rules of Criminal Procedure. 2nd ed. LC 80-10646. 1980. looseleaf with 1981 rev. pages 45.00 (ISBN 0-87632-106-6). Boardman.

Hermann, Placid, ed. see Francis of Assisi, Saint.

Hermann, Robert. Diffferential Geometry & the Calculus of Variations. 2nd ed. LC 68-14664. (Intermath Ser.: No. 17). 1977. 48.00 (ISBN 0-915692-23-6). Math Sci Pr.

Hermanns, William. Einstein & the Poet: In Search of the Cosmic Man. 1983. 16.50 (ISBN 0-8283-1851-4); pap. 10.00 (ISBN 0-8283-1873-5). Branden.

Hermans, J. J. Polymer Solution Properties: Part II, Hydrodynamics & Light Scattering. LC 78-820. (Benchmark Papers in Polymer Chemistry Ser. Vol. 2). 294p. 1978. 52.50 (ISBN 0-87933-323-5); 84.50 set (ISBN 0-87933-094-5). Hutchinson Ross.

Hermans, J. J., ed. Polymer Solution Properties: Part I, Statistics & Thermodynamics. LC 87-820. (Benchmark Papers in Polymer Chemistry: Vol. 1). 234p. 1978. 41.50 (ISBN 0-87933-322-7); 84.50 (ISBN 0-87933-094-5). Hutchinson Ross.

Hermanson, Renee. Raspberry Kingdom. LC 78-62985. 1978. pap. 4.50 (ISBN 0-8358-0374-0). Upper Room.

Hermanson, Roger H., jt. auth. see Edwards, James D.

Hermassi, Elbaki. The Third World Reassessed. LC 78-62848. 1980. 14.95x (ISBN 0-520-03764-2). U of Cal Pr.

Hermassi, Karen. Polity & Theatre in Historical Perspective. LC 76-19971. 1977. 23.00x (ISBN 0-520-03294-2). U of Cal Pr.

Hermens, W. T. Quantification of Circulating Proteins. 1983. 44.00 (ISBN 90-247-2755-3, Pub. by Martinus Nijhoff Netherlands). Kluwer Boston.

Hermes, Eberhard, ed. see Alfonsi, Petrus.

Hermes, Patricia. Nobody's Fault. 112p. (gr. 5 up). 1983. pap. 1.75 (ISBN 0-440-46523-0, YB). Dell.

--Who Will Take Care of Me? LC 82-48757. 128p. (gr. 8-12). 10.95 (ISBN 0-15-296265-4, HJ). HarBraceJ.

Hermet, Guy, et al, eds. Elections Without Choice. LC 77-16116. 256p. 1978. 29.95x o.s.i. (ISBN 0-470-99292-1). Halsted Pr.

Hermite, P. L' see L'Hermite, P. & Handtschutter, J.

Hermlin, Stephan. Evening Light. Dvorak, Paul F., tr. from Ger. Orig. Title: Abendlicht. 128p. (Orig.). 1983. pap. 6.95 (ISBN 0-940242-03-6). Fjord Pr.

Hern, Nicholas. Peter Handke. LC 76-190349. (Literature and Life Ser.). 1972. 11.95 (ISBN 0-8044-2380-6). Ungar.

Hernandez, Carrol A., et al. Chicanos: Social & Psychological Perspectives. 2nd ed. LC 75-37769. (Illus.). 376p. 1976. pap. 12.00 o.p. (ISBN 0-8016-5316-9). Mosby.

Hernandez, David & Page, Carole G. La Familia del Cirujano. 272p. Date not set. 3.25 (ISBN 0-88113-090-7). Edit Betania.

Hernandez, Ernie, Jr. Police Handbook for Applying the Systems Approach & Computer Technology. LC 82-17662. (Illus.). 231p. 1982. 26.95 (ISBN 0-910657-00-9); pap. 19.95 (ISBN 0-910657-01-7). Frontline.

Hernandez, Jose. Martin Fierro. Carrino, Frank G. & Carlos, Alberto J., eds. Ward, Catherine E., tr. LC 67-63759. (Illus., Eng. & Span.). 1967. 44.50x (ISBN 0-87395-026-7). State U NY Pr.

Hernandez, Jose A. Mutual Aid for Survival: The Case of the Mexican-American. LC 82-21246. 1983. lib. bdg. 11.50 (ISBN 0-89874-546-2). Krieger.

Hernandez, Pedro L. There Is No Tomorrow. 1978. 5.95 o.p. (ISBN 0-533-03027-7). Vantage.

Hernandez, Ramon. Something is Happening Here. LC 82-61182. 300p. (Orig.). 1983. pap. 15.00 (ISBN 0-89295-025-0). Society Sp & Sp-Am.

Hernando Fernandez, V. Fertilizers, Crop Quality & Economy. 1400p. 1975. 138.50 (ISBN 0-444-41277-8). Elsevier.

Herndon, Booton. Mary Pickford & Douglas Fairbanks: The Most Popular Couple the World Has Known. (Illus.). 1977. 9.95 o.p. (ISBN 0-393-07508-7). Norton.

--Unlikeliest Hero. (Destiny Ser.). 199p. 1982. pap. 4.95 (ISBN 0-8163-0527-7). Pacific Pr Pub Assn.

Herndon, Gene. Professor Metaphor's Weekly Bingo, No. 2. (Illus.). 128p. 1982. pap. 1.75 (ISBN 0-448-17087-6, Pub. by Tempo). Ace Bks.

Herndon, James. How to Survive in Your Native Land. 1971. 6.95 o.p. (ISBN 0-671-20864-0, Touchstone Bks). S&S.

--Sorrowless Times. 1981. 12.95 o.s.i. (ISBN 0-671-24321-7). S&S.

--Way It Spozed to Be. LC 68-12171. 1968. 6.95 o.p. (ISBN 0-671-79846-4). S&S.

--The Way It Spozed to Be. 1977. pap. 3.95 o.p. (ISBN 0-671-23028-X, Touchstone Bks). S&S.

Herndon, Venable. James Dean: A Short Life. 1975. pap. 1.50 o.p. (ISBN 0-451-06518-2, W6518, Sig). NAL.

Herndon, William H. Life of Lincoln. LC 82-73435. 511p. Repr. of 1942 ed. lib. bdg. 37.50x (ISBN 0-88116-005-9). Brenner Bks.

Hernes, Helga, ed. The Multinational Corporation: A Guide to Information Sources. LC 73-17509. (International Relations Information Guide Series: Vol. 4). 1977. 42.00x (ISBN 0-8103-1327-8). Gale.

Hernon, Peter. Use of Government Publications by Social Scientists. LC 79-16144. (Libraries & Librarianship Ser.). 1979. 22.50x (ISBN 0-89391-024-4). Ablex Pub.

Hernon, Peter, jt. auth. see Ching-hih Chen.

Hernon, Peter, ed. Communicating Public Access to Government Information. 100p. 1983. 35.00X (ISBN 0-930466-59-4). Meckler Pub.

Hernon, Peter, et al. Increased User Access to Government Publications. (Libraries & Information Science Ser.). 1983. write for info. (ISBN 0-89391-100-3). Ablex Pub.

Hero, Alfred O. & Barratt, John, eds. The American People & South Africa: Publics, Elites & Policymaking Processes. LC 80-8632. 240p. 1981. 22.95x (ISBN 0-669-04320-6). Lexington Bks.

Hero, Alfred O., Jr., jt. ed. see Beigie, Carl E.

Herold, Ann B. The Helping Day. (Illus.). 32p. (gr. k-2). 1980. 7.95 (ISBN 0-698-20492-1, Coward). Putnam Pub Group.

Herold, J. Christopher. The Battle of Waterloo. LC 67-15416. (Horizon Caravel Bks.). 154p. (YA) (gr. 7 up). 1967. 12.95 o.p. (ISBN 0-06-022307-3, HarpJ). Har-Row.

Herold, Mort. You Can Have a Near-Perfect Memory. (Illus.). 272p. 1983. pap. 7.95 (ISBN 0-8092-5942-7). Contemp Bks.

Heron, Alastair & Myers, Mary, eds. Intellectual Impairment. Date not set. price not set (ISBN 0-12-342680-4). Acad Pr.

Heron, Ann, ed. One Teenager in Ten: Writings by Gay & Lesbian Youth. 120p. (gr. 7-12). 1983. pap. 3.95 (ISBN 0-932870-26-0). Alyson Pubns.

Heron, Gayle A. Twenty-Six Species of Oncaeidae (Copepoda: Cyclopoida) from the Southwest Pacific--Antarctic Area: Paper 2 in Biology of the Antarctic Seas IV. Pawson, David L., ed. LC 77-2302. (Antarctic Research Ser.: Vol. 26). 1977. pap. 28.25 (ISBN 0-87590-130-1). Am Geophysical.

Heron, Michael, tr. see Lindgren, Astrid.

Heron, Michael, tr. see Von Daniken, Erich.

Heron, S. D., jt. auth. see Schlaifer, R.

Heron, Shaun. Aladale. 1979. pap. 2.50 o.p. (ISBN 0-451-08882-4, E8882, Sig). NAL.

Herpy, Miklos. Analog Integrated Circuits: Operational Amplifiers & Analog Multipliers. LC 77-21008. 479p. 1980. 71.95 (ISBN 0-471-99604-1, Pub. by Wiley-Interscience). Wiley.

Herr, David, jt. auth. see Haydock, Roger.

Herr, Edward, jt. auth. see Evans, Rupert.

Herr, Edwin L. Decision-Making & Vocational Development. (Guidance Monograph). pap. 2.40 o.p. (ISBN 0-395-09940-4, 9-78840). HM.

--Guidance & Counseling in the Schools: Perspective on the Past, Present & Future. 1979. 8.00 (ISBN 0-686-36370-1, 72124); nonmembers 9.25 (ISBN 0-686-37293-X). Am Personnel.

Herr, Edwin L. & Moore, Roberta. Your Working Life: A Guide to Getting & Holding a Job. LC 79-28360. Orig. Title: Career Education. (Illus.). 464p. 1980. 15.96 (ISBN 0-07-028342-7, G); tchrs. manual 3.50 (ISBN 0-07-028344-3); student wkbk. 6.96 (ISBN 0-07-028343-5). McGraw.

Herr, Edwin L., ed. Schools & Careers. (Cooperative Work Experience Education for Careers Program). (Illus.). (gr. 11-12). 1976. pap. text ed. 7.96 (ISBN 0-07-028325-7, G); tchr's manual & key 3.50 (ISBN 0-07-028326-5). McGraw.

--Vocational Guidance & Human Development. LC 81-40850. 608p. 1982. lib. bdg. 30.75 (ISBN 0-8191-1955-5); pap. text ed. 19.75 (ISBN 0-8191-1956-3). U Pr of Amer.

Herr, Edwin L., ed. see Fruehling, Rosemary T.

Herr, Edwin L., ed. see Kidwell, William M., et al.

Herr, Edwin L., ed. see Lynch, Richard L.

Herr, Edwin L., ed. see Weagraff, Patrick J. & Lynn, James J.

Herr, Edwin L., ed. see Wilson, Maurice.

Herr, Ethel. Bible Study for Busy Women. 160p. 1983. pap. 6.95 (ISBN 0-8024-0147-3). Moody.

--Chosen Families of the Bible. LC 81-9510. 96p. 1981. pap. 3.95 (ISBN 0-8024-1298-X). Moody.

--Chosen Women of the Bible. LC 75-36503. 96p. (Orig.). 1976. pap. 3.95 (ISBN 0-8024-1297-1). Moody.

--Growing up Is a Family Affair. LC 78-17581. 1978. pap. 5.95 (ISBN 0-8024-3359-6). Moody.

--Schools: How Parents Can Make a Difference. LC 81-11034. 224p. 1981. pap. 6.95 (ISBN 0-8024-1163-0). Moody.

Herr, Michael. Dispatches. 1978. pap. 2.95 (ISBN 0-380-40196-7, 58255). Avon.

Herr, Richard. An Historical Essay on Modern Spain. 1974. pap. 8.95x (ISBN 0-520-02534-2). U of Cal Pr.

Herr, Selma E. Effective Reading for Adults. 3rd ed. 304p. 1970. pap. text ed. write for info. o.p. (ISBN 0-697-06170-1). Wm C Brown.

Herr, Stanley S. Rights & Advocacy for Retarded People. LC 81-47573. 1983. write for info. (ISBN 0-669-04682-5). Lexington Bks.

Herr, Stanley S. & Arons, Stephen. Legal Rights & Mental-Health Care. Talbot, J., frwd. by. LC 81-47823. 1983. write for info. (ISBN 0-669-04910-7). Lexington Bks.

Herreid, Clyde F. Biology. (Illus.). 1978. 23.95x (ISBN 0-02-353780-9). Macmillan.

Herrera, A. O., et al. Catastrophe or New Society: A Latin American World Model. 108p. 1976. pap. 8.75 (ISBN 0-88936-083-9, IDRC64, IDRC). Unipub.

Herrera, Hayden. Frida: A Biography of Frida Kahlo. LC 80-8688. (Illus.). 256p. 1983. write for info (ISBN 0-06-011843-1, HarpT). Har-Row.

Herrera, L. Catalogue of the Orthoptera of Spain. 1982. 37.00 (ISBN 90-6193-131-2, Pub. by Junk Pubs Netherlands). Kluwer Boston.

Herrera, R., jt. auth. see Robertson, C. P.

Herrera, R. A. Anselm's Proslogion: An Introduction. LC 79-66421. 1979. pap. text ed. 9.50 (ISBN 0-8191-0825-1). U Pr of Amer.

Herreshoff, Halsey C., ed. The Sailor's Handbook. (Illus.). 224p. 1983. 14.45i (ISBN 0-316-54693-3). Little.

Herrick. Experiments in Electronic Circuits. 1968. text ed. 17.95 (ISBN 0-675-09679-0). Merrill.

Herrick, Bruce & Hudson, Barclay. Urban Poverty & Economic Development: A Case Study of Costa Rica. LC 79-29713. 1980. 25.00 (ISBN 0-312-83459-4). St Martin.

Herrick, Bruce, jt. auth. see Kindleberger, C.

Herrick, Bruce, jt. auth, see Kindleberger, Charles H.

Herrick, C. Electrical Wiring: Principles & Practices. 1975. ref. ed. 23.95 (ISBN 0-13-247676-2). P-H.

Herrick, C. N. Instruments & Measurements for Electronics. 1971. 19.05 o.p. (ISBN 0-07-028367-2, G). McGraw.

Herrick, Clyde N. Audio Systems. LC 74-9696. 1974. 21.95 (ISBN 0-87909-049-9). Reston.

--Electronic Service Instruments. (Illus.). 224p. 1974. 21.95 (ISBN 0-13-251868-6). P-H.

--Radio: Theory & Servicing. (Illus.). 288p. 1975. 18.95 (ISBN 0-87909-697-7). Reston.

Herrick, E. C., et al. Unit Process Guide to Organic Chemical Industries. LC 79-89444. (Unit Process Ser. - Organic Chemical Industries: Vol. 1). 1979. 29.95 (ISBN 0-250-40328-5). Ann Arbor Science.

Herrick, Robert. Selected Poems. Jesson-Dibley, David, ed. (Fyfield Ser.). 90p. 1980. pap. 5.25x (ISBN 0-85635-320-5, Pub. by Carcanet New Pr England). Humanities.

Herrick, Tracy G. Bank Analysts Handbook. LC 78-987. 1978. 55.00 (ISBN 0-471-02025-7, Pub. by Wiley-Interscience). Wiley.

Herrick, Virgil E. Strategies of Curriculum Development: The Works of Virgil E. Herrick. Macdonald, James & Andersen, Dan W., eds. LC 74-1781. 196p. 1975. Repr. of 1965 ed. lib. bdg. 20.50x (ISBN 0-8371-7400-7, HECD). Greenwood.

Herrick, William. Hermanos. LC 82-40437. 334p. 1983. Repr. of 1969 ed. 16.95 (ISBN 0-933256-38-8). Second Chance.

--Love & Terror. LC 80-25140. 256p. 1981. 13.95 (ISBN 0-8112-0791-9); pap. 5.95 (ISBN 0-8112-0841-9, NDP538). New Directions.

Herrigel, Gustie L. Zen in the Art of Flower Arrangement: An Introduction to the Spirit of the Japanese Art of Flower Arrangement. 1974. 12.50 (ISBN 0-7100-7941-9); pap. 6.95 (ISBN 0-7100-7942-7). Routledge & Kegan.

Herrin, Kym & Benyo, Richard. Sexercise. (Illus.). 220p. 1982. 14.95 (ISBN 0-89037-226-8). Anderson World.

Herring, Chuck & Herring, Judy. Offical GED Handbook. rev. ed. (The GED Institute's Offical GED Preparation Ser.). Orig. Title: The GED Handbook. (Illus.). 96p. (gr. 8-12). 1982. write for info (ISBN 0-937128-06-6). GED Inst.

Herring, George C. America's Longest War: The U. S. & Vietnam 1950 to 1975. LC 79-16408. (America in Crisis Ser.). 1979. text ed. 14.95 o.p. (ISBN 0-471-01546-6); pap. text ed. 9.95x o.p. (ISBN 0-471-01547-4). Wiley.

Herring, George C., ed. The Secret Diplomacy of the Vietnam War: The Negotiation Volumes of the Pentagon Papers. 928p. 1983. text ed. 47.50x (ISBN 0-292-77573-3). U of Tex Pr.

Herring, Harriet L. Welfare Work in Mill Villages: The Story of Extra-Mill Activities in North Carolina. LC 68-55773. (Criminology, Law Enforcement, & Social Problems Ser.: No. 20). 1968. Repr. of 1929 ed. 17.00x (ISBN 0-87585-020-0). Patterson Smith.

Herring, Hubert. History of Latin America. 3rd ed. (YA) 1968. l 29.95 (ISBN 0-394-42870-6); ref. 25.00 (ISBN 0-394-30247-8). Knopf.

Herring, James E. School Librarianship. 1982. 13.00 (ISBN 0-85157-347-9, Pub. by Bingley England). Shoe String.

Herring, Judy, jt. auth. see Herring, Chuck.

Herring, Marguerite B. The Wedding Organizer or How to Plan a Smooth Trip Down the Aisle. rev. ed. LC 82-81574. 157p. 1982. pap. 6.95 (ISBN 0-931948-36-3). Peachtree Pubs.

Herring, Marquetta, ed. Mesquite, Texas, U. S. A. Stories & Poems from a Rodeo Town. (Illus.). 100p. (Orig.). 1982. pap. write for info. (ISBN 0-942186-00-1). Paperbacks Plus.

Herring, R. J. & Marston, R. C. National Monetary Policies & International Financial Markets. (Contributions to Economic Analysis Ser.: Vol. 104). 1977. 59.75 (ISBN 0-7204-0519-X, North-Holland). Elsevier.

Herring, Ronald J. Land to the Tiller: The Political Economy of Agrarian Reform in South Asia. LC 82-48903. (Illus.). 336p. 1983. text ed. 30.00x (ISBN 0-300-02725-7). Yale U Pr.

Herringshaw, Thomas W., ed. Local & National Poets of America: With Interesting Biographical Sketches & Choice Selections From Over One Thousand Living American Poets. 1036p. 1982. Repr. of 1890 ed. lib. bdg. 150.00 (ISBN 0-89760-021-5). Telegraph Bks.

Herrington, M., jt. auth. see Hanson, D.

Herrington, Pat, jt. auth. see Ewens, Jim.

Herrington, Roland E. Alcohol & Drug Abuse Handbook. (Allied Health Professions Monograph). 1983. 17.00 (ISBN 0-87527-274-6). Green.

Herriot, James. All Creatures Great & Small & All Things Bright & Beautiful. (Illus.). 1976. 19.95 o.p. (ISBN 0-312-01925-4). St Martin.

--All Things Bright & Beautiful. LC 73-87407. 400p. 1974. 13.95 (ISBN 0-312-02030-9). St Martin.

--All Things Wise & Wonderful. 1977. lib. bdg. 17.95 o.p. (ISBN 0-8161-6525-4, Large Print Bks). G K Hall.

--All Things Wise & Wonderful. LC 77-76640. 1977. 13.95 (ISBN 0-312-02031-7). St Martin.

--James Herriot's Yorkshire. 1979. 17.95 (ISBN 0-312-43970-9). St Martin.

--James Herriot's Yorkshire. (Illus.). 224p. 1981. pap. 10.95 (ISBN 0-312-43971-7). St Martin.

Herriot, James, et al. Animals Tame & Wild. Phelps, Gilbert & Phelps, John, eds. LC 78-57781. (Illus.). 1979. 16.95 o.p. (ISBN 0-8069-3098-5); lib. bdg. 14.99 o.p. (ISBN 0-8069-3099-3). Sterling.

Herriot, Peter. Language & Teaching: A Psychological View. 1971. 7.50x (ISBN 0-416-65200-X); pap. 5.95x (ISBN 0-416-65210-7). Methuen Inc.

Herriot, Peter, et al. Organization & Memory. 1973. pap. 3.50x o.p. (ISBN 0-416-77590-X). Methuen Inc.

Herriott, James. Illustrated Textbook of Dog Diseases. (Illus.). 284p. 1980. 12.95 (ISBN 0-87666-733-7, PS-770). TFH Pubns.

Herriott, Peter. An Introduction to the Psychology of Language. 1976. pap. 7.95x (ISBN 0-416-85500-8). Methuen Inc.

Herriott, Robert E. & Gross, Neal, eds. The Dynamics of Planned Educational Change: Case Studies & Analyses. LC 78-61456. 1979. 21.25 (ISBN 0-8211-0761-5); text ed. 19.25 ten or more copies (ISBN 0-685-59768-7). McCutchan.

Herrmann, Dorothy. With Malice Toward All: The Quips, Lives & Loves of Some Celebrated 20th-Century American Wits. LC 81-15819. (Illus.). 235p. 1982. 14.95 (ISBN 0-399-12710-0). Putnam Pub Group.

Herrmann, Elizabeth R. & Spitz, Edna H., eds. German Women Writers of the Twentieth Century. LC 78-40139. 1978. text ed. write for info. (ISBN 0-08-021827-X). Pergamon.

Herrmann, Ernest C., Jr., ed. Conference on Antiviral Substances, Third, Vol. 284. (Annals of the New York Academy of Sciences). 720p. 1977. 58.00x (ISBN 0-89072-030-4). NY Acad Sci.

Herrmann, Frank, jt. auth. see Davies, Hunter.

Herrmann, G. & Perrone, N., eds. The Dynamic Response of Structures. 1973. 55.00 (ISBN 0-08-016850-7). Pergamon.

Herrmann, Nina. Go Out in Joy. LC 76-44972. 1977. 7.95 o.p. (ISBN 0-8042-2073-5). John Knox.

Herrmann, Robert O., jt. auth. see Jelley, Herbert M.

Herrmann, Roland, jt. auth. see Alkemade, Cornelis T.

Herrmann, Siegfried. A History of Israel in Old Testament Times. Bowden, John, tr. from Ger. LC 74-24918. 384p. 1975. 15.50x o.p. (ISBN 0-8006-0405-9, 1-405). Fortress.

Herrmann, William J., jt. auth. see Stevens, Wendelle.

Herrnstadt, Richard L., ed. Letters of A. Bronson Alcott. LC 76-76209. (Illus.). 1969. 21.50x (ISBN 0-8138-0087-0). Iowa St U Pr.

Herron, Bob. Moritz! 220p. 1983. pap. text ed. 6.95 (ISBN 0-930762-06-1). Calamus Bks.

Herron, Don. Dashiell Hammett Tour. 2nd ed. (Herron's Literary Walks in San Francisco Ser.). (Illus.). 98p. (Orig.). 1982. pap. 6.95 (ISBN 0-939790-02-5). Dawn Heron.

--San Francisco Mysteries: A Survey & Checklist 1874-1982. (Illus.). 40p. (Orig.). 1983. pap. 5.00 (ISBN 0-939790-03-3). Dawn Heron.

Herron, Dudley. Understanding Chemistry. Incl. Kean, Elizabeth. wkbk. 7.00 (ISBN 0-394-32423-4); Copes, Jane. lab manual 8.00 (ISBN 0-394-32437-4). 515p. 1981. text ed. 19.00 (ISBN 0-394-32087-5). Random.

Herron, J. Dudley. Preparation for General Chemistry. 1980. text ed. 19.00x (ISBN 0-394-32087-5). Random.

Herron, J. Dudley, et al. A Summary of Research in Science Education, 1974. (A Supplement Volume of Science Education Ser.). 1976. pap. 14.95 o.s.i. (ISBN 0-471-05189-6, Pub. by Wiley-Interscience). Wiley.

Herron, Jim, jt. auth. see Chrisman, Harry E.

Herron, Shaun. The Ruling Passion. (Orig.). 1978. pap. 2.25 o.p. (ISBN 0-451-08042-4, E8042, Sig). NAL.

Hersch, Giselle & Mann, Peggy. Giselle, Save the Children. LC 79-51194. 288p. 1980. 12.95 (ISBN 0-89696-054-4, An Everest House Book). Dodd.

Herschdoerfer, S. M. Quality Control in the Food Industry. Vol.1. 1967. 61.00 o.s.i. (ISBN 0-12-342901-3); Vol. 2. 1968. 70.50 (ISBN 0-12-342902-1); Vol. 3. 1972. 77.50 (ISBN 0-12-342903-X). Acad Pr.

Herscher, Uri D. Jewish Agricultural Utopias in America, Eighteen Eighty to Nineteen Ten. (Illus.). 214p. 1981. 15.95 (ISBN 0-8143-1678-6). Wayne St U Pr.

Herschy, R. W. Hydrometry: Principles & Practices. LC 78-4101. 1978. 105.00 (ISBN 0-471-99649-1, Pub. by Wiley-Interscience). Wiley.

Herself. Denise. (Dreams & Fantasies Ser.: No. 6). (Orig.). 1983. pap. 2.95 (ISBN 0-440-01862-5). Dell.

--Diane. 272p. 1982. pap. 2.95 (ISBN 0-440-01736-X, Emerald). Dell.

--Renee. (Dreams & Fantasies Ser.: No. 5). (Orig.). 1983. pap. 2.95 (ISBN 0-440-07476-2). Dell.

--Sharon. (Dreams & Fantasies Ser.: No. 4). (Orig.). 1983. pap. 2.95 (ISBN 0-440-08085-1, Emerald). Dell.

Hersen, Michel, jt. auth. see Bellack, Alan S.

Hersen, Michel, ed. Progress in Behavior Modification, Vols. 4-5 & 7. Incl. Vol. 4. 38.50 (ISBN 0-12-535604-8); lib. ed. 49.50 (ISBN 0-12-535680-3); microfiche 26.50 (ISBN 0-12-535681-1); Vol. 5. 38.50 (ISBN 0-12-535605-6); lib. ed. 49.50 (ISBN 0-12-535682-X); microfiche 26.50 (ISBN 0-12-535683-8); Vol. 7. 35.00 (ISBN 0-12-535607-2); lib. ed. 46.00 (ISBN 0-12-535686-2); microfiche 25.00 (ISBN 0-12-535687-0). LC 74-5697. 1977-79. Acad Pr.

Hersen, Michel & Eisler, Richard M., eds. Progress in Behavior Modification, Vol. 14. (Serial Publication). Date not set. price not set (ISBN 0-12-535614-5); price not set lib ed; price not set microfiche (ISBN 0-12-535700-1). Acad Pr.

Hersen, Michel & Kazdin, Alan E., eds. The Clinical Psychology Handbook. (General Psychology Ser.: No. 120). 1000p. Date not set. 100.00 (ISBN 0-08-028058-7); before 7/83 75.00 (ISBN 0-686-82630-2). Pergamon.

Hersen, Michel & Ollendick, Thomas H., eds. Handbook of Child Psychopathology. 538p. 1983. 50.00x (ISBN 0-306-40938-0, Plenum Pr). Plenum Pub.

Hersen, Michel, et al, eds. Progress in Behavior Modification, Vol. 11. 1981. 38.00 (ISBN 0-12-535611-0); lib. ed. 49.50 (ISBN 0-12-535694-3); microfiche 26.50 (ISBN 0-12-535695-1). Acad Pr.

--Progress in Behavior Modification, Vol. 13. (Serial Publication Ser.). 1982. 35.00 (ISBN 0-12-535613-7). Acad Pr.

Hersey, Harold B. Pulpwood Editor. LC 74-4841. 301p. 1974. Repr. of 1937 ed. lib. bdg. 18.75x (ISBN 0-8371-7490-2, HEPE). Greenwood.

Hersey, Jean. Woman's Day Book of Annuals & Perennials. LC 76-49507. 1977. 7.95 o.p. (ISBN 0-671-22508-1). S&S.

--The Woman's Day Book of Wildflowers. (Illus.). 1976. 7.95 o.p. (ISBN 0-671-22251-1). S&S.

Hersey, Jean D. Woman's Day Book of House Plants. (Illus.). 1965. 8.95 o.p. (ISBN 0-671-82535-6). S&S.

Hersey, Jerry. Pollution & Our Environment. (Science Ser.). 24p. (gr. 7 up). 1977. wkbk. 5.00 (ISBN 0-8209-0154-7, S-16). ESP.

Hersey, John. The Child Buyer. 240p. 1982. pap. 2.95 (ISBN 0-553-20937-X). Bantam.

--Wall. 1967. 6.95 o.s.i. (ISBN 0-394-60798-8, G98). Modern Lib.

Hersey, John, ed. Ralph Ellison: A Collection of Critical Essays. LC 73-16224. (Twentieth Century Views Ser). 192p. 1973. 12.95 (ISBN 0-13-274357-4, Spec); pap. 1.95 (ISBN 0-13-274340-X, Spec). P-H.

Hersey, John R. Single Pebble. (YA) 1956. 12.50 (ISBN 0-394-44562-7). Knopf.

Hersey, Mayo D. Theory & Research in Lubrication: Foundations for Future Developments. LC 66-21058. 488p. 1966. text ed. 26.50 (ISBN 0-471-37346-X, Pub. by Wiley). Krieger.

Hersey, Paul & Blanchard, Kenneth H. Management of Organizational Behavior: Utilizing Human Resources. 4th ed. (Illus.). 368p. 1982. 21.95 (ISBN 0-13-549618-7); pap. text ed. 16.95 (ISBN 0-13-549600-4). P-H.

Hersey, Paul & Stinson, John E., eds. Perspectives in Leader Effectiveness. LC 79-14646. (Illus.). vii, 175p. 1980. 11.95x (ISBN 0-8214-0411-3, 82-83004). Ohio U Pr.

Hersh, Evan M., et al, eds. Augmenting Agents in Cancer Therapy. (Progress in Cancer Research & Therapy Ser.: Vol. 16). 592p. 1981. text ed. 71.50 (ISBN 0-89004-525-9). Raven.

Hersh, S. P. The Executive Parent. 1979. 9.95 o.p. (ISBN 0-671-18428-8). Sovereign Bks.

Hersh, Seymour. My Lai Four. 10.95 (ISBN 0-394-43737-3, V450, Vin); pap. 2.45 (ISBN 0-394-71450-4). Random.

Hersh, Seymour, ed. The Price of Power: Kissinger in the Nixon White House. 480p. 1983. 16.95 (ISBN 0-671-44760-2). Summit Bks.

Hershbell, Jackson P. Pseudo-Plato, Axiochus. Hershbell, Jackson P., tr. LC 79-20127. (Society of Biblical Literature, Text & Translations: 21). 1981. pap. 13.50 (ISBN 0-89130-354-5, 06-02-04). Scholars Pr CA.

Hershberg, Theodore, ed. Philadelphia: Work, Space, Family & Group Experience in the Nineteenth Century. Essays Toward an Interdisciplinary History of the City. (Illus.). 1981. pap. 12.95 (ISBN 0-19-502753-1, 619, GB). Oxford U Pr.

Hershberger, Mary & Christner, Barbara. Miller Family History: Descendants of Solomon S. Miller. (Illus.). 6.00 (ISBN 0-686-95513-7). O R Miller.

Hershelman, N. L., jt. auth. see Davis, Phyllis.

Hershey, Daniel & Wang, Hsuan-Hsien. A New Age-Scale for Humans. LC 79-8318. 176p. 1980. 22.95x (ISBN 0-669-03374-X). Lexington Bks.

Hershey, Ed, jt. auth. see Jones, Cleon.

Hershey Foods Corporation. Hershey's 1934 Cookbook. (Illus.). 1978. 4.95 (ISBN 0-307-49269-9, Golden Pr). Western Pub.

Hershey, Gerald L., jt. auth. see Lugo, James O.

Hershey, Lester T. Lecciones Biblicas. (Span). 1954. pap. 0.50x o.p. (ISBN 0-8361-1143-5). Herald Pr.

Hershey, Nathan. Hospital Physician Relationships: Case Studies & Commentaries on Medical Staff Problems. LC 82-11359. 239p. 1982. 23.50 (ISBN 0-89443-386-5). Aspen Systems.

Hershey, Richard, ed. see Munch, Richard W.

Hershey, Robert D. Advent Landmarks: From a Preacher's Notebook. LC 75-13034. 64p. 1975. pap. 0.50 o.p. (ISBN 0-8006-1211-6, 1-1211). Fortress.

Hershey, Ronald A. Physical Therapy Examination Review Book Clinical Application, Vol. 2. 2nd ed. 1973. pap. 12.75 (ISBN 0-87488-482-9). Med Exam.

--Physical Therapy Examination Review Book: Vol. 1, Basic Sciences. 3rd ed. Seibert, Helen K., ed. 1976. pap. 12.75 (ISBN 0-87488-481-0). Med Exam.

Hershey, William E., jt. ed. see Austin, Michael J.

Hershfield, David C. The Multinational Union Challenges the Multinational Company. (Report Ser.: No. 658). 40p. (Orig.). 1975. pap. 20.00 o.p. (ISBN 0-8237-0077-1). Conference Bd.

Hershlag, Z. Y. Introduction to the Modern Economic History of the Middle East. 1980. Repr. of 1964 ed. text ed. 66.00x (ISBN 90-040-2565-0). Humanities.

Hershman, J. M. Practical Endocrinology. 284p. 1981. pap. 30.00 (ISBN 0-471-09502-8, Pub. by Wiley Med). Wiley.

Hershman, Jerome M., ed. Endrocrine Pathophysiology: A Patient-Oriented Approach. 2nd ed. LC 82-7183. (Illus.). 316p. 1982. text ed. 15.75 (ISBN 0-8121-0840-X). Lea & Febiger.

Hershon, Robert. Grocery Lists. LC 72-83393. (Illus.). 56p. 1972. 5.95 o.p. (ISBN 0-912278-28-5); pap. 2.50 o.p. (ISBN 0-912278-20-X). Crossing Pr.

Herskovits, Frances S., jt. auth. see Herskovits, Melville J.

Herskovits, Melville. Anthropometry of the American Negro. LC 73-121370. (Studies in Black History & Culture, No. 54). 1970. Repr. of 1930 ed. lib. bdg. 52.95x (ISBN 0-8383-1116-4). Haskell.

Herskovits, Melville J. Background of African Art. lim. ed. LC 67-18433. (Cooke-Daniels Lecture Ser., Denver Art Museum). (Illus.). 1945. 10.00x (ISBN 0-8196-0201-9). Biblo.

--Cultural Relativism. pap. 8.95 (ISBN 0-394-48154-2, V-879, Vin). Random.

Herskovits, Melville J. & Herskovits, Frances S. Outline of Dahomean Religious Belief. LC 34-5259. 1933. pap. 12.00 (ISBN 0-527-00540-1). Kraus Repr.

Herskowitz, G. P. & Schilling, Ronald B. Semiconductor Device Modeling for Computer-Aided Design. LC 72-5494. (Illus.). 352p. 1972. 34.50 o.p. (ISBN 0-07-028396-6, P&RB). McGraw.

Herskowitz, Irwin H. The Elements of Genetics. 25.95x (ISBN 0-02-353950-X). Macmillan.

--Principles of Genetics. 2nd ed. 672p. 1977. 28.95x (ISBN 0-02-353930-5). Macmillan.

Herskowitz, Joel & Rosman, N. Paul. Pediatrics, Neurology, & Psychiatry--Common Ground. 1982. 48.00x (ISBN 0-02-354620-4). Macmillan.

Herskowitz, Mickey & Perkins, Steve. Everything You Always Wanted to Know About Sports (but Didn't Know Where to Ask) 1977. pap. 2.50 (ISBN 0-451-11183-4, AE1183, Sig). NAL.

Herskowitz, Mickey, jt. auth. see Autry, Gene.

Herskowitz, Mickey, jt. auth. see Blanda, George.

Herskowitz, Mickey, jt. auth. see Uecker, Bob.

Hersov, L., ed. Children in Turmoil: Tomorrow's Parents. 256p. 1982. 30.00 (ISBN 0-08-027955-4). Pergamon.

Hersov, L., et al, eds. Aggression & Anti-Social Behaviour in Childhood & Adolescence. 1977. text ed. 12.00 (ISBN 0-08-021810-5). Pergamon.

Hersov, Lionel & Berg, Ian, eds. Out of School: Modern Perspectives in Truancy & School Refusal. LC 79-41725. (Studies in Child Psychiatry Ser.). 377p. 1980. 52.95 (ISBN 0-471-27743-6, Pub. by Wiley-Interscience). Wiley.

Herstein, H., et al. Challenge & Survival: The History of Canada. 1970. text ed. 14.95 (ISBN 0-13-125088-4). P-H.

Herstein, I. N. Topics in Algebra. 2nd ed. LC 74-82577. 432p. 1975. text ed. 31.95 (ISBN 0-471-01090-1). Wiley.

Herstein, I. N. & Kaplansky, Irving. Matters Mathematical. 2nd ed. LC 77-16091. 1978. 11.95 (ISBN 0-8284-0300-7). Chelsea Pub.

Herstein, Sheila & Robbins, Naomi. United States of America. (World Bibliographical Ser.: No. 16). 307p. 1982. text ed. 45.00 (ISBN 0-903450-29-1). ABC-Clio.

Hertel, Hannes. Revision Einiger Calciphiler Formenkreise der Flechtengattung Lecidea. (Illus.). 1967. pap. 24.00 (ISBN 3-7682-5424-0). Lubrecht & Cramer.

Hertel, Margaret F., jt. auth. see Jennings, Jerry E.

Herter, Lori. No Time for Love. (Orig.). 1980. pap. 1.25 o.s.i. (ISBN 0-440-16585-7). Dell.

--To Have & to Hold. (Candlelight Ecstasy Ser.: No. 118). (Orig.). 1983. pap. 1.95 (ISBN 0-440-18861-X). Dell.

--Too Close for Comfort. (Candlelight Romance Ser.: No. 669). (Orig.). 1981. pap. 1.50 o.s.i. (ISBN 0-440-18673-0). Dell.

Hertling, jt. auth. see Kessler, Randolph M.

Hertsch, Max. Famous Stamps of the World. (World in Color Ser). (Illus.). 48p. 1975. 3.95 o.p. (ISBN 0-88254-336-9). Hippocrene Bks.

Herttell, Thomas. The Demurrer; or, Proofs of Error in the Decision of the Supreme Court of the State of New York Requiring Faith in a Particular Religious Doctrine As a Legal Qualification of Witnesses. LC 70-122160. (Civil Liberties in American History Ser). 154p. 1972. Repr. of 1828 ed. lib. bdg. 19.50 (ISBN 0-306-71971-1). Da Capo.

Hertz, David & Thomas, Howard. Practical Risk Analysis: An Approach Through Case Histories. 360p. 1982. 29.95 (ISBN 0-471-10144-3, Pub. by Wiley-Interscience). Wiley.

Hertz, David B. & Thomas, Howard. Risk Analysis & Its Applications. 360p. 1982. 23.00 (ISBN 0-471-10145-1, Pub. by Wiley-Interscience). Wiley.

Hertz, Frederick. The Economic Problem of the Danubian States: A Study in Economic Nationalism. LC 68-9662. 1970. 22.50x (ISBN 0-86527-054-6). Fertig.

Hertz, Geraldine. What's in It for Mothers? LC 75-20741. 176p. (Orig.). 1975. pap. 1.75 o.p. (ISBN 0-87973-793-X). Our Sunday Visitor.

Hertz, Grete J. Hi, Daddy, Here I Am. LC 64-2541. (Foreign Lands Bks). (Illus.). (gr. k-3). 1964. PLB 3.95g (ISBN 0-8225-0351-4). Lerner Pubns.

Hertz, Hamilton & Hertz, Joan. How to Raise & Train a Standard Schnauzer. (Orig.). pap. 2.95 (ISBN 0-87666-400-1, DS1124). TFH Pubns.

Hertz, Joan, jt. auth. see Hertz, Hamilton.

Hertz, L., jt. ed. see Federoff, S.

Hertz, L., jt. ed. see Fedoroff, S.

Hertz, Leah. In Search of a Small Business Definition: An Exploration of the Small-Business Definitions of the U. S., the U.K., Israel, & the People's Republic of China. LC 81-40926. 482p. 1982. lib. bdg. 29.75 (ISBN 0-8191-2308-0); pap. text ed. 17.25 (ISBN 0-8191-2309-9). U Pr of Amer.

Hertz, Louis H. Complete Book of Building & Collecting Model Automobiles. LC 68-9100. (Illus.). 1970. 9.95 o.p. (ISBN 0-517-50225-9). Crown.

Hertz, Roy. Choriocarcinoma & Related Gestational Trophoblastic Tumors in Women. LC 75-31481. 180p. 1978. 21.50 (ISBN 0-89004-086-9). Raven.

Hertz, Susan H. The Welfare Mothers Movement: A Decade of Change for Poor Women? LC 81-40358. (Illus.). 200p. (Orig.). 1981. lib. bdg. 20.75 (ISBN 0-8191-1780-3); pap. text ed. 10.00 (ISBN 0-8191-1781-1). U Pr of Amer.

Hertzberg, A., jt. auth. see Brucknet, A. P.

Hertzberg, Arthur. Being Jewish in America: The Modern Experience. LC 78-54390. 1979. 16.95 (ISBN 0-8052-3692-9). Schocken.

Hertzberg, Arthur, ed. Zionist Idea: A Historical Analysis & Reader. LC 77-90073. (Temple Books). 1969. pap. text ed. 7.95x (ISBN 0-689-70093-8, T4). Atheneum.

Hertzberg, Hazel W. Search for an American Indian Identity: Modern Pan-Indian Movements. LC 77-140889. 1971. 18.95x (ISBN 0-8156-0076-3); pap. 10.95x (ISBN 0-8156-2245-7). Syracuse U Pr.

Hertzberg, Richard W. Deformation & Fracture Mechanics of Engineering Materials. LC 76-10812. 580p. 1976. 40.50 (ISBN 0-471-37385-0). Wiley.

--Deformation & Fracture Mechanics of Engineering Materials. 2d ed. 725p. 1983. 36.95 (ISBN 0-686-84628-1). Wiley.

Hertzberg, Robert. Elementary Developing & Printing. (Illus.). 150p. 1973. 8.95 o.p. (ISBN 0-8174-0558-5, Amphoto). Watson-Guptill.

--Photo Darkroom Guide. 5th ed. LC 67-25844. (Illus.). 128p. 1976. pap. 3.45 o.p. (ISBN 0-8174-1148-8, Amphoto). Watson-Guptill.

Hertzberg, Robert, jt. auth. see Collins, A. Frederick.

Hertzberg, Ruth, et al. Putting Food By. 2nd ed. LC 74-27454. (Illus.). 448p. 1975. 14.95 o.p. (ISBN 0-8289-0252-6); pap. 10.95 o.p. (ISBN 0-8289-0251-8). Greene.

--Putting Food by. 3rd ed. (Illus.). 550p. 1982. 18.95 (ISBN 0-8289-0468-5); pap. 11.95 (ISBN 0-8289-0469-3). Greene.

Hertzfelt, Bruce D. An Investigation into the Powers of the Conscious, the Subconscious & of the Unconscious in an Effort to Master the Essence of Man. Rev. ed. (Illus.). 114p. 1982. Repr. of 1918 ed. 61.85 (ISBN 0-89901-067-9). Found Class Reprints.

Hertzson, David. Hotel-Motel Marketing. LC 76-142509. 1971. text ed. 17.50 (ISBN 0-672-96083-4); tchr's manual 8.50 (ISBN 0-672-96085-0); wkbk. o.p. 6.95 (ISBN 0-672-96084-2). Bobbs.

Herubin, Charles. Principles of Surveying. 3rd ed. 1982. text ed. 20.95 (ISBN 0-8359-5616-4); solutions manual avail. (ISBN 0-8359-5617-2). Reston.

Herubin, Charles & Marotta, Theodore. Basic Construction Materials. 2nd ed. 1981. text ed. 21.95 (ISBN 0-8359-0362-1); solutions manual avail. (ISBN 0-8359-0363-X). Reston.

Herum, John, jt. ed. see Cummings, Donald W.

Hervas Y Panduro, L. Catalogo delle Lingue Conosciute e Notizia della Loro Affinita e Diversita. (Linguistics 13th-18th Centuries Ser.). 260p. (Fr.). 1974. Repr. of 1784 ed. lib. bdg. 70.50 o.p. (ISBN 0-8287-0427-9, 71-5047). Clearwater Pub.

Hervey, George F. & Hems, Jack. Vivarium. (YA) (gr. 9 up). 1968. 7.95 o.p. (ISBN 0-571-08039-1). Transatlantic.

Hervier, Y., jt. ed. see Barz, P. Le.

Herwig, Ellis. Amphoto Guide to Flash Photography. (Illus.). 168p. 1981. 11.95 o.p. (ISBN 0-8174-3515-8, Amphoto); pap. 7.95 (ISBN 0-8174-3516-6). Watson-Guptill.

--The Handbook of Color Photography. (Illus.). 160p. (Orig.). 1982. 21.95 (ISBN 0-8174-3952-8, Amphoto); pap. 12.95 (ISBN 0-8174-3953-6). Watson-Guptill.

--Stock Photography. (How to Shoot It, How to Sell It). (Illus.). 152p. 1981. 19.95 o.p. (ISBN 0-8174-5900-6, Amphoto); pap. 11.95 (ISBN 0-8174-5901-4). Watson-Guptill.

Herwig, Holger H. Politics of Frustration: The United States in German Naval Planning, 1889-1941. 1976. 18.00 o.p. (ISBN 0-316-35890-8). Little.

Herwig, Holger H. & Heyman, Neil M. Biographical Dictionary of World War I. LC 81-4242. (Illus.). 406p. 1982. lib. bdg. 49.95 (ISBN 0-313-21356-9, HBD/). Greenwood.

Herwitz, Stanley R. The Regeneration of Selected Tropical Tree Species in Corcovado National Park, Costa Rica. (U.C. Publications in Geography: Vol. 24). 1981. pap. 12.00x (ISBN 0-520-09631-2). U of Cal Pr.

Herz, John H. From Dictatorship to Democracy: Coping with the Legacies of Authoritarianism & Totalitarianism. LC 82-12002. (Contributions in Political Science Ser.: No. 92). (Illus.). 376p. 1983. lib. bdg. 35.00 (ISBN 0-313-23636-4, HDD/). Greenwood.

Herz, Martin F. David Bruce's "Long Telegram" of July 3, 1951. LC 78-71946. 26p. 1978. 1.50 (ISBN 0-686-83450-X, Inst Study Diplomacy). Geo U Sch For Serv.

--Making the World a Less Dangerous Place: Lessons learned from a Career in Diplomacy. LC 81-86226. 24p. 1981. 1.25 (ISBN 0-934742-15-4, Inst Study Diplomacy). Geo U Sch For Serv.

Herz, Martin F. & Krogh, Peter F. Two Hundred Fifteen Days in the Life of an American Ambassador. LC 81-13346. 1981. 9.85 (ISBN 0-934742-12-X, Inst Study Diplomacy). Geo U Sch For Serv.

Herz, Martin F., ed. Contacts with the Opposition: A Symposium. LC 79-91020. 72p. 1979. 3.00 (ISBN 0-934742-03-0, Inst Study Diplomacy). Geo U Sch For Serv.

--The Role of Embassies in Promoting Business: A Symposium. LC 81-6427. 75p. 1981. 4.50 (ISBN 0-934742-13-8, Inst Study Diplomacy). Geo U Sch For Serv.

Herz, Michael J., jt. ed. see Peeke, Harmon V.

Herz, W., et al, eds. Progress in the Chemistry of Organic Natural Products. LC 39-1015. (Vol. 37). (Illus.). 1979. 105.10 (ISBN 0-387-81528-7). Springer-Verlag.

--Progress in the Chemistry of Organic Natural Products, Vol. 42. 330p. 1983. 66.00 (ISBN 0-387-81706-9). Springer-Verlag.

Herzberg, Paul. Principles of Statistics. 600p. 1983. text ed. 21.95 (ISBN 0-471-07989-8); tchrs.' manual avail. (ISBN 0-471-87306-3). Wiley.

Herzberger, David K. Jesus Fernandez Santos. (World Authors Ser.). 168p. 1983. lib. bdg. 18.95 (ISBN 0-8057-6534-4, Twayne). G K Hall.

Herzberger, Jurgen, jt. auth. see Alefeld, Gotz.

Herzberger, Max. Modern Geometrical Optics. LC 77-9030. 516p. 1978. Repr. 27.50 (ISBN 0-88275-585-4). Krieger.

Herzen, Alexander I. De l'Autre Rive. (Nineteenth Century Russia Ser.). 252p. (Fr.). 1974. Repr. of 1870 ed. lib. bdg. 69.00x o.p. (ISBN 0-8287-0428-7, R26). Clearwater Pub.

--Du Developement des Idees Revolutionnaires en Russie par A. Iscander. (Nineteenth Century Russia Ser.). 176p. (Fr.). 1974. Repr. of 1851 ed. lib. bdg. 53.00x o.p. (ISBN 0-8287-0429-5, R17). Clearwater Pub.

--Lettres de France et d'Italie, 1847-1852. (Nineteenth Century Russia Ser.). 323p. (Fr.). 1974. Repr. of 1871 ed. lib. bdg. 84.50x o.p. (ISBN 0-8287-0430-9, R25). Clearwater Pub.

--Le Monde Russe et la Revolution, Memoires, 3 vols. (Nineteenth Century Russia Ser.). (Fr.). 1974. Repr. of 1860 ed. Set. lib. bdg. 300.00 o.p. (ISBN 0-8287-0431-7). Clearwater Pub.

--Nouvelle Phase de la Litterature Russe. (Nineteenth Century Russia Ser.). 83p. (Fr.). 1974. Repr. of 1864 ed. 24.00x o.p. (ISBN 0-8287-0432-5, R24). Clearwater Pub.

--Le Peuple Russe et le Socialisme. (Nineteenth Century Russia Ser.). 58p. (Fr.). 1974. Repr. of 1852 ed. 29.00x o.p. (ISBN 0-8287-0433-3, R18). Clearwater Pub.

Herzfeld, Thomas J. The Investor's Guide to Closed-End Funds: The Herzfeld Hedge. (Illus.). 1979. 19.50 o.p. (ISBN 0-07-028417-2). McGraw.

Herzfeld, Thomas J. & Drach, Robert F. High Return, Low-Risk Investment: Combining Market Timing, Stock Selection & Closed-End Funds. 228p. 1981. 16.95 (ISBN 0-399-12642-2). Putnam Pub Group.

Herzig, Jakub & Allen-Shore, Lena. Roots & Wings. LC 82-60602. 152p. 1982. pap. 3.95 (ISBN 0-88400-085-0); 8.95 (ISBN 0-88400-087-7). Shengold.

Herzinger, Kim A. D. H. Lawrence in His Time. LC 81-65863. 240p. 1982. 28.50 (ISBN 0-8387-5028-1). Bucknell U Pr.

Herzka, A. & Booth, R. G. Food Industry Wastes: Disposal & Recovery. 1981. 45.00 (ISBN 0-85334-957-6, Pub. by Applied Sci England). Elsevier.

Herzlinger, Regina & Kane, Nancy M. A Managerial Analysis of Federal Income Distribution Mechanisms: The Government As Factory, Insurance Company & Bank. LC 79-14524. (Illus.). 208p. 1979. prof ref 24.50x (ISBN 0-88410-368-4). Ballinger Pub.

Herzman, Ronald B., jt. auth. see Cook, William R.

Herzog, et al. Herzog's Bankruptcy Forms & Practice, 2 vols. LC 80-18209. 1980. looseleaf 150.00 (ISBN 0-87632-011-6). Boardman.

Herzog, A. Regula & Bachman, Jerald G. Sex Roles Attitudes Among High School Seniors: Views about Work & Family Roles. 272p. 1982. pap. 16.00x (ISBN 0-87944-275-1). Inst Soc Res.

Herzog, A. Reguls & Rodgers, Willard L. Subjective Well-Being among Different Age Groups. 124p. 1982. pap. 14.00x (ISBN 0-87944-283-2). Inst Soc Res.

Herzog, Arthur. Aries Rising. 352p. 1980. 12.95 (ISBN 0-399-90088-8, Marek). Putnam Pub Group.

--Earthsound. (RL 9). 1976. pap. 1.75 o.p. (ISBN 0-451-07255-3, E7255, Sig). NAL.

--Glad to Be Here. LC 79-7099. 1979. 12.45i (ISBN 0-690-01818-5). T Y Crowell.

--Heat. (RL 9). 1978. pap. 1.95 o.p. (ISBN 0-451-08115-3, J8115, Sig). NAL.

--LSITT. 1983. 14.95 (ISBN 0-87795-470-4). Arbor Hse.

--The Swarm. 1974. 6.95 o.p. (ISBN 0-671-21709-7). S&S.

Herzog, Barbara. Friends. (Illus.). 32p. (Orig.). (gr. 1-4). 1983. pap. 4.98 (ISBN 0-943194-10-5). Childwrite.

Herzog, Barbara J. ABC! Animals & Me! (Illus.). 32p. (Orig.). (gr. 1-2). 1983. pap. 4.98 (ISBN 0-943194-15-6). Childwrite.

--Here I Am! (Illus.). 16p. (Orig.). (gr. 1-3). 1983. pap. 3.98 (ISBN 0-943194-11-3). Childwrite.

--My Night Before Christmas. (Illus.). 16p. (Orig.). (gr. 1-3). 1983. pap. 3.98 (ISBN 0-943194-13-X). Childwrite.

--My Own Story & Picture Book. 32p. (Orig.). (gr. 1-4). 1983. pap. 4.98 (ISBN 0-943194-14-8). Childwrite.

--Once Upon a Rhyme. (Illus.). 48p. (Orig.). (gr. 1-3). 1983. pap. 5.98 (ISBN 0-943194-12-1). Childwrite.

Herzog, Billy Jean. Tennis Handbook. 4th ed. (Illus.). 1982. pap. text ed. 5.95 (ISBN 0-8403-2828-1). Kendall-Hunt.

Herzog, Chaim. The Arab-Israeli Wars. 1982. 20.00 (ISBN 0-394-50379-1). Random.

Herzog, David A. Mathematics Workbook for the GED Test. LC 82-20571. (Arco's Preparation for the GED Examination Ser.). 256p. 1983. pap. 5.95 (ISBN 0-668-05542-1). Arco.

--Science & Social Studies Workbook for the GED Test. (Arco's Preparation for the GED Examination Ser.). 256p. 1983. pap. 5.95 (ISBN 0-668-05541-3, 5541). Arco.

Herzog, Edgar. Psyche & Death. LC 67-10439. 1967. 8.00 o.p. (ISBN 0-913430-18-8). C G Jung Foun.

--Psyche & Death: Death-Demons in Folklore, Myth, & Modern Dreams. LC 82-63008. (Jungian Classics Ser.). 222p. 1982. pap. 13.50 (ISBN 0-88214-504-5). Spring Pubns.

Herzog, Elizabeth, jt. auth. see Zborowski, Mark.

Herzog, George, ed. see Hudson, A. P.

Herzog, H., ed. Interasma Abstracts. (Respiration Journal: Vol. 42, Suppl. 1, 1981). iv, 144p. 1981. pap. 31.75 (ISBN 3-8055-3425-6). S Karger.

Herzog, Issac. Essays Presented to Chief Rabbi Israel Brodie on the Occasion of His Seventieth Birthday. 25.00x (ISBN 0-685-01040-6). Bloch.

Herzog, Martje, tr. see Herzog, Werner.

Herzog, Richard B., jt. auth. see Drake, W. Homer, Jr.

Herzog, Richard B., jt. auth. see Zener, Robert V.

Herzog, Stephanie. Joy in the Classroom. Ray, Ann, ed. (Illus.). 1982. text ed. 6.95 (ISBN 0-916438-46-5). Univ of Trees.

Herzog, Werner. Fitzcarraldo: The Original Story. Herzog, Martje & Greenberg, Alan, trs. from German. 160p. (Orig.). 1982. pap. 8.00 (ISBN 0-940242-04-4). Fjord Pr.

Herzog, Yaacov D. The Mishnah. 15.00 (ISBN 0-686-84235-9). Bloch.

Herzstein, R. The Nazis. LC 79-24323. (World War II Ser.). PLB 19.92 (ISBN 0-8094-2535-1). Silver.

Herzstein, Robert E. The War That Hitler Won: The Most Infamous Propaganda Campaign in History. LC 77-7257. (Illus.). 1978. 15.00 o.p. (ISBN 0-399-11845-4). Putnam Pub Group.

--Western Civilization, 2 vols. Incl. Vol. 1. From the Origins Through the Seventeenth Century. 15.50 (ISBN 0-395-19370-2); Vol. 2. From the Seventeenth Century to the Present. 15.50 (ISBN 0-395-19371-0); instr's. manual 2.70 (ISBN 0-395-14043-9). 1975. Set. 23.75 (ISBN 0-395-14042-0). HM.

Heschel, Abraham J. Israel: An Echo of Eternity. (Illus.). 230p. 1969. pap. 3.95 o.p. (ISBN 0-374-50740-6, N358). FS&G.

--Israel: An Echo of Eternity. 232p. pap. 5.50 o.p. (ISBN 0-686-95159-X). ADL.

--Maimonides. Newgroschel, Joachim, tr. from German. 1983. text ed. 8.25 (ISBN 0-374-51759-2). FS&G.

--A Passion for Truth. 336p. 1973. 8.95 (ISBN 0-374-22992-9); pap. 6.95 o.p. (ISBN 0-374-51184-5). FS&G.

--Prophets, Vol. 1. 1969. pap. 5.95xi (ISBN 0-06-131421-8, TB1421, Torch). Har-Row.

--Prophets, Vol. 2. 1971. pap. 4.95xi (ISBN 0-06-131557-5, TB1557, Torch). Har-Row.

Heschel, Abraham Joshua. The Wisdom of Heschel. 368p. 1975. 10.00 (ISBN 0-374-29124-1); pap. 5.95 o.p. (ISBN 0-686-85977-4). FS&G.

Heschong, Lisa. Thermal Delight in Architecture. 1979. 13.75x (ISBN 0-262-08101-6); pap. 5.95 (ISBN 0-262-58039-X). MIT Pr.

Heschong, Naomi H. Get the Job You Want. 3rd ed. 112p. 1983. pap. text ed. cancelled (ISBN 0-8120-2354-4). Barron.

Heseltine, Janet E., jt. ed. see Harvey, Paul.

Heshusius, Lous. Meaning in Life As Experienced by Persons Labeled Retarded in a Group Home: A Participant Observation Study. (Illus.). 176p. 1981. 19.50x (ISBN 0-398-04064-8); pap. 15.75x (ISBN 0-398-04079-6). C C Thomas.

Heske, Franz. German Forestry. 1938. 49.50x (ISBN 0-686-51394-0). Elliots Bks.

Heskes, Deborah. Supportive Services for Disadvantaged Workers & Trainees. (Key Issues Ser.: No. 12). 48p. 1973. pap. 2.00 (ISBN 0-87546-225-1). ILR Pr.

Heskes, Irene, ed. see Binder, Abraham W.

Heskestad, Gunnar. Engineering Relations for Fire Plumes. Date not set. 4.65 (ISBN 0-686-37673-0, TR 82-8). Society Fire Protect.

Hesketh, Howard E. Air Pollution Control. LC 78-71429. 1979. 39.95 (ISBN 0-250-40288-2). Ann Arbor Science.

Hesketh, Howard E. & Cross, Frank L., Jr. Fugitive Emissions & Controls. LC 82-72348. (The Environment & Energy Handbook Ser.). (Illus.). 150p. 1983. 22.50 (ISBN 0-250-40448-6). Ann Arbor Science.

Hesketh, Howard E., jt. auth. see Schifftner, Kenneth C.

Heskett, J. L., et al. Business Logistics: Physical Distribution & Materials Management. 2nd ed. (Illus.). 789p. 1973. 34.95 (ISBN 0-471-06598-6); instr's manual avail. (ISBN 0-471-07468-3). Wiley.

--Case Problems in Business Logistics. 1973. 23.95 (ISBN 0-471-06599-4). Wiley.

Heskett, James L. Marketing. (Illus.). 640p. 1976. text ed. 25.95x (ISBN 0-02-353940-2). Macmillan.

Hesler, L. R. Entoloma (Rhodophyllus) in Southeastern North America. 1967. pap. 32.00 (ISBN 3-7682-5423-2). Lubrecht & Cramer.

Heslet, Frederick E., jt. auth. see Frey, David H.

Heslin, J., jt. auth. see Natow, A. B.

Heslin, Richard & Patterson, Miles. Nonverbal Behavior & Social Psychology. (Perspectives in Social Psychology Ser.). 196p. 1982. 24.50x (ISBN 0-306-40952-6, Plenum Pr). Plenum Pub.

Heslop. Cellular Recognition Systems in Plants. (Studies in Biology: No. 100). 1979. 5.95 o.p. (ISBN 0-8391-0250-X). Univ Park.

Heslop, R. B. Numerical Aspects of Inorganic Chemistry. (Illus.). 1970. 20.50 (ISBN 0-444-20060-6, Pub. by Applied Sci England). Elsevier.

Heslop, R. B. & Jones, K. Inorganic Chemistry. 4th ed. 1976. text ed. 23.50 (ISBN 0-444-41426-6). Elsevier.

Heslop, R. B. & Wild, Gillian M. SI Units in Chemistry: An Introduction. (Illus.). 1971. text ed. 12.50x (ISBN 0-85334-650-X, Pub. by Applied Sci England); pap. text ed. 12.00x (ISBN 0-85334-515-5). Burgess-Intl Ideas.

Heslop-Harrison, J. see Jackson, B. D., et al.

Hess, Amy M., jt. auth. see Gouldman, W. Clyde.

Hess, B., ed. see FEBS Meeting, Eighth.

Hess, Bartlett & Hess, Margaret. How Does Your Marriage Grow? 180p. 1983. pap. 4.95 (ISBN 0-88207-529-2). Victor Bks.

Hess, Beth B. & Markson, Elizabeth W. Aging & Old Age: An Introduction to Social Gerontology. (Illus.). 1980. text ed. 20.95x (ISBN 0-02-354100-8). Macmillan.

Hess, Beth B., et al. Sociology. 1982. text ed. 21.95x (ISBN 0-02-354120-2). Macmillan.

Hess, Donald T., jt. auth. see Clarke, Kenneth K.

Hess, Gerhard. Freshmen & Sophomores Abroad: Community Colleges & Overseas Academic Programs. 1982. text ed. 12.95x (ISBN 0-8077-2727-X). Tchrs Coll.

Hess, H. Pictures as Arguments. 30.00x (ISBN 0-686-97015-2, Pub. by Scottish Academic Pr Scotland). State Mutual Bk.

Hess, H. C. Van see Van Ness, H. C.

Hess, Herbert J. & Tucker, Charles O. Talking About Relationships. 2nd ed. 80p. 1980. pap. text ed. 3.95x (ISBN 0-917974-47-6). Waveland Pr.

Hess, Joachim. Dispositien der merkwaardigste Kerk-orgelen, welken in de zeven Vereenigde Provincien alsmede in Duytsland en Elders aangetrofen worden Gouda Seventeen Seventy-Four. (Bibliotheca Organologica Ser.: Vol. 11). 280p. 1981. Repr. of 1782 ed. 47.50 o.s.i. (ISBN 90-6027-385-0, Pub. by Frits Knuf Netherlands); wrappers 35.00 o.s.i. (ISBN 90-6027-256-0, Pub. by Frits Knuf Netherlands). Pendragon NY.

--Luister van het orgel, of nauwkeurige aanwijzinge Gouda Seventeen Seventy-Two. (Bibliotheca Organologica Ser.: Vol. 10). 1976. Repr. wrappers 22.50 o.s.i. (ISBN 90-6027-255-2, Pub. by Frits Knuf Netherlands). Pendragon NY.

Hess, John E., jt. ed. see Sinks, Thomas A.

Hess, John L. & Hess, Karen. The Taste of America. 1977. pap. 3.95 (ISBN 0-14-004535-X). Penguin.

Hess, Joseph C. Night Stick. LC 82-61732. (Illus.). 419p. 1982. pap. 7.50 (ISBN 0-89750-082-2, 419). Ohara Pubns.

--Nunchaku in Action: For Kobudo & Law Enforcement. (Illus., Orig.). 1983. pap. 7.95 (ISBN 0-89750-086-5, 423). Ohara Pubns.

Hess, Joseph W., et al, eds. Family Practice & Preventitive Medicine: Health Promotion in Primary Care. LC 82-15718. 304p. 1983. text ed. 29.95x (ISBN 0-89885-131-9). Human Sci Pr.

Hess, Karen, jt. auth. see Hess, John L.

Hess, Karen, notes by see David, Elizabeth.

Hess, Karen, et al. Dialects & Dialect Learning. 1974. 77.00 o.p. (ISBN 0-8141-1116-5); members 55.00 o.p. (ISBN 0-686-86402-6). NCTE.

Hess, Karen M. Introduction to Private Security. Wrobleski, Henry M., ed. (Criminal Justice Ser.). (Illus.). 400p. 1982. text ed. 20.95 (ISBN 0-314-63252-2). West Pub.

Hess, Karen M., jt. auth. see Bennett, Wayne W.

Hess, Karen M., jt. auth. see Wrobleski, Henry M.

Hess, L. Y. Reprocessing & Disposal of Waste Petroleum Oils. LC 79-20213. (Pollution Technology Review No. 64; Chemical Technology Review: No. 140). (Illus.). 1980. 42.00 (ISBN 0-8155-0775-5). Noyes.

Hess, Lilo. Making Friends with Guinea Pigs. LC 82-21632. (Illus.). 48p. (gr. 4-6). 11.95 (ISBN 0-684-17853-2). Scribner.

--Shetland Ponies. LC 64-10862. (Illus.). (gr. k-3). 1964. 10.53i (ISBN 0-690-73234-1, TYC-J). Har-Row.

Hess, Linda, ed. & tr. see Kabir.

Hess, M. A. & Hunt, A. Pickles & Ice Cream. 1982. 14.95 (ISBN 0-07-028419-9). McGraw.

Hess, Margaret. Esther: Courage in Crisis. 1980. pap. 3.95 (ISBN 0-88207-216-1). Victor Bks.

--Love Knows No Barriers. 1979. pap. 3.95 (ISBN 0-88207-780-5). Victor Bks.

Hess, Margaret, jt. auth. see Hess, Bartlett.

Hess, Mary, jt. auth. see Middleton, Katharine.

Hess, Mary A., jt. auth. see Middleton, Katherine.

Hess, Patricia & Day, Candra. Understanding the Aging Patient. LC 77-2596. 1977. 14.95 o.p. (ISBN 0-87618-733-5). R J Brady.

Hess, Patricia, jt. auth. see Ebersole, Priscilla.

Hess, Robert & Croft, Doreen J. Teachers of Young Children. 3rd ed. LC 80-81928. (Illus.). 528p. 1981. text ed. 20.50 (ISBN 0-395-29172-0); instr's. manual 1.00 (ISBN 0-395-29173-9). HM.

Hess, Robert & Hermalin, Jared, eds. Innovations in Prevention. (Prevention in Human Services, Vol. 2, No. 3). 128p. 1983. text ed. 19.95 (ISBN 0-86656-227-3, B227). Haworth Pr.

Hess, Robert D., jt. auth. see Croft, Doreen.

Hess, Robert P. Desk Book for Setting up the Closely - Held Corporation. LC 79-19309. 1979. 59.50 (ISBN 0-87624-113-5). Inst Busn Plan.

Hess, Stanley. The Modification of Letter-Forms. LC 72-85237. (Illus.). 1972. 9.50 (ISBN 0-910158-79-7). Art Dir.

Hess, Stanley W., jt. ed. see Hoffberg, Judith A.

Hess, Stephen. Organizing the Presidency. 1976. 18.95 (ISBN 0-8157-3588-X); pap. 7.95 (ISBN 0-8157-3587-1). Brookings.

--The Presidential Campaign. rev. ed. 1978. pap. 4.95 (ISBN 0-8157-3591-X). Brookings.

--The Washington Reporters. LC 80-70077. 275p. 1981. 18.95 (ISBN 0-8157-3594-4); pap. 7.95 (ISBN 0-8157-3593-6). Brookings.

Hess, Steven. Ramon Menendez Pidal. (World Authors Ser.). 1982. lib. bdg. 17.95 (ISBN 0-8057-6494-1, Twayne). G K Hall.

Hess, W. M., jt. auth. see Weber, Darrell J.

Hesse. Approaches to Teaching Foreign Languages. 1975. 32.00 (ISBN 0-444-11006-2, North-Holland). Elsevier.

Hesse, Alice W. Jungle Holiday. 112p. 1983. 7.00 (ISBN 0-682-49979-X). Exposition.

Hesse, Bob. The Short Season: Baseball's Spring Fling. 128p. 1982. pap. text ed. 8.95 (ISBN 0-8403-2658-0). Kendall-Hunt.

Hesse, Eva, ed. New Approaches to Ezra Pound: A Co-ordinated Investigation of Pound's Poetry & Ideas. LC 76-78928. 1969. 27.50x (ISBN 0-520-01439-1). U of Cal Pr.

Hesse, Everett & Orjuela, Hector H. Spanish Review. 5th ed. 1980. text ed. 14.95x (ISBN 0-442-25800-3); tapes 75.00 (ISBN 0-442-25799-6); cassettes 49.95 (ISBN 0-442-25798-8). Van Nos Reinhold.

Hesse, Everett W. Calderon de la Barca. (World Authors Ser.). 1968. lib. bdg. 15.95 (ISBN 0-8057-2100-2, Twayne). G K Hall.

Hesse, Everett W. & Williams, Harry F., eds. Vida de Lazarillo de Tormes y de sus fortunas y adversidades. rev. ed. 104p. 1961. pap. text ed. 6.95 (ISBN 0-299-00545-3). U of Wis Pr.

Hesse, Hermann. Demian. LC 64-18078. 1965. 11.49i (ISBN 0-06-011875-X, HarpT). Har-Row.

--Gertrude. Rosner, Hilda, tr. from Ger. 1969. 6.95 o.p. (ISBN 0-686-85972-3); pap. 2.25 (ISBN 0-374-50812-7). FS&G.

--Hours in the Garden & Other Poems. Lesser, Rika, tr. 96p. 1979. 10.95 o.p. (ISBN 0-686-85974-X); pap. 4.95 (ISBN 0-374-51423-2). FS&G.

--My Belief: Essays on Life & Art. Lindley, Denver, tr. from Ger. 384p. 1974. 14.95 o.p. (ISBN 0-374-21666-5); pap. 8.95 (ISBN 0-374-51109-8). FS&G.

--Peter Camenzind. Roloff, Michael, tr. from Ger. 208p. 1969. pap. 7.95 (ISBN 0-374-50784-8, N369). FS&G.

--Pictor's Metamorphoses: & Other Fantasies. Lesser, Rika, tr. from Ger. (Illus.). 1982. 15.95 (ISBN 0-374-23212-1); pap. 7.25 (ISBN 0-374-51723-1). FS&G.

--Wandering. Wright, James, tr. from Ger. 128p. 1972. pap. 5.95 (ISBN 0-374-50975-1, N420). FS&G.

Hesse, Manfred. Alkaloid Chemistry. LC 80-22828. 231p. 1981. 31.95x (ISBN 0-471-07973-1, Pub. by Wiley-Interscience). Wiley.

Hesse, Mary. Structure of Scientific Inference. LC 73-85373. 1974. 36.50x (ISBN 0-520-02582-2). U of Cal Pr.

Hesse, Rick & Woolsey, Gene. Applied Management Science. 384p. 1980. pap. text ed. 16.95 (ISBN 0-574-19345-6, 13-2345); instr's. guide avail. (ISBN 0-574-19346-4, 13-2346). SRA.

Hessel, Alfred. History of Libraries. LC 57-2485. 1955. 11.00 o.p. (ISBN 0-8108-0058-6). Scarecrow.

Hessel, Dieter T. Social Ministry. LC 82-6960. 1982. pap. 8.95 (ISBN 0-664-24422-X). Westminster.

Hessel, Dieter T., ed. Social Themes of the Christian Year: A Commentary on the Lectionary. 276p. (Orig.). 1983. pap. price not set (ISBN 0-664-24472-6). Westminster.

Hessel, L. W. & Krans, J. M., eds. Lipoprotein Metabolism & Endocrine Regulation. (Developments in Endocrinology: Vol. 4). 1979. 62.25 (ISBN 0-444-80102-2, Biomedical Pr). Elsevier.

Hesselgrave, David & Hesselgrave, Ronald. What in the World Has Gotten into the Church? LC 81-3921. 128p. 1981. pap. 5.95 (ISBN 0-8024-9386-6). Moody.

Hesselgrave, Ronald, jt. auth. see Hesselgrave, David.

Hesselgrave, Ruth A. Lady Miller & Batheaston Literary Circle. 1927. Limited Ed. 32.50x (ISBN 0-685-69826-2). Elliots Bks.

Hesseling, P. Effective Organization Research for Development. (Illus.). 220p. 1981. 19.95 (ISBN 0-08-024082-8). Pergamon.

Hessen, Robert, ed. Does Big Business Rule America? Critical Commentaries on Charles E. Lindblom's Politics & Markets. LC 81-9821. 75p. 1981. pap. 3.00 (ISBN 0-89633-048-6). Ethics & Public Policy.

Hessler, Gene. The Comprehensive Catalog of U.S. Paper Money. 4th ed. (Illus.). 580p. 1983. lib. bdg. 24.95 (ISBN 0-931960-11-8); pap. 17.95 (ISBN 0-931960-10-X). BNR Pr.

Hesslink, G. K. Black Neighbors: Negroes in a Northern Rural Community. 2nd ed. LC 73-8915. 345p. 1974. 10.95 o.p. (ISBN 0-672-51522-9). Bobbs.

Hess-Luttich, Ernest. Multimedial Communication, 2 Vols. 650p. 1982. Set. 59.50 (ISBN 3-87808-537-0). Benjamins North Am.

Hesson, Elizabeth C. Twentieth Century Odyssey: A Study of Heimito Von Doderer's "Die Damonen". LC 81-69885. (Studies in German Literature, Linguistics & Culture: Vol. 9). (Illus.). 220p. 1982. 18.95x (ISBN 0-938100-07-6). Camden Hse.

Hestenes, Marshall & Hill, Richard. Algebra & Trigonometry with Calculators. (Illus.). 512p. 1981. text ed. 23.95 (ISBN 0-13-021857-X). P-H.

--College Algebra with Calculators. (Illus.). 416p. 1982. 21.95 (ISBN 0-13-140806-2). P-H.

Hestenes, Marshall D. & Hill, Richard O., Jr. Trigonometry with Calculators. (Illus.). 288p. 1982. text ed. 20.95 (ISBN 0-13-930859-8). P-H.

Hestenes, Roberta & Curley, Lois, eds. Women & the Ministries of Christ. Date not set. pap. 8.95x (ISBN 0-686-94587-5). Fuller Theol Soc.

Hester, Debbie & Brewer, Bryan. The Christmas Fairy. (Illus.). 56p. (Orig.). 1982. softbound 5.00 (ISBN 0-9609834-0-6). CIRI-BETH.

Hester, George. Classic Nude. (Illus.). 1973. 19.95 o.p. (ISBN 0-8174-0554-2, Amphoto). Watson-Guptill.

--Man-Woman, 2 vols. (Illus.). 96p. 1975. slipcase 24.95 o.p. (ISBN 0-685-54049-9, Amphoto). Vol. 1, Man (ISBN 0-8174-0590-9). Vol. 2, Woman (ISBN 0-8174-0591-7). Watson-Guptill.

Hester, H. I. The Heart of Hebrew History. 1980. Repr. of 1949 ed. 10.95 (ISBN 0-8054-1217-4). Broadman.

--The Heart of the New Testament. 1980. Repr. of 1950 ed. 10.95 (ISBN 0-8054-1386-3). Broadman.

--Introduccion Al Estudio Del Nuevo Testamento. Benlliure, Felix, tr. from Eng. 366p. (Span.). 1980. pap. 7.95 (ISBN 0-311-04330-5). Casa Bautista.

Hester, R. E., jt. ed. see Clark, R. J.

Hester, Ralph, jt. auth. see Jian, Gerard.

Hester, Ralph, jt. auth. see Lenard, Yvone.

Hester, Randolph T., Jr., jt. auth. see Smith, Frank J.

Hester, Ruth L. The Wandering Muse. 1978. 5.00 o.p. (ISBN 0-8233-0280-6). Golden Quill.

Hester, Thomas R., et al. Field Methods in Archaeology. 6th ed. LC 74-33732. Orig. Title: Guide to Archaeological Field Methods. (Illus.). 408p. 1975. pap. text ed. 14.95 (ISBN 0-87484-323-5). Mayfield Pub.

Hesterman, Vicki, jt. auth. see Storrer, Carol M.

Heston, Alan W., jt. ed. see Berki, S. E.

Heston, W. L., jt. auth. see Sayyed Mohammad Ali Jamalzadeh.

Hestwood, Diana & Huseby, Edward. Crossnumber Puzzle Books, 2 bks. 1973. Bk. 1. pap. 6.85 wkbk. (ISBN 0-88488-013-3); Bk. 2. pap. 6.85 wkbk. (ISBN 0-88488-014-1). Creative Pubns.

Het PTT-BEDRIJF, The Netherlands. Human Factors in Telephone Communications International Symposium, 3rd. 1967. pap. 75.00 (ISBN 0-686-37973-X). Info-Gatekeepers.

Hetata, Sherif. The Eye with an Iron Lid. 409p. 1982. 15.00x (ISBN 0-686-82686-8). Three Continents.

Hetherington, E. M. Contemporary Readings in Child Psychology. 2nd ed. Parke, R. D. & Nave, Patricia S., eds. 448p. 1981. pap. text ed. 14.95 (ISBN 0-07-028426-1, C). McGraw.

Hetherington, E. M. & Parke, R. D. Child Psychology: A Contemporary Viewpoint. 1979. text ed. 21.95 (ISBN 0-07-028431-8); instr's. manual & study guide avail. McGraw.

Hetherington, H. Lee, jt. auth. see Frascogna, X. M., Jr.

Hetherington, John, Jr., jt. auth. see Kolker, Allan E.

Hetherington, Mavis & Parke, Ross. Contemporary Headings in Child Psychology. 1977. 15.95 (ISBN 0-07-028425-3, C). McGraw.

Hetherington, Mavis, jt. auth. see Mussen, Paul H.

Hetherington, Mavis, jt. auth. see Mussen, Paul.

Hetherington, Mavis, jt. auth. see Mussen, Paul H.

Hetrick, David L. & Weaver, Lynn E., eds. Neutron Dynamics & Control. LC 66-60098. (AEC Symposium Ser.). 612p. 1966. pap. 23.50 (ISBN 0-87079-297-0, CONF-650413); microfiche 4.50. DOE.

Hetrick, Patrick K. Webster's Real Estate Law in North Carolina. rev. ed. 1981. 60.00 (ISBN 0-87215-402-5). Michie-Bobbs.

Hetsroni, G. Handbook of Multiphase Systems. 1024p. 1981. 69.50 (ISBN 0-07-028460-1). McGraw.

Hettema, P. J. Personality & Adaptation. (Advances in Psychology Ser.: Vol. 2). 228p. 1979. 40.50 (ISBN 0-686-85934-0, North Holland). Elsevier.

Hettich, M. & Ahern, C. Looking Out. 30p. 1981. 3.00 (ISBN 0-686-38060-6). Moons Quilt Pr.

Hettich, M., ed. see Budy, Andrea H.

Hettich, M., ed. see Dragone, Carol.

Hettich, Michael, ed. see Sandy, Stephen.

Hettinger, Theodor. Physiology of Strength. (Illus.). 96p. 1961. photocopy ed. spiral 11.50x (ISBN 0-398-04281-0). C C Thomas.

Hettlinger, Richard F. Sexual Maturity. 1970. pap. 6.95x o.p. (ISBN 0-534-00258-7). Wadsworth Pub.

Hetzel, B. S. & Smith, R. M., eds. Fetal Brain Disorders: Recent Approaches to the Problem of Mental Deficiency. 1981. 131.00 (ISBN 0-444-80321-1). Elsevier.

Hetzel, Basil S. Basic Health Care in Developing Countries: An Epidemiological Perspective. (IEA & WHO Handbooks Ser.). (Illus.). 1979. pap. text ed. 24.95x (ISBN 0-19-261223-9). Oxford U Pr.

Hetzel, Howard R., jt. auth. see Ward, Jack A.

Hetzel, Nancy K. Environmental Cooperation Among Industrialized Countries: The Role of Regional Organizations. LC 79-5438. 1980. pap. text ed. 13.50 (ISBN 0-8191-0886-3). U Pr of Amer.

Hetzel, Otto & Szymanski, Michael. Housing Associations in England: A Model For Success in America. 48p. 1981. pap. text ed. 4.25 (ISBN 0-87855-885-3). Transaction Bks.

Hetzler, Stanley A. Applied Measures for Promoting Technological Growth. (International Library of Sociology Ser). 1973. 19.50x o.p. (ISBN 0-7100-7502-2). Routledge & Kegan.

Heuer, Janet, et al. Magic Kits: Meaningful Activities for the Gifted in the Classroom Through Knowledge, Interests, Training & Stimulation. (Illus.). 53p. 1980. pap. 9.95 (ISBN 0-936386-11-8). Creative Learning.

Heuer, Richards J., Jr. Quantitative Approaches to Political Intelligence: The CIA Experience. (A Westview Special Study). 1978. lib. bdg. 25.00 o.p. (ISBN 0-89158-096-4). Westview.

Heufelder, Emmanuel. The Way to God According to the Rule of Saint Benedict. Eberle, Luke, tr. from Ger. (Cistercian Studies: No. 49). 1983. price not set (ISBN 0-87907-849-9). Cistercian Pubns.

Heukensfeldt Jansen, H. P. Project Evaluation & Discounted Cash Flow: A Reassessment & an Alternative Suggestion. 1977. 47.00 (ISBN 0-7204-0480-0, North-Holland). Elsevier.

Heuman, jt. auth. see Boldy.

Heuman, William. Famous Pro Football Stars. LC 67-10443. (Illus.). (gr. 7-9). 1967. 5.95 o.p. (ISBN 0-396-05490-0). Dodd.

Heun, Linda & Heun, Richard. Developing Skills for Human Interaction. 2nd ed. (Speech & Drama Ser.). 1978. pap. text ed. 16.95x (ISBN 0-675-08396-6). Additional supplements may be obtained from publisher (ISBN 0-686-67976-8). Merrill.

Heun, Linda, jt. auth. see Heun, Richard.

Heun, Richard & Heun, Linda. Public Speaking: A New Speech Book. (Illus.). 1979. pap. text ed. 14.50 (ISBN 0-8299-0239-2); instrs.' manual avail. (ISBN 0-8299-0488-3). West Pub.

Heun, Richard, jt. auth. see Heun, Linda.

Heurck, Jan van see Von der Grun, Max.

Heurgon, Jacques. The Rise of Rome. LC 70-126762. 1973. 30.00x (ISBN 0-520-01795-1). U of Cal Pr.

Heurn, J. van. De Orgelmaaker behelzende eene uitvoerige beschrijving van alle de uit en inwendige deelen des Orgels en handleiding tot het maaken, zamenbrengen en herstellen derzelven, benevens de beschrijving en afbeelding der werktuigen welke tot deze kunst gebezigd worden, 3 vols. (Bibliotheca Organologica Ser.: Vol. 56). 1976. Repr. of 1805 ed. Set. 137.50 o.s.i. (ISBN 90-6027-257-9, Pub. by Frits Knuf Netherlands). Pendragon NY.

Heusch, Luc de. The Drunken King, or, The Origin of the State. Willis, Roy, tr. LC 81-47569. (African Systems of Thought Ser.). (Illus.). 288p. 1982. 27.50x (ISBN 0-253-31832-7). Ind U Pr.

Heusch, Luc De see De Heusch, Luc.

Heusch, Luc De see Heusch, Luc de.

Heuser, Harro G. Functional Analysis. 408p. 1981. 62.95x (ISBN 0-471-28052-6, Pub. by Wiley-Interscience); pap. 24.95 (ISBN 0-471-10069-2). Wiley.

Heusghem, Camille & Albert, Adelin, eds. Advanced Interpretation of Clinical Laboratory Data. (Clinical & Biochemical Analysis Ser.: Vol. 13). (Illus.). 448p. 1982. 55.00 (ISBN 0-8247-1744-9). Dekker.

Heuson, John C., et al, eds. Breast Cancer: Trends in Research & Treatment. LC 76-22910. (European Organization for Research on Treatment of Cancer Monograph: Vol. 2). 343p. 1976. 35.00 (ISBN 0-89004-096-6). Raven.

Heute, F. U. Isothermal Extrusion of Heavy Metals. (Illus.). 90p. 1981. pap. 30.00 (ISBN 3-88355-033-7, Pub. by DGM Metallurgy Germany). IR Pubns.

Heutte, Frederic. Fred Heutte's Gardening in the Temperate Zone. LC 77-11096. (Illus.). 1977. 9.95 o.p. (ISBN 0-915442-35-3). Donning Co.

Hevener, Natalie K. International Law & the Status of Women. (Replica Edition). 145p. 1982. lib. bdg. 20.00 (ISBN 0-86531-924-3). Westview.

Hevener, Natalie K., ed. Dynamics of Human Rights in United States Foreign Policy. LC 79-66435. 375p. 1981. 39.95 (ISBN 0-87855-347-9); pap. 19.95. Transaction Bks.

Heverly, Judith. Fraternizing in the Office: The Book the Boss Should Never Have. LC 80-10359. 1983. 14.95 (ISBN 0-87949-177-9). Ashley Bks.

Hevesi, Alan G. Legislative Politics in New York State: A Comparative Analysis. LC 74-6864. (Special Studies). 265p. 1975. 27.95 o.p. (ISBN 0-275-05520-5). Praeger.

Heward, William L. & Orlansky, Michael D. Exceptional Children: An Introductory Survey to Special Education. (Special Education Ser.). 480p. 1980. text ed. 21.95 (ISBN 0-675-08179-3). Additional supplements may be obtained from publisher. Merrill.

Heward, William L., jt. auth. see Orlansky, Michael D.

Hewat, Joanathan, jt. auth. see Hewat, Theresa.

Hewat, Sybil, jt. auth. see Cluysenaar, Anne.

Hewat, Theresa & Hewat, Joanathan. Overland & Beyond. 5th ed. 160p. 1980. 9.95 (ISBN 0-903909-13-8). Bradt Ent.

Hewes, Gordon W. see Wescott, Roger W.

Hewes, Jeremy J., jt. auth. see Fluegelman, Andrew.

Hewett, E. A. Foreign Trade Prices in the Council for Mutual Economic Assistance. LC 73-86045. (Soviet & East European Studies). (Illus.). 212p. 1974. 37.50 (ISBN 0-521-20377-5). Cambridge U Pr.

Hewett, Edgar L., jt. auth. see Bandelier, Adolph F.

Hewett, Joan. Watching Them Grow: Inside a Zoo Nursery. LC 77-15642. (Illus.). (gr. 3-7). 1979. 9.95 (ISBN 0-316-35968-8). Little.

Hewett, Robert B., ed. Political Change & the Economic Future of East Asia. 208p. 1981. pap. 10.00x (ISBN 0-8248-0750-2). UH Pr.

Hewins, Caroline M. Mid-Century Child & Her Books. LC 69-16070. 1969. Repr. of 1926 ed. 30.00x (ISBN 0-8103-3857-2). Gale.

Hewish, Mark. The Young Scientist Book of Jets. LC 78-17507. (Young Scientist Ser.). (Illus.). (gr. 4-5). 1978. text ed. 7.95 (ISBN 0-88436-527-1). EMC.

Hewish, Mark, jt. auth. see Jay, Michael.

Hewish, Mark, et al. Air Forces of the World. 1979. 24.95 o.p. (ISBN 0-671-25086-8). S&S.

Hewison, C. H. Locomotive Boiler Explosions. (Illus.). 144p. 1982. 16.50 (ISBN 0-7153-8305-1). David & Charles.

Hewison, Robert. Monty Python: The Case Against. LC 81-47631. (Illus.). 96p. (Orig.). 1981. pap. 9.95 o.s.i. (ISBN 0-394-17949-8, E787, Ever). Grove.

Hewison, William, tr. see Wodehouse, P. G.

Hewitt. Conceptual Physics: A New Introduction to Your Environment. 4th ed. 1981. text ed. 21.95 (ISBN 0-316-35969-6); tchrs'. manual avail. (ISBN 0-316-35971-8); test bank avail. (ISBN 0-316-35972-6). Little.

Hewitt, Abram. Sire Lines. 26.25 o.p. (ISBN 0-936032-09-X). Blood-Horse.

Hewitt, Elizabeth. Broken Vows. 1982. pap. 2.25 (ISBN 0-451-11514-7, AE1514, Sig). NAL.

Hewitt, Emily C. & Hiatt, Suzanne R. Women Priests: Yes or No? LC 72-81027. 128p. 1973. pap. 1.00 (ISBN 0-8164-2076-9, SP77). Seabury.

Hewitt, Geoff. Stone Soup. 61p. 1974. 3.45 (ISBN 0-87886-045-2). Ithaca Hse.

Hewitt, H. J. The Organisation of War under Edward III, 1338-62. 1966. 19.00 (ISBN 0-7190-0066-1). Manchester.

Hewitt, Helen, ed. Petrucci's Harmnica Musices Odhecation A. LC 77-25989. (Music Reprint Ser., 1978). 1978. Repr. of 1942 ed. lib. bdg. 47.50 (ISBN 0-306-77562-X). Da Capo.

Hewitt, James R. Andre Malraux. LC 70-15661. (Literature and Life Ser.). 1978. 11.95 (ISBN 0-8044-2379-2). Ungar.

--Marcel Proust. LC 74-76127. (Literature and Life Ser.). 136p. 1975. 11.95 (ISBN 0-8044-2382-2). Ungar.

Hewitt, Jean. The New York Times Heritage Cook Book. (Illus.). 1972. 7.95 o.p. (ISBN 0-399-11005-4). Putnam Pub Group.

--The New York Times New England Heritage Cook Book. (Illus.). 1977. 8.95 o.p. (ISBN 0-399-11910-8). Putnam Pub Group.

--The New York Times Southern Heritage Cook Book. LC 76-13363. (Illus.). 1976. 7.95 o.p. (ISBN 0-399-11768-7). Putnam Pub Group.

Hewitt, John, jt. auth. see Chinoy, Ely.

Hewitt, John P. Social Stratification & Deviant Behavior. 1970. pap. text ed. 7.25x (ISBN 0-394-30794-1). Phila Bk Co.

Hewitt, Karen & Haviland, William A. Educational Toys in America: Eighteen Hundred to the Present. LC 80-131686. (Illus.). 151p. (Orig.). 1979. pap. 12.50 (ISBN 0-87451-988-8). U Pr of New Eng.

Hewitt, W. P. Land & Community: European Migration to Rural Texas in the 19th Century. (Illus.). 69p. 1982. pap. text ed. 1.95 (ISBN 0-89641-101-X). American Pr.

Hewitt, W. R., jt. ed. see Plaa, G. L.

Hewlett, Crockette. Two Centuries of Art in New Hanover County. LC 76-12221. 1976. 15.000 (ISBN 0-87716-065-1, Pub. by Moore Pub Co). F Apple.

Hewlett, P. S. An Introduction to the Interpretation of Quantal Responses in Biology. 82p. 1979. pap. text ed. 12.95 o.p. (ISBN 0-8391-1386-2). Univ Park.

Hewlett-Packard Co. Series Eighty Software Catalog. 2nd ed. 1982. pap. 12.95 (ISBN 0-8359-6983-5). Reston.

Hewlett-Packard. Optoelectronics-Fiber-Optics Applications Manual. 2nd ed. (Illus.). 448p. 1981. 31.25 (ISBN 0-07-028606-X, P&RB). McGraw.

Hewlitt, P. S. & Placket, R. L. Interpretation of Quantal Responses in Biology. 88p. 1979. pap. text ed. 12.95 (ISBN 0-7131-2742-2). E Arnold.

Hexham, Irving. The Irony of Apartheid: The Struggle for National Independence of Afrikaner Calvinism Against British Imperialism. (Texts & Studies in Religion: Vol. 8). xii, 240p. 1981. soft cover 34.95x (ISBN 0-88946-904-0). E Mellen.

Hexter, J. H. Reappraisals in History: New Views on History & Society in Early Modern Europe. 2nd ed. LC 78-55041. 1979. lib. bdg. 20.00x (ISBN 0-226-33232-2); pap. 8.00x (ISBN 0-226-33233-0, P794). U of Chicago Pr.

Hexter, J. H., ed. The Traditions of the Western World. LC 80-5711. 310p. 1980. lib. bdg. 20.50 (ISBN 0-8191-1179-1); pap. text ed. 10.25 (ISBN 0-8191-1180-5). U Pr of Amer.

Hexter, R. M., jt. auth. see Decius, J. C.

Hey, A. J., jt. auth. see Aitchison, I. J.

Hey, M. H. & Embry, P. G. An Index of Mineral Species & Varieties Arranged Chemically with an Alphabetical Index of Accepted Mineral Names & Synonyms. 2nd ed. 1975. 62.50x set (ISBN 0-686-37456-8). Index (ISBN 0-565-00097-7) (ISBN 0-565-00578-2) (ISBN 0-565-00725-4). Sabbot-Natural Hist Bks.

Hey, M. H., et al. Catalogue of Meteorites with Special Reference to Those Represented in the Collection of the British Museum (Natural History) 3rd ed. 1966. 62.50 set (ISBN 0-686-37455-X). Catalog (ISBN 0-565-00464-6). Appendix to the Catalogue of Meteorites 1977 (ISBN 0-565-00789-0). Sabbot-Natural Hist Bks.

Hey, Nigel S. How We Will Explore the Outer Planets. new ed. (Illus.). 160p. (gr. 7-10). 1973. PLB 5.49 o.p. (ISBN 0-399-60763-3). Putnam Pub Group.

--The Mysterious Sun. (Illus.). (gr. 7-10). 1971. PLB 4.99 o.p. (ISBN 0-399-60482-0). Putnam Pub Group.

Hey, R. D., et al. Gravel-Bed Rivers: Fluvial Processes, Engineering & Management. 992p. 1982. 84.00 (ISBN 0-471-10139-7, Pub. by Wiley-Interscience). Wiley.

Heyck, T. W. The Transformation of Intellectual Life in Victorian England. LC 82-840. 262p. 1982. 25.00x (ISBN 0-312-81427-5). St Martin.

Heyd, Michael. Between Orthodoxy & the Enlightenment. 1983. 65.00 (ISBN 90-247-2508-9, Pub. by Martinus Nijhoff Netherlands). Kluwer Boston.

Heyde, Herbert. Floteninstrumente Karl-Marx-Universitat zu Leipzig: Musik-instrumenten-Museum, Gesamtkatalog, Band I. (The Flute Library: Vol. 20). 1979. 32.50 o.s.i. (ISBN 90-6027-261-7, Pub. by Frits Knuf Netherlands). Pendragon NY.

Heyden, Siegfried. Keep Your Heart in Shape. 96p. (Orig.). 1981. pap. 2.50 (ISBN 0-8326-2249-4, 7446). Delair.

Heydenreich, Ludwig & Lotz, Wolfgang. Architecture in Italy: 1400-1600. (Pelican History of Art Ser: No. 38). (Orig.). 1974. 50.00 o.p. (ISBN 0-670-13146-6, Pelican). Viking Pr.

Heydenryk, Henry. Art & History of Frames: An Inquiry into the Enhancement of Paintings. (Illus.). 1969. 15.00 o.p. (ISBN 0-685-11947-5). Heineman.

Heydron, Vicki A., jt. auth. see Garrett, Randall.

Heyel, Carl. Foreman's Handbook. 4th ed. 1967. 32.50 o.p. (ISBN 0-07-028627-2, P&RB). McGraw.

Heyen, William. The Trains. (Metacom Limited Edition Ser.: No. 2). 24p. 1981. ltd. 25.00x (ISBN 0-911381-01-5). Metacom Pr.

Heyer, Georgette. April Lady. (Regency Romance Ser.). 256p. 1983. pap. 2.75 (ISBN 0-515-07082-3). Jove Pubns.

--April Lady. 288p. 1973. 7.95 (ISBN 0-399-11136-0). Putnam Pub Group.

--Arabella. 1971. 7.95 (ISBN 0-399-10053-9). Putnam Pub Group.

--Barren Corn. 1976. Repr. of 1930 ed. lib. bdg. 16.95 (ISBN 0-89966-123-8). Buccaneer Bks.

--Bath Tangle. 1979. pap. 1.95 o.p. (ISBN 0-425-04251-0). Berkley Pub.

--Bath Tangle. (Regency Romance Ser.). 320p. 1983. pap. 2.75 (ISBN 0-515-06880-2). Jove Pubns.

--A Civil Contract. 1971. 7.95 (ISBN 0-399-10144-6). Putnam Pub Group.

--The Foundling. 1971. 7.95 o.s.i. (ISBN 0-399-10318-X). Putnam Pub Group.

--Friday's Child. 1971. 7.95 o.s.i. (ISBN 0-399-10327-9). Putnam Pub Group.

--The Grand Sophy. (Regency Romance Ser.). 320p. 1981. pap. 2.75 (ISBN 0-515-05928-5). Jove Pubns.

--The Grand Sophy. 1972. 7.95 o.s.i. (ISBN 0-399-10953-6). Putnam Pub Group.

--Helen. 1976. Repr. of 1928 ed. lib. bdg. 16.95 (ISBN 0-89966-120-3). Buccaneer Bks.

--Merely Murder. 369p. 1981. Repr. lib. bdg. 17.95 (ISBN 0-89966-296-X). Buccaneer Bks.

--The Quiet Gentleman. 288p. 1983. pap. 2.75 o.s.i. (ISBN 0-515-07137-4). Jove Pubns.

--The Quiet Gentlemen. 1972. 7.95 (ISBN 0-399-10921-8). Putnam Pub Group.

--The Reluctant Widow. 1971. 7.95 (ISBN 0-399-10685-5). Putnam Pub Group.

--Sprig Muslin. 256p. 1983. pap. 2.75 (ISBN 0-515-07148-X). Jove Pubns.

--Sylvester or the Wicked Uncle. 1971. 7.95 (ISBN 0-399-10784-3). Putnam Pub Group.

--The Toll Gate. 320p. 1972. 7.95 (ISBN 0-399-11029-1). Putnam Pub Group.

--The Unknown Ajax. LC 60-8471. 320p. 1974. 7.95 (ISBN 0-399-11348-7). Putnam Pub Group.

--Venetia. 308p. 1973. 7.95 (ISBN 0-399-11171-9). Putnam Pub Group.

--Venetia. 320p. 1982. pap. 2.75 (ISBN 0-515-06878-0). Jove Pubns.

Heyer, H. Einfuehrung in die Theorie Markoffacher Prozesse. 253p. 1979. pap. text ed. 14.95x. (ISBN 3-411-01564-0). Birkhauser.

--Theory of Statistical Experiments. (Springer Series in Statistics). (Illus.). 289p. 1983. 19.80 (ISBN 0-387-90785-8). Springer-Verlag.

Heyer, Herbert, ed. Probability Measures on Groups, Oberwolfach, Federal Republic of Germany, 1981: Proceedings. (Lecture Notes in Mathematics Ser.: Vol. 928). 477p. 1982. pap. 23.00 (ISBN 0-387-11501-3). Springer-Verlag.

Heyer, Robert, ed. Nuclear Disarmament: Key Statements of Popes, Bishops, Councils & Churches. 1982. pap. 7.95 (ISBN 0-8091-2456-4). Paulist Pr.

--Religious Life of the Adolescent. LC 75-10113. (New Catholic World Ser.). 80p. 1975. pap. 2.45 o.p. (ISBN 0-8091-1878-5). Paulist Pr.

Heyer, Robert J., ed. Celebrating Lent. LC 74-28634. 1975. pap. 2.45 o.s.i. (ISBN 0-8091-1864-5). Paulist Pr.

Heyerdahl, Thor. The Tigris Expedition: In Search of Our Beginnings. (Illus.). 1982. pap. 7.95 (ISBN 0-452-25358-6, Z5358, Plume). NAL.

Heyerdahl, Thor see Allen, W. S.

Heyerdahl, V., ed. Best of the Doll Reader. 250p. 1980. pap. 9.95 (ISBN 0-87588-187-4). Hobby Hse.

Heyl, Bernard C. New Bearings in Esthetics & Art Criticism: A Study in Semantics & Evaluation. 1943. text ed. 13.50x (ISBN 0-686-83646-4). Elliots Bks.

Heym, Stefan. Queen Against Defoe & Other Stories. LC 73-20380. (Illus.). 128p. 1974. 6.95 o.p. (ISBN 0-88208-041-5). Lawrence Hill.

Heym, Stefan, ed. see Twain, Mark.

Heyma, K., ed. see Allen, John.

Heyman, Anita. Final Grades. LC 82-45997. 192p. (gr. 7 up). 1983. PLB 9.95 (ISBN 0-396-08141-X). Dodd.

Heyman, D. P. & Sobel, M. J. Stochastic Models in Operations Research: Stochastic Optimization, Vol. 2. (Quantitative Methods for Management Ser.). 414p. 1983. 28.00 (ISBN 0-07-028632-9). McGraw.

Heyman, J., jt. auth. see Baker, John.

Heyman, Jacques. Elements of Stress Analysis. LC 81-15495. (Illus.). 140p. 1982. 32.50 (ISBN 0-521-24523-0). Cambridge U Pr.

--The Masonry Arch. 117p. 1982. 44.95x (ISBN 0-470-27544-8). Halsted Pr.

Heyman, Mark. Simulation Games for the Classroom. LC 74-33810. (Fastback Ser.: No. 54). (Illus., Orig.). 1975. pap. 0.75 o.p. (ISBN 0-87367-054-X). Phi Delta Kappa.

Heyman, Neil M., jt. auth. see Herwig, Holger H.

Heymann, Michael, ed. The Uganda Controversy, Vol 2. 390p. 1978. 14.95 (ISBN 0-87855-271-5). Transaction Bks.

Heymann, O. & Nguyen, O. Simulation & Analysis of Immobilized Cell Fermentors. (Progress in Solar Energy Supplements SERI Ser.). 1983. pap. text ed. 7.50x (ISBN 0-89553-091-0). Am Solar Energy.

Heymer, Armin. The Ethological Dictionary: In English, French & German. new ed. LC 77-78418. (Illus.). 238p. 1979. Repr. of 1977 ed. lib. bdg. 35.00 o.s.i. (ISBN 0-8240-7005-4, Garland STPM Pr). Garland Pub.

Heyn, Ernest V., jt. auth. see Lees, Alfred W.

Heyne & Van Winkle. Art for Young America. 1979. text ed. 18.64 (ISBN 0-87002-294-6). Bennett IL.

Heyne, Paul. The Economic Way of Thinking. 2nd ed. LC 76-21665. 1976. text ed. 12.95 o.p. (ISBN 0-574-19250-6, 13-2250); instr's guide avail. o.p. (ISBN 0-574-19251-4, 13-2251). SRA.

Heyne, Paul & Johnson, Thomas. Toward Understanding Microeconomics. LC 76-22434. 1976. pap. text ed. 13.95 (ISBN 0-574-19270-0, 13-2270); instr's guide avail. (ISBN 0-574-19256-5, 13-2256). SRA.

Heyne, Paul T. The Economic Way of Thinking. 4th ed. 208p. 1983. text ed. write for info. (ISBN 0-574-19425-8); write for info. tchr's ed. (ISBN 0-574-19426-6); write for info. student guide (ISBN 0-574-19427-4). SRA.

Heyne, Paul T. & Johnson, Thomas. Toward Economic Understanding. LC 75-31554. (Illus.). 720p. 1976. text ed. 21.95 (ISBN 0-574-19255-7, 13-2255); instr's guide avail. (ISBN 0-574-19256-5, 13-2256); study guide 7.95 (ISBN 0-574-19257-3, 13-2257). SRA.

Heyneman, Stephen P. The Evaluation of Human Capital in Malawi. (Working Paper: No. 420). vi, 101p. 1980. 5.00 (ISBN 0-686-36038-9, WP-0420). World Bank.

--Investment in Indian Education: Uneconomic? (Working Paper: No. 327). 56p. 1979. 3.00 (ISBN 0-686-36040-0, WP-0327). World Bank.

Heyneman, Stephen P. & Currie, Janice K. Schooling, Academic Performance & Occupational Attainment in a Non-Industrialized Society. LC 79-63564. 1979. pap. text ed. 9.50 (ISBN 0-8191-0729-8). U Pr of Amer.

Heynen, A. James, jt. auth. see Brinks, Herbert.

Heyns, Roger W., ed. Leadership for Higher Education. 1977. 13.50 o.p. (ISBN 0-8268-1341-0). ACE.

Heyrick, Benjamin A. Short Studies in Composition. 104p. 1982. Repr. of 1905 ed. lib. bdg. 30.00 (ISBN 0-89760-366-4). Telegraph Bks.

Heyting, A. Axiomatic Projective Geometry. 2nd ed. 1980. 38.50 (ISBN 0-444-85431-2). Elsevier.

Heyting, A., jt. auth. see Brouwer, L.

Heyting, A., ed. see Brouwer, L. E.

Heyward, Du Bose. Mamba's Daughter. new ed. LC 29-3497. 311p. 1974. 13.95 (ISBN 0-910220-59-X). Berg.

--Porgy. LC 25-17940. 1967. 9.95 (ISBN 0-910220-13-1). Berg.

Heyward, Isabel C. The Redemption of God: A Theology of Mutual Relation. LC 81-43706. 266p. (Orig.). 1982. lib. bdg. 23.25 (ISBN 0-8191-2389-7); pap. text ed. 11.50 (ISBN 0-8191-2390-0). U Pr of Amer.

Heywood, Arthur. A First Program in Mathematics. 3rd ed. 1977. 17.95x o.p. (ISBN 0-8221-0185-8). Dickenson.

Heywood, Arthur H. Arithemetic: A Programmed Worktext. 4th ed. LC 81-10231. (Mathematics). 405p. 1982. pap. text ed. 19.95 (ISBN 0-8185-0490-0). Brooks-Cole.

Heywood Brothers & Wakefield Co. Classic Wicker Furniture: The Complete 1898-1899 Illustrated Catalog of the Heywood Brothers & Wakefield Company. (Antiques Ser.). (Illus.). 128p. 1982. pap. 6.50 (ISBN 0-486-24355-9). Dover.

Heywood, Christopher, ed. & intro. by. Perspectives on African Literature. LC 71-169493. 172p. 1972. text ed. 24.50x (ISBN 0-8419-0093-0, Africana). Holmes & Meier.

Heywood, Harry. Black Bolshevik: Autobiography of an Afro-American Communist. LC 77-77464. (Illus.). 736p. 1978. 19.95 o.p. (ISBN 0-930720-52-0); pap. 9.95 o.p. (ISBN 0-930720-53-9). Liberator Pr.

Heywood, Jean S. Children in Care: The Development of the Service for the Deprived Child. rev. ed. (International Library of Sociology). 284p. 1978. 15.00 (ISBN 0-7100-8733-0). Routledge & Kegan.

Heywood, John. Pitfalls & Planning in Student Teaching. 192p. 1982. 22.50 (ISBN 0-89397-133-2). Nichols Pub.

Heywood, R. B. Photoelasticity for Designers. (International Series in Mechanical Engineering: Vol. 2). 1969. inquire for price o.p. (ISBN 0-08-013005-4). Pergamon.

Heywood, Thomas. Apology for Actors. Bd. with A Refutation of the Apology for Actors. LC 42-8174. 1978. 25.00x (ISBN 0-8201-1198-8). Schol Facsimiles.

Heywood, V. H. Plant Taxonomy. (Studies in Biology: No. 5). 64p. 1978. pap. text ed. 8.95 (ISBN 0-7131-2609-4). E Arnold.

Heywood, V. H., ed. Flowering Plants of the World. (Illus.). 1978. 13.50x (ISBN 0-19-217674-9). Oxford U Pr.

Heywood, V. H. & Clark, R. B., eds. Taxonomy in Europe: Final Report of the European Science Research Council's Ad Hoc Group on Biological Recording Systematics & Taxonomy. (European Science Research Council Review Ser.: No. 17). 170p. 1982. pap. 13.25 (ISBN 0-444-86363-X, North Holland). Elsevier.

Heywood, W. S., ed. see Ballou, Adin.

Heywood Broun, May, tr. see Valle-Inclan, Ramon.

Heyworth, P. L., ed. Medieval Studies for J. A. W. Bennett: Aetatis suae LXX. (Illus.). 438p. 1981. 65.00x (ISBN 0-19-812628-X). Oxford U Pr.

Hiaasen, Carl, jt. auth. see Monalbano, William D.

Hiaasen, Carl, jt. auth. see Montalbano, William L.

Hiang The, jt. auth. see Sin The.

Hiatsma, Julia Van see Van Hiatsma, Willard & Van Hiatsma, Julia.

Hiatsma, Willard Van see Van Hiatsma, Willard & Van Hiatsma, Julia.

Hiatt, Jane, ed. see Bignell, Steven.

Hiatt, L. R. Australian Aboriginal Concepts. LC 78-58302. 1978. text ed. 18.25x (ISBN 0-391-00887-0); pap. text ed. 11.00x (ISBN 0-391-00888-9). Humanities.

Hiatt, L. R., ed. Australian Aboriginal Mythology: Essays in Honour of W. E. H. Stanner. (AIAS Social Anthropology Ser.: No. 9). (Illus.). 1975. 19.75x (ISBN 0-85575-044-8). Humanities.

Hiatt, Mary P. Artful Balance: The Parallel Structures of Style. LC 75-11673. 192p. 1975. text ed. 14.95x (ISBN 0-8077-2487-4); pap. text ed. 7.95 (ISBN 0-8077-2486-6). Tchrs Coll.

--The Way Women Write: Sex & Style in Contemporary Prose. LC 77-14122. 1977. pap. 8.95x (ISBN 0-8077-2542-0). Tchrs Coll.

Hiatt, Suzanne R., jt. auth. see Hewitt, Emily C.

Hiatt, Thomas A. & Gerzon, Mark F., eds. The Young Internationalists. LC 70-188981. 224p. 1973. 14.00x (ISBN 0-8248-0218-7, Eastwest Ctr). UH Pr.

Hibbard, Addison & Frenz, Horst, eds. Writers of the Western World. 2nd ed. LC 67-6008. 1967. text ed. 26.50 (ISBN 0-395-04601-7). HM.

Hibbard, Caroline M. Charles I & the Popish Plot. LC 81-23075. 350p. 1983. 28.00x (ISBN 0-8078-1520-9). U of NC Pr.

Hibbard, Don & Kaleialoha, Carol. The Role of Rock: A Guide to the Social & Political Consequences of Rock Music. 252p. 1983. 14.95 (ISBN 0-13-782458-0); pap. 6.95 (ISBN 0-13-782441-6). P-H.

Hibbard, Howard. Bernini. (Illus., Orig.). 1966. pap. 6.95 (ISBN 0-14-020701-5, Pelican). Penguin.

--Caravaggio. LC 78-2145. (Icon Editions). (Illus.). 304p. 1983. write for info (ISBN 0-06-433322-1, HarpT). Har-Row.

Hibbard, Jeff. Baja Bugs & Buggies. 106p. 1982. pap. 9.95 (ISBN 0-89586-186-0). H P Bks.

Hibbard, Lester T. & Gibbons, William. Handbook of Gynecologic Emergencies. 2nd ed. 1982. pap. 13.95 (ISBN 0-87488-640-6). Med Exam.

Hibbard, P. G. & Schuman, S. A., eds. Constructing Quality Software: Proceedings of the IFIP Working Conference on Constructing Quality Software, Novosibirsk, U.S.S.R., May, 1977. 1978. 64.00 (ISBN 0-444-85106-2, North-Holland). Elsevier.

Hibbard, Wanda M. A Handbook of Nuclear Pharmacy. (Illus.). 120p. 1982. pap. 18.75x spiral (ISBN 0-398-04760-X). C C Thomas.

Hibbeler, R. C. Engineering Mechanics: Dynamics. 3rd ed. 512p. 1983. text ed. 25.95 (ISBN 0-02-354260-8). Macmillan.

--Engineering Mechanics: Statics. 2nd ed. (Illus.). 1978. 27.95 (ISBN 0-02-354020-6). Macmillan.

--Engineering Mechanics: Statics. 3rd ed. 448p. 1983. text ed. 25.95 (ISBN 0-02-354300-0). Macmillan.

Hibberd, Robert G. Integrated Circuits: A Basic Course for Engineers & Technicians. (Texas Instruments Electronics Ser.). 1969. 35.75 (ISBN 0-07-028651-5, P&RB). McGraw.

--Solid-State Electronics: A Basic Course for Engineers & Technicians. (Texas Instruments Electronics Ser.). 1968. 32.50 o.p. (ISBN 0-07-028650-7, P&RB). McGraw.

Hibbert, Albert. Smith Wigglesworth: The Secret of His Power. 112p. 1982. pap. 4.95 (ISBN 0-89274-211-9, HH-211). Harrison Hse.

Hibbert, Christopher. Chateaux of the Loire. New ed. Bayrd, Edwin, ed. (Wonders of Man Ser.). (Illus.). 176p. 1982. 19.95 (ISBN 0-88225-317-4). Newsweek.

--The Court of St. James's: The Monarch at Work from Victoria to Elizabeth II. LC 82-62185. (Illus.). 288p. 1983. pap. 6.95 (ISBN 0-688-01602-2). Quill NY.

--The Days of the French Revolution: The Day-to-Day Story of the Revolution. LC 81-9666. (Illus.). 24p. 1981. pap. 6.95 (ISBN 0-688-00746-5). Quill NY.

--Gilbert & Sullivan & Their Victorian World. LC 76-21063. (Illus.). 1976. 24.95 o.p. (ISBN 0-399-11830-6, Pub. by Am Heritage). Putnam Pub Group.

--The Great Mutiny: India, Eighteen Fifty-Seven. 472p. 1980. pap. 7.95 (ISBN 0-14-004752-2). Penguin.

--House of Medici: Its Rise & Fall. LC 79-26508. (Illus.). 364p. 1980. pap. 6.95 (ISBN 0-688-05339-4). Quill NY.

--The Pen & the Sword. (Milestones of History Ser). (Illus.). 160p. 1974. 10.00 o.p. (ISBN 0-88225-068-X). Newsweek.

--Personal History of Samuel Johnson. Repr. of 1970 ed. 10.95 o.s.i. (ISBN 0-911660-26-7). Yankee Peddler.

Hibbert, J. R., jt. auth. see Heathcote, J. G.

Hibbett, Howard, tr. see Kawabata, Yasunari.

Hibbett, Howard, tr. see Tanizaki, Junichiro.

Hibbs, A. R., jt. auth. see Feyman, P.

Hibbs, D. A., et al, eds. Contemporary Political Economy: Studies on the Interdependence of Politics & Economy. 1981. 38.50 (ISBN 0-444-86014-2). Elsevier.

Hibner, Dixie, jt. auth. see Cromwell, Liz.

Hibshman, Dan. Your Affordable Solar Home. (Tools for Today Ser.). 1983. pap. 7.95 (ISBN 0-686-84929-9). Sierra.

Hichborn, Franklin. System: As Uncovered by the San Francisco Graft Prosecution. LC 69-14933. (Criminology, Law Enforcement, & Social Problems Ser.: No. 38). 1969. Repr. of 1915 ed. 15.00x (ISBN 0-87585-038-3). Patterson Smith.

Hichens, Robert S. An Imaginative Man. LC 76-24387. (The Decadent Consciousness Ser.: Vol. 15). 1977. Repr. of 1895 ed. lib. bdg. 38.00 o.s.i. (ISBN 0-8240-2763-9). Garland Pub.

--The Londoners: An Absurdity. Fletcher, Ian & Stokes, John, eds. LC 76-24388. (Decadent Consciousness Ser.: Vol. 16). 1977. Repr. of 1898 ed. lib. bdg. 38.00 o.s.i. (ISBN 0-8240-2764-7). Garland Pub.

Hichman, Martha W. When can Daddy Come Home? (Illus.). 48p. 1983. 9.50 (ISBN 0-687-44969-3). Abingdon.

Hick, John. Classical & Contemporary Readings in the Philosophy of Religion. 2nd ed. LC 75-98092. (Philosophy Ser). 1969. text ed. 23.95 (ISBN 0-13-135269-5). P-H.

--God & the Universe of Faiths. LC 73-88027. 224p. 1974. 19.95 o.p. (ISBN 0-312-33040-5). St Martin.

--God Has Many Names. 108p. 1981. text ed. 20.00x o.p. (ISBN 0-333-27747-3, Pub. by Macmillan, England); pap. text ed. 7.50x o.p. (ISBN 0-333-27758-9). Humanities.

--God Has Many Names. LC 82-1959. 144p. 1982. pap. 7.95 (ISBN 0-664-24419-X). Westminster.

--Philosophy of Religion. 2nd ed. LC 72-5429. (Foundations of Philosophy). 144p. 1973. pap. 8.95x ref. ed. (ISBN 0-13-663948-8). P-H.

Hick, John, ed. The Myth of God Incarnate. LC 77-9965. 1978. pap. 7.95 (ISBN 0-664-24178-6). Westminster.

Hick, John H. Evil & the God of Love. rev. ed. LC 76-62953. 1977. pap. 7.64xi (ISBN 0-06-063902-4, RD219, HarpR). Har-Row.

Hicken, Victor. The World Is Coming to an End: An Irreverent Look at Modern Doomsayers. 1975. 7.95 o.p. (ISBN 0-87000-303-8, Arlington Hse). Crown.

Hickerson, Harold. Chippewa Indians IV: Ethnohistory of Chippewa in Central Minnesota. (American Indian Ethnohistory Ser: North Central & Northeastern Indians). (Illus.). lib. bdg. 42.00 o.s.i. (ISBN 0-8240-0811-1). Garland Pub.

--Sioux Indians, Vol. One: Mdewakanton Band of Sioux Indians. (American Indian Ethnohistory Ser: Plains Indians). (Illus.). lib. bdg. 42.00 o.s.i. (ISBN 0-8240-0794-8). Garland Pub.

Hickerson, J. Mel. How I Made the Sale That Did the Most for Me: Fifty Great Sales Stories by Fifty Great Salespeople. LC 81-50244. 372p. 1981. 14.95 (ISBN 0-471-07769-0, Pub. by Wiley-Interscience). Wiley.

Hickerson, Thomas F. Route Location & Design. 5th ed. (Illus.). 1967. text ed. 32.50 (ISBN 0-07-028680-9, C). McGraw.

Hickey, Bob. In the Room of Poems. (Illus.). 100p. (Orig.). 1982. pap. text ed. 7.95x (ISBN 0-939414-00-7). Ascii.

--Laundry Room Poems. (Illus.). 92p. (Orig.). pap. 2.95x (ISBN 0-9603432-1-0). Ascii.

--Mental Training. LC 79-67021. (Illus., Orig.). 1979. pap. 19.50x (ISBN 0-9603432-0-2). Ascii.

Hickey, Dave & Plagens, Peter. The Works of Edward Ruscha. LC 81-20242. (Illus.). 182p. 1982. 35.00 (ISBN 0-933920-21-0). Hudson Hills.

Hickey, Denis. Home from Exile: An Approach to Post-Existentialist Philosophizing. LC 82-20059. 504p. (Orig.). (gr. 2-5). 1983. lib. bdg. 29.50 (ISBN 0-8191-2848-1); pap. text ed. 17.75 (ISBN 0-8191-2849-X). U Pr of Amer.

Hickey, Des & Smith, Gus. Seven Days to Disaster: The Sinking of the Lusitania. (Illus.). 336p. 1982. 14.95 (ISBN 0-399-12699-6). Putnam Pub Group.

Hickey, Doralyn J., ed. see Hensel, Evelyn & Deveillette, Peter.

Hickey, H. & Villines, W. Elements of Electronics. 3rd ed. 1970. text ed. 23.10 o.p. (ISBN 0-07-028693-0, G). McGraw.

Hickey, Henry V. & Villines, William M., Jr. Elements of Electronics. 4th ed. LC 79-13830. (Illus.). 1980. text ed. 25.95 (ISBN 0-07-028695-7); ans. to problems 2.00 (ISBN 0-07-028696-5). McGraw.

Hickey, Judson C. & Zarb, George A. Boucher's Prosthodontic Treatment for Edentulous Patients. 8th ed. LC 80-11234. (Illus.). 628p. 1980. text ed. 42.95 (ISBN 0-8016-0725-6). Mosby.

Hickey, Kieran. The Light of Other Days: Irish Life at the Turn of the Century in the Photographs of Robert French. LC 74-24950. (Illus.). 172p. 1975. 40.00 (ISBN 0-87923-131-9). Godine.

Hickey, M. & King, C. One Hundred Families of Flowering Plants. LC 79-42670. (Illus.). 220p. 1981. 69.50 (ISBN 0-521-23283-X); pap. 19.95 (ISBN 0-521-29891-1). Cambridge U Pr.

Hickey, Marily. Divorce Is Not the Answer. LC 78-70663. 1979. pap. 3.95 (ISBN 0-89221-009-5). New Leaf.

Hickey, Marilyn. Fear Free Faith Filled. 176p. 1982. pap. 3.25 (ISBN 0-89274-259-3). Harrison Hse.

--God's Covenant for Your Family. 140p. (Orig.). 1982. pap. 4.95 (ISBN 0-89274-245-3). Harrison Hse.

Hickler, Holly, jt. auth. see Mack, John.

Hickling, C. F. Water As a Productive Environment. LC 75-4394. 200p. 1975. 25.00 (ISBN 0-312-85680-6). St Martin.

Hickling, Robert & Kamal, Mounir M. Engine Noise: Excitation, Vibration, & Radiation. (General Motors Research Symposia Ser.). 490p. 1982. 62.50x (ISBN 0-306-41168-7, Plenum Pr). PLenum Pub.

Hickman. Get More from your Personal Computer. 1983. text ed. 13.50 (ISBN 0-408-01131-9). Butterworth.

Hickman, B. G., et al. An Annual Growth Model of the U. S. Economy. (Contributions to Economic Analysisz: Vol. 100). 1976. 51.00 (ISBN 0-444-11013-5, North-Holland). Elsevier.

Hickman, Cleveland P., et al. Integrated Principles of Zoology. 6th ed. LC 78-27064. (Illus.). 1086p. 1979. text ed. 27.95 (ISBN 0-8016-2172-0). Mosby.

Hickman, Cleveland P., Jr., et al. Biology of Animals. 3rd ed. LC 81-14156. (Illus.). 646p. 1982. text ed. 25.95 (ISBN 0-8016-2167-4). Mosby.

Hickman, Hoyt. Word & Table. 1983. pap. 3.95 (ISBN 0-687-46127-8). Abingdon.

Hickman, Hoyt, ed. A Service of Death & Resurrection: The Ministry of the Church at Death. 1983. pap. 4.50 (ISBN 0-687-38075-8). Abingdon.

Hickman, John & Oakes, Dean. Standard Catalog of National Bank Notes. (Illus.). 1982. text ed. 75.00 (ISBN 0-87341-026-2). Krause Pubns.

Hickman, Larry. Philosophy. (College Outlines Ser.). pap. 4.95 o.p. (ISBN 0-671-08034-2). Monarch Pr.

Hickman, Mary A., jt. auth. see Butler, Eugenia W.

Hickman, William F. Ravaged & Reborn: The Iranian Military, 1979-1982. LC 82-73900. 75p. 1983. pap. 5.95 (ISBN 0-8157-3611-8). Brookings.

Hickmott, G. J. Principles & Practice of Interruption Insurance. 937p. 1981. 125.00 (ISBN 0-900886-56-0, Pub. By Witherby & Co England). State Mutual Bk.

Hickok, Floyd. Your Energy Efficient Home: Improvements to Save Utility Dollars. (Illus.). 11.95 o.p. (ISBN 0-13-978312-1, Spec); pap. text ed. 4.95 o.p. (ISBN 0-13-978304-0). P-H.

Hickok, L. P. Rational Psychology. LC 72-13798. (Hist. of Psych. Ser.). 756p. Repr. of 1849 ed. lib. bdg. 70.00x (ISBN 0-8201-1117-1). Schol Facsimiles.

Hickok, Lorena A. The Story of Helen Keller. rev. ed. LC 58-9836. (Illus.). 192p. (gr. 3-6). 1974. Repr. 3.95 o.p. (ISBN 0-448-11810-6, G&D). Putnam Pub Group.

Hickok, Ralph. The New Encyclopedia of Sports. (Illus.). 1977. 42.95 (ISBN 0-07-028705-8, P&RB). McGraw.

Hickok, Robert. Exploring Music. 3rd ed. LC 78-62545. (Illus.). 1979. text ed. 19.95 (ISBN 0-201-02929-4); instructor's manual 3.00 (ISBN 0-201-02932-4); student's wkbk. 4.95 (ISBN 0-201-02933-2); record 21.95 (ISBN 0-201-02934-0). A-W.

Hickok, Robert, ed. see American Physical Therapy Association.

Hickok, Robert J. Physical Therapy Administration & Management. 2nd ed. (Illus.). 251p. 1982. 21.00 (ISBN 0-683-03976-8). Williams & Wilkins.

Hickok, Will & Daniels, John S. Web of Gunsmoke Bound with Ute Country. 1978. pap. 1.75 o.p. (ISBN 0-451-07977-9, E7977, Sig). NAL.

Hickox, Ron G. U.S. Military Edged Weapons of the Second Seminole War 1835-1842. LC 82-62494. (Historic Byways of Florida Ser.: Vol. IX). (Illus.). 100p. 1982. pap. 10.95 (ISBN 0-941948-09-9). St Johns-Oklawaha.

Hicks, Anthony, jt. auth. see Dean, Winton.

Hicks, Cedric S. Man & Natural Resources: An Agricultural Perspective. LC 75-15274. 130p. 1975. 18.95 o.p. (ISBN 0-312-51065-9). St Martin.

Hicks, Charles E. & Standifer, James A., eds. Methods & Perspectives in Urban Music Education. LC 82-16105. (Illus.). 524p. (Orig.). 1983. lib. bdg. 28.75 (ISBN 0-8191-2760-4); pap. text ed. 16.75 (ISBN 0-8191-2761-2). U Pr of Amer.

Hicks, Clifford B. Alvin Fernald TV Anchorman: Skylark Ser. 144p. 1982. pap. 1.95 (ISBN 0-553-15157-6, Skylark). Bantam.

Hicks, Diana, et al. A Case for English Student's Book. (Cambridge English Language Learning Ser.). 112p. 1980. pap. 6.50x (ISBN 0-521-22291-5); cassette 13.95x (ISBN 0-521-22527-2); tchr's bk. 8.95x (ISBN 0-521-22526-4, 84 PAGES). Cambridge U Pr.

Hicks, Dorothy J. Patient Care Techniques. LC 74-18673. (Allied Health Ser). 1975. pap. 7.75 (ISBN 0-672-61394-8). Bobbs.

Hicks, Ellis A. Check List & Bibliography on the Occurrence of Insects in Birds' Nests. 1959. incl. 1962 1971 suppl 11.50x o.p. (ISBN 0-8138-1180-5). Iowa St U Pr.

Hicks, George L. & McNicoll, Geoffrey. The Indonesian Economy, Nineteen Fifty to Nineteen Sixty-Five: A Bibliography. LC 67-25434. (Bibliography Ser.: No. 9). x, 248p. 1967. 5.75x (ISBN 0-686-30909-X). Yale U SE Asia.

--The Indonesian Economy, Nineteen Fifty to Nineteen Sixty-Seven: Bibliographic Supplement. LC 67-25434. (Bibliography Ser.: No. 10). xii, 211p. 1968. 6.75x (ISBN 0-686-30908-1). Yale U SE Asia.

Hicks, H., et al. Modern Business Management. (Illus.). 400p. 1974. text ed. 23.95 (ISBN 0-07-028756-2, C); tchr's manual 7.95 (ISBN 0-07-028758-9); study guide 14.95 (ISBN 0-07-028757-0). McGraw.

Hicks, Herbert G. & Gullett, C. Ray. The Management of Organizations. 4th ed. (Illus.). 656p. 1981. text ed. 23.95 (ISBN 0-07-028773-2, C); instr's. manual 16.95 (ISBN 0-07-028774-0); study guide 8.95 (ISBN 0-07-028777-5). McGraw.

--Organizations: Theory & Behavior. (Management Ser.). (Illus.). 448p. 1975. text ed. 25.95 (ISBN 0-07-028730-9, C); instructors' manual by Slaughter 12.95 (ISBN 0-07-058160-6). McGraw.

Hicks, Herbert G. & Powell, James D. Management, Organizations & Human Resources: Selected Readings. 2nd ed. 1975. text ed. 15.95 (ISBN 0-07-028733-3, C). McGraw.

Hicks, Herbert G., et al. Business: An Involvement Approach. 1975. 28.00 (ISBN 0-07-028715-5, C); study guide 6.95 (ISBN 0-07-028718-X); instructor's manual 5.50 (ISBN 0-07-028716-3); transparency masters 15.00 (ISBN 0-07-028720-1). McGraw.

Hicks, J. William, ed. Exempted Transactions Under the Securities Act of 1933. LC 79-15969. 1981. 3 looseleaf vols. 210.00 (ISBN 0-87632-199-6). Boardman.

Hicks, Jack. In the Singer's Temple: Prose Fictions of Barthelme, Gaines, Brautigan, Piercy, Kesey, & Kosinski. LC 80-26074. vii, 293p. 1982. 18.50x (ISBN 0-8078-1467-9); pap. 7.95 (ISBN 0-8078-4096-3). U of NC Pr.

Hicks, James O., Jr. & Leininger, Wayne E. Accounting Information Systems. 608p. 1981. text ed. 24.95 (ISBN 0-8299-0384-4). West Pub.

Hicks, John. Capital & Growth. 1972. pap. 8.95 (ISBN 0-19-877001-4, GB375, GB). Oxford U Pr.

--The Crisis in Keynesian Economics. LC 74-79284. 85p. 1975. text ed. 12.95x (ISBN 0-465-01480-1). Basic.

Hicks, John D. Republican Ascendancy: 1921-1933. (New American Nation Ser.). 1960. 17.26x (ISBN 0-06-011885-7, HarpT). Har-Row.

Hicks, John G. Welded Joint Design. LC 78-32047. 82p. 1979. 27.95 o.s.i. (ISBN 0-470-26686-4). Halsted Pr.

Hicks, John R. Theory of Economic History. 1969. pap. 6.95x (ISBN 0-19-881163-2, OPB). Oxford U Pr.

--Theory of Wages. 2nd ed. (International Economic Assn. Ser). 1963. 25.00 o.p. (ISBN 0-312-79870-9). St Martin.

Hicks, Philip, jt. auth. see Nilsson, W. D.

Hicks, Philip E., ed. Introduction to Industrial Engineering & Management Science. (Industrial Engineering & Management Science Ser.). 1977. text ed. 29.50 (ISBN 0-07-028767-8, C); solutions manual 7.95 (ISBN 0-07-028768-6). McGraw.

Hicks, R. E., jt. auth. see Probstein, R. F.

Hicks, Richard, jt. ed. see Christian, Portia.

Hicks, Roy. Another Look at the Rapture. 120p. (Orig.). 1982. pap. 3.95 (ISBN 0-89274-246-1). Harrison Hse.

--Healing Your Insecurities. (Orig.). 1982. pap. 2.25 (ISBN 0-89274-249-6). Harrison Hse.

Hicks, Roy H. Praying Beyond God's Ability: The Enigma of Unanswered Prayer. 96p. 1977. 2.95 (ISBN 0-89274-052-3). Harrison Hse.

Hicks, Russell G., jt. auth. see Oglesby, Clarkson H.

Hicks, Tony, jt. auth. see Granger, Colin.

Hicks, Tyler. Tyler Hick's Encyclopedia of Wealth-Building Secrets. 454p. 1982. pap. 6.95 (ISBN 0-13-935247-3, Reward). P-H.

Hicks, Tyler, jt. auth. see Pippenger, John.

Hicks, Tyler G. Business Borrowers Complete Success Kit. 2nd ed. 596p. 1981. pap. 99.50 (ISBN 0-914306-68-5). Intl Wealth.

--Business Capital Sources. 2nd ed. 150p. 1983. pap. 15.00 (ISBN 0-914306-71-5). Intl Wealth.

--Directory of High-Discount Merchandise & Product Sources for Distributors & Mail-Order Wealth Builders. 2nd ed. 150p. 1983. pap. 17.50 (ISBN 0-914306-82-0). Intl Wealth.

--Fast Financing of Your Real Estate Fortune Success Kit. 2nd ed. 523p. 1983. pap. 99.50 (ISBN 0-914306-70-7). Intl Wealth.

--Financial Broker-Finder-Business Broker-Consultant Success Kit. 2nd ed. 485p. 1983. pap. 99.50 (ISBN 0-914306-62-6). Intl Wealth.

--Franchise Riches Success Kit. 2nd ed. 876p. 1983. pap. 99.50 (ISBN 0-914306-64-2). Intl Wealth.

--Go Where the Money Is: Mideast & North African Banks & Financial Institutions. 2nd ed. 150p. 1983. pap. 15.00 (ISBN 0-914306-80-4). Intl Wealth.

--How to Borrow Your Way to Real Estate Riches. 2nd ed. 150p. 1983. pap. 15.00 (ISBN 0-914306-76-6). Intl Wealth.

--How to Build a Second Income Fortune in Your Spare Time. 1965. pap. 4.95 (ISBN 0-13-402941-0, Reward). P-H.

--How to Make a Fortune Through Export Mail-Order Riches. 2nd ed. 150p. 1983. pap. 17.50 (ISBN 0-914306-81-2). Intl Wealth.

--How to Prepare & Process Export-Import Documents. 1978. 25.00 (ISBN 0-914306-51-0). Intl Wealth.

--How to Prepare & Process Export-Import Documents: A Fully Illustrated Guide. 2nd ed. 320p. 1983. pap. 25.00 (ISBN 0-914306-75-8). Intl Wealth.

--How to Start Your Own Business on a Shoestring & Make up to One Hundred Thousand Dollars a Year. 1968. 14.95 o.p. (ISBN 0-13-434936-9, Parker). P-H.

--Mail Order Riches Success Kit. 2nd ed. 927p. 1983. pap. 99.50 (ISBN 0-914306-65-0). Intl Wealth.

--Professional Achievement for Engineers & Scientists. 1963. 16.95 (ISBN 0-07-028739-2, P&RB). McGraw.

--Pump Operation & Maintenance. LC 81-20890. 328p. 1983. Repr. of 1958 ed. write for info. (ISBN 0-89874-409-1). Krieger.

--Raising Money from Grants & Other Sources Success Kit. 2nd ed. 496p. 1983. pap. 99.50 (ISBN 0-914306-69-3). Intl Wealth.

--Real Estate Riches Success Kit. 2nd ed. 466p. 1983. pap. 99.50 (ISBN 0-914306-67-7). Intl Wealth.

--Sixty Day Fully Financed Fortune. 2nd ed. 150p. 1983. pap. 29.50 (ISBN 0-914306-78-2). Intl Wealth.

--Small Business Investment Company Directory & Handbook. 2nd ed. 150p. 1983. pap. 15.00 (ISBN 0-914306-72-3). Intl Wealth.

--Starting Millionaire Success Kit. 2nd ed. 361p. 1983. pap. 99.50 (ISBN 0-914306-63-4). Intl Wealth.

--Successful Engineering Management: Modern Techniques for Effective & Profitable Direction of the Engineering Function. 1966. 19.50 o.p. (ISBN 0-07-028745-7, P&RB). McGraw.

--Worldwide Riches Opportunites, Vol. 1. 150p. 1983. pap. 25.00 (ISBN 0-914306-73-1). Intl Wealth.

--Worldwide Riches Opportunities, Vol. 2. 2nd ed. 150p. 1983. pap. 25.00 (ISBN 0-914306-74-X). Intl Wealth.

--Zero Cash Success Techniques Kit. 2nd ed. 876p. 1983. pap. 99.50 (ISBN 0-914306-66-9). Intl Wealth.

Hicks, Tyler G. & Beach, Sean C. Tyler Hicks Encyclopedia of Wealth-Building Secrets. 1980. 17.95 o.p. (ISBN 0-13-935254-6, Parker). P-H.

Hicks, Tyler G. & Edwards, T. Pump Application Engineering. 1970. 36.50 (ISBN 0-07-028741-4, P&RB). McGraw.

Hicks, Tyler G., jt. auth. see Chopey, Nicholas.

Hicks, Tyler G., jt. auth. see Pippenger, John H.

Hicks, Tyler G., ed. Standard Handbook of Engineering Calculations. LC 73-130674. (Illus.). 1216p. 1972. 39.50 (ISBN 0-07-028734-1, P&RB). McGraw.

Hicks, Warren. Managing the Building-Level School Library Media Program: School Media Centers: Focus on Trends & Issues, No. 7. LC 81-8016. 52p. 1981. pap. 6.00 (ISBN 0-8389-3262-2). ALA.

Hicks, Warren W., jt. auth. see Connor, D. Russell.

Hicks-Bruun, M. Polly's Journal. 7.50 o.p. (ISBN 0-8062-1044-3). Carlton.

Hickson, D. J. & McMillan, C. J., eds. Organization & Nation. 248p. 1981. text ed. 37.25x (ISBN 0-566-00324-4). Gower Pub Ltd.

Hidaka, Hiroyoshi, jt. ed. see Kakiuchi, Shiro.

Hidaru, Alula, ed. see African Bibliographic Center.

Hidayat, Sadiq. Sadeq Hedayat: An Anthology. LC 79-5100. 176p. 1983. 25.00x (ISBN 0-89158-387-4). Caravan Bks.

Hiddleston, J. A. Essai sur Laforgue et les Derniers Vers suivi de Laforgue et Baudelaire. LC 80-66331. (French Forum Monographs: No. 23). 132p. (Orig., Fr.). 1980. pap. 9.50x (ISBN 0-917058-22-4). French Forum.

Hiden, Martha W. How Justice Grew - Virginia Counties: An Abstract of Their Formation. (Illus.). 101p. 1957. pap. 2.95 (ISBN 0-8139-0143-X). U Pr of Va.

Hidore, John J. Physical Geography: Earth Systems. 1974. text ed. 17.95x (ISBN 0-673-07827-2). Scott F.

Hidy, Vernon S. & Sports Illustrated Editors. Sports Illustrated Fly Fishing. rev. ed. LC 74-38908. (Illus.). (YA) 1972. 5.95i (ISBN 0-397-00859-7); pap. 2.95i o.p. (ISBN 0-397-00858-9, LP-63). Har-Row.

Hieatt, A. Kent, ed. see Chaucer, Geoffrey.

Hieatt, A. Kent, tr. see Chaucer, Geoffrey.

Hieatt, Constance, ed. see Chaucer, Geoffrey.

Hieatt, Constance, tr. see Chaucer, Geoffrey.

Hieatt, Constance B., ed. Beowulf & Other Old English Poems. (Bantam Classics Ser.). 192p. (YA) (gr. 9-12). 1982. pap. 1.95 (ISBN 0-553-21109-9). Bantam.

Hieatt, Constance B., tr. Beowulf & Other Old English Poems. LC 67-25645. (Orig.). (gr. 9-12). 1967. pap. 4.95 (ISBN 0-672-63012-5). Odyssey Pr.

Hieb, Elizabeth, ed. Fund Advisors Institute, Lake Tahoe, June, 1977: Proceedings. 1977. spiral bdg. 10.50 (ISBN 0-89154-067-9). Intl Found Employ.

Hieb, Elizabeth A., ed. Textbook for Employee Benefit Plan Trustees, Administrators & Advisors, 1978: Proceedings, Vol. 20. 27.00 (ISBN 0-89154-093-8). Intl Found Employ.

--Textbook for Employee Benefit Plan Trustees, Administrators & Advisors 1981: Proceedings, Vol. 23. 322p. 1982. text ed. 30.00 (ISBN 0-89154-187-X). Intl Found Employ.

Hieb, Elizabeth A., jt. ed. see Brennan, Mary E.

Hiebert, D. Edmond. The Epistle of James. LC 78-23925. 1979. 13.95 (ISBN 0-8024-2353-1). Moody.

--First Timothy. (Everymans Bible Commentary Ser.). 1967. pap. 4.50 (ISBN 0-8024-2054-0). Moody.

--An Introduction to the New Testament: The Pauline Epistles, Vol. II. 1977. pap. 9.95 (ISBN 0-8024-4148-3). Moody.

--An Introduction to the New Testament: Vol. I-the Gospels & Acts. 1975. pap. 9.95 (ISBN 0-8024-4147-5). Moody.

--An Introduction to the New Testament: Vol. III, the Non-Pauline Epistles & Revelation. 1977. pap. 9.95 (ISBN 0-8024-4149-1). Moody.

--Mark: A Portrait of the Servant. LC 73-15084. 400p. 1974. 12.95 (ISBN 0-8024-5182-9). Moody.

--Second Timothy. (Everyman's Bible Commentary Ser). 1958. pap. 4.50 (ISBN 0-8024-2055-9). Moody.

--Thessalonian Epistles. 1971. 8.95 (ISBN 0-8024-8641-X). Moody.

Hiebert, D. Edmund. Titus & Philemon. (Everyman's Bible Commentary Ser.). 1957. pap. 4.50 (ISBN 0-8024-2056-7, MBP). Moody.

Hiebert, William, jt. auth. see Stahmann, Robert F.

Hiebert, William J., jt. ed. see Stahmann, Robert F.

Hiebsch & Branstatter. Social Psychology. Date not set. 53.25 (ISBN 0-444-86352-4). Elsevier.

Hiedemann, Robert E., ed. American Future & the Humane Tradition: The Role of the Humanities in Higher Education. LC 81-86560. (Humanities Ser.). 246p. (Orig.). 1982. pap. text ed. 16.50x (ISBN 0-86733-018-X). Assoc Faculty Pr.

Hiel, Grace L. Daphne Deane, No. 19. 192p. 1982. pap. 2.25 (ISBN 0-553-22533-2). Bantam.

Hiers, John T., et al. Today's Language: A Vocabulary Workbook. 368p. 1981. pap. text ed. 10.95 (ISBN 0-669-03078-3); cancelled (ISBN 0-669-03080-5). Heath.

Hiers, Richard H. Jesus & the Future: Unsolved Questions on Eschatology. LC 80-82189. 1981. 16.50 (ISBN 0-8042-0341-5); pap. 4.95 (ISBN 0-8042-0340-7). John Knox.

Hieshima, Grant B., jt. auth. see Tsai, Fong Y.

Hiestand, Dale L. & Ostow, Miriam, eds. Health Manpower: Data for Policy Guidance. LC 75-38687. 112p. 1976. prof ref 22.00x (ISBN 0-88410-135-5). Ballinger Pub.

Hietanen, Eino. Regulation of Serum Lipids by Physical Exercise. 192p. 1982. 64.00 (ISBN 0-8493-6330-6). CRC Pr.

Hiett, Steve. Pleasure Places. 1976. pap. 4.95 (ISBN 0-8256-3904-2, Quick Fox). Putnam Pub Group.

Hifler, Joyce S. Put your Mind at Ease. 128p. (Orig.). 1983. pap. 5.95 (ISBN 0-687-34929-X). Abingdon.

Higashi, Shinbu, tr. see Asano, Osamu & Ishiwata, Mutsuko.

Higashi, Sumiko. Virgins, Vamps & Flappers: The American Silent Movie Heroine. LC 78-74106. 1979. 17.95 o.p. (ISBN 0-88831-028-5). Eden Pr.

Higashimura, T., jt. ed. see Imahori, K.

Higasi, Ken'Ichi, et al. Quantum Organic Chemistry. LC 65-16408. 358p. 1965. text ed. 18.50 o.p. (ISBN 0-470-38690-8, Pub. by Wiley). Krieger.

Higdon, Hal. Hitting, Pitching & Fielding: Major League Players Tell How They Play Baseball. LC 77-13368. (Putnam Sports Shelf). (Illus.). 1978. PLB 6.99 (ISBN 0-399-61117-7). Putnam Pub Group.

--Johnny Rutherford: Indy Champ. (Sport Shelf Ser.). (Illus.). 128p. (gr. 5 up). 1980. PLB 6.99 (ISBN 0-399-61136-3). Putnam Pub Group.

--The Marathoners. (Illus.). (gr. 6-8). 1980. 8.95 (ISBN 0-399-20695-7). Putnam Pub Group.

--On the Run from Dogs & People. LC 79-64243. 1979. pap. 6.95 o.p. (ISBN 0-914090-59-3). Chicago Review.

--Showdown at Daytona. LC 75-43731. (Illus.). 160p. (gr. 5 up). 1976. 5.95 o.p. (ISBN 0-399-20507-1). Putnam Pub Group.

--Six Seconds to Glory: Don Prudhomme's Greatest Drag Race. LC 74-21061. (Illus.). 160p. (gr. 5 up). 1975. 6.95 o.p. (ISBN 0-399-20447-4). Putnam Pub Group.

--Summer of Triumph. LC 77-2217. 1977. 8.95 o.p. (ISBN 0-399-11911-6). Putnam Pub Group.

--Thirty Days in May: The "Indy" 500. (Putnam Sports Shelf). (Illus.). (gr. 5 up). 1971. PLB 5.29 o.p. (ISBN 0-399-60630-0). Putnam Pub Group.

Higelin, S., et al. Svenska Fur Er, Part 1. (Illus.). Set. pap. text ed. 27.50 exercise, wordlist (ISBN 9-1522-1363-3, SW174); 8 tapes 75.00x (ISBN 0-686-05370-2, SW174T); cassettes 75.00x (ISBN 0-686-05371-0, SW174C); o.p. (ISBN 91-522-1395-1); o.p. (ISBN 91-522-1363-3); o.p. (ISBN 91-522-1376-5); o.p. (ISBN 91-522-1381-1). Vanous.

--Svenska Fur Er, Part 2. (Illus.). 1971. Set. pap. text ed. 27.50x exercise wordlist (ISBN 0-686-05373-7, SW175); 4 tapes 75.00x (ISBN 0-686-05374-5, SW175T); 3 cassettes 75.00 (ISBN 0-686-05375-3, SW175C); o.p. (ISBN 0-686-05376-1); o.p. (ISBN 91-522-1424-9); o.p. (ISBN 91-522-1425-7); o.p. (ISBN 91-522-1503-2). Vanous.

Higgenbotham, Don. The War of American Independence. 515p. 1983. 24.95x (ISBN 0-930350-43-X); pap. text ed. 9.95 (ISBN 0-930350-44-8). NE U Pr.

Higgens, Judith, ed. see Beddoes, Thomas L.

Higginbotham, A. L. In the Matter of Color, Race, & the American Legal Process: The Colonial Period. (Galaxy Bks.: No. 608). (Illus.). 1978. pap. 9.95 (ISBN 0-19-502745-0). Oxford U Pr.

Higginbotham, A. Leon, Jr. In the Matter of Color, Race, & the American Legal Process: The Colonial Period, Vol. 1. LC 76-51713. (Illus.). 1978. 18.95x (ISBN 0-19-502387-0). Oxford U Pr.

Higginbotham, Bill. Carving Country Characters. 1981. pap. 2.50 o.p. (ISBN 0-486-24135-1). Dover.

--Whittling. LC 81-85041. (Illus.). 128p. 1982. pap. 6.95 (ISBN 0-8069-7598-9). Sterling.

Higginbotham, Don. Daniel Morgan: Revolutionary Rifleman. (Institute of Early American & Culture Ser.). xvi, 239p. 1979. 16.95 (ISBN 0-8078-0824-5); pap. 6.00 (ISBN 0-8078-1386-9). U of NC Pr.

--The War of American Independence: Military Attitudes, Policies & Practice,1763-1789. LC 77-74433. (Wars of the United States Ser.). (Illus.). 524p. 1977. pap. 6.95x o.p. (ISBN 0-253-28910-6). Ind U Pr.

Higginbotham, Don, ed. Reconsiderations on the Revolutionary War: Selected Essays. LC 77-84752. (Contributions in Military History: No. 14). 1978. lib. bdg. 25.00x (ISBN 0-8371-9846-1, HIA/). Greenwood.

Higginbotham, Jay. Fast Train Russia. LC 82-23514. 1983. 8.95 (ISBN 0-396-08156-8). Dodd.

--The Mobile Indians. 1966. pap. 5.95 (ISBN 0-913208-02-7). Rockwell.

Higginbotham, Virginia. Luis Bunuel. (Filmmakers Ser.). 1979. lib. bdg. 12.95 (ISBN 0-8057-9261-9, Twayne). G K Hall.

Higginbottom, J. Winslow, tr. see LeRoy, Gen.

Higgins. Organizational Policy: Strat Mgmt. 2nd ed. 1983. 26.95 (ISBN 0-03-061961-0). Dryden Pr.

Higgins & Riley. A Field Guide to the Butterflies of Britain & Europe. 29.95 (ISBN 0-686-42783-1, Collins Pub England). Greene.

Higgins, jt. auth. see Hawkins.

Higgins, A. J. The Son of Man in the Teaching of Jesus. LC 79-42824. (Society for New Testament Studies Monographs: No. 39). 186p. 1981. 27.95 (ISBN 0-521-22363-6). Cambridge U Pr.

Higgins, Afred. Common-Sense Guide to Refinishing Antiques. rev. ed. LC 76-8913. (Funk & W Bk.). (Illus.). 288p. 1976. 13.41i (ISBN 0-308-10252-5). T y Crowell.

Higgins, Alex & Elonka, Stephen M. Boiler Room Questions & Answers. 2nd ed. (Illus.). 384p. 1976. 27.50 (ISBN 0-07-028754-6, P&RB). McGraw.

Higgins, C. S. & Moss, P. D. Sounds Real: Radio in Everyday Life. LC 81-21808. (Illus.). 237p. 1983. text ed. 27.50 (ISBN 0-7022-1900-2); pap. 14.95 (ISBN 0-7022-1910-X). U of Queensland Pr.

Higgins, Charles B. & Carlsson, Erik, eds. Computerized Transmission of Tomography of the Heart: Experimental Evaluation & Clinical Application. LC 82-71767. (Illus.). 416p. 1982. 68.00 (ISBN 0-87993-180-9). Futura Pub.

Higgins, Colin. Harold & Maude. 1975. pap. 2.25 (ISBN 0-380-00385-6, 63255). Avon.

Higgins, D. S. Rider Haggard: A Biography. LC 81-48452. 288p. 1982. 19.95 (ISBN 0-8128-2860-7). Stein & Day.

Higgins, David. Designing Structured Programs. (Illus.). 240p. 1983. pap. text ed. 14.95 (ISBN 0-13-201418-1). P-H.

Higgins, Dick. Die Fabelhafte Getraume Von Taifun Willi. 64p. 1970. pap. 5.95 (ISBN 0-914162-57-8). Knowles.

--Foew & Ombwhnw. (Illus.). 1969. 16.95 (ISBN 0-685-89038-4). Printed Edns.

--Piano Album. 64p. 1980. pap. 10.00 (ISBN 0-914162-42-X). Knowles.

--Ten Ways of Looking at a Bird. 16p. 1981. pap. 10.00 (ISBN 0-914162-55-1). Knowles.

--Twenty Six Mountains for Viewing the Sunset From. 32p. 1981. pap. 12.00 (ISBN 0-914162-54-3). Knowles.

Higgins, Dick, et al. The Word & Beyond. 1982. 12.95 (ISBN 0-912292-70-9); pap. 9.95 (ISBN 0-686-83017-2). Horizon.

Higgins, E. T., jt. ed. see Zanna, M. P.

Higgins, E. Tory & Hartup, Willard W., eds. Social Cognition & Social Development: A Sociocultural Perspective. LC 82-12897. (Cambridge Studies in Social & Emotional Development: No. 5). 352p. Date not set. price not set (ISBN 0-521-24587-7). Cambridge U Pr.

Higgins, E. Tory, et al, eds. Social Cognition: The Ontario Symposium, Vol. 1. 448p. 1981. text ed. 29.95x (ISBN 0-89859-049-3). L Erlbaum Assocs.

Higgins, Earl, jt. auth. see Moracco, John.

Higgins, F. R. The Pseudo-Cleft Construction in English. Hankamer, Jorge, ed. LC 78-66547. (Outstanding Dissertations in Linguistics Ser.). 1979. lib. bdg. 44.00 o.s.i. (ISBN 0-8240-9683-5). Garland Pub.

Higgins, Hugh. Vietnam. LC 82-11787. (Studies in Modern History). (Illus.). x, 180p. (Orig.). 1982. pap. text ed. 7.50x (ISBN 0-435-31399-1). Heinemann Ed.

Higgins, J., ed. Cesar Vallejo: An Anthology of Poetry. 1970. 24.00 o.p. (ISBN 0-08-015762-9); pap. 10.75 o.p. (ISBN 0-08-015761-0). Pergamon.

Higgins, J. R. Completeness & Basis Properties of Sets of Special Functions. LC 76-19630. (Cambridge Tracts in Mathematics Ser.: No. 72). (Illus.). 1977. 52.50 (ISBN 0-521-21376-2). Cambridge U Pr.

Higgins, Jack. Day of Judgement. (General Ser.). 1979. lib. bdg. 13.95 (ISBN 0-8161-6756-7, Large Print Bks). G K Hall.

--Luciano's Luck. (General Ser.). 1982. lib. bdg. 15.50 (ISBN 0-8161-3304-2, Large Print Bks). G K Hall.

--Solo. (GenerAL Ser.). 1980. lib. bdg. 13.95 (ISBN 0-8161-3120-1, Large Print Bks). G K Hall.

--Touch the Devil. (General Ser.). 1983. lib. bdg. 16.95 (ISBN 0-8161-3484-7, Large Print Bks). G K Hall.

Higgins, James. Human Relations Skills. 518p. 1982. text ed. 24.95 (ISBN 0-394-32574-5); student activities manual 14.95 (ISBN 0-394-32587-7). Random.

Higgins, James E. Beyond Words: Mystical Fancy in Children's Literature. LC 71-96760. 1970. pap. 4.50x (ISBN 0-8077-1517-4). Tchrs Coll.

Higgins, James E., jt. auth. see Henson, Kenneth T.

Higgins, John A. Workbook Two Thousand. 300p. 1982. pap. text ed. 11.50 scp (ISBN 0-06-042813-9, HarpC); diagnostic & Achievement Test avail. (ISBN 0-06-362734-5). Har-Row.

Higgins, John J. Thomas Merton on Prayer. 200p. 1975. pap. 3.95 (ISBN 0-385-02813-X, Im). Doubleday.

Higgins, Judith H. Energy: A Multimedia Guide for Children & Young Adults. LC 78-15611. (Selection Guide Ser.: No. 2). 195p. 1979. text ed. 16.50 o.s.i. (ISBN 0-87436-266-0, Co-Pub. by Neal-Schuman). ABC-Clio.

Higgins, L. R. Cost Reduction from A to Z. 1976. 44.95 (ISBN 0-07-028765-1, P&RB). McGraw.

Higgins, L. R. & Morrow, L. C. Maintenance Engineering Handbook. 3rd ed. 1977. 59.50 (ISBN 0-07-028755-4, P&RB). McGraw.

Higgins, Lindley R. Handbook of Construction Equipment Maintenance. (Illus.). 1979. 49.50 (ISBN 0-07-028764-3, P&RB). McGraw.

Higgins, Mary, ed. see Reich, Wilhelm.

Higgins, Norman & Sullivan, Howard J. Teaching for Competence. 1983. pap. price not set (ISBN 0-8077-2725-3). Tchrs Coll.

Higgins, P. C. & Butler, R. R. Understanding Deviance. 1982. 14.95x (ISBN 0-07-028776-7). McGraw.

Higgins, P. J. An Introduction to Topological Groups. LC 74-82222. (London Mathematical Society Lecture Note Ser.: No. 15). 100p. 1974. 13.95 (ISBN 0-521-20527-1). Cambridge U Pr.

Higgins, Paul C., jt. auth. see Albrecht, Gary L.

Higgins, Raymond A. Engineering Metallurgy, 2 Vols. Incl. Vol. 1. Applied Physical Metallurgy. 576p. lib. bdg. price not set (ISBN 0-89874-567-5); Vol. 2. Metallurgical Process Technology. 480p. lib. bdg. price not set (ISBN 0-89874-568-3). LC 82-19292. 1983. lib. bdg. write for info. Krieger.

Higgins, Ris, ed. Christmas in the Country. (Illus.). 84p. 1974. pap. 5.95 (ISBN 0-89821-005-4). Reiman Assoc.

Higgins, Robert, jt. auth. see Gibson, R.

Higgins, Robert C. Analysis for Financial Management. LC 82-73628. 325p. 1983. 19.95 (ISBN 0-87094-377-4). Dow Jones-Irwin.

--Financial Management: Theory & Applications. LC 76-25053. 600p. 1981. text ed. 23.95 (ISBN 0-574-19240-9, 13-2510); instr's guide avail. (ISBN 0-574-19241-7, 13-2241). SRA.

Higgins, Ronald. The Seventh Enemy. 1978. 12.50 o.p. (ISBN 0-07-028780-5, GB). McGraw.

Higgins, Rosalyn. United Nations Peacekeeping, 1946-1967: Documents & Commentary, Africa, Vol. 3 Africa. 1980. 89.00x (ISBN 0-19-218321-4). Oxford U Pr.

--United Nations Peacekeeping, 1946-1967: Documents & Commentary Vol. 2: Asia. 1970. 94.00x (ISBN 0-19-214978-4). Oxford U Pr.

--United Nations Peacekeeping, Documents & Commentary: Vol. 4, Europe 1946-1979. (Illus.). 1981. 98.00x (ISBN 0-19-218322-2). Oxford U Pr.

Higgins, Susan. A Latin Filmography. (Latin American Culture Studies Project Ser.). ix, 1978p. 1978. pap. text ed. 5.00x (ISBN 0-86728-011-5). U TX Inst Lat Am Stud.

Higgins, Thomas. Comparing Strageties for Reducing Traffic Related Problems: The Potential for Road Pricing. 40p. (Orig.). 1978. pap. text ed. 3.50 (ISBN 0-87766-227-4). Urban Inst.

--Ethical Theories in Conflict. 1967. pap. 4.95x o.p. (ISBN 0-02-818510-2). Glencoe.

--Man as Man. 1958. 5.95 o.p. (ISBN 0-02-818480-7). Glencoe.

Higgins, Trumbull. Winston Churchill & the Second Front, 1940-1943. LC 74-14025. 281p. 1975. Repr. of 1957 ed. lib. bdg. 18.25x (ISBN 0-8371-7782-0, HIWI). Greenwood.

Higgins, W. E. Xenophon the Athenian: The Problem of the Individual & the Society of the Polis. LC 77-2392. 1977. 34.50x (ISBN 0-87395-369-X). State U NY Pr.

Higgins, William R., jt. auth. see Walton, Brian G.

Higginson, Thomas W. Army Life in a Black Regiment. (Collector's Library of the Civil War). 1982. 26.60 (ISBN 0-8094-4237-X). Silver.

Higgott, Richard A. Political Development Theory: The Contemporary Debate. LC 82-42718. 140p. 1983. 18.95x (ISBN 0-312-62225-2). St Martin.

Higgs, D., jt. auth. see Callahan, W. J.

Higgs, E. S., ed. Palaeoeconomy. LC 74-76576. (Illus.). 330p. 1975. 44.50 (ISBN 0-521-20449-6). Cambridge U Pr.

--Papers in Economic Prehistory. LC 78-180019. (Illus.). 250p. 1972. 44.50 (ISBN 0-521-08452-0). Cambridge U Pr.

Higgs, Robert J. Laurel & Thorn: The Athlete in American Literature. LC 80-51014. 208p. 1981. 15.00x (ISBN 0-8131-1412-8). U Pr of Ky.

Higgs, Roger, et al. Agricultural Mathematics. 2nd ed. 1981. 12.00 (ISBN 0-8134-2130-6); ans. bk 1.00x (ISBN 0-8134-2131-4, 2131); text ed. 8.25x (ISBN 0-686-86128-0). Interstate.

High, Dallas M., jt. ed. see Bayles, Michael D.

High Fidelity Editors. High Fidelity's Silver Anniversary Treasury. LC 76-42077. 1976. 9.95 (ISBN 0-911656-01-4). Wyeth Pr.

High Fidelity Magazine. The Recordings of Beethoven. LC 77-26057. 1978. Repr. of 1971 ed. lib. bdg. 18.25x (ISBN 0-313-20171-4, HFRB). Greenwood.

High, Monique R. Encore. 1981. 13.95 o.s.i. (ISBN 0-440-02351-3). Delacorte.

--The Four Winds of Heaven. 695p. 1980. 10.95 o.s.i. (ISBN 0-440-02573-7). Delacorte.

Higham, Charles. The Earliest Farmer & the First Cities. LC 76-22425. (Cambridge Topic Bks). (Illus.). (gr. 5-10). 1977. PLB 6.95g (ISBN 0-8225-1203-3). Lerner Pubns.

--Errol Flynn: The Untold Story. LC 78-22633. (Illus.). 1980. 12.95 o.p. (ISBN 0-385-13495-9). Doubleday.

--Kate: The Life of Katherine Hepburn. (Illus.). (RL 10). 1976. pap. 2.95 o.p. (ISBN 0-451-11153-2, AE1153, Sig). NAL.

--Life in the Old Stone Age. LC 76-22442. (Cambridge Topic Bks). (Illus.). (gr. 5-10). 1977. PLB 6.95g (ISBN 0-8225-1206-8). Lerner Pubns.

Higham, Charles & Moseley, Roy. Princess Merle: The Romantic Life of Merle Oberon. LC 82-18201. (Illus.). 304p. 1983. 14.95 (ISBN 0-698-11231-8, Coward). Putnam Pub Group.

Higham, David. Literary Gent. LC 78-6488. 1978. 12.50 o.p. (ISBN 0-698-10852-3, Coward). Putnam Pub Group.

Higham, Norman. The Library in the University: Observations on a Service. 208p. 1980. 22.50 (ISBN 0-233-97222-6, 05798-3, Pub. by Gower Pub Co England). Lexington Bks.

Higham, R. & Kipp, Jacob, eds. Soviet Aviation & Air Power: A Historical Review. LC 76-30815. (Illus.). 1978. lib. bdg. 40.00 (ISBN 0-89158-116-2). Westview.

Highberger, Ruth & Schramm, Carol. Child Development for Day Care Workers. LC 75-31008. (Illus.). 288p. 1976. text ed. 18.95 (ISBN 0-395-20631-6); resource manual 1.65 (ISBN 0-395-20632-4). HM.

Highet, Gilbert. Classical Tradition. 1949. 27.50x (ISBN 0-19-500570-8). Oxford U Pr.

--Explorations. 1971. 19.95x (ISBN 0-19-501450-2). Oxford U Pr.

--People, Places, & Books. 1953. 15.95x (ISBN 0-19-500572-4). Oxford U Pr.

--Powers of Poetry. 1960. 24.95x (ISBN 0-19-500573-2). Oxford U Pr.

Highet, Gilbert, tr. see Jaeger, Werner.

Highfield, Arnold R. The French Dialect of St. Thomas U.S. Virgin Islands: A Descriptive Grammar with Texts & Glossary. 350p. 1979. pap. 10.50 o.p. (ISBN 0-89720-026-8). Karoma.

Highfield, Beryl S. & Hale, John, eds. Europe in the Late Middle Ages. (Illus.). 522p. (Orig.). 1970. pap. 7.95 o.p. (ISBN 0-571-09413-9). Faber & Faber.

Highfield, J. R. & Jeffs, Robin, eds. The Crown & Local Communities in England & France in the Fifteenth Century. 192p. 1981. text ed. 20.25x (ISBN 0-904387-67-4, 61065); pap. text ed. 11.25x (ISBN 0-904387-79-8, 61090). Humanities.

Highfill, Philip H., Jr., et al. A Biographical Dictionary of Actors, Actresses, Musicians, Dancers, Managers, & Other Stage Personnel in London, 1660-1800, 6 vols. Incl. Vol. 1. Abaco to Belfille. 462p. 1973 (ISBN 0-8093-0517-8); Vol. 2. Belfort to Byzand. 494p. 1973 (ISBN 0-8093-0518-6); Vol. 3. Cabanel to Cory. 544p. 1975 (ISBN 0-8093-0692-1); Vol. 4. Corye to Dynion. 576p. 1975 (ISBN 0-8093-0693-X); Vol. 5. Eagan to Garrett. 504p. 1978 (ISBN 0-8093-0832-0); Vol. 6. Garrick to Gyngell. 512p. 1978 (ISBN 0-8093-0833-9); Vol. 7. Habgood to Houbert. 448p. 1982 (ISBN 0-8093-0918-1); Vol. 8. Hough to Keyse. 448p. 1982 (ISBN 0-8093-0919-X). LC 71-157068. (Biographical Dictionary of Actors Ser.). (Illus.). 40.00x ea. S Ill U Pr.

Highland. Hazardous Waste Disposal: Assessing the Problem. LC 81-86537. 325p. 1982. 49.95 (ISBN 0-250-40540-7). Ann Arbor Science.

Highland, Esther H. Business Mathematics. 2nd ed. (Illus.). 512p. 1981. text ed. 18.95 (ISBN 0-8359-0585-3); instr's manual free (ISBN 0-8359-0586-1). Reston.

Highland, Harold, ed. Winter Simulation Conference Proceedings, 1982. 1982. 48.00 (ISBN 0-686-38789-9). Soc Computer Sim.

Highland, Harold J. Flight. (How & Why Wonder Books Ser.). (gr. 4-6). deluxe ed. 1.95 o.p. (ISBN 0-448-04018-2, G&D). Putnam Pub Group.

Highland, Joseph H. Hazardous Waste: What is Being Done to Control Its Disposal? (Vital Issues Ser.: Vol. XXXI, No. IV). 0.80 (ISBN 0-686-84137-9). Ctr Info Am.

Highland, Monica. Lotus Land. 608p. 1983. 16.95 (ISBN 0-698-11202-4, Coward). Putnam Pub Gruop.

Highlights Editors. Creative Craft Activities. LC 67-28201. (Jumbo Handbooks Ser.). (gr. 1-6). 1967. text ed. 4.95 o.p. (ISBN 0-87534-554-9). Highlights.

--Tricks & Teasers. (Highlights Handbooks Ser). (Illus.). (gr. 2-6). 1965. pap. 1.95 o.p. (ISBN 0-87534-125-X). Highlights.

Highnam, K. & Hill, L. Comparative Endocrinology of the Invertebrates. 2nd ed. 1977. 36.00 (ISBN 0-444-19497-5). Elsevier.

--Comparative Endocrinology of the Vertebrates. Date not set. pap. price not set (ISBN 0-444-19496-7). Elsevier.

Highnam, Kenneth C. & Hill, Leonard. The Comparative Endocrinology of the Invertebrates. 2nd ed. LC 77-15979. (Contemporary Biology Ser). 368p. 1978. text ed. 29.50 o.p. (ISBN 0-8391-1193-2). Univ Park.

Highsmith, Patricia. Strangers on a Train. (Crime Ser.). 1979. pap. 2.95 (ISBN 0-14-003796-9). Penguin.

Highsmith, R. M., Jr., jt. auth. see Heintzelman, Oliver K.

Hight, Donald W., jt. auth. see Pettofrezzo, Anthony J.

Hight, G. A., tr. The Saga of Grettir the Strong. 1978. Repr. of 1972 ed. 9.95x (ISBN 0-460-00699-1, Evman); pap. 6.95x (ISBN 0-460-01699-7). Biblio Dist.

Highton, Jake. Reporter. (Illus.). 1978. pap. text ed. 18.00 (ISBN 0-07-028771-6). McGraw.

Highton, N. B. & Highton, R. B. The Home Book of Vegetarian Cookery. (Home Book). (Illus.). 336p. 1979. pap. 7.95 (ISBN 0-571-11391-5). Faber & Faber.

Highton, R. B., jt. auth. see Highton, N. B.

Hightower, James E., Jr. Voices from the Old Testament. LC 81-68611. (Orig.). 1983. pap. 3.95 (ISBN 0-8054-2245-5). Broadman.

Hightower, Jim, et al. Hard Tomatoes, Hard Times: The Hightower Report. new ed. 328p. 1978. pap. text ed. 11.95x (ISBN 0-87073-625-6). Schenkman.

Highwater, Jamake. ANPAO: An American Indian Odyssey. LC 77-9264. (Illus.). 256p. 1980. pap. 5.95i (ISBN 0-06-090762-2, CN 762, CN). Har-Row.

--Eyes of Darkness. LC 82-187. 192p. (gr. 6 up). 1983. 10.00 (ISBN 0-688-41993-3). Lothrop.

--Journey to the Sky. LC 78-3324. (Illus.). 1978. 11.49 (ISBN 0-690-01758-8). T Y Crowell.

--The Sun, He Dies. 1981. pap. 2.95 (ISBN 0-451-11110-9, AE1110, Sig). NAL.

Highwater, Jamake, ed. The Primal Mind: Vision & Reality in Indian America. 1982. pap. 6.95 (ISBN 0-452-00602-3, Mer). NAL.

Higman, B. W. Slave Population & the Economy of Jamaica: 1807-1834. LC 75-28627. (Illus.). 1977. 49.50 (ISBN 0-521-21053-4); pap. 12.95 (ISBN 0-521-29569-6). Cambridge U Pr.

Higman, Dennis J. Pranks. 432p. (Orig.). 1983. pap. 3.50 o.s.i. (ISBN 0-8439-1154-9, Leisure Bks). Dorchester Pub Co.

Hignett, T. P., jt. auth. see Mudahar, M. S.

Hignett, T. P., ed. Fertilizer Manual. (Reference Manual Ser.: No. R-1). (Illus.). 353p. (Orig.). 1979. pap. 25.00 (ISBN 0-88090-023-7). Intl Fertilizer.

Hignite, Haskel. Sound Advice for Everyone. LC 82-60526. 125p. 1983. pap. 4.95 (ISBN 0-88247-681-5). R & E Res Assoc.

Higson, C. W. Sources for the History of Education. 1967. lib. bdg. 37.00 o.p. (ISBN 0-85365-452-2, Pub. by Lib Assn England); lib. bdg. 37.00x suppl. 1976 o.p. (ISBN 0-85365-238-4). Oryx Pr.

Higuchi, T. & Brochmann-Hanssen, E., eds. Pharmaceutical Analysis. LC 60-16810. (Illus.). 1961. 89.95 (ISBN 0-470-39534-6, Pub. by Halsted Press). Wiley.

Higuchi, Tadahiko. The Visual & Spatial Structure of Landscapes. Terry, Charles, tr. from Japanese. (Illus.). 232p. 1983. 20.00x (ISBN 0-262-08120-2). MIT Pr.

Hihara, Koho, et al. Ikebana. (Quick & Easy Ser.). (Illus., Orig.). 1978. pap. 3.95 (ISBN 0-8048-1335-3, Pub. by Shufunotomo Co Ltd Japan). C E Tuttle.

Hijams, Willy & Schaeffer, Morris, eds. International Conference on Immunofluorescence & Related Staining Techniques, 5th. (Annals of the New York Academy of Sciences Ser.: Vol. 254). 627p. 1975. 74.00x (ISBN 0-89072-008-8). NY Acad Sci.

Hijiya, Yukihito. Ishikawa Takuboku. (World Authors Ser.). 1979. lib. bdg. 15.95 (ISBN 0-8057-6381-3, Twayne). G K Hall.

Hijuelos, Oscar. Our House in the Last World. 256p. 1983. 13.95 (ISBN 0-89255-069-4). Persea Bks.

Hiket, Nazim. The Epic of Sheik Bedreddin & Other Poems. Blasing, Randy & Konuk, Mutlu, trs. from Turk. LC 77-76663. 1978. o. p. 10.00 (ISBN 0-89255-023-6); pap. 5.95 (ISBN 0-89255-024-4). Persea Bks.

Hikmet, Nazim. Human Landscapes. Blasing, Randy & Konuk, Mutlu, trs. from Turkish. (Persea Series of Poetry in Translation). 325p. (Orig.). 1983. cancelled 16.95 (ISBN 0-89255-067-8); pap. 9.95 (ISBN 0-89255-068-6). Persea Bks.

--Moscow Symphony & Other Poems. Baybars, Taner, tr. LC 82-71496. (Poetry in Europe Ser.: No. 13). 64p. 1970. 6.95 (ISBN 0-8040-0217-7). Swallow.

--Things I Didn't Know I Loved: Selected Poems of Nazim Hikmet. Blasing, Randy & Konuk, Mutlu, trs. LC 75-10789. 96p. 1982. pap. 5.95 o.p. (ISBN 0-89255-001-5). Persea Bks.

Hilary, Richard. The Last Enemy. 192p. 1983. 10.95 (ISBN 0-312-47079-7). St Martin.

Hilber, Oswald. Die Gattung Pleurotus (Fr.) Kummer Unter Besonderer Beruecksichtigung des Pleurotus-Eryngii-Komplexes. (Bibliotheca Mycologica Ser.: Vol. 87). (Illus.). 447p. (Orig., Ger.). 1982. text ed. 80.00x (ISBN 3-7682-1335-8). Lubrecht & Cramer.

Hilberg, Raul. The Destruction of European Jews. LC 61-7931. 800p. 1979. pap. 10.95xi (ISBN 0-06-131959-7, TB 1959, Torch). Har-Row.

Hilberg, Raul & Staron, Stanislaw, eds. The Warsaw Diary of Adam Czerniakow: Prelude to Doom. 480p. Repr. 14.00 (ISBN 0-686-95101-8). ADL.

Hilberman, Elaine. The Rape Victim. LC 76-5627. 112p. 1976. pap. 5.00x (ISBN 0-89042-142-0). Am Psychiatric.

Hilberry, Conrad. Rust. LC 73-92903. 61p. 1974. 6.95 (ISBN 0-8214-0153-X, 82-83756). Ohio U Pr.

Hilbert, D., jt. auth. see Courant, R.

Hilbert, David. Foundations of Geometry. 2nd ed. Unger, Leo, tr. LC 73-110344. 226p. (Taken from the 10th german edition). 1971. 15.50 (ISBN 0-87548-163-9); pap. 9.50 (ISBN 0-87548-164-7). Open Court.

--Gesammelte Abhandlungen, 3 Vols. 3rd ed. LC 65-21834. (Ger). 1981. Set. 59.95 (ISBN 0-8284-0195-0). Chelsea Pub.

Hilbert, David & Ackermann, W. Principles of Mathematical Logic. LC 50-4784. 11.95 (ISBN 0-8284-0069-5). Chelsea Pub.

Hilbert, David & Cohn-Vossen, Stephan. Geometry & the Imagination. LC 52-2894. (gr. 9 up). 1952. text ed. 16.95 (ISBN 0-8284-0087-3). Chelsea Pub.

Hilbert, Stephen & Jaffe, Eugene. Barron's How to Prepare for the Graduate Management Admission Test (GMAT) 4th ed. LC 81-3536. 576p. 1981. pap. text ed. 7.95 (ISBN 0-8120-2350-1). Barron.

Hilborn, Ann. Personal Justice. 272p. 1982. pap. 2.95 (ISBN 0-380-81109-X, 81109). Avon.

Hilborn, Nat & Hilborn, Sam. Battleground of Freedom: South Carolina in the Revolution. LC 70-143042. (Illus.). 256p. 1970. 15.00 (ISBN 0-87844-000-3). Sandlapper Pub Co.

Hilborn, Sam, jt. auth. see Hilborn, Nat.

Hilbrink, W. R. Who Really Invented Radio? (Who Really Invented Ser.). (Illus.). (gr. 5-8). 1972. PLB 4.29 o.p. (ISBN 0-399-60722-6). Putnam Pub Group.

Hilburn, J. L. & Julich, P. Microcomputers - Microprocessors: Hardware, Software & Applications. 1976. text ed. 29.95 (ISBN 0-13-580969-X). P-H.

Hilburn, J. L., jt. auth. see Johnson, D. E.

Hilburn, John L. & Johnson, David E. Manual of Active Filter Design. (Illus.). 192p. 1973. 35.75 (ISBN 0-07-028759-7, P&RB). McGraw.

Hilburn, May S. Golden Tributes: Fraternal Ceremonies. 1982. Repr. of 1977 ed. text ed. 8.75 (ISBN 0-686-43323-8). Macoy Pub.

Hild, Walter J., ed. see Sobotta, Johannes.

Hildebidle, John. Thoreau: A Naturalist's Liberty. 192p. 1983. text ed. 15.00x (ISBN 0-674-60455-5). Harvard U Pr.

Hildebrand, D. Von. Man & Woman. LC 81-52213. Date not set. pap. 3.95 (ISBN 0-89526-883-3). Regnery-Gateway. Postponed.

Hildebrand, David, jt. auth. see Ott, Lyman.

Hildebrand, Dietrich von see Von Hildebrand, Dietrich.

Hildebrand, Francis B. Advanced Calculus for Applications. 2nd ed. (Illus.). 816p. 1976. 34.95 (ISBN 0-13-011189-9). P-H.

--Introduction to Numerical Analysis. 2nd ed. 1973. text ed. 35.00 o.p. (ISBN 0-07-028761-9, C); instructor's manual 7.95 o.p. (ISBN 0-07-028763-5). McGraw.

--Methods of Applied Mathematics. 2nd ed. 1965. ref. ed. 32.95 (ISBN 0-13-579201-0). P-H.

Hildebrand, George C., jt. auth. see Porter, Gareth.

Hildebrand, J., ed. Lesions of the Nervous System in Cancer Patients. LC 78-3000. (European Organization for Research on Treatment of Cancer Monograph: Vol. 5). 162p. 1978. 22.00 (ISBN 0-89004-269-1). Raven.

Hildebrand, J., ed. see European Organization for Research & Treatment of Cancer.

Hildebrand, Joel, et al. Regular & Related Solutions: The Solubility of Gases, Liquids & Solids. LC 79-122670. 238p. 1970. 15.95 (ISBN 0-442-15665-0). Krieger.

Hildebrand, Klaus. The Foreign Policy of the Third Reich. LC 79-149942. 1974. 26.50x (ISBN 0-520-01965-2); pap. 7.95x (ISBN 0-520-02528-8). U of Cal Pr.

Hildebrand, Milton. Analysis of Vertebrate Structure. 2nd ed. 704p. 1981. text ed. 28.50 (ISBN 0-471-09058-1). Wiley.

--Anatomical Preparations. LC 68-21891. 1968. 24.50x (ISBN 0-520-00558-9). U of Cal Pr.

Hildebrand, Peter E., jt. auth. see Andrew, Chris O.

Hildebrand, Verna. Guiding Young Children. 2nd ed. (Illus.). 1980. text ed. 21.95x (ISBN 0-02-354240-3). Macmillan.

--Introduction to Early Childhood Education. 3rd ed. 1981. text ed. 22.95x (ISBN 0-02-354290-X); lab. manual 10.95 (ISBN 0-02-354280-2). Macmillan.

--Parenting & Teaching Young Children. Newman, Carol, ed. (Illus.). 432p. (gr. 10-12). 1980. text ed. 18.56 (ISBN 0-07-028775-9, W); tchrs. manual 7.44 (ISBN 0-07-051305-8). McGraw.

Hildebrandt, jt. auth. see Carruth.

Hildebrandt, A., jt. ed. see Schmidt, E. H.

Hildebrandt, Rita. The Rita & Timonthy Hildebrandt Fantasy Cookbook. new ed. 128p. 1983. 14.95 (ISBN 0-672-52703-0). Bobbs.

Hildenbrand, Werner, ed. Advances in Econometrics. LC 81-18171. (Econometric Society Monograph in Quantitative Economics). 282p. 1983. 39.50 (ISBN 0-521-24572-9). Cambridge U Pr.

Hilderby, Robert & McNulty, Elizabeth. Treating & Caring: A Human Approach to Patient Care. 1982. text ed. 14.95 (ISBN 0-8359-7832-X); pap. text ed. 12.95 (ISBN 0-8359-7831-1). Reston.

Hildesheimer, Wolfgang. Mozart. Faber, Marion, tr. from Ger. LC 81-9719. (Illus.). 1982. 22.50 (ISBN 0-374-21483-2). FS&G.

Hildesley, Angela, jt. auth. see Cooper, Christine.

Hildick, E. W. The Case of the Felon's Fiddle. LC 82-10078. (A McGurk Mystery Ser.). (Illus.). 144p. (gr. 3-6). 1982. 9.95 (ISBN 0-02-743900-3). Macmillan.

--Case of the Invisible Dog. (A McGurk Mystery: No. 5). (Illus.). (gr. 3-5). 1978. pap. 1.95 (ISBN 0-671-44879-X). Archway.

--Case of the Nervous Newsboy. (A McGurk Mystery: No. 3). (Illus.). (gr. 3-5). 1978. pap. 1.95 (ISBN 0-671-46529-5). Archway.

--Case of the Phantom Frog. (A McGurk Mystery: No. 7). (Illus.). (gr. 3-5). 1980. pap. 1.95 (ISBN 0-671-43878-6). Archway.

--The Case of the Slingshot Sniper. LC 82-20913. (McGurk Mystery Ser.). (Illus.). 144p. (gr. 3-6). 1983. 9.95 (ISBN 0-02-743920-8). Macmillan.

--The Case of the Treetop Treasure. (A McGurk Mystery: No. 8). 1981. pap. 1.95 (ISBN 0-671-45918-X). Archway.

Hildick, E. Wallace. Top-Flight Fully Automated Junior High School Girl Detective. LC 76-42337. (gr. 4-7). 1977. 5.95a o.p. (ISBN 0-385-08259-2); PLB 5.95a (ISBN 0-385-08328-9). Doubleday.

Hildreth, Dolly, et al. The Money God. (Indian Culture Ser.). (gr. 6). 1972. 1.95 o.p. (ISBN 0-89992-031-4). MT Coun Indian.

Hildyard, R. J., jt. auth. see Oswald, Adrian.

Hileman, Josephine, jt. auth. see Coleman, Bruce.

Hileman, Sam, tr. see Fuentes, Carlos.

Hileman, Sam, tr. see Rodrigues, Jose H.

Hilen, Andrew, ed. see Longfellow, Henry W.

Hilen, Andrew R., ed. see Longfellow, Henry W.

Hiley, Michael. Frank Sutcliffe: Photographer of Whitby. LC 74-81519. (Illus.). 224p. 1975. 40.00 (ISBN 0-87923-105-X). Godine.

Hilf, E. R., jt. auth. see Baltes, H. P.

Hilfer, S. R., jt. ed. see Sheffield, J. B.

Hilgard, Ernest, ed. American Psychology in Historical Perspective: Addresses of the Presidents of the American Psychological Association. LC 78-15672. 1978. lib. bdg. 18.00x o.p. (ISBN 0-912704-05-5); pap. 15.00x o.p. (ISBN 0-912704-07-1). Am Psychol.

Hilgard, Ernest J., jt. auth. see Bower, Gordon H.

Hilgard, Ernest R. The Experience of Hypnosis. LC 68-25372. (Shorter Version of Hypnotic Susceptibility). 1968. pap. 4.95 (ISBN 0-15-629552-0, Harv). HarBraceJ.

--Hypnotic Susceptibility. 434p. 1965. text ed. 23.95 (ISBN 0-15-540523-3, HC). HarBraceJ.

Hilgartner. Hemophilia in the Child & Adult. LC 82-7780. 390p. 1982. 59.50 (ISBN 0-89302-131-8). Masson Pub.

Hilgartner, Stephen, et al. Nukespeak: The Selling of Nuclear Technology in America. (Illus.). 1983. pap. 6.95 (ISBN 0-14-006684-5). Penguin.

Hilgemann, Werner, jt. auth. see Kinder, Hermann.

Hilgenfeldt, C. L. Johann Sebastian Bachs Leben, Wirken und Werke. (Facsimiles of Early Biographies Ser.: Vol. 3). 1965. Repr. of 1850 ed. 32.50 o.s.i. (ISBN 90-6027-017-7, Pub. by Frits Knuf Netherlands). Pendragon NY.

Hilgers, J. & Sluyser, M., eds. Mammary Tumors in the Mouse. 1981. 183.50 (ISBN 0-444-80315-7). Elsevier.

Hilgert, Raymond L., et al. Cases & Policies in Human Resource Management. 3rd ed. LC 77-72903. (Illus.). 1978. pap. text ed. 10.95 o.p. (ISBN 0-395-25070-6); instr's. manual 0.80 o.p. (ISBN 0-395-25071-4). HM.

--Cases & Policies in Personnel-Human Resources Management. 4th ed. LC 81-84466. 1982. 14.50 (ISBN 0-395-31738-X); instr's manual 1.50 (ISBN 0-395-31739-8). HM.

Hilgetag, G., jt. auth. see Weygand.

Hilkemeyer, Renilda E., ed. Cancer Nursing. (M. D. Anderson Series on the Diagnosis & Management of Cancer). Date not set. price not set (ISBN 0-89004-438-4). Raven.

Hilken, Thomas J. Engineering at Cambridge University, 1783-1965. 1967. 29.95 (ISBN 0-521-05256-4). Cambridge U Pr.

Hilker, Helen-Anne. Ten First Street, Southeast: Congress Builds a Library, 1886-1897. LC 80-60780. (Illus.). iv, 102p. 1980. pap. 5.50 (ISBN 0-8444-0351-2). Lib Congress.

Hill. Cats & Kittens. 1983. 5.95 (ISBN 0-86020-645-9, 15101); pap. 2.95 (ISBN 0-86020-644-0, 15102). EDC.

--The School Business Administrator. 3rd ed. 1982. 6.50 (ISBN 0-910170-26-6). Assn Sch Busn.

--The School Business Administrator: Qualifications & Responsibilities. (Research Bulletin: No. 21). pap. 0.50 o.p. (ISBN 0-685-57187-4). Assn Sch Busn.

--Small Pets. 1983. 5.95 (ISBN 0-86020-649-1, 15121); pap. 2.95 (ISBN 0-86020-648-3, 15122). EDC.

--Where's Spot? 8.95 (ISBN 0-399-20758-9). Putnam Pub Group.

Hill & Roberts. Secret of the Star. (Arch Bks: Set 3). 1966. laminated bdg. 0.89 (ISBN 0-570-06021-4, 59-1130). Concordia.

Hill, jt. auth. see Mckay.

Hill, ed. Medical Ultrasonic Images. (International Congress Ser.: Vol. 541). 1981. 40.50 (ISBN 0-444-90199-X). Elsevier.

Hill, jt. auth. see Bannister.

Hill, A. V. First & Last Experiments in Muscle Mechanics. LC 73-96092. (Illus.). 1970. 37.50 (ISBN 0-521-07664-1). Cambridge U Pr.

Hill, A. W. see Jackson, B. D., et al.

Hill, A. W., et al. Handbook to BS 5337, 1976: The Structural Use of Concrete for Retaining Aqueous Liquids. (Viewpoint Publication Ser.). (Illus.). 60p. 1979. pap. text ed. 25.75x (ISBN 0-7210-1078-4, Pub. by C&CA London). Scholium Intl.

Hill, Adrian. What Shall We Draw? (Illus.). 80p. 1983. 8.95 (ISBN 0-87523-202-7). Emerson.

Hill, Alan G., ed. The Letters of William & Dorothy Wordsworth: The Later Years, 1835-1839, Vol. VI, Pt. 3. 2nd ed. 816p. 1982. 49.50x (ISBN 0-19-812483-X). Oxford U Pr.

Hill, Alan G. see Wordsworth, William & Wordsworth, Dorothy.

Hill, Albert F. Economic Botany. 2nd ed. (Botanical Sciences Ser.). (Illus.). 1952. text ed. 39.95 (ISBN 0-07-028789-9, C). McGraw.

Hill, Alexis. In the Arms of Love. (Candlelight Ecstasy Ser.: No. 115). (Orig.). 1983. pap. 1.95 (ISBN 0-440-14203-2). Dell.

--Passion's Slave. (Orig.). 1979. pap. 2.50 o.s.i. (ISBN 0-515-04862-3). Jove Pubns.

Hill, Alice P. Tales of the Colorado Pioneers. LC 76-28500. (Beautiful Rio Grande Classics Ser). 1976. lib. bdg. 15.00 o.s.i. (ISBN 0-87380-135-0). Rio Grande.

Hill, Ann, ed. The Visual Encyclopedia of Unconventional Medicine. 12.95 o.p. (ISBN 0-517-53613-7); pap. 6.95 o.p. (ISBN 0-517-53614-5). Crown.

Hill, Art. I Don't Care If I Never Come Back. 1980. 11.95 o.p. (ISBN 0-671-25272-0). S&S.

Hill, Arthur G. The Organ-Cases & Organs of the Middle Ages & Renaissance. (Bibliotheca Organologica Ser.: Vol. 6). (Illus.). 1975. Repr. of 1891 ed. 42.50 o.s.i. (ISBN 90-6027-026-6, Pub. by Frits Knuf Netherlands); wrappers 30.00 o.s.i. (ISBN 90-6027-262-5, Pub. Frits Knuf Netherlands). Pendragon NY.

Hill, Barbara. Graphology. LC 80-27752. (Illus.). 144p. 1981. 9.95 o.p. (ISBN 0-312-34444-9). St Martin.

Hill, Benneth D., jt. auth. see McKay, John P.

Hill, Bennett D., jt. auth. see McKay, John P.

Hill, Betty. Verbal Dyspraxia Clinical Practice. 80p. 1980. text ed. 11.95 o.p. (ISBN 0-85896-623-9). Univ Park.

Hill, Brennan. The Near-Death Experience: A Christian Approach. 66p. 1981. pap. 3.50 (ISBN 0-697-01756-7). Wm C Brown.

--Rediscovering the Sacraments. 3.95 (ISBN 0-8215-9882-1). Sadlier.

Hill, Brennan, jt. auth. see Hill, Marie.

Hill, Brennan & Newland, Mary R., eds. Theologians & Catechists in Dialogue: The Albany Forum. 64p. (Orig.). 1977. pap. 2.25 (ISBN 0-697-01671-4). Wm C Brown.

--Why Be a Catholic? 108p. (Orig.). 1979. pap. 2.00 (ISBN 0-697-01713-3). Wm C Brown.

Hill, Brian. Britain's Agricultural Industry. (Studies in British Economy). 1975. pap. text ed. 5.00x o.p. (ISBN 0-435-84565-9). Heinemann Ed.

--Faith at the Blackboard: Issues Facing the Christian Teacher. 160p. (Orig.). 1982. pap. 6.95 (ISBN 0-8028-1932-X). Eerdmans.

Hill, Brian V. Education & the Endangered Individual: A Critique of Ten Modern Thinkers. LC 73-82283. 322p. 1974. pap. text ed. 9.95x (ISBN 0-8077-2432-7). Tchrs Coll.

Hill, C. J. Introduction to the Law of Carriage of Goods by Sea. 1974. 10.00 (ISBN 0-540-07374-1). Heinman.

Hill, C. P., jt. ed. see Allen, H. C.

Hill, C. R., jt. auth. see Alvisi, C.

Hill, C. W. Edwardian Scotland. 182p. 1976. 15.00x o.p. (ISBN 0-87471-846-5). Rowman.

Hill, Cecil. Ferdinand Ries, Three Symphonies 1784-1838. (The Symphony 1720-1840 Series C: Vol. 12). 1982. lib. bdg. 90.00 (ISBN 0-8240-3817-7). Garland Pub.

Hill, Charles G., Jr. An Introduction to Chemical Engineering Kinetics & Reactor Design. LC 77-8280. 1977. 39.95 (ISBN 0-471-39609-5); Solutions Manual avail. (ISBN 0-471-05258-2). Wiley.

Hill, Charles L., tr. see Melanchthon, Philipp.

Hill, Christopher. Century of Revolution, 1603-1714. 1966. pap. 5.95x o.p. (ISBN 0-393-00365-5, Norton Lib). Norton.

--The Century of Revolution, 1603-1714. 2nd ed. 304p. 1982. 19.95 (ISBN 0-393-01573-4); pap. text ed. 4.95x (ISBN 0-393-30016-1). Norton.

--God's Englishman: Oliver Cromwell & the English Revolution. 324p. 1972. pap. 7.50xi (ISBN 0-06-131666-0, TB1666, Torch). Har-Row.

--Intellectual Origins of the English Revolution. 348p. 1980. pap. text ed. 15.95x (ISBN 0-19-822635-7). Oxford U Pr.

--Some Intellectual Consequences of the English Revolution. LC 79-5408. (Curti Lecture Ser.). 1980. 15.00 (ISBN 0-299-08140-0); pap. 6.95 (ISBN 0-299-08144-3). U of Wis Pr.

Hill, Christopher & Barber, James. The West & South Africa. (Chatham House Papers on Foreign Policy Ser.). (Orig.). 1983. pap. 10.00 (ISBN 0-7100-9232-6). Routledge & Kegan.

Hill, Christopher, ed. see Winstanley, Gerrard.
Hill, Claude. Bertolt Brecht. (World Authors Ser.). 1975. lib. bdg. 12.95 (ISBN 0-8057-2179-7, Twayne). G K Hall.
Hill, Clyde M., ed. Educational Progress & School Administration: Symposium By a Number of His Former Associates Written As a Tribute to Frank Ellsworth Spauling. 1936. text ed. 49.50x (ISBN 0-686-83532-8). Elliots Bks.
Hill, D. S. & Waller, J. M. Pests & Diseases of Tropical Crops: Principles & Methods, Vol. 1. LC 81-18561. (Illus.). 192p. (Orig.). 1982. pap. text ed. 7.95x (ISBN 0-582-60614-4). Longman.
Hill, D. W. Physics Applied to Anaesthesia. 3rd ed. 320p. 1976. 39.95 o.p. (ISBN 0-407-00039-9). Butterworth.
--Principles of Electronics in Medical Research. 2nd ed. (Illus.). 1973. 22.95 o.p. (ISBN 0-407-36401-3). Butterworth.
Hill, D. W., jt. auth. see Payne, J. P.
Hill, D. W. see Watson, B. W.
Hill, Dave. Boy Who Gave His Lunch Away. (Arch Bks: Set 4). 1967. laminated bdg. 0.89 (ISBN 0-570-06027-3, 59-1138). Concordia.
--Most Wonderful King. (Arch Bks: Set 5). (Illus.). (gr. 3-4). 1968. laminated bdg. 0.89 (ISBN 0-570-06032-X, 59-1145). Concordia.
--Walls Came Tumbling Down. (Arch Bks: Set 4). 1967. laminated bdg 0.89 (ISBN 0-570-06024-9, 59-1135). Concordia.
Hill, David. New Testament Prophecy. LC 79-16707. (New Foundations Theological Library). 260p. (Peter Toon & Ralph Martin series editors). 1980. 12.95 (ISBN 0-8042-3702-6). John Knox.
Hill, Dawn. Reaching for the Other Side. (Orig.). 1983. pap. 6.95 (ISBN 0-87877-063-1). Newcastle Pub.
--Reaching for the Other Side. 1983. Repr. of 1893 ed. lib. bdg. 13.95x (ISBN 0-89370-663-9). Borgo Pr.
Hill, Debora. Cuts from a San Francisco Rock Journal. LC 81-68393. (Illus.). 400p. (Orig.). 1981. pap. 9.95 (ISBN 0-89708-079-3). And Bks.
Hill, Deborah. House of Kingsley Merrick. LC 78-2192. 1978. 10.95 o.p. (ISBN 0-698-10866-3, Coward). Putnam Pub Group.
--Kingsland. 1981. pap. 2.95 o.p. (ISBN 0-451-11263-6, AE 1263, Sig). NAL.
--This Is the House. 1977. pap. 3.50 (ISBN 0-451-11272-5, AE1272, Sig). NAL.
Hill, Deborah A., jt. ed. see Ebeling, Nancy B.
Hill, Denis. Psychiatry in Medicine: Retrospect & Prospect. 179p. 1969. 25.00x (ISBN 0-686-96978-2, Pub. by Nuffield England). State Mutual Bk.
Hill, Devra. Rejuvenate. 1982. 6.95x (ISBN 0-686-37599-8). Cancer Control Soc.
Hill, Dick. Death & Dying. 4.25 (ISBN 0-89137-532-5). Quality Pubns.
Hill, Don. Transport Laws of the World, 2 vols. Evans, Malcolm, ed. LC 77-8397. 1977. looseleaf 340.00 (ISBN 0-379-10195-5). Set. Oceana.
Hill, Donald L., ed. see Pater, Walter.
Hill, Donna. Eerie Animals: Seven Stories. LC 82-13755. (Illus.). 160p. (gr. 4-6). 1983. 10.95 (ISBN 0-689-30956-2). Atheneum.
--Joseph Smith: The First Mormon. LC 73-15345. 1977. 17.95 o.p. (ISBN 0-385-00804-X). Doubleday.
Hill, Douglas. The Huntsman. LC 82-3959. 144p. 1982. 9.95 (ISBN 0-689-50240-0, Argo). Atheneum.
--The Illustrated Faerie Queene. Brooks, Valrie, ed. LC 80-392. (Illus.). 192p. 1980. 16.95 o.p. (ISBN 0-88225-297-6). Newsweek.
--Warriors of the Wasteland. LC 82-13896. 144p. (gr. 8 up). 1983. 9.95 (ISBN 0-689-50269-9, Argo). Atheneum.
Hill, Douglas & Williams, Pat. Supernatural. pap. 1.95 o.p. (ISBN 0-451-09265-1, J9265, Sig). NAL.
Hill, Douglas, jt. ed. see Birrell, Robert.
Hill, Draper, ed. see Gillray, James.
Hill, E. Joy. General Health Occupations Practice. LC 71-176181. 320p. 1983. 24.50 (ISBN 0-87527-108-1). Green.
Hill, Edward B. Modern French Music. LC 71-87491. (Music Reprint Ser). 1969. Repr. of 1924 ed. lib. bdg. 32.50 (ISBN 0-306-71497-3). Da Capo.
--Modern French Music. Repr. of 1924 ed. lib. bdg. 19.25x (ISBN 0-8371-3942-2, HIMF). Greenwood.
Hill, Eldon C. George Bernard Shaw. (English Authors Ser.). 1978. lib. bdg. 11.95 (ISBN 0-8057-6709-6, Twayne). G K Hall.
Hill, Elizabeth W., jt. ed. see Starr, Martha H.
Hill, Eric. The Aphrodisiac Gourmet. (Illus.). 136p. 1983. pap. 3.95 (ISBN 0-931290-74-0). Aries Pub.
--At Home. (Eric Hill's Baby Bear Bks.). (Illus.). 14p. (ps-k). 1983. pap. 1.95 (ISBN 0-394-85638-4). Random.
--My Pets. LC 82-60625. (Eric Hill's Baby Bear Bks.). (Illus.). 14p. (ps). 1983. pap. 1.95 (ISBN 0-394-85637-6). Random.
--The Park. LC 82-60615. (Eric Hill's Baby Bear Bks.). (Illus.). 14p. (ps). 1983. pap. 1.95 (ISBN 0-394-85636-8). Random.
--Puppy Love. (Illus.). 32p. 1982. 3.95 (ISBN 0-399-20935-2). Putnam Pub Group.
--Spot's Birthday Party. (Illus.). 1982. 8.95 (ISBN 0-399-20903-4). Putnam Pub Group.
--Spot's First Walk. (A Lift the Flap Bk.). (Illus.). (ps). 1981. 8.95 (ISBN 0-399-20838-0). Putnam Pub Group.
--Up There. LC 82-60626. (Eric Hill's Baby Bear Bks). (Illus.). 14p. (ps). 1983. pap. 1.95 (ISBN 0-394-85635-X). Random.
Hill, Errol, ed. see Tipling, Carmen, et al.
Hill, Eugenie. A More Innocent Time. 208p. 1981. pap. 2.25 o.p. (ISBN 0-380-54478-4, 54478). Avon.
Hill, Evan & Breen, John J. Reporting & Writing the News. 1977. pap. 12.95 (ISBN 0-316-36337-5); instructors manual avail. (ISBN 0-316-36338-3). Little.
Hill, Evan & Stekl, William. The Connecticut River. LC 72-3727. (Illus.). 144p. 1972. 15.00x (ISBN 0-8195-4051-X, Pub. by Wesleyan U Pr); pap. 8.95 (ISBN 0-8195-6042-1). Columbia U Pr.
Hill, Evelyn F. The Holtzman Inkblot Technique: A Handbook for Clinical Application. LC 74-184959. (Social & Behavioral Science Ser.). 1972. 37.95x (ISBN 0-87589-121-7). Jossey-Bass.
Hill, F. S., Jr., jt. auth. see Glorioso, Robert M.
Hill, Faith F., jt. auth. see Stollberg, Robert.
Hill, Forest. Steel. (Orig.). 1983. pap. cancelled (ISBN 0-523-40637-1). Pinnacle Bks.
Hill, Frank. The VFR Pilot Handbook. LC 82-6773. 256p. Date not set. 20.00 (ISBN 0-87668-606-4). Aronson.
Hill, Frank W. English Springer Spaniels. Foyle, Christina, ed. (Foyle's Handbks). 1973. 3.95 (ISBN 0-685-55817-7). Palmetto Pub.
Hill, Frederick J. & Peterson, Gerald R. Digital Systems: Hardware Organization & Design. 2nd ed. LC 78-7209. 1978. text ed. 36.95 (ISBN 0-471-39608-7); tchrs. ed. 6.00x (ISBN 0-471-03694-3). Wiley.
--Introduction to Switching Theory & Logical Design. 3rd ed. LC 80-20333. 617p. 1981. text ed. 33.95 (ISBN 0-471-04273-0); solutions manual avail. (ISBN 0-471-09081-6). Wiley.
Hill, Frederick P. Charles F. McKim the Man. 1950. 3.00 o.p. (ISBN 0-8338-0026-4). M Jones.
Hill, G. F. Coins of Ancient Sicily. Bd. with Catalog of Greek Coins in the British Museum: Sicily. Poole, R. S. Repr. of 1903 ed. (Illus.). 1983. Repr. of 1876 ed. lib. bdg. 50.00 (ISBN 0-915262-96-7). S J Durst.
Hill, Gene. Hill Country: Stories About Hunting & Fishing & Dogs & Guns & Such. 1978. 13.50 (ISBN 0-87690-297-2, 01311-390). Dutton.
Hill, Geoffrey. Tenebrae. 1979. 7.95 o.p. (ISBN 0-395-27610-1); pap. 4.50 o.p. (ISBN 0-395-27938-0). HM.
Hill, Geoffrey, jt. auth. see Ibsen, Henrik.
Hill, George J. Leprosy in Five Young Men. LC 79-125621. (Illus.). 1971. 15.00x (ISBN 0-87081-003-0). Colo Assoc.
Hill, George J., II. Outpatient Surgery. 2nd ed. LC 77-27749. (Illus.). 1457p. 1980. text ed. 70.00 (ISBN 0-7216-4676-X). Saunders.
Hill, George R. A Preliminary Checklist of Research on the Classic Symphony & Concerto to the Time of Beethoven (Excluding Haydn & Mozart) (Music Indexes & Bibliographies: No. 2). pap. 5.00 (ISBN 0-913574-02-3). Eur-Am Music.
--A Thematic Catalog of the Instrumental Music of Florian Leopold Gassmann. (Music Indexes & Bibliographies: No. 12). 1976. 28.00 (ISBN 0-913574-12-0). Eur-Am Music.
Hill, George R. & Gould, Murray. A Thematic Locator for Mozart's Works, As Listed in Koechel's Chronologisch Thematisches Verzeichnis. 6th ed. (Music Indexes & Bibliographies: No. 1). 1970. pap. 7.50 (ISBN 0-913574-01-5). Eur-Am Music.
Hill, Gladwin. Noise-The Most Ubiquitous of All Pollutions: What's Being Done to Tone It Down? (Vital Issues, Vol. XXVIII 1978-79: No. 3). 0.50. Ctr Info Am.
Hill, Gordon. Bikes. LC 80-50939. (Whizz Kids Ser.). 8.00 (ISBN 0-382-06432-1). Silver.
Hill, Grace L. The Head of the House. (Romance Ser.: No. 12). 256p. 1982. pap. 2.50 (ISBN 0-553-22670-3). Bantam.
--Keeper of the Faith, No. 20. 192p. 1982. pap. 2.25 (ISBN 0-553-20829-2). Bantam.
Hill, Graham & Ewart, Neil. Graham. LC 77-72299. (Illus.). 1977. 8.95 o.p. (ISBN 0-312-34212-8). St Martin.
Hill, Graham L. Ileostomy: Surgery, Physiology & Management. LC 75-44116. (Illus.). 208p. 1976. 34.00 (ISBN 0-8089-0928-2). Grune.
Hill, H. Freedom to Roam. 144p. 1981. 25.00x o.p. (ISBN 0-903485-77-X, Pub. by Moorland). State Mutual Bk.
Hill, H & Perkins, Acompiled by. New Coasts & Strange Harbors: Discovering Poems. LC 74-12343. (Illus.). 224p. (gr. 7 up). 1974. 10.95i o.p. (ISBN 0-690-00271-8, TYC-J). Har-Row.
Hill, H. A. Inorganic Biochemistry, Vol. 2. 362p. 1982. 190.00x (ISBN 0-85186-555-0, Pub. by Royal Soc Chem England). State Mutual Bk.
Hill, Hamlin, jt. auth. see Blair, Walter.
Hill, Harold. Instant Answers for King's Kids in Training. 1978. pap. 3.50 o.p. (ISBN 0-88270-277-7, Pub. by Logos). Bridge Pub.
Hill, Harold & Harrell, Irene. How Did It All Begin? LC 75-20898. 1976. pap. 2.95 (ISBN 0-88270-140-1, Pub. by Logos). Bridge Pub.
Hill, Harold & Harrell, Irene B. How to Live the Bible Like a King's Kid. (Illus.). 128p. 1980. pap. 4.95 (ISBN 0-8007-5051-9, Power Bks). Revell.
Hill, Harry G. Automotive Service & Repair Tools. LC 73-907400. 343p. 1975. pap. 13.20 (ISBN 0-8273-1035-8); instructor's guide 2.00 (ISBN 0-8273-1036-6). Delmar.
--Interpreting Automotive Systems. LC 75-19527. 1977. pap. 13.00 (ISBN 0-8273-1057-9); instructor's guide 2.75 (ISBN 0-8273-1058-7). Delmar.
Hill, Henry P., et al. Sampling in Auditing: A Simplified Guide & Statistical Tables. LC 79-23351. 180p. 1979. Repr. of 1962 ed. lib. bdg. 11.50 (ISBN 0-89874-102-5). Krieger.
Hill, Herbert. Black Labor & the American Legal System: Race, Work, & the Law. LC 75-34475. 472p. 1977. 21.50 (ISBN 0-87179-222-2). BNA.
--Roman Middle Class in the Republican Period. LC 79-136867. 226p. 1974. Repr. of 1952 ed. lib. bdg. 19.00x (ISBN 0-8371-5303-4, HIRM). Greenwood.
Hill, Herbert, jt. auth. see Hamilton, Charles V.
Hill, Herbert, jt. ed. see Ware, Gilbert.
Hill, Herminie W. Pekingese. Foyle, Christina, ed. (Foyles Handbks). 1973. 3.95 (ISBN 0-685-55813-4). Palmetto Pub.
Hill, Howard. Freedom to Roam: The Struggle for Access to Britain's Moors & Mountains. 139p. 1980. 29.75x o.p. (ISBN 0-903485-77-X, Pub. by Moorland England). State Mutual Bk.
Hill, Howard E. Nine Magic Secrets of Long Life. 1979. 14.95 o.p. (ISBN 0-13-622548-9, Parker). P-H.
Hill, Ivan. Common Sense & Everyday Ethics. 36p. 1980. write for info. Ethics Res Ctr.
Hill, Ivan & Biemiller, Carl. How to Make America More Honest. Hill, Joan, ed. LC 74-11111. 1974. pap. text ed. 1.50 o.p. (ISBN 0-916152-03-0). Ethics Res Ctr.
Hill, Ivan, ed. The Ethical Basis of Economic Freedom. LC 76-5728. 400p. 1977. 12.50 (ISBN 0-916152-02-2). Ethics Res Ctr.
--Ethical Basis of Economic Freedom. LC 87-5829. 325p. 1980. pap. 15.95 (ISBN 0-686-81709-5). Ethics Res Ctr.
Hill, J. M. Solution of Differential Equations by Means of One-Parameter Groups. (Research Notes in Mathematics Ser.: No. 63). 176p. 1982. pap. text ed. 20.95 (ISBN 0-273-08506-9). Pitman Pub MA.
Hill, J. M., jt. auth. see Chaung, Y. H.
Hill, James. Rita Hayworth. 1983. 14.95 (ISBN 0-671-43273-7). S&S.
Hill, James E. & Kedar, Ervin Y. Ecology-Environment Handbook. LC 78-57574. 1978. pap. text ed. 7.25 (ISBN 0-8191-0525-2). U Pr of Amer.
Hill, Joan, ed. see Hill, Ivan & Biemiller, Carl.
Hill, John. From Subservience to Strike: Industrial Relations in the Banking Industry. LC 82-2684. (Illus.). 296p. 1983. text ed. 32.50x (ISBN 0-7022-1830-8). U of Queensland Pr.
--Heartbeeps. 224p. (Orig.). 1981. pap. 2.50 o.s.i. (ISBN 0-515-06183-2). Jove Pubns.
--The Life & Works of Francesco Maria Veracini. Buelow, George, ed. LC 79-20453. (Studies in Musicology: No. 3). 556p. 1980. 59.95 (ISBN 0-8357-1000-9, Pub. by UMI Res Pr). Univ Microfilms.
Hill, John G., Jr., jt. auth. see O'Hara, William T.
Hill, John W. & Feigl, Dorothy M. Chemistry & Life: An Introduction to General, Organic, & Biological Chemistry. LC 77-73541. 1978. pap. text ed. 23.95x (ISBN 0-8087-3109-2). Burgess.
Hill, Joseph F., jt. ed. see Kaminsky, Stuart M.
Hill, Katherine F., et al. Movement Plus... For the Elementary School. 1976. pap. text ed. 9.50 (ISBN 0-8403-1629-1). Kendall-Hunt.
Hill, Kathleen K. Rosalia de Castro. (World Authors Ser.). lib. bdg. 15.95 (ISBN 0-8057-6282-5, Twayne). G K Hall.
Hill, L., jt. auth. see Highnam, K.
Hill, L. R., ed. see Cowan, S. T.
Hill, Lawrence F., ed. Brazil: Chapters by Manoel Cardozo & Others. LC 82-15848. (The United Nations Ser.). (Illus.). xxi, 394p. 1982. Repr. of 1947 ed. lib. bdg. 49.75x (ISBN 0-313-23503-1, HILB). Greenwood.
Hill, Leonard, jt. auth. see Highnam, Kenneth C.
Hill, Leslie A. Advanced Anecdotes in American English. (Anecdotes in American English Ser.). (Illus., Orig.). 1981. pap. text ed. 3.50x (ISBN 0-19-502603-9). Oxford U Pr.
--Advanced Stories for Reproduction. 1965. pap. 3.25x o.p. (ISBN 0-19-432543-1). Oxford U Pr.
--Elementary Anecdotes in American English. (Anecdotes in American English Ser.). (Illus.). 1980. 3.50x (ISBN 0-19-502601-2). Oxford U Pr.
--Intermediate Anecdotes in American English. (Anecdotes in American English Ser.). (Illus.). 1981. pap. 3.50x (ISBN 0-19-502602-0); cassette 6.95x (ISBN 0-19-502829-5). Oxford U Pr.
--Intermediate Stories for Reproduction. 1965. pap. 3.25x o.p. (ISBN 0-19-432542-3). Oxford U Pr.
Hill, Leslie A. & Popkin, P. R. A Second Crossword Puzzle Book. 1969. pap. text ed. 2.95x o.p. (ISBN 0-19-432552-0). Oxford U Pr.
Hill, Lorna. The Scent of Rosemary. (Aston Hall Romances Ser.: No. 109). (Orig.). 1980. pap. 1.50 o.p. (ISBN 0-523-41121-9). Pinnacle Bks.
Hill, Louis A., Jr. Structured Programming in FORTRAN. (Illus.). 512p. 1981. text ed. 17.95 (ISBN 0-13-854612-6). P-H.
Hill, Louis B. Joseph E. Brown & the Confederacy. LC 70-138612. 360p. 1973. Repr. of 1939 ed. lib. bdg. 20.75x (ISBN 0-8371-5722-6, HIJB). Greenwood.
Hill, Lowell D., ed. The Role of Government in a Market Economy. (Illus.). 1982. 12.95 (ISBN 0-8138-1576-2). Iowa St U Pr.
Hill, M. The United Nations System. LC 77-71410. (Illus.). 1978. 44.50 (ISBN 0-521-21674-5). Cambridge U Pr.
Hill, M. N., ed. The Sea: Vol. 1, Physical Oceanography. 2nd ed. LC 80-248. 880p. 1982. Repr. of 1962 ed. lib. bdg. 65.00 (ISBN 0-89874-097-5). Krieger.
Hill, M. R. The Export Marketing of Capital Goods to the Socialist Countries of Eastern Europe. 200p. 1978. text ed. 50.75x (ISBN 0-566-03004-7). Gower Pub Ltd.
Hill, Margot H. & Bucknell, Peter A. Evolution of Fashion: Pattern & Cut from 1066-1930. LC 68-10504. 240p. 25.00x (ISBN 0-89676-064-2). Drama Bk.
Hill, Marie & Hill, Brennan. Adult Catechesis: A Basic Parish Program. Ryan, Mary P., ed. LC 77-89323. (Illus.). 1977. pap. 4.95 o.p. (ISBN 0-88489-094-5). St Mary's.
Hill, Marvin, Jr. & Sinicropi, Anthony V. Evidence in Arbitration. 212p. 1980. text ed. 15.00 (ISBN 0-87179-336-9). BNA.
--Remedies in Arbitration. 372p. 1981. text ed. 20.00 (ISBN 0-87179-359-8). BNA.
Hill, Mary. Geology of the Sierra Nevada. LC 73-93053. (California Natural History Guides Ser.). (Illus.). 1975. 14.95x (ISBN 0-520-02801-5); pap. 6.95 (ISBN 0-520-02698-5). U of Cal Pr.
Hill, Mary A. Charlotte Perkins Gilman: The Making of a Radical Feminist, 1860-1896. Davis, Allen F., ed. (American Civilization Ser.). (Illus.). 376p. 1980. 29.95 (ISBN 0-87722-160-X). Temple U Pr.
Hill, MaryAnn, ed. BMDP User's Digest: BMDP Statistical Software, Inc. rev. ed. 157p. 1982. text ed. 6.00 (ISBN 0-935386-02-5). BMDP Stat.
Hill, Matthew D. Suggestions for the Repression of Crime. LC 70-172581. (Criminology, Law Enforcement, & Social Problems Ser.: No. 169). 1975. 30.00x (ISBN 0-87585-169-X). Patterson Smith.
Hill, Melvin, ed. Hannah Arendt: The Recovery of the Public World. LC 78-19393. 1979. 14.95 o.p. (ISBN 0-312-36071-1); pap. 7.95 o.p. (ISBN 0-312-36072-X). St Martin.
Hill, Melvyn A., jt. auth. see Gear, Maria C.
Hill, Morgan. Bandits in Blue. (Dan Colt Ser.: No. 5). (Orig.). 1981. pap. 1.95 o.s.i. (ISBN 0-440-10421-1). Dell.
Hill, Myron G., et al. Smith's Review of Real & Personal Property, Conveyancing & Future Interests. 3rd ed. (Smith's Review Ser.). 1978. 18.95 o.p. (ISBN 0-685-91308-2). West Pub.
Hill, Myron G., Jr., et al. Smith's Review of Real & Personal Property, Conveyancing & Future Interests. 3rd ed. LC 78-10824. (Legal Gem Ser.). 307p. 1978. pap. text ed. 9.95 (ISBN 0-8299-2018-8). West Pub.
Hill, N. The Think & Grow Rich Action Pack. 1966. 11.95 (ISBN 0-8015-7554-0, 01160-350, Hawthorn); pap. 5.95 (ISBN 0-8015-7560-5, 0577-180, Hawthorn). Dutton.
Hill, N. C. Counseling at the Workplace. Date not set. 15.95 (ISBN 0-07-028785-6). McGraw.
Hill, Nancy K. A Reformer's Art: Dickens' Picturesque & Grotesque Imagery. LC 80-23256. (Illus.). xii, 169p. 1981. text ed. 14.50x (ISBN 0-8214-0586-1, 82-83749); pap. 7.50x (ISBN 0-8214-0613-2, 82-83756). Ohio U Pr.
Hill, Nancy L. The Plutonians Are Coming! 1978. 5.95 o.p. (ISBN 0-533-03672-0). Vantage.
Hill, Napoleon. Think & Grow Rich. 11.95 (ISBN 0-685-22136-9). Wehman.
Hill, Norman. Webster's Red Seal Crossword Dictionary. 272p. 1982. pap. 2.75 (ISBN 0-446-31055-7). Warner Bks.
Hill, Norman L. Claims to Territory in International Law & Relations. LC 75-25488. (Illus.). 248p. 1976. Repr. of 1945 ed. lib. bdg. 29.25x (ISBN 0-8371-8430-4, HICT). Greenwood.
Hill, Norwood, jt. ed. see Khan, Amanullah.
Hill, O. W. Modern Trends in Psychosomatic Medicine, Vol. 3. 1976. 29.50 o.p. (ISBN 0-407-31302-8). Butterworth.
Hill, P. M. & Humphrey, P. Human Growth & Development Throughout Life: A Nursing Perspective. LC 81-16472. 496p. 1982. 19.95x (ISBN 0-471-05814-9, Pub. by Wiley Med). Wiley.
Hill, Pamela. Daneclere. LC 78-3969. 1979. 8.95 o.p. (ISBN 0-312-18215-5). St Martin.
--Fire Opal. 280p. 1980. 9.95 o.p. (ISBN 0-312-29111-6). St Martin.
--Place of Ravens. 224p. 1981. 9.95 o.p. (ISBN 0-312-61373-3). St Martin.
Hill, Percy H. Short Course in Engineering Graphics & Design. (Illus.). 1964. text ed. 8.95x (ISBN 0-02-354480-5). Macmillan.
Hill, Percy H., et al. Making Decisions: A Multi-Disciplinary Introduction. 2nd. ed. 1980. pap. text ed. 18.50 (ISBN 0-201-03103-5). A-W.

Hill, Peter. The Enthusiast. 1979. 7.95 o.p. (ISBN 0-395-27543-1). HM.

Hill, Philip G. Power Generation: Resources, Hazards, Technology & Costs. LC 76-54739. 1977. 30.00x (ISBN 0-262-08091-5). MIT Pr.

Hill, Philip G. & Peterson, C. R. Mechanics & Thermodynamics of Propulsion. 1965. 34.95 (ISBN 0-201-02838-7). A-W.

Hill, Polly. Dry Grain Farming Families: Hausaland (Nigeria) & Karnataka (India) Compared. LC 81-21610. (Illus.). 352p. 1982. 39.50 (ISBN 0-521-23370-4); pap. 16.95 (ISBN 0-521-27102-9). Cambridge U Pr.

--Migrant Cocoa Farmers of Southern Ghana. 47.95 (ISBN 0-521-05264-5). Cambridge U Pr.

--Population, Prosperity, & Poverty. LC 77-23167. (Illus.). 1977. 32.50 (ISBN 0-521-21511-0). Cambridge U Pr.

--Rural Hausa: A Village & a Setting. LC 75-161287. 1972. 37.50 (ISBN 0-521-08242-0). Cambridge U Pr.

Hill, R. Principles of Dynamics. 1964. 24.00 o.p. (ISBN 0-08-010571-8); pap. 9.75 o.p. (ISBN 0-08-013540-4). Pergamon.

Hill, R. G., jt. ed. see Matthews, B.

Hill, R. R. Descriptive Catalogue of Documents Relating to the History of the United States in the Papeles Procedentes De Cuba in the Archivo General De Indias at Seville. 1916. pap. 45.00 (ISBN 0-527-00697-1). Kraus Repr.

Hill, R. R. & Rendell, D. A. Interpretation of Infrared Spectra: A Programmed Introduction. 1975. 29.95 (ISBN 0-471-25771-0, Wiley Heyden). Wiley.

Hill, Ralph N. Contrary Country. (Illus.). pap. 5.95 (ISBN 0-939384-10-8). Shelburne.

Hill, Ralph N., ed. The College on the Hill: A Dartmouth Chronicle. LC 64-16542. (Illus.). 367p. 1964. 20.00 (ISBN 0-87451-033-3). U Pr of New Eng.

Hill, Randal C. Official Price Guide to Collectible Rock Records. 3rd ed. LC 78-72032. (Collector Ser.). (Illus.). 400p. 1980. pap. 9.95 (ISBN 0-87637-356-2, 127-06). Hse of Collectibles.

--The Official Price Guide to Collectible Rock Records 1982. 3rd ed. (Collector Ser.). (Illus.). 500p. 1981. pap. 9.95 o.p. (ISBN 0-87637-180-2). Hse of Collectibles.

Hill, Ray. Unsung Heroes of Pro Basketball. (Illus.). (gr. 5 up). 1973. 2.50 o.p. (ISBN 0-394-82415-6, BYR); PLB 3.69 (ISBN 0-394-92415-0). Random.

Hill, Raymond T., ed. see Theobaldus of Provins Saint.

Hill, Rebecca. Blue Rise. LC 82-14329. 363p. 1983. 12.95 (ISBN 0-688-01875-0). Morrow.

Hill, Reuben. Family Development in Three Generations. (gr. 10-12). 1971. text ed. 19.25 (ISBN 0-87073-088-6). Schenkman.

Hill, Richard, jt. auth. see Hestenes, Marshall.

Hill, Richard F. Energy Technology Conference Proceedings Series Vols. 1-9, 7 Vols. (Illus.). 1982. pap. 240.00 (ISBN 0-686-38761-9). Gov Insts.

--Synfuels Industry Development. LC 80-65895. (Illus.). 168p. 1980. pap. text ed. 25.00 (ISBN 0-86587-083-7). Gov Insts.

Hill, Richard O., Jr., jt. auth. see Hestenes, Marshall D.

Hill, Robert, jt. ed. see Neurath, Hans.

Hill, Robert B. Occupational Attainment: Minorities & Women in Selected Industries, 1969-1979. 150p. 1983. pap. 6.95 (ISBN 0-87855-606-0). Transaction Bks.

Hill, Robert H. Dictionary of Difficult Words. 1975. pap. 3.95 (ISBN 0-451-11803-0, AE1803, Sig). NAL.

Hill, Robert L., jt. auth. see Smith, Emil L.

Hill, Rol la B. & La Via, Mariano F., eds. Principles of Pathobiology. 3rd ed. (Illus.). 1980. 24.00x (ISBN 0-19-502660-8); pap. 14.95x (ISBN 0-19-502661-6). Oxford U Pr.

Hill, Rolla B. & Terzian, James A., eds. Environmental Pathology: An Evolving Field. LC 82-14922. 376p. 1982. 60.00 (ISBN 0-8451-0221-4). A R Liss.

Hill, Ron, jt. auth. see Wasley, John.

Hill, Ron D. Rice in Malaya: A Study in Historical Geography. 1978. 39.50x (ISBN 0-19-580335-3). Oxford U Pr.

Hill, Ronald C., jt. auth. see Brouws, Jeffrey T.

Hill, S., jt. auth. see Wray, M.

Hill, Scott, jt. auth. see Playfair, Guy.

Hill, Shirley & Barnes, B. J., eds. Young Children & Their Families: Needs of the Nineteen Nineties. LC 81-484633. 240p. 1982. 23.95x (ISBN 0-669-05372-4). Lexington Bks.

Hill, Stephen. Competition & Control at Work: A New Industrial Sociology. (Organization Studies). 288p. 1982. 27.50x (ISBN 0-262-08113-X); pap. text ed. 9.95x (ISBN 0-262-58053-5). MIT Pr.

--The Dockers: Class & Tradition in London. 1976. text ed. 37.00x o.p. (ISBN 0-435-82416-3). Heinemann Ed.

Hill, T. A. Biology of Weeds. (Studies in Biology: No. 79). 64p. 1977. pap. text ed. 8.95 (ISBN 0-7131-2637-X). E Arnold.

Hill, Thomas A. Endogenous Plant Growth Substances. (Studies in Biology: No. 40). 72p. 1980. pap. text ed. 8.95 (ISBN 0-7131-2767-8). E Arnold.

Hill, Thomas D., jt. ed. see Cross, James E.

Hill, Thomas M., et al. Institution Building in India: A Study of International Collaboration in Management Education. LC 73-75880. (Illus.). 381p. 1973. 18.50x (ISBN 0-87584-105-8). Harvard Busn.

Hill, Tomas. Rios De Tinta: Historia y Ministerio De la Casa Bautista De Publicaciones. Smith, Josie, tr. from Eng. Orig. Title: Rivers of Ink. 64p. 1980. pap. 2.50 (ISBN 0-311-29009-4). Casa Bautista.

Hill, V. L. & Black, H. L. The Properties & Performance of Materials in the Coal Gasification Environment. 1981. 68.00 (ISBN 0-87170-112-X). ASM.

Hill, W. C. Primates: Comparative Anatomy & Taxonomy. Incl. Vol. 2. 367p. 1955. 43.95 o.s.i. (ISBN 0-471-39699-0); Vol. 3. 376p. 1957. o.p. (ISBN 0-471-39732-6); Vol. 4. 523p. 1960. o.p. (ISBN 0-471-39765-2); Vol. 5. 537p. 1962. o.p. (ISBN 0-471-39798-9); Vol. 6. 757p. 1966. o.p. (ISBN 0-471-39831-4); Vol. 7. 1974. 139.95 o.s.i. (ISBN 0-471-39835-7); Vol. 8. 692p. 1970. o.p. (ISBN 0-471-39836-5). Halsted Pr.

Hill, William H., et al. Antonio Stradivari, His Life & Work (1644-1739) 2nd ed. (Illus.). 1909. pap. 6.50 (ISBN 0-486-20425-1). Dover.

Hill, William J. The Three-Personed God: The Trinity As a Mystery of Salvation. 1982. 37.95 (ISBN 0-8132-0560-3). Cath U Pr.

Hill, Winfield, jt. auth. see Horowitz, Paul.

Hill, Winston W., jt. auth. see Atchison, Thomas J.

Hillaby, Joe G. The Book of Ledbury. 1981. 39.50x o.p. (ISBN 0-86023-125-9, Pub. by Barracuda England). State Mutual Bk.

Hillard, A. & Jhaveri, S. Fish Preservation: An Annotated Bibliography. (Technical Report Ser.: No. 82). 50p. 1981. 2.00 (ISBN 0-938412-24-8, P909). URI Mas.

Hillard, A. E. & Botting, C. G. Elementary Latin Exercises: An Introduction to North & Hillard's "Latin Prose Composition". 222p. 1982. pap. text ed. 10.95x (ISBN 0-7156-1525-4, Pub. by Duckworth England). Biblio Dist.

Hillary, Anne. Compromised Love. (Candlelight Romance Ser.). (Orig.). 1981. pap. 1.50 o.s.i. (ISBN 0-440-11351-2). Dell.

--The Mismatched Lovers. (Orig.). 1980. pap. 1.50 o.s.i. (ISBN 0-440-16388-9). Dell.

Hillary, Edmund. Nothing Venture, Nothing Win. LC 74-24330. (Illus.). 1975. 12.95 o.p. (ISBN 0-698-10649-0, Coward). Putnam Pub Group.

Hillcourt, William. Fun with Nature Hobbies. (Cub Scout Project Bks.). (Illus.). (gr. 3-5). 1970. 5.95 o.p. (ISBN 0-399-20080-0). Putnam Pub Group.

--New Field Book of Nature Activities & Hobbies. rev. ed. LC 78-96211. (Putnam's Nature Field Bks.). (Illus.). 1970. 6.95 o.p. (ISBN 0-399-10290-6). Putnam Pub Group.

--The New Field Book of Nature Activities & Hobbies. LC 78-96211. (Putnam's Nature Field Bks.). (Illus.). 1978. pap. 3.95 o.p. (ISBN 0-399-12158-7). Putnam Pub Group.

Hille, E., jt. auth. see Salas, S. L.

Hille, Einar. Analytic Function Theory, 2 vols. 2nd ed. LC 73-647. 308p. 1973. 15.95 (ISBN 0-686-85788-7); Vol. 1. 15.95 (ISBN 0-8284-0269-8). Vol. 2 (ISBN 0-8284-0270-1). Chelsea Pub.

--Einar Hille: Selected Papers: Classical Analysis & Functional Analysis. Kallman, Robert R., ed. LC 74-18465. (MIT Press Mathematicians of Our Time Ser.: Vol. 2). 752p. 1975. 45.00x (ISBN 0-262-08080-X). MIT Pr.

Hille, Einar, jt. auth. see Salas, S. L.

Hilleborg, Arno. Strip Method of Design. 2nd ed. (C & CA Viewpoint Publication Ser.). (Illus.). 1976. pap. text ed. 26.50x (ISBN 0-7210-1012-1). Scholium Intl.

Hillebrandt, Alfred. Vedic Mythology, 2 vols. 2nd ed. Sharma, S. R., tr. from Ger. 492p. Date not set. Vol. 1. 20.00 (ISBN 0-89581-473-0); Vol. 2. 24.00 (ISBN 0-686-96769-0). Lancaster-Miller.

Hillegas, Mark R. The Future As Nightmare: H. G. Wells & the Anti-Utopians. LC 74-4084. (Arcturus Books Paperbacks Ser.). 212p. 1974. lib. bdg. 12.95x o.p. (ISBN 0-8093-0680-8); pap. 6.95 (ISBN 0-8093-0676-X). S Ill U Pr.

Hillegass, L. L. Taming of the Shrew Notes. (Orig.). 1971. pap. 2.25 (ISBN 0-8220-0081-4). Cliffs.

--Tempest Notes. (Orig.). 1971. pap. 2.25 (ISBN 0-8220-0083-0). Cliffs.

Hillel, jt. auth. see Silverman, Morris.

Hillel, Daniel. The Negev: Land, Water & Life in a Desert Environment. LC 82-5218. 288p. 1982. 29.95 (ISBN 0-03-062067-8); pap. 12.95 (ISBN 0-03-062068-6). Praeger.

Hillel, Daniel, ed. Advances in Irrigation, Vol. I. 302p. 1982. 37.50 (ISBN 0-12-024301-6). Acad Pr.

--Advances in Irrigation, Vol. II. Date not set. price not set (ISBN 0-12-024302-4). Acad Pr.

Hillenbrand, Martin, jt. ed. see Yergin, Daniel.

Hiller, Carl E. Caves to Cathedrals: Architecture of the Worlds Religions. (Illus.). 112p. 1974. 9.95 (ISBN 0-316-36395-2). Little.

Hiller, Catherine. Abracatabby. (A Break-of-Day Book). (Illus.). 64p. 1981. 6.99 (ISBN 0-698-30727-5, Coward). Putnam Pub Group.

--Argentaybee & the Boonie. LC 77-15643. (Illus.). (ps-2). 1979. 7.50 o.p. (ISBN 0-698-20441-7, Coward). Putnam Pub Group.

Hiller, Ferdinand. Mendelsshon: Letters & Recollections. Von Glehn, M. E., tr. LC 70-163790. 234p. Date not set. Repr. of 1874 ed. price not set. Vienna Hse.

Hiller, Ferdinand, jt. ed. see Schone, Alfred.

Hiller, H. Geometry of Coxeter Groups. (Research Notes in Mathematics Ser.: No. 54). 232p. (Orig.). 1982. pap. text ed. 21.95 (ISBN 0-273-08517-4). Pitman Pub MA.

Hiller, Lejaren A. & Isaacson, Leonard M. Experimental Music: Composition with an Electronic Computer. LC 79-21368. 1979. Repr. of 1959 ed. lib. bdg. 20.50x (ISBN 0-313-22158-8, HIEM). Greenwood.

Hiller, Marc D., ed. Medical Ethics & the Law. 496p. 1981. prof ref 35.00x (ISBN 0-88410-707-8). Ballinger Pub.

Hiller, Robert L., tr. see Christoffel von Grimmelshausen, Hans J.

Hiller, Susan, jt. auth. see Coxhead, David.

Hillerbrand, Hans. Men & Ideas in the Sixteenth Century. 1969. pap. 10.95 (ISBN 0-395-30628-0). HM.

Hillerbrand, Hans J., ed. Protestant Reformation. (Documentary History of Western Civilization Ser). (Orig.). 1968. pap. 5.95xi (ISBN 0-06-131342-4, TB 1342, Torch). Har-Row.

Hillerich, Robert L. Reading Fundamentals for Preschool and Primary Children. (Elementary Education Ser.). 1977. pap. text ed. 11.50 (ISBN 0-675-08543-8). Merrill.

Hillerman, Tony. The Blessing Way. (YA) (gr. 7 up). 1978. pap. 2.75 (ISBN 0-380-39941-5, 61606-8). Avon.

--The Boy Who Made Dragonfly. LC 72-76498. (Illus.). 144p. (gr. 5 up). 1972. PLB 9.89 (ISBN 0-06-022312-X, HarpJ). Har-Row.

--Dance Hall of the Dead. 1975. pap. 2.95 (ISBN 0-380-00217-5, 63222-5). Avon.

--The Dark Wind. 224p. 1983. pap. 2.50 (ISBN 0-380-63321-3). Avon.

--The Listening Women. LC 77-11788. (Harper Novel of Suspense Ser.). 1978. 10.53i (ISBN 0-06-011901-2, HarpT). Har-Row.

--People of Darkness. LC 80-7605. (A Harper Novel of Suspense). 208p. 1980. 10.53i (ISBN 0-06-011907-1, HarpT). Har-Row.

Hillert, Margaret. Away Go the Boats. (Just-Beginning-to-Read Ser.). 32p. 1980. PLB 4.39 (ISBN 0-695-41454-2, Dist. by Caroline Hse); pap. 1.95 (ISBN 0-695-31454-8). Follett.

--The Baby Bunny. 32p. 1980. PLB 4.39 (ISBN 0-695-41352-X, Dist. by Caroline Hse); pap. 1.95 (ISBN 0-695-31352-5). Follett.

--The Ball Book. (Just Beginning-to-Read Ser.). (Illus.). 32p. (gr. 1-6). 1981. PLB 4.39 (ISBN 0-695-41553-0, Dist. by Caroline Hse); pap. 1.95 (ISBN 0-695-31553-6). Follett.

--Birthday Car. (Beginning-to-Read Bks). (Illus.). (ps). 1966. 2.50 (ISBN 0-695-40801-1, Dist. by Caroline Hse); PLB 4.39 (ISBN 0-685-10940-2); pap. 1.95 (ISBN 0-695-30801-7). Follett.

--The Boy & the Goats. (Just Beginning-to-Read Ser.). (Illus.). 32p. (gr. 1-6). 1981. PLB 4.39 (ISBN 0-695-41545-X, Dist. by Caroline Hse); pap. 1.95 (ISBN 0-695-31545-5). Follett.

--Cinderella at the Ball. (gr. 1-4). PLB 4.39 (ISBN 0-695-40081-9, Dist. by Caroline Hse); pap. 1.95 (ISBN 0-695-30081-4). Follett.

--Circus Fun. LC 69-15968. (Beginning-to-Read Bks). (Illus.). (ps). 1969. PLB 4.39 (ISBN 0-695-41487-9, Dist. by Caroline Hse); pap. 1.95 (ISBN 0-695-81487-7). Follett.

--City Fun. (Just Beginning-to-Read Ser.). 32p. 1980. PLB 4.39 (ISBN 0-695-41457-7, Dist. by Caroline Hse); pap. 1.95 (ISBN 0-695-31457-2). Follett.

--Come Play with Me. LC 75-884. (Beginning-to-Read Bks). (Illus.). 32p. (ps). 1975. PLB 3.39 (ISBN 0-695-40587-X, Dist. by Caroline Hse); pap. 1.95 (ISBN 0-695-30587-5). Follett.

--The Cookie House. (Illus.). (gr. 1-3). 1978. PLB 4.39 (ISBN 0-695-40880-1, Dist. by Caroline Hse); pap. 1.95 (ISBN 0-695-30880-7). Follett.

--Four Good Friends. 32p. 1980. PLB 4.39 (ISBN 0-695-41356-2, Dist. by Caroline Hse); pap. 1.95 (ISBN 0-695-31356-8). Follett.

--Fun Days. (Just Beginning-to-Read Ser.). (Illus.). (gr. 1-6). 1981. PLB 4.39 (ISBN 0-695-41546-8, Dist. by Caroline Hse); pap. 1.95 (ISBN 0-695-31546-3). Follett.

--Funny Baby. (Just Beginning-to-Read Ser.). (Illus.). (ps). 1963. 2.50 o.s.i. (ISBN 0-695-83300-6, Dist. by Caroline Hse); PLB 4.39 (ISBN 0-695-43300-8); pap. 1.95 (ISBN 0-695-33300-3). Follett.

--The Funny Ride. (Just Beginning-to-Read Ser.). (Illus.). 32p. (gr. 1-6). 1981. PLB 4.39 (ISBN 0-695-41552-2, Dist. by Caroline Hse); pap. 1.95 (ISBN 0-695-31552-8). Follett.

--The Golden Goose. (Illus.). (gr. 1-3). 1978. PLB 4.39 (ISBN 0-695-40881-X, Dist. by Caroline Hse); pap. 1.95 (ISBN 0-695-30881-5). Follett.

--Happy Birthday, Dear Dragon. (Just Beginning-to-Read Ser.). (Illus.). (gr. 1-3). 1977. lib. bdg. 4.39 (ISBN 0-695-40743-0, Dist. by Caroline Hse); pap. 1.95 (ISBN 0-695-30743-6). Follett.

--Happy Easter, Dear Dragon. 32p. 1980. PLB 4.39 (ISBN 0-695-41363-5, Dist. by Caroline Hse); pap. 1.95 (ISBN 0-695-31363-0). Follett.

--House for Little Red. new ed. LC 75-85953. (Just Beginning-To-Read Ser). (Illus.). (ps). 1970. PLB 4.39 (ISBN 0-695-40082-7, Dist. by Caroline Hse); pap. 1.95 (ISBN 0-695-30082-2). Follett.

--I Like Things. (Just Beginning-to-Read Ser.). (Illus.). (gr. 1-6). 1981. 4.39 (ISBN 0-695-41554-9, Dist. by Caroline Hse); pap. 1.95 (ISBN 0-695-31554-4). Follett.

--I Love You, Dear Dragon. 32p. 1980. PLB 4.39 (ISBN 0-695-41362-7, Dist. by Caroline Hse); pap. 1.95 (ISBN 0-695-31362-2). Follett.

--It's Halloween, Dear Dragon. 1980. lib. bdg. 4.39 (ISBN 0-695-41361-9, Dist. by Caroline Hse); pap. 1.95 (ISBN 0-695-31361-4). Follett.

--Let's Go, Dear Dragon. (Illus.). 32p. 1980. PLB 4.39 (ISBN 0-695-41360-0, Dist. by Caroline Hse); pap. 1.95 (ISBN 0-695-31360-6). Follett.

--Let's Have a Play. (Just Beginning-to-Read Ser.). (Illus.). 32p. (gr. 1-6). 1981. PLB 4.39 (ISBN 0-695-41544-1, Dist. by Caroline Hse); pap. 1.95 (ISBN 0-695-31544-7). Follett.

--The Little Cookie. (Illus.). 32p. 1980. PLB 4.39 (ISBN 0-695-41355-4, Dist. by Caroline Hse); pap. 1.95 (ISBN 0-695-31355-X). Follett.

--The Little Cowboy & the Big Cowboy. (Just-Beginning-to-Read Ser.). 32p. 1980. PLB 4.39 (ISBN 0-695-41453-4, Dist. by Caroline Hse); pap. 1.95 (ISBN 0-695-31453-X). Follett.

--Little Puff. LC 73-81993. (Just Beginning to Read Ser.). (Illus.). 32p. (ps). 1973. PLB 4.39 (ISBN 0-695-40416-4, Dist. by Caroline Hse); pap. 1.95 (ISBN 0-695-30416-X). Follett.

--Little Red Riding Hood. (Just Beginning-to-Read Ser.). (Illus.). 32p. (gr. 1-6). 1981. PLB 4.39 (ISBN 0-695-41543-3, Dist. by Caroline Hse); pap. 1.95 (ISBN 0-695-31543-9). Follett.

--Little Runaway. 32p. (gr. 3-6). 1966. lib. bdg. 4.39 (ISBN 0-695-45258-4, Dist. by Caroline Hse); pap. text ed. 1.95 (ISBN 0-695-35258-X). Follett.

--Magic Beans. (Beginning-to-Read Bks.). (Illus.). (ps). 1966. PLB 4.39 (ISBN 0-695-45483-8, Dist. by Caroline Hse); pap. 1.95 (ISBN 0-695-35483-3). Follett.

--The Magic Nutcracker. (Just-Beginning-to-Read Ser.). 1980. PLB 4.39 (ISBN 0-695-41456-9, Dist. by Caroline Hse); pap. 1.95 (ISBN 0-695-31456-4). Follett.

--Merry Christmas, Dear Dragon. (Dear Dragon Ser.). (Illus.). lib. bdg. 4.39 (ISBN 0-695-41359-7, Dist. by Caroline Hse); pap. 1.95 (ISBN 0-695-31359-2). Follett.

--Not I, Not I. (Illus.). 32p. 1980. PLB 4.39 (ISBN 0-695-41353-8, Dist. by Caroline Hse); pap. 1.95 (ISBN 0-695-31353-3). Follett.

--Pinocchio. (Just Beginning-to-Read Ser.). (Illus.). 32p. (gr. 1-6). 1981. PLB 4.39 (ISBN 0-695-41551-4, Dist. by Caroline Hse); pap. 1.95 (ISBN 0-695-31551-X). Follett.

--Play Ball. (Illus.). (gr. 1-3). 1978. PLB 4.39 (ISBN 0-695-40879-8, Dist. by Caroline Hse); pap. 1.95 (ISBN 0-695-30879-3). Follett.

--The Purple Pussycat. (Just-Beginning-to-Read Ser.). 32p. (gr. k-3). 1980. PLB 4.39 (Dist. by Caroline Hse); pap. 1.95 (ISBN 0-695-31455-6). Follett.

--Run to the Rainbow. 32p. 1980. PLB 4.39 (ISBN 0-695-41354-6, Dist. by Caroline Hse); pap. 1.95 (ISBN 0-695-31354-1). Follett.

--Snow Baby. LC 69-15969. (Just Beginning-To-Read Ser). (Illus.). (ps). 1969. PLB 4.39 (ISBN 0-695-48146-0, Dist. by Caroline Hse); pap. 1.95 (ISBN 0-695-38146-6). Follett.

--Three Bears. (Beginning-to-Read Bks). (Illus.). (ps). 1963. 2.50 o.s.i. (ISBN 0-695-88710-6, Dist. by Caroline Hse); PLB 4.39 (ISBN 0-695-48710-8); pap. 1.95 (ISBN 0-695-38710-3). Follett.

--Three Goats. (Just Beginning-to-Read Ser.). (Illus.). (ps). 1963. lib. bdg. 4.39 (ISBN 0-695-48720-5, Dist. by Caroline Hse); PLB 1.95 (ISBN 0-695-38720-0). Follett.

--Three Little Pigs. (Beginning-to-Read Bks). (Illus.). (ps). 1963. PLB 4.39 (ISBN 0-695-48730-2, Dist. by Caroline Hse); pap. 1.95 (ISBN 0-695-38730-8). Follett.

--Tom Thumb. (Just Beginning-to-Read Ser.). (Illus.). 32p. (gr. 1-6). 1981. PLB 4.39 (ISBN 0-695-41542-5, Dist. by Caroline Hse); pap. 1.95 (ISBN 0-695-31542-0). Follett.

--Up, Up, & Away. (Just Beginning-to-Read Ser.). (Illus.). 32p. (gr. 1-6). 1981. PLB 4.39 (ISBN 0-695-41541-7, Dist. by Caroline Hse); pap. 1.95 (ISBN 0-695-31541-2). Follett.

--What Am I? (Beginning-to-Read Ser.). 32p. 1980. PLB 4.39 (ISBN 0-695-41351-1, Dist. by Caroline Hse); pap. 1.95 (ISBN 0-695-31351-7). Follett.

--What Is It? (gr. 1-3). 1978. PLB 4.39 (ISBN 0-695-40882-8, Dist. by Caroline Hse); pap. 1.95 (ISBN 0-695-30882-3). Follett.

--Who Goes to School? (Just Beginning-to-Read Ser.). 1980. PLB 4.39 (ISBN 0-695-41458-5, Dist. by Caroline Hse); pap. 1.95 (ISBN 0-695-31458-0). Follett.

--Why We Have Thanksgiving. (Just Beginning-to-Read Ser.). (Illus.). 32p. (gr. 1-6). 1981. PLB 4.39 (ISBN 0-695-41550-6, Dist. by Caroline Hse); pap. 1.95 (ISBN 0-695-31550-1). Follett.

--The Witch Who Went for a Walk. (Illus.). (gr. 1-6). 1981. PLB 4.39 (ISBN 0-695-41549-2, Dist. by Caroline Hse); pap. 1.95 (ISBN 0-695-31549-8). Follett.

--Yellow Boat. (Beginning-to-Read Bks). (Illus.). (ps). 1966. PLB 4.39 (ISBN 0-695-49842-8, Dist. by Caroline Hse); pap. 1.95 (ISBN 0-695-39842-3). Follett.

Hillery, Mable & Hall, Patricia. A Guide to the Use of Street-Folk-Musical Games in the Classroom: Vol. II, Chanting Games. (Street-Folk-Musical Games Ser.: Vol. II). (Illus.). 76p. (Orig.). (gr. 2-6). 1981. pap. 7.00 (ISBN 0-939632-05-5). ILM.

Hillesheim, James W. & Merrill, George D., eds. Theory & Practice in the History of American Education: A Book of Readings. LC 79-3735. 439p. 1980. Repr. of 1971 ed. 11.25 (ISBN 0-8191-0929-0). U Pr of Amer.

Hillgrove, Thomas. Hillgroves's Ball Room Guide. (Series in Dance). (Illus.). 237p. 1982. Repr. of 1864 ed. lib. bdg. 22.50 (ISBN 0-306-76113-0). Da Capo.

Hillhouse, Marion S. & Mansfield, E. A. Dress Design: Draping & Flat Pattern Making. LC 48-7554. 1948. text ed. 25.50 (ISBN 0-395-04627-0). HM.

Hilliard, John N., ed. see Downs, T. Nelson.

Hilliard, Joseph. How to Unlock the Secrets of Winning & Good Luck. (Orig.). 1982. pap. 5.95x (ISBN 0-934650-02-0). Sunnyside.

Hilliard, Robert L. & Field, Hyman H. Television & the Teacher: A Handbook for Classroom Use. (Illus.). 96p. 1975. pap. text ed. 5.95x o.s.i. (ISBN 0-8038-7157-0). Hastings.

Hillier, Carol M., jt. auth. see Lockwood, Robert S.

Hillier, Caroline, tr. see Simenon, Georges.

Hillier, Florence B. Basic Guide to Flower Arranging. (Illus.). 296p. 1974. 24.95 (ISBN 0-07-028907-7, P&RB). McGraw.

Hillier, Frederick S. & Lieberman, Gerald J. Introduction to Operations Research. 3rd ed. LC 78-54193. 848p. 1980. text ed. 32.50x (ISBN 0-8162-3867-7); solutions manual 7.50 (ISBN 0-8162-3868-5). Holden-Day.

--Operations Research. 2nd ed. LC 73-94383. 816p. 1974. text ed. 30.95x (ISBN 0-8162-3856-1); solutions manual o.p. 7.50 (ISBN 0-8162-3866-9). Holden-Day.

Hillier, J. Japanese Color Prints. (Phaidon Color Library). (Illus.). 84p. 1983. 25.00 (ISBN 0-7148-2167-5, Pub. by Salem Hse Ltd); pap. 17.95 (ISBN 0-7148-2165-9). Merrimack Bk Serv.

Hillier, Mary. Pollock's Dictionary of English Dolls. 1983. 19.95 (ISBN 0-517-54922-0). Crown.

Hillier, Paul, ed. Three Hundred Years of English Partsongs. 96p. (Orig.). 1983. pap. 5.95 (ISBN 0-571-10045-7). Faber & Faber.

Hillier, Sheila & Jewell, John. Health Care & Traditonal Medicine in China, 1800-1982. 600p. 1983. price not set (ISBN 0-7100-9425-6). Routledge & Kegan.

Hillier, Walter. An English-Chinese Dictionary of Peking Colloquial. enl. & rev. ed. 1953. 35.00 o.p. (ISBN 0-7100-1527-5). Routledge & Kegan.

Hillig, Chuck. What Are You Doing in My Universe. 1983. pap. 5.95 (ISBN 0-87877-065-8). Newcastle Pub.

--What Are You Doing in My Universe? 1983. lib. bdg. 14.95x (ISBN 0-89370-665-5). Borgo Pr.

Hillis, Dick. Not Made For Quitting. (Dimension Ser.). 144p. 1973. pap. 2.95 (ISBN 0-87123-396-7). Bethany Hse.

Hillis, Don W. Live Happily with Yourself. 1978. pap. 1.95 (ISBN 0-88207-507-1). Victor Bks.

Hillison, John & Crunkilton, John. Human Relations in Agribusiness: Career Preparation for Agriculture-Agribusiness. Moore, R., ed. (Illus.). 128p. (gr. 9-12). 1980. pap. text ed. 6.56 (ISBN 0-07-028904-2); activity guide 3.96 (ISBN 0-07-028905-0); tchrs. manual & key 4.50 (ISBN 0-07-028906-9). McGraw.

Hillix, William A. & Marx, Melvin H. Systems & Theories in Psychology: A Reader. LC 74-1203. 450p. 1974. pap. text ed. 14.95 (ISBN 0-8299-0010-1). West Pub.

Hillix, William A., jt. auth. see Marx, Melvin H.

Hill1, David B. & Luttbeg, Norman R. Trends in American Electoral Behavior. LC 79-91103. 177p. 1980. pap. text ed. 7.50 (ISBN 0-87581-251-1). Peacock Pubs.

Hillman, et al. Soul & Money. LC 81-84495. 89p. (Orig.). 1982. pap. text ed. 7.50 (ISBN 0-88214-318-2). Spring Pubns.

Hillman, Abraham P. & Alexanderson, Gerald L. A First Undergraduate Course in Abstract Algebra. 3rd ed. 512p. 1982. text ed. 30.95x (ISBN 0-534-01195-0). Wadsworth Pub.

Hillman, Anthony, jt. auth. see Shourds, Harry.

Hillman, Brenda. Coffee, Three A.M. 1982. signed 35.00x (ISBN 0-686-37137-2); pap. 17.50x (ISBN 0-686-37138-0). Penumbra Press.

Hillman, J. R., ed. Isolation of Plant Growth Substances. LC 77-83997. (Society for Experimental Biology Seminar Ser.: No. 4). (Illus.). 1978. 39.50 (ISBN 0-521-21866-7); pap. 15.95 (ISBN 0-521-29297-2). Cambridge U Pr.

Hillman, James. Archetypal Psychology: A Brief Account. 88p. (Orig.). 1983. pap. 7.50 (ISBN 0-88214-321-2). Spring Pubns.

--Healing Fiction. 164p. 1983. 16.00 (ISBN 0-930794-55-9); pap. 8.50 (ISBN 0-930794-56-7). Station Hill Press.

--Insearch: Psychology & Religion. (Jungian Classics Ser.). 1967. pap. 8.50 (ISBN 0-88214-501-0). Spring Pubns.

--Inter Views: Exchanges with Marina Beer on Psychotherapy, Biography, Love, Soul, Dreams, Imagination, Work & the State of the Culture. LC 82-48119. 192p. 1983. 13.41i (ISBN 0-06-015099-8, HarpT). Har-Row.

--Loose Ends: Primary Papers in Archetypal Psychology. 212p. 1975. pap. 9.50 (ISBN 0-88214-308-5). Spring Pubns.

--The Myth of Analysis. 1978. pap. 6.95xi (ISBN 0-06-131974-0, TB1974, Torch). Har-Row.

--Re-Visioning Psychology. 1977. pap. 5.95i (ISBN 0-06-090563-8, CN563, CN). Har-Row.

--Suicide & the Soul. (Dunquin Ser.: No. 8). 191p. 1964. 7.50 (ISBN 0-88214-208-9). Spring Pubns.

Hillman, James, ed. Spring Nineteen Seventy-Five: An Annual of Archetypal Psychology & Jungian Thought. annual 226p. 1975. pap. 12.50 (ISBN 0-88214-010-8). Spring Pubns.

Hillman, James, jt. ed. see Roscher, Wilhelm.

Hillman, Jordan J. Competition & Railroad Price Discrimination: Legal Precedent & Economic Policy. 164p. 1968. pap. 4.00 (ISBN 0-686-94031-8, Trans). Northwestern U Pr.

--The Export-Import Bank at Work: Promotional Financing in the Public Sector. LC 82-11204. (Illus.). 288p. 1982. lib. bdg. 35.00 (ISBN 0-89930-040-5, HIE/, Quorum). Greenwood.

--The Parliamentary Structuring of British Road-Rail Freight Coordination. 301p. 1973. pap. 2.50 (ISBN 0-686-94037-7, Trans). Northwestern U Pr.

Hillman, Libby. Fresh Garden Vegetables. LC 82-48667. (Great American Cooking School Ser.). (Illus.). 80p. 1983. 8.61i (ISBN 0-06-015157-9, HarpT). Har-Row.

--Menu-Cookbook for Entertaining. LC 68-8524. (Illus.). 1968. 8.95 (ISBN 0-8208-0211-5). Hearthside.

--New Lessons in Gourmet Cooking. rev. ed. (Illus.). 1971. 8.95 (ISBN 0-8208-0210-7). Hearthside.

Hillman, Priscilla. The Merry Mouse Book of Opposites. LC 82-45292. (Illus.). 14p. (gr. k-3). 1983. 3.95 (ISBN 0-385-17918-9). Doubleday.

--Merry Mouse Book of Toys. LC 82-45250. (Illus.). 14p. (gr. k-3). 1983. 3.95 (ISBN 0-385-17917-0). Doubleday.

--The Merry Mouse Counting & Colors Book. LC 81-43652. (Illus.). 14p. (gr. k-3). 1983. 3.95 (ISBN 0-385-17916-2). Doubleday.

Hillman, Robert S., jt. auth. see Hillman, Sheilah.

Hillman, Robert S., et al. Introduction to Clinical Medicine. (Illus.). 512p. 1981. pap. text ed. 14.95x (ISBN 0-07-028910-7). McGraw.

Hillman, Sheilah & Hillman, Robert S. Traveling Healthy: A Complete Guide to Medical Services in 23 Countries. (Orig.). 1980. pap. 7.95 o.p. (ISBN 0-14-046455-7). Penguin.

Hillman, William C. Commercial Loan Documentation. 357p. 1982. text ed. 40.00 (ISBN 0-686-95387-8, AL-1288). PLI.

Hillmann, Karl-Heinz. Umweltkrise und Wertwandel: Der Umwerting der Werte als Strategie des Uberlebens. 419p. Date not set. price not set. P Lang Pubs.

Hillner, K. P. Learning: A Conceptual Approach. 1978. text ed. 35.00 (ISBN 0-08-017864-2); pap. text ed. 13.25 (ISBN 0-08-017865-0). Pergamon.

Hillocks, George, Jr., ed. The English Curriculum under Fire: What Are the Real Basics. (Orig.). 1982. pap. 5.75 (ISBN 0-8141-1398-2). NCTE.

Hillquit, Morris. Loose Leaves from a Busy Life. LC 78-146160. (Civil Liberties in American History Ser). 1971. Repr. of 1934 ed. lib. bdg. 42.50 (ISBN 0-306-70102-2). Da Capo.

Hillrurn, John & Johnson, David E. Manual of Active Filter Design. 2nd ed. (Illus.). 256p. 1983. 37.50 (ISBN 0-07-028769-4, P&RB). McGraw.

Hills, A., jt. auth. see Lake, Tony.

Hills, A. W., ed. Heat & Mass Transfer in Process Metallurgy. 252p. 1967. text ed. 26.00x (ISBN 0-686-32511-7). IMM North Am.

Hills, B. A. Decompression Sickness: The Biophysical Basis of Prevention & Treatment, Vol. 1. LC 76-55806. 1977. 62.95 (ISBN 0-471-99457-X, Pub. by Wiley-Interscience). Wiley.

--Gas Transfer in the Lung. (Monographs in Experimental Biology: No. 19). (Illus.). 200p. 1974. 42.50 (ISBN 0-521-20167-5). Cambridge U Pr.

Hills, C. A. Growing Up in the Nineteen Fifties. (Growing Up Ser.). (Illus.). 72p. (gr. 7-12). 1983. 14.95 (ISBN 0-7134-1367-0, Pub. by Batsford England). David & Charles.

--The Seine. LC 80-53949. (Rivers of the World Ser.). PLB 12.68 (ISBN 0-382-06519-0). Silver.

--World Trade. (Today's World Ser.). (Illus.). 72p. (gr. 7-10). 1981. 14.95 (ISBN 0-7134-3472-4, Pub. by Batsford England). David & Charles.

Hills, Car. The Danube. LC 78-62988. (Rivers of the World Ser.). (Illus.). 1978. PLB 12.68 (ISBN 0-382-06203-5). Silver.

--The Rhine. LC 78-62989. (Rivers of the World Ser.). (Illus.). 1978. PLB 12.68 (ISBN 0-382-06202-7). Silver.

Hills, Christopher, ed. see Nakamura, Hiroshi.

Hills, E. S. Elements of Structural Geology. 2nd ed. 1972. pap. 22.95x (ISBN 0-412-20750-8, Pub. by Chapman & Hall). Methuen Inc.

Hills, F. Jackson, ed. see Little, Thomas.

Hills, George. The Battle for Madrid. LC 76-28035. 1977. 12.95 o.p. (ISBN 0-312-06965-0). St Martin.

Hills, George S. The Law of Accounting & Financial Statements. LC 82-48368. (Accountancy in Transitions Ser.). 354p. 1982. lib. bdg. 35.00 (ISBN 0-8240-5319-2). Garland Pub.

Hills, Ida. A Love to Remember. (Orig.). 1980. pap. 1.50 o.s.i. (ISBN 0-440-14293-8). Dell.

--A Love to Remember. large print ed. LC 82-5478. 222p. 1982. Repr. of 1980 ed. 9.95x (ISBN 0-89621-363-3). Thorndike Pr.

--Shalom, My Love. (Orig.). 1981. pap. 1.50 o.s.i. (ISBN 0-440-17928-9). Dell.

--Shalom, My Love. LC 82-10668. 230p. 1982. Repr. of 1981 ed. 9.95 (ISBN 0-89621-387-0). Thorndike Pr.

Hills, John R. Measurement & Evaluation. 2nd ed. (Illus.). 480p. 1981. pap. text ed. 17.95 (ISBN 0-675-08044-4). Additional supplements may be obtained from publisher. Merrill.

--Measurement & Evaluation in Schools. (Illus.). 352p. 1976. pap. text ed. 14.95 (ISBN 0-675-08632-9). Additional supplements may be obtained from publisher (ISBN 0-686-67250-X). Merrill.

Hills, M. Statistics for Comparative Studies. 1974. pap. 9.95x (ISBN 0-412-12800-4, Pub by Chapman & Hall England). Methuen Inc.

Hills, M. T. & Eisenhart, E. J., eds. Ready Reference History of the English Bible. 11th ed. 1983. pap. 2.00x (ISBN 0-8267-0326-7, 16228). United Bible.

Hills, Michael T. Telecommunications Switching Principles. (Illus.). 1979. text ed. 30.00x (ISBN 0-262-08092-3). MIT Pr.

Hills, Nicolas & Phillips, Barty. Setting up Home. (Illus.). 1978. pap. 6.95 o.p. (ISBN 0-8256-3124-6, Quick Fox). Putnam Pub Group.

Hills, P. J. The Self-Teaching Process in Higher Education. LC 75-44716. 144p. 1976. 19.95x o.s.i. (ISBN 0-470-15024-6). Halsted Pr.

Hills, P. J., ed. Dictionary of Education. (Routledge Education Bks.). 300p. 1982. 29.95 (ISBN 0-7100-0871-6). Routledge & Kegan.

Hills, P. J., ed. see Lovell, R. Bernard.

Hills, Patricia. The Genre Painting of Eastman Johnson: The Sources & Development of His Styles & Themes. LC 76-23627. (Outstanding Dissertations in the Fine Arts-American). (Illus.). 1977. Repr. of 1973 ed. lib. bdg. 48.00 o.s.i. (ISBN 0-8240-2697-7). Garland Pub.

Hills, Sally W. & Birmingham, Jacqueline J. Burn Care. LC 80-836340. (Series in Critical Care Nursing). (Illus.). 136p. (Orig.). 1980. pap. text ed. 9.95. Wiley.

Hills, Sarah Jane, jt. auth. see Hills, Theo L.

Hills, Stuart L. Demystifying Social Deviance. 1980. pap. text ed. 14.50 (ISBN 0-07-028917-4, C). McGraw.

Hills, Theo L. & Hills, Sarah Jane. Canada. rev. ed. LC 77-80448. (American Neighbors Ser.). (Illus.). 224p. (gr. 5 up). 1979. text ed. 11.20 1-4 copies, 5 or more copies 8.96 o.s.i. (ISBN 0-88296-090-3); tchrs'. guide o.s.i. 6.96 o.s.i. (ISBN 0-88296-353-8). Fideler.

Hillson, Charles J. Seaweeds: A Color-Coded, Illustrated Guide to Common Marine Plants of the East Coast of the United States. LC 76-42192. (Keystone Books). 1977. lib. bdg. 12.95x (ISBN 0-271-01239-0); pap. 7.95 (ISBN 0-271-01247-1). Pa St U Pr.

Hillson, Maurie & Bongo, Joseph. Continuous Progress Education: A Practical Approach. LC 79-130820. 1970. text ed. 11.95 o.p. (ISBN 0-574-17890-2, 13-0890); pap. text ed. 9.95 (ISBN 0-574-17891-0, 13-0891). SRA.

Hillway, Tyrus. Herman Melville. rev. ed. (United States Authors Ser.). 1979. lib. bdg. 10.95 (ISBN 0-8057-7256-1, Twayne). G K Hall.

Hilmar, Ernst & Brusatti, Otto, eds. Franz Schubert-Gedenkausstellung Nineteen Seventy-Eight. (Illus.). 1978. 27.00 (ISBN 3-7024-0128-8, 51-26230). Eur-Am Music.

Hilprecht, H. V. The Earliest Version of the Babylonian Deluge Story & the Temple Library of Nippur. (Publications of the Babylonian Section, Ser. D: Vol. 5-1). (Illus.). 65p. 1910. soft bound 1.50x (ISBN 0-686-11918-5). Univ Mus of U PA.

Hilscher, W. Problems of the Keimbahn. (Bibliotheca Anatomica Ser.: No. 24). (Illus.). 150p. 1983. pap. 58.75 (ISBN 3-8055-3614-3). S Karger.

Hilsen, R. & Kramer, M. Right Book. 1980. 11.95 (ISBN 0-13-781146-2). P-H.

Hilsman, Roger. Politics of Policy Making in Defense & Foreign Affairs. 1971. pap. text ed. 11.95 scp o.p. (ISBN 0-06-042836-8, HarpC). Har-Row.

--Strategic Intelligence & National Decisions. LC 80-29549. 187p. 1981. Repr. of 1956 ed. lib. bdg. 20.50x (ISBN 0-313-22717-9, HILI). Greenwood.

Hilsum, C. & Moss, T. S., eds. Handbook on Semiconductors, Vol. 4: Device Physics. 1981. 166.00 (ISBN 0-444-85347-2). Elsevier.

Hilt, Nancy E. & Schmitt, E. William, Jr. Pediatric Orthopedic Nursing. LC 74-13222. (Illus.). 248p. 1975. text ed. 16.95 o.p. (ISBN 0-8016-2188-7). Mosby.

Hilt, R. Gulliksen. Oslo: Info 1980-81. (Illus.). 300p. (Orig.). 1981. pap. 9.50 (ISBN 82-90182-19-8, N543, Pub. by Forfatterforlaget Norway). Vanous.

Hiltebeitel, tr. see Gauss, Karl F.

Hiltner, Judith. The Newspaper Verse of Philip Freneau. 270p. 1983. write for info (ISBN 0-87875-248-X). Whitston Pub.

Hilton, Clifford L., jt. ed. see Bluestein, Bernard R.

Hilton, David. Huladance. LC 76-6457. (New Poets Ser.). 64p. 1976. 12.95 (ISBN 0-912278-71-4); pap. 3.95 (ISBN 0-912278-72-2). Crossing Pr.

Hilton, George. The Truck System. LC 75-11877. 166p. 1975. Repr. of 1960 ed. lib. bdg. 17.00 (ISBN 0-8371-8130-5, HITS). Greenwood.

Hilton, George W. The Cable Car in America. Rev. ed. LC 81-20295. (Illus.). 484p. 1982. 30.00 (ISBN 0-8310-7145-1). Howell North.

Hilton, Ian, tr. see Kohlschmidt, Werner.

Hilton, J. Georg Buchner. 1982. 49.00x (ISBN 0-333-29109-3, Pub. by Macmillan England). State Mutual Bk.

Hilton, Jack. Quest for Carp. (Illus.). 188p. 1972. 14.00 o.s.i. (ISBN 0-7207-0582-7). Transatlantic.

Hilton, John B. The Anathema Stone. 1980. 8.95 o.p. (ISBN 0-312-03351-6). St Martin.

--Playground of Death. 224p. 1981. 9.95 o.p. (ISBN 0-312-61559-0). St Martin.

--Playground of Death. (Fingerprint Mysteries Ser.). 224p. 1983. pap. 5.95 (ISBN 0-312-61560-4). St Martin.

Hilton, Kenneth, ed. see Southampton Conf. on Short-Run Econometric Models of UK Economy.

Hilton, Nelson. Literal Imagination: Blake's Vision of Words. LC 81-19764. (Illus.). 400p. 1983. text ed. 30.00 (ISBN 0-520-04463-0). U of Cal Pr.

Hilton, Peter J. General Cohomology Theory & K. Theory. (London Mathematical Society Lecture Note Ser.: No. 1). 1970. text ed. 12.95 (ISBN 0-521-07976-4). Cambridge U Pr.

--Introduction to Homotopy Theory. (Cambridge Tracts in Mathematics & Mathematical Physics: No. 43). 1953. 23.95 (ISBN 0-521-05265-3). Cambridge U Pr.

Hilton, Peter J. & Wylie, Shaun. Homology Theory. 1961. 65.50 (ISBN 0-521-05266-1); pap. 22.95x (ISBN 0-521-09422-4). Cambridge U Pr.

Hilton, R. H. Peasants, Knights & Heretics. LC 76-1137. (Past & Present Publications Ser.). 320p. 1976. 37.50 (ISBN 0-521-21276-6); pap. 12.95 (ISBN 0-521-28019-2). Cambridge U Pr.

Hilton, Rexford B. Number One Best Seller. 1983. 6.95 (ISBN 0-533-05514-8). Vantage.

Hilton, Rodney. Bond Men Made Free: Medieval Peasant Movements & the English Rising of 1381. 1979. pap. 9.95x (ISBN 0-416-82520-6). Methuen Inc.

Hilton, Rodney H. A Medieval Society: The West Midlands at the End of the Thirteenth Century. LC 82-19732. (Past & Present Publications Ser.). 315p. Date not set. price not set (ISBN 0-521-25374-8). Cambridge U Pr.

Hilton, Ruth B. An Index to Early Music in Selected Anthologies. (Music Indexes & Bibliographies: No. 13). 1978. 28.00 (ISBN 0-913574-13-9). Eur-Am Music.

Hilton, Suzanne. Getting There: Frontier Travel Without Power. LC 79-23196. (Illus.). 1980. 10.95 (ISBN 0-664-32657-9). Westminster.

--How Do They Cope with It? LC 72-123399. (Illus.). 368p. (gr. 5 up). 1970. 5.25 o.s.i. (ISBN 0-664-32481-9). Westminster.

--It's a Model World. LC 72-76435. (Illus.). 128p. (gr. 5 up). 1972. 5.95 o.s.i. (ISBN 0-664-32515-7). Westminster.

--Who Do You Think You Are? Digging for Your Family Roots. (Illus.). (RL 6). 1978. pap. 1.75 o.p. (ISBN 0-451-07884-5, E7884, Sig). NAL.

Hilts, Philip. Scientific Temperaments. 1982. 15.95 (ISBN 0-671-22533-2). S&S.

Hilty, Hiram. North Carolina Quakers & Slavery. 120p. 1983. price not set (ISBN 0-913408-84-0). Friends United.

Hiltz, S. R. Online Communities. Shneiderman, Ben, ed. (Human-Computer Interaction Ser.). 272p. 1983. text ed. 29.50 (ISBN 0-89391-145-3). Ablex Pub.

Hiltz, Starr R. & Turoff, Murray. Network Nation: Human Communication Via Computer. 1978. text ed. 38.50 (ISBN 0-201-03140-X, Adv Bk Prog); pap. text ed. 26.50 (ISBN 0-201-03141-8). A-W.

Hiltz, Starr R., jt. auth. see Kerr, Elaine B.

Himalayan Institute. Meditation in Christianity. rev. ed. LC 79-92042. 150p. 1983. pap. 3.95 (ISBN 0-89389-085-5). Himalayan Intl Inst.

Himalayan International Institute. Joints & Glands Exercises. 2nd ed. Ballentine, Rudolph M., ed. (Illus.). 90p. (Orig.). 1982. pap. 3.95 (ISBN 0-89389-083-9). Himalayan Intl Inst.

Himelfarb, A. & Richardson, C. J. Sociology for Canadians: Images of Society. 512p. 1982. 21.95 (ISBN 0-07-548440-4). McGraw.

Himelfarb, Alexander & Richardson, C. James. People, Power & Process: A Reader. 353p. 1980. pap. text ed. 11.95 o.p. (ISBN 0-07-092349-3). McGraw.

Himes, Chester. If He Hollers, Let Him Go. 1971. pap. 0.95 o.p. (ISBN 0-451-04846-6, Q4846, Sig). NAL.

Himes, Gary K., et al. Solving Problems in Chemistry. Lappa, Ellen, ed. (Illus.). (gr. 10-12). 1979. pap. text ed. 7.00 o.p. (ISBN 0-675-06376-0). Merrill.

Himes, Norman E. Medical History of Contraception. LC 70-102799. (Illus.). 1970. pap. 4.50 o.p. (ISBN 0-8052-0246-3). Schocken.

Himler, Ronald. Glad Day & Other Classical Poems for Children. (Illus.). (gr. 1 up). 1972. PLB 3.86 o.p. (ISBN 0-399-60697-1). Putnam Pub Group.
--Wake Up, Jeremiah. LC 77-25679. (Illus.). (ps-1). 1979. 8.95 o.p. (ISBN 0-06-022323-5, HarpJ); PLB 9.89 (ISBN 0-06-022324-3). Har-Row.
Himmelblau, David M. Applied Nonlinear Programming. LC 76-148127. (Illus.). 512p. 1972. text ed. 32.00 (ISBN 0-07-028921-2, C). McGraw.
--Basic Principles & Calculations in Chemical Engineering. 4th ed. (Illus.). 656p. 1982. text ed. 31.95 (ISBN 0-13-066498-7). P-H.
--Basic Principles & Calculations in Chemical Engineering. 3rd ed. (P-H Int'l Series in Physical & Chemical Engineering Sciences). (Illus.). 544p. 1974. ref. ed. 29.95 o.p. (ISBN 0-13-066472-3). P-H.
--Process Analysis & Simulation: Deterministic Systems. (Illus.). 348p. 1968. pap. text ed. 27.95 (ISBN 0-88408-132-X). Sterling Swift.
--Process Analysis by Statistical Methods. (Illus.). 463p. 1970. pap. text ed. 29.95 (ISBN 0-88408-140-0). Sterling Swift.
Himmelfarb, Gertrude, ed. see Mill, J. S.
Himmelfarb, Milton & Baras, Victor, eds. Zero Population Growth--For Whom? Differential Fertility & Minority Group Survival. LC 77-87966. (Contributions in Sociology: No. 30). (Illus.). 1978. lib. bdg. 27.50x (ISBN 0-313-20041-6, AJC/). Greenwood.
Himmelfarb, Milton & Singer, David, eds. American Jewish Year Book 1982, Vol. 82. 450p. 1982. 23.50 (ISBN 0-8276-0204-9). Jewish Pubn.
Himmelstein, Jerome L. The Strange Career of Marihuana: Politics & Ideology of Drug Control in America. LC 82-12181. (Contributions in Political Science Ser.: No. 94). (Illus.). 208p. 1983. lib. bdg. 27.95 (ISBN 0-313-23517-1, HSC/). Greenwood.
Himstreet, et al. Business Communications. (gr. 9-12). 1982. text ed. 14.60 (ISBN 0-8224-1180-6); activities bk. 6.60 (ISBN 0-8224-1181-4); tchr's guide & keys 6.60 (ISBN 0-8224-1182-2). Pitman Learning.
Himstreet, William C. & Baty, Wayne M. Business Communications: Principles & Methods. 6th ed. Date not set. 23.95x (ISBN 0-534-00908-5). Kent Pub Co.
Himwich, Harold, jt. auth. see Himwich, Williamina.
Himwich, Harold E. Biochemistry, Schizophrenias & Affective Illnesses. LC 77-2015. (Illus.). 514p. 1977. 26.50 (ISBN 0-88275-524-2). Krieger.
Himwich, W. A. & Schade, J. P. Horizons in Neuropsychopharmacology. (Progress in Brain Research: Vol. 16). 1965. 88.00 (ISBN 0-444-40287-X, North Holland). Elsevier.
Himwich, Williamina & Himwich, Harold. Biogenic Amines. (Progress in Brain Research: Vol. 8). 1964. 65.75 (ISBN 0-444-40285-3). Elsevier.
--The Developing Brain. (Progress in Brain Research Ser.: Vol. 9). 1964. 68.00 (ISBN 0-444-40286-1, North Holland). Elsevier.
Hin, Floris. This is Knotting & Splicing. (This Is Ser.). (Illus.). 127p. 1983. 17.95 (ISBN 0-914814-35-4). Sail Bks.
Hinchcliffe, A. J., jt. auth. see Cradock, S.
Hinchcliffe, Keith, jt. auth. see Annan, Bill.
Hinchcliffe, Mary K., et al. The Melancholy Marriage: Depression in Marriage & Psychosocial Approaches to Therapy. LC 78-4526. 1978. 31.95 o.s.i. (ISBN 0-471-99650-5, Pub. by Wiley-Interscience). Wiley.
Hinchcliffe, Philip. Doctor Who & the Masque of Mandragora. (Doctor Who Ser.: No. 8). 1979. pap. 1.95 (ISBN 0-523-41975-9). Pinnacle Bks.
--Dr. Who & the Seeds of Doom. (Dr. Who Ser.: No. 10). 1980. pap. 1.95 (ISBN 0-523-41974-0). Pinnacle Bks.
Hinchey, Fred A. Introduction to Applicable Mathematics: Elementary Analysis, Vol. 1. LC 80-18569. (Ser. of Introduction to Applicable Mathematics). 288p. 1981. 19.95x o.p. (ISBN 0-470-27041-1). Halsted Pr.
Hinchliffe, Arnold P. Harold Pinter. rev. ed. (English Authors Ser.). 1981. lib. bdg. 11.95 (ISBN 0-8057-6784-3, Twayne). G K Hall.
Hinckley, Alden D. Applied Ecology: A Nontechnical Approach. (Illus.). 384p. 1976. pap. text ed. 13.95x (ISBN 0-02-354550-X). Macmillan.
Hinckley, Barbara. Congressional Elections. LC 81-2413. (CQ Politics & Public Policy). 192p. 1981. pap. 8.25 (ISBN 0-87187-171-8). Congr Quarterly.
--Outline of American Government: The Continuing Experiment. (Illus.). 288p. 1981. pap. 12.95 (ISBN 0-13-645200-0). P-H.
--Stability & Change in Congress. 2nd ed. 1978. pap. text ed. 11.95 scp o.p. (ISBN 0-06-042839-2, HarpC). Har-Row.
--Stability & Change in Congress. 3rd ed. 288p. 1983. pap. text ed. 10.95 scp (ISBN 0-06-042852-X, HarpC). Har-Row.
Hinckley, Clive. Settling and Safeguarding Estates in California Without an Attorney-with Forms. LC 79-74698. 1982. pap. 13.00 o.p. (ISBN 0-9602984-1-X). C Hinckley.
Hinckley, Edith P. Redlands & Certain Old-Timers. (Orig.). pap. 3.00 (ISBN 0-685-03407-0). Creative Pr.
--Redlands, Nineteen Fifty to Nineteen Sixty. (Orig.). pap. 2.00 (ISBN 0-685-08704-2). Creative Pr.
Hincks, W. D. A Systematic Monograph of the Dermaptera of the World, Part 1: Pygidicranidae, Subfamily Diplatyinae. (Illus.). 132p. 1955. pap. 14.50x (ISBN 0-565-00568-5, Pub. by Brit Mus Nat Hist England). Sabbot-Natural Hist Bks.
--A Systematic Monograph of the Dermaptera of the World, Part 2: Pygidicranidae, Excluding Diplatyinae. (Illus.). 218p. 1959. pap. 21.50x (ISBN 0-565-00459-X, Pub. by Brit Mus Nat Hist England). Sabbot-Natural Hist Bks.
Hind, Arthur M. Catalogue of Rembrandt's Etchings 2 Vols. in 1. 2nd ed. LC 67-27456. (Graphic Art Ser). 1967. Repr. of 1923 ed. lib. bdg. 49.50 (ISBN 0-306-70977-5). Da Capo.
--Giovanni Battista Piranesi: A Critical Study. LC 68-16238. (Illus.). 1968. Repr. of 1922 ed. lib. bdg. 35.00 o.p. (ISBN 0-306-71050-1). Da Capo.
Hinde, R. A., ed. Non-Verbal Communication. LC 75-171675. (Illus.). 464p. 1972. 54.50 (ISBN 0-521-08370-2); pap. 18.95 (ISBN 0-521-29012-0). Cambridge U Pr.
Hinde, R. A., jt. ed. see Horn, G.
Hinde, Robert A. Biological Bases of Human Social Behavior. (Illus.). 416p. 1974. text ed. 31.50 (ISBN 0-07-028932-8, C); pap. text ed. 26.50 (ISBN 0-07-028931-X). McGraw.
--Ethology: Its Nature & Relations with Others Sciences. (Illus.). 1982. 19.95x (ISBN 0-19-520370-4). Oxford U Pr.
Hinde, Thomas. Cottage Book: Manual of Maintenance, Repair, Construction. 1979. 18.95 (ISBN 0-686-84202-2, Pub. by W Heineman). David & Charles.
Hindelang, Michael J. Criminal Victimization in Eight American Cities: A Descriptive Analysis of Common Theft & Assault. LC 76-8185. 536p. 1976. prof ref 25.00x (ISBN 0-88410-225-4). Ballinger Pub.
Hindelang, Michael J., et al. Victims of Personal Crime: An Empirical Foundation for a Theory of Personal Victimization. LC 77-15981. 352p. 1978. prof ref 22.50x (ISBN 0-88410-793-0). Ballinger Pub.
Hindemith, Paul. A Concentrated Course in Traditional Harmony, Bk. 1. 1943. pap. 8.25 (ISBN 0-901938-42-4). Eur-Am Music.
--A Concentrated Course in Traditional Harmony: Bk. 2, Exercises for Advanced Students. 1953. pap. 6.50 (ISBN 0-901938-43-2). Eur-Am Music.
--The Craft of Musical Composition: Book One, Theoretical Part. 1942. pap. 10.50 (ISBN 0-901938-30-0). Eur-Am Music.
--The Craft of Musical Composition: Book Two, Exercises in Two-Part Writing. 1941. pap. 8.25 (ISBN 0-901938-41-6). Eur-Am Music.
--Elementary Training for Musicians. 1946. pap. 8.25 (ISBN 0-901938-16-5). Eur-Am Music.
Hinden, Ruth B. How to Make Grow Clothes: Fashions That Grow with Boys & Girls. (Illus.). 64p. 1981. pap. 5.95 (ISBN 0-939842-02-5). RBH Pub.
Hindenburg, Paul Von see Von Hindenburg, Paul.
Hinderschiedt, Ingeborg. Zur Heliandmetrik: Das Verhaeltnis Von Rhythmus und Satzgewicht Im Altsaechsischen. (German Language & Literature Monographs). vi, 143p. 1979. 16.00 (ISBN 90-272-4001-9, 8). Benjamins North Am.
Hindess, Barry. Parliamentary Democracy & Socialist Politics. 200p. 1983. pap. 10.95 (ISBN 0-7100-9319-5). Routledge & Kegan.
--Philosophy & Methodology in the Social Sciences. 1977. 28.50x (ISBN 0-391-00607-X); pap. 12.50x. Humanities.
--The Use of Official Statistics in Sociology: A Critique of Positivism and Ethnomethodology. (Studies in Sociology). 63p. (Orig.). 1973. pap. text ed. 3.25x o.p. (ISBN 0-333-13772-8). Humanities.
Hindess, Barry & Hirst, Paul. Mode of Production & Social Formation: An Auto-Critique of Precapitalist Modes of Production. 1977. text ed. 15.00 o. p. (ISBN 0-333-22344-6); pap. text ed. 5.50x (ISBN 0-391-00731-9). Humanities.
Hindle, Brooke. Emulation & Invention. (Illus.). 184p. 1983. pap. 5.95 (ISBN 0-393-30113-3). Norton.
Hindle, Brooke, jt. auth. see Richardson, Edgar P.
Hindle, Wilfrid. The Morning Post, Seventeen Seventy-Two to Nineteen Thirty-Seven: Portrait of a Newspaper. LC 73-16946. (Illus.). 260p. 1974. Repr. of 1937 ed. lib. bdg. 15.75x (ISBN 0-8371-7243-8, HIMP). Greenwood.
Hindler, Nelson H. & Fenton, Judith A. Coping with Chronic Pain: The Latest Treatments & Techniques for Dealing with It. 1979. 10.00 o.p. (ISBN 0-517-53440-1, C N Potter Bks). Crown.
Hindley, jt. auth. see Amery.
Hindley, Charles. History of the Catnach Press. LC 67-27867. 1969. Repr. of 1887 ed. 37.00x (ISBN 0-8103-3259-0). Gale.
--History of the Cries of London. LC 67-23948. 1969. Repr. of 1884 ed. 30.00x (ISBN 0-8103-0156-3). Gale.
--Life & Times of James Catnach, Late of Seven Dials, Ballad Monger. LC 68-20122. 1968. Repr. of 1878 ed. 42.00x (ISBN 0-8103-3412-7). Gale.
Hindley, Geoffrey. England in the Age of Caxton. LC 79-4329. (Illus.). 1979. 26.00x (ISBN 0-312-25274-9). St Martin.
--The Medieval Establishment: 1200-1500. (Putnam's Pictorial Sources Ser). (Illus.). 1970. 6.95 o.p. (ISBN 0-399-10530-1). Putnam Pub Group.
Hindley, Judy & Rumbelow, Donald. The Know How Book of Detection. LC 78-59661. (Know How Books). (gr. 4-5). 1978. text ed. 7.95 (ISBN 0-88436-532-8). EMC.
Hindley, Judy, jt. auth. see Jefferis, Tony.
Hindlin, Brian, jt. ed. see Black, John.
Hindman, Juanita L. Postpioneers. LC 73-75069. 1973. 6.95 o.p. (ISBN 0-87706-023-1). Branch-Smith.
Hinds, Bill, jt. auth. see Millar, Jeff.
Hinds, Dudley & Carn, Neil. Winning at Zoning. (Illus.). 1979. 19.95 (ISBN 0-07-028937-9, P&RB). McGraw.
Hinds, Dudley & Ordway, Nicholas. International Real Estate Investment. 320p. 1982. 35.95 (ISBN 0-88462-475-7). Real Estate Ed Co.
Hinds, Harold E., Jr. & Tatum, Charles M., eds. Studies in Latin American Popular Culture, Vol. I. 1982. pap. 25.00 (ISBN 0-686-96552-3). New Mexico St Univ.
--Studies in Latin American Popular Culture, Vol. 2. 1983. pap. 25.00 (ISBN 0-9608664-1-8). New Mexico St Univ.
Hinds, John T see Gospel Advocate.
Hinds, William C. Aerosol Technology: Properties, Behavior, & Measurement of Airborne Particles. LC 82-1889. 480p. 1982. text ed. 37.50 o.s.i. (ISBN 0-471-08726-2, Pub. by Wiley-Interscience). Wiley.
Hindson, Edward E. Isaiah's Immanuel. pap. 3.50 (ISBN 0-8010-4220-8). Baker Bk.
Hindson, Theodore T., et al. Principles of American Government: A PSI Handbook. 111p. 1978. pap. text ed. 3.95x (ISBN 0-89641-006-4). American Pr.
Hindus, Maurice. Humanity Uprooted. LC 77-159716. (Illus.). 369p. 1972. Repr. of 1929 ed. lib. bdg. 18.75x (ISBN 0-8371-6190-8, HIHU). Greenwood.
Hindus, Maurice G. Cossacks: The Story of a Warrior People. Repr. of 1945 ed. lib. bdg. 17.50x (ISBN 0-8371-3816-7, HICS). Greenwood.
Hindus, Michael S. & Hobson, Barbara. The Files of the Massachusetts Superior Court, 1859-1959: An Analysis & a Plan for Action. 1980. lib. bdg. 50.00 (ISBN 0-8161-9037-2, Univ Bks). G K Hall.
Hindus, Milton, ed. Old East Side. LC 69-19040. (Illus.). 1969. 6.00 o.p. (ISBN 0-8276-0154-9, 199). Jewish Pubn.
Hindwood, Keith. Australian Birds in Colour. (Illus.). 1967. 7.50 (ISBN 0-8248-0066-4, Eastwest Ctr). UH Pr.
Hine, Al. Brother Owl. LC 79-8966. 312p. 1980. 10.95 o.p. (ISBN 0-385-15818-1). Doubleday.
Hine, Al & Alcorn, John. A Letter to Anywhere. LC 65-10961. (Illus.). (gr. 2-5). 1965. 4.95 (ISBN 0-15-245071-8, HJ). HarBraceJ.
Hine, Darlene C. Black Victory: The Rise & Fall of the White Primary in Texas. LC 79-16511. (KTO Studies in American History). 1979. lib. bdg. 30.00 (ISBN 0-527-40758-5). Kraus Intl.
Hine, Daryl. Theocritus: Idylls & Epigrams. LC 82-71256. 144p. 1982. 17.95 (ISBN 0-689-11320-X); pap. 10.95 (ISBN 0-689-11321-8). Atheneum.
Hine, F. R., et al. Introduction to Behavioral Science in Medicine. (Illus.). 350p. 1983. pap. 22.00 (ISBN 0-387-90736-X). Springer-Verlag.
Hine, J. & Wetherill, G. B. Programmed Text in Statistics, 4 bks. 1975. pap. 10.95x ea. (Pub. by Chapman & Hall England); Bk. 1, Summarizing Data. (ISBN 0-412-13590-6); Bk. 2, Basic Theory. (ISBN 0-412-13730-5); Bk. 3, The T-text & X-squared Goodness Of Fit. (ISBN 0-412-13740-2); Bk. 4, Tests On Variance & Regression. (ISBN 0-412-13750-X). Methuen Inc.
Hine, Jack. Physical Organic Chemistry. 2nd ed. (Advanced Chemistry Ser.). 1962. text ed. 42.50 (ISBN 0-07-028929-8, C). McGraw.
Hine, Jacqui. How to Book of Salads & Summer Dishes. Daniels, Gilbert, ed. (How to Bks.). (Illus.). 96p. (Orig.). 1982. pap. 3.95 (ISBN 0-7137-1291-0, Pub. by Blandford Pr England). Sterling.
Hine, James R. Alternative to Divorce. 3rd ed. 1978. pap. 4.95x (ISBN 0-8134-2008-3, 2008). Interstate.
--Grounds for Marriage. 6th ed. 1977. pap. text ed. 4.95x (ISBN 0-8134-1976-X, 1976). Interstate.
--Marriage Counseling Kit. 14.75x (ISBN 0-8134-2096-2, 2096). Interstate.
Hine, Lewis W. Men at Work. LC 76-50337. (Illus.). 1977. pap. 4.00 (ISBN 0-486-23475-4). Dover.
Hine, Reginald L. Charles Lamb & His Hertfordshire. LC 73-13023. 374p. Repr. of 1949 ed. lib. bdg. 20.50 (ISBN 0-8371-7111-3, HICL). Greenwood.
Hine, Robert V. California Utopianism. Hundley, Norris, Jr. & Schutz, John A., eds. LC 81-66063. (Golden State Ser.). (Illus.). 100p. 1981. pap. text ed. 5.95x (ISBN 0-87835-115-9). Boyd & Fraser.
--In the Shadow of Fremont: Edward Kern & the Art of American Exploration, 1845-1860. (Illus.). 240p. 1982. Repr. of 1962 ed. 18.95 (ISBN 0-8061-1735-4). U of Okla Pr.
Hine, William C. Dietary Technician's Handbook. (Allied Health Professions Monograph). 224p. 1983. write for info. (ISBN 0-87527-275-4). Green.
Hineline, Harris D. Forms & Their Use in Patent & Trade Mark Practice in the United States & Canada. 1951. 25.00 o.p. (ISBN 0-87215-023-2). Michie-Bobbs.
Hinerman, Ivan D. Automotive Engine Repair. Vorndran, Richard A., ed. LC 77-81911. 512p. 1979. pap. text ed. 14.36 (ISBN 0-02-818600-1); instrs'. manual 7.40 (ISBN 0-686-61256-6). Glencoe.
Hinerman, Ivan D., jt. auth. see Abbott, Sheldon L.
Hines, C. O., et al, eds. Upper Atmosphere in Motion. LC 74-28234. (Geophysical Monograph Ser.: Vol. 18). (Illus.). 1974. 29.00 (ISBN 0-87590-018-6). Am Geophysical.
Hines, Charlotte. The Earl's Fancy. (Second Chance at Love Ser.: No. 93). 1982. pap. 1.74 (ISBN 0-515-06855-1). Jove Pubns.
Hines, Dolores W. Forgiveness Undenied. 1982. 8.95 (ISBN 0-533-05445-1). Vantage.
Hines, Lawrence G. The Persuasion of Price: Introductory Microeconomics. (Orig.). 1977. pap. text ed. 11.95 (ISBN 0-316-36446-0); tchr's ed. avail. (ISBN 0-316-36447-9). Little.
Hines, Mary A. Comprehensive Review for Real Estate License Examinations. 488p. Date not set. pap. 7.95 (ISBN 0-15-600075-X). HarBraceJ. Postponed.
--Real Estate Finance. LC 77-13003. (Illus.). 1978. ref. 23.95 (ISBN 0-13-762724-6). P-H.
--Real Estate Investment. (Illus.). 1980. text ed. 24.95x (ISBN 0-02-354490-2). Macmillan.
--Shopping Center Development & Investment. 394p. 1983. 34.95 (ISBN 0-471-86851-5). Ronald Pr.
Hines, R. D., jt. auth. see Jensen, C. H.
Hines, Robert S. Singers Manual of Latin Diction & Phonetics. LC 74-34130. 1975. 10.95 (ISBN 0-02-870800-8). Schirmer Bks.
Hines, Rosemary W. One Hundred One Cures for Cabin Fever or Summer Slump. Zapel, Arthur L., ed. 146p. (Orig.). 1981. pap. text ed. 8.95 (ISBN 0-916260-12-7). Meriwether Pub.
Hines, Sherman. Nova Scotia: The Lighthouse & the Annapolis Valley. (Illus.). 1980. 17.95 o.p. (ISBN 0-19-540319-3). Oxford U Pr.
Hines, Thomas M. Le Reve et l'Action: Une Etude de l'Homme a Cheval de Drieu la Rochelle. 14.00 (ISBN 0-917786-02-5). French Lit.
Hines, Thomas M., tr. see La Rochelle, Pierre Drieu.
Hines, Thomas S. Richard Neutra & the Search for Modern Architecture: A Biography & History. LC 81-22530. (Galaxy Bk.: No. 663). (Illus.). 1982. 49.95x (ISBN 0-19-503028-1); pap. 29.95x (ISBN 0-19-503029-X). Oxford U Pr.
Hines, Walker D. War History of American Railroads. LC 74-75240. (The United States in World War 1 Ser). xviii, 327p. 1974. Repr. of 1928 ed. lib. bdg. 18.95x (ISBN 0-89198-104-7). Ozer.
Hines, William W. & Montgomery, Douglas C. Probability & Statistics in Engineering & Management Science. 2nd ed. LC 79-26257. 634p. 1980. text ed. 32.95 (ISBN 0-471-04759-7); solutions manual 8.25 (ISBN 0-471-05006-7). Wiley.
Hingley, Ronald. The Undiscovered Dostoyevsky. LC 74-5549. (Illus.). 241p. 1975. Repr. of 1962 ed. lib. bdg. 18.75x (ISBN 0-8371-7506-2, HIUD). Greenwood.
Hingley, Ronald, ed. & tr. see Chekhov, Anton.
Hingley, Ronald, ed. see Dostoevsky, Feodor.
Hingley, Ronald, ed. see Dostoevsky, Fyodor.
Hingley, Ronald, tr. see Chekhov, Anton.
Hingora. The Prophecies of the Holy Quran. pap. 3.75 (ISBN 0-686-18509-9). Kazi Pubns.
Hingorani, R. C. Studies in International Law. 115p. 1981. 30.00 (ISBN 0-379-20719-2). Oceana.
Hingorani, R. C., ed. Modern International Law. 1979. lib. bdg. 17.50 (ISBN 0-379-20439-8). Oceana.
Hinke, W. J. A New Boundary Stone of Nebuchadnezzar I from Nippur. (Publications of the Babylonian Section, Ser. D: Vol. 4). (Illus.). 323p. 1907. bound 5.00xsoft (ISBN 0-686-11917-7). Univ Mus of U PA.
Hinke, William J. & Weiser, Frederick S., trs. Records of Pastoral Acts at the Lutheran & Reformed Congregations of the Muddy Creek Church: East Cocalico Township, Lancaster County, Pennsylvania, 1730-1790. (Sources & Documents of the Pennsylvania Germans Ser.: Vol. V). (Illus.). 1980. 12.50x o.p. (ISBN 0-911122-42-7). Penn German Soc.
Hinkel, Daniel F. & Dick, Richard J. Indiana Mechanic's Lien Law. 221p. 1982. 25.00 (ISBN 0-87215-416-5). Michie-Bobbs.
Hinkemeyer, Michael T. The Fields of Eden. LC 77-23754. 1977. 7.95 o.p. (ISBN 0-399-12094-7). Putnam Pub Group.
Hinkle, Charles L. & Koza, Russell C. Marketing Dynamics: Decision & Control. (Illus.). 144p. 1975. pap. text ed. 7.95 o.p. (ISBN 0-07-028960-3, C); instructors' manual 2.95 o.p. (ISBN 0-07-028961-1). McGraw.
Hinkle, Dennis, et al. Basic Behavioral Statistics. LC 81-81700. (Illus.). 416p. 1982. text ed. 19.95 (ISBN 0-395-31729-0); solutions manual 1.00 (ISBN 0-395-31730-4); study guide 2.00 (ISBN 0-395-31731-2). HM.
Hinkle, Dennis E. & Wiersma, William. Applied Statistics for the Behavioral Sciences. 1979. 23.95 (ISBN 0-395-30810-0); wkbk. 10.95 (ISBN 0-395-30812-7); solutions manual 2.70 (ISBN 0-395-30811-9). HM.

Hinkle, Gerald H. Art As an Event: An Aesthetic for the Performing Arts. 1979. pap. text ed. 8.25 (ISBN 0-8191-0764-6). U Pr of Amer.

Hinkle, J. Herbert. How to Reach Multitudes for Christ. (Resources for Black Ministries Ser.). pap. 3.50 o.p. (ISBN 0-8010-4254-2). Baker Bk.

Hinkle, Joseph & Cook, Melva. How to Minister to Families in Your Church. LC 77-82925. 1978. 7.95 (ISBN 0-8054-3224-8). Broadman.

Hinkley, D. V., jt. auth. see Cox, D. R.

Hinkley, James W. The Book of Vampires. LC 78-24070. (Easy-Read Fact Bks.). (Illus.). (gr. 2-4). 1979. PLB 8.60 (ISBN 0-531-02276-5). Watts.

Hinman, Bob. The Duck Hunter's Handbook. (Stoeger Bks). (Illus.). 272p. 1976. pap. 5.95 o.s.i. (ISBN 0-695-80683-1). Follett.

Hinman, Charlton. Printing & Proof-Reading of the First Folio of Shakespeare, 2 Vols. 1963. 110.00x (ISBN 0-19-811613-6). Oxford U Pr.

Hinman, Charlton, ed. see Shakespeare, William.

Hinman, Dorothy & Zimmerman, Ruth. Reading for Young People: The Midwest. LC 78-24479. 1979. pap. 11.00 (ISBN 0-8389-0271-5). ALA.

Hinman, Steve & Stearns, John. Conditioning for Baseball: A Guide for Athletes & Coaches. LC 81-85976. (Illus.). 176p. Date not set. pap. 6.95 (ISBN 0-88011-006-6). Leisure Pr. Postponed.

Hinmon, Dean. Loving. 1976. pap. 2.95 perfect bound (ISBN 0-685-79064-9). Awareness.

Hinnant, Charles H. Thomas Hobbes. (English Authors Ser.). 1977. lib. bdg. 13.95 (ISBN 0-8057-6684-7, Twayne). G K Hall.

--Thomas Hobbes: A Reference Guide. 1980. lib. bdg. 27.00 (ISBN 0-8161-8173-X, Hall Reference). G K Hall.

Hinnebusch, Paul. Praise: A Way of Life. 1976. pap. 3.95 o.p. (ISBN 0-89283-032-8). Servant.

Hinnebusch, Thomas J & Mirza, Sarah M. Swahili: A Foundation for Speaking, Reading & Writing. LC 78-65430. (Illus., English & Swahili). 1978. pap. 11.25 (ISBN 0-8191-0659-3). U Pr of Amer.

Hinnebusch, William A. The Dominicans: A Short History. LC 74-26562. 185p. (Orig.). 1975. pap. 3.95 o.p. (ISBN 0-8189-0301-5). Alba.

Hinnells, John R. & Sharpe, Eric J., eds. Hinduism. 1972. cased 13.00 o.p. (ISBN 0-85362-116-0, Oriel); pap. 6.50 o.p. (ISBN 0-85362-137-3). Routledge & Kegan.

Hinojoso, Ida N. Follett Vest-Pocket Dictionaries: Spanish. 320p. 1976. pap. 1.95 o.p. (ISBN 0-695-80609-2). Follett.

Hinrichs, A. F., tr. see Von Wieser, Friedrich.

Hinrichs, John R., jt. auth. see Newman, John E.

Hinrichs, Roy S. Measuring. LC 80-67036. (Industrial Arts Ser.). 98p. 1981. pap. 7.80 (ISBN 0-8273-1916-9). Delmar.

Hinrichsen, D. & Isidori, A., eds. Feedback Control of Linear & Nonlinear Systems, Bielefeld, FRG Germany, & Rome, Italy: Proceedings. (Lecture Notes in Control & Information Sciences Ser.: Vol. 39). 284p. 1982. pap. text ed. 14.00 (ISBN 0-387-11749-0). Springer-Verlag.

Hinrichsen, Dennis. The Attraction of Heavenly Bodies. 1983. 12.00x (ISBN 0-8195-2111-6); pap. 6.95X (ISBN 0-8195-1111-0). Wesleyan U Pr.

Hinselmann, M., jt. auth. see Meudt, R. O.

Hinsley, Francis H. Power & the Pursuit of Peace. (Orig.). 1968. 31.50 o.p. (ISBN 0-521-05274-2); pap. 15.95 (ISBN 0-521-09448-8). Cambridge U Pr.

Hinsley, Francis H., ed. British Foreign Policy Under Sir Edward Grey. LC 76-19631. 1977. 99.50 (ISBN 0-521-21347-9). Cambridge U Pr.

Hinsley, Francis H., et al. British Intelligence in the Second World War: Its Influence on Strategy & Operations, Vol. I. LC 79-87703. 1979. 34.50 (ISBN 0-521-22940-5). Cambridge U Pr.

Hinson, Dolores. Quilting Manual. 1970. 6.95 (ISBN 0-8208-0322-7). Hearthside.

Hinson, Dolores A. Quilting Manual. (Illus.). 1980. pap. 3.25 (ISBN 0-486-23924-1). Dover.

Hinson, E. Glenn. The Evangelization of the Roman Empire: Identity & Adaptability. LC 81-11266. 342p. 1981. 22.00x (ISBN 0-86554-014-4). Mercer Univ Pr.

--A Serious Call to a Contemplative Lifestyle. LC 74-9658. 1974. pap. 3.95 (ISBN 0-664-24992-2). Westminster.

Hinson, E. Glenn, jt. auth. see Garrett, James L., Jr.

Hinson, Elizabeth. Cuentos Folkloricos De los Candoshi. (Comunidades y Culturas Peruanas: No. 4). 56p. 1976. 1.90x (ISBN 0-88312-747-4); 1.50. Summer Inst Ling.

Hintermister, William L. How to Get Rid of a Double Chin in Six Weeks. (Illus., Orig.). 1982. pap. 2.95 (ISBN 0-933328-49-4). Delilah Bks.

Hintikka, Merrill & Harding, Sandra, eds. Discovering Reality. 1983. lib. bdg. 54.50 (ISBN 90-277-1496-7, Pub. by Reidel Holland). Kluwer Boston.

Hinton, A., jt. auth. see Endacott, G. B.

Hinton, Ann P., et al. Getting Free: Women & Psychotherapy. (A Fred Jordan Bk.). 1982. pap. 8.95 (ISBN 0-394-17982-X). Grove.

Hinton, E. & Owen, D. R. Finite Element Programming. (Computational Mathematics & Application Ser.). 1977. 48.50 o.p. (ISBN 0-12-349350-1). Acad Pr.

Hinton, H. E. Biology of Insect Eggs, 3 vols. LC 77-30390. (Illus.). 1500p. 1981. Set. 400.00 (ISBN 0-08-021539-4). Pergamon.

Hinton, Harold C. The Bear at the Gate: Chinese Policymaking Under Soviet Pressure. (AEI-Hoover Policy Studies). 1971. pap. 5.25 o.p. (ISBN 0-8447-3069-6). Am Enterprise.

--An Introduction to Chinese Politics. 2nd ed. LC 75-49. 336p. 1978. lib. bdg. 13.00 o.p. (ISBN 0-88275-719-9). Krieger.

--The People's Republic of China: A Handbook. (Illus.). 1979. lib. bdg. 35.00 (ISBN 0-89158-419-6, Dawson). Westview.

Hinton, James. Labour & Socialism: A History of the British Labour Movement, 1870-1970. LC 82-21798. 230p. 1983. lib. bdg. 22.00x (ISBN 0-87023-393-9). U of Mass Pr.

Hinton, John W. Dangerousness: Problems of Assessment & Prediction. 176p. 1983. text ed. 27.50x (ISBN 0-04-364021-4). Allen Unwin.

Hinton, Leanne. Havasupai Songs: A Linguistic Perspective. (Ars Linguistica: No. 6). 380p. 1983. pap. 44.00 (ISBN 3-87808-356-4). Benjamins North Am.

Hinton, Norman I. Essay Exam Preparation Guide. (Cliffs Test Presparation Ser.). 71p. (Orig.). 1981. pap. 2.95 (ISBN 0-8220-1471-8). Cliffs.

Hinton, R. & Dobrota, M. Density Gradient Centrifugation. (Laboratory Techniques in Biochemistry & Molecular Biology: Vol. 6, Pt. 1). 1977. pap. 24.25 (ISBN 0-7204-4217-6, North-Holland). Elsevier.

Hinton, S. E. Tex. LC 78-50448. (gr. 7 up). 1979. 10.95 (ISBN 0-440-08641-8). Delacorte.

Hinton, Susie E. That Was Then, This Is Now. (gr. 7-12). 1980. pap. 2.25 (ISBN 0-440-98652-4, LFL). Dell.

--That Was Then, This Is Now. (gr. 7 up). 1971. 10.95 (ISBN 0-670-69798-2). Viking Pr.

Hinton, William. Hundred Day War: The Cultural Revolution at Tsinghua University. LC 66-23525. 288p. 1972. 7.95 (ISBN 0-85345-238-5, CL-2385); pap. 4.50 (ISBN 0-85345-281-4, PB-2814). Monthly Rev.

Hintz, Harold F. Horse Nutrition: A Practical Guide. LC 82-16294. (Illus.). 256p. 1983. 15.95 (ISBN 0-668-05416-6). Arco.

Hintz, Martin. Norway, Enchantment of the World. LC 82-9400. (Illus.). (gr. 5-9). 1982. PLB 13.25g (ISBN 0-516-02780-8). Childrens.

Hinz, Evelyn, ed. A Woman Speaks: The Lectures, Seminars, & Interviews of Anais Nin. LC 82-73831. 270p. 1975. 13.95x (ISBN 0-8040-0693-8); pap. 6.95x (ISBN 0-8040-0694-6). Swallow.

Hinz, Walther. The Lost World of Elam: Re-creation of a Vanished Civilization. Barnes, Jennifer, tr. (Illus.). 192p. 1972. 16.50x o.p. (ISBN 0-8147-3365-4). NYU Pr.

Hinz, William J., jt. ed. see Wold, Richard J.

Hinze, J., ed. Numerical Integration of Differential Equations & Large Linear Systems: Proceedings, Bielfeld, FRG, 1980. (Lecture Notes in Mathematics Ser.: Vol. 968). 412p. 1983. pap. 20.00 (ISBN 0-387-11970-1). Springer-Verlag.

Hinze, J. O. Turbulence. 2nd ed. 1975. 45.00 (ISBN 0-07-029037-7, C). McGraw.

Hinze, Jugen, ed. Electron-Atom & Electron Molecule Collisions. (Physics of Atoms & Molecules Ser.). 362p. 1983. 49.50x (ISBN 0-306-41188-1, Plenum Pr). Plenum Pub.

Hinzen, H. & Hundsdoerfer, V. H., eds. The Tanzanian Experience: Education for Liberation & Development. (Illus.). 266p. 1979. pap. 20.75 (ISBN 0-686-94192-6, UNESCO). Unipub.

Hionides, Harry T. Paisius Ligarides. (World Authors Ser.). lib. bdg. 15.95 (ISBN 0-8057-2536-9, Twayne). G K Hall.

--Yannis Manglis. (World Authors Ser.). 1975. lib. bdg. 15.95 (ISBN 0-8057-2578-4, Twayne). G K Hall.

Hip Society. The Hip Society: The Hip, 8 vols. Incl. Vol. 1 O.p. 1973. text ed. 25.00 o.p. (ISBN 0-8016-0019-7); Vol. 2 O.p. 1974. text ed. 35.00 o.p. (ISBN 0-8016-0020-0); Vol. 3 O.p. 332p. 1975. text ed. 39.50 o.p. (ISBN 0-8016-0035-9); Vol. 4 O.p. Evarts, C. M., ed. 1976. text ed. 32.50 o.p. (ISBN 0-8016-0036-7); Vol. 5. 1977. text ed. 49.50 (ISBN 0-8016-0038-3); Vol. 6. 1978. text ed. 49.50 (ISBN 0-8016-0041-3); Vol. 7. 1979. text ed. 49.50 (ISBN 0-8016-0033-2); Vol. 8. 350p. 1980. text ed. 54.50 (ISBN 0-8016-0049-9). LC 73-7515. (Illus.). Mosby.

Hipgnosis. Hands Across the Water: Wings Tour U.S.A. LC 77-18483. (Illus.). 1978. pap. 7.95 (ISBN 0-89169-500-1). Reed Bks.

--Walk Away Rene. (Illus.). 160p. 1978. 25.00 o.s.i. (ISBN 0-89104-105-2, A & W Visual Library); pap. 10.95 o.s.i. (ISBN 0-89104-104-4, A & W Visual Library). A & W Pubs.

Hipgrave, Tony, jt. auth. see Newson, Elizabeth.

Hipona, Florencio, ed. Heart. (Multiple Imaging Procedures Ser.: Vol. 5). Date not set. price not set (ISBN 0-8089-1485-5). Grune.

Hipona, Florencio A., jt. auth. see Shapiro, Jerome H.

Hippaka, William H., jt. auth. see Pugh, J. W.

Hippe, Z., ed. Data Processing in Chemistry. (Studies in Physical & Theoretical Chemistry: Vol. 16). 1982. 64.00 (ISBN 0-444-99744-X). Elsevier.

Hippel, Arthur R. Von see Von Hippel, Arthur R.

Hippel, Ursula Von see Von Hippel, Ursula.

Hippisley, J. H. Chapters on Early English Literature. 344p. 1982. Repr. of 1837 ed. lib. bdg. 75.00 (ISBN 0-8495-2433-4). Arden Lib.

Hippius, H., jt. ed. see Grahame-Smith, D. G.

Hipple, T. W. Teaching English in the Secondary School. 1973. 19.95x (ISBN 0-02-354570-4). Macmillan.

Hipps, G. Melvin, ed. Effective Planned Change Strategies. LC 81-48481. 1982. 7.95x (ISBN 0-87589-903-X, IR-33). Jossey-Bass.

Hipsher, Edward E. American Opera & Its Composers. LC 77-25413. (Music Reprint Ser., 1978). (Illus.). 1978. Repr. of 1927 ed. lib. bdg. 42.50 (ISBN 0-306-77516-6). Da Capo.

Hirai, Hidematsu & Alpert, Elliot, eds. Carcinofetal Proteins: Biology & Chemistry, Vol. 259. (Annals of the New York Academy of Sciences). 452p. 1975. 54.50x (ISBN 0-89072-013-4). NY Acad Sci.

Hiraki, Akemi & Parlocha, Pamela Kees. Returning to School: The RN to BSN Handbook. 1983. pap. text ed. write for info. (ISBN 0-316-36460-6). Little.

Hiranandani, L. H. & Deshpande, C. K. Histopathological Study of the Middle Ear Cleft & Its Clinical Application. (Illus.). 1971. 18.95 o.p. (ISBN 0-407-19950-0). Butterworth.

Hirano, Asao, jt. auth. see Malamud, Nathan.

Hirano-Nakanishi, Marsha see Nakanishi, Don T.

Hiraoka, M. Crown Compounds: Their Characteristics & Applications. (Studies in Organic Chemistry: No. 12). 276p. 1982. 76.75 (ISBN 0-444-99692-3). Elsevier.

Hirasawa, Louise & Markstein, Linda R. Developing Reading Skills-Advanced. 1974. pap. text ed. 8.95 (ISBN 0-912066-85-7). Newbury Hse.

Hirasawa, Louise, jt. auth. see Markstein, Linda.

Hirasawa, Louise, jt. auth. see Markstein, Linda R.

Hirata, M., et al. Computer Aided Data Book of Vapor-Liquid Equilibria. 960p. 1975. 117.00 (ISBN 0-444-99855-1). Elsevier.

Hird. Introduction to Photo-Offset Lithography. 1981. text ed. 11.96 (ISBN 0-87002-336-5); student guide 4.68 (ISBN 0-87002-360-8); tchr's guide 3.96 (ISBN 0-87002-361-6). Bennett IL.

Hird, Kenneth F. Paste-up for Graphic Arts Production. (Illus.). 352p. 1982. pap. text ed. 17.95 (ISBN 0-13-652875-9). P-H.

Hiremath, S. G. Patterns of Career Mobility. 1981. text ed. 13.00x (ISBN 0-391-02256-3, Pub. by Concept India). Humanities.

Hirn, K. E. Monographie & Iconographie der Oedogoniaceen. (Illus.). 1960. pap. 80.00 (ISBN 3-7682-7056-4). Lubrecht & Cramer.

Hirn, Kathryn F., jt. auth. see Bumagin, Victoria E.

Hirnle, Robert W. Clinical Simulations in Neonatal Respiratory Therapy. LC 81-13134. 316p. 1982. pap. 15.95 (ISBN 0-471-08266-X, Pub. by Wiley Medical). Wiley.

Hiro, D. Inside the Middle East. 1983. 19.95 (ISBN 0-07-029055-5); pap. 8.95 (ISBN 0-07-029056-3). McGraw.

Hirohata, Kazushi & Morimoto, Kazuo. Ultrastructure of Bone & Joint Diseases. LC 72-1791. (Illus.). 349p. 1972. 110.00 o.p. (ISBN 0-8089-0771-9). Grune.

Hironaka, H. see Zariski, Oscar.

Hirsch, A., jt. ed. see Chretien, J.

Hirsch, Abby & Dooley, Susan. The Lessons of Love. 224p. 1983. 13.95 (ISBN 0-688-01916-1). Morrow.

Hirsch, Alison D., jt. auth. see Speth, Linda.

Hirsch, Bernard A. see Cherry, Richard L., et al.

Hirsch, Bonnie C. Reading the Weather. 1982. pap. 4.00 (ISBN 0-917652-27-4). Confluence Pr.

Hirsch, Charles S., et al. Handbook of Legal Medicine. 5th ed. LC 79-16053. (Illus.). 378p. 1979. pap. text ed. 23.95 (ISBN 0-8016-3509-8). Mosby.

Hirsch, Eli. The Persistence Objects. 80p. 1976. pap. 19.95 (ISBN 0-87722-112-X). Temple U Pr.

Hirsch, Ernest A. Joy, Woe, Hope & Fear: Thoughts About the Life of the Young & Old; the Free & Imprisoned. LC 81-40060. (Illus.). 326p. (Orig.). 1982. lib. bdg. 24.00 (ISBN 0-8191-1843-5); pap. text ed. 12.75 (ISBN 0-8191-1844-3). U Pr of Amer.

Hirsch, Ethel. Painted Decoration on the Floors of Bronze Age Structures on Crete & the Greek Mainland. (Studies in Mediterranean Archaelogy Ser.: No. LIII). (Illus.). 1977. pap. text ed. 30.00x (ISBN 91-85058-76-9). Humanities.

Hirsch, Felice L., jt. auth. see Hall, Sandra P.

Hirsch, Foster. George Kelly. (United States Authors Ser.). 1975. lib. bdg. 13.95 (ISBN 0-8057-7158-1, Twayne). G K Hall.

--Joseph Losey. (Filmmakers Ser.). 1980. lib. bdg. 12.95 (ISBN 0-8057-9257-0, Twayne). G K Hall.

--Laurence Olivier. (Filmmakers Ser.). 1979. lib. bdg. 12.95 (ISBN 0-8057-9260-0, Twayne). G K Hall.

--A Portrait of the Artist: The Plays of Tennessee Williams. (National Univ. Pubns. Literary Criticism Ser.). 1979. 11.95 o.p. (ISBN 0-8046-9230-0). Kennikat.

Hirsch, G. P., jt. auth. see Maunder, A. H.

Hirsch, H. Poverty & Politicization: Political Socialization in an American Sub-Culture. LC 74-136611. 1971. 10.95 (ISBN 0-02-914690-9). Free Pr.

Hirsch, H. J., tr. see Begemann, H. & Rastetter, J.

Hirsch, H. J., tr. see Borchard, Franz.

Hirsch, H. J., tr. see Grewe, Horst-Eberhard & Kremer, Karl.

Hirsch, Herbert. The Right of the People: An Introduction to American Politics. LC 79-47987. 531p. 1980. text ed. 23.50 o.p. (ISBN 0-8191-0990-8); pap. text ed. 13.50 (ISBN 0-8191-0991-6). U Pr of Amer.

Hirsch, Ira J. Measurement of Hearing. (Psychology Ser.). 1952. text ed. 31.50 o.p. (ISBN 0-07-029045-8, C). McGraw.

Hirsch, Julie. Family Photographs: Content, Meaning & Effect. (Illus.). 1981. 16.95x (ISBN 0-19-502889-9). Oxford U Pr.

Hirsch, Katrina De, jt. auth. see Jansky, Jeannette.

Hirsch, Linda. The Sick Story. (Illus.). (gr. k-3). 1976. 6.50 (ISBN 0-8038-6733-6). Hastings.

Hirsch, Marianne. Beyond the Single Version: Henry James, Michael Butor, Uwe Johnson. 18.00 (ISBN 0-917786-21-1). French Lit.

Hirsch, Marianne, jt. ed. see Abel, Elizabeth.

Hirsch, Maurice L., Jr. & Louderback, Joseph G. Cost Accounting: Accumulation, Analysis & Use. 960p. 1982. text ed. 27.95x (ISBN 0-534-01026-1). Kent Pub Co.

Hirsch, Max. Socialism the Slave State. 32p. pap. 0.25 (ISBN 0-911312-62-5). Schalkenbach.

Hirsch, Meyer, ed. The New Commercialist: A Review, Vol. 1. 1978. pap. cancelled (ISBN 0-917986-10-5). NFS Pr.

--The New Commercialist: A Review, Vol. 2. 1978. pap. cancelled (ISBN 0-917986-11-3). NFS Pr.

Hirsch, P. B. The Physics of Metals, Vol. 2: Defects. LC 74-14439. (Illus.). 304p. 1976. 74.50 (ISBN 0-521-20077-6). Cambridge U Pr.

Hirsch, Phil. Zany Certificates. Schneider, Meg, ed. (Illus.). 32p. (gr. 8-12). 1983. pap. 2.95 (ISBN 0-671-44462-X). Wanderer Bks.

Hirsch, Roger, jt. auth. see Nonken, Pamela.

Hirsch, S. R. Horeb, 2 Vols. Set. 19.95x (ISBN 0-900689-40-4). Bloch.

Hirsch, S. R. & Leff, J. P. Abnormalities in Parents of Schizophrenics. (Maudsley Monographs: No. 22). (Illus.). 1975. text ed. 24.95x (ISBN 0-19-712144-6). Oxford U Pr.

Hirsch, Seymour. BASIC: A Programmed Text. LC 75-6806. 496p. 1975. text ed. 22.95x (ISBN 0-471-40045-9). Wiley.

Hirsch, Sylvia. Miss Grimble Presents: Delicious Deserts. (Illus.). 256p. 1983. 14.95 (ISBN 0-02-551860-7). Macmillan.

Hirsch, Tannah, ed. see Rosenkranz, George.

Hirsch, W., jt. auth. see Zollschan, G. K.

Hirsch, Werner Z. Economics of State & Local Governments. 1970. text ed. 32.95 (ISBN 0-07-029042-3, C). McGraw.

Hirsch, Werner Z., jt. auth. see Ferber, Robert.

Hirsch, Werner Z., ed. The Economics of the Municipal Labor Market. (Monograph & Research Ser.: No. 33). 400p. 1983. write for info. (ISBN 0-89215-117-X). U Cal LA Indus Rel.

Hirsch, William J. The Contracts Management Deskbook: For Buyers & Sellers in Business, Industry, & Government. 256p. 1983. 29.95 (ISBN 0-8144-5759-2). Am Mgmt Assns.

Hirschberg, W. Black Africa. LC 64-28801. (Monumenta Ethnographica Ser.: Vol. 1). (Illus.). 106p. 1962. 187.50x (ISBN 0-8002-0798-X). Intl Pubns Serv.

Hirschberger, Johannes & Moiser, Jeremy. A Short History of Western Philosophy. LC 76-25125. 1977. lib. bdg. 24.50 o.p. (ISBN 0-89158-642-3). Westview.

Hirschel, Joseph D. Fourth Amendment Rights. LC 78-57161. (Illus.). 176p. 1979. 19.95x (ISBN 0-669-02361-2). Lexington Bks.

Hirschelmann, R. see Bekemeier, H.

Hirschfeld, Alan & Sinnott, Roger, eds. Sky Catalogue 2000.0: Volume 1: Stars to Magnitude 8.0. LC 81-17975. 684p. 1982. 49.95 (ISBN 0-521-24710-1); pap. 29.95 (ISBN 0-521-28913-0). Cambridge U Pr.

Hirschfeld, Burt. Fire Island. 1970. pap. 2.50 o.p. (ISBN 0-380-00232-9, 50427). Avon.

--Key West. 1979. 9.95 o.p. (ISBN 0-688-03416-0). Morrow.

--King of Heaven. 320p. (Orig.). 1983. pap. 3.50 (ISBN 0-345-29864-0). Ballantine.

Hirschfeld, Ronald C. & Poulos, Steve J. Embankment Dam Engineering: The Casagrande Volume. LC 72-8626. 480p. 1973. 61.95 (ISBN 0-471-40050-5, Pub by Wiley-Interscience). Wiley.

Hirschfelder, Arlene, ed. American Indian & Eskimo Authors. 112p. 1974. pap. 4.00 o.p. (ISBN 0-913456-60-8). Interbk Inc.

Hirschfelder, Arlene B. Annotated Bibliography of the Literature on American Indians Published in State Historical Society Publications: New England & Middle Atlantic States. LC 82-17213. 1982. lib. bdg. 60.00 (ISBN 0-527-40889-1). Kraus Intl.

Hirschhorn, Howard. All About Mice. (Illus.). 96p. (Orig.). 1974. pap. 3.95 (ISBN 0-87666-786-8, M-542). TFH Pubns.

--All About Rabbits. (Illus.). 96p. (Orig.). 1974. 5.95 (ISBN 0-87666-760-4, M-543). TFH Pubns.

Hirschhorn, Howard H. All About Guard Dogs. (Illus.). 128p. (Orig.). 1976. pap. 4.95 (ISBN 0-87666-775-2, HS1110). TFH Pubns.

--The Home Herbal Doctor. LC 82-6490. 215p. 1982. pap. 14.95 (ISBN 0-13-392837-3, Reward); pap. 4.95 (ISBN 0-13-392829-2). P-H.

Hirschhorn, Larry. Cutting Back: Retrenchment & Redevelopment in Human & Community Services. LC 82-49038. (Social & Behavioral Science & Management Ser.). 1983. text ed. price not set (ISBN 0-87589-568-9). Jossey-Bass.

Hirschhorn, Norbert & Lamstein, Joel. Quality of Care Assessment & Assurance: An Annotated Bibliography with a Point of View. 1978. lib. bdg. 17.50 (ISBN 0-8161-2123-0, Hall Medical). G K Hall.

Hirschi, Travis. Causes of Delinquency. LC 69-16508. 1969. 24.95x o.p. (ISBN 0-520-01487-1); pap. 6.50x (ISBN 0-520-01901-6, CAMPUS47). U of Cal Pr.

Hirschkop, Philip J., jt. auth. see Bronstein, Alvin J.

Hirschman, A. O. Latin American Issues: Essays & Comments. (Twentieth Century Fund Ser.). 1961. pap. 7.00 (ISBN 0-527-02821-5). Kraus Repr.

Hirschman, Albert O. Development Projects Observed. 1967. 14.95 (ISBN 0-8157-3650-9); pap. 5.95 (ISBN 0-8157-3649-5). Brookings.

--Exit, Voice, & Loyalty: Responses to Decline in Firms, Organizations, & States. 1970. 8.95x o.p. (ISBN 0-674-27650-7); pap. 4.95x (ISBN 0-674-27660-4). Harvard U Pr.

--Journeys Toward Progress: Studies of Economic Policy-Making in Latin America. LC 68-8620. (Illus.). 1968. Repr. of 1963 ed. lib. bdg. 17.75x (ISBN 0-8371-0106-9, HIJP). Greenwood.

Hirschman, Jack. Kameas. cancelled 4.00 (ISBN 0-686-13974-7). Tree Bks.

Hirschman, Jack, tr. see Abulafia, Abraham Ben Samuel.

Hirschman, Jack, tr. see Gogou, Katerina.

Hirschman, Joseph L., jt. auth. see Herfindal, Eric T.

Hirschmann, Fred. Yellowstone. LC 81-86038. (Illus.). 88p. (Orig.). 1982. pap. 9.95 (ISBN 0-912856-75-0). Graphic Arts Ctr.

Hirschmann, Maria Ann. Hansi, The Girl Who Left the Swastika. 1973. pap. 5.95 (ISBN 0-8423-1291-9). Tyndale.

Hirschmeier, Johannes & Yui, Tsunehiko. The Development of Japanese Business, 1600-1973. LC 74-82190. 350p. 1975. 18.50x o.p. (ISBN 0-674-20045-4). Harvard U Pr.

Hirschnorn, Nobert & Lamstein, Joel. Quality by Objectives. 1978. lib. bdg. 14.95 (ISBN 0-8161-2122-2). G K Hall.

Hirschorn, Clive, ed. The Warner Brother Story: The Complete History of Hollywood's Greatest Studio. (Illus.). 1979. 30.00 o.p. (ISBN 0-517-53834-2). Crown.

Hirschowitz, R. G. & Levy, B., eds. The Changing Mental Health Scene. LC 75-42398. 382p. 1976. 27.50x o.s.i. (ISBN 0-470-14981-7). Halsted Pr.

Hirschy, Esther E. Poems for Today. (Illus.). 96p. 1983. 7.95 (ISBN 0-89962-294-1). Todd & Honeywell.

Hirsh, Alice. From Pipes Long Cold. 1954. 4.00 (ISBN 0-910294-08-9). Brown Bk.

Hirsh, Diana. World of Turner. LC 73-78989. (Library of Art Ser.). (Illus.). (gr. 6 up). 1969. 19.92 (ISBN 0-8094-0279-3, Pub. by Time-Life). Silver.

Hirsh, Jack, jt. ed. see Colman, Robert W.

Hirsh, Marilyn. Captain Jiri & Rabbi Jacob. LC 76-6114. (Illus.). 32p. (gr. 1-4). 1976. PLB 6.95 o.p. (ISBN 0-8234-0279-7). Holiday.

--Deborah the Dybbuk: A Ghost Story. LC 77-13502. (Illus.). 40p. (gr. k-3). 1978. PLB 5.95 (ISBN 0-8234-0315-7). Holiday.

--Hannibal & His Thirty-Seven Elephants. LC 77-590. (Illus.). 32p. (gr. 1-3). 1977. PLB 5.95 (ISBN 0-8234-0300-9). Holiday.

--How the World Got Its Color. LC 70-185088. (Illus.). (ps-2). 1972. reinforced lib. bdg. 3.95 o.p. (ISBN 0-517-50334-4). Crown.

--One Little Goat: A Passover Song. LC 78-24354. (Illus.). 32p. (ps-3). 1979. PLB 7.95 o.p. (ISBN 0-8234-0345-9). Holiday.

--Potato Pancakes All Around: A Hanukkah Tale. (Illus.). 34p. (gr. 4-8). 1982. pap. 5.50 (ISBN 0-8276-0217-0). Jewish Pubn.

Hirsh, Robert O. Listening: A Way To Process Information Aurally. (Comm Comp Ser.). (Illus.). 45p. 1979. pap. text ed. 2.95 (ISBN 0-89787-316-5). Gorsuch Scarisbrick.

Hirshaut, Julien. Jewish Martyrs of Pawiak. LC 81-85301. 256p. 1982. 11.95 (ISBN 0-8052-5039-5); pap. 6.95 (ISBN 0-8052-5040-9). Holocaust Lib.

Hirshaw, Cecil F. Apology for Perfection. LC 64-22766. (Orig.). 1964. pap. 1.50 (ISBN 0-87574-138-X). Pendle Hill.

Hirshberg, Al. Basketball's Greatest Stars. (Putnam Sports Shelf). (Illus.). (gr. 6-10). 1963. PLB 6.29 o.p. (ISBN 0-399-60045-0). Putnam Pub Group.

--Basketball's Greatest Teams. (Putnam Sports Shelf). (Illus.). (gr. 5 up). 1966. PLB 6.29 o.p. (ISBN 0-399-60046-9). Putnam Pub Group.

--Bobby Orr: Fire on Ice. new ed. LC 75-10436. (Putnam Sports Shelf). 160p. (gr. 5 up). 1975. PLB 6.29 o.p. (ISBN 0-399-60954-7). Putnam Pub Group.

--Frank Howard, the Gentle Giant. new ed. (Putnam Sports Shelf). 192p. (gr. 5 up). 1973. PLB 6.29 o.p. (ISBN 0-399-60803-6). Putnam Pub Group.

--Frank Robinson: Born Leader. new ed. (Putnam Sports Shelf). 160p. (gr. 6 up). 1973. PLB 4.97 o.p. (ISBN 0-399-60826-5). Putnam Pub Group.

--The Greatest American Leaguers. (Putnam Sports Shelf). (Illus.). (gr. 5 up). 1970. PLB 5.29 o.p. (ISBN 0-399-60205-4). Putnam Pub Group.

--Henry Aaron: Quiet Superstar. rev. ed. (Putnam Sports Shelf). (gr. 5 up). 1974. PLB 6.29 o.p. (ISBN 0-399-60915-6). Putnam Pub Group.

Hirshberg, Edgar W. George Henry Lewes. (English Authors Ser.: No. 100). lib. bdg. 10.95 o.p. (ISBN 0-8057-1332-8, Twayne). G K Hall.

Hirshfeld, Alan & Sinnott, Roger W. Sky Catalogue Two Thousand. 604p. 1982. 29.97; pap. 17.97 (ISBN 0-933346-34-4). Sky Pub.

Hirshleifer, Jack. Price Theory & Applications. 2nd ed. (Illus.). 1980. text ed. 24.95 (ISBN 0-13-699710-4). P-H.

Hirshman, Howard. The Return of the Seattle Bargain. write for info. Robinson News.

--Targets: Media Guide. write for info. Robinson Pr.

Hirshman, Jack, tr. see Barron, Stephanie, et al.

Hirshmann, Linda & Applebaum, Sharon. Adventures in S. C. 1976. pap. 2.25 (ISBN 0-87844-031-3). Sandlapper Pub Co.

Hirshorn, Paul & Izenour, Steven. White Towers. (Illus.). 1979. 22.50 (ISBN 0-262-08096-6); pap. 9.95 (ISBN 0-262-58051-9). MIT Pr.

Hirson, Baruch. Year of Fire, Year of Ash - the Soweto Revolt: Roots of a Revolution? 348p. (Orig.). 1979. 35.00 (ISBN 0-905762-28-2, Pub. by Zed Pr England); pap. 9.50 (ISBN 0-905762-29-0, Pub. by Zed Pr England). Lawrence Hill.

Hirst, D. The Representative of the People? LC 75-9283. 320p. 1975. 42.50 (ISBN 0-521-20810-6). Cambridge U Pr.

Hirst, David L. Comedy of Manners. (The Critical Idiom Ser.). 1979. 14.95x (ISBN 0-416-85590-3); pap. 4.95x (ISBN 0-416-85570-9). Methuen Inc.

Hirst, David W., jt. ed. see Link, Arthur S.

Hirst, F. W., ed. see Porter, George R.

Hirst, Francis W. Consequences of the War to Great Britain. LC 35-1644. (Illus.). 1969. Repr. of 1934 ed. lib. bdg. 17.50x (ISBN 0-8371-0477-7, HICO). Greenwood.

Hirst, Francis W., jt. auth. see Redlich, Josef.

Hirst, I. R. & Reekie, W. Duncan, eds. The Consumer Society. (Social Issues in the Seventies Ser.). 1977. text ed. 29.95 o.p. (ISBN 0-422-76260-1, Pub. by Tavistock England). Methuen Inc.

Hirst, Irene, jt. auth. see Homebook, Beeton.

Hirst, Irene, ed. Continental Cookery. (Beeton Homebook Ser.). (Illus.). 13.50x (ISBN 0-392-05591-0, SpS). Sportshelf.

Hirst, Margaret E. The Quakers in Peace & War: An Account of Their Peace Principles & Practice. LC 73-137545. (Peace Movement in America Ser). 560p. 1972. Repr. of 1923 ed. lib. bdg. 29.95x (ISBN 0-89198-073-3). Ozer.

Hirst, Paul, jt. auth. see Hindess, Barry.

Hirst, R. J., ed. Philosophy: An Outline for the Intending Student. (Outlines Ser). 1968. cased 16.95x (ISBN 0-7100-2038-4); pap. 6.95 (ISBN 0-7100-6099-8). Routledge & Kegan.

Hirst, Wolf Z. John Keats. (English Author Ser.). 1981. lib. bdg. 11.95 (ISBN 0-8057-6821-1, Twayne). G K Hall.

Hirstein, Sandra J., jt. auth. see Fearon, Mary.

Hirstein, Sandra J., jt. auth. see Tully, Mary Jo.

Hirszowicz, Maria. Industrial Sociology. 280p. 1982. 27.50x (ISBN 0-312-41559-1). St Martin.

Hirt, Andrew J., jt. auth. see Dobie, Ann B.

Hirt, Geoffrey A., jt. auth. see Block, Stanley B.

Hirth, John P. & Lothe, J. Theory of Dislocations. (Materials Science & Engineering Ser.). 1968. text ed. 26.50 o.p. (ISBN 0-07-029048-2, C). McGraw.

Hirth, John P. & Lothe, Jens. Theory of Dislocations. 2nd ed. LC 81-15939. 857p. 1982. 72.95x (ISBN 0-471-09125-1, Pub. by Wiley-Interscience). Wiley.

Hirtz, jt. auth. see Garrett.

Hiscock, Eric C. Voyaging Under Sail. 2nd ed. 1970. 22.50 (ISBN 0-19-217527-0). Oxford U Pr.

Hiscocks, Richard. The Adenauer Era. LC 75-35027. 312p. 1976. Repr. of 1966 ed. lib. bdg. 19.25x (ISBN 0-8371-8569-6, HIAE). Greenwood.

Hiscox, Gardener D. Mechanical Movements, Powers & Devices. 405p. 1983. pap. 8.50 (ISBN 0-88072-018-2). Tanager Bks.

Hise, Charles Van see Van Hise, Charles R.

Hise, Richard T., et al. Basic Marketing: Concepts & Decisions. 1978. text ed. 20.95 (ISBN 0-316-36471-1); tchrs'. ed. avail. (ISBN 0-316-36474-6); study guide 8.95 (ISBN 0-316-36473-8). Little.

Hiser, Michel L., ed. Wood Energy. LC 78-65335. 1978. 20.00 o.p. (ISBN 0-250-40287-4). Ann Arbor Science.

Hiserodt, Donald. Human Relations in Marketing. 2nd ed. Dorr, Eugene, ed. (Occupational Manuals & Projects in Marketing Ser.). (Illus.). 1978. pap. text ed. 7.32 (ISBN 0-07-029052-0, G); tchr's manual & key 4.50 (ISBN 0-07-029053-9). McGraw.

Hisey, Lehmann. Keys to Inner Space. 1975. pap. 1.95 o.p. (ISBN 0-380-00411-9, 25098). Avon.

Hislop, Alexander. Proverbs of Scotland. LC 68-21774. 1968. Repr. of 1868 ed. 37.00x (ISBN 0-8103-3201-9). Gale.

Hislop, Donald L. The Nome Lackee Indian Reservation, 1854-1870. (ANCRR Occasional Publication Ser.: No. 4). 99p. 1978. 7.00 (ISBN 0-686-38935-2). Assn NC Records.

Hislop, Helen J. & Sanger, Joan. Chest Disorders in Children. LC 68-31199. 1968. pap. 3.00 cancelled (ISBN 0-912452-04-8). Am Phys Therapy Assn.

Hislop, John. Breeding for Racing. 1976. 14.95 (ISBN 0-686-83969-2, Pub by Secker & Warburg). David & Charles.

Hislop, R. Annual Art Sales Index 81-82. 1982. 140.00 (ISBN 0-686-30714-3). Apollo.

--Auction Prices American Artists, 70-78. 65.00. Apollo.

--Auction Prices American Artists, 80-82. 46.00. Apollo.

--Auction Prices of Impressionist & 20th Century Artists 1970-1980, 2 Vols. 160.00 (ISBN 0-903872-12-9). Apollo.

--Auction Prices of Old Masters. 1980. 156.00 (ISBN 0-903872-14-5). Apollo.

--Auction Prices of 19th Century Artists, 2 Vols. 1980. 176.00 (ISBN 0-903872-13-7). Apollo.

Hispanic Council see Canning House Library.

Hispanic Society of America, New York. Catalogue of the Library of the Hispanic Society of America, 10 Vols. 1962. Set. 950.00 (ISBN 0-8161-0624-X, Hall Library). G K Hall.

--Catalogue of the Library of the Hispanic Society of America, First Supplement, 4 vols. 1970. lib. bdg. 420.00 (ISBN 0-8161-0910-9, Hall Library). G K Hall.

Hisrich, Bob & Bronstein, Eugene. The MBA Career. 256p. 1983. pap. 4.95 (ISBN 0-8120-2485-0). Barron.

Hisrich, Robert D., jt. auth. see Peters, Michael P.

Historic Huntsville Foundation. Huntsville Entertains. King, Shelbie, ed. 480p. 1983. pap. 13.95 (ISBN 0-686-43262-2). Wimmer Bks.

Historic New Orleans Collection. Orleans Gallery: The Founders. (Illus.). 48p. (Orig.). 1982. pap. 5.00x (ISBN 0-917860-10-1). Historic New Orleans.

Historic Santa Fe Foundation. Old Santa Fe Today. rev. & enl. 2nd ed. LC 72-86822. (Illus.). 64p. 1972. pap. 8.95 (ISBN 0-8263-0251-3). U of NM Pr.

--Old Santa Fe Today. 3rd, enl. ed. LC 80-52287. (Illus.). 128p. 1981. pap. 9.95 (ISBN 0-8263-0562-8). U of NM Pr.

Historical Association of Kenya. Hadith: Proceedings, 7 vols. Ogot, Bethwell A., ed. (Illus.). Vol. 1. 1968. 6.25x (ISBN 0-8002-0574-X); Vol. 2. 1970. 12.50x (ISBN 0-8002-0501-4); Vol. 3. 1971. 7.50x (ISBN 0-8002-0572-3); Vol. 4. 1972. 12.50x (ISBN 0-8002-0600-2); Vol. 5. 1973. 12.50x (ISBN 0-8002-0601-0); Vol. 6. 1974. 12.50x (ISBN 0-8002-0602-9); Vol. 7. 1975. 15.00x (ISBN 0-8002-0603-7). Intl Pubns Serv.

Historical Committee Texas Surveyors Assn. Three Dollars Per Mile. (Illus.). 455p. 1981. 25.00 (ISBN 0-686-81643-9). Eakin Pubns.

Historical Committee Texas Surveys Association. One League to Each Wind. 2nd ed. (Illus.). 376p. 1973. 25.00x (ISBN 0-686-37675-7). Von-Bogckmann.

Hitch, Charles J., ed. Energy Conservation & Economic Growth. (AAAS Selected Symposium: No. 22). (Illus.). 1978. lib. bdg. 21.00 (ISBN 0-89158-354-8). Westview.

Hitchcock, Alfred. Alfred Hitchcock Presents Stories My Mother Never Told Me. 1976. pap. 1.25 o.s.i. (ISBN 0-440-18290-5). Dell.

--Alfred Hitchcock's Spellbinders in Suspense. (Illus.). (gr. 7-11). 1967. 4.95 o.p. (ISBN 0-394-81665-X, BYR); PLB 6.99 o.p. (ISBN 0-394-91665-4); pap. 2.50 (ISBN 0-394-84900-0). Random.

--Death on Arrival. 1980. pap. 1.75 o.s.i. (ISBN 0-440-11839-5). Dell.

--Games Killers Play. 1980. pap. 1.95 o.s.i. (ISBN 0-440-12790-4). Dell.

--Hangman's Dozen. 1976. pap. 1.25 o.s.i. (ISBN 0-440-13428-5). Dell.

--Murderer's Row. 1980. pap. 1.95 o.s.i. (ISBN 0-440-16036-7). Dell.

--Murders on the Half Skull. 1979. pap. 1.50 o.s.i. (ISBN 0-440-16093-6). Dell.

Hitchcock, Alfred, ed. Alfred Hitchcock & the Three Investigators in the Mystery of the Laughing Shadow. (Three Investigators Ser.: No. 12). (Illus.). (gr. 4-7). 1969. 2.95 o.p. (ISBN 0-394-81492-4, BYR); PLB 5.39 (ISBN 0-394-91492-9); pap. 1.95 o.p. (ISBN 0-394-83775-4). Random.

--Alfred Hitchcock Presents: Thirteen More They Wouldn't Let Me Do on TV. 1978. pap. 1.50 o.s.i. (ISBN 0-440-13640-7). Dell.

--Alfred Hitchcock Presents Twelve Stories for Late at Night. 1976. pap. 1.50 o.s.i. (ISBN 0-440-19178-5). Dell.

--Alfred Hitchcock's Haunted Houseful. (Illus.). (gr. 4-9). 1961. 6.95 (ISBN 0-394-81224-7, BYR); PLB 6.99 o.p. (ISBN 0-394-91224-1). Random.

--Alfred Hitchcock's Monster Museum. (gr. 6-11). 1965. 4.95 o.p. (ISBN 0-394-81230-1, BYR); PLB 6.99 o.p. (ISBN 0-394-91230-6); pap. 2.50 (ISBN 0-394-84899-3). Random.

--Alfred Hitchcock's Sinister Spies. (Illus.). (gr. 7-11). 1966. 4.95 o.p. (ISBN 0-394-81564-5, BYR); PLB 6.99 o.p. (ISBN 0-394-91564-X); pap. 2.50 (ISBN 0-394-84901-9). Random.

--Alfred Hitchcock's Solve-Them-Yourself Mysteries. (Illus.). (gr. 6-9). 1963. 6.95 (ISBN 0-394-81242-5, BYR); PLB 6.99 o.p. (ISBN 0-394-91242-X). Random.

--Alfred Hitchcock's Supernatural Tales of Terror & Suspense. LC 73-3694. (Illus.). 224p. (gr. 4 up). 1983. pap. 2.50 (ISBN 0-394-85622-8). Random.

Hitchcock, Alfred, ed. see Arden, William.

Hitchcock, Alfred, ed. see Arthur, Robert.

Hitchcock, Alfred, ed. see Carey, M. V.

Hitchcock, Alfred, ed. see West, Nick.

Hitchcock, Arthur A. & Nott, Wanda L., eds. Mid-Life Change. 1981. 3.75 (ISBN 0-686-36402-3); 4.75 (ISBN 0-686-37308-1). Am Personnel.

Hitchcock, Bert. Richard Malcolm Johnston. (United States Authors Ser.). 1978. 13.95 (ISBN 0-8057-7238-3, Twayne). G K Hall.

Hitchcock, C. Leo, et al. Vascular Plants of the Pacific Northwest, 5 pts. Incl. Pt. 1. Vascular Cryptogams, Gymnosperms, & Monocotyledons. (Illus.). 925p. 1969. 27.50 o.s.i. (ISBN 0-295-73983-5); Pt. 2. Salicaceae to Saxifragaceae. (Illus.). 597p. 1964. 27.50 o.s.i. (ISBN 0-295-73984-3); Pt. 3. Saxifragaceae to Ericaceae. (Illus.). 614p. 1961. 27.50 o.s.i. (ISBN 0-295-73985-1); Pt. 4. Ericaceae Through Companulaceae. (Illus.). 516p. 1959. 27.50 o.s.i. (ISBN 0-295-73986-X); Pt. 5. Compositae. (Illus.). 349p. 1955. 27.50 o.s.i. (ISBN 0-295-73987-8). LC 56-62679. (Publications in Biology Ser.: No. 17). U of Wash Pr.

Hitchcock, Charles J., ed. see Chandler, A. Bertram & Hoffman, Lee.

Hitchcock, George. Collected Poems, Stories, & Collages. 300p. (Orig.). 1983. 12.95 (ISBN 0-937310-04-2); pap. 7.95 (ISBN 0-937310-05-0). Panjandrum.

--The Devil Comes to Wittenberg. LC 80-7591. (New Poetic Drama Ser.: No. 1). 1980. pap. 3.50 (ISBN 0-686-81661-7). Dragons Teeth.

--Notes of the Siege Year. 1974. pap. 2.00 o.p. (ISBN 0-87711-053-0). Kayak.

Hitchcock, H. Wiley. Music in the United States: A Historical Introduction. 2nd ed. (Illus.). 288p. 1974. text ed. 15.95 (ISBN 0-13-608398-6); pap. text ed. 13.95 (ISBN 0-13-608380-3). P-H.

Hitchcock, H. Wiley, ed. The American Music Miscellany. LC 75-39731. (Earlier American Music Ser: Vol. 9). 300p. 1972. Repr. of 1798 ed. lib. bdg. 27.50 (ISBN 0-306-77309-0). Da Capo.

Hitchcock, H. Wiley, ed. see Belcher, Supply.

Hitchcock, H. Wiley, ed. see Foster, Stephen.

Hitchcock, Henry R. American Architectural Books: A List of Books, Portfolios, and Pamphlets on Architecture and Related Subjects Published in America Before 1895. LC 75-25672. (Architectural and Decorative Arts Ser.). xii, 130p. 1975. Repr. of 1962 ed. lib. bdg. 21.50 (ISBN 0-306-70742-X). Da Capo.

--In the Nature of Materials: The Buildings of Frank Lloyd Wright 1887-1941. LC 75-14322. (Architecture Paperbacks). (Illus.). 1975. pap. 12.95 (ISBN 0-306-80019-5). Da Capo.

Hitchcock, Henry-Russell. Architecture of H. H. Richardson & His Times. 2nd ed. (Illus.). 1966. pap. 9.95 (ISBN 0-262-58005-5). MIT Pr.

Hitchcock, Henry Russell. Early Victorian Architecture in Britain, 2 Vols. LC 72-151765. (Architecture & Decorative Art Ser.). 658p. 1972. Repr. of 1954 ed. Set. lib. bdg. 85.00 (ISBN 0-306-70195-2). Da Capo.

Hitchcock, Henry-Russell. In the Nature of Materials: The Buildings of Frank Lloyd Wright, 1887-1941. LC 72-75322. (Architecture & Decorative Arts Ser). 1973. Repr. of 1942 ed. lib. bdg. 35.00 (ISBN 0-306-71283-0). Da Capo.

--Rhode Island Architecture. 2nd ed. LC 68-27725. (Architecture & Decorative Art Ser.: Vol. 19). (Illus.). 1968. Repr. of 1939 ed. lib. bdg. 35.00 (ISBN 0-306-71037-4). Da Capo.

Hitchcock, James. Catholicism & Modernity: Confrontation or Capitulation? 1979. 12.95 (ISBN 0-8164-0427-5). Seabury.

--The New Enthusiasts: And What They Are Doing to the Catholic Church. 168p. 1982. pap. 7.95 (ISBN 0-88347-150-7). Thomas More.

--What Is Secular Humanism? Why Humanism Became Secular & How It Is Changing Our World. (Illus.). 180p. 1982. pap. 6.95 (ISBN 0-89283-163-4). Servant.

Hitchcock, James & Bednarski, Gloriana. Charismatics. (Catholic Perspectives Ser.). 104p. (Orig.). 1980. pap. 6.95 (ISBN 0-88347-114-0). Thomas More.

Hitchcock, James, jt. auth. see Durkin, Mary.

Hitchcock, Mary J. Foodservice Systems Administration. (Illus.). 1980. text ed. 21.95x (ISBN 0-02-354650-6). Macmillan.

Hitchcock, Raymond. Attack the Lusitania! 1980. 10.00 o.p. (ISBN 0-312-06006-8). St Martin.

--The Canaris Legacy. 196p. 1980. 10.95 o.p. (ISBN 0-312-11817-1). St Martin.

Hitchcock, Ruth H. Leaves of the Past: A Pioneer Register, Including an Overview of the History & Events of Early Tehama County. (ANCRR Occasional Paper: No. 10). Date not set. 85.00 (ISBN 0-686-38936-0). Assn NC Records.

Hitchcock, Thomas H. Monogram Close-up: Junkers 290 Airplane. (Monogram Aircraft Close-up: No. 3). 32p. 1975. pap. 5.95 (ISBN 0-914144-03-0, Pub. by Monogram). Aviation.

--Monogram Close Ups Nos. 1 & 2. Incl. No. 1. Junkers 287 Airplane. 32p (ISBN 0-914144-01-4); No. 2. Junkers 288 Airplane. 32p (ISBN 0-914144-02-2). (Monogram Aircraft Close-up Ser.). (Illus.). 1975. pap. 5.95 ea. Aviation.

Hitchener, Elizabeth see Booth, David.

Hitchfield, Elizabeth, jt. auth. see Brearley, Molly.

Hitching, Francis. World Atlas of Mysteries. (Illus.). 256p. 1980. 21.75x (ISBN 0-330-25683-1). Intl Pubns Serv.

Hitchings, G. H., ed. Inhibition of Folate Metabolism in Chemotherapy: The Origins & Uses Of Co-trixomazole. (Handbook of Experimental Pharmacology Ser.: Vol. 64). (Illus.). 457p. 1983. 150.00 (ISBN 0-387-11782-2). Springer-Verlag.

Hitchman, Michael L. Measurement of Dissolved Oxygen. LC 77-26710. (Monographs on Analytical Chemistry & Its Applications: Vol. 49). 1978. 40.95 (ISBN 0-471-03885-7, Pub. by Wiley-Interscience). Wiley.

Hitchock, Alfred. Alive & Screaming. 1980. pap. 1.95 o.s.i. (ISBN 0-440-10148-4). Dell.

Hite, Molly. Ideas of Order in the Novels of Thomas Pynchon. 220p. 1983. price not set (ISBN 0-8142-0350-7). Ohio St U Pr.

Hitiris, Theodore, jt. auth. see Burrows, Paul.

Hitner, Trevor, jt. auth. see Torrington, Derek.

Hitomi, K. Manufacturing Systems Engineering. 310p. 1978. write for info. (ISBN 0-85066-177-3, Pub. by Taylor & Francis). Intl Pubns Serv.

Hitt, Christopher, jt. auth. see Austin, James E.

Hitt, Michael A. & Middlemist, R. Dennis. Management: Concepts & Effective Practices. (Illus.). 650p. 1983. text ed. 21.95 (ISBN 0-314-69654-7); instrs.' manual avail. (ISBN 0-314-71098-1); study guide avail. (ISBN 0-314-71099-X). West Pub.

Hitt, Michael A., jt. auth. see Middlemist, R. Dennis.

Hitt, Michael A., et al. Effective Management. (Management Ser). (Illus.). 1979. text ed. 22.50 (ISBN 0-8299-0196-5); pap. study guide 8.50 (ISBN 0-8299-0246-5); instrs.' manual avail. (ISBN 0-8299-0489-1); transparency masters avail. (ISBN 0-8299-0490-5). West Pub.

Hitt, Michael A., jt. auth. see Middlemist, R. Dennis.

Hitt, Michael A., jt. auth. see Palia, Kyamas A.

Hitt, Russell T. How Christians Grow. 1979. 10.95x (ISBN 0-19-502558-X). Oxford U Pr.

Hitti, Philip K. Arabs: A Short History. 1956. pap. 6.95 (ISBN 0-89526-982-1). Regnery-Gateway.

Hittleman, Daniel. Developmental Reading. 1978. 22.95 (ISBN 0-395-30629-9); instr's. manual 1.00 (ISBN 0-395-30630-2). HM.

--Developmental Reading, K-8: Teaching from a Psycholinguistic Perspective. 2d ed. 480p. 1983. text ed. 23.95 (ISBN 0-395-32770-9, EA95); write for info. instr's. manual (ISBN 0-395-32771-7, EA96). HM.

Hittleman, Richard. Yoga for Health. 256p. (Orig.). 1983. pap. 7.95 (ISBN 0-345-30852-2). Ballantine.

Hix, Charles. Working Out. 1983. 15.95 (ISBN 0-671-45793-4). S&S.

Hixenbaugh, Paula, jt. auth. see Wall, Shavaun M.

Hixon, Thomas J., et al. Introduction to Communication Disorders. (Illus.). 1979. text ed. 25.95 (ISBN 0-13-480186-5). P-H.

Hixson, Joseph. History of the Human Body: A Five Thousand Year Mystery Told with Pictures. LC 65-17179. (Illus., Orig.). 1966. 15.00x (ISBN 0-8154-0115-9); pap. 4.95 (ISBN 0-8154-0114-0). Cooper Sq.

Hixson, S., jt. ed. see Creamer, T.

Hjelle, L. A. & Ziegler, D. J. Personality Theories: Basic Assumptions, Research & Applications. 1975. text ed. 20.50 o.p. (ISBN 0-07-029061-X, C); instructors' manual 2.95 o.p. (ISBN 0-07-029062-8). McGraw.

Hjelle, Larry A. & Ziegler, Daniel J. Personality Theories. 2nd, rev. ed. (Illus.). 512p. 1981. text ed. 24.00 (ISBN 0-07-029063-6, C); instr's manual 4.95 (ISBN 0-07-029064-4). McGraw.

Hjelm, J. Thaddeus Jones & the Dragon. LC 68-56830. (Illus.). (gr. 2-5). PLB 6.75x (ISBN 0-87783-039-8); pap. 2.95x deluxe ed. (ISBN 0-87783-110-6). Oddo.

Hjelmfelt, A. T., Jr. & Cassidy, J. J. Hydrology for Engineers & Planners. (Illus.). 1975. text ed. 15.95x (ISBN 0-8138-0795-6). Iowa St U Pr.

Hjelmslev, Louis. Resume of a Theory of Language. Whitfield, Francis J., ed. 312p. 1975. 25.00x (ISBN 0-299-07040-9). U of Wis Pr.

Hjelte, George. Administration of Public Recreation. LC 79-156192. (Illus.). 1971. Repr. of 1940 ed. lib. bdg. 20.00x (ISBN 0-8371-6141-X, HJPR). Greenwood.

Hjort, Oystein, jt. auth. see Hulten, Pontus.

Hlavacek, I., jt. auth. see Necas, J.

Hlope, Stephen S. Class, Ethnicity & Politics in Liberia: Analysis of Power Struggles in the Tubman & Tolbert Administrations from 1944-1975. LC 79-63261. 1979. pap. text ed. 12.50 (ISBN 0-8191-0721-2). U Pr of Amer.

HM Study Skills Group. HM College Study Skills Level III Student Text. 1982. pap. text ed. 4.25 (ISBN 0-88210-138-2); tchr's. guide 3.50 (ISBN 0-88210-139-0); workshop kit 12.50 (ISBN 0-88210-140-4). Natl Assn Principals.

Hnatek, E. R. Applications of Linear Integrated Circuits. 518p. 1975. 51.95 (ISBN 0-471-40111-0, Pub. by Wiley-Interscience). Wiley.

--User's Guidebook to Digital CMOS Integrated Circuits. 1981. 24.50 o.p. (ISBN 0-07-029067-9). McGraw.

Ho. Developing the Economy of the PRC. 142p. 1982. 21.95 (ISBN 0-03-062581-5). Praeger.

--Hemoglobin & Oxygen Binding. Bd. with Electron Transport & Oxygen Utilization. 1982. 135.00 (ISBN 0-444-00717-2). Elsevier.

Ho & Eaton. Electron Transport & Oxygen Utilization. 1982. 80.00 (ISBN 0-444-00644-3). Elsevier.

Ho, Beng T., et al. Serotonin in Biological Psychiatry: Advances in Biochemical Psychopharmacology, Vol. 34. 355p. 1982. text ed. 33.00 (ISBN 0-89004-803-7). Raven.

Ho, C. & Heaton, eds. Hemoglobin & Oxygen Binding. 1982. 80.00 (ISBN 0-444-00571-4). Elsevier.

Ho, C. Y., jt. auth. see Touloukian, U. S.

Ho, C. Y., jt. auth. see Touloukian, Y. S.

Ho, James K. K., ed. Black Engineers in the United States: A Directory. LC 73-84956. 308p. 1974. 24.95 (ISBN 0-88258-136-8). Howard U Pr.

Ho, Lucy. Authentic Chinese Cooking. (Dover Cook Bk.). (Illus.). 170p. 1973. pap. 3.50 (ISBN 0-486-22833-9). Dover.

Ho, P. S. & Tu, K. N. Thin Films & Interfaces. (Materials Research Society Ser.: Vol. 10). 1982. 75.00 (ISBN 0-444-00774-1). Elsevier.

Ho, Sam P. S. Small-Scale Enterprises in Korea & Taiwan. (Working Paper: No. 384). vi, 151p. 1980. 5.00 (ISBN 0-686-36187-3, WP-0384). World Bank.

Ho, Steve. How I Turned Nine Dollars into a Million in Imports in My Spare Time. LC 82-90190. 1982. 14.95 (ISBN 0-686-35868-6). S Ho.

Hoa, Nguyen D. see Linguistic Circle of Saigon & Summer Institute of Linguistics.

Hoadley, Irene B. & Clark, Alice S., eds. Quantitative Methods in Librarianship: Standards, Research, & Management. LC 73-149962. (Contributions in Librarianship & Information Science: No. 4). 256p. 1972. lib. bdg. 29.95 (ISBN 0-8371-6061-8, HOQ/). Greenwood.

Hoag, Edwin. How Business Works. LC 77-15449. (Illus.). 1978. 6.95 o.p. (ISBN 0-672-52422-8). Bobbs.

Hoag, Ernest B. & Williams, Edward H. Crime, Abnormal Minds & the Law. (Historical Foundations of Forensic Psychiatry & Psychology Ser.). 405p. 1980. Repr. of 1923 ed. lib. bdg. 39.50 (ISBN 0-306-76060-6). Da Capo.

Hoag, Philip M., jt. auth. see Pawlak, Elizabeth A.

Hoagland, Albert A. Digital Magnetic Recording. LC 82-23203. 164p. 1983. Repr. of 1963 ed. lib. bdg. write for info. (ISBN 0-89874-591-8). Krieger.

Hoagland, Clayton. Pleasures of Sketching Outdoors. rev. ed. (Illus.). 1970. pap. 5.00 (ISBN 0-486-22229-2). Dover.

Hoagland, Clayton & Hoagland, Kathleen. Thomas Wolfe Our Friend 1933-1938. Magi, Aldo P., ed. 21p. 1979. 25.00 (ISBN 0-912348-03-8). Croissant & Co.

Hoagland, Edward. Courage of Turtles. LC 78-117661. 1970. 1.25. Random.

--Red Wolves & Black Bears. 1983. pap. 5.95 (ISBN 0-14-006686-1). Penguin.

--The Tugman's Passage. 1983. pap. 5.95 (ISBN 0-14-006685-3). Penguin.

Hoagland, Kathleen, jt. auth. see Hoagland, Clayton.

Hoagland, Kathleen, ed. One Thousand Years of Irish Poetry. 884p. 1982. 12.95 (ISBN 0-517-34295-2). Devin.

Hoaglin, David C. & Mosteller, F. Understanding Robust & Exploratory Data Analysis. (Applied Probability & Math Statistics Ser.). 447p. 1983. 37.95x (ISBN 0-471-09777-2, Pub. by Wiley-Interscience). Wiley.

Hoaglund, Franklin T., jt. auth. see Leach, Robert E.

Hoak, D. E. The King's Council in the Reign of Edward VI. LC 75-9286. (Illus.). 394p. 1975. 57.50 (ISBN 0-521-20866-1). Cambridge U Pr.

Hoar, W. S., jt. auth. see Harvey, B. J.

Hoar, W. S. & Randall, D. J., eds. Fish Physiology Vol. 8: Bioenergetics & Growth. LC 76-84233. 1979. 85.00 (ISBN 0-12-350408-2); subscription 73.00 (ISBN 0-685-86991-1). Acad Pr.

Hoar, William S. General & Comparative Physiology. 2nd ed. (Illus.). 896p. 1975. 29.95 (ISBN 0-13-350272-4); lab. companion 9.95 (ISBN 0-13-347724-X). P-H.

--General & Comparative Physiology. 3rd ed. (Illus.). 928p. 1983. 30.95 (ISBN 0-13-349308-3). P-H.

Hoard, F. & Marlow, Andrew. Good Furniture You Can Make Yourself. 1972. pap. 5.95 o.p. (ISBN 0-02-080290-0, Collier). Macmillan.

Hoard, Samuel L. Satellite Services Sourcebook. LC 82-72850. 1982. 75.00 (ISBN 0-910339-00-7). Drake's Ptg & Pub.

Hoare, H. R. Project Management Using Network Analysis. 1973. 24.95 (ISBN 0-07-084436-4, P&RB). McGraw.

Hoare, Katharin L. The Art of Tatting. Kliot, Jules, ed. (Illus.). 128p. 1982. Repr. of 1910 ed. 30.00 (ISBN 0-686-97469-7). Lacis Pubns.

Hoare, Merval. Norfolk Island: An Outline of Its History, 1774-1981. 3rd ed. LC 82-4719. (Illus.). 188p. 1983. pap. 8.95 (ISBN 0-7022-1941-X). U of Queensland Pr.

Hoare, R. J., jt. auth. see Harrison, P. M.

Hoath, David C., jt. auth. see Smith, Chris.

Hoban, Brom. Skunk Lane. LC 81-47729. (Illus.). 64p. (gr. 2-4). 1983. 8.61i (ISBN 0-06-022347-2, HarpJ); PLB 8.89g (ISBN 0-06-022348-0). Har-Row.

Hoban, Gary J., jt. auth. see Culver, Carmen M.

Hoban, Lillian. Arthur's Funny Money. LC 80-7903. (I Can Read Bk.). (Illus.). 64p. (gr. k-3). 1981. 7.64i (ISBN 0-06-022343-X, HarpJ); PLB 8.89g (ISBN 0-06-022344-8). Har-Row.

--Harry's Song. LC 78-31712. (Illus.). 32p. (gr. k-3). 1980. 9.75 (ISBN 0-688-80220-6); PLB 9.36 (ISBN 0-688-84220-8). Greenwillow.

--The Sugar Snow Spring. LC 72-9866. (Illus.). 48p. (ps-3). 1973. 7.95 o.p. (ISBN 0-06-022333-2, HarpJ); PLB 9.89 (ISBN 0-06-022334-0). Har-Row.

Hoban, Lillian & Hoban, Phoebe. The Laziest Robot in Zone One. LC 82-48613. (An I Can Read Bk.). (Illus.). 64p. (gr. k-3). 1983. 7.64i (ISBN 0-06-022349-9, HarpJ); PLB 8.89g (ISBN 0-06-022352-9). Har-Row.

--Ready...Set...Robot! LC 81-47731. (An I Can Read Bk.). (Illus.). 64p. (gr. k-3). 1982. 7.64i (ISBN 0-06-022345-6, HarpJ); PLB 8.89 (ISBN 0-06-022346-4). Har-Row.

Hoban, Phoebe, jt. auth. see Hoban, Lillian.

Hoban, Russell. Arthur's New Power. LC 77-11550. (Illus.). (gr. 1-5). 1978. 9.57i (ISBN 0-690-01370-1, TYC-J); PLB 9.89 (ISBN 0-690-01371-X). Har-Row.

--Baby Sister for Frances. LC 64-15154. (Illus.). (gr. k-3). 1964. 8.61i (ISBN 0-06-022335-9, HarpJ); PLB 9.89 (ISBN 0-06-022336-7). Har-Row.

--The Battle of Zormia. 32p. 1982. 6.95 (ISBN 0-399-20882-8, Philomel). Putnam Pub Group.

--Bedtime for Frances. LC 60-8347. (Illus.). (gr. k-3). 1960. 8.61i (ISBN 0-06-022350-2, HarpJ); PLB 9.89 (ISBN 0-06-022351-0). Har-Row.

--Best Friends for Frances. LC 71-77935. (Illus.). (ps-3). 1969. 8.61i (ISBN 0-06-022327-8, HarpJ); PLB 9.89 (ISBN 0-06-022328-6). Har-Row.

--Birthday for Frances. LC 68-24321. (Illus.). (gr. k-3). 1968. 8.61i (ISBN 0-06-022338-3, HarpJ); PLB 9.89 (ISBN 0-06-022339-1). Har-Row.

--Bread & Jam for Frances. LC 64-19605. (Illus.). (gr. k-3). 1964. 8.61i (ISBN 0-06-022359-6, HarpJ); PLB 9.89 (ISBN 0-06-022360-X). Har-Row.

--Flat Cat. LC 79-21958. (Illus.). 48p. (ps-2). 1980. 6.95 (ISBN 0-399-20749-X, Philomel); PLB 6.99 (ISBN 0-399-61159-2). Putnam Pub Group.

--The Flight of Bembel Rudzuk. 32p. 1982. 6.95 (ISBN 0-399-20888-7, Philomel). Putnam Pub Group.

--The Great Gumdrop Robbery. (Illus.). 32p. 1982. 6.95 (ISBN 0-399-20819-4, Philomel); PLB 6.99 (ISBN 0-399-61184-3). Putnam Pub Group.

--Letitia Rabbit's String Song. (Illus.). 48p. (ps-3). 1973. PLB 3.99 o.p. (ISBN 0-698-30490-X, Coward). Putnam Pub Group.

--The Mouse & His Child. (Illus.). 1975. pap. 2.25 (ISBN 0-380-00910-2, 63487-2, Camelot). Avon.

--Mouse & His Child. LC 67-19624. (gr. 1-5). 1967. 10.95 (ISBN 0-06-022377-4, HarpJ); PLB 10.89 (ISBN 0-06-022378-2). Har-Row.

--A Near Thing for Captain Najork. LC 75-29464. (Illus.). (gr. k-3). 1976. PLB 7.95 o.p. (ISBN 0-689-30503-6). Atheneum.

--Pilgermann. 1983. 14.95 (ISBN 0-671-45968-6). Summit Bks.

--They Came from Aargh! (Illus.). 32p. (gr. 1-5). 1981. 6.95 (ISBN 0-399-20817-8, Philomel); lib. bdg. 6.99 (ISBN 0-399-61182-7). Putnam Pub Group.

--Turtle Diary. 1978. pap. 1.95 o.p. (ISBN 0-380-39081-7, 39081, Bard). Avon.

Hoban, Tana. A. B. See. (Illus.). (ps-3). 1982. 8.50 (ISBN 0-688-00832-1); PLB 7.63 (ISBN 0-688-00833-X). Greenwillow.

--Round & Round & Round. LC 82-11984. (Illus.). 32p. (gr. k-3). 1983. 9.00 (ISBN 0-688-01813-0); PLB 8.59 (ISBN 0-688-01814-9). Greenwillow.

Hoban, Y. Instrumental English: English for the Secretary. 1982. text ed. 6.96 (ISBN 0-07-004522-4). McGraw.

Hobar, Donald, ed. Papers of the Dictionary Society of North America, 1977. 93p. members 5.50 (ISBN 0-686-95920-5); members 7.00 (ISBN 0-686-99671-2). Ind St Univ.

Hobba, Isabel K. Needlepainting Made Easy. (Illus.). 48p. (Orig.). pap. 3.95 (ISBN 0-9609196-0-0). Wertz Pubns.

Hobbes, Thomas. De Cive or The Citizen. Lamprecht, Sterling P., ed. LC 82-11829. 211p. 1982. Repr. of 1949 ed. lib. bdg. 28.25x (ISBN 0-313-23659-3, HODE). Greenwood.

--Leviathan: On the Matter, Form & Power Of A Commonwealth Ecclesiastical & Civil. Oakeshott, Michael, ed. 1962. pap. 3.95 (ISBN 0-02-065510-X, Collier). Macmillan.

--The Metaphysical System of Hobbes. 2nd ed. xxv, 212p. 1974. 16.00 (ISBN 0-87548-044-6); pap. 6.00 (ISBN 0-87548-045-4). Open Court.

Hobbie, J. E., ed. Limnology of Tundra Ponds: Barrow, Alaska. LC 80-26373. (US-IBP Synthesis Ser.: Vol. 13). 514p. 1980. 34.00 (ISBN 0-87933-386-3). Hutchinson Ross.

Hobbie, Margaret, compiled by. Museums, Sites, & Collections of Germanic Culture in North America: An Annotated Directory of German Immigrant Culture in the United States & Canada. LC 79-6822. 184p. 1980. lib. bdg. 27.50 (ISBN 0-313-22060-3, HGC/). Greenwood.

Hobbie, Russell K. Intermediate Physics for Medicine & Biology. LC 77-27293. 1978. text ed. 32.95 (ISBN 0-471-03212-3); solns. manual 10.95 (ISBN 0-471-03684-6). Wiley.

Hobbing, Peter. Strafwurdigkeit der Selbstverletzung der Drogenkonsum Im Deutschen und Brasilianischen Recht. xv, 400p. (Ger.). 1982. write for info. (ISBN 3-8204-6278-3). P Lang Pubs.

Hobbins, John, jt. auth. see Warshaw, Joseph B.

Hobbins, John C. & Winsberg, Fred. Ultrasonography in Obstetrics & Gynecology. 2nd ed. (Illus.). 240p. 1982. lib. bdg. 32.00 o.p. (ISBN 0-683-04089-8). Williams & Wilkins.

Hobbs, jt. auth. see Constantine.

Hobbs & Paschall, eds. Teacher's Bible Commentary. LC 75-189505. 21.95 (ISBN 0-8054-1116-X). Broadman.

Hobbs, A. C. Construction of Locks & Safes. Tomlinson, Charles, ed. (Illus.). vi, 212p. 1982. Repr. of 1868 ed. 20.00 (ISBN 0-87556-126-8); stiff wrappers 15.00 (ISBN 0-686-82966-2). Saifer.

Hobbs, Albert H. Man Is Moral Choice. 1979. 12.95 o.p. (ISBN 0-87000-433-6, Arlington Hse). Crown.

Hobbs, B. E., et al. An Outline of Structural Geology. LC 75-20393. 512p. 1976. text ed. 29.95 (ISBN 0-471-40156-0). Wiley.

Hobbs, D. A. & Blank, S. J. Sociology & the Human Experience. 3rd ed. 536p. 1982. pap. 16.95 (ISBN 0-471-08281-3). Wiley.

Hobbs, F. D. Traffic Planning & Engineering. 2nd, rev. ed. 1974. text ed. 29.70 o.p. (ISBN 0-08-017926-6); pap. text ed. 17.00 o.p. (ISBN 0-08-017927-4). Pergamon.

Hobbs, F. D. & Doling, J. F. Planning for Engineers & Surveyors. LC 80-41553. (Illus.). 230p. 1981. 32.00 (ISBN 0-08-025459-4); pap. 15.75 (ISBN 0-08-025458-6). Pergamon.

Hobbs, Herschel H. The Epistles of John. 176p. 1983. 9.95 (ISBN 0-8407-5274-1). Nelson.

--John: A Study Guide Commentary. 96p. 1973. pap. 3.95 (ISBN 0-310-26113-9). Zondervan.

--What Baptists Believe. LC 64-12411. 1963. bds. 3.95 (ISBN 0-8054-8101-X). Broadman.

Hobbs, Herschell H. More Welcome Speeches. 1968. pap. 2.50 (ISBN 0-310-26121-X). Zondervan.

Hobbs, Hershel H. Welcome Speeches. pap. 2.95 (ISBN 0-310-26151-1). Zondervan.

Hobbs, Jack. Installing & Servicing Home Audio Systems. LC 75-94452. (Orig. Ils Ser.). 1969. pap. 5.95 o.p. (ISBN 0-8306-8505-7, 505). TAB Bks.

Hobbs, Laura. Cars. (Easy-Read Fact Bks.). (Illus.). (gr. 2-4). 1977. PLB 8.60 s&l (ISBN 0-531-00375-2). Watts.

Hobbs, Margie, jt. auth. see Cleaves, Cheryl.

Hobbs, Marvin. Modern Communications Switching Systems. 2nd ed. 308p. 1981. 9.95 (ISBN 0-686-98114-6). Telecom Lib.

Hobbs, Michael, compiled by. In Celebration of Golf. (Illus.). 224p. 1983. 19.95 (ISBN 0-684-17800-1, ScribT). Scribner.

Hobbs, Peter V. Ice Physics. (Illus.). 1975. 115.00x (ISBN 0-19-851936-2). Oxford U Pr.

Hobbs, Robert. Robert Smithson: Sculpture. LC 80-69989. (Illus.). 272p. 1981. 29.50 (ISBN 0-8014-1324-9); pap. write for info (ISBN 0-8014-9237-8). Cornell U Pr.

Hobbs, Ruth. The Christian Short Story. 11.30 (ISBN 0-686-32320-3). Rod & Staff.

Hobbs, W. Functions for Applied Calculas. (Finite Math Text Ser.). write for info. (ISBN 0-685-84474-9). J W Wills.

Hobbs, Walter C., ed. Government Regulation of Higher Education. LC 77-27442. 1978. 15.00 o.p. (ISBN 0-88410-183-5). Ballinger Pub.

--Understanding Academic Law. LC 81-48573. 1982. 7.95x (ISBN 0-87589-900-5, IA-16). Jossey-Bass.

Hobbs, William H. Exploring About the North Pole of the Winds. LC 68-55196. (Illus.). Repr. of 1930 ed. lib. bdg. 20.75x (ISBN 0-8371-0478-5, HONP). Greenwood.

Hobby, Charles R., jt. auth. see Peterson, Thurman S.

Hobby, Janice. Staying Back. (Illus.). (gr. k-6). 1982. 10.95 (ISBN 0-937404-00-4); pap. 6.95 (ISBN 0-937404-16-0). Triad Pub FL.

Hobby, William F. How to Say it Better: How to Speak in Public & Get Results. LC 82-60421. (Illus.). 150p. (Orig.). 1983. pap. 9.95 (ISBN 0-910159-01-7, 101-S). Man Pr TN.

Hobday, Peter. Saudi Arabia Today. LC 78-441. 1978. 20.00 (ISBN 0-312-69976-X). St Martin.

Hobday, Victor C. Sparks at the Grassroots: Municipal Distribution of TVA Electricity in Tennessee. LC 70-77845. (Illus.). 1969. 16.50x (ISBN 0-87049-099-0). U of Tenn Pr.

Hobe, Phyllis. Tapestries of Life. LC 74-4003. 1982. boxed 19.95 (ISBN 0-8054-5112-9); pap. 10.95 (ISBN 0-8054-5111-0). Broadman.

Hobe, Phyllis, ed. The Wonder of Comfort. LC 82-8322. (Small Wonders Ser.). (Illus.). 108p. (Orig.) 1982. pap. 4.95 (ISBN 0-664-26003-9, Pub. by Bridgebooks Pub.). Westminster.

--The Wonder of Love. LC 82-8376. (Small Wonders Ser.). (Illus.). 112p. 1982. pap. 4.95 (ISBN 0-664-26001-2, Pub. by Bridgebooks Pub). Westminster.

--The Wonder of Prayer. LC 82-8317. (Small Wonders Ser.). (Illus.). 112p. (Orig.). 1982. pap. 4.95 (ISBN 0-664-26002-0, Pub. by Bridgebooks Pub). Westminster.

Hoberman, J. Art of Coins & Their Photography. 1982. lib. bdg. 75.00 (ISBN 0-686-43399-8). S J Durst.

Hoberman, J. & Rosenbaum, Jonathan. Midnight Movies. LC 82-47526. (Illus.). 224p. 1983. 14.95 (ISBN 0-06-015052-1, HarpT); pap. 7.95i (ISBN 0-06-090990-0, CN-990). Har-Row.

Hoberman, John M. The Olympic Crisis: To Moscow & Beyond. 220p. 1984. lib. bdg. price not set (ISBN 0-89241-224-0); pap. price not set (ISBN 0-89241-225-9). Caratzas Bros.

Hoberman, Mary-Anne. The Cozy Book. LC 80-10916. (Illus.). 48p. (gr. k-3). 1982. 12.95 (ISBN 0-670-24447-3). Viking Pr.

Hobhouse, Christopher. Fox. pap. 2.25 o.p. (ISBN 0-7195-0461-9). Transatlantic.

Hobhouse, Janet. Dancing in the Dark. LC 82-18620. 225p. 1983. 12.95 (ISBN 0-394-52940-5). Random.

--Everybody Who Was Anybody: A Biography of Gertrude Stein. LC 75-10844. (Illus.). 1975. 17.50 o.p. (ISBN 0-399-11605-2). Putnam Pub Group.

Hobhouse, L. T. Liberalism. 1911. pap. text ed. 5.95x (ISBN 0-19-500332-2). Oxford U Pr.

Hobhouse, Leonard T. Liberalism. LC 80-10822. 130p. 1980. Repr. of 1911 ed. lib. bdg. 18.25x (ISBN 0-313-22332-7, HOLI). Greenwood.

Hobi, V., jt. auth. see Ladewig, D.

Hobley, Brian, jt. ed. see Milne, Gustave.

Hobman, David, ed. The Social Challenge of Aging. LC 77-26095. 1978. 22.50 (ISBN 0-312-73158-2). St Martin.

Hobsbaum, Phillip. A Reader's Guide to D. H. Lawrence. 160p. 1981. 19.95 (ISBN 0-500-14023-5); pap. 9.95 (ISBN 0-500-15017-6). Thames Hudson.

Hobsbawm, E. J., et al, eds. Peasants in History: Essays in Honour of Daniel Thorner. (Illus.). 1981. 19.95x (ISBN 0-19-561215-9). Oxford U Pr.

Hobshawn, Eric J. Age of Revolution: Seventeen Eighty-Nine to Eighteen Forty-Eight. (Photos). pap. 4.50 (ISBN 0-451-62179-4, ME2179, Ment). NAL.

Hobsley. Disorders of the Digestive System. (Physical Principles in Medicine Ser.). 192p. 1982. pap. text ed. 14.95 (ISBN 0-8391-1750-7). Univ Park.

Hobsley, M. Arbeitsdiagnose - Neue Wege der Chirurgischen Diagnose und Therapie. Seemann, Caroline, tr. from Eng. Orig. Title: Pathways in Surgical Management. 480p. (Ger.). 1981. pap. 58.75 (ISBN 3-8055-0747-X). S Karger.

Hobsley, M., jt. ed. see Hadfield, J.

Hobsley, Michael, jt. ed. see Hadfield, John.

Hobson. Stamp Collecting for Beginners. pap. 3.00 (ISBN 0-87980-148-4). Wilshire.

Hobson, Art. Physics & Human Affairs. LC 81-11407. 418p. 1982. text ed. 21.95 (ISBN 0-471-04746-5); tchrs.' ed. avail. (ISBN 0-471-09706-3). Wiley.

Hobson, Barbara, jt. auth. see Hindus, Michael S.

Hobson, Burton & Obojski, Robert. Illustrated Encyclopedia of World Coins. rev. & expanded ed. LC 81-43255. (Illus.). 528p. 1983. 19.95 (ISBN 0-385-17805-0). Doubleday.

Hobson, Burton, jt. auth. see Reinfeld, Fred.

Hobson, Burton H. Coin Collecting as a Hobby. Rev. ed. LC 81-85023. (Illus.). 192p. (gr. 6 up). 1982. 8.95 (ISBN 0-8069-6018-3); PLB 10.99 (ISBN 0-8069-6019-1). Sterling.

--Getting Started in Stamp Collecting. Rev. ed. LC 81-85029. (Illus.). 160p. (gr. 6 up). 1982. 8.95 (ISBN 0-8069-6076-0); PLB 10.99 (ISBN 0-8069-6077-9). Sterling.

Hobson, Burton H., jt. auth. see Reinfeld, Fred.

Hobson, Constance T., jt. auth. see Cazort, Jean.

Hobson, Dale. Second Growth. (Illus.). 36p. (Orig.). 1980. pap. 3.50 (ISBN 0-918092-09-4). Tamarack Edns.

Hobson, Edmund & Chave, Edith H. Hawaiian Reef Animals. LC 72-84060. (Illus.). 1979. pap. 12.95 (ISBN 0-8248-0653-0). UH Pr.

Hobson, Ernest W. Spherical & Ellipsoidal Harmonics. LC 55-233. 1955. 17.95 (ISBN 0-8284-0104-7). Chelsea Pub.

Hobson, Fred, ed. South-Watching: Selected Essays by Gerald W. Johnson. LC 82-2620. (Fred W. Morrison Ser. in Southern Studies). xxxiii, 207p. 1983. 19.00x (ISBN 0-8078-1531-4); pap. 8.95x (ISBN 0-8078-4094-7). U of NC Pr.

Hobson, G. D. Developments in Petroleum Geology, Vols. 1 & 2. Vol. 1, 1977. 74.00 (ISBN 0-85334-745-X, Pub. by Applied Sci England); Vol. 2, 1980. 74.00 (ISBN 0-85334-907-X). Elsevier.

Hobson, G. D. & Tiratsoo, E. N. Introduction to Petroleum Geology. 2nd ed. 360p. 1981. 43.50x (ISBN 0-87201-399-5). Gulf Pub.

Hobson, Grant D. Marketing Books to Consumers: Trends in Trade, Paperback, Book Club & Mail Order Publishing. 1980. spiral 750.00 (ISBN 0-686-42879-X). Knowledge Indus.

Hobson, J. Allan & Brazier, Mary A., eds. The Reticular Formation. (International Brain Research Organization Monograph: Vol. 6). 564p. 1979. text ed. 59.00 (ISBN 0-89004-379-5). Raven.

Hobson, John. The Sisgruder Conspiracy. 104p. (Orig.). 1982. pap. 5.95 (ISBN 0-86666-030-5). GWP.

Hobson, John A. Imperialism. 1965. pap. 8.95 (ISBN 0-472-06103-8, 103, AA). U of Mich Pr.

Hobson, Libby. Basic Skills Music Workbook. (Basic Skills Workbooks). 32p. (gr. 4-7). 1983. 0.99 (ISBN 0-8209-0542-9, MUW-1). ESP.

--What's Music All About? (Music Ser.). 24p. (gr. 3-6). 1977. wkbk. 5.00 (ISBN 0-8209-0272-1, MU-1). ESP.

Hobson, Marian. The Object of Art: The Theory of Illusion in 18th Century France. LC 81-17101. (Cambridge Studies in French). 275p. 1982. 49.50 (ISBN 0-521-24350-5). Cambridge U Pr.

Hobson, Mary. Poor Tom. 192p. 1982. 14.95 (ISBN 0-434-34022-7, Pub. by W Heinemann). David & Charles.

Hobson, P. N. & Robertson, A. M. Waste Treatment in Agriculture. 1977. 41.00 (ISBN 0-85334-736-0, Pub. by Applied Sci England). Elsevier.

Hobson, R. L. Chinese Pottery & Porcelain. LC 75-21139. (Illus.). 563p. 1976. pap. 11.95 (ISBN 0-486-23253-0). Dover.

Hobson, Robert L. Wares of the Ming Dynasty. LC 62-18358. (Illus.). 1962. Repr. of 1923 ed. 39.50 (ISBN 0-8048-0623-3). C E Tuttle.

Hobson, Robert W., II, ed. Venous Trauma: Pathophysiology Diagnosis & Surgery Management. LC 81-71800. (Illus.). 256p. 1983. 32.50 (ISBN 0-87993-155-8). Futura Pub.

Hobson, Sarah. Belts for All Occasions. (Illus.). 64p. (Orig.). 1976. 6.95 o.p. (ISBN 0-263-05599-X). Transatlantic.

Hobson, Wilder. American Jazz Music. LC 76-22565. (Roots of Jazz Ser.). 1976. Repr. of 1939 ed. lib. bdg. 22.50 (ISBN 0-306-70816-7). Da Capo.

Hobson, William, ed. The Theory & Practice of Public Health. 5th ed. (Illus.). 1980. text ed. 145.00x (ISBN 0-19-264227-8). Oxford U Pr.

Hobst, L. & Zajic, J. Anchoring in Rock & Soil. (Developments in Geotechinical Engineering: Vol. 33). Date not set. 100.00 (ISBN 0-444-99689-3). Elsevier.

Hobst, Leos & Zajic, Josef. Anchoring in Rock. LC 76-21716. (Developments in Geotechnical Engineering: Vol. 13). 1977. 68.00 (ISBN 0-444-99830-6). Elsevier.

Hobusch, Erich. Fair Game: A History of Hunting, Shooting & Animal Conservation. Michaelis-Jena, Ruth & Murray, Patrick, trs. from Ger. LC 80-19008. (Illus.). 280p. 1981. 29.95 o.p. (ISBN 0-668-05101-9, 5101). Arco.

Hobza, P. & Zahradnik, R. Weak Intermolecular Interactions in Chemistry & Biology. (Studies in Physical & Theoretical Chemistry: Vol. 3). 1980. 47.00 (ISBN 0-444-99785-7). Elsevier.

Hoccleve, Thomas. Selected Poems. O'Donoghue, Bernard, ed. (Fyfield Ser.). 128p. (Orig.). 1982. pap. text ed. 7.00x (ISBN 0-85635-321-3, Pub. by Carcanet New Pr England). Humanities.

Hoch. Sexology. (International Congress Ser.: Vol. 566). 1982. 98.00 (ISBN 0-444-90260-0). Elsevier.

Hoch, Edward D. Baffling Detective Cases. Duenewald, Doris, ed. LC 78-58885. (Inkpot Mini-Mysteries Ser.). (Illus.). (gr. 3-7). pap. 0.95 (ISBN 0-448-16370-5, G&D). Putnam Pub Group.

--Best Detective Stories of the Year, 1981: 35th Annual Collection. 224p. 1981. 12.50 o.p. (ISBN 0-525-06440-0, 01214-360). Dutton.

--Clues for Supersleuths. Duenewald, Doris, ed. LC 78-58884. (Inkpot Mini-Mysteries Ser.). (Illus.). (gr. 3-7). 1978. pap. 0.95 (ISBN 0-448-16369-1, G&D). Putnam Pub Group.

--The Monkey's Clue & The Stolen Sapphire. Duenewald, Doris, ed. LC 78-58882. (Inkpot Mini-Mysteries). (Illus.). (gr. 3-7). 1978. pap. 0.95 o.s.i. (ISBN 0-448-16367-5, G&D). Putnam Pub Group.

--Mysteries for Crime-Busters. Duenewald, Doris, ed. LC 78-58883. (Inkpot Mini-Mysteries Ser.). (Illus.). (gr. 3-7). 1978. pap. 0.95 (ISBN 0-448-16368-3, G&D). Putnam Pub Group.

Hoch, Elizabeth, tr. see David, Katalin.

Hoch, Elizabeth, tr. see Fulep, Ferenc.

Hoch, Elizabeth, tr. see Korner, Eva.

Hoch, Elizabeth, tr. see Szabadi, Judit.

Hochberg, B. Fibre Facts. LC 81-83115. (Illus.). 68p. (Orig.). 1981. pap. 5.95 (ISBN 0-9600990-6-9). B Hochberg.

--Handspindles. rev. ed. LC 76-62721. (Illus.). 68p. 1980. pap. 5.95 (ISBN 0-9600990-4-2). B Hochberg.

--Handspinner's Handbook. rev. ed. LC 76-12949. (Illus.). 68p. 1980. pap. 5.95 (ISBN 0-9600990-5-0). B Hochberg.

--Spin Span Spun: Fact & Folklore for Spinners. LC 79-89003. (Illus., Orig.). 1979. pap. 5.95 (ISBN 0-9600990-3-4). B Hochberg.

Hochberg, Bette. Handspindles. LC 76-62721. pap. cancelled o.p. (ISBN 0-9600990-2-6). B Hochberg.

--Handspinner's Handbook. 3rd rev. ed. LC 76-12949. 1978. 5.95 o.p. (ISBN 0-9600990-1-8). B Hochberg.

Hochberg, Gary M. Kant: Moral Legislation & Two Senses of "Will". LC 81-40396. 238p. (Orig.). 1982. lib. bdg. 22.25 (ISBN 0-8191-2121-5); pap. text ed. 10.75 (ISBN 0-8191-2122-3). U Pr of Amer.

Hochberg, Howard, jt. auth. see Lauersen, Neils H.

Hochberg, Julian. Perception. 2nd ed. LC 77-27274. (Foundations of Modern Psychology Ser.). (Illus.). 1978. pap. text ed. 14.95 (ISBN 0-13-657098-4). P-H.

Ho-chee-nee, see Burton, Jimalee.

Hochfield, Sylvia, ed. see Ferber, Linda S.

Ho Chi Minh, jt. auth. see Phan Boi Chau.

Hochman, ed. Kettridge's English-French - French-English Dictionary. 1971. pap. 3.50 (ISBN 0-451-11804-9, AE1804, Sig). NAL.

Hochman, Baruch. The Test of Character: On the Victorian Novel & the Modern. LC 81-71793. 224p. 1983. 27.50 (ISBN 0-8386-3122-3). Fairleigh Dickinson.

Hochman, Gloria. Heart Bypass: What Every Patient Must Know. 368p. 1983. pap. 7.95 (ISBN 0-345-30902-2). Ballantine.

Hochman, Janice M., jt. auth. see Steel, Catherine M.

Hochman, Sandra. Endangered Species. LC 77-6223. 1977. 8.95 o.p. (ISBN 0-399-11912-4). Putnam Pub Group.

--Jogging: A Love Story. LC 78-21236. 1979. 9.95 o.p. (ISBN 0-399-12189-7). Putnam Pub Group.

Hochman, Stanley. Yesterday & Today: A Dictionary of Recent American History. LC 79-12265. (Illus.). 407p. 1979. 29.95 (ISBN 0-07-029103-9). McGraw.

Hochman, Stanley, jt. auth. see DeVries, Louis.

Hochman, Stanley, ed. From Quasimodo to Scarlett O'Hara: A National Board of Review Anthology (1920-1940) LC 81-40463. 450p. 1982. 29.95 (ISBN 0-8044-2381-4); pap. 14.95 (ISBN 0-8044-6274-7). Ungar.

Hochmeister, Ludwig. The Failure of the United States as World Leadership Power. (Illus.). 109p. 1983. 93.75 (ISBN 0-86722-040-6). Inst Econ Pol.

Hochstadt, Harry. Differential Equations: A Modern Approach. LC 75-2569. (Illus.). 320p. 1975. pap. text ed. 6.00 (ISBN 0-486-61941-9). Dover.

Hochstein, Rolaine. Table Forty-Seven. LC 82-45570. 360p. 1983. 16.95 (ISBN 0-385-18242-2). Doubleday.

Hochstein, Rolaine, jt. auth. see Sugarman, Daniel A.

Hock, G., jt. ed. see Berenyi, D.

Hockel, Jack L. Orthopedic Gnathology. (Illus.). 480p. 1983. 160.00 (ISBN 0-86715-107-2). Quint Pub Co.

Hockelman, et al. Principles of Pediatrics: Health Care of the Young. (Illus.). 1978. text ed. 60.00 (ISBN 0-07-029178-0, HP). McGraw.

Hocken, Sheila. Emma & I. (RL 5). 1979. pap. 2.50 (ISBN 0-451-11254-7, AE1254, Sig). NAL.

Hocker, Harold W., Jr. Introduction to Forest Biology. LC 78-26878. 1979. text ed. 33.95 (ISBN 0-471-01978-X). Wiley.

Hockett, Betty & Abbott, Grace. Life Changing Learning for Children: Resources That Work. (C. E. Ministries Ser.). 1977. pap. 3.50 (ISBN 0-89367-020-0). Light & Life.

Hockett, Charles F. Course in Modern Linguistics. (Illus.). 1958. text ed. 22.95x (ISBN 0-02-355090-2). Macmillan.

Hockett, H. C. Western Influences on Political Parties to 1825. LC 75-87650. (American Scene Ser.). 1970. Repr. of 1917 ed. lib. bdg. 24.50 (ISBN 0-306-71777-8). Da Capo.

Hockett, Shirley. Barron's How to Prepare for the Advanced Placement Examination - Mathematics. rev. ed. (gr. 10-12). 1983. pap. text ed. 9.95 (ISBN 0-8120-2071-5). Barron.

--Basic Mathematics: What Every College Student Should Know. (Illus.). 1977. pap. 19.95 (ISBN 0-13-063446-8). P-H.

Hockey, Robert. Stress & Fatigue in Human Performance. (Studies in Human Performance Ser.). 400p. 1983. 45.95x (ISBN 0-471-10265-2, Pub. by Wiley-Interscience). Wiley.

Hockey, Robert V. Physical Fitness: The Pathway to Healthful Living. 4th ed. LC 80-28800. (Illus.). 151p. 1981. pap. text ed. 10.95 (ISBN 0-8016-2216-6). Mosby.

Hockin, T. Apex of Power: The Prime Minister & Political Leadership in Canada. 2nd ed. 1979. pap. 13.25 (ISBN 0-13-038653-7). P-H.

Hockin, Thomas A. Government in Canada. (Comparative Modern Government Ser.). (Illus.). 1976. 11.95x o.p. (ISBN 0-393-05532-9); pap. 5.95x (ISBN 0-393-09294-1). Norton.

Hocking, Brian, jt. auth. see Hocking, Drake.

Hocking, Carol, jt. auth. see Hocking, David L.

Hocking, David. Marrying Again: A Guide for Christians. 160p. 1983. 8.95 (ISBN 0-8007-1338-9). Revell.

Hocking, David L. & Hocking, Carol. Love & Marriage. LC 81-413. (Orig.). 1981. pap. 4.95 o.p. (ISBN 0-89081-291-8). Harvest Hse.

Hocking, Drake & Hocking, Brian. Skeletons for Life. 500p. 1982. 24.95 (ISBN 0-87073-927-1); pap. 14.95 (ISBN 0-87073-928-X). Schenkman.

Hocking, W. J. The Son of His Love. 5.25 (ISBN 0-88172-088-7). Believers Bkshelf.

Hocking, William E. Freedom of the Press. LC 77-39587. (Civil Liberties in American History Ser). 240p. 1972. Repr. of 1947 ed. lib. bdg. 29.50 (ISBN 0-306-70231-2). Da Capo.

--Man & the State. 1926. text ed. 19.50x (ISBN 0-686-83615-4). Elliots Bks.

Hocking, William G. Practical Hematology. (Family Practice Today: A Comprehensive Postgraduate Library). 355p. 1983. 35.00 (ISBN 0-471-09563-X, Pub. by Wiley Med). Wiley.

Hockley, Graham. Public Finance: An Introduction. (Illus.). 1979. 34.50x (ISBN 0-7100-0148-7); pap. 16.95 (ISBN 0-7100-0149-5). Routledge & Kegan.

Hockney, David. David Hockney. Stangos, Nikos, ed. LC 76-11721. (Illus.). 1977. 40.00 o.p. (ISBN 0-8109-1058-6). Abrams.

--David Hockney Photographs. 1982. 30.00 (ISBN 0-902825-15-1). Petersburg Pr.

Hockney, David, jt. auth. see Spender, Stephen.

Hockney, Monica. Meals in Minutes. 3.95 o.p. (ISBN 0-685-44121-0). Transatlantic.

Hockney, R. W. & Jesshope, C. R. Parallel Computers. 416p. 1981. 65.00x o.p. (ISBN 0-85274-422-6, Pub. by A Hilger). State Mutual Bk.

Hocmard, G., et al. The American Dream: Advanced Readings on the U. S. A. (English As a Second Language Bk.). 1982. pap. text ed. 5.95 (ISBN 0-582-79799-3). Longman.

Hocquenghem, Guy. Homosexual Desire. Dangoor, Daniella, tr. from Fr. 144p. 1980. 9.95x (ISBN 0-8052-8025-1, Pub. by Allison & Busby England); pap. 5.95 (ISBN 0-8052-8024-3, Pub. by Allison & Busby England). Schocken.

Hocutt, Charles H. & Stauffer, Jay R., Jr., eds. Biological Monitoring of Fish. LC 79-3049. 432p. 1980. 34.95x (ISBN 0-669-03309-X). Lexington Bks.

Hodder, B. K. & Lee, R. K. Economic Geography. LC 74-77770. (Field of Geography Ser.). 224p. 1974. 12.95x o.p. (ISBN 0-312-23310-8). St Martin.

Hodder, Ian. The Present Past: An Introduction to Anthropology for Archaeologists. LC 82-17437. (Illus.). 240p. 1983. text ed. 22.50x (ISBN 0-87663-736-5). Universe.

Hodder, Ian & Orton, C. Spatial Analysis in Archaeology. LC 75-44582. (New Studies in Archaeology Ser.). (Illus.). 1976. 37.50x (ISBN 0-521-21080-1). Cambridge U Pr.

--Spatial Analysis in Archaeology. LC 75-44582. (New Studies in Archaeology). (Illus.). 260p. 1980. pap. 15.95 (ISBN 0-521-29738-9). Cambridge U Pr.

Hodder, Ian, ed. Simulation Studies. LC 78-51670. (Illus.). 1979. 27.95 (ISBN 0-521-22025-4). Cambridge U Pr.

--Symbolic & Structural Archaeology. LC 81-17992. (New Directions in Archaeology Ser.). (Illus.). 250p. 1982. 39.50 (ISBN 0-521-24406-4). Cambridge U Pr.

Hodder, Ian, et al, eds. Pattern of the Past. LC 79-8497. (Illus.). 424p. 1981. 54.50 (ISBN 0-521-22763-1). Cambridge U Pr.

Hodder-Williams, Richard. Politics of U. S. Supreme Court. 224p. (Orig.). 1980. text ed. 22.50x (ISBN 0-04-328010-2); pap. text ed. 8.95x (ISBN 0-04-328011-0). Allen Unwin.

--Public Opinion Polls & British Politics. 1970. 15.00 o.p. (ISBN 0-7100-6934-0). Routledge & Kegan.

Hodeir, Andre. Jazz: Its Evolution & Essence. Noakes, David, tr. from Fr. LC 74-23387. (Roots of Jazz Ser). ix, 295p. 1975. Repr. of 1956 ed. lib. bdg. 27.50 (ISBN 0-306-70682-2). Da Capo.

--Since Debussy: A View of Contemporary Music. Burch, Noel, tr. LC 74-28310. (Illus.). 256p. 1975. Repr. of 1961 ed. lib. bdg. 25.00 (ISBN 0-306-70662-8). Da Capo.

--Toward Jazz. LC 76-7568. (The Roots of Jazz Ser.). 1976. Repr. of 1962 ed. lib. bdg. 22.50 (ISBN 0-306-70810-8). Da Capo.

Hodenc, Raoul de. Le Roman des Eles. 120p. 1982. 26.00 (ISBN 90-272-2192-8); pap. 16.00 (ISBN 90-272-2202-9). Benjamins North Am.

Hodes, Barnet & Roberson, G. Gale. The Law of Mobile Homes. 3rd ed. LC 73-92292. 952p. 1974. 25.00 (ISBN 0-87179-195-1). BNA.

Hodes, Bernard S. The Principles & Practice of Recruitment Advertising. LC 82-71746. 344p. 1982. 29.95 (ISBN 0-8119-0453-9). Fell.

Hodgart, Matthew. James Joyce: A Student's Guide. 1978. 18.00x (ISBN 0-7100-8817-5); pap. 7.95 (ISBN 0-7100-8943-0). Routledge & Kegan.

Hodge. The Queen Mother. 3.98 o.p. (ISBN 0-517-30812-6). Crown.

Hodge, A. A. Evangelical Theology. 1976. pap. 5.95 (ISBN 0-85151-236-4). Banner of Truth.

Hodge, Bartow. Computers for Engineers: Introduction to Computing Machines & Programming. (Illus.). 1969. 26.50 o.p. (ISBN 0-07-029119-5, P&RB). McGraw.

Hodge, Ben, Sr. Good Times with Football. LC 77-81703. (Illus.). 20p. (Span. & Eng.). (gr. 3-4). 1976. 4.50 (ISBN 0-912122-11-0); pap. 1.89 (ISBN 0-912122-12-9); Eng. flash cards 3.50 (ISBN 0-912122-25-0); Span. flash cards 3.50 (ISBN 0-912122-26-9). Football Hobbies.

Hodge, Billy J. & Johnson, Herbert J. Management & Organizational Behavior: A Multidimensional Approach. LC 79-26856. (Management & Administration Ser.). 552p. 1981. Repr. of 1970 ed. lib. bdg. 23.50 (ISBN 0-89874-086-X). Krieger.

Hodge, Charles. Commentary on the Epistle to the Ephesians. (Thornapple Commentaries Ser.). 1980. pap. 8.95 (ISBN 0-8010-4221-6). Baker Bk.

--Princeton Sermons. 1979. 12.95 (ISBN 0-85151-285-2). Banner of Truth.

Hodge, Charles B., Jr. Getting Involved with Jesus. LC 78-140289. (Twentieth Century Sermons Ser.). 1970. 11.95 o.p. (ISBN 0-89112-304-0). Bibl Res Pr.

Hodge, Gene M. Four Winds, Poems from Indian Rituals. LC 77-17800. 1979. pap. 4.25 (ISBN 0-913270-07-5). Sunstone Pr.

--The Kachinas Are Coming. Smith, James C., Jr., ed. (Illus.). 130p. 1983. 55.00 (ISBN 0-86534-002-1); pap. 19.95 (ISBN 0-86534-003-X). Sunstone Pr.

Hodge, Ian & Whitby, Martin. Rural Employment: Trends, Options, Choices. 272p. 1981. 33.00x (ISBN 0-416-73080-9). Methuen Inc.

Hodge, Jane A. Judas Flowering. LC 76-9768. 354p. 1976. 9.95 o.p. (ISBN 0-698-10741-1, Coward). Putnam Pub Group.

--Last Act. LC 79-10663. 1979. 8.95 (ISBN 0-698-10988-0, Coward). Putnam Pub Group.

--The Lost Garden. 320p. 1982. 13.95 (ISBN 0-698-11188-5, Coward). Putnam Pub Group.

--One Way to Venice. LC 74-79683. 1975. 7.95 o.p. (ISBN 0-698-10615-6, Coward). Putnam Pub Group.

--Red Sky at Night--Lover's Delight? 1977. 8.95 (ISBN 0-698-10841-8, Coward). Putnam Pub Group.

--Strangers in Company. 1973. 6.95 (ISBN 0-698-10499-4, Coward). Putnam Pub Group.

--Wide Is the Water. 1981. 12.95 (ISBN 0-698-11080-3, Coward). Putnam Pub Group.

Hodge, M. J., jt. auth. see Cantor, G. N.

Hodge, Marshall Bryant. Your Fear of Love. LC 67-15960. 1969. pap. 2.50 o.p. (ISBN 0-385-04372-4, C483, Dolp). Doubleday.

Hodge, P. W. Concepts of Contemporary Astronomy. 2nd ed. 1979. 23.95 (ISBN 0-07-029147-0). McGraw.

Hodge, Paul W. Concepts of the Universe. LC 69-18715. 1969. text ed. 14.95 o.p. (ISBN 0-07-029132-2, C); pap. text ed. 8.50 o.p. (ISBN 0-07-029130-6). McGraw.

Hodge, Peter. Aspects of Roman Life: Folder 1. (Illus.). 1977. folder 13.50x (ISBN 0-582-31416-X). Longman.

--The Roman Army. (Aspects of Roman Life Ser.). (Illus.). 48p. (Orig.). (gr. 7-12). 1977. pap. text ed. 3.50 (ISBN 0-582-31414-3). Longman.

--Roman Family Life. (Aspects of Roman Life Ser.). 64p. (Orig.). (gr. 7-12). 1974. pap. text ed. 3.50 (ISBN 0-582-31411-9). Longman.

--Roman House. (Aspects of Roman Life Ser.). (Illus.). 1976. pap. text ed. 2.95x o.p. Longman.

--Roman House. (Aspects of Roman Life Ser.). (Illus.). 64p. (Orig.). (gr. 7-12). 1971. pap. text ed. 3.50 (ISBN 0-582-20300-7). Longman.

--Roman Towns. (Aspects of Roman Life Ser.). (Illus.). 48p. (Orig.). (gr. 7-12). 1977. pap. text ed. 3.50 (ISBN 0-582-20301-5). Longman.

--Roman Trade & Travel. (Aspects of Roman Life Ser.). (Illus.). 48p. (Orig.). (gr. 7-12). 1978. pap. text ed. 3.50 (ISBN 0-582-31413-5). Longman.

Hodge, Peter, ed. see Buchanan, David.

Hodge, Peter, ed. see Green, Miranda.

Hodge, Peter, ed. see Massey, Michael.

Hodge, Philip G. Plastic Analysis of Structures. 1959. text ed. 19.00 o.p. (ISBN 0-07-029129-2, C). McGraw.

Hodge, R. V., ed. see Milton, John.

Hodgell, P. C. God Stalk. LC 82-1672. 228p. 1982. 13.95 (ISBN 0-689-30844-2, Argo). Atheneum.

Hodges see Andrews, M. E.

Hodges, C. Walter. The Namesake: A Story of King Alfred. (Illus.). (gr. 5-7). 1964. 6.95 o.p. (ISBN 0-698-20098-5, Coward). Putnam Pub Group.

--The Norman Conquest: Story of Britain. (Illus.). (gr. 3-7). 1966. PLB 4.99 o.p. (ISBN 0-698-30260-5, Coward). Putnam Pub Group.

--Plain Lane Christmas. LC 77-17233. (Illus.). (gr. 6-8). 1978. 8.50 o.p. (ISBN 0-698-20454-9, Coward). Putnam Pub Group.

--Playhouse Tales. LC 74-94147. (Illus.). 198p. (gr. 6-12). 1975. 7.95 o.p. (ISBN 0-698-20268-6, Coward). Putnam Pub Group.

--The Puritan Revolution: Story of Britain. (Illus.). 32p. (gr. 4-7). 1972. PLB 4.99 o.p. (ISBN 0-698-30426-8, Coward). Putnam Pub Group.

--Shakespeare & the Players. rev. ed. LC 70-118119. (Illus.). (gr. 7-12). 1970. 4.20e o.p. (ISBN 0-698-20126-4, Coward). Putnam Pub Group.

--Shakespeare's Theatre. (Illus.). 104p. (gr. 6-8). 1980. pap. 5.95 (ISBN 0-698-20511-1, Coward). Putnam Pub Group.

--Shakespeare's Theatre. (Illus.). (gr. 5-7). 1964. 7.50e o.p. (ISBN 0-698-20127-2, Coward). Putnam Pub Group.

Hodges, C. Walter, et al, eds. see Reconstruction of the Globe Playhouse Symposium.

Hodges, D. R., ed. Recent Analytical Developments in the Petroleum Industry. LC 74-23137. 337p. 1974. 64.95 o.s.i. (ISBN 0-470-40208-3). Halsted Pr.

Hodges, David A. & Jackson, Horace G. Analysis & Design of Digital Integrated Circuits. (Series in Electrical Engineering). (Illus.). 448p. 1983. 29.50x (ISBN 0-07-029153-5, C); text ed. 15.00 (ISBN 0-07-029154-3). McGraw.

Hodges, Donald & Gandy, Ross. Mexico Nineteen Ten - Nineteen Seventy Six: Reform or Revolution? 240p. (Orig.). 1980. 30.00 (ISBN 0-905762-46-0, Pub. by Zed Pr England); pap. 6.95 o.s.i. (ISBN 0-905762-47-9). Lawrence Hill.

Hodges, Donald C., jt. ed. see Fann, K. T.

Hodges, Hollis. Don't Tell Me Your Name. 192p. 1981. pap. 2.25 o.p. (ISBN 0-380-53751-6, 53751). Avon.

--Don't Tell Me Your Name. 1978. 8.95 o.p. (ISBN 0-517-53472-X). Crown.

--Why Would I Lie? 1978. pap. 2.25 o.p. (ISBN 0-380-01918-3, 50732). Avon.

Hodges, J. L., et al. Statlab. new ed. (Illus.). 384p. 1975. text ed. 27.50 (ISBN 0-07-029134-9, C); instructor's manual 15.00 (ISBN 0-07-029135-7). McGraw.

Hodges, J. L., Jr. & Lehmann, E. L. Basic Concepts of Probability & Statistics. rev. ed. 2nd ed. LC 72-104973. 1970. text ed. 21.95x (ISBN 0-8162-4004-3); ans. bk. 6.00x (ISBN 0-8162-4024-8). Holden-Day.

Hodges, L. K. The Reduction of Gold & Silver Ore. (Prospecting Ser.). 24p. Repr. of 1897 ed. pap. 2.95 (ISBN 0-8466-1993-8, SJS134D). Shorey.

Hodges, Lewis H. Building Antique Doll House Furniture from Scratch. (Orig.). 1980. 14.95 (ISBN 0-8306-9946-5); pap. 9.95 o.p. (ISBN 0-8306-1240-8, 1240). TAB Bks.

--Sixty-Six Weekend Wood Furniture Projects. (Illus.). 1977. 10.95 o.p. (ISBN 0-8306-7974-X); pap. 6.95 o.p. (ISBN 0-8306-6974-4, 974). TAB Bks.

Hodges, Mary Ann. Oral Reading. (Language Arts Ser.). 24p. (gr. 5-8). 1977. wkbk. 5.00 (ISBN 0-8209-0323-X, LA-9). ESP.

Hodges, Norman E. Breaking the Chains of Bondage. (gr. 9-12). pap. 4.50 o.p. (ISBN 0-671-18702-3). Monarch Pr.

Hodges, R. E. & Rudorf, E. Hugh. Language & Learning to Read: What Teachers Should Know About Language. LC 70-175170. 1972. pap. text ed. 14.95 (ISBN 0-395-12639-8). HM.

Hodges, Richard. The Hamwih Pottery: The Local & Improved Wares from 30 Years Excavations at Middle Saxon South Hampton & Their European Context. (CBA Research Reports Ser.: No. 37). 112p. 1981. pap. text ed. 37.50x (ISBN 0-900312-99-8, Pub. by Coun Brit Archaeology). Humanities.

Hodges, Richard E. Improving Spelling & Vocabulary in the Secondary School. (Theory & Research into Practice Ser.). (Orig.). 1982. pap. 4.00 (ISBN 0-8141-4662-7). NCTE.

Hodges, Richard E., jt. auth. see Hanna, Paul R.

Hodges, Tony. Western Sahara: Polisario's War for Independence. 320p. (Orig.). 1983. 18.95 (ISBN 0-88208-151-9); pap. 9.95 (ISBN 0-88208-152-7). Lawrence Hill.

Hodges, Wayne L., ed. see Kheel, Theodore W., et al.

Hodges, Wilfred. Logic. 1980. 4.95 (ISBN 0-14-021985-4, Pelican). Penguin.

Hodges, William F., jt. ed. see Cooper, Saul.

Hodges, William S., jt. auth. see Orwig, Gary W.

Hodges, Zane C. The Gospel Under Siege: A Study on Faith & Works. 125p. (Orig.). 1981. pap. 4.95 (ISBN 0-9607576-0-0). Redencion Viva.

Hodgett, Gerald A. A Social & Economic History of Medieval Europe. 1974. pap. 3.45xi o.p. (ISBN 0-06-131765-9, TB1765, Torch). Har-Row.

Hodgett, Gerald A. J. The Cartulary of Holy Trinity Aldgate. 1971. 50.00x (ISBN 0-686-96613-9, Pub by London Rec Soc England). State Mutual Bk.

Hodgetts, D. Combustion Processes in the Spark Ignition Engine. 1966. inquire for price o.p. (ISBN 0-08-011909-3). Pergamon.

Hodgetts, J. E. & Dwivedi, O. P. Provincial Governments As Employers: A Survey of Public Personnel Administration in Canada's Provinces. (Canadian Public Administration Ser.). 224p. 1974. 13.50 o.p. (ISBN 0-7735-0224-6); pap. 6.95 (ISBN 0-7735-0234-3). McGill-Queens U Pr.

Hodgetts, R. & Smart, T. Essentials of Economics & Free Enterprise. (gr. 9-12). 1982. pap. text ed. 19.60 (ISBN 0-201-03958-3); manual 21.20 (ISBN 0-201-03959-1). A-W.

--Fundamentals of the American Free Enterprise System. (gr. 11-12). 1978. pap. text ed. 16.00 (ISBN 0-201-02771-2, Sch Div); tchr's manual 8.08 (ISBN 0-201-02772-0). A-W.

Hodgetts, Richard M. Effective Small Business Management. 1981. 19.25 (ISBN 0-12-351050-3); study guide 6.50 (ISBN 0-12-351051-1); instr's manual 2.50 (ISBN 0-12-351052-X). Acad Pr.

--Introduction to Business. 2nd ed. LC 80-21284. (Business Ser.). (Illus.). 600p. 1981. text ed. 21.95 (ISBN 0-201-03894-3); instr's manual 9.95 (ISBN 0-201-03895-1); study guide 7.95 (ISBN 0-201-03896-X). A-W.

Hodgetts, Richard M. & Wortman, Max S. Administrative Policy: Text & Cases in Strategic Management. 2nd ed. LC 78-24528. (Management Ser.). 712p. 1979. text ed. 30.95 (ISBN 0-471-03605-6); case notes avail. (ISBN 0-471-05041-5). Wiley.

--Administrative Policy: Text & Cases in the Policy Science. 2nd ed. 712p. 1980. text ed. 30.95; suppl. materials avail. (ISBN 0-471-40216-8). Wiley.

Hodgins, Bruce W., et al, eds. Federalism in Canada & Australia: The Early Years. 318p. 1978. text ed. 13.75 o.p. (ISBN 0-88920-061-0, Pub. by Wilfrid Laurier U Pr Canada). Humanities.

Hodgkin. The Conduction of the Nervous Impulse. 108p. 1982. 50.00x (ISBN 0-85323-061-7, Pub. by Liverpool Univ England). State Mutual Bk.

Hodgkin, Alan, et al. The Pursuit of Nature. LC 76-58844. (Illus.). 1979. pap. 9.95 (ISBN 0-521-29617-X). Cambridge U Pr.

Hodgkin, Thomas. Vietnam: The Revolutionary Path. 1980. 30.00 (ISBN 0-312-84588-X). St Martin.

Hodgkins, John, jt. auth. see Love, John.

Hodgkins, John B. Thomas A. Edison & Major Frank McLaughlin: Their Quest for Gold in Butte County. (ANCRR Research Paper: No. 5). 1979. 6.00 (ISBN 0-686-38937-9). Assn NC Records.

Hodgkinson, Christopher. Towards a Philosophy of Administration. LC 78-676. 1978. 25.00 (ISBN 0-312-81036-9). St Martin.

Hodgkiss, Alan G., jt. auth. see Clarke, Colin G.

Hodgman, Ann. True Tiny Tales of Terror. (Illus.). 1982. 4.95 (ISBN 0-399-50631-4, Perige). Putnam Pub Group.

Hodgson, ed. Reviews in Biochemistry Toxicology, Vol. 4. 1982. 37.50 (ISBN 0-444-00685-0). Elsevier.

Hodgson, E. & Bend, J. R., eds. Biochemical Toxicology, No. 4. 288p. 1982. 37.50 (ISBN 0-444-00436-X, Biomedical Pr). Elsevier.

Hodgson, E., et al, eds. Reviews in Biochemical Toxicology, Vol. 3. 1981. 54.95 (ISBN 0-444-00436-X). Elsevier.

Hodgson, Godfrey. All Things to All Men: The False Promise of the Modern American Presidency from F.D.R. to Ronald Reagan. 1981. pap. 7.75 (ISBN 0-671-43165-X, Touchstone Bks). S&S.

--America in Our Time: From World War II to Nixon--What Happened & Why. 1978. pap. 6.95 (ISBN 0-394-72517-4, Vin). Random.

Hodgson, J. T. & Eade, D., eds. Information Systems in Public Administration: Their Role in Economics & Social Development. 1981. 49.00 (ISBN 0-444-86275-7). Elsevier.

Hodgson, John H. Earthquakes & Earth Structure. (Illus.). 1964. text ed. 12.95 (ISBN 0-13-222455-0). P-H.

Hodgson, John H., tr. see Nousiainen, Jaakko.

Hodgson, John S. & Herander, Mark G. International Economic Relations. (Illus.). 496p. 1982. text ed. 24.95 (ISBN 0-13-472753-3). P-H.

Hodgson, Marshall G. The Venture of Islam, 3 vols. Incl. Vol. 1. The Classical Age of Islam. pap. 12.50 (ISBN 0-226-34683-8, P716); Vol. 2. The Expansion of Islam in the Middle Period. pap. 12.50 (ISBN 0-226-34684-6, P717); Vol. 3. The Gunpowder Empire & Modern Times. pap. 9.50 (ISBN 0-226-34685-4, P718). LC 73-87243. (Illus.). 1977 (Phoen). U of Chicago Pr.

Hodgson, Moira. The Hot & Spicy Cookbook. LC 76-52464. (Illus.). 208p. 1981. pap. 6.95 (ISBN 0-448-11989-7, G&D). Putnam Pub Group.

Hodgson, Pat. Home Life. (History in Focus Ser.). (Illus.). 72p. (gr. 7-12). 1982. 14.95 (ISBN 0-7134-4451-7, Pub by Batsford England). David & Charles.

Hodgson, R., jt. auth. see Rachman, S.

Hodgson, Ray & Miller, Peter. Self-Watching: Addictions, Habits, Compulsions: What to do About Them. 1983. 17.95 (ISBN 0-87196-726-X). Facts on File.

Hodgson, William H. The House on the Borderland. LC 75-28857. (Classics of Science Fiction Ser.). xii, 300p. 1976. 21.50 (ISBN 0-88355-371-6); pap. 4.95 (ISBN 0-88355-456-9). Hyperion Conn.

Hodgson, William R. & Skinner, Paul. Hearing Aid Assessment & Use in Audiologic Rehabilitation. 2nd ed. (Illus.). 343p. 1981. 34.00 (ISBN 0-683-04092-8). Williams & Wilkins.

Hodkinson, Ken. Missing Links. (Puzzlebacks Ser.). (Illus.). 64p. (Orig.). (gr. 3-7). 1982. pap. 2.50 (ISBN 0-671-44202-3). Wanderer Bks.

--Word Salad. (Puzzleback Ser.). (Illus.). 64p. (Orig.). (gr. 3-7). 1981. pap. 1.95 o.p. (ISBN 0-671-43357-1). Wanderer Bks.

Hodl, Guenther, jt. ed. see Boehm, Eric H.

Hodl, Gunther & Boehm, Eric, eds. Austrian Historical Bibliography: Annual, 7 vols. LC 68-19156. 1968. 37.75 ea. o.p.; 1965 o.p. (ISBN 0-87436-056-0); 1966 o.p. (ISBN 0-87436-067-6); 1967 o.p. (ISBN 0-87436-100-1); 1968 o.p. (ISBN 0-87436-102-8); 1969 o.p. (ISBN 0-87436-104-4); 1970 o.p. (ISBN 0-87439-106-7); 1971 o.p. (ISBN 0-87436-108-7). ABC-Clio.

Hodlering, Michael F., et al, eds. Arbitration & the Law, 1982. (Arbitration & the Law Ser.). 472p. (Orig.). 1983. text ed. 75.00 (ISBN 0-686-37920-9). Am Arbitration.

Hodnett, Edward. Francis Barlow: First Master of English Book Illustration. LC 76-55570. 1978. 55.00x (ISBN 0-520-03409-0). U of Cal Pr.

Hodnett, Grey. Leadership in Soviet National Republics. 409p. (Orig.). 1978. pap. text ed. 45.00x (ISBN 0-686-61282-5, Pub. by K G Saur). Gale.

Hodson, Barbara W. The Assessment of Phonological Processes. (Illus.). 52p. pap. text ed. 24.95x (ISBN 0-8134-2123-3). Interstate.

Hodson, C. John & Kincaid-Smith, Priscilla, eds. Reflux Nephropathy. LC 79-84477. (Illus.). 366p. 1979. text ed. 50.00x (ISBN 0-89352-044-6). Masson Pub.

Hodson, Geoffrey. Supreme Splendour. 1969. 2.25 o.p. (ISBN 0-8356-7296-4). Theos Pub Hse.

Hodson, H. V., ed. The Annual Register of World Events' 1976. 1977. 37.50 o.p. (ISBN 0-312-04166-7). St Martin.

--Annual Register, 1980: A Record of World Events. (Illus.). 550p. 1981. 75.00x (ISBN 0-8103-2026-6, Pub. by Longman). Gale.

--Annual Register 1981. 600p. 1982. 75.00x (ISBN 0-8103-2029-0, Pub. by Longman). Gale.

--The International Foundation Directory. 2nd ed. LC 73-90303. 1980. 74.00x (ISBN 0-8103-2018-5, Europa Publication). Gale.

Hodson, H. V. & Engel, M., eds. The Business Who's Who, 1974-5. LC 73-91903. 30.00x (ISBN 0-900537-21-3, H-316, Dist. by Hippocrene Books Inc.). Leviathan Hse.

Hodson, Henry V., ed. International Foundation Directory. 2nd ed. LC 73-90303. 378p. 1979. 65.00 (ISBN 0-905118-41-3). Intl Pubns Serv.

Hodson, Paul, jt. auth. see Purkis, Andrew.

Hoe, Susanna. God Save the Tsar. LC 77-15924. 1978. 8.95 o.p. (ISBN 0-312-33032-4). St Martin.

Hoebel, E. A. Political Organizations and Law-Ways of the Comanche Indians. LC 42-13539. 1940. 13.00 (ISBN 0-527-00553-3). Kraus Repr.

Hoebel, E. Adamson & Weaver, Thomas. Anthropology & the Human Experience. 5th ed. (Illus.). 1979. text ed. 28.95 (ISBN 0-07-029140-3, C); instr's manual 13.95 (ISBN 0-07-029141-1). McGraw.

Hoebel, Edward A. Anthropology: The Study of Man. 4th ed. (Illus.). 672p. 1972. text ed. 15.95 o.p. (ISBN 0-07-029137-3, C); 3.95 o.p. (ISBN 0-07-022561-3); study guide 6.95 o.p. (ISBN 0-07-022560-5). McGraw.

Hoebel, Edward A. & Frost, E. L. Cultural & Social Anthropology. new ed. (Illus.). 1975. pap. text ed. 26.95 (ISBN 0-07-029145-4, C); instr's manual 7.95 (ISBN 0-07-022517-6). McGraw.

Hoeber, Amoretta M. The Chemistry of Defeat: Asymmetries in U. S. & Soviet Chemical Warfare Postures. LC 81-84989. (Special Report Ser.). 94p. 1981. 6.50 (ISBN 0-89549-037-4). Inst Foreign Policy Anal.

Hoeber, Daniel R. & Kasden, Lawrence N. Basic Writing: Essays for Teachers, Researchers, & Administrators. LC 80-14634. 185p. (Orig.). 1980. pap. 9.50 o.p. (ISBN 0-8141-0268-9); pap. 7.75 members o.p. (ISBN 0-686-86381-X). NCTE.

Hoeber, Francis P. Military Applications of Modeling Selected Case Studies. Leibholz, Stephhen W., ed. (Military Operations Research Ser.: Vol. 1). 240p. 1981. 65.00 (ISBN 0-677-05840-3); pap. text ed. 25.00 o.p. (ISBN 0-686-79105-3). Gordon.

Hoeber, R. C., et al. Contemporary Business Law. 2nd ed. 1982. 26.95x (ISBN 0-07-029165-9). McGraw.

Hoeber, Ralph, et al. Contemporary Business Law: Principles & Cases. Severance, Gordon, ed. (Illus.). 1980. text ed. 23.95 (ISBN 0-07-029160-8); instr's manual 25.00 (ISBN 0-07-029161-6); test bank 19.00 (ISBN 0-07-029163-2); study guide 8.95 (ISBN 0-07-029162-4); student CPA examination suppl. 3.50 (ISBN 0-07-029164-0). McGraw.

Hoeber, Thomas R., ed. California Journal Almanac of State Government & Politics, 1983-1984. (Biennial Ser.). (Illus.). 184p. (Orig.). 1983. pap. 4.95 (ISBN 0-930302-52-4). Cal Journal.

Hoeck, Mary C., tr. see Cocteau, Jean.

Hoefer, Hans. Mexico: Insight Guide. (Illus.). 384p. 1982. pap. 17.50 (ISBN 9971-925-12-5). Lee Pubs Group.

--Nepal. (Illus.). 368p. 1982. pap. 17.50 (ISBN 9971-925-10-9). Lee Pubs Group.

Hoeffken, Walther & Lanyi, Marton. Mammography. Rigler, Leo G., tr. LC 76-20936. (Illus.). 1977. text ed. 20.00 (ISBN 0-7216-4707-3). Saunders.

Hoeft, Robert D. Exhibits at a Retirement Home. 1983. pap. 2.95 (ISBN 0-939736-40-3). Wings ME.

--Tools. (Illus.). 48p. 1982. 18.00 (ISBN 0-88014-043-7). Mosaic Pr OH.

Hoeft, William G. Visual Aid for the Illinois Test of Psycholinguistic Abilities. 1972. text ed. 2.00x (ISBN 0-8134-1597-7). Interstate.

Hoegner, W. & Richter, N. Isophotometric Atlas of Comets, 2 pts. (Illus.). 1979. Pt. 1. 62.60 (ISBN 0-387-09171-8); Pt. 2. 52.00 (ISBN 0-387-09172-6). Springer-Verlag.

Hoeh, James A., Jr., jt. auth. see Lipham, James M.

Hoehling, A. A. After the Guns Fell Silent: The Appomattox Legacy. (Illus.). Date not set. write for info. (ISBN 0-498-02544-6). A S Barnes.

Hoehn, Matthew, ed. Catholic Authors: Contemporary Biographical Sketches, 1930-1947. 800p. 1981. Repr. of 1947 ed. 67.00x (ISBN 0-8103-4314-2). Gale.

Hoehnel, F. Fragmente Zur Mykologie, 2vols. 1966. 120.00 (ISBN 3-7682-0467-7). Lubrecht & Cramer.

Hoehner, Harold W. Chronological Aspects of the Life of Christ. 1976. pap. text ed. 5.95 (ISBN 0-310-26211-9). Zondervan.

Hoek, E. & Bray, J. W. Rock Slope Engineering. 3rd ed. 360p. 1981. pap. text ed. 43.25x (ISBN 0-900488-57-3). IMM North Am.

Hoek, E. & Brown, E. T. Underground Excavations in Rock. 532p. 1980. text ed. 69.00x (ISBN 0-900488-54-9); pap. text ed. 43.25x (ISBN 0-900488-55-7). IMM North Am.

Hoek, E. & Imperial College of Science & Technology, Rock Mechanics Section. KWIC Index of Rock Mechanics Literature: Pt. 1, 1870-1968. 1977. text ed. 175.00 (ISBN 0-08-022063-0). Pergamon.

Hoek, John H. Your Government & You: Simplified American Government. 1981. pap. 2.75 (ISBN 0-88323-124-7, 212); tchr's guide 1.00x (ISBN 0-88323-125-5, 213). Richards Pub.

Hoek Den, Van see Van den Hoek, C.

Hoekelman, R. A. Principles of Pediatrics Patient Management Cases Pre-Test Self-Assessment. 1981. 33.95 (ISBN 0-07-051653-7). McGraw.

Hoekema, Thomas, tr. see Fraire, Isabel.

Hoeks, Arnold P., jt. auth. see Reneman, Robert S.

Hoeksema, Herman. Wonder of Grace. LC 81-85197. 1982. pap. 3.95 (ISBN 0-8254-2847-5). Kregel.

Hoeksema, Thomas, tr. see Fraire, Isabel.

Hoekstra, Teun, et al. Lexical Grammer. 350p. 1981. 37.20x (ISBN 0-686-32123-5); pap. 21.35x (ISBN 90-70176-16-5). Foris Pubns.

Hoel, Donna, ed. see Madden, Mary J.

Hoel, L., jt. auth. see Gray, G.

Hoel, Paul, et al. Introduction to Probability Theory. LC 74-136173. 1971. text ed. 24.95 o.p. (ISBN 0-395-04636-X, 3-25650). HM.

--Introduction to Statistical Theory. LC 70-136172. 1971. text ed. 24.95 o.p. (ISBN 0-395-04637-8, 3-25652). HM.

--Introduction to Stochastic Processes. LC 79-105035. (Illus.). 1972. text ed. 25.95 (ISBN 0-395-12076-4). HM.

Hoel, Paul G. Elementary Statistics. 4th ed. LC 75-33400. (Probability & Mathematical Statistics Ser). 400p. (Arabic Translation available). 1976. text ed. 24.95 (ISBN 0-471-40302-4); solutions manual 3.00 (ISBN 0-471-40269-9); wkbk. 10.95. (ISBN 0-471-01613-6). Wiley.

--Finite Mathematics & Calculus with Applications to Business. LC 73-19505. 464p. 1974. text ed. 25.95 (ISBN 0-471-40430-6); tchrs.' manual 8.50 (ISBN 0-471-40432-2). Wiley.

--Introduction to Mathematical Statistics. 4th ed. LC 70-139277. (Ser. in Probability & Mathematical Statistics). 1971. text ed. 29.95 (ISBN 0-471-40365-2). Wiley.

Hoel, Paul G. & Jessen, Raymond J. Basic Statistics for Business & Economics. 2nd ed. LC 76-54504. (Management & Administration Ser.). 1977. 23.95x o.p. (ISBN 0-471-40268-0); study guide 10.95x o.p. (ISBN 0-471-01697-7). Wiley.

Hoel, Robert F. Marketing Now! 1973. pap. 8.95x (ISBN 0-673-07875-2). Scott F.

Hoeldtke, Clyde, jt. auth. see Richards, Lawrence O.

Hoeller, Stephen. The Gnostic Jung & the Seven Sermons to the Dead. LC 82-50220. 282p. (Orig.). 1982. 13.95 (ISBN 0-8356-0573-6, Quest); pap. 7.50 (ISBN 0-8356-0568-X). Theos Pub Hse.

Hoelscher, R. P., et al. Graphics for Engineers: Visualizations, Communication & Design. LC 67-29722. 1968. text ed. 36.95 (ISBN 0-471-40558-2); tchr's manual avail. (ISBN 0-471-40563-9). Wiley.

Hoelscher, Russ Von see Sterne, George & Von Hoelscher, Russ.

Hoelscher, Russ von see Von Hoelscher, Russ.

Hoemann, Harry & Lucafo, Rosemarie. Sign Language Flash Cards. (Vol. II). 500p. 1983. pap. text ed. 13.95x (ISBN 0-913072-52-4). Natl Assn Deaf.

Hoenig, J., tr. see Jaspers, Karl.

Hoenig, Stuart A. & Scott, Daphne H. Medical Instrumentation & Electrical Safety: The View from the Nursing Station. LC 77-5878. 1977. 24.95 (ISBN 0-471-40566-3, Pub. by Wiley Medical). Wiley.

Hoeniger, F. D., ed. see Shakespeare, William.

Hoepfner, R., jt. auth. see Guilford, Joy P.

Hoeprich, Paul D., et al, eds. Infectious Diseases: A Modern Treatise of Infectious Processes. 3rd ed. (Illus.). 1409p. 1983. text ed. 75.00 (ISBN 0-06-141197-3, Harper Medical). Lippincott.

Hoequist, Charles, Jr., jt. ed. see Urdang, Lawrence.

Hoercker, Bernard L. & Stadtman, Earl R., eds. Current Topics in Cellular Regulation, 016 vols. Incl. Vol. 1. 1969. 47.00 (ISBN 0-12-152801-4); Vol. 2. 1970. 47.00 (ISBN 0-12-152802-2); Vol. 3. 1971. 47.00 (ISBN 0-12-152803-0); Vol. 4. 1971. 47.00 (ISBN 0-12-152804-9); Vol. 5. 1972. 47.00 (ISBN 0-12-152805-7); Vol. 6. 1973. 47.00 (ISBN 0-12-152806-5); Vol. 7. 1973. 43.00 (ISBN 0-12-152807-3); Vol. 8. 1974. 55.00 (ISBN 0-12-152808-1); Vol. 9. 1975. 47.00 (ISBN 0-12-152809-X); lib ed. 60.00 (ISBN 0-12-152874-X); microfiche 34.00 (ISBN 0-12-152875-8); Vol. 10. 1974. 55.00 (ISBN 0-12-152810-3); lib ed. 68.00 (ISBN 0-12-152876-6); 42.00 (ISBN 0-12-152877-4); Vol. 11. 1974. 51.00 (ISBN 0-12-152811-1); lib. ed. 64.00 (ISBN 0-12-152878-2); microfiche 38.00 (ISBN 0-12-152879-0); Vol. 12. 1977. 51.00 (ISBN 0-12-152812-X); lib. ed. 64.00 (ISBN 0-12-152880-4); microfiche 38.00 (ISBN 0-12-152881-2); Vol. 13. 1978. 46.00 (ISBN 0-12-152813-8); lib ed. 58.50 (ISBN 0-12-152882-0); microfiche 33.50 (ISBN 0-12-152883-9); Vol. 14. 1978. **46.50 (ISBN 0-12-152814-6); lib ed. 58.50 (ISBN 0-12-152884-7); microfiche 35.00 (ISBN 0-12-152885-5); Vol. 15. 1979. 39.50 (ISBN 0-12-152815-4); lib. ed. 47.00 (ISBN 0-12-152886-3); microfiche 27.00 (ISBN 0-12-152887-1); Vol. 16. 1980. 39.50 (ISBN 0-12-152816-2); lib. ed 47.00 (ISBN 0-12-152888-X); microfiche 27.00 (ISBN 0-12-152889-8); Vol. 17. 1980. 40.00 (ISBN 0-12-152817-0); lib. ed. 45.50 (ISBN 0-12-152890-1); microfiche 24.50 (ISBN 0-12-152891-X). Acad Pr.**

Hoerder, Dick, ed. Protest, Direct Action, Repression: Dissent in American Society from Colonial Times to the Present. 434p. 1977. text ed. 48.00x (ISBN 3-7940-7009-7, Pub. by K G Saur). Gale.

Hoerder, Dirk. American Labor & Immigrant History Recent European Research. LC 81-23078. (The Working Class in American History). 360p. 1983. 26.95 (ISBN 0-252-00963-0). U of Ill Pr.

Hoerl, Bryan G., jt. auth. see Boyd, Robert F.

Hoerlein, B. F. Canine Neurology: Diagnosis & Treatment. 3rd ed. LC 77-72825. (Illus.). 1978. text ed. 39.00 o.p. (ISBN 0-7216-4712-X). Saunders.

Hoermander, L. The Analysis of Linear Partial Differential Operators II: Differential Operators with Constant Coefficients. (Illus.). 380p. 1983. 49.50 (ISBN 0-387-12139-0). Springer-Verlag.

--The Analysis of Linear Partial Differential Operators I: Distribution Theory & Fourier Analysis. (Grundlehren der Mathematischen Wissenschaften: Vol. 256). (Illus.). 380p. 1983. 39.00 (ISBN 0-387-12104-8). Springer-Verlag.

Hoernes, G. & Heilweil, M. Introduction to Boolean Algebra & Logic Design: A Program for Self-Instruction. 1964. pap. text ed. 19.95 (ISBN 0-07-029183-7, C); instructor's manual 15.00 (ISBN 0-07-029187-X). McGraw.

Hoerni, B., et al. Opportunistic Infections in Cancer Patients. Armstrong, Donald, tr. from Fr. LC 77-94828. (Illus.). 207p. 1978. text ed. 28.50 (ISBN 0-89352-014-4). Masson Pub.

Hoerr, Stanley O., jt. auth. see Cooperman, Avram M.

Hoeschele, D. Analog to Digital-Digital to Analog Conversion Techniques. LC 68-22305. 1968. 48.50x o.s.i. (ISBN 0-471-40575-2, Pub. by Wiley-Interscience). Wiley.

Hoest, Bill. Agatha Crumm. (Orig.). 1980. pap. 1.50 o.p. (ISBN 0-451-09422-0, W9422, Sig). NAL.

--Agatha Crumm, No. 3: Too Mush is Never Enough. 1982. pap. 1.95 (ISBN 0-451-11844-8, AJ1844, Sig). NAL.

--Bumper Snickers: Even More Bumper Snickers, No. 3. 1982. pap. 1.75 (ISBN 0-451-11399-3, AE1399, Sig). NAL.

--Even More Bumper Stickers. 1982. pap. 1.75 (ISBN 0-451-11399-3, AE1399, Sig). NAL.

--Is This the Steak or the Charcoal? The Lockhorns No. 4. (Orig.). 1979. pap. 1.25 o.p. (ISBN 0-451-08475-6, Y8475, Sig). NAL.

--The Lockhorns, No. 2: Loretta, the Meat Loaf Is Moving. (Orig.). 1976. pap. 1.25 o.p. (ISBN 0-451-08167-6, Y8167, Sig). NAL.

--The Lockhorns, No. 3: Who Made the Caesar Salad --Brutus ? (Orig.). 1977. pap. 0.95 o.p. (ISBN 0-451-07408-4, Q7408, Sig). NAL.

--Lockhorns, No. 4: Is This the Steak or the Charcoal? (Orig.). Date not set. pap. 1.25 o.p. (ISBN 0-686-73799-7, E8475, Sig). NAL.

--Lockhorns, No. 6: Of Course I Love You What Do I Know? (Orig.). Date not set. pap. 1.75 (ISBN 0-451-09984-2, E9984, Sig). NAL.

--The Lockhorns, No. 7: Let's Go for a Walk...And Bring your Wallet. 1982. pap. 1.75 (ISBN 0-451-11472-8, AE1472, Sig). NAL.

--The Lockhorns, No. 8: I Could Live Without These Meals...Probably Longer. 1982. pap. 1.75 (ISBN 0-451-11749-2, AE1749, Sig). NAL.

--The Lockhorns, No. 9: You Name It...I'm Guilty. 1982. pap. 1.95 (ISBN 0-451-11936-3, AJ1936, Sig). NAL.

--The Lockhorns: What's the Garbage Doing on the Stove. (Orig.). 1975. pap. 1.25 o.p. (ISBN 0-451-08166-8, Y8166, Sig). NAL.

--The Return of Agatha Crumm. 1982. pap. 1.75 (ISBN 0-451-11526-0, AE1526, Sig). NAL.

Hoet, J., et al, eds. see International Diabetes Federation.

Hoetzsch, Otto & Evans, Rhys. The Evolution of Russia. 214p. 1966. pap. text ed. 9.95 (ISBN 0-15-525100-7, HC). HarBraceJ.

Hoeveler, Diane L., jt. ed. see Wilson, Harris W.

Hoeven, James W. Van see Van Hoeven, James W.

Hoew, Abba L., et al. Brewster through the Years, 1848-1948. LC 82-15405. (Illus.). 192p. Repr. of 1948 ed. 12.00 (ISBN 0-916346-46-3). Harbor Hill Bks.

Hoexter, Joan C. & Hayes, Janice E. Curriculum in Graduate Education in Nursing: Part II-Components in the Curriculum Development Process. 64p. 1976. 4.95 (ISBN 0-686-38255-2, 15-1632). Natl League Nurse.

Hoey, Allen. Evening in the Antipodes. 48p. 1977. pap. 5.00 (ISBN 0-918092-04-3). Tamarack Edns.

--Hymns To a Tree. (Illus.). 24p. 1983. pap. 5.00 (ISBN 0-918092-38-8); signed 10.00 (ISBN 0-918092-37-X). Tamarack Edns.

Hoey, William, tr. see Oldenberg, Hermann.

Hof, M. W. van see Van Hof, M. W. & Mohn, G.

Hofacker, Erich P. Christian Morgenstern. (World Authors Ser.). 1978. 15.95 (ISBN 0-8057-6349-X, Twayne). G K Hall.

Hofacker, Winfried & Floegel, Ekkehard. The Custom Apple & Other Mysteries, Vol. I. Trap, Charles, ed. (Apple Information Ser.). 192p. (Orig.). 1982. pap. 24.95 (ISBN 0-936200-05-7). IJG Inc.

Hofdstadter, Richard, et al. The United States: Brief Edition. (Illus.). 1979. pap. text ed. 17.95 (ISBN 0-13-938860-5). P-H.

Hofeditz, Calvin A. Computers & Data Processing Made Simple. LC 78-22635. (Made Simple Books). (Illus.). 1979. pap. 4.95 (ISBN 0-385-14945-X, Made). Doubleday.

Hofeldt, Fred D. Preventing Reactive Hypoglycemia. 148p. 1983. 18.50 (ISBN 0-87527-214-2). Green.

Hofeller, Kathleen H. Battered Women, Shattered Lives. LC 82-50377. 125p. (Orig.). pap. 6.95 (ISBN 0-88247-687-4). R & E Res Assoc.

Hofer, Charles W. & Schendel, Dan E. Strategy Formulation: Analytical Concepts. (West Ser. in Business Policy & Planning). (Illus.). 1978. pap. text ed. 12.50 (ISBN 0-8299-0213-9). West Pub.

Hofer, Charles W., et al. Strategic Management: Cases in Business Policy & Planning. 1980. text ed. 24.95 (ISBN 0-8299-0331-3). West Pub.

Hofer, Jack. Sexercise: How to Exercise Your Way to Sexual Fitness. LC 78-65882. (Illus.). 128p. 1979. 14.95 o.s.i. (ISBN 0-89104-138-9, A & W Visual Library); pap. 8.95 o.s.i. (ISBN 0-89104-137-0, A & W Visual Library). A & W Pubs.

--Total Massage. 10.00 o.p. (ISBN 0-686-67791-9, G&D); pap. 5.95 o.p. (ISBN 0-448-12324-X, Today Press). Putnam Pub Group.

Hofer, Philip, intro. by. The Artist & the Book Eighteen-Sixty to Nineteen-Sixty, in Western Europe & the United States. Museum of Fine Arts, Boston & Harvard College Library. LC 81-81721. (Illus.). 332p. 1982. Repr. of 1961 ed. lib. bdg. 65.00 (ISBN 0-87817-277-7). Hacker.

Hoff, Benjamin. The Tao of Pooh. 1983. pap. 4.95 (ISBN 0-14-006747-7). Penguin.

Hoff, C. Clayton & Riedesel, Marvin L., eds. Physiological Systems in Semiarid Environments. LC 68-56229. (Illus.). 293p. 1969. 12.00x (ISBN 0-8263-0054-5). U of NM Pr.

Hoff, Ebbe C. Alcoholism: The Hidden Addiction. LC 74-13014. 1975. 4.00 (ISBN 0-8164-0248-5). Seabury.

Hoff, Marshall G., ed. see Haensel, Phyllis C.

Hoff, Nicholas J. Analysis of Structures: Based on the Minimal Principles & the Principle of Virtual Displacement. LC 56-6503. 1956. 38.95x o.p. (ISBN 0-471-40590-6, Pub. by Wiley-Interscience). Wiley.

Hoff, Syd. Amy's Dinosaur. LC 80-14082. (Illus.). 48p. (ps-2). 1980. 4.95 o.p. (ISBN 0-671-41338-4, Pub. by Windmill). S&S.

--Barkley. LC 75-6290. (Early I Can Read Bk.). (Illus.). 32p. (ps-3). 1975. 7.64i o.p. (ISBN 0-06-022447-9, HarpJ); PLB 8.89 (ISBN 0-06-022448-7). Har-Row.

--Baseball Mouse. LC 68-24515. (Illus.). (gr. k-3). 1979. pap. 2.95 (ISBN 0-399-20705-8). Putnam Pub Group.

--Baseball Mouse. (Illus.). (gr. 1-4). 1969. PLB 5.99 (ISBN 0-399-60043-4). Putnam Pub Group.

--Boss Tweed & the Man Who Drew Him. LC 78-5622. (Break-of-Day Bk.). (Illus.). (gr. k-3). 1978. PLB 6.59 o.p. (ISBN 0-698-30706-2, Coward). Putnam Pub Group.

--Gentleman Jim & the Great John L. LC 77-175. (Break-of-Day Bk.). (Illus.). (gr. k-4). 1977. PLB 6.99 o.p. (ISBN 0-698-30669-4, Coward). Putnam Pub Group.

--Giants & Other Plays for Kids. new ed. LC 72-84838. (Illus.). 64p. (gr. 2-5). 1973. PLB 4.99 o.p. (ISBN 0-399-60759-5). Putnam Pub Group.

--Happy Birthday, Henrietta! LC 82-1064. (Imagination Ser.). (Illus.). 48p. (gr. k-4). 1983. PLB write for info. (ISBN 0-8116-4423-5). Garrard.

--Henrietta, Circus Star. LC 78-58524. (Imagination Ser.). (Illus.). (gr. k-6). 1978. PLB 6.69 (ISBN 0-8116-4413-8). Garrard.

--Henrietta Goes to the Fair. LC 78-22051. (Imagination Books). (Illus.). (gr. k-6). 1979. PLB 6.69 (ISBN 0-8116-4416-2). Garrard.

--Henrietta Lays Some Eggs. LC 76-44325. (Imagination Ser.). (Illus.). (gr. k-4). 1977. lib. bdg. 6.69 (ISBN 0-8116-4406-5). Garrard.

--Henrietta, the Early Bird. LC 77-21246. (Imagination Ser.). (Illus.). (gr. k-4). 1978. PLB 6.69 (ISBN 0-8116-4410-3). Garrard.

--Henrietta's Fourth of July. LC 81-2334. (Imagination Ser.). (Illus.). 48p. (gr. k-4). 1981. lib. bdg. 6.69 (ISBN 0-8116-4422-7). Garrard.

--Henrietta's Halloween. LC 79-23729. (Imagination Ser.). (Illus.). 48p. (gr. k-4). 1980. PLB 6.69 (ISBN 0-8116-4421-9). Garrard.

--Ida the Bareback Rider. new ed. (See & Read Storybooks). (Illus.). 32p. (gr. 1-4). 1972. PLB 5.29 o.p. (ISBN 0-399-60707-2). Putnam Pub Group.

--Jokes to Enjoy, Draw & Tell. new ed. (Illus.). 96p. (gr. 3-6). 1974. PLB 5.99 (ISBN 0-399-60879-6). Putnam Pub Group.

--Kip Van Wrinkle. new ed. LC 73-83992. (See & Read Storybooks). (Illus.). 32p. (gr. 1-4). 1974. PLB 5.29 o.p. (ISBN 0-399-60868-0). Putnam Pub Group.

--Lengthy. (Illus.). (gr. 1-4). 1964. PLB 6.99 (ISBN 0-399-60345-X). Putnam Pub Group.

--Lengthy. (Illus.). (gr. 4-7). 1979. pap. 2.95 (ISBN 0-399-20704-X). Putnam Pub Group.

--The Littlest Leaguer. LC 75-25782. (Illus.). 48p. (gr. 2 up). 1976. 5.95 o.p. (ISBN 0-671-96152-7); pap. 2.50 (ISBN 0-671-42580-3). Windmill Bks.

--Mahatma. (Illus.). (gr. k-2). 1969. PLB 4.69 o.p. (ISBN 0-399-60440-5). Putnam Pub Group.

--The Man Who Loved Animals. (Break-of-Day Ser.). (Illus.). 48p. 1982. lib. bdg. 6.99 (ISBN 0-698-30737-2, Coward). Putnam Pub Group.

--Merry Christmas, Henrietta! LC 79-19787. (Imagination Ser.). (Illus.). 48p. (gr. k-4). 1980. PLB 6.69 (ISBN 0-8116-4419-7). Garrard.

--Mrs. Switch. (Illus.). (gr. 1-3). 1966. PLB 5.97 o.p. (ISBN 0-399-60480-4). Putnam Pub Group.

--Palace Bug. (See & Read Storybooks). (Illus.). (gr. 1-3). 1970. PLB 4.29 o.p. (ISBN 0-399-60503-7). Putnam Pub Group.

--Scarface Al & His Uncle Sam. (Break-of-Day Bk.). (Illus.). 48p. (gr. 3-5). 1980. PLB 6.99 (ISBN 0-698-30723-2, Coward). Putnam Pub Group.

--Slithers. LC 68-24518. (Illus.). (gr. 1-4). 1968. PLB 5.29 o.p. (ISBN 0-399-60585-1). Putnam Pub Group.

--Slugger Sal's Slump. LC 78-26338. (Illus.). 48p. (gr. 2 up). 1979. 2.50 (ISBN 0-671-96148-9). Windmill Bks.

--Syd Hoff's Joke Book. (Illus.). (gr. 4 up). 1972. PLB 5.99 (ISBN 0-399-60708-0). Putnam Pub Group.

--A Walk Past Ellen's House. LC 72-11751. (Illus.). 32p. (gr. k-3). 1973. 5.95 o.p. (ISBN 0-07-029175-6, GB); PLB 5.72 o.p. (ISBN 0-07-029176-4). McGraw.

--Walpole. LC 76-41514. (Early I Can Read Bk.). (Illus.). 32p. (gr. k-3). 1977. 7.64i (ISBN 0-06-022543-2, HarpJ); PLB 8.89 (ISBN 0-06-022544-0). Har-Row.

--Where's Prancer. LC 60-9450. (Illus.). (gr. k-3). 1960. PLB 10.89 (ISBN 0-06-022546-7, HarpJ). Har-Row.

--Wilfred the Lion. (See & Read Storybooks). (Illus.). (gr. k-3). 1970. PLB 4.89 o.p. (ISBN 0-399-60669-6). Putnam Pub Group.

--The Young Cartoonist. (Illus.). 192p. 1983. 14.95 (ISBN 0-87396-088-2). Stravon.

Hoff, Ursula. National Gallery of Victoria. (Illus.). 216p. 1974. 18.00 o.p. (ISBN 0-500-18139-X); pap. 6.95 o.p. (ISBN 0-500-20133-1). Transatlantic.

Hoffbauer, Johannes C. Tentamina Semiologica, sive quaedam generalem theoriam signorum spectantia. (Foundation of Semiotics Ser.: No. 4). 120p. 1983. 16.00 (ISBN 90-272-3274-1). Benjamins North Am.

Hoffberg, Judith A. & Hess, Stanley W., eds. Directory of Art Libraries & Visual Resource Collections in North America. 298p. 1978. text ed. 42.50 o.s.i. (ISBN 0-918212-05-7). ABC-Clio.

Hoffenber, Connie & Hoffenber, Terry. Portland Super Shopper. 162p. (Orig.). 1982. pap. 3.95 (ISBN 0-916076-59-8). Writing.

Hoffenber, Terry, jt. auth. see Hoffenber, Connie.

Hoffenberg, H. L. Nineteenth-Century South America in Photographs. (Illus.). 160p. (Orig.). 10.95 (ISBN 0-486-24133-5). Dover.

Hoffenberg, Jack. The Desperate Adversaries. 1976. pap. 1.95 o.p. (ISBN 0-380-00702-9, 29801). Avon.

--Hero for Regis. 1970. pap. 1.95 o.s.i. (ISBN 0-380-01248-0, 37259). Avon.

--A Time for Pagans. 1971. pap. 1.95 o.s.i. (ISBN 0-380-00876-9, 31435). Avon.

Hoffer. Year Book of Nuclear Medicine 1983. 1983. 45.00 (ISBN 0-8151-4527-6). Year Bk Med.

Hoffer, Alan R. Geometry. (gr. 10-12). 1979. text ed. 17.60 (ISBN 0-201-02958-8, Sch Div); tchr's ed. 22.20 (ISBN 0-201-02959-6); solutions manual 16.48 (ISBN 0-201-02960-X); test booklet 14.64 (ISBN 0-201-02961-8). A-W.

Hoffer, Alice. Gretchen's World. LC 80-83354. (Illus.). 48p. (gr. k-3). 1981. 5.95 (ISBN 0-448-16560-0, G&D); PLB 11.85 (ISBN 0-448-13491-8). Putnam Pub Group.

Hoffer, Bates L. & St. Clair, Robert N., eds. Developmental Kinesics: The Emerging Paradigm. 288p. 1981. text ed. 19.95 (ISBN 0-8391-1651-9). Univ Park.

Hoffer, Charles R. The Understanding of Music. 4th ed. 544p. 1981. text ed. 20.95x (ISBN 0-534-00915-8); wkbk. 7.95x (ISBN 0-534-00916-6); record album 27.95x (ISBN 0-534-00950-6). Wadsworth Pub.

Hoffer, Charles R. & Hoffer, Marjorie L. Teaching Music in the Elementary Classroom. 384p. 1982. text ed. 18.95 (ISBN 0-15-588809-9, HC). HarBraceJ.

Hoffer, Eric. Before the Sabbath. LC 78-69626. 1979. 11.49i (ISBN 0-06-011914-4, HarpT). Har-Row.

--Between the Devil & the Dragon: Thoughts of Men & Nature. LC 81-48140. 384p. 1982. 19.18i (ISBN 0-06-014984-1, HarpT). Har-Row.

Hoffer, Marjorie L., jt. auth. see Hoffer, Charles R.

Hoffer, Paul B., et al. Gallium-67 Imaging. LC 77-13125. (Diagnostic & Therapeutic Radiology Ser.). 1978. 52.95 (ISBN 0-471-02601-8, Pub. by Wiley Medical). Wiley.

Hoffer, Peter T. Klaus Mann. (World Authors Ser.). 1978. lib. bdg. 15.95 (ISBN 0-8057-6309-0, Twayne). G K Hall.

Hofferbert, Richard I. The Study of Public Policy. LC 73-9826. (Policy Analysis Ser). 1974. 14.50 o.p. (ISBN 0-672-51475-3); pap. text ed. 12.50 o.p. (ISBN 0-672-61062-0). Bobbs.

Hoffman. Adolescent Medicine. 1982. text ed. 38.95 (ISBN 0-201-11071-7, Med-Nurse). A-W.

--Federal Taxation - Solutions Manual: Corporations, Partnerships, Estates & Trusts. 420p. 1979. write for info. o.s.i. (ISBN 0-8299-0491-3). West Pub.

--Thermodynamic Theory of Latent Image Formation. 1982. pap. 31.95 (ISBN 0-240-51200-6). Focal Pr.

Hoffman, Abbie. Soon to Be a Major Motion Picture. 1980. 13.95 o.p. (ISBN 0-399-12561-2, Perige); pap. 6.95 o.p. (ISBN 0-399-50503-2). Putnam Pub Group.

--Square Dancing in the Ice Age: Underground Writings. 242p. 1982. 14.95 (ISBN 0-399-12701-1). Putnam Pub Group.

Hoffman, Alan M. History of an Idea. LC 80-5963. 316p. (Orig.). 1981. lib. bdg. 22.00 (ISBN 0-8191-1698-X); pap. text ed. 12.25 (ISBN 0-8191-1699-8). U Pr of Amer.

Hoffman, Alice. Angel Landing. 256p. 1980. 10.95 (ISBN 0-399-12504-3). Putnam Pub Group.

--White Horses. 256p. 1982. 12.95 (ISBN 0-399-12709-7). Putnam Pub Group.

Hoffman, Allen. Kagan's Superfecta & Other Stories. 304p. 1982. 12.95 (ISBN 0-89659-234-0); special ltd. ed. 100.00 (ISBN 0-89659-271-5). Abbeville Pr.

Hoffman, B. & Hasse, R. L. Weight Training for Athletes. (Illus.). 1961. 19.95 (ISBN 0-471-07118-8). Wiley.

Hoffman, Banesh. The Tyranny of Testing. LC 77-26028. 1978. Repr. of 1962 ed. lib. bdg. 20.75x (ISBN 0-313-20097-1, HOTT). Greenwood.

Hoffman, Banesh & Dukes, Helen. Albert Einstein, Creator & Rebel. (Illus.). 288p. 1973. pap. 4.95 (ISBN 0-452-25263-6, Z5263, Plume). NAL.

Hoffman, Bob. No One Is to Blame: Getting a Loving Divorce from Mom & Dad. LC 79-63271. 1979. pap. 6.95 (ISBN 0-8314-0057-9). Sci & Behavior.

Hoffman, Brian F. & Cranefield, Paul F. Electrophysiology of the Heart. LC 76-18003. 334p. 1976. Repr. of 1960 ed. 17.50 o.p. (ISBN 0-87993-083-7). Futura Pub.

Hoffman, Brian F., jt. ed. see Cranefield, Paul F.

Hoffman, C., tr. see Troeger, W. E.

Hoffman, Carl. Grammar of the Margi Language. LC 63-23583. 1963. 13.25x o.p. (ISBN 0-8002-0749-1). Intl Pubns Serv.

Hoffman, Carolyn. Fifty Hikes in Eastern Pennsylvania: Day Hikes & Backpacks from the Susquehanna to the Poconos. LC 82-4004. (Fifty Hikes Ser.). (Illus.). 224p. (Orig.). 1982. pap. 8.95 (ISBN 0-942440-02-1). Backcountry Pubns.

Hoffman, Charles W., et al, eds. see Kafka, Franz, et al.

Hoffman, Claire P. & Lipkin, Gladys B. Simplified Nursing. 9th ed. (Illus.). 500p. 1981. pap. text ed. 14.00 (ISBN 0-397-54364-6, Lippincott Nursing); wkbk. 9.00 (ISBN 0-686-86026-8). Lippincott.

Hoffman, Daniel. The Center of Attention. 96p. Date not set. pap. 5.95 o.p. (ISBN 0-394-74726-7, Vin). Random.

--Paul Bunyan: Last of the Frontier Demigods. LC 66-14159. 227p. 1966. 19.95x (ISBN 0-685-46410-5). Temple U Pr.

--Poe Poe Poe Poe Poe Poe Poe. 1978. pap. 2.95 o.p. (ISBN 0-380-41459-7, 41459, Discus). Avon.

Hoffman, Daniel, ed. Harvard Guide to Contemporary American Writing. 618p. 1979. 25.00 (ISBN 0-674-37535-1). Harvard U Pr.

Hoffman, Daniel N., jt. auth. see Halperin, Morton H.

Hoffman, David, jt. ed. see Zeman, Zavis P.

Hoffman, Dietrich, jt. ed. see Wynder, Ernest L.

Hoffman, Dominic M. Living Divine Love: Transformation, the Goal of Christian Life. LC 82-11552. 256p. (Orig.). 1982. pap. 7.95 (ISBN 0-8189-0443-7). Alba.

Hoffman, Donald. Frank Lloyd Wright's Fallingwater: The House & Its History. (Illus.). 12.00 (ISBN 0-8446-5774-3). Peter Smith.

Hoffman, Donna. Bucksport Vital Records. LC 82-73244. 125p. 1982. pap. 14.95 (ISBN 0-941216-03-9). Cay-Bel.

Hoffman, Douglas R., ed. see Adams, Jennifer A.

Hoffman, E. Practical Problems in Mathematics for Machinists. 2nd ed. LC 78-74432. (Mathematics Ser.). (gr. 8). 1980. 7.80 (ISBN 0-8273-1281-4); instr's. guide 4.25 (ISBN 0-8273-1282-2). Delmar.

Hoffman, E. J. The Concept of Energy: An Inquiry into Origins & Applications. LC 76-50987. 1977. 60.00 o.p. (ISBN 0-250-40153-3). Ann Arbor Science.

--Heat Transfer Rate Analysis. 702p. 1980. 63.95x (ISBN 0-87814-139-1). Pennwell Book Division.

Hoffman, Edward G. Jig & Fixture Design. LC 78-55901. 256p. pap. 13.00 (ISBN 0-8273-1694-1); instr.'s guide 2.50 (ISBN 0-686-67378-6). Delmar.

--Jig & Fixture Design. 251p. 1980. 10.95 o.p. (ISBN 0-442-20162-1). Van Nos Reinhold.

Hoffman, Edward G. & Romero, Felix. Welding Blueprint Reading. 1983. pap. text ed. 19.95 (ISBN 0-534-01431-3, Breton Pubs). Wadsworth Pub.

Hoffman, Emanuel. Fairchild's Dictionary of Home Furnishings: Furniture, Accessories, Curtains & Draperies, Fabrics, Floor Coverings. new ed. Buck, Babs F. & Small, Verna, eds. LC 70-180155. (Illus.). 384p. 1974. lib. bdg. 25.00 o.p. (ISBN 0-87005-106-7). Fairchild.

Hoffman, Enid. Develop Your Psychic Skills. 192p. (Orig.). 1981. pap. 7.95 (ISBN 0-914918-29-X). Para Res.

--Huna: A Beginner's Guide. rev. ed. LC 75-41901. Orig. Title: You Two Can Be a Kahuna. 1981. pap. 7.95 (ISBN 0-914918-03-6). Para Res.

Hoffman, Eric. Renegade Houses: A Free-Thinker's Guide to Innovative Owner-Built Homes. (Illus.). 160p. (Orig.). 1982. lib. bdg. 19.80 (ISBN 0-89471-182-2); pap. 7.95 (ISBN 0-89471-181-4). Running Pr.

Hoffman, F., jt. auth. see Fritz, N.

Hoffman, F., et al. Accounting Fundamentals: A Gregg Text-Kit for Adult Education. 3rd ed. 1980. 19.10 o.p. (ISBN 0-07-029208-6, G); instructor's manual 8.50 o.p. (ISBN 0-07-029209-4). McGraw.

Hoffman, F. G., jt. ed. see Root, W. S.

Hoffman, F. J., et al. Little Magazine: A History & a Bibliography. LC 46-17. 1946. 25.00 o.s.i. (ISBN 0-527-41500-6). Kraus Repr.

Hoffman, Felix. The Story of Christmas. LC 75-6921. (Illus.). 32p. (gr. k up). 1975. 6.95 o.p. (ISBN 0-689-50031-9, McElderry Bk). Atheneum.

Hoffman, Fred. Just a Great Thing to Do: Selected Works by Charles Garabedian. LC 81-81544. (Illus.). 74p. 1981. pap. text ed. 20.00x (ISBN 0-934418-10-1). La Jolla Mus Contemp Art.

Hoffman, Frederick J. Twenties: American Writing in the Postwar Decade. 1965. pap. text ed. 6.95 (ISBN 0-02-914780-8). Free Pr.

--William Faulkner. (United States Authors Ser.). lib. bdg. 11.95 (ISBN 0-8057-0244-X, Twayne). G K Hall.

Hoffman, Frederick J. & Vickery, Olga W. William Faulkner: Three Decades of Criticism. LC 60-11481. 1963. pap. 5.25 o.p. (ISBN 0-15-696755-3, Harv). HarBraceJ.

Hoffman, George. How to Inspect a House. (Illus.). 1979. 8.95 o.s.i. (ISBN 0-440-04366-2, Sey Lawr). Delacorte.

Hoffman, George W., et al, eds. A Geography of Europe. 4th ed. LC 77-75128. (Illus.). 671p. 1977. 31.95 (ISBN 0-471-06741-5). Wiley.

Hoffman, Glen L. & Meyer, Fred P. Parasites of Freshwater Fishes. (Illus.). 224p. 1974. pap. 19.95 (ISBN 0-87666-130-4, PS-208). TFH Pubns.

Hoffman, Gloria & Graivier, Pauline. Speak the Language of Success. LC 82-82303. 320p. (Orig.). 1983. pap. 8.95 (ISBN 0-448-16811-1, G&D). Putnam Pub Group.

Hoffman, Heinrich see Lear, Edward.

Hoffman, Horace Addison. Everyday Greek: Greek Words in English, Including Scientific Terms. (Midway Reprint). 1976. pap. 8.00x (ISBN 0-226-34787-7). U of Chicago Pr.

Hoffman, I., ed. Vectorcardiography 2. (Proceedings). 1971. 52.75 (ISBN 0-7204-4093-9, North Holland). Elsevier.

Hoffman, I & Hamby, R., eds. Vectorcardiography 3. (Proceedings). 1976. 62.25 (ISBN 0-444-10919-6). Elsevier.

Hoffman, I. & Taymor, R., eds. Vectorcariography. (Proceedings). 1966. 31.75 (ISBN 0-7204-4025-4, North Holland). Elsevier.

Hoffman, Joe D., jt. auth. see Zucrow, Maurice J.

Hoffman, John P. Introduction to Electronics for Technologists. LC 77-74381. (Illus.). 1978. text ed. 23.95 (ISBN 0-395-25115-X); solutions manual 1.50 (ISBN 0-395-25819-7). HM.

Hoffman, Joseph F., ed. Membrane Transport Processes, Vol. 1. LC 76-19934. 488p. 1978. 48.00 (ISBN 0-89004-170-9). Raven.

Hoffman, Joseph F & Giebisch, Gerhard H., eds. Membranes in Growth & Development. LC 82-7178. (Progress in Clinical & Biological Research Ser.: Vol. 91). 644p. 1982. 94.00 (ISBN 0-8451-0091-2). A R Liss.

Hoffman, K. Analysis in Euclidian Space. 1975. text ed. 32.95 (ISBN 0-13-032656-9). P-H.

Hoffman, K. & Kleiman, R., eds. Advanced Concepts in Contraception. 1968. 13.75 (ISBN 90-219-0107-2). Elsevier.

Hoffman, Kay Y., jt. auth. see Cope, Gabriele E.

Hoffman, Kenneth & Kunze, Ray. Linear Algebra. 2nd ed. LC 75-142120. (Illus.). 1971. ref. ed. 26.95 (ISBN 0-13-536797-2). P-H.

Hoffman, Kenneth E. Rx for Us-a Revitalized Constitution: Increased Democracy. LC 78-66119. 1979. pap. text ed. 9.50 (ISBN 0-8191-0686-0). U Pr of Amer.

Hoffman, L., jt. auth. see Graves, Harold F.

Hoffman, L. J. Security & Privacy in Computer Systems. LC 73-6744. 1973. 51.95 (ISBN 0-471-40611-2, Pub. by Wiley-Interscience). Wiley.

Hoffman, Lance J. Modern Methods for Computer Security & Privacy. LC 76-49896. (Illus.). 1977. 29.95 (ISBN 0-13-595207-7). P-H.

Hoffman, Laurence D. Applied Calculus. (Illus.). 640p. 1983. text ed. 25.95x (ISBN 0-07-029319-8, C); instr's manual 5.95 (ISBN 0-07-029321-X); pap. 9.50 computer supplement (ISBN 0-07-029323-6). McGraw.

--Calculus for the Social, Managerial & Life Sciences. 2nd ed. (Illus.). 1980. text ed. 23.50x (ISBN 0-07-029317-1); instructor's manual 10.95 (ISBN 0-07-029318-X). McGraw.

Hoffman, Laurence D. & Orkin, Michael. Mathematics with Applications. (Illus.). 1979. text ed. 25.00 (ISBN 0-07-029301-5, C); 7.95 (ISBN 0-07-029302-3); study guide 9.95 (ISBN 0-07-029303-1). McGraw.

Hoffman, Laurence D. & Orkin, Micheal. Finite Mathematics with Applications. (Illus.). 1979. text ed. 22.50 (ISBN 0-07-029310-4, C); instructor's manual 7.95 (ISBN 0-07-029311-2); study guide 7.95 (ISBN 0-07-029312-0). McGraw.

Hoffman, Lee, jt. auth. see Chandler, A. Bertram.

Hoffman, Lee see Daniels, John S.

Hoffman, Lois W., jt. ed. see Hoffman, Martin L.

Hoffman, Mable. Chocolate Cookery. LC 78-61007. (Illus.). 1978. pap. 7.95 (ISBN 0-89586-016-3). H P Bks.

--Deep-Fry Cookery. LC 77-83277. (Illus.). 1977. 6.95 (ISBN 0-89586-152-6); pap. 5.95 o.s.i. (ISBN 0-912656-80-8). H P Bks.

--Ice Cream. 5.95 (ISBN 0-89586-040-6). H P Bks.

Hoffman, Margaret A. & Fischer, Gerald C. Credit Department Management. LC 80-65026. (Illus.). 264p. 1980. 23.00 (ISBN 0-936742-00-3). Robt Morris Assocs.

Hoffman, Marlin A. The Power of Prayer & Fasting. 1.60 (ISBN 0-89137-535-X). Quality Pubns.

Hoffman, Marshall & Southmayd, William. Sports Health: The Complete Book of Athletic Injuries. (Illus.). 464p. 1981. pap. 14.95 (ISBN 0-8256-3205-6, Quick Fox); 24.95 (ISBN 0-8256-3263-3). Putnam Pub Group.

Hoffman, Martin L. & Hoffman, Lois W., eds. Review of Child Development Research, 2 Vols. LC 64-20472. Vol. 1, 1964, 548p. 10.95x ea. (ISBN 0-87154-384-2). Vol. 2, 1966, 598p (ISBN 0-87154-385-0). Set of 2 Vols (ISBN 0-87154-383-4). Russell Sage.

Hoffman, Michael J. Gertrude Stein. (United States Authors Ser.). 1976. lib. bdg. 11.95 (ISBN 0-8057-7168-9, Twayne). G K Hall.

Hoffman, Michael L., tr. see Guindey, Guillaume.

Hoffman, Norman S. A New World of Health. (Illus.). 1976. pap. text ed. 21.50 (ISBN 0-07-029203-5, C); instructor's manual 15.00 (ISBN 0-07-029204-3). McGraw.

Hoffman, P. Genetische Grundlagen der Artbildung in der Gattung Polyporus. (Bibliotheca Mycologica Ser.: No. 65). (Illus.). 1978. pap. text ed. 12.00x (ISBN 3-7682-1210-6). Lubrecht & Cramer.

Hoffman, Paul. Rome, the Sweet Tempestuous Life. 224p. 1982. 14.95 (ISBN 0-312-92737-1). St Martin.

Hoffman, Paul, jt. auth. see Freedman, Matt.

Hoffman, Paul E. The Spanish Crown & the Defense of the Caribbean, 1535 to 1585: Precedent, Patrilmonialism, & Royal Parsimony. LC 79-16864. xxii, 354p. 1980. 30.00x (ISBN 0-8071-0583-X). La State U Pr.

Hoffman, Paul S. The Software Legal Book. 253p. 1982. 79.95 (ISBN 0-935506-01-2). Carnegie Pr.

Hoffman, Phyllis. Play Ball with the New York Yankees. LC 82-20783. (Illus.). 48p. (Orig.). (gr. 4-7). 1983. pap. 2.95 (ISBN 0-689-70759-2, A-135, Aladdin). Atheneum.

Hoffman, Piotr. The Anatomy of Idealism: Passivity & Activity in Kant, Hegel & Marx. 1982. lib. bdg. 24.00 (ISBN 0-686-37433-9, Pub. by Martinus Nijhoff Netherlands). Kluwer Boston.

Hoffman Research Services. A Treasury of Tips for the Antiquarian Bookseller. 24p. (Orig.). 1983. pap. 7.95 (ISBN 0-910203-00-8). Hoffman Res.

Hoffman, Richard L. & Luria, Maxwell S., eds. Middle English Lyrics. (Critical Editions Ser.). (Illus.). 1974. pap. 7.95x (ISBN 0-393-09338-7). Norton.

Hoffman, Richard W. see Hass, Georg, et al.

Hoffman, Robert C. Pitfalls to Avoid: Am I Doing This Right? rev. ed. 80p. (Orig.). 1982. pap. 6.95 (ISBN 0-9610018-0-1); guide & newsletters, binder format 13.95 (ISBN 0-9610018-1-X). Financial Aid.

Hoffman, Ronald & Albert, Peter J., eds. Sovereign States n an Age of Uncertainty. LC 81-19660. 288p. 1982. 20.00x (ISBN 0-8139-0926-0). U Pr of Va.

Hoffman, Ronald, jt. ed. see Berlin, Ira.

Hoffman, Roslyn. Phoenix: A Pictorial History. Friedman, Donna R., ed. LC 80-22301. (Illus.). 208p. 1981. pap. write for info. o.p. (ISBN 0-89865-090-9). Donning Co.

Hoffman, Stanley. Gulliver's Troubles, or the Setting of American Foreign Policy. LC 68-13516. (Council on Foreign Relations). 1968. 12.95 o.p. (ISBN 0-07-029196-9, P&RB). McGraw.

Hoffman, Susanna. The Classified Man: Twenty-Two Types of Men (& What to Do About Them) LC 79-25249. (Illus.). 1980. 10.95 o.p. (ISBN 0-698-11014-5, Coward). Putnam Pub Group.

--The Classified Man: Twenty-Two Types of Men (& What to Do About Them) 1981. pap. 4.95 (ISBN 0-399-50544-X, Perige). Putnam Pub Group.

Hoffman, Taryn & Frompovich, Catherine J. The Fox in Shangri-La. (Illus.). 32p. (ps-2). 1982. pap. 3.95 (ISBN 0-935322-20-5). C J Frompovich.

Hoffman, Theodore J., jt. auth. see Cameron, Kenneth M.

Hoffman, Thomas R., jt. auth. see Davis, Gordon B.

Hoffman, W. Michael. Kant's Theory of Freedom: A Metaphysical Inquiry. LC 78-70860. 1978. pap. text ed. 8.25 (ISBN 0-8191-0651-8). U Pr of Amer.

Hoffman, W. Michael, ed. Proceedings of the Second National Conference on Business Ethics. LC 79-64514. 1979. pap. text ed. 18.00 (ISBN 0-8191-0762-X). U Pr of Amer.

Hoffman, Walter K., ed. A-O-A Hong Kong Guidebook: Official Guidebook Hong Kong Tourist Association. rev. ed. LC 78-3217. (Illus.). 1982. pap. 5.00 (ISBN 0-8048-1361-2). C E Tuttle.

Hoffman, Wayne L., jt. ed. see Dilamarter, Ronald R.

Hoffman, William, ed. New American Plays, Vol. 2. 271p. 1968. 5.95 o.p. (ISBN 0-8090-7251-3). Hill & Wang.

Hoffman, William H. Economic Recovery Tax Act of 1981: Supplement to Accompany the 1982 Annual Ed. of West's Federal Taxation. 72p. 1981. write for info. o.s.i. (ISBN 0-314-64025-8). West Pub.

--West's Federal Taxation: Corporations, Partnerships, Estates & Trusts, 1979. rev. ed. (Illus.). 1978. text ed. 17.95 o.s.i. (ISBN 0-8299-0177-9). West Pub.

--West's Federal Taxation: Corporations, Partnerships, Estates & Trusts, 1983. 916p. text ed. 26.95 (ISBN 0-314-67112-9); write for info. instr's manual (ISBN 0-314-67319-9). West Pub.

Hoffman, William H. & Willis, Eugene. West Federal Taxation: Individual Income Taxes, 1983 Annual Edition. 1068p. 1982. text ed. 24.95 (ISBN 0-314-67113-7); write for info. instr's manual (ISBN 0-314-67322-9). West Pub.

Hoffman, William H., jt. auth. see Phillips, Lawrence C.

Hoffman, William H., Jr. & Willis, Eugene. West's Federal Taxation: Comprehensive Volume, 1983. (Illus.). 1150p. 1982. text ed. 22.95 (ISBN 0-314-70648-8); student guide avail. (ISBN 0-314-72295-5); solutions manual avail. (ISBN 0-314-72296-3). West Pub.

Hoffmann, jt. auth. see Klix.

Hoffmann, Charles. The Chinese Worker. LC 74-3053. 1974. 29.50x (ISBN 0-87395-238-3). State U NY Pr.

--Depression of the Nineties: An Economic History. LC 78-90790. (Contributions in Economics & Economic History: No. 2). 1970. lib. bdg. 29.95 (ISBN 0-8371-1855-7, HOD/). Greenwood.

Hoffmann, Charles G. Ford Madox Ford. (English Authors Ser.: No. 55). lib. bdg. 10.95 o.p. (ISBN 0-8057-1200-3, Twayne). G K Hall.

Hoffmann, Christa F. Getting Ready for AACR2: The Cataloger's Guide. LC 80-15168. (Professional Librarian Ser.). 225p. 1980. pap. text ed. 24.50 (ISBN 0-914236-64-4). Knowledge Indus.

Hoffmann, Donald. Frank Lloyd Wright's Fallingwater: The House & Its History. 1978. pap. 5.95 (ISBN 0-486-23671-4). Dover.

Hoffmann, E. T. Tales of E. T. A. Hoffmann. Kent, Leonard J. & Knight, Elizabeth C., eds. Jacob. 1972. pap. 8.25 (ISBN 0-226-34789-3, P452, Phoen). U of Chicago Pr.

Hoffmann, Fritz L. & Hoffmann, Olga M. Sovereignty in Dispute: The Falklands-Malvinas. (Special Studies on Latin America & the Caribbean). 150p. 1983. lib. bdg. 18.50x (ISBN 0-86531-605-8). Westview.

Hoffmann, Helmut. The Religions of Tibet. LC 78-11420. (Illus.). 1979. Repr. of 1961 ed. lib. bdg. 19.25x (ISBN 0-313-21120-5, HORT). Greenwood.

Hoffmann, Herbert. Collecting Greek Antiquities. (Illus.). 1970. 15.00 o.p. (ISBN 0-685-92062-3, 517R01676). Crown.

Hoffmann, Laurence. Practical Calculus for the Social & Managerial Sciences. (Illus.). 448p. 1975. pap. text ed. 16.50 o.p. (ISBN 0-07-029315-5, C). McGraw.

Hoffmann, Leon-Francois. Essays on Haitian Literature. 269p. 1983. 17.00x (ISBN 0-89410-344-X); pap. 8.00x (ISBN 0-89410-345-8). Three Continents.

Hoffmann, M., et al. Polymer Analytics. Stahlberg, H., tr. from Ger. (MMI Press Polymer Monographs: Vol. 3). 623p. Date not set. 124.50 (ISBN 3-7186-0024-2). Harwood Academic.

Hoffmann, Marta. The Warp Weighted Loom. pap. 16.95 (ISBN 82-00-08094-3). Robin & Russ.

Hoffmann, Olga M., jt. auth. see Hoffmann, Fritz L.

Hoffmann, Oswald C. Hurry Home Where You Belong. LC 76-113868. 1970. 2.95 o.p. (ISBN 0-570-03004-8, 6-1140). Concordia.

Hoffmann, Peter. History of German Resistance, Nineteen Thirty-Three to Nineteen Forty-Five. Barry, Richard, tr. from Ger. 1979. 35.00x (ISBN 0-262-08088-5); pap. 9.95x (ISBN 0-262-58038-1). MIT Pr.

--Hitler's Personal Security. 1979. 20.00x (ISBN 0-262-08099-0). MIT Pr.

Hoffmann, R., jt. auth. see Woodward, R. B.

Hoffmann, Stanley. Dead Ends: American Foriegn Policy in the New Cold War. 312p. 1983. prof ref 24.50 (ISBN 0-88410-003-0). Ballinger Pub.

--Primacy or World Order: American Foreign Policy since the Cold War. 1978. 17.95 (ISBN 0-07-029205-1, P&RB). McGraw.

Hoffmann, Stanley, ed. Conditions of World Order. 1970. pap. 3.95 o.p. (ISBN 0-671-20748-2, Touchstone Bks). S&S.

Hoffmann, Thomas R. & Johnson, Brian. The World Energy Triangle: A Strategy for Cooperation. 1981. prof ref 27.50x (ISBN 0-905347-15-3). Ballinger Pub.

Hoffmann, Thomas R., jt. auth. see Davis, Gordon B.

Hoffmaster, Henry R. Financial Statements: How to Read & Interpret Them for Success in the Stock Market. (Illus.). 1980. deluxe ed. 57.85 (ISBN 0-918968-62-3). Inst Econ Finan.

Hoffmeister, Donna L. The Theater of Confinement: Language & Survival in the Milieu Plays of Marieluise Fleisser & Franz Xaver Kroetz. LC 82-72261. (Studies in German Literature, Linguistics & Culture: Vol. 11). (Illus.). 190p. 1983. 16.95x (ISBN 0-938100-12-2). Camden Hse.

Hoffmeister, F. & Stille, G., eds. Psychotropic Agents, Part Two: Anxiolytics, Gerontopsychopharmacological Agents, & Psychomotor Stimulants. (Handbook of Experimental Pharmacology Ser.: Vol. 55-II). (Illus.). 830p. 1981. 199.00 (ISBN 0-387-10300-7). Springer-Verlag.

Hoffmeister, Gerhart, ed. German Baroque Literature: The European Perspective. LC 80-5341. 400p. 1983. 35.00 (ISBN 0-8044-2394-6). Ungar.

Hoffmeister, Peter. Turkoman Carpets in Franconia. 1982. 175.00x (ISBN 0-903580-45-4, Pub. by Elements Bks). State Mutual Bk.

Hoffmeister, Werner G., jt. auth. see Weimar, Karl S.

Hoffner, Harry A., Jr. Alimenta Hethaeorum: Food Production in Hittite Asia Minor. (American Oriental Ser.: Vol. 55). 1974. 12.50x o.s.i. (ISBN 0-686-00035-8). Kraus Repr.

Hoffner, Paul E., et al, eds. Practical Labor Relations: A Collection of Readings. LC 80-5525. 183p. 1980. pap. text ed. 9.50 (ISBN 0-8191-1119-8). U Pr of Amer.

Hofling, Charles K. Custer & the Little Big Horn: A Psychobiographical Inquiry. 1981. 15.95 (ISBN 0-8143-1668-9). Wayne St U Pr.

Hofman, Peter L., jt. auth. see Anderson, Richard J.

Hofmann. Elements of Compact Semigroups. 1966. text ed. 18.95x (ISBN 0-675-09850-5). Merrill.

--LSD: My Problem Child. 1980. 9.95 o.p. (ISBN 0-07-029325-2). McGraw.

Hofmann, A. F., jt. auth. see Dowling, R. H.

Hofmann, Alan F. & Huebner, Vicky L. Bile, Bile Acid, Gallstones & Gallstone Dissolution. 340p. 1982. text ed. 39.00 (ISBN 0-85200-497-4, Pub. by MTP Pr England). Kluwer Boston.

Hofmann, Charles. American Indians Sing. LC 67-14614. (Illus.). (gr. 3-6). 1967. PLB 14.38 (ISBN 0-381-99608-5, A02600, JD-J). Har-Row.

Hofmann, Ginnie. Who Wants an Old Teddy Bear? LC 80-10445. (Picturebacks Ser.). (Illus.). 32p. (ps-3). 1980. PLB 4.99 (ISBN 0-394-93925-5); pap. 1.50 (ISBN 0-394-83925-0). Random.

Hofmann, Joseph E. History of Mathematics to Eighteen Hundred. (Quality Paperback Ser.: No. 144). 1967. pap. 4.95 (ISBN 0-8226-0144-3). Littlefield.

Hofmannsthal, Hugo Von see Strauss, Richard & Von Hofmannsthal, Hugo.

Hofmeister, W. Vergleichende Untersuchungen der Keimung Entfaltung, und Fruchtbildung Hoeherer Kryptogamen (Moose, Farne, Equisetaceen, Rhizocarpeen un Lycopodiaceen) un der Samenbildung der Coniferen. (Historia Naturalis Classica: No. 105). (Illus., Ger.). 1979. Repr. of 1851 ed. lib. bdg. 24.00 (ISBN 3-7682-1250-5). Lubrecht & Cramer.

Hofmekler, Ori. Hofmekler's People. LC 82-83651. (Illus.). 128p. 1983. pap. 9.95 (ISBN 0-03-063371-0). HR&W.

Hofner, H., ed. see International Symposium, Mannheim, 26-29 of July, 1972.

Hofrichter, Ruth. Three Poets & Reality. 1942. text ed. 11.50x (ISBN 0-686-83821-1). Elliots Bks.

Hofsinde, Robert. The Indian & His Horse. (Illus.). (gr. 3-7). 1960. PLB 8.16 (ISBN 0-688-31421-X). Morrow.

--Indian Costumes. LC 68-11895. (Illus.). (gr. 3-7). 1968. PLB 8.16 (ISBN 0-688-31614-X). Morrow.

--Indian Music Makers. (Illus.). (gr. 3-7). 1967. PLB 8.16 (ISBN 0-688-31616-6). Morrow.

--Indian Picture Writing. (Illus.). (gr. 5-9). 1959. PLB 8.16 (ISBN 0-688-31609-3). Morrow.

--Indian Sign Language. (Illus.). (gr. 5 up). 1956. PLB 8.16 (ISBN 0-688-31610-7). Morrow.

--Indian Warriors & Their Weapons. (Illus.). (gr. 4-7). 1965. PLB 8.16 (ISBN 0-688-31613-1). Morrow.

--Indians at Home. (Illus.). (gr. 3-7). 1964. PLB 8.16 (ISBN 0-688-31611-5). Morrow.

Hofsoos, Emil. What Management Should Know About Industrial Advertising. 131p. 1970. 7.95 o.p. (ISBN 0-87201-386-3). Gulf Pub.

Hofstadter, Albert, tr. see Heidegger, Martin.

Hofstadter, Dan, tr. Nostradamus: The Future Foretold. (Illus.). 64p. 1983. 3.95 (ISBN 0-88088-451-7). Peter Pauper.

Hofstadter, Douglas. Godel, Escher, Bach: An Eternal Golden Braid. LC 78-19943. 1979. 23.00 (ISBN 0-465-02685-0). Basic.

Hofstadter, Douglas R. & Dennett, Daniel C. The Mind's I: Fantasies & Reflections on Self & Soul. LC 81-66099. 280p. 1981. 16.95 (ISBN 0-465-04624-X). Basic.

Hofstadter, Douglas R. & Dennett, Daniel C., eds. The Mind's I: Fantasies & Reflections of Self & Soul. 368p. 1982. pap. 8.95 (ISBN 0-553-01412-9). Bantam.

Hofstadter, Richard. America at Seventeen-Fifty. 320p. 1973. pap. 4.95 (ISBN 0-394-71795-3, Vin). Random.

--The American Political Tradition & the Man Who Made It. 2nd ed. (YA) 1973. 15.50 (ISBN 0-394-48880-6). Knopf.

--The Idea of a Party System: The Rise of Legitimate Opposition in the United States, 1780-1840. LC 76-82377. (Jefferson Memorial Lectures). 1969. 22.50x (ISBN 0-520-01389-1); pap. 3.95 (ISBN 0-520-01754-4, CAL196). U of Cal Pr.

Hofstadter, Richard & Lipset, Seymour M., eds. Sociology & History: Methods. LC 68-22327. (Sociology of American History Ser.: Vol. 1). 1968. pap. text ed. 4.75x o.s.i. (ISBN 0-465-07994-6). Basic.

Hofstee, E. W., jt. auth. see Constandse, A. K.

Hofstetter, H. H. Solvent Processing for Textiles. 1970. 5.00 o.p. (ISBN 0-87245-140-2). Textile Bk.

Hofstetter, Richard R., ed. U. S. Immigration Policy. (Duke Press Policy Studies). 240p. Date not set. 19.75 (ISBN 0-8223-0476-7). Duke.

Hoft, R. G., jt. auth. see Bedford, Burnice D.

Hoftijzer, J., jt. ed. see Eggermont, P. H. L.

Hofvander, Tngve, jt. auth. see Cameron, Margaret.

Hogan, Charles. Bibliography of Edwin Arlington Robinson. 1936. text ed. 23.50x (ISBN 0-686-37863-6). Elliots Bks.

Hogan, Daniel B. The Regulation of Psychotherapists I: A Study in the Philosophy & Practice of Professional Regulation. LC 78-11291. (Regulation of Psychotherapists Ser.). 1978. prof ref 27.50x (ISBN 0-88410-501-6). Ballinger Pub.

--The Regulation of Psychotherapists II: A Handbook of State Licensure Laws. LC 77-28991. (Regulation of Psychotherapists Ser.). 1978. prof ref 30.00x (ISBN 0-88410-523-7). Ballinger Pub.

--The Regulation of Psychotherapists, Vol. IV: A Resource Bibliography. LC 77-28992. (The Regulation of Psychotherapists Ser.). 1979. prof ref 27.50x (ISBN 0-88410-532-6). Ballinger Pub.

--The Regulation of Psychotherapists, Vol. III: A Review of Malpractice Suits in the U.S. LC 78-23778. (The Regulation of Psychotherapists Ser.). 1979. prof ref 27.50x (ISBN 0-88410-524-5). Ballinger Pub.

Hogan, Ed, et al, eds. The Aspect Anthology: A Ten-Year Retrospective. LC 81-52957. (Illus.). 272p. 1981. pap. 4.95 (ISBN 0-939010-01-1). Zephyr Pr.

Hogan, Elizabeth. The Curse of King Tut. Uhlich, Richard, ed. (Bluejeans Paperbacks Ser.). (Illus., Orig.). (gr. 7-12). 1978. pap. text ed. 1.25 o.p. (ISBN 0-8374-0045-7). Xerox Ed Pubns.

--Stevie's Day off. (ps). 1980. 4.95 o.p. (ISBN 0-8054-4155-7). Broadman.

Hogan, Inez. A Dog for Danny. LC 72-10461. (Venture Ser). (Illus.). 40p. (gr. 1). 1973. PLB 6.69 (ISBN 0-8116-6729-4). Garrard.

Hogan, James P. The Code of the Lifemaker. 1983. 13.95 (ISBN 0-345-30925-1, Del Rey). Ballantine.

Hogan, Judy. Sun-Blazoned. 90p. 1982. pap. 5.00 (ISBN 0-686-97379-8). Carolina Wren.

Hogan, Kirk, jt. auth. see Hogan, Paula Z.

Hogan, Paul. Playgrounds for Free: The Utilization of Used & Surplus Materials in Playground Construction. 1974. pap. 9.95x (ISBN 0-262-58030-6). MIT Pr.

Hogan, Paula Z. I Hate Boys - I Hate Girls. LC 79-24056. (Life & Living from a Child's Point of View Ser.). (Illus.). (gr. k-5). 1980. PLB 13.30 (ISBN 0-8172-1358-9). Raintree Pubs.

--Sometimes I Don't Like School. LC 79-24055. (Life & Living from a Child's Point of View Ser.). (Illus.). (gr. k-5). 1980. PLB 13.30 (ISBN 0-8172-1357-0). Raintree Pubs.

--Sometimes I Get So Mad. LC 79-24057. (Life & Living from a Child's Point of View Ser.). (Illus.). (gr. k-5). 1980. PLB 13.30 (ISBN 0-8172-1359-7). Raintree Pubs.

--Will Dad Ever Move Back Home? LC 79-24058. (Life & Living from a Child's Point of View Ser.). (Illus.). (gr. k-5). 1980. PLB 13.30 (ISBN 0-8172-1356-2). Raintree Pubs.

Hogan, Paula Z. & Hogan, Kirk. The Hospital Scares Me. LC 79-23886. (Life & Living from a Child's Point of View Ser.). (Illus.). (gr. k-5). 1980. PLB 13.30 (ISBN 0-8172-1351-1). Raintree Pubs.

Hogan, Ray. Day of Reckoning. Bd. with Dead Man on a Black Horse. 1982. pap. 2.50 (ISBN 0-451-11523-6, AE1523, Sig). NAL.

--Dead Gun. 1980. pap. 1.75 o.p. (ISBN 0-451-09026-8, E9026, Sig). NAL.

--The Doomsday Bullet. 1982. pap. 1.95 (ISBN 0-451-11630-5, AJ1630, Sig). NAL.

--The Doomsday Marshall. (Large Print Bks.). 1979. lib. bdg. 10.95 o.p. (ISBN 0-8161-6754-0). G K Hall.

--The Doomsday Posse. (General Ser.). 1982. lib. bdg. 10.95 (ISBN 0-8161-3364-6, Large Print Bks). G K Hall.

--The Doomsday Trail. LC 79-15835. (Double D Western Ser.). 1979. 10.95 o.p. (ISBN 0-385-14841-0). Doubleday.

--The Glory Trail. 1979. pap. 1.75 o.p. (ISBN 0-451-08826-3, E8826, Sig). NAL.

--The Hellborn. 1979. pap. 1.50 o.p. (ISBN 0-451-08760-7, W8760, Sig). NAL.

--Lawman's Choice. 1981. pap. 1.95 (ISBN 0-451-11216-4, AE 1216, Sig). NAL.

--Man Without A Gun. (General Ser.). 1982. 10.95 (ISBN 0-8161-3363-8, Large Print Bks). G K Hall.

--Outlaw Marshall-Wolf Lawman. 1982. pap. 2.75 (ISBN 0-451-11744-1, AE1744, Sig). NAL.

--Outlaw's Pledge. (Orig.). 1981. pap. 1.95 (ISBN 0-451-09778-5, J9778, Sig). NAL.

--R the Doomsday Bullet. (General Ser.). 1983. lib. bdg. 11.95 (ISBN 0-8161-3432-4, Large Print Bks). G K Hall.

--Reagan's Law. 1981. pap. 1.95 o.p. (ISBN 0-451-11030-7, AJ1030, Sig). NAL.

--The Renegades. 1982. pap. 2.25 (ISBN 0-451-11928-2, AE1928, Sig). NAL.

--Rimrocker. Bd. with The Outlaw. 1978. pap. 1.75 o.p. (ISBN 0-451-07888-8, E7888, Sig). NAL.

--Three Cross & Deputy of Violence. (Orig.). 1978. pap. 2.50 (ISBN 0-451-11604-6, AE1604, Sig). NAL.

--The Vengeance of Fortuna West. LC 82-45612. (D. D. Western Ser.). 192p. 1983. 11.95 (ISBN 0-385-18432-8). Doubleday.

Hogan, Robert. Bernard Shaw's 'An Unsocial Socialist' (Adaptations Ser.). 6.95x (ISBN 0-912262-53-2); pap. 2.95x (ISBN 0-912262-54-0). Proscenium.

--Dion Boucicault. (U. S. Authors Ser.). 13.95 (ISBN 0-8057-0076-5, Twayne). G K Hall.

--Since O'Casey: And Other Essays on Irish Drama. LC 82-22813. (Irish Literary Studies: No. 15). 166p. 1983. text ed. 28.50x (ISBN 0-389-20346-7). B&N Imports.

Hogan, Robert, ed. Dictionary of Irish Literature. LC 78-20021. 1979. lib. bdg. 45.00 (ISBN 0-313-20718-6, HDI/). Greenwood.

Hogan, Robert L. Mallet to Mogul. (Illus.). pap. 6.95 soft bound (ISBN 0-89685-031-5). Chatham Pub CA.

Hogan, Steven, ed. Spanish Art: The Masterpieces of Spanish Art in the Great Museums of Spain. (Illus.). 93p. 1983. 87.55 (ISBN 0-86650-060-X). Gloucester Art.

Hogan, Terrence P., jt. auth. see Erickson, Gerald D.

Hogan, Thom. Discover FORTH: Learning & Programming the FORTH Language. 146p. (Orig.). 1982. pap. 14.95 (ISBN 0-931988-79-9). Osborne-McGraw.

--Osborne CP-M User Guide. rev., 2nd ed. 292p. (Orig.). 1982. pap. 15.95 (ISBN 0-931988-82-9). Osborne-McGraw.

Hogan, William T. World Steel in the 1980's: A Case for Survival. LC 75-41587. 288p. 1982. 26.95 (ISBN 0-669-00465-0). Lexington Bks.

Hogarth, C. A. Materials Used in Semiconductor Devices. LC 65-27440. 243p. 1965. text ed. 16.00 o.p. (ISBN 0-470-40614-3, Pub. by Wiley). Krieger.

Hogarth, C. J., tr. see Sienkiewicz, Henryk.

Hogarth, G. Memoirs of the Opera in Italy, France, Germany & England, 2 vols. LC 71-166101. (Music Ser.). 1972. Repr. of 1851 ed. Set. lib. bdg. 65.00 (ISBN 0-306-70256-8). Da Capo.

Hogarth, George. Musical History, Biography, & Criticism. LC 69-12685. (Music Reprint Ser). 1969. Repr. of 1848 ed. lib. bdg. 25.00 (ISBN 0-306-71234-2). Da Capo.

Hogarth, James, tr. see Taddei, Maurizio.

Hogarth, Paul. Paul Hogarth's Walking Tours of Old Philadelphia. 1976. 15.00 o.p. (ISBN 0-517-52384-1, C N Potter Bks); pap. 6.95 o.p. (ISBN 0-517-52385-X, C N Potter Bks). Crown.

Hogarth, Paul & Spender, Stephen. America Observed. 1979. 25.00 o.p. (ISBN 0-517-53080-5, C N Potter Bks). Crown.

Hogarth, Peter J. Viviparity. (Studies in Biology: No. 75). 72p. 1978. pap. text ed. 8.95 (ISBN 0-7131-2593-4). E Arnold.

Hogarth, W. D., tr. see Momigliano, Arnaldo.

Hogarth, William. The Aesthetical & Psychological Analysis of Beauty. (Illus.). 177p. 1983. Repr. of 1907 ed. 77.45 (ISBN 0-89901-108-X). Found Class Reprints.

Hogben, Lancelot. Mathematics for the Million. (Illus.). 656p. 1983. pap. 8.95 (ISBN 0-393-30035-8). Norton.

Hogbe-Nlend, H. Bornologies & Functional Analysis. (North-Holland Mathematical Studies: Vol. 26). 1977. pap. 38.50 (ISBN 0-7204-0712-5, North-Holland). Elsevier.

Hogbe-Nlend, H. & Moscatelli, V. B. Nuclear & Conuclear Spaces. (North-Holland Mathematics Studies: Vol. 52). 1981. pap. 47.00 (ISBN 0-444-86207-2). Elsevier.

Hoge, Cecil C., Sr. Mail Order Know-How. LC 82-50903. 472p. 1982. 19.95 (ISBN 0-89815-016-7); pap. 16.95 (ISBN 0-89815-015-9). Ten Speed Pr.

Hoge, James O. & West, James L., eds. Review, Vol. 2. 1980. 20.00x (ISBN 0-8139-0865-5). U Pr of Va.

--Review, Vol. 3. 1981. 20.00x (ISBN 0-8139-0910-4). U Pr of Va.

Hoge, James O., III & West, James L. W., eds. Review IV. 1983. 24.00 (ISBN 0-8139-0974-0). U Pr of Va.

Hogeland, Ronald W. Woman & Womanhood in America. (Problems in American Civilization Ser.). 1974. pap. text ed. 5.95 (ISBN 0-669-85597-9). Heath.

Hogg, A. H. Surveying for Archaeologists & Other Fieldworkers. LC 80-10396. (Illus.). 320p. 1980. 36.00 (ISBN 0-312-77727-2). St Martin.

Hogg, Anthony. The Winetaster's Guide to Europe: How to Visit over 300 Vineyards & Cellars on Your European Vacation. (Illus.). 1980. 17.50 o.p. (ISBN 0-525-93071-X); pap. 8.95 o.p. (ISBN 0-525-93084-1). Dutton.

Hogg, Gayle, ed. see Maston, T. B.

Hogg, Ian. Artillery in Color: Nineteen Twenty to Nineteen Sixty-Three. LC 80-379. (Illus.). 192p. 1980. 11.95 (ISBN 0-668-04939-1); pap. 7.95 o.p. (ISBN 0-668-04941-3). Arco.

--Fighting Tanks. LC 77-78749. (Illus.). 1978. 9.95 o.p. (ISBN 0-448-14459-X, G&D). Putnam Pub Group.

--Fortress: A History of Military Defense. LC 76-62774. 1977. 15.00 o.p. (ISBN 0-312-29977-X). St Martin.

--The History of Fortification. (Illus.). 256p. 1983. 32.50 (ISBN 0-312-37852-1). St Martin.

Hogg, Ian & Weeks, John, eds. Jane's 1982-83 Military Annual. (Illus.). 158p. 1982. 15.95 (ISBN 0-86720-633-0). Sci Bks Intl.

Hogg, Ian V. Armour in Conflict. (Illus.). 288p. 1980. 16.95 (ISBN 0-86720-587-3). Sci Bks Intl.

--The Complete Illustrated Encyclopedia of the World's Firearms. LC 78-56305. (Illus.). 320p. 1978. 24.95 o.s.i. (ISBN 0-89479-031-5). A & W Pubs.

--The Encyclopedia of Infantry Weapon of World War II. (Illus.). 192p. 1981. 9.98 o.p. (ISBN 0-89196-099-6, Bk Value Intl). Quality Bks IL.

Hogg, Ivan V. Guns & How They Work. LC 78-53013. (Illus.). 1979. 16.95 (ISBN 0-89696-023-4, An Everest House Book). Dodd.

Hogg, Ivan V. & Weeks, John. The Illustrated Encyclopedia of Military Vehicles. LC 80-8006. (Illus.). 1980. 30.00 o.p. (ISBN 0-13-450817-3). P-H.

Hogg, J. & Mittler, P. Advances in Mental Handicap Research, Vol. 1. 311p. 1980. 64.95 (ISBN 0-471-99740-4, Pub. by Wiley-Interscience). Wiley.

Hogg, James. The Peter Russell Seminar, 1981-82. (Salzburg - Poetic Drama Ser.: No. 72). 143p. 1982. pap. text ed. 25.00x (ISBN 0-391-02776-X, Pub. by Salzburg Austria). Humanities.

--Private Memoirs & Confessions of a Justified Sinner. 1970. pap. 4.95x (ISBN 0-393-00515-1, Norton Lib). Norton.

--The Scourge of Immortality: The Rev. Jeremy Collier & the Restoration Dramatists. (Salzburg Poetic Drama & Poetic Theory: 4). 1979. pap. text ed. 25.00x cancelled (ISBN 0-391-01428-5). Humanities.

--Shelley: The Critics & "The Cenci". (Salzburg Studies in English Literature: Romantic Reassessment Ser.: No. 29). 1980. pap. text ed. 25.00x cancelled (ISBN 0-391-01427-7). Humanities.

Hogg, James, ed. Elizabethan Miscellany, Vol. 3. (Salzburg-Elizabethan & Renaissance Ser.: Vol. 71: 2). 117p. 1981. pap. text ed. 25.00x (ISBN 0-391-02813-8, Pub. by Salzburg Austria). Humanities.

--Romantic Reassessment. (Salzburg Studies in English Literature: Vol. 87, No. 4). 105p. 1981. pap. text ed. 25.00x (ISBN 0-391-02759-X, 40596, Pub. by Salzburg Austria). Humanities.

--Stylistic Media of Byron's Satire. (Salzburg - Romantic Reassessment Ser.: Vol. 81, No. 3). 83p. 1982. pap. text ed. 25.00x (ISBN 0-391-02804-9, Pub. by Salzburg Austria). Humanities.

Hogg, Robert V. & Craig, Allen T. Introduction to Mathematical Statistics. 4th ed. (Illus.). 1978. text ed. 28.95x (ISBN 0-02-355710-9, 35571). Macmillan.

Hogg, Robert V. & Tanis, Elliot A. Probability & Statistical Inference. (Illus.). 1977. text ed. 25.95 (ISBN 0-02-355650-1). Macmillan.

--Probability & Statistical Inference. 2nd ed. 500p. 1983. text ed. 22.95 (ISBN 0-02-355730-3). Macmillan.

Hoggard, Kevin, ed. Summer Theatre Directory, 1980: 1980. 1980. pap. 3.50x o.p. (ISBN 0-940528-13-4). Am Theatre Assoc.

Hoggard, Stuart. David Bowie: An Illustrated Discography. (Illus.). 96p. 1981. pap. 4.95 (ISBN 0-8256-3956-5, Quick Fox). Putnam Pub Group.

Hoggarth, Pauline, jt. auth. see Gifford, Douglas.

Hoggett, Chris. Stage Crafts. LC 76-10554. (Illus.). 1977. 17.50 (ISBN 0-312-75495-7). St Martin.

Hoggett, J. G., et al. Nitration & Aromatic Reactivity. LC 76-138374. (Illus.). 1971. 44.50 (ISBN 0-521-08029-0). Cambridge U Pr.

Hogins, James B. Literature: Fiction. LC 73-90125. (Illus.). 368p. 1974. pap. text ed. 7.95 (ISBN 0-574-19130-5, 13-2130). SRA.

--Literature: Poetry. LC 73-90125. (Illus.). 368p. 1974. pap. text ed. 7.95 (ISBN 0-574-19125-9, 13-2125). SRA.

Hogins, James B. & Bryant, Gerald R., Jr. Juxtaposition, Encore! LC 74-15169. (Illus.). 304p. 1975. pap. text ed. 15.95 (ISBN 0-574-17000-6, 13-5000); instr's guide avail. (ISBN 0-574-17001-4, 13-5001). SRA.

Hogins, James B. & Yarber, Robert E. Models for Writing. LC 74-18853. (Illus.). 448p. 1975. pap. text ed. 11.95 (ISBN 0-574-18010-9, 13-5010); instructor's guide 2.25 (ISBN 0-574-22011-9, 13-5011). SRA.

--Phase Blue. rev. ed. LC 73-87858. (Illus.). 464p. 1974. pap. text ed. 8.95 o.s.i. (ISBN 0-574-18370-1, 13-1370); instr's guide avail. o.s.i. (ISBN 0-574-18371-X, 13-1371); student guide 3.95 o.s.i. (ISBN 0-574-18395-7, 13-1395); instructor's guide 2.50 o.s.i. (ISBN 0-574-18372-8, 13-1372). SRA.

--Reading, Writing & Rhetoric. 4th ed. LC 78-13940. 1979. pap. text ed. 11.95 (ISBN 0-574-22045-3, 13-5045); instr's guide avail. (ISBN 0-574-22046-1, 13-5046). SRA.

--Reading, Writing, & Rhetoric. 5th ed. 576p. 1983. pap. text ed. write for info. (ISBN 0-574-22080-1); write for info. instr's. guide (ISBN 0-574-22081-X). SRA.

--Theme & Rhetoric. LC 76-28344. 1977. pap. text ed. 11.95 (ISBN 0-574-22025-9, 13-5025); instr's guide avail. (ISBN 0-574-22026-7, 13-5026). SRA.

Hogner, Dorothy C. Birds of Prey. LC 79-81954. (Illus.). (gr. 3 up). 1969. 9.57i o.p. (ISBN 0-690-14585-3, TYC-J). Har-Row.

--Good Bugs & Bad Bugs in Your Garden: Backyard Ecology. LC 74-6235. (Illus.). 96p. (gr. 3-7). 1974. PLB 9.89 o.p. (ISBN 0-690-00120-7, TYC-J). Har-Row.

--Grasshoppers & Crickets. LC 60-9219. (Illus.). (gr. 2-5). 1960. 8.95 o.p. (ISBN 0-690-35035-X, TYC-J) (ISBN 0-690-35036-8). Har-Row.

Hogrogian, Nonny. One Fine Day. LC 75-119834. (Illus.). 32p. (ps-2). 1974. pap. 2.95 (ISBN 0-02-043620-3, Collier). Macmillan.

Hogrogian, Nonny see Kherdian, David.

Hogstel, Mildred O. Nursing Care of the Older Adult. LC 80-22985. 587p. 1981. 21.95 (ISBN 0-471-06022-4, Pub. by Wiley Med). Wiley.

Hogstel, Mildred O., ed. Management of Personnel in Long Term Care. (Illus.). 336p. 1982. text ed. 19.95 (ISBN 0-89303-231-X). R J Brady.

Hogue, Arthur R., ed. see Schurz, Carl.

Hogue, L. L. Public Health & the Law: Issues & Trends. LC 80-15041. 427p. 1980. text ed. 42.00 (ISBN 0-89443-289-3). Aspen Systems.

Hogue, W. Dickerson, jt. auth. see Farmer, Richard N.

Hogwood, Brian. Government Policy & Shipbuilding. 1979. text ed. 33.25x (ISBN 0-566-00233-7). Gower Pub Ltd.

Hogwood, Brian & Peters, Guy. Policy Dynamics. LC 82-10330. 304p. 1982. 27.50x (ISBN 0-312-62014-4). St Martin.

Hogwood, Christopher. The Trio Sonata. 1983. write for info. U of Wash Pr.

Hohenberg, Paul. A Primer on the Economic History of Europe. LC 81-40794. 254p. 1981. pap. text ed. 9.25 (ISBN 0-8191-1804-4). U Pr of Amer.

Hohenemser, K. H. & Swift, A. H. Investigation of Passive Blade Cyclic Pitch Variation using an Automatic Yaw Control System. (Progress in Solar Energy, Supplements Ser.). 112p. 1982. pap. text ed. 12.00x (ISBN 0-89553-105-4). Am Solar Energy.

Hohenemser, Kurt. Elastokinetik. LC 50-2567. (Ger). 14.95 (ISBN 0-8284-0055-5). Chelsea Pub.

Hohenshil, Thomas H. & Miles, Johnnie H. School Guidance Services: A Career Development Approach. 1979. pap. text ed. 11.95 (ISBN 0-8403-2044-2). Kendall-Hunt.

Hohenstein, C. Louis. Computer Peripherals for Minicomputers, Microprocessors & Personal Computers. (Illus.). 320p. 1980. 21.90 (ISBN 0-07-029451-8, P&RB). McGraw.

Hohfeld, Wesley N. Fundamental Legal Conceptions, As Applied in Judicial Reasoning. Wheeler, Walter C., ed. LC 75-31367. 1978. Repr. of 1964 ed. lib. bdg. 19.75x (ISBN 0-8371-8525-4, HOLC). Greenwood.

Hohler, G., ed. Solid-State Physics. LC 76-18956. (Tracts in Modern Physics: Vol. 78). (Illus.). 1976. 52.90 o.p. (ISBN 0-387-07774-X). Springer-Verlag.

Hohler, Thomas P. Imagination & Reflection: Intersubjectivity. 1983. lib. bdg. 29.50 (ISBN 90-247-2732-4, Pub. by Martinus Nijhoff Netherlands). Kluwer Boston.

Hohlfelder, Robert L. City, Town & Countryside in the Early Byzantine Era. (Brooklyn College Studies on Society in Change). 280p. 1982. 22.50x (ISBN 0-88033-013-9). East Eur Quarterly.

Hohlt, David T. Heaven Can't Wait: We've Seen Too Much of Hell. 1983. 8.95 (ISBN 0-533-05599-7). Vantage.

Hohlwein, Kathryn J., jt. auth. see Lamb, Patricia F.

Hohman, Helen F. & Field, James A., eds. Essays on Population & Other Papers. 1931. 12.50 (ISBN 0-686-33258-X). R S Barnes.

Hohman, Jo. Focus on Nurse Credentialing. LC 80-17049. 96p. (Orig.). 1980. 12.50 (ISBN 0-87258-303-1, AHA-154162). Am Hospital.

--Shared Food Services in Health Care Institutions. LC 76-13193. (Illus.). 100p. (Orig.). 1976. pap. 12.50 (ISBN 0-87258-178-0, AHA-046130). Am Hospital.

--Taft-Hartley Amendments: Implications for the Health Care Field. LC 76-29662. 136p. (Orig.). 1976. pap. 13.50 (ISBN 0-87258-181-0, AHA-112175). Am Hospital.

Hohmann, Hans-Hermann, et al, eds. The New Economic Systems of Eastern Europe. LC 74-76386. 1975. 49.75x (ISBN 0-520-02732-9). U of Cal Pr.

Hohn, Franz E. Elementary Matrix Algebra. 3rd ed. 1973. text ed. 25.95x (ISBN 0-02-355950-0). Macmillan.

Hohn, Franz E., jt. auth. see Dornhoff, Larry L.

Hoie, T. A. Performance Control: Service & Resource Control in Complex IBM Computing Centres. (Illus.). 252p. 1983. 42.75 (ISBN 0-444-86517-9, North Holland). Elsevier.

Hoig, Stan. The Humor of the American Cowboy. LC 58-5328. (Illus.). 193p. 1970. pap. 4.95 (ISBN 0-8032-5719-8, BB 520, Bison). U of Nebr Pr.

Hojnacki, Linda & Halfman, Marsha. Cardiac Rehabilitation. 1982. pap. text ed. 14.95 (ISBN 0-8359-0673-6). Reston.

Hokanson, Jack E. Introduction to the Therapeutic Process. (Illus.). 416p. Date not set. text ed. price not set (ISBN 0-201-10525-X). A-W.

Hokanson, Joseph D. Your Winning Ticket. (Illus.). 271p. 1982. info. manual 47.50 (ISBN 0-910625-00-X). Ark Val Pubns.

Hoke, Donald, ed. The Church in Asia. 650p. 1976. 15.95 o.p. (ISBN 0-8024-1543-1). Moody.

Hoke, Helen & Pitt, Valerie. Whales. LC 72-11769. (First Bks). (Illus.). 72p. (gr. 4 up). 1973. PLB 8.90 (ISBN 0-531-04196-4). Watts.

Hoke, Helen, ed. Creepies, Creepies, Creepies. LC 77-6289. (Terrific Triple Titles Ser.). (Illus.). (gr. 7 up). 1977. s&l 8.90 (ISBN 0-531-01323-5). Watts.

--Eerie, Weird & Wicked. LC 77-7252. (gr. 7 up). 1977. 7.95 o.p. (ISBN 0-525-66554-4). Lodestar Bks.

--Ghastly, Ghoulish, Gripping Tales. (Terrific Triple Titles Ser.). 176p. (gr. 7 up). 1983. PLB 8.60 (ISBN 0-531-04593-5). Watts.

--Tales of Fear & Frightening Phenomena. 160p. (gr. 7 up). 1982. 10.50 (ISBN 0-525-66789-X, 01019-310). Lodestar Bks.

Hoke, James H. I Would If I Could & I Can. LC 80-51606. 180p. 1982. 10.95 (ISBN 0-8128-2745-7); pap. 6.95 (ISBN 0-8128-6135-3). Stein & Day.

Hoke, John. Solar Energy. rev. ed. (Impact Bks.). (Illus.). (gr. 7 up). 1978. PLB 7.45 s&l o.p. (ISBN 0-531-01329-4). Watts.

Hoke, Rudolf, jt. auth. see Dilcher, Gerhard.

Hokin, L. E. see Greenberg, D. M.

Hok-Lam Chan. Li Chih (Fifteen Twenty-Seven to Sixteen Two) in Contemporary Chinese Historiography: New Light on His Life & Works. LC 79-57496. 1980. 25.00 (ISBN 0-87332-160-X). M E Sharpe.

Hol, Joh C. Horatio Vecchi's weltliche Werke: Mit einem musikalischen Anhang, bis jetzt unveroffentl Kompositionen enthaltend. (Sammlung MW. Abh. 13-1934 Ser.). iv, 94p. 25.00 o.s.i. (ISBN 90-6027-263-3, Pub. by Frits Knuf Netherlands). Pendragon NY.

Holahan, Charles J. Environmental Psychology. 448p. 1982. text ed. 24.00 (ISBN 0-394-32320-3). Random.

Holahan, John. Physician Supply, Peer Review, & Use of Health Services in Medicaid. (An Institute Paper). 70p. 1976. pap. 3.50 o.p. (ISBN 0-87766-159-6, 13800). Urban Inst.

Holahan, John, jt. auth. see Bovbjerg, Randall R.

Holand, H. R. Norse Discoveries & Explorations in America: 982-1362. (Illus.). 9.50 (ISBN 0-8446-0703-7). Peter Smith.

Holbach, Paul T. Le Bon-sens ou Idees Naturelles Opposees aux Idees Surnaturelles. (Holbach & His Friends Ser). 261p. (Fr.). 1974. Repr. of 1772 ed. lib. bdg. 71.00 o.p. (ISBN 0-8287-0436-8, 1551). Clearwater Pub.

--Le Christianisme Devoile. (Holbach & His Friends Ser). 326p. (Fr.). 1974. Repr. of 1756 ed. lib. bdg. 85.50 o.p. (ISBN 0-8287-0437-6, 1516). Clearwater Pub.

--La Contagion Sacree ou Histoire Naturelle de la Superstition, 2 vols. (Holbach & His Friends Ser). 369p. (Fr.). 1974. Repr. of 1768 ed. lib. bdg. 95.00x set o.p. (ISBN 0-8287-0438-4, 1511-2). Clearwater Pub.

--Elements de la Morale Universelle ou Catechisme de la Nature. (Holbach & His Friends Ser). 215p. (Fr.). 1974. Repr. of 1790 ed. lib. bdg. 61.00x o.s.i. (ISBN 0-8287-0439-2, 1591). Clearwater Pub.

--Essai sur l'Art de Ramper, a l'Usage des Courtisans. (Holbach & His Friends Ser). (Fr.). 1974. Repr. lib. bdg. 19.00 o.p. (ISBN 0-8287-1369-3, 1517). Clearwater Pub.

--Essai sur les Prejuges, ou de l'Influence des Opinions sur les Moeurs et sur le Bonheur des Hommes. (Holbach & His Friends Ser). 402p. (Fr.). 1974. Repr. of 1770 ed. lib. bdg. 102.50 o.p. (ISBN 0-8287-0440-6, 1508). Clearwater Pub.

--Histoire de Jesus-Christ ou, Analyse Raisonnee des Evangiles. (Holbach & His Friends Ser). 440p. (Fr.). 1974. Repr. of 1770 ed. lib. bdg. 111.00 o.p. (ISBN 0-8287-0443-0, 1505). Clearwater Pub.

--Lettre a une Dame d'un Certain Age, sur l'Etat Present de l'Opera. (Holbach & His Friends Ser). (Fr.). 1974. Repr. of 1752 ed. lib. bdg. 20.00x o.p. (ISBN 0-8287-1383-9, 1522). Clearwater Pub.

--Lettres a Eugenie ou Preservatif Contra les Prejuges, 2 vols. (Holbach & His Friends Ser). 380p. (Fr.). 1974. Repr. of 1768 ed. lib. bdg. 110.50 o.p. (ISBN 0-8287-0444-9, 1578-9). Clearwater Pub.

--La Morale Universelle ou les Devoirs de l'Homme Fondes sur sa Nature, 3 vols. (Holbach & His Friends Ser). 1042p. (Fr.). 1974. Repr. of 1776 ed. lib. bdg. 270.00x o.p. (ISBN 0-8287-0445-7, 1547-9). Clearwater Pub.

--La Politique Naturelle. (Holbach & His Friends Ser). 523p. (Fr.). 1974. Repr. of 1773 ed. lib. bdg. 129.00x o.p. (ISBN 0-8287-0446-5, 1596). Clearwater Pub.

--Systeme Social, 3 vols. (Holbach & His Friends Ser). 571p. (Fr.). 1974. Repr. of 1773 ed. lib. bdg. 166.00x o.p. (ISBN 0-8287-0447-3, 1540-2). Clearwater Pub.

--Tableau des Saints, 2 vols. (Holbach & His Friends Ser). 610p. (Fr.). 1974. Repr. of 1770 ed. lib. bdg. 161.00x o.p. (ISBN 0-8287-0448-1, 1528-9). Clearwater Pub.

--Theologie Portative ou Dictionaire de la Religion Chretienne. (Holbach & His Friends Ser). 241p. (Fr.). 1974. Repr. of 1768 ed. lib. bdg. 67.00x o.p. (ISBN 0-8287-0449-X, 1574). Clearwater Pub.

Holbach, Paul T., jt. auth. see Naigeon, Jacques-Andre.

Holbein, Hans. Dance of Death. LC 74-172180. Orig. Title: Les Simulachres & Historiees Faces Des La Mort. 1972. pap. 3.50 (ISBN 0-486-22804-5). Dover.

--Drawings in the Royal Collection. 1982. 3500.00 (ISBN 0-384-23845-9). Johnson Repr.

Holbein, Hans The Younger. The Dance of Death: A Complete Facsimile of the Original 1538 French Edition. 8.75 (ISBN 0-8446-0144-6). Peter Smith.

Holberg, L. Seven One-Act Plays. LC 50-9258. Repr. of 1950 ed. 14.00 o.s.i. (ISBN 0-527-41820-X). Kraus Repr.

Holberg, Ruth L. American Bard: The Story of Henry Wadsworth Longfellow. LC 63-15090. (Illus.). (gr. 5-9). 1963. 8.95i o.p. (ISBN 0-690-05923-X, TYC-J). Har-Row.

Holbert, Neil. Research in the Twilight Zone. LC 76-45823. (Monograph Ser.: No. 7). 1977. 5.00 (ISBN 0-87757-084-1). Am Mktg.

Holbo, Paul S. Tarnished Expansion: The Alaska Scandal, the Press, & Congress, 1867-1871. LC 82-17513. (Illus.). 170p. 1983. text ed. 12.95x (ISBN 0-87049-380-9). U of Tenn Pr.

Holborn, H. A History of Modern Germany, 3 Vols. 1982. Vol. 1, The Reformation. 30.00 (ISBN 0-691-05357-X); Vol. 1, The Reformation. pap. 7.95 (ISBN 0-691-00795-0); Vol. 2, 1648-1840. 45.00 (ISBN 0-691-05358-8); Vol. 2, 1648-1840. pap. 9.95 (ISBN 0-691-00796-9); Vol. 3, 1840-1945. 65.00 (ISBN 0-691-05359-6); Vol. 3, 1840-1945. pap. 16.50 (ISBN 0-691-00797-7). Princeton U Pr.

Holborn, Hajo. American Military Government: Its Organization & Policies. LC 77-23165. 1977. Repr. of 1947 ed. lib. bdg. 18.75x (ISBN 0-8371-9450-4, HOAMG). Greenwood.

--American Military Government: Its Organization & Policies. Kavass, Igor I. & Sprudz, Adolf, eds. LC 75-766. (International Military Law & History Ser.: Vol. 10). 1975. Repr. of 1947 ed. lib. bdg. 30.00 (ISBN 0-930342-47-X). W S Hein.

--A History of Modern Germany, 3 vols. Incl. Vol. 1. The Reformation. 1959. 20.50 o.s.i. (ISBN 0-394-42878-1); Vol. 2. 1648-1840. 20.50 o.s.i. (ISBN 0-394-42879-X); Vol. 3. 1840-1945. 20.50 o.s.i. (ISBN 0-394-42877-3). Knopf.

--The Political Collapse of Europe. LC 82-11839. 207p. 1982. Repr. of 1965 ed. lib. bdg. 27.50 (ISBN 0-313-23031-5, HOPC). Greenwood.

--Ulrich Von Hutten & the German Reformation. Bainton, Roland H., tr. LC 77-25067. (Yale Historical Publications Studies: No. XI). (Illus.). 1978. Repr. of 1937 ed. lib. bdg. 20.50x (ISBN 0-313-20125-0, HOUV). Greenwood.

Holbraad, Carsten. Superpowers & International Conflict. LC 79-9942. 1979. 26.00x (ISBN 0-312-77674-8). St Martin.

Holbrook, Becky T. Revised Handful of Ideas. 5.95 (ISBN 0-89137-611-9). Quality Pubns.

Holbrook, Becky T., jt. auth. see Holbrook, D. L.

Holbrook, D. L. God Needs Strong Men. 3.75 (ISBN 0-89137-530-9). Quality Pubns.

Holbrook, D. L. & Holbrook, Becky T. Every Step Along the Way. 3.75 (ISBN 0-89137-418-3). Quality Pubns.

--Give Them God's Way. 3.75 (ISBN 0-89137-417-5). Quality Pubns.

--Lib Movement-God's Way. 3.75 (ISBN 0-89137-419-1). Quality Pubns.

Holbrook, David. Children's Writing. 1967. 24.95 (ISBN 0-521-05284-X); pap. 9.95 (ISBN 0-521-09434-8). Cambridge U Pr.

--English for Maturity. 2nd ed. 1967. 27.95 (ISBN 0-521-05286-6); pap. 9.95x (ISBN 0-521-09465-8). Cambridge U Pr.

--English for the Rejected. (Orig.). 1964. pap. 10.95x (ISBN 0-521-09215-9). Cambridge U Pr.

--Gustav Mahler & the Courage to Be. (Illus.). 270p. 1981. Repr. of 1975 ed. lib. bdg. 29.50 (ISBN 0-306-76095-9). Da Capo.

--Maxim Gorki: Childhood. 1965. 4.50 (ISBN 0-521-05121-5). Cambridge U Pr.

--Old World New World. 3.75 o.p. (ISBN 0-85391-150-9). Transatlantic.

--Quest for Love. LC 65-24879. 376p. 1965. 21.95 o.p. (ISBN 0-8173-7305-5). U of Ala Pr.

--Thieves & Angels. 1962. text ed. 5.95x (ISBN 0-521-05302-1). Cambridge U Pr.

Holbrook, David, ed. The Case Against Pornography. LC 72-5279. 311p. 1973. 21.00x (ISBN 0-912050-28-4, Library Pr); 9.00x (ISBN 0-87548-360-7). Open Court.

Holbrook, David & Postan, Elizabeth, eds. The Apple Tree: Christmas Music from the Cambridge Hymnal. LC 76-12916. 1976. 14.95 o.p. (ISBN 0-521-21479-3); pap. 5.95 (ISBN 0-521-29116-X). Cambridge U Pr.

Holbrook, H. T. Etude Sur Pathelin. (Elliott Monographs: Vol. 5). 1917. pap. 15.00 (ISBN 0-527-02609-3). Kraus Repr.

Holbrook, J. G. Laplace Transforms for Electronic Engineers. 2nd ed. 1966. 27.00 o.p. (ISBN 0-08-011411-3). Pergamon.

Holbrook, Jay M. Vermont's First Settlers. LC 76-151555. 111p. 1976. pap. 15.00 o.p. (ISBN 0-931248-03-5). Holbrook Res.

Holbrook, Jennifer K. Gymnastics: A Movement Activity. 116p. 1975. 29.00 (ISBN 0-7121-0717-7, Pub. by Macdonald & Evans). State Mutual Bk.

Holbrook, John. A Closer Look at Elephants. LC 79-19893. (Closer Look at Ser.). (Illus.). (gr. 4-7). 1978. pap. 1.95 (ISBN 0-531-02491-1). Watts.

Holbrook, K. A., jt. auth. see Robinson, P. J.

Holbrook, Sabra. Getting to Know the Two Germanys. (Getting to Know Ser.). (Illus.). (gr. 3-5). 1966. PLB 3.97 o.p. (ISBN 0-698-30165-X, Coward). Putnam Pub Group.

Holbrook, Sally J., jt. ed. see Longacre, William A.

Holbrook, Stephen F. Effective Decision Making. revised ed. 45p. 1983. pap. text ed. 9.90 (ISBN 0-686-42968-0). PMA.

Holbrook, Stewart. Davy Crockett. (Landmark Ser.: No. 57). (Illus.). (gr. 4-6). 1955. 2.95 o.p. (ISBN 0-394-80357-4, BYR); PLB 5.99 (ISBN 0-394-90357-9). Random.

Holbrook, Stewart H. Old Post Road. 1971. pap. 3.50 o.p. (ISBN 0-07-029536-0, SP). McGraw.

Holbrook, Wallace W. Contemporary Lamps. (gr. 9 up). 1968. text ed. 15.28 (ISBN 0-87345-029-9). McKnight.

Holcenberg, John C. & Roberts, Joseph. Enzymes As Drugs. LC 80-20641. 455p. 1981. 74.95 (ISBN 0-471-05061-X, Pub. by Wiley-Interscience). Wiley.

Holcomb, Brent H. Marriages of Rowan County, North Carolina 1753-1865. LC 81-81538. 506p. 1981. 28.50 (ISBN 0-8063-0942-3). Genealog Pub.

Holcomb, M. C., jt. auth. see Kulp, G.

Holcomb Research Institute. Environmental Modeling & Decision Making: The United States Experience. LC 76-28798. 176p. 1976. 22.95 o.p. (ISBN 0-275-24190-4). Praeger.

Holcombe, A. D., jt. auth. see Pisano, Beverly.

Holcombe, Arthur N., jt. auth. see Commission to Study the Organization of Peace.

Holcombe, Arthur N., ed. see Commission to Study the Organization of Peace.

Holcombe, Henry. Patent Medicine Tax Stamps: A History of the Firms Using U.S. Private Die Proprietary Medicine Tax Stamps. LC 76-51546. 1979. 100.00x o.p. (ISBN 0-88000-098-8). Quarterman.

Holcombe, Marya & Stein, Judith. Writing for Decision Makers. LC 80-24900. 260p. 1980. text ed. 15.95 leaders manual (ISBN 0-534-97980-7). Lifetime Learn.

Holcombe, Randall G. Public Finance & Political Process. LC 82-10803. (Political & Social Economy Ser.). 208p. 1983. price not set (ISBN 0-8093-1082-1). S Ill U Pr.

Holcombe, William M. Algebraic Automata Theory. LC 81-18169. (Cambridge Studies in Advanced Mathematics 1). 250p. 1982. 29.50 (ISBN 0-521-23196-5). Cambridge U Pr.

Holcroft, M. H. The Shaping of New Zealand. LC 78-670174. (Illus.). 1974. 12.50x o.p. (ISBN 0-600-07277-0). Intl Pubns Serv.

Holcroft, Thomas. Anna St. Ives. Faulkner, Peter, ed. & intro. by. (Oxford Paperbacks Ser). 1973. pap. 5.25x o.p. (ISBN 0-19-281141-X). Oxford U Pr.

Holdcroft, Anita. Body Temperature Control: In Relation to Anaesthesia, Surgery & Intensive Care. 1980. text ed. 34.50 (ISBN 0-02-858050-8, Pub. by Bailliere-Tindall). Saunders.

Holde, K. Van see Van Holde, K.

Holden, Anthony. Prince Charles. LC 82-52176. 432p. 1983. pap. 10.95 (ISBN 0-689-70638-3, 287). Atheneum.

Holden, David. Dakota Visions: A County Approach. 391p. 1982. pap. write for info. (ISBN 0-931170-21-4). Ctr Western Studies.

Holden, David F. Analytical Index to Modern Drama. 1972. 15.00 o.p. (ISBN 0-685-64736-6). Samuel Stevens.

Holden, Donald. Art Career Guide. 4th, rev., enl. ed. 320p. 1983. 14.95 (ISBN 0-8230-0252-7). Watson-Guptill.

Holden, Edward S. A Primer of Heraldry for Americans. LC 73-2815. (Illus.). 129p. 1973. Repr. of 1898 ed. 30.00x (ISBN 0-8103-3271-X). Gale.

Holden, Frances M. Lambshead Before Interwoven. Bd. with Interwoven. Matthews, Sallie R. (Illus.). 1982. ltd. signed ed. 75.00x o.p. (ISBN 0-89096-130-1). Tex A&M Univ Pr.

Holden, Glenda, jt. auth. see Holden, Ronald.

Holden, Herbert L. Introduction to FORTRAN Four. (Illus.). 1970. pap. 14.95x (ISBN 0-02-355990-X). Macmillan.

Holden, J. T., ed. Amino Acid Pools: Distribution, Formation & Function of Free Amino Acids. 1962. 58.75 (ISBN 0-444-40288-8). Elsevier.

Holden, James P., jt. auth. see Wolfman, Bernard.

Holden, K. & Peel, D. A. An Introduction to the Econometric Modelling of the United Kingdom. 220p. 1983. text ed. 35.00x (ISBN 0-85520-519-9, Pub. by Martin Robertson England); pap. text ed. 9.95x (ISBN 0-85520-520-2, Pub. by Martin Robertson England). Biblio Dist.

Holden, M. P. A Practice of Cardiothoracic Surgery. (Illus.). 448p. 1982. text ed. 49.50 (ISBN 0-7236-0626-9). Wright-PSG.

Holden, P. E., et al. Top Management. (Illus.). 1968. text ed. 13.95 o.p. (ISBN 0-07-029545-X, C). McGraw.

Holden, Pat, ed. Women's Religious Experience. LC 82-24314. 224p. 1983. text ed. 26.50x (ISBN 0-389-20363-7). B&N Imports.

Holden, Raymond P. All About Famous Scientific Expeditions. (Allabout Ser, No. 24). (Illus.). (gr. 4-6). 1958. PLB 4.39 o.p. (ISBN 0-394-90224-6, BYR); 2.95 (ISBN 0-394-80224-1). Random.

Holden, Ronald & Holden, Glenda. Touring the Wine Country of Oregon. (Touring the Wine Country of....Ser.). (Illus.). 208p. (Orig.). pap. 6.95 (ISBN 0-910571-00-7). Holden Travel Res.

Holden, Stan. Twenty Ways to Make Money in Photography. (Illus.). 1977. 6.95 (ISBN 0-8174-2106-8, Amphoto). Watson-Guptill.

Holden, Ursula. Fallen Angels: Endless Race. 192p. 1981. pap. 2.25 o.p. (ISBN 0-523-41273-8). Pinnacle Bks.

Holden, William C. A Ranching Saga: The Lives of William Elections Halsell & Ewing Halsell, 2 vol. boxed. LC 75-9300. 569p. 1976. Trinity U Pr.

Holder, Alan. A. R. Ammons. (United States Authors Ser.). 1978. lib. bdg. 12.95 (ISBN 0-8057-7208-1, Twayne). G K Hall.

Holder, Angela R. Medical Malpractice Law. 2nd ed. LC 77-27288. 1978. 55.00 (ISBN 0-471-03882-2, Pub. by Wiley Medical). Wiley.

Holder, Leonard. Trigonometry. 288p. 1981. text ed. 21.95x (ISBN 0-534-01014-8). Wadsworth Pub.

Holder, P. A., ed. The Roman Army in Britain. LC 82-3332. (Illus.). 137p. 1982. 20.00x (ISBN 0-312-68961-6). St Martin.

Holder, Robert. You Can Analyze Your Own Handwriting. pap. 2.95 (ISBN 0-451-11542-2, AE1542, Sig). NAL.

Holder, Stephen. Collecting Stamps. LC 80-50950. (Whizz Kids Ser.). 8.00 (ISBN 0-382-06438-0). Silver.

Holder, William W. A Study of Selected Concepts for Government Financial Accounting & Reporting. LC 85-50315. 69p. 1980. pap. 5.00 (ISBN 0-686-84264-2). Municipal.

Holderlin, F. Poems & Fragments. Hamburger, M., tr. from Ger. LC 79-41382. 704p. 1980. 59.50 (ISBN 0-521-23051-9); pap. 17.95 (ISBN 0-521-29788-5). Cambridge U Pr.

Holderness, B. A. Pre-Industrial England: Economy & Society from 1500 to 1750. 244p. 1976. 17.50x o.p. (ISBN 0-87471-910-0). Rowman.

Holderness, Ginny W. The Exuberant Years: A Guide for Junior High Leaders. LC 75-13458. 128p. 1976. pap. 6.95 (ISBN 0-8042-1225-2). John Knox.

Holderness, Graham. D. H. Lawrence: History, Ideology & Fiction. 1982. 75.00x (ISBN 0-7171-1197-0, Pub. by Gill & Macmillan Ireland). State Mutual Bk.

Holdgate, M. W. A Perspective of Environmental Pollution. LC 78-8394. (Illus.). 288p. 1981. pap. 14.95 (ISBN 0-521-29972-1). Cambridge U Pr.

--A Perspective of Environmental Pollution. LC 78-8394. (Illus.). 1979. 47.50 (ISBN 0-521-22197-8). Cambridge U Pr.

Holdgate, Martin W. & White, Gilbert F., eds. Environmental Issues-Scope Report 10. LC 77-2667. 1977. 33.95 (ISBN 0-471-99503-7, Pub. by Wiley-Interscience). Wiley.

Holdich, D. M. & Jones, J. A. Tanaids. LC 82-12761. (Synopses of the British Fauna Ser.: No. 27). (Illus.). 64p. Date not set. 29.95 (ISBN 0-521-27203-3). Cambridge U Pr.

Holding, A. The Art of Royal Icing. 1980. 16.50 (ISBN 0-85334-860-X, Pub. by Applied Sci England). Elsevier.

Holding, Dennis H. Human Skills. LC 80-49977. (Studies in Human Performance Ser.). 303p. 1981. 44.95 (ISBN 0-471-27838-6, Pub. by Wiley-Interscience). Wiley.

Holding, Elisabeth S. Miss Kelly. (Illus.). (gr. 1-5). 1955. Repr. of 1947 ed. 8.50 (ISBN 0-688-21665-X). Morrow.

Holding, James. A Bottle of Pop. (See & Read Storybooks). (Illus.). (gr. 1-4). 1972. PLB 4.49 o.p. (ISBN 0-399-60067-1). Putnam Pub Group.

--The Robber of Featherbed Lane. (See & Read Storybooks). (Illus.). (gr. 1-3). 1970. PLB 3.96 o.p. (ISBN 0-399-60538-X). Putnam Pub Group.

Holdren, Bob R. Structure of a Retail Market & the Market Behavior of Retail Units. (Illus.). 1960. 7.00x o.p. (ISBN 0-8138-1605-X). Iowa St U Pr.

Holdridge, Barbara. Aubrey Beardsley Designs from the Age of Chivalry. (The International Design Libary). (Illus.). 48p. (Orig.). 1983. pap. 2.95 (ISBN 0-88045-022-3). Stemmer Hse.

Holdstock, Robert. Eye Among the Blind. 1979. pap. 1.75 o.p. (ISBN 0-451-08480-2, E8480, Sig). NAL.

Holdstock, Robert & Edwards, Malcolm. Tour of the Universe. (Illus.). 144p. 1981. 17.95 (ISBN 0-8317-8797-X, Mayflower Bks); pap. 11.95 (ISBN 0-8317-8798-8). Smith Pubs.

Holdsworth. Digital Logic Design. 1981. text ed. 49.95 (ISBN 0-408-00404-5); pap. text ed. 24.95 (ISBN 0-408-00566-1). Butterworth.

Holdsworth, Roger, ed. see Jonson, Ben.

Holdsworth, Roger, ed. see Symmons, Arthur.

Holdsworth, Roger, ed. see Symons, Arthur.

Holdsworth, Ruth. Psychology for Careers Counseling. (Psychology for Professional Groups Ser.). 320p. 1982. text ed. 23.25x (ISBN 0-333-31864-1, Pub. by Macmillan England); pap. text ed. 9.25x (ISBN 0-333-31881-1). Humanities.

Holdswoth, Ruth. Psychology for Careers Counselling. Chapman, Antony & Gale, Anthony, eds. (Psychology for Professional Groups Ser.). 320p. 1982. 49.00x (ISBN 0-333-31864-1, Pub. by Macmillan England). State Mutual Bk.

Hole, F. B. Assembly Principles. Daniel, R. P., ed. 40p. pap. 2.50 (ISBN 0-88172-141-7). Believers Bkshelf.

--Great Salvation. Daniel, R. P., ed. 72p. pap. 2.75 o.p. (ISBN 0-88172-142-5). Believers Bkshelf.

--Outlines of Truth. Daniel, R. P., ed. 73p. pap. 2.75 (ISBN 0-88172-143-3). Believers Bkshelf.

Hole, John W., Jr. Essentials of Human Anatomy & Physiology. 480p. 1982. pap. text ed. write for info. (ISBN 0-697-04730-X); write for info. instr's. manual (ISBN 0-697-04741-5); write for info. study guide (ISBN 0-697-04742-3). Wm C Brown.

Hole, Robert, ed. Parthenia In-Violata, or Mayden-Musicke for the Virginalls & Bass-Viol: Selected by Robert Hole. facsimile ed. LC 61-12304. 1961. 12.00 o.p. (ISBN 0-87104-141-3). Ny Pub Lib.

Holelson, Doug, jt. auth. see Krogman, Dane.

Holeman, Jack R. Condominium Management. (Illus.). 1980. text ed. 24.95 (ISBN 0-13-167155-3). P-H.

Holen, Harold H., jt. auth. see Hoven, Vernon.

Holesovsky, Vaclav. Economic Systems: Analysis & Comparison. 1st ed. (Illus.). 1977. text ed. 18.95 o.p. (ISBN 0-07-029557-3, C). McGraw.

Holevo, A. S. Probablistic & Statistical Aspects of Quantum Theory. (North-Holland Ser. in Statistics & Probability: Vol. 1). 316p. 1982. 95.75 (ISBN 0-444-86333-8, North Holland). Elsevier.

Holford, Ingrid. Interpreting the Weather: A Practical Guide for Householders, Gardners, Motorist and Sportsmen. (Illus.). 1973. 14.95 (ISBN 0-7153-5800-6). David & Charles.

--Weather Facts & Feats. (Illus.). 240p. 1980. 19.95 (ISBN 0-900424-75-3, Pub by Guinness Superlatives England). Sterling.

Holgate, Jack F., jt. auth. see Broussard, E. Joseph.

Holiday & Hunt. Intermediate Chemistry: Organic Chemistry. 1981. text ed. 15.95 (ISBN 0-408-70915-4). Butterworth.

Holiday, Billie & Dufty, William. Lady Sings the Blues. 1979. pap. 2.50 o.p. (ISBN 0-380-00491-7, 53173). Avon.

Holiday Editors. Holiday Guide to Ireland. 1976. pap. 3.95 (ISBN 0-394-73705-9). Random.

--Holiday Guide to Italy. 1976. pap. 3.95 (ISBN 0-394-73707-5). Random.

--The Holiday Travel Guide Series. 8th ed. Incl. Britain (ISBN 0-394-73700-8). (Illus.). 1979. Set. pap. 355.50 (ISBN 0-394-73792-X). Random.

Holiday Editors, ed. Holiday Guide to Caribbean. 1976. pap. 3.95 (ISBN 0-394-73701-6). Random.

--Holiday Guide to France. 1976. pap. 3.95 (ISBN 0-394-73702-4). Random.

--Holiday Guide to Greece & the Aegean Islands. 1976. pap. 3.95 (ISBN 0-394-73703-2). Random.

--Holiday Guide to Hawaii. 1976. pap. 3.95 (ISBN 0-394-73704-0). Random.

--Holiday Guide to Israel. 1976. pap. 3.95 (ISBN 0-394-73706-7). Random.

--Holiday Guide to London. 1976. pap. 3.95 (ISBN 0-394-73708-3). Random.

--Holiday Guide to Mexico. 1976. pap. 3.95 (ISBN 0-394-73709-1). Random.

--Holiday Guide to Paris. 1976. pap. 3.95 (ISBN 0-394-73710-5). Random.

--Holiday Guide to Rome. 1976. pap. 3.95 (ISBN 0-394-73711-3). Random.

--Holiday Guide to Scandinavia. 1976. pap. 3.95 (ISBN 0-394-73712-1). Random.

--Holiday Guide to Spain. 1976. pap. 3.95 (ISBN 0-394-73713-X). Random.

--Holiday Guide to West Germany. 1976. pap. 3.95 (ISBN 0-394-73714-8). Random.

--Travel Holiday Guide to Ireland. 1976. pap. 3.95 (ISBN 0-394-70895-4). Random.

Holinshed, Raphael. Holinshed's Chronicle. 1978. 8.95x (ISBN 0-460-00800-5, Evman). Biblio Dist.

Holisky, Dee A. Aspect & Georgian Medial Verbs. LC 81-17036. 224p. 1981. 35.00x (ISBN 0-88206-046-5). Caravan Bks.

Holister, G. S. Experimental Stress Analysis. (Cambridge Engineering Pubns.). 1967. 49.50 (ISBN 0-521-05312-9). Cambridge U Pr.

Holister, G. S., jt. auth. see Window, A. L.

Holister, G. S., ed. Developments in Composite Materials: Stress Analysis, Vol. 2. (Developments Ser.). (Illus.). 207p. 1981. 53.30 (ISBN 0-85334-966-5, Pub. by Applied Sci England). Elsevier.

--Developments in Stress Analysis, Vol. 1. (Illus.). 1979. 39.00 (ISBN 0-85334-812-X, Pub. by Applied Sci England). Elsevier.

Holl, Adelaide. ABC of Cars, Trucks & Machines. (ps-1). 1970. 8.95 o.p. (ISBN 0-07-029561-1, GB). McGraw.

--Bedtime for Bears. LC 72-10460. (Venture Ser.). (Illus.). 40p. (gr. 1). 1973. PLB 6.69 (ISBN 0-8116-6727-8). Garrard.

--Gus Gets the Message. LC 74-8179. (Venture Ser). (Illus.). 64p. (gr. 2). 1974. PLB 6.89 (ISBN 0-8116-6973-4). Garrard.

--If We Could Make Wishes. LC 76-16113. (Imagination). (Illus.). (gr. 2-6). 1977. lib. bdg. 6.69 (ISBN 0-8116-4401-4). Garrard.

--The Long Birthday. LC 74-8103. (Venture Ser). (Illus.). 64p. (gr. 2). 1974. PLB 6.89 (ISBN 0-8116-6974-2). Garrard.

--My Weekly Reader Picture Word Book. (Illus.). 128p. (ps-3). 1975. 6.95 (ISBN 0-448-11783-5, G&D). Putnam Pub Group.

--My Weekly Reader Picture Word Book. (Illus.). 128p. (ps-k). 1981. pap. 5.95 (ISBN 0-671-42542-0, Little Simon). S&S.

--The Poky Little Puppy's First Christmas. (Illus.). 24p. (ps-2). 1973. 2.95 (ISBN 0-307-10395-1, Golden Pr); PLB 7.62 (ISBN 0-307-60395-4). Western Pub.

--Small Bear & the Secret Surprise. LC 77-17204. (Small Bear Ser.). (Illus.). (gr. k-4). 1978. PLB 6.69 (ISBN 0-8116-4455-3). Garrard.

--Small Bear Builds a Playhouse. LC 77-11640. (Small Bear Adventures). (Illus.). (gr. k-4). 1978. PLB 6.69 (ISBN 0-8116-4454-5). Garrard.

--Small Bear Solves a Mystery. LC 78-16727. (Small Bear Adventures Ser.). (Illus.). (gr. k-4). 1979. PLB 6.69 (ISBN 0-8116-4456-1). Garrard.

--Small Bear's Birthday Party. LC 77-5630. (Small Bear Adventures). (Illus.). (gr. k-4). 1977. PLB 6.69 (ISBN 0-8116-4453-7). Garrard.

--Small Bear's Busy Day. LC 77-910. (Small Bear Adventures). (Illus.). (gr. k-4). 1977. 6.69 (ISBN 0-8116-4452-9). Garrard.

--Small Bear's Name Hunt. LC 76-56141. (Small Bear Adventures). (Illus.). (gr. k-4). 1977. lib. bdg. 6.69 (ISBN 0-8116-4451-0). Garrard.

--Too Fat to Fly. LC 72-12849. (Venture Ser). (Illus.). 40p. (gr. 1). 1973. PLB 6.69 (ISBN 0-8116-6731-6). Garrard.

--Wake up, Small Bear. LC 76-44318. (Small Bear Adventures). (Illus.). (gr. k-4). 1977. lib. bdg. 6.69 (ISBN 0-8116-4450-2). Garrard.

Holl, Adolf. Death & the Devil. 1976. 2.00 (ISBN 0-8164-0313-9). Seabury.

Holl, Adolf & Heinegg, Peter. The Last Christian: A Biography of Francis Assisi. LC 79-7868. 288p. 1980. 12.95 o.p. (ISBN 0-385-15499-2). Doubleday.

Holl, Kristi. Just Like a Real Family. LC 82-16239. 132p. (gr. 3-7). 1983. 9.95 (ISBN 0-689-30970-8). Atheneum.

Holladay, Carl, jt. auth. see Hayes, John H.

Holladay, John S., Jr. Cities of the Delta: Tell el Maskhuta, 1978-1979 Part III. LC 81-72087. (American Research Center in Egypt Reports: Vol. 6). xii, 220p. 1982. 26.25x (ISBN 0-89003-085-5); pap. 21.25x (ISBN 0-89003-084-7). Undena Pubns.

Holladay, Sylvia & Brown, Thomas. Options in Rhetoric: Writing & Reading. (Illus.). 416p. 1981. pap. text ed. 11.95 (ISBN 0-13-638254-1). P-H.

Holladay, Wendell G., jt. auth. see Oldenberg, Otto.

Hollaender, jt. auth. see Legator.

Hollaender, Alexander & Laskin, Allen I., eds. Basic Biology of New Developments in Biotechnology. (Basic Life Sciences Ser.: Vol. 25). 579p. 1983. 69.50x (ISBN 0-306-41244-6, Plenum Pr). Plenum Pub.

Hollaender, Alexander, jt. ed. see Fleck, Raymond F.

Hollahan, John R. & Bell, Alexis T., eds. Techniques & Applications of Plasma Chemistry. LC 74-5122. 416p. 1974. 54.95 (ISBN 0-471-40628-7, Pub. by Wiley-Interscience). Wiley.

Holland, Barron, compiled by. Popular Hinduism & Hindu Mythology: An Annotated Bibliography. LC 79-7188. 1979. lib. bdg. 35.00 (ISBN 0-313-21358-5, HPH/). Greenwood.

Holland, C. Fundamentals & Modeling of Separation Processes: Absorption, Distillation, Evaporation & Extraction. (International Ser. in Physical & Chemical Engineering Science). (Illus.). 464p. 1975. 36.95 (ISBN 0-13-344390-6). P-H.

Holland, C. D. Fundamentals of Multicomponent Distillation. 1981. text ed. 39.95 (ISBN 0-07-029567-0); solutions manual avail. McGraw.

Holland, C. H., ed. Lower Palaeozoic of the Middle East, Eastern & Southern Africa & Antarctica: With Essays on Lower Palaeozoic Trace Fossils of Africa & Lower Palaeozoic Palaeoclimatology. LC 80-41688. (Lower Palaeozoic Rocks of the World Ser.). 344p. 1981. 75.00 (ISBN 0-471-27945-5, Pub. by Wiley-Interscience). Wiley.

Holland, Celia M. Ellicot City: Maryland Mill Town. (Illus.). 1970. 14.95 (ISBN 0-686-36673-5). Md Hist.

Holland, Charles D. & Anthony, Raymond G. Fundamentals of Chemical Reaction Engineering. (International Series in the Physical & Chemical Engineering Series). (Illus.). 1979. text ed. 32.95 (ISBN 0-13-335596-9). P-H.

Holland, Clifton L., ed. World Christianity: Central America & the Caribbean. 1981. pap. 10.00 (ISBN 0-912552-36-0). Missions Adv Res Comm Ctr.

Holland, Dan. The Trout Fisherman's Bible. rev. ed. LC 78-55853. (Illus.). 1979. pap. 4.95 (ISBN 0-385-14406-7, Outdoor Bible). Doubleday.

Holland, David. If Jesus Came Back to Earth. 1968. 10.00 (ISBN 0-685-08738-7). Croydon.

--Miracle That Heals. 1956. 8.00 (ISBN 0-685-08739-5). Croydon.

Holland, David S., jt. auth. see Golembe, Carter H.

Holland, F. A. Fluid Flow for Chemical Engineers. 1973. 28.50 o.p. (ISBN 0-8206-0217-5). Chem Pub.

Holland, Faith M., jt. ed. see Dixon-Hunt, John.

Holland, Francis R., Jr. America's Lighthouses: Their Illustrated History since 1716. rev. ed. LC 74-170080. (Illus.). 240p. 1981. pap. 19.95 (ISBN 0-8289-0441-3). Greene.

Holland, Heinrich D. The Chemistry of the Atmosphere & Oceans. LC 77-28176. 1978. 43.50 (ISBN 0-471-03509-2, Pub. by Wiley-Interscience). Wiley.

Holland, I. I., jt. ed. see Anderson, David.

Holland, Isabelle. Abbie's God Book. LC 81-21845. 96p. (gr. 3-6). 1982. 7.95 (ISBN 0-664-32688-9). Westminster.

--Counterpoint. large print ed. LC 80-27954. 1981. Repr. of 1980 ed. 11.95 o.p. (ISBN 0-89621-262-9). Thorndike Pr.

--God, Mrs. Muskrat & Aunt Dot. LC 82-23794. (Illus.). 96p. (gr. 4-8). 1983. write for info. (ISBN 0-664-32703-6). Westminster.

--Grenelle. LC 80-24329. 357p. 1980. Repr. of 1976 ed. large print ed. 9.95x o.p. (ISBN 0-89621-252-1). Thorndike Pr.

--The Lost Madonna. 272p. 1983. pap. 2.95 (ISBN 0-449-20020-5, Crest). Fawcett.

--The Man Without a Face. (gr. 6-12). 1980. pap. 1.75 (ISBN 0-440-96097-5, LFL). Dell.

--Moncrief. large type ed. LC 82-10362. 431p. 1982. Repr. of 1975 ed. 10.95 (ISBN 0-89621-381-1). Thorndike Pr.

--Of Love & Death & Other Journeys. (YA) 1977. 1.50 o.p. (ISBN 0-440-96547-0, LFL). Dell.

--Perdita. 252p. (gr. 7 up). 1983. 12.00i (ISBN 0-316-37001-0). Little.

Holland, Isabelled. The Lost Madonna. large print ed. LC 82-4873. 419p. 1982. Repr. of 1982 ed. 11.95 (ISBN 0-89621-364-1). Thorndike Pr.

Holland, Jack H. Your Freedom to Be. LC 77-92780. 1977. pap. 3.50 deluxe (ISBN 0-87852-002-3). Inst Human Growth.

Holland, James & Skinner, B. F. Analysis of Behavior: A Program for Self-Instruction. 1961. pap. text ed. 18.00 (ISBN 0-07-029565-4, C). McGraw.

Holland, John. Bird Spotting. 5th rev. ed. (Illus.). 292p. 1976. 7.50 (ISBN 0-7137-0334-2). Intl Pubns Serv.

--Come to France. LC 78-68588. (Come to Ser.). (Illus.). (gr. 4-6). 1979. PLB 9.40 s&l (ISBN 0-531-09156-2, Warwick Press). Watts.

Holland, John L., jt. auth. see Gottfredson, Gary D.

Holland, Joyce. Bessie, the Messy Penguin. (Kindergarten Read-to Bks.). (Illus.). (gr. k-2). PLB 5.95 o.p. (ISBN 0-513-00300-2). Denison.

--Porter, the Pouting Pigeon. (First Grade Read-to Bks.). (Illus.). (gr. 1-3). PLB 5.95 o.p. (ISBN 0-513-00393-2). Denison.

Holland, Ken, jt. auth. see Holland, Lois.

Holland, Kenneth & Lambert, Richard D., eds. International Exchange of Persons: A Reassessment. new ed. LC 75-36473. (Annals Ser.: No. 424). 250p. 1976. 15.00 (ISBN 0-87761-198-X); pap. 7.95 (ISBN 0-87761-199-8). Am Acad Pol Soc Sci.

Holland, Lois & Holland, Ken. The Art of Solo Handbell Ringing. LC 81-70977. 1982. pap. 6.95 (ISBN 0-8054-3305-8). Broadman.

Holland, Marion. No Children, No Pets. (Illus.). (gr. 3-7). 1956. PLB 4.99 o.p. (ISBN 0-394-91447-3). Knopf.

Holland, Max. The Militarization of the Middle East. 1981. pap. 1.50 (ISBN 0-686-95356-8). Am Fr Serv Comm.

Holland, Morris K. Introductory Psychology. 656p. 1981. text ed. 21.95 (ISBN 0-669-03347-2); instr's. guide with test 1.95 (ISBN 0-669-03346-4); student guide 6.95. Heath.

--Psychology: An Introduction to Human Behavior. 2nd ed. 1978. text ed. 21.95x o.p. (ISBN 0-669-00994-6); inst. manual free o.p. (ISBN 0-669-00998-9); wkbk. 5.95x o.p. (ISBN 0-669-00995-4); indiv. prog. 6.95x o.p. (ISBN 0-669-00996-2); test item file to adopters free o.p. (ISBN 0-669-00997-0); tests for indiv. prog. free o.p. (ISBN 0-669-01161-4). Heath.

Holland, Norman N., ed. see Shakespeare, William.

Holland, P. The Ornament of Action. LC 78-1157. (Illus.). 1979. 44.50 (ISBN 0-521-22048-3). Cambridge U Pr.

Holland, Patricia G., ed. see Child, Lydia M.

Holland, Paul, ed. Test Equating. 1982. 46.00 (ISBN 0-12-352520-9). Acad Pr.

Holland, Ray. Self & Social Context. LC 77-27530. 1978. 26.00x (ISBN 0-312-71229-4). St Martin.

Holland, Richard & EerNisse, E. P. Design of Resonant Piezoelectric Devices. (Press Research Monographs: No. 56). 1969. 25.00x (ISBN 0-262-08033-8). MIT Pr.

Holland, Ron. Talk & Grow Rich. 276p. 1982. 14.95 (ISBN 0-89803-098-6). Eureka Pr.

Holland, Sarah. Deadly Angel. (Harlequin Presents Ser.). 192p. 1983. pap. 1.95 (ISBN 0-686-82655-8). Harlequin Bks.

--Fever Pitch. (Harlequin Presents Ser.). 192p. 1983. pap. 1.95 (ISBN 0-373-10601-7). Harlequin Bks.

Holland, Stuart. Capital Versus the Regions. LC 77-70277. 1977. 17.95x o.p. (ISBN 0-312-11945-3). St Martin.

--The Regional Problem. LC 77-70276. 1977. 18.95x (ISBN 0-312-66935-6). St Martin.

--Uncommon Market: Capital, Class & Power in the European Community. 1980. 25.00x (ISBN 0-312-82867-5). St Martin.

Holland, Stuart, ed. Beyond Capitalist Planning. LC 78-19586. 1979. 25.00 (ISBN 0-312-07778-5). St Martin.

Holland, Susan, ed. American Theatre Association Annual Directory 1982. (Orig.). 1982. pap. 7.00 o.p. (ISBN 0-940528-25-8). Am Theatre Assoc.

Holland, Susan S. & Ferrer, Esteban A., eds. Changing Legal Environment in Latin America. LC 74-29066. (Illus.). 370p. 1974. Vol. 2, Andean Pact, Chile, Ecuador, Peru. pap. 16.50 (ISBN 0-685-56605-6, COA#, CoA). Unipub.

Holland, Vyvyan. Son of Oscar Wilde. LC 73-5267. (Illus.). 237p. 1973. Repr. of 1954 ed. lib. bdg. 17.25x (ISBN 0-8371-6884-8, HOOW). Greenwood.

Holland, Vyvyan, tr. see Green, Julien.

Holland, Vyvyan, tr. see Koch, Rudolf.

Hollander, Annette. How to Help Your Child Have a Spiritual Life: A Parent's Guide to Inner Development. LC 79-28074. (Illus.). 224p. 1980. 12.95 o.s.i. (ISBN 0-89479-061-7). A & W Pubs.

Hollander, Bernard. Brain, Mind, & the External Signs of Intelligence. LC 78-72802. 1931. 32.50 (ISBN 0-404-60864-7). AMS Pr.

--The Psychology of Misconduct, Vice & Crime. (Historical Foundations of Forensic Psychiatry & Psychology Ser.). 220p. 1980. Repr. of 1922 ed. lib. bdg. 27.50 (ISBN 0-306-76063-0). Da Capo.

Hollander, Carlton. How to Build a Hot Tub. LC 80-52332. (Illus.). 128p. 1980. 12.95 (ISBN 0-8069-0212-4); lib. bdg. 11.69 o.p. (ISBN 0-8069-0213-2); pap. 7.95 (ISBN 0-8069-8948-3). Sterling.

--How to Build a Sauna. LC 77-90521. (Illus.). 1979. pap. 6.95 (ISBN 0-8069-8388-4). Sterling.

Hollander, Edwin P. & Hunt, Raymond G., eds. Classic Contributions to Social Psychology. 1972. pap. 13.95x (ISBN 0-19-501507-X). Oxford U Pr.

--Current Perspectives in Social Psychology. 4th ed. (Illus.). 1976. pap. text ed. 12.95x (ISBN 0-19-501998-9). Oxford U Pr.

Hollander, Jack M., jt. ed. see Harris, Jeffrey P.

Hollander, Jack M., et al, eds. Annual Review of Energy, Vol. 7. (Illus.). 560p. 1982. text ed. 22.00 (ISBN 0-8243-2307-6). Annual Reviews.

Hollander, Jacob H. Economic Library of Jacob H. Hollander. Marsh, Elsie A., ed. LC 67-14032. 1966. Repr. of 1937 ed. 34.00x (ISBN 0-8103-3103-9). Gale.

Hollander, Joe, tr. see Komarov, Boris.

Hollander, John. Powers of Thirteen. LC 82-73010. 96p. (Orig.). 1983. 12.95 (ISBN 0-689-11371-4); pap. 7.95 (ISBN 0-689-11372-2). Atheneum.

--Rhyme's Reason: A Guide to English Verse. LC 81-51342. (Illus.). 64p. 1981. text ed. 13.95 (ISBN 0-300-02735-4); pap. 4.45 (ISBN 0-300-02740-0). Yale U Pr.

--Town & Country Matters. LC 72-82864. 60p. 1972. 12.95 (ISBN 0-87923-058-4); pap. 5.95 (ISBN 0-87923-093-2). Godine.

Hollander, John, ed. Modern Poetry: Essays in Criticism. (Orig.). (YA) (gr. 9 up). 1968. pap. 9.95 (ISBN 0-19-500757-3, GB). Oxford U Pr.

Hollander, Lee M., tr. Viga-Glum's Saga & the Story of Ogmund Dytt. (International Studies & Translations Ser). lib. bdg. 8.95 o.p. (ISBN 0-8057-3381-7, Twayne). G K Hall.

Hollander, Lee M., jt. tr. see Schach, Paul.

Hollander, Lee M., tr. see Snorri Sturleson.

Hollander, Myles, jt. auth. see Brown, Byron W., Jr.

Hollander, Nicole. Hi, This is Sylvia. I'm Not at Home Right Now, So When You Hear the Beep...Hang Up. (Illus.). 128p. 1983. pap. 4.95 (ISBN 0-312-37193-4); ppk of 10 49.50 (ISBN 0-312-37194-2). St Martin.

--Ma, Can I Be a Feminist & Still Like Men? pap. 4.95 (ISBN 0-312-50170-6); pap. 49.50 prepack (ISBN 0-312-50171-4). St Martin.

--That Woman Must Be on Drugs. (Illus.). 128p. 1981. pap. 4.95 (ISBN 0-312-79510-6). St Martin.

Hollander, Patricia A. Legal Handbook for Educators. LC 77-26092. 1978. lib. bdg. 25.00 (ISBN 0-89158-420-X); pap. text ed. 13.75 (ISBN 0-86531-073-4). Westview.

Hollander, Paul. The Many Faces of Socialism & Other Essays in Comparative Sociology. 1983. write for info. Transaction Bks.

--The Many Faces of Socialism: Essays in Comparative Sociology & Politics. 371p. 1983. 29.95 (ISBN 0-87855-480-7). Transaction Bks.

--Political Pilgrims. LC 82-48394. 544p. 1983. pap. 8.61i (ISBN 0-06-091029-1, CN 1029, CN). Harper-Row.

--Sam Houston. (See & Read Biographies). (Illus.). (gr. 2-4). 1968. PLB 4.49 o.p. (ISBN 0-399-60554-1). Putnam Pub Group.

--Soviet & American Society: A Comparison. 1973. 25.00x (ISBN 0-19-501686-6). Oxford U Pr.

Hollander Publishing Co., Inc. Auto-Truck Interchange Manual, 3 vols. 48th ed. (Auto-Truck Interchange Ser.). (Illus.). 2166p. Set. 112.00 (ISBN 0-943032-22-9). Hollander Co.

--Auto-Truck Interchange Manual: Wheel Cover Supplement. 48th ed. (Auto-Truck Interchange Ser.). (Illus.). 88p. 1982. 16.00 (ISBN 0-943032-23-7). Hollander Co.

--Auto-Truck Manual: Special Wheel Supplement. 48th ed. (Auto-Truck Interchange Ser.). (Illus.). 16p. 1982. 6.00 (ISBN 0-943032-24-5). Hollander Co.

--Domestic Car Inventory Index, 1972-1982. 910p. 1982. 189.00 (ISBN 0-943032-25-3). Hollander Co.

Hollander Publishing Company Inc. Auto-Truck Interchange Manual. 16th ed. 504p. 1979. Repr. of 1949 ed. 28.50 (ISBN 0-943032-12-1). Hollander Co.

--Auto-Truck Interchange Manual. 23rd ed. 528p. 1979. Repr. of 1957 ed. 34.50 (ISBN 0-943032-13-X). Hollander Co.

--Auto-Truck Interchange Manual. 32nd ed. 1184p. 1982. Repr. of 1966 ed. 48.50 (ISBN 0-943032-08-3). Hollander Co.

--Auto-Truck Interchange Manual, 2 vols. 40th ed. 1664p. 1982. Repr. of 1974 ed. 69.50 (ISBN 0-943032-09-1). Hollander Co.

--Auto-Truck Interchange Manual, Vol. II. 40th ed. 560p. 1982. Repr. of 1974 ed. 28.50 (ISBN 0-943032-11-3). Hollander Co.

--Auto-Truck Interchange Manual. 45th ed. 1784p. Date not set. 64.50 (ISBN 0-943032-16-4). Hollander Co.

--Auto-Truck Interchange Manual, 2 vols. 46th ed. 1938p. 1980. Set. 74.50 (ISBN 0-943032-15-6). Hollander Co.

--Auto-Truck Interchange Manual, 3 vols. 47th ed. 2070p. 1981. Set. 92.50 (ISBN 0-943032-19-9). Hollander Co.

--Auto-Truck Interchange Manual, Vol. 1. 40th ed. 1104p. 1982. Repr. of 1974 ed. 48.50 (ISBN 0-943032-10-5). Hollander Co.

--Auto-Truck Interchange Manual: Body Parts. 46th ed. 462p. 1980. 15.00 (ISBN 0-943032-17-2). Hollander Co.

--Auto-Truck Interchange Manual: Group 9B. 34th ed. 234p. 1968. 12.50 (ISBN 0-943032-14-8). Hollander Co.

--Auto-Truck Interchange Manual: Wheel Covers. 46th ed. 86p. 1980. 8.00 (ISBN 0-943032-18-0). Hollander Co.

--Auto-Truck Interchange Manual: Wheel Covers. 47th ed. 88p. 1982. 15.95 (ISBN 0-943032-20-2). Hollander Co.

--Auto-Truck Interchange Manual: Wheels. 47th ed. 12p. 1981. 5.95 (ISBN 0-943032-21-0). Hollander Co.

--Clark, New Process, Warner Edition. (Truck Interchange Ser.). 244p. 1972. 35.00 (ISBN 0-943032-07-5). Hollander Co.

--Eaton Edition. (Truck Interchange Ser.). 322p. 1974. 39.50 (ISBN 0-943032-04-0). Hollander Co.

--Foreign Interchange Manual. 5th ed. 982p. 1981. 64.50 (ISBN 0-943032-00-8). Hollander Co.

--Foreign Interchange Manual. 6th ed. 1058p. 1982. 76.50 (ISBN 0-943032-01-6). Hollander Co.

--Fuller Edition. (Truck Interchange Ser.). 326p. 1979. 49.50 (ISBN 0-943032-03-2). Hollander Co.

--Rockwell Edition. (Truck Interchange Ser.). 588p. 1977. 49.50 (ISBN 0-943032-06-7). Hollander Co.

--Spicer Edition. (Truck Interchange Ser.). 420p. 1975. 39.50 (ISBN 0-943032-05-9). Hollander Co.

--Truck Parts Edition. (Truck Interchange Ser.). 510p. 1972. 43.75 (ISBN 0-943032-02-4). Hollander Co.

Hollander, Robert see Giamatti, A. Bartlett.

Hollander, Samuel. Sources of Increased Efficiency: A Study of DuPont Rayon Plants. 1965. 20.00x (ISBN 0-262-08019-2). MIT Pr.

Hollander, Xaviera. Xaviera on the Best Part of a Man. (Orig.). 1975. pap. 2.95 (ISBN 0-451-11689-5, AE1689, Sig). NAL.

--Xaviera's Fantastic Sex. (Orig.). 1978. pap. 2.95 (ISBN 0-451-11371-3, AE1371, Sig). NAL.

--Xaviera's Supersex: Her Personal Techniques for Total Lovemaking. 1978. pap. 2.25 (ISBN 0-451-11061-7, AE1061, Sig). NAL.

--Xaviera's Supersex: Her Personal Techniques for Total Lovemaking. 1976. pap. 5.95 o.p. (ISBN 0-451-79967-4, G9967, Sig). NAL.

Hollander, Zander. The Complete Book of Baseball: 1983 Edition. 1982. pap. 3.95 (ISBN 0-451-12153-8, AE2153, Sig). NAL.

--Complete Handbook of Baseball, 1980 Edition. (Orig.). (RL 7). 1980. pap. 2.50 o.p. (ISBN 0-451-09129-9, E9129, Sig). NAL.

--The Complete Handbook of Pro Basketball: 1980 Edition. (Illus., Orig.). (RL 7). 1979. pap. 2.50 o.p. (ISBN 0-451-08902-2, E8902, Sig). NAL.

--The Complete Handbook of Pro Basketball, 1981. (YA) (RL 7). 1980. pap. 2.75 o.p. (ISBN 0-451-09471-9, E9471, Sig). NAL.

--The Complete Handbook of Pro-Basketball: 1983 Edition. 1982. pap. 3.95 (ISBN 0-451-11846-4, AE1846, Sig). NAL.

--The Complete Handbook of Pro Football, 1981 Edition. (Orig.). 1981. pap. 3.50 o.p. (ISBN 0-451-09986-9, E9986, Sig). NAL.

--The Complete Handbook of Pro-Football: 1982 Edition. 1982. pap. 3.95 (ISBN 0-451-11753-0, AE1753, Sig). NAL.

--The Complete Handbook of Pro-Hockey: 1983 Edition. 1982. pap. 3.95 (ISBN 0-451-11845-6, AE1845, Sig). NAL.

--Complete Handbook of Soccer: 1980 Edition. (Orig.). 1980. pap. 2.50 o.p. (ISBN 0-451-09213-9, E9213, Sig). NAL.

--Official Pete Rose Scrapbook. 1978. pap. 4.95 o.p. (ISBN 0-451-82054-1, XE2054, Sig). NAL.

Hollander, Zander, jt. auth. see Pepe, Phil.

Hollander, Zander, ed. The American Encyclopedia of Soccer. LC 79-51205. (An Associated Features Bk.). (Illus.). 608p. 1980. 29.95 o.p. (ISBN 0-89696-057-9, An Everest House Book). Dodd.

--The Complete Handbook of Baseball - 1981 Edition. (Orig.). 1981. pap. 2.95 o.p. (ISBN 0-451-09682-7, E9682, Sig). NAL.

--Complete Handbook of College Basketball, 1981. 1980. pap. 2.75 o.p. (ISBN 0-451-09497-2, E9487, Sig). NAL.

--The Complete Handbook of College Basketball: 1980 Edition. (Illus.). (RL 7). 1979. pap. 2.50 o.p. (ISBN 0-451-08936-7, E8936, Sig). NAL.

--The Complete Handbook of Pro Football: 1980. (Illus.). 275p. (Orig.). (YA) (RL 7). 1980. pap. 2.75 o.p. (ISBN 0-451-09359-3, E9359, Sig). NAL.

--The Complete Handbook of Pro Hockey: 1980 Edition. (Illus., Orig.). (RL 7). 1979. pap. cancelled o.p. (ISBN 0-451-08903-0, E8903, Sig). NAL.

--The Complete Handbook of Pro Hockey, 1981. 1980. pap. 2.75 o.p. (ISBN 0-451-09470-0, E9470, Sig). NAL.

--Strange But True Football Stories. (NFL Punt, Pass & Kick Library: No. 8). (Illus.). (gr. 5-9). 1967. 2.95 (ISBN 0-394-80198-9, BYR); PLB 4.39 o.p. (ISBN 0-394-90198-3); pap. 0.95 o.p. (ISBN 0-394-82202-1). Random.

--Strange but True Football Stories. LC 82-13237. (Random House Sports Library). (Illus.). 144p. (gr. 5-10). 1983. pap. 1.95 (ISBN 0-394-85632-5). Random.

Hollander, Zander, jt. ed. see Collins, Bud.

Holland-Liapis. Computer Methods for Solving Dynamic Separation Problems. (Illus.). 512p. 1983. text ed. 41.50x (ISBN 0-07-029573-5, C). McGraw.

Holland-Moritz, K., jt. auth. see Siesler, H. W.

Hollands, Judith W. Non-Stop Stories. 45p. (gr. 3-10). 1983. pap. 3.95x (ISBN 0-8290-1227-3). Irvington.

Hollaway, Ida N. Loneliness: The Untapped Resource. LC 81-66557. 1982. 3.95 (ISBN 0-8054-5295-8). Broadman.

--When All the Bridges Are Down. LC 75-13365. 1975. pap. 3.25 (ISBN 0-8054-5416-0). Broadman.

Holledge, Julie. Innocent Flowers: Women in the Edwardian Theater. (Illus.). 218p. 1983. pap. 7.95 (ISBN 0-86068-071-1, Virago Pr). Merrimack Bk Serv.

Hollen, Norma, et al. Textiles. 5th ed. (Illus.). 1979. text ed. 22.95x (ISBN 0-02-356130-0). Macmillan.

Hollenbach, David. Claims in Conflict: Retrieving & Renewing the Catholic Human Rights Teaching. LC 79-84239. (Woodstock Ser.: No. 4). (Orig.). 1979. 7.95 (ISBN 0-8091-0287-0); pap. 5.95 (ISBN 0-8091-2197-2). Paulist Pr.

Hollenberg, N. K. The Haemodynamics of Nadolol. Date not set. price not set (ISBN 0-8089-1535-5). Grune.

Hollender, Betty R. Bible Stories for Little Children, Vol. 3. (Illus.). (gr. k-3). text ed. 4.00 o.p. (ISBN 0-686-82999-9). UAHC.

Hollender, Louis F. & Marrie, Alain. Highly Selective Vagotomy. LC 78-61475. (Illus.). 144p. 1979. 26.00x (ISBN 0-89352-026-8). Masson Pub.

Hollender, Marc H. The Practice of Psychoanalytic Psychotherapy. LC 65-26443. 168p. 1965. 24.25 o.p. (ISBN 0-8089-0208-3). Grune.

Hollender, Sherman. Ohio Real Property Law & Practice, 3 vols. 4th ed. 1983. Set. text ed. write for info (ISBN 0-87473-026-0). A Smith Co.

Holler, Anne. Florencewalks. LC 82-1107. (Illus.). 224p. 1983. pap. 9.95 (ISBN 0-03-059938-5). New Republic.

Holler, Frederick L. The Information Sources of Political Science. 3rd, rev. ed. LC 80-22517. 1981. 41.25 (ISBN 0-87436-179-6). ABC-Clio.

Holler, Kathy. Seasons. (Science Ser.). 24p. (gr. 3-6). 1982. wkbk. 5.00 (ISBN 0-8209-0163-6, S-25). ESP.

Holler, Rich. Dinosaur Era. (Science Ser.). 24p. (gr. 3-9). 1979. wkbk. 5.00 (ISBN 0-8209-0159-8, S-21). ESP.

Holleran, Andrew. Dancer from the Dance. LC 78-6600. 1978. 9.95 o.p. (ISBN 0-688-03357-1). Morrow.

Hollerbach, John, jt. auth. see Brady, Michael.

Hollerbach, Lew. A Sixty Minute Guide to Microcomputers. (Illus.). 137p. 1982. 12.95 (ISBN 0-13-811430-7); pap. 6.95 (ISBN 0-13-811422-6). P-H.

Hollerbach, Marion. Das Religionsgesprach Als Mittel Der Konfessionellen Und Politischen Auseinandersetzung Im Deutschland Des 16. Jahrhunderts. (Ger.). 1982. write for info (ISBN 3-8204-7015-8). P Lang Pubs.

Hollerman, Charles E. Pediatric Nephrology. (Medical Outline Ser.). 1979. pap. 25.00 (ISBN 0-87488-590-6). Med Exam.

Hollerweger, jt. ed. see Berger.

Holles, Robert. Sun Blight. 240p. 1983. 16.95 (ISBN 0-241-10733-4, Pub. by Hamish Hamilton England). David & Charles.

Holleuffer, Carol, jt. auth. see Browning, Robert.

Holley, Barbara. Pieces of a Woman. (Illus.). 12p. 1982. pap. 2.00 (ISBN 0-943696-01-1). Red Key Pr.

Holley, F. M., jt. auth. see Cunge, J. A.

Holley, Marietta. Samantha Rastles the Woman Question. Curry, Jane, ed. LC 82-13482. (Illus.). 234p. 1983. 14.95 (ISBN 0-252-01020-5). U of Ill Pr.

Holley, W., et al. Plantation South. LC 78-166955. (Research Monograph Ser.: Vol. 22). 1971. Repr. of 1940 ed. lib. bdg. 19.50 (ISBN 0-306-70354-8). Da Capo.

Holley, William H. & Jennings, Kenneth M. Personnel Management: Functions & Issues. 608p. 1983. text ed. 26.95 (ISBN 0-03-062712-5). Dryden Pr.

Holley, William S., et al. A Handbook of Civilization, Vol. 2. 2nd ed. (Illus.). 1978. pap. text ed. 12.95 (ISBN 0-8403-1834-0). Kendall-Hunt.

Holli, Melvin see Jones, Peter d'A.

Holliday, jt. auth. see Cohen.

Holliday, A. K., jt. auth. see Block, H.

Holliday, A. K., jt. auth. see Chambers, C.

Holliday, Bob. Norton Story. 1981. 19.95 (ISBN 0-85059-479-0). Aztex.

Holliday, Carl. Wit & Humor of Colonial Days Sixteen Seven to Eighteen Hundred. LC 71-148586. 1970. Repr. of 1912 ed. 27.00 o.p. (ISBN 0-8103-3592-1). Gale.

--Woman's Life in Colonial Days. LC 72-140408. 1970. Repr. of 1922 ed. 34.00x (ISBN 0-8103-3593-X). Gale.

Holliday, George D. Technology Transfer to the U. S. S. R., Nineteen Twenty-Eight to Nineteen Thirty-Seven & Nineteen Sixty-Six to Nineteen Seventy-Five: The Role of Western Development in Soviet Economic Development. (A Westview Replica Edition Ser.). 1979. lib. bdg. 25.00 o.p. (ISBN 0-89158-189-8). Westview.

Holliday, J., ed. City Centre Redevelopment. LC 73-17764. (Illus.). 244p. 1973. 34.95x o.s.i. (ISBN 0-470-40644-5). Halsted Pr.

Holliday, L., ed. Ionic Polymers. LC 74-11509. 416p. 1975. 64.95 o.p. (ISBN 0-470-40640-2). Halsted Pr.

Holliday, Paul. Fungus Diseases of Tropical Crops. LC 79-41602. (Illus.). 500p. 1980. 135.00 (ISBN 0-521-22529-9). Cambridge U Pr.

Hollies, Norman R. & Goldman, Ralph F., eds. Clothing Comfort: Interaction of Thermal Ventilation, Construction & Assessment Factors. LC 76-46024. (Illus.). 1977. 37.50 o.p. (ISBN 0-250-40159-2). Ann Arbor Science.

Hollije, Bert. How to Be Your Own Advertising Agency. LC 80-27207. (Illus.). 215p. 1981. 19.95 (ISBN 0-07-029665-0). McGraw.

Holling, C. S., ed. Adaptive Environmental Assessment & Management. LC 78-8523. (IIASA International Series on Applied Systems Analysis). 1978. 26.95 (ISBN 0-471-99632-7, Pub. by Wiley-Interscience). Wiley.

Holling, Fred, tr. see Meissner, Boris.

Holling, Holling C. Paddle to the Sea. (Illus.). (gr. 4-6). reinforced bdg. 14.95 (ISBN 0-395-15082-5); pap. 2.95 (ISBN 0-395-29203-4). HM.

Hollingdale, R. J. Western Philosophy: An Introduction. LC 79-63624. 158p. 1983. pap. 4.95 (ISBN 0-8008-8130-3). Taplinger.

Hollingdale, R. J., tr. see Loffler, Fritz.

Hollingdale, R. J., tr. see Nietzsche, Friedrich.

Hollinger, David A. Morris R. Cohen & the Scientific Ideal. 288p. 1975. pap. 5.95x (ISBN 0-262-58041-1). MIT Pr.

Hollinger, Richard C. & Clark, John P. Theft by Employees. LC 82-48028. 176p. 1983. 21.95x (ISBN 0-669-05887-4). Lexington Bks.

Hollings, Michael. Enfolded by Christ: An Encouragement to Pray. Orig. Title: Day by Day. 128p. 1976. pap. 2.50 (ISBN 0-914544-10-1). Living Flame Pr.

Hollingshead, A. B. & Redlich, F. C. Social Class & Mental Illness: A Community Study. LC 58-6076. 1958. pap. 19.95 (ISBN 0-471-40685-6). Wiley.

Hollingshead, A. B., jt. auth. see Rogler, L. H.

Hollingshead, August B. Elmtown's Youth & Elmtown Revisited. LC 74-17311. 1975. pap. text ed. 15.95 (ISBN 0-471-40655-4). Wiley.

Hollingsworth, Brian. Atlas of the World's Railways. (Illus.). 352p. 1980. 25.00 (ISBN 0-89696-043-9, An Everest House Book). Dodd.

Hollingsworth, Dorothy & Morse, Elisabeth, eds. People & Food Tomorrow: The Scientific, Economic, Political, & Social Factors Affecting Food Supplies in the Last Quarter of the 20th Century. 1976. 39.00 (ISBN 0-85334-701-8, Pub. by Applied Sci England). Elsevier.

Hollingsworth, E. P., Jr. & Launie, J. J. Commercial Property & Multiple-Lines Underwriting. LC 78-67502. 591p. 1978. pap. 14.00 o.p. (ISBN 0-89462-005-3, UND 64). IIA.

Hollingsworth, Ellen J., jt. auth. see Hollingsworth, J. Rogers.

Hollingsworth, J. Rogers & Hollingsworth, Ellen J. Dimensions in Urban History on Middle-Size American Cities: Historical & Social Science Perspectives. LC 78-65011. 192p. 1979. 25.00 (ISBN 0-299-07820-5). U of Wis Pr.

Hollingsworth, J. Rogers, ed. American Expansion in the Late Nineteenth Century: Colonialist or Anticolonialist? LC 82-10008. 128p. 1983. pap. text ed. write for info (ISBN 0-89874-531-4). Krieger.

Hollingsworth, J. Rogers & Lambert, Richard D., eds. Social Theory & Public Policy. LC 77-83259. (Annals of the American Academy of Political & Social Science: No. 434). 1977. 15.00 (ISBN 0-87761-220-X); pap. 7.95 (ISBN 0-87761-221-8). Am Acad Pol Soc Sci.

Hollingsworth, Jane. Discovering the Gospel of Mark. pap. 1.95 o.p. (ISBN 0-87784-419-4). Inter-Varsity.

Hollingsworth, Lawrence W. Zanzibar Under the Foreign Office: 1890-1913. LC 75-31770. (Illus.). 232p. 1976. Repr. of 1953 ed. lib. bdg. 16.00x (ISBN 0-8371-8447-9, HOZA). Greenwood.

Hollingsworth, M. J. & Bowler, K. Principles & Processes of Biology. 1972. 16.95x (ISBN 0-412-11000-8, Pub. by Chapman & Hall). Methuen Inc.

Hollingworth, Brian, ed. Songs of the People: Lancashire Dialect Poetry of the Industrial Revolution. 176p. 1982. pap. 6.50 (ISBN 0-7190-0906-5). Manchester.

Hollingworth, Shelagh. Traditional Knitting. (Illus.). 64p. 1983. pap. 4.95 (ISBN 0-7134-4336-7, Pub. by Batsford England). David & Charles.

Hollins, Holly. The Tall Ships Are Sailing: The Cutty Sark Tall Ships Races. (Illus.). 192p. 1981. 22.50 (ISBN 0-7153-8028-1). David & Charles.

Hollinshead, W. Henry. Anatomia Para Cirujanos Dentistas. 3rd ed. 384p. (Span.). 1982. pap. text ed. write for info. (ISBN 0-06-313376-8, Pub. by HarLA Mexico). Har-Row.

--Anatomy for Surgeons, Vol. 1: The Head & Neck. 3rd ed. (Illus.). 624p. 1982. text ed. 19.00x (ISBN 0-06-141264-3, Harper Medical). Lippincott.

--Anatomy for Surgeons, Vol. 3: The Back & Limbs. 3rd ed. (Illus.). 880p. 1982. text ed. 72.00x (ISBN 0-06-141266-X, Harper Medical). Lippincott.

--Functional Anatomy of the Limbs & Back. 4th ed. LC 75-19844. (Illus.). 430p. 1976. text ed. 18.95 o.p. (ISBN 0-7216-4757-X). Saunders.

Hollis, Alfred C. Nandi: Their Language & Folk-Lore. LC 71-76481. (Illus.). Repr. of 1909 ed. 20.00x o.p. (ISBN 0-8371-1515-9, Pub. by Negro U Pr). Greenwood.

Hollis, C. Carroll. Language & Style in Leaves of Grass. LC 82-20881. 320p. 1983. text ed. 27.50X (ISBN 0-8071-1096-5). La State U Pr.

Hollis, D. Animal Identifcation: Insects, Vol. 3. 160p. 1980. 44.95 (ISBN 0-471-27767-3, Pub. by Wiley-Interscience). Wiley.

Hollis, Daniel W., III. An Alabama Newspaper Tradition: Grover C. Hall & the Hall Family. (Illus.). 224p. 1983. text ed. 19.95 (ISBN 0-8173-0136-4). U of Ala Pr.

Hollis, Ernest V. & Taylor, Alice L. Social Work Education in the United States: The Report of a Study Made for the National Council on Social Work Education. LC 75-136070. (Illus.). 1971. Repr. of 1951 ed. lib. bdg. 20.25x (ISBN 0-8371-5220-8, HOSW). Greenwood.

Hollis, F. & Woods, M. E. Casework: A Psychological Therapy. 3rd ed. 552p. 1981. text ed. 20.00 (ISBN 0-394-32368-8). Random.

Hollis, G. L., compiled by. Surfactants Europa, Vol. 1. 1982. pap. 100.00x (ISBN 0-7114-5736-0, Pub. by Macdonald & Evans). State Mutual Bk.

Hollis, James, ed. see Pettit, Terry, et al.

Hollis, Jocelyn. Peace Poems: New Poems on Peace for the 1980s. Topham, J., ed. LC 82-13915. 24p. (Orig.). Date not set. pap. text ed. 3.95 (ISBN 0-933486-40-5). Am Poetry Pr.

--Vietnam Poems: The War Poems of Today. LC 80-65621. 37p. 1983. pap. 3.95 (ISBN 0-933486-10-3). Am Poetry Pr.

Hollis, John H., jt. ed. see Schiefelbusch, Richard L.

Hollis, Joseph & Hollis, Lucile. Organizing for Effective Guidance. 1977. text ed. 14.95 o.s.i. (ISBN 0-574-50079-0, 5-0079). SRA.

Hollis, Lucile, jt. auth. see Hollis, Joseph.

Hollis, Lucille U. Career Education & Business Education. (Guidance Monograph). 1975. pap. 2.40 o.p. (ISBN 0-395-20045-8). HM.

Hollis, Marcia & Hollis, Reginald. The Godswept Heart. 96p. 1983. pap. 5.95 (ISBN 0-8164-2410-1). Seabury.

Hollis, Martin. Models of Man. LC 76-49902. (Illus.). 1977. 34.50 (ISBN 0-521-21546-3); pap. 8.95x (ISBN 0-521-29181-X). Cambridge U Pr.

Hollis, Martin & Lukes, Steven, eds. Rationality & Relativism. 320p. 1983. 25.00x (ISBN 0-262-08130-X); pap. 12.50x (ISBN 0-262-58061-6). MIT Pr.

Hollis, Martin, jt. ed. see Hahn, Frank.

Hollis, Martin I. & Nell, Edward J. Rational Economic Man. (Illus.). 288p. 1975. 37.50x (ISBN 0-521-20408-9). Cambridge U Pr.

Hollis, Patricia, ed. Class & Conflict in Nineteenth-Century England, 1815-1850. (Birth of Modern Britain Ser). 402p. 1973. 20.00x o.p. (ISBN 0-7100-7419-0); pap. 10.00 (ISBN 0-7100-7420-4). Routledge & Kegan.

--Pressure from Without in Early Victorian England. LC 74-76016. 356p. 1974. 26.00 (ISBN 0-312-64155-9). St Martin.

Hollis, Reginald, jt. auth. see Hollis, Marcia.

Hollis, Shelia S., jt. auth. see Tomain, Joseph P.

Hollister, C. W., ed. see Smith, Lacey B.

Hollister, C. Warren. Medieval Europe: A Short History. 5th ed. LC 81-7415. 384p. 1982. text ed. 11.50 (ISBN 0-471-08447-6). Wiley.

--Odysseus to Columbus: A Synopsis of Classical & Medieval History. LC 74-2428. 352p. 1974. pap. text ed. 16.95 o.s.i. (ISBN 0-471-40689-9). Wiley.

Hollister, C. Warren, ed. Landmarks of the Western Heritage, 2 vols. 2nd ed. Incl. Vol. 1. The Ancient Near East to 1789. 544p. pap. text ed. 20.95 (ISBN 0-471-40700-3); Vol. 2. 1715 to Present. 416p. pap. text ed. 18.95 (ISBN 0-471-40704-6). LC 72-7315. (Illus.). 1973. Wiley.

Hollister, C. Warren, et al. Medieval History: A Short Sourcebook. LC 81-14747. 246p. 1982. text ed. 11.50 (ISBN 0-471-08369-0). Wiley.

--River Through Time: The Course of Western Civilization. LC 74-14972. 576p. 1975. pap. 20.95 (ISBN 0-471-40695-3); tchr's manual avail. (ISBN 0-471-40692-9). Wiley.

Hollister, Herbert. Real Estate Math Primer: Problem-Solving with the Hand-Held Calculator. (Illus.). 216p. 1983. 18.95 (ISBN 0-13-764308-X); pap. 10.95 (ISBN 0-13-764290-3). P-H.

Hollister, Leo E. Year Book of Drug Therapy 1983. 1983. 42.00 (ISBN 0-8151-4621-3). Year Bk Med.

Hollister, Paul. Glass Paperweights of the New York Historical Society. (Illus.). 192p. 1974. 25.00 o.p. (ISBN 0-517-51667-5, C N Potter Bks). Crown.

Hollister, Paul & Lanmon, Dwight P. Paperweights: Flowers Which Clothe the Meadows. LC 77-91357. 167p. 1978. 30.00 o.p. (ISBN 0-686-67962-8); pap. 20.00 o.p. (ISBN 0-87290-065-7). Corning.

Hollister, V. F., jt. ed. see Riordon, P. H.

Hollister, Victor F. Geology of the Porphyry Copper Deposits of the Western Hemisphere. LC 77-71575. (Illus.). 1978. text ed. 20.00x (ISBN 0-89520-048-1). Soc Mining Eng.

Hollister, Warren C., ed. The Impact of the Norman Conquest. 150p. 1982. 5.95 (ISBN 0-89874-470-9). Krieger.

Hollmann, Clide. Pontiac, King of the Great Lakes. LC 68-13443. (Illus.). (gr. 6-9). 1968. 7.95g o.s.i. (ISBN 0-8038-5716-0). Hastings.

Hollo, Anselm. No Complaints. LC 82-19277. (Illus.). 64p. (Orig.). 1983. 40.00 (ISBN 0-915124-68-8); pap. 8.50 (ISBN 0-915124-69-6). Toothpaste.

--With Ruth in Mind. LC 79-28147. 50p. 1980. ltd., signed ed. 20.00 (ISBN 0-930794-19-2); pap. 4.45 (ISBN 0-930794-18-4). Station Hill Pr.

Hollo, Anselm, ed. Jazz Poems. (Pocket Poems Ser.). 1963. pap. 1.25 (ISBN 0-8023-9048-X). Dufour.

--Negro Verse. (Pocket Poet Ser.). 1964. pap. 1.25 (ISBN 0-8023-9049-8). Dufour.

Hollo, Anselm, tr. see Arsan, Emmanuelle.

Hollo, Anselm, tr. see Saarikoski, Pentti.

Hollo, Reuven & Fifadara, Haresh. TI-Fifty-Nine Reservoir Engineering Manual. 220p. 1980. 59.95x (ISBN 0-87814-134-0). Pennwell Book Division.

Hollomon, J. Herbert & Grenon, Michele. Energy Research & Development. LC 74-23368. (Ford Foundation Energy Policy Project Ser.). 384p. 1975. prof ref 22.50 (ISBN 0-88410-316-1). Ballinger Pub.

Hollon, W. Eugene. Frontier Violence: Another Look. LC 73-87617. (Illus.). 288p. 1976. pap. 5.95 (ISBN 0-19-502098-7, 475, GB). Oxford U Pr.

Hollow, John. Against the Night, the Stars: The Science Fiction of Arthur C. Clarke. 224p. 14.95 (ISBN 0-15-103966-6). HarBraceJ.

Holloway, A. & Ridler, E. Information Work with Unpublished Reports. 320p. 1976. 30.50 (ISBN 0-233-96824-5, 05799-1, Pub. by Gower Pub Co England). Lexington Bks.

Holloway, David. The Soviet Union & the Arms Race. LC 82-20050. 208p. 1983. 14.95 (ISBN 0-300-02963-2). Yale U Pr.

Holloway, Elizabeth, jt. auth. see Donald, Kathleen.

Holloway, Gordon F. & Berkey, Gordon. Elementary Physics of Sound for Speech Pathology & Audiology. LC 73-571. (Illus.). 244p. 1983. 14.50 (ISBN 0-87527-190-1). Green.

Holloway, Harry. The Politics of the Southern Negro: From Exclusion to Big City Organization. 1969. text ed. 11.95x (ISBN 0-685-77213-6, 0-394-30283). Phila Bk Co.

Holloway, John. Narrative & Structure: Exploratory Essays. LC 78-20826. 1979. 24.95 (ISBN 0-521-22574-4). Cambridge U Pr.

--Social Policy Harmonisation in the European Communities. 1980. text ed. 35.50x (ISBN 0-566-00196-9). Gower Pub Ltd.

Holloway, Joseph E. Liberian Diplomacy in Africa. LC 80-6186. 256p. 1982. lib. bdg. 22.75 (ISBN 0-8191-1790-0); pap. text ed. 11.50 (ISBN 0-8191-1791-9). U Pr of Amer.

Holloway, Nancy M. Nursing the Critically Ill Adult. LC 78-21153. 1978. 25.95 (ISBN 0-201-02948-0, Med-Nurse). A-W.

Holloway, Olivia. Stolen Waters. 1978. 6.50 o.p. (ISBN 0-533-03196-6). Vantage.

Holloway, R. Ross. A View of Greek Art. LC 72-187947. (Illus.). 235p. 1973. 25.00x (ISBN 0-87057-133-8, Pub. by Brown U Pr). U Pr of New Eng.

Holloway, Richard. Signs of Glory. 96p. 1983. pap. 5.95 (ISBN 0-8164-2412-8). Seabury.

Holloway, William, ed. see Symposia on Infectious Disease, 7th & 8th, Wilmington, Del., 1970, 1971.

Holloway, William, ed. see Symposium on Infectious Disease, 9th, Wilmington, Del., 1972.

Holloway, William J., ed. see Symposium on Infectious Disease, 10th, Wilmington, Del., 1973.

Hollowell, Mary L., ed. The Cable-Broadband Communications Book, 1980-1981, Vol. 2. (Video Bookshelf Ser.). 230p. 1980. text ed. 29.95x (ISBN 0-914236-79-2). Knowledge Indus.

--The Cable-Broadband Communications Book: 1982-83, Vol. 3. 175p. 1983. 34.95 (ISBN 0-86729-042-0). Knowledge Indus.

Hollstein, Milton & Kurtz, Larry. Editing With Understanding. 342p. 1981. pap. text ed. 16.95 (ISBN 0-02-356290-0). Macmillan.

Holly, J. Hunter. Mind Traders. (YA) 6.95 (ISBN 0-685-07448-X, Avalon). Bouregy.

Holly, J. Hunter, et al. Graduated Robot & Other Stories. Elwood, Roger, ed. LC 73-21477. (Science Fiction Bks.). (Illus.). 48p. (gr. 4-8). 1974. PLB 3.95g (ISBN 0-8225-0956-3). Lerner Pubns.

Holly, Sean & Zarrop, M. B., eds. Optimal Control for Econometric Models. 1979. 37.50x (ISBN 0-312-58689-2). St Martin.

Hollyday, Frederic. Bismarck's Rival: A Political Biography of General & Admiral Albrecht Von Stosch. LC 75-40917. 316p. 1976. Repr. of 1960 ed. lib. bdg. 20.25x (ISBN 0-8371-8686-2, HOBR). Greenwood.

Hollyfield, J. P., jt. auth. see Tindell-Hopwood, A.

Hollyman, Burnes S. Glauber Rocha & the Cinema Novo in Brazil: A Study of His Films & Critical Writing. Jowett, Garth S., ed. LC 81-48354. (Dissertations on Film Ser.). 220p. 1982. lib. bdg. 25.00 (ISBN 0-8240-5103-3). Garland Pub.

Hollyn, Lynn & Goldstrom, Robert. Lynn Hollyn's Town & Country Cat. LC 82-40389. (Illus.). 144p. 1982. 16.95 (ISBN 0-89480-214-3). Workman Pub.

Holm & Kristensen. Ultrasonically Guided Puncture Technique. LC 80-54153. (Illus.). 128p. 1981. text ed. 20.00 (ISBN 0-7216-4731-6). Saunders.

Holm, Anne. North to Freedom. Kingsland, L. W., tr. from Danish. LC 73-12928. 190p. (gr. 7-9). 1974. pap. 1.25 (ISBN 0-15-666100-4, VoyB). HarBraceJ.

Holm, Bill, jt. auth. see Vaughn, Thomas.

Holm, Bill, annotations by. Soft Gold: The Fur Trade & Cultural Exchange on the Northwest Coast of America. LC 82-81739. (Illus.). 312p. (Orig.). 1982. 29.95 (ISBN 0-87595-107-4, Western Imprints); pap. 19.95 (ISBN 0-87595-108-2, Western Imprints). Oreg Hist Soc.

Holm, James N. Productive Speaking for Business & the Professions. 466p. 1982. pap. text ed. 12.95x (ISBN 0-89641-024-2). American Pr.

Holm, Jeanne. Women in the Military: An Unfinished Revolution. (Illus.). 420p. 1982. 16.95 (ISBN 0-89141-078-3). Presidio Pr.

Holm, John A. & Shilling, Alison W. The Dictionary of Bahamian English. LC 82-83045. 270p. 1982. 42.00 (ISBN 0-936368-03-9). Lexik Hse.

Holm, Leroy, et al. A Geographical Atlas of World Weeds. LC 78-24280. 1979. 48.50 (ISBN 0-471-04393-1, Pub. by Wiley-Interscience). Wiley.

Holm, LeRoy G., et al. The World's Worst Weeds: Distribution & Biology. LC 74-78866. 512p. 1977. text ed. 45.00x (ISBN 0-8248-0295-0, Eastwest Ctr). UH Pr.

Holm, Mayling M. A Forest Christmas. LC 76-58696. (Illus.). (ps-3). 1977. 9.95 o.p. (ISBN 0-06-022572-6, HarpJ); PLB 10.89 o.p. (ISBN 0-06-022573-4). Har-Row.

Holm, Nora S. Runner's Bible. 8.95 (ISBN 0-395-07806-7). HM.

Holm, R., jt. auth. see Ohnsorge, J.

Holm, R. W., jt. auth. see Ehrlich, Paul R.

Holm, Richard & Parnell, Dennis. Introduction to the Plant Sciences. (Illus.). 1979. text ed. 13.95 o.p. (ISBN 0-07-029578-6, C); write for info. instructor's manual o.p. (ISBN 0-07-029579-4). McGraw.

Holm, Vanja A. & Pipes, Peggy L., eds. Prader-Willi Syndrome. 368p. 1981. text ed. 34.50 (ISBN 0-8391-1638-1). Univ Park.

Holman, Alfred L., ed. see Ryerson, Albert W

Holman, B. L., jt. ed. see Ell, P. J.

Holman, C. Hugh. The American Novel Through Henry James. 2nd ed. LC 79-84212. (Goldentree Bibliographies in Language & Literature). 1979. text ed. 22.50x (ISBN 0-88295-576-4); pap. text ed. 13.95x (ISBN 0-88295-577-2). Harlan Davidson.

--A Handbook to Literature. 4th ed. LC 79-10061. 1980. 12.95 o.p. (ISBN 0-672-61477-4); pap. 8.95 o.p. (ISBN 0-672-61441-3). Odyssey Pr.

Holman, Donna, ed. Rhineland: Winter in a Missouri Rivertown. (Illus.). 191p. (Orig.). 1979. pap. 8.00 (ISBN 0-930552-02-4). Tech Ed Serv.

Holman, Felice. Elizabeth & the Marsh Mystery. LC 66-11105. (Illus.). 64p. (gr. k-3). 1974. pap. 0.95 o.p. (ISBN 0-02-043660-2, Collier). Macmillan.

Holman, Halsted R., jt. auth. see Fries, James F.

Holman, J. P. Heat Transfer. 5th ed. (Illus.). 672p. 1981. text ed. 34.95x (ISBN 0-07-029618-9, C); solutions manual 12.50 (ISBN 0-07-029619-7). McGraw.

Holman, Jack. Thermodynamics. 3rd ed. (Illus.). 1980. text ed. 35.50 (ISBN 0-07-029625-1, C); solutions manual 22.00 (ISBN 0-07-029626-X). McGraw.

Holman, Jack P. Experimental Methods for Engineers. 3rd ed. (Mechanical Engineering Ser). (Illus.). 1978. text ed. 34.50 (ISBN 0-07-029601-4, C); instructor's manual 19.50 (ISBN 0-07-029602-2). McGraw.

Holman, L. Bruce. Cinema Equipment You Can Build. (Illus.). 90p. 1975. pap. 8.95 (ISBN 0-686-14081-8). Walnut Pr.

--Holman's Harvest from Down on the Farm. (Illus.). 117p. 1982. 9.95 (ISBN 0-686-83875-0). Harvest Pr.

Holman, R. J., ed. Essential Fatty Acids & Prostaglandins: Golden Jubilee International Conference, Minnesota, USA, May 4-7 1980. (Illus.). 968p. 1982. 135.00 (ISBN 0-08-028011-0, H115, H125). Pergamon.

Holman, Richard, ed. see Casler, Darwin J. & Crockett, James R.

Holman, Robert. Trading in Children: A Study of Private Fostering. (International Library of Social Policy). (Illus.). 374p. 1973. 32.50x o.p. (ISBN 0-7100-7538-3). Routledge & Kegan.

Holmasen, Ingmar. Nature Photography. (Illus.). 120p. 14.95 (ISBN 0-87165-082-7, Amphoto); pap. 9.95 (ISBN 0-87165-109-2). Watson-Guptill.

Holmberg, Ingvar, jt. ed. see Andersson, Ake E.

Holme, Bryan. Advertising: Reflections of a Century. LC 82-70186. (Illus.). 324p. 1982. 45.00 (ISBN 0-670-74728-9, Studio). Viking Pr.

--Creatures of Paradise: Pictures to Grow Up With. (Illus.). (gr. 4 up). 1980. 14.95 (ISBN 0-19-520205-8). Oxford U Pr.

--Enchanted World: The Magic of Pictures. (Illus.). (gr. 7 up). 1979. 14.95 (ISBN 0-19-520130-2). Oxford U Pr.

Holme, C. Geoffrey, ed. see James, Philip.

Holme, Geoffrey. Caricature of Today. LC 73-20081. (Illus.). 136p. 1974. Repr. of 1928 ed. 31.00 o.p. (ISBN 0-8103-3969-2). Gale.

Holme, Geoffrey, ed. see Salaman, Malcolm C.

Holme, T. & Holmgren, J. Acute Enteric Infections in Children: New Prospects for Treatment & Prevention. 1982. 125.00 (ISBN 0-444-80328-9). Elsevier.

Holme, T., jt. auth. see Ghirardelli, B.

Holme, Timothy. A Funeral of Gondolas. 256p. 1982. 14.95 (ISBN 0-698-11179-6, Coward). Putnam Pub Group.

--The Neapolitan Streak. 224p. 1980. 10.95 o.p. (ISBN 0-698-11052-8, Coward). Putnam Pub Group.

Holmen, Milton G. & Docter, Richard F. Educational & Psychological Testing: A Study of the Industry & Its Practices. LC 72-132514. 218p. 1972. 9.95x (ISBN 0-87154-390-7). Russell Sage.

Holmes. Beginners Guide to Technical Illustration. 1982. text ed. 9.95 (ISBN 0-408-00582-3). Butterworth.

Holmes, A. L., jt. auth. see Harding, Robert T.

Holmes, Ann, jt. auth. see Amsterdam, Ezra.

Holmes, Ann M., jt. auth. see Amsterdam, Ezra A.

Holmes, Arthur F. All Truth Is God's Truth. LC 77-3567. 1977. pap. 3.95 o.p. (ISBN 0-8028-1701-7). Eerdmans.

--Contours of a World View. Henry, Carl F., ed. (Studies in a Christian World View: Vol. 1). 256p. 1983. pap. 8.95 (ISBN 0-8028-1957-5). Eerdmans.

Holmes, Augusta. Selected Songs. (Women Composers Ser.: No. 13). 100p. 1983. lib. bdg. 22.50 (ISBN 0-306-76170-X). Da Capo.

Holmes, B. J. Basic Programming: An Instructional Manual. 528p. 1982. pap. text ed. 11.00x (ISBN 0-905435-25-7). Verry.

Holmes, Beth. The Whipping Boy. LC 77-18732. 1978. 10.00 o.p. (ISBN 0-399-90000-4, Marek). Putnam Pub Group.

Holmes, Brian. International Handbook of Education Systems: Europe & Canada, Vol. 1. 800p. 1983. write for info. (ISBN 0-471-90078-8, Pub. by Wiley-Interscience). Wiley.

Holmes, Brian, ed. Diversity & Unity in Education. 176p. 1980. text ed. 28.50x (ISBN 0-04-370094-2). Allen Unwin.

Holmes, Bruce E. Manual of Comparative Anatomy: A Laboratory Guide & Brief Text. 416p. 1980. pap. text ed. 13.95 (ISBN 0-8403-2254-2). Kendall-Hunt.

Holmes, Burnham. The First Seeing Eye Dogs. LC 78-14804. (Famous Firsts Ser.). (Illus.). 1978. PLB 10.76 (ISBN 0-89547-045-4). Silver.

--The Mysterious Ghosts of Flight Four Hundred One. LC 78-21852. (Unsolved Mysteries of the World Ser.). PLB 11.96 (ISBN 0-686-79596-2). Silver.

--The World's First Baseball Game. LC 78-14581. (Famous Firsts Ser.). (Illus.). 1978. PLB 10.76 (ISBN 0-686-51115-8). Silver.

Holmes, Buster. Buster Holmes Restaurant: New Orleans Handmade Cookin' (Illus.). 124p. 1983. Repr. of 1980 ed. spiral bdg. 8.95 (ISBN 0-88289-374-2). Pelican.

Holmes, C. The Eastern Association in the English Civil War. LC 73-91616. (Illus.). 320p. 1974. 39.50 (ISBN 0-521-20400-3). Cambridge U Pr.

Holmes, Christine, ed. see Gilbert, George.

Holmes, Colin, jt. auth. see Pollard, Sidney

Holmes, D. L. Principles of Physical Geology. 3rd ed. LC 78-2508. text ed. cancelled o.p. (ISBN 0-471-07251-6). Wiley.

Holmes, D. R. & Rahmel, A., eds. Materials & Coatings to Resist High Temperature Corrosion. (Illus.). 1978. 90.25 (ISBN 0-85334-784-0, Pub. by Applied Sci England). Elsevier.

Holmes, Deborah. Good Apple & Daily Breaks. (gr. 3-7). 1981. 9.95 (ISBN 0-86653-048-7, GA 280). Good Apple.

Holmes, Donald B. Air Mail: An Illustrated History, 1793-1981. (Illus.). 1982. 27.95 (ISBN 0-517-54146-7, C N Potter Bks). Crown.

Holmes, E. R. Borodino Eighteen-Twelve. (Knight's Battles for Wargamers Ser.). (Illus.). 104p. 1973. 3.95 o.p. (ISBN 0-88254-209-5). Hippocrene Bks.

Holmes, Edmond. The Creed of Buddha. LC 72-9918. 260p. 1973. Repr. of 1957 ed. lib. bdg. 20.50x (ISBN 0-8371-6606-3, HOCB). Greenwood.

Holmes, Edward. An Age of Cameras. Rev. ed. LC 75-315789. (Illus.). 160p. 1978. 17.50x (ISBN 0-85242-346-2). Intl Pubns Serv.

--The Life of Mozart. (Music Reprint Ser.). 1979. Repr. of 1845 ed. lib. bdg. 35.00 (ISBN 0-306-79560-4). Da Capo.

--Ramble Among the Musicians of Germany. 2nd ed. LC 68-16239. 1969. Repr. of 1828 ed. lib. bdg. 32.50 (ISBN 0-306-71086-2). Da Capo.

Holmes, Edward & Maynard, Christopher. Great Men of Science. LC 78-68533. (Modern Knowledge Library). (Illus.). (gr. 5 up). 1979. PLB 9.90 s&l (ISBN 0-531-09150-3, Warwick Press). Watts.

Holmes, Efner T. Amy's Goose. LC 77-3027. (Illus.). (gr. 1-3). 1977. 7.64i (ISBN 0-690-03800-3, TYC-J); PLB 8.89 (ISBN 0-690-03801-1). Har-Row.

--Carrie's Gift. LC 78-8452. (Illus.). (gr. 1-4). 1978. PLB 7.95 (ISBN 0-529-05428-0, Philomel); PLB 7.99 (ISBN 0-529-05429-9). Putnam Pub Group.

Holmes, Eliazbeth A., jt. auth. see Heilman, Arthur W.

Holmes, Eric M., jt. auth. see Corley, Robert N.

Holmes, Ernest & Holmes, Fenwicke. Voice Celestial. (Illus.). 352p. Date not set. pap. 11.95 (ISBN 0-911336-70-2). Sci of Mind.

Holmes, Ernest & Kinnear, Willis. A New Design for Living. 1983. pap. 5.95 (ISBN 0-13-612259-0). P-H.

Holmes, Ernest & Smith, Alberta. Questions & Answers on the Science of Mind. 192p. 1981. pap. write for info. (ISBN 0-911336-88-5). Sci of Mind.

Holmes, Ernest S. Creative Mind. 78p. 4.00 (ISBN 0-686-38214-5). Sun Bks.

Holmes, Fenwicke & McEathron, Margaret. Philip's Cousin Jesus: The Untold Story. LC 81-65247. 425p. cancelled 15.95 (ISBN 0-914350-45-5). Reading Hse.

--Philip's Cousin Jesus: The Untold Story. LC 82-65247. 425p. 1982. pap. 9.95 (ISBN 0-87516-494-3). De Vorss.

Holmes, Fenwicke, jt. auth. see Holmes, Ernest.

Holmes, Fenwicke, jt. auth. see McEathron, Margaret.

Holmes, Fenwicke L. The Faith That Heals. 100p. 4.00 (ISBN 0-686-38218-8). Sun Bks.

Holmes, Geoffrey. Augustan England. 352p. 1983. text ed. 37.50x (ISBN 0-04-942178-6). Allen Unwin.

Holmes, Geoffrey S. British Politics in the Reign of Queen Anne. 1967. 25.00 o.p. (ISBN 0-312-10500-2). St Martin.

Holmes, George. Europe: Hierarchy & Revolt 1320-1450. 1976. pap. 6.25xi o.p. (ISBN 0-06-131908-2, TB1908, Torch). Har-Row.

--The Good Parliament. 1975. 39.00x (ISBN 0-19-822446-X). Oxford U Pr.

Holmes, Harold C. Some Random Reminiscences: The Autobiography of Harold C. Holmes. limited ed. (Illus.). 10.00 (ISBN 0-910740-01-1). Holmes.

Holmes, Helen B., et al, eds. Birth Control & Controlling Birth: Women-Centered Perspectives. Hoskins, Betty & Gross, Michael. LC 80-82173. (Contemporary Issues in Biomedicine, Ethics, & Society Ser.). 352p. 1980. 14.95 (ISBN 0-89603-022-9); pap. 7.95 (ISBN 0-89603-023-7). Humana.

Holmes, Irvin. The Christian Path of Intuitive Wisdom. 80p. (Orig.). Date not set. pap. 3.50 cancelled (ISBN 0-87516-408-0). De Vorss. Postponed.

Holmes, Ivory H. The Allocation of Time by Women Without Family Responsibilities. LC 82-20167. (Illus.). 186p. (Orig.). 1983. lib. bdg. 19.75 (ISBN 0-8191-2903-8); pap. text ed. 9.75 (ISBN 0-8191-2904-6). U Pr of Amer.

Holmes, J. W., jt. auth. see Marshall, T. J.

Holmes, J. W. & Talsma, T., eds. Land & Stream Salinity: Proceedings. (Developments in Agricultural Engineering Ser.: Vol. 2). 1981. 55.00 (ISBN 0-444-41999-3). Elsevier.

Holmes, Jack K. Coherent Spread Spectrum Systems. LC 81-4296. 624p. 1982. 64.95 (ISBN 0-471-03301-4, Pub. by Wiley-Interscience). Wiley.

Holmes, James R. & Lander, Gerald H. Profile of the Management Accountant. 140p. pap. 12.95 (ISBN 0-686-37887-3, 82139). Natl Assn Accts.

Holmes, John. Writing Poetry. 1960. 10.00 o.s.i. (ISBN 0-87116-033-1). Writer.

Holmes, John R. Refuse Recycling & Recovery. LC 80-42145. (Institution of Environmental Science Ser.). 200p. 1981. 35.95 (ISBN 0-471-27902-1, Pub. by Wiley-Interscience); pap. 15.95x (ISBN 0-471-27903-X, Pub. by Wiley-Interscience). Wiley.

Holmes, K. C. & Blow, D. M. The Use of X-Ray Diffraction in the Study of Protein & Nucleic Acid Structure. Glick, D., ed. LC 79-20293. 1979. Repr. of 1965 ed. lib. bdg. 11.50 (ISBN 0-89874-046-0). Krieger.

Holmes, K. K. & Mardh, P. Sexually Transmitted Diseases. 1216p. 1983. 65.00x (ISBN 0-07-029675-8). McGraw.

Holmes, K. K., jt. ed. see Mardh, P. A.

Holmes, Keith D. The Sound of English. Set. tchrs guide 25.00 (ISBN 0-9608250-4-5); per set, 4 disc recordings 25.00 (ISBN 0-9608250-3-7). Educ Serv Pub.

Holmes, Keith O. Seventy Steps to Vocabulary Power. rev., 2nd ed. (Illus.). 100p. (Orig.). 1983. pap. text ed. 4.95 per box (ISBN 0-9608250-1-0). Educ Serv Pub.

--Songs of the Maggodee. (Illus.). 95p. (Orig.). 1982. pap. text ed. 5.00x (ISBN 0-9608250-0-2). Educ Serv Pub.

--Student Guide to Language Skills. rev. ed. (Illus.). 95p. (Orig.). 1983. Repr. of 1960 ed. 7.75x (ISBN 0-9608250-2-9). Educ Serv Pub.

Holmes, Kenneth L., ed. Covered Wagon Women: Diaries & Letters from the Western Trails, 1840-1890. LC 82-72586. (Covered Wagon Women Ser.). (Illus.). 280p. 1983. 25.00 (ISBN 0-87062-146-7). A H Clark.

Holmes, King, jt. auth. see Wear, Jennifer.

Holmes, King K. & Mardh, Per-Anders. International Perspectives on Neglected Sexually Transmitted Diseases: Impact on Venereology, Infertility, & Maternal & Infant Health. (Illus.). 352p. 1982. text ed. 45.00 (ISBN 0-07-029676-6, HP). McGraw.

Holmes, Leonard, ed. Odhams New Motor Manual. (Illus.). 320p. 1972. 7.25x o.p. (ISBN 0-600-71800-X). Transatlantic.

Holmes, Lewis B., et al. Mental Retardation: An Atlas of Diseases with Associated Physical Abnormalities. (Illus.). 1972. text ed. 59.00x (ISBN 0-02-356470-9). Macmillan.

Holmes, Lowell D. Other Cultures, Elder Years: An Introduction to Cross Culture Gerontology. 240p. (Orig.). 1982. pap. text ed. 11.95x (ISBN 0-8087-4715-0). Burgess.

Holmes, Lowell D. & Thomson, John W. Jazz Greats: Case Studies in Creativity & Adaptability. (Illus.). 225p. 1982. cancelled (ISBN 0-8419-0750-1); pap. cancelled (ISBN 0-8419-0751-X). Holmes & Meier.

Holmes, Lowell E. & Parris, Wayne. Anthropology, an Introduction. 3rd ed. LC 80-22138. 598p. 1981. text ed. 22.95 (ISBN 0-471-08107-8). Wiley.

Holmes, Lucile B. Oaklawn Manor. (Illus.). 84p. 1983. pap. 5.00 (ISBN 0-88289-418-8). Pelican.

Holmes, M. R. Nutrition of the Oilseed Ripe Crop. 1980. 24.75 (ISBN 0-85334-900-2, Pub. by Applied Sci England). Elsevier.

Holmes, Marguerite C. & Gottlieb, Marvine I. Anatomy & Physiology. 3rd ed. (Nursing Examination Review Bk: Vol. 5). 1975. pap. 7.50 o.p. (ISBN 0-87488-505-1). Med Exam.

Holmes, Marguerite C., et al, eds. Basic Sciences. 3rd ed. (Nursing Examination Review Book Ser.: Vol. 4). 1973. spiral bdg. 7.50 o.p. (ISBN 0-87488-504-3). Med Exam.

Holmes, Marjorie. Hold Me up a Little Longer, Lord. LC 76-42338. (Illus.). 1977. 9.95 (ISBN 0-385-12403-1). Doubleday.

--Hold Me up a Little Longer, Lord. 1977. lib. bdg. 10.95 o.p. (ISBN 0-8161-6530-0, Large Print Bks). G K Hall.

--I've Got to Talk to Somebody, God. 1971. pap. 2.50 (ISBN 0-8007-8080-9, Spire Bks). Revell.

--Love & Laughter. 1978. lib. bdg. 13.50 o.p. (ISBN 0-8161-6548-3, Large Print Bks). G K Hall.

--To Help You Through the Hurting. LC 81-43571. (Illus.). 120p. 1983. 7.95 (ISBN 0-385-17842-5). Doubleday.

--Two from Galilee. 224p. 1972. pap. 5.95 (ISBN 0-8007-5089-6, Power Bks); pap. 2.95 (ISBN 0-8007-8155-4, Spire Bks). Revell.

Holmes, Michael S. The New Deal in Georgia. LC 74-289. 384p. 1975. lib. bdg. 29.95 (ISBN 0-8371-7375-2, HND/). Greenwood.

Holmes, Mike & Martin, L. H. Analysis & Design of Connection Between Elements. (Civil & Mechanical Engineering Ser.). 260p. 1983. 42.95 (ISBN 0-470-27365-8). Halsted Pr.

Holmes, N. J., et al. Gateways to Science, 6 Levels. 4th ed. Incl. Level 1. 192p. text ed. 8.92 (ISBN 0-07-029821-1); tchr's. ed. 15.76 (ISBN 0-07-029831-9); Level 2. 192p. text ed. 9.32 (ISBN 0-07-029822-X); tchr's. ed. 16.20 (ISBN 0-07-029832-7); Level 3. 320p. text ed. 10.00 (ISBN 0-07-029823-8); tchr's. ed. 16.96 (ISBN 0-07-029833-5); Level 4. 368p. text ed. 11.08 (ISBN 0-07-029824-6); tchr's. ed. 17.88 (ISBN 0-07-029834-3); Level 5. 384p. text ed. 11.76 (ISBN 0-07-029825-4); tchr's. ed. 18.80 (ISBN 0-07-029905-6); Level 6. 432p. text ed. 12.16 (ISBN 0-07-029826-2); tchr's. ed. 19.12 (ISBN 0-07-029836-X). (gr. k-6). 1983. Tchr's manual level k. 10.16 (ISBN 0-07-029820-3); Bulletin boards gr. 1-6. 16.00 ea.; Webstermaster Gr. 1-6. 40.00 ea.; Pupil's lab. bk. Gr. 3-6. 4.44 ea.; Tchr's lab. bk. Gr. 3-6. 6.00 ea.; supplementary materials avail. McGraw.

--Gateways to Science, Level 1. 1981. text ed. 8.88 (ISBN 0-07-029801-7); tchr's. ed. 17.52 (ISBN 0-07-029811-4). McGraw.

--Gateways to Science, Level 2. 3rd ed. 1981. text ed. 9.84 (ISBN 0-07-029802-5); tchr's. ed. 18.00 (ISBN 0-07-029812-2). McGraw.

--Gateways to Science, Level 3. 3rd ed. 1981. text ed. 11.04 (ISBN 0-07-029803-3); tchr's. ed. 18.84 (ISBN 0-07-029813-0). McGraw.

--Gateways to Science, Level 4. 3rd ed. 1981. text ed. 11.81 (ISBN 0-07-029804-1); tchr's. ed. 19.84 (ISBN 0-686-96774-7). McGraw.

--Gateways to Science, Level 5. 3rd ed. 1981. text ed. 12.96 (ISBN 0-07-029805-X); tch's ed 20.88 (ISBN 0-07-029815-7). McGraw.

--Gateways to Science, Level 6. 3rd ed. 1981. text ed. 13.08 (ISBN 0-07-029806-8); tchr's. ed. 21.24 (ISBN 0-07-029816-5). McGraw.

Holmes, Neal J. & Leake, John B. Gateways to Science Webstermaster Activities, Level 1. 4th ed. (Gateways to Science Ser.). 43p. 1982. pap. text ed. 40.00s (ISBN 0-07-029851-3, W). McGraw.

--Gateways to Science Webstermaster Activities, Level 2. 4th ed. Kita, M. Jane, ed. (Gateways to Science Ser.). 43p. 1982. pap. text ed. 40.00s (ISBN 0-07-029852-1, W). McGraw.

--Gateways to Science Webstermaster Activities, Level 3. 4th ed. Kita, M. Jane, ed. (Gateways to Science Ser.). 85p. 1982. pap. text ed. 40.00s (ISBN 0-07-029853-X, W). McGraw.

--Gateways to Science Webstermaster Activities, Level 4. 4th ed. Mongillo, John F., ed. (Gateways to Science Ser.). 89p. 1982. pap. text ed. 40.00s (ISBN 0-07-029854-8, W). McGraw.

--Gateways to Science Webstermaster Activities, Level 5. 4th ed. (Gateways to Science Ser.). 89p. 1982. pap. text ed. 40.00s (ISBN 0-07-029855-6, W). McGraw.

--Gateways to Science Webstermaster Activities, Level 6. Mongillo, John F., ed. (Gateways to Science Ser.). 97p. 1982. pap. text ed. 40.00 (ISBN 0-07-029856-4, W). McGraw.

Holmes, Neal J., et al. Gateways to Science. 2nd ed. Incl. Level K. tchr's. ed. 11.28 (ISBN 0-07-029679-0, W); Level 1. text ed. 8.88 (ISBN 0-07-029641-3); tchr's. ed. 17.52 (ISBN 0-07-029651-0); Level 2. text ed. 8.88 (ISBN 0-07-029642-1); tchr's. ed. 18.00 (ISBN 0-07-029652-9); Level 3. text ed. 11.04 (ISBN 0-07-029643-X); tchr's. ed. 18.84 (ISBN 0-07-029653-7); Level 4. text ed. 11.80 (ISBN 0-07-029644-8); tchr's. ed. 19.84 (ISBN 0-07-029654-5); Level 5. text ed. 12.96 (ISBN 0-07-029645-6); tchr's. ed. 20.88 (ISBN 0-07-029655-3); Level 6. text ed. 13.08 (ISBN 0-07-029646-4); tchr's. ed. 21.24 (ISBN 0-07-029656-1). (Gateways to Science Ser.). Orig. Title: Science: People, Concepts, Processes. (Illus.). 1979. kits avail. (W). McGraw.

Holmes, Oliver W. Autocrat of the Breakfast-Table. (Classics Ser). (YA) (gr. 11 up). pap. 1.95 (ISBN 0-8049-0159-7, CL-159). Airmont.

--Psychiatric Novels of Oliver Wendell Holmes. abr. ed. 2nd ed. LC 72-156193. 1971. Repr. of 1946 ed. lib. bdg. 16.00x (ISBN 0-8371-6142-8, HOPN). Greenwood.

--Ralph Waldo Emerson. LC 67-23884. 1967. Repr. of 1885 ed. 34.00 o.p. (ISBN 0-8103-3039-3). Gale.

Holmes, Oliver W. & Rohrbach, Peter T. Stagecoach East: Stagecoach Days in the East from the Colonial period to the Civil War. (Illus.). 240p. 1983. text ed. 17.50x (ISBN 0-87474-522-5). Smithsonian.

Holmes, P. J., ed. New Approaches to Nonlinear Problems in Dynamics. LC 80-52593. xii, 529p. 1980. 45.00 (ISBN 0-89871-167-3). Soc Indus-Appl Math.

Holmes, Paul C. Phonics Guidelines: An Introduction. 320p. 1980. pap. text ed. 14.95 (ISBN 0-8403-2225-9). Kendall-Hunt.

Holmes, Paul C. & Lehman, Anita J. Keys to Understanding: Receiving & Sending - the Poem. 1969. pap. text ed. 13.50 scp o.p. (ISBN 0-06-042867-8, HarpC). Har-Row.

Holmes, Peter, jt. auth. see Estrin, Saul.

Holmes, Philip. Vilhelm Moberg. (World Authors Ser.). 1980. lib. bdg. 15.95 (ISBN 0-8057-6426-7, Twayne). G K Hall.

Holmes, R. B. A Course on Optimization & Best Approximation. (Lecture Notes in Mathematics: Vol. 257). 233p. 1972. pap. 7.50 o.p. (ISBN 0-387-05764-1). Springer-Verlag.

Holmes, R. L., jt. ed. see Harrison, R. J.

Holmes, Richard W. & Kennedy-Streetman, Marrianna B. Mines & Minerals of the Great American Rift. 336p. 1982. text ed. 29.50 (ISBN 0-442-28038-6). Van Nos Reinhold.

Holmes, Roger. Legitimacy & the Politics of the Knowable. (Direct Editions Ser.). (Orig.). 1976. pap. 16.95 (ISBN 0-7100-8351-3). Routledge & Kegan.

Holmes, Stacey. Mellifluous Voice. (Illus.). 22p. 1982. pap. 10.00 (ISBN 0-910681-00-7). S Holmes Enter.

Holmes, Stewart. Meaning in Language. 1983. 6.50 (ISBN 0-686-84069-0). Intl Gen Semantics.

Holmes, T. Chretien de Troyes. (World Authors Ser.). 13.95 (ISBN 0-8057-2890-2, Twayne). G K Hall.

Holmes, Thomas, Jr. Bayou Cook Book. (Illus.). 185p. 1983. Pelican.

Holmes, Tommy. The Hawaiian Canoe. LC 82-234748. (Illus.). 191p. 1982. 35.00 (ISBN 0-9607938-1-X); deluxe ed. 100.00 (ISBN 0-9607938-0-1). Editions Ltd.

Holmes, Urban. The Priest in Community: Exploring the Roots of Ministry. LC 78-17645. 1978. 10.95 (ISBN 0-8164-0400-3). Seabury.

Holmes, Urban T. A History of Christian Spirituality: An Analytical Introduction. 176p. 1981. pap. 6.95 (ISBN 0-8164-2343-1). Seabury.

Holmes, Urban T. & Westerhoff, John H. Christain Believing. (Church's Teaching Ser.: Vol. I). 144p. 1979. 5.95 (ISBN 0-8164-0418-6); pap. 3.95 (ISBN 0-8164-2214-1). Seabury.

Holmes, Urban T. & Westerhoff, John H., III. The Church's Teaching Series, 9 Vols. 1979. Set. 45.45 (ISBN 0-8164-0453-4); Set. pap. 24.95 (ISBN 0-8164-2271-0). Seabury.

Holmes, Urban T., jt. auth. see Terwilliger, Robert E.

Holmes, Urban T., jt. ed. see Cabeen, David C.

Holmes, Urban T., III. Young Children & the Eucharist. rev. ed. 128p. 1982. pap. 6.95 (ISBN 0-8164-2425-X). Seabury.

Holmes, Urban T., 3rd, jt. ed. see Stough, Furman C.

Holmes, W. H. Archaeological Studies Among the Ancient Cities of Mexico. (Chicago Field Museum of Natural History Fieldiana Anthropology Ser). Repr. of 1895 ed. pap. 45.00 (ISBN 0-527-01861-9). Kraus Repr.

Holmes, W. H., jt. auth. see Heinlein, W. E.

Holmes, William. Grass: Its Production & Utilization. (Illus.). 304p. 1981. pap. text ed. 19.50 (ISBN 0-632-00618-8, B-2229-8). Mosby.

--La Statira by Pietro Ottobuni & Alescandro Scarlatti: The Textual Sources, with a Documentary Postscript. (The Pendragon Monographs in Musicology: No. 1). 120p. 1983. lib. bdg. 32.50x (ISBN 0-918728-18-5). Pendragon NY.

Holmgren, Frederick. The God Who Cares: A Christian Looks at Judaism. LC 78-52445. (Orig.). 1979. pap. 2.75 (ISBN 0-8042-0588-4). John Knox.

--The God Who Cares: A Christian Looks at Judaism. 144p. 4.95 (ISBN 0-686-95170-0). ADL.

Holmgren, J., jt. auth. see Holme, T.

Holmgren, John H. Purchasing for the Health Care Facility. (Illus.). 288p. 1975. 28.75x (ISBN 0-398-03399-4). C C Thomas.

Holmgren, Virginia. The Pheasant. Schroeder, Howard, ed. (Wildlife Habits & Habitat Ser.). (Illus.). 48p. (gr. 4-5). 1983. lib. bdg. 8.95 (ISBN 0-89686-222-4). Crestwood Hse.

Holmquist, Emily & Sloan, Marjorie. Depth & Scope, Guides for Curriculum in a Technical Nursing Program: A Study for the Determination & Application of Unlimited Depth & Limited Scope in a Technical Nursing Program. (League Exchange Ser.: No. 117). 89p. 1978. 6.95 (ISBN 0-686-38258-7, 23-1697). Natl League Nurse.

Holms, R., jt. auth. see Beck, L.

Holmstedt, B., jt. ed. see Costa, E.

Holmstedt, B., et al, eds. Mechanisms of Toxicity & Hazard Evaluation. (Developments in Toxicology & Environmental Science Ser.: Vol. 8). 1981. 88.00 (ISBN 0-444-80293-2). Elsevier.

Holmstedt, Bo & Liljestrand, G., eds. Readings in Pharmacology. 410p. 1981. Repr. of 1963 ed. text ed. 21.50 (ISBN 0-89004-662-X). Raven.

Holmstrom, J. E., et al. Trilingual Dictionary for Materials & Structures. 1971. inquire for price o.p. (ISBN 0-08-013370-3). Pergamon.

Holmstrom, Lynda L. & Burgess, Ann W. The Victim of Rape: Institutional Reactions. 1983. pap. 12.95 (ISBN 0-87855-932-9). Transaction Bks.

Holmstrom, Lynda Lytle & Burgess, Ann Wolbert. The Victime of Rape: Institutional Reactions. LC 77-27074. 308p. Repr. of 1978 ed. text ed. 20.95 (ISBN 0-471-40785-2). Krieger.

Holmstrom, M. South Indian Factory Workers. LC 75-46205. (Cambridge South Asian Studies: No. 20). 1977. 24.95 (ISBN 0-521-21134-4). Cambridge U Pr.

Holoch, George, tr. see Lacouture, Jean.

Holoien, Martin O. Computers & Their Societal Impact. 1977. pap. text ed. 19.50 (ISBN 0-471-02197-0). Wiley.

Holoien, Martin O. & Behforooz, Ali. Problem Solving & Structured Programming with FORTRAN 77. LC 82-24436. 560p. 1983. pap. text ed. 18.95 (ISBN 0-534-01275-2). Brooks-Cole.

Holoien, Renee A., jt. ed. see Patton, Peter C.

Holoman, D. Kern & Palisca, Claude V., eds. Musicology in the Nineteen Eighties: Methods, Goals, Opportunities. (Music Reprint Ser.). 170p. 1983. Repr. lib. bdg. 18.50 (ISBN 0-306-76188-2). Da Capo.

Holowinsky, Ivan Z. Psychology & Education of Exceptional Children & Adolescents: United States & International Perspectives. LC 82-61527. 352p. 1983. text ed. 22.95x (ISBN 0-916622-26-6). Princeton Bk Co.

Holquist, Michael, ed. see Bakhtin, M. M.

Holroyd, Michael, jt. auth. see Easton, Malcolm.

Holroyd, Michael, ed. Essays by Diverse Hands XLII. (Royal Society of Literature Ser.). 208p. 1983. text ed. 22.50x (ISBN 0-85115-173-6, Pub. by Boydell & Brewer). Biblio Dist.

Holroyd, Michael, ed. see Strachey, Lytton.

Holroyd, Sam V., jt. auth. see Requa, Barbara.

Holroyd, Stuart. Alien Intelligence. LC 78-71104. 1980. 9.95 o.p. (ISBN 0-89696-040-4, An Everest House Book). Dodd.

Holschneider, Alexander M. Hirschsprung's Disease. (Illus.). 124p. 1982. 59.00 (ISBN 0-86577-050-6). Thieme-Stratton.

Holsinger, Alden O., Jr., jt. auth. see Loomba, N. Paul.

Holsinger, Rosemary. Shasta Indian Tales. (Illus.). 48p. 1982. lib. bdg. 8.95 (ISBN 0-87961-128-6); pap. 3.95 (ISBN 0-87961-129-4). Naturegraph.

Holsinger, Terry W. A Mind In Time. LC 82-90071. 125p. (Orig.). 1982. pap. 4.95 (ISBN 0-9607966-0-6). T W Holsinger.

Holst, Auke Van see Van Holst, Auke.

Holst, Gustav, jt. auth. see Vaughan Williams, Ralph.

Holst, Gustav, jt. auth. see Williams, Ralph Vaughan.

Holst, Gustav, ed. see Williams, Ralph Vaughan & Holst, Gustav.

Holst, Imogen. Bach. LC 65-20723. (Great Composer Ser.). (Illus.). (gr. 7 up). 1965. PLB 11.89 o.p. (ISBN 0-690-11391-9, TYC-J). Har-Row.

Holst, Imogen, ed. see Vaughan Williams, Ralph & Holst, Gustav.

Holst, Phyllis. Recipes from Hidden Hills, Tried & True. 36p. pap. 3.95 (ISBN 0-941016-02-1). Penfield.

Holstein, Bjorn E., jt. auth. see Andersen, Svend E.

Holsti, K. J. International Politics: A Framework for Analysis. 4th ed. (Illus.). 512p. 1983. text ed. 22.95 (ISBN 0-13-473322-3). P-H.

Holsti, Kalvei J. International Politics: A Framework for Analysis. 3rd ed. (Illus.). 1977. 22.95 (ISBN 0-13-473371-1). P-H.

Holsti, Ole R., et al, eds. Change in the International System. 460p. 1980. lib. bdg. 30.00 (ISBN 0-89158-846-9); pap. 12.50 (ISBN 0-89158-895-7). Westview.

Holstrom, Linda L. The Two Career Family. LC 70-189095. 204p. 1972. text ed. 13.95 o.p. (ISBN 0-87073-092-4); pap. text ed. 8.95 o.p. (ISBN 0-87073-093-2). Schenkman.

Holsworth, Robert D. Public Interest Liberalism & the Crisis of Affluence: Reflections on Nader, Environmentalism, & the Politics of a Sustainable Society. 1980. lib. bdg. 17.50 (ISBN 0-8161-9032-1, Univ Bks). G K Hall.

Holsworth, Robert D. & Wray, J. Harry. American Politics & Everyday Life. LC 81-23171. 204p. 1982. pap. text ed. 9.95 (ISBN 0-471-08645-2). Wiley.

Holt, jt. auth. see Hume.

Holt, Alfred H. American Place Names. LC 68-26574. 1969. Repr. of 1938 ed. 30.00x (ISBN 0-8103-3235-3). Gale.

--Phrase & Word Origins: A Study of Familiar Expressions. 9.00 (ISBN 0-8446-2268-0). Peter Smith.

Holt, Alix, intro. by see Kollontai, Alexandra.

Holt, Arthur G. Handwriting in Psychological Interpretations. (Illus.). 276p. 1974. 21.75x (ISBN 0-398-00864-7). C C Thomas.

Holt, C. A. & Shore, R. W. Bayesian Analysis in Economic Theory & Time Series Analysis. (Studies in Bayesian Econometrics: Vol. 2). 1980. 34.00 (ISBN 0-444-85414-2). Elsevier.

Holt, Charles A. Electronic Circuits: Digital & Analog. LC 77-11654. 1978. 33.95 (ISBN 0-471-02313-2); tchr's manual avail. (ISBN 0-471-03044-9). Wiley.

Holt, Delores. Black History Biographies. LC 77-87843. (Illus.). 62p. 1978. pap. 4.00 incl. card deck (ISBN 0-913866-09-1). US Games Syst.

Holt, Dennis M. & Thompson, Keith P. Developing Competencies to Teach Music in the Elementary Classroom. (Elementary Education Ser.). 360p. 1980. spiral 12.95 (ISBN 0-675-08135-1); instr's. manual 3.95. Merrill.

Holt, Edgar A. Party Politics in Ohio Eighteen Forty-Eighteen Fifty. (Perspectives in America Hist. Ser.: No. 38). (Illus.). 449p. Repr. of 1931 ed. lib. bdg. 27.50x (ISBN 0-87991-362-2). Porcupine Pr.

Holt, Elizabeth G., ed. A Documentary History of Art, Vol. 1. pap. 3.50 ea. (Anch); Vol. 1. pap. (ISBN 0-385-09320-9); Vol. 2. pap. o.p. (ISBN 0-385-09366-7). Doubleday.

--From the Classicists to the Impressionists: A Documentary History of Art & Architecture in the 19th Century. pap. 7.95 (ISBN 0-385-06683-X, A114C, Anch). Doubleday.

--Triumph of Art for the Public: The Emerging Role of Exhibitions & Critics. LC 77-27708. 1979. pap. 6.95 (ISBN 0-385-13511-4, Anch). Doubleday.

Holt, Emily S. Ye Olden Time: English Customs in the Middle Ages. LC 72-164343. 1971. Repr. of 1884 ed. 30.00x (ISBN 0-8103-3798-3). Gale.

Holt, F. A., tr. see Von Hindenburg, Paul.

Holt, Fred C. The Pupil Personnel Team in the Elementary School. (Guidance Monograph). 1975. pap. 2.40 o.p. (ISBN 0-395-20060-1). HM.

Holt, G. Richard & Mattox, Douglas E. Decision Making in Otolaryngology: Head & Neck Surgery. 256p. 1983. text ed. 32.00 (ISBN 0-941158-09-8, D2250-6). Mosby.

Holt, Geoffrey, jt. auth. see Bull, Alan T.

Holt, Helen. One Love Lost. (Aston Hall Romances Ser.). 192p. 1981. pap. 1.75 o.p. (ISBN 0-523-41130-8). Pinnacle Bks.

Holt, J. C. Magna Carta. Reeves, Marjorie, ed. (Then & There Ser.). (Illus.). 88p. (gr. 7-12). 1961. pap. text ed. 3.10 (ISBN 0-582-20377-5). Longman.

Holt, James. The Emergence of Modern America 1890-1920. (Studies in 20th Century History Ser.). 1973. pap. text ed. 4.50x o.p. (ISBN 0-435-31177-8). Heinemann Ed.

Holt, James C. Magna Carta & the Idea of Liberty. 200p. 1982. pap. 5.95 (ISBN 0-89874-471-7). Krieger.

Holt, John. Freedom & Beyond. 1973. pap. 2.95 o.s.i. (ISBN 0-440-52755-4, Delta). Dell.

--How Children Fail. pap. text ed. 1.95 o.s.i. (ISBN 0-440-33869-7). Dell.

--How Children Learn. 1970. pap. text ed. 1.95 o.s.i. (ISBN 0-440-33871-9). Dell.

--Instead of Education. 1975. pap. 3.45 o.s.i. (ISBN 0-686-78751-X, Delta). Dell.

--Never Too Late. 1978. 10.00 o.s.i. (ISBN 0-440-06641-7, Sey Lawr). Delacorte.

--Never Too Late. 1980. pap. 4.95 o.s.i. (ISBN 0-440-56352-6, Delta). Dell.

--Teach Your Own: New & Hopeful Path for Parents & Educators. 1982. pap. 8.95 (ISBN 0-440-58539-2, Delta). Dell.

--Underachieving School. 208p. 1972. pap. 1.25 o.s.i. (ISBN 0-440-39160-1). Dell.

--Underachieving School. 1970. pap. 2.25 o.s.i. (ISBN 0-440-59324-7, Delta). Dell.

--What Do I Do Monday? 1972. pap. text ed. 5.95 o.s.i. (ISBN 0-440-59584-3, Delta). Dell.

Holt, John G. Supplement to the Index Bergeyana. 456p. 1981. 38.95 (ISBN 0-683-04106-1, 4106-1). Williams & Wilkins.

Holt, K. S., jt. ed. see Douglas, C. P.

Holt, Kenneth S. Developmental Pediatrics. (Postgraduate Pediatric Ser.). 304p. 1977. 22.95 (ISBN 0-407-00065-8). Butterworth.

Holt, Knut. Product Innovation-Models & Methods: A Workbook for Management in Industry. new ed. 1978. 29.95 (ISBN 0-408-00288-3). Butterworth.

Holt, Marion P. The Contemporary Spanish Theater, Nineteen Forty-Nine to Nineteen Sixty-Two. (World Authors Ser.). 1975. lib. bdg. 13.95 (ISBN 0-8057-2243-2, Twayne). G K Hall.

--Jose Lopez Rubio. (World Authors Ser.). 1980. lib. bdg. 15.95 (ISBN 0-8057-6395-3, Twayne). G K Hall.

Holt, Marion P. & Dueber, Julianne. One Thousand & One Pitfalls in Spanish. rev. ed. LC 75-167690. 1973. pap. 4.50 (ISBN 0-8120-0433-7). Barron.

Holt, Maurice, ed. Basic Developments in Fluid Dynamics, 2 Vols. Vol. 1. 1965. 72.00 (ISBN 0-12-354001-1); Vol. 2, 1968. 48.00 (ISBN 0-12-354002-X). Acad Pr.

Holt, Michael F. Political Crisis of the 1850's. LC 77-13564. (Critical Episodes in American Politics Ser.). 1978. text ed. 11.95 o.p. (ISBN 0-471-40840-9); pap. text ed. 9.95x o.p. (ISBN 0-471-40841-7). Wiley.

Holt, P. M., ed. The Eastern Mediterranean Lands in the Period of the Crusades. 112p. 1977. text ed. 18.00x o.p. (ISBN 0-85668-091-5, Pub. by Aris & Phillips England). Humanities.

Holt, Pat M., jt. auth. see Crabb, Cecil V.

Holt, R. C. & Hume, J. N. Fundamentals of Structured Programming Using FORTRAN with SF-K & WATFIV-S. 2nd ed. (Illus.). 1977. pap. text ed. 16.95 (ISBN 0-87909-302-1). Reston.

--Programming Standard PASCAL. (Illus.). 400p. 1980. text ed. 20.95 (ISBN 0-8359-5691-1); pap. text ed. 16.95 (ISBN 0-8359-5690-3); instructor's manual o.p. avail. Reston.

--UCSD Pascal: A Beginner's Guide to Programming Microcomputers. 368p. 1982. 18.95 (ISBN 0-8359-7915-6); pap. 14.95 (ISBN 0-8359-7913-X). Reston.

Holt, R. F., ed. The Strength of Tradition: Stories of the Immigrant Presence in Australia. LC 82-10874. 288p. 1983. 16.50 (ISBN 0-7022-1691-7); pap. 8.95 (ISBN 0-7022-1701-8). U of Queensland Pr.

Holt, Richard C., et al. Structured Concurrent Programming with Operating Systems Applications. 1978. pap. text ed. 15.95 (ISBN 0-201-02937-5). A-W.

Holt, Robert L. Bonds: How to Double Your Money Quickly & Safely. LC 80-65576. 1980. 13.95x (ISBN 0-930926-03-X, CA Finan Pubns). Calif Health.

--Hemorrhoids: A Cure & Preventative. LC 77-86391. (Illus.). 1978. pap. 7.95 (ISBN 0-930926-01-3). Calif Health.

--Hemorrhoids: A Cure & Preventive. rev. ed. LC 79-21792. 1980. pap. 4.95 (ISBN 0-688-08584-9). Quill NY.

--Publishing: A Complete Guide for Schools, Small Presses, & Entrepreneurs. LC 82-83565. (Calif. Financial Publications Ser.). 1982. 25.95 (ISBN 0-930926-08-0); pap. 19.95 (ISBN 0-930926-09-9). Calif Health.

--Straight Teeth: Orthodontics for Everyone. LC 80-10562. (Illus.). 283p. 1980. pap. 7.95 (ISBN 0-930926-07-2). Calif Health.

Holt, Robert W. Theory, Evidence & Interference: A Handbook on the Scientific Method. LC 81-40632. (Illus.). 96p. (Orig.). 1982. lib. bdg. 19.25 (ISBN 0-8191-2246-7); pap. text ed. 7.25 (ISBN 0-8191-2247-5). U Pr of Amer.

Holt, Rochelle. The Bare Tissue of Her Soul. folder ed. (Poems in Calligraphy). 1972. signed 2.00 (ISBN 0-934536-06-6); pap. 2.00 (ISBN 0-686-09149-3). Merging Media.

--Love in the Year of the Dragon. 1977. pap. 1.50 (ISBN 0-686-19060-2). Merging Media.

--A Summer of the Heart. 1977. 1.50 (ISBN 0-934536-11-2). Merging Media.

Holt, Roy D. Children Indian Captives. (Stories for Young Americans Ser.). 1980. 5.95 (ISBN 0-89015-245-4). Eakin Pubns.

Holt, S. C., jt. auth. see Farguharson, J. B.

Holt, Simma. The Other Mrs. Diefenbaker. LC 80-2860. (Illus.). 384p. 1983. 22.95 (ISBN 0-385-17089-0). Doubleday.

Holt, Smith L., ed. Inorganic Reactions in Organized Media. (ACS Symposium Ser.: No. 177). 1982. write for info. (ISBN 0-8412-0670-8). Am Chemical.

Holt, Stephen H. Laboratory Aids in Diagnosis. LC 77-136967. 196p. 1973. 12.00 (ISBN 0-88275-121-2). Krieger.

Holt, Vesta. Keys for Identification of Wild Flowers, Ferns, Trees, Shrubs, Woody Vines of Northern California. 174p. 1962. pap. 6.95 o.p. (ISBN 0-87484-072-4). Mayfield Pub.

Holt, Victoria. Curse of the Kings. LC 72-96242. 336p. 1973. 13.95 (ISBN 0-385-01153-9). Doubleday.

--Demon Lover. LC 82-45073. 384p. 1982. 14.95 (ISBN 0-385-18222-8). Doubleday.

--The Demon Lover. (General Ser.). 1983. lib. bdg. 18.95 (ISBN 0-8161-3514-2, Large Print Bks). G K Hall.

--The Devil on Horseback. LC 77-72414. 1977. 13.95 (ISBN 0-385-13209-3). Doubleday.

--The House of a Thousand Lanterns. LC 73-20514. 336p. 1974. 13.95 (ISBN 0-385-00817-1). Doubleday.

--The Judas Kiss. LC 81-43291. 408p. 1982. 13.95 (ISBN 0-385-17786-0). Doubleday.

--The Judas Kiss. (General Ser.). 1982. lib. bdg. 15.95 (ISBN 0-8161-3342-5, Large Print Bks). G K Hall.

--The Judas Kiss. 336p. 1983. pap. 3.50 (ISBN 0-449-20055-8, Crest). Fawcett.

--King of the Castle. LC 67-10974. 1967. 13.95 (ISBN 0-385-07672-X). Doubleday.

--Legend of the Seventh Virgin. 1965. 13.95 (ISBN 0-385-00609-8). Doubleday.

--Mask of the Enchantress. LC 79-6088. 356p. 1980. 13.95 (ISBN 0-385-17024-6). Doubleday.

--My Enemy the Queen. LC 77-11366. 1978. 13.95 (ISBN 0-385-14111-4). Doubleday.

--On the Night of the Seventh Moon. LC 72-76170. 360p. 1972. 13.95 (ISBN 0-385-08579-6). Doubleday.

--Queen's Confession: A Biography of Marie Antoinette. LC 68-10586. 1968. 14.95 (ISBN 0-385-08276-2). Doubleday.

--Shadow of the Lynx. LC 72-144273. 1971. 13.95 (ISBN 0-385-05427-0). Doubleday.

--The Spring of the Tiger. LC 78-22814. 1979. 13.95 (ISBN 0-385-15261-2). Doubleday.

Holt, Victoria, pseud. Will You Love Me in September. 320p. 1982. pap. 2.95 o.p. (ISBN 0-686-97231-7). Popular Lib.

Holt, W. Stull, ed. see Adams, Herbert B.

Holt, Will. Savage Snow. (Orig.). 1980. pap. 2.25 o.p. (ISBN 0-451-09019-5, E9019, Sig). NAL.

Holt, William S. Treaties Defeated by the Senate. 1964. 8.50 (ISBN 0-8446-1242-1). Peter Smith.

Holt, Wythe. Essays in Nineteenth-Century American Legal History. LC 76-27129. (Contributions in American History: No. 60). 800p. 1976. lib. bdg. 35.00 (ISBN 0-8371-9285-4, HEN/). Greenwood.

--Selected Essays in the Alabama Law of Decedent's Estates, Trusts, & Future Interests. new ed. 415p. 1975. 12.50 (ISBN 0-87215-177-8). Michie-Bobbs.

Holtan, O. I. Introduction to Theatre: A Mirror to Nature. (Theatre & Drama Ser.). (Illus.). 240p. 1976. ref. ed. 19.95 (ISBN 0-13-498741-1). P-H.

Holte, Susan & Wynar, Bohdan S., eds. Best Reference Books, 1970-1980: Titles of Lasting Value Selected from American Reference Books Annual. LC 81-5788. 480p. 1981. lib. bdg. 30.00 (ISBN 0-87287-255-6). Libs Unl.

Holten, M. Gary & Jones, Melvin E. The System of Criminal Justice. 2nd ed. 1982. text ed. 20.95 (ISBN 0-316-37171-8); tchrs' manual avail. (ISBN 0-316-37172-6). Little.

Holter, Wayne V. & Phillips, James M. Morgan Fire & Steel. LC 82-90180. (Illus.). 140p. 18.95 (ISBN 0-932572-10-3). Phillips Holter.

Holtermuller, K. H., jt. ed. see Malagalada, J. R.

Holthouse, Hector. River of Gold. (Illus.). 1968. 7.95 o.p. (ISBN 0-685-20620-3). Transatlantic.

Holtje, H., jt. auth. see Webb, M. J.

Holtje, Herbert & Stockwell, John. How to Borrow Everything You Need to Build a Great Personal Fortune. LC 73-20233. 1983. pap. 4.95 (ISBN 0-13-396572-4, Reward). P-H.

Holtje, Herbert, jt. ed. see Stockwell, John.

Holtje, Herbert F. Directory of Manufacturers' Representatives. LC 77-14580. 1978. 54.00 o.p. (ISBN 0-07-029640-5, P&RB). McGraw.

--Handbook of Exterior Home Repairs: A Practical Illustrated Guide. 218p. 1979. 12.95 o.p. (ISBN 0-686-92146-1, Parker). P-H.

--Successful Real Estate Negotiation Strategy. Christman, Donald A., ed. LC 82-8578. (Real Estate for Professional Practitioners Ser.). 190p. 1982. 18.95 (ISBN 0-471-09437-4, Pub. by Wiley-Interscience). Wiley.

Holt-Jensen, Arild. Geography its History & Concepts: A Student's Guide. Fullerton, Brian, tr. 184p. 1982. pap. 9.95x (ISBN 0-389-20262-2). B&N Imports.

Holtom, Robert B., jt. auth. see Glendenning, G. William.

Holtom, Robert B., jt. auth. see Glendenning, G. Williams.

Holton, Frances. Caverns of Danger. (YA) 1979. 6.95 (ISBN 0-686-59785-0, Avalon). Bouregy.

--Home from Hawaii. (YA) 6.95 (ISBN 0-685-19058-7, Avalon). Bouregy.

Holton, G. The Scientific Imagination. LC 76-47196. (Illus.). 1978. 42.50 (ISBN 0-521-21700-8); pap. 12.95 (ISBN 0-521-29237-9). Cambridge U Pr.

Holton, Gerald & Sopka, Katherine R. History of Modern Physics, Eighteen Hundred to Nineteen Fifty. 1983. write for info limited edition (ISBN 0-938228-05-6). Tomash Pubs.

Holton, J., et al. Spanish Review Grammar: Theory & Practice. 1977. 18.95 (ISBN 0-13-824409-X). P-H.

Holton, Milne. Cylinder of Vision: The Fiction & Journalistic Writings of Stephen Crane. LC 79-181358. 336p. 1972. 27.50x o.p. (ISBN 0-8071-0045-5). La State U Pr.

Holtrop, ed. see Newell, Adnah C.

Holtrop, W. F. Operation of Modern Woodworking Machines. 1966. pap. 6.60 o.p. (ISBN 0-02-818770-9); key 0.40 o.p. (ISBN 0-02-818680-X). Glencoe.

Holtrop, Wm., jt. auth. see Cunningham, Beryl M.

Holtsmark, Erling B. Tarzan & Tradition: Classical Myth in Popular Literature. LC 80-1023. (Contributions to the Study of Popular Culture: No. 1). (Illus.). xv, 196p. 1981. lib. bdg. 25.00 (ISBN 0-313-22530-3, HOT/). Greenwood.

Holtz, H. Directory of Federal Purchasing Offices: Where, What, How to Sell the U.S. Government. 415p. 1981. 50.50 (ISBN 0-471-08227-9, Pub. by Wiley-Interscience). Wiley.

--Mail Order Magic: Sure-Fire Techniques to Expand Any Business by Direct Mail. 256p. 1983. 15.95 (ISBN 0-07-029628-6); pap. 7.95 (ISBN 0-07-029631-6). McGraw.

--Persuasive Writing: Communicating Effectively in Business. 288p. 1983. 14.95 (ISBN 0-07-029627-8); pap. 6.95 (ISBN 0-07-029630-8). McGraw.

Holtz, Herman. How to Succeed As An Independent Consultant. LC 82-13429. 395p. 1983. 19.95 (ISBN 0-471-86742-X, Pub. by Wiley-Interscience). Wiley.

Holtz, Herman R. Two Thousand One Sources of Financing for Small Business. LC 82-11366. 192p. 1983. lib. bdg. 14.95 (ISBN 0-668-05468-9); pap. 9.95 (ISBN 0-668-05470-0). Arco.

Holtz, Herman R. & Schmidt, Terry D. The Winning Proposal: How to Write It. (Business Communication Ser.). (Illus.). 384p. 1981. text ed. 24.95x (ISBN 0-07-029649-9). McGraw.

Holtz, Lou & Hall, Wally. Lou Holtz in Hog Heaven (Arkansas Football) (College Sports Ser.). 250p. (Orig.). pap. 7.95 o.p. (ISBN 0-87397-174-4). Strode.

Holtz, Per A. Index to Simulation Literature. 300p. 1982. pap. 38.00 (ISBN 0-686-36688-3). Soc Computer Sim.

Holtz, Robert D., jt. auth. see Kovacs, William D.

Holtz, William, ed. see Lane, Rose W. & Boylston, Helen D.

Holtzclaw, Robert F. William Henry Holtzclaw: Scholar in Ebony; a History of Utica Junior College. LC 76-29278. (Illus.). 252p. 1977. 5.00 (ISBN 0-913228-19-2). Keeble Pr.

Holtzclaw, William. Black Man's Burden. LC 70-154044. (Studies in Black History & Culture, No. 54). 1971. Repr. of 1915 ed. lib. bdg. 54.95x (ISBN 0-8383-1277-2). Haskell.

Holtzman, Abraham. American Government: Ideals & Reality. (Illus.). 1980. pap. text ed. 15.95 (ISBN 0-13-027151-9). P-H.

Holtzman, Steven H. & Leich, Christopher M., eds. Wittgenstein: To Follow a Rule. (International Library of Philosophy). 250p. 1981. 25.00 (ISBN 0-7100-0760-4). Routledge & Kegan.

Holtzman, Wayne H. Introduction to Psychology. 1978. text ed. 24.50 scp o.p. (ISBN 0-06-168400-7, HarpC); 8.50 o.p. (ISBN 0-06-168418-X). Har-Row.

Holtzman, Wayne H., ed. Introductory Psychology in Depth: Developmental Topics. 1978. pap. text ed. 8.95 scp o.p. (ISBN 0-06-168415-5, HarpC). Har-Row.

--Introductory Psychology in Depth: Social Topics. 1978. pap. text ed. 8.95 scp o.p. (ISBN 0-06-168416-3, HarpC). Har-Row.

Holtzman, Will. Judy Holliday: Only Child. (Illus.). 304p. 1982. 13.95 (ISBN 0-399-12647-3). Putnam Pub Group.

Holtzmann, Adolf. Ueber Den Umlaut: Zwei Abhandlungen (1843), & Ueber Den Ablaut (1844) (Amsterdam Classics in Linguistics Ser.). xxix, 129p. 1977. 22.00 (ISBN 0-686-31498-0, ACIL 12). Benjamins North Am.

Holtzmeier, Dawn K. Applied Anatomy & Physiology: A Laboratory Manual & Workbook for Health Careers. 304p. 1983. pap. text ed. 18.50 (ISBN 0-8403-2915-6). Kendall-Hunt.

Holub, Alex. Escape from Intimacy. LC 82-83495. 144p. 1983. pap. 5.95 (ISBN 0-86666-064-X). GWP.

Holub, Steven F. & Kalick, Laura L. Hospital Tax Management. LC 82-13716. 187p. 1982. 24.00 (ISBN 0-89443-665-5). Aspen Systems.

Holub, William, ed. Ministries for the Lord: Nineteen Seventy-Nine to Nineteen Eighty Edition of the Resource Guide & Church Vocation Directory for Men. 1979. pap. 4.95 o.p. (ISBN 0-8091-2177-8). Paulist Pr.

Holum, Dianne. The Complete Handbook of Speed Skating. LC 82-18174. (Illus.). 450p. 1983. 45.00x (ISBN 0-89490-051-X). Enslow Pubs.

Holum, J. R. Elements of General & Biological Chemistry: An Introduction to the Molecular Basis of Life. 6th ed. 593p. 1979. 25.95 o.p. (ISBN 0-471-02224-1); lab manual 11.95 o.p. (ISBN 0-471-04751-1); tchr's. manual avail. o.p. (ISBN 0-471-04753-8); study guide avail. o.p. (ISBN 0-471-04752-X). Wiley.

--Elements of General & Biological Chemistry: An Introduction to the Molecular Basis of Life. 6th ed. 593p. text ed. 27.95 (ISBN 0-471-09935-X); 11.95 (ISBN 0-471-08236-8); tchr's. manual avail. (ISBN 0-471-89033-2). Wiley.

Holum, John R. Fundamentals of General, Organic, & Biological Chemistry. LC 77-10418. 1978. text ed. 24.95x o.p. (ISBN 0-471-40873-5); study guide 8.95 o.p. (ISBN 0-471-02454-6); tchrs.' manual 8.95 o.p. (ISBN 0-471-03669-2). Wiley.

--Organic & Biological Chemistry. LC 78-634. 1978. text ed. 25.95 (ISBN 0-471-40872-7). Wiley.

--Organic Chemistry: A Brief Course. LC 74-20773. (Illus.). 528p. 1975. text ed. 26.95 o.s.i. (ISBN 0-471-40849-2); solutions manual o.p. 5.95 o.p. (ISBN 0-471-40861-1); o.p. instructors' manual o.p. (ISBN 0-471-51716-X). Wiley.

Holum, John R., jt. auth. see Brady, James E.

Holweck, Frederick G. Biographical Dictionary of the Saints. LC 68-30625. 1969. Repr. of 1924 ed. 66.00x (ISBN 0-8103-3158-6). Gale.

Holy, Ladislav. Neighbours & Kinsmen: A Study of the Berti People of Darfur. LC 73-87139. 160p. 1974. 25.00 (ISBN 0-312-56350-7). St Martin.

Holy Transfiguration Monastery, ed. The Life of St. Maximus the Confessor. Birchall, Christopher, tr. from Greek, & Russian. (Illus.). 73p. (Orig.). 1982. pap. 4.50x (ISBN 0-913026-52-2). St Nectarios.

Holy Transfiguration Monastery, tr. see Chrysostom, John.

Holy Transfiguration Monastery, tr. see Sakkas, Basile.

Holyoake, George J. Among the Americans, & Stranger in America. LC 70-88508. xiv, 246p. Repr. of 1881 ed. lib. bdg. 15.00 o.p. (ISBN 0-8371-4970-3, HOAM). Greenwood.

Holyst, Brunon. Comparative Criminology. LC 81-47713. 432p. (Polish.). 1983. 35.95x (ISBN 0-669-04726-0). Lexington Bks.

Holz, Harald. Anthropodizee: Zur Inkarnation von Vernunft in Geschichte. 555p. Date not set. price not set (ISBN 3-8204-5823-9). P Lang Pubs.

--Evolution und Geist. 560p. 1981. write for info. (ISBN 3-8204-6107-8). P Lang Pubs.

Holz, K. P., et al, eds. Finite Elements in Water Resources, Hannover, Germany 1982: Proceedings. 1100p. 1982. 74.90 (ISBN 0-387-11522-6). Springer-Verlag.

Holz, Loretta. The Christmas Spider: A Puppet Play from Poland & Other Traditional Games, Crafts & Activities. (gr. 3-7). 5.95 (ISBN 0-399-20754-6, Philomel); lib. bdg. 5.99g (ISBN 0-399-61164-9). Putnam Pub Group.

Holz, R., et al. Mendes I. Hall, E. Swann & Bothmer, Bernard, eds. (American Research in Egypt, Reports Ser.: Vol. 2). xxi, 83p. 1980. 45.00 (ISBN 0-936770-02-3, Pub by Am Res Ctr Egypt). Undena Pubns.

Holz, Robert K., ed. Surveillant Science: Remote Sensing of the Environment. LC 72-7922. (Illus.). 300p. (Orig.). 1973. pap. text ed. 19.95 (ISBN 0-395-14041-2). HM.

Holzer, Eva, ed. see Messec, Jerry & Kranich, Roger.

Holzer, Hans. The Great Ghost Hunt. LC 82-9724. (Illus.). 220p. 1983. pap. 5.95 (ISBN 0-89865-177-8). Donning Co.

--Houses of Horror. 192p. 1982. pap. 2.25 (ISBN 0-8439-1143-3, Leisure Bks). Dorchester Pub Co.

--Westghosts: The Psychic World of California. LC 82-75794. Orig. Title: Ghosts of the Golden West. xiv, 233p. 1980. pap. 5.95 (ISBN 0-8040-0759-4). Swallow.

Holzman, D. Poetry & Politics: The Life & Works of Juan Chi (A.D. 210-263) LC 75-27798. (Cambridge Studies in Chinese History, Literature & Institutions). 350p. 1977. 47.50 (ISBN 0-521-20855-6). Cambridge U Pr.

Holzman, Philip S. Psychoanalysis & Psychopathology. LC 75-88883. 1970. pap. text ed. 15.50 (ISBN 0-07-029671-5, C). McGraw.

Holzman, Richard W. Impact of Nature Photography. (Illus.). 1979. 17.95 o.p. (ISBN 0-8174-2476-8, Amphoto); pap. 12.95 (ISBN 0-8174-2147-5). Watson-Guptill.

Holzman, Robert S. Estate Planning: The New Golden Opportunities. LC 82-12942. 250p. 1982. 50.00 (ISBN 0-932648-31-2). Boardroom.

--A Survival Kit for Taxpayers: How to Deal with the I.R.S. rev. ed. 192p. 1981. pap. 5.95 (ISBN 0-02-553510-2). Macmillan.

--Take It Off! 350p. 1981. pap. 8.50 o.p. (ISBN 0-06-464048-5, BN 4048, BN). B&N NY.

--Take It Off: Two Thousand Three Hundred Sixty-Three Deductions Most People Overlook. rev. & expanded ed. 1983. 16.30i (ISBN 0-06-015036-X, HarpT); pap. 8.61 (ISBN 0-06-464053-1, BN-4053). Har-Row.

--Take It Off! 2363 Tax Deductions Most People Overlook. 1983. 400p. 1982. pap. 8.61i (ISBN 0-686-37773-7, BN-4053). B&N NY.

Holzner, W. & Numata, M. Biology & Ecology of Weeds. 1982. 99.50 (ISBN 90-6193-682-9, Pub. by Junk Pubs Netherlands). Kluwer Boston.

Holzner, W. & Werger, M. J. Man's Impact on Vegetation. 1983. 98.00 (ISBN 90-6193-685-3, Pub. by Junk Pubs Netherlands). Kluwer Boston.

Hom, Ken & Steiman, Harvey. Chinese Technique: An Illustrated Guide to the Fundamental Techniques of Chinese Cooking. (Illus.). 1981. 18.25 (ISBN 0-671-25347-6). S&S.

Homan, Dianne. In Christina's Toolbox. LC 81-83958. (Illus.). 28p. (Orig.). (ps-1). 1981. pap. 2.75 (ISBN 0-914996-23-1). Lollipop Power.

Homans, George C. The Human Group. 484p. 1950. text ed. 20.95 (ISBN 0-15-540375-3, HC). HarBraceJ.

--The Nature of Social Science. LC 67-22390. (Orig.). 1967. pap. 1.95 (ISBN 0-15-665425-3, Harv). HarBraceJ.

Homberger, Conrad P. Ruckschau & Fortschritt: A Continuation Course in German. LC 68-56441. (Illus., Ger.). 1969. text ed. 13.95x o.p. (ISBN 0-669-44065-5); tapes. 7 reels 35.00 o.p. (ISBN 0-669-44073-6). Heath.

Homberger, Conrad P. & Ebelke, John F. Foundation Course in German. rev. ed. 1964. text ed. 21.95 o.p. (ISBN 0-669-29264-8); tapes 35.00 o.p. (ISBN 0-669-33993-8). Heath.

Homberger, Eric. The Art of the Real: Poetry in England & America Since 1939. 246p. 1977. 14.00x o.p. (ISBN 0-87471-938-0). Rowman.

Homburger, F., ed. Safety Evaluation & Regulation of Chemicals. (Illus.). xii, 240p. 1983. 118.75 (ISBN 3-8055-3578-3). S Karger.

--Skin Painting Techniques & in vivo Carcinogenesis Bioassays: Progress in Experimental Tumor Research Ser, Vol. 26. (Illus.). vi, 3140p. 1983. 131.75 (ISBN 3-8055-3556-2). S Karger.

Homburger, F. & Hayes, J. A., eds. A Guide to General Toxicology. (Karger Continuing Education Ser.: Vol. 5). (Illus.). 392p. 1983. 56.00 (ISBN 3-8055-3606-2). S Karger.

Homburger, Wolfgang S., jt. auth. see Carter, Everett.

Home Planners. English Tudor Homes & Other Family Plans. 1979. 1.75 (ISBN 0-918894-21-2). Home Planners.

--Home Designs. 1979. 1.50 (ISBN 0-918894-20-4). Home Planners.

--Home Plans. 1980. 1.75 (ISBN 0-918894-22-0). Home Planners.

--House Plans for Contemporary Living. 1980. 1.75 (ISBN 0-918894-12-3). Home Planners.

--Low & Medium Cost Homes. 1974. 2.00 (ISBN 0-918894-14-X). Home Planners.

--Most Popular Homes. 1980. 1.95 (ISBN 0-918894-25-5). Home Planners.

--Traditional & Contemporary Family Homes. 1979. 1.50 (ISBN 0-918894-19-0). Home Planners.

--Traditional & Contemporary Plans. 1978. 4.95 (ISBN 0-918894-15-8). Home Planners.

Home Planners, Inc. Four-Hundred & a Half & Two Story Homes. (Design Category Ser.: Vol. 1). (Illus.). 1982. pap. 5.95 o.p. (ISBN 0-918894-26-3). Home Planners.

--Three Hundred & Fifty Homes: One Story Designs Under 2,000 Square Feet. (Design Category Ser.: Vol. 3). (Illus.). 1982. pap. 4.95 o.p. (ISBN 0-918894-28-X). Home Planners.

--Two Hundred & Ten: One Story Designs Over 2,000 Sq. Ft. (Design Category Ser.: Vol. 2). (Illus.). 1982. pap. 3.95 (ISBN 0-918894-27-1). Home Planners.

Home Planners Inc. Two Twenty Three Homes: Vacation Homes. (Design Category Ser.: Vol. 5). (Illus.). 1982. pap. 4.25 (ISBN 0-918894-30-1). Home Planners.

Homebook, Beeton & Hirst, Irene. Art of the Kitchen. 13.50x (ISBN 0-392-06269-0, LTB). Sportshelf.

Homebook, Beeton & Tompkins, Dorothy. Art of the Table. 13.50x (ISBN 0-392-06241-0, LTB). Sportshelf.

Homel, David T., tr. see Caron, Louis.

Homer. Homer's Odyssey. Hull, Denison B., tr. from Gr. LC 79-106151. xxx, 281p. (gr. 7-9). 1978. text ed. 12.00x (ISBN 0-8214-0433-4, 82-83210). Ohio U Pr.

--Iliad. Rouse, William H., tr. 1954. pap. 2.25 (ISBN 0-451-62056-9, ME2056, Ment). NAL.

--La Iliada. (Span.). 9.95 (ISBN 84-241-5415-0). E Torres & Sons.

--Odyssey. Fitzgerald, Robert, tr. LC 61-8886. (Illus.). 1961. pap. 5.95 (ISBN 0-385-05040-2, A333, Anch). Doubleday.

--Odyssey. Rouse, W. H., tr. 1971. pap. 2.25 (ISBN 0-451-62200-6, ME2200, Ment). NAL.

--The Odyssey. Shewring, Walter, tr. (The World's Classics Ser.). 1981. 24.00x (ISBN 0-19-251019-3); pap. 3.95x (ISBN 0-19-281542-3). Oxford U Pr.

--Odyssey, Bks. 6 & 7. Edwards, Gerald M., ed. (Gr.). 1915. text ed. 6.50x (ISBN 0-521-05322-6). Cambridge U Pr.

--Odyssey: Critical Ed. Cook, Albert, ed. & tr. 1974. 10.00 (ISBN 0-393-04161-1); pap. 6.95x (ISBN 0-393-09971-7). Norton.

Homer, Jack A., ed. Gandhi Reader. 316p. 1983. 5.95 (ISBN 0-394-62472-6, E279, Ever). Grove.

Homer, Sidney. My Wife & I: The Story of Louise & Sidney Homer. LC 77-10561. (Music Reprint Ser.). (Illus.). 1978. Repr. of 1939 ed. lib. bdg. 32.50 (ISBN 0-306-77526-3). Da Capo.

Homer, William I. Alfred Stieglitz & the American Avant-Grade. 1979. pap. 11.95 (ISBN 0-8212-0755-5, 031933). NYGS.

--Alfred Stieglitz & the American Avant-Garde. LC 76-50068. (Illus.). 1977. 19.95 (ISBN 0-8212-0676-1, 031917). NYGS.

--Seurat & the Science of Painting. (Illus.). 1964. pap. 8.95 o.p. (ISBN 0-262-58036-5). MIT Pr.

Homer, Winslow. Winslow Homer Illustrations: Forty-Four Wood Engravings after Drawings by the Artist. (Illus.). 48p. (Orig.). 1983. pap. 2.25 (ISBN 0-486-24392-3). Dover.

Homewood, Harry. A Matter of Size. LC 74-25386. 160p. 1975. 7.95 (ISBN 0-87955-904-7). O'Hara.

--O God of Battles. 384p. 1983. 14.95 (ISBN 0-688-01915-3). Morrow.

Homma, S. Understanding the Stretch Reflex. (Progress in Brain Research Ser.: Vol. 44). 1976. 126.50 (ISBN 0-444-41456-8, North Holland). Elsevier.

Homola, Samuel, jt. auth. see Lupus, Peter.

Homsher, Lola M., ed. see Chisholm, James.

Hon, David C. Rehearsals for Armageddon, No. 1. Zapel, Arthur L., ed. (Illus.). 1973. pap. text ed. 4.95 (ISBN 0-916260-01-1). Meriwether Pub.

--Rehearsals for Armageddon, No. 2. Zapel, Arthur L., ed. LC 79-84744. (Illus.). 1976. pap. text ed. 4.95 (ISBN 0-916260-02-X). Meriwether Pub.

Honan, Park. Matthew Arnold: A Life. 512p. 1983. pap. text ed. 9.95x (ISBN 0-674-55465-5). Harvard U Pr.

Honda, Isao. The World of Origami. abr. ed. LC 65-27101. (Illus.). 200p. 1976. pap. 12.95 (ISBN 0-87040-383-4). Japan Pubns.

Honda, Masaaki. Suzuki Changed My Life. (Illus.). 1976. pap. text ed. 9.70 (ISBN 0-87487-084-4). Summy.

Honderich, Ted, ed. Social Ends & Political Means. 190p. 1976. 20.00 (ISBN 0-7100-8370-X). Routledge & Kegan.

Hone, J. Ann. For the Cause of Truth: Radicalism in London, 1795-1821. (Historical Monographs). 422p. 1982. 45.00x (ISBN 0-19-821887-7). Oxford U Pr.

Hone, Philip. Diary of Philip Hone, 1828-1851, 2 Vols. in 1. 1927. 48.00 o.s.i. (ISBN 0-527-42100-6). Kraus Repr.

Hone, William. Ancient Mysteries Described. LC 67-23905. (Illus.). 1969. Repr. of 1823 ed. 30.00x (ISBN 0-8103-3444-5). Gale.

--Every-Day Book, 2 Vols. LC 67-12945. 1967. Repr. of 1827 ed. Set. 118.00x (ISBN 0-8103-3005-9). Gale.

--Table Book, 2 Vols. LC 67-12946. Repr. of 1827 ed. Set. 54.00x (ISBN 0-8103-3006-7). Gale.

--The Year Book of Daily Recreation & Information. LC 67-12947. 1967. Repr. of 1832 ed. 54.00x (ISBN 0-8103-3007-5). Gale.

Honea, Charla, compiled by. Family Rituals. LC 81-52861. (Illus., Orig.). 1981. pap. 3.95x (ISBN 0-686-79888-0). Upper Room.

Honecker, Erich. From My Life. LC 80-41162. (Leaders of the World Ser.: Vol. 3). (Illus.). 500p. 1981. 24.00 (ISBN 0-08-024532-3). Pergamon.

Honegger, Gitta, tr. see Canetti, Elias.

Honer, Stanley M. & Hunt, Thomas C. Invitation to Philosophy. 3rd ed. 1978. pap. 11.95x o.p. (ISBN 0-534-00564-0). Wadsworth Pub.

Honerkamp, J. & Pohlmeyer, J., eds. Structural Elements in Particle Physics & Statistical Mechanics. (NATO ASI Series B, Physics: Vol. 82). 470p. 1983. 65.00x (ISBN 0-306-41038-9, Plenum Pr). Plenum Pub.

Honess, C. Brian, jt. auth. see Fleck, Robert.

Honey, Martha, jt. auth. see Avirgan, Tony.

Honey, Sandra, et al, eds. Mies Van der Rohe. LC 79-92594. (Architectural Monographs). (Illus.). 112p. (Orig.). 1981. pap. cancelled (ISBN 0-8478-0295-7). Rizzoli Intl.

Honeybone, R. C. & Long, I. L. World Geography. 1972. pap. text ed. 11.00x o.p. (ISBN 0-435-34428-5). Heinemann Ed.

Honeycombe, Gordon. Dragon Under the Hill. 1973. 7.95 o.p. (ISBN 0-671-21553-1). S&S.

--The Year of the Princess. LC 82-47969. (Illus.). 160p. 1982. 16.95 (ISBN 0-316-37212-9). Little.

Honeyman, Katrina. Origins of Enterprise: Business Leadership in the Industrial Revolution. LC 82-10441. 180p. 1982. 20.00x (ISBN 0-312-58848-8). St Martin.

Hong, Christopher C. A History of the Future: A Study of the Four Major Eschatologies. LC 81-40010. 186p. 1981. lib. bdg. 19.00 (ISBN 0-8191-1625-4); pap. text ed. 9.50 (ISBN 0-8191-1626-2). U Pr of Amer.

Hong, Edna. The Way of the Sacred Tree. LC 82-72643. 192p. 1983. pap. 8.95 (ISBN 0-8066-1949-X, 10-6958). Augsburg.

Hong, Edna H., ed. see Kierkegaard, Soren.

Hong, Edna H., tr. see Kierkegaard, Soren.

Hong, Edna H., tr. see Malantschuk, Gregor.

Hong, Howard V., ed. see Kierkegaard, Soren.

Hong, Howard V., tr. see Kierkegaard, Soren.

Hong, Howard V., tr. see Malantschuk, Gregor.

Hong, Sawon. Community Development & Human Reproductive Behavior. 196p. 1979. text ed. 10.00x (ISBN 0-8248-0685-9, Korea Devel Inst). UH Pr.

Hong, Wontack. Factor Supply & Factor Intensity of Trade in Korea. 1976. text ed. 10.00x (ISBN 0-8248-0539-9). UH Pr.

--Trade, Distortions & Employment Growth in Korea. 410p. 1979. 15.00x (ISBN 0-8248-0678-6, Korea Devel Inst). UH Pr.

Hong, Wontack & Krause, Laurence B., eds. Trade & Growth of the Advanced Developing Countries in the Pacific Basin. 650p. 1981. text ed. 24.00x (ISBN 0-8248-0791-X, Korea Devel Inst). UH Pr.

Hong, Wontack & Krueger, Anne O., eds. Trade & Development in Korea. 1975. text ed. 10.00x (ISBN 0-8248-0536-4). UH Pr.

Hong, Xiao. Selected Stories of Xiao Hong. Goldbratt, Howard, tr. from Chinese. 220p. 1982. pap. 3.50 (ISBN 0-8351-1049-4). China Bks.

Hongxun, Yang. The Classical Gardens of China: History & Design Techniques. LC 81-23974. 144p. 1982. 29.95 (ISBN 0-442-23209-8) (ISBN 0-686-83126-8). Van Nos Reinhold.

Honig, jt. ed. see Williams, Oscar.

Honig, Alice S. Playtime Learning Games for Young Children. LC 82-16794. (Illus.). 128p. 1982. pap. 9.95 (ISBN 0-8156-0178-6). Syracuse U Pr.

Honig, Donald. Baseball Between the Lines: Baseball After World War II As Told by the Men Who Played It. LC 75-34477. (Illus.). 320p. 1976. 9.95 o.p. (ISBN 0-698-10725-X, Coward). Putnam Pub Group.

--Baseball When the Grass Was Real: Baseball in the Forties, Told by the Men Who Played It. LC 74-30610. (Illus.). 320p. (YA) 1975. 12.50 o.p. (ISBN 0-698-10660-1, Coward). Putnam Pub Group.

--An End of Innocence. (gr. 4-9). 1972. 5.75 o.p. (ISBN 0-399-20254-4). Putnam Pub Group.

--Going the Distance. (Target Bks.). (Illus.). 48p. (gr. 3 up). 1976. PLB 7.90 o.p. (ISBN 0-531-02679-5). Watts.

--The Los Angeles Dodgers: An Illustrated Tribute. (Illus.). 192p. 1983. 19.95 (ISBN 0-312-49880-2). St Martin.

Honig, Donald, jt. auth. see Ritter, Lawrence S.

Honig, Edwin. Dark Conceit: The Making of Allegory. LC 72-2452. 224p. 1982. pap. text ed. 8.00x (ISBN 0-87451-222-0). U Pr of New Eng.

--Four Springs. LC 82-73112. 60p. 1972. 6.00 (ISBN 0-8040-0580-X); pap. 2.75 o.p. (ISBN 0-8040-0581-8). Swallow.

--Interrupted Praise: New & Selected Poems. LC 82-5998. (Poets Now Ser.: No. 6). 194p. 1983. 13.50 (ISBN 0-8108-1564-8). Scarecrow.

--Selected Translations. 64p. 1983. pap. 7.95 (ISBN 0-935306-22-6). Barnwood Pr.

Honig, Edwin, jt. auth. see Zaleski, Jean.

Honig, Edwin, tr. Selected Poems by Fernando Pessoa. LC 82-72593. (Poetry in Europe Ser.). 170p. 1974. pap. 6.95 (ISBN 0-8040-0521-4). Swallow.

Honig, Edwin, tr. from Port. Selected Poems by Fernando Pessoa. LC 82-72585. (Poetry in Europe Ser.). 170p. 1971. 10.95 (ISBN 0-8040-0520-6). Swallow.

Honig, J. M. Thermodynamics: Principles Characterizing Physical & Chemical Processes. (Studies in Modern Thermodynamics: Vol. 4). Date not set. 102.25 (ISBN 0-444-42092-4). Elsevier.

Honig, Werner K., ed. Operant Behavior: Areas of Research & Application. (Illus.). 1966. text ed. 39.95 o.p. (ISBN 0-13-637884-6). P-H.

Honig, Werner K. & Staddor, J., eds. Handbook of Operant Behavior. LC 76-26034. (Century Psychology Ser.). 1977. 55.00 (ISBN 0-13-380535-2). P-H.

Honigfeld, G. & Howard, A. Psychiatric Drugs: A Desk Reference. 2nd ed. 1978. 16.50 (ISBN 0-12-354860-8). Acad Pr.

Honigmann, E. A. Shakespeare's Impact on His Contemporaries. 1982. 59.00x (ISBN 0-333-26938-1, Pub. by Macmillan England). State Mutual Bk.

Honigsbaum, Frank. The Division in British Medicine: The Separation of General Practice from Hospital Care, 1911-1968. LC 79-14789. 1979. 30.00 (ISBN 0-312-21431-6). St Martin.

Honigsberg, Peter, jt. auth. see Mancuso, Anthony.

Honjo, S., ed. Ocean Biocoenosis: Microfossil Counterparts in Sediment Traps. (Micropaleontology Special Publications Ser.: No. 5). 1982. 50.00 (ISBN 0-686-84259-6). Am Mus Natl Hist.

Honnecourt, Villard de see De Honnecourt, Villard.

Honness, Elizabeth. Mystery in the Square Tower. LC 57-10325. (Illus.). (gr. 4-6). 1957. 8.95i o.p. (ISBN 0-397-30382-3, JBL-J). Har-Row.

Honnold, John O., jt. auth. see Farnsworth, E. Allan.

Honold, P. Secondary Radar. 1976. 57.95 (ISBN 0-471-25772-9, Wiley Heyden). Wiley.

Honore, M., jt. auth. see Catudal, Jr.

Honore, Tony. Ulpian. 1982. 65.00x (ISBN 0-19-825358-3). Oxford U Pr.

Honour, Hugh. Companion Guide to Venice. (Illus.). 304p. 1983. 15.95 (ISBN 0-13-154666-X); pap. 7.95 (ISBN 0-13-154658-9). P-H.

Honour, T. F. & Mainwaring, R. M. Business & Sociology. (Sociology in Practice Ser.). 224p. 1982. text ed. 28.00x (ISBN 0-7099-0333-2, Pub. by Croom Helm Ltd England). Biblio Dist.

Honrubia, Vicente & Brazier, Mary, eds. Nystagmus & Vertigo: Clinical Approach to the Patient with Dizziness. LC 82-3906. (UCLA Forum in Medical Sciences Ser.: No. 24). 320p. 1982. 26.00 (ISBN 0-12-355080-7). Acad Pr.

Honsberger, Ross. Ingenuity in Mathematics. LC 77-134351. (New Mathematical Library: No. 23). 1975. pap. 8.75 (ISBN 0-88385-623-9). Math Assn.

Hoobler, Dorothy & Hoobler, Thomas. An Album of the Seventies. LC 81-3347. (Picture Albums Ser.). (Illus.). 96p. (gr. 5 up). 1981. PLB 9.60 (ISBN 0-531-04322-3). Watts.

--An Album of World War I. LC 75-44281. (Picture Albums Ser.). (Illus.). 96p. (gr. 5 up). 1976. PLB 9.60 (ISBN 0-531-01169-0). Watts.

--An Album of World War II. LC 77-5090. (Picture Albums Ser.). (Illus.). (gr. 5 up). 1977. PLB 9.60 s&l (ISBN 0-531-02911-5). Watts.

--Photographing History: The Career of Mathew Brady. LC 77-3009. (Illus.). (gr. 5-9). 1977. 8.95 o.p. (ISBN 0-399-20602-7). Putnam Pub Group.

--Photographing the Frontier. LC 79-11130. (Illus.). (gr. 7-12). 1980. 9.95 o.p. (ISBN 0-399-20694-9). Putnam Pub Group.

--The Social Security System. (Impact Bks.). (Illus.). 96p. (gr. 7 up). 1982. PLB 8.90 (ISBN 0-531-04490-4). Watts.

--The Trenches: Fighting on the Western Front in World War I. LC 78-2698. (Illus.). (gr. 6-8). 1978. 9.95 (ISBN 0-399-20640-X). Putnam Pub Group.

--U. S. China Relations Since World War II. LC 80-25343. (Impact Bks). 1981. 8.90 (ISBN 0-531-04264-2). Watts.

Hoobler, James A., ed. Nashville Memories: Thirty-Two Historic Postcards. LC 82-23841. (Illus.). 16p. 1983. pap. 3.95 (ISBN 0-87049-385-X). U of Tenn Pr.

Hoobler, Thomas, jt. auth. see Hoobler, Dorothy.

Hoobler, Thomas, jt. auth. see Wetanson, Burt.

Hood & Shors. Closely Held Corporations in Estate Planning. LC 81-86293. 1982. write for info. (ISBN 0-316-37218-8). Little.

Hood, Christopher & Wright, Maurice, eds. Big Government in Hard Times. (Illus.). 240p. 1981. pap. 9.95x (ISBN 0-85520-417-6, Pub. by Martin Robertson England); text ed. 19.95x (ISBN 0-85520-416-8). Biblio Dist.

Hood, Christopher C. The Limits of Administration. LC 75-37850. 208p. 1976. 36.95x o.p. (ISBN 0-471-01652-7, Pub. by Wiley-Interscience). Wiley.

Hood, Donald W. Impingement of Man on the Oceans. LC 74-151728. 738p. 1971. 42.50 (ISBN 0-471-40870-0, Pub. by Wiley). Krieger.

Hood, Dora. Davidson Black: A Biography. 1964. 25.00x o.p. (ISBN 0-8020-7081-7). U of Toronto Pr.

Hood, Evelyn M. The Story of Scottish Country Dancing. 128p. 1983. pap. 7.95 (ISBN 0-00-411110-9, Collins Pub England). Greene.

Hood, Flora M. The Turquoise Horse. (Illus.). (gr. 5-9). 1972. PLB 5.29 o.p. (ISBN 0-399-60744-7). Putnam Pub Group.

Hood, Gail H. & Dincher, Judy. Medical-Surgical Nursing: Workbook for Nurses. 5th ed. LC 79-24346. (Illus.). 226p. 1980. pap. text ed. 12.50 (ISBN 0-8016-2567-X). Mosby.

--Total Patient Care: Foundations & Practice. 5th. ed. LC 79-23834. (Illus.). 916p. 1980. text ed. 24.95 (ISBN 0-8016-2574-2). Mosby.

Hood, Graham, ed. An Inventory of the Contents of the Governor's Palace Taken After the Death of Lord Botetourt. 19p. (Orig.). 1973. pap. 0.50 (ISBN 0-87935-063-6). Williamsburg.

Hood, K., jt. auth. see Gimblett, F.

Hood, Kenneth. Spice for Speakers, Sports, & Squares. LC 76-12025. 1976. 8.95x (ISBN 0-8134-1814-3, 1814). Interstate.

Hood, Leroy, et al. Immunology. 1978. 17.95 (ISBN 0-8053-4405-5). Benjamin-Cummings.

Hood, M. Ethnomusicologist. 1971. text ed. 49.95 (ISBN 0-07-029725-8). McGraw.

Hood, Mantle. The Ethnomusicologist. LC 82-14828. (Illus.). 386p. 1982. 27.50x (ISBN 0-87338-280-3). Kent St U Pr.

--The Nuclear Theme As a Determinant of Patet in Javanese Music. LC 77-5680. (Music Reprint Ser.). 1977. Repr. of 1954 ed. lib. bdg. 37.50 (ISBN 0-306-77419-4). Da Capo.

Hood, Robert E. Let's Go to a Basketball Game. new ed. LC 76-10030. (Let's Go Ser.). (Illus.). (gr. 3-5). 1976. PLB 4.29 o.p. (ISBN 0-399-61007-3). Putnam Pub Group.

--Let's Go to a Football Game. (Let's Go Ser.). (Illus.). (gr. 4-6). 1975. PLB 4.29 o.p. (ISBN 0-399-60946-6). Putnam Pub Group.

--Let's Go to a Stock Car Race. new ed. (Let's Go Ser.). (Illus.). 48p. (gr. 4-6). 1974. PLB 4.29 o.p. (ISBN 0-399-60849-4). Putnam Pub Group.

Hood, Roger, jt. auth. see Radzinowicz, Leon.

Hood, Sinclair. The Home of the Heroes: The Aegean Before the Greeks. (Illus.). 144p. 1975. pap. 7.50 o.p. (ISBN 0-500-29009-1). Transatlantic.

Hood, Stuart. The Mass Media. (Studies in Contemporary Europe). (Orig.). 1973. pap. text ed. 6.00x (ISBN 0-333-12704-8). Humanities.

Hood, Stuart, tr. see Pasolini, Pier P.

Hood, Vernon, jt. auth. see Dubisch, Roy.

Hood, W. Edmund. Home Brew HF-VHF Antenna Handbook. (Illus.). 1977. pap. 6.95 (ISBN 0-8306-6963-9, 963). TAB Bks.

Hood, William. Mole. (Espionage-Intelligence Library). 320p. 1983. pap. 3.50 (ISBN 0-345-30491-8). Ballantine.

Hooft, J. P. Advanced Dynamics of Marine Structures. (Ocean Engineering Ser.). 368p. 1982. text ed. 50.95 o.p. (ISBN 0-471-03000-7, Pub. by Wiley-Interscience). Wiley.

Hoog, Michael. Delaunay. (QLP Ser.). 1977. 7.95 (ISBN 0-517-52875-4). Crown.

Hoog, Michel, jt. auth. see Druick, Douglas.

Hoogehboom, Ari A. Outlawing the Spoils: A History of the Civil Service Movement, 1865-1883. LC 82-15507. xi, 306p. 1982. Repr. of 1968 ed. lib. bdg. 35.00x (ISBN 0-313-22821-3, H00S). Greenwood.

Hoogenboom, Ari, jt. auth. see Klein, Philip S.

Hooglund, Eric, jt. ed. see Keddie, Nikki R.

Hooglund, Eric, tr. see Behrangi, Samad.

Hooglund, Eric J. Land & Revolution in Iran, 1960-1980. (Modern Middle East Ser.: No. 7). 213p. 1982. text ed. 19.95x (ISBN 0-292-74633-4). U of Tex Pr.

Hooglund, Mary, tr. see Behrangi, Samad.

Hoogstraten, Barth, ed. Cancer Research: Impact of the Cooperative Groups. LC 80-82668. 480p. 1980. 51.00x (ISBN 0-89352-092-6). Masson Pub.

Hoogvelt, Ankie M. M. The Sociology of Developing Societies. LC 77-522. 1977. text ed. 20.00x o.p. (ISBN 0-391-00703-3); pap. text ed. 15.75x o.p. (ISBN 0-391-00704-1). Humanities.

Hook & Boren. Los Pequenos Eschuchan a Dios. Carrodeguas, Andy & Marosi, Esteban, eds. Powell, David, tr. from Eng. Orig. Title: Little Ones Listen to God. 132p. (Span.). (gr. k-3). 1982. pap. 2.50 (ISBN 0-8297-1331-X). Life Pubs Intl.

Hook, Brian, ed. The Cambridge Encyclopedia of China. (Cambridge Regional Encyclopedias). (Illus.). 1982. 35.00 (ISBN 0-521-23099-3). Cambridge U Pr.

Hook, Donal D. & Crawford, R. M. M., eds. Plant Life in Anaerobic Environments. LC 77-85085. 1978. 40.00 o.p. (ISBN 0-250-40197-5). Ann Arbor Science.

Hook, Donald D., jt. auth. see Kahn, Lothar.

Hook, Edward W., et al, eds. Current Concepts of Infectious Diseases. LC 77-4458. 1977. 52.00 (ISBN 0-471-01598-9, Pub. by Wiley Medical). Wiley.

Hook, Frances, jt. auth. see Hook, Richard.

Hook, Frances, illus. My Book of Friends. (Illus.). (gr. k-2). 1968. pap. 4.95 board cover (ISBN 0-87239-242-2, 3045). Standard Pub.

Hook, J. N. English Today: A Practical Handbook. LC 74-22538. 380p. (Orig.). 1976. pap. 9.50 (ISBN 0-471-06984-1). Krieger.

--History of the English Language. 1975. 21.95x (ISBN 0-673-15680-X). Scott F.

--Two-Word Verbs in English. 198p. (Orig.). 1981. pap. text ed. 7.95 (ISBN 0-15-592506-7, HC). HarBraceJ.

Hook, Jay M. Van see Ellul, Jacques, et al.

Hook, Jerry B., ed. Toxicology of the Kidney. (Target Organ Toxicology Ser.). 288p. 1981. 35.00 (ISBN 0-89004-475-9). Raven.

Hook, Martha & Boren, Tinka. Little Ones Listen to God. (Illus.). 128p. (gr. k-3). 1971. 5.95 o.p. (ISBN 0-310-26220-8). Zondervan.

Hook, Olle, jt. ed. see Sarno, Martha T.

Hook, Peter E. Hindi Structures: Intermediate Level. LC 79-53527. (Michigan Papers on South & Southeast Asia: No. 16). (Illus.). xxii, 338p. (Orig.). 1979. pap. 10.50x (ISBN 0-89148-016-1). Ctr S&SE Asian.

Hook, Peter E., jt. ed. see Deshpande, Madhav M.

Hook, Peter Edwin. Compound Verb in Hindi. LC 74-82629. (Michigan Papers in South & Southeast Asian Languages & Linguistics: No. 1). xxv, 318p. (Orig.). 1974. pap. 9.50x (ISBN 0-89148-051-X). Ctr S&SE Asian.

Hook, Phillip. Who Art in Heaven. 1979. pap. 3.95 o.p. (ISBN 0-310-38191-6). Zondervan.

Hook, Richard & Hook, Frances. Jesus: El Amigo De los Ninos. (Illus.). 112p. 1981. 18.95 (ISBN 0-311-38552-4, Edit Mundo); pap. 12.95 (ISBN 0-311-38553-2). Casa Bautista.

Hook, Sidney. Education & the Taming of Power. LC 72-98117. 310p. 1973. 21.00 (ISBN 0-87548-083-7). Open Court.

--Marx & the Marxists: The Ambiguous Legacy. LC 81-20921. 192p. pap. 5.95 (ISBN 0-89874-443-1). Krieger.

--Marxism & Beyond. LC 82-20542. 238p. 1983. text ed. 19.95 (ISBN 0-8476-7159-3). Rowman.

--Philosophy & Public Policy. LC 79-16825. 296p. 1980. 17.50x (ISBN 0-8093-0937-8); pap. 9.95 (ISBN 0-8093-1041-4). S Ill U Pr.

Hooke. How to Tell the Liars from the Statisticians. (Monographs & Textbooks in Statistics). 152p. 1983. write for info. (ISBN 0-8247-1817-8). Dekker.

Hooke, J. M. Historical Change In Physical Environment. 256p. 1982. text ed. 49.95 (ISBN 0-686-37995-0). Butterworth.

Hooke, S. H., tr. see Lods, Adolphe.

Hooke, Samuel H. In the Beginning. LC 78-10638. (The Clarendon Bible Old Testament Ser.: Vol. VI). (Illus.). 1979. Repr. of 1947 ed. lib. bdg. 17.50x (ISBN 0-313-21014-4, HOIB). Greenwood.

Hooker, Alan. Vegetarian Gourmet Cookery. LC 72-19332. (Illus., Orig.). 1970. pap. 5.95 o.p. (ISBN 0-912238-03-8). One Hund One Prods.

Hooker, Brian, tr. see Rostand, Edmond.

Hooker, Edward E. How Not to Make a Fool of Yourself in Wall Street. (The Recondite Sources of Stock Market Action Library). (Illus.). 134p. 1983. 65.45 (ISBN 0-86654-046-6). Inst Econ Finan.

Hooker, Edward N. see Dryden, John.

Hooker, J. D. The Botany of the Antartic Voyage of H. M. Discovery Ships Erebus & Terror in the Years 1839-43, 3 vols. (Illus.). 1963. 384.00 (ISBN 3-7682-0196-1). Lubrecht & Cramer.

--A Century of Indian Orchids. (Calutta Royal Bot. Gard. Ser.). (Illus.). 1967. 80.00 (ISBN 3-7682-0464-2). Lubrecht & Cramer.

--Himalayan Journals or Notes of a Naturalist in Bengal, 2vols. in 1. (Illus.). 15.00 (ISBN 0-934454-84-1). Lubrecht & Cramer.

Hooker, J. D., jt. auth. see Bentham, G.

Hooker, J. D. & Jackson, B. D., eds. Index Kewensis Plantarum Phanerogamarum (Linnaeus to the Year 1885, 2 vols. 1977. Repr. text ed. 424.00x set (ISBN 0-686-34413-8). Vol. 1. Vol. 2 (ISBN 3-87429-117-0). Lubrecht & Cramer.

Hooker, J. T. Mycanean Greece. (States & Cities of Ancient Greece Ser.). 330p. 1977. 25.00 (ISBN 0-7100-8379-3). Routledge & Kegan.

Hooker, Jeremy. Englishman's Road. (Carcanet New Pr England). 80p. (Orig.). 1981. pap. 6.95 o.p. (ISBN 0-85635-322-1, Pub. by Carcanet New Pr England). Humanities.

--Englishman's Road. 80p. 1980. pap. text ed. 6.95x (ISBN 0-85635-322-1, Pub. by Carcanet New Pr England). Humanities.

--The Poetry of Place. 197p. 1982. text ed. 21.00x (ISBN 0-85635-409-0, 80340, Pub. by Carcanet New Pr England). Humanities.

--Solent Shore. (Poetry Ser.). 61p. 1978. pap. 4.95x (ISBN 0-85635-249-7, Pub. by Carcanet New Pr England). Humanities.

--A View From the Source. 107p. 1982. pap. text ed. 10.50x (ISBN 0-85635-379-5, 80736, Pub. by Carcanet New Pr England). Humanities.

Hooker, M. B. Adat Law in Modern Indonesia. (East Asian Historical Monographs). 1979. 28.00x o.p. (ISBN 0-19-580394-9). Oxford U Pr.

--Legal Pluralism: An Introduction to Colonial & Neo-Colonial Laws. 1975. 54.00x (ISBN 0-19-825329-X). Oxford U Pr.

Hooker, Morna. A Preface to Paul. 1980. pap. 4.95x (ISBN 0-19-520188-4). Oxford U Pr.

Hooker, Morna D. Studying the New Testament. LC 82-70959. 224p. (Orig.). 1982. pap. 7.95 (ISBN 0-8066-1934-1, 10-6140). Augsburg.

Hooker, Richard. Of the Laws of Ecclesiastic Polity. McGrade, A. S. & Vickers, B. W., eds. LC 75-4450. 425p. 1976. 26.00 (ISBN 0-312-58240-4). St Martin.

Hooker, W. J. Icones Plantarum, 4 vols, Vols. 1-20. (Ser. 1-3). 1966. 384.00 (ISBN 3-7682-0250-X). Lubrecht & Cramer.

--Icones Plantarum: On Orchids, Vols. 21 & 22. (Ser. 4). 1967. Vol. 21. 24.00 ea. Vol. 22 (ISBN 3-7682-0853-2) (ISBN 3-7682-0854-0). Lubrecht & Cramer.

--Species Filicum, 5 vols. 1970. Repr. of 1864 ed. 200.00 (ISBN 3-7682-0690-4). Lubrecht & Cramer.

Hooker, W. J., et al. Niger Flora. (Illus.). 1966. Repr. of 1849 ed. 60.00 (ISBN 3-7682-0359-X). Lubrecht & Cramer.

Hooks, Margaret Anne. God Cares for Timothy. (ps-3). 1982. 6.25 (ISBN 0-686-36253-5). Rod & Staff.

Hooks, William, jt. auth. see Galinsky, Ellen.

Hooks, William H. Circle of Fire. LC 82-3982. 144p. (gr. 5-9). 1982. 9.95 (ISBN 0-689-50241-9, McElderry Bk). Atheneum.

--Maria's Cave. (Science Discovery Bks.). (Illus.). (gr. 3-5). 1977. 6.95 o.p. (ISBN 0-698-20403-4, Pub. by Coward). Putnam Pub Group.

--The Seventeen Gerbils of Class 4-A. LC 75-28000. (Illus.). 64p. (gr. 3-5). 1976. 6.95 (ISBN 0-698-20369-0, Coward). Putnam Pub Group.

Hool, Bryce, jt. ed. see Conrad, Robert.

Hoolahan, Michael, jt. auth. see Phillips, Jeremy.

Hoole, K. see Thomas, David J.

Hoole, W. Stanley. According to Hoole: The Collected Essays & Tales of a Scholar-Librarian & Literary Maverick. LC 74-148688. 341p. 1973. 20.00 o.p. (ISBN 0-8173-7102-8). U of Ala Pr.

Hoole, W. Stanley, ed. see Anderson, Edward C.

Hoole, William S. The Birmingham Horrors. (Illus.). 272p. (Orig.). 1980. pap. 4.95 (ISBN 0-87397-151-5). Strode.

--It's Raining Violets: The Life & Poetry of Robert Loveman. 1981. 8.95 (ISBN 0-916620-55-7). Portals Pr.

Hooley, C. Applications of Sieve Methods to the Theory of Numbers. LC 75-27796. (Cambridge Tracts in Mathematics Ser.: No. 70). 122p. 1976. 35.50 (ISBN 0-521-20915-3). Cambridge U Pr.

Hoon, Elizabeth E. Organization of the English Customs System, 1696-1786. LC 68-23298. 1968. Repr. of 1938 ed. lib. bdg. 18.50x (ISBN 0-8371-0108-5, HOEC). Greenwood.

Hooper, jt. auth. see Page.

Hooper, C., jt. auth. see Reader, C. T.

Hooper, D. A Complete Defence to IP-K4: A Study of Petroff's Defence. 1967. 11.00 o.p. (ISBN 0-08-012228-0); pap. 7.15 o.p. (ISBN 0-08-012229-9). Pergamon.

Hooper, D. E., jt. auth. see Cherry, E. M.

Hooper, David. Practical Chess Endgames. (Routledge Chess Handbooks). 152p. 1981. pap. 4.95 (ISBN 0-7100-5226-X). Routledge & Kegan.

Hooper, H. Paul. Introduction to Financial Accounting. 712p. 1982. text ed. 24.95 (ISBN 0-8299-0387-9). West Pub.

Hooper, Henry O. & Gwynne, Peter. Physics & the Physical Perspective. 2nd ed. 1980. text ed. 30.95 scp (ISBN 0-06-042912-7, HarpC); inst. manual avail. (ISBN 0-06-362982-8). Har-Row.

Hooper, I. R., jt. ed. see Umezawa, H.

Hooper, Kay. Lady Thief. (Candlelight Regency Ser.: No. 665). (Orig.). 1981. pap. 1.50 o.s.i. (ISBN 0-440-14685-2). Dell.

--On the Wings of Magic. (Candlelight Ecstasy Ser.: No. 153). (Orig.). 1983. pap. 1.95 (ISBN 0-440-16720-5). Dell.

Hooper, Patricia & Pulsinelli, Linda. Introductory Algebra. 540p. 1983. pap. text ed. 20.95 (ISBN 0-02-357100-4). Macmillan.

Hooper, Patricia, jt. auth. see Pulsinelli, Linda.

Hooper, Paul F. Elusive Destiny: The Internationalist Movement in Modern Hawaii. LC 79-24540. 1980. text ed. 15.00x (ISBN 0-8248-0631-X). UH Pr.

Hooper, Paul F., ed. Building a Pacific Community. LC 81-17252. 1982. pap. text ed. 9.95x o.p. (ISBN 0-8248-0790-1). UH Pr.

Hooper, S. S., jt. auth. see Symoens, J. J.

Hooper, Walter. Through Joy & Beyond: A Pictorial Biography of C. S. Lewis. LC 82-9884. 192p. 1982. 15.75 (ISBN 0-02-553670-2). Macmillan.

Hooper, Walter, ed. see Lewis, C. S.

Hoopes, et al. A Followup Study of Adoptions: Postplacement Functioning of Adopted Children, Vol. 2. LC 71-89863. 126p. 1970. pap. 5.75 (ISBN 0-87868-017-9, A-33). Child Welfare.

Hoopes, David S., et al, eds. Overview of Intercultural Education, Training & Research, 3 vols. Incl. Vol. I. Theory. LC 78-70690. pap. text ed. o.p. (ISBN 0-933934-01-7); Vol. 2. Training & Research. LC 78-70690. 1978. pap. text ed. o.p. (ISBN 0-933934-02-5); Vol. 3. Special Research Areas. LC 78-70690. 1978. pap. text ed. 6.50x (ISBN 0-933934-03-3). LC 78-70690. pap. Intercult Pr.

Hoopes, David T. & Tillion, Diana R. Alaska in Haiku. LC 77-182061. (Illus.). (YA) 1972. pap. 2.95 o.p. (ISBN 0-8048-0974-7). C E Tuttle.

Hoopes, Donelson F. Childe Hassam. (Illus.). 1979. 22.50 o.p. (ISBN 0-8230-0622-0). Watson-Guptill.

Hoopes, James. Oral History: An Introduction for Students. LC 78-9956. ix, 155p. 1979. 12.50 o.s.i. (ISBN 0-8078-1341-9); pap. 5.00x o.s.i. (ISBN 0-8078-1344-3). U of NC Pr.

Hoopes, James, ed. see Miller, Perry.

Hoopes, Janet L. New Publication on Adoption Offered by the Child Welfare League Prediction in Child Development: A Longitudinal Study of Adoptive & Nonadoptive Families--the Delaware Family Study. 104p. 1982. 9.50 (ISBN 0-87868-170-1). Child Welfare.

Hoopes, Lyn L. When I Was Little. LC 82-18207 (Illus.). 32p. (ps-3). 1983. 9.95 (ISBN 0-525-44053-4, 0966-290). Dutton.

Hoopes, Ned E., ed. see Henry, O.

Hoopes, Robert, jt. ed. see Stone, Wilfred.

Hoopes, Roy. Cain: The Biography of James M. Cain. LC 81-16133. 768p. 1982. 24.50 (ISBN 0-03-049331-5). HR&W.

--Political Campaigning. (Impact Ser.). (Illus.). (gr. 7 up). 1979. PLB 8.90 s&l (ISBN 0-531-02858-5). Watts.

--What the President of the U. S. Does. LC 74-5067. (Illus.). (gr. 4-10). 1974. 7.95 o.p. (ISBN 0-381-99628-X, JD-J); PLB 10.89 (ISBN 0-686-96736-4); pap. 2.50 (ISBN 0-381-99601-8). Har-Row.

Hoops, Richard A. Speech Science: Acoustics in Speech. 2nd ed. (Illus.). 164p. 1976. 12.75x o.p. (ISBN 0-398-00869-8). C C Thomas.

Hoor, Elvie T., jt. auth. see Meilach, Dona Z.

Hoos, Ida R. Systems Analysis in Public Policy: A Critique. LC 79-170723. (Institute of Governmental Studies). 300p. 1972. 35.00x (ISBN 0-520-02105-3); pap. 7.95x (ISBN 0-520-02609-8). U of Cal Pr.

--Systems Analysis in Public Policy: A Critique. rev. ed. LC 82-48766. 320p. 1983. text ed. 30.00x (ISBN 0-520-04953-5); pap. 8.95x (ISBN 0-520-04952-7). U of Cal Pr.

Hoos, Sidney, ed. Agricultural Marketing Boards: An International Perspective. LC 78-26425. 384p. 1979. prof ref 25.00 (ISBN 0-88410-367-6). Ballinger Pub.

Hooten, Ted & Ward, Richard. Supermarine Spitfire Mk. 1-16: Merline Engine. LC 78-93926. (Arco-Aircam Aviation Ser). (Illus., Orig.). 1968. pap. 3.95 (ISBN 0-668-02099-7). Arco.

Hootkins, Hirsch. Spanish Through Reading. 1950. 5.95x (ISBN 0-685-21806-6). Wahr.

Hootman, Marcia, jt. auth. see Perkins, Patt.

Hooton, Earnest A. Crime & the Man. LC 68-8738. (Illus.). 1968. Repr. of 1939 ed. lib. bdg. 20.25x (ISBN 0-8371-0482-3, HOCM). Greenwood.

Hooton, Ernest A. Indians of Pecos Pueblo. 1930. text ed. 175.00x (ISBN 0-686-83582-4). Elliots Bks.

Hooton, Ted & Ward, Richard. Supermarine Spitfire Mk. 12-24, Supermarine Seafire Mk. 1-47. LC 73-93930. (Aircam Aviation Ser). (Illus., Orig.). 1969. pap. 2.95 o.p. (ISBN 0-668-02107-1). Arco.

Hoover, Arlie J. Don't You Believe It! LC 82-8016. 1982. pap. 5.95 (ISBN 0-8024-2531-3). Moody.

Hoover, Dwight W. & Koumouledes, John T., eds. Sports & Society. (Conspectus of History Ser.). (Orig.). 1982. pap. 5.95 (ISBN 0-937994-03-0). Ball State Univ.

Hoover, Eleanor, jt. auth. see Edwards, Marie.

Hoover, Frances M. When the Lamp Is Shattered. LC 79-63517. 1979. 7.95 o.p. (ISBN 0-533-04270-4). Vantage.

Hoover, Gladys N. Nancy Harlow: Ward of the Royalls. 1977. 5.00 o.p. (ISBN 0-533-02838-8). Vantage.

Hoover, H. M. The Bell Tree. LC 82-2827. 180p. (gr. 5 up). 1982. 11.95 (ISBN 0-670-15600-0). Viking Pr.

Hoover, Helen. Gift of the Deer. (Illus.). (YA) 1966. 11.95 (ISBN 0-394-41803-4). Knopf.

--Years of the Forest. 1973. 13.95 (ISBN 0-394-47538-0). Knopf.

Hoover, Herbert. The Challenge to Liberty. LC 72-2373. (FDR & the Era of the New Deal Ser.). 212p. 1973. Repr. of 1934 ed. lib. bdg. 29.50 (ISBN 0-306-70499-4). Da Capo.

Hoover, Jan, jt. auth. see Doyle, Kathleen E.

Hoover, Janet, jt. auth. see Hanna, Barbara.

Hoover, John E., ed. Dispensing of Medication. 8th ed. 1976. 22.00 (ISBN 0-912734-07-8). Mack Pub.

Hoover, Marjorie L. Alexander Ostrovsky. (World Authors Ser.). 1981. 13.95 (ISBN 0-8057-6453-4, Twayne). G K Hall.

Hoover, Mary, jt. auth. see Ohasi, Wataru.

Hoover, Norman K. Approved Practices in Beautifying the Home Grounds. 5th ed. (Illus.). (gr. 9-12). 1979. 16.50 (ISBN 0-8134-2042-3, 2042); text ed. 12.50x. Interstate.

Hoover, Robert F. The Vascular Plants of San Luis Obispo County, California. LC 71-104883. 1970. 32.50x (ISBN 0-520-01663-7). U of Cal Pr.

Hoover, Rosalie & Murphy, Barbara. Learning About Our Five Senses. (gr. k-3). 1981. 5.95 (ISBN 0-86653-013-4, GA 241). Good Apple.

Hoover, Ryan E., ed. Library & Information Manager's Guide to Online Services. LC 80-21602. (Professional Librarian Ser.). (Illus.). 269p. 1980. text ed. 34.50x (ISBN 0-914236-60-1); pap. text ed. 27.50x (ISBN 0-914236-52-0). Knowledge Indus.

--Online Search Strategies. LC 82-17179. (Professional Librarian Ser.). 345p. 1982. text ed. 37.50 (ISBN 0-86729-005-6); pap. text ed. 29.50 (ISBN 0-86729-004-8). Knowledge Indus.

Hoover, T. W. & Schumacher, H. G. Tool & Die Drafting. LC 57-12844. 1968. 5.25x o.p. (ISBN 0-911168-09-5). Prakken.

Hoover, Thomas. The Moghul. LC 82-45146. 576p. 1983. 16.95 (ISBN 0-385-17576-0). Doubleday.

--The Zen Experience. (Illus., Orig.). 1980. pap. 5.95 (ISBN 0-452-25315-2, Z5315, Plume). NAL.

Hopcraft, Arthur. Mid-Century Men. 256p. 1982. 16.95 (ISBN 0-241-10782-2, Pub. by Hamish Hamilton England). David & Charles.

Hopcroft, John, jt. auth. see Aho, Alfred.

Hopcroft, John E. & Ullman, Jeffrey D. Introduction to Automata Theory, Languages, & Computation. LC 78-67950. 1979. text ed. 26.95 (ISBN 0-201-02988-X). A-W.

Hope, Anthony. The Prisoner of Zenda. lib. bdg. 16.95x (ISBN 0-89966-226-9). Buccaneer Bks.

--Rupert of Hentzau (Sequel to Prisoner of Zenda) lib. bdg. 16.95x (ISBN 0-89966-227-7). Buccaneer Bks.

Hope, Anthony see Allen, W. S.

Hope, Anthony see Eyre, A. G.

Hope, C. E. The Perfect Pony Owner. 14.50x (ISBN 0-273-40165-3, SpS). Sportshelf.

Hope, Christopher. A Seperate Development. 208p. 1983. pap. 4.95 (ISBN 0-686-83725-8, ScribT). Scribner.

Hope, James. The Holistic Approach to Magic: Seven Possible Ways to Perform the Impossible. LC 82-13331. (Illus.). 1982. 17.95 (ISBN 0-943224-15-2). Presto Bks.

Hope, K. Elementary Statistics: A Workbook. 1964. 14.75 o.p. (ISBN 0-08-012132-2); pap. 7.00 (ISBN 0-08-012131-4). Pergamon.

Hope, Kempe R. Development Policy in Guyana: Planning, Finance, & Administration. LC 79-5229. (Westview Replica Editions). lib. bdg. 29.50 (ISBN 0-89158-583-4). Westview.

Hope, Laura L. Bobbsey Twins' Adventure in the Country. (Bobbsey Twins Ser.: Vol. 2). (gr. 1-4). 1930. 2.95 (ISBN 0-448-08002-8, G&D). Putnam Pub Group.

--Bobbsey Twins' Adventure in Washington. rev. ed. (Bobbsey Twins Ser.: Vol. 12). (gr. 1-4). 1963. 2.95 (ISBN 0-448-08012-5, G&D). Putnam Pub Group.

--Bobbsey Twins' Adventures with Baby May. (Bobbsey Twins Ser.: Vol. 17). (Illus.). (gr. 1-4). 1968. 2.95 (ISBN 0-448-08017-6, G&D). Putnam Pub Group.

--Bobbsey Twins & Dr. Funnybone's Secret. (Bobbsey Twins Ser.). 196p. (gr. k-5). Date not set. 2.95 (ISBN 0-448-08065-6, G&D). Putnam Pub Group.

--Bobbsey Twins & the Big River Mystery. (Bobbsey Twins Ser.: Vol. 56). (gr. 1-4). 1963. 2.95 (ISBN 0-448-08056-7, G&D). Putnam Pub Group.

--Bobbsey Twins & the Cedar Camp Mystery. (Bobbsey Twins Ser.: Vol. 14). (gr. 1-4). 1967. 2.95 (ISBN 0-448-08014-1, G&D). Putnam Pub Group.

--Bobbsey Twins & the Circus Surprise. (Bobbsey Twins Ser.: Vol. 25). (gr. 1-4). 1932. 2.95 (ISBN 0-448-08025-7, G&D). Putnam Pub Group.

--Bobbsey Twins & the County Fair Mystery. (Bobbsey Twins Ser.: Vol. 15). (gr. 1-4). 1922. 2.95 (ISBN 0-448-08015-X, G&D). Putnam Pub Group.

--Bobbsey Twins & the Doodlebug Mystery. (Bobbsey Twins Ser.: Vol. 62). (Illus.). (gr. 1-4). 1969. 2.95 (ISBN 0-448-08062-1, G&D). Putnam Pub Group.

--Bobbsey Twins & the Flying Clown. (Bobbsey Twins Ser.). 196p. (gr. k-5). Date not set. 2.95 (ISBN 0-448-08067-2, G&D). Putnam Pub Group.

--Bobbsey Twins & the Four-Leaf Clover Mystery. rev. ed. (Bobbsey Twins Ser.: Vol. 19). (Illus.). (gr. 1-4). 1968. 2.95 (ISBN 0-448-08019-2, G&D). Putnam Pub Group.

--Bobbsey Twins & the Freedom Bell Mystery. (Bobbsey Twins Ser.). 196p. (gr. k-5). Date not set. 2.95 (ISBN 0-448-08069-9, G&D). Putnam Pub Group.

--Bobbsey Twins & the Goldfish Mystery. (Bobbsey Twins Ser.: Vol. 55). (Illus.). (gr. 1-4). 1962. 2.95 (ISBN 0-448-08055-9, G&D). Putnam Pub Group.

--Bobbsey Twins & the Greek Hat Mystery. (Bobbsey Twins Ser.: Vol. 57). (gr. 1-4). 1964. 2.95 (ISBN 0-448-08057-5, G&D). Putnam Pub Group.

--Bobbsey Twins & the Mystery at Snow Lodge. (Bobbsey Twins Ser.: Vol. 5). (gr. 1-4). 1930. 2.95 (ISBN 0-448-08005-2, G&D). Putnam Pub Group.

--Bobbsey Twins & the Play House Secret. rev. ed. (Bobbsey Twins Ser.: Vol. 18). (Illus.). (gr. 1-4). 1968. 2.95 (ISBN 0-448-08018-4, G&D). Putnam Pub Group.

--Bobbsey Twins & the Secret of Candy Castle. (Bobbsey Twins Ser.: No. 61). (Illus.). (gr. 1-4). 1968. 2.95 (ISBN 0-448-08061-3, G&D). Putnam Pub Group.

--The Bobbsey Twins & the Smoky Mountain Mystery. (Bobbsey Twins Ser.: Vol. 70). (Illus.). (gr. 1-4). 1977. 2.95 (ISBN 0-448-08070-2, G&D) Putnam Pub Group.

--Bobbsey Twins & the Tagalong Giraffe. (Bobbsey Twins Ser.: Vol. 66). (gr. 1-4). 2.95 (ISBN 0-448-08066-4, G&D). Putnam Pub Group.

--Bobbsey Twins & the Talking Fox Mystery. (Bobbsey Twins Ser.: No. 63). (Illus.). (gr. 1-4). 1970. 2.95 (ISBN 0-448-08063-X, G&D). Putnam Pub Group.

--Bobbsey Twins & Their Camel Adventure. (Bobbsey Twins Ser.: Vol. 59). (gr. 1-4). 1966. 2.95 (ISBN 0-448-08059-1, G&D). Putnam Pub Group.

--Bobbsey Twins at Big Bear Pond. (Bobbsey Twins Ser.: Vol. 47). (gr. 1-4). 1954. 2.95 (ISBN 0-448-08047-8, G&D). Putnam Pub Group.

--Bobbsey Twins at London Tower. (Bobbsey Twins Ser.: Vol. 52). (Illus.). (gr. 1-4). 1959. 2.95 (ISBN 0-448-08052-4, G&D). Putnam Pub Group.

--Bobbsey Twins at Pilgrim Rock. (Bobbsey Twins Ser.: Vol. 50). (gr. 1-4). 1957. 2.95 (ISBN 0-448-08050-8, G&D). Putnam Pub Group.

--Bobbsey Twins' Big Adventure at Home. (Bobbsey Twins Ser.: Vol. 8). (gr. 1-4). 1930. 2.95 (ISBN 0-448-08008-7, G&D). Putnam Pub Group.

--Bobbsey Twins: Camp Fire Mystery. (The Bobbsey Twins Ser.: No. 6). 128p. (gr. 3-8). 1982. 8.95 (ISBN 0-671-43374-1); pap. 2.95 (ISBN 0-671-43373-3). Wanderer Bks.

--Bobbsey Twins Camping Out. (Bobbsey Twins Ser.: Vol. 16). (gr. 1-4). 1923. 2.95 (ISBN 0-448-08016-8, G&D). Putnam Pub Group.

--Bobbsey Twins' Forest Adventure. (Bobbsey Twins Ser.: Vol. 51). (gr. 1-4). 1958. 2.95 (ISBN 0-448-08051-6, G&D). Putnam Pub Group.

--The Bobbsey Twins in a TV Mystery Show. LC 77-76127. (Vol. 71). (Illus.). (gr. 1-4). 1978. 2.95 (ISBN 0-448-08071-0, G&D). Putnam Pub Group.

--Bobbsey Twins in the Mystery Cave. (Bobbsey Twins Ser.: Vol. 53). (Illus.). (gr. 1-4). 1960. 2.95 (ISBN 0-448-08053-2, G&D). Putnam Pub Group.

--Bobbsey Twins in Volcano Land. (Bobbsey Twins Ser.: Vol. 54). (Illus.). (gr. 1-4). 1961. 2.95 (ISBN 0-448-08054-0, G&D). Putnam Pub Group.

--Bobbsey Twins' Mystery at Meadowbrook. rev. ed. (Bobbsey Twins Ser.: Vol. 7). (gr. 1-4). 1963. 2.95 (ISBN 0-448-08007-9, G&D). Putnam Pub Group.

--Bobbsey Twins' Mystery at School. (Bobbsey Twins Ser.: Vol. 4). (gr. 1-4). 1930. 2.95 (ISBN 0-448-08004-4, G&D). Putnam Pub Group.

--Bobbsey Twins' Mystery of the King's Puppet. (Bobbsey Twins Ser.: Vol. 60). (gr. 1-4). 1967. 2.95 (ISBN 0-448-08060-5, G&D). Putnam Pub Group.

--Bobbsey Twins' Mystery on the Deep Blue Sea. (Bobbsey Twins Ser.: Vol. 11). (gr. 1-4). 1930. 2.95 (ISBN 0-448-08011-7, G&D). Putnam Pub Group.

--Bobbsey Twins of Lakeport. (Bobbsey Twins Ser.: Vol. 1). (gr. 1-4). 1936. 2.95 (ISBN 0-448-08001-X, G&D). Putnam Pub Group.

--Bobbsey Twins on a Bicycle Trip. (Bobbsey Twins Ser.: Vol. 48). (gr. 1-4). 1955. 2.95 (ISBN 0-448-08048-6, G&D). Putnam Pub Group.

--Bobbsey Twins on a Houseboat. (Bobbsey Twins Ser.: Vol. 6). (gr. 1-4). 1930. 2.95 (ISBN 0-448-08006-0, G&D). Putnam Pub Group.

--Bobbsey Twins on Blueberry Island. (Bobbsey Twins Ser.: Vol. 10). (gr. 1-4). 1930. 2.95 (ISBN 0-448-08010-9, G&D). Putnam Pub Group.

--The Bobbsey Twins on the Sun-Moon Cruise. new ed. LC 74-10460. (Bobbsey Twins Ser.: No. 68). (Illus.). 196p. (gr. 1-4). 1975. 2.95 (ISBN 0-448-08068-0, G&D). Putnam Pub Group.

--Bobbsey Twins' Own Little Ferryboat. (Bobbsey Twins Ser.: Vol. 49). (gr. 1-4). 1956. 2.95 (ISBN 0-448-08049-4, G&D). Putnam Pub Group.

--Bobbsey Twins' Search for the Green Rooster. (Bobbsey Twins Ser.: Vol. 58). (gr. 1-4). 1965. 2.95 (ISBN 0-448-08058-3, G&D). Putnam Pub Group.

--Bobbsey Twins' Search in the Great City. (Bobbsey Twins Ser.: Vol. 9). (gr. 1-4). 1930. 2.95 (ISBN 0-448-08009-5, G&D). Putnam Pub Group.

--Bobbsey Twins' Secret at the Seashore. rev. ed. (Bobbsey Twins Ser.: Vol. 3). (gr. 1-4). 1936. 2.95 (ISBN 0-448-08003-6, G&D). Putnam Pub Group.

--The Bobbsey Twins: Secret in the Pirate's Cave. (The Bobbsey Twins Ser.: No. 2). 128p. (gr. 2-5). 1980. PLB 8.95 (ISBN 0-671-41118-7); pap. 2.95 (ISBN 0-671-41113-6). Wanderer Bks.

--The Bobbsey Twins: Seventy Fifth Anniversary Commemorative Editions, 3 vols. Incl. The Bobbsey Twins (ISBN 0-671-95665-5); The Bobbsey Twins at the Seashore (ISBN 0-671-95681-7); The Country (ISBN 0-671-95673-6). (Illus.). 1979. Set. 10.00 o.p. (ISBN 0-671-95521-7). Wanderer Bks.

--Bobbsey Twins Solve a Mystery. (Bobbsey Twins Ser.: Vol. 27). (gr. 1-4). 1934. 2.95 (ISBN 0-448-08027-3, G&D). Putnam Pub Group.

--The Bobbsey Twins: The Blue Poodle Mystery. (Bobbsey Twins Ser.: No. 1). (Illus.). 128p. (gr. 2-5). 1980. 8.95 (ISBN 0-671-95546-2); pap. 2.95 (ISBN 0-671-95554-3). Wanderer Bks.

--Bobbsey Twins: The Mystery at Cherry Corners. rev. ed. (Bobbsey Twins Ser.: No. 20). (Illus.). (gr. 1-4). 1971. 2.95 (ISBN 0-448-08020-6, G&D). Putnam Pub Group.

--Bobbsey Twins: The Red, White & Blue Mystery. (Bobbsey Twins Ser.: No. 64). (Illus.). (gr. 1-4). 1971. 2.95 (ISBN 0-448-08064-8, G&D). Putnam Pub Group.

--Bobbsey Twins: The Rose Parade Mystery. (The Bobbsey Twins Ser.: No. 5). (Illus.). 112p. (Orig.). (gr. 2-5). 1981. 8.95 (ISBN 0-671-43372-5); pap. 2.95 (ISBN 0-671-43371-7). Wanderer Bks.

--Bobbsey Twins Visit to the Great West. rev. ed. (Bobbsey Twins Ser.: Vol. 13). (gr. 1-4). 1966. 2.95 (ISBN 0-448-08013-3, G&D). Putnam Pub Group.

--Bobbsey Twins' Wonderful Winter Secret. (Bobbsey Twins Ser.: Vol. 24). (gr. 1-4). 1931. 2.95 (ISBN 0-448-08024-9, G&D). Putnam Pub Group.

--Double Trouble, No. 7. (Bobbsey Twins Ser.). (Illus.). 128p. (gr. 7-10). 1983. 8.95 (ISBN 0-671-43584-1); pap. 2.95 (ISBN 0-671-43585-X). Wanderer Bks.

Hope, Laura Lee. Bobbsey Twins: Dune Buggy Mystery. (The Bobbsey Twins Ser.: No. 3). (Illus.). 112p. (gr. 2-5). 1981. 8.95 (ISBN 0-671-42293-6); pap. 2.95 (ISBN 0-671-42294-4). Wanderer Bks.

--The Bobbsey Twins: Mystery of the Laughing Dinosaur. Barish, Wendy, ed. (The Bobbsey Twins). (Illus.). 128p. (gr. 8-12). 1983. 8.95 (ISBN 0-671-43586-8); pap. 2.95 (ISBN 0-671-43587-6). Wanderer Bks.

--Bobbsey Twins: The Missing Pony Mystery. (The Bobbsey Twins Ser.: No. 4). (Illus.). 112p. (gr. 2-5). 1981. 8.95 (ISBN 0-671-42295-2); pap. 2.95 (ISBN 0-671-42296-0). Wanderer Bks.

Hope, Q. M. Spoken French in Review. 3rd ed. 1974. 17.95x (ISBN 0-02-356950-6); wkbk. o.p. 1.95 (ISBN 0-02-357090-3). Macmillan.

Hope, Quentin M. Reading French for Comprehension. 1965. text ed. 10.95 (ISBN 0-02-357000-8). Macmillan.

Hope, Richard, tr. see Aristotle.

Hope, Robert C. Glossary of Dialectal Place-Nomenclature. LC 68-58761. 1968. Repr. of 1883 ed. 30.00x (ISBN 0-8103-3530-1). Gale.

--Legendary Lore of the Holy Wells of England. LC 68-21775. (Illus.). 1968. Repr. of 1893 ed. 30.00x (ISBN 0-8103-3445-3). Gale.

Hope, Ronald. The Seaman's World: Merchant Seamen's Reminiscences. 1982. 32.00x (ISBN 0-245-53893-3, Pub. by Ian Harrap England). State Mutual Bk.

Hopeman, Richard A. Production & Operations Management. 4th ed. (Marketing & Management Ser.). 608p. 1980. text ed. 24.95 (ISBN 0-675-08140-8). Additional supplements may be obtained from publisher. Merrill.

Hopewell, Graham, jt. auth. see Snow, Anthony.

Hopewell, Lynn, jt. auth. see Federal Communications Commission Planning Conference November 8 & 9, 1976.

Hopf, A. Strange Sex Lives in the Animal Kingdom. 1981. 8.95 (ISBN 0-07-030319-3). McGraw.

Hopf, Alice. Misplaced Animals, Plants & Other Living Creatures. LC 75-10952. 160p. (Orig.). (gr. 7-12). 1975. 7.95 (ISBN 0-07-030318-5, GB). McGraw.

Hopf, Alice L. Biography of a Giraffe. LC 76-52934. (Nature Biography Ser.). (Illus.). (gr. 2-5). 1978. PLB 6.99 (ISBN 0-399-61088-X). Putnam Pub Group.

--Biography of a Komodo Dragon. (A Nature Biography Book). (Illus.). 64p. (gr. 7-11). 1981. PLB 6.99 (ISBN 0-399-61140-1). Putnam Pub Group.

--Biography of a Rhino. new ed. (Nature Biography Ser.). (Illus.). (gr. 3-5). 1972. PLB 5.49 o.p. (ISBN 0-399-60745-5). Putnam Pub Group.

--Biography of a Snowy Owl. LC 78-16533. (Nature Biography Ser.). (Illus.). (gr. 3-6). 1979. PLB 6.99 (ISBN 0-399-61130-4). Putnam Pub Group.

--Biography of an American Reindeer. LC 76-5497. (Nature Biography Ser.). (Illus.). (gr. 3-5). 1976. PLB 5.49 o.p. (ISBN 0-399-61009-X). Putnam Pub Group.

--Biography of an Ant. new ed. (Nature Biography Ser.). (Illus.). 64p. (gr. 3-5). 1974. PLB 5.49 o.p. (ISBN 0-399-60862-1). Putnam Pub Group.

--Biography of an Armadillo. LC 74-21066. (Nature Biography Ser.). (Illus.). 64p. (gr. 3-5). 1976. PLB 6.59 o.p. (ISBN 0-399-60945-8). Putnam Pub Group.

--Biography of an Octopus. (Nature Biography Ser.). (Illus.). (gr. 2-5). 1971. PLB 5.49 o.p. (ISBN 0-399-60059-0). Putnam Pub Group.

--Biography of an Ostrich. new ed. LC 72-95562. (Nature Biography Ser.). (Illus.). 64p. (gr. 3-5). 1975. PLB 6.59 o.p. (ISBN 0-399-60839-7). Putnam Pub Group.

--Carab, the Trap Door Spider. (See & Read Science Ser). (Illus.). (gr. k-3). 1970. PLB 3.96 o.p. (ISBN 0-399-60084-1). Putnam Pub Group.

--Chickens & Their Wild Relatives. LC 82-45385. (Illus.). 128p. (gr. 6 up). 1982. PLB 9.95 (ISBN 0-396-08085-5). Dodd.

--Misunderstood Animals. new ed. LC 73-6623. (Illus.). 128p. (gr. 3-9). 1973. PLB 6.95 o.p. (ISBN 0-07-030312-6, GB). McGraw.

--Nature's Pretenders. (Illus.). (gr. 5 up). 1979. 8.95 o.p. (ISBN 0-399-20671-X). Putnam Pub Group.

--Wild Cousins of the Cat. LC 74-21077. (Illus.). 160p. (gr. 6-8). 1975. 6.95 o.p. (ISBN 0-399-20442-3). Putnam Pub Group.

--Wild Cousins of the Horse. LC 77-6710. (Illus.). 1977. 6.50 o.p. (ISBN 0-399-20581-0). Putnam Pub Group.

Hopf, H., jt. auth. see Alexandroff, Paul S.

Hopf, Peter. Designer's Guide to OSHA: A Practical Design Guide to the Occupational Safety & Health Act for Architects, Engineers, & Builders. 2nd ed. (Illus.). 1982. 39.50 (ISBN 0-07-030317-7). McGraw.

Hopf, Peter S. Designer's Guide to OSHA. (Illus.). 256p. 1975. 34.50 (ISBN 0-07-030314-2, P&RB). McGraw.

--Handbook of Building Security Planning & Design. LC 78-21636. 1979. 44.50 (ISBN 0-07-030316-9, P&RB). McGraw.

Hopfe, Lewis M. Religions of the World. 2nd ed. 368p. 1979. pap. text ed. 18.95 (ISBN 0-02-474820-X). Macmillan.

--Religions of the World. 416p. 1983. pap. text ed. 16.95 (ISBN 0-02-474740-8). Macmillan.

Hopfe, Manfred W. Mathematics: Foundations for Business. rev. ed. 1980. text ed. 22.95 (ISBN 0-574-19530-0, 13-2530); instr's. guide avail. (ISBN 0-574-19531-9, 13-2531); study guide 7.95 (ISBN 0-574-19387-1, 13-2387). SRA.

Hopfinger, A. J. Intermolecular Interactions & Biomolecular Organization. LC 76-26540. 1977. 52.50 o.s.i. (ISBN 0-471-40910-3, Pub by Wiley-Interscience). Wiley.

Hopfl, H. The Christian Polity of John Calvin. LC 81-24192. (Studies in the History & Theory of Politics). 302p. 1982. 44.50 (ISBN 0-521-24417-X). Cambridge U Pr.

Hopgood, Alan. And the Big Men Fly. (Australian Theatre Workshop Ser.). 1969. pap. text ed. 4.50x o.p. (ISBN 0-85859-010-7, 00520). Heinemann Ed.

Hopgood, James F. Settlers of Bajavista. LC 79-21191. (Papers in International Studies: Latin America Ser.: No. 7). 1979. pap. 11.00 (ISBN 0-89680-101-2, Ohio U Ctr Intl). Ohio U Pr.

Ho Ping Ti. The Ladder of Success in Imperial China. LC 76-6917. (China in the 20th Century Ser.). 1976. Repr. of 1962 ed. lib. bdg. 42.50 (ISBN 0-306-70759-4). Da Capo.

Hopke, Philip K., jt. auth. see Natusch, David F.

Hopkin, Alannah. A Joke Goes a Long Way in the Country. LC 82-73014. 160p. 1983. 10.95 (ISBN 0-689-11353-6). Atheneum.

Hopkin, John A., et al. Financial Management in Agriculture. 2nd. ed. (Illus.). 1979. 19.35 (ISBN 0-8134-2037-7); text ed. 14.50x. Interstate.

Hopkins. Elvis: The Final Years. (Illus.). 296p. 1980. 12.95 o.p. (ISBN 0-312-24384-7). St Martin.

--Life Among the Paiutes: Their Wrongs & Claims. LC 71-102992. 12.95 (ISBN 0-912494-06-9); pap. 8.95 (ISBN 0-912494-18-2). Chalfant Pr.

Hopkins & Mergers, Thomas H. Acquisitions & Divestitures: A Guide to Their Impact for Investors & Directors. LC 82-71347. 125p. 1982. 17.95 (ISBN 0-87094-200-X). Dow Jones-Irwin.

Hopkins, A. & Brassley, P. The Wildlife of Rivers & Canals. 192p. 1982. 50.00x (ISBN 0-86190-061-8, Pub. by Moorland). State Mutual Bk.

Hopkins, Adam. Crete. 250p. 1979. pap. 7.95 (ISBN 0-571-11361-3). Faber & Faber.

Hopkins, Anne E. Work & Job Satisfaction in the Public Sector. 160p. 1983. text ed. 25.00x (ISBN 0-86598-111-6). Allanheld.

Hopkins, Anthony. Epilepsy: The Facts. (The Facts Ser.). (Illus.). 1981. text ed. 12.95x (ISBN 0-19-261257-3). Oxford U Pr.

Hopkins, Antony. Understanding Music. 256p. 1982. 30.00x (ISBN 0-460-02234-2, Pub. by J M Dent). State Mutual Bk.

Hopkins, Bill, ed. & tr. see Worner, Karl H.

Hopkins, Bruce. Charity Under Siege: Government Regulation of Fund Raising. LC 80-23987. 274p. 1980. 48.95 (ISBN 0-471-08170-1, Pub. by Ronald). Wiley.

Hopkins, Bruce R. Charitable Giving & Tax-Exempt Organizations: The Impact of the 1981 Tax Act. 166p. 1982. 33.50x (ISBN 0-471-86736-5). Ronald Pr.

--The Law of Tax-Exempt Organizations. 3rd ed. LC 78-23949. 1979. 54.95 (ISBN 0-471-05122-5). Ronald Pr.

--The Law of Tax-Exempt Organizations. 3d ed. LC 80-81195. 1980. pap. 48.95x o.p. (ISBN 0-471-05122-5, Pub. by Wiley Interscience); pap. 21.95x 1980 suppl. o.p. (ISBN 0-471-08171-X); 1981 suppl. 19.95 o.p. (ISBN 0-471-09351-3). Wiley.

--The Law of Tax-Exempt Organizations. 4th ed. 650p. 1983. 49.00x (ISBN 0-471-87538-4). Ronald Pr.

--A Tax Guide for College & University Presidents. 1980. 5.00 o.p. (ISBN 0-8268-1399-2). ACE.

Hopkins, Budd. Missing Time: A Documented Study of UFO Abductions. 256p. 1981. 12.95 (ISBN 0-399-90102-7, Marek). Putnam Pub Group.

Hopkins, C. & Baur, P. V. Christian Church at Dura-Europos. (Illus.). 1934. pap. 29.50x (ISBN 0-686-50041-5). Elliots Bks.

Hopkins, C. Edward, tr. see Ellul, Jacques.

Hopkins, C. Howard, ed. see White, Ronald C., Jr.

Hopkins, Charles D. Understanding Educational Research: An Inquiry Approach. 2nd ed. (Illus.). 544p. 1980. text ed. 21.95 (ISBN 0-675-08162-9). Additional supplements may be obtained from publisher. Merrill.

Hopkins, Charles R. & Morton, Margaret A. Theory & Skill Building, Bk. 1. LC 77-80674. (Hedman Stenotype System Ser.). (Illus.). 372p. text ed. 17.00x (ISBN 0-939056-00-3). Hedman Steno.

Hopkins, Charles R., et al. General Business in Our Modern Society. Vorndran, Richard A., ed. LC 77-73296. 640p. (gr. 9-10). 1979. text ed. 13.50 (ISBN 0-02-472860-8); tchrs. manual & key 10.00 (ISBN 0-686-61260-4); student act guide 2 4.96 (ISBN 0-686-61261-2); 4.96 (ISBN 0-02-472880-2). Glencoe.

Hopkins, David M., et al, eds. Paleocology of Beringia: Symposium. LC 82-22621. 1982. 37.00 (ISBN 0-12-355860-3). Acad Pr.

Hopkins, E. Wasburn. Ethics of India. 1924. text ed. 10.50x (ISBN 0-686-83539-5). Elliots Bks.

Hopkins, Edward J. & Rimbault, Edward F. The Organ: Its History and Construction. (Bibliotheca Organologica Ser.: Vol. 4). 1981. Repr. of 1877 ed. 55.00 o.s.i. (ISBN 90-6027-145-9, Pub. by Frits Knuf Netherlands). Pendragon NY.

Hopkins, Edward S. & Bean, Elwood L. Water Purification Control. 4th ed. LC 74-21712. 346p. 1975. Repr. of 1966 ed. 19.50 (ISBN 0-88275-248-0). Krieger.

Hopkins, Edward S., et al. The Practice of Sanitation: In Its Relation to the Environment. 4th ed. 560p. 1970. 34.50 o.p. (ISBN 0-683-04140-1, Pub. by W & W). Krieger.

Hopkins, Edwin A., jt. ed. see Lohnes, Walter F.

Hopkins, Emma C. High Mysticism. 368p. 1974. Repr. pap. 8.95 (ISBN 0-87516-198-7). De Vorss.

--Scientific Christian Mental Practice. 1974. pap. 7.95 (ISBN 0-87516-199-5). De Vorss.

Hopkins, Ernest J. Our Lawless Police. LC 74-168829. (Civil Liberties in American History Ser.). 379p. 1971. Repr. of 1931 ed. lib. bdg. 45.00 (ISBN 0-306-70213-4). Da Capo.

--What Happened in the Mooney Case. LC 73-107411. (Civil Liberties in American History Ser.). 1970. Repr. of 1932 ed. lib. bdg. 32.50 (ISBN 0-306-71891-X). Da Capo.

Hopkins, Evan H. Law of Liberty in the Spiritual Life. 1968. pap. 1.50 o.p. (ISBN 0-87508-244-0). Chr Lit.

Hopkins, F. N. Business & Law for the Shipmaster. 6th ed. 908p. 1982. text ed. 65.00x (ISBN 0-85174-434-6). Sheridan.

Hopkins, Fred W., Jr. Tom Boyle, Master Privateer. 101p. 1976. pap. 4.00 (ISBN 0-686-36711-1). Md Hist.

Hopkins, G., jt. auth. see Ravasio, P.

Hopkins, G. H. & Rothschild, M. An Illustrated Catalogue of the Rothschild Collection of Fleas, Vol. V: Leptopsyllidae & Ancistropsyllidae. 530p. 1971. 180.00x (ISBN 0-686-82366-4, Pub. by Brit Mus England). State Mutual Bk.

--An Illustrated Catalogue of the Rothschild Collection of Fleas, Vol. IV: Hystrichopsyllidae (Tenophthalminae, Dinopsyllinae & Listropsyllinae) 594p. 1966. 175.00x (ISBN 0-686-82367-2, Pub. by Brit Mus England). State Mutual Bk.

--An Illustrated Catalogue of the Rothschild Collection of Fleas, Vol. III: Hystrichopsyllidae (Acedestiinae, Anamiopsyllinae, Histrichopsyllinae, Neopsyllinae, Rhadinopsyllinae & Stenoponiinae) 559p. 1962. 125.00x (ISBN 0-686-82369-9, Pub. by Brit Mus England). State Mutual Bk.

--An Illustrated Catalogue of the Rothschild Collection of Fleas, Vol. II: Coptopsyllidae, Verminpsyllidae, Sephanociridae, Tschnopsyllidae, Hypsophthalmidae & Xiphiopsyllidae. 446p. 1956. 110.00x (ISBN 0-686-82370-2, Pu b. by Brit Mus England). State Mutual Bk.

--An Illustrated Catalogue of the Rothschild Collection of Fleas, Vol. I: Tungidae & Pulicidae. 362p. 1953. 90.00x (ISBN 0-686-82372-9, Pub. by Brit Mus England). State Mutual Bk.

Hopkins, G. H. & Rothschild, Miriam. Illustrated Catalogue of the Rothschild Collection of Fleas (Siphonaptera) in the British Museum (Natural History) Incl. Vol. 1. Tungidae & Pulicidae. 362p. 1953. 43.00x (ISBN 0-565-00160-4); Vol. 2. Coptopsyllidae, Vermipsyllidae, Slephanocircidae, Ischnopsyllidae, Hypsophthalmidae & Xiphiopsyllidae. 446p. 1956. 54.00x (ISBN 0-565-00071-3); Vol.3. Hystrichopsyllidae, Acedestiinae, Anomiopsyllinae, Histrichopsyllinae, Neopsyllinae, Rhadinopsyllinae & Stenoponinae. 560p. 1962. 61.25x (ISBN 0-8277-4248-7); Vol. 4. Hystrichopsyllinae, Ctenophthalminae, Dinopsyllinae, Doratopsyllinae, & Listropsyllinae. 550p. 1966. 87.50x (ISBN 0-565-00652-5); Vol. 5. Leptopsyllidae & Ancistropsyllidae. 530p. 1971. 107.00x (ISBN 0-565-00706-8). (Illus., Pub. by Brit Mus Nat Hist). Sabbot-Natural Hist Bks.

Hopkins, Gerard M. Poems & Prose of Hopkins. Gardner, W. H., ed. (Poets Ser.). 1953. pap. 4.95 (ISBN 0-14-042015-0). Penguin.

--Wreck of the Deutschland. LC 72-157927. 1971. special ed. 6.00 (ISBN 0-87923-021-5); pap. 2.95 (ISBN 0-87923-040-1). Godine.

Hopkins, Gerard M., tr. see Bloch, Marc.

Hopkins, Gilbert N., jt. auth. see Conder, Joseph M.

Hopkins, H. G. & Sewell, M. J., eds. Mechanics of Solids: The Rodney Hill 60th Anniversary Volume. (Illus.). 720p. 1982. 100.00 (ISBN 0-08-025443-8). Pergamon.

Hopkins, Helen L. & Smith, Helen D. Willard & Spackman's Occupational Therapy. 6th ed. (Illus.). 950p. 1983. text ed. write for info. (ISBN 0-397-54361-1, Lippincott Medical). Lippincott.

Hopkins, Helen L. & Smith, Helen D., eds. Willard & Spackman's Occupational Therapy. 5th ed. LC 78-4607. 1978. text ed. 33.50 o.p. (ISBN 0-397-54216-X, Lippincott Nursing). Lippincott.

Hopkins, J., jt. auth. see Wollheim, R.

Hopkins, Jack. Latin America in World Affairs: The Politics of Inequality. Dillon, Mary, ed. LC 76-17616. (Politics of Government Ser.). 1977. pap. 4.50 (ISBN 0-8120-0497-3). Barron.

Hopkins, Jack W., ed. Latin America & Caribbean Contemporary Record, Vol. 1: 1981-82. 1000p. 1983. 149.50x (ISBN 0-8419-0754-4). Holmes & Meier.

Hopkins, James D., jt. auth. see MacCrate, Robert.

Hopkins, James F., ed. see Clay, Henry, II.

Hopkins, Jasper. Nicholas of Cusa on God As Not-Other: Translation & an Appraisal of De Li Non Aliud. 2nd ed. LC 82-73976. Date not set. Repr. of 1979 ed. text ed. 20.00 (ISBN 0-938060-26-0). Banning Pr.

Hopkins, Jeffery, ed. see Rinbochy, Khetsun S.

Hopkins, Jerry. The Hula. (Illus.). 194p. 1982. 35.00 (ISBN 9971-925-07-9). Lee Pubs Group.

Hopkins, Jerry & Sugerman, Daniel. No One Here Gets Out Alive. (Illus., Orig.). 1980. pap. 8.95 (ISBN 0-446-37015-0); pap. 3.95 (ISBN 0-446-30576-6). Warner Bks.

Hopkins, John A. Changing Technology & Employment in Agriculture. LC 73-174470. (FDR & the Era of the New Deal Ser.). 242p. 1973. Repr. of 1941 ed. lib. bdg. 29.50 (ISBN 0-306-70380-7). Da Capo.

Hopkins, John A. & Heady, Earl O. Farm Records & Accounting. 5th ed. (Illus.). 1962. 18.50x (ISBN 0-8138-0590-2). Iowa St U Pr.

Hopkins, John R., ed. James Jones: A Checklist. LC 74-20824. (Modern Authors Checklist Ser.). (Illus.). vii, 67p. 1974. 23.00x (ISBN 0-8103-0907-6, Bruccoli Clark Bk). Gale.

Hopkins, K. Conquerors & Slaves. LC 77-90209. (Sociological Studies in Roman History: No. 1). (Illus.). 272p. 1981. pap. 12.95 (ISBN 0-521-28181-4). Cambridge U Pr.

Hopkins, Keith, jt. ed. see Garnsey, Peter.

Hopkins, Kenneth D. & Glass, Gene V. Basic Statistics for the Behavioral Sciences. LC 77-10877. (Educational, Measurement, Research & Statistics Ser.). (Illus.). 1978. pap. text ed. 24.95 (ISBN 0-13-069377-4). P-H.

Hopkins, Kenneth D. & Stanley, Julian C. Educational & Psychological Measurement & Evaluation. 6th ed. (Illus.). 544p. 1981. text ed. 26.95 (ISBN 0-13-236273-2). P-H.

Hopkins, Lee, ed. City Talk. LC 74-102801. (gr. 3-7). 1970. PLB 5.99 o.s.i. (ISBN 0-394-91086-9). Knopf.

Hopkins, Lee B. How do You Make an Elephant Float? & Other Delicious Riddles. Tucker, Kathleen, ed. (Illus.). 32p. (gr. 1-5). 1983. PLB 6.50 (ISBN 0-8075-3415-3). A Whitman.

--Mama. LC 76-47628. (gr. 3 up). 1977. o. p. 4.95 o.s.i. (ISBN 0-394-83525-5); PLB 5.99 o.s.i. (ISBN 0-394-93525-X). Knopf.

--The Sky Is Full of Song. LC 82-48263. (A Charlotte Zolotow Bk.). (Illus.). 48p. (gr. 3-7). 1983. 9.57i (ISBN 0-06-022582-3, HarpJ); PLB 9.89g (ISBN 0-06-022583-1). Har-Row.

Hopkins, Lee B., ed. A Dog's Life. LC 82-974. (Illus.). 48p. (gr. 8 up). 9.95 (ISBN 0-15-223937-5, HJ). HarBraceJ.

--Merrily Comes Our Harvest In: Poems for Thanksgiving. LC 78-52804. (Illus.). (gr. k-3). 1978. 4.95 (ISBN 0-15-253179-3, HJ). HarBraceJ.

Hopkins, Lee B., ed. see Sanburg, Carl.

Hopkins, Leo N. & Long, Donlin M., eds. Clinical Management of Intracranial Aneurysms. (Seminars in Neurological Surgery Ser.). 344p. 1982. text ed. 39.00 (ISBN 0-89004-481-3). Raven.

Hopkins, Levi T. Emerging Self in School & Home. Repr. of 1954 ed. lib. bdg. 15.75x (ISBN 0-8371-2877-3, HOES). Greenwood.

Hopkins, Margaret. Corfu. 1977. 16.95 (ISBN 0-7134-0880-4, Pub by Batsford, England). David & Charles.

Hopkins, Mary. Celebrating: Family Prayer Services. LC 75-30486. 164p. 1975. pap. 7.95 o.p. (ISBN 0-8091-1893-9). Paulist Pr.

Hopkins, Mary F., jt. auth. see Long, Beverly.

Hopkins, Raymond F. & Puchala, Donald J., eds. The Global Political Economy of Food. 349p. 1979. 25.00 (ISBN 0-299-07750-0); pap. 9.95 (ISBN 0-299-07754-3). U of Wis Pr.

Hopkins, Richard L. Freedom & Education: The Beginnings of a New Philosophy. LC 79-66475. 1979. text ed. 16.75 (ISBN 0-8191-0836-7); pap. text ed. 8.50 (ISBN 0-8191-0837-5). U Pr of Amer.

Hopkins, S. J. Principal Drugs: An Alphabetical Guide to Modern Therapeutic Agents. 7th ed. 192p. (Orig.). 1983. pap. 3.95 (ISBN 0-571-18063-9). Faber & Faber.

Hopkins, Sheila V., jt. auth. see Brown, Henry P.

Hopkins, Stephen. The Rights of Colonies Examined. Campbell, Paul, ed. LC 74-20472. (Rhode Island Revolutionary Heritage Ser.: Vol. 2). (Illus.). 1975. Repr. 3.75 (ISBN 0-917012-02-X). Ri Pubns Soc.

Hopkins, Terri, ed. see Olsson, Karl.

Hopkins, Terry, ed. see Davidson, Judith.

Hopkins, Terry, ed. see Levinson, Nancy S.

Hopkins, Terry, ed. see Olsson, Kari.

Hopkins, Washburn. Legends of India. 1928. 29.50x (ISBN 0-686-51410-6). Elliots Bks.

Hopkins, William F. Murder Is My Business. 350p. 1974. pap. 4.95 (ISBN 0-913428-16-7). Landfall Pr.

Hopkinson, Ann, jt. auth. see Anderson, Fletcher.

Hopkinson, D. A., jt. auth. see Harris, H.

Hopkinson, Simon. The Crazy World of Advertising. (Australian Theatre Workshop Ser.). 1975. pap. text ed. 4.50x o.p. (ISBN 0-85859-111-1, 00527). Heinemann Ed.

Hopko, Thomas. All the Fulness of God: Essays on Orthodoxy, Ecumenism & Modern Society. LC 82-5454. 188p. (Orig.). 1982. pap. 6.95 (ISBN 0-913836-96-6). St Vladimirs.

Hopley, Catherine C. Life in the South, from the Commencement of the War: Being a Social History of Those Who Took Part in the Battles, from a Personal Acquaintance with Them in Their Own Homes, 2 vols. LC 68-16240. (American Scene Ser.). 831p. 1974. Repr. of 1863 ed. Set. lib. bdg. 85.00 (ISBN 0-306-71015-3). Da Capo.

Hopley, David. The Geomorphology of the Great Barrier Reef: Quaternary Development of Coral Reefs. LC 81-163336. 453p. 1982. 59.95x (ISBN 0-471-04562-4, Pub. by Wiley-Interscience). Wiley.

Hoplirk, Joyce. Slimmer's Cookbook. 1978. 4.95 (ISBN 0-7153-7529-6). David & Charles.

Hopman, Harry. Better Tennis for Boys & Girls. LC 76-165672. (Illus.). (gr. 7 up). 1972. PLB 6.95 (ISBN 0-396-06365-9). Dodd.

Hopp, Joyce, jt. ed. see Hamburg, Marian.

Hoppal, M., jt. auth. see Djoszegi, V.

Hoppe, H. Whittling & Wood Carving. LC 69-19488. (Little Craft Book Ser). (gr. 4 up). 1969. 6.95 (ISBN 0-8069-5126-5); PLB 8.99 (ISBN 0-8069-5127-3). Sterling.

--Whittling & Wood Carving. LC 69-19488. (Illus.). 50p. 1983. pap. 4.95 (ISBN 0-8069-7692-6). Sterling.

Hoppe, Joanne. April Spell. (gr. 7-10). 1982. pap. 2.25 (ISBN 0-671-46527-9). Archway.

Hoppel, Charles L., jt. auth. see Tandler, Bernard.

Hoppenfeld, Stanley. Orthopaedic Neurology: A Diagnostic Guide to Neurologic Levels. LC 77-9316. (Illus.). 1977. 23.50 o.p. (ISBN 0-397-50368-7, Lippincott Medical). Lippincott.

Hoppensteadt, Frank. Mathematical Theories of Populations: Demographics, Genetics & Epidemics. (CBMS Regional Conference Ser.: Vol. 20). (Illus.). viii, 72p. (Orig.). 1975. pap. text ed. 9.50 (ISBN 0-89871-017-0). Soc Indus-Appl Math.

Hopper. User Oriented Command Language. 1981. 29.95 (ISBN 0-471-25773-7, Wiley Heyden). Wiley.

Hopper, A. G. Einfuhrung in Die Statistische Qualitatskontrolle. Berchtold, W., tr. from Eng. (Lehr- und Handbucher der Ingenierwissenschaften Ser.: No. 30). 194p. (Ger.). 1971. 33.90 (ISBN 3-7643-0528-2). Birkhauser.

Hopper, Gordon E. Model A Ford Restoration Handbook. Clymer Publications, ed. (Illus.). pap. 6.00 o.p. (ISBN 0-89287-263-2, H523). Clymer Pubns.

Hopper, Jess A. Rainbow Junction. 1983. 12.95 (ISBN 0-533-05517-2). Vantage.

Hopper, Kim, jt. auth. see Baxter, Ellen.

Hopper, Kim, et al. One Year Later: The Homeless Poor in New York City. LC 82-200214. 92p. (Orig.). 1982. pap. 6.50 (ISBN 0-88156-000-6). Comm Serv Soc NY.

Hopper, Millard. Win at Backgammon. LC 72-86224. Orig. Title: Backgammon. (Illus.). 111p. 1972. pap. 1.95 (ISBN 0-486-22894-0). Dover.

--Win at Checkers. 1956. pap. 2.50 (ISBN 0-486-20363-8). Dover.

Hopper, Nancy J. Hang on, Harvey! LC 82-18253. 128p. (gr. 4-8). 1983. 9.95 (ISBN 0-525-44045-3, 0966-290). Dutton.

--Just Vernon. 128p. (gr. 7 up). 1982. 9.95 (ISBN 0-525-66788-1, 0966-290). Lodestar Bks.

--Secrets. LC 79-4667. (gr. 6). 1979. 8.95 o.p. (ISBN 0-525-66621-4). Lodestar Bks.

Hopper, Paul, ed. Syntax & Semantics: Vol. 15, Studies in Transivity. Thompson, Sandra. (Syntax & Semantics Ser.). 1982. 59.00 (ISBN 0-12-613515-0). Acad Pr.

Hopper, Paul J., ed. Studies in Descriptive & Historical Linguistics. x, 502p. 1977. 46.00 o.p. (ISBN 90-272-0905-7, CILT 4). Benjamins North Am.

--Tense-Aspect: Between Semantics & Pragmatics. (Typological Studies in Language: 1). 450p. 1982. 40.00 (ISBN 90-272-2865-5); pap. 25.00 (ISBN 90-272-2861-2). Benjamins North Am.

--Tense Aspect: Between Semantics & Pragmatics. 450p. 1982. 45.00 o.p. (ISBN 90-272-2865-5); pap. 30.00 o.p. (ISBN 90-272-2861-2). Benjamins North Am.

Hopper, Robert. Interpersonal Communication for Professionals. (Procom Ser.). 1983. pap. text ed. 8.95 (ISBN 0-673-15551-X). Scott F.

Hopper, Stanley R. & Miller, David L., eds. Interpretation: The Poetry of Meaning. LC 67-13470. (Orig.). 1967. pap. 2.25 (ISBN 0-15-644880-7, Harv). HarBraceJ.

Hopper, Vincent F. English Verb Conjugations. rev. ed. LC 75-627. 1975. pap. 4.95 (ISBN 0-8120-0557-0). Barron.

Hopper, Vincent F. & Gale, Cedric. Essentials of Writing. 3rd ed. 168p. 1983. pap. 3.95 (ISBN 0-8120-2265-3). Barron.

--Practice for Effective Writing. rev. ed. LC 61-8198. (Orig.). 1971. pap. text ed. 4.50 (ISBN 0-8120-0148-6). Barron.

Hopper, Vincent F., ed. Classic American Short Stories. rev. ed. LC 63-23444. (Orig.). 1984. text ed. 5.95 o.p. (ISBN 0-686-82868-2); pap. text ed. 2.95 (ISBN 0-8120-2334-X). Barron.

Hopper, Vincent F., ed. see Chaucer, Geoffrey.

Hoppes, Steve. Running Through Austin. Orig. Title: A Guide to Austin Running, 1976. (Illus.). 112p. 1982. pap. 4.95 (ISBN 0-938934-03-1). C&M Pubns.

Hoppin, Martha J. & Adam, Henry S. William Morris Hunt: A Memorial Exhibition. LC 79-2475. (Illus.). 88p. 1979. pap. 7.95 (ISBN 0-87846-138-8). Mus Fine Arts Boston.

Hoppin, Richard H. Medieval Music. (Introduction to Music History Ser.). (Illus.). 1978. 16.95x (ISBN 0-393-09090-6). Norton.

Hopple, Gerald W. Political Psychology & Biopolitics: Assessing & Predicting Elite Behavior in Foreign Policy Crises. (A Westview Replica Edition Ser.). 150p. 1980. lib. bdg. 22.50 (ISBN 0-89158-847-7). Westview.

Hopple, Gerald W. & Andriole, Stephen J., eds. National Security Crisis Forecasting & Management. Replica ed. Freedy, Amos. 275p. 1983. so ftcover 21.50 (ISBN 0-86531-913-8). Westview.

Hoppock, Robert. Occupational Information. 4th ed. 1975. text ed. 30.00 (ISBN 0-07-030330-4). McGraw.

Hopps, Helen, ed. see Litvak, Lawrence, et al.

Hopps, Marti & Maron, Michael P. The Child Inside of Me. 1978. pap. 3.95 o.p. (ISBN 0-448-16187-7, D&G). Putnam Pub Group.

Hopson, B. & Hayes, J. The Theory & Practice of Vocational Guidance. 1969. 37.00 o.s.i. (ISBN 0-08-013284-7); pap. 16.25 (ISBN 0-08-013391-6). Pergamon.

Hopson, Barrie & Hopson, Charlotte. Intimate Feedback: Lover's Guide to Getting in Touch with Each Other. 1976. pap. 1.50 o.p. (ISBN 0-451-06894-7, W6894, Sig). NAL.

Hopson, Barrie, jt. auth. see Loughary, John W.

Hopson, Charlotte, jt. auth. see Hopson, Barrie.

Hopson, D., Jr., et al. Juvenile Offender & the Law: A Symposium. LC 79-146557. (Symposia on Law & Society Ser). 1971. Repr. of 1968 ed. lib. bdg. 27.50 (ISBN 0-306-70095-6). Da Capo.

Hopson, Janet. Scent Signals. LC 78-21912. 1979. 7.95 o.p. (ISBN 0-688-03410-1). Morrow.

Hopson, William. Apache Kill. 256p. (YA) 1974. 6.95 (ISBN 0-685-40095-6, Avalon). Bouregy.

--Gunfighters Pay. (YA) 1973. 6.95 (ISBN 0-685-31776-5, Avalon). Bouregy.

--The Last Apaches. 256p. (YA) 1975. 6.95 (ISBN 0-685-50530-8, Avalon). Bouregy.

Hopwood, A. G., ed. Human Resource Accounting. 1977. pap. text ed. 29.00 (ISBN 0-08-021419-3). Pergamon.
Hopwood, Anthony. Accounting & Human Behavior. 1976. text ed. 10.95 ref. ed. o.p. (ISBN 0-13-002063-X); pap. text ed. 12.95 (ISBN 0-13-002055-9). P-H.
Hopwood, Derek. Egypt: Politics & Society, 1945-1981. 224p. 1982. text ed. 28.50x (ISBN 0-04-956011-5); pap. text ed. 9.95x (ISBN 0-04-956012-3). Allen Unwin.
Hopwood, Derek, ed. The Arabian Penninsula: Society & Politics. (Studies on Modern Asia & Africa). (Illus.). 1972. text ed. 32.50x (ISBN 0-04-953006-2). Allen Unwin.
Hora, jt. auth. see Lange.
Hora, Bayard, ed. Oxford Encyclopedia of Trees of the World. LC 80-40560. (Illus.). 1981. 25.00 (ISBN 0-19-217712-5). Oxford U Pr.
Hora, Heinrich. Physics of Laser Driven Plasmas. LC 80-39792. 317p. 1981. 39.95 (ISBN 0-471-07880-8, Pub. by Wiley-Interscience). Wiley.
Horace. Complete Works of Horace. Passage, Charles E., tr. from Greek. LC 81-70126. 500p. 1983. 28.50 (ISBN 0-8044-2404-7). Ungar.
--The Essential Horace: Odes, Epodes, Satires & Epistles. Raffel, Burton, tr. from Latin. LC 82-73717. 352p. 1983. 22.50 (ISBN 0-86547-111-8); pap. 13.50 (ISBN 0-86547-112-6). N Point Pr.
--Horace: Complete Odes & Epodes. Shepherd, W. G., tr. 1983. pap. price not set (ISBN 0-14-044422-X). Penguin.
--Odes & Epodes. Clancy, Joseph P., tr. LC 60-10659. 1960. pap. 6.95 (ISBN 0-226-10679-9, P47, Phoen). U of Chicago Pr.
--Opera. 2nd ed. Wickham, E. C. & Garrod, H. W., eds. (Oxford Classical Texts Ser). 1912. 11.95x (ISBN 0-19-814618-3). Oxford U Pr.
--Satires One. Gow, Andrew S., ed. (Lat). 1901. text ed. 6.95x (ISBN 0-521-05332-3). Cambridge U Pr.
Horacek, J., jt. auth. see Borchardt, D. H.
Horadam, A. F. A Guide to Undergraduate Projective Geometry. LC 71-110243. 1971. 39.00 (ISBN 0-08-017479-5). Pergamon.
Horak, Barbara. Getting from Paycheck to Paycheck-Simply. pap. 2.95 (ISBN 0-8341-0780-5). Beacon Hill.
Horak, E. Entoloma (Agaricales) in Indo-Malaysia & Australasia. (Nova Hedwigia Beiheft: No. 65). (Illus.). 1980. lib. bdg. 60.00 (ISBN 3-7682-5465-8). Lubrecht & Cramer.
--Fungi Agaracini Nova Zelandiae. 1973. 40.00 (ISBN 3-7682-5443-7). Lubrecht & Cramer.
Horak, E., jt. auth. see Moser, M.
Horak, J. & Pasek, J. Design of Industrial Chemical Reactors from Laboratory Data. 1978. casebound 31.00 (ISBN 0-686-86039-X, Pub. by Wiley Heyden). Wiley.
Horak, M. & Vitek, Antonin V. Interpretation & Processing of Vibrational Spectra. LC 78-16741. 1978. 92.95 (ISBN 0-471-99504-5, Pub. by Wiley-Interscience). Wiley.
Horak, Stephan M., ed. Guide to the Study of the Soviet Nationalities: Non-Russian Peoples of the USSR. LC 81-18657. 265p. 1982. lib. bdg. 30.00 (ISBN 0-87287-270-X). Libs Unl.
Horak, V., jt. auth. see Ma, T. S.
Horam, M. Naga Polity. LC 75-907212. 1975. 12.50x o.p. (ISBN 0-88386-699-4). South Asia Bks.
Horan, James D. The Desperate Years: A Pictorial History of the Thirties. (Illus.). 1962. 7.95 o.p. (ISBN 0-517-02684-8). Crown.
--Ginerva: The Lady of the Lightning. 1979. 12.95 o.p. (ISBN 0-517-53392-8). Crown.
--The Great American West. rev. ed. (Illus.). 1978. 14.95 o.p. (ISBN 0-517-53491-6). Crown.
Horan, James F. & Taylor, G. Thomas, Jr. Experiments in Metropolitan Government. LC 77-7816. (Praeger Special Studies). 1978. 31.95 o.p. (ISBN 0-03-022336-9). Praeger.
Horatio, Algernon. The Penny Capitalist: How to Build a Small Fortune from Next to Nothing. 1979. 10.00 o.p. (ISBN 0-87000-422-0, Arlington Hse). Crown.
Horatius Flaccus. Art of Poetry. Raffel, Burton, tr. & intro. by. LC 78-171176. 96p. (Lat. & Eng.). 1974. pap. 10.95x (ISBN 0-87395-240-5). State U NY Pr.
Horatius Flaccus, Quintus. Horace His Arte of Poetrie, Pistles, & Satyrs Englished (1567) Drant, Thomas H., tr. from Lat. LC 73-173753. 296p. 1972. Repr. of 1567 ed. 35.00x (ISBN 0-8201-1099-X). Schol Facsimiles.
Horbar, Amy, ed. see Curators at the Musei Vaticani & the Metropolitan Museum of Art.
Horblit, Marcus & Nielsen, Kaj L. Plane Geometry Problems with Solutions. (Orig.). 1947. pap. 4.95 (ISBN 0-06-460063-7, CO 63, COS). B&N NY.
Horbury, W. & McNeil, B., eds. Suffering & Martyrdom in the New Testament. LC 80-40706. 240p. 1981. 42.50 (ISBN 0-521-23482-4). Cambridge U Pr.
Horcasitas, Fernando, jt. auth. see Oettinger, Marion, Jr.
Hord, Michael. Digital Image Processing of Remotely Sensed Data. (Notes & Reports in Computer Science & Applied Math). 221p. 1982. 27.50 (ISBN 0-12-355620-1). Acad Pr.
Horden, William. Experience & Faith. LC 82-72653. 160p. 1983. pap. 8.95 (ISBN 0-8066-1960-0, 10-2133). Augsburg.
Horder, John, jt. auth. see Butrym, Zofia.
Horder, Merwyn, ed. Book of Love Songs. pap. 4.95 o.s.i. (ISBN 0-685-20577-0). Transatlantic.
Hordern, William E. Layman's Guide to Protestant Theology. rev. ed. 1968. pap. 2.95 (ISBN 0-02-085470-6). Macmillan.
Hordinsky, J. R., ed. see Basic Environmental Problems of Man in Space II, 6th International Symposium, Bonn, Germany, 3-6 November 1980.
Hordon, Harris E. Introduction to Urban Economics: Analysis & Policy. 1973. pap. text ed. 14.95 o.p. (ISBN 0-13-499491-4). P-H.
Hordyk, Margaret M., tr. see Bonger, Willem A.
Horecker, Bernard & Stadtman, E., eds. Current Topics in Cellular Regulations, Vol. 22. (Serial Publication). Date not set. price not set (ISBN 0-12-152822-7); price not set Lib. ed. (ISBN 0-12-152800-6). Acad Pr.
Horecky, H. Coling, Eighty-Two. (North Holland Linguistic Ser.: Vol. 47). Date not set. 49.00 (ISBN 0-444-86393-1, North Holland). Elsevier.
Horecky, J. P., et al. Prague Studies in Mathematical Linguistics, Vols. 5 & 6. 1977-78. Vol. 5. 47.00 (ISBN 0-7204-8034-5, North-Holland); Vol. 6. 47.00 (ISBN 0-7204-0439-8). Elsevier.
Horecky, Paul L., ed. East Central & Southeast Europe: A Handbook of Library & Archival Resources in North America. new ed. LC 76-28392. 467p. 1976. text ed. 45.00 o.p. (ISBN 0-87436-214-8). ABC-Clio.
Horeker, Bernard & Earl, R., eds. Current Topics in Cellular Regulation, Vol. 21. 306p. 1982. 43.00 (ISBN 0-12-152821-9). Acad Pr.
Horemis, Spyros. Geometrical Design Coloring Book. 1973. pap. 2.25 (ISBN 0-486-20180-5). Dover.
--Optical & Geometric Patterns & Designs. 1970. pap. 5.50 (ISBN 0-486-22214-4). Dover.
Horenstein, Henry. Black & White Photography: A Basic Manual. rev. ed. (Illus.). 256p. 1983. 19.45i (ISBN 0-316-37313-3); pap. 9.70i (ISBN 0-316-37314-1). Little.
Horgan, J. J. Criminal Investigation. 1973. 15.50 o.p. (ISBN 0-07-030337-1). McGraw.
--Criminal Investigation. 2nd ed. 1979. text ed. 21.95 (ISBN 0-07-030334-7); instr's. manual avail. McGraw.
Horgan, Joanne C., jt. auth. see Johnson, E. Verner.
Horgan, Maureen A. To Feel Is to Live. 1979. 4.95 o.p. (ISBN 0-533-03988-6). Vantage.
Horgan, Paul. Conquistadors in North American History. 320p. 1982. 20.00 (ISBN 0-87404-071-X); pap. 10.00 (ISBN 0-87404-072-8). Tex Western.
--Lamy of Santa Fe: His Life & Times. 1980. 25.00 (ISBN 0-374-18300-7); Limited Ed. 150.00 o.p. (ISBN 0-686-85975-8); pap. 12.95 (ISBN 0-374-51588-3). FS&G.
--Things as They Are. 1964. 8.95 o.p. (ISBN 0-374-27476-2). FS&G.
Hori, J. Spectral Properties of Disordered Chains & Lattices. 1969. 37.00 (ISBN 0-08-012359-7). Pergamon.
Horiuchi, A., jt. ed. see Goto, Y.
Horizon Magazine Editors. Shakespeare's England. LC 64-12231. (Horizon Caravel Bks.). 154p. (YA) (gr. 7 up). 1964. PLB 14.89 o.p. (ISBN 0-06-022591-2, HarpJ). Har-Row.
Horkheimer, Foley A. & Alley, Louis E., eds. Educators Guide to Free Health, Physical Education & Recreation Materials. 15th rev. ed. LC 68-57948. 1982. pap. 21.00 (ISBN 0-87708-129-8). Ed Prog.
Horkheimer, Mary F., jt. ed. see Diffor, John C.
Horlock, J. H. Actuator Disk Theory: Discontinuities in Thermo-Fluid Dynamics. (Illus.). 1979. 50.00 (ISBN 0-07-030360-6). McGraw.
Horlock, J. H., ed. see Benson, Rowland S.
Hormachea, Carroll R. Sourcebook in Criminalistics. LC 73-9554. (Illus.). 208p. 1974. 16.00 (ISBN 0-87909-778-7). Reston.
Hormander, L. An Introduction to Complex Analysis in Several Variables. 2nd rev. ed. LC 73-81532. (Mathematical Library: Vol. 7). 230p. 1973. 40.50 (ISBN 0-444-10523-9, North-Holland). Elsevier.
Hormasji, Nariman. Katherine Mansfield: An Appraisal. 160p. 1982. Repr. of 1967 ed. lib. bdg. 35.00 (ISBN 0-89984-703-X). Century Bookbindery.
Hormuth, W., jt. auth. see Brodhage, H.
Horn & Gleason. Beginning Structured COBOL. 450p. 1983. pap. text ed. 21.95x (ISBN 0-87835-133-7). Boyd & Fraser.
Horn, jt. auth. see Turner.
Horn, Berthold K., jt. auth. see Winston, Patrick H.
Horn, Bob. Swimming Techniques in Pictures. LC 73-22734. (Sports Handbooks Ser.). 96p. 1974. pap. 2.95 o.p. (ISBN 0-448-11636-7, G&D). Putnam Pub Group.
Horn, Carin E. & Collins, Carroll L. Com-Lit: Computer Literacy for Kids. 1983. write for info. Sterling Swift.
Horn, Carl E. Van see Van Horn, Carl E.
Horn, David J. Biology of Insects. LC 76-1217. (Illus.). 1976. text ed. 14.95 o.p. (ISBN 0-7216-4780-4, CBS C). SCP.
Horn, Delton T. Basic Electronics Theory with Projects & Experiments. LC 81-9207. (Illus.). 532p. 1981. 19.95 (ISBN 0-8306-0020-5); pap. 12.95 (ISBN 0-8306-1338-2). TAB Bks.
--Electronic Music Synthesizers. (Illus.). 168p. 1980. 11.95 (ISBN 0-8306-9722-5); pap. 6.95 (ISBN 0-8306-1167-3, 1167). TAB Bks.
--Writing Adventure Games for Your Computer. 175p. 1983. pap. price not set (ISBN 0-88056-089-4). Dilithium Pr.
Horn, Frank W. Cable, Inside & Out, Vol. V. 1978. 7.95 (ISBN 0-686-98061-1). Telecom Lib.
Horn, Frederick F. & Farah, Victor W. Trading in Commodity Futures. 2nd ed. LC 78-27235. (Illus.). 373p. 1979. 18.95 (ISBN 0-13-925941-4). NY Inst Finance.
Horn, G. & Hinde, R. A., eds. Short-Term Changes in Neural Activity & Behaviour. LC 71-121367. (Illus.). 1970. 95.00 (ISBN 0-521-07942-X). Cambridge U Pr.
Horn, Geoffrey & Cavanaugh, Arthur, eds. Bible Stories for Children. (Illus.). 1980. 12.95 o.p. (ISBN 0-686-64566-9). Macmillan.
Horn, George F. Balance & Unity. LC 75-21109. (Concepts of Design Ser.). (Illus.). 80p. (gr. 8-12). 1975. 9.95 (ISBN 0-87192-073-5). Davis Mass.
--The Crayon, a Versatile Medium for Creative Expression. LC 76-78029. (Illus.). 64p. 1969. 7.50 o.p. (ISBN 0-87192-029-8). Davis Mass.
--Texture: A Design Element. LC 74-82683. (Concepts of Design Ser). (Illus.). 72p. (gr. 7up). 1974. 9.95 (ISBN 0-87192-066-2). Davis Mass.
Horn, Huston. The Pioneers. LC 73-94242. (The Old West). (Illus.). (gr. 5 up). 1974. 17.28 (ISBN 0-8094-1477-5, Pub. by Time-Life). Silver.
Horn, Jack. Manager's Factomatic. (Illus.). 1978. 29.95 (ISBN 0-13-549295-5, Busn). P-H.
--Portfolio of Public Accountant's Forms, Reports, & Procedures. 1975. 45.00 o.p. (ISBN 0-13-685990-9, Busn). P-H.
Horn, James Van see Van Horn, James.
Horn, John L. The Education of Exceptional Children: A Consideration of Public School Problems & Policies in the Field of Differentiated Education. 343p. 1982. Repr. of 1929 ed. lib. bdg. 40.00 (ISBN 0-686-37943-8). Darby Bks.
Horn, L. Karma. 1983. 8.95 (ISBN 0-533-05669-1). Vantage.
Horn, L. Wayne, jt. auth. see Boillot, Michel.
Horn, Lyle H., jt. auth. see Trewartha, Glenn T.
Horn, Marilyn J. & Gurel, Lois M. The Second Skin: An Interdisciplinary Study of Clothing. 3rd ed. LC 80-81918. (Illus.). 480p. 1981. text ed. 22.50 (ISBN 0-395-28974-2); instr's. manual 1.60 (ISBN 0-395-28963-7). HM.
Horn, Mary. Children & Plastics: Stages 1 & 2 & Background. LC 77-83010. (Science 5-13 Ser.). 1977. pap. text ed. 12.85 (ISBN 0-356-04352-5). Raintree Pubs.
Horn, Maurice. Comics of the American West. (Illus.). 1978. pap. 7.95 o.s.i. (ISBN 0-695-80954-7). Follett.
Horn, Maurice, ed. World Encyclopedia of Cartoons, 2 vols. 787p. 1980. 78.00x (ISBN 0-8103-0183-0). Gale.
Horn, Max. Intercollegiate Socialist Society, Nineteen Hundred Five to Nineteen Twenty-One: Origins of the Modern American Student Movement. LC 79-9404. (A Westview Replica Edition Ser.). (Illus.). 1979. softcover 27.50 (ISBN 0-89158-584-2). Westview.
Horn, Pamela. Education in Rural England, 1800-1914. LC 78-58415. 1978. 27.50x (ISBN 0-312-23727-8). St Martin.
Horn, R. C., jt. auth. see Murray, T. P.
Horn, R. E. How to Write Information Mapping. 1982. 750.00 (ISBN 0-912864-05-2). Info Res Inc.
--Writing Management Reports. 1979. 375.00 (ISBN 0-686-83947-1). Info Res Inc.
Horn, Ronald C. Code of Professional Ethics of the American Institute for Property & Liability Underwriters. American Institute, ed. LC 79-50832. 86p. 1979. pap. 3.00 (ISBN 0-89463-021-0). Am Inst Property.
--On Professions, Professionals & Professional Ethics. 1978. write for info. o.p. (CPCU 10). IIA.
--On Professions, Professionals, & Professional Ethics. LC 78-67501. 114p. 1978. pap. 3.00 (ISBN 0-89463-020-2). Am Inst Property.
Horn, Royal Van see Van Horn, Royal.
Horn, Stanley F. Invisible Empire, the Story of the Ku Klux Klan, 1866-1871. 2nd, enl. ed. LC 69-16239. (Criminology, Law Enforcement, & Social Problems Ser.: No. 81). (Illus.). 1969. 15.00x (ISBN 0-87585-081-2). Patterson Smith.
Horn, Susan, tr. see Nagybakay, Peter.
Horn, Susanna, tr. see Bernath, Maria.
Horn, Susanna, tr. see Pataky-Brestyanszky, Ilona.
Horn, Susanna, tr. see Vegh, Janos.
Horn, Vivian. Composition Steps. LC 76-57147. 1977. pap. text ed. 9.95 (ISBN 0-88377-069-5); tchrs manual 2.95 (ISBN 0-88377-085-7). Newbury Hse.
Horn, Yvonne. Dozens of Ways to Make Money. LC 76-39930. (gr. 7 up). 1977. pap. 2.95 (ISBN 0-15-224185-X, VoyB). HarBraceJ.
Horn, Z., tr. see Csapodi, Csaba.
Horn, Zsuzsanna, tr. see Gero, Gyozo.
Hornak, J. E., jt. auth. see Phillips, D. A.
Hornback, Bert G. The Hero of My Life: Essays on Dickens. LC 81-565. (Illus.). xii, 159p. 1981. text ed. 18.95x (ISBN 0-8214-0587-X, 82-83764). Ohio U Pr.
--Metaphor of Chance: Vision & Technique in the Works of Thomas Hardy. LC 77-122099. viii, 177p. 1971. 12.00x (ISBN 0-8214-0077-0, 82-80810). Ohio U Pr.
--Noah's Arkitecture: A Study of Dicken's Mythology. LC 70-181681. x, 183p. 1972. 12.00x (ISBN 0-8214-0100-9, 82-81057). Ohio U Pr.
Hornblass, Albert. Tumors of the Ocular Adnexa & Orbit. LC 79-11089. (Illus.). 1979. text ed. 59.50 o.p. (ISBN 0-8016-2246-8). Mosby.
Hornblass, Albert, jt. auth. see Aston, Sherrell J.
Hornblow, Arthur, jt. auth. see Hornblow, Leonora.
Hornblow, Leonora & Hornblow, Arthur. Birds Do the Strangest Things. (Step-up Bks). (Illus.). (gr. 2-6). 1965. 3.95 (ISBN 0-394-80061-3, BYR); PLB 4.95 o.p. (ISBN 0-394-90061-8). Random.
--Insects Do the Strangest Things. LC 68-10046. (Step-up Bks). (Illus.). (gr. 2-9). 1968. 4.95 (ISBN 0-394-80072-9, BYR); PLB 4.99 (ISBN 0-394-90072-3). Random.
--Prehistoric Monsters Did the Strangest Things. LC 73-9348. (Illus.). 72p. 1974. 4.95 (ISBN 0-394-82051-7, BYR); PLB 5.99 (ISBN 0-394-92051-1). Random.
Hornblower, Jane. Hieronymus of Cardia. (Classical & Philosophical Monographs). 314p. 1981. text ed. 44.00x (ISBN 0-19-814717-1). Oxford U Pr.
Hornbogen, E. & Zum-Gahr, K. H., eds. Metallurgical Aspects of Wear: Proceedings of the Symposium, held in Bad Pyrmont, West Germany, 1979. Nicoll, A. R., tr. (Illus.). 425p. 1981. lib. bdg. 71.00 (ISBN 3-88355-046-9, Pub. by DGM Metallurgy Germany). IR Pubns.
Hornbostel, Caleb. Construction Materials: Types, Uses & Applications. LC 78-6278. 1978. 65.00 (ISBN 0-471-40940-5, Pub. by Wiley-Interscience). Wiley.
Hornbostel, Caleb & Hornung, William. Materials & Methods for Contemporary Construction. 2nd ed. (Illus.). 1982. 25.95 (ISBN 0-13-560904-6). P-H.
Hornbostel, H. & Strohmeyer, G. Internal Medicine. (International Congress Ser.: Vol. 536). 1980. 24.00 (ISBN 0-444-90178-7). Elsevier.
Hornbostel, Peter. International Banking Operations in the United States: An Update. LC 79-53556. (Corporate Law & Practice Course Handbook Ser.: 1978-1979). 1979. pap. text ed. 20.00 o.p. (ISBN 0-686-59548-3, B4-6513). PLI.
Hornbrook, John F. Glimpse of Perfection. 178p. (Orig.). 1979. pap. 5.95 (ISBN 0-89841-004-5). Zoe Pubns.
Hornbrook, John F. & Wolf, Allan C. You Are Somebody Special. 148p. (Orig.). 1980. pap. 4.95 (ISBN 0-89841-005-3). Zoe Pubns.
Hornburger. African Countries & Cultures. 1981. 13.95 (ISBN 0-679-20507-1). McKay.
Hornby, A. S., et al. Oxford Advanced Learner's Dictionary of Current English with Chinese Translations. (Illus.). 1354p. 1980. text ed. 17.50x (ISBN 0-19-580003-6). Oxford U Pr.
Hornby, George, ed. Your National Parks: A Photographic Guide to the National Parks System of the U.S. (Illus.). 1979. 19.95 o.p. (ISBN 0-517-53370-7). Crown.
Hornby, James A. Introduction to Company Law. (Repr. of 1957 ed). 1970. text ed. 6.00 (ISBN 0-09-020713-0, Hutchinson U Lib); pap. text ed. 3.75 o. p. (ISBN 0-09-020714-9, Hutchinson U Lib). Humanities.
Hornby, W. F. & Jones, M. An Introduction to Population Geography. LC 78-74536. (Illus.). 1980. pap. 12.95 (ISBN 0-521-21395-9). Cambridge U Pr.
Horne. The Structure & Function of Viruses. (Studies in Biology: No. 95). 1978. 5.95 o.p. (ISBN 0-7131-2706-1). Univ Park.
Horne, Alexander, jt. auth. see Goldman, Charles.
Horne, Alistair. The Price of Glory: Verdun Nineteen Sixteen. (Illus.). 1979. pap. 4.95 (ISBN 0-14-002215-5). Penguin.
Horne, Arthur M., jt. auth. see Fleischman, Matthew J.
Horne, Caroline. Fashion Crochet. (Illus.). 1970. 5.95 (ISBN 0-8208-0335-9). Hearthside.
Horne, Chevis F. Dynamic Preaching. LC 82-70871. (Orig.). 1983. pap. 6.95 (ISBN 0-8054-2110-6). Broadman.
Horne, D. F. Dividing, Ruling & Mask-Making. LC 74-7856. (Illus.). 315p. 1974. 62.50x o.s.i. (ISBN 0-8448-0359-6). Crane Russak Co.
--Lens Mechanism Technology. LC 75-21733. (Illus.). 266p. 1975. 79.50x o.s.i. (ISBN 0-8448-0770-2). Crane-Russak Co.
--Optical Production Technology. 599p. 1980. Repr. 87.50x o.s.i. (ISBN 0-8448-1398-2). Crane-Russak Co.
--Spectacle Lens Technology. LC 77-90820. 323p. 1978. 62.50x o.s.i. (ISBN 0-8448-1265-X). Crane-Russak Co.
Horne, Field, ed. The Diary of Mary Cooper: Life on a Long Island Farm 1768-1773. LC 81-38405. (Illus.). 84p. (Orig.). 1981. pap. 10.00 (ISBN 0-89062-108-X, Pub by Oyster Bay Historical Society). Pub Ctr Cult Res.
Horne, J. C., tr. see Madach, Imre.
Horne, James C. Van see Van Horne, James C.

Horne, Michael R. Plastic Theory of Structures. 184p. 1972. 17.50x o.p. (ISBN 0-262-08050-8). MIT Pr.

Horne, Peggy. Savannah's Battlefield Park: A Photographic Essay. LC 82-61031. (Illus.). 64p. 1982. 18.95 (ISBN 0-9609236-0-8). Regina Pr GA.

Horne, R. A. The Chemistry of Our Environment. LC 77-1156. 1978. 75.00 (ISBN 0-471-40944-8, Pub. by Wiley-Interscience). Wiley.

--Marine Chemistry: The Structure of Water & the Chemistry of the Hydrosphere. LC 69-16120. 1969. text ed. 58.50 (ISBN 0-471-40942-1, Pub. by Wiley-Interscience). Wiley.

Horne, Robert W. Structure & Function of Viruses. (Studies in Biology: No. 95). 58p. 1978. pap. text ed. 8.95 (ISBN 0-686-43111-1). E Arnold.

Horne, Ross. Health Revolution. 1980. 8.95 (ISBN 0-9594423-0-8). Cancer Control Soc.

Horne, Virginia L. Stunts & Tumbling for Girls. LC 81-19344. 230p. 1983. Repr. of 1943 ed. lib. bdg. write for info. (ISBN 0-89874-459-8). Krieger.

Hornemann, Grace V. Basic Nursing Procedures. LC 77-94835. (Illus.). 340p. 1980. pap. 13.00 (ISBN 0-8273-1320-9); instructor's guide 2.75 (ISBN 0-8273-1321-7). Delmar.

Horner, Althea J. Little Big Girl. (Illus.). 32p. 1982. 9.95 (ISBN 0-89885-098-3). Human Sci Pr.

Horner, D. M. High Command: Australia & Allied Strategy, 1939-45. 384p. 1982. text ed. 40.00x (ISBN 0-86861-084-4); pap. cancelled (ISBN 0-686-85577-9). Allen Unwin.

Horner, D. M., jt. ed. see O'Neill, Robert.

Horner, Don R. & Billionis, Cynthia. Brushing Your Teeth. (Project MORE Daily Living Skills Ser.). 32p. 1979. Repr. of 1975 ed. pap. text ed. 5.95 (ISBN 0-8331-1246-5). Hubbard Sci.

Horner, Don R., jt. auth. see Keilitz, Ingo.

Horner, Harlan H. Lincoln & Greeley. LC 74-135247. viii, 432p. Repr. of 1953 ed. lib. bdg. 20.00x o.p. (ISBN 0-8371-5166-X, HOLG). Greenwood.

Horner, Peter. Reading: An Introduction to the Teaching of Reading in the Primary School. 1972. pap. text ed. 4.50x o.p. (ISBN 0-435-80605-X). Heinemann Ed.

Horner, Tom. All About the Bull Terrier. (All About Ser.). (Illus.). 150p. 1983. 12.95 (ISBN 0-7207-1086-3, Pub by Michael Joseph). Merrimack Bk Serv.

--Jonathan Loved David: Homosexuality in Biblical Times. LC 77-15628. 1978. softcover 6.95 (ISBN 0-664-24185-9). Westminster.

Horner, William R. Bad at the Bijou. (Illus.). 168p. 1982. lib. bdg. 17.95x (ISBN 0-89950-060-9). McFarland & Co.

Horner, Winifred B., ed. The Present State of Scholarship in Historical & Contemporary Rhetoric. LC 82-20002. 240p. 1983. text ed. 25.00x (ISBN 0-8262-0398-1). U of Mo Pr.

Horney, Karen. The Adolescent Diaries of Karen Horney. LC 80-50552. (Illus.). 271p. 1980. 14.50 (ISBN 0-465-00055-X). Basic.

--Feminine Psychology. Kelman, Harold, ed. 1967. 6.95 o.p. (ISBN 0-393-01045-7); pap. 3.95, 1973 (ISBN 0-393-00686-7). Norton.

--Neurosis & Human Growth. 1970. pap. 3.95 o.s.i. (ISBN 0-393-00135-0). Norton.

--New Ways in Psychoanalysis. 1939. 8.95 o.p. (ISBN 0-393-01015-5, Norton Lib); pap. 3.95 (ISBN 0-393-00132-6). Norton.

--Our Inner Conflicts. 1945 o.p. 6.45 (ISBN 0-393-01016-3, Norton Lib); pap. 3.95 1966 (ISBN 0-393-00133-4). Norton.

--Self-Analysis. 1942, o.p. 6.50 (ISBN 0-393-01025-2); pap. 3.95, 1968 (ISBN 0-393-00134-2). Norton.

Horngren, C. Introduction to Financial Accounting. 1981. 24.95 (ISBN 0-13-483743-6); practice set 7.95 (ISBN 0-13-483701-0); working papers 10.95 (ISBN 0-13-483727-4); student guide 10.95 (ISBN 0-13-483750-9). P-H.

Horngren, Charles T. Cost Accounting: A Managerial Emphasis. 5th ed. (Illus.). 928p. 1982. 29.95 (ISBN 0-13-179671-2); wkbk. 12.95 (ISBN 0-13-179630-5). P-H.

--Introduction to Management Accounting. 5th ed. (Ser. in Accounting). (Illus.). 848p. 1981. text ed. 25.95 (ISBN 0-13-487652-0); wkbk. by Dudley W. Curry 10.95 (ISBN 0-13-487785-3). P-H.

Horngren, Charles T. & Leer, J. Arthur. CPA Problems & Approaches to Solutions, Vol. 1. 5th ed. (Illus.). 1979. 30.60 (ISBN 0-13-187898-0). P-H.

Hornick, Melvyn. The Successful Marketing of Schools. 90p. 1980. softcover 8.95 (ISBN 0-932930-38-7). Pilgrimage Inc.

Hornick, William F., jt. auth. see Enk, Gordon A.

Hornig-Rohan, Mady, jt. auth. see Locke, Steven.

Hornik, Edith L. The Drinking Woman. Date not set. 8.95 (ISBN 0-695-81160-6). Follett.

--You & Your Alcoholic Parent. (gr. 7-12). 1973. 5.95 o.s.i. (ISBN 0-8096-1881-8); pap. 2.95 o.s.i. (ISBN 0-8096-1881-8). Follett.

Horning, A. S. Readings in Contemporary Culture. 1979. text ed. 5.62 (ISBN 0-07-030352-5). McGraw.

Horning, D. H., jt. auth. see Counsell, J. N.

Horning, E. C. Organic Synthesis: Collective Vols, Vol. 3, Vols. 20-29. 890p. 1955. 49.95 (ISBN 0-471-40953-7). Wiley.

Hornnes, Esther & Magos, Eunice. Sew & Know: Puppet Project to Teach Numbers, 1-12. Sussman, Ellen, ed. (Illus.). 28p. (Orig.). (ps-1). 1982. pap. text ed. 4.95 (ISBN 0-933606-17-6, MS-615). Monkey Sisters.

Hornof, John A. Traditional Math: Restored, Simplified, Condensed, Brought up to Date, Made Relevant, Programmed & All Those Good Things. (Illus.). 1977. pap. 19.95 (ISBN 0-918094-01-1); answer bk 1.00 (ISBN 0-918094-02-X). Bedous.

Hornsby, Ken. Is That the Library Speaking? LC 78-60465. 1978. 7.95 o.p. (ISBN 0-312-43728-5). St Martin.

--The Padded Sell. 176p. 1980. 9.95 o.p. (ISBN 0-312-59406-2). St Martin.

Hornsby, Roger, ed. see Wright, John.

Hornsey, et al. Mechanics & Materials: An Individualized Approach - Reference Manual-Study Guide. LC 76-18470. (Illus.). 1977. pap. 25.50 (ISBN 0-395-24993-7); solutions manual 7.50 (ISBN 0-395-24994-5). HM.

Hornsey, A. W., ed. see Mann, Thomas.

Hornstein, H. A., jt. ed. see Deutsch, M.

Hornstein, Harvey, jt. auth. see Heilman, Madeline E.

Hornstein, Lillian H., et al, eds. The Reader's Companion to World Literature. rev. ed. 1973. pap. 4.95 (ISBN 0-451-62177-8, ME2177, Ment). NAL.

Hornstein, Marvin. The Sky is Falling! Why Buildings Fall. LC 82-72602. (Illus.). 128p. (Orig.). 1982. pap. 7.95 (ISBN 0-89708-106-4). And Bks.

Hornstra, G. Dietary Fats, Prostanoids & Arterial Thrombosis. 1983. 48.00 (ISBN 90-247-2667-0, Pub. by Martinus Nijhoff Netherlands). Kluwer Boston.

Hornung, Clarence. Antique Automoblies. (Illus.). 1978. pap. 2.00 (ISBN 0-486-22742-1). Dover.

Hornung, Clarence P. Handbook of Early Advertising Art, 2 vols. 3rd rev. ed. Incl. Vol. 1. Pictorial. (Illus.). 288p. pap. 15.00 (ISBN 0-486-20122-8); Vol. 2. Typographical & Ornamental. (Illus.). 320p. pap. 15.00 (ISBN 0-486-20123-6). 1956. Dover.

--Old-Fashioned Christmas in Illustration & Decoration. (Orig.). 1970. pap. 5.00 (ISBN 0-486-22367-1). Dover.

Hornung, Erik & Baines, John, trs. from Ger. Conceptions of God in Ancient Eygpt: The One & the Many. LC 82-71602. (Illus.). 296p. 1982. 25.00x (ISBN 0-8014-1223-4). Cornell U Pr.

Hornung, William, jt. auth. see Hornbostel, Caleb.

Hornung, William J. Builder's Vestpocket Reference Book. 1956. 6.95 o.p. (ISBN 0-13-085951-6). P-H.

--Metric Architectural Construction Drafting & Design. (Illus.). 240p. 1981. text ed. 19.95 (ISBN 0-13-579367-X). P-H.

--Plumbing & Heating. (Illus.). 224p. 1982. 15.95 (ISBN 0-13-683920-7). P-H.

Horny, J. Differentialdiagnostisches Kompendium. 3rd ed. xvi, 260p. 1982. pap. 17.00 (ISBN 3-8055-3627-5). S Karger.

Horobin, G. W., ed. Experience with Abortion. LC 73-77171. (Illus.). 280p. 1973. 75.00 (ISBN 0-521-20240-X). Cambridge U Pr.

Horobin, Gordon, jt. ed. see Davis, Alan.

Horodniceanu, Michael & Cantilli, Edmund J. Transportation-System Safety. LC 78-7126. (Illus.). 240p. 1979. 22.95x (ISBN 0-669-02467-8). Lexington Bks.

Horonjeff, R. & McKelvey, F. X. Planning & Design of Airports. 3rd ed. 640p. 1983. 49.95 (ISBN 0-07-030367-3). McGraw.

Horonjeff, Robert. Planning & Design of Airports. 2nd ed. LC 75-2187. (Illus.). 460p. 1975. 49.50 (ISBN 0-07-030366-5, P&RB). McGraw.

Horosz, William, jt. auth. see Feaver, J. Clayton.

Horoszowski, Pawel. Economic Special-Opportunity Conduct & Crime. LC 78-24829. 222p. 1980. 27.95x (ISBN 0-669-02849-5). Lexington Bks.

Horovitz, Jacques H. Top Management Control in Europe. 210p. 1980. 35.00x (ISBN 0-312-80908-5). St Martin.

Horowitz, Al. Chess for Beginners: A Picture Guide. (Illus.). 1959. pap. 4.33i (ISBN 0-06-463223-7, EH 223, EH). B&N NY.

Horowitz, Blanche. A Family Planning Library Manual. 3rd ed. LC 75-39893. (Illus.). 1976. spiral bndg. 7.50 o.p. (ISBN 0-934586-01-2). Plan Parent.

Horowitz, Blanche, jt. auth. see Roberts, Gloria A.

Horowitz, Daniel, jt. auth. see Luttwak, Edward N.

Horowitz, David. Fight Back! And Don't Get Ripped off. LC 78-19498. 1979. 8.95i o.p. (ISBN 0-06-250390-1, HarpR). Har-Row.

Horowitz, David, jt. auth. see Collier, Peter.

Horowitz, David, et al. Counter Culture & Revolution. 1972. pap. text ed. 2.95x (ISBN 0-685-55615-8, 31553). Phila Bk Co.

Horowitz, Donald L. The Courts & Social Policy. LC 76-48944. 1977. 22.95 (ISBN 0-8157-3734-3); pap. 8.95 (ISBN 0-8157-3733-5). Brookings.

Horowitz, Edward. Word Detective. 192p. (Orig.). 1978. pap. 4.95 o.s.i. (ISBN 0-89104-253-9, A & W Visual Library). A & W Pubs.

--Words Come in Families. 320p. (Orig.). 1979. pap. 5.95 (ISBN 0-89104-254-7, A & W Visual Library). A & W Pubs.

Horowitz, Ellis. Fundamentals of Programming Languages. 1983. 23.95 (ISBN 0-914894-37-4). Computer Sci.

Horowitz, Ellis & Sahni, Sartaj. Fundamentals of Computer Algorithms. LC 78-14735. 1978. text ed. 28.95x (ISBN 0-914894-22-6). Computer Sci.

--Fundamentals of Data Structures. LC 76-15250. (Illus.). 1982. text ed. 24.95x (ISBN 0-914894-20-X). Computer Sci.

Horowitz, Ellis, ed. Programming Languages: A Grand Tour. 1983. 37.95 (ISBN 0-914894-67-6). Computer Sci.

Horowitz, Frances D. Review of Child Development Research, Vol. 4. 1975. 25.00x (ISBN 0-226-35353-2). U of Chicago Pr.

Horowitz, Frances D., ed. Early Developmental Hazards: Predictors & Precautions. LC 78-352. (AAAS Selected Symposium Ser.: No. 19). 1978. lib. bdg. 16.00 o.p. (ISBN 0-89158-084-0). Westview.

Horowitz, Gene. The Ladies of Levittown. LC 79-24074. 352p. 1980. 11.95 (ISBN 0-399-90076-4, Marek). Putnam Pub Group.

Horowitz, Harvey. Non-Profit Cultural Organizations. LC 79-88855. (Patents, Copyrights, Trademards, & Literary Property Course Habndbook Ser.: 1978-1979). 1979. pap. 20.00 o.p. (ISBN 0-686-59555-6, G4-3662). PLI.

Horowitz, I. A. & Reinfeld, Fred. First Book of Chess (Bobby Fischer Celebration Issue) (Illus.). 128p. 1973. 6.95 o.p. (ISBN 0-8069-4918-X); lib. bdg. 6.69 o.p. (ISBN 0-8069-4919-8). Sterling.

Horowitz, Inge & Windmueller, Ida. Windmueller Family Chronicle. 2nd, rev. ed. Windmueller, Ida & Grausz, Ilse, trs. from Ger. LC 81-52060. (Illus.). 304p. 1981. 25.00 (ISBN 0-9605242-0-7). Windmill Pr.

Horowitz, Ira. Introduction to Quantitative Business Analysis. 2nd ed. (Illus.). 352p. 1972. text ed. 22.00 o.p. (ISBN 0-07-030398-3); solutions to problems 2.75 o.p. (ISBN 0-07-030399-1). McGraw.

Horowitz, Irving L. Beyond Empire & Revolution: Militarization & Consolidation in the Third World. 350p. 1982. 19.95 (ISBN 0-19-502931-3). Oxford U Pr.

--Ideology & Utopia in the United States, 1956-1976. 1977. pap. text ed. 9.95 (ISBN 0-19-502107-X, 477, GB). Oxford U Pr.

--Philosophy, Science & the Sociology of Knowledge. LC 76-27756. 1976. Repr. of 1961 ed. lib. bdg. 18.50x (ISBN 0-8371-9051-7, HOPS). Greenwood.

--Winners & Losers: Society, Ideology, & Politics in America. (Duke Press Policy Studies). 350p. 1983. text ed. 30.00x (ISBN 0-8223-0495-3). Duke.

Horowitz, Irving L. & Dror, Yehezkel. Terrorism, Legitimacy, & Power: The Consequences of Political Violence. Crenshaw, Martha, ed. 228p. 1982. 17.95 (ISBN 0-8195-5081-7). Wesleyan U Pr.

Horowitz, Irving L. & Katz, James E. Social Science & Public Policy in the United States. LC 74-33034. (Illus.). 206p. 1975. 27.95 o.p. (ISBN 0-275-05310-5); pap. text ed. 12.95 o.p. (ISBN 0-275-89160-7). Praeger.

Horowitz, Irving L. & Lipset, Seymour M. Dialogues on American Politics. 1978. pap. 5.95 (ISBN 0-19-502450-8, GB547, GB). Oxford U Pr.

Horowitz, Irving L., ed. El Comunismo Cubano, 1959-1979. Lugones, Noevia & Miranda, Ruben, trs. 195p. (Span.). 1980. pap. text ed. 9.95x (ISBN 84-359-0192-0). Transaction Bks.

--Equity, Income, & Policy: Comparative Studies in Three Worlds of Development. LC 76-2904. (Special Studies). 1977. text ed. 35.95 o.p. (ISBN 0-275-56570-X). Praeger.

--New Sociology: Essays in Social Science & Social Theory in Honor of C. Wright Mills. (YA) (gr. 9 up). 1965. pap. 9.95 (ISBN 0-19-500722-0, GB). Oxford U Pr.

--Science, Sin & Scholarship: The Politics of Reverend Moon & the Unification Church. 312p. 1978. 16.50x (ISBN 0-262-08100-8); pap. 6.95x (ISBN 0-262-58042-X). MIT Pr.

Horowitz, Irving L., ed. see Mills, C. Wright.

Horowitz, Israel A. Chess Openings: Theory & Practice. 1964. 19.95 o.p. (ISBN 0-671-13390-X). S&S.

Horowitz, Joel. Air Quality Analysis for Urban Transportation Planning. (Transportation Studies Ser.). (Illus.). 352p. 1982. 55.00x (ISBN 0-262-08116-4). MIT Pr.

Horowitz, Joseph. Conversations with Arrau. LC 82-47817. 1982. 17.95 (ISBN 0-394-51390-8). Knopf.

Horowitz, June A. & Hughes, Cynthia B. Parenting Reassessed: A Nursing Perspective. (Illus.). 416p. 1982. 16.95 (ISBN 0-13-650085-4). P-H.

Horowitz, Leonard. Elements of Statistics for Psychology & Education. (Psychology & Human Development in Education Ser.). (Illus.). 448p. 1974. text ed. 27.50 (ISBN 0-07-030390-8); instructor's manual 2.95 (ISBN 0-07-030391-6). McGraw.

Horowitz, Mannie. Citizen Band Transceivers: Installation & Troubleshooting. (Illus.). 1978. ref. 19.95 (ISBN 0-87909-102-9). Reston.

--How to Design & Build Audio Amplifiers, Including Digital Circuits. 2nd ed. (Illus.). 350p. (Orig.). 1980. 15.95 o.p. (ISBN 0-8306-9729-2); pap. 10.95 (ISBN 0-8306-1206-8, 1206). TAB Bks.

--How to Troubleshoot & Repair Electronic Test Equipment. LC 74-81730. (Illus.). 252p. 1974. 9.95 o.p. (ISBN 0-8306-4680-9); pap. 6.95 (ISBN 0-8306-3680-3, 680). TAB Bks.

Horowitz, Mardi J. Psychosocial Function in Epilepsy: Rehabilitation After Surgical Treatment for Temporal Lobe Epilepsy. 196p. 1970. photocopy ed. spiral 19.50x (ISBN 0-398-00872-8). C C Thomas.

Horowitz, Martin, ed. The Glycoconjugates: Glyconproteins, Glycolipides & Proteoglycans. LC 77-4086. 392p. 1982. 49.50 ea. Vol. III: Pt. A: 392 pgs (ISBN 0-12-356103-5). Vol. IV: Pt. B: 82-45134: 384 pgs (ISBN 0-12-356104-3). subscription 42.00 (ISBN 0-686-81649-8). Acad Pr.

Horowitz, Michael, ed. see Huxley, Aldous.

Horowitz, Michael, jt. ed. see Palmer, Cynthia.

Horowitz, Morris A., jt. auth. see Goldstein, Harold M.

Horowitz, Paul & Hill, Winfield. The Art of Electronics. LC 79-27170. (Illus.). 544p. 1980. 27.95 (ISBN 0-521-23151-5). Cambridge U Pr.

Horowitz, Paul & Robinson, Ian. Laboratory Manual for the Art of Electronics. (Illus.). 144p. 1981. pap. 9.95 (ISBN 0-521-28510-0). Cambridge U Pr.

Horowitz, Ruth. Honor & the American Dream: Culture & Social Identity in a Chicano Community. (Crime, Law & Deviance Ser.). 300p. 1983. 24.00 (ISBN 0-8135-0966-1); pap. 12.00 (ISBN 0-8135-0991-2). Rutgers U Pr.

Horowitz, S. H. Protective Relaying for Power Systems. LC 80-21776. 575p. 1981. 49.95 (ISBN 0-471-08968-0, Pub. by Wiley-Interscience); pap. 32.50 (ISBN 0-471-08967-2). Wiley.

Horowitz, Shel, ed. Breathe! An Anti-Smoking Anthology. (Illus.). 64p. 1981. pap. 3.00 (ISBN 0-686-36233-0). Warthog Pr.

Horr, David A., ed. see Berthrong, Donald J.

Horr, David A., ed. see Cline, Howard F.

Horr, David A., ed. see Doster, James F.

Horr, David A., ed. see Ewers, John C.

Horr, David A., ed. see Fairbanks, Charles H.

Horr, David A., ed. see Jablow, Joseph.

Horr, David A., ed. see Jicarilla Apache Tribe.

Horr, David A., ed. see Kroeber, Alfred L.

Horr, David A., ed. see Ray, Verne F., et al.

Horr, David A., ed. see Smith, G. Hubert.

Horr, David A., ed. see Williams, Stephen.

Horr, Norton T., jt. auth. see Jessel, Frederic.

Horr, Norton T. see Jessel, Frederic & Horr, Norton T.

Horrell, C. W., et al. Land Between the Rivers: The Southern Illinois Country. LC 71-156777. (Illus.). 207p. 1973. 24.95 (ISBN 0-8093-0566-6); pap. 16.95 (ISBN 0-8093-1119-4). S Ill U Pr.

Horribin, David F., ed. see Flodin, Nestor W.

Horrigan, P. & Kelly, J. Challenging Experiments in Chemistry. rev. ed. 1982. pap. 9.95 (ISBN 0-941512-00-2). Marshland Pub.

Horrigan, Philip A. The Challenge of Chemistry. rev. ed. 1980. pap. text ed. 13.95 (ISBN 0-941512-01-0). Marshland Pub.

Horrobin, D., ed. see Oparil, Suzanne & Katholi, Richard.

Horrobin, D., ed. see Ziegler, Thomas W.

Horrobin, D. F., jt. auth. see Smith, Donald F.

Horrobin, D. F., ed. Hormones, Drugs & Aggression. (Hormone Research Review Ser.: Vol. 3). 173p. 1980. Repr. of 1979 ed. 24.95 o.p. (ISBN 0-87705-959-4). Human Sci Pr.

Horrobin, D. F., ed. see Adachi, M., et al.

Horrobin, D. F., ed. see Augusteyn, R. C., et al.

Horrobin, D. F., ed. see Bremner, W. Fraser.

Horrobin, D. F., ed. see Briggs, Michael & Briggs, Maxine.

Horrobin, D. F., ed. see Carmichael, Stephen.

Horrobin, D. F., ed. see Chiodini, P. G. & Liuzzi, A.

Horrobin, D. F., ed. see Damjanov, Ivan.

Horrobin, D. F., ed. see Flodin, N. W.

Horrobin, D. F., ed. see Forsling, Mary.

Horrobin, D. F., ed. see Forsling, Mary L.

Horrobin, D. F., ed. see Fulkerson, W. J.

Horrobin, D. F., ed. see Grahame, R.

Horrobin, D. F., ed. see Hamblin, T. J.

Horrobin, D. F., ed. see Hutchinson, J. S.

Horrobin, D. F., ed. see Katzeff, I. E. & Edwards, H.

Horrobin, D. F., ed. see Lambert, Michael J.

Horrobin, D. F., ed. see McQuillan, Mary T.

Horrobin, D. F., ed. see Oparil, S., et al.

Horrobin, D. F., ed. see Oparil, Suzanne, et al.

Horrobin, D. F., ed. see Oparil, Suzanne & Katholi, Richard.

Horrobin, D. F., ed. see Reiter, Russel J.

Horrobin, D. F., ed. see Samal, Babrubahan.

Horrobin, D. F., ed. see Skrabanek, Petr & Powell, David.

Horrobin, D. F., ed. see Taylor, Clive R.

Horrobin, D. F., ed. see Wallach, Donald F.

Horrobin, D. F., ed. see Watkins, Wayne.

Horrobin, D. F., ed. see Wormsley, K. G.

Horrobin, David. Medical Hubris: A Reply to Ivan Illich. LC 80-66836. 146p. 1980. 9.95 (ISBN 0-88831-080-3); pap. 6.95 (ISBN 0-88831-086-2). Eden Pr.

--Prostaglandins: Physiology, Pharmacology & Clinical Signifiance. 1978. 21.60 (ISBN 0-88831-032-3). Eden Pr.

Horrobin, David, ed. see Reiter, Russel J.

Horrobin, David F. Medical Hubris: A Reply to Ivan Illich. 1977. 9.00 o.p. (ISBN 0-88831-001-3). Eden Pr.

--Prolactin, Vol. 2. (Annual Research Reviews Ser.). 1974. 19.20 (ISBN 0-85200-120-7). Eden Pr.

--Prolactin, Vol. 4. (Annual Research Reviews Ser.). 1976. 24.00 (ISBN 0-904406-47-4). Eden Pr.

--Prolactin, Vol. 5. LC 77-369577. (Annual Research Reviews Ser.). 1977. 24.00 (ISBN 0-88831-009-9). Eden Pr.

--Prolactin, Vol. 6. (Annual Research Reviews Ser.). 1979. 21.60 (ISBN 0-88831-041-2). Eden Pr.

--Prolactin, Vol. 7. LC 77-369577. (Annual Research Reviews Ser.). 126p. 1980. 18.00 (ISBN 0-88831-069-2). Eden Pr.

Horrobin, David F., ed. see Augusteyn, R. C. & Collin, H. B.

Horrobin, David F., ed. see Carmichael, Stephen W.

Horrobin, David F., ed. see Fulkerson, William J.

Horrobin, David F., ed. see Lamberts, Steven W. & MacLeod, Robert M.

Horrobin, David F., ed. see Smith, Cedric M.

Horrobin, David F., ed. see Watkins, Wayne B.

Horrobin, F., ed. see Reiter, Russel J.

Horrobin, Peter. Constructional Mathematics, Vol. 1. 1970. pap. 7.00 (ISBN 0-08-006890-1). Pergamon.

Horroblin, David F., jt. auth. see Hume, Wilfred.

Horrocho, Roger & Tremewan, Phillip. On Film. (Illus.). 72p. 1980. pap. 6.95 (ISBN 0-86863-356-9, Pub. by Heinemann Pubs New Zealands). Intl Schol Bk Serv.

Horrocks, David, jt. auth. see Wilkinson, Barry.

Horrocks, John E. The Psychology of Adolescence. 4th ed. LC 75-26086. (Illus.). 608p. 1976. text ed. 24.95 o.p. (ISBN 0-395-21918-3); test items 2.05 o.p. (ISBN 0-395-21922-1). HM.

Horrow, Richard B. Sports Violence: The Interaction Between Private Lawmaking & the Criminal Law. LC 80-65053. (Scholarly Monographs). 286p. 1980. 27.50 o.p. (ISBN 0-8408-0500-4); pap. 17.50 o.p. (ISBN 0-686-63392-X). Carrollton Pr.

Horry, Peter. Parson Weem's Life of Francis Marion. LC 76-21439. 1976. 15.00 (ISBN 0-937684-04-X). Tradd St Pr.

Horsburgh, E. M., ed. Handbook of the Napier Tercentary Celebration or Modern Instruments & Methods of Calculation. (The Charles Babbage Institute Reprint Series for the History of Computing: Vol. 3). (Illus.). 1982. Repr. of 1914 ed. write for info. ltd. ed. (ISBN 0-938228-10-2). Tomash Pubs.

Horsburgh, Peg. Living Light: Exploring Bioluminescence. LC 78-1684. (Illus.). 96p. (gr. 4-6). 1978. PLB 7.29 o.p. (ISBN 0-671-32849-2). Messner.

Horsfall, Bruce. Bluebirds Seven. 1978. 9.95X (ISBN 0-931686-03-2). Nature Bks Pubs.

Horsfall, J. G. & Cowling, E. R., eds. Plant Disease: An Advanced Treatise, How Pathogens Induce Disease, Vol. 4. 1979. 50.00 (ISBN 0-12-356404-2); 42.50 (ISBN 0-686-85545-0). Acad Pr.

Horsfall, James G. & Cowling, Ellis B., eds. Plant Disease: An Advanced Treatise, Vol. 3: How Plants Suffer from Disease. 1979. 50.00 (ISBN 0-12-356403-4); 42.00 (ISBN 0-686-66289-X). Acad Pr.

Horsfield, John. The Art of Leadership in War: The Royal Navy from the Age of Nelson to the End of World War II. LC 79-54059. (Contributions in Military History: No. 21). (Illus.). xiv, 240p. 1980. lib. bdg. 27.50 (ISBN 0-313-20919-7, HLE/). Greenwood.

Horsky, Charles A. The Washington Lawyer: A Series of Lectures Delivered Under the Auspices of the Julius Rosenthal Foundation at Northwestern University School of Law in April, 1952. LC 81-646. viii, 179p. 1981. Repr. of 1952 ed. lib. bdg. 20.50x (ISBN 0-313-22736-5, HOWL). Greenwood.

Horsley, Gaye. Commercial Foods Exposed! 1975. 7.95 (ISBN 0-89036-043-X); pap. 5.95 (ISBN 0-89036-131-2). Hawkes Pub Inc.

Horsley, J. A., jt. auth. see Richards, W. G.

Horsley, Jo Anne. Using Research to Improve Nursing Practice: A Guide. (Monographs in Applied Nursing Ser.). Date not set. pap. price not set (ISBN 0-8089-1510-X). Grune.

Horsley, Joanne, ed. see C.U.R.N. Project, Michigan Nurses Association.

Horsman, Reginald. The Frontier in the Formative Years, 1783-1815. LC 76-94404. (Histories of the American Frontier Ser). (Illus.). 253p. 1979. pap. 9.95x (ISBN 0-8263-0313-7). U of NM pr.

Horst. Sixth & Seventh Books of Moses. 3.95x (ISBN 0-685-22112-1). Wehman.

Horst, J. F. Ter see Ter Horst, J. F.

Horst, Robert ter see Ter Horst, Robert.

Horst, Thomas. At Home Abroad: A Study of Domestic & Foreign Operations of the American Food-Processing Industry. LC 73-18264. 120p. 1974. prof ref 17.50 (ISBN 0-88410-259-9). Ballinger Pub.

Horst, W., ed. Frontiers of Nuclear Medicine. LC 71-152727. (Illus.). 1971. 59.00 (ISBN 0-387-09895-X). Springer-Verlag.

Horswell, Jane. Bronze Sculpture of les Animaliers. (Illus.). 1971. 62.50 (ISBN 0-902028-13-8). Apollo.

Hort, A. F., jt. auth. see Hort, F. J.

Hort, Erasmus. The Bible Book: Resources for Reading the New Testament. 172p. 1983. 14.95 (ISBN 0-8245-0556-5); pap. 7.95 (ISBN 0-8245-0557-3). Crossroad NY.

Hort, F. J. & Hort, A. F. Expository & Exegetical Studies. 1980. 29.50 (ISBN 0-86524-021-3, 7103). Klock & Klock.

Horton, Arthur M., Jr., ed. Mental Health Interventions for the Aging: Psychotherapeutic Treatment Approaches. 224p. 1982. 29.95x (ISBN 0-686-86219-8). J F Bergin.

Horton, Carolyn. Cleaning & Preserving Bindings & Related Materials. 2nd ed. LC 76-95200. (LTP Publication: No. 16). (Illus.). 1969. pap. 10.00 (ISBN 0-8389-3008-5). ALA.

Horton, Casey. The Amazing Fact Book of Animals, Vol. 7. LC 8-80667. (Illus.). 32p. (Orig.). (gr. 4 up). 1980. 5.95 (ISBN 0-86550-012-6); PLB 8.95 (ISBN 0-686-96977-4); pap. 2.95 (ISBN 0-86550-013-4). A & P Bks.

--The Amazing Fact Book of Insects, Vol. 8. LC 80-80617. (Illus.). 32p. (Orig.). (gr. 4 up). 1980. 5.95 (ISBN 0-86550-014-2); PLB 8.95 (ISBN 0-686-96979-0); pap. 2.95 (ISBN 0-86550-015-0). A & P Bks.

--The Amazing Fact Book of Machines. LC 80-80666. (Illus.). 32p. (Orig.). (gr. 4 up). 1980. 5.85 (ISBN 0-86550-010-X); PLB 8.95 (ISBN 0-686-96974-X); pap. 2.95 (ISBN 0-86550-011-8). A & P Bks.

Horton, Catherine. A Closer Look at Grasslands. LC 77-10762. (Closer Look at Ser.). (Illus.). (gr. 4 up). 1979. PLB 9.40 s&l (ISBN 0-531-03411-9, Gloucester Pr). Watts.

--Grasslands & People. LC 82-50393. (Nature's Landscape Ser.). PLB 15.96 (ISBN 0-382-06672-3). Silver.

Horton, Craig, jt. ed. see Mencke, Claire.

Horton, D., jt. auth. see Pigman, W.

Horton, D., jt. ed. see Tipson, Stuart.

Horton, David L. & Turnage, Thomas W. Human Learning. (P-H Series in Experimental Psychology). (Illus.). 464p. 1976. Ref. Ed. 23.95 (ISBN 0-13-445312-3). P-H.

Horton, Derek & Tipson, Stuart, eds. Advances in Carbohydrate Chemistry & Biochemistry, Vol. 37. LC 45-11351. 1980. 54.50 (ISBN 0-12-007237-8); lib. ed. 69.00 (ISBN 0-12-007286-6); microfiche ed. 37.50 (ISBN 0-12-007287-4). Acad Pr.

Horton, Derek, jt. ed. see Pigman, Ward.

Horton, Derek, jt. ed. see Tipson, R. Stuart.

Horton, F. L. The Melchizedek Tradition. LC 75-32479. (Society for New Testament Studies Monographs: No. 30). 220p. 1976. 39.50 (ISBN 0-521-21014-3). Cambridge U Pr.

Horton, Forest W., Jr. Five Easy Steps to IRM. 75p. 1983. 29.95 (ISBN 0-9606408-2-7). Info Mgmt Pr.

--The Information Management Workbook. (Illus.). 325p. 1982. 195.00 (ISBN 0-9606408-0-0). Info Mgmt Pr.

Horton, Forest W., Jr., ed. Understanding U. S. Information Policy, 4 vols. Incl. Vol. I. The Resources for the Information Economy. LC 82-81853 (ISBN 0-942774-02-7); Vol. II. The Participants in the Information Marketplace. LC 82-81854 (ISBN 0-942774-03-5); Vol. III. The Assets of the Information Society. LC 82-81855 (ISBN 0-942774-04-3); The Information Policy Primer. LC 82-81852. 25.00 (ISBN 0-942774-01-9); with purchase of one or more volumes free. 1982. Set. 99.50 (ISBN 0-942774-07-8); 49.50 ea., any two 74.50 (ISBN 0-942774-08-6). Info Indus.

Horton, Frank E., jt. auth. see Berry, Brian J.

Horton, G. & Maradudin, A., eds. Dynamical Properties of Solids, Vol. 3: Metals, Superconductors, Magnetic Materials & Liquids. 1980. 68.00 (ISBN 0-444-85314-6). Elsevier.

--Dynamical Properties of Solids, Vol. 4: Disordered Solids, Optical Properties. 1980. 85.00 (ISBN 0-444-85315-4). Elsevier.

Horton, G. K. & Maradudin, A. A. Dynamical Properties of Solids, Vol. 1 & 2: Crystalline Solids, 2 vols. 1974-76. Vol. 1, Fundamentals. 136.25 (ISBN 0-444-10536-0, North-Holland); Vol. 2, Applications. 132.00 (ISBN 0-444-10970-6). Elsevier.

Horton, H. Mack, tr. see Fujioka, Michio.

Horton, Henry P., tr. see Lombroso, Cesare.

Horton, J. Development & Differentiation of Vertebrate Lymphocytes. (Developments in Immunology Ser.: Vol. 8). 1980. 55.50 (ISBN 0-444-80195-2). Elsevier.

Horton, J. D., jt. ed. see Solomon, J. B.

Horton, John. Scandinavian Music: A Short History. LC 73-7673. (Illus.). 180p. 1975. Repr. of 1963 ed. lib. bdg. 16.00x (ISBN 0-8371-6944-5, HOSM). Greenwood.

Horton, John B. Not Without Struggle. 1978. 6.95 o.p. (ISBN 0-533-03649-6). Vantage.

Horton, John E., et al, eds. Mechanisms of Localized Bone Loss. (Illus.). 454p. 1978. pap. 18.00 (ISBN 0-917000-03-X). IRL Pr.

Horton, John J. Yugoslavia. (World Bibliography Ser.: No. 1). 194p. 1978. text ed. 25.25 o.p. (ISBN 0-903450-09-7). ABC-Clio.

Horton, John T. James Kent: A Study in Conservatism, 1763-1847. LC 76-84189. (American Scene, Comments & Commentators Ser.). 1969. Repr. of 1939 ed. lib. bdg. 45.00 (ISBN 0-306-71502-3). Da Capo.

Horton, Lowell & Horton, Phyllis, eds. Teacher Education: Trends, Issues, Innovations. 1974 ed. LC 73-90606. pap. text ed. 6.95x (ISBN 0-8134-1626-4, 1626). Interstate.

Horton, Lucy. Country Commune Cooking. (Illus.). 224p. 1972. pap. 4.95 o.p. (ISBN 0-698-10457-9, Coward). Putnam Pub Group.

Horton, M. H. French Defence 1. (Chess Player Ser.). 1977. pap. 5.95 (ISBN 0-7134-2921-6, H-1156). Hippocrene Bks.

Horton, Marilee. Dear Momma, Please Don't Die. 1982. pap. 1.95 (ISBN 0-451-11462-0, AJ1462, Sig). NAL.

Horton, Paul B. & Horton, Robert L. Introductory Sociology. 3rd ed. (Plaid Ser.). 1982. pap. 7.95 (ISBN 0-87094-345-6). Dow Jones-Irwin.

--Plaid for Introductory Sociology. 1977. pap. 5.95 o.p. (ISBN 0-256-01987-8, 17-0302-02). Dow Jones-Irwin.

Horton, Paul B. & Hunt, Chester L. Sociology. 5th ed. (Illus.). 1979. text ed. 23.95 (ISBN 0-07-030430-0); instrs'. manual 15.00 (ISBN 0-07-030431-9); test file 20.00 (ISBN 0-07-030433-5); study guide 9.95 (ISBN 0-07-030432-7). McGraw.

--Sociology. 3rd ed. (Illus.). 560p. 1972. text ed. 19.95 (ISBN 0-07-030425-4, C); instructor's manual by E. P. Robin 4.95 (ISBN 0-07-053178-1). McGraw.

--Sociology. 4th ed. 1975. text ed. 21.95 (ISBN 0-07-030426-2, C). instr's manual o.p. 5.95 (ISBN 0-07-030427-0). McGraw.

Horton, Paul B. & Leslie, Gerald R. The Sociology of Social Problems. 7th ed. (Illus.). 672p. 1981. text ed. 22.95 (ISBN 0-13-821702-5). P-H.

Horton, Phyllis, jt. ed. see Horton, Lowell.

Horton, Raymond, jt. ed. see Brcher, Charles.

Horton, Raymond D. & Brecher, Charles, eds. Setting Municipal Priorities, 1980. LC 79-88261. 224p. Date not set. price not set o.p. Allanheld & Schram.

Horton, Raymond D., jt. ed. see Brecher, Charles.

Horton, Raymond L. The General Linear Model: Data Analysis in the Social & Behavioral Sciences. (Illus.). 1978. text ed. 37.50x (ISBN 0-07-030418-1). McGraw.

Horton, Robert L., jt. auth. see Horton, Paul B.

Horton, Rod W. & Edwards, Herbert W. Backgrounds of American Literary Thought. 3rd ed. 1974. pap. 16.95 (ISBN 0-13-056291-2). P-H.

Horton, Russell M. Lincoln Steffens. LC 74-3089. (World Leaders Ser: No. 35). 168p. 1974. lib. bdg. 9.95 o.p. (ISBN 0-8057-3721-9, Twayne). G K Hall.

Horton, Stanley M. Desire Spiritual Gifts - Earnestly. (Charismatic Bks.). 1972. pap. 0.69 o.p. (ISBN 0-88243-921-9, 02-0921). Gospel Pub.

Horton, Susan R. Thinking Through Writing. LC 81-18628. (Illus.). 217p. 1982. 25.00 (ISBN 0-686-97521-9); pap. 8.95 (ISBN 0-686-97522-7). Johns Hopkins.

Horton, Tom. Superspan. (Illus.). 96p. (Orig.). 1983. pap. 8.95 (ISBN 0-87701-277-6). Chronicle Bks.

Horton, Tom, jt. auth. see Gentry, Curt.

Horton, Wendell, et al. Long Time Predicton in Dynamics. 464p. 1982. 85.00 o.s.i. (ISBN 0-471-86447-1, Pub. by Wiley-Interscience). Wiley.

Horvat, Branko. The Political Economy of Socialism: A Marxist View. LC 81-9430. 660p. 1982. 37.50 (ISBN 0-87332-184-7). M E Sharpe.

--Towards a Theory of Planned Economy. LC 67-30957. 1964. 22.50 (ISBN 0-87332-019-0). M E Sharpe.

--The Yugoslav Economic System: The First Labor-Managed Economy in the Making. LC 75-46111. 1976. 20.00 o.p. (ISBN 0-87332-074-3); pap. 9.95 (ISBN 0-87332-175-8). M E Sharpe.

Horvat, Branko, et al, eds. Self-Governing Socialism: A Reader, 2 vols. Incl. Vol. 1. 491p. text ed. 30.50 (ISBN 0-87332-050-6); pap. 13.95 (ISBN 0-87332-060-3); Vol. 2. 329p. text ed. 27.50 (ISBN 0-87332-061-1); pap. 11.95 (ISBN 0-87332-062-X). LC 73-92805. 1975. Set (ISBN 0-87332-048-4). M E Sharpe.

Horvat, Paul. Statically Indeterminate Structures: Their Analysis & Design. (Illus.). 1953. 26.95 o.p. (ISBN 0-471-10405-1). Wiley.

Horvath, Csaba, ed. High-Performance Liquid Chromatography: Advances & Perspectives, Vol. 3. 220p. 1983. price not set (ISBN 0-12-312203-1). Acad Pr.

Horvath, E. Szivarvany Konyvek, No. 2. 1982. 9.50 (ISBN 0-936398-09-4). Framo Pub.

Horvath, K., tr. see Szejtli, J.

Horvath, Odon Von see Von Horvath, Odon.

Horvath, Patricia. Nursing Care of the Cardiac Surgical Patient. (Series in Critical Care Nursing). (Illus.). 200p. (Orig.). pap. text ed. 12.95. Wiley.

Horvitz, Leslie & Gerhard, H. Harris. The Compton Effect. 1980. pap. 2.25 o.p. (ISBN 0-451-09299-6, E9299, Sig). NAL.

Horvitz, P. Monetary Policy & the Financial System. 4th ed. 1979. 22.95 (ISBN 0-13-599944-8). P-H.

Horwath, Ernest B., et al. Hotel Accounting. 4th ed. LC 77-79169. 1978. 49.95 (ISBN 0-471-07247-8, Pub. by Wiley-Interscience). Wiley.

Horwege, Richard A., ed. see Bringas, Ernie.

Horwege, Richard A., ed. see Masson, Francois.

Horwege, Richard A., ed. see Schwartz, William F.

Horwich, George & Mitchell, Edward J., eds. Policies for Coping with Oil Supply Disruptions. 1982. 16.95 (ISBN 0-8447-2241-3); pap. 8.95 (ISBN 0-8447-2240-5). Am Enterprise.

Horwich, Kathleen, jt. auth. see Fishman, Meryl.

Horwich, Paul. Probability & Evidence. LC 81-18144. (Cambridge Studies in Philosophy). 160p. 1982. 24.50 (ISBN 0-521-23758-0). Cambridge U Pr.

Horwitz, Brewster, tr. see Osaragi, Jiro.

Horwitz, E., ed. Ways of Wildlife. 157p. 1977. pap. 2.95 o.p. (ISBN 0-590-09617-6). Wildlife Soc.

Horwitz, Elinor L. Capital Punishment, U. S. A. LC 72-13135. (Illus.). 160p. (gr. 7 up). 1973. 10.53i (ISBN 0-397-31465-5, JBL-J). Har-Row.

--Communes in America: The Place Just Right. LC 72-3685. 160p. (gr. 7 up). 1972. 10.53i (ISBN 0-397-31437-X, JBL-J). Har-Row.

--Mountain People, Mountain Crafts. LC 73-19665. (Illus.). 144p. 1974. 10.53i (ISBN 0-397-31498-1, JBL-J); pap. 3.95 (ISBN 0-397-31499-X). Har-Row.

--When the Sky Is Like Lace. LC 75-9664. 32p. (gr. k-2). 1975. 10.53i (ISBN 0-397-31550-3, HarpJ). Har-Row.

Horwitz, Henry. Welding: Principles & Practice. LC 77-76341. (Illus.). 1979. text ed. 25.95 (ISBN 0-395-24473-0); instr's. manual 1.25 (ISBN 0-395-24474-9). HM.

Horwitz, John J. Team Practice & the Specialist: An Introduction to Interdisciplinary Teamwork. 172p. 1970. 12.75x (ISBN 0-398-00873-6). C C Thomas.

Horwitz, Joshua. Doll Hospital. LC 82-14508. (Illus.). 56p. (gr. 3-7). 1983. 10.95 (ISBN 0-394-85332-6); PLB 10.99 (ISBN 0-394-95332-0). Pantheon.

Horwitz, Norman H. Post-Operative Complications in Neurosurgical Practice: Recognition, Prevention & Management. LC 66-28163. 440p. 1973. Repr. of 1967 ed. 24.50 o.p. (ISBN 0-88275-124-7). Krieger.

Horwitz, Norman H. & Rizzoli, Hugo V. Post Operative Complications of Intracranial Neurosurgery. (Illus.). 456p. 1982. lib. bdg. 55.00 (ISBN 0-683-04158-4). Williams & Wilkins.

Horwitz, Robert H. Moral Foundations of the American Republic. 3rd ed. LC 79-20387. 275p. 1982. 15.00x (ISBN 0-8139-0853-1); pap. 3.95x (ISBN 0-8139-0854-X). U Pr of Va.

Horwitz, Robert H., ed. The Moral Foundations of the American Republic. 2nd ed. LC 76-52991. (Kenyon Public Affairs Forum). 275p. 1982. 15.00x (ISBN 0-8139-0723-3); pap. 3.95 (ISBN 0-8139-0724-1). U Pr of Va.

Horwitz, Rudy J., jt. ed. see Fields, Francis R.

Horwitz, Steven N., jt. auth. see Frost, Phillip.

Horwitz, Sylvia L. Toulouse-Lautrec: His World. LC 73-5484. (Illus.). 208p. (gr. 7 up). 1973. PLB 9.89 o.p. (ISBN 0-06-022593-9, HarpJ). Har-Row.

Horwood, R. Networks. 96p. 1976. pap. 6.50x o.s.i. (ISBN 0-471-14974-8); tchrs.' manual 6.75x o.s.i. (ISBN 0-471-01481-8). Wiley.

Horwood, William. Duncton Wood. LC 79-23235. 1980. 12.95 (ISBN 0-07-030434-3). McGraw.

Hosack, John. On the Rise & Growth of the Law of Nations, as Established by General Usage & by Treaties, from the Earliest Time to the Treaty of Utrecht. xii, 394p. 1982. Repr. of 1882 ed. lib. bdg. 35.00x (ISBN 0-8377-0647-5). Rothman.

Hosch, Charles R. Official Guide to World Proof Coins. rev. 2nd ed. LC 73-94075. (Collector's Ser.). (Illus.). 1975. pap. 10.50 o.p. (ISBN 0-87637-259-0). Hse of Collectibles.

Hoseh, M. Russian-English Dictionary of Chemical Technology. 540p. 1964. 27.00 o.p. (ISBN 0-442-15553-0, Pub. by Van Nos Reinhold). Krieger.

Hosek, Chaviva, jt. ed. see Cook, Eleanor.

Hosek, William R. & Zahn, Frank. Monetary Theory, Policy & Financial Markets. (Illus.). 1977. text ed. 26.95 (ISBN 0-07-030436-X, C); instructor's manual 7.95 (ISBN 0-07-030437-8). McGraw.

Hoselitz, Bert F., jt. ed. see Lambert, Richard D.

Hosen, Harris. Clinical Allergy Based on Provocative Testing. LC 77-82572. 1978. 10.00 o.p. (ISBN 0-682-48940-9, University). Exposition.

Hosford, Bowen. Making Your Medical Decisions: Your Rights & Harsh Choices Today. LC 81-40464. 250p. 1982. 12.95 (ISBN 0-8044-5502-3). Ungar.

Hosford, Helga. The German Teacher's Companion: Development & Structure of the German Language. 352p. 1982. pap. text ed. 16.95 (ISBN 0-88377-276-0); pap. text ed. 14.95 wkbk & key (ISBN 0-686-83027-X). Newbury Hse.

Hosford, WIlliam F., jt. auth. see Caddell, Robert M.

Hosh, Koi, jt. auth. see Coffer, William E.

Hoshino, K. Encyclopedic Dictionary of Architecture & Building Construction. 535p. (Eng. & Japanese.). 1978. leatherette 75.00 (ISBN 0-686-92226-3, M-9332). French & Eur.

Hoshizaki, M. K. Teaching Mentally Retarded Children Through Music. (Illus.). 198p. 1982. 16.75x (ISBN 0-398-04739-1). C C Thomas.

Hosie, Kenneth, jt. auth. see Bullock, Spencer M.

Hosier, Helen K. It Feels Good to Forgive. ev. ed. 176p. 1980. pap. 3.95 o.p. (ISBN 0-89081-251-9). Harvest Hse.

--Suicide: A Cry for Help. LC 78-65124. 1979. pap. 2.95 o.p. (ISBN 0-89081-178-4, 1784). Harvest Hse.

Hosker, Rayford P., Jr. see Hanna, Steven R., et al.

Hoskin. William Herschel & the Construction of the Heavens. 1970. 7.80 (ISBN 0-444-19662-5). Elsevier.
Hosking, Eric. A Passion for Birds: Fifty Years of Photographing Wildlife. LC 79-10943. 1979. 25.00 o.p. (ISBN 0-698-11002-1, Coward). Putnam Pub Group.
Hosking, G. A. The Russian Constitutional Experiment Government of Duma, 1907-14. LC 72-87181. (Soviet & East European Studies). 288p. 1973. 37.50 (ISBN 0-521-20041-5). Cambridge U Pr.
Hosking, Gwilym. An Introduction to Pediatric Neurology. (Illus.). 252p. 1982. 26.50 (ISBN 0-571-11848-8); pap. 10.95 (ISBN 0-571-11849-6). Faber & Faber.
Hoskins, Betty see Holmes, Helen B., et al.
Hoskins, Brian & Pearce, Robert, eds. Large-Scale Dynamical Processes in the Atmosphere. Date not set. price not set (ISBN 0-12-356680-0). Acad Pr.
Hoskins, J. M. Virological Procedures. 1967. 19.95 o.p. (ISBN 0-407-79000-4). Butterworth.
Hoskins, Janina W., ed. Early & Rare Polonica of the 15th-17th Centuries in American Libraries: A Bibliographic Survey. 1973. lib. bdg. 24.00 (ISBN 0-8161-1002-6, Hall Reference). G K Hall.
Hoskins, Linus A. The New International Economic Order: A Bibliographic Handbook. LC 82-17640. 122p. (Orig.). 1983. lib. bdg. 17.75 (ISBN 0-8191-2789-2); pap. text ed. 7.75 (ISBN 0-8191-2790-6). U Pr of Amer.
Hoskins, Richard. Westward to Arthur. 1977. pap. 6.95 (ISBN 0-906158-00-1). Pendragon Hse.
Hoskins, Robert. The Fury Bombs. (Phoenix Force Ser.). 192p. 1983. pap. 1.95 (ISBN 0-373-61305-9, Pub. by Worldwide). Harlequin Bks.
Hoskins, Robert, et al. Survival Run. 256p. (Orig.). 1980. pap. 2.25 o.p. (ISBN 0-523-40712-2). Pinnacle Bks.
Hoskins, Robert L. Black Administrators in Higher Education: Conditions & Perceptions. LC 78-19740. 1978. 27.95 o.p. (ISBN 0-03-046611-3). Praeger.
Hoskyns, A. H. & Buckley, P. M. Basic Electronic Circuits. 168p. 1980. pap. 15.95x (ISBN 0-419-11420-3, Pub. by E & FN Spon England). Methuen Inc.
Hosler, Bellamy. Changing Aesthetic Views of Instrumental Music in 18th Century Germany. Buelow, George, ed. LC 81-4754. (Studies in Musicology: No. 42). 310p. 1981. 44.95 (ISBN 0-8357-1172-2, Pub. by UMI Res Pr). Univ Microfilms.
Hosler, Jay, jt. auth. see Gonick, Larry.
Hosler, R. J., jt. auth. see Lloyd, Alan C.
Hosler, Ray, jt. auth. see Sisson, Mark.
Hosler, Russell J., jt. auth. see Lloyd, Alan C.
Hosler, Russell J., et al. Programmed Gregg Shorthand. (Diamond Jubilee Ser). (Experimental Ed). 1969. text ed. 23.00 (ISBN 0-07-030440-8, G); instructor's handbk 5.50 (ISBN 0-07-030442-4). tests free. McGraw.
Hosler, Virginia N., jt. auth. see Fadely, Jack L.
Hosmer, G. L., jt. auth. see Breed, C. B.
Hosmer, James K. The Life of Thomas Hutchinson: Royal Governor of the Province of Massachusetts Bay. LC 70-124926. (American Scene Ser). (Illus.). 454p. 1972. Repr. of 1896 ed. lib. bdg. 55.00 (ISBN 0-306-71038-2). Da Capo.
Hosmer, La Rue T. Strategic Management: Text & Cases on Business Policy. (Illus.). 736p. 1982. 24.95 (ISBN 0-13-851063-6). P-H.
Hosmer, Rachel & Jones, Alan. Living in the Spirit. (Church's Teaching Ser.: Vol. 7). 272p. 1979. 5.95 (ISBN 0-8164-0424-0); pap. 3.95 (ISBN 0-8164-2220-6). Seabury.
Hosmer, Steven T. & Wolfe, Thomas W. Soviet Policy & Practice Towards Third-World Conflicts. 336p. 1982. 31.95x (ISBN 0-669-06054-2). Lexington Bks.
Hospers, John. Introduction to Philosophical Analysis. 2nd ed. 1967. lib. bdg. 22.95 (ISBN 0-13-491688-3). P-H.
--Understanding the Arts. (Illus.). 416p. 1982. pap. 17.95 ref. ed. (ISBN 0-13-935965-6). P-H.
Hospers, John, jt. ed. see Sellars, Wilfrid.
Hospital Financial Management Association. Cost Effectiveness Notebook. 1978. loose leaf 7.50 (ISBN 0-930228-10-3). Healthcare Fin Man Assn.
--Cost Effectiveness Notebook: Nineteen Eighty Update. 1980. write for info. (ISBN 0-930228-14-6). Healthcare Fin Man Assn.
--Cost Effectiveness Notebook: Nineteen Seventy-Nine Update. 1979. looseleaf 4.00 (ISBN 0-930228-12-X). Healthcare Fin Man Assn.
--Departmental Method Handbook. LC 79-88945. 70p. 1979. pap. 10.00 (ISBN 0-930228-11-1, 14411). Healthcare Fin Man Assn.
Hospital, Janette. The Ivory Swing. Macrae, Jack & Wells, Leslie, eds. 252p. 1983. 14.95 (ISBN 0-525-24170-1, 01451-440). Dutton.
Hospital Management Systems Society, American Hospital Association. Selection & Employment of Management Consultants for Health Care. LC 78-4971. (Illus.). 64p. 1978. pap. 12.00 (ISBN 0-87258-233-7, AHA-001105). Am Hospital.
Hossack, I. B. & Pollard, J. H. Introductory Statistics with Applications in General Insurance. LC 82-4421. 250p. Date not set. price not set (ISBN 0-521-24781-0); pap. price not set (ISBN 0-521-28957-2). Cambridge U Pr.
Hossfeld, D. K. & Engel, P., eds. Wirkung und Nebenwirkungen Von Bleomycin. (Beitraege zur Onkologie-Contributions to Oncology Ser.: Vol. 12). x, 220p. 1982. pap. 39.00 (ISBN 3-8055-3504-X). S Karger.
Host, David, ed. Citizen & the News. 1962. 4.95 o.p. (ISBN 0-87462-406-1). Marquette.
Hostage, Jacqueline. Jackie's Book of Household Charts. 112p. 1982. 5.95 (ISBN 0-932620-04-3, Pub. by Betterway Pubns). Berkshire Traveller.
--Jackie's Diet & Nutrition Charts. 128p. 1982. pap. 5.95 (ISBN 0-932620-10-8, Pub. by Betterway Pubns). Berkshire Traveller.
--Jackie's Kitchen Charts. LC 82-14680. 128p. (Orig.). 1982. pap. 5.95 (ISBN 0-932620-16-7). Betterway Pubns.
Hostage, Jacqueline, jt. auth. see Toth, Robin.
Hostage, Jacqueline, ed. see Mills, Richard G.
Hostetler, John A. Amish Life. rev. ed. (Illus.). 40p. 1981. pap. 2.95 o.p. (ISBN 0-8361-1954-1). Herald Pr.
--Amish Life. 2nd ed. LC 82-83964. (Illus.). 48p. (Orig.). 1983. pap. 4.95 (ISBN 0-8361-3326-9). Herald Pr.
--Hutterite Life. (Illus., Orig.). 1965. pap. 1.10 o.p. (ISBN 0-8361-1524-4). Herald Pr.
--Hutterite Life. 2nd ed. LC 82-83962. (Illus., Orig.). 1983. pap. 4.95 (ISBN 0-8361-3329-3). Herald Pr.
--Mennonite Life. rev. ed. (Illus., Orig.). 1959. pap. 1.50 o.p. (ISBN 0-8361-1394-2). Herald Pr.
--Mennonite Life. 2nd ed. LC 82-83963. (Illus.). 48p. 1983. pap. 4.95 (ISBN 0-8361-1995-9). Herald Pr.
Hostetler, Robert P., jt. auth. see Larson, Roland E.
Hostetler, Robert P., jt. auth. see Larson, Ronald A.
Hostetler, Ronald E. Reading Games: A Tournament for Your Mind, 5 vols. (Illus.). 87p. (gr. 2-6). 1982. pap. text ed. 9.95 ea. Vol. II (ISBN 0-9608722-7-2). Vol. III (ISBN 0-9608722-1-3). Vol. IV (ISBN 0-9608722-6-4). Vol. V (ISBN 0-9608722-0-5). Vol VI (ISBN 0-9608722-5-6). Set. pap. text ed. 44.95 (ISBN 0-9608722-8-0). Kitten Pub.
Hostettler, R. Printer's Terms Dictionary. (Illus., Eng. Fr., Ger., Ital. & Dutch.). Date not set. price not set (ISBN 0-685-12041-4). Heinman.
Hostrop, Richard W. Managing Education for Results. rev. 3rd ed. LC 74-32074. (Illus.). xii, 248p. 1983. 16.95 (ISBN 0-88280-022-1). ETC Pubns.
Ho Tai, Hue-Tam. Millenarianism & Peasant Politics in Vietnam. (Harvard East Asian Ser.: No. 99). (Illus.). 240p. 1983. text ed. 30.00x (ISBN 0-674-57555-5). Harvard U Pr.
Hotchkis, Joan, jt. auth. see Morris, Eric.
Hotchkiss, Bill. Ammahabas: A Novel. 1983. 16.50 (ISBN 0-393-01718-4). Norton.
--Jeffers: The Sivaistic Vision. 1975. 15.00 o.p. (ISBN 0-912950-22-6). Blue Oak.
Hotchkiss, Bill & Shears, Judith. Shoshone Thunder. (American Indians Ser.: No. 12). (Orig.). 1983. pap. 2.95 (ISBN 0-440-07659-5). Dell.
Hotchkiss, Burt. Have Miracles, Will Travel. 96p. 1982. pap. 4.95 (ISBN 0-8187-0047-5). Harlo Pr.
Hotchkiss, Jed. Virginia Expanded Volume: Confederate Military History. (Illus.). 1976. Repr. 40.00 (ISBN 0-89029-027-X). Pr of Morningside.
Hotchkiss, John F. Cut Glass Handbook & Price Guide. (Illus.). pap. 4.95 (ISBN 0-912220-04-X). Wallace-Homestead.
Hotchkiss, John F. & Cassidy, Joan H. Bottle Collecting Manual with Prices. rev. ed. (Illus.). 3.50 (ISBN 0-8015-0846-0). Wallace-Homestead.
Hotchner, A. E. Looking for Miracles: A Memoir About Loving. LC 73-4091. (Illus.). 158p. (YA) 1975. 12.45i (ISBN 0-06-011965-9, HarpT). Har-Row.
--The Man Who Lived at the Ritz. 360p. 1982. 13.95 (ISBN 0-399-12651-1). Putnam Pub Group.
--Papa Hemingway: The Ecstasy & Sorrow. (Illus.). 352p. 1983. Repr. 16.95 (ISBN 0-688-02041-0). Morrow.
--Papa Hemingway: The Ecstasy & Sorrow. (Illus.). 352p. 1982. pap. 8.95 (ISBN 0-688-02042-9). Quill NY.
Hoth, Iva, ed. The Picture Bible. (Illus.). 1979. 14.95 (ISBN 0-89191-224-X); pap. 10.95 (ISBN 0-89191-501-X). Cook.
Hotham, David. Turkey. LC 77-70192. (Countries Ser.). (Illus.). 1977. PLB 12.68 (ISBN 0-382-06116-0). Silver.
Hothem, Lar. Antiques-A Collector's Identification & Value Guide. 2nd ed. (Illus.). 1982. pap. 9.95 o.p. (ISBN 0-89689-034-1). Bks Americana.
--North American Indian Artifacts: A Collectors Identification & Value Guide. (Illus.). 9.95 (ISBN 0-89689-015-5). Wallace-Homestead.
Hothern, Lar. North American Indian Artifacts. 2nd ed. 1980. pap. 9.95 o.p. (ISBN 0-517-54112-2). Crown.
Hotman, Francis. Francogallia by Francis Hotman. Salmon, J. H. & Giesey, R., eds. LC 73-172835. (Cambridge Studies in the History & Theory of Politics). (Illus.). 608p. 1972. 69.50 (ISBN 0-521-08379-6). Cambridge U Pr.
Hotson, John H. International Comparisons of Money Velocity & Wage Markups. LC 68-56840. (Illus.). 1968. 25.00x (ISBN 0-678-00437-4). Kelley.
Hotson, L. Shakespeare Versus Shallow. LC 74-95430. (Studies in Shakespeare, No. 24). 1970. Repr. of 1931 ed. lib. bdg. 39.95x (ISBN 0-8383-0981-X). Haskell.
Hotson, Leslie. Mr. W. H. 328p. 1982. Repr. lib. bdg. 40.00 (ISBN 0-89987-391-X). Darby Bks.
--Shakespeare by Hilliard. LC 76-24584. 1977. 27.50x (ISBN 0-520-03313-2). U of Cal Pr.
Hottel, Althea K. & Sellin, Thorsten, eds. Women Around the World. LC 68-16155. (The Annals of the American Academy of Political & Social Science: No. 375). (Orig.). 1968. pap. 7.95 (ISBN 0-87761-104-1). Am Acad Pol Soc Sci.
Hottel, H. C. & Howard, J. B. New Energy Technology - Some Facts & Assessments. 384p. 1972. pap. 4.95x (ISBN 0-262-58019-5). MIT Pr.
Hottel, H. C. & Sarofim, A. F. Radiative Transfer. (Mechanical Engineering Ser.). 1967. text ed. 33.00 o.p. (ISBN 0-07-030450-5, C). McGraw.
Hotton, Peter. So You Want to Build an Energy-Efficient Addition. (Illus.). 256p. (Orig.). 1983. pap. 12.00i (ISBN 0-316-37385-0). Little.
Hou, H. S. Introduction to Digital Document Processing. 336p. 1983. 34.95 (ISBN 0-471-86247-9, Pub. by Wiley Interscience). Wiley.
Houben, Milton & Kropf, William. Dr. Harmful Food Additives: The Eat-Safe Guide. LC 79-13879. 1980. 11.95 (ISBN 0-87949-161-2). Ashley Bks.
Houck, Carter. Nova Scotia Patchwork Patterns: Full-Size Templates & Instructions for 12 Quilts. (Illus.). 80p. (Orig.). pap. 3.50 (ISBN 0-486-24145-9). Dover.
--One Hundred-One Folk Art Designs for Counted Cross-Stitch & Other Needlecrafts. (Crafts Ser.). (Illus.). 48p. (Orig.). 1982. pap. 1.95 (ISBN 0-486-24369-9). Dover.
--The Quilt Engagement Calendar Treasury. LC 82-72509. (Illus.). 272p. 1983. 35.95 (ISBN 0-525-93252-6, 03491-104); pap. 24.75 (ISBN 0-525-47712-8, 02403-720). Dutton.
Houck, Carter, ed. White Work: Techniques & 180 Designs. (Needlework Ser.). (Illus.). 1979. pap. 2.25 (ISBN 0-486-23695-1). Dover.
Houck, Fannie L. Promises of the Bible Puzzle Book. 48p. 1983. pap. 1.50 (ISBN 0-87239-587-1, 2785). Standard Pub.
Houck, J. C. Chemical Messengers of the Inflammatory Process. (Handbook of Inflammation: Vol. 1). 1980. 90.00 (ISBN 0-444-80134-0). Elsevier.
Houck, J. C., ed. Chalones. 1976. 142.75 (ISBN 0-444-11202-2, North-Holland). Elsevier.
Houck, James A., ed. William Hazlitt: A Reference Guide. 1977. lib. bdg. 28.00 (ISBN 0-8161-7826-7, Hall Reference). G K Hall.
Houck, John & Daugherty, Wayne. Chalones: A Tissue-Specific Approach to Mitotic Control. LC 73-21867. 70p. (Orig.). pap. 10.50 (ISBN 0-8463-0114-8). Krieger.
Houck, Lewis D., Jr. A Practical Guide to Budgetary & Management Control Systems. LC 78-14716. 272p. 1979. 24.95x (ISBN 0-669-02705-7). Lexington Bks.
Houck, Walter & New York-New Jersey Trail Conference Staff. Day Walker: Twenty-Eight Hikes in the New York Metropolitan Area. LC 79-7688. (Illus.). 192p. 1983. pap. 7.95 (ISBN 0-385-14140-8, Anch). Doubleday.
Houdin, William J., jt. auth. see Robert, Williar.
Houdini, Harry. The Right Way to do Wrong: An Expose of Successful Criminals. 96p. 1983. 12.95 (ISBN 0-943224-01-2); lib. bdg. 13.95 (ISBN 0-943224-02-0); pap. 6.95 (ISBN 0-943224-03-9). Presto Bks.
Houfe, Simon. Old Bedfordshire. 88p. 1982. 25.00x (ISBN 0-900804-15-7, Pub. by White Crescent England). State Mutual Bk.
Houfe, Simon, ed. Dictionary of British Book Illustrators & Caricaturists, Eighteen Hundred to Nineteen Fourteen. (Illus.). 520p. 1978. 125.00x (ISBN 0-902028-73-1, Pub. by Antique Collectors Club England). Gale.
Hougen, O. A., et al. Chemical Process Principles, 3 pts. Incl. Pt. 1. Material & Energy Balances. 2nd ed. 525p. 1954. 33.50x o.p. (ISBN 0-471-41283-X); Pt. 2. Thermodynamics. 2nd ed. 624p. 1959. 49.95 (ISBN 0-471-41382-8); Pt. 3. Kinetics & Catalysis. 303p. 1947. o.p. (ISBN 0-471-41415-8). LC 54-13512. Wiley.
Hough, B. J. Help! for Primary Teachers. 1981. 3.95 (ISBN 0-86653-008-8, GA 236). Good Apple.
Hough, B. K. Basic Soils Engineering. 2nd ed. LC 69-14671. (Illus.). 635p. 1969. 33.95 (ISBN 0-471-06666-4); tchrs. manual 3.00 (ISBN 0-471-07502-7). Wiley.
Hough, C. A., et al, eds. Developments in Sweeteners, Vol. 1. (Illus.). 1979. 43.00 (ISBN 0-85334-820-0, Pub. by Applied Sci England). Elsevier.
Hough, Charles W. The Unique Teacher. 1979. 6.95 o.p. (ISBN 0-533-03996-7). Vantage.
Hough, Charlotte. The Bassington Murder. 1980. 8.95 o.p. (ISBN 0-312-06917-0). St Martin.
Hough, Edith A. The Blue-Eyed Iroquois. 1967. 6.95 (ISBN 0-932052-30-4). North Country.
Hough, Emerson. The Mississippi Bubble: How the Star of Good Fortune Rose & Set & Rose Again, by a Woman's Grace, for one John Law of Lauriston. 452p. 1982. Repr. of 1902 ed. lib. bdg. 25.00 (ISBN 0-8495-2435-0). Arden Lib.
--Passing of the Frontier. 1918. text ed. 8.50x (ISBN 0-686-83683-9). Elliots Bks.
Hough, Franklin B. The Seige of Savannah. LC 77-165683. (Era of the American Revolution Ser.). 187p. 1974. Repr. of 1866 ed. lib. bdg. 27.50 (ISBN 0-306-70619-9). Da Capo.
Hough, George A. News Writing. 2nd ed. LC 79-91631. (Illus.). 1980. text ed. 18.50 (ISBN 0-395-28636-0); instr's. manual 1.00 (ISBN 0-395-28638-7); practice exercises 9.95 (ISBN 0-395-28637-9). HM.
Hough, Graham. Selected Essays. LC 77-85692. 1978. 34.50 (ISBN 0-521-21901-9). Cambridge U Pr.
--Selected Essays. 247p. 1981. pap. 10.95 (ISBN 0-521-29918-7). Cambridge U Pr.
Hough, Henry B. Country Editor. LC 40-27604. 1974. pap. 5.95 (ISBN 0-85699-091-4). Chatham Pr.
Hough, J. R. The French Economy. 1982. text ed. 29.50x (ISBN 0-8419-0821-4). Holmes & Meier.
Hough, J. S., et al. Malting & Brewing Science, Vol. 1. 2nd ed. 1981. 40.00x (ISBN 0-412-16580-5, Pub. by Chapman & Hall); Vol. 2, 1983. 63.00x (ISBN 0-412-16590-2); Set. 90.00x. Methuen Inc.
Hough, Jerry F. The Polish Crisis: American Policy Options. LC 82-72742. 80p. 1982. pap. 5.95 (ISBN 0-8157-3743-2). Brookings.
--Soviet Leadership in Transition. LC 80-67873. 175p. 1980. 18.95 (ISBN 0-8157-3742-4); pap. 7.95 (ISBN 0-8157-3741-6). Brookings.
Hough, Lindy. Changing Woman. (Illus.). 90p. 1971. pap. 20.00 (ISBN 0-913028-01-0). North Atlantic.
Hough, Richard. Fight of the Few. 1981. pap. 2.50 o.s.i. (ISBN 0-440-12771-8). Dell.
--The Potemkin Mutiny. LC 75-3797. (Illus.). 190p. 1975. Repr. of 1960 ed. lib. bdg. 16.00x (ISBN 0-8371-8075-9, HOPM). Greenwood.
--Wings Against the Sky. 1981. pap. 2.50 o.s.i. (ISBN 0-440-19591-8). Dell.
--Wings Against the Sky. LC 79-16570. (R.A.F. Trilogy Ser.). 1979. 9.95 o.p. (ISBN 0-688-03554-X). Morrow.
Hough, Richard L., jt. ed. see Kruszewski, Z. Anthony.
Houghtalen, Esther G. & Uhl, Laura C. Be Upright with a Wright, 2 bks. (Wright Genealogy Ser.). Set. 35.00 (ISBN 0-943240-02-6); Bk. 1, 138p. text ed. 25.00 (ISBN 0-943240-00-X); Bk. 2: Supplement, Jan. 1981 to Jan. 1982. pap. text ed. 10.00 (ISBN 0-943240-01-8). Uhls Pub.
Houghteling, James L., Jr., jt. auth. see Spiro, George W.
Houghton, ed. Romeo & Juliet & West Side Story. (YA) 1965. pap. 2.50 (ISBN 0-440-97483-6, LFL). Dell.
Houghton, B. & Wisdom, J. C. Non-Bibliographic On-Line Databases: An Investigation into Their Uses Within the Fields of Economics & Business Studies. 34p. 1981. pap. 30.00x (ISBN 0-905984-70-6, Pub. by Brit Lib England). State Mutual Bk.
Houghton, Bryan. Mitre & Crook. LC 78-23857. 1979. 9.95 o.p. (ISBN 0-87000-434-4, Arlington Hse). Crown.
Houghton, Diane & Wallace, Ralph G. Students' Accounting Vocabulary. 278p. 1980. pap. text ed. 15.00x (ISBN 0-566-00330-9). Gower Pub Ltd.
Houghton, E. I. & Carruthers, N. B. Aerodynamics for Engineering Students. 704p. 1982. pap. text ed. 39.50 (ISBN 0-7131-3433-X). E Arnold.
Houghton, George. Golf Addicts on Parade. 12.50x (ISBN 0-392-08197-0, SpS). Sportshelf.
--How to Be a Golf Addict. 1972. 8.75 o.p. (ISBN 0-7207-0499-5). Transatlantic.
Houghton, H. W., ed. Developments in Soft Drinks Technology, Vols. 1 & 2. Vol. 1, 1978. 53.50 (ISBN 0-85334-767-0, Pub. by Applied Sci England); Vol. 2, 1981. 45.00 (ISBN 0-85334-962-2). Elsevier.
Houghton, J. T. The Physics of Atmospheres. LC 76-26373. (Illus.). 1977. 34.50 (ISBN 0-521-21443-2). Cambridge U Pr.
--The Physics of Atmospheres. LC 76-26373. (Illus.). 1979. pap. 13.95 (ISBN 0-521-29656-0). Cambridge U Pr.
Houghton, Leighton. Guide to the British Cathedrals. (Illus.). 128p. 1974. pap. 5.95 o.p. (ISBN 0-212-97007-0). Transatlantic.
Houghton, Neal D., ed. Struggle Against History: U. S. Foreign Policy in an Age of Revolution. 1968. pap. 2.95 o.p. (ISBN 0-671-20059-3, Touchstone Bks). S&S.
Houghton, Norris. But Not Forgotten: The Adventure of the University Players. LC 79-136071. (Illus.). 1971. Repr. of 1952 ed. lib. bdg. 18.75x (ISBN 0-8371-5221-6, HONF). Greenwood.
Houghton, P. S. Ball & Roller Bearings. 1976. 98.50 (ISBN 0-85334-598-8, Pub. by Applied Sci England). Elsevier.
Houghton, R. P. Metal Complexes in Organic Chemistry. LC 78-51685. (Cambridge Texts in Chemistry & Biochemistry). 1979. 59.50 (ISBN 0-521-21992-2); pap. 21.95 (ISBN 0-521-29331-6). Cambridge U Pr.
Houghton, Richard. True Book About Nelson. (Illus.). (gr. 7 up). 12.75x (ISBN 0-392-05140-0, LTB). Sportshelf.
Houghton, S. M. Sketches from Church History. Murray, Iain, ed. (Illus.). 256p. (Orig.). 1981. pap. 10.95 (ISBN 0-85151-317-4). Banner of Truth.

Houghton, Walter E. & Stange, G. Robert. Victorian Poetry & Poetics. 2nd ed. LC 74-370. 1968. text ed. 26.50 (ISBN 0-395-04646-7). HM.

Houghton, Walter E., ed. Wellesley Index to Victorian Periodicals, 1824-1900, 3 vols. Incl. Vol. 1. 1966. 150.00x o.p. (ISBN 0-8020-1393-7); Vol. 2. 1972. 150.00x (ISBN 0-8020-1910-2); Vol. 3. 1978. 150.00x (ISBN 0-8020-2253-7). LC 66-5405. Set. 375.00x (ISBN 0-8020-2343-6). U of Toronto Pr.

Houghton-Alico, Doann & Dunning, Marcy. Mining Industry Permitting Guidelines: Coal Exploration & Production - the Western Region. 450p. 1982. 650.00 (ISBN 0-86531-463-2). Westview.

Houglum, Roger J. Electronics: Concepts, Applications & History. 1979. text ed. 23.95 (ISBN 0-534-00769-4, Breton Pubs). Wadsworth Pub.

Houk, Rose, ed. see Lister, Robert H. & Lister, Florence C.

Houk, Rose, et al, eds. see Olin, George.

Houldcroft, Peter Thomas. Welding Process Technology. LC 76-47408. (Illus.). 1977. 37.50 (ISBN 0-521-21530-7). Cambridge U Pr.

Houlden. Ethics & the New Testament. 1977. pap. 5.95 (ISBN 0-19-519958-8). Oxford U Pr.

Houlden, J. L., ed. Paul's Letters from Prison: Philippians, Colossians, Philemon & Ephesians. LC 77-24028. (Westminister Pelican Commentaries). 1978. 11.50 (ISBN 0-664-21347-2); softcover 6.95 (ISBN 0-664-24182-4). Westminster.

Houle, Paul, jt. auth. see Healy, Timothy.

Houlihan, D. F., et al, eds. Gills. LC 81-21778. (Society for Experimental Biology Seminar Ser.: No. 16). (Illus.). 250p. 1982. 49.50 (ISBN 0-521-24083-2). Cambridge U Pr.

Houlihan, William J. The Chemistry of Heterocyclic Compounds: Indoles. LC 76-154323. (Chemistry of Heterocyclic Compounds: Monographs: Vol. 25, Pt. 3). 1979. 148.50 (ISBN 0-471-05132-2, Pub. by Wiley-Interscience). Wiley.

Hoult, Thomas F. Dictionary of Modern Sociology. LC 67-10018. (Quality Paperback: No. 226). (Orig.). 1977. pap. 5.95 (ISBN 0-8226-0226-1). Littlefield.

--Sociology for a New Day: Reader. 2nd ed. 1979. pap. text ed. 8.95x o.p. (ISBN 0-394-32243-6). Random.

Hoult, Thomas F., ed. Social Justice & Its Enemies: A Normative Approach to Social Problems. 584p. 1975. text ed. 18.95 o.p. (ISBN 0-470-41530-4); pap. text ed. 9.95 o.p. (ISBN 0-470-41531-2). Halsted Pr.

Houp, Kenneth W. Reporting Technical Information. 4th ed. 547p. 1980. pap. text ed. 17.95 (ISBN 0-02-475630-X). Macmillan.

Houpis, C. H. & Lubelfeld, J. Pulse Circuits. (Technical Outlines Ser.). 1970. pap. 3.95 o.p. (ISBN 0-671-18905-0). Monarch Pr.

Houpis, Constantine, jt. auth. see D'Azzo, John.

Houpis, Constantine, jt. auth. see D'Azzo, John J.

Houppert, Joseph W. John Lyly. LC 74-20932. (English Authors Ser.: No. 177). 1975. lib. bdg. 10.95 o.p. (ISBN 0-8057-1349-2, Twayne). G K Hall.

Houpt, Jeffrey L., et al. The Importance of Mental Health Services to General Health Care. LC 79-1043. 288p. 1979. prof ref 19.50x (ISBN 0-88410-534-2). Ballinger Pub.

Hourani, Albert. The Emergence of the Modern Middle East. 1981. 32.50x (ISBN 0-520-03862-2). U of Cal Pr.

--Europe & the Middle East. LC 78-59452. 1980. 27.50x (ISBN 0-520-03742-1). U of Cal Pr.

Housden, Jack, jt. auth. see Housden, Theresa.

Housden, Theresa & Housden, Jack. How to Design & use Questionnaires. 150p. 1983. pap. 9.95 (ISBN 0-88056-115-7). Dilithium Pr.

House & Luetje, C. Acoustic Tumors: Diagnosis & Management. 318p. 1979. Vol. I (Diagnosis) text ed. 34.50 (ISBN 0-8391-1314-5); Vol. II (Management) 296 pp. text ed. 34.50 (ISBN 0-8391-1346-3). Univ Park.

House & Garden Editors. House & Garden's New Cookbook. 1967. 12.50 o.p. (ISBN 0-671-31971-X). S&S.

House, Arthur H. The U.N. in the Congo: The Political & Civilian Efforts. LC 78-56052. 1978. pap. text ed. 16.25 (ISBN 0-8191-0516-3). U Pr of Amer.

House, Charles H., jt. auth. see Wiatrowski, Claude A.

House, E. Lawrence, et al. A Systematic Approach to Neuroscience. 3rd ed. (Illus.). 1979. text ed. 38.00 (ISBN 0-07-030468-8, HP). McGraw.

House, Ernest R. The Politics of Educational Innovation. LC 74-12822. 324p. 1974. 16.50x (ISBN 0-8211-0754-2); pap. text ed. 14.50x (ISBN 0-685-57222-6). McCutchan.

House, Ernest R. & Lapan, Stephen D. Survival in the Classroom: Negotiating with Kids, Colleagues & Bosses. 1978. pap. text ed. 21.95x (ISBN 0-205-06082-X); tchr's ed. avail. (ISBN 0-685-89341-3); abridged ed. 11.95 (ISBN 0-686-96651-1). Allyn.

House, Ernest R., ed. School Evaluation: Politics & Process. LC 72-91622. 370p. 1973. 22.00x (ISBN 0-8211-0750-X); text ed. 20.20x (ISBN 0-685-28806-4). McCutchan.

House, Ernest R. & Mathison, Sandra, eds. Evaluation Studies Review Annual, 1982, Vol. 7. LC 76-15865. 736p. 1982. 37.50 (ISBN 0-8039-0386-3). Sage.

House, Floyd N. Development of Sociology. Repr. of 1936 ed. lib. bdg. 20.75x (ISBN 0-8371-4241-5, HOSO). Greenwood.

House, H., jt. auth. see Harman, Susan E.

House, Herbert O. Modern Synthetic Reactions. 2nd ed. LC 78-173958. 1972. text ed. 29.95 (ISBN 0-8053-4501-9). Benjamin-Cummings.

House, Heron. The Book of Numbers. LC 78-55109. (Illus.). 464p. 1978. 12.50 o.s.i. (ISBN 0-89479-028-5). A & W Pubs.

House, J. D. Contemporary Entrepreneurs: The Sociology of Residential Real Estate Agents. LC 76-52329. (Contributions in Sociology: No. 25). 1977. lib. bdg. 25.00 (ISBN 0-8371-9533-0, HCE/). Greenwood.

House, J. W. Frontier on the Rio Grande: A Political Geography of Development & Social Deprivation. (Illus.). 1982. 29.95 (ISBN 0-19-823237-3). Oxford U Pr.

House, James S. Occupational Stress & the Mental & Physical Health of Factory Workers. 356p. 1980. pap. 16.00x (ISBN 0-87944-254-9). Inst Soc Res.

House, John. Monet. (Phaidon Color Library). (Illus.). 84p. 1983. 25.00 (ISBN 0-7148-2162-4, Pub. by Salem Hse Ltd); pap. 17.95 (ISBN 0-7148-2160-8). Merrimack Bk Serv.

--The Wonders of Science. (Science Ser.). 24p. (gr. 3-5). 1977. wkbk. 5.00 (ISBN 0-8209-0155-5, S-17). ESP.

House, Lon W. Incorporating Wind Energy into Utility Supply Planning. (Supplement to Progress in Solar Energy Ser.). 150p. 1983. text ed. 21.50x (ISBN 0-89553-055-4). Am Solar Energy.

House, Marilyn G. Ice Skating Fundamentals. (Illus.). 1982. pap. text ed. 8.50 (ISBN 0-8403-2906-7, 40290601). Kendall-Hunt.

House, Nancy A. Van see Van House, Nancy A.

House of Collectibles. Official O. J. Simpson Price Guide to Football Cards. 2nd ed. LC 81-86222. (Collector Ser.). (Illus.). 1982. pap. 2.50 (ISBN 0-87637-323-6). Hse of Collectibles.

--Official Price Guide to Antique Jewelry. 2nd ed. LC 78-72035. (Collector Ser.). (Illus.). 500p. 1982. pap. 9.95 o.p. (ISBN 0-87637-354-6). Hse of Collectibles.

--The Official Price Guide to Baseball Cards, 1982. (Collector Ser.). (Illus.). 200p. (Orig.). 1981. pap. 2.50 o.p. (ISBN 0-87637-182-9, 182-09). Hse of Collectibles.

--The Official Price Guide to Bottles Old & New. 5th ed. (Collector Ser.). (Illus.). 500p. 1981. pap. 9.95 o.p. (ISBN 0-87637-174-8). Hse of Collectibles.

--Official Price Guide to Comic & Science Fiction Book. 4th ed. (Collector Ser.). (Illus.). 400p. 1981. pap. 9.95 o.p. (ISBN 0-87637-146-2, 146-02). Hse of Collectibles.

--Official Price Guide to Comic Books. LC 82-82257. (Collector Ser.). (Illus.). 500p. (Orig.). 1982. pap. cancelled o.p. (ISBN 0-87637-348-1). Hse of Collectibles.

--The Official Price Guide to Hummel Figurines & Plates. 2nd ed. (Collector Ser.). (Illus.). 400p. 1981. pap. 9.95 o.p. (ISBN 0-87637-178-0). Hse of Collectibles.

--Official Price Guide to Paper Collectibles. (Collector Ser.). (Illus.). 400p. 1980. pap. 9.95 o.p. (ISBN 0-87637-114-4, 114-04). Hse of Collectibles.

--Official Price Guide to Wicker Furniture. LC 82-82250. (Collector Ser.). (Illus.). 500p. (Orig.). 1982. pap. 9.95 (ISBN 0-686-83179-9). Hse of Collectibles.

House of Collectibles, Inc. Official Price Guide to Antique & Modern Firearms. (Collector Ser.). (Illus.). 400p. 1981. pap. 9.95 o.p. (ISBN 0-87637-155-1, 155-01). Hse of Collectibles.

House, Peggy A. Interactions of Science & Mathematics. (Illus.). 185p. 1982. pap. 7.50 (ISBN 0-686-94079-2). NCTM.

House, Peter A. & Steger, Wilber A. The Modern Federalism: An Analytical Dimension. LC 81-47972. 320p. 1982. pap. 29.95x (ISBN 0-669-05208-6). Lexington Bks.

House, Peter W. & Ryan, Gerard R. The Future Indefinite: Decision-Making in a Transition Economy. LC 79-2723. 192p. 1979. 23.95x (ISBN 0-669-03231-X). Lexington Bks.

House, Peter W. & Williams, Edward R. Planning & Conservation: The Emergence of the Frugal Society. LC 77-7584. (Praeger Special Studies). 1977. 32.95 o.p. (ISBN 0-03-021946-9); pap. 12.95 o.p. (ISBN 0-03-022281-8). Praeger.

House, Robert W., jt. auth. see Leonhard, Charles.

House, Suda. Artistic Photographic Processes. (Illus.). 144p. 1981. 21.95 o.p. (ISBN 0-8174-3540-9); pap. 14.95 o.p. (ISBN 0-8174-3541-7). Watson-Guptill.

House, Toni, jt. auth. see Conconi, Charles.

House, William C. Decision Support Systems. 250p. pap. 15.00 (ISBN 0-89433-208-2). Petrocelli.

--Electronic Communication Systems. 1980. 25.00 (ISBN 0-89433-098-5). Petrocelli.

--Interactive Computer Graphics Systems. (Illus.). 350p. 1982. text ed. 25.00 (ISBN 0-89433-188-4). Petrocelli.

House, William C., Jr. Sensitivity Analysis in Making Capital Investment Decisions. 7.95 (ISBN 0-86641-013-9, 6843). Natl Assn Accts.

House, William F., jt. ed. see Graham, Malcolm.

Household, Geoffrey. The Europe That Was. LC 78-20671. 1979. 8.95 o.p. (ISBN 0-312-26925-0). St Martin.

--The Last Two Weeks of Georges Rivac. (General Ser.). (gr. 7-12). 1979. lib. bdg. 12.95 (ISBN 0-8161-6744-3, Large Print Bks). G K Hall.

--Red Anger. (Crime Ser.). 1977. pap. 2.95 (ISBN 0-14-004522-8). Penguin.

--Rogue Justice. 192p. 1983. 14.00i (ISBN 0-316-37440-7, Pub. by Atlantic Monthly Pr). Little.

--Watcher in the Shadows. (Crime Ser). 1977. pap. 2.95 (ISBN 0-14-001962-6). Penguin.

Householder. Numerical Treatment of a Single Nonlinear Equation. 1970. text ed. 35.00 (ISBN 0-07-030465-3, C). McGraw.

Houseman, Gerald L. G. D. H. Cole. (English Authors Ser.). 1979. lib. bdg. 14.95 (ISBN 0-8057-6746-0, Twayne). G K Hall.

Houseman, John. Front & Center. 1979. 15.00 o.p. (ISBN 0-671-24328-4). S&S.

--Run-Through. 1981. pap. 7.95 o.s.i. (ISBN 0-671-41390-2, Touchstone Bks). S&S.

Housepian, Marjorie. Smyrna Nineteen Twenty-Two. (Illus.). 276p. 1972. 10.95 o.p. (ISBN 0-571-10108-9). Faber & Faber.

Houser, E. A. Principles of Sample Handling & Sampling System Design for Process Analysis. LC 72-85741. (Illus.). 112p. 1972. text ed. 15.00x o.p. (ISBN 0-87664-189-3). Instru Soc.

Houser, Roy. Catalogue of Chamber Music for Woodwind Instruments. LC 76-166093. (Music Ser). 1973. Repr. of 1960 ed. lib. bdg. 19.50 (ISBN 0-306-70257-6). Da Capo.

Houser, Schuyler O., jt. ed. see McNeill, William H.

Houser, Thomas. Agatha's Friends. 224p. 1983. pap. 2.50 (ISBN 0-380-82222-9, 82222-9). Avon.

Housing & Urban Development Dept. Your Guide to Energy Saving Home Improvements. 1977. pap. 2.50 o.p. (ISBN 0-448-14046-2, G&D). Putnam Pub Group.

Houslay, Miles D. & Stanley, Keith K. Dynamics of Biological Membranes: Influence on Synthesis Structure & Function. 300p. 1982. for info. 54.95rite (ISBN 0-471-10080-3, Pub. by Wiley-Interscience); pap. 21.95 (ISBN 0-471-10095-1). Wiley.

Housley, Charles E. Hospital Material Management. LC 78-14526. 368p. 1978. text ed. 39.50 (ISBN 0-89443-046-7). Aspen Systems.

--Strategies in Hospital Material Management: Case Analysis & Masterplanning. LC 82-20620. 602p. 1982. 42.50 (ISBN 0-89443-668-6). Aspen Systems.

Housley, Norman. The Italian Crusade: The Papal-Angevin Alliance & the Crusades Against Christian Lay Powers, 1254-1343. (Illus.). 308p. 1982. 44.00x (ISBN 0-19-821925-3). Oxford U Pr.

Housley, Trevor. Data Communications & Teleprocessing Systems. (P-H Data Processing Management Ser.). (Illus.). 1979. text ed. 30.00 (ISBN 0-13-197368-1). P-H.

Housman, A. E. A Shropshire Lad. 100p. 1981. Repr. lib. bdg. 11.95x (ISBN 0-89966-285-4). Buccaneer Bks.

Housman, Alfred E. Shropshire Lad. pap. 2.50 (ISBN 0-8283-1455-1, 7, IPL). Branden.

--A Shropshire Lad. LC 80-13329. 126p. 1980. Repr. of 1946 ed. lib. bdg. 15.50x (ISBN 0-313-22456-0, HOSH). Greenwood.

Housman, Gertrude H. No Trespassing & Other Poems. 80p. 1982. 7.95 (ISBN 0-9609706-0-6). Leeger Pr.

Housner, J. M., jt. ed. see Noor, A. K.

Houssiadas, L., jt. ed. see Welford, A. T.

Houston & Pankratz, eds. Staff Development & Educational Chance. 1980. 5.00 (ISBN 0-686-38077-0). Assn Tchr Ed.

Houston, jt. auth. see Andrews.

Houston, Charles S. High Altitude Physiology Study. (Illus., Orig.). 1982. 15.00 (ISBN 0-686-37171-2). Queen City VT.

Houston, Charles S., jt. ed. see Sutton, John R.

Houston, David. Ice from Space. (Tales of Tomorrow Ser.: No. 4). 208p. (Orig.). 1982. pap. 2.25 o.s.i. (ISBN 0-8439-1132-8, Leisure Bks). Nordon Pubns.

--Time Forgotten. (Tales of Tomorrow Ser.: No. 5). (Illus.). 208p. (Orig.). 1982. pap. 2.50 o.s.i. (ISBN 0-8439-1170-0, Leisure Bks). Nordon Pubns.

Houston, Douglas. The Northern Yellowstone Elk: Ecology & Management. LC 82-70079. 1982. 48.00x (ISBN 0-02-949450-8). Free Pr.

Houston, Douglas B. The Northern Yellowstone Elk. 1982. text ed. 48.00x (ISBN 0-02-949450-8). Macmillan.

Houston, Henrietta. An Improper Betrothment, No. 75. 1982. pap. 1.75 (ISBN 0-515-06686-9). Jove Pubns.

Houston, J. C., et al. A Short Textbook of Medicine. LC 82-73298. (Illus.). 772p. 1983. pap. text ed. 19.95x (ISBN 0-668-05739-4, 5739). Arco.

Houston, Jack. Basic Skills Health Workbook: Grade 7. (Basic Skills Workbook). 32p. 1982. tchrs' ed. 0.99 (ISBN 0-8209-0417-1, HW-H). ESP.

--Basic Skills Health WorkBook: Grade 8. (Basic Skills Workbook). 32p. 1982. tchrs' ed. 0.99 (ISBN 0-8209-0418-X, HW-I). ESP.

--Basic Skills Health Workbook: Grade 9. (Basic Skills Workbooks). 32p. (YA) 1982. tchr's ed. 0.99 (HW-J). ESP.

--Basic Skills Health Workbooks: Grade 6. (Basic Skills Workbooks). 32p. 1982. tchrs' ed. 0.99 (ISBN 0-8209-0416-3, HW-G). ESP.

--Basic Skills Science Workbook: Grade 3. (Basic Skills Workbooks). 32p. (gr. 3). 1982. wkbk. 0.99 (ISBN 0-8209-0402-3, SW-D). ESP.

--Basic Skills Science Workbook: Grade 5. (Basic Skills Workbooks). 32p. (gr. 5). 1982. wkbk. 0.99 (ISBN 0-8209-0404-X, SW-F). ESP.

--Basic Skills Science Workbook: Grade 6. (Basic Skills Workbooks). 32p. (gr. 6). 1982. wkbk. 0.99 (ISBN 0-8209-0405-8, SW-G). ESP.

--Basic Skills Science Workbook: Grade 7. (Basic Skills Workbooks). 32p. (gr. 7). 1982. wkbk. 0.99 (ISBN 0-8209-0406-6, SW-H). ESP.

--Jumbo Health Yearbook: Grade 5. (Jumbo Health Ser.). 96p. (gr. 5). 1979. 14.00 (ISBN 0-8209-0065-6, JHY 5). ESP.

--Jumbo Health Yearbook: Grade 6. (Jumbo Health Ser.). 96p. (gr. 6). 1979. 14.00 (ISBN 0-8209-0066-4, JHY 6). ESP.

--Jumbo Health Yearbook: Grade 7. (Jumbo Health Ser.). 96p. (gr. 7). 1979. 14.00 (ISBN 0-8209-0067-2, JHY 7). ESP.

--Jumbo Health Yearbook: Grade 8. (Jumbo Health Ser.). 96p. (gr. 8). 1979. 14.00 (ISBN 0-8209-0068-0, JHY 8). ESP.

--Jumbo Science Yearbook: Grade 3. (Jumbo Science Ser.). 96p. (gr. 3). 1978. 14.00 (ISBN 0-8209-0024-9, JSY 3). ESP.

--Jumbo Science Yearbook: Grade 5. (Jumbo Science Ser.). 96p. (gr. 5). 1979. 14.00 (ISBN 0-8209-0026-5, JSY 5). ESP.

--Jumbo Science Yearbook: Grade 6. (Jumbo Science Ser.). 96p. (gr. 6). 1979. 14.00 (ISBN 0-8209-0027-3, JSY 6). ESP.

--Jumbo Science Yearbook: Grade 7. (Jumbo Science Ser.). 96p. (gr. 7). 1981. 14.00 (ISBN 0-8209-0028-1, JSY 7). ESP.

--Jumbo Science Yearbook: Grade 8. (Jumbo Science Ser.). 96p. (gr. 8). 1982. 14.00 (ISBN 0-8209-0029-X, JSY 8). ESP.

Houston, James. Eagle Mask: A West Coast Indian Tale. LC 66-10074. (Illus.). (gr. 2-6). 1966. 5.50 o.p. (ISBN 0-15-224444-1, HJ). HarBraceJ.

--Eagle Song. (Illus.). 300p. 1983. 14.95 (ISBN 0-15-127117-8). HarBraceJ.

--The White Archer: An Eskimo Legend. LC 79-14458. (Illus.). (gr. 4-7). 1979. pap. 2.25 (ISBN 0-15-696224-1, VoyB). HarBraceJ.

--The White Dawn: An Eskimo Saga. 275p. pap. 4.95 (ISBN 0-15-696256-X, Harv). HarBraceJ.

Houston, James M., ed. see Baxter, Richard.

Houston, James M., ed. see Bernard of Clairvaux & William of St. Thierry.

Houston, James M., ed. see Owen, John.

Houston, James M., ed. see Wilberforce, William.

Houston, Jean. Lifeforce. 1980. 12.95 o.s.i. (ISBN 0-440-05011-1). Delacorte.

Houston, Jean & Loeb, Millie. The Possible Human: A Course in Extending Your Physical, Mental, and Creative Abilities. (Illus.). 229p. 1982. text ed. 16.50 (ISBN 0-87477-219-2); pap. text ed. 9.95 (ISBN 0-87477-218-4). J P Tarcher.

Houston, Jean, jt. auth. see Masters, Robert.

Houston, John. The Pursuit of Happiness. 1981. pap. text ed. 9.95x (ISBN 0-673-15421-1). Scott F.

Houston, John P. The Rhetoric of Poetry in the Renaissance & 17th Century. 344p. 1983. text ed. 32.50 (ISBN 0-8071-1066-3). La State U Pr.

--Victor Hugo. (World Authors Ser.: France). 1974. lib. bdg. 11.95 (ISBN 0-8057-2443-5, Twayne). G K Hall.

Houston, John P., jt. auth. see McCarthy, Melodie A.

Houston, John P., et al. Essentials of Psychology. 550p. 1981. 16.00 (ISBN 0-12-356858-7); study guide 6.75 (ISBN 0-12-356856-0); test blank II (1500 items) 3.50 (ISBN 0-12-356855-2); instrs.' manual 3.50 (ISBN 0-12-356842-0). Acad Pr.

Houston, Julie. The Woman's Day Great American Cookie Book. Date not set. pap. 5.95 (ISBN 0-449-90032-0, Columbine). Fawcett.

Houston, Lee. Samples...Fables from the Slope. Frauenglas, Robert A., ed. LC 82-60838. (Illus.). 48p. (Orig.). 1982. pap. 4.00 (ISBN 0-9603950-5-9). Somrie Pr.

Houston, Mary G. Ancient Egyptian, Mesopotamian & Persian Costumes & Decoration. 2nd ed. (Technical History of Costume Ser.: Vol. I). (Illus.). 190p. 1972. Repr. of 1954 ed. 26.50x (ISBN 0-06-492999-X). B&N Imports.

Houston, Neal B. & Quinn, John J. Phonetikon: A Visual Aid to Phonetic Study. 1970. 4.95x o.p. (ISBN 0-673-05889-1). Scott F.

Houston, Peyton. Occasions in a World. LC 68-58536. 1969. pap. 4.50 (ISBN 0-912330-16-3, Dist. by Inland Bk). Jargon Soc.

Houston, Ralph. Talk Does Not Cook the Rice: The Teachings of Agni Yoga, 2 vols. Phillips, Amelia, ed. 416p. Date not set. pap. 7.95 ea. (ISBN 0-87728-530-6). Vol. 1. Vol. 2 (ISBN 0-87728-535-7). Weiser.

Houston, Robert. Ararat. 400p. 1982. pap. 3.50 (ISBN 0-380-80937-0, 80937). Avon.

Houston, Robert & Howsam, Robert. Competency-Based Teacher Education: Progress, Problems, & Prospects. LC 72-83692. 1972. pap. text ed. 6.50 o.s.i. (ISBN 0-574-18360-4, 13-1360). SRA.

Houston, Robert W. Exploring Competency Based Education. LC 74-76532. 1974. 21.25x (ISBN 0-8211-0752-6); text ed. 19.25x (ISBN 0-685-42635-1). McCutchan.

Houston, Robert W., jt. auth. see Collier, Calhoun C.

Houston, S. J. James I. (Seminar Studies in History). 150p. 1974. pap. text ed. 5.95x (ISBN 0-582-35208-8). Longman.

Hout, Thomas M., jt. auth. see Magaziner, Ira C.

Houten, Franklyn B. Van see Van Houten, Franklyn B.

Houten, Lois Van see Van Houten, Lois.

Houten, Ron V., jt. auth. see Hall, R. Vance.

Houts, Paul L., ed. The Myth of Measurability. 320p. (Orig.). 1977. pap. 6.95 o.s.i. (ISBN 0-89104-240-7, A & W Visual Library). A & W Pubs.

Houtte, J. A. Van see Van Houtte, J. A.

Houwen, P. Van der see Van der Houwen, P.

Houwink, R. Sizing up Science. (Illus.). 232p. 1975. 12.50 o.p. (ISBN 0-7195-3101-2). Transatlantic.

Houwink, R., ed. Odd Book of Data. 1965. 8.50 (ISBN 0-444-40299-3). Elsevier.

Houwink, Roelof, ed. Adhesion & Adhesives, 2 vols. 2nd ed. Incl. Vol. 1. Adhesives. 1965 (ISBN 0-444-40300-0); Vol. 2. Applications. 1967 (ISBN 0-444-40301-9). Set. 159.75 (ISBN 0-686-57579-2); 85.00 ea. Elsevier.

Hovanessian, S. A. Computational Mathematics in Engineering. 272p. 1976. 34.95x (ISBN 0-669-00733-1). Lexington Bks.

Hovanessian, S. A. & Pipes, L. Digital Computer Methods in Engineering. 1969. 38.50 o.p. (ISBN 0-07-030490-4, P&RB). McGraw.

Hovannisian, Richard G. The Republic of Armenia, Vol. 2: From Versailles to London, 1919-1920. LC 72-129613. (Illus.). 570p. 1982. 35.00x (ISBN 0-520-04186-0). U of Cal Pr.

Hovda, Robert. Strong, Loving & Wise: Presiding in Liturgy. LC 76-56474. 1976. pap. 8.75 o.s.i. (ISBN 0-918208-12-2). Liturgical Conf.

Hovda, Robert W. There Are Different Ministries. 76p. 1978. pap. 5.25 (ISBN 0-918208-62-9). Liturgical Conf.

Hovde, Jeanne. A Horse Named Cinnamon. (Pennypincher Bks.). 132p. (gr. 3-6). 1982. pap. 1.75 (ISBN 0-89191-714-4). Cook.

--Winter of the White-Tail Buck. LC 75-36698. (Illus.). 192p. (gr. 5 up). 1976. pap. 1.75 o.p. (ISBN 0-912692-88-X). Cook.

Hovdhaugen, Even. Foundation of Western Linquistics. 152p. (Orig.). 1982. pap. 20.00 (ISBN 82-00-06055-1). Universitet.

Hovell, Mark. Chartist Movement. 3rd ed. Tout, T. F., ed. LC 67-4890. Repr. of 1918 ed. 25.00x (ISBN 0-678-06761-9). Kelley.

Hoven, Vernon & Holen, Harold H. Dramatic Tax Savings Through Real Estate Transactions. 208p. 1982. 27.95 (ISBN 0-13-219071-0). P-H.

Hover, Herman. How Many Three Cents Stamps in a Dozen? or How Logical Are You? 1976. pap. 1.75 (ISBN 0-8431-0408-2). Price Stern.

Hover, Margo. What Kind of Truck? LC 81-86498. (First Little Golden Bk.). (Illus.). 24p. (ps). 1983. 0.69 (ISBN 0-307-10154-1, Golden Pr). Western Pub.

Hover, Margot K. & Breidenbach, Monica E. Chrisitan Family Almanac. 128p. (Orig.). 1980. pap. 9.95 (ISBN 0-697-01740-0). Wm C Brown.

Hovet, Thomas & Chamberlin, Waldo. The Chronology & Fact Book of the United Nations: 1941-1979. 6th ed. LC 76-18777. (The Library on the United Nations). 304p. 1979. 17.50 (ISBN 0-379-20680-3); Years 1941-1969; 1941-1976. o.p. Oceana.

Hovey, Alvah. Memoir of the Life & Times of the Reverend Isaac Backus. LC 73-148598. (Era of the American Revolution Ser.). 367p. 1972. Repr. of 1858 ed. lib. bdg. 47.50 (ISBN 0-306-70415-3). Da Capo.

Hovey, Gail. Namibia's Stolen Wealth: North American Investment & South African Occupation. (Illus.). 52p. (Orig.). 1982. pap. 2.50 (ISBN 0-943428-04-1). Africa Fund.

Hoveyda, Fereydoun. The Fall of the Shah. Liddell, Roger, tr. 1980. 9.95 o.p. (ISBN 0-671-61003-1). S&S.

Hoving, Thomas. Tutankhamun: The Untold Story. 1980. pap. 5.95 o.p. (ISBN 0-671-24370-5). S&S.

Howand, Kathleen, ed. see Okada, Barbara T.

Howar, Barbara. Setting Things Straight. Date not set. 13.95 (ISBN 0-671-42564-1, Linden). S&S. Postponed.

Howard. Aerial Photo Ecology. 1971. 18.00 (ISBN 0-444-19768-0). Elsevier.

--Conan: The Devil in Iron. 6.95 o.p. (ISBN 0-448-14580-4, G&D). Putnam Pub Group.

--Fluidized Beds: Combustion & Applications. Date not set. price not set (ISBN 0-85334-177-X). Elsevier.

--Fungi Pathogenic for Humans & Animals, Vol. A. 672p. 1983. 79.50 (ISBN 0-8247-1875-5). Dekker.

--Fungi Pathogenic for Humans & Animals, Vol. B. 576p. 1983. 67.50 (ISBN 0-8247-1144-0). Dekker.

Howard & Gibat. Making Wine, Beer & Merry. Rev. ed. 178p. 1978. pap. 3.00 (ISBN 0-686-35948-8). Rutan Pub.

Howard, A., jt. auth. see Honigfeld, G.

Howard, A., jt. ed. see Ebert, M.

Howard, A. Dick. Magna Carta: Text & Commentary. LC 64-66214. (Illus.). 55p. 1978. pap. 2.95 (ISBN 0-8139-0121-9). U Pr of Va.

Howard, Alan. Ain't No Big Thing: Coping Strategies in a Hawaiian-American Community. LC 73-86029. 336p. 1974. text ed. 14.00x o.p. (ISBN 0-8248-0300-0, Eastwest Ctr). UH Pr.

--Nativity Stories. LC 79-20746. (Illus.). 96p. (gr. 5 up). 1980. 9.95 o.p. (ISBN 0-89742-027-6, Dawne-Leigh). Celestial Arts.

--Sex in the Light of Reincarnation & Freedom. 1980. pap. 6.95 (ISBN 0-916786-48-X). St George Bk Serv.

Howard, Sir Albert. The Soil & Health: A Study of Organic Agriculture. LC 70-179077. (Illus.). 335p. 1972. pap. 5.95 (ISBN 0-8052-0334-6). Schocken.

Howard, Arthur D. & Remson, Irwin. Geology in Environmental Planning. (Illus.). 1977. text ed. 37.50 (ISBN 0-07-030510-2, C). McGraw.

Howard, B. D. & Pollock, E. O. Passive Solar Space Heating Systems Performance: Comparative Reports. 260p. 1983. pap. 34.50x (ISBN 0-89934-004-0, A-021). Solar Energy Info.

Howard, C., jt. auth. see Summers, Robert S.

Howard, C., et al. Contact: A Textbook in Applied Communications. 3rd ed. 1979. pap. 12.95 (ISBN 0-13-169052-3). P-H.

Howard, C. Jeriel & Lundy, Eileen. Reprise: A Review of Basic Writing Skills. 2nd ed. 1980. pap. text ed. 12.50x (ISBN 0-673-16220-6). Scott F.

Howard, C. Jeriel, jt. auth. see Brock, Dee.

Howard, Clark. American Saturday. 1981. 13.95 (ISBN 0-399-90120-5, Marek). Putnam Pub Group.

--Brothers In Blood. 320p. 1983. 16.95 (ISBN 0-312-10610-6, Pub. by Marek). St Martin.

--A Movement Toward Eden. LC 77-88523. 1969. 10.95 (ISBN 0-87716-009-0, Pub. by Moore Pub Co). F Apple.

--The Wardens. 384p. 1981. pap. 2.75 o.p. (ISBN 0-425-04670-2). Berkley Pub.

--The Wardens. LC 78-13296. 1979. 10.95 (ISBN 0-399-90032-2, Marek). Putnam Pub Group.

--Zebra. LC 79-15985. 1979. 11.95 (ISBN 0-399-90050-0, Marek). Putnam Pub Group.

Howard, Colin. Slowmotional Meditation. 540p. 1983. 45.00 (ISBN 0-686-84355-X). Olam.

Howard, Constance. Inspiration for Embroidery. 240p. 1967. 27.50 (ISBN 0-8231-4017-2). Branford.

Howard, Daniel F., ed. The Modern Tradition: An Anthology of Short Stories. 4th ed. 1979. pap. 10.95 (ISBN 0-316-37456-3); instr's manual pap avail. (ISBN 0-316-37455-5). Little.

Howard, Darlene. Cognitive Psychology: Memory, Language, & Thought. 592p. 1983. text ed. 25.95 (ISBN 0-02-357320-1). Macmillan.

Howard, David, et al, eds. Tradition & Tolerance in Nineteenth-Century Fiction: Critical Essays on Some English & American Novels. 1966. 18.95x o.p. (ISBN 0-7100-1563-1). Routledge & Kegan.

Howard, David H. The Disequilibrium Model in a Controlled Economy. LC 78-24828. (Illus.). 128p. 1979. 17.95x (ISBN 0-669-02851-7). Lexington Bks.

Howard, David M. How Come God? LC 72-3477. 1982. pap. 2.95 o.p. (ISBN 0-8054-5902-2). Broadman.

--Student Power in World Missions. 2nd ed. LC 79-122918. (Orig.). 1979. pap. 4.95 (ISBN 0-87784-493-3). Inter-Varsity.

Howard, David S. Chinese Armorial Porcelain. 1034p. 1974. 199.00 (ISBN 0-571-09811-8). Faber & Faber.

Howard, Dick, jt. auth. see Luxemburg, Rosa.

Howard, Donald R. The Idea of the Canterbury Tales. LC 74-81433. 400p. 1976. 30.00x (ISBN 0-520-02816-3); pap. 5.95 (ISBN 0-520-03492-9). U of Cal Pr.

--Writers & Pilgrims: Medieval Pilgrimage Narratives & Their Posterity. LC 79-64480. (A Quantum Bk.). 100p. 1980. 11.95 (ISBN 0-520-03926-2). U of Cal Pr.

Howard, Donald S. The WPA & the Federal Relief Policy. LC 72-2374. (FDR & the Era of the New Deal Ser). 888p. 1973. Repr. of 1943 ed. lib. bdg. 95.00 (ISBN 0-306-70489-7). Da Capo.

Howard, Dorothy. No Longer Alone. LC 74-32603. 128p. (Orig.). 1976. pap. 1.50 o.p. (ISBN 0-912692-60-X). Cook.

Howard, E. Basic Bible Survey. Gambill, Henrietta, ed. 96p. (Orig.). 1983. pap. 2.95 (ISBN 0-87239-572-3, 3210). Standard Pub.

Howard, Ebenezer. Garden Cities of To-Morrow. (Illus.). 1965. pap. 5.95x (ISBN 0-262-58002-0). MIT Pr.

Howard, Edward. Rattlin the Reefer. Howse, Arthur, ed. (Oxford English Novels Ser). 1971. 10.50x o.p. (ISBN 0-19-255333-X). Oxford U Pr.

Howard, Edwin J. Geoffrey Chaucer. (English Authors Ser.). 1964. lib. bdg. 11.95 (ISBN 0-8057-1088-4, Twayne). G K Hall.

Howard, Elizabeth. Out of Step with the Dancers. LC 77-25928. (gr. 7 up). 1978. 10.75 (ISBN 0-688-22141-6); PLB 10.32 (ISBN 0-688-32141-0). Morrow.

--Winter on Her Own. LC 68-16625. (gr. 7 up). 1968. 9.50 (ISBN 0-688-21710-9). Morrow.

Howard, Elizabeth J. The Long View. LC 82-47563. 368p. 1982. pap. 3.37i (ISBN 0-06-080627-3, P627, PL). Har-Row.

--Odd Girl Out. LC 82-47564. 288p. 1982. pap. 3.37i (ISBN 0-06-080628-1, P628, PL). Har-Row.

Howard, Eugene R. School Discipline Desk Book: With Model Programs & Tested Procedures. (Illus.). 1977. 18.50 (ISBN 0-13-793000-3, Parker). P-H.

Howard, Fred D. Layman's Bible Book Commentary: 1, 2, 3 John, Jude, Revelation, Vol. 24. LC 80-66807. 1982. 4.75 (ISBN 0-8054-1194-1). Broadman.

Howard, G. Paul: Crisis in Galatia. LC 77-82498. (Society for New Testament Studies Monographs: No. 35). 1979. 22.95 (ISBN 0-521-21709-1). Cambridge U Pr.

Howard, G. M., jt. auth. see Poucher, W. A.

Howard, George. How We Find Out About the Sea. (Illus.). 64p. (gr. 7-9). 1974. 6.50 o.p. (ISBN 0-212-98417-9). Transatlantic.

Howard, George P., ed. Airport Economic Planning. 688p. 1974. 25.00x (ISBN 0-262-08072-9). MIT Pr.

Howard, Harold P. Sacajawea. 1971. pap. 5.95 (ISBN 0-686-95813-6). Jefferson Natl.

Howard, Helen A. American Indian Poetry. (United States Authors Ser.). 1979. lib. bdg. 13.95 (ISBN 0-8057-7271-5, Twayne). G K Hall.

Howard, Herbert H. & Kievman, Michael S. Radio & TV Programming. LC 82-6079. (Gird Series in Advertising & Journalism). 336p. 1982. text ed. 25.95 (ISBN 0-88244-251-1). Grid Pub.

Howard, I. K., tr. see Al-Mufid, Shaykh.

Howard, Ian P. Human Visual Orientation. LC 80-41689. 697p. 1981. 59.95x (ISBN 0-471-27946-3, Pub. by Wiley-Interscience). Wiley.

Howard, J. B., jt. auth. see Hottel, H. C.

Howard, J. Grant. Balancing Life's Demands: A New Perpective on Priorities. 1983. pap. write for info. (ISBN 0-88070-012-2). Multnomah.

Howard, James H. Shawnee: The Ceremonialism of a Native Indian Tribe & Its Cultural Background. LC 80-23752. (Illus.). xvi, 454p. 1981. 28.95x (ISBN 0-8214-0417-2, 82-83087); pap. 14.95 (ISBN 0-8214-0614-0, 82-83095). Ohio U Pr.

Howard, James L. Seth Harding, Mariner. 1930. 39.50x (ISBN 0-685-69827-0). Elliots Bks.

Howard, Jane. Families. 1978. 9.95 o.p. (ISBN 0-671-22536-7). S&S.

--Please Touch. 1971. pap. 3.95 o.s.i. (ISBN 0-440-56798-X, Delta). Dell.

Howard, Jessica. Prairie Flame. 320p. 2.95 (ISBN 0-515-04729-5). Jove Pubns.

--Traitor's Bridge. (Orig.). 1979. pap. 2.25 o.s.i. (ISBN 0-515-04728-7). Jove Pubns.

Howard, John. Prisons & Lazarettos, 2 vols. Incl. State of Prisons in England & Wales. 4th ed. Repr. of 1792 ed; Account of the Principal Lazarettos in Europe. 2nd ed. Repr. of 1791 ed. LC 74-129312. (Criminology, Law Enforcement, & Social Problems Ser.: No. 135). (Illus., With 45 plates & a new intro. essay). 1973. Vol. 1 (ISBN 0-685-27770-4). Vol. 2 (ISBN 0-685-27771-2). Set. 90.00x (ISBN 0-87585-135-5). Patterson Smith.

Howard, John A. Consumer Behavior: Application of Theory. (McGraw-Hill Ser. in Marketing). (Illus.). 1977. text ed. 28.95 (ISBN 0-07-030520-X, C); instructor's manual 7.95 (ISBN 0-07-030521-8). McGraw.

Howard, John R. Fourteen Decisions for Undeclared War. LC 78-62668. (Illus.). 1978. pap. text ed. 9.50 (ISBN 0-8191-0585-6). U Pr of Amer.

Howard, John R., ed. Awakening Minorities: Continuity & Change. 2nd ed. 130p. 1983. 15.95 (ISBN 0-87855-468-8); pap. text ed. 7.95 (ISBN 0-87855-911-6). Transaction Bks.

Howard, John R. & Smith, Robert C., eds. Urban Black Politics. LC 78-56922. (Annals: No. 439). 1978. 15.00 (ISBN 0-87761-230-7); pap. 7.95 (ISBN 0-87761-231-5). Am Acad Pol Soc Sci.

Howard, John T. & Lyons, James. Modern Music: A Popular Guide to Greater Musical Enjoyment. LC 78-60139. 1978. Repr. of 1957 ed. lib. bdg. 18.00x (ISBN 0-313-20556-6, HOMU). Greenwood.

Howard, John T., jt. ed. see Engel, Carl.

Howard, John Tasker. Stephen Foster, America's Throubadour. 445p. 1982. Repr. of 1943 ed. lib. bdg. 50.00 (ISBN 0-8495-2436-9). Arden Lib.

Howard, John W. Easy Company & the Bible Salesman, No. 25. 192p. 1983. pap. 2.25 (ISBN 0-515-06357-6). Jove Pubns.

--Easy Company & the Big Game Hunter, No. 28. 192p. 1983. pap. 2.25 (ISBN 0-515-06360-6). Jove Pubns.

--Easy Company & the Big Medicine. (Easy Company Ser.: No. 6). 192p. (Orig.). 1981. pap. 1.95 o.s.i. (ISBN 0-515-05947-1). Jove Pubns.

--Easy Company & the Blood Feud, No. 26. 192p. pap. 2.25 (ISBN 0-515-06358-4). Jove Pubns.

--Easy Company & the Cardsharps, No. 18. 192p. 1982. pap. 1.95 (ISBN 0-515-06350-9). Jove Pubns.

--Easy Company & the Cow Country, No. 24. 192p. 1983. pap. 2.25 (ISBN 0-515-06356-8). Jove Pubns.

--Easy Company & the Dog Soldiers. 192p. 1983. pap. 2.25 (ISBN 0-515-06359-2). Jove Pubns.

--Easy Company & the Indian Doctor, No. 19. 192p. 1982. pap. 2.25 o.s.i. (ISBN 0-515-06351-7). Jove Pubns.

--Easy Company & the Mystery Trooper, No. 23. 192p. 1982. pap. 2.25 (ISBN 0-515-06355-X). Jove Pubns.

--Easy Company & the Sheep Ranchers, No. 21. 192p. (Orig.). 1982. pap. 2.25 (ISBN 0-515-06353-3). Jove Pubns.

--Easy Company & the Twilight Sniper. 192p. 1982. pap. 2.25 (ISBN 0-515-06352-5). Jove Pubns.

--Easy Company at Hat Creek Station, No. 22. 208p. 1982. pap. 2.25 (ISBN 0-515-06354-1). Jove Pubns.

Howard, Jonathan. Darwin. Thomas, Keith, ed. (Past Masters Ser.). 1982. 8.95 (ISBN 0-8090-3758-0); pap. 3.25 (ISBN 0-8090-1418-1). Hill & Wang.

Howard, Joseph. Damien: The Omen II. (Orig.). (RL 7). 1978. pap. 2.95 (ISBN 0-451-11990-8, AE1990, Sig). NAL.

Howard, Joseph K. Montana: High, Wide & Handsome. LC 82-17667. xiv, 350p. 1983. pap. 7.50 (ISBN 0-8032-7214-6, BB 820, Bison). U of Nebr Pr.

Howard, Joy. Stormy Paradise. (Super Romances Ser.). 384p. 1983. pap. 2.95 (ISBN 0-373-70060-1, Pub. by Worldwide). Harlequin Bks.

Howard, Kathleen, ed. see Okada, Barbara T.

Howard, Kathleen, ed. see Von Bothmer, Dietrich & Mertens, Joan R.

Howard, Kenneth I., jt. auth. see Orlinsky, David O.

Howard, Kenneth S., ed. Spectacular Chess Problems. (Orig.). 1965. pap. 2.50 (ISBN 0-486-21477-X). Dover.

Howard, Lawrence. Sanctuary in Love. LC 78-66221. 1979. 5.95 o.p. (ISBN 0-533-04153-8). Vantage.

Howard, Lawrence C., jt. auth. see McKinney, Jerome B.

Howard, Leann, jt. auth. see Keltner, Autumn.

Howard, Leon. Victorian Knight-Errant: A Study of the Early Literary Career of James Russell Lowell. LC 72-136072. 1971. Repr. of 1952 ed. lib. bdg. 19.00x (ISBN 0-8371-5222-4, HOVK). Greenwood.

Howard, Leslie. Trivial Fond Records. Howard, Ronald, ed. 1982. 39.00x (ISBN 0-686-82340-0, Pub. by W Kimber). State Mutual Bk.

Howard, Leslie R. Auditing. 7th ed. 332p. (Orig.). 1978. pap. text ed. 11.95x (ISBN 0-7121-0178-0, Pub. by Macdonald & Evans England). Intl Ideas.

Howard, Leslie R., jt. auth. see Brown, J. Lewis.

Howard, Lillie P. Zora Neale Hurston. (United States Authors Ser.). 1980. lib. bdg. 10.95 (ISBN 0-8057-7296-0, Twayne). G K Hall.

Howard, Linda. Expecting Miracles. LC 79-28591. 1980. 10.95 o.p. (ISBN 0-399-12496-9). Putnam Pub Group.

Howard, Linda U. The Money, Honey. 304p. 1982. 15.95 (ISBN 0-399-12694-5). Putnam Pub Group.

Howard, Linden. The Devil's Lady. 224p. 1980. 9.95 o.p. (ISBN 0-312-19823-X). St Martin.

--Foxglove Country. LC 76-5374. 1977. 8.95 o.p. (ISBN 0-312-30205-3). St Martin.

Howard, Lowell B. Business Law: An Introduction. rev. ed. 608p. 1983. pap. text ed. 6.95 (ISBN 0-8120-2260-2). Barron.

Howard, M. Skyblazer. (Illus.). (gr. 7-9). 1966. 2.95 o.p. (ISBN 0-394-81642-0, BYR); PLB 5.69 (ISBN 0-394-91642-5). Random.

Howard, Margo. Eppie: The Story of Ann Landers. (Illus.). 256p. 1982. 13.95 (ISBN 0-399-12688-0). Putnam Pub Group.

--Eppie: The Story of Ann Landers. (Illus.). 1983. pap. 3.50 (ISBN 0-523-42016-1). Pinnacle Bks.

Howard, Maria W. Lowney's Cookbook. LC 78-71372. 410p. 1982. 11.95 (ISBN 0-88289-376-9); pap. 7.95 (ISBN 0-88289-369-6). Pelican.

Howard, Marion. Sometimes I Wonder About Me: Teen-Agers & Mental Health. 200p. 1983. 12.95 (ISBN 0-8264-0199-6). Continuum.

Howard, Marshall C. Legal Aspects of Marketing. 1964. pap. 13.95 (ISBN 0-07-030531-5, C). McGraw.

Howard, Maureen. Grace Abounding. 13.95 (ISBN 0-686-84925-6). Little.

Howard, Michael. The Franco-Prussian War: The German Invasion of France, 1870-71. LC 80-41677. 528p. 1981. pap. 11.95 (ISBN 0-416-30750-7). Methuen Inc.

--War in European History. 1976. 9.95x (ISBN 0-19-211564-2, Opus); pap. text ed. 5.95x (ISBN 0-19-289095-6). Oxford U Pr.

Howard, Michael C. Aboriginal Politics in Southwestern Australia. (Illus.). 181p. 1982. pap. text ed. 23.00 (ISBN 0-686-83950-1, Pub. by U of W Austral Pr). Intl Schol Bk Serv.

--Modern Theories of Income Distribution. LC 79-13523. 1979. 26.00x (ISBN 0-312-54244-5). St Martin.

Howard, Michael C., ed. Aboriginal Power in Australian Society. 252p. 1982. pap. text ed. 16.95x (ISBN 0-8248-0815-0). UH Pr.

Howard, Moe. Moe Howard & the Three Stooges. (Illus.). 1979. pap. 9.95 (ISBN 0-8065-0666-0). Citadel Pr.

Howard, Neale E. Standard Handbook for Telescope Making. (Illus.). 1959. 14.37i (ISBN 0-690-76784-6). T Y Crowell.

--The Telescope Handbook & Star Atlas. rev. ed. LC 75-6601. (Illus.). 226p. 1975. 21.10i (ISBN 0-690-00686-1). T Y Crowell.
Howard, Nigel. Paradoxes of Rationality: Games, Metagames & Political Behavior. 1971. 25.00x (ISBN 0-262-08046-X). MIT Pr.
Howard, Oliver O. My Life & Experiences Among Our Hostile Indians. LC 76-87436. (The American Scente Ser.). 1972. Repr. of 1907 ed. lib. bdg. 55.00 (ISBN 0-306-71506-6). Da Capo.
--Nez Perce Joseph. LC 70-39379. (Law, Politics, & History Ser). (Illus.). 274p. 1972. Repr. of 1881 ed. lib. bdg. 32.50 (ISBN 0-306-70461-7). Da Capo.
Howard, Patricia. Gluck & the Birth of Modern Opera. (Illus.). 1963. 8.95 o.p. (ISBN 0-312-32970-9). St Martin.
--The Operas of Benjamin Britten: An Introduction. LC 76-7367. 1976. Repr. of 1969 ed. lib. bdg. 17.00x (ISBN 0-8371-8867-9, HOOB). Greenwood.
Howard, Paul. Easy to Make Wooden Furniture for Children. 176p. 1981. 12.95 (ISBN 0-920510-51-5, Pub. by Personal Lib); pap. 8.95 (ISBN 0-920510-10-8). Dodd.
Howard, Philip. London's River. LC 76-28032. (Illus.). 1977. 15.00 o.p. (ISBN 0-312-49595-1). St Martin.
--New Words for Old. 1977. 12.95x (ISBN 0-19-519988-X). Oxford U Pr.
--Royal Palaces. LC 70-118211. (Illus.). 1970. 10.00 o.p. (ISBN 0-87645-031-1). Gambit.
Howard, Phillip L. Basic Liquid Scintillation Counting. LC 75-43423. (Illus.). 40p. 1976. pap. text ed. 9.00 perfect bdg. o.p. (ISBN 0-89189-021-1, 45-8-006-00). Am Soc Clinical.
Howard Press. C. Wright Mills. (World Leaders Ser.). 1978. lib. bdg. 12.95 (ISBN 0-8057-7708-3, Twayne). G K Hall.
Howard, R. C., et al. Event-Related Brain Potentials in Personality & Psychopathology: A Pavlovian Approach. (Psychophysiology Rsearch Studies). 112p. 1982. 29.95 (ISBN 0-471-10454-X, Pub. by Res Stud Pr). Wiley.
Howard, R. N., ed. Developments in Polymerisation, Vol. 3. Date not set. 59.50 (ISBN 0-85334-117-6, Pub. by Applied Sci England). Elsevier.
Howard, Richard & Moore, A. A Complete Checklist of the Birds of the World. 1981. 49.50x (ISBN 0-19-217681-1). Oxford U Pr.
Howard, Richard, tr. see Barthes, Roland.
Howard, Richard, tr. see Barthes, Ronald.
Howard, Richard, tr. see Baudelaire, Charles.
Howard, Richard, tr. see Cioran, E. M.
Howard, Richard, tr. see Gide, Andre.
Howard, Richard, tr. see Pieyre de Mandiargues, Andre.
Howard, Richard, tr. see Poliakov, Leon.
Howard, Richard, tr. see Robbe-Grillet, Alain.
Howard, Richard, tr. see Sachs, Maurice.
Howard, Richard, tr. see Tillion, Germaine.
Howard, Robert. Performance in a World of Change: Perspective on Learning Environments. LC 79-65294. 1979. pap. text ed. 10.00 (ISBN 0-8191-0785-9); lib. bdg. 19.00 (ISBN 0-8191-1275-5). U Pr of Amer.
Howard, Robert & Bumba, V. Atlas of Solar Magnetic Fields. 1967. 10.00 (ISBN 0-87279-637-X). Carnegie Inst.
Howard, Robert E. Conan of Aquilonia. (Conan Ser.: No. 11). 192p. 1982. pap. 2.25 (ISBN 0-441-11640-X, Pub. by Ace Science Fiction). Ace Bks.
--Conan of the Isles. (Conan Ser.: No. 12). 192p. 1982. pap. 2.25 (ISBN 0-441-11641-8, Pub. by Ace Science Fiction). Ace Bks.
--Conan, the Avenger. (Conan Ser.: No. 10). 192p. 1982. pap. 2.25 (ISBN 0-441-11639-6, Pub. by Ace Science Fiction). Ace Bks.
--Conan, the Warrior. De Camp, L. Sprague, ed. (Conan Ser.: No. 7). 192p. 1982. pap. 2.50 (ISBN 0-441-11636-1, Pub. by Ace Science Fiction). Ace Bks.
--Garden of Fear. pap. 4.95x (ISBN 0-685-30959-2). Wehman.
--The People of the Black Circle. LC 78-20392. 1978. 9.95 o.p. (ISBN 0-399-12147-1, Pub. by Berkley). Putnam Pub Group.
--The Tower of the Elephant. Shaw, Grace, ed. LC 78-59789. (Illus.). 1978. pap. 6.95 o.p. (ISBN 0-448-16238-5, G&D). Putnam Pub Group.
Howard, Robert E., jt. auth. see De Camp, L. Sprague.
Howard, Robert E., et al. Conan. (Conan Ser.: No. 1). 1982. pap. 2.25 (ISBN 0-441-11630-2, Pub. by Ace Science Fiction). Ace Bks.
--Conan of Cimmeria. (Conan Ser.: No. 2). 192p. 1982. pap. 2.25 (ISBN 0-441-11631-0, Pub. by Ace Science Fiction). Ace Bks.
--Conan, the Wanderer. (Conan Ser.: No. 4). 192p. 1983. pap. 2.50 (ISBN 0-686-82845-3, Pub. by Ace Science Fiction). Ace Bks.
--Conan, the Freebooter. (Conan Ser.: No. 3). 192p. 1982. pap. 2.50 (ISBN 0-441-11596-9, Pub. by Ace Science Fiction). Ace Bks.
Howard, Robert P. James R. Howard & The Farm Bureau. 224p. 1983. text ed. 18.95 (ISBN 0-8138-0886-3). Iowa St U Pr.
Howard, Ronald, ed. see Howard, Leslie.
Howard, Ronald L. A Social History of American Family Sociology, 1865-1940. Mogey, John H. & Van Leeuwen, Louis Th., eds. LC 80-1790. (Contributions in Family Studies Ser.: No. 4). xiii, 150p. 1981. lib. bdg. 25.00 (ISBN 0-313-22767-5, MOA/). Greenwood.
Howard, Ronnalie R. The Dark Glass: Vision & Technique in the Poetry of Dante Gabriel Rossetti. LC 70-158176. xiii, 218p. 1972. 12.00x (ISBN 0-8214-0099-1, 82-81040). Ohio U Pr.
Howard, Rosanne B. Nutrition in Clinical Care. 2nd ed. Herbold, Nancy H., ed. (Illus.). 800p. 1982. 24.50x (ISBN 0-07-030514-5). McGraw.
Howard, Rosanne B. & Herbold, Nancie. Nutrition in Clinical Care. (Illus.). 1977. text ed. 19.95 o.p. (ISBN 0-07-030545-5, HP). McGraw.
Howard, Ross & Perley, Michael. Acid Rain: The North American Forecast. (Illus.). 208p. 1980. 18.95 o.p. (ISBN 0-88784-082-5, Pub. by Hse Anansi Pr Canada). U of Toronto Pr.
Howard, Roy J. Three Faces of Hermeneutics: A Introduction to Current Theories of Understanding. (Campus 280 Ser.). 160p. 1982. 17.95x (ISBN 0-520-03851-7, CAMPUS 280); pap. 5.95x (ISBN 0-520-04689-7). U of Cal Pr.
Howard, Sam. Communications Machines. LC 79-27715. (Machine World Ser.). (Illus.). 32p. (gr. 2-4). 1980. PLB 13.85 (ISBN 0-8172-1335-X). Raintree Pubs.
Howard, Samuel A. Juris Imprudence. LC 76-56710. 1976. 10.95 (ISBN 0-87716-071-6, Pub. by Moore Pub Co). F Apple.
Howard, T. Dear Ruin. 1972. 5.95 (ISBN 0-87645-057-5). Gambit.
Howard, Ted, jt. auth. see Rifkin, Jeremy.
Howard, Thomas. Dialogue with a Skeptic. (Trumpet Bks). 1976. pap. 1.25 o.p. (ISBN 0-87981-060-2). Holman.
--The Novels of Charles Williams. LC 82-18902. 224p. 1983. 16.95 (ISBN 0-19-503247-0). Oxford U Pr.
Howard University Library, Washington, D.C. Dictionary Catalog of the Arthur B. Spingarn Collection of Negro Authors, 2 vols. 1970. lib. bdg. 190.00 (ISBN 0-8161-0872-2, Hall Library). G K Hall.
--Dictionary Catalog of the Jesse E. Moorland Collection of Negro Life & History, 9 vols. 1970. Set. lib. bdg. 855.00 (ISBN 0-8161-0871-4, Hall Library). G K Hall.
--Dictionary Catalog of the Jesse E. Moorland Collection of Negro Life & History, First Supplement, 3 vols. 1976. lib. bdg. 350.00 (ISBN 0-8161-0944-3, Hall Library). G K Hall.
Howard, V. A. Artistry: the Work of Artists. LC 81-6265. 228p. 1982. 13.50 (ISBN 0-915145-06-5). Hackett Pub.
Howard, Velma S., tr. see Lagerlof, Selma.
Howard, Vernon. The Esoteric Encyclopedia of Eternal Knowledge. LC 80-6203. 256p. 1981. 12.95 (ISBN 0-8128-2797-X); pap. 7.95 (ISBN 0-8128-6117-5). Stein & Day.
--Esoteric Mind Power. 196p. 1980. pap. 6.00 (ISBN 0-87516-401-3). De Vorss.
--One Hundred Games for Boys & Girls. 120p. 1974. pap. 2.50 o.p. (ISBN 0-310-26302-6). Zondervan.
--Pantomimes, Charades & Skits. rev. ed. LC 59-12983. (Illus.). 124p. (gr. 4 up). 1974. 7.95 (ISBN 0-8069-7004-9); PLB 9.99 (ISBN 0-8069-7005-7). Sterling.
--The Power of Your Supermind. 1979. pap. 6.00 (ISBN 0-87516-375-0). De Vorss.
--Psycho-Pictography: The New Way to Use the Miracle Power of Your Mind. 1968. pap. 4.95 (ISBN 0-13-732222-4, Reward). P-H.
--There Is a Way Out. LC 75-11137. 173p. 1982. pap. 6.00 (ISBN 0-87516-472-2). De Vorss.
Howard, Veronica. Rebel in Love. (Orig.). 1981. pap. 1.50 o.s.i. (ISBN 0-440-17423-6). Dell.
Howard, Victor B. Black Liberation in Kentucky: Emancipation & Freedom, 1861-1884. LC 82-40461. 240p. 1983. 23.00x (ISBN 0-8131-1433-0). U Pr of Ky.
Howard, Wayne. Veda Recitation in Varanasi. 1983. 15.00x (ISBN 0-8364-0872-1). South Asia Bks.
Howard, Wilbert F. Christianity According to St. John. (Studies in Theology: No. 46). 1943. 6.00x (ISBN 0-8401-6046-1). Allenson Breckinridge.
Howard, William. John Clare. (English Authors Ser.). 14.95 (ISBN 0-8057-6734-7, Twayne). G K Hall.
Howard, William, jt. auth. see Hamilton, Douglas.
Howard, William W. Atlas of Operative Dentistry. 3rd ed. LC 80-25063. (Illus.). 292p. 1981. pap. 22.95 (ISBN 0-8016-2282-4). Mosby.
Howard-Hall, T. H. British Bibliography & Textual Criticism: A Bibliography. (Index to British Literary Bibliography Ser.: Vols. IV & V). 1979. Set. 129.00x (ISBN 0-19-818163-9). Oxford U Pr.
Howard-Hill, T. H. British Literary Bibliography & Textual Criticism Eighteen Ninety to Nineteen Sixty-Nine, an Index. 1980. 129.00x (ISBN 0-19-818180-9). Oxford U Pr.
--Shakesperian Bibliography & Textual Criticism. (Index to British Literary Bibliography Ser). 1971. 36.00x (ISBN 0-19-818140-X). Oxford U Pr.
Howards, Melvin. Reading Diagnosis & Instruction: An Integrated Approach. (Illus.). 1980. text ed. 17.95 (ISBN 0-8359-6443-4). Reston.
Howards, Stuart S., jt. ed. see Gillenwater, Jay Y.
Howard-Williams, Jeremy. Night Intruder. 13.95 o.p. (ISBN 0-7153-7054-5). Hippocrene Bks.
Howarth, David P. The Dreadnoughts. (The Seafarers Ser.). (Illus.). 1979. lib. bdg. 19.92 (ISBN 0-8094-2712-5); 17.28 (ISBN 0-8094-2713-3). Silver.
--The Men-of-War. LC 78-18476. (The Seafarers Ser.). (Illus.). 1978. lib. bdg. 19.92 (ISBN 0-8094-2667-6). Silver.
Howarth, Herbert. Tiger's Heart: Eight Essays on Shakespeare. LC 70-106057. 1970. 7.50x (ISBN 0-19-519035-1). Oxford U Pr.
Howarth, O. J. R., jt. auth. see Dickinson, Robert E.
Howarth, P. When the Riviera Was Ours. (Illus.). 1977. 21.95 (ISBN 0-7100-8465-X). Routledge & Kegan.
Howarth, P. J., jt. auth. see Gray, C. H.
Howarth, Shirley R., ed. Directory of Corporate Art Collections. LC 82-643083. 168p. (Orig.). 1982. pap. 35.00 (ISBN 0-943488-00-1). Intl Art Alliance.
--Directory of Corporate Art Collections. 200p. 1983. pap. 35.00 (ISBN 0-943488-01-X). Intl Art Alliance.
Howarth, Tony. Twentieth Century History: The World Since Nineteen Hundred. (Illus.). 320p. (Orig.). (gr. 10-12). 1979. pap. text ed. 10.95 (ISBN 0-582-22162-5). Longman.
Howarth, W. D., ed. Comic Drama: The European Heritage. 1979. 25.00 (ISBN 0-312-15091-1). St Martin.
Howarth, W. D., et al. French Literature from Sixteen Hundred to the Present. LC 75-2864. 161p. 1974. pap. 4.95x (ISBN 0-416-81640-1). Methuen Inc.
Howarth, W. D., et al, eds. Form & Content in Seventeenth-Century French Drama. 1982. 65.00x o.p. (ISBN 0-86127-216-1, Pub. by Avebury Pub England). State Mutual Bk.
Howarth, William L., ed. The John McPhee Reader. 1977. pap. 3.95 (ISBN 0-394-72733-9, Vin). Random.
Howat, G. M. Stuart & Cromwellian Foreign Policy. LC 73-91111. 180p. 1974. 22.50 (ISBN 0-312-76895-8). St Martin.
Howat, Henry T. & Sarles, Henri, eds. The Exocrine Pancreas. LC 79-1524. (Illus.). 551p. 1979. text ed. 35.00 (ISBN 0-7216-4779-0). Saunders.
Howay, F. W., ed. see Colnett, James.
Howden, P. Ecologistics. 1982. 30.00x (ISBN 0-9507230-0-2, Pub. by Element Bks). State Mutual Bk.
--Smallternatives Too. 1982. 25.00x (ISBN 0-686-99812-X, Pub. by Element Bks). State Mutual Bk.
Howe, C. J. Acquiring Language in a Conversational Context: Behavioral Development. LC 81-66381. (A Series of Monographs). 1981. 24.50 (ISBN 0-12-356920-6). Acad Pr.
Howe, Charles W. Natural Resource Economics: Issues Analysis & Policy. LC 78-24174. 1979. text ed. 30.95 (ISBN 0-471-04527-6). Wiley.
Howe, Charles W., ed. Benefit-Cost Analysis for Water System Planning. LC 72-182565. (Water Resources Monograph: Vol. 2). (Illus.). 1971. pap. 10.00 (ISBN 0-87590-302-9). Am Geophysical.
Howe, Christopher. China's Economy: A Basic Guide. LC 77-20423. 1978. 16.95x o.p. (ISBN 0-465-01099-7, CN-5045); pap. 4.95x (ISBN 0-465-00110-6). Basic.
--Employment & Economic Growth in Urban China, 1949-57. LC 76-152641. (Contemporary China Institute Publications). (Illus.). 1971. 37.50 (ISBN 0-521-08172-6). Cambridge U Pr.
Howe, Claude L., Jr. Glimpses of Baptist Heritage. LC 80-68798. 1981. pap. 5.95 (ISBN 0-8054-6559-6). Broadman.
Howe, D. R. Data Analysis for Data Base Design. 304p. 1983. pap. text ed. price not set (ISBN 0-7131-3481-X). E Arnold.
Howe, De M. Wolfe see Howe, Mark A.
Howe, Ellic. The Magicians of the Golden Dawn. (Illus.). 1978. pap. 5.95 o.p. (ISBN 0-87728-369-9). Weiser.
Howe, F. G., jt. ed. see Edmonds, G. A.
Howe, Fanny. Alsace-Lorraine. Owen, Maureen, ed. (Summer Ser.). (Illus.). 64p. (Orig.). 1982. pap. 4.00 (ISBN 0-916382-28-1). Telephone Bks.
Howe, Florence, ed. Dialogue on Difference. 224p. 1983. 8.95 (ISBN 0-935312-22-6). Feminist Pr.
Howe, Florence & Rothermich, John A., eds. Household & Kin: Families in Flux. (Women's Lives - Women's Work Ser.). 208p. (Orig.). Date not set. pap. text ed. 8.32 (ISBN 0-07-020427-6, W). McGraw.
--Las Mujeres: Conversations from a Hispanic Community. (Women's Lives - Women's Work Ser.). 192p. (Orig.). 1980. pap. text ed. 7.44 (ISBN 0-07-020445-4, W). McGraw.
--The Sex-Role Cycle: Socialization from Infancy to Old Age. (Women's Lives - Women's Work Ser.). 192p. (Orig.). 1980. pap. text ed. 7.44 (ISBN 0-07-020425-X, W). McGraw.
--With These Hands: Women Working on the Land. (Women's Lives - Women's Work). (Orig.). pap. text ed. 11.40 (ISBN 0-07-020441-1, W). McGraw.
--Women Have Always Worked: An Historical Overview. (Women's Lives - Women's Work Ser.). 208p. (Orig.). 1980. pap. text ed. 8.32 (ISBN 0-07-020435-7, W). McGraw.
--Women's "True" Profession: Voices from the History of Teaching. (Women's Lives-Women's Work Ser.). 352p. (Orig.). 1981. pap. text ed. 11.40 (ISBN 0-07-020437-3); tchrs. guide 6.04 (ISBN 0-07-020438-1). McGraw.
Howe, Frederic R. Challenge & Response: A Handbook of Christian Apologetics. 224p. 1982. 9.95 (ISBN 0-310-45070-5). Zondervan.
Howe, Gary N., jt. auth. see McNall, Scott G.
Howe, Gary N., jt. ed. see McNall, Scott G.
Howe, George & Harrer, G. A. Handbook of Classical Mythology. LC 77-121209. 1970. Repr. of 1947 ed. 27.00 o.p. (ISBN 0-8103-3290-6). Gale.
Howe, Glenn. Dinner in the Clouds. 1980. text ed. write for info. (ISBN 0-87046-009-9, Pub. by Trans-Anglo). Interurban.
Howe, Henry, jt. auth. see Barber, John W.
Howe, Henry V. Ostracod Taxonomy. LC 62-11741. 1962. 30.00x o.p. (ISBN 0-8071-0539-2). La State U Pr.
Howe, Hubert. TRS-80 MOD III Assembly Language. 1983. price not set. P-H.
Howe, Hubert S., Jr. TRS-Eighty Model III Assembly Language Tutor. 192p. 1983. 29.95 (ISBN 0-13-931279-X); pap. 16.95 (ISBN 0-13-931261-7); software 29.95 (ISBN 0-13-931287-0). P-H.
--TRS-80 Assembly Language. (Illus.). 192p. 1981. text ed. 15.95 (ISBN 0-13-931139-4, Spec); pap. text ed. 9.95 (ISBN 0-13-931121-1, Spec). P-H.
Howe, I. & Widick, B. J. The UAW & Walter Reuther. LC 72-2375. (FDR & the Era of the New Deal Ser.). 324p. 1973. Repr. of 1949 ed. lib. bdg. 39.50 (ISBN 0-306-70485-4). Da Capo.
Howe, I., et al. Literature of America, Vol. 2. 1971. text ed. 10.95 o.p. (ISBN 0-07-030572-2, C). McGraw.
Howe, Imogen. Fatal Attraction. (Twilight Ser.). (YA) (gr. 7-12). 1982. pap. 1.95 (ISBN 0-440-92496-0, LFL). Dell.
Howe, Irving. Beyond the Welfare State. LC 81-40408. 288p. 1982. 17.95x (ISBN 0-8052-3787-9); pap. 8.95 (ISBN 0-8052-0685-X). Schocken.
--Orwell's 1984: Text, Source, Criticism. 2nd ed. 450p. 1982. pap. text ed. 9.95 (ISBN 0-15-565811-5). HarBraceJ.
--Twenty-Five Years of Dissent: An American Tradition. 1980. 17.95 (ISBN 0-416-00041-X); pap. 8.95 o.p. (ISBN 0-416-00051-7). Methuen Inc.
Howe, Irving & Coser, Lewis. The American Communist Party: A Critical History. LC 73-22072. (FDR & the Era of the New Deal Ser.). x, 612p. 1974. Repr. of 1962 ed. lib. bdg. 59.50 (ISBN 0-306-70636-9). Da Capo.
Howe, Irving & Libo, Ken. How We Lived: A Documentary History of Immigrant Jews in America, 1880-1930. LC 79-13391. (Illus.). 1979. 22.50 (ISBN 0-399-90051-9, Marek). Putnam Pub Group.
Howe, Irving, jt. auth. see Coser, Lewis.
Howe, Irving, ed. Essential Works of Socialism. LC 75-28967. 864p. 1976. 35.00x o.p. (ISBN 0-300-01976-9); pap. 10.95x o.p. (ISBN 0-300-01977-7, Y-292). Yale U Pr.
Howe, Irving & Greenberg, Eliezer, eds. A Treasury of Yiddish Poetry. LC 76-9422. 1976. pap. 6.95 (ISBN 0-8052-0546-2). Schocken.
--A Treasury of Yiddish Stories. LC 54-9599. (Illus.). 630p. 1973. pap. 8.95 (ISBN 0-8052-0400-8). Schocken.
--Voices from the Yiddish: Essays, Memoirs & Diaries. LC 75-10751. 340p. 1975. pap. 5.95 (ISBN 0-8052-0495-4). Schocken.
Howe, Irving, ed. see Orwell, George.
Howe, Irving, ed. see Peretz, I. L.
Howe, J. From the Revolution Through the Age of Jackson. 1973. pap. text ed. 13.95 (ISBN 0-13-331348-4). P-H.
Howe, James. The Case of the Missing Mother. LC 82-13287. (Muppet Press Bks.). (Illus.). 32p. (gr. 1-6). 1983. pap. 1.95 (ISBN 0-394-85729-1). Random.
--A Night Without Stars. LC 82-16278. 192p. (gr. 4-6). 1983. 10.95 (ISBN 0-689-30957-0). Atheneum.
Howe, James R. Marlowe, Tamburlaine, & Magic. LC 75-36978. x, 220p. 1976. 12.95x (ISBN 0-8214-0200-5, 82-82063). Ohio U Pr.
Howe, Jeanne. Nursing Care of Adolescents. (Illus.). 1980. text ed. 21.50 (ISBN 0-07-030585-4). McGraw.
Howe, Jeffery W. The Symbolist Art of Fernand Knopff. Foster, Stephen, ed. LC 82-4734. (Studies in Fine Arts: The Avant Garde: No. 28). 274p. 1982. 39.95 (ISBN 0-8357-1317-2, Pub. by UMI Res Pr). Univ Microfilms.
Howe, John. Choosing the Right Dog. rev. ed. LC 79-3394. (Illus.). 176p. 1980. 11.49i (ISBN 0-06-012014-2, HarpT). Har-Row.
Howe, John B. Monetary & Industrial Fallacies: A Dialogue. Repr. of 1878 ed. lib. bdg. 15.50x (ISBN 0-8371-1102-1, HOIF). Greenwood.
Howe, John W. Our Anglican Heritage. LC 77-78492. (Church Heritage Ser.). 1977. pap. 1.95 o.p. (ISBN 0-89191-079-4). Cook.
Howe, Jonathan. Multicrises: Sea Power & Global Policies in the Missile Age. 1971. 27.50x (ISBN 0-262-08043-5). MIT Pr.
Howe, Joseph. Western & Eastern Rambles: Travel Sketches of Nova Scotia. Parks, M. G., ed. LC 72-97424. (Illus.). 1973. pap. 6.50 o.p. (ISBN 0-8020-6183-4). U of Toronto Pr.

Howe, Joseph & Blakey, Walker. Assignments in Trial Practice. 4th ed. 316p. 1975. pap. 12.00 (ISBN 0-316-37571-3). Little.

Howe, K. R. The Loyalty Islands: History of Culture Contacts, 1840-1900. LC 76-50009. 1977. 12.00x (ISBN 0-8248-0451-1). UH Pr.

Howe, Leland W. & Howe, Mary M. Personalizing Education: Values Clarification & Beyond. 448p. (Orig.). 1975. pap. 8.95 o.s.i. (ISBN 0-89104-189-3, A & W Visual Library). A & W Pubs.

Howe, Leland W. & Solomon, Bernard. How to Raise Children in a TV World. (A Hart Book). 320p. (Orig.). 1979. pap. 6.95 o.s.i. (ISBN 0-89104-235-0, A & W Visual Library). A & W Pubs.

Howe, Louise K. Pink Collar Workers. 1978. pap. 3.50 (ISBN 0-380-01924-8, 63008-7). Avon.

--Pink Collar Workers: Inside the World of Women's Work. 1977. 8.95 (ISBN 0-399-11558-7). Putnam Pub Group.

Howe, M., ed. Learning from Television. Date not set. price not set (ISBN 0-12-357160-X). Acad Pr.

Howe, Marguerite, jt. auth. see Senter, Sylvia.

Howe, Marguerite B. The Art of the Self in D. H. Lawrence. LC 75-39864. 164p. 1977. 12.00x (ISBN 0-8214-0234-X, 82-82360). Ohio U Pr.

Howe, Mark A. The Boston Symphony Orchestra: 1881-1931. rev. ed. Burk, John N., ed. LC 77-16532. (Music Reprint Ser.: 1978). (Illus.). 1978. Repr. of 1931 ed. lib. bdg. 29.50 (ISBN 0-306-77533-6). Da Capo.

--Touched with Fire Civil War Letters & Diary of Oliver Wendell Holmes. LC 73-96218. (American Scene Ser). 1969. Repr. of 1947 ed. lib. bdg. 24.50 (ISBN 0-306-71825-1). Da Capo.

--Venture in Remembrance. Repr. of 1941 ed. lib. bdg. 15.75x (ISBN 0-8371-3582-6, HORE). Greenwood.

Howe, Mark A., ed. Readings in American Legal History. LC 70-155924. (American Constitutional & Legal History Ser). 1971. Repr. of 1949 ed. lib. bdg. 59.50 (ISBN 0-306-70159-6). Da Capo.

Howe, Mark D. Justice Oliver Wendell Holmes, 2 vols. Incl. Vol. 1. The Shaping Years, 1841-1870. (Illus.). 330p. 1957 (ISBN 0-674-49500-4); Vol. 2. The Proving Years, 1870-1882. (Illus.). 1963. o.p. (ISBN 0-674-49501-2). 18.00x ea. o.p. (Belknap Pr). Harvard U Pr.

Howe, Mark D., ed. see Bancroft, George.

Howe, Mary M., jt. auth. see Howe, Leland W.

Howe, Michael J. Introduction to the Psychology of Memory. 160p. 1983. pap. text ed. 9.50 scp (ISBN 0-06-042925-9, HarpC). Har-Row.

Howe, Michael J. A. Adult Learning: Psychological Research & Applications. LC 76-44226. 256p. 1977. 48.95 (ISBN 0-471-99458-8, Pub. by Wiley-Interscience). Wiley.

Howe, P. J., ed. Advanced Converters & Near Breeders: Proceedings of the Wingspread Conference, Racine, Wisconsin, 1975. 1976. text ed. 22.50 (ISBN 0-08-020523-2). Pergamon.

Howe, Raymond E., ed. Producibility Machinability of Space-Age & Conventional Materials. LC 68-56154. (Manufacturing Data Ser). (Illus., Orig.). 1968. pap. 11.00x o.p. (ISBN 0-87263-013-7). SME.

Howe, Reuel L. Miracle of Dialogue. 1963. pap. 5.95 (ISBN 0-8164-2047-5, SP9). Seabury.

Howe, Richard, jt. auth. see Rohlich, Gerard.

Howe, Robin. French Cookery. 5.50x (ISBN 0-392-06255-0, LTB). Sportshelf.

--Rice Cooking. 276p. 1973. 10.00 o.s.i. (ISBN 0-233-96364-2). Transatlantic.

Howe, Susan W., jt. auth. see Whitney, John R.

Howe, Susannah. Fever Moon. (Orig.). 1978. pap. 1.95 o.s.i. (ISBN 0-515-04550-0). Jove Pubns.

Howe, W. D., jt. auth. see Burke, W. J.

Howe, W. S. The Dundee Textiles Industry 1960-1977: Decline & Diversification. 1982. 23.00 (ISBN 0-08-028454-X). Pergamon.

Howel, Terry K. Black Heritage. 1978. 8.95 o.p. (ISBN 0-533-03171-0). Vantage.

Howell. The Lincoln Plan. 1977. 7.00 (ISBN 0-685-05647-3). Assn Sch Busn.

Howell, A. A., jt. auth. see Fletcher, H.

Howell, A. G. Ferrers, tr. see Dante Alighieri.

Howell, Benjamin F., Jr. Introduction to Geophysics. rev. ed. LC 77-814. (International Ser. in the Earth & Planetary Sciences). (Illus.). 412p. 1978. Repr. of 1959 ed. lib. bdg. 22.50 (ISBN 0-88275-540-4). Krieger.

Howell, Bert, jt. auth. see Buzan, Norma.

Howell, Clinton. Joyous Journey. LC 78-14341. 1978. 6.95 (ISBN 0-8407-5137-0). Nelson.

Howell, Clinton T., ed. Harvest of Hope. LC 78-17312. 1978. 6.95 (ISBN 0-8407-5136-2). Nelson.

Howell, David. British Social Democracy: A Study in Development & Decay. 2nd ed. 340p. 1980. 28.50 o.p. (ISBN 0-312-10536-3). St Martin.

--British Social Democracy: A Study in Development & Decay. LC 76-11701. 1976. 28.50 (ISBN 0-312-10535-5). St Martin.

--Freedom & Capital: Prospects for the Property-Owning Democracy. (Mainstream Ser.). 136p. 1981. pap. text ed. 7.95x (ISBN 0-631-13042-X, Pub. by Basil Blackwell England). Biblio Dist.

Howell, David W. Land & People in Nineteenth-Century Wales. (Studies in Economic History). (Illus.). 1978. 24.95x (ISBN 0-7100-8673-3). Routledge & Kegan.

Howell, Edward. Enzyme Nutrition. 160p. 1983. pap. 7.95 (ISBN 0-686-43191-X). Avery Pub.

--Food Enzymes for Health & Longevity. (Illus.). 154p. 1981. pap. text ed. 5.95 (ISBN 0-933278-06-3). Twen Fir Cent.

Howell, Elizabeth & Bayes, Marjorie, eds. Women & Mental Health. LC 81-66982. 448p. 1981. text ed. 27.50x (ISBN 0-465-09202-0); pap. text ed. 18.95 (ISBN 0-465-09200-4). Basic.

Howell, F. Clark. Early Man. rev. ed. LC 80-52608. (Life Nature Library). 13.40 (ISBN 0-8094-3927-1). Silver.

--Early Man. (Young Readers Library). (Illus.). 1977. PLB 6.80 (ISBN 0-8094-1364-7). Silver.

Howell, Frank M. & Frese, Wolfgang. Making Life Plans: Race, Gender & Career Decisions. LC 80-6292. (Illus.). 414p. (Orig.). 1982. lib. bdg. 28.25 (ISBN 0-8191-2580-6); pap. text ed. 15.50 (ISBN 0-8191-2581-4). U Pr of Amer.

Howell, Fred G., et al, eds. Mineral Cycling in Southeastern Ecosystems: Proceedings. LC 75-33463. (ERDA Technical Information Center Ser.). 920p. 1975. pap. 31.00 (ISBN 0-87079-022-6, CONF-740513) (ISBN 0-87079-276-8, CONF-740513). DOE.

Howell, Georgina. In Vogue: Sixty Years of International Celebrities & Fashion from British Vogue. LC 75-42970. (Illus.). 1976. 34.95 o.s.i. (ISBN 0-8052-3624-4). Schocken.

Howell, J. R., jt. auth. see Siegel, R.

Howell, J. R., et al. Solar Thermal Energy Systems: Analysis & Design. 416p. 1982. 32.95x (ISBN 0-07-030603-6). McGraw.

Howell, James. Instruction for Forine Travel 1642. Arber, Edward, tr. Date not set. pap. 12.50 (ISBN 0-87556-499-2). Saifer.

Howell, James A., jt. ed. see Boltz, David F.

Howell, James F., jt. auth. see Hay, David E.

Howell, James M. & Stamm, Charles F. Urban Fiscal Stress: A Comparative Analysis of 66 U. S. Cities. LC 79-3083. 176p. 1979. 22.95x (ISBN 0-669-03372-3). Lexington Bks.

Howell, John B. Style Manuals of the English Speaking World: A Guide. 1983. price not set (ISBN 0-89774-089-0). Oryx Pr.

Howell, John C. The Citizens Do-It-Yourself Legal Guide. (Howell Legal Guide Ser.). 256p. 1981. pap. 9.95 o.p. (ISBN 0-89648-088-7). Hamilton Pr.

--Citizens Legal Guide for Avoiding Income Taxes. (Howell Legal Guides Ser.). 160p. 1981. pap. 7.95 o.p. (ISBN 0-89648-092-5). Hamilton Pr.

--Citizens Legal Guide for Avoiding Probate & Avoiding Estate Taxes. (Howell Legal Guides Ser). 256p. (Orig.). 1981. pap. 7.95 o.p. (ISBN 0-89648-090-9). Hamilton Pr.

--Dynamics of Memory Development. 224p. (Orig.). (gr. 11 up). 1981. pap. 8.95 o.p. (ISBN 0-89648-094-1). Hamilton Pr.

--Dynamics of Vocabulary Development: 1001 Words You Ought to Know. 224p. (Orig.). (gr. 11 up). 1981. pap. 8.95 o.p. (ISBN 0-89648-096-8). Hamilton Pr.

--Equality & Submission in Marriage. LC 78-67292. 1979. 7.95 (ISBN 0-8054-5632-5). Broadman.

--Form Your Own Corporation. 128p. 1980. pap. 5.95 o.p. (ISBN 0-13-329193-6, Spec). P-H.

--Howell Encyclopedia of Business Law. (Howell Legal Guides Ser.). 560p. (Orig.). 1981. pap. 24.95 o.p. (ISBN 0-89648-082-8). Hamilton Pr.

Howell, John C., jt. auth. see Hayes, Rick S.

Howell, John R., jt. auth. see Siegel, Robert.

Howell, Joseph T. Hard Living on Clay Street. LC 73-79736. 440p. 1973. pap. 6.50 (ISBN 0-385-05317-7, Anch). Doubleday.

Howell, Kenneth. Working with the Handicapped. 250p. 1983. pap. text ed. 8.95 (ISBN 0-675-20050-4). Merrill.

Howell, Kenneth W. & Kaplan, Joseph S. Evaluating Exceptional Children: A Task Analysis Approach. 320p. 1979. text ed. 23.95 (ISBN 0-675-08389-3). Additional supplements may be obtained from publisher. Merrill.

Howell, Kenneth W., et al. Handbook for Diagnosing Basic Skills: A Handbook for Deciding What to Teach. (Special Education Ser.). 393p. 1980. pap. text ed. 23.95 (ISBN 0-675-08130-0). Merrill.

Howell, Leonore, jt. auth. see McNamara, Charlotte.

Howell, Maxwell L., jt. auth. see Bennett, Bruce L.

Howell, Michael & Ford, Peter. The True History of the Elephant Man. (Illus.). 194p. 1980. 12.95 (ISBN 0-8052-8000-6, Pub. by Allison & Busby England). Schocken.

Howell, P. A. The Judicial Committee of the Privy Council: 1833-1876. LC 78-54326. (Studies in English Legal History). (Illus.). 1979. 39.50 (ISBN 0-521-22146-3). Cambridge U Pr.

Howell, Patricia L., jt. auth. see Howell, Robert G., Jr.

Howell, Peter. A Commentary on Book One of the Epigrams of Martial. 369p. 1980. text ed. 65.00x (ISBN 0-686-86084-5, Athlone Pr). Humanities.

Howell, R. H., jt. auth. see Sauer, J. J.

Howell, Rapalje, tr. see Tarde, Gabriel.

Howell, Robert B. The Deaconship. new ed. 3.00 o.p. (ISBN 0-8170-0784-9). Judson.

Howell, Robert E., jt. ed. see Weber, Bruce.

Howell, Robert G., Jr. & Howell, Patricia L. Discipline in the Classroom: Solving the Teaching Puzzle. (Illus.). 1980. text ed. 16.95 (ISBN 0-8359-1344-9). Reston.

Howell, Ruth R. Splash & Flow. LC 73-76318. (Illus.). 48p. (gr. k-3). 1973. 4.95 o.p. (ISBN 0-689-30101-4). Atheneum.

Howell, Sandra C. Designing for Aging: Patterns of Use. (Illus.). 329p. 1980. 27.50x (ISBN 0-262-08107-5). MIT Pr.

Howell, T. A. A Flora of Northwest America. (Reprints of U. S. Floras 9 Ser.: Vol. 1). 1978. Repr. lib. bdg. 32.00 (ISBN 3-7682-1170-3). Lubrecht & Cramer.

Howell, Thomas R. Breeding Biology of the Egyptian Plover, Pluvianus aegyptius. (U. C. Publications in Zoology Ser.: Vol. 113). 1980. pap. 15.50x (ISBN 0-520-03804-5). U of Cal Pr.

Howell, William C. & Dipboye, Robert L. Essentials of Industrial & Organizational Psychology. 1982. pap. 11.95x (ISBN 0-256-02740-4). Dorsey.

Howell, William S., jt. auth. see Brembeck, Winston L.

Howell, Y. & Miller, H. Everyone's Guide to Passive Solar Design: The Inexpensive Approach to Solar Energy. 100p. 1983. write for info o.p. (ISBN 0-89934-148-9, A918); pap. 9.50 o.p. (ISBN 0-89934-149-7, A018). Solar Energy Info.

Howells. Family Psychiatry in Medical Practice. 1977. cancelled o.p. (ISBN 0-407-00112-3). Butterworth.

Howells, Coral A. Love, Mystery & Misery: Feeling in Gothic Fiction. 1978. text ed. 32.75x (ISBN 0-485-11181-0, Athlone Pr). Humanities.

Howells, Harvey. Dowsing for Everyone. LC 78-26713. (Illus.). 1979. 8.95 o.p. (ISBN 0-8289-0341-7); pap. 7.95 (ISBN 0-8289-0342-5). Greene.

--Dowsing: Mind Over Matter. (Illus.). 132p. 1982. pap. 7.95 (ISBN 0-8289-0465-0). Greene.

Howells, John G. Integral Clinical Investigation: As Aspect of Panathropic Medicine. 272p. 1982. 65.00x (ISBN 0-333-29446-7, Pub. by Macmillan England). State Mutual Bk.

Howells, John G. & Lickorish, J. R. Family Relations Indicator. 1983. write for info (ISBN 0-8236-1883-8). Intl Univs Pr.

Howells, W. D. Selected Letters of W. D. Howells: 1852-1872, Vol. 1. Arms, George, et al, eds. (Critical Editions Programs). 1979. lib. bdg. 30.00 (ISBN 0-8057-8527-2, Twayne). G K Hall.

Howells, W. W. Cranial Variation in Man: A Study by Multivariate Analysis. LC 73-77203. (Peabody Museum Papers: Vol. 67). 1973. pap. text ed. 20.00x (ISBN 0-87365-189-8). Peabody Harvard.

Howells, William. The Heathens. LC 48-5578. 5.50 o.p. (ISBN 0-385-01611-5). Natural Hist.

Howells, William D. Hazard of New Fortunes. pap. 2.95 (ISBN 0-451-51597-8, CE1597, Sig Classics). NAL.

--Imaginary Interviews. LC 69-13938. (Illus.). 358p. Repr. of 1910 ed. lib. bdg. 17.00x (ISBN 0-8371-2080-2, HOII). Greenwood.

--The Landlord at Lion's Head. (Illus.). 512p. 1983. pap. 8.95 (ISBN 0-486-24455-5). Dover.

--Literary Friends & Acquaintance: A Personal Retrospect of American Authorship. Repr. of 1911 ed. lib. bdg. 17.75x (ISBN 0-8371-4090-0, HOLF). Greenwood.

--Novels Eighteen Seventy-Five to Eighteen Eighty-Six. Cady, Edwin H., ed. LC 82-112. 1218p. 1982. 27.50 (ISBN 0-940450-04-6). Literary Classics.

--Prefaces to Contemporaries, 1882-1920. LC 57-6416. 1978. Repr. 30.00x (ISBN 0-8201-1238-0). Schol Facsimiles.

--Rise of Silas Lapham. (RL 9). pap. 2.25 (ISBN 0-451-51590-0, CE1590, Sig Classics). NAL.

--The Rise of Silas Lapham. rev. ed. Dixson, Robert J., ed. (American Classics Ser.: No. 8). 1974. pap. text ed. 3.25 (ISBN 0-88345-204-9, 18127); cassettes 40.00 (ISBN 0-685-38925-1); 40.00 o.p. tapes (ISBN 0-685-38926-X). Regents Pub.

--The Rise of Silas Lapham. 1983. pap. 4.95 (ISBN 0-14-039030-8). Penguin.

Hower, Alfred, tr. see Pereira, Antonio O.

Howery, Darryl G., jt. auth. see Malinowski, Edmund R.

Howes, Alan B. Teaching Literature to Adolescents: Plays. 1968. pap. 9.95x (ISBN 0-673-05830-1). Scott F.

Howes, Alan B., jt. auth. see Dunning, Stephen.

Howes, Barbara. Moving. LC 82-84115. 70p. (Orig.). Date not set. pap. 3.95 (ISBN 0-941692-00-0); Ltd. Sign. ed 10.00, (ISBN 0-941692-01-9). Elysian Pr.

Howes, C. Practical Upholstery. rev. ed. LC 77-18394. (Home Craftsman Bk.). (Illus.). 128p. 1980. pap. 6.95 (ISBN 0-8069-8578-X). Sterling.

Howes, Durwood, ed. American Women Nineteen Thirty-Five to Nineteen-Forty, 2 vols. LC 80-17368. (Gale Composite Biographical Dictionary Ser.: No. 6). 1500p. 1981. Set. 130.00x (ISBN 0-8103-0403-1). Gale.

Howes, F. N. Dictionary of Useful & Everyday Plants & Their Common Names. LC 73-91701. 300p. 1974. 34.50 (ISBN 0-521-08520-9). Cambridge U Pr.

Howes, Fred. This Is the Prophet Jesus. LC 82-72741. 256p. 1983. pap. 8.95 (ISBN 0-87516-497-8). De Vorss.

Howes, M. J. & Morgan, D. V. Charge Coupled Devices & Systems. 300p. 1979. 54.95 (ISBN 0-471-99665-3). Wiley.

--Large Scale Integration: Devices, Circuits & Systems. LC 80-42016. (Wiley Ser. in Solid State Devices & Circuits). 352p. 1981. 35.95x (ISBN 0-471-27988-9, Pub. by Wiley-Interscience). Wiley.

--Optical Fiber Communications: Devices, Circuits & Systems. LC 79-40512. (Wiley Series in Solid State Devices & Circuits). 1980. 56.95 (ISBN 0-471-27611-1, Pub. by Wiley-Interscience). Wiley.

--Reliability & Degradation: Semiconductor Devices & Circuits. LC 80-42310. (Wiley Series in Solid State Devices & Circuits). 424p. 1981. 55.00x (ISBN 0-471-28028-3, Pub. by Wiley-Interscience). Wiley.

Howes, M. J. & Morgan, D. V., eds. Microwave Devices: Device Circuit Interaction. LC 75-15887. (Solid State Devices & Circuits Ser.). 426p. 1976. 71.95 (ISBN 0-471-41729-7, Pub. by Wiley-Interscience). Wiley.

--Variable Impedance Devices. LC 78-4122. (Solid State Devices & Circuits Ser.). 1978. 59.95 (ISBN 0-471-99651-3, Pub. by Wiley-Interscience). Wiley.

Howes, V. M. Informal Teaching in the Open Classroom. 1974. pap. 11.95x (ISBN 0-02-357330-9). Macmillan.

Howes, Vernon E. Essentials of Mathematics: Precalculus-a Programmed Text. LC 75-9733. 1975. Bk. 1: Algebra I. text ed. 18.95x o.p. (ISBN 0-471-41736-X); Bk. 2: Algebra II. text ed. o.p. (ISBN 0-471-41737-8); Bk. 3: Trigonometric Functions & Applications. text ed. 23.95x o.p. (ISBN 0-471-41738-6); instr's manual 6.00 o.p. (ISBN 0-471-41739-4). Wiley.

Howes, Wright, ed. U. S. - Iana. 2nd ed. 1978. Repr. 47.50 (ISBN 0-8352-0103-1). Bowker.

Howett, Jerry. Building Basic Skills in Mathematics. (Orig.). 1981. pap. 5.55 (ISBN 0-8092-5877-3). Contemp Bks.

--The Cambridge Program for the GED Mathematics Test. (GED Preparation Ser.). (Illus.). 352p. (Orig.). 1981. pap. text ed. 5.87 (ISBN 0-8428-9386-5); Cambridge Exercise Book for the Mathematics Test wkbk. 96 p. 3.33 (ISBN 0-8428-9393-8). Cambridge Bk.

--Number Power: The Real World of Adult Math. Somerfield, Benita & Schenk, Brian, eds. LC 76-27723. (Orig.). 1977. wkbk. 3.85 (ISBN 0-8092-8011-6). Contemp Bks.

--Number Power 2: Fractions, Decimals, Percents. 1977. wkbk. 3.85 (ISBN 0-8092-8010-8). Contemp Bks.

Howey & Bents, eds. School-Focused Inservice: Description & Discussions. 1981. 6.00 (ISBN 0-686-38076-2). Assn Tchr Ed.

Howey, Kenneth R. & Garner, William E., eds. The Education of Teachers: A Look Ahead. LC 81-20841. (Professional Bk.). (Illus.). 240p. 1982. text ed. 25.00tx (ISBN 0-582-28354-X). Longman.

Howick, William H. Philosophies of Education. 2nd ed. xiv, 150p. 1980. pap. 8.95x (ISBN 0-8134-2146-2). Interstate.

Howie, Carl G. Ezekiel, Daniel. LC 59-10454. (Layman's Bible Commentary, Vol. 13). 1961. pap. 3.95 (ISBN 0-8042-3073-0). John Knox.

Howie, John. Perspectives for Moral Decisions. LC 80-6102. 192p. 1981. lib. bdg. 19.75 (ISBN 0-8191-1375-1); pap. text ed. 9.75 (ISBN 0-8191-1376-X). U Pr of Amer.

Howie, John, ed. Ethical Principles for Social Policy. 1982. 16.95x (ISBN 0-8093-1063-5). S Ill U Pr.

Howie, John & Buford, Thomas O., eds. Contemporary Studies in Philosophical Idealism. LC 74-76007. (Philosophy Ser.: No. 601). 285p. 1976. 15.00 (ISBN 0-89007-601-4). C Stark.

Howie, John & Rouner, Leroy, eds. The Wisdom of William Earnest Hocking. LC 78-61397. 1978. pap. text ed. 7.25 (ISBN 0-8191-0595-3). U Pr of Amer.

Howie, Patricia A. & Winkleman, Gretchen. Behavior Modification: A Practical Guide for the Classroom Teacher. 1976. 14.95 (ISBN 0-13-072678-8, Parker). P-H.

Howington, Jon. Laboratory Manual for Introductory Criminal Investigation. pap. text ed. 9.50 (ISBN 0-8191-0070-6). U Pr of Amer.

Howkes. Twentieth Century Interpretations of Macbeth. 1977. 8.95 o.p. (ISBN 0-13-541458-X, Spec); pap. 2.45 o.p. (ISBN 0-13-541441-5, Spec). P-H.

Howkins, Ben. Rich, Rare & Red: Guide to Port. (Illus.). 224p. 1983. 18.95 (ISBN 0-434-34909-7, Pub. by Heinemann England). David & Charles.

Howkins, John. New Technologies, New Policies? 74p. 1982. pap. 9.95 (ISBN 0-85170-128-0). NY Zoetrope.

Howkins, John & Stallworthy, John. Bonney's Gynaecological Survey. 8th ed. (Illus.). 1974. text ed. 37.50 o.p. (ISBN 0-02-858070-2, Pub. by Bailliere-Tindall). Saunders.

Howland, Bette. Things to Come & Go: Three Stories. LC 82-48724. 192p. 1983. 11.95 (ISBN 0-394-53032-2). Knopf.

Howland, Charles P. Survey of American Foreign Relations: 1928, 1929, 1930, 1931. Ea. 49.50x (ISBN 0-686-50174-8). Elliots Bks.

Howland, Gerald. You're in the Driver's Seat. 128p. (Orig.). 1981. pap. 6.95 (ISBN 0-8289-0418-9). Greene.

Howland, Harold. Theodore Roosevelt & His Times. 1921. text ed. 8.50x (ISBN 0-686-83813-0). Elliots Bks.

Howland, Joseph, jt. auth. see Gilbart, Helen.
Howland, Joseph W., jt. auth. see Hackworth, Robert D.
Howland, Llewellyn & Storey, Isabelle, eds. A Book for Boston. LC 79-55279. (Illus.). 1980. 17.95 (ISBN 0-87923-317-6); pap. 6.95 (ISBN 0-87923-321-4). Godine.
Howley, Robert C. & Simon, Sidney B. Composition for Personal Growth: A Teacher's Handbook of Meaningful Student Writing Experiences. 184p. (Orig.). 1983. pap. 9.95 (ISBN 0-913636-15-0). Educ Res MA.
Howorth, Beckett. Cure Your Own Backache. LC 82-17468. (Illus.). 128p. 1983. 9.95 (ISBN 0-87805-172-4). U Pr of Miss.
Howorth, Muriel. Atomic Transmutation: Memoirs of Fred Soddy. 1953. 12.50 (ISBN 0-911268-01-4). Rogers Bk.
Howsam, Robert, jt. auth. see Houston, Robert.
Howsden, Jackie L. Work & the Helpless Self: The Social Organization of a Nursing Home. LC 81-40132. (Illus.). 176p. (Orig.). 1982. lib. bdg. 20.00 (ISBN 0-8191-1750-1); pap. text ed. 9.50 (ISBN 0-8191-1751-X). U Pr of Amer.
Howse, Arthur, ed. see Howard, Edward.
Howse, Derek. Greenwich Time & the Discovery of the Longitude. (Illus.). 1980. 25.00x (ISBN 0-19-215948-8). Oxford U Pr.
Howse, P. E. Termites: A Study in Social Behavior. 1970. pap. text ed. 5.50x o.p. (ISBN 0-09-100841-7, Hutchinson U Lib). Humanities.
Howser, Harry S. Richard I in England (1189-1194) (Medieval People Ser.: Vol. 1). (Illus.). 80p. (Orig.). 1983. 19.95 (ISBN 0-86663-100-3); pap. 12.95 (ISBN 0-86663-101-1). Ide Hse.
Howson, A. G. A Handbook of Terms Used in Algebra & Analysis. LC 71-178281. (Illus.). 260p. 1972. 35.50 (ISBN 0-521-08434-2); pap. 14.95 (ISBN 0-521-09695-2). Cambridge U Pr.
--A History of Mathematics Education in England. LC 82-4175. (Illus.). 300p. 1982. 49.50 (ISBN 0-521-24206-1). Cambridge U Pr.
Howson, A. G., jt. auth. see Griffiths, H. B.
Howson, A. G., ed. Developments in Mathematical Education. (Illus.). 250p. 1973. 35.50 (ISBN 0-521-20190-X); pap. 15.95 (ISBN 0-521-09803-3). Cambridge U Pr.
Howson, A. G., et al. Curriculum Development in Mathematics. LC 80-41205. 200p. 1981. 54.50 (ISBN 0-521-23767-X); pap. 13.95 (ISBN 0-521-27053-7). Cambridge U Pr.
Howson, C., ed. Method & Appraisal in the Physical Sciences. LC 75-44580. 280p. 1976. 47.50 (ISBN 0-521-21110-7). Cambridge U Pr.
Howson, D. P. Mathematics for Electronic Technology. 280p. 1975. text ed. 31.00 o.p. (ISBN 0-08-018219-4); pap. text ed. 17.00 (ISBN 0-08-018218-6). Pergamon.
Howson, Geoffrey, ed. Children at School: Primary Education in Britain Today. LC 75-106645. (Illus.). 1970. pap. text ed. 7.25x (ISBN 0-8077-1523-9). Tchrs Coll.
Howson, Mark, tr. see Barthel, Manfred.
Howson, Rosemary J., jt. auth. see Turner, Lawrence E.
Howson, S. & Winch, D. The Economic Advisory Council 1930-1939. LC 75-38187. (Illus.). 1977. 74.50 (ISBN 0-521-21138-7). Cambridge U Pr.
Howson, Susan. Domestic Monetary Management in Britain, 1919-38. LC 75-21032. (Department of Applied Economics, Occasional Papers Ser.: No. 48). 1975. 37.50 (ISBN 0-521-21059-3); pap. 18.95 (ISBN 0-521-29026-0). Cambridge U Pr.
--Sterling's Managed Float: The Operations of the Exchange Equalisation Account, 1932-39. LC 80-23197. (Princeton Studies in International Finance: No. 46). 1980. pap. text ed. 4.50x (ISBN 0-88165-217-2). Princeton U Int Finan Econ.
Hoxa, Enver. Party of Labor of Albania, Report Submitted to the 8th Congress. 82p. 1981. pap. 2.00 (ISBN 0-86714-021-6). Marxist-Leninist.
Hoxeng, James, jt. ed. see Evans, David.
Hoxie, R. G. Command Decision & the Presidency. 1977. 15.00 (ISBN 0-07-030605-2). McGraw.
Hoxie, R. Gordon. Command Decision & the Presidency. LC 77-88416. 1977. 15.00 o.p. (ISBN 0-88349-162-1). Readers Digest Pr.
Hoy, Anne. Annie on Camera. Grubb, Nancy, ed. LC 81-20497. (Illus.). 192p. 1982. 29.95 (ISBN 0-89659-277-4); pap. 19.95 (ISBN 0-89659-278-2). Abbeville Pr.
Hoy, Cyrus. Introductions, Notes & Commentaries to Texts in the Dramatic Works of Thomas Dekker, 4 vols. Bowers, Fredson, ed. LC 77-80838. Vol. 1, Nov. 1980. 57.50 (ISBN 0-521-21786-5); Vol. 2, Nov. 1980. 57.50 (ISBN 0-521-21894-2); Vol. 3, May. 1980. 59.50 (ISBN 0-521-22336-9); Vol. 4, May 1981. 49.50 (ISBN 0-521-22506-X). Cambridge U Pr.
Hoy, David. Psychic & Other ESP Party Games. 144p. 1979. pap. 2.95 (ISBN 0-06-463485-X, EH 485, EH). B&N NY.
Hoy, David C. The Critical Circle: Literature & History in Contemporary Hermeneutics. LC 76-52028. 1978. 23.00x (ISBN 0-520-03434-1). U of Cal Pr.
Hoy, Helen, ed. Modern English-Canadian Prose: A Guide to Information Sources. LC 73-16996. (American Literature, English Literature & World Literature in English Ser.: Vol. 38). 435p. 1983. 42.00x (ISBN 0-8103-1245-X). Gale.
Hoy, James. The Cattle Guard: Its History & Lore. LC 82-9055. (Illus.). 248p. 1982. 19.95x (ISBN 0-7006-0226-7). Univ Pr KS.
Hoy, James F. & Somer, John, eds. The Language Experience. 288p. 1974. pap. 2.95 o.s.i. (ISBN 0-440-54640-0, Delta). Dell.
Hoy, John C. & Bernstein, Melvin H., eds. Business & Academia: Partners in New England's Economic Renewal. LC 80-54467. (Futures of New England Ser.). 174p. 1981. 13.50x (ISBN 0-87451-197-6). U Pr of New Eng.
--Financing Higher Education: The Public Investment. 200p. 1982. 19.95 (ISBN 0-86569-114-2). Auburn Hse.
--New England's Vital Resource: The Labor Force. LC 82-3902. 149p. 1982. 12.00. NE Board Higher Ed.
Hoy, Ken. On Nature's Trail. LC 78-65673. (Illus.). 128p. 1979. 16.95 o.s.i. (ISBN 0-89479-039-0). A & W Pubs.
Hoy, Marjorie. Recent Advances in Knowledge of the Phytoseiidae. (Illus.). 100p. (Orig.). 1983. pap. 7.00x (ISBN 0-931876-62-1). Ag Sci Pubns.
Hoy, Michael & Stevens, Michael. Chaucer's Major Tales. LC 82-10419. 192p. 1983. 15.00 (ISBN 0-8052-3844-1); pap. 5.95 (ISBN 0-8052-0734-1). Schocken.
Hoy, Michael, compiled by. Directory of Mail Drops in the United States & Canada: 1981 Edition. 1983. pap. 7.95 (ISBN 0-686-23954-7). Loompanics.
Hoy, Sharon W. Cuisine of China. LC 80-70735. (Illus.). 310p. 1982. 15.95 (ISBN 0-9607508-1-9). Benshaw Pub.
Hoy, Suellen M. & Robinson, Michael C., eds. Public Works History in the United States: A Guide to the Literature. LC 81-19114. 49.00 (ISBN 0-910050-63-5). AASLH.
Hoy, Wayne K. & Miskel, Cecil G. Educational Administration: Theory, Research, & Practice. 1978. text ed. 13.95x o.p. (ISBN 0-394-31915-X). Random.
Hoye, David. Solar-Gas. 202p. 1979. pap. 7.95 (ISBN 0-935494-00-6). Rutan Pub.
Hoyem, George A. The History & Development of Small Arms Ammunition: Cartridge Value Guide to Vols. One & Two. LC 80-67532. (Illus.). 16p. 1982. pap. 4.00x (ISBN 0-9604982-1-4). Armory Pubns.
Hoyem, T. & Kvale, O., eds. Physical, Chemical & Biological Changes in Food Caused by Thermal Processing. (Illus.). 1977. 106.75 (ISBN 0-85334-729-8, Pub. by Applied Sci England). Elsevier.
Hoyenga, Katharine B. & Hoyenga, Kermit T. The Question of Sex Differences: Psychological, Cultural & Biological Issues. 1979. text ed. 18.95 (ISBN 0-316-37597-7); tchrs' manual avail. (ISBN 0-316-37598-5). Little.
Hoyenga, Kermit T., jt. auth. see Hoyenga, Katharine B.
Hoyer, G. W. And Live under Him. (gr. 8-9). 1967. text ed. 6.45 (ISBN 0-570-06236-5, 22-2144); wkbk. 3.95 (ISBN 0-570-06237-3, 22-2145); teachers ed. 12.95 (ISBN 0-570-06238-1, 22-2146); 5 color filmstrips with record 10.00 ea. Concordia.
Hoyer, Mary. Mary Hoyer & Her Dolls. 232p. 1982. 17.95 (ISBN 0-87588-182-3). Hobby Hse.
Hoyer, S., ed. The Aging Brain: Physiological & Pathophysiological Aspects. (Experimental Brain Research Ser.: Supplementum 5). (Illus.). 281p. 1982. 45.00 (ISBN 0-387-11394-0). Springer-Verlag.
Hoyer, V., ed. see Bohr, Niels.
Hoyer, William, jt. auth. see Huyck, Margaret H.
Hoyer, William J., jt. auth. see Lopez, Martita A.
Hoyle, B. S. The Foundation of East African Geography: The Life & Work of Clement Gillman 1882-1946. 1982. 80.00x o.p. (ISBN 0-86127-303-6, Pub. by Avebury Pub England). State Mutual Bk.
--The Foundation of East African Geography: The Life & Work of Clement Gillman, 1882-1946. 240p. 1983. text ed. 35.95x (ISBN 0-86127-303-6, Pub. by Avebury England). Humanities.
Hoyle, Brian & Pinder, David, eds. Cityport Industrialization: Spatial Analysis & Planning Strategies Cityport Industrialization,15-18 Nov. 1978, Univ. Of Southampton. LC 80-40837. (Urban & Regional Planning Ser.). (Illus.). 350p. 1981. 60.00 (ISBN 0-08-025815-8). Pergamon.
Hoyle, Brian S. Spatial Aspects of Development. LC 73-2785. 372p. 1974. 49.95 (ISBN 0-471-41753-X). Wiley.
Hoyle, Edmund. Hoyle's Games. 20th, rev. ed. 1967. Repr. of 1950 ed. 15.00 (ISBN 0-7100-1566-6). Routledge & Kegan.
Hoyle, Fred. The Black Cloud. 192p. 1973. pap. 2.25 (ISBN 0-451-11432-9, AE1432, Sig). NAL.
--Evolution from Space (The Omni Lecture) And Other Papers on the Origin of Life. LC 82-8856. (Illus.). 80p. 1982. 8.95x (ISBN 0-89490-083-8). Enslow Pubs.
Hoyle, Fred & Wickramasinghe, C. Evolution from Space. 1982. 13.50 (ISBN 0-671-45031-X). S&S.
Hoyle, Fred & Wickramasinghe, Chandra. Space Travellers: The Bringers of Life. LC 82-1492. 192p. 1982. text ed. 17.50x (ISBN 0-89490-061-7). Enslow Pubs.
Hoyle, G. Electroslag Processes: Principles & Practice. (Illus.). 228p. 1982. 51.25 (ISBN 0-85334-164-8). Elsevier.
Hoyle, G., jt. auth. see Duckworth, Walter E.
Hoyle, Graham. Muscles & Their Neural Control. 672p. 1983. 59.95 (ISBN 0-471-87709-3, Pub. by Wiley-Interscience). Wiley.
Hoyle, L. Influenza Viruses. (Virology Monographs: Vol. 4). (Illus.). 1968. 59.00 (ISBN 0-387-80892-2). Springer-Verlag.
Hoyle, Ralph L. Checan. 1982. 90.00x (ISBN 0-686-94090-3, Pub. by C Skilton Scotland). State Mutual Bk.
Hoyos, Ramon R. D. Vigilia & Cantico. (Poetry Ser.). 70p. 1982. pap. 6.00 (ISBN 0-686-37370-7). Edit Asol.
Hoy Siu, Ralph Gun see Gun Hoy Siu, Ralph.
Hoyt, Charles A. Witchcraft. LC 80-24731. 160p. 1981. 19.95 o.p. (ISBN 0-8093-0964-5); pap. 10.95 (ISBN 0-8093-1015-5). S Ill U Pr.
Hoyt, David W. The Old Families of Salisbury-& Amesbury, MA. 1100p. 1981. Repr. 55.00x (ISBN 0-89725-026-5). NH Pub Co.
Hoyt, Edwin P. Airborne: The History of American Parachute Forces. (Illus.). 256p. 1982. 12.95 (ISBN 0-8128-2573-X); pap. 8.95 (ISBN 0-8128-6127-2). Stein & Day.
--The Battle of Leyte Gulf. (War Bks.). 368p. 1983. pap. 2.50 (ISBN 0-87216-629-5). Jove Pubns.
--The Destroyer Killer. LC 81-22075. 256p. Date not set. price not set (ISBN 0-8397-1942-6). Eriksson. Postponed.
--The Glory of the Solomons. LC 82-48513. 320p. 1983. 17.95. Stein & Day.
--Guadalcanal. LC 80-5433. 320p. 1981. 14.95 (ISBN 0-8128-2735-X). Stein & Day.
--Guadalcanal. 320p. 1983. pap. 3.25 (ISBN 0-515-07103-X). Jove Pubns.
--The Kamikazes. (Illus.). 1983. 16.50 (ISBN 0-87795-496-8). Arbor Hse.
--Merrill's Marauders. 160p. (Orig.). 1980. pap. 1.95 o.p. (ISBN 0-523-41590-7). Pinnacle Bks.
--Submarines at War. LC 81-40808. (Illus.). 288p. 1982. 18.95 (ISBN 0-8128-2833-X). Stein & Day.
--War in the Deep: Pacific Submarine Action in World War II. LC 77-16769. (Illus.). (gr. 6-8). 1978. 8.95 (ISBN 0-399-20629-9). Putnam Pub Group.
Hoyt, Fred, jt. auth. see Seifert, Anne.
Hoyt, Herman A. Studies in Revelation. pap. 4.95 (ISBN 0-88469-118-7). BMH Bks.
Hoyt, J. W., ed. Cavitation & Polyphase Flow Forum-Nineteen Eighty-Two. 65p. 1982. 20.00 (G00208). ASME.
Hoyt, John R. As the Pro Flies. (Illus.). 1959. 12.95 (ISBN 0-07-030610-9, GB). McGraw.
Hoyt, John S., Jr. Personal Time Management Manual. 11th ed ed. 246p. 1981. 15.00 (ISBN 0-943000-08-4). Telstar Inc.
Hoyt, John S., Sr. Personal Time Management Manual. rev. 12th ed. 246p. 1983. write for info. Telstar Inc.
Hoyt, Joseph B. Man & the Earth. 3rd ed. (Illus.). 512p. 1973. text ed. 26.95 (ISBN 0-13-550947-5). P-H.
Hoyt, Murray. Creative Retirement: Planning the Best Years Yet. LC 74-75465. 120p. 1974. 5.95 o.p. (ISBN 0-88266-034-9); pap. 3.95 o.p. (ISBN 0-88266-033-0). Garden Way Pub.
Hoyt, Nancy. Elinor Wylie: The Portrait of an Unknown Lady. LC 76-56441. (Illus.). 1977. Repr. of 1935 ed. lib. bdg. 19.75x (ISBN 0-8371-9413-X, HOEW). Greenwood.
Hoyt, Olga. Exorcism. LC 77-17084. (Illus.). (gr. 7 up). 1978. 8.90 (ISBN 0-531-01480-0). Watts.
Hoyt, Richard. The Siskiyou Two-Step. 224p. 1983. 10.95 (ISBN 0-688-01636-7). Morrow.
--Trotsky's Run. LC 82-6343. 252p. 1982. 12.50 (ISBN 0-688-01311-2). Morrow.
Hoyt, Robert S. Royal Demesne in English Constitutional History, 1066-1272. LC 68-23299. 1968. Repr. of 1968 ed. lib. bdg. 16.00x (ISBN 0-8371-0109-3, HORD). Greenwood.
Hoyt, Robert S. & Chodorow, Stanley. Europe in the Middle Ages. 3rd ed. (Illus.). 707p. 1976. pap. text ed. 23.95 (ISBN 0-15-524712-3, HC). HarBraceJ.
Hoyt, S. C., jt. auth. see Croft, B. A.
Hoyt, Samuel L. Men of Metals. 1979. 16.00 (ISBN 0-87170-059-X). ASM.
Hoyt, William Henry. The Mecklenburg Declaration of Independence. LC 76-166330. (Era of the American Revolution Ser). 284p. 1972. Repr. of 1907 ed. lib. bdg. 39.50 (ISBN 0-306-70248-7). Da Capo.
Hraba, Joseph. American Ethnicity. LC 78-61877. 1979. text ed. 16.50 (ISBN 0-87581-236-8). Peacock Pubs.
Hrabal, Shirley M. So You Want to Have a Facelift-Great! 1979. 4.95 o.p. (ISBN 0-533-04020-5). Vantage.
Hranitz, John R. & Noakes, Ann M., eds. Working with the Young Child: A Text of Readings-II. LC 78-56266. 1978. pap. text ed. 20.50 (ISBN 0-8191-0520-1). U Pr of Amer.
Hrapchak, Barbara B., jt. auth. see Sheehan, Denza C.
Hrdlicka, Ales. The Most Ancient Skeletal Remains of Man. 2nd ed. Bd. with The Skeletal Remains of Early Man. Hrdlicka, Ales. 1930. LC 78-72697. 1916. 80.00 (ISBN 0-404-18268-2, -). AMS Pr.
Hrdy, Sarah B. The Women That Never Evolved. 276p. 1983. pap. 6.95x (ISBN 0-674-95541-2). Harvard U Pr.
Hrebic, Herbert J., jt. auth. see Cahill, Robert B.
Hrebiniak, Lawrence G. Complex Organizations. (Management Ser.). 1978. text ed. 19.95 (ISBN 0-8299-0169-8). West Pub.
Hrebiniak, Lawrence G. & Joyce, William F. Implementing Strategy. 224p. Date not set. text ed. 11.95 (ISBN 0-02-357540-9). Macmillan.
Hresko, W. P., jt. auth. see Reid, D. K.
Hridayananda dasa Goswami Acaryadeva. Srimad-Bhagavatam: Eleventh Canto, Vol. 1. Gopiparanadhana dasa Adhikari, et al, eds. (Illus.). 450p. 1982. 9.95 (ISBN 0-89213-112-8); text ed. 9.95 (ISBN 0-686-98021-2). Bhaktivedanta.
Hromas, Bobi. Passport to the Bible. 1980. pap. 3.85 (ISBN 0-8423-4802-6). Tyndale.
Hromic, Alma. The Lonelier Road. 1982. 7.95 (ISBN 0-533-05220-3). Vantage.
Hrubec, C., jt. auth. see Behrman, J. R.
Hrubesh, Lawrence W., jt. auth. see Varma, Ravi.
Hsaio, David K. Systems Programming: Concepts of Operating & Data Base Systems. LC 74-30699. (Illus.). 352p. 1975. text ed. 26.95 (ISBN 0-201-02950-2). A-W.
Hsia, Linda. Speak Chinese: Supplementary Materials. 6.50 (ISBN 0-686-09999-0); tapes avail. (ISBN 0-686-10000-X). Far Eastern Pubns.
Hsia, Linda & Yue, Roger. Strange Stories from a Chinese Studio. 6.75 (ISBN 0-686-09984-2); tapes avail. (ISBN 0-686-09985-0). Far Eastern Pubns.
Hsia, Miriam, jt. auth. see Caputo, Robert.
Hsia, Tien C. System Identification: Least Squares Method. LC 75-3515. (Illus.). 192p. 1977. 29.95x (ISBN 0-669-99630-0). Lexington Bks.
Hsiacd Chun, pseud. Village in August. LC 74-3729. 313p. 1974. Repr. lib. bdg. 18.25x (ISBN 0-8371-7458-9, HSVA). Greenwood.
Hsiao. Sino-American Normalization. 300p. 1983. 27.95 (ISBN 0-03-058022-6); pap. 9.95 (ISBN 0-03-058023-4). Praeger.
Hsiao, Gene T. Foreign Trade of China: Policy, Law, & Practice. LC 76-7768. 1977. 40.00x (ISBN 0-520-03257-8). U of Cal Pr.
Hsiao, James C. & Cleaver, David S. Management Science: Quantitative Approaches to Resource Allocation & Decision Making. LC 80-80960. (Illus.). 584p. 1982. text ed. 26.95 (ISBN 0-395-29488-6); instr's. manual 3.00 (ISBN 0-395-29489-4). HM.
Hsiao, T. C. Directory of Computer Education & Research: International Education. 500p. 1983. cancelled o.p. Sci & Tech Pr.
Hsiao, T. C., ed. Computer Dissertations: First Supplement 1976-1978. LC 78-59418. 350p. 1983. 32.00x (ISBN 0-686-60280-3). Sci & Tech Pr.
--Computer Dissertations Nineteen Fifty to Nineteen Seventy-Five. LC 78-59418. 500p. 1983. 58.00x (ISBN 0-686-09239-2). Sci & Tech Pr.
--Computer Dissertations: Second Supplement, 1979-1980. LC 78-59418. 300p. 1983. 28.00x (ISBN 0-686-28922-6). Sci & Tech Pr.
--Computer Faculty Directory (International Edition) LC 81-51818. 450p. 1983. 50.00x (ISBN 0-686-30601-5). Sci & Tech Pr.
--Computer Faculty Directory (U. S. Edition) LC 81-51817. 450p. 1983. 50.00x (ISBN 0-686-28923-4). Sci & Tech Pr.
--Directory of Computer Education & Research, 2 vols. Incl. Vol. 1. Senior Colleges; Vol. 2. Junior Colleges. LC 72-91675. 1800p. 1973. 50.00x set (ISBN 0-686-05822-4). Sci & Tech Pr.
--Directory of Computer Education & Research: (U. S. Edition) LC 81-51816. 1100p. 1983. 120.00x (ISBN 0-686-28968-4). Sci & Tech Pr.
Hsiao Han see Chow Chen-Ho.
Hsie, Abraham W., et al, eds. Banbury Report 2: Mammalian Cell Mutagenesis: The Maturation of Test Systems. LC 79-21186. (Banbury Report Ser.). (Illus.). 504p. 1979. 45.00x (ISBN 0-87969-201-4). Cold Spring Harbor.
Hsieh, Alice L. Communist China's Strategy in Nuclear Era. LC 75-45069. (Illus.). 204p. 1976. Repr. of 1962 ed. lib. bdg. 16.25x (ISBN 0-8371-8654-4, HSCC). Greenwood.
Hsieh, Andrew C. K., jt. tr. see Cochran, Sherman.
Hsieh, J. S. Principles of Thermodynamics. 800p. 1974. text ed. 32.00 o.p. (ISBN 0-07-030630-3, C). McGraw.
Hsieh, R. K., jt. ed. see Brulin, O.
Hsieh, Yuan-Yu. Elementary Steel Structures. (Civil Engineering & Engineering Mechanics Ser). (Illus.). 192p. 1973. ref. ed. 29.95 (ISBN 0-13-260158-3). P-H.
--Elementary Theory of Structures. 2nd ed. (Illus.). 448p. 1982. 31.95 (ISBN 0-13-261545-2). P-H.
Hsieh Pingying. Girl Rebel: The Autobiography of Hsieh Pingying with Extracts from Her "New War Diaries". Lin, Adet & Lin, Anor, trs. from Chinese. LC 74-34583. (China in the 20th Century Ser). (Illus.). xviii, 270p. 1975. Repr. of 1940 ed. lib. bdg. 32.50 (ISBN 0-306-70691-1). Da Capo.

Hsiung, Chuan-Chih. A First Course in Differential Geometry. LC 80-22112. (Pure & Applied Mathematics Ser.). 343p. 1981. 37.50 (ISBN 0-471-07953-7, Pub. by Wiley-Interscience). Wiley.

Hsiung, G. D. Diagnostic Virology: An Illustrated Handbook. rev. enl. ed. LC 72-91298. (Illus.). 176p. 1973. text ed. 25.00x.o.p. (ISBN 0-300-01591-7). Yale U Pr.

Hsiung, James C., ed. The Logic of "Maoism". Critiques & Explication. LC 74-3515. 272p. 1974. text ed. 32.50 o.p. (ISBN 0-275-09070-1). Praeger.

Hsiung, James C., ed. see Li, Jui.

Hsiung, S. I. Lady Precious Stream. Taylor, C. W., retold by. (Oxford Progressive English Readers Ser.). (Illus.). (gr. k-6). 1971. pap. text ed. 3.50x (ISBN 0-19-638235-1). Oxford U Pr.

Hsu, F. L. Iemoto: The Heart of Japan. LC 74-5352. 260p. 1975. text ed. 11.25 o.p. (ISBN 0-470-41755-2); pap. text ed. 7.95x o.p. (ISBN 0-470-41756-0). Halsted Pr.

Hsu, Francis L. Americans & Chinese: Passage to Differences. 3rd ed. LC 81-10461. 568p. 1981. text ed. 22.50x (ISBN 0-8248-0710-3); pap. 9.95 (ISBN 0-8248-0757-X). UH Pr.

--Rugged Individualism Reconsidered: Essays in Psychological Anthropology. LC 82-13687. 544p. 1983. text ed. 34.50x (ISBN 0-87049-370-1); pap. text ed. 14.95x (ISBN 0-87049-371-X). U of Tenn Pr.

Hsu, Francis L., jt. ed. see Chu, Godwin C.

Hsu, Hsien-Wen, jt. auth. see Weissberger, Arnold.

Hsu, Hwei. Vector Analysis. (Monarch Technical Outlines). pap. 3.95 o.p. (ISBN 0-671-18907-7). Monarch Pr.

Hsu, Immanuel C. China Without Mao: The Search for a New Order. LC 82-2161. (Illus.). 224p. 1983. 19.95x (ISBN 0-19-503133-4). Oxford U Pr.

--China Without Mao: The Search for a New Order. (Illus.). 224p. 1982. pap. 7.95 (ISBN 0-19-503134-2, GB 696, GB). Oxford U Pr.

--The Rise of Modern China. 2nd ed. (Illus.). 1975. text ed. 19.95x o.p. (ISBN 0-19-501872-9). Oxford U Pr.

--The Rise of Modern China. 3rd ed. LC 81-22409. (Illus.). 1983. cancelled (ISBN 0-19-503218-7); pap. 19.95x (ISBN 0-19-503140-7). Oxford U Pr.

Hsu, K. J. Mountain Building Processes. 72.50 (ISBN 0-12-357980-5). Acad Pr.

Hsu, Kenneth J. Paleocenography of the Mesozoic Alpine-Tethys. LC 75-32124. (Special Paper: No. 170). (Illus., Orig.). 1976. pap. 7.00x (ISBN 0-8137-2170-9). Geol Soc.

Hsu, Linda, jt. auth. see Roisen, Fred J.

Hsu, P. L. Collected Papers. (Illus.). 589p. 1983. 48.00 (ISBN 0-387-90725-4). Springer-Verlag.

Hsu, Robert C. China's Agriculture: Policies & Performance Since 1949. (Special Study on China & East Asia). 125p. 1981. lib. bdg. 18.95 o.p. (ISBN 0-86531-062-9); pap. 8.95 o.p. (ISBN 0-86531-379-2). Westview.

Hsu, T. C. The Chinese Conception of the Theatre. 1983. write for info. U of Wash Pr.

Hsu, T. C., ed. Cytogenetic Assays of Environmental Mutagens. LC 79-88262. 442p. 1982. text ed. 45.00x (ISBN 0-916672-56-5). Allanheld.

Hsu, Vivian. Readings from the People's Daily. 1974. 6.25 (ISBN 0-686-10566-4). Far Eastern Pubns.

Hsu, Y. & Graham, Robert W. Transport Processes in Boiling & Two-Phase Systems Including Near-Critical Fluids. LC 75-38662. (McGraw-Hill - Hemisphere Ser. in Thermal & Fluids Engineering). (Illus.). 1976. text ed. 31.50 o.p. (ISBN 0-07-030637-0, C). McGraw.

Hsu-Balzer, Eileen, et al. China Day by Day. (Illus.). 128p. 1974. 20.00x.o.p. (ISBN 0-300-01751-0); pap. 8.95 o.p. (ISBN 0-300-01752-9). Yale U Pr.

Hsueh, Chun-tu, ed. China's Foreign Relations: New Perspectives. 160p. 1982. 20.95 (ISBN 0-03-060239-4); pap. 7.95 (ISBN 0-03-061699-9). Praeger.

--Dimensions of China's Foreign Relations. LC 76-24354. 1977. 37.95 o.p. (ISBN 0-275-56780-X). Praeger.

--Revolutionary Leaders of Modern China. (Orig.). 1971. pap. text ed. 8.95x (ISBN 0-19-501274-7). Oxford U Pr.

Hsueh, W. A., jt. ed. see Campese, V. M.

Hsueh-Chin, Tsao. Dream of the Red Chamber. LC 58-13296. pap. 5.50 (ISBN 0-385-09379-9, Anch). Doubleday.

Hsu Ying & Brown, J. Marvin. Speaking Chinese in China. LC 82-48904. 1983. text ed. 35.00 (ISBN 0-300-02955-1); pap. text ed. 9.95x (ISBN 0-300-03032-0). Yale U Pr.

Htin Aung, U. Folk Elements in Burmese Buddhism. LC 77-29231. 1978. Repr. of 1962 ed. lib. bdg. 17.50x (ISBN 0-313-20275-3, HTFE). Greenwood.

Hu, C. T. & Beach, Beatrice. Russian-Chinese-English Glossary of Education. LC 73-108419. 1970. text ed. 10.95x (ISBN 0-8077-1529-8). Tchrs Coll.

Hu, C. T., ed. Aspects of Chinese Education. LC 73-95245. 1969. pap. 5.95x (ISBN 0-8077-1528-X). Tchrs Coll.

Hu, Chenming & White, Richard M. Solar Cells: From Basic to Advanced Systems. (Series in Electrical Engineering: Power & Energy). (Illus.). 288p. 1983. text ed. 30.00 (ISBN 0-07-030745-8, C). McGraw.

Hu, John Y. Ts'ao Yu. (World Authors Ser.). lib. bdg. 15.95 (ISBN 0-8057-2894-5, Twayne). G K Hall.

Hu, S. Handbook of Industrial Energy Conservation. 1982. text ed. 39.95 (ISBN 0-442-24426-6). Van Nos Reinhold.

Hu, T. Econometrics. 1975. 12.50 o.p. (ISBN 0-8391-0706-4). Univ Park.

Hu, T. C. Combinatorial Algorithms. LC 81-15024. (Computer Science Ser.). 500p. 1981. text ed. 23.95 (ISBN 0-201-03859-5). A-W.

Hu, T. C. & Shing, M. T. A Manual of Computer Program in "Combinatorial Algorithms". 200p. 1983. pap. text ed. 15.00 (ISBN 0-201-11469-0). A-W.

Hu, Teh-Wei. Econometrics. 2nd ed. 208p. 1981. pap. text ed. 18.95 (ISBN 0-8391-1697-7). Univ Park.

Hu, William & Hyman, Virgina D. Carpets of China & Its Border Regions. LC 82-82969. (Illus.). 300p. 1982. 95.00 (ISBN 0-89344-030-2); write for info. (ISBN 0-89344-031-0). Ars Ceramica.

Hua, Ch'an Master, ed. Heart Sutra & Verses Without a Stand, With Prose Commentary. Epstein, R. B., tr. (Illus.). 160p. (Orig.). 1980. pap. 7.50 (ISBN 0-917512-27-8). Buddhist Text.

Hua, Ellen K. Meditations of the Masters. LC 76-47649. (Illus., Orig.). 1977. pap. 2.50 (ISBN 0-87407-203-4, FP-3). Thor.

--Wisdom from the East: Meditations, Reflections, Proverbs & Chants. LC 73-21886. (Illus.). 128p. (Orig.). 1974. pap. 2.50 (ISBN 0-87407-202-6, FP2). Thor.

Hua, Ellen Kei see Hua, Ellen K.

Hua, L. K. Selected Papers. (Illus.). 888p. 1983. 42.00 (ISBN 0-387-90744-0). Springer-Verlag.

Huai-Chen, Nan. Tao & Longevity: Mind Body Transformation. Kuan Chu, Wen, tr. from Chinese. 192p. (Orig.). Date not set. price not set (ISBN 0-87728-542-X); pap. 8.95 (ISBN 0-686-83010-5). Weiser.

Huang, C. C., tr. see Han, Wu.

Huang, C. L. & Daniels, V. G., eds. Companion to Gynaecology. (Companion Ser.). 120p. 1982. text ed. 18.00 (ISBN 0-85200-379-X, Pub. by MTP Pr England). Kluwer Boston.

--Companion to Obstetrics. (Companion Ser.). 1982. text ed. write for info. (ISBN 0-85200-378-1, Pub. by MTP Pr England). Kluwer Boston.

Huang, John, jt. ed. see Lamson-Scribner, Frank H., Jr.

Huang, Kerson. Statistical Mechanics. LC 63-11437. 1963. 36.95 (ISBN 0-471-41760-2). Wiley.

Huang, Lien-Fu, jt. auth. see Lee, Byung S.

Huang, P. C. & Kuo, T. T., eds. Genetic Engineering Techniques: Recent Developments (Symposium) LC 82-20687. Date not set. 28.50 (ISBN 0-12-358250-4). Acad Pr.

Huang, Parker P. Cantonese Dictionary: Cantonese-English, English-Cantonese. LC 72-110727. (Illus.). 1970. text ed. 45.00x (ISBN 0-300-01293-4). Yale U Pr.

Huang, Parker P., et al. Twenty Lectures on Chinese Culture: An Intermediary Chinese Textbook. 1967. 0.p. 13.00 (ISBN 0-300-00579-2); pap. text ed. 10.95 (ISBN 0-300-00127-4). Yale U Pr.

Huang, Parker Po-fei. Twenty Lectures on Chinese Culture: Exercise Book. LC 66-21520. 1967. pap. text ed. 12.95x (ISBN 0-300-00128-2). Yale U Pr.

Huang, Philip, et al. Chinese Communists & Rural Society, Nineteen Twenty-Seven to Nineteen Thirty-Four. LC 78-620018. (China Research Monographs: No. 13). 1978. pap. text ed. 5.00x (ISBN 0-912966-18-1). IEAS.

Huang, Philip C., ed. The Development of Underdevelopment in China: A Symposium. LC 80-51203. 1980. text ed. 17.50 (ISBN 0-87332-164-2). M E Sharpe.

Huang Po. The Zen Teaching of Huang Po: On the Transmission of the Mind. Blofeld, John, tr. 1959. pap. 9.95 (ISBN 0-394-17217-5, E171, Ever). Grove.

Huang, Po-fei. Speak Cantonese, Bk. 2. 9.75 (ISBN 0-686-11089-7); tapes avail. (ISBN 0-686-11090-0). Far Eastern Pubns.

--Speak Cantonese, Bk. 3. rev. ed. 8.50 (ISBN 0-686-11087-0); tapes avail. (ISBN 0-686-11088-9). Far Eastern Pubns.

Huang, Po-Fei & Kok, Gerard P. Speak Cantonese, Bk. 1. rev. ed. 9.75 (ISBN 0-686-11092-7); tapes avail. (ISBN 0-686-11093-5). Far Eastern Pubns.

Huang, Ray. Fifteen-Eighty-Seven, a Year of No Significance: The Ming Dynasty in Decline. LC 80-5392. (Illus.). 396p. 1981. 22.50x (ISBN 0-300-02518-1, Y-434); pap. 8.95x (ISBN 0-300-02884-9). Yale U Pr.

Huang, T. S. Picture Processing & Digital Filtering. LC 75-5770. (Illus.). 270p. 1975. 23.00 (ISBN 0-387-09339-7). Springer-Verlag.

Huang, T. S. & Tretiak, O. J. Picture Bandwidth Compression. LC 74-135062. 746p. 1972. 163.00x (ISBN 0-677-14680-9, 1468). Gordon.

Huang, T. S., ed. Two-Dimensional Digital Signal Processing I: Linear Filters. (Topics in Applied Physics Ser.: Vol. 42). (Illus.). 1981. 46.60 (ISBN 0-387-10359-7). Springer-Verlag.

Huang, Walter T. Petrology. 1962. text ed. 45.00 (ISBN 0-07-030750-4, C). McGraw.

Huang, Yang. Stability Analysis of Earth Slopes. 1983. 28.50 (ISBN 0-442-23689-1). Van Nos Reinhold.

Huang, Yukon. Nepal: Development Performance & Prospects. vii, 123p. 1979. pap. 10.00 (ISBN 0-686-36112-1, RC-7912). World Bank.

Huang Po-Fei. Exercise Book for Speak Cantonese Bk. 2. 4.75 (ISBN 0-686-15210-7). Far Eastern Pubns.

Huang Po-Fei & Kok, Gerard P. Character Text for Speak Cantonese Bk. 1. 8.75 (ISBN 0-686-15211-5). Far Eastern Pubns.

Huang Su Huei. Chinese Cuisine. Simonds, Nina, tr. from Chinese. (Illus.). 238p. 1976. Repr. of 1974 ed. 12.50 (ISBN 0-941676-02-1). Wei-Chuan's Cooking.

--Chinese Snacks. Simonds, Nina, tr. from Chinese. 178p. 1974. 12.50 (ISBN 0-941676-04-8). Wei-Chuan's Cooking.

--Meditations on Nature: The Art of Flower Arrangement. Simonds, Nina, tr. (Illus.). 184p. 1975. 12.95 (ISBN 0-941676-06-4). Wei-Chuan's Cooking.

Huard, P., ed. Point-to-Set Maps & Mathematical Programming. LC 78-23304. (Mathemartical Programming Studies: Vol. 10). 1979. 30.00 (ISBN 0-444-85243-3, North Holland). Elsevier.

Huard, Pierre & Wong, Ming. Chinese Medicine. (Illus., Orig.). 1968. pap. 2.45 o.p. (ISBN 0-07-030785-7, SP). McGraw.

Huart, C., tr. see Aflaki.

Huarte de San Juan, Juan. Examen de Ingenios: The Examination of Mens Wits. Camilli, M. Camillo & Carew, Richard, trs. LC 59-6246. (Hist. of Psych. Ser.). 1976. Repr. of 1594 ed. lib. bdg. 40.00x o.p. (ISBN 0-8201-1248-8). Schol Facsimiles.

Hubbard, B., ed. Technology Management. (Computer State of the Art Report, Series 10: No. 8). 400p. 1982. 445.00 (ISBN 0-08-028571-6). Pergamon.

Hubbard, Bela. Memorials of a Half-Century in Michigan & the Lake Region. LC 75-23322. (Illus.). 1978. Repr. of 1888 ed. 40.00x (ISBN 0-8103-4268-5). Gale.

Hubbard, Ben C., jt. auth. see Garber, Lee O.

Hubbard, Charles L., jt. auth. see Grawoig, Dennis E.

Hubbard, Cortlandt Van Dyke see Eberlein, H. D. & Van Dyke Hubbard, Cortlandt.

Hubbard, David A. The Practice of Prayer. 91p. 1983. pap. 2.95 (ISBN 0-87784-393-7). Inter-Varsity.

--Strange Heroes. (A Trumpet Book). 1977. pap. 1.50 o.p. (ISBN 0-87981-077-7). Holman.

--They Met Jesus. (Trumpet Bks). 1976. pap. 1.25 o.p. (ISBN 0-87981-057-2). Holman.

--They Met Jesus. LC 74-2312. 1982. pap. 2.95 o.p. (ISBN 0-8054-1321-9). Broadman.

--Why Do I Have to Die? LC 77-20572. 90p. 1978. pap. 2.50 o.p. (ISBN 0-8307-0618-6, 54-088-06). Regal.

Hubbard, David A., jt. auth. see Bush, Frederic W.

Hubbard, Earl. The Creative Intention. 192p. 1974. 8.75 o.p. (ISBN 0-913456-67-5); pap. 3.95 (ISBN 0-913456-68-3). Transbooks.

--Our Need for New Worlds. 58p. 1976. pap. 2.50 (ISBN 0-89192-079-X). Transbooks.

Hubbard, Elbert. Little Journeys to the Homes of American Statesmen. 436p. 1982. Repr. of 1898 ed. lib. bdg. 35.00 (ISBN 0-89984-914-8). Century Bookbindery.

Hubbard, Freeman, jt. auth. see Knapke, William F.

Hubbard, G. Art for Elementary Classrooms. 1982. 20.95 (ISBN 0-13-047274-3). P-H.

--De l'Organisation des Societes de Prevoyances ou de Secours Mutuel. (Conditions of the 19th Century French Working Class Ser.). 317p. 1974. Repr. of 1852 ed. lib. bdg. 84.00x o.p. (ISBN 0-8287-0453-8, 1020). Clearwater Pub.

Hubbard, Guy & Zimmerman, Enid. Artstrands: A Program of Individualized Art Instruction. (Illus.). 223p. 1982. pap. text ed. 12.95 (ISBN 0-917974-88-3). Waveland Pr.

Hubbard, James C., jt. auth. see Clay, Horace F.

Hubbard, L. Ron. Advanced Procedure & Axioms. 1951. 14.00 (ISBN 0-88404-021-6). Bridge Pubns Inc.

--Axioms & Logics. 1958. pap. 3.25 (ISBN 0-88404-066-6). Bridge Pubns Inc.

--Battlefield Earth: A Saga of the Year 3000. 960p. 1982. 24.00 (ISBN 0-312-06978-2). St Martin.

--Control & Mechanics of S. C. S. (Start, Change, Stop) 1951. pap. 4.50 (ISBN 0-88404-067-4). Bridge Pubns Inc.

--The Creation of Human Ability: A Handbook for Scientologists. 292p. 1954. 17.00 (ISBN 0-88404-011-9). Bridge Pubns Inc.

--Dianetica: la Ciencia Moderna De Salud Mental. spanish ed. 1976. pap. 3.95 (ISBN 0-88404-086-0). Bridge Pubns Inc.

--Dianetics & Scientology Technical Dictionary. 1975. 37.00 (ISBN 0-88404-037-2). Bridge Pubns Inc.

--Dianetics Fifty-Five. 168p. 1955. 17.00 (ISBN 0-88404-003-8). Bridge Pubns Inc.

--Dianetics: The Evolution of a Science. 110p. 1950. 6.00 (ISBN 0-88404-017-8). Bridge Pubns Inc.

--Dianetics: The Modern Science of Mental Health. 483p. 1950. 15.00 (ISBN 0-88404-000-3). Bridge Pubns Inc.

--Dianetics: The Modern Science of Mental Health. 550p. 1978. pap. 3.95 (ISBN 0-88404-108-5). Bridge Pubns Inc.

--Dianetics: The Original Thesis. 157p. 1951. 10.00 (ISBN 0-88404-002-X). Bridge Pubns Inc.

--Dianetics Today. 1975. 56.00 (ISBN 0-88404-036-4). Bridge Pubns Inc.

--The Effective Communication Course. 112p. 1980. pap. 10.00 o.p. (ISBN 0-88404-075-5). Bridge Pubns Inc.

--Final Blackout. Del Rey, Lester, ed. LC 75-411. (Library of Science Fiction). 1975. lib. bdg. 17.50 o.s.i. (ISBN 0-8240-1416-2). Garland Pub.

--Handbook for Preclears. (Illus.). 192p. 1951. 18.00 (ISBN 0-88404-016-X). Bridge Pubns Inc.

--Have You Lived Before This Life? A Study of Death & Evidence of Past Lives. 1978. 20.00 (ISBN 0-88404-055-0). Bridge Pubns Inc.

--How to Live Though an Executive: Communications Manual. 132p. 1953. 15.00 (ISBN 0-88404-010-0). Bridge Pubns Inc.

--Hubbard Communications Office Policy Letter Subject Index Under Likely Titles. Brice, Pat, ed. 1976. 30.00 (ISBN 0-88404-052-6). Bridge Pubns Inc.

--Introduction to Scientology Ethics. 74p. 1968. 15.00 (ISBN 0-88404-015-1). Bridge Pubns Inc.

--Mission into Time. 1973. 19.00 (ISBN 0-88404-023-2). Bridge Pubns Inc.

--Modern Management Technology Defined. 1977. text ed. 50.00 (ISBN 0-88404-040-2). Bridge Pubns Inc.

--Notes on the Lectures of L. Ron Hubbard. (Illus.). 160p. 1951. 17.00 (ISBN 0-88404-005-4). Bridge Pubns Inc.

--The Organization Executive Course: An Encyclopedia of Scientology Policy (1950-1951, 1953-1974, 7 vols. Incl. Vol. 0. Basic Staff Volume of the Organization Executive Course (ISBN 0-88404-025-9); Vol. 1. Hubbard Communications Office Division One of the Organization Executive Course (ISBN 0-88404-026-7); Vol. 2. Hubbard Communications Office Dissemination Division Two of the Organization Executive Course (ISBN 0-88404-027-5); Vol. 3. Treasury Division Three of the Organization Executive Course (ISBN 0-88404-028-3); Vol. 4. Technical Division Four of the Organization Executive Course (ISBN 0-88404-029-1); Vol. 5. Qualifications Division Five of the Organization Executive Course (ISBN 0-88404-030-5); Vol. 6. Distribution Division Six of the Organization Executive Course. 1971 (ISBN 0-88404-031-3); Vol. 7. Executive Division Seven: The Executive's Handbook of the Organization Executive Course (ISBN 0-88404-032-1). 1974. 390.00 set (ISBN 0-88404-033-X); 50.00 ea. Bridge Pubns Inc.

--The Phoenix Lectures. 325p. 1968. 18.00 (ISBN 0-88404-006-2). Bridge Pubns Inc.

--The Problems of Work: Scientology Applied to the Work-a-Day World. 106p. 1956. 10.00 (ISBN 0-88404-007-0). Bridge Pubns Inc.

--The Research & Discovery Ser, Vol. 2. 600p. 1980. 53.00 (ISBN 0-686-63377-6). Bridge Pubns Inc.

--Return to Tomorrow. Del Rey, Lester, ed. LC 75-412. (Library of Science Fiction). 1975. lib. bdg. 17.50 o.s.i. (ISBN 0-8240-1417-0). Garland Pub.

--Science of Survival: Prediction of Human Behavior. LC 51-5566. (Illus.). 550p. 1951. 22.00 (ISBN 0-88404-001-1). Bridge Pubns Inc.

--Scientology: A History of Man. 1952. 13.00 (ISBN 0-88404-024-0). Bridge Pubns Inc.

--Scientology: A New Slant on Life. 160p. 1965. 10.00 (ISBN 0-88404-013-5). Bridge Pubns Inc.

--Scientology: Clear Procedure Issue One. 1957. pap. 9.50 (ISBN 0-88404-069-0). Bridge Pubns Inc.

--Scientology Eight to Eight Thousand Eight. 152p. 1953. 22.00 (ISBN 0-88404-008-9). Bridge Pubns Inc.

--Scientology Eight to Eighty: The Discovery & Increase of Life Energy in the Genus Homo Sapiens. 1952. 22.00 (ISBN 0-88404-020-8). Bridge Pubns Inc.

--Scientology: The Fundamentals of Thought. 128p. 1956. 19.00 (ISBN 0-88404-018-6). Bridge Pubns Inc.

--Scientology Zero to Eight: The Book of Basics. 159p. 1950. 22.00 (ISBN 0-88404-009-7). Bridge Pubns Inc.

--Self Analysis. 254p. 1982. pap. 8.95 (ISBN 0-88404-109-3). Bridge Pubns Inc.

--Self Analysis. Date not set. 8.95 (ISBN 0-88404-109-3). Bridge Pub.

--Success Through Communication. 72p. 1980. pap. 9.00 (ISBN 0-88404-076-3). Bridge Pubns Inc.

--Technical Bulletins of Dianetics & Scientology, 12 vols. Incl. Vol. 1. 1950-53 (ISBN 0-88404-041-0); Vol. 2. 1954-56 (ISBN 0-88404-042-9); Vol. 3. 1957-59 (ISBN 0-88404-043-7); Vol. 4. 1960-61 (ISBN 0-88404-044-5); Vol. 5. 1962-64 (ISBN 0-88404-045-3); Vol. 6. 1965-69 (ISBN 0-88404-046-1); Vol. 7. 1970-71 (ISBN 0-88404-047-X); Vol. 8. 1972-76 (ISBN 0-88404-048-8); Vol. 9. Auditing Ser., 1965-75 (ISBN 0-88404-049-6); Vol. 10. Case Supervisor Ser. & Cumulative Index, 1970-75 (ISBN 0-88404-050-X); Vol. 11. 1976-78 (ISBN 0-88404-065-8); Vol. 12. 1979-80 (ISBN 0-88404-074-7). 1980. 58.00 ea. Bridge Pubns Inc.

--Volunteer Minister's Handbook. 1976. 58.00 (ISBN 0-88404-039-9). Bridge Pubns Inc.

--When in Doubt, Communicate... Minshull, Ruth & Lefson, Edward, eds. 150p. (Orig.). 1982. pap. cancelled (ISBN 0-937922-08-0). SAA Pub.

Hubbard, L. Ron, jt. auth. see Medicus.

Hubbard, L. Ron, intro. by. Child Dianetics. 1951. 18.00 (ISBN 0-88404-022-4). Bridge Pubns Inc.

Hubbard, Linda S., ed. Book Publishers Directory. 3rd ed. 1193p. 1981. 180.00x (ISBN 0-8103-0191-1). Gale.

--Book Publishers Directory. 4th ed. 1200p. 1983. 195.00x (ISBN 0-8103-0194-6). Gale.

Hubbard, Mary S. Marriage Hats. 1970. pap. 6.00 (ISBN 0-88404-068-2). Bridge Pubns Inc.

Hubbard, R., jt. auth. see Hailes, W.

Hubbard, R. H. Canadian Landscape Painting, Sixteen Seventy to Nineteen Thirty: The Artist & the Land. LC 72-11461. (Illus.). 212p. 1973. pap. 10.00x o.p. (ISBN 0-87451-104-6). U Pr of New Eng.

Hubbard, Robert, ed. see Goldingay, John.

Hubbard, Ruth & Henefin, Mary S. Women Look at Biology Looking at Women: A Collection of Feminist Critiques. 1979. lib. bdg. 17.95 (ISBN 0-8161-9000-3, Univ Bks). G K Hall.

Hubbard, Ruth & Henifin, Mary S. Biology's Woman: The Conveniant Myth. 320p. 1982. 18.95 (ISBN 0-87073-702-3); pap. 11.95 (ISBN 0-87073-703-1). Schenkman.

Hubbard, Stuart W. The Computer Graphics Glossary. 1983. price not set (ISBN 0-89774-072-6). Oryx Pr.

Hubbard, Thomas D. & Johnson, Johnny R. Auditing: Concepts, Standards, Procedures. LC 82-72439. 925p. 1983. text ed. 28.95x (ISBN 0-931920-44-2). Dame Pubns.

Hubbard, Thomas D., et al. Readings & Cases in Auditing. rev. ed. LC 79-52071. 550p. (Orig.). 1980. pap. text ed. 13.95x (ISBN 0-931920-22-1). Dame Pubns.

Hubbard, W., jt. auth. see Rosen, A.

Hubbard, W. P. & Harris, Peggy. Notorious Grizzly Bears. LC 82-73369. (Illus.). 205p. 1960. pap. 5.95 (ISBN 0-8040-0617-2, SB). Swallow.

Hubbard, William. Stack Management: A Practical Guide to Shelving & Maintaining Collections. LC 80-28468. 110p. 1981. pap. 8.00 (ISBN 0-8389-0319-3). ALA.

Hubbard, William Q. Complicity & Conviction: Steps Toward an Architecture of Convention. (Illus.). 1980. 15.00x (ISBN 0-262-08106-7); pap. 8.95 (ISBN 0-262-58057-8). MIT Pr.

Hubbell, George S. Writing Term Papers & Reports. 4th ed. (Orig.). 1969. pap. 3.50 (ISBN 0-06-460037-8, CO 37, COS). B&N NY.

Hubbell, Harold R. Stop It! Quit It! Cut It Out! Or How to Be Painfully Happy. (Orig.). Date not set. pap. price not set (ISBN 0-910093-00-8). J & C Pub.

Hubbell, Harry M. The Influence of Isocrates on Cicero, Dionysius & Aristides. 1913. 47.50x (ISBN 0-686-50045-8). Elliots Bks.

Hubbell, J. G. P.O.W. 1976. 15.00 (ISBN 0-07-030831-4). McGraw.

Hubbell, Jay B. Tales & the Raven & Other Poems of Edgar Allen Poe. (gr. 9-12). 1969. pap. text ed. 3.50x (ISBN 0-675-09530-1). Merrill.

Hubbell, John T., ed. Battles Lost & Won: Essays from Civil War History. LC 75-10045. (Contributions in American History: No. 45). 289p. 1975. lib. bdg. 27.50 (ISBN 0-8371-7959-9, HCW/); pap. 5.95 (ISBN 0-8371-8920-9). Greenwood.

Hubbell, Kenneth, ed. Fiscal Crisis in American Cities: The Federal Response. LC 79-614. 384p. 1979. prof ref 25.00x (ISBN 0-88410-491-5). Ballinger Pub.

Hubbell, Lindley W. Seventy Poems. LC 82-71918. 96p. 1965. 7.95 (ISBN 0-8040-0272-X). Swallow.

Hubbell, Robert D. Children's Language Disorders: An Integrated Approach. (Illus.). 432p. 1981. text ed. 23.95 (ISBN 0-13-132001-7). P-H.

Hubbell, Ruth. Foster Care & Families: Conflicting Values & Policies. (Family Impact Seminar Ser.). 218p. 1981. 24.95 (ISBN 0-87722-206-1). Temple U Pr.

Hubbert, William T., jt. auth. see Hagstad, Harry V.

Hubbert, William T., et al, eds. Diseases Transmitted from Animals to Man. 6th ed. (Illus.). 1236p. 1975. 79.75x (ISBN 0-398-03056-1). C C Thomas.

Hubenka, Lloyd J., ed. see Ruskin, John.

Huber & Klein. Neurogenetics & Neuro-Opthalmology. (Developments in Neurology Ser.: Vol. 5). 1982. 78.75 (ISBN 0-444-80378-5). Elsevier.

Huber, A. Probleme der Kontrazeption Bei der Jugendlichen. 1981. 47.00 (ISBN 90-219-9450-X). Elsevier.

Huber, Bruno & Huber, Louise. Life Clock: Age Progression in the Horoscope, Vol. 1. 224p. 1982. 8.95 (ISBN 0-87728-554-3). Weiser.

--Man & His World. Lore, Wallace, tr. 1983. pap. write for info. (ISBN 0-87728-413-X). Weiser.

Huber, Evelyn M., jt. auth. see Blazier, Kenneth D.

Huber, Frederic V. Apple Crunch. 1982. pap. 2.95 (ISBN 0-380-60699-2, 60699). Avon.

Huber, G. C. Stratigraphy & Uranium Deposits, Lisbon Valley District, San Juan County, Utah. Raese, Jon W., ed. (CSM Quarterly Ser.: Vol. 75, No. 2). (Illus.). 100p. (Orig.). 1980. pap. 10.00 (ISBN 0-686-63163-3). Colo Sch Mines.

Huber, George. Managerial Decision Making. 1980. pap. text ed. 10.95x (ISBN 0-673-15141-7). Scott F.

Huber, J., ed. Proceedings: First Symposium. (Journal of Chromatography Ser.: Vol. 83). 1973. 64.00 (ISBN 0-444-41170-4). Elsevier.

Huber, Jack T. & Millman, Howard L. Goals & Behavior in Psychotherapy & Counseling: Readings & Questions. LC 73-190060. 384p. 1972. pap. text ed. 15.95 (ISBN 0-675-09092-X). Merrill.

Huber, Joan & Form, William H. Income & Ideology: An Analysis of the American Political Formula. LC 73-2128. (Illus.). 1973. 14.95 (ISBN 0-02-915330-1). Free Pr.

Huber, Joan & Spitze, Glenna, eds. Stratification, Children, Housework & Jobs: Monograph. LC 82-18407. (Quantitative Studies in Social Relations). 242p. 1983. price not set (ISBN 0-12-358480-9). Acad Pr.

Huber, John E., ed. Kline Guide to the Paper Industry. 4th ed. (Illus.). 343p. 1979. pap. 110.00 (ISBN 0-917148-10-X). Kline.

Huber, K. A. Morphologisch und Entwicklungsgeschichtliche Untersuchungen an Blueten und Bluetenstaenden Von Solannaceen und Von Nolana Paradoxa Lindl: Nolanaceae. (Dissertationes Botanicae: No. 55). (Illus.). 486p. (Ger.). 1980. pap. text ed. 40.00x (ISBN 3-7682-1268-8). Lubrecht & Cramer.

Huber, Leonard, et al. New Orleans Architecture, Vol. 3: The Cemeteries. Wilson, Samuel, Jr., ed. LC 72-172272. (New Orleans Architecture Ser.). (Illus.). 208p. 1974. 22.50 (ISBN 0-88289-020-4). Pelican.

Huber, Louise, jt. auth. see Huber, Bruno.

Huber, Martin & Banbery, Alan. Patek Philippe Geneve. (Illus.). 288p. 1982. 136.50 (ISBN 0-686-84138-7). Am Reprints.

Huber, Maureen. Cherry Cobbler. 1976. 6.20 (ISBN 0-686-15735-4). Rod & Staff.

Huber, Miriam B. Story & Verse for Children. 3rd ed. (gr. k-4). 1965. 18.95x (ISBN 0-02-357500-X). Macmillan.

Huber, Norman F. Data Communications: The Business Aspects. 356p. 1982. looseleaf bound 49.95 (ISBN 0-935506-05-5). Carnegie Pr.

Huber, Peter J. Robust Statistical Procedures. (CBMS-NSF Regional Conference Ser.: Vol. 27). (Illus.). v, 56p. (Orig.). 1977. pap. text ed. 9.00 (ISBN 0-89871-024-3). Soc Indus-Appl Math.

Huber, Richard. Treasury of Fantastic & Mythological Creatures: One Thousand & Eighty-Seven Renderings from Historic Sources. 15.00 (ISBN 0-8446-5894-4). Peter Smith.

Huber, Roger, ed. Where My Money Is Going: Income & Expense Budget. (Orig.). 1980. pap. 3.95 (ISBN 0-918300-00-2); wkbk. 3.95 (ISBN 0-686-70172-0). Lankey.

Huber, Roger C. Anatomy of Success. 2nd ed. LC 76-52718. (Illus., Orig.). 1977. pap. 3.95 (ISBN 0-918300-00-2). Lankey.

Huber, Werner. James Stephens' Fruhe Romane. 304p. (Ger.). 1982. write for info. (ISBN 3-8204-5845-X). P Lang Pubs.

Huberman, A. M. Understanding Change in Education. (Experiments & Innovations in Education). (Illus., Orig.). 1973. pap. 6.25 (ISBN 92-3-101116-2, U689, UNESCO). Unipub.

Huberman, Jack, jt. auth. see Gopnik, Adam.

Huberman, Leo. Labor Spy Racket. LC 77-139201. (Civil Liberties in American History Ser). (Illus.). 1971. Repr. of 1937 ed. lib. bdg. 27.50 (ISBN 0-306-70080-8). Da Capo.

Huberman, Leo, ed. see Marx, Karl & Engels, Friedrich.

Hubert. The Mystery of Purgatory. 1974. 7.95 o.p. (ISBN 0-8199-0546-1). Franciscan Herald.

Hubert, Amelia. Sweet Dreams for Sally. (Illus.). 48p. (ps-3). 1983. 4.99 (ISBN 0-910313-01-6). Parker Bro.

Hubert, C. I. Electric Circuits AC-DC: An Integrated Approach. 576p. 1982. text ed. 29.50x (ISBN 0-07-030845-4); solns manual 14.50 (ISBN 0-07-030846-2). McGraw.

Hubert, Charles. Preventive Maintenance of Electrical Equipment. 2nd ed. 1969. 25.95 (ISBN 0-07-030839-X, G); instructor's manual 1.50 (ISBN 0-07-030840-3). McGraw.

Hubert, Henri & Mauss, Marcel. Sacrifice: Its Nature & Function. Halls, W. D., tr. LC 64-12260. 1964. 7.50x o.p. (ISBN 0-226-35678-7); pap. 11.00x (ISBN 0-226-35679-5). U of Chicago Pr.

Hubert, J. D. Moliere & the Comedy of Intellect. LC 62-18021. (California Library Reprint). 1974. 27.50x (ISBN 0-520-02520-2). U of Cal Pr.

Hubert, J. J. & Carter. Biostatistics: 1064 Answers. 64p. 1980. pap. text ed. 4.95 saddle stitched (ISBN 0-8403-2288-7). Kendall-Hunt.

--Biostatistics: 1064 Questions. LC 80-82899. 160p. 1980. pap. text ed. 7.95 (ISBN 0-8403-2287-9). Kendall-Hunt.

Hubert, John J. Bioassay. 1980. pap. text ed. 13.95 (ISBN 0-8403-2126-0). Kendall-Hunt.

Hubert, Tony see Bailey, David.

Hubert-Valleroux, P. Les Associations Cooperatives en France et a l'Etranger. (Conditions of the 19th Century French Working Class Ser.). 480p. (Fr.). 1974. Repr. of 1884 ed. lib. bdg. 120.00 o.p. (ISBN 0-8287-0454-6, 1160). Clearwater Pub.

Huberty, Ernst & Wange, Willy B. Olympics 1976. (Illus.). 1976. 10.00 o.p. (ISBN 0-517-52743-X, C N Potter Bks). Crown.

Hubin, Wilbert N. Basic Programming for Scientists & Engineers. LC 77-21343. (Illus.). 1978. pap. 16.95 ref. ed. (ISBN 0-13-066480-4). P-H.

Hu Bing. A Brief Introduction to the Science of Breathing Exercise. (Illus.). 89p. 1981. pap. 6.95 (ISBN 0-686-42861-7). China Bks.

Hubley, Faith & Towe, Kenneth M. Enter Life. LC 82-71680. (Illus.). 32p. (gr. 4 up). cancelled o.s.i. (ISBN 0-440-02357-2, E Friede). Delacorte.

Hublow, Karl. The Working of Christ in Man: The Thousand-Year Old Frescoes in the Church of St. George on the Island of Reichenau. (Illus.). 1979. 18.95 (ISBN 0-903540-28-2, Pub. by Floris Books). St George Bk Serv.

Hubmann, Franz. Habsburg Empire: The World of the Austro-Hungarian Monarchy in Original Photographs 1840-1916. Wheatcroft, Andrew, ed. LC 72-2138. (Illus.). 320p. 1972. 27.50x (ISBN 0-912050-24-1, Library Pr). Open Court.

Hubmann-Uhlich, Inge. Colloquial German. rev. ed. (Colloquial Ser.). 1980. pap. 7.95 (ISBN 0-7100-0482-6). Routledge & Kegan.

Hubschman, Lynn. Hospital Social Work Practice. 196p. 1983. 29.95 (ISBN 0-03-061926-2). Praeger.

Huchel, Peter. Poems. Hamburger, Michael, tr. from Ger. 160p. 1983. text ed. 14.75x (ISBN 0-85635-418-X, Pub. by Carcanet New Pr England). Humanities.

Huchingson, Dale. New Horizons for Human Factors in Design. (Illus.). 512p. 1981. text ed. 32.50 (ISBN 0-07-030815-2, C); instructor's guide & manual 5.95 (ISBN 0-07-030816-0). McGraw.

Huck, Gabe. A Book of Family Prayer. 1979. 9.95 (ISBN 0-8164-0415-1). Seabury.

--Liturgy Needs Community Needs Liturgy. LC 73-84360. 96p. 1974. pap. 2.45 o.p. (ISBN 0-8091-1791-6). Paulist Pr.

--Teach Me to Pray. 192p. pap. 3.95 (ISBN 0-8215-9887-2). Sadlier.

Huckabay, Loucine M. Patient Classification: A Basis for Staffing. (League Exchange Ser.: No. 131). 40p. 1981. 4.50 (ISBN 0-686-38337-0, 20-1864). Natl League Nurse.

Hucker, Charles O. China to 1850: A Short History. LC 77-79998. 1978. 8.50x (ISBN 0-8047-0957-2); pap. 2.95x (ISBN 0-8047-0958-0). Stanford U Pr.

--China's Imperial Past: An Introduction to Chinese History & Culture. LC 74-25929. (Illus.). 1975. 19.50 (ISBN 0-8047-0887-8); hardbound student ed. 11.95x (ISBN 0-8047-0979-3). Stanford U Pr.

Huckin, Thomas & Olsen, Leslie. English for Science & Technology: A Handbook for Non-Native Speakers. (Illus.). 672p. 1983. 19.95x (ISBN 0-07-030821-7); instr's manual 6.95 (ISBN 0-07-047822-8). McGraw.

Huckleberry, Alan W., jt. auth. see Strother, Edward S.

Hudak, Carolyn & Lohr, Thelma. Critical Care Nursing. 3rd ed. (Illus.). 688p. 1982. text ed. 22.50 (ISBN 0-397-54353-0, Lippincott Nursing); wkbk. 10.50 (ISBN 0-397-54380-8). Lippincott.

Hudak, Joseph. Trees for Every Purpose. (Illus.). 1980. 27.50 (ISBN 0-07-030841-1). McGraw.

Huddleston, Eugene L. Thomas Jefferson: A Reference Guide. 1982. lib. bdg. 30.00 (ISBN 0-8161-8141-1, Hall Reference). G K Hall.

Huddleston, Eugene L. & Noverr, Douglas A., eds. The Relationship of Painting & Literature: A Guide to Information Sources. LC 78-53436. (American Studies Information Guide Ser.: Vol. 4). 1978. 42.00x (ISBN 0-8103-1394-4). Gale.

Huddleston, Sisley. Back to Montparnasse: Glimpses of Broadway in Bohemia. (Illus.). 313p. 1982. Repr. of 1931 ed. lib. bdg. 40.00 (ISBN 0-89984-916-4). Century Bookbindery.

Hudec, John. An Empirical Analysis of the Circular Dichroism of Chiral Olefins. 1977. pap. text ed. write for info. (ISBN 0-08-021584-X). Pergamon.

Huden, John C. Development of State School Administration in Vermont. 277p. 1944. 2.25x o.p. (ISBN 0-934720-11-8). VT Hist Soc.

Hudes, Isidore, jt. auth. see Moriber, George.

Hudesman, Anna. Four Score & Five: Recollections & Reflections. 200p. 1981. 4.95 (ISBN 0-88437-021-6). Psych Dimensions.

Hudgens, Betty L., ed. Kurt Vonnegut, Jr. A Checklist. LC 74-13322. (Modern Authors Checklist Ser.). (Illus.). 77p. 1972. 36.00x (ISBN 0-8103-0903-3, Bruccoli Clark Book). Gale.

Hudgins, Bryce B. Educational Psychology. LC 82-81417. 690p. 1983. pap. text ed. 14.95 (ISBN 0-87581-283-X). Peacock Pubs.

Hudgins, Bryce B., jt. ed. see Smith, Louis M.

Hudgins, H. C., jt. auth. see Vacca, Richard S.

Hudlicka, O. Circulation of Skeletal Muscle. 1968. inquire for price o.p. (ISBN 0-08-012466-6). Pergamon.

Hudlicky, M. Chemistry of Organic Fluorine Compounds. 1962. 13.95x (ISBN 0-02-357750-9). Macmillan.

Hudlin, Richard A. Black Population & Representation in Selected Alabama Counties & Places. 1982. 1.00 (ISBN 0-686-38022-3). Voter Ed Proj.

--Black Population Concentrations in Southern Counties. 1982. 10.00 (ISBN 0-686-36624-7). Voter Ed Proj.

--Black Population Concentrations in Southern Counties. 1982. 1.00 (ISBN 0-686-38023-1). Voter Ed Proj.

--Black Population, Voting Age Population, & Registrants for Counties in Georgia: 1980. 1982. 1.00 (ISBN 0-686-38024-X). Voter Ed Proj.

--Directory of Southern U.S. Senators & Representatives. 1981. 1.00 (ISBN 0-686-38020-7). Voter Ed Proj.

--Profile of Georgia Black Voting Strength & Political Representation. 1982. 1.00 (ISBN 0-686-38027-4). Voter Ed Proj.

--Survey of Black School Board Members in the South. Lewis, Shelby & Kenneth, Ellis, eds. 1981. 1.00 (ISBN 0-686-38021-5). Voter Ed Proj.

--Voter Registration in Eleven Southern States, by Race: 1960-1980, in U.S. Bureau of the Census: Statistical Abstract of the United States: 1981. 1981. 0.10 ea. Voter Ed Proj.

Hudlin, Richard A. & Brimah, K. Farouk. State of Mississippi's Procurement Policies & Minority Business Enterprises. 1981. 1.00 (ISBN 0-686-38010-X). Voter Ed Proj.

--What Happened in the South: 1980. 1981. 1.00 (ISBN 0-686-38009-6). Voter Ed Proj.

Hudlin, Richard A. & Farouk, Brimah K. Barriers to Effective Political Participation. 1981. 1.00 (ISBN 0-686-38012-6). Voter Ed Proj.

--Profile of Alabama Black Voting Strength & Political Representation. 1982. 1.00 (ISBN 0-686-38026-6). Voter Ed Proj.

--Profile of Georgia's Black Voting Strength & Political Representation. 1981. 1.00 (ISBN 0-686-38015-0). Voter Ed Proj.

--Profile of Mississippi's Black Voting Strength & Political Representation. 1981. 1.00 (ISBN 0-686-38016-9). Voter Ed Proj.

--Roster of Blacks in the U.S. House & Senate: 1869 to 1981. 1981. 1.00 (ISBN 0-686-38014-2). Voter Ed Proj.

--State of North Carolina's Procurement Policies & Minority Business Enterprises. 1981. 1.00 (ISBN 0-686-38011-8). Voter Ed Proj.

--Voting Rights Act: Questions & Answers. 1981. 1.00 (ISBN 0-686-38020-7). Voter Ed Proj.

Hudlin, Richard A. & Lewis, Shelby. Survey of Black School Board Members in the South. 1981. 3.00 (ISBN 0-686-36623-9). Voter Ed Proj.

Hudlin, Richard A., jt. auth. see Farouk, Brimah K.

Hudlow, Emily E. Alabaster Chambers. 1980. pap. 2.25 o.p. (ISBN 0-451-09294-5, E9294, Sig). NAL.

Hudman, Lloyd E., jt. auth. see Jackson, Richard H.

Hudson & Weaver. Reading, Writing & Speaking: Here & Now. (Illus.). 1980. pap. 3.50x (ISBN 0-88323-160-3, 248); tchr's. key 1.00 (ISBN 0-88323-166-2, 256). Richards Pub.

Hudson, A. P. Folk Tunes from Mississippi. Herzog, George & Halpert, Herbert, eds. LC 76-58548. (Music Reprint Ser.). 1977. Repr. of 1937 ed. lib. bdg. 22.50 (ISBN 0-306-70787-X). Da Capo.

Hudson, Alvin & Nelson, Rex. University Physics. 1000p. 1982. text ed. 33.95 (ISBN 0-15-592960-7, HC); instr's. manual 3.50 (ISBN 0-15-592961-5); study guide 10.95 (ISBN 0-15-592962-3). HarBraceJ.

Hudson, Anne. Kiss the Tears Away. (Candlelight Ecstasy Ser.: No. 156). (Orig.). 1983. pap. 1.95 (ISBN 0-440-14525-2). Dell.

Hudson, Anne, ed. Wycliffite Sermons, Vol. 1. (Oxford English Texts). (Illus.). 1982. 59.00x (ISBN 0-19-812704-9). Oxford U Pr.

Hudson, B. J., ed. Developments in Food Proteins, Vol. 1. 1982. 71.75 (ISBN 0-85334-987-8, Pub. by Applied Sci England). Elsevier.

--Developments in Food Proteins, Vol. 2. Date not set. 73.80 (ISBN 0-85334-176-1, Pub. by Applied Sci England). Elsevier.

Hudson, Barbara L. Social Work with Psychiatric Patients. 240p. 1982. 39.00x (ISBN 0-333-26685-4, Pub. by Macmillan England). State Mutual Bk.

Hudson, Barclay, jt. auth. see Herrick, Bruce.

Hudson, C. S., jt. auth. see Rash, J. E.

Hudson, C. Wayne. The Marxist Philosophy of Ernest Bloch. LC 80-20438. 256p. 1982. 27.50x (ISBN 0-312-51860-9). St Martin.

Hudson, Clare Maxwell see Maxwell-Hudson, Clare.

Hudson, D. C. Your Book of Golf. (gr. 7 up). 1969. 4.95 o.p. (ISBN 0-571-08123-1). Transatlantic.

Hudson, Derek. Lewis Carroll: An Illustrated Biography. (Illus.). 1977. 12.95 o.p. (ISBN 0-517-53078-3, C N Potter Bks). Crown.

Hudson, Don. Introduction to Swimming. 64p. 1981. pap. text ed. 5.95 (ISBN 0-8403-2509-6). Kendall-Hunt.

Hudson, Donald. A Century of Moral Philosophy. 1980. 25.00 (ISBN 0-312-12777-4). St Martin.

Hudson, Eleanor. The Care Bears Help Out. LC 82-61596. (Care Bear Mini-Storybooks). (Illus.). 32p. (gr. 1-6). 1982. pap. 1.25 saddle-stitched (ISBN 0-394-85842-5). Random.

--A Whale of a Rescue. Gerver, Jane, ed. LC 82-61014. (Sea World Mini-Storybooks). (Illus.). 32p. (gr. 1-5). 1983. pap. 1.25 (ISBN 0-394-85642-2). Random.

Hudson, G. F., ed. Reform & Revolution in Asia. LC 72-85550. 300p. 1973. 25.00 (ISBN 0-312-66780-9). St Martin.

Hudson, Gladys W. Paradise Lost: A Concordance. LC 74-127413. 1971. 34.00x (ISBN 0-8103-1002-3). Gale.

Hudson, Gladys W., ed. Elizabeth Barrett Browning Concordance, 4 vols. LC 73-5735. 1973. Set. 165.00x (ISBN 0-8103-1003-1). Gale.

Hudson, H. J. Fungal Saprophytism. 2nd ed. (Studies in Biology: No. 32). 64p. 1980. pap. text ed. 8.95 (ISBN 0-7131-2792-9). E Arnold.

Hudson, H. N. Shakespeare, His Life, Art & Character: An Historical Sketch of the Origin & Growth of the Drama in England, 2 Vols. 495p. 1982. Repr. of 1880 ed. Set. lib. bdg. 100.00 (ISBN 0-89987-394-4). Darby Bks.

Hudson, Hamilton C., jt. auth. see Galaway, Burton.

Hudson, Herman & Imhoof, Maurice L. From Paragraph to Theme. Orig. Title: Understanding & Expressing Convictions Through Paragraph & Essay. (Illus.). 160p. 1972. pap. text ed. 11.95x (ISBN 0-02-357800-9). Macmillan.

Hudson, J. The Core of Walmatjari Grammar. (AIAS New Ser.: No. 2). (Illus.). 1978. pap. text ed. 14.00x (ISBN 0-391-00971-0). Humanities.

Hudson, J. A. The Excitation & Propagation of Elastic Waves. LC 79-4505. (Monographs on Mechanics & Applied Mathematics Ser.). (Illus.). 1980. 42.50 (ISBN 0-521-22777-1). Cambridge U Pr.

Hudson, J. W., jt. ed. see Hudson, R. D.

Hudson, Jack W., jt. ed. see Wang, Lawrence.

Hudson, James, jt. auth. see Rivers, Gayle.

Hudson, James F., et al. Pollution-Pricing: Industrial Response to Wastewater Charges. LC 80-8363. 240p. 1981. 25.95x (ISBN 0-669-04033-9). Lexington Bks.

Hudson, Jeffery. A Case of Need. 320p. 1974. pap. 2.50 (ISBN 0-451-09796-3, E9796, Sig). NAL.

Hudson, Joe & Galaway, Burt, eds. Victims, Offenders, & Alternative Sanctions. LC 80-7578. 224p. 1980. 23.95x (ISBN 0-669-03758-3). Lexington Bks.

Hudson, Joe, jt. ed. see Galaway, Burt.

Hudson, John. Inflation: A Theoretical Survey & Synthesis. 171p. 1983. pap. text ed. 9.95x (ISBN 0-04-339034-X). Allen Unwin.

Hudson, John L. & Rochelle, Gary T., eds. Flue Gas Desulfurization. (ACS Symposium Ser.: No. 188). 1982. write for info. (ISBN 0-8412-0722-4). Am Chemical.

Hudson, K. World Industrial Archaeology. LC 77-94225. (New Studies in Archaeology). 1979. 49.50 (ISBN 0-521-21991-4); pap. 15.50x (ISBN 0-521-29330-8). Cambridge U Pr.

Hudson, Kenneth. Help the Aged: Twenty-One Years of Experiment & Achievement. 208p. 1983. 15.95 (ISBN 0-370-30463-2, Pub. by The Bodley Head). Merrimack Bk Serv.

Hudson, Kenneth & Nicholls, Ann. Tragedy on the High Seas: A History of Shipwrecks. (Illus.). 240p. 1979. 12.50 o.s.i. (ISBN 0-89479-024-2). A & W Pubs.

Hudson, Kenneth, ed. The Good Museums Guide: The Best Museums & Art Galleries in the British Isles. 320p. 1982. 30.00x (ISBN 0-333-32763-2, Pub. by Macmillan England). State Mutual Bk.

Hudson, L. Frank & Prescott, Gordon R. Lost Treasures of Florida's Gulf Coast. LC 73-9494. (Illus.). 64p. 1973. pap. 3.95 o.p. (ISBN 0-8200-1026-X). Great Outdoors.

Hudson, Leafy. The Lost Buzzer-the Haunted Meadow. (Buzzy Byron Bumblebee Story Ser.: No. 1). (Illus.). 24p. (Orig.). (ps-4). 1982. pap. 2.50 (ISBN 0-910219-03-6). Little People.

Hudson, Marc. Island. 1977. 3.50 (ISBN 0-918116-07-4). Jawbone Pr.

Hudson, Margaret W. All About Me Books. rev. ed. 1973. pap. 1.75x boys' ed. (ISBN 0-88323-000-3, 101); pap. 1.75x girls' ed. (ISBN 0-88323-001-1, 102). Richards Pub.

--How? 1967. 1.50x (ISBN 0-88323-046-1, 145). Richards Pub.

--When? 1965. 1.50x (ISBN 0-88323-081-X, 178). Richards Pub.

--Where? 1965. 1.50x (ISBN 0-88323-082-8, 179). Richards Pub.

--Why? 1967. 1.50x (ISBN 0-88323-083-6, 180). Richards Pub.

Hudson, Margaret W. & Weaver, Ann A. Getting Ready for Pay Day, 3 bks. Incl. Bk. 1. Checking Accounts (ISBN 0-88323-028-3, 126); Bk. 2. Savings Accounts (ISBN 0-88323-029-1, 127); Bk. 3. Planning Ahead (ISBN 0-88323-030-5, 128). 1982. pap. 2.75x ea. Richards Pub.

Hudson, Margaret W., jt. auth. see Weaver, Ann A.

Hudson, Meg. Return to Rapture. (Superromances Ser.). 384p. 1983. pap. 2.50 (ISBN 0-373-70053-9, Pub. by Worldwide). Harlequin Bks.

--Though Hearts Resist. (Superromance Ser.). 295p. 1983. pap. 2.95 (ISBN 0-373-70064-4, Pub. by Worldwide). Harlequin Bks.

Hudson, Michael, jt. auth. see Panati, Charles.

Hudson, Miles. Triumph or Tragedy? Rhodesia to Zimbabwe. (Illus.). 256p. 1981. 25.00 (ISBN 0-241-10571-4, Pub. by Hamish Hamilton England). David & Charles.

Hudson, N. H. Shakespeare: His Life, Art & Characters, 2 Vols. LC 79-124395. (Studies in Shakespeare, No. 24). 1970. Repr. of 1872 ed. lib. bdg. 79.95x (ISBN 0-8383-1100-8). Haskell.

Hudson, R. A. Sociolinguistics. LC 79-51824. (Cambridge Textbooks in Linguistics Ser.). (Illus.). 1980. 42.50 (ISBN 0-521-22833-6); pap. 11.95x (ISBN 0-521-29668-4). Cambridge U Pr.

Hudson, R. D. & Hudson, J. W., eds. Infrared Detectors. LC 75-4923. (Benchmark Papers in Optics: Vol. 2). 392p. 1975. 51.50 (ISBN 0-87933-135-6). Hutchinson Ross.

Hudson, R. Lofton. Como Mejorar Sus Relaciores Humanas. De Lerin, O. S. D., tr. 1982. Repr. of 1980 ed. 1.75 (ISBN 0-311-46037-2). Casa Bautista.

--Is This Divorce Really Necessary? LC 81-86665. (Orig.). 1983. pap. 5.95 (ISBN 0-8054-5649-X). Broadman.

Hudson, Randolph H. & McGuire, Gertrude M., eds. Business Writing: Concepts & Applications. (Illus.). 332p. 1983. pap. text ed. 16.95x (ISBN 0-935732-06-3). Roxbury Pub Co.

Hudson, Robert P. Disease & It's Control: The Shaping of Modern Thought. LC 82-21135. (Contributions in Medical History: No. 12). 288p. 1983. lib. bdg. 29.95 (ISBN 0-313-23806-5, HHD/). Greenwood.

Hudson, Ronald, jt. ed. see Kelley, Philip.

Hudson Symposium, 9th, Plattsburgh, N.Y., Apr. 1976. Homoatomic Rings, Chains & Macromolecules of Main Group Elements: Proceedings. Rheingold, A. L., ed. 1977. 106.50 (ISBN 0-444-41634-X). Elsevier.

Hudson, Travis. Guide to Painted Cave. LC 82-17218. 1982. 4.50 (ISBN 0-87461-049-4). McNally.

Hudson, Travis & Blackburn, Thomas C. The Material Culture of the Chumash Interaction Sphere: Vol. I, Food Procurement & Transportation. LC 82-13832. (Ballena Press Anthropological Papers: No. 25). (Illus.). 392p. (Orig.). 1982. 34.95 (ISBN 0-87919-099-X); pap. 19.95 (ISBN 0-87919-097-3). Ballena Pr.

Hudson, Travis & Underhay, Ernest. Crystals in the Sky: An Intellectual Odyssey Involving Chumush Astronomy, Coamology & Rock Art. (Ballena Press Anthropological Papers: No. 10). 1978. pap. 8.95 o.p. (ISBN 0-87919-074-4). Ballena Pr.

Hudson, Val & Wade, Judy. First Time Family. (Illus.). 288p. 1981. pap. 7.95 (ISBN 0-8256-3186-6, Quick Fox). Putnam Pub Group.

Hudson, Virginia C. O Ye Jigs & Juleps. 1962. 7.95 (ISBN 0-02-555340-2). Macmillan.

Hudson, W. D. Modern Moral Philosophy. 1971. 14.95 o.p. (ISBN 0-312-54110-4). St Martin.

Hudson, W. D., ed. New Studies in Ethics, 2 vols. LC 74-76687. 598p. 1974. 25.00 ea. Vol. 1 o.p (ISBN 0-312-57015-5). Vol. 2 (ISBN 0-312-57050-3). St Martin.

Hudson, W. Donald. Wittgenstein & Religious Belief. LC 75-14714. (New Studies in the Philosophy of Religion Ser.). 224p. 1975. 13.95 o.p. (ISBN 0-312-88620-9). St Martin.

Hudson, W. H. The Book of a Naturalist. 360p. 1982. 30.00x (ISBN 0-7045-0408-1, Pub. by Wildwood House). State Mutual Bk.

--Far Away & Long Ago. 350p. 1981. cancelled 14.95 (ISBN 0-8180-0251-4). Horizon.

--The Lands End. 307p. 1982. 30.00x (ISBN 0-7045-0420-0, Pub. by Wildwood House). State Mutual Bk.

Hudson, W. J. Australia & the Colonial Question at the United Nations. LC 79-86488. (Illus.). 1970. 8.00x o.p. (ISBN 0-8248-0096-6, Eastwest Ctr). UH Pr.

Hudson, W. Ronald, jt. auth. see Haas, Ralph.

Hudson, William R. & Bozzini, Yvette M. I Love Parking in San Francisco. (Illus.). 80p. (Orig.). 1982. pap. 4.95 (ISBN 0-9609838-0-5). Get Happy.

Hudson-Evans, Richard. Custom Cars & Vans. (Illus.). 64p. 1983. pap. 4.95 (Pub. by Batsford England). David & Charles.

--The Lightweight Bike Book. (Illus.). 120p. 1981. 18.50 o.p. (ISBN 0-7134-1972-5, Pub. by Batsford England); pap. 11.95 (ISBN 0-7134-1973-3). David & Charles.

Hudspeth, Mary Kay. Introductory Geometry. (Illus.). 576p. Date not set. pap. text ed. 16.95 (ISBN 0-201-10690-6). A-W.

Hudspeth, Robert N. Ellery Channing. (United States Authors Ser.). 1973. lib. bdg. 12.95 (ISBN 0-8057-0131-1, Twayne). G K Hall.

Hudspeth, Ron. Southern Nights & City Lights. LC 82-61870. 179p. 1982. 9.95 (ISBN 0-931948-41-X). Peachtree Pubs.

Hudzik, John & Cordner, Gary W. Planning in Criminal Justice Organizations & Systems. 352p. 1983. text ed. 20.95 (ISBN 0-02-475170-7). Macmillan.

Hue & Van den Werve. Short Term Regulation of Liver Metabolism. 1982. 119.75 (ISBN 0-444-80333-5). Elsevier.

Huebel, Harry R. Things in the Driver's Seat. 1972. pap. 12.95 (ISBN 0-395-30633-7). HM.

Huebner, Kenneth H. Finite Element Method for Engineers. LC 74-17452. 448p. 1975. 39.95x o.p. (ISBN 0-471-41950-8, Pub. by Wiley-Interscience). Wiley.

Huebner, Kenneth H. & Thornton, Earl A. The Finite Element Method for Engineers. 2nd ed. LC 82-8379. 656p. 1982. 37.50 (ISBN 0-471-09159-6, Pub. by Wiley-Interscience). Wiley.

Huebner, Mildred H., jt. auth. see Bush, Clifford L.

Huebner, S. S., jt. auth. see Black, Kenneth, Jr.

Huebner, S. S., et al. Property & Liability Insurance. 3rd ed. (Illus.). 608p. 1982. ref. ed. 26.95 (ISBN 0-13-730978-3). P-H.

Huebner, Vicky L., jt. auth. see Hofmann, Alan F.

Huechert, Charles M., jt. auth. see Schultz, Edward W.

Huede, Henri le see Le Huede, Henri.

Hueffer, Ford M., jt. auth. see Conrad, Joseph.

Huegel, F. J. Cross of Christ, the Throne of God. 1965. pap. 2.50 o.p. (ISBN 0-87123-068-2, 210068). Bethany Hse.

--Ministry of Intercession. LC 76-15861. (Orig.). 1971. pap. 1.95 (ISBN 0-87123-365-7, 200365). Bethany Hse.

Huegli, Rich see James, Don.

Huelsman, L. P. Basic Circuit Theory with Digital Computations. (Illus.). 1972. ref. ed. 32.95 (ISBN 0-13-057430-9). P-H.

Huelsman, Lawrence P. Digital Computation in Basic Circuit Theory. (Illus.). 1968. text ed. 18.50 o.p. (ISBN 0-07-030843-8, C). McGraw.

Huelsman, Lawrence P. & Allen, Philip. Introduction to the Theory & Design of Active Filters. (Electrical Engineering Ser.). (Illus.). 1980. text ed. 34.50x (ISBN 0-07-030854-3); solutions manual 25.00 (ISBN 0-07-030855-1). McGraw.

Huelsman, Richard J. Intimacy with Jesus: An Introduction. LC 82-60587. 1983. pap. 4.95 (ISBN 0-8091-2492-0). Paulist Pr.

Huer, Jon H. Ideology & Social Character. LC 78-56917. 1978. pap. 10.25 (ISBN 0-8191-0522-8). U Pr of Amer.

--Society & Social Science. LC 79-63563. 1979. pap. text ed. 10.00 o.p. (ISBN 0-8191-0730-1). U Pr of Amer.

Hueslsman, Richard J. Pray: Participant's Handbook. pap. 3.95 o.p. (ISBN 0-8091-1976-5). Paulist Pr.

Huessler, Robert, ed. see Camerron, Donald.

Huet, Marie-Helene. Rehearsing the Revolution: The Staging of Marat's Death, 1793-1797. Hurley, Robert, tr. from Fr. LC 81-21965. (Quantum Bks.). 150p. 1982. 14.95x (ISBN 0-520-04321-9). U of Cal Pr.

Hueter, John E. Matthew, Mark, Luke, John... Now: Judas & His Redemption (In Search of the Real Judge) 1983. 17.95; pap. 9.95 (ISBN 0-8283-1874-3). Branden.

Hueting, R. New Scarcity & Economic Growth: More Welfare Through Less Production. 1980. 38.50 (ISBN 0-444-85400-2). Elsevier.

Huett, Lenora, jt. auth. see Mathes, J. H.

Huettig, Mae D. Economic Control of the Motion Picture Industry: A Study in Industrial Organization. LC 70-160235. (Moving Pictures Ser). x, 163p. 1971. Repr. of 1944 ed. lib. bdg. 12.95x (ISBN 0-89198-036-9). Ozer.

Huettinger, Edouard. Degas. (Q L P Art Ser). (Illus.). 7.95 (ISBN 0-517-00502-6). Crown.

Huey, Raymond B. & Pianka, Eric R., eds. Lizard Ecology: Studies of a Model Organism. (Illus.). 720p. 1983. text ed. 35.00x (ISBN 0-674-53673-8). Harvard U Pr.

Hueze, Francios E., jt. ed. see Goodman, Richard E.

Huf, L. M. Portrait of the Artist as a Young Woman. LC 82-40263. (Literature & Life Ser.). 200p. 1983. 13.50 (ISBN 0-8044-2406-3). Ungar.

Hufbauer, Gary C. Economic Warfare: Sanctions in Support of National Foreign Policy Goals. (Policy Analyses in International Economics Ser.: No. 6). 1983. 6.00 (ISBN 0-88132-011-0). Inst Intl Eco.

Hufbauer, Gary C. & Erb, Joanna S. Subsidies in International Trade. 200p. 1983. 20.00 (ISBN 0-88132-004-8). Inst Intl Eco.

Huff, Darrell & Geis, Irving. How to Lie with Statistics. 1954. 12.95 o.p. (ISBN 0-393-05264-8, NortonC); pap. 1.95x (ISBN 0-393-09426-X). Norton.

--How to Take a Chance. (Illus.). 1964. pap. 5.95 (ISBN 0-393-00263-2, Norton Lib). Norton.

Huff, Doug. Sports in West Virginia: A Pictorial History. LC 79-10503. (Illus.). 1979. pap. 12.95 o.p. (ISBN 0-915442-65-5). Donning Co.

Huff, Elizabeth, ed. see Fang, Chaoying.

Huff, R. W. & Pauerstein, C. J. Human Reproduction: Physiology & Pathophysiology. 497p. 1979. pap. 25.00 (ISBN 0-471-03562-9). Wiley.

Huff, Robert. The Ventriloquist: New & Selected Poems. LC 77-1338. (Virginia Commonwealth University Series for Contemporary Poetry). 58p. 1977. 8.95 (ISBN 0-8139-0725-X). U Pr of Va.

Huffaker, C. B. & Messenger, P. S., eds. Theory & Practice of Biological Control. 1977. 69.00 o.s.i. (ISBN 0-12-360350-1). Acad Pr.

Huffaker, Clair. The Cowboy & the Cossack. large type ed. LC 82-10540. 560p. 1982. Repr. of 1973 ed. 11.95 (ISBN 0-89621-385-4). Thorndike Pr.

--Seven Ways from Sundown. large print ed. LC 82-838. 212p. 1982. Repr. of 1960 ed. 9.95x (ISBN 0-89621-350-1). Thorndike Pr.

Huffaker, Robert, jt. auth. see Fowles, John.

Huffaker, Sandy. The Bald Book: Miracle Cures & More. (Illus.). 64p. 1983. pap. 3.95 (ISBN 0-87131-401-0). M Evans.

--The Dispensible Man: How to Figure Your Net Worth. LC 82-5181. (Illus.). 64p. 1982. pap. 3.95 (ISBN 0-87131-383-9). M Evans.

Huffman, Claire de C. L. see De C. L. Huffman, Claire.

Huffman, Clifford C., jt. auth. see Ribner, Irving.

Huffman, Donald R., jt. auth. see Bohren, Craig F.

Huffman, Franklin E. & Proum, Im. Cambodian-English Glossary. LC 76-50539. (Linguistic Ser.). 160p. 1981. 11.00x (ISBN 0-300-02070-8); pap. 6.95x. Yale U Pr.

--English for Speakers of Khmer. LC 82-48905. 608p. 1983. text ed. 30.00 (ISBN 0-300-02895-4); pap. text ed. 10.95x (ISBN 0-300-03031-2). Yale U Pr.

--English-Khmer Dictionary. LC 78-7705. (Linguistic Ser.). 1978. text ed. 37.50x (ISBN 0-300-02261-1). Yale U Pr.

Huffman, H. Programmed Business Mathematics, 3 bks. 3rd ed. Incl. Bk. 1. Business Mathematics Fundamental. 8.75 o.p. (ISBN 0-07-031101-3); Bk. 2. Negotiable Instruments, Discounts, Payroll & Taxes. 8.75 o.p. (ISBN 0-07-031102-1); Bk. 3. Business Ownership Depreciation, Compound Interest, Insurance & Statistics. 8.95 o.p. (ISBN 0-07-031103-X). instructor's manual & key 10.00 o.p. (ISBN 0-07-031111-0, G). McGraw.

Huffman, H., et al. Mathematics for Business Careers. 4th ed. 1974. 16.28 (ISBN 0-07-031121-8, G); tchr's manual & key 7.50 (ISBN 0-07-031124-2); performance guide 7.00 (ISBN 0-07-031122-6). McGraw.

Huffman, Harry. Programmed Business Mathematics, Bk. 1. 4th, rev. ed. 1980. pap. text ed. 11.20 (ISBN 0-07-030901-9); test bklet free (ISBN 0-07-030904-3); Bks. 1-3. instr's manual 11.20 (ISBN 0-07-030907-8). McGraw.

--Programmed Business Mathematics, Bk. 2. 4th, rev. ed. (Illus.). 256p. 1980. pap. text ed. 11.20 (ISBN 0-07-030902-7); test bklet free (ISBN 0-07-030905-1). McGraw.

--Programmed Business Mathematics, Bk. 3. 4th rev. ed. (Illus.). 192p. 1980. pap. 11.20 (ISBN 0-07-030903-5, G); test bklet free (ISBN 0-07-030906-X). McGraw.

Huffman, Harry & Fiber, Larry. Principles of Business Mathematics: Using the Electronic Calculator. (Illus.). 1978. pap. text ed. 13.50 (ISBN 0-07-030890-X, G); inst. manual & key 8.50 (ISBN 0-07-030891-8). McGraw.

Huffman, Harry & Stewart, J. R. General Recordkeeping. 7th ed. 1975. 15.84 (ISBN 0-07-031030-0, G); wkbk. pts. 1 & 2 5.96 ea. Pt. 1 (ISBN 0-07-031031-9). Pt. 2 (ISBN 0-07-031032-7). McGraw.

Huffman, Harry & Stewart, Jeffrey R. General Recordkeeping. 8th ed. (Illus.). 224p. (gr. 9-11). 1980. 15.84 (ISBN 0-07-031040-8, G); Bk. 1. tchrs. ed. activity guide & working papers 8.75 (ISBN 0-07-031043-2); Bk. 2. tchr's ed. for activity guide & working papers 7.95 (ISBN 0-07-031044-0); Bk. 1. activity guide & working papers 5.64 (ISBN 0-07-031041-6); Bk. 2. activity guide & working papers 5.64 (ISBN 0-07-031042-4). McGraw.

Huffman, Hughes & Hunt, Mark. Carols. LC 77-27739. 1978. sprial bdg. 6.95 o.p. (ISBN 0-87784-739-8); pap. 4.95 o.p. (ISBN 0-87784-748-7). Inter-Varsity.

Huffman, James L. Politics of the Meiji Press: The Life of Fukuchi Gen'ichiro. LC 79-3879. 1980. text ed. 15.00x (ISBN 0-8248-0679-4). UH Pr.

Huffman, John A., Jr. Wholly Living. 132p. 1981. pap. 4.50 (ISBN 0-89693-005-X). Victor Bks.

Huffman, Robert & Specht, Irene. Many Wonderful Things. 3rd ed. 1977. pap. 7.50 (ISBN 0-87516-027-1). De Vorss.

Huffman, Virginia, jt. auth. see Kutie, Rita.

Huffmon, H. B., et al, eds. The Quest for the Kingdom of God: Essays in Honor of George E. Mendenhall. 1983. text ed. 20.00x (ISBN 0-931464-15-3). Eisenbrauns.

Hufford, Larry, ed. Reminisicing with D. B. 192p. Date not set. write for info. (ISBN 0-931052-04-1); pap. write for info. (ISBN 0-931052-05-X). AAR-Tantalus. Postponed.

Hufford, Susan. Going All the Way. (Orig.). 1980. pap. 2.25 o.p. (ISBN 0-451-09014-4, E9014, Sig). NAL.

Huffstadt, A. J. Congenital Malformations. (Jonxis Lectures: Vol. 4). 1981. 47.75 (ISBN 0-444-90110-8). Elsevier.

Huffstickler, Albert. A Remembered Light. 32p. pap. 2.25 (ISBN 0-941720-05-5). Slough Pr TX.

Hufner, Klaus & Naumann, Jens. The United Nations System International Bibliography, Vol. 3B. new ed. (Monographs & Articles in Collective Vols. 1971-75). 692p. 1979. 78.00x (ISBN 0-686-52995-2, Pub. by K G Saur). Gale.

Hufton, Olwen H. The Poor of Eighteenth-Century France 1750-1789. (Illus.). 1979. pap. 12.95x (ISBN 0-19-822558-X). Oxford U Pr.

Hug, James E., ed. Tracing the Spirit: Communities, Social Action & Theological Reflections. LC 82-62419. (Woodstock Studies). 320p. 1983. pap. 9.95 (ISBN 0-8091-2529-3). Paulist Pr.

Hug, William E. Instructional Design & the Media Program. 1976. pap. text ed. 9.00 (ISBN 0-8389-0207-3). ALA.

Hugard, Jean & Braue, Frederick. Expert Card Technique. 480p. 1975. pap. 6.00 (ISBN 0-486-21755-8). Dover.

Hugard, Jean & Crimmins, John J. Encyclopedia of Card Tricks. (Illus.). 448p. (Orig.). 1965. pap. 8.95 (ISBN 0-571-07017-5). Faber & Faber.

Hugel, F. von. Mystical Element of Religion As Studied in St. Catherine of Genoa & Her Friends, 2 vols. 2nd ed. 1961. Repr. of 1923 ed. x set 49.50 (ISBN 0-227-67535-5). Attic Pr.

Hugel, Friedrich Von. Essays & Addresses on the Philosophy of Religion. LC 72-9828. 308p. 1974 Repr. of 1921 ed. lib. bdg. 17.00x (ISBN 0-8371-6219-X, HUPR). Greenwood.

Hugenholtz, P. G., jt. auth. see Roelandt, J.

Huges, Patricia & Ochi, Kaz. The Power of Visicalc Real Estate. 166p. 1982. pap. 14.95 (ISBN 0-13-687350-2). P-H.
--The Power of Visiplot-Visicalc-Visifile. 154p. 1982. pap. 14.95 (ISBN 0-13-687368-5). P-H.
Huggard, E. M., tr. see Giaever, John.
Huggard, E. M., tr. see Meyer, Conrad F.
Huggenvik, Theodore. We Believe. 1950. pap. 3.25 (ISBN 0-8066-0151-5, 15-7102). Augsburg.
Huggett, Joyce. Growing Into Love. LC 82-18667. 128p. pap. 3.95 (ISBN 0-87784-374-0). Inter-Varsity.
Huggins, Frank B. Of Human Bondage Notes. (Orig.). 1963. pap. 2.50 (ISBN 0-8220-0930-7). Cliffs.
Huggins, Kenneth, jt. auth. see Goodman, Joel.
Huggins, Larry. The Blood Speaks. 128p. 1982. pap. 4.95 (ISBN 0-89274-231-3, HH-231). Harrison Hse.
Huggins, Nathan I. Protestants Against Poverty: Boston's Charities, 1870-1900. (Contributions in American History: No. 9). 1970. lib. bdg. 27.50 (ISBN 0-8371-3307-6, HUP/). Greenwood.
--Slave & Citizen: The Life of Frederick Douglas. (Library of American Biography). 1980. 9.95 (ISBN 0-316-38001-6); pap. 5.95 (ISBN 0-316-38000-8). Little.
Huggins, Nathan I., ed. Voices from the Harlem Renaissance. (Illus.). 1976. pap. text ed. 11.95x0454387x (ISBN 0-19-501955-5). Oxford U Pr.
Huggins, P. J., ed. see Orion Nebula to Honor Henry Draper Symposium, Dec 4-5, 1981.
Huggins, R. A., et al, eds. Annual Review of Materials Science, Vol. 12. LC 75-172108. (Illus.). 1982. text ed. 22.00 (ISBN 0-8243-1712-2). Annual Reviews.
Huggins, Robert A., et al, eds. Annual Review of Materials Science, Vol. 5. LC 75-172108. (Illus.). 1975. text ed. 17.00 (ISBN 0-8243-1705-X). Annual Reviews.
Hugh, Kelsey, jt. auth. see Ottlik, Geza.
Hugh, Wheeler, jt. auth. see Sondheim, Stephen.
Hughart, David P. Prospects for Traditional & Non-Conventional Energy Sources in Developing Countries. (Working Paper: No. 346). ii, 132p. 1979. 5.00 (ISBN 0-686-36159-8, WP-0346). World Bank.
Hughes. Systems Programming Under CP-M80. 1982. text ed. 21.95 (ISBN 0-8359-7457-X); pap. text ed. 15.95 (ISBN 0-8359-7456-1). Reston.
Hughes & Bond. Reach. (gr. 4-9). pap. 4.59 (ISBN 0-8372-4259-2); tchr's programme 4.59 (ISBN 0-8372-4260-6); tapes avail. Bowmar-Noble.
Hughes & Stafford. Anaerobic Digestion, 1981. 1982. 73.25 (ISBN 0-444-80406-4). Elsevier.
Hughes, A. Psychology & the Political Experience. LC 74-12961. 224p. 1975. 17.95 (ISBN 0-521-20594-8). Cambridge U Pr.
Hughes, A. C., jt. auth. see Leibositz, S.
Hughes, A. Daniel. Tombstone Story: The Biography of an Arizona Pioneer. 1979. cancelled 10.00 (ISBN 0-682-49394-5, Lochinvar). Exposition.
Hughes, Alan. A Home of Your Own for the Least Cash: The Home Buyer's Guide for Today. (Illus.). 304p. 1982. pap. 8.95 (ISBN 0-686-97243-0). Acropolis.
Hughes, Albert E. What Your Handwriting Reveals. 1978. 3.00 (ISBN 0-87980-365-7). Wilshire.
Hughes, Ann J. & Grawoig, Dennis E. Linear Programming: An Emphasis on Decision Making. LC 72-1938. 1973. text ed. 26.95 (ISBN 0-201-03024-1). A-W.
--Statistics: A Foundation for Analysis. LC 76-133891. (Business & Economics Ser). 1971. text ed. 23.95 (ISBN 0-201-03021-7). A-W.
Hughes, Anne E. A Book of Sounds: A, B, C. LC 78-62981. (Learn-a-Sound). (Illus.). (gr. 1-3). 1979. PLB 13.85 (ISBN 0-8393-0188-X). Raintree Pubs.
--A Book of Sounds: Blends & Ends. LC 79-62984. (Learn-a-Sound). (Illus.). (gr. 1-3). 1979. PLB 13.85 (ISBN 0-8393-0191-X). Raintree Pubs.
--A Book of Sounds: ee, oo, ai. LC 79-62983. (Learn-a-Sound). (Illus.). (gr. 1-3). 1979. PLB 13.85 (ISBN 0-8393-0190-1). Raintree Pubs.
--A Book of Sounds: sl, ch, pr. LC 79-62982. (Learn-a-Sound). (Illus.). (gr. 1-3). 1979. PLB 13.85 (ISBN 0-8393-0189-8). Raintree Pubs.
Hughes, Arthur. English Accents & Dialects. 102p. 1979. text ed. 19.95 (ISBN 0-8391-1361-7). Univ Park.
Hughes, Arthur & Trudgill, Peter. English Accents & Dialects: An Introduction to Social & Regional Varieties of British English. 104p. 1979. pap. text ed. 9.95 (ISBN 0-7131-6129-9). E Arnold.
Hughes, Arthur F. The American Biologist Through Four Centuries. (Illus.). 432p. 1982. 32.50x (ISBN 0-398-04598-4). C C Thomas.
Hughes, Arthur J. American Government. 2nd ed. (gr. 9-12). 1974. 4.92 (ISBN 0-02-644560-3, 64448); tchr's manual 1.36 (ISBN 0-02-644490-9, 64449). Glencoe.
Hughes, B. R., jt. auth. see Lewis, Jack.
Hughes, Barbara, ed. Typing Manual. 4rd ed. 38p. 1981. pap. text ed. 10.00 (ISBN 0-935012-00-1). Edit Experts.
Hughes, Barnabas. Thinking Through Problems. (YA) 1976. wkbk 9.25 (ISBN 0-88488-056-7). Creative Pubns.
Hughes, Barnabas, ed. Regiomontanus: On Triangles. (Illus.). 308p. 1967. 35.00 (ISBN 0-299-04210-3). U of Wis Pr.
Hughes, Barry B. World Modeling: The Mesarovic-Pestel World Model in the Context of Its Contemporaries. LC 79-3252. 240p. 1980. 25.95x (ISBN 0-669-03401-0). Lexington Bks.
Hughes, C. David & Singler, Charles H. Strategic Sales Management. 352p. 1983. pap. instrs' manual avail. (ISBN 0-201-10261-7). A-W.
Hughes, C. J. Igneous Petrology. (Developments in Petrology Ser.: Vol. 7). 1982. 30.00 (ISBN 0-444-42011-8). Elsevier.
Hughes, Catharine R., ed. American Theatre Annual, 1978-1979. (Illus.). 1980. 52.00x (ISBN 0-8103-0418-X, Incorporates New York Theatre Annual). Gale.
--American Theatre Annual, 1979-80. (Illus.). 200p. 1981. 52.00x (ISBN 0-8103-0419-8). Gale.
--New York Theatre Annual: 1976-77. LC 78-50757. (Illus.). 1978. 52.00x (ISBN 0-8103-0416-3). Gale.
--New York Theatre Annual: 1977-78. LC 78-50757. (Illus.). 1978. 52.00x (ISBN 0-8103-0417-1). Gale.
Hughes, Catherine A., ed. Economic Education: A Guide to Information Sources. LC 73-17576. (Economics Information Guide Ser.: Vol. 6). 1977. 42.00x (ISBN 0-8103-1290-5). Gale.
Hughes, Charles. Guide to Texas Title Insurance. 1983. 11.95 (ISBN 0-87201-777-X). Gulf Pub.
Hughes, Charles A. Grosset's Italian Phrase Book & Dictionary for Travelers. (Orig.). 1971. pap. 2.95 (ISBN 0-448-00653-7, G&D). Putnam Pub Group.
Hughes, Charles E., et al, eds. Advanced Programming Techniques: A Second Course in Programming Using Fortran. 287p. 1978. text ed. 24.95 (ISBN 0-471-02611-5). Wiley.
Hughes, Charles Evans. Pan American Peace Plans. 1929. 24.50x (ISBN 0-685-69828-9). Elliots Bks.
Hughes, Charles W. Human Side of Music. LC 70-107871. (Music Ser). 1970. Repr. of 1948 ed. lib. bdg. 35.00 (ISBN 0-306-71895-2). Da Capo.
Hughes, Colin A., jt. auth. see Western, J. S.
Hughes, Cynthia B., jt. auth. see Horowitz, June A.
Hughes, D. E. & Rose, A. H., eds. Microbes & Biological Productivity. (Illus.). 1971. 47.50 (ISBN 0-521-08112-2). Cambridge U Pr.
Hughes, D. J. Science & Starvation. 1968. 15.50 (ISBN 0-08-012327-9); pap. 10.75 (ISBN 0-08-012326-0). Pergamon.
Hughes, D. R. & Piper, F. C. Projective Planes. 2nd ed. (Graduate Texts in Mathematics: Vol. 6). 291p. 1982. 32.00 (ISBN 0-387-90043-8). Springer-Verlag.
Hughes, David. Treatise on the Law Relating to Insurance in Three Parts: Of Marine Insurance, of Insurance on Lives & of Insurance Against Fire. Helmholz, R. H. & Reams, Bernard D., Jr., eds. LC 80-84860. (Historical Writings in Law & Jurisprudence Ser.: No. 13, Bk. 16). xxxii, 472p. 1981. Repr. of 1883 ed. lib. bdg. 38.50 (ISBN 0-89941-068-5). W S Hein.
Hughes, David, ed. see Wells, H. G.
Hughes, David G. History of European Music. (Illus.). 512p. 1974. text ed. 35.00 (ISBN 0-07-031105-6, C). McGraw.
Hughes, David G., ed. Instrumental Music: A Conference, at Isham Memorial Library, Harvard University. LC 70-166094. 152p. 1972. Repr. of 1959 ed. lib. bdg. 17.50 (ISBN 0-306-70273-8). Da Capo.
Hughes, David T. & Marshall, P. T. Human Health, Biology & Hygiene. LC 79-128501. (Illus.). 1970. text ed. 8.95x (ISBN 0-521-07731-1). Cambridge U Pr.
Hughes, Dean. Facing the Enemy. LC 82-12810. 143p. (gr. 6-12). 1982. 6.95 (ISBN 0-87747-928-3). Deseret Bk.
--Millie Willenheimer & the Chestnut Corporation. LC 82-13758. 144p. (gr. 4-6). 1983. 9.95 (ISBN 0-689-30958-9). Atheneum.
--Switching Tracks. LC 82-3899. 180p. (gr. 5-9). 1982. 10.95 (ISBN 0-689-30923-6). Atheneum.
Hughes, Denis & Bowler, Peter. The Security Survey. 154p. 1982. text ed. 34.25x (ISBN 0-566-02291-5). Gower Pub Ltd.
Hughes, Derek. Dryden's Heroic Plays. LC 80-19109. xi, 195p. 1980. 26.50x (ISBN 0-8032-2314-5). U of Nebr Pr.
Hughes, Dom A. see Abraham, Gerald.
Hughes, Dom Anselm see Abraham, Gerald, et al.
Hughes, Donna, jt. auth. see Whitney, George.
Hughes, E. R., ed. & tr. Chinese Philosophy in Classical Times. 382p. 1982. pap. text ed. 4.95 (ISBN 0-460-01973-2, Pub. by Erman). Biblio Dist.
Hughes, Eden. The Selkirks. 1982. pap. 2.95 (ISBN 0-451-11506-6, AE1506, Sig). NAL.
--The Wiltons. (Orig.). 1980. pap. 2.75 (ISBN 0-451-09520-0, E9520, Sig). NAL.
Hughes, Edward. Marcel Proust: A Study in the Quality of Awareness. LC 82-9718. 224p. Date not set. 39.50 (ISBN 0-521-24768-3). Cambridge U Pr.
--Studies in Administration & Finance, 1558-1825: With Special Reference to the History of Salt Taxation in England. LC 79-12656. Repr. of 1934 ed. lib. bdg. 35.00x (ISBN 0-87991-856-X). Porcupine Pr.
Hughes, Edward F. X., et al. Hospital Cost Containment Programs: A Policy Analysis. LC 78-13793. 168p. 1978. prof ref 22.50x (ISBN 0-88410-705-1). Ballinger Pub.
Hughes, Eric L. Gymnastics for Men: A Competitive Approach for Teacher & Coach. (Illus.). 1966. 22.95 (ISBN 0-471-07122-6). Wiley.
Hughes, Erica, jt. auth. see Watkins, Peter.
Hughes, Eugene, jt. auth. see Musselman, Vernon A.
Hughes, Evan. Banking. LC 74-76176. (The Professions Ser.). 160p. 1974. 11.50 o.p. (ISBN 0-7153-6625-4). David & Charles.
Hughes, Everett C. French Canada in Transition. 1963. pap. 2.95 o.s.i. (ISBN 0-226-35925-5, P139, Phoen). U of Chicago Pr.
--Men & Their Work. LC 80-29143. 184p. 1981. Repr. of 1958 ed. lib. bdg. 19.25x (ISBN 0-313-22791-8, HUMW). Greenwood.
Hughes, F. Quentin. Seaport: Architecture & Townscape of Liverpool. 16.00 o.p. (ISBN 0-685-20625-4). Transatlantic.
Hughes, Frederick W. OP AMP Handbook. (Illus.). 304p. 1981. text ed. 21.95 (ISBN 0-13-637298-8). P-H.
Hughes, G. Hebrews & Hermeneutics. LC 77-84806. (Society for New Testament Studies Monographs: No. 36). 1980. 24.95 (ISBN 0-521-21858-6). Cambridge U Pr.
Hughes, G. & Gaylord, E. W. Basic Equations of Engineering. (Orig.). 1964. pap. 6.95 (ISBN 0-07-031109-9, SP). McGraw.
Hughes, G. A. & Heal, G. M. Public Policy & the Tax System. (Illus.). 224p. 1980. text ed. 29.50x (ISBN 0-04-336067-X). Allen Unwin.
Hughes, G. David. Marketing Management: A Planning Approach. LC 77-83036. 1978. text ed. 25.95 (ISBN 0-201-03057-8); instr's resource manual o. p. 6.95 (ISBN 0-201-03056-X). A-W.
Hughes, G. E., ed. see Buridan, John.
Hughes, George E. & Cresswell, Maxwell J. An Introduction to Modal Logic. 388p. 1972. pap. 14.50x (ISBN 0-416-29460-X). Methuen Inc.
Hughes, George W., jt. auth. see Hayt, William.
Hughes, George W., jt. auth. see Hayt, William H., Jr.
Hughes, Gethin. The Poetry of Francisco de la Torre. (University of Toronto Romance Ser.: No. 43). 136p. 1982. 22.50x (ISBN 0-8020-2427-0). U of Toronto Pr.
Hughes, Gilbert C., jt. auth. see Neish, Gordon A.
Hughes, H. Stuart. Consciousness & Society: The Reorientation of European Social Thought 1890-1930. 1961. pap. 4.95 (ISBN 0-394-70201-8, Vin). Random.
--Contemporary Europe: A History. 5th ed. (Illus.). 656p. 1981. text ed. 23.95 (ISBN 0-13-170027-8). P-H.
--Prisoners of Hope: The Silver Age of the Italian Jews, 1924-1974. 184p. 1983. text ed. 15.00x (ISBN 0-674-70727-3). Harvard U Pr.
Hughes, Harold K. A Dictionary of Abbreviations in Medicine & the Health Sciences. 336p. 1977. 28.95x (ISBN 0-669-00688-2). Lexington Bks.
Hughes, Helen & Seng, You Poh, eds. Foreign Investment & Industrialisation in Singapore. LC 69-14301. 240p. 1969. 21.50 o.p. (ISBN 0-299-05420-9). U of Wis Pr.
Hughes, Helen M. News & the Human Interest Story. LC 80-19176. (Social Science Classics Ser.). 313p. 1980. text ed. 29.95 (ISBN 0-87855-326-6); pap. text ed. 7.95 (ISBN 0-87855-729-6). Transaction Bks.
Hughes, Irene F. ESPecially Irene: A Guide to Psychic Awareness. LC 70-189997. 160p. 1972. pap. 2.50 (ISBN 0-8334-1730-4, Steinbks). Garber Comm.
Hughes, J. & Michton, J. A Structured Approach to Programming. 1977. 24.95 (ISBN 0-13-854356-9). P-H.
Hughes, J. A., jt. auth. see Dowse, R. E.
Hughes, J. Donald. American Indian Ecology. (Illus.). 200p. 1983. 20.00 (ISBN 0-87404-070-1). Tex Western.
Hughes, J. Donald, ed. see Earthday X Colloquium, University of Denver, April 21-24, 1980.
Hughes, J. K. Structured Programming Using PL-C. LC 81-4434. 432p. 1981. text ed. 18.95 (ISBN 0-471-04969-7); tchr's manual avail. (ISBN 0-471-86939-2). Wiley.
Hughes, J. R. Industrialization & Economic History: Theses & Conjectures. 1970. pap. text ed. 17.95 o.p. (ISBN 0-07-031115-3, C). McGraw.
Hughes, J. S., jt. ed. see Eger, J. D.
Hughes, J. Trevor. Pathology of Muscle. LC 73-89178. (Major Problems in Pathology Ser.: No. 4). (Illus.). 225p. 1974. text ed. 14.00 o.p. (ISBN 0-7216-4827-4). Saunders.
Hughes, James & Bleakly, Kenneth. Urban Homesteading. LC 75-29148. (Illus.). 230p. 1975. 12.95 o.p. (ISBN 0-88285-026-1). Ctr Urban Pol Res.
Hughes, James G. Guide to the Automobile Mechanics Certification Examination. (Illus.). 1978. ref. ed. 17.95 (ISBN 0-8359-2618-4); pap. 12.95 o.p. (ISBN 0-686-96865-4). Reston.
--Synopsis of Pediatrics. 5th ed. LC 79-14927. 914p. 1979. pap. text ed. 29.95 (ISBN 0-8016-2309-X). Mosby.
Hughes, James W., jt. ed. see Sternlieb, George.
Hughes, Janet & Ireland, Brian. Costing & Calculations for Catering. 176p. 1981. 30.00x (ISBN 0-85950-493-X, Pub. by Thornes England). State Mutual Bk.
Hughes, Jennifer. An Outline of Modern Psychiatry. LC 81-16399. 1982. 27.95x (ISBN 0-471-10073-0, Pub. by Wiley-Interscience); pap. 16.50 (ISBN 0-471-10024-2). Wiley.
Hughes, Jill. Aztecs. (Gloucester Press Ser.). (gr. 4-8). 1980. PLB 9.40 (ISBN 0-531-03414-3, Gloucester Pr). Watts.
--Eskimos. LC 77-11059. (Civilization Library). (Illus.). (gr. 5-8). 1978. PLB 9.40 s&l (ISBN 0-531-01427-4). Watts.
Hughes, Joan. Programming the IBM 1130. LC 69-16045. 1969. 33.50 (ISBN 0-471-42040-9). Wiley.
Hughes, Joan K. PL-One Structured Programming. 2nd ed. LC 78-15665. 1979. text ed. 27.95 (ISBN 0-471-01908-9); tchrs. manual avail. (ISBN 0-471-03051-1). Wiley.
Hughes, John & Breckinridge, John. A Discussion: Is the Roman Catholic Religion Inimical to Civil or Religious Liberty? Is the Presbyterian Religion Inimical to Civil or Religious Liberty? LC 76-122167. (Civil Liberties in American History Ser). 1970. Repr. of 1836 ed. lib. bdg. 75.00 (ISBN 0-306-71979-7). Da Capo.
Hughes, John, jt. auth. see Choron, Sandra.
Hughes, John J. Proclaiming the Good News: Homilies for a Cycle. 156p. 1983. pap. 14.95 (ISBN 0-87973-722-0, 722). Our Sunday Visitor.
Hughes, John P. Linguistics & Language Teaching. (Orig.). 1967. pap. text ed. 3.70x (ISBN 0-685-19742-5). Phila Bk Co.
Hughes, John T. & Rozier, R. G. Natural History of Dental Disease in North Carolina: 1976-1977. 182p. 1982. lib. bdg. 27.95 o.p. (ISBN 0-89089-188-5); pap. 14.95 (ISBN 0-89089-189-3). Carolina Acad Pr.
Hughes, Jon C. The Tanyard Murder: On the Case with Lafcadio Hearn. LC 82-20280. (Illus.). 138p. (Orig.). 1983. lib. bdg. 19.50 (ISBN 0-8191-2833-3); pap. text ed. 8.25 (ISBN 0-8191-2834-1). U Pr of Amer.
Hughes, Jonathan. The Vital Few: American Economic Progress & Its Protagonists. LC 65-23202. 1973. pap. 9.95 (ISBN 0-19-519743-7, GB393, GB). Oxford U Pr.
Hughes, Jonathan R. American Economic History. 1983. text ed. 24.95x (ISBN 0-673-15338-X). Scott F.
Hughes, Joseph H., Jr. A Covenant with Honor. LC 65-26682. 12.00 (ISBN 0-8022-0757-X); pap. 10.00. Aaron-Jenkins.
Hughes, Judith M. Emotion & High Politics: Personal Relations in Late Nineteenth-Century Britain & Germany. LC 82-4737. 232p. 1983. 28.50x (ISBN 0-520-04691-9). U of Cal Pr.
Hughes, Katherine. Corporate Response to Declining Rates of Growth. LC 81-47623. 160p. 1982. 24.95x (ISBN 0-669-04698-1). Lexington Bks.
Hughes, Kathleen, ed. Good Works. 220p. 1982. pap. 25.00 (ISBN 0-936758-06-6). Ctr Responsive Law.
Hughes, Kathleen, jt. ed. see Clemoes, Peter.
Hughes, Langston. Five Plays by Langston Hughes. Smalley, Webster, ed. LC 63-7169. (Midland Bks.: No. 121). 280p. 1963. 25.00 o.p. (ISBN 0-253-32230-8); pap. 5.95 (ISBN 0-253-20121-7). Ind U Pr.
--Good Morning, Revolution: Uncollected Writings of Social Protest. Berry, Faith, ed. LC 73-81747. 160p. 1973. 8.50 (ISBN 0-88208-023-7); pap. 5.95 (ISBN 0-88208-024-5). Lawrence Hill.
--I Wonder As I Wander: An Autobiographical Journey. (Orig.). 1964. pap. 5.95 o.p. (ISBN 0-8090-0068-7, AmCen); 20.00 o.p. (ISBN 0-374-94031-2). Hill & Wang.
--Jazz. rev. ed. (First Bks). (Illus.). 96p. (gr. 7-9). 1982. PLB 8.90 (ISBN 0-531-04393-2). Watts.
--Panther & the Lash. 1967. 5.95 o.s.i. (ISBN 0-394-40417-3); pap. 5.95 o.s.i. (ISBN 0-394-40419-X). Knopf.
--Selected Poems of Langston Hughes. LC 73-14913. 1974. pap. 4.95 (ISBN 0-394-71910-7, Vin). Random.
--Simple's Uncle Sam. 1965. pap. 7.25 (ISBN 0-8090-0087-3, AmCen). Hill & Wang.
Hughes, Lawrence E. Data Communications for CP-M Based Micro-Computers. 1983. text ed. 21.95 (ISBN 0-8359-1229-9); pap. text ed. 15.95 (ISBN 0-8359-1228-0). Reston.
Hughes, Lynn. Frogs, Horses & Parrots. (Illus.). 1982. prepack 15 horses, 10 frogs, 5 parrots, 64pp. ea. 148.50 (ISBN 0-312-92213-2). Congdon & Weed.
Hughes, M. T., ed. Stochastic Processes in Control Systems. (IEE Control Engineering Ser.). (Illus.). 408p. 1981. 57.50 (ISBN 0-906048-44-3, Pub. by Peregrinus London). Inst Elect Eng.
Hughes, Mary Margaret, ed. Successful Retail Security. LC 73-91244. 320p. 1974. 18.95 (ISBN 0-913708-15-1). Butterworth.
Hughes, Maysie J. & Barnes, Charles D., eds. Neural Control of Circulation. LC 79-6784. (Research Topics in Physiology Ser.). 1980. 27.50 (ISBN 0-12-360850-3). Acad Pr.
Hughes, Merritt Y. see Milton, John.
Hughes, Monica. Hunter in the Dark. LC 82-13807. 144p. (gr. 5-9). 1983. 9.95 (ISBN 0-689-30959-7). Atheneum.
Hughes, N. F. Paleobiology of Angiosperm Origins. LC 75-3855. (Illus.). 216p. 1976. 49.50 (ISBN 0-521-20809-2). Cambridge U Pr.

Hughes, Norton J. The Airport People. (Inflation Fighter Ser.). 192p. 1982. pap. 1.50 o.s.i. (ISBN 0-8439-1149-2, Leisure Bks). Nordon Pubns.

Hughes, O. R., jt. ed. see Slocum, D. W.

Hughes, Owen F. Ship Structural Design: A Rationally-Based, Computer Aided, Optimization Approach. (Ocean Engineering Ser.). 600p. 1983. 65.00x (ISBN 0-471-03241-7, Pub. by Wiley-Interscience). Wiley.

Hughes, Patrick M., tr. see Fernandes, Florestan.

Hughes, Paul L. & Fries, Robert F. Basic Historical Documents of European Civilization. (Quality Paperback: No. 61). 1972. pap. 4.95 (ISBN 0-8226-0061-7). Littlefield.

Hughes, Philip. Commentary on the Second Epistle to the Corinthians. (New International Commentary on the New Testament). 1962. 13.95 (ISBN 0-8028-2186-3). Eerdmans.

Hughes, Philip E. Christian Ethics in Secular Society: An Introduction to Christian Ethics. 240p. 1983. 13.95 (ISBN 0-8010-4267-4). Baker Bk.

Hughes, Philip E., ed. & intro. by. Faith & Works: Cranmer & Hooker on Justification. 128p. (Orig.). 1982. pap. 5.95 (ISBN 0-8192-1315-2). Morehouse.

Hughes, Phillip. Interpreting Prophecy. 128p. (Orig.). 1976. pap. 3.95 o.p. (ISBN 0-8028-1630-4). Eerdmans.

Hughes, Phyllis. Pueblo Indian Cookbook. rev. ed. LC 77-76238. (Illus.). 1977. pap. 5.95 (ISBN 0-89013-094-9). Museum NM Pr.

Hughes, Phyllis, jt. auth. see Ely, Evelyn.

Hughes, R. C. Membrane Glycoproteins. 1976. 64.95 o.p. (ISBN 0-408-70705-4). Butterworth.

Hughes, R. N., jt. auth. see Barnes, R. S.

Hughes, Richard. The Sisters' Tragedy. Brown, Edmund R., ed. (International Pocket Library). pap. 3.00 (ISBN 0-686-77242-3). Branden.

--Theology & the Cain Complex. LC 81-43698. 148p. (Orig.). 1982. lib. bdg. 19.50 (ISBN 0-8191-2357-9); pap. text ed. 8.25 (ISBN 0-8191-2358-7). U Pr of Amer.

Hughes, Richard & Brewin, Robert. Tranquilizing of America. 1980. pap. 2.95 o.p. (ISBN 0-446-93638-3). Warner Bks.

Hughes, Richard see Brown, Edmund R.

Hughes, Richard E. The Lively Image: 4 Myths in Literature. 1975. pap. text ed. 8.95 (ISBN 0-316-38034-2). Little.

Hughes, Richard E. & Duhamel, P. A. Rhetoric: Principles & Usage. 2nd ed. 1967. text ed. 15.95 (ISBN 0-13-780718-X). P-H.

Hughes, Riley. How to Write Creatively. (gr. 7 up). 1980. PLB 8.90 (ISBN 0-531-04128-X). Watts.

Hughes, Robert. The Shock of the New: Art & the Century of Change. 423p. 1981. pap. text ed. 19.00 (ISBN 0-394-32800-0). Knopf.

Hughes, Robert, ed. see Khodasevich, Vladislav.

Hughes, Robert E., jt. auth. see Fitzgerald, Edward T.

Hughes, Robert J., jt. auth. see McKenzie, Jimmy C.

Hughes, Robert J., et al. Business. 1980. 22.95 (ISBN 0-395-30634-5); Instr's. manual 2.70 (ISBN 0-395-30636-1); study resource guide 9.50 (ISBN 0-395-30635-3). HM.

Hughes, Ronald C. & Rycus, Judith S. Child Welfare Services for Children with Development Disabilities. 1982. pap. write for info (ISBN 0-87868-200-7, DD-1). Child Welfare.

Hughes, Rowland, jt. auth. see Scalzo, Frank.

Hughes, Rupert, ed. Songs by Thirty Americans for High Voice. LC 77-1948. (Music Reprint Series). 1976. Repr. of 1904 ed. lib. bdg. 27.50 (ISBN 0-306-70824-8). Da Capo.

Hughes, Ruth P., ed. see Jacoby, G. Polly.

Hughes, S., jt. auth. see Davies, J.

Hughes, Samantha. A Silent Wonder. (Candlelight Ecstasy Ser.). (Orig.). 1983. pap. 1.95 (ISBN 0-440-18409-6). Dell.

Hughes, Serge. The Fall & Rise of Modern Italy. LC 82-18387. xiv, 322p. 1983. Repr. of 1967 ed. lib. bdg. 39.75x (ISBN 0-313-23737-9, HUFR). Greenwood.

Hughes, Shirley. Alfie Gets in First. (Illus.). 1982. 8.50 (ISBN 0-688-00848-8); PLB 7.63 (ISBN 0-688-00849-6). Lothrop.

--Alfie's Feet. LC 82-13012. (Illus.). 32p. (ps-1). 1983. 8.00 (ISBN 0-688-01658-8); PLB 7.63 (ISBN 0-688-01660-X). Lothrop.

--Moving Molly. (Illus.). (ps-2). 1979. PLB 7.95x (ISBN 0-13-604587-1); pap. 2.95 (ISBN 0-13-604579-0). P-H.

Hughes, Susan C., jt. auth. see Boskey, James B.

Hughes, T. J., jt. auth. see Denton, G. H.

Hughes, Ted. Crow: From the Life & Songs of the Crow. LC 70-125352. 1971. 8.95i (ISBN 0-06-011989-6, HarpT); pap. 3.95i (ISBN 0-06-090905-6, CN-905, HarpT). Har-Row.

--Earth-Owl & Other Moon-People. (Illus.). 46p. (gr. 2-6). 1963. 5.95 (ISBN 0-571-05627-X). Faber & Faber.

--Gaudete. LC 77-3753. 1977. 12.45i (ISBN 0-06-012007-X, HarpT). Har-Row.

--Moortown. LC 79-3396. 1980. 12.45i (ISBN 0-06-012016-9, HarpT). Har-Row.

--Moortown. LC 79-3396. (Illus.). 182p. 1983. pap. 5.72i (ISBN 0-06-091017-8, CN 1017, CN). Har-Row.

--Selected Poems: Nineteen Fifty-Seven to Nineteen Sixty-Seven. LC 72-79673. (Illus.). 128p. 1974. 13.41i (ISBN 0-06-011991-8, HarpT). Har-Row.

--Under the North Star. LC 80-17894. (Illus.). 48p. 1981. 16.95 (ISBN 0-670-73942-1, Studio). Viking Pr.

Hughes, Ted, adapted by. Seneca's Oedipus. LC 82-24204. 55p. 1983. pap. 4.95 (ISBN 0-571-09223-3). Faber & Faber.

Hughes, Ted, ed. see Dickinson, Emily.

Hughes, Ted, tr. see Pilinszky, Janos.

Hughes, Terence. The Day They Stole the Queen Mary. 348p. 1983. 13.95 (ISBN 0-688-01935-8). Morrow.

Hughes, Theodore E. & Klein, David. A Family Guide to Estate Planning, Funeral Arrangements, & Settling an Estate After Death. 240p. 1983. 13.95 (ISBN 0-686-83669-3, ScribT). Scribner.

Hughes, Thomas. Tom Brown's Schooldays. (Classics Ser). (gr. 7 up). 1968. pap. 1.50 (ISBN 0-8049-0174-0, CL-174). Airmont.

Hughes, Thomas P. Dictionary of Islam: Being a Cyclopaedia of the Doctrines, Rites, Ceremonies, & Customs, Together with the Technical & Theological Terms, of the Muhannadan Religion. (Illus.). 1977. Repr. of 1885 ed. text ed. 25.00x o.p. (ISBN 0-391-01066-2). Humanities.

Hughes, Thomas P., ed. see Smiles, Samuel.

Hughes, Trevor J. & Luard, D. E. The Economic Development of Communist China, 1949-1960. LC 75-31368. 229p. 1976. Repr. of 1961 ed. lib. bdg. 17.50x (ISBN 0-8371-8529-7, HUEDC). Greenwood.

Hughes, Vivian. The Unjust Judge. (Arch Bk Ser.: No. 15). (Illus.). (gr. k-3). 1978. 0.89 (ISBN 0-570-06119-9, 59-1237). Concordia.

Hughes, W. F. & Brighton, J. A. Fluid Dynamics. (Schaum's Outline Ser). (Orig.). 1967. pap. 7.95 (ISBN 0-07-031110-2, SP). McGraw.

Hughes, W. G. The Magdalene & Other Poems. 1979. 8.00 o.p. (ISBN 0-682-49229-9). Exposition.

Hughes, W. H. & Stewart, H. C. Concise Antibiotic Treatment. 2nd ed. 148p. 1973. text ed. 12.40 o.p. (ISBN 0-407-13881-1). Butterworth.

Hughes, Wayne C., Jr. Thoroughbred Wagering: How to Win Before You Play, Pt. II. 1983. pap. 24.00 (ISBN 0-686-38884-4). Write A Book.

Hughes, Wayne C, Jr. Throughbred Wavering: How to Win Before You Play. 141p. (Orig.). 1983. pap. 18.00 (ISBN 0-943682-01-0). Write-A-Book.

Hughes, William. Aspects of Biophysics. LC 78-8992. 1979. text ed. 33.95 (ISBN 0-471-01990-9). Wiley.

--General Music: A Comprehensive Approach-Zone 4, Book A. new ed. (University of Hawaii Music Project Ser.). (gr. 7-9). 1975. pap. text ed. 11.16 (ISBN 0-201-00817-3, Sch Div). A-W.

Hughes, William F. Introduction to Viscous Flow. LC 78-14471. (Illus.). 1979. text ed. 35.00 (ISBN 0-07-031130-7, C). McGraw.

Hughes, Zach. Killbird. (Orig.). 1980. pap. 1.75 o.p. (ISBN 0-451-09263-5, E9263, Sig). NAL.

--Thunderworld. (Orig.). 1982. pap. 2.25write for info. (ISBN 0-451-11290-3, AE1290, Sig). NAL.

Hughes-Hallett, Andrew & Rees, Hedley. Quantitative Economic Policies & Interactive Planning: A Reconstruction of the Theory of Economic Policy. LC 82-4204. 370p. Date not set. 49.50 (ISBN 0-521-23718-1). Cambridge U Pr.

Hughes-Hallett, Deborah. The Math Workshop: Algebra. 1980. text ed. 21.95x (ISBN 0-393-09030-2); tchrs'. manual avail. (ISBN 0-393-09024-8). Norton.

--The Math Workshop: Elementary Functions. 1980. text ed. 21.95x (ISBN 0-393-09033-7); tchrs'. manual avail. (ISBN 0-393-09028-0). Norton.

Hughes-Stanton, Penelope. See Inside an Ancient Chinese Town. LC 79-63367. (See Inside Bks.). (Illus.). (gr. 5 up). 1979. PLB 8.90 s&l o.p. (ISBN 0-531-09158-9, Warwick Press). Watts.

Hughey, J. D. Baptists Partnership in Europe. LC 81-66559. 1982. pap. 4.95 (ISBN 0-8054-6326-7). Broadman.

Hughey, J. D. & Johnson, Arlee W. Speech Communication: Foundation & Challenges. 1975. pap. 15.95x (ISBN 0-02-358230-8). Macmillan.

Hughey, Michael W. Civil Religion & Moral Order: Theoretical & Historical Dimensions. LC 82-15429. (Contributions in Sociology Ser.: No. 43). 256p. 1983. lib. bdg. 29.95 (ISBN 0-313-23522-8, HUR/). Greenwood.

Hugh-Jones, Christine. From the Milk River. LC 76-73126. (Cambridge Studies in Social Anthropology: No. 26). (Illus.). 1980. 29.95 (ISBN 0-521-22544-2). Cambridge U Pr.

Hugh-Jones, S. The Palm & the Pleiades. LC 78-5533. (Studies in Social Anthropology: No. 24). (Illus.). 1979. 29.95 (ISBN 0-521-21952-3). Cambridge U Pr.

Hugh-Jones, Stephens. Amazonian Indians. LC 78-24568. (Civilization Library). (Illus.). (gr. 5-8). 1979. PLB 9.40 s&l (ISBN 0-531-01448-7). Watts.

Hughley, Ella J. The Truth About Black Biblical Hebrew Israelites (Jews) (Orig.). 1982. pap. 5.00 (ISBN 0-9605150-1-1). Hughley Pubns.

Hughston, George, jt. auth. see Keller, James F.

Hughston, L. P., ed. Advances in Twistor Theory. Ward, R. S. LC 79-17800. (Research Notes in Mathematics Ser.: No. 37). 336p. (Orig.). 1979. pap. text ed. 25.00 (ISBN 0-273-08448-8). Pitman Pub MA.

Hugill, Peter J. & Doughty, Robin W., eds. Field Trip Guide: AAG San Antonio 1982. (Illus.). 165p. (Orig.). 1982. pap. 2.00 (ISBN 0-89291-165-4). Assn Am Geographers.

Hugill, Robert. I Traveled Through Spain. 12.50 (ISBN 0-392-15828-0, SpS). Sportshelf.

Huglin, M. B., ed. Light Scattering from Polymer Solutions. (Physical Chemistry Ser.: Vol. 27). 1972. 121.50 o.s.i. (ISBN 0-12-361050-8). Acad Pr.

Hugo, John. St. Augustine on Nature, Sex & Marriage. 249p. 1969. pap. 8.95 o.p. (ISBN 0-933932-23-5). Scepter Pubs.

Hugo, Richard. The Hitler Diaries. LC 82-14350. 288p. 1983. 12.95. Morrow.

--The Lady in Kicking Horse Reservoir. 96p. 1973. pap. 4.95 (ISBN 0-393-04225-1). Norton.

Hugo, Thomas. Bewick Collector, 2 Vols. LC 67-24353. (Illus.). 1968. Repr. of 1866 ed. Set Incl. Suppl. 58.00x (ISBN 0-8103-3491-7). Gale.

Hugo, Victor. Choix de Poemes. Gaudon, J., ed. (Modern French Text Ser.). 1957. pap. write for info. (ISBN 0-7190-0146-3). Manchester.

--The Hunchback of Notre Dame. abr. ed. Bair, Lowell, tr. from Fr. (Bantam Classics Ser.). (gr. 9-12). 1981. pap. 1.95 (ISBN 0-553-21032-7). Bantam.

--Hunchback of Notre Dame. Cobb, Walter J., tr. pap. 1.95 (ISBN 0-451-51683-4, CJ1683, Sig Classics). NAL.

--Les Miserables. Wilbur, Charles E., tr. 9.95 (ISBN 0-394-60489-X). Modern Lib.

--Les Miserables, 3 tomes. 1951. Set. pap. 13.80 (ISBN 0-685-11397-3). French & Eur.

--Notre Dame De Paris: The Hunchback of Notre Dame. 1979. Repr. of 1910 ed. 14.95x (ISBN 0-460-00422-0, Evman). Biblio Dist.

Hugo, Victor see Swan, D. K.

Hugo, Victor M. Journal, Eighteen Thirty to Eighteen Forty-Eight. Repr. of 1954 ed. lib. bdg. 16.25x (ISBN 0-8371-3022-0, HUJO). Greenwood.

Hugon, Paul D. The Modern Word-Finder: A Living Guide to Modern Usage, Spelling, Synonyms, Pronunciation, Grammar, Word Origins, & Authorship. LC 73-20139. 420p. 1974. Repr. of 1934 ed. 45.00x (ISBN 0-8103-3970-6). Gale.

Hugot, A. & Wunderlich, J. G. Methode de Flute. (The Flute Library: Vol. 3). 1975. Repr. of 1804 ed. 62.50 o.s.i. (ISBN 90-6027-265-X, Pub. by Frits Knuf Netherlands); wrappers 45.00 o.s.i. (ISBN 90-6027-264-1). Pendragon NY.

Hugot, E. Handbook of Cane Sugar Engineering. 2nd ed. 1972. 234.00 (ISBN 0-444-40896-7). Elsevier.

Hugstad, Paul. Business Schools in the Nineteen Eighties: Liberialism Versus Vocationalism. 172p. 1983. 24.95 (ISBN 0-03-060586-5). Praeger.

Huheey, James E. Inorganic Chemistry. 1975. 18.00 o.p. (ISBN 0-06-318045-6, IntlDept). Har-Row.

--Inorganic Chemistry: Principles of Structure & Reactivity. 2nd ed. (Illus.). 1978. text ed. 33.95 scp o.p. (ISBN 0-06-042986-0, HarpC); ans. key avail. o.p. (ISBN 0-06-362986-0). Har-Row.

--Inorganic Chemistry: Principles of Structure & Reactivity. 3rd ed. 1024p. 1983. text ed. 34.50 scp (ISBN 0-06-042987-9, HarpC); answer book avail. (ISBN 0-06-362987-9). Har-Row.

Huhn, A. P. & Schmidt, E. T. Lattice Theory. (Colloquia Mathematic Societatis Ser.: Vol.14). 1977. 85.00 (ISBN 0-7204-0498-3, North-Holland). Elsevier.

Hui, Yiu H. Human Nutrition & Diet Therapy. LC 82-20136. 900p. 1983. text ed. 25.00 (ISBN 0-534-01336-8). Brooks-Cole.

Hui Seng, et al, eds. The Buddha Speaks the Brahma Net Sutra, Vol. 1. Bhikshuni Heng Tao, et al, trs. from Chinese. (Illus.). 312p. (Orig., Bilingual Text). 1981. pap. 10.00 (ISBN 0-917512-79-0). Buddhist Text.

Huisingh, Donald & Bailey, Vicki, eds. Making Pollution Prevention Pay: Ecology with Economy as Policy. 168p. 1982. 25.00 (ISBN 0-08-029417-0). Pergamon.

Huiskes, R. Biomechanics: Principles & Applications. 1982. 65.00 (ISBN 90-247-3047-3, Pub. by Martinus Nijhoff Netherlands). Kluwer Boston.

Huisman, L. & Olsthorn, T. N. Artificial Groundwater Recharge. (Water Resources Engineering Ser.). 240p. 1983. text ed. 59.95 (ISBN 0-273-08544-1). Pitman Pub MA.

Huizenga, Jann, et al. Basic Composition for E S L. pap. text ed. 10.95x (ISBN 0-673-15489-0). Scott F.

Huizenga, John R., jt. auth. see Vandenbosch, Robert.

Huizing, Peter & Walf, Knut, eds. Electing Our Own Bishops. (Concilium Ser.: Vol. 137). 128p. (Orig.). 1980. pap. 5.95 (ISBN 0-8164-2279-6). Seabury.

Huizinga, J. Waning of the Middle Ages. LC 54-4529. pap. 5.50 (ISBN 0-385-09288-1, A42, Anch). Doubleday.

Huizinga, Johan. Waning of the Middle Ages: Study of the Forms of Life, Thought & Art in France & the Netherlands in the 14th & 15th Centuries. (Illus.). 1924. 32.50 (ISBN 0-312-85540-0). St Martin.

Hujar, Peter. Portraits in Life & Death. LC 75-46627. 1976. 22.50 (ISBN 0-306-70755-1); pap. 8.95 (ISBN 0-306-80038-1). Da Capo.

Hukins, David W. X-Ray Diffraction by Disordered & Ordered Systems: Covering X-Ray Diffraction by Gases, Liquids & Solids & Indicating How the Theory of Diffraction by These Different States of Matter Is Related & How It Can Be Used to Solve Structural Problems. (Illus.). 173p. 1981. 28.75 (ISBN 0-08-023976-5). Pergamon.

Hulbert, Archer B. Path of Inland Commerce. 1920. text ed. 8.50x (ISBN 0-686-83686-3). Elliots Bks.

Hulbert, Archer B., ed. see Pike, Zebulon M.

Hulbert, James R., jt. ed. see Craigie, William A.

Hulbert, Mark. Interlock. 256p. 1982. write for info. Dutton.

Huldebrand, Nicholas, jt. auth. see Deroche, Andre.

Hulet, Claude L. Brazilian Literature, 3 vols. Incl. Vol. 1. 1500-1880. 395p. 1974. (ISBN 0-87840-036-2); pap. (ISBN 0-87840-033-8); Vol. 2. 1880-1920. 297p. 1974. (ISBN 0-87840-037-0); pap. (ISBN 0-87840-034-6); Vol. 3. 1920-1960. 1975. (ISBN 0-87840-039-7); pap. (ISBN 0-87840-038-9). LC 74-16331. lib. bdg. 13.25 ea.; pap. 7.75 ea. Georgetown U Pr.

Hulicka, Irene M., jt. auth. see Hulicka, Karel.

Hulicka, Karel & Hulicka, Irene M. Soviet Institutions, the Individual & Society. 12.00 o.p. (ISBN 0-8158-0118-1). Chris Mass.

Hulin, Charles L. & Drasgow, Fritz. Item Response Theory: Application to Psychological Measurement. LC 82-73929. (Dorsey Professional Ser.). 300p. 1982. 22.50 (ISBN 0-87094-284-0). Dow Jones-Irwin.

Hulke, Malcolm. Dr. Who & the Dinosaur Invasion. (The Dr. Who Ser.: No. 3). 1979. pap. 1.95 (ISBN 0-523-41613-X). Pinnacle Bks.

--Dr. Who & the Doomsday Weapon. (Dr. Who Ser: No. 2). 1979. pap. 1.95 (ISBN 0-523-42005-6). Pinnacle Bks.

Hulkrantz, Ake. The Study of American Indian Religions. 176p. 1983. 12.95 (ISBN 0-8245-0558-1). Crossroad NY.

Hull, Anthony H. Charles III & the Revival of Spain. LC 80-491. (Illus.). 416p. 1980. text ed. 24.50 (ISBN 0-8191-1021-3); pap. text ed. 15.50 (ISBN 0-8191-1022-1). U Pr of Amer.

Hull, Betty. Cobwebs & Crystal: Colorado's Grand Old Hotels. (Illus.). 100p. (Orig.). 1982. pap. 7.95 (ISBN 0-87108-611-5). Pruett.

Hull, C., jt. auth. see Rhodes, R. A.

Hull, C. Hadlai & Nie, Norman. SPSS Update: New Procedures & Facilities for Releases 7-9. 1981. pap. text ed. 13.95 (ISBN 0-07-046542-8, C). McGraw.

Hull, C. Hadlai & Nie, Norman H. SPSS-Eleven: The SPSS Batch System for the DEC PDP-11. 265p. 1980. pap. text ed. 11.95 (ISBN 0-07-046537-1, C). McGraw.

--SPSS Update: New Procedures & Facilities for Releases 7 & 8. LC 79-568. 1979. pap. text ed. 6.95 o.p. (ISBN 0-07-046534-7, C). McGraw.

Hull, Cary S., jt. auth. see Veasey, William.

Hull, Clark L. Essentials of Behavior. 1951. 14.50x (ISBN 0-686-51380-0). Elliots Bks.

Hull, Clark L., et al. Mathematico-Deductive Theory of Rote Learning: A Study in Scientific Methodology. Repr. of 1940 ed. lib. bdg. 19.75x (ISBN 0-8371-3126-X, HURL). Greenwood.

Hull, David L. Philosophy of Biological Science. LC 73-12981. (Foundations of Philosophy Ser). (Illus.). 192p. 1974. pap. text ed. 9.95 (ISBN 0-13-663609-8). P-H.

Hull, Denison B., tr. from Medieval Greek. Digenis Akritas: The Two Blood Border Lord. LC 79-141384. (Illus.). xlviii, 148p. 1972. 10.00x (ISBN 0-8214-0097-5, 82-81024). Ohio U Pr.

Hull, Denison B., tr. from Gr. Homer's Ilad: A Translation with An Introduction. xxx, 361p. 1983. text ed. 13.95x (ISBN 0-8214-0709-0, 82-84788). Ohio U Pr.

Hull, Denison B., tr. see Homer.

Hull, Derek. Introduction to Dislocations. 2nd ed. 280p. 1975. text ed. 29.00 (ISBN 0-08-018129-5); pap. text ed. 14.00 (ISBN 0-08-018128-7). Pergamon.

Hull, Eleanor. Alice with Golden Hair. 1982. pap. 2.25 (ISBN 0-451-11795-6, AE1795, Sig). NAL.

Hull, Galen S. Pawns on a Chessboard: The Resource War in Southern Africa. LC 81-40602. (Illus.). 245p. (Orig.). 1982. lib. bdg. 21.75 (ISBN 0-8191-2019-7); pap. text ed. 10.75 (ISBN 0-8191-2020-0). U Pr of Amer.

Hull, Harry H. Addendum to an Approach to Rheology Through Multivariable Thermodynamics. 24p. 1982. pap. 4.00x (ISBN 0-686-83764-9). Hull.

--An Approach to Rheology Through Multi-Variable Thermodynamics. Rev. ed. 192p. 1982. text ed. 28.00 (ISBN 0-9606118-2-7). Hull.

--An Approach to Rheology Through Multi-Variable Thermodynamics: Or, Inside the Thermodynamic Black Box. 168p. 1981. text ed. 24.00x o.p. (ISBN 0-9606118-1-9); pap. text ed. 16.00x (ISBN 0-9606118-0-0). Hull.

--An Approach to Rheology Through Multivariable Thermodynamics: With Addendum. 192p. 1982. 28.00 (ISBN 0-9606118-2-7). Hull.

--An Approach to Rheology Through Multivariable Thermodynamics: Without Addendum. 158p. 1981. pap. 16.00 (ISBN 0-9606118-1-9). Hull.

Hull, Jerry. Luke, Vol. 1. (Beacon Small Group Bible Studies). 72p. (Orig.). 1980. pap. 2.25 (ISBN 0-8341-0657-4). Beacon Hill.

--Timothy One & Two; Titus. (Beacon Small Group Bible Studies). 70p. (Orig.). 1980. pap. 2.25 o.p. (ISBN 0-8341-0622-1). Beacon Hill.

Hull, Jerry, ed. Living out of the Mold. 1982. pap. 4.95 (ISBN 0-8341-0804-6). Beacon Hill.

Hull, Jesse R. Stanley's Secret Trip. Schroeder, Howard, ed. LC 81-3161. (Roundup Ser.). (Illus.). 48p. 1981. PLB 7.95 (ISBN 0-89686-157-0); pap. 3.95 (ISBN 0-89686-165-1). Crestwood Hse.

Hull, Marion. Phonics for the Teacher of Reading. 3rd ed. (Illus.). 144p. 1981. pap. text ed. 8.95 (ISBN 0-675-08074-6). Merrill.

Hull, Nancy R., ed. see Burrows, Susan G. & Gassert, Carole A.

Hull, Nancy R., ed. see Purcell, Julia A., et al.

Hull, Nancy R., ed. see Purcell, Julia Ann.

Hull, Nancy R., ed. see Purcell, Julia Ann & Johnston, Barbara.

Hull, O. Geography of Production. 1967. 17.95 o.p. (ISBN 0-312-32235-6). St Martin.

Hull, R. Modern Africa: Change & Continuity. 1980. pap. 14.95 (ISBN 0-13-586305-8). P-H.

Hull, R. F., ed. see Weber, Alfred.

Hull, Raymond. Man's Best Friend. (Illus.). 180p. 1982. Repr. of 1975 ed. pap. 5.97 (ISBN 0-88254-706-2). Hippocrene Bks.

--Successful Public Speaking. LC 74-127369. 1970. lib. bdg. 5.95 o.p. (ISBN 0-668-02395-3). Arco.

Hull, Raymond, jt. auth. see Anderson, Stanley F.

Hull, Raymond, jt. auth. see Sleight, Jack.

Hull, Richard. Murder of My Aunt. (Seagull Library of Mystery & Suspense Ser). 1968. 4.95 o.p. (ISBN 0-393-08404-3). Norton.

Hull, Sylvia. Cooking for a Baby. 1983. pap. 3.95 (ISBN 0-14-046367-4). Penguin.

Hull, T. E., ed. Studies in Optimization One. (Illus.). 137p. 1970. text ed. 12.50 (ISBN 0-89871-152-5). Soc Indus-Appl Math.

Hull, W. Frank, IV. Foreign Students in the United States of America: Coping Behavior Within the Educational Environment. LC 78-19741. 1978. 26.95 o.p. (ISBN 0-03-046151-0). Praeger.

Hull, W. Frank, IV, jt. auth. see Klineberg, Otto.

Hull, Walter & Bruchey, Stuart, eds. Practical Problems in Banking & Currency. LC 80-1151. (Rise of Commercial Banking Ser.). 1981. Repr. of 1907 ed. lib. bdg. 55.00x (ISBN 0-405-13656-0). Ayer Co.

Hull, William I. The New Peace Movement. LC 77-137546. (Peace Movement in America Ser.). xi, 216p. 1972. Repr. of 1912 ed. lib. bdg. 16.95x (ISBN 0-89198-074-1). Ozer.

Hull, William L., jt. auth. see Drawbaugh, Charles C.

Hulliung, Mark. Montesquieu & the Old Regime. 1977. 26.50x (ISBN 0-520-03108-3). U of Cal Pr.

Hulme, F. Edward. The Birth & Development of Ornament. LC 79-78173. (Illus.). xii, 340p. 1974. Repr. of 1893 ed. 38.00x (ISBN 0-8103-4026-7). Gale.

--History, Principles, & Practice of Symbolism in Christian Art. LC 68-18027. 1969. Repr. of 1891 ed. 37.00x (ISBN 0-8103-3214-0). Gale.

--Proverb Lore. LC 67-23913. 1968. Repr. of 1902 ed. 34.00x (ISBN 0-8103-3202-7). Gale.

Hulme, John, tr. Morder Guss Reims: The Gustav Leberwurst Manuscripts. 64p. 1981. 7.95 (ISBN 0-517-54559-4, C N Potter Bks). Crown.

Hulme, William. Living with Myself. LC 64-10164. 1971. pap. 4.50 (ISBN 0-8066-1129-4, 10-3990). Augsburg.

Hulme, William E. Don't Say Yes, When You Want to Say No: Dealing With Doublemindedness. LC 82-47745. 128p. (Orig.). 1982. pap. 5.72i (ISBN 0-06-064079-0, HarpR). Har-Row.

Hulme, William E., ed. see Vayhinger, John M.

Hulphers, A. Historisk Afhandling om Musik och Instrumenter sardeles om Orgwerks... An Historical Treatise on Music & Instruments Including the Arrangement of Organs in General, Together with a Brief Description of Organs in Sweden. (Bibliotheca Organologica Ser.: Vol. 35). 1972. Repr. of 1773 ed. 25.00 o.s.i. (ISBN 90-6027-146-7, Pub. by Frits Knuf Netherlands). Pendragon NY.

Huls, H., jt. auth. see Van Der Werff, A.

Hulse, et al. The Psychology of Learning. 5th, rev. ed. (Psychology Ser.). (Illus.). 480p. 1980. text ed. 25.00 (ISBN 0-07-031151-X). McGraw.

Hulse, J. H. & Laing, E. M. Nutritive Value of Triticale Protein. 183p. 1974. pap. 20.00 casebound (ISBN 0-88936-025-1, IDRC21, IDRC). Unipub.

Hulse, Michael. Knowing & Forgetting. 1981. 11.50 (ISBN 0-436-20965-9, Pub. by Secker & Warburg). David & Charles.

Hulsizer, Allan. The Indian Boy's Day's: The Indian Then & Now-His Presence & Influence on Our Culture. 64p. 1983. 5.50 (ISBN 0-682-49959-5). Exposition.

Hulsmann, Carl. Awakening of Consciousness. 1982. 18.00 (ISBN 0-86164-151-5, Pub by Momenta Publishing Ltd U. K.). Hunter Hse.

Hulst, Harry van der see Van der Hulst, Harry & Smith, Norval.

Hulsz Suarez, E., et al. Anaesthesiology. (International Congress Ser.: No. 399). (Proceedings). 1977. 136.50 (ISBN 0-444-15237-7). Elsevier.

Hulten, Charles R., ed. Depreciation, Inflation, & the Taxation of Income from Capital. LC 81-533061. 319p. 1981. text ed. 32.00 (ISBN 0-87766-311-4, URI 33800). Urban Inst.

Hulten, E. The Amphi-Atlantic Plants & Their Phytogeographic Connections. (Illus.). 1973. 96.00 (ISBN 3-87429-041-7). Lubrecht & Cramer.

Hulten, Pontus & Granath, Olle. Oyvind Fahlstrom. LC 82-60794. (Illus.). 120p. 1982. pap. 9.00 (ISBN 0-89207-035-8). S R Guggenheim.

Hulten, Pontus & Hjort, Oystein. Sleeping Beauty-Art Now. LC 82-60793. (Illus.). 136p. 1982. pap. 9.00 (ISBN 0-89207-036-6). S R Guggenheim.

Hulten, Pontus, pref. by. Marcel Duchamp Notes. (Illus.). 300p. (Fr.). 1980. lib. bdg. 295.00 (ISBN 2-85850-029-0, Pub. by Centre National d' Art France). Hacker.

Hulteng, John L. Messenger's Motive: Ethical Problems of the News Media. 250p. 1976. pap. 13.95 (ISBN 0-13-577460-8). P-H.

--The Opinion Function: Editorial & Interpretive Writing for the News Media. LC 72-12467. 1977. pap. 5.00x (ISBN 0-686-20045-4). Ridge Hse.

Hulteng, John L. & Nelson, Roy P. The Fourth Estate: An Informal Appraisal of the News & Opinion Media. 2nd ed. 464p. 1983. pap. text ed. 10.95 scp (ISBN 0-06-042991-7, HarpC). Har-Row.

Hultgren, Barbara. Ball Persons: A Trainer's Manual. (Illus.). 31p. 1981. 2.00 (ISBN 0-938822-20-9). USTA.

Hultkrantz, Ake. The Religions of the American Indians. LC 73-90661. (Hermeneutics--Studies in the History of Religions: Vol. 7). 1979. 16.95 (ISBN 0-520-02653-5); pap. 5.95 (ISBN 0-520-04239-5, CAL 463). U of Cal Pr.

Hultkrantz, Ake & Vorren, Ornulf, eds. The Hunters: Their Culture & Way of Life. 192p. (Orig.). 1982. pap. 27.00 (ISBN 0-686-83124-1). Universitet.

Hultsch, David F. & Deutsch, Francine. Adult Development & Aging. (Illus.). 448p. 1980. 23.50 (ISBN 0-07-031156-0, C); instr's manual 9.95 (ISBN 0-07-031157-9). McGraw.

Hultsch, David F., jt. auth. see Lerner, Richard M.

Hulvenstot, Luz. Irish Setters. (Illus.). 1979. 4.95 (ISBN 0-87666-691-8, KW-044). TFH Pubns.

Human Relations Area Files Inc. North Borneo, Brunei, Sarawak (British Borneo) LC 72-12329. (Illus.). 287p. 1973. Repr. of 1956 ed. lib. bdg. 18.25x (ISBN 0-8371-6735-3, HUNB). Greenwood.

Human Resource Communication Group. The Directory of Human Resource Services 1982. 128p. (Orig.). 1982. pap. 12.00x (ISBN 0-9609088-1-1). Human Res Comm.

Human Rights Foundation. Demystifying Homosexuality: A Teacher's Sourcebook about Lesbians & Gay Men. 150p. 1983. pap. 12.95x (ISBN 0-8290-1273-7). Irvington.

Humayun, Kabir. Education in New India. LC 77-8085. 1977. Repr. of 1956 ed. lib. bdg. 18.50x (ISBN 0-8371-9673-6, HUEN). Greenwood.

Humber, D. P., ed. Immunological Aspects of Leprosy, Tuberculosis & Leishmaniasis. (International Congress Ser.: No. 574). 450p. 1982. 64.25 (ISBN 0-444-90251-1). Elsevier.

Humber, James H. & Almeder, Robert, eds. Biomedical Ethics Reviews 1983. (Biomedical Ethics Reviews Ser.). 224p. 1983. tentative 24.50 (ISBN 0-89603-041-5). Humana.

Humberstone. Things That Go. (Let's Find Out about Ser.). (gr. 2-5). 1981. 5.95 (ISBN 0-86020-500-2, Usborne-Hayes); PLB 8.95 (ISBN 0-88110-020-X); pap. 2.95 (ISBN 0-86020-493-6). EDC.

Humbert, Jack & Williams, Larry. Petroleum Marketing. (Career Competencies in Marketing Ser.). (Illus.). (YA) (gr. 11-12). 1979. pap. 7.32 (ISBN 0-07-031206-0, G); tchr's manual & key 4.50 (ISBN 0-07-031207-9). McGraw.

Humbert, Roger P. Growing of Sugar Cane. 2nd ed. 1968. 117.00 (ISBN 0-444-40310-8). Elsevier.

Humbertson, James E., ed. Evangelical Sunday School Lesson Commentary 1978-79. 1979. 5.50 o.p. (ISBN 0-87148-290-8). Pathway Pr.

--Evangelical Sunday School Lesson Commentary 1980-81. 448p. 3.50 (ISBN 0-87148-294-0). Pathway Pr.

--Evangelical Sunday School Lesson Commentary, 1979-80. 448p. 1979. 3.00 (ISBN 0-87148-291-6). Pathway Pr.

Humble, B. J., ed. see Kenya Mission Team.

Humble, John. Management by Objectives in Action. 1971. 19.95 (ISBN 0-07-094217-X, P&RB). McGraw.

Humble, Lance. Gambling Times Guide to Harness Racing. (Illus., Orig.). Date not set. pap. text ed. 5.95 (ISBN 0-89746-002-2). Lyle Stuart.

Humble, Lance & Cooper, Carl. The World's Greatest Blackjack Book. LC 79-8930. (Illus.). 432p. 1980. 15.95 (ISBN 0-385-15370-8). Doubleday.

Humble, Linda. Tell Me About God. Sparks, Judith, ed. LC 81-86703. (Happy Day Bks.). (Illus.). 24p. (Orig.). (ps-3). 1982. pap. 1.29 (ISBN 0-87239-544-8, 3590). Standard Pub.

Humble, Richard. The Explorers. LC 78-1292. (The Seafarers Ser.). (Illus.). 1978. lib. bdg. 19.92 (ISBN 0-8094-2659-5). Silver.

--Marco Polo. LC 74-19870. (Illus.). 252p. 1975. 12.95 o.p. (ISBN 0-399-11517-X). Putnam Pub Group.

Humblestone, jt. auth. see Maple.

Humboldt, Wilhelm Von see Von Humboldt, Wilhelm.

Humby, E. Programs from Decision Tables. LC 72-90803. (Computer Monograph Ser.: No. 19). 700p. 1973. 16.95 (ISBN 0-444-19569-6). Elsevier.

Hume & Holt. Structured Programming Using PL-One SP-K. 2nd ed. 1980. pap. text ed. 16.95 (ISBN 0-8359-7131-7); text ed. 19.95 (ISBN 0-8359-7133-3). Reston.

Hume, Abraham. Learned Societies & Printing Clubs of the United Kingdom. LC 66-16418. 1966. Repr. of 1853 ed. 34.00x (ISBN 0-8103-3081-4). Gale.

Hume, Audrey Noel see Noel Hume, Audrey.

Hume, Charles. Raise & Train Skunks. pap. 3.95 (ISBN 0-87666-223-8, M527). TFH Pubns.

Hume, D. A. & Weidmann, M. J. Mitogenic Lymphocyte Transformation. (Research Monographs in Immunology: Vol. 2). 1981. 67.25 (ISBN 0-444-80219-3). Elsevier.

Hume, David. Dialogues Concerning Natural Religion. Popkin, Richard H., ed. LC 79-25349. 1980. lib. bdg. 12.50 (ISBN 0-915144-46-8); pap. text ed. 2.95 (ISBN 0-915144-45-X). Hackett Pub.

--Enquiries Concerning Human Understanding & Concerning the Principles of Morals. 3rd ed. Nidditch, P. H., ed. 1975. pap. text ed. 9.95x (ISBN 0-19-824536-X). Oxford U Pr.

--An Enquiry Concerning Human Understanding: and LeHer From a Gentleman to His Friend in Edinburgh. new ed. Steinberg, Eric, ed. LC 77-2600. 1977. lib. bdg. 12.50 (ISBN 0-915144-17-4); pap. text ed. 2.95 (ISBN 0-915144-16-6). Hackett Pub.

--Enquiry Concerning Human Understanding. 2nd ed. McCormack, Thomas J. & Calkins, Mary W., eds. 320p. 1966. 21.00 (ISBN 0-87548-015-2); pap. 8.50 (ISBN 0-87548-362-3). Open Court.

--Enquiry Concerning the Principles of Morals. 2nd ed. 200p. 1966. 16.00 (ISBN 0-87548-017-9); pap. 6.00 (ISBN 0-87548-018-7). Open Court.

--An Enquiry Concerning the Principles of Morals. Schneewind, J. B., ed. LC 82-11679. (HPC Philosophical Classics Ser.). 132p. lib. bdg. 13.50 (ISBN 0-915145-46-4); pap. text ed. 2.95 (ISBN 0-915145-45-6). Hackett Pub.

--Of the Standard of Taste & Other Essays. Lenz, John W., ed. LC 64-66070. 1965. pap. 7.25 (ISBN 0-672-60269-5). Bobbs.

--The Philosophical Works, 4 vols. Green, Thomas H. & Grose, Thomas H., eds. 1964. Repr. of 1882 ed. Set. 235.00x (ISBN 3-511-01210-4). Intl Pubns Serv.

Hume, Fergus W. The Mystery of a Hansom Cab. (Detective Ser.). 256p. 1982. pap. 4.00 (ISBN 0-486-21956-9). Dover.

Hume, George B. Searching for God. 1978. pap. 4.95 o.p. (ISBN 0-8192-1240-7). Morehouse.

Hume, I. D. Digestive Physiology & Nutrition of Marsupials. LC 81-17032. (Monographs on Marsupial Biology). (Illus.). 220p. 1982. 44.50 (ISBN 0-521-23892-7). Cambridge U Pr.

Hume, Ivey. Physics, 2 vols. new ed. Incl. Vol. 1. Classical Mechanics & Introductory Statistical Mechanics. 818p. 31.50x (ISBN 0-471-07173-0); Vol. 2. Relativity Electromagnetism & Quantum Physics. 500p. 28.80x (ISBN 0-8260-4724-6). (Illus.). 1974. Wiley.

Hume, Ivor Noel. Discoveries in Martin's Hundred. (Williamsburg Archaeological Ser.). (Illus.). 64p. (Orig.). 1983. pap. 2.95 (ISBN 0-87935-069-5). Williamsburg.

Hume, Ivor Noel see Noel Hume, Ivor.

Hume, J. N. & Ivey, D. G. Physics: Relativity, Electromagnatism, & Quantum Physics, Vol. 2. 1974. 31.50x o.p. (ISBN 0-471-07173-0). Wiley.

Hume, J. N., jt. auth. see Holt, R. C.

Hume, John F. Get-Rich-Quick Schemes in the Stock Market & Sound Investment Practices. (A New Stock Market Library Bk.). (Illus.). 133p. 1983. 47.75 (ISBN 0-86654-056-3). Inst Econ Finan.

Hume, L. J. Bentham & Bureaucracy. LC 80-41999. 336p. 1981. 54.50 (ISBN 0-521-23542-1). Cambridge U Pr.

Hume, Martha. Kenny Rogers: Gambler, Dreamer, Lover. (Illus.). 1980. pap. 8.95 o.p. (ISBN 0-452-25254-7, Z5254, Plume). NAL.

--You're So Cold I'm Turning Blue. LC 82-70133. (Illus.). 256p. 1982. 16.95 (ISBN 0-670-24417-1). Viking Pr.

--You're So Cold I'm Turning Blue. 1982. pap. 8.95 (ISBN 0-14-006348-X). Penguin.

Hume, Robert D. The Development of English Drama in the Late Seventeenth Century. 1976. 52.00x (ISBN 0-19-812063-X). Oxford U Pr.

--The Rakish Stage: Studies in English Drama, 1660-1800. 1983. price not set (ISBN 0-8093-1100-3). S Ill U Pr.

Hume, Robert D., ed. The London Theatre World, Sixteen Sixty to Eighteen Hundred. LC 79-20410. (Illus.). 416p. 1980. 26.95x (ISBN 0-8093-0926-2). S Ill U Pr.

Hume, Roberto E. Las Religiones Vivas. Beltroy, Manuel, tr. from Eng. Orig. Title: Living Religions of the World. 320p. (Span.). 1981. pap. 5.25 (ISBN 0-311-05758-6, Edit Mundo). Casa Bautista.

Hume, Sandy. Western Man: Photographs from the National Western Stock Show. 1980. 9.95 (ISBN 0-933472-49-8); pap. 6.95 (ISBN 0-933472-48-X). Johnson Bks.

Hume, Wilfred & Horroblin, David F. Biofeedback. LC 80-15617. (Biofeedback Research Review Ser.: Vol. III). 83p. 1981. 14.95 (ISBN 0-87705-969-1). Human Sci Pr.

Hume-Rothery, W. & Cole, B. R. Atomic Theory for Students of Metallurgy. 438p. 1969. write for info. (ISBN 0-85066-099-8, Pub. by Taylor & Francis). Intl Pubns Serv.

Humes, D. Joy. Oswald Garrison Villard, Liberal of the 1920's. LC 77-23783. (Men & Movements Ser.). (Illus.). 1977. Repr. of 1960 ed. lib. bdg. 20.25x o.p. (ISBN 0-8371-9752-X, HUOGV). Greenwood.

Humes, Harry. Winter Weeds: Poems. LC 82-11008. (Breakthrough Bks.: No.41). 64p. (Orig.). 1983. pap. 5.95 (ISBN 0-8262-0387-6). U of Mo Pr.

Humes, James C. Churchill. LC 79-3812. 360p. 1980. 12.95 (ISBN 0-8128-2710-4); pap. 9.95 (ISBN 0-8128-6151-5). Stein & Day.

Humez & Goldfrank. The Boston Basic Bicycle Book. LC 74-32579. (Godine Guides: No. I). 1979. pap. 3.95 (ISBN 0-87923-133-5). Godine.

Humiston, G. E., jt. auth. see Brady, J. E.

Humiston, Gerard E., jt. auth. see Brady, James E.

Humitz, R. Man Meets God. 1971. pap. 4.00 o.s.i. (ISBN 0-02-644500-X); tchr's manual 2.68 o.s.i. (ISBN 0-02-644520-4, 64452); tchr's ed. 6.16 o.s.i. (ISBN 0-02-644510-7). Benziger Pub Co.

Humm, W. Rehabilitation of the Lower Limb Amputee: for Nurses & Therapists. 3rd ed. 1978. text ed. 12.00 o.p. (ISBN 0-02-858090-7, Pub. by Bailliere-Tindall). Saunders.

Hummel & Seebeck. Mathematics of Finance. 3rd ed. 1970. text ed. 23.95 (ISBN 0-07-031161-7, C). McGraw.

Hummel, Anne, jt. auth. see Hummel, Charles.

Hummel, Arthur W., ed. see Ku, Chieh-Kang.

Hummel, Charles & Hummel, Anne. I Corinthians: Problems & Solutions in a Growing Church. (Fisherman Bible Studyguides). 96p. 1981. saddle-stitched 2.50 (ISBN 0-87788-137-5). Shaw Pubs.

Hummel, Charles F. A Winterthur Guide to American Chippendale Furniture: Middle Atlantic & Southern Colonies. (Winterthur Ser.). (Illus.). 1976. 6.95 o.p. (ISBN 0-517-52783-9). Crown.

Hummel, Charles F., jt. auth. see Garvan, Beatrice B.

Hummel, Dieter O. & Scholl, Friedrich. Atlas of Polymer & Plastics Analysis, 3 vols. 2nd ed. Incl. Vol. 1. Polymers, Structures, & Spectra. (Illus.). 703p. 1978. 279.50x (ISBN 0-89573-001-4); Vol. 2. Plastics, Fibres, Rubber, Resins. (Illus.). 741p. 1981. 325.00 (ISBN 0-89573-013-8); Vol. 3. Additives & Processing Aids. 325.00x (ISBN 0-89573-014-6). (Illus.). 703p. 1978. Verlag Chemie.

Hummel, Kay, jt. auth. see Zucker, Jeff.

Hummel, Nancy, tr. see Steiner, Rudolf & Steiner Von Sivers, Marie.

Hummel, Ray O. Southeastern Broadsides Before 1877: A Bibliography. (Virginia State Library). (Illus.). 501p. 1971. 15.00x o.p. (ISBN 0-88490-064-9). U Pr of Va.

Hummel, Robert P., Jr. Clinical Burn Therapy: A Management & Prevention Guide. 577p. 1982. 45.00 (ISBN 0-88416-284-2). Wright-PSG.

Hummel, Thomas J., jt. ed. see Collier, Raymond O., Jr.

Hummer, Patricia M. The Decade of Elusive Promise: Professional Women in the United States, 1920-1930. Berkhofer, Robert, ed. LC 78-27674. (Studies in American History & Culture: No. 5). 157p. 1979. 39.95 (ISBN 0-8357-0986-8, Pub. by UMI Res Pr). Univ Microfilms.

Hummingbird, Annie. How to Love a Dog. LC 82-12350. (Annie Hummingbird Bks.). (Illus.). 16p. (ps-8). 1983. pap. 1.25 saddle-wire (ISBN 0-394-85675-9). Random.

Hummon, N. P., jt. auth. see Doreian, P.

Humphresy, A. R., ed. see Shakespeare, William.

Humphrey. The Sea Shells of the West Indies. 24.95 (ISBN 0-686-42790-4, Collins Pub England). Greene.

Humphrey, C. Surgical Nursing. 399p. Date not set. 23.00x (ISBN 0-07-072993-X). McGraw.

Humphrey, Caroline, ed. see Vainshtein, Sevyan.

Humphrey, Christopher C. The Speakers of the Sun Series. 1977. pap. 20.00 (ISBN 0-914312-09-X). Thales Microuniv.

Humphrey, Clifford C. & Evans, Robert G. What's Ecology? LC 73-155286. (Illus.). 64p. (gr. 7 up). 1972. pap. 3.15 (ISBN 0-8331-1501-4). Hubbard Sci.

Humphrey, Deirdre, jt. auth. see Humphrey, Henry.

Humphrey, Donald R., jt. ed. see Talbott, Richard E.

Humphrey, E. W. Manual of Pulmonary Surgery. (Comprehensive Manuals of Surgical Specialities). (Illus.). 259p. 1983. 149.50 (ISBN 0-387-90732-7). Springer-Verlag.

Humphrey, G. A., ed. see Graphic Arts Trade Journals Int'l. Inc.

Humphrey, G. A., ed. see Graphics Arts Trade Journals International Inc.

Humphrey, G. B. Pancreatic Tumors in Children. 1983. 58.50 (ISBN 90-247-2702-2, Pub. by Martinus Nijhoff Netherlands). Kluwer Boston.

Humphrey, George, tr. see Itard, Jean-Marc-Gaspard.

Humphrey, Grace. Stories of the World's Holidays. LC 74-3023. 1974. Repr. of 1923 ed. 40.00x (ISBN 0-8103-3660-X). Gale.

Humphrey, Henry. The Farm. LC 76-23768. (gr. 1-3). 1978. 7.95a o.p. (ISBN 0-385-03447-4). Doubleday.

Humphrey, Henry & Humphrey, Deirdre. When Is Now: Experiments with Time & Timekeeping Devices. (Illus.). 80p. (gr. 6-7). 1981. 8.95a o.p. (ISBN 0-385-13215-8); 8.95a (ISBN 0-385-13216-6). Doubleday.

Humphrey, Hugh M. A Bibliography for the Gospel of Mark: 1954-1980. LC 81-78717. (Studies in the Bible & Early Christianity: Vol. 1). 176p. 1982. 39.95x (ISBN 0-88946-916-4). E Mellen.

Humphrey, J. H., jt. ed. see Taliaferro, W. H.

Humphrey, J. H. see Taliaferro, W. H. & Humphrey, J. H.

Humphrey, James H. Child Development Through Physical Education. (Illus.). 200p. 1980. 14.75 (ISBN 0-398-03561-X). C C Thomas.

Humphrey, Joseph F., jt. ed. see Haring, Joseph E.

Humphrey, Michael. Hostage Seekers: A Study of Childless & Adopting Couples. (Studies in Child Development). (Orig.). 1969. pap. text ed. 9.50x (ISBN 0-582-32438-6). Humanities.

Humphrey, Michael R. A Manual of Clay Tennis Court Maintenance. (Illus.). 74p. 1982. 7.50 (ISBN 0-9610438-0-6). Bacon St Pr.

Humphrey, Muriel, tr. see Itard, Jean-Marc-Gaspard.

Humphrey, P., jt. auth. see Hill, P. M.

Humphrey, Richard A., jt. auth. see Carroll, Mary A.

Humphrey, Rilda. Bible Story & Color Book. Mahany, Patricia, ed. (Illus.). 64p. (Orig.). (gr. k-3). 1982. pap. 1.95 (ISBN 0-87239-582-0, 2397). Standard Pub.

--Jesus Story & Color Book. Mahany, Patricia, ed. (Illus.). 64p. (Orig.). (gr. k-3). 1982. pap. 1.95 (ISBN 0-87239-583-9, 2398). Standard Pub.

Humphrey, Ted, ed. & tr. see Kant, Immanuel.

Humphrey, Thomas J. Basic Programming for the Financial Executive. LC 78-5670. 1978. 44.95 (ISBN 0-471-03020-1, Pub. by Wiley-Interscience). Wiley.

Humphrey, William. The Spawning Run. (Illus.). 1979. 7.50 o.s.i. (ISBN 0-440-08204-8, Sey Lawr); pap. 4.95 o.s.i. (ISBN 0-440-08206-4). Delacorte.

Humphrey-Hutchins, Bertha. Impressions of Monterey. LC 82-81933. (Illus.). 112p. 1982. pap. 5.95 (ISBN 0-686-36404-X). H Three.

Humphreys. Analyzing & Aiding Decision Processes. Date not set. price not set (ISBN 0-444-86522-5). Elsevier.

Humphreys & Leonard. Practical Decisions. 288p. 1983. 45.00 (ISBN 0-8247-1884-4). Dekker.

Humphreys Academy Patrons. Festival. (Illus.). 320p. 1983. pap. 10.95 (ISBN 0-9610058-0-7). Humphreys Acad.

Humphreys Academy Patrons, ed. Festival. (Illus.). 320p. 1983. pap. 10.95 (ISBN 0-686-82289-7). Wimmer Bks.

Humphreys, Alan H. & Post, Thomas R. Interdisciplinary Methods: A Thematic Approach. 1981. pap. text ed. 17.95x (ISBN 0-673-16495-0). Scott F.

Humphreys, Alice L. Three Hear the Bells. new ed. LC 78-52449. 2.49 (ISBN 0-8042-2586-9). John Knox.

Humphreys, Arthur R., ed. see Shakespeare, William.

Humphreys, Christmas. Studies in the Middle Way: Being Thoughts on Buddhism Applied. 4th rev. ed. 169p. 1982. 11.00x o.p. (ISBN 0-87471-826-0). Rowman.

--Zen Comes West: The Present & Future of Zen Buddhism in Western Society. 2nd ed. 218p. 1977. 12.50x o.p. (ISBN 0-87471-951-8). Rowman.

Humphreys, David. Miscellaneous Works. LC 68-24210. 1968. Repr. of 1804 ed. 47.00x (ISBN 0-8201-1028-0). Schol Facsimiles.

Humphreys, Dena. Animals Every Child Should Know. (Illus.). (gr. 4-6). 1962. 1.50 o.p. (ISBN 0-448-00324-4, G&D). Putnam Pub Group.

--Animals Every Child Should Know. (Illus.). 32p. (gr. k-3). 1982. 3.95 (ISBN 0-448-04245-2, G&D). Putnam Pub Group.

Humphreys, Fisher & Wise, Philip. A Dictionary of Doctrinal Terms. (Orig.). 1983. pap. 4.95 (ISBN 0-8054-1141-0). Broadman.

Humphreys, H. I., jt. auth. see Nelkon, M.

Humphreys, J. Anthony, et al. Guidance Services. 3rd ed. 1967. text ed. 14.95 o.s.i. (ISBN 0-574-50100-2, 5-0100). SRA.

Humphreys, Joel D. Vendetta. LC 81-15605. 256p. 1982. 12.95 o.p. (ISBN 0-02-557150-8). Macmillan.

Humphreys, John. The Sportsman Head to Toe. (Illus.). 96p. (Orig.). 1980. pap. 8.50x (ISBN 0-85242-733-6). Intl Pubns Serv.

Humphreys, K. K. & McMillan, B. G., eds. AACE Publications Index, 1979-1981, Vol. 2. 54p. 1982. pap. 25.00 (ISBN 0-930284-16-X). Am Assn Cost Engineers.

--Transactions of the American Association of Cost Engineers. (Illus.). 334p. 1982. 48.50 (ISBN 0-930284-15-1); pap. 38.50 (ISBN 0-930284-14-3). Am Assn Cost Engineers.

Humphreys, Robert A. Latin American History: A Guide to the Literature in English. LC 77-752. 1977. Repr. of 1958 ed. lib. bdg. 17.50x (ISBN 0-8371-9490-3, HULA). Greenwood.

Humphreys, Robert E., et al, eds. Pharmacology. 2nd ed. LC 79-83721. (Basic Sciences PreTest Self-Assessment & Review Ser.). (Illus.). 1980. 10.95 o.p. (ISBN 0-07-050965-4). McGraw-Pretest.

Humphreys, W. Lee. Crisis & Story: Introduction to the Old Testament. LC 78-64594. (Illus.). 313p. 1979. text ed. 16.95 (ISBN 0-87484-437-1). Mayfield Pub.

Humphries, Adelaide. Danger for Nurse Vivian. (YA) 1979. 6.95 (ISBN 0-686-52549-3, Avalon). Bouregy.

--Miracle for Nurse Louisa. (YA) 1978. 6.95 (ISBN 0-685-87344-7, Avalon). Bouregy.

Humphries, C. M., ed. Instrumentation for Astronomy with Large Optical Telescopes. 1982. 48.00 (ISBN 90-277-1388-X, Pub. by Reidel Holland). Kluwer Boston.

Humphries, J. D., jt. ed. see George, F. H.

Humphries, James T. & Sheets, Leslie P. Industrial Electronics. 1983. text ed. 28.95 (ISBN 0-534-01415-1, Breton). Wadsworth Pub.

Humphries, Joan R. The Application of Scientific Behaviorism to Humanistic Phenomena. 2nd ed. LC 77-18593. 1978. pap. text ed. 6.50 o.p. (ISBN 0-8191-0163-X). U Pr of Amer.

Humphries, Stephen, jt. auth. see Bild, Ian.

Humphry, Derek. Let Me Die Before I Wake: Hemlock's Book of Self-Deliverance for the Dying. 106p. 1981. pap. 10.00 (ISBN 0-9606030-0-X). Hemlock CA.

Humphry, Derek & Wickett, Ann. Jean's Way. 128p. 1981. pap. text ed. 5.95 (ISBN 0-86666-033-X, Dist. by Hemlock CA). GWP.

Hun, Hyon Jong, jt. auth. see Sik, Chai Sin.

Huna, Michael S. Havoc. 1983. 5.95 (ISBN 0-533-05541-5). Vantage.

Hunczak, Taras, ed. The Ukraine: Nineteen Seventeen to Nineteen Twenty-One: A Study in Revolution. (Ser. in Ukrainian Studies). 1978. 17.50x (ISBN 0-674-92009-0). Harvard U Pr.

Hunderfund, Richard. Wines, Spirits & Fermentations. (Illus.). 192p. (Orig.). 1983. pap. 11.95. Star Pub CA.

Hundley, Daniel R. Social Relations in Our Southern States. Cooper, William J., Jr., ed. LC 78-23811. (Library of Southern Civilization). (Illus.). 1979. text ed. 25.00x (ISBN 0-8071-0554-6); pap. text ed. 7.95x (ISBN 0-8071-0559-7). La State U Pr.

Hundley, Norris, ed. see Dasmann, Raymond F.

Hundley, Norris, ed. see Phillips, George H., Jr.

Hundley, Norris, Jr. Dividing the Waters: A Century of Controversy Between the United States & Mexico. LC 66-18468. 1966. 27.50x (ISBN 0-520-00586-4). U of Cal Pr.

Hundley, Norris, Jr., ed. The American Indian: Essays from the Pacific Historical Review. LC 74-76443. 151p. 1974. 9.75 (ISBN 0-87436-139-7); pap. text ed. 9.75 o.p. (ISBN 0-87436-140-0). ABC-Clio.

--The Asian American: The Historical Experience. LC 75-2354. 186p. 1976. text ed. 24.75 o.p. (ISBN 0-87436-219-9); pap. text ed. 11.75 o.p. (ISBN 0-87436-220-2). ABC-Clio.

Hundley, Norris, Jr., ed. see Cherny, Robert W. & Issel, William.

Hundley, Norris, Jr., ed. see Hendrick, Irving G.

Hundley, Norris, Jr., ed. see Hine, Robert V.

Hundley, Norris, Jr., ed. see Lapp, Rudolph M.

Hundley, Norris, Jr., ed. see Olin, Spencer C., Jr.

Hundley, Norris, Jr., ed. see Putnam, Jackson K.

Hundley, Norris, Jr., ed. see Rolle, Andrew, Jr.

Hundley, Norris, Jr., ed. see Selvin, David F.

Hundley, Norris, Jr., et al, eds. see Jelinek, Lawrence.

Hundley, Norris, Jr., et al, eds. see Jelinek, Lawrence J.

Hundsdoerfer, V. H., jt. ed. see Hinzen, H.

Hundt, Sheila W. Invitation to Riding. (Illus.). 320p. 1976. 12.95 o.p. (ISBN 0-671-22239-2). S&S.

Huneker, James G. Iconoclasts, a Book of Dramatists: Ibsen, Strindberg, Becque, Hauptmann, Sudermann, Hervieu, Gorky, Duse & D'Annunzio, Maeterlinck & Bernard Shaw. LC 68-57613. (Illus.). 1969. Repr. of 1905 ed. lib. bdg. 18.50x (ISBN 0-8371-0930-2, HUIC). Greenwood.

Huneycutt, James. Introduction to Probability. LC 72-97005. (gr. 9-12). 1973. text ed. 18.95 (ISBN 0-675-08960-3). Merrill.

Hung, Wellington & August, Gilbert P. Advanced Textbook of Pediatric Endocrinology. (Advanced Textbook Ser.). 1982. pap. text ed. 32.50 (ISBN 0-87488-674-0). Med Exam.

Hung, Wellington, et al. Pediatric Endocrinology. (Medical Outline Ser.). 1978. pap. 23.00 o.p. (ISBN 0-87488-674-0). Med Exam.

Hung, Y. S. & MacFarlane, A. G. Multivariable Feedback: A Quasi-Classical Approach. (Lecture Notes in Control & Information Sciences: Vol. 40). 182p. 1983. pap. 9.50 (ISBN 0-387-11902-7). Springer-Verlag.

Hunger, J. David, jt. auth. see Wheelen, Thomas L.

Hungerford, Harold, et al. English Linguistics: An Introductory Reader. 1970. pap. 10.95x (ISBN 0-673-05296-6). Scott F.

Hungerford, T. W. Algebra. (Graduate Texts in Mathematics: Vol. 73). 502p. 1981. 24.00 o.p. (ISBN 0-387-90518-9). Springer-Verlag.

Hungler, Bernadette P., jt. auth. see Polit, Denise.

Hungness, Carl. Go: The Bettenhausen Story. 512p. 1983. lib. bdg. 17.95 (ISBN 0-915088-33-9). C Hungness.

--Who's Who in Stained Glass. 284p. 1983. pap. 9.95 (ISBN 0-915088-34-7). C Hungness.

Hungness, Carl, jt. ed. see Fox, Jack.

Hunisak, John M. The Sculptor Jules Dalou: Studies in His Style & Imagery. LC 76-23629. (Outstanding Dissertations in the Fine Arts - 19th Century). (Illus.). 1977. Repr. of 1976 ed. lib. bdg. 60.00 o.s.i. (ISBN 0-8240-2699-3). Garland Pub.

Hunke, H., ed. Software Engineering Environments. 1981. 57.50 (ISBN 0-444-86133-5). Elsevier.

Hunker, Jeffrey A., ed. Structural Change in the U. S. Automobile Industry. LC 82-48529. 1983. write for info. (ISBN 0-669-06267-7). Lexington Bks.

Hunkins, Francis P. Curriculum Development: Program Planning & Improvement. (Elementary Education Ser.: No. C22). 410p. 1980. text ed. 21.95 (ISBN 0-675-08177-7). Merrill.

Hunn, David. Gymnastics. LC 80-50934. (Intersport Ser.). 13.00 (ISBN 0-382-06434-8). Silver.

Hunnicutt, R. P. Pershing: A History of the Medium Tank, T-Twenty Ser. (Illus.). 1971. 16.50 o.p. (ISBN 0-8168-7125-6). Presidio Pr.

Hunninger, Benjamin. The Origin of the Theater: An Essay. LC 77-20684. 1978. Repr. of 1961 ed. lib. bdg. 17.00x (ISBN 0-313-20007-6, HUOT). Greenwood.

Hunnisett, R. F. Editing Records for Publications. 73p. 1977. 35.00x (ISBN 0-686-98234-7, Pub. by British Records). State Mutual Bk.

Hunsaker, Jerome C. Aeronautics at the Mid-Century. 1952. 29.50x (ISBN 0-685-89732-X). Elliots Bks.

Hunsberger, I. Moyer. The Quintessential Dictionary. 512p. 1978. 15.00 o.s.i. (ISBN 0-89104-247-4). A & W Pubs.

Hunsberger, Mabel, jt. auth. see Tackett, Jo J.

Hunsinger. Correspondencia Comercial Moderna. 4th ed. 232p. 1982. 9.00 (ISBN 0-07-031282-6, G). McGraw.

Hunsinger, Doris L. Respiratory Technology: Procedure & Equipment Manual. 3rd ed. (Illus.). 448p. 1980. text ed. 22.95 (ISBN 0-8359-6670-4). Reston.

Hunsinger, Marjorie & Clarke, P. B. Modern Business Correspondence, a Text-Workbook for Colleges. 3rd ed. 1972. 10.50 o.p. (ISBN 0-07-031270-2, G); instructor's guide & key 6.75 o.p. (ISBN 0-07-031272-9); tests free o.p. McGraw.

Hunt. Encyclopedia of American Architecture. 100p. 1980. 43.95 (ISBN 0-07-031299-0). McGraw.

--Nursing Care Plans. 9.95 (ISBN 0-471-25778-8, Wiley Heyden). Wiley.

--Pathology of Injury. 29.95 (ISBN 0-471-25776-1, Wiley Heyden). Wiley.

--Plant Growth Analysis. (Studies in Biology: No. 96). 1978. 5.95 o.p. (ISBN 0-7131-2696-5). Univ Park.

--Plant Growth Curves: An Introduction to Functional Approach to Plant Growth Analysis. 256p. 1982. pap. text ed. 22.95 (ISBN 0-8391-1757-4). Univ Park.

Hunt, jt. auth. see Holiday.

Hunt see Mascona, A.

Hunt, jt. auth. see Fry, John.

Hunt, A., jt. auth. see Hess, M. A.

Hunt, A. Lee. Pocket Guide to Supervising in the Oilfield. 1983. pap. text ed. 6.95 (ISBN 0-87201-714-1). Gulf Pub.

Hunt, Alan. The Sociological Movement in Law. LC 78-4286. 186p. 1978. 29.95 (ISBN 0-87722-135-9). Temple U Pr.

Hunt, Alan, ed. Class & Class Structure. 1977. pap. text ed. 7.75x o.p. (ISBN 0-85315-402-3). Humanities.

Hunt, Alan, jt. ed. see Fryer, Bob.

Hunt, Albert. The Language of Television. 1982. 6.95x (ISBN 0-413-33740-5). Methuen Inc.

Hunt, Antonia. Little Resistance. 160p. 1982. 9.95 (ISBN 0-312-48866-1). St Martin.

Hunt, Arnold D. & Grotty, Robert B. Ethics of World Religions. (Illus.). (gr. 9-12). 1978. lib. bdg. 10.95 (ISBN 0-912616-74-1); pap. 5.95 (ISBN 0-912616-73-3). Greenhaven.

Hunt, B. The Complete How-to Book of Indian Craft. Orig. Title: Ben Hunt's Big Indian Craft Book. 1973. pap. 6.95 (ISBN 0-02-011690-X, Collier). Macmillan.

Hunt, Barbara. The Paradox of Christian Tragedy. 85p. 1983. write for info (ISBN 0-87875-251-X). Whitston Pub.

Hunt, Bernice, jt. auth. see Hunt, Morton.

Hunt, Bernice K. Apples: A Bushel of Fun & Facts. LC 75-17911. (Finding-Out Book). (Illus.). 64p. (gr. 2-4). 1976. PLB 7.95 o.p. (ISBN 0-8193-0838-2, Pub by Parents). Enslow Pubs.

--The Whatchamacallit Book. LC 76-18831. (Illus.). (gr. 3-5). 1976. PLB 4.99 o.p. (ISBN 0-399-61011-1). Putnam Pub Group.

Hunt, Cathy S. How to Search for Information: A Beginner's Guide to the Literature of Music. (Basic Tools Ser.: No. 3). 50p. Date not set. pap. text ed. price not set (ISBN 0-938376-02-0). Willowood Pr.

Hunt, Chester L. & Walker, Lewis. Ethnic Dynamics: Patterns of Intergroup Relations in Various Societies. 2nd ed. LC 78-73117. 1979. text ed. 21.95x (ISBN 0-918452-16-3); pap. text ed. 15.95 (ISBN 0-918452-17-1). Learning Pubns.

Hunt, Chester L., jt. auth. see Horton, Paul B.

Hunt, Cindy, jt. auth. see Hunt, Jim.

Hunt, Connie. Reaching. (Illus.). 96p. 1982. pap. 6.00 (ISBN 0-9609442-0-6). Pulsar Pub.

Hunt, Connie M. Mike Was Here. LC 81-68368. 1981. 4.95 (ISBN 0-8054-5648-1). Broadman.

Hunt, Daniel. Energy Conservation in Health Care Facilities. (Illus.). 300p. 1983. text ed. 36.00 (ISBN 0-915586-66-5). Fairmont Pr.

Hunt, Daniel V. Industrial Robotics Handbook. (Illus.). 300p. 1983. 32.50 (ISBN 0-8311-1148-8). Indus Pr.

--Synfuels Handbook. (Illus.). 500p. 1983. 45.00 (ISBN 0-8311-1144-5). Indus Pr.

Hunt, Dave. Peace, Prosperity & the Coming Holocaust. LC 82-84069. 224p. 1983. pap. 6.95 (ISBN 0-89081-331-0). Harvest Hse.

Hunt, David C. Legacy of the West. (Illus.). 157p. (Orig.). 1982. 34.50 (ISBN 0-936364-11-4); pap. 17.95 (ISBN 0-936364-08-4). Joslyn Art.

Hunt, Dennis D. Common Sense Industrial Relations. LC 77-89384. 1978. 14.95 o.p. (ISBN 0-7153-7453-2). David & Charles.

Hunt, Derald D. California Criminal Law Manual. 5th ed. 240p. 1980. pap. 13.95x (ISBN 0-8087-3178-5). Burgess.

Hunt, Derald D., jt. auth. see Schultz, Donald O.

Hunt, Donald. Pondering the Proverbs. (The Bible Study Textbook Ser.). (Illus.). 1974. 14.30 o.s.i. (ISBN 0-89900-018-5). College Pr Pub.

Hunt, Donald M. Texas Appellate Practice Manual. 376p. 1974. 30.00 (ISBN 0-938160-04-4, 6320). State Bar TX.

Hunt, E. K. & Sherman, Howard J. Economics: An Introduction to Traditional & Radical Views. 4th ed. 736p. 1981. pap. text ed. 20.95 scp (ISBN 0-06-043008-7, HarpC); inst. manual avail. (ISBN 0-06-363024-9). Har-Row.

Hunt, E. Stephen, jt. ed. see Lefever, Ernest W.

Hunt, Earl W. The Living Wilderness. LC 76-22449. (Adult & Young Adult Bks.). (Illus.). 1977. 7.95g (ISBN 0-8225-0760-9). Lerner Pubns.

Hunt, Edgar, ed. see Dowland, Robert.

Hunt, Edward D. Holy Land Pilgrimage in the Later Roman Empire, AD 312-460. 280p. 1982. 39.95x (ISBN 0-19-826438-0). Oxford U Pr.

Hunt, Elgin F. Social Science: An Introduction to the Study of Society. 4th ed. (Illus.). 896p. 1972. text ed. 22.95x (ISBN 0-02-358750-4). Macmillan.

Hunt, Florine E., ed. Public Utilities Information Sources. LC 65-24658. (Management Information Guide Ser.: No. 7). 1965. 42.00x (ISBN 0-8103-0807-X). Gale.

Hunt, Freeman, ed. Lives of American Merchants, 2 Vols. LC 66-21679. 1969p. Repr. of 1856 ed. 57.50x set (ISBN 0-678-00294-0). Kelley.

Hunt, G. H., jt. ed. see May, Herbert G.

Hunt, G. W., jt. auth. see Thompson, J. M.

Hunt, Gaillard. Israel Elihu & Cadwallader Washburn. LC 71-87440. (American Scene Ser.). 1969. Repr. of 1925 ed. lib. bdg. 49.50 (ISBN 0-306-71510-4). Da Capo.

--Life in America One Hundred Years Ago. LC 74-6223. (Illus.). xiv, 298p. 1976. Repr. of 1914 ed. 30.00x (ISBN 0-8103-4017-8). Gale.

Hunt, Garry & Moore, Patrick. The Planet Venus. LC 82-5045. (Illus.). 240p. 1983. 22.00 (ISBN 0-571-09050-8). Faber & Faber.

--Saturn. (The Rand Mcnally Library of Astronomical Atlases for Amateur & Professional Observers). (Illus.). 96p. 1982. 16.95 (ISBN 0-528-81545-8). Rand.

Hunt, Gary. Public Speaking. (Illus.). 386p. 1981. text ed. 16.95 (ISBN 0-13-738807-1). P-H.

Hunt, Gary T. Communication Skills in the Organization. (Illus.). 1980. text ed. 21.95 (ISBN 0-13-153296-0). P-H.

Hunt, George. John Updike & the Three Great Secret Things: Sex, Religion & Art. 1981. 13.95 (ISBN 0-8028-3539-2, 3539-2). Eerdmans.

--The Story of the U. S. Marines. (Landmark Ser.: No. 14). (gr. 4-6). 1951. PLB 5.99 o.p. (ISBN 0-394-90314-5). Random.

Hunt, Gladys. The God Who Understands Me: The Sermon on the Mount. LC 75-181992. (Fisherman Bible Studyguides). 1971. saddle-stitched 2.50 (ISBN 0-87788-316-5). Shaw Pubs.

--How to Handbook for Inductive Bible-Study Leaders. LC 73-169168. 1971. pap. 2.95 (ISBN 0-87788-396-3). Shaw Pubs.

--John: Eyewitness. LC 70-158130. (Fisherman Bible Studyguides Ser.). 1971. pap. 2.50 saddle stitch (ISBN 0-87788-245-2). Shaw Pubs.

--Relationships. (Fisherman Bible Studyguides Ser.). 80p. 1983. saddle stitched 2.50 (ISBN 0-87788-721-7). Shaw Pubs.

--Revelation: The Lamb Who Is the Lion. (Fisherman Bible Studyguides Ser.). 1973. saddle-stitched 2.50 (ISBN 0-87788-486-2). Shaw Pubs.

--Romans: Made Righteous by Faith. (Fisherman Bible Studyguides Ser.). 94p. 1980. saddle-stitched 2.50 (ISBN 0-87788-733-0). Shaw Pubs.

Hunt, Gordon. How to Audition: Advice from a Casting Director. LC 79-1796. 1979. Repr. of 1977 ed. 10.53i (ISBN 0-06-012006-1, HarpT). Har-Row.

Hunt, Greg. Dewitt's Strike. 1980. pap. 1.95 o.s.i. (ISBN 0-440-12024-1). Dell.

--John Bozeman: Mountain Journey. (American Explorers Ser.: No. 13). (Orig.). 1983. pap. 2.95 (ISBN 0-440-04340-9). Dell.

Hunt, H. Allen, jt. auth. see Barth, Peter S.

Hunt, H. Draper. The Blaine House, Home of Maine's Governors. LC 73-86843. pap. 5.95 o.p. (ISBN 0-915592-12-6). Maine Hist.

Hunt, H. R. Introductory Chemistry Laboratory Manual. 1974. pap. 10.95 (ISBN 0-02-358670-2). Macmillan.

Hunt, Harrison J. North to the Horizon. Thompson, Ruth H., ed. LC 80-69081. (Illus.). 104p. 1981. 11.95 (ISBN 0-89272-080-8, PIC451). Down East.

Hunt, Henry T. Case of Thomas J. Mooney & Warren K. Billings. LC 72-122166. (Civil Liberties in American History Ser). (Illus.). 1971. Repr. of 1929 ed. lib. bdg. 55.00 (ISBN 0-306-71976-2). Da Capo.

Hunt, Herbert J. Balzac's Comedie Humaine. 1959. pap. text ed. 13.00x o.p. (ISBN 0-485-12008-9, Athlone Pr). Humanities.

Hunt, Herbert J., tr. see Balzac, Honore de.

Hunt, Hugh, jt. auth. see O'Connor, Frank.

Hunt, Hugh, et al. Revels History of Drama in English, Vol. 7: 1880 to the Present. (The Revels History of Drama in English Ser.). (Illus.). 1978. 53.00x (ISBN 0-416-13080-1); pap. 18.95x (ISBN 0-416-81390-9). Methuen Inc.

Hunt, Inez & Draper, Wanetta. Ghost Trails to Ghost Towns. rev. ed. (Illus.). 48p. 1980. pap. 2.50 o.p. (ISBN 0-936564-17-2). Little London.

Hunt, Irene. Across Five Aprils. (gr. 7 up). 1964. 4.95 o.s.i. (ISBN 0-695-80100-7); lib. ed. 4.98 o.s.i. (ISBN 0-695-40100-9). Follett.

--Up a Road Slowly. (gr. 7 up). 1966. 4.95 o.s.i. (ISBN 0-695-89009-3); lib. ed. 4.98 (ISBN 0-695-49009-5). Follett.

--William. 192p. (gr. 6-12). 1981. pap. 1.95 (ISBN 0-686-82846-1, Pub. by Tempo). Ace Bks.

Hunt, J. A. An Outline of Features of Microprocessor-Based Controllers, 1979. 1981. 69.00x (ISBN 0-686-97138-8, Pub. by W Spring England). State Mutual Bk.

Hunt, J. A., jt. auth. see King, P. J.

Hunt, James. Readings in Sociobiology. (Illus.). 464p. 1980. pap. 15.95x (ISBN 0-07-031308-3). McGraw.

Hunt, James W. Employer's Guide to Labor Relations. rev. ed. LC 74-167769. 162p. 1979. pap. 12.00 (ISBN 0-87179-292-3). BNA.

Hunt, Janet. Simple & Speedy Wholefood Cooking. (Illus.). 128p. (Orig.). 1983. pap. 3.95 (ISBN 0-7225-0752-6, Pub. by Thorsons Pubs England). Sterling.

Hunt, Jeanne, ed. Being A Loving Wife. LC 82-48422. (Christian Reader Ser.). 128p. (Orig.). 1983. pap. 5.72i (ISBN 0-06-061386-6, HarpR). Har-Row.

--Raising a Joyful Family. LC 82-4823. (Christian Reader Ser.). 128p. (Orig.). 1983. pap. 5.72i (ISBN 0-06-061387-4, HarpR). Har-Row.

Hunt, Jena. Sweeter Than Wine, No. 78. 1982. pap. 1.75 (ISBN 0-515-06689-3). Jove Pubns.

Hunt, Jim & Hunt, Cindy. How to Live with an Alcoholic & Win. 1978. pap. 2.95 (ISBN 0-89728-018-0). Omega Pubns Or.

Hunt, John D., ed. see Switzer, Stephen.

Hunt, Joyce, jt. auth. see Selsam, Millicent.

Hunt, Joyce, jt. auth. see Selsam, Millicent E.

Hunt, Lacy H. Dynamics of Forecasting Financial Cycles: Theory, Technique & Implementation, Vol. 1. Altman, Edward I. & Walter, Ingo, eds. LC 76-5756. (Contemporary Studies in Economic & Financial Analysis). 300p. 1976. lib. bdg. 34.50 (ISBN 0-89232-002-8). Jai Pr.

Hunt, Lee M., jt. auth. see Groves, Donald G.

Hunt, Leigh, jt. auth. see Cheney, David R.

Hunt, Linda & Frasw, Marianne. Loaves & Fishes. LC 80-12165. (Illus.). 176p. (gr. 2-5). 1980. pap. 6.95 (ISBN 0-8361-1922-3). Herald Pr.

Hunt, Margaret, tr. see Grimm, Jakob L.

Hunt, Mark, jt. auth. see Huffman, Hughes.

Hunt, Michael H. The Making of a Special Relationship: The United States & China to 1914. LC 82-9753. 480p. 1983. 27.50x (ISBN 0-231-05516-1). Columbia U Pr.

Hunt, Morton. The Universe Within: A New Science Explores the Human Mind. 1982. 17.95 (ISBN 0-671-25258-5). S&S.

Hunt, Morton & Hunt, Bernice. The Divorce Experience. 1979. pap. 3.50 (ISBN 0-451-12094-9, AE2094, Sig). NAL.

Hunt, Norman J. Brass Ensemble Method: Beginning Class Instruction. 3rd ed. 174p. 1974. write for info. plastic comb. o.p. (ISBN 0-697-03498-4). Wm C Brown.

Hunt, Patricia. Snowy Owls. LC 82-7361. (Skylight Bk.). (Illus.). 64p. (gr. 2-5). 1982. PLB 7.95 (ISBN 0-396-08073-1). Dodd.

Hunt, Paul O. Cube of Art. (Illus.). 16p. 1982. pap. 1.50 o.s.i. (ISBN 0-932970-25-7). Prinit Pr.

Hunt, Percival. Samuel Pepys in the Diary. LC 78-2747. 1978. Repr. of 1958 ed. lib. bdg. 19.00x (ISBN 0-313-20363-6, HUSD). Greenwood.

Hunt, R. Pocket Guide to...BASIC. 64p. spiral bdg. 6.95 (ISBN 0-201-07744-2). A-W.

Hunt, R., jt. auth. see Rorison, I.

Hunt, R. Reed, jt. auth. see Ellis, Henry C.

Hunt, R. W. Colour Seventy Three: Survey Lectures & Abstracts of the Papers to be Presented at the Second Congress of the International Colour Association, University of York. 566p. 1973. 73.95 o.s.i. (ISBN 0-470-42130-4). Halsted Pr.

Hunt, Raymond G., jt. ed. see Hollander, Edwin P.

Hunt, Reginald. A First Harmony Book. LC 77-23413. 1977. lib. bdg. 18.75x (ISBN 0-8371-9703-1, HUFH). Greenwood.

Hunt, Richard N. The Political Ideas of Marx & Engels, (Vol. 1: Marxism & Totalitarian Democracy, 1818-1850. LC 74-13536. 1974. 19.95x (ISBN 0-8229-3285-7). U of Pittsburgh Pr.

Hunt, Rkobert D. Fruit & Vegetable Exports from the Mediterranean Area to the EEC. (Working Paper: No. 321). 90p. 1979. 5.00 (ISBN 0-686-36208-X, WP-0321). World Bank.

Hunt, Robert. Necki the African Giraffe. LC 72-736445. (Adventures of Wild Animals Book). (gr. 2-5). 1978. incl. 10 bks & one cassette 22.00 (ISBN 0-89290-030-X). Soc for Visual.

--A Popular Treatise on the Art of Photography, Including Daguerreotype, & All the New Methods of Producing Pictures by the Chemical Agency of Light. facsimile ed. LC 72-96395. lxxv, 96p. 1973. Repr. of 1841 ed. 10.00x (ISBN 0-8214-0127-0, 82-81305). Ohio U Pr.

Hunt, Robert & Mason, David. The Normandy Campaign. 1976. 14.95 o.p. (ISBN 0-85052-209-9). Hippocrene Bks.

Hunt, Robert, jt. auth. see Arras, John.

Hunt, Robert & Arras, John, eds. Ethical Issues in Modern Medicine. LC 76-56508. 524p. 1977. pap. 13.95 (ISBN 0-87484-396-0). Mayfield Pub.

Hunt, Roberta. Obstacles to Interstate Adoption. 1972. pap. 3.50 (ISBN 0-87868-100-0, A-36). Child Welfare.

Hunt, Rockwell D. California in the Making. LC 73-20904. 325p. 1974. Repr. of 1953 ed. lib. bdg. 18.50x (ISBN 0-8371-5866-4, HUCM). Greenwood.

Hunt, Roderick. Oxford Christmas Book for Children. (Illus.). 160p. 1982. 10.95 (ISBN 0-19-278104-9, Pub. by Oxford U Pr Childrens). Merrimack Bk Serv.

Hunt, Ronald D., jt. auth. see Jones, Thomas C.

Hunt, Ronald H. The Church's Pilgrimage of Pastoral Care in Mental Retardation. (Illus.). 1978. 5.95 o.p. (ISBN 0-533-03107-9). Vantage.

Hunt, S. E. Games & Sports the World Around. 3rd ed. 271p. 1964. 19.95 (ISBN 0-471-07096-3). Wiley.

Hunt, Sara M., et al. Nutrition: Principles & Clinical Practice. LC 79-25899. 1980. text ed. 29.50 (ISBN 0-471-03149-6). Wiley.

Hunt, Shane J., jt. ed. see Cortes-Conde, Roberto.

Hunt, Shelby D., jt. ed. see Bush, Ronald F.

Hunt, Tamara & Renfro, Nancy. Pocketful of Puppets: Mother Goose Rhymes. Kelley, Merily H., ed. (Puppetry in Education Ser.). (Illus.). 80p. (Orig.). 1982. pap. 7.50 (ISBN 0-931044-06-5). Renfro Studios.

--Puppetry & Early Childhood Education. Schwalb, Ann W., ed. (Puppetry in Education Ser.). (Illus.). 264p. (Orig.). 1981. pap. 13.50 (ISBN 0-931044-04-9). Renfro Studios.

Hunt, Thomas C., jt. auth. see Honer, Stanley M.

Hunt, Thomas C. & Maxson, Marilyn M., eds. Religion & Morality in American Schooling. LC 81-40154. 297p. (Orig.). 1981. lib. bdg. 20.50 (ISBN 0-8191-1584-3); pap. text ed. 11.00 (ISBN 0-8191-1585-1). U Pr of Amer.

Hunt, Thomas G., ed. Society, Culture & Schools: The American Approach. 403p. 1979. 8.95 (ISBN 0-912048-06-9). Garrett Pk.

Hunt, Violet. I Have This to Say. LC 78-64035. (Des Imagistes: Literature of the Imagist Movement). (Illus.). 344p. 1982. Repr. of 1926 ed. 35.00 (ISBN 0-404-17116-8). AMS Pr.

Hunt, W. Ben. Ben Hunt's Big Book of Whittling. 1970. 13.95 (ISBN 0-02-557430-2). Macmillan.

Hunt, William. Of the Map That Changes. LC 82-73377. (New Poetry Ser.: No. 46). 84p. 1973. 6.50 (ISBN 0-8040-0623-7). Swallow.

--The Puritan Movement: The Coming of Revolution in an English County. (Harvard Historical Studies: No. 102). (Illus.). 384p. 1983. text ed. 36.00x (ISBN 0-674-73903-5). Harvard U Pr.

Hunten, Donald M. & Colin, Lawrence, eds. Venus. 1200p. 1983. text ed. 60.00x (ISBN 0-8165-0788-0). U of Ariz Pr.

Hunter. Dramatic Identities & Cultural Tradition. 376p. 1982. 60.00x (ISBN 0-85323-443-4, Pub. by Liverpool Univ England). State Mutual Bk.

--Families Under the Flag: A Review of Military Family Literature. 320p. 1982. 33.95 (ISBN 0-03-062014-7). Praeger.

--Hunter's Lectures of Anatomy. 1972. 28.00 (ISBN 0-444-40910-6, North Holland). Elsevier.

Hunter, A. M. The Epistle to the Romans. (Student Christian Movement Press-Torch Bible Ser.). (Orig.). 1955. pap. 7.95x (ISBN 0-19-520298-8). Oxford U Pr.

--The Fifth Evangelist. (Student Christian Movement Press Ser.). 144p. (Orig.). 1980. 6.95x (ISBN 0-19-520321-6). Oxford U Pr.

--The Gospel According to St. Mark. (Student Christian Movement Press-Torch Bible Ser.). (Orig.). 1949. pap. 7.95x (ISBN 0-19-520299-6). Oxford U Pr.

--The Gospel Then & Now. (Student Christian Movement Press). (Orig.). 1978. pap. 6.95x o.p. (ISBN 0-19-520322-4). Oxford U Pr.

Hunter, Alan. Death on the Heath. (Scene of the Crime Ser.: No. 58). 1983. pap. 2.75 (ISBN 0-440-11686-4). Dell.

Hunter, Alvin J. Sea Gulls Don't Fly at Night. Date not set. 6.95 o.p. (ISBN 0-533-04098-1). Vantage.

Hunter, Archibald M. Galatians-Colossians. LC 59-10454. (Layman's Bible Commentary Ser: Vol. 22). 1959. pap. 3.95 (ISBN 0-8042-3082-X). John Knox.

--The Gospel According to St. Paul. rev. ed. LC 67-10511. Orig. Title: Interpreting Paul's Gospel. 1967. pap. 3.95 (ISBN 0-664-24742-3). Westminster.

--Interpreting the Parables. LC 61-5122. 1976. pap. 5.95 (ISBN 0-664-24746-6). Westminster.

--Introducing the New Testament. 3rd. rev. ed. LC 72-7110. 1973. pap. 5.95 (ISBN 0-664-24965-5). Westminster.

--A Pattern for Life: An Exposition of the Sermon on the Mount. rev. ed. LC 66-11517. 1966. pap. 5.95 (ISBN 0-664-24687-7). Westminster.

--The Work & Words of Jesus. rev. ed. LC 73-7559. 1973. pap. 7.95 (ISBN 0-664-24976-0). Westminster.

Hunter, B. Administration of Hospital Wards. 1972. 11.00 (ISBN 0-7190-0525-6). Manchester.

Hunter, Beatrice. The Natural Foods Cookbook. 2.75x (ISBN 0-671-20421-1). Cancer Control Soc.

Hunter, Beatrice T. Beatrice Trum Hunter's Favorite Natural Foods. 1974. 7.95 o.p. (ISBN 0-671-21820-4). S&S.

--Fact-Book on Food Additives & Your Health. rev. ed. LC 72-83521. (Pivot Original Health Book). 128p. 1980. pap. 1.95 o.p. (ISBN 0-87983-024-7). Keats.

--Gardening Without Poisons. 2nd ed. 1981. 14.95 o.s.i. (ISBN 0-686-76734-9). Regent House.

--How Safe is Food in Your Kitchen? 96p. 1982. pap. 3.95 (ISBN 0-686-97218-X, ScribT). Scribner.

--The Natural Foods Cookbook. 1980. pap. 2.75 (ISBN 0-515-05691-X, V2850). Jove Pubns.

--Natural Foods Cookbook. 1961. 6.95 (ISBN 0-671-51347-8); pap. 3.95 o.p. (ISBN 0-671-20421-1). S&S.

Hunter, Brenda. Beyond Divorce: A Personal Journey. 1978. pap. 4.95 (ISBN 0-8007-5021-7, Power Bks). Revell.

--Where Have All the Mothers Gone? 176p. 1982. 8.95 (ISBN 0-310-45550-2). Zondervan.

Hunter, Carman S. Adult Illiteracy in the United States. (Illus.). 1979. 10.95 o.p. (ISBN 0-07-031380-6, P&RB). McGraw.

Hunter, Charles. Follow Me! 184p. (Orig.). 1975. pap. 2.95 (ISBN 0-86694-020-0). Omega Pubns OR.

Hunter, Charles & Hunter, Frances. Since Jesus Passed By. 146p. (Orig.). 1973. pap. 2.95 (ISBN 0-86694-032-4). Omega Pubns OR.

Hunter, Christine, jt. auth. see Aylward, Gladys.

Hunter, Clark. The Life & Letters of Alexander Wilson. (Memoirs Ser.: Vol. 154). 1983. 40.00 (ISBN 0-87169-154-X). Am Philos.

Hunter, Claud, jt. auth. see Weathers, Thomas.

Hunter, Claud, jt. auth. see Weathers, Tom.

Hunter, D. R., ed. Precambrian of the Southern Hemisphere. (Developments in Precambrian Geology: Vol. 2). 1981. 149.00 (ISBN 0-444-41862-8). Elsevier.

Hunter, Dard. Papermaking. (Illus.). 1978. pap. 8.95 (ISBN 0-486-23619-6). Dover.

--Papermaking: The History & Technique of an Ancient Craft. LC 77-92477. 1978. lib. bdg. 17.50x (ISBN 0-88307-610-1). Gannon.

Hunter, David E. & Whitten, Phillip M. Anthropology: Contemporary Perspectives. 3rd ed. 1982. pap. 9.95 (ISBN 0-316-38266-3). Little.

Hunter, David M. Supervisory Management: Skill Building Techniques. 300p. 1981. text ed. 17.95 (ISBN 0-8359-7155-4); pap. text ed. 15.95 (ISBN 0-8359-7156-2); instr's. manual free (ISBN 0-8359-7157-0). Reston.

Hunter, Doug. Against the Odds. (Illus.). 288p. 1981. 19.95 (ISBN 0-920510-43-4, Pub. by Personal Lib). Dodd.

Hunter, Edgar H., jt. auth. see Hunter, Margaret K.

Hunter, Elizabeth. A Touch of Magic. 192p. 1981. pap. 1.50 o.s.i. (ISBN 0-671-57065-X). S&S.

Hunter, Emily. Como Ser Encantadora (Para Alumna) Mendoza De Mann, Wilma & Mariotti, F. A., trs. Orig. Title: Christian Charm Notebook. (Illus.). 56p. (Span.). 1981. pap. 2.50 (ISBN 0-311-46054-2). Casa Bautista.

Hunter, Emily, jt. auth. see Hunter, Wayne.

Hunter, Eric & Bakewell, K. G. Cataloguing. 2nd ed. 256p. 1983. 18.50 (ISBN 0-85157-358-4, Pub. by Bingley England). Shoe String.

Hunter, Eric J. The ABC of BASIC: An Introduction to Programming for Librarians. 128p. 1982. 16.00 (ISBN 0-85157-355-X, Pub. by Bingley England). Shoe String.

Hunter, Evan. The Blackboard Jungle. 1976. pap. 1.75 o.p. (ISBN 0-380-00859-9, 31260). Avon.

--Come Winter. 224p. 1974. pap. 1.50 o.p. (ISBN 0-451-05826-7, W5826, Sig). NAL.

--Every Little Crook & Nanny. 1980. pap. 1.95 o.p. (ISBN 0-451-09122-1, J9122, Sig). NAL.

--Far from the Sea. LC 82-71564. 320p. 1983. 12.95 (ISBN 0-689-11338-2). Atheneum.

--Find the Feathered Serpent. 1979. lib. bdg. 9.50 (ISBN 0-8398-2519-6, Gregg). G K Hall.

--Last Summer. 208p. 1974. pap. 1.50 o.p. (ISBN 0-451-07317-7, W7317, Sig). NAL.

--Love, Dad. 1981. 12.95 o.p. (ISBN 0-517-54411-3). Crown.

--Me & Mr. Stenner. LC 76-24810. (gr. 5-12). 1976. 9.57i (ISBN 0-397-31689-5, JBL-J). Har-Row.

--Mothers & Daughters. 1969. pap. 1.75 o.p. (ISBN 0-451-06731-2, E6731, Sig). NAL.

Hunter, Frances, jt. auth. see Hunter, Charles.

Hunter, George, 3rd. The Contagious Congregation: Frontiers in Evangelism & Church Growth. LC 78-12322. 1979. pap. 5.95 (ISBN 0-687-09490-9). Abingdon.

Hunter, Grant. The New Zealand Tramper's Handbook. (Illus.). 160p. (Orig.). 1981. pap. 12.00 (ISBN 0-589-01348-3, Pub. by Reed Books Australia). C E Tuttle.

Hunter, Guy. Modernizing Peasant Societies: A Comparative Study in Asia & Africa. (Illus.). 1969. pap. text ed. 6.95x (ISBN 0-19-500333-0). Oxford U Pr.

Hunter, Guy, et al, eds. Policy & Practice in Rural Development. LC 76-15078. 520p. 1976. text ed. 21.50x (ISBN 0-86598-002-0). Allanheld.

Hunter, Ian. Reflections of a Rock Star. LC 75-45514. (Illus.). 196p. (Orig.). 1976. pap. 3.95 o.p. (ISBN 0-8256-3905-0, Quick Fox). Putnam Pub Group.

Hunter, Ilene & Judson, Marilyn. Simple Folk Instruments to Make & Play. LC 76-50091. 1977. 10.95 o.p. (ISBN 0-671-22446-8). S&S.

--Simple Folk Instruments to Make & to Play. 1980. 4.95 o.p. (ISBN 0-671-25432-4). S&S.

Hunter, J. A. Entertaining Mathematical Teasers & How to Solve Them. 128p. (Orig.). 1983. pap. 3.50 (ISBN 0-486-24500-4). Dover.

Hunter, J. F. Sexual Morality & Personal Intimacy. LC 79-27352. 1980. cancelled (ISBN 0-312-71346-0). St Martin.

--Thinking About Sex & Love: A Philosophical Inquiry. LC 79-27352. 172p. 1980. 20.00 (ISBN 0-312-80018-5). St Martin.

Hunter, J. Paul, ed. The Norton Introduction to Poetry. 2nd. ed. (gr. 12). 1981. pap. text ed. 10.95x (ISBN 0-393-95157-X); classroom guide 1.25 (ISBN 0-393-95160-X). Norton.

Hunter, J. R., jt. auth. see Reid, John T.

Hunter, James. All the Forgotten Places. LC 81-12143. 287p. 1981. 10.95 (ISBN 0-931948-21-5). Peachtree Pubs.

--Coping with Uncertainty Policy & Politics in the National Health Service. LC 80-4170. (Social Policy Research Monographs). 292p. 1981. 55.95 (ISBN 0-471-27906-4, Pub. by Res Stud Pr). Wiley.

Hunter, James D. American Evangelicalism: Conservative Religion & the Quandary of Modernity. LC 82-317. 166p. 1983. 27.50x (ISBN 0-8135-0960-2); pap. 9.95x (ISBN 0-8135-0985-8). Rutgers U Pr.

Hunter, Jeffrey J., ed. Mathematical Techniques of Applied Probability: Vol. 1: Discrete Time Models. 518p. 1983. price not set (ISBN 0-12-361801-0). Acad Pr.

Hunter, Jim. Clemson Football. (College Sports Ser.: Football). 1983. 10.95 (ISBN 0-87397-194-9). Strode.

--Offbeat Baja. (Illus.). 5.95 o.p. (ISBN 0-87701-093-5). Chronicle Bks.

--Tom Stoppard's Plays. LC 82-47988. 272p. 1982. pap. 12.50 (ISBN 0-394-62414-9, E825, Ever). Grove.

Hunter, Joan, ed. The Independent Study Catalog: NUCEA's Guide to Independent Study Through Correspondence Instruction 1983-1985. 1983. pap. 5.95 (ISBN 0-87866-180-8, 1204). Petersons Guides.

Hunter, Joan H. Guide to Independent Study Through Correspondence Instruction, 1980-82. 112p. 1980. pap. 4.50 o.p. (ISBN 0-87866-086-0). Petersons Guides.

Hunter, Joan H., ed. Peterson's Annual Guide to Undergraduate Study, 1983. 2093p. (Orig.). 1982. pap. 13.95 (ISBN 0-87866-184-0). Petersons Guides.

Hunter, John, jt. auth. see Pace, David.

Hunter, John E. & Schmidt, Frank L. Meta-Analysis: Cumulating Research Findings Across Studies. (Studing Organizations in Methodology). 144p. 1982. 17.95 (ISBN 0-8039-1863-1); pap. 7.95 (ISBN 0-8039-1864-X). Sage.

Hunter, John M. & Foley, James W. Economic Problems of Latin America. 1975. text ed. 26.95 (ISBN 0-395-18941-1). HM.

Hunter, John M., jt. ed. see Thomas, Robert N.

Hunter, Kathryn, jt. auth. see Throop, Sara.

Hunter, Kerri C., jt. auth. see Robbins, Claude L.

Hunter, Lloyd P. Handbook of Semiconductor Electronics. 3rd ed. (Illus.). 1970. 56.65 (ISBN 0-07-031305-9, P&RB). McGraw.

Hunter, Louis C. Studies in the Economic History of the Ohio Valley. LC 72-98689. (American Scene Ser.). 1973. Repr. of 1933 ed. lib. bdg. 24.50 (ISBN 0-306-71837-5). Da Capo.

Hunter, Lynette. G. K. Chesterton: Explorations in Allegory. 1979. 25.00x (ISBN 0-312-31492-2). St Martin.

Hunter, Mac. Golf for Beginners. (Illus.). 96p. 1973. pap. 3.95 (ISBN 0-448-11538-7, G&D). Putnam Pub Group.

Hunter, Margaret K. & Hunter, Edgar H. The Indoor Garden: Design, Construction & Furnishing. LC 77-20942. 1978. 33.95 (ISBN 0-471-03016-3, Pub. by Wiley-Interscience). Wiley.

Hunter, Marvin H., et al. The Retarded Child from Birth to Five: A Multi-Disciplinary Approach for Child & Family. LC 70-179783. (John Day Bk.). 320p. 1972. 12.45i (ISBN 0-381-98127-4, A66100). T Y Crowell.

Hunter, Mary V. Sassafras. 288p. 1980. 10.95 o.p. (ISBN 0-453-00376-1, H376). NAL.

Hunter, Mary Vann see Vann Hunter, Mary.

Hunter, Michael. Science & Society in Restoration England. LC 80-41071. 224p. 1981. 42.50 (ISBN 0-521-22866-2); pap. 13.95 (ISBN 0-521-29685-4). Cambridge U Pr.

Hunter, Mollie. A Furl of Fairy Wind. LC 76-58732. (Illus.). (gr. 2-5). 1977. 8.61i (ISBN 0-06-022674-9, HarpJ); PLB 8.89 o.p. (ISBN 0-06-022675-7). Har-Row.

--Walking Stones. (Story of Suspense Ser.). (Illus.). (gr. 4 up). 1970. pap. 1.25 o.p. (ISBN 0-06-440034-4, Trophy). Har-Row.

--You Never Knew Her As I Did! LC 81-47114. 224p. (YA) (gr. 7 up). 1981. 10.10i (ISBN 0-06-022678-1, HarpJ); PLB 10.89 (ISBN 0-06-022679-X). Har-Row.

Hunter, Norman. The Wizard Book of Magic. LC 78-52333. (gr. 4-8). 1978. 6.95 o.p. (ISBN 0-8069-4586-9); PLB 6.69 o.p. (ISBN 0-8069-4587-7). Sterling.

Hunter, Paul. Mockingbird. 1981. pap. 4.00 (ISBN 0-918116-24-4). Jawbone Pr.

Hunter, Peter J. Peter Hunter's Guide to Grasses, Clovers, & Weeds. (Illus.). 80p. pap. 5.95 (ISBN 0-938670-02-6). By Hand & Foot.

Hunter, R. H. Reproduction of Farm Animals. LC 81-19318. (Longman Handbooks in Agriculture). (Illus.). 176p. (Orig.). 1982. pap. text ed. 14.95 (ISBN 0-582-45085-3). Longman.

Hunter, R. H. & Brown, T. C. Battle Coast: An Illustrated History of D-Day. (Illus.). 142p. 1974. 14.50 o.p. (ISBN 0-902875-24-8). Transatlantic.

Hunter, Richard & Macalpine, Ida. Three Hundred Years of Psychiatry, 1535-1860. xxvi, 1107p. 1982. Repr. of 1963 ed. 75.00 (ISBN 0-910177-00-7). Carlisle Pub.

Hunter, Richard S. The Measurement of Appearance. LC 75-20429. 348p. 1975. 46.00 (ISBN 0-471-42141-3, Pub. by Wiley-Interscience). Wiley.

Hunter, Rob. Camping & Backpacking Cookbook. (Venture Guides Ser.). (Illus.). 1978. pap. 2.95 o.p. (ISBN 0-904978-90-7). Hippocrene Bks.

Hunter, Rob, jt. auth. see Brown, Terry.

Hunter, Robert H. Narrative of Robert Hancock Hunter, 1813-1902. LC 81-2938. 55p. 1982. lib. bdg. 10.95 (ISBN 0-86663-426-6); pap. text ed. 6.95 (ISBN 0-86663-401-0). Ide Hse.

Hunter, Robin. The Design & Construction of Compilers. (Wiley Series in Computing). 272p. 1982. 24.95x (ISBN 0-471-28054-2, Pub. by Wiley-Interscience); pap. write for info. (ISBN 0-471-09979-1). Wiley.

Hunter, S. C. Mechanics of Continuous Media. LC 76-7923. (Mathematics & Its Applications Ser.). 567p. 1977. text ed. 79.95 o.p. (ISBN 0-470-15092-0); pap. 34.95x o.p. (ISBN 0-470-27015-2). Halsted Pr.

Hunter, S. H., jt. ed. see Levandowsky, M.

Hunter, Sam. Arnaldo Pomodoro. LC 82-6826. (Illus.). 228p. 1983. 85.00 (ISBN 0-89659-227-8). Abbeville Pr.

--Twentieth Century Painting. (Abbeville Library of Art: No. 8). (Illus.). 112p. 1980. pap. 4.95 o.p. (ISBN 0-89659-123-9). Abbeville Pr.

Hunter, Sam & Jacobus, John. American Art of the Twentieth Century. (Illus.). 580p. 1974. text ed. 27.95 (ISBN 0-13-024075-3). P-H.

Hunter, Sam, jt. auth. see Carmean, E. A., Jr.

Hunter, Susan. A Family Guide to Amusement Centers: From Disneyland to Jungle Habitat. (Illus.). 1975. 9.95 o.s.i. (ISBN 0-8027-0451-4); pap. 5.95 o.s.i. (ISBN 0-8027-7092-4). Walker & Co.

Hunter, Thomas C. Beginnings: The Patterns of Success--Twenty-Four. LC 77-27831. (Illus.). 1978. 12.45i (ISBN 0-690-01687-5). T Y Crowell.

Hunter, Thomas O'D. Softly Walks the Beast. 208p. 1982. pap. 2.75 o.p. (ISBN 0-380-80903-6, 80903). Avon.

Hunter, W. F. & La Follette, P. Building Arithmetic Skills. (Learning Skills Ser: Arithmetic). 1969. 5.88 o.p. (ISBN 0-07-031312-1, W); tchr's manual for ser. 7.00 o.p. (ISBN 0-07-031315-6). McGraw.

--Learning Skills Series: Arithmetic. 1969. 5.88 o.p. (ISBN 0-07-031314-8, W); Tchr's Manual 7.00 o.p. (ISBN 0-07-031315-6). McGraw.

Hunter, W. F., et al. Acquiring Arithmetic Skills. 2nd ed. (gr. 8-12). 1976. 7.64 (ISBN 0-07-031321-0, W); tchr's manual for series 9.56 (ISBN 0-07-031325-3). McGraw.

--Building Arithmetic Skills. 2nd ed. (gr. 8-12). 1976. 7.64 (ISBN 0-07-031322-9, W); tchr's manual for series 9.56 (ISBN 0-07-031325-3). McGraw.

--Continuing Arithmetic Skills. 2nd ed. (gr. 8-12). 1976. 7.64 (ISBN 0-07-031323-7, W); tchr's manual for series 9.56 (ISBN 0-07-031325-3). McGraw.

--Directing Arithmetic Skills. 2nd ed. (gr. 8-12). 1976. 7.64 (ISBN 0-07-031324-5, W); tchr's manual for series 9.56 (ISBN 0-07-031325-3). McGraw.

Hunter, Wayne & Hunter, Emily. Como Ser un Joven Ideal (Para Alumno) Mariotti, Federico A., tr. Orig. Title: Man in Demand. (Span.). 1980. pap. 6.95 student ed., 80p. (ISBN 0-311-46074-7); pap. 7.50 teacher ed. 1981 (ISBN 0-311-46075-5). Casa Bautista.

Hunter, Wilbur H. Bodine's Baltimore. new ed. LC 72-133334. (Illus.). 160p. 1973. 16.95 o.p. (ISBN 0-910254-05-2). Bodine.

Hunter, William. CMOS Databook. (Illus.). 1978. 9.95 o.p. (ISBN 0-8306-7984-7); pap. 8.95 (ISBN 0-8306-6984-1, 984). TAB Bks.

Hunter, WIlliam B., Jr. Milton's Comus: Family Piece. 110p. 1983. 15.00 (ISBN 0-87875-257-9). Whitston Pub.

Hunter, William F., et al. Acquiring Language Skills. (Learning Skills Ser: Language Arts). (Illus.). (gr. 7-12). 1978. pap. text ed. 6.64 o.p. (ISBN 0-07-031331-8, W); tchr's manual for series 10.60 o.p. (ISBN 0-07-031335-0). McGraw.

--Continuing Language Skills. (Learning Skills Ser: Language Arts). (Illus.). 1978. pap. text ed. 6.64 (ISBN 0-07-031333-4, W); tchr's manual for series 10.60 (ISBN 0-07-031335-0). McGraw.

--Directing Language Skills. (Learning Skill Ser: Lanugage Arts). (Illus.). 1978. pap. text ed. 6.64 (ISBN 0-07-031334-2, W); tchr's manual for series 10.60 (ISBN 0-07-031335-0). McGraw.

--Building Language Skills. (Learning Skills Ser: Language Arts). (Illus.). (gr. 7-12). 1978. pap. text ed. 6.64 (ISBN 0-07-031332-6, W); tchr's manual for series 10.60 (ISBN 0-07-031335-0). McGraw.

Hunter-Jones, P. Laboratory Studies on the Inheritance of Phase Characters in Locusts. 1958. 35.00x (ISBN 0-85135-018-6, Pub. by Centre Overseas Research). State Mutual Bk.

Huntford, Roland. Scott & Amundsen: The Race to the South Pole. 1980. 19.95 o.p. (ISBN 0-399-11960-4). Putnam Pub Group.

Hunting, Anthony L. Encyclopedia of Shampoo Ingredients. LC 82-90176. 500p. (Orig.). 1983. pap. text ed. 75.00 (ISBN 0-9608752-0-4). Micelle Pr.

Hunting, Constance & Bisset, Virgil, eds. In a Dark Time. 1983. pap. 3.95 (ISBN 0-913006-28-9). Puckerbrush.

Hunting, Constance, ed. see Nason, Thelma C.

Hunting, Constance, ed. see Phippen, Sanford.

Hunting, Constance, ed. see Young, Douglas.

Hunting, Contance, ed. May Sarton: Woman & Poet. (Man & Poet Ser.). (Illus.). 344p. (Orig.). 1982. 25.00 (ISBN 0-915032-55-4); pap. 12.95 (ISBN 0-686-83122-5). Natl Poet Foun.

Hunting, Robert. Jonathan Swift. (English Authors Ser.). 1966. lib. bdg. 11.95 (ISBN 0-8057-1520-7, Twayne). G K Hall.

Huntingford, G. W. Northern Nilo-Hamites. LC 77-408451. 1968. 10.00x (ISBN 0-85302-032-9). Intl Pubns Serv.

--Southern Nilo-Hamites. LC 54-1745. (Illus., Orig.). 1970. pap. 11.50x (ISBN 0-8002-2009-9). Intl Pubns Serv.

Huntington, Ellsworth. The Geography of Europe: A Presentation of Some Aspects of European Geography for the Use of Members of the Students Army Training Corps. 1918. pap. 19.50x (ISBN 0-686-51392-4). Elliots Bks.

--Red Man's Continent. 1919. text ed. 8.50x (ISBN 0-686-83728-2). Elliots Bks.

--Season of Birth: Its Relation to Human Abilities. 1938. 29.50 (ISBN 0-686-51307-X). Elliots Bks.

--World Power & Evolution. 1919. text ed. 13.50x (ISBN 0-686-83862-9). Elliots Bks.

Huntington Free Library & Reading Room. Dictionary Catalog of the American Indian Collection. 1977. lib. bdg. 380.00 (ISBN 0-8161-0065-9, Hall Library). G K Hall.

Huntington, Harriet E. Let's Look at Dogs. LC 76-2783. (Illus.). 1980. 8.95 o.p. (ISBN 0-385-11053-7); PLB 8.95 (ISBN 0-385-11054-5). Doubleday.

Huntington, John. The Logic of Fantasy: H. G. Wells & Science Fiction. LC 82-4593. 192p. 1982. text ed. 22.50x (ISBN 0-231-05378-9). Columbia U Pr.

Huntington, Lee. Simple Shelters. LC 78-23712. (Illus.). (gr. 3-6). 1979. PLB 5.99 (ISBN 0-698-30690-2, Coward). Putnam Pub Group.

Huntington, Lee P. Americans at Home: Four Hundred Years of American Houses. (Illus.). (gr. 6 up). 1980. 9.95 (ISBN 0-698-20530-8, Coward). Putnam Pub Group.

--The Arctic & the Antarctic. (What Lives There Ser.). (Illus.). 48p. (gr. 2-6). 1975. 5.95 o.p. (ISBN 0-698-20322-4, Coward). Putnam Pub Group.

Huntington, R. & Metcalf, P. Celebrations of Death. LC 79-478. (Illus.). 1979. 32.50 (ISBN 0-521-22531-0); pap. 9.95x (ISBN 0-521-29540-8). Cambridge U Pr.

Huntington, Samuel P., ed. The Strategic Imperative: New Policies for American Security. LC 82-8722. 376p. 1982. Prof. Ref. 27.50x (ISBN 0-88410-895-3). Ballinger Pub.

Huntington, Whitney C. & Mickadeit, Robert E. Building Construction: Materials & Types of Construction. 5th ed. LC 79-24467. 471p. 1981. text ed. 27.95 (ISBN 0-471-05354-6). Wiley.

Huntington-Vigman, Frederick K. The Collapse of Western Civilization. LC 75-32058. 224p. 1976. 8.95 o.p. (ISBN 0-8158-0332-X). Chris Mass.

Huntley, B. & Birks, H. J. An Atlas of Past & Present Pollen Maps for Europe: 0-13000 B. P. LC 82-21613. 650p. Date not set. price not set (ISBN 0-521-23735-1). Cambridge U Pr.

Huntley, B. J. & Walker, B. H., eds. Ecology of Tropical Savannas. (Ecological Studies: Vol. 42). (Illus.). 669p. 1983. 49.00 (ISBN 0-387-11885-3). Springer-Verlag.

Huntley, Frank L., ed. see Browne, Thomas.

Huntley, G. Haydn, ed. see Love, Richard H.

Huntley, Stephen V. The Good Earth Notes. 59p. (Orig.). 1974. pap. text ed. 2.50 (ISBN 0-8220-0535-2). Cliffs.

Huntsberger, Paul E. Highland Mosaic: A Critical Anthology of Ethiopian Literature in English. LC 73-620219. (Papers in International Studies: Africa: No. 19). 1973. pap. 7.00x (ISBN 0-89680-052-0, Ohio U Ctr Intl). Ohio Ctr Pr.

Huntsman, Ann J. & Binger, Jane L. Communicating Effectively. LC 80-83694. (Nursing Management Anthologies). 220p. 1981. pap. text ed. 17.50 (ISBN 0-913654-67-1). Aspen Systems.

Hunt-Triol, Gene, jt. auth. see Mueller-Triol, Ingrid.

Hunzeker, Jeanne M., jt. auth. see Stone, Helen D.

Hunzicker-Dunn, Mary, jt. ed. see Schwartz, Neena B.

Hupkes, G., jt. ed. see Polak, J. B.

Huppe, Bernard F. Reading of the Canterbury Tales. LC 64-17577. 1964. 29.50x (ISBN 0-87395-011-9); pap. 7.95x (ISBN 0-87395-022-4). State U NY Pr.

--Web of Words. LC 70-91202. (Illus.). 1970. 39.50x (ISBN 0-87395-057-7); pap. 9.95x o.p. (ISBN 0-87395-063-1). State U NY Pr.

Huq, Muhammad S. Education, Manpower, & Development in South & Southeast Asia. LC 74-19336. (Special Studies). (Illus.). 240p. 1975. 18.95 o.p. (ISBN 0-275-09120-1). Praeger.

Huray, P. Le see Le Huray, Peter.

Hurd, Archibald S. German Sea-Power, Its Rise, Progress, & Economic Basis. LC 71-110846. (Illus.). xv, 388p. Repr. of 1913 ed. lib. bdg. 18.50x (ISBN 0-8371-4513-9, HUGS). Greenwood.

Hurd, Conrad & Hurd, Phyllis. Nasioi Language Course. 283p. 1966. pap. 1.00x (ISBN 0-88312-791-1); microfiche 3.75 (ISBN 0-88312-334-7). Summer Inst Ling.

Hurd, Edith. The Mother Kangaroo. (Illus.). (gr. 1-3). 1976. 6.95 (ISBN 0-316-38326-0). Little.

Hurd, Edith T. The Black Dog Who Went into the Woods. LC 79-2000. (Illus.). (gr. k-4). 1980. 8.61i (ISBN 0-06-022683-8, HarpJ); PLB 9.89 (ISBN 0-06-022684-6). Har-Row.

--Christmas Eve. LC 61-12074. (Illus.). (gr. k-3). 1962. 6.95 o.p. (ISBN 0-06-022670-6, HarpJ); PLB 12.89 o.p. (ISBN 0-06-022671-4). Har-Row.

--Come with Me to Nursery School. (Illus.). (ps-2). 1970. PLB 5.49 o.p. (ISBN 0-698-30050-5, Coward). Putnam.

--Hurry Hurry. LC 60-9453. (I Can Read Books). (Illus.). (gr. k-3). 1960. 7.64i o.p. (ISBN 0-06-022695-1, HarpJ); PLB 7.89 o.p. (ISBN 0-06-022696-X). Har-Row.

--Look for a Bird. LC 76-58726. (A Science I Can Read Bk.). (Illus.). (gr. k-3). 1977. 7.64i (ISBN 0-06-022719-2, HarpJ); PLB 8.89 o.p. (ISBN 0-06-022720-6). Har-Row.

--The Mother Owl. (Illus.). 32p. (gr. 1-3). 1974. 6.95 (ISBN 0-316-38325-2). Little.

--Starfish. LC 62-7742. (A Let's-Read-&-Find-Out Science Bk). (Illus.). (gr. k-2). 1962. PLB 10.89 (ISBN 0-690-77069-3, TYC-J). Har-Row.

Hurd, F. K., jt. auth. see Paris, D. T.

Hurd, Florence. Night Wind at Northriding. (Orig.). 1977. pap. 1.50 o.p. (ISBN 0-451-07626-5, W7626, Sig). NAL.

--Shadows of the Heart. 400p. 1980. pap. 2.50 o.p. (ISBN 0-380-76406-7, 76406). Avon.

Hurd, Frank J. & Hurd, Rosalie. Vegetarian Natural Foods Cookbook. 1968. spiral bdg. 9.95 (ISBN 0-9603532-0-8); 3 copies 6.65 ea.; 30 copies 6.45 ea.; 100 copies 5.45 ea.; 200 copies 5.25 ea.; looseleaf binder 5.95, 3 binders 4.50 ea. (ISBN 0-9603532-1-6); chart 3.95 (ISBN 0-9603532-2-4); 3 charts 2.50 ea. Ten Talents.

Hurd, John. Pyramid. 1977. 3.50 (ISBN 0-918116-05-8). Jawbone Pr.

Hurd, John, jt. auth. see Aufrecht, Walter E.

Hurd, John C., Jr. The Origin of One Corinthians. Rev. ed. 335p. 1982. lib. bdg. 21.95x (ISBN 0-86554-046-2). Mercer Univ Pr.

Hurd, Peter. Sketch Book. LC 70-150951. (Illus.). 121p. 1971. 60.00 o.p. (ISBN 0-8040-0531-1, SB). Swallow.

Hurd, Phyllis, jt. auth. see Hurd, Conrad.

Hurd, Rollin Carlos. A Treatise on the Right of Personal Liberty & on Writ of Habeas Corpus. LC 77-37767. (American Constitutional & Legal History Ser). 670p. 1972. Repr. of 1876 ed. lib. bdg. 75.00 (ISBN 0-306-70431-5). Da Capo.

Hurd, Rosalie, jt. auth. see Hurd, Frank J.

Hurd, Thacher. Axle the Freeway Cat. LC 80-8432. (Illus.). 32p. (gr. k-3). 1981. 9.13i (ISBN 0-06-022697-8, HarpJ); PLB 9.89 (ISBN 0-06-022698-6). Har-Row.

--Mystery on the Docks. LC 82-48261. (Illus.). 32p. (ps-3). 1983. 9.57i (ISBN 0-06-022701-X, HarpJ); PLB 9.89g. (ISBN 0-06-022702-8). Har-Row.

Hurdel, J. Frank. The Biofeedback Diet: A Doctor's Revolutionary Approach. 240p. 1977. 10.95 o.p. (ISBN 0-13-076539-2, Reward); pap. 3.95 (ISBN 0-13-076422-1). P-H.

Hurding, Roger F. Christian Care & Counseling: A Practical Guide. (Illus.). 128p. (Orig.). 1983. pap. 4.95 (ISBN 0-8192-1321-7). Morehouse.

Hurdle, V. F., jt. ed. see Hauer, E.

Hurdle, William R. Ecology Experienced. 265p. 1973. text ed. 15.00 (ISBN 0-686-37064-3). Trippensee Pub.

Hureau, Jean. Morocco Today. (J. A. Editions: Today). (Illus.). 240p. 1983. 14.95 (ISBN 0-88254-539-6, Pub. by J. A. Editions France). Hippocrene Bks.

Hurewitz, J. C. Middle East Politics: The Military Dimension. (Encore Edition Ser.). 550p. 1983. softcover 32.50x (ISBN 0-86531-546-9). Westview.

Hurewitz, J. C., ed. Oil, the Arab-Israel Dispute & the Industrial World: Horizons of Crisis. LC 76-6470. (Special Studies on the Middle East Ser). 1976. 20.00x o.p. (ISBN 0-89158-043-3); pap. 12.00 o.p. (ISBN 0-89158-105-7). Westview.

Hurford, J. R. The Linguistic Theory of Numerals. LC 74-25652. (Studies in Linguistics: No. 16). 260p. 1975. 44.50 (ISBN 0-521-20735-5). Cambridge U Pr.

Hurford, N. Observations from a Helicopter of Insoluble Substances Discharged into a Ship's Wake, 1980. 1981. 40.00x (ISBN 0-686-97126-4, Pub. by W Spring England). State Mutual Bk.

--Residue Assessment Trials on Coastal Chemical Tankers, 1980. 1981. 30.00x (ISBN 0-686-97154-X, Pub. by W Spring England). State Mutual Bk.

--A Review of the IMCO Standards for Procedures & Arrangements for the of Noxious Liquid Substances from Ships, 1980. 1981. 65.00x (ISBN 0-686-97160-4, Pub. by W Spring England). State Mutual Bk.

Hurh, Won M. & Kim, Hei C. Assimilation Patterns of Immigrants in the United States: A Case Study of Korean Immigrants in the Chicago Area. LC 78-59860. (Illus.). 1978. pap. text ed. 8.25 (ISBN 0-8191-0553-8). U Pr of Amer.

Hurlburt, Allen. The Grid. 96p. 1982. pap. 10.95 (ISBN 0-442-23966-1). Van Nos Reinhold.

Hurlbut, C. S., jt. auth. see Dana, E. S.

Hurlbut, Cornelius S., Jr. & Klein, Cornelis. Manual of Mineralogy After J. D. Dana. 19th ed. LC 77-1131. 1977. 34.50 (ISBN 0-471-42226-6). Wiley.

Hurlbut, Cornelius S., Jr. & Switzer, George S. Geomology. LC 78-13262. 1979. 35.95 (ISBN 0-471-42224-X, Pub. by Wiley-Interscience). Wiley

Hurlbutt, Catherine. Adventures with Talking Birds. (Illus.). 288p. 1981. 14.95 (ISBN 0-87666-895-3, H-1029). TFH Pubns.

Hurlbutt, Robert H., jt. auth. see Dewey, Robert E.

Hurley, Andrew, tr. see Padilla, Herberto.

Hurley, Edward N. The Bridge to France. LC 74-75241. (The United States in World War 1 Ser). (Illus.). xiii, 338p. 1974. Repr. of 1927 ed. lib. bdg. 20.95x (ISBN 0-89198-105-5). Ozer.

Hurley, F. Jack. Portrait of a Decade: Roy Stryker & the Development of Documentary Photography in the Thirties. LC 72-79331. (Illus.). 224p. 1972. 17.50x (ISBN 0-8071-0235-0). La State U Pr.

Hurley, Gale E. Personal Money Management. 2nd ed. (Illus.). 528p. 1981. text ed. 20.95 (ISBN 0-13-657544-7). P-H.

Hurley, George & Hurley, Suzanne. Ocean City: A Pictorial History. LC 79-15873. (Illus.). 1979. pap. 12.95 o.p. (ISBN 0-915442-98-1). Donning Co.

--Ocean City, A Pictorial History. 191p. 1979. pap. 12.95 (ISBN 0-686-36700-6). Md Hist.

Hurley, James P. & Garrod, Claude. Principles of Physics. LC 77-75475. (Illus.). 1978. text ed. 31.95 (ISBN 0-395-25036-6); solutions manual 0.40 (ISBN 0-395-25037-4). HM.

Hurley, Leslie, jt. auth. see Osgood, William.

Hurley, Lucille. Developmental Nutrition. (Illus.). 1979. text ed. 21.95 (ISBN 0-13-207639-X). P-H.

Hurley, Mark, ed. see Vatican Council Two.

Hurley, Patrick J. A Concise Introduction to Logic. 464p. 1982. text ed. 18.95x (ISBN 0-534-01120-9); study guide 6.95x (ISBN 0-534-01121-7). Wadsworth Pub.

Hurley, Patrick M. How Old Is the Earth? LC 78-25843. (Illus.). 1979 Repr. of 1959 ed. lib. bdg. 17.50x (ISBN 0-313-20776-3, HUHO). Greenwood.

Hurley, Randle. The Sinclair ZX-81, Programming for Real Applications. 166p. 1982. pap. 9.95 (ISBN 0-88056-090-8). Dilithium Pr.

Hurley, Robert, tr. see Huet, Marie-Helene.

Hurley, Suzanne, jt. auth. see Hurley, George.

Hurlimann, Martin see Roth, Ernst.

Hurlimann, Ruth. The Proud White Cat. (Illus.). (ps-3). 1977. 9.95 (ISBN 0-688-22095-9); PLB 9.55 (ISBN 0-688-32095-3). Morrow.

Hurll, Estelle M. Life of Our Lord in Art: With Some Account of the Artistic Treatment of the Life of St. John the Baptist. LC 76-89272. 1969 Repr. of 1898 ed. 31 00 o.p. (ISBN 0-8103-3137-3) Gale.

Hurlock, Elizabeth. Child Development. 6th ed. (McGraw-Hill Psychology Ser.). (Illus.). 1977. 25.00 (ISBN 0-07-031427-6, C); instr's manual 22.95 (ISBN 0-07-031428-4). McGraw.

Hurlock, Elizabeth B. Adolescent Development. 4th ed. 1973. text ed. 26.50 (ISBN 0-07-031457-8, C). McGraw.

--Child Growth & Development. 4th ed. (gr. 10-12). 1970. text ed. 19.98 (ISBN 0-07-031436-5, W). McGraw.

--Child Growth & Development. 5th ed. (Illus.). 1977. text ed. 19.36 (ISBN 0-07-031437-3, W). McGraw.

--Developmental Psychology: A Life-Span Approach. 5th, rev. ed. (Illus.). 1980. text ed. 25.00x (ISBN 0-07-031450-0); instr's manual 15.00 (ISBN 0-07-031451-9). McGraw.

--Personality Development. (Illus.). 520p. 1973. text ed. 24.00 (ISBN 0-07-031447-0, C). McGraw.

Hurlow, Janet. Psalms from the Hills of West Virginia. LC 81-68460. (Illus.). 144p. (Orig.). 1982. pap. 7.95 (ISBN 0-939680-02-5). Bear & Co.

Hurmence, Belinda. A Girl Called Boy. 180p. (gr. 3-6). 1982. 9.95 o.p. (ISBN 0-395-31022-9, Clarion). HM.

Hurn, Russ. Not for the Boys Only. LC 80-51432. 154p. 1980. 8.95 o.p. (ISBN 0-533-04695-5). Vantage.

Hurnard, Hannah. Eagle's Wings to Higher Places. LC 82-48406. 160p. 1983. pap. 4.76i (ISBN 0-686-99871-5, HarpR). Har-Row.

--Eagle's Wings to Higher Places. 160p. 1983. pap. 4.95 (ISBN 0-686-84426-2, HarpJ). Har-Row.

--Hearing Heart. 1975. pap. 2.50 (ISBN 0-8423-1405-9). Tyndale.

--Kingdom of Love. 1975. pap. 2.50 (ISBN 0-8423-2080-6). Tyndale.

--Walking Among the Unseen. 1977. pap. 2.95 (ISBN 0-8423-7805-7). Tyndale.

--Wayfarer in the Land. 1975. pap. 2.95 (ISBN 0-8423-7823-5). Tyndale.

--Winged Life. 1975. pap. 3.50 (ISBN 0-8423-8225-9). Tyndale.

Hurok, Solomon & Goode, Ruth. Impresario: A Memoir. LC 75-8838. (Illus.). 1975. Repr. of 1946 ed. lib. bdg. 20.50x (ISBN 0-8371-8125-9, HUIM). Greenwood.

Hurov, L. Handbook of Veterinary Surgical Instruments & Glossary of Surgical Terms. LC 77-78572. (Illus.). 1978. text ed. 19.50 o.p. (ISBN 0-7216-4848-7). Saunders.

Hurry, David J., jt. auth. see Charles, David.

Hurry, Jamieson B. Woad Plant & Its Dye. LC 70-132019. (Illus.). Repr. of 1930 ed. 25.00x (ISBN 0-678-00779-9). Kelley.

Hursch-Cesar, Gerald, jt. auth. see Backstrom, Charles H.

Hurshell, Jennifer. Portland Epicure. (Epicure Ser.). (Orig.). 1982. pap. 5.95 (ISBN 0-89716-094-0). Peanut Butter.

Hurshell, Jennifer, ed. Aspen Epicure. (Epicure Ser.). 1982. pap. 2.95 (ISBN 0-89716-116-5). Peanut Butter.

--Portland Epicure 1982-83. (Epicure Ser.). 112p. 1982. pap. 5.95 (ISBN 0-89716-094-0). Peanut Butter.

Hurst, Alan. Hardy: An Illustrated Dictionary. (Illus.). 216p. 1980. 15.95 o.p. (ISBN 0-312-36220-X). St Martin.

Hurst, C. V. & Bray, F. E., eds. Russian & Japanese Prize Cases. LC 72-76352. (International Military Law & History Ser.: Vols. 6 & 7). 1972. Repr. of 1913 ed. Vol. 6, 382 Pgs. lib. bdg. 30.00 (ISBN 0-930342-43-7); Vol. 7, 476 Pgs. text ed. 30.00 (ISBN 0-930342-44-5). W S Hein.

Hurst, H. Norman. Four Elements in Literature. 192p. 1982. Repr. of 1936 ed. lib. bdg. 35.00 (ISBN 0-89984-917-2). Century Bookbindery.

Hurst, Hugo. A Search for Meaning in Love, Sex, & Marriage. rev. ed. LC 75-9961. 232p. (gr. 11-12). 1975. pap. text ed. 4.95x (ISBN 0-88489-063-5); tchr's ed. 2.50x (ISBN 0-88489-119-4). St. Marys.

Hurst, J. G., jt. auth. see Beresford, M.

Hurst, J. W. Update III: The Heart. (Illus.). 288p. 1980. text ed. 32.00 (ISBN 0-07-031492-6, HP). McGraw.

Hurst, J. W., ed. The Heart. 4th ed. (Illus.). 1978. text ed. 60.00 1 vol. ed. (ISBN 0-07-031472-1, HP); text ed. 73.00 2 vol. ed. (ISBN 0-07-031473-X); commemorator ed. 125.00 (ISBN 0-07-031474-8). McGraw.

Hurst, J. Willard. Law & the Conditions of Freedom in the Nineteenth-Century United States. 150p. 1956. pap. 7.95 (ISBN 0-299-01363-4). U of Wis Pr.

Hurst, J. Willis. Medicine for Practicing Physian. new ed. 2000p. 1983. text ed. 40.00 (ISBN 0-409-95031-9). Butterworth.

--Update II: The Heart. (Illus.). 1979. text ed. 32.00 (ISBN 0-07-031491-8). McGraw.

--Update IV: The Heart. (Updates Ser.). (Illus.). 224p. 1980. text ed. 32.00 (ISBN 0-07-031493-4, HP). McGraw.

--Update V: The Heart. (Illus.). 304p. 1981. text ed. 32.00 (ISBN 0-07-031495-0, HP). McGraw.

Hurst, J. Willis & Hurst, John W., Jr. The Heart Self-Assessment & Review with CME. (Illus.). 270p. (Orig.). 1980. 75.00 o.p. (ISBN 0-07-079066-3, HP). McGraw.

--Self-Assessment & Review of the Heart. 1978. pap. text ed. 13.95 (ISBN 0-07-031475-6, HP). McGraw.

Hurst, J. Willis & Myerburg, Robert J. Introduction to Electrocardiography. 2nd ed. (Illus.). 336p. 1973. pap. text ed. 19.95 (ISBN 0-07-031464-0, HP). McGraw.

Hurst, J. Willis & Walker, H. Kenneth. Problem-Oriented System. 302p. 1972. 18.00 (ISBN 0-686-74092-0). Krieger.

Hurst, J. Willis, ed. Update I: The Heart. 1979. text ed. 32.00 (ISBN 0-07-031490-X, HP). McGraw.

Hurst, J. Willis, et al. The Heart. 5th ed. (Illus.). 352p. 1982. 80.00 (ISBN 0-07-031481-0). McGraw.

--The Heart, 2 vol. ed. 5th ed. 2120p. 1982. Set. 82.00 (ISBN 0-07-031482-9); Vol. 1. write for info. (ISBN 0-07-031483-7); Vol.2. write for info. (ISBN 0-07-031484-5). McGraw.

Hurst, James C., jt. ed. see Morrill, Weston H.

Hurst, James W. The Growth of American Law: The Law Makers. 1950. 15.00 o.p. (ISBN 0-316-38357-0). Little.

--Law & Social Process in United States History. LC 74-173669. (American Constitutional & Legal History Ser.). 359p. 1971. Repr. of 1960 ed. lib. bdg. 42.50 (ISBN 0-306-70409-9). Da Capo.

--Law of Treason in the United States: Collected Essays. (Contributions in American History: No. 12). 1971. lib. bdg. 29.95 (ISBN 0-8371-4666-6, HLT/). Greenwood.

Hurst, John W., Jr., jt. auth. see Hurst, J. Willis.

Hurst, Leonard L., jt. auth. see Giebink, Gerald A.

Hurst, Walter E. The Movie Industry Book, Part II. Rico, Don & Kargodorian, Annette, eds. (The Entertainment Industry Ser.: Vol. 23). (Illus.). 112p. (Orig.). 1982. 20.00 (ISBN 0-911370-56-0); pap. 10.00 (ISBN 0-911370-55-2). Seven Arts.

--The Music Industry Book: Protect Yourself Before You Lose Your Rights & Royalties! Kargodorian, Annette, ed. (The Entertainment Industry Ser.: Vol. 2). (Illus.). 100p. 1981. 15.00 (ISBN 0-911370-52-8); pap. 10.00 (ISBN 0-686-96886-7). Seven Arts.

Hurst, Walter E., jt. auth. see Delson, Donn.

Hurst, William. Advances in Petroleum Engineering. 382p. 1981. 45.95x (ISBN 0-87814-147-2). Pennwell Book Division.

--Reservoir Engineering & Conformal Mapping of Oil & Gas Fields. 124p. 1979. 43.95x (ISBN 0-87814-095-6). Pennwell Pub.

Hurstfield, J., jt. ed. see Sutherland, James R.

Hurstfield, Joel, ed. The Reformation Crisis. 1966. pap. 3.45xi o.p. (ISBN 0-06-131267-3, TB1267, Torch). Har-Row.

--The Tudors. LC 73-82823. 224p. 1973. 22.50 (ISBN 0-312-82320-7). St Martin.

Hurston, Zora N. Tell My Horse. (New World Writing Ser). (Illus.). 296p. 1981. 17.95 o.p. (ISBN 0-913666-31-9); pap. 8.95 (ISBN 0-686-96902-2). Turtle Isl Foun.

Hurt, H. H., Jr. Aerodynamics for Naval Aviators. (Illus.). 1965. pap. 12.95 (ISBN 0-939158-00-0, Pub. by Flightshop). Aviation.

Hurt, J. Focus on Film & Theatre. 1974. pap. 2.95 o.p. (ISBN 0-13-314658-8, Spec). P-H.

Hurt, James. Aelfric. (English Authors Ser.: No. 131). lib. bdg. 7.95 o.p. (ISBN 0-8057-1004-3, Twayne). G K Hall.

--Catiline's Dream: An Essay on Ibsen's Plays. LC 79-186346. 224p. 1972. 14.50 o.p. (ISBN 0-252-00238-5). U of Ill Pr.

Hurt, James, jt. auth. see Beckett, Royce.

Hurt, R. Douglas. American Farm Tools: From Hand Power to Steam Power. 1982. 20.00x (ISBN 0-89745-027-2); pap. 9.95x (ISBN 0-89745-026-4). Sunflower U Pr.

Hurt, Wesley R. Sioux Indians, Vol. Two: Dakota Sioux Indians. (American Indian Ethnohistory Ser: Plains Indians). (Illus.). lib. bdg. 42.00 o.s.i. (ISBN 0-8240-0795-6). Garland Pub.

Hurt, William C. Current Therapy in Dentistry, Vol. 7. LC 78-31587. (Current Therapy Ser.). 1980. text ed. 54.50 (ISBN 0-8016-1189-X). Mosby.

Hurt, Zuelia A. Country Samplers. LC 82-60542. (Illus.). 128p. 1983. 17.26i (ISBN 0-8487-0520-3). Oxmoor Hse.

Hurtado, Mario, jt. auth. see Rivera, Francisco P.

Hurtik, Emil. Insight: A Rhetoric Reader. 3rd ed. 1976. pap. text ed. 11.50 scp (ISBN 0-397-47353-2, HarpC); instr's. manual avail. (ISBN 0-06-379314-8). Har-Row.

Hurtik, Emil & Yarber, Robert, eds. An Introduction to Short Fiction & Criticism. LC 73-138096. (Orig.). 1971. pap. text ed. 17.95x (ISBN 0-673-15681-8). Scott F.

Hurty, Walter C. & Rubinstein, M. F. Dynamics of Structures. (Illus.). 1964. 34.95 (ISBN 0-13-222075-X). P-H.

Hurvich, Leo M. Color Vision. LC 80-19077. (Illus.). 280p. 1981. text ed. 42.50x (ISBN 0-87893-336-0); pap. text ed. 29.95x (ISBN 0-87893-337-9). Sinauer Assoc.

Hurvitz, David, jt. ed. see Gay, Tim.

Hurwicz, L., jt. ed. see Arrow, K. J.

Hurwicz, Leonid, ed. see Schmookler, Jacob.

Hurwitz, Abraham B., et al. More Number Games: Mathematics Made Easy Through Play. LC 74-23849. (Funk & W Bk.). (gr. 5 up). 1977. 9.95i (ISBN 0-308-10255-X, TYC-T). T Y Crowell.

Hurwitz, Al & Madeja, Stanley. The Joyous Vision: A Sourcebook for Elementary Art Appreciation. (Illus.). 320p. 1977. text ed. 20.95 (ISBN 0-13-511600-7). P-H.

Hurwitz, Johanna. Aldo Applesauce. LC 79-16200. (Illus.). 128p. (gr. 4-6). 1979. 9.25 (ISBN 0-688-22199-8); PLB 8.88 (ISBN 0-688-32199-2). Morrow.

--Aldo Ice Cream. (Illus.). (gr. 3-5). 1982. pap. 1.75 (ISBN 0-671-43940-5). Archway.

--Aldo Ice Cream. LC 80-24371. (Illus.). 128p. (gr. 4-6). 1981. 7.95 (ISBN 0-688-00375-3); PLB 7.63 (ISBN 0-688-00376-1). Morrow.

--Baseball Fever. (gr. k-6). 1983. pap. 2.25 (ISBN 0-440-40311-1, YB). Dell.

--Busybody Nora. (gr. 3 up). 1977. pap. 1.50 (ISBN 0-440-41019-3, YB). Dell.

--Busybody Nora. LC 75-25921. (Illus.). 64p. (gr. 1-5). 1976. PLB 7.63 (ISBN 0-688-32057-0). Morrow.

--The Law of Gravity. LC 77-13656. (Illus.). (gr. 3-7). 1978. 7.50 o.p. (ISBN 0-688-22142-4); PLB 9.36 (ISBN 0-688-32142-9). Morrow.

--Much Ado About Aldo. (Illus.). (gr. 4-6). 1978. 9.75 (ISBN 0-688-22160-2); PLB 9.36 (ISBN 0-688-32160-7). Morrow.

--New Neighbors for Nora. LC 78-12631. (Illus.). (gr. k-3). 1979. 8.25 (ISBN 0-688-22173-4); PLB 7.92 (ISBN 0-688-32173-9). Morrow.

--Once I Was a Plum Tree. LC 79-23518. (Illus.). 160p. (gr. 4-6). 1980. 9.25 (ISBN 0-688-22223-4); PLB 8.88 (ISBN 0-688-32223-9). Morrow.

--Superduper Teddy. LC 80-12962. (Illus.). 80p. (gr. k-3). 1980. 8.75 (ISBN 0-688-22234-X); PLB 8.40 (ISBN 0-688-32234-4). Morrow.

Hurwitz, Ken, jt. auth. see Bugliosi, Vincent.

Hurwitz, Leon, ed. Contemporary Perspectives on European Integration: Attitudes, Nongovernmental Behavior & Collective Decision Making. LC 79-6573. (Contributions in Political Science: No. 45). (Illus.). xx, 292p. 1980. lib. bdg. 29.95 (ISBN 0-313-21357-7, HEI/). Greenwood.

Hurwitz, Sidney. Clinical Pediatric Dermatology. (Illus.). 656p. 1980. 79.00 (ISBN 0-7216-4872-X). Saunders.

Hurwood, Bernardt. My Savage Muse: The Story of My Life - Edgar A. Poe. LC 79-51196. 1980. 11.95 o.p. (ISBN 0-89696-058-7, An Everest House Book). Dodd.

Hurwood, Bernhardt J. Vampires. (Illus.). 160p. 1981. pap. 7.95 (ISBN 0-8256-3202-1, Quick Fox). Putnam Pub Group.

Hurzeler, Johannes. Contribution a L'odontologie et a la Phylogenese du Genre Pliopithecus Gervais. Bd. with Die Primatenfunde aus der miozanen Spaltenfullung von neudorf an der March, Devin ska Nova Ves, Tschechoslowakei. Zapfe, Helmuth. 1961. LC 78-72721. 1954. 79.50 (ISBN 0-404-18296-8). AMS Pr.

Husain, Ashfaq. Electral Power System. (Illus.). 400p. 1982. text ed. 35.00x (ISBN 0-7069-1765-0, Pub. by Vikas India). Advent NY.

Husain, M. Crop Combinations in India. 200p. 1982. text ed. 19.50x (ISBN 0-391-02754-9, Pub. by Concept India). Humanities.

Husain, Majid. Agricultural Geography. (Illus.). 1980. text ed. 18.25x (ISBN 0-391-01931-7). Humanities.

Husain, S. A. The Book of Thousand Lights. 5.95 (ISBN 0-686-18591-9). Kazi Pubns.

--Glorious Caliphate. 9.50 (ISBN 0-686-18626-5). Kazi Pubns.

Husain, S. S. Implications in Indian Agriculture. Date not set. text ed. price not set (ISBN 0-391-01836-1). Humanities.

Husain, Syed Arshad & Vandiver, Trish. Suicide in Children & Adolescents. 192p. 1983. text ed. 20.00 (ISBN 0-89335-190-3). SP Med & Sci Bks.

Husain, Syed H., ed. see Forster, E. M.

Husaini, S. A. Q. The Constitution of the Arab Empire. 8.00 (ISBN 0-686-18334-7). Kazi Pubns.

Husak, G. & Pahre, P. The Money Series, 11 bks. Incl. Banking. 25p. pap. text ed. 2.00 (ISBN 0-910839-18-2); Buying a House. 32p. pap. text ed. 2.00 (ISBN 0-910839-20-4); Buying Furniture for Your Home. 46p. pap. text ed. 3.00 (ISBN 0-910839-13-1); Finding a Place to Live. 28p. pap. text ed. 2.50 (ISBN 0-910839-14-X); How to Borrow Money. 39p. pap. text ed. 2.50 (ISBN 0-910839-17-4); How to Budget Your Money. 23p. pap. text ed. 2.50 (ISBN 0-910839-16-6); How to Buy Clothes. 44p. pap. text ed. 3.00 (ISBN 0-910839-12-3); How to Buy Food. 40p. pap. text ed. 3.00 (ISBN 0-910839-11-5); Insurance. 40p. pap. text ed. 2.00 (ISBN 0-910839-19-0); Where to Get Medical Help. 33p. pap. text ed. 2.50 (ISBN 0-910839-15-8). (Illus.). 28p. (gr. 7-12). 1977. tchrs' ed. 2.00 (ISBN 0-910839-21-2). Hopewell.

--The Work Series, 9 pts. Incl. Getting to Work. 55p. pap. text ed. 3.00 (ISBN 0-910839-05-0); How I Should Act at Work. 71p. pap. text ed. 3.00 (ISBN 0-910839-08-5); How to Find a Job. 60p. pap. text ed. 3.00 (ISBN 0-910839-07-7); Job Training Centers. 51p. pap. 3.00 (ISBN 0-910839-06-9); Payroll Deductions & Company Benefits. 27p. pap. text ed. 1.75 (ISBN 0-910839-02-6); Taxes. 22p. pap. 1.75 (ISBN 0-910839-04-2); Where to Get Help. 26p. pap. text ed. 1.75 (ISBN 0-910839-03-4); Work Rules. 63p. pap. text ed. 3.00 (ISBN 0-910839-01-8). (Illus.). (gr. 7-12). 1976. tchrs' ed. 2.00 (ISBN 0-910839-09-3). Hopewell.

Husak, Glen. How to Buy & Use Medicine. (The Health Ser.). (Illus.). 45p. (gr. 7-12). 1981. pap. text ed. 3.00 (ISBN 0-910839-24-7). Hopewell.

Husband, Janet. Sequels. 368p. 1982. text ed. 22.50 (ISBN 0-8389-0368-1). ALA.

Husband, Timothy & Gilmore-House, Gloria. The Wild Man: Medieval Myth & Symbolism. Shakely, Lauren, ed. LC 80-24082. (Illus.). xii, 220p. 1980. 25.00 o.s.i. (ISBN 0-87099-254-6); pap. 14.95 o.s.i. (ISBN 0-87099-255-4). Metro Mus Art.

Husbands, Charles, ed. see ASIS Annual Meeting 38th.

Husch, Bertram, et al. Forest Mensuration. 2nd ed. (Illus.). 1972. 26.95x o.p. (ISBN 0-471-06834-9). Wiley.

--Forest Mensuration. 3rd ed. LC 82-4811. 402p. 1982. text ed. 27.95 (ISBN 0-471-04423-7). Wiley.

Huse, Edgar F. Management. 2nd ed. (West Series in Management). (Illus.). 689p. 1982. text ed. 25.95 (ISBN 0-314-63256-5). West Pub.

--Organization Development & Change. LC 75-631. 448p. 1975. text ed. 18.95 o.s.i. (ISBN 0-8299-0046-2). West Pub.

--Organization Development & Change. 2nd ed. (West Series in Management Ser.). (Illus.). 500p. 1980. text ed. 23.95 (ISBN 0-8299-0300-3). West Pub.

Huse, Edgar F. & Bowditch, James L. Behavior in Organizations: A Systems Approach to Managing. 2nd ed. LC 76-9329. (Illus.). 1977. text ed. 25.95 (ISBN 0-201-02965-0). A-W.

Huse, Nancy L. The Survival Tales of John Hersey. LC 82-50825. 220p. 1983. 18.50X (ISBN 0-87875-238-2). Whitston Pub.

Huseboe, Arthur R. Sir John Vanbrugh. (English Authors Ser). 1976. lib. bdg. 14.95 (ISBN 0-8057-6665-0). G K Hall.

Huseby, Edward, jt. auth. see Hestwood, Diana.

Husemann, Friedrich, et al. The Anthroposophical Approach to Medicine, Vol. 1. (Illus.). 411p. 1983. 30.00 (ISBN 0-88010-031-1). Anthroposophic.

Husemoller, D. Fibre Bundles. 2nd ed. LC 74-23157. (Graduate Texts in Mathematics: Vol. 20). (Illus.). 340p. 1975. Repr. of 1966 ed. 29.80 (ISBN 0-387-90103-5). Springer-Verlag.

Husen, T. An Incurable Academic: Memoirs of a Professor. (Illus.). 138p. 1983. 30.00 (ISBN 0-08-027925-2). Pergamon.

Husen, Torsten & Saha, Lawrence J. Teacher Training & Student Achievement in Less Developed Countries. (Working Paper: No. 310). ii, 133p. 1978. 5.00 (ISBN 0-686-36043-5, WP-0310). World Bank.

Husen, Torsten, ed. International Study of Achievement in Mathematics, Vol. 1 & 2. (Orig.). 1967. 10.95 ea. o.p. (Pub. by Wiley Heyden). Vol. 1, 304 Pgs. Vol. 2, 368 Pgs. Wiley.

Hu Shih. My Mother's Betrothal. Rouse, Mary, ed. 3.25 (ISBN 0-686-15213-1). Far Eastern Pubns.

Husinger, Margorie & McComas, Donna C. Modern Business Correspondence. 4th ed. (Illus.). 1979. pap. text ed. 14.35 (ISBN 0-07-031275-3, G); instr's guide & key 8.40 (ISBN 0-07-031276-1). McGraw.

Huskins, David. Quality Measuring Instruments in On Line Process Analysis. 455p. 1982. 102.95X (ISBN 0-470-27521-9). Halsted Pr.

Huskisson, E. C. & Katona, G., eds. New Trends in Osteoarthritis: Internationales Symposium, Monte Carlo, Oktober 1981. (Illus.). viii, 212p. (Ger.). 1982. pap. cancelled (ISBN 3-8055-3565-1). S Karger.

Huson, F. R., jt. ed. see Carrigan, R. A., Jr.

Huson, Paul. Mastering Herbalism. LC 73-90704. 1975. pap. 10.95 (ISBN 0-8128-1847-4). Stein & Day.

Husry, Khaldun S. al see Al-Husry, Khaldun S.

Huss, Roy & Silverstein, Norman. Film Experience. 1969. pap. 6.95 (ISBN 0-440-52547-0, Delta). Dell.

Huss, Wayne D. Van see Van Huss, Wayne D., et al.

Hussain, jt. auth. see Feutchwant.

Hussain, Asaf. Islamic Movements in Egypt, Pakistan & Iran: An Annotated Bibliography. 192p. 1982. 32.00 (ISBN 0-7201-1648-1, Pub. by Mansell England). Wilson.

Hussain, F. Wives of the Prophet. 5.95 (ISBN 0-686-18463-7). Kazi Pubns.

Hussain, M. N. Islam vs, Socialism. pap. 5.50 (ISBN 0-686-18569-2). Kazi Pubns.

Husseiny. Icebergs. 350p. 1982. text ed. write for info. (ISBN 0-08-023911-0). Pergamon.

Husselbee, William. Automatic Transmission Service: A Text-Workbook. (Orig.). 1981. pap. 12.95 (ISBN 0-8359-0266-8). Reston.

--Automotive Tune up Procedures. 1982. pap. text ed. 26.95 (ISBN 0-8359-0295-1); instrs'. manual avail. (ISBN 0-8359-0296-X). Reston.

Husselbee, William K. Automatic Transmission Fundamentals. (Illus.). 1980. text ed. 19.95 (ISBN 0-8359-0257-9). Reston.

Husselman, E. M., ed. see Kammerer, W.

Husselman, Elinor. Karanis Excavations of the University of Michigan in Egypt, 1928-1935: Topography & Architecture. LC 79-16072. (Kelsey Museum of Archaeology Studies: No. 5). (Illus., Orig.). 1979. pap. 24.50 (ISBN 0-472-02713-1, IS-00085, Pub. by U of Mich Pr). Univ Microfilms.

Husserl, E. Studien zur Arithmetik und Geometrie. 1983. 91.50 (ISBN 90-247-2497-X, Pub. by Martinus Nijhoff Netherlands). Kluwer Boston.

Hussey, D. E., ed. The Truth About Corporate Planning: International Research into the Practice of Planning. (Illus.). 388p. 1983. 35.00 (ISBN 0-08-025833-6). Pergamon.

Hussey, David. Corporate Planning: Theory & Practice. 2nd ed. 468p. 35.00 (ISBN 0-686-84784-9). Work in Amer.

Hussey, David & Langham, M. J. Corporate Planning: The Human Factor. 1979. text ed. 48.00 (ISBN 0-08-022464-4); pap. text ed. 19.50 (ISBN 0-08-022475-X). Pergamon.

Hussey, David, ed. The Corporate Planners' Yearbook 1978-9. (Illus.). 1978. text ed. 39.00 (ISBN 0-08-022255-2). Pergamon.

Hussey, David E. Introducing Corporate Planning. 220p. 1973. text ed. 7.15 o.p. (ISBN 0-08-017793-X). Pergamon.

Hussey, Dyneley. Wolfgang Amadeus Mozart. LC 70-104288. (Illus.). 1971. Repr. of 1928 ed. lib. bdg. 17.75x (ISBN 0-8371-3957-0, HUWM). Greenwood.

Hussey, Harry. Venerable Ancestor: The Life & Times of Tz'u Hsi, 1835-1908, Empress of China. Repr. of 1949 ed. lib. bdg. 18.25x (ISBN 0-8371-4430-2, HUVA). Greenwood.

Hussey, M., ed. see Chaucer, Geoffrey.

Hussey, Maurice, et al, eds. see Chaucer, Geoffrey.

Hussey, S. The Literary Language of Shakespeare. LC 81-20889. 208p. (Orig.). 1982. pap. text ed. 10.95x (ISBN 0-582-49228-9). Longman.

Hussey, W. D. British Empire & Commonwealth, Fifteen Hundred to Nineteen Sixty-One. 1963. text ed. 13.95x (ISBN 0-521-05351-X). Cambridge U Pr.

--British History, Eighteen Fifteen to Nineteen Thirty-Nine. LC 79-149429. (Illus.). 1972. 13.95 (ISBN 0-521-07985-3). Cambridge U Pr.

Hussman, Lawrence E. Dreiser & His Fiction: A Twentieth-Century Quest. LC 82-40493. 224p. 1983. 22.50x (ISBN 0-8122-7875-5). U of Pa Pr.

Husson, Armand. Les Consommations de Paris. (Conditions of the 19th Century French Working Class Ser.). 531p. (Fr.). 1974. Repr. of 1856 ed. lib. bdg. 131.00 o.p. (ISBN 0-8287-0456-2, 1065). Clearwater Pub.

Hustad, Donald P. & Shorney, George H, Jr. Dictionary-Handbook to Hymns for the Living Church. LC 77-75916. 1978. 14.95 (ISBN 0-916642-09-7). Hope Pub.

Husted, Darrell. Stage Daughter. LC 81-43414. (Starlight Romance Ser.). 192p. 1982. 11.95 (ISBN 0-385-17629-5). Doubleday.

Husted, Virginia M., jt. auth. see Foreman, Kenneth E.

Hustedt, F. Die Diatomeenflora des Fluss-Systems der Weser im Gebiet der Hansestadt Bremen. 1976. pap. text ed. 40.00x (ISBN 3-87429-102-2). Lubrecht & Cramer.

Hustedt, Friedrich. Bacillariophyta: Diatomeae. (Suesswasserflora Mitteleuropas Ser.: Vol. 10). (Illus.). 466p. (Ger.). 1976. 55.20x (ISBN 3-87429-111-1). Lubrecht & Cramer.

--Die Kieselalgen, 3 vols. (Rabenhorst's Kryptogamenflora Deutschlands Etc.: Vol. 7, 1-3). 1977. Repr. of 1927 ed. Set. lib. bdg. 268.80x (ISBN 3-87429-115-4). Lubrecht & Cramer.

--Suesswasser-Diatomeen des indo-Malayischen Archipels und der Hawaii-Inseln. (Ger.). 1979. Repr. of 1942 ed. lib. bdg. 64.00x (ISBN 3-87429-162-6). Lubrecht & Cramer.

--Systematische und Oekologische Untersuchungen ueber die Diatomeenflora von Java, Bali und Sumatra. (Illus.). 709p. 1980. Repr. lib. bdg. 184.00x (ISBN 0-686-34414-6). Lubrecht & Cramer.

Huston, Harvey. The Right of Appropriation & the Colorado System of Laws in Regard to Irrigation. 334p. 1983. Repr. of 1893 ed. lib. bdg. 27.50x (ISBN 0-8377-0649-1). Rothman.

--The Roddis Line. LC 78-184838. (Illus.). 1972. 12.00 (ISBN 0-9600048-2-3). Huston.

--Thunder Lake Narrow Gauge. 2nd, rev. ed. Andrews, Ondre H. & Huston, Ondre N., eds. LC 82-82291. 168p. pap. 14.50 (ISBN 0-9600048-3-1). Huston.

Huston, Ondre N., ed. see Huston, Harvey.

Hustrulid, William A., jt. ed. see Crawford, John T., III.

Hustrulid, William A., ed. see Rapid Excavation & Tunneling Conference, 1979.

Hustrulid, William H., ed. Underground Mining Methods Handbook. LC 80-70416. (Illus.). 1754p. 1982. 120.00x (ISBN 0-89520-049-X). Soc Mining Eng.

Hustuedt, Sigurd B., tr. see Munch, Peter A. & Olsen, Magnus.

Hustvedt, Siri. Reading to You. 32p. (Orig.). 1983. pap. 3.95 (ISBN 0-940170-12-4). Open Bk Pubns.

--Reading to You. 32p. (Orig.). 1983. pap. 3.95 (ISBN 0-940170-12-4). Station Hill Pr.

Hutch, Richard A. Emerson's Optics: Biographical Process & the Dawn of Religious Leadership. 380p. (Orig.). 1983. lib. bdg. 27.25 (ISBN 0-8191-3005-2); pap. text ed. 15.75 (ISBN 0-8191-3006-0). U Pr of Amer.

Hutchenson, Richard G., Jr. The Churches & the Chaplaincy. LC 74-19970. 160p. (Orig.). 1975. 3.75 (ISBN 0-8042-1575-8). John Knox.

Hutcheon, Linda. Narcissistic Narrative: The Metafictional Paradox, Vol. 5. Dimic, Milan V., ed. (Library of the Canadian Review of Comparative Literature). 168p. 1980. text ed. 11.25x (ISBN 0-88920-102-1, Pub. by Wilfrid Laurier U Pr Canada). Humanities.

Hutcheson, Francis. Essay on the Nature & Conduct of the Passions & Affections, 1742. 3rd ed. LC 76-81361. (History of Psychology Ser). 1969. Repr. of 1742 ed. 43.00x (ISBN 0-8201-1058-2). Schol Facsimiles.

Hutcheson, Francis see McReynolds, Paul.

Hutcheson, Harold. Tench Coxe: A Study in American Economic Development. LC 77-98690. (American Scene Ser.). 1969. Repr. of 1938 ed. lib. bdg. 32.50 (ISBN 0-306-71511-2). Da Capo.

Hutcheson, John D., Jr. & Shevin, Jann. Citizen Groups in Local Politics: A Bibliographic Review. LC 76-23441. 275p. 1976. text ed. 32.50 o.p. (ISBN 0-87436-231-8). ABC-Clio.

Hutcheson, Richard G., Jr. Wheel Within the Wheel. LC 79-11481. 1979. 6.00 (ISBN 0-8042-1886-2). John Knox.

Hutchesson, P. G., jt. auth. see Wraith, R. E.

Hutchieson, J. C. Fugitive Poetry 1600-1878. 592p. 1982. Repr. of 1878 ed. lib. bdg. 45.00 (ISBN 0-89984-913-X). Century Bookbindery.

Hutchings, jt. auth. see Feirer.

Hutchings, A. Church Music in the Nineteenth Century. (Illus.). 166p. 1967. 22.00 o.s.i. (ISBN 90-6027-266-8, Pub. by Frits Knuf Netherlands). Pendragon NY.

Hutchings, Alan E., jt. ed. see Russell, Philip A.

Hutchings, Arthur. Church Music in the Nineteenth Century. (Studies in Church Music). 1977. Repr. of 1967 ed. lib. bdg. 17.50x (ISBN 0-8371-9695-7, HUCMN). Greenwood.

--Purcell. LC 81-71304. (BBC Music Guides Ser.). 87p. (Orig.). 1983. pap. 5.95 (ISBN 0-295-95927-4). U of Wash Pr.

Hutchings, Bill, ed. see Marvell, Andrew.

Hutchings, David. Edison at Work: The Thomas A. Edison Laboratory at West Orange, N.J. LC 78-98058. (Famous Museum Ser). (Illus.). (gr. 6-9). 1969. PLB 6.95 o.s.i. (ISBN 0-8038-1893-9). Hastings.

Hutchings, F. R. & Unterweiser, P. M. Failure Analysis: The British Engine Technical Reports. 1981. 92.00 (ISBN 0-87170-116-2). ASM.

Hutchings, Margaret. Button-Box Book. (Make & Play Ser.). (Illus.). 48p. 1976. pap. 1.50 o.p. (ISBN 0-685-69138-1). Transatlantic.

--Nature's Toyshop. (Illus.). 128p. 1976. 9.75 o.p. (ISBN 0-263-05595-7). Transatlantic.

--Wool-Bag Book. (Make & Play Ser.). (Illus.). 48p. (gr. 5-6). 1976. pap. 1.50 o.p. (ISBN 0-263-05911-1). Transatlantic.

Hutchings, R. S. The Western Heritage of Type Design. 130p. 1982. 35.00x (ISBN 0-284-39104-2, Pub. by C Skilton Scotland). State Mutual Bk.

Hutchings, Raymond. Soviet Economic Development. 2nd ed. 368p. 1983. text ed. 32.50x (ISBN 0-8147-3419-7, NYU Pr). Columbia U Pr.

Hutchings, William. William Cowper: A Critical Study. 208p. 1983. text ed. 25.25x (ISBN 0-7099-1249-8, Pub. by Croom Helm Ltd England). Biblio Dist.

Hutchins, Bobbie. Child Nutrition & Health. (Careers in Home Economics Ser.). (Illus.). 1979. pap. text ed. 10.96 (ISBN 0-07-031527-2, G); wkbk. 5.96 (ISBN 0-07-031528-0); tchrs' manual 4.00 (ISBN 0-07-031529-9). McGraw.

Hutchins, Carleen M. Moon Moth. (Illus.). (gr. 2-5). 1965. PLB 3.64 o.p. (ISBN 0-698-30240-0, Coward). Putnam Pub Group.

--Who Will Drown the Sound? (Science Is What & Why Ser.). (Illus.). (gr. 1-3). 1972. PLB 5.99 o.p. (ISBN 0-698-30478-0, Coward). Putnam Pub Group.

Hutchins, James S. Horse Equipment & Cavalry Accoutrements. LC 87-130398. (Illus.). 12.00 (ISBN 0-87026-042-1). Westernlore.

Hutchins, John. Hutchins' Guide to Bible Reading. (Illus.). 608p. 1983. 25.00x (ISBN 0-938386-00-X). Button Gwin.

--The Hutchins Guide to Writing Sentences. 116p. 1983. 9.95 (ISBN 0-932298-32-X). Copple Hse.

Hutchins, John G. B. Transportation & the Environment. Rose, J. & Weidner, Edward W., eds. LC 77-2350. (Environmental Studies: Vol. 5). 1977. lib. bdg. 18.00 o.p. (ISBN 0-89158-738-1). Westview.

Hutchins, Maude. Victorine. LC 82-72197. 191p. 1959. 8.95 (ISBN 0-8040-0311-4); pap. 4.95 (ISBN 0-8040-0312-2). Swallow.

Hutchins, Nigel. Restoring Old Houses. 240p. 1982. pap. 19.95 (ISBN 0-7706-0021-2). Van Nos Reinhold.

Hutchins, Pat. Happy Birthday, Sam. LC 78-1295. (Illus.). 32p. (gr. k-3). 1978. 9.75 o.p. (ISBN 0-688-80160-9); PLB 9.36 (ISBN 0-688-84160-0). Greenwillow.

Hutchins, Paul. Sugar Creek Gang & the Thousand Dollar Fish. (gr. 3-7). 1966. pap. 2.95 (ISBN 0-8024-4815-1). Moody.

Hutchins, R., jt. auth. see Martin, W. C.

Hutchins, Robert M. The Higher Learning in America. LC 78-23719. 1979. Repr. of 1962 ed. lib. bdg. 16.25x (ISBN 0-313-20713-5, HUHL). Greenwood.

--Saint Thomas & the World State. (Aquinas Lecture). 1949. 7.95 (ISBN 0-87462-114-3). Marquette.

Hutchins, Robert M. & Adler, Mortimer, eds. Great Books of the Western World, 54 Vols. (YA) (gr. 9 up). 1952. per set 829.00 (ISBN 0-85229-163-9). Ency Brit Ed.

Hutchins, Sheila. Pates & Terrines. 1979. 17.95 o.p. (ISBN 0-241-89892-7, Pub. by Hamish Hamilton England). David & Charles.

Hutchins, Thomas. Historical Narrative & Topographical Description of Louisiana & West Florida. Tregle, J. G., Jr., ed. LC 68-21657. (Floridiana Facsimile & Reprint Ser.). 1968. Repr. of 1784 ed. 7.75 o.p. (ISBN 0-8130-0119-6). U Presses Fla.

Hutchins, William M., tr. see Al-Hakim, Tawfiq.

Hutchinson & Barton. Physical Aspects of Building Science. 1977. text ed. 14.95 (ISBN 0-408-00031-7). Butterworth.

Hutchinson, Ann. FNNY Elssle's Cachucha. 1981. 9.95 (ISBN 0-87830-575-0). Theatre Arts.

Hutchinson, C. Alan, tr. see Figueroa, Jose.

Hutchinson, C. S., jt. auth. see Gobbett, D. J.

Hutchinson, D. W. & Miller, J. A. Organophosphorous Chemistry, Vol. 12. 288p. 1982. 215.00x (ISBN 0-85186-106-7, Pub. by Royal Soc Chem England). State Mutual Bk.

Hutchinson, David. Fundamentals of Computer Logic. 214p. 1981. 61.95x o.p. (ISBN 0-686-30989-8). Halsted Pr.

Hutchinson, Dorothy. Unless One Is Born Anew. LC 65-26994. (Orig.). 1965. pap. 1.50x o.p. (ISBN 0-87574-143-6). Pendle Hill.

Hutchinson, Duane. Images of Mary. (Illus.). pap. 6.95 (ISBN 0-934988-03-X). Foun Bks.

--Savidge Brothers, Sandhills Aviators. (Illus.). 332p. 1982. 19.95 (ISBN 0-934988-06-4). Foun Bks.

Hutchinson, E. C. & Acheson, E. J. Strokes: Natural History, Pathology & Surgical Treatment. LC 74-28100. (Major Problems in Neurology: Vol. 4). (Illus.). 283p. 1975. text ed. 10.00 (ISBN 0-7216-4870-3). Saunders.

Hutchinson, Eliot D. Rhymes for Our Times. LC 79-123008. 1970. 4.00 (ISBN 0-911838-05-8). Windy Row.

Hutchinson, F. Milton & the English Mind. LC 74-7187. (Studies in Milton, No. 22). 1974. lib. bdg. 36.95x (ISBN 0-8383-1906-8). Haskell.

Hutchinson, F. E., ed. see Herbert, George.

Hutchinson, G. Evelyn. A Treatise on Liminology, 3 vols. Incl. Vol. 1, 2 pts. 1975. Set. 39.50 (ISBN 0-471-42567-2); Pt. 1. Geography & Physics of Lakes. 672p. 22.50 (ISBN 0-471-42568-0); Pt. 2. Chemistry of Lakes. 474p. 21.00x (ISBN 0-471-42569-9); Vol. 2. Introduction to Lake Biology & the Limnoplankton. 1957. 99.95x (ISBN 0-471-42572-9); Vol. 3. Limnological Biology. 704p. 1975. 50.50x (ISBN 0-471-42574-5). LC 57-8888 (Pub. by Wiley-Interscience). Wiley.

Hutchinson, George E. The Enchanted Voyage, & Other Studies. LC 77-26010. (Illus.). 1978. Repr. of 1962 ed. lib. bdg. 17.25x (ISBN 0-313-20098-X, HUEV). Greenwood.

Hutchinson, Harry D. Economics & Social Goals: An Introduction. LC 72-93643. (Illus.). 514p. 1973. pap. text ed. 14.95 (ISBN 0-574-17975-5, 13-0975); instr's guide avail. (ISBN 0-574-17976-3, 13-0976). SRA.

--Money, Banking, & the U. S. Economy. 4th ed. 1980. text ed. 23.95 (ISBN 0-13-600379-6). P-H.

Hutchinson, Helene. Hutchinson Guide to Writing Research Papers. LC 72-86030. 256p. 1973. pap. text ed. 4.95x o.p. (ISBN 0-02-475050-6). Glencoe.

Hutchinson, Helene D. Horizons: Readings & Communication Activities for Vocational-Technical Students. 1975. pap. text ed. 7.50x o.p. (ISBN 0-02-475030-1, 47503); tchrs' manual free (ISBN 0-02-475040-9). Glencoe.

--Mixed Bag: Artifacts from the Contemporary Culture. 1970. text ed. 13.50x (ISBN 0-673-05250-8). Scott F.

Hutchinson, Henry N. Marriage Customs in Many Lands. LC 73-5520. (Illus.). xii, 348p. 1975. Repr. of 1897 ed. 47.00x (ISBN 0-8103-3971-4). Gale.

Hutchinson, J. The Families of Flowering Plants, Arranged According to a New System Based on Their Probable Phylogeny. 3rd ed. (Illus.). 1979. Repr. of 1973 ed. lib. bdg. 72.00x (ISBN 3-87429-160-X). Lubrecht & Cramer.

--The Genera of Flowering Plants: Angiospermae, 2 vols. 1200p. 1980. Repr. of 1964 ed. lib. bdg. Vol. I. lib. bdg. 48.00x (ISBN 3-87429-177-4); Vol. 2. lib. bdg. 48.00x (ISBN 3-87429-178-2). Lubrecht & Cramer.

--Key to the Families of Flowering Plants of the World. 1979. Repr. of 1967 ed. lib. bdg. 40.00 (ISBN 3-87429-161-8). Lubrecht & Cramer.

Hutchinson, J. S. The Hypothalamo-Pituitary Control of the Ovary, Vol. 1. Horrobin, D. F., ed. (Annual Research Reviews). 1979. 20.00 (ISBN 0-88831-064-1). Eden Pr.

--The Hypothalamo-Pituitary Control of the Ovary, Vol. 2. Horrobin, D. F., ed. (Annual Research Reviews Ser.). 215p. 1980. 28.00 (ISBN 0-88831-091-9). Eden Pr.

Hutchinson, John W., jt. ed. see Wu, Theodore Y.

Hutchinson, John Wallace. Story of the Hutchinsons, 2 vols. Mann, Charles E., ed. LC 76-56562. (Music Reprint Series). 1977. Repr. of 1896 ed. Set. lib. bdg. 75.00 (ISBN 0-306-70864-7). Da Capo.

Hutchinson, Joseph. The Challenge of the Third World. (Eddington Memorial Lecture Ser.: No. 2). 80p. 1975. 12.95 (ISBN 0-521-20853-X); pap. 4.95 (ISBN 0-521-09996-X). Cambridge U Pr.

Hutchinson, Joseph, ed. Evolutionary Studies in World Crops: Diversity & Change in the Indian Sub-Continent. (Illus.). 192p. 1974. 24.95 (ISBN 0-521-20339-2). Cambridge U Pr.

Hutchinson, Joyce. Voix d'Afrique. 5.95x (ISBN 0-521-05356-0). Cambridge U Pr.

Hutchinson, Joyce, ed. see Diop, Birago.

Hutchinson, Joyce A., ed. see Laye, Camara.

Hutchinson, P. J., jt. auth. see Ray, G. H.

Hutchinson, Peter. Evolution Explained. LC 74-81008. (Illus.). 224p. 1975. pap. 5.95 o.p. (ISBN 0-7153-6190-2). David & Charles.

Hutchinson, Robert. What One Christian Can Do About Hunger in America. LC 82-18199. xii, 115p. (Orig.). 1982. pap. 5.95 (ISBN 0-8190-0651-3, FC 145). Fides Claretian.

Hutchinson, Ron. Says I, Says He. (Phoenix Theatre Ser.). pap. 2.95x (ISBN 0-912262-69-9). Proscenium.

Hutchinson, Rosemary, jt. ed. see Burmeister, Jill.

Hutchinson, Sally A. Survival Practices of Rescue Workers: Hidden Dimensions of Watchful Readiness. LC 82-20097. 114p. (Orig.). 1983. lib. bdg. 18.50 (ISBN 0-8191-2889-9); pap. text ed. 8.00 (ISBN 0-8191-2890-2). U Pr of Amer.

Hutchinson, Stuart. Henry James: An American As Modernist. (Critical Studies). 136p. 1983. text ed. 27.00 (ISBN 0-389-20344-0). B&N Imports.

Hutchinson, T. W. On Revolutions & Progress in Economic Knowledge. LC 77-82498. 1978. 47.50 (ISBN 0-521-21805-5). Cambridge U Pr.

Hutchinson, Thomas, ed. see Wordsworth, William.

Hutchinson, Vernal. A Maine Town in the Civil War. LC 67-16827. (Illus.). 1965. pap. 2.95 (ISBN 0-87027-119-9). Cumberland Pr.

Hutchinson, Veronica S. Candlelight Stories. (Illus.). (gr. k-3). 1928. PLB 7.69 o.p. (ISBN 0-399-60081-7). Putnam Pub Group.

--Chimney Corner Fairy Tales. (Illus.). (gr. k-3). 1926. PLB 7.69 o.p. (ISBN 0-399-60090-6). Putnam Pub Group.

--Chimney Corner Stories. (Illus.). (gr. k-3). 1905. PLB 7.69 o.p. (ISBN 0-399-60091-4). Putnam Pub Group.

Hutchinson, Veronica S., ed. Henny Penny. (Illus.). 1976. 5.95 (ISBN 0-316-38400-3). Little.

Hutchinson, Warner. Jesus: An Enduring Portrait. LC 78-70651. (Illus.). cancelled o.s.i. (ISBN 0-448-16817-0, G&D); pap. cancelled o.s.i. (ISBN 0-448-16818-9). Putnam Pub Group.

--New York! (Readers Ser.: Stage 2). 1979. pap. text ed. 1.95 o.p. (ISBN 0-88377-158-6). Newbury Hse.

--The Oral Roberts Scrapbook. Shaw, Grace, ed. (Illus.). 1978. 14.95 o.p. (ISBN 0-448-16257-1, G&D); pap. 5.95 o.p. (ISBN 0-448-16259-8). Putnam Pub Group.

Hutchinson, Warner A., jt. auth. see Abrams, Richard I.

Hutchinson, William K. History of Economic Analysis. LC 73-17578. (Economics Information Guide Ser.: Vol. 3). 1976. 42.00x (ISBN 0-8103-1295-6). Gale.

Hutchinson, William K., ed. American Economic History: A Guide to Information Sources. LC 73-17577. (Economic Information Guide Ser.: Vol. 16). 250p. 1980. 42.00x (ISBN 0-8103-1287-5). Gale.

Hutchinson, William T. Cyrus Hall McCormick, 2 Vols. 2nd ed. LC 68-8127. (American Scene Ser). 1968. Repr. of 1935 ed. Set. lib. bdg. 95.00 (ISBN 0-306-71162-1). Da Capo.

Hutchison, Alan. China's African Revolution. LC 75-45233. 1976. lib. bdg. 25.00 o.p. (ISBN 0-89158-025-5). Westview.

Hutchison, Becky & Farish, Kay. Lisa. Carrodeguas, Andy & Marosi, Esteban, eds. Kjellgreen, Shily, tr. from Eng. (Span.). 1982. pap. 2.25 (ISBN 0-8297-1284-4). Life Pubs Intl.

--Lisa. Caruso, Luis, ed. Batista, Joao, tr. 191p. (Port.). 1981. pap. 1.60 (ISBN 0-8297-1205-4). Life Pubs Intl.

Hutchison, Charles S. Economic Deposits & Their Tectonic Setting. 328p. 1983. 34.95 (ISBN 0-471-87281-4, Pub. by Wiley-Interscience). Wiley.

--Laboratory Handbook of Petrographic Techniques. LC 73-17336. 544p. 1974. 49.95 o.s.i. (ISBN 0-471-42550-8, Pub. by Wiley-Interscience). Wiley.

Hutchison, Clyde A. Chemical Separation of the Uranium Isotopes. (National Nuclear Energy Ser.: Div. III, Vol. 3). 178p. 1952. pap. 17.50 (ISBN 0-87079-159-1, TID-5224); microfilm 4.50 (ISBN 0-87079-160-5, TID-5224). DOE.

Hutchison, J. B., ed. Biological Determinants of Sexual Behavior. LC 76-57753. 1978. 118.00 (ISBN 0-471-99490-1, Pub by Wiley-Interscience). Wiley.

Hutchison, John A. Living Options in World Philosophy. LC 76-46489. 1977. 15.00x (ISBN 0-8248-0455-4). UH Pr.
--Paths of Faith. 3rd ed. (Illus.). 608p. 1981. 22.00x (ISBN 0-07-031532-9). McGraw.
Hutchison, Terance W. Limitations of General Theories in Macroeconomics. pap. 3.25 (ISBN 0-8447-3390-3). Am Enterprise.
Hu Teh-Wei, et al. A Benefit-Cost Analysis of Alternative Library Delivery Systems. LC 74-5989. (Contributions in Librarianship & Information Science Ser.: No. 13). 256p. 1975. lib. bdg. 29.95 (ISBN 0-8371-7528-3, HUA/). Greenwood.
Huters, Theodore. Qian Zhongshu. (World Authors Ser.). 1982. lib. bdg. 18.95 (ISBN 0-8057-6503-4, Twayne). G K Hall.
Huth, Angela. Infidelities. 192p. 1979. 8.95 (ISBN 0-517-53874-1, C N Potter Bks). Crown.
Huth, Edward J. How to Write & Publish Papers in the Medical Sciences. (Illus.). 203p. 1982. 17.95 (ISBN 0-89495-018-5); pap. 11.95 (ISBN 0-89495-019-3). ISI Pr.
Huth, H. & Pugh, W., eds. Talleyrand in America As a Financial Promoter, 1794-96. LC 76-75323. (American Scene Ser). 1971. Repr. of 1942 ed. lib. bdg. 27.50 (ISBN 0-306-71286-5). Da Capo.
Huth, H. C. Practical Problems in Mathematics for Carpenters. LC 77-82373. 1979. pap. text ed. 7.80 (ISBN 0-686-85869-7); instr.'s guide 3.75 (ISBN 0-8273-1276-8). Delmar.
Huth, Mark. Understanding Construction Drawings. (Illus.). 304p. 1983. pap. text ed. 14.60 (ISBN 0-8273-1584-8); instr's guide 2.96 (ISBN 0-8273-1585-6). Delmar.
Huth, Mark W. Basic Construction Blueprint Reading. LC 79-50919. (gr. 9). 1980. pap. text ed. 9.80 (ISBN 0-8273-1865-0); instructor's guide 3.25 (ISBN 0-8273-1866-9). Delmar.
--Introduction to Construction. LC 78-60838. (Construction Ser.). (YA) (gr. 9-12). 1980. pap. text ed. 17.60 (ISBN 0-8273-1737-9); instr's. guide 3.75 (ISBN 0-8273-1738-7). Delmar.
Huth, Tom. Drive-A-Way Man. 1981. pap. 6.95 o.s.i. (ISBN 0-440-52149-1, Delta). Dell.
--Unnatural Axe. 1979. 8.95 o.s.i. (ISBN 0-440-09184-5). Delacorte.
--Unnatural Axe. 1979. pap. 4.95 o.s.i. (ISBN 0-440-59190-2, Delta). Dell.
Huth, Tom, jt. auth. see Ewalt, Norma.
Huth, Tricia, jt. auth. see Engelken, David.
Hutheesing, Raja, ed. The Great Peace: An Asian's Candid Report on Red China. LC 74-28428. (China in the 20th Century Ser). 246p. 1975. Repr. of 1953 ed. lib. bdg. 29.50 (ISBN 0-306-70694-6). Da Capo.
Hutmacher, Barbara. In Black & White. LC 82-6772. 208p. 1982. lib. bdg. 22.00 (ISBN 0-89093-465-7, Aletheia Bks); pap. 13.00 (ISBN 0-89093-466-5, Aletheia Bks). U Pubns Amer.
Hutner, S. H., jt. ed. see Levandowsky, Michael.
Hutnik, Russell & Davis, Grant, eds. Ecology & Reclamation of Devastated Land, 2 Vols. LC 76-122849. (Illus.). 1040p. 1973. Vol. 1, 552p. 85.00x (ISBN 0-677-15580-8); Vol. 2, 518p. 85.00x (ISBN 0-677-15590-5); Set. 152.00x (ISBN 0-677-15600-6). Gordon.
Hutschnecker, Arnold A. Hope: The Dynamics of Self-Fulfillment. 320p. 1981. 11.95 (ISBN 0-399-12589-2). Putnam Pub Group.
Hutslar, Donald, jt. auth. see Bachner, John P.
Hutson, A. B. The Navigator's Art. (Illus.). 192p. 1975. 9.95 o.p. (ISBN 0-263-05592-2). Transatlantic.
Hutson, D. H. & Roberts, T. R. Progress in Pesticide Biochemistry, Vol. 1. LC 80-41419. 360p. 1981. 66.00x (ISBN 0-471-27920-X, Pub. by Wiley-Interscience). Wiley.
--Progress in Pesticide Biochemistry, Vol. 2. 226p. 1982. text ed. 52.00x (ISBN 0-471-10118-4, Pub. by Wiley-Interscience). Wiley.
--Progress in Pesticide Biochemistry, Vol. 3. 500p. 1983. price not set (ISBN 0-471-90053-2, Pub. by Wiley Interscience). Wiley.
Hutson, Howard. Adventures in "Buyer Agency". 1982. pap. 20.95 (ISBN 0-686-84802-0). Atcom.
Hutson, Joan. Heal My Heart O Lord. LC 75-30493. 112p. 1976. pap. 2.75 (ISBN 0-87793-106-2). Ave Maria.
--The Lord's Prayer. Mahany, Patricia, ed. (Happy Day Bks.). (Illus.). 24p. (ps-2). 1983. 1.29 (ISBN 0-87239-640-1, 3560). Standard Pub.
--Love Never Ever Ends. Mahany, Patricia, ed. (Happy Day Bks.). (Illus.). 24p. (ps-2). 1983. 1.29 (ISBN 0-87239-641-X, 3561). Standard Pub.
Hutson, Sandy. Goodbye Beverly Hills. 1980. pap. 2.25 o.p. (ISBN 0-451-09300-3, E9300, Sig). NAL.
--Return to Sender. (Orig.). 1981. 2.75 o.p. (ISBN 0-451-09808-0, E9808, Sig). NAL.
Hutt, A. T. A Relational Data Base Management System. LC 79-40516. (Wiley Series in Computing). 226p. 1979. 32.95x (ISBN 0-471-27612-X, Pub. by Wiley-Interscience). Wiley.
Hutt, C., jt. ed. see Hutt, S. J.
Hutt, Frederick B. & Rasmusen, Benjamin. Animal Genetics. 2nd ed. LC 81-19671. 682p. 1982. text ed. 27.95 (ISBN 0-471-08497-2). Wiley.
Hutt, Max L. The Michigan Picture Test. rev. ed. 69p. 1980. 44.50 (ISBN 0-8089-1268-2); 50 scoring foms 10.00 (ISBN 0-8089-1286-0); manual (69pps.) 16.50 (ISBN 0-8089-1379-4); 15 picture cards 19.50 (ISBN 0-8089-1380-8). Grune.
Hutt, Michael D., jt. auth. see Moyer, Reed.
Hutt, S. J. & Hutt, C., eds. Early Human Development. (Illus.). 1973. pap. text ed. 10.95x o.p. (ISBN 0-19-857124-0). Oxford U Pr.
Hutt, W. H. A Rehabilitation of Say's Law. LC 74-82499. xiii, 150p. 1974. 10.95x (ISBN 0-8214-0164-5, 82-81651). Ohio U Pr.
--The Strike-Threat System. LC 72-91215. 1973. 11.95 o.p. (ISBN 0-87000-186-8, Arlington Hse). Crown.
Hutt, William H. & Klingman, David, eds. Individual Freedom: Selected Works of William H. Hutt. LC 75-16965. (Contributions in Economics & Economic History: No. 14). 250p. 1975. lib. bdg. 29.95 (ISBN 0-8371-8283-2, PIF/). Greenwood.
Hutten, Joan M. Short-Term Contracts in Social Work. (Library of Social Work Ser.). 1977. 20.00x (ISBN 0-7100-8584-2); pap. 8.95 (ISBN 0-7100-8585-0). Routledge & Kegan.
Huttenback, Robert A. The British Imperial Experience. LC 75-31434. (Illus.). 225p. 1976. Repr. of 1966 ed. lib. bdg. 20.00x (ISBN 0-8371-8505-X, HUBI). Greenwood.
Hutter, A. D. Death Mechanic. 1980. pap. 1.95 o.p. (ISBN 0-451-09410-7, J9410, Sig). NAL.
Hutter, Catherine. The Outnumbered. 416p. 1981. pap. 2.75 o.p. (ISBN 0-523-41108-1). Pinnacle Bks.
Hutter, Catherine, tr. see Ekert-Rotholz, Alice.
Hutter, Catherine, tr. see Von Goethe, Johann W.
Hutter, Mark. The Family & Social Change: Changing Family. LC 80-28829. 551p. 1981. text ed. 21.95 (ISBN 0-471-08394-1); tchrs.' manual 8.50 (ISBN 0-471-09287-8). Wiley.
Hutterer, Karl L., ed. Economic Exchange & Social Interaction in Southeast Asia: Perspectives from Prehistory, History, & Ethnography. LC 77-95147. (Michigan Papers on South & Southeast Asia: No. 13). (Illus.). xiv, 319p. (Orig.). 1977. pap. 9.50x (ISBN 0-89148-013-7). Ctr S&SE Asian.
Huttig, Jack. Fifteen Ways to Sharpen Your Selling Skills. 1975. pap. text ed. 24.95 (ISBN 0-686-98286-X). Sales & Mktg.
--Psycho-Sales Analysis: The New Art of Self-Taught Sales Success. (Quality Paperback: No. 263). 232p. 1978. pap. 5.95 (ISBN 0-8226-0263-6). Littlefield.
Huttman, Barbara. Code Blue: A Nurse's True Life Story. 1982. 12.50 (ISBN 0-688-00996-4). Morrow.
Huttman, Elizabeth D. Housing & Social Services for the Elderly: Social Policy Trends. LC 75-44932. (Special Studies). 1977. text ed. 33.95 o.p. (ISBN 0-275-23830-X). Praeger.
--Introduction to Social Policy. Black, Nelson W., ed. (Illus.). 368p. 1980. text ed. 23.50x (ISBN 0-07-031548-5). McGraw.
Hutto, M. Denise, jt. auth. see Lopinot, Neal H.
Hutton, jt. auth. see Clement.
Hutton, Artley O. Oh! What a Time! 1983. 10.95 (ISBN 0-533-05528-8). Vantage.
Hutton, David V. Applied Mechanical Vibrations. (Mechanical Engineering Ser.). (Illus.). 416p. 1980. text ed. 28.95x (ISBN 0-07-031549-3, C); solutions manual 16.95 (ISBN 0-07-031550-7). McGraw.
Hutton, Deane W., jt. ed. see Fleming, Malcolm L.
Hutton, G. & Rostron, M. International Directory of Computer Programs for the Construction Industry. 2nd ed. LC 77-134. (Illus.). 1979. cancelled o.p. (ISBN 0-89397-024-7). Nichols Pub.
Hutton, G. H., et al. Value in Building. 1973. 16.50 (ISBN 0-85334-547-3, Pub. by Applied Sci England). Elsevier.
Hutton, Geoffrey. Thinking About Organization. 1979. 8.50x o.p. (ISBN 0-422-74100-0, Pub. by Tavistock England). Methuen Inc.
Hutton, Graham. Source Book on Restrictive Practices in Britain. (Institute of Economic Affairs Research Monographs: No. 7). (Orig.). 1969. pap. 3.75 o.p. (ISBN 0-255-69610-8); 3.75 o.p. Transatlantic.
Hufton, Harold. Doc Middleton: Life & Legends of the Notorious Plains Outlaw. LC 82-72700. (Illus.). 290p. 1980. Repr. of 1974 ed. 15.95 (ISBN 0-8040-0532-X, SB). Swallow.
--Vigilante Days: Frontier Justice Along the Niobrara. LC 82-74078. (Illus). 365p. 1978. 17.95 (ISBN 0-8040-0738-1, SB). Swallow.
Hutton, J. F., et al, eds. Theoretical Rheology. (Illus.). xvi, 377p. 1975. 53.50 (ISBN 0-85334-638-0, Pub. by Applied Sci England). Elsevier.
Hutton, James. Theory of the Earth, 2 vols. 1960. Repr. of 1795 ed. 58.00 (ISBN 3-7682-0025-6). Lubrecht & Cramer.
Hutton, James see Aristotle.
Hutton, John H. Caste in India: Its Nature, Function, & Origins. 4th ed. 1963. 8.95x (ISBN 0-19-635206-1). Oxford U Pr.
Hutton, Richard. Bio-Revolution: DNA & the Ethics of Man-Made Life. 1978. pap. 2.25 (ISBN 0-451-61698-7, E1698, Ment). NAL.
--The Cosmic Chase. 1981. pap. 3.50 o.p. (ISBN 0-451-61925-0, ME1925, Ment). NAL.
Hutton, Richard, jt. auth. see Harsanyi, Zsolt.
Hutton, Richard H., ed. see Bagehot, Walter.
Hutton, William, jt. ed. see Fuller, Dwain.
Huttrer, Gerald W. & Roesner, Raymond E., eds. Geothermal Energy: The International Success Story. (Transaction Ser.: Vol. 5). (Illus.). 749p. 1981. 30.00 (ISBN 0-934412-55-3). Geothermal.
Hutzler, Laurie H. The Regulatory & Paperwork Maze. Incl. A Guide for Association Executives. pap. (ISBN 0-937542-03-2); A Guide for Government Personnel. pap. (ISBN 0-937542-04-0); A Guide for Small Business. pap. (ISBN 0-937542-02-4). (Illus.). 1980. pap. 12.50x ea. Legal Mgmt Serv.
Huus, Helen. The Education of Children & Youth in Norway. LC 73-7378. 247p. 1973. Repr. of 1960 ed. lib. bdg. 15.75x (ISBN 0-8371-6931-3, HUCY). Greenwood.
Huver, Charles W., compiled by. A Bibliography of the Genus Fundulus. 1973. lib. bdg. 22.00 (ISBN 0-8161-0976-1, Hall Reference). G K Hall.
Huxham, Mona. All About the Jack Russell Terrier. (All About Ser.). (Illus.). 159p. 1983. 12.95 (ISBN 0-7207-1201-7, Pub. by Michael Joseph). Merrimack Bk Serv.
Huxhold, Harry N., ed. Adventures with God. LC 66-15551. 1966. pap. 5.95 (ISBN 0-570-03736-0, 12-2640). Concordia.
Huxley, Aldous. The Art of Seeing. LC 82-70423. 160p. 1982. pap. 6.95 (ISBN 0-916870-48-0). Creative Arts Bk.
--Brave New World. LC 46-21397. 1932. 12.45i (ISBN 0-06-012035-5, HarpT); lib. bdg. 10.97i (ISBN 0-06-012037-1, HarpT). Har-Row.
--Brave New World. 1979. pap. 3.37i (ISBN 0-06-083095-6, P 3095, PL). Har-Row.
--The Devils of Loudun. 1979. pap. 5.95i o.p. (ISBN 0-06-090210-8, CN-210, CN). Har-Row.
--Doors of Perception. 1970. pap. 2.95i (ISBN 0-06-080171-9, P171, PL). Har-Row.
--Island. 1972. pap. 2.95i (ISBN 0-06-083101-4, P3101, PL). Har-Row.
--Moksha: Writings on Psychedelics & the Visionary Experience (1931-1963) Horowitz, Michael & Palmer, Cynthia, eds. 300p. 1982. pap. 7.95 (ISBN 0-87477-208-7). J P Tarcher.
--Perennial Philosophy. 1970. pap. 5.95i (ISBN 0-06-090191-8, CN191, CN). Har-Row.
--Point Counter-Point. 1928. 12.45i (ISBN 0-06-012105-X, HarpT). Har-Row.
Huxley, Aldous L. On Art & Artists. Philipson, Morris, ed. Repr. of 1960 ed. 13.00 o.s.i. (ISBN 0-527-43800-6). Kraus Repr.
--Texts & Pretexts. LC 76-16523. 1976. Repr. of 1933 ed. lib. bdg. 20.75x (ISBN 0-8371-8851-2, HUTP). Greenwood.
Huxley, Anthony, jt. auth. see Edlin, Herbert L.
Huxley, D. Making Films in Super Eight. LC 77-84809. (Illus.). 1978. pap. 10.95 (ISBN 0-521-29300-6). Cambridge U Pr.
Huxley, Elizabeth. Murder on Safari. LC 81-48172. 288p. 1982. pap. 2.84i (ISBN 0-06-080587-0, P587, PL). Har-Row.
Huxley, Elspeth. Scott of the Antarctic. LC 77-23662. 1978. 12.95 o.p. (ISBN 0-689-10861-3). Atheneum.
Huxley, Elspeth. Four Guineas: A Journey Through West Africa. LC 74-63. (Illus.). 303p. 1974. Repr. of 1954 ed. lib. bdg. 19.00x (ISBN 0-8371-7371-X, HUFG). Greenwood.
--A New Earth. LC 72-12318. (Illus.). 288p. 1973. Repr. of 1960 ed. lib. bdg. 19.00x (ISBN 0-8371-6688-8, HUNE). Greenwood.
--Settlers of Kenya. LC 74-33894. (Illus.). 126p. 1975. Repr. of 1948 ed. lib. bdg. 19.25x (ISBN 0-8371-5457-X, HUSK). Greenwood.
Huxley, Francis. The Dragon: Nature of Spirit, Spirit of Nature. (Illus.). 1979. pap. 7.95 o.s.i. (ISBN 0-02-000650-0, Collier). Macmillan.
Huxley, G. L. Early Ionians. 1966. pap. text ed. 15.00x (ISBN 0-7165-2065-6). Humanities.
Huxley, Julian. UNESCO: Its Purpose & Its Philosophy. 1979. 3.50 (ISBN 0-686-66193-1). Pub Aff Pr.
Huxley, Julian S. Religion Without Revelation. LC 78-12065. 1979. Repr. of 1967 ed. lib. bdg. 18.25x (ISBN 0-313-21225-2, HURR). Greenwood.
Huxley, Laura A. You Are Not the Target. 1976. pap. 1.95 o.p. (ISBN 0-380-00826-2, 30924). Avon.
Huxley, M. N. The Distribution of Prime Numbers: Large Sieves & Zero-Density Theorems. (Oxford Mathematical Monographs). (Illus.). 1972. text ed. 42.00x o.p. (ISBN 0-19-853518-X). Oxford U Pr.
Huxley, T. H. The Crayfish: An Introduction to the Study of Zoology. 1974. pap. 5.95x (ISBN 0-262-58034-9). MIT Pr.
Huxtable, Nils, jt. auth. see Skelton, Peter.
Huxtable, Ryan & Barbeau, Andre, eds. Taurine. LC 75-14577. 416p. 1976. 45.50 (ISBN 0-89004-064-8). Raven.
Huxtable, Ryan, jt. ed. see Barbeau, Andre.
Huybens, G., ed. see Cavaille-Coll, A.
Huybens, Gilbert. Het geestelijk em wereldijk Volksliedboek van de Zuidelijke Nederlanden, 6e - 18e eeuw - Gedrukte bronnen. (Facsimile of Dutch Songbks. Ser.: Vol. 7). 1981. write for info. o.s.i. (ISBN 90-6027-267-6, Pub. by Frits Knuf Netherlands). Pendragon NY.
Huybens, Gilbert, ed. Victor Legley-1915-1980: Commemorative Publication for His 65th Birthday. (Composers' Worklists Ser.: Vol. 4). 48p. 1980. wrappers 15.00 o.s.i. (ISBN 90-6027-287-0, Pub. by Frits Knuf Netherlands). Pendragon NY.
Huyck, Earl E., jt. ed. see Udry, J. Richard.
Huyck, Margaret H. & Hoyer, William. Adult Development & Aging. 640p. 1982. text ed. 24.95x (ISBN 0-534-01013-X). Wadsworth Pub.
Huyck, Peter & Kremenak, Nellie W. Design & Memory: Computer Programming in the 20th Century. (Illus.). 1980. 13.95 (ISBN 0-07-031554-X). McGraw.
Huyette, Marcia. John Lennon: A Real, Live Fairytale. (Illus., Orig.). pap. 12.95 (ISBN 0-942722-00-0). Hidden Studio.
Huygen, F. J. Family Medicine: The Medical Life History of Families. LC 82-12819. 224p. 1982. 20.00 (ISBN 0-87630-319-X). Brunner-Mazel.
Huygen, Wil, jt. auth. see Poortvliet, Rien.
Huyghe, Rene. Gauguin. (Q L P Art Ser). (Illus.). 1959. 7.95 (ISBN 0-517-00499-2). Crown.
--Van Gogh. (Q L P Art Ser). (Illus.). 1958. 7.95 (ISBN 0-517-00500-X). Crown.
Huyler, Jean W. Campaign Savvy-School Support. rev., 2nd ed. (Illus.). 56p. 1981. pap. 5.95 (ISBN 0-941554-02-3, LB2825.H87). Wagener News Serv.
--Crisis Communications & Communicating About Negotiations. rev., 2nd ed. Orig. Title: Crisis Communications. 92p. pap. 8.95x (ISBN 0-941554-03-1). EdCom.
--Demystifying the Media. rev., 2nd ed. (Illus.). 51p. 1981. pap. 7.95 (ISBN 0-941554-00-7, HM263.H89). Wagener News Serv.
Huynh, Sanh T., tr. see Huynh Sanh Thong.
Huynh Sanh Thong. The Tale of Kieu: A Bilingual Edition of Nauyen Du's "Truyen Kieu". Huynh, Sanh T., tr. LC 82-10979. 256p. (Chinese & Eng.). 1983. text ed. 17.50x (ISBN 0-300-02873-3). Yale U Pr.
Huys, Bernard, intro. by. Occo Codex. (Facsimilia Musica Neerlandica Ser.: Vol. 1). xxix, 154p. 1979. 72.50 o.s.i. (ISBN 90-6027-308-7, Pub. by Frits Knuf Netherlands). Pendragon NY.
Huyser, E. S., ed. Methods in Free-Radical Chemistry, Vol. 1. 1969. 39.00 o.p. (ISBN 0-8247-1310-9). Dekker.
--Methods in Free-Radical Chemistry, Vol. 2. 1969. 39.00 o.p. (ISBN 0-8247-1311-7). Dekker.
--Methods in Free-Radical Chemistry, Vol. 3. 184p. 1972. 39.00 o.p. (ISBN 0-8247-1312-5). Dekker.
--Methods in Free-Radical Chemistry, Vol. 4. 208p. 1973. 39.00 o.p. (ISBN 0-8247-6089-1). Dekker.
--Methods in Free Radical Chemistry, Vol. 5. 224p. 1974. 39.00 o.p. (ISBN 0-8247-6181-2). Dekker.
Huysmans, J. K. The Vatard Sisters. Babcock, James C., tr. & intro. by. (Studies in Romance Languages: No. 26). 192p. 1983. 16.50x (ISBN 0-8131-1426-8). U Pr of Ky.
Huysmans, Joris K. En Route. Paul, C. Kegan, tr. from Fr. LC 76-15215. xi, 313p. 1976. Repr. of 1918 ed. 21.50x (ISBN 0-86527-243-3). Fertig.
Huysmans, Joris-Karl. A Rebours. 230p. (Fr.). 1981. Repr. of 1889 ed. lib. bdg. 115.00 (ISBN 0-8287-1754-0). Clearwater Pub.
Huzan, E., jt. auth. see Carter, L. R.
Huzar, Elias. Purse & the Sword: Control of the Army by Congress Through Military Appropriations, 1933-1950. LC 72-138590. 1971. Repr. of 1950 ed. lib. bdg. 20.25x (ISBN 0-8371-5791-9, HUPS). Greenwood.
Hwang, Chun-ming. Drowning of an Old Cat & Other Stories. Goldblatt, Howard, tr. LC 80-7494. (Chinese Literature in Translation Ser.-Midland Bks: No. 253). 288p. 1980. 27.50x (ISBN 0-253-32452-1); pap. 9.95x (ISBN 0-253-20253-1). Ind U Pr.
Hwang, David H. Broken Promises: Four Chinese American Plays. 272p. 1983. pap. 3.95 (ISBN 0-380-81844-2, 81844-2, Bard). Avon.
Hwang, J. C., jt. ed. see Dancis, J.
Hwang, John & Schutzer, Daniel, eds. Selected Analytical Concepts in Command & Control. (Military Operations Research Ser.: Vol. 2). 272p. 1982. 56.00 (ISBN 0-677-16420-3). Gordon.
Hwang, Kai. Computer Arithmetic: Principles, Architecture & Design. LC 78-18922. 1979. text ed. 35.95 (ISBN 0-471-03496-7); solns. manual 6.00 (ISBN 0-471-05200-0). Wiley.
Hwang, N. Quantitative Cardiovascular Studies. 800p. 1979. text ed. 49.95 o.p. (ISBN 0-8391-1273-4). Univ Park.
Hwang, N. H. & Normann, N., eds. Cardiovascular Flow Dynamics & Measurements. (Illus.). 990p. 1977. text ed. 49.95 o.p. (ISBN 0-8391-0972-5). Univ Park.
Hwang, Ned H. Fundamentals of Hydraulic Engineering Systems. (P-H Ser. in Environmental Sciences). (Illus.). 352p. 1981. text ed. 33.95 (ISBN 0-13-340000-X). P-H.
Hwang, S. & Kammermeyer, K. Membranes in Separations, Vol. 7. (Techniques of Chemistry). 559p. 1975. 89.95 o.s.i. (ISBN 0-471-93268-X). Wiley.
Hwang, S. T. see Weissberger, A.
Hwang Sun-won. The Stars & Other Korean Short Stories. Poitrass, Edward W., tr. (Writing in Asia Ser.). 227p. (Orig., Korean.). 1980. pap. text ed. 8.95x (ISBN 0-686-98153-7). Heinemann Ed.
Hy, Ronn J. Using the Computer in the Social Sciences: A Nontechnical Approach. LC 77-956. (Illus.). 1977. pap. 12.95 (ISBN 0-444-00218-9, North Holland); pap. 12.00 (ISBN 0-444-00211-1). Elsevier.

Hyam, Ronald. Failure of South African Expansion, 1908-1948. LC 72-88093. 213p. 1972. text ed. 32.50x (ISBN 0-8419-0129-5, Africana). Holmes & Meier.
Hyams, Edward. Soil & Civilization. 1976. pap. 6.50xi o.p. (ISBN 0-06-090458-5, TB1962, Torch). Har-Row.
Hyams, Joe. Murder at the Academy Awards. 192p. 1983. 11.95 (ISBN 0-312-55284-X). St Martin.
--Zen in the Martial Arts. 144p. 1982. pap. 2.95 (ISBN 0-553-22510-3). Bantam.
Hyams, Vincent J., et al. Pathology of the Ear. LC 72-85. (Atlases of the Pathology of the Head & Neck). 24p. 1976. 90.00 (ISBN 0-89189-095-5, 15-1-017-00); microfiche ed. 22.00 (ISBN 0-89189-096-3, 17-1-017-00). Am Soc Clinical.
Hyamson, Albert M. Dictionary of English Phrases: Phraseological Allusions, Catchwords, Stereotyped Modes of Speech & Metaphors, Nicknames, Sobriquets, Derivations from Personal Names. LC 66-22673. 1970. Repr. of 1922 ed. 37.00x (ISBN 0-8103-3852-1). Gale.
--Dictionary of Universal Biography: Of All Ages & All Peoples. 2nd ed. 680p. 1981. Repr. of 1951 ed. 51.00x (ISBN 0-8103-4150-6). Gale.
--Palestine under the Mandate, 1920-1948. LC 72-593. 210p. 1976. Repr. of 1950 ed. lib. bdg. 21.00x (ISBN 0-8371-5996-2, HYPU). Greenwood.
Hyatt, jt. auth. see Regardie.
Hyatt, Betty H. The Jade Pagoda. LC 79-8433. (Romantic Suspense Ser.). 1980. 10.95 o.p. (ISBN 0-385-15746-0). Doubleday.
--The Sapphire Lotus. LC 82-45640. (Starlight Romance Ser.). 192p. 1983. 11.95 (ISBN 0-385-17909-X). Doubleday.
Hyatt, Carole. The Woman's Selling Game: How to Sell Yourself & Anything Else. 1981. pap. 5.95 (ISBN 0-446-37651-5); pap. 2.95 (ISBN 0-446-90195-4). Warner Bks.
--Women & Work: Honest Answers to Real Questions. LC 80-23984. 324p. 1980. 14.95 (ISBN 0-87131-324-3). M Evans.
Hyatt, Christopher S. Undoing Yourself with Energized Meditation & Other Devices. 114p. 1982. pap. 9.95 (ISBN 0-941404-06-4). Falcon Pr Az.
Hyatt, Christopher S. & Slaughter, S. L. Dogma Daze. 40p. 1982. pap. 2.95 (ISBN 0-941404-22-6). Falcon Pr Az.
Hyatt, Christopher S., jt. auth. see Regardie, Israel.
Hyatt, H. R. & Feldman, B. The Hand-Held Calculators: Use & Applications. 256p. 1979. pap. 16.95 o.p. (ISBN 0-471-02276-4). Wiley.
Hyatt, Herman R. & Small, Laurence. Trigonometry: A Calculator Approach. 416p. 1981. text ed. 24.95 (ISBN 0-471-07985-5); supple. to Trigonometry San. 1st 1982 avail. (ISBN 0-471-08069-1); tchr's manual avail. (ISBN 0-471-86938-4). Wiley.
Hyatt, Herman R., et al. Arithmetic with Pushbutton Accuracy. LC 76-4558. 1977. text ed. 25.95 (ISBN 0-471-22308-5); tchrs. manual 5.00 (ISBN 0-471-02395-7). Wiley.
--Introduction to Technical Mathematics: A Calculator Approach. LC 78-17016. 1979. text ed. 23.95x o.s.i. (ISBN 0-471-22240-2); tchr's manual avail. o.s.i. (ISBN 0-471-04053-3). Wiley.
Hyatt, Jessica. Summer Share. 288p. 1982. pap. 3.25 o.p. (ISBN 0-505-51862-7). Tower Bks.
Hyatt, Lillian. Bonfires at Heaven's Gate: A Biography of Dr. David Hyatt. (Illus.). 160p. (Orig.). 1983. pap. 7.95 (ISBN 0-8164-2354-7). Seabury.
Hyatt, Marshall, ed. The Afro-American Cinematic Experience: An Annotated Bibliography & Filmography. LC 82-22974. 280p. 1983. lib. bdg. 24.95 (ISBN 0-8420-2213-9). Scholarly Res Inc.
Hyatt, Ralph I. Before You Love Again. (Paperbacks Ser.). 192p. 1980. pap. 4.95 (ISBN 0-07-031555-8, GB). McGraw.
Hyatt, Stephen L., ed. The Greek Vase. LC 81-83963. (Illus.). 186p. 25.00 (ISBN 0-686-35880-5). Hudson-Mohawk.
Hybalski, Daniel H. The Flight of Thought. 1983. 6.95 (ISBN 0-533-05576-8). Vantage.
Hybels, Bill. Christians in the Marketplace. 144p. 1982. pap. 4.95 (ISBN 0-88207-314-1). Victor Bks.
Hybels, Saundra & Weaver, Richard L. Speech-Communication. 2nd ed. 256p. 1979. pap. 9.95 (ISBN 0-442-23623-9). Van Nos Reinhold.
Hyde, Albert C. & Shafritz, Jay M., eds. Government Budgeting: Theory, Process, Politics. LC 78-21866. (Orig.). 1978. pap. 12.50x (ISBN 0-935610-01-4). Moore Pub IL.
Hyde, Albert C., jt. ed. see Shafritz, Jay M.
Hyde, Bruce G., jt. auth. see Hyde, Margaret O.
Hyde, Cornelius J., III & Doiron, John. Louisiana Supplement to Modern Real Estate Practice. 110p. (Orig.). 1982. pap. 8.95 (ISBN 0-88462-293-2); pap. text ed. 6.95 (ISBN 0-686-96932-4). Real Estate Ed Co.
Hyde, D. M., jt. auth. see Elias, H.
Hyde, Douglas. Communism Today. LC 72-12639. 180p. 1973. pap. 2.95x o.p. (ISBN 0-268-00493-5). U of Notre Dame Pr.
--A Literary History of Ireland. 1980. 32.50x (ISBN 0-312-48741-X). St Martin.
--Poems from the Irish. Gibbon, Monk, ed. 1963. 4.75 (ISBN 0-685-09194-5). Dufour.
Hyde, Douglas see Schaff, Harrison H.
Hyde, Francis E. Cunard & the North Atlantic 1840-1973. 1975. text ed. 20.00x o.p. (ISBN 0-391-00384-4). Humanities.
Hyde, George E. Indians of the High Plains: From the Prehistoric Period to the Coming of Europeans. 1981. pap. 5.95 (ISBN 0-686-95781-4). Jefferson Natl.
--Life of George Bent: Written from His Letters. Lottinville, Savoie, ed. (Illus.). 389p. 1968. 14.50 o.p. (ISBN 0-8061-0769-3); pap. 14.95 o.p. (ISBN 0-8061-1577-7). U of Okla Pr.
Hyde, George E., jt. auth. see Will, George F.
Hyde, H. Montgomery. A Solitary in the Ranks: Lawrence of Arabia As Airman & Private Soldier. LC 77-88903. 1978. 11.95 o.p. (ISBN 0-689-10848-6). Atheneum.
Hyde, J. S. Understanding Human Sexuality. 2nd ed. 640p. 1982. 21.00x (ISBN 0-07-031567-1); instr's manual 1.00 (ISBN 0-07-031568-X). McGraw.
Hyde, Janet. Understanding Human Sexuality. (Illus.). 1978. text ed. 17.95 (ISBN 0-07-031558-2, C); instr's manual 15.00 (ISBN 0-07-031559-0). McGraw.
Hyde, Janet & Rosenberg, B. G. Half the Human Experience. 2nd ed. 1980. pap. text ed. 13.95x (ISBN 0-669-02500-3); instrs'. manual 1.95 (ISBN 0-669-02502-X). Heath.
Hyde, Janet S. & Rosenberg, B. G. Half the Human Experience: The Psychology of Women. 304p. 1975. pap. text ed. 7.95x o.p. (ISBN 0-669-02500-3); instr's manual free o.p. (ISBN 0-669-00370-0). Heath.
Hyde, Lewis. The Gift: Imagination & the Erotic Life of Property. LC 82-49088. 352p. 1983. pap. 7.95 (ISBN 0-394-71519-5, Vin). Random.
Hyde, Lewis, ed. see Aleixandre, Vicente.
Hyde, Lewis, tr. see Alexander, Vicente.
Hyde, Margaret O. Brainwashing & Other Forms of Mind Control. 1977. PLB 7.95 (ISBN 0-07-031639-2, GB). McGraw.
--Cloning & the New Genetics. (Illus.). 128p. (gr. 5-11). 1983. 10.95 (ISBN 0-89490-084-6). Enslow Pubs.
--Energy: The New Look. 128p. (gr. 7-9). 1981. 8.95 (ISBN 0-07-031552-3). McGraw.
--Everyone's Trash Problem: Nuclear Wastes. LC 78-23859. 1979. 8.95 (ISBN 0-07-031551-5, GB). McGraw.
--Hotline. 2nd ed. LC 74-9655. 128p. (gr. 9-12). 1976. PLB 8.95 (ISBN 0-07-031565-5, GB). McGraw.
--Is the Cat Dreaming Your Dream. LC 79-22684. (gr. 7-9). 1980. 8.95 (ISBN 0-07-031594-9). McGraw.
--Juvenile Justice & Injustice. rev. ed. (Single Title Ser.). 128p. (gr. 7 up). 1983. PLB 9.90 (ISBN 0-531-04594-3). Watts.
--Know About Alcohol. (Illus.). (gr. 4-6). 1978. 8.95 (ISBN 0-07-031621-X, GB). McGraw.
--Know About Smoking. (Know About Bks.). (gr. 4-8). 1983. 8.95 (ISBN 0-07-031671-6). McGraw.
--Mind Drugs. 3rd ed. 192p. (gr. 9 up). 1974. 7.95 o.p. (ISBN 0-07-031634-1, GB). McGraw.
--My Friend Wants to Run Away. LC 79-14517. (gr. 7-9). 1979. 8.95 (ISBN 0-07-031642-2). McGraw.
--The Rights of the Victim. (Single Title Ser.). 128p. (gr. 7 up). 1983. PLB 8.90 (ISBN 0-531-04596-X). Watts.
--VD: The Silent Epidemic. 2nd ed. 64p. (gr. 7-12). 1982. 9.95 (ISBN 0-07-031651-1). McGraw.
--VD: The Silent Epidemic. PLB 7.95 o.p. (ISBN 0-07-031638-4, GB). McGraw.
Hyde, Margaret O. & Forsyth, Elizabeth H. Suicide: The Hidden Epidemic. (gr. 9 up). 1978. PLB 8.90 s&l (ISBN 0-531-02224-2). Watts.
Hyde, Margaret O. & Hyde, Bruce G. Know About Drugs. 2nd ed. LC 79-13288. 64p. (gr. 4-6). 8.95 (ISBN 0-07-031643-0). McGraw.
Hyde, Margaret O. & Marks, Edwin S. Psychology in Action. 2nd ed. LC 75-43722. (gr. 7-12). 1976. PLB 7.95 o.p. (ISBN 0-07-031597-3, GB). McGraw.
Hyde, Margaret O., et al. Mysteries of the Mind. 160p. (gr. 9-12). 1972. PLB 6.95 o.p. (ISBN 0-07-031562-0, GB). McGraw.
Hyde, Marj. Rag Creek & Other Poems. Weine, Ruth, ed. (Illus.). 48p. 1982. pap. write for info. o.s.i. (ISBN 0-932370-44-6). Brooks Pub Co.
Hyde, Mary, ed. see Shaw, Bernard & Douglas, Alfred.
Hyde, Montgomery, ed. The Annotated Oscar Wilde. (Illus.). 480p. 1982. 25.00 (ISBN 0-517-54745-7, C N Potter Bks). Crown.
Hyde, Montgomery H. Secret Intelligence Agent. 304p. 1983. 11.95 (ISBN 0-312-70847-5). St Martin.
Hyde, R. M. & Patnode, Robert. Immunology. (Illus.). 1978. text ed. 18.95 o.p. (ISBN 0-87909-385-4); pap. text ed. 15.95 o.p. (ISBN 0-8359-3853-0). Reston.
Hyde, Robin. Check to Your King. 1977. 8.50 o.p. (ISBN 0-85558-448-3). Transatlantic.
Hyde, Sarah & Engle. The Potomac Program. 439p. 1977. 24.95 (ISBN 0-86575-037-8). Dormac.
Hyde, Stuart. Television & Radio Announcing. 4th ed. LC 82-83204. 528p. 1983. text ed. 22.50 (ISBN 0-395-32618-4); write for info. instr's. manual (ISBN 0-395-32619-2). HM.
Hyde, Stuart W. Television & Radio Announcing. 3rd ed. LC 78-69615. (Illus.). 1979. text ed. 22.50 (ISBN 0-395-27108-8). HM.
Hyde, T. A. & Draisey, T. Principles of Chemical Pathology. 1974. 33.95 o.p. (ISBN 0-407-36340-8). Butterworth.
Hydemark, David R. The Dangerous Conflict of the World Leaderships & the Possibility of a Mortal Explosion in the Destinies of Mankind. (Illus.). 141p. 1983. 71.75 (ISBN 0-86722-034-1). Inst Econ Pol.
Hyder. Picture Framing. (Pitman Art Ser.: Vol. 43). pap. 2.95 (ISBN 0-448-00552-2, G&D). Putnam Pub Group.
Hyder, Clyde K., ed. Swinburne As Critic. (The Routledge Critics Ser.). 1972. 25.00x o.p. (ISBN 0-7100-7343-7). Routledge & Kegan.
Hyder, O. Quentin. Shape Up. (Illus.). 160p. 1979. pap. 4.95 (ISBN 0-8007-0975-6). Revell.
Hyer, Paul, jt. auth. see Jagchid, Sechin.
Hyginus, et al. Fabularum Liber. LC 75-27848. (Renaissance & the Gods Ser.: Vol. 6). 1976. Repr. of 1535 ed. lib. bdg. 73.00 o.s.i. (ISBN 0-8240-2055-3). Garland Pub.
H. Y. Hou, jt. ed. see Wu Cheng Yih.
Hyland, Ann. Endurance Riding. LC 75-17774. (Illus.). 1976. 11.49i (ISBN 0-397-01082-6). Har-Row.
--Foal to Five Years. LC 80-11310. 128p. 1980. 14.95 (ISBN 0-668-04952-9, 4952-9). Arco.
Hyland, Drew A. The Virtue of Philosophy: An Interpretation of Plato's "Charmides". LC 81-38355. xii, 156p. 1981. text ed. 22.95x (ISBN 0-8214-0588-8, 82-83772). Ohio U Pr.
Hyland, M., jt. auth. see Gandy, R. D.
Hyland, Patricia A., jt. auth. see Saxton, Dolores F.
Hylander, Clarence J., ed. see Dana, William S.
Hylen, Arnold. Bunker Hill: A Los Angeles Landmark. (L.A. Miscellany Ser.: No. 7). (Illus.). 1976. 30.00 (ISBN 0-87093-172-5). Dawsons.
--Los Angeles Before the Freeways: 1850-1950, Images of a Era. (Illus.). 162p. 1981. 30.00 (ISBN 0-686-84000-3). Dawsons.
Hylton, Bill, ed. see Smyser, Carol.
Hylton, John. Reintegrating the Offender: Assessing the Impact of Community Corrections. LC 80-5730. 334p. 1981. lib. bdg. 23.25 (ISBN 0-8191-1387-5); pap. text ed. 12.75 (ISBN 0-8191-1388-3). U Pr of Amer.
Hyma, Albert. History of the Dutch in the Far East. 1953. 5.95x (ISBN 0-685-21788-4). Wahr.
Hyman, jt. ed. see Bell.
Hyman, A. A., jt. auth. see Brandstatter, A. F.
Hyman, Alan. Sullivan & His Satellites: A Survey of English Operettas 1860-1914. 1979. 22.00 o.p. (ISBN 0-903443-24-4, Pub by Hamish Hamilton). David & Charles.
Hyman, Allen & Johnson, M. Bruce, eds. Advertising & Free Speech. LC 77-5272. 1977. 17.95x (ISBN 0-669-01604-7). Lexington Bks.
Hyman, Arthur & Walsh, James J., eds. Philosophy in the Middle Ages: The Christian, Islamic & Jewish Traditions. new ed. LC 67-18445. 747p. (Orig.). 1973. 20.00 (ISBN 0-915144-06-9); pap. text ed. 15.00x (ISBN 0-915144-05-0). Hackett Pub.
Hyman, David N. Public Finance: A Contemporary Application of Theory to Policy. 689p. 1983. 28.95 (ISBN 0-686-43099-9). Dryden Pr.
Hyman, G. M., jt. auth. see Angel, S.
Hyman, Harold, ed. see McPherson, Edward.
Hyman, Harold M. A More Perfect Union. 1973. 15.00 o.s.i. (ISBN 0-394-46707-8). Knopf.
Hyman, Harold M. & Wiecek, William M. Equal Justice Under Law. LC 81-47658. (New American Nation Ser.). (Illus.). 572p. 1983. pap. 7.64i (ISBN 0-06-090929-3, CN 929, CN). Har-Row.
Hyman, Henry A. Where to Sell It. 400p. 1981. pap. 7.95 o.p. (ISBN 0-911818-21-9). World Almanac.
Hyman, Herbert H. Health Planning: A Systematic Approach. 2nd ed. LC 81-12780. 606p. 1982. text ed. 42.50 (ISBN 0-89443-379-2). Aspen Systems.
--Of Time & Widowhood: Nationwide Studies of Enduring Effects. (Duke Press Policy Studies). 150p. 1983. 20.00 (ISBN 0-8223-0504-6). Duke.
Hyman, Herbert Harvey, jt. auth. see Spiegel, Allen D.
Hyman, Irwin A. & Wise, James H., eds. Corporal Punishment in American Education: Readings in History, Practice, & Alternatives. LC 79-17. 487p. 1979. lib. bdg. 34.95 (ISBN 0-87722-147-2). Temple U Pr.
Hyman, J. D., et al. Toward Equal Opportunity in Employment, the Role of State & Local Government: Proceedings. LC 74-15228. (Symposia on Law and Society Ser.). 1971. Repr. of 1964 ed. lib. bdg. 22.50 (ISBN 0-306-70120-0). Da Capo.
Hyman, Jane & Lawrence, Patty. Beginning Phonics. Klimo, Kate, ed. (Project Teach Ser.). (Illus.). 64p. (Orig.). (ps-3). 1983. wkbk. 3.95 o.s.i. (ISBN 0-671-42541-2, Little Simon). S&S.
Hyman, Jane & Santeusanio, Joan. Learning about Math. Klimo, Kate, ed. (Project Teach). (Illus.). 64p. (Orig.). (ps-3). 1983. wkbk. 3.95 o.s.i. (ISBN 0-671-44460-3, Little Simon). S&S.
Hyman, June. Deafness. LC 80-15676. (gr. 4 up). 1980. PLB 8.90 (ISBN 0-531-02940-9). Watts.
Hyman, Mary, tr. see LeNotre, Gaston.
Hyman, Mary, tr. see Lenotre, Gaston.
Hyman, Mary, tr. see Pomiane, Edouard de.
Hyman, Mary, tr. see Senderens, Alain.
Hyman, Paula, jt. auth. see Brown, Charlotte.
Hyman, Paula, jt. ed. see Cohen, Steven M.
Hyman, Philip, tr. see LeNotre, Gaston.
Hyman, Philip, tr. see Lenotre, Gaston.
Hyman, Philip, tr. see Pomiane, Edouard de.
Hyman, Philip, tr. see Senderens, Alain.
Hyman, Ronald. Improving Discussion Leadership. 154p. (Orig.). 1980. pap. 10.95x (ISBN 0-8077-2610-9). Tchrs Coll.
Hyman, Ronald T. Paper, Pencils, Pennies: Games for Learning & Having Fun. (Illus.). 1977. 9.95 (ISBN 0-13-648436-0, Spec); pap. 3.95 o.p. (ISBN 0-13-648428-X, Spec). P-H.
--Strategic Questioning. LC 79-783. (Illus.). 1979. pap. text ed. 15.95 (ISBN 0-13-851055-5). P-H.
Hyman, Ronald T. & Thomson, Robert P. Strategies for Effective Teaching: A Basis for Creativity. 195p. 1975. 6.95 (ISBN 0-686-38277-3, 16-1538). Natl League Nurse.
Hyman, Sidney. The American President. LC 73-15166. 342p. 1974. Repr. lib. bdg. 17.50x (ISBN 0-8371-7170-9, HYAP). Greenwood.
Hyman, Sidney, ed. see Eccles, George S.
Hyman, Stanley E. The Armed Vision: A Study in the Methods of Modern Literary Criticism. LC 77-29139. 1978. Repr. of 1948 ed. lib. bdg. 39.75x (ISBN 0-313-20273-7, HYAV). Greenwood.
Hyman, Susan. Edward Lear's Birds. LC 80-80860. (Illus.). 96p. 1980. 37.95 o.p. (ISBN 0-688-03671-6). Morrow.
Hyman, Tom. Giant Killer. 320p. 1982. pap. 3.50 (ISBN 0-553-22521-9). Bantam.
--The Russian Woman. 1983. 16.95 (ISBN 0-312-69614-0, Pub. by Marek). St Martin.
Hyman, Trina S. The Sleeping Beauty. LC 75-43769. (Illus.). (gr. 1 up). 1977. 10.95 (ISBN 0-316-38702-9); pap. 3.95 o.p. (ISBN 0-316-38703-7). Little.
Hyman, Trina S., as told by. The Sleeping Beauty. 48p. (gr. 1 up). 1983. pap. 5.70i (ISBN 0-316-38708-8). Little.
Hyman, Trina S., retold by. & illu see Brothers Grimm.
Hyman, Vernon T. Giant Killer. 352p. 1981. 12.95 o.s.i. (ISBN 0-399-90099-3, Marek). Putnam Pub Group.
Hyman, Virgina D., jt. auth. see Hu, William.
Hymans, Saul H., ed. Economics & the World Around It. LC 81-21798. 256p. 1982. text ed. 18.50x o.p. (ISBN 0-472-08021-0); pap. text ed. 9.95x o.p. (ISBN 0-472-08022-9). U of Mich Pr.
Hymanson, Mary C. Connections & Contexts: A Basic Vocabulary. 372p. (Orig.). 1981. pap. text ed. 10.95 (ISBN 0-15-513260-1, HC); instr's. manual 1.95 (ISBN 0-15-513261-X). HarBraceJ.
Hymer, S. The Multinational Corporation. Cohen, R. B., et al, eds. LC 79-52327. (Illus.). 1979. 47.50 (ISBN 0-521-22695-3). Cambridge U Pr.
Hymer, S. see Kay, Geoffrey.
Hymer, Stephen H. The International Operations of National Firms: A Study of Direct Foreign Investment. LC 75-33365. (Economic Monograph Ser.). 208p. 1976. text ed. 15.95x (ISBN 0-262-08085-0). MIT Pr.
Hymers, Robert P. Professional Photographer in Practice. 4th ed. 432p. 1969. 18.50x o.p. (ISBN 0-85242-103-6). Intl Pubns Serv.
Hymes, Dell. Pidginization & Creolization of Languages: Proceedings. LC 77-123672. 1971. 42.50 o.p. (ISBN 0-521-07833-4); pap. 18.95 (ISBN 0-521-09888-2). Cambridge U Pr.
Hymes, Dell, ed. Language in Culture & Society: A Reader in Linguistics & Anthropology. 1964. text ed. 35.95 scp o.p. (ISBN 0-06-043030-3, HarpC). Har-Row.
Hymes, Dell H. Essays in the History of Linguistic Anthropology. (Studies in the History of Linguistics (SIHOL): 25). 300p. 1983. 30.00 (ISBN 90-272-4507-X). Benjamins North Am.
--Papers in the History of Linguistic Anthropology. 300p. 1982. 30.00 o.p. (ISBN 90-272-4507-X). Benjamins North Am.
Hymes, James L. Behavior & Misbehavior: A Teacher's Guide to Action. LC 78-5645. 1978. Repr. of 1955 ed. lib. bdg. 18.25x (ISBN 0-313-20427-6, HYBM). Greenwood.
--Teaching the Child Under Six. 3rd ed. (Illus.). 224p. 1981. pap. text ed. 10.95 (ISBN 0-675-08063-0). Merrill.
Hymes, James L., Jr. Teaching the Child Under Six. 2nd ed. LC 73-84784. (Education - Elementary Ser.). 192p. 1974. pap. text ed. 10.95 (ISBN 0-675-08891-7). Merrill.
Hymni. Ofte Loff-Sangen op de Christelijcke Feest-Dagen ende Ander-Sins. (Facsimile of Dutch Songbks. Ser.: Vol. 1). 1967. Repr. of 1615 ed. wrappers 20.00 o.s.i. (ISBN 90-6027-047-9, Pub. by Frits Knuf Netherlands). Pendragon NY.
Hymoff, Edward. Stig Von Bayer: International Troubleshooter for Peace. (Future Maker Ser). (Illus.). 1965. 5.95 o.p. (ISBN 0-685-11984-X). Heineman.
Hymovich, Debra & Barnard, Martha. Family Health Care, 2 vols. (Illus.). 1979. Vol. 1. pap. text ed. 15.50 (ISBN 0-07-031675-9, HP); Vol. 2. pap. text ed. 15.50. McGraw.

Hymovich, Debra P. Nursing of Children: Family-Centered Guide for Study. 2nd ed. LC 74-4568. (Illus.). 400p. 1974. 12.95 o.p. (ISBN 0-7216-4951-3). Saunders.

Hymovich, Debra P. & Chamberlin, Robert. Child & Family Development. (Illus.). 1980. text ed. 23.50 (ISBN 0-07-031650-3). McGraw.

Hymowitz, Carol & Weissman, Michaele. A History of Women in the United States. (Illus.). 416p. Repr. 2.95 (ISBN 0-686-95032-1). ADL.

Hynd, Alan. Great Crime Busters: True Stories of Crime Detection. (A Pedro Book). (Illus.). (gr. 7 up). 1967. PLB 4.69 o.p. (ISBN 0-399-60208-9). Putnam Pub Group.

Hynd, George W., ed. The School Psychologist: An Introduction. 416p. text ed. 27.00x (ISBN 0-8156-2289-9); pap. text ed. 14.95x (ISBN 0-8156-2290-2). Syracuse U Pr.

Hynding, Alan. From Frontier to Suburb: The Story of the San Mateo Peninsula. (Illus.). 400p. 1982. 24.95 (ISBN 0-89863-055-X); pap. 15.95 (ISBN 0-89863-056-8). Star Pub CA.

Hyndman, Donald, jt. auth. see Alt, David.

Hyndman, Donald W. Petrology of Igneous & Metamorphic Rocks. (Illus.). 480p. 1972. text ed. 34.95 (ISBN 0-07-031657-0, C). McGraw.

Hynds, Ernest C. American Newspapers in the Nineteen Eighties. (Studies in Media Management). 1981. 18.95 o.p. (ISBN 0-8038-0490-3); pap. 9.95 o.p. (ISBN 0-8038-0491-1). Hastings.

Hynds, Fran, jt. auth. see Bowles, Norma.

Hyne, Norman J. Geology for Petroleum Exploration, Drilling, & Production. (Illus.). 320p. 1983. 31.50 (ISBN 0-07-031659-7, P&RB). McGraw.

Hyneman, Charles S. The Supreme Court on Trial. LC 73-20501. 308p. 1974. Repr. of 1963 ed. lib. bdg. 36.50x (ISBN 0-8371-7326-4, HYSC). Greenwood.

Hynes. The Biology of Polluted Waters. 216p. 1982. 50.00x (ISBN 0-85323-200-8, Pub. by Liverpool Univ England). State Mutual Bk.

--The Ecology of Running Waters. 580p. 1982. 60.00x (ISBN 0-85323-100-1, Pub. by Liverpool Univ England). State Mutual Bk.

Hynes, Arleen. Handbook on Bibliotherapy. Date not set. 16.00 (ISBN 0-89158-950-3). Westview.

Hynes, H. B. Biology of Polluted Waters. 1970. 17.50 o.p. (ISBN 0-8020-1690-1). U of Toronto Pr.

Hynes, Millie R. Sooner or Later. (Illus.). 106p. (Orig.). 1982. pap. 4.95 (ISBN 0-939688-07-7). Directed Media.

Hynes, Richard O., ed. Surfaces of Normal & Malignant Cells. LC 78-16184. 1979. 98.00 (ISBN 0-471-99712-9, Pub. by Wiley-Interscience). Wiley.

Hynes, Samuel, ed. see Hardy, Thomas.

Hypia, Jorma. The Complete Tiffen Filter Manual. (Illus.). 136p. 1981. pap. 9.95 (ISBN 0-8174-3700-2, Amphoto). Watson-Guptill.

Hyska, June E. & Vanasse, Debra L. Changes. (Illus.). 200p. (Orig.). 1982. tchr's. ed 13.80 (ISBN 0-934696-03-9); 14.20 (ISBN 0-934696-04-7). Mosaic Pr.

Hyslop, Francis, tr. see Baudelaire, Charles P.

Hyslop, Lois, tr. see Baudelaire, Charles P.

Hyslop, Lois B. Henry Becque. (World Authors Ser.: France: No. 180). pap. 10.95 o.p. (ISBN 0-8057-2128-2, Twayne). G K Hall.

Hyslop, Lois B., ed. Baudelaire As a Love Poet & Other Essays. LC 68-8180. (Illus.). 1969. 13.95x (ISBN 0-271-00086-4). Pa St U Pr.

Hyslop, Richard S., jt. auth. see Miller, Crane S.

Hyslop, Theophilus B. Great Abnormals. LC 79-162514. xxviii, 289p. 1971. Repr. of 1925 ed. 37.00x (ISBN 0-8103-3797-5). Gale.

Hysom, John L. Business & Its Environment. Bolce, William J., ed. (Illus.). 450p. 1982. text ed. 19.95 (ISBN 0-314-63259-X); tchrs.' manual avail. (ISBN 0-314-63260-3). West Pub.

Hytten, F. E. & Chamberlain, G. V. Clinical Physiology in Obstetrics. (Illus.). 520p. 1981. 67.50 (ISBN 0-632-00654-4, B-1147-4). Mosby.

Hyun, Bong H., et al. Practical Hematology: A Lab Manual in Filmstrip. LC 75-8179. (Illus.). 384p. 1975. pap. text ed. 14.95 o.p. (ISBN 0-7216-9865-4); 72.00 o.p. (ISBN 0-7216-9864-6). Saunders.

Hyun, Judith, tr. see Memmi, Albert.

Hyvit, J., jt. auth. see Broul, M.

Hyzer, Donald V., ed. Project Implementation: Project Case Histories, Vol. 2. (Illus.). 242p. 1982. pap. 44.95 (ISBN 0-89852-402-4, 01 01 R102). TAPPI.

I

I, Jalal Huma, ed. see Ghazali.

I. P. A. New York. Government in Metropolitan Calcutta. 6.50x o.p. (ISBN 0-210-22663-3). Asia.

I. S. S. C. T. Congress, 13th, Taiwan, 1968. Proceedings. Liu, K. C., ed. 1970. 195.25 (ISBN 0-444-40738-3). Elsevier.

Iaccarino, Joseph, jt. auth. see Stephenson, Richard M.

Iacobelli, S., et al, eds. The Role of Tamoxifen in Breast Cancer. 136p. 1982. text ed. 19.00 (ISBN 0-89004-852-5). Raven.

Iacobelli, Stefano, et al, eds. Hormones & Cancer. (Progress in Cancer Research & Therapy Ser.). 589p. 1980. text ed. 70.50 (ISBN 0-89004-486-4). Raven.

Iagolnitzer, D., jt. ed. see Balian, R.

Iakovidis, S. E. Mycenae-Epidaurus. (Athenon Illustrated Guides Ser.). (Illus.). 160p. 1983. pap. 12.00 (ISBN 0-88332-302-8, 8239, Pub. by Ekdotike Athenon Greece). Larousse.

Iakovidis, Spiros. Excavations of the Necropolis at Perati. (Occasional Paper: No. 8). (Illus.). 121p. 1980. pap. 9.00 (ISBN 0-917956-19-2). UCLA Arch.

Ianelli, Richard. The Devil's New Dictionary. 320p. 1983. 14.95 (ISBN 0-8065-0791-8). Citadel Pr.

Iannaccone, Laurence, jt. ed. see Lutz, Frank W.

Ianni, Francis A. Culture, System & Behavior. LC 67-19464. 1967. pap. text ed. 6.50 o.p. (ISBN 0-574-17306-4, 13-0306). SRA.

Ianni, Francis A. & Reuss-Ianni, Elizabeth. A Family Business: Kinship & Social Control in Organized Crime. LC 72-75320. 200p. 1972. 10.00x (ISBN 0-87154-396-6). Russell Sage.

Ianni, Francis A., et al. Conflict & Change in Education. 1975. pap. 12.50x (ISBN 0-673-07750-0). Scott F.

Ianniello, Louis C., jt. ed. see Corbett, James W.

Iannone, N. Supervision of Police Personnel. 3rd ed. 1980. 20.95 (ISBN 0-13-876987-7). P-H.

Iannone, N. F. Principles of Police Patrol. 1974. 19.95 (ISBN 0-07-031667-8, G); instructor's manual 4.50 (ISBN 0-07-031669-4). McGraw.

Iannuzzi, John N. J. T. 336p. (Orig.). 1982. pap. 2.95 o.s.i. (ISBN 0-515-05528-X). Jove Pubns.

Iatrides, John O., ed. Greece in the Nineteen Forties: A Nation in Crisis. LC 80-54472. 462p. 1981. 37.50x (ISBN 0-87451-198-4). U Pr of New Eng.

Ibach, Bob & Colletti, Ned. Cub Fan Mania. LC 82-83941. (Illus.). 128p. (Orig.). pap. 5.95 (ISBN 0-88011-109-7). Leisure Pr.

Ibach, H. & Mills, L. Electron Energy Loss Spectroscopy & Surgace Vibrations. LC 81-22938. 384p. 1982. 49.00 (ISBN 0-12-369350-0). Acad Pr.

Ibadan University, Africana Catalogue of the Ibadan University Library, 2 vols. 1973. Set. 190.00 (ISBN 0-8161-0941-9, Hall Library). G K Hall.

Ibanez, V. Blasco. La Corrida: The Bullfight. Campbell, C. D., tr. from Span. 128p. 1943. 5.00 (ISBN 0-911268-52-9); pocket size avail. Rogers Bk.

Ibarguengoitia, Jorge. The Dead Girls. Zatz, Asa, tr. 160p. (Span.). 1983. pap. 2.95 (ISBN 0-380-81612-1, 81612-1, Bard). Avon.

Ibarra, F. & Da Rosa, A. M. Antologia de Autores Espanoles, Vol. 2: Modernos. 1972. text ed. 18.95x (ISBN 0-02-359400-4). Macmillan.

Ibbotson, Eva. A Countess Below Stairs. 288p. 1982. pap. 2.95 (ISBN 0-380-61374-3, 61374). Avon.

Ibero-American Institute in Berlin. Subject Catalog of the Ibero-American Institute in Berlin, Prussian Cultural Heritage Foundation. 1977. lib. bdg. 2700.00 (ISBN 0-8161-0068-3, Hall Library). G K Hall.

Ibingira, Grace S. African Upheavals Since Independence. (Westview Special Studies on Africa). 1980. lib. bdg. 29.50 (ISBN 0-89158-585-0). Westview.

Ibn-al-Hasan, Muhammad, jt. auth. see Isfandiyar, Ibn.

Ibn Isma'il, A. H. Ali see Ali ibn Isma'il, A. H., et al.

Ibn-Tahir, Abd-Al-Kahir. Moslem Schism & Sects (Pt. 2) Being the History of Various Philosophic System Developed in Islam. Halkin, A. S., tr. from Arabic. LC 78-3673. (Studies in Islamic History: No. 1). 239p. Repr. of 1935 ed. lib. bdg. 22.50x (ISBN 0-87991-450-5). Porcupine Pr.

IBP Research & Editorial Staff. How to Raise Money to Make Money. LC 80-26568. (Illus.). 432p. 1980. 99.50 (ISBN 0-87624-214-X). Inst Busn Plan.

--Lawyer's Desk Book. 6th ed. LC 79-13813. 650p. 1979. 49.50 (ISBN 0-87624-323-5). Inst Busn Plan.

--Real Estate Desk Book. 6th ed. LC 79-17735. 498p. 1979. text ed. 39.50 (ISBN 0-87624-490-8). Inst Busn Plan.

--Successful Techniques That Multiply Profits & Personal Payoff in the Closely - Held Corporation. 4th ed. LC 80-16143. (Illus.). 500p. 1980. 69.50 (ISBN 0-87624-532-7). Inst Busn Plan.

--Tax Desk Book for the Small Business. 3rd ed. 1979. 39.50 o.p. (ISBN 0-87624-560-2). Inst Busn Plan.

Ibraham, A., jt. auth. see Kelley, Joe.

IBRO Symposium, Italy, September 1978. Reflex Control of Posture & Movement: Proceedings. Granit, R. & Pompeiano, O., eds. (Progress in Brain Research Ser.: Vol. 50). 1980. 126.50 (ISBN 0-444-80099-9, North Holland). Elsevier.

Ibry, David. Know Thy Role: Happiness at Any Age. LC 81-81616. 1983. 7.95 (ISBN 0-87212-156-9). Libra.

Ibsen, Henrik. Brand. Meyer, Michael, tr. from Norwegian. 112p. 1967. pap. 6.95 (ISBN 0-413-30900-2). Methuen Inc.

--Complete Major Prose Plays of Ibsen. Fjelde, Rolf, tr. pap. 10.95 (ISBN 0-452-25300-4, Z5300, Plume). NAL.

--A Doll's House, the Wild Duck, & the Lady From the Sea. 1975. 9.95x (ISBN 0-460-00494-8, Evman); pap. 2.75x (ISBN 0-460-01494-3, Evman). Biblio Dist.

--Eight Plays. Le Gallienne, Eva, tr. Incl. Doll's House; Ghosts; Enemy of the People; Rosmersholm; Hedda Gabler; The Master Builder; The Wild Duck; The Lady from the Sea. (YA) 1981. pap. 4.95x (ISBN 0-394-30924-3, T24, Mod LibC). Modern Lib.

--Eleven Plays of Henrik Ibsen. 8.95 (ISBN 0-394-60414-8). Modern Lib.

--Four Great Plays. Sharp, R. Farquharson, tr. from Norwegian. Incl. Doll's House; Enemy of the People; Ghosts; Wild Duck. (Bantam Classics Ser.). 306p. (Orig.). (gr. 10 up). 1981. pap. 2.25 (ISBN 0-553-21040-8). Bantam.

--Four Major Plays, Vol. 1. Fjelde, Rolf, tr. Incl. Doll's House; Wild Duck; Hedda Gabler; Master Builder. 1965. pap. 2.25 (ISBN 0-451-51397-5, CL1397, Sig Classics). NAL.

--Four Major Plays, Vol. 2. Fjelde, Rolf, tr. Incl. Ghosts; Enemy of the People; Lady from the Sea; John Gabriel Borkman. 1970. pap. 2.50 (ISBN 0-451-51655-9, CE1655, Sig Classics). NAL.

--Hedda Gabler & Other Plays. Ellis-Femor, Una, tr. Incl. Pillars of the Community; Wild Duck. (Classics Ser.). (Orig.). 1951. pap. 3.50 (ISBN 0-14-044016-X). Penguin.

--The Master Builder. 1979. 7.95x o.s.i. (ISBN 0-8464-0095-2). Beekman Pubs.

--The Oxford Ibsen. McFarlane, James W., ed. Incl. Vol. 2. The Vikings at Helgeland; Love's Comedy; The Pretenders. Arup, Jens, tr. 1962. 24.00x (ISBN 0-19-211334-8); Vol. 4. The League of Youth; Emperor Galilean. McFarlane, James W. & Orton, Graham, trs. 1963. 29.00x (ISBN 0-19-211338-0); Vol. 5. Pillars of Society, a Doll's House, Ghosts. McFarlane, James W., tr. 1961. 18.50x (ISBN 0-19-211326-7); Vol. 7. The Lady from the Sea; Hedda Gabler; The Master Builder. Arup, Jens & McFarland, James W., trs. 1966. 32.00x (ISBN 0-19-211342-9); Vol. 3. Brand, Peer Gynt. Kirkup, James & Fry, Christopher, trs. 1972. 24.00x (ISBN 0-19-211360-7); Vol. 1. Early Plays. Orton, Graham, tr. 1970. 45.00x o.p. (ISBN 0-19-211357-7). Oxford U Pr.

--Wild Duck. Jurgensen, Kai & Schenkkan, Robert, eds. Jurgensen, Kai & Schenkkan, Robert, trs. LC 66-21588. 1966. pap. text ed. 3.50x (ISBN 0-88295-046-0). Harlan Davidson.

--Wild Duck. Christiani, Dounia B., ed. (Critcal Editions). (gr. 9-12). 1969. 5.00 o.p. (ISBN 0-393-04187-5, NortonC); pap. text ed. 5.95x (ISBN 0-393-09825-7). Norton.

Ibsen, Henrik & Hill, Geoffrey. Brand: A Version for the Stage. rev. 2nd ed. LC 81-16055. 160p. 1981. 15.00x (ISBN 0-8166-1002-9); pap. 5.95 (ISBN 0-8166-1005-3). U of Minn Pr.

Ibsen, Henrik see Laurel Editions Editors.

Ibsen, Henrik, jt. auth. see Strindberg, August.

ICAP Hellas (Athens), ed. ICAP Financial Directory of Greek Companies, 1980, 4 vols. 15th ed. (Illus.). 2960p. 1980. Set. pap. 180.00 o.p. (ISBN 0-8002-2762-X). Intl Pubns Serv.

Icaza, Jorge. The Villagers (Huasipungo) A Novel. Dulsey, Bernard M., tr. from Span. LC 73-9551. (Arcturus Books Paperbacks). 238p. 1973. pap. 7.95x (ISBN 0-8093-0653-0). S Ill U Pr.

Ice, Rhoderick. Thirteen Lessons on the Gospel of Mark. (Bible Student Study Guides Ser). 1977. pap. 2.95 o.s.i. (ISBN 0-89900-151-3). College Pr Pub.

Ichiishi, Tatsuro, ed. Game Theory for Economic Analysis. (Economic Theory, Econometrics & Mathematical Economics Ser.). 142p. 1982. 32.00 (ISBN 0-12-370180-5). Acad Pr.

Ichikawa, M., jt. auth. see Tamaru, K.

Ichikawa, Satomi. Let's Play. (A First Looking-& Learning Bk.). (Illus.). (ps). 1981. 9.95 o.s.i. (ISBN 0-399-20824-0, Philomel); lib. bdg. 9.99 o.s.i. (ISBN 0-399-61186-X). Putnam Pub Group.

Ichikawa, Satomi, illus. Sun Through Small Leaves: Poems of Spring. LC 79-23913. (Illus.). 32p. (gr. k-3). 1980. 8.95 (ISBN 0-529-05571-6, Philomel); PLB 8.99 (ISBN 0-529-05572-4). Putnam Pub Group.

Ichimura, Shinichi, ed. Southeast Asia: Nature, Society, & Development. LC 77-777. (Center for Southeast Asian Studies, Kyoto University). 1977. text ed. 15.00x (ISBN 0-8248-0543-7); pap. text ed. 10.00x (ISBN 0-8248-0554-2). UH Pr.

Ichimura, Shinici, ed. Economic Development of East & Southeast Asia. (Centre for Southeast Asia Studies Monographs). 1975. pap. 10.00x (ISBN 0-8248-0336-1, Eastwest Ctr). UH Pr.

Ichioka, Yuji, et al, eds. A Buried Past: An Annotated Bibliography of the Japanese American Research Project Collection. LC 73-83063. 1974. 27.50x (ISBN 0-520-02541-5). U of Cal Pr.

Ickes, Harold L. Back to Work: The Story of PWA. LC 72-7426. (FDR & the Era of the New Deal Ser.). (Illus.). 276p. 1973. Repr. of 1935 ed. lib. bdg. 39.50 (ISBN 0-306-70527-3). Da Capo.

--The Secret Diary of Harold L. Ickes, 3 vols. LC 73-21721. (FDR & the Era of the New Deal Ser.). 1974. Repr. of 1954 ed. Set. lib. bdg. 175.00 (ISBN 0-306-70626-1); lib. bdg. 79.50 ea. Vol. 1, The First Thousand Days, 1933-1936 (ISBN 0-306-70627-X). Vol. 2, The Inside Struggle, 1936-1939 (ISBN 0-306-70628-8). Vol. 3, The Lowering Clouds, 1939-1941 (ISBN 0-306-70629-6). Da Capo.

Icks, Robert J. Tanks & Armored Vehicles 1900-1945. 1974. 12.95 (ISBN 0-87364-228-7). Paladin Pr.

ICN-UCLA Symposia on Molecular & Cellular Biology. Eukaryotic Genetics Systems. Wilcox, Gary, et al, eds. 1977. 36.00 (ISBN 0-12-751550-X). Acad Pr.

ICRD see Sowby, F. D.

ICRP. Protection Against Ionizing Radiation from External Sources Used in Medicine. (ICRP Publication: No. 33). 74p. 1982. 25.00 (ISBN 0-08-029779-X). Pergamon.

--Recommendations de la Comision Internationale de Protection Radiologique. Duchene, A. & Jammet, H., eds. (ICRP Publicaton Ser.: No. 26). 63p. (Fr.). 1980. pap. 15.75 (ISBN 0-08-025529-9). Pergamon.

ICRP see Sowby, F. D.

ICTA Conference, Kyoto 1977, 5th & Chihara. Thermal Analysis: Proceedings. 1975. 114.00 (ISBN 0-471-25628-5, Wiley Heyden). Wiley.

ICTA Conference, 4th & Buzas. Thermal Analysis: Proceedings, 3 vols. 1975. Set. 415.95 (ISBN 0-471-25619-6, Wiley Heyden). Wiley.

--Thermal Analysis, Proceedings, Vol. 1: Theory - Organic Chemistry. 1975. 154.95 (ISBN 0-471-25621-8, Wiley Heyden). Wiley.

--Thermal Analysis, Proceedings, Vol. 2: Organic & Macrocolecular Chemistry, Earth Science. 1975. 154.95 (ISBN 0-471-25622-6, Wiley Heyden). Wiley.

--Thermal Analysis, Proceedings, Vol. 3: Applied Sciences - Methods & Instrumentation. 1975. 154.95 (ISBN 0-471-25623-4, Wiley Heyden). Wiley.

Idaho State Department of Education & Northwest Regional Educational Laboratory. Understanding Contracts & Legal Documents & Understanding Criminal Law. (Lifeworks Ser.). (Illus.). 1980. pap. text ed. 5.28 (ISBN 0-07-060913-6). McGraw.

Iddings, Joseph P. Problem of Volcanism. 1914. 65.00x (ISBN 0-686-50031-8). Elliots Bks.

Ide, Arthur F. Woman in Ancient Israel under the Torah & Talmud. LC 82-9184. (Women in History Ser.: Vol. 5B). (Illus.). 86p. (Orig.). 1982. cloth 18.95 (ISBN 0-86663-080-5); pap. text ed. 13.95 (ISBN 0-86663-081-3). Ide Hse.

--Woman in Greek Civilization Before 100 B.C. 2nd ed. LC 81-13468. (Woman in History Ser.: Vol. 7b). (Illus.). 83p. 1983. lib. bdg. 12.95 (ISBN 0-86663-031-7); pap. text ed. 8.25 (ISBN 0-86663-032-5). Ide Hse.

--Woman in the American Colonial South. 2nd ed. LC 79-19011. (Woman in History Ser.: Vol. 30). viii, 130p. (Orig.). 1983. 17.95 (ISBN 0-86663-078-3); pap. 13.95 (ISBN 0-86663-079-1). Ide Hse.

--Woman in the Apostolic Age (33-107 A. D.) 2nd ed. LC 79-19011. (Women in History: Vol. 8). (Illus.). 100p. (Orig.). 1983. lib. bdg. 13.95 (ISBN 0-86663-035-X); pap. 10.95 (ISBN 0-86663-036-8). Ide Hse.

--Woman: Vol. I: from the Dawn of Time to the Renaissance. (Woman in History: Synopsis I). (Illus.). 210p. (Orig.). 1983. lib. bdg. 17.95 (ISBN 0-86663-094-5); pap. text ed. 9.95 (ISBN 0-86663-095-3). Ide Hse.

Ide, Arthur F. & Ide, Charles A. Woman in the Age of Christian Martyrs (67-317 AD) 2nd ed. LC 81-13476. (Woman in History Ser.: Vol. 10). (Illus.). ix, 120p. 1983. 20.95 (ISBN 0-86663-039-2); pap. 17.95 (ISBN 0-86663-040-6). Ide Hse.

Ide, Charles A., jt. auth. see Ide, Arthur F.

Ide, H. Chandler see Kavass, Igor I. & Sprudzs, Adolf.

Ide, Richard S. & Wittreich, Joseph, eds. Milton Studies, Vol. XVII: Composite Orders: The Genres of Milton's Last Poems. LC 69-12335. 340p. 1983. 29.95x (ISBN 0-8229-3473-6). U of Pittsburgh Pr.

Ide, Sachiko, jt. auth. see Bull, Richard H.

Ideals Editors. The Book of Comfort & Joy. LC 80-1192. 96p. 1981. 9.95 (ISBN 0-385-17289-3, Galilee). Doubleday.

Idema, W. L., ed. Leyden Studies in Sinology: Papers Presented at the Conference held in Celebration of the 50th Anniversary of the Sinological Institute of Leyden University, December 8-12, 1982. (Sinica Leidensia Ser.: Vol. 15). (Illus.). ix, 234p. 1981. pap. write for info. (ISBN 90-04-06529-6). E J Brill.

Idleman, H. K. Housing, Furniture & Appliances. (Contemporary Consumer Ser.). 1974. text ed. 6.68 (ISBN 0-07-031701-1, G); tchr's manual & key 6.50 (ISBN 0-07-031702-X). McGraw.

Idleman, H. K. & McKitrick, M. O. Transportation. (Contemporary Consumer Ser.). 1974. text ed. 6.68 (ISBN 0-07-031691-0, G); tchr's. manual & key 6.50 (ISBN 0-07-031692-9). McGraw.

--Understanding the Marketplace. (Contemporary Consumer Ser.). text ed. 6.68 (ISBN 0-07-031687-2, G); tchr's manual & key 6.50 (ISBN 0-07-031688-0). McGraw.

Idleman, H. K. & Stanton, E. N. Food & Clothing. (Contemporary Consumer Ser.). 1976. text ed. 6.68 (ISBN 0-07-031689-9, G); tchr's manual & key 6.50 (ISBN 0-07-031690-2). McGraw.
--Health, Education & Recreation. (Contemporary Consumer Ser.). 1974. text ed. 6.68 (ISBN 0-07-031698-8, G); tchr's manual & key 6.50 (ISBN 0-07-031699-6). McGraw.
Idler, Ellen, jt. auth. see Levin, Lowell.
Idol, John L. & Eisiminger, Sterling. Why Can't They Write? A Symposium on the State of Written Communication. LC 78-68569. 1979. pap. text ed. 7.00 (ISBN 0-8191-0693-3). U Pr of Amer.
Idol-Maestas, Lorna. Special Educator's Consultation Handbook. 350p. 1982. 27.50 (ISBN 0-89443-926-X). Aspen Systems.
Idone, Christopher. Glorious Food. LC 82-5587. (Illus.). 256p. 1982. 40.00 (ISBN 0-941434-22-2, 8006). Stewart Tabori & Chang.
Idyll, C. P. Abyss: The Deep Sea & the Creatures That Live in It. 3rd rev. ed. (Apollo Eds.). (Illus.). pap. 6.95i o.p. (ISBN 0-8152-0400-0, A400). T Y Crowell.
--The Sea Against Hunger. new, rev. ed. LC 77-2655. (Apollo Eds.). (Illus.). 1978. pap. 6.95i (ISBN 0-8152-0422-1, A-422, TYC-T). T Y Crowell.
Idziak, Janine Marie. Divine Command Morality: Historical & Contemporary Readings. LC 79-91621. (Texts & Studies in Religion: Vol. 5). 1980. soft cover 39.95x (ISBN 0-88946-969-5). E Mellen.
IEA Staff, jt. auth. see OECD Staff.
Iechukwu, John A. Ndidi, the African Businessman. 1978. 7.95 o.p. (ISBN 0-533-03245-8). Vantage.
IES Committee on Office Lighting. American National Standard Practice for Office Lighting A132.1-1973. new ed. (Illus.). 42p. 1973. 13.50 (ISBN 0-87995-011-0); 9.00. Illum Eng.
IES Office Lighting Committee. Proposed American National Standard Practice for Office Lighting. (Illus.). 44p. 1982. Repr. 9.00 (ISBN 0-87995-011-0); 13.50 (ISBN 0-686-82676-0). Illum Eng.
IFAC. Control of Distributed Parameter Systems: Proceedings of the 3rd IFAC Symposium, 29 June-2 July 1982. Babary, J. P. & Letty, L. le, eds. 550p. 1983. 145.00 (ISBN 0-08-029361-1). Pergamon.
--Modelling & Control of Biotechnical Processes: Proceedings of the First IFAC Workshop, Helsinki, 17-19 August 1982. Halme, A., ed. (IFAC Proceedings Ser.). 350p. 1983. 85.00 (ISBN 0-08-029978-4). Pergamon.
IFAC-IFIP Workshop, Kyoto, Japan, August 31 - Sept. 2, 1981. Real Time Programming 1981: Processing. Hasegawa, T., ed. (Illus.). 150p. 1982. 45.00 (ISBN 0-08-027613-X). Pergamon.
Ifcovic, Edward, et al see Di Pietro, Robert.
Ife, Anne E., et al. Tal Como Es. LC 73-10208. 1973. pap. text ed. 5.95 (ISBN 0-912022-76-0). EMC.
IFIP Conference on Human Choice & Computers Apr. 1-5, 1974. Human Choice & Computers, 1: Proceedings. Mumford, E. & Sackman, H., eds. LC 74-24343. 358p. 1975. 53.25 (ISBN 0-444-10774-6, North-Holland). Elsevier.
IFIP-IFAC International Conference, 3rd, Univ. of Strathclyde, Scotland, June 1979. Computer Application in the Automation of Shipyard Operation & Ship Design, III: Proceedings. Kuo, C., et al, eds. (Computer Applications in Shipping & Shipbuilding Ser.: Vol. 6). 385p. 1980. 89.50 (ISBN 0-444-85337-5, North Holland). Elsevier.
IFIP TC Four Working Conference. Decision Making & Medical Care: Proceedings. De Dombal, E. T. & Gremy, F., eds. 1976. 70.25 (ISBN 0-7204-0464-9, North-Holland). Elsevier.
IFIP Working Conference on Modelling in Data Base Management Systems. Architecture & Models in Data Base Management: Proceedings. Nijssen, G. M., ed. (IFIP Ser.). 1977. 59.75 (ISBN 0-7204-0758-3, North-Holland). Elsevier.
IFIP Workshop on Methodology in Computer Graphics, France, May 1976. Methodology in Computer Graphics: Proceedings. Guedj, R. A. & Tucker, H., eds. 1979. 32.00 (ISBN 0-444-85301-4, North Holland). Elsevier.
IFIP World Conference, 2nd. Computers in Education: Proceedings. Lecarme, O. & Lewis, R., eds. 1020p. 1976. 106.50 (ISBN 0-444-10987-0, North-Holland). Elsevier.
IFIP 2nd Conference, Baden, Austria, June 1979. Human Choice & Computers, 2. Mowshowitz, A., ed. 1980. 40.50 (ISBN 0-444-85456-8). Elsevier.
IFIPtC4 Working Conference, Germany, 1976. Realization of Data Protection in Health Information Systems: Proceedings. Griesser, G, ed. LC 77-1802. 1977. 34.00 (ISBN 0-7204-0462-2, North-Holland). Elsevier.
Ifkovic, John see Weaver, Glenn.
IFORS International Conference on Operational Research, 7th, Japan, 1975 & Haley, K. B. Operational Research 1975: Proceedings. 1976. 85.00 (ISBN 0-444-11025-9, North-Holland). Elsevier.
IFPtC4 Working Conference, Amsterdam, 1976. Trends in Computer-Processed Electrocardiograms: Proceedings. Van Bemmel, J. H. & Willems, J. L., eds. LC 77-1801. 1977. 55.50 (ISBN 0-7204-0723-0, North-Holland). Elsevier.
Iftikhar-Ul-Awwal, A. Z. The Industrial Development of Bengal, 1900-1939. 336p. 1982. text ed. 35.00x (ISBN 0-7069-1579-8, Pub. by Vikas India). Advent NY.
Iga, Ken-Ichi, jt. auth. see Suematsu, Yasuharu.
Igbal, Sabiha, jt. auth. see Adams, John.
Iggers, Georg G. & Parker, Harold T., eds. International Handbook of Historical Studies: Contemporary Research & Theory. LC 79-7061. 1980. lib. bdg. 39.95 (ISBN 0-313-21367-4, ICD/). Greenwood.
Iggers, George G., tr. from Fr. & pref. by. The Doctrine of Saint-Simon: An Exposition. LC 72-80873. (Studies in the Libertarian & Utopian Tradition). 340p. 1972. 7.50x o.p. (ISBN 0-8052-3451-9); pap. 3.95 o.p. (ISBN 0-8052-0371-0). Schocken.
Iggers, Jeremy & Bovbjerg, Dana. The Joy of Cheesecake. LC 81-17014. (Illus.). 1980. 12.95 (ISBN 0-8120-5350-8). Barron.
Igglesden, Charles. Those Superstitions. LC 73-12798. 1974. Repr. of 1932 ed. 34.00x (ISBN 0-8103-3621-9). Gale.
Iggo, A. & Ilyinsky, B. Somatosensory & Visceral Receptor Mechanism. (Progress in Brain Research: Vol. 43). 1976. 83.00 (ISBN 0-444-41342-1, North Holland). Elsevier.
Iglehart, Alfreda P. Married Women & Work: Nineteen Fifty-Seven & Nineteen Seventy-Six. LC 78-75320. (Illus.). 128p. 1979. 16.95 (ISBN 0-669-02838-X). Lexington Bks.
Iglesia, Maria E. de la see De la Iglesia, Maria E.
Iglesia, Ramon. Columbus, Cortes, & Other Essays. Simpson, Lesley B., tr. LC 69-13727. 1969. 27.50x (ISBN 0-520-01469-3). U of Cal Pr.
Iglesias, Hector A. & Chirife, Jorge, eds. Handbook of Food Isotherms: Water Sorption Parameters for Food & Food Components (Monographs) (Food Science & Food Technology Ser.). 1982. 49.00 (ISBN 0-12-370380-8). Acad Pr.
Iglewicz, B. & Stoyle, J. Introduction to Mathematical Reasoning. 1973. pap. 11.95x (ISBN 0-02-359600-7). Macmillan.
Iglitzin, Lynne B., et al, eds. Women in the World: A Comparative Study. new ed. LC 74-14197. (Studies in International & Comparative Politics: No. 6). 427p. 1976. text ed. 11.75 (ISBN 0-87436-200-8); pap. text ed. 11.75 o.p. (ISBN 0-87436-201-6). ABC-Clio.
Ignarro, Louis, ed. see International Conference on Cyclic Nucleotide, 3rd, New Orleans, la., July 1977.
Ignas, Edward & Corsini, Raymond J. Alternative Educational Systems. LC 78-61883. 1979. text ed. 12.95 o.p. (ISBN 0-87581-246-5); pap. text ed. 7.95 o.p. (ISBN 0-87581-242-2). Peacock Pubs.
Ignas, Edward & Corsini, Raymond J., eds. Comparative Educational Systems. LC 80-52449. 442p. 1981. text ed. 17.95 (ISBN 0-87581-260-0). Peacock Pubs.
Ignatieff, E., tr. see Adrianov, O. S. & Mering, T. A.
Ignatow, David. Open Between Us. (Poets on Poetry Ser.). 248p. 1980. pap. 7.95 (ISBN 0-472-06314-6). U of Mich Pr.
--Whisper to the Earth. 1981. 10.95 (ISBN 0-316-41494-8, Pub. by Atlantic Monthly Pr); pap. 6.95 (ISBN 0-686-96773-9). Little.
Ignatow, Yaedi. The Flaw. 65p. 1983. pap. 7.95 (ISBN 0-935296-32-8). Sheep Meadow.
Ignition Manufacturers Institute. Automotive Emission Control & Tune-up Procedures. 3rd ed. (Illus.). 1980. text ed. 20.95 (ISBN 0-13-054791-3); pap. text ed. 15.95 (ISBN 0-13-054783-2). P-H.
Ignizio, James P. Linear Programming in Single & Multiple Objective Systems. (Illus.). 576p. 1982. 31.95 (ISBN 0-13-537027-2). P-H.
Ignoffo, Robert, jt. auth. see See-Lasley, Kay.
Iguchi, B. Convent Cat. (ps-3). 1976. 5.95 o.p. (ISBN 0-07-031703-8, GB); PLB 5.72 o.p. (ISBN 0-07-031704-6). McGraw.
Igumnov, K. N., ed. see Scriabin, Alexander.
Ihara, Saikaku. This Scheming World. Takatsuka, Masanori & Stubbs, David, trs. LC 65-17850. 1965. pap. 4.25 (ISBN 0-8048-1115-6). C E Tuttle.
Ihara, Toni, jt. auth. see Warner, Ralph.
Ihara Saikaku. Tales of Japanese Justice. Kondo, Thomas M. & Marks, Alfred H., trs. 1980. pap. text ed. 7.50x (ISBN 0-8248-0669-7). UH Pr.
Ihde, Aaron J. The Development of Modern Chemistry. (Illus.). 851p. 1983. pap. 15.00 (ISBN 0-486-64235-6). Dover.
Ihde, Don. Experimental Phenomenology: An Introduction. LC 77-8703. (Illus.). 1977. 7.95 o.p. (ISBN 0-399-11913-2); pap. 3.95 (ISBN 0-399-50373-0, Perigee). Putnam Pub Group.
--Listening & Voice: A Phenomenology of Sound. LC 76-8302. (Illus.). x, 188p. 1976. 12.00x (ISBN 0-8214-0201-3, 82-82071). Ohio U Pr.
--Listening & Voice: A Phenomenology of Sound. LC 76-8302. (Illus.). x, 188p. 1979. pap. 6.95x (ISBN 0-8214-0563-2, 82-82089). Ohio U Pr.
--Sense & Significance. LC 72-90635. (Philosophical Ser.: No. 31). 1973. text ed. 10.95x (ISBN 0-391-00313-5). Duquesne.
Ihilevich, David & Gleser, Goldine G. Evaluating Mental-Health Programs: The Progress Evaluation Scales. LC 81-48627. (Illus.). 272p. 1982. 24.95x (ISBN 0-669-05464-X). Lexington Bks.
Ihlanfeldt, William. Achieving Optimal Enrollments & Tuition Revenues: A Guide to Modern Methods of Market Research, Student Recruitment, & Institutional Pricing. LC 79-92463. (Higher Education Ser.). 1980. text ed. 16.95x (ISBN 0-87589-452-6). Jossey-Bass.
Ihle, Sandra N. Malory's Grail Quest: Invention & Adaptation in Medieval Prose Romance. LC 82-70554. (Illus.). 224p. 1983. text ed. 22.50 (ISBN 0-299-09240-2). U of Wis Pr.
Iijima, A. & Hein, J. R., eds. Siliceous Deposits in the Pacific Region. (Developments in Sedimentology Ser.: No. 36). 472p. 1982. 85.00 (ISBN 0-686-84505-6). Elsevier.
Iiyama, Patti, et al. Drug Use & Abuse Among U.S. Minorities: An Annotated Bibliography. LC 78-58481. (Special Studies). (Illus.). 220p. 1976. text ed. 19.95 o.p. (ISBN 0-275-05370-9). Praeger.
Ijiri, Y. & Simon, H. A. Skew Distributions & Sizes of Business Firms. (Studies in Mathematical & Managerial Economics: Vol. 24). 1977. 42.75 (ISBN 0-7204-0518-1, North-Holland). Elsevier.
Ijiri, Yuji, jt. auth. see Cooper, W. W.
Ijsewijn, J., ed. Companion to Neo-Latin Studies. 1977. 51.00 (ISBN 0-7204-0510-6, North-Holland). Elsevier.
Ijuri, Robert, tr. see Tal, Mikhail & Hajtun, Jozsef.
Ike, Nobutaka. Beginnings of Political Democracy in Japan. Repr. of 1950 ed. lib. bdg. 18.25x (ISBN 0-8371-1808-5, IKPD). Greenwood.
--A Theory of Japanese Democracy. LC 77-13167. (Special Studies on China & East Asia). (Illus.). 1978. lib. bdg. 18.00 o.p. (ISBN 0-89158-061-1); pap. 12.00 o.p. (ISBN 0-89158-932-5). Westview.
Ikeda, Fusaye, jt. auth. see Fellows, Hugh.
Ikeda, Kyoko. Kosher Chinese Cooking for Everyone. LC 82-11242. 1982. 4.50 (ISBN 0-86628-031-6). Ridgefield Pub.
Ikeda, N. & Watanabe, S. Stochastic Differential Equations & Diffusion Processes: North-Holland Mathematical Library, Vol. 24. 1981. 74.50 (ISBN 0-444-86172-6). Elsevier.
Ikegami, Yoshihiko, ed. The Empire of Signs: Contributions by Japanese Semioticians. (Foundations of Semiotics: 8). 320p. 1983. 32.00 (ISBN 90-272-3278-4). Benjamins North Am.
Ikels, Charlotte. Adaptation & Aging: Chinese in Hong Kong & the United States. 1983. 27.50 (ISBN 0-208-01999-5, Archon). Shoe String.
Ikemoto, Takashi, jt. ed. see Stryk, Lucien.
Ikemoto, Takashi, jt. tr. see Stryk, Lucien.
Ikenberry, Oliver S. American Education Foundations. LC 73-89294. 1974. text ed. 19.95 o.p. (ISBN 0-675-08897-6). Merrill.
Ikle, Fred C. How Nations Negotiate. LC 76-8398. 1976. Repr. of 1964 ed. 20.00 (ISBN 0-527-44220-8). Kraus Repr.
--How Nations Negotiate. LC 76-8398. 264p. 1982. Repr. of 1964 ed. 20.00 (ISBN 0-527-44220-8, Inst Study Diplomacy). Geo U Sch For Serv.
Ikle, Max. Switzerland: An International Banking & Financial Center. Schiff, Eric, tr. from Ger. LC 72-76544. 156p. 1972. text ed. 34.50 (ISBN 0-87933-002-3). Hutchinson Ross.
Ilaco, B. V. Agricultural Compendium: For Rural Development in the Tropics & Subtropics. 1981. 42.75 (ISBN 0-444-41952-7). Elsevier.
Ilardi, Frank A. Computer Circuit Analysis: Theory & Application. (Illus.). 416p. 1976. 24.95 (ISBN 0-13-165357-1). P-H.
Ilardi, Vincent, ed. Dispatches with Related Documents of Milanese Ambassadors in France Burgundy 1450-1483 (Mar. 11- June 29 1466) Fata, Frank J., tr. LC 68-20933. 1980. Vol. III, 445 p. 35.00 (ISBN 0-87580-069-6); Vol. I, 1450-1460, 390 p. (1970) 35.00 (ISBN 0-8214-0067-3). N Ill U Pr.
Ilardo, Joseph A., jt. auth. see Eisenberg, Abne M.
ILA's Board of Regents. Certified Internal Auditor Examination: May 1982-Questions & Suggested Solutions, No. 9. 51p. 1982. pap. text ed. 4.00 (ISBN 0-89413-096-X). Inst Inter Aud.
Ilchman, Warren F. & Uphoff, Norman T. The Political Economy of Change. LC 71-81743. 1969. 26.50x (ISBN 0-520-01390-5); pap. 5.95x o.p. (ISBN 0-520-02033-2, CAMPUS58). U of Cal Pr.
Iler, Ralph K. The Chemistry of Silica: Solubility, Polymerization, Colloid & Surface Properties & Biochemistry. LC 78-23960. 1979. 100.00 (ISBN 0-471-02404-X, Pub. by Wiley-Interscience). Wiley.
Iles, Frances. Malice Aforethought. LC 31-32419. 289p. 1980. pap. 2.95i (ISBN 0-06-080532-3, P 532, PL). Har-Row.
Iles, Francis. Before the Fact. 1979. lib. bdg. 9.95 (ISBN 0-8398-2539-0, Gregg). G K Hall.
--Before the Fact. LC 80-7837. 352p. 1980. pap. 2.50i (ISBN 0-06-080517-X, P 517, PL). Har-Row.
Iles, P. A. & Soclof, S. I. Solar Cells & Photodiodes. Date not set. price not set (ISBN 0-07-031714-3). McGraw.
Iles, T. D., jt. auth. see Fryer, G.
Iles, T. D., jt. auth. see Fryer, Geoffrey.
Ileto, Reynaldo C. Pasyon & Revolution: Popular Movements in the Philippines, 1840-1910. (Illus.). 345p. 1980. 20.00x o.p. (ISBN 0-686-28640-5); pap. 15.00x (ISBN 0-686-28641-3). Cellar.
Ilford, Mary, tr. see Lacour-Gayet, Robert.
Ilfrey, Jack & Reynolds, Max. Happy Jack's Go-Buggy: A WW 11 Fighter Pilot's Personal Document. 1979. 8.00 o.p. (ISBN 0-682-49236-1). Exposition.
Ilg, jt. auth. see Ames.
Ilg, Frances L. & Ames, Louise B. Child Behavior. pap. 2.84i (ISBN 0-06-080072-0, P72, PL). Har-Row.
Ilg, Frances L., jt. auth. see Ames, Louise B.
Ilg, Francis L., et al. School Readiness. rev. ed. LC 77-11826. (Illus.). 1978. 15.34i (ISBN 0-06-012146-7, HarpT). Har-Row.
Ilgan, Daniel R., jt. auth. see McCormick, Ernest J.
Ilich, John. Restaurant Finance: A Handbook for Successful Management & Operations. LC 75-22093. 142p. 1975. 19.95 (ISBN 0-86730-216-X). Lebhar Friedman.
Iliffe, J. Basic Machine Principles. 2nd ed. 1972. 10.50 (ISBN 0-444-19582-3). Elsevier.
Iliffe, John. A Modern History of Tanganyika. LC 77-95445. (African Studies Ser.: No. 25). 1979. 84.50 (ISBN 0-521-22024-6); pap. 22.95x (ISBN 0-521-29611-0). Cambridge U Pr.
--Tanganyika Under German Rule, Nineteen Five to Nineteen Twelve. LC 69-10196. 1969. 34.50 (ISBN 0-521-05371-4). Cambridge U Pr.
Iliuc, I. Tribology of Thin Layers. (Tribology Ser.: Vol. 4). 1980. 53.25 (ISBN 0-444-99768-7). Elsevier.
Illes, J. H., ed. Mechanism of Graben Formation. (Developments in Geotechtonics Ser.: Vol. 17). 1981. 57.50 (ISBN 0-444-41956-X). Elsevier.
Illica, Luigi, jt. ed. see Giacomo, Giuseppe.
Illich, Ivan. Deschooling Society. 1972. pap. 2.50i o.p. (ISBN 0-06-080381-9, P381, PL). Har-Row.
--Deschoolong Society. LC 82-48800. (World Perspective Ser.). 192p. 1983. pap. 4.76i (ISBN 0-06-091046-1, CN 1046, CN). Har-Row.
--Medical Nemesis: The Expropriation of Health. 1982. pap. 5.95 (ISBN 0-686-37141-0). Pantheon.
Illich, Ivan & Verne, Etienne. Imprisoned in the Global Classroom. (Education Ser.). 64p. (Orig.). 1980. pap. 1.25 (ISBN 0-686-30856-5). Writers & Readers.
Illich-Svitych, Vladislav M. Nominal Accentuation in Baltic & Slavic. Leed, Richard L. & Feldstein, Ronald F., trs. from Rus. 1979. text ed. 30.00x (ISBN 0-262-09018-X). MIT Pr.
Illick, Joseph E. Colonial Pennsylvania: A History. LC 75-37551. (A History of the American Colonies Ser.). 1976. lib. bdg. 30.00 (ISBN 0-527-18719-4). Kraus Intl.
Illing. Petroleum Geology of the Continental Shelf of N. W. Europe. 1980. 150.00 (ISBN 0-471-25779-6, Wiley Heyden). Wiley.
Illingsworth, Charles. The Sanguine Mystery: 'This Bloody & Butcherly Department of the Healing Art' 84p. 1970. 20.00x (ISBN 0-686-96976-6, Pub. by Nuffield England). State Mutual Bk.
Illingworth, R. S., jt. ed. see Egan, D. F.
Illinois Association For Criminal Justice. Illinois Crime Survey. Wigmore, John H., ed. LC 68-55774. (Criminology, Law Enforcement, & Social Problems Ser.: No. 9). (Complete & Unexpurgated including Organized Crime in Chicago by John Landesco). 1968. Repr. of 1929 ed. 40.00x (ISBN 0-87585-009-X). Patterson Smith.
Illis, L. S., ed. Viral Diseases of the Central Nervous System. (Illus.). 1975. text ed. 25.00 o.p. (ISBN 0-02-858110-5, Pub. by Bailliere-Tindall). Saunders.
Illis, L. S., et al. Rehabilitation of the Neurological Patient. (Illus.). 436p. 1982. pap. text ed. 45.95 (ISBN 0-632-00595-5, B2359-6). Mosby.
Illuminating Engineering Society Industrial Lighting Committee. American National Standard Practice for Industrial Lighting. rev. ed. (Illus.). 48p. 1979. 10.00 (ISBN 0-87995-001-3, RP7); member 5.00. Illum Eng.
Illyes, Elemer. National Minorities in Rumania: Change in Transylvania. (East European Monographs: No. 112). 320p. 1982. 25.00x (ISBN 0-88033-005-8). East Eur Quarterly.
Ilma, Viola. Funk & Wagnall's Guide to the World of Stamp Collecting: The Joys of Stamp Collecting for the Beginning & Advanced Philatelist. LC 78-4762. (Funk & W Bk). 1978. 15.34i (ISBN 0-308-10330-0). T y Crowell.
Ilmavirta, V. & Jones, R. I. Lakes & Water Management. 1982. 54.50 (ISBN 90-6193-758-2, Pub. by Junk Pubs Netherlands). Kluwer Boston.
Ilomechina, Chike P. Personnel Management & Industrial Relations in a United Nations Agency: History Basis & Practice in the Food & Agriculture Organization. 1983. 13.95 (ISBN 0-533-05265-3). Vantage.
Ilse, Sherokee. Empty Arms: A Guide to Help Parents & Loved Ones Cope with a Miscarriage, Stillbirth or Natural Death. Appelbaum, Arlene, ed. 64p. 1982. pap. 3.95 (ISBN 0-9609456-0-1). Sherokee.
Ilsley, Paul & Niemi, John A. Recruiting & Training Volunteers. (Adult Education Association Professional Development Ser.). (Illus.). 176p. 1980. text ed. 14.95x (ISBN 0-07-000556-7, C). McGraw.
Ilyin, Donna. Ilyin Oral Interview Test. (Illus.). 1976. test & manual 15.95 (ISBN 0-88377-057-1); 50 scoring sheets 5.50 (ISBN 0-685-57363-X). Newbury Hse.

--Listening Comprehension Group Test: Examiner's Test Manual. (Listening Comprehension Group Test Ser.). 32p. 1981. pap. text ed. 4.50 (ISBN 0-88377-212-4); LCWT answer sheets (50) 5.95 (ISBN 0-88377-214-0); keys LCPT 5.95 (ISBN 0-88377-213-2). Newbury Hse.

--Listening Comprehension Group Tests: Student Picture Booklet. (Listening Comprehension Group Test Ser.). 32p. (gr. 8-12). 1981. pap. text ed. 2.95 (ISBN 0-88377-210-8). Newbury Hse.

Ilyin, Donna & Rubin, Susan. LCGT Technical Guide. (Listening Comprehension Group Test Ser.). 24p. 1981. pap. text ed. 5.95 (ISBN 0-88377-211-6). Newbury Hse.

Ilyin, Donna, jt. auth. see Doherty, Cecelia.

Ilyin, Donna, et al. English Language Skills Assessment in a Reading Context (Elsa Test AN) 1980. 8.95 ea. (ISBN 0-88377-145-4); test material 4.95 (ISBN 0-686-86504-9). Newbury Hse.

Ilyin, M. Moscow: Monuments of Architecture, 1700-1830. (Illus.). 450p. 1980. 50.00 (ISBN 0-89893-041-3). CDP.

Ilyinsky, B., jt. auth. see Iggo, A.

Il'yuchenok, R. Pharmacology of Behavior & Memory. LC 76-11831. 216p. 1976. 22.50x o.p. (ISBN 0-470-15116-1). Halsted Pr.

Imahori, K., jt. auth. see Wood, R. D.

Imahori, K. & Higashimura, T., eds. Progress in Polymer Science, Japan, Vol. 8. LC 72-7446. 244p. 1975. 47.95 o.s.i. (ISBN 0-470-65727-8). Halsted Pr.

Imahori, Kozo. Ecology, Phytogeography & Taxonomy of the Japanese Charophyta. (Illus.). 1977. pap. text ed. 44.00x (ISBN 3-87429-126-X). Lubrecht & Cramer.

Imai, Ryukichi & Rowen, Henry S. Nuclear Energy & Nuclear Proliferation: Japanese & American Views. LC 79-16589. (Special Studies in International Relations). 1979. lib. bdg. 22.50 (ISBN 0-89158-667-9). Westview.

Imakita, Junichi. A Techno-Economic Analysis of the Port Transport System. 1978. 33.95 o.p. (ISBN 0-03-046241-X). Praeger.

Imaz, Jose L. De see De Imaz, Jose L.

Imber, Gerald & Kurtin, Stephen B. Doctors' Orders: Your Prescription for Staying Young. 228p. 1983. cancelled 12.95 o.p. (ISBN 0-89479-089-7, A & W Visual Library). A & W Pubs.

--Face Care: The Plan for Looking Younger Longer. 228p. 1983. 14.95 (ISBN 0-89479-127-3). A & W Pubs.

Imber, Gerald, jt. auth. see Wagner, Kurt J.

Imber, Steve, ed. Readings in Emotional & Behavioral Disorders. rev. ed. (Special Education Ser.). (Illus.). 224p. pap. text ed. 15.00 (ISBN 0-89568-294-X). Spec Learn Corp.

Imbert De La Platiere, S. Galerie Universelle Des Hommes Qui Se Sont Illustres: Voltaire. Repr. of 1787 ed. 28.00 o.p. (ISBN 0-8287-0457-0). Clearwater Pub.

Imbo, M. Mi Guia Telefonica. Kreps, Georgian, tr. from Eng. (Shape Board Play Book). Orig. Title: My Telephone Book. (Illus.). 14p. (Span.). (ps-3). 1981. bds. 3.50 plastic come bdg. (ISBN 0-686-69692-1, 15009). Tuffy Bks.

--Mi Querido Reloj. Kreps, Georgian, tr. from Eng. (Shape Board Lay Book). Orig. Title: The Happy Clock Book. (Illus.). 14p. (Span.). (ps-3). 1981. bds. 3.50 plastic comb bdg (ISBN 0-89828-204-7, 15008). Tuffy Bks.

IMCO-FAO-UNESCO-WMO-WHO-IAEAUN Joint Group of Experts on the Scientific Aspects of Marine Pollution, 7th Session. Report. (FAO-GESAMP Reports: No. 1). 43p. 1975. pap. 7.50 o.p. (ISBN 0-686-92784-2, F1388, FAO). Unipub.

Imdieke, Leroy F., jt. auth. see Helmkamp, John G.

Imeko, jt. auth. see International Measurement Confederation Congress, Sixth.

Imelik. Catalysis by Zeoliter: Proceedings. (Studies in Surface Science & Catalysis: Vol. 5). 1980. 64.00 (ISBN 0-444-41916-0). Elsevier.

--Metal Support & Metal Additive Effects in Catalysis. (Studies in Surface Science & Catalysis: Vol. 11). 1982. 76.75 (ISBN 0-444-42111-4). Elsevier.

Imfeld, T. N. Identification of Low Caries Risk Dietary Components. (Monographs in Oral Science: Vol. 11). (Illus.). viii, 172p. 1983. 76.25 (ISBN 3-8055-3634-8). S Karger.

Imhalep, Leonid, tr. see Oldenburg, S. S.

Imhoff, Eugene A., Jr., jt. auth. see Danos, Paul.

Imholte, John Q. First Volunteers. 10.00 (ISBN 0-87018-029-0). Ross.

Imhoof, Maurice L., jt. auth. see Hudson, Herman.

Imlay, Gilbert. Emigrants. LC 64-10668. Repr. of 1793 ed. 40.00x (ISBN 0-8201-1262-3). Schol Facsimiles.

Immegart, Glenn L. & Boyd, William L., eds. Problem-Finding in Educational Administration: Trends in Research & Theory. LC 78-19912. 320p. 1979. 25.95x (ISBN 0-669-02438-4). Lexington Bks.

Immel, Constance & Sacks, Florence. Sentence Dynamics: An English Skills Workbook. 1983. pap. text ed. 10.95x (ISBN 0-673-15805-5). Scott F.

Immelman, Klaus. Australian Finches. (Illus.). 224p. 1982. 32.95 (ISBN 0-207-14165-7). Avian Pubns.

Immelmann, Klaus, et al, eds. Behavioural Development: The Bielefeld Interdisciplinary Project. LC 80-29668. (Illus.). 768p. 1981. 69.50 (ISBN 0-521-24058-1); pap. 24.95 (ISBN 0-521-28410-4). Cambridge U Pr.

Immergut, E. H., jt. ed. see Brandrup, Johannes.

Immerman, Richard H. The C.I.A. in Guatemala: The Foreign Policy of Intervention. (Texas Pan American Ser.). 302p. 1983. pap. 9.95 (ISBN 0-292-71083-6). U of Tex Pr.

Immerwahr, Henry R. Form & Thought in Herodotus. LC 66-25319. (American Philological Association Reprint Ser.). 1981. pap. 22.50 (ISBN 0-89130-478-9, 40-00-23). Scholars Pr CA.

Immerzeel, George & Ockenga, Earl. The Calculator. (Mathematics in Our World Ser.). 1981. Bk. I. pap. text ed. 4.56 student ed. (ISBN 0-201-16075-7, Sch Div); Bk. I. tchr's. ed. 4.88 (ISBN 0-201-16076-5); Bk. II. pap. text ed. 4.04 (ISBN 0-201-16085-4); Bk. II. tchr's. manual 4.56 (ISBN 0-201-16086-2). A-W.

--Calculator Activities for the Classroom: Bk. 2. Preiss, Irene, ed. 1977. wkbk. 8.50 (ISBN 0-88488-109-1). Creative Pubns.

--Calculator Activities for the Classroom: Bk. 1. Preiss, Irene, ed. 1977. wkbk. 8.50 (ISBN 0-88488-108-3). Creative Pubns.

Immerzeel, George & Thomas, Melvin, eds. Ideas From the "Arithmetic Teacher": Grades Six to Eight, Middle School. (Illus.). 144p. (gr. 6-8). 1982. pap. 5.40 (ISBN 0-87353-200-7). NCTM.

Immroth, John P., ed. see Bloomberg, Marty & Weber, Hans.

Imms, A. D., et al. Imm's General Textbook of Entomology, 2 vols. 10th ed. 1977. Vol. 1. 45.00x (ISBN 0-412-15200-2, Pub. by Chapman & Hall England); Vol. 2. 75.00x o.p. (ISBN 0-412-15220-7); Vol. 1. pap. 17.95x o.p. (ISBN 0-412-15210-X); Vol. 2. pap. 46.00x (ISBN 0-412-15230-4). Methuen Inc.

Impe, Rexella Van see Van Impe, Rexella.

Imperato, Eleanor M., jt. auth. see Imperato, Pascal J.

Imperato, Pascal J. The Administration of a Public Health Agency: A Case Study of the New York City Department of Health. 192p. 1983. 26.95 (ISBN 0-89885-122-X). Human Sci Pr.

--Medical Detective. LC 79-15315. 1979. 10.95 o.p. (ISBN 0-399-90058-6, Marek). Putnam Pub Group.

Imperato, Pascal J. & Imperato, Eleanor M. Mali: A Handbook of Historical Statistics. 1982. lib. bdg. 75.00 (ISBN 0-8161-8147-0, Hall Reference). G K Hall.

Imperato, Pascal J., ed. Historical Dictionary of Mali. LC 76-10050. (African Historical Dictionaries Ser.: No. 11). (Illus.). 1977. 13.00 (ISBN 0-8108-1005-0). Scarecrow.

Imperial Chemical Industries Ltd. Plastics Division, ed. see Ogorkiewicz, R. M.

Imperial College, London, Sept. 9-13, 1974, 6th Symposium, et al see Marton, L.

Imperial College of Science & Technology, Rock Mechanics Section, jt. auth. see Hoek, E.

Imre, Roberta W. Knowing & Caring: Philosophical Issues in Social Work. LC 82-20209. 164p. (Orig.). 1983. lib. bdg. 18.50 (ISBN 0-8191-2859-7); pap. text ed. 8.75 (ISBN 0-8191-2860-0). U Pr of Amer.

IMS Press Staff. Ayer Directory of Publications, 1983. rev. ed. (Annual Ser.). 1983. 95.00 (ISBN 0-910190-26-7). IMS Pr.

Imwinkelried, Edward J., et al. Criminal Evidence. (Criminal Justice Ser.). 1979. pap. text ed. 21.50 (ISBN 0-8299-0221-X); tchrs.' manual avail. (ISBN 0-8299-0591-X). West Pub.

Inada, Hogitaro, jt. auth. see Koop, Albert J.

Inagaki, Yoshio & Okazaki, Renji. Chemistry of N-Thiosulfinylamines. (Sulfur Reports: Vol. 2, No. 4). 40p. 1982. 24.50 (ISBN 3-7186-0126-5). Harwood Academic.

Inamdar, F. A. Image & Symbol in Joseph Conrad's Novels. 1980. text ed. 16.25x (ISBN 0-391-01916-3). Humanities.

Inashima, O. James, jt. auth. see Johns, Marjorie P.

Inayat, Taj, et al. The Crystal Chalice: Spiritual Themes for Women. LC 79-105496. (Illus.). 152p. (Orig.). 1979. pap. 5.95 (ISBN 0-930872-08-8). Omega Pr NM.

Inayat Khan, Hazrat. Spiritual Dimensions of Psychology. LC 80-54830. (Collected Works of Hazrat Inayat Khan Ser.). 256p. (Orig.). 1981. 7.95 (ISBN 0-930872-24-X, 1012P). Omega Pr NM.

Inbar, Michael. The Vulnerable Age Phenomenon. LC 76-23365. (Social Science Frontiers Ser.). 59p. 1976. pap. 3.50x (ISBN 0-87154-397-4). Russell Sage.

Inbau, F. E., jt. auth. see Waltz, J. R.

Inbau, Fred E., et al. Scientific Police Investigation. LC 77-187837. (Inbau Law Enforcement Ser). (Illus.). 200p. 1972. 7.95x o.p. (ISBN 0-8019-5417-7). Chilton.

Inbucon Consultants. Managing Human Resources. LC 76-39984. 179p. 1976. 18.95x o.p. (ISBN 0-470-98954-8). Halsted Pr.

Incani, Albert G., et al. Coordinated Activity Programs for the Aged: A How-to-Do-It Manual. LC 75-14106. (Illus.). 168p. (Orig.). 1975. pap. 18.75 (ISBN 0-87258-162-4, AHA-175124). Am Hospital.

Ince & Mayhew. Universal Systems of Household Furniture 1762. 16.50 o.s.i. (ISBN 0-85458-618-0). Transatlantic.

Inch, Morris, jt. ed. see Youngblood, Ronald.

Inchley, Christopher. Immunobiology. (Studies in Biology: No. 128). 88p. 1981. pap. text ed. 8.95 (ISBN 0-7131-2808-9). E Arnold.

Inciardi, James A., et al. Legal & Illicit Drug Use: Acute Reactions of Emergency Room Populations. LC 78-19743. 1978. 29.95 o.p. (ISBN 0-03-046701-2). Praeger.

Incropera, Frank P. Fundamentals of Heat Transfer. DeWitt, David P., ed. LC 80-17209. 819p. 1981. text ed. 36.95 (ISBN 0-471-42711-X); solutions guide avail. (ISBN 0-471-09084-0). Wiley.

Ind. Cancer Research Foundation. Got a Horse-Get DMSO. 1981. 3.00x o.p. (ISBN 0-686-29832-2). Cancer Control Soc.

Indakwa, John. Expansion of British Rule in the Interior of Central Africa. 316p. 1977. pap. text ed. 13.25 (ISBN 0-8191-0141-9). U Pr of Amer.

--Swahili, Conversation & Grammar. 2nd ed. 517p. 1975. 14.95 (ISBN 0-87201-813-X). Gulf Pub.

Inden, Ronald B. Marriage & Rank in Bengali Culture: A History of Caste & Clan in Middle-Period Bengal. LC 73-85789. 176p. 1976. 27.50x (ISBN 0-520-02569-5). U of Cal Pr.

Independent Commission on Disarmanent & Security Issues. Common Security: A Blueprint for Survival. LC 82-5973. 202p. 1982. 10.75 (ISBN 0-671-45880-9); pap. 5.95 (ISBN 0-671-45879-5). S&S.

Indian Claims Commission. Coast Salish & Western Washington Indians, Vol. 5: Findings of Fact, & Opinion. (American Indian Ethnohistory Ser: Indians of the Northwest). (Illus.). lib. bdg. 42.00 o.s.i. (ISBN 0-8240-0787-5). Garland Pub.

--Sioux Indians, Vol. Four: Findings of Fact, & Opinion. (American Indian Ethnohistory Ser: Plains Indians). (Illus.). lib. bdg. 42.00 o.s.i. (ISBN 0-8240-0797-2). Garland Pub.

Indian Law Institute. Indian Legal System. 1979. 28.00 o.p. (ISBN 0-379-20368-5). Oceana.

Indian Ocean Fishery Commission, Executive Committee for the Implementation of the International Indian Ocean Fishing Survey & Development Programme, 1st Session. Report. (FAO Fisheries Reports: No. 105). 18p. 1971. pap. 7.50 (ISBN 0-686-93056-8, F1696, FAO). Unipub.

Indian Ocean Fishery Commission Executive Committee for the Implementation of the International Indian Ocean Fishery Survey & Development Programme, 2nd Session, Rome, 1971. Report. (FAO Fisheries Reports: No. 111). 36p. 1971. pap. 7.50 (ISBN 0-686-93070-3, F1700, FAO). Unipub.

Indian Ocean Fishery Commission Executive Committee for the Implementation of the International Indian Ocean Fishery Survey & Development Programme, 3rd Session, Columbia, Sri Lanka, 1972. Report. (FAO Fisheries Reports: No. 126). 10p. 1972. pap. 7.50 (ISBN 0-686-93082-7, F1707, FAO). Unipub.

Indian Ocean Fishery Commission, Executive Committee for the Implementation of the International Indian Ocean Fishery Survey & Development Programme, 7th Session, Rome, 1978. Report. (FAO Fisheries Reports: No. 205). 26p. 1978. pap. 7.50 (ISBN 0-686-94001-6, F1496, FAO). Unipub.

Indian Ocean Fishery Commission, Executive Committee for the Implementation of the International Indian Ocean Fishery Survey & Development Programme, 8th Session, Rome, 1979. Report. (FAO Fisheries Reports: No. 221). 14p. 1979. pap. 7.50 (ISBN 0-686-94007-5, F1828, FAO). Unipub.

Indian Ocean Fishery Commission on Management of Indian Ocean Tuna, 2nd Session, Rome, 1971, jt. auth. see Indo-Pacific Fisheries Council Special Committee on Management of Indo-Pacific Tuna, 1st Session.

Indian Ocean Fishery Commission Special Working on Party Stock Assessment of Shrimp of the Indian Ocean Area, 1st Session, Bahrain, 1971. Report. (FAO Fisheries Reports: No. 138). 44p. 1973. pap. 7.50 (ISBN 0-686-93969-7, F781, FAO). Unipub.

Indian Ocean Fishery Commission, 1st Session, Rome, 1968. Report. (FAO Fisheries Reports: No. 60). 35p. 1968. pap. 7.50 (ISBN 0-686-93015-0, F1673, FAO). Unipub.

Indian Ocean Fishery Commission, 3rd Session, Colombo, Sri Lanka, 1972. Report. (Fao Fisheries Reports: No. 130). 28p. 1973. pap. 7.50 (ISBN 0-686-93088-6, F1709, FAO). Unipub.

Indian Ocean Fishery Commission, 5th Session, Rome, 1976. Report of the Executive Committee for the Implementation of the International Indian Ocean Fishery Survey & Development Programme. (FAO Fisheries Reports: No. 180). 16p. 1976. pap. 7.50 (ISBN 0-686-93087-8, FAO). Unipub.

Indiana University, Folklore Institute, Archives of Traditional Music. A Catalog of Phonorecording of Music & Oral Data Held by the Archives of Traditional Music. 1976. lib. bdg. 30.00 (ISBN 0-8161-1120-0, Hall Reference). G K Hall.

Indiana University, Institute for Sex Research. Catalog of Periodical Literature in the Social & Behavioral Sciences Section, Library of the Institute for Sex Research, Including Supplement to Monographs, 1973-1975, 4 vols. 1976. Set. lib. bdg. 380.00 (ISBN 0-8161-0041-1, Hall Library). G K Hall.

--Catalog of the Social & Behavioral Sciences Monograph Section of the Library of the Institute for Sex Research, 4 vols. 2572p. 1975. Set. lib. bdg. 380.00 (ISBN 0-8161-1141-3, Hall Library). G K Hall.

--International Directory of Sex Research & Related Fields, 2 vols. 1976. Set. lib. bdg. 145.00 (ISBN 0-8161-0043-8, Hall Library). G K Hall.

--Sexual Nomenclature: A Thesaurus. 1976. lib. bdg. 95.00 (ISBN 0-8161-0044-6, Hall Library). G K Hall.

Indik, Bernard P. People, Groups & Organizations. LC 68-23785. 1968. text ed. 14.95x (ISBN 0-8077-1546-8). Tchrs Coll.

Indo-Pacific Fisheries Council Special Committee on Management of Indo-Pacific Tuna, 1st Session & Indian Ocean Fishery Commission on Management of Indian Ocean Tuna, 2nd Session, Rome, 1971. Report of the Joint Meeting. (FAO Fisheries Reports: No. 104). 21p. 1971. pap. 7.50 (ISBN 0-686-92734-6, F1695, FAO). Unipub.

Indo-Pacific Fishery Commission, Working Party on Aquaculture & Environment, 5th Session, Jakarta, Indonesia, 1980. Report. (FAO Fisheries Reports: No. 241). 12p. 1980. pap. 7.50 (ISBN 0-686-94015-6, F2081, FAO). Unipub.

Indochina Curriculum Group. The Vietnam Era: A Guide to Teaching Resources. 1978. pap. 5.00 (ISBN 0-686-95364-9). Am Fr Serv Comm.

Industrial Robots, International Symposium, Twelfth. Proceedings of the Twelfth International Symposium on Industrial Robots: Paris, June 9-11, 1982. 540p. 1982. 101.00 (ISBN 0-444-86471-7, North Holland). Elsevier.

Industrial Waste Symposia, 1980. Proceedings. 20.00 (ISBN 0-686-30995-2, T00053). Water Pollution.

Ineman, Kathleen. The Postal Service Guide to U. S. Stamps. 9th ed. LC 82-60322. (Illus.). 280p. 1982. pap. 3.50 (ISBN 0-9604756-2-1). USPS.

Ineson, Frank A., jt. auth. see Read, William R.

Inesse, Daniel, jt. auth. see Wright, Ezekiel.

Inez, Colette. Alive & Taking Names. LC 77-86351. 74p. 1977. 8.95x (ISBN 0-8214-0377-X, 82-82741); pap. 4.95 (ISBN 0-8214-0393-1, 82-82758). Ohio U Pr.

Infanger, jt. auth. see Casavant.

Infante, Mary S. The Clinical Laboratory in Nursing Education. LC 74-12454. 112p. 1975. text ed. 19.50 (ISBN 0-471-42715-2, Pub. by Wiley Medical). Wiley.

Infeld, Leopold. Quest: An Autobiography. LC 79-55510. viii, 361p. 1980. 14.95 (ISBN 0-8284-0309-0). Chelsea Pub.

Infield, Glenn. Big Week! 256p. 1979. pap. 1.95 o.p. (ISBN 0-523-40519-7). Pinnacle Bks.

Infield, Glenn B. Leni Riefenstahl: The Fallen Film Goddess. LC 76-7084. (Illus.). 1976. 12.45i (ISBN 0-690-01167-9, TYC-T). T Y Crowell.

Infield, Louis, tr. see Kant, Immanuel.

Infomap Inc. Atlas of Demographics: U. S. by County. (Illus.). 60p. 1982. 195.00 (ISBN 0-910471-00-2). Infomap Inc.

Inform Inc. Cleaning up Coal: A Study of Coal Cleaning & the Use of Cleaned Coal. 416p. 1982. prof. ref. 37.50x (ISBN 0-88410-913-5). Ballinger Pub.

--Energy Futures: Industry & the New Technologies. abr. ed. Orr, Leonard H., ed. LC 76-30324. 1978. prof ref 13.50x (ISBN 0-88410-617-9). Ballinger Pub.

Inform, Inc. The Scrubber Strategy: The How & Why of Flue Gas Desulfurization. 192p. 1982. prof. ref. 37.50x (ISBN 0-88410-912-7). Ballinger Pub.

Informal Consultation on Antarctic Kill, 1974. Report. (FAO Fisheries Reports: No. 153). 153p. 1974. pap. 7.50 (ISBN 0-686-93980-8, F794, FAO). Unipub.

Information Gatekeepers, Inc. The Second European Fiber Optics & Communications Exposition, 2 vols. 1982. pap. 125.00 (ISBN 0-686-38470-9). Info Gatekeepers.

--The Second Viewtext Exposition VT'82. 1981. 125.00 (ISBN 0-686-38471-7). Info Gatekeepers.

--The Sixth International Fiber Optics & Communications Exposition. 1982. 125.00 (ISBN 0-686-38469-5). Info Gatekeepers.

Information Sources, Inc. The Small Systems Software & Services Sourcebook. Koolish, Ruth K., ed. 504p. 1982. pap. 125.00 (ISBN 0-943906-00-8). Info Sources.

Infotech Ltd., ed. Computer Graphics, 2 vols. Incl. Vol. 1-Analysis. 247p; Vol. 2-Invited Papers. 301p. (Illus.). 1980. Set. 355.00x (ISBN 0-8002-3034-5). Intl Pubns Serv.

Ing, Dean. Pulling Through. 1983. pap. 2.95 (ISBN 0-441-69050-5, Pub. by Ace Science Fiction). Ace Bks.

Ingall, R. F. & Mastromarino, Anthony J., eds. Prevention of Hereditary Large Bowel Cancer. LC 82-24988. (Progress in Clinical & Biological Research Ser.: Vol. 115). 278p. 1983. 30.00 (ISBN 0-8451-0115-3). A R Liss.

Ingalls, A. Joy & Salerno, M. Constance. Maternal & Child Health Nursing. (Illus.). 800p. 1983. pap. text ed. 23.95 (ISBN 0-8016-2324-3); study guide 10.95 (ISBN 0-8016-2323-5). Mosby.

Ingalls, Jeremy, tr. see Nakagawa, Yoiche.

Ingalls, Rachel. Mediterranean Cruise. LC 73-81317. 154p. 1973. 9.95 (ISBN 0-87645-081-8). Gambit.

--Mrs. Caliban. LC 81-84459. 125p. 1983. 8.95 (ISBN 0-87645-112-1). Gambit.

--Theft & the Man Who Was Left Behind. LC 73-118212. 1970. 6.95 (ISBN 0-87645-032-X). Gambit.

Ingalls, Robert P. Hoods: The Story of the Ku Klux Klan. LC 78-11596. (Illus.). (gr. 6 up). 1979. 9.95 (ISBN 0-399-20658-2). Putnam Pub Group.

--Mental Retardation: The Changing Outlook. LC 77-23359. 1978. text ed. 27.95 (ISBN 0-471-42716-0); tchrs.' manual 5.00 (ISBN 0-471-05031-8). Wiley.

--Point of Order: A Profile of Senator Joe McCarthy. (Illus.). 1981. 9.95 (ISBN 0-399-20827-5). Putnam Pub Group.

Ingamells, Lynn & Porter, Standish. Variedades del Espanol Actual. (Illus.). 384p. (Span., Prog. Bk.). 1975. pap. text ed. 14.95x (ISBN 0-582-35026-3); of 4 tapes 60.00x set (ISBN 0-582-37394-8); tapescript 4.50x (ISBN 0-582-35027-1). Longman.

Ingard, K. U., jt. auth. see Morse, Philip M.

Inge, M. Thomas, jt. auth. see Young, Thomas D.

Inge, M. Thomas, ed. Ellen Glasgow: Centennial Essays. LC 75-15976. 232p. 1976. 13.95 (ISBN 0-8139-0620-2). U Pr of Va.

--Handbook of American Popular Culture, Vol. 3. LC 77-95357. 472p. 1981. lib. bdg. 39.25 (ISBN 0-313-22025-5, IAS/). Greenwood.

--Handbook of American Popular Culture, Vol. 1: Animation, the Automobile, Children's Literature, Comic Art, Detective & Mystery Novels, Film, Gothic Novels, Popular Music, the Pulps, Radio Science Fiction, Sports, Stage Entertainments, Television, the Western. LC 77-95357. 1979. lib. bdg. 35.00x (ISBN 0-313-20325-3, IAP/). Greenwood.

--Handbook of American Popular Culture, Vol. 2: Advertising, Best Sellers, Circus & Outdoor Entertainment, Death in Popular Culture, Editorial Cartoons, Foodways, Games & Toys, Historical Fiction, Occult & the Supernatural, Photography as Popular Culture, Popular Architecture, Popular Religion & Theories of Self-Help, Romantic Fiction, Verse & Popular Poetry, Women in Popular Culture. LC 77-95357. 1980. lib. bdg. 35.00 (ISBN 0-313-21363-1, IAQ/). Greenwood.

Inge, M. Thomas & MacDonald, Edgar E., eds. James Branch Cabell: Centennial Essays. (Southern Literary Studies). (Illus.). 230p. 1982. text ed. 15.95x (ISBN 0-8071-1028-0). La State U Pr.

Inge, Ott. The Siege of Montsegur. 1982. 14.95 (ISBN 0-903540-63-0, Pub. by Floris Books). St George Bk Serv.

Inge, William. Four Plays. Incl. Bus Stop; Come Back, Little Sheba; The Dark at the Top of the Stairs; Picnic. 1979. pap. 5.95 (ISBN 0-394-17075-X, B417, BC). Grove.

Inge, William R. Mysticism in Religion. LC 76-15407. 1976. Repr. of 1948 ed. lib. bdg. 16.25x (ISBN 0-8371-8953-5, INMR). Greenwood.

Ingebritsen, Karl J. Reston Home Owners Association: A Case Study in New Community Management. Ader-Brin, Dianne, ed. 53p. 1977. pap. text ed. 8.95 (ISBN 0-912104-26-0). Inst Real Estate.

Ingelfinger. Biostatistics in Clinical Medicine. 1983. not set 24.95 (ISBN 0-02-360010-1). Macmillan.

Ingelfinger, Franz J., et al, eds. Controversy in Internal Medicine II. LC 73-76267. (Illus.). 829p. 1974. 21.50 o.p. (ISBN 0-7216-5026-0). Saunders.

Ingelman-Sundberg, Axel & Wirsens, Claes. A Child Is Born: The Drama of Life Before Birth. rev. ed. 1977. 16.95 (ISBN 0-440-01266-X, Sey Lawr). Delacorte.

Ingelow, Jean. Allerton & Dreux; or, the War of Opinion, 1851. Wolff, Robert L., ed. LC 75-475. (Victorian Fiction Ser.). 1975. lib. bdg. 66.00 o.s.i. (ISBN 0-8240-1553-3). Garland Pub.

--Mopsa the Fairy. LC 75-32172. (Classics of Children's Literature, 1621-1932: Vol. 35). (Illus.). 1976. Repr. of 1869 ed. PLB 38.00 o.s.i. (ISBN 0-8240-2284-X). Garland Pub.

Ingels, Jack E. Landscaping: Principles & Practices. 2nd ed. (Illus.). 1983. text ed. 16.00 (ISBN 0-8273-2157-0); instrs.' guide 3.25 (ISBN 0-8273-2158-9). Delmar.

Ingenkamp, K., ed. Developments in Educational Testing, 2 Vols. 1969. Set. 115.00x (ISBN 0-677-61720-8); 65.00x ea. Vol. 1, 450p (ISBN 0-677-61700-3). Vol. 2, 504p (ISBN 0-677-61710-0). Gordon.

Ingenthron, Donita & Ferneti, Casper. Blowing Your Nose. (Project MORE Daily Living Skills Ser.). 32p. 1979. Repr. of 1975 ed. pap. text ed. 5.95 (ISBN 0-8331-1240-6). Hubbard Sci.

Inger, Robert F. The Reptiles. (Beginning-to-Read Bks). (ps). pap. 1.50 o.s.i. (ISBN 0-695-37735-3). Follett.

Ingersall, Robert G. Faith or Agnosticism. 24p. Date not set. pap. 3.00 (ISBN 0-686-83985-4). Am Atheist.

Ingersoll Engineers. The FMS Report. Mortimer, John, ed. (Illus.). 180p. 1983. pap. text ed. 89.00x (ISBN 0-903608-31-6, Pub. by IFSPUBS). Scholium Intl.

Ingersoll, Ernest. Birds in Legend, Fable & Folklore. LC 68-26576. 1968. Repr. of 1923 ed. 34.00x (ISBN 0-8103-3548-4). Gale.

Ingersoll, Gary M. Adolescents in School & Society. 480p. 1982. text ed. 19.95 (ISBN 0-669-02325-6); instr's guide 1.95 (ISBN 0-669-02326-4). Heath.

Ingersoll, Leonard R., et al. Laboratory Manual of Experiments in Physics. 6th ed. (Illus.). 1953. text ed. 8.95 o.p. (ISBN 0-07-031695-3, C). McGraw.

Ingersoll, Robert. Debates with Clergy. 47p. pap. 3.00 (ISBN 0-686-95283-9). Am Atheist.

--The Enemies of Individuality & Mental Freedom. 32p. pap. 3.00 (ISBN 0-686-95284-7). Am Atheist.

--Essays by an Agnostic & Criticisms by a Skeptic. 39p. pap. 3.00 (ISBN 0-686-95285-5). Am Atheist.

--Foundations of Faith. 24p. pap. 3.00 (ISBN 0-686-95287-1). Am Atheist.

--Some Reasons Why I am a Freethinker. 24p. pap. 3.00 (ISBN 0-686-95294-4). Am Atheist.

--What Can You Believe in the Bible. 106p. 1982. pap. 4.00 (ISBN 0-686-95299-5). Am Atheist.

Ingersoll, Robert G. A Christmas Sermon. 30p. pap. 3.00 (ISBN 0-686-83986-2). Am Atheist.

--The Trail of C. B. Reynolds. 31p. pap. 3.00 (ISBN 0-686-83988-9). Am Atheist.

--The Truth about the Holy Bible. 31p. pap. 3.00 (ISBN 0-686-83990-0). Am Atheist.

Ingersoll, William B., ed. see Burlingame, et al.

Ingerson, Earl & Bragg, Wayne G., eds. La Cienca, el Gobierno y la Industria Para el Desarrollo: El foro de Texas. LC 75-21547. (Institute of Latin American Studies-Special Publication). 470p. 1976. pap. 6.95x Span. ed. (ISBN 0-292-71035-6). U of Tex Pr.

Ingham, A. E. Sea Surveying. LC 74-3066. 1975. 124.95x (ISBN 0-471-42729-2, Pub. by Wiley-Interscience). Wiley.

Ingham, Barbara. Tropical Exports & Economic Development: New Perspectives on Producer Response in Three-Low-Income Countries. 1980. 25.00 (ISBN 0-312-81918-8). St Martin.

Ingham, Barbara & Simmons, Colin, eds. The Two World Wars & Economic Development. (Journal of World Development Ser.: No. 9). 100p. 1982. 40.00 (ISBN 0-08-028944-4). Pergamon.

Ingham, Henry L., Jr. The United States: The Destiny of a Democracy, 2 vols. 1978. Vol. 1. pap. text ed. 15.50 (ISBN 0-8191-0384-5); Vol. 2. pap. text ed. 16.50 (ISBN 0-8191-0385-3). U Pr of Amer.

Ingham, Jennie. Books & Reading Development: The Bradford Book Flood Experiment. 2nd ed. 296p. 1982. pap. text ed. 12.50x (ISBN 0-435-10451-9). Heinemann Ed.

Ingham, John N. Biographical Dictionary of American Business Leaders, 2 vols. LC 82-6113. 2496p. 1983. lib. bdg. 195.00 (ISBN 0-313-21362-3, HC102). Greenwood.

--The Iron Barons: A Social Analysis of an American Urban Elite, 1874-1965. LC 77-84761. (Illus.). 1978. lib. bdg. 27.50x (ISBN 0-8371-9891-7, IIB/). Greenwood.

Ingham, Kenneth. The Kingdom of Toro in Uganda. LC 74-31591. (Studies in African History). (Illus.). 186p. 1975. 19.95x (ISBN 0-416-80200-1); pap. 6.95x (ISBN 0-416-80210-9). Methuen Inc.

Ingham, Robert. The Dowager Empress Maria of Russia on Malta. LC 76-175240. 1983. 10.95 (ISBN 0-8315-0130-8). Speller.

Ingham, Rosemary & Covey, Liz. The Costume Designer's Handbook: A Complete Guide for Amateur & Professional Costume Designers. 272p. 1983. 24.95 (ISBN 0-13-181289-0); pap. 12.95 (ISBN 0-13-181271-8). P-H.

Ingle, David J. & Shein, Harvey M., eds. Model Systems in Biological Psychiatry. LC 74-32500. 1975. 20.00x (ISBN 0-262-09015-5). MIT Pr.

Ingle, H. L. & Ward, James A. American History: A Brief View, Vol. 1. 1978. pap. text ed. 9.95 (ISBN 0-316-41858-7); tchrs' manual free (ISBN 0-316-41859-5). Little.

Ingle, Harold N. Nesselrode & the Russian Rapprochement with Britain, 1836-1843. LC 74-79764. 1976. 28.50x (ISBN 0-520-02795-7). U of Cal Pr.

Ingle, John I. & Blair, Patricia, eds. International Dental Care Delivery Systems: Issues in Dental Health Policies. LC 78-13352. 288p. 1978. prof ref 25.00x (ISBN 0-88410-529-6). Ballinger Pub.

Ingle, Neelima, jt. auth. see Ingle, Sud.

Ingle, Stephen & Tether, Philip. Parliament & Health Policy: The Role of the MPs 1970-75. 180p. 1981. text ed. 34.25x (ISBN 0-566-00388-0). Gower Pub Ltd.

Ingle, Sud & Ingle, Neelima. Quality Circles in Service Industries: Comprehensive Guidelines for Increased Productivity & Efficiency. (Illus.). 1983. 21.95 (ISBN 0-13-745059-1); pap. 12.95 (ISBN 0-13-745042-7). P-H.

Ingledew, Robert, tr. see Taylor, Kenneth N.

Inglefield, Ruth K. Marcel Grandjany: Concert Harpist. 1977. pap. text ed. 8.25 (ISBN 0-8191-0348-9). U Pr of Amer.

Inglehart, Ronald, jt. auth. see Rabier, Jacques-Rene.

Ingles, Lloyd G. Mammals of the Pacific States: California, Oregon, Washington. (Illus.). 1965. 14.95 (ISBN 0-8047-0297-7); hardbound student ed. 11.20x (ISBN 0-8047-0298-5). Stanford U Pr.

Inglett, George E., ed. Maize: Recent Progress in Chemistry & Technology. LC 82-20711. 1982. 23.50 (ISBN 0-12-370940-7). Acad Pr.

Inglis, A. The White Women's Protection Ordinance: Sexual Anxiety & Politics in Papua. 20.00x (ISBN 0-686-97035-7, Pub. by Scottish Academic Pr Scotland). State Mutual Bk.

Inglis, Amirah. The White Women's Protection Ordinance: Sexual Anxiety & Politics in Papua, 1920-1934. LC 74-32646. 300p. 1975. 18.95 (ISBN 0-312-86800-6). St Martin.

Inglis, Brian. The Freedom of the Press in Ireland, Seventeen Eighty-Four to Eighteen Forty-One. LC 74-2554. (Studies in Irish History: Vol. 6). 256p. 1975. Repr. of 1954 ed. lib. bdg. 17.00x (ISBN 0-8371-7403-1, INFP). Greenwood.

Inglis, Fred. Ideology & Imagination. LC 74-82220. 240p. 1975. 29.95 (ISBN 0-521-20540-9); pap. 10.95x (ISBN 0-521-09886-6). Cambridge U Pr.

--The Promise of Happiness: Values & Meaning in Children's Fiction. LC 80-49986. 250p. 1982. 39.50 (ISBN 0-521-23142-6); pap. 10.95 (ISBN 0-521-27070-7). Cambridge U Pr.

Inglis, I., jt. auth. see Wright, E. N.

Inglis, J. K. A Textbook of Human Biology. 2nd rev. ed. LC 73-21696. 1974. text ed. 15.50 o.s.i. (ISBN 0-08-017846-4); pap. text ed. 6.75 (ISBN 0-08-017847-2). Pergamon.

Inglis, J. K., jt. auth. see Lee, C. M.

Inglis, K. A., ed. Energy: From Surplus to Scarcity? LC 73-22112. (Illus.). 242p. 1974. 34.95x o.s.i. (ISBN 0-470-42731-0). Halsted Pr.

Inglis, Ruth, ed. Freedom of the Movies: A Report of Self-Regulation from the Commission on Freedom of the Press. LC 74-3391. x, 240p. 1974. Repr. of 1947 ed. lib. bdg. 32.50 (ISBN 0-306-70591-5). Da Capo.

Ingmanson, Dale E. & Wallace, William J. Oceanography: An Introduction. 2nd ed. 1979. text ed. 25.95x (ISBN 0-534-00538-1); lab manual 9.95x (ISBN 0-534-00624-8). Wadsworth Pub.

Ingmire, Frances, jt. ed. see Ericson, Carolyn.

Ingoglia, Gina. Benji & the Tornado. (Golden Look-Look Bks.). (Illus.). 24p. (ps-3). 1982. PLB 5.38 (ISBN 0-307-61871-4, Golden Pr); pap. 1.25 (ISBN 0-307-11871-1). Western Pub.

--Benji, Fastest Day in the West. (Little Golden Reader Ser.). 1979. 5.77 (ISBN 0-307-60165-X). Western Pub.

--Joe Camp's Benji: Fastest Dog in the West. (A Big Picture Bk.). (Illus.). (ps-k). 1979. 2.95 (ISBN 0-307-10826-0, Golden Pr); PLB 7.62 (ISBN 0-307-60826-3). Western Pub.

Ingold. The Biology of Mucor & Its Allies. (Studies in Biology: No. 88). 1978. 5.95 o.p. (ISBN 0-7131-2680-9). Univ Park.

Ingold, Beth, jt. auth. see Windt, Theodore O.

Ingold, Tim. Hunters, Pastoralists & Ranchers. LC 78-73243. (Cambridge Studies in Social Anthropology: No. 28). (Illus.). 1980. 32.50 (ISBN 0-521-22588-4). Cambridge U Pr.

--The Skolt Lapps Today. LC 76-8289. (Changing Cultures Ser.). (Illus.). 1977. 32.50 (ISBN 0-521-21299-5); pap. 10.95x (ISBN 0-521-29090-2). Cambridge U Pr.

Ingraham, Barton. Political Crime in Europe: A Comparative Study of France, Germany, & England. LC 77-83103. 1979. 34.50x (ISBN 0-520-03562-3). U of Cal Pr.

Ingraham, Curtis. CP-M DiskGuide. (DiskGuides Ser.). 32p. (Orig.). 1983. pap. 8.95 (ISBN 0-931988-97-7). Osborne-McGraw.

Ingraham, F. & Anderson, Eric. Prince of the House of David. Orig. Title: Three Years in the Holy City. 363p. 1980. Repr. text ed. 15.95 (ISBN 0-89841-003-7). Zoe Pubns.

Ingraham, John L. & Maaloe, Ole. Growth of the Bacterial Cell. (Illus.). 375p. 1983. text ed. write for info. (ISBN 0-87893-352-2). Sinauer Assoc.

Ingraham, Larry A. The Boys in the Barracks: Observations on American Military Life. 230p. 1983. text ed. 17.50 (ISBN 0-89727-048-7). Inst Study Human.

Ingraham, Lloyd L., jt. auth. see Lowe, James N.

Ingraham, Vernon L., ed. Literature from the Irish Literary Revival: An Anthology. LC 81-40528. 350p. (Orig.). 1982. lib. bdg. 24.00 (ISBN 0-8191-2079-0); pap. text ed. 12.75 (ISBN 0-8191-2080-4). U Pr of Amer.

Ingram, A. W., jt. auth. see Avery, J. H.

Ingram, Arthur. Off Highway & Construction Trucks. (Illus.). 160p. 1980. 17.50 o.p. (ISBN 0-7137-0960-X, Pub. by Blandford Pr England). Sterling.

Ingram, Arthur, ed. Trucks of the World Highways. (Illus.). 128p. 1982. pap. 9.95 (ISBN 0-686-97927-3, Pub. by Blandford Pr England). Sterling.

Ingram, D. Phonological Disability in Children. (Studies in Language & Remediation: 2). 1976. pap. text ed. 17.50 o.p. (ISBN 0-444-19506-8). Elsevier.

Ingram, D. S. & Williams, P. H., eds. Advances in Plant Pathology, Vol. I. (Serial Publication Ser.). 1982. 36.00 (ISBN 0-12-033701-0). Acad Pr.

Ingram, Dave. The Complete Handbook of Slow Scan TV. LC 77-3735. (Illus.). 1977. 14.95 (ISBN 0-8306-7859-X); pap. 9.95 o.p. (ISBN 0-8306-6859-4, 859). TAB Bks.

--Forty-Four Electronics Projects for Hams, SWLs, CBers & Radio Experimenters. LC 80-28323. (Illus.). 181p. 1981. 10.95 (ISBN 0-8306-9643-1); pap. 5.95 (ISBN 0-8306-1258-0, 1258). TAB Bks.

--OSCAR: The Ham Radio Satellites. (Illus., K4TWJ). 1979. 8.95 (ISBN 0-8306-9805-1); pap. 4.95 o.p. (ISBN 0-8306-1120-7, 1120). TAB Bks.

Ingram, David, jt. auth. see Dale, Philip S.

Ingram, David, et al, eds. Proceedings of the First International Congress for the Study of Child Language. LC 80-7952. 668p. 1980. lib. bdg. 36.00 (ISBN 0-8191-1084-1). U Pr of Amer.

Ingram, Doreen. Time in Arabia. 1977. 10.00 o.p. (ISBN 0-7195-2050-9). Transatlantic.

Ingram, G. I., et al. Bleeding Disorders: Investigation & Management. (Illus.). 416p. 1982. text ed. 55.95 (ISBN 0-632-00867-9, B2363-4). Mosby.

Ingram, Gregory K., ed. Residential Location & Urban Housing Markets. (Studies in Income & Wealth Ser.: No. 43). 1978. prof ref 25.00x (ISBN 0-88410-479-6). Ballinger Pub.

Ingram, James, tr. see Garmonsway.

Ingram, James C. International Economic Problems. 3rd ed. LC 77-11139. (Wiley Introduction to Economic Ser.). 1978. pap. text ed. 13.95 (ISBN 0-471-02182-2). Wiley.

Ingram, K. E., ed. see International Conference, Kingston, Jamaica, April 24-29, 1972.

Ingram, Kenneth. History of the Cold War. 1955. 5.00 o.p. (ISBN 0-8022-0778-2). Philos Lib.

Ingram, Marilyn, jt. ed. see Stehle, Audrey P.

Ingram, Marilyn W. & Folse, Lois J. Dining In--Dallas. (Dining In--Ser.). 200p. 1982. pap. 8.95 (ISBN 0-89716-113-0). Peanut Butter.

Ingram, R. E., ed. see Hamilton, William R.

Ingram, R. W. John Marston. (English Authors Ser.). 1978. 14.95 (ISBN 0-8057-6725-8, Twayne). G K Hall.

Ingram, Richard T., et al. Handbook of College & University Trusteeship: A Practical Guide for Trustees, Chief Executives, & Other Leaders Responsible for Developing Effective Governing Boards. LC 79-92465. (Higher Education Ser.). 1980. text ed. 29.95x (ISBN 0-87589-450-X). Jossey-Bass.

Ingram, Robert W., jt. auth. see Copeland, Ronald M.

Ingram, W. A Review of Anatomical Neurology. (Illus.). 1976. 22.50 (ISBN 0-8391-0961-X). Univ Park.

Ingram, W. G. & Redpath, Theodore, eds. Shakespeare's Sonnets. 1978. text ed. 24.50x (ISBN 0-8419-6210-3); pap. text ed. 11.50x (ISBN 0-8419-6211-1). Holmes & Meier.

Ingram, William & Swain, Kathleen M., eds. Concordance to Milton's English Poetry. 1972. 118.00x (ISBN 0-19-811138-X). Oxford U Pr.

Ingrams, Doreen. Mosques & Minarets. LC 74-12221. (The Arab World Ser). 1974. lib. bdg. 6.95 (ISBN 0-88436-115-2); pap. 3.95 (ISBN 0-88436-116-0). EMC.

--New Ways for Ancient Lands. LC 74-14756. (The Arab World Ser). 1974. lib. bdg. 6.95 (ISBN 0-88436-117-9); pap. 3.95 (ISBN 0-88436-118-7). EMC.

--Tents to City Sidewalks. LC 74-16154. (The Arab World Ser). 1974. lib. bdg. 6.95 (ISBN 0-88436-113-6); pap. 3.95 (ISBN 0-88436-114-4). EMC.

Ingstad, Helge. Westward to Vinland. Friis, Erik J., tr. LC 67-10089. (Illus.). 1969. 8.95 o.p. (ISBN 0-312-86450-7, W19225). St Martin.

Ingwersen, Faith & Ingwersen, Niels. Martin A. Hansen. (World Authors Ser.). 1976. lib. bdg. 15.95 (ISBN 0-8057-6259-0, Twayne). G K Hall.

Ingwersen, Niels, jt. auth. see Ingwersen, Faith.

Ingwersen, Ulla. Respiratory Physical Therapy & Pulmonary Care. LC 76-27094. 1976. 29.50x o.p. (ISBN 0-471-02473-2, Pub. by Wiley Medical). Wiley.

Inhaber, Herbert. Energy Risk Assessment. 408p. 1982. 67.50 (ISBN 0-677-05980-9). Gordon.

--Physics of the Environment. LC 77-76911. 1978. 24.00 o.p. (ISBN 0-250-40187-8). Ann Arbor Science.

Inhelder, Barbel & Piaget, Jean. Early Growth of Logic in the Child: Classification & Seriation. Orig. Title: Genesedes Structures Logiques Elementaires. 1970. pap. text ed. 29.50x (ISBN 0-391-00124-8). Humanities.

--Growth of Logical Thinking: From Childhood to Adolescence. LC 58-6439. pap. text ed. 6.95x o.p. (ISBN 0-465-02772-5). Basic.

Inhelder, Barbel, jt. auth. see Piaget, Jean.

Inhorn, Stanley L., ed. Quality Assurance Practices for Health Laboratories. LC 77-17929. 1244p. 1978. 50.00x (ISBN 0-87553-083-4, 010). Am Pub Health.

Inikori, J. E., ed. Forced Migration: The Impact of the Export Slave Trade on African Societies. 352p. 1983. text ed. 22.00x (ISBN 0-8419-0795-1); pap. text ed. 13.50x (ISBN 0-8419-0799-4). Holmes & Meier.

Inkeles, Alex. Social Change in Soviet Russia. 1971. pap. 3,95 o.p. (ISBN 0-671-20950-7, Touchstone Bks). S&S.

--What Is Sociology: An Introduction to the Discipline & Profession. (Orig.). 1964. pap. 9.95 ref. ed. (ISBN 0-13-952416-9). P-H.
Inkeles, Alex, jt. auth. see Spencer, Metta.
Inkeles, Alex, et al. Exploring Individual Modernity. 448p. 1983. text ed. 24.00 (ISBN 0-231-05442-4). Columbia U Pr.
Inkeles, Gordon. The New Massage: Total Body Conditioning for People Who Exercise. 1980. 14.95 o.p. (ISBN 0-399-12455-1, Perige); pap. 7.95 (ISBN 0-399-50453-2). Putnam Pub Group.
Inken, U., jt. auth. see Gmehling, J.
Inlow, Gail. The Emergent in Curriculum. LC 72-6141. 349p. 1966. 16.50 (ISBN 0-471-42804-3, Pub. by Wiley). Krieger.
Inman, jt. auth. see Dymax.
Inman, Don. More TRS-80 Basic. LC 81-150. (Self-Teaching Guide Ser.). 280p. 1981. pap. text ed. 12.95 (ISBN 0-471-08010-1). Wiley.
Inman, Don & Inman, Kurt. Assembly Language Graphics for the TRS-80 Color Computer. 1982. text ed. 19.95 (ISBN 0-8359-0318-4); pap. text ed. 14.95 (ISBN 0-8359-0317-6). Reston.
--The Atari Assembler. 300p. 1981. 18.95 (ISBN 0-8359-0237-4); pap. 12.95 (ISBN 0-8359-0236-6). Reston.
Inman, Don, et al. Real Time BASIC for the TRS-80. Date not set. pap. 9.95 (ISBN 0-918398-05-3). Dilithium Pr.
Inman, Fred W. & Miller, Carl E. Contemporary Physics. (Illus.). 576p. 1974. text ed. 25.95x (ISBN 0-02-359700-3). Macmillan.
Inman, Henry. Old Santa Fe Trail. 1897. Repr. 15.00 o.p. (ISBN 0-87018-031-2). Ross.
Inman, James E., jt. auth. see Litka, Michael P.
Inman, Kurt, jt. auth. see Inman, Don.
Inman, Verne T. Human Walking. (Illus.). 168p. 1980. lib. bdg. 27.00 (ISBN 0-683-04348-X). Williams & Wilkins.
Inmon, Marvin, jt. auth. see Wright, Norman.
Inmon, William. Effective Data Base Design. (P-H Ser. in Data Processing Management). (Illus.). 240p. 1981. text ed. 29.95 (ISBN 0-13-241489-9). P-H.
Inmon, William H. & Friedman, L. Jeanne. Design Review Methodology for a Data Base Environment. (Prentice-Hall Ser. in Data Processing Management). (Illus.). 288p. 1982. 26.95 (ISBN 0-13-201392-4). P-H.
Inn, Martin, ed. see Lo, Benjamin P., et al.
Innes, Christopher. Holy Theatre: Ritual & the Avant Garde. (Illus.). 280p. 1981. 34.50 (ISBN 0-521-22542-6). Cambridge U Pr.
Innes, Clive. Cacti & Other Succulent Plants. (Illus.). 104p. 1982. pap. 7.95 cancelled o.p. (ISBN 0-7063-5511-3). Hippocrene Bks.
Innes, Hammond. The Last Voyage: Captain Cook's Lost Diary. LC 78-20443. 1979. 8.95 o.s.i. (ISBN 0-394-50579-4). Knopf.
--North Star. 1975. 7.95 o.s.i. (ISBN 0-394-49578-0). Knopf.
Innes, Kathleen E. Hampshire Pilgrimages: Men & Women Who Have Sojourned in Hampshire (Jane Austen, Charlotte Mary Yonge, William Cobbett. 60p. 1982. Repr. of 1982 ed. lib. bdg. 40.00 (ISBN 0-89984-927-X). Century Bookbindery.
Innes, Michael. Appleby on Ararat. LC 82-48812. 256p. 1983. pap. 2.84i (ISBN 0-06-080648-6, P648, PL). Har-Row.
--Appleby's End. LC 82-48813. 224p. 1983. pap. text ed. 2.84i (ISBN 0-06-080649-4, P 649, PL). Har-Row.
--The Case Journeying Boy. LC 82-48245. 336p. 1983. pap. 2.84i (ISBN 0-06-080632-X, P 632, PL). Har-Row.
--Lord Mullion's Secret. 1983. pap. 2.95 (ISBN 0-14-006521-0). Penguin.
--The Michael Innes Omnibus. 1983. pap. 8.95 (ISBN 0-14-006059-6). Penguin.
--Money from Holme. (Crime Ser.). 1976. pap. 2.95 (ISBN 0-14-002484-0). Penguin.
--Sheiks & Adders: A Sir John Appleby Mystery Novel. LC 82-9694. (Red Badge Novel of Suspense Ser.). 196p. 1982. 10.95 (ISBN 0-396-08063-4). Dodd.
--The Weight of the Evidence. LC 82-48246. 256p. 1983. pap. 2.84i o.p. (ISBN 0-06-080633-8, P633, HarpR). Har-Row.
--What Happened at Hazelwood. (Crime Ser.). 1976. pap. 2.95 (ISBN 0-14-002650-9). Penguin.
Innes, Stephen, jt. auth. see Breen, T. H.
Innes, William T. Innes Exotic Aquarium Fish. 8.95 (ISBN 0-87666-090-1, PS642). TFH Pubns.
Innes-Homer, William, ed. Heart's Gate: Letters Between Marsden Hartley & Horace Traubel 1906-1915. LC 81-86063. 88p. 1982. pap. 7.50 (ISBN 0-912330-48-1). Jargon Soc.
Inness, George, Jr. Life, Art, & Letters of George Inness. LC 76-87444. (Library of American Art Ser). 1969. Repr. of 1917 ed. lib. bdg. 35.00 (ISBN 0-306-71515-5). Da Capo.
Innis, George S., ed. New Directions in the Analysis of Ecological Systems. (SCS Simulation Ser.: Vol. 5, Nos. 1 & 2). 30.00 (ISBN 0-686-36670-0). Soc Computer Sim.
Innis, Harold A. & Lower, A. R., eds. Select Documents in Canadian Economic History, 2 vols. LC 77-8258. Repr. of 1933 ed. Set. lib. bdg. 67.50x (ISBN 0-87991-132-8); Vol. 1. lib. bdg. 35.00x (ISBN 0-87991-133-6); Vol. 2. lib. bdg. 45.00x (ISBN 0-87991-134-4). Porcupine Pr.
Innis, P. B. & Innis, Walter D. Gold in the Blue Ridge. 1982. 12.50 o.p. (ISBN 0-686-34608-4). Caroline Hse.
--Gold in the Blue Ridge or the True Story of the Beale Treasure. rev. ed. LC 80-144741. (Illus.). 249p. 1980. 12.50 (ISBN 0-941402-00-2). Devon Pub.
Innis, Pauline, ed. Prayer & Power in the Capital: With Prayers of the Presidents. LC 82-156801. (Illus.). 120p. 1982. 10.00 (ISBN 0-941402-02-9). Devon Pub.
Innis, Walter D., jt. auth. see Innis, P. B.
Innocent. Revision Notes on Construction Science. 1977. 3.95 o.p. (ISBN 0-408-00279-4). Butterworth.
Inns, E. G. & Marsden, E. Ordinary Level Practical Chemistry. 2nd ed. 1973. pap. text ed. 9.95x o.p. (ISBN 0-435-64466-1). Heinemann Ed.
Innvarto, Albert, et al. West Coast Plays Four: Earth Worms, Skaters, Two O'clock Feeding, Sunset-Sunrise. (Illus., Orig.). 1979. pap. text ed. 4.95 (ISBN 0-934782-03-2). West Coast Plays.
Inoue, S. & Stephens, R. E., eds. Molecules & Cell Movement. LC 75-16666. (Society of General Physiologists Ser.: Vol. 30). 460p. 1975. 39.50 (ISBN 0-89004-041-9). Raven.
Inoue, T., jt. auth. see Genoud, C.
Inoue, Yasushi. Chronicle of My Mother. Moy, Jean O., tr. LC 82-48168. Orig. Title: Waga Haha No Ki. 113p. (Japanese.). 1983. 14.95 (ISBN 0-87011-533-2). Kodansha.
Inouye, Masayori. Bacterial Outer Membranes: Biogenesis & Functions. LC 79-13999. 1980. 85.50x (ISBN 0-471-04676-0, Pub. by Wiley-Interscience). Wiley.
Inrig, Gary. Quality Friendship. LC 81-38379. 192p. (Orig.). 1981. pap. 5.95 (ISBN 0-8024-2891-6). Moody.
Inrig, Gary, ed. Hearts of Iron, Feet of Clay. 1979. 8.95 (ISBN 0-8024-3486-X); pap. 5.95 (ISBN 0-8024-3487-8). Moody.
Insdorf, Annett. Indelible Shadows: Film & the Holocaust. LC 82-48892. (Illus.). 256p. 1983. pap. 8.95 (ISBN 0-394-71464-4, Vin). Random.
Insdorf, Annette. Francois Truffaut. LC 79-66736. (Illus.). 1979. pap. 4.95 (ISBN 0-688-08586-5). Quill NY.
--Francois Truffaut. (Fillmakers Ser.). 1978. lib. bdg. 11.95 (ISBN 0-8057-9253-8, Twayne). G K Hall.
Insel, Paul M. & Roth, Walton T. Core Concepts in Health. 3rd ed. LC 81-84690. (Illus.). 555p. 1982. pap. text ed. 15.95 o.p. (ISBN 0-686-86320-8); instructor's manual avail. (ISBN 0-87484-537-8). Mayfield Pub.
--Core Concepts in Health. 2nd ed. LC 78-71611. 599p. 1979. pap. text ed. 14.95 o.p. (ISBN 0-87484-498-3). Mayfield Pub.
--Health in a Changing Society. LC 75-39358. (Illus.). 584p. 1976. text ed. 17.95 o.p. (ISBN 0-87484-361-8). Mayfield Pub.
Insel, Paul M., ed. Environmental Variables & the Prevention of Mental Illness. LC 79-3521. 240p. 1980. 28.95x (ISBN 0-669-03457-6). Lexington Bks.
Insh, George P. The Company of Scotland Trading to Africa & the Indies. (Illus.). 343p. Repr. of 1932 ed. lib. bdg. 25.00x (ISBN 0-87991-059-3). Porcupine Pr.
Insight Guides. Bali. (Illus.). 280p. 1983. pap. 14.95 (ISBN 0-13-056200-9). P-H.
--Burma. (Illus.). 336p. 1983. pap. 14.95 (ISBN 0-13-090902-5). P-H.
--Florida. (Illus.). 456p. 1983. pap. 14.95 (ISBN 0-13-322412-0). P-H.
--Hawaii. (Illus.). 418p. 1983. 18.95 (ISBN 0-13-384651-2); pap. 14.95 (ISBN 0-13-384529-X). P-H.
--Hong Kong. (Illus.). 460p. 1983. 18.95 (ISBN 0-13-394643-6); pap. 14.95 (ISBN 0-13-394635-5). P-H.
--Jamaica. (Illus.). 320p. 1983. pap. 14.95 (ISBN 0-13-509000-8). P-H.
--Java. (Illus.). 300p. 1983. 18.95 (ISBN 0-686-84573-0); pap. 14.95 (ISBN 0-13-509976-5). P-H.
--Korea. (Illus.). 378p. 1983. 18.95 (ISBN 0-13-516633-0); pap. 14.95 (ISBN 0-13-516641-1). P-H.
--Malaysia. (Illus.). 304p. 1983. 18.95 (ISBN 0-13-548040-X); pap. 14.95 (ISBN 0-13-547992-4). P-H.
--Mexico. (Illus.). 432p. 1983. pap. 14.95 (ISBN 0-13-579524-9). P-H.
--Nepal. (Illus.). 384p. 1983. pap. 14.95 (ISBN 0-13-611038-X). P-H.
--Philippines. (Illus.). 338p. 1983. 18.95 (ISBN 0-13-662205-4); pap. 14.95 (ISBN 0-13-662197-X). P-H.
--Singapore. (Illus.). 240p. 1983. 18.95 (ISBN 0-13-810994-X); pap. 14.95 (ISBN 0-13-810713-0). P-H.
--Sri Lanka. (Illus.). 384p. 1983. pap. 14.95 (ISBN 0-13-839944-1). P-H.
--Thailand. (Illus.). 334p. 1983. 18.95 (ISBN 0-13-912618-X); pap. 14.95 (ISBN 0-13-912600-7). P-H.
Institue of Petroleum. Model Code of Safe Practice, Pt. 13: Pressure Piping Systems Inspection Safety Code. 1978. 19.95 (ISBN 0-471-25789-3, Wiley Heyden). Wiley.
Institut de Droit international, ed. Session D'Athens Nineteen Seventy-Nine: Travaux Preparatoires, 2 vols, Vol. 58. xxii, 640p. 1980. Set. pap. 320.00 (ISBN 3-8055-0070-X). S Karger.
--Session de Zagreb 1971. (Institut de Droit international Annuaire: Vol. 54, 1-2). xciv, 1392p. 1971. pap. 450.00 (ISBN 3-8055-1537-5). S Karger.
--Session d'Edimbourg 1969. (Institut de Droit international Annuaire: Vol. 53, 1-2). xcii, 1238p. 1969. pap. 179.75 (ISBN 3-8055-1534-0). S Karger.
--Session d'Oslo 1977. (Institut de Droit international Annuaire: Vol. 57, 1-2). lx, 416p. 1978. pap. 320.50 (ISBN 3-8055-2956-2). S Karger.
--Session du Centenaire, Rome 1973. (Institut de Droit international Annuaire: Vol. 55). xcviii, 916p. 1973. pap. 296.50 (ISBN 3-8055-2175-8). S Karger.
Institut Des Etudes Augustiniennes, Paris. Fichier Augustinien, 4 vols. (Augustine Bibliography). 1972. Set. 340.00 (ISBN 0-8161-0947-8, Hall Library). G K Hall.
--Fichier Augustinien, First Supplement. 1981. lib. bdg. 120.00 (ISBN 0-8161-0365-8, Hall Library). G K Hall.
Institut Dominicain d'Etudes Orientales du Caire. Melanes: French-Arabic Text, Vol. 14. 1980. 40.00x (ISBN 0-86685-284-0). Intl Bk Ctr.
--Melanges: Tables Generales Tomes 1-13 (1954-1977) (French, Arabic.). 1980. 13.00x (ISBN 0-86685-283-2). Intl Bk Ctr.
Institut du Petrole Francaise, ed. Drilling Data Handbook. 412p. 1980. 99.95 (ISBN 0-87201-204-2). Gulf Pub.
Institut Francais De Pertrole. Manual of Economic Analysis of Chemical Processes. Miller, Ryle & Miller, Ethel B., trs. (Illus.). 1980. 41.75 (ISBN 0-07-031745-3). McGraw.
Institut Francais d'Histoire Sociale, Paris. L Anarchisme (Anarchism) 1982. 27.00 (ISBN 3-598-10442-1, Pub. by K G Saur). Shoe String.
Institut national de la statistique et des etudes economiques. Annuaire Statistique de la France 1980: Statistical Yearbook of France 1980. 85th ed. LC 7-39039. (Illus.). 913p. (Fr.). 1980. 80.00x (ISBN 0-8002-3010-8). Intl Pubns Serv.
--Annuaire Statistique de la France 1981: Statistical Yearbook of France 1981. 86th ed. LC 7-39079. (Illus.). 862p. (Fr.). 1981. 80.00x (ISBN 0-8002-3011-6). Intl Pubns Serv.
Institut Voor Sociale Geschiedenis. Alfabetische Catalogus Van De Boeken En Brochures Van Het International: Alphabetical Catalog of the Books & Pamphlets of the International Institute of Social History, 12 vols. 1970. Set. lib. bdg. 1170.00 (ISBN 0-8161-0807-2, Hall Library). G K Hall.
Institut Voor Sociale Geschiedenis, (Amsterdam) Alfabetische Catalogus Van De Bocken En Brochures Van Het Internationaal Instituut Voor Sociale Geschiedenis (Alphabetical Catalog of the Books & Pamphlets of the International Institute of Social History) Amsterdam, 1st Suppl, 2 vols. 1975. Set. lib. bdg. 240.00 (ISBN 0-8161-1033-6, Hall Library). G K Hall.
Institute for Advanced Study of Human Sexuality. Sex & the Married Woman. 224p. 1983. pap. 8.95 (ISBN 0-671-47283-6, Wallaby). S&S.
Institute for Communication Research, Stanford University. The Role of the Telephone in Economic Development. 1980. 50.00 (ISBN 0-686-37965-9). Info Gatekeepers.
Institute for Contemporary History, Munich. Catalog for the Institute for Contemporary History, 4 pts. Incl. Pt. 1. Alphabetical Catalog, 5 vols. Set. 400.00 (ISBN 0-8161-0724-6); Pt. 2. Subject Catalog, 2 Vols. Set. 520.00 (ISBN 0-8161-0176-0); Pt. 3. Regional Catalog, 2 vols. Set. 140.00 (ISBN 0-8161-0177-9); Pt. 4. Biographical Catalog. 95.00 (ISBN 0-8161-0178-7). 1967 (Hall Library). G K Hall.
--Catalog of the Library of the Institute for Contemporary History, First Supplement. 1973. lib. bdg. 130.00 alphabetical catalog (ISBN 0-8161-0920-6, Hall Library); lib. bdg. 245.00 subject catalog (2 vols.) (ISBN 0-8161-0179-5); lib. bdg. 115.00 biographical catalog & regional catalog (ISBN 0-8161-1075-1). G K Hall.
Institute for Energy Analysis. Economic & Environmental Impacts of a U. S. Nuclear Moratorium. Weinberg, Alvin M., ed. 1979. 25.00x (ISBN 0-262-23093-3). MIT Pr.
Institute for Environmental Education & Association of New Jersey Environmental Commissions. Tuning the Green Machine, An Integrated View of Environmental Systems. LC 77-17902. (Illus.). 320p. 1978. lib. bdg. 12.50 (ISBN 0-379-00811-4). Oceana.
Institute for Food & Develop Policy. Removing the Obstacles. Millikan, Brent & Kinley, David, eds. 45p. (Orig.). 1983. pap. 2.95 (ISBN 0-935028-15-3). Inst Food & Develop.
Institute for Language Study. Vest Pocket Arabic. LC 74-17006. (Illus.). 252p. (Arabic.). 1979. pap. 3.50 (ISBN 0-06-464907-5, BN 4907, BN). B&N NY.
--Vest Pocket English. LC 58-59519. (Illus.). 188p. 1979. pap. 2.95 (ISBN 0-06-464908-3, BN 4908, BN). B&N NY.
--Vest Pocket German. LC 58-8920. (Illus.). 128p. (Ger.). 1979. pap. 2.45 (ISBN 0-06-464902-4, BN 4902, BN). B&N NY.
--Vest Pocket Italian. LC 58-8919. (Illus.). 128p. (Ital.). 1979. pap. 2.45 (ISBN 0-06-464903-2, BN 4903, BN). B&N NY.
--Vest Pocket Japanese. (Illus.). 240p. (Japanese.). 1979. pap. 2.95 (ISBN 0-06-464906-7, BN 4906, BN). B&N NY.
--Vest Pocket Modern Greek. LC 60-53247. (Illus.). 184p. (Modern Greek.). 1979. pap. 2.95 (ISBN 0-06-464904-0, BN4904, BN). B&N NY.
--Vest Pocket Spanish. (Illus.). 128p. (Span.). 1979. pap. 2.45 (ISBN 0-06-464900-8, BN 4900, BN). B&N NY.
Institute for Policy Analysis. The Warsaw Pact: Arms, Doctrine & Strategy. Lewis, William J., ed. (Illus.). 512p. 1982. 29.95 (ISBN 0-07-031746-1, P&RB). McGraw.
Institute for Research in Social Science, the Comparative Urban Studies Program. HABITAT: A Southern Perspective. LC 77-22022. (Comparative Urban Studies Ser.: No. 6). 1977. pap. text ed. 3.00 (ISBN 0-89143-049-0). U NC Inst Res Soc Sci.
Institute for Sex Research, Indiana University. Sex Studies Index: 1980. 1982. lib. bdg. 45.00 (ISBN 0-8161-0386-0, Pub by Hall Library). G K Hall.
Institute for the History of Art, Florence. Kunsthistorischen Institut - Florence. Katalog Des Kunsthistorischen Instituts in Florenz, Catalogue of the Institute for the History of Art, Florence, 9 vols. 1964. Set. 855.00 (ISBN 0-8161-0696-7, Pub. by Hall Libray); 1st suppl. 2 vols. (1968) 210.00 (ISBN 0-8161-0763-7); 2nd suppl. 2 vols. (1972) 200.00 (ISBN 0-8161-0905-2); 3rd suppl, 2 vols. (1977) 220.00 (ISBN 0-8161-0052-7). G K Hall.
Institute for the Study of Conflict, London. Annual of Power & Conflict, 1980-81. 10th ed. LC 77-370326. 465p. 1981. 65.00x (ISBN 0-8002-2888-X). Intl Pubns Serv.
--Annual of Power & Conflict, 1981-82. 11th ed. LC 77-370326. 485p. 1982. 77.50x (ISBN 0-8002-3061-2). Intl Pubns Serv.
Institute for the Study of Labor & Economic Crisis. Grassroots Politics in the Nineteen Eighties: A Case Study. LC 82-7329. (Orig.). 1982. pap. 5.00 (ISBN 0-89935-017-8). Synthesis Pubns.
Institute for the Study of Labor and Economic Crisis. The Iron Fist & the Velvet Glove: Analysis of the U. S. Police. 3d ed. LC 82-60574. (Illus.). 1982. pap. 6.00 (ISBN 0-935206-02-7). Crime & Soc Justice.
Institute for the Study of Labor & Economic Crisis. Worker's Report on the Conditions of Labor & Their Effect on Patient Care at San Francisco General Hospital. 42p. (Orig.). 1979. pap. 2.00 (ISBN 0-89935-006-2). Synthesis Pubns.
Institute for World Economics, Kiel, Germany. Catalog of the Library of the Institute for World Economics, 7 pts. Incl. Pt. 1. Bibliographical Catalog of Persons, 30 vols. 1966. Set. 2850.00 (ISBN 0-8161-0677-0); Pt. 2. Catalog of Administrative Authorities, 10 vols. 1967. Set. 950.00 (ISBN 0-8161-0189-2); Pt. 3. Catalog of Corporations, 13 vols. 1967. Set. 1235.00 (ISBN 0-8161-0190-6); Pt. 4. Regional Catalog, 52 vols. 1967. Set. 4940.00 (ISBN 0-8161-0191-4); Pt. 5. Subject Catalog, 83 vols. 1968. Set. 6800.00 (ISBN 0-8161-0192-2); Pt. 6. Shelf List of Periodical Holdings, 6 vols. 4734p. 1968. Set. 570.00 (ISBN 0-8161-0193-0); Pt. 7. Title Catalog, 13 vols. 1968. Set. 1235.00 (ISBN 0-8161-0194-9). Hall Library). G K Hall.
Institute of Advanced Legal Studies, University of London. Catalogue of the Library of the Institute of Advanced Legal Studies, 6 vols. 1978. lib. bdg. 570.00 (ISBN 0-8161-0099-3, Hall Library). G K Hall.
Institute of C. F. A. Readings in Financial Analysis. 5th ed. 1981. pap. 12.00x (ISBN 0-256-02583-5). Irwin.
Institute of Criminology, University of Cambridge, England. The Library Catalogue of the Radzinowicz Library, 6 vols. Perry, R., ed. (Library Catalogs Bib.Guides). 1979. Set. lib. bdg. 590.00 (ISBN 0-8161-0242-2, Hall Library). G K Hall.
Institute of Economics, Academia Sinica. Agricultural Development in China, Japan, & Korea. 1036p. 1983. 40.00 (ISBN 0-295-95997-5, Pub. by Inst Econ Acad Sinica Taiwan). U of Wash Pr.
Institute of Electrical & Electronics Engineers. CAMAC Instrumentation & Interface Standards. (IEEE Reprint Ser.). 1976. 19.95x o.p. (ISBN 0-471-02307-8, Pub. by Wiley-Interscience). Wiley.
Institute of Electrical & Electronics Engineers, Inc. Recommended Practice for Grounding of Industrial & Commercial Power Systems. (IEEE Ser.). 95p. 1972. 7.95x o.p. (ISBN 0-471-42632-6). Wiley.
Institute of Endicrinology, Gunma University. Phylogenic Aspects of Thyroid Hormone Actions. 199p. 1983. text ed. 28.00 (ISBN 0-686-84820-9, Pub. by Japan Sci Soc Japan). Intl Schol Bk Serv.

Institute of Environmental Sciences. Shuttle Plus One - A New View of Space: Proceedings of the 12th Conference on Space Simulation, May 1982, Pasadena, California. 363p. 1982. 12.00 (ISBN 0-686-92542-4). Inst Environ Sci.
Institute of Financial Lending. Income Property Lending. LC 82-73629. 175p. 1983. 29.95 (ISBN 0-87094-402-9). Dow Jones-Irwin.
Institute of Judicial Investigations. Legal Protection of the Environment in Developing Countries. Prieto, Ignacio C. & Nocedal, Raul, eds. 1976. lib. bdg. 22.50 o.p. (ISBN 0-379-20295-6). Oceana.
Institute of Marine Engineers. Glossary of Marine Technology Terms. 178p. 1980. pap. 15.00x (ISBN 0-434-90840-1). Sheridan.
Institute of Medicine. Assessment of Medical Care for Children. (Contrasts in Health Status Ser.). (Illus.). 224p. 1974. 12.00 (ISBN 0-309-02145-6); pap. 9.50 (ISBN 0-309-02145-6). Natl Acad Pr.
Institute of Operations Research, Sponsored by IBM, University of Bonn, Germany, Sept. 8-12, 1975. Studies in Integer Programming: Proceedings of a Workshop Held in Bonn. Hammer, P. L., ed. (Annals of Discrete Mathematics: Vol. 1). 1977. 95.75 (ISBN 0-7204-0765-6, North-Holland). Elsevier.
Institute of Personnel Management. Staff Status for All. LC 78-301269. 1977. pap. 25.00x (ISBN 0-85292-150-0). Intl Pubns Serv.
Institute of Personnel Management, ed. Practical Participation & Involvement: Vol. IV Meeting Education & Training Needs. 144p. 1982. pap. text ed. 44.00x (ISBN 0-85292-292-2, Pub. by Inst Personnel Mgmt England). Renouf.
--Practical Participation & Involvement: Vol. III The Individual & the Job. 197p. 1982. pap. 35.50x (ISBN 0-85292-290-6, Pub. by Inst Personnel Mgmt England). Renouf.
Institute of Petroleum. Airfields Safety Code. 1971. 16.50 (ISBN 0-444-39969-0). Elsevier.
--Application of Computer Techniques in Chemical Research. 1971. 59.95x (ISBN 0-471-26163-7, Pub. by Wiley Heyden). Wiley.
--Aviation Hydrant Pit Systems. 1980. 16.95x (ISBN 0-471-25800-8, Pub. by Wiley Heyden). Wiley.
--Chemisorption & Catalysis. 1970. 47.95x (ISBN 0-471-26164-5, Pub. by Wiley Heyden). Wiley.
--Code of Practice for Metal Working Fluids. 1978. 19.95x (ISBN 0-471-25788-5, Pub. by Wiley Heyden). Wiley.
--Code of Practice for the Use of Oil Slick Dispersants. 1979. 19.95x (ISBN 0-471-25783-4, Pub. by Wiley Heyden). Wiley.
--The Effective Use of Petroleum. 1979. 42.95 (ISBN 0-471-25792-3, Pub. by Wiley Heyden). Wiley.
--Health & Safety in the Oil Industry. 1978. 76.50 o.p. (ISBN 0-85501-308-7). Wiley.
--Mechanical Systems for the Recovery of Oil Spilled on Water. (Illus.). 1975. 33.00 (ISBN 0-85334-451-5, Pub. by Applied Sci England). Elsevier.
--Methods for Analysis & Testing, Vol. 1, Pt. 1. 1982. 145.00x (ISBN 0-471-26146-7, Pub. by Wiley Heyden). Wiley.
--Model Code of Safe Practice: Bitumen Safety Code, Pt. 11. 1979. 19.95 (ISBN 0-471-25787-7, Wiley Heyden). Wiley.
--Model Code of Safe Practice: Drilling & Production, Pt. 4. 3rd ed. 1980. 29.95 (ISBN 0-471-25809-1, Wiley Heyden). Wiley.
--Model Code of Safe Practice: Drilling, Production & Pipeline Operations in Marine Areas, Pt. 8. 2nd ed. 1980. 23.95x (ISBN 0-471-25809-1). Wiley.
--Model Code of Safe Practice, Pt. 12: Pressure Vessel Inspection Safety Code, Pt. 12. 1976. 29.95 (ISBN 0-471-25785-0, Wiley Heyden). Wiley.
--Model Code of Safe Practice, Pt. 14: Inspection & Testing of Protective Instrumentation Systems. 19.95 (ISBN 0-471-25815-6, Wiley Heyden). Wiley.
--Model Code of Safe Practices for the Petroleum Industry: The Petroleum Pipeline, Pt. 6. 1982. write for info. (ISBN 0-471-26139-4, Pub. by Wiley Interscience). Wiley.
--North Sea Development: Experiences & Challenges. 1979. 35.95 (ISBN 0-471-25796-6, Wiley Heyden). Wiley.
--Petroleum Development & the Environment: 1979 Annual Conf. 1980. 49.95 (ISBN 0-471-25797-4, Wiley Heyden). Wiley.
--Petroleum Measurement Manual: Automatic Tank Gauging, Pt. VI. 1982. 41.95x (ISBN 0-471-26147-5, Pub. by Wiley Interscience). Wiley.
--Petroleum Measurement Manual: Calculation of Oil Quantities, Pt. I. 1980. 18.00x (ISBN 0-471-25807-5). Wiley.
--Petroleum Measurement Manual: Fidelity & Security of Measurement - Data Transmission Systems Section 1, Pt. XIII. 1977. 29.95x (ISBN 0-471-25782-6). Wiley.
--Petroleum Measurement Manual: Section 1: Positive Displacement Meters, Pt. IX. 1980. 19.95x (ISBN 0-471-25806-7). Wiley.
--Road Tank Vehicle Workshop Code. 1980. 16.95 (ISBN 0-471-25799-0, Wiley Heyden). Wiley.
--Road Tank Wagon Design Notes. 1980. 16.95 (ISBN 0-471-25798-2, Wiley Heyden). Wiley.
Institute of Petroleum, jt. auth. see Hepple, P.
Institute of Petroleum, jt. ed. see Kendrick, E.
Institute of Petroleum, jt. ed. see Mead, W. L.
Institute of Petroleum Oil Pollution Analysis Committee, London. Marine Pollution by Oil. (Illus.). 1974. 39.00 (ISBN 0-85334-452-3, Pub. by Applied Sci England). Elsevier.
Institute of Real Estate Management, jt. auth. see U. S. Dept. of Energy.
Institute of Real Estate Management. The Condominium Community. 2nd ed. (Illus.). 350p. 1983. price not set (ISBN 0-912104-61-9). Inst Real Estate.
--Expense Analysis: Condominiums, Cooperatives, & Planned Unit Developments - 1981 Edition. Anderson, Kenneth R., ed. 125p. 1981. pap. text ed. 15.00 (ISBN 0-912104-57-0). Inst Real Estate.
Institute of Real Estate Management Staff. How To Write an Operations Manual: A Guide for Apartment Management. Kirk, Nancye J., ed. LC 78-61862. 138p. 1978. pap. text ed. 21.95 (ISBN 0-912104-35-X). Inst Real Estate.
Institute of Real Estate Management. Income-Expense Analysis: Apartments, 1981. Anderson, Kenneth R., ed. 220p. 1981. pap. text ed. 24.50 (ISBN 0-912104-55-4). Inst Real Estate.
--Managing the Shopping Center. Glickson, Jeannie L., ed. LC 82-84485. (Illus.). 350p. 1983. text ed. 24.95x (ISBN 0-912104-60-0). Inst Real Estate.
--Property Management's Role in Real Estate Investment Strategy. Kirk, Nancye J., ed. (Illus.). 400p. 1982. text ed. cancelled (ISBN 0-912104-59-7). Inst Real Estate.
Institute of Recreation Management, ed. Recreational Management Handbook. 1980. 40.00x (ISBN 0-419-11620-6, Pub. by E & FN Spon England). Methuen Inc.
Institute of Southeast Asia Studies. Southeast Asia Affairs 1982. x, 396p. 1982. text ed. 40.00x (ISBN 0-686-83754-1, 00155). Heinemann Ed.
Institute of Southeast Asian Studies Singapore, ed. Southeast Asian Affairs 1981. 1981. text ed. 32.50x (ISBN 0-686-79039-1, 00150). Heinemann Ed.
Institute of Transportation Engineers. Manual of Traffic Signal Design. (Illus.). 304p. 1982. 39.95 (ISBN 0-13-554360-6). P-H.
Institute Publishing Company. Thoughts for Buffets. 1958. 14.95 (ISBN 0-395-07825-3). HM.
Institution of Chemical Engineers. Design Eighty-Two: Proceedings of the Symposium Organised by the Institution of Chemical Engineers at the University of Aston in Birmingham, UK, 22-23 September 1982. (Institution of Chemical Engineers Symposium Ser.: No. 76). 425p. 1982. 63.00 (ISBN 0-08-028773-5). Pergamon.
--Energy-Money, Materials & Engineering: Proceedings of the Symposium Organised by the Institution of Chemical Engineers (in Conjunction with the American Institute of Chemical Engineers & Deutsche Vereinigung fur Chemie-und Verfahrenstechnik), London, UK, 12-15 October 1982. (Institution of Chemical Engineers Symposium Ser.: No. 78). 475p. 1982. 72.00 (ISBN 0-08-028774-3). Pergamon.
--The Jubilee Chemical Engineering Symposium: Proceedings of the Symposium Organised by the Institution of Chemical Engineers, Imperial College, London, UK, April 1982. (Institution of Chemical Engineers Symposium Ser.: Vol. 73). 678p. 1982. 90.00 (ISBN 0-08-028770-0). Pergamon.
--Management & Conservation of Resources: Proceedings of the Conference Organised by the Institution of Chemical Engineers at the University of Salford, UK, April 1982. (Institution of Chemical Engineers Symposium Ser.: No. 72). 206p. 1982. 45.00 (ISBN 0-08-028769-7). Pergamon.
Institution of Engineering Australia. Manufacturing Engineering International Conference, 1980. 622p. (Orig.). 1980. pap. text ed. 60.00x (ISBN 0-85825-132-9, Pub. by Inst Engineering Australia). Renouf.
Insull, Robert & Sumner, Jeanne, eds. Multi-State Information System: Proceedings of the Seventh Annual National Users Group Conference. 280p. 1982. pap. 10.00 (ISBN 0-936934-03-4). Rockland Resea.
Insull, Thomas. Transport by Sea. Redmayne, Paul, ed. (Changing Shape of Things Ser). (Illus.). 1971. 8.95 o.p. (ISBN 0-7195-2213-7). Transatlantic.
Insurance Institute of America. Accident Prevention. 1980. 20.00 o.p. (ISBN 0-686-95942-6). IIA.
Integral Yoga Institutes. Integral Yoga Hatha Booklet & Tape. 1979. 6.95 (ISBN 0-932040-23-3). Integral Yoga Pubns.
Intel Marketing Corporations. The Semiconductor Memory Book. LC 78-3741. (Intel Ser.). 1978. 24.95x (ISBN 0-471-03567-X, Pub. by Wiley-Interscience). Wiley.
Inter-Governmental Meeting on the Impact of the Current Energy Crisis on the Economy of the ESCAP Region. Proceedings. (Energy Resources Development Ser.: No. 13). pap. 12.00 (ISBN 0-686-92913-6, UN75/2F7, UN). Unipub.
Inter Technology - Solar Corporation. Photosynthesis Energy Factory: Analysis Synthesis, & Demonstration - Final Report. 518p. 1983. pap. 54.50 (ISBN 0-89934-141-1, P044, Pub. by B-T Bks). Solar Energy Info.
Inter-Varsity Staff. Rough Edges of the Christian Life. pap. 2.50 (ISBN 0-87784-442-9). Inter-Varsity.
Interafrican Committee for Hydraulic Studies. Catalog of the Documentation Center Interafrican Committee for Hydraulic Studies. 1977. lib. bdg. 190.00 (ISBN 0-8161-0091-8, Hall Library). G K Hall.
Interchurch World Movement. Report on the Steel Strike of 1919. LC 73-139200. (Civil Liberties in American History Ser). (Illus.). 1971. Repr. of 1920 ed. lib. bdg. 37.50 (ISBN 0-306-70081-6). Da Capo.
Interchurch World Movement, Commission of Inquiry. Public Opinion & the Steel Strike. LC 77-119052. (Civil Liberties in American History Ser.). 1970. Repr. of 1921 ed. lib. bdg. 47.50 (ISBN 0-306-71938-X). Da Capo.
Interdisciplinary Conference -1st. Biology of Hard Tissues: Proceedings. Budy, A. M., ed. 580p. 1967. 65.00x (ISBN 0-677-65000-0). Gordon.
Interdisciplinary Conference - 2nd. Origins of Life: Proceedings, Vol. 2. Margulis, Lynn, ed. 246p. 1971. 51.00x (ISBN 0-677-13630-7). Gordon.
Interdisciplinary Conference - 3rd. Biology of Hard Tissues: Proceedings. Budy, A. M., ed. 580p. 1970. 108.00x (ISBN 0-677-13620-X). Gordon.
Interdisciplinary Conference-5th. Cellular Dynamics: Vol. 5. Peachey, L. D., ed. 1969. Vols. 1 & 2. 63.00x (ISBN 0-677-65010-8); Vols. 3 & 4. 42.00x (ISBN 0-677-65020-5); Vol. 5. 92.00x (ISBN 0-677-13300-6). Gordon.
Interdisciplinary Research Conference - 1961. Physiological Correlates of Psychological Disorders: Proceedings. Roessler, Robert & Greenfield, Norman S., eds. (Illus.). 294p. 1962. 20.00x (ISBN 0-299-02650-7). U of Wis Pr.
Intergovernmental Group on Oilseeds, Oils & Fats, 13th Session. Report to the Committee on Commodity Problems. 34p. 1979. pap. 7.00 (ISBN 0-686-93098-3, F1639, FAO). Unipub.
Intergovernmental Oceanographic Commission Assembly, 10th Session, Paris, 1977. Bruun Memorial Lectures, 1977. (IOC Technical Ser.: No. 19). (Illus.). 1979. pap. 3.25 (ISBN 92-3-101746-2, U61, UNESCO). Unipub.
Intermed Comuunications Editors, ed. Assessment. LC 82-11760. (Nurse's Reference Library). (Illus.). 1024p. 1982. text ed. 23.95 (ISBN 0-916730-39-5). InterMed Comm.
International Academy of Oral Pathology. Proceedings, Vol. 4. Cahn, L. R., ed. 256p. 1970. 60.00 (ISBN 0-677-62260-0). Gordon.
International African Institute. Cumulative Bibliography of African Studies, International African Institute,London Author Catalog, 2 vols. 1973. Set. lib. bdg. 190.00 (ISBN 0-8161-1045-X, Hall Library). G K Hall.
--Cumulative Bibliography of African Studies, International African Institute, London Classified Catalog, 3 vols. 1973. Set. lib. bdg. 285.00 (ISBN 0-8161-1076-X, Hall Library). G K Hall.
International Agency for the Prevention of Blindness, jt. auth. see Wilson, John.
International Assn. for Analog Computation. Proceedings of the Third International Analog Computation Meetings, Opatija, Yugoslavia, Sept. 5-8, 1961. 712p. 1961. 186.00 (ISBN 0-677-10195-3). Gordon.
International Association for Hydraulic Research. Fundamentals of Transport Phenomena in Porous Media. LC 71-183910. (Developments in Soil Science: Vol. 2). 1972. 76.75 (ISBN 0-444-99897-7). Elsevier.
International Association for Philosophy of Law & Social Philosophy. Equality & Freedom, Vols. 1-3. LC 77-76800. 1977. Set. 105.00 (ISBN 0-379-00657-X). Oceana.
International Association of Briologists, Taxonomic Workshop, 1979. Bryophyte Taxonomy: Methods, Practices & Floristic Exploration: Proceedings. Geissler, P. & Greene, S. W., eds. (Beiheft zu Nova Hedwigia Ser.: No. 71). (Illus.). 600p. 1982. 80.00 (ISBN 3-7682-5471-2). Lubrecht & Cramer.
International Association of Business Communications. Excellence in Communication 1981. McGoon, Cliff, et al, eds. 1981. pap. 9.50 (ISBN 0-686-37161-5). Intl Assn Busn Comm.
International Association of Business Communicators. Nonprofit CEOs Speak Out on Importance of Communications. (Orig.). 1982. pap. 22.50 o.p. (ISBN 0-686-37162-3). Intl Assn Busn Comm.
--Without Bias: A Guidebook for Nondiscriminatory Communication. LC 81-16457. 200p. 1982. pap. text ed. 12.95x (ISBN 0-471-08561-8). Wiley.
International Association of Fish & Wildlife Agencies. Proceedings of the Sixty-Ninth Convention. Blouch, Ralph I., ed. (Orig.). 1980. pap. 11.00 (ISBN 0-932108-04-0). IAFWA.
International Association of Music Libraries. Guide for Dating Early Published Music: A Manual of Bibliographical Practices. Krummel, Don W., ed. (Illus.). 1974. 26.00 (ISBN 0-913574-25-2, 05KRUM). Eur-Am Music.
International Association of Music Libraries & International Musicological Society. Terminorum Musicae Index Septen Linguis Redactus. Leuchtmann, Horst, ed. (Illus.). 1978. 89.50 o.p. (ISBN 3-7618-0553-5). Eur-Am Music.
International Astronautical Congress, 27th, Anaheim, Ca., Oct. 1976, jt. auth. see Napolitano, Luigi G.
International Astronomical Union Symposium, 44th, Uppsala, Sweden, 1970. External Galaxies & Quasi-Stellar Objects: Proceedings. Evans, D. S., ed. LC 77-154736. (Illus.). 549p. 1972. 46.00 o.p. (ISBN 0-387-91092-1). Springer-Verlag.
International Astronomical Union Symposium, 45th, Leningrad, 1970. The Motion, Evolution of Orbits, & Origin of Comets. Chebotarev, E. I., et al, eds. LC 73-179895. (Illus.). xxiii, 521p. 1972. 57.00 o.p. (ISBN 0-387-91103-0). Springer-Verlag.
International Astronomical Union Symposium, 35th, Budapest, Hungary, 1967. Structure & Development of Solar Active Regions. Kiepenheuer, K. O., ed. 1968. 37.70 o.p. (ISBN 0-387-91020-4). Springer-Verlag.
International Biological Programme Section PM (Productivity Marine) Bibliography on Methods of Studying the Marine Beaches. (FAO Fisheries Technical Papers: No. 98). 102p. 1970. pap. 7.50 (ISBN 0-686-93103-3, F1745, FAO). Unipub.
International Brain Research Organization. Psychophysiological Mechanisms of Hypnosis: Proceedings. Chertok, L., ed. (Illus.). 1969. 29.00 o.p. (ISBN 0-387-04678-X). Springer-Verlag.
International Brecht Society. Beyond Brecht: Brecht Yearbook, Vol. 11. Fuegi, John & Bahr, Gisela, eds. 250p. 1982. 20.00 (ISBN 0-8143-1735-9). Wayne St U Pr.
International Burn Seminar Shanghai, June 1981. The Treatment of Research in Burns: Proceedings. Ji-Xiang Shi & Zhi-Yong Sheng, eds. 500p. 1983. 50.00x (ISBN 0-471-87328-4, Pub. by Wiley Med). Wiley.
International Business & Management Institute. Little Known Business Secrets & Shortcuts for Entrepreneurs & Managers. (Illus.). 110p. (Orig.). pap. 25.00x looselesf (ISBN 0-935402-03-9); lib. bdg. 26.00x (ISBN 0-935402-10-1). Intl Comm Serv.
International Cancer Congress, 11th, October 1974. Proceedings, 6 vols. Bucalossi, P., ed. Incl. Vol. 1. Cell Biology & Tumor Immunology. 381p (ISBN 0-444-15132-X); Vol. 2. Chemical & Viral Oncogenesis. 305p (ISBN 0-444-15170-2); Vol. 3. Cancer Epidemiology, Environmental Factors. 348p (ISBN 0-444-15171-0); Vol. 4. Cancer Campaigns, Detection, Rehabilitation, Clinical Classification. 279p (ISBN 0-444-15169-9); Vol. 5. Surgery, Radiotherapy & Chemotherapy of Cancer. 386p (ISBN 0-444-15171-0); Vol. 6. Tumors of Specific Sites. 446p (ISBN 0-444-15172-9). (International Congress Ser: Nos. 349-354). 1975. pap. 45.75 ea. o.p. (ISBN 0-685-55274-8); Set. pap. 206.00 o.p. (ISBN 0-685-55275-6). Elsevier.
International Centre for Settlement of Investment Disputes. Investment Laws of the World: The Developing Nations, 10 vols. LC 77-72048. 1973-79. looseleaf 75.00 ea. (ISBN 0-379-00650-2); index 75.00 (ISBN 0-686-96819-0); Set incl. index & 4 releases. 800.00. Oceana.
International Cheerleading Foundation Staff & Neil, Randy L. The Official Cheerleading Manual. (Illus.). 96p. (Orig.). (gr. 7 up). 1982. pap. 2.95 (ISBN 0-671-44542-1). Wanderer Bks.
International City Management Association. Effective Supervisory Practices. LC 77-28712. (Municipal Management Ser.). (Orig.). 1978. pap. text ed. 22.50 (ISBN 0-87326-019-8). Intl City Mgt.
International College of Surgeons, Biennial World Congress. Abstracts: Twentieth Congress, Athens, 1976. Louros, N., ed. (International Congress Ser.: No. 389). 1976. pap. 31.25. Elsevier.
International Colloquium, June 25-July 1, 1973. Infinite & Finite Sets: Proceedings, 3 vols. Hajnal, A., et al, eds. (Colloquia Mathematica Societatis Janos Bolyai Ser.: Vol. 10). 1975. Set. 159.75 (ISBN 0-444-10732-0, North-Holland). Elsevier.
International Commercial Services Consulting Group. Business Survival & Success Techniques for Managers & Entrepreneurs. (Illus.). 100p. (Orig.). 1982. pap. 25.00x looseleaf (ISBN 0-935402-07-1); lib. bdg. 26.00x (ISBN 0-935402-08-X). Intl Comm Serv.
International Commission for the Conservation of Atlantic Tunas, 1st Meeting, Rome 1969. Report. (FAO Fisheries Reports: No. 84). 47p. 1970. pap. 7.50 (ISBN 0-686-93046-0, F1686, FAO). Unipub.
International Commission on Radiation Units & Measurements. Cameras for Image Intensifier Fluorography. LC 73-97641. 8.00 (ISBN 0-913394-08-4). Intl Comm Rad Meas.
--Certification of Standardized Radioactive Sources. LC 68-58199. 5.00 (ISBN 0-913394-05-X). Intl Comm Rad Meas.
--The Conceptual Basis for the Determination of Dose Equivalent. LC 76-24373. 1976. 9.00 (ISBN 0-913394-19-X). Intl Comm Rad Meas.
--Determination of Absorbed Dose in a Patient Irradiated by Beams of X or Gamma Rays in Radiotherapy. LC 76-22297. 1976. 10.00 (ISBN 0-913394-18-1). Intl Comm Rad Meas.
--Dose Equivalent: Supplement to ICRU Report 19. LC 68-56968. (Illus.). iv, 5p. 1973. 3.00 o.p. (ISBN 0-913394-17-3). Intl Comm Rad Meas.

International Commission on Radiation Units and Measurements. Linear Energy Transfer. LC 72-113962. (Illus.). viii, 51p. 1972. 10.00 (ISBN 0-913394-09-2). Intl Comm Rad Meas.

International Commission on Radiation Units & Measurements. Measurement of Absorbed Dose in a Phantom Irradiated by a Single Beam of X or Gamma Rays. LC 72-97332. 10.00 (ISBN 0-913394-16-5). Intl Comm Rad Meas.

--Measurement of Low-Level Radioactivity. LC 71-186876. (Illus.). v, 66p. 1972. 11.50 (ISBN 0-913394-15-7). Intl Comm Rad Meas.

International Commission on Radiation Units and Measurements. Neutron Fluence, Neutron Spectra & Kerma. LC 75-97639. (Illus.). viii, 57p. 1969. 9.00 (ISBN 0-913394-06-8). Intl Comm Rad Meas.

--Radiation Dosimetry: Electrons with Initial Energies Between 1 & 50 MeV. LC 76-190452. (Illus.). v, 64p. 1972. 13.00 (ISBN 0-913394-14-9). Intl Comm Rad Meas.

International Commission on Radiation Units & Measurements. Radiation Dosimetry: X Rays & Gamma Rays with Maximum Photon Energies Between 0.6 & 50 MeV. LC 70-97640. 8.00 (ISBN 0-913394-07-6). Intl Comm Rad Meas.

--Radiation Dosimetry: X Rays Generated at Potentials of 5 to 150 kV. LC 74-126755. 9.00 (ISBN 0-913394-10-6). Intl Comm Rad Meas.

International Commission on Radiation Units and Measurements. Radiation Protection Instrumentation & Its Application. LC 70-177297. (Illus.). v, 60p. 1971. 11.50x (ISBN 0-913394-13-0). Intl Comm Rad Meas.

International Commission on Radiation Units & Measurements. Specification of High Activity Gamma-Ray Sources. LC 72-131967. 9.00 (ISBN 0-913394-11-4). Intl Comm Rad Meas.

International Commission on Radiological Protection, jt. ed. see Sowby, F. D.

International Commission on Radiology Protection, jt. ed. see Sowby, F. D.

International Commission on Radiological Protection. Radiation Protection - Recommendations of the ICRP. (ICRP Publication Ser.: No. 9). 1966. pap. 7.15 (ISBN 0-08-013160-3). Pergamon.

International Committee for Social Sciences Information & Documentation (UNESCO), ed. International Bibliography of Economics - Bibliographie Internationale de Science Economique, Vol. 28. LC 55-2317. (International Bibliography of the Social Sciences - Bibliographie Internationale des Sciences Sociales). 502p. 1981. 90.00x (ISBN 0-422-80900-4). Intl Pubns Serv.

International Committee for Social Science Information & Documentation (UNESCO), ed. International Bibliography of Economics, 1978, Vol. 27. LC 55-2317. (International Bibliography of the Social Sciences). 526p. 1980. 90.00x o.p. (ISBN 0-422-80890-3). Intl Pubns Serv.

--International Bibliography of Political Science - Bibliographie Internation ale de Science Politique, Vol. 28. LC 54-14355. (International Bibliogarphy of the Social Science Ser.). 451p. 1981. 90.00x (ISBN 0-422-80920-9). Intl Pubns Serv.

--International Bibliography of Political Science, 1978, Vol. 27. LC 54-14355. (International Bibliography of the Social Sciences). 405p. 1980. 85.00x o.p. (ISBN 0-422-80880-6). Intl Pubns Serv.

--International Bibliography of Social & Cultural Anthropology - Bibliographie Internationale D'Anthropologie Sociale et Culturelie, Vol. 24. LC 58-4366. (International Bibliography of the Social Sciences - Bibliographie Internationale des Sciences Sociales). 393p. 1981. 90.00x (ISBN 0-422-80930-6). Intl Pubns Serv.

--International Bibliography of Social & Cultural Anthropology, 1977, Vol. 23. LC 58-4366. (International Bibliography of the Social Sciences). 569p. 1981. 90.00x o.p. (ISBN 0-422-80860-1). Intl Pubns Serv.

International Committee for Social Science Information & Documentation. International Bibliography of the Social Sciences A: Anthropology, Vols. VI-XXV. Incl. Vol. VI. 1960. 80.00x (ISBN 0-422-80040-6); Vol. VII. 1961. 80.00x (ISBN 0-422-80080-5); Vol. VIII. 1964. 80.00x (ISBN 0-422-80120-8); Vol. IX. 1964. 80.00x (ISBN 0-422-80160-7); Vol. X. 1965. 80.00x (ISBN 0-422-80200-X); Vol. XI. 1967. 80.00x (ISBN 0-422-80240-9); Vol. XII. 1968. 80.00x (ISBN 0-422-80280-8); Vol. XIII. 1969. 80.00x (ISBN 0-422-80400-2); Vol. XIV. 1970. 80.00x (ISBN 0-422-80500-9); Vol. XV. 1971. 80.00x (ISBN 0-422-80620-X); Vol. XVI. 1972. 80.00x (ISBN 0-422-80750-8); Vol. XVII. 1973. 80.00x (ISBN 0-422-74190-6); Vol. XVIII. 1974. 80.00x (ISBN 0-422-74400-X); Vol. XIX. 1975. 80.00x (ISBN 0-422-74770-X); Vol. XX. 1976. 80.00x (ISBN 0-422-80770-2); Vol. XXI. 1978. 80.00x (ISBN 0-422-76250-4); Vol. XXII. 1979. 80.00x (ISBN 0-422-80820-2); Vol. XXIII. 80.00x (ISBN 0-422-80860-1); Vol. XXIV. 1982. 80.00x (ISBN 0-422-80930-6); Vol. XXV. 80.00x (ISBN 0-422-80940-3). **Pub. by Tavistock England). Methuen Inc.**

International Committee for Social Science Information & Documentation. International Bibliography of the Social Sciences B: Economics, Vols. IX-XXIX. Incl. Vol. IX. 1960. 80.00x (ISBN 0-422-80010-4); Vol. X. 1960. 80.00x (ISBN 0-422-80050-3); Vol. XI. 1964. 80.00x (ISBN 0-422-80090-2); Vol. XII. 1964. 80.00x (ISBN 0-422-80150-X); Vol. XIII. 1965. 80.00x (ISBN 0-422-80190-9); Vol. XIV. 1966. 80.00x (ISBN 0-422-80230-1); Vol. XV. 1968. 80.00x (ISBN 0-422-80270-0); Vol. XVI. 1969. 80.00x (ISBN 0-422-80410-X); Vol. XVII. 1970. 80.00x (ISBN 0-422-80510-6); Vol. XVIII. 1971. 80.00x (ISBN 0-422-80630-7); Vol. XIX. 1972. 60.00x (ISBN 0-422-80740-0); Vol. XX. 1973. 80.00x (ISBN 0-422-74180-9); Vol. XXI. 1974. 80.00x (ISBN 0-422-74390-9); Vol. XXII. 1975. 80.00x (ISBN 0-422-74790-4); Vol. XXIII. 1976. 80.00x (ISBN 0-422-80790-7); Vol. XXIV. 1977. 79.00x o.p. (ISBN 0-422-76220-2); Vol. XXV. 1978. 80.00x (ISBN 0-422-80800-8); Vol. XXVI. 1979. 80.00x (ISBN 0-422-80850-4); Vol. XXVII. 1980. 80.00x (ISBN 0-422-80890-3); Vol. XXVIII. 1982. 80.00x (ISBN 0-422-**80900-4); Vol. XXIX. 1983. 80.00x (ISBN 0-422-81000-2). Pub. by Tavistock England). Methuen Inc.**

--International Bibliography of the Social Sciences C: Political Science, Vols. IX-XXIX. Incl. Vol. IX. 1960. 80.00x (ISBN 0-686-66148-6); Vol. X. 1961. 80.00x (ISBN 0-422-80060-0); Vol. XI. (No bound stock available); Vol. XII. 1965. 80.00x (ISBN 0-422-80140-2); Vol. XIII. 1965. 80.00x (ISBN 0-422-80180-1); Vol. XIV. 1966. 80.00x (ISBN 0-422-80220-4); Vol. XV. 1968. 80.00x (ISBN 0-422-80260-3); Vol. XVI. 1969. 80.00x (ISBN 0-422-80420-7); Vol. XVII. 1970. 80.00x (ISBN 0-422-80520-3); Vol. XVIII. 1971. 80.00x (ISBN 0-422-80640-4); Vol. XIX. 1972. 80.00x (ISBN 0-422-80730-3); Vol. XX. 1973. 80.00x (ISBN 0-422-74170-1); Vol. XXI. 1974. 80.00x (ISBN 0-422-74380-1); Vol. XXII. 1975. 80.00x (ISBN 0-422-74780-7); Vol. XXIII. 1976. 80.00x (ISBN 0-422-80760-5); Vol. XXIV. 1977. 75.00x (ISBN 0-422-76240-7); Vol. XXV. 1978. 80.00x (ISBN 0-422-80810-5); Vol. XXVI. 1979. 80.00x (ISBN 0-422-80840-7); Vol. XXVII. 1980. 80.00 (ISBN 0-422-80870-9); Vol. XXVIII. 1981. 80.00x (ISBN 0-422-80920-9); Vol. XXIX. 80.00x (ISBN 0-422-80990-X). Pub. by Tavistock England). Methuen Inc.

--International Bibliography of the Social Sciences D: Sociology, Vols. X-XXX. Incl. Vol. X. 1960. 80.00x (ISBN 0-422-80030-9); Vol. XI. 1961. 80.00x (ISBN 0-422-80070-8); Vol. XII. 1964. 80.00x (ISBN 0-422-80110-0); Vol. XIII. 1965. 80.00x (ISBN 0-422-80130-5); Vol. XIV. 1965. 80.00x (ISBN 0-422-80170-4); Vol. XV. 1965. 80.00x (ISBN 0-422-80210-7); Vol. XVI. 1968. 80.00x (ISBN 0-422-80250-6); Vol. XVII. 1969. 80.00x (ISBN 0-422-80430-4); Vol. XVIII. 1970. 80.00x (ISBN 0-422-80530-0); Vol. XIX. 1971. 80.00x (ISBN 0-422-80650-1); Vol. XX. 1972. 80.00x (ISBN 0-422-80720-6); Vol. XXI. (No bound stock available). 75.00x (ISBN 0-686-86353-4); Vol. XXII. 1974. 80.00x (ISBN 0-422-74370-4); Vol. XXIII. 1975. 80.00x (ISBN 0-422-74800-5); Vol. XXIV. 1976. 80.00x (ISBN 0-422-80780-X); Vol. XXV. 1977. 80.00x (ISBN 0-422-76230-X); Vol. XXVI. 1978. 80.00x (ISBN 0-422-76560-0); Vol. XXVII. 1979. 80.00x (ISBN 0-422-80830-X); Vol. XXIX. 1981. 80.00x (ISBN 0-422-80910-1); Vol. XXX. 1982. 80.00x (ISBN 0-422-80970-5). Pub. by Tavistock England). Methuen Inc.

International Committee on English in the Liturgy. Documents on the Liturgy, 1963-1979: Conciliar, Papal & Curial Texts. O'Brien, Thomas C., ed. LC 82-83580. 1496p. 1983. text ed. 45.00 (ISBN 0-8146-1281-4). Liturgical Pr.

International Computer Programs, Inc. ICP Software Directory - United Kingdom: Software Products, Services & Suppliers. Spangler, Richard J., ed. 1982. pap. 125.00 (ISBN 0-88094-012-3). Intl Computer.

--ICP Software Directory: Cross Industry Applications. rev. ed. Spangler, Richard J., ed. 1983. pap. 150.00 (ISBN 0-686-82214-5). Intl Computer.

--ICP Software Directory: Directory of Business Applications for Microcomputers. (Illus.). 320p. 1983. 26.95 (ISBN 0-89303-533-5); pap. 19.95 (ISBN 0-89303-532-7). R J Brady.

--ICP Software Directory: Industry Specific Applications. rev. ed. Spangler, Richard J., ed. 1983. pap. 150.00 (ISBN 0-88094-015-8). Intl Computer.

International Computer Programs Inc. ICP Software Directory: Mini-Small Business Systems: Cross Industry. Spangler, Richard J., ed. 1982. pap. 85.00 (ISBN 0-88094-005-0). Intl Computer.

--ICP Software Directory: Mini Small Business Systems: Industry Specific. Spangler, Richard J., ed. 1982. pap. 85.00 (ISBN 0-88094-006-9). Intl Computer.

--ICP Software Directory: Software Product & Service Suppliers. Spangler, Richard J., ed. 1982. pap. 125.00 (ISBN 0-88094-007-7). Intl Computer.

International Computer Programs, Inc. ICP Software Directory: Software Product & Service Suppliers. rev. ed. Spangler, Richard J., ed. 1983. pap. 150.00 (ISBN 0-88094-016-6). Intl Computer.

--ICP Software Directory: Systems Software. rev. ed. Spangler, Richard J., ed. 1983. pap. 150.00 (ISBN 0-88094-013-1). Intl Computer.

International Computer Programs Inc. ICP Software Reference Series. Spangler, Richard J., ed. 1982. pap. 65.00 (ISBN 0-88094-000-X). Intl Computer.

--ICP Software Reference Series: For Data General Small Computers. Spangler, Richard J., ed. 1982. pap. 65.00 (ISBN 0-88094-002-6). Intl Computer.

--ICP Software Reference Series: For Dec Small Computers. Spangler, Richard J., ed. 1982. pap. 65.00 (ISBN 0-88094-004-2). Intl Computer.

International Computers Programs Inc. ICP Software Reference Series: For Hewlett-Packard Computers. Spangler, Richard J., ed. 1982. pap. 65.00 (ISBN 0-88094-003-4). Intl Computer.

--ICP Software Reference Series: For IBM Small Computers. Spangler, Richard J., ed. 1982. pap. 65.00 (ISBN 0-88094-001-8). Intl Computer.

International Conference at the Calouste Gulbenkian Foundation Centre, Lisbon, Portugal, April 8-24, 1974, jt. auth. see Birks, J. B.

International Conference, Brighton, United Kingsom, March 1982 & Jerrard. Electro-Optics Laser International, 82: Proceedings. 1982. text ed. write for info. (ISBN 0-408-01235-8). Butterworth.

International Conference Held in Bangkok, Jan. 7-9, 1980 & Karasudhi, Pisidhi. Engineering for Protection from Natural Disasters: Proceedings. Kanok-Nukulchai, Worsak, ed. LC 80-4169. 1981. 113.00x (ISBN 0-471-27895-5, Pub. by Wiley-Interscience). Wiley.

International Conference, Kingston, Jamaica, April 24-29, 1972. Libraries & the Challenge of Change: Proceedings. Ingram, K. E. & Jefferson, Albertina A., eds. LC 76-351890. 276p. 1975. 24.00 o.p. (ISBN 0-7201-0523-4, Pub. by Mansell England). Wilson.

International Conference on Alternative Energy Sources, 3rd, Miami Beach, 1980. Alternative Energy Sources Three: Proceedings. Veziroglu, T. Nejat, ed. LC 82-9181. 1983. text ed. 597.00 (ISBN 0-89116-226-7). Hemisphere Pub.

International Conference on Atherosclerosis, Milan, November 1977. Proceedings. Carlson, Lars A., et al, eds. LC 78-66345. 796p. 1978. 71.50 (ISBN 0-89004-267-5). Raven.

International Conference on Biomass 1st, Brighton, England, November, 1980. Energy from Biomass: Proceedings. Palz, W., et al, eds. (Illus.). 982p. 1981. 88.25 (ISBN 0-85334-970-3, Pub. by Applied Sci England). Elsevier.

International Conference on Civil Liability for Nuclear Damage, Vienna, 1963. Civil Liability for Nuclear Damage: Official Records. (Legal Ser.: No. 2). 522p. (Fr., Rus. & Span. eds. also avail.). 1964. pap. o.p. (ISBN 92-0-176064-7, STI-PUB-54, IAEA). Unipub.

International Conference on Computational Methods in Nonlinear Mechanics, 2nd, Univ. of Texas at Austin. Computational Methods in Nonlinear Mechanics: Selected Papers. Oden, J. T., ed. 160p. 1980. pap. 41.25 (ISBN 0-08-025068-8). Pergamon.

International Conference on Cyclic Amp, 2nd, July, 1974. Advances in Cyclic Nucleotide Research: Proceedings. Drummond, G. I., et al, eds. LC 74-24679. (Advances in Cyclic Nucleotide Research Ser.: Vol. 5). 886p. 1975. 74.00 (ISBN 0-89004-021-4). Raven.

International Conference on Cyclic Nucleotide, 3rd, New Orleans, la., July 1977. Advances in Cyclic Nucleotide Research: Proceedings, Vol. 9. George, William J. & Ignarro, Louis, eds. LC 77-84555. 831p. 1978. 80.00 (ISBN 0-89004-240-3). Raven.

International Conference on Energy Storage, Brighton, England, April 1981. Energy Storage: Proceedings. 1982. 150.00x (ISBN 0-686-97034-9, Pub. by BHRA Fluid England). State Mutual Bk.

International Conference on Environment Future, 2nd. Growth Without Ecodisasters: Proceedings. Polunin, Nicholas, ed. LC 78-26933. 1979. 69.95x o.p. (ISBN 0-470-26615-5). Halsted Pr.

International Conference on High-Energy Physics & Nuclear Structure, 5th. High Energy Physics& Nuclear Structure: Proceedings. Tibell, G., ed. 1974. 68.00 (ISBN 0-444-10688-X, North-Holland). Elsevier.

International Conference on Investment in Fisheries, Rome, 1969. Report. (FAO Fisheries Reports: No. 83, Vol. 1). 78p. 1970. pap. 7.50 (ISBN 0-686-93042-8, F1685, FAO). Unipub.

International Conference on Lasers, Beijing-Shanghai, May, 1980. Proceedings. 1000p. 1983. 100.00 (ISBN 0-471-87093-5, Pub. by Wiley-Interscience). Wiley.

International Conference on Low Lying Lattice Vibrational Modes & Their Relationship to Superconductivity & Ferroelectricity, Puerto Rico, 1975 & Lefkowitz, I. Proceedings, 2 vols. 472p. 1977. Set. pap. 278.00x (ISBN 0-677-15535-2). Gordon.

International Conference on Marketing Systems for Developing Countries. Agricultural Marketing for Developing Countries: Proceedings, Vol. 2. Izaeli, D. N. & Messner, F., eds. 1977. 54.95x o.p. (ISBN 0-470-15095-5). Halsted Pr.

--Marketing Systems for Developing Countries: Proceedings, Vol. 1. Izraeli, D. N. & Messner, F., eds. LC 76-8243. 1977. 43.95x o.p. (ISBN 0-470-15094-7). Halsted Pr.

International Conference on Mechanical Behavior of Materials, 2nd. Proceedings. 1976. Condensed Vol. 15.00 o.p. (ISBN 0-686-95119-0). ASM.

--Proceedings. 1978. Special Vol. 35.00 o.p. (ISBN 0-686-95120-4). ASM.

International Conference on Noise Control Engineering. The Inter-Noise Eighty-Two: Proceedings, 2 Vol. set. 55.00 (ISBN 0-686-37431-2). Noise Control.

International Conference on Operator Theory, Timisoara & Herculane, Romania, June 2-12, 1980. Topics in Modern Operator Theory. Gohberg, I., ed. (Operator Theory, Advances & Applications Ser.: 2). 335p. 1981. text ed. 30.80x (ISBN 3-7643-1244-0). Birkhauser.

International Conference on Parkinson's Disease, No. 6. The Extrapyramidal System & Its Disorders. Poirier, Louis J., et al, eds. LC 78-57817. (Advances in Neurology Ser.: Vol. 24). 551p. 1979. text ed. 58.50 (ISBN 0-89004-369-8). Raven.

International Conference on Plant Pathogenic Bacteria, 3rd. Proceedings. 1972. 45.00 o.p. (ISBN 9-0220-0357-4, PUDOC). Unipub.

International Conference on Pressure Vessel Technology. Discussions, Pt. III. 257p. 1970. text ed. 20.00 o.p. (ISBN 0-685-41498-1, G00064). ASME.

International Conference on Production Disease in Farm Animals, Third, Wageningen, the Netherlands, 13-16 Sept., 1976. Proceedings. 1977. pap. 32.00 o.p. (ISBN 90-220-0630-1, Pub. by PUDOC). Unipub.

International Conference on the Synapse, Czechoslovakia, May, 1978. The Cholinergic Synapse: Proceedings. Tucek, S., et al, eds. LC 79-577. (Progress in Brain Research Ser.: Vol. 49). 1979. 96.75 (ISBN 0-444-80105-7, North Holland). Elsevier.

International Conference on the Theory of Groups, 1969. Proceedings. Neumann, B. H. & Kovacs, L. G., eds. 414p. 1967. 60.00 (ISBN 0-677-10780-3). Gordon.

International Conference on Tonnage Measurement of Ships, 1969. Proceedings. 83p. 1970. pap. 7.00 (ISBN 0-686-93967-0, IMCO39, IMCO). Unipub.

International Conference on Underwater Education, 11th. Proceedings. Boone, Cheri, ed. Date not set. pap. 17.00 (ISBN 0-916974-32-4); Incl. addendum to proceedings, 147p. NAUI.

International Conference Sixth Vienna, 1974. Advances in Input-Output Analysis. Polenske, Karen & Skolka, Jiri, eds. LC 75-19295. 656p. 1976. prof ref 45.00x (ISBN 0-88410-277-7). Ballinger Pub.

International Conference, 1st, Stratford-upon-Avon, UK June 2-4, 1981. Automated Guided Vehicle Systems: Proceedings. 231p. 1981. pap. text ed. 88.00x (ISBN 0-903608-18-9). Scholium Intl.

International Conference, 1st Stratford-upon-Avon, UK April 1-3, 1981. Robot Vision & Sensory Controls: Proceedings. 348p. 1981. pap. text ed. 90.00x (ISBN 0-903608-15-4). Scholium Intl.

International Conference, 2nd, Tokyo, 1972. The Properties of Liquid Metals: Proceedings. Takeuchi, S. & Takeuchi, S., eds. LC 73-1286. 640p. 1973. 54.95x o.p. (ISBN 0-470-84414-0). Halsted Pr.

International Conference, 5th, Baden-Baden, Sep. 10-13, 1975. Plutonium & Other Actinides: Proceedings, 1975. Blank, H. & Lindner, R., eds. 1976. 76.75 (ISBN 0-444-11050-X, North-Holland). Elsevier.

International Conference, 7th, Tel Aviv, June 23-28, 1974. General Relativity & Gravitation: Proceedings. Shaviv, G., ed. LC 75-33824. 1976. 64.95x o.p. (ISBN 0-470-77939-X). Halsted Pr.

International Congress of Acarology-2nd. Proceedings. Evans, Owen, ed. 652p. 1969. 32.50x o.p. (ISBN 0-8002-1861-2). Intl Pubns Serv.

International Congress of Allergology. Abstracts: Eighth Conference, Tokyo, 1973. Munro-Ashman, D. & Pugh, D., eds. (International Congress Ser.: No. 300). 1974. pap. 14.25 (ISBN 0-444-15066-8). Elsevier.

International Congress of Ecology, 1st, the Hague, Netherlands, Sept. 1974. Proceedings. 250p. 1975. pap. 40.00 o.p. (ISBN 9-0220-0525-9, Pub. by PUDOC). Unipub.

International Congress of Food & Science Technology-1st-London, 1962. Food & Science Technology, 5 vols. Leitch, J. M., ed. Incl. Vol. 1. Chemical & Physical Aspects of Foods. 1969; Vol. 2. Biological & Microbiological Aspects of Foods. 1969; Vol. 3. Quality Analysis & Composition of Foods. 1969; Vol. 4. Manufacture & Distribution of Foods. 1969; Vol. 5. Proceedings. 1969. (Illus.). 3456p. Set. 736.00x (ISBN 0-677-10290-9). Gordon.

International Congress of Game Biologists, Thirteenth, Atlanta, Ga., March 11-15, 1977. Proceedings. Peterle, Tony J., ed. (Illus.). 538p. (Orig.). 1978. pap. 5.00 (ISBN 0-933564-04-X). Wildlife Soc.

International Congress of Pesticides Chemistry, 4th, Zurich, July 1978. World Food Production--Environment--Pesticides: Plenary Lectures. Geissbuehler, H., et al, eds. (IUPAC Symposia). 1979. text ed. 32.00 (ISBN 0-08-022374-5). Pergamon.

International Congress of Pharmacology, 7th, Reims, 1978. Satellite Symposium. Marihuana-Biological Effects, Analysis, Metabolism, Cellular Responses, Reproduction & Brain: Proceedings. Nahas, Gabriel G. & Paton, William D., eds. (Illus.). 1979. text ed. 80.00 (ISBN 0-08-023759-2). Pergamon.

International Congress of Pharmacology. Toward Chronopharmacology: Proceedings of Satellite Symposium to the 8th International Congress of Pharmacology, Nagasaki, Japan, 27-28 July 1981. Takahashi, R. & Halberg, F., eds. (Illus.). 456p. 1982. 80.00 (ISBN 0-08-027977-5). Pergamon.

International Congress of Pure & Applied Chemistry 28th, Vancouver, BC, Canada, 16-22 August 1981. Frontiers in Chemistry: Proceedings. Laidler, ed. (IUPAC Symposium Ser.). (Illus.). 350p. 1982. 85.00 (ISBN 0-08-026220-1). Pergamon.

International Congress of Rheumatology, et al. Abstracts: Thirteenth Congress, Kyoto, Japan, 1977. Dixon, A., ed. (International Congress Ser.: No. 299). 1974. 16.00 (ISBN 0-444-15065-X). Elsevier.

International Congress on Archives, 8th. Proceedings, Archivum, Vol. 26. International Council on Archives, ed. 207p. 1979. 35.00x (ISBN 0-89664-135-X, Pub. by K G Saur). Gale.

International Congress on Biblical Studies, 6th, Oxford, 3-7 April,1978. Studia Biblica Nineteen Seventy-Eight, III: Papers on Paul & Other New Testament Authors. Livingstone, E. A., ed. (Journal for the Study of the New Testament, Supplement Ser.: No. 3). 468p. 1981. text ed. 37.50x (ISBN 0-905774-27-2, Pub. by JSOT Pr England). Eisenbrauns.

International Congress on Biblical Studies. Studia Biblica Nineteen Seventy-Eight II: Papers on the Gospels. Livingston, E. A., ed. (Journal for the Study of the New Testament Supplement Ser.: No. 2). 350p. 1980. text ed. 37.50x (ISBN 0-905774-22-1, Pub. by JSOT Pr England). Eisenbrauns.

International Congress on Catalysis - Philadelphia - 1956 see Frankenburg, W. G., et al.

International Congress On Chemotherapy- 6th. Progress in Antimicrobial & Anticancer Chemotherapy: Proceedings, 2 Vols. Umezawa, Hamao, ed. (Illus.). 1970. Set. 75.00 o.p. (ISBN 0-8391-0033-7). Univ Park.

International Congress on Child Abuse & Neglect, 2nd, London, 1978. Selected Papers, Vol. 3. Kempe, C. H., et al, eds. 1100p. 1980. 138.00 (ISBN 0-08-023430-5). Pergamon.

International Congress on Electro Cardiology, Lisbon, 7th, June 1980 & De Padua, Fernando. New Frontiers of Electrocardiology: Proceedings. Macfarlane, Peter W., ed. 562p. 1981. 69.95x (ISBN 0-471-10041-2, Pub. by Res. Stud Pr). Wiley.

International Congress on Mathematical Education Staff, Fourth. C. I. M. E Lectures: Proceedings. Zweng, M., ed. 700p. Date not set. text ed. price not set (ISBN 3-7643-3082-1). Birkhauser.

International Congress on Programming & Control, 1st. Proceedings. Neustadt, L. W., ed. 261p. 1966. 22.00 (ISBN 0-89871-155-X). Soc Indus-Appl Math.

International Congress on Technology & Blindness, 1st, 1962. Proceedings, 4 vols. Clark, Leslie L., ed. Incl. Vol. 1. Man-Machine Systems (ISBN 0-89128-025-1, PTR025); Vol. 2. Living Systems (ISBN 0-89128-026-X, PTR026); Vol. 3. Sound Recording & Reproduction: Adapted & Special Purpose Devices (ISBN 0-89128-027-8, PTR027); Vol. 4. Catalog Appendix (ISBN 0-89128-028-6, PTR028). 1963. Set. pap. 12.00 o.p. (ISBN 0-686-63979-0); pap. 4.00 ea. o.p. Am Foun Blind.

International Congress on Thrombosis, 7th, Valencia, Spain, October, 1982. Abstracts: Journal-Haemostasis, Vol. 12, Nos. 1-2. Aznar, J., ed. 240p. 1982. pap. 58.25 (ISBN 3-8055-3617-8). S Karger.

International Cooperative Alliance. Cooperative Leadership in South-East Asia. 1963. 6.00x o.p. (ISBN 0-210-34055-X). Asia.

--Readings in Consumer Cooperation. 1973. 8.95x (ISBN 0-210-22348-0). Asia.

International Council for Building Research Studies & Documentation. Directory of Building Research, Information & Development Organizations. 4th ed. 215p. 1981. pap. 42.00x (ISBN 0-419-12550-7, Pub by E&FN Spon England). Methuen Inc.

International Council of Museums General Conference, 7th, 1970. Training of Museum Personnel. 242p. Date not set. pap. 6.50 (ISBN 0-686-93882-8, MISC13, ICOM). Unipub.

International Council of Shopping Centers, ed. Leasing Opportunities, 1983. 144p. 1982. pap. 39.00 (ISBN 0-913598-14-3). Intl Coun Shop.

International Council on Archives, ed. see International Congress on Archives, 8th.

International Diabetes Federation. Abstracts: Eighth Congress. Hoet, J., et al, eds. (International Congress Ser.: No. 280). 1973. pap. 29.50 (ISBN 0-444-15064-1). Elsevier.

International Economic Association. Theory of Interest Rates: Proceedings. Hahn, F. H. & Brechling, F. P., eds. 1965. 25.00 o.p. (ISBN 0-312-79835-0). St Martin.

International Economic Association Conference, Tokyo. The Economics of Health & Medical Care: Proceedings. Perlman, Mark, ed. LC 73-20107. 547p. 1974. 44.95x o.p. (ISBN 0-470-68051-2). Halsted Pr.

International Economic Association, Conference, Turin, Italy & Feldstein, M. S. The Economics of Public Services: Proceedings. LC 75-37750. 529p. 1977. 64.95x o.p. (ISBN 0-470-01374-5). Halsted Pr.

International Economic Studies Institute & Stanley, Timothy W. Raw Materials & Foreign Policy. (Illus.). 1977. lib. bdg. 25.00 o.p. (ISBN 0-89158-340-8); pap. text ed. 12.50 o.p. (ISBN 0-89158-446-3). Westview.

International Federation of Surveyors. Multilingual Dictionary of the International Federation of Surveyors. Date not set. 78.75 (ISBN 0-444-40795-2). Elsevier.

International Film Bureau Inc., ed. Deutsche Kulturfilme. (European Studies-Germany). 32p. 1982. 3.00x (ISBN 0-8354-2547-9). Intl Film.

International Gas Union, ed. Elsevier's Dictionary of the Gas Industry, 2 vols. (Polyglot). 1961. Set. 95.75 (ISBN 0-444-40758-8); Incl. suppl. pap. 138.50 (ISBN 0-686-85926-X). Elsevier.

International Gas Union, compiled by. Supplement to Elsevier's Dictionary of the Gas Industry: Polygot. LC 61-8851. 216p. 1973. 42.75 (ISBN 0-444-40757-X). Elsevier.

International Geographical Union, ed. Orbis Geographicus, 1980-84: World Directory of Geography. 5th ed. 962p. (Orig.). 1982. pap. 50.00x (ISBN 0-686-84541-2). Intl Pubns Serv.

International Heat Pipe Conference, Iv, London, 7-10 Sepbember 1981. Heat Pipes & Thermosyphons for Heat Recovery: Selected Papers. Reay, D. A., ed. 64p. 1982. pap. 25.00 (ISBN 0-08-028693-3). Pergamon.

International Hotel Association, ed. International Hotel Guide 1979. 32nd ed. LC 52-16324. 1979. pap. 22.50x o.p. (ISBN 0-8002-0838-2). Intl Pubns Serv.

International Hydrographic Bureau, Symposium on Tides, Monaco, 1967. Proceedings. 204p. (Eng. & Fr.). 1969. pap. 22.50 o.p. (ISBN 0-686-94168-3, UNESCO). Unipub.

International Institute for Applied Syetem Analysis, jt. ed. see Hafele, Wolf.

International Institute for Applied Systems Analysis, jt. ed. see Hafele, Wolf.

International Institute for Educational Planning. Planning the Development of Universities - 4. Onushkin, Victor G., tr. (Illus.). 439p. 1975. pap. 20.75 o.p. (ISBN 92-803-1068-2, U460, UNESCO). Unipub.

International Institute for Environment & Development (I.I.E.D.) United Nations Conference on Human Settlements, Vancouver, B. C., 1976: Human Settlements, National Reports: Summaries & Reference Guides. Anglemeyer, Mary & Ottersen, Signe R., eds. LC 76-14569. 1976. pap. text ed. 40.00 (ISBN 0-08-021243-3). Pergamon.

International Institute for Strategic Studies, ed. The Military Balance, Nineteen Seventy-Nine to Nineteen Eighty. LC 76-617319. (Illus.). 120p. 1980. lib. bdg. 12.50 o.p. (ISBN 0-86079-032-0). Westview.

International Institute for Strategic Studies. Strategic Survey 1975. LC 76-24927. 1976. 20.00 o.p. (ISBN 0-89158-545-1). Westview.

--Strategic Survey 1976. (Illus.). 1977. pap. 9.25 o.p. (ISBN 0-86079-006-1). Westview.

International Institute for Strategic Studies, ed. Strategic Survey 1978. LC 76-24927. 140p. 1980. pap. 11.50 o.p. (ISBN 0-86079-026-6). Westview.

International Institute for the Unification of Private Law. Digest of Legal Activities of International Organizations & Other Institutions. 4th ed. LC 74-19327. 1982. 85.00 (ISBN 0-379-00525-5); suppplement 1977 o.p. 15.00 (ISBN 0-686-96816-6). Oceana.

International Institute for the Unification of Private Law (UNIDROIT) New Directions in International Trade Law: Acts & Proceedings of the Second International Congress on Private Law, Vol. I & II. LC 77-10129. 1977. 85.00 set (ISBN 0-379-00670-7). Oceana.

International Institute of Public Finance, 35th Congress, 1979. Reforms of Tax Systems: Proceedings. Roskamp, Karl W. & Forte, Francesco, eds. 1981. 30.00 (ISBN 0-8143-1675-1). Wayne St U Pr.

International Institute of Refrigeration. The New International Dictionary of Refrigeration in English, French, Russian, German, Italian, Spanish, & Norwegian. 550p. 1977. text ed. write for info. (ISBN 0-08-020368-X). Pergamon.

International Institute of Social History, Amsterdam. Alphabetical Catalog of the Books & Pamphlets of the International Institute of Social History: Library Catalogs-Bib. Guides. 1979. lib. bdg. 390.00 (ISBN 0-8161-0297-X, Hall Library). G K Hall.

International Institute of Strategic Studies. Strategic Survey 1979. (Illus.). 144p. 1980. lib. bdg. 12.50 (ISBN 0-86079-037-1, International Institute for Strategic Studies). Westview.

International IUPAC Congress-2nd. Pesticide Chemistry: Proceedings, 6 vols. Tahori, A. S., ed. 1971. Set. 384.00x (ISBN 0-677-12120-2); Vol. 1, 506p. 92.00x (ISBN 0-677-12130-X); Vol. 2, 310p. 60.00x (ISBN 0-677-12140-7); Vol. 3, 236p. 54.00x (ISBN 0-677-12150-4); Vol. 4, 616p. 112.00x (ISBN 0-677-12160-1); Vol. 5, 576p. 107.00x (ISBN 0-677-12170-9); Vol. 6, 582p. 105.00x (ISBN 0-677-12180-6). Gordon.

International Journal of Quantum Chemisty-Symposium, 15th. Atomic, Molecular & Solid-State Theory, Collision Phenomena & Computational Quantum Chemistry: Proceedings. Lowdin, P. O., ed. 1982. 70.00x (ISBN 0-471-86672-5, Pub. by Wiley-Interscience). Wiley.

International Journal of Quantum Chemistry Symposium, 8th. Quantum Biology & Quantum Pharmacology: Proceedings. 1982. pap. 50.00x (ISBN 0-471-86671-7, Pub. by Wiley-Interscience). Wiley.

International Journal of Quantum Chemistry-Quantum Biology Symposium, 7th. Quantum Biology & Quantum Pharmacology: Proceedings. 438p. 1981. pap. 49.95x (ISBN 0-471-09190-1, Pub. by Wiley-Interscience). Wiley.

International Labour Conference, 59th session, Geneva, 1974. Apartheid: Tenth Special Report of the Director-General on the Application of the Declaration cooncerning the Policy of "Apartheid" of the Republic of South Africa. 68p. 8.55 (ISBN 92-2-100967-X, ILC 59/1/SPECIAL REPORT). Intl Labour Office.

International Labour Conference, 60th session, 1975. Apartheid: Eleventh Special Report of the Director-General on the Application of the Declaration Concerning the Policy of "Apartheid" of the Republic of South Africa. 51p. 7.15 (ISBN 92-2-100968-8, ILC 60/1/SPECIAL REPORT). Intl Labour Office.

International Labour Conference, 63rd session, 1977. Apartheid: Thirteenth Special Report of the Director-General on the Application of the Declaration Concerning the Policy of "Apartheid" of the Republic of South Africa. 56p. 8.55 (ILC 63/1). Intl Labour Office.

International Labour Conference, 64th session, 1978. Apartheid: Fourteenth Special Report of the Director-General on the Application of the Declaration Concerning the Policy of "Apartheid" of the Republic of South Africa. 54p. 8.55 (ILC 64/1). Intl Labour Office.

International Labour Conference, 65th session, 1979. Apartheid: Fifteenth Special Report of the Director-General on the Application of the Declaration Concerning the Policy of "Apartheid"of the Republic of South Africa. iii, 48p. 8.55 (ISBN 92-2-101971-3, ILC 65/1/SPECIAL REPORT). Intl Labour Office.

International Labour Conference, 68th session. Apartheid: Eighteenth Special Report of the Director-General on the Application of the Declaration Concerning the Policy of Apartheid of the Republic of South Africa. 1982. write for info. (ILC 68/SPECIAL REPORT). Intl Labour Office.

International Labour Office. Education & Training Policies in Occupational Safety & Health & Ergonomics: International Symposium. (Occupational Safety & Health Ser.: No. 47). viii, 389p. (Orig., Eng., Fr., & Span.). 1982. pap. 19.95 (ISBN 92-2-003002-0). Intl Labour Office.

--Family Living Studies: A Symposium. LC 74-2684. (International Labour Office Studies & Reports: No. 63). 280p. 1974. Repr. of 1961 ed. lib. bdg. 19.00x (ISBN 0-8371-7423-6, INFA). Greenwood.

--Guidelines for the Use of ILO International Classification of Radiographs of Pneumoconioses. (Occupational Safety & Health Ser.: No. 22). (Orig.). 1980. pap. 2.30. Intl Labour Office.

--The ILO-Norway African Regional Training Course for Senior Social Security Managers & Administrative Officials. iii, 333p. (Orig.). 1982. pap. 19.95. Intl Labour Office.

--International Labour Conventions & Recommendations, 1919-1981. Arranged by Subject Matter. xxxiv, 1167p. 1982. 39.90 (ISBN 92-2-102934-4). Intl Labour Office.

--Labour Relations & Development: Country Studies on Japan, the Philippines, Singapore & Sri Lanka. (Labour Management Relations Ser.). 153p. 1982. pap. 11.40. Intl Labour Office.

--Labour Relations in Southern Africa: Proceedings of & Documents Submitted to a Seminar, Gaborone, 2-4 December 1981. (Labour-Management Relations Ser.: No. 61). 58p. (Orig.). 1982. pap. 7.15 (ISBN 92-2-103005-9). Intl Labour Office.

--Sixth International Report on the Prevention & Suppression of Dust in Mining, Tunnelling, & Quarrying, 1973-1977. International Labour Office, ed. (Occupational Safety & Health Ser.: No. 48). viii, 152p. 1982. pap. 10.00 (ISBN 92-2-103006-7). Intl Labour Office.

--Small-scale Processing of Fish. (Technology Series Technical Memorandum: No. 3). xi, 118p. (Orig.). 1982. pap. 8.55 (ISBN 92-2-103205-1). Intl Labour Office.

--Vocational Rehabilitation of Leprosy Patients Report on the ILO-DANIDA Asian Seminar Bombay, India (26 October-6 November, 1981) iii, 126p. 1982. pap. 8.55 (ISBN 92-2-103047-4). Intl Labour Office.

--Vocational Rehabilitation Services for Disabled Persons. ii, 120p. 1982. pap. 10.00 (ISBN 92-2-103015-6). Intl Labour Office.

International Labour Office, ed. see Fraser, T. M.

International Labour Office, ed. see Jobs & Skills Programme for Afica, Addis Ababa.

International Labour Office, ed. see Kurian, Rachel.

International Labour Office, ed. see Molyneux, Maxine.

International Labour Office, ed. see Paul, Samuel.

International Labour Office, ed. see Phongpaichit, Pasuk.

International Labour Office, ed. see Schregle, Johannes.

International Labour Office, ed. see Standing, Guy.

International Labour Office, ed. see Takezawa, S., et al.

International Labour Office, Central Library, Geneva. International Labour Documentation, Cumulative Edition, 1965-1969, 8 vols. 5334p. 1970. Set. lib. bdg. 840.00 (ISBN 0-8161-0902-8, Hall Library). G K Hall.

--International Labour Documentation: Cumulative Edition 1970-71, 2 vols. 1972. Set. lib. bdg. 210.00 (ISBN 0-685-24887-9, Hall Library). G K Hall.

--Subject Index to International Labour Documentation, 1957-1964, 2 Vols. 1967. Set. 80.00 (ISBN 0-8161-0785-8, Hall Library). G K Hall.

International Labour Office staff. Year Book of Labour Statistics, 1982. 42nd ed. xv, 760p. 1983. text ed. 63.00 (ISBN 92-2-003262-7). Intl Labour Office.

International Labour Office, 67th session, 1981. Seventeenth Special Report of the Director-General on the Application of the Declaration Concerning the Policy of Apartheid of the Republic of South Africa. 102p. (Orig.). 1981. pap. 10.00 (ISBN 92-2-102395-8). Intl Labour Office.

International Labour Organisation (Geneva), ed. Yearbook of Labor Statistics, 1981. 41st ed. LC 36-130. (Illus.). 704p. 1982. 75.00 (ISBN 92-2-002850-6). Intl Pubns Serv.

International Labour Organisation, 5th Conference of American States Members,Petropolis. Application & Supervision of Labour Legislation in Agriculture: Report I. 56p. 1952. 3.40 (ISBN 0-686-84712-1, CRA 1952/5/I). Intl Labour Office.

International Labour Organization. Encyclopedia of Occupational Health, 2 vols. LC 74-39329. (Illus.). 1972. Set. 68.50 o.p. (ISBN 0-07-079555-X, P&RB). McGraw.

International Machine Tool Design & Research Conference, 15th. Proceedings. Tobias, S. A. & Koenigsberger, F., eds. 738p. 1975. 199.95x o.p. (ISBN 0-470-87532-1, EM15 02). Halsted Pr.

International Machine Tool Design & Research Conference, 20th. Proceedings. Tobias, S. A., ed. 638p. 1980. 184.95x o.p. (ISBN 0-470-27062-4, EM15 05). Halsted Pr.

International Maritime Organization, ed. International Maritime Dangerous Goods Code (IMDC, 5 vols. 1982. English ed. 300.00x (ISBN 0-686-96589-2, Pub. by Intl Maritime England); French ed. 395.00x (ISBN 0-686-99792-1). State Mutual Bk.

International Mathematic Union, ed. World Dictionary of Mathematics 1982. 7th ed. 728p. 23.00 (ISBN 0-686-84619-2, WRLDIR/7). Am Math.

International Measurement Confederation Congress, Sixth & Imeko. Measurement & Instrumentation: Proceedings, 3 vols. 1975. Set. 138.50 (ISBN 0-444-10685-5, North-Holland). Elsevier.

International Meeting of the Societe de chimie physique, Thiais, 27th, 1975. Lasers in Physical Chemistry & Biophysics: Proceedings. Joussot-Dubien, J., ed. LC 75-29093. 1975. 95.75 (ISBN 0-444-41388-X). Elsevier.

International Meeting of the Societe de Chimie Physique, 25th, July, 1974. Reaction Kinetics in Heterogeneous Chemical Systems: Proceedings. Barret, P., ed. LC 75-31672. 1975. 76.75 (ISBN 0-444-41351-0). Elsevier.

International Mine Ventilation Congress, 2nd. Proceedings. Mousset-Jones, Pierre, ed. LC 80-52943. (Illus.). 864p. 1980. 38.00x (ISBN 0-89520-271-9). Soc Mining Eng.

International Monetary Fund Staff. World Economic Outlook: 1982 Edition. 1982. 11.00 (ISBN 0-686-97773-4). Intl Monetary.

International Peace Academy Conference, Nov. 1979, New Paltz, New York. Negotiating the End of Conflicts: Namibia & Zimbabwe. (IPA Reports: No. 7). 54p. 1980. 2.00 (ISBN 0-686-36944-0). Intl Peace.

International Peace Academy Conference, Oct. 31-Nov. 2, 1980, New Paltz, New York. The Organization of African Unity: A Role for the Eighties. (IPA Peace Ser.: No. 10). 48p. 1980. 3.00x (ISBN 0-686-36947-5). Intl Peace.

International Peace Academy, Feb. 12-17, 1978, New Delhi, India. Regional Colloquium on Disarmament & Arms Control: A Report. (IPA Reports Ser.: No. 5). 88p. 1978. 1.50x (ISBN 0-686-36942-4). Intl Peace.

International Peace Academy Symposium, Nov. 6-8, 1979, Warrenton, Virginia. Weapons of Peace: How New Technology Can Revitalize Peacekeeping. (IPA Reports Ser.: No. 8). 59p. 1980. 3.00x (ISBN 0-686-36945-9). Intl Peace.

International Physicians for the Prevention of Nuclear War. Last Aid: The Medical Dimensions of Nuclear War. Chivian, Eric, et al, eds. LC 82-13472. (Illus.). 224p. 1982. 19.95 (ISBN 0-7167-1434-5); pap. 9.95 (ISBN 0-7167-1435-3). W H Freeman.

International Project for Soft Energy Paths, jt. auth. see Harding, Jim.

International Project for Soft Energy Paths Network. Tools for the Soft Path. (Illus.). 288p. (Orig.). 1982. pap. 11.95 (ISBN 0-686-83030-X). Brick Hse Pub.

International Resource Development Inc. Staff, ed. Electronic Mail: Executives Directory. 200p. 1982. 95.00 (ISBN 0-686-82647-7). Knowledge Indus.

International Rice Commission, Working Party on Fertilizers, 3rd Meeting, Bangkok, 1953. Report. (FAO Agricultural Development Papers: No. 39). 46p. 1953. pap. 4.50 (ISBN 0-686-92869-5, F1920, FAO). Unipub.

International Rice Commission, Working Party on Fertilizers, 4t, Tokyo, 1954. Report. (FAO Agricultural Development Papers: No. 48). 48p. 1955. pap. 4.75 (ISBN 0-686-92892-X, F192, FAO). Unipub.

International Rice Research Institute. Annual Report, 1977. pap. 49.00 (ISBN 0-686-93104-1, RQ88, IRRI). Unipub.

International School of Elementary Particle Physics, Herceg-Novi. Methods in Subnuclear Physics: Proceedings, 1965-1969, Vols. 1-4. Nikolic, M., ed. Incl. Vol. 1. 516p. 1968. 96.00 (ISBN 0-677-11950-X); Vol. 2. 858p. 1968. 141.00 (ISBN 0-677-11960-7); Vol. 3. 882p. 1969. 156.00 (ISBN 0-677-12790-1); Vol. 4. 1970. Part 1. 103.00 (ISBN 0-677-14340-0); Part 2. 83.00 (ISBN 0-677-14350-8); Part 3. 103.00 (ISBN 0-677-14360-5); Three Part Set. 235.00 (ISBN 0-677-13530-0); Vol. 5. 1977. Pt. 1. (ISBN 0-677-15910-2); Pt. 2. (ISBN 0-677-15920-X); Two Part Set. 180.00 (ISBN 0-677-15960-9). Gordon.

International School of Nuclear Physics, Sept 23-30, 1974. The Investigation of Nuclear Structure by Scattering Processes at High Energies: Proceedings. Schopper, H., ed. 360p. 1975. 34.00 (ISBN 0-444-10887-4, North-Holland). Elsevier.

International School of Physics. Problems of the Foundations of Physics: Proceedings. Di Francia, G. Toraldo, ed. (Enrico Fermi Course: No. 72). 1979. 98.00 (ISBN 0-444-85285-9, North Holland). Elsevier.

International School of Physics "Enrico Fermi" Course LXI, Varenna, July 8-20, 1974. Atomic Structure & Mechanical Properties of Metals: Proceedings. Caglioti, G., ed. 1976. 149.00 (ISBN 0-7204-0490-8, North-Holland) (ISBN 0-685-74299-7). Elsevier.

International School of Physics "Enrico Fermi" Course 66 & Baarli. Health & Medical Physics: Proceedings. 1978. 115.00 (ISBN 0-7204-0728-1, North-Holland). Elsevier.

International School of Physics "Enrico Fermi" Course LIX, Varenna on Lake Como, July 9-21 1973. Local Properties at Phase Transitions: Proceedings. Mueller, K. A. & Rigamonti, A., eds. 1976. 161.75 (ISBN 0-7204-0448-7, North-Holland). Elsevier.

International Science & Technology, Inc. Report on the Potential Use of Small Dams to Produce Power for Low-Income Communities. Allen, Mary M., ed. (Illus.). 1979. 20.00 (ISBN 0-936130-02-4). Intl Sci Tech.

International Seaweed Symposium, 7th, Sappora, Japan, Aug. 1971. Proceedings. Science Council of Japan, ed. 607p. 1973. 67.95x o.p. (ISBN 0-470-77090-2). Halsted Pr.

International Seminar, Imperial College of Science & Technology, UK. Finite Element Methods in Radiation Physics: Proceedings. Goddard, A. J., ed. Williams. 160p. 1981. pap. 37.00 (ISBN 0-08-028694-1). Pergamon.

International Seminar on Approval & Gathering Plans in Large & Medium Size Academic Libraries, 3rd. Economics of Approval Plans: Proceedings. Spyers-Duran, Peter & Gore, Daniel, eds. LC 72-836. 134p. 1972. lib. bdg. 25.00 (ISBN 0-8371-6405-2, SAJ/). Greenwood.

International Seminar on Energy Conservation & Use of Renewable Energies in the Bio-Industries, Trinity College, Oxford, UK, 2nd 6-10 Sept. 1982. Energy Conservation & Use of Renewable Energies in the Bio-Industries: Proceedings. Vogt, F., ed. (Illus.). 750p. 1982. 100.00 (ISBN 0-08-029781-1). Pergamon.

International Society for Artificial Organs. International Society for Artificial Organs, 3rd, Paris, July 8-10, 1981: Proceeding, Supplement to Vol. 5. Funck, J. L. & Bretano, eds. LC 78-640817. (Illus.). 864p. 1982. text ed. 90.00 (ISBN 0-936022-06-X); pap. text ed. 115.00 (ISBN 0-936022-05-1). Intl Soc Artificial Organs.

International Society for Artificial Organs, 2nd, New York, April 18-19, 1979, et al. Proceedings, Suppl. To Vol. 3. Friedman, Eli A. & Beyer, Monica M., eds. LC 81-13627. (Illus.). 512p. 1980. text ed. 80.00 (ISBN 0-936022-02-7); pap. text ed. 65.00x (ISBN 0-936022-01-9). Intl Soc Artifical Organs.

International Society for Paediatric Ophthalmology, 2nd Meeting. Paediatric Ophtalmology: Proceedings. Francois, J. & Maione, M., eds. 600p. 1982. 45.00x (ISBN 0-471-10040-4, Pub. by Wiley-Interscience). Wiley.

International Society for Tropical Root Crops, 1st Triennial Root Crops Symposium, Ibadan, Nigeria, 1980. Tropical Root Crops: Research Strategies for the 1980's, Proceedings. 279p. 1981. pap. 18.00 (ISBN 0-686-93946-8, IDRC163, IDRC). Unipub.

International Solar Energy Society. International Solar Energy Congress, Sun II: Proceedings Held May 28 to June 1,1979, Atlanta, Georgia, 3 vols. Boer, ed. 1980. 385.00 (ISBN 0-08-025074-2); pap. 275.00 o.p. (ISBN 0-08-025075-0). Pergamon.

International Solar Energy Society American Section Annual Meeting, Orlando Fla., 1977. Proceedings, 3 vols. 1977. Set. pap. text ed. 115.00x (ISBN 0-89553-004-X). Am Solar Energy.

International Solar Energy Society American Section Annual Meeting, Phoenix, 1980. Proceedings, 2 vols. Franta, Gregory E. & Glenn, Barbara H., eds. 1980. Set. pap. text ed. 150.00x (ISBN 0-89553-021-X). Am Solar Energy.

International Solar Energy Society, American Section, Annual Meeting, Denver, 1978. Solar Diversification: Proceedings, 2 vols. Boer, Karl W. & Franta, Gregory E., eds. 1978. Set. pap. text ed. 115.00x (ISBN 0-89553-011-2). Am Solar Energy.

International Solar Energy Society, American Section. Solar Energy Symposia: Bio-Chemistry, Physics, Wind, & "On the Rise", a Program on State & Local Government Initiatives. Boer, Karl W. & Jenkins, Alec F., eds. 1978. pap. text ed. 27.00 (ISBN 0-89553-014-7). Am Solar Energy.

International Solar Energy Society, American Section, Annual Meeting, Philadelphia, 1981. Solar Rising: Proceedings, 2 vols. Glenn, Barbara H. & Franta, Gregroy E., eds. LC 77-79643. (Illus.). 1982. Set. pap. text ed. 150.00x (ISBN 0-89553-030-9). Am Solar Energy.

International Solar Energy Society, American Section. A Summary of the Basics in Solar Energy: Supplement-Tutorials to the 1978 Annual Meeting of the American Section of the International Solar Energy Society. Boer, Karl W., ed. 1978. pap. text ed. 18.00x (ISBN 0-89553-013-9). Am Solar Energy.

--To Will One Thing: Solar Action at the Local Level. Jenkins, Alec F., ed. 1979. pap. text ed. 30.00x (ISBN 0-89553-022-8). Am Solar Energy.

International Solvay Conference on Physics, XVII, et al. Order & Fluctuations in Equilibrium & Nonequilibrium Statistical Mechanics: Proceedings. LC 80-13215. 374p. 1981. 66.00x (ISBN 0-471-05927-7, Pub. by Wiley Interscience). Wiley.

International Spring School on Crystal Growth, 2nd, Japan, 1974. Crystal Growth & Characterization: Proceedings. Ueda, R. & Mullin, J. B., eds. 1976. 68.00 (ISBN 0-444-11061-5, North-Holland). Elsevier.

International Symposium, Fourth, Wright State University, June, 1975 & Krishnaiah, P. R. Multivariate Analysis 4: Proceedings. 1977. 85.00 (ISBN 0-7204-0520-3, North-Holland). Elsevier.

International Symposium in Chemical Synthesis of Nucleic Acids, Egestorf, West Germany, May 1980. Nucleic Acid Synthesis: Applications to Molecular Biology & Genetic Engineering. (Nucleic Acids Symposium Ser.: No. 7). 396p. 1980. 40.00 (ISBN 0-904147-27-4). IRL Pr.

International Symposium, Louvain, Sept., 1978. Preparation of Catalysts II: Scientific Basis for the Preparation of Heterogeneous Catalysts; Proceedings. Delmon, B., et al, eds. (Studies in Surface Science & Catalysts: Vol. 3). 1979. 106.50 (ISBN 0-444-41733-8). Elsevier.

International Symposium, Mannheim, 26-29 of July, 1972. The Roots of Evaluation, the Epidemiological Basis for Planning Psychiatric Services: Proceedings. Wing, J. H. & Hofner, H., eds. 1973. 32.50x o.p. (ISBN 0-19-721375-8). Oxford U Pr.

International Symposium of Physiology, New Delhi-Patiala, Oct. 1974. Advances in Exercise Physiology: Proceedings. Jokl, E., et al, eds. (Medicine & Sport: Vol. 9). 160p. 1976. 57.00 (ISBN 3-8055-2291-6). S Karger.

International Symposium of the French Institute for Health & Medical Research (Neurosciences), Marseilles, May 13-16, 1975. Advances in Cerebral Angiography: Anatomy, Stereotaxy, Embolization, Computerized Axial Tomography. Salamon, G., ed. (Illus.). 430p. 1976. 36.00 o.p. (ISBN 0-387-07569-0). Springer-Verlag.

International Symposium on Analysis, Chemistry, & Biology, No. 2. Polynuclear Aromatic Hydrocarbons. Jones, Peter W. & Freudenthal, Ralph I., eds. LC 77-87456. (Carcinogenesis-A Comprehensive Survey Ser.: Vol. 3). 507p. 1978. 54.00 (ISBN 0-89004-241-1). Raven.

International Symposium on Cancer Detection & Prevention. Abstracts: Second Symposium, Bologna, 1973. Maltoni, C., et al, eds. (International Congress Ser.: No. 275). 1973. pap. 29.00 (ISBN 0-686-43412-9). Elsevier.

International Symposium on Cell Biology & Cytopharmacology, First. Advances in Cytopharmacology, Vol. 1. Clementi, F. & Ceccarelli, B., eds. LC 70-84115. (Illus.). 493p. 1971. 53.00 (ISBN 0-911216-09-X). Raven.

International Symposium on Coenzyme Q, Lake Yamanaka, Japan, 1976 & 1979. Biomedical & Clinical Aspects of Coenzyme Q: Proceedings, Vols. 1 & 2. Folkers, K., et al, eds. 1977. Vol. 1. 67.00 (ISBN 0-444-41576-9, North Holland); Vol. 2. 68.00 (ISBN 0-444-80238-X). Elsevier.

International Symposium on Macromolecules. Proceedings. Mano, E. B., ed. 1974. 51.00 (ISBN 0-444-41278-6). Elsevier.

International Symposium on Medicinal Chemistry, Brighton, U. K., 6th, Sept. 4-7, 1978 & Simkins, M. A. Medicinal Chemistry: Proceedings, Vol. 6. 477p. 1981. 105.95x (ISBN 0-471-27990-0, Pub. by Res Stud Pr). Wiley.

International Symposium on Microtubule Inhibitors, Belgium, 1975. Microtubules & Microtubule Inhibitors: Proceedings. Borgers, M., ed. De Brabander, M. 1976. 133.25 (ISBN 0-444-11041-0, North-Holland). Elsevier.

International Symposium on Modern Developments in Fluid Dynamics. Proceedings. Rom, J., ed. LC 77-73178. (Illus.). xvii, 398p. 1977. text ed. 43.50 (ISBN 0-89871-035-9). Soc Indus-Appl Math.

International Symposium on Neurophysiology. Recent Contributions to Neurophysiology: Proceedings. Cordeau, J., ed. Gloor, P. (Supplements to Electroencephalography & Clinical Neurophysiology: Vol. 31). 1972. 38.50 (ISBN 0-444-40963-7, North Holland). Elsevier.

International Symposium on Olfaction & Taste, 6th, Gif Sur Yvette, France, 1977. Olfaction & Taste VI: Proceedings. LeMagnen, J. & Macleod, P., eds. 500p. 25.00 (ISBN 0-904147-08-8). IRL Pr.

International Symposium on Olfaction & Taste, 7th, the Netherlands 1980. Olfaction & Taste VII: Proceedings. Van der Starre, H., ed. x, 500p. 1980. 50.00 (ISBN 0-904147-20-7). IRL Pr.

International Symposium On Poly-A-Amino Acids - 1st - University Of Wisconsin - 1961. Polyamino Acids, Polypeptides, & Proteins: Proceedings. Stahmann, Mark, ed. (Illus.). 412p. 1962. 45.00 (ISBN 0-299-02620-5). U of Wis Pr.

International Symposium on Pre-Harvest Sprouting in Cereals. Proceedings. Kruger, James E. & LaBerge, Donald E., eds. 320p. 1982. lib. bdg. 22.00 (ISBN 0-86531-535-3). Westview.

International Symposium on Protein Metabolism & Nutrition, 2nd, the Netherlands, May 2-6, 1977. Proceedings. (European Association for Animal Production (EAAP) Ser.: No. 20). 1977. pap. 28.00 o.p. (ISBN 9-0220-0634-4, Pub. by PUDOC). Unipub.

International Symposium on Quantitative Mass Spectrometry in Life Sciences, 1st, State University of Ghent Belgium June 16-18 1976. Quantitative Mass Spectrometry in Life Sciences: Proceedings. DeLeenheer, A. P. & Roncucci, Romeo R, eds. LC 77-3404. 1977. 64.00 (ISBN 0-444-41557-2). Elsevier.

International Symposium on Quantum Biology & Quantum Pharmacology. Proceedings. (International Journal of Quantum Chemistry-Quantum Biology Symposium: No. 5). 472p. 1978. 62.95x (ISBN 0-471-05635-9). Wiley.

--Proceedings. Lowdin, Per-Olav & Sabin, John R., eds. 430p. 1982. 64.95 (ISBN 0-471-89123-1, Pub. by Wiley-Interscience). Wiley.

International Symposium on Rarefied Gas Dynamics - 2nd see Von Mises, Richard & Von Karman, Theodore.

International Symposium on Rarefied Gas Dynamics - 3rd see Von Mises, Richard & Von Karman, Theodore.

International Symposium on Rarefied Gas Dynamics - 4th see Von Mises, Richard & Von Karman, Theodore.

International Symposium on Rarefied Gas Dynamics - 5th see Von Mises, Richard & Von Karman, Theodore.

International Symposium on Rarefied Gas Dynamics - 6th see Von Mises, Richard & Von Karman, Theodore.

International Symposium on Shipboard Acoustics. International Symposium on Shipboard Acoustics: Proceeedings, 1976. Janssen, J. H., ed. 1977. 85.00 (ISBN 0-444-41650-1). Elsevier.

International Symposium on Solar Terrestrial Physics. Physics of Solar Planetary Environments: Proceedings, 2 vols. Williams, Donald J., ed. LC 76-29443. (Illus.). 1976. pap. 10.00 (ISBN 0-87590-204-9). Am Geophysical.

International Symposium on Statistical Design & Linear Models, March 19-23, 1973. A Survey of Statistical Design & Linear Models: Proceedings. Srivastava, J. N., ed. 750p. 1975. 78.00 (ISBN 0-444-10590-5, North-Holland). Elsevier.

International Symposium on the Brattleboro Rat, Sept. 4-7, 1981. The Brattleboro Rat: Proceedings, Vol. 394. Sokol, Hilda W. & Valtin, Heinz, eds. 828p. 1982. 150.00 (ISBN 0-89766-178-8). NY Acad Sci.

International Symposium on the Early Life History of Fish, Obun, Scotland, 1973. Report. (FAO Fisheries Reports: No. 141). 61p. 1973. pap. 7.50 (ISBN 0-686-93971-9, F786, FAO). Unipub.

International Symposium on the Future of Union Catalogue, University of Toronto, May 21-22 1981. The Future of the Union Catalogue: Proceedings of the International Symposium on the Future of Union Catalogue, University of Toronto, May 21-22 1981. Cook, C. Donald, ed. LC 82-6238. (Cataloging & Classification Quarterly Ser.: Vol. 2, Nos. 1 & 2). 136p. 1982. text ed. 19.95 (ISBN 0-86656-175-7, B175). Haworth Pr.

International Symposium on the German Democratic Republic, 6th. Studies in GDR Culture & Society: Proceedings. Gerber, Margy, et al, eds. LC 80-6255. 324p. (Orig.). 1981. lib. bdg. 25.25 (ISBN 0-8191-1735-8); pap. text ed. 13.50 (ISBN 0-8191-1736-6). U Pr of Amer.

International Symposium on the Kittay Scientific Foundation, 4th. New Trends of Psychiatry in the Community: Proceedings. Serban, George, ed. LC 77-6322. 1977. prof ref 20.00x (ISBN 0-88410-516-4). Ballinger Pub.

International Symposium on the Relations Between Heterogeneous & Homogeneous Catalytic Phenomena, Brussels, 1974. Catalysis: Heterogeneous & Homogeneous: Proceedings. Delmon, B. & Jannes, G., eds. 1975. 106.50 (ISBN 0-444-41346-4). Elsevier.

International Symposium, Switzerland, Sept. 1978. Development & Chemical Specificity Neurons: Proceedings. Cuenod, M., et al, eds. (Progress in Brain Research Ser.: Vol. 51). 1980. 111.00 (ISBN 0-444-80128-6, North Holland). Elsevier.

International Symposium, 12th, Paris, 1976. Atmospheric Pollution, 1976: Proceedings. Benarie, Michel, ed. 1976. 63.00 (ISBN 0-444-41497-5). Elsevier.

International Symposium, 2nd, Cambridge, Sept. 1976. Rapid Methods & Automation in Microbiology: Proceedings. Johnston, H. H. & Newsom, S. W., eds. 1977. 25.95 (ISBN 0-471-09397-1). Res Stud Pr.

International Symposium, 2nd, Tokyo, 1972. Atherogenesis II: Proceedings. Shimamoto, et al, eds. (International Congress Ser.: No. 269). 1973. 78.00 (ISBN 0-444-15007-2, Excerpta Medica). Elsevier.

International Symposium, 3rd, Amsterdam, Sept. 1976. Analytical Pryolysis: Proceedings. Jones, C. E. & Cramers, C. A., eds. 1977. 76.75 (ISBN 0-444-41558-0). Elsevier.

International Textiles of Amsterdam, ed. Dutch Textiles. (A Survey of World Textiles: No. 16). (Illus.). 1960. text ed. 15.00x (ISBN 0-85317-620-5, Pub. by A & C Black England). Humanities.

International Thermal Spraying Conference, 8th. Papers. American Welding Society, ed. 25.00 o.p. (ISBN 0-686-50108-X). Am Welding.

--Raporteur's Reports & Seminar Papers. American Welding Society, ed. 10.00 o.p. (ISBN 0-686-50107-1). Am Welding.

International Union Against Cancer Staff. Manual of Clinical Oncology. 3rd, enl. ed. (Illus.). 370p. 1982. pap. 18.00 (ISBN 0-387-11746-6). Springer-Verlag.

International Union of Pure & Applied Chemistry. Classification & Nomenclature of Electroanalytical Techniques. 1977. pap. text ed. 10.75 (ISBN 0-08-021226-3). Pergamon.

--Membership Lists & Report: 1982. 180p. 1982. pap. 13.00 (ISBN 0-08-029241-0). Pergamon.

--Nomenclature of Inorganic Chemistry. 2nd ed. 122p. 1976. text ed. 14.85 o.p. (ISBN 0-08-020834-7). Pergamon.

--Nomenclature of Organic Chemistry: Sections A, B & C. 352p. 1976. text ed. 40.00 o.p. (ISBN 0-08-020835-5). Pergamon.

--Stability Constants of Metal Complexes: Critical Survey of Stability Constants of EDTA Complexes, Vol. 14. Anderegg, G., ed. 1977. text ed. 13.00 (ISBN 0-08-022009-6). Pergamon.

--Standard Methods for the Analysis of Oils, Fats & Soaps. 5th ed. Suppl. 2, 1976. pap. text ed. 13.75 o.p. (ISBN 0-08-020839-8); Suppl. 3. 1976. pap. 5.50 o.p. (ISBN 0-08-020838-X); Suppl. 4. 1977. pap. 13.75 o.p. (ISBN 0-08-020955-6). Pergamon.

International Urinary Stone Conference, Australia, 1979, et al. Urinary Calculus. Finlayson, B., ed. LC 80-11704. 518p. 1981. text ed. 42.50 o.p. (ISBN 0-88416-294-X). Wright-PSG.

International Workshop, IIASA, Laxenburg, Austria, 28-31 January 1980. Planning for Rare Events: Nuclear Accident Preparedness & Management-Proceedings. Lathrop, J. W., ed. (IIASA Proceedings Ser.: Vol. 14). (Illus.). 280p. 1981. 30.00 (ISBN 0-08-028703-4). Pergamon.

International Workshop, World Hydrocarbon Markets. World Hydrocarbon Markets-Current Status, Projected Prospects & Future Trends: Proceedings of the International Workshop, Mexico City, April 1982. Wionczek, M. S., ed. (Illus.). 225p. 1982. 40.00 (ISBN 0-08-029962-8). Pergamon.

Internationalen Jugendbibliothek,(International Youth Library) Kataloge der Internationale Jugendbibliothek,(Catalogs of the International Youth Library, 5 pts. Incl. Pt. 1. Alphabetischer Katalog, (Alphabetical, 5 vols. 2634p. Set. 365.00 (ISBN 0-8161-0759-9); Pt. 2. Laenderkatalog, (Language Sections Catalog, 4 vols. 2493p. Set. 320.00 (ISBN 0-8161-0110-8); Pt. 3. Systematischer Katalog, (Classified, 2 vols. 1140p. Set. 170.00 (ISBN 0-8161-0108-6); Pt. 4. Titelkatalog, (Title, 4 vols. 2274p. Set. 335.00 (ISBN 0-8161-0111-6); Pt. 5. Illustratorenkatalog, (Catalog of Illustrators, 3 vols. 1487p. Set. 235.00 (ISBN 0-8161-0109-4). 1968. G K Hall.

Interregional Seminar on Problems of Early School Leavers. Report. pap. 5.00 (ISBN 0-686-94405-4, UN74/4/5, UN). Unipub.

Interregional Seminar on the Financing of Housing & Urban Development. Report. pap. 3.50 (ISBN 0-686-94401-1, UN72/4/5, UN). Unipub.

Interregional Seminar on the Mobilization of Personal Savings in Developing Countries. Report. pap. 3.00 (ISBN 0-686-94385-6, UN72/2A7, UN). Unipub.

Intersociety Committee on Pathology Information, Inc. Directory of Pathology Training Programs, 1981-82. 13th ed. Graves, Judy, ed. (Illus.). 1980. 15.00 o.p. (ISBN 0-686-26820-2). Intersoc Comm Path Info.

Intersociety Energy Conversion Engineering Conference, 16th. Proceeding, 3 Vols. 2608p. 1981. Set. 165.00 (H00179). ASME.

Interstate Bureau of Regulations. Political Action Register. Alperin, David S., ed. 2500p. 1982. 249.50 (ISBN 0-911693-02-5). IBR Pub.

InterTechnology Corp. Analysis of the Economic Potential of Solar Thermal Energy to Provide Industrial Process Heat: Executive Summary Report. 120p. 1979. pap. 17.95x (ISBN 0-930978-49-8). Solar Energy Info.

Intia, Peria S. Three Tales from Bicol. (Illus.). 45p. (Orig.). (gr. 4-6). 1982. pap. 3.50 (ISBN 971-10-0029-6, Pub. by New Day Philippines). Cellar.

Intriligator, jt. auth. see Arrow.

Intriligator, M. D., jt. ed. see Griliches, A.

Intriligator, Michael D. Econometric Models, Techniques & Applications. (Illus.). 1978. pap. 27.95 ref. (ISBN 0-13-223255-3). P-H.

--Mathematical Optimization & Economic Theory. (Mathematical Economics Ser.). 1971. text ed. 25.95 (ISBN 0-13-561753-7). P-H.

Intriligator, Michael D., jt. ed. see Brodie, Bernard.

Inui, Naomichi, ed. Mutation, Promotion & Transformation in Vitro. 260p. 1982. text ed. 40.00 (ISBN 0-686-98396-3, Pub. by Japan Sci Soc Japan). Intl Schol Bk Serv.

Inumara, Kazuo. Tan Tan's Hat. Date not set. 6.95 (ISBN 0-686-95235-9). Bradbury Pr.

Inwood, Robert & Bruyere, Christian. In Harmony with Nature. LC 80-54351. (Illus.). 224p. 1981. pap. 8.95 (ISBN 0-8069-7504-0). Sterling.

Inwood, Robert, jt. auth. see Bruyere, Christian.

Ioachim, H. L., ed. Pathobiology Annual. LC 75-151816. 442p. 1978. 45.00 (ISBN 0-89004-277-2). Raven.

Ioachim, Harry L. Lymph Node Biopsy. (Illus.). 368p. 1982. text ed. 75.00x (ISBN 0-397-50413-6, Lippincott Medical). Lippincott.

Ioachim, Harry L., ed. Pathobiology Annual, 1979. LC 75-151816. 414p. 1979. text ed. 46.00 (ISBN 0-89004-360-4). Raven.

--Pathobiology Annual, 1980. 336p. 1980. text ed. 41.00 (ISBN 0-89004-437-6). Raven.

--Pathobiology Annual, 1981. 432p. 1981. text ed. 47.00 (ISBN 0-89004-571-2). Raven.

--Pathobiology Annual, 1982. 1982. text ed. write for info. (ISBN 0-89004-724-3). Raven.

Ioannou, P. A. & Kokotovic, P. V. Adaptive Systems with Reduced Models. (Lecture Notes in Control & Information Sciences Ser.: Vol. 47). 162p. 1983. pap. 10.00 (ISBN 0-387-12150-1). Springer-Verlag.

Iocolano, Mark. Nikon F-Two. (Amphoto Pocket Companion Ser.). (Illus.). 1980. pap. 4.95 (ISBN 0-8174-2182-3, Amphoto). Watson-Guptill.

--Nikon FM & FE. (Amphoto Pocket Companion Ser.). (Illus.). 1980. pap. 4.95 (ISBN 0-8174-2181-5, Amphoto). Watson-Guptill.

Ioffe, A. D. & Tihomirov, V. M. Theory of Extremal Problems. (Studies in Mathematics & Its Applications: Vol. 6). 1979. 85.00 (ISBN 0-444-85167-4, North Holland). Elsevier.

Iohvidov, I. S. Hankel Toeplitz Matrices & Forms. 244p. 1982. text ed. 24.95 (ISBN 3-7643-3090-2). Birkhauser.

Ion, Sam. Advice to the Working Woman. 256p. 1981. 10.95 (ISBN 0-920510-55-8, Pub. by Personal Lib). Dodd.

Ionasescu, Victor & Zellweger, Hans. Genetics in Neurology. 1982. text ed. write for info. (ISBN 0-89004-775-8). Raven.

Ionesco, Eugene. Macbett. Marowitz, Charles, tr. from Fr. LC 73-6644. 1973. pap. 5.95 (ISBN 0-394-17805-X, E614, Ever). Grove.

--Victimes du Devoir. Lee, Vera G., ed. LC 72-4875. (Illus.). 178p. (Orig.). 1973. pap. text ed. 7.50 o.p. (ISBN 0-395-12745-9, 3-32658). HM.

Ionesco, Eugene, jt. auth. see Benamou, Michael.

Ionesco, Eugene see Moon, Samuel.

Ionescu, G., ed. Between Sovereignty & Integration. LC 73-19586. 192p. 1973. text ed. 22.95x o.p. (ISBN 0-470-42800-7). Halsted Pr.

Ionescu, Ghita. The New Politics of European Integration. LC 72-80483. 250p. 1972. 22.50 (ISBN 0-312-56875-4). St Martin.

Ioose, G. Bifurcation of Maps & Applications. (North-Holland Mathematics Studies: Vol. 36). 1979. 40.50 (ISBN 0-444-85304-9, North Holland). Elsevier.

Iordan, Iorgu. Introduction to Romance Linguistics, Its Schools & Scholars. Orr, John, ed. Repr. of 1937 ed. lib. bdg. 20.50x (ISBN 0-8371-4244-X, IORL). Greenwood.

Iorillo, Nino R., jt. auth. see Diaz, Andres C.

Iorio, Dominick A. Nicolas Malebranche: Dialogue Between a Christian Philosopher & a Chinese Philosopher on the Existence & Nature of God. LC 80-5045. 115p. 1980. text ed. 18.25 (ISBN 0-8191-1027-2); pap. text ed. 8.25 (ISBN 0-8191-1028-0). U Pr of Amer.

Iorizzo, Luciano J. & Mondello, Salvatore. The Italian-Americans. (Immigrant Heritage of America Ser.). lib. bdg. 9.95 o.p. (ISBN 0-8057-3234-9, Twayne). G K Hall.

--The Italian-Americans. rev. ed. (Immigrant Heritage of America Ser.). 1980. lib. bdg. 11.95 (ISBN 0-8057-8416-0, Twayne). G K Hall.

Iosa, Ann, compiled by. & illus. Witches. LC 80-85256. (Illus.). 48p. (ps-3). 1981. 6.95 (ISBN 0-448-42002-3, G&D). Putnam Pub Group.

Iosifescu, Marius. Finite Markov Processes & Applications. LC 79-42726. 250p. 1980. 41.95x (ISBN 0-471-27677-4). Wiley.

Iotti, R. C., jt. ed. see Berstein, M. D.

Iowa State University - Center For Agricultural And Economic Development. Alternatives for Balancing World Food Production & Needs. 1967. 6.95x o.p. (ISBN 0-8138-1797-8). Iowa St U Pr.

--Research & Education for Regional & Area Development. (Illus.). 1966. 7.50x (ISBN 0-8138-1350-6). Iowa St U Pr.

Iowa State University of Science & Technology Center for Agricultural & Economic Adjustment. Labor Mobility & Population in Agriculture. LC 74-7535. 1977. Repr. of 1961 ed. lib. bdg. 18.50x (ISBN 0-8371-7584-4, IOLM). Greenwood.

IP International Conference. A Guide to North Sea Oil & Gas Technology. 1978. casebound 38.00 (ISBN 0-471-25786-9, Pub. by Wiley Heyden). Wiley.

Ipcar, Dahlov. The Biggest Fish in the Sea. (Illus.). 48p. (gr. k-3). 1972. PLB 10.95 (ISBN 0-670-16541-7). Viking Pr.

--Black & White. (Illus.). (gr. k-3). 1963. PLB 4.99 o.s.i. (ISBN 0-394-90954-2). Knopf.

--Bug City. LC 74-34389. (Illus.). 32p. (ps-3). 1975. PLB 6.95 (ISBN 0-8234-0258-4). Holiday.

--Hard Scrabble Harvest. 32p. (gr. k-3). 1976. PLB 8.95 (ISBN 0-385-00777-9). Doubleday.

--Ten Big Farms. (Illus.). (gr. k-4). 1958. PLB 5.99 o.s.i. (ISBN 0-394-90770-1). Knopf.

IPCP Group of Experts on the Indian Ocean, Rome, 1967. The Present Status of Fisheries & Assessment of Potential Resources of the Indian Ocean & Adjacent Seas. (FAO Fisheries Reports: No. 54). 33p. 1967. pap. 7.50 (ISBN 0-686-92888-1, F1679, FAO). Unipub.

IPFC Ad Hoc Committee to Review the Functions & Responsibilities of IPFC, Bagnou, 1975. Report. (FAO Fisheries Reports: No. 181). 21p. 1976. pap. 7.50 (ISBN 0-686-93991-3, F829, FAO). Unipub.

IPFC-IOFC Ad Hoc Working Party of Scientists on Assessment of Tuna, Rome, 1972. Report. (FAO Fisheries Reports: No. 137). 20p. 1973. pap. 7.50 (ISBN 0-686-93097-5, F783, FAO). Unipub.

IPFC-IOFC Ad Hoc Working Party of Scientists on Stock Assessment of Tuna, 2nd Session, Nantes, 1974. Report. (FAO Fisheries Reports: No. 152). 22p. 1974. pap. 7.50 (ISBN 0-686-93979-4, F793, FAO). Unipub.

IPFC-IOFC Joint Working Party of Experts on Indian Ocean & Western Pacific Fishery Statistics, Bangkok, 1971. Report. (FAO Fisheries Reports: No. 120). 14p. 1971. pap. 6.00 (ISBN 0-686-93077-0, F1703, FAO). Unipub.

IPFC-IOFC Joint Working Party of Experts on Indian Ocean & Western Pacific Fishery Statistics, 4th Session, Colombo, Sri Lanka, 1976. Report. (FAO Fisheries Reports: No. 189). 19p. 1977. pap. 7.50 (ISBN 0-686-93994-8, F837, FAO). Unipub.

IPFC-OIFC Joint Working of Experts on Indian Ocean & Western Pacific Fishery Statistics, 5th Session, Manila, 1978. Report. (FAO Fisheries Reports: No. 218). 23p. 1979. pap. 7.50 (ISBN 0-686-94006-7, F1827, FAO). Unipub.

Ippen, A. T. Estuary & Coastline Hydrodynamics. (Engineering Societies Monographs). 1966. text ed. 42.50 (ISBN 0-07-032015-2, C). McGraw.

Ippolito, Dennis S. & Walker, Thomas G. Political Parties: Interest Groups & Public Policy: Group Influence in American Politics. 431p. 1980. text ed. 22.95 (ISBN 0-13-684357-3). P-H.

Ipsen, David C. Issac Newton: Reluctant Genius. (Illus.). 96p. 1983. 9.95 (ISBN 0-89490-090-0). Enslow Pubs.

Iqbal, A. Culture of Islam. 1981. 9.95 (ISBN 0-686-97867-6). Kazi Pubns.

Iqbal, Afzal. The Life & Times of Mohammad Ali: An Analysis of the Hopes, Fears & Aspirations of Muslim India from 1778-1931. LC 75-930033. 1974. 12.50x o.p. (ISBN 0-88386-630-7). South Asia Bks.

--The Prophet's Diplomacy: The Art of Negotiation As Conceived & Developed by the Prophet of Islam. rev. ed. LC 74-20174. (God Ser.: No. 801). 164p. 1975. 8.00 (ISBN 0-89007-006-7). C Stark.

Iqbal, M. The Reconstruction of Religious Thoughts in Islam. 5.95 (ISBN 0-686-18482-3). Kazi Pubns.

Iqbal, M. A., ed. see Atkins Research & Development Corp.

Iranzo, Carmen. Antonio Garcia Gutierrez. (World Authors Ser.). 1980. lib. bdg. 15.95 (ISBN 0-8057-6407-0, Twayne). G K Hall.

--Juan Eugenio Hartzenbusch. (World Authors Ser.). 1978. 15.95 (ISBN 0-8057-6342-2, Twayne). G K Hall.

Irby, James A. Backdoor at Bagdad. (Southwest Studies Ser.: No. 53). 1977. 3.00 (ISBN 0-87404-110-4). Tex Western.

Ireland & Law. The Economics of the Labor-Managed Enterprises. LC 82-42615. 240p. 1982. 25.00x (ISBN 0-312-23431-7). St Martin.

Ireland, jt. auth. see Gottlieb.

Ireland, Alexander. Book-Lover's Enchiridion. LC 78-76113. 1969. Repr. of 1888 ed. 34.00x (ISBN 0-8103-3895-5). Gale.

Ireland, Brian, jt. auth. see Hughes, Janet.

Ireland, David. A Woman of the Future. pap. 3.95 (ISBN 0-686-43341-6). Bantam.

Ireland, Glen E. Automotive Fuel, Ignition, & Emission Control Systems. 1980. pap. 15.95x (ISBN 0-534-00866-6, Breton Pubs). Wadsworth Pub.

Ireland, John. Word Attack Skills. LC 77-82988. (Teaching 5 to 13 Reading Ser.). (Illus.). 1977. pap. text ed. 9.85 (ISBN 0-356-05055-6). Raintree Pubs.

Ireland, LaVern H. The Small Business Expense Planner. 49p. 1982. pap. write for info. Petervin Pr.

Ireland, LaVerne H. The Teacher's & Librarian's Alternative Job Hunt Helper: An Annotated List of Transferable Job Skills & Alternative Career Possibilities. Date not set. 3.00 (ISBN 0-686-37851-2). Petervin Pr.

Ireland, Patrick J. Fashion Design Drawing. LC 73-134681. 127p. 1972. pap. 14.95x o.s.i. (ISBN 0-470-42837-6). Halsted Pr.

Irele, F. A., ed. Selected Poems of Leopold Sedar Senghor. LC 76-16919. 1977. 24.95 (ISBN 0-521-21339-8); pap. 9.95 (ISBN 0-521-29111-9). Cambridge U Pr.

Iremonger, Valentin, tr. see MacAmhlaigh, Donall.

Irenaeus, St. Excerpts from the Works of St. Irenaeus (c. 130 to c. 202). rev. ed. Roberts, Alexander & Robinson, J. Armitage, trs. (Excerpts from the Saints Ser.). 60p. 1973. pap. 0.65 (ISBN 0-88263-030-X). St Charles Hse.

Ireson, Barbara. Cottage Crafts. (Illus.). 112p. 1976. 7.50 o.p. (ISBN 0-571-10752-4). Transatlantic.

Ireson, Barbara, ed. Faber Book of Nursery Stories. (gr. k-3). 1967. O.S.I. 8.95 (ISBN 0-571-06623-2). Transatlantic.

--Tales Out of Time. 224p. (gr. 10 up). 1981. 9.95 (ISBN 0-399-20786-4, Philomel). Putnam Pub Group.

Ireson, W. Grant & Grant, Eugene, eds. Handbook of Industrial Engineering & Management. 2nd ed. LC 71-139954. 1971. 42.95 (ISBN 0-13-378463-0). P-H.

Ireson, William G. Reliability Handbook. 1966. 55.00 o.p. (ISBN 0-07-032040-3, P&RB). McGraw.

Ireys, Alice R. Small Gardens for City & Country: A Guide to Designing & Planting Your Own Property. (Illus.). 1977. 14.95 o.p. (ISBN 0-13-813063-9, Spec); pap. 8.95 (ISBN 0-13-813055-8, Spec). P-H.

Ireys, Katharine. Finishing & Mounting Your Needlepoint Pieces. (Illus.). 232p. 1973. 14.37i (ISBN 0-690-00085-5). T Y Crowell.

Irgolic, K. Organic Chemistry of Tellurium. LC 73-84669. 466p. 1974. 80.00 (ISBN 0-677-04110-1). Gordon.

Irgolic, Kurt & Peck, Larry. Fundamentals of Chemistry in the Laboratory. 2nd ed. 1977. text ed. 23.50 scp o.p. (ISBN 0-06-044874-1, HarpC); pap. text ed. 11.95 scp o.p. (ISBN 0-06-043219-5). Har-Row.

Irick, Tina. The First Price Guide to Antique & Vintage Clothes: Styles for Women. (Illus.). 128p. 1983. pap. 13.95 (ISBN 0-525-48050-1, 01354-410). Dutton.

Irion, Clyde. Profit & Loss of Dying. 4.95 (ISBN 0-87516-030-1). De Vorss.

Irion, Paul E. Cremation. LC 68-10291. 160p. 1968. pap. 3.95x o.p. (ISBN 0-8006-1067-9, 1-1067). Fortress.

Irish, Donald P., ed. Multinational Corporations in Latin America: Private Rights & Public Responsibilities. LC 77-620055. (Papers in International Studies: Latin America: No. 2). (Illus.). 1977. pap. 9.00x (ISBN 0-89680-067-9, Ohio U Ctr Intl). Ohio U Pr.

Irish Genealogical Foundation. Geographical Guide to Ireland. 1982. pap. 15.00 (ISBN 0-940134-13-6). Irish Genealog.

--Three Hundred Great Families of Ireland. (Irish Genealogical Ser.). (Illus.). 380p. 1981. text ed. 29.95 (ISBN 0-940134-11-X). Irish Genealog.

Irish, Marian D., et al. The Politics of American Democracy. 7th ed. (Illus.). 544p. 1981. text ed. 22.95 (ISBN 0-13-685156-8). P-H.

Irish, Marion D. & Frank, Elke. Introduction to Comparative Politics: Thirteen Nation States. 2nd ed. LC 77-22021. (Illus.). 1978. ref. ed. 22.95 (ISBN 0-13-500991-X). P-H.

Irish, Marion D., et al. Politics of American Democracy. 6th ed. (Illus.). 1977. text ed. 20.95 o.p. (ISBN 0-13-685453-2). P-H.

Irish, Richard K. Go Hire Yourself an Employer. rev. expanded ed. LC 77-15159. 1978. pap. 6.95 (ISBN 0-385-13638-2, Anch). Doubleday.

--If Things Don't Improve Soon I'm Going to Ask You to Fire Me: The Management Book for Everyone Who Works. LC 74-12710. 240p. 1975. pap. 4.95 o.p. (ISBN 0-385-11637-3, Anch). Doubleday.

Iritani, Chika. I Know an Animal Doctor. (Community Helper Bks.). (Illus.). (gr. 2-4). 1971. PLB 4.29 o.p. (ISBN 0-399-60275-5). Putnam Pub Group.

Iritani, Toshio. The Value of Children: a Cross-National Study: Japan, Vol. 6. LC 75-8934. 1979. pap. text ed. 3.00x o.p. (ISBN 0-8248-0387-6, Eastwest Ctr). UH Pr.

Iriye, Akira. Power & Culture: The Japanese-American War, 1941-1945. LC 80-23536. (Illus.). 336p. 1981. text ed. 22.00x (ISBN 0-674-69580-1); pap. text ed. 8.95x (ISBN 0-674-69582-8). Harvard U Pr.

Irizarry, Carmen. Spain. LC 75-44868. (Macdonald Countries). (Illus.). (gr. 6 up). 1976. PLB 12.68 (ISBN 0-382-06100-4, Pub. by Macdonald Ed). Silver.

Irizarry, Estelle. Enrique A. Laguerre. (World Authors Ser.). 1982. lib. bdg. 15.95 (ISBN 0-8057-6489-5, Twayne). G K Hall.

--Francisco Ayala. (World Authors Ser.). 1977. lib. bdg. 15.95 (ISBN 0-8057-6287-6, Twayne). G K Hall.

--Rafael Dieste. (World Authors Ser.). 1979. lib. bdg. 15.95 (ISBN 0-8057-6396-1, Twayne). G K Hall.

Irland, Lloyd C. Wilderness Economics & Policy. LC 78-24791. 256p. 1979. 22.95x (ISBN 0-669-02821-5). Lexington Bks.

Irland, Nancy. Aren't You Glad? Mahany, Patricia, ed. (Cut & Color Bks.). (Illus.). 16p. (Orig.). (gr. k-3). 1982. pap. 0.89 (ISBN 0-87239-584-7, 2388). Standard Pub.

--Baby Jesus' Birthday. Mahany, Patricia, ed. (Cut & Color Bks.). (Illus.). 16p. (Orig.). (gr. k-3). 1982. pap. 0.89 (ISBN 0-87239-585-5, 2389). Standard Pub.

Irle, Martin & Katz, Lawrence B., eds. Studies in Decision Making. 917p. 1982. 88.00x (ISBN 0-686-97632-0). De Gruyter.

Iroaganachi, John, jt. auth. see Achebe, Chinua.

Iroh, Eddie. The Siren in the Night. (African Writers Ser.). 207p. 1982. pap. 6.00x (ISBN 0-435-90255-5). Heinemann Ed.

Iron-Eyes Cody. Iron Eyes: My Life As a Hollywood Indian. (Illus.). 384p. 1982. 14.95 (ISBN 0-89696-111-7, An Everest House Book). Dodd.

Ironmonger, D. S. New Commodities & Consumer Behaviour. new ed. LC 75-163056. (Department of Applied Economics Monographs: No. 20). (Illus.). 1972. 37.50 (ISBN 0-521-08337-0). Cambridge U Pr.

Irons, Greg, jt. auth. see Gygax, E. Gary.

Irons, Owen G. Back to Texas. (YA) 1978. 6.95 (ISBN 0-685-85776-X, Avalon). Bouregy.

--Guns of the Hawk. (YA) 1976. 6.95 (ISBN 0-685-69050-4, Avalon). Bouregy.

--The Marshal from Texas. 192p. (YA) 1975. 6.95 (ISBN 0-685-53496-0, Avalon). Bouregy.

--Outlaw Town. (YA) 1979. 6.95 (ISBN 0-685-65273-4, Avalon). Bouregy.

Irons, Patricia. Psychotropic Drugs & Nursing Intervention. (Illus.). 1978. pap. text ed. 12.95 (ISBN 0-07-032052-7, HP). McGraw.

Ironside, H. A. Colossians, Lectures. 6.25 o.p. (ISBN 0-87213-352-4). Loizeaux.

--The Daily Sacrifice: Daily Meditations on the Word of God. 370p. 1982. pap. 4.95 (ISBN 0-87213-356-7). Loizeaux.

--Daniel the Prophet. 1911. with chart 8.25 (ISBN 0-87213-357-5); chart only 0.15 (ISBN 0-87213-358-3). Loizeaux.

--Galatians, Ephesians (in the Heavenlies) 11.95 (ISBN 0-87213-397-4). Loizeaux.

--Holiness: The False & the True. 4.75 (ISBN 0-87213-364-8); pap. 3.25 (ISBN 0-87213-365-6) Loizeaux.

--Philippians, Notes. 1922. 5.75 o.p. (ISBN 0-87213-381-8). Loizeaux.

--Revelation. 1920. 9.25 (ISBN 0-87213-384-2); 0.15, chart only (ISBN 0-87213-385-0). Loizeaux.

--Thessalonians. 5.50 o.p. (ISBN 0-87213-390-7). Loizeaux.

Ironside, Harry A. Full Assurance. 1937. pap. 2.95 (ISBN 0-8024-2896-7). Moody.

Irschick, Eugene F. Politics & Social Conflict in South India: The Non-Brahman Movement & Tamil Separatism, 1916-1929. LC 69-31595. (Center for South & Southeast Asia Studies, UC Berkeley). (Illus.). 1969. 32.50x (ISBN 0-520-00596-1). U of Cal Pr.

Irsigler, Karl, et al, eds. New Approaches to Insulin Therapy. 588p. 1981. text ed. 39.50 (ISBN 0-8391-1650-0). Univ Park.

Irukayama, K., jt. ed. see Tsubaki, T.

Irvin, Carol K. & Irvin, James D. Ohio Real Estate Law. 2nd ed. (Illus.). 464p. 1982. pap. text ed. 22.95 (ISBN 0-89787-904-X). Gorsuch Scarisbrick.

Irvin, D. Power Tool Maintenance. 1971. 24.95 (ISBN 0-07-032050-0, G). McGraw.

Irvin, J. L., ed. see Fisher, J. & Downey, J.

Irvin, J. L., ed. see Fisher, J. & Dryer, R.

Irvin, J. L., ed. see Gosen, Patricia E.

Irvin, James D., jt. auth. see Irvin, Carol K.

Irvin, Judith L. & Downey, Joan M. Los Angeles Studies Program: Activity Manual. Yockstick, Elizabeth, ed. Martinez-Miller, Orlando, tr. (Illus.). 73p. (Spanish.). (gr. 3). 1981. 49.00 (ISBN 0-943068-41-X). Graphic Learning.

Irvin, Marjory, jt. auth. see Borroff, Edith.

Irvin, Maurice R. Eternally Named. 1975. 1.75 (ISBN 0-87509-079-6). Chr Pubns.

Irvin, Richard F., jt. auth. see Roy, Steven P.

Irvine, Betty J. & Fry, P. Eileen. Slide Libraries: A Guide for Academic Institutions, Museums, & Special Collections. 2nd ed. LC 79-17354. (Illus.). 1979. lib. bdg. 27.50 (ISBN 0-87287-202-5). Libs Unl.

Irvine, Demar. Writing About Music: A Style Book for Reports & Theses. rev. enl. ed. LC 56-13245. (Illus.). 220p. 1968. pap. 8.95 (ISBN 0-295-78558-6). U of Wash Pr.

Irvine, Demar, jt. ed. see Moldenhauer, Hans.

Irvine, Georgeanne. Alberta the Gorilla. LC 82-9446. (Zoo Babies Ser.). (Illus.). (gr. k-4). 1982. PLB 7.95g (ISBN 0-516-09301-0). Childrens.

--Nanuch the Polar Bear. LC 82-9463. (Zoo Babies Ser.). (Illus.). (gr. k-4). 1982. PLB 7.95g (ISBN 0-516-09302-9). Childrens.

--Sasha the Cheetah. LC 82-9450. (Zoo Babies Ser.). (Illus.). (gr. k-4). 1982. PLB 7.95g (ISBN 0-516-09303-7). Childrens.

--Sydney the Koala. LC 82-9452. (Zoo Babies). (Illus.). (gr. k-4). 1982. PLB 7.95g (ISBN 0-516-09304-5). Childrens.

--Wilbur & Orville the Otter Twins. LC 82-4576. (Zoo Babies Ser.). (Illus.). (gr. k-4). 1982. PLB 7.95g (ISBN 0-516-09305-3). Childrens.

Irvine, H. M. Cable Structures. (Illus.). 304p. 1981. 45.00x (ISBN 0-262-09023-6). MIT Pr.

Irvine, J. M. Nuclear Structure Theory. 492p. 1972. text ed. 59.00 o.s.i. (ISBN 0-08-016401-3); pap. text ed. 34.00 (ISBN 0-08-018991-1). Pergamon.

Irvine, Keith, ed. see Ayensu, Edward S.

Irvine, Keith, ed. see Dickerson, Robert B., Jr.

Irvine, Keith, ed. see Koykka, Arthur S.

Irvine, Linda M., jt. auth. see Dixon, Peter S.

Irvine, Robert G. Operational Amplifier Characteristics & Applications. (Illus.). 416p. 1981. text ed. 27.95 (ISBN 0-13-637751-3). P-H.

Irvine, S. H. & Sanders, J. T., eds. Cultural Adaptation Within Modern Africa. LC 79-171692. 1972. text ed. 10.95x (ISBN 0-8077-1550-6). Tchrs Coll.

Irvine, T. F. & Hartnett, J. P., eds. Advances in Heat Transfer, Vol. 15. 1982. 54.00 (ISBN 0-12-020015-5); lib. ed. 70.50 (ISBN 0-12-020082-1); microfiche 38.00 (ISBN 0-12-020083-X). Acad Pr.

Irvine, Theodora U. How to Pronounce the Names in Shakespeare. LC 74-7114. 1974. Repr. of 1919 ed. 37.00x (ISBN 0-8103-3653-7). Gale.

Irvine, W. James, ed. Medical Immunology. (Illus.). 506p. 1980. pap. text ed. 28.00x (ISBN 0-07-032049-7, HP). McGraw.

Irvine, W. M., tr. see Sobolev, V. V.

Irvine, W. T. Modern Trends in Surgery-3. 1971. 14.95 o.p. (ISBN 0-407-31703-1). Butterworth.

Irving, Blanche M. Five Deer on Old Loco Mountain Road. Hausman, Gerald, ed. (Illus.). 64p. 1982. 25.00 (ISBN 0-86534-012-9). Sunstone Pr.

Irving, Clifford. Fake: The Story of Elmer De Hory, the Greatest Art Forger of Our Time. 1969. 7.95 o.p. (ISBN 0-07-032047-0, GB). McGraw.

Irving, Clive. Promise the Earth. LC 82-47789. 402p. 1982. 15.34i (ISBN 0-06-015063-7, HarpT). Har-Row.

Irving, David. The Secret Diaries of Hitler's Doctor. 320p. 1983. 15.95 (ISBN 0-02-558250-X). Macmillan.

--The War Between the Generals. (Illus.). 480p. 1981. 17.95 o.p. (ISBN 0-312-92920-X). St Martin.

--The War Between the Generals: Inside the Allied High Command. LC 80-68916. (Illus.). 384p. 1983. 17.95 (ISBN 0-312-92920-X); pap. 9.95 (ISBN 0-312-92921-8). Congdon & Weed.

Irving, F. G. An Introduction to the Longitudinal Static Stability of Low-Speed Aircraft. 1965. inquire for price o.p. (ISBN 0-08-010741-9). Pergamon.

Irving, J. & Searl, C. Knots, Ties & Splices: A Handbook for Seafarers, Travellers, & All Who Use Cordage. rev. ed. 1978. pap. 6.95 (ISBN 0-7100-8671-7). Routledge & Kegan.

Irving, John. The Hotel New Hampshire. LC 81-2610. 480p. 1981. 9.50 (ISBN 0-525-12800-X, Henry Robbins Bk). Dutton.

Irving, Luella. Nurse Patsy's Last Chance. (YA) 1980. 6.95 (ISBN 0-686-59798-2, Avalon). Bouregy.

Irving, Lynn. Pocketful of Puppets: Poems for Church School. Keller, Merilu H., ed. (Puppetry in Education ser.). (Illus.). 48p. (Orig.). 1982. pap. 5.50 (ISBN 0-931044-05-7). Renfro Studios.

Irving, Mary B., jt. auth. see Robbins, Maurice.

Irving, Pierre M. The Life & Letters of Washington Irving, 4 vols. LC 67-23893. 1967. Repr. of 1863 ed. 74.00x set (ISBN 0-8103-3044-X). Gale.

Irving, R. J. The North Eastern Railway 1870-1914: An Economic History. 1976. text ed. 28.75x o.p. (ISBN 0-7185-1141-7, Leicester). Humanities.

Irving, Robert. Electronics. (Illus.). (gr. 7 up). 1961. PLB 5.39 o.p. (ISBN 0-394-91116-4). Knopf.

--Volcanoes & Earthquakes. (Illus.). (gr. 4-7). 1962. PLB 5.39 o.p. (ISBN 0-394-91796-0). Knopf.

Irving, T. B. Tide of Islam. 5.95 (ISBN 0-686-83887-4). Kazi Pubns.

Irving, W. Ronald, jt. auth. see Jackson, Frank.

Irving, Washington. The Complete Works of Washington Irving -- the Sketch Book of Geoffrey Crayon, Gentleman. Springer, Haskell S., ed. (Critical Editions Program). 1978. lib. bdg. 25.00 (ISBN 0-8057-8510-8, Twayne). G K Hall.

--The Complete Works of Washington Irving--Astoria; or, Anecdotes of an Enterprize Beyond the Rocky Mountains. Rust, Richard D., ed. (Critical Editions Program). 1976. lib. bdg. 25.00 (ISBN 0-8057-8507-8, Twayne). G K Hall.

--The Complete Works of Washington Irving--Adventures of Captain Bonneville. Rees, Robert A. & Sandy, Alan, eds. (Critical Editions Program). 1977. lib. bdg. 25.00 (ISBN 0-8057-8508-6, Twayne). G K Hall.

--Complete Works of Washington Irving, Journals & Notebooks, Vol. 2: 1807-1822. Schlissel, Lillian & Reichart, Walter A., eds. (Critical Editions Program). 1981. 32.00 (ISBN 0-8057-8501-9, Twayne). G K Hall.

--The Complete Works of Washington Irving-Oliver Goldsmith: A Biography & Poetical Remains of the Late Margaret Davidson. West, Elsie L., ed. (Critical Editions Program). 1978. lib. bdg. 25.00 (ISBN 0-8057-8521-3, Twayne). G K Hall.

--Letters of Jonathan Oldstyle, Gent, & Salmagundi; or, the Whim-Whams & Opinions of Launcelot Langstaff, Esq., & Others: Complete Works of W. Irving. Granger, Bruce I. & Hartzog, Martha, trs. (Critical Editions Program). 1977. lib. bdg. 25.00 (ISBN 0-8057-8509-4, Twayne). G K Hall.

--Rip Van Winkle. (Illus.). 1982. 12.50 (ISBN 0-434-95859-X, Pub. by Heinemann). David & Charles.

--Rip Van Winkle Coloring Book. (Illus.). 48p. (Orig.). (gr. 3 up). 1983. pap. 2.25 (ISBN 0-486-24479-2). Dover.

--Rip Van Winkle, the Legend of Sleepy Hollow & Other Tales. (Companion Lib.). (Illus.). (gr. 6 up). 2.95 (ISBN 0-448-05482-5, G&D). Putnam Pub Group.

--Sketch Book. (RL 5). pap. 2.95 (ISBN 0-451-51614-1, CE1614, Sig Classics). NAL.

--A Tour of the Praries. (Classics of the Old West Ser.). 1983. lib. bdg. 17.28 (ISBN 0-8094-4034-2). Silver.

Irving, Washington see Swan, D. K.

Irwin. Analytic Pyrolysis. (Chromatographic Science Ser.: Vol. 22). 432p. 1982. 69.50 (ISBN 0-686-83024-5). Dekker.

Irwin, Constance. Strange Footprints on the Land. LC 78-19519. (Illus.). 192p. (gr. 7 up). 1980. 10.95 o.p. (ISBN 0-06-022772-9, HarpJ); PLB 11.89 (ISBN 0-06-022773-7). Har-Row.

Irwin, Godfrey. American Tramp & Underworld Slang. LC 75-149783. 1971. Repr. of 1931 ed. 34.00x (ISBN 0-8103-3748-7). Gale.

Irwin, H. S., jt. auth. see Goodland, R. J.

Irwin, Inez. The Story of Alice Paul. cancelled o.p. (ISBN 0-87714-058-8). Green Hill.

Irwin, J. & Marge, M. Principles of Childhood Language Disabilities. 1972. 25.95 (ISBN 0-13-708180-4). P-H.

Irwin, J. David & Graf, Edward R. Industrial Noise & Vibration Control. LC 78-7786. (Illus.). 1979. ref. 34.00 (ISBN 0-13-461574-3). P-H.

Irwin, J. G. Odour Removal by Catalytic Oxidation Nineteen Seventy Eight. 1982. 75.00x (ISBN 0-686-97132-9, Pub. by W Spring England). State Mutual Bk.

Irwin, James B. More Than Earthlings. 1983. 5.95 (ISBN 0-8054-5255-9). Broadman.

Irwin, James B., Jr. & Emerson, W. A. Un Astronauta y la Lumbrera De la Noche. 1981. Repr. of 1978 ed. 4.25 (ISBN 0-311-01066-0). Casa Bautista.

Irwin, James W., ed. Hatch Act Decisions (Political Activity Cases) of the United States Civil Service Commission. viii, 304p. 1981. Repr. of 1949 ed. lib. bdg. 26.00x (ISBN 0-8377-0639-4). Rothman.

Irwin, John. Ancient Indian Cosmogony. Kuiper, F. B., ed. 257p. 1983. text ed. 37.50x (ISBN 0-7069-1370-1, Pub. by Vikas India). Advent NY.

Irwin, John R. Baskets & Basket Makers of Southern Appalachia. LC 81-86386. (Illus.). 192p. 1982. 22.50 (ISBN 0-916838-60-9); pap. 14.95 (ISBN 0-916838-61-7). Schiffer.

--Guns & Gunmaking Tools of Southern Appalachia. 2nd ed. (Illus.). 120p. 1983. pap. 9.95 (ISBN 0-916838-81-1). Schiffer.

--Musical Instruments of the Southern Appalachian Mountains. (Illus.). 108p. 1983. pap. 8.50 (ISBN 0-916838-80-3). Schiffer.

Irwin, John V. & Wong, Seok P., eds. Phonological Development in Children 18 to 72 Months. LC 82-5893. 1983. write for info. (ISBN 0-8093-1057-0). S Ill U Pr.

Irwin, Joseph J. M. G. Lewis. (English Author Ser.). 1976. lib. bdg. 13.95 (ISBN 0-8057-6670-7, Twayne). G K Hall.

Irwin, Kevin W. Sunday Worship. 1983. pap. 14.95 (ISBN 0-916134-52-0). Pueblo Pub Co.

Irwin, Leonard B. Pacific Railways & Nationalism in the Canadian American Northwest, 1845-1873. LC 69-10107. 1969. Repr. of 1939 ed. lib. bdg. 17.50x (ISBN 0-8371-0495-5, IRPR). Greenwood.

Irwin, Margaret. Elizabeth & the Prince of Spain. 1975. Repr. of 1953 ed. 13.95 o.p. (ISBN 0-7011-0847-9). Dufour.

--Royal Flush. 368p. 1983. 13.95 (ISBN 0-312-69471-7). St Martin.

Irwin, Mark, tr. see Denis, Philippe.

Irwin, Mark, tr. see Stanescu, Nichita.

Irwin, Martin, jt. auth. see Schulman, Jerome L.

Irwin, Mary & Harris, Madalene. The Moon Is Not Enough. 1978. pap. 4.95 o.p. (ISBN 0-310-37051-5). Zondervan.

Irwin, Robert. How to Buy a Home at a Reasonable Price. LC 78-23828. (Illus.). 1979. 18.95 (ISBN 0-07-032060-8, P&RB); pap. 5.95 (ISBN 0-07-032058-6). McGraw.

--How to Buy & Sell Real Estate at a Profit. 1975. 24.95 (ISBN 0-07-032063-2, P&RB). McGraw.

--The One Hundred Thousand Dollar Decision: The Older American's Guide to Selling a Home & Choosing Retirement Housing. LC 80-28974. (Illus.). 208p. 1981. 14.95 o.p. (ISBN 0-07-032070-5, P&RB). McGraw.

--Protect Yourself in Real Estate. 1977. 18.95 o.p. (ISBN 0-07-032064-0, P&RB). McGraw.

--Riches in Real Estate. LC 80-16252. (Illus.). 224p. 1980. 15.95 (ISBN 0-07-032062-4, P&RB). McGraw.

--Smart Money Real Estate for the 80's: New Profits in Big Properties. 240p. 1982. 14.00 (ISBN 0-936602-41-4). Harbor Pub CA.

--Timeshare Properties: What Every Buyer Must Know! LC 82-17185. (Illus.). 224p. 1983. 19.95 (ISBN 0-07-032082-9, P&RB). McGraw.

Irwin, Robert & Brickman, Richard. The Real Estate Agent's & Investor's Tax Book. (Illus.). 1980. 19.95 (ISBN 0-07-032061-6). McGraw.

Irwin, Stevens. Dictionary of Pipe Organ Stops. rev. ed. 1965. pap. 10.95 o.s.i. (ISBN 0-02-871130-0). Schirmer Bks.

--Dictionary of Pipe Organ Stops. 2nd ed. 1983. 20.00 (ISBN 0-02-871150-5). Schirmer Bks.

Irwin, Terence. Plato's Moral Theory: The Early & Middle Dialogues. 1977. pap. 13.50x (ISBN 0-19-824614-5). Oxford U Pr.

Irwin, Walter. The Best of Trek: From the Magazine for Star Trek Fans, No. 2. (Illus., Orig.). 1980. pap. 2.50 (ISBN 0-451-09836-6, E9836, Sig). NAL.

Irwin, Walter & Love, G. B., eds. The Best of Trek. (Illus., Orig.). (RL 10). 1978. pap. 2.50 (ISBN 0-451-11682-8, AE1682, Sig). NAL.

--The Best of Trek, No. 4. (Illus., Orig.). 1981. pap. 2.75 (ISBN 0-451-12356-5, AE2356, Sig). NAL.

--The Best of Trek, No. 5. 1982. pap. 2.75 (ISBN 0-451-11751-4, AE1751, Sig). NAL.

--The Best of Trek No. 3. 1981. pap. 2.50 (ISBN 0-451-11807-3, AE1807, Sig). NAL.

Irwin, William J. Analytical Pyrolysis: A Comprehensive Guide. (Chromatographic Science Ser.: Vol. 22). (Illus.). 600p. 1982. 69.50 (ISBN 0-686-82221-8). Dekker.

Irwin, Yukiko & Wagenvoord, James. Shiatzu: Japanese Finger Pressure for Energy. (Illus.). 240p. 1976. 9.50 o.p. (ISBN 0-397-01054-0); pap. 7.95 (ISBN 0-397-01107-5, LP-093). Har-Row.

ISA Conference & Exhibit, 31st, Houston, 1976. Advances in Instrumentation: Proceedings, 4 pts, Vol. 31. LC 52-29277. 1976. pap. text ed. 37.50 ea. o.p. Pt. 1 (ISBN 0-87664-302-0). Pt. 2 (ISBN 0-87664-303-9). Pt. 3 (ISBN 0-87664-304-7). Pt. 4 (ISBN 0-87664-305-5). Set. pap. text ed. 125.00x o.p. (ISBN 0-87664-647-X). Instru Soc.

ISA Instrument Maintenance Management Symposium, 9th, Newark, 1974. Instrument Maintenance Management: Proceedings, Vol. 9. LC 67-13017. 42p. pap. text ed. 7.00 o.p. (ISBN 0-87664-241-5). Instru Soc.

Isaac, G. & McCown, E. Human Evolution: Louis Leakey & the East African Experience. 1976. pap. 16.95 (ISBN 0-8053-9942-9). Benjamin-Cummings.

Isaac, Rondall. Stories of the Unforseen. 1979. 6.95 o.p. (ISBN 0-533-04170-8). Vantage.

Isaac, Stephen. Songs from the House of Pilgrimage. LC 77-169595. 1971. 8.50 (ISBN 0-8283-1334-2). Christward.

Isaacman, Allen. The Tradition of Resistance in Mozambique: The Zambesi Valley. LC 75-17292. 1977. 34.50x (ISBN 0-520-03065-6). U of Cal Pr.

Isaacman, Allen & Isaacman, Barbara. Mozambique: Sowing the Seeds of Revolution. 160p. 1983. lib. bdg. price not set (ISBN 0-86531-210-9). Westview.

Isaacman, Barbara, jt. auth. see Isaacman, Allen.

Isaacs. Darwin to Double Helix: The Biological Theme in Science Fiction. (Siscon Ser.). 1977. 3.95 o.p. (ISBN 0-408-71302-X). Butterworth.

Isaacs, A. D. & Post, F. Studies in Geriatric Psychiatry. LC 77-9990. 1978. 57.95x (ISBN 0-471-99550-9, Pub. by Wiley-Interscience). Wiley.

Isaacs, A. D., jt. auth. see Leff, J. P.

Isaacs, Benno & Kobler, Jay. The Nickolaus Technique: What It Takes to Feel Good. LC 79-6559. (Illus.). 162p. 1980. pap. 5.95 o.s.i. (ISBN 0-89104-173-7, A & W Visual Library). A & W Pubs.

Isaacs, Elizabeth. An Introduction to the Poetry of Yvor Winters. LC 82-75067. xiv, 216p. 1981. 16.95x (ISBN 0-8040-0353-X). Swallow.

Isaacs, H. D., ed. see Ghazali.

Isaacs, Harold R. Scratches or Our Minds: American Views of China & India. LC 80-65695. 1980. pap. 9.95 (ISBN 0-87332-161-8). M E Sharpe.

Isaacs, Harold R., ed. & intro. by. Straw Sandals: Chinese Stories of Social Realism. 432p. 1974. 17.50x (ISBN 0-262-09014-7); pap. 5.95 (ISBN 0-262-59006-9). MIT Pr.

Isaacs, Ken. How to Build Your Own Living Structures. (Illus.). 144p. 1974. 9.95 o.p. (ISBN 0-517-50562-2); spiral bound 4.95 o.p. (ISBN 0-517-50559-2). Crown.

Isaacs, Marty. Marty's Walking Tours of Biblical Jerusalem. (Illus.). 128p. 1982. pap. 4.95 (ISBN 0-686-43008-5, Carta Maps & Guides Pub Isreal). Hippocrene Bks.

Isaacs, Nathan. A Brief Introduction to Piaget. LC 74-9738. 118p. 1974. pap. 4.95 (ISBN 0-8052-0456-3). Schocken.

Isaacs, Neil. Reactive Intermediates in Organic Chemistry. LC 73-8194. 560p. 1974. 72.95 o.p. (ISBN 0-471-42861-2, Pub. by Wiley-Interscience); pap. 33.95x (ISBN 0-471-42859-0, Pub. by Wiley-Interscience). Wiley.

Isaacs, Neil D. & Motta, Dick. Sports Illustrated Basketball. rev. ed. LC 80-7896. (Illus.). 160p. 1981. 9.95i (ISBN 0-06-015006-8, CN-865, HarpT); pap. 5.95i (ISBN 0-06-090865-3, CN-865). Har-Row.

Isaacs, Neil S. Liquid Phase High Pressure Chemistry. LC 80-40844. 414p. 1981. 101.00x (ISBN 0-471-27849-1, Pub. by Wiley-Interscience). Wiley.

Isaacs, Susan. Children We Teach: Seven to Eleven Years. LC 75-139841. 1971. pap. 3.45 o.p. (ISBN 0-8052-0288-9). Schocken.

--Close Relations. LC 80-7858. 288p. 1980. 12.45i (ISBN 0-690-01940-8). Har-Row.

--Compromising Positions. (Orig.). pap. 3.25 (ISBN 0-515-06488-2). Jove Pubns.

--Troubles of Children & Parents. LC 72-95661. 252p. 1973. pap. 2.95 o.p. (ISBN 0-8052-0383-4). Schocken.

Isaacs, Susan, jt. auth. see Klein, Melanie.

Isaacson, Dorris A. Maine: A Guide Downeast. (Illus.). 1970. 6.50 o.p. (ISBN 0-913764-06-X). Maine St Mus.

Isaacson, E. & Isaacson, M. Dimensional Methods in Physics: Reference Sets & Their Extensions. LC 75-8311. 220p. 1975. 38.95x o.s.i. (ISBN 0-470-42866-X). Halsted Pr.

Isaacson, Eugene & Keller, H. B. The Analysis of Numerical Methods. LC 66-17630. 1966. 38.50x (ISBN 0-471-42865-5). Wiley.

Isaacson, Leonard M., jt. auth. see Hiller, Lejaren A.

Isaacson, M., jt. auth. see Isaacson, E.

Isaacson, Marshall. An Answer to Spiritual Hunger. 64p. 1972. pap. 2.00 o.p. (ISBN 0-89036-019-7). Hawkes Pub Inc.

Isaacson, Martin J. & Rennie, Dorothy A. A Treasury of Stencil Designs for Artists & Craftsmen. 8.00 (ISBN 0-8446-5469-8). Peter Smith.

Isaak, David T., jt. auth. see Fesharaki, Fereidum.

Isaak, Samuel & Manougian, Manoug. Basic Concepts of Linear Algebra. 416p. 1976. text ed. 19.95x (ISBN 0-393-09199-6). Norton.

Isaaman. Battlegames. 1983. pap. 4.95 (ISBN 0-86020-685-8, 24052). EDC.

--Spacegames. 1983. pap. 4.95 (ISBN 0-86020-683-1, 24062). EDC.

Isaccson, Robert L. & Spear, Norman, eds. The Expression of Knowledge: Neurobehavioral Transformation into Action. LC 82-13253. 442p. 1982. 39.50 (ISBN 0-306-40927-5, Plenum Pr). Plenum Pub.

Isacson, Orjan, jt. ed. see Rideout, Edward H.

Isadora, Rachel. Ben's Trumpet. LC 78-12885. (Illus.). 32p. (gr. k-3). 1979. 9.25 (ISBN 0-688-80194-3). Greenwillow.

--No, Agatha. LC 79-26734. (Illus.). 32p. (ps-3). 1980. 9.75 (ISBN 0-688-80274-5); PLB 9.36 (ISBN 0-688-84274-7). Greenwillow

Isakson, Hans R. & Cantwell, Donald W. Real Estate Principles: The Texas Supplement. 96p. 1982. pap. text ed. 9.95 (ISBN 0-8403-2738-2). Kendall-Hunt.
Isaksson, A. J., jt. ed. see Peterson, H. E.
Isaksson, Hans. Lars Gyllensten. (World Authors Ser.). 1978. lib. bdg. 15.95 (ISBN 0-8057-6314-7, Twayne). G K Hall.
Isard, Walter. Introduction to Regional Science. (Illus.). 544p. 1975. ref. ed. 24.95 (ISBN 0-13-493841-0). P-H.
Isard, Walter & Langford, Thomas. Regional Input-Output Study: Recollections, Reflections & Diverse Notes on the Philadelphia Experience. (Regional Science Studies Ser: No. 10). 1971. 20.00x (ISBN 0-262-09013-9). MIT Pr.
Isard, Walter & Smith, Christine. Conflict Analysis & Practical Conflict Management Procedures: An Introduction to Peace Science. LC 82-11626. (Peace Science Studies Ser.). 656p. 1982. prof ref 35.00x (ISBN 0-88410-899-6). Ballinger Pub.
Isard, Walter, ed. International & Regional Conflict: Analytic Approaches. Nagao, Yoshimi. (Peace Science Studies Sers.). 240p. 1983. prof ref 36.00x (ISBN 0-88410-030-8). Ballinger Pub.
Isbell, Harold. Last Poets of Imperial Rome. 1983. pap. 5.95 (ISBN 0-14-044246-4). Penguin.
Isbell, Lyn, jt. auth. see Dougan, Terrell.
Isberg, Lynne, jt. ed. see Haycock, Ken.
Isby, David. Weapons & Tactics of the Soviet Army. (Illus.). 320p. 1981. 34.95 (ISBN 0-86720-568-7). Sci Bks Intl.
Iscan, M. Yasar, ed. A Topical Guide to the American Journal of Physical Anthropology. LC 82-21696. 234p. 1983. 24.00 (ISBN 0-8451-0224-9). A R Liss.
Isdebsky-Pritchard, Aline. The Art of Mikhail Vrubel (1856-1920) Foster, Stephen, ed. LC 82-8439. (Studies in Fine Arts; The Avant-Garde: No. 35). 316p. 1982. 44.95 (ISBN 0-8357-1363-6, Pub. by UMI Res Pr). Univ Microfilms.
Isele, Elizabeth. Pooks. LC 82-48462. (Illus.). 32p. (ps-3). 1983. 8.61i (ISBN 0-397-32044-2, JBL-J); PLB 8.95g (ISBN 0-397-32045-0). Har-Row.
Iselin, Fred & Spectorsky, A. C. Invitation to Modern Skiing. 1965. 7.95 o.p. (ISBN 0-671-38460-0). S&S.
Isely, Duane. Leguminosae of the United States Pt. III: Subfamily Papilionoideae - Tribes Sophoreae, Podalyreae, Loteae. (Memoirs of the New York Botanical Garden Ser.: Vol. 25, No. 3). (Illus.). 1981. pap. write for info. o.p. (ISBN 0-89327-232-9). NY Botanical.
Isen, jt. auth. see Hastorf.
Isenbart, Hans-Heinrich. A Duckling Is Born. (Illus.). 40p. (gr. 1-4). 1981. 9.95 (ISBN 0-399-20778-3). Putnam Pub Group.
--A Foal Is Born. LC 76-2605. (Illus.). 48p. (gr. k-5). 1976. 7.95 (ISBN 0-399-20517-9). Putnam Pub Group.
Isenberg, Anita & Isenberg, Seymour. How to Work in Beveled Glass: Forming, Designing, & Fabricating. LC 81-69047. 240p. 1982. 19.95 (ISBN 0-8019-7103-9); pap. 14.95 (ISBN 0-8019-7104-7). Chilton.
Isenberg, Barbara. California Theatre Annual: 1982. (California Theatre Annual Ser.). (Illus.). 400p. 1982. 35.00 (ISBN 0-942230-02-7). Perf Arts Network.
Isenberg, Barbara & Wolf, Susan. The Adventures of Albert, the Running Bear. (Illus.). 32p. (ps-2). 1982. 11.50 (ISBN 0-89919-113-4, Clarion); pap. 3.95 (ISBN 0-89919-125-8). HM.
Isenberg, Seymour. Keep Your Kids Thin. 176p. 1982. 11.95 (ISBN 0-312-45100-8). St Martin.
Isenberg, Seymour, jt. auth. see Isenberg, Anita.
Isenhour, Judith C. Knoxville: A Pictorial History. LC 78-1489. (Illus.). 1978. pap. 13.95 (ISBN 0-915442-46-9). Donning Co.
Isenhour, T. L. & Pederson, L. G. Passing Freshman Chemistry: Prerequesite Skills & Concepts. 177p. (Orig.). 1981. pap. text ed. 9.95 spiralbound (ISBN 0-15-568230-X); instructor's manual 3.95 (ISBN 0-15-568231-8). HarBraceJ.
Isenhour, T. L., jt. ed. see Justice, J. B.
Isern, Thomas D. Custom Combining on the Great Plains: A History. LC 81-2781. (Illus.). 304p. 1982. 17.95 (ISBN 0-8061-1681-1). U of Okla Pr.
Isert, Paul E. Voyages en Guinee et dans les Isles Caraibes, en Amerique. (Bibliotheque Africaine Ser.). 400p. (Fr.). 1974. Repr. of 1793 ed. lib. bdg. 101.50 o.p. (ISBN 0-8287-0458-9, 72-2116). Clearwater Pub.
Isfandiyar, Ibn & Ibn-al-Hasan, Muhammad. An Abridged Translation of the History of Tabaristan. Browne, Edward G., tr. (Studies in Islamic History: No. 23). xiv, 356p. lib. bdg. 35.00x (ISBN 0-87991-470-X). Porcupine Pr.
Isham, C. J., jt. ed. see Duff, M. J.
Isham, C. J., et al, eds. Quantum Gravity Two: A Second Oxford Symposium. (Illus.). 39.95x (ISBN 0-19-851952-4). Oxford U Pr.
Isham, Norman M. Early American Houses & a Glossary of Colonial Architectural Terms, 2 vols. LC 67-27458. (Architecture & Decorative Art Ser). 1967. Repr. of 1939 ed. lib. bdg. 19.50 (ISBN 0-306-70973-2). Da Capo.
Isham, V., jt. auth. see Cox, D. R.
Ishaq, I. The Life of Muhammad: A Translation of Ishaq's Sirat Rasul Allah. Guillaume, A., intro. by. 1979. pap. text ed. 19.95x (ISBN 0-19-636034-X). Oxford U Pr.
Ishee, John A. Design for Living: The Sermon on the Mount. 36p. 1982. pap. 3.50 (ISBN 0-939298-07-4). J M Prods.
--Everyman's Gospel: Studies in Romans. 32p. (Orig.). 1983. pap. 3.50 (ISBN 0-939298-19-8). J M Prods.
--God's Purpose-God's People: Studies in Ephesians. 36p. 1982. pap. 3.50 (ISBN 0-939298-03-1). J M Prods.
--God's Wisdom-God's Way: Studies in 1 Corinthians. 32p. (Orig.). 1983. pap. 3.50 (ISBN 0-939298-20-1). J M Prods.
--New Beginning: Studies in John's Gospel. 32p. (Orig.). 1982. pap. 3.50 (ISBN 0-939298-13-9, 139). J. M. Prods.
--What Every Person Should Know About God: Bible Study for New Christians. 36p. 1982. pap. 3.50 (ISBN 0-939298-05-8). J M Prods.
Isherwood, C., tr. see Bhagavad-Gita.
Isherwood, Christopher. All the Conspirators. LC 58-12798. 1979. pap. 6.95 (ISBN 0-8112-0725-0, NDP480). New Directions.
--Kathleen & Frank. LC 70-156155. 1971. 10.00 o.p. (ISBN 0-671-20991-4). S&S.
--People One Ought to Know. LC 81-43424. (Illus.). 64p. 1982. 12.95 (ISBN 0-385-17536-1). Doubleday.
--Prater Violet. 1978. pap. 2.75 (ISBN 0-380-01836-5, 63016-8, Bard). Avon.
--Ramakrishna & His Disciples. 1970. pap. 4.95 o.p. (ISBN 0-671-20740-7, Touchstone Bks). S&S.
Isherwood, Christopher, ed. Great English Short Stories. 1957. pap. 2.25 o.p. (ISBN 0-440-33084-X, LE). Dell.
Isherwood, Margaret. Lodestars for the Journey of Life. 91p. 1980. pap. text ed. 6.50 (ISBN 0-227-67840-0). Attic Pr.
Ishida, Eiichiro. Japanese Culture: A Study of Origins & Characteristics. Kachi, Teruko, tr. from Japanese. LC 73-92494. Orig. Title: Nihon Bunka Ron. 156p. 1974. 10.00x o.p. (ISBN 0-8248-0325-6, Eastwest Ctr). UH Pr.
Ishida, T., ed. Studies in the Period of David & Solomon & Other Essays. LC 82-11183. 409p. 1982. text ed. 35.00x (ISBN 0-931464-16-1). Eisenbrauns.
Ishida, Takeshi. Japanese Political Culture: Change & Continuity. LC 82-10957. 186p. 1983. 24.95 (ISBN 0-87855-465-3). Transaction Bks.
--Japanese Society. LC 81-40790. 158p. 1981. pap. text ed. 7.00 (ISBN 0-8191-1814-1). U Pr of Amer.
Ishigai, S., jt. auth. see Bergles, A. F.
Ishiguro, Kazou. A Pale View of the Hills. 1983. pap. 4.95 (ISBN 0-14-006260-2). Penguin.
Ishiguro, Kazuo. A Pale View of Hills. 192p. 1982. 11.95 (ISBN 0-399-12718-6). Putnam Pub Group.
Ishihara, Akira & Levy, Howard S. Tao of Sex: A Chinese Introduction to the Bedroom Arts. 2nd ed. (Japanese Special Supplement). 1969. 20.00 (ISBN 0-910878-09-9, Pub. by Langstaff-Levy); 1st signed ed. 25.00 (ISBN 0-686-34399-9). Oriental Bk Store.
Ishii, Yoneo, ed. Thailand: A Rice-Growing Society. LC 78-3839. (Center for Southeast Asian Studies, Kyoto University Monograph). 1978. text ed. 20.00x (ISBN 0-8248-0625-5); pap. text ed. 13.00x (ISBN 0-8248-0626-3). UH Pr.
Ishikawa, ed. Lung Cancer: Proceedings of the Tokyo Meeting, May, 1982. (International Congress Ser.: Vol. 569). 1982. 49.00 (ISBN 0-444-90238-4). Elsevier.
Ishimoto, Tatsuo. The Art of Driftwood & Dried Arrangements. (Illus.). 144p. 1951. 4.50 o.p. (ISBN 0-517-02565-5). Crown.
Ishimura, Y., jt. ed. see Hayaischi, O.
Ishino, Iwao, jt. auth. see Bennett, John W.
Ishiwata, Mutsuko, jt. ed. see Asano, Osamu.
Ishizaka, K., et al, eds. Recent Trends in Allergen & Complement Research: Progress in Allergy, Vol. 30. (Illus.). xiv, 234p. 1982. 79.75 (ISBN 3-8055-2580-X). S Karger.
Ishizaki, Hatsuo & Chiu, Arthur, eds. Wind Effects on Structures. LC 76-45584. 1976. text ed. 35.00x (ISBN 0-8248-0523-2). UH Pr.
Ish-Kishor, Sulamith. Our Eddie. (Windward Bks.). (gr. 7 up). 1969. 4.95 (ISBN 0-394-81455-X, BYR); PLB 5.99 (ISBN 0-394-91455-4). Random.
Ishumi, A. G., jt. auth. see Maliyamkono, T. L.
Isichei, Elizabeth. A History of Nigeria. LC 81-12342. (Illus., Orig.). 1983. text ed. 35.00x (ISBN 0-582-64331-7); pap. text ed. 10.95x (ISBN 0-582-64330-9). Longman.
--A History of the Igbo People. LC 75-14713. 200p. 1976. text ed. 21.50 o.p. (ISBN 0-312-37975-7). St Martin.
Isichel, Elizabeth, ed. Studies in the History of the Plateau State, Nigeria. 224p. 1981. 75.00x (ISBN 0-333-26931-4, Pub. by Macmillan England). State Mutual Bk.
Isidori, A., jt. ed. see Hinrichsen, D.
Iskandar, A. & Moulton, D. The Learning Fund: Income Generation Through NFE. 21p. (Orig.). 1982. pap. 1.00 (ISBN 0-932288-68-5). Ctr Intl Ed U of MA.
Iskander, Fazil. Sandro of Chegem. Brownsberger, Susan, tr. from Russian. LC 82-13219. 416p. (Orig.). 1983. pap. 8.95 (ISBN 0-394-71516-0, Vin). Random.
Iskander, I. K. Modeling Wastewater Renovation: Land Treatment. LC 80-39879. (Environmental Science & Technology: a Wiley-Interscience Series of Texts & Monographs). 802p. 1981. 72.00x (ISBN 0-471-08128-0, Pub. by Wiley-Interscience). Wiley.
Islam, A. K. A Revision of the Genus Stigeoclonium. (Illus.). 1963. pap. 24.00 (ISBN 3-7682-5410-0). Lubrecht & Cramer.
Islam, Jumal N. The Ultimate Fate of the Universe. LC 82-14558. 150p. Date not set. price not set (ISBN 0-521-24814-0). Cambridge U Pr.
Islam, K. M. Spectacle of Death. pap. 10.50 (ISBN 0-686-63915-4). Kazi Pubns.
Islam, M Anisul, jt. auth. see Gupta, Kanhaya L.
Islam, M. M. Bengal Agriculture Nineteen Twenty to Nineteen Forty-Six. LC 76-57098. (Cambridge South Asian Studies: No. 22). 1979. 44.50 (ISBN 0-521-21579-X). Cambridge U Pr.
Islam, Nural. Development Strategy of Bangladesh. 1978. text ed. 20.00 (ISBN 0-08-021840-7). Pergamon.
Islam, Shamsul. Kipling's Law: A Study of His Philosophy of Life. LC 75-24793. 300p. 1975. 18.95 o.p. (ISBN 0-312-45675-1). St Martin.
Ismael, Tareq Y. Iraq & Iran: Roots of Conflict. LC 82-1562. (Contemporary Issues in the Middle East Ser.). (Illus.). 280p. 1982. 24.00x (ISBN 0-8156-2279-1); pap. 12.95x (ISBN 0-8156-2280-5). Syracuse U Pr.
Isma'il, A. H. Ali Ibn see Ali ibn Isma'il, A. H., et al.
Ismail, V. Muhammad: The Last Prophet. 4.95 (ISBN 0-686-83579-4). Kazi Pubns.
Isnard, Achille N. Observations sur le Principe Qui a Produit les Revolutions de France, de Geneve et D'amerique. (Rousseauism, 1788-1797). 1978. Repr. lib. bdg. 30.00x o.p. (ISBN 0-8287-0459-7). Clearwater Pub.
Isom, Joan S. Fox Grapes, Cherokee Verse. (Wild & Woolly West Ser: No.33). (Illus.). 1977. 7.00 o.p. (ISBN 0-910584-45-1); pap. 1.50 o.p. (ISBN 0-910584-67-2). Filter.
--Foxgrapes: Poems of the Plains & the People. rev. ed. (Illus.): 55p. 1983. pap. 4.50 (ISBN 0-938604-03-1). Foxmoor.
Isom, Joan S., ed. Sun-Catcher: Children of Earth. (Illus.). 118p. (Orig.). 1982. pap. 5.50 (ISBN 0-938604-02-3). Foxmoor.
Ison, Barry, jt. auth. see Students, Expressive Arts Dept., Sogeri National High School, Papua New Guinea.
Ison, H. C., jt. auth. see Butler, G.
Ispa, Jean. Exploring Careers in Child Care Services. (Careers in Depth Ser.). 140p. 1983. lib. bdg. 7.97 (ISBN 0-8239-0556-X). Rosen Pr.
Israel, Calvin, ed. Discoveries & Considerations: Papers on Early American Literature & Aesthetics Presented to Harold Jantz. LC 76-5424. (Illus.). 1976. 29.50x (ISBN 0-87395-340-1). State U NY Pr.
Israel, Elaine. Up, Over, Under & Around: The New Explorers. LC 80-19618. (Illus.). 96p. (gr. 4 up). 1980. PLB 7.79 o.p. (ISBN 0-671-34002-6). Messner.
Israel, Jerold H., jt. auth. see Kerper, Hazel B.
Israel, John & Klein, Donald. Rebels & Bureaucrats: China's December 9ers. LC 74-18757. 1976. 32.50x (ISBN 0-520-02861-9). U of Cal Pr.
Israel, Jonathan I. The Dutch Republic & the Hispanic World, 1606 to 1661. 1982. 54.00x (ISBN 0-19-826534-4). Oxford U Pr.
Israel, Lee. Kilgallen. (Illus.). 1979. 12.95 o.s.i. (ISBN 0-440-04522-3). Delacorte.
Israel, Lucien. Decision Making: The Modern Doctor's Dilemma. 1982. 11.50 (ISBN 0-394-51528-5). Random.
--Decision Making: The Modern Doctor's Dilemma. Feeny, Mary, tr. 1982. 11.50 (ISBN 0-394-51528-5). Knopf.
Israel, Martin. Living Alone. Kelsey, Morton T., intro. by. 144p. (Orig.). 1983. pap. 7.95 (ISBN 0-8245-0503-4). Crossroad NY.
Israel, Milton, ed. Pax Britannica. LC 68-113032. (Selections from History Today Ser.: No. 9). (Illus.). 1968. 7.95 (ISBN 0-05-001653-9); pap. 3.95 o.p. (ISBN 0-685-09189-9). Dufour.
Israel - State Of - Ministry Of Justice. Selected Judgments of the Supreme Court of Israel, 4 vols. 1976. 30.00 ea. Vol. 1 (ISBN 0-379-13901-4). Vol. 2 (ISBN 0-379-13902-2). Vol. 3 (ISBN 0-379-13903-0). Vol. 4 (ISBN 0-379-13904-9). Vol. 5 o.p (ISBN 0-379-13905-7). Oceana.
Israel, W., jt. ed. see Hawking, Stephen.
Israeli Govt. Atlas of Israel. 1970. 276.75 (ISBN 0-444-40740-5). Elsevier.
Israels, M. G. & Delamore, I. W. Haematological Aspects of Systemic Disease. LC 76-26782. (Illus.). 1976. text ed. 12.00 (ISBN 0-7216-5047-3). Saunders.
Israelsen, O. W., jt. auth. see Hansen, V. E.
Issacharoff, Michael & Vilquin, Jean-Claude, eds. Sartre et la Mise En Signe. LC 81-68003. (French Forum Monographs: No. 30). 168p. (Orig.). 1982. pap. 12.50x (ISBN 0-917058-29-1). French Forum.
Issacs, Susan. The Sex Information Trap. Graver, Fred, ed. 288p. cancelled o.s.i. (ISBN 0-87131-350-2). M Evans.
Issaev. Practive & Prospects of Multi-Regional Economic Modelling. (Studies in Regional Science: Vol. 9). 1982. 51.00 (ISBN 0-444-86485-7). Elsevier.
Issel, William, jt. auth. see Cherny, Robert W.
Isselbacher, K. J., et al. Harrison's Principles of Internal Medicine. 9th ed. 1979. 2 vol. ed. 80.00 (ISBN 0-07-032069-1); 1 vol. ed. 65.00 (ISBN 0-07-032068-3). McGraw.
Isselbacher, Kurt J. & Adams, Raymond D. Harrison's Principles of Internal Medicine: Update 4. 9th ed. (Updates to Harrison's Principles of Internal Medicine Ser.). (Illus.). 320p. 1982. text ed. 32.00x (ISBN 0-07-032134-5, HP). McGraw.
Isselbacher, Kurt J., et al. Harrison's Principles of Internal Medicine: Update One. 9th ed. (Illus.). 304p. 1981. text ed. 32.00 (ISBN 0-07-032131-0). McGraw.
Isselhard, Donald E., jt. auth. see Brand, Richard W.
ISSS Working Group on Soil Information Systems 2nd Varna-Sofia, Bulgaria, 30 May - 4 June, 1977. Developments in Soil Information Systems: Proceedings. Sadovsky, A. D. & Bie, S. W., eds. 119p. 1978. pap. 14.00 (ISBN 0-686-93147-5, PDC107, Pudoc). Unipub.
Istvan, Donald F. & Avery, Clarence G. Accounting Principles. (Illus.). 1095p. 1979. text ed. 23.95 (ISBN 0-15-500420-4, HC); study guide 8.95 (ISBN 0-15-500423-9); practice set A 6.95 (ISBN 0-15-500431-X); practice set A with business papers 8.95 (ISBN 0-15-500434-4); practice set B 6.95 (ISBN 0-15-500432-8); practice set C 6.95 (ISBN 0-15-500433-6); working papers (1) 7.95 (ISBN 0-15-500429-8); working papers (2) 7.95 (ISBN 0-15-500430-1); solutions manual & tranparencies avail. HarBraceJ.
Iswolsky, Helene, tr. see Bakhtin, M.
Italian National Institute of Higher Mathematics Conventions. Symposia Mathematica: Proceedings. Incl. Vol. 1. Group Theory. 1970. 68.50 (ISBN 0-12-612201-6); Vol. 2. Functional Analysis & Geometry. 1970. 65.00 (ISBN 0-12-612202-4); Vol. 3. Problems in the Evolution of the Solar System. 1970. 79.00 (ISBN 0-12-612203-2); Vol. 4. 1971. 73.50 (ISBN 0-12-612204-0); Vol. 5. 1971. 73.50 (ISBN 0-12-612205-9); Vol. 6. 1971. 62.50 (ISBN 0-12-612206-7); Vol. 7. 1972. 78.00 (ISBN 0-12-612207-5); Vol. 8. 1972. 44.50 (ISBN 0-12-612208-3); Vol. 9. 1972. 82.50 (ISBN 0-12-612209-1); Vol. 10. 1973. 64.50 (ISBN 0-12-612210-5); Vol. 18. 1977. 78.00 (ISBN 0-12-612218-0); Vol. 19. 1977. 60.50 (ISBN 0-12-612219-9). Acad Pr.
Itard, Jean-Marc-Gaspard. Wild Boy of Aveyron. Humphrey, George & Humphrey, Muriel, trs. 1962. pap. 8.95x (ISBN 0-13-959494-9). P-H.
Itaya, Kikuo. Tengu Child. 1983. 15.95 (ISBN 0-8093-1081-3). S Ill U Pr.
ITC-U. S. A. Conference, Los Angeles, 1974. International Telemetering Conference: Proceedings, Vol. X. (Illus.). 617p. 1974. text ed. 50.00x o.p. (ISBN 0-87664-258-X). Instru Soc.
--International Telemetering Conference: Proceedings, Vol. XII. 737p. 1976. text ed. 50.00x o.p. (ISBN 0-87664-321-7). Instru Soc.
ITC-U. S. A. Conference, Los Angeles, 1977. International Telemetering Conference: Proceedings, Vol. XIII. LC 66-4573. 482p. 1977. text ed. 65.00x (ISBN 0-87664-375-6). Instru Soc.
ITC-U. S. A. Conference, San Diego 1979. International Telemetering Conference: Proceedings, Vol. XV. LC 66-4573. 568p. 1979. text ed. 95.00x (ISBN 0-87664-459-0). Instru Soc.
ITC-U. S. A. Conference, San Diego 1980. International Telemetering Conference: Proceedings, Vol. XVI. 670p. 1980. text ed. 100.00x o.p. (ISBN 0-87664-494-9). Instru Soc.
ITC-U. S. A. Conference, San Diego 1981, XVIIth. International Telemetering Conference: Proceedings, Vol. XVII. 1504p. 1981. text ed. 245.00x o.p. (ISBN 0-87664-516-3). Instru Soc.
ITC-U. S. A. Conference, Washington, D.C., 1975. International Telemetering Conference: Proceedings, Vol. XI. LC 66-4573. 652p. 1975. text ed. 50.00x (ISBN 0-87664-286-5). Instru Soc.
Iterson, S. R. Van see Van Iterson, S. R.
Itkis, U. Control Systems of Variable Structure. LC 76-4870. 214p. 1976. 59.95x o.s.i. (ISBN 0-470-15072-6). Halsted Pr.
Ito, Dee, jt. auth. see Das, Swami Harihar.
Ito, Haruyoshi, tr. see Aoki, Hiroyuki.
Ito, Kiyosi, ed. Proceedings of the International Symposium on Stochastic Differential Equations, Kyoto, 1976. LC 78-19655. 1978. 64.95x (ISBN 0-471-05375-9, Pub. by Wiley-Interscience). Wiley.
Ito, M. Integrative Control Functions of the Brain, Vol. 2. 1980. 98.75 (ISBN 0-444-80193-6). Elsevier.
--Integrative Control Functions of the Brain, Vol. 3. 1981. 101.50 (ISBN 0-444-80314-9). Elsevier.
Ito, Toshio & Komura, Hirotsugu. Kites: The Science & the Wonder. (Illus.). 176p. (Orig.). 1983. pap. 11.95 (ISBN 0-87040-526-8). Kodansha.
Ito, Y. Comparative Ecology. 2nd ed. Kikkawa, J., ed. LC 79-41581. (Illus.). 350p. 1981. text ed. 60.00 (ISBN 0-521-22977-4); pap. text ed. 22.95 (ISBN 0-521-29845-8). Cambridge U Pr.

Ito, Z., et al. Cerebral Ischemia: An Update. (International Congress Ser.: No. 599). Date not set. 64.00 (ISBN 0-444-90290-2). Elsevier.

Ito, Zentaro. Microsurgery of Cerebral Aneurysms. (Illus.). 350p. 1982. 279.00 (ISBN 0-444-90267-8, Excerpta Medica). Elsevier.

Itoh, Teiji & Futagawa, Yukio. Traditional Japanese Houses. (Illus.). 360p. 1983. 75.00 (ISBN 0-8478-0479-8). Rizzoli Intl.

Itono, H. Studies on the Ceramiaceous Algae (Rhodophyta) from Southern Parts of Japan. (Bibliotheca Phycologica Ser.: No. 35). 1977. lib. bdg. 60.00x (ISBN 3-7682-1148-7). Lubrecht & Cramer.

ITT Educational Services Inc. This Is Electronics, 2 bks. Incl. Bk. 1. Basic Principles (ISBN 0-672-97619-6); Bk. 2. Circuits & Applications (ISBN 0-672-97620-X). LC 74-105093. 1978. text ed. 26.95 ea. Set. Bobbs.

Ittaman, K. P. Amini Islanders: Social Structure & Change. LC 76-901759. 1976. 13.00x o.p. (ISBN 0-88386-844-X). South Asia Bks.

Itzhak, Benjamin Avi see Vardi, Joseph & Avi-Itzhak, Benjamin.

Itzkoff, Seymour W. Ernst Cassirer. (World Leaders Ser.). 1977. lib. bdg. 13.95 (ISBN 0-8057-7712-1, Twayne). G K Hall.

Iuppa, Nicholas V. A Practical Guide to Interactive Video Design. 175p. 1983. 32.95 (ISBN 0-86729-041-2). Knowledge Indus.

IUTAM International Congress, 14th. Theoretical & Applied Mechanics: Proceedings. Koiter, W. T., ed. 1977. 85.00 (ISBN 0-7204-0549-1, North-Holland). Elsevier.

Ivan, Dan, jt. auth. see Demura, Fumio.

Ivan, Leslie P. & Bruce, Derek A. COMA: Physiopathology, Diagnosis & Management. (Illus.). 304p. 1982. 38.75x (ISBN 0-398-04683-2). C C Thomas.

Ivancevich, John, jt. auth. see Matteson, Michael.

Ivancevich, John M. & Lyon, Herbert L. Introduction to Business. 2nd ed. (Illus.). 700p. 1983. text ed. 22.95 (ISBN 0-314-69656-3); tchrs. ed avail. (ISBN 0-314-71100-7); study guide avail. (ISBN 0-314-71101-5). West Pub.

Ivancevich, John M. & Matteson, Michael T. Stress & Work: A Managerial Perspective. 1981. pap. text ed. 10.95x (ISBN 0-673-15381-9). Scott F.

Ivancevich, John M., et al. Business in a Dynamic Environment. (Illus.). 1979. text ed. 21.95 (ISBN 0-8299-0180-9); study guide by Curtis Q. Mason 8.50 (ISBN 0-8299-0257-0); instrs.' manual avail. (ISBN 0-8299-0494-8); transparency masters avail. (ISBN 0-8299-0495-6). West Pub.

Ivanoff, Pierre. Maya. Nannicini, Guiuliana & Bowman, John, eds. Mondadori, tr. from It. LC 74-170260. (Monuments of Civilization Ser.). Orig. Title: Cita Maya. (Illus.). 192p. 1973. 25.00 o.p. (ISBN 0-448-02020-3, G&D). Putnam Pub Group.

Ivanov, M. V. & Freney, J. R. The Global Biogeochemical Sulphur Cycle Scope 19. (Scientific Committee on Problems of the Environment Ser.). 350p. 1983. price not set (ISBN 0-471-10492-2, Pub. by Wiley-Interscience). Wiley.

Ivanov, Vladimir, jt. auth. see Faensen, Hubert.

Ivanov, Vladimir A. Ismaili Tradition Concerning the Rise of the FATamids. (Studies in Islamic History Ser.). xxii, 337p. Repr. of 1942 ed. lib. bdg. 37.50x (ISBN 0-87991-471-8). Porcupine Pr.

Ivany, J. W. Today's Science: A Professional Approach to Teaching Elementary School Science. LC 74-17745. (Illus.). 416p. 1975. pap. text ed. 15.95 (ISBN 0-574-19600-5, 13-6010). SRA.

Ivarie, Theodore W. Tower Typing: Using Sears, Roebuck & Co. Business Forms. 1978. pap. text ed. 9.75 o.p. (ISBN 0-07-032066-7, G); inst. manual & key 3.50 o.p. (ISBN 0-07-032067-5). McGraw.

Ivenbaum, Elliott. Drawing People. LC 79-14246. (gr. 4 up). 1980. PLB 8.90 (ISBN 0-531-02283-8, A46). Watts.

Ivener, Martin H. & Rosefsky, Robert S. Telecourse Study Guide for Personal Finance & Money Management. 1978. pap. text ed. 11.50 (ISBN 0-471-03797-4); Set. 27.95 o.p. (ISBN 0-471-03796-6). Wiley.

Ivens, Dorothy & Massee, Bill. Just Tell Me What I Want to Know About Wine. LC 78-73319. 1981. pap. write for info. (ISBN 0-448-16055-2, G&D). Putnam Pub Group.

Ivens, Dorothy & Massee, William E. Just Tell Me What I Want to Know About Wine. LC 78-73319. 1980. pap. 6.95 o.p. (ISBN 0-686-58203-9, G&D). Putnam Pub Group.

Ivens, T. C. Still Water Fly Fishing: A Modern Guide to Angling in Reservoirs & Lakes. 3rd ed. (Illus.). 1971. 12.50 o.p. (ISBN 0-233-96128-3). Transatlantic.

Iversen, Gudmund R. Statistics for Sociology. 400p. 1979. text ed. write for info. (ISBN 0-697-07557-5); solutions man. avail. (ISBN 0-697-07597-4). Wm C Brown.

Iversen, Gudmund R., jt. auth. see Boyd, Lawrence H.

Iversen, Leslie & Iversen, Susan, eds. Handbook of Psychopharmacology, New Techniques in Psychopharmacology. (Vol. 15). 440p. 1982. 55.00x (ISBN 0-306-40975-5, Plenum Pr). Plenum Pub.

Iversen, Leslie L. Uptake & Storage of Noradrenaline in Sympathic Nerves. 1967. 44.50 (ISBN 0-521-05390-0). Cambridge U Pr.

Iversen, Leslie L., jt. auth. see Iversen, Susan D.

Iversen, Leslie L. & Iversen, Susan D., eds. Handbook of Psychopharmacology: Neuropeptides, Vol. 16. 594p. 1983. 65.00x (ISBN 0-306-41048-6, Plenum Pr). Plenum Pub.

Iversen, Leslie L., jt. ed. see Iversen, Susan D.

Iversen, Susan, jt. ed. see Iversen, Leslie.

Iversen, Susan D. & Iversen, Leslie L. Behavioral Pharmacology. 2nd ed. (Illus.). 1981. text ed. 21.95x (ISBN 0-19-502778-7); pap. text ed. 12.95x (ISBN 0-19-502779-5). Oxford U Pr.

Iversen, Susan D. & Iversen, Leslie L., eds. Handbook of Psychopharmacology: Biochemical Studies of CNS Receptors, Vol. 17. 420p. 1983. 55.00x (ISBN 0-306-41145-8, Plenum Pr). Plenum Pub.

Iversen, Susan D., jt. ed. see Iversen, Leslie L.

Iverson, Genie. Jacques Cousteau. LC 75-25822. (See& Read Biographies Ser.). 64p. (gr. k-4). 1976. PLB 5.99 (ISBN 0-399-60987-3). Putnam Pub Group.

--Louis Armstrong. LC 76-4975. (Biography Ser.). (Illus.). 40p. (gr. 1-4). 1976. PLB 10.89 (ISBN 0-690-01127-X, TYC-J). Har-Row.

--Margaret Bourke-White. (People to Remember Ser.). 32p. (gr. 4-12). 1980. PLB 7.95 (ISBN 0-87191-743-2). Creative Ed.

Iverson, I. B. Pythagoras & the Quantum World. 1982. 9.75 (ISBN 0-8062-1935-1). Carlton.

Iverson, K. E. A Programming Language. 286p. 1962. 30.95x (ISBN 0-471-43014-5). Wiley.

Iverson, Peter. Carlos Montezuma & the Changing World of American Indians. (Illus.). 240p. 1982. 17.50 (ISBN 0-8263-0641-1). U of NM Pr.

--The Navajo Nation. LC 80-1024. (Contributions in Ethnic Studies: No. 3). (Illus.). xxxii, 273p. 1981. lib. bdg. 29.95 (ISBN 0-313-22309-2, INN/). Greenwood.

Iverson, R., tr. see Trakl, Georg.

Iverson, William, jt. auth. see Sebesta, Sam L.

Ives, Charles. The Isles of Summer: Or Nassau & the Bahamas. (Illus.). Repr. of 1880 ed. 49.50x (ISBN 0-685-39987-7). Elliots Bks.

Ives, Charles E. Charles E. Ives: Memos. Kirkpatrick, John E., ed. (Illus.). 1972. 15.00x o.p. (ISBN 0-393-02153-X). Norton.

Ives, E. W. The Common Lawyers of Pre-Reformation England: Thomas Kebell, A Case Study. LC 82-1297. (Cambridge Studies in English Legal History). (Illus.). 512p. Date not set. 79.50 (ISBN 0-521-24011-5). Cambridge U Pr.

Ives, George. History of Penal Methods: Criminals, Witches & Lunatics. LC 70-108241. (Criminology, Law Enforcement, & Social Problems Ser.: No. 124). 1970. Repr. of 1914 ed. 17.00x (ISBN 0-87585-124-X). Patterson Smith.

Ives, Howard C. & Kissam, P. Highway Curves. 4th ed. LC 52-9033. 1952. 36.95x (ISBN 0-471-43032-3, Pub. by Wiley-Interscience). Wiley.

Ives, Jack, jt. auth. see Vigdorchik, Michael.

Ives, Jack D., ed. Geocology of the Front Range: A Study of Alpine & Subalpine Environments. (INSTAAR Studies in High Altitude Geoecology). (Illus.). 484p. 1980. lib. bdg. 30.00 (ISBN 0-89158-993-7). Westview.

Ives, Joseph C. Report Upon the Colorado River of the West. LC 69-18459. (American Scene Ser). (Illus.). 1969. Repr. of 1861 ed. lib. bdg. 52.50 (ISBN 0-686-85847-6). Da Capo.

Ives, Josephine & Bursak, Laura Z. Word Identification Techniques. 1979. pap. 10.50 (ISBN 0-395-30638-8). HM.

Ives, Kenneth H. Nurturing Spiritual Development: Stages, Structure, Style. (Studies in Quakerism: No. 8). 60p. (Orig.). 1982. pap. 3.00 (ISBN 0-89670-011-9). Progresiv Pub.

Ives, M. B., ed. Materials Engineering in the Arctic. (Illus., TA 407.m36). 1977. 46.00 o.p. (ISBN 0-87170-050-6). ASM.

Ives, Ronald, et al. Audio Frequency Testers. Cole, Sandy, ed. (Seventy-Three Test Equipment Library: Vol. 2). 78p. 1976. pap. 4.95 o.p. (ISBN 0-88006-011-5, LB 7360). Green Pub Inc.

Ivey, Allen E. Counseling & Psychotherapy: Skills, Theories & Practices. (Illus.). 1980. text ed. 24.95 (ISBN 0-13-183152-6). P-H.

--Intentional Interviewing & Counseling. LC 82-14689. (Counseling Ser.). 320p. 1982. pap. text ed. 13.95 (ISBN 0-534-01331-7). Brooks-Cole.

Ivey, D. G., jt. auth. see Hume, J. N.

Ivey, Henry F. see Marton, L.

Ivey, Jessie. Yes I Remember. 21p. Date not set. pap. 2.00 (ISBN 0-686-97738-6). Ivey Pubns.

Ivic, jt. auth. see De Koninck.

Ivin, K. J., ed. Structural Studies of Macromolecules by Spectroscopic Methods. LC 75-19355. 1976. 84.95x (ISBN 0-471-43120-6, Pub. by Wiley-Interscience). Wiley.

Ivin, Kenneth J., tr. see Braun, D., et al.

Ivins, Dan. Main Events. LC 82-70869. (Orig.). (gr. 7-12). 1983. pap. 4.50 (ISBN 0-8054-5339-3). Broadman.

Ivins, David. The Complete Book of Woodburning Stoves. LC 78-56961. (Illus.). 1978. pap. 6.95 o.p. (ISBN 0-8069-8242-X). Sterling.

Ivins, John C., jt. auth. see Chao, Edmund Y.

Ivins, William M., Jr. Notes on Prints. LC 67-25544. (Graphic Art Ser). 1967. Repr. of 1930 ed. lib. bdg. 32.50 (ISBN 0-306-70957-0). Da Capo.

--Notes on Prints. 1969. pap. 5.95 (ISBN 0-262-59003-4). MIT Pr.

--Prints & Books. LC 76-75295. (Graphic Art Ser). 1969. Repr. of 1927 ed. lib. bdg. 37.50 (ISBN 0-306-71288-1). Da Capo.

--Prints & Visual Communication. LC 68-31583. (Graphic Art Ser). (Illus.). 1969. Repr. of 1953 ed. lib. bdg. 29.50 (ISBN 0-306-71159-1). Da Capo.

Ivins, Williams, Jr. On the Rationalization of Sight: De Artificiali Perspectiva. 2nd ed. LC 68-54843. (Graphic Arts Ser). 1973. Repr. of 1938 ed. lib. bdg. 32.50 (ISBN 0-306-71189-3). Da Capo.

Ivison. Electrical Circuit Theory. 1977. 21.95 o.p. (ISBN 0-442-30201-0); pap. 9.10x (ISBN 0-442-30202-9). Van Nos Reinhold.

Ivlev, V. S. Experimental Ecology & the Feeding of Fishes. 1961. 32.50x o.p. (ISBN 0-685-89751-6). Elliots Bks.

Ivory, Thomas P., ed. see Archdiocese of Newark.

Ivy, Robert H., Jr. see Roach, William.

Iwago, Mitsuaki. Puppies II. (Illus.). 76p. (Orig.). 1983. pap. 7.95 (ISBN 0-89346-202-0). Heian Intl.

Iwamura, Kazuo. Tan Tan's Suspenders. 40p. Date not set. 6.95 (ISBN 0-686-95237-5). Bradbury Pr.

Iwamura, Susan. The Verbal Games of Pre-School Children. LC 79-22384. 1979. 25.00x (ISBN 0-312-83877-8). St Martin.

Iwasaki, C. What's Fun Without a Friend. (gr. 2-4). 1975. 5.95 o.p. (ISBN 0-07-032088-8, GB); PLB 5.72 o.p. (ISBN 0-07-032089-6). McGraw.

Ixer, Joyce. The Alsatian. 1977. pap. 2.50 (ISBN 0-7028-1044-4). Palmetto Pub.

Iyanaga, S. The Theory of Numbers. (North-Holland Mathematical Library: Vol. 8). 1976. 93.75 (ISBN 0-444-10678-2, North-Holland). Elsevier.

Iyanaga, Shokichi & Kawada, Yukiyosi, eds. Encyclopedic Dictionary of Mathematics, 2 vols. 1977. Set. text ed. 175.00x (ISBN 0-262-09016-3); pap. text ed. 50.00x (ISBN 0-262-59010-7). MIT Pr.

Iyayi, Festus. Violence. 316p. (Orig.). 1979. 10.00 o.s.i. (ISBN 0-89410-105-6); pap. 5.00 o.s.i. (ISBN 0-89410-104-8). Three Continents.

Iyengar, B. K. The Concise Light on Yoga. LC 82-5473. (Illus.). 256p. 1982. 12.95x (ISBN 0-8052-3831-X); pap. 7.95 spiral (ISBN 0-8052-0723-6). Schocken.

--Light on Yoga. rev. ed. LC 76-48857. (Illus.). 1977. 12.50x (ISBN 0-8052-3653-8); pap. 8.95 (ISBN 0-8052-0610-8). Schocken.

Iyengar, K. T. & Ramu, S. Anantha. Design Tables for Beams on Elastic Foundations & Related Structural Problems. (Illus.). 1979. 38.90x (ISBN 0-85334-841-3, Pub. by Applied Sci England). Elsevier.

Iyer, Raghavan. The Descent of the Gods: Mystical Writings of A. E. Raghavan Iyer & Nandini Iyer. (Collected Edition of the Writings of G.W. Russell III). Date not set. text ed. price not set (ISBN 0-391-01143-X). Humanities.

Izaeli, D. N., ed. see International Conference on Marketing Systems for Developing Countries.

Izakowitz, David, jt. ed. see Leverett, James.

Izant, Grace G. Ohio Scenes & Citizens. LC 64-12464. 254p. 1973. Repr. of 1964 ed. 9.95 (ISBN 0-913428-10-8). Landfall Pr.

Izard, Janet W. The Mandala Coloring Book. 1972. pap. 1.75 pad bound o.s.i. (ISBN 0-913858-00-5). Ducks Bks.

Izard, Ralph S., et al. Fundamentals of News Reporting. 4th ed. LC 70-145615. 1982. perfect bdg. 11.95 (ISBN 0-8403-2770-6, 40277001). Kendall-Hunt.

Izatt, Reed M. & Christensen, James J. Progess in Macrocyclic Chemistry, Vol. 2. (Progress in Macrocyclic Chemistry Ser.). 347p. 1981. 56.50x (ISBN 0-471-05178-0, Pub. by Wiley-Interscience). Wiley.

--Progress in Macrocyclic Chemistry. LC 78-14354. (Progress in Macrocyclic Chemistry Ser.). 1979. Vol. 1. 45.95x (ISBN 0-471-03477-0, Pub by Wiley-Interscience); Vol. 2. 56.50x (ISBN 0-686-86904-4). Wiley.

--Progress in Macrocyclic Chemistry, Vol. 2. 300p. 1981. 50.00 o.p. (ISBN 0-471-05178-0, Pub. by Wiley-Interscience). Wiley.

Izawa, T., illus. Preschool Puppet Board Books. new ed. Incl. Farm Animals (9730); Cars & Trucks. o.s.i. (9734); Puppies (9731); Airplanes (9733); Pandas (9732); Colors (9735). (Puppet Board Books Ser.). (Illus.). 7p. (ps-2). 1973. 2.50 ea. (G&D). Putnam Pub Group.

--Preschool Puppet Board Books. Incl. Bunnies (ISBN 0-448-09737-0); Dinosaurs (ISBN 0-448-09739-7); Pets. o.s.i. (ISBN 0-448-09738-9); Kittens (ISBN 0-448-09736-2); Wild Animals. o.s.i. (ISBN 0-448-09740-0); Koala Bears & Kangaroos. o.s.i. (ISBN 0-448-09741-9); The Tortoise & the Hare, & the Lion & the Mouse (ISBN 0-448-09742-7); Rhymes (ISBN 0-448-09743-5); City Mouse & the Country Mouse (ISBN 0-448-09744-3); Owl & the Pussycat. o.s.i. (ISBN 0-448-09745-1). (Puppet Board Books Ser.). (Illus.). (gr. k-2). 1975. 2.50 ea. (G&D). Putnam Pub Group.

Izawa, T. & Hijkata, S., illus. Hansel & Gretel. (Puppet Storybooks). (Illus.). 18p. (gr. k-2). 1981. 3.50 (ISBN 0-448-09754-0, G&D). Putnam Pub Group.

--Jack & the Beanstalk. (Puppet Storybooks). (Illus.). 18p. (gr. k-2). 1981. 3.50 (ISBN 0-448-09758-3, G&D). Putnam Pub Group.

--The Little Red Hen. (Puppet Storybooks). (Illus.). 18p. (gr. k-2). 1981. 3.50 (ISBN 0-448-09756-7, G&D). Putnam Pub Group.

--Peter Rabbit. (Puppet Storybooks). (Illus.). 18p. (gr. k-2). 1981. 3.50 (ISBN 0-448-09755-9, G&D). Putnam Pub Group.

--Snow White & the Seven Dwarfs. (Puppet Storybooks). (Illus.). 18p. (gr. k-2). 1981. 3.50 (ISBN 0-448-09757-5, G&D). Putnam Pub Group.

--What Time Is It? (Puppet Storybooks). (Illus.). 18p. (gr. k-2). 1981. 3.50 (ISBN 0-448-09753-2, G&D). Putnam Pub Group.

Izawa, Tadasu & Hijikata, Shigemi, illus. A Puppet Treasure Book of Fairy Tales. (Illus.). 98p. (ps-1). 1981. 5.95 (ISBN 0-448-12290-1, G&D). Putnam Pub Group.

--A Puppet Treasure Book of Nursery Rhymes. (Illus.). 96p. (ps-1). 1981. 5.95 (ISBN 0-448-12288-X, G&D). Putnam Pub Group.

--A Puppet Treasure Book of Nursery Tales. (Illus.). 94p. (ps-1). 1981. 5.95 (ISBN 0-448-12289-8, G&D). Putnam Pub Group.

Izenour, G. C. Theater Design. 1977. 175.00 (ISBN 0-07-032086-1, P&RB). McGraw.

Izenour, Steven, jt. auth. see Hirshorn, Paul.

Izerghina, A., intro. by. Henri Matisse. Rosengrant, R. J., et al, trs. 1979. 45.00 (ISBN 0-89893-031-6). CDP.

Izmidlian, Georges. Oriental Rugs & Carpets Today. LC 77-174. (Illus.). 1978. 12.95 (ISBN 0-88254-442-X); pap. 11.95 o.p. (ISBN 0-88254-486-1). Hippocrene Bks.

--Oriental Rugs & Carpets Today: How to Choose & Enjoy Them. (Illus.). 128p. 1983. 19.95 (ISBN 0-88254-800-X); pap. 11.95 (ISBN 0-88254-801-8). Hippocrene Bks.

Izraeli, D. & Zif, J. Societal Marketing Boards. LC 77-10606. 265p. 1978. 59.95x o.p. (ISBN 0-470-99308-1). Halsted Pr.

Izraeli, D. N., ed. see International Conference on Marketing Systems for Developing Countries.

Izumiya, Nobuo. Synthetic Aspects of Biologically Active Cyclic Peptides: Gramicidei S & Tyrocidres. LC 79-19998. 166p. 1979. 44.95x o.s.i. (ISBN 0-470-26863-8). Halsted Pr.

Izutsu, Toshihiku, tr. see Sabzavari, Hadi Ibn Mahdi.

Izzard, Sebastian. Hiroshige: An Exhibition of Selected Prints. (Illus.). 116p. 1983. pap. 20.00 (ISBN 0-9610398-0-9). Ukiyo-e Soc.

Izzi, Guglielmo. Photographing People: The Creative Photographer's Guide to Equipment & Technique. (Illus.). 256p. 1982. 19.95 (ISBN 0-8174-5431-4, Amphoto). Watson-Guptill.

Izzidien, Mouel Y. Nisab Al Ihtisab. Quinlan, Hamid, ed. LC 82-70458. 230p. (Orig.). 1982. pap. 5.00 (ISBN 0-89259-031-9). Am Trust Pubns.

Izzidien, Movel Y., tr. see Sabiq, Sayyed.

Izzo, Alberto, jt. auth. see Gubitosi, Camillo.

Izzo, Barbara & Keefe, Marie. Speak English, Text 4. (Speak English Ser.). (Illus.). 80p. (Orig.). 1983. pap. text ed. 4.95 (ISBN 0-88499-657-3). Inst Mod Lang.

Izzo, Herbert J., ed. Italic & Romance: Linguistic Studies in Honor of Ernst Pulgram. (Current Issues in Linguistic Theory Ser.). xxi, 338p. 1980. 35.00 (ISBN 90-272-3511-2, 18). Benjamins North Am.

Izzo, Suzanne. Second Language Learning: A Review of Related Studies. LC 81-82494. 56p. (Orig.). 1981. pap. 6.00 (ISBN 0-89763-058-0). Natl Clearinghse Bilingual Ed.

J

J. Bruce Carruthers II, Business Info. Display, Inc. The Energy Decade: Nineteen Seventy to Nineteen Eighty. LC 81-22884. 558p. 1982. prof ref 125.00x (ISBN 0-88410-873-2). Ballinger Pub.

J. J. Keller & Associates, Inc. Driver's Guide to Low Underpasses. 3rd ed. LC 75-26145. (6h). 1981. pap. 6.00 perfect bdg (ISBN 0-934674-16-7). J J Keller.

--Parcel Shipments Distribution Manual. LC 82-84710. 400p. 1983. loose-leaf 60.00 (ISBN 0-934674-46-9). J J Keller.

J, Mr. Still More of the World's Best Dirty Jokes. (Illus.). 120p. 1983. pap. 3.95 (ISBN 0-8065-0834-5). Citadel Pr.

Jaag, O., et al, eds. Water Pollution Research: Proceedings of the Second International Conference. 2nd ed. 1966. Set. 221.00 (ISBN 0-08-011438-5). Pergamon.

Jabay, Earl. The God Players. 4.95 o.p. (ISBN 0-686-92325-1, 6380). Hazelden.

Jabbari, Ahmad. A Practical Guide to the Persian Alphabet. (Illus.). 66p. (Orig.). 1982. pap. text ed. 7.95 (ISBN 0-939214-12-1). Mazda Pubs.

Jabbari, Ahmad, ed. see Bahar, Mehrdad.

Jabbari, Ahmad, ed. & tr. see Farjam, Farideh.

Jabbari, Ahmad, ed. & tr. see Farjam, Farideh & Azaad, Meyer.

Jabbari, Ahmad, ed. see Taleqani, Mahmood.
Jabbari, Ahmad, tr. see Taleqani, Mahmood.
Jabbour, J. T., et al, eds. Pediatric Neurology Handbook. 2nd ed. (Illus.). 1976. pap. 24.95 (ISBN 0-87488-636-8). Med Exam.
Jaber, Faiz S. Abu- see Abu-Jaber, Faiz S.
Jaber, William. Whatever Happened to the Dinosaurs? LC 78-15939. (Illus.). 160p. (gr. 7 up). 1978. PLB 7.79 o.p. (ISBN 0-671-32872-7). Messner.
Jaberg, Gene & Wargo, Louis G., Jr. The Video Pencil: Cable Communications for Church & Community. LC 80-7951. 156p. 1980. lib. bdg. 18.75 (ISBN 0-8191-1085-X); pap. text ed. 8.50 (ISBN 0-8191-1086-8). U Pr of Amer.
Jabes, Edmond. The Book of Questions: Yael, Elya, Aely. Waldrop, Rosmarie, tr. 256p. 25.95 (ISBN 0-8195-5086-8). Wesleyan U Pr.
Jabes, Jak. Individual Processes in Organizational Behavior. MacKenzie, Kenneth D., ed. LC 77-86012. (Organizational Behavior Ser.). 1978. pap. text ed. 13.95x (ISBN 0-88295-450-4). Harlan Davidson.
Jablon, Howard. Crossroads of Decision: The State Department & Foreign Policy, 1933-1937. LC 82-40459. 192p. 1983. 16.00x (ISBN 0-8131-1483-7). U Pr of Ky.
Jablons, Beverly. Dance Time. 1981. pap. 2.25 o.p. (ISBN 0-425-04797-0). Berkley Pub.
--Dance Time. LC 79-15755. 1979. 8.95 o.p. (ISBN 0-688-03517-5). Morrow.
Jablonski, D., jt. ed. see Fairbridge, R. W.
Jablonski, Donna M. & Crawford, Mark H., eds. Federal Coal Leases: Marketing, Management & Financial Profiles. LC 80-85184. 236p. (Orig.). pap. 97.00 o.p. (ISBN 0-07-606719-X). McGraw.
Jablonski, E. America in the Air War. LC 82-5539. (Epic of Flight Ser.). lib. bdg. 19.96 (ISBN 0-8094-3342-7, Pub. by Time-Life). Silver.
Jablonski, Edward. Encyclopedia of American Music. LC 77-16925. 648p. 1982. 24.95 (ISBN 0-385-08088-3). Doubleday.
--Man with Wings: A Pictorial History of Aviation. LC 77-25596. (Illus.). 1980. 19.95 o.p. (ISBN 0-385-14107-6). Doubleday.
--A Pictorial History of the World War Two Years. LC 77-73328. (Illus.). 1978. 17.95 (ISBN 0-385-12350-7). Doubleday.
Jablonski, Ramona. The Chinese Cut-Out Design Coloring Book: Designs from the World of Nature. (The International Design Library). (Illus.). 48p. 1980. pap. 2.95 (ISBN 0-916144-55-0). Stemmer Hse.
--Medieval Garden Designs. (The International Design Library). (Illus.). 1982. pap. 2.95 (ISBN 0-88045-011-8). Stemmer Hse.
--Victorian Wallpaper Design Coloring Book. (International Design Library). (Illus.). 1981. pap. 2.95 (ISBN 0-916144-89-5). Stemmer Hse.
Jablonski, Ronald, jt. auth. see Moore, Franklin G.
Jablow, Alta. Yes & No: The Intimate Folklore of Africa. LC 72-13867. 223p. 1973. Repr. of 1961 ed. lib. bdg. 17.75x (ISBN 0-8371-6757-4, JAYN). Greenwood.
Jablow, Joseph. Indians of Illinois & Indiana: Illinois, Kickapoo & Potawatomi Indians. Horr, David A., ed. (American Indian Ethnohistory Ser.: North Central & Northeastern Indians). 1974. lib. bdg. 42.00 o.s.i. (ISBN 0-8240-0805-7). Garland Pub.
Jablow, Martha Moraghan see Moraghan Jablow, Martha.
Jabs, Carolyn. Re-Uses: Two Thousand One Hundred Thirty-Three Ways to Recycle & Reuse the Things You Ordinarily Throw Away. 1982. 18.95 (ISBN 0-517-54663-9); pap. 9.95 (ISBN 0-517-54363-X). Crown.
Jabusch, David M. & Littlejohn, Stephen. Elements of Speech Communication: Achieving Competency. LC 80-82760. (Illus.). 464p. 1981. pap. text ed. 14.50 (ISBN 0-395-29730-3); instrs' manual 1.00 (ISBN 0-395-29731-1). HM.
Jaccoma, Richard. Yellow Peril: The Adventures of Sir John Weymouth-Smythe. 1978. 8.95 o.p. (ISBN 0-399-90007-1, Marek). Putnam Pub Group.
Jaciow, Douglas M., jt. auth. see Moore, Gary S.
Jack. Sociology for Community Nurses. 1981. write for info. (ISBN 0-471-25824-5, Wiley Heyden). Wiley.
Jack, Adrienne. Witches & Witchcraft. LC 79-26834. (Easy-Read Fact Bks). (gr. 2-4). 1981. 8.60 (ISBN 0-531-03249-3). Watts.
Jack, Alex, jt. auth. see Kushi, Michio.
Jack, Brian, jt. auth. see Bassett, G. W.
Jack, Ian. English Literature, Eighteen Fifteen to Eighteen Thirty-Two. (Oxford History of English Literature Ser.). 1963. 39.50x (ISBN 0-19-500168-0). Oxford U Pr.
Jack, Ian & Smith, Margaret, eds. The Poetical Works of Robert Browning, 2 Vols. (Oxford English Texts). 1982. Vol. 1, 450 p. 69.00x (ISBN 0-19-811893-7); Vol. 2, 450 p. 69.00x (ISBN 0-19-812317-5). Oxford U Pr.
Jack, Ion, ed. see Bronte, Emily.
Jack, Jane, ed. see Defoe, Daniel.
Jack, M. A., jt. auth. see Mavor, J.
Jack, Robert L., jt. auth. see Little, Hunter.
Jack, Susan, ed. see Dietz, Tim.
Jack, Susan, ed. see Ferriss, Lloyd.
Jack, Susan, ed. see Snow, John.
Jack, Susan, ed. see Swenson, Peter J.
Jackendoff, Nathaniel. Money, Flow of Funds, & Economic Policy. LC 68-30892. (Illus.). 523p. 1968. 27.95x o.p. (ISBN 0-471-06632-X). Wiley
Jackendoff, Ray, jt. auth. see Lerdahl, Fred.
Jackendoff, Ray S. Semantic Interpretation in Generative Grammar. (Studies in Linguistics). 384p. 1972. 30.00x (ISBN 0-262-10013-4); pap. 10.95x (ISBN 0-262-60007-2). MIT Pr.
Jackins, Harvey. Einfurung in das Co-Counseling: Handbuch Fur Co-Counseling - Grundlehrgange. (Ger.). 1974. pap. 5.00 o.p. (ISBN 0-911214-30-5). Rational Isl.
--Elementaer Medradgivnings Handbog. Einhorn, Vibeke, tr. (Danish.). 1976. pap. 5.00 o.p. (ISBN 0-911214-55-0). Rational Isl.
--Fundamentals of Co-Counseling Manual: Greek Translation. Anastassatos, Popi, tr. (Greek.). 1979. pap. 5.00 (ISBN 0-911214-71-2). Rational Isl.
--Fundamentals of Co-Counseling Manual: Hebrew Translation. (Orig., Hebrew.). 1979. pap. 5.00 (ISBN 0-911214-70-4). Rational Isl.
Jackins, Harvey, ed. Human Side of Human Beings: Chinese Translation. Sung See Whai, tr. (Chinese.). pap. 3.00 (ISBN 0-911214-84-4). Rational Isl.
Jacklin, Judith. Blues Brother Private. (Illus.). 128p. 1980. pap. 7.95 (ISBN 0-399-50476-1, Perige). Putnam Pub Group.
--The Blues Brothers: Private. 1980. pap. 7.95 (ISBN 0-686-64416-6, Perigre). Putnam Pub Group.
Jackman, Abraham I. The Paranoid Homosexual Basis of Anti-Semitism. 1979. 8.95 o.p. (ISBN 0-533-03340-3). Vantage.
Jackman, Brian & Evans, Harold. We Learned to Ski. (Illus.). 255p. 1982. pap. 9.95 (ISBN 0-312-85859-0). St Martin.
Jackman, Brian, et al. We Learned to Ski. rev. ed. 1979. pap. 8.95 o.p. (ISBN 0-312-85858-2). St Martin.
Jackman, E. R. & Long, R. A. The Oregon Desert. LC 64-15389. (Illus.). 1964. 14.95 (ISBN 0-87004-074-X). Caxton.
Jackman, Jarrell C. & Borden, Carla M., eds. The Muses Flee Hitler: Cultural Transfer & Adaptation, 1930-1945. (Illus.). 340p. 1983. 17.50 (ISBN 0-87474-554-3); pap. 8.95 (ISBN 0-87474-555-1). Smithsonian.
Jackman, Mary R. & Jackman, Robert W. Class Awareness in the United States. LC 82-2766. 300p. 1982. 24.50x (ISBN 0-520-04674-9). U of Cal Pr.
Jackman, Michael. Political Quotations: Over Twenty-Five Hundred Lively Quotes from Plato to Reagan. 1982. 15.95 o.p. (ISBN 0-686-97695-9). Crown.
Jackman, Oliver. Saw the House in Half: A Novel. LC 73-88971. 352p. 1974. 7.95 (ISBN 0-88258-010-8). Howard U Pr.
Jackman, Raymond J. & Beahrs, Oliver H. Tumors of the Large Bowel. LC 28-23685. (Major Problems in Clinical Surgery Ser.: Vol. 8). (Illus.). 1968. 16.00 o.p. (ISBN 0-7216-5060-0). Saunders.
Jackman, Robert W. Politics & Social Equality: A Comparative Analysis. LC 74-24725. (Comparative Studies in Behavioral Science Ser). 256p. 1975. 33.94x (ISBN 0-471-43128-1, Pub. by Wiley-Interscience). Wiley.
Jackman, Robert W., jt. auth. see Jackman, Mary R.
Jackman, Stuart. The Davidson File. LC 82-13443. 128p. 1983. pap. 7.95 (ISBN 0-664-24459-9). Westminster.
Jack-Roller & Snodrass, Jon. The Jack-Roller at Seventy. LC 81-47825. 192p. 1982. 17.95 (ISBN 0-669-04912-3). Lexington Bks.
Jacks, ed. Associative Information Techniques. (Proceedings). 1971. 17.50 (ISBN 0-444-00089-5). Elsevier.
Jacks, E. High Rupturing Capacity Fuses: Design & Application for Safety in Electrical Systems. 1975. 29.95x (ISBN 0-419-10900-5, Pub. by E & FN Span). Methuen Inc.
Jacks, Elaine B., jt. auth. see Lauter, Leah.
Jacks, L. P. Responsibility & Culture. 1924. 22.50x (ISBN 0-685-89778-8). Elliots Bks.
Jacks, Oliver. Autumn Heroes. LC 77-4629. 1977. 8.95 o.p. (ISBN 0-312-06238-9). St Martin.
Jacks, William, Jr. Supercrip. 180p. (Orig.). 1981. pap. 5.00 (ISBN 0-930012-30-5). Bandanna Bks.
Jackson. Blacks in America: Nineteen Fifty-Four to Nineteen Seventy-Nine. (gr. 6 up). 1980. PLB 6.90 o.p. (ISBN 0-531-02176-9, E09). Watts.
--Concepts of Atomic Physics. 1972. pap. text ed. 7.50 o.p. (ISBN 0-07-094160-2, I). McGraw.
--The Concise Dictionaty of Artist's Signatures. 1981. 50.00 (ISBN 0-933516-39-8). Apollo.
--Newnes Book of Audio. (Illus.). 1979. 16.50 (ISBN 0-408-00429-0). Focal Pr.
--Newnes Book of Video. (Illus.). 1980. 16.50 (ISBN 0-408-00475-4). Focal Pr.
--Newnes Book of Video. 2nd ed. (Illus.). 1983. write for info. (ISBN 0-408-01319-2). Focal Pr.
Jackson & Mac Low. Asymmetries 1-260. 1981. pap. 19.95 (ISBN 0-914162-43-8); pap. 6.95 (ISBN 0-686-86242-2). Knowles.
Jackson, jt. auth. see Gill.
Jackson, A. B. As I See Ghent, a Visual Essay. LC 76-43065. (Illus.). 1979. 29.95 o.p. (ISBN 0-915442-22-1); pap. 16.95 o.p. (ISBN 0-915442-72-8). Donning Co.
Jackson, A. D., jt. auth. see Brown, G. E.
Jackson, A. J. Air Travel. LC 80-50960. (New Reference Library Ser.). PLB 11.96 (ISBN 0-382-06392-9). Silver.
Jackson, Albert & Day, David. Better Than New: A Practical Guide to Renovating Furniture. LC 83-370. (Illus.). 144p. (Orig.). 1983. pap. 8.95 (ISBN 0-8069-7730-2). Sterling.
--The Modelmaker's Handbook. LC 80-2702. (Illus.). 352p. 1981. 21.95 (ISBN 0-394-50788-6). Knopf.
Jackson, Albert S. Analog Computation. 1960. text ed. 35.50 o.p. (ISBN 0-07-032115-9, C). McGraw.
Jackson, Andrew S., jt. auth. see Baugmartner, Ted A.
Jackson, Anthony. A Place Called Home: A History of Low Cost Housing in Manhattan. LC 76-17659. 1976. 22.00x (ISBN 0-262-10017-7). MIT Pr.
Jackson, Arthur, jt. auth. see Clarke, J. Christopher.
Jackson, B., jt. auth. see Lees, R.
Jackson, B. D., jt. ed. see Hooker, J. D.
Jackson, B. D. see Jackson, B. D., et al.
Jackson, B. D., et al, eds. Index Kewensis Supplements. Incl. Vol. 1. 1866-1895. Durand, T. & Jackson, B. D., eds. 1901-06. o.p. (ISBN 0-19-854310-7); Vol. 4. 1906-1910. Prain, D., ed. 1913. o.p. (ISBN 0-19-854313-1); Vol. 6. 1916-1920. Hill, A. W., ed. 1926. 63.00x (ISBN 0-19-854315-8); Vol. 7. 1921-1925. Hill, A. W., ed. 1929. 63.00x (ISBN 0-19-854316-6); Vol. 8. 1926-1930. Hill, A. W., ed. 1933. 63.00x (ISBN 0-19-854317-4); Vol. 10. 1936-1940. Hill, A. W. & Salisbury, E. J., eds. 1947. o.p. (ISBN 0-19-854319-0); Vol. 12. 1951-1955. Taylor, George, ed. 1959. o.p. (ISBN 0-19-854321-2); Vol. 13. 1956-1960. Taylor, George, ed. 1966. 63.00x (ISBN 0-19-854354-9); Vol. 14. 1961-1965. Taylor, George, ed. 1970. 63.00x (ISBN 0-19-854370-0); Vol. 15. 1966-1970. Heslop-Harrison, J., compiled by. 1973. 63.00x (ISBN 0-19-854382-4); Vol. 16. 1971-1976. Brenan, J. P., ed. 1980. 129.00x (ISBN 0-19-854531-2). Oxford U Pr.
Jackson, B. E., jt. auth. see Berkeley, S. G.
Jackson, Barbara, jt. auth. see Blondis, Marion N.
Jackson, Barbara B., jt. ed. see Fiering, Myron B.
Jackson, Barbara E., jt. auth. see Blondis, Marion N.
Jackson, Barbara G., jt. auth. see Benward, Bruce.
Jackson, Barbara W. Policy for the West. Repr. of 1951 ed. lib. bdg. 15.50x (ISBN 0-8371-3428-5, JAPW). Greenwood.
Jackson, Basil. State of Emergency, A Novel. 1982. 13.95 (ISBN 0-393-01605-6). Norton.
Jackson, Betty & Snowden, Derek. Powdered Vegetable Drugs. 1968. 21.95 (ISBN 0-444-19903-9). Elsevier.
Jackson, Blair. The Grateful Dead: The Music Never Stopped. (Illus.). 160p. (Orig.). 1983. pap. 9.95 (ISBN 0-933328-61-3). Delilah Bks.
Jackson, Bonnie F., jt. auth. see Monroe, James I.
Jackson, Brian. Streaming: An Educational System in Miniature. 156p. 1964. pap. 8.95 (ISBN 0-7100-3926-3). Routledge & Kegan.
Jackson, Bruce. Get Your Ass in the Water & Swim Like Me: Narrative Poetry from Black Oral Tradition. LC 74-81626. 1974. 13.50x (ISBN 0-674-35420-6); pap. 6.95x o.p. (ISBN 0-674-35421-4). Harvard U Pr.
--Outside the Law: A Thief's Primer. LC 79-186713. Orig. Title: Thief's Primer: Life of an American Character. 243p. 1972. pap. 5.95 (ISBN 0-87855-531-5). Transaction Bks.
Jackson, Bruce & Christian, Diane. Death Row. (Illus.). 312p. 1980. 19.95 (ISBN 0-686-97234-1). Transaction Bks.
Jackson, Bruce & Jackson, Michael. Doing Drugs. 320p. 1983. pap. 6.95 (ISBN 0-686-42931-1, Pub. by Marek). St Martin.
Jackson, Bruce, ed. see Jackson, Michael & Jackson, Jessica.
Jackson, C. Paul. Rose Bowl Pro. LC 79-125002. (gr. 6-9). 1970. PLB 6.95 o.p. (ISBN 0-8038-6313-6). Hastings.
Jackson, Carl T. The Oriental Religious & American Thought: Nineteenth-Century Explorations. LC 80-25478. (Contributions in American Studies: No. 55). 296p. 1981. lib. bdg. 29.95 (ISBN 0-313-22491-9, JOR/). Greenwood.
Jackson, Carlton. The Dreadful Month. LC 82-72582. (Illus.). 161p. 1982. 16.95 (ISBN 0-87972-205-3); pap. 7.95 (ISBN 0-87972-206-1). Bowling Green Univ.
--Zane Grey. (United States Authors Ser.). 1973. lib. bdg. 11.95 (ISBN 0-8057-0338-1, Twayne). G K Hall.
Jackson, Carolyn, tr. see Garin, Eugenio.
Jackson, Charles. The Practical Vibration Primer. (Illus.). 120p. 1979. 29.95x (ISBN 0-87201-891-1). Gulf Pub.
Jackson, Charles J. English Goldsmiths & Their Marks. 25.00 (ISBN 0-486-21206-8). Dover.
Jackson, Charles O. Passing: The Vision of Death in America. (Contributions in Family Studies: No. 2). 1977. lib. bdg. 27.50 (ISBN 0-8371-9757-0, JPA/). Greenwood.
Jackson, Charles R. How to Buy a Used Car. LC 67-30501. (Illus.). 90p. (gr. 9 up). 1967. 4.25 o.p. (ISBN 0-8019-5292-1). Chilton.
Jackson, Cherry R. Agate Eyes. (Illus., Orig.). 1978. pap. text ed. 4.00 (ISBN 0-9605208-1-3). Sea Urchin.
Jackson, Clyde O. Let the Record Show. 112p. 1983. 7.50 (ISBN 0-682-49985-4). Exposition.
Jackson, D. D. & Wood, P. The Sierra Madre. LC 75-21613. (American Wilderness Ser.). (Illus.). (gr. 6 up). 1975. PLB 15.96 (ISBN 0-8094-1339-6, Pub. by Time-Life). Silver.
Jackson, D. E., jt. auth. see Lyons, Malcom C.
Jackson, D. L. Australian Agricultural Plants. 1982. 20.00 (ISBN 0-686-15350-2, Pub. by Sydney U Pr). Intl Schol Bk Serv.
Jackson, Daphne F., jt. auth. see Barrett, Roger C.
Jackson, Dave. Dial 911: Peaceful Christians & Urban Violence. LC 81-2541. 160p. 1981. pap. text ed. 5.95 (ISBN 0-8361-1952-5). Herald Pr.
Jackson, David & Schuster, Danny. Grape Growing & Wine Making: A Handbook for Cool Climates. (Illus.). 194p. 1981. 27.50 (ISBN 0-9607896-0-X). Altarinda Bks.
Jackson, David A. & Stitch, Stephen P. Recombinant DNA Debate. 1979. text ed. 29.95 (ISBN 0-13-767442-2). P-H.
Jackson, David C., et al, eds. World Shipping Laws. LC 79-18789. 1979. Set incl. binder & 3 releases. looseleaf 340.00 (ISBN 0-379-10165-3). Oceana.
Jackson, David H. The Microeconomics of the Timber Industry. (Replica Edition Ser.). (Illus.). 136p. 1980. softcover 18.50x (ISBN 0-89158-887-6). Westview.
Jackson, David M. Curriculum Development for the Gifted. (Special Education Series). (Illus.). 1980. pap. text ed. 15.00 (ISBN 0-89568-188-9). Spec Learn Corp.
--Foundations of Gifted Education. (Special Education Ser.). (Illus.). 1980. pap. text ed. 15.00 (ISBN 0-89568-189-7). Spec Learn Corp.
Jackson, Diane. August in Abiquiu. LC 80-11214. (Illus.). 64p. (Orig.). 1980. pap. 6.95 (ISBN 0-913270-87-3, Sundial Bks). Sunstone Pr.
Jackson, Don D., ed. Communication, Family & Marriage. LC 68-21576. (The Human Communication Ser.: Vol. 1). (Orig.). 1968. pap. 6.95x (ISBN 0-8314-0015-3). Sci & Behavior.
--Therapy, Communication & Change. LC 68-21577. (The Human Communication Ser: Vol. 2). 1968. pap. 6.95x (ISBN 0-8314-0016-1). Sci & Behavior.
Jackson, Donald. Sagebrush Country. LC 74-32622. (American Wilderness Ser.). (Illus.). 184p. (gr. 6 up). 1975. PLB 15.96 (ISBN 0-8094-1218-7). Silver.
--Underground Worlds. (Planet Earth Ser.). 1982. lib. bdg. 19.92 (ISBN 0-8094-4321-X, Pub. by Time-Life). Silver.
Jackson, Donald A., jt. auth. see Jackson, Nancy F.
Jackson, Donald D. The Aeronauts. (Epic of Flight Ser.). lib. bdg. 19.96 (ISBN 0-8094-3267-6). Silver.
--Flying the Mail. LC 82-2020. (Epic of Flight Ser.). lib. bdg. 19.96 (ISBN 0-8094-3330-3, Pub. by Time-Life). Silver.
Jackson, Dorothy. Backward Glance. 240p. 1983. 12.00 (ISBN 0-682-49964-1). Exposition.
Jackson, Douglas W. Soviet Union. rev. ed. LC 83-80051. (World Cultures Ser). (Illus.). 168p. (gr. 6 up). 1983. text ed. 11.20 ea.1-4 copies,5 or more copies 8.96 ea. (ISBN 0-88296-196-9); tchr's ed 8.96 (ISBN 0-88296-369-4); skills manual incl. (ISBN 0-685-54535-0). Fideler.
Jackson, Douglas W. & Pescar, Susan C. The Young Athlete's Health Handbook. 352p. 1981. 15.95 (ISBN 0-89696-118-4, An Everest House Book); pap. 9.95 (ISBN 0-89696-124-9). Dodd.
Jackson, E. B. & Jackson, R. L. Industrial Information Systems: A Manual for Higher Managements & Their Information-Librarian Associates. LC 78-15890. (The Information Sciences Ser.). 314p. 1979. 45.00 (ISBN 0-87933-328-6). Hutchinson Ross.
Jackson, Edgar N. The Many Faces of Grief. 7.95 o.p. (ISBN 0-686-92379-0, 6238). Hazelden.
--A Psychology for Preaching. LC 81-47430. (Harper's Ministers Paperback Library). 208p. 1981. pap. 6.01i (ISBN 0-06-064111-8, RD366, HarpR). Har-Row.
--Telling a Child About Death. 1965. pap. 4.95 (ISBN 0-8015-7494-3, 0481-140, Hawthorn). Dutton.
--Understanding Prayer. LC 81-47845. 224p. pap. 7.21i (ISBN 0-06-064112-6, RD 377, HarpR). Har-Row.
--You & Your Grief. 1961. 4.25 (ISBN 0-8015-9036-1, 0413-120, Hawthorn). Dutton.
Jackson, Elaine. Lufkin: From Sawdust to Oil. 1982. 24.95 (ISBN 0-87201-437-1). Gulf Pub.
Jackson, Elinor & Dundon, H. Dwyer, eds. Occupational Therapy Examination Review Book, Vol. 1. 3rd ed. 1974. pap. 12.79 (ISBN 0-87488-475-6). Med Exam.
Jackson, Elizabeth R., ed. see Peret, Benjamin.
Jackson, Ellen. Subject Guide to Major United States Government Publications. LC 68-25844. 1968. 9.00 (ISBN 0-8389-0056-9). ALA.
Jackson, Emily. The History of Hand Made Lace: Dealing with the Origin of Lace, the Growth of the Great Lace Centres, Etc. LC 70-136558. (Tower Bks.). (Illus.). xiv, 245p. 1972. Repr. of 1900 ed. 47.00x (ISBN 0-8103-3935-8). Gale.
Jackson, Erika, tr. see Bumke, Joachim.
Jackson, Eugene & Geiger, Adolph. German Made Simple. LC 65-10615. pap. 4.95 (ISBN 0-385-00129-0, Made). Doubleday.
Jackson, Eugene & LoPreato, Joseph. Italian Made Simple. pap. 4.95 (ISBN 0-385-00736-1, Made). Doubleday.

Jackson, Eugene & Rubio, Antonio. French Made Simple. LC 73-9033. pap. 4.95 (ISBN 0-385-08691-1, Made). Doubleday.

--Spanish Made Simple. pap. 4.95 (ISBN 0-385-01212-8, Made). Doubleday.

Jackson, Forrest W., compiled by. Bible Studies for Special Occasions in Youth Ministry. LC 82-70109. 1982. pap. 4.95 (ISBN 0-8054-3617-0). Broadman.

Jackson, Frank & Irving, W. Ronald. Border Terriers. (Foyle's Handbks). 1969. 3.95 (ISBN 0-685-55815-0). Palmetto Pub.

Jackson, Geoffrey. Concorde Diplomacy: The Ambassador's Role in the World Today. 254p. 1982. 23.50 (ISBN 0-241-10524-2, Pub. by Hamish Hamilton England). David & Charles.

Jackson, George. COBOL. (Illus.). 294p. 1982. 16.95 (ISBN 0-8306-0051-5, 1398); pap. 9.95 (ISBN 0-8306-1398-6). TAB Bks.

--Soledad Brother: The Prison Letters of George Jackson. 1970. 7.95 o.p. (ISBN 0-698-10347-5, Coward). Putnam Pub Group.

Jackson, George P. White & Negro Spirituals, Their Life Span & Kinship. (Music Reprint Ser). (Illus.). xii, 349p. 1975. Repr. of 1944 ed. lib. bdg. 35.00 (ISBN 0-306-70667-9). Da Capo.

Jackson, George P., ed. Down-East Spirituals & Others: Three Hundred Songs Supplementary to the Author's "Spiritual Folk-Songs of Early America". LC 74-34317. (Music Reprint Ser). (Illus.). 296p. 1975. Repr. of 1943 ed. lib. bdg. 29.50 (ISBN 0-306-70666-0). Da Capo.

Jackson, Gordon. The Prison Expose & Muldergate: A Case Study in Changing Government-Press Relations in South Africa. (Graduate Student Paper Competition Ser.: No. 3). 25p. (Orig.). 1980. pap. text ed. 2.00 (ISBN 0-941934-31-4). Ind U Afro-Amer Arts.

Jackson, Gordon E. Pastoral Care & Process Theology. LC 81-40159. 266p. (Orig.). 1981. lib. bdg. 23.50 (ISBN 0-8191-1710-2); pap. text ed. 12.50 (ISBN 0-8191-1711-0). U Pr of Amer.

Jackson, H. C. The Good 'Uns: A Memoir of H.C. "Bud" Jackson. (Illus.). 280p. 1980. 17.95 o.p. (ISBN 0-914330-38-1). Pioneer Pub Co.

Jackson, H. L. Teaching of New Topics in Informatics. 1982. 36.25 (ISBN 0-444-86364-8). Elsevier.

Jackson, H. L. & Wiechers, G., eds. Post-Secondary & Vocational Education in Data Processing. 186p. 1980. 38.50 (ISBN 0-444-85398-7, North Holland). Elsevier.

Jackson, Harry F. & O'Donnell, Thomas F. Back Home in Oneida: Hermon Clarke & His Letters. LC 64-23344. 1965. 10.00 (ISBN 0-8156-0041-0). Syracuse U Pr.

Jackson, Hartley H. Mammals of Wisconsin. (Illus.). 518p. 1961. 27.50t (ISBN 0-299-02150-5). U of Wis Pr.

Jackson, Haywood. An Act of God. 1979. pap. 1.00 o.p. (ISBN 0-686-26167-4). Samisdat.

Jackson, Helen H. Ramona. 1970. pap. 3.50 (ISBN 0-380-00383-X, 59303-1). Avon.

Jackson, Henry F. The FLN in Algeria: Party Development in a Revolutionary Society. LC 76-47889. (Contributions in Afro-American & African Studies: No. 30). (Illus.). 1977. lib. bdg. 29.95 (ISBN 0-8371-9401-6, JFA/). Greenwood.

Jackson, Herbert L. Basic Nuclear Physics for Medical Personnel. (Illus.). 164p. 1973. 13.75x o.p. (ISBN 0-398-02663-7). C C Thomas.

Jackson, Herbert W. Introduction to Electric Circuits. 5th ed. (Illus.). 736p. 1981. text ed. 25.95 (ISBN 0-13-481432-0). P-H.

Jackson, Holbrook. The Complete Nonsense of Edward Lear. 288p. 1982. Repr. of 1947 ed. lib. bdg. 30.00 (ISBN 0-8495-3400-3). Arden Lib.

--The Fear of Books. LC 82-15785. x, 199p. 1982. Repr. of 1932 ed. lib. bdg. 29.75x (ISBN 0-313-23738-7, JAFB). Greenwood.

Jackson, Holdrook, ed. see Lear, Edward.

Jackson, Horace G., jt. auth. see Hodges, David A.

Jackson, Ian, ed. see Mabogunje, A. L., et al.

Jackson, Ian T., et al. Atlas of Craniomaxillofacial Surgery. LC 81-14193. (Illus.). 752p. 1982. text ed. 110.50 (ISBN 0-8016-4295-7). Mosby.

Jackson, Irene V., compiled by. Afro-American Religious Music: A Bibliography & a Catalogue of Gospel Music. LC 78-60527. (Illus.). 1979. lib. bdg. 29.95 (ISBN 0-313-20560-4, JGM/). Greenwood.

Jackson, J. D. Classical Electrodynamics. 2nd ed. LC 75-9962. 864p. 1975. text ed. 36.95x (ISBN 0-471-43132-X). Wiley.

Jackson, J. D., et al, eds. Annual Review of Nuclear & Particle Science, Vol. 32. LC 53-995. (Illus.). 1982. text ed. 25.00 (ISBN 0-8243-1532-4). Annual Reviews.

Jackson, J. H. The Eternal Flame: The Story of a Preaching Mission in Russia. 1956. 2.50 (ISBN 0-686-42985-0). Townsend Pr.

--Many But One: The Ecumenics of Charity. LC 64-19899. 1964. 4.50 (ISBN 0-686-42984-2). Townsend Pr.

--Nairobi: A Joke, a Junket, or a Journey? LC 76-27046. 1976. 5.50 (ISBN 0-935990-03-8). Townsend Pr.

--A Short History of France from Early Times to 1972. 2nd ed. (Illus.). 260p. 1974. 39.50 (ISBN 0-521-20485-2); pap. 10.95 (ISBN 0-521-09864-5). Cambridge U Pr.

--Stars in the Night: Report on a Visit to Germany. 1950. 1.50 (ISBN 0-686-42986-9). Townsend Pr.

--A Story of Christian Activism: History of the National Baptist Convention U. S. A., Inc. LC 80-17408. (Illus.). 790p. 1980. 19.95 (ISBN 0-935990-01-1). Townsend Pr.

--Unholy Shadows & Freedom's Holy Light. LC 67-29805. 1967. 5.00 (ISBN 0-935990-05-4). Townsend Pr.

Jackson, J. H., tr. see Shih Nai-An.

Jackson, J. Hampden. England since the Industrial Revolution, 1815-1848. LC 75-7239. (Illus.). 298p. 1975. Repr. of 1949 ed. lib. bdg. 17.75x (ISBN 0-8371-8102-X, JAES). Greenwood.

Jackson, J. Mark, Jr., jt. auth. see Bellante, Donald M.

Jackson, J. W. Cardiothoracic Surgery. 3rd ed. (Operative Surgery Ser.). 1978. 130.00 (ISBN 0-407-00604-4). Butterworth.

Jackson, Jack. Comanche Moon. LC 79-88142. 1979. pap. 2.95 (ISBN 0-89620-079-5). Tex St Hist Assn.

--Comanche Moon. (Illus.). 128p. (Orig.). 1979. pap. 6.95 (ISBN 0-89620-079-5). Rip Off.

Jackson, Jacqueline. The Ghost Boat. LC 69-11783. (Illus.). (gr. 4-6). 1969. 4.95 o.p. (ISBN 0-316-45479-6). Little.

--Turn Not Pale, Beloved Snail: A Book About Writing & Other Things. 192p. 1974. 8.95 (ISBN 0-316-45481-8). Little.

Jackson, James J. Steam Boiler Operation: Principles & Practice. (Illus.). 1980. text ed. 19.95 (ISBN 0-13-846311-5). P-H.

Jackson, James L., ed. Three Elizabethan Fencing Manuals, 3 vols. in one. Incl. True Arte of Defence. Di Grassi, Giacomo. Repr. of 1594 ed; His Practice. Saviolo, Vincentio. Repr. of 1595 ed; Paradoxes of Defence. Silver, George. Repr. of 1599 ed. LC 72-6321. 640p. 1972. Repr. 70.00x (ISBN 0-8201-1107-4). Schol Facsimiles.

Jackson, James R. Method & Imagination in Coleridge's Criticism. LC 77-400918. 1969. 10.00x (ISBN 0-674-57135-5). Harvard U Pr.

Jackson, Jane F. & Jackson, Joseph H. Infant Culture. LC 78-4351. 1979. pap. 4.95 o.p. (ISBN 0-452-25221-0, Z5221, Plume). NAL.

Jackson, Jeremy C. No Other Foundation. LC 79-92017. 384p. 1979. 12.95 (ISBN 0-89107-169-5, Crossway Bks). Good News.

Jackson, Jerome A. The Mid-South Bird Notes of Ben B. Coffey, Jr. (Special Publications: No. 1). 127p. (Orig.). 1981. pap. 10.00 (ISBN 0-686-37622-6). Mississippi Orni.

Jackson, Jessica, jt. auth. see Jackson, Michael.

Jackson, Joan S., jt. ed. see De Ford, Miriam A.

Jackson, John A., ed. Migration. LC 70-85720. (Sociological Studies: No. 2). (Illus.). 1969. 27.95 (ISBN 0-521-07645-5). Cambridge U Pr.

--Professions & Professionalization. LC 75-123346. (Sociological Studies: No. 3). 1970. 34.50 (ISBN 0-521-07982-9). Cambridge U Pr.

--Role. (Cambridge Sociological Studies: No. 4). (Illus.). 1971. 24.95 (ISBN 0-521-08307-9). Cambridge U Pr.

Jackson, John E., ed. Public Needs & Private Behavior in Metropolitan Areas. LC 75-6732. 1975. prof ref 19.50x (ISBN 0-88410-035-9). Ballinger Pub.

Jackson, John H. & Morgan, Cyril P. Organization Theory: A Macro Perspective for Management. 2nd ed. (Illus.). 432p. 1982. 23.95 (ISBN 0-13-641415-X). P-H.

Jackson, John H., jt. auth. see Mathis, Robert L.

Jackson, John N. Surveys for Town & Country Planning. LC 76-7580. 1976. Repr. of 1963 ed. lib. bdg. 18.00x (ISBN 0-8371-8866-0, JAST). Greenwood.

Jackson, John P. & Dichtl, Rudolph J. The Science & the Art of Hot Air Ballooning. LC 76-24774. (Reference Library of Science & Technology Ser.: Vol. 7). (Illus.). 1977. lib. bdg. 12.00 o.s.i. (ISBN 0-8240-9903-6). Garland Pub.

Jackson, John W. With the British Army in Philadelphia, 1777-1778. LC 78-10657. (Illus.). 1978. 16.95 o.p. (ISBN 0-89141-057-0). Presidio Pr.

Jackson, Jonathan. The Teenage Chef. LC 82-20144. (Illus.). 96p. (gr. 12 up). 1983. 10.95 (ISBN 0-7232-6219-5); pap. 5.95 (ISBN 0-7232-6248-9). Warne.

Jackson, Joseph F. Louise Colet et Ses Amis Litteraires. 1937. text ed. 16.50x (ISBN 0-686-83609-X). Elliots Bks.

Jackson, Joseph H. Anybody's Gold. LC 70-133990. (Illus.). 320p. (Orig.). 1982. pap. 7.95 (ISBN 0-87701-273-3). Chronicle Bks.

Jackson, Joseph H., jt. auth. see Jackson, Jane F.

Jackson, Judith, II & Robson, Graham. Man & the Automobile. LC 79-14104. (Illus.). 1979. 24.95 o.p. (ISBN 0-07-032119-1). McGraw.

Jackson, K. A., et al, eds. Crystal Growth 1974. LC 74-82900. 708p. 1975. 127.75 (ISBN 0-444-10703-7, North-Holland). Elsevier.

Jackson, K. C. Textbook of Lithology. 1970. text ed. 38.50 (ISBN 0-07-032143-4, C). McGraw.

Jackson, K. F. The Art of Solving Problems. LC 74-83579. 262p. 1975. 10.00 o.p. (ISBN 0-312-05460-2). St Martin.

Jackson, K. G. Dictionary of Electrical Engineering. 1975. text ed. 12.95 o.p. (ISBN 0-600-41060-9). Butterworth.

Jackson, Karl D. Traditional Authority, Islam & Rebellion: A Study of Indonesian Political Behavior. 1980. 33.00x (ISBN 0-520-03769-3). U of Cal Pr.

Jackson, Kathryn. The Animals' Merry Christmas. (Illus.). 72p. (ps-3). 1950. PLB 12.23 (ISBN 0-307-63773-5, Golden Pr); pap. 4.95 (ISBN 0-307-13773-2). Western Pub.

--Golden Book of Three Hundred Sixty-Five Stories. 1955. 8.05 (ISBN 0-307-15557-9, Golden Pr); PLB 12.23 o.p. (ISBN 0-307-65575-X). Western Pub.

Jackson, Kenneth. Gaelic Notes in the Book of Deer. LC 78-161293. 1972. 42.50 (ISBN 0-521-08264-1). Cambridge U Pr.

Jackson, Kenneth T. Ku Klux Klan in the City, 1915-1930. (Urban Life in America Ser.). 1967. 17.95 o.p. (ISBN 0-19-500591-0); pap. text ed. 7.95x (ISBN 0-19-500918-5). Oxford U Pr.

Jackson, Kenneth T., jt. ed. see Dinnerstein, Leonard.

Jackson, Livia. Elli: Coming of Age in the Holocaust. 1983. pap. 6.95 (ISBN 0-8129-6327-X). Times Bks.

Jackson, M. Recruiting, Interviewing & Selecting: A Manual for Line Managers. 1973. 21.95 o.p. (ISBN 0-07-084406-2, P&RB). McGraw.

Jackson, M. & Berger, G. Vaginal Contraception. 1980. lib. bdg. 32.50 (ISBN 0-8161-2211-3, Pub. by Hall Medical). G K Hall.

Jackson, M. P. & Hanby, V. Work Creation. 1979. text ed. 29.75x (ISBN 0-566-00287-6). Gower Pub Ltd.

Jackson, M. P., jt. auth. see Dix, Owen R.

Jackson, MacDonald P. The Revenger's Tragedy: A Facsimile of the 1607-8 Quarto-Attributed to Thomas Middleton. LC 81-72052. 120p. 1983. 19.50 (ISBN 0-8386-3131-2). Fairleigh Dickinson.

Jackson, Mark, jt. auth. see Bellante, Donald.

Jackson, Martin, jt. auth. see Cassel, Don.

Jackson, Mary H. Guide to Correspondence in Spanish. 64p. 1981. 25.00x (ISBN 0-85950-335-6, Pub. by Thornes England). State Mutual Bk.

--How Does Your Garden Grow? (Illus.). 64p. 1980. 4.95 (ISBN 0-517-54027-4, C N Potter Bks) (ISBN 0-517-54118-1). Crown.

Jackson, Mason. Pictorial Press, Its Origin & Progress. LC 68-21776. (Illus.). 1968. Repr. of 1885 ed. 30.00x (ISBN 0-8103-3355-4). Gale.

Jackson, Michael. Allegories of the Wilderness: Ethics & Ambiguity in Kuranko Narratives. LC 81-47772. (African Systems of Thought Ser.). 336p. 1982. 30.00x (ISBN 0-253-30471-7). Ind U Pr.

--The Kuranko: Dimensions of Social Reality in a West African Society. LC 77-70341. 1977. 26.00 (ISBN 0-312-46112-7). St Martin.

--The Pocket Guide to Beer. 144p. 1982. pap. 5.95 (ISBN 0-399-50578-4, Perige). Putnam Pub Group.

Jackson, Michael & Jackson, Jessica. Your Father's Not Coming Home Anymore: Children Tell How They Survive Divorce. Jackson, Bruce, ed. 324p. 1981. 12.95 (ISBN 0-399-90109-4, Marek). Putnam Pub Group.

Jackson, Michael, jt. auth. see Jackson, Bruce.

Jackson, Michael M. & Liebman, Bonnie. Salt: The Complete Brand Name Guide to Sodium Content. LC 82-40505. 224p. 1983. pap. 4.95 (ISBN 0-89480-361-1). Workman Pub.

Jackson, Michael P. & Hanby, Victor J. British Work Creation Programmes. 87p. 1982. pap. text ed. 23.50x (ISBN 0-566-00523-9). Gower Pub Ltd.

Jackson, Michael P. & Valencia, B. Michael. Financial Aid Through Social Work. (Library of Social Work Ser.). 1979. 18.00x (ISBN 0-7100-0176-2). Routledge & Kegan.

Jackson, Miles M., ed. Comparative & International Librarianship. LC 77-98710. 1970. lib. bdg. 29.95x (ISBN 0-8371-3327-0, JAL/). Greenwood.

--Contemporary Developments in Librarianship: An International Handbook. (Illus.). 688p. 1982. lib. bdg. write for info. (ISBN 0-85365-834-X, Pub. by Lib Assn England). Oryx Pr.

Jackson, N. Civil Engineering Materials. 2nd ed. (Engineering Text Ser). (Illus.). 338p. 1982. text ed. 40.00x (ISBN 0-333-28959-5). Scholium Intl.

--Civil Engineering Materials. 2nd ed. LC 76-381536. (Illus.). 1980. pap. 19.50x (ISBN 0-686-96883-2). Scholium Intl.

Jackson, Nancy F. & Jackson, Donald A. Getting along with Others: Teaching Social Effectiveness to Children, 2 Vol. (Skill Lessons & Activities Ser.). 150p. 1983. write for info. spiral bdg. Res Press.

Jackson, Nell. The Coaches Collection of Women's Track Drills. LC 81-85974. (Illus.). 160p. Date not set. pap. 6.95 (ISBN 0-918438-97-7). Leisure Pr.

Jackson, Neta. A New Way to Live. LC 82-83392. 104p. (Orig.). 1982. pap. 4.95 (ISBN 0-8361-3323-4). Herald Pr.

Jackson, P. B. & Ribbinck, Tony. Mbunas, Malawi Cichlids. (Illus.). 128p. (Orig.). 1975. pap. 6.95 o.p. (ISBN 0-87666-454-0, PS-740). TFH Pubns.

Jackson, P. M. The Political Economy of Bureaucracy. LC 82-22674. 304p. 1983. text ed. 27.50x (ISBN 0-389-20352-1). B&N Imports.

Jackson, P. M., jt. auth. see Brown, C. V.

Jackson, Paul T. Collectors' Contact Guide. 2nd ed. (Record Collectors' Source Bk.: No. 3). 58p. 1975. pap. 3.00x o.p. (ISBN 0-916262-02-2). Recorded Sound.

Jackson, Philip W. The Teacher & the Machine. LC 68-12729. (Horace Mann Lecture Ser.). 1968. 4.95x o.p. (ISBN 0-8229-3142-7). U of Pittsburgh Pr.

Jackson, Philip W., et al. Perspectives on Inequality. (Reprint Ser.: No. 8). 5.50 (ISBN 0-916690-08-3). Harvard Educ Rev.

Jackson, R. Comparison of SAT Score Trends in Selected Schools Judged to Have Traditional or Experimental Orientations. 1977. 2.00 o.p. (ISBN 0-87447-021-8, 251715). College Bd.

--Transport in Porous Catalysts. (Chemical Engineering Monographs: Vol. 4). 1977. 51.00 (ISBN 0-444-41593-9). Elsevier.

Jackson, R. H. Children, the Environment & Accidents. (Illus.). 164p. 1977. 40.00x (ISBN 0-272-79406-6, Pub. by Pitman Bks England); text ed. 18.00x (ISBN 0-686-96893-X). State Mutual Bk.

--Land Use In America. (Scripta Geography Ser.). 226p. 1982. 22.95x (ISBN 0-470-27363-1). Halsted Pr.

Jackson, R. L., jt. auth. see Jackson, E. B.

Jackson, Richard. Acts of Mind: Conversations with Contemporary Poets. LC 82-4767. 232p. 1983. text ed. 19.95 (ISBN 0-8173-0122-4). U of Ala Pr.

--Part of the Story. Pack, Robert, ed. (Grove Press Poetry Ser.). 96p. 1983. 12.50 (ISBN 0-394-53133-7, GP863). Grove.

--Part of the Story. Pack, Robert, ed. (Grove Press Poetry Ser.). 96p. 1983. pap. 5.95 (ISBN 0-394-62451-3, Ever). Grove.

Jackson, Richard H. Land Use in America. LC 80-20184. (Scripta Ser. in Geography). 226p. 1981. 29.95x o.p. (ISBN 0-470-27063-2). Halsted Pr.

Jackson, Richard H. & Hudman, Lloyd E. World Regional Geography: Issues for Today. LC 81-16430. 534p. 1982. text ed. 26.95 (ISBN 0-471-06214-6); tchr's. ed. 10.00 (ISBN 0-471-06212-X). Wiley.

Jackson, Richard M. The Machinery of Justice in England. 7th ed. LC 77-4401. 1978. 74.50 (ISBN 0-521-21688-5); pap. 29.95 (ISBN 0-521-29231-X). Cambridge U Pr.

Jackson, Robert. Dunkirk. LC 76-11705. 1977. 8.95 o.p. (ISBN 0-312-22190-8). St Martin.

--Fighter Pilots of World War II. (Inflation Fighters Ser.). 176p. 1982. pap. cancelled o.s.i. (ISBN 0-8439-1138-7, Leisure Bks). Nordon Pubns.

--The Jet Age. 176p. 1980. 9.95 o.p. (ISBN 0-312-44221-1). St Martin.

Jackson, Robert H. & Rosberg, Carl G. Personal Rule in Black Africa: Prince, Autocrat, Prophet, Tyrant. LC 80-25439. 350p. 1981. 25.00x (ISBN 0-520-04185-2); pap. 10.95 (ISBN 0-520-04209-3). U of Cal Pr.

Jackson, Robert J. Rebels & Whips: An Analysis of Dissension, Discipline & Cohesion in British Political Parties. LC 68-19078. 1968. 25.00 (ISBN 0-312-66570-9). St Martin.

Jackson, Ronald. China Clipper. LC 79-51191. (Illus.). 1980. 11.95 (ISBN 0-89696-061-7, An Everest House Book). Dodd.

--The Power of Progaganda. (Illus.). 224p. 1983. 13.00 (ISBN 0-682-49942-0). Exposition.

Jackson, Rope. Bonfire. 112p. 1983. 7.00 (ISBN 0-682-49947-1). Exposition.

Jackson, Rosemary. Fantasy: The Literature of Subversion. 1981. 15.95x (ISBN 0-416-71170-7); pap. 7.50x (ISBN 0-416-71180-4). Methuen Inc.

Jackson, Russell, ed. see Jones, Henry A.

Jackson, Russell, ed. see Wilde, Oscar.

Jackson, Ruth A. Combing the Coast II: Santa Cruz to Carmel. LC 82-4327. (Illus.). 120p. 1982. pap. 6.95 (ISBN 0-87701-236-9). Chronicle Bks.

Jackson, S. M. & Lane, S. Personal & Community Health. 1982. 25.00x (ISBN 0-7020-0576-2, Pub. by Cas sell England). State Mutual Bk.

Jackson, Sarah & Patterson, Mary Ann. A Children's History of Texas: Text & Coloring Book. (Illus.). (gr. 1-6). 1972. 3.95 (ISBN 0-89015-056-7). Eakin Pubns.

Jackson, Shirley. Haunting of Hill House. 176p. 1982. pap. 2.75 (ISBN 0-446-31036-0). Warner Bks.

--The Lottery: Or The Adventures of James Harris. (Illus.). 306p. 1949. pap. 7.95 (ISBN 0-374-51681-2). FS&G.

--Witchcraft of Salem Village. (gr. 4-6). 1956. 2.95 (ISBN 0-394-80369-8, BYR); PLB 5.99 (ISBN 0-394-90369-2). Random.

Jackson, Sidney, et al, eds. A Century of Service. LC 76-41815. 1976. text ed. 30.00 (ISBN 0-8389-0220-0). ALA.

Jackson, Stanley. J. P. Morgan. LC 81-40333. 464p. 1983. 22.95 (ISBN 0-8128-2824-0). Stein & Day.

Jackson, T. Sturges, ed. Logs of the Great Sea Fights: 1794-1805, 2 vols. 1981. Repr. text ed. 35.00x ea. Vol. 1, 346pp (ISBN 0-85937-266-9). Vol. 2, 348pp (ISBN 0-85937-267-7). Set. text ed. 65.00x (ISBN 0-911378-40-5). Sheridan.

Jackson, Timothy. Friends Are for Signing. (Illus.). 34p. (Orig.). (YA) (gr. 7-9). 1982. pap. 1.95x (ISBN 0-913072-51-6). Natl Assn Deaf.

Jackson, Tom. Guerrilla Tactics in the Job Market. 288p. 1982. pap. 3.50 (ISBN 0-553-23160-X). Bantam.

--The Perfect Resume. LC 79-7802. (Illus.). 160p. 1981. pap. 8.95 (ISBN 0-385-15027-X, Anch). Doubleday.

Jackson, Tom, ed. see Simon, Anne, et al.

Jackson, Tony, ed. Learning Through Theatre: Essays & Casebooks on Theatre in Education. 240p. 1982. 20.00 (ISBN 0-7190-0789-5). Manchester.

Jackson, W. A. Douglas see Creed, Virginia & Douglas Jackson, W. A.

Jackson, W. H., ed. Knighthood in Medieval Literature. 112p. 1981. text ed. 25.00x (ISBN 0-85991-094-6, Pub. by Boydell & Brewer). Biblio Dist.

Jackson, Wallace. Vision & Re-vision in Alexander Pope. 204p. 1983. 17.95 (ISBN 0-8143-1729-4). Wayne St U Pr.

Jackson, Walter C., jt. auth. see White, Newman I.

Jackson, William Eric. The Structure of Local Government in England & Wales. 4th ed. LC 74-29792. 1976. Repr. of 1960 ed. lib. bdg. 20.50x (ISBN 0-8371-8001-5, JASL). Greenwood.

Jackson, William F., jt. auth. see Snyder, Llewellyn R.

Jacob, Diane B. & Arnold, Judith M. A Virginia Military Institute Album, 1839-1910. LC 82-1865. (Illus.). 112p. 1982. 14.95x (ISBN 0-8139-0947-3). U Pr of Va.

Jacob, Ellen. Dance in New York. (Illus.). 1980. pap. 6.95 (ISBN 0-8256-3147-5, Quick Fox). Putnam Pub Group.

Jacob, Francois. The Logic of Life: A History of Heredity. Spillman, Betty E., tr. from Fr. 1976. 10.00 (ISBN 0-394-47246-2, Vin); pap. 7.95 (ISBN 0-394-71007-X). Random.

Jacob, Gordon. Orchestral Technique: A Manual for Students. 2nd ed. 1940. 7.95x o.p. (ISBN 0-19-318201-7). Oxford U Pr.

--Orchestral Technique: A Manual for Students. 100p. 1982. pap. 11.25 (ISBN 0-19-318204-1). Oxford U Pr.

Jacob, H. Crime & Justice in Urban America. 1980. pap. 11.95 (ISBN 0-13-192849-X). P-H.

Jacob, Herbert. Urban Justice: Law & Order in American Cities. 160p. 1973. pap. 10.95 ref. ed. (ISBN 0-13-938944-X). P-H.

Jacob, Herbert & Weissberg, Robert. Elementary Political Analysis. 2nd ed. (Illus.). 320p. 1975. text ed. 18.95 (ISBN 0-07-032136-1, C). McGraw.

Jacob, Herbert, jt. auth. see Eisenstein, James.

Jacob, John & Jacob, Meera. Fruit & Vegatable Carving. revised ed. 99p. 1983. 25.00 (ISBN 0-686-42989-3). Hippocrene Bks.

Jacob, M., ed. CERN: 25 Years of Physics, Vol. 4. (Physics Reports Reprint Bk.). 1981. 68.00 (ISBN 0-444-86146-7). Elsevier.

--Dual Theory. LC 74-83266. (Physics Reports Reprint Book Ser.: Vol. 1). 399p. 1975. 30.00 (ISBN 0-444-10743-6, North-Holland). Elsevier.

Jacob, Max. The Dice Cup: Selected Prose Poems. Brownstein, Michael, ed. Ashbery, John, et al, trs. LC 79-26610. 122p. (Orig.). 1980. pap. 6.00 (ISBN 0-915342-32-4). SUN.

Jacob, Meera, jt. auth. see Jacob, John.

Jacob, Morris B., jt. auth. see Scheflan, Leopold.

Jacob, Nina, jt. auth. see Oftedal, Laura.

Jacob, Stanley. DMSO: The True Story. 1981. 10.95x (ISBN 0-688-00716-3). Cancer Control Soc.

Jacob, Stanley W., et al. Structure & Function in Man. 4th ed. LC 77-84673. (Illus.). 678p. 1978. text ed. 16.95 o.p. (ISBN 0-7216-5098-8); 9.95 o.p. (ISBN 0-7216-5099-6). Saunders.

Jacobi, Charles A. Textbook of Anatomy & Physiology in Radiologic Technology. 2nd ed. LC 74-20889. 438p. 1975. text ed. 19.95 o.p. (ISBN 0-8016-2390-1). Mosby.

Jacobi, Charles T. The Printers' Vocabulary. LC 68-30613. 1975. Repr. of 1888 ed. 30.00x (ISBN 0-8103-3309-0). Gale.

Jacobi, Henry. Building Your Best Voice. 271p. 1982. 17.95 (ISBN 0-13-086595-8); pap. 8.95 (ISBN 0-13-086587-7). P-H.

Jacobi, Karl G. Gesammelte Werke, 8 vols. 2nd ed. LC 68-31427. (Illus., Ger., Includes Supplementband Vorlesugen Uber Dynamik). 1969. Vols. 1-7. 215.00 (ISBN 0-8284-0226-4); Vol. 8. 20.00 (ISBN 0-8284-0227-2). Chelsea Pub.

Jacobi, Lotte. Theatre & Dance Photographs. 46p. (Orig.). 1982. pap. 10.95 (ISBN 0-914378-93-7). Countryman.

Jacobi, Peter. The Messiah Book: The Life & Times of G. F. Handel's Greatest Hit. (Illus.). 169p. 1982. 10.95 (ISBN 0-312-53072-2). St Martin.

--Writing with Style: The News Story & the Feature. LC 82-62576. (Communications Library). 111p. (Orig.). 1982. pap. 15.00 (ISBN 0-931368-12-X). Ragan Comm.

Jacobowitz, Henry. Electricity Made Simple. pap. 4.95 (ISBN 0-385-00436-2, Made). Doubleday.

--Electronics Made Simple. rev. ed. LC 64-20579. pap. 4.95 (ISBN 0-385-01227-6, Made). Doubleday.

Jacobs. Metal Microstructures in Zeolites. (Studies in Surface Science & Catalysis: Vol. 12). 1982. 70.25 (ISBN 0-444-42112-2). Elsevier.

Jacobs, et al. PPBES Show & Tell Handbook. (Research Bulletin: No. 18). 2.00 (ISBN 0-685-57173-4). Assn Sch Busn.

Jacobs, A. G. Basketball Rules in Pictures. rev. ed. pap. 3.95 (ISBN 0-448-01592-7, G&D). Putnam Pub Group.

Jacobs, Albert L. Patent & Trademark Forms, 4 vols. LC 76-448212. 1977. looseleaf with 1979 rev. pages 265.00 (ISBN 0-87632-218-6); Vols. 4 & 4A. 140.00 (ISBN 0-686-77279-2); Vols. 4B & 4C. 140.00 (ISBN 0-686-77280-6); Vols. 4, 4A, 4B, & 4C. 265.00 (ISBN 0-686-77281-4). Boardman.

Jacobs, Allan, jt. auth. see Jacobs, Leland.

Jacobs, Allan B. Making City Planning Work. LC 78-72577. 323p. (Orig.). 1978. pap. 15.95 (ISBN 0-918286-12-3). Planners Pr.

Jacobs, Allan D. & Jacobs, Leland B., eds. Sports & Games in Verse & Rhyme. LC 74-18274. (Poetry Ser.). (Illus.). 64p. (gr. 2-5). 1975. PLB 6.69 (ISBN 0-8116-4118-X). Garrard.

Jacobs, Anita. Where Has Deedie Wooster Been All These Years? 240p. (YA) (gr. 7-12). 1983. pap. 2.25 (ISBN 0-440-98955-8, LFL). Dell.

Jacobs, Arnold S. The Impact of Rule 10b-5, 3 vols. LC 74-27270. 1974. cancelled (ISBN 0-87632-093-0). Boardman.

--Litigation & Practice Under Rule 10B-5, 2 Vols. 2nd ed. LC 81-15493. 1982. 70.00 ea., looseleaf (ISBN 0-87632-093-0). Boardman.

--Manual of Corporate Forms for Securities Practice. LC 81-3857. 1981. 75.00 (ISBN 0-87632-302-6). Boardman.

--Opinion Letters in Securities Matters: Text-Clauses-Law. LC 79-24005. 1980. looseleaf 75.00 (ISBN 0-87632-301-8). Boardman.

Jacobs, Arthur, ed. Choral Music. 1979. pap. 4.95 o.p. (ISBN 0-14-020533-0, Pelican). Penguin.

Jacobs, Ava. And Nobody Came. 210p. Date not set. cancelled (ISBN 0-89733-057-9). Academy Chi Ltd.

Jacobs, Barbara S., jt. ed. see Gay, James.

Jacobs, Barry G. Guide to Federal Housing Programs. 297p. pap. text ed. 20.00 (ISBN 0-87179-275-3). BNA.

Jacobs, Barry L. & Gelperin, Alan, eds. Serotonin Neurotransmission & Behavior. 430p. 1981. text ed. 49.50x (ISBN 0-262-10023-1). MIT Pr.

Jacobs, Bill. Thank You for My Wife & Kid. pap. 1.50 o.p. (ISBN 0-686-79562-8). Paulist Pr.

Jacobs, C. O. & Harrell, W. R. Agricultural Power & Machinery. 480p. 1983. text ed. 19.96 (ISBN 0-07-032210-4); write for info tchr's manual & key (ISBN 0-07-032212-0); write for info activity guide (ISBN 0-07-032211-2). Mcgraw.

Jacobs, Charles M., et al. Measuring the Quality of Patient Care: The Rationale for Outcome Audit. LC 75-29234. 1976. prof ref 22.50x (ISBN 0-88410-128-2). Ballinger Pub.

Jacobs, Clyde. Justice Frankfurter & Civil Liberties. LC 74-1331. (Civil Liberties in American History Ser.). 265p. 1974. Repr. of 1961 ed. lib. bdg. 35.00 (ISBN 0-306-70585-0). Da Capo.

Jacobs, Clyde E. The Eleventh Amendment & Sovereign Immunity. LC 71-149959. (Contributions in American History: No. 19). 1972. lib. bdg. 25.00 (ISBN 0-8371-6058-8, JAE/). Greenwood.

--Law Writers & the Courts. LC 73-251. (American Constitutional & Legal History Ser.). 234p. 1973. Repr. of 1954 ed. lib. bdg. 29.50 (ISBN 0-306-70570-2). Da Capo.

Jacobs, D., jt. ed. see Ogra, P. L.

Jacobs, D. G. Sources of Tritium & Its Behavior upon Release to the Environment. LC 68-67209. (AEC Critical Review Ser.). 90p. 1968. pap. 10.25 (ISBN 0-87079-345-4, TID-24635); microfiche 4.50 (ISBN 0-87079-346-2, TID-24635). DOE.

Jacobs, Dan N. & Paul, Ellen F., eds. Studies of the Third Wave: Recent Migration of Soviet Jews to the United States. (Replica Edition Ser.). 176p. 1981. lib. bdg. 22.00 (ISBN 0-86531-143-9). Westview.

Jacobs, Dan N., et al. Comparative Politics: Introduction to the Politics of the United Kingdom, France, Germany, & the Soviet Union. 384p. 1983. pap. text ed. 14.95x (ISBN 0-934540-05-5). Chatham Hse Pubs.

Jacobs, David. An American Conscience: Woodrow Wilson's Search for World Peace. LC 71-135770. (Illus.). (gr. 5-9). 10.95 (ISBN 0-06-022794-X, HarpJ). Har-Row.

--Architecture. LC 73-89394. (World of Culture Ser). (Illus.). 12.95 o.p. (ISBN 0-88225-107-4). Newsweek.

--Master Builders of the Middle Ages. LC 69-13692. (Horizon Caravel Bks.). 154p. (YA) (gr. 7 up). 1969. 12.95i (ISBN 0-06-022803-2, HarpJ); PLB 14.89 (ISBN 0-06-022804-0). Har-Row.

Jacobs, Diane. Hollywood Renaissance. 1980. pap. 6.95 o.s.i. (ISBN 0-440-53382-1, Delta). Dell.

Jacobs, Donald M. Antebellum Black Newspapers: Indices to New York Freedom's Journal (1827-1829), Rights of All (1829) The Weekly Advocate (1837) & The Colored American (1837-1841) LC 76-2119. 600p. (Orig.). 1976. lib. bdg. 45.00 (ISBN 0-8371-8824-5, JWA/). Greenwood.

Jacobs, Donald P., ed. Regulating Business: The Search for an Optimum. LC 78-50678. 261p. 1978. pap. text ed. 6.95 (ISBN 0-917616-27-8). ICS Pr.

Jacobs, Donald R. Pilgrimage in Mission. 168p. (Orig.). 1983. pap. 6.50 (ISBN 0-8361-3324-2). Herald Pr.

Jacobs, Eric. European Trade Unionism. LC 73-84698. 180p. 1973. text ed. 24.50x (ISBN 0-8419-0106-6). Holmes & Meier.

Jacobs, Everett M., ed. The Organization of Agriculture in the Soviet Union & Eastern Europe. LC 79-3807. (Studies in East European & Soviet Russian Agrarian Policy: Vol. 2). 500p. 1983. text ed. 49.50x (ISBN 0-916672-41-7). Allanheld.

--Soviet Local Politics & Government. (Illus.). 224p. 1983. text ed. 28.50x (ISBN 0-04-329042-6). Allen Unwin.

Jacobs, Everett M., ed. see Wadekin, Karl-Eugen.

Jacobs, F. G., ed. Yearbook of European Law 1981. 1982. 89.00x (ISBN 0-19-825384-2). Oxford U Pr.

Jacobs, Flora G. Doll's Houses in America: Historic Preservation in Minature. (Illus.). 395p. 1974. pap. 16.95 (ISBN 0-686-37145-3). Wash Dolls Hse.

--The Nineteen Hundred Seven Mace Toy Catalogue. (Illus.). 126p. 1977. pap. 6.00 (ISBN 0-686-35939-9). Wash Dolls Hse.

--The Toy Shop Mystery. (Illus.). (gr. k-3). 1960. PLB 4.99 o.p. (ISBN 0-698-30375-X, Coward). Putnam Pub Group.

Jacobs, Francine. Africa's Flamingo Lake. LC 79-13117. (Illus.). 96p. (gr. 4-6). 1979. 7.75 (ISBN 0-688-22197-1); PLB 7.44 (ISBN 0-688-32197-6). Morrow.

--Bermuda Petrel: The Bird That Would Not Die. LC 80-20466. (Illus.). 40p. (gr. k-3). 1981. 8.95 (ISBN 0-688-00240-4); PLB 8.59 (ISBN 0-688-00244-7). Morrow.

--Coral. (See & Read Book). (Illus.). 48p. (gr. 1-4). 1980. PLB 6.99 (ISBN 0-399-61145-2). Putnam Pub Group.

--Cosmic Countdown: What Astronomers Have Learned About the Life of the Universe. (Illus.). 192p. 1983. 9.95 (ISBN 0-87131-404-5). M Evans.

--Fire Snake: The Railroad That Changed East Africa. LC 80-13840. (Illus.). 96p. (gr. 4-6). 1980. 9.25 (ISBN 0-688-22232-3); PLB 8.88 (ISBN 0-688-32232-8). Morrow.

--The Freshwater Eel. LC 72-9697. (Illus.). 64p. (gr. 3-7). 1973. 7.95 (ISBN 0-688-20066-4). Morrow.

--The Legs of the Moon. (Illus.). (gr. k-3). 1971. PLB 4.39 o.p. (ISBN 0-698-30214-1, Coward). Putnam Pub Group.

--Nature's Light: The Story of Bioluminescence. LC 73-18326. (Illus.). 96p. (gr. 3-7). 1974. 8.95 (ISBN 0-688-20115-6); PLB 8.59 (ISBN 0-688-30115-0). Morrow.

--The Red Sea. (Illus.). (gr. 4-6). 1978. 8.75 (ISBN 0-688-22150-5); PLB 8.40 (ISBN 0-688-32150-X). Morrow.

--A Secret Language of Animals, Communication by Pheromones. LC 75-42409. (gr. 4-6). 1976. 7.95 (ISBN 0-688-22071-1); PLB 7.63 (ISBN 0-688-32071-6). Morrow.

--Sounds in the Sea. LC 77-345. (Illus.). (gr. 3-7). 1977. 7.95 (ISBN 0-688-22113-0); PLB 7.63 (ISBN 0-688-32113-5). Morrow.

--Supersaurus. (Illus.). 48p. 1982. PLB 6.99 (ISBN 0-399-61150-9). Putnam Pub Group.

Jacobs, Frank. Mad for Better or Verse. (Orig.). pap. 0.75 o.p. (ISBN 0-451-05069-X, T5069, Sig). Nal.

--The Mad World of William M. Gaines. 1973. 7.95 o.p. (ISBN 0-8184-0054-4). Lyle Stuart.

Jacobs, Frank & Davis, Jack. The Mad Jock Book. (Illus.). 192p. 1983. pap. 1.95 (ISBN 0-446-30079-9). Warner Bks.

Jacobs, Frederic & Allen, Richard J., eds. Experiential Learning & the Missions of Graduate & Professional Education. LC 81-48478. 1982. 7.95x (ISBN 0-87589-891-2, EL-15). Jossey-Bass.

Jacobs, Gabriel. When Children Think: Using Journals to Encourage Creative Thinking. LC 71-78837. 1970. pap. text ed. 4.95 (ISBN 0-8077-1558-1). Tchrs Coll.

Jacobs, Glenn, jt. ed. see Gerstl, Joel.

Jacobs, Harriet B. see Brent, Linda, pseud.

Jacobs, Henry. Cymbeline: An Annotated Bibliography. Godshalk, William, ed. LC 82-48082. (Garland Shakespeare Bibliographies). 590p. 1982. lib. bdg. 60.00 (ISBN 0-8240-9258-9). Garland Pub.

Jacobs, Holly, et al. Testing ESL Composition: A Practical Approach. 160p. 1981. pap. 13.95 (ISBN 0-88377-225-6). Newbury Hse.

Jacobs, Howard, ed. see Trosclair.

Jacobs, I. M., jt. auth. see Wozencraft, John M.

Jacobs, J. Celtic Fairy Tales. (Illus.). 8.50 (ISBN 0-8446-2302-4). Peter Smith.

--Connla & the Fairy Maiden. (Illus.). 8p. (Orig.). 1982. pap. 2.50 (ISBN 0-914676-71-7, Pub. by Envelope Bks). Green Tiger Pr.

Jacobs, J. A. The Earth's Core & Geomagnetism. 1963. inquire for price o.p. (ISBN 0-08-010340-5); pap. 5.50 o.p. (ISBN 0-08-010339-1). Pergamon.

--A Textbook of Geonomy. LC 74-9662. 328p. (Orig.). 23.00 o.p. (ISBN 0-470-43445-7). Krieger.

Jacobs, James B. New Perspectives on Prisons & Imprisonment. 264p. 1983. text ed. 29.50x (ISBN 0-8014-1586-1); pap. 10.95x (ISBN 0-8014-9248-3). Cornell U Pr.

--Stateville: The Penitentiary in Mass Society-Studies in Crime & Justice. LC 76-22957. 1978. pap. 7.95 (ISBN 0-226-38977-4, P788, Phoen). U of Chicago Pr.

Jacobs, James B. & Crotty, Norma M. Guard Unions & the Future of the Prisons. LC 78-62007. (Institute of Public Employment Monograph: No. 9). 60p. 1978. pap. 3.50 (ISBN 0-87546-070-4). ILR Pr.

Jacobs, Jane. Economy of Cities. 1970. pap. 3.95 (ISBN 0-394-70584-X, Vin). Random.

Jacobs, Jay. Color Encyclopedia of World Art. (Illus.). 324p. (YA) 1975. 25.00 o.p. (ISBN 0-517-52208-X). Crown.

--Cooking for All It's Worth: Making the Most of Every Morsel of Food You Buy. 1983. 14.95 (ISBN 0-07-032155-8). McGraw.

Jacobs, Jerald A. Association Law Handbook. 368p. 1981. text ed. 40.00 (ISBN 0-87179-366-0). BNA.

Jacobs, Jerome L. Interplay. 1979. 10.00 o.p. (ISBN 0-07-032146-9). Readers Digest Pr.

Jacobs, Jerry. The Moral Justification of Suicide. (Illus.). 144p. 1982. pap. 12.75x (ISBN 0-398-04725-1). C C Thomas.

--The Search for Help: A Study of the Retarded Child in the Community. LC 82-13535. 150p. 1983. pap. text ed. 8.25 (ISBN 0-8191-2680-2). U Pr of Amer.

--Social Problems Through Social Theory: A Selective View. rev. ed. 1983. text ed. 14.95x (ISBN 0-88105-013-X); pap. text ed. 9.95x (ISBN 0-88105-014-8). Cap & Gown.

Jacobs, Jerry, jt. auth. see Schwartz, Howard.

Jacobs, John & Aultman, Dick. Quick Cures for Weekend Golfers. (Illus.). 1979. 10.95 o.p. (ISBN 0-671-22658-4). S&S.

Jacobs, John & Bowden, Ken. Practical Golf. LC 82-73277. 192p. 1983. pap. 10.95 (ISBN 0-689-70634-0). Atheneum.

Jacobs, John A., et al. Physics & Geology. 2nd ed. (International Ser. in the Earth & Planetary Sciences). (Illus.). 448p. 1974. text ed. 27.50 (ISBN 0-07-032148-5, C). McGraw.

Jacobs, John J., jt. auth. see Tobin, Charles E.

Jacobs, Joseph. Johnny Cake. (Illus.). (gr. 1-3). 1967. PLB 4.29 o.p. (ISBN 0-399-60324-7). Putnam Pub Group.

--More English Folk & Fairy Tales. (Illus.). (gr. 3-6). 1904. 5.00 o.p. (ISBN 0-399-20172-6). Putnam Pub Group.

--The Story of the Three Little Pigs. (Illus.). 32p. (Orig.). (ps-3). 1980. 8.95 (ISBN 0-399-20733-3); pap. 3.95 (ISBN 0-399-20732-5). Putnam Pub Group.

Jacobs, Joseph, ed. The Fables of Aesop. LC 66-24908. (Illus.). (gr. k up). 1966. 8.95x (ISBN 0-8052-3068-8); pap. 4.95 (ISBN 0-8052-0138-6). Schocken.

--The Most Delectable History of Reynard the Fox. LC 67-15750. (gr. 4 up). 1967. 3.95x o.p. (ISBN 0-8052-3225-7); pap. 1.95 o.p. (ISBN 0-8052-0151-3). Schocken.

Jacobs, Joseph, ed. see Painter, William.

Jacobs, Joy. They Were Women, Too. LC 1-67319. 375p. 1981. pap. 9.95 (ISBN 0-87509-304-3). Chr Pubns.

Jacobs, Judy, jt. auth. see Enteen, Shellie.

Jacobs, Lawrence, et al. Computerized Tomography of the Orbit & Sella Turcica. 376p. 1980. text ed. 98.00 (ISBN 0-685-95340-8). Raven.

Jacobs, Leland. Monkey & the Bee. (Golden Beginning Readers). (ps-2). 1969. PLB 6.08 (ISBN 0-307-61158-2, Golden Pr). Western Pub.

Jacobs, Leland & Jacobs, Allan. Behind the Circus Tent. LC 67-15703. (General Juvenile Bks). (Illus.). (gr. k-5). 1967. PLB 3.95g (ISBN 0-8225-0259-3). Lerner Pubns.

Jacobs, Leland B. April Fool! LC 72-10677. (Venture Ser). (Illus.). 40p. (gr. 1). 1973. PLB 6.69 (ISBN 0-8116-6728-6). Garrard.

--Hello, Pleasant Places! LC 72-77470. (Venture Ser.). (Illus.). 64p. (gr. 2). 1972. PLB 6.89 (ISBN 0-8116-6951-3). Garrard.

--Hello, Year! LC 72-77468. (Venture Ser.). (Illus.). 64p. (gr. 2). 1972. PLB 6.89 (ISBN 0-8116-6954-8). Garrard.

--I Don't I Do. LC 79-155570. (Venture Ser). (Illus.). (gr. 1). 1971. PLB 6.69 (ISBN 0-8116-6705-7). Garrard.

--Teeny-Tiny. LC 75-6550. (Easy Venture Ser). (Illus.). 32p. (gr. k-2). 1976. PLB 6.69 (ISBN 0-8116-6070-2). Garrard.

--What Would You Do? LC 72-1772. (Venture Ser). (Illus.). 64p. (gr. 2). 1972. PLB 6.89 (ISBN 0-8116-6963-7). Garrard.

Jacobs, Leland B., ed. All About Me: Verses I Can Read. LC 73-155566. (Venture Ser.). (Illus.). (gr. 1). 1971. 6.09 o.p. (ISBN 0-8116-6701-4). Garrard.

--Funny Bone Ticklers in Verse & Rhyme. LC 73-3178. (Poetry Ser.). (Illus.). 64p. (gr. 2-5). 1973. PLB 6.69 (ISBN 0-8116-4115-5). Garrard.

--Playtime in the City. LC 70-155565. (Venture Ser). (Illus.). (gr. 1). 1971. PLB 6.69 (ISBN 0-8116-6700-6). Garrard.

--Poetry for Chuckles & Grins. LC 68-16162. (Poetry Ser.). (Illus.). (gr. 2-5). 1968. PLB 6.69 (ISBN 0-8116-4101-5). Garrard.

--Poetry of Witches, Elves & Goblins. LC 70-99767. (Poetry Ser.). (Illus.). (gr. 2-5). 1970. PLB 6.69 (ISBN 0-8116-4105-8). Garrard.

Jacobs, Leland B., jt. ed. see Jacobs, Allan D.

Jacobs, Leland B., et al. Individualizing Reading Practices. LC 58-8337. 1958. pap. 4.95x (ISBN 0-8077-1554-9). Tchrs Coll.

Jacobs, Lenworth M. & Bennett, Barbara R. Emergency Medical Technician (EMT) Solidus Paramedic Training: Perspectives on Status & Trends. (Emergency Health Services Quarterly Ser.: Vol. 2, No. 1). 80p. 1983. pap. text ed. 15.00 (ISBN 0-917724-51-8, B51). Haworth Pr.

Jacobs, Lewis. Rise of the American Film: A Critical History with an Essay "Experimental Cinema in America 1921-1947". LC 68-25845. (Illus.). 1968. text ed. 24.95x (ISBN 0-8077-1556-5); pap. 15.95x (ISBN 0-8077-1555-7). Tchrs Coll.

Jacobs, Lewis, ed. The Movies As Medium. LC 71-97611. (Illus.). 352p. 1970. pap. 7.95 o.p. (ISBN 0-374-50852-6, N388). FS&G.

Jacobs, Linda. Annemarie Proell: Queen of the Mountain. LC 75-4501. (Women Who Win Ser.: No. 3). 1974. lib. bdg. 6.95 (ISBN 0-88436-170-5); pap. 3.95 (ISBN 0-88436-171-3). EMC.

--Arthur Ashe: Alone in the Crowd. LC 76-15. (Black American Athletes Ser.). (Illus.). 40p. 1976. PLB 6.95 (ISBN 0-88436-263-9); pap. 3.95 (ISBN 0-88436-264-7). EMC.

--Barbara Jordan: Keeping Faith. LC 78-9550. (Headliners II). (gr. 3-5). 1978. text ed. 6.95 (ISBN 0-88436-432-1). EMC.

--A Candle, a Feather, a Wooden Spoon. LC 74-23770. (Really Me! Ser). (gr. 6-9). 1974. PLB 6.95 (ISBN 0-88436-150-0); pap. 3.95 (ISBN 0-88436-151-9). EMC.

--Cathy Rigby: On the Beam. LC 74-31424. (Women Who Win Ser.: No. 2). 1975. lib. bdg. 6.95 (ISBN 0-88436-168-3); pap. 3.50 o.p. (ISBN 0-88436-169-1). EMC.

--Checkmate, Julie. LC 74-23756. (Really Me! Ser). (gr. 6-9). 1974. PLB 6.95 (ISBN 0-88436-154-3); pap. 3.95 (ISBN 0-88436-155-1). EMC.

--Cher: Simply Cher. LC 75-15552. (Women Behind the Bright Lights Ser.). (Illus.). 40p. (gr. 4 up). 1975. PLB 6.95 (ISBN 0-88436-186-1); pap. 3.95 (ISBN 0-88436-187-X). EMC.

--Chris Evert, Tennis Pro. LC 74-2300. (Women Who Win Ser.: No. 1). 1974. 6.95 (ISBN 0-88436-128-4); pap. 3.95 (ISBN 0-88436-129-2). EMC.

--Cindy Nelson: North Country Skier. LC 76-7592. (Women Who Win Ser.: No. 4). (Illus.). 40p. 1976. PLB 6.95 (ISBN 0-88436-232-9); pap. 3.95 (ISBN 0-88436-233-7). EMC.

--Elton John: Reginald Dwight & Company. LC 75-26990. (Men Behind the Bright Lights Ser.). (Illus.). 40p. (gr. 4 up). 1976. PLB 6.95 (ISBN 0-88436-213-2); pap. 3.50 o.p. (ISBN 0-88436-214-0). EMC.

--Everyone's Watching Tammy. LC 74-23759. (Really Me! Ser). (gr. 6-9). 1974. PLB 6.95 (ISBN 0-88436-152-7); pap. 3.95 (ISBN 0-88436-153-5). EMC.

--Evonne Goolagong: Smiles & Smashes. LC 74-31267. (Women Who Win Ser.: No. 2). 1975. lib. bdg. 6.95 (ISBN 0-88436-158-6); pap. 3.95 (ISBN 0-88436-159-4). EMC.

--Gabe Kaplan: A Spirit of Laughter. LC 78-28232. (Headliners 1). (gr. 3-5). 1978. text ed. 6.95 (ISBN 0-88436-428-3); pap. 3.95 (ISBN 0-88436-429-1). EMC.

--Jane Pauley: A Heartland Style. LC 77-27805. (Headliners 1). (gr. 3-5). 1978. text ed. 6.95 (ISBN 0-88436-474-7); pap. 3.95 (ISBN 0-88436-425-9). EMC.

--Janet Lynn, Sunshine on Ice. LC 74-2133. (Women Who Win Ser.: No. 1). 1974. 6.95 (ISBN 0-88436-122-5); pap. 3.95 (ISBN 0-88436-123-3). EMC.

--Jim Croce: The Feeling Lives On. LC 75-26984. (Men Behind the Bright Lights Ser.). (Illus.). 40p. (gr. 4 up). 1976. PLB 6.95 (ISBN 0-88436-215-9); pap. 3.50 o.p. (ISBN 0-88436-216-7). EMC.

--Jimmie Walker: Funny Is Where It's At. LC 77-24950. (Center Stage Ser.). 40p. (gr. 4-12). 1977. PLB 6.95 (ISBN 0-88436-416-X); pap. 3.95 (ISBN 0-88436-417-8). EMC.

--Joan Moore Rice: The Olympic Dream. LC 75-5519. (Women Who Win Ser.: No. 3). 1974. lib. bdg. 6.95 (ISBN 0-88436-164-0); pap. 3.95 (ISBN 0-88436-165-9). EMC.

--John Denver: A Natural High. LC 75-26649. (Men Behind the Bright Lights). (Illus.). 40p. (gr. 4 up). 1976. PLB 6.95 (ISBN 0-88436-211-6); pap. 3.95 (ISBN 0-88436-212-4). EMC.

--John Travolta: Making an Impact. LC 77-24995. (Center Stage Ser.). (Illus.). 40p. (gr. 4-12). 1977. PLB 6.95 (ISBN 0-88436-412-7); pap. 3.95 (ISBN 0-88436-413-5). EMC.

--Julius Erving: Doctor J & Julius W. LC 76-86. (Black American Athletes Ser.). (Illus.). 40p. (gr. 4-6). 1976. PLB 6.95 (ISBN 0-88436-265-5); pap. 3.95 (ISBN 0-88436-266-3). EMC.

--Laura Baugh: Golf's Golden Girl. LC 74-31187. (Women Who Win Ser.: No. 2). 1974. lib. bdg. 6.95 (ISBN 0-88436-160-8); pap. 3.95 (ISBN 0-88436-161-6). EMC.

--Lee Elder: The Daring Dream. LC 75-45429. (Black American Athletes Ser.). (Illus.). 40p. (gr. 4-6). 1976. PLB 6.95 (ISBN 0-88436-267-1); pap. 3.95 (ISBN 0-88436-268-X). EMC.

--Lindsay Wagner: Her Own Way. LC 77-22955. (Center Stage Ser.). (Illus.). 40p. (gr. 4-12). 1977. PLB 6.95 (ISBN 0-88436-414-3); pap. 3.95 (ISBN 0-88436-415-1). EMC.

--Madeline Manning Jackson: Running on Faith. LC 76-16. (Black American Athletes Ser.). (Illus.). 40p. (gr. 4-6). 1976. PLB 6.95 (ISBN 0-88436-261-2); pap. 3.95 (ISBN 0-88436-262-0). Emc.

--Martina Navratilova: Tennis Fury. LC 76-8421. (Women Who Win Ser.). (Illus.). 40p. (gr. 4-6). 1976. PLB 6.95 (ISBN 0-88436-236-1); pap. 3.95 (ISBN 0-88436-237-X). EMC.

--Mary Decker: Speed Records & Spaghetti. LC 75-2225. (Women Who Win Ser.: No. 3). 1974. lib. bdg. 6.95 (ISBN 0-88436-162-4); pap. 3.95 (ISBN 0-88436-163-2). EMC.

--Natalie Cole: Star Child. LC 77-23114. (Center Stage Ser.). (Illus.). 40p. (gr. 4-12). 1977. PLB 6.95 (ISBN 0-88436-410-0); pap. 3.95 (ISBN 0-88436-411-9). EMC.

--Olga Korbut, Tears & Triumph. LC 74-2384. (Women Who Win Ser.: No.1). 1974. 6.95 (ISBN 0-88436-124-1); pap. 3.50 o.p. (ISBN 0-88436-125-X). EMC.

--Olivia Newton John: Sunshine Supergirl. LC 75-15757. (Women Behind the Bright Lights). (Illus.). 40p. (gr. 4 up). 1975. PLB 6.95 (ISBN 0-88436-184-5); pap. 3.95 (ISBN 0-88436-185-3). EMC.

--Roberta Flack: Sound of Velvet Melting. LC 75-15627. (Women Behind the Bright Lights). (Illus.). 40p. (gr. 4 up). 1975. PLB 6.95 (ISBN 0-88436-188-8); pap. 3.95 (ISBN 0-88436-189-6). EMC.

--Robin Campbell: Joy in the Morning. LC 76-8446. (Women Who Win Ser.: No.4). (Illus.). 40p. (gr. 4-6). 1976. PLB 6.95 (ISBN 0-88436-238-8); pap. 3.95 (ISBN 0-88436-239-6). EMC.

--Robyn Smith: In Silks. LC 76-8489. (Women Who Win Ser.: No. 4). (Illus.). 40p. (gr. 4-6). 1976. PLB 6.95 (ISBN 0-88436-234-5); pap. 3.95 (ISBN 0-88436-235-3). EMC.

--Rosemary Casals: The Rebel Rosebud. LC 75-4646. (Women Who Win Ser.: No. 3). 1974. lib. bdg. 6.95 (ISBN 0-88436-166-7); pap. 3.95 (ISBN 0-88436-167-5). EMC.

--Shane Gould, Olympic Swimmer. LC 74-2228. (Women Who Win Ser.: No.1). 1974. 6.95 (ISBN 0-88436-126-8); pap. 3.50 o.p. (ISBN 0-88436-127-6). EMC.

--Stevie Wonder: Sunshine in the Shadows. LC 75-33012. (Men Behind the Bright Lights). (Illus.). 1976. text ed. 6.95 (ISBN 0-88436-257-4); pap. text ed. 3.50 o.p. (ISBN 0-88436-258-2). EMC.

--Valerie Harper: The Unforgettable Snowflake. LC 75-15661. (Women Behind the Bright Lights). (Illus.). 40p. (gr. 4 up). 1975. PLB 6.95 (ISBN 0-88436-190-X); pap. 3.95 (ISBN 0-88436-191-8). EMC.

--Will the Real Jeannie Murphy Please Stand up? LC 74-23758. (Really Me! Ser). (gr. 6-9). 1974. PLB 6.95 (ISBN 0-88436-156-X); pap. 3.95 (ISBN 0-88436-157-8). EMC.

--Wilma Rudolph: Run for Glory. LC 74-31084. (Women Who Win Ser.: No. 2). 1975. lib. bdg. 6.95 (ISBN 0-88436-172-1); pap. 3.50 o.p. (ISBN 0-88436-173-X). EMC.

Jacobs, Lou. Electronic Flash. 2nd. ed. (Illus.). 1971. 4.95 o.p. (ISBN 0-8174-0447-3, Amphoto). Watson-Guptill.

--The Shapes of Our Land. LC 73-111526. (Illus.). (gr. 7-12). 1970. PLB 3.86 o.p. (ISBN 0-399-60579-7). Putnam Pub Group.

Jacobs, Lou, Jr. Amphoto Guide to Lighting. (Illus.). 1979. pap. text ed. 10.95 o.p. (ISBN 0-8174-2467-9, Amphoto); pap. 7.95 (ISBN 0-8174-2140-8). Watson-Guptill.

--Amphoto Guide to Selling Photographs: Rates & Rights. (Illus.). 1979. 10.95 o.p. (ISBN 0-8174-2481-4, Amphoto); pap. 7.95 (ISBN 0-8174-2153-X). Watson-Guptill.

--Expressive Photography. LC 78-15600. (Illus.). 1979. 24.50x (ISBN 0-673-16333-4). Scott F.

--Konica Autoreflex Manual. 1974. 11.95 o.p. (ISBN 0-8174-0551-8, Amphoto). Watson-Guptill.

--The Konica Guide. rev. ed. (Modern Camera Guide Ser.). (Illus.). 128p. 1980. 11.95 o.p. (ISBN 0-8174-4124-7, Amphoto); pap. 7.95 (ISBN 0-8174-4125-5). Watson-Guptill.

--The Konica Guide. (Modern Camera Guides Ser.). (Illus.). 1978. 11.95 o.p. (ISBN 0-8174-2501-2, Amphoto); pap. 6.95 o.p. (ISBN 0-8174-2121-1). Watson-Guptill.

--Olympus OM Camera Manual. LC 76-16459. (Illus.). 1977. 11.95 o.p. (ISBN 0-8174-2412-1, Amphoto). Watson-Guptill.

--Photography Today for Personal Expression: Principles, Equipment, Techniques. LC 76-42205. (Illus.). 1977. text ed. 20.95x (ISBN 0-673-16515-9). Scott F.

--The Photography Workbook. (Illus.). 136p. 1980. pap. 9.95 (ISBN 0-8174-5518-3, Amphoto). Watson-Guptill.

Jacobs, Louis, ed. Aspects of Vertebrate History. 1980. 22.00 o.p. (ISBN 0-89734-052-3); pap. 9.95 (ISBN 0-89734-053-1). Mus Northern Ariz.

Jacobs, Maeona K., jt. auth. see Chinn, Peggy L.

Jacobs, Marcia, jt. auth. see Greenburg, Dan.

Jacobs, Mark. Jumping Up & Down on the Roof Throwing Bags of Water on People. LC 79-7495. (Illus.). 160p. 1980. pap. 10.95 o.p. (ISBN 0-385-15282-5, Dolp). Doubleday.

Jacobs, Mark & Kokrda, Ken. Photography in Focus. LC 75-20872. (Illus.). 181p. 1976. pap. 9.25 o.p. (ISBN 0-8174-2901-8, Amphoto). Watson-Guptill.

--Photography in Focus. rev ed. LC 75-20872. (Illus.). 181p. 1981. pap. 12.95 (ISBN 0-8174-5405-5, Amphoto). Watson-Guptill.

Jacobs, Martina M., et al, eds. see McGinnis, Helen J.

Jacobs, Mildred Spires. Come Unto Me. (Illus.). 56p. (Orig.). (gr. 5-6). 1982. pap. 2.95 (ISBN 0-9609612-0-8). Enrichment.

Jacobs, Mitchell, et al. Massachusetts Taxation: The Law & the Lore. LC 81-81903. 491p. 1982. 50.00 (ISBN 0-316-45539-3). Little.

Jacobs, Morris B., jt. auth. see Brookes, Vincent J.

Jacobs, Nancy F., jt. auth. see Willoughby, William E.

Jacobs, Nancy R., jt. ed. see Siegel, Mark A.

Jacobs, Nicolas, jt. auth. see Schmidt, A. V.

Jacobs, Paul I., jt. auth. see Meirowitz, Marcus.

Jacobs, Peter A., ed. Carboniogenic Activity of Zeolites. LC 77-1788. 1977. 55.50 (ISBN 0-444-41556-4). Elsevier.

Jacobs, Philip. Economics of Health & Medical Care. 328p. 1980. pap. text ed. 17.95 (ISBN 0-8391-1526-1). Univ Park.

Jacobs, Robert L., tr. Wagner Rehearsing the Ring: An Eye-Witness Account of the Stage Rehearsals of the First Bayeuth Festival. (Illus.). 145p. 1983. 19.95 (ISBN 0-686-84715-6). Cambridge U Pr.

Jacobs, Robert L., tr. see Wagner, Richard.

Jacobs, Roderick A. & Rosenbaum, Peter S. English Transformational Grammar. 1968. text ed. 25.50x (ISBN 0-673-15682-6). Scott F.

Jacobs, Roderick A., jt. auth. see Jacobs, Suzanne.

Jacobs, Roderick A. & Rosenbaum, Peter S., eds. Transformations, Style & Meaning. LC 70-138978. (Orig.). 1971. pap. text ed. 14.50x (ISBN 0-673-15684-2). Scott F.

Jacobs, Russell, ed. see Kressen, David C.

Jacobs, Suzanne & Jacobs, Roderick A. The College Writer's Handbook. 2nd ed. 1976. pap. text ed. 14.50x (ISBN 0-673-15683-4). Scott F.

Jacobs, Sylvia M. The African Nexus: Black American Perspectives on the European Partitioning of Africa, 1880-1920. LC 80-660. (Contributions in Afro-American & African Studies: No. 55). (Illus.). xiv, 311p. 1981. lib. bdg. 29.95 (ISBN 0-313-22312-2, JEP/). Greenwood.

Jacobs, Valerie. Black & White Shaded Drawing. (Illus.). 64p. 1975. pap. 5.50 (ISBN 0-85440-295-0, Pub. by Steinerbooks). Anthroposophic.

Jacobs, W. W. Cargoes: Famous Stories of the Sea. (Orig.). pap. 2.50 (ISBN 0-8283-1430-6, 26, IPL). Branden.

Jacobs, William J. Mother, Aunt Susan, & Me: The First Fight for Woman's Rights. LC 78-25715. (Illus.). (gr. 3-5). 1979. 7.95 o.p. (ISBN 0-698-20480-8, Coward). Putnam Pub Group.

Jacobs, William P. Plant Hormones & Plant Development. LC 78-54580. (Illus.). 1979. 19.95 (ISBN 0-521-22062-9). Cambridge U Pr.

Jacobsen, Carl G. The Nuclear Era: Its History, Its Implications. LC 82-8077. 160p. 1982. 20.00 (ISBN 0-89946-158-1). Oelgeschlager.

Jacobsen, David, et al. Methods for Teaching: A Skills Approach. (Illus.). 304p. 1981. pap. text ed. 15.95 (ISBN 0-675-08079-7). Merrill.

Jacobsen, Gertrude A. William Blathwayt. (Yale Historical Studies, Miscellany: No. XXI). 1932. 57.50x (ISBN 0-685-69829-7). Elliots Bks.

Jacobsen, Hans-Adolf & Smith, Arthur L., Jr. World War Two: Policy & Strategy--Selected Documents with Commentary. LC 79-11507. (Illus.). 505p. 1979. text ed. 24.95 (ISBN 0-87436-291-1); pap. text ed. 13.95 (ISBN 0-87436-348-9). ABC-Clio.

Jacobsen, Henry. The Acts: Then & Now. LC 72-96738. 224p. 1973. pap. 4.50 (ISBN 0-88207-239-0). Victor Bks.

--The Good Life. LC 68-11556. 96p. 1968. pap. 4.50 (ISBN 0-88207-018-5). Victor Bks.

Jacobsen, J. P. Marie Grubbe. Larsen, Hanna A., tr. from Danish. (International Studies & Translations Ser.,: Scandinavian). 1975. lib. bdg. 9.95 o.p. (ISBN 0-8057-8151-X, Twayne). G K Hall.

Jacobsen, Johan A. Alaskan Voyage, 1881-1883: An Expedition to the Northwest Coast of America. Gunther, Erna, tr. from Ger. LC 77-78066. (Illus.). 1977. Repr. of 1884 ed. 17.50x o.s.i. (ISBN 0-226-39032-2). U of Chicago Pr.

Jacobsen, Johann A. Alaskan Voyage, Eighteen Eighty-One to Eighteen Eighty-Three: An Expedition to the Northwest Coast of America. Gunther, Erna, tr. (Illus.). xiv, 266p. 1977. pap. 12.50 (ISBN 0-226-39033-0). U of Chicago Pr.

Jacobsen, Karen. Farm Animals. LC 81-7686. (The New True Bks.). (Illus.). 48p. (gr. k-4). 1981. PLB 9.25 (ISBN 0-516-01619-9). Childrens.

--Health. LC 81-6193. (The New True Bks.). (Illus.). 48p. (gr. k-4). 1981. PLB 9.25 (ISBN 0-516-01622-9). Childrens.

--Japan. LC 82-4445. (New True Bks.). (Illus.). (gr. k-4). 1982. PLB 9.25g (ISBN 0-516-01630-X). Childrens.

Jacobsen, Quentin. Solitary in Johannesburg. 256p. 1974. 9.50 o.p. (ISBN 0-7181-1109-5). Transatlantic.

Jacobsen, Richard J. & Avellani, Pamela B. A Review of Placement Services Within a Comprehensive Rehabilitation Framework: Survey Report. LC 78-72067. 76p. 1978. 8.25 (ISBN 0-686-38818-6). Human Res Ctr.

Jacobsen, Richard J., jt. auth. see Schroedel, John G.

Jacobsen, Richard J., jt. auth. see Vandergoot, David.

Jacobsen, Sally-Ann, jt. auth. see Duke, Charles R.

Jacobsen, Steve. The Best Team Money Could Buy: The Turmoil & Triumph of the 1977 New York Yankees. (RL 7). 1978. pap. 1.95 o.p. (ISBN 0-451-08002-5, J8002, Sig). NAL.

Jacobsen, T., tr. see Landsberger, B.

Jacobsen, Thorkild. Salinity & Irrigation Agriculture in Antiquity: Diyala Basin Archaeological Projects, Report on Essential Results, 1957-58. (Bibliotheca Mesopotamica Ser.: Vol. 14). (Illus.). xii, 129p. 1982. 24.00x (ISBN 0-89003-093-6); pap. 18.50x (ISBN 0-89003-092-8). Undena Pubns.

Jacobson. Focalguide to Home Processing. 2nd ed. (Focalguide Ser.). (Illus.). 1982. pap. 7.95 (ISBN 0-240-51017-8). Focal Pr.

Jacobson & Reinert. International Directory of Psychologists Exclusive of the U. S. A. 3rd ed. 1980. 53.25 (ISBN 0-444-85492-4). Elsevier.

Jacobson, Adrienne C., jt. auth. see Emery, Jared M.

Jacobson, B. Transformational-Generative Grammar. 2nd ed. (North Holland Linguistic Ser.: Vol. 17). 1978. 47.00 (ISBN 0-444-85240-9, North Holland). Elsevier.

Jacobson, Bernard. Singers On Singing: Opera. 224p. 1983. 18.95 (ISBN 0-914366-09-2). Vanguard.

Jacobson, Bertil & Webster, John G. Medicine & Clinical Engineering. LC 76-13842. (Illus.). 1977. text ed. 34.95 (ISBN 0-13-572966-1). P-H.

Jacobson, C. I. Developing: The Technique of the Negative. 18th rev. ed. 392p. 1976. 19.95 (ISBN 0-240-44770-0). Focal Pr.

Jacobson, C. I. & Mannheim, L. A. Enlarging: The Technique of the Positive. 22nd rev. ed. 164p. 1975. 19.95 (ISBN 0-240-50913-7). Focal Pr.

Jacobson, Dan. The Story of the Stories: The Chosen People & Its God. LC 81-48154. 192p. 1982. 11.49i (ISBN 0-06-014986-8, HarpT). Har-Row.

Jacobson, David B. Program for Revision: A Practical Guide. (Illus.). 352p. 1973. pap. text ed. 12.95 (ISBN 0-13-730671-7). P-H.

Jacobson, Doranne & Wadley, Susan. Women in India: Two Perspectives. 1977. 7.00x o.p. (ISBN 0-8364-0012-7); pap. text ed. 5.00x o.p. (ISBN 0-8364-0013-5). South Asia Bks.

Jacobson, Edmund, jt. auth. see Orleans, Jacob S.

Jacobson, Eric, jt. ed. see Jacobson, Sally.

Jacobson, Eugene, jt. auth. see Sernka, Thomas.

Jacobson, Eugene D., jt. auth. see Sernka, Thomas J.

Jacobson, Gary C., jt. auth. see Crotty, William J.

Jacobson, Gerald. The Multiple Crises of Marital Separation & Divorce. (Seminars in Psychiatry Ser.). Date not set. price not set (ISBN 0-8089-1483-9). Grune.

Jacobson, Gerald F. & Portuges, Stephen H. The Multiple Crisis of Marital Separation & Divorce. (A Seminars in Psychiatry Monograph). 1982. 38.50 (792159). Grune.

Jacobson, Harold K. America's Foreign Policy. pap. text ed. 7.95x (ISBN 0-685-77199-7). Phila Bk Co.

--Networks of Interdependence: International Organizations & the Global Political System. 1979. text ed. 23.00 (ISBN 0-394-32153-7). Knopf.

Jacobson, Harold K., jt. auth. see Kay, David A.

Jacobson, Howard. The Exagoge of Ezekiel. LC 82-4410. 240p. 1983. 44.50 (ISBN 0-521-24580-X). Cambridge U Pr.

--Ovid's Heroides. LC 73-16754. 425p. 1974. 39.00x o.p. (ISBN 0-691-06271-4). Princeton U Pr.

--Racewalk to Fitness. 1980. 11.95 o.p. (ISBN 0-671-24938-X). S&S.

Jacobson, James A. Woodturning Music Boxes. (Illus.). 192p. (Orig.). 1983. pap. 10.95 (ISBN 0-8069-7726-4). Sterling.

Jacobson, Jerry. The Secret of Life: Perspectivism in Science. 1983. 9.95 (ISBN 0-8022-2400-8). Philos Lib.

Jacobson, Jerry I. Perspectivism in Art. LC 73-77403. (Illus.). 160p. 1974. 8.75 o.p. (ISBN 0-8022-2116-5). Philos Lib.

Jacobson, Julius, jt. auth. see Jacobson, Phyllis.

Jacobson, K. I. & Jacobson, R. E. Imaging Systems: Mechanism & Applications of Established & New Photosensitive Processes. LC 76-23144. 319p. 1976. 44.95 o.s.i. (ISBN 0-470-98905-X). Halsted Pr.

Jacobson, Karen. Mexico. LC 82-4437. (New True Bks.). (Illus.). (gr. k-4). 1982. PLB 9.25g (ISBN 0-516-01632-6). Childrens.

--Television. LC 82-4456. (New True Bks.). (Illus.). (gr. k-4). 1982. PLB 9.25g (ISBN 0-516-01659-8). Childrens.

--Zoos. LC 82-9545. (New True Bks.). (Illus.). (gr. k-4). 1982. PLB 9.25g (ISBN 0-516-01664-4). Childrens.

Jacobson, Katherine, jt. auth. see Crandall-Stotler, Barbara.

Jacobson, Lenore, jt. auth. see Rosenthal, Robert.

Jacobson, M. Statistical Analysis of Counting Processes. (Lecture Notes in Statistics Ser.: Vol. 12). 226p. 1983. pap. 14.80 (ISBN 0-387-90769-6). Springer-Verlag.

Jacobson, Michael, jt. auth. see Bunin, Greta.

Jacobson, Michael, ed. see Lipske, Michael & Center for Science in the Public Interest Staff.

Jacobson, Michael F. Eater's Digest: The Consumer's Factbook of Food Additives. LC 75-186030. 1972. pap. 4.95 (ISBN 0-385-05341-X, Anch). Doubleday.

--Eater's Digest: The Consumer's Factbook of Food Additives. 1982. 5.00 (ISBN 0-686-95497-1). Ctr Sci Public.
--Nutrition Scoreboard. 1975. pap. 2.25 o.p. (ISBN 0-380-00534-4, 44537). Avon.
Jacobson, Michael G. Nutrition Scoreboard. 1975. 2.25x (ISBN 0-380-00534-4, Avon). Formur Intl.
Jacobson, Morris K. & Franz, David R. Wonders of Snails & Slugs. LC 79-6646. (Wonders Ser.). (Illus.). (gr. 5 up). 1980. 7.95 (ISBN 0-396-07815-X). Dodd.
Jacobson, Nolan P. Buddhism & the Contemporary World: Change & Self Correction. 1982. 18.95x (ISBN 0-8093-1052-X); pap. 9.95 (ISBN 0-8093-1071-6). S Ill U Pr.
--Buddhism: The Religion of Analysis. LC 66-71124. (Arcturus Books Paperbacks). 202p. 1970. pap. 6.95 (ISBN 0-8093-0463-5). S Ill U Pr.
Jacobson, Norman. Pride & Solace: The Functions & Limits of Political Theory. LC 76-52029. 1978. 15.95x (ISBN 0-520-03438-4). U of Cal Pr.
Jacobson, Paul B., et al. The Principalship: New Perspectives. 512p. 1973. ref. ed. 25.95 (ISBN 0-13-700856-2). P-H.
Jacobson, Phyllis & Jacobson, Julius. Socialist Perspectives, Vol. 1. 220p. 1983. 29.95 (ISBN 0-943828-51-1). Karz-Cohl Pub.
--Socialist Perspectives, Vol. 1. 220p. (Orig.). 1983. pap. 9.95 (ISBN 0-943828-52-X). Karz-Cohl Pub.
Jacobson, R. E. El Revelado Amateur. Torres, Elena, tr. from Eng. (Focalguide Ser.). 210p. (Span.). 1976. pap. 8.95 o.p. (ISBN 0-240-51093-3, Pub. by Ediciones Spain). Focal Pr.
Jacobson, R. E., jt. auth. see Jacobson, K. I.
Jacobson, R. E., et al. The Manual of Photography. 7th ed. 1978. 20.95 (ISBN 0-240-50957-9). Focal Pr.
Jacobson, Robert E. Municipal Control of Cable Communications. LC 77-7815. (Praeger Special Studies). 1977. 26.95 o.p. (ISBN 0-03-021831-4). Praeger.
Jacobson, Robert M, jt. auth. see Steiner, Christian.
Jacobson, Sally & Jacobson, Eric, eds. The Dance Horizons Travel Guide to Six of the World's Dance Capitals: New York, Washington, London, Paris, Leningrad & Moscow. LC 78-54983. 316p. 1978. pap. 7.95 o.p. (ISBN 0-87127-105-2). Dance Horiz.
Jacobson, Sharol F. & McCrath, H. Marie. Nurses Under Stress. 320p. 1983. 14.95 (ISBN 0-471-07899-9, Pub. by Wiley Med). Wiley.
Jacobson, Sherwood A. The Post Traumatic Syndrome Following Head Injury: Mechanisms & Treatment. (Illus.). 106p. 1963. photocopy ed. spiral 11.75x (ISBN 0-398-00913-9). C C Thomas.
Jacobson, Walter & Lowe, Walter, Jr. A Hard Night's News... (Illus.). 280p. cancelled 9.95 (ISBN 0-89803-051-X). Green Hill.
Jacobson, Willard & Bergman, Abby. Science Activities for Children. (Illus.). 256p. 1983. 16.95 (ISBN 0-13-794594-9). P-H.
Jacobson, Willard, ed. see Anderson, O. Roger.
Jacobstein, J. Myron & Pimsleur, Meira. Law Books in Print: Through 1969, 4 vols. LC 76-12173. 1974. Set. lib. bdg. 75.00 Set (ISBN 0-87802-010-1). Glanville.
Jacobstein, J. Myron, ed. see Jeaffreson, John C.
Jacobstein, J. Myron, ed. see Van Santvoord, George.
Jacob see Hoffmann, E. T.
Jacobus. Texas Real Estate Law. 3rd ed. text ed. 21.95 (ISBN 0-8359-7573-8). Reston.
Jacobus & Harwood. Texas Real Estate. 2nd ed. (Illus.). 672p. 1980. ref. ed. 19.95 (ISBN 0-8359-7553-3). Reston.
Jacobus, jt. auth. see Harwood.
Jacobus, Charles. Texas Real Estate Law. 2nd ed. 1981. text ed. 19.95 (ISBN 0-8359-7571-1); instrs' manual free (ISBN 0-8359-7572-X). Reston.
Jacobus, John, jt. auth. see Hunter, Sam.
Jacobus, L. A. Aesthetics & the Arts. 1968. pap. text ed. 9.95 o.p. (ISBN 0-07-032215-5, C). McGraw.
Jacobus, Lee, jt. auth. see Martin, David.
Jacobus, Lee A. Developing College Reading. 2nd ed. 343p. 1979. text ed. 12.95 (ISBN 0-15-517602-1, HC); instr's. key 0.75 (ISBN 0-15-517603-X). HarBraceJ.
--John Cleveland. (English Authors Ser.). 1979. lib. bdg. 14.95 (ISBN 0-8057-1095-7, Twayne). G K Hall.
Jacobus, Lee A., jt. auth. see Martin, F. David.
Jacobus, Mary. Tradition & Experiment in Wordsworth's Lyrical Ballads (1798) 1976. 32.50x (ISBN 0-19-812069-9). Oxford U Pr.
Jacoby, E. H., jt. auth. see Moral-Lopez, P.
Jacoby, Ed. Applied Techniques in Track & Field. LC 82-81819. (Illus.). 192p. (Orig.). 1983. pap. 9.95 (ISBN 0-88011-050-3). Leisure Pr.
Jacoby, Erich H. Agrarian Reconstruction. 1968. pap. 4.75 o.p. (ISBN 0-685-09369-7, FAO). Unipub.
--Agrarian Unrest in Southeast Asia. LC 75-75. (Illus.). 279p. 1975. Repr. of 1961 ed. lib. bdg. 17.25x (ISBN 0-8371-8014-7, JAAU). Greenwood.
Jacoby, G. Polly. Preparing for a Home Economics Career. Hughes, Ruth P., ed. (Careers in Home Economics Ser.). 1979. pap. text ed. 15.96 (ISBN 0-07-032240-6, G); tchr's manual & key 4.00 (ISBN 0-07-032241-4); wkbk 6.96 (ISBN 0-07-032242-2). McGraw.
Jacoby, H. How to Know Oriental Carpets & Rugs. 2nd ed. 1967. 23.50x (ISBN 0-87245-151-8). Textile Bk.
Jacoby, H. J., jt. ed. see Bullock, R. L.
Jacoby, Henry. The Bureaucratization of the World. LC 74-166224. 1973. 37.50x (ISBN 0-520-02083-9); pap. 8.95 (ISBN 0-520-03044-3). U of Cal Pr.
Jacoby, Henry D. & Steinbruner, John. Clearing the Air: Federal Policy on Automotive Emissions Control. LC 73-10393. 232p. 1973. prof ref 20.00 (ISBN 0-88410-301-3). Ballinger Pub.
Jacoby, Henry D., jt. auth. see Neff, Thomas L.
Jacoby, Hilla & Jacoby, Max, photos by. The Land of Israel. (Illus.). 1978. 40.00 (ISBN 0-500-24101-5). Thames Hudson.
Jacoby, J. H. & Lytle, L. D., eds. Serotonin Neurotoxins. (Annals of the New York Academy of Sciences: Vol. 305). 702p. 1978. pap. 68.00x (ISBN 0-89072-061-4). NY Acad Sci.
Jacoby, James W. How to Prepare Managerial Communications. 230p. 1983. text ed. 20.00 (ISBN 0-87179-388-1). BNA.
Jacoby, Joan E. The American Prosecutor: A Search for Identity. LC 79-2795. 336p. 1980. 31.95x (ISBN 0-669-03291-3). Lexington Bks.
Jacoby, Joseph E., ed. Classics of Criminology. LC 79-15697. (Classics Ser.). (Orig.). 1979. pap. 11.00x (ISBN 0-935610-08-1). Moore Pub IL.
Jacoby, Oswald, jt. auth. see Benson, William H.
Jacoby, Susan. Inside Soviet Schools. LC 75-10786. 254p. 1975. pap. 4.95 (ISBN 0-8052-0494-6). Schocken.
Jacolev, Leon, jt. auth. see DeVries, Louis.
Jaconelli, Joseph. Enacting a Bill of Rights: The Legal Problems. 1980. text ed. 44.00x (ISBN 0-19-825351-6). Oxford U Pr.
Jacot, Guillardmod A. Flora of Lesotho (Basutoland) 1971. 60.00 (ISBN 3-7682-0719-6). Lubrecht & Cramer.
Jacox, Ada. A Primary Care Process Measure: The Nurse Practitioner Rating Form. LC 81-80621. 144p. 1981. Repr. spiral bd. 24.00 (ISBN 0-913654-75-2). Aspen Systems.
Jacque, Laurent L. Management of Foreign Exchange Risks: Theory & Proxis. LC 77-12281. (Illus.). 320p. 1978. 26.95x (ISBN 0-669-01954-2). Lexington Bks.
Jacquemart, Nicolas-Francois. Reflexions d'un Cultivateur Americain sur le Projet d'Abolir l'Esclavage et la Traite des Negres. (Slave Trade in France, 1744-1848, Ser.). 103p. (Fr.). 1974. Repr. of 1788 ed. lib. bdg. 32.00x o.p. (ISBN 0-8287-0460-0, TN109). Clearwater Pub.
Jacques Cattell Press. Who Was Who on Screen. 3rd ed. 1983. 65.00 (ISBN 0-8352-1578-4). Bowker.
Jacques Cattell Press, ed. American Men & Women of Science Cumulative Index: Vols. 1-14. 900p. 125.00 (ISBN 0-686-83438-0). Bowker.
Jacques, Hylah. Departure Point. 12p. (Orig.). 1981. 5.00 (ISBN 0-686-38170-X). Seal Pr WA.
Jacques, Hylah, jt. auth. see Aliesan, Jody.
Jacques, J. A. Respiratory Physiology. 1979. text ed. 27.95 (ISBN 0-07-032247-3). McGraw.
Jacques, Jean, et al. Enantiomers, Racemates & Resolutions. LC 81-1604. 447p. 1981. 52.50x (ISBN 0-471-08058-6, Pub. by Wiley-Interscience). Wiley.
Jacques, M., jt. auth. see Hall, S.
Jacques, Reginald & Willcocks, David. Carols for Choirs: Fifty Christmas Carols, Bk. 1. (YA) (gr. 9 up). 1961. 12.00 (ISBN 0-19-353221-2); pap. 6.00 (ISBN 0-19-353222-0). Oxford U Pr.
Jacques-Garvey, Amy, ed. see Garvey, Marcus.
Jacquet, Constant H., Jr. Yearbook of American & Canadian Churches, 1983. 304p. (Orig.). 1983. pap. 17.95 (ISBN 0-687-46638-5). Abingdon.
Jacquette, Jane, jt. ed. see Staudt, Kathleen.
Jaczewski, J. Logical Systems for Industrial Applications. (Studies in Automation & Control: Vol. 1). 1978. 64.00 (ISBN 0-444-99804-7). Elsevier.
Jaech, John L. Statistical Methods in Nuclear Material Control. LC 73-600241. (AEC Technical Information Center Ser.). 409p. 1973. pap. 18.25 (ISBN 0-87079-343-8, TID-26298); microfiche 4.50 (ISBN 0-87079-344-6, TID-26298). DOE.
Jaeger, A. & Sauerbeck, F. Genera et Species Muscorum Systematice Disposita Seu Adumbratio Florae Muscorum Totius Orbis Terrarum, 2 vols. Repr. of 1870 ed. Set. lib. bdg. 80.00x (ISBN 3-7682-1157-6). Lubrecht & Cramer.
Jaeger, C. Rock Mechanics & Engineering. 2nd ed. LC 77-85700. (Illus.). 1979. 99.50 (ISBN 0-521-21898-5). Cambridge U Pr.
Jaeger, Edmund C. Desert Wild Flowers. rev. ed. LC 41-22485. (Illus.). 1941. 9.95 (ISBN 0-8047-0364-7); pap. 6.95 (ISBN 0-8047-0365-5, SP81). Stanford U Pr.
Jaeger, Edward A., jt. ed. see Duane, Thomas D.
Jaeger, J. C. Elasticity, Fracture & Flow: With Engineering & Geological Applications. 3rd ed. 1971. pap. 10.50x (ISBN 0-412-20890-3, Pub. by Chapman & Hall). Methuen Inc.
Jaeger, L. G. Elementary Theory of Elastic Plates. 1964. 17.75 o.p. (ISBN 0-08-010342-1); pap. 7.75 o.p. (ISBN 0-08-010341-3). Pergamon.
Jaeger, Marietta. The Lost Child. 128p. 1983. pap. 4.95 (ISBN 0-310-45811-0). Zondervan.
Jaeger, Richard M. & Tittle, Carol K., eds. Minimum Competency Achievement Testing: Motives, Models, Measures & Consequences. LC 79-88823. 1980. 24.25 (ISBN 0-685-96790-5); text ed. 22.00 in copies of 10 (ISBN 0-685-96791-3). McCutchan.
Jaeger, T. A. & Baley, B. A., eds. Structural Mechanics in Reactor Technology, 13 vols. 5821p. 1979. Set. pap. 298.00 (ISBN 0-444-85356-1, North Holland). Elsevier.
Jaeger, T. A. & Roley, B. A., eds. International Conference on Structural Mechanics in Reactor Technology: Third Proceedings, London, 1975, 8 pts. in 5 vols. 1976. Set. pap. 213.00 (ISBN 0-444-10974-9). Elsevier.
Jaeger, T. A. & Roleyr, B. A., eds. International Conference on Structural Mechanics in Reactor Technology: Proceedings, Fourth, San Francisco, 1977, 13 Vols. (SMIRT 1977). 1978. Set. pap. 298.00 (ISBN 0-686-43416-1). Elsevier.
Jaeger, Werner. Humanism & Theology. (Aquinas Lecture). 1943. 7.95 (ISBN 0-87462-107-0). Marquette.
--Paideia: The Ideals of Greek Culture, 3 vols. Highet, Gilbert, tr. from Ger. Incl. Vol. 1. Archaic Greece; The Mind of Athens. 2nd ed. 1945 (ISBN 0-19-500399-3); Vol. 2. In Search of the Divine Center. 1943 (ISBN 0-19-500592-9); Vol. 3. The Conflict of Cultural Ideals in the Age of Plato. 1944 (ISBN 0-19-500593-7). 29.50 ea. Oxford U Pr.
Jaeggli, Osvaldo. Topics in Romance Syntax. 240p. 1981. 34.75x (ISBN 90-70176-34-3); pap. 19.75x (ISBN 90-70176-23-8). Foris Pubns.
Jaemko, Matt, jt. ed. see Meichenbaum, Donald.
Jaenicke, ed. Protein Folding. 1980. 92.00 (ISBN 0-444-80197-9). Elsevier.
Jaenicke, Henry R., jt. auth. see Johnson, Kenneth P.
Jaenicke, L., ed. Biochemistry of Differentiation & Morphogenosis. (Collequium Mosbach Ser.: Vol. 33). (Illus.). 301p. 1983. 37.00 (ISBN 0-387-12010-6). Springer-Verlag.
Jaenisch, R., jt. ed. see Graf, T.
Jaensch, D., jt. auth. see Loveday, P.
Jaensch, Dean. The Australian Party System. 234p. 1983. text ed. 28.50x (ISBN 0-86861-077-1). Allen Unwin.
Jaeschke, W., jt. ed. see Georgii, H. W.
Jaffa, Harry V., jt. auth. see Bloom, Allen.
Jaffa, Herbert C. Kenneth Slessor. (World Authors Ser.: Australia: No. 145). lib. bdg. 10.95 o.p. (ISBN 0-8057-2838-4, Twayne). G K Hall.
Jaffa, Herbert C., ed. Modern Australian Poetry: A Guide to Information Sources. LC 74-11535. (The American Literature, English Literature, & World Literatures in English Information Guide Ser.: Vol. 24). 1979. 42.00x (ISBN 0-8103-1242-5). Gale.
Jaffe. Property Management in Real Estate Investment Decision-Making. (Special Ser. in Real Estate & Urban Land Economics). (Illus.). 192p. 1979. 23.95x (ISBN 0-669-02453-8). Lexington Bks.
Jaffe, Alfred I. Insurance Producer's Handbook, 2 vols. 1980. Set. 109.00 (ISBN 0-686-73129-8). Inst Busn Plan.
--Insurance Producer's Handbook, Vol. 1. LC 78-58728. 1978. 49.50 (ISBN 0-87624-253-0). Inst Busn Plan.
--Insurance Producer's Handbook, Vol. 2. LC 78-58728. 1980. 65.00 (ISBN 0-87624-254-9). Inst Busn Plan.
Jaffe, Andrew. Jazz Theory. 350p. 1983. pap. text ed. write for info. (ISBN 0-697-03549-2); write for info. instr's. supplement (ISBN 0-697-03563-8). Wm C Brown.
Jaffe, Aniela. Apparitions: An Archetypal Approach to Death Dreams & Ghosts. rev. ed. (Jungian Classics Ser.). 214p. 1978. pap. text ed. 12.00 (ISBN 0-88214-500-2). Spring Pubns.
Jaffe, Bernard. Crucibles: The Story of Chemistry from Ancient Alchemy to Nuclear Fission. 4th rev. ed. 10.00 (ISBN 0-8446-5486-8). Peter Smith.
--Michelson & the Speed of Light. LC 78-25969. (Illus.). 1979. Repr. of 1960 ed. lib. bdg. 18.50x (ISBN 0-313-20777-1, JAMI). Greenwood.
Jaffe, Dan & Knoepfle, John, eds. Frontier Literature: Images of the American West. (Patterns in Literary Art). (gr. 9-12). 1979. pap. text ed. 9.16 (ISBN 0-07-032187-6, W); tchrs' manual 2.08 (ISBN 0-07-032188-4). McGraw.
Jaffe, David. The Stormy Petrel & the Whale: Some Origins of Moby-Dick. LC 81-43745. (Illus.). 84p. 1982. lib. bdg. 18.00 (ISBN 0-8191-2175-4); pap. text ed. 7.00 (ISBN 0-8191-2176-2). U Pr of Amer.
Jaffe, Dennis T. Healing from Within. 288p. 1982. pap. 3.50 (ISBN 0-553-22537-5). Bantam.
Jaffe, Eliezer D. Israelis in Institutions: Studies in Child Placement, Practice & Policy. (Special Aspects of Education Ser.: Vol. 2). 324p. 1982. 52.75 (ISBN 0-677-05960-4). Gordon.
Jaffe, Eliezer F. Child Welfare in Israel. Gilbert, Neil & Specht, Harry, eds. (Studies in Social Welfare). 336p. 1982. 27.95 (ISBN 0-03-057752-7). Praeger.
Jaffe, Eugene, jt. auth. see Hilbert, Stephen.
Jaffe, Frederick S., et al. Abortion Politics: Private Morality & Public Policy. LC 80-17035. 224p. 1980. 17.95 (ISBN 0-07-032189-2, P&RB). McGraw.
Jaffe, Fredericks S., jt. auth. see Cutright, Phillips.
Jaffe, H. H. & Orchin, Milton M. Symmetry in Chemistry. LC 76-7534. 206p. 1976. pap. text ed. 7.50 (ISBN 0-88275-414-9). Krieger.
Jaffe, H. H., jt. auth. see Orchin, Milton.
Jaffe, Harold. Dos Indios. 161p. 1983. 14.95 (ISBN 0-938410-11-3); pap. 8.95 (ISBN 0-938410-10-5). Thunder's Mouth.
--Mourning Crazy Horse. rev. ed. LC 81-71645. 224p. (Orig.). 1982. 11.95 (ISBN 0-914590-72-3); pap. 5.95 (ISBN 0-914590-73-1). Fiction Coll.
Jaffe, Harold, jt. ed. see Tytell, J.
Jaffe, Hilde & Relis, Nurie. Draping for Fashion Design. (Illus.). 176p. 1975. 17.95 (ISBN 0-87909-210-6). Reston.
Jaffe, Joseph, jt. auth. see Dahlberg, Charles C.
Jaffe, Louis L. English & American Judges As Lawmakers. 1969. 24.95x (ISBN 0-19-825193-9). Oxford U Pr.
Jaffe, Louis L. & Nathanson, Nathaniel L. Administrative Law: Cases & Materials. 4th ed. 1976. 26.00 (ISBN 0-316-45606-3). Little.
Jaffe, Margaret S. Clinical Simulations for Students of Medicine. 148p. 1982. 24.95 (ISBN 0-8151-4852-6). Year Bk Med.
Jaffe, N. Jay. Inward Image. (Illus.). 24p. 1981. pap. 3.00 (ISBN 0-87273-083-2). Bklyn Mus.
Jaffe, Nora C., jt. ed. see Skarda, Patricia L.
Jaffe, Norman S. Cataract Surgery & Its Complications. 3rd ed. LC 80-19355. (Illus.). 611p. 1981. text ed. 84.50 (ISBN 0-8016-2404-5). Mosby.
Jaffe, Norman S., jt. auth. see Clayman, Henry M.
Jaffe, Philip M. & Maglio, Rodolfo. Technical Mathematics. 1979. text ed. 21.95x (ISBN 0-673-15111-5). Scott F.
Jaffe, Rona. The Best of Everything. 1976. pap. 2.75 o.p. (ISBN 0-380-00581-6, 54221). Avon.
--Class Reunion. 1979. 11.95 o.s.i. (ISBN 0-440-01408-5). Delacorte.
--Mazes & Monsters. 1981. 13.95 o.s.i. (ISBN 0-440-05536-9). Delacorte.
Jaffe, S. M. Broker-Dealers & Securities Markets. 1977. 40.00 (ISBN 0-07-032218-X). McGraw.
Jaffe, Sherril. The Unexamined Wife. 150p. 1983. 14.00 (ISBN 0-87685-570-2); pap. 8.50 (ISBN 0-87685-569-9); signed ed. 25.00 (ISBN 0-87685-571-0). Black Sparrow.
Jaffe, Susanne. The Other Anne Fletcher. 1980. 9.95 o.p. (ISBN 0-453-00386-9, H386). NAL.
Jaffee, Al. Al Jaffee Blows a Fuse. (Orig.). 1980. pap. 1.75 (ISBN 0-451-09549-9, E9549, Sig). NAL.
--Al Jaffee Blows His Mind. (Orig.). 1975. pap. 2.25 (ISBN 0-451-11190-7, AE1190, Sig). NAL.
--Al Jaffee Bombs Again. (Orig.). 1978. pap. 1.75 (ISBN 0-451-11606-2, AE1606, Sig). NAL.
--Al Jaffee: Dead or Alive. 1980. pap. 2.25 (ISBN 0-451-12340-9, AE2340, Sig). NAL.
--Al Jaffee Draws a Crowd. (Orig.). 1978. pap. 2.25 (ISBN 0-451-08226-5, Y8226, Sig). NAL.
--Al Jaffee Fowls His Nest. 1981. pap. 1.95 (ISBN 0-451-09741-6, J9741, Sig). NAL.
--Al Jaffee Gags. (Orig.). 1974. pap. 1.75 (ISBN 0-451-09546-4, E9546, Sig). NAL.
--Al Jaffee Gags Again. (Orig.). 1975. pap. 1.75 (ISBN 0-451-09583-9, E9583, Sig). NAL.
--Al Jaffee Gets His Just Desserts. (Orig.). 1980. pap. 1.95 (ISBN 0-451-09838-2, J9838, Sig). NAL.
--Al Jaffee Goes Bananas. (Orig.). 1982. pap. 2.25 (ISBN 0-451-12201-1, AE2201, Sig). NAL.
--Al Jaffee Hogs the Show. (Orig.). 1981. pap. 1.95 (ISBN 0-451-09908-7, J9908, Sig). NAL.
--Al Jaffee Meets His End. (Orig.). 1979. pap. 1.95 (ISBN 0-451-11317-9, AJ1317, Sig). NAL.
--Al Jaffee Meets Willie Weirdie. (Orig.). 1981. pap. 2.25 (ISBN 0-451-12310-7, AE2310, Sig). NAL.
--Al Jaffee Shoots His Mouth Off. 1982. pap. 1.95 (ISBN 0-451-11569-4, AJ1569, Sig). NAL.
--Al Jaffee Sinks to a New Low. (Orig.). 1978. pap. 2.25 (ISBN 0-451-12366-2, AE2366, Sig). NAL.
--Al Jaffee's Next Book. (Orig.). 1977. pap. 1.95 (ISBN 0-451-11377-2, AJ1377, Sig). NAL.
--The Ghoulish Book of Weird Records. (Orig.). 1979. pap. 1.95 (ISBN 0-451-11234-2, J1234, Sig). NAL.
--Mad Book of Magic & Other Dirty Tricks. (Illus., Orig.). 1970. pap. 1.25 o.p. (ISBN 0-451-06743-6, Y6743, Sig). NAL.
--Mad's Vastly Overrated Al Jaffee. 160p. 1983. pap. 5.95 (ISBN 0-446-37584-5). Warner Bks.
--Still More Snappy Answers to Stupid Questions. (Illus.). 192p. 1976. pap. 1.95 (ISBN 0-446-30443-3). Warner Bks.
--Willie Weirdie, No. 2: Willie Weirdie Scares the Pants off Al Jaffee. 1982. pap. 2.25 (ISBN 0-451-11881-2, AE1881, Sig). NAL.
Jaffee, Annette W. Adult Education. 240p. 1982. pap. 6.95 (ISBN 0-446-37192-0). Warner Bks.
Jaffray, Angela, ed. see Shaw, Joan.
Jaffray, G., jt. auth. see Gruenberger, F. J.
Jaffrey, Madhur. An Invitation to Indian Cooking. LC 74-14951. (Illus.). 1975. pap. 5.95 (ISBN 0-394-71191-2, Vin). Random.
Jafolla, Richard. Soul Surgery: The Ultimate Self-Healing. LC 81-71018. 176p. (Orig.). 1982. pap. 5.95 (ISBN 0-87516-473-0). De Vorss.
Jagannathan, V. R., jt. auth. see Bahri, Vijal S.
Jagchid, Sechin & Hyer, Paul. Mongolia's Culture & Society. LC 79-1438. (Illus.). 461p. 1980. 37.50 (ISBN 0-89158-390-4); text ed. 15.00. Westview.
Jagdfeld, G., jt. auth. see Gernyet, N.

Jagendorf, Moritz. Puppets for Beginners. (gr. 4-6). 1952. 10.00 (ISBN 0-8238-0072-5). Plays.

Jagendorf, Moritz A. Tales from the First Americans. LC 78-56057. (The World Folktale Library). (Illus.). 1979. PLB 12.68 (ISBN 0-382-03348-5). Silver.

--Tales of Mystery. LC 78-56056. (The World Folktale Library). (Illus.). 1979. PLB 12.68 (ISBN 0-382-03356-6). Silver.

Jageneau. Noninvasive Methods on Cardiovascular Haemodynamics. (Janssen Research Foundation Ser.: Vol. 5). 1982. 93.75 (ISBN 0-444-80399-8). Elsevier.

Jager, E. M., jt. auth. see Martini, R.

Jager, E. M. see Eckhaus, W. & De Jager, E. M.

Jager, Susan G., jt. auth. see Fencl, Shirley.

Jager, T. Soil of the Serengeti Woodlands. 253p. 1981. pap. 29.25 (ISBN 0-686-93178-5, PDC239, Pudoc). Unipub.

Jagers, D. P. Branching Processes with Biological Applications. LC 74-32296. (Wiley Series in Probability & Mathematical Statistics). 276p. 1975. 71.95x (ISBN 0-471-43652-6). Wiley.

Jagersma, Henk. A History of Israel in the Old Testament Period. Bowden, John, tr. LC 82-48548. 320p. 1983. pap. text ed. 13.95 (ISBN 0-8006-1692-8). Fortress.

Jaggar, Alison & Struhl, Paula R. Feminist Frameworks. 1977. pap. text ed. 16.50 (ISBN 0-07-032250-3, C). McGraw.

Jaggar, Alison M. Feminist Politics & Human Nature. (Philosophy & Society Ser.). 220p. 1983. text ed. 19.95x (ISBN 0-8476-7181-X). Rowman.

Jaggard, W. Shakespeare Once a Printer & Bookman. LC 70-181003. (Studies in Shakespeare, No. 24). 34p. 1972. Repr. of 1933 ed. 40.95x (ISBN 0-8383-1372-8). Haskell.

Jagger, Brenda. Verity. LC 79-6656. 1980. 12.95 o.p. (ISBN 0-385-15887-4). Doubleday.

--Verity. 1981. pap. 2.95 o.p. (ISBN 0-451-09718-1, E9718, Sig). NAL.

Jagger, Peter J. Clouded Witness: Initiation in the Church of England in the Mid-Victorian Period 1850-1875. (Pittsburgh Theological Monographs New Ser.: No. 1). vii, 221p. (Orig.). 1982. pap. 16.50 (ISBN 0-915138-51-4). Pickwick.

Jaggi, O. P. A Concise History of Science: Science in India. LC 78-670091. (Illus.). 1974. 12.50x o.p. (ISBN 0-8002-0240-6). Intl Pubns Serv.

Jagner, D., jt. auth. see Whitfield, M.

Jago, Charles. Aristocracy & Social Change in Early Modern Europe. (Pre-Industrial Europe Ser.: No. 6). Date not set. text ed. price not set (ISBN 0-391-01043-3). Humanities.

Jahadhmy, Ali. Kusanyiko la Mashairi. (Swahili Literature). (Orig., Swahili.). 1978. pap. text ed. 3.25x o.p. (ISBN 0-686-74448-9, 00615). Heinemann Ed.

Jahan, Rounaq & Papanek, Hanna, eds. Women & Development: Perspectives from South & Southeast Asia. 1980. pap. 14.00x (ISBN 0-8364-0596-X, Pub. by Bangladesh Inst Law India). South Asia Bks.

Jahn, G. Application of Vegetation Science to Forestry. 1982. 79.50 (ISBN 90-6193-193-2, Pub. by Junk Pubs Netherlands). KLuwer Boston.

Jahn, H. Mitteleuropaeische Porlinge (Poly. S. Lato) & Ihr Vorkommen in Westfalen. (Illus.). 1970. pap. 12.00 (ISBN 3-7682-0698-X). Lubrecht & Cramer.

Jahn, Melvin E., tr. see Beringer, Johann B.

Jahn, R. G. The Role of Consciousness in the Physical World. (AAAS Selected Symposium: No. 57). 136p. 1981. lib. bdg. 18.50 (ISBN 0-89158-955-4). Westview.

Jahn, Rudiger. Skiing Skills. LC 81-47706. (Illus.). 160p. 1981. pap. 10.95 (ISBN 0-448-11988-9, G&D). Putnam Pub Group.

Jahnel, Franz. Manual of Guitar Technology. (Illus.). 240p. 1981. Repr. of 1963 ed. 80.00 (ISBN 0-686-74791-7). Bold Strummer Ltd.

Jahnsmann, Alan H. It's All About Jesus. LC 74-21233. 160p. (ps-7). 1975. 7.95 (ISBN 0-570-03025-0, 6-1153); pap. 5.95 (ISBN 0-570-03031-5, 6-1157). Concordia.

Jahoda, G. Psychology & Anthropology: A Psychological Perspective. 1982. 29.50 (ISBN 0-12-379820-5). Acad Pr.

Jahoda, Gerald, jt. auth. see Needham, William L.

Jahoda, Gustav. The Psychology of Superstition. LC 74-9667. 158p. 1974. Repr. 17.50x o.s.i. (ISBN 0-87668-185-2). Aronson.

Jahoda, Marie. Employment & Unemployment: A Social-Psychology Analysis. LC 82-4165. (The Psychology of Social Issues Ser.). 128p. 1982. 19.50 (ISBN 0-521-24294-0); pap. 6.95 (ISBN 0-521-28586-0). Cambridge U Pr.

Jahsmann, Allan H. & Simon, Martin P. Little Visits with God. (gr. k-3). 1957. 7.95 (ISBN 0-570-03016-1, 6-1055); pap. 5.95 (ISBN 0-570-03032-3, 6-1158). Concordia.

Jahss, Melvin H. Disorders of the Foot, 2 Vols. (Illus.). 1771p. 1982. 165.00 set (ISBN 0-686-97304-6); Vol. 1 82.50 (ISBN 0-7216-5106-2); Vol. 2 82.50 (ISBN 0-7216-5107-0). Saunders.

Jain, Chaman L., jt. auth. see Migliaro, Al.

Jain, Devaki. Woman's Quest for Power. LC 80-901719. (Illus.). 272p. 1980. 12.50x (ISBN 0-7069-1021-4). Intl Pubns Serv.

Jain, J. P. China, Pakistan & Bangladesh, Vol. 1. LC 74-900810. vii, 270p. 1974. 14.00x o.p. (ISBN 0-88386-461-4). South Asia Bks.

--China, Pakistan & Bangladesh, Vol. 2, Documents, Vol. 2, Documents. 1976. 15.00x o.p. (ISBN 0-88386-769-9). South Asia Bks.

Jain, Jagdish P. After Mao What? LC 75-31534. 1976. lib. bdg. 24.50x o.p. (ISBN 0-89158-528-1). Westview.

Jain, M. K. Handbook of Enzyme Inhibitors. 800p. 1982. 100.00x (ISBN 0-471-86727-6, Pub. by Wiley-Interscience). Wiley.

--Numerical Solution of Differential Equations. LC 78-26649. 443p. 1979. 27.95x o.s.i. (ISBN 0-470-26609-0). Halsted Pr.

--Numerical Solution of Differential Equations. 2nd ed. 1983. 29.95 (ISBN 0-470-27389-5). Halsted Pr.

Jain, N. K., ed. Muslims in India: A Biographical Dictionary, 1857-1976. 1980. 38.00x o.p. (ISBN 0-88386-886-5). South Asia Bks.

Jain, Nemi C., ed. International & Intercultural Communication Annual, Vol. VI. 150p. (Orig.). 1983. pap. text ed. 9.50x (ISBN 0-933662-22-X). Intercult Pr.

Jain, P. C. Socio-Economic Exploration of Medieval India. LC 76-904842. 1976. 17.50x o.p. (ISBN 0-88386-884-9). South Asia Bks.

Jain, R. B., jt. ed. see Bain, J. S.

Jain, R. C., tr. see Castro, R. & De Cadenet, J. J.

Jain, R. K. China & Japan Nineteen Forty-Nine to Nineteen Eighty. rev. ed. LC 77-70008. 1981. text ed. 26.00x (ISBN 0-391-00749-1). Humanities.

--Japan's Postwar Peace Settlements. 1978. text ed. 19.00x (ISBN 0-391-00870-6). Humanities.

--Soviet South Asian Relations Nineteen Fourty-Seven to Nineteen Seventy-Eight: The Kashmir Question 1952-1964, 2 vols. Incl. Vol. 1. The Dutch Conflict Indo-Pak Conflict of 1965 Bangladesh Crisis & Indo-Pak War of 1971 India; Vol. 2. Pakistan, Bangladesh, Nepal. 1979. Set. 57.75x set (ISBN 0-391-00974-5). Humanities.

--The U. S. S. R. & Japan, Nineteen Forty-Five to Nineteen-Eighty. 400p. 1980. text ed. 26.00x (ISBN 0-391-01898-1). Humanities.

Jain, Rakesh K. & Gullino, Pietro M., eds. Thermal Characteristics of Tumors: Applications in Detection & Treatment. LC 80-13379. (N.Y. Academy of Sciences Annals: Vol. 335). 542p. 1980. 97.00x (ISBN 0-89766-046-3). NY Acad Sci.

Jain, S. C. & Radhakrishna, S. Physics of Semiconductor Devices Proceedings of the International Workshop. 803p. 1982. 54.95x (ISBN 0-470-27512-X). Halsted Pr.

Jain, S. K. Glimpses of Indian Ethnobotany. 344p. 1980. 69.00 (ISBN 0-686-84454-8, Pub. by Oxford & I B H India). State Mutual Bk.

Jain, S. K., jt. auth. see Bhattacharya, P. B.

Jain, S. R. The Social Structure of Hindu-Muslim Community. LC 75-902037. 1975. 11.00x o.p. (ISBN 0-88386-621-8). South Asia Bks.

Jain, Sagar C., ed. Policy Issues in Personal Health Services: Current Perspectives. 500p. 1983. price not set (ISBN 0-89443-672-4). Aspen Systems.

Jain, Sager C., ed. Role of State & Local Governments in Relation to Personal Health Services. 259p. 1980. 4.00x (ISBN 0-87553-097-4, 062). Am Pub Health.

Jain, Subhash C. & Tucker, Lewis R. International Marketing: Managerial Perspectives. LC 78-31876. 518p. 1979. pap. text ed. 12.95x (ISBN 0-8436-0903-6). Kent Pub Co.

Jain, Sunita. John Steinbeck's Concept of Man: A Critical Study of His Novels. 1980. text ed. 10.50x (ISBN 0-391-01730-6). Humanities.

Jain-Neubauer, Jutta. The Stepwells of Gujarat: In Art - Historical Perspective. 118p. 1981. text ed. 65.00x (ISBN 0-391-02284-9). Humanities.

Jairazbhoy, R. A. Ancient Egyptians & Chinese in America. (Old World Origins of American Civilization Ser). (Illus.). 135p. 1974. 16.50 o.p. (ISBN 0-87471-571-7). Rowman.

Jaiswal, N. K., ed. Scientific Management of Transport Systems. 1981. 55.50 (ISBN 0-444-86205-6). Elsevier.

Jakab, I., ed. Mental Retardation. (Karger Continuing Education Ser.: Vol. 2). (Illus.). xx, 508p. 1982. 56.00 (ISBN 3-8055-3433-7). S Karger.

Jakeman, Alan. Getting to Know Japan. (Getting to Know Ser.). (Illus.). (gr. 3-5). 1971. PLB 3.97 o.p. (ISBN 0-698-30131-5, Coward). Putnam Pub Group.

Jakes, John. The Bastard, No. 1. (Kent Family Chronicles). 1978. pap. 3.50 (ISBN 0-515-06483-1). Jove Pubns.

--The Furies. (Kent Family Chronicle: No. 4). (Orig.). 1976. pap. 3.95 (ISBN 0-515-07144-7). Jove Pubns.

--The Imposter. 224p. 1981. pap. 2.25 o.p. (ISBN 0-523-48020-2). Pinnacle Bks.

--A Night for Treason. 224p. 1982. pap. 2.25 o.p. (ISBN 0-523-48023-7). Pinnacle Bks.

--North & South. 1983. pap. 4.95 (ISBN 0-440-16204-1). Dell.

--The Seekers, No. 3. (The Kent Family Chronicles). (Orig.). 1979. pap. 3.50 (ISBN 0-515-06588-9). Jove Pubns.

--The Seventh Man. 224p. 1981. pap. 2.25 o.p. (ISBN 0-523-48018-0). Pinnacle Bks.

--Time Gate. (RL 6). 1978. pap. 1.25 o.p. (ISBN 0-451-07889-6, Y7889, Sig). NAL.

--The Warriors. (Kent Family Chronicles: No. 6). (Orig.). 1977. pap. 3.95 (ISBN 0-515-07264-8). Jove Pubns.

Jakes, John, photos by. The Bastard Photostory. (Orig.). 1980. pap. 2.75 o.s.i. (ISBN 0-515-05433-X). Jove Pubns.

Jaki, Stanley L. Angels, Apes & Men. 136p. (Orig.). 1982. pap. 4.95 (ISBN 0-89385-017-9). Sugden.

--Brain, Mind & Computers. LC 72-76283. 1978. pap. 5.95 (ISBN 0-89526-907-4). Regnery-Gateway.

--The Origin of Science & the Science of Its Origin. LC 78-74439. 1979. 12.95 o.p. (ISBN 0-89526-684-9); pap. 5.95 (ISBN 0-89526-903-1). Regnery-Gateway.

--Planets & Planetarians: A History of Theories of the Origin of Planetary Systems. LC 77-4200. 266p. 1978. 32.95x o.s.i. (ISBN 0-470-99149-6). Halsted Pr.

Jakob, Max & Hawkins, G. A. Elements of Heat Transfer. 3rd ed. LC 57-12230. 1957. text ed. 38.50x (ISBN 0-471-43725-5). Wiley.

Jakobiec, Frederick A., ed. Ocular Anatomy, Embryology, & Teratology. (Illus.). 1200p. 1982. 125.00 (ISBN 0-06-141336-4, Harper Medical). Lippincott.

Jakobovits, Immanuel. The Timely & the Timeless. 1977. 15.95 o.p. (ISBN 0-85303-189-4). Bloch.

Jakobovits, L. A., jt. auth. see Steinberg, D. D.

Jakobson, Roman. Selected Writings: Poetry of Grammar, Grammar of Poerty, Vol. 3. Rudy, Stephan, ed. 814p. 1981. 114.00x (ISBN 90-279-3178-X). Mouton.

--Six Lectures on Sound & Meaning. Mepham, John, tr. from Fr. 1978. text ed. 17.50x (ISBN 0-262-10019-3); pap. 5.95 (ISBN 0-262-60010-2). MIT Pr.

Jakobson, Roman, et al. Preliminaries to Speech Analysis: The Distinctive Features & Their Correlates. 1961. pap. 3.95x o.p. (ISBN 0-262-60001-3). MIT Pr.

Jakoby, William B., jt. ed. see Caldwell, John.

Jakopic, R. R. Jakopic. (Illus.). 230p. 1981. 50.00 (ISBN 0-89893-170-3). CDP.

Jakoubek, B. Brain Function & Macromolecular Synthesis. (Advanced Biochemistry Ser.). 156p. 1974. 15.00x (ISBN 0-85086-043-1, Pub. by Pion England). Methuen Inc.

Jakovljevic, B. New International Status of Civil Defence. 1982. lib. bdg. 34.50 (ISBN 90-247-2567-4, Pub. by Martinus Nijhoff Netherlands). Kluwer Boston.

Jakowlew, B. & Szymanski, A., eds. Synthetic Materials for Electronics. (Materials Science Monograph: Vol. 8). 1982. 70.25 (ISBN 0-444-99741-5). Elsevier.

Jaksic, B., ed. Lectures on High Energy Physics. (Nuclear Physics Ser). 530p. 1965. 123.00 (ISBN 0-677-10770-6). Gordon.

Jakubowski, Franz. Ideology & Superstructure. LC 75-32930. 144p. 1976. 18.95 (ISBN 0-312-40460-3). St Martin.

Jakubowski, Patricia & Lange, Arthur J. The Assertive Option. pap. 9.95 (ISBN 0-686-36682-4). Inst Rat Liv.

Jakubowsky, Frank. The Psychological Patterns of Jesus Christ. 342p. (Orig.). 1982. pap. 14.95 (ISBN 0-932588-02-6). Jakubowsky.

Jalland, Patricia. The Liberals & Ireland: The Ulster Question in British Politics to 1914. LC 79-26719. 250p. 1980. 27.50x (ISBN 0-312-48347-3). St Martin.

Jameelah, M. Islam & Modernism. pap. 6.95 (ISBN 0-686-18574-9). Kazi Pubns.

--Islam & Orientalism. pap. 5.50 (ISBN 0-686-18573-0). Kazi Pubns.

--Islam in Theory & Practice. pap. 9.95 (ISBN 0-686-18501-3). Kazi Pubns.

--Islam vs. Ahl-al-Kitab, Past & Present. pap. 12.00 (ISBN 0-686-18570-6). Kazi Pubns.

James, jt. auth. see Cusack.

James, A. & Evison, Lilian. Biological Indicators of Water Quality. LC 79-557. 1979. 64.95x (ISBN 0-471-27590-5, Pub. by Wiley-Interscience). Wiley.

James, A., ed. Mathematical Models in Water Pollution Control. LC 77-7214. 1978. 71.95x (ISBN 0-471-99471-5, Pub. by Wiley-Interscience). Wiley.

James, A. Everette, jt. auth. see Fleischer, Arthur C.

James, A. Everette see Squire, Lucy F., et al.

James, A. Everette, ed. Legal Medicine with Special Reference to Diagnostic Imaging. LC 79-19277. (Illus.). 412p. 1980. text ed. 35.00 (ISBN 0-8067-0951-0). Urban & S.

James, A. Everette, et al. Pediatric Nuclear Medicine. LC 72-97912. (Illus.). 560p. 1974. text ed. 35.00 o.p. (ISBN 0-7216-5108-9). Saunders.

James, A. T., jt. auth. see Gurr, M. I.

James, Albert. Like & Unlike: Stages 1, 2, & 3. LC 77-83007. (Science 5-13 Ser.). (Illus.). 1977. pap. text ed. 11.55 (ISBN 0-356-04350-9). Raintree Pubs.

--Structures & Forces: Stage 3. LC 77-82991. (Science 5-13 Ser.). (Illus.). 1977. pap. text ed. 11.55 (ISBN 0-356-04107-7). Raintree Pubs.

--Structures & Forces: Stages 1 & 2. LC 77-82991. (Science 5-13 Ser.). (Illus.). 1977. pap. text ed. 11.55 (ISBN 0-356-04007-0). Raintree Pubs.

James, Allan & Kettermann, Bernhard, eds. Dialaktphonologie und Fremdsprachenerwerb (Dialect Phonology & Foreign Language Acquisition) (Ger.). 1983. pap. write for info. (ISBN 3-87808-574-5). Benjamins North Am.

James, Allen. Touring on Two Wheels. LC 78-24723. (Illus.). 1979. cancelled o.p. (ISBN 0-89196-056-2, Domus Bks); pap. cancelled o.p. (ISBN 0-89196-055-4). Quality Bks IL.

James, Anna. The Darker Side of Love. (Orig.). 1979. pap. 2.50 o.s.i. (ISBN 0-515-05096-2). Jove Pubns.

--The Day Beyond Destiny. 480p. (Orig.). 1981. pap. 2.75 o.s.i. (ISBN 0-515-05320-1). Jove Pubns.

James, Arthur M. A Dictionary of Thermodynamics. LC 76-5472. 262p. 1976. 29.95x o.s.i. (ISBN 0-470-15035-1). Halsted Pr.

James B. & Peters, Joseph P. Strategic Thinking: New Frontier for Hospital Management. 1983. pap. write for info. (ISBN 0-87258-404-6). Am Hospital.

James, Barrie G. The Future of the Multinational Pharmaceutical Industries to 1990. LC 77-72268. 283p. 1977. 49.95x o.s.i. (ISBN 0-470-99130-5). Halsted Pr.

James, Barry. Call Me Mister. 1974. 17.25 (ISBN 0-87350-178-0); instructor's manual 14.95 (ISBN 0-87350-153-5). Milady.

--Man's Guide to Business & Social Success. 1969. 17.25 (ISBN 0-87350-151-9); instructor's manual 14.95 (ISBN 0-87350-153-5). Milady.

James, Bessie R. Anne Royall's U. S. A. 1972. 35.00 (ISBN 0-8135-0732-4). Rutgers U Pr.

James, Bill. The Bill James Baseball Abstract 1983. 224p. (Orig.). 1983. pap. 6.95 (ISBN 0-345-30367-9). Ballantine.

James, Brian, ed. A Catalogue of the Tract Collection of Saint David's University College, Lampeter. LC 76-353069. 336p. 1975. 56.00 o.p. (ISBN 0-7201-0538-2, Pub. by Mansell England). Wilson.

James, C. C. M. & Lassman, L. P. Spinal Dysraphism: Spina Bifida Occulta. (Illus.). 1972. 16.95 o.p. (ISBN 0-407-39870-8). Butterworth.

James, C. D. Twentieth Century French Reader. 1967. 8.00 (ISBN 0-08-011232-3); pap. 6.70 (ISBN 0-08-011231-5). Pergamon.

James, C. Vaughan. Soviet Socialist Realism. LC 73-87878. 192p. 1974. 15.95 o.p. (ISBN 0-312-74900-7). St Martin.

James, Carl. Contrastive Analysis. (Applied Linguistics & Language Study Ser.). 1980. pap. text ed. 10.75x (ISBN 0-582-55370-9). Longman.

James, Charity. Young Lives at Stake: The Education of Adolescents. LC 77-166550. 221p. 1973. pap. 2.95 o.p. (ISBN 0-8052-0395-8). Schocken.

James, Charles F. Documentary History of the Struggle for Religious Liberty in Virginia. LC 70-121101. (Civil Liberties in American History Ser). 1971. Repr. of 1900 ed. lib. bdg. 37.50 (ISBN 0-306-71977-0). Da Capo.

James, Clifford L. Principles of Economics. rev. 9th ed. (Orig.). 1972. pap. 5.50 (ISBN 0-06-460008-4, CO 8, COS). B&N NY.

James, Columba, tr. see Musset, Lucien.

James, D. E. Student's Guide to Efficient Study. 1967. text ed. 7.50 o.s.i. (ISBN 0-08-012321-X); pap. 6.25 (ISBN 0-686-86593-6). Pergamon.

James, D. E., et al. Economic Approaches to Environmental Problems: Techniques & Results of Empirical Analysis. (Fundamental Aspects of Pollution Control & Environmental Sciences Ser.: Vol. 3). 1978. 51.00 (ISBN 0-444-41716-8). Elsevier.

James, D. W., et al. Modern Irrigated Soils. 256p. 1982. 30.00x (ISBN 0-471-06351-7, Pub. by Wiley-Interscience). Wiley.

James, Dan. Gunsmoke Mesa. 256p. (YA) 1974. 6.95 (ISBN 0-685-49094-7, Avalon). Bouregy.

--Shadow Guns. (YA) 1972. 6.95 (ISBN 0-685-24999-9, Avalon). Bouregy.

--Trouble at Choctaw Bend. (YA) 1972. 6.95 (ISBN 0-685-28626-6, Avalon). Bouregy.

James, Dave. Volleyball for Schools. (Illus.). 1977. 12.95 o.p. (ISBN 0-7207-0886-9). Transatlantic.

James, Dilmus D., jt. ed. see Street, James H.

James, Don, ed. Conditioning for Football: The Washington Way. Huegli, Rich. LC 80-82967. (Illus.). 136p. (Orig.). 1982. pap. text ed. 5.95 (ISBN 0-88011-016-3). Leisure Pr.

James, Don L., et al. Retailing Today. 2nd ed. 543p. 1981. text ed. 22.95 (ISBN 0-15-576672-4, HC); instr's. manual 3.95 (ISBN 0-15-576673-2). HarBraceJ.

James, Donald. The Fall of the Russian Empire. LC 81-21175. 336p. 1982. 13.95 (ISBN 0-399-12689-9). Putnam Pub Group.

James, Dorothy. Poverty, Politics & Change. (Illus.). 224p. 1972. pap. text ed. 12.95 (ISBN 0-13-686584-4). P-H.

James, Dorothy, ed. The Political Science of Poverty & Welfare. 1974. pap. 6.00 (ISBN 0-918592-06-2). Policy Studies.

James, Dorothy B. The Contemporary Presidency. 2nd ed. LC 73-19657. 350p. 1974. pap. 8.75 (ISBN 0-672-63716-2). Pegasus.

James, E. K., tr. see Rivera, Jose E.

James, Edgar. Day of the Lamb. 132p. 1980. pap. 4.50 (ISBN 0-88207-793-7). Victor Bks.

James, Edgar C. Arabs, Oil & Energy. LC 77-26112. 128p. 1982. pap. 4.95 (ISBN 0-8024-0296-8). Moody.

--Arabs, Oil, & Energy. 1978. pap. 2.50 o.p. (ISBN 0-8024-0294-1). Moody.
--Armageddon. 128p. 1981. pap. 4.95 (ISBN 0-8024-0297-6). Moody.
James, Edward. The Origins of France: From Clovis to the Capetians, AD 500-1000. LC 82-10691. 288p. 1982. 25.00x (ISBN 0-312-58862-3). St Martin.
James, Edward, tr. see Musset, Lucien.
James, Edward T. & James, Janet W., eds. Notable American Women, 1607-1950: A Biographical Dictionary, 3 Vols. LC 76-152274. 2141p. 1971. 90.00x o.p. (ISBN 0-674-62731-8, Belknap Pr); Set. pap. 32.50 (ISBN 0-674-62734-2). Harvard U Pr.
James, Elizabeth M. Political Theory: An Introduction to Interpretation. LC 81-40791. 104p. 1982. pap. text ed. 8.25 (ISBN 0-8191-2008-1). U Pr of Amer.
James, Fannie B. Dawning Truth. 1968. pap. 1.95 (ISBN 0-686-24357-9). Divine Sci Fed.
--Truth & Health. 1970. 8.95 (ISBN 0-686-24356-0). Divine Sci Fed.
James, Fannie B., compiled by. Divine Science: Its Principle & Practice. 1957. pap. 7.50 (ISBN 0-686-24361-7). Divine Sci Fed.
James, Felix. The American Addition: History of a Black Community. LC 78-65427. (Illus.). 1979. pap. 9.25 (ISBN 0-8191-0663-1). U Pr of Amer.
James, Fleming, Jr. & Hazard, Geoffrey. Civil Procedure. 2nd ed. 1977. 19.95 (ISBN 0-316-45689-6). Little.
James, Fleming, Jr., jt. auth. see Harper, Fowler V.
James, Frances W. The Iron Age at Beth-Shan: A Study of Levels VI-IV. (Museum Monographs). (Illus.). 369p. 1966. soft bound 8.00x (ISBN 0-934718-20-2). Univ Mus of U PA.
James, Francis, jt. auth. see Gray, Michael.
James, Francis G. North Country Bishop: A Biography of William Nicolson. 1956. 49.50x (ISBN 0-686-51425-4). Elliots Bks.
James, Francisco J. The Electronic Industry Game. (Business Adventures Ser.). (Orig.). 1978. pap. 50.00 o.s.i. (ISBN 0-933836-02-3); 4.95 (ISBN 0-933836-09-0). Simtek.
--The Pocket Calculator Boom. (Business Adventures Ser.). (Orig.). 1978. pap. 50.00 o.s.i. (ISBN 0-933836-01-5); 4.95 (ISBN 0-933836-08-2). Simtek.
James, Frank L. Years of Discontent: Dr. Frank L. James in Arkansas, 1877-1878. Baird, W. David, intro. by. LC 76-40025. (Memphis State University Press Primary Source Ser.). 1977. pap. 6.95x o.p. (ISBN 0-87870-037-4). Memphis St Univ.
James, G. V., jt. auth. see Smith, R.
James, Gene, ed. The Unification Church & The Family. (Conference Ser.: No. 17). 1983. pap. text ed. price not set (ISBN 0-932894-17-8). Unif Theol Seminary.
James, George W., ed. Airline Economics. (Illus.). 352p. 1981. 35.95x (ISBN 0-669-04909-3). Lexington Bks.
James, Glenn D. Energy Potpourri. (Illus.). 1977. pap. 8.80x (ISBN 0-916898-01-6). Sono Pubs.
James, H. Question of Speech-The Lesson of Balzac: Two Lectures. LC 72-334. (Studies of Henry James, No. 17). 1972. Repr. of 1905 ed. lib. bdg. 27.95x (ISBN 0-8383-1411-2). Haskell.
James, Henry. The Ambassadors. 1971. pap. 1.95x (ISBN 0-460-01987-2, Evman). Biblio Dist.
--Ambassadors. pap. 3.50 (ISBN 0-451-51746-6, CE1746, Sig Classics). NAL.
--Americans. pap. 3.50 (ISBN 0-451-51709-1, CE1709, Sig Classics). NAL.
--Aspern Papers. Bd. with The Turn of the Screw; The Liar; The Two Faces. LC 76-158791. (Novels & Tales of Henry James: Vol. 12). xxiii, 412p. Repr. of 1908 ed. 25.00x (ISBN 0-678-02811-7). Kelley.
--Confidence, Eighteen Eighty. Ruhm, Herbert, ed. LC 76-39775. 1977. Repr. of 1962 ed. lib. bdg. 20.00x (ISBN 0-8371-9296-X, JACO). Greenwood.
--Daisy Miller & Other Stories. 1983. pap. price not set (ISBN 0-14-006721-3). Penguin.
--Eight Tales from the Major Phase. 1969. pap. 7.95 (ISBN 0-393-00286-1, Norton Lib). Norton.
--The Europeans. 176p. 1976. Repr. of 1878 ed. lib. bdg. 15.95x (ISBN 0-89244-018-X). Queens Hse.
--Great Short Works of Henry James. Flower, Dean, ed. pap. 3.95i (ISBN 0-06-083040-9, P3040, PL). Har-Row.
--In the Cage & Other Stories. 1983. pap. 2.95 (ISBN 0-14-003500-1). Penguin.
--International Episodes. 1982. pap. cancelled (ISBN 0-14-004641-0). Penguin.
--Novels & Tales of Henry James, 26 Vols. (New york edition). Repr. of 1907 ed. lib. bdg. 494.00x (ISBN 0-678-02800-1). Kelley.
--The Other House. 228p. 1976. Repr. of 1896 ed. lib. bdg. 16.95x (ISBN 0-89244-083-X). Queens Hse.
--The Outcry. LC 80-17012. xiv, 267p. 1982. Repr. of 1911 ed. 22.50 (ISBN 0-86527-335-9). Fertig.
--Partial Portraits. Repr. of 1888 ed. lib. bdg. 18.25x (ISBN 0-8371-2797-1, JAPA). Greenwood.
--Portrait of a Lady. (Orig.). pap. 3.50 (ISBN 0-451-51605-2, CE1605, Sig Classics). NAL.
--The Portrait of a Lady. Bamberg, Robert D., ed. (Norton Critical Edition Ser.). 1975. pap. text ed. 9.95x (ISBN 0-393-09259-3). Norton.
--The Portrait of a Lady. rev. ed. Dixson, Robert J., ed. (American Classics Ser.: Bk. 7). (gr. 9 up). 1974. pap. text ed. 3.25 (ISBN 0-88345-203-0, 18126); cassettes 40.00 (ISBN 0-685-38927-8); o.p tapes 40.00 (ISBN 0-685-38928-6). Regents Pub.
--The Portrait of a Lady. (World's Classics Ser.). 1981. pap. 4.95 (ISBN 0-19-281514-8). Oxford U Pr.
--The Portrait of a Lady. LC 82-42867. 8.95 (ISBN 0-394-60432-6). Modern Lib.
--The Princess Casamassima. 1977. pap. 4.50 (ISBN 0-14-004102-8). Penguin.
--The Princess Casamassima. (Apollo Eds.). 608p. 1976. pap. 5.95i (ISBN 0-8152-0381-0, A-395, TYC-T). T Y Crowell.
--Princess Casamassima, Vol. 2. LC 70-158784. (Novels & Tales of Henry James: Vol. 6). Repr. of 1908 ed. lib. bdg. 22.50x (ISBN 0-678-02806-0). Kelley.
--Richard Olney & His Public Service. LC 70-87445. (American Scene Ser). (Illus.). 1971. Repr. of 1923 ed. lib. bdg. 39.50 (ISBN 0-306-71516-3). Da Capo.
--Roderick Hudson. (World's Classics Ser.). 1980. pap. 4.95 (ISBN 0-19-281547-4). Oxford U Pr.
--Selected Literary Criticism. Shapira, Morris, ed. LC 80-49685. 350p. 1981. pap. 16.95 (ISBN 0-521-28365-5). Cambridge U Pr.
--Selected Short Stories. Incl. Daisy Miller; Last of the Valerii; Real Thing; Lesson of the Mastery. (YA) (gr. 9 up). 1963. pap. 2.50 (ISBN 0-14-001919-7). Penguin.
--The Spoils of Poynton. 1977. pap. 2.95 (ISBN 0-14-001922-7). Penguin.
--The Spoils of Poynton. Richards, Bernard, ed. (The World's Classics Ser.). 224p. 1983. pap. 4.50 (ISBN 0-19-281605-5, GB). Oxford U Pr.
--Tales of Henry James: Vol. 1, 1864-1869. Aziz, Maqbool, ed. (Illus.). 1973. 39.00x (ISBN 0-19-812457-0). Oxford U Pr.
--Turn of the Screw. 1975. 8.95x (ISBN 0-460-00912-5, Evman); pap. 1.95x (ISBN 0-460-01912-0, Evman). Biblio Dist.
--Turn of the Screw. Bd. with Daisy Miller. 1956. pap. 2.50 (ISBN 0-440-39154-7, LE). Dell.
--The Turn of the Screw. 1977. Repr. of 1898 ed. lib. bdg. 15.95x (ISBN 0-89244-046-5). Queens Hse.
--Turn of the Screw & Other Short Novels. (Orig.). pap. 1.95 (ISBN 0-451-51669-9, CJ1669, Sig Classics). NAL.
--Washington Square. (Classics Ser). (gr. 10 up). 1969. pap. 1.50 (ISBN 0-8049-0210-0, CL-210). Airmont.
--Washington Square. pap. 2.25 (ISBN 0-451-51766-0, CE1766, Sig Classics). NAL.
--Washington Square. Le Fanu, Mark, ed. (The World's Classics Ser.). 224p. 1983. pap. 2.95 (ISBN 0-19-281611-X, GB). Oxford U Pr.
--What Maisie Knew. Jefferson, Douglas & Grant, Douglas, eds. (World's Classics Paperback Ser.). 1980. pap. 2.95 (ISBN 0-19-281533-4). Oxford U Pr.
--What Maisie Knew. 1974. pap. 3.50 (ISBN 0-14-002448-4). Penguin.
--William Wetmore Story & His Friends, 2 vols. in one. LC 69-18460. (Library of American Art Ser). 1969. Repr. of 1903 ed. lib. bdg. 55.00 (ISBN 0-306-71249-0). Da Capo.
--Wings of the Dove. pap. 3.50 (ISBN 0-451-51691-5, CE1691, Sig Classics). NAL.
James, Henry see Hawthorne, Nathaniel.
James, Henry E. Long White Mountain or a Journey in Manchuria, with Some Account of the History, People, Administration & Religion of That Country. LC 68-55199. (Illus.). Repr. of 1888 ed. lib. bdg. cancelled o.p. (ISBN 0-8371-0497-1, JALW). Greenwood.
James, I. M. The Topology of Stiefel Manifolds. LC 76-9646. (London Mathematical Society Lecture Notes Ser.: No. 24). 1977. 15.95x (ISBN 0-521-21334-7). Cambridge U Pr.
James, J. Perspective Drawing. 1981. pap. 13.95 (ISBN 0-13-660357-2). P-H.
James, Jack & Fayers, Heather. Probate Guide for Alberta. 99p. 1976. 9.95 (ISBN 0-88908-210-3); Forms 11.95 (ISBN 0-686-35992-5). Self Counsel Pr.
James, Jack D. Divorce Guide for Ontario. 5th ed. 105p. 1982. write for info. (ISBN 0-88908-333-9); forms 14.50 (ISBN 0-686-35996-8). Self Counsel Pr.
James, Janet W. Changing Ideas about Women in the United States, 1776-1825. Freidel, Frank, ed. LC 80-8474. (Modern American History Ser.). 369p. 1982. lib. bdg. 45.00 (ISBN 0-8240-4858-X). Garland Pub.
James, Janet W., jt. ed. see James, Edward T.
James, Janice. A Lady of Repute. LC 78-20079. 264p. 1980. 10.95 o.p. (ISBN 0-385-13507-6). Doubleday.
James, Jean M., tr. see Lao She.
James, John. Chartres: The Masons Who Built a Legend. (Illus.). 224p. 1982. 39.95 (ISBN 0-7100-0886-4). Routledge & Kegan.
James, John, jt. ed. see Ardell, Donald.
James, John D., et al. A Guide to Drug Interaction. (Illus.). 1978. pap. text ed. 17.95 (ISBN 0-07-032262-7, HP). McGraw.
James, K., jt. auth. see Dinda, S.
James, K. W., jt. auth. see Ngan, H.
James, Kenneth see Allen, W. S.
James, L. D. & Lee. Economics of Water Resources Planning. 1970. 36.50 (ISBN 0-07-032263-5, C). McGraw.
James, L. S., jt. ed. see Bloom, Arthur D.
James, Lawrence R. & Mulaik, Stanley A. Causal Analysis: Assumptions, Models, & Data: Studying Organizations: Innovations in Methodology. 144p. 1982. 17.95 (ISBN 0-8039-1867-4); pap. 7.95 (ISBN 0-8039-1868-2). Sage.
James, Leigh F. Flight of the Hawk, No. 4. 352p. 1982. pap. 3.50 (ISBN 0-553-22578-2). Bantam.
James, Livia. The Emerald Land. 368p. (Orig.). 1983. pap. 2.95 (ISBN 0-449-12410-X, GM). Fawcett.
James, M. L., et al. Applied Numerical Methods for Digital Computation with Fortran & CSMP. 2nd ed. 1977. text ed. 32.95 scp (ISBN 0-7002-2499-8, HarpC); solution manual avail. (ISBN 0-06-363255-1). Har-Row.
James, M. Lynn & Schreck, James O. General, Organic & Biological Chemistry: A Brief Introduction. short ed. 560p. 1982. text ed. 25.95 (ISBN 0-669-03862-8); lab guide 8.95 (ISBN 0-669-03864-4); student guide 7.95 (ISBN 0-669-03865-2); instr's guide 1.95 (ISBN 0-669-03866-0). Heath.
James, M. Lynn, et al. General, Organic & Biological Chemistry: Chemistry for the Living System. 1980. text ed. 27.95 (ISBN 0-669-01329-3); lab. guide 9.95 (ISBN 0-669-01332-3); study guide 8.95 (ISBN 0-669-01331-5); instrs'. guide 1.95 (ISBN 0-669-01330-7). Heath.
James, M. R. John Rylands University Library, Manchester: Catalogue of the Latin Manuscripts in the John Rylands University Library, Manchester. Repr. of 1921 ed. lib. bdg. 140.00 2 Vols. in One (ISBN 3-601-00246-9). Kraus Intl.
James, Margaret. Footsteps in the Fog. 182p. 1980. 8.95 o.p. (ISBN 0-312-29782-3). St Martin.
--Marionette. (General Ser.). 1980. lib. bdg. 11.95 (ISBN 0-8161-3113-9, Large Print Bks). G K Hall.
--Ring the Bell Softly. 1980. pap. 1.25 o.s.i. (ISBN 0-440-17626-3). Dell.
--A Voice in the Darkness. (General Ser.). (gr. 7-12). 1979. lib. bdg. 10.95 (ISBN 0-8161-6749-4, Large Print Bks). G K Hall.
James, Marquis. The Raven: A Biography of Sam Houston. LC 29-22644. (Maps, Photos). 1970. 14.95 (ISBN 0-910220-15-8). Berg.
--They Had Their Hour: Benjamin Franklin, Thomas Jefferson. 324p. 1982. Repr. of 1926 ed. lib. bdg. 40.00 (ISBN 0-8495-2802-X). Arden Lib.
James, Maynard. I Believe in the Holy Spirit. LC 23-9036. Orig. Title: I Believe in the Holy Ghost. 176p. 1965. pap. 1.95 o.p. (ISBN 0-87123-241-3, 200241). Bethany Hse.
James, Melanie. Love Forever. 192p. (Orig.). 1983. pap. 2.50 (ISBN 0-449-12409-6, GM). Fawcett.
James, Michael. The Second Quiltmaker's Handbook. (Creative Handcrafts Ser.). 208p. 1981. 19.95 (ISBN 0-13-797795-6, Spec); pap. 10.95 (ISBN 0-13-797787-5). P-H.
James, Michael, tr. see Delaunay, Charles.
James, Muriel & Jongeward, Dorothy. Born to Win. 1978. pap. 3.50 (ISBN 0-451-11152-4, AE1152, Sig). NAL.
--Born to Win. 6.95 o.p. (ISBN 0-686-92308-1, 6370). Hazelden.
--The People Book: Transactional Analysis for Students. new ed. 1975. pap. text ed. 10.64 (ISBN 0-201-03279-1, Sch Div); tchr's ed. 3.32 (ISBN 0-201-03280-5). A-W.
James, Naomi. Alone Around the World. LC 79-1403. (Illus.). 1979. 9.95 o.p. (ISBN 0-698-10986-4, Coward). Putnam Pub Group.
James, Otis. Dolly Parton. (Illus.). 1978. pap. 3.95 (ISBN 0-8256-3922-0, Quick Fox). Putnam Pub Group.
--Dolly Parton: A Photo-Bio. (Orig.). pap. 1.95 o.s.i. (ISBN 0-515-05157-8). Jove Pubns.
James, P. D. The Black Tower. 288p. 1982. pap. 2.95 (ISBN 0-446-31001-8). Warner Bks.
--Cover Her Face. (General Ser.). 1979. lib. bdg. 12.95 (ISBN 0-8161-6793-1, Large Print Bks). G K Hall.
--Cover Her Face. 256p. 1982. pap. 2.95. Warner Bks.
--Death of an Expert Witness. 1978. lib. bdg. 13.95 o.p. (ISBN 0-8161-6600-5, Large Print Bks). G K Hall.
--Death of an Expert Witness. 1982. pap. 2.95 (ISBN 0-446-31003-4). Warner Bks.
--Innocent Blood. 349p. 1982. pap. 3.50 (ISBN 0-446-31004-2). Warner Bks.
--A Mind to Murder. 256p. 1982. pap. 2.95 (ISBN 0-446-31005-0). Warner Bks.
--Murder in Triplicate. 720p. 1982. pap. 12.95 (ISBN 0-684-17646-7, ScribT). Scribner.
--A Shroud for a Nightingale. 288p. 1982. pap. 2.95 (ISBN 0-446-31006-9). Warner Bks.
--Unnatural Causes. (General Ser.). 1980. lib. bdg. 12.95 (ISBN 0-8161-3106-6, Large Print Bks). G K Hall.
--Unnatural Causes. 256p. 1982. pap. 2.95 (ISBN 0-446-31007-7). Warner Bks.
--An Unsuitable Job for a Woman. 288p. 1982. pap. 2.95 (ISBN 0-446-31008-5). Warner Bks.
James, Peter. The Future of Coal. 296p. 1982. 19.50x (ISBN 0-8448-1412-1). Crane-Russak Co.
James, Philip. Children's Books of Yesterday. Holme, C. Geoffrey, ed. LC 79-174059. (Illus.). 128p. 1976. Repr. of 1933 ed. 40.00x (ISBN 0-8103-4135-2). Gale.
James, Preston E. & Martin, Geoffrey J. All Possible Worlds, a History of Geographical Ideas. 2nd ed. LC 80-25021. 508p. 1981. text ed. 27.95x (ISBN 0-471-06121-2). Wiley.
James, Preston E. & Webb, Kempton. One World Divided: A Geographer Looks at the Modern World. 3rd ed. LC 79-12136. 1980. text ed. 29.95 (ISBN 0-471-02687-5). Wiley.
James, R. & Claus, Karen E. Handbook of Signage & Sign Legislation. (Illus.). 1976. 25.00 o.p. (ISBN 0-685-51822-1). Signs of Times.
James, R., et al. Laboratory Manual for Criminalistics. 1980. 14.95 (ISBN 0-13-519819-4). P-H.
James, R. W. The Optical Principles of the Diffraction of X-Rays. LC 82-80706. 1982. Repr. of 1948 ed. 55.00 (ISBN 0-918024-23-4). Ox Bow.
James, Rebecca. Tomorrow Is Mine. LC 77-25597. 1979. 10.95 o.p. (ISBN 0-385-12675-1). Doubleday.
James, Rob. Ocean Sailing. (Illus.). 224p. 1980. 24.95 (ISBN 0-686-95471-8). Sheridan.
James, Robert R. The British Revolution 1880-1939. 1977. 17.95 o.s.i. (ISBN 0-394-40761-X). Knopf.
James Second, King of Great Britain. The Memoirs of James Second: His Campaigns As Duke of York, 1652-1660. Sells, A. Lytton, tr. LC 71-163544. 301p. 1962. Repr. lib. bdg. 17.00x (ISBN 0-8371-6209-2, JAME). Greenwood.
James, Selma, jt. auth. see DallaCosta, Mariarosa.
James, Selma, jt. auth. see Hall, Ruth.
James, Sidney V. Colonial Rhode Island: A History. LC 75-9685. (A History of the American Colonies Ser.). 1975. lib. bdg. 30.00 (ISBN 0-527-18720-8). Kraus Intl.
James, Stewart. Abbott's Encyclopedia of Rope Tricks for Magicians. (Illus.). 9.00 (ISBN 0-8446-5206-7). Peter Smith.
James, Stuart. Lacrosse for Beginners. LC 80-27810. (Illus.). 128p. (gr. 7 up). 1981. PLB 8.79 o.p. (ISBN 0-671-34050-6). Messner.
James, Susannah. A Distant Shore. 1982. pap. 2.95 (ISBN 0-451-11264-4, AE1264, Sig). NAL.
--The Jeweled Birdcage. (Orig.). 1982. pap. 2.95 o.p. (ISBN 0-451-11264-4, Sig). NAL.
James, T. B., jt. ed. see Richardson, R. C.
James, T. G., ed. Excavating in Egypt: The Egypt Exploration Society 1882-1982. 194p. 1982. 45.00x (ISBN 0-7141-0932-0, Pub. by Brit Mus Pubns England). State Mutual Bk.
James, T. H., ed. Theory of the Photographic Process. 4th ed. 1977. 68.95 (ISBN 0-02-360190-6, 36019). Macmillan.
James, Terry, jt. auth. see Poulton, G. A.
James, Theodore, Jr. The Gourmet Garden: How to Grow Vegetables, Fruits & Herbs for Today's Cuisine. (Illus.). 256p. 1983. 15.95 (ISBN 0-525-93264-X, 01549-460); pap. 9.95 (ISBN 0-525-48044-7, 0966-290). Dutton.
James, Timothy A. The Messiah's Return: Delayed, Fulfilled, or Double-fulfillment? (Studies in Biblical Prophecy). (Orig.). pap. 2.50 (ISBN 0-9608478-0-4). James T A.
James, V. H., jt. ed. see Gray, C. H.
James, V. H., jt. ed. see Martini, L.
James, V. H., jt. ed. see Martini, Luciano.
James, V. H., et al, eds. see Symposium at University of Florence, Italy.
James, Vivian H., ed. The Adrenal Gland. LC 77-85870. 342p. 1979. 38.00 (ISBN 0-89004-297-7). Raven.
James, W. C. Television in Transition. LC 82-73647. 200p. 1982. 74.95 (ISBN 0-87251-079-4). Crain Bks.
James, Wendy. Kwanim Pa: The Making of the Uduk People; an Ethnographic Study of Survival in the Sudan-Ethiopian Borderlands. (Illus.). 1979. text ed. 45.00x (ISBN 0-19-823194-6). Oxford U Pr.
James, Will. The American Cowboy. (Westerns Ser.). 1981. lib. bdg. cancelled o.s.i. (ISBN 0-8398-2681-8, Gregg). G K Hall.
James, William. Essays in Psychology. Burkhardt, Frederick & Bowers, Fredson, eds. (The Works of William James: Eleventh Title: Vol. 13). (Illus.). 512p. 1983. text ed. 40.00x (ISBN 0-674-26714-1). Harvard U Pr.
--Memories & Studies. LC 68-19276. 1968. Repr. of 1911 ed. lib. bdg. 18.00x (ISBN 0-8371-0496-3, JAMS). Greenwood.
--Pragmatism. Kuklick, Bruce, ed. (Philosophical Classics Ser.). 152p. 1980. lib. bdg. 13.50 (ISBN 0-915145-04-9); pap. text ed. 3.25 (ISBN 0-915145-05-7). Hackett Pub.
--Pragmatism & Other Essays. Blau, J. L., ed. 1983. pap. 4.95 (ISBN 0-671-46629-1). WSP.
--Talks to Teachers on Psychology & to Students on Some of Life's Ideals. 1958. pap. 4.95 (ISBN 0-393-00165-2, Norton Lib). Norton.
--Talks to Teachers on Psychology: And to Students on Some of Life's Ideals. Burkhardt, Frederick & Bowers, Redson, eds. (Works of William James: Tenth Title). (Illus.). 384p. 1983. text ed. 25.00x (ISBN 0-674-86785-8). Harvard U Pr.
--Varieties of Religious Experience. pap. 3.50 (ISBN 0-451-62069-0, ME2069, Ment). NAL.

--The Varieties of Religious Experience: A Study in Human Nature. Marty, Martin, ed. (American Library). 1982. pap. 4.95 (ISBN 0-14-039034-0). Penguin.

--Will to Believe & Other Essays in Popular Philosophy & Human Immortality. 9.50 (ISBN 0-8446-2313-X). Peter Smith.

--Writings of William James. McDermott, John J., ed. 1968. 5.95 o.s.i. (ISBN 0-394-60796-1, G96). Modern Lib.

James, William M. All Blood Is Red. (The Apache Ser.: No. 10). (Orig.). 1977. pap. 1.50 o.p. (ISBN 0-523-40559-6). Pinnacle Bks.

--Apache, No. 3: Duel to the Death. 192p. (Orig.). 1975. pap. 1.50 o.p. (ISBN 0-523-40552-9). Pinnacle Bks.

--Apache No. 8: Blood on the Tracks. (The Apache Ser). (Orig.). 1977. pap. 1.50 o.p. (ISBN 0-523-40557-X). Pinnacle Bks.

--Blood Brother. (Apache Ser.: No. 17). 160p. (Orig.). 1980. pap. 1.50 o.p. (ISBN 0-523-40694-0). Pinnacle Bks.

--Blood Line. (Apache No. 7). 1976. pap. 1.50 o.p. (ISBN 0-523-40556-1). Pinnacle Bks.

--Death Ride. (Apache Ser.: No. 24). 208p. (Orig.). 1983. pap. 1.95 (ISBN 0-523-41675-X). Pinnacle Bks.

--Death Valley. (Apache Ser.: No. 23). 208p. (Orig.). 1983. pap. 1.95 (ISBN 0-523-41025-5). Pinnacle Bks.

--Fort Treachery. (Apache Ser.: No. 5). 192p. 1975. pap. 1.50 o.p. (ISBN 0-523-40554-5). Pinnacle Bks.

--Knife in the Night. (Apache Ser., No. 2). 160p. 1974. pap. 1.50 o.p. (ISBN 0-523-40551-0). Pinnacle Bks.

--Sonora Slaughter. (Apache Ser.: No. 6). 160p. 1976. pap. 1.50 o.p. (ISBN 0-523-40555-3). Pinnacle Bks.

--Texas Killing. (Apache Ser.: No. 16). (Orig.). 1980. pap. 1.50 o.p. (ISBN 0-523-40593-6). Pinnacle Bks.

James, Williams. The Selected Letters of William James. Hardwick, Elizabeth, ed. LC 80-66463. 304p. 1981. pap. 8.95 (ISBN 0-87923-348-6, Nonpareil Bks). Godine.

James-Gerth, W., tr. see Gijsen, Marnix.

Jameson, Anna B. The History of Our Lord As Exemplified in Works of Art; with That of His Type; St. John the Baptist; & Other Persons of the Old & New Testament, 2 vols. LC 92-167006. (Illus.). 1976. Repr. of 1890 ed. Set. 60.00x (ISBN 0-8103-4304-5). Gale.

--Legends of the Madonna, As Represented in the Fine Arts. LC 70-89273. (Tower Bks). (Illus.). lxxvi, 344p. 1972. Repr. of 1890 ed. 42.00x (ISBN 0-8103-3114-4). Gale.

Jameson, Cynthia. Catofy the Clever. (Illus.). 1972. PLB 4.69 o.p. (ISBN 0-698-30038-6, Coward). Putnam Pub Group.

--The Clay Pot Boy. (Break of Day Bk.). (Illus.). (gr. 1-3). 1973. PLB 6.99 o.p. (ISBN 0-698-30479-9, Coward). Putnam Pub Group.

--A Day with Whisker Wickles. (Illus.). 48p. (gr. k-2). 1975. 6.95 o.p. (ISBN 0-698-20316-X, Coward). Putnam Pub Group.

--The House of the Five Bears. LC 78-18519. (See & Read Storybooks). (Illus.). (gr. k-3). 1978. PLB 6.99 (ISBN 0-399-61122-3). Putnam Pub Group.

--Mr. Wolf Gets Ready for Supper. LC 74-21071. (Break-of-Day Bk). (Illus.). 66p. (gr. 1-7). 1975. PLB 6.59 o.p. (ISBN 0-698-30573-6, Coward). Putnam Pub Group.

--The Secret of the Royal Mounds: Henry Layard & the First Cities of Assyria. (Science Discovery Bk.). (Illus.). 64p. (gr. 6-8). 1980. PLB 5.99 (ISBN 0-698-30710-0, Coward). Putnam Pub Group.

--Tales from the Steppes. (Illus.). 64p. (gr. 3-7). 1975. 5.95 o.p. (ISBN 0-698-20330-5, Coward). Putnam Pub Group.

--Winter Hut. (A Break of Day Bk.). (Illus.). 48p. (gr. 1-3). 1973. PLB 6.59 o.p. (ISBN 0-698-30500-0, Coward). Putnam Pub Group.

Jameson, D. L. Genetics of Speciation. (Benchmark Papers in Genetics: Vol. 9). 1977. 46.50 (ISBN 0-12-786756-2). Acad Pr.

Jameson, E. C. Thermal Machining Processes. LC 79-62917. (Manufacturing Update Ser.). (Illus.). 29.00 (ISBN 0-87263-049-8). SME.

Jameson, Fredric. Fables of Aggression: Wyndham Lewis, the Modernist As Fascist. LC 78-64462. 1979. 17.95x (ISBN 0-520-03792-8); pap. 5.95 (ISBN 0-520-04398-7, CAL 496). U of Cal Pr.

--The Political Unconscious: Narrative As a Socially Symbolic Act. LC 80-21459. 320p. 1981. 24.50x (ISBN 0-8014-1233-1); pap. 7.95x (ISBN 0-8014-9222-X). Cornell U Pr.

Jameson, G. J. First Course Complex Functions. 1970. pap. 11.95x (ISBN 0-412-09710-9, Pub. by Chapman & Hill England). Methuen Inc.

Jameson, J. The Picture Life of O. J. Simpson. 1978. pap. 1.95 (ISBN 0-380-01906-X, 60962, Camelot). Avon.

Jameson, J. Franklin. Dictionary of United States History: Alphabetical, Chronological, Statistical. rev. ed. McKinley, Albert E., ed. LC 68-30658. (Illus.). 1971. Repr. of 1931 ed. 55.00x (ISBN 0-8103-3332-5). Gale.

--Essays on the Constitutional History of the United States in the Formative Period, 1775-1789. LC 78-99473. (American Constitutional & Legal History Ser.). 1970. Repr. of 1889 ed. lib. bdg. 39.50 (ISBN 0-306-71856-1). Da Capo.

Jameson, John A. Treatise on Constitutional Conventions Their History, Powers & Modes of Proceeding. LC 73-166332. (American Constitutional & Legal History Ser). 1972. Repr. of 1887 ed. lib. bdg. 75.00 (ISBN 0-306-70243-6). Da Capo.

Jameson, John F. History of Historical Writing in America. Repr. of 1961 ed. lib. bdg. 15.00x o.p. (ISBN 0-8371-1150-1, JAHW). Greenwood.

Jameson, John F., ed. Privateering & Piracy in the Colonial Period. LC 68-22375. Repr. of 1923 ed. lib. bdg. 37.50x (ISBN 0-678-00668-7). Kelley.

Jameson, Jon. Monsters of the Mountains. (Easy-Read Facts Bks.). (Illus.). (gr. 2-4). 1979. PLB 8.60 s&l (ISBN 0-531-02269-2). Watts.

Jameson, K. P., jt. ed. see Wilber, C. K.

Jameson, Kenneth, jt. auth. see Weaver, James.

Jameson, Kenneth P., jt. auth. see Wilber, Charles K.

Jameson, Kenneth P. & Wilber, Charles K., eds. Religious Values & Development. (Illus.). 154p. 1981. 40.00 (ISBN 0-08-026107-8). Pergamon.

Jameson, Kenneth P. & Wilbur, Charles K., eds. Directions in Economic Development. LC 78-63299. 268p. 1980. 14.95 o.p. (ISBN 0-268-00846-9); pap. 4.95 o.p. (ISBN 0-686-65786-1). U of Notre Dame Pr.

Jameson, Michael see Sophocles.

Jameson, Storm. The Writer's Situation, & Other Essays. LC 77-21842. 1977. Repr. of 1950 ed. lib. bdg. 18.00x (ISBN 0-8371-9794-5, JAWS). Greenwood.

Jameson, W. J., Jr., ed. Studies in Numerical Analysis, One. (Illus.). 133p. 1966. text ed. 13.00 (ISBN 0-89871-042-1). Soc Indus-Appl Math.

Jamgotch, Nish, Jr., ed. Thinking the Thinkable: Investment in Human Survival. LC 77-18592. 1978. pap. text ed. 12.00 o.p. (ISBN 0-8191-0402-7). U Pr of Amer.

Jamieson, A. M. & Rippon, W. B. Instrumental Methods for Characterization of Biological Macromolecules. Date not set. price not set (ISBN 0-685-84733-0). Elsevier.

Jamieson, Alfred. Latin America, 4 bks. (Culture Studies Program). (gr. 7-12). 1979. pap. text ed. 7.32 (ISBN 0-201-42669-2, Sch Div); tchr's ed. 3.32 (ISBN 0-201-42670-6). A-W.

Jamieson, Archibald. Introduction to Quality Control. 1981. text ed. 20.95 (ISBN 0-8359-3264-8); instr's. manual free (ISBN 0-8359-3265-6). Reston.

Jamieson, G. A. & Robinson, D. M., eds. Mammalian Cell Membranes, 5 vols. (Illus.). 1977. text ed. 159.95 set o.p. (ISBN 0-686-25573-9). Butterworth.

Jamieson, Graham A. & Scipio, Alice R. Interaction of Platelets & Tumor Cells, Vol. 89. LC 82-6530. (Progress in Clinical & Biological Research Ser.). 510p. 1982. 48.00 (ISBN 0-8451-0089-0). A R Liss.

Jamieson, Ian. Capitalism & Culture. 256p. 1980. text ed. 36.75x (ISBN 0-566-00356-2). Gower Pub Ltd.

Jamieson, Kathleen H. & Campbell, Karlyn K. The Interplay of Influence: Mass Media & Their Public in News, Advertising, Politics. 304p. 1982. pap. text ed. 11.95x (ISBN 0-534-01267-1). Wadsworth Pub.

Jamieson, Paul, ed. The Adirondack Reader. 2nd ed. 544p. 1983. 29.50 (ISBN 0-935272-21-6); pap. 18.50 (ISBN 0-935272-22-4). ADK Mtn Club.

Jamieson, Robert H. Exercises for the Elderly. (Illus.). 160p. 1982. 12.95 (ISBN 0-87523-198-5). Emerson.

Jamieson, T. H. Optimization of Techniques in Lens Design. (Applied Optics Monographs: No. 5). 1971. 27.95 o.p. (ISBN 0-444-19590-4). Elsevier.

Jamison, Bill. Santa Fe: An Intimate View. LC 82-81390. (Illus., Orig.). 1982. pap. 7.95 (ISBN 0-9608504-0-6). Milagro Co.

Jamison, Colleen B., jt. auth. see Attwell, Arthur A.

Jamison, Dean T., jt. ed. see Froomkin, Joseph.

Jamison, P. L. & Seguras, S. L., eds. The Eskimo of Northwestern Alaska: A Biological Perspective. LC 77-18941. (US-IBP Synthesis Ser.: Vol. 8). 319p. 1978. 46.00 (ISBN 0-87933-319-7). Hutchinson Ross.

Jamison, Rex L. & Kriz, Wilhelm. Urinary Concentrating Mechanism: Structure & Function. (Illus.). 1982. text ed. 45.00x (ISBN 0-19-502801-5). Oxford U Pr.

Jamison, Robert V. Fortran IV Programming: Based on the IBM System 1130. LC 70-96241. (Illus.). 1970. text ed. 232.05 (ISBN 0-07-032270-8, G); instructor's manual 3.95 (ISBN 0-07-032274-0). McGraw.

Jamison, Ted, Jr. George Monck & the Restoration: Victor Without Bloodshed. LC 74-28945. (History & Culture Monograph Ser., No. 11). 1975. pap. 6.00x (ISBN 0-912646-04-7). Tex Christian.

Jammers, Ewald. Der Gregorianische Rhythmus: Antiphonals Studien mit einer Ubertragung der Introitus und Offiziumsantiphonen des 1 Tones. (Sammlung Mw. Abh. 25-1937 Ser.). 248p. 40.00 o.s.i. (ISBN 90-6027-269-2, Pub. by Frits Knuf Netherlands). Pendragon NY.

--Das Karlsoffizium "Regali Natus". Einfuhrung, Text und Ubertragung in Moderne Notenschrift. (Sammlung Mw. Abh. 14-1934 Ser.). 193p. 40.00 o.s.i. (ISBN 90-6027-268-4, Pub. by Frits Knuf Netherlands). Pendragon NY.

Jammet, H., ed. see ICRP.

Jamous, R. Honneur et Baraka. LC 78-54581. (Atelier d'Anthropologie Sociale). (Illus.). 280p. 1981. 52.50 (ISBN 0-521-22318-0). Cambridge U Pr.

Jamplis, R. W., jt. auth. see Lillington, Glen A.

Jamplis, Robert W., jt. auth. see Lillington, Glen A.

Jampolsky, Gerald. Love Is Letting Go of Fear. 144p. 1982. pap. 2.95 (ISBN 0-553-23079-4). Bantam.

Jampolsky, Gerald G., et al, eds. Children as Teachers of Peace. pap. 7.95 (ISBN 0-89087-362-3). Celestial Arts.

Jamshidi. Large-Scale Systems: Modeling & Control. (Systems Science & Engineering Ser.: Vol. 8). Date not set. 42.50 (ISBN 0-444-00706-7). Elsevier.

Jan. Does Your Child Have Epilepsy? 256p. 1982. pap. text ed. write for info. (ISBN 0-8391-1758-2). Univ Park.

Janacek, Leos. Janacek: Leaves from His Life. Tausky, Vilem & Tausky, Margaret, trs. from Czech. LC 81-52424. (Illus.). 160p. 1982. 11.95 (ISBN 0-8008-4299-5, Crescendo). Taplinger.

Janaro, Richard P. Philosophy: Something to Believe in. 1975. pap. text ed. 12.95x (ISBN 0-02-475800-0, 47580). Macmillan.

Janaro, Richard P. & Altshuler, Thelma. The Art of Being Human: The Humanities As a Technique for Living. 1979. text ed. 21.50 scp (ISBN 0-06-044427-4, HarpC); instr's. manual avail. (ISBN 0-06-364425-8); scp study guide 10.50 (ISBN 0-06-044428-2). Har-Row.

Jancel, R. Foundations of Classical & Quantum Statistical Mechanics. 1969. 54.00 (ISBN 0-08-012823-8). Pergamon.

Jancic, S. J., ed. Industrial Crystallization, 1981. 1982. 64.00 (ISBN 0-444-86402-4). Elsevier.

Jancic, S. J., jt. ed. see De Jong, E. J.

Janda. Diagnosis of Dysfunction in Normal Muscles. Date not set. text ed. price not set (ISBN 0-407-00201-4). Butterworth.

Janda, James. Nobody Stop by to See. LC 77-80807. 144p. 1977. pap. 2.95 o.p. (ISBN 0-8091-2040-2). Paulist Pr.

Janda, Kenneth. Comparative Political Parties Data, 1950-1962. LC 79-90467. 1980. write for info. (ISBN 0-89138-966-0). ICPSR.

Janda, Louis & Klenke-Hamel, Karen. Exploring Human Sexuality. (Orig.). 1980. pap. 9.95 (ISBN 0-442-25869-0); instr's. manual 2.50 (ISBN 0-442-25732-5). Van Nos Reinhold.

Janda, Louis, jt. auth. see Derlega, Valerian J.

Janda, Louis H. & Klenke-Hamel, Karin E. Psychology: Its Study & Uses. LC 81-51857. 636p. 1982. text ed. 22.95 (ISBN 0-312-65241-0); Study guide 7.95 (ISBN 0-312-65243-7); instr's. manual avail. St Martin.

Janda, Louis H., jt. auth. see Derlega, Valerian.

Jander, Klaus H. & Mertin, Dietz. Zur Gruendung und Fuehrung von Tochtergesellschaften in den U. S. A. German American Chamber of Commerce, Inc., ed. 200p. (Ger.). 1982. text ed. 29.00 (ISBN 0-86640-008-7). German Am Chamber.

Jane, Fred T., ed. Jane's Fighting Ships, 1906-07. facsimile ed. LC 69-14519. 19.95 o.p. (ISBN 0-668-02019-9). Arco.

Janeczko, Paul B., ed. Don't Forget to Fly. LC 81-10220. 160p. (YA) 1981. 10.95 (ISBN 0-02-747780-0). Bradbury Pr.

--Poetspeak. 160p. (gr. 7-12). 1983. 11.95 (ISBN 0-02-747770-3). Bradbury Pr.

--Postcard Poems: A Collection of Poetry for Sharing. LC 79-14192. 144p. (YA) 1979. 9.95 (ISBN 0-02-747750-9). Bradbury Pr.

Janell, Paul A., jt. auth. see Dascher, Paul E.

Janelle, Pierre, ed. see Gardiner, Stephen.

Janelli, Dawnhee Y., jt. auth. see Janelli, Roger L.

Janelli, Roger L. & Janelli, Dawnhee Y. Ancestor Worship & Korean Society. LC 81-51757. (Illus.). 248p. 1982. 25.00x (ISBN 0-8047-1135-6). Stanford U Pr.

Janericco, Terence. The Book of Great Breakfasts & Brunches. 272p. 1983. 16.95 (ISBN 0-8436-2264-4). CBI Pub.

Janes, E. C. The First Book of Camping. rev. ed. LC 76-47479. (First Bks.). (Illus.). 72p. (gr. 3-6). 1977. PLB 7.40 o.s.i. (ISBN 0-531-00494-5). Watts.

Jane's Pocket Books. Jane's Pocket Book of Major Combat Aircraft. Taylor, John, ed. (Jane's Pocket Bks). (Illus.). 280p. 1974. pap. 9.95 (ISBN 0-02-080470-9, Collier). Macmillan.

--Jane's Pocket Book of Major Warships. Moore, John E., ed. LC 73-9329. (Jane's Pocket Bks). (Illus.). 280p. (Orig.). 1974. pap. 5.95 o.p. (ISBN 0-02-080520-9, Collier). Macmillan.

--Jane's Pocket Book of Military Transport Aircraft. Taylor, John, ed. (Jane's Pocket Bks). 1974. pap. 5.95 o.p. (ISBN 0-02-080490-3, Collier). Macmillan.

--Jane's Pocket Book of Submarine Development. Moore, John E., ed. (Jane's Pocket Bks). (Illus.). 264p. 1976. pap. 5.95 o.p. (ISBN 0-02-080420-2, Collier). Macmillan.

Janeschitz-Kriegl, H. Polymer Melt Rheology & Flow Birefringence. (Polymers-Properties & Applications Ser.: Vol. 6). (Illus.). 524p. 1983. 41.00 (ISBN 0-387-11928-0). Springer-Verlag.

Jane's Pocket Books Staff, ed. Jane's Pocket Book of Helicopters. (Illus.). 260p. 1981. pap. 8.95 (ISBN 0-686-69548-8, Collier). Macmillan.

Janeway, Elizabeth. Cross Sections: From a Decade of Change. LC 82-3485. 324p. 1982. 14.95 (ISBN 0-688-01024-5). Morrow.

--Man's World Woman's Place. 1972. pap. 5.95 o.s.i. (ISBN 0-440-55163-3, Delta). Dell.

--Man's World, Woman's Place: A Study in Social Mythology. 1971. 8.95 o.p. (ISBN 0-688-02047-X). Morrow.

--Powers of the Weak: The Book That Explodes the Mystique of Power. LC 81-9672. 350p. 1981. pap. 6.95 (ISBN 0-688-00747-3). Quill NY.

Janeway, Harriet. This Passionate Land. (Orig.). 1979. pap. 2.25 o.p. (ISBN 0-451-08462-4, E8462, Sig). NAL.

Janich, Klaus, jt. auth. see Brocker, Theodor.

Janics, Kalman. Czechoslovak Policy & the Hungarian Minority: 1945-1948. Borsody, Stephen, tr. from Hungarian. & intro. by. LC 80-67487. (Brooklyn College Studies on Society in Change). 288p. 1982. 25.00x (ISBN 0-914710-99-0). East Eur Quarterly.

--Czechoslovak Policy & the Hungarian Minority, 1945-1948. 288p. 1982. 25.00 (ISBN 0-686-82241-2). Columbia U Pr.

Janik, Allan & Towlmin, Stephen. Wittgenstein's Vienna. (Illus.). 1974. pap. 8.50 (ISBN 0-671-21725-9, Touchstone Bks). S&S.

Janik, Carolyn. The Woman's Guide to Selling Residential Real Estate Successfully. 288p. 1982. 11.95 (ISBN 0-686-30966-9, An Everest House Book). Dodd.

Janik, Del Ivan, jt. ed. see Rhodes, Robert E.

Janis, Arthur, jt. auth. see Miller, Morris.

Janis, Irving. Victims of Groupthink: A Psychological Study of Foreign-Policy Decisions & Fiascoes. 1973. pap. text ed. 11.95 o.p. (ISBN 0-395-14044-7). HM.

Janis, Irving L. Air War & Emotional Stress. LC 76-1958. 280p. 1976. Repr. of 1951 ed. lib. bdg. 25.00x (ISBN 0-8371-8666-8, JAAW). Greenwood.

--Stress: Attitudes & Decisions. 366p. 1982. 28.95 (ISBN 0-03-059036-1). Praeger.

Janis, J. Harold. College Writing: A Rhetoric & Handbook. (Illus.). 1977. kivar 13.95x (ISBN 0-02-360230-9). Macmillan.

--Writing & Communication in Business. 3rd ed. (Illus.). 500p. 1978. text ed. 22.95x (ISBN 0-02-360300-3, 36030). Macmillan.

Janitch, Valerie. Dolls for Sale. (Illus.). 116p. 1980. pap. 6.95 (ISBN 0-571-11536-5). Faber & Faber.

--Paper Flowers. (Creative Crafts Ser.). (Illus.). 1977. 11.95 o.p. (ISBN 0-8019-6414-8); pap. 6.95 o.p. (ISBN 0-8019-6415-6). Chilton.

Janke, W, ed. Response Variability to Psychotropic Drugs. (International Series in Experimental Psychology). (Illus.). 272p. 1983. 37.00 (ISBN 0-08-028907-X). Pergamon.

Janko, Richard. Homer, Hesiod & the Hymns: Diachronic Development in Epic Diction. LC 81-7666. (Cambridge Classical Studies). 200p. 1982. 44.50 (ISBN 0-521-23869-2). Cambridge U Pr.

Jankowiak, James. The Prosperous Gardener. Breslow, Lori, ed. LC 77-18089. 1978. 8.95 o.p. (ISBN 0-87857-204-X). Rodale Pr Inc.

Jankowski, Thaddeus, jt. auth. see Franklin, Douglas.

Jankowski, William C., jt. auth. see Johnson, Leroy F.

Janna, William S. Introduction to Fluid Mechanics. LC 82-17734. (Mechanical Engineering Ser.). 512p. 1982. text ed. 28.95 (ISBN 0-534-01238-8). Brooks-Cole.

Jannequin, Claude. Voyage de Lybie au Senegal, le Long du Niger. (Bibliotheque Africaine Ser.) 243p. (Fr.). 1974. Repr. of 1643 ed. lib. bdg. 67.00x o.p. (ISBN 0-8287-0461-9, 72-2102). Clearwater Pub.

Jannersten, Eric. Find the Mistakes. (Master Bridge Ser.). (Illus.). 160p. 1982. 16.50 (ISBN 0-575-03172-7, Pub. by Gollancz England). David & Charles.

Jannes, G., ed. see International Symposium on the Relations Between Heterogeneous & Homogeneous Catalytic Phenomena, Brussels, 1974.

Jannis, C. Paul, et al. Managing & Accounting for Inventories: Control, Income Recognition, & Tax Strategy. 3rd ed. 1979. 52.50x (ISBN 0-471-05016-4, Pub by Ronald Pr). Wiley.

Jannott, Paul F. Teller World. LC 82-18497. 122p. 1983. 19.95 (ISBN 0-87267-040-6). Bankers.

Janos, Andrew C. & Slottman, William B., eds. Revolution in Perspective: Essays on the Hungarian Soviet Republic. LC 74-138510. 1971. 30.00x (ISBN 0-520-01920-2). U of Cal Pr.

Janosik, Ellen, jt. auth. see Miller, Jean R.

Janosik, G. Edward, jt. auth. see Cooke, Edward F.

Janossy, Ferenc. The End of the Economic Miracle: Appearance & Reality in Economic Development. Jellinek, Hedy D., tr. from German. LC 68-14425. (Illus.). 269p. 1971. text ed. 20.00 (ISBN 0-87332-001-8). M E Sharpe.

Janossy, L. Theory of Relativity Based on Physical Reality. 317p. 1971. 22.50x (ISBN 0-8002-2080-3). Intl Pubns Serv.

Janota, M. S., jt. auth. see Watson, N.

Janov, Arthur. Imprints: The Lifelong Effects of the Birth Experience. 416p. 1983. 17.95 (ISBN 0-698-11183-4, Coward). Putnam Pub Group.
--The Primal Scream. 448p. 1981. pap. 6.95 (ISBN 0-399-50537-7, Perige). Putnam Pub Group.
Janovic, Florence, jt. auth. see Nierenberg, Judith.
Janower, Murray L., jt. auth. see Dreyfuss, Jack R.
Janowitz, M. Intermediate Algebra. 1976. 14.95 (ISBN 0-13-469528-3). P-H.
--Social Control of the Welfare State. 1976. 22.50 (ISBN 0-444-99020-8). Elsevier.
Janowitz, Morris. Institution Building in Urban Education. LC 72-81407. 126p. 1969. 6.50x (ISBN 0-87154-400-8); pap. 4.50x (ISBN 0-87154-401-6). Russell Sage.
--Military Institutions & Coercion in the Developing Nations: An Essay in Comparative Analysis. expanded ed. LC 76-50462. (Orig.). 1977. lib. bdg. 12.50x (ISBN 0-226-39309-7); pap. 8.00 (ISBN 0-226-39310-0, P174, Phoen). U of Chicago Pr.
Janowitz, Morris & Wesbrook, Stephen D. The Political Education of Soldiers. (Sage Research Progress Series on War, Revolution, & Peacekeeping: Vol. 11). 320p. 1982. 25.00 (ISBN 0-8039-1020-7). Sage.
Janowitz, Phyliss. Visiting Rites. 1982. 10.95 (ISBN 0-691-06523-3); pap. 5.95 (ISBN 0-691-01398-5). Princeton U Pr.
Janowitz, Phyllis. Rites of Strangers. Beacham, Walton, ed. LC 78-16729. (Associated Writing Programs Series for Contemporary Poetry). 68p. 1978. 8.95 (ISBN 0-8139-0797-7). U Pr of Va.
Janowitz, Tama. American Dad. 256p. 1981. 11.95 (ISBN 0-399-12585-X). Putnam Pub Group.
Janowka, T. B. Clavis ad Thesaurum Magnae Artis Musicae. (Dictionarium Musicum Ser.: Vol. 2). 1973. Repr. of 1701 ed. wrappers 37.50 o.s.i. (ISBN 90-6027-270-6, Pub. by Frits Knuf Netherlands). Pendragon NY.
Janowski, et al. SJIS State of the Art, Nineteen Eighty. 500p. 1980. pap. 8.00 o.p. (ISBN 0-89656-047-3, F-006). Natl Ctr St Courts.
Janscha, Laurens & Ziegler, Johann. Vues Du Rhin. 2500.00x (ISBN 0-686-97101-9, Pub. by P Harris England). State Mutual Bk.
Jansen. Working with the Doctor. (Library of Health). 13.95 o.p. (ISBN 0-686-79856-2). Silver.
Jansen, C. J. Readings in the Sociology of Migration. LC 72-105954. 1970. 23.00 (ISBN 0-08-006915-0); pap. 11.25 o.p. (ISBN 0-08-006914-2). Pergamon.
Jansen, Elly, ed. The Therapeutic Community: Outside the Hospital. 392p. 1980. 31.50x o.p. (ISBN 0-85664-967-8, Pub. by Croom Helm Ltd England). Biblio Dist.
Jansen, F. J. Ludvig Holberg. (World Authors Ser.). 136p. 1974. lib. bdg. 15.95 (ISBN 0-8057-2431-1, Twayne). G K Hall.
Jansen, G. Existential Approach to Theology. (Orig.). 1966. pap. 2.50 o.p. (ISBN 0-685-07630-X, 80326). Glencoe.
Jansen, G. R., et al, eds. New Developments in Modelling Travel Demand & Urban Systems. 1979. 45.75x (ISBN 0-566-00269-8). Gower Pub Ltd.
Jansen, Godfrey. Militant Islam. LC 79-2623. 1980. 8.95i (ISBN 0-06-012202-1, CN-759, HarpT); 3.95i (ISBN 0-06-090759-2). Har-Row.
Jansen, J. F. Calvin's "Doctrine of the Work of Christ". 120p. 1956. 16.50 (ISBN 0-227-67425-1). Attic Pr.
Jansen, Karen, ed. Monetarism, Economic Crisis & the Third World. 224p. 1983. text ed. 30.00x (ISBN 0-7146-3222-8, F Cass Co). Biblio Dist.
Jansen, Mariuse, et al. Japan in the Nineteen Thirtys. Waldner, George, ed. LC 82-80791. (Papers on International Issues: No.3). 1982. free. Southern Ctr Intl Stud.
Jansen, Michael. The Battle of Beirut: Why Israel Invaded Lebanon. 160p. 1983. 17.50 (ISBN 0-89608-174-5); pap. 6.50 (ISBN 0-89608-173-7). South End Pr.
Jansen, P. P., et al. Principles of River Engineering: The Non-Tidal Alluvial River. LC 79-40141. (Water Resources Engineering Ser.). 509p. 1979. text ed. 131.95 (ISBN 0-273-01139-1). Pitman Pub MA.
Jansen, Scott. The Right to Kill. 192p. (Orig.). Date not set. pap. (ISBN 0-505-51711-6). Tower Bks.
Jansen, Will. The Bassoon: Its History, Construction, Makers, Players & Music, 4 vols. (Illus.). 2500p. 1981. Set. 487.50 o.p. (ISBN 90-6027-271-4, Pub. by Frits Knuf Netherlands). Pendragon NY.
Jansky, Jeannette & Hirsch, Katrina De. Preventing Reading Failure: Prediction, Diagnosis, Intervention. LC 72-79674. (Illus.). 256p. 1972. 12.45i (ISBN 0-06-012171-8, HarpT). Har-Row.
Jansma, Paul, jt. auth. see French, Ronald.
Jansma, Paul, ed. The Psychomotor Domain & the Seriously Handicapped. LC 80-6299. (Illus.). 502p. (Orig.). 1981. lib. bdg. 32.00 (ISBN 0-8191-1718-8); pap. text ed. 20.25 (ISBN 0-8191-1719-6). U Pr of Amer.
Janson. History of Art. 2nd ed. 1977. 24.95 (ISBN 0-13-389296-4). P-H.
Janson, H., ed. see Held, Julius & Posner, Donald.
Janson, H. W., ed. Paris Salon de 1874. LC 77-24778. (Catalogues of the Paris Salon, 1673 to 1881: Vol. 53). 1978. lib. bdg. 50.00 o.s.i. (ISBN 0-8240-1877-X). Garland Pub.
Janson, H. W., et al. A Basic History of Art. 2nd ed. (Illus.). 444p. 1981. pap. text ed. 18.95 (ISBN 0-13-062356-3). P-H.
Janson, P., jt. ed. see West, A.
Janssen, Al, jt. auth. see Thornton, Andre.
Janssen, Arlo T. International Stories: A Conversation Reader to Improve Your English. (English As a Second Language Ser.). (Illus.). 160p. 1980. pap. text ed. 9.95 (ISBN 0-13-470856-3); tapes 40.00 (ISBN 0-13-470864-4). P-H.
Janssen, J. H., ed. see International Symposium on Shipboard Acoustics.
Janssen, J. M., et al, eds. Dynamic Modelling & Control of National Economies: Third IFAC - IFORS Conference, Warsaw, Poland, 16-19 June 1980. (International Federation of Automatic Control). (Illus.). 410p. 1981. 90.00 (ISBN 0-08-024485-8). Pergamon.
Janssen, L. P. Twin Screw Extrusion. (Chemical Engineering Monographs: Vol. 7). 1977. 44.75 (ISBN 0-444-41629-3). Elsevier.
Janssen, Raymond E. Some Fossil Plant Types of Illinois. (Scientific Papers Ser.: Vol. I). (Illus.). 124p. 1940. 2.50x (ISBN 0-89792-094-5); pap. 2.00x (ISBN 0-89792-000-7). Ill St Museum.
Janssens, Jacques. Ensor: Q.L.P. (Illus.). 7.95 (ISBN 0-517-53284-0). Crown.
Jansson, Tove. Comet in Moominland. (gr. 3-5). 1975. pap. 1.95 o.p. (ISBN 0-380-00436-4, 52100, Camelot). Avon.
--Sun City. 1977. pap. 1.95 o.p. (ISBN 0-380-00955-2, 32318, Bard). Avon.
Jantsch, Erich & Waddington, Conrad H., eds. Evolution & Consciousness: Human Systems in Transition. (Illus.). 1976. 29.50 (ISBN 0-201-03438-7, Adv Bk Prog); pap. 22.50 (ISBN 0-201-03439-5). A-W.
Jantscher, Gerald R. Bread upon the Waters: Federal Aids to the Maritime Industries. (Studies in the Regulation of Economic Activity). 164p. 1975. 13.95 (ISBN 0-8157-4574-5). Brookings.
Jantzen, Dan, ed. see Swedish Academy of Engineering.
Januz, Lauren R. & Jones, Susan K. Time Management for Executives. (Illus.). 240p. 1982. pap. 6.95 (ISBN 0-686-83727-4, ScribT). Scribner.
Janvier, Jeannine. Fantastic Fish You Can Make. LC 76-19819. (Illus.). (gr. 4 up). 1976. 5.95 o.p. (ISBN 0-8069-5406-X); PLB 5.89 o.p. (ISBN 0-8069-5407-8). Sterling.
Janz, Denis, ed. Three Reformation Catechisms: Catholic, Anabaptist, Lutheran. (Texts & Studies in Religion: Vol. 13). viii, 224p. 1982. 34.95x (ISBN 0-88946-800-1). E Mellen.
Janz, Dieter, et al, eds. Epilepsy, Pregnancy, & the Child. 576p. 1982. text ed. 53.00 (ISBN 0-89004-654-9). Raven.
Janzen, Danies H. Ecology of Plants in the Tropics. (Studies in Biology: No. 58). 72p. 1975. pap. text ed. 8.95 (ISBN 0-7131-2482-2). E Arnold.
Janzen, J. M., ed. Causality & Classification in African Medicine & Health. 280p. 1983. 22.50 (ISBN 0-08-028134-6). Pergamon.
Janzen, John M. The Quest for Therapy in Lower Zaire. (Comparative Studies of Health Systems & Medical Care). 1978. 34.50x (ISBN 0-520-03295-0). U of Cal Pr.
Janzen, William B., jt. auth. see Melvin, Kenneth B.
Japan Chamber of Commerce & Industry. Standard Trade Index of Japan, 1983-84. 27th ed. LC 55-36368. 1500p. 1983. 135.00x (ISBN 0-8002-3006-X). Intl Pubns Serv.
Japan Culture Institute Staff. Discover Japan: Words, Customs & Concepts, Vol. 1. LC 82-48294. (Discover Japan Ser.). (Illus.). 208p. 1983. Repr. of 1975 ed. 17.95 (ISBN 0-87011-546-4). Kodansha.
--Discover Japan: Words, Customs, & Concepts, Vol.2. LC 82-48294. (Discover Japan Ser.). (Illus.). 216p. 1983. 17.95 (ISBN 0-686-84483-1). Kodansha.
Japan External Trade Organization. White Paper on International Trade: Japan, 1981. 33rd ed. LC 52-36099. (Illus.). 419p. 1981. pap. 45.00 (ISBN 4-8224-0113-8). Intl Pubns Ser.
Japan External Trade Organization (JETRO), ed. White Paper on International Trade: Japan 1980. 32nd ed. LC 52-36099. (Illus.). 299p. (Orig.). 1981. pap. 42.50x (ISBN 0-8002-2912-6). Intl Pubns Serv.
Japan Graphic Designers Association. Graphic Design in Japan, Vol. 2. (Graphic Design in Japan Ser.). (Illus.). 288p. 1983. 59.50 (ISBN 0-87011-552-9). Kodansha.
Japan Industrial Robot Association. The Robotics Industry of Japan: Today & Tomorrow. 592p. 1982. pap. 525.00 (ISBN 0-13-782102-6). P-H.
Japan Information Processing Development Center. Fifth Generation Computer Systems. 1982. 49.00 (ISBN 0-444-86440-7). Elsevier.
Japan Institute of International Affairs, ed. White Papers of Japan, 1978-79: Annual Abstract of Official Reports & Statistics of the Japanese Government. LC 72-620531. (Illus.). 228p. (Orig.). 1980. pap. 37.50x o.p. (ISBN 0-8002-2734-4). Intl Pubns Serv.
Japan Institute of International Affairs, Tokyo, ed. White Papers of Japan, 1979-80: Annual Abstract of Official Reports & Statistics of the Japanese Government. LC 72-620531. (Illus.). 220p. (Orig.). 1981. pap. 40.00x o.p. (ISBN 0-8002-2911-8). Intl Pubns Serv.
Japan Institute of International Affairs, Tokyo. White Papers of Japan, 1980-81: Annual Abstract of Official Reports & Statistics of the Japanese Government. LC 72-620531. (Illus.). 232p. 1982. pap. 40.00x (ISBN 0-8002-3058-2). Intl Pubns Ser.
Japan Motor Industrial Federation. Guide to the Motor Industry of Japan, 1982. 22nd ed. LC 73-648715. (Illus.). 263p. (Orig.). 1982. pap. 45.00x (ISBN 0-8002-3101-5). Intl Pubns Serv.
Japan Pharmaceutical Association, ed. Modern Pharmaceuticals of Japan, 1981. 6th ed. LC 73-165508. (Illus.). 128p. 1980. pap. 35.00x (ISBN 0-8002-3064-7). Intl Pubns Serv.
Japan-United States Seminar on Minimal Submanifolds, Including Geodesics, Tokyo, 1977. Minimal Submanifolds & Geodesics: Proceedings. Obata, M., ed. 1979. 64.00 (ISBN 0-444-85327-8, North Holland). Elsevier.
Japananda, K. Yoga, You, Your New Life. (Illus.). 208p. pap. 5.95 spiral bdg. (ISBN 0-686-37620-X). E Ruffer.
Japanese American Anthology Committee. Ayumi: A Journey. 320p. 1980. 9.00 o.p. (ISBN 0-9603222-0-5). Volcano Pr.
Japanese Culture Institute. A Hundred Things Japanese. (Illus.). 216p. 1976. 15.50 o.p. (ISBN 0-87040-364-8). Japan Pubns.
Japikse, Carl, jt. auth. see Leichtman, Robert R.
Jappinen, Rae, jt. auth. see Ryan, Tim.
Jappinen, Roe, jt. auth. see Ryal, Tim.
Jaques Cattell Press, compiled by. American Book Trade Directory. 27th ed. 1243p. 1981. 69.95 o.p. (ISBN 0-8352-1359-5). Bowker.
Jaques Cattell Press, ed. American Book Trade Directory. 28th ed. 1300p. 1982. 89.95 (ISBN 0-8352-1498-2). Bowker.
Jaques Cattell Press, compiled by. American Library Directory. 34th ed. 1872p. 1981. 67.50 o.p. (ISBN 0-8352-1358-7). Bowker.
Jaques Cattell Press, ed. American Library Directory 1980. 33rd ed. LC 23-3581. 1836p. 1980. 54.95 o.p. (ISBN 0-8352-1251-3). Bowker.
--Directory of American Scholars, 4 vols. 8th ed. Incl. Vol. 1. History (ISBN 0-8352-1478-8); Vol. II. English, Speech, Drama (ISBN 0-8352-1479-6); Vol. III. Foreign Language, Linguistics, & Philology (ISBN 0-8352-1481-8); Vol. IV. Philosophy, Religion & Law (ISBN 0-8352-1482-6). 2900p. Set. 295.00 (ISBN 0-8352-1476-1); 90.00 ea. Bowker.
--Industrial Research Laboratories of the U. S. 16th ed. LC 21-26022. 1979. 75.00 o.p. (ISBN 0-8352-1135-5). Bowker.
--Library Journal Book Review, 1979. LC 68-59515. 769p. 1980. 35.00 o.p. (ISBN 0-8352-1272-6). Bowker.
--Who's Who in American Art 1980. 14th ed. LC 36-27014. 1980. 50.00 o.p. (ISBN 0-8352-1258-0). Bowker.
Jaques, E. Measurement of Responsibility: A Study of Work, Payment & Individual Capacity. LC 72-5856. 144p. 1972. 16.95x o.s.i. (ISBN 0-470-44020-1). Halsted Pr.
Jaques, Elliott. General Theory of Bureaucracy. 1981. pap. text ed. 10.00x (ISBN 0-435-82478-3). Heinemann Ed.
--Measurement of Responsibility: A Study of Work, Payment, & Individual Capacity. 144p. (Orig.). 1972. 9.50 (ISBN 0-435-85480-1). Krieger.
--Time Span Handbook. (Glacier Project Ser). 143p. 1964. 6.95x o.p. (ISBN 0-8093-0375-2). S Ill U Pr.
Jaques, Faith. Kidnap in Willowbank Wood. (Illus.). 40p. (ps-2). 1983. 11.00 (ISBN 0-434-94442-4, Pub. by Heinemann England). David & Charles.
Jaques, H. E., jt. auth. see Bland, Roger G.
Jaquette, Jane S., ed. Women in Politics. LC 74-1037. 384p. 1974. 38.50x (ISBN 0-471-44022-1, Pub. by Wiley-Interscience). Wiley.
Jaquith, Priscilla. Bo Rabbit Smart for True: Folktales from the Gullah. (Illus.). 64p. (gr. 6-12). 1981. 9.95 (ISBN 0-399-20793-7, Philomel); PLB 9.99 (ISBN 0-399-61179-7). Putnam Pub Group.
Jaramillo, Barbara L. Conventions in the Mechanics of Writing: A Language Laboratory Manual for Foreign Students. (Pitt Series in English as A Second Language). 1974. pap. text ed. 4.95x (ISBN 0-8229-8202-1). U of Pittsburgh Pr.
Jarausch, Konrad. The Transformation of Higher Learning, Eighteen Sixty to Nineteen Thirty: Expansion, Diversification, Social Opening, & Professionalization in England, Germany, Russia, & the United States. LC 82-17629. 376p. 1983. lib. bdg. 30.00x (ISBN 0-226-39367-4). U of Chicago Pr.
Jaray, Cornell, ed. Historic Chronicles of New Amsterdam, Colonial New York & Early Long Island, First & Second Series. LC 68-18355. (Empire State Historical Publications Ser.: Nos. 35 & 36). ser. 1. 9.00 o.p. (ISBN 0-87198-035-5); ser. 2. 9.00 o.p. (ISBN 0-87198-036-3). Friedman.
Jardim, Anne. First Henry Ford: A Study in Personality & Business Leadership. 1970. 15.00x o.p. (ISBN 0-262-10008-8); pap. 4.95 (ISBN 0-262-60005-6). MIT Pr.
Jardim, Anne, jt. auth. see Hennig, Margaret.
Jardin, Rosamond Du see Du Jardin, Rosamond.
Jardine, A. K., jt. auth. see Greensted, C. S.
Jardine, Alice, jt. auth. see Eisenstein, Hester.
Jardine, D. A., ed. see Share Working Conference on Data Base Management Systems, 2nd, Canada, 1977.
Jardine, Rodney G. How to Make a Smashing Success in a Business of Your Own. (The International Council for Excellence in Management Library). (Illus.). 109p. 1980. plastic spiral bdg. 38.95 (ISBN 0-686-61850-5). Am Classical Coll Pr.
Jardon, Carl F., ed. Tropical Ecology. LC 81-4260. (Benchmark Papers in Ecology Ser.: Vol. 10). 356p. 1981. 45.00 (ISBN 0-87933-398-7). Hutchinson Ross.
Jaremko, Matt E. Cognitive-Behavioral Reflections on Some Dimensions of Personality. LC 79-6602. 1980. pap. text ed. 10.00 o.p. (ISBN 0-8191-0924-X). U Pr of Amer.
Jarett, Irwin M. Computer Graphics & Reporting Financial Data. 250p. 1983. price not set (ISBN 0-471-86761-6). Ronald Pr.
Jargocki, Christopher P. More Science Braintwisters & Paradoxes. 192p. 1983. 14.95 (ISBN 0-442-24524-6). Van Nos Reinhold.
Jarman, Cathy. Atlas of Animal Migration. LC 72-1748. (John Day Bk.). (Illus.). 128p. 1974. 14.37i (ISBN 0-381-98129-0, A06030). T Y Crowell.
Jarman, Christopher. The Development of Handwriting Skills: A Book of Resources for Teachers. 150p. 1979. 17.95x o.p. (ISBN 0-631-19240-9, Pub. by Basil Blackwell); pap. 9.95x o.p. (ISBN 0-631-19230-1). Biblio Dist.
Jarman, Colin. Coastal Cruising. (Illus.). 280p. 1976. 18.50 o.p. (ISBN 0-7136-1569-9). Transatlantic.
Jarman, Douglas. The Music of Alban Berg. (Illus.). 278p. 1983. pap. 11.95 (ISBN 0-520-04954-3, CAL 623). U of Cal Pr.
Jarman, M. R, et al. Early European Agriculture: Its Foundations & Development. LC 81-17960. 280p. 1982. 42.50 (ISBN 0-521-24359-9). Cambridge U Pr.
Jarman, Rosemary H. The Courts of Illusion. 384p. 1983. 15.45i (ISBN 0-316-45784-1). Little.
Jarman, T. L. The Rise & Fall of Nazi Germany. LC 56-9548. 388p. 1956. cusa 19.50x o.p. (ISBN 0-8147-0217-1). NYU Pr.
Jarman, T. L., jt. auth. see Derry, T. K.
Jarman, Tom & Hanley, Reid. Wrestling for Beginners. (Illus.). 192p. (Orig.). 1983. 15.00 (ISBN 0-8092-5657-6); pap. 7.95 (ISBN 0-8092-5656-8). Contemp Bks.
Jarmon, Charles. The Nkrumah Regime: An Evaluation of the Role of Charismatic Authority. Nyang, Sulayman S., ed. (Third World Monograph Ser.). 24p. (Orig.). 1981. pap. 1.50x o.p. (ISBN 0-931494-05-2). Brunswick Pub.
Jarmon, Charles & Rutledge, Dennis. Afro-Americans: A Social Science Perspective. 1977. pap. text ed. 13.00 o.p. (ISBN 0-8191-0000-5). U Pr of Amer.
Jarmul, Seymour. The Architect's Guide to Energy Conservation. (Illus.). 1980. 27.95 (ISBN 0-07-032296-1). McGraw.
Jarnagin, Jutta F. The Raging. 245p. 1982. pap. 3.50 (ISBN 0-8423-5128-0). Tyndale.
Jarnow, J. A. & Judelle, B. Inside the Fashion Business: Text & Readings. 1965. 21.99x (ISBN 0-87245-154-2). Textile Bk.
Jarnow, Jeannette A. Inside the Fashion Business: Text & Readings. 3rd ed. LC 80-25000. 427p. 1981. text ed. 22.95x (ISBN 0-471-06038-0). Wiley.
Jarnow, Jill. The Complete Book of Pillow Stitchery. 1979. 12.95 o.p. (ISBN 0-671-22538-3). S&S.
--Sampler Stitchery. LC 80-2415. (Illus.). 224p. 1982. 15.95 (ISBN 0-385-18531-6). Doubleday.
Jarolimek, John. Social Studies Competencies & Skills: Learning to Teach As an Intern. (Illus.). 1977. pap. text ed. 10.95 (ISBN 0-02-360380-1). Macmillan.
--Social Studies In Elementary Education. 6th ed. 1982. text ed. 22.95x (ISBN 0-02-360440-9). Macmillan.
Jarolimek, John & Foster, Clifford E. Teaching & Learning in the Elementary School. 2nd ed. 401p. 1981. text ed. 20.95 (ISBN 0-02-360400-X). Macmillan.
Jaros, C. G. Elementary Medical Biophysics. 1978. 16.95 o.p. (ISBN 0-409-08271-6). Butterworth.
Jaros, Dean & Grant, Lawrence V. Political Behavior: Choices & Perspectives. 416p. (Orig.). 1974. 19.95 o.p. (ISBN 0-312-62090-X); pap. text ed. 12.95 (ISBN 0-312-62125-6). St Martin.
Jaros, G. G., jt. auth. see Brown, J. M.
Jarreau, Leslie. Hanky Panky. 224p. (Orig.). 1982. pap. 2.50 (ISBN 0-523-41843-4). Pinnacle Bks.
Jarrell, Randall. The Complete Poems. LC 68-29469. 507p. 1969. 25.00 (ISBN 0-374-12716-6); pap. 12.95 (ISBN 0-374-51305-8). FS&G.
--Kipling, Auden & Co. Essays & Reviews, 1935-1964. 1980. 17.95 (ISBN 0-374-18153-5); pap. 9.95 (ISBN 0-374-51668-5). FS&G.
Jarrell, Randall, tr. see Grimm, Jacob & Grimm, Wilhelm.
Jarrett, A., ed. The Psychology & Pathophysiology of the Skin, Vol. 7. 272p. 48.50 (ISBN 0-12-380607-0). Acad Pr.

Jarrett, Amanda J. The Passion & the Fury. (Southerners Ser.: No. 4). (Orig.). 1983. pap. 3.50 (ISBN 0-440-06849-5, Emerald). Dell.

--Red Roses Forever. (The Southerners Ser.: No. 5). (Orig.). 1983. pap. 3.50 (ISBN 0-440-07456-8). Dell.

--This Traitor Moon. 320p. 1983. pap. 3.50 (ISBN 0-440-08813-5, Bryans). Dell.

--Where My Love Lies Dreaming. (Southerners Ser.: No. 3). (Orig.). 1983. pap. 3.50 (ISBN 0-686-82202-1). Dell.

Jarrett, Beverly, jt. auth. see Clegg, Holly Berkowitz.

Jarrett, Dennis, ed. The Electronic Office. 176p. 1982. text ed. 32.00x (ISBN 0-566-03409-3). Gower Pub Ltd.

Jarrett, Fred. Stamps of British North America. LC 74-82308. (Illus.). 624p. 1975. Repr. 40.00x o.p. (ISBN 0-88000-052-X). Quarterman.

Jarrett, Henry, et al. Science & Resources: Prospects & Implications of Technological Advance. LC 77-23132. (Resources for the Future, Inc.). (Illus.). 1977. Repr. of 1959 ed. lib. bdg. 18.75x (ISBN 0-8371-9470-9, JASR). Greenwood.

Jarrett, James L., ed. Educational Theories of the Sophists. LC 71-108882. 1969. text ed. 10.50 (ISBN 0-8077-1565-4); pap. text ed. 5.50x (ISBN 0-8077-1564-6). Tchrs Coll.

Jarrett, John, jt. auth. see Keen, Harry.

Jarrett, Patricia. Roland Batchelor: A Twentieth-Century View of the Human Comedy. 88p. 1982. 50.00x (ISBN 0-284-98613-5, Pub. by C Skilton Scotland). State Mutual Bk.

Jarrett, R. J. Nutrition & Disease. 224p. 1979. text ed. 19.95 o.p. (ISBN 0-8391-1366-8). Univ Park.

Jarry, Alfred. The Ubu Plays. Connolly, Cyril & Taylor, Simon W., trs. Incl. Ubu Rex; Ubu Cuckolded; Ubu Enchained. 1969. pap. 7.95 (ISBN 0-394-17485-2, E496, Ever). Grove.

Jarry, M. Carpets of Aubusson. 1969. 33.50x (ISBN 0-87245-155-0). Textile Bk.

--Carpets of the Manufacture de la Savonnerie. 33.50x (ISBN 0-87245-156-9). Textile Bk.

Jarry, Madeleine. The Carpets of Aubusson. (Illus.). 68p. 1969. text ed. 25.00x (ISBN 0-686-86082-9, Pub. by A & C Black England). Humanities.

Jarvella, Robert J. & Klein, Wolfgang. Speech, Place & Action: Studies in Deixis & Related Topics. 384p. 1982. 51.95x (ISBN 0-471-10045-5, Pub. by Wiley-Interscience). Wiley.

Jarvenpa, Aili. Tuohela. (Illus.). 48p. (Orig.). 1982. pap. 3.50 (ISBN 0-87839-037-5). North Star.

Jarves, James J. Art Thoughts: The Experiences & Observations of an American Amateur in Europe. Weinberg, H. Barbara, ed. LC 75-28866. (Art Experience in Late 19th Century America Ser.: Vol. 2). (Illus.). 1976. Repr. of 1869 ed. lib. bdg. 37.50x o.s.i. (ISBN 0-8240-2226-2). Garland Pub.

--A Glimpse at the Art of Japan. LC 82-50327. (Illus.). 288p. 1983. pap. 6.50 (ISBN 0-8048-1446-5). C E Tuttle.

Jarvey, Paulette S. Let's Dough It Again. (Illus.). 80p. (Orig.). 1982. pap. 6.95 (ISBN 0-9605904-1-2). Hot Off Pr.

Jarvi, Edith, jt. auth. see McLean, Isabel.

Jarvie, I. C. Concepts & Society. (International Library of Sociology). 230p. 1972. 21.50x (ISBN 0-7100-7265-1). Routledge & Kegan.

--The Revolution in Anthropology. LC 72-97621. 280p. 1969. pap. 5.95 (ISBN 0-89526-973-2). Regnery-Gateway.

Jarvik, L. F., et al, eds. Clinical Pharmacology & the Aged Patient. (Aging Ser.: Vol. 16). 264p. 1981. 31.50 (ISBN 0-89004-340-X, 349). Raven.

Jarvinen. Finite & Infinite Dimensional Linear Spaces. (Lecture Notes in Pure & Applied Mathematics Ser.: Vol. 66). 185p. 1981. write for info. (ISBN 0-8247-1172-6). Dekker.

Jarvis, A. C., jt. auth. see Mee, A. J.

Jarvis, Ana C. & Lebredo, Raquel. Aventuras Literarias. 256p. 1983. pap. 9.95 (ISBN 0-686-82410-5). Heath.

--Basic Spanish Grammar. (Orig.). 1980. pap. text ed. 14.95 (ISBN 0-669-03086-4); Business & Finance wkbk. 8.95 (ISBN 0-669-03089-9); spanish for communication wkbk. 8.95 (ISBN 0-669-03592-0); wkbk. for Medical Personnel 8.95 (ISBN 0-669-03090-2); wkbk. for Law Enforcement Personnel 7.95 (ISBN 0-669-03593-9); social sciences wkbk. (isbn 0-699-03593-9) 7.95, inst. guide 1.00 to adopters (ISBN 0-686-65955-4); business cassettes 20.00 (ISBN 0-669-03465-7); medical cassettes 20.00 (ISBN 0-669-03466-5); social sciences cassettes (isbn 0-669-03464 9) 20.00, spanish for communications cassettes, 20.00 (ISBN 0-669-03634-X). Heath.

--Business & Economics Workbook. 256p. 1983. pap. 7.95 (ISBN 0-669-05337-6). Heath.

--Continuemos: Curso Intermedio de Espanol. 320p. 1982. pap. 14.95 (ISBN 0-669-05335-X). Heath.

--Nuestro Mundo. 256p. 1983. pap. 9.95 (ISBN 0-669-05340-6). Heath.

Jarvis, Ana C., et al. Continuemos: Curso Intermedio De Espanol. 1979. text ed. 20.95x (ISBN 0-669-01830-9); wkbk.-lab. manual 7.95 (ISBN 0-669-01831-7); reel tapeset 65.00 (ISBN 0-669-01833-3); cassette tapeset 50.00 (ISBN 0-669-01835-X). Heath.

--Como Se Dice. 2nd ed. 448p. 1982. text ed. 21.95 (ISBN 0-669-04495-4); wkbk. lab manual 8.95 (ISBN 0-669-04496-2); instr's guide 1.95 (ISBN 0-669-04497-0); reels 40.00 (ISBN 0-669-04500-4); cassettes 20.00 (ISBN 0-686-86034-9). Heath.

--Como Se Dice. 1976. text ed. 17.95x o.p. (ISBN 0-669-00192-9); instr's manual 1.95 o.p. (ISBN 0-669-00357-3); wkbk. 6.95x o.p. (ISBN 0-669-00189-9); reels 70.00 o.p. (ISBN 0-669-00191-0); cassettes 70.00 o.p. (ISBN 0-669-00358-1); transcripts avail. o.p. Heath.

Jarvis, Charles A. Jewelry Manufacture & Repair. (Illus.). 3.98 o.p. (ISBN 0-517-30587-9). Crown.

Jarvis, D. C. Arthritis & Folk Medicine. 2.25x (ISBN 0-449-23042-2). Cancer Control Soc.

--Folk Medicine. Date not set. pap. 5.95 (ISBN 0-449-90066-5, Columbine). Fawcett.

--Institutional Treatment of the Offender. 1977. text ed. 21.95 (ISBN 0-07-032308-9); tchr's. manual & key avail. McGraw.

Jarvis, F. J., jt. auth. see Herbert, W. L.

Jarvis, F. Washington. Prophets, Poets, Priests, & Kings: The Old Testament Story. 288p. 1975. pap. 6.95 (ISBN 0-8164-2089-0). Seabury.

Jarvis, Fred, jt. auth. see Merrill, Robert.

Jarvis, John J., jt. auth. see Bazaraa, Mokhtar S.

Jarvis, Peter. Professional Education. (New Patterns of Learning Ser.). 192p. 1983. text ed. 27.25x (ISBN 0-7099-1409-1, Pub. by Croom Helm Ltd England). Biblio Dist.

Jarvis, R. C. & Craig, R. Liverpool Registry of Merchant Ships. 278p. 1967. 22.50 (ISBN 0-7190-1114-0). Manchester.

Jarvis-Sladky, Kay. Un Grabado de Goya: Reader 3. LC 81-7783. (A la Aventura! Ser.). (Illus.). 40p. (Orig., Span.). (gr. 7-12). 1982. pap. 1.95 (ISBN 0-88436-860-2, 70261). EMC.

--La Guitarra Misteriosa: Reader 1. LC 81-7785. (A la Adventura! Ser.). (Illus.). 40p. (Orig., Span.). (gr. 7-12). 1982. pap. 1.95 (ISBN 0-88436-858-0, 70259). EMC.

--El Penitente Elusivo: Reader 4. LC 81-7842. (A la Aventura! Ser.). (Illus., Orig., Span.). (gr. 7-12). 1982. pap. 1.95 (ISBN 0-88436-861-0, 70262). EMC.

--Secretos de Famalia: Reader 2. LC 81-7780. (A la Aventura! Ser.). (Illus.). 40p. (Orig., Span.). (gr. 7-12). 1982. pap. 1.95 (ISBN 0-88436-859-9, 70260). EMC.

Jarymowycz, Mary, tr. see Smereczynska, Anastasia.

Jaschek, C. & Heintz, W., eds. Automated Data Retrieval in Astronomy. 1982. 48.00 (ISBN 90-277-1435-5, Pub. by Reidel Holland). Kluwer Boston.

Jasentuliyana, Nandasiri & Lee, S. K. Manual on Space Law: Travaux Preparatoires & Related Documents, 4 vols. (Manual on Space Law Ser.). 1981. lib. bdg. 200.00 set (ISBN 0-379-20263-8). Oceana.

Jashemski, Wilhelmina F. The Gardens of Pompeii, Herculaneum & the Villas Destroyed by Vesuvius: Appendices Including Illustrations, Bibliography & Complete Indices, Vol. II. (Illus.). 288p. 1983. write for info (ISBN 0-89241-125-2). Caratzas Bros.

Jasik, Henry. Antenna Engineering Handbook. 1961. 65.95 (ISBN 0-07-032290-2, P&RB). McGraw.

Jasik, Henry & Johnson, Richard C. Antenna Engineering Handbook. 1408p. 1984. 96.00 (ISBN 0-07-032291-0). McGraw.

Jaske, Carl R., et al. Corrosion Fatigue of Metals in Marine Environments. 245p. 49.95 (ISBN 0-387-90656-8). Springer-Verlag.

Jaslyn, Richard & Johnson, Janet. Setups: Campaign '80-The Public & the Presidential Selection Process. 1983. pap. 5.00 (ISBN 0-915654-52-0). Am Political.

Jasmin, Barbara Dalia, ed. The Captain's Lady: Cookbook-Personal Journal Circa Massachusetts 1837-1917, Vol. II. LC 82-90816. (Illus.). 192p. pap. 10.95 (ISBN 0-9609534-0-X). Captains Lady.

Jasmin, Sylvia & Trygstad, Louise. Behavioral Concepts & the Nursing Process. LC 78-26960. (Illus.). 194p. 1979. pap. text ed. 10.50 (ISBN 0-8016-2435-5). Mosby.

Jasny, Naum. Soviet Economists of the Twenties: Names to Be Remembered. Kaser, M., ed. LC 77-168894. (Soviet & East European Studies). 1972. 32.50 (ISBN 0-521-08302-8). Cambridge U Pr.

Jason, Kathryn & McMahon, J. J. The Power to Change Your Life. LC 81-43118. 240p. 1982. 13.95 (ISBN 0-385-17736-4). Doubleday.

Jason, Leonard A., jt. ed. see Felner, Robert D.

Jason, Paul & Sager, Jeffrey. Entangled. 272p. 1982. 14.95 (ISBN 0-453-00414-8, H414). NAL.

Jason, Philip K. Thawing Out. LC 79-15901. pap. 3.75 (ISBN 0-931848-27-X). Dryad Pr.

Jason, Philip K., ed. Anais Nin Reader. LC 82-73211. 316p. 1973. 10.00 o.p. (ISBN 0-8040-0595-8); pap. 7.95 (ISBN 0-8040-0596-6). Swallow.

Jason, Stuart. Butcher, No. Eight: Fire Bomb. 192p. 1973. pap. 1.25 o.p. (ISBN 0-523-22608-X). Pinnacle Bks.

--Butcher, No. Eighteen: The U.N. Affair. 192p. 1976. pap. 1.25 o.p. (ISBN 0-523-22843-0). Pinnacle Bks.

--Butcher, No. One: Kill Quick or Die. 1970. pap. 1.75 (ISBN 0-523-40678-9). Pinnacle Bks.

--The Corporate Caper. (Butcher Ser: No. 25). (Orig.). 1977. pap. 1.25 o.p. (ISBN 0-523-40055-1, 40-523-6). Pinnacle Bks.

--Instant Dead. (Butcher Ser.: No. 21). 1976. pap. 1.25 o.p. (ISBN 0-523-22923-2). Pinnacle Bks.

--Kill Them Silently. (Butcher Ser.: No. 29). 192p. (Orig.). 1980. pap. 1.75 o.p. (ISBN 0-523-40727-0). Pinnacle Bks.

Jason, Veronica. So Wild a Heart. (Orig.). 1981. pap. 2.95 (ISBN 0-451-11067-6, AE1067, Sig). NAL.

--Wild Winds of Love. 1982. pap. 3.50 (ISBN 0-451-11911-8, AE1911, Sig). NAL.

Jasper, James & Morgan, Edith. Developing Listening Skills. (gr. k-6). 1981. 5.95 (ISBN 0-86653-005-3, GA233). Good Apple.

Jasper, R. C. & Cuming, G. J., eds. Prayers of the Eucharist: Early & Reformed. 2nd ed. 1980. 15.95x (ISBN 0-19-520140-X); pap. 5.95 (ISBN 0-19-520141-8). Oxford U Pr.

Jasper, Ronald & Winstone, Harold, eds. Prayers We Have in Common. (Orig.). 1975. pap. 0.50 o.p. (ISBN 0-8006-1207-8, 1-1207). Fortress.

Jaspers, Karl. Anselm & Nicholas of Cusa. Arendt, Hannah, ed. Manheim, Ralph, tr. from Ger. LC 74-4484. (From the Great Philosophers: Vol. No. 2). 208p. 1974. pap. 3.50 o.p. (ISBN 0-15-607600-4, HB289, Harv). HarBraceJ.

--The Nature of Psychotherapy: A Critical Appraisal. Hoenig, J. & Hamilton, Marian W., trs. LC 75-34897. (Midway Reprint Ser). xii, 52p. 1975. pap. text ed. 3.00x o.s.i. (ISBN 0-226-39482-4). U of Chicago Pr.

--The Question of German Guilt. LC 78-5401. 1978. Repr. of 1947 ed. lib. bdg. 18.50x (ISBN 0-8371-9305-2, JAQG). Greenwood.

--Reason & Existenz. Earle, William, tr. from Ger. 116p. pap. 3.95 o.p. (ISBN 0-374-50060-6, N117). FS&G.

--Strindberg & Van Gogh. Grunow, Oskar & Woloshin, David, trs. LC 76-26386. 1977. text ed. 12.50x o.s.i. (ISBN 0-8165-0608-6); pap. text ed. 4.95x (ISBN 0-8165-0434-2). U of Ariz Pr.

Jaspersen, Frederick. Adjustment Experience & Growth Prospects of the Semi-Industrial Countries. (Working Paper: No. 477). 52p. 1981. 5.00 (ISBN 0-686-36162-8, WP-0477). World Bank.

Jaspersohn, William. A Day in the Life of a Marine Biologist. (Illus.). 96p. (gr. 5 up). 1982. 10.95 (ISBN 0-316-45814-7). Little.

--A Day in the Life of a Veterinarian. LC 78-13584. (Illus.). (gr. 3-7). 1978. 8.95 (ISBN 0-316-45810-4). Little.

--Magazine: A Week Behind the Scenes at Sports Illustrated. LC 82-21703. (Illus.). 128p. (gr. 7 up). 1983. 12.45i (ISBN 0-316-45815-5). Little.

Jastak, J. Theodore & Yagiela, John A. Regional Anesthesia of the Oral Cavity. 1st ed. LC 81-961. (Illus.). 212p. 1981. text ed. 22.95 (ISBN 0-8016-2434-7). Mosby.

Jaster, Robert S. Southern Africa in Conflict. 1982. pap. 4.75 (ISBN 0-8447-1098-9). Am Enterprise.

Jastram, Roy W. The Golden Constant: The English & American Experience, 1560-1976. LC 77-15034. 1977. 32.95x (ISBN 0-471-02303-5, Pub. by Wiley-Interscience). Wiley.

--Silver: The Restless Metal. LC 80-28361. 224p. 1981. 29.95x (ISBN 0-471-03912-8, Pub. by Wiley-Interscience). Wiley.

Jastrow, Rachel S., tr. see Saleilles, Raymond.

Jastrow, Robert. The Enchanted Loom. 1983. pap. write for info. (ISBN 0-671-47068-X, Touchstone Bks). S&S.

--Red Giants & White Dwarfs: Man's Descent from the Stars. 1971. pap. 1.95 o.p. (ISBN 0-451-08270-2, J8270, Sig). NAL.

Jastrow, Robert & Thompson, Malcolm H. Astronomy: Fundamentals & Frontiers. 3rd ed. LC 76-46622. 1977. text ed. 27.95 (ISBN 0-471-01845-7); tchr's manual 7.00 (ISBN 0-471-02728-6); study guide 8.95 (ISBN 0-471-03035-X). Wiley.

Jastrzebski, Zbigniew D. The Nature & Properties of Engineering Materials. 2nd ed. LC 75-20431. 656p. 1975. text ed. 37.95x (ISBN 0-471-44089-2). Wiley.

--The Nature & Properties of Engineering Materials: SI Version. 2nd ed. LC 77-83735. 1977. text ed. 36.95x (ISBN 0-471-02859-2); solutions manual 7.95x (ISBN 0-471-03671-4); solution matls. 6.00x (ISBN 0-471-01600-4). Wiley.

Jaswon, M. A. & Rose, M. A. Crystal Symmetry: The Theory of Colour Crystallography. (Mathematics & Its Applications Ser.). 150p. 1983. 47.95x (ISBN 0-470-27353-4). Halsted Pr.

Jauncey, J. H. La Ciencia Retorna a Dios. Swenson, Ana M., tr. Moore, J. N. 110p. (Sp.). 1981. pap. 2.25 (ISBN 0-311-05004-2). Casa Bautista.

Jaunez-Sponville, Pierre-Ignace & Bugnet, Nicolas. La Philosophie de Ruravebohni, 2 vols. (Utopias in the Enlightenment Ser.). 575p. (Fr.). 1974. Repr. of 1809 ed. Set. lib. bdg. 154.00x o.p. (ISBN 0-8287-0462-7). Clearwater Pub.

Jauss, Hans R. Aesthetic Experience & Literary Hermeneutics. Shaw, Michael, tr. LC 82-4786. (Theory & History of Literature Ser.: Vol. 3). 384p. 1982. 29.50x (ISBN 0-8166-1003-7); pap. 12.95 (ISBN 0-8166-1006-1). U of Minn Pr.

Jaussi, Laureen & Chaston, Gloria. Genealogical Records of Utah. LC 73-87713. 336p. 1974. 5.95 (ISBN 0-87747-507-5). Deseret Bk.

Javadi, Hasan, tr. see Farrokhzad, Forugh.

Javadpour, Nasser. Principles & Management of Urologic Cancer. (Illus.). 544p. 1979. pap. 43.00 (ISBN 0-683-04352-8). Williams & Wilkins.

Javarek, Vera, ed. Serbo-Croatian Prose & Verse. 1958. text ed. 19.00x (ISBN 0-485-17506-1, Athlone Pr). Humanities.

Javid, M., jt. auth. see Brenner, Egon.

Javid, Mansour & Brenner, Egon. Analysis, Transmission, & Filtering of Signals. LC 77-23951. 476p. 1978. Repr. of 1963 ed. lib. bdg. 25.00 (ISBN 0-88275-599-4). Krieger.

Javitt, N. Liver & Biliary Tract Physiology I. 384p. 1980. text ed. 39.50 o.p. (ISBN 0-8391-1554-7). Univ Park.

Javna, Gordon, jt. auth. see Javna, John.

Javna, John & Javna, Gordon. Sixties! (Illus.). 1983. pap. 12.95 (ISBN 0-312-72752-6). St Martin.

Javor. Discrete Simulation & Related Fields. 1982. 32.00 (ISBN 0-444-86429-6). Elsevier.

Javor, F. A. Rim-World Legacy. pap. 1.50 o.p. (ISBN 0-451-08424-1, W8424, Sig). NAL.

Jawin, Ann & Heimlich, Milton. Where is the Money for College? 250p. Date not set. 5.95 (ISBN 0-15-600018-0). HarBraceJ. Postponed.

Jaworski, Leon. After Fifteen Years. 167p. 1961. 9.95 (ISBN 0-87201-017-1). Gulf Pub.

--The Right & the Power: The Prosecution of Watergate. 316p. 1976. 12.95 (ISBN 0-87201-792-3). Gulf Pub.

Jaworski, Leon & Schneider, Dick. Encrucijadas. Date not set. 3.50 (ISBN 0-88113-082-6). Edit Betania.

Jay, Charlotte. The Voice of the Crab. (Adult Ser.). 1975. Repr. lib. bdg. 8.95 o.p. (ISBN 0-8161-6270-0, Large Print Bks). G K Hall.

Jay, David. How to Play the Moonlighting Game. LC 82-18364. 224p. 1983. 14.95 (ISBN 0-87196-131-8). Facts on File.

Jay, Hilda L. Stimulating Student Search: Library Media Classroom Teacher Techniques. 160p. 1983. 18.50 (ISBN 0-208-01936-7, Lib Prof Pubns); pap. 14.50 (ISBN 0-208-01926-X). Shoe String.

Jay, John, jt. ed. see Rieber, Robert W.

Jay, Karla & Young, Allen. The Gay Report. LC 78-24056. 1979. 14.95 o.p. (ISBN 0-671-40013-4). Summit Bks.

--Lavender Culture. (Orig.). 1979. pap. 2.50 o.s.i. (ISBN 0-515-04462-8). Jove Pubns.

--Out of the Closets, Voices of Gay Liberation. 1977. pap. 1.95 o.s.i. (ISBN 0-515-04497-0). Jove Pubns.

Jay, Michael. Spacecraft. (Easy-Read Fact Bks.). (Illus.). 32p. (gr. 2-4). 1983. PLB 8.60 (ISBN 0-531-04512-9). Watts.

Jay, Michael & Henbest, Nigel. The Moon. (Easy-Read Fact Bks.). (Illus.). 32p. (gr. 2-4). 1982. PLB 8.60 (ISBN 0-531-04373-8). Watts.

Jay, Michael & Hewish, Mark. Airports. (Easy-Read Fact Bks). 32p. (gr. 2-4). 1982. PLB 8.60 (ISBN 0-531-04370-3). Watts.

Jay, Peter, ed. & intro. by. The Greek Anthology & Other Ancient Greek Epigrams. 1973. 19.95x (ISBN 0-19-519745-3). Oxford U Pr.

Jay, W., jt. auth. see Gray, Willaim.

Jay, William. Autobiography of William Jay. 1974. 11.95 (ISBN 0-85151-177-5). Banner of Truth.

--War & Peace: The Evils of the First, & a Plan for Preserving the Last. LC 70-137547. (Peace Movement in America Ser.). xiv, 69p. 1972. Repr. of 1919 ed. lib. bdg. 9.95x (ISBN 0-89198-075-X). Ozer.

Jayadeva. The Gita Govinda of Jayadeva. Varma, Monika, tr. 106p. (Sanskrit.). 1974. 10.00 (ISBN 0-88253-704-0); pap. 6.75 (ISBN 0-89253-620-9). Ind-US Inc.

Jayakanthan, D. A Literary Man's Political Experiences. 1976. text ed. 12.95x o.p. (ISBN 0-7069-0407-9, Pub. by Vikas India). Advent NY.

Jayakumar, V., jt. auth. see Johnson, David E.

Jayana, Sheth. Munshi: Self-Sculptor. 1982. 18.50x (ISBN 0-8364-0857-8, Pub by Bharatiya Bhavan). South Asia Bk.

Jayant, N. S., ed. Waveform Quantization & Coding. LC 75-44651. 1976. 43.95 (ISBN 0-87942-073-1). Inst Electrical.

Jayarajah, Carl A. Bangladesh: Current Trends & Development Issues. x, 116p. 1979. 10.00 (ISBN 0-686-36100-8, RC-7904). World Bank.

Jayatilaka, Ayal De S. Fracture of Engineering Brittle Materials. (Illus.). 1979. 69.75x (ISBN 0-85334-825-1, Pub. by Applied Sci England). Elsevier.

Jayawant, B. V. Electromagnetic Levitation & Suspension Techniques. 144p. 1981. pap. text ed. 24.50 (ISBN 0-7131-3428-3). E Arnold.

Jaye, Walter, jt. auth. see Patterson, Jerry L.

Jayne, A. G., tr. see Bojer, Johan.

Jayne, H. H. Archaic Chinese Jades: Special Exhibition. (Illus.). 58p. 1940. soft bound 2.00x (ISBN 0-686-11896-0). Univ Mus of U PA.

Jayne, Sears R. John Colet & Marsilio Ficino. LC 80-17262. (Illus.). 172p. 1980. Repr. of 1963 ed. lib. bdg. 20.75x (ISBN 0-313-22606-7, JACF). Greenwood.

Jayne, Sears R., tr. Commentary on Plato's Symposium on Love by Marsilio Ficino. 2nd rev. ed. 300p. (Latin.). Date not set. pap. price not set (ISBN 0-88214-600-9). Spring Pubns.

Jaynes, Julian. The Origin of Consciousness in the Breakdown of the Bicameral Mind. 1977. 19.95 (ISBN 0-395-20729-0). HM.

Jayson, Malcolm. Total Hip Replacement. 152p. 1971. 30.00 (ISBN 0-686-97968-0, Pub. by Pitman Bks England). State Mutual Bk.

Jayson, Malcolm I. Back Pain: The Facts. (The Facts Ser.). (Illus.). 1981. text ed. 12.95x (ISBN 0-19-261285-9). Oxford U Pr.

Jazani, Bizhan. Capitalism & Revolution in Iran: Selected Writings. 1981. 25.00 (ISBN 0-905762-82-7, Pub. by Zed Pr England); pap. 8.50 (ISBN 0-905762-57-6, Pub. by Zed Pr England). Lawrence Hill.

Jazbi, ed. Pediatric Otorhinolaryngology. (International Congress Ser.: Vol. 509). 1980. 63.50 (ISBN 0-444-90115-9). Elsevier.

Jeaffreson, John C. Pleasantries of English Courts & Lawyers. Mersky, Roy M. & Jacobstein, J. Myron, eds. LC 74-82120. (Classics in Legal History Reprint Ser.: Vol. 23). 328p. 1974. Repr. lib. bdg. 30.00 (ISBN 0-89941-022-7). W S Hein.

--The Real Shelley: New Views of the Poet's Life, 2 Vols. 478p. 1982. Repr. of 1885 ed. lib. bdg. 250.00 set (ISBN 0-8495-2801-1). Arden Lib.

Jeakle, William T., jt. auth. see Reardon, Eugene F.

Jeal, Tim. A Marriage of Convenience. 1979. 11.95 o.p. (ISBN 0-671-22872-2). S&S.

Jean, B. & Mouret, F. Montaigne, Descartes et Pascal. 1971. pap. 10.00 (ISBN 0-7190-0422-5). Manchester.

Jeanin, Paule. A Coeur-Menteur. (Collection Colombine Ser.). 192p. 1983. pap. 1.95 (ISBN 0-373-48059-8). Harlequin Bks.

Jeanloz, Roger W. & Balazs, Endre A., eds. The Amino Sugars: The Chemistry & Biology of Compounds Containing Amino Sugars, 2 vols. Incl. Vol. 1, Pt. A. 1969. 59.50 (ISBN 0-12-381801-X); by subscription 59.50 (ISBN 0-686-85500-0); Vol. 2, Pt. A. 1965. 69.50 (ISBN 0-12-381802-8); Vol. 2, Pt. B. 1966. 67.50 (ISBN 0-12-381842-7). Acad Pr.

Jeanneret, Charles E., pseud. Etude Sur Le Mouvement D'art Decoratif En Allemagne. LC 68-26652. (Architecture & Decorative Art Ser). (Fr). 1968. Repr. of 1912 ed. lib. bdg. 25.00 (ISBN 0-306-71147-8). Da Capo.

Jeanneret, Charles E. see Le Corbusier, pseud.

Jeanneret, O., ed. Alcohol & Youth. (Child Health & Development Ser.: Vol. 2). (Illus.). x, 200p. 1982. 78.00 (ISBN 3-8055-3655-0). S Karger.

Jeannet, Angela M. & Barnett, Louise K., eds. New World Journeys: Contemporary Italian Writers & the Experience of America. (Contributions in American Studies: No. 33). 1977. lib. bdg. 27.50 (ISBN 0-8371-9758-9, BAT/). Greenwood.

Jeanpierre, Wendell A., tr. see Senghor, Leopold S.

Jeans, James. Physics & Philosophy. 232p. 1981. pap. 4.00 (ISBN 0-486-24117-3). Dover.

Jeans, James S. An Introduction to the Kinetic Theory of Gases. LC 40-3353. (Cambridge Science Classics). 319p. 1982. pap. 15.95 (ISBN 0-521-09232-9). Cambridge U Pr.

Jeansonne, Louis O., jt. auth. see Waring, William W.

Jeary. Engineering Drawing Two Checkbook Limp. 1982. text ed. 19.95 (ISBN 0-408-00683-8); pap. text ed. 9.95. Butterworth.

Jeavons, John. How to Grow More Vegetables Than You Ever Thought Possible on Less Land Than You Can Imagine. rev. ed. LC 82-50212. (Illus.). 144p. 1982. 10.95 (ISBN 0-89815-074-4); pap. 7.95 (ISBN 0-89815-073-6). Ten Speed Pr.

Jeavons, John & Griffin, J. Morgodor. The Backyard Homestead, Mini-Farm & Garden Log Book. 224p. (Orig.). 1983. pap. 8.95 (ISBN 0-89815-093-0). Ten Speed Pr.

Jebb, R. C., ed. Selections from the Attic Orators: Antiphon, Andocides, Lysias, Isocrates & Isaeus. 1983. 25.00 (ISBN 0-89241-360-3); pap. 12.50 (ISBN 0-89241-129-5). Caratzas Bros.

Jebb, Richard C., tr. see Hadas, Moses.

Jech, T. Axiom of Choice. (Studies in Logic: Vol. 75). 1973. 19.50 (ISBN 0-444-10484-4). Elsevier.

Jedamus, Paul & Frame, R. Business Decision Theory. LC 69-13609. (Illus.). 1969. text ed. 24.95 (ISBN 0-07-032307-0, C); instructor's manual 5.50 (ISBN 0-07-032311-9). McGraw.

Jedamus, Paul, et al. Statistical Analysis for Business Decisions. new ed. (Illus.). 1976. text ed. 24.95 (ISBN 0-07-032302-X, C). McGraw.

Jedin, Hubert & Dolan, John, eds. Reformation & Counter-Reformation. 1980. 37.50 (ISBN 0-686-95526-9). Crossroad NY.

Jedlicka, Allen D. Organization for Rural Development: Risk Taking & Appropriate Technology. LC 77-10757. (Praeger Special Studies). 1977. 26.95 o.p. (ISBN 0-03-022341-5). Praeger.

Jedruch, Jacek. Constitutions, Elections & Legislatures of Poland, 1493-1977: A Guide to Their History. LC 81-40301. (Illus.). 612p. (Orig.). 1982. PLB 33.75 (ISBN 0-8191-2508-3); pap. text ed. 22.50 (ISBN 0-8191-2509-1). U Pr of Amer.

Jedrzejewicz, Waclaw. Jozef Pilsudski: A Life for Poland. LC 81-86441. (Illus.). 232p. 1982. 22.50 (ISBN 0-88254-633-3). Hippocrene Bks.

Jeejeebhoy, Khursheed N. Gastrointestinal Diseases: Focus on Clinical Diagnosis. 1979. pap. 24.50 (ISBN 0-87488-831-X). Med Exam.

Jeep, Elizabeth. Classroom Creativity: An Idea Book for Religion Teachers. LC 77-24719. 1977. pap. 5.95 (ISBN 0-8164-2160-9). Seabury.

Jeeves, Malcolm. Experimental Psychology. (Studies in Biology: No. 47). 64p. 1978. pap. text ed. 8.95 (ISBN 0-7131-2448-2). E Arnold.

Jeffares, A. Norman. Anglo-Irish Literature. LC 82-5753. (History of Literature Ser.). (Illus.). 360p. 1982. 33.50x (ISBN 0-8052-3828-X). Schocken.

--Politics, Society & Nationhood, Vol. 1. (Collected Edition of the Writings of G. W. Russell Ser.: VI-1). Date not set. text ed. price not set (ISBN 0-391-01185-5). Humanities.

--Politics, Society & Nationhood, Vol. 2. (Collected Edition of the Writings of G. W. Russell Ser.: VI-2). Date not set. text ed. price not set (ISBN 0-391-01183-9). Humanities.

--W. B. Yeats: Man & Poet. 365p. 1949. 22.50 (ISBN 0-686-84516-1). Routledge & Kegan.

Jeffares, A. Norman, ed. see Blamires, Harry.

Jeffares, A. Norman, ed. see Yeats, William B.

Jeffcoate, N. Principles of Gynecology. 4th ed. 1975. 74.95 (ISBN 0-407-00000-3). Butterworth.

Jeffcoate, S. L. Androgens & Anti-Androgen Therapy. (Current Topics in Reproductive Endocrinology Ser.). 250p. 1983. 43.95 (ISBN 0-471-10154-0, Pub. by Wiley Med). Wiley.

Jeffcoate, S. L. & Sandler, M. Progress Towards a Male Contraceptive. (Current Topics in Reproductive Endocrinology Ser.). 220p. 1983. 45.00 (ISBN 0-471-10417-5, Pub. by Wiley Med). Wiley.

Jeffcott, L. B., jt. ed. see Archer, R. K.

Jefferds, Vince. The Elegant Disney ABC Book. Klimo, Kate, ed. (Illus.). 96p. Date not set. 10.25 (ISBN 0-671-45571-0, Little Simon). S&S. Postponed.

Jefferies, Lawrence. Air, Air, Air. LC 82-15808. (Question & Answer Bks.). (Illus.). 32p. (gr. 3-6). 1983. PLB 8.59 (ISBN 0-89375-880-9); pap. text ed. 1.95 (ISBN 0-89375-881-7). Troll Assocs.

--All About Stars. LC 82-20027. (Question & Answer Bks.). (Illus.). 32p. (gr. 3-6). PLB 8.59 (ISBN 0-89375-888-4); pap. text ed. 1.95 (ISBN 0-89375-889-2). Troll Assocs.

--Amazing World of Animals. LC 82-20061. (Question & Answer Bks.). (Illus.). 32p. (gr. 3-6). 1983. PLB 8.59 (ISBN 0-89375-898-1); pap. text ed. 1.95 (ISBN 0-89375-899-X). Troll Assocs.

Jefferies, Richard. Bevis: The Story of a Boy. 1981. pap. 4.95x (ISBN 0-460-01850-7, Evman). Biblio Dist.

--Wood Magic. LC 74-82725. 1974. 8.95 (ISBN 0-89388-177-5). Okpaku Communications.

Jefferis, David & Gatland, Kenneth. Robots. LC 82-50066. (Easy-Read Fact Bks.). (Illus.). (gr. 2-4). 1982. PLB 8.60 (ISBN 0-531-04448-3). Watts.

Jefferis, Tony & Hindley, Judy. Farm Animals. LC 82-50065. (Easy-Read Fact Bks.). (Illus.). 32p. (gr. 2-4). 1982. PLB 8.60 (ISBN 0-531-04447-5). Watts.

Jeffers. Introduction to Systems Analysis with Ecological Implications. 208p. 1978. text ed. 27.95 o.p. (ISBN 0-8391-1305-6). Univ Park.

Jeffers, Coleman R., jt. ed. see Dobrian, Walter A.

Jeffers, J. H. & Tait, R. J., eds. Physical Chemistry of Process Metallurgy: The Richarson Conference. 266p. 1974. text ed. 72.00x (ISBN 0-900488-22-0). IMM North Am.

Jeffers, Robert J. & Lehiste, Ilse. Principles & Methods for Historical Linguistics. (Illus.). 1979. text ed. 13.95x o.p. (ISBN 0-262-10020-7); pap. text ed. 6.95x (ISBN 0-262-60011-0). MIT Pr.

Jeffers, Robinson. Dear Judas. 1977. 12.95 (ISBN 0-87140-624-1); pap. 3.95 (ISBN 0-87140-113-4). Liveright.

--The Double Axe. 1977. 12.95 (ISBN 0-87140-625-X); pap. 5.95 (ISBN 0-87140-114-2). Liveright.

--Selected Poems. 1965. pap. 2.95 (ISBN 0-394-70295-6, Vin). Random.

--The Woman at Point Sur. 1977. 12.95 (ISBN 0-87140-626-8); pap. 3.95 (ISBN 0-87140-115-0). Liveright.

Jeffers, Susan. If Wishes Were Horses: Mother Goose Rhymes. LC 79-9986. (Illus.). (ps-3). 1979. 9.95 (ISBN 0-525-32531-X, 0966-290). Dutton.

--Three Jovial Huntsmen. LC 70-122739. (Illus.). 32p. (ps-1). 1973. 10.95 (ISBN 0-02-747690-1). Bradbury Pr.

Jeffers, Thomas L. Samuel Butler Revalued. LC 80-24904. 152p. 1981. 13.75x (ISBN 0-271-00281-6). Pa St U Pr.

Jefferson. The Invasive Adeomas of the Anterior Pituitary. 76p. 1982. 50.00x (ISBN 0-85323-471-X, Pub. by Liverpool Univ England). State Mutual Bk.

Jefferson, Alan. Delius. (Master Musicians Ser). (Illus.). 189p. 1972. 7.95x o.p. (ISBN 0-460-03131-7, Pub. by J. M. Dent England). Biblio Dist.

--The Glory of Opera. LC 76-5917. (Illus.). 1976. 20.00 o.p. (ISBN 0-399-11771-7). Putnam Pub Group.

Jefferson, Albertina A., ed. see International Conference, Kingston, Jamaica, April 24-29, 1972.

Jefferson, Ann. The Nouveau Roman & the Poetics of Fiction. LC 79-41507. 225p. 1980. 29.95 (ISBN 0-521-22239-7). Cambridge U Pr.

Jefferson, Christina. Dendroglyphs of the Chatham Islands. (Illus.). 1956. 8.00x (ISBN 0-8248-0586-0). UH Pr.

Jefferson, Douglas, ed. see James, Henry.

Jefferson, George. Library Co-operation. 192p. 1977. 20.00 (ISBN 0-233-96851-2, 05800-9, Pub. by Gower Pub Co England). Lexington Bks.

Jefferson, James W. & Greist, John H. Lithium Encyclopedia for Clinical Practice. (Illus.). 185p. 1983. spiral bdg. 17.00x (ISBN 0-88048-011-4). Am Psychiatric.

Jefferson, James W., jt. ed. see Greist, John H.

Jefferson, K. & Rees, S. Clinical Cardiac Radiology. 1973. 39.95 o.p. (ISBN 0-407-13575-8). Butterworth.

Jefferson, Keith. Clinical Cardiac Radiology. 2nd ed. LC 79-40913. (Illus.). 1980. text ed. 49.95 (ISBN 0-407-13576-6). Butterworth.

--The Hyena Reader. LC 75-39158. 1976. pap. 1.50 (ISBN 0-916692-00-0). Black River.

Jefferson National Expansion Historical Association. Gateway to the West. 36p. 1975. pap. 2.00 (ISBN 0-686-95728-8). Jefferson Natl.

Jefferson, Thomas. Complete Annals of Thomas Jefferson. Sawvel, Franklin R., ed. LC 70-75272. (Amer. Public Figures Ser.). 1970. Repr. of 1903 ed. lib. bdg. 37.50 (ISBN 0-306-71311-X). Da Capo.

--Correspondence Between Thomas Jefferson & Pierre Samuel Du Pont De Nemours, 1798-1817. Malone, Dumas, ed. Lehmann, Linwood, tr. LC 78-75282. (The American Scene Ser.). 1970. Repr. of 1930 ed. lib. bdg. 42.50 (ISBN 0-306-71301-2). Da Capo.

--Life & Selected Writings. 1944. 9.95 (ISBN 0-394-60454-7). Modern Lib.

--Reports of Cases Determined in the General Court of Virgina from 1730-1740, 1768-1772. LC 81-84431. viii, 145p. 1981. Repr. of 1829 ed. lib. bdg. 28.50 (ISBN 0-89941-143-6). W S Hein.

Jeffery, Barbara. Wedding Speeches & Toasts. 1980. 3.95x o.p. (ISBN 0-685-22158-X). Wehman.

Jeffery, E. A., jt. auth. see Mole, T.

Jeffery, Keith & Hennesy, Peter. State of Emergency: British Governments & Strikebreaking Since 1919. 280p. 1983. 29.95 (ISBN 0-7100-9464-7); pap. write for info. (ISBN 0-7100-9474-4). Routledge & Kegan.

Jeffery, L. H. Archaic Greece. LC 75-10758. (Illus.). 300p. 1976. 27.50 (ISBN 0-312-04760-6). St Martin.

Jeffery, Patricia. Migrants & Refugees. LC 75-25428. (Illus.). 200p. 1976. 24.95 (ISBN 0-521-21070-4). Cambridge U Pr.

Jeffery, V. M., tr. see Pirandello, Luigi.

Jefferys, William H. & Robbins, Ralph. Discovering Astronomy. 1980. text ed. 28.95 (ISBN 0-471-44125-2); tchr's. manual 8.95 (ISBN 0-471-05666-9). Wiley.

Jeffree, C. E., jt. auth. see Juniper, B. E.

Jeffrey, A. & Kawahara, T. Asymptotic Methods in Nonlinear Wave Theory. (Applicable Mathematics Ser.). 256p. (Orig.). 1982. pap. text ed. 43.95 (ISBN 0-273-08509-3). Pitman Pub MA.

Jeffrey, A., ed. see Taniuti, T. & Nishihara, K.

Jeffrey, Alan. Quasilinear Hyperbolic Systems & Waves. (Research Notes in Mathematics Ser.: No. 5). 203p. (Orig.). 1976. pap. text ed. 20.95 (ISBN 0-273-00102-7). Pitman Pub MA.

Jeffrey, C. An Introduction to Plant Taxonomy. 2nd ed. LC 81-17090. 100p. 1982. 24.95 (ISBN 0-521-24542-7); pap. 12.50 (ISBN 0-521-28775-8). Cambridge U Pr.

Jeffrey, C., tr. see Takhtajan, A.

Jeffrey, Harry R. Wood Finishing. (gr. 9-12). 1957. pap. text ed. 9.80 (ISBN 0-87002-012-9). Bennett IL.

Jeffrey, Lloyd N. Thomas Hood. (English Authors Ser.). lib. bdg. 13.95 (ISBN 0-8057-1268-2, Twayne). G K Hall.

Jeffrey, Patricia. Frogs in a Well: Indian Women in Purdah. 192p. (Orig.). 1979. 20.00 (ISBN 0-905762-20-7, Pub. by Zed Pr England); pap. 9.50 (ISBN 0-905762-32-0, Pub. by Zed Pr England). Lawrence Hill.

Jeffrey, R. The Decline of Nayar Dominance. Society & Politics in Travancore, 1847-1908. 40.00x (ISBN 0-686-96994-4, Pub. by Scottish Academic Scotland). State Mutual Bk.

Jeffrey, R. C., jt. auth. see Boolos, G. S.

Jeffrey, Richard C. Formal Logic: Its Scope & Limits. 2nd ed. (Illus.). 256p. 1981. text ed. 21.00 (ISBN 0-07-032321-6, C); instr's manual 10.95 (ISBN 0-07-032322-4). McGraw.

--The Logic of Decision. 2nd ed. LC 82-13465. 1983. lib. bdg. 19.00x (ISBN 0-226-39581-2). U of Chicago Pr.

Jeffrey, Richard C., ed. Studies in Inductive Logic & Probability, Vol. II. 312p. 1980. 28.50x (ISBN 0-520-03826-6). U of Cal Pr.

Jeffrey, Robert C. & Peterson, Owen. Speech: A Basic Text. 2nd ed. 412p. 1982. pap. text ed. 14.50 scp (ISBN 0-06-043279-9, HarpC); instr's manual avail. (ISBN 0-06-363274-8). Har-Row.

Jeffrey, Robin. Decline of Nayar Dominance: Society & Politics in Travancore 1847-1908. LC 74-22112. 1976. 39.50x (ISBN 0-8419-0184-8). Holmes & Meier.

Jeffrey, Sara. Who Lives Here? LC 78-72121. (Illus.). (ps). 1979. 6.75 (ISBN 0-89799-145-1); pap. 3.50 (ISBN 0-89799-009-9). Dandelion Pr.

Jeffreys, A. E., ed. The Art of the Librarian: A Collection of Original Papers from the Library of the University of Newcastle Upon Tyne. 200p. 1976. 14.95 o.p. (ISBN 0-85362-151-9, Oriel). Routledge & Kegan.

Jeffreys, Bertha S., jt. auth. see Jeffreys, Harold.

Jeffreys, H. B. Collected Papers of Sir Harold Jeffrey's on Geophysics & Other Sciences, 6 vols. Incl. Vol. I. 558p. 1971. 98.00x (ISBN 0-677-03170-X); Vol. II. 718p. 1973. 123.00 (ISBN 0-677-03180-7); Vol. III. 680p. 1974. 115.00 (ISBN 0-677-03190-4); Vol. IV. 542p. 1975. 98.00 (ISBN 0-677-03200-5); Vol. V. 512p. 1976. 98.00 (ISBN 0-677-03210-2); Vol. VI. 640p. 1977. 115.00x (ISBN 0-677-03220-X). Set. 580.00x (ISBN 0-677-03230-7). Gordon.

Jeffreys, Harold. Cartesian Tensors. (Orig.). 1931-1962. 18.95 (ISBN 0-521-05423-0); pap. 8.95 (ISBN 0-521-09191-8). Cambridge U Pr.

--The Earth. 6th ed. LC 74-19527. (Illus.). 600p. 1976. 95.00 (ISBN 0-521-20648-0). Cambridge U Pr.

--Scientific Inference. 3rd ed. LC 71-179159. (Illus.). 280p. 1973. 45.00 (ISBN 0-521-08446-6). Cambridge U Pr.

Jeffreys, Harold & Jeffreys, Bertha S. Methods of Mathematical Physics. 3rd ed. (Illus.). 1956. pap. 27.95 (ISBN 0-521-09723-1). Cambridge U Pr.

Jeffreys, J. G. Suicide Most Foul. 204p. 1983. pap. 2.95 (ISBN 0-8027-3019-1). Walker & Co.

Jeffreys, T. E., et al. Disorders of the Cervical Spine. (Illus.). 1980. text ed. 69.95 (ISBN 0-407-00158-1). Butterworth.

Jeffri, Joan. Arts Money: Raising It, Saving It, & Earning It. 250p. 1983. pap. 17.95 (ISBN 0-918212-68-5). Neal-Schuman.

Jeffries & Mabey, Richard. The Open Air. 270p. 1982. 30.00x (ISBN 0-686-81704-4, Pub. by Wildwood House). State Mutual Bk.

Jeffries, jt. auth. see Gatland.

Jeffries, C. D. & Meldysh, L. V. Electron-Hole Droplets in Semiconductors. Date not set. price not set (ISBN 0-444-86530-6). Elsevier.

Jeffries, Ian, ed. The Industrial Enterprise in Eastern Europe. 176p. 1981. 25.95 (ISBN 0-03-059323-9). Praeger.

Jeffries, Julia. The Chadwick Ring. (Orig.). 1982. pap. 2.25 (ISBN 0-451-11346-2, AE1346, Sig). NAL.

Jeffries, N. P., jt. auth. see Shell, R. L.

Jeffries, Paul, jt. auth. see Liebers, Arthur.

Jeffries, R. Class, Power & Ideology in Ghana. LC 77-22872. (African Studies: No. 22). (Illus.). 1978. 37.50 (ISBN 0-521-21806-3). Cambridge U Pr.

Jeffries, Roderic. Just Deserts. 208p. 1981. 9.95 o.p. (ISBN 0-312-44942-9). St Martin.

--Patrol Car. LC 67-3934. (gr. 5 up). 1967. PLB 8.79 o.p. (ISBN 0-06-022818-0, HarpJ). Har-Row.

--Police Dog. (gr. 5 up). 1977. pap. 1.50 o.p. (ISBN 0-06-440083-2, Trophy). Har-Row.

Jeffries, Ron. PET Fun & Games. (Orig.). 1982. pap. 11.95 (ISBN 0-931988-70-5). Osborne-McGraw.

Jeffs, Angela, ed. Creative Crafts. (Illus.). 1977. 35.00 o.p. (ISBN 0-8069-5378-0); lib. bdg. 32.99 o.p. (ISBN 0-8069-5379-9). Sterling.

--Wild Knitting. LC 79-51988. (Illus.). 144p. 1979. 19.95 o.s.i. (ISBN 0-89479-054-4). A & W Pubs.

Jeffs, Julian. Sherry. (Faber Wine Books Ser.). 320p. 17.95 (ISBN 0-571-18047-7); pap. 7.95 (ISBN 0-571-11799-6). Faber & Faber.

Jeffs, Robin, jt. ed. see Highfield, J. R.

Jeffus, Larry. Safety for Welders. LC 78-73579. (Metalworking Ser.). (gr. 8). 1980. pap. text ed. 5.80 (ISBN 0-8273-1684-4); instructor's guide 2.75 (ISBN 0-8273-1685-2). Delmar.

Jefkins, F. W. Marketing & PR Media Planning. LC 74-618347. 1974. text ed. 30.00 o.p. (ISBN 0-08-018086-8); pap. text ed. 13.25 (ISBN 0-08-018085-X). Pergamon.

Jefkins, Frank. Advertisement Writing. 256p. 1976. 25.00x (ISBN 0-7121-0138-1, Pub. by Macdonald & Evans). State Mutual Bk.

Jegede, Oluremi. Bibliography on the Constitutions of Nigeria. LC 81-83448. 72p. 1981. pap. 15.00 (ISBN 0-379-20739-7). Oceana.

Jegede, Oluremi, compiled by. Nigerian Legal Bibliography. 320p. Date not set. lib. bdg. 50.00 (ISBN 0-379-20801-6). Oceana.

Jeger, M. & Eckmann, M. Einfuhrung in Die Vektorielle Geometrie und Lineare Algebra Fur Ingenieure und Naturwissenschafter. 252p. (Ger.). 1967. 36.30x (ISBN 3-7643-0198-8). Birkhauser.

Jeger, Max, jt. auth. see Rueff, Marcel.

Jehle, Faustin F. Complete & Easy Guide to Social Security & Medicare. 1982. pap. 6.95 (ISBN 0-440-01129-9, Dell Trade Pbks). Dell.

Jehu, Derek. Sexual Dysfunction: A Behavioral Approach to Causation, Assessment & Treatment. LC 79-40582. 1979. 64.95x (ISBN 0-471-99756-0, Pub. by Wiley-Interscience); pap. 27.95x (ISBN 0-471-27597-2, Pub. by Wiley-Interscience). Wiley.

Jeier, Thomas & Wallman, Jeffrey M. Return to Canta Lupe. LC 82-45327. (Science Fiction Ser.). 192p. 1983. 11.95 (ISBN 0-385-18257-0). Doubleday.

Jeiven, Helene. Checklist for a Perfect Bar Mitzvah (& a Bat Mitzvah) LC 82-45929. (Illus.). 220p. 1983. pap. 3.95 (ISBN 0-385-18134-5, Dolp). Doubleday.

Jekel, Pamela. Sea Star: The Private Life of Anne Bonny, Pirate Queen. 1983. pap. 5.95 (ISBN 0-517-54946-8, Harmony). Crown.

Jekyll, Gertrude. Children & Gardens. (Illus.). 192p. 1982. 29.50 (ISBN 0-907462-27-8). Antique Collect.

--Flower Decoration in the House. (Illus.). 1982. 29.50 (ISBN 0-907462-31-6). Antique Collect.

--A Gardener's Testament. (Illus.). 336p. 1982. 29.50 (ISBN 0-907462-29-4). Antique Collect.

--Home & the Garden. (Illus.). 390p. 1982. 29.50 (ISBN 0-907462-18-9). Antique Collect.

--Lilies for English Gardens. (Illus.). 156p. 1982. 29.50 (ISBN 0-907462-28-6). Antique Collect.

--Old English Household Life: Some Account of Cottage Objects & Country Folk. 2nd ed. (Illus.). 218p. 1975. 11.50x o.p. (ISBN 0-87471-791-4). Rowman.

--Roses for English Gardens. (Illus.). 392p. 1982. 29.50 (ISBN 0-907462-24-3). Antique Collect.

--Wall, Water & Woodland Gardens. (Illus.). 380p. 1982. 29.50 (ISBN 0-907462-26-X). Antique Collect.

Jelen, F. C. Cost & Optimization Engineering. 1970. text ed. 33.00 (ISBN 0-07-032323-2, C); solutions manual 25.00. McGraw.

Jelen, Frederic C. & Black, James. Cost & Optimization Engineering. 2nd ed. (Illus.). 560p. 1982. text ed. 33.00x (ISBN 0-07-032331-3, C); solutions manual 21.00 (ISBN 0-07-032332-1). McGraw.

Jelenko, C. & Frey, C. F. Emergency Medical Services. LC 76-7422. (Illus.). 1976. 24.95 o.p. (ISBN 0-87618-702-5). R J Brady.

Jelinek, Lawrence. Harvest Empire. Hundley, Norris, Jr., et al, eds. (Golden State Ser.). 120p. 1982. pap. cancelled (ISBN 0-686-91738-3). Boyd & Fraser.

Jelinek, Lawrence J. Harvest Empire. 2nd ed. Hundley, Norris, Jr., et al, eds. (Golden States Ser.). 130p. (gr. 12). 1982. pap. text ed. 5.95x (ISBN 0-87835-131-0). Boyd & Fraser.

Jelinek, Mariann, ed. Career Management for the Organization: The Individual. 1979. pap. text ed. 18.95x (ISBN 0-471-06233-2); teacher's manual o.p. (ISBN 0-471-06292-8). Wiley.

Jelinski, Lynn W., jt. ed. see Bovey, Frank A.

Jeljackzewicz, Janusz, et al, eds. Bacteria & Cancer. Date not set. 39.50 (ISBN 0-12-383820-7). Acad Pr.

Jeljaszewicz, J., jt. ed. see Easmon, C. S.

Jellema, Rod. Something Tugging the Line. 2nd ed. Date not set. pap. 4.50 o.p. (ISBN 0-931848-41-5). Dryad Pr.

Jelley, Herbert M. & Herrmann, Robert O. The American Consumer: Issues & Decisions. (Illus.). 512p. (gr. 11-12). 1973. text ed. 13.96 (ISBN 0-07-032325-9, G); tchr's. manual & key 6.50 (ISBN 0-07-032327-5); student activity guide 7.20 (ISBN 0-07-032326-7). McGraw.

--The American Consumer: Issues & Decisions. 2nd ed. (gr. 11-12). 1978. pap. text ed. 16.24 (ISBN 0-07-032341-0, G); student activity guide 7.20 (ISBN 0-07-032342-9); tchrs. manual & key 7.95 (ISBN 0-07-032343-7). McGraw.

Jellicoe, Ann & Mayne, Roger. Devon: A Shell Guide. (Shell Guide Ser.). (Illus.). 180p. 1975. 12.95 o.p. (ISBN 0-571-04836-6). Faber & Faber.

Jelliffe, D. B. & Stanfield, J. P., eds. Diseases of Children in the Subtropics & Tropics. 1070p. 1978. text ed. 89.50 (ISBN 0-7131-4277-4). E Arnold.

Jelliffe, Derrick B. & Jelliffe, E. F. Human Milk in the Modern World: Psychosocial, Nutritional & Economic Significance. (Illus.). 1981. Repr. of 1978 ed. 29.95x (ISBN 0-19-264921-3). Oxford U Pr.

Jelliffe, Derrick B., jt. auth. see Williams, Cicely D.

Jelliffe, E. F., jt. auth. see Jelliffe, Derrick B.

Jellinek, E. M. Alcohol Addiction & Chronic Alcoholism. 1942. text ed. 29.50x (ISBN 0-686-83459-3). Elliots Bks.

--The Disease Concept of Alcoholism. 8.50 o.p. (ISBN 0-686-92186-0, 4236). Hazelden.

Jellinek, Frank, tr. see Aron, Raymond.

Jellinek, Frank, tr. see Foucault, Michel.

Jellinek, Hedy D., tr. see Janossy, Ferenc.

Jellinek, J. Stephan. The Use of Fragrance in Consumer Products. LC 75-2106. 219p. 1975. 40.00x (ISBN 0-471-44151-1, Pub. by Wiley-Interscience). Wiley.

Jellinek, S. Formulation & Function of Cosmetics. Fenton, G. L., tr. from Ger. LC 74-110170. 1970. 79.00x (ISBN 0-471-44150-3, Pub. by Wiley-Interscience). Wiley.

Jellink, H. H. Aspects of Degradation & Stabilization of Polymers. 1978. 149.00 (ISBN 0-444-41563-7). Elsevier.

Jencks, Charles. The Language of Post-Modern Architecture. 3rd, rev. & enlarged ed. (Illus.). 152p. 1981. pap. 18.50 o.s.i. (ISBN 0-8478-0288-4). Rizzoli Intl.

--Modern Movements in Architecture. (Illus.). 432p. 1973. pap. 9.95 (ISBN 0-385-02554-8, Anch). Doubleday.

Jencks, Charles & Chaitkin, William. Architecture Today. LC 80-27124. (Illus.). 359p. 1982. 65.00 (ISBN 0-8109-0669-4). Abrams.

Jencks, Charles, ed. Post-Modern Classicism: The New Synthesis. 1981. pap. 19.95 (ISBN 0-8478-5334-9). Rizzoli Intl.

Jencks, Charles, et al. New Chicago Architecture. (Illus.). 200p. 1982. pap. 17.50 (ISBN 0-8478-0411-9). Rizzoli Intl.

Jencks, Lance. The Wisdom of Southern California. 68p. (Orig.). 1982. pap. 5.95 (ISBN 0-9609678-1-8). Lindenhof Pr.

Jencks, William P. Catalysis in Chemistry & Enzymology. LC 68-31661. (Advanced Chemistry Ser). (Illus.). 1969. text ed. 42.50 (ISBN 0-07-032305-4, C). McGraw.

Jendricke, Bernhard. Die Nachkriegszeit Im Spiegel der Satire. 388p. (Ger.). 1982. write for info. (ISBN 3-8204-6268-6). P Lang Pubs.

Jeneid, Michael & Martens, Tom. Five Easy Turns: A Guide to Cross-Country Ski Turns. (Illus.). 72p. 1980. pap. 7.95 (ISBN 0-9610410-0-5). Nordic Ski.

Jenis, Edwin H. & Lowenthal, David T. Kidney Biopsy Interpretation. LC 76-30870. (Illus.). 286p. 1977. text ed. 27.50x o.p. (ISBN 0-8036-4990-8). Davis Co.

Jenish, Daniel. Philosophisch-Kritische-Vergleichung und Wurdigung von vierzehn altern und neuren SPRACHENS EUROPENS. (Linguistics 13th-18th Centuries Ser.). 504p. (Ger.). 1974. Repr. of 1796 ed. lib. bdg. 114.00 o.p. (ISBN 0-8287-0464-3, 5184). Clearwater Pub.

Jenkin, Hamilton. Cornwall & Its People. (Illus.). 224p. 1983. 27.50 (ISBN 0-7153-4702-0). David & Charles.

Jenkins, A. L., ed. see American College of Emergency Physicians.

Jenkins, Alan. The Rich Rich: The Story of the Big Spenders. LC 77-89624. (Illus.). 1978. 12.50 o.p. (ISBN 0-399-12062-9). Putnam Pub Group.

Jenkins, Alec F., ed. see International Solar Energy Society, American Section.

Jenkins, Anita, jt. auth. see Gordon, Marcy.

Jenkins, Annibel. Nicholas Rowe. (English Authors Ser.). 1977. lib. bdg. 14.95 (ISBN 0-8057-6663-4, Twayne). G K Hall.

Jenkins, Arthur H., ed. see Smith, Adam.

Jenkins, Barbara, jt. auth. see Jenkins, Peter.

Jenkins, Betty. Bulletin Board Book No. 2. (gr. k-3). 1979. 5.95 (ISBN 0-916456-14-5, GA73). Good Apple.

Jenkins, Betty L. & Phillis, Susan, eds. The Black Separatism Controversy: An Annotated Bibliography. LC 75-23866. 163p. 1976. lib. bdg. 25.00 (ISBN 0-8371-8378-2, MBN/). Greenwood.

Jenkins, C., et al. How to Prepare for the New High School Equivalency Examination. (Illus.). 1978. pap. 7.95 (ISBN 0-07-032350-X, SP). McGraw.

Jenkins, C. B., jt. auth. see Deubert, L. W.

Jenkins, Carol & Savage, John. Activities for Integrating the Language Arts. (Illus.). 224p. 1983. 16.95 (ISBN 0-13-003699-4); pap. 12.95 (ISBN 0-13-003681-1). P-H.

Jenkins, Cecil. Practical Chemistry for Schools. 1958. text ed. 6.95x (ISBN 0-521-05427-3). Cambridge U Pr.

Jenkins, Christie. Buns: A Woman Looks at Men's. (Illus.). 96p. 1980. pap. 5.95 (ISBN 0-399-50500-8, Perige). Putnam Pub Group.

Jenkins, Christopher, et al, trs. see Phan Boi Chau & Ho Chi Minh.

Jenkins, Clive. Power at the Top: A Critical Survey of the Nationalized Industries. LC 75-45383. 292p. 1976. Repr. of 1959 ed. lib. bdg. 18.50x (ISBN 0-8371-8661-7, JEPT). Greenwood.

Jenkins, Clive & Sherman, Barrie. Collective Bargaining: What You Always Wanted to Know About Trade Unions & Never Dared to Ask. 1977. 18.95 (ISBN 0-7100-8690-3); pap. 8.95 (ISBN 0-7100-8691-1). Routledge & Kegan.

Jenkins, Creed H. Modern Warehouse Management. LC 68-20991. 1968. 44.95 (ISBN 0-07-032360-7, P&RB). McGraw.

Jenkins, D. L., tr. see Desoutter, D. M.

Jenkins, D. T. Taxonomic & Nomenclatural Study of the Genus Amanita Section Amanita for North America. (Bibliotheca Mycologica Ser.: No. 57). (Illus.). 1977. lib. bdg. 24.00x (ISBN 3-7682-1132-0). Lubrecht & Cramer.

Jenkins, Dan. Semi-Tough: Movie Edition. (Illus.). 1977. pap. 1.95 (ISBN 0-451-08184-6, J8184, Sig). NAL.

Jenkins, Daniel. Believing in God. LC 56-9576. (Layman's Theological Library). 1965. pap. 1.45 (ISBN 0-664-24004-6). Westminster.

Jenkins, Dave. The Dinghy-Owner's Handbook. (Illus.). 224p. 1976. 14.00 o.p. (ISBN 0-370-10243-6); pap. 9.95 o.p. (ISBN 0-370-10346-7). Transatlantic.

Jenkins, David, jt. auth. see Ponting, K. G.

Jenkins, David, jt. auth. see Snoeyink, Vernon L.

Jenkins, Donald C. Hymns & Gospel Songs for the Classical Guitar. 37p. 1981. pap. 3.95 (ISBN 0-89323-020-0). BMA Pr.

Jenkins, Dorothy H., jt. auth. see Gaines, Edith.

Jenkins, Elizabeth. Dr. Gully's Story. 400p. 1972. 7.95 o.p. (ISBN 0-698-10103-0; Coward). Putnam Pub Group.

--Elizabeth the Great. (Illus.). 1959. 8.95 o.p. (ISBN 0-698-10110-3, Coward). Putnam Pub Group.

--The Mystery of King Arthur. LC 74-29396. (Illus.). 240p. 1975. 20.00 o.p. (ISBN 0-698-10676-8, Coward). Putnam Pub Group.

--The Princes in the Tower. LC 78-14459. (Illus.). 1978. 10.95 o.p. (ISBN 0-698-10842-6, Coward). Putnam Pub Group.

--The Shadow & the Light. (Illus.). 352p. 1983. 32.95 (ISBN 0-241-10892-6, Pub. By Hamish Hamilton England). David & Charles.

Jenkins, Esther, jt. auth. see Austin, Mary.

Jenkins, Ferguson. Inside Pitching. (Inside Sports Ser.). (Illus.). 96p. 1972. 7.95 o.p. (ISBN 0-8092-8847-8); PLB avail o.p. (ISBN 0-685-28677-0); pap. 4.95 o.p. (ISBN 0-8092-8845-1). Contemp Bks.

Jenkins, Francis A. Fundamentals of Optics. 4th ed. (Illus.). 672p. 1976. 36.00 (ISBN 0-07-032330-5, C); solutions manual 15.00 (ISBN 0-07-032334-8). McGraw.

Jenkins, G. D., jt. auth. see Post, K. W.

Jenkins, G. H. Introduction to Cane Sugar Technology. 1966. 83.00 (ISBN 0-444-40319-1). Elsevier.

Jenkins, G. M. & Kawamura, K. Polymeric Carbons - Carbon Fibre, Glass & Char. LC 74-16995. (Illus.). 140p. 1976. 34.50 (ISBN 0-521-20693-6). Cambridge U Pr.

Jenkins, Gerald & Wild, Anne. Mathematical Curiosities, Vol. III. 28p. 1983. pap. 3.95 (ISBN 0-13-561225-X). P-H.

--Mathematical Curiosities I. (Illus.). 32p. 1982. pap. 3.95 (ISBN 0-13-561209-8). P-H.

--Mathematical Curiosities II. (Illus.). 28p. 1982. pap. 3.95 (ISBN 0-13-561217-9). P-H.

Jenkins, Gilbert. Oil Economists' Handbook. 1977. 55.50 (ISBN 0-85334-728-X, Pub. by Applied Sci England). Elsevier.

Jenkins, Gladys G. Helping Children Reach Their Potential: A Teachers' Resource Book. rev. ed. 1971. pap. 4.95x (ISBN 0-673-08610-0). Scott F.

Jenkins, Gladys G. & Shacter, Helen S. These Are Your Children. 4th ed. 366p. 1975. pap. 13.50x (ISBN 0-673-07931-7). Scott F.

Jenkins, Glenn P., jt. auth. see Glenday, Graham.

Jenkins, Gwilym, jt. auth. see Box, George E.

Jenkins, Gwilym M. & Watts, Donald G. Spectral Analysis & Its Applications. LC 67-13840. 1968. pap. 38.50x (ISBN 0-8162-4464-2). Holden-Day.

Jenkins, Harold, ed. see Shakespeare, William.

Jenkins, Harold R. The Management of a Public Library. Stueart, Robert D., ed. LC 76-13957. (Foundations in Library & Information Science: Vol. 8). 1980. lib. bdg. 37.50 (ISBN 0-89232-038-9). Jai Pr.

Jenkins, Herbert. Keeping the Peace: A Police Chief Looks at His Job. 205p. 3.50 (ISBN 0-686-95018-6); pap. 1.50 (ISBN 0-686-99450-7). ADL.

Jenkins, Herbert T. Crime in Georgia: Interviews with Georgia Top Law Enforcement Officials. Jenkins, James, ed. LC 82-73850. 217p. 1982. pap. write for info. (ISBN 0-89937-035-7). Ctr Res Soc Chg.

--Forty Years on the Force: Nineteen Thirty-Two to Nineteen Seventy-Two. LC 73-91480. (Illus.). 1974. pap. 4.95 o.p. (ISBN 0-89937-015-2). Ctr Res Soc Chg.

Jenkins, Hugh M. Educating Students from Other Nations: American Colleges & Universities in International Educational Interchange. LC 82-49043. (Higher Education Ser.). 1983. text ed. price not set (ISBN 0-87589-559-X). Jossey-Bass.

Jenkins, J. International Directory of Musical Instrument Collections. 1978. 35.00 o.s.i. (ISBN 90-6027-378-8, Pub. by Frits Knuf Netherlands); wrappers 22.00 o.s.i. (ISBN 90-6027-276-5, Pub. by Frits Knuf Netherlands). Pendragon NY.

Jenkins, J. J. Understanding Locke. 192p. 1982. 10.00x (ISBN 0-85224-442-8, Pub. by Edinburgh U Pr Scotland). Columbia U Pr.

Jenkins, James, ed. see Jenkins, Herbert T.

Jenkins, James J., jt. auth. see Dember, William N.

Jenkins, Janet, jt. auth. see Mauck, Diane.

Jenkins, Jerry. Erin. LC 81-22368. (Margo Ser.: No. 6). 160p. 1982. pap. 2.95 (ISBN 0-8024-4316-8). Moody.

--Janell. (Margo Mystery Ser.). 128p. 1983. pap. 2.95 (ISBN 0-8024-4322-2). Moody.

--Light on the Heavy. 1978. pap. 3.50 (ISBN 0-88207-769-4). Victor Bks.

--Margo. 1979. pap. 2.95 (ISBN 0-686-95480-7). Omega Pubns Or.

--Shannon. LC 82-8070. (Margo Mystery Ser.: No. 7). 1982. pap. 2.95 (ISBN 0-8024-4317-6). Moody.

Jenkins, Jerry, jt. auth. see Tippit, Sammy.

Jenkins, Jerry, jt. auth. see Williams, Pat.

Jenkins, Jerry B. Lindsey. (Margo Mystery Ser.). 128p. (Orig.). 1983. pap. 2.95 (ISBN 0-8024-4318-4). Moody.

--Meaghan. (Margo Mystery Ser.). 128p. (Orig.). 1983. pap. 2.95 (ISBN 0-8024-4321-4). Moody.

Jenkins, John B., jt. auth. see Corwin, Harry O.

Jenkins, John D., jt. auth. see Dennis, Ervin A.

Jenkins, John D., jt. auth. see Dennis, Erwin A.

Jenkins, Loa T., jt. auth. see Eliason, Claudia.

Jenkins, M. F., tr. see Voltaire.

Jenkins, Marilyn, ed. Islamic Art in the Kuwait National Museum. (Illus.). 200p. 1983. text ed. 39.95x (ISBN 0-85667-174-6, Pub. by Sotheby Pubns England). Biblio Dist.

Jenkins, Michael, ed. see Newton, Margaret.

Jenkins, Michael D. & Sexton, Donald L. Starting & Operating a Business in Texas. 200p. 1983. 27.95 (ISBN 0-686-43310-6, Oasis Pr). Pub Serv Inc.

Jenkins, Michael D. & Warner, Jonathan H. Starting & Operating a Business in Florida. 200p. 1983. 27.95 (ISBN 0-916378-25-X, Oasis Pr). Pub Serv Inc.

Jenkins, Mildred R. Fundamentals of English Grammar. (Illus.). 208p. 1982. 10.50 (ISBN 0-682-49904-8). Exposition.

Jenkins, Morton. Seashore Studies. (Practical Ecology Ser.). (Illus.). 104p. 1983. pap. text ed. 8.50x (ISBN 0-04-574019-4). Allen Unwin.

Jenkins, Morton, jt. auth. see Rowlinson, Pat.

Jenkins, Myra E. & Schroeder, Albert H. A Brief History of New Mexico. LC 74-21917. (Illus.). 89p. (Orig.). 1974. pap. 4.95 (ISBN 0-8263-0370-6). U of NM Pr.

Jenkins, Ned J. see Oakley, Carey.

Jenkins, Ned. J. see Oakley, Carey.

Jenkins, Peter. A Walk Across America. (General Ser.). 1982. lib. bdg. 15.95 (ISBN 0-8161-3459-6, Large Print Bks). G K Hall.

Jenkins, Peter & Jenkins, Barbara. The Walk West: A Walk Across America II. (General Ser.). 1983. lib. bdg. 18.95 (ISBN 0-8161-3460-X, Large Print Bks). G K Hall.

--The Walk West: A Walk Across America 2. 1983. pap. 3.95 (ISBN 0-449-20022-1, Crest). Fawcett.

Jenkins, Philip. Focalguide to Movie Titling. (Focal Guide Ser.). (Illus.). 160p. 1980. pap. 7.95 (ISBN 0-240-51011-9). Focal Pr.

--The Making of a Ruling Class: The Glamorgan Gentry 1640-1790. LC 82-14703. 336p. Date not set. 44.50 (ISBN 0-521-25003-X). Cambridge U Pr.

Jenkins, R. An Introduction to X-Ray Spectrometry. 1974. 35.95 (ISBN 0-471-25826-1, Wiley Heyden). Wiley.

Jenkins, Reva C. Resource Guide to Preschool & Primary Programs for the Gifted & Talented. 86p. 1979. pap. 9.95 (ISBN 0-936386-06-1). Creative Learning.

Jenkins, Rhys O. Dependent Industrialization in Latin America: The Automotive Industry in Argentina, Chile, & Mexico. LC 76-25352. (Illus.). 1976. 31.95 o.p. (ISBN 0-275-23220-4). Praeger.

Jenkins, Richard L. & Harms, Ernest, eds. Understanding Disturbed Children: Professional Insights into Their Psychiatric & Developmental Problems. LC 74-84846. 1976. text ed. 18.15 o.p. (ISBN 0-87562-057-4); pap. 12.00x o.p. (ISBN 0-87562-054-X). Spec Child.

Jenkins, Roy. The Role of the European Community in World Affairs. LC 81-13340. 20p. 1981. 1.25 (ISBN 0-934742-09-X, Inst Study Diplomacy). Geo U Sch For Serv.

Jenkins, W. I. Policy Analysis: A Political & Organizational Perspective. LC 78-422. 1978. 26.00x (ISBN 0-312-61998-7). St Martin.

Jenkins-Murphy, Andrew. The Language of Agriculture in English. (English for Careers Ser.). (Illus.). 108p. (gr. 10 up). 1981. pap. text ed. 3.75 (ISBN 0-88345-350-9, 18524). Regents Pub.

Jenkins-Murphy, Andrew, jt. auth. see Flowers, James L.

Jenkinson, Dennis. The Automobile Year Book of Sports Car Racing 1953-1972. (Illus.). 1983. 39.50 (ISBN 0-686-43390-4, Pub. by Edita Switerland). Norton.

Jenkinson, Edward B. Censors in the Classroom: The Mind Benders. LC 79-17417. 206p. 1979. 15.95 (ISBN 0-8093-0929-7). S Ill U Pr.

Jenkinson, Hilary. Manual of Archive Administration. 20.00 o.s.i. (ISBN 0-85331-072-6). Transatlantic.

Jenkinson, Michael. Beasts Beyond the Fire. (Illus.). 1980. 14.95 o.p. (ISBN 0-525-06177-0). Dutton.

--Wild Rivers of North America. updated ed. (Illus.). 411p. 1981. pap. 11.50 o.p. (ISBN 0-525-47679-2, 01117-330). Dutton.

Jenks, Albert E. Minnesota's Browns Valley Man and Associated Burial Artifacts. LC 38-22478. 1937. pap. 8.00 (ISBN 0-527-00548-7). Kraus Repr.

Jenks, James M., ed. see Alexader Hamilton Institute, Inc.

Jenks, James M., ed. see Alexander Hamilton Institute, Inc.

Jenks, James M., ed. see Alexander Institute, Inc.

Jenks, Jamess M., ed. see Alexander Institute, Inc.

Jenks, Jeremiah, et al. Questions of Public Policy. 1913. 29.50x (ISBN 0-686-51295-2). Elliots Bks.

Jenks, Jorian. The Stuff We're Made of: The Positive Approach to Health through Nutrition. 1959. 5.00 (ISBN 0-8159-6829-9). Devin.

Jenks, William A. Francis Joseph & the Italians: 1849-1859. LC 78-5727. 1978. 13.95x (ISBN 0-8139-0758-6). U Pr of Va.

Jenne, Frank H. & Greene, Walter H. Turner's School Health & Health Education. 7th ed. LC 75-43985. (Illus.). 358p. 1976. 15.95 o.p. (ISBN 0-8016-5134-4). Mosby.

Jenner, F. A., jt. ed. see De Koning, A. J.

Jenner, Philip N. Southeast Asian Literatures in Translation: A Preliminary Bibliography. LC 72-619667. (Asian Studies at Hawaii Ser.: No. 9). 224p. (Orig.). 1973. pap. text ed. 4.50x o.p. (ISBN 0-8248-0261-6). UH Pr.

Jenner, Philip N., ed. Mon-Khmer Studies IX-X. 592p. 1982. 20.00x (ISBN 0-8248-0727-8). UH Pr.

--Mon-Khmer Studies VI. 1977. pap. text ed. 8.00x (ISBN 0-8248-0602-6). UH Pr.

Jenner, Philip N. & Thompson, Lawrence C., eds. Austroasiatic Studies, 2 vols. (Oceanic Linguistics Special Publication: No. 13). 1328p. 1976. pap. text ed. 25.00x o.p. (ISBN 0-8248-0280-2). UH Pr.

Jenner, Thomas. Emblem Books of Thomas Jenner. 1983. write for info. (ISBN 0-8201-1389-1). Schol Facsimiles.

Jenner, W. J. F., tr. see Lu Xun.

Jennergren, L. Peter, jt. auth. see Dirickx, Yvo M.

Jeneness, Aylette. The Bakery Factory. LC 77-8094. (Illus.). (gr. 3-7). 1978. 6.95i (ISBN 0-690-03805-4, TYC-J); PLB 8.89 (ISBN 0-690-01338-8). Har-Row.

Jennett, Sean. The Loire. (Batsford Countries Ser.). (Illus.). 216p. 1975. 11.95 (ISBN 0-8038-4293-7). Hastings.

Jennings, A., jt. auth. see Wangerin, W., Jr.

Jennings, A. R. Financial Accounting: An Instructional Manual. 580p. (Orig.). 1982. pap. text ed. 13.00 (ISBN 0-905435-23-0). Verry.

Jennings, Anne. Amrah & the Living Water. (Arch Bks: No. 13). (Illus.). 32p. (ps-3). 1976. pap. 0.89 (ISBN 0-570-06100-8, 59-1218). Concordia.

--A Story for Obed. (Arch Book Ser., No. 11). (Illus.). 32p. (gr. 1-4). 1974. pap. 0.89 (ISBN 0-570-06082-6, 59-1202). Concordia.

Jennings, Anthony, jt. auth. see Weiss, Thomas G.

Jennings, Bill, jt. ed. see Ting, I. P.

Jennings, Bruce, jt. ed. see Callahan, Daniel.

Jennings, Edward H., jt. auth. see Stevenson, Richard A.

Jennings, Elizabeth. Celebrations & Elegies. 64p. 1982. pap. text ed. 7.00x (ISBN 0-85635-360-4, 60561, Pub. by Carcanet New Pr England). Humanities.

--Consequently I Rejoice. 70p. 1980. 7.95 o.p. (ISBN 0-85635-218-7, Pub. by Carcanet New Pr England); pap. 4.95 o.p. (ISBN 0-85635-219-5). Humanities.

--Consequently I Rejoice. 70p. 1977. text ed. 8.50x (ISBN 0-85635-218-7, Pub. by Carcanet New Pr England); pap. text ed. 6.25x (ISBN 0-85635-219-5). Humanities.

--Growing Points. (Poetry Ser.). 1979. pap. 3.95 o.p. (ISBN 0-85635-123-7, Pub. by Carcanet NewPr England). Humanities.

--Moments of Grace. 64p. (Orig.). 1980. pap. 6.95 o.p. (ISBN 0-85635-281-0, Pub. by Carcanet New Pr England). Humanities.

--Moments of Grace. 62p. 1979. pap. text ed. 6.95x (ISBN 0-85635-281-0, Pub. by Carcanet New Pr England). Humanities.

--Selected Poems. 122p. (Orig.). 1980. pap. 6.95 o.p. (ISBN 0-85635-282-9, Pub. by Carcanet New Pr England). Humanities.

Jennings, Eugene E. An Anatomy of Leadership: Princes, Heroes & Supermen. 1972. pap. 4.95 (ISBN 0-07-032449-2, SP). McGraw.

--Executive in Crisis. LC 65-64648. 1972. pap. 2.95 o.p. (ISBN 0-07-032446-8, SP). McGraw.

--Mobile Manager. LC 67-65498. 1971. pap. 4.95 (ISBN 0-07-032450-6, SP). McGraw.

--Routes to the Executive Suite. LC 70-134596. (McGraw-Hill Paperbacks). 1976. pap. 5.95 (ISBN 0-07-032444-1, SP). McGraw.

Jennings, F. C. Meditations on Ecclesiastes. 143p. 4.75 (ISBN 0-88172-090-9). Believers Bkshelf.

Jennings, Francis. The Invasion of America: Indians, Colonialism, & the Cant of Conquest. (Illus.). 384p. 1976. pap. 6.95 (ISBN 0-393-00830-4, Norton Lib). Norton.

Jennings, Gary. March of the Demons. (Illus.). (gr. 5 up). 1978. 8.95 o.s.i. (ISBN 0-695-81106-1). Follett.

--March of the Gods. (Illus.). (YA) 1976. 7.95 o.s.i. (ISBN 0-8096-1912-1). Follett.

--March of the Heroes: The Folk Hero Through the Ages. (Illus.). 224p. 1975. 7.95 o.s.i. (ISBN 0-8096-1895-8). Follett.

Jennings, Herbert S. Universe & Life. 1933. text ed. 8.50x (ISBN 0-686-83841-6). Elliots Bks.

Jennings, Ivor. British Constitution. 5th ed. (English Institution Ser). (Illus.). 1961. pap. 11.95 (ISBN 0-521-09136-5). Cambridge U Pr.

--Cabinet Government. 3rd ed. 1969. 59.50 (ISBN 0-521-05430-3); pap. 19.95 (ISBN 0-521-09570-0). Cambridge U Pr.

--Parliament. 2nd ed. 1969. 59.50 (ISBN 0-521-07056-2); pap. 14.95 (ISBN 0-521-09532-8). Cambridge U Pr.

Jennings, J. B. Feeding, Digestion & Assimilation in Animals. 2nd ed. LC 72-90021. 1973. 17.95 o.p. (ISBN 0-312-28630-9). St Martin.

Jennings, J. H. Elementary Map Interpretation. 1960. text ed. 6.95 (ISBN 0-521-20899-8). Cambridge U Pr.

Jennings, J. N. Karst. (Introduction to Systematic Geomorphology Ser). 1971. 16.50x (ISBN 0-262-10011-8). MIT Pr.

Jennings, Jane. Why Joy? Learning to Love My Special Child. LC 77-90122. 1978. 6.95 o.p. (ISBN 0-915684-35-7). Christian Herald.

Jennings, Jerry E. & Hertel, Margaret F. China. rev. ed. LC 83-80050. (World Cultures Ser.). (Illus.). (gr. 6 up). 1983. text ed. 11.20 ea. 1-4 copies (ISBN 0-88296-275-2); text ed. 8.96 5 or more copies (ISBN 0-686-96716-X); tchrs'. guide 8.96 (ISBN 0-88296-375-9). Fideler.

Jennings, Jerry E., et al, eds. Great Americans & Great Ideas. LC 78-54257. (American History & Culture Ser.). (Illus.). (gr. 4 up). 1979. text ed. 8.70 1-4 copies, 5 or more 6.96 (ISBN 0-88296-483-6); tchrs'. annotated ed. 8.70 (ISBN 0-88296-489-5). Fideler.

Jennings, Jesse D. Prehistory of North America. 2nd ed. (Illus.). 320p. 1974. text ed. 39.95 (ISBN 0-07-032454-9, C). McGraw.

Jennings, Joseph, jt. auth. see Theriault, Jean Y.

Jennings, K. & Miller, V. Growing Fuchsias. (Illus.). 170p. 1980. Repr. of 1979 ed. 17.50x o.p. (ISBN 0-85664-890-6, Pub. by Croom Helm LTD England). Biblio Dist.

--Growing Fuchsias. (Illus.). 170p. 1982. 14.95 (ISBN 0-85664-890-6). Timber.

Jennings, Kenneth M., jt. auth. see Holley, William H.

Jennings, Kenneth M., Jr., et al. Labor Relations in a Public Service Industry: Unions, Management, & the Public Interest in Mass Transit. LC 77-13717. (Praeger Special Studies). 1978. 36.95 o.p. (ISBN 0-03-040866-0). Praeger.

Jennings, Louis B. The Function of Religion: An Introduction. LC 79-53368. 1979. pap. text ed. 13.50 (ISBN 0-8191-0789-1). U Pr of Amer.

Jennings, Lucy M. Secretarial & Administrative Procedures. LC 77-5743. (Illus.). 1978. 20.95 (ISBN 0-13-797654-2). P-H.

--Secretarial & General Office Procedures. (Illus.). 400p. 1981. pap. text ed. 18.95 (ISBN 0-13-797803-0). P-H.

Jennings, M. K. High School Seniors Cohort Study, 1965 & 1973. LC 79-91209. 1980. write for info. (ISBN 0-89138-964-4). ICPSR.

Jennings, M. Kent & Niemi, Richard G. Youth-Parent Socialization Study, 1965 & 1973, 2 vols. LC 81-81765. 1981. Set. write for info. (ISBN 0-89138-947-4); Vol. 1. (ISBN 0-89138-948-2); Vol. 2. (ISBN 0-89138-949-0). ICPSR.

Jennings, Margaret, ed. Library & Reference Facilities in the Area of the District of Columbia. 10th ed. LC 44-41159. (American Society for Information Science Ser.). 1979. text ed. 19.50x softcover (ISBN 0-914236-35-0). Knowledge Indus.

Jennings, Margaret, compiled by. Library & Reference Facilities in the Area of the District of Columbia. 11th ed. 285p. 1983. pap. 39.50 (ISBN 0-86729-021-8). Knowledge Indus.

Jennings, Mary L., ed. see Kraus, William.

Jennings, Peter R., jt. auth. see Maxwell, Fowden G.

Jennings, Preston. Book of Trout Flies. Lyons, Nick, ed. (Illus.). 1970. 7.50 o.p. (ISBN 0-517-50204-6). Crown.

Jennings, R. & Sidwell, E. H. Graphics for Engineers. (Illus.). 1968. text ed. 21.00x (ISBN 0-7131-3169-1). Intl Ideas.

Jennings, R. Y. & Brownlie, Ian, eds. The British Year Book of International Law 1978, Vol. XLIX. (British Year Book of International Law). (Illus.). 1980. 94.00x (ISBN 0-19-818178-7). Oxford U Pr.

Jennings, R. Y. see Royal Institute of International Affairs.

Jennings, Richard W. & Marsh, Harold, Jr. Securities Regulation, Cases & Materials. 5th ed. LC 82-11075. (University Casebook Ser.). 1432p. 1982. text ed. write for info. (ISBN 0-88277-054-3). Foundation Pr.

--Selected Statutes, Rules & Forms under the Federal Securities Laws, 1982. 927p. 1982. pap. write for info. (ISBN 0-88277-081-0). Foundation Pr.

Jennings, Robert E. Education & Politics. 1976. 27.00 o.p. (ISBN 0-7134-0474-4, Pub. by Batsford England); pap. 14.95 (ISBN 0-7134-0475-2). David & Charles.

Jennings, Robert M. & Trout, Andrew P. The Tontine: From the Reign of Louis XIV to the French Revolutionary Era. LC 82-81028. (S. S. Huebner Foundation Monograph Ser.). 96p. (Orig.). 1982. pap. 14.95 (ISBN 0-918930-12-X). Huebner Foun Insur.

Jennings, Royalston F. Gas & A.C. Arc Welding & Cutting. 3rd ed. (gr. 7 up). 1956. pap. text ed. 6.64 (ISBN 0-87345-119-8). McKnight.

Jennings, T. Studying Birds in the Garden. 1975. 8.90 (ISBN 0-08-017802-2). Pergamon.

Jennings, Terry. Your Book of Pre-Historic Animals. lst ed. (Your Book Ser.). (Illus.). 64p. (gr. 4-7). 1982. pap. 4.95 (ISBN 0-571-12509-3). Faber & Faber.

Jennings, Theodore W., Jr. Introduction to Theology: An Invitation to Reflection Upon the Christian Mythos. LC 76-7867. 192p. 1976. pap. 3.00 o.p. (ISBN 0-8006-1234-5, 1-1234). Fortress.

Jennings, William D. The Ronin. 160p. 1975. pap. 1.25 o.p. (ISBN 0-451-06673-1, Y6673, Sig). NAL.

Jennings, William I. Constitutional Problems in Pakistan. LC 72-8240. 378p. 1973. Repr. of 1957 ed. lib. bdg. 20.75x (ISBN 0-8371-6540-7, JECP). Greenwood.

Jennison, Peter S., jt. auth. see Tree, Christina.

Jensen, et al. Basic Drafting Problems. Breskin, Myrna, ed. 96p. 1981. wkbk. 6.95 (ISBN 0-07-032521-9); solutions manual 4.00 (ISBN 0-07-032523-5). McGraw.

Jensen, A. Traffic, Operational Research, Futurology: A Collection of Papers Published on Occasion of the Author's 60th Birthday. 1980. 53.25 (ISBN 0-444-85425-8). Elsevier.

Jensen, A. & Chenoweth, H. H. Applied Engineering Mechanics. 4th ed. 464p. 23.95x (ISBN 0-07-032492-1). McGraw.

Jensen, A. C. & Chenoweth, H. Statics & Strength of Materials. 4th ed. 656p. 1982. 27.95 (ISBN 0-07-032494-8, G). McGraw.

Jensen, A. C. & Chenowith, H. Applied Strength of Materials. 4th ed. 384p. 1982. text ed. 23.95x (ISBN 0-07-032490-5, C); solutions manual 2.95 (ISBN 0-07-032491-3). McGraw.

Jensen, Alfred & Chenoweth, Harry H. Applied Strength of Materials. 3rd ed. LC 74-18384. (Illus.). 374p. 1975. text ed. 23.95 (ISBN 0-07-032471-9, G). McGraw.

Jensen, Alfred D. Contexts for Ethical Discussion. (Philosophy Ser.). 1977. pap. text ed. 8.95 (ISBN 0-675-08491-1). Merrill.

Jensen, Alfred D., jt. auth. see Dew, Donald.

Jensen, Alfred E. & Chenoweth, H. Applied Engineering Mechanics. 3rd ed. 1971. 23.95 (ISBN 0-07-032480-8, G); problem answers 1.50 (ISBN 0-07-032481-6). McGraw.

Jensen, Alfred E. & Chenoweth, Harry H. Statics & Strength of Materials. 3rd ed. LC 75-8820. (Illus.). 608p. 1975. text ed. 26.95 (ISBN 0-07-032472-7, G). McGraw.

Jensen, Arthur R. Educational Differences. 1973. 42.00x (ISBN 0-416-75980-7). Methuen Inc.

Jensen, B. S. Migration Phenomena of Radionuclides into the Geosphere: A Critical Review of the Available Information; Radioactive Waste Management. (A Series of Monographs & Tracts: Vol. 5). 200p. 1982. write for info. (ISBN 3-7186-0120-6). Harwood Academic.

Jensen, Bernard. Iridology: Science & Practice in the Healing Arts, Vol. II. 608p. 1982. write for info. (ISBN 0-9608360-6-3). B Jensen.

Jensen, Bernard D. Iridology Simplified. 4.50x (ISBN 0-686-29758-X). Cancer Control Soc.

Jensen, C. & Helsel, J. Fundamentals of Engineering Drawin g. 1979. 17.60 (ISBN 0-07-032517-0). McGraw.

Jensen, C. & Viosinet, D. Advanced Design Problems: To Accompany Engineering Drawing & Designs. 2nd ed. 1982. 6.95 (ISBN 0-07-032522-7); solutions manual 4.00 (ISBN 0-07-032530-8). McGraw.

Jensen, C. H. Interpreting Engineering Drawings. LC 70-92052. 241p. 1972. 12.80 (ISBN 0-8273-0061-1); instructor's guide 3.25 (ISBN 0-8273-0062-X). Delmar.

Jensen, C. H. & Hines, R. D. Interpreting Engineering Drawings: Metric Edition. LC 77-78175. 1979. pap. text ed. 13.20 (ISBN 0-8273-1061-7); instructor's guide 4.25 (ISBN 0-8273-1062-5). Delmar.

Jensen, C. H. & Mason, F. H. Fundamentos de Dibujo Mecanico. 1970. text ed. 14.95 (ISBN 0-07-091605-5, G). McGraw.

Jensen, C. W., jt. auth. see Fisher, Eugene.

Jensen, Cecil & Helsel, Jay. Engineering Drawing & Design. 2nd ed. (Illus.). 1979. text ed. 24.75x (ISBN 0-07-032516-2, G); worksheet sets 1 & 2 11.95 ea.; solution manual 4.00 (ISBN 0-07-032520-0). McGraw.

Jensen, Clayne & Schultz, Gordon. Applied Kinesiology. 3rd ed. (Illus.). 352p. text ed. 24.95x (ISBN 0-07-032469-7, C). McGraw.

Jensen, Clayne, jt. auth. see Tucker, Karl.

Jensen, Clayne R. Administrative Management of Physical Education & Athletic Programs. LC 82-23933. (Illus.). 375p. 1983. write for info (ISBN 0-8121-0817-5). Lea & Febiger.

--Outdoor Recreation in America: Trends, Problems, & Opportunities. 3rd ed. LC 76-52662. 1977. text ed. 15.95x (ISBN 0-8087-1035-4). Burgess.

Jensen, Clayne R. & Schultz, Gordon W. Applied Kinesiology. 2nd ed. (McGraw-Hill Ser. in Health Ed., Phys. Ed., & Recreation). (Illus.). 1976. text ed. 23.95 (ISBN 0-07-032463-8, C). McGraw.

Jensen, Clayne R., jt. auth. see Tucker, Karl.

Jensen, David L. The Role of Cluster Analysis in Computer Assisted Mass Appraisal. (Lincoln Institute Monograph: No. 77-7). 1977. pap. 3.00 o.p. (ISBN 0-686-22984-3). Lincoln Inst Land.

Jensen, De Lamar. Reformation Europe: Age of Reform & Revolution. 480p. 1981. pap. text ed. 11.95 (ISBN 0-669-03626-9). Heath.

--Renaissance Europe: Age of Recovery & Reconciliation. 416p. 1981. pap. text ed. 11.95 (ISBN 0-669-51722-4). Heath.

Jensen, DeLamar. Renaissance World. 1979. pap. text ed. 2.95x. Forum Pr IL.

Jensen, DeLamar, et al. World of Europe to Eighteen Fifteen, Vol. 2. 1979. pap. text ed. 10.95x. Forum Pr IL.

Jensen, Dwight W. Discovering Idaho, A History. LC 77-24010. (Illus.). 1977. text ed. 11.95x (ISBN 0-87004-261-0); wkbk. 3.00x (ISBN 0-87004-262-9). Caxton.

Jensen, F. B. & Walter, I., eds. Readings in International Economic Relations. 1966. 16.95x o.p. (ISBN 0-471-06636-2). Wiley.

Jensen, Finn & Petersen, Niels E. Burn-In: An Engineering Approach to the Design & Analysis of Burn-In Procedures. 180p. 1982. 39.95x (ISBN 0-471-10215-6, Pub. by Wiley-Interscience). Wiley.

Jensen, Gary F. & Rojek, Dean G. Delinquency: A Sociological View. 1980. text ed. 18.95 (ISBN 0-669-00045-0). Heath.

--Readings in Juvenile Delinquency. 448p. 1982. pap. text ed. 14.95 (ISBN 0-669-03763-X). Heath.

Jensen, Irving. Irving Jensen's Do-It-Yourself Bible Study: Mark. 120p. (Orig.). 1983. wkbk 3.95 (ISBN 0-89840-035-X). Heres Life.

Jensen, Irving L. Acts: An Inductive Study. 256p. 1973. pap. 7.95 (ISBN 0-8024-0138-4). Moody.

--Disfrute Su Biblia. Mercado, Benjamin E., tr. 128p. 1981. pap. 2.95 (ISBN 0-8024-2354-X). Moody.

--Enjoy Your Bible. 1969. pap. 3.95 (ISBN 0-8024-2350-7); 5.95 (ISBN 0-8024-2347-7). Moody.

--Genesis. (Bible Self-Study Ser.). 1967. pap. 2.95 (ISBN 0-8024-1001-4). Moody.

--Independent Bible Study. LC 68-12114. 1972. pap. 5.95 (ISBN 0-8024-4050-9). Moody.

--Jensen's Survey of the New Testament. 608p. 1981. text ed. 18.95 (ISBN 0-8024-4308-7). Moody.

--Jensen's Survey of the Old Testament. 1978. text ed. 18.95 (ISBN 0-8024-4307-9). Moody.

--Jeremiah & Lamentations. (Everyman' Bible Commentary Ser.). (Orig.). 1966. pap. 4.50 (ISBN 0-8024-2024-9). Moody.

--Joshua: Rest-Land Won. (Everyman's Bible Commentary Ser.). (Orig.). 1966. pap. 4.50 (ISBN 0-8024-2006-0). Moody.

--Numbers: Journey to God's Rest-Land. (Everyman's Bible Commentary Series). 1968. pap. 4.50 (ISBN 0-8024-2004-4). Moody.

--Proverbs. (Bible Self-Study Guide Ser.). (Illus.). 96p. 1976. pap. 2.95 (ISBN 0-8024-1020-0). Moody.

Jensen, J. T. & Ferren, William P. College General Chemistry. LC 70-97561. 1971. text ed. 16.95x (ISBN 0-675-09400-3). Merrill.

Jensen, J. Trygve. Physics for the Health Professions. 3rd ed. LC 82-70068. 329p. 1982. 14.95 (ISBN 0-471-08696-7, Pub. by Wiley Med). Wiley.

Jensen, James R., jt. auth. see Schwarzrock, Shirley P.

Jensen, Jens A. & Rowland, John H. Methods of Computation: The Linear Space Approach to Numerical Analysis. 1975. text ed. 19.95x (ISBN 0-673-05394-6). Scott F.

Jensen, Joan M., jt. ed. see Scharf, Lois.

Jensen, Johannes. Energy Storage. (Illus.). 1979. text ed. 21.95 (ISBN 0-408-00390-1). Butterworth.

Jensen, John T., et al. Yapese-English Dictionary. LC 76-47495. (Pali Language Texts: Micronesia). (Orig.). 1977. pap. text ed. 8.00x (ISBN 0-8248-0517-8). UH Pr.

--Yapese Reference Grammar. LC 76-40952. (PALI Language Texts: Micronesia). (Orig.). 1977. pap. text ed. 15.00x (ISBN 0-8248-0476-7). UH Pr.

Jensen, Joyce D. & Cooley, Stella G. A Handbook of Career Education Activities: For Use by Secondary Counselors & Classroom Teachers. 114p. 1982. pap. 14.50x spiral (ISBN 0-398-04768-5). C C Thomas.

Jensen, K. & Wirth, N. PASCAL-User Manual & Report. 2nd ed. LC 75-16462. (Springer Study Edition). 180p. 1975. pap. 4.47 (ISBN 0-387-90144-2). Springer-Verlag.

Jensen, L. E., et al. Automotive Science. LC 76-3940. 1977. pap. 9.80 (ISBN 0-8273-1302-0); instructor's guide 2.50 (ISBN 0-8273-1303-9). Delmar.

Jensen, Larry. The Movie Railroads. (Illus.). 34.95 (ISBN 0-933506-05-8). Darwin Pubns.

Jensen, Larry C. & Knight, Richard S. Moral Education: Historical Perspectives. LC 80-5896. 174p. (Orig.). 1982. lib. bdg. 21.25 (ISBN 0-8191-1919-9); pap. text ed. 10.25 (ISBN 0-8191-1920-2). U Pr of Amer.

Jensen, Line, et al, eds. Contemporary Danish Poetry. (International Studies & Translations Program). 1977. lib. bdg. 12.50 (ISBN 0-8057-8157-9, Twayne). G K Hall.

Jensen, Lloyd. Explaining Foreign Policy. 272p. (Orig.). 1982. pap. 12.95 reference (ISBN 0-13-295600-4). P-H.

Jensen, M. L. & Bateman, A. M. Economic Mineral Deposits. 3rd rev. ed. LC 78-9852. 593p. 1981. text ed. 28.95 (ISBN 0-471-09043-3). Wiley.

Jensen, Margaret & Bobak, Irene. Handbook of Maternity Care: A Guide for Nursing Practice. LC 79-18163. 294p. 1980. pap. text ed. 13.95 (ISBN 0-8016-2490-8). Mosby.

Jensen, Margaret D., jt. auth. see Bobak, Irene M.

Jensen, Margaret D., et al. Maternity Care: The Nurse & the Family. 2nd ed. LC 80-270023. (Illus.). 1013p. 1981. text ed. 32.95 (ISBN 0-8016-2492-4). Mosby.

Jensen, Margaret M. Seaside Kisses. 1982. pap. 6.95 (ISBN 0-686-84711-3, Avalon). Bouregy.

Jensen, Margie C., ed. Blue Ribbon Breads. (Blue Ribbon Cookbks: No. 6). (Illus.). 1978. pap. 3.95 o.s.i. (ISBN 0-695-80896-6). Follett.

--Blue Ribbon Cakes. (Blue Ribbon Cookbks: No. 6). (Illus.). 1978. pap. 3.95 o.s.i. (ISBN 0-695-80947-4). Follett.

--Blue Ribbon Candies. (Blue Ribbon Cookbks: No. 6). (Illus.). 1978. pap. 3.95 o.s.i. (ISBN 0-695-80950-4). Follett.

--Blue Ribbon Cookies. (Blue Ribbon Cookbks: No. 6). (Illus.). 1978. pap. 3.95 o.s.i. (ISBN 0-695-80948-2). Follett.

--Blue Ribbon Jams & Jellies, Pickles & Relishes. (Blue Ribbon Cookbks: No. 6). (Illus.). 1978. pap. 3.95 o.s.i. (ISBN 0-695-80894-X). Follett.

--Blue Ribbon Pies. (Blue Ribbon Cookbks: No. 6). (Illus.). 1978. pap. 3.95 o.s.i. (ISBN 0-695-80949-0). Follett.

Jensen, Marilyn. Formerly Married: Learning to Live with Yourself. 120p. 1983. price not set (ISBN 0-664-27010-7). Westminster.

Jensen, Merrill. The New Nation: A History of the United States During the Confederation 1781-1789. LC 80-39976. 446p. 1981. text ed. 24.95x (ISBN 0-930350-15-4); pap. text ed. 9.95x (ISBN 0-930350-14-6). NE U Pr.

Jensen, Merrill, ed. Tracts of the American Revolution, 1763-1776. LC 66-26805. (Orig.). 1967. pap. 11.95 (ISBN 0-672-60046-3, AHS35). Bobbs.

Jensen, Merrill, ed. see Wisconsin University.

Jensen, Niels L. Jens Peter Jacobsen. (World Authors Ser.). 1980. lib. bdg. 15.95 (ISBN 0-8057-6415-1, Twayne). G K Hall.

Jensen, Paul A. & Barnes, J. Wesley. Network Flow Programming. LC 79-26939. (Industrial Engineering Ser.). 408p. 1980. text ed. 33.50x (ISBN 0-471-04471-7); solutions manual 7.00x (ISBN 0-471-06063-1). Wiley.

Jensen, R. & Tonies, C. Software Engineering. 1979. 35.00 (ISBN 0-13-822130-8). P-H.

Jensen, R. J. Such a Good Baby. 320p. (Orig.). 1982. pap. 2.75 o.p. (ISBN 0-523-48022-9). Pinnacle Bks.

Jensen, Richard A. Telling the Story: Variety & Imagination in Preaching. LC 79-54113. 190p. (Orig.). 1979. pap. 6.95 (ISBN 0-8066-1766-7, 10-6232). Augsburg.

Jensen, Richard J., et al. Rhetorical Perspectives on Communication & Mass Media. 176p. 1980. pap. text ed. 9.95 (ISBN 0-8403-2258-5, 40225801). Kendall-Hunt.

Jensen, Robert & Conway, Patricia. Ornamentalism: The New Decorativeness in Architecture & Design. (Illus.). 312p. 1982. 40.00 (ISBN 0-517-54383-4, C N Potter Bks). Crown.

Jensen, Robert G., jt. auth. see Brockerhoff, Hans.

Jensen, Rolf. Cities of Vision. (Illus.). 1974. 45.00x (ISBN 0-85334-569-4, Pub. by Applied Sci England). Elsevier.

Jensen, Rosalie. Exploring Mathematical Concepts & Skills in the Elementary School. LC 72-91083. (gr. 2-6). 1973. text ed. 18.95 (ISBN 0-675-09029-6). Merrill.

Jensen, Ruby J. Hear the Children Cry. 288p. 1981. pap. 2.50 (ISBN 0-8439-0968-4, Leisure Bks). Nordon Pubns.

Jensen, Sheila R., ed. Pearls. LC 78-54741. 1979. pap. 3.00 (ISBN 0-932044-21-2). M O Pub Co.

--Touchstone. LC 78-54742. (Illus.). 1978. pap. 3.00 (ISBN 0-932044-14-X). M O Pub Co.

Jensen, Sheila R., ed. see Abel, et al.

Jensen, Sheila R., ed. see Amadeo, et al.

Jensen, Sheila R., ed. see Barker, et al.

Jensen, Sheila R., ed. Gems. LC 78-714444. 1979. pap. 3.00 (ISBN 0-932044-25-5). M O Pub Co.

--Poemscapes. LC 79-87822. 1979. pap. 3.00 (ISBN 0-932044-23-9). M O Pub Co.

--Threshold. (Illus.). 1979. pap. 3.00 (ISBN 0-932044-22-0). M O Pub Co.

Jensen, Steven A. Paramedic Handbook. 120p. 1983. pap. write for info. (ISBN 0-940122-05-7). Mosby.

--Paramedic Handbook. LC 82-42830. 176p. (Orig.). 1983. pap. 7.95 (ISBN 0-940122-05-7). Multi Media CO.

Jensen, Tom & Clee, Suzanne. Skylights: The Definitive Guide to Planning, Installing, Maintaining Skylights & Natural Light Systems. (Illus.). 192p. (Orig.). 1983. lib. bdg. 19.80 (ISBN 0-89471-195-4); pap. 8.95 (ISBN 0-89471-194-6). Running Pr.

Jensen, Vernon. Argumentation: Reasoning in Communication. 1980. text ed. 15.95 (ISBN 0-442-25396-6); instr's. manual 2.00 (ISBN 0-442-24213-1). Van Nos Reinhold.

Jensen, Vernon H. Decasualization & Modernization of Dock Work in London. LC 72-632773. (ILR Paperback Ser.: No. 9). 112p. 1971. pap. 3.50 (ISBN 0-87546-040-2); pap. 6.50 special hard bdg. (ISBN 0-87546-276-6). ILR Pr.

--Heritage of Conflict: Labor Relations in the Nonferrous Metals Industry up to 1930. 512p. 1950. pap. 1.25 o.p. (ISBN 0-87546-018-6); pap. 4.25 special hard bdg. o.p. (ISBN 0-87546-268-5). ILR Pr.

Jensen, Virginia A. & Edman, Polly. Red Thread Riddles. LC 79-28168. (Illus.). 24p. (Orig.). (ps). 1980. pap. 10.95 (ISBN 0-529-05604-6, Philomel). Putnam Pub Group.

Jensen, Virginia A. & Haller, Dorcas W. What's That? (Illus.). (ps-4). 10.95 (ISBN 0-399-20760-0, Philomel). Putnam Pub Group.

Jensen, Virginia A., tr. see Martin, Sarah C.

Jensen, William B. The Lewis Acid-Base Concepts: An Overview. LC 79-15561. 364p. 1980. 42.50x (ISBN 0-471-03902-0, Pub. by Wiley-Interscience). Wiley.

Jentoft, Clyde W. Sir Thomas Wyatt & Henry Howard, Earl of Surrey: A Reference Guide. 1980. lib. bdg. 24.00 (ISBN 0-8161-8176-4, Hall Reference). G K Hall.

Jentz, Barry C. & Wofford, Joan W. Leadership & Learning: Personal Change in a Professional Setting. 1979. text ed. 15.95 (ISBN 0-07-032497-2, P&RB). McGraw.

Jentz, John B., jt. ed. see Keil, Hartmut.

Jen-Yu Wang & Barger, Gerald L., eds. Bibliography of Agricultural Meteorology. 686p. 1962. 45.00x (ISBN 0-299-02510-1). U of Wis Pr.

Jeon, Sang-Woon. Science & Technology in Korea: Traditional Instruments & Techniques. (East Asian Science Ser). 448p. 1974. 25.00x (ISBN 0-262-10014-2). MIT Pr.

Jeong, Tung Hon. International Exhibition of Holography. Croydon, Michael, compiled by. LC 82-83046. 26p. (Orig.). 1982. pap. text ed. 7.00 (ISBN 0-910535-00-0). Lake Forest.

Jephcott, E. F., tr. see Adorno, Theodor.

Jephcott, Edmund, tr. see Elias, Norbert.

Jepperson, jt. auth. see Electric Power Research Institute.

Jeppesen, Knud. Counterpoint: The Polyphonic Vocal Style of the Sixteenth Century. Haydon, G., tr. 1939. ref. ed. 22.95 (ISBN 0-13-183608-0). P-H.

Jeppesen Sanderson. Aviation-Aerospace Fundamentals Instructors Guide. (Illus.). 322p. 1979. text ed. 35.65 3-ring binder ed. o.p. (ISBN 0-88487-031-6, SA418077). Jeppesen Sanderson.

Jeppesen Sanderson, ed. see Gunby, R. A.

Jeppson, Lee R., et al. Mites Injurious to Economic Plants. LC 72-93523. (Illus.). 1975. 67.50x (ISBN 0-520-02381-1). U of Cal Pr.

Jeppson, Roland W. Analysis of Flow in Pipe Networks. LC 75-36280. 1976. 29.95 (ISBN 0-250-40119-3). Ann Arbor Science.

Jepsen, Stanley M. The Gentle Giants: The Story of Draft Horses. LC 72-92315. (Illus.). 1971. 9.95 o.p. (ISBN 0-668-02765-7). Arco.

Jepson, J. W. El Amor: La Base de Todo. 128p. Date not set. 2.50 (ISBN 0-88113-008-7). Edit Betania.

Jepson, Willis L. A Manual of the Flowering Plants of California. (Illus.). 1925. 50.00x (ISBN 0-520-00606-2). U of Cal Pr.

Jereb, Elza, tr. see Krzisnik, Zoran.

Jereb, Elza, tr. see Stele, France.

Jeremiah, David. Abraham: Twenty-Six Daily Bible Studies. (Steps to Higher Ground Ser.). 1982. pap. 1.50 (ISBN 0-86508-201-4). BCM Pubns.

--John I, II, III: Twenty-Six Daily Bible Studies. (Steps to Higher Ground Ser.). 1983. pap. 1.50 (ISBN 0-86508-206-5). BCM Pubns.

--Malachi: Twenty-Six Daily Bible Studies. (Steps to Higher Ground Ser.). 1983. pap. 1.50 (ISBN 0-86508-207-3). BCM Pubns.

--Philippians: Twenty-Six Daily Bible Studies. (Steps to Higher Ground Ser.). 1983. pap. 1.50 (ISBN 0-86508-208-1). BCM Pubns.

Jeremiah, Maryalyce. Coaching Basketball: Ten Winning Concepts. LC 78-12292. 247p. 1979. text ed. 23.95x (ISBN 0-471-04090-8). Wiley.

Jeremiah, Rosemary W. How You Can Make Money in the Hairdressing Business. 112p. 1982. 29.00x (ISBN 0-85950-330-5, Pub. by Thornes England). State Mutual Bk.

Jeremy, David J. Transatlantic Industrial Revolution: The Diffusion of Textile Technologies Between Britain & America, 1790-1830. (Illus.). 384p. 1981. text ed. 35.00x (ISBN 0-262-10022-3). MIT Pr.

Jeresaty, Robert M. Mitral Valve Prolapse. LC 78-66350. 263p. 1979. 32.00 (ISBN 0-89004-230-6). Raven.

Jergensen, Gerald V., III, jt. ed. see Mular, Andrew L.

Jerger, James, jt. auth. see Jerger, Susan.

Jerger, Susan & Jerger, James. Audiologic Tests of Central Auditory Function. 1983. pap. text ed. 13.95 (ISBN 0-8391-1801-5, 15644). Univ Park.

Jerison, Harry J. Evolution of the Brain & Intelligence. 1973. 59.50 (ISBN 0-12-385250-1). Acad Pr.

Jerison, M., jt. auth. see Gillman, L.

Jerlov, N. G. Marine Optics. 2nd rev. & enl. ed. (Elsevier's Oceanography Ser: Vol. 14). 1976. 57.50 (ISBN 0-444-41490-8). Elsevier.

Jerman, Max E. & Beardslee, Edward C. Elementary Mathematics Method. (Illus.). 1978. text ed. 27.50 (ISBN 0-07-032531-6, C); 15.00 (ISBN 0-07-032532-4). McGraw.

Jermann, William. Structure & Programming of Microcomputers. (Illus.). 368p. 1982. pap. text ed. 19.95 (ISBN 0-88284-175-0); avail. instructor's manual. Alfred Pub.

Jermy, A. C. & Crabbe, J. A., eds. The Island of Mull, a Survey of It's Flora & Environment. (Illus.). 1978. 100.00x (ISBN 0-565-00791-2, Pub. by Brit Mus Nat Hist). Sabbot-Natural Hist Bks.

Jernick, Ruth. Housewife. 1981. 9.95 (ISBN 0-698-11081-1, Coward). Putnam Pub Group.

Jernigan, E. Jay. Henry Demarest Lloyd. LC 76-17104. (U.S. Authors Ser.: No. 277). 1976. lib. bdg. 13.95 (ISBN 0-8057-7177-8, Twayne). G K Hall.

Jernudd, Bjorn H., jt. auth. see Rubin, Joan.

Jernudd, Bjorn H., jt. ed. see Rubin, Joan.

Jerome, Chris, jt. auth. see McDole, Brad.

Jerome, Helen. Fine Art of Cooking. rev. ed. (YA) 1968. 13.50 (ISBN 0-392-02934-0, SpS). Sportshelf.

--Housewife Book of Cakemaking. pap. 5.00x (ISBN 0-392-06224-0, SpS). Sportshelf.

Jerome, Jerome K. Diary of a Pilgrimage. (Illus.). 160p. 1982. pap. text ed. 4.95x (ISBN 0-86299-010-6, Pub. by Sutton England). Humanities.

--Evergreens & Other Short Stories. 128p. 1982. pap. text ed. 3.25x (ISBN 0-86299-011-4, Pub. by Sutton England). Humanities.

--Idle Thoughts of an Idle Fellow. 144p. 1982. pap. text ed. 4.25x (ISBN 0-686-84443-2, Pub. by Sutton England). Humanities.

--Three Men in a Boat. 192p. 1982. pap. text ed. 4.25x (ISBN 0-86299-028-9, Pub. by Sutton England). Humanities.

--Three Men on the Bummel. 192p. 1982. pap. text ed. 4.25x (ISBN 0-86299-029-7, Pub. by Sutton England). Humanities.

Jerome, Jerome K see Eyre, A. G.

Jerome, John, jt. auth. see Sports Illustrated Editors.

Jerome, Joseph. Approximation of Nonlinear Evolution Systems. (Mathematics in Science & Engineering Ser.). 244p. 1982. write for info. o.s.i. (ISBN 0-12-384680-3). Acad Pr.

Jerome, Norge W., et al, eds. Nutritional Anthropology. 1982. pap. 12.80 o.p. (ISBN 0-913178-55-1, Pub. by Redgrave Pub. Co.). Hippocrene Bks.

Jerram, C. S. Lucian Vera Historia. 104p. Date not set. Repr. of 1879 ed. 5.00x (ISBN 0-86516-019-8). Bolchazy-Carducci.

Jerrard, jt. auth. see International Conference, Brighton, United Kingsom, March 1982.

Jerrold, Blanchard. Life of Gustave Dore. LC 69-17492. (Illus.). 1969. Repr. of 1891 ed. 42.00x (ISBN 0-8103-3532-8). Gale.

Jerrold, Walter C. A Book of Famous Wits. LC 77-155086. 1971. Repr. of 1912 ed. 40.00x (ISBN 0-8103-3757-6). Gale.

--A Descriptive Index to Shakespeare's Characters, in Shakespeare's Words. LC 74-23634. xvi, 176p. 1975. Repr. of 1905 ed. 42.00x (ISBN 0-8103-4097-6). Gale.

--Thomas Hood: His Life & Times. Repr. of 1907 ed. lib. bdg. 18.75x (ISBN 0-8371-1043-2, JETH). Greenwood.

Jerrold, Walter C. & Leonard, R. M. Century of Parody & Imitation. LC 68-30585. 1968. Repr. of 1913 ed. 37.00x (ISBN 0-8103-3215-9). Gale.

Jerse, Dorothy W. & Stedman, Judith, eds. On the Banks of the Wabash: A Photograph Album of Greater Terre Haute, 1900-1950. LC 82-47955. (Illus.). 128p. (Orig.). 1983. 20.00x (ISBN 0-253-19035-5); pap. 12.95 (ISBN 0-253-20309-0). Ind U Pr.

Jersild, Arthur T. Child Development & the Curriculum. 274p. 1982. Repr. of 1946 ed. lib. bdg. 50.00 (ISBN 0-89987-434-7). Darby Bks.

--Psychology of Adolescence. 3rd ed. (Illus.). 1978. text ed. 22.95x (ISBN 0-02-360610-X, 36061). Macmillan.

Jersild, Paul T. Invitation to Faith: Christian Belief Today. LC 77-84097. 1978. 8.95 (ISBN 0-8066-1622-9, 10-3396); pap. 5.50 (ISBN 0-8066-1623-7, 10-3395). Augsburg.

Jervey, Phyllis. Rice & Spice: Rice Recipes from East to West. LC 57-10198. (Illus.). 1957. pap. 5.25 (ISBN 0-8048-1078-8). C E Tuttle.

Jervey, Theodore D. Robert Y. Hayne & His Times. LC 73-104330. (American Scene Ser). (Illus.). 1970. Repr. of 1909 ed. lib. bdg. 65.00 (ISBN 0-306-71870-7). Da Capo.

Jervis, Alice D., tr. see Mazzini, Giuseppe.

Jerzy, George B. & Sherlock, Paul, eds. Progress in Gastroenterology. (Vol. 4). write for info. Grune.

Jesch, F., jt. auth. see Peter, K.

Jeschke, Herbert, tr. see Muir, John.

Jeschke, Marlin. Believers Baptism for Children of the Church. 160p. (Orig.). 1983. pap. 7.95 (ISBN 0-8361-3318-8). Herald Pr.

Jeske, Richard L. Revelation for Today: Images of Hope. LC 82-16079. 144p. 1983. pap. 6.95 (ISBN 0-8006-1693-6). Fortress.

Jess, John D. Reflections for Busy People. 1982. pap. 3.95 (ISBN 0-8423-5399-2). Tyndale.

Jesse, F. Tennyson. A Pin to See the Peep Show. 1975. pap. 1.95 o.p. (ISBN 0-380-00720-7, 25627). Avon.

Jesse, John. Strength, Power & Muscular Endurance for Runners & Hurdlers. LC 73-131245. (gr. 10-12). 1971. pap. 4.95 o.p. (ISBN 0-87095-036-3). Athletic.

Jessee, Jill. Perfume Album. LC 74-13588. 194p. 1974. Repr. of 1951 ed. 11.50 (ISBN 0-88275-216-2). Krieger.

Jessel, Camilla. Life at the Royal Ballet School. LC 79-12162. (Illus.). (gr. 4 up). 1979. 12.95 (ISBN 0-416-86320-5). Methuen Inc.

Jessel, Frederic & Horr, Norton T. Bibliographies of Works on Playing Cards & Gaming. Incl. Bibliography of Works in English on Playing Cards & Gaming. Jessel, Frederic. Repr. of 1905 ed; Bibliography of Card Games & of the History of Playing Cards. Horr, Norton T. Repr. of 1892 ed. LC 77-129310. (Criminology, Law Enforcement, & Social Problems Ser., No. 132). 1972. 20.00x (ISBN 0-87585-132-0). Patterson Smith.

Jessen, Kenneth C. Railroads of Northern Colorado. (Illus.). 300p. 1982. 34.95 (ISBN 0-87108-599-2). Pruett.

Jessen, Peter. Masterpieces of Calligraphy: Two Hundred & Sixty-One Examples, 1500-1800. (Illus.). 1981. pap. 6.50 (ISBN 0-486-24100-9). Dover.

Jessen, Raymond J., jt. auth. see Hoel, Paul G.

Jesshope, C. R., jt. auth. see Hockney, R. W.

Jessie, Karen. O. T. Books of the Bible. Sparks, Judith A., ed. 48p. (Orig.). (gr. 7 up). 1983. 1.50 (ISBN 0-87239-674-6, 2774). Standard Pub.

Jessie, Karen, jt. auth. see Bruno, Angela.

Jesson-Dibley, David, ed. see Herrick, Robert.

Jessop, Ann L. Nurse-Patient Communication: A Skills Approach. (Illus.). 1979. pap. text ed. 8.95 (ISBN 0-917276-05-1). Microtraining Assocs.

Jessop, Bob. The Capitalist State: Marxist Theories & Methods. 320p. 1982. 27.50 (ISBN 0-8147-4163-0); pap. 8.50 (ISBN 0-8147-4164-9). Columbia U Pr.

Jessop, Charles H. Treatise on the Line Complex. LC 68-55945. 1969. Repr. of 1903 ed. 14.95 (ISBN 0-8284-0223-X). Chelsea Pub.

Jessop, H. T. & Harris, F. C. Photoelasticity: Principles & Methods. (Illus.). 1950. pap. text ed. 3.00 o.p. (ISBN 0-486-60720-8). Dover.

Jessor, Richard, et al. Society, Personality & Deviant Behavior: A Study of a Tri-Ethnic Community. LC 75-20249. 512p. 1975. Repr. of 1968 ed. 22.50 (ISBN 0-88275-339-8). Krieger.

Jessup, Bertram & Rader, M. Art & Human Values. (Illus.). 1976. 19.95 (ISBN 0-13-046821-5). P-H.

Jessup, Gilbert & Jessup, Helen. Selection & Assessment at Work. (Essential Psychology Ser.). 1975. pap. 4.95x (ISBN 0-416-82270-3). Methuen Inc.

Jessup, Helen, jt. auth. see Jessup, Gilbert.

Jessup, Kathryn. Transplant. LC 82-60721. (Karen Evans, M.D. Ser.: No. 4). 256p. 1983. pap. 2.75 (ISBN 0-86721-239-X). Playboy Pbks.

Jessup, P. C. The Use of International Law. LC 79-173670. 164p. 1971. Repr. of 1959 ed. lib. bdg. 27.50 (ISBN 0-306-70407-2). Da Capo.

Jessup, Paul F. Modern Bank Management. 300p. 1980. text ed. 24.95 (ISBN 0-8299-0330-5). West Pub.

--Modern Bank Management: A Casebook. 1978. text ed. 19.95 (ISBN 0-8299-0207-4); instrs.' maual avail. (ISBN 0-8299-0496-4). West Pub.

Jessup, Philip C. Transnational Law. 1956. 29.50x (ISBN 0-685-89792-3). Elliots Bks.

Jessup, Philip C., ed. Atoms for Power. LC 58-6048. 1957. 3.00; pap. 1.00 (ISBN 0-936904-01-1). Am Assembly.

Jessup, Philip C., jt. ed. see Deak, Francis.

Jessup, Philip C., et al. International Regulation of Economic & Social Questions: International Organization by Joseph L. Chamberlain. LC 77-18933. (Illus.). 1978. Repr. of 1955 ed. lib. bdg. 18.50x (ISBN 0-313-20206-0, JEIR). Greenwood.

Jessup, Richard. Threat. 1982. pap. 2.75 (ISBN 0-451-11411-6, AE1411, Sig). NAL.

Jeste, Dilip & Wyatt, Richard J. Understanding & Treating Tardive Dyskinesia. LC 81-7059. (Foundations in Modern Psychiatry Ser.). 365p. 1982. 29.50 (ISBN 0-89862-175-5). Guilford Pr.

Jester, Pat. Microwave Cookbook: The Complete Guide. (Illus.). 1982. ring bdg. 24.95 (ISBN 0-89586-169-0). H P Bks.

Jesuale, Nancy J. & Smith, Ralph L., eds. The CTIC Cablebooks, 2 Vols. 240p. (Orig.). 1982. pap. 27.00 (ISBN 0-943336-02-3); pap. 15.00 ea. Cable TV Info Ctr.

Jesuale, Nancy J. & Smith, Ralph Lee, eds. The CTIC Cablebooks. Incl. The Community Medium. Vol. I (ISBN 0-943336-00-7); A Guide for Local Policy. Vol. II (ISBN 0-943336-01-5). LC 82-71509. 240p. (Orig.). 1982. Set. pap. 27.00 (ISBN 0-943336-02-3); pap. 15.00 ea. Cable TV Info Ctr.

Jesus, Ed. C. de see McCoy, Alfred W. & De Jesus, Ed. C.

Jesus d' Elbee, Jean du Couer de see Couer de Jesus d' Elbee, Jean du.

Jetly, Nancy. India-China Relations Nineteen Forty-Seven to Nineteen Seventy-Seven: A Study of Parliament's Role in the Making of Foreign Policy. 1979. text ed. 19.50x (ISBN 0-391-00986-9). Humanities.

Jevnikar, Jana M. Video Service Profiles. 60p. (Orig.). 1983. pap. 6.00 o.p. (ISBN 0-935654-02-X, Pub. by Ctr for Arts Info). Pub Ctr Cult Res.

Jevons, William S. The Papers & Correspondence of William Stanley Jevons, 7 vols. LC 72-77230. 1981. Vol. 1. lib. bdg. 25.00x (ISBN 0-678-07012-1); Vol. 2. 30.00x (ISBN 0-678-07011-3); Vols. 3-7. 22.50 ea. Vol. 3 (ISBN 0-333-10253-3). Vol. 4 (ISBN 0-333-19977-4). Vol. 5 (ISBN 0-333-19978-2). Vol. 6 (ISBN 0-333-10258-4). Vol. 8 (ISBN 0-333-19979-0). Kelley.

Jewell, Diana L., jt. auth. see Fiedorek, Mary B.

Jewell, Don. Public Assembly Facilities: Planning & Management. LC 77-16524. 208p. Repr. of 1978 ed. text ed. 28.95 (ISBN 0-471-02437-6). Krieger.

Jewell, John, jt. auth. see Hillier, Sheila.

Jewell, Linda N. & Reitz, H. Joseph. Group Effectiveness in Organizations. (Organizational Behavior & Psychology Ser.). 1981. pap. text ed. 10.95x (ISBN 0-673-15334-7). Scott F.

Jewell, Malcolm E. & Patterson, Samuel. The Legislative Process in the United States. 3rd ed. 1977. 20.00 (ISBN 0-394-31265-1, RanC). Random.

Jewell, Malcolm E., ed. The Politics of Reapportionment. LC 82-18695. (The Atherton Press Political Science Ser.). xii, 334p. 1982. Repr. of 1962 ed. lib. bdg. 39.75x (ISBN 0-313-23317-9, JERA). Greenwood.

Jewell, Nancy. Try & Catch Me. LC 72-80368. (Illus.). (ps-3). 1972. 5.95 o.p. (ISBN 0-06-022831-8, HarpJ); PLB 5.79 o.p. (ISBN 0-06-022832-6). Har-Row.

Jewell, Richard B. The RKO Story. Harbin, Vernon, ed. LC 81-22100. (Illus.). 320p. 1982. 35.00 (ISBN 0-517-54656-6, Arlington Hse). Crown.

Jewell, W. J., ed. Energy, Agriculture & Waste Management: Proceedings. LC 75-22898. (Illus.). 1977. 47.50 o.p. (ISBN 0-250-40113-4). Ann Arbor Science.

Jewett, Claudia L. Helping Children Cope with Separation & Loss. LC 82-11823. 146p. 1982. 11.95 (ISBN 0-916782-27-1). Harvard Common.

Jewett, Cora-Mae. Patchwork Sampler: More Doodles in Verse. 1983. 5.95 (ISBN 0-533-05515-6). Vantage.

Jewett, Don L. & McCarroll, H. Relton, Jr. Nerve Repair & Regeneration: Its Clinical & Experimental Basis. LC 79-19276. 372p. 1979. pap. text ed. 59.50 o.p. (ISBN 0-8016-2507-6). Mosby.

Jewett, Frank I., jt. auth. see Ruprecht, Theodore K.

Jewett, Iran B. Alexander W. Kinglake. (English Authors Ser.). 1981. lib. bdg. 13.95 (ISBN 0-8057-6812-2, Twayne). G K Hall.

--Edward FitzGerald. (English Authors Ser.). 1977. lib. bdg. 13.95 (ISBN 0-8057-6675-8, Twayne). G K Hall.

Jewett, Jim & Shrago, Jackie. Designing Optimal Voice Networks for Business, Government & Telephone Companies. 240p. 1980. 39.95 (ISBN 0-686-98044-1). Telecom Lib.

--Traffic Engineering Tables: The Complete Practical Encyclopedia. 480p. 1980. 125.00 (ISBN 0-686-98045-X). Telecom Lib.

Jewett, Robert. The Captain America Complex. 264p. pap. 6.95 (ISBN 0-939680-09-2). Bear & Co.

--Christian Tolerance: Paul's Message to the Modern Church. LC 82-13480. (Biblical Perspectives on Current Issues Ser.). pap. 9.95 (ISBN 0-664-24444-0). Westminster.

Jewish Agency for Israel. Memorandum Submitted to the Palestine Royal Commission on Behalf of the Jewish Agency for Palestine. LC 71-97287. 323p. 1975. Repr. of 1936 ed. lib. bdg. 15.75x (ISBN 0-8371-2610-X, JEAP). Greenwood.

Jewkes, Wilfred T., et al. Literature As a Mode of Travel: Five Essays & a Postscript. LC 63-23262. (Orig.). 1964. pap. 5.00 o.p. (ISBN 0-87104-109-X). NY Pub Lib.

Jewler, A. Jerome. Creative Strategy in Advertising: What the Copy-Editor Should Know About the Creative Side of the Business. 240p. 1980. pap. text ed. 16.95x (ISBN 0-534-00824-0). Wadsworth Pub.

Jewsbury, Geraldine E. Zoe: The History of Two Lives 1845. Wolff, Robert L., ed. LC 75-1518. (Victorian Fiction Ser.). 1975. lib. bdg. 66.00 o.s.i. (ISBN 0-8240-1591-6). Garland Pub.

Jeynes, B. J., jt. auth. see Warren, B. A.

Jha, Akhileshwar. Sexual Designs in Indian Culture. 1979. text ed. 13.00x (ISBN 0-7069-0744-2). Humanities.

Jha, Ganganath. Foreign Policy of Thailand, Nineteen Fifty-Four to Nineteen Seventy-One. 1979. text ed. 15.25x (ISBN 0-391-01012-3). Humanities.

Jha, L. K. North South Debate. 153p. 1982. text ed. 10.75x (ISBN 0-391-02769-7, 41257). Humanities.

--North South Debate. 1982. 14.00x (ISBN 0-8364-0907-8, Pub. by Heritage India). South Asia Bks.

Jha, P. Political Representation in India. 1976. 11.00x o.p. (ISBN 0-88386-774-5). South Asia Bks.

Jha, Prem S. India: A Political Economy of Stagnation. (Illus.). 1980. 17.50x (ISBN 0-19-561153-5). Oxford U Pr.

Jhabvala, Ruth P. A Backward Place. (Orient Paperbacks Ser.). 236p. 1965. pap. 3.00 o.p. (ISBN 0-86578-078-1). Ind-US Inc.

--Heat & Dust. 1977. pap. 1.95i o.p. (ISBN 0-06-080431-9, P431, PL). Har-Row.

--In Search of Love & Beauty. 384p. 1983. 12.95 (ISBN 0-688-02035-6). Morrow.

Jhaveri, S. & Montecalvo, J., Jr. Abstracts of Methods Used to Assess Fish Quality. (Technical Report Ser.: No. 69). 104p. 1978. 3.00 o.p. (ISBN 0-686-36990-4, P777). URI Mas.

Jhaveri, S., jt. auth. see Hillard, A.

Jhigan, M. L. Micro Economic Theory. 2nd ed. 775p. 1982. text ed. 45.00x (ISBN 0-7069-1803-7, Pub. by Vikas India). Advent NY.

Jhingan, M. L. The Economics of Development & Planning. 15th ed. 600p. 1982. text ed. 40.00x (ISBN 0-7069-2057-0, Pub. by Vikas India). Advent NY.

Jhon, Mu S., jt. auth. see Eyring, Henry.

Jian, Gerard & Hester, Ralph. Decouvert et Creation. 3rd ed. 1981. 22.95 (ISBN 0-395-30987-5); instr's manual 1.95 (ISBN 0-395-30989-1); Exercises de Laboratoire 7.95 (ISBN 0-395-30988-3); tapes 150.00 (ISBN 0-395-30990-5). HM.

Jiang, Boju. Lectures on Nielsen Fixed Point Theory. LC 82-20756. (Contemporary Mathematics Ser.: Vol. 14). 16.00 (ISBN 0-8218-5014-8, CONM/14). Am Math.

Jiasan, Yang, ed. The Way to Locate Acu-Points. Xiankun, Meng & Xuewu, Li, trs. from Chinese. (Illus.). 72p. (Orig.). 1982. pap. 12.95 (ISBN 0-8351-1028-1). China Bks.

Jicarilla Apache Tribe. Apache Indians VII. Horr, David A., ed. (American Indian Ethnohistory Ser.). 1978. lib. bdg. 42.00 o.s.i. (ISBN 0-8240-0709-3). Garland Pub.

Jick, Leon A. The Americanization of the Synagogue, 1820-1870. LC 75-18213. (Illus.). 260p. 1976. text ed. 18.00x (ISBN 0-87451-119-4). U Pr of New Eng.

Jiggins, Janice. Caste & Family in the Politics of the Sinhalese. LC 78-54715. (Illus.). 1979. 32.50 (ISBN 0-521-22069-6). Cambridge U Pr.

Jilling, Michael. Foreign Exchange Risk Management in U. S. Multinational Corporations. Dufey, Gunter, ed. LC 78-24052. (Research for Business Decisions Ser.: No. 6). 364p. 1978. 44.95 (ISBN 0-8357-0952-3, Pub. by UMI Res Pr). Univ Microfilms.

Jillson, Joyce. Real Women Don't Pump Gas: A Guide to All That Is Divinely Feminine. (Illus., Orig.). 1982. pap. 3.95 (ISBN 0-671-46309-8). PB.

Jimenez, Francisco. Mosaico De la Vida: Prosa Chicana, Cubana, y Puertorriquena. 1981. pap. text ed. 8.95 (ISBN 0-15-564090-9, HC). HarBraceJ.

Jimenez, Francisco, jt. auth. see Keller, Gary D.

Jimenez, Francisco, ed. The Identification & Analysis of Chicano Literature. LC 78-67287. (Studies in the Language & Literature of United States Hispanos). 1979. lib. bdg. 19.95x (ISBN 0-916950-12-3); pap. text ed. 11.95x (ISBN 0-916950-11-5). Bilingual Pr.

Jimenez, Francisco, jt. ed. see Keller, Gary D.

Jimenez, Nilda, compiled by. The Bible & the Poetry of Christina Rossetti: A Concordance. LC 78-74651. 1979. lib. bdg. 45.00 (ISBN 0-313-21196-5, JBR/). Greenwood.

Jimenez, Sherry L. Childbearing: A Guide for Pregnant Parents. (Illus.). 176p. 1980. 12.95 (ISBN 0-13-130328-7, Spec); pap. 5.95 (ISBN 0-13-130310-4). P-H.

--The Pregnant Woman's Comfort Guide. (Illus.). 192p. 1983. 14.95 (ISBN 0-13-694919-3); pap. 7.95 (ISBN 0-13-694901-0). P-H.

Jimenez de Asua, L., ed. Control Mechanisms in Animal Cells: Specific Growth Factors. 406p. 1980. text ed. 40.00 (ISBN 0-89004-509-7). Raven.

Jimenez-Fajardo, Salvador. Claude Simon. (World Authors Ser.). 1975. lib. bdg. 13.95 (ISBN 0-8057-2828-7, Twayne). G K Hall.

--Luis Cernuda. (World Authors Ser.). 1978. lib. bdg. 15.95 (ISBN 0-8057-6292-2, Twayne). G K Hall.

Jimerson, H. C., jt. auth. see Rowe, K. L.

Jiminez, Jose O. La Presencia de Antonio Machado en la Poesia Espanola de Posguerra. 230p. 1983. pap. 25.00 (ISBN 0-89295-024-2). Society Sp & Sp-Am.

Jinadu, L. Adele. Structure & Choice in African Politics. (Hans Wolff Memorial Lecture Ser.). 52p. (Orig.). 1979. pap. text ed. 3.00 (ISBN 0-941934-23-3). Ind U Afro-Amer Arts.

Jing, Bao-Shan, jt. auth. see Dodd, Gerald D.

Jinhai, He. Mount Taishan. (Illus.). 120p. (Orig.). 1982. pap. 7.95 (ISBN 0-8351-0979-8). China Bks.

Jinich, Horacio, tr. see Bruguera, Miquel, et al.

Jinkins, Dana, jt. auth. see Bobrow, Jill.

Jinks, William. The Celluloid Literature: Film in the Humanities. 2nd ed. LC 73-7361. (Illus.). 208p. 1974. pap. text ed. 11.95x (ISBN 0-02-474910-9, 47490). Macmillan.

JIRA, see Japan Industrial Robot Association.

Jirjees, Jassim M., jt. auth. see Myers, Marcia J.

Jirsch, Dennis. Frontiers in General Surgery. LC 81-71140. (Illus.). 390p. 1982. text ed. 35.00x (ISBN 0-8036-5028-0). Davis Co.

Ji-Xiang Shi, ed. see International Burn Seminar Shanghai, June 1981.

Jo, Yung-Hwan & Pi, Ying-Hsien. Russia Versus China & What Next? LC 80-1404. 164p. 1980. lib. bdg. 19.00 (ISBN 0-8191-1237-2); pap. text ed. 9.50 (ISBN 0-8191-1238-0). U Pr of Amer.

Joachain, C. J. Quantum Collision Theory. 1976. One Vol. Ed. 106.50 (ISBN 0-444-10662-6, North-Holland); Set, 2 Pts. pap. 61.75 (ISBN 0-444-85235-2); Pt. 1. pap. 36.25 (ISBN 0-444-85233-6); Pt. 2. pap. 36.25 (ISBN 0-444-85234-4). Elsevier.

Joachim, Harold H. Descartes's Rules for the Direction of the Mind. Harris, Errol E., ed. LC 79-9958. 1979. Repr. of 1957 ed. lib. bdg. 16.25x (ISBN 0-313-21263-5, JODE). Greenwood.

--Study of the Ethics of Spinoza. LC 64-11845. 1964. Repr. of 1901 ed. 12.00x (ISBN 0-8462-0418-5). Russell.

Joad, Cyril E. The Present & Future of Religion. LC 77-109756. 310p. 1974. Repr. of 1930 ed. lib. bdg. 16.25x (ISBN 0-8371-4246-6, JOPF). Greenwood.

--The Recovery of Belief: A Restatement of Christian Philosophy. LC 76-26097. 1976. Repr. of 1952 ed. lib. bdg. 19.25x (ISBN 0-8371-9022-3, JORB). Greenwood.

Joan, jt. auth. see Willadeene.

Joao Teixeira de Medeiros. Do Tempo e De Mim. Almeida, Onesimo T., ed. LC 82-81459. 148p. (Port.). 1982. pap. 3.50 (ISBN 0-686-35846-5). Gavea-Brown.

Joaquin, Nick. Tropical Gothic. (Asian & Pacific Writing Ser.: No. 2). 284p. 1972. 14.95x (ISBN 0-7022-0775-6); pap. 8.50 (ISBN 0-7022-0776-4). U of Queensland Pr.

Job, Glenn T., ed. Parent's Guide to Accredited Camps. 1983. pap. 4.50 (ISBN 0-87603-070-3). Am Camping.

Jobb, Jamie. The Complete Book of Community Gardening. LC 78-23840. (Illus.). 1979. 14.95 o.s.i. (ISBN 0-688-03409-8); pap. 7.95 o.p. (ISBN 0-688-08409-5). Morrow.

--The Night Sky Book. (Brown Paper School Ser.). (gr. 5 up). 1977. 9.95 (ISBN 0-316-46551-8); pap. 6.70i (ISBN 0-316-46552-6). Little.

Jobe, Bobbie C. Striving for Holiness. write for info. (ISBN 0-89137-423-X). Quality Pubns.

Jobs & Skills Programme for Afica, Addis Ababa. Ensuring Equitable Growth: A Strategy for Increasing Employment Equity & Basic Needs Satisfaction in Sierra Leone. Report to Government of Sierra Leone by a JASPA Employment Advisory Mission. International Labour Office, ed. xxxv, 314p. (Orig.). 1981. pap. 14.00 (ISBN 92-2-102776-7). Intl Labour Office.

Jobson, John. The Complete Book of Practical Camping. (Illus.). 1977. pap. 5.95 o.s.i. (ISBN 0-695-80736-6). Follett.

--The Complete Book of Practical Camping. (Illus.). 288p. pap. 5.95 o.p. (ISBN 0-88317-026-4). Stoeger Pub Co.

Jocano, F. Landa. Sulod Society. 1968. 5.00x (ISBN 0-8248-0438-4). UH Pr.

Jocelyn, John. Meditations on the Signs of Zodiac. LC 76-125796. 288p. 1981. Repr. of 1976 ed. 14.00 (ISBN 0-89345-027-8, Spiritual Sci Lib). Garber Comm.

Jocher, Willy. Live Foods for Aquarium & Terrarium Animals. Vevers, Gwynne, tr. (Illus.). 1973. pap. 8.95 (ISBN 0-87666-097-9, PS-309). TFH Pubns.

--Spawning Problem Fishes. Incl. Book 1 (ISBN 0-87666-146-0, PS-302); Book 2 (ISBN 0-87666-147-9, PS-303). (Illus.). 1972. pap. 4.95 ea. TFH Pubns.

--Turtles for Home & Garden. (Illus.). 1973. 6.95 (ISBN 0-87666-777-9, PS-307). TFH Pubns.

Jochim, H. & Ziegler, B. Interaction Studies in Nuclei. LC 75-23218. 1975. 74.50 (ISBN 0-444-10963-3, North-Holland). Elsevier.

Jochmans, Joey R. Rolling Thunder: The Coming Earth Changes. (Illus.). 240p. (Orig.). 1980. pap. 7.50 (ISBN 0-89540-058-8). Sun Pub.

Jochnowitz, Carol. Careers in Medicine for the New Woman. (Choosing Careers & Life-Styles Ser.). (Illus.). (gr. 7 up). 1978. PLB 8.90 s&l (ISBN 0-531-01444-4). Watts.

Jochum, Helen P. Alaskan Journey. LC 80-51526. (Illus.). 153p. 1980. 11.25 (ISBN 0-9606206-0-5). Jochum.

J. Odo Op, Den Orth see Op Den Orth, J. Odo.

Jodorowsky, Alexandro. El Topo: A Book of the Film. LC 70-182697. (Illus.). 1972. 5.95 o.p. (ISBN 0-8256-3403-2, Quick Fox); pap. 3.95 o.p. (ISBN 0-8256-3402-4, Douglas-Links). Putnam Pub Group.

Jody, Ruth, jt. auth. see Cohen, Robert D.

Joe, Barbara. Public Policies Toward Adoption. 84p. 1979. pap. text ed. 5.00 (ISBN 0-87766-253-3). Urban Inst.

Joehnk, Michael D., jt. auth. see Gitman, Lawrence J.

Joekes, A. M., et al, eds. Radionuclides in Nephrology: Proceedings of the International Symposium, 5th, London, 1981. 1982. 36.00 (ISBN 0-8089-1521-5). Grune.

Joel, A. E. Electronic, Switching Systems: Central Office Systems of the World. (IEEE Press Selected Reprint Ser.). 279p. 1976. pap. 17.00x (ISBN 0-471-02391-4). Wiley.

Joel, A. E., Jr. Switching Technology 1925-1975: A History of Engineering & Science in the Bell System. Schindler, G. E., ed. (Illus.). 600p. 1982. 25.00 (ISBN 0-686-83987-0). Bell Telephone.

Joel, Amos E. Electronic Switching: Digital Central Office Systems of the World. 268p. 1982. 30.95x (ISBN 0-471-86884-1, Pub. by Wiley-Interscience); pap. 20.00x (ISBN 0-471-86883-3). Wiley.

Joel, Amos E., Jr., ed. Electronic Switching: Central Office Systems of the World. LC 76-11448. 1976. 11.95 o.p. (ISBN 0-87942-080-4). Inst Electrical.

Joel, J. F., ed. Electronic Switching: Digital Control Office Systems of the World. LC 81-20041. 1981. 30.95 (ISBN 0-87942-159-2). Inst Electrical.

Joel, Lucille A. & Collins, Doris L. Psychiatric Nursing: Theory & Application. (Illus.). 1978. text ed. 25.00 (ISBN 0-07-032537-5, HP). McGraw.

Joelson, M. R., jt. auth. see Kintner, E. W.

Joens. Basic Drafting Skills. (Technical Drafting Ser.). 1977. 6.95 o.p. (ISBN 0-87618-888-9). R J Brady.

--Multiview Drawings. LC 77-13562. (Technical & Drafting Ser.). 1978. pap. 7.95 o.p. (ISBN 0-87618-889-7). R J Brady.

Joens, Clifford J. Technical Drafting, 4 bks. LC 77-12932. 686p. 1977. Set. pap. text ed. 19.95 o.p. (ISBN 0-87619-853-1). R J Brady.

Joerger, Pauline K., ed. see Dampier, Robert.

Joers, Lawrence. Call Collect. Tyson-Flyn, Juanita, ed. (Redwood Ser.). 96p. pap. 3.95 (ISBN 0-8163-0458-0). Pacific Pr Pub Assn.

Joes, Anthony J. Fascism in the Contemporary World: Ideology, Evolution, Resurgence. LC 77-14141. (A Westview Special Study Ser.). 1978. lib. bdg. 23.50 o.p. (ISBN 0-89158-448-X); pap. 12.95 (ISBN 0-89158-159-6). Westview.

Joesting, Edward. Hawaii: An Uncommon History. (Illus.). 353p. 1972. 10.95 o.p. (ISBN 0-393-05382-2); pap. 5.95 (ISBN 0-393-00907-6). Norton.

Joffe, C. David. Practical Echocardiography. LC 77-8494. (Illus.). 193p. 1978. pap. text ed. 24.95 o.p. (ISBN 0-913486-82-5). Charles.

Joffe, Carole E. Friendly Intruders: Childcare Professionals & Family Life. LC 74-27281. 1977. 19.95x (ISBN 0-520-02925-9); pap. 3.95 (ISBN 0-520-03934-3). U of Cal Pr.

Joffe, Irwin. Achieving Success in College. 256p. 1981. pap. text ed. 9.95x (ISBN 0-534-01032-6). Wadsworth Pub.

Joffe, Justin M. & Albee, George W., eds. Prevention Through Political Action & Social Change. LC 80-51504. (Primary Prevention of Psychopathology Ser.: Vol. 5). 376p. 1981. 27.50x (ISBN 0-87451-187-9). U Pr of New Eng.

Joffe, Justin M., jt. ed. see Albee, George W.

Joffe, Justin M., jt. ed. see Bond, Lynne A.

Joglekar, Rajani & Clerman, Robert J. Biotechnology in Industry: Selected Applications & Unit Operations. LC 82-48642. (Illus.). 200p. 1983. 27.50 (ISBN 0-250-40605-5). Ann Arbor Science.

Joglekar, Rajani, jt. auth. see Clerman, Robert J.

Johan, Z., jt. auth. see Picot, P.

Johann Gottfried Herder Institut. Alphabetischer Katalog der Bibliothek des Johann Gottfried Herder-Instituts: Second Supplement. 1981. lib. bdg. 350.00 (ISBN 0-8161-0277-5, Hall Library). G K Hall.

Johann Gottfried Herder-Instituts, Marburg, Lahn. Alphabetischer Katalog der Bibliothek, 5 Vols. 1964. Set. lib. bdg. 380.00 (ISBN 0-8161-0698-3, Hall Library); First Suppl. 1971. 2 Vol. Set. lib. bdg. 215.00 (ISBN 0-8161-0808-0). G K Hall.

Johann, Robert. Meaning of Love. LC 66-22053. 162p. 1966. pap. 1.95 o.p. (ISBN 0-8091-1633-2). Paulist Pr.

Johann, Robert O. Pragmatic Meaning of God. (Aquinas Lecture). 1966. 7.95 (ISBN 0-87462-131-3). Marquette.

Johannesen, Richard L. Ethics in Human Communication. LC 80-54107. 176p. 1981. pap. text ed. 5.95x o.p. (ISBN 0-917974-58-1). Waveland Pr.

--Ethics in Human Communications. 2nd ed. 244p. 1983. pap. text ed. 8.95X (ISBN 0-88133-009-4). Waveland Pr.

Johannesen, Richard L., jt. auth. see Buehler, Ezra C.

Johannessen, J. V. Electron Microscopy in Human Medicine, Vol. 7: Digestive System. 1980. text ed. 69.00 (ISBN 0-07-032507-3). McGraw.

Johannessen, J. V., jt. auth. see Lapis, K.

Johannessen, J. V., ed. Electron Microscopy in Human Medicine, Vol. 11: The Skin - Special Applications. Date not set. text ed. price not set (ISBN 0-07-032510-3). McGraw.

Johannessen, Jan V. Diagnostic Electron Microscopy. 210p. 1982. text ed. 34.50 (ISBN 0-07-032543-X, Co-Pub. by Hemisphere Pub). McGraw.

--Electron Microscopy in Human Medicine: Vol. I, Instrumentation & Techniques. (Electron Microscopy in Human Medicine). (Illus.). 1978. text ed. 60.00 (ISBN 0-07-032501-4, HP). McGraw.

--Electron Microscopy in Human Medicine: Vol. 2, Cellular Pathology. (Illus.). 1978. text ed. 51.00 (ISBN 0-07-032502-2, HP). McGraw.

--Electron Microscopy in Human Medicine: Vol. 6, Nervous System, Sensory Organs, & Respiratory Tract. (Electron Microscopy in Human Medicine Ser.). (Illus.). 368p. 1980. text ed. 78.00 (ISBN 0-07-032506-5, HP). McGraw.

--Electron Microscopy in Human Medicine: Vol. 8, the Liver, Gallbladder & Biliary Ducts. (Illus.). 1979. text ed. 65.00 (ISBN 0-07-032499-9). McGraw.

Johannessen, Jans V. Electron Microscopy in Human Medicine: Vol. 9, Urogenital System & Breast. (Illus.). 396p. 1980. text ed. 79.00 (ISBN 0-07-032508-1, HP). McGraw.

Johannessen, Larry & Kahn, Elizabeth. Designing & Sequencing Prewriting Activites. 45p. 1982. 4.00 (ISBN 0-686-95289-8); members 3.50 (ISBN 0-686-99486-8). NCTE.

Johannessen, Svein, et al, eds. Antiepileptic Therapy: Advances in Drug Monitoring. 456p. 1980. text ed. 46.00 (ISBN 0-89004-407-4). Raven.

Johannesson, Eric O. The Novels of August Strindberg: A Study in Theme & Structure. LC 68-29156. 1968. 30.00x (ISBN 0-520-00607-0). U of Cal Pr.

Johanningmeier, Robert. The Art of Investing While Collecting: An Authoritative Guide to Quality, Value & All Aspects of Collecting -Fine Art & Tangibles. LC 82-70884. (Illus.). 234p. 1982. pap. 14.95 (ISBN 0-943188-07-5). Art & Comm.

Johanningmeir, Edwin V. Americans & Their Schools. 328p. 1980. pap. 15.50 (ISBN 0-395-30640-X). HM.

Johannsen, Chris J. & Sanders, James L., eds. Remote Sensing for Resource Management. (Illus.). 688p. 1982. text ed. 45.00 (ISBN 0-935734-08-2). Soil Conservation.

Johannsen, Elizabeth, jt. auth. see Johannsen, Neil.

Johannsen, Elizabeth, ed. The Alaska Catalog: Living, Working & Traveling in the Northland. LC 77-76351. (Illus.). 1977. pap. 6.95x (ISBN 0-918792-01-0). Polar Palm.

Johannsen, Neil & Johannsen, Elizabeth. Exploring Alaska's Prince William Sound. LC 75-1912. (Illus.). 1975. 7.50 o.p. (ISBN 0-914164-03-1). Alaska Travel.

Johannsen, Robert W. Stephen A. Douglas. (Illus.). 1973. 35.00x (ISBN 0-19-501620-3). Oxford U Pr.

Johannsen, Robert W., ed. Union in Crisis, Eighteen Fifty to Eighteen Seventy-Seven. LC 65-11899. (Orig.). 1965. pap. text ed. 4.95. Free Pr.

Johannsen, Robert W., ed. see Lincoln, Abraham & Douglas, Stephen.

Johansen, Bruce & Maestas, Roberto. Wasi'chu: The Continuing Indian Wars. LC 79-10153. (Illus.). 268p. 1980. pap. 6.95 (ISBN 0-85345-507-4, PB5074). Monthly Rev.

Johansen, Bruce E. The Forgotten Founders: Benjamin Franklin, the Iroquois & the Rationale for American Revolution. LC 81-83027. 167p. 1982. 10.95 (ISBN 0-87645-111-3). Gambit.

Johansen, Bruce E & Maestas, Roberto F. El Pueblo: The Gallegos Family's American Journey. LC 82-48036. (Illus.). 256p. 1983. 20.00 (ISBN 0-85345-611-9, CL6119); pap. 10.00 (ISBN 0-85345-612-7, PB6127). Monthly Rev.

Johansen, Donald A. Plant Microtechnique. (Botanical Sciences Ser.). 1940. text ed. 49.95 (ISBN 0-07-032540-5, C). McGraw.

Johansen, Harley & Fugitt, Glenn V. The Changing Rural Village of America. 160p. 1983. 25.00x (ISBN 0-88410-692-6). Ballinger Pub.

Johansen, L. Lectures on Macroeconomic Planning, 2 pts. 1977-78. Pt. 1: General Aspects. 38.50 (ISBN 0-7204-0565-3, North-Holland); Pt. 2: Centralization, Decentralization & Planning Under Uncertainty. 47.00 (ISBN 0-444-85119-4). Elsevier.

--Public Economics. 1971. Repr. 42.75 (ISBN 0-444-10075-X, North-Holland). Elsevier.

Johansen, Robert & Vallee, Jacques. Electronic Meetings: Technical Alternatives & Social Choices. 244p. 1979. 16.95 (ISBN 0-686-98116-2). Telecom Lib.

Johansen, Robert, et al. Electronic Meetings: Technical Alternatives. 1979. text ed. 23.95 (ISBN 0-201-03478-6). A-W.

Johanson, Stanley, jt. auth. see Dukeminier, Jesse.

Johanson, Stanley M., jt. auth. see Dukeminier, Jesse, Jr.

Johansson, Bertil. The Adapter Adapted: A Study of Sir John Vanbrugh's Comedy the Mistake, Its Predecessors & Successors. (Stockholm Studies in English Ser.: No. 41). 1977. 12.75x o.p. (ISBN 9-1220-0097-6). Humanities.

Johansson, Gunn, jt. auth. see Gardell, Bertil.

Johansson, S. G., jt. ed. see Manell, P.

Johansson, Stig. Studies of Error Gravity: Native Reactions to Errors Produced by Swedish Learners of English. (Gothenburg Studies in English: No. 44). 1978. pap. text ed. 25.50x o.p. (ISBN 91-7346-054-0). Humanities.

Johany, Ali D. The Myth of the OPEC Cartel: The Role of Saudi Arabia. LC 80-40959. 107p. 1980. 42.95x (ISBN 0-471-27864-5, Pub. by Wiley-Interscience). Wiley.

Johari, Harish. Leela: Game of Knowledge. (Illus.). 170p. (Orig.). 1983. pap. 14.95 (ISBN 0-7100-0689-6). Routledge & Kegan.

--Leela: The Game of Self-Knowledge. (Illus.). 256p. 1975. pap. 4.95 o.p. (ISBN 0-698-10647-4, Coward). Putnam Pub Group.

Johari, O., et al, eds. Studies of Food Microstructure. LC 81-84080. (Illus.). x, 342p. 1981. 49.00 (ISBN 0-931288-22-3). Scanning Electron.

Johari, Om & Albrecht, R. M, eds. Scanning Electron Microscopy 1981, Vol. IV. LC 72-626068. viii, 312p. 1982. 53.00 (ISBN 0-931288-20-7). SEM Inc.

Johari, Om & Zaluzec, N. J., eds. Scanning Electron Microscopy 1981, Vol. I. (Illus.). xiv, 666p. 1982. 53.00 (ISBN 0-931288-17-7); Set of 4 parts 109.00 (ISBN 0-931288-21-5). SEM Inc.

John, B. S., jt. auth. see Sugden, D. E.

John, Bernard. Population Cytogenetics. (Studies in Biology: No. 70). 80p. 1976. pap. text ed. 8.95 (ISBN 0-7131-2597-7). E Arnold.

John, Bernard & Lewis, Kenneth. The Meiotic Mechanism. Head, J. J., ed. LC 76-29381. (Carolina Biology Readers Ser.). (Illus.). 32p. 1983. pap. text ed. 2.00 (ISBN 0-89278-265-X, 45-9665). Carolina Biological.

John, Brian. The Winters of the World: Earth Under the Ice Ages. 256p. 1979. 29.95x o.p. (ISBN 0-470-26844-1). Halsted Pr.

John Crerar Library. List of Books on the History of Industry & the Industrial Arts. LC 67-14030. 1966. Repr. of 1915 ed. 40.00x (ISBN 0-8103-3104-7). Gale.

John Crerar Library - Chicago. Author-Title Catalog, 35 Vols. 1967. Set. 3325.00 (ISBN 0-8161-0728-9, Hall Library). G K Hall.

--Classified Subject Catalog, 42 Vols. 1967. incl. subject index 3990.00 (ISBN 0-8161-0195-7, Hall Library); subject index 95.00 (ISBN 0-8161-0196-5). G K Hall.

John, D. M., jt. auth. see Lawson, G. W.

John, David & Moody, Richard. Evolution of Life. (World of Knowledge Ser.). PLB 16.72 (ISBN 0-382-06511-5). Silver.

--Prehistoric World. (World of Knowledge Ser.). PLB 16.72 (ISBN 0-382-06512-3). Silver.

John Dewey Society. Yearbook (Second) Educational Freedom & Democracy. Alberty, H. B. & Bode, B. H., eds. LC 76-150367. 292p. 1972. Repr. of 1938 ed. lib. bdg. 15.50x (ISBN 0-8371-6063-4, JDSY). Greenwood.

John, E. Roy. Functional Neuroscience, Neurometrics: Clinical Applications of Quantitative Electrophysiology, Vol. 2. 320p. 1977. text ed. 29.95 (ISBN 0-89859-125-2). L Erlbaum Assocs.

John, E. Roy, jt. auth. see Thatcher, Robert W.

John, Errol. Moon on a Rainbow Shawl. 86p. 1958. pap. 4.95 o.p. (ISBN 0-571-05403-X). Faber & Faber.

John, F. Lectures on Advanced Numerical Analysis. (Notes on Mathematics & Its Applications Ser). 1967. 24.00 (ISBN 0-677-00315-3). Gordon.

John, Fritz, jt. auth. see Courant, Richard.

John I. Goodlad & Associates. Curriculum Inquiry: The Study of Curriculum Practice. (Illus.). 1979. text ed. 22.95 (ISBN 0-07-023530-9). McGraw.

John, J. & Haberman, W. Introduction to Fluid Mechanics. 2nd ed. 1980. 31.95 (ISBN 0-13-483941-2). P-H.

John M. Wing Foundation, Newberry Library. Dictionary Catalogue of the History of Printing from the John M. Wing Foundation, Second Supplement. 1981. lib. bdg. 435.00 (ISBN 0-8161-0326-7, Hall Library). G K Hall.

John, McNicol. McNicol's Bible Survey, 4 vols. in 1. LC 76-25079. 1982. 12.95 (ISBN 0-8254-3210-3). Kregel.

John, Mar, jt. auth. see Wolff, Charles E.

John, Martha T. Teaching & Loving the Elderly. 274p. 1983. pap. text ed. 19.75 (ISBN 0-398-04812-6). C C Thomas.

John, Michael St. see St. John, Michael.

John, P. W. Statistical Design & Analysis of Experiments. 1971. 22.95x (ISBN 0-02-360820-X). Macmillan.

John, Patricia St. see St. John, Patricia.

John R. Zabka Associates, Inc. Compensation Report on Hospital-Based Physicians, 1982-83. (Annual Report Ser.). 230p. 1982. 92.50 (ISBN 0-939326-06-X). Hosp Compensation.

--Compensation Report on Hospital-Based Physicians 1981-82: 6th Annual Report. 220p. 1981. 92.50 o.p. (ISBN 0-939326-02-7). Hosp Compensation.

--Compensation Report, 1982: Management Employers in Hospital Management Companies. (Annual Report Ser.). 20p. 1982. spiral binding 112.50 o.p. (ISBN 0-939326-04-3). Hosp Compensation.

--Hospital Salary Survey Report, 1982-83: Twelfth Annual Report. 200p. (Orig.). 1982. 92.50 (ISBN 0-939326-05-1). Hosp Compensation.

--Hospital Salary Survey Report 1982-83: 12th Annual Report. 200p. 1981. 92.50 o.p. (ISBN 0-939326-01-9). Hosp Compensation.

John R. Zabka Assocs., Inc. Nursing Home Salary & Benefits Report 1982. (Annual Report Ser.). 250p. 1982. spiral bdg. 87.50 o.p. (ISBN 0-939326-03-5). Hosp Compensation.

John, Sue. The Bread Basket Cookbook. (Illus.). 32p. 1982. pap. 6.95 (ISBN 0-399-20862-3, Philomel). Putnam Pub Group.

--The Special Days Cookbook. (Illus.). 32p. 1982. pap. 6.95 (ISBN 0-399-20865-8, Philomel). Putnam Pub Group.

John, Timothy. A Great Song Book. Hankey, John & Hankey, John, eds. (gr. 1 up). 1978. 14.95 o.p. (ISBN 0-385-13328-6). Doubleday.

John, Tommy, jt. auth. see Smith, Robert.

John, Tommy, et al. The Tommy John Story. 1979. 8.95 o.p. (ISBN 0-8007-0923-3). Revell.

John Chrysostom, St. Homilies, 48-88. (Fathers of the Church Ser.: Vol. 41). 1960. 25.00 (ISBN 0-8132-0041-5). Cath U Pr.

Johnk, Carl T. Engineering Electromagnetic Fields & Waves. LC 74-13567. 655p. 1975. 34.95x (ISBN 0-471-44289-5, Pub. by Wiley-Interscience). Wiley.

John Lame Deer & Erdoes, Richard. Lame Deer Seeker of Visions: The Life of a Sioux Medicine Man. 288p. 1976. pap. 3.95 (ISBN 0-671-45586-9, 80391). WSP.

Johnne, A. S. A Study in Contrast. LC 78-68946. 1979. 6.95 o.p. (ISBN 0-533-04208-9). Vantage.

John Of The Cross. Dark Night of the Soul. Zimmerman, Benedict, tr. 1974. pap. 10.95 (ISBN 0-227-67807-9). Attic Pr.

John Paul II, Pope Day by Day With Pope John Paul II. 1982. pap. 5.95 (ISBN 0-8091-2458-0). Paulist Pr.

--Healing & Hope. 266p. 1982. 5.00 (ISBN 0-8198-3317-7, EP0545); pap. 3.50 (ISBN 0-8198-3318-5). Dghtrs St Paul.

Johns, Bruce, jt. auth. see Hart-Johns, Martha.

Johns, Catherine. Sex or Symbol: Erotic Images of Greece & Rome. 192p. 1982. 80.00x o.p. (ISBN 0-7141-8042-4, Pub. by Brit Mus Pubns England). State Mutual Bk.

Johns, Corydon T. An Introduction to Liability Claims Adjusting Book. 3rd, rev. ed. LC 82-61231. 672p. 1982. text ed. 25.00 (ISBN 0-87218-320-3). Natl Underwriter.

Johns, E. A. The Sociology of Organizational Change. LC 73-8972. 182p. 1973. text ed. 27.00 o.p. (ISBN 0-08-017601-1); pap. text ed. 12.75 (ISBN 0-08-017602-X). Pergamon.

Johns, E. A., jt. auth. see Green, B. S.

Johns, Edward B., et al. Health for Effective Living. 6th ed. (Illus.). 512p. 1975. pap. text ed. 24.00 (ISBN 0-07-032572-3, C); 10.00 (ISBN 0-07-032574-X). McGraw.

Johns, Eric, ed. Theatre Review 1973. (Illus.). 240p. 1974. 12.50 o.p. (ISBN 0-491-01231-4). Transatlantic.

Johns, Gary. Organizational Behavior: Understanding Life at Work. 1983. text ed. 24.95 (ISBN 0-673-15366-5). Scott F.

Johns, Harold E. & Cunningham, John R. The Physics of Radiology. 4th ed. (Illus.). 1000p. 1983. 49.50x (ISBN 0-398-04669-7). C C Thomas.

Johns, J. Murray & Compton, Bill. Guadalcanal Twice-Told. 1978. 5.95 o.p. (ISBN 0-533-03380-2). Vantage.

Johns, Kenneth. True Book About Space Travel. (Illus.). (gr. 7 up). 12.75 (ISBN 0-392-06627-0, LTB). Sportshelf.

Johns, Marjorie P. & Inashima, O. James. Drug Therapy & Nursing Care. 1979. text ed. 26.95x (ISBN 0-02-360800-5). Macmillan.

Johns, Marjorie P., et al. Case Studies in Drug Therapy. 1979. pap. text ed. 11.95x (ISBN 0-02-360860-9). Macmillan.

Johns, R. B., jt. auth. see Rowe, A. H.

Johns, Richard A. Tax Havens & Offshore Finance: A Study of Transnational Economic Development. LC 82-10755. 270p. 1983. 32.50x (ISBN 0-312-78641-7). St Martin.

Johns, Roe L. Full State Funding of Education: Evolution & Implications. LC 72-91863. (Horace Mann Lecture Ser.). 1973. 4.95x o.p. (ISBN 0-8229-3258-X). U of Pittsburgh Pr.

Johns, Roe L. & Morphet, Edgar L. The Economics & Financing of Education: A Systems Approach. 3rd ed. LC 74-30213. (Illus.). 496p. 1975. ref. ed. 25.95 (ISBN 0-13-229898-8). P-H.

Johns, Row, et al. Financing Education: Fiscal & Legal Alternatives. 1972. text ed. 23.95 (ISBN 0-675-09071-7). Merrill.

Johns, T., jt. auth. see Ross, C. T.

Johns, Trevor W. & Hendry, Norman J. English Through Projects. 1970. Bk. 1. pap. text ed. 4.00x o.p. (ISBN 0-435-10480-2); Bk. 2. pap. text ed. 4.00x o.p. (ISBN 0-435-10482-9); tchrs' ed. 2.50x o.p. (ISBN 0-435-10481-0). Heinemann Ed.

Johns, Virginia J. Dining In: Vancouver, B.C. (Dining in Ser.). (Orig.). 1982. pap. 8.95 (ISBN 0-89716-084-3). Peanut Butter.

Johns, William D., tr. see Engelhardt, W. V., et al.

Johns-Brian, Ann. Make Your Choice: 80 Things to Make for Yourself & the Home. (Illus.). 127p. 1975. 7.50 o.p. (ISBN 0-263-05515-9). Transatlantic.

Johnsen, Frederick. B-Twenty-Nine Book. (Illus.). 1978. pap. 4.95 (ISBN 0-911721-40-1, Pub. by Bomber). Aviation.

Johnsen, Frederick A. Bomber Barons: History of the 5th Bomb Group. (Illus.). 28p. 1982. pap. 4.95 (ISBN 0-686-84257-X, Pub. by Bomber). Aviation.

--Thundering Peacemaker: The B-36 Story. (Illus.). 1978. pap. 4.50 (ISBN 0-911721-31-2, Pub. by Bomber). Aviation.

Johnsen, Montfort A. Aerosol Handbook. 2nd ed. 1982. 62.50x (ISBN 0-9603250-3-4). Dorland Pub Co.

Johnsgard, Karin, jt. auth. see Johnsgard, Paul.

Johnsgard, Paul & Johnsgard, Karin. Dragons & Unicorns: A Natural History. LC 82-5630. 160p. 1982. 9.95 (ISBN 0-312-21895-8). St Martin.

Johnsgard, Paul A. Hummingbirds of North America. (Illus.). 384p. 1983. 29.95 (ISBN 0-87474-562-4). Smithsonian.

Johnson. A Brief History of Student Teaching. 1968. 9.95 (ISBN 0-686-38069-X). Assn Tchr Ed.

--Development in Mammals, Vol. 4. 1981. 55.50 (ISBN 0-444-80274-6). Elsevier.

--Education & Society in England, 1780-1870. (Studies in Economic & Social History). 1980. pap. text ed. 11.50x o.p. (ISBN 0-391-01131-6). Humanities.

--An Essay on West African Therapeutics. (Traditional Healing Ser.: No. 7). 1982. 17.50 o.p. (ISBN 0-686-76824-8, Trado-Medic Bks.); lib. bdg. 39.50 deluxe ed. (ISBN 0-932426-19-0). Conch Mag.

--Manufacturing Process. 1979. text ed. 26.00 (ISBN 0-87002-299-7); study guide 6.60 (ISBN 0-87002-044-7). Bennett IL.

--The Social Evolution of Industrial Britain. 188p. 1982. 49.00x (ISBN 0-85323-073-0, Pub. by Liverpool Univ England). State Mutual Bk.

--Technical Metals. (gr. 9-12). 1981. text ed. 21.52 (ISBN 0-87002-313-6); student guide 4.72 (ISBN 0-87002-322-5). Bennett IL.

--Variation Research. 1964. 8.50 (ISBN 0-444-40323-X). Elsevier.

--Your Guide to Better Health, Greater Energy. 1944. 2.00 (ISBN 0-910140-28-6). Anthony.

Johnson & Wood. Contemporary Physical Distribution & Logistics. 1981. 23.95x (ISBN 0-87814-152-9). Pennwell Books Division.

Johnson, jt. auth. see Cluff.

Johnson, jt. auth. see Gruetzner.

Johnson, jt. auth. see Quible.

Johnson & Lemuel, A., eds. Toward Defining the African Aesthetic. Cailler, Bernadette, et al. (Annual Selected Papers of the ALA). 140p. 1983. 22.00X (ISBN 0-89410-356-3); pap. 14.00X (ISBN 0-89410-357-1). Three Continents.

Johnson, jt. ed. see Johnson, Robert B.

Johnson, A. C., jt. auth. see Schulz, R.

Johnson, A. E., tr. see Perrault, Charles.

Johnson, A. F. Type Designs: Their Historical Development. 192p. 1966. 12.50 (ISBN 0-233-95869-X, 05802-5, Pub. by Gower Pub Co England). Lexington Bks.

Johnson, A. H. Philosophers in Action. (Philosophy Ser.). 1977. text ed. 12.95 (ISBN 0-675-08490-3). Merrill.

Johnson, A. H., ed. see Whitehead, Alfred N.

Johnson, A. J., illus. Eighteen Sixty-Three A. J. Johnson Map of Florida. (Illus.). 1p. Date not set. Repr. of 1863 ed. map 2.95 (ISBN 0-941948-13-7). St Johns-Oklawaha.

Johnson, A. M. Styles of Folding: Mechanics & Mechanisms of Folding of Natural Elastic Materials. (Developments in Geotectonics: Vol. 11). 1977. 70.25 (ISBN 0-444-41496-7). Elsevier.

--Taxonomy of the Flowering Plants. (Illus.). 1977. Repr. of 1931 ed. lib. bdg. 60.00x (ISBN 3-7682-1169-X). Lubrecht & Cramer.

Johnson, A. P. Organization & Management of Hospital Laboratories. (Illus.). 1969. 6.95 o.p. (ISBN 0-407-34650-3). Butterworth.

Johnson, A. Ross. The Transformation of Communist Idealogy: The Yugoslav Case, 1945-1953. Griffith, William E., ed. (Studies in Communism, Revisionism & Revolution). 304p. 1973. 20.00x (ISBN 0-262-10012-6). MIT Pr.

Johnson, A. Wetherall. Created for Commitment. Date not set. 9.95 (ISBN 0-8423-0484-3). Tyndale.

Johnson, Alan F. Romans: The Freedom Letter, 2 vols. (Everyman's Bible Commentary Ser.). 1976. pap. 4.50 ea. Vol. 1 (ISBN 0-8024-2063-X). Vol. 2 (ISBN 0-8024-2064-8). Moody.

Johnson, Alan F., jt. ed. see Gundry, Stanley N.

Johnson, Alexander B. Guide to the Right Understanding of Our American Union. Repr. of 1957 ed. lib. bdg. 20.00x o.p. (ISBN 0-8371-0500-5, JOGU). Greenwood.

--Meaning of Words. Repr. of 1862 ed. lib. bdg. 15.75x (ISBN 0-8371-0501-3, JOMW). Greenwood.

--The Meaning of Words: Analysed into Words & Unverbal Things, & Unverbal Things Classified into Intellections, Sensations & Emotions. 1948. 12.50x (ISBN 0-686-30224-9). R S Barnes.

Johnson, Allan G. Social Statistics Without Tears. (Illus.). 1976. text ed. 19.95 (ISBN 0-07-032601-0, C); instructor's manual 15.00 (ISBN 0-07-032602-9). McGraw.

Johnson, Allen. Jefferson & His Colleagues. 1921. text ed. 8.50x (ISBN 0-686-83595-6). Elliots Bks.

--Stephen A. Douglas: A Study in American Politics. LC 77-98690. (American Scene Ser). 1970. Repr. of 1908 ed. lib. bdg. 55.00 (ISBN 0-306-71836-7). Da Capo.

Johnson, Alton C., jt. auth. see Schulz, Rockwell.

Johnson & Johnson Baby Products Company. The First Wondrous Year: You & Your Baby. (Illus.). 1979. 16.95 (ISBN 0-02-559530-X); pap. 11.95 (ISBN 0-02-077100-2). Macmillan.

Johnson, Andrew. Trial of Andrew Johnson, President of the U.S, 3 vols. in 2. LC 69-11326. (Law, Politics, & History Ser). 1970. Repr. of 1868 ed. Set. lib. bdg. 145.00 (ISBN 0-306-71184-2). Da Capo.

Johnson, Ann D., jt. auth. see Johnson, Spencer.

Johnson, Annabel & Johnson, Edgar. Bearcat. LC 60-9458. (gr. 7 up). 1960. PLB 10.89 (ISBN 0-06-022836-9, HarpJ). Har-Row.

--Black Symbol. LC 58-9780. (gr. 7 up). 1959. PLB 10.89 (ISBN 0-06-022846-6, HarpJ). Har-Row.

--Golden Touch. LC 63-10592. (gr. 7 up). 1963. PLB 10.89 (ISBN 0-06-022856-3, HarpJ). Har-Row.

--The Grizzly. LC 64-11831. (Illus.). (gr. 5-9). 1964. PLB 9.89 (ISBN 0-06-022871-7, HarpJ). Har-Row.

Johnson, Anne. Mosses of Singapore & Malaysia. 126p. 1980. pap. 7.50 o.p. (ISBN 0-8214-0547-0). Swallow.

Johnson, Arlee W., jt. auth. see Hughey, J. D.

Johnson, Arthur M. The Challenge of Change: The Sun Oil Company 1945-1977. (Illus.). 500p. 1983. 30.00x (ISBN 0-8142-0340-X). Ohio St U Pr.

Johnson, Arthur W. T H Manual of Bookbinding. (Illus.). 224p. 1981. pap. 9.95 (ISBN 0-393-56801-6). Norton.

Johnson, Audrey P. Nurse of the Thousand Islands. (YA) 1978. 6.95 (ISBN 0-685-85780-8, Avalon). Bouregy.

Johnson, Audreye E., ed. The Black Experience: Considerations for Health & Human Services. LC 82-84461. (Dialogue Bks.). 160p. 1983. 9.75 (ISBN 0-89881-014-0). Intl Dialogue Pr.

Johnson, B. C. The Atheist Debater's Handbook: Skeptics Bookshelf Ser. LC 81-80487. 135p. 1981. 10.95 (ISBN 0-87975-152-5); pap. 6.95 (ISBN 0-87975-210-6). Prometheus Bks.

Johnson, B. Lamar, ed. General Education in Two-Year Colleges. LC 81-48568. 1982. 7.95x (ISBN 0-87589-886-6, CC-40). Jossey-Bass.

Johnson, B. W. & DeWelt, Don. The Gospel of Mark. LC 76-1069. (The Bible Study Textbook Ser.). (Illus.). 1965. 14.30 o.s.i. (ISBN 0-89900-033-9). College Pr Pub.

Johnson, B. W., ed. People's New Testament with Notes, 1 vol. 12.95 (ISBN 0-89225-141-7). Gospel Advocate.

Johnson, Barbara, tr. see Derrida, Jacques.

Johnson, Barbara F. Delta Blood. 1977. pap. 3.50 (ISBN 0-380-00989-7, 63867-3). Avon.

--Echoes From the Hills. 464p. 1983. pap. 3.50 (ISBN 0-446-90834-7). Warner Bks.
--Homeward Winds the River. 1979. pap. 3.50 (ISBN 0-380-42952-7, 82016-1). Avon.
--Tara's Song. 1978. pap. 3.50 (ISBN 0-380-39123-6, 79954-5). Avon.
Johnson, Barbara M. Pilgrim on a Bicycle. LC 81-68637. 144p. 1982. 4.95 (ISBN 0-86693-001-9). B M Johnson.
Johnson, Barry L. & Garcia, Mary J. Conditioning: Fitness & Performance for Everyone. rev. ed. (Illus.). 1978. pap. text ed. 5.95 o.p. (ISBN 0-88408-104-4). Sterling Swift.
Johnson, Ben see Morrell, Janet M.
Johnson, Ben, tr. see Svevo, Italo.
Johnson, Ben C. An Evangelism Primer. LC 82-49021. 120p. 1983. pap. 4.95 (ISBN 0-8042-2039-5). John Knox.
Johnson, Ben E. How to Read Better & Enjoy It More. rev. ed. LC 80-81475. 228p. 1980. pap. 4.95 (ISBN 0-89081-257-8). Harvest Hse.
Johnson, Beryl. Advanced Embroidery Techniques. (Illus.). 144p. 1983. 22.50 (ISBN 0-7134-0085-4, Pub. by Batsford England). David & Charles.
Johnson, Bob & Bragg, Patricia. The Complete Triathlon Swim-Bike-Run: Distance Training Manual. (Illus.). 600p. 1982. 24.95 (ISBN 0-87790-029-9). Health Sci.
Johnson, Bonnie M. Communication: The Process of Organizing. 404p. 1981. pap. text ed. 12.95x (ISBN 0-89641-089-7). American Pr.
Johnson, Brad L. The Comic Collector's Handbook. LC 81-51037. (Illus.). 130p. (Orig.). 1983. pap. 5.95 (ISBN 0-686-30135-8). Zanon Pubns.
Johnson, Bradley T. Reports of Cases Decided by Chief Justice Chase in the Circuit Court of the United States for the Fourth Circuit: 1865-1869. facsimile ed. LC 75-75292. (American Constitutional & Legal History Ser.). 1972. Repr. of 1876 ed. lib. bdg. 75.00 (ISBN 0-306-71291-1). Da Capo.
Johnson, Brian & Hefferman, Terry. A Most Secret Place: Boscombe Down 1939-45. (Illus.). 288p. 1983. 19.95 (ISBN 0-86720-641-1). Sci Bks Intl.
Johnson, Brian, jt. auth. see Hoffmann, Thomas R.
Johnson, Brian, jt. auth. see Stein, Robert E.
Johnson, Brian F., ed. Transition Metal Clusters. LC 80-40496. 681p. 1980. 96.95x (ISBN 0-471-27817-3, Pub. by Wiley-Interscience). Wiley.
Johnson, Brooks. Andre Kertesz, Master of Photography. LC 82-72323. (Illus.). 64p. 1982. pap. 7.50 (ISBN 0-940744-38-4). Chrysler Museum.
Johnson, Brooks & Styron, Thomas. Still Modern After All These Years. LC 82-83632. (Illus.). 48p. (Orig.). 1982. pap. 6.00 (ISBN 0-940744-40-6). Chrysler Museum.
Johnson, Bruce. A Child's Comfort: Baby & Doll Quilts in American Folk Art. LC 76-24707. (Illus.). 1977. pap. 6.95 o.p. (ISBN 0-15-117185-8, Harv). HarBraceJ.
Johnson, Bruce, jt. auth. see Gillmer, Thomas.
Johnson, Bruce G., et al. Basic Steel Design. 2nd ed. 1980. text ed. 31.95 (ISBN 0-13-069344-8). P-H.
Johnson, Bruce L. Chinese Wand Exercise. LC 77-3534. (Illus.). 1979. pap. 4.50 o.p. (ISBN 0-688-08183-5, Quill). Morrow.
Johnson, Byron L. & Ewegen, Robert. B.S.-The Bureaucratic Syndrome. LC 82-3410. 176p. 1982. 10.95 (ISBN 0-88427-051-3, Dist. by Everest Hse). North River.
Johnson, C. Natural World: Chaos & Conservation. 1971. text ed. 11.50 o.p. (ISBN 0-07-032591-X, C); pap. text ed. 8.50 o.p. (ISBN 0-07-032590-1). McGraw.
--Practical Arithmetic: The Third "R". (Illus.). 1977. pap. 19.95 (ISBN 0-13-689273-6). P-H.
Johnson, C. C., jt. auth. see Durney, C. H.
Johnson, C. D. The Hammett Equation. LC 72-93140. (Chemistry Texts Ser). (Illus.). 180p. 1973. 29.95 (ISBN 0-521-20138-1). Cambridge U Pr.
Johnson, C. L. Analog Computer Techniques. 2nd ed. 1963. text ed. 24.50 o.p. (ISBN 0-07-032641-X, C). McGraw.
Johnson, C. R. Organic Synthesis, Vol. 57. 153p. 1977. 20.95 o.s.i. (ISBN 0-471-03235-2, Pub. by Wiley-Interscience). Wiley.
Johnson, C. W., et al. Basic Psychopathology: A Programmed Text. (Illus.). 350p. (Orig.). 1981. pap. 15.95 (ISBN 0-89335-155-5). SP Med & Sci Bks.
--Basic Psychopathology: A Programmed Text. 605p. 1981. soft bound 14.95 (ISBN 0-89335-155-5). Spectrum Pub.
--Basic Psychotherapeutics: A Programmed Text. 605p. 1980. pap. 17.50 (ISBN 0-89335-128-8). Spectrum Pub.
Johnson, Caesar, compiled by. To See a World in a Grain of Sand. LC 72-179257. (Illus.). 96p. 1972. boxed 5.50 (ISBN 0-8378-1789-7). Gibson.
Johnson, Carl, jt. auth. see Pasto, Daniel.
Johnson, Carl E., jt. auth. see Sparks, J. E.
Johnson, Carl G. Preaching Helps: Sermon Outlines, Illustrations & Poems. (Pocket Pulpit Library Ser). 1978. pap. 2.95 (ISBN 0-8010-5050-2). Baker Bk.
Johnson, Carlean. Six Ingredients or Less. (Illus.). 224p. pap. 8.95 (ISBN 0-942878-00-0). C J Bks.
Johnson, Carol R., jt. auth. see Pasto, Daniel J.
Johnson, Carolyn E. & Thew, Carol L., eds. Proceedings of the Second International Congress for the Study of Child Language, Vol. I. LC 82-16145. (Illus.). 614p. (Orig.). 1983. lib. bdg. 34.50 (ISBN 0-8191-2738-8); pap. text ed. 22.50 (ISBN 0-8191-2739-6). U Pr of Amer.
Johnson, Carroll B. Inside Guzman De Alfarache. (Publications in Modern Philology Ser.: Vol. 111). 1978. pap. 16.50x (ISBN 0-520-09569-3). U of Cal Pr.
--Madness & Lust: A Psychoanalytic Approach to Don Quixote. LC 82-10916. 252p. 1983. text ed. 22.50 (ISBN 0-520-04752-4). U of Cal Pr.
Johnson, Catherine E. TV Guide Index: 1978 to 1980 Supplement. LC 82-80797. 113p. 1982. pap. text ed. 41.00 (ISBN 0-9603684-1-8). Triangle Pubns.
--TV Guide Index: 1981 Supplement. LC 82-74385. 50p. 1983. pap. text ed. write for info. (ISBN 0-9603684-2-6). Triangle Pubns.
Johnson, Chalmers. Autopsy on People's War. LC 73-81201. (Quantum Bk.). 1974. 16.95x (ISBN 0-520-02516-4); pap. 2.85 (ISBN 0-520-02518-0). U of Cal Pr.
--Conspiracy at Matsukawa. LC 73-161998. (Illus.). 1972. 35.75x (ISBN 0-520-02063-4). U of Cal Pr.
--Revolutionary Change. 2nd ed. LC 81-85448. 232p. 1982. 17.50x (ISBN 0-8047-1144-5); pap. 6.95 (ISBN 0-8047-1145-3). Stanford U Pr.
Johnson, Charles W. The Nature of Vermont: Introduction & Guide to a New England Environment. LC 79-56774. (Illus.). 288p. 1980. text ed. 15.00x (ISBN 0-87451-182-8); pap. 9.95 (ISBN 0-87451-183-6). U Pr of New Eng.
Johnson, Chuck. The Greatest Packers of Them All. (Putnam Sports Shelf). (Illus.). (gr. 5 up). 1968. PLB 4.97 o.p. (ISBN 0-399-60215-1). Putnam Pub Group.
Johnson, Claudia D. & Johnson, Vernon E. Nineteenth-Century Theatrical Memoirs. LC 82-15576. 285p. 1982. lib. bdg. 35.00 (ISBN 0-313-23644-5, JNT/). Greenwood.
Johnson, Clay, jt. auth. see Christy, Joe.
Johnson, Clifford L., jt. auth. see Fulwood, Robinson.
Johnson, Clifton. Old Time Schools & School Books. (Illus.). 381p. 1982. Repr. of 1935 ed. 27.00x (ISBN 0-8103-4273-1). Gale.
Johnson, Crisfield. History of Washington County, New York Seventeen Thirty-Seven to Eighteen Seventy-Eight. 1979. Repr. of 1878 ed. deluxe ed. 30.00 o.p. (ISBN 0-932334-20-2). Heart of the Lakes.
Johnson, Crockett. Harold & the Purple Crayon. LC 55-7683. (Illus.). (gr. k-3). 1958. 7.64i (ISBN 0-06-022935-7, HarpJ); PLB 8.89 (ISBN 0-06-022936-5). Har-Row.
Johnson, Curt. The Morning Light. LC 76-50958. (Illus., Orig.). 1977. pap. 5.95x (ISBN 0-914140-02-7). Carpenter Pr.
Johnson, Curt & McLaughlin, Mark. Civil War Battles. (Illus.). 1977. 15.95 o.p. (ISBN 0-517-52633-6, 526336). Crown.
Johnson, Curtis D. Process Control Instrumentation Technology. 2nd ed. LC 81-10488. (Electronic Technology Ser.). 561p. 1982. text ed. 27.95x (ISBN 0-471-05789-4); solns. manual 11.00x (ISBN 0-471-86317-3). Wiley.
Johnson, Curtiss. Raymond E. Baldwin, Connecticut Statesman. Devaney, Sally, ed. LC 91-183874. 1972. deluxe edition 25.00 (ISBN 0-686-96724-0). Globe Pequot.
Johnson, D. French Society & the Revolution. LC 76-1136. (Past and Present Publications Ser.). 300p. 1976. 32.50 (ISBN 0-521-21275-8). Cambridge U Pr.
Johnson, D. & Johnson, J. Introductory Electric Circuit Analysis. 1981. 25.95 (ISBN 0-13-500835-2). P-H.
Johnson, D., jt. auth. see Rifenbark, Richard K.
Johnson, D. C., jt. auth. see Bishop, R. E.
Johnson, D. C. & Tinsley, J. D., eds. Informatics & Mathematics in Secondary Schools: Proceedings of the IFIP TC3 Working Conference, Bulgaria. 1978. 39.50 (ISBN 0-444-85160-7, North-Holland). Elsevier.
Johnson, D. E. & Hilburn, J. L. Rapid Practical Designs of Active Filters. LC 75-14074. 264p. 1975. 34.95x (ISBN 0-471-44304-2, Pub. by Wiley-Interscience). Wiley.
Johnson, D. E. & Johnson, J. R. Graph Theory: With Engineering Applications. 392p. 1972. 45.00x o.p. (ISBN 0-471-06709-1, Pub. by Wiley-Interscience). Wiley.
Johnson, D. G. Medieval Chinese Oligarchy. LC 76-44875. (Westview Special Studies on China & East Asia & Studies of the East Asian Institute, Columbia University). 1977. lib. bdg. 28.00x o.p. (ISBN 0-89158-140-5). Westview.
Johnson, D. Gale. The Soviet Impact on World Grain Trade. LC 77-78146. (British-North American Committee Ser.). 72p. 1977. 3.00 (ISBN 0-902594-30-3). Natl Planning.
--World Food Problems & Prospects. 1975. pap. 4.25 (ISBN 0-8447-3165-X). Am Enterprise.
Johnson, D. Gale & Brooks, Karen M. Prospects for Soviet Agriculture in the 1980's. LC 82-48625. (Publication Series on the Soviet Union in the 1980's). 224p. 1983. 15.00 (ISBN 0-253-34619-3). Ind U Pr.
--Prospects for Soviet Agriculture in the 1980's. LC 82-48625. (Midland Bks.: No. 300). 224p. 1983. pap. 7.95 (ISBN 0-253-20300-7). Ind U Pr.
Johnson, D. J. Topics in the Theory of Group Presentations. (London Mathematical Society Lecture Note Ser.: No. 42). (Illus.). 230p. (Orig.). 1980. pap. 32.50x (ISBN 0-521-23108-6). Cambridge U Pr.
Johnson, Dale L., ed. Class & Social Development: A New Theory of the Middle Class. (Class, State & Development Ser.: Vol. 1). (Illus.). 336p. 1982. 25.00 (ISBN 0-8039-0070-8). Sage.
Johnson, Dale L., jt. ed. see Chilcote, Ronald H.
Johnson, Dale S., ed. Readings in Financial Services: Environment & Professions. (Huebner School Ser.). 322p. (Orig.). 1982. pap. text ed. 12.00 (ISBN 0-943590-01-9). Amer College.
Johnson, Dallas, ed. see Read, Jenny.
Johnson, Daniel L. Starting Right, Staying Strong: A Guide to Effective Ministry. LC 82-22383. 108p. (Orig.). 1983. pap. 5.95 (ISBN 0-8298-0648-2). Pilgrim NY.
Johnson, Daphne & Ransom, Elizabeth. Family & School. 192p. 1983. text ed. 24.50x (ISBN 0-7099-2236-1, Pub. by Croom Helm Ltd England). Biblio Dist.
Johnson, Dave, ed. see Zimmerman, M. G.
Johnson, David E. Introduction to Filter Theory. (Illus.). 336p. 1976. 32.95 (ISBN 0-13-483776-2). P-H.
Johnson, David E. & Jayakumar, V. Operational Amplifier Circuits Design & Applications. (Illus.). 272p. 1982. 25.95 (ISBN 0-13-637447-6). P-H.
Johnson, David E. & Johnson, Johnny R. Mathematical Methods in Engineering & Physics. 208p. 1982. 29.95 (ISBN 0-13-561126-1). P-H.
Johnson, David E., jt. auth. see Hilburn, John L.
Johnson, David E., jt. auth. see Hillrurn, John.
Johnson, David E., et al. Basic Electric Circuit Analysis. LC 77-24210. (Illus.). 1978. ref. 32.95x (ISBN 0-13-060137-3). P-H.
--Digital Circuits & Microcomputers. LC 78-13244. (Illus.). 1979. ref. ed. 28.95 (ISBN 0-13-214015-2). P-H.
--A Handbook of Active Filters. (Illus.). 1980. text ed. 26.00 (ISBN 0-13-372409-3). P-H.
Johnson, David G., jt. ed. see Bressler, Rubin.
Johnson, David L. Structured Assembly Language for IBM Computers. (Illus.). 613p. 1982. pap. text ed. 19.95 (ISBN 0-88284-172-6); study guide 8.95 (ISBN 0-88284-182-3); instructor's manual avail. Alfred Pub.
Johnson, David N. Organ Teacher's Guide. 48p. 1971. pap. 2.75 (ISBN 0-8066-1119-7, 11-9326). Augsburg.
Johnson, David P., jt. auth. see Wortman, Julie A.
Johnson, David R. Policing the Urban Underworld: The Impact of Crime on the Development of the American Police, 1800-1887. LC 78-31220. 1979. 27.95 (ISBN 0-87722-148-0). Temple U Pr.
Johnson, David W. Educational Psychology. (Illus.). 1979. pap. 24.95 ref. ed. (ISBN 0-13-236760-2). P-H.
--Human Relations & Your Career: A Guide to Interpersonal Skills. (Illus.). 1978. 18.95 (ISBN 0-13-445601-7). P-H.
--Reaching Out: Interpersonal Effectiveness & Self-Actualization. 2nd ed. (Illus.). 320p. 1981. text ed. 20.95 (ISBN 0-13-753327-6); pap. text ed. 16.95 (ISBN 0-13-753319-5). P-H.
Johnson, David W. & Johnson, Frank P. Joining Together: Group Theory & Group Skills. 2nd ed. LC 74-23698. 480p. 1982. 17.95 (ISBN 0-13-510396-7). P-H.
Johnson, David W. & Johnson, Roger T. Learning Together & Alone: Cooperation, Competition, & Individualization. (Illus.). 224p. 1975. pap. text ed. 16.95 (ISBN 0-13-527945-3). P-H.
Johnson, David W., jt. auth. see Tjosvold, Dean.
Johnson, Deborah H., jt. auth. see Gelso, Charles J.
Johnson, Denis. The Incognito Lounge. 1982. 10.50 (ISBN 0-394-52347-4); pap. 5.95 (ISBN 0-394-70677-3). Random.
Johnson, Dennis, jt. auth. see Ruddle, Kenneth.
Johnson, Dewayne & Parks, Barbara A. Field Hockey. (Illus.). 79p. 1983. pap. text ed. 2.95x (ISBN 0-89641-091-9). American Pr.
Johnson, Dewayne J. & Haines, Joey. Track & Field. (Illus.). 78p. (Orig.). 1982. pap. text ed. 2.95x (ISBN 0-89641-093-5). American Pr.
Johnson, Dewayne J. & Oliver, Robert A. Racquetball. (Illus.). 75p. 1980. pap. text ed. 2.95x (ISBN 0-89641-045-5). American Pr.
Johnson, Dewayne J. & Riggs, Charles. Conditioning. (Illus.). 77p. 1982. pap. text ed. 2.95 (ISBN 0-89641-090-0). American Pr.
Johnson, Dewayne J., jt. auth. see Johnson, M. L.
Johnson, Diana L. Fantastic Illustration & Design in Britain: 1850-1930. (Illus.). 1980. 25.00 (ISBN 0-262-10021-5). MIT Pr.
Johnson, Diana L. & Landow, George P. Fantastic Illustration & Design in Britain, Eighteen Fifty to Nineteen Thirty. LC 78-70652. (Illus.). 1979. 25.00 o.p. (ISBN 0-686-25091-5); pap. 12.00 o.p. (ISBN 0-686-26247-6). Mus of Art RI.
Johnson, Diane. Lying Low. LC 82-40418. 304p. 1983. pap. 3.95 (ISBN 0-394-71376-1, Vin). Random.
--Terrorists & Novelists. LC 82-47818. 1982. 14.50 (ISBN 0-394-52161-7). Knopf.
Johnson, Don. Protean Body: A Rolfer's View of Human Flexibility. (Orig.). 1977. pap. 6.95i o.p. (ISBN 0-06-090552-2, CN 552, CN). Har-Row.
Johnson, Don & Patterson, Jack. Inside Bowling. LC 73-6476. (Inside Sports Ser.). (Illus.). 96p. 1973. 7.95 o.p. (ISBN 0-8092-8902-4); pap. 6.95 (ISBN 0-8092-8901-6). Contemp Bks.
Johnson, Donald C. Index to Southeast Asian Journals, 1975-1979: A Guide to Articles, Book Reviews, & Composite Works. 1982. lib. bdg. 38.00 (ISBN 0-8161-8564-6, Hall Reference). G K Hall.
--Index to Southeast Asian Journals, 1960-1974: A Guide to Articles, Book Reviews & Composite Works. 1977. lib. bdg. 57.00 (ISBN 0-8161-7891-7, Hall Reference). G K Hall.
Johnson, Donald J. Disinfection-Water & Wastewater. LC 74-14425. 1975. 39.95 o.p. (ISBN 0-250-40042-1). Ann Arbor Science.
Johnson, Donovan A. & Rising, Gerald R. Guidelines for Teaching Mathematics. 2nd ed. 560p. 1972. 21.95x o.p. (ISBN 0-534-00189-0). Wadsworth Pub.
Johnson, Dora E., jt. auth. see Smith, Robert E.
Johnson, Doris, jt. ed. see Myklebust, Helmer R.
Johnson, Doris M. Children's Toys & Books: Choosing the Best for All Ages from Infancy to Adolescence. (Illus.). 192p. 1982. 12.95 (ISBN 0-684-17767-6, ScribT). Scribner.
Johnson, Doris V., tr. see Mochulsky, Konstantin.
Johnson, Dorothy E. & King, Imogene M. Theory Development: What, Why, How? 86p. 1978. 5.95 (ISBN 0-686-38281-1, 15-1708). Natl League Nurse.
Johnson, Dorothy E. & Vestermark, Mary J. Barriers & Hazards in Counseling. LC 73-14990. (Orig.). 1970. pap. text ed. 12.95 (ISBN 0-395-04694-7). HM.
Johnson, Dorothy M. The Bloody Bozeman. 384p. 1983. pap. 9.95 (ISBN 0-87842-152-1). Mountain Pr.
--Bloody Bozeman: The Perilous Trail to Montana's Gold. Stewart, Robert, ed. (Illus.). 1977. 9.95 o.p. (ISBN 0-07-032576-6, GB). McGraw.
--The Hanging Tree. 1980. lib. bdg. 9.95 (ISBN 0-8398-2616-8, Gregg). G K Hall.
--Indian Country. 1979. 9.95 (ISBN 0-8398-2586-2, Gregg). G K Hall.
--Montana. LC 72-106927. (States of the Nation Bks). (Illus.). (gr. 7-11). 1971. PLB 5.99 o.p. (ISBN 0-698-30238-9, Coward). Putnam Pub Group.
--When You & I Were Young, Whitefish. 192p. 1982. 13.95 (ISBN 0-87842-149-1). Mountain Pr.
Johnson, Douglas, jt. auth. see Mettam, Roger S.
Johnson, Douglas E. & Samuels, Melvin L., eds. Cancer of the Genitourinary Tract: M. D. Anderson Clinical Conference on Cancer, 23rd. LC 79-2070. 338p. 1979. text ed. 38.00 (ISBN 0-89004-383-3). Raven.
Johnson, Douglass W., jt. auth. see Johnson, R. Winifred.
Johnson, Doyle P. Sociological Theory: Classical Founders & Contemporary Perspectives. LC 80-23441. 597p. 1981. text ed. 22.95 (ISBN 0-471-02915-7) tchrs.' ed. 4.50 (ISBN 0-471-08958-3). Wiley.
Johnson, E. Research Methods in Criminology & Criminal Justice. 1981. 22.95 (ISBN 0-13-774349-1). P-H.
Johnson, E. D. Charles Dickens: An Introduction to the Reading of His Novels. (Orig.). 1969. pap. text ed. 3.95 (ISBN 0-685-19710-7). Phila Bk Co.
Johnson, E. L. Integer Programming. LC 79-93152. (CBMS-NSF Regional Conference Ser.: No. 32). vii, 68p. 1980. pap. 10.00 (ISBN 0-89871-162-2). Soc Indus-Appl Math.
Johnson, E. M. & Kochhar, D. M., eds. Teratogenesis & Reproductive Toxicology. (Handbook of Experimental Pharmacology Ser.: Vol. 65). (Illus.). 400p. 1983. 116.00 (ISBN 0-387-11906-X). Springer-Verlag.
Johnson, E. Verner & Horgan, Joanne C. Museum Collection Storage. (Technical Handbooks for Museums & Monuments Ser.: No. 2). (Illus.). 56p. 1979. pap. 7.00 (ISBN 92-3-101632-6, U978, UNESCO). Unipub.
Johnson, Earl, Jr. Justice & Reform: The Formative Years of the OEO Legal Services Program. LC 73-83890. 456p. 1974. 14.50x (ISBN 0-87154-399-0). Russell Sage.
Johnson, Earl S. The Humanistic Teaching of Earl S. Johnson. Haas, John, ed. (The Academy of Independent Scholars Retrospections Ser.). 210p. 1983. lib. bdg. 20.00X (ISBN 0-86531-542-6). Westview.
Johnson, Earvin & Levin, Richard. Magic. (Illus.). 256p. 1983. 13.50 (ISBN 0-670-44804-4). Viking Pr.
Johnson, Ed. Old House Woodwork Restoration: How to Restore Doors, Windows, Walls, Stairs, Decorative Trim to Their Original Beauty. (Illus.). 208p. 1982. 19.95 (ISBN 0-13-634022-9); pap. 10.95 (ISBN 0-13-634014-8). P-H.
Johnson, Edgar, jt. auth. see Johnson, Annabel.
Johnson, Edgar, ed. see Dickens, Charles.
Johnson, Edna, et al. Anthology of Children's Literature. 5th ed. 1977. text ed. 25.50 (ISBN 0-395-24554-0). HM.

Johnson, Edward. Wonder-Working Providence of Sions Saviour in New England (1654) LC 74-5118. 256p. 1974. lib. bdg. 30.00x (ISBN 0-8201-1130-9). Schol Facsimiles.

Johnson, Edward D. The Washington Square Press: Handbook of Good English. Orig. Title: A Grammar Book. 320p. (Orig.). 1983. pap. 4.95 (ISBN 0-671-44294-5). WSP.

Johnson, Edward M. see Nelson, Robert S.

Johnson, Edward R. & Mann, Stuart H. Organization Development for Academic Libraries: An Evaluation of the Management Review & Analysis Program. LC 79-8289. (Contributions in Librarianship & Information Science: No. 28). (Illus.). 1980. lib. bdg. 25.00 (ISBN 0-313-21373-9, JMA/). Greenwood.

Johnson, Edwin. Restoring Antique Furniture. LC 81-50987. (Illus.). 160p. 1981. 12.95 (ISBN 0-8069-5430-2); lib. bdg. 15.69 (ISBN 0-8069-5431-0); pap. 6.95 (ISBN 0-8069-8998-X). Sterling.

Johnson, Elissa W. The Soul of Wit. 1978. 4.50 o.p. (ISBN 0-533-03169-9). Vantage.

Johnson, Ellen, ed. The Toy Library: A How-To Handbook. 82p. (Orig.). pap. text ed. 9.95 (ISBN 0-934140-18-9). Toys N Things.

Johnson, Ellen H., ed. American Artists on Art from 1940-1980. LC 80-8702. (Icon Editions Ser.). (Illus.). 256p. 1982. 17.25i (ISBN 0-06-433426-0, HarpT); pap. 9.95i (ISBN 0-06-430112-5, IN112, HarpT). Har-Row.

Johnson, Elmer D. Communication: An Introduction to the History of Writing, Printing, Books & Libraries. 4th ed. LC 73-83. 1973. 12.00 o.p. (ISBN 0-8108-0588-X). Scarecrow.

Johnson, Elmer H., ed. International Handbook of Contemporary Developments in Criminology, Vol. I: General Issues & the Americas; Volume II, Europe, Africa, the Middle East & Asia, 2 Vols. LC 82-6164. (Illus.). lib. bdg. 95.00 (ISBN 0-313-21059-4, JCR/). Greenwood.

Johnson, Elmer S. At Least Once. 1983. 9.95 (ISBN 0-533-05566-0). Vantage.

Johnson, Emilie. My China Odyssey. (Illus.). 192p. (Orig.). 1981. pap. 8.95x (ISBN 0-9605910-0-1). Silver Fox.

Johnson, Ernest F. Automatic Process Control. (Chemical Engineering Ser.). (Illus.). 1967. text ed. 23.00 o.p. (ISBN 0-07-032636-3, C). McGraw.

Johnson, Ernest N. Practical Electromyography. (Rehabilitation Medicine Library Ser.). (Illus.). 457p. 1980. lib. bdg. 41.00 o.p. (ISBN 0-683-04464-8). Williams & Wilkins.

Johnson, Eugene J. S. Andrea in Mantua: The Building. LC 74-30085. (Illus.). 220p. 1975. 36.50x (ISBN 0-271-01186-6). Pa St U Pr.

Johnson, Evelyne. Cow in the Kitchen. Klimo, Kate, ed. (Illus.). 24p. 1983. 5.75 (ISBN 0-671-46086-2, Little). S&S.

Johnson, Evelyne & Santoro, Christopher. A First Cookbook for Children: With Illustrations to Color. (Illus.). 48p. (Orig.). (gr. 4 up). 1983. pap. 2.25 (ISBN 0-486-24275-7). Dover.

Johnson, Ferne, ed. Start Early for an Early Start: You & the Young Child. LC 76-44237. 1976. pap. 8.00 o.p. (ISBN 0-8389-3185-5). ALA.

Johnson, Frank P., jt. auth. see Johnson, David W.

Johnson, Frederick, jt. ed. see MacNeish, Richard S.

Johnson, Fridolf. Mythical Beasts Coloring Book. (Illus.). 1976. pap. 2.00 (ISBN 0-486-23353-7). Dover.

Johnson, Fridolf, ed. Rockwell Kent. LC 81-47477. (Illus.). 352p. 1982. 60.00 (ISBN 0-394-41771-2). Knopf.

--Treasury of American Pen & Ink Illustration: 222 Drawings by 99 Artists, 1890-1930. (Illus.). 176p. 1982. pap. 6.00 (ISBN 0-486-24280-3). Dover.

Johnson, G. & Gentry, J. Finney & Miller's Principles of Accounting, Advanced. 6th ed. 1971. 29.95 (ISBN 0-13-317578-2). P-H.

--Finney & Miller's Principles of Accounting, Introductory. 8th ed. 1980. 25.95 (ISBN 0-13-317370-4); Pt. 1. working papers 10.95 (ISBN 0-13-317594-4); Part 2. working papers 10.95 (ISBN 0-13-317602-9); practice set 10.95 (ISBN 0-13-317636-3); student guide 10.95 (ISBN 0-13-317628-2). P-H.

Johnson, G. David. The Limits & Relationships of the Lutjanidae & Associated Families, Vol. 24. (Bulletin of the Scripps Institute of Oceanography). 1981. pap. 9.00x (ISBN 0-520-09642-8). U of Cal Pr.

Johnson, G. E., jt. auth. see Eary, Donald F.

Johnson, G. M., jt. ed. see Emerson.

Johnson, G. Orville, jt. auth. see Cruickshank, William M.

Johnson, Gail. Fabriscapes. (Illus.). 18p. 1981. pap. 5.00 (ISBN 0-943574-06-4). That Patchwork.

Johnson, Gale D. World Agriculture in Disarray. LC 72-94818. 304p. 1973. 18.95 o.p. (ISBN 0-312-89040-0). St Martin.

Johnson, Gary L. Son Songs for Christian Folk, 2 vols. Incl. Vol. I. pap. 1.50 (ISBN 0-87123-509-9, 280509); Vol. II. pap. 1.50 (ISBN 0-87123-532-3, 280532). 1975. pap. Bethany Hse.

Johnson, George C. Writing for the Twilight Zone. Mayer, Frederick J., ed. (Illus.). 130p. (Orig.). 1980. pap. 10.00 (ISBN 0-9605404-0-7); special limited edition, signed 50.00 (ISBN 0-686-36857-6). Outre House.

Johnson, Gerald W. America Grows Up: A History for Peter. (Illus.). (gr. 5 up). 1960. 10.50 (ISBN 0-688-21015-5). Morrow.

--The Cabinet. (Illus.). (gr. 7 up). 1966. PLB 9.12 (ISBN 0-688-31136-9). Morrow.

--Honorable Titan, a Biographical Study of Adolph S. Ochs. Repr. of 1946 ed. lib. bdg. 15.75x (ISBN 0-8371-3836-1, JOHT). Greenwood.

Johnson, Gilbert, ed. see Demura, Fumio & Ivan, Dan.

Johnson, Glen R. & Walker, Fred M. Army Staff Officer's Guide. 313p. 1975. 16.95 (ISBN 0-87201-046-5). Gulf Pub.

Johnson, Glenn & Maunder, Allen, eds. Rural Change: The Challenge for Agricultural Economists. LC 80-27966. 1981. 38.50x (ISBN 0-86598-043-8). Allanheld.

Johnson, Gordon H., jt. auth. see Hagen, Willis W.

Johnson, Guy. Save the Stratford Canal! (Illus.). 168p. 1983. 17.50 (ISBN 0-7153-8424-4). David & Charles.

Johnson, Guy B. Folk Culture on St. Helena Island, South Carolina. LC 68-5945. xxiv, 183p. Repr. of 1930 ed. 30.00x (ISBN 0-8103-5015-7). Gale.

Johnson, H. The International Book of Trees. (Illus.). 15.95 o.p. (ISBN 0-517-32257-9). Crown.

--Patterns of Pulmonary Interstitial Disease. (Illus.). 320p. 1983. 15.00 (ISBN 0-87527-218-5). Green.

Johnson, H. Earle. Hallelujah, Amen! The Story of the Handel & Haydn Society of Boston. (Music Ser.). (Illus.). 256p. 1981. Repr. of 1965 ed. lib. bdg. 25.00 (ISBN 0-306-79598-1). Da Capo.

Johnson, H. G. & Nobay, A. R., eds. Issues in Monetary Economics Proceedings of the 1972 Money Study Group Conference. (Illus.). 1974. 37.50x (ISBN 0-19-877021-9). Oxford U Pr.

Johnson, H. Wayne, ed. Rural Human Services: A Book of Readings. LC 79-91102. 228p. 1980. pap. text ed. 9.95 (ISBN 0-87581-248-1). Peacock Pubs.

Johnson, Harold V. General-Industrial Machine Shop. 1979. text ed. 21.20 (ISBN 0-87002-293-8); student guide 4.20 (ISBN 0-87002-295-4); visual masters 15.96 (ISBN 0-87002-054-4). Bennett IL.

--Technical Metals. rev. ed. (gr. 10-12). 1973. text ed. 19.96 (ISBN 0-87002-139-7); 6.40 o.p. wrbk. (ISBN 0-87002-147-8). Bennett IL.

Johnson, Harold V., ed. see Ray, J. Edgar.

Johnson, Harriett S., ed. see Coyne, Marla & Smith, Nancy.

Johnson, Harriett S., ed. see Schneck, Joshua J.

Johnson, Harriette C. & Goldberg, Gertrude S. Government Money for Everyday People. 1982. pap. 10.00 (ISBN 0-536-03867-8). Adelphi Univ.

Johnson, Harry, ed. Negotiating the Mainstream. 1978. text ed. 15.00 o.p. (ISBN 0-8389-0254-5). ALA.

Johnson, Harry G. On Economics & Society. LC 74-11625. xii, 356p. 1975. 21.00x (ISBN 0-226-40162-6); pap. 9.95 (ISBN 0-226-40163-4). U of Chicago Pr.

--Technology & Economic Interdependence. LC 75-34703. 200p. 1976. 25.00 (ISBN 0-312-78855-X). St Martin.

Johnson, Harry G. & Nobay, A. R. The Current Inflation. LC 73-171602. 1971. text ed. 26.00 (ISBN 0-312-17920-0). St Martin.

Johnson, Harry G., ed. The New Mercantilism. LC 74-82533. 128p. 1975. 26.00 (ISBN 0-312-56840-1). St Martin.

Johnson, Harry L., ed. State & Local Tax Problems. LC 69-10113. 1969. 14.50x (ISBN 0-87049-089-3). U of Tenn Pr.

Johnson, Helen, jt. auth. see Sussman, Ellen.

Johnson, Herbert J., jt. auth. see Hodge, Billy J.

Johnson, Honor. Small as a Resurrection. (Poetry Ser.: No. 20). 60p. 1982. pap. 5.95 (ISBN 0-918786-23-1). Lost Roads.

Johnson, Howard M. Planning & Financial Management for the School Principal. 1982. text ed. 24.95x (ISBN 0-8077-2719-9). Tchrs Coll.

Johnson, Hubert R. Who Then Is Paul? Chevy Chase Manuscripts, ed. LC 80-1406. 272p. 1981. lib. bdg. 22.25 (ISBN 0-8191-1364-6); pap. text ed. 11.75 (ISBN 0-8191-1365-4). U Pr of Amer.

Johnson, Hugh. Hugh Johnson's Modern Encyclopedia of Wine. (Illus.). Date not set. 25.95 (ISBN 0-671-45134-0). S&S.

--International Book of Trees. 1973. 29.95 o.p. (ISBN 0-671-21607-4). S&S.

--The Principles of Gardening. 1979. 29.95 o.p. (ISBN 0-671-24273-3). S&S.

--Wine. rev. ed. 1975. 17.95 (ISBN 0-671-21997-9). S&S.

--World Atlas of Wine. rev. ed. (Illus.). 1978. 35.00 (ISBN 0-671-24552-X). S&S.

Johnson, I., jt. auth. see Jorgensen, S. E.

Johnson, I. D. Advances in Clinical Nutrition. 500p. 1982. text ed. 49.00 (ISBN 0-85200-496-6, Pub. by MTP Pr England). Kluwer Boston.

Johnson, Ida Mae. Developing the Listening Skills. 1974. 5.95 (ISBN 0-914296-18-3). Activity Rec.

Johnson Institute. Chemical Dependency & Recovery Are a Family Affair. 1.95 o.p. (ISBN 0-686-92588-2). Hazelden.

Johnson, Irene. Prophecy Foretold-Fulfilled: Puzzle Book. (Illus.). 48p. 1983. pap. 1.50 (ISBN 0-87239-590-1, 2788). Standard Pub.

Johnson, Irene L. The Apostle Peter & His Writing. Sparks, Judith, ed. 48p. (Orig.). (gr. 7 up). 1983. pap. 1.50 (ISBN 0-87239-672-X, 2772). Standard Pub.

Johnson, Irvin E. Instant Mortgage-Equity: Extended Tables of Overall Rates. LC 80-7729. (Lexington Books Real Estate & Urban Land Economics Special Ser.). 464p. 1980. 24.95x (ISBN 0-669-03808-3). Lexington Bks.

--The Instant Mortgage Equity Technique. LC 72-6464. (Special Ser. in Real Estate & Urban Land Economics). 400p. 1972. 20.95x (ISBN 0-669-84749-6). Lexington Bks.

--Selling Real Estate by Mortgage Equity Analysis: Tools & Techniques for Marketing Investment Properties. LC 74-15543. (Special Ser. in Real Estate & Urban Land Economics). (Illus.). 544p. 1976. 20.95x (ISBN 0-669-95588-4). Lexington Bks.

Johnson, J., jt. auth. see Johnson, D.

Johnson, J. A. Automotive Diagnosis & Tune-Up. 1972. 13.95 o.p. (ISBN 0-07-032578-2, G); instructors' manual 2.00 o.p. (ISBN 0-07-032579-0). McGraw.

Johnson, J. C., ed. Plant Growth Regulators & Herbicide Antagonists: Recent Advances. LC 82-7966. (Chemical Technology Rev. 212). (Illus.). 303p. 1983. 45.00 (ISBN 0-8155-0915-4). Noyes.

Johnson, J. Douglas. Advertising Today. LC 78-15897. 416p. 1978. pap. text ed. 19.95 (ISBN 0-574-19355-3, 13-2355); instr's guide avail. (ISBN 0-574-19356-1, 13-2356). SRA.

Johnson, J. H. Urban Geography. 2nd ed. 217p. 1972. text ed. 18.50 (ISBN 0-08-016927-9); pap. text ed. 7.00 (ISBN 0-08-016928-7). Pergamon.

Johnson, J. M., jt. ed. see Douglas, J. D.

Johnson, J. R., jt. auth. see Johnson, D. E.

Johnson, Jack. Jack Johnson in the Ring & Out. LC 72-162515. (Illus.). ix, 259p. 1975. Repr. of 1927 ed. 27.00 o.p. (ISBN 0-8103-4047-X). Gale.

Johnson, James. Loneliness Is Not Forever. LC 79-368. 1979. 7.95 (ISBN 0-8024-4949-2). Moody.

--Profits, Power & Piety: An Inside Look at What Goes on Behind the Velvet Curtains of Christian Business. LC 72-83881. 1980. pap. 2.50 o.p. (ISBN 0-89081-240-3). Harvest Hse.

Johnson, James A. Automotive Diagnosis & Tune-up: A Text-Workbook. 2nd ed. (Automotive Technology Ser.). (Illus.). 1977. pap. text ed. 19.95 (ISBN 0-07-032593-6, G); instructor's manual 4.50 (ISBN 0-07-032594-4). McGraw.

--Group Therapy: A Practical Approach. 1963. 22.00 o.p. (ISBN 0-07-032632-0, HP). McGraw.

Johnson, James B. Daystar & Shadow. (Science Fiction Ser.). 1981. pap. 2.25 o.p. (ISBN 0-87997-605-5, UE1605, DAW Bks). DAW Bks.

Johnson, James B., jt. ed. see Comer, John C.

Johnson, James C., jt. auth. see Wood, Donald F.

Johnson, James F., et al. Applied Mathematics. 4th ed. 1975. text ed. 8.96 o.p. (ISBN 0-02-819070-X); tchr's ed. 11.40 o.p. (ISBN 0-02-819080-7). Glencoe.

Johnson, James H., jt. auth. see Williams, Thomas A.

Johnson, James L. Kinetics of Coal Gasification. LC 79-10439. 324p. 1979. 38.50x (ISBN 0-471-05575-1, Pub. by Wiley-Interscience). Wiley.

--Sepastian Agente Secreto. Lievano, Francisco, tr. 200p. 1977. pap. 3.95 (ISBN 0-311-37021-7). Casa Bautista.

Johnson, James W. Along This Way: The Autobiography of James Weldon Johnson. LC 72-8404. (Civil Liberties in American History). (Illus.). 450p. 1973. Repr. of 1933 ed. lib. bdg. 49.50 (ISBN 0-306-70539-7). Da Capo.

--Negro Americans, What Now? LC 72-8355. 103p. 1973. Repr. of 1934 ed. lib. bdg. 19.50 (ISBN 0-306-70531-1). Da Capo.

Johnson, James W., ed. Book of American Negro Poetry. rev. ed. LC 67-99475. 1969. pap. 1.45 (ISBN 0-15-613539-6, Harv). HarBraceJ.

Johnson, Jane. Maroni De Chypre. (Studies in Mediterranean Archaeology Ser.: LIX). 1980. text ed. 45.00x (ISBN 91-85058-94-7). Humanities.

--Sybil & the Blue Rabbit. LC 79-7904. (Illus.). 32p. (gr. 1-3). 1980. 8.95a o.p. (ISBN 0-385-15757-6); PLB 8.95a (ISBN 0-385-15758-4). Doubleday.

Johnson, Janeen A. Games to Improve Perceptual Skills of Pre-Schoolers: Ideas for Parents & Teachers. 1978. pap. text ed. 0.25 (ISBN 0-8134-2049-0, 2049); for 25 copies 4.38 (ISBN 0-686-82922-0). Interstate.

Johnson, Janet, jt. auth. see Jaslyn, Richard.

Johnson, Janet H., jt. auth. see Whitcomb, Donald D.

Johnson, Janet H., jt. auth. see Whitcomb, Donald S.

Johnson, Jeff, jt. ed. see Stokely, Jim.

Johnson, Jeffrey, jt. auth. see Childs, David.

Johnson, Jerrilou. Living Language: U. S. A. Culture Capsules for English As a Second Language Students. 1979. pap. text ed. 8.95 (ISBN 0-88377-152-7). Newbury Hse.

Johnson, Jerry M. Country Scrapbook. 1978. 16.95 o.p. (ISBN 0-671-22848-X); pap. 5.95 o.p. (ISBN 0-671-22895-1). S&S.

Johnson, Jim. Lasers. LC 80-17871. (A Look Inside Ser.). (Illus.). 48p. (gr. 4-12). 1981. PLB 14.25 (ISBN 0-8172-1400-3). Raintree Pubs.

Johnson, Joan. Excellent Cassandra: The Life & Times of the Dutchess of Chandos. 160p. 1981. text ed. 18.00x (ISBN 0-904387-76-3, 61071, Pub. by Sutton England). Humanities.

Johnson, Joan D. & Xanthos, Paul. Tennis. 5th ed. (Exploring Sports Ser.). 1983. pap. text ed. write for info. o.p. (ISBN 0-697-07071-9). Wm C Brown.

Johnson, Joe, jt. auth. see Racina, Thom.

Johnson, Joe D. The Granite, the Possible, & the Bending Fern. 38p. 1982. pap. 3.00 (ISBN 0-915564-01-7). Joe D Johnson.

Johnson, John E., jt. auth. see Salmon, Charles G.

Johnson, John E., illus. My First Book of Things. LC 78-64609. (Board Bks). (ps). 1979. 3.50 (ISBN 0-394-84128-X, BYR). Random.

Johnson, John E, Jr., ed. Current Trends in Morphological Techniques, Vols. II & III. 272p. 1981. Vol. II, 288p. 84.50 (ISBN 0-686-73486-6); Vol. III, 296p. 84.50 (ISBN 0-686-82889-5). CRC Pr.

Johnson, John M., jt. ed. see Douglas, Jack D.

Johnson, John W. American Legal Culture, 1908-1940. LC 80-1027. (Contributions in Legal Studies: No. 16). x, 185p. 1981. lib. bdg. 25.00 (ISBN 0-313-22337-8, JAM/). Greenwood.

Johnson, Johnny R., jt. auth. see Johnson, David E.

Johnson, Johnny R., jt. auth. see Hubbard, Thomas D.

Johnson, Joseph C., II. Scholars Before School. LC 74-140951. 1970. 9.95 (ISBN 0-87716-029-5, Pub. by Moore Pub Co). F Apple.

Johnson, Joseph E., III, jt. auth. see Cluff, Leighton E.

Johnson, Joseph T. Location & Trade Theory: Industrial Location, Comparative Advantage, & the Geographic Pattern of Production in the United States. (University of Chicago, Department of Geography Research Papers Ser.: No. 198). (Illus.). 107p. 1981. pap. 8.00 (ISBN 0-89065-105-1). U Chicago Dept Geog.

Johnson, Josephine W. Inland Island. LC 69-12090. 1969. 5.00 o.p. (ISBN 0-671-20177-8). S&S.

--Now in November. 1970. 5.95 o.p. (ISBN 0-671-20489-0). S&S.

--Seven Houses: A Memoir of Time & Places. (Illus.). 1973. 5.95 o.p. (ISBN 0-671-21454-3). S&S.

Johnson, Jotham. Inscriptions: Republican Magistri. (Excavations at Minturnae Ser.: Vol. 2). (Illus.). 138p. 1933. soft bound 7.00x (ISBN 0-686-11906-1). Univ Mus of U PA.

--Monuments of the Republican Forum. (Excavations at Minturnae Ser.: Vol. 1). (Illus.). 122p. 1935. bound 10.00xsoft (ISBN 0-686-11905-3). Univ Mus of U PA.

Johnson, Joy. Use of Groups in Schools: A Practical Manual for Everyone Who Works in Elementary & Secondary Schools. 137p. 1977. pap. text ed. 8.25 (ISBN 0-8191-0099-4). U Pr of Amer.

Johnson, Joyce. Bad Connections. LC 77-16367. 1978. 8.95 o.p. (ISBN 0-399-12122-6). Putnam Pub Group.

--Minor Characters. 262p. 1983. 13.95 (ISBN 0-395-32513-7). HM.

Johnson, Judith M. Victorian House-Keeping: A Combined Study of Restoration & Photography. Smith, Linda H., ed. 1978. pap. 4.95 (ISBN 0-936386-05-3). Creative Learning.

Johnson, June. Eight-Hundred Thirty Eight Ways to Amuse a Child: Crafts, Hobbies & Creative Ideas for the Child from Six to Twelve. Rev ed. LC 82-48801. 224p. (gr. 1-6). 1983. pap. 4.76i (ISBN 0-06-091047-X, CN 1047, CN). Har-Row.

Johnson, K. Research Designs in General Semantics. 298p. 1974. 58.00x (ISBN 0-677-14370-2). Gordon.

Johnson, K., jt. auth. see Morrow, K.

Johnson, Karen, jt. auth. see Korn, Errol R.

Johnson, Keith. Communicate in Writing: A Functional Approach to Writing Through Reading Comprehension. (English As a Second Language Bk.). 1981. pap. text ed. 5.50x (ISBN 0-582-74811-9); tchr's bk. 5.75x (ISBN 0-582-74848-8). Longman.

--Communicative Language Teaching: Problems of Syllabus Design & Methodology. (Illus.). 160p. 1981. pap. 11.95 (ISBN 0-08-025355-5). Pergamon.

Johnson, Ken. The Cheshire Cat. 336p. (Orig.). 1983. pap. 3.50 (ISBN 0-440-01264-3, Emerald). Dell.

Johnson, Kenneth A., ed. see American Academy of Orthopaedic Surgeons.

Johnson, Kenneth F. & Ogle, Nina M. Illegal Mexican Aliens in the United States: A Teaching Manual on Impact Dimensions & Alternative Futures. LC 78-62177. 1978. pap. text ed. 10.25 (ISBN 0-8191-0575-9). U Pr of Amer.

Johnson, Kenneth G., ed. see Conference on Research Designs in General Semantics, 1st, Pennsylvania State University.

Johnson, Kenneth G., et al. Nothing Never Happens: Exercises to Trigger Group Discussion & Promote Self-Discovery with Selected Readings. LC 72-91270. 352p. 1974. pap. text ed. 14.95x (ISBN 0-02-475140-5); tchr's ed. 12.95x (ISBN 0-02-475130-8). Macmillan.

Johnson, Kenneth M. Population & Retail Services in Nonmetropolitan America. (Rural Studies). 350p. 1983. softcover 25.00x (ISBN 0-86531-584-1). Westview.

Johnson, Kenneth P. & Jaenicke, Henry R. Evaluating Internal Control: Concepts, Guidelines, Procedures, Documentation. LC 79-23172. 649p. 1980. 55.95x (ISBN 0-471-05620-0, Ronald). Ronald Pr.

Johnson, Kent R. Behavioral Instruction: An Evaluative Review. LC 77-9258. 1977. pap. 5.00 o.p. (ISBN 0-912704-04-7). Am Psychol.
Johnson, L. D. Layman's Bible Book Commentary: Proverbs, Ecclesiastes, Song of Solomon, Vol. 9. LC 80-66543. 1982. 4.75 (ISBN 0-8054-1179-8). Broadman.
Johnson, L. M., jt. auth. see Steffensen, Arnold J.
Johnson, L. M., jt. auth. see Steffensen, Arnold R.
Johnson, L. Murphy, jt. auth. see Steffensen, Arnold R.
Johnson, Larry, jt. auth. see Toboldt, William K.
Johnson, Laura R. The Teddy Bear ABC. (Illus.). 1982. pap. 6.95 (ISBN 0-914676-86-5, Star & Eleph Bks). Green Tiger Pr.
Johnson, Lee A. Mary Hallock Foote. (United States Author Ser.). 1980. lib. bdg. 12.95 (ISBN 0-8057-7231-6, Twayne). G K Hall.
Johnson, Lee W. & Riess, R. Dean. Introduction to Linear Algebra. LC 80-19984. (Mathematics Ser.). (Illus.). 352p. 1981. text ed. 21.95 (ISBN 0-201-03392-5). A-W.
--Numerical Analysis. LC 81-15019. (Mathematics Ser.). (Illus.). 448p. 1982. text ed. 25.95 (ISBN 0-201-10392-3). A-W.
Johnson, Leland G. Biology. 1983. text ed. write for info. (ISBN 0-697-04706-7); instr's. manual avail. (ISBN 0-697-04732-6); study guide avail. (ISBN 0-697-04733-4); lab manual (complete version) avail. (ISBN 0-697-04721-0); lab manual (short version) avail. (ISBN 0-697-04736-9); transparencies avail. (ISBN 0-697-04908-6); slides avail. (ISBN 0-697-04909-4). Wm C Brown.
Johnson, Leon J. Introductory Soil Science: A Study Guide & Laboratory Manual. (Illus.). 1979. pap. text ed. 11.95x (ISBN 0-02-361120-0). Macmillan.
Johnson, Leonard R. Gastrointestinal Physiology. 2nd ed. LC 80-25206. (Illus.). 173p. 1981. text ed. 16.95 (ISBN 0-8016-2532-7). Mosby.
Johnson, Leroy F. & Cooper, Rodney H. File Techniques for Data Base Organization in Cobol. (P-H Software Ser.). (Illus.). 384p. 1981. text ed. 24.95 (ISBN 0-13-314039-3). P-H.
Johnson, Leroy F. & Jankowski, William C. Carbon-Thirteen: NMR Spectra. LC 78-14357. (Illus.). 500p. 1978. Repr. of 1972 ed. lib. bdg. 34.00 (ISBN 0-88275-733-4). Krieger.
Johnson, Leslie & Schade, Charlene. Rhythmic Aerobex: Workbook. 98p. 1982. 22.95 (ISBN 0-9610234-0-6). Rhythmic Aerobex.
Johnson, Lewis D., jt. auth. see Gravanis, Michael B.
Johnson, Lois. Lollipop Lexicon. 1979. 4.50 o.p. (ISBN 0-682-49338-4). Exposition.
Johnson, Lois V., jt. auth. see Bany, Mary A.
Johnson, Lois W. Aaron's Christmas Donkey. LC 74-79364. (Illus.). 32p. (gr. 1 up). 1974. 3.95 o.p. (ISBN 0-8066-1425-0, 10-0120). Augsburg.
Johnson, Luke T. Decision Making in the Church: A Biblical Model. LC 82-17675. 112p. 1983. pap. 5.95 (ISBN 0-8006-1694-4). Fortress.
Johnson, Lynwood A. & Montgomery, Douglas C. Operations Research in Production Planning, Scheduling, & Inventory Control. LC 73-17331. 525p. 1974. text ed. 38.50x (ISBN 0-471-44618-1). Wiley.
Johnson, Lynwood A., jt. auth. see Montgomery, Douglas C.
Johnson, M. Bruce, jt. auth. see Machan, Tibor R.
Johnson, M. Bruce, ed. Resolving the Housing Crisis. (Pacific Institute on Public Policy Research Ser.). 448p. 1982. prof ref 26.00x (ISBN 0-88410-381-1). Ballinger Pub.
Johnson, M. Bruce, jt. ed. see Hyman, Allen.
Johnson, M. Clemens. A Review of Research Methods in Education. 1977. 24.50 (ISBN 0-395-30641-8); Instr's. manual 1.90 (ISBN 0-395-30642-6). HM.
Johnson, M. H., jt. ed. see Edinin, M.
Johnson, M. H., jt. ed. see Edwards, R. G.
Johnson, M. L. & Johnson, Dewayne J. Badminton. (Illus.). 67p. 1981. pap. text ed. 2.95x (ISBN 0-89641-061-7). American Pr.
--Volleyball. (Illus.). 51p. 1981. pap. text ed. 2.95x (ISBN 0-89641-057-9). American Pr.
Johnson, Manly. Virginia Woolf. LC 72-79944. (Literature and Life Ser.). 1973. 11.95 (ISBN 0-8044-2424-1). Ungar.
Johnson, Margaret. Divorce Is A Family Affair. 128p. 1983. pap. 4.95 (ISBN 0-310-45831-5). Zondervan.
--Eighteen: No Time to Waste. 144p. (gr. 10 up). 1971. pap. 2.75 (ISBN 0-310-26672-6). Zondervan.
Johnson, Margaret, jt. auth. see Hawes, Carolyn.
Johnson, Margaret H., jt. auth. see Quible, Zane K.
Johnson, Margo & Wertheimer, Michael. The Psychology Teacher's Resource Book: First Course. 3rd ed. (Orig.). 1979. pap. 14.50x (ISBN 0-912704-52-7). Am Psychol.
Johnson, Marilyn E. see Riley, Matilda W., et al.
Johnson, Marion. A Personal Bouquet: An Idea Book for Miniature Flower Arrangements. 1983. 12.95 (ISBN 0-517-54788-0, C N Potter Bks). Crown.
Johnson, Marion L. Functional Administration in Physical & Health Education. LC 76-13089. (Illus.). 1977. text ed. 21.95 o.p. (ISBN 0-395-20635-9); instr's. manual 1.35 o.p. (ISBN 0-395-20636-7); study guide 10.50 o.p. (ISBN 0-395-20637-5). HM.
Johnson, Mark, jt. auth. see Lakoff, George.
Johnson, Marlys C. & Thompson, Linda J. Dollars for Scholars Student Aid Catalog: New Hampshire Edition. Citizen's Scholarship Foundation of America, ed. (Dollars for Scholars Student Aid Catalogs Ser.). 100p. (Orig.). 1982. pap. text ed. 5.95 (ISBN 0-87866-193-X, 6193). Petersons Guides.
Johnson, Martha P. Mystery at Winter Lodge. Schroeder, Howard, ed. LC 81-3303. (Roundup Ser.). (Illus.). 48p. (gr. 3 up). 1981. lib. bdg. 7.95 (ISBN 0-89686-152-X); pap. 3.95 (ISBN 0-89686-160-0). Crestwood Hse.
Johnson, Martha S., jt. auth. see Lahey, Benjamin B.
Johnson, Martin. Safari: A Saga of the African Blue. LC 72-170251. (Tower Bks). (Illus.). x, 294p. 1972. Repr. of 1928 ed. 34.00x (ISBN 0-8103-3934-X). Gale.
--Through the South Seas with Jack London. (Illus.). 1976. Repr. of 1913 ed. 15.00 (ISBN 0-915046-07-5). Wolf Hse.
Johnson, Martin L., jt. auth. see Ashlock, Robert B.
Johnson, Mary F. Visual Workouts: A Collection of Art-Making Problems. (Illus.). 160p. 1983. pap. text ed. 13.95 (ISBN 0-13-942664-7). P-H.
Johnson, Mary M. & Forbes, Judy. Historic Colonial French Dress: A Guide to Re-Creating North American French Clothing. (Illus.). 140p. (Orig.). 1982. pap. 7.50 (ISBN 0-9609026-0-0). Ouabache Pr.
Johnson, Maxwell O. The Military as an Instrument of U.S. Policy in Southwest Asia: The Rapid Deployment Joint Task Force, 1979-1982. (Replica Edition Ser.). 135p. 1982. softcover 16.00x (ISBN 0-86531-952-9). Westview.
Johnson, Merle D. A Bibliography of the Works of Mark Twain, Samuel Langhorne Clemens. rev. & enl. ed. LC 71-138153. (Illus.). 274p. 1972. Repr. of 1935 ed. lib. bdg. 25.00x (ISBN 0-8371-5610-6, JOMT). Greenwood.
Johnson, Michael & Mackworth-Young, Robin. Tune & Repair Your Own Piano. LC 78-51046. (Illus.). 1978. 3.95 (ISBN 0-15-191383-8). HarBraceJ.
Johnson, Michael A. The Earth Spins While I Stand Still. 1981. cancelled 4.50 (ISBN 0-8062-1756-1). Carlton.
Johnson, Mike, ed. Poland, Solidarity & Self-Management. 216p. (Orig.). 1982. cancelled (ISBN 0-946097-03-8); pap. cancelled (ISBN 0-946097-01-1). Heretic Bks.
Johnson, Mildred. How to Solve Word Problems in Algebra: A Solved Problem Approach. (Orig.). 1976. pap. 4.95 (ISBN 0-07-032620-7, SP). McGraw.
Johnson, Miriam M., jt. auth. see Stockard, Jean.
Johnson, Mohamed I. The World & the Sickle Cell Gene: A Study in Health Education. (Illus.). 150p. 1982. 15.00 (ISBN 0-932426-15-8); pap. text ed. 7.50 (ISBN 0-932426-16-6). Trado-Medic.
Johnson, Mohamed L. World & the Sickle Cell Gene: A Study in Health Education. (Illus.). 150p. 1982. 15.00x (ISBN 0-932426-15-8, Trado-Medic Bks); pap. 7.50 (ISBN 0-932426-16-6, Trado-Medic Bks). Conch Mag.
Johnson, N. State & Government in the Federal Republic of Germany: The Executive at Work. (Governments of Western Europe Ser.). 240p. 1983. 35.00 (ISBN 0-08-030188-6); pap. 17.50 (ISBN 0-08-030190-8). Pergamon.
Johnson, N. L., jt. auth. see Elderton, W. P.
Johnson, Nancy. How to Insure Your Child's Success in School. Taylor, Judy, ed. LC 82-62372. (Illus.). 200p. 1983. pap. 15.00 (ISBN 0-911625-00-3). M Murach & Assoc.
Johnson, Nancy, jt. auth. see Sterbenz, Carol E.
Johnson, Nancy A. Current Topics in Language: Introductory Readings. (Orig.). 1976. pap. text ed. 11.95 (ISBN 0-316-46761-8). Little.
Johnson, Nancy P. Sources of Compiled Legislative Histories: Bibliography of Government Documents, Periodical Articles & Books, 1st Congress - 96th Congress. (AALL Publications Ser.: No. 14). iv, 146p. 1979. loose-leaf in vinyl, 3-ring binder 35.00x (ISBN 0-8377-0112-0). Rothman.
Johnson, Ned K. Character Variation & Evolution of Sibling Species in the Empidonax Difficilis-Flavescens Complex (Aves: Tyrannidae) (University of California Publications in Zoology: Vol. 112). 1980. monograph 15.00x (ISBN 0-520-09599-5). U of Cal Pr.
Johnson, Nels. Islam & the Meaning of Politics in Palestine Nationalism. 200p. 1983. 19.50 (ISBN 0-7103-0021-2). Routledge & Kegan.
Johnson, Nora. You Can Go Home Again: An Intimate Journey. LC 82-45252. 288p. 1982. 15.95 (ISBN 0-385-15856-4). Doubleday.
Johnson, Norman & Kotz, Samuel. Urn Models & Their Application: An Approach to Modern Discrete Probability Theory. LC 76-58846. (Wiley Series in Probability & Mathematical Statistics). 402p. 1977. 49.95x (ISBN 0-471-44630-0, Pub. by Wiley-Interscience). Wiley.
Johnson, Norman H. & Galin, Saul. The Complete Kitten & Cat Book. LC 78-20168. (Illus.). 1979. 13.95i o.p. (ISBN 0-06-012134-3, HarpT). Har-Row.
Johnson, Norman L., jt. auth. see Elandt-Johnson, Regina C.
Johnson, Norman L., jt. auth. see Kotz, Samuel.
Johnson, O. An Essay on West African Therapeutics. Singer, Philip & Titus, Elizabeth A., eds. 1982. 17.50 o.p. (ISBN 0-932426-09-3); lib. bdg. 39.50 (ISBN 0-932426-19-0). Trado-Medic.
Johnson, O. C. Robert Owen in the United States. (Historical Ser.: No. 6). 5.00 o.p. (ISBN 0-89977-043-6). Am Inst Marxist.
Johnson, O. H., jt. auth. see Elonka, Stephen M.
Johnson, Olaf A. Fluid Power for Industrial Use: Hydraulics, 2 Vols. LC 80-12953. 224p. 1981. Vol. I. 9.50 (ISBN 0-89874-243-9); Vol. II. lib. bdg. write for info (ISBN 0-89874-048-7). Krieger.
Johnson, Oliver A. Skepticism & Cognitivism: A Study in the Foundations of Knowledge. LC 77-91743. 1979. 23.75x (ISBN 0-520-03620-4). U of Cal Pr.
Johnson, Oliver A., jt. auth. see Beatty, J. L.
Johnson, Overton. Route Across the Rocky Mountains. Winter, William H., ed. LC 77-87648. (The American Scene Ser). (Illus.). 200p. 1972. Repr. of 1932 ed. lib. bdg. 29.50 (ISBN 0-306-71780-8). Da Capo.
Johnson, Owen. Lawrenceville Stories. LC 67-25392. (gr. 5 up). 1967. 7.50 o.p. (ISBN 0-671-41074-1). S&S.
Johnson, P. & Stolberg, D., eds. Teacher's Manual to P-H Sports Series. 1973. pap. 1.25 o.p. (ISBN 0-13-696005-7). P-H.
Johnson, P., jt. ed. see Crook, M. A.
Johnson, P. S. Co-Operative Research in Industry: An Economic Study. 232p. 1973. 18.95x o.s.i. (ISBN 0-470-44620-X). Halsted Pr.
Johnson, Pat & Van Tuyl, Barbara. Horse Called Bonnie. (Orig.). (RL 5). 1971. pap. 1.95 (ISBN 0-451-11982-7, AJ1982, Sig). NAL.
Johnson, Patricia H., ed. see Van Tuyl, Barbara.
Johnson, Patricia J., jt. auth. see Burns, Kenneth R.
Johnson, Paul. Enemies of Society. LC 76-54230. 1977. 9.95 o.p. (ISBN 0-689-10798-6). Atheneum.
--Ireland: Land of Troubles. (Illus.). 224p. 1982. 14.50 (ISBN 0-8419-0758-7). Holmes & Meier.
--Modern Times. LC 82-48836. 544p. 1983. 22.07 (ISBN 0-06-015159-5, HarpT). Har-Row.
--The National Trust Book of British Castles. LC 77-10261. (Illus.). 1978. 20.00 o.p. (ISBN 0-399-12091-2). Putnam Pub Group.
Johnson, Paul, jt. auth. see Richards, Larry.
Johnson, Paul B. From Sticks & Stones: Personal Adventures in Mathematics. LC 74-23322. (Illus.). 552p. 1975. text ed. 20.95 (ISBN 0-574-19115-1, 13-6005); instr's guide avail. (ISBN 0-574-19116-X, 13-6006). SRA.
Johnson, Paul C. Peripheral Circulation. LC 77-26858. 369p. 1978. 60.00 o.p. (ISBN 0-471-44637-8, Pub. by Wiley Medical). Wiley.
Johnson, Paul C. & Reinhardt, Richard W. San Francisco-As It Is, As It Was. LC 77-80891. (Illus.). 1979. 19.95 o.p. (ISBN 0-385-09882-0). Doubleday.
Johnson, Paul E. A Shopkeeper's Millennium: Society & Revivals in Rochester, N. Y. 1815 to 1837. 1979. 10.95 (ISBN 0-8090-8654-9, AmCen); pap. 5.25 (ISBN 0-8090-0136-5). Hill & Wang.
Johnson, Paul R. Quotations from Chairman Falwell. (Illus.). 34p. (Orig.). 1983. pap. 1.95x (ISBN 0-910097-01-1). Marco & Johnson.
Johnson, Paul R. & Eaves, Thomas F. Gays & the New Right: A Debate. Garrison, Clay, ed. (Illus.). 145p. (Orig.). 1983. 4.95x (ISBN 0-910097-03-8); pap. 4.95. Marco & Johnson.
Johnson, Peter. Boating Facts & Feats. LC 76-1163. (Illus.). 1979. pap. 7.95 o.p. (ISBN 0-8069-8860-6). Sterling.
Johnson, Peter, jt. auth. see Bannister, Anthony.
Johnson, Peter, jt. auth. see Dupain, Max.
Johnson, Phillip E. Elements of Criminal Due Process. (Criminal Justice Ser.). 1975. pap. text ed. 13.95 o.s.i. (ISBN 0-685-99579-8); pap. text ed. write for info o.s.i. (ISBN 0-8299-0620-7). West Pub.
Johnson, Phyllis, jt. auth. see Martin, David.
Johnson, Phyllis, tr. see Giono, Jean.
Johnson, R. Condemned to Die: Life Under Sentence of Death. 1981. pap. 15.00 (ISBN 0-444-99089-5). Elsevier.
--Jane Austen: Her Life, Work, Family & Critics. LC 74-6375. (Jane Austen Ser., No. 69). 1974. lib. bdg. 45.95x (ISBN 0-8383-1748-0). Haskell.
--Shelley-Leigh Hunt: How Friendship Made History. LC 72-3431. (Studies in Shelley, No. 25). 1972. Repr. of 1929 ed. lib. bdg. 56.95x (ISBN 0-8383-1536-4). Haskell.
--Volcanism in Australasia. 1976. 57.50 (ISBN 0-444-41462-2). Elsevier.
--The Women Novelists. LC 72-3467. (Studies in Fiction, No. 34). 1972. Repr. of 1918 ed. lib. bdg. 37.95x (ISBN 0-8383-1496-1). Haskell.
Johnson, R. & Cox, R. Electrical Wiring: Design & Construction. 1981. Repr. 21.95 (ISBN 0-13-247650-9). P-H.
Johnson, R., jt. auth. see Camille, A.
Johnson, R., jt. auth. see Comyn, J.
Johnson, R., ed. Leigh Hunt. LC 73-115182. (English Literature Ser., No. 33). 1970. Repr. of 1896 ed. lib. bdg. 45.95x (ISBN 0-8383-1010-9). Haskell.
Johnson, R., et al. Critical Issues in Modern Religion. 1973. pap. 16.95 (ISBN 0-13-193979-3). P-H.
Johnson, R. E. Juvenile Delinquency & Its Origins. LC 78-67263. (ASA Rose Monograph). (Illus.). 1979. 27.95 (ISBN 0-521-22477-2); pap. 8.95 (ISBN 0-521-29516-5). Cambridge U Pr.
Johnson, R. H. & Blair, J. A. Logical Self Defense. 1980. pap. text ed. 9.95 o.p. (ISBN 0-07-082348-0). McGraw.
Johnson, R. H. & Spalding, J. M. Disorders of the Autonomic Nervous System. (Contemporary Neurology Ser.: No. 11). 300p. 1974. 25.00x o.p. (ISBN 0-8036-5030-2). Davis Co.
Johnson, R. H., jt. auth. see Forrest, E.
Johnson, R. W. The Long March of the French Left. 350p. 1981. 26.00x (ISBN 0-312-49645-1). St Martin.
Johnson, R. W., jt. ed. see Allen, Christopher.
Johnson, R. W., jt. ed. see Lee, R. D.
Johnson, R. Winifred & Johnson, Douglass W. Introduction to Nursing Care. 1976. text ed. 13.95 (ISBN 0-07-032595-2, G); manual 5.00tchr's (ISBN 0-07-032596-0). McGraw.
Johnson, Ralph W. & Brown, Gardner M. Cleaning Up Europe's Waters: Economics, Management, Policies. LC 76-23193. 1976. 39.95 o.p. (ISBN 0-275-56930-6). Praeger.
Johnson, Ramond. The Rio Grande. LC 80-53849. (Rivers of the World Ser.). PLB 12.68 (ISBN 0-382-06521-2). Silver.
Johnson, Ray C. Mechanical Design Synthesis: Creative Design & Optimization. 2nd ed. LC 77-10974. 360p. 1978. lib. bdg. 21.50 (ISBN 0-88275-612-5). Krieger.
Johnson, Ray E., ed. The Politics of Division, Partition, & Unification. LC 75-23973. (Special Studies). (Illus.). 1976. 25.95 o.p. (ISBN 0-275-55660-3). Praeger.
Johnson, Raymond B., jt. ed. see Lukash, William M.
Johnson, Rees. Wills-Probate Procedure for Oregon. 2nd ed. (Illus.). 1983. pap. write for info (ISBN 0-88908-814-4). Self Counsel Pr.
Johnson, Rex. Communication: Key to Your Parents. LC 78-61874. 1978. pap. 2.95 (ISBN 0-89081-157-1, 1571). Harvest Hse.
Johnson, Richard & McLennan, Gregor, eds. Making Histories: Studies in History Writing & Politics. 384p. 1982. 35.00x (ISBN 0-8166-1164-5); pap. 15.95 (ISBN 0-8166-1165-3). U of Minn Pr.
Johnson, Richard, et al. Algebra One: A Two Part Course. (gr. 9-12). 1977. First Book. text ed. 15.20 (ISBN 0-201-14300-3, Sch Div); Second Book. text ed. 15.20 (ISBN 0-201-14302-X); Course A. tchr's guide 19.76 (ISBN 0-201-14301-1); Course B. tchr's guide 19.76 (ISBN 0-201-14303-8); blackline masters avail. A-W.
Johnson, Richard A. & Wichern, Dean W. Applied Multivariate Statistical Analysis. 750p. 1982. 38.95 (ISBN 0-13-041400-X). P-H.
Johnson, Richard A., jt. auth. see Bhattacharyya, Gouri K.
Johnson, Richard A., et al. Theory & Management of Systems. 3rd ed. (Management Ser). (Illus.). 544p. 1973. text ed. 26.95 (ISBN 0-07-032634-7, C); instructor's manual 25.00 (ISBN 0-07-032635-5). McGraw.
Johnson, Richard B., et al. Town Meeting Time: A Handbook of Parliamentary Law. 1962. 8.95 o.p. (ISBN 0-316-46736-7). Little.
Johnson, Richard C., jt. auth. see Jasik, Henry.
Johnson, Richard E., et al. Elementary Algebra. 1981. 21.95 (ISBN 0-8053-5052-7); study guide by Lucille Groenke 8.95 (ISBN 0-8053-5054-3, 800A00); instr's. guide 4.95 (ISBN 0-8053-5053-5). Benjamin-Cummings.
--Algebra & Trigonometry: With Answers. (gr. 9-12). 1975. text ed. 18.04 (ISBN 0-201-03423-9, Sch Div); tchr's ed. 22.56 (ISBN 0-201-03424-7). A-W.
--Algebra: With Answers. rev. ed. (gr. 9-12). 1975. text ed. 18.04 (ISBN 0-201-04652-0, Sch Div); tchr's ed. 22.56 (ISBN 0-201-03422-0). A-W.
--College Algebra. 2nd ed. LC 72-94886. 562p. 1973. pap. text ed. 21.95 (ISBN 0-8465-3396-0); tchr's guide 4.95 (ISBN 0-8465-3397-9, 53397); study guide 4.95 (ISBN 0-8465-0297-6). Benjamin-Cummings.
Johnson, Richard R., ed. Directory of Evaluation Consultants. LC 80-67499. (Orig.). 1981. pap. 8.95 o.p. (ISBN 0-87954-035-4). Foundation Ctr.
Johnson, Rita B., jt. auth. see Johnson, Stuart R.
Johnson, Robert & Toch, Hans, eds. The Pains of Imprisonment. (Illus.). 352p. 1982. 25.00 (ISBN 0-8039-1902-6); pap. 12.50 (ISBN 0-8039-1903-4). Sage.
Johnson, Robert, jt. ed. see Sheahan, Desmond.
Johnson, Robert A. He: Understanding Masculine Psychology. 1977. pap. 2.84i (ISBN 0-06-080415-7, P415, PL). Har-Row.
--Mechanical Filters in Electronics. (Series on Filters: Design, Manufacturing & Applications). 400p. 1983. 39.50x (ISBN 0-471-08919-2, Pub. by Wiley-Interscience). Wiley.
Johnson, Robert A. & Pease, Ralph W. Police Report Writing. (HBJ Criminal Justice Ser.). 160p. 1982. pap. text ed. 9.95 (ISBN 0-15-570708-6, HC). HarBraceJ.
Johnson, Robert B. Henry de Montherlant. (World Authors Ser.: No. 37). 15.95 (ISBN 0-8057-2626-8, Twayne). G K Hall.

Johnson, Robert B. & Johnson, eds. The Black Resource Guide: A National Black Directory. 3rd ed. LC 82-83692. (Illus., Orig.). 1983. pap. 15.00 (ISBN 0-9608374-0-X). Black Resource.

Johnson, Robert C. John Heywood. (English Authors Ser.). 13.95 (ISBN 0-8057-1260-7, Twayne). G K Hall.

Johnson, Robert C., et al, eds. Commons Debates 1628, 4 vols. Incl. Introduction & Reference Materials,Vol.1. 18.50x (ISBN 0-300-02033-3); Vol. II. 17 March-19 April 1628. 45.00x (ISBN 0-300-01946-7); Vol. III. 21 April-27 May 1628. 50.00x (ISBN 0-300-02048-1); Vol. IV. May 28 - June 26, 1628. (Illus.). 1978. 50.00x (ISBN 0-300-02050-3). LC 75-43321. 1977. Set. 113.50x (ISBN 0-300-02161-5). Yale U Pr.

Johnson, Robert F. Subjective Realities: Seven Bay Area Artists. LC 82-71808. (Illus.). 46p. 1982. pap. 7.00 o.p. (ISBN 0-88401-041-4). Fine Arts Mus.

Johnson, Robert K. Francis Ford Coppola. (Filmmakers Ser.). 1977. lib. bdg. 11.95 (ISBN 0-8057-9252-X, Twayne). G K Hall.

--Neil Simon. (United States Authors Ser.). 228p. 1983. lib. bdg. 15.95 (ISBN 0-8057-7387-8, Twayne). G K Hall.

Johnson, Robert M. & Tibbits, Patricia. Basic Industrial Mathematics, Metric Edition. (Illus.). 1979. pap. text ed. 17.95 (ISBN 0-07-032671-1, G); answers to even numbered problems 6.00 (ISBN 0-07-032672-X). McGraw.

Johnson, Robert S. Messiaen. LC 74-81434. (Illus.). 1975. 36.50x (ISBN 0-520-02812-0). U of Cal Pr.

Johnson, Roberta. Carmen Laforet. (World Authors Ser.). 1981. lib. bdg. 14.95 (ISBN 0-8057-6443-7, Twayne). G K Hall.

Johnson, Rodney D. & Siskin, Bernard R. Quantitative Techniques for Business Decisions. (Illus.). 544p. 1976. 26.95 (ISBN 0-13-746990-X). P-H.

Johnson, Roger, commentary by. Scores: An Anthology of New Music. LC 80-53302. (Illus.). 450p. 1981. pap. text ed. 18.95 (ISBN 0-02-871190-4). Schirmer Bks.

Johnson, Roger A., ed. Views from the Pews: Christian Beliefs & Attitudes. LC 82-18237. 272p. 1983. pap. 14.95 (ISBN 0-8006-1695-2, 1-1695). Fortress.

Johnson, Roger T., jt. auth. see Johnson, David W.

Johnson, Ron. The Early Sculpture of Picasso, 1901-1914. LC 75-23795. (Outstanding Dissertations in the Fine Arts - 20th Century). (Illus.). 1976. lib. bdg. 41.00 o.s.i. (ISBN 0-8240-1990-3). Garland Pub.

Johnson, Ron & Bone, Jan. Understanding the Film. LC 75-20875. (Illus.). 248p. 1976. pap. 9.25 (ISBN 0-8174-2903-4, Amphoto). Watson-Guptill.

--Understanding the Film: An Introduction to Film Appreciation. (Illus.). 296p. 1981. pap. 11.95 (ISBN 0-8174-6330-5, Amphoto). Waston-Guptill.

Johnson, Ronald. Eyes & Objects. LC 75-37296. pap. 4.00 (ISBN 0-912330-34-1, Dist. by Inland Bk). Jargon Soc.

Johnson, Ronald C. George Gascoigne. (English Authors Ser.). lib. bdg. 13.95 (ISBN 0-8057-1212-7, Twayne). G K Hall.

Johnson, Ronald C. & Medinnus, Gene R. Child Psychology: Behavior & Development. 3rd ed. LC 73-22298. 562p. 1974. text ed. 26.95x (ISBN 0-471-44624-6); tests 7.95x (ISBN 0-471-44631-9). Wiley.

Johnson, Ronald C., jt. auth. see Day, R. A., Jr.

Johnson, Ronald C., jt. auth. see Medinnus, Gene R.

Johnson, Ross H. & Winn, Paul R. Quantitative Methods for Management. LC 75-25239. (Illus.). 448p. 1976. text ed. 26.50 (ISBN 0-395-20633-2); instr's. manual with solutions 5.50 (ISBN 0-395-20634-0). HM.

Johnson, Ross H., jt. auth. see Ficek, Edmund F.

Johnson, Rossiter, ed. A Dictionary of Biographies of Authors Represented in the Authors Digest Series: With a Supplemental List of Later Titles & a Supplementary Biographical Section. LC 71-167011. 476p. 1974. Repr. of 1927 ed. 47.00x (ISBN 0-8103-3876-9). Gale.

--A Dictionary of Famous Names in Fiction, Drama, Poetry, History & Art. LC 75-167012. 1974. Repr. of 1908 ed. 47.00x (ISBN 0-8103-3875-0). Gale.

Johnson, Roxanna M. The Picture Communication Symbols. 3rd ed. (Illus.). 118p. 1982. 3 ring bdg. 36.00 (ISBN 0-9609160-0-8). Mayer-Johnson.

Johnson, Ruby E. From the Heart of a Mother. LC 82-8218. 1982. pap. 3.95 (ISBN 0-8024-5090-3). Moody.

Johnson, Rudolph, Jr. Opium. (Novel - Adventure Ser.). 232p. 1981. 11.95 (ISBN 0-938952-00-5). Mona Pub.

Johnson, Russell T., et al, eds. Advances in Sugarbeet Production: Principles & Practices. LC 75-137094. 1971. 16.50x (ISBN 0-8138-1415-4). Iowa St U Pr.

Johnson, Sahnny. Getting to Know the Japanese. Sebeok, Thomas, ed. (Non-Verbal Communication Ser.). 128p. (gr. 10-12). 1982. pap. text ed. 12.95 o.p. (ISBN 0-88377-241-8). Newbury Hse.

Johnson, Sally P., ed. Princesses: Sixteen Stories about Princesses. LC 62-14318. (Illus.). (ps-3). 1962. PLB 10.89 o.p. (ISBN 0-06-023041-X, HarpJ). Har-Row.

Johnson, Samuel. Diaries, Prayers & Annals. McAdam, E. L., Jr., et al, eds. (Works of Samuel Johnson Ser.: Vol. 1). 1958. 37.50x (ISBN 0-300-00733-7). Yale U Pr.

--Idler & the Adventurer. Bate, W. J., et al, eds. (Works of Samuel Johnson Ser.: Vol. 2). (Illus.). 1963. 45.00x (ISBN 0-300-00294-7). Yale U Pr.

--Johnson on Shakespeare, 2 vols. Sherbo, Arthur, ed. (Works of Samuel Johnson Ser.: Vol. 7 & 8). 1968. Set. 75.00x (ISBN 0-300-00605-5). Yale U Pr.

--Journey to the Western Islands of Scotland. Lascelles, Mary, ed. LC 57-11918. (Works of Samuel Johnson Ser.: Vol. 9). 1971. 22.50x (ISBN 0-300-01251-9). Yale U Pr.

--Lives of the English Poets, 2 vols. (World's Classics Ser.). Vol. 1. 14.95 (ISBN 0-19-250083-X); Vol. 2. 8.95 o.p. (ISBN 0-19-250084-8). Oxford U Pr.

--Poems. McAdam, E. L., Jr. & Milne, George, eds. (Works of Samuel Johnson Ser.: Vol. 6). (Illus.). 1965. 37.50x (ISBN 0-300-00734-5). Yale U Pr.

--The Poems of Samuel Johnson. 2nd ed. Smith, David N. & McAdam, Edward, eds. (Oxford English Texts Ser.). 1974. 37.95x (ISBN 0-19-812702-2). Oxford U Pr.

--Political Writings: The Works of Samuel Johnson, Vol. 10. Greene, Donald J., ed. LC 57-11918. (Illus.). 1977. 45.00x (ISBN 0-300-01593-3). Yale U Pr.

--Rambler, 3 Vols. Bate, W. J. & Strauss, Albrecht, eds. (Works of Samuel Johnson Ser.: Nos. 3, 4 & 5). 1969. Set. 80.00x (ISBN 0-300-01157-1). Yale U Pr.

--Rasselas & Essays. Peake, Charles, ed. (Routledge English Texts). 1971. pap. 4.95 (ISBN 0-7100-4507-7). Routledge & Kegan.

--Samuel Johnson: Selected Writings. Cruttwell, Patrick, ed. 1982. pap. 5.95 (ISBN 0-14-043033-4). Penguin.

--Selected Essays from the Rambler, Adventurer & Idler. Bate, W. J., ed. LC 68-27747. (Works of Samuel Johnson Ser). 1968. 35.00x (ISBN 0-300-00364-1); pap. 6.95x (ISBN 0-300-00016-2, Y207). Yale U Pr.

Johnson, Samuel see Boswell, James.

Johnson, Sandee S. Cadences: The Jody Call Book, No. 1. 180p. (Orig.). 1983. lib. bdg. 10.95 (ISBN 0-938936-13-1). Daring Pr.

Johnson, Sandra. The CUPPI (Circumstances Undetermined Pending Police Investigaion) 1979. 8.95 o.s.i. (ISBN 0-440-01190-6, E Friede). Delacorte.

Johnson, Sandy. Walk a Winter Beach. 1983. pap. 3.50 (ISBN 0-440-19485-7). Dell.

Johnson, Scott D. A Computer System for Checking Proofs. Stone, Harold, ed. LC 82-6990. (Computer Science: Artificial Intelligence Ser.: No. 12). 280p. 1983. 44.95 (ISBN 0-8357-1343-1, Pub. by UMI Res Pr). Univ Microfilms.

Johnson, Sheila K. Idle Haven: Community Building Among the Working-Class Retired. LC 72-145786. (California Studies in Urbanization & Environmental Studies). 1971. 27.50x (ISBN 0-520-01909-1). U of Cal Pr.

Johnson, Sherman E. The Year of the Lord's Favor: Preaching the Three-Year Lectionary. 300p. 1983. pap. 13.95 (ISBN 0-8164-2359-8). Seabury.

Johnson, Sidney M. & Kavanagh, Thomas C. Design of Foundations for Buildings. LC 68-18576. (Modern Structure Ser.). 1968. 32.00 o.p. (ISBN 0-07-032583-9, P&RB). McGraw.

Johnson, Simon, jt. auth. see Sherman, Theodore A.

Johnson, Skip. Offering. 1979. pap. 3.50 (ISBN 0-934040-03-6). Quality Ohio.

Johnson, Sonia. From Housewife to Heretic. LC 80-2964. 408p. 1983. pap. 8.95 (ISBN 0-385-17494-2, Anch). Doubleday.

Johnson, Spencer & Johnson, Ann D. Value of Caring. 1979. 12.23 (ISBN 0-686-98163-4). Western Pub.

--Value of Courage. 1979. 12.23 (ISBN 0-686-98164-2). Western Pub.

--Value of Dedication. 1979. 12.23 (ISBN 0-686-98165-0). Western Pub.

--Value of Determination. 1979. 12.23 (ISBN 0-686-98166-9). Western Pub.

--Value of Fantasy. 1979. 12.23 (ISBN 0-686-98167-7). Western Pub.

--Value of Foresight. 1979. 12.23 (ISBN 0-686-98168-5). Western Pub.

--Value of Friendship. 1979. 12.23 (ISBN 0-686-98169-3). Western Pub.

--Value of Giving. 1979. 12.23 (ISBN 0-686-98170-7). Western Pub.

--Value of Helping. 1979. 12.23 (ISBN 0-686-98171-5). Western Pub.

--Value of Honesty. 1979. 12.23 (ISBN 0-686-98172-3). Western Pub.

--Value of Humor. 1979. 12.23 (ISBN 0-686-98173-1). Western Pub.

--Value of Kindness. 1979. 12.23 (ISBN 0-686-98174-X). Western Pub.

--Value of Learning. 1979. 12.23 (ISBN 0-686-98175-8). Western Pub.

--Value of Love. 1979. 12.23 (ISBN 0-686-98177-4). Western Pub.

--Value of Patience. 1979. 12.23 (ISBN 0-686-98178-2). Western Pub.

--Value of Saving. 1979. 12.23 (ISBN 0-686-98179-0). Western Pub.

--Value of Understanding. 1979. 12.23 (ISBN 0-686-98180-4). Western Pub.

Johnson, Spencer, jt. auth. see Blanchard, Kenneth.

Johnson, Stanley R. & Hassan, Zahair A. Demand Systems Estimation: Methods & Applications. (Illus.). 152p. 1983. pap. text ed. 15.00 (ISBN 0-8138-0431-0). Iowa St U Pr.

Johnson, Stephen. First Person Singular: Living the Good Life Alone. 1978. pap. 2.95 (ISBN 0-451-11350-0, AE1350, Sig). NAL.

--The Roman Forts of the Saxon Shore. LC 76-1301. (Illus.). 224p. 1976. 21.50 o.p. (ISBN 0-312-68985-3). St Martin.

Johnson, Stuart E. The Military Equation in Northeast Asia. (Studies in Defense Policy). 1979. pap. 4.95 (ISBN 0-8157-4689-X). Brookings.

Johnson, Stuart R. & Johnson, Rita B. Developing Individualized Instructional Material. pap. text ed. cancelled o.p. (ISBN 0-88250-403-7). Westinghouse Learn.

Johnson, Susan. First Aid for Kids. (Illus.). 128p. 1981. spiral bound 7.95 (ISBN 0-8256-3227-7, Quick Fox). Putnam Pub Group.

Johnson, Sylvia A. Animals of the Deserts. LC 75-27754. (Wildlife Library). (Illus.). 28p. (gr. 4 up). 1976. PLB 5.95g (ISBN 0-8225-1279-3). Lerner Pubns.

--Animals of the Grasslands. LC 75-27755. (Wildlife Library). (Illus.). 28p. (gr. 4 up). 1976. PLB 5.95g (ISBN 0-8225-1280-7). Lerner Pubns.

--Animals of the Mountains. LC 75-27756. (Wildlife Library). (Illus.). 28p. (gr. 4 up). 1976. PLB 5.95g (ISBN 0-8225-1277-7). Lerner Pubns.

--Animals of the Polar Regions. LC 75-27753. (Wildlife Library). (Illus.). 28p. (gr. 4 up). 1976. PLB 5.95g (ISBN 0-8225-1281-5). Lerner Pubns.

--Animals of the Temperate Forests. LC 75-27757. (Wildlife Library). (Illus.). 28p. (gr. 4 up). 1976. PLB 5.95g (ISBN 0-8225-1276-9). Lerner Pubns.

--Animals of the Tropical Forests. LC 75-27758. (Wildlife Library). (Illus.). 28p. (gr. 4 up). 1976. PLB 5.95g (ISBN 0-8225-1278-5). Lerner Pubns.

--Beetles. LC 82-7230. (Lerner Natural Science Bks.). (Illus.). 48p. (gr. 4-10). 1982. lib. bdg. 8.95g (ISBN 0-8225-1476-1). Lerner Pubns.

--Crabs. LC 82-10056. (Natural Science Bks.). (Illus.). 48p. (gr. 4-10). 1982. PLB 8.95g (ISBN 0-8225-1471-0). Lerner Pubns.

--Inside an Egg. LC 81-17235. (Lerner Natural Science Bks.). (Illus.). 48p. (gr. 4-10). 1982. PLB 8.95g (ISBN 0-8225-1472-9). Lerner Pubns.

--Mushrooms. LC 82-212. (Lerner Natural Science Bks.). (Illus.). 48p. (gr. 4-10). 1982. PLB 8.95g (ISBN 0-8225-1473-7). Lerner Pubns.

--Penguins. LC 80-28180. (Lerner Natural Science Bks.). (gr. 4-10). 1981. PLB 8.95g (ISBN 0-8225-1453-2). Lerner Pubns.

--Silkworms. LC 82-250. (Lerner Natural Science Bks.). (Illus.). 48p. (gr. 4-8). 1982. PLB 8.95g (ISBN 0-8225-1478-8). Lerner Pubns.

--Snails. LC 82-10086. (Lerner Natural Science Bks.). (Illus.). 48p. (gr. 4-10). 1982. PLB 8.95g (ISBN 0-8225-1475-3). Lerner Pubns.

Johnson, Sylvia A., jt. auth. see Dallinger, Jane.

Johnson, Sylvia L., ed. see Lovelace, Alice.

Johnson, T. B. & Barnes, R. J., eds. Application of Computers & Operations in the Mineral Industry: 17th International Symposium. LC 82-70016. (Illus.). 806p. 1982. text ed. 35.00x (ISBN 0-89520-293-X). Soc Mining Eng.

Johnson, T. H., jt. auth. see Miller, Perry.

Johnson, T. W., Jr. & Sparrow, F. K., Jr. Fungi in Oceans & Estuaries. (Illus.). 1970. pap. 40.00 (ISBN 3-7682-0076-0). Lubrecht & Cramer.

Johnson, Tharveal T. Neo-Slaves. 1979. 4.50 o.p. (ISBN 0-533-03825-1). Vantage.

Johnson, Theodore O. An Analytical Survey of the Fifteen Two-Part Inventions by J. S. Bach. LC 81-43826. (Illus.). 108p. (Orig.). 1982. lib. bdg. 18.25 (ISBN 0-8191-2582-2); pap. text ed. 7.00 (ISBN 0-8191-2583-0). U Pr of Amer.

Johnson, Thomas, jt. auth. see Heyne, Paul.

Johnson, Thomas, jt. auth. see Heyne, Paul T.

Johnson, Thomas A. & Misner, Gordon. The Police & Society: An Environment for Collaboration & Confrontation. (Illus.). 416p. 1982. 20.95 (ISBN 0-13-684076-0). P-H.

Johnson, Thomas C. The Life of Robert Lewis Dabney. 1977. 15.95 (ISBN 0-85151-253-4). Banner of Truth.

Johnson, Thomas H., jt. ed. see Miller, Perry.

Johnson, Thomas M. Collecting the Edged Weapons of the Third Reich, 4 vols. Bradach, Wilfrid, tr. LC 75-15486. (Illus.). Vol. 1. 25.00 (ISBN 0-9600906-1-4); Vol.1. pap. 15.00 (ISBN 0-686-96899-9); Vol. 2. 18.50 (ISBN 0-9600906-2-2); Vol. 3. 20.00 (ISBN 0-9600906-3-0); Vol. 4. 25.00 (ISBN 0-9600906-4-9). T M Johnson.

--World War II German War Booty. LC 82-90691. (Illus.). 1982. pap. 15.00 (ISBN 0-9600906-7-3). T M Johnson.

Johnson, Thomas W. & Stinson, John E. Managing Today & Tomorrow. LC 77-76123. (Illus.). 1978. text ed. 19.95 (ISBN 0-201-03487-5); instr's man. 3.95 (ISBN 0-201-03488-3). A-W.

Johnson, Thomas W., jt. auth. see Christenson, Christina.

Johnson, Thompson. Endocrine Surgery: BIMR 2. 1983. text ed. 39.95 (ISBN 0-407-02317-8). Butterworth.

Johnson, Timothy E. Investment Principles. LC 77-13345. (Illus.). 1978. ref. 22.95 (ISBN 0-13-504506-1). P-H.

--Investment Principles. 2nd ed. (Illus.). 480p. 1983. 23.95 (ISBN 0-13-504522-3). P-H.

Johnson, Toni O. Synge: The Medieval & the Grotesque. LC 82-8762. (Irish Literary Studies: No. 11). 218p. 1983. text ed. 27.50x (ISBN 0-389-20307-6). B&N Imports.

Johnson, U. Alexis & Packard, George R. The Common Security Interests of Japan, The United States & NATO. 38p. pap. 6.00x (ISBN 0-87855-873-X). Transaction Bks.

Johnson, Una, et al. Krishna Reddy: A Retrospective. (Illus.). 78p. (Orig.). 1981. pap. 10.00 (ISBN 0-89062-138-1, Pub by Bronx Museum Arts). Pub Ctr Cult Res.

Johnson, Uwe. Third Book About Achim. LC 67-12273. (Helen & Kurt Wolff Bk). 1967. 5.75 o.p. (ISBN 0-15-189901-0). HarBraceJ.

Johnson, V. A. Karl Lark-Horovitz, Pioneer in Solid State Physics. LC 77-91464. (Men of Physics Ser.). 1969. 24.00 (ISBN 0-08-006581-3); pap. 10.75 (ISBN 0-08-006580-5). Pergamon.

Johnson, Vance. Heaven's Tableland: The Dust Bowl Story. LC 73-20453. (FDR & the Era of the New Deal Ser.). (Illus.). 288p. 1974. Repr. of 1947 ed. lib. bdg. 37.50 (ISBN 0-306-70606-7). Da Capo.

Johnson, Vernon. I'll Quit Tomorrow. Rev. ed. 10.95 o.p. (ISBN 0-686-92259-X, 8021). Hazelden.

Johnson, Vernon E., jt. auth. see Johnson, Claudia D.

Johnson, Vicki, jt. auth. see Adams, Patricia.

Johnson, Vivienne. What Makes Arith-Me-Tick? (gr. 3-6). 1982. 6.95 (ISBN 0-86653-086-X, GA 437). Good Apple.

Johnson, W., jt. auth. see Clement, Preston.

Johnson, W. R. Darkness Visible: A Study of Vergil's Aeneid. LC 74-82845. 1976. 23.00x (ISBN 0-520-02942-9); pap. 7.50x (ISBN 0-520-03848-7). U of Cal Pr.

--The Idea of Lyric: Lyric Modes in Ancient & Modern Poetry. Rosenmeyer, Thomas G., ed. LC 81-3384. (Eidos; Studies in Classical Kinds: Vol. 1). 214p. 1983. pap. 7.95 (ISBN 0-520-04821-0). U of Cal Pr.

Johnson, W. W. The Spanish West. LC 76-1423. (The Old West). (Illus.). (gr. 5 up). 1976. 17.28 (ISBN 0-8094-1535-6, Pub. by Time-Life). Silver.

Johnson, Wallace. A Fresh Look at Patriotism. 131p. 1976. pap. 3.95 (ISBN 0-8159-5515-4). Devin.

Johnson, Walter. August Strindberg. (World Authors Ser.). 1976. lib. bdg. 12.95 (ISBN 0-8057-6250-7, Twayne). G K Hall.

--The Battle Against Isolation. LC 72-3376. (FDR & the Era of the New Deal Ser.). 270p. 1973. Repr. of 1944 ed. lib. bdg. 35.00 (ISBN 0-306-70480-3). Da Capo.

Johnson, Walter, ed. Journals of Gilbert White. 1st u.s. ed. 1971. pap. 4.95 o.p. (ISBN 0-262-60003-X). MIT Pr.

Johnson, Walter, tr. see Strindberg, August.

Johnson, Walter, tr. & intros by see Strindberg, August.

Johnson, Walter, tr. see Strindberg, August.

Johnson, Walter C. Transmission Lines & Networks. (Electronic & Electrical Engineering Ser.). 1950. text ed. 35.00 (ISBN 0-07-032580-4, C). McGraw.

Johnson, Walter C., jt. auth. see Clement, Preston R.

Johnson, Walter D., jt. ed. see Blumhagen, Kathleen O.

Johnson, Walter K., ed. National Conference on Environmental Engineering, 1982. LC 82-72214. 784p. 1982. pap. text ed. 56.00 (ISBN 0-87262-311-4). Am Soc Civil Eng.

Johnson, Walter R. Fires of Oakhurst. 1980. pap. 2.95 (ISBN 0-451-11100-1, AE1100, Sig). NAL.

--The Lion of Oakhurst. (Orig.). 1979. pap. 2.95 (ISBN 0-451-11686-0, AE1686, Sig). NAL.

--Oakhurst. (Orig.). 1978. pap. 2.50 (ISBN 0-451-11480-9, AE1480, Sig). NAL.

Johnson, Ward. Caring Is What Counts. (Illus.). 40p. (ps-3). Date not set. 5.95 (ISBN 0-910313-05-9). Parker Bro.

Johnson, Wayne & Olson, Richard P. Each Day a Gift. LC 82-8043. 224p. 1982. 10.50 (ISBN 0-688-01331-7). Morrow.

Johnson, Wayne G. Theological Method in Luther & Tillich: Law-Gospel & Correlation. LC 80-5691. 204p. 1982. lib. bdg. 21.75 (ISBN 0-8191-1895-8); pap. text ed. 10.75 (ISBN 0-8191-1896-6). U Pr of Amer.

Johnson, Wayne L. Ray Bradbury. LC 79-4825. (Recognitions Ser.). 1980. 11.95 (ISBN 0-8044-2426-8); pap. 5.95 (ISBN 0-8044-6318-2). Ungar.

Johnson, Wendell S., jt. auth. see Danziger, Marlies K.

Johnson, Wendell S., jt. ed. see Danziger, Marlies K.

Johnson, Wesley M. & Maxwell, John A. Rock & Mineral Analysis. 2nd ed. LC 81-1659. (Chemical Analysis Ser.). 489p. 1981. 63.00x (ISBN 0-471-02743-X, Pub. by Wiley-Interscience). Wiley.

Johnson, Willard E. & Sherwood, Peter B., eds. Geothermal Energy: Turn on the Power! (Transactions Ser.: Vol. 6). (Illus.). 546p. 1982. 33.00 (ISBN 0-934412-56-1). Geothermal.

Johnson, Willard, Jr. Poetry & Speculation of the Rg Veda. LC 80-14040. 175p. 1981. 21.75x (ISBN 0-520-02560-1). U of Cal Pr.

Johnson, Willard L., jt. auth. see Robinson, Richard.

Johnson, William. Baja California. LC 72-85157. (American Wilderness Ser). (Illus.). (gr. 6 up). 1972. lib. bdg. 15.96 (ISBN 0-8094-1161-X, Pub. by Time-Life). Silver.

--Sketches of the Life & Correspondences of Nathanael Green, 2 vols. LC 78-119063. 516p. 1973. Repr. of 1822 ed. Set. lib. bdg. 65.00 o.p. (ISBN 0-306-71953-3). Da Capo.

Johnson, William W. The Forty-Niners. LC 73-88997. (The Old West). (Illus.). (gr. 5 up). 1974. 17.00 (ISBN 0-8094-1472-4, Pub. by Time-Life). Silver.

Johnson, Willis L., ed. Directory of Special Programs for Minority Group Members: Career Information Services, Employment Skills Banks, Financial Aid. 3rd. ed. 612p. 1980. pap. 9.75 o.p. (ISBN 0-686-82904-2). Garrett Pk.

--Directory of Special Programs for Minority Group Members: Career Information, Service, Employment Skills Banks, Financial Aid Services. 612p. 1980. 19.95. Impact VA.

Johnson, Willoughby & Davis, Thomas M. College Reading & College Writing. rev. ed. 1971. pap. 7.95x o.p. (ISBN 0-673-07503-6). Scott F.

Johnson-Laird, P. N. & Wason, P. C., eds. Thinking: Readings in Cognitive Science. LC 77-78887. (Illus.). 1978. 52.00 (ISBN 0-521-21756-3); pap. 15.95x (ISBN 0-521-29267-0). Cambridge U Pr.

Johnstad, Jack & Johnstad, Lois. Attaining Financial Peace of Mind: A Practical Guide for the Thinking Person. LC 80-67104. (Illus.). 320p. 1980. pap. 8.95 o.p. (ISBN 0-937346-00-4). Bright Spirit.

--The Power of Prosperus Thinking: A Practical & Inspirational Guide to Making, Managing, & Multiplying Your Money. (Illus.). 256p. 1982. 12.95 (ISBN 0-312-63431-5); pap. 5.95 (ISBN 0-312-63432-3). St Martin.

Johnstad, Lois, jt. auth. see Johnstad, Jack.

Johnston & Bacon. Great Britain, Road Atlas. (Illus.). 372p. 1978. 17.95 o.p. (ISBN 0-7179-4239-2). Bradt Ent.

Johnston & Casserly. Locomotives at the Grouping, Great Western Railway. 18.50x (ISBN 0-392-08054-0, SpS). Sportshelf.

Johnston, jt. auth. see Cox.

Johnston, Annie F. The Little Colonel. new ed. (Illus.). 1974. 6.95 (ISBN 0-88289-050-6). Pelican.

Johnston, Arthur. The Battle for World Evangelism. 1978. pap. 5.95 (ISBN 0-8423-0101-1). Tyndale.

Johnston, B. F. Manual on Food & Nutrition Policy. (FAO Nutritional Studies, No. 22; FAO Food & Nutrition: No. 15). 95p. 1969. pap. 4.75 (ISBN 0-686-93240-4, F265, FAO). Unipub.

Johnston, Barbara. Beauty from the Inside Out. 1977. text ed. 7.95 o.p. (ISBN 0-914094-03-3). Symphony.

Johnston, Barbara, jt. auth. see Purcell, Julia Ann.

Johnston, Benjamin H. And In Creating, Live: The Early Life of Nikola Tesla. (Illus.). 200p. (Orig.). 1983. price not set (ISBN 0-910077-03-7); pap. price not set (ISBN 0-910077-02-9). Hart Bro Pub.

Johnston, Brian. The Ibsen Cycle. (International Studies & Translations Ser.). 1975. lib. bdg. 17.50 o.p. (ISBN 0-8057-3313-2, Twayne). G K Hall.

--Middlemarch Notes. (Orig.). 1967. pap. 2.95 (ISBN 0-8220-0825-4). Cliffs.

Johnston, Bruce F. & Kilby, Peter. Agriculture & Structural Transformation: Economic Strategies in Late-Developing Countries. (Economic Development Ser.). (Illus.). 1975. pap. text ed. 12.50x (ISBN 0-19-501870-2). Oxford U Pr.

Johnston, Bruce G. Guide to Stability Design Criteria for Metal Structures. 3rd ed. LC 75-40155. 616p. 1976. 59.50x (ISBN 0-471-44629-7, Pub. by Wiley-Interscience). Wiley.

Johnston, C. Christopher, jt. auth. see Buchan, Robert J.

Johnston, C. S. Oily Water Discharges. 1980. 41.00 (ISBN 0-85334-876-6, Pub. by Applied Sci England). Elsevier.

Johnston, Carol. Plane Trigonometry: A New Approach. 2nd ed. LC 77-16841. 1978. text ed. 20.95 (ISBN 0-13-677666-3). P-H.

Johnston, D. A. Surgical Aspects of Hyperparathyroidism. (Illus.). 1977. text ed. write for info o.p. (ISBN 0-7216-5190-9). Saunders.

Johnston, D. R., ed. Factors Affecting Aerial Application of Microencapsulated Pheromone Formulation for Control of Pectinophora Gossypiella (Saunders) by Communication Disruption on Cotton in Egypt. 1982. 35.00x (ISBN 0-686-82424-5, Pub. by Centre Overseas Research). State Mutual Bk.

Johnston, David. Surgery of Peptic Ulcer. LC 74-4571. (Illus.). 1976. text ed. write for info o.p. (ISBN 0-7216-5176-3). Saunders.

Johnston, Denis. The Dramatic Works of Denis Johnston, 2 vols. Incl. Vol. 1. 1977. text ed. 30.00x (ISBN 0-686-86086-1); Vol. 2. 1978. text ed. 36.50x (ISBN 0-901072-53-2). Humanities.

--In Search of Swift. 240p. 1982. Repr. of 1959 ed. lib. bdg. 50.00 (ISBN 0-89984-912-1). Century Bookbindery.

Johnston, Donald. A Copyright Handbook. 1978. 18.50 o.p. (ISBN 0-8352-0951-2). Bowker.

Johnston, Douglas, ed. see Law of the Sea Institute 11th. Annual Conference.

Johnston, E. R., jt. auth. see Beer, F. P.

Johnston, E. R., jt. auth. see Beer, Ferdinand P.

Johnston, E. R., Jr., jt. auth. see Beer, Ferdinand P.

Johnston, E. Russell, Jr., jt. auth. see Beer, Ferdinand P.

Johnston, Ellen T. So What Happened to You? LC 74-14960. (Illus.). 70p. 1974. 7.95 (ISBN 0-87716-057-0, Pub. by Moore Pub Co). F Apple.

--We Don't Do Nothin' in Here. LC 76-46776. 1976. 7.95 (ISBN 0-87716-076-7, Pub. by Moore Pub Co). F Apple.

Johnston, Francis. Alexandrina: The Agony & the Glory. (Illus.). 120p. 1982. pap. 2.50 (ISBN 0-686-81622-6). TAN Bks Pubs.

Johnston, Francis E. Physical Anthropology. 496p. 1982. pap. text ed. write for info. (ISBN 0-697-07564-8); instrs.' manual avail. (ISBN 0-697-07566-4). Wm C Brown.

Johnston, G. A., ed. Selections from the Scottish Philosophy of Common Sense. 274p. 17.00 (ISBN 0-87548-365-8). Open Court.

Johnston, G. H. Permafrost: Engineering Design & Construction. 540p. 1981. 47.95x (ISBN 0-471-79918-1, Pub. by Wiley-Interscience). Wiley.

Johnston, Gary & Grant, C. D., eds. New Rain, Vol. 2. (Illus.). 72p. 1982. pap. 4.25 (ISBN 0-940738-04-X). Blind Beggar.

Johnston, H. B. Annotated Catalogue of African Grasshoppers: Supplement. 1968. 45.00x (ISBN 0-521-05443-5, Pub. by Centre Overseas Research). State Mutual Bk.

Johnston, H. B. & Buxton, D. R. Field Observations on Locusts in Eastern Africa. 1949. 35.00x (ISBN 0-85135-008-9, Pub. by Centre Overseas Research). State Mutual Bk.

Johnston, H. B., jt. auth. see Davey, J. T.

Johnston, H. H. & Newsom, S. Rapid Methods & Automation in Microbiology. 318p. 1981. 80.95 o.p. (ISBN 0-471-28018-6, Pub. by Res Stud Pr). Wiley.

Johnston, H. H., ed. see International Symposium, 2nd, Cambridge, Sept. 1976.

Johnston, Hank. Railroads of the Yosemite Valley. rev. 3rd ed. (Illus.). 1980. 17.95 (ISBN 0-87046-055-2). Trans-Anglo.

Johnston, Harold W. The Private Life of the Romans. LC 72-94075. (Illus.). 430p. 1973. Repr. of 1932 ed. lib. bdg. 27.50x o.p. (ISBN 0-8154-0453-0). Cooper Sq.

Johnston, Henry P. Campaign of Seventeen Seventy-Six Around New York & Brooklyn. LC 74-157827. (Era of the American Revolution Ser). 1971. Repr. of 1878 ed. lib. bdg. 59.50 (ISBN 0-306-70169-3). Da Capo.

--Storming of Stony Point on the Hudson, Midnight, July 15, 1779. LC 70-146150. (Era of the American Revolution Ser). 1971. Repr. of 1900 ed. lib. bdg. 29.50 (ISBN 0-306-70141-3). Da Capo.

--Yorktown Campaign & the Surrender of Cornwallis, 1781. LC 75-146149. (Era of the American Revolution Ser). 1971. Repr. of 1881 ed. lib. bdg. 27.50 (ISBN 0-306-70142-1). Da Capo.

Johnston, Henry P., ed. Correspondence & Public Papers of John Jay, 1763-1781. LC 69-16639. (American Public Figures Ser). 1971. Repr. of 1890 ed. lib. bdg. 72.50 (ISBN 0-306-71124-9). Da Capo.

Johnston, J. Phillips. Success in a Small Business is a Laughing Matter. 2nd rev. ed. (Illus.). 224p. 1982. 14.95 (ISBN 0-939710-11-0). Meridional Pubns.

--Success in Small Business Is a Laughing Matter. LC 78-60481. 1978. 14.95 (ISBN 0-87716-093-7, Pub. by Moore Pub Co). F Apple.

Johnston, James O., jt. auth. see Spatz, Chris.

Johnston, Jane, jt. auth. see Ridenour, Dian M.

Johnston, Jerom, et al. An Evaluation of Freestyle: A Television Series to Reduce Sex-Role Stereotypes. 308p. 1980. pap. 16.00 (ISBN 0-87944-256-5). Inst Soc Res.

Johnston, Jill. Gullibles Travels. (Illus.). 11.95 (ISBN 0-8256-3036-3, Quick Fox); pap. 4.95 (ISBN 0-8256-3025-8). Putnam Pub Group.

--The Lesbian Nation. LC 72-83934. 1973. 7.95 o.p. (ISBN 0-671-21433-0). S&S.

--Mother Bound. LC 82-48592. 200p. 1983. 12.95 (ISBN 0-394-52757-7). Knopf.

Johnston, Joe & Rodis-Jamero, Nilo. Return of the Jedi Sketchbook. 96p. (Orig.). 1983. pap. 5.95 (ISBN 0-345-30959-6). Ballantine.

Johnston, Johanna. Edie Changes Her Mind. (Illus.). (gr. 1-4). 1964. PLB 5.97 o.p. (ISBN 0-399-60145-7). Putnam Pub Group.

--Speak up, Edie! LC 73-82025. (Illus.). 48p. (gr. 1-4). 1974. PLB 5.29 o.p. (ISBN 0-399-60864-8). Putnam Pub Group.

--That's Right Edie. (Illus.). (gr. 1-2). 1967. PLB 5.99 o.p. (ISBN 0-399-60627-0). Putnam Pub Group.

Johnston, John. Econometric Methods. 2nd ed. 1971. text ed. 27.95 (ISBN 0-07-032679-7, C). McGraw.

Johnston, John E. Site Control of Materials: Handling, Storage, & Security. (Illus.). 1981. text ed. 25.95 (ISBN 0-408-00377-4). Butterworth.

Johnston, John K., et al. Wrestling: Coaching to Win. (Illus.). 1979. pap. 6.25 (ISBN 0-8015-8933-9, 0607-180, Hawthorn). Dutton.

Johnston, John L., jt. auth. see Jones, Elmer W.

Johnston, Kenneth S., jt. auth. see Gray, Jack C.

Johnston, Leonard, tr. see Van Steenberghen, Fernand.

Johnston, Lloyd. Drugs & American Youth. LC 71-190022. 287p. 1973. cloth 16.00x (ISBN 0-87944-133-X); pap. 10.00x (ISBN 0-87944-120-8). Inst Soc Res.

Johnston, Lloyd D. & Bachman, Jerald G. Monitoring the Future: Questionnaire Responses from the Nation's High School Seniors. LC 79-640937. lib. bdg. 20.00 (ISBN 0-87944-261-1, 1979 266); text ed. 25.00 (ISBN 0-87944-269-7, 1980 266); pap. 30.00 (ISBN 0-87944-276-X, 1981 266). Inst Soc Res.

Johnston, Lloyd D., et al. Monitoring the Future: Questionnaire Responses from the Nation's High School Seniors, Annual Vols., 7 vol. set 175.00x, (ISBN 0-87944-277-8); 1975, 188p. 25.00x (ISBN 0-87944-235-2); 1976, 264p. 30.00x (ISBN 0-87944-236-0); 1977, 266p. 30.00 (ISBN 0-87944-237-9); 1978, 266p. 30.00x (ISBN 0-87944-238-7); 1979, 266p. 30.00x (ISBN 0-87944-261-1); 1980, 266p. 30.00 (ISBN 0-87944-269-7); 1981, 272p. 30.00x (ISBN 0-87944-276-X). Inst Soc Res.

Johnston, Lynn. Is This "One of Those Days," Daddy? LC 82-72417. (Illus.). 128p. (gr. 5 up). 1982. pap. 5.95 (ISBN 0-8362-1197-9). Andrews & McMeel.

--Who's Afraid of the I.R.S? 250p. Date not set. 14.50 (ISBN 0-916728-54-4). Bks in Focus.

Johnston, M., ed. Ireland Under the Ascendancy, 1688-1800. 280p. 1982. 49.00x (ISBN 0-7171-0896-1, Pub. by Macmillan England). State Mutual Bk.

Johnston, Mary. Pioneers of the Old South. 1918. text ed. 8.50x (ISBN 0-686-83699-5). Elliots Bks.

--Prisoners of Hope: A Tale of Colonial Virginia. 378p. 1982. Repr. of 1899 ed. lib. bdg. 40.00 (ISBN 0-89987-435-5). Darby Bks.

--Roman Life. 1957. text ed. 20.95x (ISBN 0-673-05069-6). Scott F.

Johnston, Mary A. Sing Me a Song. LC 76-57727. (Illus.). (ps-3). 1977. 5.95 (ISBN 0-913778-81-8). Childs World.

Johnston, Michael L., jt. auth. see Vanderleest, Henry W.

Johnston, Mireille. The Cuisine of the Rose: Classical French Cooking from Burgundy & Lyonnais. 321p. 1982. 16.95 (ISBN 0-394-42565-0). Random.

--The Cuisine of the Sun: Classic Recipes from Nice & the South of France. 1976. 6.95. Random.

--The Cuisine of the Sun: Classical French Cooking from Nice & Provence. LC 78-21922. (Illus.). 1979. pap. 6.95 (ISBN 0-394-72824-6, Vin). Random.

Johnston, Norma. Timewarp Summer. LC 82-16240. 180p. (gr. 7 up). 1983. 10.95 (ISBN 0-689-30960-0). Atheneum.

Johnston, Norman & Savitz, Leonard D. Legal Process & Corrections. LC 81-12970. 352p. 1982. pap. text ed. 11.95 (ISBN 0-471-08337-2). Wiley.

Johnston, Norman, jt. auth. see Savitz, Leonard D.

Johnston, Norman J. Cities in the Round: The Planned Circular City Tradition. LC 81-21984. (Illus.). 144p. 1983. 29.95 (ISBN 0-295-95918-5). U of Wash Pr.

Johnston, O. R., tr. see Luther, Martin.

Johnston, Ollie, jt. auth. see Thomas, Frank.

Johnston, P. M. & Liebowitz, M. Basic Sheet Metal Skills. LC 76-14085. 1977. pap. text ed. 13.40 (ISBN 0-8273-1237-7); instructor's guide 4.75 (ISBN 0-8273-1238-5). Delmar.

Johnston, Patricia C. Eastman Johnson's Lake Superior Indians. (Illus., Orig.). 1983. price not set (ISBN 0-942934-30-X); pap. price not set (ISBN 0-942934-29-6). Johnston Pub.

--Pretty Red Wing, Minnesota Rivertown. (Illus.). 96p. (Orig.). 1983. price not set (ISBN 0-942934-28-8); pap. price not set (ISBN 0-942934-27-X). Johnston Pub.

Johnston, Patricia I., ed. Perspectives on a Grafted Tree. (Illus.). 1983. 12.95 (ISBN 0-9609504-0-0). Perspect Indiana.

Johnston, Philip M. & Liebowitz, Murray. Advanced Sheet Metal Skills. LC 76-14088. 1978. pap. 13.80 (ISBN 0-686-85865-4); instr's. guide 4.75 (ISBN 0-8273-1240-7). Delmar.

Johnston, R. Geography & Geographers. 272p. 1983. pap. text ed. write for info. (ISBN 0-7131-6387-9). E Arnold.

Johnston, R. B. The Economics of the Euro-Market: History, Theory & Policy. LC 82-10300. 296p. 1982. 27.50x (ISBN 0-312-23295-0). St Martin.

Johnston, R. J. Geography & the State. LC 82-10483. 304p. 1982. 27.50x (ISBN 0-312-32172-4). St Martin.

--Spatial Structures. LC 73-86665. (Illus.). 128p. 1973. 14.95 o.p. (ISBN 0-312-75040-4). St Martin.

--The World Trade System: Some Inquiries into Its Spatial Structure. LC 76-6744. 250p. 1976. 26.00x (ISBN 0-312-89250-0). St Martin.

Johnston, R. J., jt. auth. see Herbert, D. T.

Johnston, R. T., jt. auth. see Herbert, D. T.

Johnston, Richard F., et al, eds. Annual Review of Ecology & Systematics, Vol. 3. LC 71-135616. (Illus.). 1972. text ed. 17.00 (ISBN 0-8243-1403-4). Annual Reviews.

--Annual Review of Ecology & Systematics, Vol. 4. LC 71-135616. (Illus.). 1973. text ed. 17.00 (ISBN 0-8243-1404-2). Annual Reviews.

--Annual Review of Ecology & Systematics, Vol. 13. LC 71-135616. (Illus.). 500p. 1982. text ed. 22.00 (ISBN 0-8243-1413-1). Annual Reviews.

Johnston, Richard J. Getting to Know the Two Koreas. (Getting to Know Ser.). (Illus.). (gr. 3-5). 1965. PLB 3.97 o.p. (ISBN 0-698-30166-8, Coward). Putnam Pub Group.

Johnston, Robert. Psalms for God's People. LC 82-5344. (Bible Commentary for Laymen Ser.). 160p. 1982. pap. 2.95 (ISBN 0-8307-0820-0, $362105). Regal.

Johnston, Robert A., jt. auth. see Aeschylus.

Johnston, Robert B & Magrab, Phyllis R., eds. Development Disorders: Assessment, Treatment, Education. (Illus.). 544p. 1976. text ed. 22.95 (ISBN 0-8391-0825-7). Univ Park.

Johnston, Robert K. Evangelicals at an Impasse: Biblical Authority in Practice. LC 78-71048. (Orig.). 1979. pap. 7.95 (ISBN 0-8042-2038-7). John Knox.

Johnston, Robert L. Numerical Methods: A Software Approach. LC 81-12974. 276p. 1982. text ed. 25.95x (ISBN 0-471-09397-1). Wiley.

Johnston, Robert M. The Napoleonic Empire in Southern Italy & the Rise of the Secret Societies, 2 vols. in 1. LC 77-156852. (Europe 1815-1945 Ser). 640p. 1973. Repr. of 1904 ed. lib. bdg. 59.50 (ISBN 0-306-70558-3). Da Capo.

Johnston, Ron. Philosophy & Human Geography: An Introduction to Contemporary Approaches. 1983. pap. text ed. 19.95 (ISBN 0-686-43072-7). E Arnold.

Johnston, Ron & Gummett, Philip, eds. Directing Technology: Policies for Promotion & Control. LC 78-26073. 1979. 30.00 (ISBN 0-312-21218-6). St Martin.

Johnston, Ronald J. The Geography of Federal Spending in the U.S.A. LC 80-40954. (Geographical Research Studies). 179p. 1980. 54.95x (ISBN 0-471-27865-3, Pub. by Res Stud Pr). Wiley.

Johnston, Russ. God Can Make It Happen. 144p. 1976. pap. 4.95 (ISBN 0-88207-741-4). Victor Bks.

Johnston, Russell. Life of Marion Harper. 256p. 1982. 19.95 (ISBN 0-87251-073-5). Crain Bks.

Johnston, Susan. Fashion Paper Dolls from Godey's Lady's Book: 1840-1854. (Illus.). 1977. pap. 3.00 (ISBN 0-486-23511-4). Dover.

--Patchwork Quilt Coloring Book. (Illus.). Date not set. pap. 1.75 (ISBN 0-486-23845-8). Dover. Postponed.

--Tangram ABC Kit. 1979. pap. 2.25 (ISBN 0-486-23853-9). Dover.

Johnston, T. H. & Greig, C. Music with Your Project. 1982. pap. 8.50 (ISBN 0-08-025761-5). Pergamon.

Johnston, Terry. Carry the Wind. 1982. 13.95 (ISBN 0-89803-106-0). Green Hill.

Johnston, Terry C. Carry the Wind. 1982. 13.95 (ISBN 0-89803-106-0). Caroline Hse.

Johnston, Tony. The Adventures of Mole & Troll. (See & Read Storybooks). (Illus.). (gr. 1-3). 1972. PLB 6.29 o.p. (ISBN 0-399-60747-1). Putnam Pub Group.

--Fig Tale. new ed. LC 74-79873. (Illus.). 32p. (gr. k-3). 1974. PLB 5.49 o.p. (ISBN 0-399-60908-3). Putnam Pub Group.

--Five Little Foxes & the Snow. LC 76-50579. (Illus.). (gr. k-4). 1977. pap. 4.95 (ISBN 0-399-20841-0). Putnam Pub Group.

--Four Scary Stories. LC 77-13027. (Illus.). 1978. 7.95 (ISBN 0-399-20614-0). Putnam Pub Group.

--Four Scary Stories. LC 77-13027. (Illus.). 32p. (gr. 3-5). 1980. pap. 2.95 (ISBN 0-399-20727-9, Peppercorn). Putnam Pub Group.

--Happy Birthday, Mole & Troll. LC 78-25717. (A See & Read Storybook). (Illus.). (gr. 1-4). 1979. PLB 6.99g (ISBN 0-399-61137-1). Putnam Pub Group.

--Little Mouse Nibbling. LC 78-24265. (Illus.). 1979. 7.95 (ISBN 0-399-20673-6). Putnam Pub Group.

--Mole & Troll Trim the Tree. new ed. LC 73-82024. (Illus.). 32p. (gr. k-3). 1980. 6.99 (ISBN 0-399-60909-1). Putnam Pub Group.

--Night Noises & Other Mole & Troll Stories. LC 76-3653. (See & Read Storybooks). (Illus.). (gr. k-4). 1977. PLB 6.99 (ISBN 0-399-61016-2). Putnam Pub Group.

--Odd Jobs. LC 76-39794. (See & Read Storybooks). (Illus.). (gr. k-4). 1977. PLB 4.99 o.p. (ISBN 0-399-61048-0). Putnam Pub Group.

--Odd Jobs & Friends. 48p. 1982. lib. bdg. 6.99 (ISBN 0-399-61204-1). Putnam Pub Group.

Johnston, Trude. Home Book of Viennese Cookery. 190p. 1978. pap. 6.95 (ISBN 0-571-11178-5). Faber & Faber.

Johnston, Velda. Deveron Hall. 1978. pap. 1.75 o.p. (ISBN 0-451-08018-1, E8018, Sig). NAL.

--The Etruscan Smile. 1980. pap. 2.25 o.p. (ISBN 0-451-09020-9, E9020, Sig). NAL.

--The Frenchman. 1977. pap. 1.50 o.p. (ISBN 0-451-07519-6, W7519, Sig). NAL.

--The Hour Before Midnight. 192p. 1980. pap. 2.25 o.p. (ISBN 0-451-09343-7, E9343, Sig). NAL.

--House above Hollywood. 1983. pap. 2.95 (ISBN 0-396-08162-2). Dodd.

--I Came to the Highlands. 1978. pap. 1.95 o.p. (ISBN 0-451-08218-4, J8218, Sig). NAL.

--A Presence in an Empty Room. LC 79-25431. 256p. 1980. 8.95 o.p. (ISBN 0-396-07796-X). Dodd.

--A Room with Dark Mirrors. 1976. Repr. lib. bdg. 10.95 o.p. (ISBN 0-8161-6344-8, Large Print Bks). G K Hall.

--The Stone Maiden. 192p. 1982. pap. 2.50 (ISBN 0-553-20667-2). Bantam.

Johnston, Verle B. Legions of Babel: The International Brigades in the Spanish Civil War. LC 67-16196. (Illus.). 1967. 17.50x (ISBN 0-271-73115-X). Pa St U Pr.

Johnston, W. D. History of the Library of Congress, Vol. 1. 1800-1864. 1904. 33.00 o.p. (ISBN 0-527-46540-2). Kraus Repr.

Johnston, W. H., tr. see Erhard, Ludwig.

Johnston, W. H., tr. see Tschuppik, Karl.

Johnston, William. Silent Music: The Science of Meditation. LC 73-18688. 1979. pap. 6.95i (ISBN 0-06-064196-7, RD 293, HarpR). Har-Row.

Johnston, William, jt. auth. see Beiderman, Charles.

Johnston, William, ed. The Cloud of Unknowing & the Book of Privy Counselling. LC 73-79737. 200p. 1973. pap. 3.50 (ISBN 0-385-03097-5, Im). Doubleday.

Johnston, William L. Pontiac. Benson, Robert, ed. (Chapbook: No. 8). 21p. 1981. pap. 2.50 (ISBN 0-932884-07-5). Red Herring.

Johnston, William L., ed. see Gerstein, Marvin.

Johnston, William M. The Austrian Mind: An Intellectual & Social History. LC 75-111418. (California Library Reprint). 1976. 47.50x (ISBN 0-520-03182-2). U of Cal Pr.

--The Austrian Mind: An Intellectual & Social History. (Illus.). 531p. 1983. pap. 10.95 (ISBN 0-520-04955-1, CAL 624). U of Cal Pr.

--Vienna, Vienna: The Golden Age, 1815-1914. 336p. 1981. 30.00 (ISBN 0-517-54555-1, C N Potter Bks). Crown.

Johnston, William R. The Nineteenth Century Paintings in the Walters Art Gallery. (Illus.). 208p. 1982. 40.00 (ISBN 0-911886-25-7). Walters Art.

Johnston, William W. & Frable, William J. Diagnostic Respiratory Cytopathology. LC 79-84478. (Masson Monographs in Diagnostic Cytopathology: Vol. 1). 328p. 1979. 47.75x (ISBN 0-89352-047-0). Masson Pub.

Johnston, William W., jt. auth. see Bigner, Sandra H.

Johnstone, Charles & Giles, Lionel, trs. Selections from the Upanishads & the Tao Te King. 142p. 1951. 3.00 (ISBN 0-938998-15-3). Theosophy.

Johnstone, Henry W., Jr. Philosophy & Argument. LC 59-11217. 1959. 11.75x (ISBN 0-271-00002-3). Pa St U Pr.

--Problem of the Self. LC 71-84666. 1970. 12.00 (ISBN 0-271-00102-X). Pa St U Pr.

Johnstone, Iain. The Man with No Name: A Biography of Clint Eastwood. LC 81-82550. (Illus.). 1981. pap. 7.95 (ISBN 0-688-00643-4). Quill NY.

Johnstone, Kathleen. Collecting Seashells. LC 68-29980. (Illus.). (gr. 4 up). 1977. pap. 3.95 o.p. (ISBN 0-448-14078-0, G&D). Putnam Pub Group.

Johnstone, Mark, intro. by. New Landscapes. LC 80-70583. (Untitled Ser.: No. 24). (Illus.). 56p. 1980. pap. 8.95 o.p. (ISBN 0-933286-22-8). Friends Photography.

Johnstone, N., tr. see Alpatov, M. V.

Johnstone, Parker L. Mission Presidio Diary: San Francisco, 1776. 1976. 7.95 (ISBN 0-912748-00-1). Mission Dolores.

Johnstone, Peter. Stone Spaces. LC 82-4506. (Cambridge Studies in Advanced Mathematics: No. 3). 300p. Date not set. price not set (ISBN 0-521-23893-5). Cambridge U Pr.

Johnstone, R. A., jt. auth. see Rose, M. E.

Johnstone, Robert. Lectures on the Book of Philippians. 1977. 18.25 (ISBN 0-86524-108-2, 5001). Klock & Klock.

--Lectures on the Epistle of James. 1977. 16.50 (ISBN 0-86524-111-2, 5901). Klock & Klock.

Johnstone, Ronald L. Religion in Society: A Sociology of Religion. 2nd ed. (Illus.). 320p. 1983. text ed. 21.95 (ISBN 0-13-773077-2). P-H.

Johnstone, Sally, ed. & illus. Sam & Company. LC 82-83034. (Illus.). 32p. (Orig.). (ps). 1982. pap. 4.95 (ISBN 0-914766-87-2, 0268). IWP Pub.

Johnstone, Sandy. Enemy in the Sky: My 1940 Diary. LC 78-31793. (Illus.). 1979. 12.95 o.p. (ISBN 0-89141-086-4). Presidio Pr.

Johnstone, T. M., ed. Jibbale Lexicon. 366p. 1981. text ed. 65.00x (ISBN 0-19-713602-8). Oxford U Pr.

Johnstone, William W. Out of the Ashes. 1983. pap. 3.50 (ISBN 0-8217-1137-7). Zebra.

John Thomas, David St. see St. John Thomas, David.

John Twenty-Third, Pope Pacem in Terris. study club ed. (Orig.). pap. 1.95 o.p. (ISBN 0-8091-5106-5). Paulist Pr.

Joiner, Charles A. The Politics of Massacre: Political Processes in South Vietnam. LC 72-95882. 362p. 1974. 19.95 (ISBN 0-87722-060-3). Temple U Pr.

Joiner, Elizabeth & Westphal, Patricia, eds. Developing Communication Skills: General Considerations & Specific Techniques. LC 78-16787. 1978. pap. text ed. 10.95 (ISBN 0-88377-118-7). Newbury Hse.

Joiner, Jasper N. Foliage Plant Production. (Illus.). 608p. 1981. text ed. 28.95 (ISBN 0-13-322867-3). P-H.

Joint Bank-Fund Library (Washington, D. C.) The Developing Areas: A Classed Bibliography of the Joint Bank-Fund Library, World Bank Group & International Monetary Fund, 3 vols. Incl. Vol. 1. Latin America & the Caribbean. lib. bdg. 75.00 (ISBN 0-8161-0023-3); Vol. 2. Africa & the Middle East. lib. bdg. 85.00 (ISBN 0-8161-0024-1); Vol. 3. Asia & Oceania. lib. bdg. 85.00 (ISBN 0-8161-0025-X). 1976. Set. lib. bdg. 225.00 (ISBN 0-8161-0003-9, Hall Library). G K Hall.

Joint Bank-Fund Library, Washington, D.C. Economics & Finance: Index to Periodical Articles, 1975-1976-1977. 1979. lib. bdg. 95.00 (ISBN 0-8161-0302-X, Hall Library). G K Hall.

--Economics & Finance: Index to Periodical Articles, 1972-1973-1974 Bank-Fund Library (Washington, D.C.), First Supplement. 1976. lib. bdg. 105.00 (ISBN 0-8161-1064-6, Hall Library). G K Hall.

Joint Bank-Fund Library (Washington, D. C.) Economics, Finance & Development: List of Subjects Used in the Main Catalog of the Joint Bank-Fund Library. 1979. lib. bdg. 88.00 (ISBN 0-8161-0276-7, Hall Library). G K Hall.

Joint Commission on Accreditation of Hospitals. Accreditation Manual for Psychiatric Facilities. 20.00 o.p. (ISBN 0-686-92175-5, 4212). Hazelden.

Joint Committee of the American Bar Association & the American Medical Association on Narcotic Drugs. Drug Addiction: Crime or Disease? Interim & Final Reports of the Joint Committee of the American Bar Association & the American Medical Association on Narcotic Drugs. LC 61-9838. 192p. 1961. 7.50x o.p. (ISBN 0-253-11850-6). Ind U Pr.

Joint Council On Economic Education. Business & the Public Interest. 1972. 4.00 o.p. (ISBN 0-07-032721-1, G). McGraw.

--Introduction to Economics & Business Enterprise. 1972. 4.00 o.p. (ISBN 0-07-032722-X, G). McGraw.

Joint FAO-USSR International Symposium of Forest Influences & Watershed Management, Moscow, 1970. Proceedings. (Forestry Ser.: No. 1). 452p. 1970. pap. 34.00 o.p. (ISBN 0-686-92965-9, F1437, FAO). Unipub.

Joint ISMAR-AMPERE International Conference on Magnetic Resonance. Proceedings. Smidt, J., ed. 1981. 30.00 (ISBN 0-686-77674-7). Franklin Inst Pr.

Joint Organizing Committee, Eleventh Session. GARP Report. (Illus.). 1976. pap. 40.00 o.p. (ISBN 0-685-66360-4, WMO). Unipub.

Joint Publications Research Service. Modern Communist Chinese Usage: Chinese English Dictionary. 2nd ed. pap. 58.00 (ISBN 0-686-23791-9, JPRS 20904). Natl Tech Info.

Jokl, E., et al, eds. see International Symposium of Physiology, New Delhi-Patiala, Oct. 1974.

Jolicoeur, Pamela M., jt. auth. see Rich, Harvey E.

Joll, Caroline & McKenna, Chris. Developments in Labour Market Analysis. (Illus.). 40p. 1983. text ed. 29.95x (ISBN 0-04-331089-3); pap. text ed. 16.50x (ISBN 0-04-331090-7). Allen Unwin.

Joll, Caroline, jt. auth. see George, K. D.

Joll, James. The Second International 1889-1914. 2nd ed. 1975. 23.00x (ISBN 0-7100-7966-4). Routledge & Kean.

Jolley, Moya, jt. auth. see Allan, Peta.

Jolley, Robert L., et al, eds. Water Chlorination: Environmental Impact & Health Effects, 2 bks, Vol. 4. LC 77-92588. (Illus.). 700p. 1983. Set. 45.00 (ISBN 0-250-40582-2); 27.50 ea. Bk. 1, Chemistry & Water Treatment (ISBN 0-250-40519-9). Bk. 2, Environment, Health & Risk (ISBN 0-250-40581-4). Ann Arbor Science.

Jollie, Malcolm. Chordate Morphology. LC 62-17800. 492p. 1973. Repr. of 1962 ed. 22.00 (ISBN 0-88275-090-9). Krieger.

Jolliffe, F. R. Commonsense Statistics for Economists & Others. (Students Library of Economics Ser.). 1974. 12.95x (ISBN 0-7100-7952-4); pap. 6.95 (ISBN 0-7100-7953-2). Routledge & Kegan.

Jolliffe, H. R. Tales from the Greek Drama. xi, 320p. 8.50 (ISBN 0-86516-013-9). Bolchazy-Carducci.

Jollivet, Th. M. Historique de la Traite et du Droit de Visite. (Slave Trade in France Ser., 1744-1848). 35p. (Fr.). 1974. Repr. of 1841 ed. 26.00x o.p. (ISBN 0-8287-0465-1, TN 151). Clearwater Pub.

Jolly, Alison. The Evolution of Primate Behavior. (Illus.). 352p. 1972. text ed. 13.95x (ISBN 0-02-361130-8). Macmillan.

Jolly, Brad. Videotaping Local History. LC 82-8730. (Illus.). 1982. pap. 11.95 (ISBN 0-910050-57-0). AASLH.

Jolly, Clifford & Plog, Fred. Physical Anthropology & Archeology. 3rd ed. 1978. pap. text ed. 15.95 (ISBN 0-394-32672-5). Knopf.

Jolly, Clifford, ed. Early Hominids of Africa. LC 78-54136. (Illus.). 1978. 56.00 (ISBN 0-312-22461-3). St Martin.

Jolly, Clifford, et al. Anthropology: Decisions, Adaptation & Evolution. 564p. 1980. text ed. 19.00 o.p. (ISBN 0-394-32095-6). Knopf.

Jolly, Erin, pseud. Flowers of Stone. LC 68-28068. 1968. 4.00 o.p. (ISBN 0-8233-0049-8). Golden Quill.

Jolly, Grace, ed. see Linguistic Association of Canada & the U. S.

Jolly, Hugh. Diseases of Children. 4th. ed. (Illus.). 760p. 1981. text ed. 32.50 (ISBN 0-632-00707-9, B 2531-9). Mosby.

Jolly, Julius, ed. The Institutes of Vishnu. (Sacred Bks. of the East: Vol. 7). 11.00 (ISBN 0-686-97480-8). Lancaster-Miller.

Jolly, Richard, jt. ed. see Cassen, Robert.

Jolly, Sonny, jt. auth. see Crowder, Vernon.

Jolly, Stephen, tr. see Langer, Jiri.

Jolly, W. L. The Principles of Inorganic Chemistry. 1975. text ed. 30.00 (ISBN 0-07-032758-0, C). McGraw.

Jolly, William L. Encounters in Experimental Chemistry. (Illus.). 157p. 1972. pap. text ed. 12.95 (ISBN 0-15-522591-X, HC); solutions manual avail. (ISBN 0-15-522592-8, HC). HarBraceJ.

Jolson, Marvin A. Marketing Management: Integrated Text, Readings & Cases. (Illus.). 1978. text ed. 24.95x (ISBN 0-02-361180-4). Macmillan.

Joly, Charles J., ed. see Hamilton, William R.

Jonaitis, Aldona, jt. auth. see Mathews, Zena.

Jonas, Ann. Two Bear Cubs. LC 82-2860. (Illus.). 24p. (gr. k-3). 1982. 8.00 (ISBN 0-688-01407-0); PLB 7.63 (ISBN 0-688-01408-9). Greenwillow.

--Two Bear Cubs. (ps-1). 1982. 8.50 (ISBN 0-688-01407-0); PLB 7.63 (ISBN 0-688-01408-9). Morrow.

--When You Were a Baby. (Illus.). (ps). 1982. 9.50 (ISBN 0-688-00863-1); PLB 8.59 (ISBN 0-688-00864-X). Morrow.

Jonas, Gerald. Stuttering: The Disorder of Many Theories. 64p. 1977. 5.95 o.p. (ISBN 0-374-27118-6); pap. 2.95 (ISBN 0-374-51429-1). FS&G.

Jonas, Hans. Gnostic Religion. 1963. pap. 7.64 (ISBN 0-8070-5799-1, BP259). Beacon Pr.

--The Phenomenon of Life: Toward a Philosphical Biology. LC 82-13437. xii, 304p. 1983. pap. 8.95 (ISBN 0-226-40595-8). U of Chicago Pr.

Jonas, Klaus W., ed. The World of Somerset Maugham: An Anthology. LC 73-156196. 200p. 1972. Repr. of 1959 ed. lib. bdg. 20.75x (ISBN 0-8371-6147-9, JOSM). Greenwood.

Jonas, Paul. Canon Manual. (Illus.). 1976. 10.95 o.p. (ISBN 0-8174-1486-X, Amphoto). Watson-Guptill.

--Manual of Darkroom Procedures & Techniques. 4th ed. (Illus.). 160p. 1971. 10.95 o.p. (ISBN 0-8174-0541-0, Amphoto). Watson-Guptill.

--Photographic Composition Simplified. (Illus.). 96p. 1975. pap. 4.95 (ISBN 0-8174-1149-6, Amphoto); Spanish Ed. pap. 6.95 (ISBN 0-8174-0320-5). Watson-Guptill.

--Taxation of Multinationals in Communist Countries. LC 77-13886. (Praeger Special Studies). 1978. 26.95 o.p. (ISBN 0-03-040676-5). Praeger.

Jonas, Susanne, jt. ed. see Dixon, Marlene.

Jonassen, Christen T. Value Systems & Personality in a Western Civilization: Norwegians in Europe & America. 400p. 1983. write for info (ISBN 0-8142-0347-7). Ohio St U Pr.

Jonathan, Stephen. The Diploma Was Death. Ashton, Sylvia, ed. LC 74-77472. 1975. 7.95 o.p. (ISBN 0-87949-032-2). Ashley Bks.

Jondorf, Gillian. Robert Garnier & the Themes of Political Tragedy. LC 69-11027. 1969. 37.50 (ISBN 0-521-07386-3). Cambridge U Pr.

Jone, Bryan J., et al see Weissberger, A.

Jones. Biochemical Development of the Fetus & Neonate. Date not set. 200.00 (ISBN 0-444-80423-4). Elsevier.

--Concrete Technology. 1982. text ed. 22.50 (ISBN 0-408-00673-0); pap. text ed. 9.95 (ISBN 0-408-00643-9). Butterworth.

--Criminal Justice Administration. (Annuals of Public Adminstrations Ser.). 144p. 1983. 32.75 (ISBN 0-8247-1808-9). Dekker.

--Going to School. LC 68-56811. (Illus.). (ps-1). 1968. PLB 6.75x (ISBN 0-87783-015-0). Oddo.

--Making TV Commercials. (Illus.). 1983. 33.95x (ISBN 0-240-51195-6). Focal Pr.

--World War Two: A Chronicle of Soldiering. 9.95 (ISBN 0-448-11896-3, G&D). Putnam Pub Group.

Jones see Borchardt, Jack A., et al.

Jones, jt. auth. see Joshua.

Jones, jt. auth. see Moncrief.

Jones, et al. Practicing Texas Politics. 5th ed. 1982. 8.50 (ISBN 0-686-84651-6); supplementary materials avail. HM.

--Family History for Fun & Profit: A How to-Do It Guide for Genealogy Research. 6.95 o.p. (ISBN 0-686-21717-9). Promised Land.

Jones, A., jt. auth. see Williams, H. H.

Jones, A. H. Were Ancient Heresies Disguised Social Movements? Lee, Clarence L., ed. LC 66-11534. (Facet Bks.). 1966. pap. 0.50 o.p. (ISBN 0-8006-3023-8, 1-3023). Fortress.

Jones, A. J. Principles of Guidance. 6th ed. (Guidance Counseling & Student Personnel in Education Ser.). 1970. text ed. 22.50 o.p. (ISBN 0-07-032999-0, C). McGraw.

Jones, A. J., jt. auth. see El-Agra, A. M.

Jones, A. R., jt. auth. see Bayvel, L. P.

Jones, Adrienne. The Hawks of Chelney. LC 77-11855. (Illus.). 1978. 10.95 (ISBN 0-06-023057-6, HarpJ); PLB 10.89 (ISBN 0-06-023058-4). Har-Row.

Jones, Alan & Botsford, Keith. Driving Ambition. LC 82-45166. 184p. 1982. 12.95 (ISBN 0-689-11308-0). Atheneum.

Jones, Alan, jt. auth. see Hosmer, Rachel.

Jones, Alan W. Lyulph Stanley: A Study in Educational Politics. 194p. 1979. text ed. 11.00x (ISBN 0-88920-074-2, Pub. by Wilfrid Laurier U Pr Canada). Humanities.

Jones, Alex. Seven Mansions of Color. LC 82-73248. 160p. 1983. pap. 7.50 (ISBN 0-87516-500-1). De Vorss.

Jones, Alexander, ed. Jerusalem Bible. new ed. LC 66-24278. 1967. 21.95 (ISBN 0-385-06932-4); thumb-indexed 24.95 (ISBN 0-385-01140-7). Doubleday.

--The Old Testamant of the Jerusalem Bible: Reader's Edition. Incl. Vol. 1. Genesis Through Ruth. 520p (ISBN 0-385-06697-X); Vol. 2. First Samuel Through Second Maccabees. 560p. o.p. (ISBN 0-385-06967-7); Vol. 3. Job Through Ecclesiasticus. 560p (ISBN 0-385-07036-5); Vol. 4. The Prophets Through Malachi. o.p. (ISBN 0-385-07052-7). 1973. pap. 1.95 ea. (Im). Doubleday.

--Old Testament of the Jerusalem Bible. 19.95 (ISBN 0-385-03665-5). Doubleday.

Jones, Alick R. The Ciliates. LC 73-87077. (Illus.). 160p. 1974. 18.95 (ISBN 0-312-13860-1). St Martin.

Jones, Allen. World Protein Resources. LC 74-11219. 381p. 1974. 31.95 o.p. (ISBN 0-470-44935-7). Halsted Pr.

Jones, Andrew N. & Cooper, Cary L. Combating Managerial Obsolescence. LC 80-16307. xii, 176p. 1980. lib. bdg. 25.00 (ISBN 0-86003-509-3, JCO/). Greenwood.

Jones, Ann. Career Color-Cut-Out Book for Girls & Boys. (Coloring Experience Ser.). (Illus.). (gr. 3-12). 1978. pap. 1.95 o.s.i. (ISBN 0-8431-0239-X). Price Stern.

--Uncle Tom's Campus. 1974. pap. 2.95 o.p. (ISBN 0-671-21721-6, Touchstone Bks). S&S.

Jones, Archer, jt. auth. see Hattaway, Herman.

Jones, Arthur. Decline of Capital. LC 75-35953. 256p. 1976. 10.53 (ISBN 0-690-01045-1). T Y Crowell.

Jones, Arthur E., jt. auth. see Francuch, Peter D.

Jones, Arthur F. The Art of Paul Sawyier. LC 75-41988. (Illus.). 208p. 1976. 31.00 (ISBN 0-8131-1340-7). U Pr of Ky.

Jones, Aubrey. I Speak BASIC to My Pet. (I Speak BASIC Ser.). 224p. 1982. pap. text ed. 7.45 (ISBN 0-8104-6176-5); tchr's. manual 16.20 (ISBN 0-8104-6166-8); exam set 12.50 (ISBN 0-8104-6186-2); classroom set (tchr's. manual, 20 student texts & exam set) 156.25 (ISBN 0-8104-6156-0). Hayden.

Jones, Augustus J., Jr. Law, Bureaucracy & Politics: The Implementation of Title VI of the Civil Rights Act of 1964. LC 81-40871. (Illus.). 316p. (Orig.). 1982. lib. bdg. 25.25 (ISBN 0-8191-2154-1); pap. text ed. 12.75 (ISBN 0-8191-2155-X). U Pr of Amer.

Jones, B. & Kavanagh, D. British Politics Today. 155p. 1979. pap. 3.50 (ISBN 0-7190-0736-4). Manchester.

Jones, B. E., ed. Instrument Science & Technology, Vol. 1. 120p. 1982. 30.00x o.p. (ISBN 0-85274-438-2, Pub. by A Hilger). State Mutual Bk.

Jones, B. J. Let's Learn Korean. LC 82-82601. (Illus.). 62p. 1982. 14.50 (ISBN 0-930878-27-2); cassette incl. Hollym Intl.

--Standard English-Korean Dictionary for Foreigners. LC 81-84204. 386p. 1982. 7.95 (ISBN 0-930878-21-3). Hollym Intl.

Jones, B. W. & Keynes, Milton. The Solar System. (Illus.). 400p. 1983. 45.00 (ISBN 0-08-026496-4); pap. 22.50 (ISBN 0-08-026495-6). Pergamon.

Jones, Barbara C., ed. see Fannin County Historical Commission.

Jones, Barbara S., jt. auth. see Morscher, Betsey.

Jones, Barbara S., jt. auth. see Robbins, James G.

Jones, Barry. Sleepers, Wake! Technology & the Future of Work. (Illus.). 302p. 1983. pap. 9.95 (ISBN 0-19-554270-3, GB). Oxford U Pr.

Jones, Barry O. Sleepers, Wake! Technology & the Future of Work. (Illus.). 302p. 1983. 24.95 (ISBN 0-19-554343-2). Oxford U Pr.

Jones, Bessie. For the Ancestors: Autobiographical Memories. Stewart, John, ed. LC 82-8593. (Illus.). 211p. 1983. 14.95 (ISBN 0-252-00959-2). U of Ill Pr.

Jones, Billy M., jt. auth. see Christy, Ron.

Jones, Boisfeuillet, ed. Health of Americans. LC 70-120793. 1970. 5.95 o.p. (ISBN 0-13-385070-6); pap. 2.45 o.p. (ISBN 0-13-385062-5). Am Assembly.

Jones, Bonzo. Train Your Human: A Manual for Caring Dogs. LC 79-52365. (Illus.). 1979. 10.50 o.p. (ISBN 0-7153-7678-0). David & Charles.

Jones, Brian. The Island Normal. 80p. (Orig.). pap. 7.95 o.p. (ISBN 0-85635-340-X, Pub. by Carcanet New Pr England). Humanities.

Jones, Brian, jt. auth. see Whitehorne, John.

Jones, Bryan. The Farming Game. LC 82-2842. (Illus.). 221p. 1982. 15.95 (ISBN 0-8032-2559-8). U of Nebr Pr.

Jones, Burton W. The Arithmetic Theory of Quadratic Forms. (Carus Monograph: No. 10). 212p. 1950. 16.50 o.s.i. (ISBN 0-88385-010-9). Math Assn.

--Linear Algebra. LC 72-83244. 1973. text ed. 21.95x (ISBN 0-8162-4544-4). Holden-Day.

Jones, Byron W. Inflation in Engineering Economic Analysis. LC 81-13038. 216p. 1982. 29.95x (ISBN 0-471-09048-4, Pub. by Wiley-Interscience). Wiley.

Jones, C. Software Development: A Rigorous Approach. 1980. 34.95 (ISBN 0-13-821884-6). P-H.

Jones, C. E. Science & the Car. Thomas, R. W. & Lowrie, R. S., eds. (gr. 7-12). 1976. 2.75 o.p. (ISBN 0-08-018283-6). Pergamon.

Jones, C. E., ed. see International Symposium, 3rd, Amsterdam, Sept. 1976.

Jones, C. L., jt. auth. see Coxon, A. P.

Jones, C. M. Tennis: How to Become a Champion. (gr. 9 up). 1968. 12.00 (ISBN 0-571-04714-9); pap. 6.50 o. p. (ISBN 0-571-09415-5). Transatlantic.

--Your Book of Tennis. (gr. 4 up). 1970. 7.95 o.p. (ISBN 0-571-08767-1). Transatlantic.

Jones, C. M. & Buxton, Angela. Starting Tennis. (Illus.). 96p. 1976. 7.50 o.p. (ISBN 0-7063-1972-9). Transatlantic.

Jones, C. M., jt. auth. see Davidson, Owen.

Jones, C. R., jt. auth. see Eyre, S. R.

Jones, C. W. Biological Energy Conservation. 2nd ed. (Outline Studies in Biology). 1981. pap. 6.50x (ISBN 0-412-13970-7, Pub. by Chapman & Hall). Methuen Inc.

Jones, Carelton. Baltimore: A Picture History. (Illus.). 208p. Date not set. 19.95o.p. (ISBN 0-910254-03-6); pap. 14.95 (ISBN 0-910254-22-2). Bodine.

Jones, Carleton. Lost Baltimore Landmarks. LC 82-60385. (Illus.). 64p. (Orig.). 1982. pap. 7.95 (ISBN 0-940776-04-9). Marclay Assoc.

--Maryland, A Picture History. (Illus.). 176p. 1976. 19.95 (ISBN 0-686-36829-0). Md Hist.

Jones, Catherine. Immigration & Social Policy in Britain. 275p. 1980. pap. 13.95x (ISBN 0-422-74680-0, Pub. by Tavistock England). Methuen Inc.

Jones, Catherine, jt. auth. see Stevenson, June.

Jones, Catherine & Stevenson, June, eds. The Yearbook of Social Policy in Britain 1980-1981. 239p. 1982. 35.00 (ISBN 0-7100-9083-8). Routledge & Kegan.

Jones, Charles C., Jr. Negro Myths from the Georgia Coast. LC 68-21779. 1969. Repr. of 1888 ed. 34.00x (ISBN 0-8103-3836-X). Gale.

Jones, Charles E. Guide to the Study of the Holiness Movement. LC 74-659. (ATLA Bibliography Ser.: No. 1). 1974. 40.00 o.p. (ISBN 0-8108-0703-3). Scarecrow.

Jones, Charles K. & Greenwich, Lorenzo K. A Choice Collection of the Works of Francis Johnson: America's First Native-Born Master of Music, Vol. 1. LC 82-62078. (Illus.). 150p. 1983. 24.95 (ISBN 0-911073-00-0). Point Two.

Jones, Charles L., jt. auth. see Coxon, Anthony P.

Jones, Charles P., jt. auth. see Poindexter, J. C.

Jones, Charles P., et al. Essentials of Modern Investments. LC 77-71239. 450p. 1977. 31.95x (ISBN 0-471-06745-8); tchr's. manual 3.00x (ISBN 0-471-07470-5). Wiley.

Jones, Cheslyn & Wainwright, Geoffrey, eds. The Study of Liturgy. 1978. 25.95x (ISBN 0-19-520075-6); pap. 11.95x (ISBN 0-19-520076-4). Oxford U Pr.

Jones, Christopher & Satterthwaite, Linton. The Monuments & Inscriptions of Tikal, Pt. A: The Carved Monuments. LC 83-1086. (Tikal Reports Ser.: No. 33). (Illus.). 364p. 1982. 55.00 (ISBN 0-934718-07-5). Univ Mus of U PA.

Jones, Christopher G., jt. auth. see Timm, Paul R.

Jones, Chuck. Rikki-Tikki-Tavi. (Good Friends Ser.). (Illus.). 48p. (gr. k-6). 1982. 4.95 (ISBN 0-8249-8041-7). Ideals.

Jones, Chuck, ed. see Kipling, Rudyard.

Jones, Claire, et al. Pollution: The Balance of Nature. LC 78-178674. (Real World of Pollution Ser). (Illus.). (gr. 5-11). 1972. PLB 4.95g (ISBN 0-8225-0632-7). Lerner Pubns.

--Pollution: The Food We Eat. LC 74-178673. (Real World of Pollution Ser). (Illus.). (gr. 5-11). 1972. PLB 4.95g (ISBN 0-8225-0634-3). Lerner Pubns.

--Pollution: The Noise We Hear. LC 79-165323. (Real World of Pollution Ser.). (Illus.). (gr. 5-12). 1972. PLB 4.95g (ISBN 0-8225-0631-9). Lerner Pubns.

Jones, Clara S., ed. Public Library Information & Referral Services. 300p. 1976. pap. 12.50 o.s.i. (ISBN 0-915794-06-3). Gaylord Prof Pubns.

Jones, Cleon & Hershey, Ed. Cleon. 1970. 5.95 o.p. (ISBN 0-698-10057-3, Coward). Putnam Pub Group.

Jones, Cordelia. Cat Called Camouflage. LC 79-166339. (Illus.). (gr. 7 up). 1971. 10.95 (ISBN 0-87599-189-0). S G Phillips.

Jones, Cornelia & Way, Olivia R. British Children's Authors. LC 76-44494. 1976. text ed. 12.00 (ISBN 0-8389-0224-3). ALA.

Jones, Craig. Fatal Attraction: A Novel. 1983. 12.95 (ISBN 0-517-54926-3). Crown.

Jones, Crate. Out of the Crate. LC 79-90650. 1979. 7.95 (ISBN 0-87716-113-5, Pub. by Moore Pub Co). F Apple.

Jones, D. An Outline of the Phonetics of English. 9th ed. LC 75-26274. (Illus.). 378p. 1975. 33.50 (ISBN 0-521-21098-4); pap. 15.95 (ISBN 0-521-29041-4). Cambridge U Pr.

--The Phoneme: Its Nature & Use. 3rd ed. LC 70-377868. 1976. Repr. of 1976 ed. 32.50 (ISBN 0-521-21351-7). Cambridge U Pr.

Jones, D. & Goodfellow, M. Bacterial Taxonomy. (Outline Studies in Biology). 1983. pap. 5.95x (ISBN 0-412-13140-4, Pub. by Chapman & Hall England). Methuen Inc.

Jones, D. & Ward, Dennis. Phonetics of Russian. 1969. text ed. 59.50 (ISBN 0-521-06736-7). Cambridge U Pr.

Jones, D., ed. Design, Construction & Rehabilitation of Public Transit Facilities. LC 82-72778. 416p. 1982. pap. text ed. 29.00 (ISBN 0-87262-315-7). Am Soc Civil Eng.

Jones, D., jt. ed. see Elithorn, A.

Jones, D. A. & Lepley, M. Nursing Assessment Across the Life Span. 600p. 1983. 28.95x (ISBN 0-07-032805-6). McGraw.

Jones, D. G. Neurons & Synapses. (Studies in Biology: No. 135). 64p. 1981. pap. text ed. 8.95 (ISBN 0-7131-2825-9). E Arnold.

--Synapses & Synaptosomes: Morphological Aspects. 1975. 66.00x (ISBN 0-412-11270-1, Pub. by Chapman & Hall). Methuen Inc.

Jones, D. S. Electrical & Mechanical Oscillations. (Library of Mathematics). 1968. pap. 5.00 o.p. (ISBN 0-7100-4346-5). Routledge & Kegan.

Jones, Daisy M. Curriculum Targets in the Elementary School. 1977. text ed. 23.95 (ISBN 0-13-196337-6). P-H.

Jones, Dallas L., ed. see National Academy Of Arbitrators - 18th Meeting.

Jones, Dallas L., ed. see National Academy of Arbitrators-20th Annual Meeting.

Jones, Daniel. Pronunciation of English. 4th ed. 1956. 29.50 (ISBN 0-521-05448-6); pap. 11.95x (ISBN 0-521-09369-4). Cambridge U Pr.

Jones, Dave. Making & Repairing Western Saddles. LC 81-19106. (Illus.). 160p. 1982. 14.95 (ISBN 0-668-04906-5). Arco.

--Practical Western Training. LC 72-485. (Illus.). 176p. 1968. 6.95 o.p. (ISBN 0-668-02537-9). Arco.

--The Western Trainer. LC 73-92075. (Illus.). 1979. pap. 5.95 o.p. (ISBN 0-668-04791-7, 4791). Arco.

Jones, David. Chartism & the Chartists. LC 75-4179. 256p. 1975. text ed. 18.95 o.p. (ISBN 0-312-13090-2). St Martin.

--Roman Quarry & Other Sequences. 300p. 1982. 27.50 (ISBN 0-935296-25-5); pap. 14.95 (ISBN 0-935296-24-7). Sheep Meadow.

--Sleeping Lord & Other Fragments. 111p. 1974. 11.95 (ISBN 0-571-10350-2). Faber & Faber.

Jones, David & Mayo, Marjorie. Community Work: Two. 1975. 16.95 (ISBN 0-7100-8191-X). Routledge & Kegan.

Jones, David A. Blow Molding. rev. ed. LC 61-18585. 220p. 1971. Repr. of 1961 ed. 9.95 (ISBN 0-88275-027-5). Krieger.

--Crime Without Punishment. LC 78-19538. 304p. 1979. 24.95x (ISBN 0-669-02512-7). Lexington Bks.

--The Law of Criminal Procedure: An Analysis & Critique. 600p. 1981. text ed. 19.95 (ISBN 0-316-47283-2). Little.

Jones, David A., jt. auth. see O'Donnell, William J.

Jones, David B. Practical Palmistry. 95p. 1981. 40.00x (ISBN 0-686-97045-4, Pub. by Rider England). State Mutual Bk.

Jones, David L. Paraguay: A Bibliography. LC 77-83382. (Reference Library of Humanities Ser.). 1979. lib. bdg. 52.00 o.s.i. (ISBN 0-8240-9825-0). Garland Pub.

Jones, David O., jt. auth. see Perone, Sam P.

Jones, David P. Peking. (The Great Cities Ser.). (Illus.). 1978. lib. bdg. 12.00 (ISBN 0-8094-2328-6). Silver.

Jones, David R., ed. Soviet Armed Forces Review Annual. (SAFRA Ser.: Vol. 6). 47.00 (ISBN 0-87569-075-0). Academic Intl.

Jones, Dean. Under Running Laughter. (Illus.). 208p. 1982. 12.95 (ISBN 0-310-60320-X). Chosen Bks Pub.

Jones, Derek C. & Svejnar, Jan, eds. Participatory & Self-Managed Firms: Evaluating Economic Performance. LC 80-8612. (Illus.). 416p. 1982. 35.95x (ISBN 0-669-04328-1). Lexington Bks.

Jones, Derek L. Everywoman: A Gynaecological Guide for Life. 3rd ed. (Illus.). 1982. 16.95 (ISBN 0-571-18062-0); pap. 4.95 (ISBN 0-686-83077-6). Faber & Faber.

Jones, Derek Llewellyn see Llewellyn-Jones, Derek.

Jones, Diana. Patterns for Canvas Embroidery. 1977. 19.95 o.p. (ISBN 0-7134-3285-3, Pub. by Batsford England). David & Charles.

Jones, Diana W. Power of Three. LC 77-3028. 250p. (gr. 5-9). 1977. 9.95 (ISBN 0-688-80106-4); PLB 9.55 (ISBN 0-688-84106-6). Greenwillow.

Jones, Diane. When You Least Expect Love. (YA) 1978. 6.95 (ISBN 0-685-84750-0, Avalon). Bouregy.

Jones, Diane W. Witch Week. (gr. 5-9). 1982. 9.50 (ISBN 0-688-01534-4). Greenwillow.

Jones, Dolores B., ed. Children's Literature Awards & Winners: A Directory of Prizes, Authors, & Illustrators. 1st ed. 1983. 65.00x (ISBN 0-8103-0171-7, Co-pub. by Neal-Schuman). Gale.

Jones, Don. Miss Liberty Meet Crazyhorse. 62p. 1972. 5.00 o.p. (ISBN 0-8040-0584-2); pap. 3.25 (ISBN 0-8040-0585-0). Swallow.

--Ultra Plot. (Illus.). 60p. 1981. pap. text ed. 19.95 (ISBN 0-930182-23-5). Avant-Garde CR.

--Ultra Plot: Complete Mailing. (Label & Filing System Interface Ser.). (Illus.). 50p. 1981. pap. text ed. 15.95 (ISBN 0-930182-25-1). Avant-Garde CR.

Jones, Donald G., ed. Business, Religion & Ethics: Inquiry & Encounter. LC 82-14479. 288p. 1982. 25.00 (ISBN 0-89946-164-6); pap. text ed. 12.95 (ISBN 0-89946-166-2). Oelgeschlager.

--Doing Ethics in Business: New Ventures in Management Development. LC 82-8294. 224p. 1982. text ed. 22.50 (ISBN 0-89946-159-X); pap. text ed. 12.95 (ISBN 0-89946-167-0). Oelgeschlager.

Jones, Donald G. & Troy, Helen, eds. A Bibliography of Business Ethics, Nineteen Seventy-Six to Nineteen Eighty. LC 81-16003. (Publications of the Colgate Darden Graduate School of Business Administration, University of Virginia). 220p. 1982. 14.95x (ISBN 0-8139-0921-X). U Pr of Va.

Jones, Donald K. The Making of the Education System, 1851-1881. (Students Library of Education). 1978. 14.95x (ISBN 0-7100-8707-1). Routledge & Kegan.

Jones, Dorothy, et al. Medical Surgical Nursing: A Conceptual Approach. (Illus.). 1978. text ed. 37.50 (ISBN 0-07-032785-8, HP); instructors manual 7.95 (ISBN 0-07-032786-6). McGraw.

Jones, Dorothy A., et al. Medical Surgical Nursing: A Conceptual Approach. 2nd ed. (Illus.). 1632p. 1982. 37.95x (ISBN 0-07-032787-4). McGraw.

Jones, Dorothy K. A Century of Servitude: Pribilof Aleuts Under U. S. Rule. LC 80-1407. 198p. 1980. lib. bdg. 20.00 (ISBN 0-8191-1348-4); pap. text ed. 9.75 (ISBN 0-8191-1349-2). U Pr of Amer.

Jones, Douglas C. Arrest Sitting Bull. 1978. lib. bdg. 13.50 o.p. (ISBN 0-8161-6555-6, Large Print Bks). G K Hall.

Jones, Douglas L., jt. ed. see Levy, Leonard W.

Jones, E. E. & Sinclair, D. J. Atlas of London. 1968. 220.00 (ISBN 0-08-013255-3). Pergamon.

Jones, E. Alfred. The Loyalists of New Jersey: Their Memorials, Petitions, Claims, etc., from English Records, Vol. 10. 346p. 1927. 12.50 (ISBN 0-686-81824-5). NJ Hist Soc.

Jones, E. B. Instrument Technology, Vol. 1. 3rd ed. 1973. text ed. 32.95 (ISBN 0-408-70535-3). Butterworth.

Jones, E. D., ed. English Critical Essays, Sixteenth to Eighteenth Centuries. (World's Classics Ser: No. 240). 16.95 (ISBN 0-19-250240-9, WC240). Oxford U Pr.

Jones, E. G., ed. Guide to Science & Technology in Eastern Europe: A Reference Guide to Science & Technology in Eastern Europe. (Illus.). 320p. 150.00x (ISBN 0-686-75637-1, Pub. by Longman). Gale.

Jones, E. L. Agriculture & the Industrial Revolution. LC 74-2400. 233p. 1974. 24.95x o.s.i. (ISBN 0-470-44870-9). Halsted Pr.

--The European Miracle: Environments, Economies & Geopolitics in the History of Europe & Asia. 274p. 1981. text ed. 32.50 (ISBN 0-521-23588-X); pap. text ed. 9.95 (ISBN 0-521-28055-9). Cambridge U Pr.

Jones, E. L., jt. auth. see Curran, R. C.

Jones, E. R. The Business Guide to Selling Information by Mail. (Illus.). 110p. 1982. 15.00 (ISBN 0-9600934-4-3). E R Jones.

--How to Promote Your Own Product As a Wholesaler. (Illus.). 100p. 1983. 25.00 (ISBN 0-9600934-5-1). E R Jones.

--Simplified Inventory System: For Collectors, Investors & Dealers. (Illus.). 68p. 1982. 6.75 (ISBN 0-9600934-3-5). E R Jones.

Jones, E. Sherwood. Essential Intensive Care. (Illus.). 1978. text ed. 24.00x (ISBN 0-397-58236-6, Lippincott Medical). Lippincott.

Jones, E. Stanley. Abundant Living. (Festival Bks.). 1976. pap. 3.95 (ISBN 0-687-00689-9). Abingdon.

--Cristo y el Comunismo. Gattinoni, C. T., tr. from Eng. Orig. Title: Christ's Alternative to Communism. 96p. (Span.). 1981. pap. 1.95 (ISBN 0-311-05040-9, Edit Mundo). Casa Bautista.

--The Divine Yes. LC 74-17119. 160p. 1975. 5.95 o.p. (ISBN 0-687-10988-4). Abingdon.

--Divine Yes. 1976. pap. write for info (ISBN 0-89616-154-4). Jove Pubns.

Jones, Edward D. Economic Crises. LC 79-51862. 1983. Repr. of 1900 ed. 21.50 (ISBN 0-88355-955-2). Hyperion Conn.

Jones, Edward L. Black Orator's Workbook. 1982. pap. 12.95 (ISBN 0-9602458-4-7). Ed-Lynne Jones.

Jones, Edward T. L. P. Hartley. (English Author Ser.). 1978. 14.95 (ISBN 0-8057-6703-7, Twayne). G K Hall.

Jones, Edward V. Reading Instruction for the Adult Illiterate. LC 80-23063. 182p. 1981. 15.00 (ISBN 0-8389-0317-7). ALA.

Jones, Eldred, ed. African Literature Today: Focus on Criticism, No. 7. LC 72-75254. 192p. 1975. text ed. 19.50x (ISBN 0-8419-0168-6, Africana). Holmes & Meier.

--African Literature Today: Poetry in Africa, No. 6. LC 72-75254. 1973. text ed. 24.50x (ISBN 0-8419-0133-3, Africana); pap. 17.50x (Africana). Holmes & Meier.

--African Literature Today: The Novel in Africa, No. 5. LC 72-75254. 156p. 1971. pap. 17.50x (ISBN 0-8419-0227-5, Africana). Holmes & Meier.

Jones, Eldred D. Wole Soyinka. (World Authors Ser.). 1971. lib. bdg. 13.95 (ISBN 0-8057-2852-X, Twayne). G K Hall.

Jones, Eldred D., ed. African Literature Today: Myth, History & the Contemporary Writer, Vol. 11. LC 72-75254. 240p. 1980. text ed. 32.95x (ISBN 0-8419-0577-0, Africana); pap. text ed. 18.00x (ISBN 0-8419-0652-1). Holmes & Meier.

Jones, Eldred D. & Palmer, Eustace, eds. Africa Literature Today: No. 12, New Writing, New Approaches. 256p. 1982. 32.50 (ISBN 0-8419-0719-6); pap. 14.95 (ISBN 0-8419-0720-X). Holmes & Meier.

Jones, Elinor. Lucetta. 1979. pap. 2.25 o.p. (ISBN 0-451-08698-8, E8698, Sig). NAL.

--Tamara. 1980. pap. 2.75 o.p. (ISBN 0-451-09450-6, E9450, Sig). NAL.

Jones, Elizabeth, ed. Declassified Documents Reference System Retrospective Collection. LC 76-39673. 1977. 3151.00 (ISBN 0-8408-0029-0). Res Pubns Conn.

--Declassified Documents Reference System: 1979 Annual Collection. 1979. 425.00 (ISBN 0-8408-0329-X). Res Pubns Conn.

--Declassified Documents Reference System: 1977 Annual Collection. 1978. lib. bdg. 425.00 (ISBN 0-8408-0328-1). Res Pubns Conn.

--Declassified Documents Reference System: 1978 Annual Collection. 1978. 425.00 (ISBN 0-8408-0327-3). Res Pubns Conn.

Jones, Elmer W. Fundamentals of Applied Electricity. 1956. 7.00 o.p. (ISBN 0-685-07634-2). Glencoe.

Jones, Elmer W. & Johnston, John L. Adequate Wiring for Home & Farm. 1963. 7.00 o.p. (ISBN 0-02-819260-5). Glencoe.

Jones, Elwyn. Barlow Exposed. LC 76-28040. 1977. 7.95 o.p. (ISBN 0-312-06685-6). St Martin.

Jones, Emrys. Scenic Form in Shakespeare. 1971. 28.95x (ISBN 0-19-812012-5). Oxford U Pr.

Jones, Emrys & Eyles, John. An Introduction to Social Geography. 1977. text ed. 37.50x o.p. (ISBN 0-19-874062-X); pap. 12.95x (ISBN 0-19-874063-8). Oxford U Pr.

Jones, Ernest. The Life & Work of Sigmund Freud, 3 vols. Incl. Vol. 1. The Formative Years & the Great Discoveries, 1856-1900. 428p. 1953 (ISBN 0-465-04016-0); Vol. 2. Years of Maturity, 1901-1919. 512p. 1955 (ISBN 0-465-04017-9); Vol. 3. The Last Phase, 1919-1939. 537p. 1957 (ISBN 0-465-04018-7). LC 53-8700. (Illus.). 75.00x set (ISBN 0-465-04015-2); 25.95x ea. Basic.

Jones, Ernest, ed. see Freud, Sigmund.

Jones, Eugene W. & Brown, Lyle C. Practising Texas Politics. 5th ed. LC 82-81521. 576p. 1982. pap. text ed. 12.95 (ISBN 0-395-32793-8); instrs.' guide avail. (ISBN 0-395-32795-4). HM.

Jones, Eugene W., et al. Practicing Texas Politics. 4th ed. LC 79-88888. 1980. pap. text ed. 12.50 (ISBN 0-395-28257-8); instr's. manual 1.35 (ISBN 0-395-28258-6); study guide 7.95 (ISBN 0-395-28259-4). HM.

Jones, Evan. American Food. 2nd ed. 1981. 20.50 (ISBN 0-394-50848-3); pap. 9.95 (ISBN 0-394-74646-5, Vin). Random.

Jones, Evan, jt. auth. see Brady, Terence.

Jones, Evans, jt. auth. see Jones, Judith.

Jones, Ezra E., jt. auth. see Anderson, James D.

Jones, F. Chapter Three - Transfer Printing. 75.00x (ISBN 0-686-98205-3, Pub. by Soc Dyers & Colour); pap. 50.00x (ISBN 0-686-98206-1). State Mutual Bk.

Jones, F. G. & Jones, Margaret G. Pests of Field Crops. 2nd ed. LC 74-75834. 448p. 1974. 32.50 (ISBN 0-312-60305-3). St Martin.

Jones, F. Margaret. Language Disability in Children. 270p. 1980. text ed. 24.95 o.p. (ISBN 0-8391-1479-6). Univ Park.

Jones, F. O., ed. Handbook of American Music & Musicians. LC 76-155355. (Music Ser). 1971. Repr. of 1886 ed. lib. bdg. 22.50 (ISBN 0-306-70163-4). Da Capo.

Jones, Frances M. Defusing Censorship: The Librarian's Guide to Handling Censorship Conflicts. 150p. 1983. lib. bdg. 24.95 (ISBN 0-89774-027-0); pap. 18.50 (ISBN 0-89774-022-X). Oryx Pr.

Jones, Franklin. The Pleasure of Painting. 1981. pap. 13.95 (ISBN 0-89134-047-5). North Light Pub.

Jones, Franklin D. Jig & Fixture Design. 4th ed. (Illus.). 1955. text ed. 37.50 (ISBN 0-8311-1098-8). Indus Pr.

Jones, Fred R. & Aldred, William H. Farm Power & Tractors. 5th ed. (Illus.). 480p. 1980. text ed. 32.50x (ISBN 0-07-032781-5). McGraw.

Jones, G., jt. auth. see Williams, D. A.

Jones, G. A. The Properties of Nuclei. (Oxford Physics Ser.). (Illus.). 1977. 24.00x (ISBN 0-19-851828-5). Oxford U Pr.

Jones, G. A., jt. auth. see Grundy, P. J.

Jones, G. B. & Grealey, S., eds. Roman Manchester. 1974. pap. 6.50 (ISBN 0-7190-0670-8). Manchester.

Jones, G. Lloyd. The Discovery of Hebrew in Tudor England: A Third Language. 300p. 1982. 35.00 (ISBN 0-7190-0875-1). Manchester.

Jones, G. W. & Richter, H. V. Population Resettlement Programs in Southeast Asia. LC 82-73138. (Development Studies Centre Monograph: No. 30). 189p. (Orig.). 1982. pap. text ed. 17.95 (ISBN 0-909150-73-7, 1230). Bks Australia.

Jones, Gareth. The Gentry & the Elizabethan State. (A New History of Wales). (Illus.). 1977. text ed. 7.75x o.p. (ISBN 0-7154-0303-6). Humanities.

Jones, Garth N., et al, eds. Planning, Development, & Change: A Bibliography on Development Administration. 1970. pap. text ed. 12.00x (ISBN 0-8248-0099-0, Eastwest Ctr). UH Pr.

Jones, Gavin W. Review of the Integration of Population & Development Policies & Programs in Asia. (Development Studies Centre Occaisional Papers: No. 30). 53p. (Orig.). 1982. pap. text ed. 4.95 (ISBN 0-909150-83-4, 1231). Bks Australia.

Jones, George, ed. New Approaches to the Study of Central-Local Government Relationships. 200p. 1980. text ed. 32.00x (ISBN 0-566-00332-5). Gower Pub Ltd.

Jones, George F. Oswald Von Wolkenstein. (World Authors Ser.). 1973. lib. bdg. 15.95 (ISBN 0-8057-2992-5, Twayne). G K Hall.

--Walther von der Vogelweide. (World Authors Ser.). 13.95 (ISBN 0-8057-2972-0, Twayne). G K Hall.

Jones, George F. & Savalle, Don, eds. Detailed Reports on the Salzburger Emigrants Who Settled in America, Vol. 7, 1740. (Wormsloe Foundation Ser.). 328p. 1983. 25.00x (ISBN 0-8203-0664-9). U of Ga Pr.

Jones, George T. Music Theory. (Illus.). 288p. (Orig.). 1974. pap. 4.95 (ISBN 0-06-460137-4, CO 137, COS). B&N NY.

Jones, Gerre. How to Market Professional Design Services. 2nd ed. (Illus.). 384p. 1983. text ed. 32.50 (ISBN 0-07-032802-1, P&RB). McGraw.

--Public Relations for the Design Professional. (Illus.). 288p. 1980. 29.95 (ISBN 0-07-032815-3). McGraw.

Jones, Gerre L. How to Market Professional Design Services. (Illus.). 384p. 1973. 31.50 (ISBN 0-07-032800-5, P&RB). McGraw.

--How to Prepare Professional Design Brochures. 1976. 31.50 (ISBN 0-07-032801-3, P&RB). McGraw.

Jones, Graham. Financial Practice & Control. 250p. 1982. pap. text ed. 12.95x (ISBN 0-7121-0640-5). Intl Ideas.

Jones, Grant D., ed. Anthropology & History in Yucatan. (Texas Pan American Ser.). 368p. 1977. text ed. 22.50x o.p. (ISBN 0-292-70314-7). U of Tex Pr.

Jones, Greta, et al. The Presentation of Science by the Media. 1978. 25.00x (ISBN 0-686-96959-6, Pub. by Primary Com England). State Mutual Bk.

Jones, Griffith. Unsolved Mysteries of Time & Place & Space. LC 80-13473. (Monsters & Mysteries Ser.). (gr. 4-10). 1980. pap. 2.25 (ISBN 0-88436-764-9). EMC.

Jones, Gurnos. Quinoline & Its Derivatives. LC 76-26941. (The Chemistry of Heterocyclic Compounds Ser.: Vol. 32, Pt. 1). 898p. 1977. 213.00x (ISBN 0-471-99437-5, Pub. by Wiley-Interscience). Wiley.

Jones, Gurnos, ed. Chemistry of Heteocyclic Compounds: Quinolines - A Series of Monographs, 2 pts, Vol. 32. rev. ed. (Orig.). 1982. Pt. 1, 898 P. 213.00x (ISBN 0-471-99437-5, Pub. by Wiley-Interscience); Pt. 2, 685p. 166.00x (ISBN 0-471-28055-0). Wiley.

Jones, Gwendolyn, ed. Packaging Information Sources. LC 67-18370. (Management Information Guide Ser.: No. 10). 1967. 42.00x (ISBN 0-8103-0811-8). Gale.

Jones, Gwyn. Kings, Beasts, & Heroes. 1972. 15.00x (ISBN 0-19-215181-9). Oxford U Pr.

--Scandinavian Legends & Folk-Tales. (Oxford Myths & Legends Ser.). (Illus.). (gr. 4 up). 1979. 14.95 (ISBN 0-19-274124-1). Oxford U Pr.

Jones, Gwyn, ed. Eirik the Red & Other Icelandic Sagas. (World's Classics Paperback Ser.). 1980. pap. 3.95 (ISBN 0-19-281528-8). Oxford U Pr.

--The Oxford Book of Welsh Verse in English. 1977. 18.95x (ISBN 0-19-211858-7). Oxford U Pr.

Jones, Gwyn & Jones, Thomas, trs. The Mabinogion. 1975. 9.95x (ISBN 0-460-00097-7, Evman); pap. 2.50x (ISBN 0-460-01097-2, Evman). Biblio Dist.

Jones, Gwyn E. & Rolls, Maurice J. Progress in Rural Extension & Community Development: Extension & Relative Advantage in Rural Development, Vol. 1. LC 81-13064. 336p. 1982. 45.00x (ISBN 0-471-10038-2, Pub. by Wiley-Interscience). Wiley.

Jones, H. Theory of Brillouin Zones & Electronic States in Crystals. 2nd rev. ed. 1975. 68.00 (ISBN 0-444-10218-3, North-Holland). Elsevier.

Jones, H., jt. auth. see Hall, G.

Jones, H. B. & Jones, Helen C. Sensual Drugs. LC 76-8154. (Illus.). 1977. 34.50 (ISBN 0-521-21247-2); pap. 9.95 (ISBN 0-521-29077-5). Cambridge U Pr.

Jones, H. G. Local Government Records: An Introduction to Their Management, Preservation, & Use. LC 79-24743. (Illus.). 208p. (Orig.). 1980. pap. text ed. 8.95 (ISBN 0-910050-42-2). AASLH.

Jones, H. G., jt. auth. see Mitchell, Brian R.

Jones, H. Wendy. First Ladies of Alaska, Vol. I. 7.95 (ISBN 0-686-38765-1). W Jones.

--Welcome Aboard Wendy's World. 5.95 (ISBN 0-686-38767-8). W Jones.

--Wendy's Windows. 4.95 (ISBN 0-686-38766-X). W Jones.

Jones, Helen C., jt. auth. see Jones, H. B.

Jones, Henry A. Plays by Henry Arthur Jones: The Silver King, The Case of Rebellious Susan, The Liars. Jackson, Russell, ed. LC 81-18047. (British & American Playwrights 1750-1920). (Illus.). 236p. 1982. 34.50 (ISBN 0-521-23369-0); pap. 12.95 (ISBN 0-521-29936-5). Cambridge U Pr.

Jones, Henry L. Sixty Years in Australia. 1983. 7.95 (ISBN 0-533-05580-6). Vantage.

Jones, Herbert. Sebago Lane Land. (Illus.). 136p. 1982. pap. 6.95 (ISBN 0-87027-152-0). Cumberland Pr.

Jones, Hettie. I Hate to Talk About Your Mother. LC 79-53601. (YA) (gr. 9 up). 1980. 8.95 o.s.i. (ISBN 0-440-04572-X). Delacorte.

Jones, Howard. Uncle Tom's Cabin. LC 74-92333. (gr. 6-8). 1969. pap. text ed. 3.50x o.p. (ISBN 0-675-09414-3). Merrill.

Jones, Howard M. Howard Mumford Jones: An Autobiography. LC 78-65013. 304p. 1979. 25.00 (ISBN 0-299-07770-5). U of Wis Pr.

--Jeffersonianism & the American Novel. LC 66-28267. (Orig.). 1966. text ed. 9.50x o.p. (ISBN 0-8077-1593-X); pap. text ed. 4.50x o.p. (ISBN 0-8077-1590-5). Tchrs Coll.

Jones, Howard M., ed. Emerson on Education: Selections. LC 66-11655. (Orig.). text ed. 9.50 o.p. (ISBN 0-8077-1587-5); pap. text ed. 5.50x (ISBN 0-8077-1584-0). Tchrs Coll.

Jones, Howard M., ed. see Anderson, Sherwood.

Jones, Howard M., tr. see Heine, Heinrich.

Jones, Howard W., Jr. & Rock, John A. Reparative & Constructive Surgery of the Female Generative Tract. (Illus.). 386p. 1982. 49.95 (ISBN 0-683-04470-2). Williams & Wilkins.

Jones, Hugh Percy, ed. Dictionary of Foreign Phrases & Classical Quotations. 552p. 1983. pap. 12.95 (ISBN 0-88072-017-4). Tanager Bks.

Jones, Huw R. A Population Geography. 330p. 1982. pap. text ed. 14.95 scp (ISBN 0-06-043443-0, Harp C). Har-Row.

Jones, I. S. Urban Transport Appraisal. LC 76-54811. 144p. 1977. 34.95 o.s.i. (ISBN 0-470-99032-5). Halsted Pr.

Jones, Ilene. Jobs for Teenagers. 176p. (Orig.). 1983. pap. 2.25 (ISBN 0-345-30905-7). Ballantine.

Jones, J. A. King John & the Magna Carta. (Illus.). 1971. pap. text ed. 5.95x (ISBN 0-582-31463-1). Longman.

Jones, J. A., jt. auth. see Holdich, D. M.

Jones, J. B. A Rebel War Clerk's Diary, Vol. I. (Collector's Library of the Old West). 1982. 26.60 (ISBN 0-8094-4212-4). Silver.

--A Rebel War Clerk's Diary, Vol. II. (Collector's Library of the Civil War). 1982. 26.60 (ISBN 0-8094-4241-8). Silver.

Jones, J. B., et al. Techniques of Chemistry: Vol. 10 Applications of Biochemical Systems in Organic Chemistry, 2 pts. 522p. 1976. Pt. 1. 65.95x o.p. (ISBN 0-471-93267-1); Pt. 2, 575pp. 72.95x o.p. (ISBN 0-471-93270-1); Set. 117.95x (ISBN 0-471-02279-9). Wiley.

Jones, J. Christopher. Design Methods: Seeds of Human Futures 1980 Edition a Review of New Topics. LC 80-41757. 448p. 1981. 25.95x (ISBN 0-471-27958-7, Pub. by Wiley Interscience). Wiley.

Jones, J. Emlyn, intro. by. Alpine Club Library Catalogue: Books & Periodicals. vii, 580p. (Orig.). 1982. pap. 95.00x (ISBN 0-686-82671-X). Heinemann Ed.

Jones, J. Farragut. Tracking the Wolfpack. (The Silent Service Ser.: No. 5). (Orig.). 1981. pap. 2.95 (ISBN 0-440-18589-0). Dell.

Jones, J. G., ed. The Biological Efficiency of Protein Production. LC 72-93672. (Illus.). 400p. 1973. 60.00 (ISBN 0-521-20179-9). Cambridge U Pr.

Jones, J. Knox, Jr., jt. ed. see Anderson, Sydney.

Jones, J. Knox, Jr., et al. Mammals of the Northern Great Plains. LC 82-2693. (Illus.). 422p. 1983. 32.50x (ISBN 0-8032-2557-1). U of Nebr Pr.

Jones, J. Sydney. Hitler in Vienna, 1907-1913: Clues to the Future. LC 81-48454. (Illus.). 1982. 19.95 (ISBN 0-8128-2855-0). Stein & Day.

Jones, J. W., jt. auth. see Stoecker, W. F.

Jones, Jack Colvard. The Anatomy of the Grasshopper: Romalea Microptera. (Illus.). 292p. 1981. spiral 27.50x (ISBN 0-398-04126-1). C C Thomas.

Jones, Jack P. Manual of Professional Remodeling. 400p. (Orig.). 1982. pap. 18.75 (ISBN 0-910460-98-1). Craftsman.

Jones, James. Whistle. 1978. 10.95 o.s.i. (ISBN 0-440-09548-4). Delacorte.

Jones, James A. Counseling Principles for Christian Leaders. 5.95 (ISBN 0-89137-534-1). Quality Pubns.

--I Never Thought It Would Be This Way. 5.95 (ISBN 0-89137-533-3). Quality Pubns.

Jones, James B. & Hawkins, George A. Engineering Thermodynamics: An Introductory Textbook. LC 60-10316. (Illus.). 724p. 1960. text ed. 40.50x (ISBN 0-471-44946-6). Wiley.

Jones, James E., Jr., ed. Reference Supplement: Discrimination in Employment, Unit R-2. LC 79-20411. (Labor Relations & Social Problems Ser.). 304p. 1979. pap. text ed. 4.00 o.p. (ISBN 0-87179-311-3). BNA.

Jones, James E., Jr. see Labor Law Group.

Jones, James H. Bad Blood: The Tuskegee Syphilis Experiment. 1982. 7.95 (ISBN 0-686-81884-9). Free Pr.

Jones, James P. John A. Logan: Stalwart Republican From Illinois. LC 82-2663. (Illus.). xiv, 292p. 1982. 20.00 (ISBN 0-8130-0729-1). U Presses Fla.

Jones, James W. The Texture of Knowledge: An Essay on Religion & Science. LC 80-69036. 112p. 1981. lib. bdg. 18.00 (ISBN 0-8191-1360-3); pap. text ed. 7.25 (ISBN 0-8191-1361-1). U Pr of Amer.

Jones, Jean, ed. see Digrande, Joseph.

Jones, Jean, ed. see King, Bill.

Jones, Jean, ed. see Richardson, Allen G.

Jones, Jean C., ed. see APA Library.

Jones, Jean R., ed. see Mueller, Ellen C.

Jones, Jean R., ed. see Thompson, Edith M. & Thompson, William L.

Jones, Jeanne. Diet for a Happy Heart. LC 75-6713. (Illus.). 192p. 1975. pap. 5.95 o.p. (ISBN 0-912238-57-7). One Hund One Prods.

--Diet for a Happy Heart: A Low-Cholesterol, Low-Saturated Fat, Low Calorie Cookbook. rev. ed. LC 80-25796. (Illus.). 192p. 1981. pap. 6.95 (ISBN 0-89286-183-5). One Hund One Prods.

--Fabulous Fiber Cookbook. rev. ed. LC 77-742. (Illus.). 1979. pap. 6.95 o.p. (ISBN 0-89286-155-X). One Hund One Prods.

--Jeanne Jones' Food Lover's Diet. 240p. 1982. 12.95 (ISBN 0-684-17795-1, ScribT). Scribner.

--More Calculated Cooking: Practical Recipes for Diabetics & Dieters. LC 80-25179. 192p. (Orig.). 1981. pap. 6.95 (ISBN 0-89286-184-3). One Hund One Prods.

--Secrets of Salt-Free Cooking: A Complete Low Sodium Cookbook. LC 79-343. (Illus.). 1979. pap. 6.95 (ISBN 0-89286-147-9). One Hund One Prods.

--Stuffed Spuds: One Hundred Meals in a Potato. 132p. (Orig.). 1982. 11.95 (ISBN 0-87131-392-8); pap. 5.95 (ISBN 0-87131-385-5). M Evans.

Jones, Jeanne & Duffy, Dick. Best Restaurants San Diego County. (Best Restaurants Ser.). 200p. 1983. pap. 4.95 (ISBN 0-89286-215-7). One Hund One Prods.

Jones, Jeanne & Swajeski, Donna. The Love in the Afternoon Cookbook: Recipes from Your Favorite ABC-TV Soap Operas - Ryans Hope, One Life to Live, All My Children, General Hospital. (Illus.). 192p. 1983. pap. 7.95 (ISBN 0-87131-405-3). M Evans.

Jones, Jeff. Yesterday's Lily. (Illus.). 80p. 1980. pap. 8.95 (ISBN 0-8256-9552-X, Quick Fox). Putnam Pub Group.

Jones, Jesse H. Fifty Billion Dollars: My Thirteen Years with the RFC (1932-1945) LC 74-31415. (FDR & the Era of the New Deal Ser.). (Illus.). xvi, 631p. 1975. Repr. of 1951 ed. lib. bdg. 75.00 (ISBN 0-306-70715-2). Da Capo.

Jones, Jo, et al. Paintings & Drawings of the Gypsies of Granada. LC 78-8842. (Illus.). 1969. 34.00x (ISBN 0-8103-5003-3). Gale.

Jones, Jo, jt. auth. see Grant, Neil.

Jones, Joan D., jt. ed. see Baumhover, Lorin S.

Jones, Johanna, jt. auth. see Jones, Joseph.

Jones, John. On Aristotle & Greek Tragedy. LC 80-50895. 288p. 1962. 16.50x (ISBN 0-8047-1092-9); pap. 6.95 (ISBN 0-8047-1093-7, SP11). Stanford U Pr.

Jones, John E. The Greeks. (Young Archeologist Ser.). (Illus.). (gr. 6-9). 1972. PLB 4.49 o.p. (ISBN 0-399-60709-9). Putnam Pub Group.

Jones, John E., jt. auth. see Pfeiffer, J. William.

Jones, John E. & Pfeiffer, J. William, eds. Annual Handbook for Group Facilitators, 1973. LC 73-92841. (Series in Human Relations Training). 292p. 1973. pap. 21.50 (ISBN 0-88390-073-4); looseleaf ntbk. 49.50 (ISBN 0-88390-081-5). Univ Assocs.

--The Annual Handbook for Group Facilitators, 1979. LC 73-92841. (Ser. in Human Relations Training). 295p. 1979. pap. 21.50 (ISBN 0-88390-095-5); looseleaf notebook 49.50 (ISBN 0-88390-093-9). Univ Assocs.

--Annual Handbook for Group Facilitators, 1977. LC 73-92841. (Series in Human Relations Training). 289p. 1977. pap. 21.50 (ISBN 0-88390-091-2); looseleaf ntbk. 49.50 (ISBN 0-88390-090-4). Univ Assocs.

--The Annual Handbook for Group Facilitators, 1981. LC 73-92841. (Series in Human Relations Training). 296p. (Orig.). 1981. pap. 21.50 (ISBN 0-88390-004-1); looseleaf ntbk. 49.50 (ISBN 0-88390-003-3). Univ Assocs.

--Annual Handbook for Group Facilitators,1975. LC 73-92841. (Series in Human Relations Training). 289p. 1975. pap. 21.50 (ISBN 0-88390-079-3); looseleaf 49.50 (ISBN 0-88390-078-5). Univ Assocs.

Jones, John E., jt. ed. see Pfeiffer, J. William.

Jones, John F., jt. auth. see Gibbons, Don C.

Jones, John G. The Amityville Horror II. 400p. (Orig.). 1982. pap. 3.95 (ISBN 0-446-30615-0). Warner Bks.

Jones, John G., ed. Mississippi Writers Talking, Vol. 2. LC 81-23057. (Illus.). 228p. 1983. 15.00 (ISBN 0-87805-174-0); pap. 8.95 (ISBN 0-87805-175-9). U Pr of Miss.

Jones, John I., tr. see Roberts, Kate.

Jones, John P. Modern Reporter's Handbook. Repr. of 1949 ed. lib. bdg. 19.75x (ISBN 0-8371-3964-3, JORH). Greenwood.

Jones, John Paul. Memoirs of Rear-Admiral Paul Jones. LC 77-166333. (Era of the American Revolution Ser.). (Illus.). 1972. Repr. of 1830 ed. lib. bdg. 65.00 (ISBN 0-306-70247-9). Da Capo.

Jones, Joseph & Jones, Johanna. Canadian Fiction. (World Authors Ser.). 1981. lib. bdg. 15.95 (ISBN 0-8057-6473-9, Twayne). G K Hall.

Jones, Joseph F. Studies in Christian Stewardship. (Living Word Paperback Ser.). (Orig.). 1968. pap. 2.95 cancelled (ISBN 0-8344-0014-6). Sweet.

Jones, Joseph J. Life on Waller Creek: A Palaver about History as Pure & Applied Education. (Illus.). 331p. 1982. 17.95 (ISBN 0-931052-06-8); pap. write for info. (ISBN 0-931052-07-6). AAR-Tantalus.

Jones, Joseph M. The Fifteen Weeks. LC 55-8923. 1965. pap. 3.45 (ISBN 0-15-630699-9, H047, Harv). HarBraceJ.

Jones, Joseph R. Antonio de Guevara. (World Authors Ser.). 1975. lib. bdg. 15.95 (ISBN 0-8057-2409-5, Twayne). G K Hall.

Jones, Joyce M. Jungian Psychology in Literary Analysis: A Demonstration Using T. S. Eliot's Poetry. LC 79-66227. 1979. pap. text ed. 6.50 (ISBN 0-8191-0810-3). U Pr of Amer.

Jones, Judith & Jones, Evans. The Book of Bread. LC 82-47527. (Illus.). 352p. 1982. 15.34i (ISBN 0-06-181434-2, HarpT). Har-Row.

Jones, Judith & Nance, Guinevera. Philip Roth. LC 80-53701. (Literature and Life Ser.). 160p. 1981. 11.95 (ISBN 0-8044-2438-1); pap. 4.95 (ISBN 0-8044-6320-4). Ungar.

Jones, Judith, jt. auth. see Nance, Guinevera A.

Jones, Judith P. Thomas More. (English Authors Ser.). 1979. lib. bdg. 12.95 (ISBN 0-8057-6711-8, Twayne). G K Hall.

Jones, K., jt. auth. see Cook, B. W.

Jones, K., jt. auth. see Heslop, R. B.

Jones, K. D., jt. auth. see Bole, A. G.

Jones, K. R. Pierre De Ronsard. (World Authors Ser.: No. 132). Date not set. 12.50 o.p. (ISBN 0-8057-2778-7, Twayne). G K Hall.

Jones, Katherine, ed. see Freud, Sigmund.

Jones, Kathleen. Opening the Door: A Study of New Policies for the Mentally Handicapped. (International Library of Social Policy Ser.). 1975. 24.00x (ISBN 0-7100-8139-1). Routledge & Kegan.

Jones, Kathleen & Brown, John. Issues in Social Policy. 2nd ed. 208p. 1983. pap. price not set (ISBN 0-7100-9440-X). Routledge & Kegan.

Jones, Kathleen, ed. Living the Faith: A Call to the Church. 1980. text ed. 18.95 (ISBN 0-19-213233-4). Oxford U Pr.

--The Year Book of Social Policy in Britain, 1976. 1978. 33.00x o.p. (ISBN 0-7100-8765-9). Routledge & Kegan.

Jones, Kathleen & Baldwin, Sally, eds. The Year Book of Social Policy in Britain, 1975. 1976. 33.00x o.p. (ISBN 0-7100-8380-7). Routledge & Kegan.

Jones, Ken & Welton, Pat. Soccer Skills & Tactics. 1977. 15.95 o.p. (ISBN 0-517-52594-1); pap. 6.95 o.p. (ISBN 0-517-52914-9). Crown.

Jones, Kenneth, jt. auth. see Yawkey, Thomas.

Jones, Kenneth C. & Gaudin, Anthony J. Introductory Biology. LC 76-45648. 619p. 1977. text ed. 27.95x (ISBN 0-471-44875-3); instr's manual 6.50 (ISBN 0-471-02381-7); study guide avail. Wiley.

Jones, Kenneth G., jt. ed. see Webb Society.

Jones, Kenneth L., jt. ed. see Nyhan, William L.

Jones, Kenneth L., et al. Dimensions: A Changing Concept of Health. 5th ed. 532p. 1982. text ed. 19.50 scp (ISBN 0-06-043442-2, HarpC); instr's resource bk. avail. (ISBN 0-06-363419-8); test bank avail. (ISBN 0-06-363418-X). Har-Row.

Jones, Kenneth P. U. S. Diplomats in Europe Nineteen Hundred Nineteen-Nineteen Hundred Forty-One. (Illus.). 240p. 1983. Repr. lib. bdg. 35.00 (ISBN 0-87436-349-7); pap. text ed. 12.75 (ISBN 0-87436-351-9). ABC-Clio.

--U. S. Diplomats: In Europe, 1919-1941. LC 81-829. (Illus.). 240p. 1981. 35.00 (ISBN 0-87436-311-X). ABC-Clio.

Jones, Kenneth W. Arya Dharm: Hindu Consciousness in Nineteenth-Century Punjab. LC 74-27290. 350p. 1976. 33.00x (ISBN 0-520-02919-4). U of Cal Pr.

--Railways for Pleasure: The Complete Guide to Steam & Scenic Lines in Great Britain & Ireland. (Illus.). 160p. 1982. pap. 12.95 (ISBN 0-7188-2446-6, Pub. by Salem Hse Ltd.). Merrimack Bk Serv.

Jones, L. & Vaughan, J. Scientific & Technical Information on the Metals Industry: Report of the Metals Information Review Committee. 1982. 50.00x (ISBN 0-7123-3008-9, Pub. by Brit Lib England). State Mutual Bk.

Jones, L. Meyer, et al. Veterinary Pharmacology & Therapeutics. 4th ed. (Illus.). 1977. 61.50x o.p. (ISBN 0-8138-1740-4). Iowa St U Pr.

Jones, Landon Y. Great Expectations: America & the Baby Boom Generation. 512p. 1980. 15.95 (ISBN 0-698-11049-8, Coward). Putnam Pub Group.

Jones, Larry. Build a Brand New You. 1983. pap. 2.50 (ISBN 0-686-82529-2). Tyndale.

--Practice to Win. Date not set. pap. 3.95 (ISBN 0-8423-4887-5). Tyndale.

Jones, Larry & Winslow, George. Encyclopedia of Cliches. 276p. 1982. pap. 10.95 (ISBN 0-89893-511-3). CDP.

Jones, Leonard A., ed. Index to Legal Periodical Literature, 1888-1899, 2 Vols. 1963. 40.00 o.s.i. (ISBN 0-379-20008-2). Oceana.

Jones, LeRoi & Abernathy, Billy. In Our Terribleness: Pictures of the Hip World. LC 76-81290. 1969. 7.95 o.p. (ISBN 0-672-50875-3). Bobbs.

Jones, Leroy P. Public Enterprise & Economic Development: The Korea Case. 1975. text ed. 12.00x (ISBN 0-8248-0538-0). UH Pr.

Jones, Leroy P., ed. Public Enterprise in Less-Developed Countries. LC 82-1206. 420p. 1982. 39.50 (ISBN 0-521-24821-3). Cambridge U Pr.

Jones, Lewis see Allen, W. S.

Jones, Linda K., jt. ed. see Longacre, Robert E.

Jones, Lloyd. Healing Forces. 1969. pap. 2.00 (ISBN 0-910140-25-1). Anthony.

Jones, Louis C. Cooperstown. 6.50 (ISBN 0-917334-11-6). Fenimore Bk.

--Things That Go Bump in the Night. (York State Bks.). (Illus.). 220p. 1983. pap. 9.95 (ISBN 0-8156-0184-0). Syracuse U Pr.

--Three Eyes on the Past: Exploring New York State Folk Life. LC 82-7334. (York State Bks.). (Illus.). 240p. (Orig.). 1982. pap. 12.95 (ISBN 0-8156-0179-4). Syracuse U Pr.

Jones, Lynn L., jt. auth. see Case, Kenneth E.

Jones, M. Australian Local Government: Organizational & Social Planning. LC 79-301985. 1978. pap. text ed. 14.95x o.p. (ISBN 0-686-65324-6, 00512). Heinemann Ed.

Jones, M., jt. auth. see Hornby, W. F.

Jones, M., ed. New Essays on Tolstoy. LC 78-1158. (Illus.). 1979. 34.50 (ISBN 0-521-22091-2). Cambridge U Pr.

Jones, M. E. Logistic Support: Subsea Oil Production. 1983. text ed. 35.95 (ISBN 0-87201-434-7). Gulf Pub.

Jones, M. H. A Practical Introduction to Electric Circuits. LC 76-11083. (Illus.). 1977. 44.50 (ISBN 0-521-21291-X); pap. 14.95x (ISBN 0-521-29087-2). Cambridge U Pr.

Jones, M. H. & Woodcock, J. T. Ultraviolet Spectometry of Floatation Reagents With Special Reference to the Determination of Xanthate in Flotation Liquors. 28p. 1973. 11.50 (ISBN 0-900488-20-4). IMM North Am.

Jones, M. J., ed. Advances in Extractive Metallurgy & Refining. 635p. 1972. text ed. 40.25x (ISBN 0-900488-06-9). IMM North Am.

--Commonwealth Mining & Metallurgical Congress, Hong Kong, 11th, 1978: Proceedings. (Commonwealth Mining & Metallurgical Congresses Ser.). 818p. 1979. text ed. 118.00x (ISBN 0-900488-45-X). IMM North Am.

--Complex Metallurgy Seventy-Eight. 143p. (Orig.). 1978. pap. text ed. 63.25x (ISBN 0-900488-42-5). IMM North Am.

--Complex Sulphide Ores. 278p. (Orig.). 1980. pap. text ed. 161.00x (ISBN 0-900488-51-4). IMM North Am.

--Geology, Mining & Extractive Processing of Uranium. 171p. (Orig.). 1975. pap. text ed. 63.25x (ISBN 0-900488-35-2). IMM North Am.

--International Mineral Processing Congress 1973. 10th ed. 1209p. 1974. text ed. 72.00x (ISBN 0-900488-24-7). IMM North Am.

--Mineral Processing & Extractive Metallurgy. (Proceedings of the Ninth Commonwealth Mining & Metallurgical Congress 1969: Vol. 3). 938p. 1970. text ed. 51.75x (ISBN 0-900488-05-0). IMM North Am.

--Minerals & the Environment. 803p. 1975. text ed. 86.25x (ISBN 0-900488-28-X). IMM North Am.

--Mining & Petroleum Geology. (Proceedings of the Ninth Commonwealth Mining & Metallurgical Congress 1969: Vol. 2). 774p. 1970. text ed. 46.00x (ISBN 0-900488-03-4). IMM North Am.

--Mining & Petroleum Technology. (Proceedings of the Ninth Commonwealth Mining & Metallurgical Congress 1969: Vol. 1). 1059p. 1970. text ed. 51.75x (ISBN 0-900488-04-2). IMM North Am.

--National & International Management of Mineral Resources. 350p. (Orig.). 1981. pap. text ed. 132.25x (ISBN 0-900488-58-1). IMM North Am.

--Physical & Fabrication Metallurgy. (Proceedings of the Ninth Commonwealth Mining & Metallurgical Congress 1969: Vol. 4). 561p. 1970. text ed. 46.00x (ISBN 0-900488-01-8). IMM North Am.

--Process Engineering of Pyrometallurgy. 105p. (Orig.). 1974. pap. text ed. 28.75x (ISBN 0-900488-23-9). IMM North Am.

--Tunnelling Eighty-Two. (Orig.). 1982. pap. text ed. 110.00x (ISBN 0-900488-62-X). IMM North Am.

--Tunnelling '76. 455p. 1977. text ed. 95.00x (ISBN 0-900488-34-4). IMM North Am.

--Tunnelling '79. 408p. 1979. text ed. 100.00x (ISBN 0-900488-47-6). IMM North Am.

Jones, M. J. & Oblatt, R., eds. Tours Guidebook, Eleventh CMMC. 76p. (Orig.). 1978. pap. text ed. 21.75x (ISBN 0-900488-40-9). IMM North Am.

Jones, M. N. Biological Interfaces. LC 74-21860. 240p. 1975. 85.00 (ISBN 0-444-41293-X, North Holland); pap. text ed. 16.75 (ISBN 0-444-41306-5, North Holland). Elsevier.

Jones, M. N., ed. Biochemical Thermodynamics. (Studies in Modern Thermodynamics: Vol. 1). 1979. 74.50 (ISBN 0-444-41761-3). Elsevier.

Jones, Mablen. Taking Care of Clothes: An Owner's Manual for Care, Repair, & Spot Removal. LC 82-5599. (Illus.). 288p. 1982. 16.95 (ISBN 0-312-78373-6); pap. 9.95 (ISBN 0-312-78374-4). St Martin.

Jones, Mablen, jt. auth. see Silberstein-Storfer, Muriel.

Jones, Mack M. Shopwork on the Farm. 2nd ed. (Test Ed.). 1955. text ed. 23.32x (ISBN 0-07-032868-4, W). McGraw.

Jones, Maitland & Moss, Robert A. Reactive Intermediates, Vol. II. (A Serial Publication Ser.). 380p. 1981. 54.95x (ISBN 0-471-01875-9, Pub. by Wiley-Interscience). Wiley.

Jones, Maitland, jt. ed. see Moss, Robert A., Jr.

Jones, Maitland, Jr., jt. auth. see Moss, Robert A., Jr.

Jones, Maitland, Jr. & Moss, Robert A., eds. Reactive Intermediates: A Serial Publication, 2 vols. (Reactive Intermediates: a Serial Publication). 349p. 1978. Vol. 1. 37.95x o.p. (ISBN 0-471-01874-0, Pub. by Wiley-Interscience); Vol. 2. 54.95x (ISBN 0-471-01875-9). Wiley.

Jones, Malcolm, jt. auth. see Kiernan, Chris.

Jones, Malcolm V. & Terry, Garth M., eds. New Essays on Dostoyevsky. LC 82-14566. 256p. Date not set. 39.50 (ISBN 0-521-24890-6). Cambridge U Pr.

Jones, Maldwyn A. American Immigration. LC 60-8301. (Chicago History of American Civilization Ser). (Illus.). 1960. 15.00x (ISBN 0-226-40631-8); pap. 6.95 (ISBN 0-226-40632-6, CHAC11). U of Chicago Pr.

Jones, Marc E. Marc Edmund Jones Five Hundred, Vol. 2. 1984. lib. bdg. 10.95 (ISBN 0-88231-046-1); pap. 7.95 (ISBN 0-685-59808-X). ASI Pubs Inc. Postponed.

Jones, Margaret B., jt. auth. see Nessel, Denise D.

Jones, Margaret E. Dolores Medio. (World Authors Ser.). 1974. lib. bdg. 15.95 (ISBN 0-8057-2610-1, Twayne). G K Hall.

Jones, Margaret G., jt. auth. see Jones, F. G.

Jones, Margaret H., jt. auth. see Carterette, Edward C.

Jones, Marian. Bonds of Enchantment. (Superromances Ser.). 384p. 1983. pap. 2.95 (ISBN 0-373-70068-7, Pub. by Worldwide). Harlequin Bks.

Jones, Marilyn P., jt. auth. see Moorman, Lawrence.

Jones, Mark. A Catalogue of the French Medals in the British Museum: Vol. 1, AD 1402-1610. 288p. 1982. 129.00x (ISBN 0-7141-0855-3, Pub. by Brit Mus Pubns England). State Mutual Bk.

Jones, Mary A. Tell Me About Jesus. rev. ed. (Illus.). (ps-3). 1967. pap. 3.95 o.s.i. (ISBN 0-528-87657-0). Rand.

Jones, Mary Ann, et al. A Second Chance for Families: Evaluation of a Program to Reduce Foster Care. LC 76-1518. (Orig.). 1976. pap. text ed. 7.20 (ISBN 0-87868-158-2, F-54). Child Welfare.

Jones, Mary E. The Eastern Way of Love. LC 76-50636. 1977. 9.95 o.p. (ISBN 0-671-22448-4). S&S.

Jones, Mary H. Swords into Ploughshares. LC 70-109757. (Illus.). 1971. Repr. of 1937 ed. lib. bdg. 18.50x (ISBN 0-8371-4247-4, JOSP). Greenwood.

Jones, Mary L. Better Soybean Recipes. 1964. pap. 2.95 (ISBN 0-911080-13-9). Outdoor Pict.

Jones, Maxwell. The Process of Change: From a Closed to an Open System in a Mental Hospital. (Therapeutic Communities Section, International Library of Group Psychotherapy & Group Processes). 220p. 1982. 20.00x (ISBN 0-7100-9255-5). Routledge & Kegan.

Jones, Melvin E., jt. auth. see Holten, M. Gary.

Jones, Mervyn. Twilight of the Day. 384p. 1974. 8.95 o.p. (ISBN 0-671-21815-8). S&S.

Jones, Michael, ed. Prayers & Graces. 1980. 7.50 (ISBN 0-903540-33-9, Pub. by Floris Books). St George Bk Serv.

Jones, Michael E. Deep Water Oil Production & Manned Underwater Structures. (Illus.). 245p. 1981. 55.00x (ISBN 0-8448-1401-6). Crane-Russak Co.

--Deepwater Oil Production & Manned Underwater Structures. 260p. cancelled (ISBN 0-87201-167-4). Gulf Pub.

--The Logistic Support of Subsea Oil Production. 116p. 1983. 40.00x (ISBN 0-8448-1433-4). Crane-Russak.

Jones, Michael J. Eurotunnel '80. 156p. (Orig.). 1980. pap. text ed. 77.75x (ISBN 0-900488-50-6). IMM North Am.

Jones, Michael O. The Hand Made Object & Its Maker. LC 73-93055. (Illus.). 288p. 1975. 22.50x o.s.i. (ISBN 0-520-02697-7). U of Cal Pr.

Jones, Michael O., jt. auth. see Georges, Robert A.

Jones, Michael W. The Cartoon History of the American Revolution. LC 75-6876. (Illus.). 192p. 1975. 20.00 o.p. (ISBN 0-399-11598-6). Putnam Pub Group.

Jones, Michael W., jt. auth. see Flower, Raymond.

Jones, Mike. Sometimes I Wonder How to Thank Him. LC 75-26325. (Stories That Win Ser.). 1976. pap. 0.95 o.p. (ISBN 0-8163-0266-9, 19424-1). Pacific Pr Pub Assn.

Jones, Mike H. Supremacy & Subordination of Labour: The Hierarchy of Work in the Early Labour Movement. xi, 220p. 1982. text ed. 27.00x (ISBN 0-435-82417-1). Heinemann Ed.

Jones, N. S. British Cumaceans: Arthropoda: Crustacea: Keys & Notes for the Identification of the Species. (Synopses of the British Fauna Ser.). 1976. pap. 8.00 o.s.i. (ISBN 0-12-389350-X). Acad Pr.

Jones, Nathan. The Childrens Choir Christmas Book. 31p. 1982. 9.95 (ISBN 0-943586-00-3). N Allen Pub.

Jones, Neil D., jt. auth. see Muchnick, Steven S.

Jones, Norman. Faith by Statute: Parliament & the Settlement of Religion, 1559. (Royal Historical Society Studies in History: No. 32). 246p. 1982. text ed. 33.25x (ISBN 0-391-02689-5, Pub. by Swiftbks England). Humanities.

--Keep in Touch: How to Communicate Better by Responding to the Feelings Instead of the Event. 142p. 1981. 10.95 (ISBN 0-13-514778-6); pap. 4.95 (ISBN 0-13-514760-3). P-H.

Jones, Norman L. & Campbell, Moran. Clinical Exercise Testing. 2nd ed. (Illus.). 268p. 1982. 32.50 (ISBN 0-7216-5225-5). Saunders.

Jones, O. C., Jr. & Bankoff, S. G., eds. Symposium on the Thermal & Hydraulic Aspects of Nuclear Reactor Safety-Liquid Metal Fast Breeder Reactors, Vol. 2. 1977. pap. text ed. 25.00 o.p. (ISBN 0-685-86879-6, G00128). ASME.

Jones, O. Garfield. Parliamentary Procedure at a Glance. (gr. 9 up). 1971. pap. 4.50 (ISBN 0-8015-5766-6, 0437-130, Hawthorn). Dutton.

Jones, O. R., ed. Private Language Argument. LC 76-124949. (Controversies in Philosophy Ser). 1971. 18.95 o.p. (ISBN 0-312-64715-8). St Martin.

Jones, Olive, tr. see Rettich, Margret.

Jones, Owen. Chinese Design & Pattern in Full Color. 48p. 1981. pap. 6.95 (ISBN 0-486-24204-8). Dover.

Jones, P., jt. ed. see Covington, A. K.

Jones, P. M., jt. ed. see Lucas, St. John.

Jones, P. V., ed. Tacitus Histories Handbook. (Latin Texts Ser). 80p. 1975. pap. text ed. 5.95 (ISBN 0-521-20489-5). Cambridge U Pr.

--Tacitus: Selections from the Histories. (Latin Texts Ser.). (Illus.). 48p. 1974. 3.25x (ISBN 0-521-20435-6). Cambridge U Pr.

Jones, Patricia. Mythologizing Always. 12p. 1981. pap. 2.00 (ISBN 0-916382-26-5). Telephone Bks.

Jones, Patricia & Oertel, William. Developing Patient Teaching Objectives & Techniques: A Self-Instructional Program. 1978. pap. 6.95 (ISBN 0-89443-801-8). Aspen Systems.

Jones, Paul, ed. Robotics for Safety & Profit. (Illus.). 1981. 20.00 (ISBN 0-686-97647-9). P-P Pubns.

Jones, Peggy, jt. auth. see Young, Pam.

Jones, Pei Te Hurinui. King Potatau: An Account of the Life of Potataute Wherowhero, the First Maori King. 1959. text ed. 7.00x o.p. (ISBN 0-8248-0587-9). UH Pr.

Jones, Penelope. Holding Together. LC 80-27101. 176p. (gr. 3-5). 1981. 9.95 (ISBN 0-02-747880-7). Bradbury Pr.

--I Didn't Want to Be Nice. LC 76-57907. (Illus.). 32p. (ps-2). 1977. 7.95 (ISBN 0-02-747890-4). Bradbury Pr.

--I'm Not Moving. LC 79-13062. (Illus.). 32p. (ps-2). 1980. 8.95 (ISBN 0-02-747900-5). Bradbury Pr.

--The Stealing Thing. LC 82-22653. 144p. (gr. 2-4). 1983. 9.95 (ISBN 0-02-747870-X). Bradbury Pr.

Jones, Peter. The Complete Book of Home Plumbing. (Illus.). 128p. 1983. pap. 10.95 (ISBN 0-686-83787-8, ScribT). Scribner.

--Fasteners, Joints & Adhesives: A Guide to Engineering Solid Constructions. 416p. 1983. 24.95 (ISBN 0-13-307694-6); pap. 14.95 (ISBN 0-13-307686-5). P-H.

--The Garden End: New & Selected Poems. (Poetry Ser.). 1979. 6.95 o.p. (ISBN 0-85635-170-9, Pub. by Carcanet New Pr England). Humanities.

--The Garden End: New & Selected Poems. 116p. 1977. Repr. of 1969 ed. text ed. 8.50x (ISBN 0-85635-170-9, Pub. by Carcanet New Pr England). Humanities.

--Hume's Sentiments: Their Ciceronian & French Context. 224p. 1982. 24.00 (ISBN 0-85224-443-6, Pub. by Edinburgh U Pr Scotland). Columbia U Pr.

--Residential Electricity. 416p. 1983. 24.95 (ISBN 0-13-774638-5); pap. 14.95 (ISBN 0-13-774620-2). P-H.

Jones, Peter & Farness, Jay. College Writing Skills. 339p. 1982. pap. text ed. 8.95 (ISBN 0-15-511740-8, HC). HarBraceJ.

Jones, Peter, jt. ed. see Freudenthal, Ralph I.

Jones, Peter d'A., ed. Ethnic Chicago. Holli, Melvin. 1981. pap. 12.95 (ISBN 0-8028-1807-2, 1807-2). Eerdmans.

Jones, Peter W. & Leber, Philip, eds. Polynuclear Aromatic Hydrocarbons: Chemistry, Biology, Carcinogenesis, Methodology. LC 79-642622. (Illus.). 1979. 69.95 (ISBN 0-250-40317-X). Ann Arbor Science.

Jones, Peter W., ed. see International Symposium on Analysis, Chemistry, & Biology, No. 2.

Jones, Philip, tr. see Luzzalto, Gino.

Jones, Philip R. Doctors & the SMA: The Study of Collective Action. 192p. 1981. text ed. 34.25x (ISBN 0-566-00338-4). Gower Pub Ltd.

Jones, Phyllis M., ed. English Critical Essays: Twentieth Century. (World's Classics Ser.). 9.95 (ISBN 0-19-250405-3). Oxford U Pr.

Jones, Proctor. Idylls of France. (Illus.). 126p. write for info (ISBN 0-9608860-0-1). P Jones Pub Co.

Jones, R. Construction Estimating. 152p. 1967. pap. 16.00 (ISBN 0-8273-0108-1); instructor's guide 4.95 (ISBN 0-8273-0109-X). Delmar.

--Framing, Sheathing & Insulation. LC 73-1847. 227p. 1973. pap. 9.80 (ISBN 0-8273-0096-4); answer book 2.75 (ISBN 0-8273-0097-2). Delmar.

--Templet Development for the Pipe Trades. LC 63-22021. (Illus.). 166p. 1963. pap. 10.80 (ISBN 0-8273-0077-8); instr.'s guide 2.75 (ISBN 0-8273-0078-6). Delmar.

Jones, R. & Wykes, C. M. Holographic & Speckle Interferometry. LC 82-1338. 250p. Date not set. price not set (ISBN 0-521-23268-6). Cambridge U Pr.

Jones, R., jt. auth. see Reed, E.

Jones, R., ed. see Balcomb, J. Douglas, et al.

Jones, R., ed. see Nikolskii, G. V.

Jones, R., tr. see Von Kleist, Heinrich.

Jones, R. A. Physical & Mechanistic Organic Chemistry. LC 78-27739. (Cambridge Texts in Chemistry & Biochemistry Ser.). (Illus.). 1980. 65.00 (ISBN 0-521-22642-2); pap. 21.95 (ISBN 0-521-29596-3). Cambridge U Pr.

Jones, R. I., jt. auth. see Ilmavirta, V.

Jones, R. J. & Laws, K. G. Speed Sensing in Belt Weighing, 1979. 1981. 95.00x (ISBN 0-686-97162-0, Pub. by W Spring England). State Mutual Bk.

Jones, R. N. & Rees, H. B Chromosomes. 1982. 44.50 (ISBN 0-12-390060-3). Acad Pr.

Jones, R. P., et al. Meteorological Problems in the Design & Operation of Supersonic Aircraft. (Technical Note Ser.). 1967. pap. 9.00 (ISBN 0-685-22321-3, W55, WMO). Unipub.

Jones, R. Page. The Man Who Killed Hitler. 256p. (Orig.). 1980. pap. 2.25 o.s.i. (ISBN 0-515-04855-0). Jove Pubns.

Jones, R. S. Asthma in Children. LC 76-12027. (Illus.). 278p. 1976. 22.50 o.p. (ISBN 0-88416-028-9). Wright-PSG.

Jones, R. T. George Eliot. LC 75-114602. (British Authors Ser.). 1971. 22.50 (ISBN 0-521-07832-6); pap. 7.95 (ISBN 0-521-09613-8). Cambridge U Pr.

Jones, R. T., jt. auth. see Trump, B. F.

Jones, R. V. The Wizard War: Britiish Scientific Intelligence, 1939-1945. new ed. LC 77-17984. 1978. 12.95 o.p. (ISBN 0-698-10896-5, Coward). Putnam Pub Group.

Jones, R. W. International Trade: Essays in Theory, Vol. 4. (Studies in International Economics). 1979. 47.00 (ISBN 0-444-85226-3, North Holland). Elsevier.

Jones, Ralph E. & Rarey, George H. The Fighting Tanks: 1916-1933. (Illus.). 1970. 8.95 (ISBN 0-87364-197-3, Paladin Press). Paladin Pr.

Jones, Randall L., jt. ed. see Guttman, Samuel.

Jones, Raymond A. The British Diplomatic Service, 1815-1914. 315p. 1982. text ed. 11.50x (ISBN 0-88920-124-2, 40810, Pub. by Laurier U Pr). Humanities.

Jones, Raymond F. Radar: How It Works. LC 79-169248. (How It Works Ser.). (Illus.). (gr. 5 up). 1972. PLB 4.49 o.p. (ISBN 0-399-60748-X). Putnam Pub Group.

Jones, Raymond T., jt. ed. see Trump, Benjamin F.

Jones, Rebecca C. The Biggest, Meanest, Ugliest Dog in the Whole Wide World. LC 82-6612. (Illus.). 32p. (ps-2). 1982. 8.95 (ISBN 0-02-747800-9). Macmillan.

Jones, Reginald L. Problems & Issues in the Education of Exceptional Children. LC 74-142329. 1971. pap. text ed. 14.50 o.p. (ISBN 0-395-11228-1, 3-28340). HM.

Jones, Rhodri. An ABC of English Teaching. (Orig.). 1980. pap. text ed. 9.00x (ISBN 0-435-10490-X). Heinemann Ed.

Jones, Richard. The Dream Poet. 1979. lib. bdg. 16.00 (ISBN 0-8161-9014-3, Univ Bks). G K Hall.

Jones, Richard F. Ancients & Moderns: A Study of the Rise of the Scientific Movement in Seventeenth-Century England. 384p. 1982. pap. 6.50 (ISBN 0-486-24414-8). Dover.

Jones, Richard M. Experiment at Evergreen. LC 81-391. 176p. 1981. text ed. 15.25 o.p. (ISBN 0-87073-838-0); pap. text ed. 7.95 (ISBN 0-87073-839-9). Schenkman.

Jones, Richard O. & Harwood, Bruce. Colorado Real Estate: An Introduction to the Profession. LC 79-939. (Illus.). 1979. text ed. 21.95 (ISBN 0-8359-0883-6). Reston.

Jones, Richard W. Principles of Biological Regulation: An Introduction to Feedback Systems. 1973. 42.50 (ISBN 0-12-389950-8). Acad Pr.

Jones, Robert. George Washington. (World Leaders Ser.). 1979. lib. bdg. 13.95 (ISBN 0-8057-7726-1, Twayne). G K Hall.

Jones, Robert & Seligman, Gustav L. The Sweep of American History, Vol. 1. 3rd ed. LC 80-39484. 400p. 1981. pap. text ed. 13.50 (ISBN 0-471-07898-0). Wiley.

--The Sweep of American History, Vol. 2. 3rd ed. LC 80-39484. 424p. 1981. pap. text ed. 13.50 (ISBN 0-471-07897-2). Wiley.

Jones, Robert A., ed. Knowledge & Society: Studies in the Sociology of Culture Past & Present, Vol. 1. 1978. lib. bdg. 40.00 (ISBN 0-89232-026-5). Jai Pr.

Jones, Robert A. & Kuklick, Henrika, eds. Knowledge & Society, Vol. 3. (Studies in the Sociology of Culture Past & Present). 300p. 1981. 42.50 (ISBN 0-89232-161-X). Jai Pr.

--Knowledge & Society: Studies in the Sociology of Culture Past & Present, Vol. 2. (Orig.). 1979. lib. bdg. 40.00 (ISBN 0-89232-123-7). Jai Pr.

Jones, Robert C. The Central Vermont Railway: A Yankee Tradition, Vol. VI. Date not set. 19.50 (ISBN 0-686-82375-3). Sundance.

Jones, Robert F. Blood Sport. 1974. 7.95 o.p. (ISBN 0-671-21696-1). S&S.

--Slade's Glacier. 1981. 12.95 (ISBN 0-671-25306-9). S&S.

Jones, Robert H. Disrupted Decades: The Civil War & Reconstruction Years. LC 78-27422. 560p. 1979. Repr. of 1973 ed. 14.50 (ISBN 0-88275-714-8). Krieger.

Jones, Robert M. Mechanics of Composite Materials. (Illus.). 350p. 1975. text ed. 38.00 (ISBN 0-07-032790-4, C). McGraw.

Jones, Robert N., jt. auth. see Rees, Hubert.

Jones, Robin, jt. auth. see Stewart, Ian.

Jones, Robin F., jt. ed. see Grunmann-Gaudet, Minnette.

Jones, Rochelle. The Other Generation: The New Power of Older People. LC 77-22306. 1977. 10.95 o.p. (ISBN 0-13-643064-3, Spec); pap. 4.95 o.p. (ISBN 0-13-643056-2, Spec). P-H.

Jones, Romelle M. The Birthday Wish. 1979. 4.50 o.p. (ISBN 0-533-04115-5). Vantage.

Jones, Ronald E. Focus on Photography. Kirchem, Ronald, ed. (Illus.). 256p. (gr. 9-12). 1980. text ed. 16.84 (ISBN 0-07-033020-4, W). McGraw.

Jones, Rosemary D. Francesco Vettori: Florentine Citizen & Medici Servant. (University of London Historical Studies: No. 34). 366p. 1972. text ed. 39.00x o.p. (ISBN 0-485-13134-X, Athlone Pr). Humanities.

Jones, Roy. Primary School Management. 160p. 1980. 14.95 o.p. (ISBN 0-7153-7843-0). David & Charles.

Jones, Roy E. Nuclear Deterrence: A Short Political Analysis. (Library of Political Studies). 1968. text ed. 6.25x o.p. (ISBN 0-7100-6537-X). Humanities.

--Principles of Foreign Policy: The Civil State in Its World Setting. LC 79-9835. 1979. 26.00x (ISBN 0-312-64561-9). St Martin.

Jones, Rufus M. Thou Dost Open up My Life. LC 63-11819. (Orig.). 1963. pap. 1.50x (ISBN 0-87574-127-4). Pendle Hill.

Jones, Russell A., et al. Social Psychology. LC 78-20857. (Illus.). 1979. text ed. 17.95x (ISBN 0-87893-367-0); wkbk. o.p. (ISBN 0-87893-686-6). Sinauer Assoc.

Jones, Russell B. Gold from Golgotha. (Orig.). 1978. pap. 1.50 (ISBN 0-89228-024-7). Impact Bks MO.

Jones, Ruth D., jt. auth. see McMillan, Mary L.

Jones, Ruth D., jt. auth. see Mc Millan, Mary L.

Jones, Ruth D., jt. auth. see McMillan, Mary L.

Jones, Samuel & Luchsinger, Arlene E. Introduction to Plant Systematics. Vastyan, James E., ed. (Organismic Ser.). (Illus.). 1979. text ed. 26.50 (ISBN 0-07-032795-5, C). McGraw.

Jones, Samuel A. Thoreau Amongst Friends & Philistines & Other Thoreauviana. Hendrick, George, ed. & LC 82-6444. xxvi, 241p. 1983. 23.95 (ISBN 0-8214-0675-2, 82-84432). Ohio U Pr.

Jones, Samuel S. Scandinavian States & the League of Nations. Repr. of 1939 ed. lib. bdg. 17.00x (ISBN 0-8371-0974-4, JOSS). Greenwood.

Jones, Seaborn. Drowning from the Inside Out. LC 80-20642. 88p. 1982. 12.00x o.p. (ISBN 0-916156-53-2); pap. 4.00x o.p. (ISBN 0-916156-52-4). Cherry Valley.

Jones, Seymour & Cohen, M. Bruce. The Emerging Business: Managing for Growth. 448p. 1983. 34.95 (ISBN 0-471-09800-0). Ronald Pr.

Jones, Sonia. Alfonsina Storni. (World Authors Ser.). 1979. 15.95 (ISBN 0-8057-6360-0, Twayne). G K Hall.

Jones, Sonia & Ruiz-Salvador, Antonio. Spanish One. 2nd ed. 416p. 1979. text ed. 14.95 (ISBN 0-442-24184-9); instructor's manual 2.50 (ISBN 0-442-24188-7); wkbk. 4.95x (ISBN 0-442-24185-2); tapes 95.00 (ISBN 0-442-24186-0); cassettes 59.95 (ISBN 0-442-24187-9). Van Nos Reinhold.

Jones, Susan K., jt. auth. see Janus, Lauren R.

Jones, Susan L. Family Therapy: A Comparison of Approaches. new ed. LC 80-10161. (Illus.). 1980. text ed. 17.95 (ISBN 0-87619-625-3). R J Brady.

Jones, Susan S. Nutrition & Exercise for the Over Fifty's. Passwater, Richard A. & Mindell, Earl R., eds. (Good Health Guide Ser.). 32p. 1983. pap. 1.45 (ISBN 0-87983-305-X). Keats.

Jones, Suzanne S. The Low-Cholesterol Food Processor Cookbook. LC 78-22329. (Illus.). 1980. 9.95 o.p. (ISBN 0-385-14745-7). Doubleday.

Jones, T. Canby. The Biblical Basis of Conscientious Objection. 0.50 (ISBN 0-910082-09-X). Am Pr Serv Comm.

Jones, T. F. Building Measurement Three Checkbook. 1983. text ed. write for info. (ISBN 0-408-00652-8). Butterworth.

Jones, Taffy. Whistle-Stop Puppet Theatre. LC 82-23931. (Illus.). 180p. (Orig.). 1983. pap. 13.95x (ISBN 0-89950-072-2). McFarland & Co.

Jones, Thomas, jt. tr. see Jones, Gwyn.

Jones, Thomas C. & Hunt, Ronald D. Veterinary Pathology. 5th ed. LC 81-20820. (Illus.). 1750p. 1983. text ed. write for info (ISBN 0-8121-0789-6). Lea & Febiger.

Jones, Tim. The Last Great Race. LC 82-13045. (Illus.). 272p. 1982. 14.95 (ISBN 0-914842-90-0). Madrona Pubs.

Jones, Timothy, jt. auth. see Ockenden, Michael.

Jones, Tom B. South America Rediscovered. LC 69-10111. (Illus.). Repr. of 1949 ed. lib. bdg. 16.00x (ISBN 0-8371-0122-0, JOSA). Greenwood.

Jones, Tom B., jt. auth. see Rothrock, George A.

Jones, Tony. Encyclopedia of Pet Mice. (Illus.). 224p. 1979. 12.95 (ISBN 0-87666-910-0, H-973). TFH Pubns.

Jones, Trevor. Ghana's First Republic: The Pursuit of the Political Kingdom. (Studies in African History). 1976. 15.95x (ISBN 0-416-84430-8); pap. 9.50x (ISBN 0-416-84440-5). Methuen Inc.

Jones, Tristan. Adrif. 288p. 1983. pap. 2.95 (ISBN 0-380-62455-9, Discus). Avon.

--Ice. 1980. pap. 3.50 (ISBN 0-380-63248-9, 50757). Avon.

--One Hand for Yourself, One Hand for the Ship: The Essentials of Single-Handed Sailing. 160p. 1982. 14.95 (ISBN 0-02-559880-5). Macmillan.

--Saga of a Wayward Sailor. 272p. 1980. pap. 3.50 (ISBN 0-380-52985-8, 62190-8). Avon.

--A Steady Trade: A Boyhood at Sea. (Illus.). 288p. 1982. 15.95 (ISBN 0-312-76138-4). St Martin.

--Yarns. 250p. 1983. 14.95 (ISBN 0-914814-41-9). Sail Bks.

Jones, Ulysses. Fertilizers & Soil Fertility. 2nd ed. 464p. 1982. text ed. 20.95 (ISBN 0-8359-1962-5); instr's. manual free (ISBN 0-8359-1963-3). Reston.

Jones, Vauncille, jt. auth. see Zimmer, Kenneth.

Jones, Victor, ed. see Bayes, Jane H.

Jones, Virgil C. Gray Ghosts & Rebel Raiders. LC 56-10512. 1982. pap. 2.95 (ISBN 0-89176-016-4, 6016). Mockingbird Bks.

Jones, W. B., ed. Analytic Theory of Continued Fractions, Leon, Norway 1981: Proceedings. (Lecture Notes in Mathematics Ser.: Vol. 932). 240p. 1982. pap. 12.50 (ISBN 0-387-11567-6). Springer-Verlag.

Jones, W. Glyn. William Heinesen. (World Authors Ser.). 1974. lib. bdg. 15.95 (ISBN 0-8057-2418-4, Twayne). G K Hall.

Jones, W. Landis, ed. see Ford, Wendell H.

Jones, W. M., ed. Chief Justice John Marshall: A Reappraisal. LC 70-152688. (American Constitutional & Legal History Ser). 1971. Repr. of 1956 ed. lib. bdg. 27.50 (ISBN 0-306-70132-4). Da Capo.

Jones, Warren W. & Solnit, Albert. What Do I Do Next? A Manual for People Just Entering Government Service. LC 80-67754. (Illus.). 128p. (Orig.). 1980. pap. 10.95 (ISBN 0-918286-20-4). Planners Pr.

Jones, William. Credulities Past & Present. LC 67-24355. 1968. Repr. of 1880 ed. 40.00x (ISBN 0-8103-3447-X). Gale.

--Crowns & Coronations, a History of Regalia. LC 67-24356. (Illus.). 1968. Repr. of 1902 ed. 45.00x (ISBN 0-8103-3448-8). Gale.

--Finger-Ring Lore. LC 67-24357. 1968. Repr. of 1890 ed. 44.00x (ISBN 0-8103-3449-6). Gale.

--History & Mystery of Precious Stones. LC 68-22031. 1968. Repr. of 1880 ed. 34.00x (ISBN 0-8103-3450-X). Gale.

Jones, William, jt. auth. see Wilson, Richard.

Jones, William, et al. Approaches to Ethics: Representative Selection from Classic Times to the Present. 3rd ed. (Illus.). 1977. text ed. 23.50 (ISBN 0-07-033005-0, C). McGraw.

Jones, William B. Programming Concepts: A Second Course. (Illus.). 336p. 1982. text ed. 21.95 (ISBN 0-13-729970-2). P-H.

Jones, William B. & Thron, W. J. Continued Fractions: Analytic Theory & Applications. (Encyclopedia of Mathematics & Applications Ser.: Vol. II). (Illus.). 450p. 1980. 39.50 (ISBN 0-201-13510-8). A-W.

Jones, William M. John Steinbeck, Great American Novelist & Playwright. Rahmas, Sigurd C., ed. (Outstanding Personalities Ser.: No. 89). 32p. (gr. 9-12). 1982. 2.95 (ISBN 0-87157-589-2); pap. text ed. 1.95 (ISBN 0-87157-089-0). SamHar Pr.

Jones, William R., ed. see Thornton, J. Quinn.

Jones, William S., jt. auth. see Finkle, Robert B.

Jones, Willie G., Sr. Fannie Foe: Phase I. 1978. 5.95 o.p. (ISBN 0-533-03461-2). Vantage.

Jones, Wilson E. Next Station Will Be.., Vol. 7. LC 82-62628. (Illus.). 60p. 1982. pap. 8.50 (ISBN 0-941652-00-9). Railroadians.

Jones, Wyatt C., jt. auth. see Freeman, Howard E.

Jones-Griffith, Philip. Vietnam, Inc. Sandum, Howard, ed. (Illus.). 1971. pap. 3.95 o.p. (ISBN 0-02-080400-8). Macmillan.

Jones-Lee, M. W., ed. The Value of Life & Safety: Proceedings of a Conference Held by the Geneva Association. 310p. 1982. 55.50 (ISBN 0-444-86439-3, North Holland). Elsevier.

Jones-Witters, Patricia, jt. auth. see Witters, Weldon L.

Jong, Erica. Fear of Flying. 1974. pap. 3.50 (AE1329, Sig). NAL.

--Witches. (Illus.). 1982. pap. 12.50 (ISBN 0-452-25357-8, Z5357, Plume). NAL.

Jong, Kees A. De see De Jong, Kees A. & Scholten, Robert.

Jong, M. T. Methods of Discrete Signal & System Analysis. 1982. 34.50 (ISBN 0-07-033025-5); solutions manual 15.00 (ISBN 0-07-033026-3). McGraw.

Jong, Russell De see Dejong, Russell N.

Jong, W. De see De Jong, W., et al.

Jonge, Alex de see De Jonge, Alex.

Jonge, Alex De see De Jonge, Alex.

Jonge, Alex de see De Jonge, Alex.

Jongeward, Dorothy, jt. auth. see James, Muriel.

Jongh, Brian de see De Jongh, Brian.

Jonk, Clarence. Ma Poos & the Fabulous Whimplegoose. (Third Grade Bk.). (Illus.). (gr. 3-4). PLB 5.95 o.p. (ISBN 0-513-00374-6). Denison.

--Old Angus, the Unhappy Baker. (Second Grade Bk.). (Illus.). (gr. 2-3). PLB 5.95 o.p. (ISBN 0-513-00385-1). Denison.

Jonkers, J. R., jt. auth. see Van der Kleijn, E.

Jonnes, Alexandre M. De see De Jonnes, Alexandre M.

Jonnes, J. Merryn. Organisational Aspects of Police Behaviour. 182p. 1980. 35.25x (ISBN 0-566-00402-X). Gower Pub Ltd.

Jonovic, Donald J. The Second Generation Boss: A Successor's Guide to Becoming the Next Owner-Manager of a Successful Family Business. LC 82-10973. 1982. 19.95 (ISBN 0-9603614-4-8). Univ Pr OH.

Jonovic, Donald J., jt. auth. see Danco, Leon A.

Jonscher, A. K., jt. ed. see Ferrari, R. L.

Jonsen, Albert R. Christian Decision & Action. (Faith & Life Bk). 1970. pap. 3.50 o.p. (ISBN 0-02-803430-9). Glencoe.

Jonsen, George. Favorite Tales of Monsters & Trolls. LC 76-24182. (Pictureback Library Editions). (ps-2). 1978. PLB 4.99 (ISBN 0-394-93477-6, BYR); 1.50 (ISBN 0-394-83477-1). Random.

Jonson, Ben. The Alchemist. Holdsworth, Roger, ed. (Plays in Performance Ser.). (Illus.). 224p. 1983. text ed. 19.50x (ISBN 0-389-20179-0). B&N Imports.

--Alchemist. 1967 ed. Steane, J. B., ed. text ed. 6.95x (ISBN 0-521-06945-9). Cambridge U Pr.

--The Alchemist. Bentley, Gerald E., ed. LC 47-4460. (Crofts Classics Ser.). 1947. pap. text ed. 3.50x (ISBN 0-88295-048-7). Harlan Davidson.

--The Alchemist. Mares, F. M., ed. 1978. pap. 7.95 (ISBN 0-416-71830-2). Methuen Inc.

--The Alchemist. Kernan, Alvin B., ed. LC 73-86901. 1974. 22.50x (ISBN 0-300-01704-9); pap. 6.95x (ISBN 0-300-01736-7, Y-268). Yale U Pr.

--The Case Is Altered. Selin, W. E., ed. 1917. pap. 39.50x (ISBN 0-685-89739-7). Elliots Bks.

--A Score for Lovers Made Men, A Masque by Ben Johnson: The Music Adapted & Arranged for Dramatic Performance from Compositart by Nicholas Lanier, Alphonso Ferrabosco, & Their Contemporaries. Sabol, Andrew J., ed. LC 63-8400. (Illus.). 117p. 1963. pap. 10.00x (ISBN 0-87057-073-0, Pub. by Brown U Pr). U Pr of New Eng.

--Work of Ben Jonson. Herford, C. H., et al, eds. Incl. Vol. 1. 47.00x (ISBN 0-19-811352-8); Vol. 2. 47.00x (ISBN 0-19-811353-6); Vol. 5. 46.50x (ISBN 0-19-811356-0); Vol. 7. 49.00x (ISBN 0-19-811358-7); Vol. 8. 49.00x (ISBN 0-19-811359-5); Vol. 10. 49.00x (ISBN 0-19-811361-7); Vol. 11. 49.00x (ISBN 0-19-811362-5). 1925-52. Oxford U Pr.

--The Works of Ben Jonson, with a Memoir by William Gifford. 817p. 1982. Repr. of 1838 ed. lib. bdg. 100.00 (ISBN 0-89760-416-4). Telegraph Bks.

Jonson, G. C. A. Handbook to Chopin's Works. 278p. 1983. pap. 7.25 (ISBN 0-88072-004-2). Tanager Bks.

Jonson, Wilfrid. Magic Tricks & Card Tricks. (Illus.). pap. 2.75 (ISBN 0-486-20909-1). Dover.

Jonsson, Hannes. Friends in Conflict the Anglo-Icelandic Cod Wars & Their Influence on the Law of the Sea. 1982. 34.00 (ISBN 0-208-02000-4). Shoe String.

Joo, Jalaleddin S. An Empirical Evaluation of FASB 33 "Financial Reporting & Changing Prices". Farmer, Richard N., ed. LC 82-16062. (Research for Business Decisions Ser.: No. 55). 114p. 1982. 34.95 (ISBN 0-8357-1385-7). Univ Microfilms.

Joo, Jalaleddin S. see Joo, Jalaleddin S.

Joode, Ton de see De Joode, Ton & Stolk, Anthonie.

Joohnson, Kenneth & Senatore, John. Nothing Never Happens. 1983. 17.75 (ISBN 0-686-84063-1). Intl Gen Semantics.

Joo Ok Koo, see Dudewicz, Edward J. & Koo, Joo O.

Joos, Martin. The Five Clocks. LC 62-62715. 1967. pap. 3.95 (ISBN 0-15-631380-4, Harv). HarBraceJ.

Joosse, Barbara M. Spiders in the Fruit Cellar. LC 82-4694. (Illus.). 36p. (gr. k-2). 1983. 9.95 (ISBN 0-394-85327-X); lib. bdg. 9.99 (ISBN 0-394-95327-4). Knopf.

Joplin, B. & Pattillo, J. Effective Accounting Reports. Orig. Title: Accounting Reports. (Illus.). 1969. 32.95 o.p. (ISBN 0-13-240721-3). P-H.

Joplin, Scott. Collected Piano Works. Lawrence, Vera B., ed. pap. 15.95 (ISBN 0-486-23106-2). Dover.

--The Collected Works of Scott Joplin. Lawrence, Vera Brodsky, ed. Incl. Vol. 1. Works for Piano. Blesh, Rudi, intro. by. 305p. 30.00 o.p. (ISBN 0-87104-231-2); Vol. 2. Works for Voice. Blesh, Rudi, intro. by. 30.00 o.p. (ISBN 0-87104-232-0). LC 78-164697. (Americana Collection Music Ser., No. 1). (Illus.). 1972. Set. 50.00 o.p. (ISBN 0-87104-238-X). NY Pub Lib.

Jopling, Samuel H., jt. auth. see Dougherty, Frank P.

Joralemon, Ira B. Adventure Beacons. Joralemon, Peter, ed. LC 76-19746. (Illus.). 1976. 18.00x (ISBN 0-89520-041-4). Soc Mining Eng.

Joralemon, Peter, ed. see Joralemon, Ira B.

Joravsky, David, ed. see Medvedev, Roy A.

Jordak, Francis E. A Bibliographical Survey for a Foundation in Philosophy. LC 78-64564. 1978. pap. text ed. 16.25 (ISBN 0-8191-0635-6). U Pr of Amer.

Jordan, A. C. Towards an African Literature: The Emergence of Literary Form in Xhosa. LC 75-165235. (Perspectives on Southern Africa: No. 6). 1973. 23.00x (ISBN 0-520-02079-0). U of Cal Pr.

Jordan, A. C., retold by. Tales from Southern Africa. (Perspectives on Southern Africa: No. 4). (Illus.), 1973. 27.50x (ISBN 0-520-01911-3); pap. 3.95 (ISBN 0-520-03638-7). U of Cal Pr.

Jordan, Alan H. The Encyclopedia of Telephone Cost Reduction Techniques. 2nd ed. 245p. 1982. 99.00 (ISBN 0-686-98055-7). Telecom Lib.

Jordan & Sons Ltd. Gore-Browne on Companies: Main Work & Three Supplements. 43rd ed. 1982. 350.00x (ISBN 0-686-82304-4, Pub. by Jordan & Sons England); 3rd supplement 65.00. State Mutual Bk.

Jordan, Bill. Freedom & the Welfare State. 1978. 18.00 (ISBN 0-7100-8425-0); pap. 7.95 (ISBN 0-7100-8910-4). Routledge & Kegan.

--Poor Parents: Social Policy & the Cycle of Deprivation. 1974. 16.95x (ISBN 0-7100-7852-8); pap. 9.95 (ISBN 0-7100-7853-6). Routledge & Kegan.

Jordan, Brigitte. Birth in Four Cultures: A Cross-Cultural Investigation of Childbirth in Yucatan, Holland, Sweden & the United States. 2nd ed. (Illus.). 128p. 1980. pap. 6.95 (ISBN 0-920792-05-7). Eden Pr.

--Birth in Four Cultures: A Cross-Cultural Investigation of Childbirth in Yucatan, Holland, Sweden & the United States. (Illus.). 1978. 14.95 o.p. (ISBN 0-88831-024-2). Eden Pr.

Jordan, Charles. Calculus of Finite Differences. 3rd ed. LC 65-29977. 24.95 (ISBN 0-8284-0033-4). Chelsea Pub.

Jordan, Dale R. Dyslexia in the Classroom. 2nd ed. (Elementary Education Ser.). 1977. pap. text ed. 12.95 (ISBN 0-675-08466-0). Merrill.

Jordan, Daniel P. Political Leadership in Jefferson's Virginia. LC 82-23867. 274p. 1983. price not set (ISBN 0-8139-0967-8). U Pr of Va.

Jordan, David, jt. ed. see Brock, Van K.

Jordan, David K., jt. auth. see Swartz, Marc J.

Jordan, David P. The King's Trial: Louis XVI vs. the French Revolution. LC 78-54797. 1979. 16.95x (ISBN 0-520-03684-0); pap. 5.95 (ISBN 0-520-04399-5, CAL 497). U of Cal Pr.

Jordan, Donald A. The Northern Expedition: China's National Revolution of 1926-1928. LC 75-40309. 336p. 1976. text ed. 16.00x (ISBN 0-8248-0352-3). UH Pr.

Jordan, E. G. The Nucleolus. rev. ed. Head, J. J., ed. LC 76-29375. (Carolina Biology Readers Ser.). (Illus.). 16p. (gr. 11 up). 1978. pap. 1.60 (ISBN 0-89278-216-1, 45-9616). Carolina Biological.

Jordan, Edward C. & Balmain, K. G. Electromagnetic Waves & Radiating Systems. 2nd ed. 1968. ref. ed. 33.95 (ISBN 0-13-249995-9). P-H.

Jordan, Ethel T. Scissor Magic. (ps-4). 1982. 5.95 (ISBN 0-86653-097-5, GA 424). Good Apple.

Jordan, Fred, ed. see Nicosia, Gerald.

Jordan, Fred S. & Jordan, Jim M. Sharing the Victory (the Twenty-Five Year History of the Fellowship of Christian Athletes. (Illus.). 1980. 12.95 (ISBN 0-8256-3173-4, Quick Fox). Putnam Pub Group.

Jordan, Frederick S., jt. auth. see Jordan, James M., IV.

Jordan, Hamilton. Crisis: The Last Year of the Carter Presidency. 1982. 16.95 (ISBN 0-399-12738-0). Putnam Pub Group.

Jordan, Helene J. How a Seed Grows. LC 60-11541. (A Let's-Read-&-Find-Out Science Bk). (Illus.). (gr. k-3). 1960. PLB 10.89 (ISBN 0-690-40645-2, TYC-J). Har-Row.

--Seeds by Wind & Water. LC 62-12820. (A Let's-Read-&-Find-Out Science Bk). (Illus.). (gr. k-3). 1962 (ISBN 0-690-72452-7, TYC-J). PLB 10.89 (ISBN 0-690-72453-5). Har-Row.

Jordan, Henry, et al. Eating Is Okay: A Radical Approach to Weight Loss. Gelman, Steve, ed. 1978. pap. 1.95 (ISBN 0-451-11062-5, AJ1062, Sig). NAL.

Jordan, Henry A. & Berland, Theodore. The Doctor's Calories-Plus Diet. 1982. pap. 2.50 (ISBN 0-451-11515-5, AE1515, Sig). NAL.

Jordan, Hope. Road to Romance. 1982. pap. 6.95 (ISBN 0-686-84749-0, Avalon). Bouregy.

Jordan, Howard E. Energy Efficient Electric Motors & Their Applications. 176p. 1983. text ed. 24.50 (ISBN 0-442-24523-8). Van Nos Reinhold.

Jordan, Inge, et al, trs. see Reich, Wilhelm.

Jordan, James B., ed. The Failure of the American Baptist Culture. (Christianity & Civilization Ser.: No. 1). xiv, 304p. (Orig.). 1982. pap. 9.95 (ISBN 0-939404-04-4). Geneva Divinity.

Jordan, James M. & Alcorn, George T., eds. The Wildfowler's Heritage. LC 80-85153. (Illus.). 120p. 1983. 46.50 (ISBN 0-938694-03-0); deluxe ed. 125.00 (ISBN 0-686-70001-5); deluxe ed. with remarque 175.00 (ISBN 0-686-70002-3). JCP Corp VA.

Jordan, James M., IV & Jordan, Frederick S. Virginia Beach: A Pictorial History. Rev. ed. LC 74-22354. (Illus.). 240p. 1983. 19.95 (ISBN 0-9610354-0-4). Jordan Assoc.

Jordan, Jerry M. One More Brown Bag. 53p. 1983. pap. 5.95 (ISBN 0-8298-0645-8). Pilgrim NY.

Jordan, Jim M., jt. auth. see Jordan, Fred S.

Jordan, John. An Illustrated Guide to the Modern Soviet Navy. LC 81-71939. (Illustrated Military Guides Ser.). (Illus.). 160p. 1983. 9.95 (ISBN 0-668-05504-9, 5504). Arco.

--An Illustrated Guide to the Modern U. S. Navy. LC 81-71937. (Illustrated Military Guides Ser.). (Illus.). 160p. 1983. 9.95 (ISBN 0-668-05505-7, 5505). Arco.

Jordan, John E. Why the Lyrical Ballads? LC 75-27926. 1976. 23.00x (ISBN 0-520-03124-5). U of Cal Pr.

Jordan, Joseph A. & Singer, Albert, eds. The Cervix. LC 76-8579. (Illus.). 529p. 1976. text ed. 12.00 (ISBN 0-7216-5227-1). Saunders.

Jordan, Julie. The Wings of Life: Whole Vegetarian Cookery. LC 76-43075. (Cookbook Ser.). (Illus.). 200p. 1976. 16.95 (ISBN 0-912278-82-X); pap. 7.95 (ISBN 0-912278-77-3). Crossing Pr.

Jordan, June. Things That I Do in the Dark: Selected Poems. 1977. 7.95 (ISBN 0-394-40937-X); pap. 4.95 (ISBN 0-394-73327-4). Random.

Jordan, Juno. Numerology: The Romance in Your Name. 1977. pap. 6.95 (ISBN 0-87516-227-4). De Vorss.

Jordan, K. Forbis, ed. Perspectives in State School Support Programs. 408p. (American Education Finance Association). 1981. prof ref 32.50x (ISBN 0-88410-197-5). Ballinger Pub.

Jordan, Lee. Cat's Eyes. 224p. 1982. 12.95 (ISBN 0-453-00416-4, H416). NAL.

Jordan, Margie. God Riches at Christ Expense. 1980. 4.95 o.p. (ISBN 0-8062-0957-7). Carlton.

Jordan, Martin, jt. auth. see Jordan, Tanis.

Jordan, Mildred. The Distelfink Country of the Pennsylvania Dutch. (Illus.). 1978. 12.95 o.p. (ISBN 0-517-53260-3). Crown.

Jordan, Nehemiah. The Wisdom of Plato: An Attempt at an Outline, 2 vols. LC 80-1409. (Orig.). 1981. Set. lib. bdg. 50.75 (ISBN 0-8191-1408-1); Set. pap. 34.75 (ISBN 0-8191-1409-X). Vol. 1, 544p. Vol. 2, 536p. U Pr of Amer.

Jordan, Novella P. Makers of Music. LC 82-71216. (gr. 2-12). 1982. pap. 5.95 (ISBN 0-8054-6810-2). Broadman.

Jordan, Pat. Sports Illustrated Pitching. LC 76-43003. (Sports Illustrated Ser.). (Illus.). 1977. 5.95i (ISBN 0-397-01123-7); pap. 2.95i (LP-105). Har-Row.

Jordan, Pat, jt. auth. see Covino, Marge.

Jordan, Patricia. District Nurse. LC 77-17785. 1978. 7.95 o.p. (ISBN 0-312-21358-1). St Martin.

Jordan, Penny. The Flawed Marriage. (Harlequin Presents Ser.). 192p. 1983. pap. 1.95 (ISBN 0-373-10584-3). Harlequin Bks.

--Phantom Marriage. (Harlequin Presents Ser.). 192p. 1983. pap. 1.95 (ISBN 0-373-10591-6). Harlequin Bks.

--Rescue Operation. (Harlequin Presents Ser.). 192p. 1983. pap. 1.95 (ISBN 0-373-10602-5). Harlequin Bks.

Jordan, Philip D. Fiddlefoot Jones of the North Woods. LC 57-7687. (Illus.). (gr. 4-7). 6.95 o.s.i. (ISBN 0-8149-0340-1). Vanguard.

Jordan, Randolph E. & Payne, James R. Fate & Weathering of Petroleum Spills in the Marine Enviroment: A Literature Review & Synopsis. LC 80-66473. 170p. 1980. 27.50 (ISBN 0-250-40381-1). Ann Arbor Science.

Jordan, Robert S. Political Leadership in NATO: A Study in Multilateral Diplomacy. 1979. lib. bdg. 32.00 (ISBN 0-89158-355-6). Westview.

Jordan, Ronald J., jt. auth. see Fischer, Donald E.

Jordan, Ruth. Daughter of the Waves: Memories of Growing up in Pre-War Palestine. LC 80-39526. (Illus.). 224p. 1983. 12.95 (ISBN 0-8008-2120-3). Taplinger.

Jordan, S., et al. Handbook of Technical Writing Practices, 2 vols. 1971. Set. 1399p. 119.95x, (ISBN 0-471-45062-6); Vol. 1. 746p. 66.50x, (ISBN 0-471-45060-X); Vol. 2. 653p. 64.50x, (ISBN 0-471-45059-6). Wiley.

Jordan, Tanis & Jordan, Martin. South America River Trips, Vol. II. (Illus.). 128p. 1982. pap. 9.95 (ISBN 0-933982-24-0). Bradt Ent.

--South America River Trips, Vol. III. (Illus.). 144p. (Orig.). 1983. pap. 11.95 (ISBN 0-933982-31-3). Bradt Ent.

Jordan, Terry G. Environment & Environmental Perceptions in Texas. Rosenbaum, Robert J., ed. (Texas History Ser.). (Illus.). 36p. 1981. pap. text ed. 1.95x (ISBN 0-89641-059-5). American Pr.

--Immigration to Texas. Rosenbaum, Robert J., ed. (Texas History Ser.). (Illus.). 39p. 1981. pap. text ed. 1.95x (ISBN 0-89641-051-X). American Pr.

--Texas Log Buildings: A Folk Architecture. LC 77-24559. (Illus.). 240p. 1982. o. p. 0.00; pap. 9.95 (ISBN 0-292-78051-6). U of Tex Pr.

Jordan, Terry G. & Bean, John L., Jr. Texas. (Geographies of the U. S.). 450p. 1983. lib. bdg. 35.00 (ISBN 0-86531-088-2); pap. text ed. 18.00 (ISBN 0-86531-481-0). Westview.

Jordan, Terry G. & Rowntree, Lester. The Human Mosaic: A Thematic Introduction to Cultural Geography. 3rd ed. 444p. 1982. text ed. 27.00 scp (ISBN 0-06-043461-9, HarpC); scp student guide 8.95 (ISBN 0-06-044073-2); instr's manual avail. (ISBN 0-06-363458-9). Har-Row.

--The Human Mosaic: A Thematic Introduction to Cultural Geography. 2nd ed. 1979. text ed. 22.95 scp o.p. (ISBN 0-06-384386-2, HarpC); instr. manual avail. o.p. (ISBN 0-06-373435-4). Har-Row.

Jordan, Thomas E. Child Development, Information, & the Formation of Public Policy: An International Perspective. (Illus.). 316p. 1982. 24.75x (ISBN 0-398-04685-9). C C Thomas.

--Development in the Preschool Years: Birth to Age Five. LC 79-51678. (Educational Psychology Ser.). 1980. 22.00 (ISBN 0-12-390450-1). Acad Pr.

Jordan, Thomas F. Linear Operators for Quantum Mechanics. LC 79-64993. 144p. 8.00 (ISBN 0-9602762-0-3). T F Jordan.

Jordan, Tristram F. The Jordan Memorial. Jordan, William B., Jr., frwd. by. LC 82-81274. (Illus.). 488p. 1982. Repr. of 1882 ed. 35.00x (ISBN 0-89725-030-3). NE History.

Jordan, V. L. Acoustical Design of Concert Halls & Theatres. (Illus.). xiv, 225p. 1980. 65.50 (ISBN 0-85334-853-7, Pub. by Applied Sci England). Elsevier.

Jordan, William. Client-Worker Transactions. (Library of Social Work). 1970. 8.95 o.p. (ISBN 0-7100-6836-0). Routledge & Kegan.

Jordan, William B., jt. ed. see Felton, Craig.

Jordan, William B., Jr., frwd. by see Jordan, Tristram F.

Jordan, William S., Jr. Community Medicine in the United Kingdom: Medical Education & an Emerging Specialty Within the Reorganized National Health Service. LC 78-4226. (Health Care & Society Ser.: Vol. 3). 1978. text ed. 23.95 o.s.i. (ISBN 0-8261-2410-0). Springer Pub.

Jordan, Winthrop. White Man's Burden: Historical Origins of Racism in the United States. 1974. 17.95x (ISBN 0-19-501742-0). Oxford U Pr.

Jordan, Winthrop, et al. The United States, Vols. 1 & 2, Combined Ed. (Illus.). 896p. 1982. text ed. 23.95 (ISBN 0-13-937946-0). P-H.

Jordan, Z. A. Evolution of Dialectical Materialism. 1967. 19.95 o.p. (ISBN 0-312-27265-0). St Martin.

Jordans, ed. Britain's Top Three Hundred Printing Companies. 42p. 1982. 175.00x (ISBN 0-85938-163-3, Pub. by Jordans House England). State Mutual Bk.

Jorde, Paula. The Kids Do It Book: An Illustrated Handbook of Imaginative Activities for Children. LC 76-796. 104p. 1976. pap. 3.95 o.p. (ISBN 0-912078-47-2). Volcano Pr.

Jorden, Eleanor H. Reading Japanese. 607p. Date not set. includes 17 cassettes 185.00x (ISBN 0-88432-096-0, J450). J Norton Pubs.

Jorden, Eleanor H. & Chaplin, Hamako I. Beginning Japanese, Pt. 2. (Linguistic Ser). (Illus.). 1963. text ed. 35.00x cloth o.p. (ISBN 0-300-00610-1); pap. text ed. 9.95x (ISBN 0-300-00136-3). Yale U Pr.

Jorden, Eleanor H., ed. Japanese Self-Instruction Program, 2 vols. (Japanese.). 1979. Vol. 1, 408p. 8 cassettes incl. 125.00x (ISBN 0-88432-030-8, J401); Vol. 2, 410p. 16 cassettes incl. 175.00x (ISBN 0-88432-031-6, J409). J Norton Pubs.

Jordon, Penny. Escape from Desire. (Harlequin Presents Ser.). 192p. 1983. pap. 1.75 (ISBN 0-373-10569-X). Harlequin Bks.

Jordon, Robert S., ed. Dag Hammarskjold Revisited: The UN Secretary-General As a Force in World Politics. LC 81-70434. (Illus.). 208p. 1982. lib. bdg. 19.95 (ISBN 0-89089-233-4). Carolina Acad Pr.

Jordon, Wendy A. By the Light of the Qulliq. 44p. 1980. pap. 5.95 (ISBN 0-86528-000-2). Stemmer Hse.

Jordon, Winthrop, et al. The United States, 2 vols. 5th ed. (Illus.). 1982. Vol. I, 480p. pap. text ed. 16.95 ea. (ISBN 0-13-937920-7). Vol II, 512p (ISBN 0-13-937938-X). P-H.

Jordy, Sarah S. see Keller, Mark.

Jordy, Sarah S., et al see Keller, Mark.

Jordy, William H., jt. auth. see Pierson, William H.

Jordy, William H. see Pierson, William H. & Jordy, William H.

Joreskog, K. G. & Wold, H. Systems Under Indirect Observation: Casualty Structure Prediction, 2 vols. (Contributions to Economic Analysis Ser.: Vol. 139). Date not set. 117.00 (ISBN 0-444-86301-X). Elsevier.

Joreskog, Karl G. & Sorbom, Dag. EFAP Two: Exploratory Factor Analysis Program. pap. 4.25 (ISBN 0-89498-007-6). Natl Ed Res.

Jorg, E. W. God's Message to His Chosen Earthly People of Israel. 1978. 6.50 o.p. (ISBN 0-533-03165-6). Vantage.

Jorge, Antonio, et al, eds. Foreign Debt & Latin American Economic Development. 200p. 1982. 30.00 (ISBN 0-08-029411-1). Pergamon.

Jorge de Sena. In Crete With the Minotaur & Other Poems. Monteiro, George, tr. 77p. (Orig., Port.). 1980. pap. 6.00 (ISBN 0-686-35845-7). Gavea-Brown.

Jorgens, K. Linear Integral Operators. Roach, G. F., tr. (Survey & Reference in Mathematics Ser.: No. 7). 1982. text ed. 66.00 (ISBN 0-273-08523-9). Pitman Pub MA.

Jorgensen, Eric, ed. Dodge Aspen: 1976-1979 Shop Manual. (Illus.). pap. text ed. 11.95 o.p. (ISBN 0-89287-311-6, A199). Clymer Pubns.

--Fiat Service-Repair Handbook: 131 Series, 1975-1977. (Illus.). pap. 11.95 o.p. (ISBN 0-89287-197-0, A158). Clymer Pubns.

--Honda CX & GL Five Hundred Twins 1978-1982 Service Repair Maintenance. pap. text ed. 10.95 (ISBN 0-89287-295-0, M335). Clymer Pubns.

--Honda XR-Seventy Five & XR-Eighty Singles: Service, Repair, Performance, 1975-82. (Illus.). pap. 10.95 (ISBN 0-89287-215-2, M312). Clymer Pubns.

--Kawasaki: 250-750cc Triples 1969-1979--Service, Repair, Maintenance Handbook. 4th ed. (Illus.). pap. 10.95 o.p. (ISBN 0-89287-192-X, M353). Clymer Pubns.

--Mustang 1979-1982 Includes Turbo Shop Manual. (Illus.). 336p. (Orig.). pap. text ed. 11.95 (ISBN 0-89287-335-3, A291). Clymer Pubns.

--Pinto Service Repair Handbook: All Models 1971-1980. (Illus.). pap. 11.95 o.p. (ISBN 0-89287-211-X, A171). Clymer Pubns.

--Plymouth Volare: 1976-1979 Shop Manual. (Illus.). 328p. (Orig.). pap. text ed. 11.95 o.p. (ISBN 0-89287-312-4, A236). Clymer Pubns.

--Suzuki GS850 & GS1000 Fours, 1979-1980: Service, Repair, Maintenance. (Illus.). 295p. (Orig.). pap. text ed. 10.95 (ISBN 0-89287-305-1, M376). Clymer Pubns.

--Triumph Service-Repair Handbook: TR 7 Series, 1975-1978. (Illus.). pap. 11.95 o.p. (ISBN 0-89287-206-3, A211). Clymer Pubns.

Jorgensen, Eric, ed. see Clymer Publications.

Jorgensen, Eric, ed. see Vesely, Anton.

Jorgensen, Erik. Successful Real Estate Sales Agreements. 3rd ed. 352p. (Orig.). 1982. 17.95 (ISBN 0-933800-02-9); pap. 14.95 (ISBN 0-933800-01-0). Axiom Pr.

Jorgensen, Heidi. The Shard. LC 81-86420. 256p. 1983. pap. 8.95 (ISBN 0-86666-048-8). GWP.

Jorgensen, James. A Woman's Guide to Retirement Planning. 96p. Date not set. pap. 5.00 (ISBN 0-943340-00-4). Jorg Pubns CA. Postponed.

Jorgensen, Johannes. Saint Francis of Assisi. pap. 4.95 (ISBN 0-385-02875-X, D22, Im). Doubleday.

Jorgensen, Joseph G., ed. Native Americans & Energy Development II. rev. 2nd ed. LC 78-72986. (Orig.). 1983. pap. 12.00 (ISBN 0-932978-06-1). Anthropology Res.

Jorgensen, Ove, et al. Modeling & Simulation of the Performance of Solar Heating & Cooling Systems. (Progress in Solar Energy Supplements IEA Ser.). 1983. pap. text ed. 21.00x (ISBN 0-89553-051-1). Am Solar Energy.

Jorgensen, Paul A. Our Naked Frailties: Sensational Art & Meaning in Macbeth. LC 70-145788. 1971. 22.50x (ISBN 0-520-01915-6). U of Cal Pr.

--Shakespeare's Military World. LC 56-9673. (California Library Reprint). 1974. 36.50x (ISBN 0-520-02519-9). U of Cal Pr.

Jorgensen, Poul. Poul Jorgensen's Modern Trout Flies and How to Tie Them. LC 79-3897. (Illus.). 1979. 12.95 o.p. (ISBN 0-385-15346-5); pap. 9.95 (ISBN 0-385-15347-3). Doubleday.

Jorgensen, Rich see Shan, Han.

Jorgensen, S. E. Application of Ecological Modelling in Enviromental Management. (Developments in Enviromental Modelling Ser.: Vol. 4A). Date not set. 125.75 (ISBN 0-444-42155-6). Elsevier.

Jorgensen, S. E. & Johnson, I. Principles of Environmental Science & Technology. (Studies in Environmental Science: Vol. 14). 1981. 53.25 (ISBN 0-444-99721-0). Elsevier.

Jorgensen, S. E., ed. Industrial Waste Water Management. (Studies in Environmental Science: Vol. 5). 388p. 1979. 59.75 (ISBN 0-444-41795-8). Elsevier.

Jorgensen-Dahl, Arnfinn. Regional Organisation & Order in South-East Asia. 200p. 1982. 60.00x (ISBN 0-333-30663-5, Pub. by Macmillan England). State Mutual Bk.

Jorgenson, D. W. Econometric Studies of U. S. Energy Policy. (Data Resources Ser.: Vol. 1). 1976. 42.75 (ISBN 0-444-10904-8, North-Holland). Elsevier.

Jorgenson, D. W., et al. Optimal Replacement Policy. (Studies in Mathematical & Managerial Economics: Vol. 8). 1971. 21.50 (ISBN 0-444-10219-1, North-Holland). Elsevier.

Jorgenson, Eric, ed. Ford Pinto & Mercury Bobcat: 1971-1980. pap. 11.95 (ISBN 0-89287-211-X). Clymer Pubns.

--Jeep All Models: 1969-1978, 4-Wheel Drive Maintenance. (Illus.). pap. 8.95 o.p. (ISBN 0-89287-291-8, A234). Clymer Pubns.

Jorgenson, Paul A., jt. auth. see Carey, Gary.

Jorgenson, Theodore. Norwegian Literature in Medieval & Early Modern Times. LC 77-27602. 1978. Repr. of 1952 ed. lib. bdg. 19.00x (ISBN 0-313-20073-4, JONL). Greenwood.

Joris, David. Een Geestelijck Liedt-Boexcken: Inholdende Veel Schoone Sinrijcke Christelijcke Liedekens - Dock Troostlijcke Nieuwe-Jaren - Claech Unde Lof-Sanghen-Ter Eeren Godes. (Mennonite Songbooks, Dutch Ser.: Vol. 1). 1971. 20.00 o.s.i. (ISBN 90-6027-242-0, Pub. by Frits Knuf Netherlands). Pendragon NY.

Jorning, P. J., jt. auth. see Kootstra, G.

Jorns, Auguste. Quakers As Pioneers in Social Work. Brown, Thomas K., tr. LC 69-14934. (Criminology, Law Enforcement, & Social Problems Ser.: No. 27). 1969. Repr. of 1931 ed. 8.50x (ISBN 0-87585-027-8). Patterson Smith.

Jorstad, Erling. Evangelicals in the White House: The Cultural Maturation of Born-Again Christianity, 1960-1981. (Studies in American Religion: Vol. 4). 171p. 1981. hard cover 29.50x; pap. 14.95x (ISBN 0-88946-881-8). E Mellen.

Jortner, J., jt. auth. see Levine, R. D.

Jortner, J., ed. Thermomechanical Behavior of High Temperature Composites. (AD-04 Ser.). 1982. 30.00 (H00248). ASME.

Jortner, Joshua, et al, eds. Photoselective Chemistry, Pt. 1. (Advances in Chemical Physics Ser.). 769p. 1981. 99.00 (ISBN 0-471-06275-8, Pub. by Wiley-Interscience). Wiley.

--Photoselective Chemistry, Pt. 2. (Advances in Chemical Physics Ser.). 718p. 1981. 87.00 (ISBN 0-471-06274-X, Pub. by Wiley-Interscience). Wiley.

Joscelyn, Archie. Gunman. 256p. (YA) 1975. 6.95 (ISBN 0-685-51236-3, Avalon). Bouregy.

--Kiowa Pass. 192p. (YA) 1976. 6.95 (ISBN 0-685-66480-5, Avalon). Bouregy.

--The Lost Herd. (YA) 1978. 6.95 (ISBN 0-685-86409-X, Avalon). Bouregy.

--Lost River Canyon. 192p. (YA) 1976. 6.95 (ISBN 0-685-62024-7, Avalon). Bouregy.

--Ride to Blizzard. 256p. (YA) 1973. 6.95 (ISBN 0-685-30372-1, Avalon). Bouregy.

--The Trail to Dismal River. 192p. (YA) 1975. 6.95 (ISBN 0-685-53494-4, Avalon). Bouregy.

Josef, Kolmas, ed. Tibetan Books & Newspapers (Chinese Collection) (Asiatische Forschungen Ser.: Band 62). 133p. 1978. pap. 30.00x (ISBN 3-447-01961-1). Intl Pubns Serv.

Josefowitz, Natasha. In a Nutshell: Feminine-Feminist Verse. Date not set. 4.95x (ISBN 0-9607812-0-X). Prestwick Pub.

Joseph, et al. Illustrated Guide to Textiles. 3rd ed. (Illus.). 160p. 1981. 10.95x (ISBN 0-8087-3435-0); 100 swatches 9.95x (ISBN 0-8087-3423-7); 150 swatches 13.95x (ISBN 0-8087-3413-X). Burgess.

Joseph, Alaine, et al. Best of Pandora. new ed. Wickstrom, Lois, ed. (Illus., Orig.). Date not set. pap. cancelled (ISBN 0-916176-09-6). Sproing.

Joseph, Alexander, et al. Physics for Engineering Technology. 2nd ed. LC 76-55696. 1978. 28.95 (ISBN 0-471-45075-8). Wiley.

Joseph, Alice. Chamorros & Carolinians of Saipan: Personality Studies. LC 70-138592. (Illus.). xi, 381p. Repr. of 1951 ed. lib. bdg. 20.00x (ISBN 0-8371-5793-5, JOCC). Greenwood.

Joseph, Bernard. Nationality: Its Nature & Problems. 1923. 37.50x o.p. (ISBN 0-686-51422-X). Elliots Bks.

Joseph, Howard, et al, eds. Truth & Compassion: Essays on Judaism & Religion for Rabbi Dr. Solomon Frank at Eighty. 250p. 1982. text ed. 11.50x (ISBN 0-919812-17-1, 40948, Pub. by Laurier U Pr). Humanities.

Joseph, J. Textbook of Regional Anatomy. 624p. 1982. 70.00x (ISBN 0-333-28911-0, Pub. by Macmillan England). State Mutual Bk.

Joseph, James. Here Is Your Hobby: Snowmobiling. (Here Is Your Hobby Ser.). (Illus.). (gr. 4-7). 1972. PLB 5.29 o.p. (ISBN 0-399-60724-2). Putnam Pub Group.

Joseph, Jenny. Beyond Descartes. 64p. 1983. 12.50 (ISBN 0-436-22801-7, Pub. by Secker & Warburg). David & Charles.

Joseph, Joan. A World for the Taking. (Orig.). 1983. pap. 3.95 (ISBN 0-440-18822-9). Dell.

Joseph, John. Muslim-Christian Relations & Inter-Christian Rivalries in the Middle East: The Case of the Jacobites in an Age of Transition. LC 82-870. 320p. 1983. 44.50x (ISBN 0-87395-600-1); pap. 14.95x (ISBN 0-87395-601-X). State U NY Pr.

Joseph, John & Pierce, Enneking. The Boston Anthenaeum Art Exhibition Index, 1827-1874. 1980. 75.00 (ISBN 0-686-43152-9). Apollo.

Joseph, Joseph M. & Lippincott, Sarah L. Point to the Stars. 2nd ed. (Illus.). (gr. 4-9). 1977. PLB 8.95 (ISBN 0-07-033050-6, GB). McGraw.

Joseph, Lawrence. Shouting at No One. LC 82-20052. (Pitt Poetry Ser.). 1983. 10.95 (ISBN 0-8229-3478-7); pap. 4.95 (ISBN 0-8229-5350-1). U of Pittsburgh Pr.

Joseph, Lou & Novick, Oscar. Doctor Discusses Children's Colds. (Illus.). 1979. pap. 2.50 o.p. (ISBN 0-686-65549-4). Budlong.

Joseph, Marie. The Listening Silence. 160p. 1983. 10.95 (ISBN 0-312-48739-8). St Martin.

Joseph, Marilyn S., jt. auth. see Williams, Preston P.

Joseph, Marjory & Joseph, William D. Research Fundamentals in Home Economics. LC 79-88756. (The Plycon Home Economics Ser.). 403p. 1979. pap. text ed. 15.95x (ISBN 0-8087-3415-6). Burgess.

Joseph, Samantha. Advances. 320p. 1983. 14.95 (ISBN 0-02-559890-2). Macmillan.

Joseph, Samuel. History of the Baron DeHirsch Fund: The Americanization of the Jewish Immigrant. LC 76-52987. (Illus.). Repr. of 1935 ed. lib. bdg. 22.50x (ISBN 0-678-01151-6). Kelley.

Joseph, Stephen. New Theatre Forms. LC 68-13407. (Illus.). 1968. 3.15 o.s.i. (ISBN 0-87830-091-0). Theatre Arts.

Joseph, Suad & Pillsbury, Barbara L., eds. Muslim-Christian Conflict: Political, Social & Economic Origins. 1979. lib. bdg. 27.00x o.p. (ISBN 0-89158-256-8). Westview.

Joseph, William D., jt. auth. see Joseph, Marjory.

Josephs, Ernest H., Jr., jt. auth. see Wicks, Robert J.

Josephs, Lewis S. Palauan Reference Grammar. LC 74-76377. (PALI Language Texts: Micronesia). 448p. (Orig.). 1975. pap. text ed. 14.00x (ISBN 0-8248-0331-0). UH Pr.

Josephs, Nancy, jt. auth. see Hatcher, Robert A.

Josephson, Elmer A. God's Key to Health & Happiness. 224p. 1976. pap. 5.95 (ISBN 0-8007-5018-7, Power Bks). Revell.

Josephson, Eric, ed. Drug Use: Epidemiological & Sociological Approaches. LC 74-19056. (General Psychiatry Ser.). 381p. 1974. 13.50x o.s.i. (ISBN 0-470-45082-7). Halsted Pr.

Josephson, Halsey D. The Tired Tirade. rev. ed. LC 68-54555. 1976. pap. 6.95 (ISBN 0-87863-132-1). Farnswth Pub.

Josephson, Hannah, tr. see Stendhal, Henri.

Josephson, Mark E. Ventricular Tachycardia: Mechanisms & Management. LC 82-83342. 320p. 1982. 49.50 (ISBN 0-87993-181-7). Futura Pub.

Josephson, Matthew. The Money Lords. pap. 1.95 o.p. (ISBN 0-451-61241-8, MJ1241, Ment). NAL.

--The President Makers: The Culture of Politics in an Age of Enlightenment. (Capricorn Bks.). 1979. pap. 6.95 o.p. (ISBN 0-399-50387-0, Perigee). Putnam Pub Group.

--Victor Hugo: A Realistic Biography of the Great Romantic. 514p. 1982. Repr. of 1942 ed. lib. bdg. 45.00 (ISBN 0-89760-415-6). Telegraph Bks.

Josephson, Matthew, tr. see Stendhal, Henri.

Josephus, Flavius. Second Jewish Commonwealth: From the Maccabaean Rebellion to the Outbreak of the Judaeo-Roman War. Glatzer, Nahum N., ed. Whitson, William, tr. LC 77-148714. Orig. Title: Antiquities, Books 12-20. 1971. 12.50x o.p. (ISBN 0-8052-3395-4); pap. 4.50 o.p. (ISBN 0-8052-0296-X). Schocken.

Josephy, Alvin. On the Hill. 1980. pap. 6.95 o.p. (ISBN 0-671-41389-9, Touchstone). S&S.

Josephy, Alvin, Jr. Now That the Buffalo's Gone. LC 82-47797. 304p. 1982. 15.95 (ISBN 0-394-46672-1). Knopf.

Josephy, Alvin M., jt. auth. see Weisberger, Bernard A.

Josephy, Alvin M., Jr. Indian Heritage of America. (Illus.). (YA) 1968. 20.00 (ISBN 0-394-43049-2). Knopf.

--The Indian Heritage of America. (Illus.). 307p. pap. 1.95 (ISBN 0-686-95020-8). ADL.

--The Nez Perce Indians & the Opening of the Northwest. abridged ed. LC 79-14847. (Illus.). xvi, 667p. 1979. 29.50x (ISBN 0-8032-2555-5); pap. 11.95 (ISBN 0-8032-7551-X, BB 718, Bison). U of Nebr Pr.

--On the Hill: A History of the American, Congress. 1979. 14.95 o.p. (ISBN 0-671-25048-5). S&S.

--Patriot Chiefs: A Chronicle of American Indian Resistance. (Illus.). 1969. pap. 4.95 (ISBN 0-14-004219-9). Penguin.

Jose-Shaw, Marie. Memory Development. (Sound Filmstrip Kits Ser.). 1p. (gr. 4-8). 1981. 24.00 (ISBN 0-8209-0448-1, FCW-25). ESP.

Josey, E. J., ed. The Information Society: Issues & Answers. LC 78-17708. (Neal-Schuman Professional Bk). 1978. lib. bdg. 27.50x (ISBN 0-912700-16-5). Oryx Pr.

--Libraries in the Political Process. (Neal-Schuman Professional Books Ser.). 1980. lib. bdg. 27.50x (ISBN 0-912700-25-4). Oryx Pr.

Josey, E. J. & DeLoach, Marva L., eds. Ethnic Collections in Libraries. 1983. 24.95 (ISBN 0-918212-63-4). Neal-Schuman.

Josey, E. J. & Shockley, A. A., eds. Handbook of Black Librarianship. LC 77-21817. 392p. 1977. lib. bdg. 25.00x o.p. (ISBN 0-87287-179-7). Libs Unl.

Joshi, Aravind, et al. Elements of Discourse Understanding. LC 80-29393. (Illus.). 352p. 1981. 34.50 (ISBN 0-521-23327-5). Cambridge U Pr.

Joshi, C. N., jt. tr. see Kane, P. V.

Joshi, Nirmala. Foundation of Indo-Soviet Relations. LC 75-906116. 1975. 9.00x o.p. (ISBN 0-88386-671-4). South Asia Bks.

Joshi, S. T. H. P. Lovecraft. (Starmont Reader's Guide Ser.: No. 13). 84p. 1982. Repr. lib. bdg. 11.95x (ISBN 0-89370-044-4). Borgo Pr.

--An Index to the Selected Letters of H. P. Lovecraft. 5.95 o.p. (ISBN 0-686-31241-4). Necronomicon.

--Reader's Guide to H. P. Lovecraft. Schlobin, Roger C., ed. (Reader's Guides to Contemporary Science Fiction & Fantasy Authors Ser.: Vol. 13). (Illus., Orig.). 1982. 11.95x (ISBN 0-916732-36-3); pap. text ed. 5.95x (ISBN 0-916732-35-5). Starmont Hse.

Joshi, S. T., ed. H. P. Lovecraft: Four Decades of Criticism. LC 80-11535. xvi, 247p. 1981. pap. 8.95 (ISBN 0-8214-0577-2, 82-83301). Ohio U Pr.

--H. P. Lovecraft: Four Decades of Criticism. LC 80-11535. xvi, 247p. 1980. 16.95x (ISBN 0-8214-0442-3, 82-83319). Ohio U Pr.

Joshi, V. C., jt. ed. see Nanda, B. R.

Joshua & Jones. Reproductive Clinical Problems in the Dog. 176p. 1982. 20.00 (ISBN 0-7236-0656-0). Wright-PSG.

Joshua, Joan, jt. auth. see White, Kay.

Joshua, Joan O. Cat Owner's Encyclopedia of Veterinary Medicine. (Illus.). 1977. pap. 12.95 (ISBN 0-87666-852-X, H-985). TFH Pubns.

Josipovici, Gabriel. Writing & the Body. LC 82-9042. (Illus.). 160p. 1983. 17.50x (ISBN 0-691-06550-0). Princeton U Pr.

Josipovici, Gabriel, ed. The Sirens' Song: Selected Essays of Maurice Blanchot. Rabinovitch, Sacha, tr. LC 81-48510. 264p. 1982. 22.50 (ISBN 0-253-35255-X). Ind U Pr.

Joske, W. D. Material Objects. 1967. 22.50 (ISBN 0-312-52150-2). St Martin.

Joskow, Paul L. Controlling Hospital Costs: The Role of Government Regulation. (Health & Public Policy). 224p. 1981. 27.50x (ISBN 0-262-10024-X). MIT Pr.

Joslin, Sesyle & Barry, Katharina. There Is a Bull on My Balcony. LC 66-11202. (Illus.). (gr. 1-6). 1966. 5.95 o.p. (ISBN 0-15-285057-0, HJ). HarBraceJ.

Josling, Timothy. Problems & Prospects for U. S. Agriculture in World Markets. LC 81-83300. (Committee on Changing International Realities Ser.). 68p. 1981. 6.00 (ISBN 0-89068-057-4). Natl Planning.

Jospe, Alfred, ed. Tradition & Contemporary Experience: Essays on Jewish Thought & Life. LC 77-110609. 1970. 8.50x o.p. (ISBN 0-8052-3349-0); pap. 3.45 o.p. (ISBN 0-8052-0275-7). Schocken.

Jospe, Michael, et al. Psychological Factors in Health Care: A Practitioner's Manual. Cohen, Barry D., ed. LC 77-11395. 512p. 1980. 31.95x (ISBN 0-669-02076-1). Lexington Bks.

Jospe, Michael L. The Placebo Effect in Healing. LC 77-6582. 192p. 1978. 21.95x (ISBN 0-669-01611-X). Lexington Bks.

Joss, Jean, tr. see Meyer, Charles.

Joss, John. Sierra Sierra. LC 77-82561. (Illus.). 1978. 8.95 o.p. (ISBN 0-688-03368-7). Morrow.

Joss, John, ed. Soaramerica. (Illus.). 216p. 1976. pap. 2.50 (ISBN 0-930514-06-8, Pub. by Soaring); pap. 6.95 o.p. (ISBN 0-686-96667-8). Aviation.

Josserand, Frank B. Richard Wagner: Patriot & Politician. LC 80-5638. 351p. (Orig.). 1981. lib. bdg. 23.00 (ISBN 0-8191-1418-9); pap. text ed. 12.75 (ISBN 0-8191-1419-7). U Pr of Amer.

Jossua, Jean-Pierre, jt. auth. see Geffre, Claude.

Jossua, Jean-pierre, jt. ed. see Geffre, Claude.

Jost, Ekkehard. Free Jazz. (Studies in Jazz Research: No. 4). 1975. pap. 27.00 o.p. (ISBN 3-7024-0013-3, 51-26654). Eur-Am Music.

Jost, Patricia C. & Griffith, O. Hayes. Lipid-Protein Interactions, Vol. 1. 338p. 1982. 75.00x (ISBN 0-471-06457-2, Pub. by Wiley-Interscience). Wiley.

--Lipid-Protein Interactions, Vol. 2. LC 81-16157. 307p. 1982. 70.00x (ISBN 0-471-06456-4, Pub. by Wiley-Interscience). Wiley.

Jost, W. see Eyring, H., et al.

Jotterand-Bellomo, Martine & Klinger, H. P., eds. The Robert Malthey Dedication. (Cytogenetics & Cell Genetics Ser.: Vol. 34, Nos. 1-2). (Illus.). iv, 188p. 1982. pap. 96.00 (ISBN 3-8055-3650-X). S Karger.

Jotwani, Motilal, ed. Contemporary Indian Literature & Society. 1979. 15.00x o.p. (ISBN 0-8364-0527-7). South Asia Bks.

Joubert, Joseph. The Notebooks of Joseph Joubert: A Selection. Auster, Paul, ed. & tr. from Fr. LC 82-73711. 176p. 1983. pap. 13.50 (ISBN 0-86547-108-8). N Point Pr.

Joubert, Philip. Rocket. 1958. 6.00 o.p. (ISBN 0-8022-0817-7). Philos Lib.

Joudry, Patricia. And the Children Played. LC 75-2790. 1975. 9.95 o.p. (ISBN 0-912766-16-6). Tundra Bks.

Jouklova, Z. Technical Dictionary: English, Czech, English. 510p. (Czech.). 1970. 20.00x (ISBN 0-89918-301-8). Vanous.

Joumblat, Kamal. I Speak for Lebanon. 128p. 1982. 20.00 (ISBN 0-86232-097-6, Pub. by Zed Pr England); pap. 8.50 (ISBN 0-86232-048-8, Pub. by Zed Pr England). Lawrence Hill.

Jourard, Sidney M. Self Disclosure: An Experimental Analysis of the Transparent Self. LC 78-10576. 264p. 1979. Repr. of 1971 ed. lib. bdg. 16.00 (ISBN 0-88275-767-9). Krieger.

Jourard, Sidney M. & Landsman, Ted. Healthy Personality: An Approach from the Viewpoint of Humanistic Psychology. 4th ed. (Illus.). 1980. text ed. 20.95x (ISBN 0-02-361390-4). Macmillan.

Jourdain, M. Old Lace: A Handbook for Collectors; an Account of the Different Styles of Lace, Their History, Characteristics & Manufacture. (Illus.). 121p. 1981. Repr. of 1908 ed. 30.00x (ISBN 0-8103-4310-X). Gale.

Jourdain, P. E., tr. see Cantor, Georg.

Jourdain, Patrick, jt. auth. see Reese, Terence.

Jourdain, Philip E., tr. see Cantor, Georg.

Jourdain, Sylvester, jt. auth. see Strachey, William.

Jourdain, Victor. La Legislation Francaise sur les Coalitions Ouvrieres, son Evolution au 19th Siecle (These) (Conditions of the 19th Century French Working Class Ser.). 180p. (Fr.). 1974. Repr. of 1898 ed. lib. bdg. 53.00x o.p. (ISBN 0-8287-0466-X, 1119). Clearwater Pub.

Jourdier, Auguste. De l'Emancipation des Serfs en Russie. (Nineteenth Century Russia Ser.). 80p. (Fr.). 1974. Repr. of 1861 ed. lib. bdg. 31.00x o.p. (ISBN 0-8287-0467-8, R28). Clearwater Pub.

--Des Forces Productives, Destructives et Improductives De la Russe. (Nineteenth Century Russia Ser.). 303p. (Fr.). 1974. Repr. of 1860 ed. lib. bdg. 80.50x o.p. (ISBN 0-8287-0468-6, R27). Clearwater Pub.

Jourlet, Maria De see De Jourlet, Marie.

Jourlet, Marie De see De Jourlet, Marie.

Jourlet, Marie de see De Jourlet, Marie.

Jourlet, Marie De see De Jourlet, Marie.

Jourlet, Marie de see De Jourlet, Marie.

Journal of Nursing Administration. Clinical Specialists & Nurse Clinicians. LC 75-41601. 46p. 1976. Repr. pap. 12.95 (ISBN 0-913654-22-1). Aspen Systems.

--Staffing, Vol. II. LC 75-1675. 47p. 1975. pap. 12.95 (ISBN 0-913654-06-X). Aspen Systems.

--Staffing, Vol. III. LC 75-43268. 43p. 1976. pap. 12.95 (ISBN 0-913654-21-3). Aspen Systems.

--The Techniques of Nursing Management, Vol. 2. LC 75-1674. 46p. 1976. pap. 12.95 (ISBN 0-913654-32-9). Aspen Systems.

Journal of Nursing Administration, ed. Primary Nursing. LC 77-18356. 44p. 1977. pap. text ed. 12.95 (ISBN 0-913654-38-8). Aspen Systems.

--Quality Control & Performance Appraisal, Vol. 3. LC 77-85307. 44p. 1977. pap. 12.95 (ISBN 0-913654-37-X). Aspen Systems.

--Staff Development, Vol. 1. LC 75-3506. 91p. 1975. pap. text ed. 12.95 (ISBN 0-913654-08-6). Aspen Systems.

--Staff Development, Vol. 2. LC 77-85308. 61p. 1977. pap. 12.95 (ISBN 0-913654-40-X). Aspen Systems.

Journal of Nursing Administration Staff. Clinical Ladders & Professional Advancement. LC 77-18357. 53p. 1977. pap. 12.95 (ISBN 0-913654-39-6). Aspen Systems.

Journalism Reseach Fellows of 1982. Juvenile Justice: Myths & Realities. Farkas, Susan, ed. 96p. (Orig.). 1983. pap. 7.50 (ISBN 0-937846-96-1). Inst Educ Lead.

Jousse, John. Catechism of Music. 1891. pap. 3.95 (ISBN 0-02-871180-7). Schirmer Bks.

Joussot-Dubien, J., ed. see International Meeting of the Societe de chimie physique, Thiais, 27th, 1975.

Jouvancy, Joseph De see De Jouvancy, Joseph.

Jouve, Nicole W. Baudelaire: A Fire to Conquer Darkness. LC 79-14978. 1980. 25.00 (ISBN 0-312-07005-5). St Martin.

--Shades of Grey. 176p. 1983. pap. 5.95 (ISBN 0-86068-229-3, Virago Pr). Merrimack Bk Serv.

Jouve, Pierre J. An Idiom of Night. Bosley, Keith, tr. LC 82-70936. (Poetry Europe Ser.: No. 9). 80p. 1969. 7.95 (ISBN 0-8040-0150-2). Swallow.

Jovanovich, William, intro. by see Brandwein, Paul F.

Jowers, Lawrence V. Places & Visions Shared: The Collected Poems of Lawrence V. Jowers. Westburg, John E., ed. 64p. pap. 10.00 (ISBN 0-87423-032-2). Westburg.

Jowett, Benjamin, ed. see Pattison, Mark.

Jowett, Benjamin, tr. see Plato.

Jowett, C. E. Compatibility & Testing of Electronic Components. LC 72-7039. 345p. 1972. 39.95x o.s.i. (ISBN 0-470-45170-X). Halsted Pr.

--Materials & Process in Electronics. 329p. 1982. text ed. 43.50x (ISBN 0-09-145100-0). Sheridan.

Jowett, Garth S., ed. see Hollyman, Burnes S.

Jowett, S. Young Disabled People: Their Further Education, Training & Employment. 148p. 1982. pap. text ed. 15.25x (ISBN 0-7005-0508-3, NFER). Humanities.

Jowitt, Glenn. Race Day. (Illus.). 96p. 1982. 24.95 (ISBN 0-00-216998-3, Pub. by W Collins Australia). Intl Schol Bk Serv.

Jowitt, Kenneth. Revolutionary Breakthroughs & National Development: The Case of Romania, 1944-1965. LC 71-123625. 1971. 36.50x (ISBN 0-520-01762-5). U of Cal Pr.

Joy, Charles R. Getting to Know the River Amazon. (Getting to Know Ser). (Illus.). (gr. 3-5). 1963. PLB 3.97 o.p. (ISBN 0-698-30147-1, Coward). Putnam Pub Group.

--Getting to Know the Sahara. (Getting to Know Ser.). (Illus.). (gr. 3-5). 1963. PLB 4.49 o.p. (ISBN 0-698-30149-8, Pub. by Coward). Putnam Pub Group.

Joy, D. C., jt. ed. see Cullis, A. G.

Joy, Donald M., ed. Moral Development Foundations: Judeo-Christian Alternatives to Piaget-Kohlberg. 240p. (Orig.). 1983. pap. 12.95 (ISBN 0-687-27177-0). Abingdon.

Joy, Leonard, ed. Nutrition Planning. new ed. 154p. Date not set. text ed. price not set (ISBN 0-86103-007-9). Butterworth.

Joy, Margaret. Monday Magic. (Illus.). 128p. (ps-8). 1982. 8.95 (ISBN 0-571-11924-7). Faber & Faber.

Joy, Robert O., jt. auth. see Pack, Alice C.

Joyce, jt. auth. see Lawson-Wood, Denis.

Joyce, Bruce, jt. auth. see Weil, Marsha.

Joyce, Bruce R. New Strategies for Social Education. LC 73-172886. (Illus.). 1972. text ed. 19.95 (ISBN 0-574-17801-5, 13-0801); instructor's guide 1.20 (ISBN 0-574-17803-1, 13-0803); basic teaching skills manual 7.95 (ISBN 0-574-17802-3, 13-0802); three teaching strategies manual 6.95 (ISBN 0-574-17832-5, 13-0832, 13-0830). strategies filmstrips-tapes 100.00 (ISBN 0-686-66971-1, 13-0831). SRA.

Joyce, Bruce R. & Weil, Marsha. Models of Teaching. 2nd ed. (Illus.). 1980. text ed. 23.95 (ISBN 0-13-586164-0). P-H.

Joyce, Bruce R., et al. Basic Teaching Skills. 1972. pap. 5.95 manual (ISBN 0-574-17802-3, 13-0801); Set. 19.95 (ISBN 0-574-17801-5, 13-0830). SRA.

--Three Teaching Strategies for the Social Sciences. 1972. pap. text ed. 6.95 o.s.i. (ISBN 0-574-17832-5, 13-0832); strategies filmstrips-tapes 100.00 o.s.i. (ISBN 0-686-60812-7, 13-0831). SRA.

Joyce, Davis D. History & Historians: Some Essays. LC 82-21865. 116p. (Orig.). 1983. lib. bdg. 18.75 (ISBN 0-8191-2936-4); pap. text ed. 8.25 (ISBN 0-8191-2937-2). U Pr of Amer.

Joyce, Deborah. In the Arms of a Stranger. (Second Chance at Love Ser.: No. 109). 1.75 (ISBN 0-515-06873-X). Jove Pubns.

--A Questing Heart. (Super Romances Ser.). 384p. 1983. pap. 2.95 (ISBN 0-373-70061-X, Pub. by Worldwide). Harlequin Bks.

Joyce, Ernest. Encyclopedia of Furniture Making. LC 76-49087. (Illus.). 1979. 19.95 (ISBN 0-8069-8302-7); PLB 16.79 o.p. (ISBN 0-8069-8303-5). Sterling.

Joyce, Frank. Local Government, Environmental Planning & Control. 301p. 1982. text ed. 39.00x (ISBN 0-566-00440-2). Gower Pub Ltd.

Joyce, George & Govoni, Norman A., eds. Black Consumer, Dimensions of Power & Strategy. 1971. pap. text ed. 5.95x (ISBN 0-394-31130-2). Phila Bk Co.

Joyce, James. The Boarding House. (Creative's Classics Ser.). 32p. (gr. 1-7). 1982. lib. bdg. 6.95 (ISBN 0-87191-895-1). Creative Ed.

--Dubliners. LC 25-23228. 1926. 5.95 (ISBN 0-394-60464-4). Modern Lib.

--Dubliners. (Centennial Editions). 1982. 17.50 (ISBN 0-670-28586-2). Viking Pr.

--The Encounter. (Creative's Classics Ser.). 32p. (gr. 1-7). 1982. lib. bdg. 6.95 (ISBN 0-87191-896-X). Creative Ed.

--Finnegans Wake. Centennial ed. 1982. 30.00 (ISBN 0-670-31538-9). Viking Pr.

--Finnegans Wake, Chapter I: The Illnesstraited Colossick Idition. LC 82-20202. (Illus.). 96p. 1983. 7.95 (ISBN 0-295-95991-6). U of Wash Pr.

--Giacomo Joyce. 1968. 25.00 (ISBN 0-670-33827-3). Viking Pr.

--A Portrait of the Artist As a Young Man: A Facsimile of the Manuscript Fragments of Stephen Hero. Groden, Michael, ed. LC 78-12105. (James Joyce Archive Ser.: Vol. 7-10). 1979. lib. bdg. 415.00 o.s.i. (ISBN 0-8240-2807-4). Garland Pub.

--Portrait of the Artist As a Young Man. Centennial ed. Ellmann, Richard, ed. 1982. 17.50 (ISBN 0-670-56683-7). Viking Pr.

--A Starchamber Quiry: A James Joyce Centennial Volume. Epstein, Edmund L., ed. 1982. 15.95 o.p. (ISBN 0-416-31560-7). Methuen Inc.

--Ulysses. 1940. 12.95 (ISBN 0-394-60486-5). Modern Lib.

--Ulysses. 1967. pap. 9.95 (ISBN 0-394-70380-4, Vin). Random.

--Ulysses: Notes & "Telemachus" - "Scylla" & "Charybdis": A Facsimile of Notes for the Book & Mauscripts for Episodes 1-9. Groden, Michael, ed. LC 78-16032. (James Joyce Archive Ser.). 1978. lib. bdg. 104.00 o.s.i. (ISBN 0-8240-2822-8). Garland Pub.

Joyce, James A. The New Politics of Human Rights. LC 78-13333. 1979. 26.00x (ISBN 0-312-56880-0). St Martin.

--World Labour Rights & Their Protection. 192p. 1980. 25.00 (ISBN 0-312-89137-7). St Martin.

Joyce, Jean, ed. see Frederick, J. George.

Joyce, Joan M. Handbook of Critical Care Nursing. Gardner, Alvin f., ed. (Allied Professions Monograph Ser.). 1983. 35.00 (ISBN 0-87527-318-1). Green.

Joyce, Jon L. Beatitudes for Moderns. (Orig.). 1981. pap. 2.00 (ISBN 0-686-97816-1). JLJ Pubs.

--That Incredible First Day. (Orig.). 1980. pap. 2.00 (ISBN 0-937172-15-4). JLJ Pubs.

--To Bring a Sword. (Orig.). 1981. pap. 2.00 (ISBN 0-937172-23-5). JLJ Pubs.

--When the Angels Go Away. (Orig.). 1980. pap. 2.00 (ISBN 0-937172-14-6). JLJ Pubs.

Joyce, M., et al. Nutritional Aspects of Cancer Care. 1982. text ed. 16.95 (ISBN 0-8359-5077-8); pap. text ed. 13.95 (ISBN 0-8359-5076-X); instrs.' manual o.p. free (ISBN 0-8359-5078-6). Reston.

Joyce, Mary. First Steps in Teaching Creative Dance to Children. 2nd ed. LC 79-91834. (Illus.). 226p. 1980. pap. 9.95 (ISBN 0-87484-510-6). Mayfield Pub.

Joyce, Michael. The War Outside Ireland. LC 82-80497. 192p. (Orig.). 1982. pap. 8.50 (ISBN 0-943608-01-5). Tinkers Dam Pr.

Joyce, Patrick. The History of Morden College Blackheath, 1695 to the Present. 1982. 50.00 (ISBN 0-686-84446-7, Pub. By Gresham England). State Mutual Bk.

Joyce, Patrick W. English As We Speak It in Ireland. LC 68-26579. 1971. Repr. of 1910 ed. 42.00x (ISBN 0-8103-3356-2). Gale.

Joyce, R. D. Encounters in Organizational Behavior: Problem Situations. 1974. text ed. 20.00 (ISBN 0-08-017013-7); pap. text ed. 9.25 (ISBN 0-08-017116-8). Pergamon.

Joyce, R. J. The Ecology of Grasshoppers in Cast Central Sudan. 1952. 35.00x (ISBN 0-85135-019-4, Pub. by Centre Overseas Research). State Mutual Bk.

Joyce, Robert E. Human Sexual Ecology. LC 79-6727. 421p. 1981. lib. bdg. 25.25 (ISBN 0-8191-1359-X); pap. text ed. 14.00 (ISBN 0-8191-0937-1). U Pr of Amer.

Joyce, Rosemary O. A Woman's Place: The Life History of a Rural Ohio Grandmother. (Illus.). 225p. 1983. pns 0.00 (ISBN 0-8142-0344-2). Ohio St U Pr.

Joyce, T. A. Mexican Archaeology. Repr. of 1920 ed. 24.00 o.p. (ISBN 0-527-46850-9). Kraus Repr.

Joyce, William F., jt. auth. see Hrebiniak, Lawrence G.

Joyce, William F., jt. ed. see Van De Ven, Andrew H.

Joyce, William L. & Hall, David D., eds. Printing & Society in Early America. 1983. text ed. price not set (ISBN 0-912296-55-0, Dist. by U Pr of VA). Am Antiquarian.

Joyce, William W. & Ryan, Frank L., eds. Social Studies & the Elementary Teacher: Promises & Practices. LC 77-93070. (Bulletin Ser.: No. 53). 1977. pap. 7.25 (ISBN 0-87986-014-6, 498-15264). Coun Soc Studies.

Joyce St. Iprimavera, Elise Peter see St. Peter, Joyce.

Joyner, Claude, jt. auth. see Linhart, Joseph W.

Joyner, Russell, jt. auth. see Lipman, Michael.

Joynson, R. B. Psychology & Common Sense. 1974. 10.00x (ISBN 0-7100-7827-7); pap. 7.95 (ISBN 0-7100-7899-4). Routledge & Kegan.

Joys, Joanne. The Wild Animal Trainer in America. (Illus.). 200p. 1982. 25.00 (ISBN 0-87108-621-2). Pruett.

Joyson, David C. Better Rugby for Boys: Better Sports Ser. 3rd rev. ed. LC 70-21463. (Illus.). 95p. 1978. 8.50x (ISBN 0-7182-1460-9). Intl Pubns Serv.

Jrade, Cathy L. Ruben Dario & the Romantic Search for Unity: The Modernist Recourse to Esoteric Tradition. (Texas Pan American Ser.). 192p. 1983. text ed. 19.95x (ISBN 0-292-75075-7). U of Tex Pr.

Juan, E. San see San Juan, E., Jr.

Juan, San P. see San Juan, P. & Chiswick, Barry.

Juarez, Bill, jt. auth. see Boyle, Pat.

Juayl, B. N. Integrated Economic Planning. Date not set. text ed. price not set (ISBN 0-391-01837-X). Humanities.

Juba, Robert D. Flights...Into Time. Gray, Charles, ed. LC 82-81680. (Illus.). 1982. pap. 7.95 (ISBN 0-686-81837-7). Joyful Noise.

Jubb, R. A. Nothobranchius. (Illus.). 64p. 1981. 4.95 (ISBN 0-87666-534-2, KW-083). TFH Pubns.

Jubiz, W. Endocrinology: A Logical Approach for Clinicians. 1980. 18.95 (ISBN 0-07-033066-2). McGraw.

Jubiz, William. Endocrinology: A Logical Approach for Clinicians. (Illus.). 1979. text ed. 28.00 (ISBN 0-07-033065-4, HP). McGraw.

Juch, Bert. Personal Development: The Roundabout Climb. 200p. 1983. 29.95 (ISBN 0-471-10458-2, Pub. by Wiley-Interscience). Wiley.

Jucker, E., ed. Progress in Drug Research, Vol. 25. 500p. 1981. text ed. 120.00x (ISBN 3-7643-1179-7). Birkhauser.

Jucker, Ernst, ed. Progress in Drug Research, Vol. 26. 412p. 1982. text ed. 98.95 (ISBN 3-7643-1261-0). Birkhauser.

Jud, Gustav D. Inflation & the Use of Indexing in Developing Countries. LC 76-12859. (Praeger Special Studies). 1978. 29.95 o.p. (ISBN 0-275-23840-7). Praeger.

Juda, Lawrence. Ocean Space Rights: Developing U.S. Policy. LC 74-1732. (Special Studies). 318p. 1975. text ed. 39.95 o.p. (ISBN 0-275-09240-2). Praeger.

Judah, Charles & Smith, George W. The Unchosen. 1962. 5.95 o.p. (ISBN 0-698-10381-5, Coward). Putnam Pub Group.

Judd. Questions & Answers: CB Radio. (Illus.). 1982. pap. 6.95 (ISBN 0-408-01216-1). Focal Pr.

--Use of Files. 2nd ed. 1976. 22.95 (ISBN 0-444-19452-5). Elsevier.

Judd, jt. auth. see Phillips.

Judd, Alan. A Breed of Heroes. 1981. 13.95 (ISBN 0-698-11087-0, Coward). Putnam Pub Group.

Judd, Amos F., ed. see Blee, Ben W.

Judd, Bernice. Voyages to Hawaii Before 1860. LC 74-78864. 1974. text ed. 12.00x (ISBN 0-8248-0329-9). UH Pr.

Judd, Bernice, et al, eds. Hawaiian Language Imprints, 1822-1899: A Bibliography. LC 77-21295. 1978. text ed. 12.00x (ISBN 0-8248-0529-1). UH Pr.

Judd, Denis. The Life & Times of George V. Fraser, Antonia, ed. (Kings & Queens of England Ser.). (Illus.). 224p. 1973. text ed. 17.50x (ISBN 0-297-76578-7, Pub. by Weidenfeld & Nicolson England). Biblio Dist.

Judd, Dennis, et al. State Government Policy. (Orig.). 1981. pap. 6.00 (ISBN 0-918592-49-6). Policy Studies.

Judd, Eloise W. Nursing Care of the Adult. (Illus.). 700p. 1983. 21.50 (ISBN 0-8036-5136-8). Davis Co.

Judd, Gerrit P. Doctor Judd, Hawaii's Friend: A Biography of Gerrit Parmele Judd, 1803-1873. (Illus.). 1960. 14.00 (ISBN 0-87022-385-2). UH Pr.

--Hawaii. LC 66-17588. (Orig.). 1966. pap. 2.95 o.p. (ISBN 0-8077-1596-4). Tchrs Coll.

Judd, H. Stanley. How to Play Golf the Easy Way: A Weekender's Guide to Successful Shotmaking. LC 79-3832. (Illus., Orig.). 1980. pap. 4.95i (ISBN 0-06-090766-5, CN 766, CN). Har-Row.

Judd, J. H. U. S. Pattern, Experimental & Trial Pieces. 7th ed. (Illus.). 1982. lib. bdg. 20.00 (ISBN 0-915262-99-1). S J Durst.

Judd, John, jt. ed. see Beck, Malcolm.

Judd, Leslie J., et al. Exhibition Gymnastics. (Illus.). 1969. 15.00 o.s.i. (ISBN 0-8096-1704-8, Assn Pr). Follett.

Judd, M. D., jt. auth. see Pope, M. I.

Judd, Mary T. Love & Lifestyles. LC 80-54285. (Illus.). 200p. (Orig.). (gr. 12). 1981. pap. text ed. 5.50x (ISBN 0-88489-132-1); teacher's guide 7.00x (ISBN 0-88489-134-8). St Mary's.

Judd, Stanley H. Think Rich. 1980. pap. 2.50 o.s.i. (ISBN 0-440-18653-6). Dell.

Judd, Sylvester. The History of Hadley, Mass. LC 75-29635. 784p. 1976. Repr. of 1905 ed. 35.00x (ISBN 0-912274-57-3). NH Pub Co.

--A Moral Review of the Revolutionary War; or, Some of the Evils of That Event Considered. LC 74-137548. (Peace Movement in America Ser). 1972. Repr. of 1842 ed. lib. bdg. 10.95x (ISBN 0-89198-076-8). Ozer.

Judd, W., jt. auth. see Miller, S.

Judd, W. John & Barnes, Asa, Jr., eds. The Clinical & Serologic Aspects of Transfusion Reactions. 141p. 1982. 19.00 (ISBN 0-914404-74-1); non-members 21.00 (ISBN 0-686-83046-6). Am Assn Blood.

Judd, William R., jt. auth. see Krynine, Dimitri P.

Jude, Albert C. Cat Genetics. new ed. (Illus.). 1977. 12.95 (ISBN 0-87666-172-X, AP4600). TFH Pubns.

Judelle, B., jt. auth. see Jarnow, J. A.

Judenko, E. Analytical Method for Assessing Yield Losses Caused by Pests on Cereal Crops with & Without Pesticides. 1973. 35.00x (ISBN 0-85135-061-5, Pub. by Centre Overseas Research). State Mutual Bk.

Judge, Anne & Healy, F. G. A Reference Grammar of Modern French. 550p. 1983. text ed. price not set (ISBN 0-7131-6285-6). E Arnold.

Judge, G. G. & Bock, M. E. The Statistical Implications of Pre-Test & Stein-Rule Estimators in Econometrics. (Studies in Mathematical & Managerial Economics: Vol. 25). 1978. 59.75 (ISBN 0-7204-0729-X, North-Holland). Elsevier.

Judge, George G., et al. Introduction to the Theory & Practice of Econometrics. (Probability & Mathematical Statistics Ser.). 750p. 1981. 35.95 (ISBN 0-471-05938-2, Pub. by Wiley-Interscience); solutions manual 37.50 (ISBN 0-471-09962-7, Pub. by Wiley-Interscience). Wiley.

Judge, Harry. American Graduate Schools of Education: A View from Abroad: A Report to the Ford Foundation. 69p. (Orig.). 1982. pap. text ed. 4.50 (ISBN 0-916584-21-6). Ford Found.

Judge, Ken. Rationing Social Services: A Study of Resource Allocation in the Personal Social Services. (Studies in Social Policy & Welfare). 1978. text ed. 17.00x (ISBN 0-435-82485-6). Heinemann Ed.

Judge, Michael. Saturday Night Women. (Contemporary Drama Ser.). pap. 2.50x (ISBN 0-912262-42-7). Proscenium.

Judge, Richard D. & Zuidema, George D. Clinical Diagnosis: A Physiologic Approach. 4th ed. 1982. text ed. 29.95 (ISBN 0-316-47589-0). Little.

Judge, Richard D. & Zuidema, George D., eds. Methods of Clinical Examination: A Physiologic Approach. 3rd ed. 1974. 19.95 o.p. (ISBN 0-316-47587-4); pap. 14.95 o.p. (ISBN 0-316-47588-2). Little.

Judge, William Q. Echoes of the Orient, Vol. II. (Illus.). 1980. 12.00 (ISBN 0-913004-34-0). Point Loma Pub.

--Echoes of the Orient: Collected Writings, Vol. 1. Eklund, Dara, ed. (Illus.). 678p. 1975. 12.00 (ISBN 0-913004-28-6, 913004-28). Point Loma Pub.

Judine, Sr., ed. Guide for Evaluating Student Composition. 1965. pap. 5.40 (ISBN 0-8141-1925-5); pap. 3.85 members (ISBN 0-686-86416-6). NCTE.

Judkins, David C. Ben Jonson's Non-Dramatic Works: A Reference Guide. 1982. lib. bdg. 32.00 (ISBN 0-8161-8036-9, Hall Reference). G K Hall.

Judkins, Joseph F. & Benefield, Larry D. Process Chemisty for Water & Wastewater Treatment. (Illus.). 528p. 1982. 32.95 (ISBN 0-13-722975-5). P-H.

Judrin, Claudie, intro. by. Rodin: Drawings & Watercolors. (Illus.). 1983. slipcased 75.00 (ISBN 0-500-23368-3). Thames Hudson.

Judson, Clara I. George Washington. (Beginning-to-Read Bks.). (Illus.). (gr. 3). 1.95 (ISBN 0-695-33350-X, Dist. by Caroline House). Follett.

Judson, David, ed. Caving & Potholding Manual. (Illus.). 224p. 1983. 23.95 (ISBN 0-7153-8155-5). David & Charles.

Judson, Frederick N. The Judiciary & the People. (William Storrs Lectures). 270p. 1982. Repr. of 1913 ed. lib. bdg. 24.00x (ISBN 0-8377-0740-4). Rothman.

Judson, Harry P. Caesar's Army: A Study of the Military Art of the Romans in the Last Days of the Republic. LC 61-12877. (Illus.). 127p. (gr. 7 up). 1888. 10.00x (ISBN 0-8196-0113-6). Biblo.

Judson, Horace. The Eighth Day of Creation. 1979. 15.95 o.p. (ISBN 0-671-22540-5). S&S.

--The Eighth Day of Creation. 12.50 (ISBN 0-671-25410-3, 25410, Touchstone). S&S.

Judson, Jeanne. Legacy of Redfern. (YA) 6.95 (ISBN 0-685-07441-2, Avalon). Bouregy.

--Treasure of Wycliffe House. (YA) 6.95 (ISBN 0-685-07462-5, Avalon). Bouregy.

Judson, John. The Carrabassett, Sweet William, Was My River. (Inland Sea Ser.: No. 2). 16.00 (ISBN 0-686-79784-1); signed ed. 30.00; pap. 9.00. Juniper Pr WI.

Judson, Lyman. The Shadows. 200p. 1982. 25.00 (ISBN 0-916146-04-9). APEX U Pr.

Judson, Marilyn, jt. auth. see Hunter, Ilene.

Judson, S., et al. Physical Geology. (Illus.). 592p. 1976. text ed. 27.95 (ISBN 0-13-669655-4); study guide 5.95 (ISBN 0-13-669630-9). P-H.

Judson, Walter W. Living Light. (Illus.). 280p. Date not set. 25.00 (ISBN 0-498-02558-6). A S Barnes.

Judson, William. Cold River. (RL 7). 1976. pap. 2.50 (ISBN 0-451-12308-5, AE2308, Sig). NAL.

Judt, T. Socialism in Provence Eighteen Seventy-One to Nineteen Fourteen. LC 78-16419. (Illus.). 1979. 47.50 (ISBN 0-521-22172-2); pap. 16.95x (ISBN 0-521-29598-X). Cambridge U Pr.

Judt, Tony. La Reconstruction Du Parti Socialiste 1921-1926. (Travaux et Recherches: No. 39). (Fr.). 1977. lib. bdg. 28.75 o.p. (ISBN 2-7246-0345-1, Pub. by Presses de la Fondation Nationale Des Sciences Politiques); pap. text ed. 21.25x o.p. (ISBN 2-7246-0338-9). Clearwater Pub.

Judy, Robert, et al. Fonemas Del Movima: Con Atencion Especial a la Serie Glotal y Apuntes sobre Etnografia Beniano. (Notas Linguisticas De Bolivia Ser.: No. 5). 36p. 1962. pap. 0.35 o.p. (ISBN 0-88312-762-8); 1.50 o.p. (ISBN 0-88312-387-8). Summer Inst Ling.

Judy, Stephen. The Burg-O-Rama Man. (YA) (gr. 7-12). 1983. pap. 2.50 (ISBN 0-440-90872-8, LFL). Dell.

--Teaching English: Reflections on the State of the Art. LC 79-17965. 120p. 1979. pap. text ed. 5.75 (ISBN 0-8104-6041-6). Boynton Cook Pubs.

Judy, Stephen N. ABC's of Literacy: A Guide for Parents & Educators. LC 79-4475. 1980. 19.95x (ISBN 0-19-502587-3). Oxford U Pr.

--The ABC's of Literacy: A Guide for Parents & Educators. 1981. pap. 7.95 (ISBN 0-19-502988-7, GB 651, GB). Oxford U Pr.

Judy, Stephen N. & Judy, Susan J. The English Teacher's Handbook: Ideas & Resources for Teaching English. (Orig.). 1979. text ed. 18.95 (ISBN 0-316-47590-4); pap. text ed. 11.95 (ISBN 0-316-47591-2). Little.

--An Introduction to the Teaching of Writing. LC 80-25163. 208p. 1981. pap. text ed. 13.50x (ISBN 0-673-15685-0). Scott F.

Judy, Stephen N., ed. Publishing in English Education. LC 81-15525. 208p. (Orig.). 1981. pap. 9.00 (ISBN 0-86709-011-1). Boynton Cook Pub.

Judy, Susan J., jt. auth. see Judy, Stephen N.

Juel, Donald H. Living a Biblical Faith. Date not set. price not set. Geneva Divinity.

--Living a Biblical Faith, Vol. 6. LC 82-8652. (Library of Living Faith Ser.). 118p. 1982. pap. 5.95 (ISBN 0-664-24429-7). Westminster.

Jueneke, Klaus. Huts of the High Country. LC 82-71656. 251p. 1982. pap. text ed. 34.95 (ISBN 0-7081-1389-3, 1233). Bks Australia.

Juergensmeyer, Julian & Wadley, James. Agricultural Law. LC 81-82512. 1345p. 1982. Vol. 1. 140.00 (ISBN 0-316-47610-2). Vol. 2 (ISBN 0-316-47611-0). Little.

Juergenson, E. M. Handbook of Livestock Equipment. 2nd ed. (Illus.). 266p. 1979. 16.50 (ISBN 0-8134-2030-X, 2030); text ed. 12.50x. Interstate.

Juergenson, E. M., jt. auth. see Baker, J. K.

Juergenson, E. M., jt. auth. see Scheer, Arnold H.

Juergenson, Edward M., ed. Approved Practices in Beef Cattle Production. 5th ed. (Illus.). (gr. 9-12). 1980. 16.50 (ISBN 0-8134-2093-8, 2093); text ed. 12.50x. Interstate.

Juergenson, Elwood M. & Mortenson, William P. Approved Practices in Dairying. 4th ed. LC 77-74120. (Illus.). (gr. 9-12). 1977. 16.50 (ISBN 0-8134-1954-9, 1954); text ed. 12.50x. Interstate.

Juergenson, Elwood M., jt. auth. see Cassard, Daniel W.

Juet, Robert. Juet's Journal, The Voyage of the Half Moon from 4 April to 7 November 1609, Vol. 12. 37p. 1959. pap. 4.00 (ISBN 0-686-81823-7). NJ Hist Soc.

Jugenheimer, Donald W. & Turk, Peter B. Advertising Media. LC 79-23007. (Grid Ser. in Advertising-Journalism). 1980. text ed. 22.95 o.p. (ISBN 0-88244-210-4). Grid Pub.

Jugenheimer, Donald W. & White, Gordon E. Basic Advertising. 2nd ed. 500p. 1980. text ed. 26.95 (ISBN 0-471-86993-7); tchr's ed. 6.00 (ISBN 0-471-86994-5); wkbk. 10.95 (ISBN 0-471-86998-8); tests 15.95 (ISBN 0-471-86995-3); transparency masters 10.95 (ISBN 0-471-86997-X); cassettes & tapes 29.95 (ISBN 0-471-86996-1). Wiley.

Jugenheimer, Robert W. Corn: Improvement, Seed Production, & Uses. LC 75-32414. 670p. 1976. 62.50x (ISBN 0-471-45315-3, Pub. by Wiley-Interscience). Wiley.

Juhasz, Jack R., jt. auth. see Shelton, Jack.

Juhasz, Suzanne, intro. by. Feminist Critics Read Emily Dickinson. LC 82-48265. 192p. 1983. 17.50x (ISBN 0-253-32170-0). Ind U Pr.

Juhr, Gerald, tr. see Asten, H. Keller-von.

Juillerat, Lee, jt. auth. see Warfield, Ronald G.

Jules, Charles. Beating the Bill Collector-Legally. LC 82-82304. 160p. (Orig.). 1983. pap. 6.95 (ISBN 0-448-16609-7, G&D). Putnam Pub Group.

Julian, Desmond, jt. ed. see Resnekov, Leon.

Julian, Faye D., jt. auth. see Ambrester, Marcus L.

Julian, Helen. Key to Abundant Living. 1977. tchr's manual 2.50 (ISBN 0-87509-099-0); student manual 1.50 (ISBN 0-87509-100-8). Chr Pubns.

Julian, James. Chelatin: Prevent Heart Attack & Stroke. 1981. 5.00x (ISBN 0-686-36342-6). Cancer Control Soc.

Julian, John. Dictionary of Hymnology, 2 vols. 1786p. 1983. Repr. 120.00 (ISBN 0-8254-2960-9); prepub. 89.95. Kregel.

Julian, Joseph. Social Problems. 3rd ed. (P-H Ser. in Sociology). (Illus.). 1980. text ed. 22.95 (ISBN 0-13-816777-X); wkbk & study guide 7.95 (ISBN 0-13-816801-6). P-H.

--Social Problems. 4th ed. 608p. 1983. text ed. 23.95 (ISBN 0-13-816819-9). P-H.

Julian, Joseph, jt. auth. see Bates, Alan P.

Julian, W. G., jt. auth. see Smith, P. R.

Juliano, Annette. Treasures of China. (Illus.). 192p. 1981. 35.00 (ISBN 0-399-90105-1, Marek). Putnam Pub Group.

Juliano, R. L., ed. Drug Delivery Systems: Characteristics & Biomedical Applications. (Illus.). 1980. text ed. 35.00x (ISBN 0-19-502700-0). Oxford U Pr.

Julian of Norwich. Revelations of Divine Love. Roberts, Roger L., ed. LC 82-80471. (Treasures from the Spiritual Classics Ser.). 64p. 1982. pap. 2.95 (ISBN 0-8192-1308-X). Morehouse.

Julich, P., jt. auth. see Hilburn, J. L.

Julien, Edouard. Toulouse-Lautrec. (Q L P Art Ser). (Illus.). 1959. 7.95 (ISBN 0-517-03718-1). Crown.

Julien, Eileen, jt. ed. see Wylie, Hal.

Julio, Mary A. de see De Julio, Mary A.

Jullian, Philippe & O'Neill, John P. La Belle Epoque. (Illus.). 48p. 1982. pap. 6.95 (ISBN 0-87099-329-1). Metro Mus Art.

Jullien, Adolphe. Richard Wagner: His Life & Works. Hall, Florence P., tr. from Fr. (Illus.). 512p. 1981. Repr. of 1892 ed. 19.95 (ISBN 0-87666-579-2, Z-48). Paganiniana Pubns.

Julme, William E., ed. see Mace, David.

Julstrom, Bryant, jt. auth. see King, Ronald.

Jumikis, Alfreds R. Soil Mechanics: Based on Intro to Soil Mechanics. LC 79-12978. 1983. Repr. lib. bdg. 38.00 (ISBN 0-88275-969-8). Krieger.

Jumonville, Florence M., ed. Bound to Please: Selected Rare Books about Louisiana from the Historic New Orleans Collection. LC 82-83113. (Illus.). 98p. 1982. pap. 16.00x (ISBN 0-917860-11-X). Historic New Orleans.

Jump, John, ed. see Byron.

Jump, John, ed. see Marlowe, Christopher.

Jump, John D. Burlesque. (Critical Idiom Ser.). 1972. pap. 4.95x (ISBN 0-416-66660-4). Methuen Inc.

--The Ode. (Critical Idiom Ser.). 1974. pap. 4.95x (ISBN 0-416-78820-3). Methuen Inc.

Jump, John D., ed. see Byron, George G.

Jump, John D., ed. see Marlowe, Christopher.

Jump, John D., ed. see Tennyson, Alfred.

Jumper, Andrew A. Chosen to Serve: The Deacon. LC 61-18257. (Orig.). 1961. pap. 3.50 (ISBN 0-8042-3912-6). John Knox.

--The Noble Task: The Elder. rev. ed. LC 65-14420. 1965. pap. 3.50 (ISBN 0-8042-3992-4). John Knox.

Jumper, S., et al. Economic Growth & Disparities: A World View. 1980. 29.95 (ISBN 0-13-225680-0). P-H.

Jumsai, M. L. Understanding Thai Buddhism. 124p. 1971. 5.50x o.p. (ISBN 0-8188-0167-0). Paragon.

Jun, Jong S. & Storm, William B. Tomorrow's Organizations: Challenges & Strategies. 1973. pap. 10.95x (ISBN 0-673-07796-9). Scott F.

Junaluska Historical Society. Junaluska Joy. Cornwell, Mary & Cornwell, Ada, eds. (Illus.). 388p. 1982. pap. 9.95 (ISBN 0-686-82093-2). Wimmer Bks.

Juncos, Luis I. Physiological Basis of Diuretic Therapy: A Programmed Course. (Illus.). 84p. 1979. spiral 11.75x (ISBN 0-398-03888-0). C C Thomas.

Juneau, Patricia S. Dimensions of Practical Nursing. 1979. pap. text ed. 11.95x (ISBN 0-02-361520-6). Macmillan.

--Fundamentals of Nursing Care. (Illus.). 1979. text ed. 24.95x (ISBN 0-02-361540-0); instrs'. manual avail. Macmillan.

--Maternal & Child Nursing-Associate. 1979. text ed. 23.95x (ISBN 0-02-361530-3). Macmillan.

--Medical-Surgical Nursing. (Illus.). 1980. text ed. 23.95x (ISBN 0-02-361570-2). Macmillan.
Jung, Carl G. The Visions Seminars. (Seminar Ser.: No. 11). 534p. 1976. pap. 30.00 set (ISBN 0-88214-111-2). Spring Pubns.
Jung, Emma. Animus & Anima. Baynes, Cary F. & Nagel, Hildegard, trs. 94p. 1957. pap. text ed. 7.50 (ISBN 0-88214-301-8). Spring Pubns.
Jung, John. The Experimenter's Challenge: Methods & Issues in Psychological Research. 1982. text ed. 21.95x (ISBN 0-02-361510-9). Macmillan.
--Understanding Human Motivation: A Cognitive Approach. (Illus.). 1978. text ed. 24.95x (ISBN 0-02-361550-8). Macmillan.
Jung, M. A Review of Annulation. Barton, D. H., ed. 1976. pap. text ed. 12.75 o.p. (ISBN 0-08-020621-2). Pergamon.
Jung, M. J., jt. ed. see Seiler, N.
Jung, N. An Approach to the Study of the Quran. pap. 3.95 (ISBN 0-686-18520-X). Kazi Pubns.
Jungclaus, David G. City Beneath the Bermuda Triangle. LC 81-86421. 80p. 1983. pap. 5.95 (ISBN 0-86666-047-X). GWP.
Jungel, Eberhard. The Doctrine of the Trinity. 1977. 6.50 o.p. (ISBN 0-8028-3490-6). Eerdmans.
--God As the Mystery of the World: On the Foundation of the Theology of the Crucified One in the Dispute Between Theism & Atheism. Guder, Darrell L., tr. 428p. (Ger.). 1983. 24.95 (ISBN 0-8028-3586-4). Eerdmans.
Jungels, Georgiana. To Be Remembered: Art & the Older Adult in Therapeutic Settings. (Illus.). Date not set. pap. 4.95 (ISBN 0-932910-43-2). Potentials Development.
Junger, Ernst. The Storm of Steel. Creighton, B., tr. from Ger. LC 75-22372. xiii, 319p. 1975. Repr. of 1929 ed. 15.00x (ISBN 0-86527-310-3). Fertig.
Jungherr, E. L., jt. ed. see Brandly, C. A.
Jungjohan, Barbara, jt. auth. see McGeough, Charles.
Jungk, Robert. The New Tyranny: How Nuclear Power Enslaves Us. 1979. 10.00 o.p. (ISBN 0-448-15161-8, G&D). Putnam Pub Group.
--The New Tyranny: How Nuclear Power Enslaves Us. 1979. pap. 2.50 o.p. (ISBN 0-446-91351-0). Warner Bks.
Jungk, Robert, et al. China & the West: Mankind Evolving. (Teilhard Study Library). 1970. text ed. 10.00x (ISBN 0-391-00023-3). Humanities.
Jungkuntz, Theodore R. Formulators of the Formula of Concord. 1977. pap. 7.95 (ISBN 0-570-03740-9, 12-2644). Concordia.
Jungmann, Joseph. The Mass of the Roman Rite. 25.00 o.p. (ISBN 0-87061-054-6). Chr Classics.
Jungnickel, D. H. & Vedder, K., eds. Combinatorial Theory: Proceedings, Schloss Rauischholzhausen, FRG, 1982. (Lecture Notes in Mathematics Ser.: Vol. 969). 326p. 1983. pap. 16.00 (ISBN 0-387-11971-X). Springer-Verlag.
Jung Young Lee. Sokdam: Capsules of Eastern Wisdom. (Illus.). 1977. pap. 4.95 (ISBN 0-918972-00-0). Far Eastern Cult.
Junior League of Asheville. Mountain Elegance Cookbook. 340p. 1982. 11.95 (ISBN 0-686-97705-X). Jr League Asheville.
Junior League of Ashville. Mountain Elegance. 11.95 (ISBN 0-686-36865-7). Mntn Elegance.
Junior League of Birmingham, Alabama, et al, eds. Magic. 348p. 1982. 9.95 (ISBN 0-686-43391-2). Magic.
Junior League of Chicago. Soupcon II. (Illus.). 384p. 1981. 11.95 (ISBN 0-686-32504-4). JLC Inc.
Junior League of Jackson, Mississippi. Southern Sideboards. Copeland, Clyde X. & Scanlon, Patrick H., eds. 414p. 1978. 11.95 (ISBN 0-9606886-0-9). Jr League Jackson.
Junior League of Nashville. Nashville Encore. McInnis, Donna, ed. 502p. 1982. pap. 12.50 (ISBN 0-939114-68-2). Wimmer Bks.
Junior League of New Orleans. The Plantation Cookbook. LC 72-84921. 256p. 1972. 17.95 (ISBN 0-385-01157-1). Doubleday.
Junior League of Newport Harbor. R. S. V. P. 1982. 14.95 (ISBN 0-9608306-0-X). Jun League NH.
Junior League of Omaha, Inc. Amber Waves. (Illus.). 1983. 11.95 (ISBN 0-686-38106-8). Omaha Print.
Junior League of Rochester, Inc. Applehood & Motherpie. Kessler, Tracy K., ed. 330p. 1981. 14.95 (ISBN 0-9605612-0-X). Jr League Rochester.
Junior League of San Antonio. Flavors: The Junior League of San Antonio. LC 77-88731. (Illus.). 426p. 1982. 14.95 (ISBN 0-9610416-0-9). Jr League Antonio.
Junior League of Sarasota FL, Inc. Fare by the Sea. Stewart, Sandra & Mathew, Jan, eds. (Illus., Orig.). 1983. pap. text ed. 10.95 (ISBN 0-686-38134-3). Moran Pub FL.
Junior League of the Palm Beaches, Inc. Palm Beach Entertains: Then & Now. LC 76-16002. (Illus.). 256p. 1976. 9.95 o.p. (ISBN 0-698-10748-9, Coward). Putnam Pub Group.
Junior League of Tyler, Inc., ed. Cooking Through Rose Colored Glasses. (Illus.). 426p. 1975. pap. 7.95 (ISBN 0-9607122-0-8). Jr League Tyler.
Junior Service League of Brooksville Florida. A Pinch of Sunshine. Bartos, Beth, ed. (Illus.). 336p. 1982. pap. 9.95 (ISBN 0-939114-63-1). Wimmer Bks.
Junior Welfare League of Enid, OK., Inc. & Sailors, Ruth A. Stir-Ups. (Cookbook Ser.). 1982. pap. 12.95 (ISBN 0-9609340-0-6). Jr Welfare Enid.
Juniper, B. E. & Jeffree, C. E. Plant Surfaces. 128p. 1983. pap. text ed. 13.95 (ISBN 0-7131-2856-9). E Arnold.
Juniper, B. E., jt. auth. see Martin, J. T.
Junke, N. Sex & Love Today. 536p. 25.00x o.p. (ISBN 0-85435-373-9, Pub. by Spearman England). State Mutual England.
Junker, John M. Standards Relating to Juvenile Delinquency & Sanctions. LC 76-27864. (IJA-ABA Juvenile Justice Standards Project Ser.). 64p. 1980. prof ref 14.00x (ISBN 0-88410-235-1); pap. 7.00x (ISBN 0-88410-829-5). Ballinger Pub.
Junkin, Daniel P., jt. auth. see Broce, Thomas E.
Junkins, David R. & Deeny, Kevin J. The Activated Sludge Process. LC 82-70699. (Illus.). 260p. 1983. 29.95 (ISBN 0-250-40506-7). Ann Arbor Science.
Junod, Mae A. The W-O-T Position or Self-Actualization for Women. 287p. 1981. 14.95x (ISBN 0-938968-00-9). Impact MI.
Junor, Penny. Diana, Princess of Wales. LC 82-45832. (Illus.). 224p. 1983. 14.95 (ISBN 0-385-19007-7). Doubleday.
--Newspaper. LC 79-65030. (Careers Ser.). PLB 12.68 (ISBN 0-382-06302-3). Silver.
Junta del Acuerdo de Cartagena. Andean Pact Technology Policies. 58p. 1976. pap. 5.00 (ISBN 0-88936-077-4, IDRC60, IDRC). Unipub.
Junwen, Lin. Beijing: China's Ancient & Modern Capital. (Illus.). 254p. (Orig.). 1982. pap. 5.95 (ISBN 0-8351-0979-8). China Bks.
Jupe, Margaret, ed. see Department of American Decorative Arts & Sculpture & Fairbanks, Jonathan L.
Jupp, T. C. & Milne, John. Basic Writing Skills in English. (Orig.). 1981. pap. text ed. 4.50x (ISBN 0-435-28496-7); tchr's ed 6.00x (ISBN 0-435-28494-0); wkbk. 2.00x (ISBN 0-686-72736-3). Heinemann Ed.
Jurade, Rafael L., tr. see Palacio, Alfredo.
Juran, Joseph M. Managerial Breakthrough: A New Concept of the Manager's Job. (Illus.). 1964. 27.50 (ISBN 0-07-033172-3, P&RB). McGraw.
--Quality Control Handbook. rev. 3rd ed. 1600p. 1974. 59.95 (ISBN 0-07-033175-8, P&RB). McGraw.
Juran, Joseph M. & Gryna, Frank M., Jr. Quality Planning & Analysis: From Product Development Through Use. 2nd ed. (Illus.). 1980. text ed. 37.00 (ISBN 0-07-033178-2); instr's manual 25.00 (ISBN 0-07-033179-0). McGraw.
Jurand, A. & Selman, G. G. Anatomy of Paramecium Aurelia. LC 75-82437. (Illus.). 1969. 25.00 o.p. (ISBN 0-312-03500-4). St Martin.
Jurd, K. H. Yacht Construction. 2nd rev. ed. Orig. Title: Practical Yacht Construction. (Illus.). 1970. text ed. 14.25x o.p. (ISBN 0-229-97485-6). Humanities.
Jurd, Ron. Wooden Boat Construction. (Questions & Answers Ser.). (Illus.). 92p. (Orig.). 1979. pap. 7.50 o.s.i. (ISBN 0-408-00315-4). Transatlantic.
Jurek, B. Optical Surfaces. 1976. 53.25 (ISBN 0-444-99868-3). Elsevier.
Juretic, Miro, et al. Herpetic Infections of Man. LC 77-75516. (National Library of Medicine Ser.). (Illus.). 202p. 1980. text ed. 20.00x (ISBN 0-87451-151-8). U Pr of New Eng.
Jurgensen, Barbara. How to Live Better on Less: A Guide for Waste Watchers. 3.95 (ISBN 0-686-95848-9). Alternatives.
Jurgensen, Genevieve. The Madness of Others. Boulanger, Ghislaine, tr. 1975. 7.95 o.p. (ISBN 0-685-52102-8). Macmillan.
Jurgensen, Kai, ed. see Ibsen, Henrik.
Jurgensen, Kai, tr. see Ibsen, Henrik.
Jurgensen, Manfred. Frauenliteratur. 230p. (Ger.). 1982. write for info. (ISBN 3-261-05013-6). P Lang Pubs.
Juris, Hervey A. & Roomkin, Myron, eds. The Shrinking Perimeter: Unionism & Labor Relations in the Manufacturing Sector. LC 79-1864. 240p. 1980. 24.95x (ISBN 0-669-02939-4). Lexington Bks.
Jurisic, N. K., ed. see Latin School of Physics, 14th Caracas, Venezuela July 10-28, 1972.
Jurmain, et al. Understanding Physical Anthropology & Archaeology. (Illus.). 1981. pap. text ed. 20.95 (ISBN 0-8299-0388-7). West Pub.
Jurmain, Robert, jt. auth. see Nelson, Harry.
Jurnior League of Beaumont, Inc. Lagniappe, a Little Something Extra. 350p. write for info stacon bdg. (ISBN 0-9609604-0-6). Jr League Beau.
Juroe, Bonnie B., jt. auth. see Juroe, David J.
Juroe, David J. & Juroe, Bonnie B. Successful Stepparenting. 192p. 1983. 9.95 (ISBN 0-8007-1339-7). Revell.
Jury, Eliahu I. Theory & Application of the Z-Transform Method. LC 64-17145. 344p. 1973. Repr. of 1964 ed. 20.50 (ISBN 0-88275-122-0). Krieger.
Jussawala, M. C., ed. see Spenser, Edmund.
Jussieu, A. L. Genera Plantarum Secundum Ordines Naturales Disposita. 1964. Repr. of 1789 ed. 40.00 (ISBN 3-7682-7107-2). Lubrecht & Cramer.
Jussim, Estelle. Visual Communication & the Graphic Arts. pap. 24.95 (ISBN 0-8352-1674-8). Bowker.
Just, H. & Bussmann, W. D., eds. Vasidilators in Chronic Heart Failure. (Illus.). 240p. 1983. 22.00 (ISBN 0-387-11616-8). Springer-Verlag.
Just, Richard, jt. auth. see Feder, Gersgon.
Juster, F. Thomas, ed. The Distribution of Economic Well-Being. NBER Studies in Income & Health. LC 76-58909. (Vol. 41). 704p. 1978. prof ref 30.00x (ISBN 0-88410-478-8). Ballinger Pub.
--The Economic & Political Impact of General Revenue Sharing. LC 76-620084. 308p. 1977. 20.00x (ISBN 0-87944-217-4). Inst Soc Res.
Juster, Norton. Otter Nonsense. (Illus.). 64p. 1982. 8.95 (ISBN 0-399-20932-8, Philomel); pap. 3.95 (ISBN 0-399-20931-X). Putnam Pub Group.
--So Sweet to Labor: The Voices of Rural Women 1865-1895. (Illus.). 1979. 19.95 (ISBN 0-670-65483-3). Viking Pr.
Justice, Betty W. Unions, Workers, & the Law. (George Meany Center for Labor Studies Ser.: No. 2). 280p. 1983. text ed. 17.50 (ISBN 0-87179-393-8); pap. text ed. 12.50 (ISBN 0-87179-400-4). BNA.
Justice, Blair. Violence in the City. 1969. 10.00x (ISBN 0-912646-34-9). Tex Christian.
Justice, J. B. & Isenhour, T. L., eds. Digital Computers in Analytical Chemistry, 2 pts. LC 81-2933. (Benchmark Papers in Analytical Chemistry: Vol. 3). 1981. Pt. 1, 1950-1969. 56.00 (ISBN 0-87933-061-9); Pt. 2, 1970-1978. 56.00 (ISBN 0-87933-095-3); 100.00 set. Hutchinson Ross.
Justis, Robert T. Dynamics of American Business. (Illus.). 608p. 1982. text ed. 23.95 (ISBN 0-13-221440-7). P-H.
--Managing Your Small Business. (Illus.). 288p. 1981. text ed. 22.954 (ISBN 0-686-68607-1). P-H.
Justus. Jumping Jack. LC 73-87803. (Illus.). (gr. k-3). 1974. PLB 6.75x (ISBN 0-87783-123-8); pap. 2.95x deluxe ed. (ISBN 0-87783-124-6); cassette 5.95x (ISBN 0-87783-189-0). Oddo.
Justus, Fred. Algebra. (Math Ser.). 24p. (gr. 7-11). 1979. wkbk. 5.00 (ISBN 0-8209-0101-6, A-11). ESP.
--Alphabet Sequence. (Early Education Ser.). 24p. (gr. 1). 1980. wkbk. 5.00 (ISBN 0-686-42826-9). ESP.
--Animals: Males, Females & Babies. (Early Education Ser.). 24p. (ps-1). 1981. wkbk. 5.00 (ISBN 0-8209-0226-8, K-28). ESP.
--Applied Mathematics for Business & Home. (Math Ser.). 24p. (gr. 6 up). 1979. wkbk. 5.00 (ISBN 0-8209-0117-2, A-27). ESP.
--Arithmetic Exercises: Grade Eight. (Math Ser.). 24p. (gr. 8). 1978. wkbk. 5.00 (ISBN 0-8209-0098-2, A-8). ESP.
--Arithmetic Exercises: Grade Five. (Math Ser.). 24p. (gr. 5). 1979. wkbk. 5.00 (ISBN 0-8209-0095-8, A-5). ESP.
--Arithmetic Exercises: Grade Four. (Math Ser.). 24p. (gr. 4). 1979. wkbk. 5.00 (ISBN 0-8209-0094-X, A-4). ESP.
--Arithmetic Exercises: Grade Seven. (Math Ser.). 24p. (gr. 7). 1979. wkbk. 5.00 (ISBN 0-8209-0097-4, A-7). ESP.
--Arithmetic Exercises: Grade Six. (Math Ser.). 24p. (gr. 6). 1977. wkbk. 5.00 (ISBN 0-8209-0096-6, A-6). ESP.
--Auditory Discrimination. (Language Arts Ser.). (gr. 1-2). 1977. wkbk. 5.00 (LA-6). ESP.
--Basic Arithmetic Fundamentals. (Math Ser.). 24p. (gr. 3-6). 1977. wkbk. 5.00 (ISBN 0-8209-0116-4, A-26). ESP.
--Basic Skills Auditory Discrimination Workbook. (Basic Skills Workbooks). 32p. (gr. 1-2). 1983. 0.99 (ISBN 0-8209-0545-3). ESP.
--Basic Skills Counting Money Workbook. (Basic Skills Workbooks). 32p. (gr. 2-4). 1983. 0.99 (ISBN 0-8209-0569-0, MW-2). ESP.
--Basic Skills Counting Workbook. (Basic Skills Workbooks). 32p. (gr. k-1). 1983. 0.99 (ISBN 0-8209-0564-X, EEW-5). ESP.
--Basic Skills Famous Quotations Workbook. (Basic Skills Workbooks). 32p. (gr. 4-7). 1983. 0.99 (ISBN 0-8209-0559-3, SSW-7). ESP.
--Basic Skills First Aid Workbook. (Basic Skills Workbooks). 32p. (gr. 5-9). 1983. 0.99 (ISBN 0-8209-0576-3, HW-3). ESP.
--Basic Skills Government Workbook. (Basic Skills Workbooks). 32p. (gr. 7-12). 1983. 0.99 (ISBN 0-8209-0538-0, SSW-2). ESP.
--Basic Skills Look, Hear, & Make Words Workbook. (Basic Skills Workbooks). 32p. (gr. k-1). 1983. 0.99 (ISBN 0-8209-0578-X, EEW-8). ESP.
--Basic Skills Mathematics Workbook: Grade 1. (Basic Skills Workbooks). 32p. (gr. 1). 1982. tchrs' ed. 0.99 (ISBN 0-8209-0388-4, MW-B). ESP.
--Basic Skills Metrics I Workbook. (Basic Skills Workbooks). 32p. (gr. 3-4). 1983. 0.99 (ISBN 0-8209-0571-2, MW-4). ESP.
--Basic Skills Metrics II Workbook. (Basic Skills Workbooks). 32p. (gr. 4-5). 1983. 0.99 (ISBN 0-8209-0572-0, MW-5). ESP.
--Basic Skills Metrics III Workbook. (Basic Skills Workbooks). 32p. (gr. 5-6). 1983. 0.99 (ISBN 0-8209-0573-9, MW-6). ESP.
--Basic Skills Seatwork Workbook. (Basic Skills Workbooks). 32p. (gr. k-1). 1983. 0.99 (ISBN 0-8209-0550-X, EEW-1). ESP.
--Basic Skills Visual Discrimination Workbook. (Basic Skills Workbooks). 32p. (gr. 1-2). 1983. 0.99 (ISBN 0-8209-0544-5, PW-4). ESP.
--Basic Skills Vocabulary Workbook: Grade 1. (Basic Skills Workbooks). 32p. (gr. 1). 1982. wkbk. 0.99 (ISBN 0-8209-0377-9, VW-B). ESP.
--Basic Skills Writing Capital & Small Letters Workbook. (Basic Skills Workbooks). 32p. (gr. k-1). 1983. 0.99 (ISBN 0-8209-0563-1, EEW-4). ESP.
--Beginner's Seatwork. (Early Education Ser.). 24p. (ps-1). 1979. wkbk. 5.00 (K-3). ESP.
--Beginning Language. (English Ser.). 24p. (ps). 1978. wkbk. 5.00 (ISBN 0-8209-0172-5, E-R). ESP.
--Beginning Metrics. (Math Ser.). 24p. (gr. 1-3). 1977. wkbk. 5.00 (ISBN 0-8209-0103-2, A-13). ESP.
--Beginning Numbers. (Math Ser.). 24p. (ps-1). 1980. wkbk. 5.00 (ISBN 0-8209-0090-7, A-R). ESP.
--Beyond Our Solar System. (Science Ser.). 24p. (gr. 8). 1976. wkbk. 5.00 (ISBN 0-8209-0146-6, S-8). ESP.
--Clock & Time Related Problems. (Math Ser.). 24p. (gr. 4-8). 1976. wkbk. 5.00 (ISBN 0-8209-0115-6, A-25). ESP.
--Counting Money. (Math Ser.). 24p. (gr. 2-4). 1979. wkbk. 5.00 (ISBN 0-8209-0113-X, A-23). ESP.
--Crossword Puzzles. (Puzzles Ser.). 24p. (gr. 5). 1980. wkbk. 5.00 (ISBN 0-8209-0295-0, PU-9). ESP.
--Crossword Puzzles Using Rhyming Words. (Puzzles Ser.). 24p. (gr. 5-7). 1980. wkbk. 5.00 (ISBN 0-8209-0299-3, PU-13). ESP.
--Developmental Metrics. (Math Ser.). 24p. (gr. 2-4). 1978. wkbk. 5.00 (ISBN 0-8209-0105-9, A-15). ESP.
--Drills & Tests: Grades Seven to Ten. (Math Ser.). 24p. 1979. wkbk. 5.00 (ISBN 0-8209-0100-8, A-10). ESP.
--Drills & Tests: Grades Six to Nine. (Math Ser.). 24p. 1979. wkbk. 5.00 (ISBN 0-8209-0099-0, A-9). ESP.
--Elementary Metrics. (Math Ser.). 24p. (gr. 1-3). 1978. wkbk. 5.00 (ISBN 0-8209-0104-0, A-14). ESP.
--English at Work: Grade Eight. (English Ser.). 24p. 1977. wkbk. 5.00 (ISBN 0-8209-0180-6, E-8). ESP.
--English at Work: Grade Five. (English Ser.). 24p. 1980. wkbk. 5.00 (ISBN 0-8209-0177-6, E-5). ESP.
--English at Work: Grade Seven. (English Ser.). 24p. 1979. wkbk. 5.00 (ISBN 0-8209-0179-2, E-7). ESP.
--English at Work: Grade Six. (English Ser.). 24p. 1979. wkbk. 5.00 (ISBN 0-8209-0178-4, E-6). ESP.
--Everyday Science. (Science Ser.). 24p. (gr. 3). 1977. wkbk. 5.00 (ISBN 0-8209-0141-5, S-3). ESP.
--Famous Quotes Puzzles. (Puzzles Ser.). 24p. (gr. 6). 1980. wkbk. 5.00 (ISBN 0-8209-0287-X, PU-1). ESP.
--First Aid. (Science Ser.). 24p. (gr. 5-9). 1980. wkbk. 5.00 (ISBN 0-8209-0164-4, FA-1). ESP.
--Four-Letter Words. (Puzzles Ser.). 24p. (gr. 4-6). 1980. wkbk. 5.00 (ISBN 0-8209-0300-0, PU-14). ESP.
--Geometric Figures & Concepts. (Math Ser.). 24p. (gr. 4-9). 1976. wkbk. 5.00 (ISBN 0-8209-0114-8, A-24). ESP.
--Geometry. (Math Ser.). 24p. (gr. 7-11). 1979. wkbk. 5.00 (ISBN 0-8209-0102-4, A-12). ESP.
--Getting a Head Start in School. (Early Education Ser.). 24p. (gr. 1-2). 1975. wkbk. 5.00 (ISBN 0-8209-0206-3, K-8). ESP.
--Grammar Crossword Puzzles. (Puzzles Ser.). 24p. (gr. 5-9). 1980. wkbk. 5.00 (ISBN 0-8209-0288-8, PU-2). ESP.
--Graphic Mathematics. (Math Ser.). 24p. (gr. 5-9). 1976. wkbk. 5.00 (ISBN 0-8209-0119-9, A-29). ESP.
--The Human Body. (Health Ser.). 24p. (gr. 3-5). 1977. wkbk. 5.00 (ISBN 0-8209-0344-2, H-5). ESP.
--Intermediate Metrics. (Math Ser.). 24p. (gr. 2-4). 1978. wkbk. 5.00 (ISBN 0-8209-0106-7, A-16). ESP.
--JUmbo Math Yearbook: Grade 1. (Jumbo Math Ser.). 96p. (gr. 1). 1980. 14.00 (ISBN 0-8209-0030-3, JMY 1). ESP.
--Jumbo Vocabulary Development Yearbook: Grade 1. (Jumbo Vocabulary Ser.). 96p. (gr. 1). 1979. 14.00 (ISBN 0-8209-0050-8, JVDY 1). ESP.
--Jumbo Vocabulary Development Yearbook: Grade 2. (Jumbo Vocabulary Ser.). 96p. (gr. 2). 1980. 14.00 (ISBN 0-8209-0051-6, JVDY 2). ESP.
--Jumbo Vocabulary Fun Yearbook. (Jumbo Vocabulary Ser.). 96p. (gr. 3). 1980. 14.00 (ISBN 0-8209-0058-3, JVFY 3). ESP.
--Learning Directions. (Early Education Ser.). 24p. (gr. 1). 1981. wkbk. 5.00 (ISBN 0-8209-0225-X, K-27). ESP.
--Learning English: Grade 1. (English Ser.). 24p. 1975. wkbk. 5.00 (ISBN 0-8209-0173-3, E-1). ESP.
--Learning English: Grade 2. (English Ser.). 24p. 1978. wkbk. 5.00 (ISBN 0-8209-0174-1, E-2). ESP.
--Learning English: Grade 3. (English Ser.). 24p. 1980. 5.00 (ISBN 0-8209-0175-X, E-3). ESP.
--Learning English: Grade 4. (English Ser.). 24p. 1980. wkbk. 5.00 (ISBN 0-8209-0176-8, E-4). ESP.
--Learning Metrics. (Math Ser.). 24p. (gr. 3-6). 1978. wkbk. 5.00 (ISBN 0-8209-0107-5, A-17). ESP.
--Look, Hear, & Make Words. (Early Education Ser.). 24p. (gr. 1). 1980. wkbk. 5.00 (ISBN 0-8209-0224-1, K-26). ESP.
--Look, Read, & Write. (Early Education Ser.). 24p. (gr. 1). 1982. wkbk. 5.00 (ISBN 0-8209-0219-5, K-21). ESP.
--Measuring Devices & Instruments. (Math Ser.). 24p. (gr. 4-6). 1976. wkbk. 5.00 (ISBN 0-8209-0118-0, A-28). ESP.

--The Melting Pot. (Social Studies Ser.). 24p. (gr. 5-9). 1978. wkbk. 5.00 (ISBN 0-8209-0255-1, SS-22). ESP.
--Metrics We Use. (Math Ser.). 24p. (gr. 3-6). 1978. wkbk. 5.00 (ISBN 0-8209-0108-3, A-18). ESP.
--Mixty Maxty Puzzles. (Puzzles Ser.). 24p. (gr. 3-5). 1979. wkbk. 5.00 (ISBN 0-8209-0283-7, MMP-1). ESP.
--Mixty Maxty Puzzles. (Puzzles Ser.). 24p. (gr. 5-6). 1979. wkbk. 5.00 (ISBN 0-8209-0284-5, MMP-2). ESP.
--Mixty Maxty Puzzles. (Puzzles Ser.). 24p. (gr. 5-7). 1979. wkbk. 5.00 (ISBN 0-8209-0285-3, MMP-3). ESP.
--Mixty Maxty Puzzles. (Puzzles Ser.). 24p. (gr. 8-12). 1979. wkbk. 5.00 (ISBN 0-8209-0286-1, MMP-4). ESP.
--My First Number Book. (Early Education Ser.). 24p. (gr. 1). 1981. wkbk. 5.00 (ISBN 0-8209-0216-0, K-18). ESP.
--Number Exercises: Grade 1. (Math Ser.). 24p. 1980. wkbk. 5.00 (ISBN 0-8209-0091-5, A-1). ESP.
--Number Exercises: Grade 2. (Math Ser.). 24p. 1977. wkbk. 5.00 (ISBN 0-8209-0092-3, A-2). ESP.
--Number Exercises: Grade 3. (Math Ser.). 24p. 1976. wkbk. 5.00 (ISBN 0-8209-0093-1, A-3). ESP.
--Nursery Rhymes. (Early Education Ser.). 24p. (gr. k-1). 1979. wkbk. 5.00 (ISBN 0-686-42865-X, K-2). ESP.
--One & One More. (Math Ser.). 24p. (gr. 1). 1980. wkbk. 5.00 (ISBN 0-8209-0088-5, A-0). ESP.
--Our Constitution & Government. (Social Studies). 24p. (gr. 5 up). 1979. wkbk. 5.00 (ISBN 0-8209-0244-6, SS-11). ESP.
--Our Environment. (Science Ser.). 24p. (gr. 2). 1979. wkbk. 5.00 (ISBN 0-8209-0140-7, S-2). ESP.
--Our Solar System. (Science Ser.). 24p. (gr. 7). 1979. wkbk. 5.00 (ISBN 0-8209-0145-8, S-7). ESP.
--Our State. (Social Studies Ser.). 24p. (gr. 3-4). 1980. wkbk. 5.00 (ISBN 0-8209-0237-3, SS-4). ESP.
--Our World of Science. (Science Ser.). 24p. (gr. 2-6). 1980. wkbk. 5.00 (ISBN 0-8209-0147-4, S-9). ESP.
--Phonetic Puzzles: Grade 3. (Puzzles Ser.). 24p. 1980. wkbk. 5.00 (ISBN 0-8209-0289-6, PU-3). ESP.
--Phonetic Puzzles: Grade 4. (Puzzles Ser.). 24p. 1980. 5.00 (ISBN 0-8209-0290-X, PU-4). ESP.
--Phonetic Puzzles: Grade 5. (Puzzles Ser.). 24p. 1980. wkbk. 5.00 (ISBN 0-8209-0291-8, PU-5). ESP.
--Phonetic Puzzles: Grade 6. (Puzzles Ser.). 24p. 1980. 5.00 (ISBN 0-8209-0292-6, PU-6). ESP.
--Phonetic Puzzles: Grade 7. (Puzzles Ser.). 24p. 1980. wkbk. 5.00 (ISBN 0-8209-0293-4, PU-7). ESP.
--Phonetic Puzzles: Grade 8. (Puzzles Ser.). 24p. 1980. wkbk. 5.00 (ISBN 0-8209-0294-2, PU-8). ESP.
--Products of America. (Social Studies Ser.). 24p. (gr. 3-6). 1979. wkbk. 5.00 (ISBN 0-8209-0267-5, POA-1). ESP.
--Programmed Math: Grade 1. (Math Ser.). 24p. 1976. wkbk. 5.00 (ISBN 0-8209-0127-X, PM-1). ESP.
--Programmed Math: Grade 2. (Math Ser.). 24p. 1976. wkbk. 5.00 (ISBN 0-8209-0128-8, PM-2). ESP.
--Programmed Math: Grade 3. (Math Ser.). 24p. 1980. wkbk. 5.00 (ISBN 0-8209-0129-6, PM-3). ESP.
--Programmed Math: Grade 4. (Math Ser.). 24p. wkbk. 5.00 (ISBN 0-8209-0130-X, PM-4). ESP.
--Programmed Math: Grade 5. (Math Ser.). 24p. 1977. wkbk. 5.00 (ISBN 0-8209-0131-8, PM-5). ESP.
--Programmed Math: Grade 6. (Math Ser.). 24p. 1979. wkbk. 5.00 (ISBN 0-8209-0132-6, PM-6). ESP.
--Programmed Math: Grade 7. (Math Ser.). 24p. 1977. 5.00 (ISBN 0-8209-0133-4, PM-7). ESP.
--Programmed Math: Grade 8. (Math Ser.). 24p. 1977. wkbk. 5.00 (ISBN 0-8209-0134-2, PM-8). ESP.
--Programmed Math: Kindergarten. (Math Ser.). 24p. 1977. wkbk. 5.00 (ISBN 0-8209-0126-1, PM-R). ESP.
--Remedial Arithmetic. (Math Ser.). 24p. (gr. 3-5). 1979. wkbk. 5.00 (ISBN 0-8209-0112-1, A-22). ESP.
--Remedial Arithmetic 1A. (Math Ser.). 24p. (gr. 2-3). 1978. wkbk. 5.00 (ISBN 0-8209-0109-1, A-19). ESP.
--Remedial Arithmetic 1B. (Math Ser.). 24p. (gr. 2-4). 1978. wkbk. 5.00 (ISBN 0-8209-0110-5, A-20). ESP.
--Remedial Arithmetic 1C. (Math Ser.). 24p. (gr. 3-5). 1978. wkbk. 5.00 (ISBN 0-8209-0111-3, A-21). ESP.
--Science Adventures. (Science Ser.). 24p. (gr. 4). 1977. wkbk. 5.00 (ISBN 0-8209-0142-3, S-4). ESP.
--Science Facts. (Science Ser.). 24p. (gr. 6). 1978. wkbk. 5.00 (ISBN 0-8209-0144-X, S-6). ESP.
--Science Facts Puzzles. (Puzzles Ser.). 24p. (gr. 6). 1980. wkbk. 5.00 (ISBN 0-8209-0298-5, PU-12). ESP.
--Science Goals. (Science Ser.). 24p. (gr. 5). 1980. wkbk. 5.00 (ISBN 0-8209-0143-1, S-5). ESP.
--The Science World. (Science Ser.). 24p. (gr. 4-7). 1978. wkbk. 5.00 (ISBN 0-8209-0156-3, S-18). ESP.
--Secret Messages: Add.-Subt. (Puzzles Ser.). 24p. (gr. 3-5). 1980. wkbk. 5.00 (ISBN 0-8209-0301-9, PU-15). ESP.
--Secret Messages: Mult.-Div. (Puzzles Ser.). 24p. (gr. 3-5). 1980. wkbk. 5.00 (ISBN 0-8209-0302-7, PU-16). ESP.
--Simple Additon & Subtraction. (Math Ser.). 24p. (gr. k-1). 1982. wkbk. 5.00 (ISBN 0-8209-0089-3, A-K). ESP.
--Spatial Relationships. (Early Education Ser.). 24p. (gr. k-1). 1981. wkbk. 5.00 (ISBN 0-8209-0221-7, K-23). ESP.
--Things & Words. (Early Education Ser.). 24p. (ps-1). 1978. wkbk. 5.00 (ISBN 0-8209-0203-9, K-5). ESP.
--Things Around Us. (Science Ser.). 24p. (ps). 1975. wkbk. 5.00 (ISBN 0-8209-0138-5, S-R). ESP.
--Think & Write. (Early Education Ser.). 24p. (gr. 1). 1982. wkbk. 5.00 (ISBN 0-8209-0220-9, K-22). ESP.
--Thinking Development. (Early Education Ser.). 24p. (gr. k). 1981. wkbk. 5.00 (ISBN 0-8209-0213-6, K-15). ESP.
--Unified Reading. (Early Education Ser.). 24p. (gr. 2). 1981. wkbk. 5.00 (ISBN 0-8209-0212-8, K-14). ESP.
--Units of Measure. (Math Ser.). 24p. (gr. 3-5). 1979. wkbk. 5.00 (ISBN 0-8209-0120-2, A-30). ESP.
--Visual Discrimination. (Language Arts Ser.). 24p. (gr. 1-2). 1979. wkbk. 5.00 (ISBN 0-8209-0319-1, LA-5). ESP.
--Word Picture Puzzles. (Puzzles Ser.). 24p. (gr. 1). 1980. wkbk. 5.00 (ISBN 0-8209-0296-9, PU-10). ESP.
--Word Scan Puzzles. (Puzzles Ser.). 24p. (gr. 3). 1980. wkbk. 5.00 (ISBN 0-8209-0297-7, PU-11). ESP.
--Writing Capital & Small Letters. (Early Education Ser.). 24p. (gr. 1). 1981. wkbk. 5.00 (ISBN 0-8209-0223-3, K-25). ESP.
--Written Problems in Math: Grade 2. (Math Ser.). 24p. 1980. wkbk. 5.00 (ISBN 0-8209-0122-9, A-32). ESP.

Justus, John R., jt. auth. see Henry, Charlier H.

Justus, May. Surprise for Perky Pup. LC 74-155569. (Venture Ser). (Illus.). (gr. 1). 1971. PLB 6.69 (ISBN 0-8116-6704-9). Garrard.
--You're Sure Silly, Billy. LC 72-1077. (Venture Ser). (Illus.). 64p. (gr. 2). 1972. PLB 6.89 (ISBN 0-8116-6958-0). Garrard.

Juszli, Frank L. & Rodgers, Charles A. Elementary Technical Mathematics. 3rd ed. (Illus.). 1980. text ed. 20.95 (ISBN 0-13-260869-3). P-H.
--Elementary Technical Mathematics with Calculus. 2nd ed. 1980. 23.95 (ISBN 0-686-64437-9). P-H.

Jutikkala, E., jt. auth. see Gissel, Sven.

Jutkovitz, Serena. SJ's Winners: An Exceptional Approach to Round-the-World Wining & Dining in the San Francisco Area. LC 82-99898. 278p. (Orig.). 1982. pap. 8.50 (ISBN 0-9608968-0-5). Russian Hill Hse.

Jutte, Rudiger. The Future of International Organization. 1981. 26.00 (ISBN 0-312-31476-0). St Martin.

Juvenal. Satires: With the Satires of Persius. Gifford, William, Jr., tr. 1954. 9.95x (ISBN 0-460-00997-4, Evman). Biblio Dist.
--Sixteen Satires upon the Ancient Harlot. Robison, S., tr. 128p. 1983. text ed. 14.75x (ISBN 0-85635-324-8, Pub. by Carcanet Pr England). Humanities.

Juvigny, F. Leonard de see Fair, D. E. & De Juvigny, F. Leonard.

Juvinall, Robert C. Engineering Considerations of Stress, Strain, & Strength. (Illus.). 1967. text ed. 35.50 (ISBN 0-07-033180-4, C); instructor's manual 23.00 (ISBN 0-07-033181-2). McGraw.
--Fundamentals of Machine Component Design. 700p. 1983. text ed. 29.95 (ISBN 0-471-06485-8); tchr's. manual avail. (ISBN 0-471-89556-3). Wiley.

Juynboll, G. H., ed. Studies on the First Century of Islamic Society. LC 81-21225. 303p. 1982. 20.00x (ISBN 0-8093-1062-7). S Ill U Pr.

Juzzinno, Carlo. The Friendly U.F.O. 1983. 5.95 (ISBN 0-533-05575-X). Vantage.

Jyoti, Swami Amar. Retreat Into Eternity: an Upanishad - Book of Aphorisms. LC 80-54236. (Illus.). 128p. (Orig.). 1981. pap. 12.95 (ISBN 0-933572-03-4). Truth Consciousness.

Jyotirmayi-devi dasa, jt. auth. see Yogesvara dasa.

K

Kaam, Adrian V. Formative Spirituality: Introduction, Vol. I. (Formative Spirituality Ser.). 320p. 1983. 17.50 (ISBN 0-8245-0544-1). Crossroad NY.

Kaam, Adrian van see Van Kaam, Adrian.

Kaasa, Harris, tr. see Nelson, E. Clifford.

Kaatz, Evelyn. Race Car Driver. LC 79-14766. (Illus.). (gr. 5 up). 1979. 7.95 (ISBN 0-316-47751-6). Little.

Kaatz, Ron. Cable: An Advertiser's Guide. 160p. 1982. pap. 14.95 (ISBN 0-87251-076-X). Crain Bks.

Kaback, Michael. Genetic Issues in Pediatric, Obstetric & Gynecologic Practice. 1981. 59.75 (ISBN 0-8151-4952-2). Year Bk Med.

Kabanov, V., ed. see Polymer Science Symposium, 67th.

Kabaservice, Thomas P. Applied Microelectronics. (Electrical Engineering Ser.). (Illus.). 1977. text ed. 27.50 (ISBN 0-8299-0143-4). West Pub.

Kabat, Carl, tr. see Comblin, Jose.

Kabat, Elvin A. Experimental Immunochemistry. 2nd ed. (Illus.). 920p. 1971. photocopy ed. spiral 89.50x (ISBN 0-398-00956-2). C C Thomas.

Kabat, Herman. Herniated Cervical Disc: Instruction Manual for Patients. 144p. 1983. 16.50 (ISBN 0-87527-299-1). Green.

Kabata, Z. Diseases of Fishes, Book 1: Crustaceans. 19.95 (ISBN 0-87666-039-1, PS200). TFH Pubns.

Kabbe, Frederick & Kabbe, Lois. Chemistry, Energy, & Human Ecology. LC 75-27126. (Illus.). 464p. 1976. pap. text ed. 22.95 (ISBN 0-395-19833-X); instr's. manual 1.10 (ISBN 0-395-19831-3); slides o.p. 11.25 (ISBN 0-395-19832-1). HM.

Kabbe, Lois, jt. auth. see Kabbe, Frederick.

Kaberlein, Joseph J. Air Conditioning Sheet Metal Layout. 3rd ed. 1973. 17.95 (ISBN 0-02-819360-1). Glencoe.
--Short-Cuts for Round Layouts. 3rd ed. 1973. 17.95 (ISBN 0-02-819390-3). Glencoe.
--Triangulation Short-Cut Layouts. 3rd ed. (gr. 9 up). 1973. 17.95 (ISBN 0-02-819410-1). Glencoe.

Kaberry, Phyllis M., ed. see Malinowski, Bronislaw.

Kabir. The Bijak of Kabir. Hess, Linda, ed. & tr. from Hindi. LC 82-73716. 208p. (Orig.). 1983. pap. 12.50 (ISBN 0-86547-114-2). N Point Pr.

Kabir, Humayun. Men & Rivers: A Novel. 228p. 1981. pap. text ed. 4.25x (ISBN 0-86131-262-7, Pub. by Orient Longman Ltd India). Apt Bks.

Kabisch, Klaus & Hemmerling, Joachim. Small Ponds, Lakes & Pools. (Illus.). 261p. 1983. 14.95 (ISBN 0-668-05674-6, 5674). Arco.

Kable, William. Three Early American Novels. LC 72-95305. (Literary Text Series). 1970. pap. text ed. 4.95x o.p. (ISBN 0-675-09406-2). Merrill.

Kabotie, Fred. Designs from the Ancient Mimbrenos With Hopi Interpretation. LC 82-80587. (Illus.). 100p. 1982. 40.00 (ISBN 0-87358-308-6); Limited edition 125.00 (ISBN 0-686-97963-X). Northland.
--Fred Kabotie: Hopi Indian Artist. 1977. 35.00 (ISBN 0-87358-164-4). Mus Northern Ariz.

Kabotie, Michael, et al, eds. Hopi Voices & Visions. 80p. (Orig.). 1983. pap. 7.50 (ISBN 0-935252-32-0). Street Pr.

Kabwasa, Antoine & Kaunda, Martin. Correspondence Education in Africa. 1973. 21.50x (ISBN 0-7100-7681-9). Routledge & Kegan.

Kac, Arthur W. The Messiahship of Jesus. LC 16-18. 350p. 1980. pap. 9.95 (ISBN 0-8024-5421-6). Moody.

Kac, Mark. Mark Kac: Probability, Number Theory, & Statistical Physics: Selected Papers. Baclawski, K. & Donsker, M. D., eds. (Mathematicians of Our Time Ser.). 1979. 50.00x (ISBN 0-262-11067-9). MIT Pr.

Kachi, Teruko, tr. see Ishida, Eiichiro.

Kachigan, Sam K. Statistical Analysis: An Interdisciplinary Introduction. (Illus.). 610p. Date not set. text ed. 24.95x (ISBN 0-942154-99-1). Radius Pr.

Kachru, B. The Other Tongue: English Across Culture. (World Language English Ser.). 358p. 1983. pap. 13.95 (ISBN 0-08-029469-3). Pergamon.

Kachru, Braj B. The Indianization of English: The English Language in India. (Illus.). 1982. 14.95x (ISBN 0-19-561353-8). Oxford U Pr.

Kadambi, V. & Prasad, Manchar. An Introduction to Energy Conversion, 3 vols. Incl. Vol. 1. Basic Thermodynamics. 1976. o.p. (ISBN 0-470-50925-2); Vol. 2. Energy Conversion Cycles. 1974 (ISBN 0-470-50926-0); Vol. 3. Principles of Turbomachinery. 1978. o.p. (ISBN 0-470-99157-7). LC 74-13881. 17.95x ea. o.p. Halsted Pr.

Kadans, Joseph M. Doctor Kadans' Herbal Weight Loss Diet. LC 82-7944. 1982. 14.95 (ISBN 0-13-216523-6, Parker); pap. 4.95 (ISBN 0-13-216531-7, Reward). P-H.

Kadar, Bela. Problems of Economic Growth in Latin America. Felix, Pal, tr. from Hungarian. LC 79-17824. 1979. Repr. of 1977 ed. 32.50x (ISBN 0-312-64758-1). St Martin.

Kadarkay, Arpad. Human Rights in American & Russian Political Thought. LC 81-43910. (Illus.). 252p. (Orig.). 1982. PLB 24.25 (ISBN 0-8191-2481-8); pap. text ed. 10.75 (ISBN 0-8191-2482-6). U Pr of Amer.

Kadarkay, Arpad, tr. see Farkas, Sandor B.

Kadas, Sotiris. Mount Athos. (Athenon Illustrated Guides Ser.). (Illus.). 200p. 1983. pap. 16.00 (ISBN 0-88332-304-4, 8237, Pub. by Ekdotike Athenon Greece). Larousse.

Kaden, Vera. The Illustration of Plants & Gardens, 1500-1850. (Illus.). 113p. 1982. pap. 15.00 (ISBN 0-686-43333-5). Intl Pubns Serv.

Kadin, Marshall E., jt. auth. see Newcom, Samuel R.

Kadir, Djelal. Juan Carlos Onetti. (World Authors Ser.). 1977. lib. bdg. 15.95 (ISBN 0-8057-6310-4, Twayne). G K Hall.

Kadiroglu, Osman, et al, eds. Nuclear Energy & Alternatives: Proceedings of the International Scientific Forum on an Acceptable Nuclear Energy Future of the World. LC 78-16007. 768p. 1978. prof ref 45.00x (ISBN 0-88410-081-2). Ballinger Pub.

Kadis, Leslie B. & McClendon, Ruth A. Chocolate Pudding & Other Approaches to Intensive Family Therapy. 1983. 12.95. Sci & Behavior.

Kadis, Leslie B., jt. ed. see Katz, Jordon.

Kadish & Paulsen. Criminal Law & Its Processes. 4th ed. LC 82-81495. 1982. text ed. 30.00 (ISBN 0-316-47812-1). Little.

Kadish, Alon. The Oxford Economics in the Late Nineteenth Century. (Oxford Historical Monographs). 1982. 46.00x (ISBN 0-19-821886-9). Oxford U Pr.

Kadish, Sanford H. & Paulsen, Monrad G. Criminal Law & Its Processes. 3rd ed. 1975. 28.00 o.p. (ISBN 0-316-47805-9); 1980 supplement 7.95 o.p. (ISBN 0-686-86279-1). Little.

Kadison, Richard V., ed. Operations Algebras & Applications, 2 pts. (Proceedings of Symposia in Pure Mathematics Ser.: Vol. 38). Set. 80.00 (ISBN 0-8218-1445-1, PSPUM/38); Part one. 46.00 (ISBN 0-8218-1441-9, PSPUM/38.1); 46.00 (ISBN 0-8218-1444-3, PSPUM/38.2). Am Math.

Kadison, Richard V. & Ringrose, John R., eds. Fundamentals of the Theory of Operator Algebras, Vol. 1. LC 82-13768. Date not set. price not set (ISBN 0-12-393301-3). Acad Pr.

Kadlec, J., jt. auth. see Kufner, A.

Kadloubovsky, Palmer, tr. see Chariton, Igumen.

Kadloubowsky, E. Early Fathers from the Philokalia. Palmer, G. E., tr. 454p. 1954. 18.95 (ISBN 0-571-03794-1). Faber & Faber.

Kadow, H., jt. auth. see Lammich, G.

Kadt, Ellen De see Medvedev, Roy A.

Kadt, Ellen De, tr. see Medvedev, Roy A.

Kaduck, John, jt. auth. see Kaduck, Margaret.

Kaduck, John M. Rare & Expensive Postcards, Bk. II. Rev. ed. 9.95 (ISBN 0-87069-407-3). Wallace-Homestead.
--Sleepers That Have a Future. (Illus.). 48p. 1972. spiral bdg. 4.95 o.p. (ISBN 0-517-10418-0). Crown.

Kaduck, Margaret & Kaduck, John. Rare & Expensive Postcards: Bk. II. (Illus.). pap. 9.95 (ISBN 0-87069-267-4). Wallace-Homestead.

Kadushin, Alfred. Child Welfare Services. 3rd ed. (Illus.). 1980. text ed. 24.95x (ISBN 0-02-361810-8). Macmillan.

Kadushin, Max. Rabbinic Mind. 3rd ed. LC 75-189016. 1972. 9.75x (ISBN 0-8197-0007-X); pap. 7.95 (ISBN 0-685-30561-9). Bloch.

Kadushin, Phineas. This Is Psychotherapy: For Those Considering It, For Those Involved in It, & for the Curious. LC 82-61943. 320p. 1983. 16.95 (ISBN 0-9610000-0-7). Tip-Top.

Kadzin, Alan E. Single-Case Research Designs: Methods for Clinical & Applied Settings. (Illus.). 382p. 1982. text ed. 27.50x (ISBN 0-19-503020-6); pap. text ed. 14.95x (ISBN 0-19-503021-4). Oxford U Pr.

Kaegi, C. E., ed. see Piaget, Jean.

Kael, Pauline. Deeper into Movies. 1980. pap. 2.95 o.p. (ISBN 0-446-93525-5). Warner Bks.

Kaelin, E. F. Man & Value: Essays in Honor of William H. Werkmeister. Florida State University, Dept. of Philosophy, ed. LC 80-27314. (A Florida State University Book). 1981. 19.25 (ISBN 0-686-31645-2, IS-00139, Pub. by U Pr of FL). Univ Microfilms.

Kaempfer, H. M. Ukiyo-E Studies & Pleasures: A Collection of Essays on the Art of Japanese Prints. 1979. text ed. 25.25x (ISBN 90-70216-01-9). Humanities.

Kaempfer, H. M. & Sickinghe, Jhr. W., eds. The Fascinating World of the Japanese Artist: A Collection of Essays on Japanese Art. 1979. text ed. 20.00x o.p. (ISBN 0-686-86089-6). Humanities.

Kaestle, Carl. Pillars of the Republic: Common Schools & American Society, 1790-1860. Foner, Eric, ed. 1983. 17.50 (ISBN 0-8090-7620-9); pap. 7.25 (ISBN 0-8090-0154-3). Hill & Wang.

Kaestle, Carl F. Joseph Lancaster & the Monitorial School Movement: A Documentary History. LC 72-97206. 200p. 1973. text ed. 11.50 (ISBN 0-8077-2375-4); pap. text ed. 6.00x (ISBN 0-8077-2380-0). Tchrs Coll.

Kaestner. Mein Onkel Franz. (Easy Reader, A). pap. 2.95 (ISBN 0-88436-037-7, 45259). EMC.

Kaestner, Erich. Kleine Grenzverkehr. LC 56-9989. 4.95 (ISBN 0-8044-0241-8); pap. 2.95 o.p. (ISBN 0-8044-6335-2). Ungar.
--Verschwundene Miniatur. new ed. Schinnerer, Otto P., ed. (Illus.). 1962. text ed. 7.95x o.p. (ISBN 0-669-29488-8). Heath.

Kafe, Joseph K., compiled by. Ghana: An Annotated Bibliography of Academic Theses, 1920-1970 in the Commonwealth, the Republic of Ireland & the United States of America. 1973. lib. bdg. 24.00 (ISBN 0-8161-1034-4, Hall Reference). G K Hall.

Kaffarnick, H., jt. auth. see Schneider, J.

Kafka, Barbara. American Food & California Wine. LC 82-47863. (The Great American Cooking Schools Ser.). (Illus.). 84p. 1982. 8.61i (ISBN 0-06-015066-1, HarpT). Har-Row.

Kafka, Doris M., jt. auth. see Bauer, Robert F.

Kafka, Francis J., jt. auth. see Eisenberg, James.

Kafka, Franz. The Basic Kafka. Heller, Erich, ed. 1983. pap. 3.95 (ISBN 0-671-82561-5). WSP.
--The Basic Writings of C. G. Jung. Muir, Willa & Muir, Edwin, trs. LC 52-9771. 6.95 (ISBN 0-394-60422-9). Modern Lib.
--Briefe on Milena. (Ger.). 1952. 14.50 (ISBN 0-8052-3022-X). Schocken.

--Castle. 1969. 4.95 (ISBN 0-394-60388-5). Modern Lib.
--The Castle. 1974. pap. 5.95 (ISBN 0-394-71991-3, Vin). Random.
--The Castle. Muir, Willa, et al, trs. LC 73-90729. 481p. (Definitive edition). 1976. pap. 5.95 (ISBN 0-8052-0415-6). Schocken.
--The Complete Stories. Glatzer, Nahum N., ed. LC 75-161559. 1976. 14.50x (ISBN 0-8052-3419-5); pap. 7.95 (ISBN 0-8052-0423-7). Schocken.
--The Complete Stories. Glatzer, Nahum N., ed. 128p. deluxe ed. 22.50 (ISBN 0-8052-3863-8). Schocken.
--Dearest Father. Brod, Max, ed. LC 54-12097. 1954. 20.00x (ISBN 0-8052-3050-5). Schocken.
--Diaries of Franz Kafka, Vol. 1: 1910-1913. Brod, Max, ed. Kresh, Joseph, tr. LC 48-6432. (Illus.). 1965. 10.50x (ISBN 0-8052-3054-8); pap. 7.50 (ISBN 0-8052-0424-5). Schocken.
--Diaries of Franz Kafka, Vol. 2: 1914-1923. Brod, Max, ed. Greenberg, Martin, tr. LC 48-6432. (Illus.). 1965. 10.50x (ISBN 0-8052-3055-6); pap. 4.95 (ISBN 0-8052-0425-3). Schocken.
--The Great Wall of China: Stories & Reflections. Muir, Willa & Muir, Edwin, trs. LC 46-8109. 1970. pap. 4.95 (ISBN 0-8052-0419-9). Schocken.
--I Am a Memory Come Alive: Autobiographical Writings. Glatzer, Nahum N., ed. LC 74-8781. 277p. 1976. 10.00 o.p. (ISBN 0-8052-3556-6); pap. 5.95 (ISBN 0-8052-0428-8). Schocken.
--Letter to His Father: Brief an Den Vater. LC 66-14874. (Bilingual). 1966. 6.00x (ISBN 0-8052-3144-7); pap. 4.95 (ISBN 0-8052-0426-1). Schocken.
--Letters to Felice. Heller, Erich & Born, Juergen, eds. Stern, James & Duckworth, Elisabeth, trs. LC 72-88262. (Illus.). 624p. 1973. 17.50 (ISBN 0-8052-3500-0). Schocken.
--Letters to Milena. LC 62-13139. 1962. 7.50x (ISBN 0-8052-3145-5); pap. 5.95 (ISBN 0-8052-0427-X). Schocken.
--Parables & Paradoxes: Parabeln Und Paradoxe. LC 61-14917. (Eng. & Ger.). (YA) 1961. pap. 5.95 (ISBN 0-8052-0422-9). Schocken.
--Trial. rev. ed. (YA) 1937. 13.50 (ISBN 0-394-44955-X). Knopf.
--Trial. 1951. 3.95 o.s.i. (ISBN 0-394-60318-4, M318). Modern Lib.
--The Trial. LC 68-59195. (Illus., Definitive edition with Kafka's own drawings). 1968. pap. 4.95 (ISBN 0-8052-0416-4). Schocken.
Kafka, Franz, et al. Erzahlungen. Hoffman, Charles W., et al, eds. (Ger). 1970. pap. 8.95x (ISBN 0-393-09937-7, NortonC). Norton.
Kafka, Sherry. I Need a Friend. (Illus.). (gr. k-2). 1971. PLB 4.29 o.p. (ISBN 0-399-60300-X). Putnam Pub Group.
Kafker, Frank A. The French Revolution: Conflicting Interpretations. 3rd ed. Laux, James M., ed. LC 82-9878. 286p. 1982. pap. 9.50 (ISBN 0-89874-517-9). Krieger.
Kagan, A. Robert & Miles, John W. Head & Neck Oncology: Controversies in Cancer Treatment. 1981. lib. bdg. 55.00 (ISBN 0-8161-2169-9, Pub. by Hall Medical Bks). G K Hall.
Kagan, A. Robert, jt. auth. see Steckel, Richard J.
Kagan, Andrew A. Paul Klee-Art & Music. (Illus.). 1982. 22.50 (ISBN 0-8014-1500-4). Cornell U Pr.
Kagan, B. A., jt. auth. see Marchuk, G. I.
Kagan, Benjamin M., jt. auth. see Gellis, Sydney S.
Kagan, C. Coping with College. 1982. 9.95x (ISBN 0-07-033191-X). McGraw.
Kagan, D. Problems in Ancient History, Vol.1. 2nd ed. 1975. pap. 14.95x (ISBN 0-02-361820-5). Macmillan.
Kagan, D., ed. Studies in the Greek Historians. LC 74-12982. (Yale Classical Studies: No. 24). 256p. 1975. 37.50 (ISBN 0-521-20587-5). Cambridge U Pr.
Kagan, Donald. End of the Roman Empire. 2nd ed. (Problems in European Civilization Ser.). 1978. pap. text ed. 5.50 (ISBN 0-669-01828-7). Heath.
--Problems in Ancient History, Vol. 2. 2nd ed. (Illus.). 464p. 1975. pap. text ed. 14.95x (ISBN 0-02-361830-2). Macmillan.
Kagan, Doreen V., jt. ed. see Morgan, John P.
Kagan, Jerome & Havemann, Ernest. Psychology: An Introduction. 4th ed. 647p. 1980. text ed. 22.95 (ISBN 0-15-572625-0, HC); instructor's manual avail. (ISBN 0-15-572627-7); study guide 7.95 (ISBN 0-686-77637-2); test items avail. HarBraceJ.
Kagan, Jerome & Moss, Howard. Birth to Maturity. LC 62-19148. 1983. text ed. 25.00x (ISBN 0-300-02998-5); pap. 8.95 (ISBN 0-300-03029-0). Yale U Pr.
Kagan, Jerome, jt. ed. see Brim, Orville G., Jr.
Kagan, Lynn W. Renal Disease: A Manual of Patient Care. (Illus.). 1979. text ed. 27.50 (ISBN 0-07-033190-1, HP). McGraw.
Kagan, M. H., jt. auth. see Gabel, D. L.
Kagan, Robert A. Regulatory Justice: Implementing a Wage-Price Freeze. LC 77-72498. 200p. 1978. 11.95x (ISBN 0-87154-425-3). Russell Sage.
Kagan, Robert A., jt. auth. see Bardach, Eugene.
Kagan, Robert A., jt. auth. see Gilbert, Harvey A.
Kagan, Robert A., jt. ed. see Bardach, Eugene.
Kagan, Robert A., jt. ed. see Steckel, R.
Kaganoff. Guide to America Holy Land Studies, 1620-1948, Vol. 2. 234p. 1982. 26.95 (ISBN 0-03-062812-1). Praeger.
Kagawa, Yasuo, jt. ed. see Sato, Ryo.
Kagay, Michael. What's Happening to Voter Turnout in American Presidential Elections? (Vital Issues, Vol. XXIX 1979-80: No. 4). 0.60 (ISBN 0-686-81609-9). Ctr Info Am.
Kagel, Sam. Anatomy of a Labor Arbitration. LC 61-10554. 192p. 1961. 15.00 (ISBN 0-87179-025-4). BNA.
Kagiwada, Harriet H., et al. Multiple Scattering Processes: Inverse & Direct. LC 75-22363. (Applied Mathematics & Computation Ser.: No. 8). 336p. 1975. text ed. 28.50 (ISBN 0-201-04104-9, Adv Bk Prog); pap. text ed. 19.50 (ISBN 0-201-04105-7, Adv Bk Prog). A-W.
Kagle, Stephen. American Diary Literature. (United States Author Ser.). 1979. lib. bdg. 13.95 (ISBN 0-8057-7280-4, Twayne). G K Hall.
Kagler, S. H. Spectroscopic & Chromatographic Analysis of Mineral Oil, 3 vols. LC 72-4105. 559p. 1973. Set. 89.95 o.s.i. (ISBN 0-470-45425-3). Halsted Pr.
Kaguei, S., jt. auth. see Wakao, N.
Kagy, Fred E. Graphic Arts. LC 81-6737. (Illus.). 128p. 1982. text ed. 5.80 (ISBN 0-87006-395-2). Goodheart.
Kagy, Frederick D. Graphic Arts. LC 78-5456. (Illus.). 1978. text ed. 5.80 o.p. (ISBN 0-87006-252-2). Goodheart.
Kagy, Frederick D. & Adams, J. Michael. Graphic Arts Photography. 1983. text ed. 25.95 (ISBN 0-534-01295-7). Breton Pubs.
Kahan, Jerome H. Security in the Nuclear Age: Developing U.S. Strategic Arms Policy. 351p. 1975. 23.95 (ISBN 0-8157-4818-3); pap. 9.95 (ISBN 0-8157-4817-5). Brookings.
Kahan, Steven. Intermediate Algebra. 588p. 1981. text ed. 20.95 (ISBN 0-15-541530-1, HC); instructor's manual avail. 2.95 (ISBN 0-15-541531-X); trigonometry suppl. avail. 2.95 (ISBN 0-15-541532-8). HarBraceJ.
Kahan, Stuart. Expectant Father's Survival Kit. LC 77-17919. 1979. 8.95 o.p. (ISBN 0-671-18371-0); pap. 3.95 (ISBN 0-671-18345-1). Sovereign Bks.
Kahan, Stuart, jt. auth. see Cavallo, Robert M.
Kahana, K. Case for Jewish Civil Law in the Jewish State. 6.25x (ISBN 0-685-01037-6). Bloch.
Kahananui, Dorothy M. & Anthony, Alberta P. Let's Speak Hawaiian - E Kama'ilio Hawai'i Kakou. rev. ed. (Illus.). 1974. pap. text ed. 8.00x (ISBN 0-8248-0283-7). UH Pr.
Kahane, Howard. Logic & Contemporary Rhetoric. 3rd ed. 288p. 1980. pap. text ed. 12.95x (ISBN 0-534-00850-X). Wadsworth Pub.
--Logic & Philosophy. 3rd ed. 1978. text ed. 20.95x o.p. (ISBN 0-534-00555-1). Wadsworth Pub.
--Logic & Philosophy. 4th ed. 448p. 1982. text ed. 21.95x (ISBN 0-534-01088-1). Wadsworth Pub.
Kahane, Meir. They Must Go. LC 81-47705. 288p. 1981. 14.95 (ISBN 0-448-12026-7, G&D). Putnam Pub Group.
--Why Be Jewish? Intermarriage, Assimilation, & Alienation. LC 77-8774. 264p. 1982. pap. 7.95 (ISBN 0-8128-6129-9). Stein & Day.
Kahane, Reuven. Legitimation & Integration in Developing Societies: The Case of India. (Replica Edition). 175p. 1982. soft cover 18.00 (ISBN 0-86531-921-9). Westview.
Kahapea, Alexander. Statute of Limitations on Malpractice. (Illus.). 320p. 1983. 25.00 (ISBN 0-89962-295-X). Todd & Honeywell.
Kahin, Audrey, jt. ed. see Anderson, Benedict.
Kahl, Gunter & Schell, Josef, eds. Molecular Biology of Plant Tumors. (Molecular Biology Ser.). 1982. 69.50 (ISBN 0-12-394380-9). Acad Pr.
Kahl, Joseph. Modernization, Exploitation & Dependency in Latin America. LC 75-43190. 215p. 1976. pap. text ed. 9.95 (ISBN 0-87855-584-6). Transaction Bks.
Kahl, Willi. Selbstbiographien Deutscher Musiker Des XVIII. (Facsimiles of Early Biographies Ser.: Vol. 5). 1972. Repr. of 1948 ed. 37.50 o.s.i. (ISBN 90-6027-277-3, Pub. by Frits Knuf Netherlands); wrappers 25.00 o.s.i. (ISBN 90-6027-133-5). Pendragon NY.
Kahle, Jane B. Double Dilemma: Minorities & Women in Science Education. LC 81-84383. (Illus.). 181p. (Orig.). 1982. pap. 5.95 (ISBN 0-931682-13-4). Purdue.
Kahlenberg, Mary H. & Schwartz, Mark. The Book of Grass Crafts: Its Beauty & Uses. (Illus.). 1983. 24.75 (ISBN 0-525-06983-6, 02403-720); pap. 14.50 (ISBN 0-525-47630-X, 01408-420). Dutton.
Kahler, Erich Von see Von Kahler, Erich.
Kahlili, Nader. Racing Alone: Houses Made with Earth & Fire. LC 82-48419. 224p. 1983. 14.37 (ISBN 0-686-82602-7, HarpR). Har-Row.
Kahm, H. S. Fifty Big Money Ideas You Can Start & Run with 250 to 5,000 Dollars. LC 81-43741. 264p. 1983. pap. 7.95 (ISBN 0-385-17829-8, Dolp). Doubleday.
--One Hundred & One Businesses You Can Start & Run with Less Than One Thousand Dollars. LC 72-96277. 240p. 1973. pap. 3.95 (ISBN 0-385-02271-9, Dolp). Doubleday.
Kahn, Ada P. Arthritis. (Help Yourself to Health Ser.). 96p. (Orig.). 1983. pap. 3.95 (ISBN 0-8092-5598-7). Contemp Bks.
--Diabetes. (Help Yourself to Health Ser.). 96p. (Orig.). 1983. pap. 3.95 (ISBN 0-8092-5601-0). Contemp Bks.
--Headaches. (Help Yourself to Health Ser.). 96p. (Orig.). 1983. pap. 3.95 (ISBN 0-8092-5600-2). Contemp Bks.
--High Blood Pressure. (Help Yourself to Health Ser.). 96p. (Orig.). 1983. pap. 3.95 (ISBN 0-8092-5599-5). Contemp Bks.
Kahn, Alfred E. The Economics of Regulation, 2 vols. Incl. Vol. 1. Economic Principles. 1970. text ed. 29.95x (ISBN 0-471-45430-3); Vol. 2. Institutional Issues. 1971. text ed. 30.95x (ISBN 0-471-45431-1). LC 74-116769. Wiley.
Kahn, Alfred E., jt. auth. see De Chazeau, Melvin G.
Kahn, Alfred J. Theory & Practice of Social Planning. LC 79-81406. 360p. 1969. 10.50x (ISBN 0-87154-430-X). Russell Sage.
Kahn, Alfred J. & Kamerman, Sheila B. Helping America's Families. 266p. 1982. 27.95 (ISBN 0-87722-212-6); pap. 10.95 (ISBN 0-87722-213-4). Temple U Pr.
--Not for the Poor Alone: European Social Services. LC 75-14690. 197p. 1975. 14.95 (ISBN 0-87722-045-X). Temple U Pr.
Kahn, Alfred J., jt. auth. see Kamerman, Sheila B.
Kahn, Arnold. Filing Systems & Records Management. LC 78-31509. 1979. 16.50 (ISBN 0-07-033228-2, P&RB). McGraw.
Kahn, Arnold D. Family Security Through Estate Planning. 2nd ed. LC 82-4673. 224p. 1983. 19.95 (ISBN 0-07-033216-9, P&RB). McGraw.
Kahn, Azizur R., jt. ed. see Griffin, Keith.
Kahn, Charles H., ed. The Art & Thought of Heraclitus: An Edition of the Fragments with Translation & Commentary. LC 77-82499. 368p. 1981. pap. 16.95 (ISBN 0-521-28645-X). Cambridge U Pr.
Kahn, Charles H., et al. Going Places with Your Personality: A Guide to Successful Living. (gr. 4-12,RL 2.7). 1971. pap. 3.20 (ISBN 0-8224-3495-4); tchr's. manual free (ISBN 0-8224-3496-2). Pitman Learning.
Kahn, Coppelia. Man's Estate: Masculine Identity in Shakespeare. 1981. 18.50x (ISBN 0-520-03899-1). U of Cal Pr.
Kahn, David. Codebreakers. 1967. 35.00 o.p. (ISBN 0-02-560460-0). Macmillan.
Kahn, Douglas. John Heartfield: The Cutting Edge. 150p. (Orig.). 1983. 15.95 (ISBN 0-934378-27-4); pap. 7.95 (ISBN 0-934378-28-2). Tanam Pr.
Kahn, Douglas & Waggoner, Lawrence. Federal Taxation of Gifts, Trusts & Estates. 848p. 1977. text ed. 22.00 o.p. (ISBN 0-316-48199-8). Little.
--Federal Taxation of Gifts, Trusts & Estates. 2nd ed. LC 81-86689. 1982. text ed. 25.00 (ISBN 0-316-48208-0). Little.
Kahn, Douglas A. Basic Corporate Taxation - Nineteen Eighty-Two Pocket Part. 3rd ed. 87p. 1982. pocket part (ISBN 0-314-68840-4); 1982 supplement 4.95 (ISBN 0-314-67869-7). West Pub.
Kahn, Douglas A. & Waggoner, Laurence W. Provisions of the Internal Revenue Code & Treasury Regulations: 1982 Supplement. 1982. 12.95 (ISBN 0-316-48209-9). Little.
Kahn, Douglas A. & Waggoner, Lawrence W. Economic Recovery Act of Nineteen Eighty-One. suppl. ed. LC 81-80761. 80p. 1981. pap. 3.50 (ISBN 0-316-48206-4). Little.
Kahn, E. J. About the New Yorker & Me: A Sentimental Journal. LC 78-11497. 1979. 12.95 o.p. (ISBN 0-399-12300-8). Putnam Pub Group.
Kahn, E. J., Jr. Far-Flung & Footloose: Pieces from the New Yorker 1937-1978. LC 79-15636. 1980. 12.95 o.p. (ISBN 0-399-12428-4). Putnam Pub Group.
Kahn, Elizabeth, jt. auth. see Johannessen, Larry.
Kahn, Emil. Conducting Guide to Selected Scores. 2nd ed. LC 75-30288. (Illus.). 1976. pap. text ed. 15.95 (ISBN 0-02-871030-4). Schirmer Bks.
--Elements of Conducting. 2nd ed. LC 75-4317. (Illus.). 1975. pap. text ed. 15.50 (ISBN 0-02-871050-9). Schirmer Bks.
Kahn, Eugen, jt. auth. see Dodge, Raymond.
Kahn, F., ed. Documents of American Broadcasting. 3rd ed. 1978. 22.95 (ISBN 0-13-217067-1). P-H.
Kahn, G., jt. auth. see Meehan, James R.
Kahn, Gilbert. Business Data Processing: Basic Principles & Applications. 1966. text ed. 8.64 (ISBN 0-07-033201-0, G); tchr's ed. 7.95 (ISBN 0-07-033202-9). McGraw.
Kahn, Gilbert & Mulkerne, Donald J. The Wordbook. 1975. pap. text ed. 6.95x (ISBN 0-02-474780-7, 47478). Glencoe.
Kahn, Gilbert, jt. auth. see Stewart, Jeffrey R., Jr.
Kahn, Gilbert, et al. Filing Systems & Records Management. 2nd ed. 1971. text ed. 15.25 (ISBN 0-07-033231-2, G); tests 3.55 (ISBN 0-07-033238-X); practice materials 10.50 (ISBN 0-07-033232-0); instructors guide & key 8.00 (ISBN 0-07-033241-X). McGraw.
--Gregg Quick Filing Practice. 1965. text ed. 5.76 o.p. (ISBN 0-07-033233-9, G); tchr's manual & visual key 6.95 o.p. (ISBN 0-07-033234-7). McGraw.
--Progressive Filing. 8th ed. 1968. text ed. 11.72 (ISBN 0-07-033225-8, G); tchr's manual 7.08 (ISBN 0-07-033227-4); tests 1.80 (ISBN 0-07-033226-6); supplies pad 4.16 (ISBN 0-07-033220-7); practice set 9.28 (ISBN 0-07-033230-4). McGraw.
Kahn, Gilbert R., jt. auth. see Ehrenkranz, Lois B.
Kahn, Hazrat I. Nature Meditations. LC 80-50829. (Collected Works of Hazrat Inayat Khan Ser.). (Illus.). 128p. (Orig.). 1980. pap. 5.00 o.s.i. (ISBN 0-930872-12-6). Omega Pr NM.
Kahn, Herman. The Coming Boom. 1982. 14.95 (ISBN 0-671-44262-7). S&S.
--Emerging Japanese Superstate: Challenge & Response. 1971. pap. 2.45 o.p. (ISBN 0-13-274670-0, P2, Spec). P-H.
Kahn, Herman & Passin, Herbert. The Japanese Challenge: The Success & Failure of Economic Success. LC 78-69520. 1979. 10.95i o.p. (ISBN 0-690-01784-7). T Y Crowell.
Kahn, Herman & Pepper, Thomas. The Japanese Challenge: The Success & Failure of Economic Success. LC 80-15432. 162p. 1980. pap. 4.95 o.p. (ISBN 0-688-08710-8). Quill NY.
Kahn, Herman, et al. World Economic Development: Projections from 1979 to the Year 2000. LC 79-1737. 1979. pap. 7.95 (ISBN 0-688-03479-9). Quill NY.
Kahn, J. H. & Nursten, J. P. Unwillingly to School. 2nd ed. 1968. 12.25 o.p. (ISBN 0-08-013304-5); pap. 6.50 o.p. (ISBN 0-08-013295-2). Pergamon.
Kahn, James. Return of the Jedi: Illustrated Edition. 224p. (Orig.). 1983. pap. 5.95 (ISBN 0-345-30960-X). Ballantine.
Kahn, Joan. Seesaw. LC 64-19716. (Illus.). (ps-1). 1964. PLB 4.79 o.p. (ISBN 0-06-023081-9, HarpJ). Har-Row.
Kahn, Joan, ed. Some Things Dark & Dangerous. 224p. 1982. pap. 2.25 (ISBN 0-380-01556-0, 61168, Flare). Avon.
--Some Things Fierce & Fatal. 176p. 1982. pap. 2.25 (ISBN 0-380-00388-0, 61176, Flare). Avon.
--Some Things Strange & Sinister. 224p. 1982. pap. 2.25 (ISBN 0-380-00084-9, 61184, Flare). Avon.
Kahn, Joel S. Minangkabau Social Formations: Indonesian Peasants & the World Economy. LC 79-7650. (Cambridge Studies in Social Anthropology: No. 30). (Illus.). 260p. 1981. 41.50 (ISBN 0-521-22993-6). Cambridge U Pr.
Kahn, Kathy. Fruits of Our Labor: U. S. & Soviet Workers Talk about Making a Living. LC 81-22708. 372p. 1982. 14.95 (ISBN 0-399-12698-8). Putnam Pub Group.
--Hillbilly Women. 1974. pap. 2.75 o.p. (ISBN 0-380-00171-3, 48371, Discus). Avon.
Kahn, Lloyd, ed. see Anderson, Bob.
Kahn, Lloyd, Jr., ed. Shelter. LC 73-5415. (Illus.). 1973. 20.00 (ISBN 0-394-48829-6); pap. 6.00 o.p. (ISBN 0-394-70991-8). Random.
Kahn, Lothar & Hook, Donald D. Conversational German One. 2nd ed. 1976. text ed. 11.95 (ISBN 0-442-22913-5); tapes 95.00 (ISBN 0-442-22914-3); cassettes 59.95 (ISBN 0-442-22917-8). Van Nos Reinhold.
--Intermediate Conversational German. 3rd ed. 1973. text ed. 11.95 (ISBN 0-442-22915-1); 18 tapes 80.00 (ISBN 0-442-22919-4). Van Nos Reinhold.
Kahn, Louis I. The Notebooks & Drawings of Louis I. Kahn. 2nd ed. Wurman, Richard S. & Feldman, Eugene, eds. 1974. 22.50 (ISBN 0-262-23065-8). MIT Pr.
Kahn, Mark L., ed. see National Academy of Arbitrators-15th Annual Meeting.
Kahn, Mark L., ed. see National Academy of Arbitrators-16th Annual Meeting.
Kahn, Mark L., ed. see National Academy of Arbitrators-17th Annual Meeting.
Kahn, Norma. More Learning in Less Time: A Guide to Effective Study. 2nd, rev. ed. 96p. (gr. 9-12). 1983. pap. text ed. 4.25x (ISBN 0-86709-037-5). Boynton Cook Pubs.
Kahn, Peggy. The Care Bears & the New Baby. LC 82-61961. (Care Bear Mini-Storybooks). (Illus.). 32p. (gr. 1-6). 1983. pap. 1.25 saddle-stitched (ISBN 0-394-85845-X). Random.
--The Care Bears' Book of ABC's. LC 82-18538. (Care Bear Mini-Storybooks). (Illus.). 40p. (ps-2). 1982. PLB 4.99 (ISBN 0-394-95808-X); pap. 3.95 (ISBN 0-394-85808-5). Random.
Kahn, R. L. & Cannell, C. F. Dynamics of Interviewing: Theory, Technique & Cases. 368p. 1957. 29.95x o.p. (ISBN 0-471-45441-9). Wiley.
Kahn, Richard. Selected Essays on Employment & Growth. LC 78-187079. 240p. 1972. 42.50 (ISBN 0-521-08493-8). Cambridge U Pr.
Kahn, Robert L. Work & Health. LC 81-11545. (Series on Organizational Assessment & Change). 216p. 1981. 21.95x (ISBN 0-471-05749-5, Pub. by Wiley-Interscience). Wiley.
Kahn, Robert L. & Cannell, Charles F. The Dynamics of Interviewing: Theory, Technique, & Cases. LC 82-9892. 378p. 1983. Repr. of 1957 ed. lib. bdg. write for info (ISBN 0-89874-493-8). Krieger.
Kahn, Robert L., jt. auth. see Katz, Daniel.
Kahn, Roger. The Boys of Summer. (RL 9). 1973. pap. 2.95 (ISBN 0-451-09954-0, E9954, Sig). NAL.
--The Seventh Game. 1983. pap. 3.50 (Sig). NAL.
Kahn, S. How People Get Power: Organizing Oppressed Communities for Action. 1970. pap. 3.95 (ISBN 0-07-033198-7, SP). McGraw.
Kahn, S. Benham, ed. Concepts in Cancer Medicine. Date not set. price not set (ISBN 0-8089-1486-3). Grune.
--Core Cancer Textbook. 1982. 39.50 (792227). Grune.

Kahn, Sanders A. & Case, Frederick E. Real Estate Appraisal & Investment. 2nd ed. LC 76-22316. 575p. 1977. 35.95x (ISBN 0-471-06566-8, Pub. by Wiley-Hamilton). Wiley.

Kahn, Sanford R., et al. Problems & Solutions in Introductory Accounting. 1979. pap. text ed. 8.95 (ISBN 0-8403-1957-6, 40195701). Kendall-Hunt.

Kahn, Waggoner. Provisions of the Internal Revenue Code & Treasury Regulations Pertaining to the Federal Taxation of Gifts, Trusts, & Estates 1983. 1983. pap. write for info. Little.

Kahn, Wolf. Pastel Light. LC 82-19152. (Contemporary Artists Ser.: No. 1). (Illus.). 50p. (Orig.). 1983. 10.95 (ISBN 0-930794-80-X). Station Hill Pr.

Kahoe, Walter. Arthur Morgan: A Biography & Memoir. LC 77-84817. (Illus.). 180p. 1977. 7.95 (ISBN 0-916178-01-3). Whimsie Pr.

Kahr, Madlyn M. Velazquez: The Art of Painting. LC 75-39563. (Icon Editions). (Illus.). 224p. 1976. 20.00i (ISBN 0-06-433575-5, HarpT); pap. 7.95i o. p. (ISBN 0-06-430079-X, IN-79, HarpT). Har-Row.

Kahrl, William L. Food Preparation. LC 78-57194. 1978. 6.95 (ISBN 0-86730-207-0). Lebhar Friedman.

--Food Service Cost Control. LC 78-57196. 1978. 6.95 (ISBN 0-86730-206-2). Lebhar Friedman.

--Food Service Equipment. LC 77-95260. 1977. 6.95 (ISBN 0-86730-203-8). Lebhar Friedman.

--Food Service Sanitation-Safety. LC 78-57192. 1978. 6.95 (ISBN 0-86730-205-4). Lebhar Friedman.

--Food Service Warehandling. LC 78-50680. 1978. 6.95 (ISBN 0-86730-204-6). Lebhar Friedman.

--Improving Food Service. LC 78-57193. 1978. 6.95 (ISBN 0-86730-209-7). Lebhar Friedman.

--Increasing Productivity & Sales. LC 80-81944. 1980. 6.95 (ISBN 0-86730-234-8). Lebhar Friedman.

--Meeting Challenges in Food Service. LC 74-15996. 224p. 1974. 18.95 (ISBN 0-86730-218-6). Lebhar Friedman.

--Menu Planning Merchandising. LC 78-57195. 1978. 6.95 (ISBN 0-912016-71-X). Lebhar Friedman.

--Modern Food Service Planning. LC 75-15518. (The Managing for Profit Ser.). 1975. pap. 6.95 (ISBN 0-86730-202-X). Lebhar Friedman.

--Wage Cost Control. LC 80-81945. 1980. 6.95 (ISBN 0-86730-233-X). Lebhar Friedman.

Kahrl, William L., ed. see California Governor's Office of Planning & Research.

Kai, Motonari, tr. see Soseki, Natsume.

Kaihara, S., jt. auth. see Lindberg, D. A.

Kailath, T. Lectures on Linear Least-Squares Estimation. (CISM International Centre for Mechanical Sciences: Vol. 140). (Illus.). 1979. pap. 17.20 (ISBN 0-387-81386-1). Springer-Verlag.

--Lectures on Wiener & Kalman Filtering. (CISM-International Centre for Mechanical Sciences Ser.: Vol. 140). 187p. 1982. pap. 16.90 (ISBN 0-387-81664-X). Springer-Verlag.

Kailath, Thomas. Linear Systems. (Information & Systems Sciences Ser.). (Illus.). 1980. text ed. 34.95 (ISBN 0-13-536961-4). P-H.

Kain, John F., et al. Essays on Urban Spatial Structure. LC 75-6871. 256p. 1975. prof ref 22.50x (ISBN 0-88410-411-7). Ballinger Pub.

Kain, Richard M. Dublin in the Age of William Butler Yeats & James Joyce. (Centers of Civilization Ser: No. 7). (Illus.). 1967. Repr. of 1962 ed. 8.95x (ISBN 0-8061-0535-6). U of Okla Pr.

Kain, Roger. Planning for Conservation: An International Perspective. 1981. 32.50 (ISBN 0-312-61400-4). St Martin.

Kainen, Paul C., jt. auth. see Saaty, Thomas L.

Kainz, Howard P. Hegel's Phenomenology: The Evolution of Ethical & Religious Consciousness to the Dialectical Standpoint. 260p. 1983. text ed. 23.95x (ISBN 0-8214-0677-9, 82-84457); pap. 12.95 (ISBN 0-8214-0738-4, 82-85074). Ohio U Pr.

--Wittenberg, Revisited: A Polymorphous Critique of Religion & Theology. LC 81-40729. 236p. (Orig.). 1982. lib. bdg. 21.75 (ISBN 0-8191-1949-0); pap. text ed. 10.75 (ISBN 0-8191-1950-4). U Pr of Amer.

Kairys, David, ed. The Politics of Law: A Progressive Critique. 1982. 22.50 (ISBN 0-686-37139-9); pap. 9.95 (ISBN 0-394-71110-6). Pantheon.

Kaiser, Ann, ed. Another Christmas in the Country. 108p. 1976. pap. 5.95 (ISBN 0-89821-015-1). Reiman Assocs.

--Cooking'n Crafts: Just for Kids. (Illus.). 84p. 1976. pap. 3.50 (ISBN 0-89821-014-3). Reiman Assoc.

--Crafts from the Country. (Illus.). 104p. 1978. pap. 7.95 (ISBN 0-89821-021-6). Reiman Assoc.

Kaiser, Carl W. History of the Academic Protectionist--Free Trade Controversy in America Before 1860. (Perspectives in American History Ser.: No. 60). 153p. Repr. of 1939 ed. lib. bdg. 17.50x (ISBN 0-87991-082-8). Porcupine Pr.

Kaiser, E. & Gabl, F., eds. Eleventh International Congress of Clinical Chemistry. (Illus.). xx, 1575p. 1982. 160.00x (ISBN 3-11-008447-3). De Gruyter.

--Sixth International Congress of Clinical Chemistry. xx, 1575p. 1982. 160.00x (ISBN 3-11-008447-3). De Gruyter.

Kaiser, E. T. & Kevan, L. Radical Ions. LC 67-20263. 800p. 1969. text ed. 41.00 (ISBN 0-470-45490-3, Pub. by Wiley). Krieger.

Kaiser, Georg. Gas One: A Play. Scheffauer, Herman, tr. LC 56-12398. (Coral Trilogy, Pt. 2). 8.00 o.p. (ISBN 0-8044-2450-0); pap. 3.95 (ISBN 0-8044-6343-3). Ungar.

Kaiser, Hannah, jt. auth. see Kaiser, Robert.

Kaiser, Hans E. Neoplasms - Comparative Pathology of Growth in Animals, Plants & Man. (Illus.). 900p. 1981. lib. bdg. 125.00 (ISBN 0-683-04503-2). Williams & Wilkins.

Kaiser, Joan E. A Comparison of Students: Practical Nursing Programs & Students in Associate Degree Nursing Programs. (League Exchange Ser.: No. 109). 78p. 1976. 5.50 (ISBN 0-686-38364-8, 23-1592). Natl League Nurse.

Kaiser, Karl & Schwartz, Hans-Peter, eds. America & Western Europe: Problems & Prospects. LC 78-19242. 448p. 1979. 16.95x (ISBN 0-669-02450-3). Lexington Bks.

Kaiser, M. A., jt. auth. see Grob, R. L.

Kaiser, Marjorie M., ed. Essays on Career Education & English: K-12. 132p. 1980. pap. 7.70 (ISBN 0-8141-1585-3, 79-21408); pap. 5.50 members (ISBN 0-686-86409-3). NCTE.

Kaiser, O'Neil. Impact of Federal Funding on Small School Districts. (Bulletin 20). 1976. 4.00 (ISBN 0-685-05658-9); member 4.00 (ISBN 0-685-05659-7). Assn Sch Busn.

Kaiser, Questa. That Reminds Me... LC 81-67424. 230p. (Orig.). (gr. 9-12). 1982. pap. text ed. 7.50x (ISBN 0-9603118-9-0). Davenport.

--That Reminds Me... 230p. 1982. 7.50x (ISBN 0-9603118-7-4). MD Bks.

Kaiser, Robert & Kaiser, Hannah. Russia from the Inside. (Illus.). 1980. 17.95 o.p. (ISBN 0-525-14886-8); pap. 10.95 o.p. (ISBN 0-525-47632-6). Dutton.

Kaiser, Robert B., jt. auth. see Haden, Pat.

Kaiser, Robert L., jt. ed. see Clark, David W.

Kaiser, W. A., ed. From Electronics to Microelectronics. 1980. 74.50 (ISBN 0-444-85481-9). Elsevier.

Kaiser, Walter C. A Biblical Approach to Personal Suffering. LC 82-2232. 1982. pap. 5.95 (ISBN 0-8024-4634-5). Moody.

Kaiser, Walter C., Jr. Classical Evangelical Essays in Old Testament Interpretation. 1972. pap. 8.95 (ISBN 0-8010-5314-5). Baker Bk.

--Ecclesiastes: Total Life. (Everyman's Bible Commentary Ser.). 1979. pap. text ed. 4.50 (ISBN 0-8024-2022-2). Moody.

--Old Testament in Contemporary Preaching. 1973. pap. 5.95 (ISBN 0-8010-5331-5). Baker Bk.

Kaisler, Stephen H. The Design of Operating Systems for Small Computer Systems. 800p. 1982. 32.00x o.s.i. (ISBN 0-471-07774-7, Pub. by Wiley-Interscience). Wiley.

Kai-yu Hsu. Wen I-to. (World Authors Ser.). 1980. lib. bdg. 15.95 (ISBN 0-8057-6422-4, Twayne). G K Hall.

Kajiya, F. & Kodama, S., eds. Comparmental Analysis. 200p. 1983. 79.25 (ISBN 3-8055-3696-8). S Karger.

Kakabadse, Andrew. Culture of the Social Services. 199p. 1982. text ed. 33.00x (ISBN 0-566-00366-X). Gower Pub Ltd.

--People & Organisations. 143p. 1982. text ed. 32.00x (ISBN 0-566-00373-2). Gower Pub Ltd.

Kakabadse, George, ed. Chemistry of Effluent Treatment. (Illus.). 1979. 33.00x (ISBN 0-85334-840-5, Pub. by Applied Sci England). Elsevier.

Kakac, Sadik & Yener, Yaman. Convective Heat Transfer. (Illus.). 512p. (Orig.). 1982. pap. text ed. 20.00 (ISBN 0-89116-347-6). Hemisphere Pub.

--Convective Heat Transfer. (Illus.). 512p. (Orig.). 1982. pap. text ed. 19.95 (ISBN 0-89116-347-6, Pub. by Middle East Tech U Turkey). Hemisphere Pub.

--Heat Conduction. (Illus.). 431p. (Orig.). 1982. pap. text ed. 20.00 (ISBN 0-89116-346-8, Pub. by Middle East Tech U Turkey). Hemisphere Pub.

Kakac, Sadik & Shah, Ramesh K., eds. Low Reynolds Number Flow Heat Exchangers. LC 82-3036. 1100p. 1983. text ed. 145.00 (ISBN 0-89116-254-2). Hemisphere Pub.

Kakak, S., et al. Heat Exchangers: Thermal-Hydraulic Fundamentals & Design. 1981. 60.00 (ISBN 0-07-033284-3). McGraw.

Kakalik, James S., jt. auth. see Brewer, Garry D.

Kakar, H. S. The Persistent Self: An Approach to Middlemarch. 1977. text ed. 8.50x (ISBN 0-391-01098-0). Humanities.

Kakar, Sudhir. Frederick Taylor: A Study in Personality & Innovation. 1970. 17.00x o.p. (ISBN 0-262-11039-3); pap. 4.95 (ISBN 0-262-61011-6). MIT Pr.

Kakavelakis, Demetris. Massa Confusa: A Vision for America. Anagnostopoulos, Athan, tr. from Gr. 70p. (Orig.). Date not set. pap. text ed. 7.95 (ISBN 0-916586-88-X). Hellenic Coll Pr.

Kakinuki, Nobulco. Adventures in Oriental Cooking. LC 72-79646. 231p. 1973. 8.25 o.p. (ISBN 0-87040-002-9). Japan Pubns.

Kakisu, Tsuneaki. The Family Tree of Painting. LC 81-22753. 154p. 1982. 10.95 (ISBN 0-686-97745-9). Philos Lib.

Kakiuchi, Shiro & Hidaka, Hiroyoshi, eds. Calmodulin & Intracellular Ca-Plus-Plus Receptors. 475p. 1982. 49.50x (ISBN 0-306-41109-1, Plenum Pr). Plenum Pub.

Kakkar, K. C., jt. auth. see Sethi, G. S.

Kakonis, Thomas E. & Scally, John. Writing in an Age of Technology. (Illus.). 1978. pap. text ed. 12.95x (ISBN 0-02-361890-6). Macmillan.

Kakonis, Tom E. & Hanzek, Donald. A Practical Guide to Police Report Writing. 1978. pap. text ed. 12.95 (ISBN 0-07-033246-0, G); teacher manual & key 4.00 (ISBN 0-07-033247-9). McGraw.

Kaku, Michio, ed. Nuclear Power, Both Sides: The Best Arguments for & Against the Most Controversial Technology. (Illus.). 384p. 1982. 14.95 (ISBN 0-393-01631-5). Norton.

Kakwani, Nanak. Income Inequality & Poverty: Methods of Estimation & Policy Applications. (World Bank Research Publications). (Illus.). 1980. 19.95 o.p. (ISBN 0-19-520126-4); pap. 12.95x (ISBN 0-19-520227-9). Oxford U Pr.

Kala, S. C. Terracottas of Allahabad Museum. 123p. 1981. text ed. 63.00x (ISBN 0-391-02234-2, Pub. by Abhinav India). Humanities.

Kalakian, Leonard H. & Eichstaedt, Carl B. Developmental Adapted Physical Education: Making Ability Count. LC 81-69952. 1982. text ed. 20.95x (ISBN 0-8087-1161-X). Burgess.

Kalan, P., jt. auth. see Bajec, A.

Kalashnikov, N. P. & Remizovich, V. S. Collisions of Fast Charged Particles in Solids. Erastov, Konstantin, tr. from Rus. 450p. 1983. price not set (ISBN 0-677-06080-7). Gordon.

Kalb, Marvin & Koppel, Ted. In the National Interest. 1977. 10.00 o.p. (ISBN 0-671-22656-8). S&S.

Kalbeck, Max, ed. Johannes Brahms: The Herzogenberg Correspondence. Bryant, Hannah, tr. LC 78-163787. 425p. Date not set. Repr. of 1909 ed. price not set. Vienna Hse.

Kalbus, Barbara H., jt. auth. see Neal, Kenneth G.

Kalbus, Barbara N. & Neal, Kenneth G. A Laboratory Manual for Human Physiology. 2nd ed. 1978. pap. text ed. 12.95x (ISBN 0-8087-1141-5). Burgess.

Kaldate, S. V. Society, Deinquent & Juvenile Court. 1982. 18.00x (ISBN 0-8364-0911-6, Pub. by Ajanta). South Asia Bks.

Kaldis, E., ed. Current Topics in Material Science, Vol. 9. 520p. 1982. 109.25 (ISBN 0-444-86274-9, North Holland). Elsevier.

--Current Topics in Materials Science, Vols. 1-6. 1978-80. Vol. 1. 127.75 (ISBN 0-7204-0708-7, North-Holland); Vol. 2. 163.00 (ISBN 0-7204-0740-0); Vol. 3. 117.00 (ISBN 0-444-85245-X); Vol. 4. 98.00 (ISBN 0-444-85348-0); Vol. 5. 93.75 (ISBN 0-444-85389-8); Vol. 6. 76.75 (ISBN 0-444-85420-7). Elsevier.

--Current Topics in Materials Science, Vol. 7. 1981. 127.75 (ISBN 0-444-86024-X, North Holland). Elsevier.

--Current Topics in Materials Science, Vol. 8. 1982. 104.25 (ISBN 0-444-86273-0). Elsevier.

--Current Topics in Materials Science, Vol. 10. 550p. 1982. 106.50 (ISBN 0-444-86321-4). Elsevier.

Kaldor. Clinical Enzymology. 256p. 1983. 27.50 (ISBN 0-03-063217-X). Praeger.

Kaldor, George & DiBattista, William J., eds. Aging: Aging in Muscle, Vol. 6. LC 78-4356. 244p. 1978. 24.00 (ISBN 0-89004-097-4). Raven.

Kaldor, Mary. The Baroque Arsenal. 1981. 14.95 (ISBN 0-8090-2812-3); pap. 7.25 (ISBN 0-8090-1501-3). Hill & Wang.

Kaldor, Nicholas. Strategic Factors in Economic Development. LC 67-65424. (Pierce Ser.: No. 1). 96p. 1967. 2.50 (ISBN 0-87546-024-0). ILR Pr.

Kale, Herbert W. Ecology & Bioenergetics of the Long-billed Marsh Wren Telmatodytes Palustris griseus (Brewster) in Georgia Salt Marshes. (Illus.). 142p. 1965. 8.00 (ISBN 0-686-35791-4). Nuttall Ornithological.

Kalechofsky, Roberta. George Orwell. LC 73-77054. (Literature & Life Ser.). 1973. 11.95 (ISBN 0-8044-2480-2). Ungar.

Kalecki, Michael. Selected Essays on the Dynamics of the Capitalist Economy, 1933-1970. LC 78-123667. (Illus.). 1971. 34.50 (ISBN 0-521-07983-7). Cambridge U Pr.

--Selected Essays on the Economic Growth of the Socialist & Mixed Economy, Vol. 2. LC 73-179162. (Illus.). 188p. 1972. 32.50 (ISBN 0-521-08447-4). Cambridge U Pr.

Kalecki, Michal. Introduction to the Theory of Growth in a Socialist Economy. Sadowski, Zdzislaw, tr. vi, 125p. Repr. of 1969 ed. pap. 5.95 (ISBN 0-87991-849-7). Porcupine Pr.

Kalectaca, Milo & Langacker, Ronald W. Lessons in Hopi. LC 77-20279. 1978. pap. 11.95x (ISBN 0-8165-0617-5). U of Ariz Pr.

Kaledin, Eugenia. The Education of Mrs. Henry Adams. LC 81-9431. (American Civilization Ser.). (Illus.). 306p. 1982. 24.95 (ISBN 0-87722-230-4). Temple U Pr.

Kaleialoha, Carol, jt. auth. see Hibbard, Don.

Kalellis, Peter M. Wedded or Wedlocked? LC 78-73624. (Illus., Orig.). 1979. pap. 2.75 o.p. (ISBN 0-8189-1157-3, 157, Pub. by Alba Bks). Alba.

Kaler, David, ed. see Raymond, Alex.

Kales, Frederick. Between Dawn & Dark. 1958. pap. 1.25 (ISBN 0-8358-0098-9). Upper Room.

Kalet, Beth. Kris Kristofferson. 1979. pap. 4.95 (ISBN 0-8256-3932-8, Quick Fox). Putnam Pub Group.

Kalewold, Alaka I. Traditional Ethiopian Church Education. LC 70-93506. pap. text ed. 4.95x (ISBN 0-8077-1597-2). Tchrs Coll.

Kaley, G. & Altura, B. M. Microcirculation, 3 vols. (Illus.). 1978. Vol. I 544 pp. text ed. 64.50 o.p. (ISBN 0-8391-0966-0); Vol. II 544 pp. text ed. 64.50 o.p. (ISBN 0-8391-0980-6); Vol. III 552 pp. text ed. 64.50 (ISBN 0-8391-0981-4). Univ Park.

Kaleya, Tana, photos by. Les Hommes. (Illus.). 104p. 1975. 19.95 o.p. (ISBN 0-517-52437-6). Crown.

Kalf, H., jt. auth. see Eastham, M. S.

Kalia & Vashista. Melting, Localization & Choas. 1982. 60.00 (ISBN 0-444-00695-8). Elsevier.

Kalian, Linda, jt. auth. see Kalian, Robert.

Kalian, Robert & Kalian, Linda. A Few Thousand of the Best Free Things in America. (Illus.). 1982. pap. 3.50. Roblin Enterprises.

Kalick, Laura L., jt. auth. see Holub, Steven F.

Kalicki, J. H. The Pattern of Sino-American Crises. LC 74-12967. (International Studies). (Illus.). 256p. 1975. 34.50 (ISBN 0-521-20600-6). Cambridge U Pr.

Kalimtgis, Konstandinos, et al. Dope, Inc. Britain's Opium War Against the U. S. Spannaus, N. & Frommer, L., eds. LC 78-26712. (Illus.). 400p. 1979. pap. 5.00 (ISBN 0-933488-00-9). New Benjamin.

--Dope, Inc. Britain's Opium War Against the U. S. 2nd ed. 1981. pap. 6.00 (ISBN 0-686-30565-5). New Benjamin.

Kalin, Berkeley & Robinson, Clayton, eds. Myths & Realities: Conflicting Values in America. (Mississippi Valley Collection Bulletin, No. 5). 78p. 1972. pap. 5.95x o.p. (ISBN 0-87870-081-1). Memphis St Univ.

Kalin, Everett R., tr. see Hengel, Martin.

Kalin, Walter. Das Prinzip des Non-Refoulement. 393p. (Ger.). 1982. write for info. (ISBN 3-261-05041-1). P Lang Pubs.

Kalinich, David B. The Inmate Economy. LC 79-9627. 128p. 1980. 16.95x (ISBN 0-669-03595-5). Lexington Bks.

Kalinnikova, Elena J. Indian-English Literature: A Survey. 248p. 1981. text ed. 15.25x (ISBN 0-391-02539-2). Humanities.

Kalir, Joseph. Introduction to Judaism. LC 79-6758. 170p. 1980. text ed. 19.75 (ISBN 0-8191-0948-7); pap. text ed. 9.50 (ISBN 0-8191-0949-5). U Pr of Amer.

Kalisch, Beatrice, jt. auth. see Kalisch, Philip A.

Kalisch, Beatrice, ed. see Alexander, Jeffrey A.

Kalisch, Beatrice, ed. see Buehler, Janice A.

Kalisch, Beatrice, ed. see Goodrich, Nancy M.

Kalisch, Beatrice, ed. see Halbur, Bernice T.

Kalisch, Beatrice, ed. see Kirchhoff, Karin T.

Kalisch, Beatrice, ed. see Minnick, Ann.

Kalisch, Beatrice, ed. see Rademaker, Analie J.

Kalisch, Beatrice, ed. see Redfearn, David J.

Kalisch, Beatrice, ed. see Zacur, Susan R.

Kalisch, Beatrice J. Child Abuse & Neglect: An Annotated Bibliography. LC 78-3123. (Contemporary Problems of Childhood: No. 2). 1978. lib. bdg. 39.95 (ISBN 0-313-20376-8, KBA/). Greenwood.

Kalisch, Beatrice J. & Kalisch, Philip A. Politics of Nursing. (Illus.). 544p. 1981. pap. text ed. 14.50 (ISBN 0-397-54245-3, Lippincott Nursing). Lippincott.

Kalisch, Philip, ed. see Alexander, Jeffrey A.

Kalisch, Philip, ed. see Buehler, Janice A.

Kalisch, Philip, ed. see Goodrich, Nancy M.

Kalisch, Philip, ed. see Halbur, Bernice T.

Kalisch, Philip, ed. see Kirchhoff, Karin T.

Kalisch, Philip, ed. see Minnick, Ann.

Kalisch, Philip, ed. see Rademaker, Analie J.

Kalisch, Philip, ed. see Redfearn, David J.

Kalisch, Philip, ed. see Zacur, Susan R.

Kalisch, Philip A. & Kalisch, Beatrice. Images of Nurses on Television. 1983. text ed. 22.50 (ISBN 0-8261-3870-5). Springer Pub.

Kalisch, Philip A., jt. auth. see Kalisch, Beatrice J.

Kalish, Harry I. From Behavioral Science to Behavior Modification. (Illus.). 448p. 1980. 23.95 (ISBN 0-07-033245-2). McGraw.

Kalish, Rafael, jt. auth. see Goldring, Gvirol.

Kalish, Richard A. Death, Grief & Caring Relationships. LC 80-18938. 350p. 1981. text ed. 18.95 (ISBN 0-8185-0417-X). Brooks-Cole.

--Guide to Effective Study. LC 78-32025. 1979. pap. text ed. 8.95 (ISBN 0-8185-0338-6). Brooks-Cole.

--The Psychology of Human Behavior. 5th ed. LC 82-12851. (Psychology Ser.). 500p. 1982. text ed. 21.95 (ISBN 0-534-01219-1). Brooks-Cole.

--Study Guide for the Psychology of Human Behavior. 5th ed. (Psychology Ser.). 144p. 1982. pap. text ed. 7.95 study guide (ISBN 0-534-01220-5). Brooks-Cole.

Kalish, Susan E., ed. see Schneiter, Paul H. & Nelson, Donald T.

Kalish, Susan S. Oriental Rugs in Needlepoint: Ten Charted Designs. (Illus.). 127p. 1982. 24.95 (ISBN 0-442-27420-3). Van Nos Reinhold.

Kaliske, G. Dictionary of Plastics Technology in English, German, French & Russian. 384p. 74.50 (ISBN 0-444-99687-7). Elsevier.

Kaliski, Burton S. Business Mathematics. 2nd ed. 1977. text ed. 16.95 o.p. (ISBN 0-15-505636-0, HC); instructor's manual with tests incl. o.p. (ISBN 0-15-505637-9); wkbk. 7.50 o.p. (ISBN 0-15-505638-7). HarBraceJ.

--Today's Business Math: A Text Workbook. 1975. pap. text ed. 12.95 o.p. (ISBN 0-15-592160-6, HC); instructor's manual avail. o.p. (ISBN 0-15-592161-4). HarBraceJ.

Kalita, Dwight & Philpott, William. Victory Over Diabetes. 275p. 1983. text ed. 18.95 (ISBN 0-87983-318-1). Keats.

Kalitina, N. Van Gogh. (Illus.). 1978. pap. 3.95 o.p. (ISBN 0-8109-2094-8). Abrams.

Kalkman, Markian E. & Davis, Anne B. New Dimensions in Mental Health-Psychiatric Nursing. 5th ed. 1979. text ed. 26.00 (ISBN 0-07-033253-3). McGraw.

Kall, Peter, jt. auth. see Feichtinger, Gustav.

Kallaher, M. J., ed. Affine Planes with Transitive Collineation Groups. 1981. 39.50 (ISBN 0-444-00620-6). Elsevier.

Kallai, Gyula. The People's Front Movement in Hungary. Gulyas, Gyula, tr. from Hungarian. 304p. (Orig.). 1979. pap. 7.50x (ISBN 963-13-0839-1). Intl Pubns Serv.

Kallas, James. Story of Paul. LC 66-19206. (Orig.). 1966. pap. 3.50 (ISBN 0-8066-0608-8, 10-6055). Augsburg.

Kallen, D., et al, eds. Social Science Research & Public Policy Making: A Re-Appraisal. (NFER Research Ser.). 370p. 1982. pap. text ed. 16.75x (ISBN 0-85633-246-1, NFER). Humanities.

Kallen, Horace M. Toward a Philosophy of the Seas. LC 72-97788. 70p. 1973. pap. 1.50x o.p. (ISBN 0-8139-0487-0). U Pr of Va.

--Zionism & World Politics: A Study in History & Social Psychology. LC 72-594. 345p. 1975. Repr. of 1921 ed. lib. bdg. 15.75x (ISBN 0-8371-5997-0, KAZI). Greenwood.

Kallen, Horace M., jt. auth. see Dewey, John.

Kallen, Horace M., tr. see Gross, Hans.

Kallen, Howard P. Handbook of Instrumentation & Controls: A Practice Design & Applications Manual for the Mechanical Services. 1983. Repr. of 1961 ed. cancelled o.p. (ISBN 0-89874-359-1). Krieger.

Kallen, Lucille. C. B. Greenfield: No Lady in the House. large print ed. LC 82-4903. 374p. 1982. Repr. of 1982 ed. 10.95 (ISBN 0-89621-365-X). Thorndike Pr.

--C. B. Greenfield: No Lady in the House. 208p. 1983. pap. 2.50 (ISBN 0-345-30870-0). Ballantine.

Kallenbach, Jessamine S., jt. auth. see Kallenbach, Joseph E.

Kallenbach, Joseph E. & Kallenbach, Jessamine S. American State Governors, 1776-1976, 3 vols. LC 76-51519. 1977. lib. bdg. 45.00 ea. (ISBN 0-379-00665-0). Oceana.

Kallet, Marilyn. Devils Live So Near. 75p. 1977. 3.50 o.p. (ISBN 0-87886-083-5). Ithaca Hse.

Kalley, Jacqueline A. The Transkei Region of Southern Africa, 1877-1978: An Annotated Bibliography. 1980. lib. bdg. 32.00 (ISBN 0-8161-8297-3, Hall Reference). G K Hall.

Kallgren, Joyce K., ed. The People's Republic of China After Thirty Years: An Overview. LC 79-89491. (China Research Monographs: No. 15). 1979. pap. 5.00x o.p. (ISBN 0-912966-21-1). IEAS.

Kallianpur, G., et al, eds. Statistics & Probability: Essays in Honour of C. R. Rao. 720p. 1982. 132.00 (ISBN 0-444-86130-0). Elsevier.

Kallick, Maureen, et al. Survey of American Gambling Attitudes & Behavior. 560p. 1979. pap. 22.00x (ISBN 0-87944-245-X). Inst Soc Res.

Kallio, Elmer, jt. auth. see Keiser, Ralph J.

Kallir, Jane. Austria's Expressionism. (Illus.). 100p. 1982. pap. 17.50 (ISBN 0-8478-0389-9). Rizzoli Intl.

--Grandma Moses: The Artist Behind the Myth. (Illus.). 1982. 25.00 (ISBN 0-517-54748-1, C N Potter Bks). Crown.

--Grandma Moses: The Artist Behind the Myth. (Illus.). 160p. (Orig.). pap. 15.00 (ISBN 0-910810-21-4). Johannes.

Kallir, Otto. Egon Schiele. 1968. 75.00 o.p. (ISBN 0-517-51324-2). Crown.

Kallman, Chester, jt. auth. see Auden, W. H.

Kallman, Chester, tr. see Brecht, Bertolt.

Kallman, Robert R., ed. see Hille, Einar.

Kallmann, Helmut, et al, eds. Encyclopedia of Music in Canada. 1100p. 1981. 85.00 (ISBN 0-8020-5509-5). U of Toronto Pr.

Kallo, D., jt. ed. see Szabo, Z. G.

Kallos, P., ed. Immunity & Concomitant Immunity in Infectious Diseases. (Progress in Allergy: Vol. 31). (Illus.). xvi, 364p. 1982. 118.75 (ISBN 3-8055-3464-7). S Karger.

Kallos, P., jt. ed. see Hanson, L. A.

Kalman, Harold & Roaf, John. Exploring Ottawa: An Architectural Guide to the Nation's Capital. (Illus.). 208p. (Orig.). 1983. pap. 10.95 (ISBN 0-8020-6395-0). U of Toronto Pr.

Kalman, Natalie & Waughfield, Claire. Mental Health Concepts. LC 81-70853. (Illus.). 256p. (Orig.). 1983. pap. text ed. 13.00 (ISBN 0-8273-1706-9); 3.25 (ISBN 0-8273-1707-7). Delmar.

Kalman, R. & Martinez, J. Computer Applications in Food Production & Agricultural Engineering. 1982. 42.75 (ISBN 0-444-86382-6). Elsevier.

Kalman, R. E., jt. ed. see Bennett, J. M.

Kalman, Sumner M. & Clark, Dennis R. Drug Assay: The Strategy of Therapeutic Drug Monitoring. LC 79-63201. 210p. 1979. 26.00x (ISBN 0-89352-053-5). Masson Pub.

Kalman, T. I., jt. ed. see Bardos, T. J.

Kalmanson, Kenneth & Kenschaft, Patricia C. Calculus: A Practical Approach. 2nd ed. LC 77-81756. (Illus.). xiv, 335p. 1978. text ed. 24.95x (ISBN 0-87901-083-5). Worth.

--Mathematics: A Practical Approach. LC 77-81755. (Illus.). 1978. text ed. 25.95x (ISBN 0-87901-085-1). Worth.

Kalmar, Gregory. Gandhism. LC 81-182559. (Studies of Developing Countries: No. 104). 82p. (Orig.). 1980. pap. 13.50x (ISBN 963-301-063-2). Intl Pubns Serv.

Kalodner, Howard I. & Fishman, James J. Limits of Justice: Courts' Role in School Desegregation. LC 77-1848. 1977. prof ref 25.00x (ISBN 0-88410-226-2). Ballinger Pub.

Kalpage, F. S. Tropical Soils: Classification, Fertility & Management. LC 75-20866. 300p. 1976. 25.00 (ISBN 0-312-81935-8). St Martin.

Kalpakgian, Mitchell. The Marvellous in Fielding's Novels. LC 80-1411. 243p. 1981. lib. bdg. 21.25 (ISBN 0-8191-1505-3); pap. text ed. 10.25 (ISBN 0-8191-1506-1). U Pr of Amer.

Kals, W. S. Land Navigation Handbook: The Sierra Club Guide to Map & Compass. LC 82-16917. (Outdoor Activities Guide Ser.). (Illus.). 288p. 1983. pap. 8.95 (ISBN 0-87156-331-2). Sierra.

--The Stargazer's Bible. LC 77-25598. (Outdoor Bible Ser.). (Illus.). 1980. pap. 4.95 (ISBN 0-385-13057-0). Doubleday.

Kalsner, Stanley, ed. The Coronary Artery. (Illus.). 784p. 1982. text ed. 75.00 (ISBN 0-19-520398-4). Oxford U Pr.

Kalson, Albert E., jt. auth. see De Vitis, A. A.

Kalstone, David. Five Temperaments: Elizabeth Bishop, Robert Lowell, James Merrill, Adrienne Rich, John Ashbery. LC 76-42655. 1977. 17.95x (ISBN 0-19-502260-2). Oxford U Pr.

Kalstone, David, ed. Selected Poetry & Prose of Sidney. pap. 1.25 o.p. (ISBN 0-685-47615-4, CY498, Sig Classics). NAL.

Kalstone, Shirlee & McNamara, Walter. First Aid for Dogs. LC 80-111390. (Illus.). 416p. 1980. 11.95 o.p. (ISBN 0-668-04863-8). Arco.

Kalt, Joseph P. The Economics & Politics of Oil Price Regulation: Federal Policy in the Post-Embargo Era. (Regulation of Economic Activity Ser.: No. 4). 336p. 1981. 40.00x (ISBN 0-262-11079-2). MIT Pr.

Kalt, Nathan. Introduction to the Hospitality Industry. LC 71-142505. 1971. text ed. 16.50 (ISBN 0-672-96086-9); tchr's manual 6.67 (ISBN 0-672-96088-5); wkbk. 7.95 (ISBN 0-672-96087-7). Bobbs.

Kaltenbach, G. E. Dictionary of Pronunciation of Artists' Names. 2nd ed. 74p. 1935. pap. text ed. 1.25 (ISBN 0-86559-000-1). Art Inst Chi.

Kalter, Joanmarie. Actors on Acting. LC 79-65062. (Illus.). 1981. pap. 8.95 (ISBN 0-8069-8976-9). Sterling.

--Actors on Acting: Performing in Theatre & Film Today. LC 79-65062. (Illus.). 1979. 13.95 (ISBN 0-8069-7026-X); lib. bdg. 16.79 (ISBN 0-8069-7027-8). Sterling.

Kalter, Suzy. Instant Parent. 312p. 1979. 12.95 o.s.i. (ISBN 0-89479-030-7). A & W Pubs.

Kalthoff, Robert J. & Lee, Leonard S. Productivity & Records Automation. (Illus.). 400p. 1981. text ed. 28.00 (ISBN 0-13-725234-X). P-H.

Kalton, G. Introduction to Statistical Ideas for Social Scientists. 1966. pap. 4.50x (ISBN 0-412-08460-0, Pub. by Chapman & Hall England). Methuen Inc.

Kaltsournis, T. Teaching Social Studies in the Elementary School: The Basics for Citizenship. 1979. 23.95 (ISBN 0-13-895631-6). P-H.

Kaluger. Profiles in Human Development. LC 75-37505. (Illus.). 236p. 1976. pap. 8.50 o.p. (ISBN 0-8016-2607-2). Mosby.

Kaluger, George & Kaluger, Merieum F. Human Development: The Span of Life. 2nd ed. LC 78-12022. (Illus.). 1979. 22.95 (ISBN 0-8016-2610-2). Mosby.

Kaluger, George & Kolson, Clifford. Reading & Learning Disabilities. 2nd ed. (Special Education Ser.). 1978. text ed. 23.95 (ISBN 0-675-08524-1). Merrill.

Kaluger, Merieum F., jt. auth. see Kaluger, George.

Kalupahana, David J. Buddhist Philosophy: A Historical Analysis. LC 75-20040. 224p. 1976. text ed. 10.00x o.p. (ISBN 0-8248-0360-4, Eastwest Ctr); pap. 4.95x (ISBN 0-8248-0392-2). UH Pr.

--Causality: The Central Philosophy of Buddhism. LC 74-76378. 320p. 1975. text ed. 12.00x (ISBN 0-8248-0298-5). UH Pr.

Kaluzny, Arnold D. & Veney, James E. Health Service Organizations: Research & Assessment of Health Services. LC 78-71810. (Health Care Ser.). 1979. 25.00 (ISBN 0-8211-1017-9); text ed. 22.95 ten or more copies (ISBN 0-685-63682-8). McCutchan.

Kaluzny, Arnold D., jt. auth. see Smith, David B.

Kalvelage, Carl & Segal, Morley. Research Guide in Political Science. 2nd ed. 1976. pap. text ed. 8.95x (ISBN 0-673-15298-7). Scott F.

Kalven, Bruce, et al. Value Development: A Practical Guide. 1982. pap. 10.00 (ISBN 0-8091-2445-9). Paulist Pr.

Kalven, H., Jr. & Clark, R.intro. by. Contempt: Transcript of the Contempt Citations, Sentences & Responses of the Chicago Conspiracy 10. LC 82-70399. 254p. (Orig.). 1970. 10.00 o.p. (ISBN 0-8040-0056-5); pap. 5.95x (ISBN 0-8040-0057-3). Swallow.

Kalven, Harry, Jr., jt. auth. see Gregory, Charles O.

Kalvius, G. M. & Tebble, R. S. Experimental Magnetism, Vol. 1. LC 79-50036. 346p. 1979. 76.95x (ISBN 0-471-99702-1, Pub. by Wiley-Interscience). Wiley.

Kalvoda, Josef. Czechoslovakia's Role in Soviet Strategy. LC 77-18499. 1978. pap. text ed. 13.50 (ISBN 0-8191-0413-2). U Pr of Amer.

Kalyanam, N. P. Common Insects of India. 1967. pap. 4.50x o.p. (ISBN 0-210-27166-3). Asia.

Kalyanaraman, A. Aryatarangini: The Saga of the Indo-Aryans, Vol. 1. 1969. 16.00x o.p. (ISBN 0-210-22271-9). Asia.

Kamakau, S. M. Ka Po'e Kahiko: The People of Old. Barrere, Dorothy B., ed. Pukui, Mary K., tr. (Special Publication Ser.: No. 51). (Illus.). 174p. 1964. pap. 8.00 (ISBN 0-910240-32-9). Bishop Mus.

--The Works of the People of Old: Na Hana A Ka Po'e Kahiko. Barrere, Dorothy B., ed. Pukui, Mary K., tr. LC 75-21315. (Special Publication Ser.: No. 61). (Illus.). 178p. 1976. pap. 8.00 (ISBN 0-910240-18-3). Bishop Mus.

Kamal, A. A. Everyday Fiqh, 2 vols. Set. pap. 14.95 (ISBN 0-686-63899-9). Kazi Pubns.

Kamal, M. H. & Wolf, J. A., Jr. Computational Methods In Ground Transportation Systems. (AMD Ser.: Vol. 50). 1982. 40.00 (H00234). ASME.

Kamal, Mounir M., jt. auth. see Hickling, Robert.

Kamali, S. A. Tahafatul Falasifa. 8.95 (ISBN 0-686-18600-1). Kazi Pubns.

Kamaraju, V., jt. auth. see Naidu, N. S.

Kamata, Satoshi. Japan in the Passing Lane: An Insider's Shocking Account of Life in A Japanese Auto Factory. LC 82-47881. 256p. 1983. 14.50 (ISBN 0-394-52718-6). Pantheon.

Kamath, M. V. The Journalist's Handbook. 240p. 1982. text ed. write for info. (ISBN 0-7069-1431-7, Pub. by Vikas India). Advent NY.

Kamath, Madhav V. The United States & India: Bicentennial Commemorative 1776-1976. LC 76-39929. lib. bdg. 25.00x slip case o.p. (ISBN 0-210-40588-0). Asia.

Kamath, S. U., jt. auth. see Murthy, H. V.

Kambe, H. & Garn, Paul D., eds. Thermal Analysis: Comparative Studies in Materials. LC 74-11511. 326p. 1975. 29.95x o.s.i. (ISBN 0-470-45567-5). Halsted Pr.

Kamen, Betty & Kamen, Sid. Kids Are What They Eat: What Every Parent Needs to Know about Nutrition. LC 82-18404. (Illus.). 1983. 12.95 (ISBN 0-668-05563-4, 5563). Arco.

Kamen, Gloria. Charlie Chaplin. LC 82-1674. (Illus.). 96p. (gr. 3-6). 1982. 10.95 (ISBN 0-689-30925-2). Atheneum.

Kamen, Henry. Spanish Inquisition. pap. 4.95 o.p. (ISBN 0-452-00493-4, F493, Mer). NAL.

Kamen, Sid, jt. auth. see Kamen, Betty.

Kamenetsky, Ihor. Nationalism and Human Rights: Processes of Modernization in the USSR. LC 77-1257. (Series in Issues Studies (USSR & East Europe): No. 1). 1977. lib. bdg. 18.50 (ISBN 0-87287-143-6). Libs Unl.

Kamenetz, Herman L. Dictionary of Rehabilitation Medicine. 1983. text ed. 21.95 (ISBN 0-8261-3320-7). Springer Pub.

Kamenka, E. & Neale, R. S. Feudalism Capitalism & Beyond. LC 75-32936. 1976. 16.95x o.p. (ISBN 0-312-28805-0). St Martin.

Kamenka, Eugene. Community As a Social Idea. LC 82-16850. 180p. 1983. 22.50x (ISBN 0-312-15302-3). St Martin.

--The Portable Karl Marx. 1983. 18.75 (ISBN 0-670-41173-6). Viking Pr.

Kamenka, Eugene, ed. Nationalism. LC 76-15051. 1976. 18.95x (ISBN 0-312-55965-8). St Martin.

Kamenka, Eugene & Erh-Soon Tay, Alice, eds. Human Rights. LC 78-4469. (Ideas & Ideologies Ser.). 1978. 16.50x o.p. (ISBN 0-312-39960-X). St Martin.

Kamenka, Eugene & Krygier, Martin, eds. Bureaucracy: The Career of a Concept. 1979. 22.50 (ISBN 0-312-10803-6). St Martin.

Kamenka, Eugene & Neale, R. S., eds. Vandalism, Capitalism & Beyond. LC 75-32936. 160p. 1976. 15.95 o.p. (ISBN 0-312-28805-0). St Martin.

Kamenka, Eugene, ed. see Marx, Karl.

Kamenka, Eugene, et al, eds. Law & Society: The Crisis in Legal Ideals. LC 78-7421. (Ideas & Ideologies Ser.). 1978. 22.50x (ISBN 0-312-47545-4). St Martin.

Kamenkay, Eugene & Smith, F. B. Intellectuals & Revolution. 22.50 (ISBN 0-312-41893-0). St Martin.

Kamenkovich, J. M. Fundamentals of Ocean Dynamics. (Elsevier Oceanography Ser.: Vol. 16). 1977. 70.25 (ISBN 0-444-41546-7). Elsevier.

Kamensky, Dennis. Winning on Your Income Taxes. 192p. 1982. 9.95 (ISBN 0-448-12329-0, G&D). Putnam Pub Group.

Kamerkar, Mani. British Paramountcy: British-Baroda Relations, 1818-1848. 253p. 1980. 34.50 (ISBN 0-940500-75-2, Pub by Popular Prakashan India). Asia Bk Corp.

Kamerman, Jack B. & Martorella, Rosanne, eds. Performers & Performances: The Social Organization of Artistic Work. (Illus.). 320p. 1983. text ed. 25.95x (ISBN 0-686-78911-3). J F Bergin.

Kamerman, Sheila B. & Kahn, Alfred J. Social Services in the United States: Policies & Programs. LC 75-35492. 573p. 1976. 17.50 (ISBN 0-87722-065-4); pap. text ed. 11.95 (ISBN 0-87722-066-2). Temple U Pr.

Kamerman, Sheila B., jt. auth. see Kahn, Alfred J.

Kamerman, Sylvia E., ed. Christmas Play Favorites for Young People. (Orig.). (gr. 4-12). 1982. pap. 7.95 (ISBN 0-8238-0257-4). Plays.

--Little Plays for Little Players. rev. ed. (gr. 1-6). 1969. 12.00 o.p. (ISBN 0-8238-0035-0). Plays.

Kamerschen, David R., jt. ed. see Danielson, Albert L.

Kamien, Marcia & Novak, Rose. Choices. 384p. (Orig.). 1982. pap. 2.95 (ISBN 0-345-29151-4). Ballantine.

Kamien, Max. The Dark People of Bourke: A Study of Planned Social Change. LC 78-64899. (AIAS Now Ser.: No. 1). (Illus.). 1978. text ed. 15.50x (ISBN 0-391-00947-8); pap. text ed. 11.25x (ISBN 0-391-00949-4). Humanities.

Kamien, R. Music: An Appreciation. 2nd ed. 1979. text ed. 23.50 (ISBN 0-07-033279-7); supplementary material avail. McGraw.

Kamien, Roger. Music: An Appreciation. 1976. text ed. 23.00 (ISBN 0-07-033266-5, C). McGraw.

Kamieniecki, Sheldon. Public Representation in Environmental Policymaking: The Case of Water Quality Management. (A Westview Replica Edition Ser.). 132p. 1980. lib. bdg. 20.00 (ISBN 0-89158-849-3). Westview.

Kamii, Constance. Number in Preschool & Kindergarten: Educational Implications of Piaget's Theory. 92p. 1982. pap. text ed. 6.50 (ISBN 0-912674-80-6, 103). Natl Assn Child Ed.

Kamii, Constance & DeVries, Rheta. Physical Knowledge in Preschool Education: Implications of Piaget's Theory. (Illus.). 1978. ref. ed. 22.95 (ISBN 0-13-669804-2). P-H.

--Piaget, Children & Number. new ed. LC 76-12224. (Illus.). 1976. pap. text ed. 2.00 o.p. (ISBN 0-912674-49-0). Natl Assn Child Ed.

Kamijo, ed. Monoamine Oxidase. (International Congress Ser.: Vol. 564). 1982. 91.50 (ISBN 0-444-90235-X). Elsevier.

Kamil, Michael L., jt. auth. see Gentile, Lance M.

Kamin, Franz. Ann Margaret Loves You & Other Psychotopological Diversions. LC 80-15325. 96p. 1980. ltd., signed ed. 20.00 (ISBN 0-930794-33-8); pap. 4.45 (ISBN 0-930794-32-X). Station Hill Pr.

Kamin, John. Hyperinflation: How You Can Come Out Ahead & Your Personal Financial Success Program. 32p. 1977. 5.00 (ISBN 0-911353-04-6). Forecaster Pub.

--The IMF-Engine of Inflation: How You Can Profit. 32p. 1979. 5.00 (ISBN 0-911353-05-4). Forecaster Pub.

Kamin, John V. Best Hope for the Young Investor to Become Financially Independent & Wealthy. 16p. 1975. 3.50 (ISBN 0-911353-08-9). Forecaster Pub.

--The Detroit Insider: How to Buy Three & Four Year Old Cars at Four Hundred & Less-How to Buy a New Car at Lowest Possible Prices-Classic Cars for Fun & Profit. Incl. How to Buy Three-Four Year Old Cars at Four Hundred Dollars & Less; How to Buy a New Car at Lowest Possible Prices; Classic Cars for Fun & Profit. 38p. 1981. pap. 6.00 (ISBN 0-911353-09-7). Forecaster Pub Co.

--How to Make Money Fast Speculating in Distressed Property. rev. ed. 343p. 1982. Repr. of 1976 ed. 15.00 (ISBN 0-911353-00-3). Forecaster Pub.

--How to Make Money in Coins. 312p. 1976. 15.00 (ISBN 0-911353-01-1). Forecaster Pub.

--How to Negotiate for Profit: Twenty-Five Ways to Buy Cheaper, Sell for More Money & Improve Your Lifestyle Through Better, Easier Negotiating. 32p. 1981. 6.00 (ISBN 0-911353-02-X). Forecaster Pub.

--How to Retire in Your Forties Financially Independent. rev. ed. 15p. 1979. 5.00 (ISBN 0-911353-03-8). Forecaster Pub.

--Power Secrets to Fast Money. 112p. 1975. 10.00 (ISBN 0-911353-06-2). Forecaster Pub.

--Up Your Gas: Sixty-One Ways to Cut Gas Consumption, Increase Your Mileage, Chop Costs & Minimize Waiting in Gas Lines! Plus Eleven Ways to Find a Good Mechanic & Save Money! Incl. Sixty-One Ways to Cut Gas Consumption; Increase Your Mileage, Chop Costs & Minimize Waiting in Gas Lines; Eleven Ways to Find a Good Mechanic & Save Money. 52p. 1979. lib. bdg. 6.00 (ISBN 0-911353-07-0). Forecaster Pub Co.

Kaminer, B. Search & Discovery: A Tribute to Albert Szent Gyorgy. 1977. 42.50 (ISBN 0-12-395150-X). Acad Pr.

Kamins, Robert M., jt. auth. see Ebel, Robert D.

Kamins, S. & Waite, M. Apple Backpack. 208p. 1982. 24.95 (ISBN 0-07-033356-4). McGraw.

Kamins, Theodore I., jt. auth. see Muller, Richard S.

Kaminska, Ruth T. I Don't Want to Be Brave Anymore. LC 78-17417. (Illus.). 1978. 10.95 (ISBN 0-915220-42-3). New Republic.

Kaminskaya, Dina. Final Judgment: My Life as a Soviet Defense Attorney. Glenny, Michael, tr. from Russian. 416p. 1983. 18.95 (ISBN 0-671-24739-5). S&S.

Kaminski, Patricia A., ed. see Flower Essence Society.

Kaminsky, Alice R. Chaucer's "Troilus & Criseyde" & the Critics. LC 79-27535. xiv, 245p. 1980. 17.95x (ISBN 0-8214-0428-8, 82-83178). Ohio U Pr.

Kaminsky, David B. Aspiration Biopsy for the Community Hospital. LC 81-11720. (Masson Monographs in Diagnostic Cytopathology: Vol. 2). (Illus.). 264p. 1981. 52.00x (ISBN 0-89352-154-X). Masson Pub.

Kaminsky, F. C., jt. auth. see Coleman, J. R.

Kaminsky, Howard. Simon De Cramaud & The Great Schism. 363p. Date not set. 35.00 (ISBN 0-8135-0949-1). Rutgers U Pr.

Kaminsky, Jack. Hegel on Art: An Interpretation of Hegel's Aesthetics. LC 61-14335. 1962. 14.00 o.p. (ISBN 0-87395-007-0); pap. 11.95x (ISBN 0-686-96895-6). State U NY Pr.

--Language & Ontology. LC 69-11516. 330p. 1969. 12.50x o.p. (ISBN 0-8093-0367-1). S Ill U Pr.

Kaminsky, Marc. All That Eyes Haved Witnessed: Aging, Reminiscence, Creating. 1981. cancelled 14.95 (ISBN 0-8180-2002-4). Horizon.

--A Table with People. LC 81-8913. 117p. (Orig.). 1982. pap. 6.00 (ISBN 0-915342-36-7). SUN.

Kaminsky, Marc & Supraner, Leon. Daily Bread. LC 82-7057. 160p. 1982. 14.95 (ISBN 0-252-01000-0). U of Ill Pr.

Kaminsky, Peter, jt. auth. see O'Rourke, P. S.

Kaminsky, Stuart. He Done Her Wrong: A Toby Peters Mystery. 192p. 1983. 10.95 (ISBN 0-312-36491-1). St Martin.

--High Midnight. 160p. 1981. 9.95 o.p. (ISBN 0-312-37234-5). St Martin.

Kaminsky, Stuart M. & Hill, Joseph F., eds. Ingmar Bergman: Essays in Criticism. (Illus., Orig.). 1975. pap. 8.95 (ISBN 0-19-501926-1, GB432, GB). Oxford U Pr.

Kamisar, Yale. Police Interrogation & Confessions: Essays in Law & Policy. 1980. 19.95x (ISBN 0-472-09318-5). U of Mich Pr.

Kamisar, Yale & LaFave, Wayne. Modern Criminal Procedure & Basic Criminal Procedure, 1982 Supplement. 5th ed. (American Casebook Ser.). 314p. 1982. pap. text ed. write for info. (ISBN 0-314-70397-7). West Pub.

Kamisar, Yale, et al. Basic Criminal Procedure, Cases, Comments & Questions. 5th ed. LC 52-52950. (American Casebook Ser.). 889p. 1980. pap. text ed. 20.95 (ISBN 0-8299-2109-5). West Pub.

Kamitses, Zoe. Moondreamer. 224p. 1983. 15.00i (ISBN 0-316-48260-9). Little.

Kamiya, Fuji, jt. ed. see Weinstein, Franklin B.

Kamke, Erich. Differentialgleichungen: Loesungsmethoden und Loesungen, Vol. 2: Partielle Differentialgleichungen Erster Ordnung Fuer eine Gesuchte Funktion. LC 49-5862. 243p. 1974. Repr. of 1967 ed. text ed. 14.95 (ISBN 0-8284-0277-9). Chelsea Pub.

Kamler, Howard. Communication: Sharing Our Stories of Experience. 300p. 1983. 24.95 (ISBN 0-937668-01-X). Psych Pr WA.

Kamm, Adrian Van see Van Kamm, Adrian & Healy, Kathleen.

Kamm, Adrian van see Van Kamm, Adrian & Muto, Susan A.

Kamm, Robert B. Leadership for Leadership: Number One Priority for Presidents & Other University Administrators. LC 81-43485. 184p. (Orig.). 1982. lib. bdg. 22.50 (ISBN 0-8191-2305-6); pap. text ed. 10.00 (ISBN 0-8191-2306-4). U Pr of Amer.

Kamman, Madeleine. Dinner Against the Clock. LC 72-94248. 1973. 10.00 o.p. (ISBN 0-689-10545-2). Atheneum.

--The Making of a Cook. LC 75-162974. 1978. pap. 9.95 (ISBN 0-689-70559-X, 238). Atheneum.

--When French Women Cook: A Gastronomic Memoir. LC 76-11582. 1976. 13.95 o.p. (ISBN 0-689-10747-1). Atheneum.

Kamman, Madeleine, jt. auth. see Gerard, Jacqueline.

Kammash, Terry. Fusion Reactor Physics: Principles & Technology. LC 74-14430. 1975. 39.95 (ISBN 0-250-40076-6). Ann Arbor Science.

Kammeier, Mary L. Profile of Hazelden Patients Discharged in 1976. 1.95 (ISBN 0-89486-068-2, 1406B). Hazelden.

Kammen, Michael. Colonial New York: A History. LC 75-5693. (A History of the American Colonies Ser.). 1975. lib. bdg. 30.00 (ISBN 0-527-18717-8). Kraus Intl.

--Deputyes & Libertyes: The Origins of Representative Government in the Colonial America. 1969. pap. text ed. 2.95x (ISBN 0-685-69589-1). Phila Bk Co.

--The Past Before Us: Contemporary Historical Writing in the United States. LC 79-25785. 552p. 1980. 29.95x (ISBN 0-8014-1224-2). Cornell U Pr.

--People of Paradox: An Inquiry Concerning the Origins of American Civilization. (Illus.). 1980. pap. 6.95 (ISBN 0-19-502803-1, GB 616). Oxford U Pr.

--A Season of Youth: The American Revolution & the Historical Imagination. (Illus.). 1980. pap. 7.95 (ISBN 0-19-502707-8, GB 597, GB). Oxford U Pr.

Kammer, Charles L., 3rd. The Kingdom Revisited: An Essay on Christian Social Ethics. LC 81-40045. 188p. (Orig.). 1981. lib. bdg. 20.75 (ISBN 0-8191-1737-4); pap. text ed. 10.75 (ISBN 0-8191-1738-2). U Pr of Amer.

Kammer, Jerry. The Second Long Walk: The Navajo-Hopi Land Dispute. 1982. pap. 9.95 (ISBN 0-8263-0642-X, S-70P). U of NM Pr.

Kammerer, Percy G. Unmarried Mother: A Study of 500 Cases. LC 69-14935. (Criminology, Law Enforcement, & Social Problems Ser.: No. 58). 1969. Repr. of 1918 ed. 15.00x (ISBN 0-87585-058-8). Patterson Smith.

Kammerer, W. Coptic Bibliography. Husselman, E. M. & Shier, L. A., eds. LC 50-9819. Repr. of 1950 ed. 22.00 o.s.i. (ISBN 0-527-47300-6). Kraus Repr.

Kammerer, William & Gross, Richard. Medical Consultation: Role of Internist on Surgical, Obstetrical & Psychiatric Services. 582p. 1983. lib. bdg. price not set (ISBN 0-683-04507-5). Williams & Wilkins.

Kammermeyer, K., jt. auth. see Hwang, S.

Kammermeyer, K. see Weissberger, A.

Kammerud, Jody. The Crow & the Fox: A Rebus Reader. 16p. 1982. 6.95 (ISBN 0-943124-03-4, Pub. by Third Century Pr). Educ Prog Dev.

--The Frog & the Bull: A Rebus Reader. 16p. 1982. 6.95 (ISBN 0-943124-02-6, Pub. by Third Century Pr). Educ Prog Dev.

--The Wolf & the Dog: A Rebus Reader. 16p. 1982. 6.95 (ISBN 0-943124-04-2, Pub. by Third Century Pr). Educ Prog Dev.

Kamoche, Jidlaph G. Imperial Trusteeship & Political Evolution in Kenya, 1923-1963: A Study of the Official Views & the Road to Decolonization. LC 81-40056. 462p. 1982. lib. bdg. 29.25 (ISBN 0-8191-1863-X); pap. text ed. 17.25 (ISBN 0-8191-1864-8). U Pr of Amer.

Kamoroff, Bernard. Small Time Operator: How to Start Your Own Small Business, Keep Your Books, Pay Your Taxes & Stay Out of Trouble. rev. ed. LC 76-29817. (Illus.). 1983. 14.00 (ISBN 0-917510-01-1); pap. 8.95 (ISBN 0-917510-00-3). Bell Springs Pub.

Kamp, Leo J. Vander see De Gruijter, Dato N. & Van Der Kamp, Leo. J.

Kamp, Leo Van der see Van Der Kamp, Leo J., et al.

Kampe, Livia. How to Learn Spanish the Easy Way. LC 79-6769. 192p. 1980. pap. text ed. 10.00 (ISBN 0-8191-0950-9). U Pr of Amer.

Kampen, N. G. van see Van Kampen, N. G.

Kampen, V. van see Van Kampen, V.

Kampf, Louis. On Modernism: The Prospects for Literature & Freedom. 1967. 17.50x (ISBN 0-262-11020-2). MIT Pr.

Kamps, Charles T. Peripheral Campaigns & the Principles of War: The British Experience, 1914-1918. 1982. 20.00 (ISBN 0-686-96384-9). MA-AH Pub.

Kamps, K. H., et al, eds. Category Theory, Applications to Algebra, Logic, & Topology: Proceedings, Gummersbach, FRG, 1981. (Lecture Notes in Mathematics Ser.: Vol. 962). 322p. 1983. pap. 16.00 (ISBN 0-387-11961-2). Springer-Verlag.

Kamrany, Nake, ed. The New Economics of the Less Developed Countries: Changing Perceptions in the North-South Dialogue. LC 77-14602. (Westview Special Studies in Social Political, & Economic Development Ser.). 1978. lib. bdg. 32.50 (ISBN 0-89158-449-8). Westview.

Kamrany, Nake M. U. S. Options for Energy Independence. LC 81-48394. 208p. 1982. 19.95x (ISBN 0-669-05361-9). Lexington Bks.

Kamrat, Mordechai & Samuel, Edwin, eds. Roots: A Hebrew-English Word List. (Illus.). 308p. 1982. pap. text ed. 7.50 (ISBN 0-686-38122-X). K Sefer.

Kamrin, Benjamin B. & Kamrin, Michael A. Handbook of Oral Diagnostic Concepts & Cues. LC 78-51141. 1978. pap. text ed. 10.50 (ISBN 0-8191-0472-8). U Pr of Amer.

Kamrin, Michael A., jt. auth. see Kamrin, Benjamin B.

Kan, Esther J., jt. auth. see Goodman, Kraines M.

Kanach, Sharon, tr. see Xenakis, Iannis.

Kanafani, A. & Sperling, D., eds. National Transportation Planning. 1982. lib. bdg. 27.50 (ISBN 90-247-2636-0, Pub. by Martinus Nijhoff Netherlands). Kluwer Boston.

Kanahele, George S., ed. Hawaiian Music & Musicians: An Illustrated History. LC 79-14233. (Illus.). 1979. 25.00 (ISBN 0-8248-0578-X). UH Pr.

Kanai, H. Classic Mauritiue. 175.00 (ISBN 0-85259-251-5). StanGib Ltd.

Kanai, Kiyoshi. Engineering Seismology. 250p. 1983. 34.50 (ISBN 0-86008-326-8, Pub. by U of Tokyo Japan). Columbia U Pr.

Kanal, L., jt. auth. see Krishnaiah, P. R.

Kanal, L. N. & Rosenfeld, A., eds. Progress in Pattern Recognition, Vol. 1. 1982. 53.25 (ISBN 0-444-86325-7). Elsevier.

Kanawada, Leo V., Jr. Franklin D. Roosevelt's Diplomacy & American Catholics, Italians, & Jews. Berkhofer, Robert, ed. LC 82-16077. (Studies in American History & Culture: No. 37). 194p. 1982. 39.95 (ISBN 0-8357-1382-2). Univ Microfilms.

Kanawati, N. The Rock Tombs of El-Hawawish: The Cemetery of Akhmim, Vol. 2. (Illus.). 51p. 1982. pap. text ed. 52.00x (Pub. by Aris & Phillips England). Humanities.

Kandel, Issac L. The Impact of the War Upon American Education. LC 73-17930. 285p. 1974. Repr. of 1949 ed. lib. bdg. 15.50x (ISBN 0-8371-7274-8, KAIW). Greenwood.

Kandel, Michael, tr. see Lem, Stanislaw.

Kandinsky, Wassily. Concerning the Spiritual in Art. 8.25 (ISBN 0-8446-5588-0). Peter Smith.

--Kandinsky: Complete Writings on Art, 2 Vols. Lindsay, Kenneth C. & Vergo, Peter, eds. LC 81-12798. (Documents of Twentieth Century Art Ser.). 1982. 60.00 (ISBN 0-8057-9950-8, Twayne). G K Hall.

Kandpal, T. C., jt. auth. see Mathur, S. S.

Kane, Andy. Tenant's Revenge: How to Tame Your Landlord. (Illus.). 96p. 1982. pap. 6.95 (ISBN 0-87364-258-9). Paladin Ent.

Kane, Barbara W., jt. auth. see Kane, Robert B.

Kane, Basil. The Official Chicago Sting Book. (Illus.). 160p. (Orig.). 1983. pap. 8.95 (ISBN 0-8092-5634-7). Contemp Bks.

Kane, Basil, jt. auth. see Chinaglia, Giorgio.

Kane, Basil, jt. auth. see Rote, Kyle, Jr.

Kane, Basil G. How to Play Soccer. rev. ed. LC 73-4460. (Illus.). 80p. 1976. pap. 3.95 o.p. (ISBN 0-448-12038-0, G&D). Putnam Pub Group.

Kane, Bernard. Retail Development Planning. 138p. 1982. 15.00 (ISBN 0-87005-411-2). Fairchild.

Kane, Betty. Ow & the Crystal Clear. LC 78-11753. (Illus.). (ps-3). 1979. 6.95 o.p. (ISBN 0-89742-021-7, Dawne-Leigh); pap. 4.95 o.p. (ISBN 0-89742-008-X). Celestial Arts.

Kane, Cornelius T. Habit: A Theological & Psychological Analysis. LC 78-64370. 1978. pap. text ed. 6.50 o.p. (ISBN 0-8191-0630-5). U Pr of Amer.

Kane, Daniel. The Eurodollar Market & the Years of Crisis. LC 82-16828. 224p. 1983. 25.00x (ISBN 0-312-26735-5). St Martin.

Kane, Dorothy N. Environmental Hazards to Small Children. 336p. 1983. 25.00 (ISBN 0-89946-150-6). Oelgeschlager.

Kane, Edward. Whisperings With Love. (Illus.). 64p. 1983. 6.95 (ISBN 0-89962-316-6). Todd & Honeywell.

Kane, G. R. Instant Navigation. (Illus.). 1977. pap. 7.95 o.p. (ISBN 0-87799-081-6). Aztex.

Kane, George. Piers Plowman: The Evidence for Authorship. 1965. text ed. 94.50x (ISBN 0-485-13502-7, Athlone Pr). Humanities.

Kane, Gerry. The CRT Controller Handbook. 224p. (Orig.). 1980. pap. 9.95 (ISBN 0-931988-45-4). Osborne-McGraw.

--The Sixty-Eight Thousand Microprocessor Handbook. 200p. (Orig.). 1981. pap. 9.95 (ISBN 0-931988-41-1). Osborne-McGraw.

Kane, Gerry, jt. auth. see Levinthal, Lance.

Kane, H. H. The Bicycle as a Factor in Genito Urinary Diseases, Prostratis, Prostatorrhea, or Prostatic Catarrh. 24p. Date not set. pap. 5.00 (ISBN 0-87556-575-1). Saifer.

Kane, H. Victor. Devotions for Dieters. 1973. pap. 1.95 o.p. (ISBN 0-8007-8108-2, Spire Bks). Revell.

Kane, Henry. The Tripoli Documents. 1976. 7.95 o.p. (ISBN 0-671-22334-8). S&S.

Kane, J. E., ed. Movement Studies & Physical Education: A Handbook for Teachers. 1978. 22.95x (ISBN 0-7100-8775-6); pap. 10.50 (ISBN 0-7100-8684-9). Routledge & Kegan.

Kane, J. Herbert. A Concise History of the Christian World Mission. 2nd ed. 1978. 7.95 (ISBN 0-8010-5395-1). Baker Bk.

--Global View of Christian Missions. 1971. 17.95 (ISBN 0-8010-5308-0). Baker Bk.

--Life & Work on the Mission Field. LC 80-65010. 1980. 14.95 (ISBN 0-8010-5406-0). Baker Bk.

--The Making of a Missionary. 160p. 1975. pap. 4.95 (ISBN 0-8010-5358-7). Baker Bk.

Kane, J. L. Operation Firelight. 1983. 8.95 (ISBN 0-533-05374-9). Vantage.

Kane, J. W. & Sternheim, M. M. Life Science Physics. 644p. 1978. 28.50 o.p. (ISBN 0-471-03137-2); tchrs' manual 8.00 o.p. (ISBN 0-471-03712-5); study guide 8.95 o.p. (ISBN 0-471-05432-1). Wiley.

Kane, Jack. Buzzard Bait. 192p. (YA) 1975. 6.95 (ISBN 0-685-54482-6, Avalon). Bouregy.

Kane, Jason, jt. auth. see Taylor, Charles G.

Kane, Jerry, jt. auth. see Osborne, Adam.

Kane, Joanne E., ed. see Mongillo, John F., et al.

Kane, John F. Pluralism & Truth in Religion. Dietrich, Wendell, ed. LC 80-20659. (American Academy of Religion Dissertation Ser.). 1981. 13.95 (ISBN 0-89130-413-4, 01-01-33); pap. 9.95 (ISBN 0-89130-414-2). Scholars Pr CA.

Kane, John R., jt. auth. see Baird, Joseph L.

Kane, Joseph N. Facts About the Presidents. 4th ed. 464p. 1981. 28.00 (ISBN 0-8242-0612-6). Wilson.

--Famous First Facts. 4th ed. 1350p. 1981. 60.00 (ISBN 0-8242-0661-4). Wilson.

Kane, Joseph W. & Sternheim, Morton M. Physics. 2nd ed. 752p. 1983. text ed. 28.50 (ISBN 0-471-08323-2). Wiley.

--Physics, SI Version. LC 80-17205. 664p. 1980. text ed. 30.95x (ISBN 0-471-08036-5); tchr's manual 13.50 (ISBN 0-471-08038-1). Wiley

Kane, Les A., ed. Process Control & Optimization Handbook for the Hydrocarbon Processing Industries. 248p. (Orig.). 1980. pap. 19.95x (ISBN 0-87201-144-5). Gulf Pub.

Kane, Lucile M. Guide to the Care & Administration of Manuscripts. 2nd ed. (Illus.). 1966. pap. 5.00 (ISBN 0-910050-02-3). AASLH.

Kane, Michael T. & Laskevich, Leonarda A. From Concept to Standardized Test. 48p. 1979. 3.95 (ISBN 0-686-38300-1, 17-1796). Natl League Nurse.

Kane, Michael T., jt. auth. see Sachs, Lorraine P.

Kane, Nancy M., jt. auth. see Herzlinger, Regina.

Kane, P. V. & Joshi, C. N., trs. Uttara Ramacharita of Bhavabhuti. 5th ed. 1971. pap. 16.95 (ISBN 0-89684-331-9). Orient Bk Dist.

Kane, Pandurang V. History of Dharmasastra, 5 vols. LC 43-20693. 1973. Set. 220.00x (ISBN 0-8002-0928-1). Intl Pubns Serv.

Kane, Patricia E., jt. auth. see Battison, Edward A.

Kane, Philip F. & Larrabee, Graydon B. Characterization of Semiconductor Materials. LC 79-81607. (Texas Instruments Electronics Ser.). 1970. 37.50 o.p. (ISBN 0-07-033273-8, P&RB). McGraw.

Kane, Robert B. & Kane, Barbara W. Frieghter Voyaging. LC 82-51070. (Illus.). 120p. (Orig.). 1982. pap. 7.95 (ISBN 0-910711-00-3). Voyaging Pr.

Kane, Robert L., jt. auth. see Kane, Rosalie A.

Kane, Robert L., ed. The Challenges of Community Medicine. LC 73-92198. (Illus.). 300p. 1974. text ed. 15.00 o.p. (ISBN 0-8261-1670-1). Springer Pub.

Kane, Robert L. & Kane, Rosalie A., eds. Values & Long-Term Care. LC 81-47581. 320p. 1982. 33.95x (ISBN 0-669-04685-X). Lexington Bks.

Kane, Robert L., et al. Geriatrics in the United States: Manpower Projections & Training Considerations. LC 80-8840. (Illus.). 208p. 1981. 21.95x (ISBN 0-669-04386-9). Lexington Bks.

Kane, Robert L., et al, eds. The Health Gap: Medical Services & the Poor. LC 75-30563. 1976. pap. text ed. 11.95 o.p. (ISBN 0-8261-1861-5). Springer Pub.

Kane, Rosalie A. & Kane, Robert L. Assessing the Elderly: A Practical Guide to Measurement. LC 81-47065. (A Rand Corporation Research Study). 320p. 1981. 19.95x (ISBN 0-669-04551-9). Lexington Bks.

Kane, Rosalie A., jt. ed. see Kane, Robert L.

Kane, Rosalyn & Wistreich, George. Biology for Survival: Text & Readings. LC 73-7358. (Illus.). 480p. 1974. pap. text ed. 15.95 (ISBN 0-02-475270-3). Macmillan.

Kane, Sandy, ed. see Vrooman, Christine W.

Kane, Thomas L. Ethiopian Literature in Amharic. 304p. (Orig.). 1975. pap. 37.50 (ISBN 3-447-01675-2). Intl Pubns Serv.

Kane, Thomas S. The Oxford Guide to Writing. Sommers, Nancy, ed. (Illus.). 650p. 1983. 14.95 (ISBN 0-19-503245-4). Oxford U Pr.

Kane, Tricky R. Wordy Gurdy, No. 2. 160p. (gr. 6 up). 1982. pap. 1.95 (ISBN 0-441-90896-9). Ace Bks.

Kaneko, Akitomo. Olympic Gymnastics. LC 76-1171. (Illus.). 256p. 1980. pap. 9.95 (ISBN 0-8069-8926-2). Sterling.

Kaneko, Erika & Melichar, Herbert. Pura Mutuzuma: Archaeological Work on Miyako Island, Ryukyus. (Social Science & Linguistics Institute Special Publications). (Illus.). 144p. 1972. pap. 6.00s (ISBN 0-8248-0245-4). UH Pr.

Kaneko, Takeo, et al, eds. Synthetic Production & Utilization of Amino Acids. LC 74-9924. 312p. 1974. 39.95x o.s.i. (ISBN 0-470-45590-X). Halsted Pr.

Kanely, Edna A. Cumulative Index to Hickcox's Monthly Catalog of U. S. Government Publications, 1885-1894, 3 vols. 1978. lib. bdg. 275.00 (ISBN 0-8408-0018-5). Res Pubns Conn.

--Cumulative Subject Index to the Monthly Catalog of U. S. Government Publications, 1895-1899, 2 vols. LC 77-93744. 1978. Set. lib. bdg. 195.00 (ISBN 0-8408-0016-9). Res Pubns Conn.

Kaner, N., tr. see Emanuel, N. M. & Evseenko, D. S.

Kaner, N., tr. see Kiselev, A. V. & Lygin, V. I.

Kaner, N., tr. see Kurtsin, I. T.

Kaner, N., tr. see Vinogradov, A. P. & Udintsev, G. B.

Kanet, Roger E. Soviet & East European Foreign Policy: A Bibliography of English & Russian-Language Publications, 1967-1971. LC 74-76444. 208p. 1974. text ed. 21.75 o.p. (ISBN 0-87436-137-0). ABC-Clio.

Kanet, Roger E. & Simon, Maurice D. Background to Crisis: Policy & Politics in Gierek's Poland. (Westview Replica Edition). 1980. lib. bdg. 18.75 (ISBN 0-89158-393-9). Westview.

Kanet, Roger E., ed. Soviet Foreign Policy & East-West Relations. LC 82-3649. (Pergamon Policy Studies on International Politics.Ser.). 212p. 1982. 25.00 (ISBN 0-08-029366-2, K125). Pergamon.

--Soviet Foreign Policy in the 1980's. 378p. 1982. 31.95 (ISBN 0-03-059314-X); pap. 13.95 (ISBN 0-03-059316-6). Praeger.

Kanetzke, Howard W. Airplanes & Balloons. LC 77-27532. (Read About Science Ser.). (Illus.). (gr. k-3). 1978. PLB 13.30 (ISBN 0-8393-0090-5). Raintree Pubs.

--Story of Cars. LC 77-27533. (Read About Science Ser.). (Illus.). (gr. k-3). 1978. PLB 13.30 (ISBN 0-8393-0086-7). Raintree Pubs.

--Trains & Railroads. LC 77-27599. (Read About Science Ser.). (Illus.). (gr. k-3). 1978. PLB 13.30 (ISBN 0-8393-0087-5). Raintree Pubs.

Kanfer, F. H. & Goldstein, A. P. Helping People Change. 1975. 23.10 o.p. (ISBN 0-08-018272-0); pap. 10.45 o.p. (ISBN 0-08-018271-2). Pergamon.

Kanfer, Stefan. Fear Itself. 216p. 1981. 12.95 (ISBN 0-399-12607-4). Putnam Pub Group.

Kang, C. H. & Nelson, Ethel. The Discovery of Genesis. 1979. pap. 5.95 (ISBN 0-570-03792-1, 12-2755). Concordia.

Kang, Tai S., ed. Nationalism & the Crises of Ethnic Minorities in Asia. LC 78-19295. (Contributions in Sociology Ser.: No. 34). (Illus.). 1979. lib. bdg. 25.00x (ISBN 0-313-20623-6, KNA/). Greenwood.

Kangas, Robert. Making Money As a Bartender in Your Spare Time. (Illus.). 144p. (Orig.). 1982. pap. 4.76i (ISBN 0-06-463557-0, EH 557, EH). B&N NY.

--The Old House Rescue Book: Buying & Renovating on a Budget. 330p. 1982. 19.95 (ISBN 0-8359-5213-4); pap. 12.95 (ISBN 0-686-96870-0). Reston.

Kanger, S., ed. see Symposium, Scandinavian Logic, 3rd.

Kanin, David B. A Political History of the Olympic Games. (Replica Edition Ser.). 160p. 1981. lib. bdg. 18.00 (ISBN 0-86531-109-9). Westview.

Kanin, Garson. Moviola. 1979. 9.95 o.p. (ISBN 0-671-24822-7). S&S.

--Together Again! the Great Movie Teams. Date not set. 19.95 o.p. (ISBN 0-448-14307-0, G&D). Putnam Pub Group. Postponed.

Kanis, A., jt. auth. see Croft, J. R.

Kanitkar, Helen & Kanitkar, Hemant. Asoka & Indian Civilization. Yapp, Malcolm, et al, eds. (World History Ser.). (Illus.). 32p. (gr. 10). 1980. Repr. lib. bdg. 6.95 (ISBN 0-89908-035-9); pap. text ed. 2.25 (ISBN 0-89908-010-3). Greenhaven.

Kanitkar, Hemant, jt. auth. see Kanitkar, Helen.

Kanitkar, Tara, jt. auth. see Rele, J. R.

Kanitz, H. Mike, jt. auth. see Morris, Kenneth T.

Kann. The American Left: Failures & Fortunes. 256p. 1982. 26.95 (ISBN 0-03-061772-3). Praeger.

Kann, Edward. The Currencies of China. (Illus.). 1978. Repr. of 1926 ed. lib. bdg. 39.50 (ISBN 0-915262-22-3). S J Durst.

Kann, Kenneth. Joe Rapoport: The Life of a Jewish Radical. (Illus.). 350p. 1980. 29.95 (ISBN 0-87722-208-8). Temple U Pr.

Kann, Mark E. Thinking About Politics: Two Political Sciences. 1980. pap. text ed. 11.50 (ISBN 0-8299-0314-3). West Pub.

Kann, Mark E., ed. The Future of American Democracy: Views from the Left. 1983. write for info. (ISBN 0-87722-288-6). Temple U Pr.

Kann, Mark E., jt. ed. see Diggins, John P.

Kann, Robert A. A History of the Habsburg Empire, 1526-1918. LC 72-97733. 1974. 55.00x (ISBN 0-520-02408-7); pap. 11.95x (ISBN 0-520-04206-9, CAMPUS 265). U of Cal Pr.

Kann, Robert A. & David, Zdenek V. The Peoples of the Eastern Habsburg Lands, 1526-1918. 1983. write for info. U of Wash Pr.

Kannan. Downsizing Detroit. 202p. 1982. 28.95 (ISBN 0-03-060597-0). Praeger.

Kannappan, Subbiah. Employment Problems & the Urban Labor Market in Developing Nations. (Illus.). 260p. (Orig.). 1983. pap. price not set (ISBN 0-87712-224-5). U Mich Busn Div Res.

Kannenstine, Louis F. The Art of Djuna Barnes: Duality & Damnation. LC 76-55152. 1977. 19.50x (ISBN 0-8147-4564-4); pap. 9.50x (ISBN 0-8147-4565-2). NYU Pr.

Kanner, L. Childhood Psychosis: Initial Studies & New Insights. LC 73-2855. 283p. 1973. 10.95x o.s.i. (ISBN 0-470-45610-8). Halsted Pr.

Kanno, C. K. & Scheidemandel, P. L. Psychiatric Treatment in the Community. 1974. 4.00 o.p. (ISBN 0-685-65572-5, 207). Am Psychiatric.

Kanno, Charles & Scheidemandel, Patricia L. The Mentally Ill Offender: A Survey of Treatment Programs. 76p. 1969. pap. 3.00 o.p. (ISBN 0-685-24860-7, P244-0). Am Psychiatric.

Kanno, Charles K. & Scheidemandel, Patricia L. Salary Ranges of Personnel Employed in State Mental Hospitals & Community Mental Health Centers-1970. pap. 5.00 o.p. (ISBN 0-685-24871-2, P156-0). Am Psychiatric.

Kanno, T., ed. Paraneurons: Their Features & Functions. (International Congress Ser.: No. 552). 1981. 45.75 (ISBN 0-444-90194-9). Elsevier.

Kanocz, Otto. Career & Occupational Literature: A Current Annotated Bibliography & Resource for Occupations. LC 79-88880. 1979. pap. 2.00 o.p. (ISBN 0-934186-00-6). Fed Employ & Guidance.

Kanok-Nukulchai, Worsak, ed. see International Conference Held in Bangkok, Jan. 7-9, 1980 & Karasudhi, Pisidhi.

Kanowitz, Leo. Equal Rights: The Male Stake. LC 81-52056. 168p. 1981. 19.95o.p. (ISBN 0-8263-0594-6); pap. 9.95 (ISBN 0-8263-0595-4). U of NM Pr.

--Sex Roles in Law & Society: 1974 Supplement. LC 72-94656. 1974. pap. 4.00x o.p. (ISBN 0-8263-0328-5). U of NM Pr.

--Women & the Law: The Unfinished Revolution. LC 70-78551. 1969. pap. 7.95x o.p. (ISBN 0-8263-0173-8). U of NM Pr.

Kansas State Historical Society Staff & Miller, Nyle H. Kansas: The Thirty-Fourth Star. LC 76-4385. (Illus.). 1977. 6.00 o.p. (ISBN 0-87726-003-6). Kansas St Hist.

Kansas State University. Practical Cookery: A Compilation of Principles of Cookery & Recipes. 24th ed. LC 20-21946. 281p. 1976. text ed. 23.95x (ISBN 0-471-45641-1). Wiley.

Kansky, Karel J. Urbanization Under Socialism: The Case of Czechslovakia. LC 75-44934. (Special Studies). (Illus.). 334p. 1976. 37.95 o.p. (ISBN 0-275-56770-2). Praeger.

Kansler, Connie, jt. ed. see Green, Lawrence.

Kant, Immanuel. The Basic Foundations of Transcendental Logic. (The Essential Library of the Great Philosophers). (Illus.). 109p. 1983. Repr. of 1888 ed. 87.45 (ISBN 0-89901-083-0). Found Class Reprints.

--Critique of Practical Reason. Beck, Lewis W., tr. LC 56-2993. 1956. pap. 5.95 (ISBN 0-672-60223-7, LLA52). Bobbs.

--Critique of Pure Reason. Smith, Norman K., ed. 1969. 19.95 o.p. (ISBN 0-312-45045-1); pap. 9.95 (ISBN 0-312-45010-9). St Martin.

--Foundations of the Metaphysics of Morals. Beck, Lewis W., tr. Bd. with What Is Enlightenment. LC 59-11679. 1959. pap. 3.95 (ISBN 0-672-60312-8, LLA113). Bobbs.

--Grounding for the Metaphysics of Morals. Ellington, James W., tr. from Ger. (HPC Philosophical Classics Ser.). 125p. 1981. lib. bdg. 12.50 (ISBN 0-915145-01-4); pap. text ed. 2.95 (ISBN 0-915145-00-6). Hackett Pub.

--The Idea & the Ideal of Beauty. (Illus.). 121p. 1983. 79.85 (ISBN 0-89901-107-1). Found Class Reprints.

--Kant's Cosmogony: As in His Essay on Retardation of the Rotation of the Earth. Hastie, W., tr. (Contributions in Philosophy, No. 1). 1968. lib. bdg. 25.00 (ISBN 0-8371-1500-0, KAH/). Greenwood.

--Kant's Ethical Philosophy. Ellington, James W., tr. LC 82-1086. (HPC Philosophical Classics Ser.). 324p. 1982. lib. bdg. 19.50 (ISBN 0-915145-44-8); pap. text ed. 7.50 (ISBN 0-915145-43-X). Hackett Pub.

--Kant's Theory of the Summum Bonum. (The Essential Library of the Great Philosophers). (Illus.). 103p. 1983. Repr. of 1888 ed. 81.75 (ISBN 0-89901-084-9). Found Class Reprints.

--Lectures on Ethics. Infield, Louis, tr. from Ger. (ISBN 0-915144-26-3). pap. text ed. 6.95. Hackett Pub.

--On History. Beck, Lewis W., ed. Beck, L. W., et al, trs. LC 62-22315. (Orig.). 1963. pap. 4.95 (ISBN 0-672-60387-X, LLA162). Bobbs.

--Perpetual Peace. Smith, Campbell, tr. (Most Meaningful Classics in World Culture Ser.). (Illus.). 111p. 1983. 69.85 (ISBN 0-89266-386-3). Am Classical Coll Pr.

--Perpetual Peace & Other Essays on Politics, History, & Morals. Humphrey, Ted, ed. & tr. from Ger. LC 82-11748. (HPC Philosophical Classics Ser.). 152p. 1982. lib. bdg. 13.50 (ISBN 0-915145-48-0); pap. text ed. 2.95 (ISBN 0-915145-47-2). Hackett Pub.

--Philosophy of Law. Hastie, W., tr. LC 77-146882. 265p. Repr. of 1887 ed. lib. bdg. 19.50x (ISBN 0-678-01152-4). Kelley.

--Prolegomena to Any Future Metaphysics That Will Be Able to Come Forward As Science. new ed. Ellington, J. W., ed. Carus, Paul, tr. LC 76-51051. 1977. 12.50 (ISBN 0-915144-33-6); pap. 2.95 (ISBN 0-915144-25-5). Hackett Pub.

Kant, Sharad. Practical Approach to Cobol Programming. 250p. 1983. 19.95 (ISBN 0-470-27392-5). Halsted Pr.

Kanta, A. The Late Minoan III Period in Crete: A Survey of Sites, Pottery & Their Distribution. (Studies in Mediterranean Archaeology: Vol. 58). (Illus.). 540p. 1980. pap. text ed. 119.75x (ISBN 91-85058-95-5). Humanities.

Kantar, Edwin. Test Your Bridge Play. 1974. pap. 5.00 (ISBN 0-87980-286-3). Wilshire.

Kanter, Arnold. Defense Politics: A Budgetary Perspective, the Ounce of Prevention Fund. LC 78-21848. (Illus.). viii, 152p. 1983. pap. 5.95 (ISBN 0-226-42374-3). U of Chicago Pr.

Kanter, Arnold B. The Secret Memoranda of Stanley J. Fairweather: As Purloined from the Files of the Law Firm of Fairweather, Winters & Sommmers. LC 82-79796. 134p. 1981. pap. 4.95 (ISBN 0-8040-0420-X). Swallow.

Kanter, Marianne, jt. auth. see Segal, Brenda L.

Kanter, Rosabeth M. The Changemasters: Innovation for Productivity in the American Corporation. 1983. 16.50 (ISBN 0-671-42802-0). S&S.

--Work & Family in the United States: A Critical Review & Agenda for Research & Policy. LC 76-46870. (Social Science Frontiers Ser.). 120p. 1977. pap. 4.00x (ISBN 0-87154-433-4). Russell Sage.

Kanter, Sanford, jt. auth. see Quinn, Sandra L.

Kanter, Sanford B., jt. auth. see Quinn, Sandra L.

Kantin & Mehra. Wonderland Nepal. 1980. pap. 9.95 (ISBN 0-933982-27-5, Lascelles). Bradt Ent.

Kantor, MacKinlay. Gentle Annie. 1980. lib. bdg. 10.95 (ISBN 0-8398-2688-5, Gregg). G K Hall.

--The Voice of Bugle Ann & the Daughter of Bugle Ann. 192p. 1980. pap. 1.95 o.s.i. (ISBN 0-515-05458-5). Jove Pubns.

Kantor, MacKinley. Andersonville. 1971. pap. 3.95 (ISBN 0-451-11324-1, AE1324, Sig). NAL.

Kantor, Michael, jt. auth. see Earle, Olive L.

Kantor, Seth. Who Was Jack Ruby? LC 78-54078. 1978. 10.95 (ISBN 0-89696-004-8, An Everest House Book). Dodd.

Kantor-Gukovskaya, Asia. Gauguin. (Illus.). 1978. pap. 4.95 o.p. (ISBN 0-8109-2153-7). Abrams.

Kantorovich, L. V. & Akilov, G. P. Functional Analysis. 2nd ed. LC 80-41734. 600p. 1982. 100.00 (ISBN 0-08-023036-9, D125); pap. 25.00 (ISBN 0-08-026486-7). Pergamon.

Kantowicz, E., jt. auth. see Walzer, Michael.

Kantowicz, Edward. Corporation Sole: Cardinal Mundelein & Chicago Catholicism. LC 82-13420. (Notre Dame Studies in American Catholicism). 320p. 1983. text ed. 19.95 (ISBN 0-268-00738-1); pap. text ed. 9.95 (ISBN 0-268-00739-X). U of Notre Dame Pr.

Kantowitz, Barry H. & Roediger, Henry L., III. Experimental Psychology. 1978. 24.50 (ISBN 0-395-30814-3); Instr's. manual 3.00. HM.

Kantowitz, Barry H. & Sorkin, Robert D. Human Factors: Understanding People-System Relationships. 600p. 1983. text ed. 30.95x (ISBN 0-471-09594-X); tchr's. manual avail. (ISBN 0-471-87201-6); lab. manual avail. (ISBN 0-471-87200-8). Wiley.

Kantowitz, Barry H., ed. Human Information Processing: Tutorials in Performance & Cognition. LC 74-19028. (Experimental Psychology Ser.). 365p. 1974. 19.95x o.s.i. (ISBN 0-470-45674-4). Halsted Pr.

Kantrovich, Jerald M. Riffle the Deck. (Illus., Orig.). 1978. pap. text ed. 5.55 o.p. (ISBN 0-933282-03-6). Stack the Deck.

Kantrowitz, Arnie. Under the Rainbow: Growing up Gay. LC 76-30442. (Illus.). 1977. 8.95 o.p. (ISBN 0-688-03191-9). Morrow.

Kantrowitz, Barbara, jt. auth. see Haber, Michelle I.

Kantrowitz, Martin P., et al. Que Paso? An English-Spanish Guide for Medical Personnel. 3rd ed. LC 78-55709. (Illus.). 1978. pap. 3.95 (ISBN 0-8263-0488-5). U of NM Pr.

Kantrowitz, Walter & Eisenberg, Howard. How to Be Your Own Lawyer (Sometimes) LC 78-5053. 1979. 12.95 o.p. (ISBN 0-399-11985-X). Putnam Pub Group.

--How to Be Your Own Lawyer (Sometimes) 1980. pap. 6.95 (ISBN 0-399-50457-5, Perigee). Putnam Pub Group.

Kantzer, Kenneth, jt. auth. see Nicholls, Bruce.

Kanuk, Leslie L., jt. auth. see Schiffman, Leon G.

Kany, Charles E. The Beginnings of the Epistolatory Novel in France, Italy, & Spain. (Studies in Comparative Literature: No. 6). (Illus.). 158p. Repr. of 1937 ed. lib. bdg. 17.50x (ISBN 0-87991-505-6). Porcupine Pr.

Kany, Charles K., jt. auth. see Speroni, Charles.

Kanyeihamba, G. W. & McAuslan, J. P., eds. Studies of Law in Social Change & Development: Urban Legal Problems in Eastern Africa, No. 2. 15.00 (ISBN 0-686-35896-1); pap. 10.00 (ISBN 0-686-37200-X). Intl Ctr Law.

Kanza, Thomas R. Africa Must Change: An African Manifesto. LC 78-21067. 25p. 1979. text ed. 2.50 o.p. (ISBN 0-87073-914-X); pap. text ed. 1.00 (ISBN 0-87073-915-8). Schenkman.

Kao, C. K. Optical Fiber Technology II. LC 80-25665. 343p. 1981. 29.95x (ISBN 0-471-09169-3, Pub. by Wiley-Interscience); pap. 19.50x (ISBN 0-471-09171-5, Pub. by Wiley-Interscience). Wiley.

Kao, Charles C. Psychological & Religious Development: Maturity & Maturation. LC 80-5852. 382p. (Orig.). 1981. lib. bdg. 23.75 (ISBN 0-8191-1759-5); pap. text ed. 13.50 (ISBN 0-8191-1760-9). U Pr of Amer.

Kao, Frederick. An Introduction to Respiratory Physiology. 1973. 77.00 (ISBN 0-444-10376-7, North Holland). Elsevier.

Kao, Hsin-sheng C. Li Ju-Chen. (World Authors Ser.). 1981. lib. bdg. 15.95 (ISBN 0-8057-6450-X, Twayne). G K Hall.

Kapanka, Tom. The Fate of Freeman. 1981. pap. 1.50 (ISBN 0-686-37156-9). Eldridge Pub.

Kapany, Narinder S., ed. Finance & Utilization of Solar Energy: Supplement. (Progress in Solar Energy Ser.). 1983. pap. text ed. 45.00 (ISBN 0-89553-121-6). Am Solar Energy.

Kapel, Priscilla. The Body Says Yes. 1982. pap. 17.95 (ISBN 0-917086-31-7, Pub. by Astro Comp Serv). Para Res.

Kapenzi, Geoffrey Z. The Clash of Cultures: Christian Missionaries & the Shona of Rhodesia. LC 78-68799. 1979. pap. text ed. 8.50 (ISBN 0-8191-0704-2). U Pr of Amer.

Kaper, H. G. & Lekkerkerker, C. J., eds. Spectral Methods in Linear Transport Theory. (Operator Theory, Advances & Applications Ser.: Vol. 5). 360p. 1982. text ed. 29.95 (ISBN 3-7643-1372-2) Birkhauser.

Kapera, Z. J. Kinyras: Bibliography of Ancient Cyprus for the Year 1979. (Studies in Mediterranean Archaeology Pocketbooks Ser.: No. 18). 68p. 1982. pap. text ed. 23.00x (ISBN 91-86098-06-3, Pub. by Astroms Sweden). Humanities.

Kapetanovic, Alojzije & Kapetanovic, Ruzica. The Best of Slavic Cooking. 276p. 1982. 10.95 (ISBN 0-910164-04-5); pap. 7.95 (ISBN 0-910164-06-1). Assoc Bk Pubs Guidance.

Kapetanovic, Ruzica, jt. auth. see Kapetanovic, Alojzije.

Kapferer, Bruce. A Celebration of Demons. LC 81-48677. (Illus.). 352p. (Orig.). 1983. 32.50x (ISBN 0-253-31326-0); pap. 18.50x (ISBN 0-253-20304-X). Ind U Pr.

Kapit, Wynn & Elson, Lawrence. The Anatomy Coloring Book. 1981. pap. text ed. 8.95 scp (ISBN 0-06-453914-8, HarpC). Har-Row.

Kapitanoff, Lorraine T., tr. see Kobishchanov, Yuri M.

Kapitza, P. L. Collected Papers of P. L. Kapitza, 2 vols. Ter Haar, D., ed. Vol. 1. 1965. inquire for price o.p. (ISBN 0-08-010744-3); Vol. 2. 1965. o.p. (ISBN 0-08-010973-X). Pergamon.

Kaplan. Cognition & Environment. 304p. 1982. 29.95 (ISBN 0-03-062344-8); pap. 13.95 (ISBN 0-03-062346-4). Praeger.

--Site of Lesion Testing. 320p. 1983. pap. text ed. 29.95 (ISBN 0-8391-4145-9). Univ Park.

Kaplan, rev. by. Barron's Regents Exams & Answers 9th Year Mathematics: Elementary Algebra. rev. ed. LC 58-33441. 1982. pap. 4.50 (ISBN 0-8120-3175-X). Barron.

Kaplan, Abraham. Love...& Death: Talks on Contemporary & Perennial Themes. LC 72-93402. (Illus.). 112p. 1973. 7.95 o.p. (ISBN 0-472-50465-7). U of Mich Pr.

--New World of Philosophy. 1961. pap. 4.95 (ISBN 0-394-70235-2, V235, Vin). Random.

Kaplan, Albert S. Organization & Replication of Viral DNA. 208p. 1982. 67.00 (ISBN 0-8493-6405-1). CRC Pr.

Kaplan, Alex & Szabo, LaVerne. Clinical Chemistry: Interpretation & Techniques. 2nd ed. LC 82-17249. (Illus.). 470p. 1983. text ed. write for info. (ISBN 0-8121-0873-6). Lea & Febiger.

Kaplan, Arthur M., jt. ed. see Sharpley, J. Miles.

Kaplan, Barbara J. Preparation of the Normal Giemsa-Trypsin-Banded Karyotype. Evans, Leonard A., ed. LC 81-720284. (Illus.). 56p. 1982. tchrs. ed. 85.00 (ISBN 0-89189-148-X, 21-9-016-00); 18.00 (ISBN 0-89189-149-8, 21-9016-20). Am Soc Clinical.

Kaplan, Barry J. That Wilder Woman. 1983. pap. 3.50 (ISBN 0-553-22922-2). Bantam.

Kaplan, Bess. The Empty Chair. LC 77-11852. 1978. 7.95 o.p. (ISBN 0-06-023092-4, HarpJ); PLB 10.89 (ISBN 0-06-023093-2). Har-Row.

Kaplan, Carol, ed. Capacity Management Case Studies: Technical Notes. 200p. 1982. Repr. 250.00 (ISBN 0-931900-04-2). Inst Software Eng.

Kaplan, Charles & Natale, Peter, eds. Paddings & Strappings of the Foot. LC 82-82871. (Illus.). 256p. 1982. pap. 31.00 (ISBN 0-87993-185-X). Futura Pub.

Kaplan, Colin, ed. Rabies: The Facts. (Illus.). 1977. text ed. 12.95x (ISBN 0-19-264918-3). Oxford U Pr.

Kaplan, David & Manners, Robert. Culture Theory. 224p. 1972. pap. 10.95 (ISBN 0-13-195511-X). P-H.

Kaplan, David & Phillips, Marcia. Smiles. (Inspirational Ser.). (Illus.). 100p. 1982. pap. 4.95 (ISBN 0-939944-05-7). Marmac Pub.

Kaplan, David, jt. auth. see Dickneider, William C., Jr.

Kaplan, Don. See with Your Ears: The Creative Music Book. LC 82-81463. (Illus.). 128p. (Orig.). (gr. 1-7). 1982. pap. 6.95 (ISBN 0-938530-09-7, 09-7); tchr's guide 2.00 (ISBN 0-938530-20-8, 20-8). Lexikos.

Kaplan, Donald & Bellink, Alan. Diners of the Northeast. (Orig.). 1980. pap. 7.95 o.p. (ISBN 0-912944-64-1). Berkshire Traveller.

Kaplan, Dorothy. The Comprehensive Diabetic Cookbook. rev. ed. LC 81-1550. 272p. 1983. 14.95 (ISBN 0-8119-0427-X); pap. 8.95 (ISBN 0-8119-0490-3). Fell.

Kaplan, E. Ann. Fritz Lang: A Guide to References & Resources. 1981. lib. bdg. 45.00 (ISBN 0-8161-8035-0, Hall Reference). G K Hall.

Kaplan, Edgar & Sheinwold, Alfred. K-S System of Winning Bridge. 2nd ed. LC 63-20332. 282p. Date not set. pap. 7.95 cancelled (ISBN 0-8303-0009-0). Fleet.

Kaplan, Edward. Zero Station. (Stone Country Poetry Ser.: No. 8). (Orig.). 1979. pap. 4.50 (ISBN 0-930020-07-3). Stone Country.

Kaplan, Edward H., tr. see Chin-Sheng, Chou.

Kaplan, Edward H., tr. see P'eng Hsin-wei.

Kaplan, Eugene H. Experiences in Life Science: A Laboratory Guide. 2nd ed. (Illus.). 256p. 1976. pap. text ed. 14.95x (ISBN 0-02-361770-5). Macmillan.

--Problem Solving in Biology. 3rd ed. 448p. 1983. pap. text ed. 13.95 (ISBN 0-02-362050-1). Macmillan.

Kaplan, Fred. The Wizards of Armageddon: Strategists of the Nuclear Age. 1983. price not set (ISBN 0-671-42444-0). S&S.

Kaplan, Fred, jt. ed. see Timko, Michael.

Kaplan, Fredric M. & Dekeijzer, Arne J. The China Guidebook 1983. X ed. (Illus.). 528p. (Orig.). pap. 12.95 (ISBN 0-932030-15-7). Eurasia Pr NJ.

Kaplan, George W., jt. auth. see Belman, A. Barry.

Kaplan, Glenn. The Big Time. 288p. 1982. 16.95 (ISBN 0-312-92052-0). Congdon & Weed.

Kaplan, H. Roy. Lottery Winners: How They Won & How Winning Changed Their Lives. LC 78-2143. 1978. 10.53i (ISBN 0-06-012257-9, HarpT). Har-Row.

Kaplan, Harold. The Passive Voice: An Approach to Modern Fiction. LC 66-11300. xi, 239p. 1966. 14.00x (ISBN 0-8214-0017-7, 82-80182). Ohio U Pr.

--The Passive Voice: An Approach to Modern Fiction. LC 66-11300. xi, 239p. 1979. pap. 6.95x (ISBN 0-8214-0434-2, 82-81190). Ohio U Pr.

Kaplan, Harold I. & Sadock, Benjamin J. Comprehensive Group Psychotherapy. 2nd ed. 408p. 1982. lib. bdg. 49.95 (ISBN 0-683-04521-0). Williams & Wilkins.

Kaplan, Harold I., jt. auth. see Freedman, Alfred M.

Kaplan, Harold I, et al. Modern Synopsis of Comprehensive Textbook of Psychiatry. 3rd ed. 1080p. 1981. 34.00 (ISBN 0-683-04512-1); pap. 31.00 o. p (ISBN 0-683-03371-9). Williams & Wilkins.

Kaplan, Harold M. Anatomy & Physiology of Speech. 2nd ed. (Speech Ser.). 544p. 1971. text ed. 38.50 (ISBN 0-07-033282-7, C). McGraw.

--Anatomy & Physiology of Speech: Laboratory Textbook. LC 80-82927. (Illus.). 180p. 1981. text ed. 21.50x (ISBN 0-932126-04-9); pap. text ed. 18.00x (ISBN 0-932126-05-7). Graceway.

Kaplan, Harriet, jt. auth. see Lloyd, Lyle L.

Kaplan, Harry & Ford, Donald H. The Brain Vascular System. 1966. 22.00 (ISBN 0-444-40329-9). Elsevier.

Kaplan, Helen S. Disorders of Sexual Desire. LC 79-18908. 1979. 22.50 (ISBN 0-87630-212-6). Brunner-Mazel.

--Disorders of Sexual Desire. 1979. 17.50 o.p. (ISBN 0-671-25362-X). S&S.

--The Evaluation of Sexual Disorders: Psychological & Medical Aspects. 352p. 1983. 25.00 (ISBN 0-87630-329-7). Brunner-Mazel.

--Making Sense of Sex. 1979. 10.95 o.p. (ISBN 0-671-25131-7). S&S.

--The New Sex Therapy: Active Treatment of Sexual Dysfunctions. LC 73-87724. 1974. 22.50 (ISBN 0-87630-083-2, Dist. by Quadrangle). Brunner-Mazel.

Kaplan, Helen S., jt. auth. see Sager, Clifford J.

Kaplan, Herman J. Peptic Ulcer. (Contemporary Patient Management Ser.). 1982. text ed. 19.50 (ISBN 0-87488-879-4). Med Exam.

Kaplan, J. G. The Molecular Basis of Immune Cell Function. 780p. 1979. 90.00 (ISBN 0-444-80168-5, North Holland). Elsevier.

Kaplan, Joel A., ed. Cardiac Anesthesia: Cardiovascular Pharmacology. (Clinical Cardiology Monograph: Vol. 2). write for info (ISBN 0-8089-1567-3). Grune.

Kaplan, John. The Court Martial of the Kaohsiung Defendants. (Research Papers & Policy Studies: No. 2). 75p. (Orig.). 1981. pap. 5.00x (ISBN 0-912966-35-1). IEAS.

--The Hardest Drug: Heroin & Public Policy. LC 82-17514. (Studies in Crime & Justice). 1983. 20.00. U of Chicago Pr.

Kaplan, John & Skolnick, Jerome H. Criminal Justice: Introductory Cases & Materials. 3rd ed. LC 81-17480. 665p. 1981. text ed. 19.00 (ISBN 0-88277-053-5); pap. text ed. write for info. tchr's manual (ISBN 0-88277-123-X). Foundation Pr.

Kaplan, John, jt. auth. see Waltz, Jon R.

Kaplan, Joseph S., jt. auth. see Howell, Kenneth W.

Kaplan, Julius D. The Art of Gustave Moreau: Theory, Style & Content. Foster, Stephen, ed. LC 82-6980. (Studies in Fine Arts: The Avant Garde: No. 33). 221p. 1982. 39.95 (ISBN 0-8357-1350-4, Pub. by UMI Res Pr). Univ Microfilms.

Kaplan, Justin. Mr. Clemens & Mark Twain. 1983. pap. write for info. (ISBN 0-671-47071-X, Touchstone Bks). S&S.

--Mister Clemens & Mark Twain: A Biography. 1966. 12.95 o.p. (ISBN 0-671-49520-8); pap. 5.95 (ISBN 0-671-20707-5). S&S.

Kaplan, Justin, ed. Poetry & Prose: Walt Whitman. LC 81-20768. 1392p. 1982. 27.50 (ISBN 0-940450-02-X). Literary Classics.

Kaplan, Justin, ed. see Aristotle.

Kaplan, Justin, ed. see Twain, Mark.

Kaplan, Justin D. Walt Whitman: A Life. (Illus.). 1980. 16.95 o.s.i. (ISBN 0-671-22542-1). S&S.

Kaplan, L. C., tr. see Ramos, Graciliano.

Kaplan, L. C., tr. see Verissimo, Erico.

Kaplan, Larry. Infantry: Cumulative Index by Author, Title, & Subject. 30.00 (ISBN 0-89126-111-7). MA AH Pub.

Kaplan, Lawrence J. Elementary Statistics for Economics & Business. (FLMI Insurance Education Program Ser.). 1966. pap. text ed. 10.00 (ISBN 0-915322-04-8). LOMA.

Kaplan, Lawrence S. Jefferson & France: An Essay on Politics & Political Ideas. LC 79-27698. (Yale Historical Publications, the Wallace Notestein Essays: No. 5). ix, 175p. 1980. Repr. of 1967 ed. lib. bdg. 19.00x (ISBN 0-313-22154-5, KAJF). Greenwood.

Kaplan, Lawrence S. & Clawson, Robert W. NATO After Thirty Years. LC 80-53885. 262p. 1981. lib. bdg. 19.95 (ISBN 0-8420-2172-8); pap. 9.95 (ISBN 0-8420-2184-1). Scholarly Res Inc.

Kaplan, Lawrence S., jt. auth. see Heald, Morrell.

Kaplan, Louise. Oneness & Separtness. 1978. 9.95 o.p. (ISBN 0-671-22854-4). S&S.

Kaplan, M. L., et al. The Structural Approach in Psychological Testing. LC 70-93755. 1971. 23.00 (ISBN 0-08-006867-7). Pergamon.

Kaplan, Marion. Focus Africa: A Photojournalist Perspective. LC 80-1812. (Illus.). 480p. 1982. 29.95 (ISBN 0-385-15030-X). Doubleday.

--The Jewish Feminist Movement in Germany: The Campaigns of the Judischer Frauenbund, 1904-1938. LC 78-67567. (Contributions in Women's Studies: No. 8). (Illus.). lib. bdg. 17.50 (ISBN 0-313-20736-4, KGJ/). Greenwood.

Kaplan, Marshall, jt. auth. see Eichler, Edward P.

Kaplan, Marshall, jt. auth. see Frieden, Bernard J.

Kaplan, Marshall H. Modern Spacecraft Dynamics & Control. LC 76-14859. 415p. 1976. text ed. 40.50x (ISBN 0-471-45703-5). Wiley.

Kaplan, Martin, ed. The Monday Morning Imagination: Report from the Boyer Workshop on State University Systems. (Special Studies). 1977. text ed. 26.95 o.p. (ISBN 0-03-021481-5). Praeger.

Kaplan, Martin M., jt. ed. see Moorhead, Paul S.

Kaplan, Meyer A. Varmint Hunting. (Monarch Illustrated Guide Ser.). 1977. pap. 2.95 o.p. (ISBN 0-671-18766-X). Monarch Pr.

--Water Sports. (Monarch Illustrated Guide Ser.). (Illus.). 1977. pap. 2.95 o.p. (ISBN 0-671-18762-7). Monarch Pr.

Kaplan, Michael. Otto Mears: Paradoxical Pathfinder. Nossaman, Allen, ed. 296p. 1982. 14.95 (ISBN 0-9608000-3-4); pap. 9.95 (ISBN 0-9608000-2-6). San Juan County.

Kaplan, Mike, ed. Variety: International Motion Picture Marketplace, 1982-1983. LC 82-9182. 430p. 1982. 50.00 (ISBN 0-8240-9378-X). Garland Pub.

Kaplan, Nathan O. & Robinson, Arthur, eds. From Cyclotrons to Cytochromes: Essays in Molecular Biology & Chemistry. LC 82-1785. 1982. 64.00 (ISBN 0-12-397580-8). Acad Pr.

Kaplan, Nathan O., jt. ed. see Colowich, Sidney P.

Kaplan, Nathan O., jt. ed. see Colowick, Sidney P.

Kaplan, Neil A., et al, eds. Parallel Grand Jury & Administrative Agency Investigations. 1000p. 1981. softbound 65.00 (ISBN 0-686-96980-4). Amer Bar Assn.

Kaplan, Norman M. Clinical Hypertension. 3rd ed. (Illus.). 464p. 1982. lib. bdg. 45.00 (ISBN 0-683-04514-8). Williams & Wilkins.

--Clinical Hypertension. 2nd ed. (Illus.). 405p. 1978. 32.00 o.p. (ISBN 0-683-04519-9). Williams & Wilkins.

Kaplan, Norman N. Prevent Your Heart Attack. (Illus.). 192p. 1983. 12.95 (ISBN 0-684-17797-8, ScribT). Scribner.

Kaplan, Patricia & Manso, Susan, eds. Major European Art Movements Nineteen Hundred to Nineteen Forty-Five: A Critical Anthology. 1977. pap. 10.95 (ISBN 0-525-47462-5, 01063-320). Dutton.

Kaplan, Paul E. & Materson, Richard S. The Practice of Rehabilitation Medicine. (Illus.). 560p. 1982. 45.50x (ISBN 0-398-04553-4). C C Thomas.

Kaplan, Richard. Great Linebackers of the NFL. (NFL Punt, Pass & Kick Library: No. 12). (Illus.). (gr. 5-9). 1970. 2.50 o.p. (ISBN 0-394-80152-0, BYR); PLB 3.69 o.p. (ISBN 0-394-90152-5). Random.

Kaplan, Robert & Dimatteo, M. Robin. Serious Illness: Psychosocial Issues in the Process of Adjustment. cancelled (ISBN 0-88410-744-2). Ballinger Pub.

Kaplan, Robert, ed. Annual Review of Applied Linguistics. 216p. 1980. lib. bdg. 17.95 (ISBN 0-88377-201-9); pap. text ed. 14.95. Newbury Hse.

Kaplan, Robert, et al, eds. Annual Review of Applied Linguistics, 1981. 280p. 1982. pap. text ed. 17.95 (ISBN 0-88377-258-2). Newbury Hse.

Kaplan, Robert B. Catcher in the Rye Notes. (Orig.). 1965. pap. 2.50 (ISBN 0-8220-0301-5). Cliffs.

Kaplan, Robert B., ed. On the Scope of Applied Linguistics. 1980. pap. text ed. 8.95 (ISBN 0-88377-140-3). Newbury Hse.

Kaplan, Robert M. & Saccuzzo, Dennis P. Psychological Testing: Principles, Applications & Issues. LC 81-38461. (Psychology Ser.). 1150p. 1982. text ed. 25.95 (ISBN 0-8185-0494-3). Brooks-Cole.

Kaplan, Robert M., jt. auth. see Harari, Herbert.

Kaplan, Robert S. Advanced Management Accounting. (Illus.). 640p. 1982. 30.95 (ISBN 0-13-011403-0). P-H.

Kaplan, Roger. Running after Red. LC 82-62442. 1983. 11.95 (ISBN 0-89526-628-8). Regnery-Gateway.

Kaplan, Samuel, jt. auth. see Lichtenberg, Joseph D.

Kaplan, Samuel, jt. ed. see Lichtenberg, Joseph D.

Kaplan, Seymour. Energy, Economics, & the Environment. (Illus.). 448p. 1983. 29.95x (ISBN 0-07-033286-X); write for info solutions manual (ISBN 0-07-033287-8). McGraw.

Kaplan, Seymour R., jt. ed. see Talbott, John A.

Kaplan, Sheila. Solar Energy. (A Look Inside Ser.). (Illus.). 48p. (gr. 4 up). 1983. PLB 14.25 (ISBN 0-8172-1415-1). Raintree Pubs.

Kaplan, Sherman. Best Restaurants Chicago & Environs: A Revised & Greatly Expanded Edition. LC 79-12230. (Best Restaurant Ser.). (Illus.). 269p. 1979. pap. 3.95 o.p. (ISBN 0-89286-151-7). One Hund One Prods.

Kaplan, Sidney O., jt. ed. see Colowick, Sidney P.

Kaplan, Stanley & Peters, Max, eds. Barron's Regents Exams & Answers 10th. Year Mathematics. rev. ed. LC 58-18006. 300p. (gr. 9-12). 1982. pap. text ed. 4.50 (ISBN 0-8120-3179-2). Barron.

Kaplan, Stanley, et al, eds. Barron's Regents Exams & Answers - 11th. Year Mathematics. rev. ed. LC 57-58722. 250p. 1982. pap. text ed. 4.50 (ISBN 0-8120-3118-0). Barron.

Kaplan, Stephen S., jt. auth. see Blechman, Barry M.

Kaplan, Stuart R. El Tarot. (Illus.). 256p. 1982. pap. 4.95 (ISBN 84-01-47101-X). US Games Syst.

--Tarot Classic. LC 74-183028. (Illus.). 240p. 1972. 8.95 o.p. (ISBN 0-913866-05-9); pap. 6.95 (ISBN 0-913866-17-2). US Games Syst.

--Tarot Classic Gift Set. LC 74-183028. (Illus.). 240p. 1972. pap. 15.00 card deck incl. (ISBN 0-913866-55-5). US Games Syst.

--Tarot of the Witches Book. LC 73-80526. (Illus.). 96p. 1981. pap. 4.95 (ISBN 0-913866-40-7). US Games Syst.

--Visconti-Sforza Instructions. (Illus.). 38p. 1975. pap. 30.00 incl. card deck (ISBN 0-913866-06-7). US Games Syst.

Kaplan, Susan, jt. auth. see Fitzhugh, William W.

Kaplan, Sylvia R., jt. auth. see Levi, Shonie B.

Kaplan, Wilfred. Advanced Calculus. 2nd ed. LC 77-184161. 1973. text ed. 30.95 (ISBN 0-201-03611-8). A-W.

--Advanced Mathematics for Engineers. LC 80-19492. (Mathematics Ser.). (Illus.). 960p. 1981. text ed. 30.95 (ISBN 0-201-03773-4). A-W.

Kaplan-Fitzgerald, Karen. Reach Me, Teach Me. 1977. pap. text ed. 5.00x o.p. (ISBN 0-87879-171-X). Acad Therapy.

Kaplan-Sanoff, Margot & Magid, Renee. Exploring Early Childhood Education. 1981. pap. text ed. 14.95x (ISBN 0-02-361940-6). Macmillan.

Kaplansky, Irving. Linear Algebra & Geometry: A Second Course. LC 74-2393. xiv, 143p. 1974. Repr. of 1969 ed. text ed. 11.95 (ISBN 0-8284-0279-5). Chelsea Pub.

--Set Theory & Metric Spaces. 2nd ed. LC 77-7344. 1977. text ed. 9.50 (ISBN 0-8284-0298-1). Chelsea Pub.

Kaplansky, Irving, jt. auth. see Herstein, I. N.

Kapleau, Phillip. To Cherish All Life: A Buddhist Case for Becoming Vegetarian. LC 82-47746. (Illus.). 112p. 1982. pap. 5.72 (ISBN 0-06-250440-1, HarpR). Har-Row.

Kaplow, Julian, ed. see Hansen, Terrence L., et al.

Kaplow, Robert. Two in the City. (gr. 7 up). 1979. 6.95 o.p. (ISBN 0-395-27813-9). HM.

Kaplowitz, Richard A. Selecting Academic Administrators: The Search Committee. 1973. 10 copies 7.50 o.p. (ISBN 0-8268-1388-7). ACE.

Kapoor, Ashok, jt. auth. see Fayerweather, John.

Kapp, K. William. The Social Costs of Private Enterprise. LC 79-144788. (Illus.). 1971. pap. 4.95 (ISBN 0-8052-0299-4). Schocken.

Kapp, Robert A., ed. see Murray, Douglas P. & Lubman, Stanley B.

Kapp, Ronald O. How to Know Pollen & Spores. (Pictured Key Nature Ser.). 260p. 1969. text ed. write for info. o.p. (ISBN 0-697-04849-7); text ed. write for info. o.p. Wm C Brown.

Kapp, Yvonne, tr. see Ehrenburg, Ilya.

Kappang, N, jt. auth. see Armstrong, D.

Kappas, A., ed. Progress in Environmental Mutagenesis & Carminogenesis. (Progress in Mutation Research Ser.: Vol. 2). 1981. 82.75 (ISBN 0-444-80334-3). Elsevier.

Kappel, F. & Schappacher, W. Abstract Cauchy Problems & Functional Differential Equations. LC 80-22557. (Research Notes in Mathematics Ser.: No. 48). 240p. (Orig.). 1981. pap. text ed. 26.50 (ISBN 0-273-08494-1). Pitman Pub MA.

Kappel, F. & Schappacher, W., eds. Evolution Equations & Their Applications. (Research Notes In Mathematics: No. 68). 250p. 1982. pap. text ed. 26.50 (ISBN 0-273-08567-0). Pitman Pub MA.

Kappel, Frederick R. Vitality in a Business Enterprise. 1960. 12.95 o.p. (ISBN 0-07-033290-8, P&RB). McGraw.

Kappeler, Max. The Christ idea. 30p. 1975. pap. 3.50 (ISBN 0-85241-079-4). Kappeler Inst Pub.

--The Development of the Christian Science Idea & Practice. 78p. 1970. pap. 6.50 (ISBN 0-85241-092-1). Kappeler Inst Pub.

--Epitomes for the Structural Interpretation of the Christian Science Textbook. LC 82-82377. 120p. 1982. write for info. (ISBN 0-942958-06-3). Kappeler Inst Pub.

--Notes on Handling Evil. 10p. 1948. pap. 1.75 (ISBN 0-85241-039-5). Kappeler Inst Pub.

--The Science of Oneness in the Christian Science Textbook. LC 82-81131. 300p. 1983. 16.00 (ISBN 0-942958-03-9). Kappeler Inst Pub.

--Why Study Christian Science as a Science? 30p. 1973. pap. 3.50 (ISBN 0-85241-040-9). Kappeler Inst Pub.

Kappeler, Susanne & Bryson, Norman, eds. Teaching the Text. 200p. (Orig.). 1983. pap. price not set (ISBN 0-7100-9412-4). Routledge & Kegan.

Kappelman, Murray, jt. auth. see Ackerman, Paul.

Kapralov, Yuri. Castle Dubrava. 280p. 1982. 13.95 (ISBN 0-525-24143-4, 01354-410). Dutton.

Kapraun, Donald F. An Illustrated Guide to the Benthic Marine Algae of Coastal North Carolina, II: Chlorophyta Phycologica. (Bibliotheca Phycologica: No. 58). (Illus.). 250p. 1983. lib. bdg. 20.00x (ISBN 3-7682-1326-9). Lubrecht & Cramer.

Kapsian, D. B. The Baileaus of Desert Home. 8.50 (ISBN 0-392-08474-0, SpS). Sportshelf.

Kapsner, Oliver L., ed. A Benedictine Bibliography: An Author-Subject Union List. LC 81-20790. 832p. 1982. first suppl. 29.95 (ISBN 0-8146-1258-X). Liturgical Pr.

Kaptchuk, Ted J. The Web That Has No Weaver: Understanding Chinese Medicine. LC 82-2511. 1983. pap. 19.95 (ISBN 0-312-92932-3). Congdon & Weed.

Kapteyn & Kooijmans. International Organisation & Integration, Vol. 1A. 1982. lib. bdg. 195.00 (ISBN 90-247-2579-8, Pub. by Martinus Nijhoff Netherlands). Kluwer Boston.

Kapteyn & Koomans. International Organisation & Integration, Vol. 1B. 1982. lib. bdg. 99.00 (ISBN 90-247-2657-3, Pub. by Martinus Nijhoff Netherlands). Kluwer Boston.

Kapteyn & Kooymans. International Organisation & Integration, Vol. IIA. 1982. lib. bdg. 99.00 (ISBN 90-247-2587-9, Pub. by Martinus Nijhoff Netherlands). Kluwer Boston.

Kapur. The Indian Ocean: Regional & International Power Politics. 256p. 1983. 29.95 (ISBN 0-03-058641-0). Praeger.

Kapur, Bahadur. Regimental Colours & Ceremonials. (Illus.). 1982. text ed. write for info. (ISBN 0-7069-1969-6, Pub. by Vikas India). Advent NY.

Kapur, Gopal K. IBM 360 Assembler Language Programming. LC 76-12572. 560p. 1971. 30.95x (ISBN 0-471-45840-6). Wiley.

--Programming in Standard COBOL. LC 72-97018. (Illus.). 330p. 1973. pap. text ed. 16.95 (ISBN 0-574-17980-1, 13-0980). SRA.

Kapur, K. C. & Lamberson, L. K. Reliability in Engineering Design. LC 76-1304. 586p. 1977. text ed. 41.95x (ISBN 0-471-51191-9). Wiley.

Kapur, R. L., jt. auth. see Carstairs, G. M.

Kapur, Tribhuwan. Hippies: A Study of Their Drug habits & Sexual Customs. 221p. 1981. 21.00x (ISBN 0-7069-1296-9). Intl Pubns Serv.

Kapuscinski, Ryszard. The Emperor: Downfall of an Autocrat. Brand, William R. & Mroczkowska-Brand, Katarzyna, trs. LC 82-47670. (A Helen & Kurt Wolff Bk.). 180p. 1983. 12.95 (ISBN 0-15-128771-6). HarBraceJ.

Kapusta, E. C., et al. Thailand Strategy for Fertilizer Development a Prefeasibility Study. (Technical Bulletin Ser.: T-17). (Illus., Orig.). 1980. pap. 4.00 (ISBN 0-88090-016-4). Intl Fertilizer.

Kar, Chintamoni. Classical Indian Sculpture. (Illus.). 112p. 1974. pap. 6.95 o.s.i. (ISBN 0-685-50124-8). Transatlantic.

Karabel, Jerome & Halsey, A. H., eds. Power & Ideology in Education. 1977. text ed. 23.95x (ISBN 0-19-502138-X); pap. text ed. 15.95x (ISBN 0-19-502139-8). Oxford U Pr.

Karacan, I., jt. auth. see Williams, R. L.

Karacuba, A. A., jt. auth. see Steklov Institute of Mathematics.

Karageorghis, Vassos. The Archaeology of Cyprus. (Illus.). 192p. 1982. 22.50 (ISBN 0-8071-0998-3). La State U Pr.

--Cypress Museum & Archaeological Sites of Cypurs. (Athenon Illustrated Guides Ser.). (Illus.). 56p. 1983. pap. 9.00 (ISBN 0-88332-312-5, 8247, Pub. by Ekdotike Athenon Greece). Larousse.

--Cyprus: Its Archaeology & Early History from the Stone Age to the Romans. LC 81-86679. (Ancient People & Places Ser.). (Illus.). 1982. 19.95 (ISBN 0-500-02102-3). Thames & Hudson.

Karalova, Z. K., jt. auth. see Nemodruk, A. A.

Karalus, Karl E. & Eckert, Allan W. Owls of North America: All the Species & Subspecies Illustrated in Full Color & Fully Described. LC 73-83629. (Illus.). 394p. 1974. 19.95 o.p. collector's ed. (ISBN 0-385-04818-1); limited ed. 200.00 (ISBN 0-385-04828-9). Doubleday.

Karam, Emil. Spoken Arabic: The Language of Lebanon. LC 82-5513. 1982. pap. 8.95 (ISBN 0-932506-18-6); pap. 16.50 with cassette (90 min.). St Bedes Pubns.

Karam, N. H., tr. Banking Laws of Kuwait. 275p. 1979. 75.00x (ISBN 0-86010-139-8, Pub.by Graham & Trotman England). State Mutual Bk.

Karamanski, Theodore J. Fur Trade & Exploration: Opening the Far Northwest, Eighteen Twenty-One to Eighteen Fifty-Two. LC 82-40453. (Illus.). 360p. 1983. 22.95 (ISBN 0-8061-1833-4). U of Okla Pr.

Karandikar, Maheshwar A. Islam in India's Transition to Modernity. 1972. lib. bdg. 35.00 (ISBN 0-8371-2337-2, KAI/). Greenwood.

Karanganis, Jerome J., jt. auth. see Thompson, William F.

Karapet'Yants, M. Khand & Karapet'Yants, M. L. Handbook of Thermodynamic Constants of Inorganic & Organic Compounds. LC 72-122509. 461p. 1968. 49.95 o.s.i. (ISBN 0-470-45850-X). Halsted Pr.

Karapet'Yants, M. L., jt. auth. see Karapet'Yants, M. Khand.

Karas, Nicholas. Complete Book of the Striped Bass. (Stoeger Bks). 384p. 1976. pap. 5.95 o.s.i. (ISBN 0-695-80661-0). Follett.

--The Complete Book of the Striped Bass. (Illus.). 384p. pap. 7.95 (ISBN 0-88317-062-0). Stoeger Pub Co.

Karas, Nick, jt. auth. see Missildine, Fred.

Karas, Phyllis. A Life Worth Living. 392p. 1981. 13.95 o.p. (ISBN 0-312-48503-4). St Martin.

Karas, Thomas. The New High Ground: Systems & Weapons of Space Age War. 1983. 15.95 (ISBN 0-671-47025-6). S&S.

Karaska, Gerald J. & Bramhall, David F., eds. Locational Analysis for Manufacturing: A Selection of Readings. (Regional Science Studies Ser.: No. 7). 1969. 25.00x (ISBN 0-262-11026-1). MIT Pr.

Karassi, Arthur H. Acute Myocardial Infarction. (Illus.). 559p. 1980. text ed. 59.00 (ISBN 0-07-033296-7, HP). McGraw.

Karassik, Igor J. Centrifugal Pumps. 1960. 65.45 o.p. (ISBN 0-07-033359-9, P&RB). McGraw.

Karassik, Igor J. & Krutzch, William C. Pump Handbook. 1000p. 1976. 52.00 (ISBN 0-07-033301-7, P&RB). McGraw.

Karasudhi, Pisidhi, jt. auth. see International Conference Held in Bangkok, Jan. 7-9, 1980.

Karasz, Ilonka. Twelve Days of Christmas. LC 49-11875. (Illus.). (gr. 3-6). 1949. 8.95 o.p. (ISBN 0-06-023090-8, HarpJ); PLB 9.89 o.p. (ISBN 0-06-023091-6). Har-Row.

Karatnycky, Adrian & Motyl, Alexander. Workers Rights, East & West. 130p. 1980. pap. 4.59 (ISBN 0-87855-867-5). Transaction Bks.

Karatzas, Theodoros & Ready, Nigel. The Greek Code of Private Maritime Law. 1982. lib. bdg. 32.50 (ISBN 90-247-2586-0, Pub. by Martinus Nijhoff Netherlands). Kluwer Boston.

Karavasil, Josie, ed. Love You, Hate You, Just Don't Know. 112p. 1982. 32.00x (ISBN 0-237-45510-2, Pub. by Evans Bros). State Mutual Bk.

Karbowiak, A. E. Trunk Waveguide Communication. 208p. 1965. text ed. 8.95x o.p. (ISBN 0-412-07940-2, Pub. by Chapman & Hall England). Methuen Inc.

Karch, Nathan J., jt. auth. see Nisbet, Ian C.

Karch, Pat. Fifty-One Paper Craft Projects. LC 79-91249. (Illus.). 64p. (Orig.). 1979. pap. 3.95 (ISBN 0-87239-391-7, 2139). Standard Pub.

Karcher, Joseph T. New Guide to Building a One Hundred Thousand Dollar Law Practice. LC 81-13180. 427p. 1981. 49.50 (ISBN 0-87624-402-9). Inst Busn Plan.

Karcz, George, ed. see Wadekin, Karl-Eugen.

Kardesduncer, Heyrettin. Social Consequences of Engineering. LC 78-23667. 1979. lib. bdg. 18.00x (ISBN 0-87835-074-8); pap. 12.95x (ISBN 0-87835-073-X). Boyd & Fraser.

Kardestuncer, Hayrettin. Elementary Matrix Analysis of Structures. (Illus.). 448p. 1974. text ed. 32.00 o.p. (ISBN 0-07-033318-1, C). McGraw.

Kardiner, Abram & Ovesey, Lionel. Mark of Oppression: Explorations in the Personality of the American Negro. pap. 3.95 o.p. (ISBN 0-452-00141-2, FM141, Mer). NAL.

Kardos, Louis T., jt. ed. see Sopper, William E.

Kare, Morley, jt. auth. see Fregly, Melvin.

Karelitz, Samuel. When Your Child Is Ill. rev. ed. LC 69-16463. 1969. 7.95 (ISBN 0-394-45168-6); pap. 1.75 (ISBN 0-446-59964-6). Random.

Karen, Robert, jt. auth. see Rosenblum, Ralph.

Karen, Ruth. Questionable Practices. LC 79-2650. 1980. 12.45i (ISBN 0-06-012293-5, HarpT). Har-Row.

Karg, H. & Schallenberger, E. Factors Influencing Fertility in the Post-Partum Cow. 1982. 76.00 (ISBN 90-247-2715-4, Pub. by Martinus Nijhoff Netherlands). Kluwer Boston.

Karger, Delmar W. & Murdick, Robert G. Managing Engineering & Research. 3rd ed. LC 79-10595. (Illus.). 534p. 1980. 29.50x o.p. (ISBN 0-8311-1125-9). Indus Pr.

Kargere, Audrey. Color & Personality. pap. 4.95 (ISBN 0-87728-478-4). Weiser.

Kargilis, G., jt. auth. see Pactor, P.

Kargodorian, Annette, ed. see Hurst, Walter E.

Kari, James M. Navajo Verb Prefix Phonology. LC 75-25117. (American Indian Linguistics Ser.). 1976. lib. bdg. 42.00 o.s.i. (ISBN 0-8240-1968-7). Garland Pub.

Karim, A. Common English Words & Idioms with Their Equivalents in Bahasa Indonesia. 1978. pap. 8.50 (ISBN 0-8048-1283-7). C E Tuttle.

--What to Say in Bahasa Indonesia: Bahasa Indonesia Phrase Book for Travellers. 1978. pap. 5.50 (ISBN 0-8048-1282-9). C E Tuttle.

Karim, F. Al-Hadith, 4 vols. Set. 35.00 (ISBN 0-686-18379-7). Kazi Pubns.

--Heroes of Islam. Incl. Bk. 1. Muhammad; Bk. 2. Abu Bakr; Bk. 3. Umar; Bk. 4. Othman; Bk. 5. Ali; Bk. 6. Khalid Bin Walid; Bk. 7. Mohammad Bin Qasim; Bk. 8. Mahmood of Ghazni; Bk. 9. Mohyuddin; Bk. 10. Sultan Tipu; Bk. 11. Aisha the Truthful; Bk. 12. Hussain the Martyr; Bk. 13. Some Companions of the Prophet - I; Bk. 14. Some Companions of the Prophet - II; Bk. 15. Some Companions of the Prophet - III. pap. 30.00 complete set (ISBN 0-686-18393-2); pap. 2.00 ea bk. Kazi Pubns.

--The Ideal World Prophet. 5.95 o.p. (ISBN 0-686-18423-8). Kazi Pubns.

Karim, S. M. Practical Applications of Prostaglandins & Their Synthesis Inhibitors. 472p. 1979. text ed. 39.50 o.p. (ISBN 0-8391-1426-5). Univ Park.

Karimi-Hakkak, Ahmad, tr. Anthology of Modern Persian Poetry. LC 78-58473. (Modern Persian Literature Ser.). 204p. 1983. 25.00x (ISBN 0-89158-181-2). Caravan Bks.

Kariuki, Josiah M. Mau Mau Detainee: The Account by a Kenya African of His Experiences in Detention Camps 1953-1960. (Illus.). 1975. pap. 7.00x o.p. (ISBN 0-19-572381-3). Oxford U Pr.

Karkainen, Paul A. Narnia Explored. 192p. 1979. 5.95 o.p. (ISBN 0-8007-1057-6). Revell.

Karkavitsas, Andreas. The Beggar. 352p. 17.50 (ISBN 0-89241-372-7). Caratzas Bros.

Karki, Chandra B., tr. see Verma, Bhagwati C.

Karki, N., ed. Mechanisms of Toxity & Metabolism: Proceedings of the 6th International Congress of Pharmacology, Helsinki, 1975, Vol. 6. 240p. 1976. text ed. write for info. (ISBN 0-08-020544-5). Pergamon.

Karkoschka, Erhard. Notation in New Music: A Critical Guide to Interpretation & Realisation. Koenig, Rush, tr. from Ger. LC 75-134522. Orig. Title: Das Schriftbild der Neuen Musik. 1972. 31.25 o.p. (ISBN 0-900938-28-5, 50-26902). Eur-Am Music.

Karl, Frederick R., jt. auth. see Hamalian, Leo.

Karl, Frederick R., jt. ed. see Hamalian, Leo.

Karl, Jean. But We Are Not of Earth. LC 80-21849. (gr. 4-7). 1981. 10.25 (ISBN 0-525-27342-5, 0995-300). Dutton.

Karl, Jean E. Beloved Benjamin Is Waiting. (gr. k-3). 1978. 10.75 (ISBN 0-525-26372-1, 01044-310). Dutton.

Karle, Jerome, jt. auth. see Hauptman, Herbert.

Karlekar, Bhalchandra V. & Desmond, Robert M. Engineering Heat Transfer. (Illus., Orig.). 1977. text ed. 29.95 (ISBN 0-8299-0054-3); solutions manual avail. (ISBN 0-8299-0497-2). West Pub.

--Heat Transfer. 2nd ed. (Illus.). 826p. 1982. text ed. 29.95 (ISBN 0-314-63261-1). West Pub.

Karlekar, Malavika. Poverty & Work Roles: A Study of Sweeper Women in Delhi. 1982. text ed. write for info. (ISBN 0-7069-1968-8, Pub. by Vikas India). Advent NY.

Karlen, Arno, jt. auth. see Diamond, Milton.

Karlen, Arno, jt. ed. see Lief, Harold I.

Karlen, Arno, jt. ed. see Orkin, Ruth.

Karlen, Arno, compiled by see Steinhacker, Charles.

Karlen, Delmar. Citizen in Court: Litigant, Witness, Juror, Judge. LC 73-19739. (American Constitutional & Legal History Ser.). 211p. 1974. Repr. of 1964 ed. lib. bdg. 27.50 (ISBN 0-306-70614-8). Da Capo.

Karlen, Harvey M. The Patterns of American Government. 2nd ed. 1975. pap. text ed. 14.95x (ISBN 0-02-475320-3, 47532); tchrs' manual free (ISBN 0-02-475330-0). Macmillan.

Karlgren, Bernard. Legends & Cults in Ancient China. (Perspectives in Asian History Ser.: No. 7). 167p. Repr. of 1946 ed. lib. bdg. 19.50x (ISBN 0-87991-478-5). Porcupine Pr.

Karlgren, Bernhard. Analytic Dictionary of Chinese & Sino-Japanese. 11.00 (ISBN 0-8446-5208-3). Peter Smith.

Karli, David. Keep a Cool Head & a Warm Bosom. LC 82-72722. 180p. (Orig.). 1982. pap. 4.00 (ISBN 0-931494-27-3). Brunswick Pub.

Karlin, Bernie. I Love-Hate New York. LC 82-5151. (Illus.). 64p. (Orig.). 1982. pap. 3.95 (ISBN 0-87131-390-1). M Evans.

Karlin, Kenneth D. & Zubieta, Jon, eds. Copper & Coordination Chemistry: Biochemical & Inorganic Perspectives. (Illus.). 500p. 1983. text ed. 65.00 (ISBN 0-940030-03-9). Adenine Pr.

Karlin, Leonard & Karlin, Muriel S. Your Career in Allied Dental Professions. LC 81-20484. (Arco's Career Guidance Ser.). 128p. 1982. lib. bdg. 7.95 (ISBN 0-668-05286-4); pap. 4.50 (ISBN 0-668-05291-0). Arco.

Karlin, Muriel S. Make Your Child a Success: Career Guidance from Kindergarten to College. LC 82-82109. 192p. 1983. pap. 6.95 (ISBN 0-448-12056-9, G&D). Putnam Pub Group.

Karlin, Muriel S., jt. auth. see Karlin, Leonard.

Karling, J. S. Chytridiomycetarum Iconographia: Illustrated & Descriptive Guide to the Chytridiomycetous Genera with a Suppl. of the Hyphochytriomycetes. (Illus.). 1978. lib. bdg. 80.00 (ISBN 3-7682-1111-8). Lubrecht & Cramer.

--The Simple Biflagellate Holocarpic Phycomycetes. 2nd ed. (Illus.). 1981. lib. bdg. 60.00x (ISBN 0-686-31663-0). Lubrecht & Cramer.

Karlins, Mark. The Courtyard of Continuous Returning. 50p. 1981. pap. 3.50 (ISBN 0-930794-46-X); ltd., signed ed. o. p. 7.00 (ISBN 0-930794-77-X). Station Hill Pr.

Karlins, Marvin. The Human Use of Human Resources. (Illus.). 208p. (Orig.). 1981. 15.95 (ISBN 0-07-033298-3); pap. text ed. 9.95 (ISBN 0-07-033297-5). McGraw.

--Psyching Out Vegas. (Illus.). 280p. 1983. 12.00 (ISBN 0-914314-03-3). Lyle Stuart.

Karlinsky, Simon. Marina Cvetaeva: Her Life & Art. LC 66-19102. 1966. 25.00x o.p. (ISBN 0-520-00632-1). U of Cal Pr.

Karlinsky, Simon, ed. The Nabokov-Wilson Letters: Correspondence Between Vladimir Nabokov & Edmund Wilson, 1940-1971. LC 78-69627. 1979. 16.30i (ISBN 0-06-012262-5, HarpT). Har-Row.

Karlinsky, Simon, ed. see Poplavskii, Boris I.

Karlinsky, Simon, ed. see Zlobin, Vladimir.

Karman, Theodore Von see Von Mises, Richard & Von Karman, Theodore.

Karmanova, Ida G. Evolution of Sleep. (Illus.). xii, 164p. 1982. 57.75 (ISBN 3-8055-3530-9). S Karger.

Karmel, Louis J. Measurement & Evaluation in the School. 2nd ed. (Illus.). 1978. text ed. 22.95x (ISBN 0-02-362000-5, 36200). Macmillan.

Karmel, Marjorie. Thank You Dr. Lamaze. rev. ed. LC 80-8372. 192p. 1981. 12.45i (ISBN 0-06-014831-4, HarpT). Har-Row.

--Thank You, Dr. Lamaze. LC 80-8372. 192p. 1983. pap. 4.76i (ISBN 0-06-090996-X, CN 996, CN). Har-Row.

Karmel, Mel, jt. auth. see Schnessel, S. Michael.

Karmel, Pepe, tr. see Apollinaire, Guillaume.

Karmel, Roberta S. Regulation by Prosecution: The Securities & Exchange Commission vs. Corporate America. 1982. 19.95 (ISBN 0-671-43408-X). S&S.

Karmiloff-Smith, A. A Functional Approach to Child Language. LC 78-15450. (Cambridge Studies in Linguistics: No. 24). (Illus.). 1981. 42.50 (ISBN 0-521-22416-0); pap. 13.95 (ISBN 0-521-28549-6). Cambridge U Pr.

Karmon, Yehuda. Ports Around the World. (Illus.). 1979. 15.95 o.p. (ISBN 0-517-53378-2). Crown.

Karmos, Joe, et al. Help for Job Hunters. LC 80-69041. 188p. (Orig.). 1982. lib. bdg. 19.75 (ISBN 0-8191-2281-5); pap. text ed. 8.00 (ISBN 0-8191-2282-3). U Pr of Amer.

Karn, George, jt. auth. see Galbraith, Judy.

Karn, Joan & Markle, Geraldine. Reading Consultant. (Michigan Learning Module Ser.: No. 33). 1979. write for info. (ISBN 0-914004-36-0). Ulrich.

Karn, V. Retiring to the Seaside. (International Library of Social Policy). 1977. 22.75x o.p. (ISBN 0-7100-8418-8). Routledge & Kegan.

Karn, Valerie, jt. ed. see Ungerson, Clare.

Karna, M. Studies in Bihar's Economy & Society. 135p. 1981. text ed. 16.50x (ISBN 0-391-02276-8, Pub. by Concept India). Humanities.

Karnani, Chetan. Criticism, Aesthetics & Psychology: A Study of the Writings of I.A. Richards. 1977. text ed. 8.25x (ISBN 0-391-01064-6). Humanities.

--Nirad C. Chaudhuri. (World Authors Ser.). 1980. lib. bdg. 15.95 (ISBN 0-8057-6245-0, Twayne). G K Hall.

Karnehm, Jack. Billiards & Snooker. (Illus.). 120p. 1973. 11.50 o.p. (ISBN 0-7207-0360-3). Transatlantic.

Karnes, M. Ray, jt. auth. see Micheels, William M.

Karney, David L., jt. auth. see Gregory, Robert.

Karni, Karen & Viskochil, Karen, eds. Clinical Laboratory Management: A Guide for Clinical Laboratory Scientists. 1982. text ed. 24.95 (ISBN 0-316-48275-7). Little.

Karnik, K., ed. see Unispace International Round Table, New York, 8-10 March 1982.

Karnoff, Jean N., tr. see Verissimo, Erico.

Karnopp, D., jt. auth. see Rosenberg, R.

Karnopp, Dean C., jt. auth. see Crandall, Stephen H.

Karnovsky, Manfred L. & Bolis, Lian, eds. Phagocytosis: Past & Future. LC 82-11461. 586p. 1982. 47.50 (ISBN 0-12-400050-9). Acad Pr.

Karo, Wolf, jt. auth. see Sandler, Stanley R.

Karol. Chemical Grouting. (Civil Engineering Ser.). 344p. 1983. 45.00 (ISBN 0-8247-1835-6). Dekker.

Karol, N. H. & Ginsburg, S. G. Managing the Higher Education Enterprise. 269p. 1980. 39.50x (ISBN 0-471-05022-9). Ronald Pr.

Karolak, S., jt. auth. see Bisko, W.

Karolevitz, Robert F. & Fenn, Ross S. Flight of Eagles. 281p. 1974. 11.95 o.p. (ISBN 0-88498-022-7). Brown Bk.

Karoly, Paul & Steffen, John J., eds. Improving Children's Competence: Advances in Child Behavioral Analysis & Therapy, Vol. I. LC 82-47798. (Advances in Child Behavior Analysis & Therapy Ser.). 336p. 1982. 28.95x (ISBN 0-669-05640-5). Lexington Bks.

Karoly, Paul, jt. ed. see Steffen, John J.

Karoly, Paul, et al, eds. Child Health Psychology: Concepts & Issues. (Pergamon General Psychology Ser.: No. 113). (Illus.). 288p. 1982. 26.50 (ISBN 0-08-029368-9, J115). Pergamon.

Karouzou, Semni. The National Museum. (Athenon Illustrated Guides Ser.). (Illus.). 174p. 1983. pap. 12.00 (ISBN 0-88332-297-8, 8241, Pub by Ekdotike Athenon Greece). Larousse.

Karp, Abraham J., ed. The Jewish Experience in America: Selected Studies from the Publications of the American Jewish Historical Society, 5 vols. Incl. The Colonial Period. 455p; Vol. II. The Early Republic. 420p; The Emerging Community. 417p; The Era of Immigration. 522p; At Home in America. 440p. 59.50 set o.p. (ISBN 0-686-95133-6). ADL.

Karp, Abraham J., intro. by. Beginnings: Early American Judaica a Collection of Ten Publications in Facsimile, Illustrative of the Religious, Communal, Cultural & Political Life of American Jewry, 1761-1845. LC 75-23405. (Illus.). 1975. 20.00 (ISBN 0-8276-0076-3, 376). Jewish Pubn.

Karp, David A. & Yoels, William C. Experiencing the Life Cycle: A Social Psychology of Aging. (Illus.). 224p. 1982. pap. 14.75x (ISBN 0-398-04708-1). C C Thomas.

Karp, David A., et al. Being Urban: A Social Psychological View of City Life. 1977. pap. text ed. 10.95 (ISBN 0-669-95703-8). Heath.

Karp, Deborah. Heroes of American Jewish History. Effron, Benjamin, ed. 155p. pap. 6.00 (ISBN 0-686-95130-1). ADL.

Karp, Gerald. Cell Biology. (Illus.). 1979. text ed. 28.95 (ISBN 0-07-033341-6, C). McGraw.

Karp, Gerald & Berrill, N. J. Development. 2nd ed. (Illus.). 640p. 1981. text ed. 27.95 (ISBN 0-07-033340-8, C). McGraw.

Karp, Harry. Practical Applications of Data Communications: A User's Guide. (Electronics Book Ser.). 424p. 1980. 30.50 (ISBN 0-07-033342-4). McGraw.

Karp, Harry R., jt. auth. see Folts, Harold C.

Karp, Harry R., ed. see Electronics Magazine.

Karp, Richard A. Proving Operating Systems Correct. Stone, Harold, ed. LC 82-13378. (Computer Science: System Programming Ser.: No. 16). 1983. 34.95 (ISBN 0-8357-1365-2, Pub. by UMI Res Pr). Univ Microfilms.

Karp, Sherman, jt. auth. see Gagliardi, Robert M.

Karp, Walter. Charles Darwin & the Origin of Species. LC 68-12439. (Horizon Caravel Bks.). 154p. (YA) (gr. 7 up). 1968. 9.95 o.p. (ISBN 0-06-023094-0, HarpJ); PLB 12.89 (ISBN 0-06-023095-9). Har-Row.

--The Politics of War: The Story of Two Wars Which Altered Forever the Political Life of the American Republic (1890-1920) LC 78-20170. 1979. 16.30i (ISBN 0-06-012265-X, HarpT). Har-Row.

Karpat, K. H. The Gecekondu: Rural Migration & Urbanization in Turkey. LC 75-12159. (Illus.). 1976. 44.50 (ISBN 0-521-20954-4). Cambridge U Pr.

Karpati, G., jt. ed. see Aguayo, A. G.

Karpel, Mark A., jt. auth. see Strauss, Eric S.

Karpeles, Maud & Sharp, Cecil J., eds. Eighty Appalachian Folk Songs. LC 82-24252. 112p. 1983. pap. 5.95 (ISBN 0-571-10049-X). Faber & Faber.

Karpinski, Jakub. Countdown: The Polish Upheavals of 1956, 1968, 1970, 1976, 1980. Amsterdamska, Olga & Moore, Gene, trs. from Pol. 256p. 1982. text ed. 29.95x (ISBN 0-918294-14-2); pap. 9.95x (ISBN 0-918294-15-0). Karz-Cohl Pub.

Karples, Maud & Shaw, Pat, eds. The Crystal Spring, 2 vols. 1975. Vol. 1. pap. 8.50 o.p. (ISBN 0-19-330516-X); Vol. 2. pap. 9.50 (ISBN 0-19-330517-8). Oxford U Pr.

Karplus, Walter, jt. auth. see Vemuri, V.

Karplus, Walter J., jt. auth. see Tomovic, Rajko.

Karplus, Walter J., ed. Peripheral Array Processors. (Simulation Ser.: Vol. 11, No. 1). 170p. 1982. 30.00 (ISBN 0-686-38787-2). Soc Computer Sim.

Karpman, V. I. Non-Linear Waves in Dispersive Media. Cap, Ferdinand, tr. 1975. text ed. 32.00 (ISBN 0-08-017720-4). Pergamon.

Karpodini-Dimitriadi, E. Greece. (Athenon Illustrated Guides Ser.). (Illus.). 212p. 1983. pap. 20.00 (ISBN 0-686-43392-0, 8234, Pub. by Ekdotike Athenon Greece). Larousse.

--The Peloponnese. (Athenon Illustrated Guides Ser.). (Illus.). 208p. 1983. pap. 20.00 (ISBN 0-88332-306-0, 8243, Pub. by Ekdotike Athenon Greece). Larousse.

Karpoff, Arnold J. Biology One Hundred Two: An Introduction to the Biological Sciences. 152p. 1982. pap. text ed. 11.95 (ISBN 0-8403-2931-8). Kendall-Hunt.

Karpovick, P., jt. auth. see Murray, J.

Karr, Clarence, Jr., ed. Analytical Methods for Coal & Coal Products, 2 vols. LC 78-4928. 66.50 ea. Vol. 1, 1978 (ISBN 0-12-399901-4). Vol. 2, 1979 (ISBN 0-12-399902-2). Set. 104.00 (ISBN 0-686-85501-9). Acad Pr.

Karr, Phyllis A. Frostflower & Thorn. 1980. pap. 2.25 o.p. (ISBN 0-425-04540-4). Berkley Pub.

--Frostflower & Windbourne. 240p. 1982. pap. 2.50 o.p. (ISBN 0-425-05591-4). Berkley Pub.

--The King Arthur Companion. (Illus.). 192p. 1983. 15.95 (ISBN 0-686-84044-5). Reston.

--Lady Susan. 320p. (Based on the unfinished novel by Jane Austen). 1980. 11.95 o.p. (ISBN 0-89696-074-9, An Everest House Book). Dodd.

Karran, S. J. Practical Nutritional Support. LC 79-56645. 351p. 1980. 40.00x (ISBN 0-471-08024-1, Pub. by Wiley Medical). Wiley.

Karras, Alex. Even Big Guys Cry. 1978. pap. 2.50 (ISBN 0-451-09627-4, E9627, Sig). NAL.

Karrass, Chester L. Give & Take: The Complete Guide to Negotiating Strategies & Tactics. LC 74-4360. 1974. 12.45i (ISBN 0-690-00566-0). T Y Crowell.

--Negotiating Game: How to Get What You Want. LC 74-1440. 1970. 12.45i (ISBN 0-690-00359-5). T Y Crowell.

Karren, Kieth J., jt. auth. see Hafen, Brent Q.

Karrenbrock, Marilyn H., jt. auth. see Lucas, Linda.

Karrer, W., jt. ed. see Bruck, P.

Karris, Robert J., jt. auth. see Getty, Mary A.

Karris, Robert J., jt. auth. see Havener, Ivan.

Karris, Robert J., jt. auth. see Kurz, William S.

Karris, Robert J., jt. auth. see Pilch, John J.

Karris, Robert J., ed. Collegeville Bible Commentary Series, 11 Vols. 1983. Set. pap. 25.00. Liturgical Pr.
Karris, Robert J., ed. see Flanagan, Neal M.
Karris, Robert J., ed. see Harrington, Daniel J.
Karris, Robert J., ed. see Kodell, Jerome.
Karris, Robert J., ed. see MacRae, George W.
Karris, Robert J., ed. see Neyrey, Jerome H.
Karris, Robert J., ed. see Perkins, Pheme.
Karris, Robert J., ed. see Van Linden, Philip.
Karris, Robert J., tr. see Lohse, Eduard.
Karrow, Paul F., jt. auth. see Legget, Robert.
Karsavina, Jean, ed. & tr. see Ochorowicz-Monatowa, Marja.
Karsen, Sonja. Jaime Torres Bodet. (World Authors Ser.). lib. bdg. 15.95 (ISBN 0-8057-2156-8, Twayne). G K Hall.
Karsh, Jeff, jt. auth. see Swanson, Jack W.
Karshen, S., ed. The Natural Approach: Language Acquisition in the Classroom. Terrell, T. (Language Teaching Methodology Ser.). (Illus.). 160p. 1982. 11.95 (ISBN 0-08-028651-8). Pergamon.
Karshner, Roger. Thirty Modern Schemes. 4.00 (ISBN 0-573-60079-1). French.
Karsk, Roger & Thomas, Bill. Working with Men's Groups, Vol. 1. 1979. pap. 7.00 (ISBN 0-934698-03-1). New Comm Pr.
Karsk, Roger S. Teenagers in the Next America. 1977. pap. 6.95 (ISBN 0-934698-07-4). New Comm Pr.
Karssen, Gien. Getting the Most Out of Being Single. rev. ed. LC 82-62240. 1983. pap. 3.95 (ISBN 0-89109-505-5). NavPress.
Karsten, P. A. Mycologia Fennica: 1871-78, 4 parts in 1 vol. 1967. 144.00 (ISBN 3-7682-0353-0). Lubrecht & Cramer.
--Symbolae Ad Mycologiam Fennicam. 1966. Repr. of 1895 ed. 64.00 (ISBN 3-7682-0352-2). Lubrecht & Cramer.
Karsten, Peter. Law, Soldiers, & Combat. LC 77-87976. (Contributions in Legal Studies: No. 3). (Illus.). 1978. lib. bdg. 27.50 (ISBN 0-313-20042-4, KSL/). Greenwood.
--Soldiers & Society: The Effects of Military Service & War on American Life. LC 77-87973. (Grass Roots Perspectives on American History: No. 1). (Illus.). 1978. lib. bdg. 29.95x (ISBN 0-313-20056-4, KAM/). Greenwood.
Karsten, Rafael. Toba Indians of the Bolivian Gran Chaco. 1967. text ed. 12.50x (ISBN 90-6234-023-7). Humanities.
Karter, Michael J. Fire Facts. Carwile, Ruth H., ed. LC 81-85437. (Illus.). 86p. (Orig.). Date not set. pap. text ed. 8.95 o.p. (ISBN 0-87765-211-2). Natl Fire Prot.
Kartezi. Bolyai Appendix. Date not set. price not set (ISBN 0-444-86528-4). Elsevier.
Kartha. Dosimetry Workbook. 1982. 16.95 (ISBN 0-8151-4983-2). Year Bk Med.
Kartiganer, Donald M. & Griffith, Malcolm A. Theories of American Literature: The Critical Perspective. 480p. 1972. pap. text ed. 12.95x (ISBN 0-02-362040-4). Macmillan.
Karttunen, Frances. An Analytical Dictionary of Nahuatl. (Texas Linguistics Ser.). 385p. 1983. text ed. 35.00x (ISBN 0-292-70365-1). U of Tex Pr.
Kartzman, Elaine. Smart Secretary's Guide to Earning More Than Just a Salary. (Illus.). 1980. 7.95 (ISBN 0-913814-25-3). Nevada Pubns.
Karuna Jemal, Sophia. The Story of Joy. (Illus.). 1978. pap. 3.00 (ISBN 0-932286-00-3). Suratao.
Karunakaran, K. P. Democracy in India. 1978. 14.00x o.p. (ISBN 0-8364-0132-8). South Asia Bks.
Karush, Aaron, et al. Psychotherapy in Chronic Ulcerative Colitis. (Illus., LC 76-028939). 1977. text ed. 13.75 o.p. (ISBN 0-7216-5293-X). Saunders.
Karve, D. D. & McDonald, Ellen E. The New Brahmans: Five Maharashtrian Families. LC 63-11389. 1963. 34.50x (ISBN 0-520-00635-6). U of Cal Pr.
Karweit, Nancy L., jt. ed. see Epstein, Joyce L.
Kasahara, K. Earthquake Mechanics. LC 79-50624. (Cambridge Earth Science Ser.). (Illus.). 256p. 1980. 59.50 (ISBN 0-521-22736-4). Cambridge U Pr.
Kasahara, Kunihiko. Creative Origami. LC 67-87040. (Illus.). 1977. pap. 14.60 (ISBN 0-87040-411-3). Japan Pubns.
--Origami Made Easy. LC 73-83956. (Illus.). 128p. 1973. pap. 5.25 (ISBN 0-87040-253-6). Japan Pubns.
Kasakov. Goluboe i Zelenoe. (Easy Reader, C). 1972. pap. 3.95 (ISBN 0-88436-053-9, 65253). EMC.
Kasarda, John D., jt. auth. see Berry, Brian J.
Kasch, Fred W. & Boyer, John L. Adult Fitness: Principles & Practice. (Illus.). 147p. 1968. pap. 6.95 (ISBN 0-87484-200-X). Mayfield Pub.
Kaschmitter, William A. The Spirituality of the Catholic Church. 980p. 1982. 30.00 (ISBN 0-912414-33-2). Lumen Christi.
Kaschnitz, Marie L. Kurzgeschichten. (Easy Readers, Ser. B). 72p. (German.). 1976. pap. text ed. 3.95 (ISBN 0-88436-277-9, 45267). EMC.
Kasdan, Sara. So It Was Just a Simple Wedding. LC 61-13280. 8.95 o.s.i. (ISBN 0-8149-0133-6). Vanguard.
Kasden, Lawrence N., jt. auth. see Hoeber, Daniel R.
Kase, Ronald J., ed. The Human Services. LC 79-2341. 1979. 24.50 (ISBN 0-404-16048-4); pap. 8.95 (ISBN 0-686-96656-2). AMS Pr.
Kasell, Walter. Marcel Proust & the Strategy of Reading. (Purdue Monographs in Romance Languages). x, 125p. 1980. 19.00 (ISBN 90-272-1714-9, 4). Benjamins North Am.
Kasemann, Ernst. Perspectives on Paul. LC 79-157540. 184p. 1982. pap. 7.50 (ISBN 0-8006-1730-4, 1-1730). Fortress.
Kasemets, Udo, jt. ed. see Beckwith, John.
Kasendorf, E., jt. auth. see Hauser, Stuart T.
Kaser, David. Directory of the Book & Printing Industries in Ante-Bellum Nashville. LC 66-17837. 1966. pap. 7.50 o.p. (ISBN 0-87104-061-1). NY Pub Lib.
Kaser, M., ed. see Jasny, Naum.
Kaser, M. C. The Economic History of Eastern Europe 1919-1975. (Illus.). 1982. 65.00x (ISBN 0-19-828445-4). Oxford U Pr.
Kaser, M. C. & Radice, E. A., eds. The Economic History of Eastern Europe, 1919-75: Economic Structure & Performance Between the Two Wars, Vol. 1. 576p. 1982. 39.95x (ISBN 0-19-828444-6). Oxford U Pr.
Kaser, Michael, jt. ed. see Brown, Archie.
Kaser, Michael C., ed. Economic Development in Eastern Europe. (Illus.). 1969. 25.00 o.p. (ISBN 0-312-22855-4). St Martin.
Kaserand, Michael & Zielinski, J. Planning in East Europe. 1971. 7.50 o.p. (ISBN 0-370-00397-7). Transatlantic.
Kash, Marilynn M. & Borich, Gary D. Teacher Behavior & Pupil Self-Conce pt. LC 77-79452. (Education Ser.). (Illus.). 1978. text ed. 14.95 (ISBN 0-201-00843-2). A-W.
Kashani, Jamal. Iran's Men of Destiny. 1983. 12.50 (ISBN 0-533-05375-7). Vantage.
Kasher, Menachem M. Israel Passover Haggadah. LC 64-17316. (Illus.). 1983. Repr. of 1964 ed. 13.95 (ISBN 0-88400-018-4). Shengold.
Kashima, Tetsuden. Buddhism in America: The Social Organization of an Ethnic Religious Institution. LC 76-57837. (Contributions in Sociology: No. 26). (Illus.). 1977. lib. bdg. 29.95 (ISBN 0-8371-9534-9, KSO/). Greenwood.
Kashner, Rita. Bed Rest. 288p. 1982. pap. 3.25 (ISBN 0-441-05285-1). Ace Bks.
Kashyap, L., jt. auth. see Dash, Bhagwan.
Kashyap, L., jt. ed. see Dash, V.
Kashyap, Lalitesh, jt. auth. see Dash, Bhagan.
Kasimow, Harold. Divine-Human Encounter: A Study of Abraham Joshua Heschel. LC 79-63562. 1979. pap. text ed. 8.25 (ISBN 0-8191-0731-X). U Pr of Amer.
Kaskell, jt. auth. see Morse.
Kaskie, Shirli. A Woman's Golf Game. (Illus.). 208p. 1983. pap. 7.95 (ISBN 0-8092-5756-4). Contemp Bks.
Kasl, Elizabeth, jt. auth. see Anderson, Richard E.
Kasle, Myron J. & Langlais, Robert. Basic Principles of Oral Radiography. (Exercises in Dental Radiology Ser.: Vol. 4). (Illus.). 200p. 1981. text ed. 18.00 (ISBN 0-7216-5291-3). Saunders.
Kaslof, Leslie J., ed. Wholistic Dimensions in Healing: A Resource Guide. LC 76-50874. 1978. 12.95 o.p. (ISBN 0-385-12628-X, Dolp). Doubleday.
Kaslow, Arthur. Freedom from Chronic Disease. 1979. 10.95x (ISBN 0-87477-112-9). Cancer Control Soc.
Kaslow, Florence & Sussman, Marvin B., eds. Cults & the Family. LC 81-20264. (Marriage & Family Review Ser.: Vol. 4, Nos. 3 & 4). 200p. 1982. text ed. 24.95 (ISBN 0-917724-55-0, B55); pap. text ed. 15.00 (ISBN 0-917724-81-X, B81). Haworth Pr.
Kaslow, Florence W., ed. The International Book of Family Therapy. LC 82-45472. 500p. 1982. 30.00 (ISBN 0-87630-316-5). Brunner-Mazel.
Kasner & Newman. Mathematics & the Imagination. 1962. pap. 4.95 o.p. (ISBN 0-671-20855-1, Touchstone Bks). S&S.
Kasner, Erick. Essentials of Engineering Economics. (Illus.). 1979. text ed. 23.95 (ISBN 0-07-033323-8, G). McGraw.
Kasper, Joseph & Feller, Steven. Digital Integrated Circuits. 197p. 1983. 19.95 (ISBN 0-13-213587-6); pap. 12.95 (ISBN 0-13-213579-5). P-H.
Kasper, Keith, jt. auth. see Haag, Kimberley.
Kasper, W. & Goebell, H., eds. Colon & Nutrition. (Illus.). 350p. 1982. text ed. 75.00 (ISBN 0-85200-444-3, Pub. by MTP Pr England). Kluwer Boston.
Kasper, Walter. Theology of Christian Marriage. 112p. 1983. pap. 5.95 (ISBN 0-8245-0559-X). Crossroad NY.
Kasperson, Roger E. & Berberian, Miriam, eds. Equity Issues in Radioactive Waste Management. LC 81-18702. 416p. 1983. text ed. 25.00 (ISBN 0-89946-055-0). Oelgeschlager.
Kaşra, Parichehr, tr. see Omar Khayyam.
Kass, E., ed. Voltaren-New Findings: Proceedings of an International Symposium on Voltaren Held in Paris on 22nd June 1981 During the 15th International Congress of Rheumatology. (Illus.). 93p. Date not set. pap. text ed. 12.00 (ISBN 3-456-81205-1, Pub. by Hans Huber Switzerland). J K Burgess.
Kass, Edward H. & Platt, Richard. Current Therapy of Infectious Disease. 400p. 1983. text ed. 44.00 (ISBN 0-941158-06-3, D2621-8). Mosby.
Kass, Iiana. Soviet Involvement in the Middle East: Policy Formulation, 1966-1973. LC 77-8279. 273p. 1978. 30.00 (ISBN 0-89158-063-8). Westview.
Kass, Jonathan F. Hellcopter. LC 81-81946. 144p. 1983. 9.95 (ISBN 0-86666-041-0). GWP.
Kass, Lawrence. Pernicious Anemia. LC 75-8180. (Major Problems in Internal Medicine: Vol. 7). (Illus.). 335p. 1976. text ed. 18.00 o.p. (ISBN 0-7216-5295-6). Saunders.
Kass, Louis A. New York Civil Practice & Procedure. 150p. 1982. 6.50 (ISBN 0-87526-093-4). Gould.
--New York Landlord-Tenant. 1964. pap. 4.00x (ISBN 0-87526-043-8). Gould.
Kass, Ray. Morris Graves: Vision of the Inner Eye. (Illus.). 176p. (Orig.). 1983. 35.00 (ISBN 0-8076-1068-2); pap. 15.00 (ISBN 0-8076-1069-0). Braziller.
Kassack, Nancy, jt. ed. see Moore, Lou.
Kassakowski & Obudhowski. Progress in the Psychology of Personality. Date not set. 40.50 (ISBN 0-444-86347-8). Elsevier.
Kassam, S. A. & Thomas, J. B., eds. Nonparametric Detection: Theory & Applications. LC 79-22557. (Benchmark Papers in Electrical Engineering & Computer Science Ser.: Vol. 23). 349p. 1980. 55.00. Hutchinson Ross.
Kass-Annese, Barbara & Danzer, Hal C. Patterns. 1981. pap. 9.95 (ISBN 0-941304-02-7). Hunter Hse.
Kassarjian, Harold & Robertson, Thomas. Perspectives in Consumer Behavior. 3rd ed. 1981. pap. text ed. 15.50x (ISBN 0-673-15394-0). Scott F.
Kasschau. Information Technology & Psychology. 272p. 1982. 29.95 (ISBN 0-03-061771-5). Praeger.
Kasschau, Patricia L. Aging & Social Policy: Leadership Planning. LC 78-15481. 1978. 31.95 o.p. (ISBN 0-03-046411-0). Praeger.
Kassem, Mahmoud M., et al, eds. see Averroes, Rushd Ibn.
Kassin, E., et al. Lev Tolstoy & Yasnaya Polyana. 253p. 1982. 25.00 (ISBN 0-8285-2226-X, Pub. by Progress Pubs USSR). Imported Pubns.
Kassin, Saul J. The Light of the Law. LC 80-51979. 288p. 1981. 16.95 o.p. (ISBN 0-88400-069-9). Shengold.
Kassis, Hanna E. A Concordance of the Qur'an. LC 82-40100. 1400p. 1982. 75.00 o.p. (ISBN 0-520-04327-8). U of Cal Pr.
Kassity, K. J., ed. Manual of Ambulatory Surgery. (Comprehensive Manuals of Surgical Specialties Ser.). (Illus.). 266p. 1982. 125.00 (ISBN 0-387-90700-9). Springer-Verlag.
Kasson, John F. Civilizing the Machine: Technology & Republican Values in America 1776-1900. 1977. pap. 4.95 (ISBN 0-14-004415-9). Penguin.
Kassorla, Irene. Nice Girls Do. LC 80-53202. 1980. 9.95 (ISBN 0-936906-01-4). Stratford Pr.
--Winner Take All. 330p. Date not set. 14.95 (ISBN 0-686-37555-6). Delacorte.
Kast, Fremont & Rosenzweig, James. Experiential Exercises & Cases in Management. (Illus.). 1976. text ed. 19.95 (ISBN 0-07-033343-2); instructor's manual 18.00 (ISBN 0-07-033344-0). McGraw.
--Organization & Management: A Systems & Contingency Approach. 3rd rev. ed. (Management Ser.). (Illus.). 1979. text ed. 27.50x (ISBN 0-07-033346-7, C); instructor's manual 20.00 (ISBN 0-07-033347-5). McGraw.
Kast, Fremont E. & Rosenzweig, James E. Contingency Views of Organization & Management. LC 73-75421. (Illus.). 355p. 1973. pap. text ed. 11.95 (ISBN 0-574-17135-5, 13-0135). SRA.
Kastan, David S. Shakespeare & the Shapes of Time. LC 82-40337. 200p. 1982. text ed. 25.00x (ISBN 0-87451-237-9). U Pr of New Eng.
Kastein, Shulamith, jt. auth. see Michal-Smith, Harold.
Kastein, Shulamith, et al. Raising the Young Blind Child: A Guide for Parents & Educators. LC 79-17820. 208p. 1980. text ed. 19.95 (ISBN 0-87705-422-3). Human Sci Pr.
Kasten, Frederick H., jt. auth. see Clark, George.
Kasten, L. A., ed. see Alfonso X.
Kasten, Lloyd & Anderson, Jean. Concordance to the Celestina (1499) 338p. 1976. 12.50 (ISBN 0-942260-10-4). Hispanic Seminary.
Kasten, Lloyd & Nitti, John. Concordances & Texts of the Royal Scriptorium Manuscripts of Alfonso X, el Sabio, 2 vols. (Spanish Ser.: No. 2). 1978. 150.00x (ISBN 0-686-27739-2). Hispanic Seminary.
Kasten, Lloyd, jt. auth. see Nitti, John.
Kasten, Lloyd, ed. see Aristotele, Pseudo.
Kastenbaum, Robert. Between Life & Death. LC 79-17760. (Death & Suicide Ser.: Vol. 1). 1979. text ed. 19.95 (ISBN 0-8261-2540-9); pap. text ed. 9.95 (ISBN 0-8261-2541-7). Springer Pub.
Kastenbaum, Robert J. Death, Society, & Human Experience. 2nd ed. 316p. 1981. pap. text ed. 15.95 (ISBN 0-8016-2640-4). Mosby.
Kastenbaum, Robert J., et al. Old, Sick & Helpless: Where Therapy Begins. 240p. 1981. prof ref 24.50x (ISBN 0-88410-717-5). Ballinger Pub.
Kastenbaum, Roberts, jt. auth. see Brustman, Barbara.
Kastens, U., et al. GAG: A Practical Compiler Generator. (Lecture Notes in Computer Science: Vol. 141). 156p. 1983. pap. 10.00 (ISBN 0-387-11591-9). Springer-Verlag.
Kaster, Lewis R., ed. Sale-Leasebacks: Economics, Tax Aspects, & Lease Terms. LC 79-87444. 1979. text ed. 25.00 (ISBN 0-685-95818-3, N2-1314). PLI.
Kasterine, Omitri. England & the English. 1981. 24.95 (ISBN 0-437-08050-1, Pub. by World's Work). David & Charles.
Kastinger Riley, Helene M. Das Bild der Antike in der Deutschen Romantik. (German Language & Literature Monographs: No. 10). xvi, 288p. (Ger.). 1981. 30.00 (ISBN 90-272-4003-5). Benjamins North Am.
Kastle, Herbert. Ladies of the Valley. 1980. pap. 2.75 o.s.i. (ISBN 0-440-14776-X). Dell.
--Sunset People. 384p. (Orig.). 1980. pap. 2.75 o.s.i. (ISBN 0-515-05488-7). Jove Pubns.
Kastler, D., ed. C-Algebras & Their Applications in Statistical Mechanics & Quantum Field Theory. (Enrico Fermi Summer School Ser.: Vol. 6). 1976. 59.75 (ISBN 0-7204-0449-5, North-Holland). Elsevier.
Kastner. Drei Manner Im Schnee. (Easy Reader, C). pap. 3.95 (ISBN 0-88436-038-5, 45271). EMC.
Kastner, Emerich. Chronologisches Verzeichniss der Von und Uber Richard Wagner Erschienenen Schriften, Musikwerke. (Composers' Worklists Ser.: Vol. 1). 1966. Repr. of 1878 ed. wrappers 20.00 o.s.i. (ISBN 90-6027-008-8, Pub. by Frits Knuf Netherlands). Pendragon NY.
Kastner, Erich. Emil und die Detektive. (Easy Readers, B). 1969. pap. 3.95 (ISBN 0-88436-297-3). EMC.
Kastor, Frank S. Giles & Phineas Fletcher. (English Authors Ser.: No. 225). 1978. lib. bdg. 14.95 (ISBN 0-8057-6696-0, Twayne). G K Hall.
Kastrup, Erwin K. & Boyd, James R., eds. Facts & Comparisons: Drug Information, 1982 Edition. 1925p. 1981. text ed. 59.50 o.p. (ISBN 0-932686-82-6, Lippincott Medical); write for info. loose leaf ed. o.p. (ISBN 0-932686-00-1); Microfiche Ed. 59.00 o.p. (ISBN 0-686-97931-1). Lippincott.
Kasulis, T. P. Zen Action-Zen Person. LC 80-27858. 192p. 1980. text ed. 12.95x (ISBN 0-8248-0702-2). UH Pr.
Kaswan, Jaques W., jt. auth. see Love, Lenore R.
Kaswell, E. R. Handbook of Industrial Textile. Sears, Wellington, ed. 1963. 33.00x (ISBN 0-87245-160-7). Textile Bk.
Kaszonyi, Kay, jt. auth. see Lowman, Kaye.
Kaszubski, Marek, jt. ed. see Wasserman, Paul.
Kata, Elizabeth. Patch of Blue. 144p. 1975. pap. 2.25 (ISBN 0-445-00303-0). Juniper.
Kataev, Valentin. The Small Farm in the Steppe. Bostock, Anna, tr. from Russ. LC 74-10362. 1976. Repr. of 1958 ed. lib. bdg. 19.75x (ISBN 0-8371-7674-3, KASF). Greenwood.
Katahn, Martin. The Two Hundred Calorie Solution: How to Burn an Extra 200 Calories a Day & Lose Weight. 320p. 1983. pap. 3.50 (ISBN 0-425-06065-9). Berkley Pub.
Katahn, Martin & Robins, Arthur J. Pathways to a Career in Mental Health. 350p. Date not set. 9.75 o.p. (ISBN 0-88437-007-0). Psych Dimensions.
Katan, Norma J. & Mintz, Barbara. Hieroglyphs: The Writing of Ancient Egypt. LC 80-13576. (Illus.). (gr. 4-7). 1981. 9.95 (ISBN 0-689-50176-5, McElderry Bk). Atheneum.
Kataoka, Tetsuya. Resistance & Revolution in China: The Communists & the Second United Front. LC 73-84386. (Illus.). 1974. 38.50x (ISBN 0-520-02553-9). U of Cal Pr.
Kataria, R. D. A Sailor Remembers. 1983. text ed. write for info. (ISBN 0-7069-2064-3, Pub. by Vikas India). Advent NY.
Katch, Frank I. & McArdle, William D. Nutrition, Weight Control, & Exercise. LC 82-25873. (Illus.). 300p. 1983. text ed. price not set (ISBN 0-8121-0867-1). Lea & Febiger.
Katch, Frank I., et al. Getting in Shape: An Optimum Approach to Fitness & Weight Control. 1979. 7.95 o.p. (ISBN 0-395-27782-5). HM.
Katcha Goodwon. The Complete Thinking Man's Guide to Handicapping & Training. 232p. (Orig.). 1983. 19.95 (ISBN 0-932896-05-7). Westcliff Pub.
Katchalsky, Aharon, et al. Dynamic Patterns of Brain Cell Assemblies. 1974. 20.00x (ISBN 0-262-11056-3). MIT Pr.
Katcher, Aaron, jt. ed. see Beck, Alan.
Katcher, Brian S. & Young, Lloyd Y., eds. Applied Therapeutics: The Clinical Use of Drugs. (Illus.). 1983. pap. 54.00 (ISBN 0-915486-05-9). Applied Therapeutics.
Katcher, Brian S., jt. ed. see Koda-Kimble, Mary Anne.
Kateman, G. & Pijpers, F. W. Quality Control in Analytical Chemistry. LC 80-23146. (Chemical Analysis Ser.). 276p. 1981. 48.00x (ISBN 0-471-46020-6, Pub. by Wiley-Interscience). Wiley.
Katen, Thomas E. Doing Philosophy. (Illus.). 368p. 1973. text ed. 19.95 (ISBN 0-13-217570-3). P-H.
Kater, John. Another Letter of John to James. (Illus.). 64p. (Orig.). (gr. k-5). 1982. pap. 3.95 (ISBN 0-8164-2376-8). Seabury.
--The Letter of John to James. (Illus.). 64p. (Orig.). (gr. k-5). 1981. pap. 3.95 (ISBN 0-8164-2344-X). Seabury.

Kater, Michael H. The Nazi Party: A Social Profile of Members & Leaders, 1919-1945. (Illus.). 400p. 1983. text ed. 25.00x (ISBN 0-674-60655-8). Harvard U Pr.

Kates, Dan B. Restricting Handguns: The Liberal Sceptics Speak Out. 7.95 (ISBN 0-88427-033-5). Green Hill.

Kates, Don B., Jr. Firearms & Violence: Issues of Regulation. (Pacific Institute on Public Policy Research Ser.). 1983. prof ref 38.00x (ISBN 0-88410-922-4). Ballinger Pub.

Kates, George N. The Years That Were Fat: The Last of Old China. 1967. 15.00 (ISBN 0-262-11063-6). MIT Pr.

Kates, M. Techniques of Lipidology. (Laboratory Techniques in Biochemistry & Molecular Biology: Vol. 3, Pt. 2). 1972. pap. 26.00 (ISBN 0-444-10350-3, North-Holland). Elsevier.

Kates, R. W. Risk Assessment of Environmental Hazard Scope Report 8. 112p. 1981. 22.95x (ISBN 0-471-09983-X, Pub. by Wiley-Interscience). Wiley.

Kates, Robert W. Risk Assessment of Environmental Hazard: Scope Report 8. LC 77-12909. (Scientific Committee on Problems of the Environment). 112p. 1978. 19.95x (ISBN 0-471-99582-7, Pub. by Wiley-Interscience). Wiley.

Kates, Robert W., jt. auth. see Burton, Ian.

Kates, Steve. Encyclopedia of Cockatoos. (Illus.). 221p. 1980. 20.00 o.p. (ISBN 0-87666-896-1, H-1023). TFH Pubns.

Katholi, Richard, jt. auth. see Oparil, Suzanne.

Katkousky, Walter & Gorlow, Leon. The Psychology of Adjustment: Current Concepts & Applications. 3rd ed. LC 75-17619. (Illus.). 1975. pap. text ed. 23.00 (ISBN 0-07-033345-9, C). McGraw.

Kato, Hidetoshi. Japanese Research on Mass Communication: Selected Abstracts. LC 74-81141. (Orig.). 1974. pap. 4.50x (ISBN 0-8248-0345-0, Eastwest Ctr). UH Pr.

Kato, Ryuichi, jt. auth. see Sato, Ryo.

Kato, S. & Roper, R. G. Electric Current & Atmospheric Motion. (Advances in Earth & Planetary Sciences Ser.: No. 7). 294p. 1980. 24.50x (ISBN 0-89955-314-1, Pub. by Japan Sci Soc Japan). Intl Schol Bk Serv.

Katoh, jt. ed. see Miyachi.

Katok, A., ed. Ergodic Theory & Dynamical Systems Eleven. (Progress in Mathematics Ser.: Vol. 21). 210p. 1982. text ed. 15.00x (ISBN 3-7643-3096-1). Birkhauser.

Katona, Anna B. Mihaly Vitez Csokonai. (World Authors Ser.). 1980. lib. bdg. 15.95 (ISBN 0-8057-6421-6, Twayne). G K Hall.

Katona, G., jt. ed. see Huskisson, E. C.

Katona, George. Essays on Behavioral Economics. LC 80-15510. (Illus.). 100p. 1980. 10.50x (ISBN 0-87944-257-3). Inst Soc Res.

--Private Pensions & Individual Saving. LC 65-64300. 114p. 1965. pap. 5.00x (ISBN 0-87944-043-0). Inst Soc Res.

Katona, George, et al. Survey of Consumer Finances. Incl. 1960. 330p. pap. 6.00x (ISBN 0-87944-096-1); 1961. 168p. 10.50x; pap. 6.00x (ISBN 0-87944-097-X); 1965. 284p. pap. 6.00x (ISBN 0-87944-101-1); 1966. 328p. pap. 6.00x (ISBN 0-87944-102-X); 1967. 362p. pap. 6.00x (ISBN 0-87944-103-8); 1968. 304p. 10.50x (ISBN 0-87944-105-4); pap. 6.00x (ISBN 0-87944-104-6); 1969. 341p. pap. 6.00x (ISBN 0-87944-106-2); 1970. 346p. 10.50x (ISBN 0-87944-001-5); pap. 6.00x (ISBN 0-87944-000-7). LC 50-39941. pap. Inst Soc Res.

Katona, Steve & Richardson, David. A Field Guide to the Whales, Porpoises, & Seals of the Gulf of Maine & Eastern Canada: Cape Cod to Labrador. (Illus.). 224p. 1983. 17.95 (ISBN 0-686-83664-2, ScribT); pap. 9.95 (ISBN 0-686-83665-0). Scribner.

Katrak, N. N., jt. auth. see Khory, R. N.

Katrin, Susan. The Impact of the Women's Movement on Counseling & Psychotherapy. 10p. 1981. pap. 2.95 (ISBN 0-932930-37-9). Pilgrimage Inc.

Katritsky. Physical Methods in Heterocyclic Chemistry, Vol. 6. 1974. 57.00 (ISBN 0-12-401106-3). Acad Pr.

Katritsky, Alan, ed. Advances in Heterocyclic Chemistry, Vol. 32. 396p. 1982. 74.50 (ISBN 0-12-020632-3); lib. ed. 97.00 (ISBN 0-12-020738-9); microfiche 52.50 (ISBN 0-12-020739-7). Acad Pr.

Katritzky, A. R., ed. Advances in Heterocyclic Chemistry, Vol. 28. (Serial Publication Ser.). 1981. 59.50 (ISBN 0-12-020628-5); lib. ed. 77.00 (ISBN 0-12-020730-3); microfiche 42.50 (ISBN 0-12-020731-1). Acad Pr.

Katritzky, A. R. & Boulton, A. J., eds. Advances in Heterocyclic Chemistry, Vol. 29. LC 62-13037. (Serial Publication). 1981. o.s. 62.50 (ISBN 0-12-020629-3); lib. ed. 81.50 (ISBN 0-12-020732-X); microfiche ed. 44.00 (ISBN 0-12-020733-8). Acad Pr.

--Advances in Heterocyclic Chemistry Supplement, No. 2. 432p. 1982. 59.50 (ISBN 0-12-020652-8); 77.50 (ISBN 0-12-020693-5); 42.00 (ISBN 0-12-020694-3). Acad Pr.

Katritzky, Alan. Advances in Heterocyclic Chemistry, Vol. 31. (Serial Publication). 1982. 68.00 (ISBN 0-12-020631-5); lib. ed. 88.50 (ISBN 0-12-020736-2); microfiche 48.00 (ISBN 0-12-020737-0). Acad Pr.

Katritzky, Alan R., ed. Advances in Heterocyclic Chemistry, Vol. 30. (Serial Publication). 1982. 76.50 (ISBN 0-12-020630-7); Lib ed 88.00 (ISBN 0-12-020734-6); microfiche .65.00 (ISBN 0-12-020735-4). Acad Pr.

--Advances in Heterocyclic Chemistry, Vol. 33. (Serial Publication). Date not set. price not set (ISBN 0-12-020633-1); price not set (ISBN 0-12-020740-0); price not set Microfiche (ISBN 0-12-020741-9). Acad Pr.

Katsaris, Kenneth, ed. Evidence & Procedure in the Administration of Justice. LC 74-17285. (Administration of Justice Ser.). 401p. 1975. text ed. 23.95x (ISBN 0-471-46025-7). Wiley.

Katsaros, Thomas & Schiro, George J. A Brief History of the Western World. LC 78-62178. 1978. pap. text ed. 14.75 (ISBN 0-8191-0466-3). U Pr of Amer.

Katsaros, Thomas & Teluk, John. Capitalism: A Cooperative Venture. LC 80-8163. 161p. 1981. lib. bdg. 19.75 (ISBN 0-8191-1484-7); pap. text ed. 9.00 (ISBN 0-8191-1485-5). U Pr of Amer.

Katsh, Abraham I., ed. Bar Mitzvah Illustrated. 8th ed. LC 76-23713. (Illus.). 1976. 13.95 (ISBN 0-88400-048-6). Shengold.

Katsigris, Costas & Porter, Mary. The Bar & Beverage Book: Basics of Profitable Management. (Service Management Ser.). 480p. 1983. pap. text ed. 23.95x (ISBN 0-471-08264-3). Wiley.

Katsimbalis, George, tr. see Palamas, Kostes.

Katsuki, S., et al, eds. Neurology: Proceedings of the World Congress of Neurology, Twelfth, Kyoto, Japan, September 20-25, 1981. (International Congress Ser.: No. 568). 452p. 1982. 121.00 (ISBN 0-444-90237-6, Excerpta Medica). Elsevier.

Katsuki, Yasuji & Norgren, Ralph. Brain Mechanisms of Sensation. LC 81-2320. 329p. 1981. 35.95 (ISBN 0-471-08148-5, Pub. by Wiley Med). Wiley.

Katsuyama, Allen M., ed. see Food Processors Institute.

Kattell, Ted, jt. auth. see McCarty, Diane.

Kattenburg, Paul M. The Vietnam Trauma in American Foreign Policy 1945-1975. LC 79-66437. 354p. 1980. 19.95 o.p. (ISBN 0-87855-378-9). Transaction Bks.

Katter, Reuben L. The Creation: Its Basis, Essence & Source of Life, the Word-Energy-System Which "Made & Upholds" All Things. 1983. pap. 7.95t (ISBN 0-911806-02-4). Theotes.

--Creationism: The Scientific Evidence of Creator Plan & Purpose for Mankind in His Universe. 1979. pap. 5.95 (ISBN 0-685-96810-3, TX346-483). Theotes.

--History of Creation & Origin of the Species: A Scientific Theological Viewpoint. 3rd ed. 1967. 14.95t (ISBN 0-911806-01-6, C13374); pap. 9.95t (ISBN 0-911806-00-8). Theotes.

--Jesus Christ: The Divine Executive; Architect of the Universe. 1982. 19.95t (ISBN 0-911806-04-0). Theotes.

Katunuma, Nobuhiko, jt. ed. see Schimke, Robert T.

Katz. The Release of Neural Transmitter Substances. 70p. 1982. 50.00x (ISBN 0-85323-060-9, Pub. by Liverpool Univ England). State Mutual Bk.

Katz, Adele T. Challenge to Musical Tradition. LC 79-180046. 408p. 1972. Repr. of 1945 ed. lib. bdg. 35.00 (ISBN 0-306-70428-5). Da Capo.

Katz, Albert M. & Katz, Virginia T. Foundations of Nonverbal Communication: Readings, Exercises, & Commentary. LC 82-10729. (Orig.). 1983. pap. price not set (ISBN 0-8093-1070-8). S Ill U Pr.

Katz, Alfred H. Hemophilia: A Study in Hope & Reality. (Illus.). 176p. 1970. 11.50x (ISBN 0-398-00978-3). C C Thomas.

--Parents of the Handicapped: Self-Organized Parents' & Relatives' Groups for Treatment of Ill & Handicapped Children. 168p. 1961. photocopy ed. spiral 14.95x (ISBN 0-398-00979-1). C C Thomas.

Katz, Alfred H. & Martin, Knute. A Handbook of Services for the Handicapped. LC 81-20314. 1982. lib. bdg. 35.00 (ISBN 0-313-21385-2, KSH/). Greenwood.

Katz, Alfred H. & Smith, David H. Self-Help Group & Voluntary Action: Some International Perspectives. 250p. 1983. text ed. 24.50x (ISBN 0-8290-1274-5). Irvington.

Katz, Arnie & Kunkel, Bill. The Home Video Games Handbook. (Illus.). 224p. 1982. pap. 5.95 cancelled (ISBN 0-201-13337-7). A-W.

Katz, Arnold, ed. Cardiac Arrhythmias. LC 82-19480. (Illus.). 160p. 1983. text ed. 17.95x (ISBN 0-87893-417-0). Sinauer Assoc.

Katz, Arnold M. Physiology of the Heart. LC 75-14580. 464p. 1977. o. p. 31.00 (ISBN 0-89004-053-2); pap. 16.95 (ISBN 0-686-67627-0). Raven.

Katz, Arthur. Reality. 1977. pap. 4.95 (ISBN 0-88270-225-4, Pub. by Logos). Bridge Pub.

Katz, Arthur M. Life After Nuclear War: The Economic & Social Impacts of Nuclear Attacks on the United States. LC 81-1300. 464p. 1981. 27.50x (ISBN 0-88410-096-0); pap. 14.95 (ISBN 0-88410-907-0). Ballinger Pub.

Katz, Barry. Herbert Marcuse & The Art of Liberation: An Intellectual Biography. 240p. 1982. 22.50 (ISBN 0-8052-7126-0, Pub by NLB England); pap. 8.50 (ISBN 0-8052-7127-9). Nichols Pub.

Katz, Bernard. Nerve, Muscle & Synapse. (New Biology Ser.). 1966. text ed. 10.95 o.p. (ISBN 0-07-033374-2, C); pap. text ed. 14.95 o.p. (ISBN 0-07-033383-1). McGraw.

Katz, Bill, ed. Ethics & Reference Services. LC 82-11862. (The Reference Librarian Ser.: No. 4). 183p. 1982. text ed. 24.00 (ISBN 0-86656-211-7, B211). Haworth Pr.

--Reference Services Administration & Management. LC 82-1085. (The Reference Librarian Ser.: No. 3). 159p. 1982. text ed. 24.00 (ISBN 0-86656-164-1, B164); pap. 15.00 (ISBN 0-86656-111-0, B111). Haworth Pr.

--Reference Services for Children & Young Adults. (The Reference Librarian Ser.: Nos. 7 & 8). 168p. 1983. text ed. 14.95 (ISBN 0-86656-201-X, B201). Haworth Pr.

Katz, Bill & Fraley, Ruth A., eds. Video to Online Reference Services & the New Technology. LC 82-232920. (The Reference Librarian: No. 56). 170p. 1983. text ed. 14.95 (ISBN 0-86656-202-8). Haworth Pr.

Katz, D. L. Handbook of Natural Gas Engineering. 1959. 87.00 (ISBN 0-07-033384-X, P&RB). McGraw.

Katz, Daniel & Kahn, Robert L. The Social Psychology of Organizations. 2nd ed. LC 77-18764. 838p. 1978. text ed. 32.95x (ISBN 0-471-02355-8). Wiley.

Katz, Daniel, et al. Bureaucratic Encounters: A Pilot Study in the Evaluation of Government Services. LC 74-620202. 270p. 1975. 16.00x (ISBN 0-87944-173-9); pap. 7.00 o.p. (ISBN 0-87944-172-0). Inst Soc Res.

Katz, David A. Econometric Theory & Applications. (Illus.). 304p. 1982. 25.95 (ISBN 0-13-223313-4). P-H.

Katz, Dori, tr. see Yourcenar, Marguerite.

Katz, Elias. Retarded Adult at Home. LC 74-123867. (Illus., Orig.). 1970. pap. 6.50 o.p. (ISBN 0-87562-019-1). Spec Child.

Katz, Elizabeth. This Is the Pekingese. 1962. 12.95 (ISBN 0-87666-347-1, PS615). TFH Pubns.

Katz, Ephraim. The Film Encyclopedia. 1280p. 1982. pap. 14.95 (ISBN 0-399-50601-2, Perige). Putnam Pub Group.

Katz, Eve, ed. La France En Metamorphose. 224p. 1976. pap. text ed. 12.95 scp (ISBN 0-06-043564-X, HarpC). Har-Row.

Katz, Fred E. Autonomy & Organization: The Limits of Social Control. 1968. text ed. 6.95x (ISBN 0-685-19686-0). Phila Bk Co.

--Contemporary Sociological Theory. 1971. pap. text ed. 10.95x (ISBN 0-394-30332-6). Phila Bk Co.

Katz, Gerald & Mitchell, Abby. Ambulatory Care & Regionalization in Multi Institutional Systems. LC 82-8815. 227p. 1982. 24.95 (ISBN 0-89443-697-X). Aspen Systems.

Katz, Harriet. Harvey's Last Chance. 144p. (gr. 3-7). 1983. pap. 2.50 (ISBN 0-671-44444-1). Wanderer Bks.

Katz, Harvey A. & Warrick, Patricia. Introductory Psychology Through Science Fiction. 2nd ed. 1977. pap. 14.95 (ISBN 0-395-30816-X). HM.

Katz, Harvey P. Telephone Manual of Pediatric Care. LC 82-8497. 184p. 1982. 19.50 (ISBN 0-471-09923-6, Pub. by Wiley Med). Wiley.

Katz, Irvin W. How to Prepare for the American College Testing Program (ACT) 488p. Date not set. 6.95 (ISBN 0-15-600001-6). HarBraceJ. Postponed.

Katz, J. J. Propositional Structure & Illocutionary Force: A Study of the Contribution of Sentence Meaning to Speech Arts. 1977. text ed. 31.50 scp o.p. (ISBN 0-690-00883-X, HarpC). Har-Row.

Katz, Jack. Poor People's Lawyers in Transition. (Crime, Law, & Deviance Ser.). 288p. 1982. 25.00 (ISBN 0-8135-0943-2). Rutgers U Pr.

Katz, Jack, jt. ed. see Lasky, Elaine Z.

Katz, Jacob. The Art of Electrostatic Precipitation. (Illus.). 350p. 1980. text ed. 47.50x (ISBN 0-9603986-1-9, Pub. by Precipitator). Scholium Intl.

--Common Orthopedic Problems in Children. 210p. 1981. 25.00 (ISBN 0-89004-273-X, 298). Raven.

--Exclusiveness & Tolerance. 208p. 1983. pap. 7.95x (ISBN 0-87441-365-6). Behrman.

--Out of the Ghetto: The Social Background of Jewish Emancipation, 1770-1870. 1978. pap. 6.95 (ISBN 0-8052-0601-9). Schocken.

--Tradition & Crisis: Jewish Society at the End of the Middle Ages. LC 61-9168. 1971. pap. 5.95 o.p. (ISBN 0-8052-0316-8). Schocken.

Katz, Jacob F. & Siffert, Robert S., eds. Management of Hip Disorders in Children. (Illus.). 304p. 1982. text ed. 49.00 (ISBN 0-397-50522-1, Lippincott Medical). Lippincott.

Katz, James E. Presidential Politics & Science Policy. LC 77-14024. (Praeger Special Studies). 1978. 29.95 o.p. (ISBN 0-03-040941-1). Praeger.

Katz, James E. & Marwah, Onkar S. Nuclear Power in Developing Countries: An Analysis of Decision Making. LC 81-47622. 384p. 1982. 29.95x (ISBN 0-669-04700-7). Lexington Bks.

Katz, James E., jt. auth. see Horowitz, Irving L.

Katz, Jane. Artists in Exile: American Odyssey. LC 81-48457. 288p. 1983. 17.95 (ISBN 0-8128-2851-8). Stein & Day.

--Swimming Through Your Pregnancy. LC 82-45296. (Illus.). 224p. 1983. pap. 10.95 (ISBN 0-385-18059-4, Dolp). Doubleday.

Katz, Jane & Bruning, Nancy P. Swimming for Total Fitness: A Progressive Aerobic Program. LC 80-708. (Illus.). 380p. 1981. pap. 11.95 (ISBN 0-385-15932-3, Dolp). Doubleday.

Katz, Jane B., ed. Let Me Be a Free Man: A Documentary History of Indian Resistance. LC 74-11910. (Voices of the American Indian Ser.). (Illus.). 184p. (gr. 6 up). 1975. PLB 6.95g (ISBN 0-8225-0640-8). Lerner Pubns.

--We Rode the Wind: Recollections of 19th-Century Tribal Life. LC 74-11909. (Voices of the American Indian Ser.). (Illus.). 112p. (gr. 7 up). 1975. PLB 6.95g (ISBN 0-8225-0639-4). Lerner Pubns.

Katz, Jay. Experimentation with Human Beings: The Authority of the Investigator, Subject, Professions, & State in the Human Experimentation Process. LC 70-188394. 1160p. 1972. 22.50x (ISBN 0-87154-438-5). Russell Sage.

Katz, Jay & Capron, Alexander M. Catastrophic Diseases: Who Decides What? A Psychosocial & Legal Analysis of the Problems Posed by Hemodialysis & Organ Transplantation. LC 75-7175. 280p. 1975. 11.00x (ISBN 0-87154-439-3). Russell Sage.

Katz, Jeffrey, jt. auth. see Freudenthal, Juan R.

Katz, Jeffrey A. Capital Flows & Developing Country Debt. (Working Paper: No. 352). 51p. 1979. 3.00 (ISBN 0-686-36168-7, WP-0352). World Bank.

Katz, Jerrold J. Language & Other Abstract Objects. LC 80-19156. 262p. 1981. 25.00x (ISBN 0-8476-6912-2); pap. 9.95x (ISBN 0-8476-6913-0). Rowman.

Katz, Jerrold J. & Postal, Paul M. An Integrated Theory of Linguistic Descriptions. LC 64-17356. 1964. pap. text ed. 5.95x (ISBN 0-262-61021-3). MIT Pr.

Katz, Jonathan N. Gay-Lesbian Almanac. LC 81-48237. (Illus.). 812p. 1983. write for info. (ISBN 0-06-014968-X, HarpT); pap. write for info. (ISBN 0-06-090966-8, CN-0966, HarpT). Har-Row.

Katz, Jordan, et al. Anesthesia & Uncommon Diseases: Pathophysiologic & Clinical Correlations. 2nd ed. (Illus.). 807p. 1981. text ed. 55.00 (ISBN 0-7216-5302-2). Saunders.

Katz, Jordon & Kadis, Leslie B., eds. Anesthesia & Uncommon Diseases: Pathophysiologic & Clinical Correlations. LC 77-173336. (Illus.). 543p. 1973. text ed. 30.00 o.p. (ISBN 0-7216-5299-9). Saunders.

Katz, Joseph & Hartnett, Rodney T., eds. Scholars in the Making: The Development of Graduate & Professional Students. LC 76-12820. 304p. 1976. prof ref 17.50x (ISBN 0-88410-166-5). Ballinger Pub.

Katz, Julian, jt. auth. see Stapleton, Thomas.

Katz, Kitty. Play with Me. (Platt & Munk Peggy Cloth Playtime Bks.). (Illus.). 8p. (ps). 1982. 4.95 (ISBN 0-448-46830-1, G&D). Putnam Pub Group.

Katz, Lawrence B., jt. ed. see Irle, Martin.

Katz, Leon. The Making of Americans: An Opera & a Play from the Novel by Gertrude Stein. LC 76-76850. 1973. 15.00 (ISBN 0-87110-108-4); pap. 6.00 (ISBN 0-87110-110-6). Ultramarine Pub.

Katz, Leon, jt. auth. see Aidala, Joseph B.

Katz, Leon see Lion, Eugene & Ball, David.

Katz, Leslie G., intro. by. Fairy Tales for Computers. LC 78-58450. 1978. pap. 8.95 (ISBN 0-87923-245-5, Nonpareil Bk). Godine.

Katz, Lilian, ed. Current Topics in Early Childhood Education, Vol. 4. 256p. 1982. text ed. 27.50 (ISBN 0-89391-109-7); pap. text ed. 16.95 (ISBN 0-89391-110-0). Ablex Pub.

Katz, Lilian G., ed. Current Topics in Early Childhood Education: Vol. 1. (Illus.). 1977. text ed. 22.50 (ISBN 0-89391-000-7); pap. 16.95 (ISBN 0-89391-073-2). Ablex Pub.

--Current Topics in Early Childhood Education, Vol. 2. 1979. 24.50 (ISBN 0-89391-015-5); pap. 16.95 (ISBN 0-89391-074-0). Ablex Pub.

--Current Topics in Early Childhood Education, Vol. 3. 304p. 1981. text ed. 19.50 (ISBN 0-89391-057-0); pap. 16.95x (ISBN 0-89391-066-X). Ablex Pub.

Katz, Louis N., jt. auth. see Silber, Earl N.

Katz, M., et al. Parasitic Diseases. (Illus.). 264p. 1983. 27.75 (ISBN 0-387-90689-4). Springer-Verlag.

Katz, M. Barry. Leon Battista Alberti & the Humanist Theory of the Arts. 1977. pap. text ed. 7.00 (ISBN 0-8191-0279-2). U Pr of Amer.

Katz, Michael B. Irony of Early School Reform: Educational Innovation in Mid-19th Century Massachusetts. 1970. pap. 5.95x o.p. (ISBN 0-8070-3187-9, BP367). Beacon Pr.

Katz, Michael B., ed. Poverty & Policy in American History: Monograph. (Studies in Social Discontinuity). 226p. 1983. price not set (ISBN 0-12-401760-6); pap. price not set (ISBN 0-12-401762-2). Acad Pr.

Katz, Milton, jt. auth. see Bromberg, Murray.

Katz, Nancy B. The Mostly Vegetable Menu Cookbook. LC 82-82316. 224p. 1982. 12.95 (ISBN 0-448-12331-2, G&D). Putnam Pub Group.

Katz, Nathan, ed. Buddhist & Western Psychology. LC 81-84342. 300p. (Orig.). 1983. pap. 15.00 (ISBN 0-87773-758-4, Prajna). Great Eastern.

Katz, Ralph. Career Issues in Human Resource Management. (Applied Management Ser.). (Illus.). 224p. 1982. 18.95 (ISBN 0-13-114819-2). P-H.

Katz, Richard A., ed. see Flower Essence Society.

Katz, Richard S., jt. auth. see Mulcahy, Kevin V.

Katz, Richard W., jt. ed. see Murphy, Allan H.

Katz, Rita E., ed. see Byalin, Joan.

Katz, Robert. The Spoils of Ararat. 1978. 8.95 o.p. (ISBN 0-395-25702-6). HM.

--Ziggurat. 1977. 7.95 o.p. (ISBN 0-395-25352-7). HM.

Katz, Robert L. Management of the Total Enterprise: Cases & Concepts in Business Policy. 1970. ref. ed. 24.95 (ISBN 0-13-548933-4). P-H.

Katz, Roger C. & Zlutnik, Steven, eds. Behavior Therapy & Health Care. LC 74-7331. 1975. 25.00 (ISBN 0-686-77052-8); text ed. 19.80 o.s.i. (ISBN 0-08-017829-4); pap. text ed. 14.50 (ISBN 0-08-017828-6). Pergamon.

Katz, S. Stanley. External Assistance & Indian Economic Growth. 5.00x o.p. (ISBN 0-210-98137-7). Asia.

Katz, Samuel L., jt. auth. see Krugman, Saul.

Katz, Sanford, jt. auth. see Meezan, William.

Katz, Sanford N., jt. auth. see Weyrauch, Walter O.

Katz, Sanford N., ed. Creativity in Social Work: Selected Writings of Lydia Rapoport. LC 75-13637. 254p. 1975. 24.95 (ISBN 0-87722-043-3). Temple U Pr.

Katz, Sedelle & Mazur, Mary Ann. Understanding the Rape Victim: A Synthesis of Research Findings. LC 78-25704. (Personality Processes Ser.). 340p. 1979. 33.95x (ISBN 0-471-03573-4, Pub. by Wiley-Interscience). Wiley.

Katz, Shelley. The Lucifer Child. (Orig.). 1980. pap. 2.50 o.s.i. (ISBN 0-440-15076-0). Dell.

Katz, Sidney B., et al. Resources for Writing for Publication in Education. LC 79-27127. 1980. pap. text ed. 6.95x (ISBN 0-8077-2579-X). Tchrs Coll.

Katz, Steve. Cheyenne River Wild Track. 1973. 4.95 (ISBN 0-87886-033-9); pap. 2.95 (ISBN 0-87886-034-7). Ithaca Hse.

Katz, Steven T. Jewish Ideas & Concepts. LC 77-75285. 1979. pap. 6.95 o.p. (ISBN 0-8052-0629-9). Schocken.

--Mysticism & Philosophical Analysis. 1978. 17.95x (ISBN 0-19-520010-1); pap. 6.95 (ISBN 0-19-520011-X, GB 538). Oxford U Pr.

--Mysticism & Religious Traditions. 250p. 1983. 19.95x (ISBN 0-19-503313-2); pap. 9.95 (ISBN 0-19-503314-0). Oxford U Pr.

Katz, Susan. The Lawrence Welk Scrapbook. LC 78-55542. (Illus.). 1978. 12.95 o.p. (ISBN 0-448-16051-X, G&D); pap. 5.95 o.p. (ISBN 0-448-16054-4, Today Press). Putnam Pub Group.

Katz, Viktor. One Thousand Years of Bohemian Coinage. (Illus.). 1980. Repr. of 1929 ed. softcover 8.00 (ISBN 0-915262-55-X). S J Durst.

Katz, Virginia T., jt. auth. see Katz, Albert M.

Katz, W. Introduction to Reference Work, Vol. I: Basic Information Services. 4th ed. 1982. 22.50x (ISBN 0-07-033333-5). McGraw.

--Introduction to Reference Work, Vol. II: Reference Services & Reference Processes. 4th ed. 1982. 23.50x (ISBN 0-07-033334-3). McGraw.

Katz, William. An Album of the Depression. LC 77-14361. (Picture Albums Ser.). (Illus.). (gr. 5 up). 1978. PLB 8.90 s&l (ISBN 0-531-02914-X). Watts.

Katz, William A. Introduction to Reference Work, 2 vols. 3rd ed. Incl. Vol. I. Basic Information Sources. text ed. 20.95 (ISBN 0-07-033331-9); Vol. II. Reference Services & Reference Processes. text ed. 20.95. (McGraw-Hill Ser. in Library Education). 1978 (C). McGraw.

Katz, William A. & Tarr, Andrea. Reference & Information Services: A Reader. LC 77-20698. 1978. 15.00 o.p. (ISBN 0-8108-1091-3). Scarecrow.

Katz, William L. An Album of Nazism. LC 78-12723. (Picture Album Ser.). (Illus.). (gr. 5 up). 1979. PLB 9.60 s&l (ISBN 0-531-01500-9). Watts.

--An Album of the Civil War. LC 73-11031. (Picture Albums Ser.). (Illus.). 96p. (gr. 4-7). 1974. PLB 9.60 (ISBN 0-531-01518-1). Watts.

--The Black West. rev. ed. LC 72-93397. (Illus.). 352p. 1973. 10.95 (ISBN 0-385-00380-3, Anch). Doubleday.

--Teacher's Guide to American Negro History. 192p. 6.95 o.p. (ISBN 0-686-95029-1); pap. 3.95 o.p. (ISBN 0-686-99451-5). ADL.

Katzan, Harry. Microprogramming Primer. Feigenbaum, Edward, ed. (Computer Science Ser). (Illus.). 1977. text ed. 33.95 (ISBN 0-07-033387-4, C); instructor's manual 8.95 (ISBN 0-07-033388-2). McGraw.

Katzan, Harry, Jr. Computer Systems Organization & Programming. LC 75-23320. (Computer Science Ser.). (Illus.). 416p. 1976. text ed. 23.95 (ISBN 0-574-21080-6, 13-4080). SRA.

--Introduction to Computers & Data Processing. 580p. 1979. text ed. 17.95 (ISBN 0-442-23422-8). Van Nos Reinhold.

Katzarova-Kukudova, Raina & Djenev, Kiril. Bulgarian Folk Dances. (Illus.). 1976. soft cover 7.95 (ISBN 0-89357-029-X). Slavica.

Katzburg, Nathaniel. Hungary & the Jews: Policy & Legislation 1920-1943. 299p. 1981. 18.00 (ISBN 965-226-020-7). Hermon.

Katzeff, I. E. & Edwards, H. Angina Pectoris, Vol. 1. (Annual Research Reviews). 1978. 26.40 (ISBN 0-88831-023-4). Eden Pr.

--Angina Pectoris, Vol. 2. Horrobin, D. F., ed. (Annual Research Reviews). 1980. 36.00 (ISBN 0-88831-067-6). Eden Pr.

Katzeff, Paul. Full Moons. LC 80-20922. 327p. 1983. 12.95 (ISBN 0-8065-0737-3); pap. 6.95 (ISBN 0-8065-0832-9). Citadel Pr.

Katzell, Raymond A., et al, eds. A Guide to Worker Productivity Experiments in the United States: 1971-75. LC 77-76042. pap. text ed. 14.50 o.p. (ISBN 0-86670-003-X). Work in Amer.

Katzen, May, ed. Multi-Media Communications. LC 82-3023. 168p. 1982. lib. bdg. 25.00 (ISBN 0-313-23565-1, KAC/). Greenwood.

Katzen, Mollie. The Enchanted Broccoli Forest: And Other Timeless Delicacies. LC 82-50667. (Illus.). 320p. 1982. 16.95 (ISBN 0-89815-079-5); pap. 11.95 (ISBN 0-89815-078-7). Ten Speed Pr.

Katzenberg, Dena S. Baltimore Album Quilts. 124p. 1981. pap. 19.50 (ISBN 0-686-36475-9). Md Hist.

Katzenelson, Susan, jt. ed. see Szabo, Denis.

Katzenstein, Peter. Disjoined Partners: Austria & Germany Since 1815. LC 74-30526. 1976. 32.50x (ISBN 0-520-02945-3). U of Cal Pr.

Katzin, Herbert M., jt. auth. see Klein, Richard.

Katzin, Leonard I., ed. Production & Separation of U-233: Collected Papers. (National Nuclear Energy Ser.: Div. IV, Vol. 17b). 743p. 1952. pap. 50.50 (ISBN 0-87079-383-7, TID-5223); microfilm 4.50 (ISBN 0-87079-341-1, TID-5223). DOE.

Katzin, Leonard I., jt. ed. see Seaborg, Glenn.

Katz-Levine, Judy. The Umpire & Other Masks. (Illus.). 12.00 (ISBN 0-686-23236-4); pap. 3.50 (ISBN 0-686-23237-2). Five Trees.

Katzman, David M. Seven Days a Week: Women & Domestic Service in Industrializing America. 1978. 19.95x (ISBN 0-19-502368-4). Oxford U Pr.

Katzman, Robert & Terry, Robert D. The Neurology of Aging. LC 82-14921. (Contemporary Neurology Ser.: No. 22). (Illus.). 249p. 1983. text ed. 40.00 (ISBN 0-8036-5231-3). Davis Co.

Katzman, Robert, ed. Congenital & Acquired Cognitive Disorders. LC 77-87458. (Association of Research in Nervous & Mental Disease Research Publication Ser.: Vol. 57). 326p. 1979. 32.00 (ISBN 0-89004-255-1). Raven.

Katzman, Robert, et al, eds. Alzheimer's Disease: Senile Dementia & Related Disorders. (Aging Ser.: Vol. 7). 703p. 1978. text ed. 58.50 (ISBN 0-89004-225-X). Raven.

Katzmann, Robert A. Regulatory Bureaucracy: The Federal Trade Commission & Antitrust Policy. (Studies in American Politics & Public Policy: No. 6). 1980. 22.00x (ISBN 0-262-11072-5); pap. 7.95x (ISBN 0-262-61034-5). MIT Pr.

Katznelson, Alexander & Nerubay, Jacobo, eds. Osteosarcoma: New Trends in Diagnosis & Treatment. LC 82-4679. (Progress in Clinical & Biological Research Ser.: Vol. 99). 164p. 1982. 25.00 (ISBN 0-8451-0099-8). A R Liss.

Katznelson, Ira. City Trenches: Urban Politics & the Patterning of Class in the United States. LC 82-8392. xvii, 268p. 1982. 8.95 (ISBN 0-226-42673-4). U of Chicago Pr.

Katzner, Donald W. Analysis Without Measurement. LC 82-4469. 366p. Date not set. price not set (ISBN 0-521-24847-7). Cambridge U Pr.

Katzner, Kenneth. Languages of the World. (Funk & W Bk.). 384p. 1974. 15.34i (ISBN 0-308-10120-0, TYC-T). T Y Crowell.

Katzung, Bertram G., et al, eds. Basic & Clinical Pharmacology. 7th ed. LC 80-82744. (Illus.). 815p. 1982. lexotone cover 23.50 (ISBN 0-87041-260-4). Lange.

Kau, James B., jt. auth. see Sirmans, C. F.

Kauchak, Donald P. & Eggen, Paul. Exploring Science in the Elementary School. 1980. pap. 15.50 (ISBN 0-395-30643-4); Instr's. manual 1.00 (ISBN 0-395-30644-2). HM.

Kauf, Robert & McCluney, Daniel C. Proben Deutscher Prosa. 1970. text ed. 6.95x o.s.i. (ISBN 0-393-09911-3, NortonC); free tchrs. ed. (ISBN 0-393-09985-7); tapes 85.00 (ISBN 0-393-99117-2). Norton.

Kaufelt, David. Silver Rose. Large Print ed. LC 82-16749. 394p. 1982. Repr. of 1982 ed. 10.95 (ISBN 0-89621-391-9). Thorndike Pr.

Kaufelt, David A. Midnight Movies. 1980. 9.95 o.s.i. (ISBN 0-440-05244-0). Delacorte.

Kaufert, Joseph M., jt. ed. see Tuckett, David.

Kauffman. Inorganic Chemical Complexes. 29.95x (ISBN 0-471-26099-1, Pub. by Wiley Heyden); pap. 19.95 (ISBN 0-471-26100-9). Wiley.

Kauffman, Christmas C. For One Moment. 1964. pap. 4.95 (ISBN 0-8024-3808-3). Moody.

--Lucy Winchester. LC 72-75018. 540p. 1974. pap. 5.95 (ISBN 0-8024-5040-7). Moody.

--Not Regina. LC 54-10828. (Illus.). 1971. pap. 3.95 (ISBN 0-8024-0072-8). Moody.

--Search to Belong. LC 63-7538. 1967. pap. 4.95 (ISBN 0-8024-3817-2). Moody.

Kauffman, Christopher J. Ministry of Healing: The History of the Alexian Brothers from the French Revolution to the Present. 1978. 7.50 (ISBN 0-8164-0387-2). Seabury.

Kauffman, Draper L., Jr. Teaching the Future: A Guide to Future-Oriented Education. LC 75-15636. (Education Futures Ser.: No. 4). (Illus., Orig.). 1976. 14.95 (ISBN 0-88280-024-8); pap. 9.95 (ISBN 0-88280-025-6). ETC Pubns.

Kauffman, J., jt. auth. see Hallahan, D.

Kauffman, James M. Characteristics of Children's Behavior Disorders. 1977. text ed. 20.95 o.p. (ISBN 0-675-08557-8). Merrill.

--Characteristics of Children's Behavior Disorders. 2nd ed. (Special Education Ser.). (Illus.). 352p. 1981. pap. text ed. 22.95 (ISBN 0-675-08055-X). Additional supplements may be obtained from publisher. Merrill.

Kauffman, James M., jt. auth. see Hallahan, Daniel P.

Kauffman, James M., jt. auth. see Wallace, Gerald M.

Kauffman, James M., jt. auth. see Payne, James S.

Kauffman, Joseph. Education. LC 66-14225. (U.S.A. Survey Ser.). (Illus.). 120p. 1966. 4.95 (ISBN 0-87107-003-0). Potomac.

Kauffman, Karen, compiled by. Mighty Fortress Is Our God. 1982. 3.95 (ISBN 0-8378-2031-6). Gibson.

Kauffman, Richard A. Pilgrimage in Mission Study Guide. 60p. 1983. pap. 4.95 (ISBN 0-8361-1260-1). Herald Pr.

Kauffman, Samuel H., jt. auth. see Reisman, Fredericka K.

Kauffman, Sandra. The Cowboy Catalog. (Illus.). 192p. 1980. 22.50 (ISBN 0-517-53950-0, C N Potter); pap. 10.95 (ISBN 0-517-54035-5, C N Potter Bks). Crown.

--Kauffmans Manual of Riding Safety. (Illus.). 1978. 7.95 (ISBN 0-517-53293-X, C N Potter Bks). Crown.

Kauffmann, C. M. A History of Manuscripts Illuminated in the British Isles: Romanesque Manuscripts 1066-1190, Vol. 3. (Illus.). 1975. 74.00x (ISBN 0-19-921010-1). Oxford U Pr.

Kauffmann, Stanley. Before My Eyes: Film Criticism & Comment. LC 78-20171. 1980. 17.26i (ISBN 0-06-012298-6, HarpT). Har-Row.

--Before My Eyes: Film Criticism & Comment. (Quality Paperbacks Ser.). (Illus.). 460p. 1982. pap. 9.95 (ISBN 0-306-80179-5). Da Capo.

Kaufman, jt. auth. see Kiver.

Kaufman, jt. auth. see Strauss.

Kaufman, A. A. Magnetotelluric Sounding Method. (Methods in Geochemistry & Geophysics Ser.: Vol. 15). 1981. 125.75 (ISBN 0-444-41863-6). Elsevier.

Kaufman, Aileen, tr. see Kloppenburg-Versteegh, J.

Kaufman, Allen. Capitalism, Slavery, & Republican Values: Antebellum Political Economists, 1819-1848. 219p. 1983. text ed. 25.00x (ISBN 0-292-76019-1). U of Tex Pr.

Kaufman, Andrew L. Problems in Professional Responsibility. 1976. 24.00 (ISBN 0-316-48344-3); suppl. 5.95 (ISBN 0-316-48343-5). Little.

Kaufman, Andrew L., jt. auth. see Countryman, Vern.

Kaufman, Arnold S. Radical Liberal. 1970. pap. 1.95 o.p. (ISBN 0-671-20576-5, Touchstone Bks). S&S.

Kaufman, B., ed. see Woollcott, Alexander.

Kaufman, Barry N. Giant Steps. LC 78-10687. 1979. 9.95 o.p. (ISBN 0-698-10956-2, Coward). Putnam Pub Group.

--The Premonition: A Psychic Odyssey. 320p. 1983. 14.95 (ISBN 0-440-06935-1). Delacorte.

--A Sense of Warning. 1983. 15.95 (ISBN 0-440-07782-6, E Friede). Delacorte.

--Son-Rise. (Illus.). 1977. pap. 3.50 (ISBN 0-446-30645-2). Warner Bks.

--To Love Is to Be Happy with: The First Book of the Option Process. 1977. 8.95 o.p. (ISBN 0-698-10779-9, Coward). Putnam Pub Group.

Kaufman, Barry N. & Kaufman, Suzy L. A Land Beyond Tears: A Guided Journey of One Family's Celebration of Life in the Face of Death. LC 81-43144. 150p. 1982. 13.95 (ISBN 0-385-17655-4). Doubleday.

Kaufman, Bel. Up the Down Staircase. (gr. 7 up). 1964. 8.95 o.p. (ISBN 0-13-939140-1). P-H.

Kaufman, Burton. Efficiency & Expansion: Foreign Trade Organization in the Wilson Administration, 1913-1921. LC 73-20971. (Contributions in American History: No. 34). 1974. lib. bdg. 29.95 (ISBN 0-8371-7338-8, KEX/). Greenwood.

Kaufman, Burton I. The Oil Cartel Case: A Documentary Study of Antitrust Activity in the Cold War Era. LC 77-87963. (Contributions in American History: No. 72). (Illus.). 1978. lib. bdg. 25.00 (ISBN 0-313-20043-2, KOC/). Greenwood.

Kaufman, Charles H. Music in New Jersey, 1655-1860. LC 78-75180. 304p. 1981. 35.00 o.p. (ISBN 0-8386-2270-4); 65.00 (ISBN 0-686-96713-5). Fairleigh Dickinson.

Kaufman, Daniel. Ireland: Presences. (Illus.). 112p. 1980. 19.95 o.p. (ISBN 0-312-43591-6). St Martin.

Kaufman, Daniel, jt. auth. see Goldberg, Phillip.

Kaufman, Donald D. What Belongs to Caesar? LC 70-109939. (Christian Peace Shelf Ser.). (Orig.). 1970. pap. 3.95 (ISBN 0-8361-1621-6). Herald Pr.

Kaufman, Edgar & Raeburn, Ben, eds. Frank Lloyd Wright: Writings & Buildings. (Illus.). pap. 7.50 (ISBN 0-452-00595-7, F595, Mer). NAL.

Kaufman, Edward. The Market for Executive Talent. 1978. 11.00 (ISBN 0-07-033421-8, P&RB). McGraw.

Kaufman, Edy. The Super Powers & Their Spheres of Influence. LC 76-24651. 1977. 25.00x (ISBN 0-312-77630-6). St Martin.

Kaufman, Erle & Hazel, Joseph, eds. Concepts & Methods of Biostratigraphy. 658p. 1977. 65.00 (ISBN 0-87933-246-8). Hutchinson Ross.

Kaufman, G. A., jt. auth. see Adelman, M. A.

Kaufman, George & Rosen, Kenneth T., eds. The Property Tax Revolt: The Case of Proposition 13. (Real Estate & Urban Economics Ser.). 256p. 1981. prof ref 27.50x (ISBN 0-88410-693-4). Ballinger Pub.

Kaufman, George G. Efficiency in the Municipal Bond Market: The Use of Tax Exempt Financing for "Private" Purposes, Vol. 30. Altman, Edward I. & Walter, Ingo, eds. LC 80-82481. (Contemporary Studies in Economic & Financial Analysis). 275p. 1981. 40.00 (ISBN 0-89232-168-7). Jai Pr.

--Money, the Financial System & the Economy. 3rd ed. 24.50 (ISBN 0-395-30817-8); Instr's. manual 1.25 (ISBN 0-395-30818-6). HM.

--The U. S. Financial System: Money, Markets, & Institutions. 2nd ed. (Illus.). 624p. 1983. text ed. 24.95 (ISBN 0-13-938126-0). P-H.

Kaufman, Gerald. How to Be a Minister. 204p. 1982. 15.95 (ISBN 0-283-98685-9, Pub. by Sidgwick & Jackson). Merrimack Bk Serv.

Kaufman, Gloria & Blakely, Mary K., eds. Pulling Our Own Strings: Feminist Humor & Satire. LC 79-3382. (Midland Bks.: No. 251). 192p. 1980. 20.00x (ISBN 0-253-13034-4); pap. 8.95 (ISBN 0-253-20251-5). Ind U Pr.

Kaufman, H. G. Career Management: A Guide to Combating Obsolescence. LC 75-8088. 441p. 1975. 29.95x (ISBN 0-471-46057-5); pap. text ed. 19.50x o.p. (ISBN 0-471-46058-3, Pub. by Wiley-Interscience). Wiley.

Kaufman, Hal & Schrocter, Bob. Hocus Focus, No. 3. 1982. pap. 1.50 (ISBN 0-451-11649-6, AW1649, Sig). NAL.

Kaufman, Harold, ed. Career Management: A Guide to Combating Obsolescence. LC 75-8088. 1975. 14.95 (ISBN 0-87942-054-5). Inst Electrical.

Kaufman, Henry J. Easy-to-Make Wooden Candlesticks, Chandeliers & Lamps. (Illus.). 48p. pap. 1.75 (ISBN 0-486-24309-5). Dover.

Kaufman, Herbert. Administrative Feedback: Monitoring Subordinates' Behavior. 1973. 12.95 (ISBN 0-8157-4838-8); pap. 4.95 (ISBN 0-8157-4837-X). Brookings.

--Are Government Organizations Immortal? 1976. pap. 4.95 (ISBN 0-8157-4839-6). Brookings.

--Red Tape: Its Origins, Uses & Abuses. 1977. 12.95 (ISBN 0-8157-4842-6); pap. 4.95 (ISBN 0-8157-4841-8). Brookings.

Kaufman, Herbert, jt. auth. see Sayre, Wallace S.

Kaufman, Herbert, tr. see Salmen, Walter.

Kaufman, Herbert E. & Zimmerman. Current Concepts in Ophthalmology, Vol. 6. (Illus.). 242p. 1979. text ed. 49.50 o.p. (ISBN 0-8016-2628-5). Mosby.

Kaufman, Herbert J., ed. see Lefebvre, Jacques.

Kaufman, Howard K. Attitude Research: The Theoretical Basis & Some Problems of Application in Rural Thailand. (PdR Press Publications in Social Psychology: No. 1). (Illus.). 1976. pap. 2.25x o.p. (ISBN 903-1600-68-7). Humanities.

Kaufman, Irving, jt. auth. see Reiner, Beatrice S.

Kaufman, Jerome E. Elementary Algebra. (Math Ser.). 480p. 1982. text ed. write for info. (ISBN 0-87150-337-9, 2701). Prindle.

--Intermediate Algebra. (Math Ser.). 550p. 1982. text ed. write for info. (ISBN 0-87150-340-9, 2721). Prindle.

Kaufman, Jerome E., jt. auth. see Devine, Donald F.

Kaufman, Joan. A Billion & Counting: Family Planning Campaigns & Policies in the People's Republic of China. LC 82-50312. (Illus.). 1983. pap. 7.50 (ISBN 0-911302-43-5). San Francisco Pr.

Kaufman, Joe. About the Big Sky, About the High Hills, About the Rich Earth & the Deep Sea. (Illus.). (gr. 1-7). 1978. 6.95 (ISBN 0-307-16805-0); PLB 12.23 (ISBN 0-307-66805-3, Golden Pr). Western Pub.

Kaufman, John E., ed. IES Lighting Handbook: Student Reference. abr. ed. (Illus.). 125p. 1982. pap. 15.00 (ISBN 0-87995-010-2). Illum Eng.

--IES Lighting Handbook-1981: Application Volume. (Illus.). 532p. 1981. 58.50x (ISBN 0-87995-008-0); member 48.50; Set. 107.00; member 87.00. Illum Eng.

--IES Lighting Handbook-1981: Reference Volume. (Illus.). 488p. 1981. 58.50x (ISBN 0-87995-007-2); member 48.50; Set. 107.00; member 87.00. Illum Eng.

Kaufman, Kenneth. Of Trees, Leaves, & Ponds: Studies in Photo-Impressionism. 64p. 1981. pap. 11.50 (ISBN 0-525-47678-4, 01117-330). Dutton.

Kaufman, Kenneth, jt. auth. see Marano, Joseph.

Kaufman, L. & Sumner, E. Medizinische Probleme in der Anaesthesie. (Illus.). x, 170p. 1983. 54.00 (ISBN 3-8055-3581-3). S Karger.

Kaufman, Leonard, jt. auth. see Massart, D. L.

Kaufman, Lloyd. Perception: The World Transformed. (Illus.). 1979. 25.00x (ISBN 0-19-502464-8); text ed. 19.95x (ISBN 0-19-502463-X). Oxford U Pr.

--Sight & Mind: An Introduction to Visual Perception. (Illus.). 1974. text ed. 22.00x (ISBN 0-19-501763-3). Oxford U Pr.

Kaufman, Louis. Essentials of Advertising. 575p. 1980. text ed. 19.95 o.p. (ISBN 0-15-524101-X, HC); instructor's manual avail. o.p. HarBraceJ.

Kaufman, Mal & Schrocter, Bob. Hocus-Focus, No. 2. 1982. pap. 1.50 (ISBN 0-451-11527-9, AW1527, Sig). NAL.

Kaufman, Martin. American Medical Education: The Formative Years, 1765-1910. LC 75-35346. 224p. 1976. lib. bdg. 25.00 (ISBN 0-8371-8590-4, KME/). Greenwood.

Kaufman, Milton & Seidman, A. Handbook for Electronic Engineering Technicians. 1976. 32.90 (ISBN 0-07-033401-3, P&RB). McGraw.

Kaufman, Milton & Seidman, Arthur H. Handbook of Electronics Calculations. (Illus.). 1979. 32.00 (ISBN 0-07-033392-0, P&RB). McGraw.

Kaufman, Milton & Wilson, J. A. Basic Electricity: Theory & Practice. 1973. pap. text ed. 23.95 (ISBN 0-07-033402-1, G). McGraw.

Kaufman, Milton, jt. auth. see Duff, John R.

Kaufman, Milton, jt. auth. see Stout, David F.

Kaufman, Milton, jt. auth. see Wilson, J. A.

Kaufman, P. J. Technical Analysis in Commodities. LC 79-19513. 227p. 1980. 42.50x (ISBN 0-471-05627-8, Pub by Ronald Pr). Wiley.

Kaufman, Paul. Community Library: A Chapter in English Social History. LC 67-28642. (Transactions Ser.: Vol. 57, Pt. 7). (Illus.). 1967. pap. 1.00 o.p. (ISBN 0-87169-577-4). Am Philos.

Kaufman, Peter. Practical Botany. 1982. text ed. 18.95 (ISBN 0-686-32081-6); instrs.' manual free. Reston.

Kaufman, Peter B. & La Croix, Don, eds. Plants, People, & Environment. 1979. text ed. 22.95x (ISBN 0-02-362120-6). Macmillan.

Kaufman, Peter I. Augustinian Piety & Catholic Reform: Augustine, Colet, & Erasmus. LC 82-12491. 128p. 1982. text ed. 9.45 (ISBN 0-86554-047-0). Mercer Univ Pr.

Kaufman, Raymond H., jt. auth. see Gardner, Herman L.

Kaufman, Robert J. Cost-Effective Telecommunications Management: Turning Telephone Costs Into Profits. 288p. 1983. 24.95 (ISBN 0-8436-1609-1). CBI Pub.

Kaufman, Roger. Educational System Planning. LC 70-178159. (Educational Administration Ser). (Illus.). 176p. 1972. ref. ed. 18.95 (ISBN 0-13-237818-3). P-H.

--Identifying & Solving Problems: A System Approach. 3rd ed. LC 76-5702. (Illus.). 163p. 1982. pap. 10.00 (ISBN 0-88390-050-5). Univ Assocs.

--Identifying & Solving Problems: A System Approach. 3rd ed. LC 76-5702. (Illus.). 164p. 1982. pap. 12.50 o.p. (ISBN 0-88390-051-3). Univ Assocs.

Kaufman, Roger & Stone, Bruce. Planning for Organizational Success: A Practical Guide. 288p. 1983. pap. text ed. 12.95 (ISBN 0-471-87698-4). Wiley.

Kaufman, Roger, jt. auth. see Stakenas, Robert G.

Kaufman, S. H., jt. auth. see Burns, R. C.

Kaufman, S. L. Investors Legal Guide. 2nd ed. LC 79-19499. (Legal Almanac Ser.: No. 42). 117p. 1979. 5.95 (ISBN 0-379-11126-8). Oceana.

Kaufman, Schima. Mendelssohn: A Second Elijah. LC 78-110829. (Illus.). 1971. Repr. of 1934 ed. lib. bdg. 19.75x (ISBN 0-8371-3229-0, KAME). Greenwood.

Kaufman, Sheilah. Sheilah's Easy Ways to Elegant Cooking. 1979. 10.95 o.s.i. (ISBN 0-440-07959-4, E Friede). Delacorte.

Kaufman, Shirley, tr. see Kovner, Abba.

Kaufman, Stanley. Practical & Legal Manual for the Investor. LC 56-5060. (Legal Almanac Ser: No. 42). (Orig.). 1956. 4.95 o.p. (ISBN 0-379-11042-3). Oceana.

Kaufman, Stuart B. Samuel Gompers & the Origins of the American Federation of Labor, 1848-1896. LC 76-176430. (Contributions in Economics and Economic History: No. 8). 1973. lib. bdg. 29.95 (ISBN 0-8371-6277-7, KAP/). Greenwood.

Kaufman, Suzy L., jt. auth. see Kaufman, Barry N.

Kaufman, Sy, jt. auth. see Blake, Sylvia.

Kaufman, Tanya & Wishny, Judith. School Events. Piltch, Benjamin, ed. 64p. (gr. 2-5). 1982. 4.00 (ISBN 0-934618-04-6). Skyview Pub.

Kaufman, Thomas C., jt. auth. see Raff, Rudolf A.

Kaufman, Walter, tr. see Nietzsche, Friedrich.

Kaufman, William E. Contemporary Jewish Philosophies. LC 75-30761. 388p. (Orig.). 1976. pap. text ed. 6.95x o.p. (ISBN 0-87441-238-2, Jewish Restructionist Press). Behrman.

Kaufman, William I. Calorie Counter for Six Quick-Loss Diets. 1973. pap. 1.95 (ISBN 0-515-07146-3, 9137). Jove Pubns.

--Calorie Guide to Brand Names. 1973. pap. 1.95 (ISBN 0-515-07092-0, 9177). Jove Pubns.

--Pocket Encyclopedia of California Wine. 212p. 1983. pap. 4.95 (ISBN 0-932664-24-5). Wine Appreciation.

Kaufman, William I., ed. Great Television Plays. (Orig.). 1969. pap. 2.75 (ISBN 0-440-33207-9, LE). Dell.

Kaufman, William J. Astronomy: The Structure of the Universe. (Illus.). 1977. 23.95x (ISBN 0-02-362130-3). Macmillan.

--Exploration of the Solar System. (Illus.). 1978. 23.95 (ISBN 0-02-362140-0). Macmillan.

Kaufmann, Helen L. The Home Book of Music Appreciation. 324p. 1983. Repr. of 1940 ed. lib. bdg. 30.00 (ISBN 0-8495-3140-3). Arden Lib.

Kaufmann, Herbert, tr. see Birzle, Hermann, et al.

Kaufmann, Herbert J., ed. see Lefebvre, Jacques.

Kaufmann, Jerome E., jt. auth. see Devine, Donald F.

Kaufmann, John. Birds Are Flying. LC 78-22510. (Let's-Read-&-Find-Out Science Bk.). (Illus.). (gr. k-3). 1979. 10.53i (ISBN 0-690-03941-7, TYC-J); PLB 10.89 (ISBN 0-690-03942-5). Har-Row.

--Fish Hawk. (gr. 3-7). 1967. 7.75 (ISBN 0-688-21298-0); PLB 6.48 (ISBN 0-688-31298-5). Morrow.

--Fly It: Making & Flying Your Own Kites, Boomerangs, Helicopters, Hang Gliders & Hand-Launched Gliders. LC 78-60292. (Illus.). (gr. 4-5). 1980. 9.95 o.p. (ISBN 0-385-14292-7); PLB 9.95 (ISBN 0-385-14293-5). Doubleday.

--Flying Reptiles, in the Age of Dinosaurs. LC 76-1919. (Illus.). 40p. (gr. 1-5). 1976. 5.75 o.p. (ISBN 0-688-22073-8); PLB 7.63 (ISBN 0-688-32073-2). Morrow.

--Insect Travelers. (Illus.). 128p. (gr. 7 up). 1972. 9.50 (ISBN 0-688-20036-2); PLB 9.12 (ISBN 0-688-30036-7). Morrow.

--Little Dinosaurs & Early Birds. LC 75-37575. (Let's Read & Find Out Science Book Ser.). (Illus.). (gr. k-3). 1977. PLB 10.89 (ISBN 0-690-01110-5, TYC-J). Har-Row.

--Robins Fly North, Robins Fly South. LC 70-109907. (Illus.). (gr. 2-5). 1970. PLB 10.89 (ISBN 0-690-70643-X, TYC-J). Har-Row.

Kaufmann, John & Meng, Heinz. Falcons Return: Restoring an Endangered Species. (Illus.). 128p. (gr. 7 up). 1975. PLB 9.55 (ISBN 0-688-32027-9). Morrow.

Kaufmann, L., jt. auth. see Hebblethwaite, P.

Kaufmann, Ludwig, jt. auth. see Hebblethwaite, Peter.

Kaufmann, M., et al. Understanding Radio Electronics. 4th ed. 1972. text ed. 22.95 (ISBN 0-07-033399-8, G). McGraw.

Kaufmann, Tohko. The Six-Legged Friends I've Met. 1983. 7.95 (ISBN 0-8062-2131-3). Carlton.

Kaufmann, W. & Krause, D., eds. Central Nervous Control of Na plus Balance. LC 76-28606. (Illus.). 212p. 1976. 25.00 o.p. (ISBN 0-88416-143-9). Wright-PSG.

Kaufmann, Walter. Discovering the Mind, Vol. 3: Freud Versus Adler & Jung. LC 80-25767. 1981. 17.95 (ISBN 0-07-033313-0). McGraw.

--Existentialism from Dostoevsky to Sartre. (Orig.). 1956. pap. 6.95 (ISBN 0-452-00596-5, F596, Mer). NAL.

--Hegel: Texts & Commentary. LC 77-89763. 1977. pap. text ed. 4.45x (ISBN 0-268-01069-2). U of Notre Dame Pr.

--Life at the Limits. (Illus.). 1978. pap. 10.00 o.p. (ISBN 0-07-033315-7, GB). McGraw.

--Philosophic Classics, 2 vols. 2nd ed. Incl. Vol. 1. Thales to Ockham. text ed. 23.95 (ISBN 0-13-662403-0); Vol. 2. Bacon to Kant. text ed. 22.95 (ISBN 0-13-662411-1). LC 68-15350. 1968. text ed. (ISBN 0-685-73716-0). P-H.

--The Ragas of North India. (Music Reprint Ser.). (Illus.). ix, 625p. 1983. Repr. of 1968 ed. lib. bdg. 65.00 (ISBN 0-306-76169-6). Da Capo.

--Time Is an Artist. 1978. pap. 7.50 o.p. (ISBN 0-07-033317-3, GB). McGraw.

--What Is Man? 1978. pap. 10.00 o.p. (ISBN 0-07-033316-5, GB). McGraw.

Kaufmann, Walter, ed. Religion from Tolstoy to Camus: Basic Writings on Religious Truth & Morals. pap. 8.95xi o.p. (ISBN 0-06-130123-X, TB123, Torch). Har-Row.

Kaufmann, Walter, ed. & tr. see Nietzsche, Friedrich.

Kaufmann, Walter, tr. see Nietzsche, Friedrich.

Kaufmann, William J., 3rd. Relatividad y Cosmologia. 2nd ed. Carriazo, Eduardo, tr. from Eng. 1978. text ed. 7.80 o.p. (ISBN 0-06-314475-1, IntlDept). Har-Row.

Kaul, Man M. The Philippines & Southeast Asia. 1978. text ed. 15.25x (ISBN 0-391-01010-7). Humanities.

Kaul, T. N. Reminiscences: Discreet & Indiscreet. (Illus.). 312p. 1982. 42.50 (ISBN 0-686-42809-9, Pub by Lancer India). Asia Bk Corp.

Kaul, Tej K., jt. auth. see Fox, Karl A.

Kaula, Edna M. Land & People of Kenya. rev. ed. LC 68-24413. (Portraits of the Nations Ser). (Illus.). (gr. 7 up). 1973. 8.95 o.p. (ISBN 0-686-96733-X, JBL-J); PLB 9.89 (ISBN 0-397-31482-5). Har-Row.

--Land and People of Rhodesia. LC 67-19263. (Portraits of the Nations Ser). (Illus.). (gr. 7 up). 1967. 9.57i o.p. (ISBN 0-397-31543-0, JBL-J). Har-Row.

--The Land & People of Tanzania. LC 72-5660. (Portraits of the Nations Ser). 160p. (gr. 7 up). 1972. 8.95 o.p. (ISBN 0-686-96734-8, JBL-J); PLB 9.89 (ISBN 0-397-31544-9). Har-Row.

Kaulla, K. N. Von see Von Kaulla, K. N. & Davidson, J. F.

Kaunda, Martin, jt. auth. see Kabwasa, Antoine.

Kaung, Stephen, tr. see Nee, Watchman.

Kaung, Stephen, tr. see Watchman Nee.

Kaupelis, Robert. Learning to Draw. (Illus.). 1966. 13.50 o.p. (ISBN 0-8230-2675-2). Watson-Guptill.

--Learning to Draw: A Creative Approach to Drawing. (Illus.). 144p. (Orig.). 1983. pap. text ed. 12.95 (ISBN 0-8230-2676-0). Watson-Guptill.

Kauper, P. G. Frontiers of Constitutional Liberty. LC 70-173668. (American Constitutional & Legal History Ser.). 252p. 1971. Repr. of 1956 ed. lib. bdg. 29.50 (ISBN 0-306-70408-0). Da Capo.

Kauper, P. G., et al. Article Five Convention Process: A Symposium. LC 70-150510. (Symposia on Law & Society Ser). 1971. Repr. lib. bdg. 25.00 (ISBN 0-306-70185-5). Da Capo.

Kauper, Paul & Beytagh, Francis. Constitutional Law, Cases & Materials. 5th ed. 1980. text ed. 32.00 (ISBN 0-316-48354-0); 1982 supplement 8.95 (ISBN 0-316-48355-9). Little.

Kauppi, Mark V. & Nation, Craig R., eds. The Soviet Union & the Middle East in the Nineteen-Eighties: Opportunities, Constraints, & Dilemmas. LC 82-48097. 1983. price not set (ISBN 0-669-05966-8). Lexington Bks.

Kaura, Uma. Muslims & Indian Nationalism, 1828-40. LC 77-74487. 1977. 11.50x o.p. (ISBN 0-88386-888-1). South Asia Bks.

Kaushall, Philip & Munshi, Kiki S. The Growing Years: A Study Guide for the Televised Course. 3rd ed. 320p. 1982. text ed. 10.95x (ISBN 0-07-011463-3); print pkg. 32.90x (ISBN 0-07-079308-5). McGraw.

Kaushall, Phillip & Skagen-Munshi, Kiki. The Growing Years: A Study Guide for the Televised Course. 2nd ed. (Illus.). 1979. pap. text ed. 9.50 (ISBN 0-07-033459-5, C). McGraw.

Kausler, Donald H. Experimental Psychology & Human Aging. LC 81-21972. 720p. 1982. 27.95 (ISBN 0-471-08163-9). Wiley.

Kautsky, John H. Moscow & the Communist Party of India: A Study in the Post War Evolution of International Communist Strategy. LC 82-11859. 200p. 1982. Repr. of 1956 ed. lib. bdg. 29.75x (ISBN 0-313-23568-6, KAMO). Greenwood.

Kautsky, Karl. Are the Jews a Race? LC 72-97288. 255p. 1972. Repr. of 1926 ed. lib. bdg. 17.75x (ISBN 0-8371-2609-6, KAJR). Greenwood.

Kautz, William C., Jr. Shelby. LC 79-89272. 192p. (Orig.). 1979. pap. 2.75 (ISBN 0-934620-00-8). Brady Pr.

Kautzky, R. Neuroradiology: A Neuropathological Approach. Boehm, W. M. & Kellet, V. B., trs. from Ger. 400p. 1982. 98.00 (ISBN 0-387-10934-X). Springer-Verlag.

Kauz, Herman. The Martial Spirit: An Introduction to the Origin, Philosophy & Psychology of the Martial Arts. LC 77-77808. (Illus.). 1978. 13.95 (ISBN 0-87951-067-6). Overlook Pr.

Kavaas, Igor I. & Granier, Jacqueline P., eds. Human Rights, the Helsinki Accords & the United States, 3 vols in 9. LC 82-81319. 1982. lib. bdg. 360.00 (ISBN 0-89941-152-5). W S Hein.

Kavaler, Florence & Swire, Margaret R. Foster-Child Health Care. LC 81-47184. 1983. price not set (ISBN 0-669-04561-6). Lexington Bks.

Kavaler, Lucy E. Green Magic: Algae Rediscovered. LC 81-43872. (Illus.). 128p. (gr. 5 up). 1983. 10.53i (ISBN 0-690-04221-3, TYC-J); PLB 10.89g (ISBN 0-690-04222-1). Har-Row.

Kavalsky, Basil. Portugal: Current & Prospective Economic Trends. vi, 52p. 1978. 10.00 (ISBN 0-686-36118-0, RC-7804). World Bank.

Kavan, Anna. Eagle's Nest. 180p. 1982. 12.95 (ISBN 0-7206-2835-0, Pub. by Peter Owen). Merrimack Bk Serv.

--Sleep Has His House. 1980. 11.95 (ISBN 0-935576-01-0); pap. 6.95 (ISBN 0-686-96762-3). Kesend Pub Ltd.

--Who Are You? 117p. 1982. 12.95 (ISBN 0-7206-0074-X, Pub. by Peter Owen). Merrimack Bk Serv.

Kavanagh, B. & Rigden, B. En Groupe. (On y Va Ser: No. 2). 1967. 4.50x o.p. (ISBN 0-7100-5104-2); pap. 2.50 o.p. (ISBN 0-7100-5103-4). Routledge & Kegan.

--En Savoie. (On y Va Ser: No. 3). 1968. 4.50 o.p. (ISBN 0-7100-5106-9); pap. 2.50 o.p. (ISBN 0-7100-5105-0). Routledge & Kegan.

Kavanagh, D., jt. auth. see Jones, B.

Kavanagh, Dennis, jt. auth. see Butler, David.

Kavanagh, James F. Orthography, Reading & Dyslexia. 352p. 1980. text ed. 29.95 (ISBN 0-8391-1559-8). Univ Park.

Kavanagh, James F. & Cutting, James E., eds. The Role of Speech in Language. 1975. 25.00 (ISBN 0-262-11059-8). MIT Pr.

Kavanagh, James F. & Mattingly, Ignatius G., eds. Language by Ear & by Eye: The Relationships Between Speech & Reading. 1972. 23.00x o.p. (ISBN 0-262-11044-X); pap. 10.95x (ISBN 0-262-61015-9). MIT Pr.

Kavanagh, James F. & Strange, Winifred, eds. Speech & Language in the Laboratory, School & Clinic. 1978. 32.50x (ISBN 0-262-11065-2). MIT Pr.

Kavanagh, Joseph T., ed. see Mid-Atlantic Conference.

Kavanagh, P. J., ed. see Gurney, Ivor.

Kavanagh, Thomas C., jt. auth. see Johnson, Sidney M.

Kavanagh, Thomas C., et al. Construction Management: A Professional Approach. (Modern Structures Ser.). (Illus.). 1978. 31.95 (ISBN 0-07-033386-6, P&RB). McGraw.

Kavanau, J. Lee. Curves & Symmetry, Vol. 1. 448p. 1982. 21.95 (ISBN 0-937292-01-X). Science Software.

--Symmetry: An Analytical Treatment. 656p. 1980. 29.95 (ISBN 0-937292-00-1). Science Software.

Kavanaugh, Aidan. Elements of Rite. 110p. (Orig.). 1982. pap. 7.95 (ISBN 0-916134-54-7). Pueblo Pub CO.

Kavanaugh, Ian. Far from the Blessed Land. (O'Donnell's Ser.: No. 3). (Orig.). 1983. pap. 3.50 (ISBN 0-440-02483-8, Emerald). Dell.

--From the Shamrock Shore. 1982. pap. 3.50 (ISBN 0-440-02798-5, Emerald). Dell.

--A Waltz on the Wind. (The O'Donnells Ser.). (Orig.). 1983. pap. 3.50 (ISBN 0-440-09487-9). Dell.

Kavanaugh, James. Celebrate the Sun. 1973. 9.95 (ISBN 0-87690-163-1, 0966-290). Dutton.

--A Fable. (Illus.). 64p. 1980. 8.95 o.p. (ISBN 0-525-93154-6). Dutton.

--There Are Men Too Gentle. 1970. 7.95 (ISBN 0-87690-165-8, 0772-230). Dutton.

--Walk Easy on the Earth. (Illus.). 1979. 9.95 (ISBN 0-525-93078-7, 0966-290). Dutton.

Kavanaugh, Kieran & Rodrigues, Otilio, trs. from Span. Teresa of Avila: The Interior Castle. LC 79-66484. (Classics of Western Spirituality Ser.). 256p. 1979. 11.95 (ISBN 0-8091-0289-7); pap. 7.95 (ISBN 0-8091-2227-8). Paulist Pr.

Kavanaugh, Patrick & O'Connor, P. J. Tarry Flynn. Nemo, John, ed. (Abbey Theatre Ser.). pap. 2.50x (ISBN 0-912262-40-0). Proscenium.

Kavanaugh-Baran, Kathryn, jt. auth. see Adams, Bruce.

Kavass, Igor I. & Blake, Michael J., eds. United States Legislation on Foreign Relations & International Commerce: 1789-1969, 4 vols. LC 76-51898. 1977-78. Set. lib. bdg. 295.00 (ISBN 0-930342-00-3). W S Hein.

Kavass, Igor I. & Sprudzs, Adolf, eds. History of the Petroleum Administration for War: 1941-1945. Frey, John W. & Ide, H. Chandler. LC 74-77638. (International Military Law & History Ser.: Vol. 8). 436p. 1974. Repr. of 1946 ed. lib. bdg. 30.00 (ISBN 0-930342-45-3). W S Hein.

Kavass, Igor I., ed. see Holborn, Hajo.

Kavenaugh, Michele. When I Grow up: Structured Experiences for Expanding Male & Female Roles, Vol. II. new ed. LC 78-56486. 1978. pap. 14.95 (ISBN 0-89334-017-0). Humanics Ltd.

--When I Grow up: Structured Experiences for Expanding Male & Female Roles, Vol. I. new ed. LC 78-56486. 206p. 1978. pap. 14.95 (ISBN 0-89334-016-2). Humanics Ltd.

Kavina, George, jt. auth. see Saville, Anthony.

Kawabata, Yasunari. Beauty & Sadness. Hibbet, Howard, tr. from Jap. (Perigee Japanese Library). 224p. 1981. pap. 4.95 (ISBN 0-399-50529-6, Perige). Putnam Pub Group.

--The Master of Go. Seidensticker, Edward G., tr. from Jap. (Perigee Japanese Library). 196p. 1981. pap. 4.95 (ISBN 0-399-50528-8, Perige). Putnam Pub Group.

--Snow Country. Seidensticker, Edward G., tr. from Jap. (Perigee Japanese Library). 192p. 1981. pap. 4.95 (ISBN 0-399-50525-3, Perige). Putnam Pub Group.

--The Sound of the Mountain. Seidensticker, Edward G., tr. from Jap. (Perigee Japanese Library). 288p. 1981. pap. 4.95 (ISBN 0-399-50527-X, Perige). Putnam Pub Group.

--Thousand Cranes. Seidensticker, Edward G., tr. from Jap. (Perigee Japanese Library). 160p. 1981. pap. 4.95 (ISBN 0-399-50526-1, Perige). Putnam Pub Group.

Kawada, Yukiyosi, jt. ed. see Iyanaga, Shokichi.

Kawaguchi, Keizaburo & Kyuma, Kazutake. Lowland Rice Soils in Malaya. (Center for Southeast Asian Studies Monographs, Kyoto University). 1969. text ed. 10.00x o.p. (ISBN 0-8248-0374-4). UH Pr.

--Lowland Rice Soils in Thailand. (Center for Southeast Asian Studies Monographs, Kyoto University). 1969. text ed. 15.00x o.p. (ISBN 0-8248-0373-6). UH Pr.

--Paddy Soils in Tropical Asia: Their Material Nature & Fertility. (Center for Southeast Asian Studies, Kyoto University). (Illus.). 1978. 15.00x (ISBN 0-8248-0570-4); pap. text ed. 10.00x (ISBN 0-8248-0571-2). UH Pr.

Kawahara, F. K., jt. ed. see Yen, T. F.

Kawahara, T., jt. auth. see Jeffrey, A.

Kawai, T., ed. Finite Element Flow Analysis: Proceedings of the Fourth International Symposium on Finite Element Methods in Flow Problems, Held at Chuo University, Tokyo, July, 1982. 1096p. 1982. 95.00 (North Holland). Elsevier.

Kawaishi, M. The Complete Seven Katas of Judo. Harrison, E. J., tr. from Japanese. LC 82-3470. (Illus.). 208p. 1982. 15.95 (ISBN 0-87951-156-7). Overlook Pr.

Kawakami, Yukiko, jt. auth. see Yano, Shigeko.

Kawamura, H., ed. see U. S.-Japan Seminar or Inelastic Light Scattering, Santa Monica, California. January 22-25, 1979.

Kawamura, K., jt. auth. see Jenkins, G. M.

Kawamura, Leslie, jt. ed. see Coward, Harold.

Kawamura, Y., ed. Oral Sensory Mechanisms. (Frontiers of Oral Physiology Ser.: Vol. 4). (Illus.). 200p. 1983. 72.00 (ISBN 3-8055-3576-7). S Karger.

Kawamura, Yojiro, ed. Oral-Facial Sensory & Motor Functions. Dubner, Ronald. (Illus.). 354p. 1981. 72.00 (ISBN 4-87417-077-3). Quint Pub Co.

Kawashima, Yasuhide. Puritan Justice & the Indian: White Man's Law in Massachusetts, 1630-1763. (Illus.). xii, 258p. 1983. 26.95 (ISBN 0-8195-5068-X). Wesleyan U Pr.

Kawata, K. & Akasaka, T., eds. Composite Materials: Mechanics, Mechanical Properties & Fabrication. (Illus.). xi, 562p. 1982. 69.75 (ISBN 0-85334-144-3, Pub. by Applied Sci England). Elsevier.

Kawata, Sukiyuki, ed. Japan's Iron & Steel Industry 1979. 28th ed. LC 55-33803. (Illus.). 1979. pap. 27.50x o.p. (ISBN 0-8002-2382-9). Intl Pubns Serv.

Kawatani, Michiko, jt. tr. see Levy, Howard S.

Kawazoe, A., jt. auth. see Eliot, J. N.

Kawin, Bruce F. Faulkner & Film. LC 77-2519. (Ungar Fil Library). (Illus.). 1977. 11.95 (ISBN 0-8044-2454-3); pap. 4.95 (ISBN 0-8044-6347-6). Ungar.

Kay, Catherine. Dawn of Passion. (Super Romances Ser.). 384p. 1982. pap. 2.50 (ISBN 0-373-70045-8, Pub. by Worldwide). Harlequin Bks.

Kay, David. Bantams. (Illus.). 96p. 1983. 12.50 (ISBN 0-7153-8395-7). David & Charles.

--Poultry Keeping for Beginners. 1977. 11.95 o.p. (ISBN 0-7153-7395-1). David & Charles.

Kay, David A. The United Nations Political System. LC 67-29937. (Illus.). 419p. 1967. text ed. 15.50 (ISBN 0-471-46110-5, Pub. by Wiley); pap. 7.50 (ISBN 0-471-46111-3). Krieger.

Kay, David A. & Jacobson, Harold K. Environmental Protection: The International Dimension. LC 81-65020. 352p. 1983. text ed. 39.50x (ISBN 0-86598-034-9). Allanheld.

Kay, David A., ed. The Changing United Nations: Options for the United States. LC 77-89037. (Special Studies). 1978. 28.95 o.p. (ISBN 0-03-043706-7). Praeger.

Kay, Donald, ed. A Provision of Human Nature: Essays on Fielding & Others in Honor of Miriam Austin Locke. LC 76-40469. xiii, 224p. 1977. 8.50 o.p. (ISBN 0-8173-7425-6). U of Ala Pr.

Kay, Donald, jt. ed. see Burke, John J., Jr.

Kay, E. Alison, ed. Natural History of the Hawaiian Islands: Selected Readings. (Illus.). 665p. 1972. pap. 15.00x (ISBN 0-8248-0203-9). UH Pr.

Kay, Ernest, ed. Dictionary of International Biography 1982. 17th ed. LC 64-1109. 885p. 1982. 72.50x (ISBN 0-900332-57-3). Intl Pubns Serv.

Kay, F. George. London. LC 79-89188. (A Rand McNally Pocket Guide). (Illus., Orig.). 1983. pap. 4.95 (ISBN 0-528-84272-2). Rand.

Kay, Geoffrey. Development, Underdevelopment & the Law of Value: A Marxist Analysis. LC 74-22889. 208p. 1975. 17.95 o.p. (ISBN 0-312-19740-3). St Martin.

--The Economic Theory of the Working Class. 1979. 25.00x (ISBN 0-312-23668-9). St Martin.

Kay, Geoffrey, ed. Political Economy of Colonialism in Ghana: A Collection of Documents & Statistics, 1900-1960. Hymer, S. (Illus.). 1971. 49.50 (ISBN 0-521-07952-7). Cambridge U Pr.

Kay, J. E., jt. ed. see Ling, N. R.

Kay, J. M. & Nedderman, R. M. An Introduction to Fluid Mechanics & Heat Transfer. 3rd. rev. ed. LC 74-77383. 300p. 1975. 49.50 (ISBN 0-521-20533-6); pap. 18.95x (ISBN 0-521-09880-7). Cambridge U Pr.

Kay, James T. De see De Kay, James T.

Kay, John, ed. Budget, Nineteen Eighty-Two. (Illus.). 156p. 1982. text ed. 15.00x (ISBN 0-631-13153-1, Pub. by Basil Blackwell England); pap. text ed. 6.50x (ISBN 0-631-13154-X, Pub. by Basil Blackwell England). Biblio Dist.

Kay, Karyn, jt. ed. see Peary, Gerald.

Kay, Kenneth & Goldberg, Marshall. The Man Who Must Not Die. 336p. (Orig.). 1982. pap. 3.50 o.s.i. (ISBN 0-8439-1174-3, Leisure Bks). Nordon Pubns.

Kay, Lona. Dialogue with a Demon. 1979. 7.95 o.p. (ISBN 0-533-03784-0). Vantage.

Kay, Margarita. Southwestern Medical Dictionary: Spanish-English & English-Spanish. LC 76-54591. 1977. pap. text ed. 4.50 (ISBN 0-8165-0529-2). U of Ariz Pr.

Kay, Margarita A. Anthropologyof Human Birth. LC 81-9776. (Illus.). 445p. 1981. text ed. 25.00x (ISBN 0-8036-5240-2). Davis Co.

Kay, Marguerite, et al, eds. Aging, Immunity & Arthritic Diseases. (Aging Ser.: Vol. 11). 275p. 1980. text ed. 30.00 (ISBN 0-89004-382-5). Raven.

Kay, Marshall & Colbert, E. H., eds. Stratigraphy & Life History. LC 64-20072. 736p. 1965. 31.50x (ISBN 0-471-46105-9). Wiley.

Kay, Martin, jt. auth. see Sparck Jones, Karen.

Kay, Neil M. The Innovating Firm: A Behavioral Theory of Corporate R & D. 1979. 29.00x (ISBN 0-312-41809-4). St Martin.

Kay, Norman & Silador, Sidney. The Complete Book of Duplicate Bridge. (Illus.). 1965. 7.95 (ISBN 0-399-10159-4). Putnam Pub Group.

Kay, Ormonde De see De Kay, Ormonde, Jr.

Kay, Paul, jt. auth. see Berlin, Brent.

Kay, Peg, jt. auth. see Nay, Joe N.

Kay, R., jt. ed. see Baum, M.

Kay, Reed. Painter's Guide to Studio Methods & Materials. (Illus.). 352p. 1982. 19.95 (ISBN 0-13-647958-8); pap. 12.95 (ISBN 0-13-647941-3). P-H.

Kay, Robert S. & Terry, Robert A., eds. How to Stay in College: A Learning Guide for Students. LC 78-61683. 1978. pap. text ed. 7.00 (ISBN 0-8191-0623-2). U Pr of Amer.

Kay, Ronald D. Farm Management. Vastyan, James E., ed. (Agricultural Sciences Publications). (Illus.). 384p. 1981. 22.50x (ISBN 0-07-033462-5). McGraw.

Kay, Shirley. The Bedouin. LC 77-88175. (This Changing World Ser.). 159p. 1978. 14.50x (ISBN 0-8448-1228-5). Crane-Russak Co.

Kay, Sophie. One-Dish Meals. (Illus.). 64p. 1982. pap. 3.25 (ISBN 0-8249-3012-6). Ideals.

Kayal, Joseph M., jt. auth. see Kayal, Philip M.

Kayal, Philip M. & Kayal, Joseph M. The Syrian-Lebanese in America. (Immigrant Heritage of America Ser.). 1975. lib. bdg. 13.95 (ISBN 0-8057-8412-8, Twayne). G K Hall.

Kayden, Eugene, tr. see Pasternak, Boris.

Kayden, Xandra. Campaign Organization. 1978. pap. text ed. 8.95x (ISBN 0-669-01782-5). Heath.

Kaye & Street. Die Casting Metallurgy. 1982. text ed. 49.95 (ISBN 0-408-10717-0). Butterworth.

Kaye, A. A., jt. auth. see Tozoni, O. V.

Kaye, Alan S. A Dictionary of Nigerian Arabic. LC 81-71736. (Bibliotheca Afroasiatica Ser.: Vol. 1). 104p. (Orig., Nigerian Arabic.). 1982. 24.50x (ISBN 0-89003-100-2); pap. 19.50x (ISBN 0-89003-101-0). Undena Pubns.

Kaye, Bernard L. & Gradinger, Gilbert P. Problems & Complications in Aesthetic Facial Plastic Surgery: A Symposium, Vol. XXIII. (Illus.). 400p. 1983. text ed. 65.00 (ISBN 0-8016-2624-2). Mosby.

Kaye, Brian H. Direct Characterization of Fineparticles. LC 81-1734. (Chemical Analysis: A Series of Monographs on Analytic Chemistry & Its Applications). 398p. 1981. 72.00x (ISBN 0-471-46150-4, Pub. by Wiley-Interscience). Wiley.

Kaye, Cecil. Communism in India: With Unpublished Documents from the National Archives of India, 1919-1924. Roy, Subodh, ed. LC 70-928934. 1971. deluxe ed. 9.50x o.p. (ISBN 0-8364-0392-4). South Asia Bks.

Kaye, David. The Book of Grimsby. 1981. 39.50x o.p. (ISBN 0-86023-137-2, Pub. by Barracuda England). State Mutual Bk.

Kaye, Donald & Rose, Louis F. Fundamentals of Internal Medicine. LC 82-3600. (Illus.). 1434p. 1983. text ed. 34.95 (ISBN 0-8016-2622-6). Mosby.

Kaye, Donald, jt. auth. see Rose, Louis F.

Kaye, Evelyn. Crosscurrents: Children, Families, & Religion. 256p. 1980. 11.95 o.p. (ISBN 0-517-53292-1, C N Potter Bks). Crown.

Kaye, Geraldine. Tim & the Red Indian Headdress. LC 75-41377. (Stepping Stones Ser.). (Illus.). 24p. (gr. k-3). 1976. 7.00 (ISBN 0-516-03594-0). Childrens.

Kaye, Hilary, jt. auth. see Koopowitz, Harold.

Kaye, Kenneth. The Mental & Social Life of Babies: How Parents Create Persons. LC 82-6965. (Illus.). 288p. 1982. lib. bdg. 22.50x (ISBN 0-226-42847-8). U of Chicago Pr.

Kaye, M. M. Death in Zanzibar. 240p. 1983. 12.95 (ISBN 0-312-18623-1). St Martin.

--Trade Wind. 1982. pap. 3.95 (ISBN 0-553-20901-9). Bantam.

Kaye, Marvin & Godwin, Parke. Wintermind. LC 81-43111. 212p. 1982. 15.95 (ISBN 0-385-14891-7). Doubleday.

Kaye, Phyllis J., ed. National Playwrights Directory. 2nd ed. LC 81-14097. 1982. 35.00 (ISBN 0-9605160-0-X). E O'Neill.

--National Playwrights Directory. 2nd ed. LC 77-83135. (Illus.). 1981. 44.00x (ISBN 0-685-87023-5, O'Neill Theater Center). Gale.

--National Playwrights Directory. 2nd ed. 400p. 1982. 44.00x (ISBN 0-686-81469-X, Pub. by O'Neill Theatre Ctr). Gale.

Kaye, Robert & Oski, Frank A., eds. Core Textbook of Pediatrics. 2nd ed. (Illus.). 542p. 1982. pap. text ed. 22.50 (ISBN 0-397-52097-2, Lippincott Medical). Lippincott.

Kaye, Robin. Lanai Folks. LC 81-19799. (Illus.). 128p. 1982. pap. 14.95 (ISBN 0-8248-0623-9). UH Pr.

Kaynak. Marketing in the Third World. 320p. 1982. 29.95 (ISBN 0-03-062179-8). Praeger.

Kayne, Richard S. French Syntax: The Transformational Cycle. LC 75-4681. (Current Studies in Linguistics: No. 6). 464p. 1975. text ed. 30.00x (ISBN 0-262-11055-5). MIT Pr.

Kay-Robinson, Denys. The First Mrs. Thomas Hardy. LC 79-14065. (Illus.). 1979. 25.00x (ISBN 0-312-29246-5). St Martin.

Kays, John M. The Horse. 3rd ed. LC 82-114961. (Illus.). 488p. 1982. 19.95 (ISBN 0-668-05469-7). Arco.

--The Horse. LC 68-27248. (Illus.). 1977. 12.95 o.p. (ISBN 0-668-02770-3). Arco.

Kays, William B. Construction of Linings for Reservoirs, Tanks, & Pollution Control Facilties. LC 77-3944. (Wiley Series of Practical Construction Guides). 379p. 1977. 52.95x (ISBN 0-471-02110-5, Pub. by Wiley-Interscience). Wiley.

Kays, William M. & Crawford, Michael. Convective Heat & Mass Transfer. 2nd ed. (Mechanical Engineering Ser.). (Illus.). 1980. text ed. 37.50 (ISBN 0-07-033457-9); solutions manual 12.00 (ISBN 0-07-033458-7). McGraw.

Kays, William M. & London, A. L. Compact Heat Exchangers. 2nd ed. (Mechanical Engineering Ser.). 1964. text ed. 39.50 (ISBN 0-07-033391-2, P&RB). McGraw.

Kaysen, Carl, jt. auth. see Tavoulareas, William.

Kayser, F. H., jt. auth. see Van Rens.

Kayser, Rita. I'm Glad I'm Not an Alligator. Mahany, Patricia, ed. (Happy Day Bks.). (Illus.). 24p. (ps-2). 1983. 1.29 (ISBN 0-87239-636-3, 3556). Standard Pub.

Kayser, Rudolf. Spinoza: Portrait of a Spiritual Hero. Repr. of 1946 ed. lib. bdg. cancelled o.p. (ISBN 0-8371-0124-7, KASP). Greenwood.

Kay-Shuttleworth, James P. Memorandum on Popular Education. LC 72-5887. (Social History of Education). Repr. of 1868 ed. 12.50x (ISBN 0-678-08457-2). Kelley.

Kaysing, Bill. Fell's Beginner's Guide to Motorcycling. LC 76-17052. 192p. 1976. 8.95 o.p. (ISBN 0-8119-0272-2); pap. 4.95 (ISBN 0-8119-0365-6). Fell.

Kazam, Benjamin, ed. Advances in Image Pickup & Display, Vol. 5. 298p. 1982. 56.00 (ISBN 0-12-022105-5). Acad Pr.

Kazamias, Andreas M. & Massialas, Byron G. Tradition & Change in Education: A Comparative Study. 1965. 15.95 (ISBN 0-13-925982-1). P-H.

Kazamias, Andreas M., ed. Herbert Spencer on Education. LC 66-17068. 1966. text ed. 10.50 (ISBN 0-8077-1602-2); pap. text ed. 5.50x (ISBN 0-8077-1599-9). Tchrs Coll.

Kazan, Benjamin, ed. Advances in Image Pickup & Display, Vol. 6. (Serial Publication). Date not set. price not set (ISBN 0-12-022106-3). Acad Pr.

Kazan, Elia. The Arrangement. 576p. 1976. pap. 2.75 o.p. (ISBN 0-446-95229-X). Warner Bks.

--The Understudy. 1976. pap. 2.50 o.p. (ISBN 0-446-81646-9). Warner Bks.

Kazanas & Klein. Technology of Industrial Materials. 1979. pap. 15.72 (ISBN 0-87002-301-2); lab manual 6.32 (ISBN 0-87002-170-2). Bennett IL.

Kazanas, H., et al. Manufacturing Processes. 1981. 18.95 (ISBN 0-07-033465-X); instr's manual avail. McGraw.

Kazanas, H. C. Properties & Uses of Ferrous & Nonferrous Metals. rev. ed. LC 78-70035. (Illus.). 1979. pap. 4.75x (ISBN 0-911168-39-7); instrs'. guide & answer bk. 1.50x (ISBN 0-911168-40-0). Prakken.

Kazanas, Hercules. Readings in Career Education. 1981. pap. text ed. 13.28 (ISBN 0-87002-308-X). Bennett IL.

Kazanjian, Dolores P., jt. auth. see McMurray, Georgia L.

Kazanjian, Gary, jt. auth. see Rosenthal, Robert.

Kazantzaki. Zorba. (Arabic.). pap. 8.95x o.s.i. (ISBN 0-86685-146-1). Intl Bk Ctr.

Kazantzakis, Nikos. Alexander the Great: A Novel. Vasils, Theodora, tr. from Greek. LC 81-11307. (Illus.). x, 222p. 1982. text ed. 20.95x (ISBN 0-8214-0654-X, 82-84234); pap. 11.95 (ISBN 0-8214-0663-9, 82-84242). Ohio U Pr.

--Buddha. Friar, Kimon & Dallas-Damis, Athena, trs. from Greek. LC 81-71164. (Orig.). 1983. pap. 11.95 (ISBN 0-932238-14-9). Avant Bks.

--Greek Passion. 1953. 9.95 o.p. (ISBN 0-671-29100-9). S&S.

--The Greek Passion. 1959. pap. 8.95 (ISBN 0-671-21216-8, Touchstone Bks). S&S.

--Last Temptation of Christ. 1960. 14.95 o.p. (ISBN 0-671-40710-4). S&S.

--The Last Temptation of Christ. 1966. pap. 7.75 (ISBN 0-671-21170-6, Touchstone Bks). S&S.

--Odyssey: A Modern Sequel. 1961. pap. 9.95 (ISBN 0-671-20247-2, Touchstone Bks). S&S.

--Rock Garden. 1969. pap. 3.95 o.p. (ISBN 0-671-20340-1, Touchstone Bks). S&S.

--Saviors of God. 1960. 5.95 o.p. (ISBN 0-671-63485-2). S&S.

--Spain: A Journal of Two Voyages Before & During the Spanish Civil War. LC 63-15059. 260p. pap. 7.95 (ISBN 0-916870-54-5). Creative Arts Bk.

--Zorba the Greek. 1953. 12.95 o.p. (ISBN 0-671-85100-4). S&S.

--Zorba the Greek. 1959. pap. 5.75 (ISBN 0-671-21132-3, Touchstone Bks). S&S.

Kazdin, Alan. History of Behavior Modification. LC 77-25180. 480p. 1978. text ed. 34.95 (ISBN 0-8391-1205-X). Univ Park.

Kazdin, Alan, jt. ed. see Lahey, Benjamin B.

Kazdin, Alan E., jt. ed. see Hersen, Michel.

Kazee, Buell H. Faith is the Victory. 1983. pap. 4.95 (ISBN 0-8423-0844-X). Tyndale.

Kazemi, Homayoun, jt. auth. see Miller, Lawrence G.

Kazemzadeh, Firuz. The Baha'i Faith: A Summary Reprinted from the Encyclopedia Britannica. 1977. o.s. 0.60 (ISBN 0-87743-121-3, 340-379-10); write for info. (ISBN 0-87743-152-3, 340-080-10). Baha'i.

Kazimiroff, Theodore L. The Last Algonquin. 1982. 12.95 (ISBN 0-8027-0698-3). Walker & Co.

Kazin, Alfred. Contemporaries, from the Nineteenth Century to the Present. rev. ed. 500p. 1981. pap. 9.95 (ISBN 0-8180-1132-7). Horizon.

--The Inmost Leaf: A Selection of Essays. LC 73-17921. 273p. Repr. of 1955 ed. lib. bdg. 17.50x (ISBN 0-8371-7281-0, KAIN). Greenwood.

--On Native Grounds. LC 42-24811. 541p. 1972. pap. 5.95 o.p. (ISBN 0-15-668750-X, HB237, Harv). HarBraceJ.

Kazin, Alfred, ed. see Whitman, Walt.

Kazmer, Daniel R. & Kazmer, Vera, eds. Russian Economic History: A Guide to Information Sources. LC 73-17588. (Economics Information Guide Ser: Vol. 4). 550p. 1977. 42.00x (ISBN 0-8103-1304-9). Gale.

Kazmer, Vera, jt. ed. see Kazmer, Daniel R.

Kazmier, L. J., jt. auth. see Philippakis, A. S.

Kazmier, Leonard, jt. auth. see Philippakis, Andreas.

Kazmier, Leonard J. Basic Statistics for Business & Economics. (Illus.). 1979. text ed. 24.95 (ISBN 0-07-033445-5, C); wkbk. 11.95 (ISBN 0-07-033446-3); instructor's manual 25.00 (ISBN 0-07-033447-1). McGraw.

--Management: A Programmed Approach with Cases & Applications. 4th, rev. ed. (Illus.). 1980. pap. text ed. 19.95 (ISBN 0-07-033453-6); instrs'. manual 19.50 (ISBN 0-07-033454-4). McGraw.

--Outline of Business Statistics. (Schaum's Outline Ser.). (Orig.). 1976. pap. 7.95 (ISBN 0-07-033460-9, SP). McGraw.

--Principles of Management: A Programmed-Instructional Approach. (Illus.). 480p. 1974. text ed. 15.95 o.p. (ISBN 0-07-033450-1, C); pap. text ed. 10.95 o.p. (ISBN 0-07-033451-X); instructors' manual 4.95 o.p. (ISBN 0-07-033452-8). McGraw.

--Statistical Analysis for Business & Economics. (Illus.). 1978. pap. text ed. 19.95 (ISBN 0-07-033439-0, C); instructors manual 19.95 (ISBN 0-07-033440-4). McGraw.

Kazmier, Leonard J. & Philippakis, A. S. Fundamentals of EDP & FORTRAN. 1970. text ed. 13.50 o.p. (ISBN 0-07-033416-1, C); 1.95 o.p. instructor's manual (ISBN 0-07-033419-6). McGraw.

Kazmier, Leonard J., jt. auth. see Philippakis, Andreas S.

Kazner, E., et al, eds. Computed Tomography in Intracranial Tumors: Differential Diagnosis & Clinical Aspects. Dougherty, F. C., tr. from Ger. (Illus.). 548p. 1982. 198.00 (ISBN 0-387-10815-7). Springer-Verlag.

Kazovsky, L. G. Transmission of Information in the Optical Waveband. LC 77-28102. 121p. 1978. 29.95x o.s.i. (ISBN 0-470-26294-X). Halsted Pr.

Kazziha, Walid. Revolutionary Transformation in the Arab World: Habash & His Comrades from Nationalism to Marxism. LC 74-21751. 128p. 1975. 14.95 o.p. (ISBN 0-312-68040-6). St Martin.

KDaneke, Gregory A. & Garcia, Margot W., eds. Public Involvement & Social Impact Assessment. (Social Impact Assessment Series: No. 9). 300p. 1983. lib. bdg. 27.50x (ISBN 0-86531-624-4). Westview.

Ke, Bacon, ed. Newer Methods of Polymer Characterization. LC 64-13218. 722p. 1964. text ed. 32.50 (ISBN 0-470-46215-9, Pub. by Wiley). Krieger.

Kea, Ray A. Settlements, Trade & Polities in the Seventeenth-Century Gold Coast. LC 81-23609. (Johns Hopkins University Studies in Atlantic History & Culture). 315p. 1982. text ed. 29.50x (ISBN 0-8018-2310-2). Johns Hopkins.

Keagan, Warren J. Mulitnational Marketing Management. 2nd ed. (Illus.). 1980. text ed. 26.95 (ISBN 0-13-605055-7). P-H.

Keagy, Robert D., jt. auth. see Bunch, Wilton H.

Keairns, D. L. see Davidson, J. F.

Kealey, Edward J. Roger of Salisbury, Viceroy of England. LC 78-92681. (Illus.). 350p. 1972. 33.00x (ISBN 0-520-01985-7). U of Cal Pr.

Kealey, Gregory S. & Palmer, Bryan D. Dreaming of What Might Be: The Knights of Labor in Ontario, 1880-1900. LC 81-21615. (Illus.). 464p. 1982. 49.50 (ISBN 0-521-24430-7). Cambridge U Pr.

Kean, A. Essays in Air Law. 1982. lib. bdg. 74.00 (ISBN 90-247-2543-7, Pub. by Martinus Nijhoff Netherlands). Kluwer Boston.

Kean, Beverly W. All the Empty Palaces: The Great Merchant Patrons of Modern Art in Pre-Revolutionary Russia. LC 82-8536. (Illus.). 336p. 1983. 29.50 (ISBN 0-87663-412-9). Universe.

Kean, Eccleston A., ed. see Symposium, Kingston, Jamaica.

Kean, Elizabeth see Herron, Dudley.

Kean, Mary-Louise, jt. ed. see Aronoff, Mark.

Kean, P. M. Chaucer & the Making of English Poetry, 2 vols. Incl. Vol. 1. Love Vision & Debate. 18.95 (ISBN 0-7100-7046-2); Vol. 2. The Art of Narrative. 18.95 (ISBN 0-7100-7250-3). (Illus.). 1972. Set. 35.00 (ISBN 0-685-25613-8). Routledge & Kegan.

Kean, Roslyn. Australian Art Guide. 1981. 5.95 (ISBN 0-9507160-3-0, Pub. by Art Guide England). Morgan.

Keane, A. H., ed. see Streeter, Edwin W.

Keane, Bil. Eggheads. 128p. 1983. pap. 1.95 (ISBN 0-449-12456-8, GM). Fawcett.

--I'm Already Tucked In. 128p. (Orig.). 1983. pap. 1.95 (ISBN 0-449-12381-2, GM). Fawcett.

--Love: The Family Circus. 104p. 1983. pap. 3.95 (ISBN 0-8362-2007-2). Andrews & McMeel.

Keane, Claire. Management Essentials in Nursing. 1980. text ed. 17.95 (ISBN 0-8359-4203-1); pap. text ed. 14.95 (ISBN 0-8359-4202-3). Reston.

Keane, Claire B. Essentials of Nursing: A Medical Surgical Text for Practical Nurses. 4th ed. (Illus.). 558p. 1979. text ed. 19.95 (ISBN 0-7216-5313-8). Saunders.

--Medical-Surgical Nursing for Practical Nurse: Study Guide & Workbook. LC 74-4573. 1974. pap. 9.95 o.p. (ISBN 0-7216-5331-6). Saunders.

--Saunders Review for Practical Nurses. LC 76-41537. (Illus.). 1977. pap. text ed. 10.95 o.p. (ISBN 0-7216-5327-8). Saunders.

--Saunders Review For Practical Nurses. 4th ed. (Illus.). 457p. 1982. 16.95 (ISBN 0-7216-5328-6). Saunders.

Keane, Claire B. & Fletcher, Sybil M. Drugs & Solutions: A Programed Introduction. 4th ed. (Illus.). 166p. 1980. soft cover 9.95 (ISBN 0-7216-5343-X). Saunders.

Keane, Claire B., jt. auth. see Miller, Benjamin F.

Keane, John B. The Good Thing. (Irish Play Ser.). pap. 2.50x (ISBN 0-912262-45-1). Proscenium.

Keane, Molly. Good Behaviour. 256p. 1983. pap. 6.95 (ISBN 0-525-48051-X, 0675-200, Obelisk). Dutton.

Keane, Noel P. & Breo, Dennis L. The Surrogate Mother. 256p. 1981. 14.95 (ISBN 0-89696-113-3, An Everest House Book); pap. 8.95 (ISBN 0-686-85939-1). Dodd.

Keane, Patrick J. A Wild Civility: Interactions in the Poetry & Thought of Robert Graves. LC 79-5428. 128p. 1980. pap. 6.95 (ISBN 0-8262-0296-9). U of Mo Pr.

Kear & Gearson, eds. Rapidly Solidified Amorphous & Crystalline Alloys. (Materials Research Society Symposia Ser.: Vol. 8). 1982. 85.00 (ISBN 0-444-00698-2). Elsevier.

Kear, Dennis J., jt. auth. see Silvaroli, Nicholas J.

Kearins, John. Yankee Revenooer. LC 70-79094. 1969. 9.95 (ISBN 0-87716-007-4, Pub. by Moore Pub Co). F Apple.

Kearney, Elizabeth I., jt. auth. see Fitzgerald, Louise S.

Kearney, Hugh. Science & Change. LC 76-96433. (World University Library Ser.). (Illus., Orig.). 1971. pap. 5.95 (ISBN 0-07-033425-0, SP). McGraw.

Kearney, Michael. World View. Langness, L. L. & Edgerton, Robert B., eds. (Publications in Anthropology & Related Fields Ser.). (Illus.). 256p. (Orig.). 1983. pap. text ed. 7.95x (ISBN 0-88316-551-1). Chandler & Sharp.

Kearney, Patrick J. A History of Erotic Literature. 216p. 1982. 75.00x (ISBN 0-333-34126-0, Pub. by Macmillan England). State Mutual Bk.

Kearney, Robert H. Communalism & Language in the Politics of Ceylon: Program in Comparative Studies on Southern Asia No. 2. LC 67-28068. 1967. 10.50 o.p. (ISBN 0-8223-0094-X). Duke.

Kearney, Robert N. Trade Unions & Politics in Ceylon. LC 76-115495. (Center for South & Southeast Asia Studies, UC Berkeley). 1971. 32.50x (ISBN 0-520-01713-7). U of Cal Pr.

Kearney, Robert N., ed. Politics & Modernization in South & Southeast Asia. LC 74-13637. (States & Societies of the Third World Ser.). 277p. 1975. 16.50x o.s.i. (ISBN 0-470-46232-9); pap. 7.95x o.s.i. (ISBN 0-470-46233-7). Halsted Pr.

--Politics & Modernization in South & Southeast Asia. 277p. 1975. 15.00 o.p. (ISBN 0-87073-117-3); pap. 7.95x (ISBN 0-87073-118-1). Schenkman.

Kearney, Robert N., jt. ed. see Fernando, Tissa.

Kearney, Thomas H., et al. Arizona Flora. 2nd rev. ed. (Illus.). 1960. 35.00x (ISBN 0-520-00637-2). U of Cal Pr.

Kearns, E. J. Ideas in Seventeenth Century France. LC 79-16610. 1979. 25.00x (ISBN 0-312-40445-X). St Martin.

Kearns, George, ed. Literature of the World. 2nd ed. (Illus.). 416p. (gr. 10). 1974. pap. text ed. 17.12 (ISBN 0-07-033437-4, W). McGraw.

Kearns, James, jt. auth. see Rodman, Selden.

Kearns, Kevin C. Georgian Dublin: Ireland's Imperilled Architectural Heritage. (Illus.). 224p. 1983. 31.50 (ISBN 0-7153-8440-6). David & Charles.

Kearns, Thomas, jt. auth. see Dietrich, Frank H., II.

Kearny, Mary Ann & Baker, James. Life, Liberty & the Pursuit of Happiness. (Readers Ser.: Stage 6). 1978. pap. text ed. 8.95 (ISBN 0-88377-111-X). Newbury Hse.

Kearon, Thomas P., jt. auth. see DiLorenzo-Kearon, Maria A.

Kearon DiLorenzo, Maria see DiLorenzo-Kearon, Maria.

Kearse, Amalya. Bridge at Your Fingertips. LC 79-88566. 320p. (Orig.). 1980. pap. 7.95 o.s.i. (ISBN 0-89104-159-1, A & W Visual Library). A & W Pubs.

Kearsley, G. P. Costs, Benefits, & Productivity in Training Systems. LC 82-22846. (Illus.). 160p. 1982. text ed. 16.95 (ISBN 0-201-10332-X). A-W.

Kearsley, Joseph E. Complete Real Estate Exchange & Acquisition Handbook. LC 82-496. 234p. 1982. 29.50 (ISBN 0-13-162420-2, Busn). P-H.

Keasey, Merritt S. The Saquaro Book. 72p. 1981. pap. text ed. 6.60 (ISBN 0-8403-2392-1). Kendall-Hunt.

Keast, Allen & Morton, Eugene S., eds. Migrant Birds in the Neotropics: Ecology, Behavior, Distribution & Conservation. LC 80-607031. (Symposia of the National Zoological Park: No. 5). 576p. (Orig.). 1980. text ed. 35.00x (ISBN 0-87474-660-4); pap. text ed. 22.50x (ISBN 0-87474-661-2). Smithsonian.

Keast, William R., ed. Seventeenth Century English Poetry. rev ed. 1971. pap. 11.95 (ISBN 0-19-501391-3, GB). Oxford U Pr.

Keat, Donald B. Fundamentals of Child Counseling. 300p. 1974. text ed. 23.95 o.p. (ISBN 0-395-17827-4); instr's. manual 2.95 o.p. (ISBN 0-395-17859-2). HM.

Keat, Donald B. & Guerney, Louise. Helping Your Child. 204p. 1980. 9.75 (ISBN 0-686-36393-0); 11.25 (ISBN 0-686-37303-0). Am Personnel.

Keat, Russell & Urry, John. Social Theory as Science. rev. ed. (International Library of Sociology Ser.). 288p. 1983. pap. 11.95 (ISBN 0-7100-9431-0). Routledge & Kegan.

Keates, Jonathan. Companion Guide to the Shakespeare Country. (Illus.). 352p. 1983. 15.95 (ISBN 0-13-154625-2); pap. 7.95 (ISBN 0-13-154617-1). P-H.

Keating, Bern & Keating, Franke. Mississippi. (Illus.). 192p. 1982. 25.00 (ISBN 0-87805-165-1). U Pr of Miss.

Keating, Charles J. The Heart of the Christian Message. school ed. flexible bdg 3.50 (ISBN 0-686-14274-8, 246-05-SD). Catholic Bk Pub.

--The Leadership Book. rev. ed. LC 77-99300. 144p. 1982. pap. 4.95 (ISBN 0-8091-2090-9). Paulist Pr.

Keating, Franke, jt. auth. see Keating, Bern.

Keating, J. M. & Vedder, O. F. History of the City of Memphis & Shelby County Tennessee, 2 vols. (Illus.). 1397p. 1977. Repr. of 1888 ed. Set. ltd. boxed ed. 85.00 (ISBN 0-937130-04-4). Burke's Bk Store.

Keating, James W. Competition & Playful Activities. LC 78-62741. 1978. pap. text ed. 9.50 (ISBN 0-8191-0589-9). U Pr of Amer.

Keating, Jeffrey, jt. auth. see Long, Mark.

Keating, Joni. Is There Room for Me? (gr. 3-8). 1981. 5.95 (ISBN 0-86653-020-7, GA 252). Good Apple.

--Suit Yourself. (gr. 3-8). 1981. 5.95 (ISBN 0-86653-021-5, GA 250). Good Apple.

--Use It, Don't Lose It. (gr. 3-8). 1981. 5.95 (ISBN 0-86653-051-7, GA 248). Good Apple.

--Watt's Happening. (gr. 3-8). 1981. 5.95 (ISBN 0-86653-019-3, GA 249). Good Apple.

Keating, Kathleen. Hug Therapy. (Illus.). 72p. (Orig.). 1983. pap. 6.95 (ISBN 0-89638-065-3). CompCare.

Keating, L. Clark. Andre Maurois. (World Authors Ser.: No. 53). 10.95 o.p. (ISBN 0-8057-2608-X, Twayne). G K Hall.

--Etienne Pasquier. (World Authors Ser.). lib. bdg. 15.95 (ISBN 0-8057-2674-8, Twayne). G K Hall.

--Joachim du Bellay. (World Authors Ser.). lib. bdg. 13.95 (ISBN 0-8057-2132-0, Twayne). G K Hall.

Keating, L. Clark & Moraud, Marcel I. Cultural Graded Readers, Elementary Series, 3 vols. Incl. Lafitte. 1958. pap. 2.50x o.p. (ISBN 0-442-21813-3); Moliere. 1958. pap. text ed. 2.50x (ISBN 0-442-31815-4); Voltaire. 1968. pap. text ed. 2.50x (ISBN 0-442-21816-8). (Fr.). pap. Van Nos Reinhold.

Keating, L. Clark, ed. see Borges, Jorge L. & De Torres, Esther Z.

Keating, L. Clark, tr. see Borges, Jorge L. & De Torres, Esther Z.

Keating, Louise J. & Silvergleid, Arthur J., eds. Hepatitis. (Illus.). 147p. 1981. 25.00 (ISBN 0-914404-65-2). Am Assn Blood.

Keating, Thomas. And the Word was Made Flesh. 144p. 1983. 6.95 (ISBN 0-8245-0505-0). Crossroad NY.

--Crisis of Faith. LC 79-13036. 1979. pap. 4.00 (ISBN 0-932506-05-4). St Bedes Pubns.

Keating, Thomas, et al. Finding Grace at the Center. rev. ed. LC 78-10514. 1979. pap. 2.50 (ISBN 0-932506-00-3). St Bedes Pubns.

Keating, W. G. & Bolza, Eleanor. Characteristics, Properties & Uses of Timbers: Southeast Asia, Northern Australia & the Pacific, Vol. I. LC 82-45895. (Illus.). 391p. 1983. 39.50x (ISBN 0-89096-141-7). Tex A&M Univ Pr.

--Characteristics, Properties & Uses of Timber: South-East Asia, Northern Australia & the Pacific, Vol. 1. 1982. lib. bdg. cancelled o.p. (ISBN 0-89874-580-2). Krieger.

Keatking, Joni. The Circle Game. (gr. 3-8). 1981. 5.95 (ISBN 0-86653-022-3, GA251). Good Apple.

Keaton, Birchfield & Keaton, Henry F. Workbook for Short Term Planning. 58p. 1973. 15.00 (ISBN 0-686-68579-2, 14913). Healthcare Fin Man Assn.

Keaton, Buster & Samuels, Charles. Buster Keaton: My Wonderful World of Slapstick. (Quality Paperbacks Ser.). (Illus.). 282p. 1983. pap. 7.95 (ISBN 0-306-80178-7). Da Capo.

Keaton, Henry F., jt. auth. see Keaton, Birchfield.

Keats, Bronya J. Linkage & Chromosome Mapping in Man. LC 81-81399. 266p. 1981. text ed. 35.00x (ISBN 0-8248-0780-4, Population Gene Lab). UH Pr.

Keats, Charles. Magnificent Masquerade. LC 82-48369. (Accountancy in Transition Ser.). 292p. 1982. lib. bdg. 30.00 (ISBN 0-8240-5322-2). Garland Pub.

Keats, Ezra J. Clementina's Cactus. LC 82-2630. (Illus.). 32p. (gr. 4-8). 1982. 11.95 (ISBN 0-670-22517-7). Viking Pr.

--Letter to Amy. LC 68-24329. (Illus.). (gr. k-3). 1968. 10.53i (ISBN 0-06-023108-4, HarpJ); PLB 10.89 (ISBN 0-06-023109-2). Har-Row.

--The Snowy Day. (Illus.). (ps-1). 1962. PLB 10.95 (ISBN 0-670-65400-0). Viking Pr.

Keats, J. A., et al, eds. Cognitive Development: Research Based on a Neo-Piagetian Approach. 458p. 1978. 62.95x (ISBN 0-471-99505-3, Pub. by Wiley-Interscience). Wiley.

Keats, Jack E. The Snowy Day. (Picture Puffins Ser.). (Illus.). 1976. pap. 3.50 (ISBN 0-14-050182-7, Puffin). Penguin.

Keats, John. John Keats: Complete Poems. Stillinger, Jack, ed. (Illus.). 544p. 1982. text ed. 20.00x (ISBN 0-674-15430-4); pap. 9.95 (ISBN 0-674-15431-2). Harvard U Pr.

--Poetical Works of John Keats. Garrod, Heathcote W., ed. (Oxford Standard Authors Ser.). 1956. 24.9506940985x (ISBN 0-19-254132-3). Oxford U Pr.

--Selected Poetry of Keats. Artos, John, ed. pap. 1.95 (ISBN 0-451-51326-6, CJ1326, Sig Classics). NAL.

--The Texts of Keat's Poems. Stillinger, Jack, ed. LC 73-86940. 320p. 1974. text ed. 16.50x (ISBN 0-674-87511-7). Harvard U Pr.

Keats-Shelley Memorial House, Rome. Catalog of Books & Manuscripts at the Keats-Shelley Memorial House in Rome. 1969. lib. bdg. 75.00 (ISBN 0-8161-0856-0, Hall Library). G K Hall.

Keattch, C. J. & Dollimore, D. An Introduction to Thermogravimetry. 1975. 29.95 (ISBN 0-471-25834-2, Wiley Heyden). Wiley.

Keaveney, Raymond, jt. auth. see Potterton, Homan.

Keaveney, Sydney S. American Painting: A Guide to Information Sources. LC 73-17522. (Art & Architecture Information Guide Ser.: Vol. 1). 296p. 1974. 42.00x (ISBN 0-8103-1200-X). Gale.

Keaveny, Timothy J., jt. auth. see Allen, Robert E.

Keavy, William T., tr. see Elbaz, Jean S. & Flageul, G.

Kebabian, Paul B. & Lipke, William C., eds. Tools & Technologies: America's Wooden Age. (Illus.). 119p. (Orig.). 1979. pap. 12.50 (ISBN 0-87451-987-X). U Pr of New Eng.

Kebart, Richard C., et al. Self-Assessment of Current Knowledge in Radiologic Technology. 2nd ed. 1979. pap. 12.75 (ISBN 0-87488-274-5). Med Exam.

Kebart, Richard C., et al, eds. X-Ray Technology Examination Review Book, Vol. 3. 2nd ed. 1976. spiral bdg. 12.75 (ISBN 0-87488-443-8). Med Exam.

Kebbe, Charles. Profitable Public Speaking. LC 82-45167. 128p. 1983. 8.95 (ISBN 0-689-11309-9). Atheneum.

Kebbede, Girma. Basic Geographic Techniques in the Analysis of Public Policy. (Learning Packages in the Policy Sciences Ser.: No. 18). (Illus.). 46p. (Orig.). 1978. pap. text ed. 2.50x (ISBN 0-936826-07-X). Pol Stud Assocs.

Keble, John. The Christian Year: Thoughts in Verse for the Sundays & Holidays Throughout the Year. LC 70-167019. (Illus.). 291p. 1975. Repr. of 1896 ed. 37.00x (ISBN 0-8103-4095-X). Gale.

Kechely, Raymond O. The Rush to Ruin. LC 77-89817. 1977. 5.00 o.s.i. (ISBN 0-930202-01-5). R O Kechely.

Keck, Caroline K. Handbook on the Care of Paintings. LC 67-13743. (Illus.). 1965. pap. 8.00 (ISBN 0-910050-00-7). AASLH.

Keck, David D., jt. auth. see Munz, Philip A.

Keck, Florence, ed. see Educational Research Council of America.

Keck, Otto. Policy-Making in a Nuclear Program: The Case of the West German Fast-Breeder Reactor. LC 79-3831. 304p. 1981. 29.95x (ISBN 0-669-03519-X). Lexington Bks.

Kedar, Ervin Y., jt. auth. see Hill, James E.

Kedda, Helena. Stained Glass Cook Book. (Illus.). 56p. (Orig.). 1982. pap. 4.95 (ISBN 0-9608958-0-9). Paw-Print.

Keddie, Nikki. The Middle East & Beyond. 1983. 29.50x (ISBN 0-7146-3151-5, F Cass Co). Biblio Dist.

Keddie, Nikki R. Religion & Politics in Iran: Shi'ism from Quietism to Revolution. LC 82-17351. 288p. 1983. text ed. 22.50x (ISBN 0-300-02874-1). Yale U Pr.

Keddie, Nikki R. & Yann, Richard. Roots of Revolution: An Interpretive History of Modern Iran. LC 81-40438. (Illus.). 316p. 1981. text ed. 30.00 (ISBN 0-300-02606-4); pap. 7.95 (ISBN 0-300-02611-0, YF-24). Yale U Pr.

Keddie, Nikki R. & Hooglund, Eric, eds. The Iranian Revolution & the Islamic Republic: Proceedings of a Conference Held at the Woodrow Wilson International Center for Scholars, May 21-22, 1982. LC 82-62038. 210p. (Orig.). 1982. pap. 7.50 (ISBN 0-916808-19-X). Mid East Inst.

Keddie, Nikki R., jt. ed. see Bonine, Michael E.

Keddie, William, ed. Cyclopaedia of Literary & Scientific Anecdote: Illustrative of the Characters, Habits, & Conversation of Men of Letters & Science. LC 74-156925. 1971. Repr. of 1859 ed. 45.00x (ISBN 0-8103-3730-4). Gale.

Kedourie, E. In the Anglo-Arab Labyrinth. LC 75-3975. (Studies in the History & Theory of Politics). (Illus.). 370p. 1976. 49.50 (ISBN 0-521-20826-2). Cambridge U Pr.

Kedourie, Elie, ed. The Jewish World: History & Culture of the Jewish People. LC 78-31363. (Illus.). 1979. 45.00 (ISBN 0-8109-1154-X). Abrams.

Kedzie, Daniel P., jt. auth. see Sommer, Armand.

Kedzior, K., jt. ed. see Morecki, A.

Kee, Howard, ed. see Rhyne, C. Thomas.

Kee, Howard C. Christian Origins in Sociological Perspective: Methods & Resources. LC 79-26668. 1980. soft cover 9.95 (ISBN 0-664-24307-X). Westminster.

--Jesus in History: An Approach to the Study of the Gospels. 2nd ed. LC 77-75349. 312p. 1977. pap. text ed. 12.95 (ISBN 0-15-547382-4, HC). HarBraceJ.

--The Origins of Christianity: Sources & Documents. LC 73-4830. 320p. 1973. 13.95 (ISBN 0-13-642553-4). P-H.

--Understanding the New Testament. 4th ed. (Illus.). 464p. 1983. text ed. 21.95 (ISBN 0-13-936591-5). P-H.

Kee, Howard C., et al. Understanding the New Testament. 3rd ed. (Illus.). 496p. 1973. 21.95 (ISBN 0-13-936104-9). P-H.

Kee, J. L. Fluids & Electrolytes with Clinical Applications. 2nd ed. LC 77-27911. 605p. 1978. pap. 14.00 o.p. (ISBN 0-471-03678-1, Pub. by Wiley Medical). Wiley.

Kee, Joyce L. Fluids & Electrolytes with Clinical Applications: A Programmed Approach. 3rd ed. LC 82-1883. 526p. 1982. 16.95 (ISBN 0-471-08989-3, Pub. by Wiley Med). Wiley.

Keeble, N. H. Richard Baxter: Puritan Man of Letters. 1982. 34.50x (ISBN 0-19-811716-7). Oxford U Pr.

Keebler, Catherine M. & Reagan, James W. A Manual of Cytotechnology. (Illus.). 1983. text ed. 50.00 (ISBN 0-89189-168-4, 16-3-005-00). Am Soc Clinical.

Keebler, Catherine M. & Reagan, James W., eds. A Manual of Cytotechnology. 5th rev ed. LC 77-9249. (Illus.). 325p. 1977. binder 50.00 o.p. (ISBN 0-89189-034-3, 45-3-001-00). Am Soc Clinical.

Keech, L. Is There a Difference Between a Khazar Jew & a Palestinian Jew? 1982. lib. bdg. 59.95 (ISBN 0-87700-335-1). Revisionist Pr.

Keech, William R. & Matthews, Donald R. The Party's Choice with an Epilogue on the 1976 Nominations. (Studies in Presidential Selection). 1977. 18.95 (ISBN 0-8157-4852-3); pap. 7.95 (ISBN 0-8157-4851-5). Brookings.

Keedy, M. & Smith, S. Applying Mathematics. (gr. 10-12). 1983. 16.20 (ISBN 0-201-05072-2, Sch Div); 18.50 (ISBN 0-201-05073-0) (ISBN 0-201-05075-7). Skills Bk. write for info. (ISBN 0-201-05074-9). A-W.

Keedy, M. L. Algebra: An Intermediate Course. 512p. 1983. text ed. 18.95 (ISBN 0-201-14799-8). A-W.

--Algebra: An Introductory Course. (Illus.). 512p. 1983. text ed. 18.95 (ISBN 0-201-14798-X). A-W.

Keedy, M. L. & Bittinger, M. L. Algebra & Trigonometry: A Functions Approach. 3rd ed. 1982. pap. 21.95 (ISBN 0-201-13404-7); Stu-Sol 3.95 (ISBN 0-201-13405-5); test 4.00 (ISBN 0-201-13406-3); Aws 2.00 (ISBN 0-201-13407-1). A-W.

--College Algebra: A Functions Approach. 3rd ed. 1982. pap. 19.95 (ISBN 0-201-13400-4); Stu Sol. (ISBN 0-201-13401-2); test booklet 3.50 (ISBN 0-201-13402-0); 2.00 (ISBN 0-201-13403-9). A-W.

Keedy, Mervin L. Arithmetic. 4th ed. (Illus.). 560p. 1983. pap. text ed. 18.95 (ISBN 0-201-14780-7). A-W.

--Introductory Algebra. 4th ed. LC 82-13771. (Illus.). 566p. pap. text ed. 18.95 (ISBN 0-686-82170-X). A-W.

Keedy, Mervin L. & Bittinger, Marcin L. Intermediate Algebra. 3rd ed. LC 78-67452. 1979. pap. text ed. 19.95 (ISBN 0-201-03880-3); student sol. manual 5.95 (ISBN 0-686-85481-0). A-W.

Keedy, Mervin L. & Bittinger, Marvin L. Arithmetic. 3rd ed. LC 78-18648. 1979. pap. text ed. 19.95 (ISBN 0-201-03791-2); avail. instructor's manual with tests (ISBN 0-201-03792-0); test book 9.95 (ISBN 0-201-03795-5); student's guide to margin exercises 4.95 (ISBN 0-201-03794-7). A-W.

--Essential Mathematics. 3rd ed. 1980. pap. text ed. 20.95 (ISBN 0-201-03837-4). A-W.

--Fundamental Algebra & Trigonometry. 2nd ed. (Mathematics-Remedial & Precalculus Ser.). (Illus.). 576p. 1981. text ed. 21.95 (ISBN 0-201-03839-0); test bk 4.00 (ISBN 0-201-03844-7); answer bk 2.00 (ISBN 0-201-03843-9); student suppl. A-W.

--Fundamental College Algebra. 2nd ed. (Mathematics-Remedial & Precalculus Ser.). 480p. 1981. text ed. 19.95 (ISBN 0-201-03847-1); student sol. manual 4.95 (ISBN 0-201-03848-X); answer bk 2.00 (ISBN 0-201-03849-8); test bk 4.00 (ISBN 0-201-03855-2). A-W.

--Introductory Algebra. 3rd ed. LC 78-55821. (Illus.). 1979. pap. text ed. 19.95 (ISBN 0-201-03874-9); instr's man. 3.50 (ISBN 0-201-03875-7); answer book 3.50 (ISBN 0-201-03876-5); student sol. manual 5.95 (ISBN 0-201-03877-3). A-W.

Keedy, Mervin L., et al. Algebra One. (gr. 9). 1978. text ed. 18.36 (ISBN 0-201-03831-5, Sch Div); tchr's ed. 22.56 (ISBN 0-201-03832-3); solutions manual 14.44 (ISBN 0-201-03834-X); test bklet. 14.44 (ISBN 0-201-03833-1). A-W.

--Algebra Two. (gr. 11-12). 1978. text ed. 18.36 (ISBN 0-201-03841-2, Sch Div); tchr's ed. 22.56 (ISBN 0-201-03842-0). A-W.

--Algebra Two with Trigonometry. (gr. 12). 1978. text ed. 18.36 (ISBN 0-201-03851-X, Sch Div); tchr's ed. 22.56 (ISBN 0-201-03852-8); solutions manual 14.44 (ISBN 0-201-03854-4); test bklet. 14.44 (ISBN 0-201-03853-6). A-W.

Keefe, Carolyn B., et al. Introduction to Debate. 1982. text ed. 22.95x (ISBN 0-02-362430-2). Macmillan.

Keefe, J. F., jt. auth. see Boudewyns, P.

Keefe, John & Leute, George. Exploring Careers in the Sunbelt. (Careers in Depth Ser.). 140p. 1983. lib. bdg. 7.97 (ISBN 0-8239-0602-7). Rosen Pr.

Keefe, John W., ed. The Antiquarian Society: The First Hundred Years. LC 76-51596. (Illus., Orig.). 1977. pap. 15.00 (ISBN 0-86559-024-9). Art Inst Chi.

Keefe, John W. & Wise, Susan, eds. Selected Works of Eighteenth Century French Art in the Collections of the Art Institute of Chicago. LC 76-410. (Illus.). 219p. (Orig.). 1976. pap. 12.50x (ISBN 0-86559-019-2). Art Inst Chi.

Keefe, Marie, jt. auth. see Izzo, Barbara.

Keefe, Thomas & Maypole, Donald E. Relationships in Social Service Practice: Context & Skills. LC 82-20693. (Psychology Ser.). 320p. 1983. text ed. 18.95 (ISBN 0-534-01322-8). Brooks-Cole.

Keefe, William J. Congress & the American People. (Illus.). 1980. pap. text ed. 11.95 (ISBN 0-13-167569-9). P-H.

Keefe-Burg, Kathleen. The Womanly Art of Self Defense. LC 78-71037. (Illus.). 192p. 1979. 9.95 o.s.i. (ISBN 0-89104-131-1, A & W Visual Library); pap. 5.95 o.s.i. (ISBN 0-89104-120-6). A & W Pubs.

Keefer, George, jt. auth. see Cromwell, Paul F., Jr.

Keefer, Raymond M., jt. auth. see Allen, Thomas L.

Keefer, Truman F. Philip Wylie. (United States Authors Ser.). 1977. lib. bdg. 13.95 (ISBN 0-8057-7187-5, Twayne). G K Hall.

Keegan, B. F. & Ceidigh, P. O., eds. Biology of Benthic Organisms: 11th European Symposium on Marine Biology, Galway, Ireland. 1977. text ed. write for info. (ISBN 0-08-021378-2). Pergamon.

Keegan, John. Blitzkrieg. LC 78-64559. (Illus.). cancelled (ISBN 0-89169-542-7). Reed Bks.

--The Face of Battle. LC 76-10611. (Illus.). 1976. 13.95 o.p. (ISBN 0-670-30432-8). Viking Pr.

--The Face of Battle. 1983. pap. 5.95 (ISBN 0-14-004897-9). Penguin.

--The Face of Battle: A Study of Agincourt, Waterloo & The Somme. 1977. pap. 5.95 o.p. (ISBN 0-394-72403-8, Vin). Random.

--Six Armies in Normandy: From D-Day to the Liberation of Paris. 1983. pap. 6.95 (ISBN 0-14-005293-3). Penguin.

Keegan, Marcia. The Taos Indians & Their Sacred Blue Lake. LC 72-1426. (Illus.). 64p. (gr. 3-6). 1972. PLB 5.29 o.p. (ISBN 0-671-32536-1). Messner.

Keehn, J. D., ed. The Ethics of Psychological Research. 84p. 1982. 22.50 (ISBN 0-08-028116-8, J125). Pergamon.

Keehner, et al. Pupil Transportation Management Bibliography. (Research Bulletin: No. 12). pap. 1.00 with film guide supplement o.p. (ISBN 0-685-57178-5). Assn Sch Busn.

Keele, Cyril A., ed. see Wright, Samson.

Keele, Doman K. The Developmentally Disabled Child: A Manual for Primary Physicians. (Illus.). 250p. 1983. text ed. 19.95 (ISBN 0-87489-271-6). Med Economics.

Keele, Kenneth D. Leonardo da Vinci's Elements of the Science of Man: monograph. Date not set. price not set (ISBN 0-12-403980-4). Acad Pr.

Keeler, Greg. Spring Catch. 1982. pap. 4.50 (ISBN 0-917652-30-4). Confluence Pr.

Keeler, Mary F. Bibliography of British History: Stuart Period, Sixteen Hundred to Seventeen-Fourteen. 2nd ed. (Bibliography of British History Ser). 1970. 89.00x (ISBN 0-19-821371-9). Oxford U Pr.

Keeler, Mary F. & Cole, Maija J., eds. Proceedings in Parliament Sixteen Twenty-Eight. LC 75-43321. (Proceedings in Parliament 1628 Ser.). 700p. 1983. Vol. V: Lords Proceedings Sixteen Twenty-Eight. text ed. 85.00x (ISBN 0-300-02051-1); Vol. VI: Appendixes & Indexes. text ed. 55.00x (ISBN 0-300-02467-3). Yale U Pr.

Keeler, Theodore E. Railroads, Freight, & Public Policy. LC 82-45985. (Regulation of Economic Activity Ser.). 250p. 1983. 24.95 (ISBN 0-8157-4856-6); pap. 9.95 (ISBN 0-8157-4855-8). Brookings.

Keeley, E. Higgins. Isaiah: The Book of Earth's Future. 1978. 7.95 o.p. (ISBN 0-533-03361-6). Vantage.

Keeley, Edmund, tr. see Ritsos, Yannis.

Keeley, James, jt. auth. see Boardman, Robert.

Keeley, Steve, jt. auth. see Wright, Shannon.

Keeling, Jill A. The Old English Sheepdog. LC 76-9848. (Illus.). 1976. bds. 2.25 o.p. (ISBN 0-668-03973-6). Arco.

--The Old English Sheepdog. Foyle, Christina, ed. (Foyle's Handbks). 1973. 3.95 (ISBN 0-685-55799-5). Palmetto Pub.

Keely, Robin. Eerdmans' Handbook of Christian Belief. (Illus.). 480p. 1982. 24.95 (ISBN 0-8028-3577-5). Eerdmans.

Keely, Stuart M., jt. auth. see Browne, M. Neil.

Keen, Benjamin. David Curtis De Forest & the Revolution of Buenos Aires. Repr. of 1947 ed. lib. bdg. 15.00x o.p. (ISBN 0-8371-3970-8, KEDF). Greenwood.

--David Curtis Deforest & the Revolution of Buenos Aires. 1947. 14.50x (ISBN 0-686-51369-X). Elliots Bks.

Keen, Benjamin & Wasserman, Mark. A Short History of Latin America. 1980. pap. text ed. 17.95 (ISBN 0-395-27838-4). HM.

Keen, Benjamin, ed. Latin American Civilization, 2 vols. 3rd ed. (The Colonial Origins Ser.). 1974. Vol. 1. pap. text ed. 13.95 (ISBN 0-395-17582-8); Vol. 2. pap. text ed. 14.95 (ISBN 0-395-17583-6). HM.

Keen, Benjamin, tr. see Bennassar, Bartolome.

Keen, C. E. Crustal Properties Across Passive Margins. (Developments in Grotectonics Ser.: Vol. 15). 1980. 85.00 (ISBN 0-444-41852-0). Elsevier.

Keen, Clifford P., et al. Championship Wrestling. rev ed. LC 72-91940. (Sports Library). (Illus.). 230p. 1973. pap. 5.95 (ISBN 0-668-02721-5). Arco.

Keen, D. Related Subjects for Motor Vehicle Mechanics. Incl. Vols. 1 to 3 (Omnibus) 1972. pap. text ed. 6.50x o.p. (ISBN 0-435-72105-4); Vol. 4. Calculations & Drawing. 1968. pap. text ed. 3.95x o.p. (ISBN 0-435-72103-8); Vol. 5. Science & Electricity. 1968. pap. text ed. 3.95x o.p. (ISBN 0-435-72104-6). pap. Heinemann Ed.

Keen, Ernest. A Primer in Phenomenological Psychology. LC 81-40901. (Illus.). 192p. 1982. pap. text ed. 9.25 (ISBN 0-8191-2262-9). U Pr of Amer.

Keen, Harry & Jarrett, John. Complications of Diabetes. 344p. 1982. text ed. 64.50 (ISBN 0-7131-4409-2). E Arnold.

Keen, Jeffrey S. Managing Systems Development. LC 80-49976. (Information Processing). 343p. 1981. 33.95x (ISBN 0-471-27839-4, Pub. by Wiley-Interscience). Wiley.

Keen, John & Smith, Vernon, eds. Visual Handicap in Children. (Clinics in Developmental Medicine Ser.: Vol. 73). 182p. 1979. text ed. 29.00 (ISBN 0-433-30652-1, Pub. by Spastics Intl England). Lippincott.

Keen, M. H. England in the Later Middle Ages. 455p. 1972. 45.00x (ISBN 0-416-75990-4); pap. 16.95 (ISBN 0-416-83570-8). Methuen Inc.

Keen, Martin L. Be a Rockhound. LC 79-1769. (Illus.). 64p. (gr. 3 up). 1979. PLB 7.59 o.p. (ISBN 0-671-32820-4). Messner.

--Magnets & Magnetism. (How & Why Wonder Books Ser.). (gr. 4-6). deluxe ed. 1.95 o.p. (ISBN 0-448-04045-X, G&D). Putnam Pub Group.

--Microscope. (How & Why Wonder Books Ser.). (gr. 4-6). deluxe ed. 1.95 o.p. (ISBN 0-448-04016-6, G&D). Putnam Pub Group.

--Prehistoric Mammals. (How & Why Wonder Books Ser.). (Illus., Orig.). (gr. 4-6). deluxe ed. 1.95 o.p. (ISBN 0-448-04032-8, G&D). Putnam Pub Group.

--Science Experiments. (How & Why Wonder Books Ser.). (Illus., Orig.). (gr. 4-6). 1962. deluxe ed. 1.95 o.p. (ISBN 0-448-04033-6, G&D). Putnam Pub Group.

--The World Beneath Our Feet: The Story of Soil. LC 74-7148. (Illus.). 96p. (gr. 4-6). 1974. PLB 6.64 o.p. (ISBN 0-671-32674-0). Messner.

Keen, Maurice. The Outlaws of Medieval Legend. (Studies in Social History). 235p. 1977. 25.00 (ISBN 0-7100-8682-2). Routledge & Kegan.

Keen, Peter F. & Scott-Morton, Michael S. Decision Support Systems: An Organizational Perspective. 1978. text ed. 23.95 (ISBN 0-201-03667-3). A-W.

Keen, Sam. Apology for Wonder. LC 69-17017. 1969. pap. 6.95i (ISBN 0-06-064261-0, RD 58, HarpR). Har-Row.

Keenan, Charles W., et al. General College Chemistry. 6th ed. 1980. text ed. 31.95 scp (ISBN 0-06-043615-8, HarpC); instr's. manual avail. (ISBN 0-06-363613-1); scp study guide 11.50 (ISBN 0-06-043706-5); scp lab. manual 13.50 (ISBN 0-06-046298-1); instr's manual & storeroom guide for lab manual avail. (ISBN 0-06-366308-2). Har-Row.

Keenan, Denis. Contract of Employment. 128p. 1979. 25.00x (ISBN 0-906501-12-1, Pub. by Keenan England). State Mutual Bk.

--The Law of Contract: Multiple-Choice Tests. 2nd ed. 96p. 1980. 25.00x (ISBN 0-906501-00-8, Pub. by Keenan England). State Mutual Bk.

--Partnerships. 72p. 1980. 25.00x (ISBN 0-906501-14-8, Pub. by Keenan England). State Mutual Bk.

--Trusts. 96p. 1979. 25.00x (ISBN 0-906501-13-X, Pub. by Keenan England). State Mutual Bk.

Keenan, E. L., ed. Formal Semantics of Natural Language. LC 74-25657. 456p. 1975. 69.50 (ISBN 0-521-20697-9). Cambridge U Pr.

Keenan, Edward J., jt. auth. see Thomas, John A.

Keenan, Edward P. & Gantert, Ann X. Integrated Mathematics: Course III. (Orig.). 1982. text ed. 19.58 (ISBN 0-87720-253-2); pap. text ed. 12.50 (ISBN 0-87720-252-4). AMSCO Sch.

Keenan, Jeremy. The Tuareg: People of Ahaggar. LC 77-77139. (Illus.). 1978. 19.95x o.p. (ISBN 0-312-82200-6). St Martin.

Keenan, John. Feel Free to Write: A Guide for Business & Professional People. LC 81-16431. 190p. 1982. pap. 11.50 (ISBN 0-471-09696-2, Pub. by Wiley-Interscience). Wiley.

Keenan, Joseph H. Thermodynamics. 1970. pap. 5.95x o.p. (ISBN 0-262-61008-6). MIT Pr.

Keenan, Linda, ed. Educators Index of Free Materials. 91st rev. ed. LC 44-32700. 1982. 39.75 (ISBN 0-87708-120-4). Ed Prog.

Keenan, Martha. The Mannerly Adventures of Little Mouse. LC 76-41397. (Illus.). (gr. k-2). 1977. reinforced lib. bdg. 6.95 o.p. (ISBN 0-517-52845-2). Crown.

Keenan, Michael & White, Lawrence J., eds. Mergers & Acquisitions: Current Problems in Perspective. LC 81-47691. 368p. 1982. 33.95x (ISBN 0-669-04719-8). Lexington Bks.

Keenan, Stella, ed. Key Papers on the Use of Computer-Based Bibliographic Services. LC 73-88744. (Key Papers Ser). 1973. 10.00 (ISBN 0-87715-105-9). Am Soc Info Sci.

Keene, Arthur S., jt. ed. see Moore, James A.

Keene, Carolyn. Bungalow Mystery. (Nancy Drew Ser.: Vol. 3). (gr. 4-7). 1930. 2.95 (ISBN 0-448-09503-3, D&G). Putnam Pub Group.

--Clue in the Ancient Disguise, No. 69. (Nancy Drew Ser.). (Illus.). 192p. (gr. 8-12). 1982. 8.95 (ISBN 0-671-45553-2); pap. 2.95 (ISBN 0-671-45552-4). Wanderer Bks.

--The Clue in the Crossword Cipher. (Nancy Drew Ser.: Vol. 44). (gr. 4-7). 1967. 2.95 (ISBN 0-448-09544-0, G&D). Putnam Pub Group.

--The Clue in the Crumbling Wall. (Nancy Drew Ser.: Vol. 22). (Illus.). 192p. (gr. 4-7). 1945. 2.95 (ISBN 0-448-09522-X, G&D). Putnam Pub Group.

--Clue in the Diary. (Nancy Drew Ser.: Vol. 7). (gr. 4-7). 1932. 2.95 (ISBN 0-448-09507-6, G&D). Putnam Pub Group.

--The Clue in the Jewel Box. (Nancy Drew Ser.: Vol. 20). (Illus.). 196p. (gr. 4-7). 1943. 2.95 (ISBN 0-448-09520-3, G&D). Putnam Pub Group.

--Clue in the Old Album. (Nancy Drew Ser.: Vol. 24). (gr. 4-7). 1947. 2.95 (ISBN 0-448-09524-6, G&D). Putnam Pub Group.

--Clue in the Old Stagecoach. (Nancy Drew Ser.: Vol. 37). (gr. 4-7). 1960. 2.95 (ISBN 0-448-09537-8, G&D). Putnam Pub Group.

--Clue of the Black Keys. rev. ed. LC 68-21715. (Nancy Drew Ser.: Vol. 28). (Illus.). (gr. 4-7). 1951. 2.95 (ISBN 0-448-09528-9, G&D). Putnam Pub Group.

--Clue of the Broken Locket. (Nancy Drew Ser.: Vol. 11). (gr. 4-7). 1943. 2.95 (ISBN 0-448-09511-4, G&D). Putnam Pub Group.

--Clue of the Dancing Puppet. (Nancy Drew Ser.: Vol. 39). (Illus.). (gr. 4-7). 1962. 2.95 (ISBN 0-448-09539-4, G&D). Putnam Pub Group.

--Clue of the Leaning Chimney. (Nancy Drew Ser: Vol. 26). (gr. 4-7). 1949. 2.95 (ISBN 0-448-09526-2, G&D). Putnam Pub Group.

--Clue of the Tapping Heels. LC 71-86679. (Nancy Drew Ser.: Vol. 16). (Illus.). (gr. 4-7). 1939. 2.95 (ISBN 0-448-09516-5, G&D). Putnam Pub Group.

--Clue of the Velvet Mask. (Nancy Drew Ser.: Vol. 30). (Illus.). (gr. 4-7). 1953. 2.95 (ISBN 0-448-09530-0, G&D). Putnam Pub Group.

--Clue of the Whistling Bagpipes. (Nancy Drew Ser.: Vol. 41). (gr. 4-7). 1964. 2.95 (ISBN 0-448-09541-6, G&D). Putnam Pub Group.

--The Crooked Banister. LC 77-130336. (Nancy Drew Ser.: Vol. 48). (Illus.). (gr. 4-7). 1971. 2.95 (ISBN 0-448-09548-3, G&D). Putnam Pub Group.

--The Curious Coronation. LC 75-1581. (Dana Girls Ser.: Vol. 14). (Illus.). 196p. (gr. 4-7). 1976. 2.95 (ISBN 0-448-09094-5, G&D). Putnam Pub Group.

--The Double Jinx Mystery. LC 72-90826. (Nancy Drew Ser.: Vol. 50). (Illus.). 196p. (gr. 4-7). 1973. 2.95 (ISBN 0-448-09550-5, G&D). Putnam Pub Group.

--Ghost of Blackwood Hall. (Nancy Drew Ser: Vol. 25). (gr. 4-7). 1948. 2.95 (ISBN 0-448-09525-4, G&D). Putnam Pub Group.

--Ghosts in the Gallery. LC 74-10467. (Dana Girls Ser.: Vol. 13). (Illus.). 196p. (gr. 4-7). 1975. 2.95 (ISBN 0-448-09093-7, G&D). Putnam Pub Group.

--The Haunted Bridge. (Nancy Drew Ser.: Vol. 15). (Illus.). 196p. (gr. 4-7). 1938. 2.95 (ISBN 0-448-09515-7, G&D). Putnam Pub Group.

--The Haunted Lagoon. rev ed. LC 72-90828. (Dana Girls Ser.: Vol. 8). (Illus.). 196p. (gr. 4-7). 1973. 2.95 (ISBN 0-448-09088-0, G&D). Putnam Pub Group.

--The Haunted Showboat. (Nancy Drew Ser.: Vol. 35). (gr. 4-7). 1958. 2.95 (ISBN 0-448-09535-1, G&D). Putnam Pub Group.

--Hidden Staircase. (Nancy Drew Ser.: Vol. 2). (gr. 4-7). 1930. 2.95 (ISBN 0-448-09502-5, G&D). Putnam Pub Group.

--The Hidden Window Mystery. rev. ed. LC 75-1582. (Nancy Drew Ser.: Vol. 34). (Illus.). 196p. (gr. 4-7). 1975. 2.95 (ISBN 0-448-09534-3, G&D). Putnam Pub Group.

--The Invisible Intruder. (Nancy Drew Ser.: Vol. 46). (Illus.). (gr. 4-7). 1969. 2.95 (ISBN 0-448-09546-7, G&D). Putnam Pub Group.

--The Message in the Hollow Oak. LC 78-181844. (Nancy Drew Ser.: Vol. 12). (Illus.). 196p. (gr. 4-7). 1935. 2.95 (ISBN 0-448-09512-2, 9512, G&D). Putnam Pub Group.

--Moonstone Castle Mystery. (Nancy Drew Ser.: Vol. 40). (gr. 4-7). 1963. 2.95 (ISBN 0-448-09540-8, G&D). Putnam Pub Group.

--The Mountain-Peak Mystery. LC 77-76133. (Dana Girl Ser.: Vol. 16). (Illus.). (gr. 4-7). 1978. 2.95 (ISBN 0-448-09096-1, G&D). Putnam Pub Group.

--Mysterious Mannequin. LC 77-100115. (Nancy Drew Ser.: Vol. 47). (Illus.). (gr. 4-7). 1970. 2.95 (ISBN 0-448-09547-5, G&D). Putnam Pub Group.

--Mystery at Lilac Inn. (Nancy Drew Ser.: Vol. 4). (gr. 4-7). 1930. 2.95 (ISBN 0-448-09504-1, G&D). Putnam Pub Group.

--Mystery at the Moss-Covered Mansion. (Nancy Drew Ser.: Vol. 18). (Illus.). (gr. 4-7). 1971. 2.95 (ISBN 0-448-09518-1, G&D). Putnam Pub Group.

--Mystery at the Ski Jump. rev. ed. (Nancy Drew Ser.: Vol. 29). (Illus.). (gr. 4-7). 1968. 2.95 (ISBN 0-448-09529-7, G&D). Putnam Pub Group.

--Mystery of Crocodile Island. LC 77-76128. (Nancy Drew Ser.: Vol. 55). (Illus.). (gr. 4-7). 1978. 2.95 (ISBN 0-448-09555-6, G&D); PLB 7.25 (ISBN 0-448-19555-0). Putnam Pub Group.

--Mystery of the Bamboo Bird. new ed. (Dana Girls Ser.: Vol. 9). (Illus.). 192p. (gr. 4-7). 1973. 2.95 (ISBN 0-448-09089-9, G&D). Putnam Pub Group.

--Mystery of the Brass Bound Trunk. (Nancy Drew Mystery Stories). 2.95 (ISBN 0-448-09517-3, D&G). Putnam Pub Group.

--Mystery of the Fire Dragon. (Nancy Drew Ser.: Vol. 38). (gr. 4-7). 1961. 2.95 (ISBN 0-448-09538-6, G&D). Putnam Pub Group.

--The Mystery of the Glowing Eye. (Nancy Drew Ser.: Vol. 51). (Illus.). 192p. (gr. 4-7). 1974. 2.95 (ISBN 0-448-09551-3, G&D). Putnam Pub Group.

--Mystery of the Ivory Charm. LC 74-3868. (Nancy Drew Ser.: Vol. 13). (Illus.). 196p. (gr. 4-7). 1974. Repr. of 1936 ed. 2.95 (ISBN 0-448-09513-0, G&D). Putnam Pub Group.

--Mystery of the Lost Dogs. LC 77-75664. (Nancy Drew Picture Book Ser.). (Illus.). 1977. 2.95 (ISBN 0-448-14900-1, G&D); PLB 3.99 (ISBN 0-448-13900-6). Putnam Pub Group.

--Mystery of the Ninety-Nine Steps. (Nancy Drew Ser.: Vol. 43). (gr. 4-7). 1965. 2.95 (ISBN 0-448-09543-2, G&D). Putnam Pub Group.

--Mystery of the Stone Tiger. (Dana Girls Ser.: Vol. 1). (Illus.). 192p. (gr. 4-7). 1972. 2.95 (ISBN 0-448-09081-3, G&D). Putnam Pub Group.

--Mystery of the Tolling Bell. (Nancy Drew Ser.: Vol. 23). (Illus.). 192p. (gr. 4-7). 1973. Repr. 2.95 (ISBN 0-448-09523-8, G&D). Putnam Pub Group.

--Mystery of the Wax Queen. (Dana Girls Ser.: Vol. 4). (Illus.). 192p. (gr. 4-7). 1972. 2.95 (ISBN 0-448-09084-8, G&D). Putnam Pub Group.

--The Nancy Drew Cookbook. (Nancy Drew Ser.). 160p. (gr. 4-7). 1973. 3.95 (ISBN 0-448-02856-5, G&D). Putnam Pub Group.

--Nancy Drew: Flying Saucer Mystery. (Nancy Drew Mystery Stories Ser.: No. 58). (Illus.). (gr. 3-7). 1980. 8.95 (ISBN 0-671-95514-4); pap. 2.95 (ISBN 0-671-95601-9). Wanderer Bks.

--Nancy Drew: Mystery of the Winged Lion. (Nancy Drew Mystery Stories Ser.: No. 65). (Illus.). 192p. (gr. 3-7). 1982. 8.95 (ISBN 0-671-42370-3); pap. 2.95 (ISBN 0-671-42371-1). Wanderer Bks.

--Nancy Drew: Race Against Time. (Nancy Drew Mystery Stories Ser.: No. 66). (Illus.). 208p. (gr. 3-7). 1982. 8.95 (ISBN 0-671-42372-X); pap. 2.95 (ISBN 0-671-42373-8). Wanderer Bks.

--Nancy Drew Sleuth Book Clues to Good Sleuthing. LC 78-58209. (Illus.). (gr. 3-7). 1979. 4.95 (ISBN 0-448-15459-5, G&D); PLB 9.15 (ISBN 0-448-13600-7). Putnam Pub Group.

--Nancy Drew: The Captive Witness. (Nancy Drew Mysteries Stories Ser.: No. 64). (Illus.). 192p. (gr. 3-7). 1981. 8.95 (ISBN 0-671-42360-6); pap. 2.95 (ISBN 0-671-42361-4). Wanderer Bks.

--Nancy Drew: The Elusive Heiress. (Nancy Drew Mystery Stories Ser.: No. 68). (Illus.). 192p. (gr. 3-7). 1982. 8.95 (ISBN 0-671-44555-3); pap. 2.95 (ISBN 0-671-44553-7). Wanderer Bks.

--Nancy Drew: The Greek Symbol Mystery. (Nancy Drew Ser.: No. 60). (Illus.). 192p. (gr. 3-7). 1981. lib. bdg. 8.95 (ISBN 0-671-42297-9); pap. 2.95 (ISBN 0-671-42298-7). Wanderer Bks.

--Nancy Drew: The Kachina Doll Mystery. (Nancy Drew Mystery Stories Ser.: No. 62). (Illus.). 192p. (gr. 3-7). 1981. 8.95 (ISBN 0-671-42346-0); pap. 2.95 (ISBN 0-671-42347-9). Wanderer Bks.

--Nancy Drew: The Secret in the Old Lace. (Nancy Drew Mystery Stories: No. 59). (Illus.). 192p. (gr. 3-7). 1980. PLB 8.95 (ISBN 0-671-41119-5); pap. 2.95 (ISBN 0-671-41114-4). Wanderer Bks.

--Nancy Drew: The Sinister Omen. (Nancy Drew Mystery Stories Ser.: No. 67). (Illus.). 192p. (gr. 3-7). 1982. 8.95 (ISBN 0-671-44554-5); pap. 2.95 (ISBN 0-671-44552-9). Wanderer Bks.

--Nancy Drew: The Twin Dilemma. (Nancy Drew Mystery Stories Ser.: No. 63). (Illus.). 192p. (gr. 3-7). 1981. 8.95 (ISBN 0-671-42358-4); pap. 2.95 (ISBN 0-671-42359-2). Wanderer Bks.

--Nancy's Mysterious Letter. (Nancy Drew Ser.: Vol. 8). (gr. 4-7). 1963. 2.95 (ISBN 0-448-09508-4, G&D). Putnam Pub Group.

--The One Hundred Year Mystery. (Dana Girls Ser.: Vol. 15). (gr. 4-7). 2.95 (ISBN 0-448-09095-3, G&D). Putnam Pub Group.

--Password to Larkspur Lane. (Nancy Drew Ser.: Vol. 10). (gr. 4-7). 1960. 2.95 (ISBN 0-448-09510-6, G&D). Putnam Pub Group.

--Phantom of Pine Hill. (Nancy Drew Ser.: Vol. 42). (gr. 4-7). 1965. 2.95 (ISBN 0-448-09542-4, G&D). Putnam Pub Group.

--The Phantom Surfer. (Dana Girls Ser.: Vol. 6). (Illus.). 192p. (gr. 4-7). 1972. 2.95 (ISBN 0-448-09086-4, G&D). Putnam Pub Group.

--Quest of the Missing Map. LC 70-86692. (Nancy Drew Ser.: Vol. 19). (Illus.). (gr. 4-7). 1942. 2.95 (ISBN 0-448-09519-X, G&D). Putnam Pub Group.

--The Riddle of the Frozen Fountain. (Dana Girls Ser.: Vol. 2). (Illus.). 192p. (gr. 4-7). 1972. 2.95 (ISBN 0-448-09082-1, G&D). Putnam Pub Group.

--The Ringmaster's Secret. rev. ed. LC 74-3867. (Nancy Drew Ser.: Vol. 31). (Illus.). 196p. (gr. 4-7). 1974. Repr. of 1954 ed. 2.95 (ISBN 0-448-09531-9, G&D). Putnam Pub Group.

--The Scarlet Slipper Mystery. rev. ed. LC 74-3869. (Nancy Drew Ser.: Vol. 32). (Illus.). 196p. (gr. 4-7). 1955. 2.95 (ISBN 0-448-09532-7, G&D). Putnam Pub Group.

--Secret at Shadow Ranch. (Nancy Drew Ser: Vol. 5). (gr. 4-7). 1931. 2.95 (ISBN 0-448-09505-X, G&D). Putnam Pub Group.

--The Secret in the Old Attic. rev. ed. LC 78-100118. (Nancy Drew Ser.: Vol. 21). (Illus.). (gr. 4-7). 1955. 2.95 (ISBN 0-448-09521-1, G&D). Putnam Pub Group.

--The Secret of Mirror Bay. (Nancy Drew Ser.: Vol. 49). (Illus.). 196p. (gr. 4-7). 1972. 2.95 (ISBN 0-448-09549-1, G&D). Putnam Pub Group.

--Secret of Red Gate Farm. (Nancy Drew Ser.: Vol. 6). (gr. 4-7). 1931. 2.95 (ISBN 0-448-09506-8, G&D). Putnam Pub Group.

--The Secret of the Forgotten City. new ed. LC 74-10461. (Nancy Drew Ser.: Vol. 52). (Illus.). 196p. (gr. 4-7). 1975. 2.95 (ISBN 0-448-09552-1, G&D). Putnam Pub Group.

--Secret of the Golden Pavilion. (Nancy Drew Ser.: Vol. 36). (Illus.). (gr. 4-7). 1959. 2.95 (ISBN 0-448-09536-X, G&D). Putnam Pub Group.

--The Secret of the Lost Lake. (Dana Girls Ser.: Vol. 11). (gr. 4-7). 2.95 (ISBN 0-448-09091-0, G&D). Putnam Pub Group.

--The Secret of the Minstrel's Guitar. (Dana Girls Ser.: Vol. 5). (Illus.). 192p. (gr. 4-7). 1972. 2.95 (ISBN 0-448-09085-6, G&D). Putnam Pub Group.

--Secret of the Old Clock. (Nancy Drew Ser.: Vol. 1). (gr. 4-7). 1930. 2.95 (ISBN 0-448-09501-7, G&D). Putnam Pub Group.

--The Secret of the Silver Dolphin. (Dana Girls Ser.: Vol. 3). (Illus.). 192p. (gr. 4-7). 1972. 2.95 (ISBN 0-448-09083-X, G&D). Putnam Pub Group.

--The Secret of the Swiss Chalet. rev ed. LC 72-90827. (Dana Girls Ser.: Vol. 7). (Illus.). 196p. (gr. 4-7). 1973. 2.95 (ISBN 0-448-09087-2, G&D). Putnam Pub Group.

--The Secret of the Twin Puppets. LC 77-76857. (Nancy Drew Picture Book Ser.). 1977. 2.95 (ISBN 0-448-14901-X, G&D); PLB 7.25 (ISBN 0-448-13901-4). Putnam Pub Group.

--Secret of the Wooden Lady. (Nancy Drew Ser.: Vol. 27). (gr. 4-7). 1950. 2.95 (ISBN 0-448-09527-0, G&D). Putnam Pub Group.

--The Sierra Gold Mystery. new ed. (Dana Girls Ser.: Vol. 10). (Illus.). 192p. (gr. 4-7). 1973. 2.95 (ISBN 0-448-09090-2, G&D). Putnam Pub Group.

--Sign of the Twisted Candles. rev. ed. (Nancy Drew Ser: Vol. 9). (Illus.). (gr. 4-7). 1959. 2.95 (ISBN 0-448-09509-2, G&D). Putnam Pub Group.

--Spider Sapphire Mystery. (Nancy Drew Ser.: Vol. 45). (Illus.). (gr. 4-7). 1968. 2.95 (ISBN 0-448-09545-9, G&D). Putnam Pub Group.

--Strange Message in the Parchment. (Nancy Drew Ser.: Vol. 54). (gr. 4-7). 1977. 2.95 (ISBN 0-448-09554-8, G&D). Putnam Pub Group.

--The Thirteenth Pearl. LC 78-57931. (Nancy Drew Ser.: Vol. 56). (Illus.). (gr. 3-7). 1979. 2.95 (ISBN 0-448-09556-4, G&D); lib. bdg. 7.25 (ISBN 0-448-19556-9). Putnam Pub Group.

--Triple Hoax. (Nancy Drew Ser.: No. 57). (Illus.). 192p. (gr. 3-7). 1979. 8.95 (ISBN 0-671-95490-3); pap. 2.95 (ISBN 0-671-95512-8). Wanderer Bks.

--Whispering Statue. LC 72-106316. (Nancy Drew Ser.: Vol. 14). (Illus.). (gr. 4-7). 1937. 2.95 (ISBN 0-448-09514-9, G&D). Putnam Pub Group.

--The Winking Ruby Mystery. (Dana Girls Ser.: Vol. 12). (Illus.). 192p. (gr. 4-7). 1974. 2.95 (ISBN 0-448-09092-9, G&D). Putnam Pub Group.

--The Witch Tree Symbol. rev. ed. LC 75-1580. (Nancy Drew Ser.: Vol. 33). (Illus.). 196p. (gr. 4-7). 1975. 2.95 (ISBN 0-448-09533-5, G&D). Putnam Pub Group.

--The Witch's Omen. LC 78-57929. (The Dana Girls Ser.: No. 17). (Illus.). (gr. 2-6). Date not set. 2.95 (ISBN 0-448-09097-X, G&D). Putnam Pub Group.

Keene, Carolyn & Dixon, Franklin W. The Nancy Drew & the Hardy Boys Super Sleuths: Seven New Mysteries. (Illus.). 192p. (Orig.). (gr. 3-7). 1981. 8.95 o.p. (ISBN 0-671-44429-8); pap. 2.95 o.p. (ISBN 0-671-43375-X). Wanderer Bks.

Keene, D. J. Winchester Studies, Vol. 2: Survey of Medieval Winchester. (Illus.). 750p. 1982. 169.00 (ISBN 0-19-813181-X). Oxford U Pr.

Keene, Dathy, jt. auth. see Keene, Donna.

Keene, Donald, ed. Modern Japanese Literature: An Anthology. 1956. pap. 12.50 (ISBN 0-394-17254-X, E573, Ever). Grove.

Keene, Donald, tr. see Abe, Kobo.

Keene, Donald, tr. see Mishima, Yukio.

Keene, Donna & Keene, Dathy. Wellspring. Bachelis, Faren, ed. (Illus.). 64p. 1982. 8.00 (ISBN 0-931724-19-8). Dandy Lion.

Keene, Frances, tr. see Vittorini, Elio.

Keene, G. B. First-Order Functional Calculus. (Monographs in Modern Logic). 1967. pap. 3.75 o.p. (ISBN 0-7100-3805-4). Routledge & Kegan.

Keene, R. D. How to Play the King's Indian, Saemisch Variation. (Chess Player Ser.). 1977. pap. 5.95 o.p. (ISBN 0-900928-44-1, H-1169). Hippocrene Bks.

Keene, R. D. & Levy, D. N. Haifa Chess Olympiad 1976. (Chess Player Ser.). 1977. pap. 8.95 o.p. (ISBN 0-906042-02-X, H-1315). Hippocrene Bks.

Keene, Raymond. World Chess Championship: Korchnoi vs Karpov. 1978. 6.95 o.p. (ISBN 0-671-24647-X); pap. 2.95 o.p. (ISBN 0-671-24648-8). S&S.

Keene, Sherman. Practical Techniques for the Recording Engineer. 2nd ed. LC 81-148444. (Illus.). 1981. text ed. 29.75 (ISBN 0-942080-00-9); tchr's. manual 45.00 (ISBN 0-942080-03-3); students wkbk 9.85 (ISBN 0-942080-04-1). Sherman Keene.

Keene, Tom & Haynes, Brian. Spyship. LC 79-20241. 1980. 11.95 (ISBN 0-399-90068-3, Marek). Putnam Pub Group.

Keene, William B. California Superior Court Criminal Trial Judges' Benchbook: 1982 Edition. 750p. 1982. pap. text ed. 33.00 (ISBN 0-314-68805-6). West Pub.

Keener, Frederick M. The Chain of Becoming: The Philosophical Tale, the Novel & a Neglected Realism of the Enlightenment: Swift, Montesquieu, Voltaire, Johnson & Austen. LC 82-12878. 376p. 1983. 30.00x (ISBN 0-231-04001-6); pap. 15.00 (ISBN 0-231-05573-0). Columbia U Pr.

Keener, Joseph. Music Series. (gr. 4-5). 1982. pap. 16.55 (ISBN 0-686-37780-X). Rod & Staff.

Keeney. Ocular Examination: Basis & Technique. 2nd ed. LC 76-7518. (Illus.). 322p. 1976. 28.50 o.p. (ISBN 0-8016-2634-X). Mosby.

Keeney, Bradford P., jt. ed. see Hansen, James C.

Keeney, Ralph L. & Raiffa, Howard. Decisions with Multiple Objectives: Preferences & Value Tradeoffs. LC 76-7895. (Probability & Mathematical Statistics Ser.). 569p. 1976. 34.95x (ISBN 0-471-46510-0, Pub by Wiley-Interscience). Wiley.

Keens, William. Dear Anyone. 1976. pap. 12.50x o.p. (ISBN 0-686-16130-0). Penumbra Press.

Keeny, Spurgeon M., Jr. Nuclear Power Issues & Choices. LC 77-693. 1977. pap. 12.00x prof ref (ISBN 0-88410-065-0). Ballinger Pub.

Keep, Pieter A. van see Van Keep, Pieter A. & Utian, Wulf H.

Keepers, Terry D., jt. auth. see Babcock, Dorothy E.

Keeping, Charles. Miss Emily & the Bird of Make-Believe. 32p. 1981. 15.95x (ISBN 0-686-97158-2, Pub. by Andersen-Hutchinson England). State Mutual Bk.

Keeran, James, ed. The McLean County Almanac Nineteen Eighty-Three. (Illus.). 300p. 1983. pap. 4.95 (ISBN 0-943782-02-3, Pantagraph Bks). Evergreen Comm.

Keers, Robert Y. Pulmonary Tuberculosis: A Journey Down the Centuries. 1979. text ed. 27.50 (ISBN 0-02-858250-0, Pub. by Bailliere-Tindall). Saunders.

Kees, Weldon, jt. auth. see Ruesch, Jurgen.

Keese, Parton. The Measure of Greatness. LC 80-17027. (Illus.). 162p. 1981. 9.95 o.p. (ISBN 0-13-567800-5). P-H.

Kesee, Allan P. Commercial Laws of the Middle East, 7 binders. 1980. Set. loose-leaf 665.00 (ISBN 0-379-20467-3). Oceana.

Keesee, Allen P. Commercial Laws of the Middle East, 8 vols. Incl. Algeria. LC 80-18047. 1981; Egypt, Arab Republic of Egypt. 1981 (ISBN 0-379-20467-3); Iran. Vafai, G. H. 1982 (ISBN 0-379-22904-8); Kuwait. 1980 (ISBN 0-379-22905-6); Oman. 1982 (ISBN 0-379-22906-4); United Arab Emirates. 1982; Saudi Arabia. 1981 (ISBN 0-379-22907-2); Sudan. 1981 (ISBN 0-379-22908-0). 1980. Set. 760.00 (ISBN 0-379-22900-5); 125.00 ea. Oceana.

Keesing, Donald B. Trade Policy for Developing Countries. (Working Paper: No. 353). vii, 264p. 1979. 5.00 (ISBN 0-686-36211-X, WP-0353). World Bank.

--World Trade & Output of Manufactures: Structural Trends & Developing Countries' Exports. (Working Paper: No. 316). v, 69p. 1979. 5.00 (ISBN 0-686-36214-4, WP-0316). World Bank.

Keesing, Donald B., jt. auth. see Chenery, Hollis.

Keesing, Felix M. Social Anthropology in Polynesia: A Review of Research. LC 80-17490. x, 126p. 1980. Repr. of 1953 ed. lib. bdg. 19.25x (ISBN 0-313-22498-6, KESO). Greenwood.

Keesing, Nancy, ed. Gold Fever: The Australian Goldfields 1851-1890's. (Illus.). 1968. 15.00 o.p. (ISBN 0-685-20588-6). Transatlantic.

Keesing, Roger M. Elota's Story: The Life & Times of a Solomon Islands Big Man. LC 77-20603. (Illus.). 1978. 18.95 (ISBN 0-312-24378-2). St Martin.

--Kwaio Religion: The Living & the Dead in a Solomon Island Community. 256p. 1982. 27.50x (ISBN 0-231-05340-1); pap. 13.50x (ISBN 0-231-05341-X). Columbia U Pr.

Keeslar, Oreon. Financial Aids for Higher Education Catalog, 1981-2. 10th ed. 1000p. 1982. pap. text ed. write for info. (ISBN 0-697-06129-9). Wm C Brown.

Keetman, Gunild. Elementaria, First Acquaintance with Orff-Schulwerk. LC 75-1152. (Illus.). 1974. 18.00 (ISBN 0-901938-04-1). Eur-Am Music.

Keeton, G. W. & Schwarzenberger, G. Yearbook of World Affairs 1977. LC 47-29156. 1977. lib. bdg. 42.00 o.p. (ISBN 0-89158-814-0). Westview.

Keeton, George W. & Scharzenberger, Georg, eds. The Yearbook of World Affairs, 1979. 1979. lib. bdg. 42.00 o.p. (ISBN 0-89158-551-6). Westview.

Keeton, George W. & Schwarzenberger, Georg, eds. The Year Book of World Affairs, 1980. LC 47-29156. 300p. 1980. 42.00 (ISBN 0-89158-876-0). Westview.

--The Year Book of World Affairs, 1981. 285p. 1981. lib. bdg. 42.00 (ISBN 0-86531-150-1). Westview.

--The Yearbook of World Affairs, 1978. LC 47-29156. 1978. lib. bdg. 42.00 o.p. (ISBN 0-89158-824-8). Westview.

Keeton, Morris T., jt. auth. see Titus, Harold H.

Keeton, Robert E. Basic Expressions for Trial Lawyers Nineteen Seventy Nine: Supplement to "Trial Tactics". 4.95 (ISBN 0-316-48581-0). Little.

--Trial Tactics & Methods. 2nd ed. 438p. 1973. 17.95 (ISBN 0-316-48572-1). Little.

Keeton, William T. Biological Science. 3rd ed. (Illus.). 1980. text ed. 25.95x (ISBN 0-393-95021-2); pap. 2.95x tchr's manual (ISBN 0-393-95031-X); study guide 7.95x (ISBN 0-393-95028-X). Norton.

Keeton, William T. & McFadden, Carol H. Elements of Biological Science. 3rd ed. 1983. pap. 24.95x (ISBN 0-393-95255-X); study guide avail. (ISBN 0-393-95259-2); tchr's. man. avail. (ISBN 0-393-95262-2). Norton.

Keeton, William T. & McFaddon, Carol H. Laboratory Guide for Biological Science. 2nd ed. 1983. pap. write for info (ISBN 0-393-95260-6). Norton.

Keeton, William T., et al. Laboratory Guide for Biological Science. (Orig.). 1968. pap. text ed. 10.95x (ISBN 0-393-09823-0, NortonC). Norton.

Keevers, William R. Gambling Times Guide to Jai Alai. (Illus., Orig.). 1983. pap. text ed. 5.95 (ISBN 0-89746-010-3). Gambling Times.

Keevil, Walter, jt. ed. see Carlson, Norman.

Keey, R. B. Drying: Principles & Practice. 1973. text ed. write for info. (ISBN 0-08-016903-1). Pergamon.

Kefgen, Mary & Touchie-Specht, Phyllis. Individuality in Clothing & Appearance. 3rd ed. 1981. text ed. 22.95x (ISBN 0-02-362150-8). Macmillan.

KeGan, Frank R. Intro to the Xray I, Links the Objective Patterns of Astrology & the Process Symbolism of the I Ching. (Illus.). 1982. pap. 5.00 (ISBN 0-933646-20-8). Aries Pr.

--Stars & Dice: Pythagorean Astrology. (Illus.). 1983. pap. 5.00t (ISBN 0-933646-22-4). Aries Pr.

Kegan, Stephanie. Places to Go with Children in Southern California. LC 81-18052. (Illus.). 160p. (Orig.). 1982. pap. 6.95 (ISBN 0-87701-194-X). Chronicle Bks.

Kegham-Keghag, tr. see Boyadjian, Knarig.

Kegley, Charles W. & Kegley, Jacquelyn A. Introduction to Logic. (Philosophy Ser.). 1978. text ed. 19.95 (ISBN 0-675-08358-3); media pkg. 75.00 (ISBN 0-675-08357-5). Additional supplements may be obtained from publisher. Merrill.

Kegley, Charles W., Jr. & Wittkopf, Eugene R. American Foreign Policy: Pattern & Process. LC 78-65249. 1979. text ed. 16.95 o.p. (ISBN 0-312-02326-X); pap. text ed. 10.95x o.p. (ISBN 0-312-02327-8). St Martin.

--World Politics: Trend & Transformation. 500p. 1981. text ed. 18.95 (ISBN 0-312-89246-2); pap. text ed. 12.95 (ISBN 0-312-89245-4); instructor's manual available (ISBN 0-312-89247-0). St Martin.

Kegley, Charles W., Jr. & McGowan, Pat, eds. Foreign Policy: U.S.A.-USSR. (Sage International Yearbook of Foreign Policy Studies: Vol. 7). (Illus.). 320p. 1982. 25.00 (ISBN 0-8039-1841-0); pap. 9.95 (ISBN 0-8039-1842-9). Sage.

Kegley, Jacquelyn A., jt. auth. see Kegley, Charles W.

Kegley, Jacquelyn A., ed. The Humanistic Delivery of Services to Families in a Changing & Technological Age. LC 81-43815. 270p. (Orig.). 1982. lib. bdg. 24.00 (ISBN 0-8191-2497-4); pap. text ed. 11.50 (ISBN 0-8191-2498-2). U Pr of Amer.

Kehde, Ned, ed. American Left Nineteen Fifty-Five to Nineteen-Seventy: A National Union Catalog of Pamphlets Published in the United States & Canada. LC 76-8002. 526p. (Orig.). 1976. lib. bdg. 45.00 (ISBN 0-8371-8282-4, KTA/). Greenwood.

Kehl, D. G. Control Yourself. Date not set. 11.95 o.p. (ISBN 0-310-45000-4). Zondervan.

Kehl, George L. Principles of Metallographic Laboratory Practice. 3rd ed. (Metallurgy & Metallurgical Engineering Ser.). (Illus.). 1949. text ed. 36.50 (ISBN 0-07-033479-X, C). McGraw.

Kehl, H. Chemistry & Biology of Hydroxamic Acids. xii, 192p. 1982. 142.50 (ISBN 3-8055-3453-1). S Karger.

Kehl, James A. Boss Rule in the Gilded Age: Matt Quay of Pennsylvania. LC 80-5254. (Illus.). 315p. 1981. 24.95 (ISBN 0-8229-3426-4). U of Pittsburgh Pr.

Kehle, Roberta. The Blooming of the Flame Tree. 144p. 1983. pap. 3.95 (ISBN 0-89107-275-6, Crossway Bks). Good News.

Kehoe, K. Theology of God: Sources. 1971. pap. 4.75 o.p. (ISBN 0-02-816670-1). Glencoe.

Kehoe, Michael. The Puzzle of Books. LC 81-17115. (Illus.). 32p. (gr. 1-5). 1982. PLB 7.95g (ISBN 0-87614-169-6). Carolrhoda Bks.

--Road Closed. LC 82-1312. (Illus.). 32p. (gr. 1-4). 1982. lib. bdg. 7.95g (ISBN 0-87614-192-0). Carolrhoda Bks.

--The Rock Quarry Book. LC 80-28165. (Illus.). 32p. (gr. k-3). 1981. PLB 7.95g (ISBN 0-87614-142-4, AACR1). Carolrhoda Bks.

Kehoe, Patrick E. Cooperatives & Condominiums. LC 74-8270. (Legal Almanac Ser.: No. 72). 124p. 1974. lib. bdg. 5.95 (ISBN 0-379-11091-1). Oceana.

Kehoe, Vincent J. The Technique of Film & Television Make-up: For Color & Black & White. rev. ed. 1969. 26.95 o.s.i. (ISBN 0-240-44942-8). Focal Pr.

--The Technique of Film & Television Make-up: For Color & Black & White. rev. ed. (Library of Communication Techniques). 29.50 o.p. (ISBN 0-8038-7087-6). Hastings.

Kehr, Eckart. Economic Interest, Militarism, & Foreign Policy: Essays on German History. Craig, Gordon A., ed. Heinz, Grete, tr. from Ger. LC 74-22964. 1977. 27.50x (ISBN 0-520-02880-5). U of Cal Pr.

Kehret, Peg. Vows of Love & Marriage. Zapel, Arthur L., ed. (Illus.). 106p. 1980. 9.95 (ISBN 0-916260-07-0). Meriwether Pub.

Keidel, Albert, 3rd. Korean Regional Farm Product & Income: 1910-1975. 251p. 1981. text ed. 13.00x (ISBN 0-8248-0758-8, Korea Devel Inst). UH Pr.

Keidel, Eudene. African Fables, Bk. 2. LC 77-15709. (Illus.). 112p. 1981. pap. 3.25 (ISBN 0-8361-1945-2). Herald Pr.

Keidel, Wolfgang D. The Physiological Basis of Hearing. (Illus.). 272p. 1983. 25.00 (ISBN 0-86577-072-7). Thieme-Stratton.

Keifer, Ralph. Blessed & Broken: An Exploration of the Contemporary Experience of God in Eucharistic Celebration. 1982. 9.95 (ISBN 0-89453-267-7); pap. 6.95 (ISBN 0-686-32778-0). M Glazier.

Keifetz, Norman. The Sensation. 1976. pap. 1.50 o.p. (ISBN 0-451-06828-9, W6828, Sig). NAL.

--Welcome Sundays. LC 78-23744. 1979. 10.95 o.p. (ISBN 0-399-12318-0). Putnam Pub Group.

Keiffer, E. Weather Information for Boaters, Cape Cod to Watch Hill. (Marine Bulletin Ser.: No. 47). 32p. 1981. 2.00 (ISBN 0-938412-27-2, P905). URI Mas.

Keiffer, Mildred & Smith, Harold. Pathways in Mathematics. Incl. Level One. rev. ed. (gr. 7). 1977. pap. text ed. 6.64 (ISBN 0-913688-31-2); tchr's guide 6.00 (ISBN 0-913688-33-9); Level Two. rev. ed. (gr. 8). 1977 (ISBN 0-913688-32-0). tchr's guide (ISBN 0-913688-34-7). pap. text ed. 7.26 ea.; guide 6.00 tchr's (ISBN 0-685-77480-5). Pawnee Pub.

Keiffer, Mildred, jt. auth. see Smith, Harold.

Keightley. The Fairy Mythology. LC 74-16410. 1975. Repr. of 1870 ed. 54.00x (ISBN 0-8103-3466-6). Gale.

Keightley, David, et al, eds. Early China, No. 5. 131p. 1980. pap. 7.00x (ISBN 0-912966-26-2). IEAS.

--Early China, No. Six. 146p. 1981. pap. 7.00x (ISBN 0-912966-37-8). IEAS.

Keightley, David N. The Origins of Chinese Civilization. LC 81-4595. (Illus.). 555p. 1983. 45.00x (ISBN 0-520-04229-8); pap. 15.00x (ISBN 0-520-04230-1, CAMPUS 296). U of Cal Pr.

--Sources of Shang History: The Oracle-Bone Inscriptions of Bronze Age China. LC 74-29806. 1979. 47.50x (ISBN 0-520-02969-0). U of Cal Pr.

Keightley, Thomas. The Fairy Mythology. 560p. 1982. 30.00x (Pub. by Wildwood House). State Mutual Bk.

--The Fairy Mythology. 560p. 1983. pap. 9.95 (ISBN 0-7045-0446-4, Pub. by Salem Hse Ltd). Merrimack Bk Serv.

Keigwin, R. P., ed. Hans Christian Andersen: Eighty Fairy Tales. Date not set. 14.95 (ISBN 0-686-37608-0). Pantheon.

Keigwin, R. P., tr. see Andersen, Hans Christian.

Keijbets, M. J. Pectic Substances in the Cell Wall & the Intercellular Cohesion of Potato Tuber Tissue During Cooking. (Agricultural Research Reports: No. 827). (Illus.). viii, 161p. 1975. pap. 22.00 (ISBN 90-220-0536-4, PDC64, Pub. by PUDOC). Unipub.

Keil, Charles. The TIV Song: The Sociology of Art in a Classless Society. LC 78-3178. (Illus.). xiv, 302p. 1983. pap. 9.95 (ISBN 0-226-42963-6). U of Chicago Pr.

Keil, E. C. Performance Appraisal & the Manager. LC 77-79343. 1977. text ed. 19.95 (ISBN 0-86730-520-7). Lebhar Friedman.

Keil, Hartmut & Jentz, John B., eds. German Workers in Industrial Chicago, 1850-1910: A Comparative Perspective. (Illus.). 300p. 1983. text ed. price not set (ISBN 0-87580-089-0). N Ill U Pr.

Keilin, David. History of Cell Respiration & Cytochrome. 1966. 65.00 (ISBN 0-521-05470-2). Cambridge U Pr.

Keilitz, Ingo & Horner, Don R. Taking Care Of Your Complexion. (Project MORE Daily Living Skills Ser.). 48p. 1979. Repr. of 1979 ed. pap. text ed. 7.95 (ISBN 0-8331-1239-2). Hubbard Sci.

Keillor, Garrison. Happy to Be Here: Stories & Comic Pieces. 1983. pap. 4.95 (ISBN 0-14-006482-6). Penguin.

Keilty, Ed. Doodlebug Country. Sebree, Mac, ed. (Special Ser.: No. 77). (Illus.). 184p. 1982. 28.95 (ISBN 0-916374-50-5). Interurban.

Keily, Danile. Programmed Basic Chemistry for Allied Health Students. LC 77-10774. (Illus.). 210p. 1978. pap. text ed. 12.95 o.p. (ISBN 0-8016-2637-4). Mosby.

Keim, Abe. Complete Guide: How to Raise, Train & Sell Puppies Successfully. Printing, Lelli, ed. 104p. (Orig.). Date not set. pap. price not set. A Keim.

Keim, Charles J., jt. auth. see Waugh, Hal.

Keim, Curtis A. & Brown, Howard. Missions in Africa: Relevant or Relic? A Conference. (African Humanities Ser.). 89p. (Orig.). 1980. pap. text ed. 5.00 (ISBN 0-941934-30-6). Ind U Afro-Amer Arts.

Keim, Hugo A. The Adolescent Spine. LC 75-32566. (Illus.). 240p. 1976. 39.50 o.p. (ISBN 0-8089-0923-1). Grune.

Keim, Marie J. Out of the Depths. 1978. 4.50 o.p. (ISBN 0-533-03348-9). Vantage.

Keintz, Rita M., ed. Health Care Costs & Financing: A Guide to Information Sources. LC 80-23862. (Health Affairs Information Guide Ser.: Vol. 6). 400p. 1981. 42.00x (ISBN 0-8103-1482-7). Gale.

Keir, Jack & Lundy, Carl P. Fundamentals of Estate Planning. rev. ed. Snyder, Bernhart R., rev. by. LC 79-92663. 1982. 7.95 (ISBN 0-87863-037-6). Farnswth Pub.

Keir, Jack C. & Lundy, Carl P. Fundamentals of Estate Planning. 4th, rev. ed. 1982. pap. 8.95 (ISBN 0-87863-037-6). Farnswth Pub.

Keir, Malcolm. March of Commerce. 1927. text ed. 22.50x. Elliots Bks.

Keiser, Beatrice. All Our Hearts Are Trump. LC 76-1455. 1976. 10.95 (ISBN 0-87716-066-X, Pub. by Moore Pub Co). F Apple.

Keiser, Gerd. Optical Fiber Communications. (Series in Electrical Engineering). (Illus.). 480p. 1983. text ed. 35.95 (ISBN 0-07-033467-6, C); solutions manual 18.00 (ISBN 0-07-033468-4). McGraw.

Keiser, Marjorie B. Housing: An Environment for Living. (Illus.). text ed. 23.95x (ISBN 0-02-362230-X). Macmillan.

Keiser, Ralph J. & Kallio, Elmer. Controlling & Analyzing Costs in Food Service Operations. LC 73-20156. 291p. 1974. text ed. 27.95x (ISBN 0-471-46710-3). Wiley.

Keisler, H. J., jt. ed. see Barwise, J.

Keisling, Bill. The Homeowner's Handbook of Solar Water Heating Systems: How to Build or Buy Systems to Heat Your Water, Your Swimming Pool, Hot Tub, or Spa. Halpin, Anne, ed. (Illus.). 256p. 1983. 16.95 (ISBN 0-87857-444-1, 14-166-0); pap. 12.95 (ISBN 0-87857-445-X, 14-166-1). Rodale Pr Inc.

Keiss, Helmut. Camera Sensitive Electrophotography. (Illus.). 100p. 1980. 27.95 (ISBN 0-240-51067-4). Focal Pr.

Keister, Elinore. Marya. LC 82-3489. 1982. pap. 5.95 (ISBN 0-8024-5199-3). Moody.

Keister, M. E. Child Care: A Handbook for Village Workers & Leaders. 58p. 1967. pap. 10.00 (ISBN 0-686-93152-1, F91, FAO). Unipub.

Keith & Gooders. Collins Bird Guide. pap. 19.95 (ISBN 0-686-42724-6, Collins Pub England). Greene.

Keith, A. B. The Veda of the Black Yajus School: Taittiriya Sanhita, 2 vols. 1967. Repr. Set. 22.00 (ISBN 0-89684-334-3). Orient Bk Dist.

Keith, A. Berriedale. Indian Mythology & Iranian Mythology. Bd. with Carnoy, Albert J. LC 63-19091. (Mythology of All Races Ser.: Vol. 6). (Illus.). Repr. of 1932 ed. 27.50x (ISBN 0-8154-0126-4). Cooper Sq.

Keith, Arthur B. Indian Logic & Atomism: An Exposition of the Nyaya & Vaicesika Systems. LC 68-54422. 1968. Repr. of 1921 ed. lib. bdg. 15.50x (ISBN 0-8371-0509-9, KEIL). Greenwood.

Keith, Arthur B., tr. from Sanskirt. Rigveda Brahmanas: The Aitareya & kausitaki of the Rigveda. LC 73-929544. 555p. 1981. Repr. of 1920 ed. 20.00x (ISBN 0-8002-3060-4). Intl Pubns Serv.

Keith, Brendan, jt. auth. see Cook, Chris.

Keith, C. & Wilbur, M. D. Revolutionary Medicine, Seventeen Hundred to Eighteen Hundred. LC 80-82790. (Illus.). 88p. (Orig.). 1980. pap. 8.95 (ISBN 0-87106-041-8). Globe Pequot.

Keith, David. Man & the Natural World. LC 82-14384. (Illus.). 432p. 1983. 19.95 (ISBN 0-394-49945-X). Pantheon.

Keith, Eros. In the Land of Enchantment: A Panorama of Fairy Tales. LC 75-654436. (Illus.). (ps-3). 1972. 8.95 (ISBN 0-02-749640-6). Bradbury Pr.

--RRRA-AH. LC 78-93086. (Illus.). 32p. (ps-1). 1969. 6.95 (ISBN 0-02-749650-3). Bradbury Pr.

--A Small Lot. LC 68-9054. (Illus.). 32p. (ps-1). 1968. 5.95 (ISBN 0-02-749660-0). Bradbury Pr.

Keith, Harold. Sports & Games. 6th ed. LC 76-17585. (Illus.). (gr. 4 up). 1976. 14.95i o.p. (ISBN 0-690-01254-3, TYC-J). Har-Row.

--Susy's Scoundrel. LC 74-1052. (Illus.). 160p. (gr. 5 up). 1974. 8.95i (ISBN 0-690-00496-6, TYC-J). Har-Row.

Keith, Henry & Hayes, Robert, eds. Perspectives on Armed Politics in Brazil. LC 76-988. 1976. 15.00x o.p. (ISBN 0-87918-030-7); pap. 7.95x o.p. (ISBN 0-87918-024-2). ASU Lat Am St.

Keith, Jennie. Old Peoples, New Lives: Community Creation in a Retirement Residence with a new Preface. LC 82-8642. xii, 228p. 1982. pap. 6.95 (ISBN 0-226-42965-2). U of Chicago Pr.

--Older People As People: Social & Cultural Influences on Aging & Old Age. (Orig.). 1982. text ed. 13.95 (ISBN 0-316-48631-0); pap. text ed. 7.95 (ISBN 0-316-48632-9). Little.

Keith, John D., jt. auth. see Kidd, B. S.

Keith, John D., et al. Heart Disease in Infancy & Childhood. 3rd ed. (Illus.). 1978. text ed. 75.00x (ISBN 0-02-362220-2). Macmillan.

Keith, Judith. I Haven't a Thing to Wear! 320p. 1981. pap. 7.95 (ISBN 0-380-62604-7, 55574). Avon.

Keith, L. & Brittain, J. Sexually Transmitted Diseases. rev. ed. LC 77-93222. 100p. 1981. 7.95 (ISBN 0-917634-01-2). Creative Infomatics.

Keith, L. A. & Gubellini, C. E. Introduction to Business Enterprise. 4th ed. 1975. text ed. 25.95 (ISBN 0-07-033485-4, C); instructor's manual 20.00 (ISBN 0-07-033487-0); study guide 9.95 (ISBN 0-07-033486-2). McGraw.

Keith, Lawrence H. Advances in the Identification & Analysis of Organic Pollutants in Water, 2 vols. LC 81-68031. 1214p. 1981. text ed. 39.95 ea. Vol. 1 (ISBN 0-250-40397-8). Vol. 2 (ISBN 0-250-40398-6). Set. text ed. 79.90 (ISBN 0-250-40472-9). Ann Arbor Science.

--Identification & Analysis of Organic Pollutants in Water. LC 76-1730. (Illus.). 1976. 45.00 (ISBN 0-250-40131-2). Ann Arbor Science.

Keith, Lawrence H., ed. Energy & Environmental Chemistry, 2 vols. LC 81-69255. (Illus.). 1982. Set. text ed. 75.00 (ISBN 0-250-40486-9); text ed. 37.50 ea. Vol. 1: Fossil Fuels, 425p (ISBN 0-250-40401-X). Vol. 2: Acid Rain, 350p (ISBN 0-250-40402-8). Ann Arbor Science.

Keith, Louis G., ed. see Theroux, Rosemary & Tingley, Josephine.

Keith, Lyman. Accounting: A Management Perspective. (Illus.). 1980. text ed. 23.95 (ISBN 0-13-001214-9). P-H.

Keith, Marilyn. Practical Medical Terminology. (Illus.). 350p. pap. text ed. write for info o.p. (ISBN 0-397-50538-8, Lippincott Medical). Lippincott.

Keith, Noel. Paul's Message for Today. 1970. 0.75 o.p. (ISBN 0-912646-31-4); pap. 4.50 (ISBN 0-912646-30-6). Tex Christian.

Keith, Pat M., jt. auth. see Smith, Louis M.

Keith, Robert I. Handbook for the Laryngectomee. 2nd ed. 1983p. 1983. pap. text ed. write for info. (ISBN 0-8134-2290-6). Interstate.

Keith, Robert L. Speech & Language Rehabilitation: A Workbook for the Neurologically Impaired & Language Delayed, Vol.1. 2nd ed. (Illus.). 400p. 1980. pap. text ed. 7.95x (ISBN 0-8134-2117-9). Interstate.

--Speech & Language Rehabilitation: A Workbook for the Neurologically Impaired, Vol. 2. xvi, 256p. 1977. pap. text ed. 7.95x (ISBN 0-8134-1949-2). Interstate.

Keith, Robert M., jt. auth. see Smith, Jack L.

Keith, Ronald. Bush Pilot with a Briefcase: The Happy-go-lucky Story of Grant McConachie. (Airlines History Project Ser.). (Illus.). Date not set. price not set (ISBN 0-404-19326-9). AMS PR.

Keith, Sam & Proenneke, Richard. One Man's Wilderness: An Alaskan Odyssey. LC 72-92089. (Illus.). 116p. 1973. 14.95x o.p. (ISBN 0-88240-092-4); pap. 9.95 (ISBN 0-88240-013-4). Alaska Northwest.

Keitner, Wendy. Ralph Gustafson. (World Authors Ser.: No. 531). 1979. lib. bdg. 15.95 (ISBN 0-8057-6373-2, Twayne). G K Hall.

Kekes, John. A Justification of Rationality. LC 76-16069. 1976. 34.50x (ISBN 0-87395-350-9). State U NY Pr.

Kekkonen, Urho. A President's View. 132p. (Orig.). 1982. 16.50 (ISBN 0-434-39705-9, Pub. by W Heinemann). David & Charles.

Kelaart, Piers. Midas. 1982. pap. 2.50 (ISBN 0-451-11618-6, AE1618, Sig). NAL.

Kelalis, Panayotis P., et al, eds. Clinical Pediatric Urology, 2 vols. LC 75-14782. (Illus.). 1107p. 1976. text ed. 70.00 set o.p. (ISBN 0-686-67914-8); Vol. 1. text ed. 40.00 o.p. (ISBN 0-7216-5350-2); Vol. 2. text ed. 40.00 o.p. (ISBN 0-7216-5351-0). Saunders.

Kelber, Werner H. Mark's Story of Jesus. LC 78-14668. 96p. 1979. pap. 3.50 (ISBN 0-8006-1355-4, 1-1355). Fortress.

--The Oral & the Written Gospel: The Hermeneutics of Speaking & Writing in the Synoptic Tradition, Mark, Paul, & Q. LC 82-7450. 272p. 1983. 22.95 (ISBN 0-8006-0689-2, 1-689). Fortress.

Kelber, Werner H., jt. auth. see Allison, C. Fitzsimons.

Kelburn, Richard & Rippery, Elizabeth. Sea Shells of Southern Africa. (Illus.). 264p. 1982. 49.95 (ISBN 0-686-83938-2, Pub. by Macmillan S Africa). Intl Schol Bk Serv.

Kelch, Maxwell. Simple Celestial Navigation. LC 74-33188. (Illus.). 1975. pap. 5.95 o.s.i. (ISBN 0-87799-051-4). Aztex.

Kelch, Ray A. Newcastle: A Duke Without Money; Thomas Pelham-Holles, 1693-1768. LC 73-83064. 1974. 33.00x (ISBN 0-520-02537-7). U of Cal Pr.

Kelcy, Raymond C. Second Corinthians. (Living Word Paperback Ser.). (Orig.). 1957. pap. 2.95 cancelled (ISBN 0-8344-0016-2). Sweet.

Kelder, Diane. French Impressionists. LC 79-57411. (Abbeville Library of Art: No. 2). (Illus.). 112p. 1980. pap. 4.95 o.p. (ISBN 0-89659-093-3). Abbeville Pr.

--Great Masters of French Impressionism. (Illus.). 1978. 17.95 o.p. (ISBN 0-517-53447-9). Crown.

Keleman, Stanley. The Human Ground. 193p. 1975. 9.95 (ISBN 0-934320-04-7); pap. 5.95 (ISBN 0-934320-02-0). Center Pr.

--The Human Ground: Sexuality, Self & Survival. LC 75-12453. 1975. pap. 6.95 (ISBN 0-8314-0047-1). Sci & Behavior.

Kelemen, E. Physiopathology & Therapy of Human Blood Diseases. LC 68-18525. 1969. 97.00 (ISBN 0-08-012786-X). Pergamon.

Kelemon, Stanley. Somatic Reality. LC 79-88485. 1979. 7.95 (ISBN 0-686-82345-1). Sci & Behavior.

Kelen, Betty. Muhammad: The Messenger of God. LC 75-5792. 224p. 1975. 7.95 o.p. (ISBN 0-525-66440-8). Lodestar Bks.

Kelen, Tibor. Polymer Degradation. 224p. 1982. text ed. 37.50 (ISBN 0-442-24837-7). Van Nos Reinhold.

Kelf-Cohen, R. British Nationalization: Nineteen Forty-Five to Nineteen Seventy-Three. LC 73-86069. 1974. 25.00 (ISBN 0-312-10360-3). St Martin.

--Twenty Years of Nationalization: British Experience. LC 69-13689. 1969. 22.50 (ISBN 0-312-82460-2). St Martin.

Kelidar, Abbas, ed. Integration of Modern Iraq. 1979. 26.00x (ISBN 0-312-41891-4). St Martin.

Kelikian, H. Congenital Deformities of the Hand & Forearm. LC 73-89181. (Illus.). 1025p. 1974. text ed. 40.00 o.p. (ISBN 0-7216-5358-8). Saunders.

Kell, Carl & Corts, Paul. Let's Talk Business: Improving Communications Skills. (Illus.). 288p. (Orig.). 1983. pap. text ed. 11.95i (ISBN 0-316-48646-9); avail.tchrs'. manual (ISBN 0-316-48647-7). Little.

Kell, Carl L. & Corts, Paul R. Fundamentals of Effective Group Communication. (Illus.). 1980. pap. text ed. 10.95 (ISBN 0-02-362280-6). Macmillan.

Kell, Walter & Ziegler, Richard. Modern Auditing. LC 79-5472. 785p. 1980. text ed. 19.75 o.p. (ISBN 0-88262-390-7); wkbk. 7.50 o.p. (ISBN 0-88262-451-2). Wiley.

Kellam, jt. auth. see Shaw.

Kelland, Frank & Kelland, Marilyn. New Jersey: Garden or Suburb? (Regional Georgraphy Ser.). (Illus.). 1978. pap. text ed. 13.95 (ISBN 0-8403-1839-1). Kendall-Hunt.

Kelland, Marilyn, jt. auth. see Kelland, Frank.

Kellar, H. A., ed. Solon Robinson, Pioneer & Agriculturalist, 2 Vols. LC 68-16242. (American Scene Ser). (Illus.). 1968. Repr. of 1936 ed. Set. lib. bdg. 95.00 (ISBN 0-306-71017-X). Da Capo.

Kellar, Jane C. & Miller, E. Selected Receipts of a Van Rensselaer Family, 1785-1835. LC 77-85726. (Illus.). 99p. 1976. pap. 5.00 (ISBN 0-943366-02-X). Hist-Cherry Hill.

Kellar, Jane C. & Miller, Ellen. Selected Receipts of a Van Rensselaer Family: 1785-1835. LC 77-85726. (Illus.). 110p. 1976. pap. 6.00 o.p. (ISBN 0-89062-026-1, Pub. by Historic Cherry). Pub Ctr Cult Res.

Kellas, J. G. The Scottish Political System. 2nd ed. LC 75-2733. (Illus.). 1975. o.p. 33.95 (ISBN 0-521-20864-5); pap. 12.95 (ISBN 0-521-09972-2). Cambridge U Pr.

Kellaway, P. & Petersen, I., eds. Automation of Clinical Electroencephalography. LC 72-96334. (Illus.). 326p. 1973. 38.00 (ISBN 0-911216-45-6). Raven.

Kellaway, Peter & Petersen, Ingemar S., eds. Quantitative Analytic Studies in Epilepsy. LC 76-22912. 588p. 1976. 53.00 (ISBN 0-89004-133-4). Raven.

Kellaway, William. The New England Company, 1649-1776. LC 74-33895. (Illus.). 303p. 1975. Repr. of 1961 ed. lib. bdg. 17.75x (ISBN 0-8371-7995-5, KENE). Greenwood.

Kellaway, William, jt. ed. see Chew, Helena M.

Kelleam, Joseph E. Hunters of Space. (YA) 6.95 (ISBN 0-685-07436-6, Avalon). Bouregy.

--Their Tributes Were Tears. 1979. 10.95 o.p. (ISBN 0-533-03917-7). Vantage.

Kelleher, Hugh, jt. auth. see Marston, Garth.

Kellejian, Robert. Applied Electronic Communication: Circuits, Systems, Transmission. rev. ed. 608p. 1982. 25.95 (ISBN 0-574-21580-8, 13-4580); instr's. guide 3.95 (ISBN 0-574-21581-6). SRA.

Keller, A. G., ed. see Sumner, William G.

Keller, Abraham C., ed. see Atkinson, Geoffroy.

Keller, Albert G. Man's Rough Road. 1932. 37.50x o.p. (ISBN 0-685-69831-9). Elliots Bks.

--Net Impressions. 1942. 19.50x (ISBN 0-686-51423-8). Elliots Bks.

--Societal Evolution: A Study of the Evolutionary Basis of the Science of Society. 1931. 32.50x o.p. (ISBN 0-686-51315-0). Elliots Bks.

--Starting Points in Social Science. 1925. 14.50x (ISBN 0-686-51316-9). Elliots Bks.

Keller, Albrecht, ed. see Schmidt, Franz.

Keller, Beverly. The Bee Sneeze. (gr. 7-10). 1982. pap. 6.99 (ISBN 0-698-30740-2, Coward). Putnam Pub Group.

--The Beetle Bush. LC 75-28180. (Break-of-Day Bk.). (Illus.). 64p. (gr. k-3). 1976. PLB 6.99 (ISBN 0-698-30618-X, Coward). Putnam Pub Group.

--Don't Throw Another One, Dover. LC 76-14813. (Break-of-Day Bk.). (Illus.). (gr. k-3). 1976. PLB 6.59 o.p. (ISBN 0-698-30638-4, Coward). Putnam Pub Group.

--Fiona's Bee. (Break-of-Day Bk.). (Illus.). 48p. (gr. 1-4). 1975. 6.99 (ISBN 0-698-30595-7, Coward). Putnam Pub Group.

--Fiona's Flea. (Illus.). 64p. (gr. 7-10). 1981. PLB 6.99 (ISBN 0-698-30719-4, Coward). Putnam Pub Group.

--The Genuine, Ingenious, Thrift Shop Genie, Clarissa Mae Bean & Me. LC 77-24050. (Illus.). (gr. 3-6). 1977. 6.95 o.p. (ISBN 0-698-20433-6, Coward). Putnam Pub Group.

--My Awful Cousin Norbert. (Illus.). (gr. 1-5). 1982. 8.50 (ISBN 0-688-00742-2); PLB 7.63 (ISBN 0-688-00743-0). Lothrop.

--No Beasts! No Children! LC 82-14011. 128p. (gr. 3-6). 1983. 8.00 (ISBN 0-688-01678-2). Lothrop.

--Pimm's Place. LC 77-27053. (Break-of-Day Bk.). (Illus.). (gr. k-3). 1978. PLB 6.59 o.p. (ISBN 0-698-30689-9, Coward). Putnam Pub Group.

Keller, C. Ballpoint-Bananas & Other Jokes for Children. (gr. 3-7). 1973. 4.95 o.p. (ISBN 0-13-055350-6). P-H.

Keller, Charles. Little Witch Presents a Monster Joke Book. (Illus.). 48p. (ps-4). 1983. pap. 4.95 (ISBN 0-13-537811-7). P-H.

--News Breaks. (Illus.). (gr. 2-6). 1981. 7.95 o.p. (ISBN 0-13-620583-6). P-H.

--Norma Lee I Don't Knock on Doors. (Illus.). 64p. (gr. 3-7). 1983. 7.95 (ISBN 0-13-623587-5). P-H.

--Ohm on the Range: Robot & Computer Jokes. (Illus.). 48p. (gr. 3-7). 1982. 7.95 (ISBN 0-13-633552-7). P-H.

Keller, Charles L. & Robinson, Douglas H. Up Ship! U. S. Navy Rigid Airships, Nineteen Nineteen to Nineteen Thirty-Five. LC 82-6374. (Illus.). 360p. 1982. 29.95 (ISBN 0-87021-738-0). Naval Inst Pr.

Keller, Clair, jt. auth. see Bartlett, Richard.

Keller, Clara. American Library Resources Cumulative Index, 1870-1970. 96p. 1981. text ed. 25.00 (ISBN 0-8389-0341-X). ALA.

Keller, Clifton & Appel, Jeanette. Science Activities for Christian Children. 100p. (gr. k-6). 1982. pap. 5.95 (ISBN 0-930192-11-7). Gazelle Pubns.

Keller, Dick & Keller, Irene. The Thingumajig Christmas. (Good Friends Ser.). (Illus.). 48p. (gr. k-6). 1982. 4.95 (ISBN 0-8249-8045-X). Ideals.

Keller, Edward A. Environmental Geology. 3rd ed. 544p. 1982. text ed. 24.95 (ISBN 0-675-09915-3). Merrill.

Keller, Edward A., jt. auth. see Botkin, Daniel B.

Keller, G. V., jt. ed. see Rapolla, A.

Keller, Gary D. Leo y Entiendo. (Bilingual Education Ser.). (Orig.). (gr. 1-3). 1983. Bk. A. pap. text ed. 5.70 (ISBN 0-8077-5995-3); Bk. B. pap. text ed. 5.70 (ISBN 0-8077-5996-1); Bk. C. pap. text ed. 5.70 (ISBN 0-8077-5997-X); Bk. A. pap. text ed. 5.70; Bk. C. tchrs manual 12.45 (ISBN 0-8077-6028-5). Tchrs Coll.

--The Significance & Impact of Gregorio Maranon. LC 76-45295. 1977. lib. bdg. 15.95x (ISBN 0-916950-04-2); pap. 8.95x (ISBN 0-916950-18-2). Bilingual Pr.

Keller, Gary D. & Jimenez, Francisco. Viva la lengua! (Illus.). 90p. (Orig., Sp.). 1975. pap. text ed. 8.95 (ISBN 0-15-594938-1, HC). HarBraceJ.

Keller, Gary D. & Jimenez, Francisco, eds. Hispanics in the United States: An Anthology of Creative Literature. LC 80-66273. 176p. 1980. pap. 10.00x (ISBN 0-916950-19-0). Bilingual Pr.

Keller, Gary D., et al, eds. Bilingualism in the Bicentennial & Beyond. LC 76-45292. 1976. lib. bdg. 14.95x (ISBN 0-916950-01-8); pap. 8.95x (ISBN 0-916950-15-8). Bilingual Pr.

Keller, Gunter. Discus. (Illus., Orig.). 1976. pap. 3.95 (ISBN 0-87666-770-1, PS-314). TFH Pubns.

Keller, H. B., jt. auth. see Isaacson, Eugene.

Keller, Hans, jt. ed. see Mitchell, Donald.

Keller, Heide, jt. ed. see Voss, Hans-Georg.

Keller, Helen. Story of My Life. LC 54-11951. (Illus.). 1954. 15.95 (ISBN 0-385-04453-4). Doubleday.

--Teacher: Anne Sullivan Macy, a Tribute by the Foster-Child of Her Mind. 1982. Repr. of 1955 ed. 17.00 (ISBN 0-89783-025-3). Larlin Corp.

Keller, Herbert B. Numerical Solution of Two Point Boundary Value Problems. (CBMS Regional Conference Ser.: Vol. 24). viii, 61p. (Orig.). 1976. pap. text ed. 9.00 (ISBN 0-89871-021-9). Soc Indus-Appl Math.

Keller, Holly. Too Big. LC 82-15653. (Illus.). 32p. (gr. k-3). 9.00 (ISBN 0-688-01998-6); PLB 8.59 (ISBN 0-688-01999-4). Greenwillow.

Keller, Irene, jt. auth. see Keller, Dick.

Keller, Irvin A. The Interscholastic Coach. 400p. 1982. 18.95 (ISBN 0-13-475707-6). P-H.

Keller, J. J. Pesticides Guide. Kleinhans, James, ed. LC 79-54216. (22g). 1982. 90.00 (ISBN 0-934674-12-4, 22G). J J Keller.

Keller, J. J., & Assocs., Inc. Fleet Safety Compliance Manual. McDowell, George B., ed. LC 78-71720. (8m). 1982. 65.00 (ISBN 0-934674-24-8). J J Keller.

--Freight Claims Manual. Seybert, Michael, ed. LC 78-71118. (6m). 1981. 45.00 (ISBN 0-934674-22-1). J J Keller.
--Freight Security Manual. Seybert, Michael, ed. LC 79-64975. (7m). 1981. 45.00 (ISBN 0-934674-23-X). J J Keller.
--Occupational Exposure Guide. Kleinhans, James, ed. LC 79-54214. (23g). 1982. 95.00 (ISBN 0-934674-13-2). J J Keller.
--Toxic Substances Control Guide. Kleinhans, James, ed. LC 79-54215. (21g). 1982. 95.00 (ISBN 0-934674-11-6). J J Keller.
Keller, James F. & Hughston, George. Counseling the Elderly: A Systems Approach. (Illus.). 168p. 1980. text ed. 17.95 scp (ISBN 0-06-453511-8, HarpC). Har-Row.
Keller, John E. Gonzalo de Berceo. (World Authors Ser.: Spain: No. 187). lib. bdg. 15.95 (ISBN 0-8057-2144-4, Twayne). G K Hall.
--Ministering to Alcoholics. 5.50 o.p. (ISBN 0-686-92206-9, 6560). Hazelden.
Keller, John G. Krispin's Fair. (Illus.). (gr. k-3). 4.95g o.p. (ISBN 0-316-48652-3). Little.
Keller, John J. Federal Motor Carrier Safety Regulations Pocketbook. rev. ed. McDowell, George B., et al, eds. LC 75-32244. (ORS7A). 110p. 1982. 1.95 (ISBN 0-934674-28-0). J J Keller.
--Interstate Motor Carrier Forms Manual: Private, Contract, Exempt. rev. ed. Seybert, Michael, et al, eds. LC 76-7194. (2g). 1982. 85.00 (ISBN 0-686-16913-1). J J Keller.
--Metrication Handbook. Laux, Patricia, et al, eds. (19h). (Illus.). 144p. 1976. spiral bdg 15.00 (ISBN 0-934674-32-9). J J Keller.
--Truck Broker Directory. 13th ed. Seybert, Michael, ed. LC 75-25256. (15h). (Illus., Prog. Bk.). 1983. spiral bdg 25.00 (ISBN 0-934674-18-3). J J Keller.
--Trucking Permit Guide: Private, Contract, Common, Exempt. rev. ed. Seybert, Michael, et al, eds. LC 75-16944. (1g). 1982. loose-leaf 119.00 (ISBN 0-934674-00-0). J J Keller.
--Trucking Safety Guide: Driver, Vehicles, Cargo, Highway. rev. ed. Newsome, Claire, et al, eds. LC 74-3865. (8g). 1982. loose-leaf 119.00 (ISBN 0-934674-03-5). J J Keller.
--Vehicle Sizes & Weights Manual: Limitations, Oversize & Overweight Mobile Homes. rev ed. Nelson, Harold C., et al, eds. LC 74-31863. (1m). 586p. (Prog. Bk.). 1982. looseleaf 85.00 (ISBN 0-934674-21-3). J J Keller.
Keller, Kathryn. Instrumental Articulatory Phonetics. (Publications in Linguistics Ser.: No. 31). (Illus.). 145p. 1971. pap. 5.50x (ISBN 0-88312-033-X); microfiche 2.25 (ISBN 0-88312-433-5). Summer Inst Ling.
Keller, M. H., ed. see Balcomb, J. D., et al.
Keller, Marion & Zant, James H. Basic Mathematics. 3rd ed. LC 78-69602. (Illus.). 1979. pap. text ed. 20.95 (ISBN 0-395-27050-2); pap. 21.95 instr's annotated ed. (ISBN 0-395-27051-0). HM.
Keller, Marion W. Intermediate Algebra: A Text Workbook. LC 74-171526. pap. text ed. 17.50 (ISBN 0-395-12643-6); test ans. & problems 3.20 (ISBN 0-395-12644-4). HM.
Keller, Mark, ed. International Bibliography of Studies on Alcohol, 3 vols. Incl. Vol. 1. References, 1901-1950. Jordy, Sarah S., compiled by. 1966. 50.00x (ISBN 0-911290-34-6); Vol. 2. Indexes, 1901-1950. Efron, Vera & Jordy, Sarah S. 1968. 50.00x (ISBN 0-911290-35-4); Vol. 3. References, 1951-1960; Indexes, 1951-1960. Jordy, Sarah S., et al. 1980. 100.00x (ISBN 0-911290-40-0). LC 60-14437. Set of Vols. 1 & 2. 95.00x (ISBN 0-911290-07-9). Rutgers Ctr Alcohol.
Keller, Merilu H., ed. see Irving, Lynn.
Keller, Merily H., ed. see Sullivan, Debbie.
Keller, Merily H., ed. see Winez, Yvonne.
Keller, Mollie. Golda Meir. (Impact Biography Ser.). (Illus.). 128p. (gr. 7 up). 1983. PLB 8.90 (ISBN 0-531-04591-9). Watts.
Keller, Morton. The Art & Politics of Thomas Nast. LC 68-19762. (Illus.). 365p. 1975. pap. 12.95 (ISBN 0-19-501929-6, GB437, GB). Oxford U Pr.
Keller, Paul T., jt. auth. see Brown, Charles T.
Keller, Peter A. & Murray, Dennis J., eds. Handbook of Rural Community Mental Health. LC 81-7048. (Illus.). 252p. 1982. 29.95x (ISBN 0-89885-065-7). Human Sci Pr.
Keller, Peter D. & Freudiger, Ullrich D. Atlas of Hematology of the Dog & Cat. 120p. (Ger., Fr., Eng., Span., & Ital.). 1983. lib. bdg. 78.00 (ISBN 0-686-37181-X). Parey Sci Pubs.
Keller, Phillip. La Vida en el Redil. Vargas, Carlos A., tr. from Eng. LC 76-14500. 141p. (Span.). 1976. pap. 2.50 o.s.i. (ISBN 0-89922-073-8). Edit Caribe.
Keller, Phyllis. Getting at the Core: Curricular Reform at Harvard. 1982. text ed. 15.00x (ISBN 0-674-35418-4). Harvard U Pr.
Keller, R. E. German Dialects. 408p. 1961. pap. 10.00 (ISBN 0-7190-0762-3). Manchester.
Keller, Robert H., Jr. American Prostestantism & United States Indian Policy, 1869-82. LC 82-8514. (Illus.). xiv, 354p. 1983. 27.95x (ISBN 0-8032-2706-X). U of Nebr Pr.
Keller, Rosemary S. & Queen, Louise L., eds. Women in New Worlds, Vol. 2. 448p. (Orig.). 1982. pap. 13.95 (ISBN 0-687-45969-9). Abingdon.
Keller, Rosemary S., jt. ed. see Thomas, Hilah F.
Keller, S. P. & Moss, T. S. Handbook on Semiconductors, Vol. 3: Materials & Preparation. 1980. 161.75 (ISBN 0-444-85274-3). Elsevier.
Keller, Sally. English-Khmer Medical Dictionary. (Workpapers of North Dakota: Vol. XX, Suppl. 2). 190p. 1976. pap. 4.50x (ISBN 0-88312-744-X); microfiche 3.00x (ISBN 0-88312-341-X). Summer Inst Ling.
Keller, Suzanne, ed. Building for Women. LC 80-8783. 240p. 1981. 25.95x (ISBN 0-669-04368-0). Lexington Bks.
Keller, T. F. & Zeff, S. A. Financial Accounting Theory Two: Issues & Controversies. 1969. pap. text ed. 14.95 (ISBN 0-07-033496-X, C). McGraw.
Keller, Thomas F., jt. auth. see Zeff, Stephen A.
Keller, Ulrich, ed. The Building of the Panama Canal in Historic Photographs. (Photography Ser.). (Illus.). 176p. (Orig.). 1983. pap. 12.50 (ISBN 0-486-24408-3). Dover.
Keller, W. D. Common Rocks & Minerals of Missouri. rev. ed. LC 67-66173. (Illus.). 78p. 1961. pap. 5.00x (ISBN 0-8262-0585-2). U of Mo Pr.
Keller, W. J. Tax Incidence: A General Equilibrium Approach. (Contributions to Economic Analysis Ser.: Vol. 134). 1980. 55.50 (ISBN 0-444-86057-6). Elsevier.
Keller, W. Philip. Il Buon Pastore E Le Sue Pecore. Arcangeli, Gianfranco, ed. (Ital.). 1980. pap. 1.60 (ISBN 0-8297-0970-3). Life Pubs Intl.
Keller, W. Phillip. A Layman Looks at the Lamb of God. 122p. (Orig.). 1982. 7.95 (ISBN 0-87123-313-4, 230314); pap. 3.95 (ISBN 0-87123-314-2, 210314). Bethany Hse.
--A Layman Looks at the Lord's Prayer. 160p. 1976. 4.95 (ISBN 0-8024-4643-4); pap. 5.95 (ISBN 0-8024-4644-2); study ed. 7.95 (ISBN 0-8024-4647-7). Moody.
--Lessons from a Sheepdog. 1983. 6.95 (ISBN 0-8499-0335-1). Word Pub.
--Ocean Glory. (Illus.). 160p. 1980. 24.95 o.p. (ISBN 0-8007-1104-1). Revell.
--Rabboni. 256p. pap. 5.95 (ISBN 0-8007-5053-5, Power Bks). Revell.
--Wonder O' the Wind. 1982. 9.95 (ISBN 0-8499-0337-8). Word Pub.
Keller, Wayne H. Achieving & Receiving Intimacy. 30p. (Orig.). 1982. pap. text ed. 4.95x (ISBN 0-686-35961-5). Scorpion Pr.
Keller, Wilhelm. Introduction to Music for Children. Kennedy, Susan, tr. from Ger. (Orff-Schulwerk). 1974. pap. 5.50 (ISBN 0-930448-10-3, 70-00271). Eur-Am Music.
Keller-Grimm, M., ed. see Grimm, George.
Kellerman, Eli. Jewish Ceremonial: A Guide to Jewish Prayer & Ritual. 69p. 1983. pap. 9.95 (ISBN 965-220-038-7, Carta Maps & Guides Pub Isreal). Hippocrene Bks.
Kellerman, Henry, jt. ed. see Plutchik, Robert.
Kellermann, J. J., ed. Comprehensive Cardiac Rehabilitation, 2nd World Congress, Jerusalem, 1981. (Advances in Cardiology: Vol. 31). (Illus.). x, 246p. 1982. 72.00 (ISBN 3-8055-3539-2). S Karger.
Kellermeyer, Robert, jt. auth. see Harris, John W.
Keller-von Asten, H. see Asten, H. Keller-von.
Kellet, V. B., tr. see Kautzky, R.
Kellett, Michael. Memory Power. LC 80-52338. (Illus.). 128p. (Orig.). 1980. 12.95 (ISBN 0-8069-0210-8); lib. bdg. 15.69 (ISBN 0-8069-0211-6); pap. 6.95 (ISBN 0-8069-8946-7). Sterling.
Kelley, Alberta. Lenses, Spectacles, & Contacts: The Story of Vision Aids. LC 78-14827. (Illus.). (gr. 6 up). 1979. 8.95 (ISBN 0-525-66617-6). Lodestar Bks.
Kelley, Barbara & Tomacci, Toni M. The Vacations & Weekends Learning Guide: Ideas & Activities to Help Children Learn Throughout the Year. 208p. 1983. 14.95 (ISBN 0-13-940130-X); pap. 8.95 (ISBN 0-13-940122-9). P-H.
Kelley, Beverly F., jt. auth. see Fox, Charles P.
Kelley, David & Donway, Roger. Laissez Parler: Freedom in the Electronic Media. (Studies in Social Philosophy & Policy: No. 1). 96p. 1982. pap. 4.00 (ISBN 0-935756-99-X). BGSU Dept Phil.
Kelley, David H. Deciphering the Maya Script. LC 75-17989. (Illus.). 352p. 1976. 55.00x (ISBN 0-292-71504-8). U of Tex Pr.
Kelley, David L. Kinesiology: Fundamentals of Motion Description. LC 79-144098. (Physical Education Ser). 1971. text ed. 22.95 (ISBN 0-13-516260-2). P-H.
Kelley, David W. How to Talk Your Way Out of a Traffic Ticket. (Illus.). 80p. (Orig.). 1982. pap. 5.00 (ISBN 0-9609982-0-9). Mark III Prods.
Kelley, Donald R. The Beginning of Ideology: Consciousness & Society in the French Reformation. LC 80-41237. 366p. Date not set. pap. 14.95 (ISBN 0-521-27483-4). Cambridge U Pr.
Kelley, Donald R., ed. The Energy Crisis & the Environment: An International Perspective. LC 76-24355. (Praeger Special Studies). 1977. text ed. 31.95 o.p. (ISBN 0-275-23850-4). Praeger.
Kelley, Edward N. Practical Apartment Management. 2nd ed. Kirk, Nancye J., ed. LC 81-80947. 347p. 1981. 21.95 (ISBN 0-912104-49-X). Inst Real Estate.
Kelley, Edward P., Jr., jt. auth. see Angell, George W.
Kelley, F. Beverly. It Was Better Than Work. Franzwa, Gregory M., ed. LC 82-24556. xii, 287p. 1983. 14.95 (ISBN 0-935284-25-7). Patrice Pr.
Kelley, Frances. Better Than I Was. LC 79-1095. 1979. pap. 4.95 (ISBN 0-8407-5671-2). Nelson.
Kelley, Francis E. Quaestio Disputata de Unitate Formae: Richard Knapwell. 100p. 1983. 12.00 (ISBN 0-86698-022-9). Medieval & Renaissance NY.
Kelley, Harold H. & Thibaut, John W. Interpersonal Relations: A Theory of Interdependence. LC 78-164. 341p. 1978. 39.50x (ISBN 0-471-03473-8, Pub. by Wiley-Interscience). Wiley.
Kelley, Harold H., jt. auth. see Thibaut, John W.
Kelley, J. H. see World Hydrogen Energy Conference, Fourth.
Kelley, J. Roland, jt. auth. see McKenzie, Jimmy C.
Kelley, Jain. Darkroom Two. LC 78-69948. (Illus.). 160p. (Orig.). 1979. pap. 17.95 (ISBN 0-912810-21-1). Lustrum Pr.
Kelley, James E., Jr. The IBM Personal Computer User's Guide. 352p. 1983. spiral bdg., shrink-wrapped, incl. a programmed floppy disk 29.95 (ISBN 0-440-03946-0, Banbury). Dell.
Kelley, Janet. Bankers & Borders: The Case of American Banks in Britain. 1976. 35.00x (ISBN 0-88410-459-1). Ballinger Pub.
Kelley, Jean, jt. auth. see Torres, Gertrude.
Kelley, Jean, jt. auth. see Connolly, Arlene F.
Kelley, Jean A., jt. auth. see Stevens, Barbara J.
Kelley, Joe & Ibraham, A. How Managers Manage. (Illus.). 1980. 15.95 (ISBN 0-13-423756-0, Spec); pap. 7.95 (ISBN 0-13-423749-8, Spec); study guide 5.95 (ISBN 0-13-423731-5). P-H.
Kelley, John H., jt. auth. see DeGravelles, William D.
Kelley, Lane, jt. auth. see Whatley, Arthur.
Kelley, Leo P. Fantasy: The Literature of the Marvelous. (Patterns in Literary Art Ser). 324p. (gr. 9-12). 1973. pap. text ed. 9.16 (ISBN 0-07-033502-8, W). McGraw.
--Luke Sutton: Outlaw. 1982. pap. 1.95 (ISBN 0-451-11522-8, AJ1522, Sig). NAL.
--Themes in Science Fiction. (Patterns in Literary Art Ser). 432p. (gr. 10-12). 1972. pap. text ed. 9.16 (ISBN 0-07-033504-4, W). McGraw.
Kelley, Leo P., ed. The Supernatural in Fiction. (Patterns in Literary Art Ser.). 324p. (gr. 10-12). 1973. pap. text ed. 9.16 (ISBN 0-07-033497-8, W). McGraw.
Kelley, Louise H. & Straw, Dorothy, eds. Vital Records, Town of Harwich Masschusetts, 1694 to 1850. 616p. 1982. write for info. (ISBN 0-88492-040-2). W S Sullwold.
Kelley, Maurice see Milton, John.
Kelley, Merily H., ed. see Hunt, Tamara & Renfro, Nancy.
Kelley, Michael R. Television: A Teacher in Our Midst. 160p. 1983. pap. text ed. 8.95x (ISBN 0-471-87132-X). Wiley.
Kelley, N. Edmund. The Contemporary Ecology of Arroyo Hondo, New Mexico. LC 79-21351. (Arroyo Hondo Archaeological Ser.: Vol. 1). (Illus., Orig.). 1979. pap. 7.50 (ISBN 0-933452-01-2). Schol Am Res.
Kelley, Nancy L., jt. auth. see Pollak, Otto.
Kelley, Nelson L. & Whatley, Arthur A. Personnel Management in Action: Skill Building Experiences. 2nd ed. (West Ser. in Management). 324p. 1980. pap. text ed. 15.95 (ISBN 0-8299-0389-5). West Pub.
Kelley, Patricia, jt. auth. see Orr, Carolyn.
Kelley, Philip & Hudson, Ronald, eds. Diary by E. B. B. LC 68-18390. 1969. 17.50x (ISBN 0-8214-0047-9, 82-80521). Ohio U Pr.
Kelley, Richard E., jt. auth. see Desmond, Glenn M.
Kelley, Richard N., jt. auth. see Billmeyer, Fred W.
Kelley, Robert. The Shaping of the American Past. 2nd ed. Incl. Combined Edition. 1978. text ed. 24.95 (ISBN 0-13-808105-0); Vol. 1. To 1877. 1978. pap. text ed. 15.95 (ISBN 0-13-808113-1); study guide 7.95 (ISBN 0-13-808089-5); Vol. 2. 1865 to Pesent. 1978. pap. text ed. 16.95 (ISBN 0-13-808121-2); study guide 7.95 (ISBN 0-13-808097-6). (Illus.). P-H.
Kelley, Robert K. Courtship, Marriage, & the Family. 3rd ed. 650p. 1979. text ed. 19.95 (ISBN 0-15-515338-2, HC); student guidebk. o.p. 6.95 (ISBN 0-15-516120-2); instructor's manual avail. (ISBN 0-15-516121-0). HarBraceJ.
--Guidebook for Marriage & the Family. 147p. 1979. pap. text ed. 4.95 (ISBN 0-15-515340-4, HC). HarBraceJ.
Kelley, Robert O. & Goetnick, Paul F., eds. Limb Development & Regeneration, Pt. B. LC 82-20391. (Progress in Clinical & Biological Research Ser.: Vol. 110B). 434p. 1982. 46.00 (ISBN 0-8451-0171-4). A R Liss.
Kelley, Susan & Segal, Robert. The ABZ'S of Word Processing: A Primer for Executives, Professionals, & Other Principals Who Submit Work to Word Processing. (Illus.). 64p. 1983. pap. 10.95 (ISBN 0-87396-097-1). Stravon.
Kelley, Thomas M., jt. auth. see Seitzinger, Jack M.
Kelley, True. Sunshine & Sculpture. (Scribbler Play Bks.). 20p. (ps). 1983. pap. write for info. (ISBN 0-307-20326-3). Western Pub.
Kelley, Vicent C., ed. see Loose Leaf Reference Services.
Kelley, Vincent C. Metabolic Endocrine & Genetic Disorders of Children, 3 vols. (Illus.). 1974. 150.00x o.p. (ISBN 0-06-141428-X, Harper Medical). Lippincott.
Kelley, William M. Dancers on the Shore. (Howard University Press Library of Contemporary Literature). 201p. 1983. pap. 6.95 (ISBN 0-88258-114-7). Howard U Pr.
--Different Drummer. LC 62-11453. 1969. pap. 2.50 (ISBN 0-385-01079-6, Anch). Doubleday.
Kelley, William N., et al. Textbook of Rheumatology. 2080p. 1980. text ed. 65.00 (ISBN 0-7216-5353-7). Vol. 1 (ISBN 0-7216-5354-5). Vol. 2. text ed. 65.00 (ISBN 0-7216-5357-X). Saunders.
Kelley, Win. Breaking the Barriers in Public Speaking. 1978. pap. text ed. 9.95 (ISBN 0-8403-1848-0). Kendall-Hunt.
Kelliher, Hilton. Andrew Marvell: Poet & Politician 1621-78. 128p. 1981. 40.00x (ISBN 0-7141-0395-0, Pub. by Brit Lib England); pap. 25.00x (ISBN 0-686-82972-7). State Mutual Bk.
Kelling, Furn F. Prayer Is... (Illus.). (gr. k-3). 1979. 4.95 (ISBN 0-8054-4256-1). Broadman.
Kelling, G., jt. ed. see Stanley, D. J.
Kelling, Harold D., jt. ed. see Frazer, Ray.
Kellman, Martin C. Plant Geography. 1980. pap. 12.50x (ISBN 0-416-73860-5). Methuen Inc.
--Plant Geography. 2nd ed. LC 80-5079. 1980. 26.00 (ISBN 0-312-61461-6). St Martin.
--Plant Geography. LC 74-83967. (Illus.). 144p. 1975. 14.95 o.p. (ISBN 0-312-61460-8). St Martin.
Kellner, Bruce, compiled by. A Bibliography of the Work of Carl Van Vechten. LC 79-8409. (Illus.). 1980. lib. bdg. 35.00 (ISBN 0-313-20767-4, KBV/). Greenwood.
Kellner, Bruce, ed. Keep a-Inchin' Along: Selected Writings of Carl Van Vechten About Black Art & Letters. LC 78-67912. (Contributions in Afro-American & African Studies: No. 45). 1979. lib. bdg. 29.95 (ISBN 0-313-21091-8, KIA/). Greenwood.
Kellner, Douglas, jt. ed. see Bronner, Stephen.
Kellner, Esther. Animals Come to My House: A Story Guide to the Care of Small Wild Animals. LC 75-37937. (Illus.). 160p. (gr. 5 up). 1976. 7.95 o.p. (ISBN 0-399-20500-4). Putnam Pub Group.
Kellner, Hugo M., tr. see Ekrutt, Joachim W.
Kellner, Leon. Restoring Shakespeare: A Critical Analysis of the Misreadings in Shakespeare's Works. LC 78-77027. (Illus.). 1969. Repr. of 1925 ed. 9.00x (ISBN 0-8196-0244-2). Biblo.
Kellock, Harold. Parson Weems of the Cherry-Tree. LC 75-107137. 1971. Repr. of 1928 ed. 30.00x (ISBN 0-8103-3785-1). Gale.
Kellog, Steven. The Orchard Cat. (Illus.). 40p. (ps-3). 1983. pap. 3.95 (ISBN 0-8037-6481-2, 0383-120). Dial Bks Young.
--Pinkerton, Behave! (Pied Piper Bks.). (Illus.). 32p. (gr. k-3). 1982. pap. 3.95 (ISBN 0-8037-7250-5). Dial.
Kellog, Stuart, ed. Literary Visions of Homosexuality: Homosexuality in Literature. (Journal of Homosexuality Ser.: Vol. 8, no. 3-4). 200p. 1983. text ed. 18.95 (ISBN 0-686-83516-6). Haworth Pr.
Kellog, William O. Barron's How to Prepare for the Advanced Placement Examination: American History. LC 76-13515. 1977. pap. 6.95 (ISBN 0-8120-0489-2). Barron.
Kellogg, Carolyn J. & Sullivan, Barbara P., eds. Current Perspectives in Oncologic Nursing, Vol. II. LC 78-492. (Current Perspectives Ser.). (Illus.). 1978. 12.50 (ISBN 0-8016-3794-5); pap. 9.50 (ISBN 0-8016-3795-3). Mosby.
Kellogg, Clara L. Memoirs of an American Prima Donna. LC 77-16534. (Music Reprint Ser., 1978). (Illus.). 1978. Repr. of 1913 ed. lib. bdg. 35.00 (ISBN 0-306-77527-1). Da Capo.
Kellogg Company. Design of Piping Systems. rev. 2nd ed. 385p. 1964. 52.95x (ISBN 0-471-46795-2, Pub. by Wiley-Interscience). Wiley.
Kellogg, Jefferson B. & Walker, Robert H., eds. Sources for American Studies. LC 82-11701. (Contributions in American Studies: No. 64). (Illus.). 581p. 1983. lib. bdg. 45.00 (ISBN 0-313-22555-9, WTO/). Greenwood.
Kellogg, John W. Dog Training Made Easy & Fun. pap. 4.00 (ISBN 0-87980-028-3). Wilshire.
Kellogg, Louise P. American Colonial Charter. LC 71-75291. (Era of the American Revolution Ser). 1971. Repr. of 1904 ed. lib. bdg. 19.50 (ISBN 0-306-71292-X). Da Capo.
Kellogg, Louise P., ed. see Cole, Harry E.
Kellogg, Louise T. British Regime in Wisconsin & the Northwest. LC 74-124927. (American Scene Ser). (Illus.). 1971. Repr. of 1935 ed. lib. bdg. 45.00 (ISBN 0-306-71047-1). Da Capo.
Kellogg, Marion S. Putting Management Theories to Work. LC 68-5675. 286p. 1968. 14.95 o.p. (ISBN 0-87201-463-0). Gulf Pub.
--Talking with Employees: A Guide for Managers. 175p. 1979. 19.95 (ISBN 0-87201-825-3). Gulf Pub.
Kellogg, Robert, jt. auth. see Scholes, Robert.
Kellogg, S. H. Grammar of the Hindi Language. 30.00 (ISBN 0-685-47302-3). Heinman.
Kellogg, Samuel H. The Book of Leviticus. 1978. 21.00 (ISBN 0-86524-132-5, 0301). Klock & Klock.

Kellogg, Steven. The Mysterious Tadpole. LC 77-71517. (Illus.). (ps-3). 1977. 9.89 (ISBN 0-8037-6245-3); PLB 6.46 (ISBN 0-8037-6246-1). Dial.

Kellogg, W. W. Meteorological Soundings in the Upper Atmosphere. (Technical Note Ser.). 1964. pap. 8.00 (ISBN 0-685-22322-1, W28, WMO). Unipub.

Kellogg, Walter G. Conscientious Objector. LC 77-107412. (Civil Liberties in American History Ser). 1970. Repr. of 1919 ed. lib. bdg. 19.50 (ISBN 0-306-71893-6). Da Capo.

Kellogg, William G. The Conscientious Objector. LC 78-143430. (The Peace movement in America Ser). xviii, 141p. 1972. Repr. of 1919 ed. lib. bdg. 12.95x (ISBN 0-89198-077-6). Ozer.

Kellogg, William W. & Schware, Robert. Climate Change & Society: Consequences of Increasing Atmospheric Carbon Dioxide. (Special Study Ser.). 170p. (Orig.). 1981. lib. bdg. 18.50 (ISBN 0-86531-179-X); pap. 8.00 (ISBN 0-86531-180-3). Westview.

Kellough, Richard D., jt. auth. see Kim, Eugene C.

Kells, Lyman M. Differential Equations: A Brief Course with Applications. 1968. pap. text ed. 22.50 (ISBN 0-07-033532-X, C). McGraw.

--Elementary Differential Equations. 6th ed. 1965. text ed. 34.00 (ISBN 0-07-033530-3, C). McGraw.

Kelly. Readings in the Philosophy of Man. 1972. 17.50 (ISBN 0-07-033882-5, C). McGraw.

Kelly, jt. auth. see Blenkin.

Kelly, jt. auth. see Henderson.

Kelly, A. Strong Solids. 2nd ed. (Monographs on the Physics & Chemistry of Materials Ser.). (Illus.). 1973. 59.00x (ISBN 0-19-851350-X). Oxford U Pr.

Kelly, A. & Mileiko, S. T., eds. Fabrication of Composites, Vol. IV. (Handbook of Composites Ser.). 500p. 1983. 95.75 (ISBN 0-444-86447-4, North Holland). Elsevier.

Kelly, A. V., jt. auth. see Blenkin, Geva.

Kelly, Alexander. Jack the Ripper: A Bibliography & Review of the Literature. 1979. 10.00x o.p. (ISBN 0-902248-03-0, Pub. by AALSED England). State Mutual Bk.

Kelly, Alfred H. & Harbison, Winfred A. American Constitution: Its Origin & Development. 6th ed. 1982. pap. text ed. 19.95x (ISBN 0-393-95204-5). Norton.

Kelly, Alison, ed. The Missing Half: Girls & Science Education. 416p. 1982. 25.00 (ISBN 0-7190-0753-4). Manchester.

Kelly, Anthony & Harris, M. J. Management of Industrial Maintenance. (Illus.). 1978. 29.95 (ISBN 0-408-00297-2). Butterworth.

Kelly, B. T. Physics of Graphite. 1981. 104.75 (ISBN 0-85334-960-6, Pub. by Applied Sci England). Elsevier.

Kelly, Balmer H., et al, eds. see Foreman, Kenneth J., et al.

Kelly, Barbara, jt. auth. see Elliot, Len.

Kelly, Brian, jt. auth. see Grimes, Dennis.

Kelly, Bruce, et al. Art of the Olmstead Landscape, 2 vols. LC 81-83950. (Illus.). 176p. 1982. Set. pap. 35.00 o.p. (ISBN 0-8390-0287-4). Allanheld & Schram.

Kelly, Clarence. Conspiracy Against God & Man. 264p. 1982. 7.95 (ISBN 0-88279-131-1). Western Islands.

Kelly, Curtis, ed. see Mayer, Allan J.

Kelly, D. R. The Beginning of Ideology: Consciousness & Society in the French Reformation. 358p. 1981. 54.50 (ISBN 0-521-23504-9). Cambridge U Pr.

Kelly, Dave. Filming Assassinations. LC 79-17783. 80p. 1979. 4.00 (ISBN 0-87886-106-8). Ithaca Hse.

Kelly, Delos, ed. Deviant Behavior: Readings in the Sociology of Deviance. LC 78-65242. 1979. pap. text ed. 12.95 (ISBN 0-312-19758-6). St Martin.

Kelly, Delos H., ed. Criminal Behavior: Readings in Criminology. 583p. 1980. text ed. 18.95 (ISBN 0-312-17211-7); pap. text ed. 12.95 (ISBN 0-312-17212-5). St Martin.

Kelly, Derek A. Documenting Computer Application Systems. (Illus.). 192p. 1983. 19.95 (ISBN 0-89433-206-6). Petrocelli.

Kelly, Dianne H., ed. see Allen, John.

Kelly, E. & Stone, P., eds. Computer Recognition of English Word Senses. (Linguistic Ser.: Vol. 13). 269p. 1975. pap. 32.00 (ISBN 0-444-10831-9, North-Holland). Elsevier.

Kelly, E., ed. see Winstanley, David.

Kelly, Edward, ed. see Defoe, Daniel.

Kelly, Eric P. The Trumpeter of Krakow. LC 66-16712. 288p. (gr. 5-9). 1973. pap. 3.95 (ISBN 0-02-044150-9, Collier). Macmillan.

Kelly, Errol G., jt. auth. see Spottiswood, David J.

Kelly, Eugene. Max Scheler. (World Leaders Ser.). 1977. lib. bdg. 13.95 (ISBN 0-8057-7707-5, Twayne). G K Hall.

Kelly, Eugene see Capaldi, Nicholas, et al.

Kelly, Eugene, jt. ed. see Navia, Luis E.

Kelly, Eugene W. Beyond Schooling: Education in a Broader Context. LC 82-60798. (Fastback Ser.: No. 177). 50p. 1982. pap. 0.75 (ISBN 0-87367-177-5). Phi Delta Kappa.

Kelly, Eugene W., Jr. Effective Interpersonal Communication: A Manual for Skill Development. 1977. pap. text ed. 8.00 (ISBN 0-8191-0125-7). U Pr of Amer.

Kelly, Everett L. & Fiske, Donald W. Prediction of Performance in Clinical Psychology. LC 69-10113. (Illus.). 1969. Repr. of 1951 ed. lib. bdg. 17.50x (ISBN 0-8371-0914-0, KECP). Greenwood.

Kelly, F. M. Shakespearian Costume. 2nd rev. ed. Mansfield, A., ed. LC 76-123629. (Illus.). 1970. 19.95 o.s.i. (ISBN 0-87830-117-8). Theatre Arts.

Kelly, F. P. Reversibility & Stochastic Networks. LC 79-40515. (Wiley Series in Probability & Mathematical Statistics). 230p. 1979. 61.95x (ISBN 0-471-27601-4, Pub. by Wiley-Interscience). Wiley.

Kelly, Fred C. George Ade: Warmhearted Satirist. LC 76-52441. (Illus.). 1977. Repr. of 1947 ed. lib. bdg. 20.75x (ISBN 0-8371-9443-1, KEGA). Greenwood.

Kelly, Gail P. & Elliot, Carolyn M., eds. Women's Education in the Third World: Comparative Perspectives. 356p. 1982. 39.50x (ISBN 0-87395-619-2); pap. 10.95x (ISBN 0-87395-620-6). State U NY Pr.

Kelly, Gary. Learning about Sex: The Contemporary Guide for Young Adults. 3rd ed. LC 77-7058. 1977. 10.95 (ISBN 0-8120-5171-8); pap. 4.95 (ISBN 0-8120-0890-1). Barron.

Kelly, Gary F. Good Sex: A Healthy Man's Guide to Sexual Fulfillment. LC 78-22257. 1979. 8.95 o.p. (ISBN 0-15-136685-3). HarBraceJ.

Kelly, George A. The Battle for the American Church. LC 77-12858. 1979. 14.95 o.p. (ISBN 0-385-13266-2). Doubleday.

--Idealism, Politics & History. LC 72-85721. (Studies in the History & Theory of Politics). 1969. 39.50 (ISBN 0-521-07510-6). Cambridge U Pr.

--Lost Soldiers: The French Army & Empire in Crises, 1947-1962. 1965. 20.00x o.p. (ISBN 0-262-11014-8). MIT Pr.

--The New Biblical Theorists: Raymond E. Brown & Beyond. 1983. write for info. (ISBN 0-89283-166-9). Servant.

--Theory of Personality: The Psychology of Personal Constructs. 1963. pap. 4.95 (ISBN 0-393-00152-0, Norton Lib). Norton.

Kelly, George W., jt. auth. see Friar, John G.

Kelly, Henry A. Canon Law & the Archpriest of Hita. 1983. write for info. (ISBN 0-86698-058-X). Medieval & Renaissance NY.

--Divine Providence in the England of Shakespeare's Histories. LC 75-111485. 1970. 18.50x (ISBN 0-674-21292-4). Harvard U Pr.

Kelly, Hugh J. Food Service Purchasing: Principles & Practice. new ed. LC 76-49750. 176p. 1976. 20.95 (ISBN 0-86730-213-5). Lebhar Friedman.

Kelly, J., jt. auth. see Horrigan, P.

Kelly, J. C., jt. auth. see Townsend, P. D.

Kelly, J. M., tr. see Kunkel, Wolfgang.

Kelly, J. Roland, et al. Business Mathematics. 1982. 20.95 (ISBN 0-395-30670-1); 1.25 (ISBN 0-395-30671-X). HM.

Kelly, J. W., jt. auth. see Davis, Raymond E.

Kelly, Jack. Unexpected Peace. LC 69-13266. 1968. 5.95 (ISBN 0-87645-019-2). Gambit.

--The Unexpected Peace. 240p. 1982. pap. 2.50 o.p. (ISBN 0-505-51849-X). Tower Bks.

--The Unexpected Peace. 240p. 1983. pap. 2.50 (ISBN 0-8439-2003-3, Leisure Bks). Dorchester Pub Co.

Kelly, Jain. Nude: Theory. LC 79-2427. (Illus.). 176p. 1979. 35.00 (ISBN 0-912810-24-6); pap. 19.95 (ISBN 0-912810-33-5). Lustrum Pr.

Kelly, Jain, ed. Darkroom Two. (Illus.). 1979. pap. 17.50 o.p. (ISBN 0-912810-21-1, Amphoto). Watson-Guptill.

Kelly, James C. & Baker, William C. The Sword of the Lord & Gideon. LC 80-15899. 1980. pap. 2.95 (ISBN 0-686-37452-5). Appalach Consortium.

Kelly, James J. The Sculptural Idea. 3rd ed. (Illus.). 219p. 1981. pap. text ed. 13.95x (ISBN 0-8087-1142-3). Burgess.

Kelly, James L., jt. auth. see Downey, John C.

Kelly, James L., ed. The Successful Teacher: Essays in Secondary School Instruction. 176p. 1982. pap. text ed. 6.95x (ISBN 0-8138-0196-6). Iowa St U Pr.

Kelly, Jeanne, tr. see Ch'ien Chung-shu.

Kelly, Jeffrey. Solving Your Child's Behavior Problems: An Everyday Guide for Parents. 224p. 1983. 15.45 (ISBN 0-316-48696-5); pap. 6.70 (ISBN 0-316-48695-7). Little.

Kelly, Jim. Flor de Estrella. span. ed. (Small Star Stories). (Illus.). 1975. 5.95 o.p. (ISBN 0-02-645730-X, 64573). Glencoe.

--El Hoyo Secreto. span. ed. (Small Star Stories). (Illus.). 1975. 5.95 o.p. (ISBN 0-02-645760-1, 64576). Glencoe.

--Little Neighbor. (Small Star Stories). (Illus.). 1975. 5.95 o.p. (ISBN 0-02-645480-7, 64548); cassette 6.95 o.p. (ISBN 0-02-645490-4, 64549). Glencoe.

--Neighbors. (Small Star Stories). (Illus.). 5.95 o.p. (ISBN 0-02-645450-5, 64545); cassette 6.95 o.p. (ISBN 0-02-645460-2, 64546). Glencoe.

--El Pequeno Vencinito. span. ed. (Small Star Stories). (Illus.). 1975. 5.95 o.p. (ISBN 0-02-645500-5, 64550). Glencoe.

--The Secret Hole. (Small Star Stories). (Illus.). 1975. 5.95 o.p. (ISBN 0-02-645740-7, 64574); cassette 6.95 o.p. (ISBN 0-02-645750-4, 64575). Glencoe.

--Star Flower. (Small Star Stories). (Illus.). 1975. 5.95 o.p. (ISBN 0-02-645710-5, 64571); cassette 6.95 o.p. (ISBN 0-02-645720-2, 64572). Glencoe.

--Wads' & Gina's Songbook. (Small Star Stories). (Illus.). 1975. 3.96 o.p. (ISBN 0-02-645790-3, 64579). Glencoe.

Kelly, Joan & Chamberlain, Valerie. Survival: A Guide to Living on Your Own. (Illus.). 1980. text ed. 17.24 (ISBN 0-07-033870-1, G); tchrs. ed. 5.76 (ISBN 0-07-033871-X). McGraw.

Kelly, Joan, jt. auth. see Chamberlain, Valerie.

Kelly, Joan, jt. auth. see Chamberlain, Valerie M.

Kelly, Joan B., jt. auth. see Wallerstein, Judith S.

Kelly, John. Successful Glamour Photography. (Illus.). 176p. 1981. 25.00 (ISBN 0-87165-117-3, Amphoto). Watson-Guptill.

Kelly, John & McConnell, Jeff. The CIA in America. LC 78-24776. 256p. 1983. 16.95 (ISBN 0-88208-102-0); pap. 9.95 (ISBN 0-88208-103-9). Lawrence Hill.

Kelly, John, jt. auth. see Verny, Thomas.

Kelly, John, jt. auth. see Steer, Charles.

Kelly, John C. Discovery Learning in Trigonometry. (A Software Microcomputer Program Ser.). 1982. student guide scp 5.95 (ISBN 0-06-043626-3, HarpC); complete package scp 75.00 (ISBN 0-06-043625-5). Har-Row.

Kelly, John D., jt. auth. see Resenberg, Richard.

Kelly, John R. Leisure: An Introduction. (Illus.). 450p. 1982. 20.95 (ISBN 0-13-530055-X). P-H.

--Pedro Prado. (World Authors Ser.). 1974. lib. bdg. 15.95 (ISBN 0-8057-2712-4, Twayne). G K Hall.

Kelly, John W., tr. see Wells, Roger, Jr.

Kelly, Joyce. The Complete Visitor's Guide to Mesoamerican Ruins. (Illus.). 480p. 1981. 39.95 (ISBN 0-8061-1566-1). U of Okla Pr.

Kelly, K. B. Grains of Wheat. (Illus.). 128p. (Orig.). 1981. pap. 2.50 (ISBN 0-914544-32-2). Living Flame Pr.

Kelly, Karin. Careers with the Circus. LC 74-11902. (Early Career Bks.). (Illus.). 36p. (gr. 2-5). 1975. PLB 5.95g (ISBN 0-8225-0326-3). Lerner Pubns.

--Carpentry. LC 72-13342. (Early Craft Bks). (Illus.). 32p. (gr. 1-4). 1974. PLB 3.95g (ISBN 0-8225-0857-5). Lerner Pubns.

--Doll Houses. LC 72-13338. (Early Craft Bks). (Illus.). 32p. (gr. 1-4). 1974. PLB 3.95g (ISBN 0-8225-0854-0). Lerner Pubns.

--Let's Bake Cookies! LC 74-33530. (Early Craft Bks). (Illus.). 32p. (gr. 1-4). 1975. PLB 3.95g (ISBN 0-8225-0873-7). Lerner Pubns.

--Let's Make Sandwiches! LC 76-12063. (Early Craft Books). (Illus.). (gr. k-3). 1977. PLB 3.95g (ISBN 0-8225-0884-2). Lerner Pubns.

--Soup's On. LC 73-7663. (Early Craft Bks). (Illus.). 32p. (gr. 1-4). 1974. PLB 3.95g (ISBN 0-8225-0863-X). Lerner Pubns.

--Weaving. LC 72-13336. (Early Crafts Bks.). (Illus.). 36p. (gr. 1-4). 1973. PLB 3.95g (ISBN 0-8225-0861-3). Lerner Pubns.

Kelly, Kate. How to Set Your Fees & Get Them. 79p. 1982. pap. 15.00 (ISBN 0-9603740-2-7). Visibility Ent.

Kelly, Kathryn, jt. auth. see Byrne, Donn.

Kelly, L. G. The True Interpreter: A History of Translation Theory & Practice in the West. LC 79-4179. 1979. 36.00x (ISBN 0-312-82057-7). St Martin.

Kelly, L. G., tr. Quastiones Alberti de Modis Significandi: Psuedo-Albertus Magnus. (Studies in the History of Linguistics Ser.). xxxvii, 191p. 1977. 30.00 (ISBN 0-686-37787-7, 15). Benjamins North Am.

Kelly, Laurence, intro. by. St. Petersburg: A Traveller's Companion. LC 82-20575. (Illus.). 304p. (Orig.). 1983. pap. 7.95 (ISBN 0-689-70645-6, 294). Atheneum.

Kelly, Leo P. Luke Sutton: Avenger. LC 82-455560. (D. D. Western Ser.). 192p. 1983. 11.95 (ISBN 0-385-18396-8). Doubleday.

Kelly, Lori D. The Life & Works of Elizabeth Stuart Phelps: Victorian Feminist Writer. 120p. 1983. 15.00 (ISBN 0-686-97440-9). Whitston Pub.

Kelly, Lou. From Dialogue to Discourse: An Open Approach to Competence & Creativity. 371p. 1972. pap. 8.95x (ISBN 0-673-07821-3). Scott F.

Kelly, Louis G. Twenty Five Centuries of Language Teaching. 1969. pap. 12.95 (ISBN 0-912066-00-8). Newbury Hse.

Kelly, Lucie Y. Dimensions of Professional Nursing. 4th ed. (Illus.). 1981. text ed. 24.95x (ISBN 0-02-362270-9). Macmillan.

Kelly, Marion, jt. auth. see Devaney, Dennis M.

Kelly, Mary. Post-Partum Document. (Illus.). 172p. (Orig.). 1983. pap. price not set (ISBN 0-7100-9495-7). Routledge & Kegan.

--The Spoilt Kill. LC 81-47812. 240p. 1982. pap. 2.40i (ISBN 0-06-080565-X, P 565, PL). Har-Row.

Kelly, Mary P., jt. auth. see Cepeda, Orlando.

Kelly, Matthew A., ed. see Kheel, Theodore W., et al.

Kelly, Michael. Reminiscences of Michael Kelly of the King's Theatre & Theatre Royal Drury Lane 2 Vols. 2nd ed. LC 68-16243. (Music Ser). 1968. Repr. of 1826 ed. Set. lib. bdg. 55.00 (ISBN 0-306-71094-3). Da Capo.

Kelly, O., jt. auth. see Saffer, T. H.

Kelly, Orly, ed. see Berry, Joy W.

Kelly, Orly, et al, eds. see Berry, Joy W.

Kelly, Orville & Murray, W. Cotter. Make Today Count. 1975. 8.95 o.s.i. (ISBN 0-440-05256-4); pap. 4.95 o.s.i. (ISBN 0-440-05257-2). Delacorte.

Kelly, Orville E. Until Tomorrow Comes. LC 78-74582. 1979. 9.95 o.p. (ISBN 0-89696-031-5, An Everest House Book). Dodd.

Kelly, Orville E., jt. auth. see Saffer, Thomas H.

Kelly, P. H., ed. William Molyneux of Dublin: 1656-1698. Simms, J. G. (Illus.). 176p. Date not set. 25.00x (ISBN 0-7165-0096-5, Pub. by Irish Academic Pr Ireland). Biblio Dist. Postponed.

Kelly, Patrick. Irish Family Names. LC 68-26580. 1975. Repr. of 1939 ed. 40.00x (ISBN 0-8103-4146-8). Gale.

Kelly, Paul J. & Weiss, Max L. Geometry & Convexity: A Study in Mathematical Methods. LC 78-21919. (Pure & Applied Mathematics: Texts, Monographs & Tracts). 261p. 1979. 39.95x (ISBN 0-471-04637-X, Pub. by Wiley-Interscience). Wiley.

Kelly, Phil. The Elderly: A Guide for Counselors. 1.25 (ISBN 0-89486-122-0). Hazelden.

Kelly, R. Gordon. Mother Was a Lady. LC 72-5451. (Illus.). 233p. 1974. lib. bdg. 25.00 (ISBN 0-8371-6451-6, KEM/). Greenwood.

Kelly, Reaney J., jt. auth. see Andrews, Lewis R.

Kelly, Richard. George DuMaurier. (English Authors Ser.). 200p. 1983. lib. bdg. 16.95 (ISBN 0-8057-6841-6, Twayne). G K Hall.

--Lewis Carroll. (English Authors Ser.). 1977. lib. bdg. 11.95 (ISBN 0-8057-6681-2, Twayne). G K Hall.

Kelly, Richard M. Douglas Jerrold. (English Authors Ser.). lib. bdg. 14.95 (ISBN 0-8057-1292-5, Twayne). G K Hall.

Kelly, Robert. Micro-Model Railways. (Illus.). 96p. 1982. 14.95 (ISBN 0-7153-8326-4). David & Charles.

Kelly, Rosalie. The Great Toozy Takeover. LC 74-21084. (Illus.). 128p. (gr. 6 up). 1975. 5.95 o.p. (ISBN 0-399-20452-0). Putnam Pub Group.

Kelly, Sally Jolly see Jolly, Erin, pseud.

Kelly, Sean, jt. auth. see Hendra, Tony.

Kelly, T., ed. see Winstanley, David.

Kelly, Thomas. Reality of the Spiritual World. LC 76-9644. (Orig.). 1942. pap. 1.50x (ISBN 0-87574-021-9). Pendle Hill.

Kelly, Thomas R. Testament of Devotion. 1941. 9.95i (ISBN 0-06-064370-6, HarpR). Har-Row.

Kelly, Tim. Don't Rock the Boat. 1983. pap. 2.50 (ISBN 0-686-38377-X). Eldridge Pub.

--Lost in Space & the Mortgage Due. 1979. pap. 2.50 (ISBN 0-686-38382-6). Eldridge Pub.

Kelly, Tom. The Imperial Post: The Meyers, the Grahams & the Paper that Rules Washington. (Illus.). 304p. 1983. 14.95 (ISBN 0-688-01919-6). Morrow.

Kelly, W. Christ Tempted & Sympathizing. 2.95 (ISBN 0-88172-091-7). Believers Bkshelf.

--Collections of Selected Pamphlets. pap. text ed. 5.50 (ISBN 0-88172-093-3). Believers Bkshelf.

--Exposition of the Epistles of John. 5.25 (ISBN 0-88172-100-X). Believers Bkshelf.

--Exposition of the Gospel of Luke. 5.25 (ISBN 0-88172-102-6). Believers Bkshelf.

--Exposition of the Gospel of Mark. 4.50 (ISBN 0-88172-103-4). Believers Bkshelf.

--Introductory Lecture Series, 4 vols. 5.50 ea. o.p. Believers Bkshelf.

--Lectures on the Church of God. 4.75 (ISBN 0-88172-092-5). Believers Bkshelf.

--Lectures on the Doctrine of the Holy Spirit. 5.25 (ISBN 0-88172-095-X). Believers Bkshelf.

--Lectures on the Epistle of Jude. 6.95 (ISBN 0-88172-101-8). Believers Bkshelf.

--Lectures on the Gospel of Matthew. 5.50 (ISBN 0-88172-104-2). Believers Bkshelf.

--Notes on Romans. 6.25 (ISBN 0-88172-107-7). Believers Bkshelf.

--Notes on 1 Corinthians. 7.25 (ISBN 0-88172-094-1). Believers Bkshelf.

--Preaching to the Spirits in Prison. pap. 3.75 (ISBN 0-88172-105-0). Believers Bkshelf.

--Revelation Expounded. 4.50 (ISBN 0-88172-106-9). Believers Bkshelf.

--Three Prophetic Gems. 5.50 (ISBN 0-88172-109-3). Believers Bkshelf.

--Titus & Philemon. 4.75 (ISBN 0-88172-110-7). Believers Bkshelf.

Kelly, Walt. Gone Pogo. 1977. Repr. lib. bdg. 9.95 o.p. (ISBN 0-8398-2391-6, Gregg). G K Hall.

--I Go Pogo. 1977. Repr. lib. bdg. 9.95 o.p. (ISBN 0-8398-2384-3, Gregg). G K Hall.

--The Incompleat Pogo. 1977. Repr. lib. bdg. 9.95 (ISBN 0-8398-2387-8, Gregg). G K Hall.

--Pogo. 1977. Repr. lib. bdg. 9.95 (ISBN 0-8398-2383-5, Gregg). G K Hall.

--Pogo a la Sundae. 1977. Repr. lib. bdg. 9.95 o.p. (ISBN 0-8398-2392-4, Gregg). G K Hall.

--The Pogo Papers. 1977. Repr. lib. bdg. 9.95 o.p. (ISBN 0-8398-2386-X, Gregg). G K Hall.

--The Pogo Peek-a-Book. 1977. Repr. lib. bdg. 9.95 o.p. (ISBN 0-8398-2389-4, Gregg). G K hall.

--Pogo Series. 1977. 85.00 o.p. (ISBN 0-686-74239-7, Gregg). G K Hall.

--The Pogo Stepmother Goose. 1977. Repr. lib. bdg. 9.95 o.p. (ISBN 0-8398-2390-8, Gregg). G K Hall.

--Potluck Pogo. 1977. lib. bdg. 9.95 o.p. (ISBN 0-8398-2385-1, Gregg). G K Hall.

--Uncle Pogo So-So Stories. 1977. Repr. lib. bdg. 9.95 o.p. (ISBN 0-8398-2388-6, Gregg). G K Hall.

Kelly, Walter K. Curiosities of Indo-European Tradition & Folk-Lore. LC 68-22032. 1969. Repr. of 1863 ed. 34.00x (ISBN 0-8103-3837-8). Gale.

Kelly, William. The Acts, Catholic Epistles & Revelation. (Introductory Lecture Ser.). 580p. 5.50 (ISBN 0-88172-096-8). Believers Bkshelf.
--An Exposition of the Book of Isaiah. 1979. 15.25 (ISBN 0-86524-003-5, 2301). Klock & Klock.
--The Gospel of Luke. 1981. 18.50 (ISBN 0-86524-046-9, 4201). Klock & Klock.
--The Gospels. (Introductory Lecture Ser.). 567p. 5.50 (ISBN 0-88172-097-6). Believers Bkshelf.
--The Pauline Epistles. (Introductory Lecture Ser.). 551p. 5.50 (ISBN 0-88172-098-4). Believers Bkshelf.
--The Pentateuch. (Introductory Lecture Ser.). 524p. 5.50 (ISBN 0-88172-099-2). Believers Bkshelf.
--The Second Coming. 375p. 5.25 (ISBN 0-88172-108-5). Believers Bkshelf.

Kelly, William A., Jr. Macroeconomics. (Illus.). 496p. 1981. text ed. 23.95 (ISBN 0-13-542761-4). P-H.

Kelly, William C., jt. auth. see Thompson, Homer C.

Kelly-Jones, Nancy & Hamilton, Harley. Signs Everywhere: A Collection of Signs for Towns, Cities, States, & Provinces in the United States, Canada, & Mexico. LC 81-80388. (Illus.). 280p. (Orig.). pap. 12.00 (ISBN 0-916708-05-5). Modern Signs.

Kelman, Alistair & Sizer, Richard. The Computer in Court. 104p. 1982. text ed. 33.50x (ISBN 0-566-03419-0). Gower Pub Ltd.

Kelman, Barbara & Mall, Jeanette, eds. Keeping Warm. (Illus.). 1978. 12.95 o.p. (ISBN 0-8256-3082-7, Quick Fox); pap. 7.95 o.p. (ISBN 0-8256-3079-7). Putnam Pub Group.

Kelman, Charles D. Cataracts: What You Must Know about Them. 96p. 1982. 9.95 (ISBN 0-517-54850-X). Crown.

Kelman, Harold, ed. see Horney, Karen.

Kelman, Peter & Key, Newton E., eds. Classroom Computer News Directory of Educational Computing Resources, 1983. (Illus.). 160p. (Orig.). 1982. pap. 14.95 (ISBN 0-9607970-0-9). Intentional Ed.

Kelman, Steven. Push Comes to Shove: The Escalation of Student Protest. 287p. pap. 2.95 o.p. (ISBN 0-686-95048-8). ADL.
--Regulating America, Regulating Sweden: A Comparative Study of Occupational Safety & Health Policy. 280p. 1981. text ed. 22.50x (ISBN 0-262-11076-8). MIT Pr.

Kelman, Stuart. Prayer Transparencies. 32p. (Orig.). 1982. 29.95x (ISBN 0-686-81835-0). Arbit.

Kelsall, Charles. Horae Viaticae. LC 79-18052. 1979. Repr. of 1839 ed. 53.00x (ISBN 0-8201-1333-6). Schol Facsimiles.

Kelsen, Hans. Peace Through Law. LC 76-147757. (Library of War & Peace; International Law). lib. bdg. 38.00 o.s.i. (ISBN 0-8240-0492-2). Garland Pub.
--Pure Theory of Law. Knight, Max, tr. from Ger. LC 67-10234. (Library Reprint Ser.: Vol. 94). 1978. pap. text ed. 37.50x (ISBN 0-520-03692-1). U of Cal Pr.
--What Is Justice? & Justice, Law, & Politics in the Mirror of Science. (California Library Reprint Series: No. 20). 1971. 37.50x (ISBN 0-520-01925-3). U of Cal Pr.

Kelsey, Benjamin S. The Dragon's Teeth: The Creation of United States Air Power for World War II. (Illus.). 148p. 1982. 15.00 (ISBN 0-87474-574-8). Smithsonian.

Kelsey, Charles A. Radiation Safety for Laboratory Technicians. Gardner, Alvin F., ed. (Allied Health Professions Monographs). 1983. write for info. (ISBN 0-87527-319-X). Green.

Kelsey, Gladys H. The Baroque: A Lifestyle. 1978. 6.95 o.p. (ISBN 0-533-03250-4). Vantage.

Kelsey, H. W. The Needle Match. 192p. 1982. 15.95 (ISBN 0-571-11872-0). Faber & Faber.

Kelsey, Hugh. Instant Guide to Bridge. 1975. pap. 6.95 (ISBN 0-575-02638-3, Pub. by Gollancz England). David & Charles.
--Start Bridge the Easy Way. (Master Bridge Ser.). 96p. 1983. pap. 8.95 (ISBN 0-575-03254-5, Pub. by Gollancz England). David & Charles.
--Test Your Card Reading. (Master Bridge Ser.). (Illus.). 80p. 1982. pap. 6.95 (ISBN 0-575-03170-0, Pub. by Gollancz England). David & Charles.
--Test Your Communications. (Master Bridge Ser.). (Illus.). 80p. 1982. pap. 6.95 (ISBN 0-575-03171-9, Pub. by Gollancz England). David & Charles.
--Winning Card Play. 1979. pap. 13.95 (ISBN 0-575-02609-X, Pub. by Gollancz England). David & Charles.

Kelsey, Hugh & Glauert, Michael. Bridge Odds for Practical Players. 1980. pap. 9.50 (ISBN 0-575-02799-1, Pub. by Gollancz England). David & Charles.

Kelsey, Hugh & Matheson, John. Improve Your Opening Leads. 1979. pap. 8.50 (ISBN 0-575-02657-X, Pub. by Gollancz England). David & Charles.

Kelsey, Jennifer L. Epidemiology of Musculoskeletal Disorders. (Monographs in Epidemiology & Biostatistics). (Illus.). 1982. text ed. 35.00x (ISBN 0-19-503117-2). Oxford U Pr.

Kelsey, Michael R. Utah Mountaineering Guide & Including the Best Canyon Hikes. (Illus.). 162p. (Orig.). 1983. pap. 9.95 (ISBN 0-9605824-1-X). Kelsey Pub.

Kelsey, Morton. Christo-Psychology. 212p. 1982. 12.95 (ISBN 0-8245-0506-9). Crossroad NY.
--Encounter with God: A Theology of Christian Experience. 304p. 1972. pap. 7.95 (ISBN 0-87123-123-9, 210123); study guide 1.25 (ISBN 0-87123-506-4, 210506). Bethany Hse.

Kelsey, Morton T. Companions on the Inner Way: The Art of Spiritual Guidance. 250p. 1983. 17.50 (ISBN 0-8245-0585-9); pap. 8.95 (ISBN 0-8245-0560-3). Crossroad NY.

Kelsey, Morton T., intro. by see Israel, Martin.

Kelsey, W. Michael. Konjaku Monogatari-Shu. (World Authors Ser.). 1982. lib. bdg. 18.95 (ISBN 0-8057-6463-1, Twayne). G K Hall.

Kelso, J. A., ed. Human Motor Behavior: An Introduction. (Illus.). 320p. 1982. text ed. 24.95 (ISBN 0-89859-188-0). L Erlbaum Assocs.

Kelso, James L. The Excavation of Bethel,1934-1960. (American Schools of Oriental Research Ser.: Vol. 39). 128p. 1968. text ed. 6.00x (ISBN 0-89757-039-1, Am Sch Orient Res). Eisenbrauns.

Kelso, James L. & Baramki, Dimitri. Excavations at New Testament Jericho & Khirbet en-Nitla. (American Schools of Oriental Research. Ser.: Vols. 29 & 30). 60p. 1955. text ed. 10.00x (ISBN 0-89757-030-8, Am Sch Orient Res). Eisenbrauns.

Kelso, Robert W. History of Public Poor Relief in Massachusetts: 1620-1920. LC 69-14936. (Criminology, Law Enforcement, & Social Problems Ser.: No. 31). 1969. Repr. of 1922 ed. 10.00x (ISBN 0-87585-031-6). Patterson Smith.

Kelso, William A. American Democratic Theory: Pluralism & Its Critics. LC 77-83894. (Contributions in Political Science Ser.: No.1). 1978. lib. bdg. 27.50 (ISBN 0-8371-9825-9, KAD/). Greenwood.

Kelson, Allen H. & Spiselman, Anne. Chicago Magazine's Guide to Chicago. (Illus.). 416p. (Orig.). 1983. pap. 8.95 (ISBN 0-8092-5893-5). Contemp Bks.

Keltner, Autumn & Howard, Leann. Basic English for Adult Competency. 112p. 1983. pap. text ed. 4.95 (ISBN 0-13-060418-6). P-H.
--Basic English for Adult Competency: Teacher's Edition. 112p. 1983. pap. text ed. 10.95 (ISBN 0-13-060426-7). P-H.

Keltner, Chester W. How to Make Money in Commodities. 1960. 12.50 o.p. (ISBN 0-686-00670-4). Keltner.

Keltner, John W. Elements of Interpersonal Communication. 1973. pap. 12.95x (ISBN 0-534-00290-0). Wadsworth Pub.
--Group Discussion Processes. LC 74-6112. (Illus.). 373p. 1974. Repr. of 1957 ed. lib. bdg. 20.00x (ISBN 0-8371-7493-7). Greenwood.

Kelton, David, jt. auth. see Law, Averill M.

Kelton, Elmer. Horsehead Crossing. 144p. 1982. pap. 1.95 (ISBN 0-553-20845-4). Bantam.
--Wagontongue. 1982. pap. 1.95 (ISBN 0-553-22525-1). Bantam.
--The Wolf & the Buffalo. 384p. 1982. pap. 2.95 (ISBN 0-553-22659-2). Bantam.

Kelty, Jean McClure. If You Have a Duck. (Illus.). 104p. 1982. write for info. G Whittell Mem.

Kelty, Matthew. Flute Solo: Reflections of a Trappist Hermit. LC 80-918. 128p. 1980. pap. 3.50 o.p. (ISBN 0-385-17173-0, Im). Doubleday.

Kelvin, Norman, jt. auth. see Gross, Theodore.

Kelz, Rochelle. Conversational Spanish for Medical Personnel. LC 76-55722. 322p. 1977. pap. text ed. 15.95 o.p. (ISBN 0-471-02154-7, Pub. by Wiley Medical). Wiley.

Kelz, Rochelle K. Conversational Spanish for Medical Personnel. 2nd ed. 550p. 1982. 16.95 (ISBN 0-471-09240-1, Pub. by Wiley Med). Wiley.

Kemal, Hashar. The Undying Grass. 1978. 10.95 o.p. (ISBN 0-688-03306-7). Morrow.

Kember, N. F. Introduction to Computer Applications in Medicine. 176p. 1982. pap. text ed. 17.95 (ISBN 0-7131-4414-9). E Arnold.

Kemble, C. Robert. The Image of the Army Officer in America. LC 72-814. (Contributions in Military History: No. 5). 289p. 1973. lib. bdg. 29.95 (ISBN 0-8371-6383-8, KAO/). Greenwood.

Kemble, John Haskell. The Panama Route. LC 79-139195. (The American Scene Ser). (Illus.). 316p. 1972. Repr. of 1943 ed. lib. bdg. 37.50 (ISBN 0-306-70083-2). Da Capo.

Kemble, Stephen. The Kemble Papers: Collections 1883, 1884, 2 vols. LC 1-13394. (New York Historical Society Collections Ser.). Set. 20.00x o.p. (ISBN 0-685-73904-X). U Pr of Va.

Kemelman, Harry. Friday the Rabbi Slept Late. 1964. 4.95 o.p. (ISBN 0-517-50691-2). Crown.
--Monday the Rabbi Took off. 288p. 1972. 5.95 o.p. (ISBN 0-399-10550-6). Putnam Pub Group.
--Thursday the Rabbi Walked Out. 1979. lib. bdg. 13.95 o.p. (ISBN 0-8161-6663-3, Large Print Bks). G K Hall.

Kemenes, I., tr. see Gombos, Karoly.

Kemenka, Eugene & Tay, Alice E. Justice. LC 79-22174. 1980. 19.95x (ISBN 0-312-44945-3). St Martin.

Kemeny, Gabor. Hungarista: Ways of Hungarian Foreign Politics. 40p. pap. 3.50 (ISBN 0-935484-07-8). Universe Pub Co.

Kemeny, John & Snell, J. Laurie. Mathematical Models in the Social Sciences. 1972. pap. 6.95x (ISBN 0-262-61030-2). MIT Pr.

Kemeny, John G. Philosopher Looks at Science. (Illus.). 1959. pap. text ed. 7.95 (ISBN 0-442-04324-4). Van Nos Reinhold.

Kemeny, John G. & Kurtz, Thomas E. Basic Programming. 3rd ed. LC 79-20683. 334p. 1980. pap. text ed. 19.95x (ISBN 0-471-01863-5); solutions manual 7.95 (ISBN 0-471-07830-1). Wiley.

Kemeny, John G., et al. Finite Mathematics with Business Applications. 2nd ed. (Quantitative Analysis for Business Ser). 1972. ref. ed. 23.95 (ISBN 0-13-317321-6). P-H.
--Introduction to Finite Mathematics. 3rd ed. 512p. 1974. ref. ed. 25.95 (ISBN 0-13-483834-3); answers 1.00 (ISBN 0-13-468835-X). P-H.

Kemerer, Frank R. Understanding Faculty Unions & Collective Bargaining. 1976. pap. 6.50 o.p. (ISBN 0-934338-32-9). NAIS.

Kemme, Douglas H., jt. auth. see Conte, Sylvester B.

Kemmer, N. Vector Analysis. LC 75-36025. (Illus.). 230p. 1977. 53.50 (ISBN 0-521-21158-1); pap. 16.95x (ISBN 0-521-29064-3). Cambridge U Pr.

Kemmer, Rick. A Guide to Paddle Adventure: How to Buy Canoes & Kayaks & Where to Travel. LC 75-386. 384p. 1975. 10.00 o.s.i. (ISBN 0-8149-0760-1); pap. 6.95 o.p. (ISBN 0-685-52406-X). Vanguard.

Kemmerer, Richard A. Formal Verification of an Operating Systems Security Kernel. Stone, Harold, ed. LC 82-4805. (Computer Science: Systems Programming Ser.: No. 2). 332p. 1982. 49.95 (ISBN 0-8357-1322-9, Pub. by UMI Res Pr). Univ Microfilms.

Kemmerly, Jack, jt. auth. see Hayt, William.

Kemp, Anthony. The Maginot Line: Myth & Reality. LC 80-6260. (Illus.). 128p. 1982. 15.95 (ISBN 0-8128-2811-9). Stein & Day.

Kemp, Anthony & Haythornthwaite, Philip. Weapons & Equipment Series, 3 vols. (Illus.). 525p. 1982. boxed set 50.00 (ISBN 0-7137-1296-1, Pub. by Blandford Pr England). Sterling.

Kemp, C. Gratton. Perspectives on the Group Process: A Foundation for Counseling with Groups. 2nd ed. LC 64-346. 1970. text ed. 24.50 (ISBN 0-395-04723-4). HM.

Kemp, Daniel S. & Vellaccio, Frank. Organic Chemistry. 1980. 32.95 (ISBN 0-87901-123-8); wkbk. & solutions manual 15.95 (ISBN 0-87901-124-6). Worth.

Kemp, Edward C. Manuscript Solicitation for Libraries, Special Collections, Museums & Archives. LC 77-29015. 204p. 1978. lib. bdg. 20.00 (ISBN 0-87287-183-5). Libs Unl.

Kemp, Fred & Buttle, Bernard. Looking Ahead: A Guide to Retirement. 128p. 1981. 19.00x (ISBN 0-7121-1250-2, Pub. by Macdonald & Evans). State Mutual Bk.

Kemp, Gene. The Clock Tower Ghost. (Illus.). 96p. (gr. 4-9). 1981. 9.95 (ISBN 0-571-11767-8). Faber & Faber.

Kemp, J. F. & Young, P. Business Notes for Shipmasters. 4th ed. (Kemp & Young Ser.). 130p. 1980. pap. 9.95x (ISBN 0-540-07346-6). Sheridan.
--Electricity & General Magnetism. 2nd ed. (Kemp & Young Ser.). 142p. 1971. pap. 9.95x (ISBN 0-540-00366-2). Sheridan.
--Notes on Cargo Work. 5th ed. (Kemp & Young Ser.). (Illus.). 112p. (Orig.). 1983. pap. text ed. 9.95x (ISBN 0-540-07356-3). Sheridan.
--Notes on Compass Work. (Kemp & Young Ser.). 112p. 1972. pap. 9.95x (ISBN 0-540-00362-X). Sheridan.
--Notes on Meteorology. 3rd ed. (Young & Kemp Ser.). 88p. 1971. pap. 9.95x (ISBN 0-540-00369-7). Sheridan.
--Seamanship Notes. 3rd ed. (Kemp & Young Ser.). 104p. 1977. pap. 9.95x (ISBN 0-540-07331-8). Sheridan.
--Ship Construction: Sketches & Notes. 3rd ed. (Kemp & Young Ser.). 136p. 1977. pap. 9.95x (ISBN 0-540-00360-3). Sheridan.
--Ship Stability: Notes & Examples. 2nd ed. (Kemp & Young Ser.). 132p. 1971. pap. 9.95x (ISBN 0-540-00361-1). Sheridan.

Kemp, Jack. American Renaissance: A Strategy for the Nineteen Eighties. LC 78-19825. 1979. 11.49i (ISBN 0-06-012283-8, HarpT). Har-Row.

Kemp, Jerrold E. Determining the Plus & Minus Outcomes of Innovation in Nursing Education. 47p. 1977. 4.50 (ISBN 0-686-38261-7, 23-1682). Natl League Nurse.
--Planning & Producing Audiovisual Materials. 4th ed. (Illus.). 304p. 1980. text ed. 24.50 scp (ISBN 0-06-043587-9, HarpC). Har-Row.

Kemp, Lysander, tr. see Dario, Ruben.

Kemp, Lysander, tr. see Fuentes, Carlos.

Kemp, Lysander, tr. see Paz, Octavio.

Kemp, Lysander, tr. see Pozas, Ricardo.

Kemp, Lysander, tr. see Rulfo, Juan.

Kemp, Lysander, tr. see Vargas Llosa, Mario.

Kemp, M. C. Three Topics in the Theory of International Trade. (Studies in International Economics: Vol. 2). 1976. text ed. 51.00 (ISBN 0-444-10967-6, North-Holland); pap. text ed. 32.00 (ISBN 0-444-11083-6). Elsevier.

Kemp, Murray, ed. Production Sets. (Economic Theory, Econometrics & Mathematical Economics Ser.). 158p. 1982. 32.00 (ISBN 0-12-404140-X). Acad Pr.

Kemp, P. True Book About Royal Navy. (Illus.). (gr. 7 up). 12.75x (ISBN 0-392-05168-0, LTB). Sportshelf.

Kemp, P. J. Care of the World: Poems. (Illus.). 12p. 1981. pap. 1.00 o.p. (ISBN 0-686-30665-1). Samisdat.
--Elemental Connection. 12p. 1982. pap. 1.00 (ISBN 0-686-37936-5). Samisdat.

Kemp, Peter. H. G. Wells & the Culminating Ape: Biological Themes & Imaginative Obsessions. LC 81-13598. 240p. 1982. 22.50x (ISBN 0-312-35592-0). St Martin.

Kemp, R. Pascal for Students. 256p. 1982. pap. text ed. 14.95 (ISBN 0-7131-3447-X). E Arnold.

Kemp, Raymond. A Journey in Faith. pap. 4.95 (ISBN 0-8215-9329-3). Sadlier.

Kemp, Robert. A History of the Old Folks' Concerts. (Music Reprint Ser.). 254p. 1982. Repr. of 1868 ed. lib. bdg. 27.50 (ISBN 0-306-76174-2). Da Capo.

Kemp, Roger. Cell Division & Heredity. 1971. text ed. 14.95 o.p. (ISBN 0-312-12635-2). St Martin.
--Cell Division & Heredity. (Studies in Biology: No. 21). 64p. 1970. pap. text ed. 8.95 (ISBN 0-7131-2282-X). E Arnold.

Kemp, Roger L. Coping with Proposition Thirteen. LC 80-8188. 256p. 1980. 23.95x (ISBN 0-669-03974-8). Lexington Bks.

Kemp, T. J., jt. auth. see Cox, A.

Kemp, T. S., ed. Mammal-Like Reptiles & the Origins of Mammals. 384p. 1982. 44.50 (ISBN 0-12-404120-5). Acad Pr.

Kemp, Thomas J., ed. Connecticut Researchers Handbook. (Genealogy & Local History Ser.: Vol. 12). 350p. 1982. 42.00x (ISBN 0-686-72830-0). Gale.

Kemp, Tom. The French Economy: Nineteen-Thirteen to Nineteen Thirty-Nine. LC 79-189810. 176p. 1972. 22.50 (ISBN 0-312-30450-1). St Martin.
--Industrialisation of the Non Western World. 206p. (Orig.). 1983. pap. text ed. 11.95 (ISBN 0-582-49234-3). Longman.

Kempczinski & Yao. Practical Noninvasive Vascular Diagnosis. 1982. 42.95 (ISBN 0-8151-5012-1). Year Bk Med.

Kempe, C. H., et al, eds. see International Congress on Child Abuse & Neglect, 2nd, London, 1978.

Kempe, C. Henry & Helfer, Ray E. The Battered Child. 3rd rev. enl. ed. LC 80-14329. (Illus.). xviii, 440p. 1982. pap. 14.00 (ISBN 0-226-43039-1). U of Chicago Pr.
--The Battered Child. 3rd rev. ed. LC 80-14329. (Illus.). 1980. 27.50 (ISBN 0-226-43038-3). U of Chicago Pr.

Kempe, C. Henry, jt. ed. see Helfer, Ray E.

Kempe, L. G. Operative Neurosurgery, 2 vols. Incl. Vol. 1. Cranial, Cerebral & Intracranial Vascular Disease. (Illus.). xiii, 269p. 1968. 129.80 (ISBN 0-387-04208-3); Vol. 2. Posterior Fossa, Spinal Cord & Peripheral Nerve Disease. (Illus.). viii, 281p. 1970. 115.00 (ISBN 0-387-04890-1). Springer-Verlag.

Kemper, A. Chemistry Experiments. (Science Experiments Ser). (Illus.). 1965. 17.50x o.p. (ISBN 0-222-69371-1). Intl Pubns Serv.

Kemper, A. M. Architectural Handbook: Environmental Analysis, Architectural Programming, Design & Technology, & Construction. 591p. 1979. 59.95x (ISBN 0-471-02697-2). Wiley.

Kemper, Alfred M. Drawings by American Architects. LC 72-13428. 613p. 1973. 68.95 (ISBN 0-471-46845-2, Pub. by Wiley-Interscience). Wiley.
--Presentation Drawings by American Architects. LC 76-40891. 380p. 1977. 51.50x (ISBN 0-471-01369-2, Pub. by Wiley-Interscience). Wiley.

Kemper, J., jt. auth. see Ostrowski, R.

Kemper, Peter, jt. auth. see Quigley, John M.

Kemper, R. W. The Pentecost Cycle. LC 12-2965. 1982. pap. 7.95 (ISBN 0-570-03872-3). Concordia.

Kemper, Rachel H. Costume. Berger, Kathleen & Bayrd, Ned, eds. LC 77-78799. (World of Culture Ser.). (Illus.). 1978. 7.95 (ISBN 0-88225-137-6). Newsweek.

Kemper, Robert G. An Elephant's Ballet. LC 77-22165. 1977. 4.00 (ISBN 0-8164-0373-2). Seabury.

Kemper, Theodore D. A Social Interactional Theory of Emotions. LC 78-8020. 459p. 1978. 36.95x (ISBN 0-471-01405-2, Pub. by Wiley-Interscience). Wiley.

Kemperman, Steve. Lord of the Second Advent. LC 80-54091. 176p. 1981. text ed. 8.95 (ISBN 0-8307-0780-8, 5109307); pap. text ed. 4.95 (ISBN 0-8307-0868-5). Regal.

Kempers, Roger D., jt. auth. see Wallach, Edward E.

Kempf, Albert F. & Richards, Thomas J. The Metric System Made Simple. LC 75-36631. 144p. 1977. 4.95 (ISBN 0-385-11032-4, Made). Doubleday.

Kempin, Frederick G., Jr. & Wiesen, Jeremy L. Legal Aspects of the Management. 3rd ed. (Illus.). 850p. 1983. text ed. 23.95 (ISBN 0-314-69658-X); instrs.' manual avail. (ISBN 0-314-71103-1). West Pub.

Kempis, Thomas A see Thomas A Kempis.

Kempis, Thomas a see Thomas a Kempis, Saint.

Kempler, Susan & Rappaport, Doreen. A Man Can Be. LC 80-25356. (Illus.). 32p. (gr. 4-8). 1981. 9.95 (ISBN 0-89885-046-0). Human Sci Pr.

Kempler, Susan, et al. A Man Can Be... LC 80-25356. 32p. 1981. 9.95 o.p. (ISBN 0-89885-046-0). Human Sci Pr.

Kemppainen, Rudolph C., jt. auth. see Benjamin, Robert C.

Kempson, Richard L., jt. auth. see Hendrickson, Michael R.

Kempson, Ruth M. Presupposition & the Delimitation of Semantics. LC 74-25078. (Studies in Linguistics Monographs: No. 15). 260p. 1975. 44.50 (ISBN 0-521-20733-9); pap. 13.95 (ISBN 0-521-09938-2). Cambridge U Pr.

Kempster, A. J. & Cuthbertson, A., eds. Carcase Evaluation in Livestone Breeding, Production & Marketing. 250p. 1982. lib. bdg. 40.00 (ISBN 0-86531-531-0). Westview.

Kempthorne, Oscar. The Design & Analysis of Experiments. LC 51-13460. 652p. 1975. Repr. of 1952 ed. write for info (ISBN 0-88275-105-0). Krieger.

Kempton, Rudolf T., jt. auth. see Brown, Fred.

Kemsley, William, ed. The Whole Hiker's Handbook. (Illus.). 1979. pap. 12.95 (ISBN 0-688-08476-1). Quill NY.

Kenamore, Jane A. & Wilson, Michael E., eds. Manuscript Sources in the Rosenberg Library: A Selective Guide. LC 82-45896. (Illus.). 184p. 1983. 20.00x (ISBN 0-89096-146-8). Tex A&M Univ Pr.

Kenan, Lucette R. A Changing Scene. 253p. 1982. pap. text ed. 9.95 (ISBN 0-15-505900-9, HC). HarBraceJ.

Kench, John. Cape Dutuch Homesteads. (Illus.). 144p. 1981. 32.50x (ISBN 0-86977-140-X). Intl Pubns Serv.

Kenda, Margaret E. & Williams, Phyliss S. The Natural Baby Food Cookbook. 1973. pap. 4.95 o.p. (ISBN 0-380-00824-6, 60640-2). Avon.

Kendall, A. Harold, jt. auth. see Pappas, Joan.

Kendall, Alan. Beethoven & His World. LC 80-68211. (Great Masters Ser.). 13.00 (ISBN 0-686-79426-5). Silver.

--Elizabeth One. LC 77-304. (History Makers Ser.). (Illus.). 1977. 6.95 o.p. (ISBN 0-312-24247-6). St Martin.

--Medieval Pilgrims. (Putnam Documentary History Ser.). (Illus.). 1970. 6.95 o.p. (ISBN 0-399-10531-X). Putnam Pub Group.

--Paganini. (Illus.). 160p. 1982. 24.95 (ISBN 0-241-10845-4, Pub. by Hamish Hamilton England). David & Charles.

Kendall, Aubyn. The Art & Archaeology of Pre-Columbian Middle America: An Annotated Bibliography of Works in English. 1977. lib. bdg. 30.00 (ISBN 0-8161-8093-8, Hall Reference). G K Hall.

Kendall, Carl & Hawkins, John, eds. Heritage of Conquest: Thirty Years Later. 320p. 1982. 27.50 (ISBN 0-8263-0639-X). U of NM Pr.

Kendall, David N. Applied Infrared Spectroscopy. LC 65-29169. 576p. 1966. 31.00 (ISBN 0-442-15073-3, Pub. by Van Nos Reinhold). Krieger.

Kendall, Elaine. Peculiar Institutions: An Informal History of the Seven Sister Colleges. LC 75-39801. (Illus.). 1976. 8.95 o.p. (ISBN 0-399-11619-2). Putnam Pub Group.

Kendall, Florence P. & Wadsworth, Gladys. Muscles: Testing & Function. (Illus.). 329p. 1983. lib. bdg. price not set (ISBN 0-683-04575-X). Williams & Wilkins.

Kendall, Harry H., jt. auth. see Long, Nguyen.

Kendall, Henry O., et al. Muscles: Testing & Function. 2nd ed. (Illus.). 294p. 1971. 29.95 o.p. (ISBN 0-683-04574-1). Williams & Wilkins.

--Posture & Pain. 212p. 1971. Repr. of 1952 ed. 18.50 (ISBN 0-88275-031-3). Krieger.

Kendall, Henry W., ed. Energy Strategies: Toward a Solar Future. Nadis, Steven J. LC 79-23757. 352p. 1979. prof ref 22.50x (ISBN 0-88410-622-5). Ballinger Pub.

Kendall, John D. Suzuki Violin Method in American Music Education. rev. ed. LC 72-96899. 32p. 1978. pap. 2.50x (ISBN 0-940796-20-1, 1049). Music Ed.

Kendall, Katherine A., compiled by. Social Casework: Cumulative Index 1920-1979. 704p. 1981. 95.00 (ISBN 0-89232-194-6). Jai Pr.

Kendall, Lace. Houdini: Master of Escape. (gr. 7-9). 1960. 6.50 (ISBN 0-8255-5075-0). Macrae.

Kendall, Lane C. The Business of Shipping. 4th ed. LC 82-72001. (Illus.). 488p. 1983. text ed. 18.50x (ISBN 0-87033-296-1). Cornell Maritime.

Kendall, Leon T. The Savings & Loan Business: Its Purpose, Functions & Economic Justification. LC 77-14207. (Trade Association Monographs). (Illus.). 1977. Repr. of 1963 ed. lib. bdg. 20.50x (ISBN 0-8371-9843-7, KESAL). Greenwood.

Kendall, Lyle H., Jr., jt. auth. see Corder, Jim W.

Kendall, M. G. Cost Benefit Analysis. 1971. 27.95 (ISBN 0-444-19641-2). Elsevier.

Kendall, Maurice. The Advanced Theory of Statistics. 484p. 1977. 88.00x (ISBN 0-85264-242-3, Pub. by Griffin England). State Mutual Bk.

Kendall, Maurice & Stuart, Alan. The Advanced Theory of Statistics: Vol. 2, Influence & Relationship. 758p. 1979. 88.00x (ISBN 0-85264-255-5, Pub. by Griffin England). State Mutual Bk.

--The Advanced Theory of Statistics: Vol. 3, Design, Analysis & Time-Series. 595p. 1976. 88.00x (ISBN 0-85264-239-3, Pub. by Griffin England). State Mutual Bk.

Kendall, Maurice & Stuart, Allan. Advanced Theory of Statistics, Vol. 4. 700p. 1983. 65.00 (ISBN 0-02-847860-6). Free Pr.

Kendall, Merriam. Medvedb's Journal. 24p. 1982. pap. 3.00 (ISBN 0-910477-00-0). LoonBooks.

Kendall, Paul. Led Zeppelin: A Visual Documentary. (Illus.). 96p. (Orig.). 1983. pap. 12.95 (ISBN 0-399-41010-4). Delilah Bks.

Kendall, Philip C. & Butcher, James N. Handbook of Research Methods in Clinical Psychology. (Personality Processes Ser.). 800p. 1982. 49.95 (ISBN 0-471-07980-4, Pub. by Wiley-Interscience). Wiley.

Kendall, Philip C. & Norton-Ford, Julian D. Clinical Psychology: Scientific & Professional Dimensions. LC 81-16035. 699p. 1982. text ed. 23.95x (ISBN 0-471-04350-8); avail. tests. Wiley.

Kendall, Philip C., ed. Advances in Cognitive Behavioral Research & Therapy, Vol. 2. (Serial Publication). Date not set. price not set (ISBN 0-12-010602-7). Acad Pr.

Kendall, R. T. Calvin & English Calvinism to Sixteen Forty-Nine. (Oxford Theological Monographs). 1979. pap. 10.95x (ISBN 0-19-826720-7). Oxford U Pr.

Kendall, Robert. White Teacher in a Black School. 1980. pap. 6.95 (ISBN 0-8159-7210-5). Devin.

Kendall, Timothy. Kush: Lost Kingdom of the Nile: A Loan Exhibition from the Museum of Fine Arts Boston. LC 82-73157. (Illus.). 64p. (Orig.). 1982. pap. 7.00 (ISBN 0-934358-11-7). Brockton Art.

Kendall, Willmoore, tr. see Rousseau, Jean-Jacques.

Kendall, Willmore, tr. see Rousseau, Jean Jacques.

Kendeigh, S. C., jt. ed. see Pinowski, J.

Kendeigh, S. Charles, ed. Symposium on the House Sparrow (Passer domesticus) & European Tree Sparrow (P. montanus) in North America. 121p. 1973. 6.00 (ISBN 0-943610-14-1). Am Ornithologists.

Kender, Joseph P., jt. ed. see Castaldi, Alfred J.

Kendig, Hal. New Life for Old Suburbs. LC 78-74190. 1979. text ed. 22.50x (ISBN 0-86861-392-4); pap. text ed. 9.50x (ISBN 0-86861-001-1). Allen Unwin.

Kendig, Lane. Performance Zoning. LC 79-93346. (Illus.). 358p. (Orig.). 1980. 39.95 (ISBN 0-918286-18-2). Planners Pr.

Kendler, Howard H. Basic Psychology: Brief Version. 3rd ed. LC 76-20875. (Illus.). 1977. pap. text ed. 19.95 (ISBN 0-8053-5195-7); instr's guide 4.95 (ISBN 0-8053-5196-5). Benjamin-Cummings.

--Psychology: A Science in Conflict. (Illus.). 1981. text ed. 22.00x (ISBN 0-19-502900-3); pap. text ed. 12.95x (ISBN 0-19-502901-1). Oxford U Pr.

Kendrick, David. Stochastic Control for Economic Models. (Economic Handbook Ser.). (Illus.). 288p. 1981. text ed. 39.95 (ISBN 0-07-033962-7, C). McGraw.

Kendrick, E. & Institute of Petroleum, eds. Advances in Mass Spectrometry, Vol. 4. 1968. 80.00 (ISBN 0-444-39942-9). Elsevier.

Kendrick, Richard & Frankland, Barry. Phytochrome & Plant Growth. (Studies in Biology: No. 68). 64p. 1978. pap. text ed. 8.95 (ISBN 0-7131-2561-6). E Arnold.

Kendris, Christopher. Beginning to Write in French: A Workbook in French Composition. rev. ed. 1983. pap. text ed. 3.50 (ISBN 0-8120-2261-0). Barron. Postponed.

--Dictionary of Five Hundred & One French Verbs: Fully Conjugated in All Tenses. LC 73-90072. 1970. 10.75 o.p. (ISBN 0-8120-6077-6); pap. 4.95 o.p. (ISBN 0-8120-0395-0). Barron.

--Dictionary of Five Hundred & One Spanish Verbs: Fully Conjugated in All Tenses. LC 78-162826. 1971. pap. text ed. 4.95 o.p. (ISBN 0-8120-0421-3). Barron.

--Five Hundred One French Verbs. 560p. (gr. 9-12). 1982. pap. 5.95 (ISBN 0-8120-2601-2). Barron.

--Five Hundred One Spanish Verbs. 560p. (gr. 7-12). 1982. pap. 5.95 (ISBN 0-8120-2602-0). Barron.

--French Card Guide. 12p. (gr. 9-12). 1983. 2.95 (ISBN 0-8120-5476-8). Barron.

--French the Easy Way, Bk. 1. (Easy Way Ser.). 160p. (gr. 9-12). 1982. pap. 5.95 (ISBN 0-8120-2635-7). Barron.

--Spanish Card Guide. (Barrons Vocabulary Card Guides). 12p. (gr. 9-12). 1983. 2.95 (ISBN 0-8120-5477-6). Barron.

--Spanish the Easy Way, Bk.2. (Easy Way Ser.). 160p. 1983. pap. write for info. (ISBN 0-8120-2636-5). Barron.

--Two Hundred & One French Verbs Fully Conjugated in All the Tenses. LC 62-18770. (Orig.). 1963. text ed. 6.50 o.p. (ISBN 0-8120-6046-6); pap. text ed. 2.50 o.p. (ISBN 0-8120-0209-1). Barron.

--Two Hundred & One Spanish Verbs Fully Conjugated in All the Tenses. LC 62-18769. 1963. text ed. 6.50 o.p. (ISBN 0-8120-6047-4); pap. text ed. 2.50 o.p. (ISBN 0-8120-0212-1). Barron.

--Two Thousand & One Words You Need to Know to Pass Any Spanish Test. 1984. pap. 2.95 (ISBN 0-8120-2537-7). Barron.

Kendris, Christopher & Newmark, Maxim, eds. Barron's Regents Exams & Answers: French, Level 3. rev ed. LC 58-47141. 250p. (gr. 9-12). 1982. pap. 3.95 (ISBN 0-8120-3147-4). Barron.

--Barron's Regents Exams & Answers: Spanish. rev. ed. LC 58-31609. 250p. (gr. 10-12). 1981. pap. text ed. 3.95 (ISBN 0-8120-3153-9). Barron.

Kendzierski, Lotti H., tr. see Thomas Aquinas, Saint.

Kendzierski, Lottie & Wade, S. J., trs. Cajetan: Commentary on St. Thomas Aquinas on Being & Essence. (Medieval Philosophical Texts in Translation Ser.: No. 14). 1965. pap. 14.95 (ISBN 0-87462-214-X). Marquette.

Keneally, Thomas. Ned Kelly & the City of the Bees. LC 80-66217. (Illus.). 128p. (gr. 2-7). 1981. 10.95 (ISBN 0-87923-338-9). Godine.

--Passenger. LC 78-22258. 1979. 8.95 o.p. (ISBN 0-15-171282-4). HarBraceJ.

--Schindler's List. 1982. 16.95 (ISBN 0-671-44977-X). S&S.

Kenedy, P. J., & Sons. New American Bible. 1970. 10.00 (ISBN 0-02-641650-6); deluxe ed. 17.95 lea. o.p. (ISBN 0-02-839570-0); text ed. 4.68 kivar bdg. o.p. (ISBN 0-02-839560-3); pap. 5.95 o.p. (ISBN 0-02-839540-9). Glencoe.

Kenedy, R. C. Collected Poems, Nineteen Forty-Eight to Nineteen Sixty-One. 150p. (Orig.). Date not set. pap. 5.00 (ISBN 0-940066-03-3). Dalmas & Ricour. Postponed.

Kenefick, Madeleine. Positively Pregnant. (Illus.). 224p. 1981. pap. 3.50 (ISBN 0-523-41777-2). Pinnacle Bks.

Kenemans, P., jt. auth. see Hafez, E. S.

Kenen, Peter, et al, eds. The International Monetary System Under Flexible Exchange Rates: Global, Regional, & National. 336p. 1982. professional reference 38.00x (ISBN 0-88410-853-8). Ballinger Pub.

Kenen, Peter B., jt. auth. see Allen, Polly R.

Kenen, Peter B., ed. International Trade & Finance. LC 75-2717. (Illus.). 580p. 1976. 39.50 (ISBN 0-521-20719-3). Cambridge U Pr.

Kenez, Peter. Civil War in South Russia, 1918: The First Year of the Volunteer Army. LC 78-114339. 1971. 32.00x (ISBN 0-520-01709-9). U of Cal Pr.

--Civil War in South Russia, 1919-1920: The Defeat of the Whites. LC 76-47998. 1978. 32.00x (ISBN 0-520-03346-9). U of Cal Pr.

Keniston, Kenneth. The Uncommitted: Alienated Youth in American Society. 1967. pap. 2.45 o.s.i. (ISBN 0-440-59237-2, Delta). Dell.

Kenkel, J. L. Dynamic Linear Economic Models. LC 73-85833. 400p. 1974. 49.00x (ISBN 0-677-04950-1). Gordon.

Kenkel, William F. The Family in Perspective. 4th ed. LC 76-21491. 1977. text ed. 21.95x o.p. (ISBN 0-673-16305-9). Scott F.

Kenmare, Dallas. Love the Unknown. 8.95 o.p. (ISBN 0-85307-067-9). Transatlantic.

Kenna, V. E. Corpus of Cypriote Antiquities No. 3: Catalogue of the Cypriote Seals of the Bronze Age in the British Museum. (Studies in Mediterranean Archaeology Ser.: No. XX, Pt. 3). (Illus.). 1971. pap. text ed. 19.75x (ISBN 91-85058-23-8). Humanities.

Kennamer, Lorrin, jt. auth. see Reese, James V.

Kennan, Elizabeth T., jt. tr. see Anderson, John D.

Kennan, George F. American Diplomacy: Nineteen Hundred to Nineteen Fifty. 1952. pap. 1.50 o.p. (ISBN 0-451-61168-3, MW1811, Ment). NAL.

--American Diplomacy: Nineteen Hundred to Nineteen Fifty. LC 51-12883. 1969. Slipcased Ed. 8.95 (ISBN 0-226-43143-6). U of Chicago Pr.

--The Cloud of Danger: Current Realities of American Foreign Policy. 1977. 10.95 (ISBN 0-316-48844-5, Pub. by Atlantic Monthly Pr). Little.

--The Nuclear Delusion: Soviet-American Relations in the Atomic Age. 1982. 13.95 (ISBN 0-394-52946-4). Pantheon.

--Realities of American Foreign Policy. 1966. pap. 2.95 o.p. (ISBN 0-393-00320-5, Norton Lib). Norton.

--Russia & the West Under Lenin & Stalin. pap. 3.50 (ISBN 0-451-62027-5, ME2027, Ment). NAL.

Kennan, Kent. Technique of Orchestration. 2nd ed. (Music Ser). (Illus.). 1970. 22.95 (ISBN 0-13-900316-9); wkbk. 2 8.95 (ISBN 0-13-900340-1); wkbk. 6.95 (ISBN 0-13-900332-0). P-H.

Kennan, Kent & Grantham, Donald. The Technique of Orchestration. 3rd ed. (Illus.). 416p. 1983. 20.95 (ISBN 0-13-900308-8). P-H.

Kennan, Kent W. Cassette Supplement for "The Technique of Orchestration". 1981. cassette 8.95x (ISBN 0-292-71070-4). U of Tex Pr.

Kennard, A. M. French Pistols & Sporting Guns. (Country Life Collector's Guides Ser). 1972. 4.95 o.p. (ISBN 0-600-43594-6). Transatlantic.

Kenneally, James J. Women & American Trade Unions. 2nd ed. 256p. 1981. pap. 8.95 (ISBN 0-920792-10-3). Eden Pr.

--Women & American Trade Unions. LC 77-9240. 1978. 17.95 o.p. (ISBN 0-88831-026-9). Eden Pr.

Kennedy, A. Six Dramatists in Search of a Language. LC 74-76572. 288p. 1975. 45.00 (ISBN 0-521-20492-5); pap. 12.95 (ISBN 0-521-09866-1). Cambridge U Pr.

Kennedy, Adam. Debt of Honor. 1981. 12.95 o.s.i. (ISBN 0-440-00012-2). Delacorte.

--Domino Principle: Movie Edition. (RL 7). 1977. pap. 1.95 o.p. (ISBN 0-451-07389-4, J7389, Sig). NAL.

--In a Far Country. 464p. 1983. 16.95 (ISBN 0-440-04217-8). Delacorte.

Kennedy, Adrienne see Harrison, Paul C.

Kennedy, Alan. Meaning & Signs in Fiction. LC 78-24284. 1979. 25.00x (ISBN 0-312-52380-7). St Martin.

Kennedy, Albert J., jt. auth. see Woods, Robert A.

Kennedy, Mrs. Alexander, tr. see Mantegazza, Paolo.

Kennedy, Andrew K. Dramatic Dialogue: The Dialogue of Personal Encounter. LC 82-4257. 304p. 45.00 (ISBN 0-521-24620-2); pap. 13.95 (ISBN 0-521-28845-2). Cambridge U Pr.

Kennedy, Benjamin H. Kennedy's Revised Latin Primer. 1962. pap. text ed. 6.25x (ISBN 0-582-36240-7). Longman.

Kennedy, C. R., ed. Ecological Aspects of Parasitology. 1976. 123.00 (ISBN 0-7204-0602-1, North-Holland). Elsevier.

Kennedy, Carroll E. Human Development: The Adult Years & Aging. (Illus.). 1978. text ed. 21.95x (ISBN 0-02-362450-7). Macmillan.

Kennedy, Charles W., ed. Anthology of Old English Poetry. 1960. pap. 8.95x (ISBN 0-19-500928-2). Oxford U Pr.

Kennedy, Charles W., tr. Beowulf: The Oldest English Epic, Translated into Alliterative Verse with a Critical Introduction. 1978. pap. 4.95 (ISBN 0-19-502435-4, GB 550, GB). Oxford U Pr.

Kennedy, Cody, Jr. The Conquering Clan. 400p. (Orig.). 1980. pap. 2.50 o.p. (ISBN 0-446-91114-3). Warner Bks.

--Warrior Flame. 1980. pap. 2.50 o.p. (ISBN 0-446-81676-0). Warner Bks.

Kennedy, D. G. Incarnational Elements in Hilton's Spirituality. (Salzburg-Elizabethan Studies: Vol. 92, No. 3). 312p. 1982. pap. text ed. 25.00x (ISBN 0-391-02732-8, 41225, Pub. by Salzburg Austria). Humanities.

Kennedy, D. J. Pourquoi Je Crois. Cosson, Annie, ed. Schneider, Michele, tr. from Eng. Orig. Title: Why I Believe. 173p. (Fr.). 1982. pap. 2.00 (ISBN 0-8297-1238-0). Life Pubs Intl.

Kennedy, David M. Over Here: The First World War & American Society. 1980. pap. 8.95 (ISBN 0-19-503209-8, GB). Oxford U Pr.

Kennedy, David M., jt. auth. see Bailey, Thomas A.

Kennedy, David W., jt. auth. see Steiner, Barry R.

Kennedy, Diana. The Tortilla Book. LC 75-6343. (Illus.). 158p. (YA) 1975. o. p. 12.95i (ISBN 0-06-012346-X, HarpT); pap. 5.95i (ISBN 0-06-090888-2, CN 888, HarpT). Har-Row.

Kennedy, Don H. Little Sparrow: A Partrait of Sophia Kovalevsky. LC 82-12405. (Illus.). 341p. 1982. text ed. 25.95x (ISBN 0-8214-0692-2, 82-84614); pap. 12.95 (ISBN 0-8214-0703-1, 82-84721). Ohio U Pr.

Kennedy, Dorothy M., jt. auth. see Kennedy, X. J.

Kennedy, E. Cooking for Love...& Money. 176p. 1982. 10.95 (ISBN 0-932620-12-4, Pub. by Betterway Pubns); pap. 6.95 (ISBN 0-932620-11-6). Berkshire Traveller.

Kennedy, E. C., ed. Scenes from Euripides' Iphigenia in Aulis & Iphigenia in Tauris. 1954. 2.95 o.p. (ISBN 0-312-43575-4). St Martin.

Kennedy, E. C., ed. see Martial & Pliny.

Kennedy, E. S., ed. see Hashimi, Ali Ibn Sulayman al.

Kennedy, Eberhard C. Roman Poetry & Prose. 1957. text ed. 7.95x (ISBN 0-521-05880-5). Cambridge U Pr.

Kennedy, Eberhard C., ed. Four Latin Authors. 1940. text ed. 7.95x (ISBN 0-521-05881-3). Cambridge U Pr.

Kennedy, Eddie C. Classroom Approaches to Remedial Reading. 2nd ed. LC 76-53238. 1977. text ed. 18.95 (ISBN 0-87581-210-4, 210). Peacock Pubs.

Kennedy, Edward C. Methods in Teaching Developmental Reading. 2nd ed. LC 80-52445. 354p. 1981. pap. text ed. 12.95 (ISBN 0-87581-258-9). Peacock Pubs.

Kennedy, Edward G., compiled by. The Etched Work of Whistler, 4 vols. in 3. LC 72-1778. (Library of American Art Ser.). (Illus.). 1974. Repr. of 1910 ed. lib. bdg. 395.00 (ISBN 0-306-70503-6). Da Capo.

Kennedy, Ellen C., tr. see Kesteloot, Lilyan.

Kennedy, Eugene. Father's Day: A Novel of Power, Passion & Conscience. LC 80-2560. 504p. 1981. 14.95 o.p. (ISBN 0-385-15415-1). Doubleday.

--If You Really Knew Me, Would You Still Like Me? 2.95 o.p. (ISBN 0-686-92366-9, 6474). Hazelden.

--St. Patrick's Day with Mayor Daley & Other Things Too Good to Miss. LC 75-44379. 220p. 1976. 8.95 o.p. (ISBN 0-8264-0157-0). Continuum.

Kennedy, Eugene C. Believing. LC 73-79681. 1977. pap. 3.95 (ISBN 0-385-12614-X, Im). Doubleday.

--The Joy of Being Human: Reflections for Every Day of the Year. 360p. 1976. pap. 5.50 (ISBN 0-385-00943-7, Im). Doubleday.

--The New Sexuality: Myths, Fables & Hang-Ups. LC 77-180907. 160p. 1973. pap. 3.50 (ISBN 0-385-06357-1, Im). Doubleday.

--A Sense of Life, a Sense of Sin. 200p. 1976. pap. 3.50 (ISBN 0-385-12070-2, Im). Doubleday.

--Time for Love. LC 75-121952. 1972. pap. 3.50 o.p. (ISBN 0-385-09481-7, Im). Doubleday.

Kennedy, F. E., jt. auth. see Chang, C. M.

Kennedy, Fern. Exploring Photography. 2nd ed. (Illus.). 1979. 17.95 o.p. (ISBN 0-8174-2465-2, Amphoto); pap. 11.95 o.p. (ISBN 0-8174-2136-X). Watson-Guptill.

--Exploring Photography. rev. ed. (Illus.). 448p. 1980. 22.50 o.p. (ISBN 0-8174-2529-2, Amphoto); pap. 12.95 o.p. (ISBN 0-8174-2194-7). Watson-Guptill.

Kennedy, Florynce, jt. auth. see Schulder, Diane.

Kennedy, Florynce R., jt. auth. see Pepper, William F.

Kennedy, G. E. Paleoanthropology. 1980. 24.95 (ISBN 0-07-034046-3). McGraw.

Kennedy, Gavin. Burden Sharing in NATO. LC 79-12140. 1981. text ed. 24.95x (ISBN 0-8419-0515-0). Holmes & Meier.

Kennedy, Gavin, ed. see Barrow, Sir John.

Kennedy, George. Electronic Communication Systems. 2nd ed. (Illus.). 1977. text ed. 24.50 (ISBN 0-07-034052-8, G); instructor's manual 3.50 (ISBN 0-07-034053-6). McGraw.

Kennedy, George A. Chinese Reading for Beginners. 3.25 (ISBN 0-686-09965-6). Far Eastern Pubns.

--Greek Rhetoric under Christian Emperors: A History of Rhetoric, Vol. III. LC 82-51044. 330p. 1983. 32.00x (ISBN 0-691-03565-2); pap. 11.50 (ISBN 0-691-10145-0). Princeton U Pr.

--Simple Chinese Stories. 2.25 (ISBN 0-686-09966-4). Far Eastern Pubns.

Kennedy, George A., jt. ed. see Rouse, Mary.

Kennedy, Gower A. Welding Technology. 2nd ed. 598p. 1982. text ed. 27.50 (ISBN 0-672-97778-8); student manual 9.95 (ISBN 0-672-97990-X). Bobbs.

--Welding Technology Student's Manual. LC 77-4673. (gr. 11-12). 1978. pap. text ed. 8.95 (ISBN 0-672-97109-7); tchr's manual 6.67 (ISBN 0-672-97158-5). Bobbs.

Kennedy, Gregory P. Vengeance Weapon 2: The V-2 Guided Missile. (Illus.). 144p. 1983. pap. text ed. 9.95x (ISBN 0-87474-573-X). Smithsonian.

Kennedy, H. E., ed. see Masaryk, Tomas G.

Kennedy, H. W., et al. Symposium on Air Pollution. LC 75-152831. (Symposia on Law & Society Ser). 1971. Repr. of 1968 ed. lib. bdg. 22.50 (ISBN 0-306-70143-X). Da Capo.

Kennedy, Harold J. No Pickle, No Performance. 1979. pap. 2.25 o.p. (ISBN 0-425-04148-4). Berkley Pub.

Kennedy, Helen. Systematics & Pollination of the "Closed Flowered" Species of Calathea (Mar-Antaceae) (Publications in Botany: No. 71). 1978. pap. 12.50x (ISBN 0-520-09572-3). U of Cal Pr.

Kennedy, J. F. Proteoglycans - Biological & Chemical Aspects in Human Life. (Studies in Organic Chemistry: Vol. 2). 490p. 1980. 76.75 (ISBN 0-444-41794-X). Elsevier.

Kennedy, J. F. & White, C. A. Bioactive Carbohydrates in Chemistry, Biochemistry & Biology. 280p. 1983. 79.95X (ISBN 0-470-27527-8). Halsted Pr.

Kennedy, James. Evangelism Explosion. deluxe ed. 12.95 (ISBN 0-8423-0780-X). Tyndale.

Kennedy, James G. Herbert Spencer. (English Author Ser.). 1978. 13.95 (ISBN 0-8057-6688-X, Twayne). G K Hall.

Kennedy, John. Stem Dictionary of the English Language. LC 78-142547. 1971. Repr. of 1870 ed. 45.00x (ISBN 0-8103-3377-5). Gale.

--Torch of the Testimony. (Orig.). Date not set. pap. 6.95 (ISBN 0-940232-12-X). Christian Bks.

Kennedy, John F. Nation of Immigrants. rev. & enl. ed. (Illus.). (gr. 10 up). 1964. pap. 3.95xi (ISBN 0-06-131118-9, TB1118, Torch). Har-Row.

--A Nation of Immigrants. 111p. pap. 2.95 (ISBN 0-686-95021-6). ADL.

Kennedy, John G. The Tarahumara of the Sierra Madre: Beer, Ecology & Social Organization. LC 77-86044. (Worlds of Man Ser.). (Illus.). 1978. text ed. 16.95x (ISBN 0-88295-614-0); pap. text ed. 8.95x (ISBN 0-88295-615-9). Harlan Davidson.

Kennedy, John J. Analyzing Qualitative Data: Introductory Log-Linear Analysis for Behavioral Research. 288p. 1983. 30.00 (ISBN 0-03-060422-2). Praeger.

--An Introduction to the Design & Analysis of Experiments in Education & Psychology. 1978. pap. text ed. 17.75 (ISBN 0-8191-0372-1). U Pr of Amer.

Kennedy, John L. Fundamentals of Drilling. 252p. 1982. 32.50x (ISBN 0-87814-200-2). Pennwell Books DIvision.

Kennedy, Joseph. Asian Nationalism in the Twentieth Century. (Illus.). 1968. text ed. 18.95 (ISBN 0-312-05635-4). St Martin.

Kennedy, Joseph P. & Marechal, Ernest. Carbocationic Polymerization. LC 80-26366. 510p. 1982. 75.00x (ISBN 0-471-01787-6, Pub. by Wiley-Interscience). Wiley.

Kennedy, Joseph P., ed. The Story of Films. LC 74-160236. (Moving Pictures Ser). xxi, 377p. 1971. Repr. of 1927 ed. lib. bdg. 21.95x (ISBN 0-89198-037-7). Ozer.

Kennedy, Judy, jt. auth. see Babcock, Judy.

Kennedy, Ken. Man on a Trestle. 285p. (Orig.). 1982. pap. 6.75 (ISBN 0-9608864-0-0). Saguaro.

Kennedy, Lena. Autumn Alley. 384p. 1982. pap. 3.50 (ISBN 0-671-42559-5). PB.

Kennedy, Leonard. The Universal Treatise of Nicholas of Autrecourt. (Medieval Philosophical Texts in Translation: No. 20). 172p. 1971. pap. 7.95 (ISBN 0-87462-220-4). Marquette.

Kennedy, Leonard M. Guiding Children to Mathematical Discovery. 3rd ed. 544p. 1979. text ed. 22.95x (ISBN 0-534-00757-0). Wadsworth Pub.

Kennedy, M. Carlos, intro. by. Digital Video Two. (Illus.). 162p. (Orig.). 1982. pap. text ed. 25.00 (ISBN 0-940690-03-9). Soc Motion Pic & TV Engrs.

Kennedy, M. Thomas. European Labor Relations: Text & Cases. LC 78-14155. 448p. 1980. 32.95x (ISBN 0-669-02663-8). Lexington Bks.

Kennedy, Margaret. Where Stands a Winged Sentry. 1941. 24.50x (ISBN 0-685-69832-7). Elliots Bks.

Kennedy, Margaretta. Considering Marriage? 12p. 1982. pap. 0.15 (ISBN 0-686-36261-6). Faith Pub Hse.

Kennedy, Marge. The Mystery of Hypnosis. LC 78-23613. (Unsolved Mysteries of the World Ser.). PLB 11.96 (ISBN 0-89547-071-3). Silver.

Kennedy, Mary-Lou. Bill S: Shakespeare for Kids. (Tomorrow's Books for Today's Children). (Illus.). 82p. 1983. 7.95 (ISBN 0-935326-10-3). Gallopade Pub Group.

Kennedy, Michael. The Halle: A History of the Orchestra from 1858-1983. 1983. write for info. (ISBN 0-7190-0921-9). Manchester.

--Portrait of Elgar. 2nd ed. 1982. 34.95x (ISBN 0-19-315449-8); pap. 16.50x (ISBN 0-19-315448-X). Oxford U Pr.

--Richard Strauss. (Master Musicians Ser). (Illus.). 274p. 1976. 11.00x o.p. (ISBN 0-460-03148-1, Pub. by J. M. Dent England). Biblio Dist.

Kennedy, Michael & Soloman, Martin B. PASCAL: Program Development with Ten Instruction Pascal Subset (Tips) & Standard Pascal. (Illus.). 512p. 1982. text ed. 19.95 (ISBN 0-13-652735-3). P-H.

Kennedy, Michael & Solomon, Martin B. Structured PL-Zero PL-One. (Illus.). 1977. pap. 17.95 (ISBN 0-13-854901-X). P-H.

--Ten Statement FORTRAN Plus FORTRAN Four. 2nd ed. (Illus.). 400p. 1975. pap. text ed. 17.95 (ISBN 0-13-903385-8). P-H.

Kennedy, Michael, ed. The Autobiography of Charles Halle: With Correspondence & Diaries. (Illus.). 216p. 1981. Repr. of 1972 ed. lib. bdg. 25.00 (ISBN 0-306-76094-0). Da Capo.

--The Concise Oxford Dictionary of Music. 3rd ed. (Illus.). 1980. 22.50 (ISBN 0-19-311315-5); pap. 9.95 (ISBN 0-19-311320-1). Oxford U Pr.

Kennedy, Michael H. Elysian. LC 80-16570. 1983. pap. 9.95 (ISBN 0-87949-186-8). Ashley Bks.

Kennedy, Patrick. Legendary Fictions of the Irish Celts. LC 68-25518. 1968. Repr. of 1866 ed. 34.00x (ISBN 0-8103-3467-4). Gale.

Kennedy, Paul E. American Wild Flowers Coloring Book. (Illus.). 48p. 1971. pap. 2.00 (ISBN 0-486-20095-7). Dover.

--Modern Display Alphabets: One Hundred Complete Fonts. LC 74-79330. 1974. lib. bdg. 12.50x (ISBN 0-88307-607-1). Gannon.

Kennedy, R. A. & Wilkes, Alan, eds. Studies in Long Term Memory. LC 74-13149. 358p. 1975. 64.95x (ISBN 0-471-46905-X, Pub. by Wiley-Interscience). Wiley.

Kennedy, R. B., ed. Blake: Songs of Innocence & of Experience, & Other Works. 272p. 1975. 20.00x (ISBN 0-7121-0150-0, Pub. by Macdonald & Evans). State Mutual Bk.

Kennedy, Raymond. The Flower of the Republic. 128p. 1983. 12.50 (ISBN 0-394-52539-6). Knopf.

--Herpes: How to Live with It, How to Treat It, How Not to Treat It. 1983. pap. 10.95 (ISBN 0-911411-12-7). Am Med Pub.

Kennedy, Richard. Come Again in the Spring. LC 76-3830. (Illus.). 48p. (gr. 1-6). 1976. PLB 8.89 o.p. (ISBN 0-06-023129-7, HarpJ). Har-Row.

--Inside My Feet: The Story of a Giant. LC 78-19479. (Illus.). 80p. (gr. 2-6). 1979. 8.61i o.p. (ISBN 0-06-023118-1, HarpJ); PLB 8.89 (ISBN 0-06-023119-X). Har-Row.

--The Leprechaun's Story. LC 79-11410. (Illus.). (ps-3). 1979. 10.00 (ISBN 0-525-33472-6, 0971-290, Unicorn Bk.). Dutton.

--Oliver Hyde's Dishcloth Concert. (gr. 2-5). 1977. 6.95g o.p. (ISBN 0-316-48902-6). Little.

--The Porcelain Man. (Illus.). (gr. 1-3). 1976. 6.95 o.p. (ISBN 0-316-48901-8, Pub by Atlantic Monthly Pr). Little.

--The Rise & Fall of Ben Gizzard. LC 78-1816. (Illus.). (gr. 2-5). 1978. 5.95 o.p. (ISBN 0-316-48903-4, Pub. by Atlantic Monthly Pr). Little.

Kennedy, Richard S. Dreams in the Mirror: A Biography of E. E. Cummings. 1982. pap. 8.95 (ISBN 0-686-86970-2). Norton.

--For the Record: The Unpublished Poems of e. e. cummings. Firmage, George J., ed. Date not set. 35.00 (ISBN 0-87140-645-4). Liveright.

Kennedy, Richard S., jt. ed. see Firmage, George J.

Kennedy, Richard S., ed. see Wolfe, Thomas.

Kennedy, Robert. Hardcore Bodybuilding. LC 82-50549. (Illus.). 192p. 1982. 18.79 (ISBN 0-8069-4166-9); lib. bdg. 18.79 (ISBN 0-8069-4167-7); pap. 8.95 (ISBN 0-8069-7646-2). Sterling.

--Natural Body Building for Everyone. LC 79-91395. (Illus.). 160p. 1980. 13.95 (ISBN 0-8069-4144-8); lib. bdg. 16.79 (ISBN 0-8069-4145-6); pap. 7.95 (ISBN 0-8069-8920-3). Sterling.

--Thirteen Days. (RL 8). pap. 2.95 (ISBN 0-451-12033-7, AE2093, Sig). NAL.

Kennedy, Robert & Weinsteiln, John M., eds. The Defense of the West: Strategic & European Security Issues Reappraised. 350p. 1983. price not set (ISBN 0-86531-612-0). Westview.

Kennedy, Robert E., Jr. The Irish: Emigration, Marriage, & Fertility. LC 70-187740. 304p. 1973. 23.75x o.p. (ISBN 0-520-01987-3); pap. 6.50x (ISBN 0-520-02896-1). U of Cal Pr.

Kennedy, Robert F. To Seek a Newer World. LC 68-12767. 1967. 4.95 (ISBN 0-385-01699-9). Doubleday.

Kennedy, Robert F., Jr. Judge Frank M. Johnson Jr. A Biography. LC 77-27540. 1978. 10.95 (ISBN 0-399-12123-4). Putnam Pub Group.

Kennedy, Roger. American Churches. (Illus.). 296p. 1982. 50.00 (ISBN 0-686-97840-4). Crossroad NY.

Kennedy, Roger G. American Churches. (Illus.). 296p. 50.00 (ISBN 0-941434-17-6, IBM 8005). Stewart Tabori & Chang.

Kennedy, Ruby J., ed. Papers of Maurice R. Davie. 1961. text ed. 47.50x (ISBN 0-686-83676-6). Elliots Bks.

Kennedy, Scott. Making Pressed Flower Pictures. (Illus.). 120p. 1982. pap. 5.95 (ISBN 0-486-24422-9). Dover.

Kennedy, Sloane W. John Greenleaf Whittier, His Life, Genius & Writings. 373p. 1982. Repr. of 1903 ed. lib. bdg. 25.00 (ISBN 0-8495-3139-X). Arden Lib.

Kennedy, Stan. Why Did They Shave My Pubic Hair? 1979. 5.95 o.p. (ISBN 0-533-04124-4). Vantage.

Kennedy, Susan, tr. see Keller, Wilhelm.

Kennedy, T. A., ed. The Illustrated Treasury of Fairy Tales. LC 82-81327. (Illus.). 192p. 1982. 9.95 (ISBN 0-448-16578-3, G&D). Putnam Pub Group.

Kennedy, Theodore. You Gotta Deal with It: Black Family Relations in a Southern Community. (Illus.). 1980. 15.95x (ISBN 0-19-502591-1). Oxford U Pr.

Kennedy, Theodore R. You Gotta Deal with It: Black Family Relations in a Southern Community. (Illus.). 1980. pap. text ed. 7.95x (ISBN 0-19-502592-X). Oxford U Pr.

Kennedy, Thomas L. The Arms of Kiangnan: Modernization in the Chinese Ordnance Industry 1860-1895. 1978. lib. bdg. 27.50 o.p. (ISBN 0-89158-258-4). Westview.

Kennedy, Timothy, jt. auth. see Miniear, Judy.

Kennedy, Timothy, jt. auth. see Twombly, Gerald.

Kennedy, Tom & Simon, Charles E. An Examination of Questionable Payments & Practices. LC 78-14195. (Praeger Special Studies). 1978. 39.95 o.p. (ISBN 0-03-046321-1). Praeger.

Kennedy, Victor S., ed. Esturarine Comparisons: Symposium. 1982. 37.00 (ISBN 0-12-404070-5). Acad Pr.

Kennedy, William. Billy Phelan's Greatest Game. 1983. pap. 5.95 (ISBN 0-14-006340-4). Penguin.

--Ironweed. 256p. 1983. 14.75 (ISBN 0-670-40176-5). Viking Pr.

--Legs. LC 74-30596. 322p. 1975. 8.95 o.p. (ISBN 0-698-10672-5, Coward). Putnam Pub Group.

--Legs. 1983. pap. 5.95 (ISBN 0-14-006484-2). Penguin.

Kennedy, William F. Humanist Versus Economist: The Economic Thought of Samuel Taylor Coleridge. LC 78-1589. (University of California Publicatons in Economics Ser.: Vol. 17). 1978. Repr. of 1958 ed. lib. bdg. 17.50x (ISBN 0-313-20352-0, KEHV). Greenwood.

Kennedy, William H., tr. see Von Franz, Marie-Louise.

Kennedy, William J. Adventures in Anthropology: A Reader in Physical Anthropology. (Illus.). 1977. pap. text ed. 13.50 (ISBN 0-8299-0094-2). West Pub.

Kennedy, X. J. Did Adam Name the Vinegarroon. LC 80-83964. (Illus.). 32p. 1982. 10.95 (ISBN 0-87923-389-3). Godine.

Kennedy, X J. Introduction to Poetry. 5th ed. 1982. pap. text ed. 10.95 (ISBN 0-316-48906-9); tchrs.' manual avail. (ISBN 0-316-48907-7). Little.

Kennedy, X. J. & Kennedy, Dorothy M. Knock at a Star: A Child's Introduction to Poetry. LC 82-47914. 144p. (gr. 3-7). 1982. PLB 12.95 (ISBN 0-316-48853-4). Little.

Kennedy, X. J., ed. Messages: A Thematic Anthology of Poetry. 1973. pap. 9.95 (ISBN 0-316-48858-5); Instructor's Manual avail. (ISBN 0-316-48859-3). Little.

Kennedy-Streetman, Marrianna B., jt. auth. see Holmes, Richard W.

Kennehan, Ann, jt. auth. see Kyle, Robert C.

Kennel, C. F., et al, eds. Solar Systems, Plasma Physics, 3 vols. 1979. Set. 223.50 (ISBN 0-444-85268-9, North Holland); Vol. 1. 97.75 (ISBN 0-444-85115-1); Vol. 2. 89.50 (ISBN 0-444-85266-2); Vol. 3. 89.50 (ISBN 0-444-85267-0). Elsevier.

Kennell, jt. auth. see Klaus.

Kennell, John H., jt. auth. see Klaus, Marshall H.

Kennelly, R. & Neal, R. E. Chemistry: With Selected Principles of Physics. 1971. 22.50 (ISBN 0-07-034060-9, HP). McGraw.

Kennemore, Tim. The Fortunate Few. 1982. 8.95 (ISBN 0-698-20555-3, Coward). Putnam Pub Group.

--Wall of Words. 160p. (gr. 5-8). 1983. 10.95 (ISBN 0-571-11856-9). Faber & Faber.

Kenner, Charles T. & Busch, Kenneth W. Quantitative Analysis. 1979. text ed. 31.95x (ISBN 0-02-362490-6). Macmillan.

Kenner, H., ed. T.S. Eliot: A Collection of Critical Essays. 1962. pap. 4.95 (ISBN 0-13-274324-8, Spec). P-H.

Kenner, Hugh. A Colder Eye: The Modern Irish Writers. LC 82-48723. 1983. 16.95. Knopf.

--Joyce's Voices. LC 76-38887. (Quantum Book Ser.). 1978. 13.00x (ISBN 0-520-03206-3, CAL 426); pap. 2.95 (ISBN 0-520-03935-1). U of Cal Pr.

--The Pound Era. LC 72-138349. 1971. 32.50x (ISBN 0-520-01860-5); pap. 10.95 (ISBN 0-520-02427-3). U of Cal Pr.

--Samuel Beckett: A Critical Study. (California Library Reprint Ser.). 1974. 22.50x (ISBN 0-520-02563-6); pap. 2.45 (ISBN 0-520-00641-0, CAL159). U of Cal Pr.

Kennerly, Karen, ed. Hesitant Wolf, Scrupulous Fox: Fables Selected from World Literature. LC 82-3328. (Illus.). 352p. 1983. pap. 9.95 (ISBN 0-8052-0717-1). Schocken.

Kennet, W. The Futures of Europe. LC 76-9541. (Illus.). 1976. 29.95 (ISBN 0-521-21326-6). Cambridge U Pr.

Kenneth, Ellis, ed. see Hudlin, Richard A.

Kennett, B. L. Seismic Wave Propagation in Stratified Media. LC 82-4242. (Cambridge Monographs on Mechanics & Applied Mathematics). (Illus.). 320p. Date not set. price not set (ISBN 0-521-23933-8). Cambridge U Pr.

Kennett, Frances. The Collector's Book of Fashion. (Illus.). 1983. 22.50 (ISBN 0-517-54860-7). Crown.

Kennett, James P. Marine Geology. (Illus.). 832p. 1982. 36.95 (ISBN 0-13-556936-2). P-H.

Kennett, James P., ed. Magnetic Stratigraphy of Sediments. LC 79-13662. (Benchmark Papers in Geology Ser.: Vol. 54). 464p. 1980. 45.50 (ISBN 0-87933-354-5). Hutchinson Ross.

Kennett, Lee. The French Forces in America: 1780-1783. LC 77-81860. (Contributions in American History: No. 65). (Illus.). 1977. lib. bdg. 25.00 (ISBN 0-8371-9544-6, KFF/). Greenwood.

--A History of Strategic Bombing. (Illus.). 224p. 1983. 15.95 (ISBN 0-684-17781-1, SCribT). Scribner.

Kenneway, Eric. Making Pop-up Greeting Cards. (gr. 9-12). 8.95 o.p. (ISBN 0-263-05065-3). Transatlantic.

Kenney. Physiology of Aging: A Synopsis. 1982. 14.95 (ISBN 0-8151-5016-4). Year Bk Med.

Kenney, Alice P. Access to the Past: Museum Programs & Handicapped Visitors. LC 80-24106. x, 131p. (Orig.). 1980. pap. 8.95 (ISBN 0-910050-45-7). AASLH.

Kenney, Bradford. Aesthetics of Change. (Guilford Family Therapy Ser.). 227p. 1983. 19.50x (ISBN 0-89862-043-0). Guilford Pr.

Kenney, Brigitte L., ed. Cable for Information Delivery: A Guide for Librarians, Educators & Cable Professionals. 175p. 1983. 34.50 (ISBN 0-86729-056-0); pap. 27.50 (ISBN 0-86729-055-2). Knowledge Indus.

Kenney, Charles L. A Memoir of Michael William Balfe. LC 77-13360. (Music Reprint Ser., 1978). (Illus.). 1978. Repr. of 1875 ed. lib. bdg. 29.50 (ISBN 0-306-77528-X). Da Capo.

Kenney, D. E., jt. auth. see Cullertson, Alan N.

Kenney, E. J. The Classical Text: Aspects of Editing in the Age of the Printed Book. 1975. 22.50x (ISBN 0-520-02711-6). U of Cal Pr.

Kenney, Ed, ed. see Lucretius.

Kenney, John P. & More, Harry W., Jr. Principles of Investigation. (Criminal Justice Ser.). (Illus.). 1979. text ed. 21.95 (ISBN 0-8299-0284-8); wkbk. 7.95 (ISBN 0-8299-0289-9); instrs. manual avail. (ISBN 0-8299-0592-8). West Pub.

Kenney, John P. & Pursuit, Dan G. Police Work with Juveniles & the Administration of Juvenile Justice. 5th ed. (Illus.). 496p. 1978. 15.25x o.p. (ISBN 0-398-03392-7). C C Thomas.

Kenney, John P., jt. auth. see Gabard, E. C.

Kennick, W. E., ed. Art & Philosophy: Readings in Aesthetics. 2nd ed. LC 78-65213. 1979. text ed. 18.95x (ISBN 0-312-05391-6). St Martin.

Kennington, Donald & Read, Danny L. The Literature of Jazz. 2nd ed. LC 80-19837. 248p. 1981. pap. 12.00 (ISBN 0-8389-0313-4). ALA.

Kennon, Noel F. Patterns in Crystals. LC 78-4531. 197p. 1978. text ed. 41.95x (ISBN 0-471-99748-X); pap. text ed. 18.00x (ISBN 0-471-99652-1, Pub. by Wiley-Interscience). Wiley.

Kenny, A. J., tr. see Wittgenstein, Ludwig.

Kenny, Anthony. Wittgenstein. 1983. pap. 4.95 (ISBN 0-14-021581-6). Penguin.

Kenny, Carolyn B. The Mythic Artery: The Magic of Music Therapy. xiv, 154p. (Orig.). 1982. lib. bdg. 24.00 (ISBN 0-917930-74-6); pap. 7.50x (ISBN 0-917930-60-6). Ridgeview.

Kenny, Clara, jt. auth. see Kenny, John B.

Kenny, Hugh, jt. auth. see Newcomb, Ellsworth.

Kenny, John. Business of Diving. 1972p. text ed. 37.00x (ISBN 0-87201-183-6). Gulf Pub.

Kenny, John B. & Kenny, Clara. Creating Ceramic Miniatures. 1979. 12.95 o.p. (ISBN 0-686-82890-9); pap. 8.95 (ISBN 0-517-53592-0). Crown.

Kenny, Katherine, jt. auth. see Campbell, Julie.

Kenny, L. W., jt. auth. see Blair, R. D.

Kenny, Maurice, ed. Greyhounding This America. (Illus., Orig.). 1983. pap. 7.95 (ISBN 0-918606-07-1). Heidelberg Graphics.

Kenny, Michael & Kertzer, David I., eds. Urban Life in Mediterranean Europe: Anthropological Perspectives. LC 82-1890. 344p. 1983. 35.00 (ISBN 0-252-00958-4); pap. 9.95 (ISBN 0-252-00990-8). U of Ill Pr.

Kenny, Shirley S. & Backscheider, P. R., eds. The Performers & Their Plays. LC 78-66655. (Eighteenth Century English Drama Ser.). lib. bdg. 50.00 (ISBN 0-8240-3577-1). Garland Pub.

Kenny, Shirley S., ed. see Steele, Richard.

Kenny, Vincent S. Paul Green. (United States Authors Ser.). lib. bdg. 13.95 (ISBN 0-8057-0336-5, Twayne). G K Hall.

Kenrick, Tony. Eighty-First Sight. 1981. pap. 2.75 o.p. (ISBN 0-451-09600-2, E9600, Sig). NAL.

--Eighty-First Site. 1980. 10.00 o.p. (ISBN 0-453-00379-6, H379). NAL.

--The Nightime Guy. LC 78-12899. 1979. 8.95 o.p. (ISBN 0-688-03414-4). Morrow.

--The Nightime Guy. 1980. pap. 2.75 o.p. (ISBN 0-451-09111-6, E9111, Sig). NAL.

--Two for the Price of One. 1981. pap. 2.50 o.p. (ISBN 0-451-09809-9, E9809, Sig). NAL.

--Two Lucky People. 1981. pap. 2.50 o.p. (ISBN 0-451-09725-4, E9725, Sig). NAL.

Kenschaft, Patricia C. Linear Mathematics: A Practical Approach. LC 77-81757. (Illus.). 1978. text ed. 16.95x (ISBN 0-87901-084-3). Worth.

Kenschaft, Patricia C., jt. auth. see Kalmanson, Kenneth.

Kensicki, Peter R., jt. auth. see Smith, Robert S.

Kent & Lancour. Encyclopedia of Library & Information Science, Vol. 37, (Suppl. 1) 1983. price not set (ISBN 0-8247-2037-7). Dekker.

Kent, ed. see Tolstoy, Leo.

Kent, et al. Encyclopedia of Library & Information Science, Vol. 36. 368p. 1983. price not set (ISBN 0-8247-2036-9). Dekker.

--Encyclopedia of Library & Information Science, Vol. 34. 1983. write for info (ISBN 0-8247-2034-2). Dekker.

--Encyclopedia of Library & Information Science, Vol. 35. 1983. write for info. Dekker.

Kent, Alexander. Command a King's Ship. 320p. 1973. 6.95 o.p. (ISBN 0-399-11278-2). Putnam Pub Group.

--Enemy in Sight. pap. 2.95 (ISBN 0-515-06732-6). Jove Pubns.

--Enemy in Sight! pap. 1.95 (ISBN 0-515-05375-9). Jove Pubns.

--Form Line of Battle. 288p. 1983. pap. 2.95 (ISBN 0-515-06804-7). Jove Pubns.

--In Gallant Company. 1978. pap. 1.95 o.p. (ISBN 0-425-03987-0, Dist. by Putnam). Berkley Pub.

--In Gallant Company. LC 77-3988. 1977. 8.95 o.s.i. (ISBN 0-399-11987-6). Putnam Pub Group.

--The Inshore Squadron. LC 78-15222. 1979. 8.95 o.s.i. (ISBN 0-399-12303-2). Putnam Pub Group.

--Midshipman Bolitho & the Avenger. LC 78-9127. (gr. 6-8). 1978. 6.95 o.p. (ISBN 0-399-20652-3). Putnam Pub Group.

--Passage to Mutiny. 352p. 1983. pap. 2.95 (ISBN 0-515-06746-6). Jove Pubns.

--Passage to Mutiny. LC 76-14819. 1976. 8.95 (ISBN 0-399-11772-5). Putnam Pub Group.

--Richard Bolitho--Midshipman. LC 76-4921. 160p. (gr. 6 up). 1976. 6.95 o.p. (ISBN 0-399-20514-4). Putnam Pub Group.

--Signal - Close Action. 352p. 1983. pap. 2.95 (ISBN 0-515-06883-7). Jove Pubns.

--Signal--Close Action! LC 74-16603. 320p. 1974. 7.95 (ISBN 0-399-11448-3). Putnam Pub Group.

--Sloop of War. 1972. 6.95 (ISBN 0-399-10975-7). Putnam Pub Group.

--Stand into Danger. 300p. 1981. 10.95 (ISBN 0-399-12539-6). Putnam Pub Group.

--Stand into Danger. 272p. 1983. pap. 2.95 (ISBN 0-515-06888-8). Jove Pubns.

--To Glory We Steer. 288p. 1983. pap. 2.95 (ISBN 0-515-06892-6). Jove Pubns.

--A Tradition of Victory. 304p. 1982. 12.95 (ISBN 0-399-12706-2). Putnam Pub Group.

Kent, Allen. Information Analysis & Retrieval. LC 70-155120. (Information Science Ser). 367p. 1971. 39.95x (ISBN 0-471-46995-5). Wiley.

Kent, Allen & Galvin, Thomas J., eds. Information Technology: Critical Choices for Library Decision-Makers. (Bks in Library & Informtion Science: Vol. 40). 504p. 1982. 57.50 (ISBN 0-686-82222-6). Dekker.

Kent, Amanda. The Ardent Protector: Regency. (Second Chance at Love Ser.: No. 111). pap. 1.75 (ISBN 0-515-06899-3). Jove Pubns.

Kent, Charles W., ed. Elene: An Old English Poem. 149p. 1982. lib. bdg. 35.00 (ISBN 0-89760-433-4). Telegraph Bks.

Kent, Dale & Kent, F. W. Neighbors & Neighborhood in Renaissance Florence: The District of the Red Lion in the Fifteenth Century. LC 82-70335. 1982. 22.00 (ISBN 0-686-92326-X). J J Augustin.

Kent, Donald H. Iroquois Indians, Vol. 1: History of Pennsylvania Purchases from the Indians. (American Indian Ethnohistory Series: North Central & Northeastern Indians). (Illus.). lib. bdg. 42.00 o.s.i. (ISBN 0-8240-0768-9). Garland Pub.

Kent, Edward A., ed. Law & Philosophy: Readings in Legal Philosophy. 1970. text ed. 24.95 (ISBN 0-13-526459-6). P-H.

Kent, Ernest W. The Brains of Men & Machines. 1980. 18.95 (ISBN 0-07-034123-0, BYTE Bks); pap. 8.95 o.p. (ISBN 0-07-034122-2). McGraw.

Kent, F. W., jt. auth. see Kent, Dale.

Kent, Frank R. The Story of Maryland Politics: An Outline History of the Big Political Battles of the State from 1864 to 1910, with Sketches & Incidents of the Men & Measures That Figured As Factors, & the Names of Most of Those Who Held Office in That Period. LC 68-31444. xiv, 439p. Repr. of 1911 ed. 34.00x (ISBN 0-8103-5035-1). Gale.

Kent, Frederick C. & Kent, Maude E. Compound Interest & Annuity Tables. 1963. pap. 4.95 (ISBN 0-07-034121-4, SP). McGraw.

Kent, George. Anatomy of the Vertebrates: A Laboratory Guide. 3rd ed. LC 77-16049. (Illus.). 1978. pap. 8.50 lab manual o.p. (ISBN 0-8016-2644-7). Mosby.

--The Politics of Pacific Islands Fisheries. (Westview Replica Edition Ser.). 1980. lib. bdg. 25.50 (ISBN 0-89158-683-0). Westview.

Kent, George C. Comparative Anatomy of the Vertebrates. 5th ed. LC 82-2078. (Illus.). 604p. 1983. pap. text ed. 26.50 (ISBN 0-8016-2651-X). Mosby.

--Comparative Anatomy of the Vertebrates. 4th ed. LC 77-13588. (Illus.). 466p. 1978. 23.95 o.p. (ISBN 0-8016-2650-1). Mosby.

Kent, George O. Bismarck & His Times. LC 78-2547. 192p. 1978. 12.50x o.p. (ISBN 0-8093-0858-4); pap. 6.95 (ISBN 0-8093-0859-2). S Ill U Pr.

Kent, H. S. War & Trade in the Northern Seas: Anglo-Scandinavian Economic Relations in the Mid-Eighteenth Century. LC 72-75304. (Cambridge Studies in Economic History Ser.). (Illus.). 288p. 1973. 44.50 (ISBN 0-521-08579-9). Cambridge U Pr.

Kent, Homer A. The Pastoral Epistles. LC 81-18873. 1982. pap. 9.95 (ISBN 0-8024-6357-6). Moody.

Kent, Homer A., Jr. Ephesians, the Glory of the Church. pap. 4.95 (ISBN 0-88469-078-4). BMH Bks.

--Pastoral Epistles. 320p. 1982. pap. 9.95 (ISBN 0-88469-075-X). BMH Bks.

Kent, Homer A., Sr. Conquering Frontiers. 8.95 (ISBN 0-88469-018-0); pap. 6.95 (ISBN 0-88469-017-2). BMH Bks.

--The Pastor & His Work. pap. 8.95 (ISBN 0-88469-079-2). BMH Bks.

Kent, Homer, Jr. Ephesians: The Glory of the Church. (Everyman's Bible Commentary Ser.). 1971. pap. 4.50 (ISBN 0-8024-2049-4). Moody.

Kent, J. Commentaries on American Law, 4 Vols. LC 78-75290. (American Constitutional & Legal History Ser). 1971. Repr. of 1826 ed. Set. lib. bdg. 245.00 (ISBN 0-306-71293-8). Da Capo.

Kent, Jack. The Caterpillar & the Polliwog. (Illus.). 32p. (ps-3). 1982. 8.95 (ISBN 0-13-120469-6). P-H.

--Floyd, the Tiniest Elephant. LC 78-4708. (gr. 1-3). 1979. 6.95 o.p. (ISBN 0-385-14099-1); PLB 6.95 o.p. (ISBN 0-385-14100-9). Doubleday.

--Jack Kent's Happy-Ever-After Book. LC 75-43289. (Illus.). (ps-3). 1976. 4.95 o.p. (ISBN 0-394-83135-7, BYR); PLB 5.99 (ISBN 0-394-93135-1). Random.

--The Once-Upon-a-Time Dragon. (Illus.). (ps-3). 10.95 (ISBN 0-15-257885-4). HarBraceJ.

--Silly Goose. (Illus.). 32p. (ps-3). 1983. 9.95 (ISBN 0-13-809947-2). P-H.

Kent, James. Memoirs & Letters of James Kent. Kent, William, ed. LC 78-99481. (American Public Figures Ser). 1970. Repr. of 1898 ed. lib. bdg. 42.50 (ISBN 0-306-71847-2). Da Capo.

Kent, James T. Lectures on Homeopathic Philosophy. 1979. 5.95x (ISBN 0-913028-61-4, Pub. by North Atlantic Books). Formur Intl.

Kent, Kate P. Puelo Indian Textiles: A Living Tradition. (Studies in American Indian Art). (Illus.). 136p. 1983. write for info. (ISBN 0-933452-07-1); pap. write for info. (ISBN 0-933452-08-X). Schol Am Res.

--Textiles of the Prehistoric Southwest. LC 81-52057. (Indian Arts Ser.). (Illus.). 416p. 1983. 45.00x (ISBN 0-8263-0591-1). U of NM Pr.

Kent, Kathryn. The Good Housekeeping Complete Guide to Traditional American Decorating. (Illus.). 1982. 27.45 (ISBN 0-87851-212-8). Hearst Bks.

Kent, Leona M., jt. auth. see Staub, George E.

Kent, Leonard J., ed. see Hoffmann, E. T.

Kent, Martha W. & Rolf, Jon E., eds. Social Competence in Children. LC 78-63587. (Primary Prevention of Psychopathology Ser.: Vol. 3). (Illus.). 351p. 1979. text ed. 25.00x (ISBN 0-87451-155-0). U Pr of New Eng.

Kent, Maude E., jt. auth. see Kent, Frederick C.

Kent, N. L. Technology of Cereals: An Introduction for Students of Food Science & Agriculture. 3rd ed. (Illus.). 200p. 1983. 40.00 (ISBN 0-08-029801-X); pap. 15.00 (ISBN 0-08-029800-1). Pergamon.

Kent, Noel J. Islands Under the Influence: Hawaii & Two Centuries of Dependent Development. LC 82-48038. (Illus.). 416p. 1982. 22.00 (ISBN 0-85345-617-8, CL6178). Monthly Rev.

Kent, P. W., ed. International Aspects of the Provision of Medical Care. 224p. 1976. 25.00 (ISBN 0-85362-160-8, Oriel). Routledge & Kegan.

--Membrane Mediated Information, Vols. 1 & 2. 1974. Vol. 1. 24.95 ea. (ISBN 0-444-19540-8); Vol. 2. 22.50 (ISBN 0-444-19539-4). Elsevier.

Kent, Peter. The Pope & the Duce. 1981. 25.00 (ISBN 0-312-63024-7). St Martin.

Kent, Peter, ed. see Royal Society of London.

Kent, R. T. Mechanical Engineers Handbook, 2 pts. 12th ed. Incl. Pt. 1. Design & Production. Carmichael, C., ed. 1611p. 59.95x (ISBN 0-471-46959-9); Pt. 2. Power. Salisbury, J. K., ed. 1409p. 64.95x (ISBN 0-471-46992-0). 1950 (Pub. by Wiley-Interscience). Wiley.

Kent, Raymond. A History of British Empirical Sociology. 228p. 1981. text ed. 41.50x (ISBN 0-566-00415-1). Gower Pub Ltd.

Kent, Raymond D., jt. auth. see Shriberg, Lawrence D.

Kent, Richard S., ed. see Canton, Alan N.

Kent, Rockwell. It's Me, O Lord: The Autobiography of Rockwell Kent. LC 77-5590. (Graphic Arts Ser.). (Illus.). 1977. Repr. of 1955 ed. lib. bdg. 65.00 (ISBN 0-306-77412-7). Da Capo.

--Wilderness: A Journal of Quiet Adventure in Alaska. (Illus.). 260p. 1983. pap. 8.95 (ISBN 0-918172-12-8). Leetes Isl.

Kent, Roland G. Old Persian Grammar Texts Lexicon. 2nd rev. ed. (American Oriental Ser.: Vol. 33). 1953. 17.00 (ISBN 0-940490-33-1). Am Orient Soc.

Kent, Rolly, ed. Southside: Twenty-One Poems by Children from Tucson's South Side. (Illus.). 28p. 1982. pap. 5.00 (ISBN 0-9608370-1-9). Friends Tucson Library.

Kent, Saul. The Life-Extension Revolution: The Source Book for Optimum Health & Maximum Lifespan. (Illus.). 480p. 1983. pap. 7.95 (ISBN 0-688-01952-8). Quill NY.

Kent, W. Data & Reality: Basic Assumptions in Data Processing Reconsidered. 1978. 34.00 (ISBN 0-444-85187-9). Elsevier.

Kent, William, ed. see Kent, James.

Kent, William W. Hooked Rug. LC 78-172437. (Tower Bks). (Illus.). 1971. Repr. of 1941 ed. 34.00x (ISBN 0-8103-3914-5). Gale.

Kenter, Adriana A. see Baker, Keith A.

Kentner, Bernice. A Rainbow in Your Eyes-Yes You Can Find Your Colors & for Others Too. (Illus.). 146p. 1982. 14.95x (ISBN 0-941522-01-6). Ken Kra Pubs.

--Tie Me up with Rainbows: A Guide to Beauty & Color. (Illus.). 126p. 1983. pap. 9.95 (ISBN 0-941522-02-4, 788-156). Ken Kra Pubs.

Kenton, Walter S., Jr. How Life Insurance Companies Rob You & What You Can Do About It. (Illus.). 1983. 13.95 (ISBN 0-394-51197-2). Random.

Kenton, Warren. Stage Properties & How to Make Them. new rev. ed. LC 74-8056. (Illus.). 1978. pap. text ed. 7.95x (ISBN 0-910482-97-7). Drama Bk.

--Stage Properties & How to Make Them. (Illus.). 119p. pap. 13.50x (ISBN 0-273-43888-3, LTB). Sportshelf.

Kentzer, Michael. Cold. LC 79-65902. (Young Scientist Ser.). PLB 11.96 (ISBN 0-382-06350-3). Silver.

--Heat. LC 79-65898. (Young Scientist Ser.). PLB 11.96 (ISBN 0-382-06347-3). Silver.

--Power. LC 79-65901. (Young Scientist Ser.). PLB 11.96 (ISBN 0-382-06351-1). Silver.

--Space. LC 79-65900. (Young Scientist Ser.). PLB 11.96 (ISBN 0-382-06353-8). Silver.

--Strength. LC 79-65899. (Young Scientist Ser.). PLB 11.96 (ISBN 0-382-06348-1). Silver.

--Waves. LC 79-6897. (Young Scientist Ser.). PLB 11.96 (ISBN 0-382-06346-5). Silver.

Kenward, Harry & Hall, Allan, eds. Environmental Archaeology in the Urban Context. (CBA Research Report: No. 43). 140p. 1982. pap. text ed. 32.95x (ISBN 0-906780-12-8, Pub. by Coun Brit Archaeology England). Humanities.

Kenward, Jean. Ragdolly Anna Stories. (Illus.). (gr. 3-6). 1980. 6.95 o.p. (ISBN 0-7232-2278-9). Warne.

Kenward, M. Potential Energy. LC 75-36174. (Illus.). 256p. 1976. 39.50 (ISBN 0-521-21086-0); pap. 12.95 (ISBN 0-521-29056-2). Cambridge U Pr.

Kenwood, A. G. & Lougheed, A. L. The Growth of the International Economy, 1820-1980: An Introductory Text. 320p. 1983. pap. text ed. 12.95x (ISBN 0-04-330332-3). Allen Unwin.

--The Growth of the International Economy, 1820-1960. LC 70-171174. 328p. 1971. 39.50x (ISBN 0-87395-137-9). State U NY Pr.

Kenwood, A. G. & Loughheed, A. L. The Growth of the International Economy 1820-1960. 1971. pap. text ed. 9.95x o.p. (ISBN 0-04-330175-4). Allen Unwin.

Kenworthy, Catherine. Best Friends. LC 82-82285. (Little Golden Bks.). (Illus.). 24p. (ps-2). 1983. 0.89 (ISBN 0-307-02096-7, Golden Pr); PLB price not set (ISBN 0-307-60197-8). Western Pr.

--Little Squirt the Fire Engine. LC 82-83382. (First Little Golden Bk.). (Illus.). (ps). 1983. 0.69 (ISBN 0-307-10144-4, Golden Pr); PLB price not set. Western Pub.

--Visit from Grandma & Grandpa. LC 81-86495. (First Little Golden Bk.). (Illus.). 24p. (ps). 1982. 0.69 (ISBN 0-307-10155-X, Golden Pr); PLB write for info. Western Pub.

Kenworthy, Leonard. Studying China. LC 74-23808. 1975. pap. text ed. 4.95x (ISBN 0-8077-2456-4). Tchrs Coll.

--Studying India. LC 74-23809. 1975. pap. text ed. 4.95x (ISBN 0-8077-2457-2). Tchrs Coll.

--Studying Japan. LC 74-23896. 1975. pap. text ed. 4.95x (ISBN 0-8077-2455-6). Tchrs Coll.

Kenworthy, Leonard S. Free & Inexpensive Materials on World Affairs. LC 68-56447. 1969. pap. text ed. 3.95x (ISBN 0-8077-1608-1). Tchrs Coll.

--Hats, Caps, & Crowns. LC 77-23800. (Illus.). 64p. (gr. 3-5). 1977. PLB 6.64 o.p. (ISBN 0-671-32874-3). Messner.

--Social Studies for the Eighties: In Elementary & Middle Schools. 3rd ed. LC 80-19096. 541p. 1981. text ed. 20.95 (ISBN 0-471-05983-8). Wiley.

--The Story of Rice. LC 79-14906. (Illus.). 64p. (gr. 3-5). 1979. PLB 6.97 o.p. (ISBN 0-671-33035-7). Messner.

--Studying Africa in Elementary & Secondary Schools. rev. ed. LC 70-105869. (Illus.). 1970. pap. text ed. 3.95x (ISBN 0-8077-1606-5). Tchrs Coll.

--Studying South America in Elementary & Secondary Schools. rev. ed. LC 65-19211. (Illus.). 1965. pap. text ed. 3.95x (ISBN 0-8077-1614-6). Tchrs Coll.

--Studying the U.S.S.R. in Elementary & Secondary Schools. LC 77-94510. 1970. pap. text ed. 3.95x (ISBN 0-8077-1615-4). Tchrs Coll.

Kenya Mission Team. Church Planting, Watering & Increasing in Kenya. Humble, B. J., ed. (Illus.). 130p. 1981. pap. 2.95 (ISBN 0-88027-002-0). Firm Foun Pub.

Kenyon, Alfred. Currency Risk Management. 200p. 1981. 26.95x (ISBN 0-471-10003-X, Pub. by Wiley-Interscience). Wiley.

Kenyon Critics. Gerard Manley Hopkins. LC 77-28228. 1978. Repr. of 1945 ed. lib. bdg. 19.75x (ISBN 0-313-20255-9, HOKC). Greenwood.

Kenyon, D. & Steinman, G. D. Biochemical Predestination. (Illus.). 1969. text ed. 14.50 o.p. (ISBN 0-07-034126-5, HP). McGraw.

Kenyon, Don J. The Double Mind. LC 1-67321. 95p. 1981. pap. 2.50 o.p. (ISBN 0-87509-288-8). Chr Lit.

--The Double Mind. 95p. 1981. pap. 2.50 (ISBN 0-87509-288-8). Chr Pubns.

--Romans, 2 vols. Incl. Vol. 1. Triumph of Truth. pap. text ed. 3.95 (ISBN 0-87509-147-4); leader's guide 2.95 (ISBN 0-87509-265-9); Vol 2. Glory of Grace. pap. text ed. 3.95 (ISBN 0-87509-148-2); leader's guide 2.95 (ISBN 0-87509-266-7). 1978. pap. Chr Pubns.

Kenyon, J. P., ed. A Dictionary of British History. LC 82-42759. 415p. 1983. 20.00 (ISBN 0-8128-2910-7). Stein & Day.

Kenyon, J. R. Stuart England. LC 78-52750. 1978. 18.95x (ISBN 0-312-76909-1). St Martin.

Kenyon, Joan, ed. see Brill, Steven.

Kenyon, John P. Stuart Constitution, Sixteen Three to Sixteen Eighty-Eight: Documents & Commentary. (Orig.). 1966. 69.50 (ISBN 0-521-05884-8); pap. 19.95 (ISBN 0-521-09370-8). Cambridge U Pr.

Kenyon, John S. American Pronunciation. 10th ed. 1958. 6.95x o.p. (ISBN 0-685-21774-4); pap. 7.50x (ISBN 0-685-21775-2). Wahr.

Kenyon, Karen. Sunshower. 320p. 1981. 12.95 (ISBN 0-399-90130-2, Marek). Putnam Pub Group.

Kenyon, Michael. The Elgar Variation. 360p. 1981. 13.95 o.p. (ISBN 0-698-11057-9, Coward). Putnam Pub Group.

--A Free Range Wife. LC 82-23480. (Crime Club Ser.). (Illus.). 192p. 1983. pap. 11.95 (ISBN 0-385-18838-2). Doubleday.

--The Molehill File. LC 77-16707. 1978. 7.95 o.p. (ISBN 0-698-10862-0, Coward). Putnam Pub Group.

Kenyon, Raymond G. I Can Learn About Calculators & Computers. LC 61-5771. (Illus.). (gr. 5 up). 1961. PLB 9.89 o.p. (ISBN 0-06-023141-6, HarpJ). Har-Row.

Kenyon, Richard A., jt. auth. see Bober, William.

Kenyon, Robert L. Gold Coins of England. LC 77-111204. (Illus.). Repr. of 1884 ed. 20.00x (ISBN 0-678-08014-3). Kelley.

--Gold Coins of England. updated ed. LC 77-74031. (Illus.). 1983. Repr. of 1884 ed. lib. bdg. 30.00 (ISBN 0-915262-13-4). S J Durst.

Kenzie, Peggy, jt. ed. see Nemeth, Doris I.

Keodel, R. Craig. South Jersey Heritage: A Social, Economic & Cultural History. 190p. 1977. pap. text ed. 9.75 (ISBN 0-8191-0246-6). U Pr of Amer.

Keogh, Barbara, ed. Advances in Special Education: Annual, Vol. 2. 350p. (Orig.). 1980. lib. bdg. 40.00 (ISBN 0-89232-149-0). Jai Pr.

Keogh, Barbara K., ed. Advances in Special Education, Vol. 1. (Orig.). 1980. lib. bdg. 40.00 (ISBN 0-89232-077-X). Jai Pr.

--Advances in Special Education, Vol. 3. 325p. 1981. 40.00 (ISBN 0-89232-202-0). Jai Pr.

Keogh, James & Koster, John. Burglarproof: A Complete Guide to Home Security. (Illus.). 1977. 16.95 (ISBN 0-07-034146-X, P&RB). McGraw.

Keogh, R. N., jt. auth. see Weisz, Paul B.

Keogh, Richard N., jt. auth. see Weisz, Paul B.

Keohane, Nannerl O. & Rosaldo, Michelle Z., eds. Feminist Theory: A Critique of Ideology. 312p. 1983. pap. 7.95 (ISBN 0-226-43163-0). U of Chicago Pr.

Keonjian, Edward, ed. Microelectronics: Theory, Design, & Fabrication. (Illus.). 1963. 43.50 (ISBN 0-07-034135-4, P&RB). McGraw.

Keough, Carol & Prevention Magazine Editors. Natural Relief for Arthritis. (Illus.). 320p. 1983. 15.95 (ISBN 0-87857-456-5, 05-901-0). Rodale Pr Inc.

Keough, Lawrence, jt. auth. see Wicks, Robert G.

Keown, Ian M. Lover's Guide to America. (Illus.). 384p. 1974. 8.95 o.p. (ISBN 0-02-562300-1). Macmillan.

Keown, Robert, jt. auth. see Faires, Virgil M.

Keown, Robert M., jt. auth. see Faires, Virgil M.

Kepes. Meningiomas: Pathology, Diagnosis & Treatment. LC 81-18659. (Masson Monographs in Diagnostic Pathology: Vol. 4). 200p. 1982. 52.00x (ISBN 0-89352-136-1). Masson Pub.

Kepes, Gyorgy. The New Landscape. (Illus.). 1956. 18.50x (ISBN 0-911498-01-X). Theobald.

Kepes, Juliet. The Story of a Bragging Duck. LC 82-6180. (Illus.). 32p. (gr. k-3). 1982. 8.95 (ISBN 0-395-32863-2). HM.

Kephart, Horace. Camping & Woodcraft. (Illus.). 1948. 10.95 o.p. (ISBN 0-02-562680-9). Macmillan.

Kephart, Newell. Slow Learner in the Classroom. 2nd ed. LC 77-158613. 1971. text ed. 22.95x (ISBN 0-675-09196-9). Merrill.

Kephart, Newell C., jt. auth. see Radler, Don H.

Kephart, William M. Extraordinary Groups: The Sociology of Unconventional Life-Styles. 2nd ed. LC 81-51860. 325p. 1982. 16.95 (ISBN 0-312-27861-6); pap. text ed. 8.95 (ISBN 0-312-27862-4). St Martin.

--The Family, Society, & the Individual. 5th ed. LC 80-81847. (Illus.). 624p. 1981. text ed. 21.95 (ISBN 0-395-29760-5); manual 01.00instr's. (ISBN 0-395-29761-3). HM.

Kepler, Angela K. Comparative Study of Todies (Todidae), with Emphasis on the Puerto Rican Tody, Todus Mexicanus. (Illus.). 206p. 1977. 11.75 (ISBN 0-686-35805-8). Nuttall Ornithogical.

Kepler, Cameron B. Breeding Biology of the Blue-faced Booby Sula Dactylatra Personata on Green Island, Kure Atoll. (Illus.). 97p. 1969. 6.50 (ISBN 0-686-35795-7). Nuttall Ornithological.

Kepler, Frank R., jt. auth. see Fryklund, Verne C.

Kepler, Harold B. Basic Graphical Kinematics. 2nd ed. (Illus.). 384p. 1973. text ed. 26.95 (ISBN 0-07-034171-0, G); problems 10.95 (ISBN 0-07-034173-7); solutions for problems 4.00 (ISBN 0-07-034172-9); solutions manual 4.00 (ISBN 0-07-034174-5). McGraw.

Kepler, Johannes. Epitome of Copernican Astronomy, Books 4 & 5, 2 Vols. in 1. 1939. 19.00 o.p. (ISBN 0-527-48900-X). Kraus Repr.

Kepler, Thomas S., ed. Contemporary Thinking about Jesus, an Anthology. Repr. of 1944 ed. lib. bdg. 17.75x (ISBN 0-8371-2553-7, KEAJ). Greenwood.

Keplinger, H. F. Without Fear or Favor. Date not set. 19.95 (ISBN 0-87201-917-9). Gulf Pub.

Kepner, Charles H. & Tregoe, Benjamin. The Rational Manager. LC 65-21586. 240p. 1976. Repr. of 1965 ed. 14.95 (ISBN 0-686-38777-5). Kepner-Tregoe.

Kepner, Charles H. & Tregoe, Benjamin B. The New Rational Manager. 220p. Date not set. 14.95 (ISBN 0-686-82623-X). Princeton Res Inst.

Kepner, G. R., ed. Cell Membrane Permeability & Transport. LC 79-11930. (Benchmark Papers in Human Physiology: Vol. 12). 410p. 1979. 50.00 (ISBN 0-87933-352-9). Hutchinson Ross.

Keppel, Geoffrey. Design & Analysis: A Researcher's Handbook. 2nd ed. (Illus.). 624p. 1982. text ed. 28.95 (ISBN 0-13-200048-2). P-H.

--Design & Analysis: A Researcher's Handbook. LC 72-6434. (Illus.). 640p. 1973. ref. ed. 28.95 (ISBN 0-13-200030-X). P-H.

Keppel, Geoffrey, jt. ed. see Postman, Leo.

Keppes, Gyorgy, ed. The Nature & Art of Motion. LC 65-10807. (Vision & Value Ser). 12.50 o.s.i. (ISBN 0-8076-0289-2). Braziller.

Kepple, Robert J. Reference Works for Theological Research: An Annotated Selective Bibliographical Guide. 2nd ed. LC 81-40350. 298p. 1981. lib. bdg. 23.00 (ISBN 0-8191-1679-3); pap. text ed. 12.25 (ISBN 0-8191-1680-7). U Pr of Amer.

Keppler, Herbert. Asahi Pentax Way. rev., new, 11th ed. (Camera Way Bks.). (Illus.). 1978. 24.95 o.p. (ISBN 0-8038-0466-0). Focal Pr.

--The Nikon-Nikkormat Way. 3rd ed. (Camera Way Bks.). (Illus.). 1982. 29.95 (ISBN 0-240-51185-9). Focal Pr.

Ker, Neil R., ed. Medieval Manuscripts in British Libraries, Vol. 1. 1969. 47.00x (ISBN 0-19-818219-8). Oxford U Pr.

Ker, William. Sir Walter Scott. LC 74-7282. (Sir Walter Scott Ser, No. 73). 1974. lib. bdg. 22.95x (ISBN 0-8383-1937-8). Haskell.

Kerbo, Ronal C. Caves. LC 81-4514. (Geo Bks.). (Illus.). 48p. (gr. 3 up). 1981. PLB 10.00 (ISBN 0-516-07638-8); pap. 3.95 (ISBN 0-516-47638-6). Childrens.

Kerby, Robert L. The Confederate Invasion of New Mexico & Arizona 1861-1862. LC 58-14001. (Illus.). 8.95 (ISBN 0-87026-055-3). Westernlore.

Kerby, William F. A Proud Profession: Memoirs of a Wall Street Journal Reporter, Editor & Publisher. LC 80-70438. 225p. 1981. 12.95 o.p. (ISBN 0-87094-235-2). Dow Jones-Irwin.

Kercher, Leonard C. The Kenya Penal System: Past, Present & Prospect. LC 80-1417. (Illus.). 334p. (Orig.). 1981. lib. bdg. 25.00 (ISBN 0-8191-1619-X); pap. text ed. 14.00 (ISBN 0-8191-1620-3). U Pr of Amer.

Kerckhoff, Alan C., ed. Research in Sociology of Education & Socialization, Vol. 1. (Orig.). 1979. lib. bdg. 42.50 (ISBN 0-89232-122-9). Jai Pr.

Kerek, Andrew. Hungarian Metrics: Some Linguistic Aspects of Iambic Verse. (Uralic & Altaic Ser: Vol. 117). (Orig., Hung). 1971. pap. text ed. 11.00x o.p. (ISBN 0-87750-163-7). Res Ctr Lang Semiotic.

Kerenyi, C. The Gods of the Greeks. (Illus.). 1980. pap. 8.95 (ISBN 0-500-27048-1). Thames Hudson.

Kerenyi, Karl. Goddesses of Sun & Moon: Circe, Aphrodite, Medea, Niobe. Stein, Murray, tr. from Ger. (Dunquin Ser.: No. 11). 84p. 1979. pap. text ed. 7.00 (ISBN 0-88214-211-9). Spring Pubns.

Keres. Practical Chess Endings. 1981. Repr. 11.50 o.p. (ISBN 0-7134-1061-2, Pub. by Batsford England). David & Charles.

Keres, Paul. Grandmaster of Chess: The Complete Games of Paul Keres. Golombeck, Harry, tr. LC 72-642. 1972. pap. 3.95 (ISBN 0-668-02645-6). Arco.

Keresztes, Paul. Constantine-A Great Christian Monarch & Apostle. (London Studies in Classical Philology Ser.). 218p. 1981. pap. text ed. 19.00x (ISBN 90-70265-03-6, Pub. by Gieben Holland). Humanities.

Keresztesi, Michael & Cocozzoli, Gary, eds. German American History & Life: A Guide to Information Sources. LC 79-24065. (Ethnic Studies Information Guide Ser.: Vol. 4). 1980. 42.00x (ISBN 0-8103-1459-2). Gale.

Kerff, G. Photographing Landscape. (Illus.). 139p. 1979. 20.95 (ISBN 0-240-51041-0). Focal Pr.

Kerfoot, Franklin H. Parliamentary Law. 1941. 7.95 (ISBN 0-8054-7901-5). Broadman.

Kerfoot, H. F. Reglas Parlamentarias. Sanchez, Jose M., tr. from Eng. 88p. (Span.). 1981. Repr. of 1957 ed. 1.80 (ISBN 0-311-11012-6). Casa Bautista.

Kerfoot, John Barrett. American Pewter. LC 75-29215. (Illus.). xxii, 236p. 1976. Repr. of 1924 ed. 58.00x (ISBN 0-8103-4147-6). Gale.

Kerfoot, W. Charles, ed. Evolution & Ecology of Zooplankton Communities. LC 80-50491. (Illus.). 817p. 1980. text ed. 65.00x (ISBN 0-87451-180-1). U Pr of New Eng.

Kerigan, Florence. Headline, Romance! (YA) 1978. 6.95 (ISBN 0-685-05587-6, Avalon). Bouregy.

Kerkhof, J. Studies in the Language of Geoffrey Chaucer. 2nd, rev. enl. ed. (Leidse Germanistische en Anglistische Reeks Ser.: Vol. 5). xii, 503p. 1982. pap. write for info. (ISBN 90-04-06789-2). E J Brill.

Kerkhofs, J., ed. Catholic Pentecostals Now. LC 76-52071. (Orig.). 1977. pap. 1.75 o.p. (ISBN 0-8189-1148-4, 148, Pub. by Alba Bks). Alba.

Kerkut, G. A., ed. Laboratory Exercises in Comparative Biochemistry & Physiology. Incl. Vol. 1. 1968. 56.00 o.p. (ISBN 0-12-404650-9); Vol. 2. 1969. o.p. (ISBN 0-12-404652-5); Vol. 3. 1970. 79.50 (ISBN 0-12-404653-3); Vol. 4. 1971. 61.50 (ISBN 0-12-404654-1); Vol. 5. 1972. 55.00 (ISBN 0-12-404655-X); Vol. 6. 1972. 54.00 (ISBN 0-12-404656-8). Acad Pr.

--Progress in Neurobiology, Vol. 13, Complete. (Illus.). 440p. 1980. 103.00 (ISBN 0-08-026039-X). Pergamon.

Kerkvliet, Benedict J. The Huk Rebelion: A Study of Peasant Revolt in the Philippines. 333p. 1982. pap. 9.95x (ISBN 0-520-04635-8). U of Cal Pr.

--The Huk Rebellion: A Study of Peasant Revolt in the Philippines. LC 75-22656. 1977. 33.00x (ISBN 0-520-03106-7). U of Cal Pr.

Kerl, Mary A. Where Are You, Lord? LC 82-70949. 112p. (Orig.). 1982. pap. 3.50 (ISBN 0-8066-1924-4, 10-7069). Augsburg.

Kerlinger, Fred N., ed. Review of Research in Education, One. LC 72-89719. (AERA Ser.). 354p. 1973. text ed. 25.00 o.p. (ISBN 0-87581-135-3). Peacock Pubs.

Kerman, A., ed. Modern American Theatre: A Collection of Critical Essays. 1967. 12.95t (ISBN 0-13-586289-2, Spec). P-H.

Kerman, Cynthia E. Creative Tension: The Life & Thought of Kenneth Boulding. LC 72-94762. (Illus.). 398p. 1974. 12.50 o.p. (ISBN 0-472-51500-4). U of Mich Pr.

Kerman, Joseph. Listen. 3rd ed. 1980. 20.95x (ISBN 0-87901-127-0); single record 4.50x (ISBN 0-686-31791-2); 10 record set 31.95x (ISBN 0-686-31792-0). Worth.

--The Music of William Byrd, Volume 1: Latin Masses & Motets. (California Studies in Nineteenth-Century Music Ser.). 1980. 48.50x (ISBN 0-520-04033-3). U of Cal Pr.

Kermode, D. G. Devolution at Work. 1979. text ed. 29.00x (ISBN 0-566-00237-X). Gower Pub Ltd.

Kermode, Frank. The Genesis of Secrecy: On the Interpretation of Narrative. LC 78-23403. (Charles Elliot Norton Lectures Ser.). 1979. text ed. 10.00x (ISBN 0-674-34525-8); pap. 4.95 (ISBN 0-686-82913-1). Harvard U Pr.

--Sense of an Ending: Studies in the Theory of Fiction. (YA) (gr. 10 up). 1968. pap. 6.95 (ISBN 0-19-500770-0, GB). Oxford U Pr.

Kermode, Frank, ed. Shakespeare, Spenser, Donne: Renaissance Essays. 304p. 1971. 18.95 (ISBN 0-7100-7003-9). Routledge & Kegan.

Kermode, Frank & Poirier, Richard, eds. Oxford Reader: Varieties of Contemporary Discourse. (Orig.). 1971. text ed. 13.95x (ISBN 0-19-501365-4); pap. 9.95x (ISBN 0-19-501366-2); pap. 6.95x shorter ed. o.p. (ISBN 0-19-501402-2). Oxford U Pr.

Kermode, Frank, ed. see Shakespeare, William.

Kermode, Frank, et al, eds. The Oxford Anthology of English Literature. Incl. Vol. 1. Middle Ages Through the Eighteenth Century. (ISBN 0-19-501659-9); pap. (ISBN 0-19-501657-2); Vol. 2. 1800 to the Present. (ISBN 0-19-501660-2); pap. (ISBN 0-19-501658-0). (Illus.). 1973. 24.95x ea.; pap. 17.95x ea. Oxford U Pr.

Kern, Alice M. Harmonization-Transposition at the Keyboard. rev. ed. 1968. pap. 14.95 (ISBN 0-87487-059-3). Summy.

Kern, Ann T., ed. see Cruz, Manny & Symington, Nikki.

Kern, Barbara & Kern, Ken. The Earth Sheltered: Owner-Built Home. LC 82-99912. (Illus.). 272p. (Orig.). 1982. pap. 9.95 (ISBN 0-910225-00-1). Owner-Builder.

--Ken Kern's Homestead Workshop. (Illus.). 176p. 1982. pap. 9.95 (ISBN 0-686-83731-2, ScribT). Scribner.

Kern, Dale R., ed. Engineering & Construction Projects: The Emerging Management Roles. LC 82-70492. 336p. 1982. pap. text ed. 28.50 (ISBN 0-87262-299-1). Am Soc Civil Eng.

Kern, Dick, ed. & illus. see Van Esterik, Penny.

Kern, Donald Q. Process Heat Transfer. 1950. text ed. 42.00 (ISBN 0-07-034190-7, C). McGraw.

Kern, Florence. Captain William Cooke Pease: Coast Guard Pioneer. 1983. 4.95 (ISBN 0-686-38462-8). Alised.

--James Montgomery's U. S. Revenue Cutter General Green, 1971-1979. 1779. 3.75 (ISBN 0-686-10943-0). Alised.

--William Cooke's U. S. Revenue Cutter Diligence, 1792-1798. 1979. 3.75 (ISBN 0-686-25728-6). Alised.

Kern, Francis G. German Shepherd Dogs. (Illus.). 1979. 4.95 (ISBN 0-87666-697-7, KW-008). TFH Pubns.

Kern, Frank D. A Revised Taxonomic Account of Gymnosporangium. new ed. LC 79-165358. (Illus.). 136p. 1973. 14.95x (ISBN 0-271-01105-X). Pa St U Pr.

Kern, Gary. Zamyatin We: A Collection of Critical Essays. 200p. 1983. 25.00 (ISBN 0-88233-804-8); pap. 5.00 (ISBN 0-686-82224-2). Ardis Pubs.

Kern, Gary, tr. see Kopelev, Lev.

Kern, Jean B. Dramatic Satire in the Age of Walpole, 1720-1750. replica ed. 1976. pap. 7.95x o.p. (ISBN 0-8138-0450-7). Iowa St U Pr.

Kern, Ken, jt. auth. see Kern, Barbara.

Kern, Louis J. An Ordered Love: Sex Roles & Sexuality in Victorian Utopias--the Shakers, the Mormons, & the Oneida Community. LC 80-10763. xv, 430p. 1981. 24.00x (ISBN 0-8078-1443-1); pap. 9.95x (ISBN 0-8078-4074-2). U of NC Pr.

Kern, Marna E. The Complete Book of Handcrafted Paper. (Illus.). 1980. 12.95 (ISBN 0-698-10989-6, Coward). Putnam Pub Group.

--An Introduction to Breadcraft. LC 77-24981. 1978. 11.95 o.p. (ISBN 0-395-25770-0); pap. 5.95 o.p. (ISBN 0-395-25951-7). HM.

Kern, Raymond & Weisbrod, Alain. Thermodynamics for Geologists. McKie, Duncan, tr. from Fr. LC 67-22353. 304p. 1967. pap. 12.50x (ISBN 0-87735-305-0). Freeman C.

Kern, Rochelle, jt. ed. see Conrad, Peter.

Kern, Stephen. Anatomy & Destiny: A Cultural History of the Human Body. LC 74-17651. (Illus.). 320p. 1975. 10.95 o.p. (ISBN 0-672-52091-5). Bobbs.

Kernaghan, Salvinija G., ed. Delivery of Health Care in Urban Underserved Areas. LC 79-21168. 128p. 1979. pap. 13.25 o.p. (ISBN 0-87258-278-7, 067165). Am Hospital.

Kernahan, Desmond A. & Thomson, Hugh G. Symposium on Pediatric Plastic Surgery, Vol. 21. Bauer, Bruce S., ed. LC 81-14074. (Illus.). 453p. 1982. text ed. 89.50 (ISBN 0-8016-2691-9). Mosby.

Kernan, Alvin, ed. see Shakespeare, William.

Kernan, Alvin B., ed. see Jonson, Ben.

Kernan, D. Steps to English, Bks. 1-2. 1974. Bk. 1. text ed. 10.00x (ISBN 0-07-034151-6); Bk. 2. text ed. 10.00x (ISBN 0-07-034156-7). wkbk. 3.53 (ISBN 0-686-76804-3); tchr's ed. 11.08 ea. (ISBN 0-686-66128-1); cassettes 199.80 ea. (ISBN 0-07-034153-2). McGraw.

--Steps to English, Bk. 4. 1976. 10.00 (ISBN 0-07-034180-X, W); tchr's ed. 11.08 (ISBN 0-07-034184-2); cassettes 199.80 (ISBN 0-07-034182-6); cue cards 63.28 (ISBN 0-07-034183-4); wkbk. 5.16 (ISBN 0-07-034181-8). McGraw.

Kernan, D., jt. auth. see Woodford, P.

Kernan, D., ed. see Kernan, Doris.

Kernan, Doris. Steps to English, Bk. 3. (Illus.). 288p. (gr. 5-6). 1975. pap. text ed. 10.00x (ISBN 0-07-034163-X, W); tchr's ed. 11.08 (ISBN 0-07-034167-2); wkbk. 5.16 (ISBN 0-07-034164-8); cassettes 199.80 (ISBN 0-07-034165-6); cue card 53.28 (ISBN 0-07-034166-4). McGraw.

--Steps to English, Bk. 6. 2nd ed. Kernan, D., ed. (Illus.). 128p. (gr. 6). 1983. pap. text ed. write for info (ISBN 0-07-033106-5, W); write for info teacher's ed. (ISBN 0-07-033116-2); write for info wkbk. (ISBN 0-07-033126-X). McGraw.

Kernan, Roderick P. Cell Potassium. LC 80-133320. (Transport in the Life Sciences Ser.). 200p. 1980. 46.50x (ISBN 0-471-04806-2, Pub. by Wiley-Interscience). Wiley.

Kernen, D. Steps to English, 5 Levels. 2nd ed. (gr. 1-5). 1982. Level 1, 128p. text ed. 5.40 (ISBN 0-07-033101-4); Level 2, 128p. text ed. 5.40 (ISBN 0-07-033102-2); Level 3, 160p. text ed. 6.84 (ISBN 0-07-033103-0); Level 4, 160p. text ed. 6.84 (ISBN 0-07-033104-9); Level 5, 160p. text ed. 6.84 (ISBN 0-07-033105-7); tchr's ed., wkbks., cue cards, & tests avail. McGraw.

Kerner, Edward H. Theory of Action-at-a-Distance in Relativistic Particle Dynamics. (International Science Review Ser.). 220p. 1972. 56.00x (ISBN 0-677-13990-X). Gordon.

Kerner, John A. Manual of Pediatric Parenteral Nutrition. 550p. 1983. 29.95 (ISBN 0-471-09291-6, Pub. by Wiley Med). Wiley.

Kerner, Martin, jt. auth. see Evanovich, Peter.

Kerner, Nora, tr. see Vargh, Georgy.

Kerner, Robert J. Bohemia in the Eighteenth Century. 20.00 (ISBN 0-87569-007-6). Academic Intl.

Kernes, Steven T. & Kuehn, Lowell L. The Criminal Investigator's Guide. (Illus.). 170p. 1982. pap. 16.75x spiral (ISBN 0-398-04693-X). C C Thomas.

Kernevez, J. P. Enzyme Mathematics. (Studies in Mathematics & Its Applications: Vol. 10). 1980. 53.25 (ISBN 0-444-86122-X). Elsevier.

Kerney & Cameron. A Field Guide to the Land Snails of Britain & North West Europe. 29.95 (ISBN 0-686-42776-9, Collins Pub England). Greene.

Kernicki, Jeanette & Weiler, Kathi. Electocardiography for Nurses: Physiological Correlates. LC 80-28705. 262p. 1981. 21.95 (ISBN 0-471-05752-5, Pub. by Wiley Med). Wiley.

Kernicki, Jeannette & Bullock, Barbara. Cardiovascular Nursing: Rationale for Therapy & Nursing Approach. (Illus.). 1971. 9.75 o.p. (ISBN 0-399-40004-4). Putnam Pub Group.

Kernighan, B. W. & Plauger, P. J. The Elements of Programming Style. 160p. 1974. pap. text ed. 5.95 o.p. (ISBN 0-07-034199-0, C). McGraw.

Kernighan, Brian W. & Plauger, P. J. The Elements of Programming Style. 2nd ed. 1978. pap. text ed. 14.95 (ISBN 0-07-034207-5, C). McGraw.

--Software Tools in Pascal. 1981. pap. 18.95 (ISBN 0-201-10342-7); tape 65.00 (ISBN 0-201-03668-1). A-W.

Kernighan, Brian W. & Ritchie, Dennis M. The C Programming Language. LC 77-28983. (Prentice-Hall Software Ser.). 1978. pap. 19.95 ref. ed. (ISBN 0-13-110163-3). P-H.

Kernodle, George & Kernodle, Portia. Invitation to the Theatre. 2nd, abr. ed. (Illus.). 370p. 1978. pap. text ed. 14.95 (ISBN 0-15-546923-1, HC). HarBraceJ.

Kernodle, Portia, jt. auth. see Kernodle, George.

Kernohan, R. D. Scotland's Life & Work. pap. 12.50 (ISBN 0-7152-0421-1). Outlook.

Kerns, Frances C. The Winter Heart: A Colorado Epic. (Orig.). 1978. pap. 2.50 o.p. (ISBN 0-446-81431-8). Warner Bks.

Kerns, Phil. Fake It Til You Make It. (Illus.). 182p. (Orig.). pap. 5.95 (ISBN 0-9609908-0-1). Victory Pr.

Kerns, Robert L. Photojournalism: Photography with a Purpose. (Illus.). 1980. text ed. 20.95 (ISBN 0-13-665695-1). P-H.

Kerns, Virginia. Women & the Ancestors: Black Carib Kinship & Ritual. LC 82-2601. (Illus.). 256p. 1983. 17.95 (ISBN 0-252-00982-7). U of Ill Pr.

Kernut, G. A. & Phillus, J. W., eds. Progress in Neurobiology, Vol. 17. 289p. 1983. 115.00 (ISBN 0-08-029697-1). Pergamon.

Keronode, Dale & Lensner, Gordon, eds. Harris Industrial Sales Atlas for Cleveland & Cuyahoga County Ohio. (Illus.). 322p. 1982. 59.50 (ISBN 0-916512-82-7). Harris Pub.

Kerouac, Jack. Dear Carolyn: (Letters to Carolyn Cassady) Knight, Arthur & Knight, Kit, eds. 1983. pap. 5.00 ltd. ed. (ISBN 0-934660-06-9). TUVOTI.

--Dharma Bums. 192p. 1976. lib. bdg. 14.95x (ISBN 0-89966-135-1). Buccaneer Bks.

--Dharma Bums. pap. 2.50 (ISBN 0-451-12313-1, AE2313, Sig). NAL.

--Doctor Sax. 245p. 1976. lib. bdg. 14.95x (ISBN 0-89966-133-5). Buccaneer Bks.

--Heaven & Other Poems. Allen, Donald, ed. LC 77-6233. 72p. 1977. pap. 3.95 (ISBN 0-912516-31-3). Grey Fox.

--Maggie Cassidy. 1978. pap. 4.95 (ISBN 0-07-034203-2, SP). McGraw.

--On the Road. 310p. 1976. lib. bdg. 16.95 (ISBN 0-89966-134-3). Buccaneer Bks.

--On the Road. pap. 2.95 (ISBN 0-451-12290-9, AE2290, Sig). NAL.

--Pic. LC 71-166459. 1971. pap. 4.95 (ISBN 0-394-62440-8, E839, Ever). Grove.

--Scattered Poems. (Pocket Poets Ser.: No. 28). 1971. pap. 3.50 (ISBN 0-87286-064-7). City Lights.

--Visions of Cody. LC 73-3847. (McGraw-Hill Paperbacks). 416p. 1974. pap. 5.95 (ISBN 0-07-034202-4, SP). McGraw.

--Visions of Gerard. (McGraw-Hill Paperbacks). 1976. pap. 4.95 (ISBN 0-07-034204-0, SP). McGraw.

Kerovac, Jan. Baby Driver. LC 82-15503. 304p. 1983. pap. 4.95 (ISBN 0-03-062538-6). HR&W.

Kerovak, Jack. Tristessa. (McGraw-Hill Paperbacks Ser.). 1978. pap. 3.95 (ISBN 0-07-034205-9, SP). McGraw.

Kerpelman, Leonard. Divorce: A Man's Guide. 1983. price not set (ISBN 0-89651-151-0). Icarus.

Kerper, Hazel B. & Israel, Jerold H. Introduction to the Criminal Justice System. 2nd ed. (Criminal Justice Ser.). (Illus.). 1979. text ed. 22.95 (ISBN 0-8299-0276-7); pap. study guide 7.95 (ISBN 0-8299-0260-0); instrs.' manual avail. (ISBN 0-8299-0593-6). West Pub.

Kerper, Hazel B. & Kerper, Janeen. Legal Rights of the Convicted. (Criminal Justice Ser.). 1974. text ed. 18.95 o.s.i. (ISBN 0-8299-0622-3); pap. text ed. write for info. o.s.i. West Pub.

Kerper, Janeen, jt. auth. see Kerper, Hazel B.

Kerr. Focalguide to the Home Studio. (Focalguide Ser.). (Illus.). 1983. pap. 8.95x (ISBN 0-240-50986-2). Focal Pr.

Kerr, Alex, ed. Resources & Development in the Indian Ocean Region. 256p. 1981. lib. bdg. 29.75 (ISBN 0-86531-123-4). Westview.

Kerr, Baine. Jumping off Place & Other Stories. LC 80-14023. (Breakthrough Bks.). 80p. 1981. text ed. 9.95 (ISBN 0-8262-0311-6). U of Mo Pr.

Kerr, Caroline V., tr. & ed. The Story of Bayreuth As Told in "The Bayreuth Letters of Richard Wagner". LC 78-163795. 364p. Date not set. Repr. of 1912 ed. price not set. Vienna Hse.

Kerr, Charles H., tr. see Labriola, Antonio.

Kerr, Clark. Labor Markets & Wage Determination: The Balkanization of Labor Markets & Other Essays. LC 75-17291. 1977. 22.50x (ISBN 0-520-03070-2). U of Cal Pr.

--Marshall, Marx & Modern Times. LC 75-92249. 1969. 14.95 (ISBN 0-521-07665-X). Cambridge U Pr.

--The Uses of the University. rev. ed. LC 63-20770. (Godkin Lectures Ser: 1963). 1972. 8.95x o.p. (ISBN 0-674-93165-3). Harvard U Pr.

Kerr, Donal A. Peel, Priests & Politics: Sir Robert Peel's Administration & the Roman Catholic Church in Ireland, 1841-1846. (Oxford Historical Monographs). 1982. 49.50x (ISBN 0-19-821891-5). Oxford U Pr.

Kerr, Donald A. & Ash, Major M., Jr. Oral Diagnosis. 6th ed. LC 82-6291. (Illus.). 383p. 1983. text ed. 32.50 (ISBN 0-8016-2656-0). Mosby.

Kerr, Donald R. Basic Mathematics: Arithmetic with an Introduction to Algebra. (Illus.). 1979. pap. text ed. 18.50 (ISBN 0-07-034230-X, C); instructors manual 19.95 (ISBN 0-07-034231-8). McGraw.

--Elementary Algebra. (Illus.). 1979. pap. text ed. 17.50 (ISBN 0-07-034221-0, C); instructor's manual 19.95 (ISBN 0-07-034222-9). McGraw.

Kerr, Elaine B. & Hiltz, Starr R. Computer-Mediated Communication Systems: Status & Evaluation. (Human Communication Research Ser.). 1982. 26.50 (ISBN 0-12-404980-X). Acad Pr.

Kerr, Elizabeth M. William Faulkner's Gothic Domain. LC 78-27795. (National University Pubns., Literary Criticism Ser.). 1979. 19.50 (ISBN 0-8046-9228-9). Kennikat.

Kerr, Francis K., jt. ed. see Kerr, Kathleen W.

Kerr, George. Formosa Betrayed. LC 76-10805. (China in the 20th Century Ser.). 1976. Repr. of 1965 ed. lib. bdg. 55.00 (ISBN 0-306-70762-4). Da Capo.

Kerr, George H. Formosa: Licensed Revolution & the Home Rule Movement, 1895-1945. LC 73-91458. 256p. 1974. 14.00x (ISBN 0-8248-0323-X). UH Pr.

--Okinawa: The History of an Island People. LC 58-12283. (Illus.). 542p. 1975. Repr. of 1958 ed. 22.50 (ISBN 0-8048-0437-0). C E Tuttle.

Kerr, Graham. The Complete Galloping Gourmet Cookbook. (Illus.). 680p. 1972. 12.95 (ISBN 0-448-01322-3, G&D). Putnam Pub Group.

--The Love Feast. (Illus.). 1978. 8.95 o.p. (ISBN 0-671-24052-8). S&S.

Kerr, Harland, jt. ed. see Pittman, Richard.

Kerr, Herminia J., jt. auth. see Azevedo, Milton M.

Kerr, Horace L. How to Minister to Senior Adults in Your Church. LC 77-80944. 1980. 7.95 (ISBN 0-8054-3222-1). Broadman.

Kerr, Howard & Crow, Charles L., eds. The Occult in America. LC 82-24770. (Illus.). 234p. 1983. 16.95 (ISBN 0-252-00983-5). U of Ill Pr.

Kerr, Hugh T., Jr., ed. Compend of Luther's Theology. 1966. pap. 5.95 (ISBN 0-664-24729-6). Westminster.

Kerr, J. Ernest. Imprint of the Maritimes. (Illus.). 1959. 4.00 o.p. (ISBN 0-8158-0122-X). Chris Mass.

Kerr, James S. Dandy, the Dime. (First Grade Read-to Bks.). (Illus.). (gr. 1-3). PLB 5.95 o.p. (ISBN 0-513-00317-7). Denison.

Kerr, Jan. Reach Out & Touch Someone. 1979. 6.50 o.p. (ISBN 0-533-04040-X). Vantage.

Kerr, Jean. How I Got to Be Perfect. LC 78-1008. 1978. 10.95 o.p. (ISBN 0-385-13502-5). Doubleday.

--Please Don't Eat the Daisies. LC 57-12467. (Illus.). 1959. 4.95 (ISBN 0-385-04860-2). Doubleday.

Kerr, Jessica. Shakespeare's Flowers. LC 68-13585. (Illus.). (gr. 7 up). 1969. 12.45i (ISBN 0-690-73163-9, TYC-J). Har-Row.

--Shakespeare's Flowers. LC 68-13585. (Illus.). 96p. (YA) (gr. 7 up). 1982. pap. 6.68i (ISBN 0-690-04320-1, TYC-J). Har-Row.

Kerr, Joan, jt. auth. see Falkus, Hugh.

Kerr, John. Matters for Judgment: An Autobiography. 1979. 26.00x (ISBN 0-312-52305-X). St Martin.

Kerr, John G. Naturalist in the Gran Chaco. LC 68-55200. (Illus.). 1968. Repr. of 1950 ed. lib. bdg. 18.50x (ISBN 0-8371-0511-0, KEGC). Greenwood.

Kerr, Judith. Mog's Christmas. LC 77-78121. (Illus.). (ps-3). 1977. 5.95 o.s.i. (ISBN 0-529-05376-4, Philomel). Putnam Pub Group.

--The Other Way Round. LC 75-4254. 256p. (gr. 6 up). 1975. 8.95 (ISBN 0-698-20335-6, Coward). Putnam Pub Group.

--A Small Person Far Away. LC 78-13195. (gr. 6-8). 1979. 8.95 (ISBN 0-698-20472-7, Coward). Putnam Pub Group.

--When Hitler Stole Pink Rabbit. (gr. 6 up). 1972. 8.95 (ISBN 0-698-20182-5, Coward). Putnam Pub Group.

--When Hitler Stole Pink Rabbit. (gr. 3 up). 1973. pap. 1.50 o.p. (ISBN 0-440-49017-0, YB). Dell.

Kerr, Kathleen W. & Kerr, Francis K., eds. Cost Data for Landscape Construction, 1982. 4th ed. (Illus.). 264p. 1983. pap. 27.50 (ISBN 0-937890-03-0). Kerr Assoc.

Kerr, M. E. Dinky Hocker Shoots Smack. LC 72-80366. 190p. (gr. 7 up). 1972. 9.95 o.p. (ISBN 0-06-023150-5, HarpJ); PLB 10.89 (ISBN 0-06-023151-3). Har-Row.

--If I Love You, Am I Trapped Forever? 1974. pap. 2.25 (ISBN 0-440-94320-5, LFL). Dell.

--Me Me Me Me Me: Not a Novel. LC 82-48521. (A Charlotte Zolotow Bk.). 224p. (YA) (gr. 7 up). 1983. 9.57i (ISBN 0-06-023192-0, HarpJ); PLB 9.89g (ISBN 0-06-023193-9). Har-Row.

--The Son of Someone Famous. LC 73-14338. 176p. (gr. 7 up). 1974. PLB 10.89 (ISBN 0-06-023147-5, HarpJ). Har-Row.

Kerr, Malcolm. Arab Cold War, Nineteen Fifty-Eight to Nineteen Seventy: A Study of Ideology in Politics. 3rd ed. 1971. pap. text ed. 5.95 (ISBN 0-19-501475-8, GB358, GB). Oxford U Pr.

Kerr, Malcolm H., ed. see Kouri, Fred, et al.

Kerr, Mary H. Warren County, North Carolina, Records: Abstracted Records of Colonial Bute County, North Carolina, 1764-1779, & Bute County Marriages, Vol. I. LC 82-20498. 104p. 1983. Repr. of 1967 ed. 25.00 (ISBN 0-87152-366-3). Reprint.

Kerr, Mary M. & Nelson, C. Michael. Strategies for Managing Behavior Problems. 448p. 1983. text ed. 14.95 (ISBN 0-675-20032-6). Merrill.

Kerr, Norm. Technique of Photographic Lighting. (Illus.). 1979. 18.95 o.p. (ISBN 0-8174-2455-5, Amphoto). Watson-Guptill.

--Techniques of Photographic Lighting. New ed. (Illus.). 208p. 1982. pap. 9.95 (ISBN 0-8174-6024-1, Amphoto). Watson-Guptill.

Kerr, Paul E. Optical Mineralogy. 4th ed. (Illus.). 1977. text ed. 39.95 (ISBN 0-07-034218-0, C). McGraw.

Kerr, Paul F., jt. auth. see Vanders, Iris.

Kerr, Rosalie see Bates, Martin & Dudley-Evans, Tony.

Kerr, Stanley E. The Lions of Marash: Personal Experiences with American Near East Relief, 1919-1922. LC 75-38001. 122p. 1973. 39.50x (ISBN 0-87395-200-6). State U NY Pr.

Kerr, Thomas J. Civil Defense in the United States: Band-Aid for a Holocaust? 250p. 1983. lib. bdg. 23.50x (ISBN 0-86531-586-8). Westview.

Kerr, Walter. The Secret of Stalingrad. (War Bks.). 288p. 1980. pap. 2.50 (ISBN 0-86721-089-3). Jove Pubns.

--The Shabunin Affair: An Episode in the Life of Leo Tolstoy. LC 81-70715. (Illus.). 192p. 1982. 14.95 (ISBN 0-8014-1461-X). Cornell U Pr.

Kerr, Wilfrid B. The Reign of Terror Seventeen Ninety-Three to Seventeen Ninety-Four: The Experiment of the Democratic Republic & the Rise of the Bourgeoisie. (Perspectives in European History: No. 24). (Illus.). Repr. of 1927 ed. lib. bdg. 35.00x (ISBN 0-87991-631-1). Porcupine Pr.

Kerr, William W. A Treatise on the Law & Practice of Injunctions. LC 81-81500. 743p. 1981. Repr. of 1927 ed. lib. bdg. 75.00x (ISBN 0-912004-16-9). W W Gaunt.

Kerrane, Kevin & Grossinger, Richard. Baseball Diamonds: Tales, Traces Visions & Voodoo from a Native American Rite. LC 79-7601. (Illus.). 1980. pap. 11.95 o.p. (ISBN 0-385-14950-6, Anch). Doubleday.

Kerrebrock, Jack L. Aircraft Engines & Gas Turbines. LC 77-4428. 1977. 27.50x (ISBN 0-262-11064-4). MIT Pr.

Kerri, James N. Unwilling Urbanites: The Life of Canadian Indians in a Prairie City. LC 78-63272. 1978. pap. text ed. 9.25 o.p. (ISBN 0-8191-0622-4). U Pr of Amer.

Kerrich, G. J., et al, eds. Key Words to the Fauna & Flora of the British Isles & Northwestern Europe. (Systematic Association Special Ser.). 1978. 31.50 (ISBN 0-12-405550-8). Acad Pr.

Kerridge, E., jt. auth. see Bankes, J.

Kerrigan, A., ed. see De Unamuno, M.

Kerrigan, Anthony, ed. & intro. by see Borges, Jorge L.

Kerrigan, Anthony & Lacy, Allen, trs. from Span. Peace in War: A Novel: Selected Works of Miguel de Unamuno, Vol. 1. LC 82-61390. (Bollingen Ser.: No. LXXXV-1). 300p. 1983. 35.00x (ISBN 0-691-09926-X). Princeton U Pr.

Kerrigan, Anthony, tr. see Ortega Y Gasset, Jose.

Kerrigan, H. D., jt. auth. see Livingstone, J. L.

Kerrigan, John. The Phoenix Assault. (Orig.). 1980. pap. 2.50 o.p. (ISBN 0-451-09522-7, E9522, Sig). NAL.

Kerrod, Robin. Metals. LC 82-50388. (Visual Science Ser.). PLB 13.00 (ISBN 0-382-06661-8). Silver.

--See Inside a Space Station. LC 78-66168. (See Inside Bks.). (Illus.). (gr. 5 up). 1979. PLB 9.40 s&l (ISBN 0-531-09122-8, Warwick Press). Watts.

Kersaudy, Francois. Churchill & DeGaulle. LC 81-69154. 480p. 1983. pap. 11.95 (ISBN 0-689-70641-3, 290). Atheneum.

Kerschner, Velma L. Nutrition & Diet Therapy. 3rd ed. LC 82-22120. 350p. 1983. pap. text ed. 11.95 (ISBN 0-8036-5302-6). Davis Co.

Kershaw, Andrew. Modern Combat Aircraft & Insignia. LC 79-12626. (Arco Fact Guides in Color). (Illus.). 1979. 6.95 o.p. (ISBN 0-668-04807-7). Arco.

Kershaw, F. & Russon, S. German for Business Studies. 1971. pap. text ed. 4.50x (ISBN 0-582-36186-9). Longman.

Kershaw, Ian. Popular Opinion & Political Dissent in the Third Reich: Bavaria 1933-1945. 450p. 1983. 49.50 (ISBN 0-19-821922-9). Oxford U Pr.

Kershaw, John D. Microprocessor Technology. 1980. text ed. 24.95x (ISBN 0-534-00748-1, Breton Pubs). Wadsworth Pub.

Kershaw, John K. Digital Electronics: Logic & Systems. 2nd ed. 1983. text ed. 27.95 (ISBN 0-534-01471-2, Breton Pubs). Wadsworth Pub.

Kershaw, Patricia. Trapped in the Old Cabin. (The Pathfinder Ser.). (Illus.). 208p. 1980. pap. 3.95 (ISBN 0-310-37861-3). Zondervan.

Kershen, Harry, ed. Collective Bargaining by Government Workers: The Public Employee. (Public Sector Contemporary Issues Ser.: Vol. 3). 264p. 1983. pap. text ed. 16.50 (ISBN 0-89503-032-2). Baywood Pub.

--Labor-Management Relations among Government Employees. (Public Sector Contemporary Issues Ser.: Vol. 2). 224p. 1983. pap. text ed. 13.95X (ISBN 0-89503-033-0). Baywood Pub.

Kershner, Howard E. Dividing the Wealth: Are You Getting Your Share. 1980. pap. 5.95 (ISBN 0-8159-5308-9). Devin.

Kershner, William K. & O'Kelley, Genie R. The Student Pilot's Study Guide. (Illus.). 104p. (gr. 10-12). 1983. pap. 9.95 (ISBN 0-8138-0821-9). Iowa St U Pr.

Kerslake, D. M. The Stress of Hot Environments. LC 74-168896. (Physiological Society Monographs: No. 29). (Illus.). 300p. 1972. 75.00 (ISBN 0-521-08343-5). Cambridge U Pr.

Kerslake, John. Early Georgian Portraits, 2 vols. (Illus.). 800p. Set. 160.00 (ISBN 0-312-22476-1). St Martin.

Kersnowski, Frank. Outsiders: Poets of Contemporary Ireland. LC 74-21131. (History & Culture Monograph Ser.: No. 12). 1975. pap. 10.00x (ISBN 0-912646-03-9). Tex Christian.

Kerst, Friedrich. Beethoven: The Man & the Artist As Revealed in His Own Words. Krehbiel, Henry E., tr. 1905. pap. 2.50 (ISBN 0-486-21261-0). Dover.

Kerstan, Reinhold. Sangre y Honor. Carrodeguas, Andy & Marosi, Esteban, eds. Romanenghi de Powell, Elsa, tr. 190p. (Span.). (gr. 4-6). 1982. pap. 3.00 (ISBN 0-686-84510-2). Life Pubs Intl.

Kerstein, Morris D. Aneurysms. (Illus.). 276p. 1983. lib. bdg. price not set (ISBN 0-683-04598-9). Williams & Wilkins.

Kerstin, A. F. Prospect of London. 15.50 (ISBN 0-392-04294-0, SpS). Sportshelf.

Kerstrat, Francoise, jt. auth. see Crawford, Williame.

Kert, Bernice. The Hemingway Women. (Illus.). 1983. 20.00 (ISBN 0-393-01720-6). Norton.

Kertes. Alkali- & Alkaline-Earth Metal Oxides & Hydroxides in Water: Solubilities of Solids. (Solubility Data Ser.). 1985. 100.01 (ISBN 0-08-023920-X). Pergamon. Postponed.

--Alkali-Metal Chlorides (Binary Systems) Solubilities of Solids. (IUPAC Solubility Data Ser.). 1984. 100.01 (ISBN 0-08-023918-8). Pergamon. Postponed.

--Alkali Metal Halides in Organic Solvents (Amides) Solubilities of Solids. (Solubility Data Ser.: Vol. 11). 1980. 100.00 o.p. (ISBN 0-08-023917-X). Pergamon.

--Alkaline-Earth Sulfates in All Solvents: Solubilities of Solids. (IUPAC Solubility Data Ser.). Date not set. 100.00 (ISBN 0-08-023916-1). Pergamon. Postponed.

--Halogenated Benzenes: Mutual Solubility of Liquids. (Solubility Data Ser.). 1983. 100.01 (ISBN 0-08-023926-9). Pergamon.

--Hydrogen & Deuterium, 2 Vols. (IUPAC Solubility Data Series: Vol. 5 & 6). 670p. 1981. 200.00 (ISBN 0-08-023927-7). Pergamon.

--Nitrogen & Air: Gas Solubilities. LC 82-15046. (Solubility Data Ser.: Vol. 10). 1982. 100.00 (ISBN 0-08-023922-6). Pergamon.

--Oxides of Nitrogen, Sulfur & Chlorine: Gas Solubilities. (IUPAC Solubility Data Ser.: Vol. 8). 1981. 100.00 (ISBN 0-08-023924-2). Pergamon.

--Oxygen & Ozone: Gas Solubilities. (Solubility Data Ser.). 1981. 100.00 (ISBN 0-08-023915-3). Pergamon.

--Tetraphenylborates. (IUPAC Solubility Data Ser.). 260p. 1981. 100.00 (ISBN 0-08-023928-5). Pergamon.

Kertes & Gerrard, W. Hydrogen Halides in Non-Aqueous Solvents: Gas Solubilities. (Solubility Data Ser.). 1983. 100.01 (ISBN 0-08-023925-0). Pergamon.

Kertes & Guminsky, C. Metals in Mercury: Solubilities of Solids. (Solubility Data Ser.). 1984. 100.01 (ISBN 0-08-023921-8). Pergamon. Postponed.

Kertes & Vincent, Colin A., eds. Alkali Metal, Alkaline-Earth Metal & Ammonium Halides in Amide Solvents. (IUPAC Solubility Data Ser.: Vol. 11). 374p. 1980. 100.00 (ISBN 0-08-023917-X). Pergamon.

Kertes, jt. ed. see Hayduk, W.

Kertes, H. Lawrence. Argon: Gas Solubilities. (IUPAC Solubility Data Ser.: Vol. 4). (Illus.). 348p. 1980. 100.00 (ISBN 0-08-022353-2). Pergamon.

--Helium & Neon: Gas Solubilities. (Solubility Data Ser.: Vol. 1). 1979. 100.00 (ISBN 0-08-022351-6). Pergamon.

--Krypton, Xenon, & Radon: Gas Solubilities. (Solubility Data Ser.: Vol. 2). 1979. 100.00 (ISBN 0-08-022352-4). Pergamon.

Kertesz, Andre. Andre Kertesz: A Lifetime of Perception. LC 82-70745. 260p. 1982. 45.00 (ISBN 0-8109-1207-4). Abrams.

--Hungarian Memories: Nineteen Twelve to Nineteen Twenty-Five. 1982. 49.95 (ISBN 0-8212-1508-6). NYGS.

Kertesz, Stephen D. Diplomacy in a Whirlpool. LC 74-7431. (Illus.). 273p. 1974. Repr. of 1953 ed. lib. bdg. 18.25x (ISBN 0-8371-7540-2, KEDW). Greenwood.

Kertis, Joan & Davis, Nina, eds. English Language & Orientation Programs in the United States. LC 78-101308. 144p. 1982. pap. 8.95 (ISBN 0-87206-101-9). Inst Intl Educ.

Kertz, George J. The Nature & Application of Mathematics. LC 78-20979. (Illus.). 1979. pap. 23.50x (ISBN 0-673-16241-9). Scott F.

Kertzer, David I. Comrades & Christians. LC 79-15313. (Illus.). 1980. 37.50 (ISBN 0-521-22879-4); pap. 9.95 (ISBN 0-521-29700-1). Cambridge U Pr.

Kertzer, David I., jt. ed. see Kenny, Michael.

Kerval, Alastor de, pseud. Amrita-Liber CCCXLIII. LC 77-8311. 1983. 45.00 (ISBN 0-913576-18-2); deluxe ed. (ISBN 0-913576-19-0). Thelema Pubns.

Kerwood, Lewis O., jt. ed. see Britton, James A., Jr.

Kery, Patricia F. Great Magazine Covers of the World. LC 81-19066. (Illus.). 384p. 1982. 75.00 (ISBN 0-89659-225-1). Abbeville Pr.

Kesey, Ken. Kesey's Garage Sale. LC 77-186734. (Illus.). 1973. pap. 5.95 o.p. (ISBN 0-670-00346-8). Penguin.

--Kesey's Garage Sale. LC 77-186734. (Illus.). 256p. 1973. 8.95 o.p. (ISBN 0-670-41268-6). Viking Pr.

--One Flew Over the Cuckoo's Nest. 1975. pap. 2.95 (ISBN 0-451-12140-6, AE2140, Sig). NAL.

Keshavamurthy, R. N., jt. auth. see Miller, Forrest R.

Keshokov, A. Starlit Hours: Selected Poems. 287p. 6.00 (ISBN 0-8285-2287-1, Pub. by Progress Pubs USSR). Imported Pubns.

Kesler, Jackson, ed. Theatrical Costume: A Guide to Information Sources. LC 79-22881. (Performing Arts Information Guide Ser.: Vol. 6). 1979. 42.00x (ISBN 0-8103-1455-X). Gale.

Kesler, S. E. Our Finite Resources. 1975. 12.95 (ISBN 0-07-034245-8, C). McGraw.

Kessel. Le Lion. (Easy Reader, C). pap. 3.95 (ISBN 0-88436-112-8, 40277). EMC.

Kessel, David & Dougherty, Thomas J., eds. Porphyrin Photosensitization. (Advances in Experimental Medicine & Biology Ser.: Vol. 160). 304p. 1983. 42.50x (ISBN 0-306-41193-8, Plenum Pr). Plenum Pub.

Kessel, Joseph. The Road Back: A Report on Alcoholics Anonymous. LC 78-9948. 1979. Repr. of 1962 ed. lib. bdg. 20.50x (ISBN 0-313-21097-7, KERB). Greenwood.

Kessel, Joyce K. Halloween. LC 80-15890. (Carolrhoda on My Own Bks.). (Illus.). 48p. (gr. k-3). 1980. PLB 6.95g (ISBN 0-87614-132-7). Carolrhoda Bks.

--St. Patrick's Day. LC 82-1254. (Carolrhoda On My Own Bks.). (Illus.). 48p. (gr. 1-4). 1983. lib. bdg. 6.95g (ISBN 0-87614-193-9). Carolrhoda Bks.

--Squanto & the First Thanksgiving. LC 82-10313. (Carolrhoda On My Own Bks). (Illus.). 48p. (gr. k-3). 1983. PLB 6.95g (ISBN 0-87614-199-8). Carolrhoda Bks.

--Valentine's Day. LC 81-3842. (Carolrhoda on My Own Bks.). (Illus.). 48p. (gr. k-3). 1981. PLB 6.95g (ISBN 0-87614-166-1, AACRZ). Carolrhoda Bks.

Kesselman, Judi R. I Can Use Tools. LC 80-26387. (Illus.). 32p. (gr. k-4). 1982. 5.95 (ISBN 0-525-66275-3). Dandelion Pr.

Kesselman, Wendy. Emma. LC 77-15161. (Illus.). 32p. (gr. k-3). 1980. 8.95a (ISBN 0-385-13461-4); PLB o.p. (ISBN 0-385-13462-2). Doubleday.

--Flick. LC 80-8435. 160p. (YA) (gr. 7 up). 1983. 10.53i (ISBN 0-06-023182-3, HarpJ); PLB 10.89g (ISBN 0-06-023183-1). Har-Row.

Kesselman-Turkel, Judi, jt. auth. see Peterson, Franklynn.

Kesselring, Joseph see Freedley, George.

Kessen, W. The Child. LC 65-14253. (Perspectives in Psychology Ser.). 301p. 1965. pap. 15.95x (ISBN 0-471-47306-5, Pub. by Wiley-Interscience). Wiley.

Kessen, William, jt. auth. see Mandler, George.

Kessinger, Mark. Exploded View. 44p. 1983. pap. 4.50 (ISBN 0-914946-34-X). Cleveland St Univ Poetry Ctr.

Kessinger, Tom G. Vilyatpur 1848-1968: Social & Economic Change in a North Indian Village. LC 72-89788. (Illus.). 1974. 30.00x (ISBN 0-520-02340-4). U of Cal Pr.

Kessler, Carol F. Elizabeth Stuart Phelps. (United States Authors Ser.). 1982. lib. bdg. 14.95 (ISBN 0-8057-7374-6, Twayne). G K Hall.

Kessler, Carolyn, jt. ed. see Hayes, Curtis.

Kessler, Carolyn, ed. see Streiff, Virginia.

Kessler, D. P., jt. auth. see GreenKorn, R. A.

Kessler, David. The Falashas. (Illus.). 1982. text ed. 24.50x o.p. (ISBN 0-8419-0791-9). Holmes & Meier.

Kessler, Edward. Images of Wallace Stevens. 275p. 1982. Repr. of 1972 ed. 13.50x (ISBN 0-87752-226-X). Gordian.

Kessler, Francis P. The Dilemmas of Presidential Leadership: Of Caretakers & Kings. LC 81-10731. (Illus.). 404p. 1982. pap. 14.95 reference (ISBN 0-13-214593-6). P-H.

Kessler, Friedrich & Gilmore, Grant. Contracts: Cases & Materials. 2nd ed. 1396p. 1976. 29.95 (ISBN 0-316-49016-4). Little.

Kessler, G. Nuclear Fission Reactors: Potential Role & Risk of Converters & Breeders. (Topics in Energy Ser.). (Illus.). 257p. 1983. 37.00 (ISBN 0-387-81713-1). Springer-Verlag.

Kessler, Gail, jt. auth. see Gutin, Brenard.

Kessler, Heilgard. Individuum und Gesellschaft In Den Romanen der Doris Lessing. 188p. (Ger.). 1982. write for info. (ISBN 3-8204-6272-4). P Lang Pubs.

Kessler, Hermann. Deutsch Fuer Auslaender: Grundstufe. Incl. Pt. 1. Leichter Anfang (Lehrbuch) pap. text ed. 9.75x (ISBN 0-685-47452-6); Pt. 1a. Leichte Aufgaben (Arbeitsheft) pap. text ed. 5.20x (ISBN 0-685-47453-4); Part 1 & Part 1a in One Volume. text ed. o.p. (ISBN 0-685-47454-2); Pt. 1b. Leichte Erzaelungen (Leseband) pap. text ed. 3.90x (ISBN 0-685-47455-0); Pt. 1c. Sprachlaboruebungen. 3.90x (ISBN 0-685-47456-9); Tonbaender fuer das Sprachlabor. 11 tapes, 9.5 cm/s 260.00x (ISBN 0-685-47457-7); Tonband mit Lehrbuchtexten. tape, 9.5 cm/s 29.25 (ISBN 0-685-47458-5). pap. Schoenhof.

--Deutsch Fuer Auslaender: Mittelstufe. Incl. Pt. 2. Schneller Fortgang (Lehrbuch) pap. text ed. 9.75x (ISBN 0-685-47459-3); Pt. 2a. Kurze Uebungen (Arbeitsheft) 5.20x (ISBN 0-685-47460-7); Part 2 & Part 2a in One Volume. text ed. o.p. (ISBN 0-685-47461-5); Pt. 2b. Kurze Geschichten (Leseband) pap. text ed. 3.90x (ISBN 0-685-47462-3); Pt. 2c. Sprachlaboruebungen. 3.90x (ISBN 0-685-47463-1); Tonbaender fuer das Sprachlabor. 10 tapes, 9.5 cm/s 260.00x (ISBN 0-685-47464-X); Tonband mit Lehrbuchtexten. tape 29.25x (ISBN 0-685-47465-8). Schoenhof.

--Deutsch Fuer Auslaender: Oberstufe. Incl. Pt. 3. Deutschlandkunde (Lehrbuch) pap. text ed. 13.00 (ISBN 0-685-47466-6); Pt. 3b. Moderne Dichtungen (Leseband) pap. text ed. 5.20x (ISBN 0-685-47467-4); tonband 29.25x, tape, 9.5 cm/s (ISBN 0-685-47468-2); Pt. 3d. Dichter unserer Zeit. pap. text ed. 5.20x (ISBN 0-685-47469-0); tonband 29.25x, tape, 9.5 cm/s (ISBN 0-685-47470-4). pap. Schoenhof.

Kessler, I. Cancer Control. 314p. 1980. text ed. 29.95 (ISBN 0-8391-1539-3). Univ Park.

Kessler, James C., jt. auth. see Shillingburg, Herbert T., Jr.

Kessler, Jane W. Psychopathology of Childhood. (Illus.). 1966. text ed. 23.95 (ISBN 0-13-736751-1). P-H.

Kessler, Jascha, tr. see Farrukhzad, Furugh.

Kessler, Leonard. The Big Mile Race. LC 82-9274. (Greenwillow Read-Alone Bks.). (Illus.). 56p. (gr. 1-3). 1983. 7.00 (ISBN 0-688-01420-8); PLB 6.67 (ISBN 0-688-01421-6). Greenwillow.

--Do You Have Any Carrots? LC 79-23708. (Easy Venture Bks.). (Illus.). (gr. k-2). 1979. PLB 6.69 (ISBN 0-8116-6074-5). Garrard.

--The Forgetful Pirate. LC 74-5026. (Venture Ser). (Illus.). 64p. (gr. 2). 1974. PLB 6.89 (ISBN 0-8116-6972-6). Garrard.

--Hey Diddle Diddle. LC 79-18966. (Young Mother Goose Bks.). (Illus.). 32p. (gr. k-3). 1980. PLB 7.12 (ISBN 0-8116-7403-7). Garrard.

--Hickory Dickory Dock. LC 79-18775. (Young Mother Goose Bks.). (Illus.). 32p. (gr. k-3). 1980. PLB 7.12 (ISBN 0-8116-7400-2). Garrard.

--Mr. Pine's Storybook. LC 81-80827. (Illus.). 48p. (gr. k-2). 1982. 5.95 (ISBN 0-448-12036-4, G&D). Putnam Pub Group.

--Mixed-up Mother Goose. LC 79-23357. (Young Mother Goose Bks.). (Illus.). 32p. (gr. k-3). 1980. PLB 7.12 (ISBN 0-8116-7404-5). Garrard.

--The Mother Goose Game. LC 79-18989. (Young Mother Goose Bks.). (Illus.). 32p. 1980. PLB 7.12 (ISBN 0-8116-7402-9). Garrard.

--Old Turtle's Baseball Stories. (Illus.). (gr. 1-4). 1982. 6.50 (ISBN 0-688-00723-6); PLB 5.71 (ISBN 0-688-00724-4). Greenwillow.

--On Your Mark, Get Set, Go. LC 72-76516. (Sports I Can Read Books). (Illus.). 64p. (gr. k-3). 1972. 6.95 o.p. (ISBN 0-06-023152-1, HarpJ); PLB 8.89 o.p. (ISBN 0-06-023153-X). Har-Row.

--The Pirates' Adventure on Spooky Island. LC 78-12379. (Imagination Bks.). (Illus.). (gr. k-6). 1979. PLB 6.69 (ISBN 0-8116-4414-6). Garrard.

--Riddles That Rhyme for Halloween Time. LC 77-13140. (Imagination Ser.). (Illus.). (gr. 1-5). 1978. PLB 6.69 (ISBN 0-8116-4409-X). Garrard.

--The Silly Mother Hubbard. LC 79-18776. (Young Mother Goose Bks.). (Illus.). 32p. (gr. k-3). 1980. PLB 7.12 (ISBN 0-8116-7401-0). Garrard.

--Tricks for Treats on Halloween. LC 78-21942. (Easy Venture Bks.). (Illus.). (gr. k-2). 1979. PLB 6.69 (ISBN 0-8116-6075-3). Garrard.

Kessler, Leonard, jt. auth. see Pape, Donna L.

Kessler, Randolph M. & Hertling. Physical Therapy in the Management of Common Musculoskeletal Disorders. (Illus.). 400p. 1983. text ed. 27.50 (ISBN 0-06-141429-8, Harper Medical). Lippincott.

Kessler, Robert & Anderson, Rodney U. Handbook of Urologic Emergencies. 1976. spiral bdg. 11.95 o.p. (ISBN 0-87488-647-3). Med Exam.

Kessler, Suzanne & McKenna, Wendy. Gender, an Ethnomethodological Approach. LC 77-15957. 233p. 1978. 32.95x (ISBN 0-471-58445-2, Pub. by Wiley-Interscience). Wiley.

Kessler, Tracy K., ed. see Junior League of Rochester, Inc.

Kessner, Thomas. The Golden Door: Italian & Jewish Immigrant Mobility in New York City, 1880-1915. 1977. text ed. 17.95x (ISBN 0-19-502116-9); pap. 6.95x (ISBN 0-19-502161-4). Oxford U Pr.

Kessner, Thomas & Caroli, Betty B. Today's Immigrants, Their Stories: A New Look at the Newest Americans. (Illus.). 330p. 1983. pap. 7.95 (ISBN 0-19-503270-5, GB 728, GB). Oxford U Pr.

Kesteloot, Lilyan. Black Writers in French: A Literary History of Negritude. Kennedy, Ellen C., tr. from Fr. LC 73-79479. (Illus.). 431p. 1974. 29.95 (ISBN 0-87722-056-5). Temple U Pr.

Kesten, Harry. Percolation Theory for Mathematicians. (Progress in Probability & Statistics Ser.: Vol. 2). 432p. 1982. text ed. 30.00 (ISBN 3-7643-3107-0). Birkhauser.

Kestenbaum, Victor, ed. The Humanity of the Ill: Phenomenological Perspectives. LC 82-2628. 256p. 1982. text ed. 21.95x (ISBN 0-87049-354-X). U of Tenn Pr.

Kester, Dale E., jt. auth. see Hartmann, Hudson T.

Kester, Dana R. & Ketchum, Bostwick H. Wastes in the Ocean: Dredged Material Disposal in the Ocean, Vol. 2. (Environmental Science & Technology Ser.). 320p. 1983. 39.95x (ISBN 0-471-09771-3, Pub. by Wiley-Interscience). Wiley.

Kester, Ellen. Climbing Rope. (Bro-Kee Ser.). (gr. 5-9). 1978. pap. 3.50 (ISBN 0-570-07760-5, 39-1106). Concordia.

Kester, Paul. Tales of the Real Gypsy. LC 77-142004. 1971. Repr. of 1897 ed. 34.00x (ISBN 0-8103-3633-2). Gale.

Kesterson, David. Merrill Studies in The Marble Faun. LC 74-15279. 1971. pap. text ed. 2.50x o.p. (ISBN 0-675-09199-3). Merrill.

Kesterson, David B. Bill Nye (Edgar Wilson Nye) (United States Authors Ser.). 1981. lib. bdg. 12.95 (ISBN 0-8057-7332-0, Twayne). G K Hall.

--Josh Billings (Henry W. Shaw) (United States Authors Ser.). 1974. lib. bdg. 13.95 (ISBN 0-8057-0058-7, Twayne). G K Hall.

Kestin, J. A Course in Thermodynamics, 2 Vols. 1979. Vol. 1. 38.50 (ISBN 0-07-034281-4); Vol. 2. 38.50 (ISBN 0-07-034282-2). McGraw.

Kestin, J., tr. see Schlichting, Hermann.

Ketcham, Charles. Federico Fellini: The Search for a New Mythology. pap. 3.95 o.p. (ISBN 0-8091-1957-9). Paulist Pr.

Ketcham, Hank. Supercharged & Ever Ready. 128p. 1983. pap. 1.95 (ISBN 0-449-12391-X, GM). Fawcett.

--Well, God, I Goofed Again. LC 75-10852. (Illus.). pap. 4.95 (ISBN 0-915696-08-8). Determined Prods.

Ketcham, Katherine & Mueller, Ann. Eating Right to Stay Sober. 260p. 1983. 14.95 (ISBN 0-914842-97-8). Madrona Pubs.

Ketcham, Robert T. I Shall Not Want. 1953. pap. 2.95 (ISBN 0-8024-0130-9). Moody.

Ketchian, S. & Desbrandes, R. Technical Petroleum Dictionary of Well-Logging, Drilling & Production Terms. 366p. 1965. 99.00x (ISBN 2-7108-0046-2, Pub. by Graham & Trotman England). State Mutual Bk.

Ketchian, Sonia, ed. Technical Petroleum Dictionary of Well-Logging, Drilling & Production Terms: Russian-French-English-German. LC 65-74805. (Illus.). 366p. 1965. 75.00x (ISBN 0-8002-2076-5). Intl Pubns Serv.

Ketchum, Bostwick H. The Water's Edge: Critical Problems of the Coastal Zone. 1972. 20.00x (ISBN 0-262-11048-2). MIT Pr.

Ketchum, Bostwick H., jt. auth. see Kester, Dana R.

Ketchum, Hank. Someone's in the Kitchen with Dennis. (Illus.). (gr. 5 up). 1978. 2.95 o.p. (ISBN 0-531-01342-1); PLB 6.90 o.p. (ISBN 0-531-00127-X). Watts.

Ketchum, Lynne, jt. auth. see Beaudry, Jo.

Ketchum, William C. Auction! The Guide to Bidding, Buying, Bargaining, Selling, Exhibiting & Making a Profit. LC 80-52588. (Illus.). 192p. 1980. 14.95 (ISBN 0-8069-0202-7); lib. bdg. 17.69 (ISBN 0-8069-0203-5); pap. 7.95 (ISBN 0-8069-7568-7). Sterling.

Ketchum, William C., Jr. The Catalog of American Antiques: 1983. 2nd, Rev. ed. (Illus.). 460p. 1982. pap. 12.95 (ISBN 0-88332-109-2, 8147). Larousse.

--Chests, Cupboards, Desks & Other Pieces. (Collector's Guides to American Antiques Ser.). pap. 13.95 (ISBN 0-394-71270-6). Knopf.

--The Collector's Book of American Crafts. 1979. 9.95 o.p. (ISBN 0-671-24823-5). S&S.

--The Family Treasury of Antiques. (Illus.). 240p. 1978. 22.50 o.s.i. (ISBN 0-89479-033-1). A & W Pubs.

--Pottery & Porcelain. LC 82-48946. 1983. 13.95 (ISBN 0-394-71494-6). Knopf.

Ketels, Hank & McDowell, Jack. Sports Illustrated Scuba Diving. 1979. 9.95i (ISBN 0-397-01304-3); pap. 5.95 (ISBN 0-397-01305-1, LP-136). Har-Row.

Ketkar, S., tr. see Winternitz, Maurice.

Kett, Merriellyn & Underwood, Virginia. How to Avoid Sexism: A Guide for Writers, Editors & Publishers. 1978. pap. 10.00 (ISBN 0-931368-01-4). Ragan Comm.

Kett, Merriellyn, jt. auth. see Underwood, Virginia.

Kettelkamp, Larry. Astrology, Wisdom of the Stars. (Illus.). 128p. (gr. 5-9). 1973. PLB 9.12 (ISBN 0-688-30085-5). Morrow.

--Dreams. (Illus.). (gr. 5-9). 1968. PLB 8.59 (ISBN 0-688-31245-4). Morrow.

--Drums, Rattles, & Bells. (Illus.). (gr. 3-7). 1960. PLB 9.12 (ISBN 0-688-31247-0). Morrow.

--Haunted Houses. (Illus.). (gr. 5-9). 1969. 8.95 (ISBN 0-688-21377-4); PLB 8.59 (ISBN 0-688-31377-9). Morrow.

--The Healing Arts. (gr. 4-6). 1978. 8.75 (ISBN 0-688-22161-0); PLB 8.40 (ISBN 0-688-32161-5). Morrow.

--Hypnosis: the Wakeful Sleep. LC 75-17605. (Illus.). 96p. (gr. 5-9). 1975. 8.95 (ISBN 0-688-22045-2); PLB 8.59 (ISBN 0-688-32045-7). Morrow.

--Investigating Psychics: Five Life Histories. (Illus.). (gr. 5-9). 1977. 8.95 (ISBN 0-688-22123-8); PLB 8.59 (ISBN 0-688-32123-2). Morrow.

--Investigating UFO's. LC 77-155993. (Illus.). (gr. 5-9). 1971. PLB 8.59 (ISBN 0-688-31768-5). Morrow.

--Lasers, the Miracle Light. LC 79-17486. (Illus.). 128p. (gr. 4-6). 1979. 8.75 (ISBN 0-688-22207-2); PLB 8.40 (ISBN 0-688-32207-7). Morrow.

--Magic Made Easy. (Illus.). (gr. 3-7). 1981. 8.75 (ISBN 0-688-00458-X); PLB 8.40 (ISBN 0-688-00377-X). Morrow.

--Mischievous Ghosts: The Poltergeist & PK. LC 80-17138. (Illus.). 128p. (gr. 4-6). 1980. 8.75 (ISBN 0-688-22243-9); PLB 8.40 (ISBN 0-688-32243-3). Morrow.

--A Partnership of Mind & Body: Biofeedback. LC 76-24818. (Illus.). (gr. 5-9). 1976. 7.25 o.s.i. (ISBN 0-688-22088-6); PLB 8.59 (ISBN 0-688-32088-0). Morrow.

--Religions East & West. (Illus.). 128p. (gr. 5-9). 1972. PLB 8.59 (ISBN 0-688-31926-2). Morrow.

--Sixth Sense. (Illus.). (gr. 5-9). 1970. PLB 8.59 (ISBN 0-688-31463-5). Morrow.

--Song, Speech & Ventriloquism. (Illus.). (gr. 5-9). 1967. PLB 8.59 (ISBN 0-688-31799-5). Morrow.

--Spinning Tops. (Illus.). (gr. 3-7). 1966. 8.95 (ISBN 0-688-21585-8); PLB 8.59 (ISBN 0-688-31585-2). Morrow.

--Tricks of Eye & Mind, the Story of Optical Illusion: The Story of Optical Illusion. LC 74-5935. (Illus.). 128p. (gr. 5-9). 1974. PLB 8.59 (ISBN 0-688-31829-0). Morrow.

Kettell, Brian. Gold. 192p. 1981. 25.00 (ISBN 0-88410-857-0). Ballinger Pub.

Kettell, Brian & Bell, Steven. Foreign Exchange Handbook. LC 82-23053. (Illus.). 250p. 1983. lib. bdg. 39.95 (ISBN 0-89930-054-5, KFM/, Quorum). Greenwood.

Kettell, Brian, jt. auth. see Bell, Steven.

Kettell, Russell H., ed. Early American Rooms Sixteen Fifty-Sixteen Fifty-Eight. (Illus.). 1966. pap. 10.95 (ISBN 0-486-21633-0). Dover.

Ketter, Robert, et al. Structural Analysis & Design. (Illus.). 1979. text ed. 36.50 (ISBN 0-07-034291-1, C); solutions manual 20.50 (ISBN 0-07-034292-X). McGraw.

Ketter, Robert L. & Prawel, Sherwood, Jr. Modern Methods of Engineering Computation. LC 72-81608. (Illus.). 1969. text ed. 35.00 (ISBN 0-07-034423-X, C). McGraw.

Kettering, Alison M. The Dutch Arcadia: Pastoral Art & Its Audience in the Golden Age. (Illus.). 272p. 1983. text ed. 58.50x (ISBN 0-8390-0278-5). Allanheld & Schram.

Kettering, Charles F., jt. auth. see Piety, Patricia.

Kettering, Ronald C., jt. auth. see Edwards, Donald E.

Ketterman, Grace H. You & Your Child's Problems: How to Understand & Solve Them. 352p. 1983. 14.95 (ISBN 0-8007-1355-9). Revell.

Kettermann, Bernhard, jt. ed. see James, Allan.

Ketterson, J. B., jt. ed. see Benneman, K. H.

Ketterson, J. B., jt. ed. see Bennemann, Karl H.

Ketting, Kees & Peeters, Henk. Two Hundred Fishing Tips: Zander. (Illus.). 88p. (Orig.). 1980. pap. 5.00x (ISBN 0-85242-615-1). Intl Pubns Serv.

Kettle, Arnold. Introduction to the English Novel, 2 vols. Incl. Vol. 1. Up to George Eliot. text ed. o.p. (ISBN 0-09-031603-7); pap. text ed. 9.00x (ISBN 0-09-031604-5); Vol. 2. Henry James to the Present. text ed. 12.50 o. p. (ISBN 0-09-048543-2); pap. text ed. 10.50x (ISBN 0-09-048544-0). 1974 (Hutchinson U Lib). Humanities.

Kettle, Russell, compiled by. Deloitte & Co., 1845-1956: Bound with Fifty Seven Years in an Accountants Office. LC 82-48359. (Accountancy in Transition Ser.). 206p. 1982. lib. bdg. 25.00 (ISBN 0-8240-5311-7). Garland Pub.

Kettridge, J. O. French-English & English-French Dictionary of Technical Terms & Phrases, 2 vols. Incl. Vol. 1. French-English. 47.50 (ISBN 0-7100-1672-7); Vol. 2. English-French. 47.50 (ISBN 0-7100-1673-5). 1970. Repr. of 1959 ed. Set. 70.00 (ISBN 0-685-25619-7). Routledge & Kegan.

Ketz, J. Edward, jt. auth. see Wyman, Harold E.

Ketzner, R. & Rights, R. Fundamentals of Civil Engineering Graphics. 1975. pap. text ed. 10.80x (ISBN 0-87563-089-8). Stipes.

Keul, Michael, jt. ed. see Francois, Michal.

Keulemans, A. I., jt. ed. see Krugers, J.

Kevan, L., jt. auth. see Kaiser, E. T.

Kevan, Larry. Time Domain Electron Spin Resonance. Schwartz, Robert N., ed. LC 78-31128. 324p. 1979. 49.50x (ISBN 0-471-03814-8, Pub. by Wiley-Interscience). Wiley.

Kevan, Larry & Kispert, Lowell D. Electron Spin Double Resonance Spectroscopy. LC 75-44418. 427p. 1976. 47.95x o.s.i. (ISBN 0-471-47340-5, Pub. by Wiley-Interscience). Wiley.

Kevan, Martin. Racing Tides. 283p. 1983. 16.95 (ISBN 0-8253-0121-1). Beaufort Bks NY.

Keve, P. W. Introduction to Corrections. 506p. 1981. 24.95 (ISBN 0-471-03004-X). Wiley.

Keverling Buisman, J., ed. Strategy in Drug Research. (Pharmaco-Chemistry Library: Vol. 4). 420p. 1982. 70.25 (ISBN 0-444-42053-3). Elsevier.

Keverling Buisman, K. A., ed. Biological Activity & Chemical Structure. (Pharmaco-Chemistry Library: Vol. 2). 1978. 61.75 (ISBN 0-444-41659-5). Elsevier.

Kevorkian, George. Business Mathematics. (Business and Economics Ser.). 288p. 1976. text ed. 14.95 (ISBN 0-675-08587-X); wkbk. 6.95 (ISBN 0-675-08586-1). Additional supplements may be obtained from publisher. Merrill.

Kewman, Donald, jt. auth. see Fadiman, James.

Key, Alexander. Escape to Witch Mountain. (Illus.). (gr. 5-7). 1973. pap. 1.95 (ISBN 0-671-42453-X). Archway.

--The Forgotten Door. LC 65-10170. (gr. 7 up). 1965. 9.95 (ISBN 0-664-32342-1). Westminster.

--The Magic Meadow. LC 74-19194. (gr. 4-7). 1975. 5.50 o.s.i. (ISBN 0-664-32561-0). Westminster.

--Return from Witch Mountain. LC 77-26992. 1981. 9.95 (ISBN 0-664-32630-7). Westminster.

--The Sword of Aradel. LC 76-54893. (gr. 5-9). 1977. 7.50 o.s.i. (ISBN 0-664-32609-9). Westminster.

Key, Bernard, jt. ed. see Ohkawa, Kazushi.

Key, Harold & Key, Mary. Bolivian Indian Tribes. (Publications in Linguistics & Related Fields Ser.: No. 15). 128p. 1967. pap. 2.00x (ISBN 0-88312-015-1); microfiche 2.25 (ISBN 0-88312-415-7). Summer Inst Ling.

Key, Jack D. & Keys, Thomas E., eds. Classics & Other Selected Readings in Medical Librarianship. LC 78-9040. 768p. 1980. lib. bdg. 31.50 (ISBN 0-88275-691-5). Krieger.

Key, L. J. The Spawn. (Orig.). 1983. pap. 3.50 (ISBN 0-440-19043-6). Dell.

Key, Mary, jt. auth. see Key, Harold.

Key, Newton E., jt. ed. see Kelman, Peter.

Key, Pierre V. & Zirato, Bruno. Enrico Caruso: A Biography. LC 72-81091. 455p. Date not set. Repr. of 1922 ed. price not set. Vienna Hse.

Key, Ted. The Cat from Outer Space. (gr. 5-7). 1978. pap. 1.95 (ISBN 0-671-43289-3). Archway.

Key, V. O., Jr. Public Opinion & American Democracy. 1961. text ed. 9.50x (ISBN 0-685-77210-1, 0-394-30322). Phila Bk Co.

Key, Vladimer O., Jr. American State Politics: An Introduction. (Illus.). 1959. text ed. 7.95x (ISBN 0-685-13685-X). Phila Bk Co.

Key, William H., jt. auth. see Drabek, Thomas E.

Key, Wilson B. The Clam Plate Orgy & Other Subliminal Techniques for Manipulating Your Behavior. (Illus.). 1981. pap. 2.95 (ISBN 0-451-11479-5, AE1479, Sig). NAL.

--The Clam-Plate Orgy: And Other Subliminals the Media Use to Manipulate Your Behavior. LC 79-24638. (Illus.). 1980. 9.95 o.p. (ISBN 0-13-135038-2). P-H.

--Media Sexploitation. (Illus.). (RL 10). 1977. pap. 2.75 (ISBN 0-451-11675-5, AE1675, Sig). NAL.

Keyes, C. D., ed. see Mueller, Gustav E.

Keyes, Charles F. & Daniel, E. Valentine. Karma: An Anthropological Inquiry. LC 81-19719. 328p. 1983. text ed. 27.50x (ISBN 0-520-04429-0). U of Cal Pr.

Keyes, D. D. Four Types of Value Destruction: A Search for the Good Through an Ethical Analysis of Everyday Experience. 1978. pap. text ed. 8.00 (ISBN 0-8191-0395-0). U Pr of Amer.

Keyes, Daniel. The Minds of Billy Milligan. LC 81-40229. (Illus.). 424p. 1981. 15.50 (ISBN 0-394-51943-4). Random.

--The Minds of Billy Milligan. 1982. pap. 3.95 (ISBN 0-553-22585-5). Bantam.

Keyes, Donald D., et al. The White Mountains: Place & Perceptions. LC 80-68935. (Illus.). 150p. 1980. 12.50x (ISBN 0-87451-190-9). U Pr of New Eng.

Keyes, Frances P. The Restless Land & Other Stories. 1982. pap. 2.95 (ISBN 0-451-11416-7, AE1416, Sig). NAL.

Keyes, Karl, ed. Pressworking: Stampings & Dies. LC 80-53009. (Manufacturing Update Ser.). (Illus.). 260p. 1980. 32.00 (ISBN 0-87263-061-7). SME.

Keyes, Karl A., ed. Innovations in Die Design. LC 81-84032. (Manufacturing Update Ser.). (Illus.). 250p. 1982. text ed. 32.00 (ISBN 0-87263-073-0). SME.

Keyes, Ken. Your Heart's Desire. 150p. 1983. pap. 2.75 (ISBN 0-915972-05-0). Living Love.

Keyes, Ken, Jr. Taming Your Mind. LC 75-4297. Orig. Title: How to Develop Your Thinking Ability. (Illus.). 264p. (Orig.). 1971. 5.95 (ISBN 0-9600688-7-2). Living Love.

Keyes, King, jt. auth. see Doane, Doris C.

Keyes, Lawrence E. Last Age of Missions. (Illus.). 256p. (Orig.). 1982. pap. 10.95 (ISBN 0-87808-435-5). William Carey Lib.

Keyes, Margaret F. Inward Journey: Art as Therapy. rev. ed. (Reality of the Psyche Ser.). (Illus.). 144p. (Orig.). 1983. pap. 8.95 (ISBN 0-87548-368-2). Open Court.

Keyes, Nelson B. El Fascinante Mundo De la Biblia. Orig. Title: Story of the Bible World. (Illus.). 216p. (Span.). 1980. 19.95 (ISBN 0-311-03664-3, Edit Mundo); pap. 16.95 (ISBN 0-311-03665-1, Edit Mundo). Casa Bautista.

Keyes, Ralph. The Height of Your Life. 344p. 1982. pap. 2.95 (ISBN 0-446-30499-9). Warner Bks.

--Is There Life after High School? (Illus.). 1976. 8.95 (ISBN 0-316-49130-6). Little.

Keyes, Sharrel. Luke: Following Jesus. (Fisherman Bible Studyguides Ser.). 80p. 1983. pap. 2.50 (ISBN 0-87788-539-7). Shaw Pubs.

Keyes, Sharrel, jt. auth. see Fromer, Margaret.

Keyes, Sharrel, jt. ed. see Frenchak, David.

Keyfitz, Nathan. Applied Mathematical Demography. LC 77-1360. 388p. 1977. 37.95x (ISBN 0-471-47350-2, Pub. by Wiley-Interscience). Wiley.

Keyhae, Donald. Aliens from Space. Date not set. pap. 1.95 o.p. (ISBN 0-451-08968-5, J8968, Sig). NAL.

Keyishian, Harry. Michael Arlen. (English Author Ser.: No. 174). 1975. lib. bdg. 9.95 o.p. (ISBN 0-8057-1011-6, Twayne). G K Hall.

Keymer, I. F., jt. auth. see Arnall, L.

Keynes, Darwin R., ed. The Beagle Record. LC 77-82500. (Illus.). 1979. 85.00 (ISBN 0-521-21822-5). Cambridge U Pr.

Keynes, Geoffrey. A Bibliography of George Berkeley, Bishop of Cloyne: His Work & His Critics in the Eighteenth Century. (Soho Bibliography Ser.). 1976. 25.00x o.p. (ISBN 0-19-818161-2). U of Pittsburgh Pr.

--A Bibliography of Henry King. (Illus.). 117p. 1977. 30.00 (ISBN 0-906795-18-4, Pub. by St Pauls Biblios England). U Pr of Va.

--Bibliography of William Hazlitt. (Illus.). 150p. 1982. 32.50x (ISBN 0-906795-01-X, Pub. by St Pauls Biblios England). U Pr of Va.

Keynes, Geoffrey, ed. see Blake, William.

Keynes, Geoffrey, intro. by see Blake, William.

Keynes, Geoffrey, ed. see Brown, Thomas.

Keynes, Geoffrey L. Bibliography of William Blake. LC 22-14055. (Illus.). 1968. Repr. of 1921 ed. 67.00 o.s.i. (ISBN 0-527-49500-X). Kraus Repr.

Keynes, Geoffrey L. & Wolf, Edwin, 2nd, eds. William Blake's Illuminated Books: A Census. LC 53-4181. 1968. Repr. of 1953 ed. 28.00 o.p. (ISBN 0-527-49520-4). Kraus Repr.

Keynes, John M. The Collected Writings, 30 vols. Incl. Vol. 1. Indian Currency & Finance. 184p. 1971. Repr. of 1913 ed (ISBN 0-521-22093-9); Vol. 2. The Economic Consequences of the Peace. LC 76-133449. 192p. 1971. Repr. of 1919 ed (ISBN 0-521-22094-7); Vol. 3. Revision of the Treaty. LC 76-133449. 158p. 1972 (ISBN 0-521-22095-5); Vol. 4. Tract on Monetary Reform. LC 76-133449. 172p. 1972 (ISBN 0-521-22096-3); Vol. 5. Pt. 1. Treatise on Money, the Pure Theory of Money. 336p. 1972 (ISBN 0-521-22097-1); Vol. 6, Pt.2. Treatise on Money, the Applied Theory of Money. 390p. 1972 (ISBN 0-521-22098-X); Vol. 7. The General Theory of Employment, Interest, & Money. 428p. 1973 (ISBN 0-521-22099-8). pap. 8.95 (ISBN 0-521-29382-0); Vol. 8. Treatise on Probability. 514p. 1972 (ISBN 0-521-22100-5); Vol. 9. Essays & Persuasions. 451p. 1972 (ISBN 0-521-22101-3); Vol. 10. Essays in Biography. 460p. 1972 (ISBN 0-521-22102-1); Vol. 13. The General Theory & After, Pt. One: Preparation. 653p. 1973 (ISBN 0-521-22103-X); **Vol. 14. The General Theory & After, Pt. Two: Defence & Development. 584p. 1973 (ISBN 0-521-22104-8); Vol. 15. Activities: Nineteen-Six to Nineteen-Fourteen: India & Cambridge. 312p. 1971 (ISBN 0-521-22105-6); Vol. 16. Activities, Nineteen-Fourteen to Nineteen-Nineteen: The Treasury & Versailles. 488p. 1971 (ISBN 0-521-22106-4); Vol. 17. Activities Nineteen Twenty to Twenty-Two: Treaty Revision & Reconstruction. 1978 (ISBN 0-521-21874-8); Vol. 18. Activities Nineteen Twenty-Two to Thirty-Two: The End of Reparations. 1978 (ISBN 0-521-21875-6); Vol. 19. Activities Nineteen Twenty-Two to Twenty-Nine: The Return to Gold & Industrial Policy, 2 vols. 519p. 1981. Set. 99.00 (ISBN 0-521-23071-3); Vol. 20. Activities Nineteen Twenty-Nine to Thirty-One: Rethinking Employment & Unemployment Policies. 330p. 1979 (ISBN 0-521-23072-1); Vol. 21. Activities Nineteen Thirty-One to Thirty Nine: World Crises & Policies in Britain & America. 688p. 1979 (ISBN 0-521-23073-X); Vol. 22. Activities Nineteen Thirty-Nine to Forty-Five: Internal War Finance (ISBN 0-521-21876-4); Vol. 23. Activities Nineteen Forty to Forty-Three: External War Finance. 368p. 1980 (ISBN 0-521-22016-5); Vol. 24. Activities Nineteen Forty-Four to Forty-Six: The Transition to Peace (ISBN 0-521-22017-3). 49.50 ea. Cambridge U Pr.**

--Essays in Persuasion. 1963. pap. 7.95 (ISBN 0-393-00190-3, Norton Lib). Norton.

--General Theory of Employment, Interest & Money. LC 36-27176. 1965. pap. 5.95 (ISBN 0-15-634711-3, Harv). HarBraceJ.

Keynes, Milo, ed. Essays on John Maynard Keynes. LC 74-12975. (Illus.). 304p. 1975. 44.50 (ISBN 0-521-20534-4). Cambridge U Pr.

--Essays on John Maynard Keynes. LC 74-12975. (Illus.). 1980. pap. 13.95 (ISBN 0-521-29696-X). Cambridge U Pr.

Keynes, Milton, jt. auth. see Jones, B. W.

Keynes, Simon. The Diplomas of King Aethelred 'the Unready' 978 to 1016. LC 79-7651. (Studies in Medieval Life & Thought Ser.: No. 13). (Illus.). 1980. 47.50 (ISBN 0-521-22718-6). Cambridge U Pr.

Keys, B., jt. auth. see Scanlan, B. K.

Keys, Bernard, jt. auth. see Scanlan, Burt.

Keys, Donald. Earth at Omega: Passage to Planetization. (International Peace Ser.). 1983. text ed. 12.95 (ISBN 0-8283-1743-7); pap. 9.95 (ISBN 0-8283-1745-3). Branden.

Keys, Gerry. Practical Navigation by Calculator. (Illus.). 176p. 1982. pap. text ed. 14.95x (ISBN 0-540-07410-1). Sheridan.

Keys, J. Bernard, jt. auth. see Scanlan, Burt.

Keys, James. Only Two Can Play This Game. LC 72-80667. 152p. 1972. 6.00 o.p. (ISBN 0-517-52778-2). Crown.

Keys, Paul, jt. auth. see Beaumont, John R.

Keys, Romey T., ed. see Evans, Mari.

Keys, Thomas E. & Willius, Fredrick A., eds. Classics of Cardiology, 3 vols. LC 82-7830. 1983. Repr. of 1941 ed. Vol. 1. write for info. (ISBN 0-89874-514-4); Vol. 2. write for info. (ISBN 0-89874-515-2); Vol. 3. write for info. (ISBN 0-89874-516-0). Krieger.

Keys, Thomas E., jt. ed. see Key, Jack D.

Keys, W., jt. auth. see Cashman, T.

Keyser. Materials Science in Engineering. 3rd ed. (Engineering Ser.). 488p. 1980. text ed. 27.95 (ISBN 0-675-08182-3). Additional supplements may be obtained from publisher. Merrill.

Keyser, Corinne, tr. see Adorjan, Carol M.

Keyser, Ignace de, jt. auth. see Haine, Malou.

Keyser, J. W. Human Plasma Proteins: Their Investigation in Pathological Conditions. LC 79-1089. 320p. 1979. 76.95x (ISBN 0-471-27598-0, Pub. by Wiley-Interscience). Wiley.

Keyser, S. Jay, ed. see Kiparsky, R. P.

Keyser, Samuel J. & Postal, Paul M. Beginning English Grammar. 480p. 1976. text ed. 23.50 scp o.p. (ISBN 0-06-045254-4, HarpC). Har-Row.

Keysor, Charles W. Forgiveness Is a Two-Way Street. 132p. 1981. pap. 4.50 (ISBN 0-88207-338-9). Victor Bks.

Kezdi, A. Soil Physics. LC 73-85223. (Handbook of Soil Mechanics: Vol. 1). 256p. 1974. 68.00 (ISBN 0-444-99890-X). Elsevier.

--Soil Testing: Soil Mechanics of Earthworks, Foundations, & Road Construction. (Handbook of Soil Mechanics: Vol. 2). 1979. 68.00 (ISBN 0-444-99778-4). Elsevier.

--Stabilized Earth Roads. (Developments in Geotechnical Engineering Ser.: Vol. 19). 1979. 68.00 (ISBN 0-444-99786-5). Elsevier.

Kezdi, A., ed. see Fourth Budapest Conference on Soil Mechanics & Foundation Engineering.

Kezilihabi, Euphrase. Kichomi. (Swahili Literature). (Orig., Swahili.). 1978. pap. text ed. 2.95x o.p. (ISBN 0-686-74447-0, 00612). Heinemann Ed.

Kezirian, Richard. American History: Major Controversies Reviewed. 192p. 1983. pap. text ed. 13.95 (ISBN 0-8403-2921-0). Kendall-Hunt.

KGB Chicken. From Scratch. new ed. 1978. pap. 6.95 (ISBN 0-89325-012-0). Joyce Pr.

Khachaturian, Narbey & Gurfinkel, German. Prestressed Concrete. 1969. text ed. 27.00 o.p. (ISBN 0-07-034465-5, C). McGraw.

Khachaturyan, A. G. Theory of Phase Transformations in Alloys. 620p. 1983. 59.95x (ISBN 0-471-07873-5, Pub. by Wiley-Interscience). Wiley.

Khadem, Hassan El, ed. Anthracycline Antibiotics (Symposium) 1982. 25.00 (ISBN 0-12-238040-1). Acad Pr.

Khailany, A. Business Programming in FORTRAN VI & ANSI FORTRAN: A Structured Approach. 1981. pap. 16.95 (ISBN 0-13-107607-8). P-H.

Khailany, Asad & Duplissey, Claude. Cobol for Medium & Small Sized Computers. LC 75-23647. (Illus.). 400p. 1976. pap. text ed. 19.50 o.p. (ISBN 0-395-18921-7). HM.

Khaing, Mi Mi. Cook & Entertain the Burmese Way. (Illus.). 190p. 1978. 4.95 o.p. (ISBN 0-89720-017-9). Karoma.

Khairallah. This Is Lebanon. 6.00x (ISBN 0-86685-017-1). Intl Bk Ctr.

Khairzada, Faiz & Magnus, Ralph H. Afghanistan: From Independence to Occupation. 1984. 24.00 (ISBN 0-86531-200-1). Westview.

Khalaf, Roseanne. Once Upon a Time in Lebanon. LC 82-1193. 1982. 10.00x (ISBN 0-88206-051-1). Caravan Bks.

Khalatnikov, I. M. Physics Reviews. (Soviet Scientific Reviews Ser.: Vol. 3). 603p. 1981. 144.00 (ISBN 3-7186-0068-4). Harwood Academic.

Khalatnikov, I. M., ed. Soviet Scientific Reviews: Physics Reviews, Vol. 2, Section A. 496p. 1980. lib. bdg. 119.00 (ISBN 3-7186-0017-X). Harwood Academic.

Khalidi, Tarif. Islamic Historiography: The Histories of Masudi. LC 75-5933. 1975. 34.50x (ISBN 0-87395-282-0). State U NY Pr.

Khalifa, R. A. Quran Times Hadith Equals Zero. 85p. (Orig.). 1983. 9.50 (ISBN 0-934894-35-3). Islamic Prods.

Khalifa, Rashad. Quran: Visual Presentation of the Miracle. (Illus.). 252p. (Orig.). 1983. 19.00 (ISBN 0-934894-30-2). Islamic Prods.

Khalil, H. M. & Carberry, M. S. Introductory Computer Science Textbook. 1983. text ed. p.n.s. Computer Sci.

Khalsa, Dayal K. Baabee Books, 4 Bks. (Illus.). 1983. Set. 12.95 (ISBN 0-686-43199-5). Bk. 1 (ISBN 0-88776-136-4). Bk. 2 (ISBN 0-88776-137-2). Bk. 3 (ISBN 0-88776-138-0). Bk. 4 (ISBN 0-88776-139-9). Tundra Bks.

Khambata, Adi J. Microprocessors-Microcomputers: Architecture, Software & Systems. LC 81-11360. (Electronic Technology Ser.). 577p. 1982. text ed. 26.95x (ISBN 0-471-06490-4); tchr's. manual 20.00x (ISBN 0-471-86316-5). Wiley.

Khambata, Farida, jt. auth. see Anderson, Dennis.

Khan, A. A. Physiology & Biochemistry of Seed Development, Dormancy & Germination. Date not set. 119.25 (ISBN 0-686-43200-2). Elsevier.

Khan, A. A., ed. The Physiology & Biochemistry of Seed Dormancy & Germination. 1977. 101.50 (ISBN 0-7204-0643-9, North-Holland). Elsevier.

Khan, Abdul M. Transition in Bengal, 1756-1775: A Study of Saiyid Muhammed Reza Khan. LC 69-29329. (South Asian Studies Ser.: No. 7). (Illus.). 1969. 44.50 (ISBN 0-521-07124-0). Cambridge U Pr.

Khan, Amanullah & Hill, Norwood, eds. Human Lymphokines. 1982. 54.00 (ISBN 0-12-406080-3). Acad Pr.

Khan, Azizur R. & Ghai, Dharam. Collective Agriculture & Rural Development in Soviet Central Asia. LC 79-15807. 1979. 25.00 (ISBN 0-312-14975-1). St Martin.

Khan, Hazrat I. Gayan, Vadan, Nirtan. LC 80-52801. (The Collected Works of Hazrat Inayat Khan Ser.). 304p. 1980. 10.00 (ISBN 0-930872-21-5, 1006H); pap. 5.95 (ISBN 0-930872-16-9, 1006P). Omega Pr NM.

--Mastery Through Accomplishment. LC 79-101639. (The Collected Works of Hazrat Inayat Khan Ser.). 320p. 1978. 8.95 (ISBN 0-930872-06-1); pap. 5.95 (ISBN 0-930872-07-X). Omega Pr NM.

--The Music of Life. LC 82-61068. (The Collected Works of Hazrat Inayat Khan Ser.). (Illus.). 368p. 1983. pap. 11.95 (ISBN 0-930872-31-2). Omega Pr NM.

--Personality: The Art of Being & Becoming. LC 82-60284. (The Collected Works of Hazrat Inayat Khan Ser.). (Illus.). 304p. (Orig.). 1982. pap. 10.95 (ISBN 0-930872-29-0, 1016P). Omega Pr NM.

--The Soul Whence & Whither. LC 77-15697. (The Collected Works of Hazrat Inayat Khan Ser.). 190p. 1977. 6.95 o.p. (ISBN 0-930872-00-2); pap. 4.95 (ISBN 0-930872-01-0). Omega Pr NM.

--Tales Told by Hazrat Inayat Khan. LC 80-52548. (The Collected Works of Hazrat Inayat Khan). (Illus.). 288p. (Orig.). 1980. pap. 7.95 (ISBN 0-930872-15-0). Omega Pr NM.

--The Unity of Religious Ideals. (The Collected Works of Hazrat Inayat Khan Ser.). 264p. 1979. 8.95 (ISBN 0-930872-09-6); pap. 5.95 (ISBN 0-930872-10-X). Omega Pr NM.

Khan, Inayat. The Complete Sayings of Hazrat Inayat Khan. LC 77-94684. (The Collected Works of Hazrat Inayat Khan Ser.). 299p. 1978. 7.95 (ISBN 0-930872-02-9). Omega Pr NM.

--Mystical Psychology. 1983. pap. 4.95 (ISBN 0-900217-16-2, Pub. by Sufi Pub Co England). Hunter Hse.

--Sacred Readings: The Gathas. (Sufi Message of Hazrat Inayat Khan Ser.: Vol. 13). 1982. 14.95 (ISBN 90-6325-021-5, Pub. by Servire BV Netherlands). Hunter Hse.

Khan, Inayat H. Music. 1982. pap. 3.95 (ISBN 0-87728-372-9). Weiser.

Khan, K. The Secrets of Anal-Haqq. 1981. 7.95 (ISBN 0-686-97864-1). Kazi Pubns.

Khan, K. R. The Law & Organisation of International Community Agreements. 1982. lib. bdg. 74.00 (ISBN 90-247-2554-2, Pub. by Martinus Nijhoff Netherlands). Kluwer Boston.

Khan, M. A. Sociological Aspects of Child Development: A Study of Rural Karnataka. 212p. 1980. text ed. 16.50x (ISBN 0-391-02127-3). Humanities.

Khan, M. A. R. Muslim Contribution to Science & Culture. pap. 2.00 (ISBN 0-686-18449-1). Kazi Pubns.

Khan, M. E. & Prasad, C. V. People's Perception About Family Planning: A Study of Andhra Pradesh & Bihar. 156p. 1980. text ed. 10.50x (ISBN 0-391-02131-1). Humanities.

Khan, Mahmood H. The Economics of the Green Revolution in Pakistan. LC 75-19796. (Special Studies). (Illus.). 248p. 1975. 28.95 o.p. (ISBN 0-275-55680-8). Praeger.

--Underdevelopment & Agrarian Structure in Pakistan. (Replica Edition Ser.). 275p. 1981. lib. bdg. 24.50 (ISBN 0-86531-134-X). Westview.

Khan, Pir Vilayat I. Introducing Spirituality into Counseling & Therapy. LC 82-60367. 176p. (Orig.). 1982. pap. 6.95 (ISBN 0-930872-30-4, 1017P). Omega Pr NM.

Khan, R., et al. Story of Life. 6.50x o.p. (ISBN 0-210-27034-9). Asia.

Khan, R. A. The Economy of Bangladesh. LC 72-88005. 1972. 25.00 (ISBN 0-312-22715-9). St Martin.

Khan, S. U., jt. ed. see Schnitzer, M.

Khan, Zafar, jt. auth. see Lerner, Judith.

Khan, Zillur. Leadership in the Least Developed Nation: Bangladesh. (Foreign & Comparative Studies Program, South Asian Ser., No. 8). (Orig.). 1983. pap. write for info (ISBN 0-915984-85-7). Syracuse U Foreign Comp.

Khanbegian. Painting Sea & Sky. (Pitman Art Ser.: Vol. 57). pap. 1.95 (ISBN 0-448-00566-2, G&D). Putnam Pub Group.

Khani, Muhammad B. Tarikh-I-Muhammadi. 110p. 1973. pap. text ed. 5.00x o.p. (ISBN 0-210-40545-7). Asia.

Khanin, Ya, jt. auth. see Fain, V. M.

Khanna, H. R. Judicial Review or Confrontation. 1977. 3.75x o.p. (ISBN 0-8364-0024-0). South Asia Bks.

Khanna, J. L., ed. New Treatment Approaches to Juvenile Delinquency. (Illus.). 164p. 1975. 15.75x o.p. (ISBN 0-398-03184-3). C C Thomas.

Khanna, K. C. & Dayal, Raghubir. Modern World History. 250p. 1982. pap. text ed. 8.95x (ISBN 0-86131-074-8, Pub. by Orient Longman Ltd India). Apt Bks.

Khanna, L. S., jt. auth. see Prakash, Ram.

Kharasch, N. Mechanisms of Reactions of Sulfur Compounds, 5 vols. 1971. Set. 229.00x (ISBN 0-677-65300-X); Vol. 1 1967, 286p. 65.00x (ISBN 0-677-65310-7); Vol. 2. 1968, 284p. 65.00x (ISBN 0-677-65320-4); Vol. 3. 1969, 180p. 42.00x (ISBN 0-677-65330-1); Vol. 4 1970, 190p. 43.00x (ISBN 0-677-65340-9); Vol. 5 1971, 186p. 43.00 (ISBN 0-677-65350-6). Gordon.

Kharasch, Norman, ed. Trace Metals in Health & Disease. 330p. 1979. 35.00 (ISBN 0-89004-389-2). Raven.

Kharbanda, O. P. & Stallworth, E. A. Project Cost Control in Action. (Illus.). 304p. 1981. text ed. 24.95 (ISBN 0-13-730812-4). P-H.

Kharbanda, O. P. & Stallworthy, E. A. Project Cost Control in Action. 273p. 1980. text ed. 34.00x (ISBN 0-566-02164-1). Gower Pub Ltd.

Kharbas, Datta S. India Maharashtra & the Marathas: A Comprehensive Bibliography. 1976. lib. bdg. 32.00 o.p. (ISBN 0-8161-1186-3, Biblio Guides). G K Hall.

Kharkevich, D. A., ed. Ganglion-Blocking & Ganglion-Stimulating Agents. 1967. inquire for price o.p. (ISBN 0-08-011929-8). Pergamon.

Khashab, A. Heating, Ventilating & Air Conditioning Estimating Manual. (Illus.). 1977. 26.50 (ISBN 0-07-034535-X, P&RB). McGraw.

Khashab, A. G. El see El Khashab, A. G.

Khatena, Joe. Educational Psychology of the Gifted. LC 81-11452. 480p. 1982. text ed. 23.50 (ISBN 0-471-05078-4). Wiley.

Khatib, Ahmad. Arabic-English Dictionary of Agricultural Terms. pap. 10.00x (ISBN 0-86685-274-3). Intl Bk Ctr.

Khatkhate, Deena R., Jr., jt. ed. see Coats, Warren L.

Khawen, Rene R. The Subtle Ruse: The Book of Arabic Wisdom & Guile. 353p. 1982. 17.95 (ISBN 0-85692-035-5, Pub. by Salem Hse Ltd.). Merrimack Bk Serv.

Khayat, Marie. Food from the Arab World. pap. 6.00x (ISBN 2-9028-7400-6). Intl Bk Ctr.

Khayyam, Omar. The Rubaiyat of Omar Khayyam. (Illus.). pap. 4.95 o.p. (ISBN 0-448-16801-4, G&D). Putnam Pub Group.

Khazanie, Ramakant G. Elementary Statistics. LC 78-25636. (Illus.). 1979. 23.50x (ISBN 0-673-16061-0); incl. study guide 10.95x (ISBN 0-673-16233-8). Scott F.

Kheel, Theodore W., et al. Technological Change & Human Development: An International Conference. Hodges, Wayne L. & Kelly, Matthew A., eds. LC 78-629733. 404p. 1970. pap. 8.00 (ISBN 0-87546-043-7). ILR Pr.

Kheng-Lian Koh. Straits in International Navigation: Contemporary Issues. LC 81-18977. 225p. 1982. lib. bdg. 35.00 (ISBN 0-379-20465-7). Oceana.

Kher, S. B., ed. see Gandhi, M. K.

Kherdian, David. Beyond Two Rivers. LC 81-1915. 128p. (gr. 5 up). 1981. 8.95 (ISBN 0-688-00567-5). Greenwillow.

--An Evening With Saroyan. pap. 2.00 (ISBN 0-686-97753-X). Giligia.

Kherdian, David, tr. Pigs Never See the Stars: Proverbs from the Armenian. Hogrogian, Nonny. 1982. 15.00 (ISBN 0-89756-009-4). Two Rivers.

Khiel, Alois. Kommunailwirtschaft und Wirtschaftsordnung. 161p. (Ger.). 1982. write for info. (ISBN 3-8204-5788-7). P Lang Pubs.

Khilnani, N. M. Panorama of Indian Diplomacy. 314p. 1981. 27.50x (ISBN 0-940500-74-4, Pub by S Chand India). Asia Bk Corp.

Khinchin, Alexander I. Mathematical Foundations of Information Theory. 1957. pap. text ed. 2.95 (ISBN 0-486-60434-9). Dover.

Khisty, C. J. Structural Steel Tables. 1976. pap. 2.00 o.p. (ISBN 0-210-22240-9). Asia.

Khma, Andres T. Wisdom of Sidereal Astrology. (Illus.). 503p. 1983. pap. 18.00 (ISBN 0-89540-127-4). Sun Pub.

Khodasevich, Vladislav. Sobranie Sochinenii V 5-i Tomakh, Vol 1. Hughes, Robert & Malmstad, John, eds. 330p. (Rus.). 1983. 25.00 (ISBN 0-88233-686-X). Ardis Pubs.

Khodashova, K. S., jt. ed. see Zlotin, R. I.

Khokar, Mohan. Kathak, Kathak. 200p. 1982. 52.00x (ISBN 0-686-94076-8, Pub. by Garlandfold England). State Mutual Bk.

Kholodny, Mykola. On the Soul in Song & Song in Soul. LC 81-508656. (Ukrainian Ser.). 139p. 1981. pap. 7.95 (ISBN 0-914834-33-9). Smoloskyp.

Khomskaia. Brain & Activation. (National Library of Medicine Ser.). 380p. 1983. text ed. 18.50 (ISBN 0-08-025993-6). Pergamon.

Khory, R. N. & Katrak, N. N. Materia Medica of India & Their Therapeutics. 809p. 1981. Repr. of 1903 ed. text ed. 59.00x (ISBN 0-391-02264-4, Pub. by Concept India). Humanities.

Khosla, G. D. Grim Fairy Tales & Other Facts & Fancies. 1966. 4.50x o.p. (ISBN 0-210-26885-9). Asia.

--The Murder of the Mahatma & Other Cases from a Judge's Notebook. 276p. 1965. pap. 2.95 (ISBN 0-88253-051-8). Ind-US Inc.

Khosla, Sarla. Gupta Civilization. 1982. 38.00x (ISBN 0-686-81734-6, Pub. by Intellectual India). South Asia Bks.

Khouri, Mounah A. & Algar, Hamid, eds. An Anthology of Modern Arabic Poetry. Khouri, Mounah A. & Algar, Hamid, trs. LC 77-189220. 1974. 23.75x o.p. (ISBN 0-520-02234-3); pap. 3.95 (ISBN 0-520-02898-8). U of Cal Pr.

Khouri, Mounah A., tr. see Khouri, Mounah A. & Algar, Hamid.

Khoury, George H., jt. auth. see Schmidt, Roland.

Khoury, Robert M., ed. The Sociology of the Offbeat: Essays in the Science of Human Social Behavior. LC 81-40726. (Illus.). 418p. (Orig.). 1982. PLB 26.25 (ISBN 0-8191-2457-5); pap. text ed. 14.50 (ISBN 0-8191-2458-3). U Pr of Amer.

Khoury, Sarkis J. Investment Management: Theory & Application. 656p. 1983. text ed. 31.95 (ISBN 0-02-362440-X). Macmillan.

--Transnational Mergers & Acquisitions in the United States. LC 80-8117. 320p. 1980. 30.95x (ISBN 0-669-03960-8). Lexington Bks.

Khrenov, L. S. Six-Figure Tables of Trigonometric Functions. 1964. 50.00 o.p. (ISBN 0-08-010101-1). Pergamon.

Khrushchev, Nikita S. Disarmament & Colonial Freedom. LC 74-31868. (Illus.). 299p. 1975. Repr. of 1960 ed. lib. bdg. 17.00x (ISBN 0-8371-7945-9, KHDI). Greenwood.

--Khrushchev Remembers. Talbot, Strobe, ed. & tr. (Illus.). 1971. 15.00 o.p. (ISBN 0-316-83140-9). Little.

Khubchandani, Lachman M. Plural Languages, Plural Cultures. 224p. 1983. pap. text ed. 15.00x (ISBN 0-8248-0639-5). UH Pr.

Khurana, I. P. S., jt. auth. see Rattan, S. S.

Khuro, Hamida. Sind Through the Centuries. (Illus.). 1982. 49.95x (ISBN 0-19-577250-4). Oxford U Pr.

Khushalani, Y. The Dignity & Honour of Women As Basic & Fundamental Human Right. 1982. lib. bdg. 39.50 (ISBN 90-247-2585-2, Pub. by Martinus Nijhoff Netherlands). Kluwer Boston.

Khvylovy, Mykola. Works in Five Volumes, Vol. 3. Kostiuk, Hryhoriy, ed. LC 78-66383. (Ukrainian Ser.). 505p. 1982. 20.00 (ISBN 0-914834-20-7). Smoloskyp.

Kiang, Yen-Hsiung & Metry, Amir. Hazardous Waste Processing Technology. LC 81-69070. (Illus.). 549p. 1982. text ed. 44.95 (ISBN 0-250-40411-7). Ann Arbor Science.

Kibbe, Constance V. Standard Textbook of Cosmetology. rev. ed. (Illus.). 1981. 17.85 (ISBN 0-87350-096-2). Milady.

Kibbe, Pat. The Hocus-Pocus Dilemma. LC 78-9906. (gr. 4-7). 1979. 5.95 o.p. (ISBN 0-394-84058-5); PLB 5.99 (ISBN 0-394-94058-X). Knopf.

Kibbe, Richard R. & Neely, John E. Machine Tool Practices. 2nd ed. LC-81-7606. 806p. 1982. text ed. 24.95 (ISBN 0-471-05788-6); student wkbk. 7.95 (ISBN 0-471-86652-0); solutions manual. Wiley.

Kibildis, Ralph. Turning Road. 112p. (Orig.). 1981. 2.50 (ISBN 0-914544-34-9). Living Flame Pr.

Kibler, James, ed. American Novelists Since World War II: Second Series. (Dictionary of Literary Biography Ser.: Vol. 6). (Illus.). 300p. 1980. 74.00x (ISBN 0-8103-0908-4, Bruccoli Clark). Gale.

Kibler, James E., Jr., jt. auth. see Butterworth, Keen.

Kibler, L. & Noris, M. Giorno per Giorno: Italian in Review. 1971. text ed. 17.95x (ISBN 0-02-362860-X). Macmillan.

Kibler, Robert J., jt. ed. see Barker, Larry L.

Kibler, William W., ed. see De Troyes, Chretien.

Kibling, Mary L. Twenty-Five Walks in the Dartmouth-Lake Sunapee Region of New Hampshire. LC 78-74156. (Twenty-Five Walks Ser.). (Illus.). 128p. 1979. pap. 4.95 (ISBN 0-89725-003-6). Backcountry Pubns.

Kice, J. L. & Marvell, E. N. Modern Principles of Organic Chemistry: An Introduction. 2nd ed. 1974. 24.95x (ISBN 0-02-362890-1). Macmillan.

Kichenside, Geoffrey. A Picture History of British Rail: Diesels & Electrics in Action. (Railway History in Pictures Ser.). (Illus.). 96p. 1976. 11.50 o.p. (ISBN 0-7153-7168-1). David & Charles.

Kickert, W. J. Organization of Decision Making. 1980. 49.00 (ISBN 0-444-85429-0). Elsevier.

Kicklighter, Clois E. Architecture: Residential Drawing & Design. rev. ed. Baird, Ronald J., ed. LC 80-28319. (Illus.). 492p. 1981. text ed. 18.00 (ISBN 0-87006-321-9). Goodheart.

Kicklighter, Richard H., jt. auth. see Richmond, Bert O.

Kidd, B. S. & Keith, John D. The Natural History & Progress in Treatment of Congenital Heart Defects. (Illus.). 360p. 1971. 26.50x o.p. (ISBN 0-398-02174-0). C C Thomas.

Kidd, Charles & Montague-Smith, Patrick. Debrett's Book of Royal Children. LC 82-8043. (Illus.). 208p. 1982. 20.00 (ISBN 0-688-01380-5). Morrow.

Kidd, D. M. & Leighbody, G. B. Methods of Teaching Shop & Technical Subjects. LC 66-26821. 1968. pap. text ed. 8.80 (ISBN 0-8273-0360-2). Delmar.

Kidd, Dusty, ed. see Levin, Paul.

Kidd, Flora. Dans Le Murmure Des Vagues. (Collection Harlequin). 192p. 1983. pap. 1.95 (ISBN 0-373-49334-7). Harlequin Bks.

--Dark Seduction. (Harlequin Presents Ser.). 192p. 1983. pap. 1.95 (ISBN 0-686-38745-7). Harlequin Bks.

--Love is Fire, Remedy for Love & The Legend of The Swans. (Harlequin Romances (3-in-1) Ser.). 576p. 1983. pap. 3.95 (ISBN 0-373-20071-4). Harlequin Bks.

--Serenade Pour Anne. (Collection Harlequin). 192p. 1983. pap. 1.95 (ISBN 0-373-49324-X). Harlequin Bks.

--Tempted To Love: Harlequin Presents Ser. 192p. 1983. pap. 1.95 (ISBN 0-373-10577-0). Harlequin Bks.

Kidd, J. R. How Adults Learn. 324p. 1972. 16.95 (ISBN 0-695-81171-1). Follett.

Kidd, James W., jt. auth. see Kidd, Sunnie D.

Kidd, James W., jt. auth. see Sunnie, D.

Kidd, Jane. A Festival of Dressage. LC 82-8780. (Illus.). 144p. 1983. 16.95 (ISBN 0-668-05654-1, 5654). Arco.

Kidd, Kenneth E. Excavation of Ste Marie First. LC 50-2617. (Illus.). xiv, 191p. 1972. Repr. of 1949 ed. 17.50x o.p. (ISBN 0-8020-7030-2). U of Toronto Pr.

Kidd, Kenneth P., et al. The Laboratory Approach to Mathematics. 1970. pap. text ed. 14.95 (ISBN 0-574-34790-9, 3-4790). SRA.

Kidd, Roby, jt. ed. see Hall, Bud L.

Kidd, Ronald. Dunker. (Illus.). 160p. (gr. 7 up). 1982. 9.95 (ISBN 0-525-66762-8, 0966-290). Lodestar Bks.

--Who Is Felix the Great? 160p. (gr. 7 up). 1983. 9.95 (ISBN 0-525-66778-4, 0966-290). Lodestar Bks.

Kidd, Sunnie D. & Kidd, James W. Brother Jerry's Stories: Following the Inspiration of the Holy Spirit. 34p. 1982. pap. text ed. 2.50 (ISBN 0-910727-00-7). Golden Phoenix.

--The Dynamic Aspects of Inspiration. 38p. (Orig.). 1982. pap. 2.50 (ISBN 0-910727-02-3). Golden Phoenix.

Kidder, Alfred V. Pottery of the Pajarito Plateau & of Some Adjacent Regions in New Mexico. LC 16-15195. 1915. pap. 12.00 (ISBN 0-527-00511-8). Kraus Repr.

Kidder, Frank E. & Parker, Harry. Architects' & Builders' Handbook. 18th ed. 2315p. 1931. 95.95x (ISBN 0-471-47421-5, Pub. by Wiley-Interscience). Wiley.

Kidder, Harvey. Illustrated Chess for Children: Simple, New Approach. LC 71-116220. 8.95 o.p. (ISBN 0-385-05764-4). Doubleday.

Kidder, Louise H. & Stewart, V. Mary. The Psychology of Intergroup Relations. (Psychology & the Problems of Society). (Illus.). 156p. 1974. pap. text ed. 12.95 (ISBN 0-07-034545-7, C). McGraw.

Kidder, Louise H., jt. ed. see Brinberg, David.

Kidder, Robert. Connecting Law & Society: An Introduction to Research & Theory. 304p. 1983. 21.95 (ISBN 0-13-167809-4). P-H.

Kiddle, L. B., ed. see Alfonso X.

Kiddle, Lawrence B., jt. ed. see Anderson-Imbert, Enrique.

Kideman, A. D., et al, eds. New Approaches to Nerve & Muscle Disorders: Basic & Applied Contributions. (International Congress Ser.: No. 546). 1981. 75.75 (ISBN 0-444-90213-9). Elsevier.

Kidman, A. D. & Tomkins, J., eds. Muscle, Nerve & Brain Degeneration. (International Congress Ser.: Vol. 473). 1980. 47.75 (ISBN 0-444-90094-2). Elsevier.

Kidner, D. Psalms One-Seventy-Two. LC 75-23852. 1973. 10.95 (ISBN 0-87784-868-8); pap. 5.95 (ISBN 0-87784-264-7). Inter-Varsity.

Kidner, Derek. Psalms Seventy-Three - One Hundred Fifty. Wiseman, D. J., ed. LC 75-7247. (Tyndale Old Testament Commentary Ser). 240p. 1975. 10.95 (ISBN 0-87784-959-5); pap. 5.95 (ISBN 0-87784-265-5). Inter-Varsity.

--A Time to Mourn, & a Time to Dance. LC 76-21460. (The Bible Speaks Today Ser.). (Orig.). 1976. pap. 4.50 (ISBN 0-87784-647-2). Inter-Varsity.

Kidney, Dorothy. The Mystery of the Old Clock Shop. (Orig.). (gr. 4-6). 1981. pap. 2.50 (ISBN 0-8341-0728-7). Beacon Hill.

Kidney, Walter C., jt. auth. see Ziegler, Arthur P.

Kidson, C. & Tooley, M. J. The Quaternary History of the Irish Sea: Geological Journal Special Issue, No. 7. (Liverpool Geological Society & the Manchester Geological Association). 356p. 1980. 82.95x (ISBN 0-471-27754-1, Pub. by Wiley-Interscience). Wiley.

Kidson, Frank. Beggar's Opera: Its Predecessors & Successors. Repr. of 1922 ed. lib. bdg. 18.25x (ISBN 0-8371-4250-4, KIBE). Greenwood.

Kidwell, Catherine. Dear Stranger. 416p. 1983. pap. 15.50 (ISBN 0-446-51247-8). Warner Bks.

Kidwell, Connie, et al. Pandora Seven: Role Expanding Science Fiction & Fantasy. Wickstrom, Lois, ed. (Illus.). 48p. 1981. 2.25 (ISBN 0-916176-12-6). Sproing.

Kidwell, R. J. & DeWelt, Don. Ecclesiastes; Song of Solomon. LC 78-301088. (The Bible Study Textbook Ser.). 1977. 14.30 o.s.i. (ISBN 0-89900-019-3). College Pr Pub.

Kidwell, William M., et al. Knowing Your Self. Herr, Edwin L., ed. (Cooperative Work Experience Education for Careers Program). (Illus.). (gr. 11-12). 1976. pap. text ed. 7.96 (ISBN 0-07-028327-3, G); tchr's manual & key 3.50 (ISBN 0-07-028328-1). McGraw.

Kieburtz, Richard B. Structured Programming & Problem Solving with Algol W. (Illus.). 384p. 1975. 17.95 (ISBN 0-13-854737-8). P-H.

--Structured Programming & Problem Solving with Pascal. (Illus.). 1978. Cloth. 22.95 (ISBN 0-13-854877-3); pap. 17.95 (ISBN 0-13-854869-2). P-H.

--Structured Programming & Problem Solving with PL-One. (Illus.). 1977. 18.95 o.p. (ISBN 0-686-60837-2); pap. 17.95 (ISBN 0-13-854943-5). P-H.

Kieckhefer, Richard. European Witch Trials: Their Foundations in Popular Learned Culture, 1300-1500. 1976. 32.00x (ISBN 0-520-02967-4). U of Cal Pr.

Kiefaber, Mark, jt. auth. see Procaccini, Joseph.

Kiefer, Ferenc. On Emphasis & Word Order in Hungarian. LC 66-64930. (Uralic & Altaic Ser: Vol. 76). 1967. pap. text ed. 8.50x o.p. (ISBN 0-87750-027-4). Res Ctr Lang Semiotic.

Kiefer, Ferenc, ed. Hungarian General Linguistics. (Linguistic & Literary Studies in Eastern Europe: No. 4). iv, 588p. 1982. 60.00 (ISBN 90-272-1508-1). Benjamins North Am.

Kiefer, Frederick. Fortune & Elizabethan Tragedy. LC 82-15836. (Illus.). 283p. 1982. 18.00 (ISBN 0-87328-122-5). Huntington Lib.

Kiefer, Irene. Energy for America. LC 79-14656. (Illus.). (gr. 5-9). 1979. 11.95 (ISBN 0-689-30713-6). Atheneum.

--Nuclear Energy at the Crossroads. LC 82-1681. (Illus.). 160p. (gr. 5 up). 1982. 10.95 (ISBN 0-689-30926-0). Atheneum.

--Underground Furnaces, the Story of Geothermal Energy. LC 76-3606. (Illus.). (gr. 3-7). 1976. PLB 7.63 (ISBN 0-688-32075-9). Morrow.

Kiefer, Kathleen E. Making Writing Work: Effective Paragraphs. 224p. 1983. pap. text ed. 9.95 (ISBN 0-07-034541-4, C); instructor's manual 4.95 (ISBN 0-07-034542-2). McGraw.

Kiefer, Louis J. How to Win Custody. LC 82-14153. 308p. 1982. pap. 8.95 (ISBN 0-346-12579-0). Cornerstone.

Kiefer, Nicholas M. The Economic Benefits from Four Employment & Training Programs. LC 78-75061. (Outstanding Dissertations in Economics Ser.). 1979. lib. bdg. 15.00 o.s.i. (ISBN 0-8240-4138-0). Garland Pub.

Kiefer, Ralph W., jt. auth. see Lillesand, Thomas M.

Kiefer, Velma B. Stories to Tell in Children's Church. (Paperback Program Ser.). Orig. Title: Please Tell Me a Story. 1976. pap. 4.50 (ISBN 0-8010-5371-4). Baker Bk.

Kiefer, Warren. The Pontius Pilate Papers. 1977. pap. write for info (ISBN 0-515-09396-3). Jove Pubns.

Kieffer & Sherman, N. Mental Health & Industry: Planning for the 1980's. LC 80-18057. 210p. 1980. 24.95 (ISBN 0-87705-085-6). Human Sci Pr.

Kieffer, Chester L. Maligned General: A Biography of Thomas S. Jesup. LC 77-73552. (Illus.). 1979. 16.95 o.p. (ISBN 0-89141-027-9). Presidio Pr.

Kieffer, Elizabeth C. Henry Harbaugh: Pennsylvania Dutchman: 1817 to 1867, Vol. 51. 30.00 (ISBN 0-911122-13-3). Penn German Soc.

Kieffer, Jarold A. Gaining the Dividends of Longer Life: A New Strategy. 250p. 1983. lib. bdg. 22.50 (ISBN 0-86531-083-1); pap. text ed. 11.50X (ISBN 0-86531-174-9). Westview.

Kieffer, Sherman, et al see Carone, Pasquale.

Kieft, Ruth M. Vande see Vande Kieft, Ruth M.

Kiehl, Charles, jt. auth. see Gallo, Michael.

Kielhofner, Gary. Health Through Occupation: Theory & Practice in Occupational Therapy. LC 82-18255. 350p. 1983. 22.00 (ISBN 0-8036-5317-4). Davis Co.

Kielhorn, F. A Grammar of the Sanskrit Language. 266p. 1976. Repr. of 1880 ed. 19.50 (ISBN 0-89684-162-6, Pub. by Cosmo Pubns India). Orient Bk Dist.

Kielkopf, Charles F. Formal Sentential Entailment. 1977. pap. text ed. 16.50 (ISBN 0-8191-0313-6). U Pr of Amer.

Kiely, Benedict. The State of Ireland: A Novella & Seventeen Short Stories. LC 79-92210. 352p. 1980. 16.95 (ISBN 0-87923-320-6). Godine.

Kiely, Dennis K. Essentials of Music for New Musicians. (Illus.). 192p. 1975. pap. text ed. 13.95 (ISBN 0-13-286492-4). P-H.

Kiene, Paul F. The Tabernacle of God in the Wilderness of Sinai. 1977. 16.95 o.p. (ISBN 0-310-36200-8). Zondervan.

Kiene, Richard H., ed. see American Academy of Orthopaedic Surgeons.

Kienel, Paul A. Christian School: Why It Is Right for Your Child. LC 74-77320. 1974. pap. 3.95 (ISBN 0-88207-703-1). Victor Bks.

Kieniewicz, Teresa. Men, Women, & the Novelist: Fact & Fiction in the American Novel of the 1870s & 1880s. LC 81-40727. 176p. (Orig.). 1982. lib. bdg. 21.25 (ISBN 0-8191-2044-8); pap. text ed. 10.00 (ISBN 0-8191-2045-6). U Pr of Amer.

Kienzle, William. Assault with Intent. 320p. 1983. pap. 2.95 (ISBN 0-345-30817-2). Ballantine.

Kienzle, William X. Mind over Murder. 1982. pap. 2.95 (ISBN 0-553-20666-4). Bantam.

--Shadow of Death. 264p. 1983. 10.95 (ISBN 0-8362-6119-4). Andrews & McMeel.

Kiepenheuer, K. O., ed. see International Astronomical Union Symposium, 35th, Budapest, Hungary, 1967.

Kieran, John. A Natural History of New York City. 2nd ed. (Illus.). pap. 9.95 (ISBN 0-8232-1086-3). Fordham.

Kierkegaard, Soren. Fear & Trembling & Repetition, 2 vols. in 1. Hong, Howard V. & Hong, Edna H., eds. Hong, Howard V. & Hong, Edna H., trs. LC 82-9006. (Kierkegaard's Writings Ser.: No. VI). 432p. 1983. 32.50x (ISBN 0-691-07237-X); pap. 6.95 (ISBN 0-691-02026-4). Princeton U Pr.

--The Point of View for My Work As an Author. 1977. pap. 3.95xi o.p. (ISBN 0-06-130088-8, TB88, Torch). Har-Row.

--Purity of Heart. Steere, Douglas, tr. pap. 5.95xi (ISBN 0-06-130004-7, TB4, Torch). Har-Row.

--Soren Kierkegaard's Journals & Papers, 7 vols. Hong, Howard V. & Hong, Edna H., eds. Incl. Vol. 1. A-E. 572p. 1967. 40.00x (ISBN 0-253-18240-9); Vol. 2. F-K. 640p. 1970. 47.50x (ISBN 0-253-18241-7); Vol. 3. L-R. 944p. 1976. 60.00x (ISBN 0-253-18242-5); Vol. 4. S-Z. 800p. 1976. 50.00x (ISBN 0-253-18243-3); Vol. 5. Autobiographical, Part One, 1829-1848. 576p. 1978. 47.50x (ISBN 0-253-18244-1); Vol. 6. Autobiographical, Part Two, 1848-1855. 648p. 1978. 50.00x (ISBN 0-253-18245-X); Vol. 7. Index & Composite Collation. 160p. 1978. 30.00x (ISBN 0-253-18246-8). Ind U Pr.

--Works of Love: Some Christian Reflections in the Form of Discourses. Long, tr. 1962. 12.00 (ISBN 0-8446-2373-3). Peter Smith.

Kierman, Frank A., Jr., tr. see Maspero, Henri.

Kierman, V. G. Marxism & Imperialism. LC 74-17723. 288p. 1975. 25.00 (ISBN 0-312-51835-8). St Martin.

Kiernan, Ben & Boua, Chanthou, eds. Peasants & Communists in Kampuchea: 1942-1979. Date not set. cancelled 30.00 (ISBN 0-905762-60-6, Pub. by Zed Pr England). Lawrence Hill.

--Peasants & Politics in Kampuchea: 1942-1981. LC 82-5451. (Illus.). 416p. 1982. 35.00 (ISBN 0-87332-217-7); pap. 14.95 (ISBN 0-87332-224-X). M E Sharpe.

Kiernan, Ben, jt. ed. see Chandler, David.

Kiernan, Brian. Patrick White. LC 80-5098. 150p. 1980. 20.00 (ISBN 0-312-59807-6). St Martin.

Kiernan, C. C. & Woodford, F. P., eds. Behaviour Modification with the Severely Retarded. (The Institute for Research into Mental & Multiple Handicap Study Group: Vol. 8). 1976. 45.00 (ISBN 0-444-15191-5, Excerpta Medica). Elsevier.

Kiernan, Chris & Jones, Malcolm. Behaviour Assessment Battery. (General Ser.). 1977. pap. text ed. 19.25x (ISBN 0-7005-0490-7, NFER). Humanities.

Kiernan, John A., jt. auth. see Barr, Murray L.

Kiernan, Joseph. Lots of Funny Riddles. 128p. (Orig.). 1981. pap. 1.75 o.p. (ISBN 0-446-94928-0). Warner Bks.

Kiernan, R. H. The Unveiling of Arabia: The Story of Arabian Travel & Discovery. (Illus.). 360p. 1983. Repr. of 1937 ed. 29.50x (ISBN 0-7146-1990-6, F Cass Co). Biblio Dist.

Kiernan, Robert F. American Writing since Nineteen Forty-Five: A Critical Survey. 200p. 1983. 14.95 (ISBN 0-8044-2458-6); pap. 7.95 (ISBN 0-8044-6359-X). Ungar.

--Gore Vidal. LC 81-70962. (Literature and Life Ser.). 160p. 1982. 11.95 (ISBN 0-8044-2461-6); pap. 5.95 (ISBN 0-8044-6360-3). Ungar.

Kiernan, Thomas. Jane: An Intimate Biography of Jane Fonda. (Illus.). 384p. 1973. 7.95 o.p. (ISBN 0-399-11207-3). Putnam Pub Group.

--Jane Fonda: Heroine for Our Time. (Illus.). 312p. (Orig.). 1982. pap. 8.95 (ISBN 0-933328-21-4). Delilah Bks.

Kiernan, Thomas, jt. auth. see Forman, Brenda.

Kiernan, Thomas, jt. auth. see Root, Leon.

Kiernan, Thomas J. The White Hound of the Mountain. (Illus.). 1962. 9.95 (ISBN 0-8159-7208-3). Devin.

Kiernan, V. G. America: The New Imperialism. 306p. 1981. 32.00 (ISBN 0-905762-18-5, Pub. by Zed Pr. England); pap. 12.50 (ISBN 0-905762-76-2, Pub. by Zed Pr England). Lawrence Hill.

--From Conquest to Collapse: European Empires from Eighteen Fifteen to Nineteen Sixty. LC 82-47883. 285p. 1982. 16.50 (ISBN 0-394-50959-5). Pantheon.

Kiernan, Victor. State & Society in Europe Fifteen Fifty to Sixteen Fifty. 1980. 26.00 (ISBN 0-312-75607-0). St Martin.

Kiers, Luc. The American Steel Industry: Problems, Challenges, Perspectives. (A Westview Special Study). (Illus.). 183p. 1980. lib. bdg. 30.00 (ISBN 0-89158-684-9). Westview.

Kiersch, George A., et al, eds. Engineering Geology Case Histories, Nos. 6-10 In One Volume. LC 74-77141. (Illus.). 1974. 12.50x (ISBN 0-8137-4202-1). Geol Soc.

Kies, Cosette. Projecting a Positive Image Through Public Relations. (School Media Centers: Focus on Issues & Trends: No. 2). 1979. pap. 6.00 (ISBN 0-8389-3219-3). ALA.

Kiesewetter, Raphael G. History of the Christian Music of Western Europe: From the First Century of the Christian Era to the Present Day. LC 74-140375. (Music Ser). 354p. 1973. Repr. of 1848 ed. lib. bdg. 29.5001624660x (ISBN 0-306-70089-1). Da Capo.

Kiesler, Charles A., et al. Attitude Change: A Critical Analysis of Theoretical Approaches. LC 81-19348. 398p. 1983. Repr. of 1969 ed. 24.95 (ISBN 0-89874-432-6). Krieger.

--Psychology & National Health Insurance: A Source Book. (Orig.). 1979. lib. bdg. 19.50x o.p. (ISBN 0-686-85625-2); pap. 15.00x o.p. (ISBN 0-912704-11-X). Am Psychol.

Kiesler, Sara B. Interpersonal Processes in Groups & Organizations. Mackenzie, Kenneth D., ed. LC 77-86018. (Organizational Behavior Ser.). 1978. pap. text ed. 13.95 (ISBN 0-88295-451-2). Harlan Davidson.

Kieslich, K. Microbial Tranformation of Non-Steroid Cyclic Compounds. 1976. 225.00x (ISBN 0-471-01812-0, Pub. by Wiley-Interscience). Wiley.

Kiesling, Stephen. The Shell Game: Reflections on Rowing & the Pursuit of Excellence. 208p. 1983. pap. 7.95 (ISBN 0-8092-5570-7). Contemp Bks.

Kieso, Donald E. & Weygandt, Jerry J. Intermediate Accounting. 3rd ed. 1290p. 1980. text ed. 35.95 (ISBN 0-471-04819-4); study guide 15.50 (ISBN 0-471-04821-6); FASB 1981 supple. o.p. 1.00 (ISBN 0-471-09356-4); practice set 9.50 (ISBN 0-471-06441-6); transparencies 450.00 (ISBN 0-471-04824-0); FASB 1981 supple. solutions o.p. 2.50 (ISBN 0-471-86408-0); tchrs. manual 9.95 (ISBN 0-471-04822-4); tests 29.95 (ISBN 0-471-04827-5); working papers (ISBN 0-471-04823-2): 3.00 checklist (ISBN 0-471-06437-8): 17.00 Expanded Solutions Manual (ISBN 0-471-05580-8) 16.95 (ISBN 0-686-91550-X). Wiley.

Kietzel, F. Von see Von Kietzel, F.

Kiev, ed. Future of Mental Health Services. (International Congress Ser.: Vol. 504). 1980. 58.50 (ISBN 0-444-90127-2). Elsevier.

Kiev, Ari. Active Loving. LC 79-7090. 1979. 8.95i o.p. (ISBN 0-690-01785-5). T Y Crowell.

--The Courage to Live. LC 78-69517. 1979. 7.95i o.p. (ISBN 0-690-01801-0). T Y Crowell.

--How to Keep Love Alive. 224p. 1982. 13.41i (ISBN 0-06-014941-8, HarpT). Har-Row.

--Recovery from Depression: A Self-Help Strategy, 120p. 1982. 6.75 (ISBN 0-525-93239-9). Dutton.

--Riding Through the Downers, Hassles, Snags & Funks. 96p. 1980. 7.95 o.p. (ISBN 0-525-93138-4). Dutton.

--Transcultural Psychiatry. LC 73-163235. 1973. 14.95 (ISBN 0-02-917180-6); pap. 4.95 (ISBN 0-02-917170-9). Free Pr.

Kieval, Gershon R. Party Politics in Israel & the Occupied Terrorities. LC 82-12000. (Contributions in Political Science Ser.: No. 95). 288p. 1983. lib. bdg. 35.00 (ISBN 0-313-23325-X, KIP/). Greenwood.

Kievman, Michael S., jt. auth. see Howard, Herbert H.

Kiewiet, D. Roderick. Macroeconomics & Micropolitics: The Electoral Effects of Economic Issues. LC 82-21985. (Illus.). 160p. 1983. lib. bdg. 16.00x (ISBN 0-226-43532-6). U of Chicago Pr.

Kiewitt, Eva L. Evaluating Information Retrieval Systems: The PROBE Program. LC 78-55322. 1978. lib. bdg. 25.00 (ISBN 0-313-20521-3, KPC/). Greenwood.

Kifer, R. S. & Stewart, H. L. Farming Hazards in the Drought Area. LC 78-165600. (Research Monograph Ser.: Vol. 26). 1971. Repr. of 1938 ed. lib. bdg. 29.50 (ISBN 0-306-70348-3). Da Capo.

Kiger, John, jt. auth. see Ayala, Francisco.

Kigin, Denis J. Teacher Liability in School-Shop Accidents. rev. ed. LC 82-61688. 1983. 6.95x (ISBN 0-911168-51-6); pap. 4.50x O.p. (ISBN 0-911168-29-X); pap. 6.95 O.p. (ISBN 0-686-86660-6). Prakken.

Kihara, H. Wheat Studies: Retrospects & Prospects. The Birthplace of Genetical Research on Wheat. (Developments in Crop Science: Vol. 3). 1982. 68.00 (ISBN 0-444-99695-8). Elsevier.

Kihara, T. Intermolecular Forces. LC 77-12353. 182p. 1978. 41.95x (ISBN 0-471-99583-5, Pub. by Wiley-Interscience). Wiley.

Kihl, Kim R. Port Tobacco: A Transformed Community. LC 82-60383. (Illus.). 102p. (Orig.). 1982. pap. 5.95 (ISBN 0-940776-03-0). Maclay Assoc.

Kihlman, B. A. Caffeine & Chromosomes. 1977. 111.00 (ISBN 0-444-41491-6, North Holland). Elsevier.

Kihlstrom, jt. auth. see Boyer.

Kihlstrom, April. A Choice of Cousins. (Orig.). 1982. pap. 2.25 (ISBN 0-451-11347-0, AE1347, Sig). NAL.

Kihlstrom, April L. Paris Summer. (YA) 1977. 6.95 (ISBN 0-685-74270-9, Avalon). Bouregy.

Kihlstrom, April Lynn. Trondelaine Castle. (YA) 1979. 6.95 (ISBN 0-685-90729-5, Avalon). Bouregy.

Kijek, Jean C., jt. auth. see Murray, Rosemary.

Kikkawa, J., ed. see Ito, Y.

Kikkoman. The Kikkoman Cookbook: Your Way to Better Flavor. 1973. pap. 9.95x o.p. (ISBN 0-442-24409-6). Van Nos Reinhold.

Kikumura, Akemi. Through Harsh Winters: The Life of a Japanese Immigrant Woman. LC 81-15534. 176p. 1981. 10.95 (ISBN 0-88316-544-9); pap. 6.95x (ISBN 0-88316-543-0). Chandler & Sharp.

Kilani-Schoch, Marianne. Processus Phonologiques, Processus Morphologiques et Lapsus Dans un Corpus Aphasique. xvii, 568p. (Fr.). 1982. write for info. (ISBN 3-8204-6211-2). P Lang Pubs.

Kilbey, B. J., et al, eds. Handbook of Mutagenicity Test Procedures. 1977. 98.75 (ISBN 0-444-41338-3, North Holland). Elsevier.

Kilbride-Jones, H. E. Celtic Craftsmanship in Bronze. LC 80-10520. (Illus.). 320p. 1980. 37.50 (ISBN 0-312-12698-0). St Martin.

Kilbury, James. The Development of Morphophonemic Theory. (Studies in History of Linguistics Ser.: No. 10). viii, 155p. 1976. 19.00 (ISBN 90-272-0951-0). Benjamins North Am.

Kilby, B. A., jt. ed. see Candy, D. J.

Kilby, Clyde. Tolkien & The Silmarillion. LC 76-1340. (Wheaton Literary Ser.). 96p. 1976. 4.95 (ISBN 0-87788-816-7). Shaw Pubs.

Kilby, Clyde S. Tolkien & the Silmarillion. 90p. 1982. 4.95 o.p. (ISBN 0-89191-816-7, 52365). Cook.

Kilby, Clyde S., ed. see Lewis, Warren H.

Kilby, Jan E. Career Education & English, K-12: Ideas for Teaching. 99p. 1980. pap. 7.00 (ISBN 0-8141-0437-1, 80-13157); pap. 5.00 members (ISBN 0-686-86384-4). NCTE.

Kilby, Peter, jt. auth. see Johnston, Bruce F.

Kilchenman, A., ed. Quantitative & Theoretical Geography. 100p. 1975. pap. text ed. write for info. (ISBN 0-08-019680-2). Pergamon.

Kildow, Judith T., ed. Deepsea Mining: Selected Papers from a Series of Seminars Held at MIT in December 1979 & January 1979. 1980. text ed. 22.50x (ISBN 0-262-11075-X). MIT Pr.

Kiley, Dan. Dr. Dan's Prescriptions: 1001 Nonmedical Hints for Solving Parenting Problems. 256p. 1982. 12.95 (ISBN 0-698-11175-3, Coward). Putnam Pub Group.

--Keeping Kids Out of Trouble. Orig. Title: Nobody Said It Would Be Easy. 1979. pap. 2.50 o.p. (ISBN 0-446-81445-8). Warner Bks.

--Keeping Parents Out of Trouble. (Orig.). 1982. 11.95 (ISBN 0-446-51221-4); pap. 3.50 (ISBN 0-446-90524-0). Warner Bks.

Kiley, Denise. Biggest Machines. LC 80-383. (Machine World Ser.). (Illus.). 32p. (gr. 2-4). 1980. PLB 13.85 (ISBN 0-8172-1332-5). Raintree Pubs.

Kiley, John C. Self Rescue. 1977. 7.95 o.p. (ISBN 0-07-034550-3, GB). McGraw.

Kiley-Worthington, M. & De La Plain, S. The Social Behaviour & Management of Cattle. (Animal Management Ser.). 112p. Date not set. price not set (ISBN 3-7643-1265-3). Birkhauser.

Kilgannon, Pete. Business Data Processing & Systems Analysts. 336p. 1980. pap. text ed. 17.95 (ISBN 0-7131-2755-4). E Arnold.

Kilgore, Hermina G. A Dean's Days. (Illus.). 64p. (Orig.). 1977. pap. 2.50 (ISBN 0-9609280-2-2). Kilgore.

--Rough Road in the Rockies. LC 61-16173. (Illus.). 135p. 1975. 5.50 (ISBN 0-9609280-0-6); pap. 3.95 (ISBN 0-9609280-1-4). Kilgore.

Kilgore, James C. African Violet: Poem for a Black Woman. 76p. pap. 5.00 (ISBN 0-916418-46-4). Lotus.

Kilgore, Kathleen. The Wolfman of Beacon Hill. LC 82-47910. 192p. (gr. 7 up). 1982. 11.95 (ISBN 0-316-49306-6). Little.

Kilgour, Gordon. Fundamentals of Biochemistry. Date not set. text ed. 21.95 o.s.i. (ISBN 0-442-25756-2); instr's. manual 2.00 o.s.i. (ISBN 0-442-25757-0). Van Nos Reinhold.

Kilgour, O. F. An Introduction to Science for Catering & Homecraft Students. 416p. 1976. pap. 30.00x (ISBN 0-686-92008-2, Pub. by Heinemann England). State Mutual Bk.

Kilian, Crawford. Eyas. 144p. 1982. 2.50 (ISBN 0-553-20930-2). Bantam.

Kilian, Michael. Northern Exposure. 352p. 1983. 14.95 (ISBN 0-312-57896-2). St Martin.

Kilias, H. Revision Gesteinsbewohnender Sippen der Flechtengattung Catillaria Mass in Europa(Lecanorales, Lecideaceae) (Illus.). 240p. (Ger.). 1981. pap. text ed. 12.00 (ISBN 3-7682-1318-8). Lubrecht & Cramer.

Kiliper, R. Smith, jt. auth. see Schulz, Charles M.

Killam, G. D. The Novels of Chinua Achebe. LC 73-95190. 1969. 9.50x (ISBN 0-8419-0023-X, Africana); pap. 6.50x (ISBN 0-8419-0024-8, Africana). Holmes & Meier.

Killeen, Jacqueline, jt. auth. see Castle, Coralie.

Killeen, Jacqueline, et al. Best Restaurants San Francisco Bay Area. (Best Restaurants Ser.). 200p. 1983. pap. 4.95 (ISBN 0-89286-216-5). One Hund One Prods.

--Country Inns of the Far West: A Revised & Expanded Guide to the Inns of California, Oregon, Washington & British Columbia. LC 78-4816. (Illus.). 1979. pap. 4.95 o.p. (ISBN 0-89286-149-5). One Hund One Prods.

Killeen, Roy, illus. Best Restaurants Chicago & Suburbs Revised. rev. ed. LC 82-8173. (Best Restaurants Ser.). (Illus.). 272p. (Orig.). 1983. pap. 4.95 (ISBN 0-89286-201-7). One Hund One Prods.

Killeen, Veronica A., jt. auth. see Hayes, Walter M.

Killen, James E. Mathematical Programming Methods for Geographers & Planners. LC 82-42839. 384p. 1983. 35.00x (ISBN 0-312-50133-1). St Martin.

Killens, John O. And Then We Heard the Thunder. (Howard University Press Library of Contemporary Literature). 485p. 1983. pap. 7.95 (ISBN 0-88258-115-5). Howard U Pr.

Killgallon, James J., jt. auth. see Weber, Gerard P.

Killian, James R., Jr. Sputnik, Scientists, & Eisenhower: A Memoir of the First Special Assistant to the President for Science & Technology. LC 77-21560. 1977. 20.00x (ISBN 0-262-11066-0); pap. 8.95 (1982) (ISBN 0-262-61035-3). MIT Pr.

Killian, James R., Jr., jt. auth. see Edgerton, Harold E.

Killian, James R., Jr., ed. Proceedings of the Atoms for Peace Awards, 1957-1969: A Memorial to Henry Ford & Edsel Ford. 1978. text ed. 20.00x (ISBN 0-262-11068-7). MIT Pr.

Killian, Kathryn W., jt. auth. see Moak, Lennox L.

Killian, Lewis, jt. auth. see Turner, Ralph.

Killick. Development Economics in Action: A Study of Economic Policies in Ghana. LC 77-74764. 1978. 22.50 (ISBN 0-312-19682-2). St Martin.

Killick, Anthony. The Economies of East Africa. 1976. lib. bdg. 15.00 (ISBN 0-8161-7916-6, Hall Reference). G K Hall.

Killikelly, Sarah H. Curious Questions in History, Literature, Art, & Social Life, 3 Vols. LC 68-26581. 1968. Repr. of 1900 ed. Set. 86.00x (ISBN 0-8103-3091-1). Gale.

Killilea, Marie, jt. ed. see Schulberg, Herbert C.

Killingbeck, J. P. Techniques of Applied Quantum Mechanics. 300p. 1975. 21.95 o.p. (ISBN 0-408-70715-1). Butterworth.

Killinger, D. K., jt. auth. see Mooradian, A.

Killinger, George G. & Cromwell, Paul F., Jr. Corrections in the Community. 2nd ed. (Criminal Justice Ser.). 1978. pap. text ed. 17.50 (ISBN 0-8299-0155-8). West Pub.

--Introductions to Corrections: Selected Readings. (Criminal Justice Ser.). (Illus.). 1978. pap. text ed. 16.50 (ISBN 0-8299-0208-2). West Pub.

Killinger, George G., et al. Penology: The Evolution of Corrections in America. 2nd ed. (Criminal Justice Ser.). (Illus.). 1979. pap. text ed. 17.50 (ISBN 0-8299-0277-5). West Pub.

Killinger, John. The Cup & the Waterfall. LC 82-61421. 1983. pap. 3.95 (ISBN 0-8091-2515-3). Paulist Pr.

Killinger, Margaret, ed. see Painter, Desmond & Shepard, John.

Killingley, Carl A., jt. auth. see Long, Charles A.

Killingray, David. The Atom Bomb. Yapp, Malcolm, et al, eds. (World History Ser.). (Illus.). 32p. (gr. 10). 1980. Repr. of 1977 ed. lib. bdg. 6.95 (ISBN 0-89908-235-1); pap. text ed. 2.25 (ISBN 0-89908-210-6). Greenhaven.

--Nyerere & Nkrumah. Yapp, Malcolm & Killingray, Margaret, eds. (World History Ser.). (Illus.). 32p. (gr. 10). 1980. Repr. of 1977 ed. lib. bdg. 6.95 (ISBN 0-89908-129-0); pap. text ed. 2.25 (ISBN 0-89908-104-5). Greenhaven.

--Population. O'Connor, Edmund, ed. (World History Ser.). (Illus.). 32p. (gr. 10). 1980. Repr. of 1977 ed. lib. bdg. 6.95 (ISBN 0-89908-141-X); pap. text ed. 2.25 (ISBN 0-89908-116-9). Greenhaven.

--The Russian Revolution. Yapp, Malcolm, et al, eds. (World History Ser.). (Illus.). (gr. 10). 1980. Repr. of 1977 ed. lib. bdg. 6.95 (ISBN 0-89908-138-X); pap. text ed. 2.25 (ISBN 0-89908-113-4). Greenhaven.

--The Slave Trade. Yapp, Malcolm & Killingray, Margaret, eds. (World History Ser.). (Illus.). (gr. 10). 1980. Repr. of 1977 ed. lib. bdg. 6.95 (ISBN 0-89908-149-5); pap. text ed. 2.25 (ISBN 0-89908-124-X). Greenhaven.

--The Two World Wars. Yapp, Malcolm & Killlingray, Margaret, eds. (World History Ser.). (Illus.). 32p. (gr. 10). 1980. Repr. of 1977 ed. lib. bdg. 6.95 (ISBN 0-89908-234-3); pap. text ed. 2.25 (ISBN 0-89908-209-2). Greenhaven.

--A World Economy. Yapp, Malcolm, et al, eds. (World History Ser.). (Illus.). 32p. (gr. 10). 1980. Repr. of 1977 ed. lib. bdg. 6.95 (ISBN 0-89908-143-6); pap. text ed. 2.25 (ISBN 0-89908-118-5). Greenhaven.

Killingray, David, jt. auth. see Cook, Chris.

Killingray, David, et al. Stalin. Yapp, Malcolm, et al, eds. (World History Ser.). (Illus.). 32p. (gr. 10). 1980. Repr. of 1977 ed. lib. bdg. 6.95 (ISBN 0-89908-126-6); pap. text ed. 2.25 (ISBN 0-89908-101-0). Greenhaven.

Killingray, Margaret. The Agricultural Revolution. Yapp, Malcolm & O'Connor, Edmund, eds. (World History Ser.). (Illus.). 32p. (gr. 10). 1980. Repr. of 1977 ed. lib. bdg. 6.95 (ISBN 0-89908-131-2); pap. text ed. 2.25 (ISBN 0-89908-106-1). Greenhaven.

--Ancient Greece. Yapp, Malcolm & O'Connor, Edmund, eds. (World History Ser.). Orig. Title: The Mediterranean. (Illus.). 32p. (gr. 10). 1980. Repr. of 1977 ed. lib. bdg. 6.95 (ISBN 0-89908-026-X); pap. text ed. 2.25 (ISBN 0-89908-001-4). Greenhaven.

--Constantine. Yapp, Malcolm, et al, eds. (Greenhaven World History Ser.). (Illus.). 32p. (gr. 10). 1980. lib. bdg. 6.95 (ISBN 0-89908-040-5); pap. text ed. 2.25 (ISBN 0-89908-015-4). Greenhaven.

Killingray, Margaret, ed. see Addison, John, et al.

Killingray, Margaret, ed. see Booth, Martin, et al.

Killingray, Margaret, ed. see Doncaster, Islay.

Killingray, Margaret, ed. see Duckworth, John, et al.

Killingray, Margaret, ed. see Harrison, John, et al.

Killingray, Margaret, ed. see Heater, Derek & Owen, Gwyneth.

Killingray, Margaret, ed. see Killingray, David.

Killingray, Margaret, ed. see O'Connor, Edmund.

Killingray, Margaret, ed. see Painter, Desmond.

Killingray, Margaret, ed. see Pearson, Eileen.

Killingray, Margaret, ed. see Read, James & Yapp, Malcolm.

Killingray, Margaret, ed. see Tames, Richard.

Killingray, Margaret, ed. see Yapp, Malcolm.

Killingray, Margaret, et al, eds. see Guyatt, John.

Killingray, Margaret, et al, eds. see Tames, Richard.

Killingray, Margaret, et al, eds. see Townson, Duncan.

Killingray, Margaret, et al, eds. see Vapp, Malcolm.

Killingray, Margaret, et al, eds. see Yapp, Malcolm.

Killingray, Marget, ed. see O'Connor, Edmund.

Killingsworth, Cleve, jt. auth. see Mullner, Ross.

Killion, Tom. Fortress Marin. LC 78-31439. (Illus.). 1979. pap. 7.95 o.p. (ISBN 0-89141-083-X). Presidio Pr.

Killy, Jean-Claude. One-Hundred & Thirty-Three Ski Lessons by Jean-Claude Killy. 80p. 1975. pap. 3.95 o.s.i. (ISBN 0-695-80628-9). Follett.

--One Hundred Thirty Three Skiing Lessons. Covino, Frank, ed. 80p. 1975. pap. 3.95 (ISBN 0-695-80628-9). DBI Bks.

Kilmann, Peter R. & Mills, Katherine H. All About Sex Therapy. 250p. 1983. 15.95x (ISBN 0-306-41317-5, Plenum Pr). Plenum Pub.

Kilmartin, Angela. Cystitis: The Complete Self-Help Guide. LC 79-26425. (Illus.). 224p. (Orig.). 1980. 9.95 (ISBN 0-446-51203-6); pap. 6.95 (ISBN 0-446-37735-X). Warner Bks.

Kilmartin, Terence, tr. see Proust, Marcel.

Kilmarx, Robert A., jt. auth. see Mikesell, Raymond F.

Kilmer, Joyce. Trees & Other Poems. LC 82-14061. 72p. 1982. Repr. of 1914 ed. 12.00 (ISBN 0-89783-024-5). Larlin Corp.

Kilmer, Nicholas, ed. see Ronsard, Pierre De.

Kilmer, Sally, ed. Advances in Early Education & Day Care, Vol. 1. 225p. (Orig.). 1980. lib. bdg. 40.00 (ISBN 0-89232-127-X). Jai Pr.

--Advances in Early Education & Day Care, Vol. 2. 300p. 1981. 40.00 (ISBN 0-89232-149-0). Jai Pr.

Kilmer, Victor J., ed. Handbook of Soils & Climate in Agriculture. 456p. 1982. 94.00 (ISBN 0-686-84130-1). CRC Pr.

Kilmister, Anthony, ed. The Good Church Guide. 320p. 1982. 39.00x (ISBN 0-85634-120-7, Pub. by Muller Ltd). State Mutual Bk.

Kilmister, C. W. Special Theory of Relativity. 1970. 38.00 o.p. (ISBN 0-08-006996-7); pap. 11.25 o.p. (ISBN 0-08-006995-9). Pergamon.

Kiloh, L. G. & McComas, A. J. Clinical Electroencephalography. 3rd ed. (Illus.). 252p. 1972. 29.95 o.p. (ISBN 0-407-13602-9). Butterworth.

Kiloh, L. G., jt. auth. see Girgis, M.

Kilpatrick. Light & Lighting. (Photographer's Library). (Illus.). 1983. pap. 12.95x (ISBN 0-240-51203-0). Focal Pr.

Kilpatrick, Bob, ed. see Mueller, Ellen C.

Kilpatrick, Cathy. The Animal World. LC 80-50337. (World of Knowledge Ser.). PLB 16.72 (ISBN 0-382-06403-8). Silver.

--Birds of Prey. (Scimitar Ser.). (Illus.). 32p. (Orig.). (gr. 4 up). 1978. PLB 0.99 (ISBN 0-686-96995-2, Pub. by Archon Pr England). A & P Bks.

Kilpatrick, David. Creative Thirty-Five Millimeter Photography: How to Use Equipment & Techniques for More Exciting Pictures. 256p. 1983. 24.95 (ISBN 0-8174-3713-4, Amphoto). Watson-Guptill.

Kilpatrick, F. & Matchett, D., eds. Water & Energy: Technical & Policy Issues. LC 82-71351. 672p. 1982. pap. text ed. 52.00 (ISBN 0-87262-308-4). Am Soc Civil Eng.

Kilpatrick, Harold. Functional Dental Assisting. LC 76-28940. (Illus.). 1977. pap. text ed. 12.95 (ISBN 0-7216-5424-X). Saunders.

Kilpatrick, James J. The Smut Peddlers. LC 72-7506. (Illus.). 323p. 1973. Repr. of 1960 ed. lib. bdg. 20.75x (ISBN 0-8371-6515-6, KISP). Greenwood.

Kilpatrick, Jeremy, jt. auth. see Polya, George.

Kilpatrick, John A., Jr., jt. auth. see Aegerter, Ernest E.

Kilpatrick, Paula & Dudley, Cliff. The Ninth Floor. LC 81-80942. 128p. 1981. pap. 4.95 (ISBN 0-89221-085-0). New Leaf.

Kilpatrick, William K. Identity & Intimacy. 272p. 1975. pap. 4.95 o.s.i. (ISBN 0-440-54576-5, Delta). Dell.

--Psychological Seduction. 228p. 1983. pap. 5.95 (ISBN 0-8407-5843-X). Nelson.

Kilson, Marion D. African Urban Kinsman: The Ga of Central Accra. LC 74-79128. 1975. 25.00 (ISBN 0-312-01050-8). St Martin.

Kim. Competitive Economics: Equilibrium & Arbitration. Date not set. price not set (ISBN 0-444-86497-0). Elsevier.

Kim, Ashida. Ninja Death Touch. (Illus.). 108p. 1982. pap. 10.00 (ISBN 0-87364-257-0). Paladin Ent.

Kim, Bok-Lim C. Asian Americans: Changing Patterns, Changing Needs. xxiii, 271p. 1978. 12.00 (ISBN 0-932014-03-8). AKCS.

Kim, Byong-suh & Lee, Sang Hyun, eds. The Korean Immigrant in America. x, 175p. 1980. 7.00 (ISBN 0-932014-05-4). AKCS.

Kim, Byong-suh, jt. ed. see Kim, Dong Soo.

Kim, C. I., jt. auth. see Zifing, Lawrence.

Kim, Carolynn, ed. see Ridgley, Marlene.

Kim, Chaiho. Quantitative Analysis for Managerial Decisions. LC 75-372. (Illus.). 448p. 1975. text ed. 23.95 (ISBN 0-201-03739-4). A-W.

Kim, Charles W., ed. Microbiology Review. 7th ed. LC 80-20088. 1980. pap. 11.95 (ISBN 0-87488-203-6). Med Exam.

Kim, Chin. Selected Writings on Asian Law. LC 82-21490. xiii, 573p. 1982. lib. bdg. 37.50x (ISBN 0-8377-0741-2). Rothman.

Kim, Chin, tr. from Chinese. China: The Criminal Code of the People's Republic of China. (American Series of Foreign Penal Codes: No. 25). xv, 74p. 1982. text ed. 18.50x (ISBN 0-8377-0045-0). Rothman.

Kim, Chong Lim & Barkan, Joel D. The Legislative Process in Developing Countries: Kenya, Korea, & Turkey. (Duke Press Policy Studies). (Illus.). 400p. 1983. prepub. 35.00 (ISBN 0-8223-0534-8). Duke.

Kim, Chong Lim & Merkl, Peter, eds. Political Participation in Korea: Democracy, Mobilization & Stability. LC 79-19711. (Studies in International & Comparative Politics: No. 15). (Illus.). 238p. 1980. text ed. 28.50 (ISBN 0-87436-296-2). ABC-Clio.

Kim, Choong H. Books by Mail: A Handbook for Libraries. LC 76-15335. (Illus.). 1977. lib. bdg. 35.00 (ISBN 0-8371-9029-0, KBM/). Greenwood.

Kim, Choong S. An Asian Anthropologist in the South: Field Experiences with Blacks, Indians, & Whites. LC 76-49448. 1977. 12.50x (ISBN 0-87049-201-2). U of Tenn Pr.

Kim, Chuk Kyo, ed. Industrial & Social Development Issues: Essays on the Korean Economy, Vol.2. 1977. text ed. 12.00x (ISBN 0-8248-0547-X, Korea Development Institute Bk). UH Pr.

--Planning Model & Macroeconomic Policy Issues: Essays on the Korean Economy, Vol.1. 1977. text ed. 14.00x (ISBN 0-8248-0546-1, Korea Development Institute Bk). UH Pr.

Kim, Daeshik & Leland, Tom W. Karate. 3rd ed. (Exploring Sports Ser.). 1983. pap. write for info. (ISBN 0-697-09976-8). Wm C Brown.

Kim, Dong S., jt. ed. see Sunoo, Harold H.

Kim, Dong Soo & Kim, Byong-suh, eds. Human Rights in Minority Perspectives. xviii, 292p. 1979. 8.00 (ISBN 0-932014-04-6). AKCS.

Kim, Elaine. With Silk Wings: Asian American Women at Work. (Illus.). 150p. 1983. pap. 10.95 (ISBN 0-936434-06-6). SF Stud Ctr.

Kim, Elaine, intro. by see Wong, Diane Yen-Mei.

Kim, Elaine H. Asian American Literature: An Introduction to the Writings & Their Social Context. 350p. 1982. 29.95 (ISBN 0-87722-260-6). Temple U Pr.

Kim, Eugene C. & Kellough, Richard D. A Resource Guide For Secondary School Teaching: Planning For Competence. 256p. 1983. pap. text ed. 13.95 (ISBN 0-02-363810-9). Macmillan.

Kim, Han Kyo, ed. Essays on Modern Politics & History. LC 75-91958. xiv, 255p. 1969. 13.95x (ISBN 0-8214-0079-7, 82-80836). Ohio U Pr.

Kim, Han-Kyo, ed. Studies on Korea: A Scholar's Guide. LC 79-26491. 576p. 1980. text ed. 25.00x (ISBN 0-8248-0673-5). UH Pr.

Kim, Hei C., jt. auth. see Hurh, Won M.

Kim, Ilpyong. The Politics of Chinese Communism: Kiangi Under Soviet Rule. LC 73-76101. 1974. 30.00x (ISBN 0-520-02438-9). U of Cal Pr.

Kim, Ilpyong J. Communist Politics in North Korea. LC 72-92887. (Special Studies). 140p. 1975. text ed. 28.95 o.p. (ISBN 0-275-09190-2). Praeger.

Kim, Jai-Hyup. The Garrison State in Prewar Japan & Post-War Korea: A Comparative Analysis of Military Politics. LC 77-26344. 1978. 12.50 (ISBN 0-8191-0416-7). U Pr of Amer.

Kim, Jeong-Hak. The Prehistory of Korea. Pearson, Richard J. & Pearson, Kazue, trs. from Japanese. LC 77-28056. 1979. text ed. 17.50x (ISBN 0-8248-0552-6). UH Pr.

Kim, Key-Hiuk. The Last Phase of the East Asian World Order: Korea, Japan, & the Chinese Empire, 1860-1882. LC 77-83106. 1980. 27.50x (ISBN 0-520-03556-9). U of Cal Pr.

Kim, Mi J. & Moritz, Derry A., eds. Classification of Nursing Diagnoses: Proceedings of the Third & Fourth National Conferences. (Illus.). 448p. 1982. pap. 17.50x (ISBN 0-07-034547-3). McGraw.

Kim, Paul K. & Wilson, Constance P., eds. Toward Mental Health of the Rural Elderly. LC 80-6071. 428p. 1981. lib. bdg. 25.25 (ISBN 0-8191-1613-0); pap. text ed. 15.50 (ISBN 0-8191-1614-9). U Pr of Amer.

Kim, Q. Y. The Fall of Syngman Rhee. (Korea Research Monographs: No. 7). (Illus.). 255p. (Orig.). 1982. pap. 12.00 (ISBN 0-912966-54-8). IEAS.

Kim, Ronald C., ed. Metabolic & Degenerative Diseases of the Nervous System. LC 76-720135. (Neuropathology: An Illustrated Course). 24p. 1977. 100.00x (ISBN 0-8036-2914-1); cassette & slides incl. Davis Co.

Kim, Roy U., ed. see Ginsburgs, George.

Kim, S. K. & Strait, E. N. Modern Physics for Scientists & Engineers. (Illus.). 1978. text ed. 28.95x (ISBN 0-02-363780-3). Macmillan.

Kim, Samuel S., jt. ed. see Falk, Richard A.

Kim, Scott. Inversions: A Catalog of Calligraphic Cartwheels. 122p. 1981. pap. 8.95 (ISBN 0-07-034546-5). McGraw.

Kim, Seung H. & Miller, Stephen W. Competitive Structure of the International Banking Industry. Miossi, Alfred F., ed. LC 81-47970. 256p. 1983. 25.95x (ISBN 0-669-05189-6). Lexington Bks.

Kim, Seyoon. The Origin of Paul's Gospel. 403p. (Orig.). 1982. pap. 14.95 (ISBN 0-8028-1933-8). Eerdmans.

Kim, Suk H. An Introduction to International Financial Management. LC 80-5203. 302p. 1980. pap. text ed. 11.50 (ISBN 0-8191-1054-X). U Pr of Amer.

Kim, Suk H. & Guithues, Henry J. Capital Expenditure Analysis. LC 80-6070. 338p. 1981. 22.25 (ISBN 0-8191-1462-6); pap. 12.00 (ISBN 0-8191-1463-4). U Pr of Amer.

Kim, Yong Choon. Oriental Thought: An Introduction to the Philosophical & Religious Thought of Asia. LC 80-39672. 144p. 1981. Repr. of 1973 ed. 8.95x (ISBN 0-8476-6972-6). Rowman.

Kim, Young C., jt. auth. see Sigur, Gastonz.

Kimambo, Isaria, jt. ed. see Ranger, T. O.

Kimball, Bonnie-Jean. Aftercare: Blueprint for a Richer Life. 1.25 (ISBN 0-89486-005-4, 1130B). Hazelden.

--Alcoholic Woman's Mad, Mad World of Denial & Mind Games. LC 77-94793. (Orig.). 1978. pap. 4.00 (ISBN 0-89486-048-8). Hazelden.

Kimball, C. P., jt. ed. see Krakowski, A. J.

Kimball, Chase P. The Biopsychosocial Approach to the Patient. (Illus.). 382p. 1981. soft cover 21.00 (ISBN 0-686-69562-3, 4616-0). Williams & Wilkins.

Kimball, David & Kimball, Jim. Market Hunter. LC 75-91355. 1969. 4.95 o.p. (ISBN 0-87518-011-6). Dillon.

Kimball, Donald L. I Remember Mamie. LC 81-85247. (Illus.). 235p. 1981. 13.95 (ISBN 0-942698-00-2). Trends & Events.

Kimball, Edward W. The Powerful, Impressive Art of Diego Rodriguez de Silva Velasquez. (The Art Library of the Great Masters of the World). (Illus.). 103p. 1983. 47.85 (ISBN 0-86650-049-9). Gloucester Art.

Kimball, Everett. The Public Life of Joseph Dudley: A Study of the Colonial Policy of the Stuarts in New England, 1660-1715. (Perspectives in American History Ser.). vii, 239p. Repr. of 1911 ed. lib. bdg. 19.50x (ISBN 0-87991-106-9). Porcupine Pr.

Kimball, Fiske. Thomas Jefferson: Architect. 2nd ed. LC 67-27459. (Architecture & Decorative Art Ser). 1968. lib. bdg. 85.00 (ISBN 0-306-70965-1); pap. 29.50 o.p. (ISBN 0-306-70464-1). Da Capo.

Kimball, Gayle. The Fifty-Fifty Marriage. LC 82-70571. 256p. 1983. 12.98 (ISBN 0-8070-2726-X). Beacon Pr.

--The Religious Ideas of Harriet Beecher Stowe: Her Gospel of Womanhood. (Studies in Women & Religion: Vol. 8). 216p. 1982. 34.95x (ISBN 0-88946-544-4). E Mellen.

Kimball, Gertrude S. Providence in Colonial Times. LC 76-87452. (The American Scene Ser.). (Illus.). 391p. 1972. Repr. of 1912 ed. lib. bdg. 65.00 (ISBN 0-306-71524-4). Da Capo.

Kimball, Gitele. Whatever Became of Gitele? Ashton, Sylvia, ed. LC 77-70298. 1977. 8.95 o.p. (ISBN 0-87949-094-2). Ashley Bks.

Kimball, Janet. The Economic Doctrines of John Gray Seventeen Ninety-Seven to Eighteen Eighty-Three. Repr. of 1948 ed. lib. bdg. 17.50x (ISBN 0-87991-801-2). Porcupine Pr.

Kimball, Jim, jt. auth. see Kimball, David.

Kimball, John. Biology. 4th ed. LC 77-74322. (Life Sciences Ser.). 1978. text ed. 27.95 (ISBN 0-201-03761-0); lab manual 10.95 (ISBN 0-201-03692-4); study guide 8.95 (ISBN 0-201-03764-5). A-W.

Kimball, John W. Biology. 5th ed. LC 82-11636. (Biology Ser.). (Illus.). 875p. 1983. text ed. 24.95 (ISBN 0-201-10245-5); Instrs' Manual avail. (ISBN 0-201-10247-1); Study Guide avail. (ISBN 0-201-10246-3); Transparencies avail. (ISBN 0-201-10249-8); Test Bank avail. (ISBN 0-201-10265-X). A-W.

--Introduction to Immunology. 496p. 1983. text ed. 23.95 (ISBN 0-02-363820-6). Macmillan.

Kimball, Judith A. Children's Caravan: A Reading Activities Idea Book for Use with Children. (A Fun with Reading Bk.). (Orig.). 1983. pap. text ed. 18.50 (ISBN 0-89774-043-2). Oryx Pr.

Kimball, Margot C., jt. auth. see Palmer, Adrian S.

Kimball, Marie. Thomas Jefferson's Cook Book. 2nd ed. LC 76-22698. 1979. Repr. of 1976 ed. 9.95 (ISBN 0-8139-0706-3). U Pr of Va.

Kimball, Paul, jt. auth. see Fraenkel-Conrat, Heinz.

Kimball, Robert C., ed. see Tillich, Paul.

Kimball, Robert E. & Simon, Alfred E. The Gershwins. LC 73-80749. (Illus.). 1973. 25.00 o.p. (ISBN 0-689-10569-X). Atheneum.

Kimball, Solon T. Culture & the Educative Process. LC 73-21760. 285p. 1974. text ed. 10.25x (ISBN 0-8077-2422-X); pap. text ed. 6.50x (ISBN 0-8077-2434-3). Tchrs Coll.

Kimball, Spencer W. Tragedy or Destiny. 1977. pap. 0.95 o.p. (ISBN 0-87747-652-7). Deseret Bk.

Kimball, Theodora, jt. ed. see Olmstead, Frederick L., Jr.

Kimball, Warren F., ed. American Diplomacy in the Twentieth Century. LC 78-81060. 1980. pap. text ed. 6.95 (ISBN 0-88273-020-7). Forum Pr IL.

Kimball, Yeffe & Anderson, Jean. Art of American Indian Cooking. LC 65-19860. 1965. 7.95 o.p. (ISBN 0-385-04260-4). Doubleday.

Kimbark, E. W. Power System Stability, 2 Vols. Vol. 1. 355p. 41.50x, (ISBN 0-471-47586-6); Vol. 2. 39.50x (ISBN 0-471-47619-6, Pub. by Wiley-Interscience). Wiley.

Kimbark, E. W., jt. ed. see Byerly, R. T.

Kimbark, Edward W., jt. ed. see Byerly, Richard T.

Kimbell Art Museum. Kimbell Art Museum: A Catalogue of the Collection. LC 73-177945. (Illus.). 336p. 1972. 25.00 (ISBN 0-912804-00-9). Kimbell Art.

--Kimbell Art Museum: Handbook of the Collection. Robb, David M., ed. LC 80-82892. (Illus.). 275p. (Orig.). 1981. 15.00 (ISBN 0-686-35839-2); pap. 9.75 (ISBN 0-686-37178-X). Kimbell Art.

Kimbell, Richard. Design Education: The Foundation Years. (Routledge Education Bks.). (Illus.). 196p. (Orig.). 1982. pap. 15.95 (ISBN 0-7100-9018-8). Routledge & Kegan.

Kimber, Jean, tr. see Merimee, Prosper.

Kimberling, C. Ronald. Kenneth Burke's Dramatism & Popular Arts. LC 81-85522. 108p. 1982. 11.95 (ISBN 0-87972-195-2); pap. 5.95 (ISBN 0-87972-196-0). Bowling Green Univ.

Kimble, D. P., ed. see Conference on Learning, Remembering & Forgetting, 3rd.

Kimble, Daniel Porter. Psychology As a Biological Science. 2d ed. LC 76-21497. (Illus.). 1977. text ed. 21.95x (ISBN 0-673-16196-X). Scott F.

Kimble, Gregory A., et al. Principles of General Psychology. 5th ed. LC 79-23269. 590p. 1980. text ed. 23.95 (ISBN 0-471-04469-5, Pub by Ronald Pr); sampler 5.00 (ISBN 0-471-07944-8); study guide 10.95 (ISBN 0-471-06447-5); tchrs. manual 7.00 (ISBN 0-471-07792-5); tests 6.00 (ISBN 0-471-07690-2); supp. tests 20.00 (ISBN 0-471-08921-4); tchrs. manual supp. 4.00 (ISBN 0-471-09282-7). Wiley.

Kimbler, Frank S. & Narsavage, Robert J., Jr. New Mexico Rocks & Minerals Guide. (Illus.). 128p. (Orig.). 1981. pap. 8.95 (ISBN 0-913270-97-0). Sunstone Pr.

Kimbrall, Grady. Introduction to Business & Office Careers. (gr. 7-10). 1975. pap. text ed. 7.33 activity ed. (ISBN 0-87345-181-3). McKnight.

Kimbrall, Mary E. Introduction to Health Careers. (gr. 7-10). 1975. pap. text ed. 7.33 activity ed (ISBN 0-87345-179-1). McKnight.

Kimbrell, Grady & Vineyard, Ben S. Activities for Succeeding in the World of Work. 1981. pap. 6.64 (ISBN 0-87345-537-1). McKnight.

--Individualized Related Instruction for Succeeding in the World of Work. pap. 6.64 (ISBN 0-87345-547-9). McKnight.

--Strategies for Implementing Work Experience Programs. 400p. 1975. text ed. 44.00 (ISBN 0-87345-528-2). McKnight.

--Succeeding in the World of Work. rev. ed. (gr. 10-12). 1981. text ed. 17.96 (ISBN 0-87345-536-3); filmstrip set 407.00 (ISBN 0-686-31670-3). McKnight.

Kimbro, Harriet. Tamotzu in Haiku. LC 77-10844. (Illus.). 1977. pap. 4.95 (ISBN 0-913270-78-4). Sunstone Pr.

Kimbrough, M. The Joy & Adventure of Growing Younger. 1983. pap. 4.95 (ISBN 0-570-03876-6). Concordia.

Kimbrough, R. D. Halogenated Biphenyls, Terphenyls, Naphthalenes, Dibenzodioxines & Related Products. (Topics in Environmental Health Ser.: Vol. 4). 1981. 101.50 (ISBN 0-444-80253-3). Elsevier.

Kimbrough, Ralph B. & Nunnery, Michael Y. Educational Administration: An Introduction. 2nd ed. 512p. 1983. text ed. 25.95 (ISBN 0-02-363980-6). Macmillan.

--Politics, Power, Polls, & School Elections. LC 70-146308. 1971. 19.00x (ISBN 0-8211-1012-8); text ed. 16.95x (ISBN 0-685-04201-4). McCutchan.

Kimbrough, Robert. Sir Philip Sidney. (English Authors Ser.: No. 114). lib. bdg. 12.95 o.p. (ISBN 0-8057-1492-8, Twayne). G K Hall.

Kimbrough, Robert, ed. Sir Philip Sidney: Selected Prose & Poetry. 2nd ed. LC 82-51093. 576p. 1983. 25.00 (ISBN 0-299-09130-9); pap. 9.95 (ISBN 0-299-09134-1). U of Wis Pr.

Kimbrough, Victoria & Palmer, Michael. Odyssey: A Communicative Course in English. Incl. 128p. teacher's manual 5.50 (ISBN 0-582-79835-3); 32p. student's workbook 2.30 (ISBN 0-582-79850-7). 96p. (Orig.). (gr. 7-12). 1983. pap. text ed. 3.90 (ISBN 0-582-79811-6). Longman.

Kimbrough, Victoria, jt. auth. see Castro, Oscar.

Kimche, Jon. Seven Fallen Pillars. LC 76-6848. (The Middle East in the 20th Century). 1976. Repr. of 1950 ed. lib. bdg. 49.50 (ISBN 0-306-70820-5). Da Capo.

Kime, Helen R. & Wynkoop, Shari H. Getting Ready for Your Baby. 1978. pap. text ed. 3.25x (ISBN 0-88323-143-3, 233). Richards Pub.

Kime, R., et al. Health Instruction: An Action Approach. 1977. text ed. 20.95 (ISBN 0-13-385252-0). P-H.

Kime, Wayne R., ed. Washington Irving Miscellaneous Writings, 1803-1859: The Complete Works of W. Irving, 2 vols. (Critical Editions Program). 1981. lib. bdg. 75.00 (ISBN 0-8057-8520-5, Twayne). G K Hall.

Kimenyi, Alexandre. Linguistics: A Relational Grammar of Kinyarwanda. (UC Publications in Linguistics: Vol. 91). 1980. 17.50x (ISBN 0-520-09598-7). U of Cal Pr.

Kimmel, Arthur S. A Critical Edition of the Old Provencal Epic "Daurel et Beton" with Notes & Prolegomena. (Studies in the Romance Languages & Literatures: No. 108). 236p. 1971. pap. 13.50x (ISBN 0-8078-9108-8). U of NC Pr.

Kimmel, Carole A. & Buelke-Sam, Judith, eds. Developmental Toxicology. (Target Organ Toxicology Ser.). 354p. 1981. 42.50 (ISBN 0-686-77677-1). Raven.

Kimmel, Douglas C. Adulthood & Aging: An Interdisciplinary Developmental View. 2nd ed. LC 79-24037. 574p. 1980. text ed. 26.95x (ISBN 0-471-05229-9); o.p. tchrs. manual (ISBN 0-471-05237-X). Wiley.

Kimmel, Eric A. Mishka, Pishka & Fishka: And Other Galician Tales. LC 75-43898. (Illus.). 64p. (gr. 3-7). 1976. 5.95 o.p. (ISBN 0-698-20370-4, Coward). Putnam Pub Group.

--The Tartar's Sword. LC 73-89758. 288p. (gr. 6 up). 1974. 6.95 o.p. (ISBN 0-698-20243-0, Coward). Putnam Pub Group.

Kimmel, Margaret M. Magic in the Mist. LC 74-18186. (Illus.). 32p. (ps-3). 1975. 10.95 (ISBN 0-689-50026-2, McElderry Bk). Atheneum.

Kimmelman, Elaine. Dark Comet. 1983. pap. 3.50 (ISBN 0-380-81828-0, 81828). Avon.

Kimmerling, Baruch. Zionism & Territory: The Socio-Territorial Dimensions of Zionist Politics. (Illus.). xii, 288p. 1983. pap. 12.50x (ISBN 0-87725-151-7). U of Cal Intl St.

Kimmey, John L. Experience & Expression: Reading & Responding to Short Fiction. 1976. pap. 9.95x (ISBN 0-673-15016-X). Scott F.

Kimmey, John L., jt. auth. see Brown, Ashley.

Kimmich, Christoph M. German Foreign Policy, Nineteen Eighteen to Nineteen Forty-Five: A Guide to Research & Research Materials. LC 80-53889. 293p. 1981. lib. bdg. 17.50 (ISBN 0-8420-2167-1). Scholarly Res Inc.

Kimmich, Christoph M., ed. see Baer, George W.

Kimmich, Christoph M., ed. see Young, Robert J.

Kimmins, James P. Forest Ecology. 896p. 1984. text ed. 29.95 (ISBN 0-686-83138-1). Macmillan.

Kimsey, Lynn S. Systematics of Bees of the Genus Eufriesea (Hymenoptera, Apidae) LC 81-7400. (University of California Publications in Entomology: Vol. 95). 136p. 1982. 12.50x (ISBN 0-520-09643-6). U of Cal Pr.

Kimura, E., jt. ed. see Lichtlen, P. R.

Kimura, H. & Maddin, R. Quench Hardening in Metals. LC 74-140489. (Defects in Crystalline Solids Ser.: Vol. 3). (Illus.). 133p. 1971. 17.00 (ISBN 0-444-10114-4, North-Holland). Elsevier.

Kimura, Jun. Electrodiagnosis in Diseases of Nerve & Muscle: Principles & Practice. LC 82-17973. (Illus.). 735p. 1983. 65.00 (ISBN 0-8036-5341-7). Davis Co.

Kimura, Katsumi. Handbook of Hei Photoelectron Spectra of Fundamental Organic Molecules. LC 81-6449. 268p. 1981. 44.95x o.p. (ISBN 0-470-27200-7). Halsted Pr.

Kimura, Ken-Ichi. Scientific Basis of Air Conditioning. (Illus.). 1977. 51.25x (ISBN 0-85334-732-8, Pub. by Applied Sci England). Elsevier.

Kimura, Yasuko. Fergus. (Illus.). (ps-3). 1976. 5.95 (ISBN 0-07-034556-2, GB); PLB 7.95 (ISBN 0-07-034557-0). McGraw.

--Fergus & the Sea Monster. (Illus.). (ps-3). 1978. 6.95 o.p. (ISBN 0-07-034558-9, GB); PLB 7.95 o.p. (ISBN 0-07-034559-7). McGraw.

Kimzey, Bruce W. Reaganomics. (Illus.). 118p. 1983. pap. text ed. 4.90 (ISBN 0-314-73187-3). West Pub.

Kinard, Jesse & Owens, Janice B. Child Development Associate Self-Assessment Manual. (Orig.). 1983. pap. 14.95 (ISBN 0-89334-041-3). Humanics Ltd.

Kincade, jt. auth. see Bertram.

Kincaid, A. N., ed. see Buck, George.

Kincaid, Charles A. Deccan Nursery Tales; or, Fairy Tales from the South. LC 76-78183. xiv, 135p. 1972. Repr. of 1914 ed. 34.00x (ISBN 0-8103-3815-7). Gale.

Kincaid, David, jt. auth. see Cheney, Ward.

Kincaid, Diane D., ed. see Caraway, Hattie W.

Kincaid, Jim. Notes to My Friends. Friedman, Robert S., ed. LC 82-5031. 178p. 10.95 (ISBN 0-89865-267-7, AACR2); pap. 6.95 (ISBN 0-89865-208-1). Donning Co.

Kincaid, Joseph J. Cristobal de Villalon. (World Authors Ser.). 1971. lib. bdg. 15.95 (ISBN 0-8057-2963-1, Twayne). G K Hall.

Kincaid, Nell. Love on Any Terms. (Candlelight Ecstasy Ser.: No. 129). (Orig.). 1983. pap. 1.95 (ISBN 0-440-11927-8). Dell.

--With Every Loving Touch. (Candlelight Ecstasy Ser.: No. 149). (Orig.). 1983. pap. 1.95 (ISBN 0-440-19661-2). Dell.

Kincaid, Stephanie. Highland Love Song. 1979. pap. 1.25 o.s.i. (ISBN 0-440-13469-2). Dell.

Kincaid-Smith, P. S. & Whitworth, J. A., eds. Hypertension: Mechanisms & Management. 200p. 1982. text ed. 15.00 (ISBN 0-86792-005-X, Pub by Adis Pr Australia). Wright-PSG.

Kincaid-Smith, Priscilla, jt. ed. see Hodson, C. John.

Kince, Eli. Visual Puns in Design: The Humorous Image As a Communications Tool. (Illus.). 168p. 1982. 23.95 (ISBN 0-8230-7490-0). Watson-Guptill.

Kinch, John. Introduction to Social Psychology. (Illus.). 256p. 1973. text ed. 17.50 (ISBN 0-07-034569-4, C); pap. text ed. 16.95 (ISBN 0-07-034570-8); instructor's manual 15.00 (ISBN 0-07-034571-6). McGraw.

Kinch, Michael P. Forestry Theses Accepted by Colleges & Universities in the United States: July 1976-June 1981. (Bibliographic Ser.: No. 19). Date not set. price not set. Oreg St U Pr. Postponed.

Kinchen, Oscar A. Lord Russell's Canadian Policy: A Study in British Heritage & Colonial Freedom. (Perspectives in Canadian History Ser.: No. 8). v, 238p. lib. bdg. 17.50x (ISBN 0-87991-115-8). Porcupine Pr.

Kindem, Gorham, ed. The American Movie Industry: The Business of Motion Pictures. LC 81-23317. 348p. 1982. 30.00x (ISBN 0-8093-1036-8); pap. 16.95x (ISBN 0-8093-1037-6). S Ill U Pr.

Kinder, Alice J. Papa's Neighbors. 120p. 1979. pap. 2.50 (ISBN 0-8341-0581-0). Beacon Hill.

Kinder, E. F., jt. auth. see Riesen, Austin H.

Kinder, Faye & Green, Nancy R. Meal Management. 5th ed. (Illus.). 576p. 1978. text ed. 21.95x (ISBN 0-02-364080-4, 36408). Macmillan.

Kinder, Gary. Victim: The Other Side of Murder. 1983. pap. 3.95 (ISBN 0-440-19704-X). Dell.

Kinder, Hermann & Hilgemann, Werner. The Anchor Atlas of World History, Vol. I: From the Stone Age to the Eve of the French Revolution. Menze, Ernest A., tr. LC 72-84971. (Illus.). 304p. 1975. pap. 6.95 (ISBN 0-385-06178-1, Anch). Doubleday.

Kinder, Jack. School Public Relations: Communicating to the Community. LC 82-60802. (Fastback Ser.: No. 182). 50p. 1982. pap. 0.75 (ISBN 0-87367-182-1). Phi Delta Kappa.

Kinder, James S. Using Instructional Media. 1973. pap. text ed. 6.95x (ISBN 0-442-24405-3). Van Nos Reinhold.

Kinderman, E. M. & Goen, R. L. Potential Markets for U.S. Solar & Conservation Technologies in Argentina, Chile & Colombia: Supplement. (Progress in Solar Energy Ser.). 175p. 1983. pap. text ed. 15.00 (ISBN 0-89553-117-8). Am Solar Energy.

Kindersley, David. Eric Gill: Further Thoughts by an Apprentice. (Illus.). 60p. 1982. pap. 13.50 (ISBN 0-913720-35-6). Beil F C.

Kindig, Joe, Jr. Thoughts on the Kentucky Rifle in Its Golden Age. annotated 2nd ed. LC 61-23719. (Illus.). 561p. 1983. casebound 75.00 (ISBN 0-87387-084-0). Shumway.

Kindle, Joseph H. Analytic Geometry. (Orig.). 1950. pap. 4.95 (ISBN 0-07-034575-9, SP). McGraw.

Kindleberger, C. & Herrick, Bruce. Economic Development. 4th ed. 560p. 1983. 25.95x (ISBN 0-07-034584-8). McGraw.

Kindleberger, C. P., jt. ed. see Chipman, J. S.

Kindleberger, Charles & Shonfield, Andrew, eds. North American & Western European Economic Policies. LC 75-144220. 1971. 32.50 (ISBN 0-312-57890-3). St Martin.

Kindleberger, Charles H. & Herrick, Bruce. Economic Development. 3rd ed. (Economic Handbook Ser.). (Illus.). 1977. text ed. 25.95 (ISBN 0-07-034583-X, C). McGraw.

Kindleberger, Charles P. Power & Money: The Politics of International Economics & the Economics of International Politics. LC 70-116852. 1970. pap. 4.95x o.p. (ISBN 0-465-06140-0). Basic.

Kindleberger, Charles P. & De Tella, G., eds. Economics in the Long View: Models & Methodology, 3 vols. 288p. 1982. Vol. 1; Models & Methodology. per vol. 74.50x (ISBN 0-8147-4582-2); Vol. 2: Application & Cases (1) (ISBN 0-8147-4580-6); Vol. 3: Application & Cases (2) NYU Pr.

Kindleberger, Charles P., jt. ed. see Agmon, Tamir.

Kindler, Leonard I. Get Top Dollar for Your Stamps. iv, 26p. 1981. pap. 4.95 (ISBN 0-943502-01-2). Kindler.

--Philatelic Agencies, 1982. ii, 20p. (Orig.). 1982. pap. 3.95 (ISBN 0-943502-02-0). Kindler.

Kindregan, Charles P. Theology of Marriage. (Contemporary Theology Series). 1967. pap. 2.95x o.p. (ISBN 0-02-819720-8). Glencoe.

Kindrick, Robert, et al. A New Classical Rhetoric. 160p. (Orig.). 1980. pap. text ed. 7.95 (ISBN 0-8403-2184-8). Kendall-Hunt.

Kindrick, Robert L. Robert Henryson. (English Authors Ser.). 1979. 14.95 (ISBN 0-8057-6758-4, Twayne). G K Hall.

Kindrick, Shirley A., jt. auth. see Addanki, Sam.

Kinell, P. O., et al. ESR Applications to Polymer Research. (Nobel Symposium Ser.). 312p. 1973. 27.95x o.p. (ISBN 0-470-47770-9). Halsted Pr.

King. Audio Handbook. (Illus.). 1975. 24.95 (ISBN 0-408-00150-X). Focal Pr.

--Beginner's Guide to Color TV. 2nd ed. (Illus.). 1978. pap. 9.95 (ISBN 0-408-00101-1). Focal Pr.

--Beginner's Guide to Radio. 8th ed. (Illus.). 1977. pap. 9.95 (ISBN 0-408-00275-1). Focal Pr.

--British Seaspiders: Arthropoda-Pycnogonida-Keys & Notes for the Identification of the Species. 1974. 7.00 o.s.i. (ISBN 0-12-407950-4). Acad Pr.

--Indian Silverwork of the Southwest, Vol. 2. LC 61-1677. (Illus.). 1977. 8.95 (ISBN 0-912762-24-1); pap. 4.95 (ISBN 0-912762-23-3). King.

--The Shining. 1980. pap. 3.95 (ISBN 0-451-11967-3, AE1967, Sig). NAL.

King & Trundle. Beginner's Guide to TV. 6th ed. 1983. pap. write for info. (ISBN 0-408-01215-3). Focal Pr.

King & Woodcock. A Field Guide to the Birds of South East Asia. 29.95 (ISBN 0-686-42761-0, Collins Pub England). Greene.

King, jt. auth. see Cleland.

King, jt. auth. see Ferguson.

King, jt. auth. see Gerhardt.

King, A. & Nicol, C. Venereal Diseases. 4th ed. 1980. text ed. 45.00 o.p. (ISBN 0-02-858270-5, Pub. by Bailliere-Tindall). Saunders.

King, A., jt. auth. see Butler, David E.

King, Aileen. Better Cookery. 14.50 (ISBN 0-392-06174-0, LTB). Sportshelf.

King, Alan G. & Wheildon, William M., Jr. Ceramics in Machining Processes. 1966. 63.00 (ISBN 0-12-407650-5). Acad Pr.

King, Alec H. A Wealth of Music. 250p. 1983. price not set (ISBN 0-85157-330-4, Pub. by Bingley England). Shoe String.

King, Alexander. Mozart in Retrospect. LC 76-1016. 278p. 1976. Repr. of 1970 ed. lib. bdg. 29.50x (ISBN 0-8371-8760-5, KIMR). Greenwood.

King, Alexander H. Chamber Music. LC 78-60140. (Illus.). 1979. Repr. of 1948 ed. lib. bdg. 17.25x (ISBN 0-313-20546-9, KICM). Greenwood.

King, Alma S. Alexander Brook (1898-1980) Looking Back. (Important American Artists, Limited Ed. Exhibition Catalogues Ser.). (Illus.). 32p. (Orig.). 1982. PLB 35.00 (ISBN 0-941430-01-4); pap. 16.00 (ISBN 0-941430-00-6). Santa Fe E Gallery.

--Bernique Longley: A Retrospective. LC 82-6025. (Illus.). 80p. (Orig.). 1982. pap. 20.00 (ISBN 0-941430-03-0). Santa Fe E Gallery.

--An Exhibition of Paintings by American Impressionists. (Illus.). 64p. (Orig.). 1982. pap. 5.00 (ISBN 0-941430-04-9). Santa Fe E Gallery.

--Five American Women Impressionists. (Important American Artists - Limited Ed. Exhibition Catalogues Ser.). (Illus.). 40p. (Orig.). 1982. pap. 2.00 (ISBN 0-941430-02-2). Santa Fe E Gallery.

--Max Weber: An Exhibition of Works. (Illus.). 24p. (Orig.). 1982. pap. 7.50 (ISBN 0-941430-05-7). Santa Fe E Gallery.

King, Andrew J., ed. see Webster, Daniel.

King, Anna-Kria. The Goldmine in Your Files. 1983. pap. 9.95 (ISBN 0-917086-41-4, Pub. by Astro Comp Serv). Para Res.

King, Anne, jt. auth. see Zwanenberg, R. M. van.

King, Anny & Lansdell, Gwen. Adult French Course. (Illus.). 228p. 1979. pap. text ed. 9.95x (ISBN 0-582-33131-5); study supplement 5.50x (ISBN 0-582-33132-3). Longman.

King, Anthony. British Members of Parliament: A Self Portrait. 128p. 1975. 12.50 o.p. (ISBN 0-333-17170-5). Transatlantic.

King, Barry G. & Showers, Mary Jane. Human Anatomy & Physiology. 6th ed. LC 69-17819. (Illus.). 1969. 12.00x o.p. (ISBN 0-7216-5431-2). Saunders.

King, Bart. How to Raise & Train a Gordon Setter. (Orig.). 1965. pap. 2.95 (ISBN 0-87666-307-2, DS1082). TFH Pubns.

King, Bert. Cocker Spaniels. (Illus.). 1979. 4.95 (ISBN 0-87666-692-6, KW-043). TFH Pubns.

King, Bill. Rodeo Trails. Jones, Jean, ed. (Illus.). 224p. (Orig.). 1982. 16.50 (ISBN 0-936204-38-9); pap. 9.95 (ISBN 0-936204-37-0). Jelm Mtn.

King, Billie-Jean, et al. How to Play Mixed Doubles. 1980. 9.95 o.p. (ISBN 0-671-24620-8). S&S.

King, Bob, ed. see Phifer, Keith R.

King, Bruce. The New English Literatures: Cultural Nationalism in a Changing World. 1980. 26.00 (ISBN 0-312-56655-7). St Martin.

King, Bruce, ed. Literatures of the World in English. 1974. 17.95x (ISBN 0-7100-7787-4). Routledge & Kegan.

King, C., jt. auth. see Hickey, M.

King, C. A. Beaches & Coasts. 2nd ed. LC-74-187106. 1972. 37.50 (ISBN 0-312-07035-7). St Martin.

King, C. A., jt. auth. see Embleton, C.

King, C. D. What's That You're Eating? Food Label Language & What it Means to you. Grubb, Mary L & Grubb, John D., eds. LC 82-90187. (Illus.). 62p. 1982. pap. 3.95 (ISBN 0-9608862-0-6). C King.

King, C. Judson. Separation Processes. 2nd ed. (Chemical Engineering Ser.). (Illus.). 1979. text ed. 35.50 (ISBN 0-07-034612-7); solutions manual 19.00 (ISBN 0-07-034613-5). McGraw.

King, C. S. Horace Mann: Seventeen Ninety-Six to Eighteen Fifty-Nine Bibliography. LC 66-11926. 453p. 1966. 17.50 (ISBN 0-379-00258-2). Oceana.

King, C. Wendell. Social Movements in the United States. 1956. pap. text ed. 3.10x (ISBN 0-394-30753-4). Phila Bk Co.

King, Carl. Model T Days: Florida or Bust. 1983. 12.95 (ISBN 0-932298-37-0). Copple Hse.

King, Carol. Finding a Job. 3rd ed. (gr. 7-12). 1983. pap. 4.40 (ISBN 0-8224-3373-7). Pitman Learning.

King, Carol S., et al. Professional On-Site Apartment Manager. Glickson, Jeannie L., ed. 300p. 1983. text ed. price not set (ISBN 0-912104-62-7). Inst Real Estate.

King, Carole, et al. Basic Science Nursing Review. LC 80-22950. 208p. (Orig.). 1981. pap. text ed. 8.00x (ISBN 0-668-05133-7, 5133). Arco.

King, Charles. The Colonel's Daughter. (Western Fiction Ser.). 1981. lib. bdg. cancelled o.s.i. (ISBN 0-8398-2699-0, Gregg). G K Hall.

--Hieroglyphs to Alphabets. LC 76-52867. 1977. 12.95x o.p. (ISBN 0-8448-1034-7). Crane-Russak Co.

King, Charles E., jt. auth. see Dawson, Peter S.

King, Charles H., Jr. Fire in My Bones. 232p. (Orig.). 1983. pap. 12.95 (ISBN 0-8028-3570-8). Eerdmans.

King, Charles L. Ramon J. Sender. (World Authors Ser.). 1974. lib. bdg. 15.95 (ISBN 0-8057-2815-5, Twayne). G K Hall.

King, Charles R., ed. see King, Rufus.

King, Clarence. Battle for the Mind. 1980. pap. 1.50 o.s.i. (ISBN 0-89274-172-4). Harrison Hse.

--Jehovah Rapha. 1978. pap. 2.50 o.s.i. (ISBN 0-89274-099-X). Harrison Hse.

--Speak to the Mountain. 54p. 1980. pap. 1.95 o.s.i. (ISBN 0-89274-156-2). Harrison Hse.

King, Clive. The Birds from Africa. LC 80-52518. (Starters Ser.). PLB 8.00 (ISBN 0-382-06496-8). Silver.

King, Clyde S., compiled by. Psychic & Religious Phenomena Limited: A Bibliographical Index. 1978. lib. bdg. 35.00x (ISBN 0-313-20616-3, KPR/). Greenwood.

King, Condon, ed. Middle East, 4 bks. rev ed. (Culture Studies Program). (gr. 7-12). 1979. tchr's. manual 3.32 (ISBN 0-201-42672-2, Sch Div); text ed. 7.32 (ISBN 0-201-42671-4). A-W.

King, Constance E. Antique Toys & Dolls. LC 79-90699. (Illus.). 256p. 1980. 40.00 (ISBN 0-8478-0278-7). Rizzoli Intl.

King, Cuchlaine A. Northern England. (Geomorphology of the British Isles Ser.). 216p. 1976. pap. 10.95x (ISBN 0-416-84460-X, 2842). Methuen Inc.

King, Cynthia. Beggars & Choosers. 1980. 10.95 o.p. (ISBN 0-670-59758-9). Viking Pr.

--Sailing Home. 192p. 1982. 9.95 (ISBN 0-399-20872-0). Putnam Pub Group.

King, D. A. & Woodruff, D. P. Chemical Physics of Solid Surfaces & Hetrogeneous Catalysis. (Fundamental Studies of Hetrogeneous Catalysis: Vol. 4). 1982. 136.25 (ISBN 0-444-41987-X). Elsevier.

--Clean Solid Surfaces. (Chemical Physics of Solid Surfaces & Heterogeneous Catalysis Ser.: Vol. 1). 1981. 98.00 (ISBN 0-444-41924-1). Elsevier.

King, D. J. Cathcart. Castellarium Anglicanum, 2 Vols. LC 81-20812. 1982. lib. bdg. 150.00 (ISBN 0-527-50110-7). Kraus Intl.

King, David, jt. auth. see Thomas, Justine.

King, David, jt. auth. see Wyndham, Francis.

King, David A. Catalogue of the Scientific Manuscripts in the Egyptian National Library, Pt. 1. (Catalogs Ser.: Vol. 2). (Arabic.). 1981. pap. 40.00 (ISBN 0-686-84036-4, Pub. by Am Res Ctr Egypt). Undena Pubns.

--Mathematical Astronomy in Medieval Yemen: A Biobibliographical Survey. LC 81-71733. (American Research Center in Egypt, Catalogs Ser.: Vol. 4). (Illus.). xiv, 108p. (Orig.). 1983. 21.00x (ISBN 0-89003-099-5); pap. 16.00 (ISBN 0-89003-098-7). Undena Pubns.

King, Deborah. Sirius & Saba. (Illus.). 32p. (gr. 3-6). 1982. 10.95 (ISBN 0-241-10599-4, Pub. by Hamish Hamilton England). David & Charles.

King, Denise S., ed. see Heath, Mary L.

King, Dennis A. The Underground Buying Guide for Hams, CBers, Experimenters, & Compute Hobbyists. 1977. pap. 5.95 o.p. (ISBN 0-918504-01-5). PMS King.

King, Donald & Rix, David, trs. Desiderius Erasmus of Rotterdam: On Copia of Words & Ideas. (Medieval Philosophical Texts in Translation: No. 12). 1963. pap. 7.95 (ISBN 0-87462-212-3). Marquette.

King, Donald W. & Fenoglio, Cecilia M. General Pathology: Principles & Dynamics. LC 82-14883. (Illus.). 575p. 1983. write for info (ISBN 0-8121-0845-0). Lea & Febiger.

King, Donald W., ed. Key Papers in the Design & Evaluation of Information Systems. LC 78-23449. (Illus.). 1978. text ed. 25.00 (ISBN 0-914236-31-8). Knowledge Indus.

King, Donald W., et al. Survey of Pathology: With Color Microfiche, Illustrations, & Instructional Objectives. (Illus.). 1976. pap. text ed. 27.95x (ISBN 0-19-502104-5). Oxford U Pr.

--Telecommunications & Libraries. LC 81-6040. (Professional Librarian Ser.). 160p. 1981. text ed. 32.50 (ISBN 0-914236-88-1); pap. text ed. 24.50 (ISBN 0-914236-51-2). Knowledge Indus.

--Scientific Journals in the United States: Their Production, Use & Economics. LC 80-25945. 336p. 1981. 34.00 (ISBN 0-87933-380-4). Hutchinson Ross.

King, Donald W., et al, eds. Key Papers in the Economics of Information. 380p. 1982. 29.95 (ISBN 0-86729-040-4). Knowledge Indus.

King, Dorothy, ed. Check List of the Incunabula in the William Allan Neilson Library. (Illus.). 20p. 1975. pap. 1.50 (ISBN 0-87391-026-5). Smith Coll.

King, Duane H., ed. The Cherokee Indian Nation: A Troubled History. LC 78-13222. (Illus.). 1979. 13.50 (ISBN 0-87049-227-6). U of Tenn Pr.

King, Dwight Y. Interest Groups & Political Linkage in Indonesia. (Special Report Ser.: No. 20). 176p. (Orig.). 1982. pap. 12.50 (ISBN 0-686-37563-7, Pub. by U Cal Ctr S&SE Asian Stud). Cellar.

King, E. J. Education & Social Change. 1966. text ed. 16.25 o.s.i. (ISBN 0-08-012059-8); pap. text ed. 7.75 (ISBN 0-08-012058-X). Pergamon.

--The Teacher & the Needs of Society in Evolution. 1970. text ed. inquire for price (ISBN 0-08-016102-2); pap. text ed. 11.25 (ISBN 0-08-016103-0); write for info. xerox copyflo avail. Pergamon.

King, Edmund F., ed. Ten Thousand Wonderful Things. LC 75-124587. 1970. Repr. of 1860 ed. 44.00x (ISBN 0-8103-3009-1). Gale.

King, Edward L. Chemistry. 1100p. 1981. text ed. 28.00 (ISBN 0-394-32761-6). Random.

--How Chemical Reactions Occur. (Orig.). (YA) (gr. 9-12). 1963. pap. 13.95 (ISBN 0-8053-5401-8, 5401). Benjamin-Cummings.

King, Eleanor A. Bible Plants for American Gardens. LC 75-3646. (Illus.). 224p. 1975. pap. 4.25 (ISBN 0-486-23188-7). Dover.

King, Elizabeth A., jt. auth. see Abravanel, Eliott D.

King, Ernest & Whitehill, Walter. Fleet Admiral King. LC 78-11889. (Politics and Strategy of World War II Ser.). 1976. Repr. of 1952 ed. lib. bdg. 59.50 (ISBN 0-306-70772-1). Da Capo.

King, Eunice M. & Wieck, Lynn. Quick Reference to Adult Nursing Procedures. (Quick Reference for Nurses Ser.). (Illus.). 674p. 1982. pap. text ed. 12.75 (ISBN 0-397-54409-X, Lippincott Nursing). Lippincott.

--Quick Reference to Pediatric Nursing Procedures. (Quick Reference for Nurses Ser.). (Illus.). 329p. 1982. pap. text ed. 12.75 (ISBN 0-397-54410-3, Lippincott Nursing). Lippincott.

King, Everard H. James Beattie. (English Authors Ser.). 1977. lib. bdg. 14.95 (ISBN 0-8057-6653-7, Twayne). G K Hall.

King, Everett M. History of Maries County, Missouri. rev. ed. (Illus.). 1967. 12.50 o.p. (ISBN 0-911208-05-4). Ramfre.

King, F. Wayne & Behler, John. The Audubon Society Field Guide to North American Reptiles & Amphibians. LC 79-2217. (Illus.). 1979. flexible bdg. 12.50 (ISBN 0-394-50824-6). Knopf.

King, Felicity, jt. auth. see King, Maurice.

King, Francis. The Magical World of Aleister Crowley. LC 77-13610. (Illus.). 1978. 8.95 o.p. (ISBN 0-698-10884-1, Coward). Putnam Pub Group.

--Sexuality, Magic & Perversion. 208p. 15.00x o.p. (ISBN 0-686-75477-8, Pub. by Spearman England). State Mutual Bk.

King, Francis H. Classical & Foreign Quotations. 3rd ed. LC 68-30647. 1968. Repr. of 1904 ed. 34.00x (ISBN 0-8103-3185-3). Gale.

King, Francis S. Advertising Practices. LC 81-68551. (Illus.). 240p. (Orig.). 1983. pap. text ed. 14.80 (ISBN 0-8273-1702-6); instr's guide 3.00 (ISBN 0-8273-1703-4). Delmar.

King, Frank. Down & Dirty. 1978. 8.95 o.p. (ISBN 0-399-90005-5, Marek). Putnam Pub Group.

--Down & Dirty. 1979. pap. 1.95 o.p. (ISBN 0-451-08699-6, J8699, Sig). NAL.

--Night Vision. LC 78-24599. 1979. 10.95 o.p. (ISBN 0-399-90041-1, Marek). Putnam Pub Group.

--Raya. LC 79-26869. 260p. 1980. 10.95 (ISBN 0-399-90078-0, Marek). Putnam Pub Group.

King, Frank P., ed. Oceania & Beyond: Essays on the Pacific Since 1945. LC 76-5261. (Illus., Orig.). 1976. lib. bdg. 29.95 (ISBN 0-8371-8904-7, KOB/). Greenwood.

King, Fred D. Palmer Method Cursive, Consumable. new ed. (Palmer Method Easy to Teach Ser.). (Illus.). (gr. 6). 1979. wkbk. 3.08 (ISBN 0-914268-68-6, 79-6C); tchr's ed. 5.60 (ISBN 0-914268-69-4, 79-6CTE). A N Palmer.

King, Fred M. Palmer Method Cursive, Consumable. new ed. (Palmer Method Easy to Teach Ser.). (Illus.). (gr. 4). 1979. wkbk 3.08 (ISBN 0-914268-64-3, 79-4C); tchr's ed. 5.60 (ISBN 0-914268-65-1, 79-4CTE). A N Palmer.

--Palmer Method Cursive, Consumable. (Palmer Method Easy to Teach Ser.). (Illus.). (gr. 4). 1976. wkbk. 3.08 (ISBN 0-914268-31-7, 76-4C); tchr's ed 5.60 (ISBN 0-914268-32-5, 76-4C-TE). A N Palmer.

--Palmer Method Cursive, Consumable. (Palmer Method Easy to Teach Ser.). (Illus.). (gr. 5). 1976. wkbk 3.08 (ISBN 0-914268-33-3, 76-5C); tchr's ed. 5.60 (ISBN 0-914268-34-1, 76-5C-TE). A N Palmer.

--Palmer Method Cursive, Consumable. (Palmer Method Easy to Teach Ser.). (Illus.). (gr. 6). 1976. wkbk. 3.08 (ISBN 0-914268-35-X, 76-6C); tchr's ed. 5.60 (ISBN 0-914268-36-8, 76-6C-TE). A N Palmer.

--Palmer Method Cursive, Grade 5, Consumable. new ed. (Palmer Method Easy to Teach Ser.). (Illus.). (gr. 5). 1979. wkbk. 3.08 (ISBN 0-914268-66-X, 79-5C); tchr's ed 5.60 (ISBN 0-914268-67-8, 79-5CTE). A N Palmer.

--Palmer Method Cursive, Non-Consumable. (Palmer Method Easy to Teach Ser.). (gr. 8). 1979. wkbk 3.80 (ISBN 0-914268-86-4, N79-SL2); tchr's ed. 5.60 (ISBN 0-914268-87-2, N79-SL2TE). A N Palmer.

--Palmer Method Cursive, Non-Consumable. (Palmer Method Easy to Teach Ser.). (Illus.). 1979. wkbk 3.80 (ISBN 0-914268-84-8, N79-SL1); tchr's ed. 5.60 (ISBN 0-914268-85-6, N79-SL1TE). A N Palmer.

--Palmer Method Cursive, Non-Consumable. new ed. (Palmer Method Easy to Teach Ser.). (Illus.). (gr. 6). 1979. wkbk. 3.80 (ISBN 0-914268-82-1, N79-6C); tchr's ed. 5.60 (ISBN 0-914268-83-X, N79-6CTE). A N Palmer.

--Palmer Method Cursive, Non-Consumable. new ed. (Palmer Method Easy to Teach Ser.). 1979. wkbk. 3.80 (ISBN 0-914268-80-5, N79-5C); tchr's ed. 5.60 (ISBN 0-914268-81-3, N79-5CTE). A N Palmer.

--Palmer Method Cursive, Non-Consumable. (Palmer Method Easy to Teach Ser.). (Illus.). (gr. 4). 1975. wkbk. 3.80 (ISBN 0-914268-45-7, N75-4C); tchr's ed. 5.60 (ISBN 0-914268-46-5, N75-4C-TE). A N Palmer.

--Palmer Method Cursive, Non-Consumable. (Palmer Method Easy to Teach Ser.). (Illus.). (gr. 5). 1975. wkbk. 3.80 (ISBN 0-914268-47-3, N75-5C); tchr's ed. 5.60 (ISBN 0-914268-48-1, N75-5C-TE). A N Palmer.

--Palmer Method Cursive, Non-Consumable. (Palmer Method Easy to Teach Ser.). (Illus.). (gr. 6). 1975. wkbk. 3.80 (ISBN 0-914268-49-X, N75-6C); tchr's ed. 5.60 (ISBN 0-914268-50-3, N75-6C-TE). A N Palmer.

--Palmer Method Cursive, Non-Consumable. (Palmer Method Easy to Teach Ser.). (Illus.). (gr. 7). 1976. wkbk. 3.80 (ISBN 0-914268-51-1, N75-SL1); tchr's ed. 5.60 (ISBN 0-914268-52-X, N75-SL1-TE). A N Palmer.

--Palmer Method Cursive, Non-Consumable. (Palmer Method Easy to Teach Ser.). (Illus.). (gr. 8). 1976. wkbk. 3.80 (ISBN 0-914268-53-8, N75-SL2); tchr's ed. 5.60 (ISBN 0-914268-54-6, N75-SL2-TE). A N Palmer.

--Palmer Method Manuscript, Consumable. new ed. (Palmer Method Easy to Teach Ser.). (Illus.). (gr. 2). 1979. wkbk. 3.08 (ISBN 0-914268-58-9, 79-2M); tchr's ed. 5.60 (ISBN 0-914268-59-7, 79-2MTE). A N Palmer.

--Palmer Method Manuscript, Consumable. new ed. (Palmer Method Easy to Teach Ser.). (Illus.). (gr. 1). 1979. 3.08 (ISBN 0-914268-56-2, 79-1M); tchr's ed. 5.60 (ISBN 0-914268-57-0, 79-1MTE). A N Palmer.

--Palmer Method Manuscript, Consumable. (Palmer Method Easy to Teach Ser.). (Illus.). (gr. 1). 1976. tchr's ed. 5.60 (ISBN 0-914268-24-4, 76-IM-TE); wkbk. 3.08 (ISBN 0-914268-23-6, 76-1M). A N Palmer.

--Palmer Method Manuscript, Consumable. (Palmer Method Easy to Teach Ser.). (Illus.). (gr. 2). 1976. wkbk. 3.08 (ISBN 0-914268-25-2, 76-2M); tchr's manual 5.60 (ISBN 0-914268-26-0, 76-2M TE). A N Palmer.

--Palmer Method Manuscript, Non-Consumable. new ed. (Palmer Method Easy to Teach Ser.). (Illus.). (gr. 2). 1979. wkbk. 3.80 (ISBN 0-914268-72-4, N79-2M); tchr's ed. 5.60 (ISBN 0-914268-73-2, N79-2MTE). A N Palmer.

--Palmer Method Manuscript, Non-Consumable. new ed. (Palmer Method Easy to Teach Ser.). (Illus.). (gr. 1). 1979. wkbk. 3.80 (ISBN 0-914268-70-8, N79-1M); tchr's ed. 5.60 (ISBN 0-914268-71-6, N79-1MTE). A N Palmer.

--Palmer Method Manuscript, Non-Consumable. (Palmer Method Easy to Teach Ser.). (Illus.). (gr. 1). 1976. wkbk. 3.80 (ISBN 0-914268-37-6, N75-1M); tchr's ed. 5.60 (ISBN 0-914268-38-4, N75-1M-TE). A N Palmer.

--Palmer Method Manuscript, Non-Consumable. (Palmer Method Easy to Teach Ser.). (Illus.). (gr. 2). 1976. wkbk. 3.80 (ISBN 0-914268-39-2, N75-2M); tchr's ed. 5.60 (ISBN 0-914268-40-6, N75-2M-TE). A N Palmer.

--Palmer Method Transition on Cursive, Consumable. (Palmer Method Easy to Teach Ser.). (Illus.). (gr. 3). 1976. wkbk. 3.08 (ISBN 0-914268-29-5, 76-3TC); tchr's ed. 5.60 (ISBN 0-914268-30-9, 76-3TC-TE). A N Palmer.

--Palmer Method Transition on Cursive, Non-Consumable. (Palmer Method Easy to Teach Ser.). (gr. 3). 1979. wkbk. 3.80 (ISBN 0-914268-76-7, N79-3TC); tchr's ed. 5.60 (ISBN 0-914268-77-5, N79-3TC TE). A N Palmer.

--Palmer Method Transition to Cursive, Consumable. new ed. (Palmer Method Easy to Teach Ser.). (Illus.). (gr. 2). 1979. wkbk. 3.08 (ISBN 0-914268-60-0, 79-2TC); tchr's ed. 5.60 (ISBN 0-914268-61-9, 79-2TCTE). A N Palmer.

--Palmer Method Transition to Cursive Consumable. (Palmer Method Easy to Teach Ser.). (Illus.). (gr. 2). 1976. tchr's ed. 5.60 (ISBN 0-914268-28-7, 76-2TC-TE); wkbk. 3.08 (ISBN 0-914268-27-9, 76-2TC). A N Palmer.

--Palmer Method Transition to Cursive, Non-Consumable. new ed. (Palmer Method Easy to Teach Ser.). (Illus.). (gr. 2). 1979. wkbk. 3.80 (ISBN 0-914268-74-0, N79-2TC); tchr's ed. 5.60 (ISBN 0-914268-75-9, N79-2TCTE). A N Palmer.

--Palmer Method Transition to Cursive, Non-Consumable. (Palmer Method Easy to Teach Ser.). (Illus.). (gr. 2). 1976. wkbk. 3.80 (ISBN 0-914268-41-4, N75-2TC); tchr's ed. 5.60 (ISBN 0-914268-42-2, N75-2TC-TE). A N Palmer.

--Palmer Method Transition to Cursive, Non-Consumable. (Palmer Method Easy to Teach Ser.). (Illus.). (gr. 3). 1975. 3.80 (ISBN 0-914268-43-0, N75-3TC); tchr's ed. 5.60 (ISBN 0-914268-44-9, N75-3TC-TE). A N Palmer.

--Palmer Method Writing Readiness, Consumable. new ed. (Illus.). (gr. k-1). 1979. wkbk. 3.08 (ISBN 0-914268-55-4, 79-WR). A N Palmer.

--Palmer Method Writing Readiness, Consumable. (Palmer Method Easy to Teach Ser.). (Illus.). (gr. k-1). 1976. wkbk. 3.08 (ISBN 0-914268-22-8, 76-WR). A N Palmer.

King, G. The Species of Ficus of the Indo-Malayan & Chinese Countries. (Illus.). 1969. Repr. 200.00 (ISBN 3-7682-0609-2). Lubrecht & Cramer.

King, G. see Blau, K.

King, G. Brooks & Caldwell, William E. Laboratory Experiments in College Chemistry. 4th ed. 1979. pap. 8.95 (ISBN 0-442-24412-6). Van Nos Reinhold.

King, G. R. Modern Refrigeration Practice. 1966. 26.95 (ISBN 0-07-034689-5, G); instructor's guide 4.00 (ISBN 0-07-034690-9). McGraw.

King, George. Student Guide for Law & the Life Insurance Contract. rev. ed. (FLMI Insurance Education Program Ser.). 1976. pap. 6.00 workbook (ISBN 0-915322-19-6). LOMA.

King, Gordon J. Audio Equipment Tests. (Illus.). 1979. text ed. 20.00 (ISBN 0-408-00336-7). Butterworth.

King, H. & Nield, D. Building Techniques, 2 vols. Vol. 1: Structure, 2nd Ed., 1976. 11.95x (ISBN 0-412-21330-3, Pub. by Chapman & Hall); Vol. 2: Services, 3rd Ed., 1980. 11.95x (ISBN 0-412-21780-5). Methuen Inc.

King, H. Gill, jt. auth. see Aceves, Joseph B.

King, H. V. English Sentence Structure Review. LC 76-49150. 1977. pap. 3.95x (ISBN 0-472-08504-2). U of Mich Pr.

King, Harold. Closing Ceremonies. LC 79-10582. 1979. 10.95 (ISBN 0-698-10950-3, Coward). Putnam Pub Group.

--Components. (Mitchell's Building Ser.). (Illus.). 200p. 1971. 31.50 o.p. (ISBN 0-7134-3332-9, Pub. by Batsford England); pap. 17.50 (ISBN 0-7134-3333-7, Pub. by Batsford England). David & Charles.

--The Taskmaster. 1977. 8.95 (ISBN 0-698-10827-2, Coward). Putnam Pub Group.

King, Harold & Marek, Richard. Code of Arms. 1981. 12.95 (ISBN 0-399-90029-2, Pub. by Coward). Putnam Pub Group.

King, Harold V. & Campbell, Russell N. English Reading Test. 1956. pap. 17.50 set of 20 tests (ISBN 0-87789-029-3); pap. 0.75 eRT answer key (ISBN 0-87789-030-7). Eng Language.

King, Heather. Morning to Night. (Scribbler Play Bks.). (Illus.). 20p. (ps). 1983. pap. write for info. (ISBN 0-307-20325-5). Western Pub.

King, Helen H. Let's Save the Children. Williams, ed. (Jackson Five Ser.). (Illus.). 22p. (gr. k-8). pap. 3.00 (ISBN 0-686-28488-7). Let's Save Children.

King, Horace M. Songs in the Night: A Study of the Book of Job. (Illus.). 1969. pap. 2.95 o.p. (ISBN 0-685-20632-7). Transatlantic.

King, Imogene M., jt. auth. see Johnson, Dorothy E.

King, J. Greatest Gift Guide Ever. (Illus.). 190p. 1982. pap. 5.95 (ISBN 0-932620-15-9, Pub. by Betterway Pubns). Berkshire Traveller.

King, J. A., et al. Amination Processes: Pollutant Discharges Identification. LC 79-88964. (Unit Process Ser. - Organic Chemical Industries: Vol. 2). 1979. 29.95 (ISBN 0-250-40329-3). Ann Arbor Science.

King, J. B. Practical Commerce. 2nd ed. 1975. 5.20 o.p. (ISBN 0-08-018295-X); pap. 3.60 o.p. (ISBN 0-08-016078-6). Pergamon.

King, J. Charles & McGilvray, James A. Political & Social Philosophy: Traditional & Contemporary Readings. LC 72-3993. 544p. 1972. text ed. 25.00 (ISBN 0-07-034630-5, C). McGraw.

King, J. E., jt. auth. see Dutton, H. I.

King, J. N. & McManus, T. Transition Element Chemistry. (Experimental Chemistry Ser.). 1976. pap. text ed. 4.00x o.p. (ISBN 0-435-65956-1); tchr's ed. 5.00x o.p. (ISBN 0-435-65957-X). Heinemann Ed.

King, J. Norman. The God of Forgiveness & Healing in the Theology of Karl Rahner. LC 81-40932. 100p. (Orig.). 1982. lib. bdg. 18.75 (ISBN 0-8191-2237-8); pap. text ed. 7.00 (ISBN 0-8191-2238-6). U Pr of Amer.

King, J. O. An Introduction to Animal Husbandry. LC 78-4883. 1978. pap. 34.95x o.s.i. (ISBN 0-470-26338-5). Halsted Pr.

King, J. R. Production Planning & Control: An Introduction to Quantitative Methods. 1974. text ed. write for info. (ISBN 0-08-017721-2). Pergamon.

King, J. R., ed. Managing Liability. LC 82-70764. 96p. 1982. pap. text ed. 16.00 (ISBN 0-87262-304-1). Am Soc Civil Eng.

King, J. R., Jr., ed. Engineering & Business-Converting Engineers to Businessmen. LC 82-83563. 1982. pap. text ed. 11.00 (ISBN 0-87262-342-4). Am Soc Civil Eng.

King, J. W. War-Ships & Navies of the World 1880. LC 82-81753. (Illus.). 768p. 1982. 24.95 (ISBN 0-87021-943-X). Naval Inst Pr.

King, Jack. Going Public. 1981. 5.95 (ISBN 0-917530-12-8); pap. fiction (ISBN 0-685-97205-4). Pig Iron Pr.

King, Jack L., jt. auth. see Wallace, Robert A.

King, James, ed. see Cowper, William.

King, James, jt. ed. see Fobes, James.

King, James C. The Biology of Race. rev. ed. (Illus.). 192p. 1982. 15.95 (ISBN 0-520-04223-9); pap. 6.95 (ISBN 0-520-04224-7). U of Cal Pr.

King, James R. The Literary Moment as a Lens on Reality. LC 82-17319. 224p. 1983. text ed. 20.00x (ISBN 0-8262-0393-0). U of Mo Pr.

King, Janet K., tr. see Raabe, Wilhelm.

King, Jeannette M. Tragedy of the Victorian Novel. LC 77-77762. 1978. 37.50 (ISBN 0-521-21670-2). Cambridge U Pr.

King, Jere C. Generals & Politicians: Conflict Between France's High Command, Parliament, & Government, 1914-1918. LC 74-112325. 1971. Repr. of 1951 ed. lib. bdg. 20.50x (ISBN 0-8371-4713-1, KIGP). Greenwood.

King, Joan. Impressionist: A Novel of Mary Cassatt. 303p. 1983. 16.95 (ISBN 0-8253-0125-4). Beaufort Bks NY.

King, John A., jt. auth. see Ouellette, Robert P.

King, John H. & Wadsworth, Joseph A. An Atlas of Ophthalmic Surgery. 3rd ed. 1980. text ed. 82.50 o.p. (ISBN 0-397-50481-0, Lippincott Medical). Lippincott.

King, John L. Human Behavior & Wall Street. LC 82-72957. 226p. 1972. 12.95 (ISBN 0-8040-0562-1). Swallow.

King, John L., jt. ed. see Kraemer, Kenneth L.

King, John O. The Iron of Melancholy. 464p. 1983. 25.95 (ISBN 0-8195-5070-1). Wesleyan U Pr.

King, Jonathan & Marans, Robert W. The Physical Environment & the Learning Process: A Survey of Recent Research. 92p. 1979. pap. 10.00x (ISBN 0-87944-239-5). Inst Soc Res.

King, Joseph H. Yet Speaketh. 3.50 o.p. (ISBN 0-911866-56-6). Advocate.

King, Judith. The Greatest Gift Guide Ever. LC 79-65184. (Illus.). 188p. (Orig.). 1980. pap. 4.00 (ISBN 0-9602776-0-9). Variety Pr.

--The Greatest Gift Guide Ever. LC 82-14682. 188p. 1982. pap. 5.95 (ISBN 0-932620-15-9). Betterway Pubns.

King, K. Introductory Algebra & Related Topics for Technicians. 1979. pap. 14.95 (ISBN 0-13-501585-5). P-H.

King, K. G., jt. auth. see Bird, B. M.

King, Kathleen. Cricket Sings: A Novel of Pre-Columbian Cahokia. LC 82-8046. 172p. 1983. 15.95 (ISBN 0-8214-0704-X, 82-84747); pap. 8.95 (ISBN 0-8214-0705-8, 82-84754). Ohio U Pr.

King, Kenneth. The African Artisan: Education & the Informal Sector in Kenya. LC 76-58316. 1977. pap. text ed. 9.50x (ISBN 0-8077-8023-5). Tchrs Coll.

--U. S. Monetary Policy & European Responses in the 1980's. (Chatham House Papers in Foreign Policy Ser.). 128p. (Orig.). 1982. pap. 10.00 (ISBN 0-7100-9337-3). Routledge & Kegan.

King, Kimball. Ten Modern American Playwrights: An Annotated Bibliography. LC 80-8498. (American Literature Catalogue Ser.). 251p. 1982. lib. bdg. 33.00 (ISBN 0-8240-9489-1). Garland Pub.

King, L. L., intro. by see Simpson, A. B.

King, L. Thomas. Problem Solving in a Project Environment. LC 80-20063. 204p. 1981. 23.95x (ISBN 0-471-08115-9, Pub. by Wiley-Interscience). Wiley.

King, Leroy O. One Hundred Years of Capital Traction: The Story of Streetcars in the Nation's Capital. LC 72-97549. (Illus.). 1972. 25.00 o.p. (ISBN 0-9600938-1-8). L O King.

King, LeRoy O., Jr., ed. see Myers, Johnnie J.

King, Lester S. The Medical World of the Eighteenth Century. LC 58-7332. 366p. 1971. Repr. of 1958 ed. lib. bdg. 14.00 o.p. (ISBN 0-88275-032-1). Krieger.

King, Louise T. & Wirker, Stewart. The Martha's Vineyard Cookbook. 320p. 1983. pap. 8.95 (ISBN 0-686-42851-X). Globe Pequot.

King, M., ed. Parsing Natural Language. Date not set. price not set (ISBN 0-12-408280-7). Acad Pr.

King, Margaret L. & Rabil, Albert, Jr., eds. Her Immaculate Hand: Selected Works by & About the Women Humanists of Quattrocento Italy. 208p. 1983. 13.50 (ISBN 0-86698-023-7). Medieval & Renaissance NY.

King, Martin L. Stride Toward Freedom. LC 58-7099. 1958. 12.45i (ISBN 0-06-064690-X, HarpR). Har-Row.

King, Maurice & King, Felicity. Primary Child Care: A Manual for Health Workers. (Illus.). 1978. pap. text ed. 9.95x (ISBN 0-19-264229-4). Oxford U Pr.

King, Maurice, et al. Primary Child Care: Book Two: a Guide for the Community Teacher, Manager & Teacher. (Illus.). 1980. pap. text ed. 12.95x (ISBN 0-19-264230-8). Oxford U Pr.

King, Maurice H., ed. Medical Care in Developing Countries. (Illus., Orig.). 1966. pap. 17.95x (ISBN 0-19-644018-1). Oxford U Pr.

King, Maurice H., et al. Nutrition for Developing Countries: With Special Reference to the Maize, Cassava & Millet Areas of Africa. (Illus.). 1973. pap. text ed. 17.95x (ISBN 0-19-572244-2). Oxford U Pr.

King, Melissa. Speak English, Text 6. (Speak English Ser.). (Illus.). 80p. (Orig.). 1983. pap. 4.95 (ISBN 0-88499-661-1). Inst Mod Lang.

King, Michael. New Zealand in Color. (Illus.). 112p. 1983. 19.95 (ISBN 0-312-57169-0). St Martin.

--New Zealanders at War. (Illus.). 307p. 1982. 19.95 (ISBN 0-86863-399-2, Pub. by Heinemann Pubs New Zealand). Intl Schol Bk Serv.

King, Michael & Ziegler, Michael. Research Projects in Social Psychology: An Introduction to Methods. LC 75-11365. 1975. pap. text ed. 12.95 (ISBN 0-8185-0167-7). Brooks-Cole.
King, Michael, et al, eds. see Pound, Ezra.
King, Nancy. Theatre Movement: The Actor & His Space. LC 73-166533. (Illus.). 1971. pap. 7.95x (ISBN 0-910482-38-1). Drama Bk.
King, Nancy R. Movement Approach to Acting. (P-H Ser. in Theatre & Drama). (Illus.). 288p. 1981. text ed. 18.95 (ISBN 0-13-604637-1). P-H.
King, Noel, tr. see Battuta, Ibn.
King, Norman. Turn Your House Into a Money Factory. 1982. 6.50 (ISBN 0-688-01376-7). Morrow.
--Turn Your House into a Money Factory. LC 82-10202. 225p. 1982. pap. 6.50 (ISBN 0-688-01376-7). Quill NY.
King, Norman, jt. auth. see Adler, Bill.
King, Ouida M. Care of the Cardiac Surgical Patient. LC 75-2460. (Illus.). 276p. 1975. text ed. 16.50 o.p. (ISBN 0-8016-3434-2). Mosby.
King, P. & Parekh, B. C., eds. Politics & Experience. 49.50 (ISBN 0-521-07333-2). Cambridge U Pr.
King, P. E. Pycnogonids. LC 73-87076. (Illus.). 150p. 1974. 17.95 o.p. (ISBN 0-312-65730-7). St Martin.
King, P. E., jt. auth. see Morgan, C. I.
King, P. J. & Hunt, J. A. The Application of Microprocessors for Control in the Food Industry, 1980. 1981. 30.00x (ISBN 0-686-97026-8, Pub. by W Spring England). State Mutual Bk.
King, Pat. Forgiving One Another. 32p. 1978. pap. 0.75 o.p. (ISBN 0-930756-38-X, 4240-F0). Women's Aglow.
--How Do You Find the Time. 176p. 1975. 3.95 o.p. (ISBN 0-930756-12-6, 4230-KI3). Women's Aglow.
King, Patricia. Mabel the Whale. (Illus.). (gr. 1-3). 1958. 4.39 (ISBN 0-695-45443-9, Dist. by Caroline Hse); PLB 1.95. Follett.
King, Patricia O. Solo. LC 82-23483. (Illus.). 90p. 1983. 5.95 (ISBN 0-87747-965-8). Deseret Bk.
King, Paul. Hermana Sam. 1977. 8.95 o.p. (ISBN 0-698-10795-0, Coward). Putnam PubGroup.
King, Paul A. National Construction Estimator 1983. 416p. (Orig.). 1982. pap. 14.75 (ISBN 0-910460-95-7). Craftsman.
King, Paula. Your Employee Assistance Program. 1.50 (ISBN 0-89486-092-5, 1938B). Hazelden.
King, Pauline, ed. see Gregg, David L.
King, Peter. Multatuli. (World Authors Ser.). lib. bdg. 15.95 (ISBN 0-8057-2642-X, Twayne). G K Hall.
King, Peter, ed. Australia's Vietnam: Australia in the Second Indo-China War. 288p. 1983. text ed. 28.50x (ISBN 0-86861-037-2). Allen Unwin.
King, Philip J. American Archaeology in the Mideast: A History of the American Schools of Oriental Research. (Illus.). 310p. 1983. text ed. 15.00x (ISBN 0-89757-508-3, Pub. by Am Sch Orient Res). Eisenbrauns.
King, Preston. Toleration. LC 75-21969. 230p. 1976. 18.95 o.p. (ISBN 0-312-80780-5). St Martin.
King, R. School & College: Studies of Post-Sixteen Education. 1976. 18.00x (ISBN 0-7100-8359-9); pap. 9.50 (ISBN 0-7100-8360-2). Routledge & Kegan.
King, R., jt. auth. see Seyferth, D.
King, R., jt. ed. see Seyferth, D.
King, R. A. Electronic Circuits & Systems. LC 74-31175. 355p. 1975. 24.95x o.p. (ISBN 0-470-47779-2). Halsted Pr.
--Reading for an Introduction to Psychology. 3rd ed. (Psychology Ser.). 1971. text ed. 9.95 o.p. (ISBN 0-07-034615-1, C). McGraw.
King, R. B., jt. ed. see Seyferth, D.
King, R. C., ed. see Crocker, Sabin.
King, R. D. Developments in Food Analysis, Vols. 1 & 2. Vol. 1, 1978. 69.75 (ISBN 0-85334-755-7, Pub. by Applied Sci England); Vol. 2, 1980. 49.25 (ISBN 0-85334-921-5). Elsevier.
King, R. D. & Morgan, R. A Taste of Prison: Custodial Conditions for Trial & Remand Prisoners. (Direct Edition Ser.). (Orig.). 1976. pap. 9.95 (ISBN 0-7100-8407-2). Routledge & Kegan.
King, R. P. Lincoln in Numismatics. (Illus.). 1983. pap. 15.00 (ISBN 0-942666-01-1). S J Durst.
King, R. W., et al. Arrays of Cylindrical Dipoles. LC 67-26069. (Illus.). 1968. 72.50 (ISBN 0-521-05887-2). Cambridge U Pr.
King, Richard A., jt. auth. see Morgan, Clifford T.
King, Richard H. A Southern Renaissance: The Cultural Awakening of the American South, 1930-1955. 1980. 19.95x (ISBN 0-19-502664-0). Oxford U Pr.
King, Richard L., ed. Business Serials of the U. S. Government. LC 77-22078. 1978. pap. text ed. 3.00 o.p. (ISBN 0-8389-3200-2). ALA.
King, Robert C. Genetics. 2nd ed. (Illus.). 1965. 12.50x (ISBN 0-19-500932-0). Oxford U Pr.
King, Robert G. & Di Michael, Eleanor M. Articulation & Voice: Improving Oral Communication. (Illus.). 1978. pap. 13.95x (ISBN 0-02-364250-5). Macmillan.
King, Robert R. & Brown, James F., eds. Eastern Europe's Uncertain Future: A Selection of Radio Free Europe Research Reports. LC 77-10666. (Praeger Special Studies). 384p. 1977. 39.95 o.p. (ISBN 0-03-040861-X). Praeger.
King, Roger T. Perspectives in Bank Management: A Book of Readings. LC 79-63851. 1979. pap. text ed. 11.50 (ISBN 0-8191-0745-X). U Pr of Amer.
King, Roma A., Jr., et al, eds. see Browning, Robert.
King, Ronald. All Things Bright & Beautiful? A Sociological Study of Infants' Classrooms. LC 78-4518. 155p. 1978. 31.00x o.p. (ISBN 0-471-99653-X, Pub. by Wiley-Interscience). Wiley.
--Botanical Illustration. (Illus.). 1979. 14.95 (ISBN 0-517-53525-4, C N Potter Bks); pap. 6.95 (ISBN 0-517-53526-2, C N Potter). Crown.
--School Organization & Pupil Involvement: A Study of Secondary Schools. (International Library of Sociology). (Illus.). 266p. 1973. 24.00x (ISBN 0-7100-7610-X). Routledge & Kegan.
King, Ronald & Julstrom, Bryant. Applied Statistics Using the Computer. (Illus.). 477p. 1982. text ed. 19.95 (ISBN 0-88284-174-2); wkbk 8.95 (ISBN 0-88284-179-3); instructor's manual avail. Alfred Pub.
King, Ronold W., et al. Antennas in Matter: Fundamentals, Theory & Applications. 784p. 1981. 75.00x (ISBN 0-262-11074-1). MIT Pr.
King, Roy D., et al. The Future of the Prison System. 240p. 1980. text ed. 34.25x (ISBN 0-566-00348-1). Gower Pub Ltd.
King, Rufus. The Life & Correspondence of Rufus King, 6 vols. King, Charles R., ed. LC 69-16653. (American Public Figures Ser.). 1971. Repr. of 1894 ed. Set. lib. bdg. 295.00 (ISBN 0-306-71125-7). Da Capo.
King, Russel, ed. see Bethemont, Jacques & Pelletier, Jean.
King, Russell. Land Reform: A World Survey. LC 77-24633. (Advanced Economic Geography Ser.). (Illus.). 1978. lib. bdg. 21.00 o.p. (ISBN 0-89158-819-1). Westview.
King, Ruth & Hart, Anita. The Ivy League Cookbook. (Illus.). 96p. (Orig.). 1982. pap. 3.95 (ISBN 0-8329-0145-8). New Century.
King, Samuel P., tr. see Korschelt, O.
King, Scottie, ed. see Cameron, Sheila M.
King, Serge. Kahuna Healing. LC 82-42704. 212p. (Orig.). 1983. pap. 6.75 (ISBN 0-8356-0572-8, Quest). Theos Pub Hse.
King, Shelbie, ed. see Historic Huntsville Foundation.
King, Stanley F. The International Dolls House Book. (Illus.). 1977. pap. 4.95 o.p. (ISBN 0-517-52943-2). Crown.
King, Stella, jt. ed. see Ferguson, Rosemary.
King, Stephen. Carrie: Movie Edition. 1976. pap. 2.95 (ISBN 0-451-11963-0, AE1963, Sig). NAL.
--Christine. 600p. 1983. 17.75 (ISBN 0-670-22026-4). Viking Pr.
--Cujo. 1982. pap. 3.95 (ISBN 0-451-11729-8, AE1729, Sig). NAL.
--The Dark Tower: The Gunslinger. (Illus.). 224p. 1982. 20.00 o.s.i. (ISBN 0-937986-50-X); 60.00 o.s.i. (ISBN 0-937986-51-8). D M Grant.
--The Dead Zone. 1980. pap. 3.95 (ISBN 0-451-11961-4, AE1961, Sig). NAL.
--Salem's Lot. (Illus.). (RL 10). 1979. pap. 3.95 (ISBN 0-451-12158-9, AE2158, Sig). NAL.
--The Shining. (RL 6). 1978. pap. 3.50 o.p. (ISBN 0-451-11334-9, AE1334, Sig). NAL.
--The Stand. 1980. pap. 4.50 (ISBN 0-451-12159-7, AE2159, Sig). NAL.
--Stephen King's Danse Macabre. 1981. 13.95 (ISBN 0-89696-076-5, An Everest House Book). Dodd.
King, Stephen W., jt. auth. see Samovar, Larry A.
King, T. E., et al, eds. Cytochrome Oxidases. (Developments in Biochemistry: Vol. 5). 1979. 77.00 (ISBN 0-444-80100-6, Biomedical Pr). Elsevier.
King, T. J. see Abercrombie, M. & Brachet, J.
King, Teri. Love, Sex & Astrology. (Illus.). 256p. 1973. pap. 4.50 (BN 4000, BN). B&N NY.
King, The Reverend Martin Luther & Riley, Clayton. Daddy King: The Autobiography of Martin Luther King, Sr. LC 80-17411. (Illus.). 256p. 1980. 10.95 o.p. (ISBN 0-688-03699-6). Morrow.
King, Thomas M. & Salmon, James F., eds. Teilhard & the Unity of Knowledge. LC 82-60590. 1983. pap. 8.95 (ISBN 0-8091-2491-2). Paulist Pr.
King, Timothy, jt. auth. see Barkin, David.
King, Timothy, ed. Education & Income. (Working Paper: No. 402). viii, 315p. 1980. 5.00 (ISBN 0-686-36035-4, WP-0402). World Bank.
King, Tobitha. Small World. 1982. pap. 3.50 (ISBN 0-451-11408-6, AE1408, Sig). NAL.
King, Tony. The Moving Alphabet Book. (Illus.). 14p. 1982. 9.95 (ISBN 0-399-20923-9). Putnam Pub Group.
King, Virginia G. & Gerwig, Norma A. Humanizing Nursing Education: A Confluent Approach Through Group Process. LC 80-83678. 206p. 1981. Repr. 19.95 (ISBN 0-913654-69-8). Aspen Systems.
King, W. J. The British Isles. 576p. 1975. 35.00x (ISBN 0-7121-0246-9, Pub. by Macdonald & Evans). State Mutual Bk.
--Cotton in the Gambia: Report on the Cotton Development Project 1975 to 1978. 1980. 35.00x (ISBN 0-85135-109-3, Pub. by Centre Overseas Research). State Mutual Bk.
King, W. J., jt. auth. see Tunstall, J. P.
King, W. R., jt. auth. see Cleland, D. I.
King, William R. Quantitative Analysis for Marketing Management. 1968. text ed. 26.00 o.p. (ISBN 0-07-034605-4, C). McGraw.
King, William R., jt. auth. see Cleland, David I.
King, Winston L. In the Hope of Nibbana: The Ethics of Theravada Buddhism. LC 62-9575. 308p. 1964. 21.00x (ISBN 0-87548-230-9); pap. 9.00x (ISBN 0-87548-231-7, P93). Open Court.
King, Woodie, Jr. Black Theatre Present Condition. LC 81-14141. (Illus.). 102p. (Orig.). pap. 7.95 (ISBN 0-89062-133-0, Pub by National Black Theatre Touring Circuit). Pub Ctr Cult Res.
Kingdom, Jonathan. East African Mammals, Vol. IIIC. 1982. 92.50 (ISBN 0-12-408344-7). Acad Pr.
Kingdon, Donald R. Matrix Organization: Managing Information Technologies. 240p. 1973. 17.95x (ISBN 0-422-73990-1, Pub. by Tavistock England). Methuen Inc.
Kingdon, R., ed. see Palmer, H. E.
Kingery, Margaret. The Whirlwind. 1979. pap. 1.00 o.p. (ISBN 0-686-24541-5). Samisdat.
Kingford, Dr. Treatment of Exotic Marine Fish Diseases. LC 75-26516. 1975. 5.95 (ISBN 0-915096-03-X). Palmetto Pub.
King-Hall, Stephen. The Communist Conspiracy. LC 79-2907. 239p. 1983. Repr. of 1953 ed. 19.75 (ISBN 0-8305-0077-4). Hyperion Conn.
Kingham, H. G., ed. U. K. Tomato Manual. 228p. 1974. text ed. 37.50x o.p. (ISBN 0-901361-14-3). Scholium Intl.
Kinghorn, Kenneth C. Dynamic Discipleship. 160p. 1975. pap. 4.95 (ISBN 0-8010-5357-9). Baker Bk.
Kingman, Daniel. American Music: A Panorama. LC 78-22782. 1979. pap. text ed. 12.95 (ISBN 0-02-871260-9). Schirmer Bks.
Kingman, J. F. Mathematics of Genetic Diversity. LC 80-51290. (CBMS-NSF Regional Conference Ser.: No. 34). vii, 70p. 1980. pap. 14.50 (ISBN 0-89871-166-5). Soc Indus-Appl Math.
Kingman, John F & Taylor, S. J. Introduction to Measure & Probability. 1966. 52.50 (ISBN 0-521-05888-0). Cambridge U Pr.
Kingman, Lee. Peter Pan Bag. LC 78-98520. (gr. 9-12). 1970. 5.95 o.p. (ISBN 0-395-06866-5). HM.
--Peter's Long Walk. (gr. k-3). 1953. PLB 5.95 o.p. (ISBN 0-385-07747-5). Doubleday.
Kingman, Russ. A Pictorial Life of Jack London. 288p. 1981. 16.95 (ISBN 0-517-53163-1); pap. 9.95 (ISBN 0-517-54093-2). Crown.
Kings, John, ed. see Wilson, Bob.
Kingsbury, A. A. Introduction to Security & Crime Prevention Surveys. (Illus.). 384p. 1973. 16.75x o.p. (ISBN 0-398-02836-2); pap. 11.95x (ISBN 0-398-02893-1). C C Thomas.
Kingsbury, John M. Poisonous Plants of the United States & Canada. 3rd ed. 1964. 30.95 (ISBN 0-13-685016-2). P-H.
Kingsbury, Ray see Allen, W. S.
Kingsbury, Robert, jt. auth. see Taaffe, Robert N.
Kingsbury, Roy & O'Shea, Patrick. Sunday Afternoons. 1974. tchrs notes 2.95x (ISBN 0-582-55226-5); record 14.00x (ISBN 0-582-56732-7); cassette 15.50x (ISBN 0-582-56755-6). Longman.
Kingsford. Marine Aquarium Compatibility Guide. LC 78-25989. 1978. 9.95 (ISBN 0-915096-07-2). Palmetto Pub.
Kingsford, Anna & Maitland, Edward. Clothed With the Sun. 248p. 11.50 (ISBN 0-686-38213-7). Sun Bks.
Kingsford, Peter. The Hunger Marchers in Britain, 1920-1940. 230p. 1982. text ed. 26.50x (ISBN 0-85315-555-0, Pub. by Lawrence & Wishart Ltd England). Humanities.
Kingsford, R. J. Publishers Association, Eighteen Ninety-Six - Nineteen Forty-Six. LC 74-101445. 1970. 34.50 (ISBN 0-521-07756-7). Cambridge U Pr.
Kingsland, L. W., tr. see Holm, Anne.
Kingsley, B., et al. Advances in Non-Invasive Diagnostic Cardiology. LC 76-367. 1976. 40.00x o.p. (ISBN 0-913590-29-0). Slack Inc.
Kingsley, Charles. Hypatia: New Foes with an Old Face. LC 82-82474. 410p. 1982. Repr. of 1882 ed. 14.00 (ISBN 0-89345-405-2, Spirit Fiction). Garber Comm.
--The Water Babies. (Childrens Illustrated Classics Ser). (Illus.). 200p. 1983. Repr. of 1957 ed. 11.95 o.p. (ISBN 0-460-05037-0, Pub. by J. M. Dent England). Biblio Dist.
Kingsley, Henry. Portable Henry Kingsley. Mellick, J. S., ed. LC 81-19990. (Portable Australian Authors Ser.). 603p. (YA) 1982. text ed. 30.00 (ISBN 0-7022-1750-6); pap. 14.95 (ISBN 0-7022-1760-3). U of Queensland Pr.
--Ravenshoe. 1970. Repr. of 1906 ed. 9.95x (ISBN 0-460-00028-4, Evman). Biblio Dist.
Kingsley, Mary. Travels in West Africa: Congo Francais, Corisco & Cameroons. 742p. 1983. pap. 10.95 (ISBN 0-86068-267-6, Virago Pr). Merrimack Bk Serv.
Kingsley, Philip. The Complete Hair Book: The Ultimate Guide to Your Hair's Health & Beauty. (A Fred Jordan Bk.). (Illus.). 1979. 12.95 o.p. (ISBN 0-448-15175-8, G&D). Putnam Pub Group.
Kingsley, Sidney see Freedley, George.
Kingsmill, Allison, jt. ed. see Cameron, Angus.
Kingsnorth, G. W., jt. auth. see Marsh, Zoe.
Kingstather, W. & Parish, W. Today's Business World. 1978. 19.95 (ISBN 0-8359-7761-7); study guide 8.95 (ISBN 0-8359-7762-5); instrs' manual avail. (ISBN 0-8359-7763-3). Reston.
Kingston, Beryl. You Can Relieve Menstrual Problems. 126p. 1982. 10.95 (ISBN 0-13-976795-9); pap. 4.95 (ISBN 0-13-976787-8). P-H.
Kingston, Irene, jt. ed. see Benjamin, William A.
Kingston, J. M. Mathematics for Teachers of the Middle Grades. LC 65-26847. 322p. 1966. text ed. 14.00 (ISBN 0-471-47960-8, Pub. by Wiley). Krieger.
Kingston, Maxine H. China Men. LC 81-69903. (Illus.). 1982. pap. 3.50 (ISBN 0-394-29482-3, Vin). Random.
Kingston, Meredith. Aloha, Yesterday. (Second Chance at Love Contemporary Ser.: No. 10). 192p. (Orig.). 1981. pap. 1.75 o.s.i. (ISBN 0-515-05907-2). Jove Pubns.
--Mixed Doubles, No. 72. 1982. pap. 1.75 (ISBN 0-515-06683-4). Jove Pubns.
Kingstone, Brett M. The Student Entrepreneur's Guide. LC 81-50251. 159p. (Orig.). 1981. pap. 4.95 (ISBN 0-89815-045-0). Ten Speed Pr.
King-Taylor, L. Not by Bread Alone: An Appreciation of Job Enrichment. 1973. 15.00x (ISBN 0-8464-0678-0). Beekman Pubs.
Kington, Miles. Let's Parler Franglais. 1982. pap. 3.95 (ISBN 0-14-005625-4). Penguin.
--Miles & Miles. (Illus.). 128p. 1982. 12.50 (ISBN 0-241-10901-9, Pub by Hamish Hamilton England). David & Charles.
Kini, Sudha R., jt. auth. see Miller, J. Martin.
Kinkead, Eugene. A Concrete Look at Nature. (Illus.). 242p. 1974. 7.95 (ISBN 0-8129-0471-0, QH105.N7K55). E Kinkead.
--Squirrel Book. (Illus.). 160p. 1980. 13.95 o.p. (ISBN 0-525-93137-6). Dutton.
--Squirrel Book. (Illus.). 147p. 1980. 8.00 (ISBN 0-686-84639-7). E Kinkead.
--Wildness Is All Around Us. (Illus.). 178p. 1978. 10.00x (ISBN 0-87690-277-8, QH541.5.C6K56). E Kinkead.
Kinkead, Mary A. Elementary Labanotation. LC 81-81276. (Illus.). 126p. 1981. spiral bdg. 7.95 (ISBN 0-87484-545-9). Mayfield Pub.
Kinkeldey, H. & Stockmair, W., trs. The New German Patent Law: 1981. 199p. (Eng. & Ger.). 1981. 28.80x (ISBN 3-527-25936-8). Verlag Chemie.
Kinkle, Roger D. The Complete Encyclopedia of Popular Music & Jazz 1900-1950, 4 vols. 1974. 100.00 o.p. (ISBN 0-517-54805-4, Arlington Hse). Crown.
Kinklighter, Clois E. Modern Masonry. LC 80-17966. (Illus.). 256p. 1980. text ed. 13.20 (ISBN 0-87006-296-4). Goodheart.
Kinlaw, Dennis C. Listening & Communicating Skills: A Facilitator's Package. LC 80-54159. 131p. (Orig.). 1981. 3-ring binder with cassette 49.95 (ISBN 0-88390-163-3). Univ Assocs.
Kinley, David, jt. auth. see Bello, Walden.
Kinley, David, ed. see Institute for Food & Develop Policy.
Kinloch, Graham C. The Dynamics of Race Relations: A Sociological Analysis. (Illus.). 352p. 1974. pap. text ed. 18.95 (ISBN 0-07-034735-2, C). McGraw.
--Racial Conflict in Rhodesia: A Socio-Historical Study. LC 78-64823. 1978. pap. text ed. 12.75 (ISBN 0-8191-0642-9). U Pr of Amer.
--Sociological Theory: Its Development & Major Paradigms. 1976. text ed. 26.50 (ISBN 0-07-034738-7, C). McGraw.
Kinmonth, J. B. The Lymphatics: Surgery, Lymphography & Diseases of the Chyle & Lymph Systems. 432p. 1982. text ed. 14.95 (ISBN 0-7131-4410-6). E Arnold.
Kinn, Mary E. Student Review Manual for the Medical Office Assistant. 2nd ed. (Illus.). 298p. 1981. wkbk. 10.95 (ISBN 0-7216-5439-8). Saunders.
Kinn, Mary E. & Bradley, Hila M. Student Workbook to Accompany the Medical Office Assistant. 233p. 1976. 8.95 o.p. (ISBN 0-7216-5438-X). Saunders.
Kinn, Mary E., jt. auth. see Frederick, Portia M.
Kinnaird, John. Reader's Guide to Olaf Stapledon. Schlobin, Roger C., ed. (Reader's Guides to Contemporary Science Fiction & Fantasy Authors Ser.: Vol. 21). (Illus., Orig.). 1983. 10.95x (ISBN 0-916732-55-X); pap. text ed. 4.95x (ISBN 0-916732-54-1). Starmont Hse.
Kinnamon, Keneth, jt. auth. see Barksdale, Richard.
Kinnamon, Kenneth, ed. James Baldwin: A Collection of Critical Essays. LC 74-6175. (Twentieth Century Views Ser.). 192p. 1973. 12.95 o.p. (ISBN 0-13-055566-5, Spec). P-H.
Kinnard, Douglas. The Secretary of Defense. LC 80-5178. 264p. 1981. 19.50x (ISBN 0-8131-1434-9). U Pr of Ky.
Kinnard, William N. Income Property Valuation: Principles & Techniques of Appraising Income-Producing Real Estate. (Special Ser. in Real Estate & Urban Land Economics). 520p. 1971. text ed. 15.95x (ISBN 0-669-74245-7). Lexington Bks.
Kinnard, William N., Jr. & Messner, Stephen D. Industrial Real Estate. 2nd ed. 8.00 (ISBN 0-686-37024-4). Soc Industrial Realtors.

Kinne, O. Marine Ecology: A Comprehensive Integrated Treatise on Life in Oceans & Coastal Waters, Vols. 1-4. Incl. Vol. 1, 3 pts. 1970. Pt. 1. 84.95x (ISBN 0-471-48001-0); Pt. 2. 64.50 o.p. (ISBN 0-471-48002-9); Pt. 3. 69.95 o.p. (ISBN 0-471-48003-7); Vol. 2, 2 pts. 1975. Pt. 1. 79.95x (ISBN 0-471-48004-5); Pt. 2. 83.95 o.p. (ISBN 0-471-48006-1); Vol. 3, 3 pts. 1976. Pt. 1. 87.25 o.p. (ISBN 0-471-48005-3); Pt. 2. 131.95x (ISBN 0-471-01577-6); Pt. 3. 64.95x (ISBN 0-471-48007-X); Vol. 4. 1978. Pt. 1. 126.95x (ISBN 0-471-48008-8). LC 79-221779 (Pub. by Wiley-Interscience). Wiley.

Kinne, O. & Bulnheim, H. P. Cultivation of Marine Organisms & Its Importance for Marine Biology. (International Symposium Helgoland 1969 Ser.). (Illus.). 722p. 1973. pap. text ed. 72.00x (ISBN 3-87429-059-X). Lubrecht & Cramer.

Kinne, Otto. Diseases of Marine Animals: General Aspects, Protozoa to Gastropoda, Vol. 1. LC 79-40580. 466p. 1980. 81.95x (ISBN 0-471-99584-3, Pub. by Wiley-Interscience). Wiley.

Kinne, Russ. Complete Book of Nature Photography. rev ed. (Illus.). 1980. 16.95 (ISBN 0-8174-2470-9, Amphoto). Watson-Guptill.

Kinne, Wisner P. George Pierce Baker & the American Theatre. LC 68-8741. (Illus.). 1968. Repr. of 1954 ed. lib. bdg. 20.00x (ISBN 0-8371-0129-8, KIGB). Greenwood.

Kinnear, Angus. Changed into His Likeness. 1978. pap. 3.95 (ISBN 0-8423-0228-X). Tyndale.

--Love Not the World. 1978. pap. 2.95 (ISBN 0-8423-3850-0). Tyndale.

--A Table in the Wilderness. 1978. pap. 4.95 (ISBN 0-8423-6900-7). Tyndale.

--What Shall This Man Do? 1978. pap. 3.95 (ISBN 0-8423-7910-X). Tyndale.

Kinnear, Mary. Daughters of Time: Women in the Western Tradition. (Women & Culture Ser.). (Illus.). 256p. 1982. pap. text ed. 13.50x (ISBN 0-472-08029-6). U of Mich Pr.

Kinnear, Thomas C. & Bernhardt, Kenneth L. Dynamics of Marketing Principles: A Reader. 1983. pap. text ed. 12.95x (ISBN 0-673-15846-2). Scott F.

--Principles of Marketing. 1982. text ed. 24.95x (ISBN 0-673-15486-6). Scott F.

Kinnear, Thomas C. & Taylor, James R. Marketing Research: An Applied Approach. (Marketing Ser.). 1979. text ed. 24.95 (ISBN 0-07-034741-7, C); instructor's manual 11.00 (ISBN 0-07-034742-5); exercises 9.95 (ISBN 0-07-034743-3); transparency masters 22.50 (ISBN 0-07-034744-1). McGraw.

--Marketing Research: An Applied Approach. 2nd ed. (McGraw-Hill Ser. in Marketing). (Illus.). 720p. 1983. text ed. 24.95x (ISBN 0-07-034745-X, C); exercises 10.95 (ISBN 0-07-034747-6); write for info. instr's manual (ISBN 0-07-034746-8). McGraw.

Kinnear, Willis, jt. auth. see Holmes, Ernest.

Kinneir, Joan. The Artist by Himself. 1979. 9.98 (ISBN 0-312-05498-X). St Martin.

Kinnell, Galaway, tr. see Goll, Yvan.

Kinnell, Galway. Black Light. rev. ed. LC 80-16114. 128p. 1980. pap. 6.00 (ISBN 0-86547-016-2). N Point Pr.

--Book of Nightmares. 1971. pap. 6.95 (ISBN 0-395-12098-5). HM.

--How the Alligator Missed Breakfast. (Illus.). (gr. k-3). 1982. PLB 8.95 (ISBN 0-395-32436-X); 8.70. HM.

--Walking Down the Stairs. Hall, Donald, ed. LC 77-23752. (Poets on Poetry Ser.). pap. 7.95 (ISBN 0-472-52530-1). U of Mich Pr.

Kinney, Arthur, jt. ed. see Salamon, Linda.

Kinney, Arthur F. Critical Essays on William Faulkner: The Compson Family. (Critical Essays on American Literature Ser.). 1982. lib. bdg. 32.00 (ISBN 0-8161-8464-X). G K Hall.

--Dorothy Parker. (United States Authors Ser.). 1978. 11.95 (ISBN 0-8057-7241-3, Twayne). G K Hall.

Kinney, Cle, jt. auth. see Kinney, Jean.

Kinney, Francis S. You Are First: The Story of Olin & Rod Stephens of Sparkman & Stephens, Inc. LC 78-8148. (Illus.). 1978. 17.95 o.p. (ISBN 0-396-07567-3). Dodd.

Kinney, Gilbert F. Engineering Properties & Applications of Plastics. LC 57-10808. 278p. 1957. text ed. 15.00 (ISBN 0-471-48015-0, Pub. by Wiley). Krieger.

Kinney, Jean & Kinney, Cle. Twenty One Kinds of American Folk Art & How to Make Each One. LC 70-175556. (Illus.). (gr. 4-6). 1972. 6.95 o.p. (ISBN 0-689-30030-1). Atheneum.

Kinney, Jean & Leaton, Gwen. Loosening the Grip: A Handbook of Alcohol Information. 2nd ed. LC 82-6319. (Illus.). 353p. 1983. pap. text ed. 13.95 (ISBN 0-8016-2688-9). Mosby.

--Loosening the Grip: A Handbook of Alcohol Information. 15.95 o.p. (ISBN 0-686-92201-8, 4281). Hazelden.

--Understanding Alcohol. LC 81-22557. (Medical Library). (Illus.). 268p. 1982. pap. 8.95 (ISBN 0-452-25338-1, 2706-0). Mosby.

Kinney, John M., ed. see Committee on Pre & Postoperative Care American College of Surgeons.

Kinney, John M., et al, eds. see American College of Surgeons Committee on Pre & Postoperative Care.

Kinney, Marguerite, et al. AACN's Reference for Critical Care Nursing. (Illus.). 1981. text ed. 56.50 (ISBN 0-07-001133-8). McGraw.

Kinney, William P. The Monetary Maze: Gold, the International Monetary System, & the Emerging World Economy. LC 76-52187. 1977. pap. text ed. 6.95 (ISBN 0-8403-1700-X). Kendall-Hunt.

Kinnibugh, William, jt. auth. see Short, Andrew.

Kinori, B. Z. Manual of Surface Drainage Engineering, Vol. 1. 1970. 51.00 (ISBN 0-444-40851-7). Elsevier.

Kinrade, F., jt. auth. see Darnbrough, A.

Kinross, Lord. The Windsor Years. (Illus.). 1980. pap. 9.95 o.p. (ISBN 0-14-005527-4). Penguin.

Kinsbourne, M., ed. Asymmetrical Function of the Brain. LC 77-8633. (Illus.). 1978. 54.50 (ISBN 0-521-21481-5). Cambridge U Pr.

Kinsell, Laurance W. Adipose Tissue as an Organ: Proceedings of the Duel Conference on Lipids. (Illus.). 292p. 1962. photocopy ed. spiral 27.75x (ISBN 0-398-04311-6). C C Thomas.

Kinsella, Paul. The Techniques of Writing. 3rd ed. 364p. 1981. pap. text ed. 10.95 (ISBN 0-15-589728-4, HC); answer key avail. 1.50 (ISBN 0-15-589729-2). HarBraceJ.

Kinsella, Valerie, ed. Surveys 1: Eight State-of-the Art Articles on Key Areas in Language Teaching. LC 82-4332. (Cambridge Language Teaching Surveys 1 Ser.). 168p. 1983. 19.95 (ISBN 0-521-24886-8); pap. 8.95 (ISBN 0-521-27046-4). Cambridge U Pr.

--Surveys 2: Eight State-of-the Art Articles on Key Areas in Language Teaching. LC 82-45961. (Cambridge Language Teaching Surveys 2 Ser.). 168p. Date not set. 19.95 (ISBN 0-521-24887-6); pap. 8.95 (ISBN 0-521-27047-2). Cambridge U Pr.

Kinsella, W. P. Shoeless Joe. 224p. 1983. pap. 2.95 (ISBN 0-345-30921-9). Ballantine.

Kinser, Charleen. Outdoor Art for Kids. LC 74-18133. (Illus.). (gr. 3 up). 1975. 6.95 o.s.i. (ISBN 0-695-80533-9); PLB 6.99 o.s.i. (ISBN 0-695-40533-0). Follett.

Kinsey, Alfred C. Sex Studies Index: 1981. 1983. lib. bdg. 85.00 (ISBN 0-8161-0394-1, Hall Library). G K Hall.

Kinsey, Bill, jt. auth. see Deboeck, Guido.

Kinsey, Thomas D. Learn to Double Your Income Legitimately in Four Years or Less. 64p. 1983. pap. text ed. 10.00 (ISBN 0-941046-06-0). ERGO Business Bks.

Kinsky, Georg. Die Originalausgaben der Werke Johann Sebastian Bachs: Ein Beitrag Zur Musikbibliographie. (Composers' Worklists Ser.: Vol. 2). 1968. Repr. of 1937 ed. 22.50 o.s.i. (ISBN 90-6027-048-7, Pub. by Frits Knuf Netherlands). Pendragon NY.

Kinsler, Lawrence E., et al. Fundamentals of Acoustics. 3rd ed. LC 81-7463. 480p. 1982. text ed. 31.95x (ISBN 0-471-02933-5); avail. answers (ISBN 0-471-09743-8). Wiley.

Kinsley, David. Hinduism: A Cultural Perspective. (Illus.). 200p. 1982. 9.95 (ISBN 0-13-388975-0). P-H.

Kinsley, David R. The Sword & the Flute - Kali & Krsna: Dark Visions of the Terrible & the Sublime in Hindu Mythology. LC 73-91669. 175p. 1975. 27.50x (ISBN 0-520-02675-6); pap. 2.95 (ISBN 0-520-03510-0). U of Cal Pr.

Kinsley, James, ed. The Oxford Book of Ballads. 1982. pap. 9.95 (ISBN 0-19-281330-7). Oxford U Pr.

Kinsley, James, ed. see Burns, Robert.

Kinsley, James, ed. see Dryden, John.

Kinslow, William E., jt. auth. see Harwell, Edward M.

Kinsman, Barbara. I've Been Thinking. Lawrence, Leslie & Weingartner, Ronald, eds. (Bright Beginnings I). (Illus.). 48p. (Orig.). (gr. 1-3). pap. 1.69 (ISBN 0-88049-032-2, 7395). Milton Bradley Co.

--Numbers for All Reasons. Lawrence, Leslie & Wiengartner, Ronald, eds. (Bright Beginnings I). (Illus.). 48p. (Orig.). (gr. 1-3). pap. 1.69 (ISBN 0-88049-031-4, 7394). Milton Bradley Co.

Kinsman, Donald M. International Meat Science Dictionary. (Illus.). 282p. 1979. pap. 10.95x (ISBN 0-89641-029-3). American Pr.

Kinsman, Robert. Your New Swiss Bank Book. rev. ed. 285p. 1983. pap. 8.95 (ISBN 0-87094-416-9). Dow Jones-Irwin.

Kinsman, Robert S. Darker Vision of the Renaissance: Beyond the Fields of Reason. LC 72-78939. 1975. 30.00x (ISBN 0-520-02259-9). U of Cal Pr.

Kinsolving, William. Born with the Century. LC 78-27078. 1979. 12.50 o.p. (ISBN 0-399-12270-2). Putnam Pub Group.

--Raven. 448p. 1983. 15.95 (ISBN 0-399-12755-0). Putnam Pub Group.

Kinsthita, Louise & Sanderson, Joyce. The Rainbow Path: Healing Ourselves. 78p. 1982. pap. 6.95 (ISBN 0-942494-27-X). Coleman Graphics.

Kinter, Earl W. A Robinson-Patman Primer: A Businessman's Guide to the Law Against Price Discrimination. 2nd ed. (Illus.). 1981. 22.95x (ISBN 0-02-364370-6). Macmillan.

Kinter, Judith. Cross-Country Caper. Schroeder, Howard, ed. LC 81-3398. (Roundup Ser.). (Illus.). 48p. (gr. 3 up). 1981. PLB 7.95 (ISBN 0-89686-155-4); pap. text ed. 3.95 (ISBN 0-89686-163-5). Crestwood Hse.

Kintgen, Eugene R. The Perception of Poetry. LC 82-48387. 288p. 1983. 22.50x (ISBN 0-253-34345-3). Ind U Pr.

Kintner, E. W. & Joelson, M. R. International Anti-Trust Primer: A Businessman's Guide to the International Aspects of U.S. Antitrust Law & to Key Foreign Antitrust Laws. 1974. 15.95x (ISBN 0-02-364380-3). Macmillan.

Kintner, Earl W. Anti-Trust Primer. 2nd ed. (Illus.). 370p. 1973. text ed. 19.95x (ISBN 0-02-364450-8). Macmillan.

--Primer on the Law of Mergers: A Guide for the Businessman. (Illus.). 480p. 1973. 16.95x (ISBN 0-02-364420-6). Macmillan.

Kintner, William R. & Copper, John F. A Matter of Two Chinas: The China-Taiwan Issue in U. S. Foreign Policy. 127p. 1979. pap. 6.00 (ISBN 0-910191-04-2). For Policy Res.

Kintsch, W., jt. auth. see Le Ny, J. F.

Kintsch, W., jt. ed. see Flammer, A.

Kintz, B. L., jt. auth. see Bruning, James L.

Kinvig. A History of the Isle of Man. 208p. 1982. 49.00x (ISBN 0-85323-483-3, Pub. by Liverpool Univ England). State Mutual Bk.

Kinyatti, Maina W., ed. Thunder from the Mountain: Mau Mau Patriotic Songs. 128p. (Orig.). 1980. 19.95 (ISBN 0-905762-83-5, Pub. by Zed Pr England); pap. cancelled (ISBN 0-905762-84-3). Lawrence Hill.

Kinzer, David M. Health Controls Out of Control. 194p. 9.75 (ISBN 0-686-68584-9, 14918). Healthcare Fin Man Assn.

Kinzer, Mark. Taming the Tongue: Why Christians Should Care about What They Say. (Living as a Christian Ser.). 1982. pap. 2.50 (ISBN 0-89283-165-0). Servant.

Kinzer, Mark, jt. auth. see Ghezzi, Bert.

Kinzer, Stephen & Schlesinger, Stephen. Bitter Fruit: The Untold Story of the American Coup in Guatemala. (Illus.). 312p. 1983. pap. 8.95 (ISBN 0-385-18354-2, Anch). Doubleday.

Kinzey, Bert. F-16A & B Fighting Falcon in Detail & Scale. (Design & Scale Ser.). (Illus.). 72p. 1982. pap. 6.95 (ISBN 0-686-97272-4). Aero.

--U. S. Air Force Aggressor Squadrons. 1982. pap. write for info. (ISBN 0-8168-1100-8). Aero.

Kinzey, Bertram Y., Jr. & Sharp, H. M. Environmental Technologies in Architecture. (Illus.). 1963. ref. ed. 36.95 (ISBN 0-13-283226-7). P-H.

Kinzie, Mary. The Threshold of the Year: Poems. LC 81-69836. (Breakthrough Ser.: No. 36). 64p. pap. 5.95 (ISBN 0-8262-0361-2). U of Mo Pr.

Kiong & Draeger. Shantung Black Tiger. 1976. 7.95 (ISBN 0-685-83535-9). Wehman.

Kip, Arthur F. Fundamentals of Electricity & Magnetism. 2nd ed. (Fundamentals of Physics Ser.). 1968. text ed. 35.00 (ISBN 0-07-034780-8, C); instr.'s manual 15.00 (ISBN 0-07-034781-6). McGraw.

Kiparsky, Carol, jt. auth. see Burt, Marina K.

Kiparsky, Paul. Explanation in Phonology. 300p. 1981. 39.25x (ISBN 0-686-32124-3); pap. 24.25x (ISBN 90-70176-24-6). Foris Pubns.

Kiparsky, R. P. Panini As a Variationist. Keyser, S. Jay, ed. (Current Studies in Linguistics Ser.). 1980. text ed. 27.50x (ISBN 0-262-11070-9). MIT Pr.

Kipling, Rudyard. American Notes: Rudyard Kipling's West. rev. ed. Gibson, Arrell M., ed. LC 81-40289. (The Western Frontier Library: Vol. 54). (Illus.). 256p. 1981. Repr. 11.95 (ISBN 0-8061-1682-X). U of Okla Pr.

--Captains Courageous. (RL 6). pap. 1.95 (ISBN 0-451-51751-2, CJ1751, Sig Classics). NAL.

--Captains Courageous. (Bantam Classics Ser.). 160p. 1982. pap. 1.50 (ISBN 0-553-21077-7). Bantam.

--Favorite Just So Stories. (Illus.). (gr. 4-6). 1957. 2.95 (ISBN 0-448-02893-X, D&G). Putnam Pub Group.

--Favorite Just So Stories. LC 76-14697. (Elephant Books). (Illus.). (gr. k-5). 1976. pap. 2.95 (ISBN 0-448-12691-5, G&D). Putnam Pub Group.

--How the Leopard Got His Spots. LC 72-81373. (Just So Ser.). (Illus.). 32p. (gr. 2 up). 1972. 7.95 (ISBN 0-8027-6111-9); PLB 7.85 o.s.i. (ISBN 0-8027-6112-7). Walker & Co.

--If. 1959. pap. 2.50 (ISBN 0-385-04217-5, Dolp). Doubleday.

--Jungle Book. (Illus.). (gr. 4-6). 1950. deluxe ed. 8.95 (ISBN 0-448-06014-0, D&G); pap. 5.95 (ISBN 0-448-11014-8, D&G); 2.95 (ISBN 0-448-05464-7, D&G). Putnam Pub Group.

--The Jungle Book. (RL 4). pap. 2.95 (ISBN 0-451-51716-4, CE1716, Sig Classics). NAL.

--The Jungle Book: Mowgli & His Brothers. (Doubleday Classics Ser.). 3.50 (ISBN 0-385-07345-3). Doubleday.

--Just So Stories. 1965. 2.95 (ISBN 0-448-05475-2 G&D). Putnam Pub Group.

--Just So Stories. LC 65-27041. (Illus.). (gr. k up). 1966. pap. 4.95 o.p. (ISBN 0-8052-0113-0). Schocken.

--Just So Stories. (Illus.). 64p. (gr. 4 up). 1982. 10.95 (ISBN 0-528-82422-8); PLB 10.97 (ISBN 0-528-80077-9). Rand.

--Just So Stories: Anniversary Edition. LC 79-170932. 112p. (gr. 2-5). 1972. 15.95 (ISBN 0-385-07225-2); PLB o.p. (ISBN 0-385-07443-3). Doubleday.

--Kim. pap. 2.25 (ISBN 0-440-94500-3, LFL). Dell.

--New Illustrated Just So Stories. (gr. 1-7). 9.95 (ISBN 0-385-02129-1); PLB o.p. (ISBN 0-385-02180-1). Doubleday.

--Second Jungle Book. (gr. 7-11). 1923. 4.50 o.p. (ISBN 0-385-07483-2). Doubleday.

--The Seven Seas. 220p. 1983. pap. 6.95 (ISBN 0-88072-015-8). Tanager Bks.

--Two Tales: Man Who Would Be King & Without Benefit of Clergy. pap. 2.50 (ISBN 0-8283-1460-8, 2, IPL). Branden.

--The White Seal. Jones, Chuck, ed. (Illus.). 48p. (gr. k-6). 1982. 4.95 (ISBN 0-8249-8042-5). Ideals.

Kipnees, Jerome J., jt. auth. see Friedman, Walter F.

Kipnis, Kenneth. Philosophical Issues in Law: Cases & Materials. 1977. pap. text ed. 16.95 (ISBN 0-13-662296-8). P-H.

Kipp, Jacob, jt. ed. see Higham, R.

Kipp, Kenneth E., jt. auth. see Benson, Harold J.

Kipp, Thomas E. Starlight. (Illus.). 75p. 1983. 5.50 (ISBN 0-682-49946-3). Exposition.

Kippenhahn, Rudolf. One Hundred Billion Suns: The Birth, Life, & Death of the Stars. (Illus.). 256p. 1983. 25.00 (ISBN 0-465-05263-0). Basic.

Kippley, John F. & Kippley, Sheila K. The Art of Natural Family Planning. 2nd ed. (Illus.). 1982. 10.95 (ISBN 0-9601036-5-1). Couple to Couple.

Kippley, Sheila K., jt. auth. see Kippley, John F.

Kipps, M. S. Production of Field Crops. 6th ed. (Agricultural Science Ser.). 1970. text ed. 35.95 (ISBN 0-07-034783-2, C). McGraw.

Kippur, Stephen A. Jules Michelet: A Study of Mind & Sensibility. 320p. (Orig.). 1980. 44.50x (ISBN 0-87395-430-0); pap. 14.95x (ISBN 0-87395-431-9). State U NY Pr.

Kiraly, Bela. Ferenc Deak. Brown, Arthur W., et al, eds. (World Leaders Ser.). 1975. lib. bdg. 14.95 (ISBN 0-8057-3030-3, Twayne). G K Hall.

Kiraly, Bela K., jt. auth. see Rothenberg, Gunther E.

Kirban, Salem. How to Keep Healthy & Happy by Fasting. (Illus.). 1976. 6.95 (ISBN 0-912582-23-5); pap. 2.95 (ISBN 0-686-96763-1). Kirban.

Kirby. Glamour Photography. (Photographer's Library). (Illus.). 1983. pap. 12.95x (ISBN 0-240-51116-6). Focal Pr.

Kirby, A. J. The Anomeric Effect & Related Stereoelectronic Effects at Oxygen. (Reactivity & Structure: Vol. 15). (Illus.). 200p. 1982. 51.00 (ISBN 0-387-11684-2). Springer-Verlag.

Kirby, Anthony J. & Warren. The Organic Chemistry of Phosphorus. (Reaction Mechanisms in Organic Chemistry Ser.: Vol. 5). 1967. 70.00 (ISBN 0-444-40333-7). Elsevier.

Kirby, D. P. The Making of Early England. LC 68-11534. (Fabric of British History Ser.). 1968. 10.00x o.p. (ISBN 0-8052-3151-X). Schocken.

Kirby, Dan & Liner, Tom. Inside Out: Developmental Strategies for Teaching Writing. LC 81-10073. 256p. (Orig.). 1981. pap. text ed. 9.00x (ISBN 0-86709-007-3). Boynton Cook Pub.

Kirby, David. Grace King. (United States Authors Ser.: No. 357). 1980. lib. bdg. 13.95 (ISBN 0-8057-7214-6, Twayne). G K Hall.

--The Opera Lover. pap. 3.00 o.s.i. (ISBN 0-686-81809-1). Anhinga Pr.

--Sarah Bernhardt's Leg. 70p. (Orig.). 1983. pap. 5.00 (ISBN 0-914946-36-6). Cleveland St Univ Poetry Ctr.

Kirby, David & Dawson, John. Small Scale Retailing in the United Kingdom. 1979. text ed. 33.25 (ISBN 0-566-00164-0). Gower Pub Ltd.

Kirby, David K., ed. American Fiction to Nineteen Hundred: A Guide to Information Sources. LC 73-16982. (American Literature, English Literature, & World Literatures in English Information Guide Ser.: Vol. 4). 260p. 1975. 42.00x (ISBN 0-8103-1210-7). Gale.

Kirby, E. S. The Soviet Far East. LC 70-175931. 1971. 19.95 o.p. (ISBN 0-312-74830-2). St Martin.

Kirby, E. Stuart. Russian Studies of Japan: An Exploratory Survey. LC 80-18128. 200p. 1981. 26.00 (ISBN 0-312-69610-8). St Martin.

Kirby, Edward. Saga of Butch Cassidy. (Wild & Woolly West Ser: No. 32). (Illus.). 1977. 10.00 o.p. (ISBN 0-910584-46-X); pap. 6.00 o.p. (ISBN 0-910584-88-5). Filter.

Kirby, F. E. Introduction to Western Music. LC 69-15248. 1970. text ed. 12.95 (ISBN 0-02-917360-4). Free Pr.

--Music in the Classic Period: An Anthology with Commentary. LC 77-84939. 1979. pap. text ed. 19.95 (ISBN 0-02-870710-9). Schirmer Bks.

Kirby, G. W., jt. auth. see Bentley, K. W.

Kirby, G. W. see Weissberger, A.

Kirby, George. Jujitsu: Basic Techniques of the Gentle Art. (Illus., Orig.). 1983. pap. 6.95 (ISBN 0-89750-088-1, 425). Ohara Pubns.

--Looking at Germany. LC 77-37629. (Looking at Other Countries Ser.). (Illus.). (gr. 4-6). 1972. 10.57i (ISBN 0-397-31337-3, JBL-J). Har-Row.

Kirby, George & Sullivan, George. Soccer. LC 71-118966. (All-Star Sports Bks). (Illus.). (gr. 3 up). 1971. lib. ed. 5.97 o.s.i. (ISBN 0-695-40147-5); pap. 3.95 o.s.i. (ISBN 0-695-80147-3). Follett.

Kirby, George, jt. auth. see Richmond, Garland.

Kirby, J. C. Retrospect. 1979. 5.00 o.p. (ISBN 0-682-49498-4). Exposition.

Kirby, Jonell, jt. ed. see West, John D.

Kirby, Kay. Autumn Beginning. (Adventures in Love Ser.: No. 31). 1982. pap. 1.75 (ISBN 0-451-11785-9, AE1785, Sig). NAL.

--Summertime Love. (Adventures in Love Ser.: No. 25). 1982. pap. 1.75 (ISBN 0-451-11567-8, AE1567, Sig). NAL.

--Winter Interlude. (Adventures in Love Ser.: No. 37). 1982. pap. 1.95 (ISBN 0-451-11930-4, AJ1930, Sig). NAL.

Kirby, Keith E., jt. auth. see Bell, Irene W.

Kirby, Lee & Scarry, John. From Writers to Writing. 1978. pap. text ed. 16.50x (ISBN 0-673-15693-1). Scott F.

Kirby, M. J. & Morgan, R. P. Soil Erosion. 312p. 1981. 72.95x (ISBN 0-471-27802-5, Pub. by Wiley-Interscience). Wiley.

Kirby, R. S. Early Years of Modern Civil Engineering. 1932. 57.50x (ISBN 0-685-69833-5). Elliots Bks.

Kirby, Ronald, et al. An Assessment of Short-Range Transit Planning in Selected U. S. Cities. 82p. (Orig.). 1979. pap. text ed. 4.00 (ISBN 0-87766-274-6). Urban Inst.

Kirby, Sandra. On Your Mark: Self-Assessment for General Nurses. (Illus.). 300p. 1982. text ed. 24.00 (ISBN 0-86792-002-5, Pub by Adis Pr Australia). Wright-PSG.

Kirby, Sheldon, jt. auth. see Brewer, Donald J.

Kirby, Susan E. Blizzard of the Heart. 1982. 6.95 (ISBN 0-686-84180-8, Avalon). Bouregy.

--Chasing a Dream. 1982. 6.95 (ISBN 0-686-84185-9, Avalon). Bouregy.

--Lessons for the Heart. 1982. 6.95 (ISBN 0-686-84168-9, Avalon). Bouregy.

--The Maple Princess. 1982. pap. 6.95 (ISBN 0-686-84737-7, Avalon). Bouregy.

Kirby, Tess, jt. auth. see Ashley, Ruth.

Kirchem, Ronald, ed. see Jones, Ronald E.

Kirchenbaum, Daniel S., jt. auth. see Grasha, Anthony F.

Kirchenmann, Jorg C. & Muschalek, Christian. Residential Districts. (Illus.). 192p. 1980. 32.50 (ISBN 0-8230-7491-9, Whitney Lib). Watson-Guptill.

Kircher, Christopher, jt. ed. see Barnes, C. D.

Kircher, John F. & Bowman, Richard E. Effects of Radiation on Materials & Components. LC 64-16977. 702p. (Orig.). 1964. 32.00 (ISBN 0-686-81277-8). Krieger.

Kirchherr, Eugene C. Abyssinia to Zimbabwe: A Guide to the Political Units of Africa in the Period 1947-1978. 3rd ed. LC 79-19046. (Papers in International Studies: Africa Ser.: No. 25). (Orig.). 1979. pap. 8.00 (ISBN 0-89680-100-4, Ohio U Ctr Intl). Ohio U Pr.

--Abyssinia to Zona Al Sur Del Draa. LC 75-620026. (Papers in International Studies: Africa: No. 25). (Illus.). 1975. pap. 4.00 o.p. (ISBN 0-89680-058-X, Ohio U Ctr Intl). Ohio U Pr.

Kirchhoff, Frederick. William Morris. (English Authors Ser.). 1979. lib. bdg. 14.95 (ISBN 0-8057-6723-1, Twayne). G K Hall.

Kirchhoff, Karin T. Coronary Precautions: A Diffusion Survey. Kalisch, Philip & Kalisch, Beatrice, eds. LC 82-17613. (Studies in Nursing Management: No. 8). 128p. 1982. 34.95 (ISBN 0-8357-1377-6). Univ Microfilms.

Kirchhoff, Theodore. Handbook of Insanity for Practitioners & Students. 362p. 1982. Repr. of 1895 ed. lib. bdg. 85.00 (ISBN 0-8495-3138-1). Arden Lib.

Kirchmayer, Leon K. Economic Operation of Power Systems. LC 58-12710. (Illus.). 260p. 1958. 37.00 o.p. (ISBN 0-471-48180-7, Pub. by Wiley-Interscience). Wiley.

Kirchner, Emil & Schwaiger, Konrad. Role of Interest Groups in the European Community. 1979. text ed. 34.25x (ISBN 0-566-00257-4). Gower Pub Ltd.

Kirchner, H. Immunobiology of Infection With Herpes Simplex Virus. (Monographs in Virology: Vol. 13). viii, 104p. 1982. 39.00 (ISBN 3-8055-3517-1). S Karger.

Kirchner, H., jt. auth. see Resch, K.

Kirchner, Justus G. Techniques of Chemistry: Thin Layer Chromatography. 2nd ed. LC 78-9163. (Techniques of Chemistry Ser.: Vol. 14). 1137p. 1978. 121.95x (ISBN 0-471-93264-7, Pub. by Wiley-Interscience). Wiley.

Kirchner, Peter T., ed. Nuclear Medicine Review Syllabus. LC 79-92990. (Illus.). 630p. 1980. pap. text ed. 30.00 (ISBN 0-932004-04-0). Soc Nuclear Med.

Kirchner, Sandra G., et al. Emergency Radiology of the Shoulder, Arm & Hand. LC 81-52309. (Illus.). 153p. 1981. pap. text ed. 19.95 (ISBN 0-7216-5457-6). Saunders.

Kirchner, Walther. History of Russia. rev. 6th ed. LC 72-5830. (Illus.). 403p. 1976. pap. 5.95 (ISBN 0-06-460169-2, 169, COS). B&N NY.

--Western Civilization Since Fifteen Hundred. 2nd ed. (gr. 9-12). 1975. pap. 5.50 (ISBN 0-06-460111-0, CO 111, COS). B&N NY.

--Western Civilization to Fifteen Hundred. (gr. 9-12). 1960. pap. 5.25 (ISBN 0-06-460110-2, CO 110, COS). B&N NY.

Kirchow, Evelyn, jt. auth. see Van D'Elden, Karl H.

Kirgis, Frederic L. Prior Consultation in International Law. LC 82-17354. (Procedural Aspects of International Law Ser.: Vol. 16). 736p. 1983. write for info. (ISBN 0-8139-0971-6). U Pr of Va.

Kirichenko, E. Moscow: Architectural Monuments of the 1830's -1910's. Meerovich, B., tr. (Illus.). 377p. 1980. 30.00 (ISBN 0-89893-039-1). CDP.

Kirk, Cooper. William Lauderdale, General Andrew Jackson's Warrior. (Illus.). 300p. 1982. 14.95 (ISBN 0-686-84231-6). Banyan Bks.

Kirk, D. Optimal Control Theory: An Introduction. 1970. ref. ed. 34.00 (ISBN 0-13-638098-0). P-H.

Kirk, Dan, illus. The Dukes of Hazzard Punch-Out Fun. (Punch-Out Bks.). (Illus.). 32p. (gr. 2). Date not set. pap. 3.95 (ISBN 0-394-85506-X). Random.

Kirk, David L. Biology Today. 3rd ed. 1036p. 1980. text ed. 28.00 (ISBN 0-394-32096-4); wkbk. 6.95 (ISBN 0-394-32452-8). Random.

Kirk, Elizabeth D., jt. ed. see Carruthers, Mary J.

Kirk, Francis G. Total System Development for Information Systems. LC 73-4359. (Business Data Processing: A Wiley Ser.). 284p. 1973. 39.95x (ISBN 0-471-48260-9, Pub. by Wiley-Interscience). Wiley.

Kirk, G. S. The Bacchae of Euripides. LC 78-31827. 1979. 21.95 (ISBN 0-521-22675-9); pap. 6.50 (ISBN 0-521-29613-7). Cambridge U Pr.

--Homer & the Oral Tradition. LC 76-7806. 1977. 29.95 (ISBN 0-521-21309-6). Cambridge U Pr.

--Myth: Its Meaning & Functions in Ancient & Other Cultures. LC 72-628267. (Sather Classical Lectures: No. 40). 1970. 27.50x (ISBN 0-520-01651-3); pap. 7.95x (ISBN 0-520-02389-7). U of Cal Pr.

--The Nature of Greek Myths. LC 74-21683. 336p. 1975. 18.95 (ISBN 0-87951-031-5). Overlook Pr.

Kirk, G. S., ed. see Heraclitus.

Kirk, Geoffrey S. Homer & the Epic. abr. ed. Orig. Title: Songs of Homer, Il. pap. 9.95 (ISBN 0-521-09356-2). Cambridge U Pr.

--Songs of Homer. 1962. 59.50 (ISBN 0-521-05890-2). Cambridge U Pr.

Kirk, Geoffrey S. & Raven, John E. Presocratic Philosophers. 1957. 49.50 (ISBN 0-521-05891-0); pap. 11.95 (ISBN 0-521-09169-1). Cambridge U Pr.

Kirk, Grayson L. Philippine Independence: Motives, Problems & Prospects. LC 72-2377. (FDR & the Era of the New Deal Ser.). 278p. 1974. Repr. of 1936 ed. lib. bdg. 37.50 (ISBN 0-306-70486-2). Da Capo.

Kirk, Irina. Anton Chekhov. (World Authors Ser.). 1981. 12.95 (ISBN 0-8057-6410-0, Twayne). G K Hall.

Kirk, J. Andrew. Liberation Theology: An Evangelical View from the Third World. LC 79-5212. (New Foundations Theological Library). 246p. (Peter toon & Ralph Martin series editor). 1980. 12.95 (ISBN 0-8042-3704-2). John Knox.

Kirk, J. T. & Tilney-Basset, R. A. The Plastids: Their Chemistry, Structure, Growth & Inheritance. 1979. 178.75 (ISBN 0-444-80022-0, Biomedical Pr). Elsevier.

Kirk, John F. Supplement to Allibone's Critical Dictionary of English Literature & British & American Authors, 2 Vols. LC 67-296. 1965. Repr. of 1891 ed. 112.00x (ISBN 0-8103-3018-0). Gale.

Kirk, John M. Jose Marti: Mentor of the Cuban Nation. LC 82-15920. 1983. 17.95 (ISBN 0-8130-0736-4). U Presses Fla.

Kirk, John T. American Furniture & British Tradition to Eighteen Thirty. LC 82-15201. 1983. 45.00 (ISBN 0-394-40038-0). Knopf.

--The Impecunious Collector's Guide to American Antiques. 1975. pap. 10.95 (ISBN 0-394-73096-8). Knopf.

Kirk, Larry R. & Kirk, Phylys E. Congress-The Drum Corps Science Fiction. LC 82-70928. (In Congress & Prelude to Congress Ser.: No. 1). (Illus.). 332p. (Orig.). 1982. pap. 8.00 (ISBN 0-9608212-0-1). Ebaesy.

Kirk, Michael. Cargo Risk. LC 80-1123. (Crime Club Ser.). 1980. 10.95 o.p. (ISBN 0-385-17272-9). Doubleday.

Kirk, Nancy, jt. auth. see Conway, Madeleine.

Kirk, Nancye J., ed. Alternatives to Master Metering in Multifamily Housing. LC 80-84530. 133p. 1981. pap. 10.95 (ISBN 0-912104-50-3). Inst Real Estate.

--Forms for Apartment Management. LC 78-61861. 155p. 1978. 35.00 (ISBN 0-912104-30-9). Inst Real Estate.

Kirk, Nancye J., ed. see Berkeley Planning Associates Inc. & Energyworks Inc.

Kirk, Nancye J., ed. see Downs, James, Jr.

Kirk, Nancye J., ed. see Institute of Real Estate Management.

Kirk, Nancye J., ed. see Institute of Real Estate Management Staff.

Kirk, Nancye J., ed. see Kelley, Edward N.

Kirk, Nancye J., ed. see U. S. Dept. of Energy & Institute of Real Estate Management.

Kirk, Nancye J., ed. see Walters, William, Jr.

Kirk, Norman A. Panda Zoo. 96p. 1983. 20.00 (ISBN 0-686-38727-9); pap. 10.00 (ISBN 0-911155-00-7). Bitterroot-West.

Kirk, P. L. Fire Investigation: Including Fire-Related Phenomena: Arson, Explosion, Asphyxiation. LC 69-19240. 255p. 1969. 23.95x (ISBN 0-471-48860-7). Wiley.

Kirk, P. W. Morphogenesis & Microscopic Cytochemistry of Marine Pyrenomycete Ascospores. (Illus.). 1966. pap. 16.00 (ISBN 3-7682-5422-4). Lubrecht & Cramer.

Kirk, Paul L., et al. Crime Investigation. 2nd ed. LC 73-19854. 508p. 1974. text ed. 29.95x (ISBN 0-471-48247-1). Wiley.

Kirk, Philip. Dead Fall. (Butler Ser.: No. 8). 240p. (Orig.). 1983. pap. 2.50 o.s.i. (ISBN 0-8439-1103-4, Leisure Bks). Dorchester Pub Co.

--The Killer Virus. (Butler Ser.: No. 9). 240p. (Orig.). 1983. pap. 2.50 (ISBN 0-8439-1130-1, Leisure Bks). Dorchester Pub Co.

--Laser Shuttle. (Butler Ser.: No. 7). 240p. (Orig.). 1982. pap. 2.50 (ISBN 0-8439-1076-3, Leisure Bks). Dorchester Pub Co.

--The Paris Kill. (Butler Ser.: No. 10). 240p. 1983. pap. 2.50 o.s.i. (ISBN 0-8439-1087-9, Leisure Bks). Dorchester Pub Co.

Kirk, Phylys E., jt. auth. see Kirk, Larry R.

Kirk, Robert H. & Ellison, Jack S. First Aid & Emergency Care: Guide to Understanding & Action. 2nd ed. 240p. 1980. pap. text ed. 9.95 (ISBN 0-8403-2189-9). Kendall-Hunt.

Kirk, Robert H. & Wallace, Bill C. Human Sexuality: Selected Readings & Workbook, Revised Printing. 1979. pap. text ed. 10.95 (ISBN 0-8403-1991-6). Kendall-Hunt.

Kirk, Robert W. First Aid for Pets: The Pet Owner's Complete Guide to Emergency Care of Dogs, Cats & Other Small Animals. 1978. 10.95 (ISBN 0-87690-265-4); pap. 8.95 (ISBN 0-87690-275-1, 0869-260). Dutton.

Kirk, Robert W. & Bistner, Stephen I. Handbook of Veterinary Procedures & Emergency Treatment. 2nd ed. LC 74-4574. (Illus.). 515p. 1975. pap. 20.00 o.p. (ISBN 0-7216-5473-8). Saunders.

--Handbook of Veterinary Procedures & Emergency Treatment. 3rd ed. (Illus.). 928p. 1981. text ed. 29.00 (ISBN 0-7216-5475-4). Saunders.

Kirk, Robert W., jt. auth. see Muller, George H.

Kirk, Robert W., ed. Current Veterinary Therapy VI: Small Animal Practice. LC 64-10489. (Illus.). 1977. text ed. 37.50 o.p. (ISBN 0-7216-5470-3). Saunders.

--Current Veterinary Therapy VII: Small Animal Practice. LC 64-10489. (Illus.). 1360p. 1980. text ed. 53.00 (ISBN 0-7216-5471-1). Saunders.

Kirk, Roger E. Experimental Design. 2nd ed. (Statistics Ser.). (Illus.). 850p. 1982. text ed. 39.95 (ISBN 0-8185-0286-X). Brooks-Cole.

Kirk, Russell. Academic Freedom: An Essay in Definition. LC 77-3073. 1977. Repr. of 1955 ed. lib. bdg. 18.50x (ISBN 0-8371-9566-7, KIAF). Greenwood.

--Eliot & His Age: T. S. Eliot's Moral Imagination in the Twentieth Century. 490p. 1983. pap. 9.95 (ISBN 0-89385-020-9). Sugden.

--Enemies of the Permanent Things: Observations of Abnormity in Literature & Politics. 316p. pap. 8.95 (ISBN 0-89385-021-7). Sugden.

Kirk, Russell, ed. The Portable Conservative Reader. 1982. pap. 6.95 (ISBN 0-14-015095-1). Penguin.

Kirk, Ruth. Badlands. 1976. pap. 2.15 o.s.i. (ISBN 0-685-88171-7). Badlands Natl Hist.

--Exploring Death Valley. rev. ed. LC 76-48022. (Illus.). 1981. pap. 4.95 (ISBN 0-8047-0943-2). Stanford U Pr.

--Exploring the Olympic Peninsula. 3rd rev. ed. LC 80-51073. (Illus.). 128p. 1980. 8.95 (ISBN 0-295-95750-6). U of Wash Pr.

--Snow. LC 77-14997. (Illus.). 1980. pap. 5.95 (ISBN 0-688-08268-8). Quill NY.

--Washington State: National Parks, Historic Sites, Recreation Areas, & Natural Landmarks. LC 74-6020. (Illus.). 64p. 1974. pap. 3.95 (ISBN 0-295-95323-3). U of Wash Pr.

Kirk, Ruth & Daugherty, Richard D. Hunters of the Whale, an Adventure in Northwest Coast Archaeology. LC 73-17317. (Illus.). 160p. (gr. 5-9). 1974. 9.95 (ISBN 0-688-30109-6); PLB 9.55 (ISBN 0-688-20109-1). Morrow.

Kirk, Samuel A. & Gallagher, James J. Educating Exceptional Children. 3rd ed. LC 78-69609. (Illus.). 1979. text ed. 22.95 (ISBN 0-395-26526-6); instr's. manual 2.00 (ISBN 0-395-26529-0); test item suppl. 1.00 (ISBN 0-395-28699-9); study guide 7.95 (ISBN 0-395-28690-5). HM.

--Educating Exceptional Children. 4th ed. 560p. 1983. text ed. 22.95 (ISBN 0-395-32772-5); write for info. instr's. manual (ISBN 0-395-32774-1); study guide 8.95 (ISBN 0-395-32773-3). HM.

Kirk, Samuel A. & McCarthy, Jeanne M. Learning Disabilies: Selected ACLD Papers. LC 74-20857. 1975. 20.95 (ISBN 0-395-20200-0). HM.

Kirk, Samuel A., et al. Teaching Reading to Slow & Disabled Learners. LC 77-77655. (Illus.). 1978. text ed. 22.95 (ISBN 0-395-25821-9). HM.

Kirk, Stephen J., jt. auth. see Dell'Isola, Alphonse.

Kirk, Sylvia Van see Van Kirk, Sylvia.

Kirk, Tim, ed. Ghosts & Goblins. LC 81-84019. (Platt & Munk Deluxe Illustrated Bks.). (Illus.). 48p. (gr. 1-3). 1982. 6.95 (ISBN 0-448-49599-6, G&D). Putnam Pub Group.

Kirk, Ursula, ed. Neuropsychology of Language, Reading & Spelling. (Educational Psychology Ser.). 293p. 1982. 29.00 (ISBN 0-12-409680-8). Acad Pr.

Kirk, W. Richard. Aim for a Job in Hospital Work. LC 74-114137. (Career Guidance Ser.). 124p. 1971. pap. 4.50 (ISBN 0-668-02230-2). Arco.

Kirkari, Abu B., tr. see Nabi, Malik B.

Kirkbright, G. F., ed. Eighth International Conference on Atomic Spectroscopy. 284p. 1980. 61.95x (ISBN 0-471-25836-9). Wiley.

Kirkby, D. One Hundred Questions in Auditing with Suggested Answers for Accountancy Examinees. 1968. o.s.i. (ISBN 0-08-012901-3); pap. 7.75 o.p. (ISBN 0-08-012900-5). Pergamon.

Kirkby, M. J., jt. auth. see Carson, M. A.

Kirkby, M. J., ed. Hillslope Hydrology. LC 77-2669. (Landscape Systems-A Series in Geomorphology). 389p. 1978. 84.95x (ISBN 0-471-99510-X, Pub. by Wiley-Interscience). Wiley.

Kirkeby, Ed. Ain't Misbehavin: The Story of Fats Waller. LC 75-14123. (Roots of Jazz Ser). 248p. 1975. lib. bdg. 25.00 (ISBN 0-306-70683-0); pap. 6.95 (ISBN 0-306-80015-2). Da Capo.

Kirkendall, Richard S. A Global Power: America since the Age of Roosevelt. 2nd ed. 358p. 1980. pap. text ed. 7.50 (ISBN 0-394-32145-6). Knopf.

--Social Scientists & Farm Politics in the Age of Roosevelt. 1982. pap. text ed. 12.95 (ISBN 0-8138-1681-5). Iowa St U Pr.

--United States, Nineteen Twenty-Nine to Nineteen Forty-Five: Years of Crisis & Change. (Modern America Ser.). (Illus.). 320p. 1974. text ed. 16.50 (ISBN 0-07-034806-5, C); pap. text ed. 15.95 (ISBN 0-07-034805-7). McGraw.

Kirkendall, Richard S., jt. auth. see Schutz, John A.

Kirk-Greene, A. H., ed. West Africa Portraits: A Biographical Dictionary of West African Personalities, 1947-1977. 1983. 35.00x (ISBN 0-7146-3112-4, F Cass Co). Biblio Dist.

Kirk-Greene, A. H. M. African Administrators in Action. rev. ed. 1983. 32.50x (ISBN 0-7146-3134-5, F Cass Co). Biblio Dist.

Kirk-Greene, Anthony H. Mutumin Kirkii: The Concept of the Good Man in Hausa. (Hans Wolff Memorial Lecture Ser.). (Orig.). 1974. pap. text ed. 3.00 (ISBN 0-941934-08-X). Ind U Afro-Amer Arts.

Kirkham, E. Bruce & Fink, John W. Indices to American Literary Annuals & Gift Books. LC 75-35636. 628p. 1975. 75.00 (ISBN 0-89235-001-6). Res Pubns Conn.

Kirkham, Margaret. Jane Austen, Feminism & Fiction. LC 82-13937. 208p. 1983. text ed. 22.50x (ISBN 0-389-20336-X). B&N Imports.

Kirkland, David, ed. see Martin, Ernest T.

Kirkland, Dianna K. I Have a Stepfamily but... (It's Not the End of the World Ser.). (Illus.). 40p. (Orig.). (ps-5). 1981. pap. 5.00 (ISBN 0-940370-05-0); counleling activity guide-stepfamilies 5.00 (ISBN 0-686-96649-X). Aid-U Pub.

Kirkland, Douglas W., ed. Marine Evaporites: Origin, Diagenesis & Geochemistry. Evans, Robert. LC 73-11151. (Benchmark Papers in Geology Ser.). 448p. 1973. text ed. 54.00 o.p. (ISBN 0-12-786850-X). Acad Pr.

Kirkland, Elithe H. Divine Average. 1979. pap. 2.25 o.p. (ISBN 0-380-41764-2, 41764). Avon.

Kirkland, Frazar. Cyclopaedia of Commerical & Business Ancedotes: Comprising Interesting Reminiscences & Facts, Remarkable Traits & Humors, & Notable Sayings, Dealings, Experiences & Witticisms of Merehants, Etc, 2 vols. LC 73-95777. (Illus.). 1969. Repr. of 1864 ed. 63.00x (ISBN 0-8103-3131-4). Gale.

Kirkland, J. J., jt. auth. see Snyder, L. R.

Kirkland, James W. & Dowell, Paul W. Fiction: The Narrative Art. 1977. pap. text ed. 13.95 (ISBN 0-13-314310-4). P-H.

Kirkland, John F. & Sebree, Mac. Dawn of the Diesel Age. 200p. 1983. price not set (ISBN 0-916374-52-1). Interurban.

Kirkley, George & Goodbody, John, eds. Manual of Weighttraining. Rev. ed. (Illus.). 187p. 1983. pap. text ed. 18.50x (ISBN 0-09-147821-9, SpS). Sportshelf.

Kirkman, John, jt. auth. see Turk, Christopher.

Kirkman, Kay & Stinnett, Roger. Joplin: A Pictorial History. Friedman, Donna R., ed. LC 80-20530. (Illus.). 192p. 1980. pap. 13.95 o.p. (ISBN 0-89865-070-4). Donning Co.

Kirkman, Patrick. Modern Credit Management: A Study of the Management of Trade Credit Under Inflationary Conditions. 1978. pap. text ed. 9.95x (ISBN 0-04-658226-6). Allen Unwin.

Kirkpatrick, A. F. The Book of Psalms. (Thornapple Commentaries Ser.). 964p. 1982. pap. 19.95 (ISBN 0-8010-5453-2). Baker Bk.

Kirkpatrick, Anita M. & Nakamura, Robert M. Alpha-Fetoprotein: Laboratory Procedures & Clinical Applications. LC 80-28890. (Illus.). 160p. 1981. 28.50x (ISBN 0-89352-130-2). Masson Pub.

Kirkpatrick, B. J., ed. A Catalogue of the Library of Sir Richard Burton. 1979. 97.00x (ISBN 0-686-98248-7, Pub. by Royal Anthro Ireland). State Mutual Bk.

Kirkpatrick, C. A., jt. auth. see Levin, R. I.

Kirkpatrick, C. A., jt. auth. see Levin, Richard I.

Kirkpatrick, Charles A. & Russ, Frederick A. Business. 2nd ed. LC 77-13460. 544p. 1978. pap. text ed. 16.95 (ISBN 0-574-19365-0, 13-2365); instr's guide avail. (ISBN 0-574-19366-9, 13-2366); study guide 7.95 (ISBN 0-574-19367-7, 13-2367); trans. mstrs. 30.00 (ISBN 0-686-60861-5, 13-2369); test booklet 6.50 (ISBN 0-574-19368-5, 13-2368); instructor's presentation notebook 49.95 (ISBN 0-686-52458-6, 13-2309). SRA.

Kirkpatrick, Charles A., jt. auth. see Levin, Richard I.

Kirkpatrick, Charles A., jt. auth. see Russ, Frederick A.

Kirkpatrick, D. L., ed. Twentieth-Century Children's Writers. LC 77-76661. 1978. 40.00 (ISBN 0-312-82413-0). St Martin.
Kirkpatrick, D. L., jt. ed. see Vinson, James.
Kirkpatrick, Daniel, jt. ed. see Vinson, James.
Kirkpatrick, Daniel, jt. ed. see Vinson, Jim.
Kirkpatrick, David L. A Practical Guide for Supervisory Training & Development. 2nd ed. (Illus.). 224p. 1983. text ed. 24.95 (ISBN 0-201-13435-7). A-W.
Kirkpatrick, Diane, ed. see Boker, Carlos.
Kirkpatrick, Diane, ed. see Gabriel, Teshome H.
Kirkpatrick, Diane, ed. see Lellis, George.
Kirkpatrick, Diane, ed. see Schatz, Thomas G.
Kirkpatrick, J. S. The Magic of Structure. 248p. 1981. binder 17.00 (ISBN 0-934586-06-3). Plan Parent.
Kirkpatrick, Jeane. Leader & Vanguard: A Study of Peronist Argentina. 1971. 25.00x (ISBN 0-262-11041-5). MIT Pr.
--The New Presidential Elite: Men & Women in National Politics. LC 76-1816. 606p. 1976. 13.95x (ISBN 0-87154-475-X). Russell Sage.
Kirkpatrick, Jeane J. Dictatorships & Double Standards: Rationalism & Reason in Politics. 1982. 14.50 (ISBN 0-671-43836-0). S&S.
Kirkpatrick, Joanne. Mathematics for Water & Wastewater Treatment Plant Operators, 2 vols. Incl. Bk. 1. Fundamentals. 24.50 (ISBN 0-250-40043-X); Bk. 2. Advances. 24.50 (ISBN 0-250-40047-2). LC 73-87788. 1973. 33.00 (ISBN 0-250-40095-2). Ann Arbor Science.
Kirkpatrick, John E., ed. see Ives, Charles E.
Kirkpatrick, Larry, jt. auth. see Wheeler, Gerald.
Kirkpatrick, R. Dante's Paradiso & the Limitations of Modern Criticism. LC 77-80839. 1978. 37.50 (ISBN 0-521-21785-7). Cambridge U Pr.
Kirkpatrick, Rena K. Look at Flowers. LC 77-27433. (Look at Science Ser.). (Illus.). (gr. k-3). 1978. PLB 13.30 (ISBN 0-8393-0061-1). Raintree Pubs.
--Look at Insects. LC 77-27130. (Look at Science Ser.). (Illus.). (gr. k-3). 1978. PLB 13.30 (ISBN 0-8393-0062-X). Raintree Pubs.
--Look at Leaves. LC 77-26662. (Look at Science Ser.). (Illus.). (gr. k-3). 1978. PLB 13.30 (ISBN 0-8393-0060-3). Raintree Pubs.
--Look at Magnets. LC 77-26665. (Look at Science Ser.). (Illus.). (gr. k-3). 1978. PLB 13.30 (ISBN 0-8393-0063-8). Raintree Pubs.
--Look at Pond Life. LC 77-27243. (Look at Science Ser.). (Illus.). (gr. k-3). 1978. PLB 13.30 (ISBN 0-8393-0059-X). Raintree Pubs.
--Look at Rainbow Colors. LC 77-27593. (Look at Science Ser.). (Illus.). (gr. k-3). 1978. PLB 13.30 (ISBN 0-8393-0064-6). Raintree Pubs.
--Look at Seeds & Weeds. LC 77-27459. (Look at Science Ser.). (Illus.). (gr. k-3). 1978. PLB 13.30 (ISBN 0-8393-0065-4). Raintree Pubs.
--Look at Shore Life. LC 77-27589. (Look at Science Ser.). (Illus.). (gr. k-3). 1978. PLB 13.30 (ISBN 0-8393-0067-0). Raintree Pubs.
--Look at Trees. LC 77-27242. (Look at Science Ser.). (Illus.). (gr. k-3). 1978. PLB 13.30 (ISBN 0-8393-0066-2). Raintree Pubs.
--Look at Weather. LC 78-6815. (Look at Science Ser.). (Illus.). (gr. k-3). 1978. PLB 13.30 (ISBN 0-8393-0069-7). Raintree Pubs.
Kirkpatrick, Samuel A. Quantitative Analysis of Political Data. LC 73-8265. 1974. text ed. 18.95x (ISBN 0-675-08903-4). Merrill.
Kirkup, James, tr. see Dumitriu, Petru.
Kirkup, James see Ibsen, Henrik.
Kirkup, James, tr. see Kpomassie, Tete-Michel.
Kirkup, James, et al, trs. see Laye, Camara.
Kirkwood, jt. auth. see Shaw.
Kirkwood, G. M., ed. see Aristotle.
Kirkwood, Gordon M. Selections from Pindar: An Introduction & Commentary. LC 80-23801. 1982. 52.50 (ISBN 0-89130-430-4, 400307). Scholars Pr CA.
Kirkwood, James. Hit Me with a Rainbow. 1980. 9.95 o.s.i. (ISBN 0-440-03397-7). Delacorte.
--P. S. Your Cat Is Dead. 224p. 1973. pap. 3.50 (ISBN 0-446-30705-X). Warner Bks.
--Some Kind of Hero. 1976. pap. 2.75 (ISBN 0-451-11576-7, AE1576, Sig). NAL.
Kirkwood, John G. Theory of Solutions. Salsburg, Z. W. & Poirier, J., eds. (Documents on Modern Physics Ser.). 314p. (Orig.). 1968. 54.00x (ISBN 0-677-01030-3). Gordon.
Kirkwood, R. C., jt. auth. see Fletcher, W. W.
Kirkwood, Thomas & Finne, Geir. The Svalbard Passage. (Illus.). 307p. 1981. 13.95 o.p. (ISBN 0-02-563560-3). Macmillan.
Kirlin, Betty A., jt. auth. see Browne, J. A.
Kirlin, John J. The Political Economy of Fiscal Limits. LC 79-3180. 160p. 1982. 19.95x (ISBN 0-669-03390-1). Lexington Bks.
Kirman, B. H. Mental Retardation. 1968. 3.75 o.p. (ISBN 0-08-013371-1). Pergamon.
Kirmmse, Bruce, tr. see Nordentoft, Kresten.
Kirn, Arthur G. & Kirn, Marie O. Life Work Planning. 4th ed. (Illus.). 1978. 25.00 o.p. (ISBN 0-07-034838-3, C); pap. text ed. 18.95 o.p. (ISBN 0-07-034835-9); leader's guide 10.00 o.p. (ISBN 0-07-034839-1). McGraw.
Kirn, Elaine, ed. Regents Illustrated Classics Series. rev. ed. 1982. pap. text ed. 2.25 o.p. (ISBN 0-686-95094-1); 3.95 o.p. (ISBN 0-686-99463-9). Regents Pub.
Kirn, H. Elaine. All Spelled Out: Basic Spelling Patterns for Learners of English. (Illus.). 94p. (Orig.). (gr. 7 up). 1981. pap. text ed. 3.95 (ISBN 0-89285-153-8); tchrs. guide & answer key 2.00 (ISBN 0-87789-207-5); cassettes 16.95 (ISBN 0-87789-217-2). English Lang.
Kirn, Marie O., jt. auth. see Kirn, Arthur G.
Kirp, David L. Doing Good by Doing Little: Race & Schooling in Britain. LC 78-62824. 1979. 17.50x (ISBN 0-520-03740-5). U of Cal Pr.
Kirp, David L. & Yudof, Mark G. Educational Policy & the Law. LC 73-17609. 1974. 33.60 o.p. (ISBN 0-8211-1015-2); text ed. 30.45x o.p. (ISBN 0-685-42636-X). McCutchan.
Kirp, David L., et al. Educational Policy & the Law. 2nd ed. LC 81-81727. (Education Ser.). 900p. 1982. 32.75x (ISBN 0-8211-1019-5); text ed. 29.50x (ISBN 0-686-97400-X). McCutchan.
Kirrane, Diane E., ed. The School Personnel Management System: 1982. 2nd, Rev. ed. 500p. write for info (ISBN 0-88364-117-8). Natl Sch Boards.
Kirsch, A., jt. auth. see Peacock, J.
Kirsch, Debbie, jt. auth. see Menditto, Joseph.
Kirsch, Dietrich & Kirsch-Korn, Jutta. Make Your Own Rugs. 1970. 12.95 o.p. (ISBN 0-7134-2461-3, Pub. by Batsford England). David & Charles.
Kirsch, James. The Reluctant Prophet: An Exploration of Prophecy & Dreams. LC 72-96516. 214p. 1973. 7.50 (ISBN 0-8202-0156-1). Sherbourne.
Kirsch, Jonathan. Bad Moon Rising. (Orig.). 1978. pap. 1.75 o.p. (ISBN 0-451-07877-2, E7877, Sig). NAL.
Kirsch, Leonard J. Soviet Wages: Changes in Structure & Administration Since 1956. 256p. 1972. 20.00x (ISBN 0-262-11045-8). MIT Pr.
Kirsch, Leonard J., ed. see Raitsin, V. I.
Kirsch, Paul J. We Christians & Jews. 160p. pap. 3.95 (ISBN 0-686-95187-5). ADL.
Kirsch, Uri. Optimum Structural Design. (Illus.). 448p. 1981. text ed. 37.50 (ISBN 0-07-034844-8, C); solutions manual 14.95 (ISBN 0-07-034845-6). McGraw.
Kirschaum, R., tr. see Heim, U., et al.
Kirschen, Jerry. Huckelberry Finn. (Grow-up Books Ser.). (gr. 4-8). 1970. 1.95 o.p. (ISBN 0-448-02235-4, G&D). Putnam Pub Group.
Kirschenbaum, Howard & Stensrud, Rockwell. The Wedding Book: Alternative Ways to Celebrate Marriage. LC 73-17901. 1974. pap. 5.95 (ISBN 0-8164-2090-4). Seabury.
Kirschenbaum, Howard, et al. Wad-Ja-Get? 320p. (Orig.). 1971. pap. 6.95 o.s.i. (ISBN 0-89104-187-7, A & W Visual Library). A & W Pubs.
Kirschenbaum, Martin, jt. auth. see Luthman, Shirley.
Kirschenbaum, Michael, jt. auth. see Bricker, Neal S.
Kirschenbaum, Michael A. Practical Diagnosis: Renal Disease. (Illus.). 1978. kroydenflex 25.00 (ISBN 0-471-09485-4, Pub. by Wiley Med). Wiley.
Kirsch-Korn, Jutta, jt. auth. see Kirsch, Dietrich.
Kirschmann, John D., ed. Nutrition Almanac. rev. ed. (Illus.). 1979. pap. 12.95 (ISBN 0-07-034849-9, SP); pap. 8.95 (ISBN 0-07-034848-0). McGraw.
Kirschner, Allen & Kirschner, Linda, eds. Journalism: Readings in the Mass Media. LC 76-158976. 1971. pap. 8.75 (ISBN 0-672-73224-6). Odyssey Pr.
Kirschner, Don S. City & Country: Rural Responses to Urbanization in the 1920's. LC 78-95510. (Contributions in American History: No. 4). 1970. lib. bdg. 29.95 (ISBN 0-8371-2345-3, KIC/). Greenwood.
Kirschner, E. & Stone, K. Electronics Drafting Workbook. 3rd ed. (Illus.). 1977. pap. text ed. 17.95 (ISBN 0-07-034890-1, G); solutions manual 2.00 (ISBN 0-07-034891-X). McGraw.
Kirschner, H. E. & White, H. C. Are You What You Eat? 1960. 2.00x (ISBN 0-686-36335-3). Cancer Control Soc.
Kirschner, L. H., jt. auth. see Folsom, M. M.
Kirschner, Linda, jt. ed. see Kirschner, Allen.
Kirschner, M. J. Yoga All Your Life. Donat, Lilian K., tr. from Ger. LC 77-75286. (Illus.). 1979. pap. 4.95 (ISBN 0-8052-0638-8). Schocken.
Kirschner, Stephen M., jt. auth. see Pavelec, Barry J.
Kirshenblatt-Gimblett, Barbara, jt. auth. see Dobroszycki, Lucjan.
Kirshner, Alan M., jt. auth. see DeWitt, Howard A.
Kirshner, C. & Stone, K. Electronics Drafting Workbook. 2nd ed. 1973. 17.95 (ISBN 0-07-034868-5, G); solutions manual o.p. 2.00 (ISBN 0-07-034869-3). McGraw.
Kirshner, Joseph M. Fluid Amplifiers. 1966. 43.95 (ISBN 0-07-034861-8, P&RB). McGraw.
Kirsner, Gary. The Mettlach Book: Illustrated Catalog, Current Prices, & Collector's Information. Gruhl, Jim, ed. (Illus.). 263p. (Orig.). 1983. pap. 25.00 (ISBN 0-911403-18-3). Seven Hills Bks.
Kirsner, Joseph B., jt. auth. see Schachter, Howard.
Kirsner, R. S. The Problem of Presentative Sentences in Modern Dutch. (North Holland Linguistic Ser.: Vol. 43). 215p. 1979. 38.50 (ISBN 0-444-85404-5, North Holland). Elsevier.
Kirst, Hans H. The Affairs of the Generals. LC 78-12394. 1979. 9.95 o.p. (ISBN 0-698-10923-6, Coward). Putnam Pub Group.
--Everything Has Its Price. LC 75-37124. 288p. 1976. 8.95 o.p. (ISBN 0-698-10719-5, Coward). Putnam Pub Group.
--The Night of the Long Knives. LC 76-25006. 1976. 8.95 o.p. (ISBN 0-698-10760-8, Coward). Putnam Pub Group.
Kirst, Michael, jt. auth. see Wirt, Frederick.
Kirst, Michael W. Politics of Education at the Local, State & Federal Levels. LC 75-100956. 1971. 24.25 (ISBN 0-8211-1009-8); text ed. 22.00x (ISBN 0-685-14294-9). McCutchan.
Kirstein, Lincoln. The Classic Ballet. (Illus.). 1952. 17.50 (ISBN 0-394-40820-9). Knopf.
Kirszner, Laurie & Mandell, Stephen R. Basic College Writing. 2nd ed. 1981. pap. text ed. 9.95x (ISBN 0-393-95180-4); instrs'. guide avail. (ISBN 0-393-95184-7). Norton.
Kirtland, John C., ed. see Ritchie, F.
Kirtland, Suzanne. Easy Answers to Hard Questions. (Grosset Non-Fiction Ser.). (Illus.). 48p. (gr. k-3). 1976. pap. 2.95 (ISBN 0-448-12409-2, G&D). Putnam Pub Group.
Kirtley, Bacil. Motif-Index of Traditional Polynesian Narratives. (Orig.). 1971. pap. text ed. 10.00x (ISBN 0-87022-416-6). UH Pr.
Kirvan, John. Thy Kingdom Come. LC 77-14826. (Emmaus Book). 1978. pap. 1.95 o.p. (ISBN 0-8091-2077-1). Paulist Pr.
Kirvan, John J. Restless Believers. LC 66-29818. 120p. (Orig.). 1966. pap. 2.45 o.p. (ISBN 0-8091-1673-1, Deus). Paulist Pr.
Kirwan, David see Bates, Martin & Dudley-Evans, Tony.
Kirwin, Gerald J. & Grodzinsky, Stephen. Basic Circuit Analysis. LC 79-88449. (Illus.). 1980. text ed. 34.95 (ISBN 0-395-28488-0); solutions manual 1.00 (ISBN 0-395-28489-9). HM.
Kirzner, Israel M. Competition & Entrepreneurship. x, 246p. 1978. pap. 7.95 (ISBN 0-226-43776-0, P787, Phoen). U of Chicago Pr.
Kirzner, Israel M., ed. Method, Process, & Austrian Economics: Essays in Honor of Ludvig von Mises. LC 82-47573. 272p. 1982. 27.95x (ISBN 0-669-05545-X). Lexington Bks.
Kis, Nicholas. Haiman. 75.00 (ISBN 0-910760-12-8). John Howell Bks.
Kisdegi-Kirimi, Iren, intro. by. Still-Lifes in the Hungarian National Gallery. Halapy, Lily, tr. (Illus.). 102p. 1980. 15.95 (ISBN 0-89893-155-X). CDP.
Kiselev, A. V. & Lygin, V. I. Infrared Spectra of Surface Compounds. Slutzkin, D., ed. Kaner, N., tr. from Rus. LC 75-15866. 384p. 1975. 69.95x o.s.i. (ISBN 0-470-48905-7). Halsted Pr.
Kiser, George, jt. auth. see Elder, Ann.
Kish, C. B. Business English Thirty. 1980. text ed. 7.96 (ISBN 0-07-034842-1); tchr's manual & key avail. McGraw.
Kish, George. Bibliography of International Geographical Congresses, 1871-1976. 1979. lib. bdg. 35.00 (ISBN 0-8161-8226-4, Hall Reference). G K Hall.
--Economic Atlas of the Soviet Union. 2nd, rev. ed. (Illus.). 96p. 1971. 12.50 o.p. (ISBN 0-472-52534-4). U of Mich Pr.
Kish, Leslie. Survey Sampling. LC 65-19479. 643p. 1965. 33.95x (ISBN 0-471-48900-X). Wiley.
Kishel, Gregory F. & Kishel, Paricia G. Your Business is a Success: Now What? (Small Business Ser.). 224p. 1983. pap. text ed. 8.95. Wiley.
Kishel, Gregory F. & Kishel, Patricia G. One Hundred One Ways to Save Money. (Illus.). 24p. 1982. pap. 3.95 (ISBN 0-935346-01-5). K & K Enter.
Kishel, Paricia G., jt. auth. see Kishel, Gregory F.
Kishel, Patricia G., jt. auth. see Kishel, Gregory F.
Kishi, Asako, jt. auth. see Watanade, Tokuji.
Kishida, K. Mazeland. 100p. 1983. 9.95 (ISBN 0-13-566612-0); pap. 3.95 (ISBN 0-13-566604-X). P-H.
Kishlansky, Mark A. The Rise of the New Model Army. LC 79-4285. 1979. 27.95 (ISBN 0-521-22751-8). Cambridge U Pr.
--The Rise of the New Model Army. LC 79-4285. (Cambridge Paperback Library). 337p. Date not set. pap. 14.95 (ISBN 0-521-27377-3). Cambridge U Pr.
Kishtainy, Khalid. The Prostitute in Progressive Literature. 192p. 1983. 16.00 (ISBN 0-8052-8134-7, Pub. by Allison & Busby England). Schocken.
Kisker, George W. The Disorganized Personality. 3rd ed. 1977. text ed. 28.50 (ISBN 0-07-034878-2, C); instructor's manual 15.00 (ISBN 0-07-034879-0). McGraw.
Kisker, George W., ed. World Tension: The Psychopathology of International Relations. LC 69-10114. 1969. Repr. of 1951 ed. lib. bdg. 17.50x (ISBN 0-8371-0516-1, KIIR). Greenwood.
Kisling, Jeffrey A., jt. ed. see Schreiner, Richard L.
Kispert, Lowell D., jt. auth. see Kevan, Larry.
Kiss, George T. Diagnosis & Management of Pulmonary Disease. 1981. 26.95 (ISBN 0-201-10606-X, 10606, Med-Nurse). A-W.
Kissack, Keith. The River Severn. 160p. 1982. 35.00x (ISBN 0-86138-004-5, Pub. by Terence Dalton England). State Mutual Bk.
Kissam, P., jt. auth. see Ives, Howard C.
Kissam, Philip. Surveying for Civil Engineers. 2nd ed. 1981. 34.50 (ISBN 0-07-034882-0, C); solutions manual avail. (ISBN 0-07-034883-9). McGraw.
--Surveying: Instruments & Methods for Surveys of Limited Extent. 2nd ed. 1956. text ed. 30.50 (ISBN 0-07-034889-8, C); solutions manual free (ISBN 0-07-034887-1). McGraw.
--Surveying Practice. 2nd ed. 1971. 22.05 (ISBN 0-07-034893-6, G). McGraw.
--Surveying Practice. 3rd ed. (Illus.). 1977. text ed. 23.95 (ISBN 0-07-034901-0, G); solutions manual to odd-numbered problems 1.50 (ISBN 0-07-034902-9). McGraw.
Kissane, James D. Alfred Tennyson. (English Authors Ser.). lib. bdg. 11.95 (ISBN 0-8057-1544-4, Twayne). G K Hall.
Kissane, John M. & Smith, Margaret G. Pathology of Infancy & Childhood. 2nd ed. LC 74-10824. (Illus.). 1208p. 1975. 74.50 o.p. (ISBN 0-8016-2671-4). Mosby.
Kissane, John M., jt. auth. see Anderson, W. A. D.
Kissel, Irwin R. & Grun. How to Handle Claims & Returns: A Manual for Manufacturers & Retailers. (Illus.). 160p. 1973. 26.50 (ISBN 0-07-034897-9, P&RB). McGraw.
Kissel, P., et al. The Neurocristopathies. LC 79-84479. (Illus.). 1980. 66.50x (ISBN 0-89352-039-X). Masson Pub.
Kissel, Stanley. Private Practice for the Mental Health Clinician. 1983. write for info. (ISBN 0-89443-849-2). Aspen Systems.
Kisselbach, Theo. Leica CL. (Illus.). 1978. 15.00 (ISBN 3-77632-550-X, 4550). Hove Camera.
Kissell, Mary L. Basketry of the Papago & Pima Indians: Anthropological Papers of the American Museum of Natural History, Vol. 17, Pt. 4. LC 72-8827. (Beautiful Rio Grande Classics Ser). lib. bdg. 12.00 (ISBN 0-87380-095-8); pap. 8.00 (ISBN 0-87380-133-4). Rio Grande.
Kisselle & Mazzeo. Aerobic Dance: A Way to Fitness. (Illus.). 192p. 1983. pap. text ed. 7.95x (ISBN 0-89582-094-3). Morton Pub.
Kissemeyer-Nielsen, F., jt. ed. see Dick, H. M.
Kissen, M. From Group Dynamics to Group Psychoanalysis: The Therapeutic Application of Group Dynamics Understanding. LC 76-14844. (Series in Classical & Community Psychology). 362p. 1976. 21.95x o.s.i. (ISBN 0-470-15132-3). Halsted Pr.
Kissin, Benjamin, jt. ed. see Begleiter, Henry.
Kissin, Benjamin, jt. ed. see Begleiterr, Henry.
Kissin, Benjamin, et al, eds. Recent Developments in Chemotherapy of Narcotic Addiction, Vol. 311. (Annals of the New York Academy of Sciences). 1978. 42.00x (ISBN 0-89766-004-8); pap. 42.00x (ISBN 0-89072-067-3). NY Acad Sci.
Kissin, S. F. Farewell to Revolution: Marxist Philosophy & the Modern World. LC 78-18948. 1978. 20.00x (ISBN 0-312-28267-2). St Martin.
Kissinger, Henry A. The Troubled Partnership: A Re-appraisal of the Atlantic Alliance. LC 82-15533. xii, 266p. 1982. Repr. of 1965 ed. lib. bdg. 25.00x (ISBN 0-313-23219-9, KIPA). Greenwood.
Kissock, Craig. Curriculum Planning for Social Studies & Teaching Cultural Approach. LC 80-40960. 125p. 1981. 25.00 o.p. (ISBN 0-471-27868-8, Pub. by Wiley Interscience). Wiley.
Kister, Kenneth F. Kister's Atlas Buying Guide: A Consumer Guide to Major National, World & Thematic Atlases in Print. 200p. 1983. lib. bdg. write for info (ISBN 0-912700-62-9). Oryx Pr.
Kister, M. J., ed. Israel Oriental Studies, 8 vols. Incl. Vol. 1. 315p. 1971 (ISBN 0-87855-212-X); Vol. 2. 473p. 1972 (ISBN 0-87855-213-8); Vol. 3. 293p. 1973 (ISBN 0-87855-214-6); Vol. 4. 286p. 1974 (ISBN 0-87855-215-4); Vol. 5. 298p. 1975 (ISBN 0-87855-216-2); Vol. 6. 307p. 1976 (ISBN 0-87855-243-X); Vol. 7. 300p. 1977 (ISBN 0-87855-334-7); Vol. 8. 332p. 1981 (ISBN 0-87855-395-9). 39.95 ea.; Set. casebound 235.00 (ISBN 0-87855-220-0). Transaction Bks.
Kistler, Edgar P. Your Life on Planet Earth. 1982. 8.75 (ISBN 0-8062-1923-8). Carlton.
Kistler, Mark O. Drama of the Storm & Stress. (World Authors Ser.). 15.95 (ISBN 0-8057-2268-8, Twayne). G K Hall.
Kistler, Robert C., jt. auth. see Crider, Charles C.
Kistner, Robert W. & Patton, Grant W. Atlas of Infertility Surgery. (Illus.). 180p. 1975. 45.00 (ISBN 0-316-49670-7). Little.
Kita, M. Jane, ed. see Holmes, Neal J. & Leake, John B.
Kitagawa, Joseph M. Religions of the East. enl. ed. LC 60-7742. 1968. pap. 7.95 (ISBN 0-664-24837-3). Westminster.
Kitagawa, Joseph M., ed. see Wach, Joachim.
KitaGawa, Masao. Neo-Lineamenta Florae Manshuricae. or: Enumeration of the Spontaneous Vascular Plants of Manchuria. (Flora et Vegetatio Mundi Ser.: No. 4). 1979. lib. bdg. 80.00 (ISBN 3-7682-1113-4). Lubrecht & Cramer.
Kitahata, Luke M. Narcotic Analgesics in Anesthesiology. (Illus.). 208p. 1981. lib. bdg. 34.00 (ISBN 0-683-04619-5). Williams & Wilkins.
Kitamura, K. & Newton, T. H. Recent Advances in Diagnostic Neuroradiology. (Illus.). 1976. 55.00 o.p. (ISBN 0-8151-5905-6). Year Bk Med.
Kitano, Harry H. Race Relations. 2nd ed. (Ser. in Sociology). (Illus.). 1980. text ed. 22.95 (ISBN 0-13-750091-2). P-H.
Kitano, Harry H., jt. auth. see Daniels, Roger.
Kitay, William. Understanding Arthritis. (Illus., Orig.). 1977. pap. 2.95 o.p. (ISBN 0-671-18089-4). Monarch Pr.
Kitchen. Suppiluliuma & the Amarna Pharoahs. 72p. 1982. 50.00x (ISBN 0-85323-133-8, Pub. by Liverpool Univ England). State Mutual Bk.

--U. S. Interests in Africa in the Eighties. 128p. 1983. write for info. Praeger.

Kitchen, Andrew. BASIC by Design: Structured Computer Programming in BASIC. (Software Ser.). (Illus.). 528p. pap. text ed. 18.95 (ISBN 0-13-060269-8). P-H.

Kitchen, Helen, jt. auth. see Commission on Critical Choices.

Kitchen, Hermine B., jt. auth. see Fenton, Carroll L.

Kitchen, Kenneth A. Ancient Orient & Old Testament. LC 66-30697. 1966. 7.95 (ISBN 0-87784-907-2). Inter-Varsity.

Kitchen Ladies of America, jt. auth. see Pantry Press.

Kitchen, Paddy. The Way to Write Novels. 96p. 1982. 16.50 o.p. (ISBN 0-241-10648-6, Pub. by Hamish Hamilton England); pap. 10.50 (ISBN 0-241-10649-4). David & Charles.

Kitchens, Ben E. Tomatoes in the Treetops: Collected Tales of Harry Rhine. 73p. 1982. pap. 5.95 (ISBN 0-943054-39-7). Thornwood Bk.

Kitchens, James A. & Estrada, Leo. Individuals in Society: A Modern Introduction to Sociology. LC 73-88244. 1974. text ed. 10.95x o.p. (ISBN 0-675-08858-5); manual 3.95 (ISBN 0-675-08786-4); instr's. manual o.p. 3.95 (ISBN 0-686-66915-0). Merrill.

Kitchens, James A. & Muessig, Raymond H. The Study & Teaching of Sociology. 2nd ed. (Social Science Seminar, Secondary Education Ser.: No. C28). 104p. 1980. pap. text ed. 7.95 (ISBN 0-675-08194-7). Merrill.

Kitchenside, G. M. Isle of Wight Album. 18.50x (ISBN 0-392-07969-0, SpS). Sportshelf.

Kitcher, Phillip. The Nature of Mathematical Knowledge. 273p. 1983. 18.95 (ISBN 0-19-503149-0). Oxford U Pr.

Kitchin, Frances. Granny's Cookery Book. LC 78-66798. (Illus.). 1978. 8.95 o.p. (ISBN 0-7153-7721-3). David & Charles.

Kitching, C. J., ed. London & Middlessex Chantry Certificate, 1548. 1980. 50.00x (ISBN 0-686-96605-8, Pub by London Rec Soc England). State Mutual Bk.

Kitching, Frances & Dowell, Susan S. Mrs. Kitching's Smith Island Cookbook. (Illus.). 127p. 1981. 9.50 (ISBN 0-686-36733-2). Md Hist.

Kitching, Gavin. Class & Economic Change in Kenya: The Making of an African Petite Bourgeoisie, 1905-1970. LC 79-21804. 448p. 1980. text ed. 45.00x (ISBN 0-300-02385-5, Y-444); pap. text ed. 14.95x (ISBN 0-300-02929-2). Yale U Pr.

--Development & Underdevelopment in Historical Perspective. 1982. 19.95x (ISBN 0-416-73130-9); pap. 8.95x (ISBN 0-416-73140-6). Methuen Inc.

Kitsao, jt. ed. see Zani.

Kitson, Charles H. The Art of Counterpoint. LC 75-4973. (Music Reprint Ser.). 344p. 1975. Repr. of 1924 ed. lib. bdg. 35.00 (ISBN 0-306-70668-7). Da Capo.

--The Elements of Fugal Construction. LC 81-6409. (Illus.). 76p. 1981. Repr. of 1929 ed. lib. bdg. 20.75x (ISBN 0-313-23099-4, KIEF). Greenwood.

Kitson, Michael. Rembrandt. (Phaidon Color Library). (Illus.). 84p. 1983. 27.50 (ISBN 0-7148-2228-0, Pub. by Salem Hse Ltd); pap. 18.95 (ISBN 0-7148-2241-8). Merrimack Bk Serv.

Kitsuse, John L., jt. auth. see Broom, Leonard.

Kittel, Charles. Elementary Statistical Physics. LC 58-12495. (Illus.). 228p. 1958. 26.95x (ISBN 0-471-49005-9). Wiley.

--Introduction to Solid State Physics. 5th ed. LC 75-25936. 599p. 1976. text ed. 34.95x (ISBN 0-471-49024-5); tchr's manual 4.00 (ISBN 0-471-01407-9). Wiley.

--Quantum Theory of Solids. LC 63-20633. 435p. 1963. 33.95x (ISBN 0-471-49025-3). Wiley.

Kittel, Gerhard & Friedrich, Gerhard, eds. Theological Dictionary of the New Testament, 10 vols. Incl. Vol. 1. 1964. 27.50 (ISBN 0-8028-2243-6); Vol. 2. 1965. 27.50 (ISBN 0-8028-2244-4); Vol. 3. 1966. 29.95 (ISBN 0-8028-2245-2); Vol. 4. 1967. 27.50 (ISBN 0-8028-2246-0); Vol. 5. 1968. 29.95 (ISBN 0-8028-2247-9); Vol. 6. 1969. 27.50 (ISBN 0-8028-2248-7); Vol. 7. 1970. 29.95 (ISBN 0-8028-2249-5); Vol. 8. 1972. 25.00 (ISBN 0-8028-2250-9); Vol. 9. 1973. 27.50 (ISBN 0-8028-2322-X); Vol. 10. 1976. 25.00 (ISBN 0-8028-2323-8). 279.80 set (ISBN 0-8028-2324-6). Eerdmans.

Kittel, Johann C. Der Angehende Praktische Organist, Oder Anweisung Zum Zweckmassigen Gebrauch der Orgel Bei Gottesverehrungen in Beispielen: Erfurt 1801-1831. (Bibliotheca Organologica: Vol. 72). 75.00 o.s.i. (ISBN 90-6027-278-1, Pub. by Frits Knuf Netherlands). Pendragon NY.

Kittel, Joseph P. Understanding DC & AC Circuits Through Analogies. LC 79-65896. (Illus.). viii, 416p. (Orig.). 1983. pap. text ed. 14.95 (ISBN 0-9603198-0-8). B Royal Pr.

Kittel, Muriel, tr. see Cipolla, Carlo M.

Kittick, J. A. Acid Sulfate Weathering. 1982. 12.50 (ISBN 0-89118-770-7). Soil Sci Soc Am.

Kitto, H. D., tr. see Sophocles.

Kitton, F. G., jt. auth. see Dickens, Charles.

Kittredge, George L., ed. Hamlet. 1966. pap. text ed. 6.95x (ISBN 0-673-15702-4). Scott F.

--Henry IV, Part I. 1966. pap. text ed. 6.95x (ISBN 0-673-15703-2). Scott F.

--Henry IV, Part II. 1966. pap. text ed. 6.95x (ISBN 0-673-15704-0). Scott F.

--Romeo & Juliet. 1966. pap. text ed. 6.95x (ISBN 0-673-15717-2). Scott F.

--The Tempest. 1966. pap. text ed. 6.95x (ISBN 0-673-15720-2). Scott F.

--Twelfth Night. 1966. pap. text ed. 5.95x o.p. (ISBN 0-673-15721-0). Scott F.

Kittredge, George L. & Riberner, Irving, eds. Merchant of Venice: William Shakespeare. 1966. pap. text ed. 6.95x (ISBN 0-673-15712-1). Scott F.

Kittredge, George L. & Ribner, Irving, eds. Macbeth: William Shakespeare. rev. ed. 1966. pap. 6.95x (ISBN 0-471-00521-5). Scott F.

--A Midsummer Night's Dream: William Shakespeare. rev. ed. 1966. pap. text ed. 6.95x (ISBN 0-673-15713-X). Scott F.

--Othello: William Shakespeare. 1966. pap. text ed. 6.95x (ISBN 0-673-15714-8). Scott F.

--Richard II: William Shakespeare. 1966. pap. text ed. 6.95x (ISBN 0-673-15715-6). Scott F.

Kittredge, George L., ed. see Shakespeare, William.

Kittrie, Nicholas N. & Susman, Jackwell, eds. Legality, Morality, & Ethics in Criminal Justice. (Praeger Special Studies). 1979. 29.95 o.p. (ISBN 0-03-047521-X). Praeger.

Kitts, Kent D., jt. auth. see Eliason, Alan.

Kitzing, Donald R. Credit & Collections for Small Business: An Easy-to-Read Guide to Effective Collections. (Illus.). 174p. 1981. 17.95 (ISBN 0-07-034915-0). McGraw.

Kitzinger, Sheila. Birth at Home. (Illus.). 1979. 16.95x (ISBN 0-19-261160-7). Oxford U Pr.

--The Birth Diary. (Illus.). 160p. (Orig.). 1981. pap. 7.95 (ISBN 0-448-12248-0, G&D). Putnam Pub Group.

--Women As Mothers. LC 79-4853. 1979. 8.95 o.p. (ISBN 0-394-50651-0); pap. 2.95 (ISBN 0-394-74079-3). Random.

Kitzinger, Sheila & Davis, John A., eds. The Place of Birth. (Illus.). 1978. text ed. 32.50x (ISBN 0-19-261125-9); pap. text ed. 17.95x (ISBN 0-19-261238-7). Oxford U Pr.

Kitzinger, Uwe, jt. auth. see Butler, David.

Kitzinger, Uwe W. The Politics & Economics of European Integration. LC 75-25491. (Illus.). 246p. 1976. Repr. of 1963 ed. lib. bdg. 15.50x (ISBN 0-8371-8418-5, KIEI). Greenwood.

Kitzmiller. Cytogenetics & Genetics of Vectors. Date not set. 64.25 (ISBN 0-444-80382-3). Elsevier.

Kitzmillev, James B. Thomas Say Foundation Publications, Vol. 8: Anopheline Names - Their Derivations & Histories. 26.50 (ISBN 0-938522-17-5). Entomol Soc.

Kiver & Kaufman. Television Electronics: Theory & Servicing. 8th ed. 768p. 1983. text ed. 27.00 (ISBN 0-8273-1328-4). Delmar.

Kiver, M. S., jt. auth. see Grob, Bernard.

Kiver, Milton S. Transistor & Integrated Electronics. 4th ed. 1972. 24.95 (ISBN 0-07-034942-8, G). McGraw.

Kivnick, Helen Q. The Meaning of Grandparenthood. Nathan, Peter, ed. LC 82-17567. (Studies in Clinical Psychology: No. 3). 252p. 1982. 39.95 (ISBN 0-8357-1383-0). Univ Microfilms.

Kiwanuka, S. History of Buganda from the Foundation of the Kingdom to 1900. LC 75-180672. 336p. 1972. text ed. 37.50x (ISBN 0-8419-0114-7, Africana). Holmes & Meier.

Kiyosaki, Wayne S. North Korea's Foreign Relations: The Politics of Accomodation, 1945-75. LC 76-19548. (Special Studies). 1976. 28.95 o.p. (ISBN 0-275-23490-8). Praeger.

Kiyose, Gisaburo N., jt. auth. see Uehara, Toyoaki.

Kiyota, Minoru. Gedatsukai: Its Theory & Practice a Study of a Shinto-Buddhist Syncretic School in Contemporary Japan. LC 82-9433. (Illus.). 1982. 12.95 (ISBN 0-914910-75-2). Buddhist Bks.

--Mahayana Buddhist Meditation: Theory & Practice. 1978. text ed. 17.50x (ISBN 0-8248-0556-9). UH Pr.

Kizer, Carolyn. Knock Upon Silence. LC 65-19901. 1965. 2.95 (ISBN 0-385-04580-8). Doubleday.

Ki-Zerbo, J., ed. African Traditional Medicine & Pharmacopia. (Traditional Healing Ser.). 750p. 1983. 100.00 (ISBN 0-932426-22-0). Trado-Medic.

Kjekshus, Helge. Ecology Control & Economic Developement in East African History: The Case of Tanganyika 1850-1950. LC 76-50250. 1977. 27.50x (ISBN 0-520-03384-1). U of Cal Pr.

Kjeldsberg, P. A. Musikinstrumenter Ved Ringve Museum: The Collection of Musical Instruments of the Ringve Museum. 1976. wrappers 17.50 o.s.i. (ISBN 90-6027-280-3, Pub. by Frits Knuf Netherlands). Pendragon NY.

Kjelgaard, Jim. Big Red. (Illus.). 254p. (gr. 7-9). 1956. 10.95 (ISBN 0-8234-0007-7). Holiday.

--Irish Red. (Illus.). 224p. (gr. 7 up). 1951. 10.95 (ISBN 0-8234-0060-3). Holiday.

--A Nose for Trouble. (Skylark Ser.). 208p. 1982. pap. 1.95 (ISBN 0-553-15124-X, Skylark). Bantam.

--Outlaw Red. 230p. (gr. 7 up). 1953. 10.95 (ISBN 0-8234-0084-0). Holiday.

Kjelgaard, Jim A. Explorations of Pere Marquette. (Landmark Ser.: No. 17). (Illus.). (gr. 4-6). 1951. PLB 5.99 o.s.i. (ISBN 0-394-90317-X). Random.

Kjellerup, Hope R. The Adventures of Emperor Jones, an Independent Cat. 1982. 5.95 (ISBN 0-533-05451-6). Vantage.

Kjellgreen, Shily, tr. see BOyer, Orlando.

Kjellgreen, Shily, tr. see Boyer, Orlando.

Kjellgreen, Shily, tr. see Gossett, Don.

Kjellgreen, Shily, tr. see Hutchison, Becky & Farish, Kay.

Kjellgreen, Shily, tr. see Raburn, Terry.

Kjellstrand, C. M., ed. The Belding H. Scribner Festschrift. (Journal: Nephron: Vol. 33, No. 2). (Illus.). 96p. 1983. pap. write for info. (ISBN 3-8055-3675-5). S Karger.

Kjelson & Tait, Malcom. Comprehensive Musicianship Through Choral Performance: Zone 4, Bk. A. (University of Hawaii Music Project Ser.). (gr. 7-9). 1976. pap. text ed. 10.92 o.p. (ISBN 0-201-00819-X, Sch Div). A-W.

Kjerfve, Bjorn, ed. Estuarine Transport Processes. LC 78-2741. xx, 332p. 1978. lib. bdg. 34.95x o.s.i. (ISBN 0-87249-371-7). U of SC Pr.

Klaas, Joe. The Twelve Steps to Happiness. 4.95 (ISBN 0-89486-156-5). Hazelden.

Klaassen, W. T., et al, eds. The Dynamics of Urban Development. 1981. 30.00x (ISBN 0-312-22373-0). St Martin.

Klaeber, F., ed. Beowulf & the Fight at Finnsburg. 3rd ed. 1936. pap. 20.95 (ISBN 0-669-21212-1). Heath.

Klafs, Carl E. & Arnheim, Daniel D. Modern Principles of Athletic Training: The Science of Sports Injury Prevention. 5th ed. LC 80-39524. (Illus.). 576p. 1981. text ed. 23.95 (ISBN 0-8016-2682-X). Mosby.

Klafs, Carl E., jt. auth. see Arnheim, Daniel D.

Klahr, D. & Wallace, J. G. Cognitive Developments: An Information-Processing View. LC 76-13901. 244p. 1976. 12.95x o.p. (ISBN 0-470-15128-5). Halsted Pr.

Klahr, Saulo, ed. The Kidney & Body Fluids in Health & Disease. 616p. 1982. 9.50x (ISBN 0-306-41062-1, Plenum Med Bk). Plenum Pub.

Klainer, Albert S., jt. auth. see Klainer, Jo-Ann.

Klainer, Jo-Ann & Klainer, Albert S. The Judas Gene. LC 79-18104. 1980. 11.95 o.p. (ISBN 0-399-90067-5, Marek). Putnam Pub Group.

Klambauer, G. Real Analysis. LC 72-93078. 416p. 1973. 25.00 (ISBN 0-444-00133-6, North Holland). Elsevier.

Klamkin, Charles, jt. auth. see Fetterman, Elsie.

Klamkin, Charles, jt. auth. see Klamkin, Marian.

Klamkin, Marian. The Carnival Glass Collector's Price Guide. LC 77-92365. (Illus., Orig.). 1978. pap. 5.95 (ISBN 0-8015-1094-5, 0578-150, Hawthorn). Dutton.

--The Collector's Guide to Carnival Glass. 224p. 1976. pap. 14.95 (ISBN 0-8015-1397-9, 01451-440, Hawthorn). Dutton.

--The Collector's Guide to Depression Glass. (Illus.). 288p. 1973. pap. 15.00 (ISBN 0-8015-1399-5, 01456-440, Hawthorn). Dutton.

Klamkin, Marian & Klamkin, Charles. Collectibles: A Compendium. LC 77-27677. (Illus.). 288p. 1981. 22.50 (ISBN 0-385-17715-1, Dolp); pap. 11.95 (ISBN 0-385-12176-8). Doubleday.

Klamkin, Mavian. Made in Occupied Japan: A Collector's Guide. (Illus.). 1976. pap. 6.95 o.p. (ISBN 0-517-52661-1). Crown.

Klammer, jt. auth. see Bell.

Klammer, Thomas, jt. auth. see Bell, Arthur.

Klaniaczay, Tibor. History of Hungarian Literature. 14.95 o.p. (ISBN 0-392-13237-0, SpS). Sportshelf.

Klapman, J. W. Group Psychotherapy. 2nd rev. ed. LC 58-11400. 312p. 1959. 33.50 o.p. (ISBN 0-8089-0233-4). Grune.

Klapp, O. E. Opening & Closing. LC 77-87382. (American Sociological Association Rose Monograph). (Illus.). 1978. 27.95 (ISBN 0-521-21923-X); pap. 8.95 (ISBN 0-521-29311-1). Cambridge U Pr.

Klapper, C. F. London's Lost Railways. (Illus.). 1976. 19.95 (ISBN 0-7100-8378-5). Routledge & Kegan.

Klapper, Jacob & Frankle, John T. Phase Lock & Frequency Feedback Systems: Principles & Techniques. (Electrical Science Ser.). 1972. 68.50 o.s.i. (ISBN 0-12-410850-4). Acad Pr.

Klapper, Marvin. Fabric Almanac. 2nd ed. LC 72-132144. (Illus.). 1971. 6.95 o.p. (ISBN 0-87005-092-3). Fairchild.

Klapthor, Margaret B. The First Ladies Hall. LC 73-8675. (Illus.). pap. 2.95 (ISBN 0-87474-133-5). Smithsonian.

Klare, G. R., jt. auth. see Games, Paul A.

Klarner, Walter E., et al. Writing by Design. LC 76-14652. (Illus.). 1977. pap. text ed. 13.50 (ISBN 0-395-24428-5); instr's. manual 1.00 (ISBN 0-395-24429-3). HM.

Klarwein, A. Mati. Milk 'n Honey. 1973. pap. 5.00 o.p. (ISBN 0-517-50453-7, C N Potter Bks). Crown.

Klarwein, Mati. God Jokes-the Art of Mati Klarwein. 1977. pap. 4.95 o.p. (ISBN 0-517-52647-6, Harmony). Crown.

--Inscapes: Real Estate Paintings by Mati Klarwein. 1983. pap. 8.95 (ISBN 0-517-54955-7, Harmony). Crown.

Klas, Rodger H., jt. auth. see Egan, M. David.

Klasne, William. Street Cops. LC 79-36745. 1980. 10.95 o.p. (ISBN 0-13-851568-9). P-H.

Klass, Dennis, jt. auth. see Gordon, Audrey.

Klass, Donald L. & Emert, George H., eds. Fuels from Biomass & Wastes. LC 81-68245. (Illus.). 592p. 1981. 39.95 (ISBN 0-250-40418-4). Ann Arbor Science.

Klass, Donald W. & Daly, David D., eds. Current Practice of Clinical Electroencephalography. LC 75-32088. 544p. 1979. text ed. 54.95 (ISBN 0-89004-088-5). Raven.

Klass, Lance J. & Lionni, Paolo. The Leipzig Connection: A Report on the Origins & Growth of Educational Psychology. 2nd ed. (Illus.). 1982. pap. write for info. o.p. (ISBN 0-89739-001-6). Heron Bks.

Klass, Michael W., ed. see Landis, Robin C.

Klass, Philip J. UFOs: The Public Deceived. 250p. 1983. 17.95 (ISBN 0-87975-203-3). Prometheus Bks.

Klass, Sheila S. To See My Mother Dance. 160p. 1983. pap. 1.95 (ISBN 0-449-70052-6, Juniper). Fawcett.

Klassen, Peter. The Reformation. LC 79-54030. (Problems in Civilization Ser.). (Orig.). 1980. pap. text ed. 4.25 (ISBN 0-88273-408-3). Forum Pr IL.

Klassen, Randolph J. Meditations for Lovers. (Illus.). 1974. 4.95 o.p. (ISBN 0-910452-21-0). Covenant.

Klassen, Walter. The Radical Reformers: "Selected Works". (Classics of Western Spirituality Ser.). 1982. 11.95 (ISBN 0-8091-0290-0); pap. 7.95 (ISBN 0-8091-2228-6). Paulist Pr.

Klastersky, J., ed. Infections in Cancer Patients. (European Organization for Research on Treatment of Cancer (EORTC) Monographs: Vol. 10). 232p. 1982. text ed. 27.50 (ISBN 0-89004-627-1). Raven.

Klastersky, J. & Staquet, M., eds. Combination Antibiotic Therapy in the Compromised Host. (European Organization for Research on Treatment of Cancer (EORTC) Monographs: Vol. 9). 260p. 1981. text ed. 31.50 (ISBN 0-89004-658-1). Raven.

Klastersky, Jean & Staquet, Maurice J., eds. Medical Complications in Cancer Patients. (European Organization for Research on Treatment of Cancer (EORTC), Monograph: Vol. 7). Orig. Title: Medical Disorders in Cancer Patients. 323p. 1981. text ed. 39.50 (ISBN 0-89004-519-4). Raven.

Klaurens, M. K. Economics of Marketing. (Occupational Manuals & Projects in Marketing). 1971. text ed. 6.56 (ISBN 0-07-035018-3, G); tchr's manual & key o.p. 3.50 (ISBN 0-07-035019-1). McGraw.

Klaurens, Mary. The Economics of Marketing. 2nd ed. Dorr, Eugene L., ed. (Occupational Manuals & Projects in Marketing). (gr. 11-12). 1978. pap. text ed. 7.32 (ISBN 0-07-035020-5, G); tchr's manual & key 4.50 (ISBN 0-07-035021-3). McGraw.

Klaus & Kennell. Maternal-Infant Bonding: The Impact of Early Separation or Loss on Family Development. LC 76-5397. Orig. Title: Care of the Family of the Normal or Sick Newborn. (Illus.). 257p. 1976. text ed. 14.95 o.p. (ISBN 0-8016-2631-5); pap. 11.95 o.p. (ISBN 0-8016-2630-7). Mosby.

Klaus, Billie & Raish, Peggy. Physical Assessment & Diagnosis in Primary Care. (Illus.). 704p. 1982. text ed. 24.95 o.p. (ISBN 0-86542-003-3). Blackwell Sci.

Klaus, Billie J. Protocols Handbook for Nurse Practitioners. LC 79-14389. 240p. 1979. 20.00x (ISBN 0-471-05219-1, Pub. by Wiley-Medical). Wiley.

Klaus, Carl H., jt. auth. see Scholes, Robert.

Klaus, Carl H. & Gilbert, Miriam A., trs. Stages of Drama. 1981. pap. text ed. 20.95x (ISBN 0-673-15686-9). Scott F.

Klaus, Marshall & Robertson, Martha O., eds. Birth, Interaction & Attachment. (Pediatric Round Table Ser.: No. 6). 141p. (Orig.). Date not set. pap. 5.00 (ISBN 0-686-97520-0). Johnson & Johnson.

Klaus, Marshall H. & Kennell, John H. Bonding: The Beginnings of Parent to Infant Attachment. (Medical Attachment Ser.). (Illus.). 256p. 1983. pap. price not set (ISBN 0-452-25402-7, 2696-X). Mosby.

Klaus, Samuel, ed. Milligan Case. LC 78-118031. (Civil Liberties in American History Ser.). 1970. Repr. of 1929 ed. lib. bdg. 55.00 (ISBN 0-306-71945-2). Da Capo.

Klausen, Klaus & Hemmingsen, Ib. Basic Sport Science. Burke, Edmund J., tr. 1982. text ed. 15.95 (ISBN 0-686-38846-1); pap. 9.95 (ISBN 0-686-38847-X). Mouvment Pubns.

Klausmeier, Herbert. Psicologia Educativa. (Span.). 1978. pap. text ed. 16.60 o.p. (ISBN 0-06-315050-6, IntlDept); wkbk. 5.00 o.p. (ISBN 0-06-315051-4). Har-Row.

Klausmeier, Herbert J., et al. Cognitive Learning & Development: Piagetian & Information-Processing Perspectives. LC 79-11448. (Illus.). 384p. 1979. prof ref 29.00x (ISBN 0-88410-188-6). Ballinger Pub.

Klausner, Carla L. & Schultz, Joseph P. From Destruction to Rebirth: The Holocaust & the State of Israel. LC 78-62262. 1978. pap. text ed. 12.50 (ISBN 0-8191-0574-0). U Pr of Amer.

Klausner, Larry. Son of Sam: Based on the Authorized Transcription of the Tapes, Official Documents & Diaries of David Berkowitz. (Illus.). 400p. 1980. 12.95 o.p. (ISBN 0-07-035027-2). McGraw.

Klausner, Samuel Z. Eskimo Capitalists: Oil, Politics & Alcohol. LC 80-67391. (Illus.). 360p. 1982. text ed. 35.00x (ISBN 0-916672-69-7). Allanheld.

Klauss, Rudi & Bass, Bernard, eds. Interpersonal Communication in Organizations. (Organizational & Occupational Psychology Ser.). 1982. 23.00 (ISBN 0-12-411650-7). Acad Pr.

Klaustermeyer, William B. Practical Allergy & Immunology: Family Practice Today-A Comprehensive Postgraduate Library. 216p. 1983. 14.95 (ISBN 0-471-09564-8, Pub. by Wiley Med). Wiley.

Klawans, Harold L. Clinical Neuropharmacology, Vol. 4. 238p. 1979. 27.00 (ISBN 0-89004-350-7). Raven.

--The Medicine History: From Paracles to Freud. 248p. Date not set. text ed. 19.50 (ISBN 0-89004-684-0). Raven.

Klawans, Harold L., ed. Clinical Neuropharmacology, Vol. 1. LC 75-14581. 238p. 1976. 28.50 (ISBN 0-89004-035-4). Raven.

--Clinical Neuropharmacology, Vol. 2. LC 75-14581. 218p. 1977. 26.50 (ISBN 0-89004-171-7). Raven.

--Clinical Neuropharmacology, Vol. 3. LC 75-14581. 221p. 1978. 27.00 (ISBN 0-89004-266-7). Raven.

Klawans, Harold L., et al. Textbook of Clinical Neuropharmacology. 382p. 1981. text ed. 36.00 (ISBN 0-89004-430-9). Raven.

Klawans, Z. Reading & Dating Roman Imperial Coins. (Illus.). 1982. Repr. of 1977 ed. softcover 10.00 (ISBN 0-686-79427-3). S J Durst.

Klay, Grace Vander see Vander Klay, Grace.

Klay, Ruedi, jt. auth. see Schmid, Otto.

Klayman, Daniel L. & Gunther, Wolfgang H. Organic Selenium Compounds: Their Chemistry & Biology. LC 72-5448. (Organometallic Compounds Ser.). 1188p. 1972. 150.00 (ISBN 0-471-49032-6, Pub. by Wiley-Interscience). Wiley.

Klebahn, H. Haupt-und Nebenfruchtforman der Askomyzeten. (Bibl. Myco. Ser: No.14). 1968. pap. 40.00 (ISBN 3-7682-0559-2). Lubrecht & Cramer.

Klebanoff, S. & Clark, R. A. The Neutrophil: Function & Clinical Disorders. 1978. 172.50 (ISBN 0-444-80020-4, Biomedical Pr). Elsevier.

Kleber, John E., ed. The Public Papers of Governor Lawrence W. Wetherby, 1950-1955. LC 82-40182. (The Public Papers of the Governors of Kentucky Ser.). 344p. 1983. 28.00x (ISBN 0-8131-0606-0). U Pr of Ky.

Kleberger, Ilse. Grandmother Oma. LC 67-10459. (Illus.). (gr. 2-5). 1967. PLB 5.95 (ISBN 0-689-20201-6). Atheneum.

Klechkovskii, V. M., et al. Radioecology. LC 73-4697. 371p. 1973. 67.95x o.s.i. (ISBN 0-470-49035-7). Halsted Pr.

Klecka, W., et al. SPSS Primer. 1975. text ed. 13.50 (ISBN 0-07-035023-X, C). McGraw.

Kleckner, Simone-Marie, tr. from Romanian. Romania: The Penal Code of the Romanian Socialist Republic. LC 76-17385. (American Series of Foreign Penal Codes: Vol. 20). xvi, 143p. 1976. text ed. 17.50x (ISBN 0-8377-0040-X). Rothman.

Klee, Albert J. Quantitative Decision-Making, Vol. 3. Vesilind, P. Aarne, ed. LC 80-67973. (Design & Management for Resource Recovery Ser.). 1980. 29.95 (ISBN 0-250-40313-7). Ann Arbor Science.

Klee, James B. Points of Departure: Aspects of the Tao. LC 82-72609. 336p. (Orig.). 1982. pap. 8.95 (ISBN 0-89708-105-6). And Bks.

Klee, Manfred, et al, eds. Physiology & Pharmacology of Epileptogenic Phenomena. 430p. 1982. text ed. 54.50 (ISBN 0-89004-599-2). Raven.

Kleefeld, Carolyn M. Satan Sleeps with the Holy: Word Paintings. LC 82-80785. 110p. 1982. 11.95 (ISBN 0-9602214-9-2); pap. 7.95 (ISBN 0-9602214-8-4). Horse & Bird.

Kleeman, Charles R., jt. ed. see Maxwell, Morton H.

Kleene, S. C. Introduction to Metamathematics. 1971. text ed. 42.75 (ISBN 0-444-10088-1, North-Holland). Elsevier.

Klei, Herbert E., jt. auth. see Sundstrom, Donald W.

Kleiber, Kenneth & Lemire, Deacon H. Deacons: Permanent or Passing? 70p. 1982. 6.95 (ISBN 0-911519-02-5). Richelieu Court.

Kleiber, Max. Fire of Life: An Introduction to Animal Energetics. rev. ed. LC 75-4729. 478p. 1975. Repr. of 1961 ed. 26.50 (ISBN 0-88275-161-1). Krieger.

Kleiber, Michael, jt. auth. see Krummes, Daniel.

Kleid, Jack J. Medical Examination Review: Textbook Study Guide of Internal Medicine, Vol. 2B. 4th ed. 1982. pap. text ed. 13.95 (ISBN 0-87488-130-7). Med Exam.

Kleid, Jack J., ed. Textbook Study Guide of Internal Medicine. 4th ed. (Medical Examination Review Book: Vol. 2B). 1982. pap. 13.95 (ISBN 0-87488-130-7). Med Exam.

Kleijn, E. Van der see Van der Kleijn, E. & Jonkers, J. R.

Kleijn, E. Van Der. see Turakka, H. & Van der Kleijn, E.

Kleiman, Carol. Women's Networks. 1980. 12.45i (ISBN 0-690-01868-1); pap. 5.95i (ISBN 0-690-01869-X). Har-Row.

Kleiman, D. G., jt. ed. see Eisenberg, J. F.

Kleiman, M. B., ed. Social Gerontology: Interdisciplinary Topics in Gerontology, Vol. 17. (Illus.). viii, 200p. 1983. pap. 78.00 (ISBN 3-8055-3649-6). S Karger.

Kleiman, R., jt. ed. see Hoffman, K.

Klein & Wolman. Beat Inflation Strategy. 1975. 9.95 o.p. (ISBN 0-671-22063-2). S&S.

Klein, jt. auth. see Huber.

Klein, jt. auth. see Kazanas.

Klein, A. M. Short Stories. Steinberg, M. W., ed. (Collected Works of A. M. Klein Ser.). 344p. 1983. 35.00 (ISBN 0-8020-5598-2). U of Toronto Pr.

Klein, Aaron E. & Klein, Cynthia L. The Better Mousetrap: A Miscellany of Gadgets, Labor-Saving Devices, & Inventions That Intrigue. LC 81-3796. (Illus.). 400p. 1982. 19.95 (ISBN 0-8253-0030-4). Beaufort Bks NY.

--Mind Trips: The Story of Consciousness-Raising Movements. LC 78-22331. 1979. 7.95a o.p. (ISBN 0-385-12759-6); PLB (ISBN 0-385-12760-X). Doubleday.

Klein, Aaron E., jt. auth. see DeWaard, E. John.

Klein, Anne, ed. see Rinbochy, Khetsun S.

Klein, Arthur H., jt. auth. see Klein, Mina C.

Klein, Barbara & Roscow, Judith. Dining In: Pittsburgh. rev. ed. (Dining in Ser.). 192p. 1981. pap. 7.95 (ISBN 0-89716-103-3). Peanut Butter.

Klein, Barry. Electronic Music Circuits. Date not set. pap. 16.95 (ISBN 0-686-82323-0). Sams.

Klein, Bob. Wounded Men, Broken Promises. 300p. 1981. 13.95 o.s.i. (ISBN 0-02-563930-7). Macmillan.

Klein, Charlotte. Anti-Judaism in Christian Theology. Quinn, Edward, tr. LC 76-62600. 192p. 1978. 4.50 (ISBN 0-8006-0488-1, 1-488). Fortress.

Klein, Chuck. So You Want to Lead Students. 96p. 1982. pap. 3.95 (ISBN 0-8423-6084-0). Tyndale.

--So You Want to Set the Pace. 96p. 1982. pap. 4.95 (ISBN 0-8423-6083-2). Tyndale.

Klein, Cornelis, jt. auth. see Hurlbut, Cornelius S., Jr.

Klein, Cynthia L., jt. auth. see Klein, Aaron E.

Klein, D. C. Community Dynamics & Mental Health. LC 68-8105. 224p. 1968. 26.50x o.p. (ISBN 0-471-49050-4, Pub. by Wiley-Interscience). Wiley.

Klein, D. C., ed. Melatonin Rhythm Generating System: Developmental Aspects. (Illus.). x, 254p. 1983. 94.75 (ISBN 3-8055-3460-4). S Karger.

Klein, Dave. The Game of Their Lives. (Illus.). (RL 7). 1977. pap. 1.95 o.p. (ISBN 0-451-07532-3, J7532, Sig). NAL.

--The Pro Football Mystique. (Orig.). 1978. pap. 1.95 o.p. (ISBN 0-451-08353-9, J8353, Sig). NAL.

Klein, David & Klein, Marymae E. Yourself Ten Years from Now: A Career Planning Guide. LC 77-76438. (Illus.). 152p. (gr. 7 up). 1977. 7.95 o.p. (ISBN 0-15-299940-X, HJ). HarBraceJ.

Klein, David, jt. auth. see Hughes, Theodore E.

Klein, Dennis A. Peter & Anthony Shaffer: A Reference Guide. 1982. lib. bdg. 20.00 (ISBN 0-8161-8574-3, Hall Reference). G K Hall.

--Peter Shaffer. (English Authors Ser.). 1979. lib. bdg. 13.95 (ISBN 0-8057-6738-X, Twayne). G K Hall.

Klein, Diane & Badalamenti, Rosalyn T. Eating Right for Two: The Complete Nutrition Guide & Cookbook for a Healthy Pregnancy. 320p. (Orig.). 1983. pap. 7.95 (ISBN 0-345-30915-4). Ballantine.

Klein, Donald, jt. auth. see Israel, John.

Klein, Donald F. & Davis, John M. Diagnosis & Drug Treatment of Psychiatric Disorders. LC 69-14459. 480p. 1969. 21.00 (ISBN 0-686-65354-8). Krieger.

Klein, Donald F., jt. auth. see Wender, Paul H.

Klein, Donald F. & Rabkin, Judith G., eds. Anxiety: New Research & Changing Concepts. (American Psychopathological Association Ser.). 454p. 1981. 54.50 (ISBN 0-686-69136-9). Raven.

Klein, Donald F., jt. ed. see Spitzer, Robert L.

Klein, E. L., ed. see Strode Publishers.

Klein, Elinor & Landey, Dora. Dazzle. LC 79-13656. 1980. 10.95 (ISBN 0-399-12343-1). Putnam Pub Group.

Klein, Elinor, jt. auth. see Landey, Dora.

Klein, Ernest. Comprehensive Etymological Dictionary of the English Language. 1971. 85.00 (ISBN 0-444-40930-0). Elsevier.

Klein, F., jt. auth. see Grove, A. T.

Klein, F. J. & Lee, J. S., eds. Selected Writings of A. T. Vanderbilt, 2 vols. LC 65-14216. (Classic Ser.). 1965. 15.00 ea. (ISBN 0-379-00226-4); Set. 30.00. Oceana.

Klein, Fannie J. The Administration of Justice in the Courts: A Selected Annotated Bibliography, 2 vols. LC 76-2627. 1976. text-ed. 80.00x set (ISBN 0-686-96810-7); Vol. 1. text ed. (ISBN 0-379-10137-8); Vol. 2. text ed. (ISBN 0-379-10138-6). Oceana.

--Bar Admission Rules & Student Practice Rules. LC 77-17177. 1232p. 1978. prof ref 95.00x (ISBN 0-88410-791-4). Ballinger Pub.

Klein, Fannie J., et al. Federal & State Court Systems: A Guide. LC 76-47480. 328p. 1977. prof ref 27.50x (ISBN 0-88410-219-X); pap. 12.95x (ISBN 0-88410-795-7). Ballinger Pub.

Klein, Felix. Entwicklung Der Mathematik Im Neunzehnten Jahrhundert, 2 Vols. in 1. (Ger). 24.95 (ISBN 0-8284-0074-1). Chelsea Pub.

--Famous Problems of Elementary Geometry & Other Monographs, 4 vols. in 1. Incl. From Determinant to Tensor. Sheppard, William F; Introduction to Combinatory Analysis. MacMahon, Percy A; Fermat's Last Theorem. Mordell, Louis J; Famous Problems of Elementary Geometry. Klein, Felix. (gr. 9 up). 1956. 11.95 (ISBN 0-8284-0108-X); pap. text ed. 3.95 o.p. (ISBN 0-8284-0166-7). Chelsea Pub.

--Nicht-Euklidische Geometrie. LC 59-10281. (Ger). 14.95 (ISBN 0-8284-0129-2). Chelsea Pub.

Klein, George & Weinhouse, Sidney. Advances in Cancer Research, Vol. 37. 382p. 1982. 52.00 (ISBN 0-12-006637-8). Acad Pr.

Klein, George, ed. Oncogene Studies, Vol. 1. (Advances in Viral Oncology Ser.: Vol. 1). 285p. 1982. text ed. 55.00 (ISBN 0-89004-692-1). Raven.

--The Transformation: Associated Cellular P53 Protein. (Advances in Viral Oncology Ser.: Vol. 2). 175p. 1982. text ed. 32.00 (ISBN 0-89004-857-6). Raven.

--Viral Oncology. 860p. 1980. text ed. 98.00 (ISBN 0-89004-390-6). Raven.

Klein, George S. Perception, Motives & Personality. pap. text ed. write for info. (ISBN 0-685-69599-9). Phila Bk Co.

Klein, Gerard. The Day Before Tomorrow. 1982. pap. 1.95 (ISBN 0-87997-767-1, UJ1767). DAW Bks.

Klein, H. Arthur & Klein, M. C. Surf's Up. (Illus.). (gr. 6 up). 1966. 5.95 o.p. (ISBN 0-672-50522-3). Bobbs.

Klein, H. Arthur, jt. ed. see Klein, Nina C.

Klein, Herbert S. Parties & Political Change in Bolivia 1880-1952. LC 77-85722. (Latin American Studies: No. 5). (Illus.). 1969. 44.50 (ISBN 0-521-07614-5). Cambridge U Pr.

Klein, Herbert S., jt. auth. see TePaske, John J.

Klein, Herman. The Golden Age of Opera. (Music Reprint Ser.). 1979. Repr. of 1933 ed. 32.50 (ISBN 0-306-70840-X). Da Capo.

--The Reign of Patti. LC 77-17874. (Music Reprint Ser.: 1978). (Illus.). 1978. Repr. of 1920 ed. lib. bdg. 39.50 (ISBN 0-306-77530-1). Da Capo.

Klein, Hermann. Thirty Years of Musical Life in London. LC 78-2565. (Music Reprint Ser., 1978). (Illus.). 1978. Repr. of 1903 ed. lib. bdg. 37.50 (ISBN 0-306-77586-7). Da Capo.

Klein, Hilary D., ed. Craft Digest. 2nd ed. (Illus.). 1977. pap. 7.95 o.s.i. (ISBN 0-695-80765-X). Follett.

Klein, Hilary D., jt. ed. see Adell, Judith.

Klein, Irving J. Law of Evidence for Police. 2nd ed. (Criminal Justice Ser.). 1978. text ed. 21.95 (ISBN 0-8299-0149-3); instrs.' manual avail. West Pub.

Klein, Jan. Immunology: The Science of Self-Nonself Discrimination. 1248p. 1982. 70.00x (ISBN 0-471-05124-1, Pub. by Wiley-Interscience). Wiley.

Klein, Jeffery A. & Ch'Uan-K'Ai Leung, Kenneth. Environmental Control Industry: An Analysis of Conditions & Prospects for the Pollution Control Equipment Industry. LC 76-1439. 157p. 1976. text ed. 14.50x (ISBN 0-916672-02-6). Allanheld.

Klein, Jerry. Father's Day. 133p. 1981. 12.95 (ISBN 0-933180-27-6); pap. 12.95 (ISBN 0-933180-24-1). Kickapoo.

Klein, John F. & Montague, Arthur. Check-Forgers. LC 77-14869. 176p. 1978. 18.95x (ISBN 0-669-01993-3). Lexington Bks.

Klein, Judy G. The Office Book. Pile, John & Duffy, Frank, eds. 288p. 1982. 40.00x (ISBN 0-87196-499-6). Facts on File.

Klein, K. E., ed. see Basic Environmental Problems of Man in Space II, 6th International Symposium, Bonn, Germany, 3-6 November 1980.

Klein, Kenneth. Getting Better. 1982. pap. 2.25 (ISBN 0-451-11558-9, AE1558, Sig). NAL.

Klein, Larry. Jim Brown: The Running Back. (Putnam Sports Shelf Ser.). (Illus.). (gr. 5-8). 1965. PLB 6.29 o.p. (ISBN 0-399-60316-6). Putnam Pub Group.

Klein, Lawrence R. & Goldberger, Arthur S. Econometric Model of the U. S., 1929-1952. (Orig.). 1964. text ed. 16.25x o.p. (ISBN 0-7204-3117-4, Pub. by North Holland). Humanities.

Klein, Lawrence R., jt. ed. see Adams, F. Gerald.

Klein, Leonard S., ed. Encyclopedia of World Literature in the Twentieth Century, 3 vols. 2nd ed. LC 81-3357. (Illus.). 1983. Vol. 1, A-D, 0-8044-3135-3. 90.00 ea. Vol. 2, E-K, 0-8044-3136-1. Vol. 3, L-Q, 0-8044-3137-X. Ungar.

Klein, Leonore. Old, Older, Oldest. (Illus.). 48p. (ps-3). 1983. 9.95 (ISBN 0-8038-5396-3). Hastings.

--Only One Ant. 32p. (gr. k-3). 1971. 6.95g o.s.i. (ISBN 0-8038-5362-9). Hastings.

Klein, M. C., jt. auth. see Klein, H. Arthur.

Klein, Mary. A New View of Cathedral Window. (Illus.). 40p. 1983. 5.00 (ISBN 0-943574-20-X). That Patchwork.

Klein, Marymae E., jt. auth. see Klein, David.

Klein, Maury D. Operating O & O-27 Trains: A Comprehensive Guide to the Design, Construction & Operation of a Layout for Lionel Trains. rev. ed. (Illus.). 240p. 1978. pap. 6.50 perfect bnd. (ISBN 0-934580-01-4). MDK Inc.

Klein, Maury D., jt. auth. see Ruocchio, Albert C.

Klein, Maury D., ed. Complete Service Manual for American Flyer Trains. (Illus.). 402p. 1978. lib. bdg. 25.00 sewn (ISBN 0-934580-06-5, K-3). MDK Inc.

Klein, Maury D & Greenberg, Bruce C., eds. Operating Zero & Zero-Twenty Seven Trains: A Comprehensive Guide to the Design, Construction & Operation of a Layout for Lionel Trains. 1977. pap. 4.95 o.p. (ISBN 0-517-52988-2). Crown.

Klein, Mavis. Lives People Live: A Textbook of Transactional Analysis. LC 79-40737. (Wiley Series on Methods in Psychotherapy). 183p. 1980. 44.95x (ISBN 0-471-27648-0, Pub. by Wiley-Interscience); pap. 22.95x (ISBN 0-471-27649-9). Wiley.

Klein, Maxine. Time: Space & Designs for Actors. 1975. pap. text ed. 16.50 (ISBN 0-395-18612-9). HM.

Klein, Melanie. Eny & Gratitude & Other Works: 1946-1963, Vol. 4. 1977. pap. 3.95 o.s.i. (ISBN 0-440-52424-5, Delta). Dell.

--Love, Guilt & Reparation & Others Work, Vol. 3. 1977. 4.95 o.s.i. (ISBN 0-440-55114-5, Delta). Dell.

--Narrative of a Child Analysis. 1976. pap. 4.95 o.s.i. (ISBN 0-440-56195-7, Delta). Dell.

--The Psychoanalysis of Children. 1976. pap. 3.95 o.s.i. (ISBN 0-440-57152-9, Delta). Dell.

Klein, Melanie & Isaacs, Susan. Developments in Psycho-Analysis. (Psychoanalysis Examined & Re-Examined Ser.). 368p. 1982. Repr. of 1952 ed. lib. bdg. 29.50 (ISBN 0-306-79711-9). Da Capo.

Klein, Michael & Parker, Gillian, eds. The English Novel & the Movies. LC 80-5342. (Ungar Film Library). (Illus.). 350p. 1980. 14.95 (ISBN 0-8044-2472-1); pap. 6.95 (ISBN 0-8044-6358-1). Ungar.

Klein, Michael J. Planning for Tomorrow. LC 79-11308. 1979. 3-ring binder 35.00 (ISBN 0-07-035032-9, T&D); leader's guide 1.95 (ISBN 0-07-035031-0). McGraw.

Klein, Michael R. & Stearns, Robert. Tableaux: Nine Contemporary Sculptors. (Illus.). 1983. write for info. (ISBN 0-917562-23-2). Contemp Arts.

Klein, Miles V. Optics. LC 73-107584. 647p. 1970. 39.95x (ISBN 0-471-49080-6). Wiley.

Klein, Mina C. & Klein, Arthur H. Kathe Kollwitz: Life in Art. LC 75-10858. (Illus.). 208p. 1975. pap. 8.95 (ISBN 0-8052-0504-7). Schocken.

Klein, Nina C. & Klein, H. Arthur, eds. The Kidnapped Saint & Other Stories by B. Traven. LC 74-9349. 1977. 8.95 (ISBN 0-88208-049-0); pap. 5.95 o.s.i. (ISBN 0-88208-074-1). Lawrence Hill.

Klein, Norma. Coming to Life. 1976. pap. 1.50 o.p. (ISBN 0-451-06864-5, W6864, Sig). NAL.

--Coming to Life. 208p. (Orig.). 1983. pap. 2.50 (ISBN 0-449-20101-5, Crest). Fawcett.

--Girls Can Be Anything. (Illus.). 32p. (ps-1). 1975. 8.95 (ISBN 0-525-30662-5, 0869-260); pap. 3.95 (ISBN 0-525-45029-7, 0383-120, Anytime Bks). Dutton.

--Sextet in A Minor: A Novella & Thirteen Stories. 224p. 1983. 12.95 (ISBN 0-312-71348-7). St Martin.

Klein, Norman, jt. auth. see Diller, Phyllis.

Klein, Paul, et al. Inside the TV Business. LC 78-66318. 1979. 14.95 o.p. (ISBN 0-8069-0142-X); lib. bdg. 13.29 o.p. (ISBN 0-8069-0143-8). Sterling.

Klein, Philip S. & Hoogenboom, Ari. A History of Pennsylvania. 2nd enlarged ed. LC 79-1731. (Illus.). 620p. 1980. 22.50x (ISBN 0-271-00216-6). Pa St U Pr.

Klein, Raymond L., jt. auth. see Clark, Leonard H.

Klein, Richard & Katzin, Herbert M. Microsurgery of the Vitreous: Comparisons of Instrumentation, Techniques, & Philosophies. (Handbook in Ophthalmology Ser.). (Illus.). 216p. 1978. 27.00 (ISBN 0-683-04654-3). Williams & Wilkins.

Klein, Richard L., et al, eds. Neurotransmitter Vesicles. 1982. 61.50 (ISBN 0-12-413680-X). Acad Pr.

Klein, Robert. Thing. (Illus.). 32p. (gr. 3-5). 1983. bds. 7.95 (ISBN 0-19-554330-0, Pub by Oxford U Pr Childrens). Merrimack Bk Serv.

Klein, Robert, jt. auth. see Eastman, Susan Tyler.

Klein, Rose B. The Joy of Living. 1978. 4.50 o.p. (ISBN 0-533-03257-1). Vantage.

Klein, S. B. Motivation: Biosocial Approaches. 576p. 1982. 25.00x (ISBN 0-07-035051-5). McGraw.

Klein, Sonia, jt. ed. see Adams, F. Gerard.

Klein, Stanley, jt. ed. see Aylesworth, Thomas C.

Klein, Stuart M. & Ritti, Richard R. Understanding Organizational Behavior. 592p. 1980. text ed. 22.95x (ISBN 0-534-00755-4, Kent Pub.). Kent Pub Co.

Klein, Thomas A. Social Costs & Benefits of Business. 1977. 12.95 o.p. (ISBN 0-13-815837-1); pap. 12.95 (ISBN 0-13-815829-0). P-H.

Klein, Viola. The Feminine Character: History of an Ideology. LC 72-83482. 240p. 1972. pap. 5.95 o.p. (ISBN 0-252-00298-9). U of Ill Pr.

Klein, W. C., tr. see Ali ibn Isma'il, A. H., et al.

Klein, Wolfgang, jt. auth. see Jarvella, Robert J.

Klein, Wolfgang, jt. ed. see Weissenborn, Juergen.

Klein, Wolfgang, jt. ed. see Weissenborn, Jurgen.

Klein-Andreu, Flora, ed. Discourse Perspectives on Syntax. Date not set. price not set (ISBN 0-12-413720-2). Acad Pr.

Kleinbach, Russell L. Marx Via Process: Whitehead's Potential Contribution to Marxian Social Theory. LC 81-40667. 212p. (Orig.). 1982. lib. bdg. 23.00 (ISBN 0-8191-2273-4); pap. text ed. 10.75 (ISBN 0-8191-2274-2). U Pr of Amer.

Kleinbauer, W. E. & Slavens, Thomas P. Research Guide to the History of Western Art. 240p. 1982. text ed. 20.00 (ISBN 0-8389-0329-0). ALA.

Kleinbaum, David G. & Kupper, Lawrence L. Solutions Manual for Epidemiologic Research: Principles & Quantitative Methods. (Research Methods Ser.). 58p. 1982. pap. 4.95 (ISBN 0-534-97935-1). Lifetime Learn.

Kleinbaum, David G., et al. Epidemiologic Research: Principles & Quantitative Methods. (Research Methods Ser.). (Illus.). 480p. 1982. 38.50 (ISBN 0-534-97950-5). Lifetime Learn.

Kleinberg, Benjamin. American Society in the Postindustrial Age: Technocracy, Power, & the End of Ideology. LC 72-89898. 1973. pap. text ed. 6.95x o.p. (ISBN 0-675-09034-2). Merrill.

Kleinberg, Eugene M., jt. auth. see Henle, James M.

Kleinberg, I, ed. Saliva & Dental Cavies. LC 79-83655. (Illus.). 576p. 1979. pap. text ed. 20.00 o.p. (ISBN 0-917000-06-4). IRL Pr.

Kleinberger, A. F. Society, Schools & Progress in Israel. LC 73-92460. 1969. 27.00 o.p. (ISBN 0-08-006494-9); pap. write for info. (ISBN 0-08-006493-0). Pergamon.

Kleinberger, G. & Deutsch, E., eds. New Aspects of Clinical Nutrition. (Illus.). x, 662p. 1983. pap. 74.25 (ISBN 3-8055-3683-6). S Karger.

Kleindienst, V. K. & Weston, A. Recreational Sports Program: Schools...Colleges...Communities. LC 77-16808. 1978. 20.95 (ISBN 0-13-767905-X). P-H.

Kleindienst, Walter, tr. see Moll, Helmut.

Kleindorfer, P. R., jt. auth. see Bensousan, A.

Kleindorfer, Paul R., jt. auth. see Crew, Michael A.

Kleindorfer, Paul R., jt. ed. see Mitchell, Bridger M.

Kleine, Lawrence J. & Warren, Roger G. Mosby's Fundamentals of Animal Health Technology: Vol. III: Small Animal Radiography. LC 82-6353. (Illus.). 184p. 1983. pap. text ed. 16.95 (ISBN 0-8016-5400-9). Mosby.

Kleiner, Art. Robots. LC 80-11681. (Look Inside Ser.). (Illus.). 48p. (gr. 4-12). 1981. PLB 14.25 (ISBN 0-8172-1401-1). Raintree Pubs.

Kleinerman, Samuel N. The Cohomology of Chevalley Groups of Exceptional Lie Type. LC 82-11545. (Memoirs of the American Mathematical Society Ser.: No. 268). 5.00 (ISBN 0-8218-2268-3). Am Math.

Kleinfeld, ed. see Newmyer, Joseph, Jr. & Klentos, Gus.

Kleinfeld, Judith S. Eskimo School on the Andreafsky: A Study of Effective Bicultural Education. LC 79-4520. 209p. 1979. 26.95 (ISBN 0-03-048366-2). Praeger.

Kleinfield, Herbert L., jt. ed. see Aderman, Ralph M.

Kleinfield, Sonny. The Biggest Commpany on Earth: A Profile of AT&T. 319p. 1981. 14.95 (ISBN 0-686-98111-1). Telecom Lib.

Kleinhammer, Edward. Art of Trombone Playing. (Illus.). 1963. pap. 12.95 (ISBN 0-87487-058-5). Summy.

Kleinhans, James, ed. Hazardous Waste Audit Program (10m) LC 8-86197. 1982. 3-ring binder 65.00 (ISBN 0-934674-41-8). J J Keller.

--Hazardous Waste Regulatory Guide (26g) LC 81-86200. 450p. 1982. 3-ring binder 95.00 (ISBN 0-934674-44-2). J J Keller.

Kleinhans, James, ed. see Keller, J. J.

Kleinhans, James, ed. see Keller, J. J., & Assocs., Inc.

Kleinig, John. Philosophical Issues in Education. LC 82-50084. 1982. 29.95x (ISBN 0-312-60524-2). St Martin.

Kleinjnen, Jack P. Computers & Profits: Quantifying Financial Benefits of Information. LC 79-14097. 1980. text ed. 22.95 (ISBN 0-201-03813-7). A-W.

Kleinman, A. Handbook of Personal Computer Terms. 1982. pap. 9.95 (ISBN 0-686-81783-4). Devin.

Kleinman, Arthur. Patients & Healers in the Context of Culture: An Exploration of the Borderland Between Anthropology, Medicine, & Psychiatry. LC 78-57311. (Comparative Studies of Health Systems & Medical Care). 1979. 32.50x o.p. (ISBN 0-520-03706-5); pap. 9.95 (ISBN 0-520-04511-4, CAMPUS 284). U of Cal Pr.

Kleinman, Arthur, et al, eds. Culture & Healing in Asian Societies. (University Books Program). 1978. lib. bdg. 25.00 o.p. (ISBN 0-8161-8248-5, Univ Bks). G K Hall.

Kleinman, Arthur M., jt. ed. see Manschreck, Theo C.

Kleinman, David S. Human Adaptation & Population Growth: A Non-Malthusian Perspective. LC 78-59176. 296p. 1981. text ed. 23.50x (ISBN 0-916672-18-2); pap. text ed. 9.95x (ISBN 0-86598-064-0). Allanheld.

Kleinman, Matthew. The Acquisition of Motor Skill. LC 81-84597. 256p. 1983. text ed. 18.95x (ISBN 0-916622-24-X). Princeton Bk Co.

Kleinman, Robert L., ed. Directory of Contraceptives-Repertoire des Contraceptifs-Guia de Anticonceptivos. 3rd ed. (International Planned Parenthood Federation Medical Publications). 95p. (Orig., Eng., Fr. & Span.). 1981. pap. 12.50x (ISBN 0-86089-043-0). Intl Pubns Serv.

Kleinmuntz, Benjamin. Personality Measurement: An Introduction. LC 75-17673. 478p. 1975. Repr. of 1967 ed. 25.00 (ISBN 0-88275-337-1). Krieger.

Kleinrock, Leonard. Queueing Systems, 2 vols. Incl. Vol. 1. Theory. 417p. 34.95x (ISBN 0-471-49110-1); Vol. 2. Computer Applications. 549p. 38.95x (ISBN 0-471-49111-X). LC 44-9846. 1975-76 (Pub. by Wiley-Interscience). Wiley.

Kleinsasser, Jacob, et al. For the Sake of Divine Truth: 1974 Visit of Four Brothers to Central Europe. LC 74-23787. 1974. pap. 1.00 (ISBN 0-87486-146-2). Plough.

Kleinschmidt, Robert, jt. auth. see Dickenson, Harry.

Kleinschmidt, William, jt. auth. see Tomeski, Edward A.

Kleinschrod, Walter & Kruk, Leonard. Word Information Processing: Administration & Office Automation. 2nd ed. 288p. 1983. text ed. 23.95 (ISBN 0-672-98442-3); instr's. guide 6.67 (ISBN 0-672-98443-1). Bobbs.

Kleinsinger, Irene J. Wine Log. (Illus.). 96p. 1982. leather cover 19.95 (ISBN 0-9605146-4-3); suede cover 11.75 (ISBN 0-9605146-3-5); vinyl cover 5.50 (ISBN 0-9605146-2-7). Kleinsinger.

Kleinsmith, Lewis J., ed. see Symposium, University of Florida, Gainsville, March, 1975.

Kleinzeller, Annost, jt. ed. see Bronner, Felix.

Kleinzeller, Arnost, jt. ed. see Bronner, Felix.

Kleiser, Greenville. Make Your Life Worth Living. 209p. 1982. pap. 5.95 (ISBN 0-13-545772-6). P-H.

Kleiser, Grenville. How to Improve Your Conversation: An Aid to Social & Business Success. 267p. 1982. Repr. of 1932 ed. lib. bdg. 25.00 (ISBN 0-8495-3136-5). Arden Lib.

Kleiss, Peter. Georg Herweghs Literaturkritik. 172p. (Ger.). 1982. write for info. (ISBN 3-8204-6292-9). P Lang Pubs.

Kleist, Heinrich von see Von Kleist, Heinrich.

Klekamp, Robert C., jt. auth. see Thierauf, Robert J.

Klekowski, Edward J., Jr., ed. Environmental Mutagenesis, Carcinogenesis, & Plant Biology, 2. 208p. 1982. 21.50 ea. (ISBN 0-03-057953-8) (ISBN 0-03-061601-8). Praeger.

Klem, Joan R. & Rademacher, Susan C. Rottweilers. (Illus.). 125p. 1981. 4.95 (ISBN 0-87666-726-4, KW-116). TFH Pubns.

Klem, Joan R. & Rodemacher, P. G. How to Raise & Train a Rottweiler. (Orig.). pap. 2.95 (ISBN 0-87666-373-0, DS1110). TFH Pubns.

Klem, Kaye W. Mirrors. 1982. pap. 3.50 (ISBN 0-451-11862-6, AE1862, Sig). NAL.

Kleman, M. Points, Lines & Walls: Liquid Crystals, Magnetic Systems & Various Ordered Media. LC 81-21976. 322p. 1982. 54.95 (ISBN 0-471-10194-X, Pub. by Wiley-Interscience). Wiley.

Klement, A. W. & Schultz, V., eds. Freshwater & Terrestrial Radioecology: A Selected Bibliography. LC 80-22169. 587p. 1980. 46.00 (ISBN 0-87933-389-8). Hutchinson Ross.

Klement, Alfred W., Jr., ed. Radioactive Fallout from Nuclear Weapons Tests: Proceedings. LC 65-62945. (AEC Symposium Ser.). 965p. 1965. pap. 32.25 (ISBN 0-87079-323-3, CONF-765); microfiche 4.50 (ISBN 0-87079-324-1, CONF-765). DOE.

Klemin, Diana. Art of Art for Children's Books. (Illus.). 1966. 6.95 o.p. (ISBN 0-517-02438-1, C N Potter Bks). Crown.

--The Illustrated Book: Its Art & Craft. 1970. 10.00 o.p. (ISBN 0-517-11039-3, C N Potter Bks). Crown.

Klemin, Diana, compiled by. Christmas Sampler of Feasts: Menus & Recipes for the Twelve Days of Christmas. LC 82-45447. 64p. 1982. pap. 2.50 (ISBN 0-385-18325-9); prepack of 12 30.00 (ISBN 0-385-18368-2). Doubleday.

Klemke, E. D., ed. Essays on Frege. LC 68-18205. 1968. 15.00 o.p. (ISBN 0-252-78401-4); pap. 8.95 o.p. (ISBN 0-252-72435-6). U of Ill Pr.

--The Meaning of Life. 1981. pap. text ed. 8.95x (ISBN 0-19-502871-6). Oxford U Pr.

Klemke, E. D., et al, eds. Introductory Readings in the Philosophy of Science. LC 80-65940. 373p. 1980. pap. text ed. 13.95 (ISBN 0-87975-134-7). Prometheus Bks.

Klemmack, David L., jt. auth. see Atherton, Charles R.

Klemperer, D., tr. see Welder, G.

Klemperer, O. E. & Barnett, M. E. Electron Optics. 3rd ed. LC 74-118065. (Cambridge Physics Monographs). (Illus.). 1970. 72.50 (ISBN 0-521-07928-4). Cambridge U Pr.

Klenck, Robert H. Words Fitly Spoken: Reflections & Prayers. LC 79-13449. 1979. 10.95 (ISBN 0-934878-35-8, 07764-1, Dist. by W.W. Norton). Dembner Bks.

Klenicki, Leon, jt. ed. see Croner, Helga.

Klenk, Robert W. & Ryan, Robert M. Practice of Social Work. 2nd ed. 1974. pap. 11.95x o.p. (ISBN 0-534-00341-9). Wadsworth Pub.

Klenk, Virginia. Understanding Symbolic Logic. (Illus.). 480p. 1983. 21.95 (ISBN 0-13-936468-4). P-H.

Klenke, William W. Art of Wood Turning. (gr. 7-12). 1954. 15.80 (ISBN 0-87002-104-4). Bennett IL.

Klenke-Hamel, Karen, jt. auth. see Janda, Louis.

Klenke-Hamel, Karin E., jt. auth. see Janda, Louis H.

Klentos, Gus & Newmyer, Joseph, Jr. Elementary Functions: Algebra & Analytic Geometry. 448p. 1975. pap. text ed. 20.95 (ISBN 0-675-08827-5); media: audiocassettes 160.00 (ISBN 0-675-08774-0). Additional supplements may be obtained from publisher. Merrill.

--Elementary Functions: Trigonometry. LC 73-87838. 1974. text ed. 19.95 (ISBN 0-675-08864-X); media: audiocassettes 140.00 (ISBN 0-675-08865-8). Additional supplements may be obtained from publisher. Merrill.

Klentos, Gus, jt. auth. see Newmyer, Joseph.

Klentos, Gus, jt. auth. see Newmyer, Joseph, Jr.

Klenze, Camillo Von. From Goethe to Hauptmann: Studies in a Changing Culture. LC 66-23519. 1926. 10.00x (ISBN 0-8196-0178-0). Biblo.

Klepec, Lou. William Scott: Drawings. LC 75-684. 1975. 12.00 (ISBN 0-685-56530-0, Dist. by David Anderson Gallery). D Anderson.

Kleper, Michael L. Illustrated Dictionary of Typographic Communication. (Illus.). 208p. (Orig.). 1983. pap. 19.00 (ISBN 0-89938-008-5). Tech & Ed Ctr Graph Arts RIT.

Klepfisz, Irena. Keeper of Accounts. LC 82-18910. 108p. 1982. pap. 5.95 (ISBN 0-930436-17-2). Persephone.

Kleppner, Daniel & Kolenkow, Robert J. An Introduction to Mechanics. (Illus.). 736p. 1973. text ed. 37.50 (ISBN 0-07-035048-5, C); solutions manual 25.00 (ISBN 0-07-035049-3). McGraw.

Kleppner, Otto & Settel, Irving, eds. Exploring Advertising. (Illus.). 1969. pap. text ed. 14.95 (ISBN 0-13-296020-6). P-H.

Kleppner, Paul. Who Voted: The Dynamics of Electoral Turnout, 1870-1980. Pomper, Gerald M., ed. (American Political Parties & Elections Ser.). 254p. 1982. 27.95 (ISBN 0-03-058933-9). Praeger.

Kleps, Arthur J. Boo Hoo Bible: The Neo-American Church Catechism & Handbook. rev. ed. LC 73-29356. Orig. Title: Neo-American Church Catechism. (Illus.). 218p. 1971. pap. 5.00 (ISBN 0-9600388-1-7). Neo-Am Church.

Klerk, M. Muziek-Karikaturen: Music-Caricatures. (Haags Gemeentemuseum, Kijkboekjes Ser.: Vol. 2). 60p. 1981. wrappers 15.00 o.s.i. (ISBN 90-6027-282-X, Pub. by Frits Knuf Netherlands). Pendragon NY.

Klerk, M. & Mensink, O. Japanse Preten Met Muziek: Japanese Woodcuts with Music. (Haags Gemeentemuseum, Kijkboekjes Ser.: Vol. 1). 1976. wrappers 15.00 o.s.i. (ISBN 90-6027-281-1, Pub. by Frits Knuf Netherlands). Pendragon NY.

Klerman, Gerald & Weissman, Myrna. Interpersonal Psychotherapy of Depression. 1983. text ed. 20.95x (ISBN 0-465-03396-2). Basic.

Klesney, S. P., jt. ed. see Rigaudy, J.

Klesnil, M. & Lukas, P. Fatigue of Metallic Materials. (Materials Science Monograph: Vol. 7). 1980. 57.50 (ISBN 0-444-99762-8). Elsevier.

Klevan, Jacob B. Modeling of Available Egress Time from Assembly Spaces or Estimating the Advance of the Fire Threat. Date not set. 4.65 (ISBN 0-686-37666-8, TR 82-2). Society Fire Protect.

Klevins, Gil. Your Career in Office Occupations. LC 77-17377. (Arco Career Guidance Ser.). (Illus.). 1978. lib. bdg. 7.95 (ISBN 0-668-04449-7); pap. 4.50 (ISBN 0-668-04434-9). Arco.

Kleyn, A. H. Seismic Reflection Interpretation. (Illus.). xii, 265p. 1983. 57.50 (ISBN 0-85334-161-3, Pub. by Applied Sci England). Elsevier.

Kliban, B. Cat. LC 75-8980. (Illus.). 160p. (Orig.). 1975. pap. 3.95 (ISBN 0-911104-54-2). Workman Pub.

--Cat. deluxe ed. LC 76-25536. (Illus.). 164p. 1976. 4.95 o.s.i. (ISBN 0-911104-87-9). Workman Pub.

--Cat Calendar Cats. LC 80-54619. (Illus.). 144p. 1981. 17.50 o.p. (ISBN 0-89480-169-4). Workman Pub.

--Kliban in a Bigger Box. (Illus.). 1979. 4 slipcased bks. 13.95 o.s.i. (ISBN 0-89480-105-8). Workman Pub.

--Tiny Footprints. LC 77-94086. (Illus.). 160p. 1978. pap. 3.95 (ISBN 0-89480-031-0). Workman Pub.

--Whack Your Porcupine & Other Drawings. LC 76-52861. (Illus.). 160p. 1977. pap. 3.95 (ISBN 0-911104-92-5). Workman Pub.

Klibbe, Lawrence & Storey, Wayne. Italian Grammar. 156p. (Orig.). 1982. pap. 4.95 (ISBN 0-06-460199-4, CO 1991). B&N NY.

Klibbe, Lawrence H. Fernan Caballero. (World Authors Ser.). 1971. lib. bdg. 15.85 (ISBN 0-8057-2187-8, Twayne). G K Hall.

--Jose Maria de Pereda. (World Authors Ser.). 15.95 (ISBN 0-686-75274-0, Twayne). G K Hall.

Kliebard, Herbert E., jt. ed. see Bellack, Arno A.

Klieneberger-Nobel, E. Focus on Bacteria. 1965. 25.00 o.s.i. (ISBN 0-12-414950-2). Acad Pr.

Kliewer, Evelyn. Please, God, Help Me Get Well in Your Spare Time. LC 79-17683. 128p. 1979. pap. 3.95 (ISBN 0-87123-027-5, 210027). Bethany Hse.

Kliewer, Vernon L. Music Reading: A Comprehensive Approach, Vol. 1. LC 72-3870. (Illus.). 352p. 1973. pap. text ed. 15.95 (ISBN 0-13-607903-2). P-H.

Kliewer, Warren. Moralities & Miracles. 1962. 3.00 o.p. (ISBN 0-8233-0054-4). Golden Quill.

--Violators. 3.00 o.p. (ISBN 0-8338-0037-X). M Jones.

Kligman, Albert M. & Leyden, James L., eds. Assessment of Safety & Efficacy of Topical Drugs & Cosmetics. 432p. Date not set. 39.50 (ISBN 0-8089-1527-4). Grune.

Klika, Thom. Rainbows. LC 78-21416. (Illus.). 1979. 10.95 o.p. (ISBN 0-312-66293-9); pap. 7.95 (ISBN 0-312-66294-7). St Martin.

--Ten Thousand Rainbows. (Illus.). 80p. 1983. pap. 6.95 (ISBN 0-312-79096-1); pap. 69.50 prepack of 10 (ISBN 0-312-79098-8). St Martin.

Klima, Jon. The Solar Controls Book: Fundamentals of Domestic Hot Water & Space Heating Solar Controls, 4 vols. (Illus.). 1982. Set. 39.95 (ISBN 0-940894-04-1); tchr's. guide, solutions manual 5.95 (ISBN 0-940894-05-X). Solar Training.

Kliman, Gilbert W. & Rosenfeld, Albert. Responsible Parenthood. LC 79-3437. 360p. 1983. pap. 8.95 (ISBN 0-03-063537-3). HR&W.

Kliman, M. Two Cents Pieces & Varieties. (Illus.). 1983. softcover 10.00 (ISBN 0-915262-84-3). S J Durst.

Klimburg-Salter, Deborah E. Buddist Art & Culture of the Hindu Kush. (Illus.). 256p. 1983. 35.00 (ISBN 0-87773-765-7). Great Eastern.

Klimet, Stephen A. Creative Communications for a Successful Design Practice. 1977. 24.95 (ISBN 0-8230-7133-2, Whitney Lib). Watson-Guptill.

Klimkeit, Hans-Joachim. Manichaean Art & Calligraphy. (Iconography of Religion: Vol. XX). (Illus.). xii, 50p. 1982. pap. write for info. (ISBN 90-04-06478-8). E J Brill.

Klimley, April. Here Is Your Career: Banking, Money & Finance. LC 77-28281. (Here Is Your Career Ser.). (Illus.). (gr. 6 up). 1978. 7.95 o.p. (ISBN 0-399-20628-0). Putnam Pub Group.

Klimo, Kate, ed. Fly Away with E.T. (Tubbies Ser.). (Illus.). 10p. 1983. 2.95 (ISBN 0-671-46437-X, Little). S&S.

--Look at Plants with E.T. (Illus.). 14p. 1982. 3.50 (ISBN 0-671-46435-3, Little). S&S.

--Meet Baby Animals with E.T. (Illus.). 14p. 1982. 3.50 (ISBN 0-671-46434-5, Little). S&S.

--Meet E.T. the Extra-Terrestrial. (Tubbies Ser.). (Illus.). 10p. 1982. 2.95 (ISBN 0-671-46436-1, Little). S&S.

Klimo, Kate, ed. see Alda, Arlene.

Klimo, Kate, ed. see Boynton, Sandra.

Klimo, Kate, ed. see Goodman, Joan E.

Klimo, Kate, ed. see Henry, Lawrence.

Klimo, Kate, ed. see Hyman, Jane & Lawrence, Patty.

Klimo, Kate, ed. see Hyman, Jane & Santeusanio, Joan.

Klimo, Kate, ed. see Jefferds, Vince.

Klimo, Kate, ed. see Johnson, Evelyne.

Klimo, Kate, ed. see Marshall, Ray & Paul, Korkey.

Klimo, Kate, ed. see Marshall, Ray & Paul, Korky.

Klimo, Kate, ed. see Miller, Suzanne S.

Klimo, Kate, ed. see Moskowitz, Stewart.

Klimo, Kate, ed. see Pienkowski, Jan.

Klimo, Kate, ed. see Rose, Dorothy.

Klimo, Kate, ed. see Schongut, Emanuel.

Klimo, Kate, ed. see Walt Disney Productions.

Klimo, Kate, ed. see Walt Disney Studios.

Klimo, Kate, ed. see Williams, Margery.

Klimo, Kate, ed. see Yeatman, Linda.

Klimo, Kate, ed. see Zokeisha.

Klimontovich, Yu L. The Kinetic Theory of Electromagnetic Processes. (Springer Series in Synergetics: Vol. 10). 320p. 1983. 44.50 (ISBN 0-387-11458-0). Springer-Verlag.

--Kinetic Theory of Nonideal Gases & Nonideal Plasmas, Vol. 105. Bakescu, R., tr. LC 82-9044. (International Series in Natural Philosophy). (Illus.). 328p. 1982. 65.00 (ISBN 0-08-021671-4). Pergamon.

Klimova, Nina T. Folk Embroidery of the U. S. S. R. LC 80-15453. (Illus.). 128p. 1981. 19.95 (ISBN 0-442-24464-9). Van Nos Reinhold.

Klimt, Gustav. One Hundred Drawings. (Orig.). 1972. pap. 5.00 (ISBN 0-486-22446-5). Dover.

--Twenty Five Drawings. 1964. Bound. 105.00x o.p. (ISBN 3-201-00373-5). Intl Pubns Serv.

Kline, jt. auth. see Eadie.

Kline, A. Burt, Jr., ed. The Environmental & Ecological Forum, 1970-1971. AEC Technical Information Center. LC 72-600120. (AEC Technical Information Center Ser.). 194p. 1972. pap. 12.75 (ISBN 0-87079-197-4, TID-25857); microfiche 4.50 (ISBN 0-87079-198-2, TID-25857). DOE.

Kline, Adam. Marriage & Family Law in Washington. 187p. 1979. 4.50 (ISBN 0-88908-708-3). Self Counsel Pr.

Kline, David. Kampuchea: A Photo Record from the First American Visit to Cambodia Since the End of the War. LC 78-64664. 1979. 15.95x (ISBN 0-930720-55-5); pap. 6.95 (ISBN 0-930720-56-3). Liberator Pr.

Kline, Gary, jt. auth. see Agee, Anne.

Kline, Harvey F. Columbia. (Nations of Contemporary Latin America). 144p. 1983. lib. bdg. 16.50 (ISBN 0-89158-941-4). Westview.

Kline, Harvey F., jt. auth. see Wiarda, Howard.

Kline, John M. State Government Influence in U. S. International Economic Policy. LC 82-48473. 288p. 1983. 27.95x (ISBN 0-669-06141-7). Lexington Bks.

Kline, Linda & Feinstein, Lloyd. Career Changing: The Worry-Free Guide. 1982. pap. 10.95 (ISBN 0-316-49858-0). Little.

Kline, Linda J. & Carhart, Jane M., eds. Multi-State Information System: Proceedings of the Sixth Annual National Users Group Conference. (May 4, 5 & 6, 1981 Orangeburg, NY). 225p. (Orig.). 1982. pap. 10.00 (ISBN 0-936934-02-6). Rockland Resea.

Kline, Mary-Jo & Ryan, Joanne W., eds. Political Correspondence & Public Papers of Aaron Burr, 2 vols. LC 82-61396. (Illus.). 1228p. 1983. 125.00x (ISBN 0-691-04685-9). Princeton U Pr.

Kline, Morris. Calculus: An Intuitive & Physical Approach. 2nd ed. LC 76-22760. 943p. 1977. text ed. 35.95 (ISBN 0-471-49116-0); solutions manual avail. (ISBN 0-471-02396-5). Wiley.

--Mathematics in Western Culture. (Illus.). 1964. pap. 12.95 (ISBN 0-19-500714-X, GB). Oxford U Pr.

--Mathematics: The Loss of Certainty. (Illus.). 1980. 22.50 (ISBN 0-19-502754-X). Oxford U Pr.

--Why the Professor Can't Teach: Mathematics & the Dilemma of American Undergraduate Education. LC 76-62777. (Illus.). 256p. 1977. 10.00 o.p. (ISBN 0-312-87867-2). St Martin.

Kline, Naomi R. Castles: An Enduring Fantasy. (Illus.). 224p. 1983. 30.00 (ISBN 0-89241-374-3). Caratzas Bros.

Kline, Nathan S. From Sad to Glad: Kline on Depression. LC 74-79652. 288p. 1974. 7.95 o.p. (ISBN 0-399-11372-X). Putnam Pub Group.

Kline, Nathan S., ed. Factors in Depression. LC 74-77571. 284p. 1974. 27.00 (ISBN 0-911216-79-0). Raven.

Kline, Raymond. Structured Digital Design Including MSI-LSI Components & Microprocessors. (Illus.). 544p. 1983. text ed. 28.95 (ISBN 0-13-854554-5). P-H.

Kline, Raymond M. Digital Computer Design. (Illus.). 1977. 31.95 (ISBN 0-13-214205-8). P-H.

Kline, Robert D., jt. ed. see Murphy, Thomas P.

Kline, Tilde S. Handbook of Fine Needle Aspiration Biopsy Cytology. LC 81-38371. (Illus.). 319p. 1981. text ed. 49.50 (ISBN 0-8016-2701-X). Mosby.

Klineberg, Otto. Race Differences. LC 74-5777. 367p. 1974. Repr. of 1935 ed. lib. bdg. 20.25x (ISBN 0-8371-7519-4, KLRD). Greenwood.

Klineberg, Otto & Hull, W. Frank, IV. At a Foreign University: An International Study of Adaptation & Coping. 223p. 26.95 (ISBN 0-03-052486-5). Praeger.

Klinefelter, Walter. A Display of Old Maps & Plans, Third. LC 73-86565. 80p. 1973. 5.00 (ISBN 0-911462-10-4). Sumac.

--A Fourth Display of Old Maps & Plans. LC 77-94176. 1978. 6.00 (ISBN 0-911462-11-2). Sumac.

--The Origins of Sherlock Holmes. LC 81-85167. (Illus.). 88p. 1983. 10.95 (ISBN 0-934468-13-3). Gaslight.

Klinefelter, Walter, et al. The ABC Books of the Pennsylvania Germans: Bd. with Abraham Harley Cassel, Nineteenth Century Pennsylvania-German American Book Collector; and Marriages Performed at the Evangelical Lutheran Church...1748-1767, Vol. VII. LC 68-4243. 1973. 15.00 (ISBN 0-911122-29-X). Penn German Soc.

Kline-Graber, Georgia & Graber, Benjamin. Woman's Orgasm: A Guide to Sexual Satisfaction. 240p. 1983. pap. 3.50 (ISBN 0-446-31123-5). Warner Bks.

Klineman, George, et al. The Cult That Died: The Tragedy of Jim Jones & the People's Temple. 456p. 1980. 14.95 o.p. (ISBN 0-399-12540-X). Putnam Pub Group.

Kling, Arthur, jt. ed. see Smith, W. Lynn.

Kling, Blair B. Partner in Empire: Dwarkanath Tagore & the Age of Enterprise in Eastern India. LC 74-27293. 1977. 28.50x (ISBN 0-520-02927-5). U of Cal Pr.

Kling, Blair B. & Pearson, M. N., eds. The Age of Partnership: Europeans in Asia Before Dominion. LC 78-31650. 1979. text ed. 14.00x (ISBN 0-8248-0495-3). UH Pr.

Klingaman, David & Vedder, Richard, eds. Essays in Nineteenth Century Economic History: The Old Northwest. LC 74-80811. xiv, 356p. 1975. 18.00x (ISBN 0-8214-0170-X, 82-81693). Ohio U Pr.

Klingberg, F. J. & Klingberg, F. W. The Correspondence Between Henry Stephens Randall & Hugh Blair Grigsby 1856-1861. LC 73-37530. (The American Scene Ser). 196p. 1972. Repr. of 1952 ed. lib. bdg. 29.50 (ISBN 0-306-70429-3). Da Capo.

Klingberg, F. W., jt. auth. see Klingberg, F. J.

Klingborg, Arne, jt. auth. see Biesantz, Hagen.

Klingborg, Arne, jt. auth. see Raab, Rex.

Klinge, Peter & McConkey, Lee. Introduction to Film Structure. LC 81-40837. 234p. (Orig.). 1982. lib. bdg. 21.75 (ISBN 0-8191-2553-9); pap. text ed. 10.75 (ISBN 0-8191-2554-7). U Pr of Amer.

Klinge, Peter L., jt. auth. see Ulloth, Dana R.

Klingemann, Hans D. & Pappi, Franz Urban. German Pre-& Post-Election Study, 1969. 1974. codebk. write for info. (ISBN 0-89138-102-3). ICPSR.

Klingenberg, Allen J., jt. auth. see Genck, Fredric H.

Klingender, Francis D. Animals in Art & Thought to the End of the Middle Ages. Antal, Evelyn & Harthan, John, eds. 1971. 50.00x o.p. (ISBN 0-262-11040-7). MIT Pr.

Klinger, A., jt. ed. see Tanimoto, S.

Klinger, David S., ed. Ultrasensitive Spectroscopic Techniques. LC 82-18417. (Quantum Electronics Ser.). Date not set. 55.00 (ISBN 0-12-414980-4). Acad Pr.

Klinger, H. P., jt. ed. see Jotterand-Bellomo, Martine.

Klinger, H. P., et al, eds. Chromosome Mutations: Their Potential Relevance to the Genetic Risks in Man. (Journal: Cytogenetics & Cell Genetics: Vol. 33, No. 1-2). (Illus.). 220p. 1982. pap. 76.75 (ISBN 3-8055-3569-4). S Karger.

Klinger, M., jt. auth. see Rinne, U. K.

Klinger, Ron. Basic Bridge. 1978. pap. 9.50 (ISBN 0-575-02637-5, Pub. by Gollancz England). David & Charles.

--Bridge Without Error. (Master Bridge Ser.). (Illus.). 128p. 1981. pap. 9.50 (ISBN 0-575-02946-3, Pub. by Gollancz England). David & Charles.

--Winning Bridge: Trick by Trick. 1980. pap. 9.50 (ISBN 0-575-02798-3, Pub. by Gollancz England). David & Charles.

--World Championship Pairs Bridge. 160p. 1983. 16.50 (ISBN 0-575-03233-2, Pub. by Gollancz England). David & Charles.

Klinghoffer, Arthur J. The Angolan War: A Study in Soviet Foreign Policy in the Third World. (Westview Special Studies on Africa). 235p. 1980. lib. bdg. 25.00 (ISBN 0-86531-022-X). Westview.

Klingman, David, jt. ed. see Hutt, William H.

Klingman, Ed. Microprocessor Systems Design. LC 76-45190. (Illus.). 1977. 32.95 (ISBN 0-13-581413-8). P-H.

Klingman, Glenn C. & Ashton, Floyd M. Weed Science: Principles & Practices. LC 75-8908. 431p. 1975. 24.00x o.p. (ISBN 0-471-49171-3, Pub. by Wiley-Interscience). Wiley.

--Weed Science: Principles & Practices. 2nd ed. 449p. 1982. text ed. 24.50x (ISBN 0-471-08487-5, Pub. by Wiley-Interscience). Wiley.

Klingner. Public Administration: A Management Approach. 1982. 16.95 (ISBN 0-686-84652-4); supplementary materials avail. HM.

Klingner, Donald. Public Administration: A Management Approach. 432p. 1983. text ed. 16.95 (ISBN 0-395-32796-2); instrs.' manual avail. (ISBN 0-395-32797-0). HM.

--Public Personnel Management: Contexts & Strategies. (Illus.). 1980. text ed. 23.95 (ISBN 0-13-737981-1). P-H.

Klingner, Donald E., ed. Public Personnel Management: Readings in Contexts & Strategies. LC 80-84019. (Illus.). 422p. 1981. pap. 14.95 (ISBN 0-87484-517-3). Mayfield Pub.

Klingsberg, E. Pyridine & Its Derivatives. 711p. 1964. 236.95x (ISBN 0-470-38016-0, Pub. by Wiley-Interscience). Wiley.

Klingstedt, John P., jt. auth. see Brock, Horace R.

Klink, J. J. Real Estate Accounting & Reporting: A Guide for Developers, Investors & Lenders. 277p. 1980. 44.95x (ISBN 0-471-06041-0). Ronald Pr.

Klink, William. Maxwell Anderson & S. N. Behrman: A Reference Guide. 1977. lib. bdg. 16.50 (ISBN 0-8161-7824-0, Hall Reference). G K Hall.

--Sentence Writing. LC 80-5805. (Illus.). 141p. (Orig.). 1981. pap. text ed. 8.25 (ISBN 0-8191-1430-8). U Pr of Amer.

Klink, William R. The Arts of Twentieth Century America. LC 80-1423. 240p. 1980. pap. 10.25 (ISBN 0-8191-1133-3). U Pr of Amer.

Klinke, H. Reichenbach see Reichenbach-Klinke, H. & Elkan, E.

Klinkenborg, Verlyn, ed. British Literary Manuscripts: Series I. 259p. 1981. pap. 12.50 (ISBN 0-486-24124-6). Dover.

Klinkowitz, Jerome. Kurt Vonnegut. (Contemporary Writers Ser.). 1982. pap. 4.25 (ISBN 0-416-33480-6). Methuen Inc.

--Vonnegut in America. 1977. 3.95 o.s.i. (ISBN 0-440-59244-5, Delta). Dell.

Klinkowitz, Jerome & Lawler, Donald L. Vonnegut in America. (Illus.). 1977. 8.95 o.s.i. (ISBN 0-440-09343-0, Sey Lawr). Delacorte.

Klinkowitz, Jerome, jt. auth. see Pieratt, Asa B., Jr.

Klinkowitz, Jerome, jt. auth. see Somer, John.

Klinkowitz, Jerome, ed. see Vonnegut, Kurt.

Klinowski, Jacek, jt. auth. see Garbicz, Adam.

Klinzing, Dene, jt. auth. see Klinzing, Dennis.

Klinzing, Dennis & Klinzing, Dene. The Hospitalized Child: Communication Techniques for Health Personnel. (Illus.). 1977. pap. text ed. 12.95 (ISBN 0-13-394817-X). P-H.

Klinzing, George E. Gas-Solid Transport. (Chemical Engineering Ser.). (Illus.). 358p. 1981. text ed. 37.50 (ISBN 0-07-035047-7, C). McGraw.

Klinzing, James E., jt. auth. see Melograno, Vincent J.

Kliot, Jules, jt. auth. see Kliot, Kaethe.

Kliot, Jules, ed. see Hoare, Katharin L.

Kliot, Jules, ed. see Tashjian, Nouvart.

Kliot, Kaethe & Kliot, Jules. Bobbin Lace: Form by the Twisting of Cords. (Arts & Crafts Ser.). (Illus.). 264p. 1973. pap. 4.95 o.p. (ISBN 0-517-50593-2). Crown.

Kliot, Kaethe, ed. see Tashjian, Nouvart.

Klir, George J. Introduction to the Methodology of Switching Circuits. 1972. text ed. 15.95x o.p. (ISBN 0-442-24463-0). Van Nos Reinhold.

Klir, George J., ed. Trends in General Systems Theory. LC 71-178143. 462p. 1972. 47.95x (ISBN 0-471-49190-X, Pub. by Wiley-Interscience). Wiley.

Klitgaard, Robert E. On the Economics of Integrated Rural Development. (Lincoln Institute Monograph Ser. No. 81-6). 58p. 1981. pap. text ed. 4.00 (ISBN 0-686-35841-4). Lincoln Inst Land.

Kliuchevskii, V. O. Istoriia Soslovii V Rossii. (Russian Ser.: Vol. 16). Repr. of 1918 ed. 22.00 (ISBN 0-87569-012-2). Academic Intl.

Klix & Hoffmann. Cognition & Memory. (Advances in Psychology Ser.: Vol. 5). 1981. 53.25 (ISBN 0-444-86041-X). Elsevier.

Klix, et al. Cognitive Research in Psychology. Date not set. 47.00 (ISBN 0-444-86350-8). Elsevier.

Klix, F., ed. Human & Artificial Intelligence. (Fundamental Studies in Computer Science: Vol. 8). 1979. 42.75 (ISBN 0-444-85173-9, North Holland). Elsevier.

Klock, David R., jt. auth. see Pfeffer, Irving.

Klockars, C. B. Thinking about Police: Contemporary Readings. (Criminology & Criminal Justice Ser.). 592p. 1983. 15.95 (ISBN 0-07-035054-X, C). McGraw.

Klocker, Harry. God & the Empiricists. (Horizons in Philosophy Ser.). 1968. pap. 1.95x o.p. (ISBN 0-02-819840-9, 81982). Glencoe.

Klocker, Harry R. The God Within. LC 81-40598. 158p. (Orig.). 1982. lib. bdg. 20.25 (ISBN 0-8191-2031-6); pap. text ed. 9.75 (ISBN 0-8191-2032-4). U Pr of Amer.

Kloe, Donald R. Understanding the Spanish Subjunctive. LC 77-88205. 1977. pap. text ed. 5.50 (ISBN 0-87716-084-8, Pub. by Moore Pub Co). F Apple.

Kloefkorn, William. Alvin Turner As Farmer. 1977. pap. 4.95 (ISBN 0-931534-02-X). Windflower Pr.

--Uncertain the Final Run to Winter. 1977. pap. 4.95 (ISBN 0-931534-01-1). Windflower Pr.

Kloefkorn, William & Kooser, Ted. Cottonwood County. 1980. pap. 3.00 o.p. (ISBN 0-931534-08-9). Windflower Pr.

Kloep, Marion. Zur Psychologie der Aufgabenschwierigkeit. vi, 355p. (Ger.). 1982. write for info. (ISBN 3-8204-5833-6). P Lang Pubs.

Kloepfel, Don V., frwd. by. Motion Picture Projection & Theatre Presentation Manual. (Illus.). 166p. 1982. pap. text ed. 20.00 (ISBN 0-940690-01-2). Soc Motion Pic & TV Engrs.

Kloepfer, Marquerite. The Heart & the Scarab. 288p. 1981. pap. 2.50 o.p. (ISBN 0-380-77610-3, 77610). Avon.

Kloesel, Christian J., jt. ed. see Fisch, Max H.

Klohn, Charles H., jt. ed. see American Society of Civil Engineers.

Klohn, Sabine. Helene Simon. 650p. (Ger.). 1982. write for info (ISBN 3-8204-6249-X). P Lang Pubs.

Klohr, M. C., jt. auth. see Goodyear, Margaret.

Kloidt, M. & Lysek, G. Die Epiphylle Pilzfora von Acer Platanoides L. (Bibliotheca Mycologica 86 Ser.). 144p. (Orig.). 1982. pap. text ed. 22.50 (ISBN 3-7682-1332-3). Lubrecht & Cramer.

Kloman, Erasmus H., ed. Cases in Accountability: The Work of the Gao. 1979. lib. bdg. 26.50 (ISBN 0-89158-395-5); pap. text ed. 11.00 (ISBN 0-89158-494-3). Westview.

Klonsky, Milton. Speaking Pictures: A Gallery of Pictorial Poetry. (Illus.). 352p. (YA) 1975. 12.00 o.p. (ISBN 0-517-52376-0, Harmony). Crown.

Kloos, Peter. Maroni River Caribs of Surinam. (Studies of Developing Countries). 1971. pap. text ed. 26.50x o.p. (ISBN 90-232-0903-6). Humanities.

Kloosterboer, Willemina. Involuntary Labour Since the Abolition of Slavery. LC 76-9771. 1976. Repr. of 1960 ed. lib. bdg. 18.00x (ISBN 0-8371-8887-3, KLIL). Greenwood.

Klopfer, Bruno & Davidson, Helen H. Rorschach Technique: An Introductory Manual. (Illus.). 245p. 1962. text ed. 30.95 (ISBN 0-15-577873-0, HC). HarBraceJ.

Klopfer, Bruno, et al. Developments in the Rorschach Technique, 3 vols. Incl. Vol. 1. Techniques & Theory. 726p (ISBN 0-15-517626-9); Vol. 2. Fields of Application. 828p (ISBN 0-15-517627-7); Vol. 3. Aspects of Personality Structure. 446p (ISBN 0-15-517628-5). 1970. 30.95 ea. (HC). HarBraceJ.

Klopfer, Leo E., jt. auth. see Champagne, Audrey B.

Klopfer, Peter H., jt. ed. see Bateson, P. P.

Kloppenburg-Versteegh, J. The Traditional Use of Malay Plants & Herbs. Kaufman, Aileen, tr. from Dutch. LC 79-89939. Orig. Title: Het Gebruik Van Indische Planten. (Illus.). 1984. 39.95 (ISBN 0-86164-152-3, Pub by Momenta Publishing Ltd U. K.). Hunter Hse.

Klopper, A., ed. Immunology of the Human Placenta: Supplement to the Quarterly Journal "Placenta", Vol. 4. 136p. 1982. 35.00 (ISBN 0-03-062117-8). Praeger.

Klopper, A., jt. ed. see Van Der Molen, H. J.

Klopper, Arnold, jt. ed. see Fuchs, Fritz.

Klopsch, Louis. Daily Light on the Daily Path. 1959. 2.95 o.p. (ISBN 0-448-01638-9, D&G). Putnam Pub Group.

--Daily Light on the Daily Path. 384p. 1983. 6.95 (ISBN 0-8407-5278-4). Nelson.

Klos, J., jt. auth. see Wittman, A.

Klose, Al P. Democracy, Technology, Collision. (ITT Key Issues Lecture Ser.). 1980. pap. 6.50 (ISBN 0-672-97676-5). Bobbs.

Klose, Nelson. Concise Study Guide to the American Frontier. LC 64-15180. (Illus.). 1964. 18.50x o.p. (ISBN 0-8032-0093-5); pap. 4.95x o.p. (ISBN 0-8032-5110-6). U of Nebr Pr.

--U. S. History, 2 vols. rev. ed. 480p. (gr. 9-12). 1983. Vol. 1. pap. text ed. 5.75 (ISBN 0-8120-2250-5); Vol. 2. pap. text ed. 5.75 (ISBN 0-8120-2251-3). Barron.

Kloss, Heinz. The American Bilingual Tradition. 1977. pap. 15.95 o.p. (ISBN 0-912066-06-7). Newbury Hse.

Kloss, Jethro. Back to Eden. LC 81-70187. (Illus.). 704p. pap. 4.95 (ISBN 0-912800-92-5). Woodbridge Pr.

Kloss, Phillips. Gene Kloss Etchings. Hausman, Gerald, ed. LC 81-16773. (Illus.). 190p. 1981. 37.95 (ISBN 0-86534-008-0). Sunstone Pr.

--The Great Kiva. LC 79-21344. (Illus.). 1980. 37.50 (ISBN 0-913270-82-2); pap. 14.95 (ISBN 0-913270-84-9). Sunstone Pr.

--Selected Poems of Phillips Kloss. Hausman, Gerald, ed. LC 82-19131. 128p. 1983. 10.95 (ISBN 0-686-82374-5). Sunstone Pr.

Klossowski de Rola, Stanislas. Balthus. LC 82-48579. (Icon Editions Ser.). (Illus.). 1983. 24.04i (ISBN 0-06-431275-5, HarpT). Har-Row.

Klotman, Robert H. The School Music Administrator & Supervisor: Catalysts for Change in Music Education. LC 72-6635. (Illus.). 256p. 1973. ref. ed. 17.95 (ISBN 0-13-793711-3). P-H.

Klots, Alexander B. & Klots, Elsie B. One Thousand One Questions Answered About Insects. (Illus.). 1977. pap. 5.00 (ISBN 0-486-23470-3). Dover.

Klots, Alfred P. & Colwill, Stiles T. The Lives & Paintings of Alfred Partridge Klots & His Son, Trafford Partridge Klots. (Illus.). 136p. 1979. 9.50 (ISBN 0-686-36495-3). Md Hist.

Klots, Elsie B. The New Field Book of Freshwater Life. LC 66-15583. (Putnam's Nature Field Bks.). (Illus.). 1966. 7.95 o.p. (ISBN 0-399-10288-4); pap. 4.50 o.p. (ISBN 0-399-12155-2). Putnam Pub Group.

Klots, Elsie B., jt. auth. see Klots, Alexander B.

Klotter, James C. & Sehlinger, Peter J., eds. Kentucky Profiles: Biographical Essays in Honor of Holman Hamilton. LC 82-81154. (Illus.). 224p. 1982. 19.95 (ISBN 0-916968-11-1). Kentucky Hist.

Klotter, John C. & Rosenfeld, Joseph. Criminal Justice Instructional Techniques. (Illus.). 216p. 1979. 16.75x (ISBN 0-398-03887-2); pap. 7.50x student workbook, 80p. (ISBN 0-398-03892-9). C C Thomas.

Klotz, Alexander H. Macrophysics & Geometry: From Einstein's Unified field Theory to Cosmology. LC 81-3849. 160p. 1982. 39.50 (ISBN 0-521-23938-9). Cambridge U Pr.

Klotz, Irving M. & Rosenberg, R. M. Chemical Thermodynamics. 3rd ed. 1972. 26.95 (ISBN 0-8053-5506-5). Benjamin-Cummings.

Klotz, Lynn, jt. auth. see Sylvester, Ed.

Klotz, Marvin, jt. ed. see Abcarian, Richard.

Klotz, Saadi, ed. see Lewis, Samuel L.

Klovdahl, Alden S. Social Networks: Selected References for Course Design & Research Planning. (Public Administration Ser.: P 79). 1978. pap. 7.50 o.p. (ISBN 0-88066-008-2). Vance Biblios.

Kluback, William, tr. see Perelman, Chaim.

Kluckhohn, Clyde & Wyman, L. C. Introduction to Navaho Chant Practice. LC 42-2722. 1940. pap. 23.00 (ISBN 0-527-00552-5). Kraus Repr.

Kluckhohn, Clyde, jt. auth. see Wyman, L. C.

Kluckhohn, Frank L. Lyndon's Legacy: A Candid Look at Some Presidential Policymakers. 1964. 6.95 (ISBN 0-8159-6113-8). Devin.

Klug, Anthony, jt. ed. see Tsichritzis, Dennis.

Klug, Eugene F. Getting into the Formula of Concord. 1977. pap. 3.50 (ISBN 0-570-03742-5, 12-2646). Concordia.

Klug, Harold P. & Alexander, Leroy E. X-Ray Diffraction Procedures: For Polycrystalline & Amorphous Materials. 2nd ed. LC 73-21936. (Illus.). 966p. 1974. 90.00x (ISBN 0-471-49369-4, Pub. by Wiley-Interscience). Wiley.

Klug, Jay, jt. ed. see Brown, Barbara B.

Klug, Ron. Growing in Joy: God's Way to Increase Joy in All of Life. LC 82-72637. 128p. 1983. pap. 4.95 (ISBN 0-8066-1943-0, 10-2902). Augsburg.

--Job: God's Answer to Suffering. (Fisherman Bible Studyguides). 80p. 1982. saddle-stitched 2.50 (ISBN 0-87788-430-7). Shaw Pubs.

--Psalms: A Guide to Prayer & Praise. (Fisherman Bible Studyguides Ser.). 1978. saddle stitch 2.50 (ISBN 0-87788-699-7). Shaw Pubs.

--Strange Young Man in the Desert: John the Baptist. (Arch Bks: Set 8). (Illus., Orig.). (ps-4). 1971. pap. 0.89 (ISBN 0-570-06057-5, 59-1174). Concordia.

Klug, Ron & Lyn, Klug. Jesus Lives. LC 82-72848. 32p. (Orig.). (ps). 1983. pap. 3.50 (ISBN 0-8066-1952-X, 10-3527). Augsburg.

Klug, Ronald. My Prayer Journal. LC 12-2964. 1982. pap. 3.95 (ISBN 0-570-03871-5). Concordia.

Klug, William S. & Cummings, Michael R. Concepts of Genetics. 1983. text ed. 22.95 (ISBN 0-675-20010-5). Additional supplements may be obtained from publisher. Merrill.

Kluger, Marilyn. Joy of Spinning. LC 72-139634. 1971. 10.95 o.p. (ISBN 0-671-20859-4). S&S.

Kluger, Richard. Star Witness. LC 78-7760. 1979. 10.95 o.p. (ISBN 0-385-13505-X). Doubleday.

Kluger, Ruth & Mann, Peggy. The Secret Ship. LC 76-2804. (Signal Bks.). (gr. 7 up). 1978. 5.95 (ISBN 0-385-11328-5). Doubleday.

Klugh, Henry E. Statistics: The Essentials for Research. 2nd ed. LC 73-16182. 426p. 1974. text ed. 27.50x (ISBN 0-471-49372-4). Wiley.

Klumpp, Gerhard. Reactivity in Organic Chemistry. LC 81-16437. 502p. 1982. 49.95x (ISBN 0-471-06285-5, Pub. by Wiley-Interscience). Wiley.

Klungness, Elizabeth J. & Klungness, James G. The Nongolfer's Cookbook. (Illus.). 160p. Date not set. pap. 5.95 (ISBN 0-910431-00-0). Tower Ent.

Klungness, James G., jt. auth. see Klungness, Elizabeth J.

Klunzinger, C. B. Synopsis der Fische Des Rothen Meeres, 2 parts in 1 vol. (Illus.). 1964. Repr. of 1871 ed. 40.00 (ISBN 3-7682-7115-3). Lubrecht & Cramer.

Klusen, Ernst A. Johann Wilhelm Wilms (1772-1847) und das Amsterdamer Musikleben Seiner Zeit. (Composers' Worklists Ser.: Vol. 3). 1975. wrappers 30.00 o.s.i. (ISBN 90-6027-283-8, Pub. by Frits Knuf Netherlands). Pendragon NY.

Klust, Gerhard. Netting Materials for Fishing Gear. 2nd ed. (Illus.). 173p. (Orig.). 1974. pap. 25.25 (ISBN 0-686-77007-2, FN98, FNB). Unipub.

Klutznick, Philip M., jt. auth. see Greene, Joseph N., Jr.

Kluver, Heinrich. Mescal & Mechanisms of Hallucinations. LC 66-20593. xviii, 108p. 1966. pap. 1.50 o.s.i. (ISBN 0-226-44506-2, P531, Phoen). U of Chicago Pr.

Kmenta, J. Elements of Econometrics. 1971. 28.95x (ISBN 0-02-365060-5). Macmillan.

Kmenta, J. & Ramsey, J. B., eds. Large-Scale Macro-Econometric Models: Theory & Practice. (Contributions to Economic Analysis Ser.: Vol. 141). 1981. 51.00 (ISBN 0-444-86295-1). Elsevier.

Kmetz, Yoko Sakakibara, jt. auth. see Brown, Jan.

Knab, Linda Z. Day is Waiting. pap. cancelled o.s.i. (ISBN 0-14-050395-1). Penguin.

Knabe, Peter E. & Rolshoven, Juergen, eds. Le Sacre. (Etudes Litteraires Francaises Ser.: No. 21). 136p. (Orig., Fr.). 1982. pap. 21.50 (ISBN 0-686-37111-9). Benjamins North Am.

Knabe, Peter E. & Rolshoven, Jurgen, eds. Le Sacre. 1982. pap. 21.50 o.p. (ISBN 0-686-36247-0). Benjamins North Am.

Knable, Alvin H. Electrical Power Systems Engineering. 1967. 39.50 o.p. (ISBN 0-07-035073-6, P&RB). McGraw.

--Electrical Power Systems Engineering: Problems & Solutions. LC 82-14801. 256p. 1983. lib. bdg. 22.50 (ISBN 0-89874-549-7). Krieger.

Knap, Jerome. The Digest Book of Hunging Tips. (The Sports & Leisure Library). (Illus.). 96p. 1979. pap. 2.95 o.s.i. (ISBN 0-695-81326-9). Follett.

--The Digest Book of Hunting Dogs. (The Sports & Leisure Library). (Illus.). 96p. 1979. pap. 2.95 o.s.i. (ISBN 0-695-81323-4). Follett.

--Your Fishing. (Illus.). 1978. 8.95 (ISBN 0-517-53320-0). Crown.

Knapke, William F. & Hubbard, Freeman. Railroad Caboose. LC 67-28316. (Illus.). (gr. 10 up). 1968. 15.95 (ISBN 0-87095-011-8). Golden West.

Knaplund, Paul. James Stephen & the British Colonial System, 1813-1847. LC 74-7611. 315p. 1974. Repr. of 1953 ed. lib. bdg. 19.25x (ISBN 0-8371-7590-9, KNJS). Greenwood.

Knapman, C. E. Developments in Chromatography, Vols. 1 & 2. 1978-80. Vol. 1. 33.00 (ISBN 0-85334-748-4, Pub. by Applied Sci England); Vol. 2. 33.00 (ISBN 0-85334-871-5). Elsevier.

Knapp, B. J. Soil Processes. (Process in Physical Geography Ser.: No. 2). (Illus.). 1979. pap. text ed. 6.95x (ISBN 0-04-631011-8). Allen Unwin.

Knapp, B. J., ed. Practical Foundations of Physical Geography. (Illus.). 152p. 1981. pap. text ed. 14.95x (ISBN 0-04-551035-0); tchr's ed. o.p. 13.50x (ISBN 0-04-551034-2). Allen Unwin.

Knapp, Barbara. Skill in Sport: The Attainment of Proficiency. 7th ed. (Illus.). 1979. pap. text ed. 22.50x (ISBN 0-7100-8562-1, SpS). Sportshelf.

Knapp, Barbara, jt. auth. see Chatham, Margaret.

Knapp, Bettina L. Anais Nin. LC 78-57692. (Literature and Life Ser.). 1978. 11.95 (ISBN 0-8044-2481-0); pap. 4.95 (ISBN 0-8044-6371-9). Ungar.

--Antonin Artaud: Man of Vision. LC 82-75968. 233p. 1980. pap. 5.95 (ISBN 0-8040-0809-4). Swallow.

--Emile Zola. LC 79-48079. (Literature and Life Ser.). 160p. 1980. 11.95 (ISBN 0-8044-2482-9). Ungar.

--Fernand Crommelynck. (World Authors Ser.). 1978. lib. bdg. 15.95 (ISBN 0-8057-6286-8, Twayne). G K Hall.

--Georges Duhamel. (World Authors Ser.). lib. bdg. 15.95 (ISBN 0-8057-2272-6, Twayne). G K Hall.

--Jean Racine: Mythos & Renewal in Modern Theater. LC 77-148686. 286p. 1971. 19.50 o.s.i. (ISBN 0-8173-7604-6). U of Ala Pr.

--Lewis Mumford-David Liebovitz Letters. 120p. 1983. 20.00 (ISBN 0-87875-250-1). Whitston Pub.

--Maurice Maeterlinck. (World Authors Ser.). 1975. lib. bdg. 15.95 (ISBN 0-8057-2562-8, Twayne). G K Hall.

--Paul Claudel. LC 81-40465. (Literature and Life Ser.). 220p. 1982. 11.95 (ISBN 0-8044-2479-9). Ungar.

--Sacha Guitry. (Filmmakers Ser.). 1981. lib. bdg. 14.95 (ISBN 0-8057-9278-3, Twayne). G K Hall.

Knapp, Brian. Earth & Man. (Illus.). 1982. pap. text ed. 12.50x o.p. (ISBN 0-04-551055-5). Allen Unwin.

Knapp, C. A Fruitful Bough. pap. 3.75 (ISBN 0-88172-112-3). Believers Bkshelf.

--Samuel the Prophet. 5.50 (ISBN 0-88172-113-1). Believers Bkshelf.

Knapp, Charles C. Problems in Contract Law: Cases & Materials. 1976. 29.95 (ISBN 0-316-49922-6). Little.

Knapp, Christopher. Kings of Judah & Israel. 1942. 5.50 (ISBN 0-87213-460-1). Loizeaux.

Knapp, Daniel R. Handbook of Analytical Derivatization Reactions. LC 78-12944. 741p. 1979. 69.00x (ISBN 0-471-03469-X, Pub. by Wiley-Interscience). Wiley.

Knapp, David A., jt. auth. see Smith, Mickey C.

Knapp, Frank A. Life of Sebastian Lerdo De Tejada, 1823-1889: A Study of Influence & Obscurity. LC 68-23305. 1968. Repr. of 1951 ed. lib. bdg. 19.75x (ISBN 0-8371-0132-8, KNLT). Greenwood.

Knapp, H. & Doring, R. Vapor-Liquid Equilibra for Mixtures of Low Boiling Substances. Berhens, D. & Eckermann, R., eds. (Dechema Chemistry Data Ser.). (Illus.). 910p. 1982. 142.50x (ISBN 0-686-43225-8, Pub. by Dechema Germany). Scholium Intl.

Knapp, Herbert, jt. auth. see Knapp, Mary.

Knapp, J. Merrill. The Magic of Opera. (Music Reprint Ser.). 371p. 1983. Repr. of 1973 ed. lib. bdg. 29.50 (ISBN 0-306-76148-3). Da Capo.

Knapp, James F. Ezra Pound. (United States Author Ser.). 1979. 11.95 (ISBN 0-8057-7286-3, Twayne). G K Hall.

Knapp, Joseph G. The Advance of American Cooperative Enterprise. (Illus.). 646p. 1973. text ed. 9.95x (ISBN 0-8134-1536-5). Interstate.

Knapp, Sr. Justina. Christian Symbols & How to Use Them. LC 74-8172. (Illus.). 164p. 1975. Repr. of 1935 ed. 37.00x (ISBN 0-8103-4050-X). Gale.

Knapp, Ken. Idaho Fishing Guide. 320p. 1983. pap. 9.95 (ISBN 0-87842-156-4). Mountain Pr.

Knapp, Kenneth W. Trees of the Oregon Campus: University of Oregon at Eugene. 1980. pap. 5.95x o.p. (ISBN 0-88246-152-4). Oreg St U Bkstrs.

Knapp, Mary & Knapp, Herbert. One Potato, Two Potato: The Folklore of American Children. 1978. pap. text ed. 6.95x (ISBN 0-393-09039-6). Norton.

--One Potato, Two Potato: The Secret Education of American Children. (Illus.). 1976. 9.95 o.p. (ISBN 0-393-08745-X). Norton.

Knapp, Peggy A., ed. Assays: Critical Approaches to Medieval & Renaissance Texts, Vol. II. 160p. 1983. 14.95x (ISBN 0-8229-3468-X). U of Pittsburgh Pr.

Knapp, Rebecca G. Basic Statistics for Nurses. LC 77-26950. 308p. 1978. pap. 12.95 (ISBN 0-471-03545-9, Wiley Medical). Wiley.

Knapp, Rebecca G., jt. auth. see Duncan, Robert C.

Knapp, Rebecca G., jt. auth. see Miller, M. Clinton.

Knapp, Richard B. The Gift of Surgery to Mankind: A History of Modern Anesthesiology. (Illus.). 144p. 1983. text ed. price not set (ISBN 0-398-04817-7). C C Thomas.

Knapp, Robert C., jt. auth. see Agnew, Jeanne.

Knapp, Ronald G., ed. China's Island Frontier: Studies in the Historical Geography of Taiwan. LC 80-18578. 368p. 1980. text ed. 20.00x (ISBN 0-8248-0705-7). UH Pr.

Knapp, Samuel L. American Cultural History, 1607-1829. LC 60-6514. 1977. Repr. of 1829 ed. 37.00x (ISBN 0-8201-1257-7). Schol Facsimiles.

Knapp, Vincent J. Austrian Social Democracy, Eighteen Eighty-Nine to Nineteen Fourteen. LC 79-5509. 1980. text ed. 22.25 (ISBN 0-8191-0906-1); pap. text ed. 12.25 (ISBN 0-8191-0907-X). U Pr of Amer.

Knapp, Wilfrid F. History of War & Peace, 1939-1965. (Royal Institute of Int'l Affairs Ser). 1967. 12.95x o.p. (ISBN 0-19-500340-3). Oxford U Pr.

Knapp, William I. Life, Writings & Correspondence of George Borrow, 2 Vols. LC 67-23870. 1967. Repr. of 1899 ed. Set. 47.00x (ISBN 0-8103-3051-2). Gale.

Knapper, Arno F. & Newcomb, Loda I. A Style Manual for Written Communication. 2nd ed. LC 82-6053. 230p. 1983. pap. text ed. 10.95 (ISBN 0-88244-248-1). Grid Pub.

Knapton, James & Evans, Bertrand. Teaching a Literature-Centered English Program. (Orig.). 1967. pap. text ed. 3.65 (ISBN 0-685-19776-X). Phila Bk Co.

Knaster, Meri. Women in Spanish America: An Annotated Bibliography From Pre-Conquest to Contemporary Times. 1977. lib. bdg. 38.00 (ISBN 0-8161-7865-8, Hall Reference). G K Hall.

Knaub, Richard K., jt. auth. see Dolman, John, Jr.

Knauff, Ellen R. The Ellen Knauff Story. LC 73-21679. (Civil Liberties in American History Ser.). 242p. 1974. Repr. of 1952 ed. lib. bdg. 35.00 (ISBN 0-306-70238-X). Da Capo.

Knauff, Thomas. Glider Basics from First Flight to Solo. Northcut, Allan & Northcut, Debbie, eds. LC 80-81375. (Illus.). 155p. 1980. text ed. 16.95 o.p. (ISBN 0-9605676-0-7). Knauff.

Knaus, James O., Jr. Social Conditions Among the Pennsylvania Germans in the Eighteenth Century, Vol. 29. 20.00 o.p. (ISBN 0-911122-08-7). Penn German Soc.

Knaus, William. Do It Now: How to Stop Procrastinating. (Illus.). 1979. text ed. 11.95 (ISBN 0-13-216614-3, Spec); pap. text ed. 5.95 (ISBN 0-13-206660-2). P-H.

Knaus, William, jt. auth. see Ellis, Albert.

Knaus, William A. Inside Russian Medicine. 416p. 1981. 14.95 (ISBN 0-89696-115-X, An Everest House Book). Dodd.

--Inside Russian Medicine. LC 79-50420. 1980. 10.95 (ISBN 0-448-14958-3, G&D). Putnam Pub Group.

Knaus, William J. How to Get Out of a Rut. (Illus.). 268p. 1982. 13.95 (ISBN 0-13-409318-6); pap. 6.95 (ISBN 0-13-409300-3). P-H.

Knaus, william J., jt. auth. see Ellis, Albert.

Knauss, John A. Introduction to Physical Oceanography. (Illus.). 1978. 36.95 (ISBN 0-13-493015-0). P-H.

Knauss, Robert L., jt. auth. see Conard, Alfred F.

Knauth, Christopher R. & Leuzzi, J. P., eds. U. S. Aviation Reports, 1968-1980, 29 vols. LC 29-3034. (Write for info. on vols. avail.). 1974. lib. bdg. 42.50 per vol. (ISBN 0-379-14100-0). Oceana.

Knauth, Percy. The North Woods. LC 72-88525. (American Wilderness Ser). (Illus.). (gr. 6 up). 1972. lib. bdg. 15.96 (ISBN 0-8094-1165-2, Pub. by Time-Life). Silver.

Kneale, Martha, jt. auth. see Kneale, William.

Kneale, William & Kneale, Martha. Development of Logic. (Illus.). 1962. 45.00x (ISBN 0-19-824183-6). Oxford U Pr.

Kneberg, Madeline, jt. auth. see Lewis, Thomas M.

Knecht, Charles D., et al. Fundamental Techniques Veterinary Surgery. 2nd ed. (Illus.). 250p. 1981. text ed. 27.50 (ISBN 0-7216-5463-0). Saunders.

--Fundamental Techniques in Veterinary Surgery. LC 74-25478. (Illus.). 200p. 1975. text ed. 19.95 o.p. (ISBN 0-7216-5482-7). Saunders.

Knecht, Ken. Introduction to FORTH. Date not set. pap. 9.95 (ISBN 0-672-21842-9). Sams.

--Microsoft BASIC. 2nd ed. LC 79-53476. 225p. 1982. pap. 15.95 (ISBN 0-88056-056-8). Dilithium Pr.

--Using & Programming the Timex Sinclair Computer. Willis, Jerry, ed. 240p. (Orig.). 1983. pap. 9.95 (ISBN 0-88056-107-6). Dilithium Pr.

Knechtges, D. R. The Han Rhapsody. LC 73-94354. (Studies in Chinese History, Literature & Institutions). 200p. 1976. 39.50 (ISBN 0-521-20458-5). Cambridge U Pr.

Knee, Allan. Second Avenue Rag. (Phoenix Theatre Ser.). pap. 2.95x (ISBN 0-912262-71-0). Proscenium.

Knee, Allan, ed. Idylls of the King: Selections. Bd. with Camelot. 1967. pap. 2.50 (ISBN 0-440-93948-8, LE). Dell.

Kneebone, P., jt. auth. see Trim, J. L.

Kneedler, Rebecca D. & Tarver, Sara G. Changing Perspectives in Special Education. 1977. pap. text ed. 15.95 (ISBN 0-675-08529-2). Merrill.

Kneeland, George J. Commercialized Prostitution in New York City. LC 69-14937. (Criminology, Law Enforcement, & Social Problems Ser.: No. 52). 1969. Repr. of 1917 ed. 15.00x (ISBN 0-87585-052-9). Patterson Smith.

Kneeland, Terry, ed. The Organic Gardening Nineteen Eighty-Three Planning Guide & Country Calendar. (Illus.). 96p. 1982. pap. 5.95 (ISBN 0-87857-387-9, 01-057-1). Rodale Pr Inc.

Kneer, Marian, ed. see Grenlee, Geraldine, et al.

Kneer, Marian, ed. see Haywood, Kathleen, et al.

Kneer, Marian, ed. see Oglesby, Carole A., et al.

Kneer, Marian, ed. see Riggs, Maida L., et al.

Kneer, Marian, ed. see Rothstein, Anne, et al.

Kneer, Marian, ed. see Studer, Ginny L., et al.

Kneer, Marian E., ed. see Svobda, Milan, et al.

Kneer, Marian E., et al. Adolescence. (Basic Stuff Ser.: No. II, 3 of 3). 94p. (Orig.). 1981. pap. text ed. 6.25 (ISBN 0-88314-023-3). AAHPERD.

Kneer, Marion, ed. see Trimble, R. Thomas, et al.

Kneer, N., jt. auth. see Heitman, H.

Kneese, Allen V. & Schultze, Charles L. Pollution, Prices & Public Policy. 125p. 1975. 14.95 (ISBN 0-8157-4994-5); pap. 5.95 (ISBN 0-8157-4993-7). Brookings.

Kneese, Allen V., jt. auth. see Bohm, Peter.

Kneip, T. J. & Lippmann, Morton, eds. The New York Summer Aerosol Study, Nineteen Seventy-Six. (Annals of the New York Academy of Sciences: Vol. 322). (Orig.). 1979. 32.00x (ISBN 0-89766-012-9). NY Acad Sci.

Kneip, Theo J. & Lioy, Paul J., eds. Aerosols: Anthropogenic & Natural, Sources & Transport. LC 80-12891. (Annals of New York Academy of Sciences: Vol. 338). 618p. 1980. 110.00x (ISBN 0-89766-064-1); pap. 108.00x (ISBN 0-89766-065-X). NY Acad Sci.

Knei-Paz, Baruch. The Social & Political Thought of Leon Trotsky. 1978. pap. 12.95x (ISBN 0-19-827234-0). Oxford U Pr.

Kneisl, Carol R., jt. auth. see Wilson, Holly S.

Knell, A. J., jt. auth. see Brod, J.

Kneller, G. E. Educational Philosophy of National Socialism. 1941. 49.50x (ISBN 0-685-69834-3). Elliots Bks.

Kneller, George F. Education & Economic Thought. LC 68-22890. 139p. 1968. cloth 9.50 o.p. (ISBN 0-471-49525-5); pap. text ed. o.p. (ISBN 0-471-49526-3, Pub. by Wiley). Krieger.

--Introduction to the Philosophy of Education. 2nd ed. LC 78-168637. 118p. 1971. pap. text ed. 11.95x (ISBN 0-471-49515-8). Wiley.

Kneller, George F., ed. Foundations of Education. 3rd ed. LC 78-138913. 674p. 1971. text ed. 27.95x (ISBN 0-471-49505-0); tchr's. manual 8.50 (ISBN 0-471-49506-9). Wiley.

Kneller, J. W., jt. auth. see Grubbs, H. A.

Knepler, Myrna. Let's Talk About It. 160p. (Orig.). 1982. pap. text ed. 8.95 (ISBN 0-15-550585-8, HC). HarBraceJ.

Knepper, William E. Liability of Corporate Officers & Directors. 3rd ed. 1979. text ed. 45.00x incl. 1982 supplement (ISBN 0-87473-118-6). A Smith Co.

Knessel, Dave. Free Publicity: A Step-by-Step Guide. LC 81-85027. (Illus.). 160p. 1982. 13.95 (ISBN 0-8069-0240-X); lib. bdg. 16.79 (ISBN 0-8069-0241-8); pap. 7.95 (ISBN 0-8069-7588-1). Sterling.

Knetsch, Jack L., ed. Outdoor Recreation and Water Resources Planning. LC 73-92765. (Water Resources Monograph Ser.: Vol. 3). (Illus.). 1974. pap. 10.00 (ISBN 0-87590-304-5). Am Geophysical.

Knevel, Adelbert M. & DiGangi, Frank E. Jenkin's Quantitative Pharmaceutical Chemistry. 7th ed. (Illus.). 1977. text ed. 27.00 o.p. (ISBN 0-07-035087-6, HP). McGraw.

Knewstubb, P. F. Mass Spectrometry & Ion-Molecule Reactions. LC 69-16282. (Cambridge Chemistry Textbooks Ser). (Illus.). 1969. 29.95 (ISBN 0-521-07489-4); pap. 12.95x (ISBN 0-521-09563-8). Cambridge U Pr.

Knezevich, Stephen J. Program Budgeting. LC 72-5703. 1973. 20.75x o.p. (ISBN 0-8211-1014-4); text ed. 18.95x o.p. (ISBN 0-685-36206-X). McCutchan.

Kniazeva, V., jt. auth. see Pruzham, I.

Knick, Allison, jt. ed. see Dahl, A. M.

Knickerbocker, Frederick T. Oligopolistic Reaction & Multinational Enterprise. LC 72-94361. 230p. 1973. 12.50x (ISBN 0-87584-102-3). Harvard Busn.

Knickerbocker, K. L., ed. see Browning, Robert.

Knief, Ronald A. Nuclear Energy Technology. (Illus.). 624p. 1981. text ed. 35.50 (ISBN 0-07-035086-8, Co-Pub by Hemisphere Pub); solutions manual 20.00 (ISBN 0-07-035088-4). McGraw.

Knies, Earl A. The Art of Charlotte Bronte. LC 69-15917. x, 234p. 1969. 12.95x (ISBN 0-8214-0059-2, 82-80653). Ohio U Pr.

Kniesner, Thomas J., jt. auth. see Fleisher, Belton M.

Knievel, Helen A., ed. Cooperative Services: A Guide to Policies & Procedures in Library Systems. LC 81-22406. 275p. 1982. 24.95 (ISBN 0-918212-56-1). Neal-Schuman.

Knigge, R. Silver Spurs. LC 75-10111. 1973. 4.95 (ISBN 0-915614-01-4); incl. record 6.95 (ISBN 0-685-57207-2). Knollwood Pub.

Knight. Liposomes. (Research Monographs in Cell & Tissue Physiology: Vol. 7). 1982. 119.75 (ISBN 0-444-80320-3). Elsevier.

Knight, jt. auth. see Reddihough.

Knight, et al, eds. see Energy Resources Center.

Knight, A., ed. Allergology. (International Congress Ser.: No. 144). (Abstracts - 6th Congress). 1967. 14.75 (ISBN 90-219-1161-2, Excerpta Medica). Elsevier.

Knight, Allen W. & Simmons, Mary Ann, eds. Water Pollution: A Guide to Information Sources. LC 73-17537. (Man & the Environment Information Guide Ser.: Vol. 9). 1980. 42.00x (ISBN 0-8103-1346-4). Gale.

Knight, Arthur, ed. see Kerouac, Jack.

Knight, Arthur W. & Knight, Glee. Until the Lights in Us Come on. 24p. 1975. pap. 1.25x (ISBN 0-914994-01-8). Cider Pr.

Knight, Bernard. Madoc: Prince of America. LC 76-4653. 1977. 7.95 o.p. (ISBN 0-312-50400-4). St Martin.

Knight, Bernard, jt. auth. see Helpern, Milton.

Knight, C. & Newman, J. Contemporary Africa: Geography & Change. 1976. 28.95 (ISBN 0-13-170035-9). P-H.

Knight, C. A. Molecular Virology. (Illus.). 256p. 1974. text ed. 18.95 (ISBN 0-07-035112-0, C); pap. text ed. 16.95 (ISBN 0-07-035113-9). McGraw.

Knight, C. Gregory, ed. see Furuseth, Owen J. & Pierce, John T.

Knight, C. Gregory, ed. see Smith, Christopher J. & Hanham, Robert Q.

Knight, Clayton S. Big Book of Helicopters. (Illus.). (gr. 4-6). 1971. 1.95 (ISBN 0-448-02253-2, G&D). Putnam Pub Group.

Knight, D. P., jt. auth. see Lewis, P. R.

Knight, Damon. A for Anything. 1980. pap. 1.95 o.s.i. (ISBN 0-380-48553-2, 48553). Avon.

--First Contact. 1978. pap. 1.50 o.p. (ISBN 0-523-40354-2). Pinnacle Bks.

--The World & Thorinn. (Illus.). 276p. 1981. 12.95 o.s.i. (ISBN 0-399-12470-5). Putnam Pub group.

Knight, David. Colonies in Orbit: The Coming Age of Human Settlements in Space. (gr. 5-9). 1977. 6.25 o.p. (ISBN 0-688-22096-7); PLB 8.59 (ISBN 0-688-32096-1). Morrow.

--Eavesdropping on Space: The Quest of Radio Astronomy. LC 74-19285. (Illus.). 96p. (gr. 5-9). 1975. PLB 8.59 (ISBN 0-688-32019-8). Morrow.

--Harnessing the Sun: The Story of Solar Energy. (Illus.). 128p. (gr. 5-9). 1976. PLB 8.59 (ISBN 0-688-32070-8). Morrow.

--Lift Your Eyes to the Mountain. 8.95 (ISBN 0-87193-137-0); pap. 5.95 (ISBN 0-87193-190-7). Dimension Bks.

--Tiny Planets: Asteroids of Our Solar System. (Illus.). 96p. (gr. 3-7). 1973. PLB 7.63 o.p. (ISBN 0-688-30072-3). Morrow.

Knight, David C. All About Sound. LC 82-17387. (Question & Answer Bks.). (Illus.). 32p. (gr. 3-6). 1983. PLB 8.59 (ISBN 0-89375-878-7); pap. text ed. 1.95 (ISBN 0-89375-879-5). Troll Assocs.

--Galaxies, Islands in Space. (Illus.). (gr. 4-6). 1979. 8.25 (ISBN 0-688-22180-7); PLB 7.92 (ISBN 0-688-32180-1). Morrow.

--The Moons of Our Solar System. rev ed. LC 80-369. (Illus.). 128p. (gr. 7-9). 1980. PLB 8.40 (ISBN 0-688-32230-1). Morrow.
--Robotics. (Illus.). (gr. 3-7). 1983. 7.00 (ISBN 0-688-01490-9). Morrow.
--Silent Sound: The World of Ultrasonics. LC 80-19118. (Illus.). 96p. (gr. 4-6). 1980. 8.75 (ISBN 0-688-22244-7); PLB 8.40 (ISBN 0-688-32244-1). Morrow.
--The Spy Who Never Was & Other True Spy Stories. LC 77-15162. (Signal Bks.). (gr. 9 up). 1978. 6.95 (ISBN 0-385-13108-9). Doubleday.
--UFO's: A Pictorial History from Antiquity to the Present. LC 78-23653. (Illus.). 1979. 13.95 (ISBN 0-07-035103-1). McGraw.
--Your Body's Defenses. LC 74-11083. (Illus.). 64p. (gr. 5-8). 1975. PLB 8.95 (ISBN 0-07-035105-8, GB). McGraw.
Knight, Douglas, jt. ed. see Tucker, Gene.
Knight, E. V. Critique & Society. LC 82-73478. 90p. (Orig.). pap. 6.95 (ISBN 0-931494-34-6). Brunswick Pub.
Knight, Elizabeth C., ed. see Hoffmann, E. T.
Knight, Etheridge. Born of a Woman: Selected & New Poems. 1980. 10.95 o.s.i. (ISBN 0-395-29199-2); pap. text ed. 5.95 o.s.i. (ISBN 0-395-29200-X). HM.
Knight, Frank H. Freedom & Reform. LC 81-83237. 502p. 1982. 14.00 (ISBN 0-86597-004-1); pap. 6.50 (ISBN 0-86597-005-X). Liberty Fund.
Knight, Franklin W. The Caribbean: The Genesis of a Fragmented Nationalism. (Latin American History Ser.). 1978. 18.95x (ISBN 0-19-502242-4); pap. 6.95x (ISBN 0-19-502243-2). Oxford U Pr.
--Slave Society in Cuba During the Nineteenth Century. LC 76-121770. (Illus.). 250p. 1970. 25.00 (ISBN 0-299-05790-9); pap. 9.95 (ISBN 0-299-05794-1). U of Wis Pr.
Knight, Fred, et al, eds. Telecommunications for Local Government. LC 82-15617. (Practical Management Ser.). (Illus.). 224p. (Orig.). 1982. 19.50 (ISBN 0-87326-036-8). Intl City Mgt.
Knight, Fred B. & Heikkenen, Herman J. Knight-Heikkenen: Principles of Forest Entomology. 5th ed. (Forestry Ser.). (Illus.). 480p. 1980. text ed. 32.50 (ISBN 0-07-035095-7). McGraw.
Knight, G. Wilson. Lord Byron's Marriage: The Evidence of Asterisks. 1957. 25.00 o.p. (ISBN 0-7100-1693-X). Routledge & Kegan.
--Poets of Action. LC 81-43479. 320p. 1982. lib. bdg. 23.75 (ISBN 0-8191-2073-1); pap. text ed. 12.75 (ISBN 0-8191-2074-X). U Pr of Amer.
--Shakespeare's Dramatic Challenge: On the Rise of Shakespeare's Tragic Heroes. LC 81-40251. (Illus.). 190p. 1982. lib. bdg. 20.75 (ISBN 0-8191-1911-3); pap. text ed. 10.00 (ISBN 0-8191-1912-1). U Pr of Amer.
--Shakespearian Production: With Especial Reference to the Tragedies. LC 81-40250. (Illus.). 346p. 1982. lib. bdg. 22.00 (ISBN 0-8191-1964-4); pap. text ed. 12.25 (ISBN 0-8191-1965-2). U Pr of Amer.
--Symbol of Man. LC 81-40003. (Illus.). 194p. 1981. lib. bdg. 19.00 (ISBN 0-8191-1588-6); pap. text ed. 9.50 (ISBN 0-8191-1589-4). U Pr of Amer.
Knight, George A. I Am: This is my Name. 96p. 1983. pap. 4.95 (ISBN 0-8028-1958-3). Eerdmans.
--Leviticus: Daily Study Bible. LC 81-3007. 1981. 12.95 (ISBN 0-664-21802-4); pap. 6.95 (ISBN 0-664-24569-2). Westminster.
--Psalms: Vol. 1, Psalms 1 to 72. LC 82-20134. (The Daily Study Bible-Old Testament). 350p. 1982. 12.95 (ISBN 0-664-21805-9); pap. 6.95 (ISBN 0-664-24572-2). Westminster.
Knight, George R. Philosophy & Education: An Introduction in Christian Perspective. (Illus.). xii, 244p. 1980. pap. text ed. 8.95 (ISBN 0-943872-79-0). Andrews Univ Pr.
Knight, George W. Church Bulletin Bits. 160p. 1976. pap. 3.95 (ISBN 0-8010-5368-4). Baker Bk.
Knight, Glee, jt. auth. see Knight, Arthur W.
Knight, H. Gary, et al, eds. Ocean Thermal Energy Conversion: Legal, Political & Institutional Aspects. LC 77-2049. 272p. 1977. 25.95x (ISBN 0-669-01441-9). Lexington Bks.
Knight, Hans, jt. auth. see Laping, Francis.
Knight, Harold, tr. see Brunner, Heinrich E.
Knight, Hilary, jt. auth. see Maiden, Cecil.
Knight, James T. Commutative Algebra. LC 76-152625. (London Mathematical Society Lecture Notes Ser.: No. 5). (Illus.). 1971. pap. 15.95 (ISBN 0-521-08193-9). Cambridge U Pr.
Knight, Jane, jt. auth. see Westland, Cor.
Knight, Judyth. Ballet & Its Music. 1973. 21.00 (ISBN 0-901938-03-3, 75-A11151). Eur-Am Music.
Knight, K. G. & Norman, F. Hauptmann Centenary Lectures. 167p. 1964. 60.00x (ISBN 0-85457-021-7, Pub. by Inst Germanic Stud England). State Mutual Bk.
Knight, Kenneth, jt. auth. see Guest, David.
Knight, Kit, ed. see Kerouac, Jack.
Knight, Lucian L., ed. Biographical Dictionary of Southern Authors. LC 75-26631. (Library of Southern Literature). (Illus.). 1978. Repr. of 1929 ed. 60.00x (ISBN 0-8103-4269-3). Gale.
Knight, Margaret. Morals Without Religion. 124p. 1981. 25.00x (ISBN 0-686-97044-6, Pub. by Dobson Bks England). State Mutual Bk.
Knight, Max, ed. The Original Blue Danube Cookbook: Fine Recipes of the Old Austrian Empire. (Illus.). 1979. 8.95 o.p. (ISBN 0-89581-008-5). Lancaster-Miller.
Knight, Max, ed. see Maenchen-Helfen, Otto J.
Knight, Max, tr. see Kelsen, Hans.
Knight, Melinda, jt. auth. see Brannon, Lil.
Knight, Melvin M., tr. see See, Henri.
Knight, Morris H., jt. auth. see Sherman, Robert W.
Knight, Paul, tr. see Wallraff, Gunter.
Knight, Peter T. & Colletta, Nat J. Implementing Programs of Human Development. (Working Paper: No. 403). iv, 372p. 1980. 5.00 (ISBN 0-686-36130-X, WP-0403). World Bank.
Knight, Peter T. & Moran, Ricardo. Brazil: Human Resources Report. xii, 548p. 1979. pap. 20.00 (ISBN 0-686-36101-6, RC-7909). World Bank.
Knight, Peter T. & Moran, Ricardo J. Brazil. 98p. 1981. 5.00 (ISBN 0-686-36128-8, BN-8103). World Bank.
Knight, Raymond M., jt. auth. see Rice, Harold S.
Knight, Richard A. Boys' Book of Gun Handling. (Illus.). (gr. 5 up). 1964. PLB 5.49 o.p. (ISBN 0-399-60069-8). Putnam Pub Group.
Knight, Richard P. Ancient Art & Mythology. (Illus.). 119p. 1982. Repr. 57.85 (ISBN 0-686-83055-5). Found Class Reprints.
Knight, Richard S., jt. auth. see Jensen, Larry C.
Knight, Richard V., jt. auth. see Gappert, Gary.
Knight, S. Rotorcraft-Helicopter Private: Commercial FAA Written Test Guide. 150p. 1982. 19.95X (ISBN 0-686-43382-3, Progressive Pilot Sem.). Aviation.
Knight, S. A. Electrical Principles Two. (Illus.). 1978. pap. 14.95 (ISBN 0-408-00325-1). Butterworth.
Knight, Stephen A. Electronics for Technicians Two. (TEC Technicians Ser.). (Illus.). 1978. pap. 12.95 (ISBN 0-408-00324-3). Butterworth.
Knight, Susan E., jt. auth. see Bullard, David G.
Knight, Tanis & Lewin, Larry. Open the Deck. Carmichael, Standrod, ed. (Writing Program Ser.). 1982. pap. 4.50 (ISBN 0-933282-07-9). Stack the Deck.
Knight, Thomas J. Technology's Future: The Hague Congress Technology Assessment. LC 80-22913. 566p. 1982. Repr. of 1976 ed. text ed. 14.50 (ISBN 0-89874-283-8). Krieger.
Knight, U. G. Power Systems Engineering & Mathematics. 304p. 1975. pap. 26.00 (ISBN 0-08-018294-1). Pergamon.
Knightley, Phillip. The First Casualty: From the Crimea to Vietnam: The War Correspondent As Hero, Propagandist, & Myth Maker. LC 75-11684. (Illus.). 465p. 1975. 12.95 o.p. (ISBN 0-15-131264-8). HarBraceJ.
Knighton, William M., jt. auth. see Rosenthal, Douglas E.
Knights, B. The Idea of the Clerisy, in the Nineteenth Century. LC 77-80840. 1978. 42.50 (ISBN 0-521-21798-9). Cambridge U Pr.
Knights, Jack. Sail Racer. (Illus.). 235p. 1974. 15.00 o.p. (ISBN 0-229-98674-9). Transatlantic.
Knights, L. C. Explorations Three. LC 75-29654. 1976. 10.95x o.p. (ISBN 0-8229-1125-6). U of Pittsburgh Pr.
Knights, Lionel C. Explorations: Essays in Criticism, Mainly on the Literature of the Seventeenth Century. LC 75-32459. 219p. 1976. Repr. of 1964 ed. lib. bdg. 15.50x (ISBN 0-8371-8548-3, KNEX). Greenwood.
Knights of the Square Table, jt. auth. see Dornfeldt, Jeanne.
Knights, R. Treatment of Hyperactivity & Learning Disorders. 448p. 1979. text ed. 18.95 (ISBN 0-8391-1515-6). Univ Park.
Knights, Robert M. & Bakker, Dirk J., eds. The Neuropsychology of Learning Disorders: Theoretical Approaches. (Illus.). 351p. 1976. text ed. 18.95 (ISBN 0-8391-0951-2). Univ Park.
Kniker, Charles. You & Values Education. (Educational Foundations Ser.). 1977. pap. text ed. 8.95 (ISBN 0-675-08516-0). Merrill.
Kniker, Charles R. & Naylor, Natalie A. Teaching Today & Tomorrow. (Special Education Ser.). (Orig.). 1981. pap. text ed. 18.95 (ISBN 0-675-08034-7). Additional supplements may be obtained from publisher. Merrill.
Knill, R. J., et al, eds. Harmonic Maps, Tulane: 1980, Proceedings. (Lecture Notes in Mathematics Ser.: Vol. 949). 158p. 1983. pap. 10.00 (ISBN 0-387-11595-1). Springer-Verlag.
Knipe, A. C. & Watts, W. Organic Reaction Mechanisms 1980: An Annual Survey Covering the Literature Dated December 1979 Through November 1980. LC 66-23143. 718p. 1981. 166.00x (ISBN 0-471-10004-8, Pub. by Wiley-Interscience). Wiley.
Knipe, A. C. & Watts, W. E. Organic Reaction Mechanisms 1977: An Annual Survey Covering the Literature Dated December 1976 Through November 1977, Vol. 13. LC 66-23143. 741p. 1979. 184.00x (ISBN 0-471-99666-1, Pub. by Wiley-Interscience). Wiley.
Kniseley, Ralph M. & Andrews, Gould A., eds. Progress in Medical Radioisotope Scanning: Proceedings. (AEC Symposium Ser.). 539p. 1963. microfiche 4.50 (ISBN 0-87079-314-4, TID-7673). DOE.
Kniseley, Ralph M., et al, eds. Dynamic Clinical Studies with Radioisotopes: Proceedings. (AEC Symposium Ser.). 658p. 1964. pap. 24.50 (ISBN 0-87079-181-8, TID-7678); microfiche 4.50 (ISBN 0-87079-182-6, TID-7678). DOE.
Knittel, Patricia, ed. Selected Bibliography: Printing Inks, Vol. I. (Orig.). 1982. pap. 15.00 (ISBN 0-89938-010-7). Tech & Ed Ctr Graph Arts RIT.
--Selected Bibliography: Quality Control, Vol. II. (Orig.). 1982. pap. 15.00 (ISBN 0-89938-009-3). Tech & Ed Ctr Graph Arts RIT.
Knittl, Z. Optics of Thin Films: An Optional Multilayer Theory. LC 73-20896. (Wiley Series in Pure & Applied Optics). 548p. 1975. 94.95x (ISBN 0-471-49531-X, Pub. by Wiley-Interscience). Wiley.
Knobel, Edward. Field Guide to the Grasses, Sedges & Rushes of the United States. LC 77-72531. (Illus.). 1977. pap. 2.25 (ISBN 0-486-23505-X). Dover.
Knobf, Mary K. & Lewis, Keith P. Cancer Chemotherapy: Treatment & Care. 1981. lib. bdg. 24.95 (ISBN 0-8161-2224-5, Pub. by Hall Medical). G K Hall.
Knoblauch, C. H., jt. auth. see Van Nostrand, A. D.
Knobloch, Ferdinand & Knobloch, Jirina. Integrated Psychotherapy. LC 77-74851. 1979. 30.00x o.s.i. (ISBN 0-87668-297-2). Aronson.
Knobloch, Jirina, jt. auth. see Knobloch, Ferdinand.
Knoblock, Peter. Teaching Emotionally Disturbed Children. LC 82-83370. 448p. 1982. text ed. 24.95 (ISBN 0-395-29708-7); write for info. instr's. manual (ISBN 0-395-29709-5). HM.
Knoch, A E., ed. Concordant Greek Text. rev. ed. 1975. leather bdg. 20.00 (ISBN 0-910424-32-2). Concordant.
Knoche, Carl H. The German Immigrant Press in Milwaukee. Cordasco, Francesco, ed. LC 80-871. (American Ethnic Groups Ser.). 1981. lib. bdg. 29.00x (ISBN 0-405-13433-9). Ayer Co.
Knoche, Gerald. The Creative Task. (Preacher's Workshop Ser.). 48p. 1977. pap. text ed. 2.50 (ISBN 0-570-07404-5, 12-2676). Concordia.
Knoche, H. Flora Balearica Etude Phytogeographique Sur les Iles Baleares, 4vols. (Illus.). 192.00 (ISBN 3-87429-061-1). Lubrecht & Cramer.
Knoche, Philip B. Has God Given You Up? (Uplook Ser). 1970. pap. 0.75 (ISBN 0-8163-0257-X, 08165-3). Pacific Pr Pub Assn.
Knock, N. A. Dispositien der Merkwaadigste Kerk-Orgelen, Welken in De Provincie Friesland, Groningen En Elders Aangetroffen Worden. (Bibliotheca Organologica: Vol. 24). 1972. Repr. of 1788 ed. 20.00 o.s.i. (ISBN 90-6027-147-5, Pub. by Frits Knuf Netherlands). Pendragon NY.
Knoefel, Peter K., et al. Absorption, Distribution, Transformation & Excretion of Drugs. (Illus.). 220p. 1972. 18.75x (ISBN 0-398-02518-5). C C Thomas.
Knoepfel & Farber. Look! I'm Growing Up. Mahany, Patricia, ed. (Happy Day Bks.). (Illus.). 24p. (ps-2). 1983. 1.29 (ISBN 0-87239-639-8, 3559). Standard Pub.
Knoepfle, John. A Gathering of Voices. 1978. pap. 1.50 o.p. (ISBN 0-916684-30-X, Scrimshaw Editions). Rook Pr.
--Thinking of Offerings: Poems Nineteen Seventy - Nineteen Seventy-Three. 1979. 10.00 o.p. (ISBN 0-686-65851-5); pap. 4.50 o.p. (ISBN 0-686-61893-9). Juniper Pr WI.
Knoepfle, John, jt. ed. see Jaffe, Dan.
Knoepflmacher, U. C. Laughter & Despair: Readings in Ten Novels of the Victorian Era. LC 73-145789. 1973. 27.50x (ISBN 0-520-01907-5); pap. 4.50x (ISBN 0-520-02352-8). U of Cal Pr.
Knoepflmacher, U. C., jt. ed. see Levine, George.
Knof, Hans. Thermodynamics of Irreversible Processes in Liquid Metals. 1966. 6.75x o.p. (ISBN 0-408-00131-3). Transatlantic.
Knoff, Gerald E. The World Sunday School Movement: The Story of a Broadening Mission. 304p. 1979. 8.00 (ISBN 0-8164-0416-X). Seabury.
Knoke, David & Kuklinski, James H. Network Analysis. (Sage University Papers: Quantitative Applications in the Social Sciences: Vol. 28). 88p. pap. 4.50 (ISBN 0-8039-1914-X). Sage.
Knoke, David, jt. auth. see Bohrnstedt, George W.
Knoll, Anne P. Food Service Management: A Human Relations Approach. 1975. 13.95 (ISBN 0-07-035183-X, G); instructor's manual & key 4.50 (ISBN 0-07-035184-8). McGraw.
Knoll, Bertha, ed. Symposium on Pharmacology of Learning & Retention, Vol. 4. (Hungarian Pharmacological Society, First Congress Ser.). (Illus.). 103p. 1974. 10.00x (ISBN 963-05-0192-9). Intl Pubns Serv.
Knoll, G. F. Radiation Detection & Measurement. 816p. 1979. 41.95x (ISBN 0-471-49545-X). Wiley.
Knoll, Robert E. Christopher Marlowe. LC 68-17237. (English Authors Ser.). 1969. lib. bdg. 11.95 (ISBN 0-8057-1376-X, Twayne). G K Hall.
Knoll, Robert E., ed. Conversations with Wright Morris: Critical Views & Responses. LC 76-25497. (Illus.). xiv, 211p. 1977. 15.95x (ISBN 0-8032-0904-5); pap. 4.95x (ISBN 0-8032-5854-2, BB 630, Bison). U of Nebr Pr.
Knoll, Tricia. Becoming Americans: Asian Sojourners, Immigrants & Refugees in the Western United States. LC 82-4539. (Illus.). 354p. 1982. 22.50 (ISBN 0-9602664-3-7); pap. 14.50 (ISBN 0-9602664-4-5). Coast to Coast.
Knopf, Alfred A. Publishing Then & Now: 1912-1964. (Bowker Lectures Ser., No. 21). 1965. pap. 3.00 o.p. (ISBN 0-87104-153-7). NY Pub Lib.
Knopf, Howard & Dunaway, Kate A. Bragon the Dragon Presents Primary Patterns. (ps-3). 1982. 4.95 (ISBN 0-86653-098-3, GA 439). Good Apple.
--Good Apple & Creative Writing Fun. (gr. 3-7). 1981. 9.95 (ISBN 0-86653-054-1, GA 255). Good Apple.
Knopf, Irwin J. Childhood Psychopathology: A Developmental Approach. (Illus.). 1979. text ed. 23.95 (ISBN 0-13-130336-8). P-H.
Knopf, Lucille. RNs One & Five Years after Graduation. 113p. 1975. 6.95 (ISBN 0-686-38368-0, 19-1535). Natl League Nurse.
Knopf, Mildred O. Perfect Hostess Cook Book. 1950. 10.95 o.p. (ISBN 0-394-40162-X). Knopf.
Knopoff, L., et al, eds. The Crust & Upper Mantle of the Pacific Area. LC 68-61439. (Geophysical Monograph Ser.: Vol. 12). 1968. 31.00 (ISBN 0-87590-012-7). Am Geophysical.
Knopper, Rob, ed. Woordstructurr. 140p. (Dutch.). pap. 13.75x (ISBN 90-70176-56-4). Foris Pubns.
Knops, R. J., ed. Nonlinear Analysis & Mechanics: Heriot-Watt Symposium, Vol. 3. (Research Notes in Mathematics Ser.: No. 30). 173p. (Orig.). 1979. pap. text ed. 20.95 (ISBN 0-273-08432-1). Pitman Pub MA.
--Nonlinear Analysis & Mechanics: Heriot-Watt Symposium, Vol. 4. LC 78-309110. (Research Notes in Mathematics Ser.: No. 39). 212p. (Orig.). 1979. pap. text ed. 21.95 (ISBN 0-273-08461-5). Pitman Pub MA.
--Nonlinear Analysis & Mechanics: Heriot-Watt Symposium, Vol. 1. (Research Notes in Mathematics Ser.: No. 17). (Orig.). 1977. pap. text ed. 20.95 (ISBN 0-273-01128-6). Pitman Pub MA.
--Nonlinear Analysis & Mechanics: Heriot-Watt Symposium, Vol. 2. (Research Notes in Mathematics Ser.: No. 27). 285p. (Orig.). 1978. pap. text ed. 26.50 (ISBN 0-273-80420-0). Pitman Pub MA.
--Trends in Applications of Pure Mathematics to Mechanics, Vol. III. LC 77-351685. (Monographs & Studies: No. 11). 243p. 1981. text ed. 77.00 (ISBN 0-686-31381-X). Pitman Pub MA.
Knorr, Dietrich. Sustainable Food Systems. (Illus.). 1983. pap. text ed. 23.50 (ISBN 0-87055-398-4). AVI.
Knorr, Klaus. Military Power & Potential. 1970. pap. text ed. 4.95x o.p. (ISBN 0-669-58115-1). Heath.
Knorr, Klaus & Morgan, Patrick. Strategic Military Surprise: Incentives & Opportunities. 350p. (Orig.). 1983. pap. 14.95 (ISBN 0-87855-912-4). Transaction Bks.
Knorr, Klaus, ed. Power, Strategy, & Security: A World Politics Reader. LC 82-48561. 270p. 1983. 32.00x (ISBN 0-686-43257-6); pap. 8.95 (ISBN 0-691-01071-4). Princeton U Pr.
Knorr, Klaus E., ed. What Price Economic Growth? Baumol, William J. LC 77-781. (Illus.). 1977. Repr. of 1961 ed. lib. bdg. 16.25x (ISBN 0-8371-9356-7, KNWP). Greenwood.
Knorr, Klaus E. & Verba, Sidney, eds. The International System: Theoretical Essays. LC 82-6268. viii, 240p. 1982. Repr. of 1960 ed. lib. bdg. 35.00x (ISBN 0-313-23617-8, KNIN). Greenwood.
Knorr, L. C. Citrus Diseases & Disorders: An Alphabetized Compendium with Particular Reference to Florida. LC 73-17462. (Illus.). 163p. 1973. 10.00 o.p. (ISBN 0-8130-0383-0). U Presses Fla.
Knorre, D. G., jt. auth. see Emanuel, N. M.
Knorre, Marty, et al. Puntas de Partida: An Invitation to Spanish. Incl. Arana, Alice & Arana, Oswaldo. 224p. wkbk. 6.95 (ISBN 0-394-32629-6); Yates, Maria S. 196p. lab manual 8.00 (ISBN 0-394-32630-X). 608p. 1981. text ed. 21.00 (ISBN 0-394-32618-0). Random.
Knott, Bill. Becos. LC 82-48897. 96p. 1983. pap. 5.95 (ISBN 0-394-71444-X, Vin). Random.
--Becos: Poems. LC 82-16712. 60p. 1983. 10.00 (ISBN 0-394-52924-3). Random.
--Selected & Collected Poems. LC 77-3473. 1977. 10.00 (ISBN 0-915342-17-0); pap. 6.00 (ISBN 0-915342-16-2). SUN.
Knott, Jack H. Managing the German Economy: Budgetary Politics in a Federal State. LC 80-8888. (Illus.). 240p. 1981. 24.95x (ISBN 0-669-04401-6). Lexington Bks.
Knott, Leonard. Before You Die. 112p. 1982. 9.95 (ISBN 0-920510-59-0, Pub. by Personal Lib). Dodd.
Knott, Leonard L. Writing for the Joy. 204p. 1983. 11.95 (ISBN 0-89879-106-5). Writers Digest.
Knott, Susan, ed. see Conway, Martin R.
Knott, Thomas A., jt. auth. see Moore, Samuel.
Knott, Will C. The Golden Mountain. (Orig.). 1980. pap. 1.75 o.p. (ISBN 0-425-04597-8). Berkley Pub.
--Killer's Canyon. 1978. lib. bdg. 10.95 o.p. (ISBN 0-8161-6615-3, Large Print Bks). G K Hall.
--Lyncher's Moon. 1980. pap. 1.75 o.p. (ISBN 0-425-04598-6). Berkley Pub.
--Red Skies Over Wyoming. 1980. pap. 1.75 o.p. (ISBN 0-425-04599-4). Berkley Pub.

--The Return of Zach Stewart. 1980. pap. 1.75 o.p. (ISBN 0-425-04600-1). Berkley Pub.

Knott, William. How to Write & Publish Your Novel. 1982. pap. text ed. 11.95 (ISBN 0-8359-2989-2). Reston.

Knotts, G. R. & McGovern, J. P. School Health Problems. (Illus.). 352p. 1976. 26.75x (ISBN 0-398-03220-3). C C Thomas.

Knotts, Howard. The Lost Christmas. LC 78-1903. (A Let Me Read Bk). (Illus.). (gr. k-4). pap. 1.75 (ISBN 0-15-653648-X, VoyB). HarBraceJ.

--The Winter Cat. LC 72-26525. (Illus.). (ps-3). 1972. 8.95 o.p. (ISBN 0-06-023166-1, HarpJ); PLB 6.89 o.p. (ISBN 0-06-023167-X). Har-Row.

Knotts, Judith, jt. auth. see Gregg, Elizabeth.

Know, Katherine M. The Sharples. LC 70-87456. (Library of American Art Ser.). 133p. 1972. Repr. of 1930 ed. lib. bdg. 37.50 (ISBN 0-306-71529-5). Da Capo.

Knowledge Industry Publications Editors. International Business Travel & Relocation Directory: The Who, What & Where Handbook. rev. 2nd ed. LC 81-20111. 1982. 200.00x (ISBN 0-8103-1137-2). Gale.

Knowles, A., jt. auth. see Burgess, C.

Knowles, A. V. Turgenev's Letters. 320p. 1983. 30.00 (ISBN 0-686-83682-0, ScribT). Scribner.

Knowles, Alison. More by Alison Knowles. 38p. 1979. pap. 8.00 (ISBN 0-914162-41-1). Knowles.

--Natural Assemblages & the True Crow. 80p. (Orig.). 1980. pap. 8.00 (ISBN 0-914162-47-0). Knowles.

Knowles, Barbara, jt. ed. see Damjanov, Ivan.

Knowles, Christopher J. Diversity of Bacterial Respiratory Systems, 2 vols. 1980. vol. 1, 272 pgs. 65.95 (ISBN 0-8493-5399-8); Vol. 2, 256 Pgs. 65.95 (ISBN 0-686-96695-3). CRC Pr.

Knowles, D. Christian Monasticism. (World University Library). (Illus., Orig.). 1969. 4.95 o.p. (ISBN 0-07-035192-9, SP); pap. 3.95 (ISBN 0-07-035191-0). McGraw.

Knowles, David. Evolution of Medieval Thought. 1964. pap. 4.95 (ISBN 0-394-70246-8, Vin). Random.

--Monastic Order in England. 2nd ed. 1963. 79.50 (ISBN 0-521-05479-6). Cambridge U Pr.

--Religious Orders in England. Incl. Vol. 1. The Old Orders. 1948. 54.50 (ISBN 0-521-05480-X); pap. 16.95 (ISBN 0-521-29566-1); Vol. 2. End of the Middle Ages. 1955. 59.50 (ISBN 0-521-05481-8); pap. 19.95 (ISBN 0-521-29567-X); Vol. 3. The Tudor Age. Knowles, David. 1979. 64.50 (ISBN 0-521-05482-6); pap. 21.95 (ISBN 0-521-29568-8). Cambridge U Pr.

Knowles, David & Hadcock, R. Neville. Medieval Religious Houses in England & Wales. 2nd ed. 1972. 29.95x o.p. (ISBN 0-312-52780-2). St Martin.

Knowles, E. W. & Lewis, R. T., eds. Spectral Theory of Differential Operators. (North-Holland Mathematics Studies: Vol. 55). 1981. 53.25 (ISBN 0-444-86277-3). Elsevier.

Knowles, Frederic. Kipling Primer. LC 73-17092. (English Literature Ser., No. 33). 1974. lib. bdg. 33.95x (ISBN 0-8383-1729-4). Haskell.

Knowles, Helen. How to Succeed in Fund Raising Today. LC 74-20200. 256p. 1975. 10.95 (ISBN 0-87027-151-2); pap. 6.95 (ISBN 0-87027-150-4). Cumberland Pr.

Knowles, Henry P. & Saxberg, Borje O. Personality & Leadership Behavior. LC 73-125609. (Business Ser). (Illus.). 1971. pap. text ed. 12.95 (ISBN 0-201-03781-5); 13.95 (ISBN 0-686-96630-9). A-W.

Knowles, Hulda, jt. auth. see Knowles, Malcolm.

Knowles, John. Peace Breaks Out. 192p. 1982. pap. 2.95 (ISBN 0-553-22580-4). Bantam.

--Separate Peace. (gr. 9 up). 1960. 13.95 (ISBN 0-02-564840-3); large print ed. o.p. 6.95 (ISBN 0-02-489390-0). Macmillan.

--A Stolen Past. LC 82-15472. 264p. 1983. 14.95 (ISBN 0-03-062209-3). HR&W.

Knowles, John H., ed. Teaching Hospital: Evolution & Contemporary Issues. LC 66-21338. 1966. 8.95x o.p. (ISBN 0-674-86955-9). Harvard U Pr.

Knowles, Leo. Candidates for Sainthood. LC 78-55247. 1978. 8.95 (ISBN 0-89310-035-8); pap. 3.95 o.p. (ISBN 0-89310-036-6). Carillon Bks.

--Saints Who Changed Things. 1977. 6.95 (ISBN 0-89310-022-6); pap. 3.95 o.p. (ISBN 0-89310-023-4). Carillon Bks.

Knowles, Malcolm. The Adult Education Movement in the U. S. rev. ed. LC 75-31825. 442p. 1977. Repr. of 1962 ed. 20.50 (ISBN 0-88275-366-5). Krieger.

Knowles, Malcolm & Knowles, Hulda. Introduction to Group Dynamics. 96p. 1972. 4.95 o.s.i. (ISBN 0-695-81080-4, T1080). Follett.

Knowles, Malcolm M. Self-Directed Learning: A Guide for Learners & Teachers. 144p. 1975. pap. 6.95 (ISBN 0-695-81116-9). Follett.

Knowles, Malcolm S. The Adult Learner: A Neglected Species. 2nd ed. (Building Blocks of Human Potential Ser.). 254p. 1978. 14.95 (ISBN 0-87201-004-X). Gulf Pub.

--The Modern Practice of Adult Education: Andragogy Versus Pedagogy. rev. ed. 400p. 1980. 17.95 (ISBN 0-695-81472-9). Follett.

--Modern Practice of Adult Education: Andragogy Versus Pedagogy. (Illus.). 1970. 14.95 o.s.i. (ISBN 0-8096-1756-0, Assn Pr). Follett.

Knowles, Michael. Organizational Functioning: A Behavioural Analysis. 1979. text ed. 29.00x (ISBN 0-566-00329-5). Gower Pub Ltd.

Knowles, P. R. Composite Steel & Concrete Construction. 200p. 1973. 34.95x o.p. (ISBN 0-470-49580-4). Halsted Pr.

Knowles, Peter F., et al. Magnetic Resonance of Biomolecules: An Introduction to the Theory & Practice of NMR & ESR in Biological Systems. LC 75-4872. 343p. 1976. 49.95x (ISBN 0-471-49575-1, Pub. by Wiley-Interscience); pap. 24.95x (ISBN 0-471-01672-1). Wiley.

Knowles, R. Automatic Testing. 1976. 11.20 (ISBN 0-07-084461-5, P&RB). McGraw.

Knowles, Ralph L. Energy & Form: An Ecological Approach to Urban Growth. LC 74-3003. 1975. 30.00x o.p. (ISBN 0-262-11050-4); pap. 9.95 (ISBN 0-262-61025-6). MIT Pr.

Knowles, Ruth S. America's Oil Famine: How It Happened & When It Will End. LC 74-93769. 1975. 8.95 o.p. (ISBN 0-698-10592-3, 74-93769, Coward). Putnam Pub Group.

--The First Pictorial History of the American Oil & Gas Industry, 1859-1983. (Illus.). 177p. 1983. 15.95 (ISBN 0-8214-0693-0, 82-84622). Ohio U Pr.

--The Greatest Gamblers: The Epic of American Oil Exploration. 2d ed. LC 78-21382. (Illus.). 1979. 14.95 (ISBN 0-8061-1513-0); pap. 9.95 (ISBN 0-8061-1654-4). U of Okla Pr.

Knowles, Tillie M. Sue & Mindy Find a New Friend. LC 73-86469. (gr. 4-6). 1973. 6.95 (ISBN 0-87716-047-3, Pub. by Moore Pub Co). F Apple.

Knowlson, T. Sharper. The Origins of Popular Superstitions & Customs. new ed. 1972. pap. 4.95 o.p. (ISBN 0-87877-013-5, W-13). Newcastle Pub.

--The Origins of Popular Superstitions & Customs. LC 80-329. 242p. 1980. Repr. of 1972 ed. lib. bdg. 12.95x (ISBN 0-89370-613-2). Borgo Pr.

Knowlson, Thomas S. Origins of Popular Superstitions & Customs. LC 68-30946. 1968. Repr. of 1910 ed. 31.00x (ISBN 0-8103-3357-0). Gale.

Knowlton, D. C. Motion Pictures in History Teaching. 1929. 39.50x (ISBN 0-685-69835-1). Elliots Bks.

Knowlton, Derrick. Naturalist in the Hebrides. 1977. 8.95 o.p. (ISBN 0-7153-7446-X). David & Charles.

Knowlton, Edgar, Jr., jt. auth. see Day, A. Grove.

Knowlton, K., et al. Technical Freehand Drawing & Sketching. 1976. 19.95 (ISBN 0-07-035207-0, G). McGraw.

Knox, Alan B., ed. Leadership Strategies for Meeting New Challenges. LC 81-48475. 1982. 7.95x (ISBN 0-87589-887-4, CE-13). Jossey-Bass.

Knox, Bernard M. The Heroic Temper: Studies in Sophoclean Tragedy. LC 64-21864. (Sather Classical Lectures Ser.: No. 35). 1965. 18.50x o.s.i. (ISBN 0-520-00661-5). U of Cal Pr.

--The Heroic Temper: Studies in Sophoclean Tragedy. (Cal Sather Classical Lecture Ser.). 224p. 1983. pap. 7.95 (ISBN 0-520-04957-8, CAL 625). U of Cal Pr.

Knox, Bill. Bloodtide. LC 82-45622. (Crime Club Ser.). 192p. 1983. 11.95 (ISBN 0-385-18452-2). Doubleday.

Knox, D. Marriage: Who, When & Why? 1974. pap. 13.95 (ISBN 0-13-559336-0). P-H.

Knox, D. B. Doctrine of Faith in the Reign of Henry Eighth. 304p. 1961. 17.50 (ISBN 0-227-67444-8). Attic Pr.

Knox, D. M. The Neolithic Revolution. Yapp, Malcolm, et al, eds. (World History Ser.). (Illus.). 32p. (gr. 10). 1980. lib. bdg. 6.95 (ISBN 0-89908-130-4); pap. text ed. 2.25 (ISBN 0-89908-105-3). Greenhaven.

Knox, David. Exploring Marriage & the Family. 1979. text ed. 18.95x o.p. (ISBN 0-673-15046-1). Scott F.

Knox, Diana. The Industrial Revolution. Yapp, Malcolm, et al, eds. (World History Ser.). (Illus.). (gr. 10). PLB 6.95 (ISBN 0-89908-108-8); pap. text ed. 2.25 (ISBN 0-89908-133-9). Greenhaven.

Knox, Donald. Death March: The Survivors of Bataan. (Illus.). 512p. pap. 8.95 (ISBN 0-15-625224-4, Harv). HarBraceJ.

Knox, Edward. Jean de la Bruyere. (World Authors Ser.). 1973. lib. bdg. 15.95 (ISBN 0-8057-2507-5, Twayne). G K Hall.

Knox, Edward C. Patterns of Person: Studies in Style and Form from Corneille to Laclos. LC 82-82430. (French Forum Monographs: No. 41). 177p. (Orig.). 1983. pap. 12.50x (ISBN 0-917058-40-2). French Forum.

Knox, Francis. Labour Supply in Economic Development. 1979. text ed. 31.25x (ISBN 0-566-00238-8). Gower Pub Ltd.

Knox, George. Epidemiology: Uses in Health Care Planning. (IEA & WHO Handbooks Ser.). 1979. pap. text ed. 17.95x (ISBN 0-19-261221-2). Oxford U Pr.

Knox, Ian P. Above or Within? The Supernatural in Religious Education. LC 76-55589. (Orig.). 1977. lib. bdg. 9.95 (ISBN 0-89135-010-1); pap. 9.95 (ISBN 0-89135-006-3). Religious Educ.

Knox, John. Humanity & Divinity of Christ. (Orig.). 22.95 (ISBN 0-521-05486-9); pap. 7.95 (ISBN 0-521-09414-3). Cambridge U Pr.

--Siege of Quebec. 1980. pap. 7.95 (ISBN 0-686-60409-1). Pendragon Hse.

Knox, John H. Molecular Thermodynamics: An Introduction to Statistical Mechanics for Chemists. rev. ed. LC 70-147399. 246p. 1978. 29.95x (ISBN 0-471-99621-1, Pub. by Wiley-Interscience). Wiley.

Knox, John J. United States Notes. LC 78-54681. 1978. Repr. of 1885 ed. lib. bdg. 25.00 supplement included (ISBN 0-915262-17-7). S J Durst.

Knox, Malcolm. Layman's Quest. (Muirhead Library of Philosophy). 1969. text ed. 15.00x (ISBN 0-04-201014-4). Humanities.

Knox, Richard. Experiments in Astronomy for Amateurs. (Illus.). 1979. pap. 4.95 (ISBN 0-312-27686-9). St Martin.

Knox, Richard A. Experiments in Astronomy for Amateurs. LC 75-34748. (Illus.). 256p. 1976. 8.95 o.p. (ISBN 0-312-27685-0). St Martin.

Knox, Robert. Ancient China. LC 78-63101. (Modern Knowledge Library). (Illus.). (gr. 5 up). 1979. PLB 9.90 s&l (ISBN 0-531-09111-2, Warwick Pr). Watts.

Knox, Ronald A. The Footsteps at the Lock. 256p. 1983. pap. 4.50 (ISBN 0-486-24493-8). Dover.

--Literary Distractions. LC 74-20678. 232p. 1975. Repr. of 1958 ed. lib. bdg. 16.25x (ISBN 0-8371-7840-1, KNLD). Greenwood.

Knox, T. M., ed. see Collingwood, Robin G.

Knox, T. M., tr. see Hegel, G. W.

Knox, Thomas W. Camp-Fire & Cotton-Field. LC 75-84186. (American Scene Ser.). 1969. Repr. of 1865 ed. lib. bdg. 59.50 (ISBN 0-306-71782-4). Da Capo.

Knox, Vera H., ed. Public Finance Information Sources. LC 64-16503. (Management Information Guide Ser.: No. 3). 1964. 42.00x (ISBN 0-8103-0803-7). Gale.

Knox-Johnson, Robin. The Twilight of Sail. LC 78-19584. (Illus.). 1979. 14.95 o.p. (ISBN 0-399-12307-5). Putnam Pub Group.

Knox-Thompson, Elaine & Dickens, Susanne. The Young Horse. (Illus.). 160p. 1979. 12.95 (ISBN 0-00-195081-9, Pub. by W Collins Australia). Intl Schol Bk Serv.

Knudsen Corporation. Dairy Food Cookery. LC 77-88223. (Illus.). 1977. 5.95 (ISBN 0-89586-153-4). H P Bks.

Knudsen, James. Just Friends. 1982. pap. 2.25 (ISBN 0-380-80481-6, 80481-6, Flare). Avon.

Knudsen, Johannes. The Formation of the Lutheran Church in America. LC 77-15235. 132p. 1978. 3.00 o.p. (ISBN 0-8006-0517-9, 1-517). Fortress.

Knudsen, Mark & Passey, Neil. Utah! Gateway to Nevada. (Illus.). 100p. (Orig.). 1983. pap. 6.00 (ISBN 0-942688-05-8). Dream Garden.

Knudsen, Odin K. Economics of Supplemental Feeding of Malnourished Children: Leakages, Costs, & Benefits. (Working Paper: No. 451). iv, 76p. 1981. 5.00 (ISBN 0-686-36190-3, WP-0451). World Bank.

Knudsen, Odin K. & Scandizzo, Pasquale L. Nutrition & Food Needs in Developing Countries. (Working Paper: No. 328). 73p. 1979. 3.00 (ISBN 0-686-36199-7, WP-0328). World Bank.

Knudson, Douglas M. Outdoor Recreation. (Illus.). 1980. text ed. 24.95x (ISBN 0-02-365350-7). Macmillan.

Knudson, Harry R. & Woodworth, Robert T. Management: An Experiential Approach. 2nd ed. (Management Ser.). (Illus.). 1978. pap. text ed. 16.95 (ISBN 0-07-035243-7, C); instructor's manual 7.95 (ISBN 0-07-035244-5). McGraw.

Knudson, R. R. Just Another Love Story. 172p. (gr. 7 up). 1983. 9.95 (ISBN 0-374-33967-8). FS&G.

--Muscles! (Illus.). 96p. 1983. pap. 1.95 (ISBN 0-380-82172-9, 82172-9, Camelot). Avon.

--Punch! (Illus.). 96p. 1983. pap. 1.95 (ISBN 0-380-82164-8, 82164-8, Camelot). Avon.

--Rinehart Lifts. LC 80-66825. 192p. (gr. 4 up). 1980. 9.95 (ISBN 0-374-36294-7). FS&G.

--Speed. (Illus.). 80p. (gr. 2 up). 1983. 8.95 (ISBN 0-525-44052-6, 0869-260, Skinny Bk). Dutton.

--Zanboomer. (gr. 7-12). 1980. pap. 2.25 (ISBN 0-440-99908-1, LFL). Dell.

Knudson, Richard L. Classic Sports Cars. LC 79-4641. (Superwheels & Thrill Sports Books). (Illus.). (gr. 4 up). 1978. PLB 7.95g (ISBN 0-8225-0427-8). Lerner Pubns.

--Fabulous Cars of the 1920s & 1930s. LC 81-343. (Superwheels & Thrill Sports Bks.). (Illus.). (gr. 4 up). 1981. PLB 7.95g (ISBN 0-8225-0504-5, AACR1). Lerner Pubns.

--Racing Yesterday's Cars. (Superwheels & Thrill Sports Bks.). (Illus.). 48p. (gr. 4up). 1983. PLB 7.95g (ISBN 0-8225-0512-6). Lerner Pubns.

--Restoring Yesterday's Cars. LC 82-24966. (Superwheels & Thrill Sports Bks.). (Illus.). 48p. (gr. 4up). 1983. PLB 7.95g (ISBN 0-8225-0440-5). Lerner Pubns.

Knudson, S. J. Culture in Retrospect. 1978. 23.95 (ISBN 0-395-30647-7). HM.

Knudsvig, Glenn M., jt. auth. see Sweet, Waldo E.

Knudsvig, Glenn M., et al. Latin for Reading: A Beginner's Textbook with Exercises. LC 82-51023. 376p. 1982. pap. text ed. 12.95x (ISBN 0-472-08038-5). U of Mich Pr.

Knudten, Richard D., jt. ed. see Schafer, Stephen.

Knudtsen, Molly F. Under the Mountain. LC 82-8552. (Illus.). 130p. 1982. 10.50 (ISBN 0-87417-072-9). U of Nev Pr.

Knust, H. Texte und Ubungen: Intermediate Readings & Exercises. 1977. pap. 12.95 (ISBN 0-13-903526-5). P-H.

Knust, Herbert, jt. ed. see Mews, Siegfried.

Knust, Louise H., jt. auth. see Fortenbaug, Doris.

Knuth, D., jt. ed. see Greene, D.

Knuth, Eldon L. Introduction to Statistical Thermodynamics. 1966. text ed. 19.50 o.p. (ISBN 0-07-035262-3, C). McGraw.

Knuth, Priscilla. Picturesque Frontier: The Army's Fort Dalles. 2nd ed. (Illus.). 112p. 1983. pap. write for info. (ISBN 0-87595-140-6, Western Imprints). Oreg Hist Soc.

Knutson, Andie L. The Individual, Society & Health Behavior. LC 65-21057. 534p. 1965. 12.00x (ISBN 0-87154-482-2). Russell Sage.

--The Individual, Society & Health Behavior. LC 80-20075. 534p. (Orig.). Date not set. pap. 6.95 (ISBN 0-87855-685-0). Transaction Bks. Postponed.

Knutson, Donald, jt. auth. see Calvin, Clyde L.

Knutson, Donald C., ed. Homosexuality & the Law. LC 79-23673. (Research on Homosexuality Ser.: No. 1). 1979. text ed. 19.95 (ISBN 0-917724-14-3, B14); pap. text ed. 12.95 (ISBN 0-917724-15-1, B15). Haworth Pr.

Knutson, Jeanne N., ed. Handbook of Political Psychology. LC 72-5893. (Social & Behavioral Science Ser.). 1973. 29.95x (ISBN 0-87589-174-8). Jossey-Bass.

Knutson, Kathleen. The Garden of Edra. (Illus.). 128p. 1981. pap. 6.95 (ISBN 0-939398-01-X). Fox River.

Knutson, Kent S. The Shape of the Question: The Mission of the Church in a Secular Age. LC 72-78558. 128p. (Orig.). 1972. pap. 3.50 o.p. (ISBN 0-8066-1225-8, 10-5750). Augsburg.

Knutson, Ronald & Penn, J. B. Agricultural & Food Policy. (Illus.). 384p. 1983. text ed. 25.95 (ISBN 0-13-018911-1). P-H.

Knuttgen, Howard, ed. Biochemistry of Exericise. (International Series on Sport Sciences). 1983. text ed. price not set (ISBN 0-931250-41-2). Human Kinetics.

Knuttgen, Howard G., ed. Neuromuscular Mechanisms for Therapeutic & Conditioning Exercise. (Illus.). 158p. 1976. pap. text ed. 14.95 (ISBN 0-8391-0954-7). Univ Park.

Kobal, Don, compiled by. Fifty Superstars. 176p. (YA) 1974. spiral bdg. 9.95 o.p. (ISBN 0-517-51591-1). Crown.

Kobal, John. Foyer Pleasure: Fifty Colourful Years of Cinema Lobby Cards. 160p. 1982. 32.00x (ISBN 0-906053-33-1, Pub. by Cave Pubns England). State Mutual Bk.

Kobal, John, jt. auth. see Blum, Daniel.

Kobal, John, ed. Movie-Star Portraits of the Forties: 163 Glamour Photos. LC 77-80118. (Illus.). 1977. pap. 6.50 (ISBN 0-486-23546-7). Dover.

Kobasa, Suzanne, jt. auth. see Maddi, Salvatore R.

Kobayashi, Hisashi. Modeling & Analysis: An Introduction to System Performance Evaluation Methodology. LC 77-73946. (IBM Ser.). (Illus.). 1978. text ed. 27.95 (ISBN 0-201-14457-3). A-W.

Kobayashi, Kando, jt. ed. see Matsui, Hideji.

Kobayashi, Kazumasa, jt. ed. see Cho, Lee-Jay.

Kobayashi, Kenzo. Two Little Ducks. Blakely, Peggy, tr. from Ger. LC 82-18786. (Picture Book Studio Ser.). 28p. (gr. k-3). 1983. 8.95 (ISBN 0-907234-07-0). Neugebauer Pr.

Kobayashi, M. Azosulfones: Versatile Precursors for Aryl Free Radicals & Aryl Cations. (Sulfur Reports Ser.). 28p. Date not set. price not set flexicover (ISBN 3-7186-0040-4). Harwood Academic.

Kobayashi, Shoshichi & Nomizu, K. Foundations of Differential Geometry, 2 pts. LC 63-19209. (Pure & Applied Mathematics Ser.: Vol. 15). 329p. 1963. Pt. 1. 43.50x (ISBN 0-470-49647-9); Pt. 2. 47.50x (ISBN 0-470-49648-7, Pub. by Wiley-Interscience). Wiley.

Kobberling, J. & Tattersall, Robert. The Genetics of Diabetes Mellitus. (Serono Symposia Ser.: No. 47). 46.50 (ISBN 0-12-417280-6). Acad Pr.

Koberg, Don & Bagnall, Jim. Values Tech: A Portable School for Self-Assessment & Self-Enhancement. 2nd ed. (Illus.). 243p. 1982. pap. 8.95 (ISBN 0-87576-016-0). W Kaufmann.

--Values Tech: The Polytechnic School of Values: a Portable School for Self-Discovery & Self-Enhancement. LC 75-19488. (Illus.). 242p. 1976. 8.95 (ISBN 0-913232-23-8); pap. 6.95 o.p. (ISBN 0-913232-24-6). W Kaufmann.

Kobishchanov, Yuri M. Axum. Michels, Joseph W., ed. Kapitanoff, Lorraine T., tr. from Rus. LC 77-88469. (Illus.). 1979. text ed. 24.50x (ISBN 0-271-00531-9). Pa St U Pr.

Kobler, Franz, ed. see Plato.

Kobler, Jay, jt. auth. see Isaacs, Benno.

Kobler, John. Damned in Paradise: A Life of John Barrymore. LC 77-76752. (Illus.). 1977. 12.95 o.p. (ISBN 0-689-10814-1). Atheneum.

--The Life & World of Al Capone. (Illus.). 416p. 1982. pap. 8.95 (ISBN 0-02-004200-0). Macmillan.

Koblinsky, Majorie A., jt. ed. see Greep, Roy O.

Koblitz, N. P-Adic Analysis. (London Mathematical Society Lecture Note Ser.: No. 46). 150p. 1980. pap. 15.95 (ISBN 0-521-28060-5). Cambridge U Pr.

Koblitz, Neal, ed. Modern Trends in Number Theory Related to Fermat's Last Theorem. (Progress in Mathematics Ser.: Vol. 26). 470p. 1982. text ed. 30.00 (ISBN 3-7643-3104-6). Birkhauser.

Kobre, Ken. Photojournalism: The Professionals' Approach. (Illus.). 368p. (Orig.). 1980. 24.95 (ISBN 0-930764-16-1); pap. text ed. 16.95 (ISBN 0-930764-15-3). Curtin & London.

Kobre, Kenneth. How to Photograph Friends & Strangers. (Illus.). 202p. 1982. pap. 17.95 (ISBN 0-930764-36-6). Curtin & London.

Kobre, Sidney. Foundations of American Journalism. Repr. of 1958 ed. lib. bdg. 17.75x (ISBN 0-8371-3117-0, KOAJ). Greenwood.

--Reporting News in Depth. LC 80-1424. (Illus.). 405p. 1981. lib. bdg. 24.00 (ISBN 0-8191-1596-7); pap. text ed. 14.00 (ISBN 0-8191-1597-5). U Pr of Amer.

Kobrin, David. Negotiable Instruments. 96p. 1980. 25.00x (ISBN 0-906501-15-6, Pub. by Keenan England). State Mutual Bk.

Kobrin, Frances E. & Goldscheider, Calvin. The Ethnic Factor in Family Structure & Mobility. LC 77-25838. 280p. 1978. prof ref 19.00x (ISBN 0-88410-358-7). Ballinger Pub.

Kobrin, Stephen J. Foreign Direct Investment, Industrialization & Social Change. Altman, Edward I. & Walter, Ingo, eds. LC 76-10401. (Contemporary Studies in Economic & Financial Analysis: Vol. 9). 325p. 1977. lib. bdg. 36.50 (ISBN 0-89232-013-3). Jai Pr.

Kobs, Jim. Profitable Direct Marketing. LC 79-53509. 1979. 24.95 (ISBN 0-87251-037-9). Crain Bks.

Kobus, Helmut. Hydraulic Modelling. (Water Resoures Engineering Ser.). 323p. 1980. pap. text ed. 27.50 (ISBN 0-273-08519-0). Pitman Pub MA.

Koc, Richard A. The German Gesellschaftsroman at the Turn of the Century: A Comparison of the Works of Theodor Fontane & Edward von Keyserling. 263p. 1982. write for info. (ISBN 3-261-05037-3). P Lang Pubs.

Kocaoglu, Dundar F., jt. auth. see Cleland, David I.

Koch, ed. Psychology, Vol. 3, Formulations Of The Person & The Social Context. 1959. text ed. 30.00 o.p. (ISBN 0-07-035273-9, C). McGraw.

--Psychology: Vol. 6, Investigations of Man as Socius, Their Place in Psychology, in the Social Sciences. 1963. text ed. 45.00 (ISBN 0-07-035277-1, C). McGraw.

Koch, jt. auth. see Levande.

Koch, Adrienne. Jefferson & Madison: The Great Collaboration. 1964. pap. 9.95 (ISBN 0-19-500420-5, GB). Oxford U Pr.

--The Philosophy of Thomas Jefferson. 8.50 (ISBN 0-8446-1270-7). Peter Smith.

Koch, Arthur, jt. auth. see Felber, Stanley B.

Koch, C. J. Year of Living Dangerously. 1983. pap. 3.95 (ISBN 0-14-006535-0). Penguin.

Koch, Charles H., jt. auth. see Rothschild, Donald P.

Koch, Charlotte, jt. auth. see Koch, Raymond.

Koch, Donald W. An Endless Vista: A Guide to Colorado's Recreational Lands. (Illus.). 144p. 1982. 17.50 (ISBN 0-87108-612-3). Pruett.

Koch, E. E., et al, eds. Vacuum Ultraviolet Radiation Physics: Proceedings of the 4th International Conference. 848p. 1975. text ed. 135.00 (ISBN 0-08-018942-3). Pergamon.

Koch, Elisabeth & Wagner, Gerard. The Individuality of Colour. Stebbing, Peter, tr. from Ger. & intro. by. (Illus.). 108p. 1980. 28.95 (ISBN 0-85440-365-5, Pub. by Steinerbooks). Anthroposophic.

Koch, Frank D. Avocado Grower's Handbook. Thomson, Paul H., ed. LC 82-83667. 440p. 1983. pap. 25.00 (ISBN 0-9602066-2-0). Bonsall Pub.

Koch, Fred C. The Volga Germans: In Russia & the Americas, 1763 to the Present. LC 76-41155. 1977. 18.95x (ISBN 0-271-01236-6). Pa St U Pr.

Koch, G. & Spizzichino, F. Exchangability in Probability & Statistics. Date not set. 59.75 (ISBN 0-444-86403-2). Elsevier.

Koch, H. Von. see Conference on Instruments & Measurements.

Koch, H. W. President's Guide to People: Power Strategies. 1982. 89.50 (ISBN 0-13-697557-7). Exec Reports.

Koch, Harry W. California Real Estate License Examinations. 2nd ed. 1982. pap. 8.00 (ISBN 0-913164-92-5). Ken-Bks.

--Janitorial & Maintenance Examinations. 2nd ed. 1975. 6.00 (ISBN 0-913164-54-2). Ken-Bks.

--Probation & Parole Examinations. 2nd ed. 1975. 6.00 (ISBN 0-913164-57-7). Ken-Bks.

--The Professional & Administrative Career Examination. 1974. pap. 6.00 o.p. (ISBN 0-913164-41-0). Ken-Bks.

Koch, Hugh. Drug Utilization in Office-Based Practice: A Summary of Findings National Ambulatory Medical Care United States, 1980, Ser.13-72. Shipp, Audrey, ed. 55p. 1982. pap. text ed. 1.95 (ISBN 0-8406-0270-7). Natl Ctr Health Stats.

Koch, James H. Profits from Country Property: How to Select, Buy, Improve & Maintain Your Country Property. (Illus.). 320p. 1981. 21.95 (ISBN 0-07-035248-8, P&RB). McGraw.

Koch, James V. Industrial Organization & Prices. 2nd ed. (Illus.). 1980. text ed. 24.95 (ISBN 0-13-462481-5). P-H.

Koch, James V., jt. auth. see Ostrosky, Anthony L., Jr.

Koch, Joanne, jt. auth. see Clarke-Stewart, Alison.

Koch, Joanne, jt. auth. see Koch, Lew.

Koch, Joanne B., jt. auth. see Levande, Diane I.

Koch, John. A Detailed Comparison of the Eight Manuscripts of Chaucer's Canterbury Tales. LC 75-350848. 427p. 1968. Repr. of 1913 ed. 72.50x (ISBN 0-8002-1252-5). Intl Pubns Serv.

Koch, K. M., jt. ed. see Baldamus, C. A.

Koch, Karen. A Special Look. 1973. pap. 1.25x (ISBN 0-88323-115-8, 220). Richards Pub.

Koch, Kenneth. The Art of Love. 1975. pap. 1.95 o.p. (ISBN 0-394-71508-X, Vin). Random.

--The Burning Mystery of Ana in Nineteen Fifty-One. LC 78-21608. 1979. 8.95 o.p. (ISBN 0-394-50473-9); 4.95 (ISBN 0-394-73693-1). Random.

--Days & Nights. 1982. 10.50 (ISBN 0-394-52480-2); pap. 5.95 (ISBN 0-394-71003-7). Random.

--The Red Robins. (Orig.). pap. 5.95 o.p. (ISBN 0-394-71467-9, V-467, Vin). Random.

Koch, Kenneth & Berrigan, Ted. ZZZZZZ. Elmslie, Kenward, ed. (Illus.). 1978. pap. 5.00 (ISBN 0-915990-11-3). Z Pr.

Koch, Kenneth & Farrell, Kate. Sleeping on the Wing: An Anthology of Modern Poetry with Essays on Reading & Writing. LC 80-5278. 336p. 1982. 15.00 (ISBN 0-394-49041-X, Vin); pap. 3.95 (ISBN 0-394-74364-4). Random.

Koch, Kenneth, tr. see Roussel, Raymond.

Koch, Klaus. The Prophets. Kohl, Margaret, tr. from Ger. LC 79-8894. 224p. 1982. pap. 10.95 (ISBN 0-8006-1648-0, 1-1648). Vol. 1, The Assyrian Age. Fortress.

--The Rediscovery of Apocalyptic. (Student Christian Movement Press Ser.). (Orig.). 1972. pap. 10.95x (ISBN 0-19-520325-9). Oxford U Pr.

Koch, Lew & Koch, Joanne. The Marriage Savers. LC 75-10479. 288p. 1976. 8.95 o.p. (ISBN 0-698-10692-X, Coward). Putnam Pub Group.

Koch, Marianna & Barbata, Jean. Figures That Count: Mathematics for Nurses. (Quality Paperback: No. 301). (Orig.). 1974. pap. 3.50 (ISBN 0-8226-0301-2). Littlefield.

Koch, Raymond & Koch, Charlotte. Educational Commune: The Story of Commonwealth College. LC 72-80036. (Illus.). 247p. 1972. 6.95x o.p. (ISBN 0-8052-3464-0). Schocken.

Koch, Robert. Louis C. Tiffany: Rebel in Glass. 3rd ed. 1982. 17.95 o.p. (ISBN 0-686-91705-7). Crown.

--What You Should Know About Business Writing. LC 67-10893. (Business Almanac Ser.: No. 9). 92p. 1967. 5.95 (ISBN 0-379-11209-4). Oceana.

Koch, Robert, jt. auth. see Gerfin, Richard.

Koch, Ronald P. Dress Clothing of the Plains Indians. LC 76-46947. (Civilization of the American Indian Ser.: Vol. 140). (Illus.). 1977. 14.95 (ISBN 0-8061-1372-3). U of Okla Pr.

Koch, Rudolf. Book of Signs. Holland, Vyvyan, tr. 1930. pap. 2.75 (ISBN 0-486-20162-7). Dover.

--Little ABC Book of Rudolf Koch. LC 76-14224. (Illus.). 1977. pap. 6.95 (ISBN 0-87923-295-1). Godine.

--The Little ABC Book of Rudolf Koch. LC 76-14224. (Illus.). 64p. 1976. 12.95 (ISBN 0-87923-196-3). Godine.

Koch, Rudolph, illus. Life of Jesus. (Illus.). 10.00 (ISBN 0-8159-6110-3). Devin.

Koch, Susan. Body Dynamics: The Body Shape-Up Book for Women. LC 82-83947. (Illus.). 192p. (Orig.). 1983. pap. 7.95 (ISBN 0-88011-115-1). Leisure Pr.

Koch, William. Immunity & Oxidative Therapy. 6.00x (ISBN 0-943080-15-0). Cancer Control Soc.

Koch, William J. Plants in the Laboratory. Stewart, Charles E., ed. (Illus.). 416p. 1973. pap. text ed. 12.95x (ISBN 0-02-365470-8). Macmillan.

Kochan, Lionel. Russia & the Weimar Republic. LC 78-17679. 1978. Repr. of 1954 ed. lib. bdg. 20.75x (ISBN 0-313-20503-5, KORW). Greenwood.

Kochan, Miriam. Life in Russia Under Catherine the Great. (European Life Ser). (Illus.). (gr. 7-11). 1969. 6.75 o.p. (ISBN 0-399-20138-6). Putnam Pub Group.

Kochar, A. K. & Burns, N. D. Microprocessors & Their Manufacturing Applications. 300p. 1983. text ed. 27.50 (ISBN 0-7131-3470-4). E Arnold.

Kochar, Mahendr S. Textbook of General Medicine. LC 82-8437. 688p. 1982. 25.95 (ISBN 0-471-09645-8, Pub. by Wiley Med). Wiley.

Kochar, Mahendra S. & Daniels, Lynda M. Hypertension Control for Nurses & Other Health Professionals. LC 78-3750. 252p. 1978. pap. text ed. 14.95 (ISBN 0-8016-2717-6). Mosby.

Kochen, Manfred. The Growth of Knowledge: Readings on Organization & Retrieval of Knowledge. LC 67-13526. 394p. 1967. text ed. 19.50 (ISBN 0-471-49695-2, Pub. by Wiley). Krieger.

--Integrative Mechanisms in Literature Growth. LC 72-815. (Contributions in Librarianship & Information Science: No. 9). 1974. lib. bdg. 29.95 (ISBN 0-8371-6384-6, KIM/). Greenwood.

--Principles of Information Retrieval. LC 74-1204. (Information Sciences Ser). 203p. 1974. 33.95x o.s.i. (ISBN 0-471-49697-9, Pub. by Wiley-Interscience). Wiley.

Kochen, Manfred, jt. ed. see Donohue, Joseph C.

Kocher, David C. Radioactive Decay Data Tables. LC 81-607800. (DOE Technical Information Center Ser.). 227p. 1981. pap. 13.75 (ISBN 0-87079-124-9, DOE/TIC-11026); microfiche 4.50 (ISBN 0-87079-496-5, DOE/TIC-11026). DOE.

Kocher, Helen R. & Ross, Alec. Success with Sentences. (Orig.). 1966. pap. text ed. 7.95x (ISBN 0-02-365490-2). Macmillan.

Kocher, Paul H. Master of Middle-Earth: The Fiction of J. R. R. Tolkien. 1972. 9.95 o.s.i. (ISBN 0-395-14097-8); pap. 3.95 (ISBN 0-395-17701-4). HM.

Kochersperger, Richard H. Food Warehousing & Transportation. LC 78-65886. 1978. 21.95 (ISBN 0-86730-302-6). Lebhar Friedman.

Kocheshkov, K., jt. auth. see Nesmeyanov, A.

Kochetkova, Natalya. Nikolay Karamzin. (World Authors Ser.). 1974. lib. bdg. 15.95 (ISBN 0-8057-2488-5, Twayne). G K Hall.

Kochetkova, Veronika I. Paleoneurology. (Scripta Ser. in Behavioral Sciences). 340p. 1978. 24.95x o.p. (ISBN 0-470-26355-5). Halsted Pr.

Kochevitsky, George. Art of Piano Playing: A Scientific Approach. (Illus.). (gr. 9 up). 1967. pap. text ed. 9.50 (ISBN 0-87487-068-2). Summy.

Kochhar, D. M., jt. ed. see Johnson, E. M.

Kochva, E., jt. ed. see Devries, A.

Koch-Weser, Jan, ed. Reprints of Articles on Drug Therapy, 6 Vols. Incl. Vol. 6. (Illus.). 215p. 1980. Repr. of 1980 ed. pap. 7.50 (ISBN 0-910133-12-3); Vol. 5. (Illus.). 1980. Repr. of 1980 ed. pap. 7.50 (ISBN 0-910133-11-5); Vol. 4. (Illus.). 141p. 1977. Repr. of 1976 ed. pap. 6.00 (ISBN 0-910133-10-7); Vol. 3. (Illus.). 197p. 1976. Repr. of 1972 ed. pap. 6.00 (ISBN 0-910133-09-3); Vol. 2. (Illus.). 167p. 1976. Repr. of 1973 ed. pap. text ed. 6.00 (ISBN 0-910133-08-5); Vol. 1. (Illus.). 163p. 1976. Repr. of 1972 ed. pap. text ed. 6.00 (ISBN 0-910133-07-7). (Orig.). pap. MA Med Soc.

Koci, Marta. Blackie & Marie. Crawford, Elizabeth D., tr. from Ger. (Junior Bks.). Orig. Title: Schwarzack. (Illus.). 32p. (gr. k-3). 1980. 9.95 (ISBN 0-688-00217-X); PLB 9.55 (ISBN 0-688-00236-6). Morrow.

--Katie's Kitten. (Picture Book Studio Ser.). (Illus.). 28p. (Eng.). 1982. 9.95 (ISBN 0-907234-21-6). Neugebauer Pr.

Kocinski, J. & Wojtczak, L. Critical Scattering Theory: An Introduction. (Phase Transition Phenomena Ser.: Vol. 1). 1979. 53.25 (ISBN 0-444-99795-4). Elsevier.

Kock, Anders. Synthetic Differential Geometry. LC 81-6099. (London Mathematical Society Lecture Note Ser.: No. 51). 328p. 1981. pap. 29.95 (ISBN 0-521-24138-3). Cambridge U Pr.

Kock, Gerald L. Georgia Commercial Practice, with 1982 Supplement. 1964. 40.00 (ISBN 0-87215-092-5); 1982 suppl. 17.50 (ISBN 0-87215-232-4). Michie-Bobbs.

Kockelman, W. J. & Leviton, A. E. San Francisco Bay: Use & Protection. LC 82-71291. 310p. (Orig.). 1982. 17.95 (ISBN 0-934394-04-0). AAASPD.

Kockelmans, Joseph J. World in Science & Philosophy. 1969. pap. text ed. 3.95 o.p. (ISBN 0-02-819880-8). Glencoe.

Kockelmans, Joseph J., ed. Interdisciplinarity & Higher Education. LC 78-50066. 1979. 22.50x (ISBN 0-271-00200-X). Pa St U Pr.

Kockman, Stanely D. The Symplectic Corbordism Ring II. LC 79-27872. (Memoirs of thr American Mathematical Society Ser.: No. 271). 10.00 (ISBN 0-8218-2271-3, MEMO/271). Am Math.

Koconda-Brons, Angela. Jorinda & Joringel. (Illus.). 17p. (gr. 2-3). 1981. pap. 15.95 (ISBN 0-88010-052-4, Pub. by Verlag Walter Keller Switzerland). Anthroposophic.

Kocsis, Miklos. High Speed Silicon Planar-Epitaxial Switching Diodes. LC 75-19391. 1976. 43.95 o.p. (ISBN 0-470-49707-6). Halsted Pr.

Koda-Kimble, Mary Anne & Katcher, Brian S., eds. Applied Therapeutics for Clinical Pharmacists. LC 78-72533. (Illus.). 1978. 32.00 o.p. (ISBN 0-915486-02-4). Applied Therapeutics.

Kodama, S., jt. ed. see Kajiya, F.

Kodansha International Ltd. Moscow, Vol. 5. LC 68-26554. (This Beautiful World Ser.). (Illus.). 146p. (Orig.). 1968. pap. 4.95 (ISBN 0-686-91928-9). Kodansha.

Kodell, Jerome. The Gospel According to Luke, No. 3. Karris, Robert J., ed. LC 82-20350. (Collegeville Bible Commentary Ser.). (Illus.). 128p. 1983. pap. 2.50 (ISBN 0-8146-1303-9). Liturgical Pr.

--Lamentations, Haggai, Zechariah, Second Zechariah, Malachi, Obadiah, Joel, Baruch, Vol. 14. 1982. 10.95 (ISBN 0-89453-248-0); pap. 7.95 (ISBN 0-686-32767-5). M Glazier.

Kodij, J. Ambiguity in Natural Language. 1973. pap. 17.00 (ISBN 0-444-10508-5). Elsevier.

Kodikari, S. Foreign Policy of Sri Lanka. 240p. 1982. text ed. 15.75x (ISBN 0-391-02763-8, Pub. by Chanaky India). Humanities.

Kodjak, Andrej. Alexander Solzhenitsyn. (World Author Ser.). 1978. lib. bdg. 12.95 (ISBN 0-8057-6320-1, Twayne). G K Hall.

--Pushkin's I. P. Belkin. 112p. 1979. pap. 8.95 (ISBN 0-89357-057-5). Slavica.

Kodjak, Andrej, et al, eds. Alexander Pushkin Symposium II. (New York University Slavic Papers Ser.: Vol. III). (Illus.). 131p. (Orig.). 1980. pap. 9.95 (ISBN 0-89357-067-2). Slavica.

Koebner, Hans K. Lasers in Medicine, Vol. 1. LC 79-40525. 274p. 1980. 116.00x (ISBN 0-471-27602-2, Pub. by Wiley-Interscience). Wiley.

Koedam, A. & Margaris, N. Aromatic Plants. 1982. text ed. 41.50 (ISBN 90-247-2720-0, Pub. by Martinus Nijhoff Netherlands). Kluwer Boston.

Koefoed, O. Geosounding Principles, I. LC 79-14798. (Methods in Geochemistry & Geophysics Ser.: Vol. 14A). 272p. 1979. 64.00 (ISBN 0-444-41704-4). Elsevier.

Koegler, Horst. The Concise Oxford Dictionary of Ballet. LC 76-9257. 1977. 17.95 o.p. (ISBN 0-19-311314-7). Oxford U Pr.

--The Concise Oxford Dictionary of Ballet. 2nd ed. (Illus.). 1982. pap. 14.95 (ISBN 0-19-311330-9). Oxford U Pr.

Koegler, Horst, jt. auth. see Spatt, Leslie.

Koehl, Robert L. The Black Corps: The Structure & Power Struggles of the Nazi SS. LC 81-69824. (Illus.). 448p. 1983. 27.50 (ISBN 0-299-09190-2). U of Wis Pr.

Koehle, Ruth, jt. auth. see Goldensohn, Eli S.

Koehler, Bart, jt. ed. see Foreman, Dave.

Koehler, Henry M., tr. see Scharer, Peter & Rinn, L. A.

Koehler, Jerry W. & Sisco, John I. Public Communication in Business & the Professions. 225p. 1981. text ed. 14.50 (ISBN 0-8299-0417-4). West Pub.

Koehler, Jerry W., et al. Public Communication: Behavioral Perspectives. (Illus.). 1978. pap. text ed. 13.95x (ISBN 0-02-365610-7). Macmillan.

Koehler, Margaret. A Visitors Guide to Cape Cod National Seashore. LC 72-92014. (Illus.). 80p. (Orig.). 1973. pap. 4.95 (ISBN 0-85699-066-3). Chatham Pr.

Koehler, Robert E., ed. Personnel Practice Handbook. rev. ed. 1978. pap. 12.00x (ISBN 0-913962-22-8). Am Inst Arch.

Koehler, Robert E., jt. ed. see Class, Robert A.

Koehler, Stephen, jt. auth. see Clark, Randy.

Koehn, Constance, ed. Books for Public Libraries. 3rd. ed. 381p. 1981. text ed. 20.00 (ISBN 0-8389-0328-2). ALA.

Koehn, Michael F. Bankruptcy Risk in Financial Depository Intermediaries: Assessing Regulatory Effects. LC 79-2411. (Arthur D. Little Bk.). (Illus.). 176p. 1979. 23.95x (ISBN 0-669-03169-0). Lexington Bks.

Koehn, Richard K., jt. ed. see Nei, Masatoshi.

Koelbel, Fritz, jt. auth. see Philbin, Tom.

Koelle, Dietrich E., jt. ed. see Bainum, Peter M.

Koellhoffer, Leonard. Shielded Metal Arc Welding. LC 82-8629. 271p. 1983. pap. text ed. 15.95x (ISBN 0-471-05048-2); wkbk. 8.95 (ISBN 0-471-09884-1). Wiley.

Koelling, Caryl. Animal Mix & Match. LC 79-90788. (Mix & Match Bks.). (Illus.). (ps-2). 1980. 4.95 o.s.i. (ISBN 0-440-00015-7). Delacorte.

--Mad Monsters Mix & Match. LC 79-90790. (Mix & Match Bks.). (Illus.). (ps-2). 1980. 4.95 o.s.i. (ISBN 0-440-05141-X). Delacorte.

--Molly Mouse Goes Shopping. (Surprise Bks). (Illus.). 22p. (ps). 1982. 4.95 (ISBN 0-8431-0628-X). Price Stern.

--Silly Stories Mix & Match. LC 79-90789. (Mix & Match Bks.). (Illus.). (ps-2). 1980. 4.95 o.s.i. (ISBN 0-440-07845-8). Delacorte.

Koelsch, Francine, jt. auth. see Aarons, Trudy.

Koelzow, D. & Maharam-Stone, D., eds. Measure Theory, Oberwolfach FRG Nineteen Eighty-One: Proceedings. (Lecture Notes in Mathematics: No. 945). 945p. 1983. pap. 20.50 (ISBN 0-387-11580-3). Springer-Verlag.

Koeman, J. H., jt. ed. see Strik, J. J.

Koenig, Alfred E., et al, eds. Philosophy of the Humanistic Society. LC 80-1425. 290p. (Orig.). 1981. lib. bdg. 24.00 (ISBN 0-8191-1414-6); pap. text ed. 12.25 (ISBN 0-8191-1415-4). U Pr of Amer.

Koenig, Constance R., jt. auth. see Bucher, Charles A.

Koenig, Denes. Endlichen und Unendlichen Graphen. LC 51-3002. (Ger). 15.95 (ISBN 0-8284-0072-5). Chelsea Pub.

Koenig, Edna, jt. auth. see Koenig, Henry.

Koenig, Erich W. Quotations & Observations. 1978. 5.95 o.p. (ISBN 0-533-03502-3). Vantage.

Koenig, F. Are You Really In... Formed? pap. 0.60 (ISBN 0-88172-111-5). Believers Bkshelf.

Koenig, George. The Lost Death Valley Forty-Niner Journal of Louis Nusbaumer. LC 74-20026. (Illus.). 72p. 1974. pap. 3.75 (ISBN 0-912494-13-1). Chalfant Pr.

Koenig, Gloria K. Patent Invalidity: A Statistical & Substantive Analysis. LC 73-89532. 1974. cancelled (ISBN 0-87632-127-9). Boardman.

Koenig, Henry & Koenig, Edna. Two Hundred & Fifteen: The Bird House. 6.95 o.p. (ISBN 0-686-16955-7). Wisconsin Audubon.

Koenig, John. Charismata: God's Gift for God's People. LC 77-12700. (Biblical Perspectives on Current Issues). 1978. softcover 5.95 (ISBN 0-664-24176-X). Westminster.

--Jews & Christians in Dialogue: New Testament Foundations. LC 79-17583. 1979. pap. 8.95 (ISBN 0-664-24280-4). Westminster.

Koenig, Linda L. The Vagabonds: America's Oldest Little Theater. LC 81-72057. 200p. 1982. 22.50 (ISBN 0-8386-3124-X). Fairleigh Dickinson.

Koenig, Louis W. The Chief Executive. 4th ed. 472p. 1981. pap. text ed. write for info (ISBN 0-15-506673-0, HC). HarBraceJ.

Koenig, Marion & Speirs, Gill. Making Rugs for Pleasure & Profit. LC 80-17110. (Illus.). 80p. 1980. 10.95 o.p. (ISBN 0-668-05079-9, 5079-9). Arco.

Koenig, Marion, tr. see Beisert, Heide H.

Koenig, Rush, tr. see Karkoschka, Erhard.

Koenig, Ruth, tr. see Eimert, Herbert & Stockhausen, Karlheinz.

Koenig, Teresa, jt. auth. see Bell, Rivian.

Koenig, William. Americans at War. 352p. 1983. 14.95 (ISBN 0-8119-0478-4, Pub. by Bison Bks.). Fell.

Koenigsbergen, T., jt. auth. see Tobias, S. A.

Koenigsberger, F., ed. see International Machine Tool Design & Research Conference, 15th.

Koenigsberger, F., jt. ed. see Tobias, S. A.

Koenigsberger, H. G., ed. see Oestreich, Gerhard.

Koenigsberger, O. H., et al, eds. Work of Charles Abrams: Housing & Urban Renewal in the U. S. A. & the Third World. (Illus.). 264p. 1981. 70.00 (ISBN 0-08-026111-6). Pergamon.

Koenigsberger, Otto, et al, eds. Review of Land Policies. 200p. 1981. 70.00 (ISBN 0-08-026078-0). Pergamon.

Koenigsberger, T. & Tobias, S. A., eds. Proceedings of the Sixteenth Machine Tool Design & Research Conference. LC 76-5219. (International Machine Tool Design & Research Conference Ser.). 599p. 1976. text ed. 129.95 o.s.i. (ISBN 0-470-15100-5). Halsted Pr.

Koening, William. Americans at War: From the Colonial Times to Vietnam. LC 79-51034. (Illus.). 1980. 28.95 o.p. (ISBN 0-399-12401-2). Putnam Pub Group.

Koeninger, Jimmy & Hephner, Thomas. Jeffrey's Department Store: A Retailing Simulation-Employee's Guide. (Illus.). (gr. 11-12). 1978. pap. text ed. 8.48x (ISBN 0-07-035231-3, G); replacement forms 90.00x (ISBN 0-07-086511-6); general mgr's manual 8.50x (ISBN 0-07-035230-5); store box 175.00x (ISBN 0-07-086510-8). McGraw.

Koeper, Frederick, jt. auth. see Whiffen, Marcus.

Koerner, E. F. Bibliographie Sausserienne, 1876-1976. 1983. 40.00 (ISBN 90-272-0999-5). Benjamins North Am.

Koerner, E. F. & Tajima, Matsuji. Noam Chomsky: A Personal Bibliography. 125p. 1983. 14.00 (ISBN 90-272-1000-4). Benjamins North Am.

Koerner, E. Konrad. Toward a Historiography of Linguistics: Selected Essays. (Studies in the History of Linguistics Ser.). xx, 222p. 1978. 25.00 (ISBN 90-272-0960-X, 19). Benjamins North Am.

--Western Histories of Linquistic Thought: An Annotated Chronological Bibliography, 1822-1976. (Studies in the History of Linguistics Ser.). x, 113p. 1978. 16.00 (ISBN 90-272-0952-9, 11). Benjamins North Am.

Koerner, E. Konrad, ed. Progress in Linguistic Historiography: Papers from the International Conference on the History of the Language Sciences, Ottawa, 28-31 August 1978. (Studies in History of Linguistics Ser.: 20). xiv, 421p. 1980. 40.00 (ISBN 90-272-4501-0, 20). Benjamins North Am.

--The Transformational-Generative Paradigm & Modern Linguistic Theory. (Current Issues in Linguistic Theory Ser.: No. 1). viii, 462p. 1975. 46.00 o.p. (ISBN 90-272-0902-2); pap. 40.00 (ISBN 90-272-0902-2). Benjamins North Am.

Koerner, Friedrich & Glawischnig, Dieter. Jazz Research (Jazzforschung, Vol. 1. (Ger.). 1970. pap. 61.00 (ISBN 3-7024-0032-X, 51-26601). Eur-Am Music.

--Jazz Research (Jazzforschung, Vol. 2. (Ger.). 1970. pap. 61.00 (ISBN 3-7024-0033-8, 51-26602). Eur-Am Music.

--Jazz Research (Jazzforschung, Vol. 3-4. (Ger.). 1973. pap. 69.00 (ISBN 3-7024-0040-0, 51-26603). Eur-Am Music.

--Jazz Research (Jazzforschung, Vol. 5. (Ger.). 1974. pap. 61.00 (ISBN 3-7024-0072-9, 51-26605). Eur-Am Music.

Koerner, James. Hoffer's America. LC 73-82782. 143p. 1973. 12.00x (ISBN 0-912050-45-4, Library Pr). Open Court.

Koerner, Konrad, jt. ed. see Maher, J. Peter.

Koerner, Robert M. & Welsh, Joseph P. Construction & Geotechnical Engineering Using Synthetic Fabrics. LC 79-21733. (Ser. on Practical Construction Guides). 267p. 1980. 36.50x (ISBN 0-471-04776-7, Pub. by Wiley-Interscience). Wiley.

Koerner, Thomas F., ed. Student Learning Styles & Brain Behavior. 256p. (Orig.). 1982. pap. text ed. 10.00 (ISBN 0-88210-142-0). Natl Assn Principals.

Koerner, Wolfgang. The Green Frontier. Crampton, Patricia, tr. from Ger. (gr. 7 up). 1977. 9.95 (ISBN 0-688-22124-6); lib. bdg. 9.55 (ISBN 0-688-32124-0). Morrow.

Koersted, Hand. Recherches Sur L'identitie Des Forces Chimiques et Electriques. Repr. of 1813 ed. 82.00 o.p. (ISBN 0-8287-1408-8). Clearwater Pub.

Koertge, Noretta, ed. The Nature & Causes of Homosexuality: A Philosophic & Scientific Inquiry. LC 81-6960. (Research on Homosexuality Ser.: No. 3). 108p. 1982. text ed. 15.00 (ISBN 0-86656-148-X, B148). Haworth Pr.

Koertge, Ronald. Fresh Meat. (Illus.). 32p. 1981. 15.00 (ISBN 0-918298-06-7). Kenmore.

Koestenbaum, Peter. The New Image of the Person: The Theory & Practice of Clinical Philosophy. LC 77-84764. (Contributions in Philosophy: No. 9). 1978. lib. bdg. 29.95 (ISBN 0-8371-9888-7, KNI/). Greenwood.

--Vitality of Death: Essays in Existential Psychology & Philosophy. (Contributions in Philosophy: No. 5). 1971. lib. bdg. 29.95 (ISBN 0-8371-3319-X, KOV/). Greenwood.

Koester, Arthur R. The Cymbidium List; Species, Hybrids, & Awards, Vol. II, 1977-1980. LC 79-84474. 64p. (Orig.). 1982. pap. 7.00x (ISBN 0-9602558-1-8). A R Koester Bks.

Koester, Helmut. Introduction to the New Testament: History & Literature of Early Christianity, Vol. II. LC 82-71828. 400p. 1982. text ed. 22.95 (ISBN 0-8006-2101-8, 1-2101). Fortress.

--Introduction to the New Testament: History, Culture, & Religion of the Hellenistic Age, Vol. I. LC 82-71828. 448p. 1982. 24.95 (ISBN 0-8006-2100-X, 1-2100). Fortress.

Koester, Helmut, ed. see Lohse, Eduard.

Koester, John, jt. ed. see Byrne, John H.

Koester, Robert. Advance Oil & Gas Accounting. 1982. 38.00 (ISBN 0-89419-241-8). Inst Energy.

--Oil & Gas Accounting. 1981. 40.00. Inst Energy.

--Oil & Gas Accounting-Intermediate. 1981. cancelled 30.00 (ISBN 0-89419-144-6). Inst Energy.

Koester, Robert, ed. Oil & Gas Accounting for the Non-Financial Executive. 1982p. 35.00 (ISBN 0-89419-206-X). Inst Energy.

Koestler, A. Darkness at Noon. 1941. 15.95x (ISBN 0-02-565200-1). Macmillan.

Koestler, Arthur. The Case of the Midwife Toad. 1972. 2.45 (ISBN 0-394-71823-2). Random.

--The Ghost in the Machine. 1982. 15.00 (ISBN 0-394-52472-1). Random.

--Janus: A Summing Up. LC 78-23626. 1979. pap. 4.95 (ISBN 0-394-72886-6, Vin). Random.

--Sleepwalkers. 1963. pap. 6.95 o.p. (ISBN 0-448-00159-4, G&D). Putnam Pub Group.

Koestler, Arthur, ed. see Whyte, L. L.

Koestlime, Henry. Dating for Singles Over Thirty. LC 82-62514. 112p. (Orig.). 1983. pap. 6.50 (ISBN 0-935834-10-9). Rainbow-Betty.

Koestline, K. Henry. What Jesus Said About It. pap. 2.25 (ISBN 0-451-12196-1, AE2196, Sig). NAL.

Koethe, G. Topological Vector Spaces One. Garling, D. J. H., tr. (Grundlehren der Mathematischen Wissenshaften: Vol. 159). 456p. (Second Revised Printing). 1983. 47.00 (ISBN 0-387-04509-0). Springer-Verlag.

Koetter, Fred, jt. auth. see Rowe, Colin.

Koetting, Michael. Nursing-Home Organization & Efficiency: Profit Versus Non Profit. LC 79-2796. 160p. 1980. 22.95 (ISBN 0-669-03290-5). Lexington Bks.

Koetzle, T. F., ed. Structure & Bonding: Relationships Between Quantum Chemistry & Crystallography. Date not set. pap. 7.50 (ISBN 0-937140-25-2). Polycrystal Bk Serv.

Kofahl, Robert E. & Segraves, Kelly L. The Creation Explanation. LC 75-7639. 1975. pap. 5.95 o.p. (ISBN 0-87788-141-3). Shaw Pubs.

Kofele-Kale, Ndiva. Tribesmen & Patriots: Political Culture in a Poly-Ethnic African State. LC 80-5734. 375p. 1981. lib. bdg. 23.50 (ISBN 0-8191-1395-6); pap. text ed. 13.50 (ISBN 0-8191-1396-4). U Pr of Amer.

Kofele-Kale, Ndiva, ed. An African Experiment in Nation Building: The Bilingual Cameroon Republic. (Westview Special Studies on Africa). 1980. lib. bdg. 32.00 (ISBN 0-89158-685-7). Westview.

Koff, Raymond S. Viral Hepatitis. LC 78-17013. (Clinical Gastroenterology Monographs). 242p. 1978. 40.00x (ISBN 0-471-03695-1, Pub. by Wiley Medical). Wiley.

Koff, Richard M. How Does It Work. 304p. (RL 5). 1973. pap. 1.50 o.p. (ISBN 0-451-06920-X, W6920, Sig). NAL.

Koff, Theodore H. Long Term Care: An Approach to Serving the Frail Elderly. (Orig.). 1982. text ed. 13.95 (ISBN 0-316-50092-5); pap. text ed. 7.95 (ISBN 0-316-50093-3). Little.

Koffka, Kurt. Growth of the Mind. LC 80-50103. (Social Science Classics Ser.). 383p. 1980. text ed. 29.95 (ISBN 0-87855-360-6); pap. text ed. 7.95 (ISBN 0-87855-784-9). Transaction Bks.

--Principles of Gestalt Psychology. LC 35-7711. 1967. pap. 6.95 o.p. (ISBN 0-15-674460-0, Harv). HarBraceJ.

Koffman, E. Problem Solving & Structured Programming in PASCAL. 1981. 18.95 (ISBN 0-201-03893-5). A-W.

Koffman, E. B., jt. auth. see Friedman, F. L.

Koffman, Elliot, jt. auth. see Friedman, Frank.

Koffman, Elliot B. & Friedman, Frank L. Problem Solving & Structured Programming in BASIC. LC 78-65355. 1979. pap. text ed. 18.95 (ISBN 0-201-03888-9). A-W.

Kofoid, C. A. The Plankton of the Illinois River, 1894-99. (Bibliotheca Phycologica Ser.: No. 29). 1977. Repr. of 1903 ed. lib. bdg. 60.00x (ISBN 3-7682-1104-5). Lubrecht & Cramer.

Kofoid, C. A. & Swezy, Olive. Free-Living Unarmoured Dinoflagellata. (Univ. of California Memoirs Ser.). (Illus.). 540p. 1974. Repr. of 1921 ed. lib. bdg. 84.00 (ISBN 3-87429-066-2). Lubrecht & Cramer.

Kofstad, Per. Nonstoichiometry, Diffusion, & Electrical Conductivity in Binary Metal Oxides. LC 74-177885. 382p. 1972. 31.50 o.p. (ISBN 0-471-49776-2, Pub. by Wiley). Krieger.

--Nonstoichiometry, Diffusion & Electrical Conductivity in Binary Metal Oxides. LC 82-20336. 394p. 1983. Repr. of 1972 ed. lib. bdg. write for info. (ISBN 0-89874-569-1). Krieger.

Kogan, David & Kogan, Maurice. The Battle for the Labour Party. 160p. 1982. 20.00x (ISBN 0-312-06958-8). St Martin.

Kogan, Herman, jt. auth. see Wendt, Lloyd.

Kogan, Maurice. The Politics of Educational Change. LC 78-66344. 172p. 1978. 21.95 o.p. (ISBN 0-03-046246-0). Praeger.

Kogan, Maurice, jt. auth. see Becher, Tony.

Kogan, Maurice, jt. auth. see Kogan, David.

Kogan, Vivian. The Flowers of Fiction: Time & Space in Raymond Queneau's Les Fleurs bleues. LC 81-68141. (French Forum Monographs: No. 29). 170p. (Orig.). 1982. pap. 15.00x (ISBN 0-917058-28-3). French Forum.

Kogbetliantz, E. G. Fundamentals of Mathematics from an Advanced Viewpoint, 4 vols. in 2. Incl. Vols. 1 & 2. Algebra & Analysis: Evolution of the Number Concept & Determinants-Equations-Logarithms-Limits. 592p. 1968. 97.00x (ISBN 0-677-02000-7); Vols. 3 & 4. Geometry & Geometric Analysis & Solid Geometry & Spherical Trigonometry. 498p. 1969. 97.00x (ISBN 0-677-02010-4). complete set 174.00x (ISBN 0-677-00470-2); pap. 174.00 (ISBN 0-677-00475-3). Gordon.

--Handbook of First Complex Prime Numbers, 2 vol. set. LC 78-142082. 1010p. 1971. 161.00x (ISBN 0-677-02920-9). Gordon.

Kogelschatz, Deane E. Financial & Physical Survival. (Illus.). 1976. 12.95 (ISBN 0-87364-054-3). Paladin Pr.

Kogge, Peter M. The Architecture of Pipelined Computers. LC 80-26122. (Advanced Computer Science Ser.). (Illus.). 352p. 1981. text ed. 42.00 (ISBN 0-07-035237-2, Co-Pub by Hemisphere Pub). McGraw.

Kohan, A., jt. auth. see Elonka, Stephen M.

Kohan, Melvin J. Nylon Plastics. LC 73-9606. (Society of Plastics Engineers Monographs). 683p. 1973. 73.50x (ISBN 0-471-49780-0, Pub. by Wiley-Interscience). Wiley.

Kohan, Rhea. Hand-Me-Downs. (Orig.). 1982. pap. 3.50 (ISBN 0-515-06431-9). Jove Pubns.

Kohavi, Zvi. Switching & Finite Automata Theory. 2nd ed. Feigenbaum & Hamming, eds. (McGraw-Hill Computer Science Ser.). (Illus.). 1978. text ed. 39.95 (ISBN 0-07-035310-7, C); solutions to problems 16.50 (ISBN 0-07-035311-5). McGraw.

Kohen-Raz, Reuven. Disadvantaged Post-Adolescents: Approaches to Education & Rehabilitation. (Special Aspects of Education Ser.: Vol. 1). 210p. 1982. write for info. (ISBN 0-677-06010-6). Gordon.

Kohl, Herb & Lindsay, Len. Atari Games & Recreation. 1982. 18.95 (ISBN 0-8359-0298-6); pap. text ed. 14.95 (ISBN 0-8359-0242-0). Reston.

Kohl, Herbert, jt. auth. see Kohl, Judith.

Kohl, Herbert R. The Age of Complexity. LC 76-10983. 1977. Repr. of 1965 ed. lib. bdg. 18.75x (ISBN 0-8371-8354-5, KOAC). Greenwood.

Kohl, Irene, jt. auth. see Kohl, Kenneth.

Kohl, Irene C., jt. auth. see Kohl, Kenneth A.

Kohl, Judith & Kohl, Herbert. Pack, Band & Colony: The World of Social Animals. (Illus.). 132p. (gr. 6 up). 1983. 10.95 (ISBN 0-686-81645-5). FS&G.

Kohl, Kenneth & Kohl, Irene. Financing College Education. rev ed. LC 80-8712. 240p. 1981. pap. 5.95i o.p. (ISBN 0-06-090861-0, CN861, CN). Har-Row.

--Financing College Education. 3rd ed. LC 82-48232. 288p. 1983. pap. 5.72i (ISBN 0-06-090994-3, CN 994, CN). Har-Row.

Kohl, Kenneth A. & Kohl, Irene C. Financing College Education: A Handbook for Students & Families. LC 78-20172. 1980. 13.41i (ISBN 0-06-012427-X, HarpT). Har-Row.

Kohl, M, tr. see Pannenberg, Wolfhart.

Kohl, Margaret, tr. see Koch, Klaus.

Kohl, Marvin, ed. Infanticide & the Value of Life. LC 77-26376. 252p. 1978. 15.95 (ISBN 0-87975-100-2); pap. 9.95 (ISBN 0-87975-214-9). Prometheus Bks.

Kohl, Philip L., ed. & tr. from Rus. The Bronze Age Civilization of Central Asia: Recent Soviet Discoveries. LC 80-5454. (Illus.). 440p. 1981. 40.00 (ISBN 0-87332-169-3). M E Sharpe.

Kohl, Sam. All About Dog Shows. (Illus.). 128p. 1981. 7.95 (ISBN 0-87666-672-1, PS-778). TFH Pubns.

Kohl, Sam & Goldstein, Catherine. All Breed Dog Grooming Guide. LC 72-86425. (Illus.). 288p. 1973. spiral bdg. 14.95 (ISBN 0-668-02729-0). Arco.

--The All Breed Dog Grooming Guide. LC 82-18446. (Illus.). 272p. 1983. spiral bdg. 16.95 (ISBN 0-668-05573-1, 5573). Arco.

Kohl, Sam & Riley, Tom. Your Career in Animal Services. LC 77-1990. (Illus.). 1977. lib. bdg. 7.95 (ISBN 0-668-04261-3); pap. 4.50 (ISBN 0-668-04259-1). Arco.

Kohl, Wilfied L. & Basevi, Giorgio. West Germany: A European & Global Power. (Illus.). 240p. 1980. 19.95x (ISBN 0-669-03162-3). Lexington Bks.

Kohl, Wilfred L., ed. Economic Foreign Policies of Industrial States. LC 76-43584. 272p. 1977. 23.95x (ISBN 0-669-00958-X). Lexington Bks.

Kohl, Wilfrid L. After the Second Oil Crisis: Energy Policies in Europe, America, & Japan. LC 81-47023. 256p. 1982. 29.95x (ISBN 0-669-04547-0). Lexington Bks.

Kohland, William. Mineral Identification. LC 77-73455. 1977. 9.00 (ISBN 0-910042-31-4); pap. 4.50 (ISBN 0-910042-30-6). Allegheny.

Kohlas, Jurg. Stochastic Methods of Operations Research. LC 81-21574. 160p. 1982. 34.50 (ISBN 0-521-23899-4); pap. 13.95 (ISBN 0-521-28292-6). Cambridge U Pr.

Kohlenberg, Robert J. Migraine Relief: A Personal Treatment Program. 1983. pap. write for info. (ISBN 0-06-091026-7, CN-1026). Har-Row.

Kohlenberger, John R., III, jt. auth. see Goodrick, Edward W.

Kohler, Carl. History of Costume. Schardt, Emma Von, ed. (Illus.). pap. 6.50 (ISBN 0-486-21030-8). Dover.

Kohler, Carolyn & Westfall, Gloria. Documentation of Intergovernmental Organizations: Proceedings of the Workshop, Indiana U., 24-26 May 1978. 70p. 1980. 32.00 (ISBN 0-08-024670-2). Pergamon.

Kohler, Eric L. Dictionary for Accountants. 5th ed. (Illus.). 528p. 1975. 39.95 (ISBN 0-13-209783-4). P-H.

Kohler, Heinz. Intermediate Microeconomics: Theory & Applications. 1982. text ed. 24.50x (ISBN 0-673-15277-4). Scott F.

--Scarcity & Freedom: An Introduction to Economics. 2nd ed. 1977. pap. text ed. 17.95x (ISBN 0-669-91140-2); instr's manual 1.95 (ISBN 0-669-00147-3). Heath.

Kohler, K., ed. Pitch Analysis: Journal: Phonetica, Vol. 39, No. 4-5, 1982. (Illus.). 156p. 1982. pap. 56.50 (ISBN 3-8055-3670-4). S Karger.

Kohler, Mary C. Young People Learning to Care: Making a Difference through Youth Participation. 160p. 1983. pap. 8.95 (ISBN 0-8164-2429-2). Seabury.

Kohler, Peter A. & Zacher, Hans F. The Evolution of Social Insurance, Eighteen Eighty-One to Nineteen Eighty-One: Studies of Great Britain, France, Switzerland, Austria, & Germany. LC 81-23258. 500p. 1982. 35.00x (ISBN 0-312-27285-5). St Martin.

Kohler, Wolfgang. Gestalt Psychology. 224p. 1974. pap. 1.50 o.p. (ISBN 0-451-61432-1, MW1432, Ment). NAL.

Kohli, Daniel R, jt. auth. see Whatmore, George B.

Kohli, M. S. Nine Atop Everest: Story of the Indian Ascent. 1969. 17.50 o.p. (ISBN 0-8046-8813-3). Kennikat.

Kohlmann, M. & Christopeit, N., eds. Stochastic Differential Systems, Bad Honnef, FRG 1982: Proceedings. (Lecture Notes in Control & Information Sciences Ser.: Vol. 43). 377p. 1983. pap. 17.50 (ISBN 0-387-12061-0). Springer-Verlag.

Kohlmeier, Louis, et al, eds. Reporting on Business & the Economy. 336p. 1981. text ed. 21.95 (ISBN 0-13-773879-X). P-H.

Kohlmeyer, E., jt. auth. see Kohlmeyer, J.

Kohlmeyer, J. Index Alphabeticus Klotzschii & Rabenhorstii Herbarii Mycologici. 1962. pap. 16.00 (ISBN 3-7682-5404-6). Lubrecht & Cramer.

Kohlmeyer, J. & Kohlmeyer, E. Synoptic Plates of Higher Marine Fungi. 3rd rev. ed. 1971. 14.00 o.p. (ISBN 3-7682-0218-6). Lubrecht & Cramer.

Kohlmeyer, J. E. Icones Fungorum Maris, 7 parts. 1969. 80.00 (ISBN 3-7682-2000-1). Lubrecht & Cramer.

Kohlrausch, K. W. Ramanspektren. 1972. 107.00 (ISBN 0-471-25837-7, Wiley Heyden). Wiley.

Kohls, Richard L. & Uhl, Joseph N. The Marketing of Agriculture Products. 5th ed. (Illus.). 1980. text ed. 28.95x (ISBN 0-02-365640-9). Macmillan.

Kohlschmidt, Werner. A History of German Literature, 1760-1805. Hilton, Ian, tr. from Ger. LC 74-32062. 420p. 1975. text ed. 44.50x (ISBN 0-8419-0195-3). Holmes & Meier.

Kohn, Barry & Matusow, Alice. Barry & Alice: Portrait of a Bisexual Marriage. LC 79-24551. 1980. 10.95 o.p. (ISBN 0-13-056150-9). P-H.

Kohn, Bernice. Look-It-up Book of Transportation. LC 68-23655. (Look-It-up Books Ser.). (Illus.). (gr. 3-5). 1968. PLB 5.99 o.p. (ISBN 0-394-90766-3, BYR). Random.

--One Day It Rained Cats & Dogs. (Illus.). (gr. 3 up). 1965. PLB 3.99 o.p. (ISBN 0-698-30269-9, Coward). Putnam Pub Group.

Kohn, H., tr. see Winternitz, Maurice.

Kohn, Hans. The Age of Nationalism: The First Era of Global History. LC 76-27696. (World Perspectives: Vol. 28). 1976. Repr. of 1962 ed. lib. bdg. 19.75x (ISBN 0-8371-9087-8, KOAN). Greenwood.

--Living in a World Revolution: My Encounters with History. 1970. pap. 2.95 o.p. (ISBN 0-671-20719-9, Touchstone Bks). S&S.

--Nationalism & Liberty: The Swiss Example. LC 77-28360. 1978. Repr. of 1956 ed. lib. bdg. 16.00x (ISBN 0-313-20233-8, KONL). Greenwood.
--Nationalism: Its Meaning & History. LC 82-163. (Anvil Ser.). 192p. 1982. pap. text ed. 5.95 (ISBN 0-89874-479-2). Krieger.
Kohn, Kate H., et al. Medical Examination Review: Physical Medicine & Rehabilitation, Vol. 20. 4th ed. (Medical Exam Review Bks.). 1983. pap. text ed. 26.00 (ISBN 0-87488-128-5). Med Exam.
--Physical Medicine & Rehabilitation. 3rd ed. (Medical Examination Review Bk.: Vol. 20). 1979. spiral bdg. 26.00 (ISBN 0-87488-128-5). Med Exam.
Kohn, L. D. Hormone Receptors. (Horizons in Biochemistry & Biophysics Ser.: Vol. 6). 404p. 1982. 67.95x (ISBN 0-471-10049-8, Pub. by Wiley-Interscience). Wiley.
Kohn, M. J., jt. auth. see Atkinson, L. J.
Kohn, Martin. Social Competence, Symptoms, & Underachivement in Childhood: A Longitudinal Perspective. LC 77-5011. 188p. 1977. 18.95x o.p. (ISBN 0-470-99151-8). Halsted Pr.
Kohn, Melvin L. & Schooler, Carmi. Work & Personality: An Inquiry into the Impact of Social Stratification. 1983. write for info. (ISBN 0-89391-121-6). Ablex Pub.
Kohn, Murray J. The Voice of My Blood Cries Out. LC 78-66108. 1979. 10.95 o.p. (ISBN 0-88400-063-X). Shengold.
Kohn, Robert & White, Kerr L., eds. Health Care: An International Study. (Illus.). 1976. text ed. 75.00x (ISBN 0-19-264226-X). Oxford U Pr.
Kohn, Robert E. A Linear Programming Model for Air Pollution Control. 1978. 30.00x (ISBN 0-262-11062-8). MIT Pr.
Kohn, Robert R. Principles of Mammalian Aging. 2nd ed. (Illus.). 1978. 24.95 (ISBN 0-13-709352-7). P-H.
Kohn, S. & Meyendorff, Alexander F. The Cost of the War to Russia. 22.50x (ISBN 0-86527-034-1). Fertig.
Kohnert, Gerald V., jt. auth. see Kolstad, C. Kenneth.
Kohnke, Helmut. Soil Physics. LC 68-21846. 1968. text ed. 21.95 o.p. (ISBN 0-07-035299-2, C). McGraw.
Kohnke, Helmut & Bertrand, A. R. Soil Conservation. (Agricultural Ser.). 1959. text ed. 35.95 (ISBN 0-07-035285-2, C). McGraw.
Kohnke, Mary F. Advocacy: Risk & Reality. LC 82-6460. (Illus.). 204p. 1982. pap. text ed. 11.95 (ISBN 0-8016-2721-4). Mosby.
Kohnstamm, M. & Hager, W. A Nation Writ Large? Foreign-Policy Problems Before European Community. LC 73-6817. 275p. (Orig.). 1973. 20.00 o.p. (ISBN 0-470-49795-5). Krieger.
Kohonen, Tuevo. Digital Circuits & Devices. (Illus.). 576p. 1972. ref. ed. 32.95 (ISBN 0-13-214122-1). P-H.
Kohout, Frank J. Statistics for Social Scientists: A Coordinated Learning System. LC 73-21843. 452p. 1974. text ed. 26.50x (ISBN 0-471-49800-9). Wiley.
Kohout, Pavel. Hangwoman. 512p. 1981. 14.95 o.s.i. (ISBN 0-399-12416-0). Putnam Pub Group.
Kohs, Ellis B. Musical Form: Studies in Analysis & Synthesis. 1976. text ed. 26.50 (ISBN 0-395-18613-7). HM.
Kohsaka, M. & Shokmori, T. Advances in Dopamine: Proceedings of a Satellite Symposium to the 8th International Congress of Pharmacology, Okayama, Japan, July 26-28, 1981. (Illus.). 464p. 1982. 70.00 (ISBN 0-08-027391-2, H130); firm 35.00 (ISBN 0-686-97494-8). Pergamon.
Koht, H. Old Norse Sagas. (Lowell Institute Lectures Ser). Repr. of 1931 ed. 14.00 o.s.i. (ISBN 0-527-52400-X). Kraus Repr.
Kohut, Jeraldine J., jt. auth. see Kohut, Sylvester, Jr.
Kohut, Rebekah. His Father's House: The Story of George Alexander Kohut. 1938. 47.50x (ISBN 0-686-51400-9). Elliots Bks.
Kohut, Sylvester, Jr. & Kohut, Jeraldine J. Reality Orientation for the Elderly. 2nd ed. 1982. pap. 12.95 (ISBN 0-87489-304-6). Med Economics.
Koike, Yujiro. Electron Tubes. (Eng.). 1972. 37.50x o.p. (ISBN 0-8002-1389-0). Intl Pubns Serv.
Koita, Mamadou, jt. auth. see Bird, Charles.
Koiter, W. T. & Mikhailov, G. K., eds. Theory of Shells. 1980. 102.25 (ISBN 0-444-85338-3). Elsevier.
Koiter, W. T., ed. see IUTAM International Congress, 14th.
Koiter, W. T., ed. see Renyi, A.
Kojima, K. & Tochigi, K. Prediction of Vapor-Liquid Equilibria by the ASOG Method. (Physical Science Data Ser.: Vol. 3). 264p. 1980. 61.75 (ISBN 0-444-99773-3). Elsevier.
Kojima, Kiyoshi. Direct Foreign Investment: A Japanese Model of Multinational Business Operations. LC 78-61337. (Praeger Special Studies). 1979. 31.95 o.p. (ISBN 0-03-047471-X). Praeger.
Kojima, Naomi. Mr. & Mrs. Thief. LC 79-7902. (Illus.). 32p. (gr. k-4). 1980. 6.95i o.p. (ISBN 0-690-04021-0, TYC-J); PLB 6.89 (ISBN 0-690-04022-9). Har-Row.
Kojm, Christopher A., ed. U. S. Defense Policy. (The Reference Shelf: Vol. 54, No. 2). 224p. 1982. pap. text ed. 6.25 (ISBN 0-8242-0666-5). Wilson.
Kok, Gerard P., jt. auth. see Huang, Po-Fei.
Kok, Gerard P., jt. auth. see Huang Po-Fei.
Kokaska, Charles J., jt. auth. see Brolin, Donn E.
Kokeritz, Helge. Shakespeare's Pronunciation. 1953. text ed. 49.50x (ISBN 0-686-83738-X). Elliots Bks.
Kok Liang Lee. Flowers in the Sky. (Writing in Asia Ser.). (Orig.). 1982. pap. text ed. 5.50x (ISBN 0-686-83873-4, 00268). Heinemann Ed.
Kokosalakis, N. Ethnic Identity & Religion: Tradition & Change in Liverpool Jewry. LC 82-13609. (Illus.). 276p. 1983. lib. bdg. 23.50 (ISBN 0-8191-2732-9); pap. text ed. 11.50 (ISBN 0-8191-2733-7). U Pr of Amer.
Kokotovic, P. V., jt. auth. see Ioannou, P. A.
Kokrda, Ken, jt. auth. see Jacobs, Mark.
Kokus, J., jt. auth. see Estes, Jack C.
Kokusaiho, Gakkai. Japan & the United Nations. LC 74-7433. (National Studies on International Organization-Carnegie Endowment for International Peace). 246p. 1974. Repr. of 1958 ed. lib. bdg. 15.50x (ISBN 0-8371-7538-0, KOJU). Greenwood.
Kolaczyk, Anne M. The Bartered Bride. 1979. pap. 1.50 o.s.i. (ISBN 0-440-10912-4). Dell.
Kolaja, Jiri. A Polish Factory. LC 73-10736. 157p. 1973. Repr. of 1960 ed. lib. bdg. 17.25x (ISBN 0-8371-7026-5, KOPF). Greenwood.
Kolakowski, Donald, jt. auth. see Bock, R. Darrell.
Kolakowski, Leszek. Religion. LC 81-85135. 1982. 19.95x (ISBN 0-19-520372-0). Oxford U Pr.
Kolars, John F. & Nystuen, John D. Human Geography: Spatial Design in World Society. (Illus.). 288p. 1974. text ed. 16.00 o.p. (ISBN 0-07-035327-1, C). McGraw.
Kolasa, Blair, jt. auth. see Meyer, Bernadine.
Kolasa, Blair J. Responsibility in Business: Issues & Problems. LC 72-170645. 1972. pap. text ed. 13.95 (ISBN 0-13-773739-4). P-H.
Kolatch, Alfred J. The Dictionary of First Names. 540p. 1981. pap. 6.95 (ISBN 0-399-50570-9, Perige). Putnam Pub Group.
--The Jewish Book of Why. 1981. 11.95 (ISBN 0-8246-0256-0). Jonathan David.
--The Name Dictionary. rev. ed. LC 66-25122. 432p. 1973. 9.95 (ISBN 0-8246-0060-6). Jonathan David.
Kolb, Albert. East Asia: China, Japan, Korea, Vietnam; Geography of a Cultural Region. Sym, C. A., tr. (Illus.). 591p. 1971. 42.50x o.p. (ISBN 0-416-08420-6); pap. 19.95x o.p. (ISBN 0-416-70780-7). Methuen Inc.
Kolb, Annette. Mozart. LC 74-29634. (Illus.). 299p. 1975. Repr. of 1956 ed. lib. bdg. 20.50x (ISBN 0-8371-7977-7, KOMO). Greenwood.
Kolb, Annette, jt. auth. see Gould, John.
Kolb, B. Applied Headspace Gas Chromatography. 200p. 1980. 42.95 (ISBN 0-471-25838-5, Pub. by Wiley Heyden). Wiley.
Kolb, D., et al. Organizational Psychology: An Experimental Approach. 3rd ed. 1979. pap. 18.95 (ISBN 0-13-641258-0). P-H.
Kolb, David A. & McIntyre, James M. Organizational Psychology: A Book of Readings. (Behavior Sciences in Business Ser.). 1979. text ed. 15.95 (ISBN 0-13-641274-2). P-H.
Kolb, Helga, jt. auth. see DeVries, Louis.
Kolb, Jack, ed. The Letters of Arthur Henry Hallam. LC 79-13490. (Illus.). 856p. 1981. 45.00x (ISBN 0-8142-0300-0). Ohio St U Pr.
Kolb, John & Ross, Steven S. Product Safety & Liability: A Desk Reference. (Illus.). 1979. 34.95 (ISBN 0-07-035380-8). McGraw.
Kolb, John H., jt. auth. see Brunner, Edmund.
Kolb, Lawrence C. Modern Clinical Psychiatry. 9th ed. LC 76-45962. (Illus.). 1977. 25.00 o.p. (ISBN 0-7216-5483-5). Saunders.
--The Painful Phantom-Psychology, Physiology & Treatment. (Illus.). 64p. 1954. photocopy ed. spiral 6.75x (ISBN 0-398-04315-9). C C Thomas.
Kolb, Patricia A. H.I.T. A Manual for the Classification, Filing, & Retrieval of Palmprints. (Illus.). 112p. 1979. spiral 16.50x (ISBN 0-398-03855-4). C C Thomas.
Kolb, Philip, ed. see Proust, Marcel.
Kolb, R. & Lumpp, D. Martin Luther: Companion of the Contemporary Christian. LC 12-2959. 1982. pap. 8.95 (ISBN 0-686-99857-X). Concordia.
Kolb, Robert. Andreae & the Formula of Concord. 1977. pap. 7.95 (ISBN 0-570-03741-7, 12-2645). Concordia.
Kolb, W. J., jt. auth. see Gould, Julius.
Kolbas, Grace H. Ecology: Cycle & Recycle. LC 72-81035. (Basic Biology in Color Ser.). (Illus.). 192p. (gr. 9 up). 1972. 14.95 (ISBN 0-8069-3558-8); PLB 17.79 (ISBN 0-8069-3559-6). Sterling.
Kolbe, Parke R. The Colleges in War Time & After: A Contemporary Account of the Effect of the War Upon Higher Education in America. LC 74-75247. (The United States in World War 1 Ser). (Illus.). xx, 320p. 1974. Repr. of 1919 ed. lib. bdg. 19.95x (ISBN 0-89198-106-3). Ozer.
Kolbe, Pierre. Description du Cap de Bonne-Esperance, 3 vols. (Bibliotheque Africaine Ser.). (Fr.). 1974. Repr. of 1741 ed. Set. lib. bdg. 252.50x o.p. (ISBN 0-8287-0472-4). Clearwater Pub.
Kolber, Alan R. & Wong, Thomas K., eds. In Vitro Toxicity Testing of Environmental Agents, Current & Future Possibilities: Part A-Survey of Test Systems. (NATO Conference Ser.: No. I, Ecology). 574p. 1983. 69.50x (ISBN 0-306-41123-7, Plenum Pr). Plenum Pub.
--In Vitro Toxicity Testing of Environmental Agents, Current & Future Possibilities: Part B-Development of Risk Assessment Guidelines. (NATO Conference Series I, Ecology: Vol. 5B). 566p. 1983. 69.50x (ISBN 0-306-41124-5). Plenum Pub.
Kolberg, Glenn C. The Kondratieff Theory: Historically Valid or a Pitiful Humbug? (Illus.). 129p. 1982. 77.35 (ISBN 0-86654-030-X). Inst Econ Finan.
Kolbick, Loyal. The Man Who Changed His Name. (Arch Bks.: Set 9). (Illus.). 32p. (ps-4). 1972. pap. 0.89 (ISBN 0-570-06066-4, 59-1184). Concordia.
Kolbrek, Loyal. The Day God Made It Rain. (Arch Books Series Fourteen). (gr. k-2). 1977. pap. 0.89 (ISBN 0-570-06108-3, 59-1226). Concordia.
Kolbrek, Loyal & Larsen, Chris. Samson's Secret. (Arch Bks.: Set 8). (Orig.). (ps-4). 1970. pap. 0.89 (ISBN 0-570-06052-4, 59-1168). Concordia.
Kolchin, Peter. First Freedom: The Responses of Alabama's Blacks to Emancipation & Reconstruction. (Contributions in American History: No. 20). (Illus.). 1972. lib. bdg. 25.00 (ISBN 0-8371-6385-4, KAB/). Greenwood.
Kolde, E. International Business Enterprise. 2nd ed. LC 78-37518. (Illus.). 672p. 1973. ref. ed. 25.95 (ISBN 0-13-472381-3). P-H.
Kolde, Endel-Jakob. Environment of International Business: Concepts, Structures, & Strategies. LC 81-17122. 483p. 1981. instr's. manual 24.95x (ISBN 0-534-01038-5). Kent Pub Co.
Kolden, Marc. Called by the Gospel. LC 82-72651. 112p. 1983. pap. 4.95 (10-0967). Augsburg.
Kolenda, Konstantin. Philosophy in Literature: Metaphysical Darkness & Ethical Light. LC 81-7979. 250p. 1982. 28.75x (ISBN 0-389-20224-X). B&N Imports.
--Religion Without God. LC 76-19349. (Skeptic's Bookshelf Ser.). 125p. 1976. 9.95 (ISBN 0-87975-066-9). Prometheus Bks.
Kolenkow, Robert J., jt. auth. see Kleppner, Daniel.
Koleshnik, Eugene, et al, eds. The Encyclopedia of Ships & Seafaring. (Illus.). 256p. 1980. 15.95 o.p. (ISBN 0-517-53738-9, Michelman Bks). Crown.
Kolesnik, Eugene M., jt. auth. see Ventry, Lord.
Kolesnik, Walter B. Mental Discipline in Modern Education. 1958. pap. 4.75 (ISBN 0-299-01674-9). U of Wis Pr.
Kolig, E. The Changing Law: Religious Organization & Western Influence Among Aborigines of the Fitzroy Area, Southern Kinberleys. Date not set. price not set (ISBN 0-391-01126-X). Humanities.
Kolin, Michael J. & De La Rosa, Denise M. The Custom Bicycle: Buying, Setting Up & Riding the Quality Bicycle. 14.95 (ISBN 0-87857-254-6); pap. 10.95 (ISBN 0-87857-255-4). Rodale Pr Inc.
Kolin, Philip C. Successful Writing at Work. 352p. 1982. pap. text ed. 13.95 (ISBN 0-669-03507-6). Heath.
Kolins, Jerry & Britten, Anthony F., eds. Plasma Products: Use & Management. 129p. 1982. 19.00 (ISBN 0-914404-72-5); non-members 21.00 (ISBN 0-686-83048-2). Am Assn Blood.
Kolinsky, Martin. Continuity & Change in European Society. LC 74-13674. 192p. 1974. 22.50 o.p. (ISBN 0-312-16870-5). St Martin.
Kolinsky, Martin & Paterson, William, eds. Social & Political Movements in Western Europe. LC 76-6010. 1976. 22.50 o.p. (ISBN 0-312-73150-7). St Martin.
Koliopoulos, John S. Greece & the British Connection, 1935-1941. 1978. 34.95x o.p. (ISBN 0-19-822523-7). Oxford U Pr.
Kolisko, E. & Kolisko, L. Agriculture of Tomorrow. 2nd ed. (Illus.). 1978. 29.50x (ISBN 0-906492-00-9, Pub. by Kolisko Archive Publications); pap. 15.95x (ISBN 0-906492-44-0). St George Bk Serv.
Kolisko, Eugen. Reincarnation & Other Essays. 1979. Repr. of 1940 ed. 9.50x (ISBN 0-906492-14-9, Pub. by Kolisko Archives). St George Bk Serv.
Kolisko, Eugen & Kolisko, Lily. Silver & Its Connection with the Human Organism. 1978. pap. 3.95x (ISBN 0-906492-10-6, Pub by Kolisko Archives). St George Bk Serv.
Kolisko, L., jt. auth. see Kolisko, E.
Kolisko, Lily, jt. auth. see Kolisko, Eugen.
Kolker, Allan E. & Hetherington, John, Jr. Becker-Shaffer's Diagnosis & Therapy of the Glaucomas. (Illus.). 576p. 1983. text ed. 55.00 (ISBN 0-8016-2723-0). Mosby.
Kolker, Robert P. The Altering Eye: Contemporary International Cinema. LC 81-22488. (Illus.). 1983. 29.95 (ISBN 0-19-503126-1); pap. 10.95 (ISBN 0-19-503302-7). Oxford U Pr.
--A Cinema of Loneliness: Penn, Kubrick, Coppola, Scorsese, Altman. LC 79-978. (Illus.). 1980. 19.95x (ISBN 0-19-502588-1). Oxford U Pr.
Kolkey, Jonathan M. The New Right, Nineteen Sixty to Nineteen Sixty-Eight: With Epilogue, 1969-1980. LC 82-23821. 416p. (Orig.). 1983. lib. bdg. 26.75 (ISBN 0-8191-2993-3); pap. text ed. 15.50 (ISBN 0-8191-2994-1). U Pr of Amer.
Koll, Elsie. The Golden Thread: Diary of Mrs. Elsie Koll, Missionary to China. SCales, John L., ed. (Illus.). 180p. (Orig.). 1982. pap. 4.95 (ISBN 0-942504-00-3). Overcomer Pr.
Koll, F. & Cohen, Edward. Handbook of Structural Concrete. 1936p. 1983. 85.86 (ISBN 0-07-011573-7, P&RB). McGraw.
Koll, Michael, ed. see Grau, T., et al.
Kollar, Nathan R., ed. Options in Roman Catholicism: An Introduction. LC 82-21823. 224p. (Orig.). 1983. lib. bdg. 21.50 (ISBN 0-8191-2958-5); pap. text ed. 10.75 (ISBN 0-8191-2959-3). U Pr of Amer.
Kollenborn, Tom, jt. auth. see Swanson, James.
Koller, John M. The Indian Way. 1982. text ed. 10.95 (ISBN 0-02-365800-2). Macmillan.
Koller, Marvin. Families: A Multigenerational Approach. (Illus.). 320p. 1974. pap. text ed. 10.95 o.p. (ISBN 0-07-035331-X, C). McGraw.
Koller, Marvin R. Social Gerontology. 1968. pap. text ed. 7.50 (ISBN 0-685-55616-6, 30337). Phila Bk Co.
Koller, Marvin R. & Ritchie, Oscar W. Sociology of Childhood. 2nd ed. LC 77-13314. (P-H Ser. in Sociology). (Illus.). 1978. text ed. 22.95 (ISBN 0-13-821074-8). P-H.
Koller, William. Your Career in Computer-Related Occupations. LC 78-13700. 1979. lib. bdg. 7.95 (ISBN 0-668-04610-4); pap. 4.50 (ISBN 0-668-04622-8). Arco.
--Your Career in Construction. LC 77-17396. (Arco Career Guidance Ser.). (Illus.). 1978. lib. bdg. 7.95 (ISBN 0-668-04453-5); pap. 4.50 (ISBN 0-668-04435-7). Arco.
Kollerstrom, Nick, jt. auth. see Best, Simon.
Kollewijn, Roeland D. American-Dutch Private International Law. 2nd ed. LC 61-18187. (Bilateral Studies in Private International Law: No. 3). 111p. 1962. 15.00 (ISBN 0-379-11403-8). Oceana.
Kollman, W. Prediction Methods for Turbulent Flows. 1980. text ed. 47.50 (ISBN 0-07-035259-3). McGraw.
Kollmann, Augustus F. Essay on Practical Musical Composition. 2nd ed. LC 70-75288. (Music Reprint Ser). 1973. Repr. of 1799 ed. lib. bdg. 27.50 (ISBN 0-306-71295-4). Da Capo.
Kollmann, Wolfgang, jt. auth. see Eversley, David.
Kolln, Martha. Understanding English Grammar. 1982. text ed. 19.95x (ISBN 0-02-365850-9). Macmillan.
Kollock, John. The Long Afternoon. 8.95 (ISBN 0-932298-01-X). Copple Hse.
--Meg's World. 1981. pap. 4.95 (ISBN 0-932298-15-X). Copple Hse.
--These Gentle Hills. 14.95 (ISBN 0-932298-14-1); pap. 8.95 (ISBN 0-932298-17-6). Copple Hse.
Kollontai, Alexandra. Selected Writings of Alexandra Kollontai. Holt, Alix, intro. by. 336p. 1980. pap. 6.95 (ISBN 0-393-00974-2). Norton.
Kolman, B., jt. auth. see Belinfante, J. G.
Kolman, B., jt. ed. see Anton, Howard.
Kolman, Bernard. Elementary Linear Algebra. 3rd ed. 368p. 1982. text ed. 24.95 (ISBN 0-02-365990-4). Macmillan.
--Introductory Linear Algebra with Applications. 2nd ed. (Illus.). 1980. text ed. 23.95x (ISBN 0-02-365970-X). Macmillan.
Kolman, Bernard & Shapiro, Arnold. Algebra for College Students. 1980. text ed. 21.75 (ISBN 0-12-417880-4); instr's manual 3.00 (ISBN 0-12-417885-5). Acad Pr.
--College Algebra. 1981. 24.00 (ISBN 0-12-417884-7); instructor's manual 3.50 (ISBN 0-12-417886-3); study guide 7.75 (ISBN 0-12-417887-1). Acad Pr.
Kolman, Bernard, jt. auth. see Anton, Howard.
Kolman, Bernard, jt. auth. see Trench, William F.
Kolman, Bernard & Shapiro, Arnold, eds. Test Bank for College Algebra. 1982. 2.50 (ISBN 0-12-417888-X); Test Bank for College Alegebra & Trigonometry. 2.50 (ISBN 0-12-417846-4). Acad Pr.
Kolman, John A. A Guide to the Development of Special Weapons & Tactics Teams. (Illus.). 212p. 1982. 19.75x (ISBN 0-398-04667-0). C C Thomas.
Kolmogorov, A. N., jt. auth. see Gnedenko, B. V.
Kolmogorov, Andrei N. Foundations of the Theory of Probability. 2nd ed. LC 56-11512. 9.50 (ISBN 0-8284-0023-7). Chelsea Pub.
Kolodziej, Edward, jt. auth. see Harkavy, Robert.
Kolodziej, Edward, jt. ed. see Harkavey, Robert.
Kolokolov, G. S., tr. see Kube, Alfred N.
Kolovakos, Gregory, tr. see Vargas Llosa, Mario.
Kolowrat, Ernest, et al. What You Should Know About Medical Lab Tests. LC 79-7092. (Illus.). 1979. 12.45i (ISBN 0-690-01831-2). T Y Crowell.
Kolpas, Norman. The Chocolate Lover's Companion. (Illus.). 1978. pap. 6.95 (ISBN 0-8256-3126-2, Quick Fox). Putnam Pub Group.
--The Gourmet's Lexicon. 1982. 5.95 (ISBN 0-686-83115-2, Perige). Putnam Pub Group.
Kolson, Clifford, jt. auth. see Kaluger, George.
Kolstad, C. Kenneth & Kohnert, Gerald V. Rapid Electrical Estimating & Pricing: A Handy, Quick Method of Directly Determining the Selling Prices of Electrical Construction Work. 3rd ed. (Illus.). 1979. 38.50 (ISBN 0-07-035129-5). McGraw.
Kolstad, P. & Stafl, A. Atlas of Colposcopy. 2nd ed. (Illus.). 152p. 1977. text ed. 49.95 o.p. (ISBN 0-8391-1109-6). Univ Park.
Kolstee, Hans M. Motion & Power. (Illus.). 256p. 1982. text ed. 20.95 (ISBN 0-13-602953-1). P-H.
Kolthoff, I. & Elving, P. Treatise on Analytical Chemistry, Pt. 1, Vol. 7. 2nd ed. LC 78-1707. (Treatise on Analytical Chemistry Ser.). 816p. 1981. 77.95x (ISBN 0-471-07996-0, Pub. by Wiley-Interscience). Wiley.

--Treatise on Analytical Chemistry, Pt. 1, Vol. 5. 2nd ed. (Treatise on Analytical Chemistry Ser.). 816p. 1982. 78.00x (ISBN 0-471-01837-6, Pub. by Wiley-Interscience). Wiley.

Kolthoff, I. M. & Elving, P. J. Treatise on Analytical Chemistry, 3 pts. Incl. Pt. 1, Vols. 10-12. Theory & Practice of Analytical Chemistry. Vol. 11, 1975. 87.00 (ISBN 0-471-49967-6); Vol. 12, 1976. 48.00 o.s.i. (ISBN 0-471-49968-4); Pt. 2, Vols. 4, 10, 12 & 14-15. Analytical Chemistry of the Elements & of Inorganic & Organic Compounds. Vol. 4, 1966, 452p. 45.00 o.p. (ISBN 0-470-49986-9); Vol. 10, 1978. 71.95 (ISBN 0-471-49998-6). Vol. 14, 1971. 51.00 (ISBN 0-471-50005-4); Vol. 15, 1976. 72.00 (ISBN 0-471-50009-7); Pt. 3, Vols. 3-4. Analytical Chemistry in Industry. 86.50 (ISBN 0-471-50012-7); 86.50 (ISBN 0-471-02765-0). LC 59-12439 (Pub. by Wiley-Interscience). Wiley.

Kolthoff, I. M. & Elving, Philip J. Treatise on Analytical Chemistry, Vol. 10, Pt. 1. 372p. 1982. 65.00 (ISBN 0-471-89688-8, Pub. by Wiley-Interscience). Wiley.

--Treatise on Analytical Chemistry, Vol. 12, Pt. 1. 2nd ed. 567p. 1983. price not set (ISBN 0-471-89653-5, Pub. by Wiley-Interscience). Wiley.

--Treatise on Analytical Chemistry: Part I: Theory & Practice, Vol. 3. 2nd ed. 592p. 1983. 70.00 (ISBN 0-471-49969-2, Pub. by Wiley-Interscience). Wiley.

Kolthoff, I. M. & Stenger, V. A. Volumetric Analysis: Theoretical Fundamentals, Vol. 1. 1942. 23.00 o.p. (ISBN 0-470-50050-6, Pub. by Wiley). Krieger.

Kolthoff, Isaak M., et al. Quantitative Chemical Analysis. 4th ed. (Illus.). 1969. text ed. 34.95x (ISBN 0-02-366000-7). Macmillan.

Koltun, Daniel S., jt. auth. see Eisenberg, Judah M.

Kolumban, Nicholas, ed. Turmoil in Hungary: An Anthology of Twentieth Century Hungarian Poetry. LC 82-81365. (Illus.). 186p. 1982. pap. 6.00 (ISBN 0-89823-039-X). New Rivers Pr.

Kolve, Carolee K. How to Buy (& Survive!) Your First Computer. (Illus.). 224p. 1983. 14.95 (ISBN 0-07-035130-9). McGraw.

Kolvin, I. Bladder Control & Enuresis. MacKeith, R. C., ed. (Clinics in Developmental Medicine Ser.: Vols. 48 & 49). 328p. 1973. 32.00 (ISBN 0-433-18825-1, Pub. by Spastics Intl England). Lippincott.

Kolvin, I., et al. Help Starts Here: The Maladjusted Child in the Ordinary School. LC 81-14184. (Illus.). 320p. 1981. 52.00x (ISBN 0-422-77380-8, Pub by Tavistock England). Methuen Inc.

Kolzow, L. V. I.D.E.A. Power for Reading Comprehension. 336p. 1976. pap. text ed. 12.95 (ISBN 0-13-450551-4). P-H.

Kolzow, Lee & Lehman, Jane. College Reading: Strategies for Success. (Illus.). 352p. 1981. pap. text ed. 12.95 (ISBN 0-13-150052-X). P-H.

Komac & Skeri, J. Modern Dictionary Slovene-English, English-Slovene. 787p. 1981. leatherette 17.50 (ISBN 0-686-97403-4, M-9701). French & Eur.

Komaitai, Rusiate T., jt. auth. see Schutz, Albert J.

Komar, Kathleen L. Pattern & Chaos: A Structural Analysis of Novels by Doeblin, Koeppen, Dos Passos, & Faulkner. LC 82-73875. (Studies in German Literature, Linguistics, & Culture: Vol. 14). (Illus.). 160p. 1983. 20.00x (ISBN 0-938100-19-X). Camden Hse.

Komar, Paul D. Beach Processes & Sedimentation. (Illus.). 464p. 1976. 36.95 (ISBN 0-13-072595-1). P-H.

Komarkova, V. Alpine Vegetation of the Indian Peaks Area, Front Range, Colorado Rocky Mountains. (Flora et Vegetatio Mundi: No. 7). (Illus.). 1979. lib. bdg. 80.00x (ISBN 3-7682-1208-4). Lubrecht & Cramer.

Komaroff, Anthony L. & Winickoff, Richard N. Common Acute Illnesses: A Problem-Oriented Textbook with Protocols. 1977. pap. text ed. 15.95 o.p. (ISBN 0-316-50157-3, Little Med Div). Little.

Komarov, Boris. The Destruction of Nature in the Soviet Union. Vale, Michel & Hollander, Joe, trs. from Rus. LC 80-5452. Orig. Title: Unichtozhenie Prioroda Obostrenie Ekologicheskogo Krizisa V SSSR. 192p. 1980. 20.00 (ISBN 0-87332-157-X). M E Sharpe.

Komarov, F., jt. auth. see Kumakhov, M.

Komarovich, V. L., ed. Kitezhskaia Legenda: Opyt Izuchenilia Mestnykh Legend. (Monuments of Early Russian Literature: Vol. 5). 184p. (Russian.). 1982. pap. 9.50 (ISBN 0-686-84208-1). Berkeley Slavic.

Komarovsky, Mirra. Blue-Collar Marriage. 1964. pap. 4.95 (ISBN 0-394-70361-8, Vin). Random.

Komarsky, E. G., jt. auth. see Glebov, I. A.

Komi, P. V., ed. Biomechanics V. (International Series on Biomechanics: Vol. Va & Vb). (Illus.). 700p. 1976. 44.50 (ISBN 0-686-86846-3); 49.50; Vol. VA. o.p. (ISBN 0-8391-0947-4). Vol. VB (ISBN 0-8391-0946-6). Univ Park.

Kommerell, B., jt. auth. see Faulstich, H.

Komnenich, Pauline, et al, eds. The Menstrual Cycle, Vol. 2: Research & Implications for Women's Health. 256p. 1981. text ed. 25.50 (ISBN 0-8261-2980-3); text ed. 48.00 vol. 1-2 set. Springer Pub.

Komp, R. J., jt. auth. see Davidson, Joel.

Kompfner, Rudolf. The Invention of the Traveling-wave Tube. LC 64-21124. (History of Technology Monographs). (Illus.). 1964. 3.50 (ISBN 0-911302-01-8). San Francisco Pr.

Komroff, Manuel. The Travels of Marco Polo. 1983. pap. 4.95 (ISBN 0-87140-132-0). Liveright.

Komura, Hirotsugu, jt. auth. see Ito, Toshio.

Komurjian, Eremya. The Jewish Bride (Armeno-Turkish Poem) Sanjian, Avedis K. & Tietze, Andreas, eds. 197p. 1981. pap. 45.00x (ISBN 3-447-02092-X). Intl Pubns Serv.

Kon, S. K. & Cowie, Alfred T., eds. Milk: The Mammary Gland & Its Secretion, 2 Vols. (Illus.). 1961. Vol. 1. o.p. (ISBN 0-12-418701-3); Vol. 2. 60.00 (ISBN 0-12-418702-1); Set. 60.00 (ISBN 0-12-418702-1). Acad Pr.

Konczacki, J. M., jt. ed. see Konczacki, Z. A.

Konczacki, Z. A. & Konczacki, J. M., eds. An Economic & Social History of Southern Africa, Vol. 3. 198p. 1983. 30.00x (ISBN 0-7146-3099-3, F Cass Co). Biblio Dist.

Kondo, K. Elsevier's Dictionary of Automobile Engineering. 1977. 127.75 (ISBN 0-444-41590-4). Elsevier.

Kondo, Riki H. Birds. (Instant Nature Guides). (Illus.). 1979. pap. 2.95 (ISBN 0-448-12672-9, G&D). Putnam Pub Group.

--Fishes. (Instant Nature Guides). (Illus.). 1979. pap. 2.95 (ISBN 0-448-12677-X, G&D). Putnam Pub Group.

--Insects. (Instant Nature Guides). (Illus.). 1979. pap. 2.95 (ISBN 0-448-12673-7, G&D). Putnam Pub Group.

--Reptiles & Amphibians. (Instant Nature Guides). (Illus.). 1979. pap. 2.95 (ISBN 0-448-12675-3, G&D). Putnam Pub Group.

--Rocks & Minerals. (Instant Nature Guides). (Illus.). 1979. pap. 2.95 (ISBN 0-448-12676-1, G&D). Putnam Pub Group.

--Trees. (Instant Nature Guides). (Illus.). 1979. pap. 2.95 (ISBN 0-448-12674-5, G&D). Putnam Pub Group.

Kondo, Sohei, jt. ed. see Sugimura, Takashi.

Kondo, Thomas M., tr. see Ihara Saikaku.

Kondor, R., tr. see Emanuel, N. M. & Knorre, D. G.

Kondor, R., tr. see Entelis, S. G. & Tiger, R. P.

Kondor, R., tr. see Kozhevnikov, A. V.

Kondor, R., tr. see Lipatov, Yu. S & Sergeeva, L. M.

Kondrashov, S. The Life & Death of Martin Luther King. 261p. 1981. pap. 1.95 (ISBN 0-8285-2043-7, Pub. by Progress Pubs USSR). Imported Pubns.

Kondratyev, K. Ya. Radiation Processes in the Atmosphere. (Illus.). 214p. 1972. pap. 50.00 (ISBN 0-685-29206-1, W111, WMO). Unipub.

Kone, Eugene E., ed. Yale Men Who Died in the Second World War: A Memorial Volume of Biographical Sketches. 1951. 49.50x (ISBN 0-685-89794-X). Elliots Bks.

Konecsni, Johnemery. A Philosophy for Living: A Sketch of Aquinate Philosophy. 184p. 1977. pap. text ed. 9.75 (ISBN 0-8191-0138-9). U Pr of Amer.

Konefsky, Alfred S., ed. see Webster, Daniel.

Konefsky, Samuel J. The Legacy of Holmes & Brandeis. LC 78-157828. (American Constitutional & Legal History, Ser.). 316p. 1974. Repr. of 1956 ed. lib. bdg. 37.50 (ISBN 0-306-70215-0). Da Capo.

Konek, Carol & Walters, Dorothy, eds. I Hear My Sisters Saying. LC 76-4973. 256p. 1976. 12.45i (ISBN 0-690-01107-5); pap. 4.95 o.p. (ISBN 0-690-01092-3). T y Crowell.

Koneman, Elmer. Color Atlas & Textbook of Diagnostic Microbiology. 1979. text ed. 42.00 o.p. (ISBN 0-397-50405-5, Lippincott Medical). Lippincott.

Koneman, Elmer W., et al. Practical Laboratory Mycology. 2nd ed. (Illus.). 1978. pap. 17.95 o.p. (ISBN 0-683-04745-0). Williams & Wilkins.

Konenigsber, ed. Technology & Development. 332p. 1981. pap. 32.00 (ISBN 0-08-028146-X). Pergamon.

Konetzni, Albert H., Jr. & Mack, William P. Command at Sea. 4th ed. LC 81-85469. (Illus.). 320p. 1982. 15.95x (ISBN 0-87021-130-7). Naval Inst Pr.

Konezny, Lorette, et al. Writing Script 1981. (gr. 2 up). 1981. 10.00 (ISBN 0-939564-00-9). Pen Notes.

Kong, Bucksam. The Tiger-Crane Form of Hung Gar Kung-Fu. (Illus., Orig.). 1983. pap. 6.95 (ISBN 0-89750-087-3, 424). Ohara Pubns.

Kong, J. A. Research Topics in Electromagnetic Wave Theory. LC 80-2874. 355p. 1981. 34.95x (ISBN 0-471-08782-3, Pub. by Wiley-Interscience). Wiley.

Kong, J. A., jt. auth. see Shen, Liang.

Konheim, Alan G. Crytography: A Primer. LC 80-24978. 432p. 1981. 38.95x (ISBN 0-471-08132-9, Pub. by Wiley-Interscience). Wiley.

Konig, Adrio. Here Am I: A Believer's Reflection on God. 272p. (Orig.). 1982. pap. 8.95 (ISBN 0-8028-1911-7). Eerdmans.

Konig, H., et al, eds. Mathematical Programming at Oberwolfach. (Mathematical Programming Studies: Vol. 14). 1981. pap. 30.00 (ISBN 0-444-86136-X). Elsevier.

Konig, Hans-Jost. Geheime Mission. LC 75-2362. 1975. pap. 4.95 (ISBN 0-88436-181-0). EMC.

Konigsberg, Irwin R., jt. ed. see Subtelny, Stephen.

Koning, A. J. De see De Koning, A. J. & Jenner, F. A.

Koning, Hans. America Made Me. 160p. 1983. 13.95 (ISBN 0-938410-09-1); pap. 8.95 (ISBN 0-938410-08-3). Thunder's Mouth.

--Amsterdam. (The Great Cities Ser.). (Illus.). 1977. lib. bdg. 12.00 (ISBN 0-8094-2291-3). Silver.

--World of Vermeer. LC 67-15299. (Library of Art Ser.). (Illus.). (gr. 6 up). 1967. 19.92 (ISBN 0-8094-0266-1, Pub. by Time-Life). Silver.

Koning, Hans, tr. see Alberts, A.

Koning, Hans, tr. see Dermout, Maria.

Koningsberger, H. The Revolutionary. 212p. 1967. 4.95 (ISBN 0-374-24984-9). FS&G.

Konizeski, Dick. Montananas' Fishing Guide: Vol. II: Waters East of the Continental Divide. Rev. ed. (Illus.). 300p. 1982. pap. 9.95 (ISBN 0-87842-144-0). Mountain Pr.

Konkle, Dan. F., ed. Principles of Speech Audiometry. (Perspectives in Audiology Ser.). (Illus.). 412p. 1982. text ed. 39.95 (ISBN 0-8391-1767-1). Univ Park.

Konner, Alfred. Jolli. LC 67-14951. (Foreign Lands Bks). (Illus.). (gr. k-3). 1967. PLB 3.95g (ISBN 0-8225-0359-X). Lerner Pubns.

Konnyu, Leslie. Hungarian Transylvania. (Illus.). 1983. 16.00x (ISBN 0-686-95911-6); pap. 11.00x (ISBN 0-686-99667-4). Hungarian Rev.

Kono, Shigemi & Shio, Mitsuru. Inter-Prefectural Migration in Japan, 1956-1961. 1965. 5.25x o.p. (ISBN 0-210-27141-8). Asia.

Kononenko, Konstantyn. Ukraine & Russia: A History of the Economic Relations Between Ukraine & Russia, 1654-1917. Olesnicki, Roman, tr. 1958. 16.95 (ISBN 0-87462-301-4); pap. 12.95 (ISBN 0-87462-303-0). Marquette.

Konopinski, Emil. Electromagnetic Fields & Relativistic Particles. (International Series in Pure & Applied Physics). (Illus.). 640p. 1981. text ed. 32.50x (ISBN 0-07-035264-X, C). McGraw.

Konopka, G. Adolescent Girl in Conflict. 1966. pap. 4.95 (ISBN 0-13-008672-X, Spec). P-H.

Konopka, Gisela. Social Group Work: A Helping Process. 3rd ed. 256p. 1983. 18.95 (ISBN 0-13-815787-1). P-H.

--Young Girls: A Portrait of Adolescence. 1976. 8.95 (ISBN 0-13-977215-4, Spec); pap. 3.45 o.p. (ISBN 0-13-977207-3, Spec). P-H.

Konopleva, N. P. & Popov, V. N. Gauge Fields. 274p. 1982. 75.00 (ISBN 3-7186-0045-5). Harwood Academic.

Konraad, Sandor. The Tarot-Numerology Connection. 1983. pap. 9.95 (ISBN 0-914918-45-1). Para Res.

Konrad, George. The Loser. Sanders, Ivan, tr. from Hungarian. LC 82-47669. (A Helen & Kurt Wolff Bk.). 320p. 1982. 14.95 (ISBN 0-15-153442-X). HarBraceJ.

--The Loser. Sanders, Ivan, tr. LC 82-47669. (A Helen & Kurt Wolff Bk.). 336p. 1982. pap. 7.95 (ISBN 0-15-653584-X, Harv). HarBraceJ.

Konrad, George & Szelenyi, Ivan. The Road of the Intellectuals to Class Power: A Sociological Study of the Role of the Intelligentsi in Socialism. Arato, Andrew & Allen, Richard E., trs. LC 77-92547. 1979. 10.00 (ISBN 0-15-177860-4). HarBraceJ.

Konrad, Patricia & Ertl, John. Pediatric Oncology. (Medical Outline Ser.). 1978. spiral 20.00 (ISBN 0-87488-673-2). Med Exam.

Konrad, Roselinde. Reviewing German Grammar & Building Vocabulary. LC 80-6238. 415p. 1981. pap. text ed. 19.75 (ISBN 0-8191-1605-X). U Pr of Amer.

Konsalik, Heinz G. Strike Force Ten. 320p. 1981. 12.95 (ISBN 0-399-12615-5). Putnam Pub Group.

Konsler, Runelle. Capitalization Critters & Punctuation Pals. (gr. 2-5). 1982. 7.95 (ISBN 0-86653-090-8, GA 441). Good Apple.

Konsler, Runelle & Mirabella, Lauren. Math Activities with a Porpoise. 1980. pap. text ed. 8.95x (ISBN 0-673-16394-6). Scott F.

Kontio, A. Loren. Zoocollage. LC 71-173451. 1974. pap. 5.000 o.p. (ISBN 0-87812-035-1). Pendell Pub.

Kontos, P. G. & Murphy, J. L. Teaching Urban Youth. LC 67-25427. 346p. 1967. text ed. 14.00 o.p. (ISBN 0-471-50220-0, Pub. by Wiley). Krieger.

Konuk, Mutlu, tr. see Hiket, Nazim.

Konuk, Mutlu, tr. see Hikmet, Nazim.

Konvitz, Milton, ed. see Pekelis, Alexander H.

Konvitz, Milton R. Civil Rights in Immigration. LC 77-2605. (Cornell Studies in Civil Liberty). 1977. Repr. of 1953 ed. lib. bdg. 18.50x (ISBN 0-8371-9556-X, KOCR). Greenwood.

Konvitz, Milton R. & Whichler, Stephen E., eds. Emerson: A Collection of Critical Essays. LC 78-5739. 1978. Repr. of 1962 ed. lib. bdg. 24.50x (ISBN 0-313-20469-1, KOEM). Greenwood.

Konwicki, Tadeusz. Anthropos-Specter-Beast. Korwin-Rodziszewski, George & Korwin-Rodziszewski, Audrey, trs. from Pol. LC 77-13500. 320p. (gr. 9 up). 1977. 10.95 (ISBN 0-87599-218-8). S G Phillips.

--The Polish Complex. 1983. pap. 4.95 (ISBN 0-14-006590-3). Penguin.

Konwicki, Taducz. A Minor Apocalypse. Lourie, Richard, tr. 1983. 16.50 (ISBN 0-374-20928-6). FS&G.

Konz, Stephan A. Work Design: Industrial Ergonomics. 2nd ed. LC 82-3041. (Grid Series in Industrial Engineering). 636p. 1983. text ed. 29.95 (ISBN 0-88244-249-X). Grid Pub.

Koo, Anthony Y. Land Market Distortion & Tenure Reform. (Illus.). 184p. 1982. text ed. 14.50 (ISBN 0-8138-1078-7). Iowa St U Pr.

Koo, Delia, et al. First Course in Modern Algebra. LC 62-18160. 14.50 (ISBN 0-8044-4561-3); 0.00 o.p. answer book & teacher's commentary pap (ISBN 0-8044-4562-1). Ungar.

Koo, Joo O., jt. auth. see Dudewicz, Edward J.

Kooche, Gerald P., jt. ed. see Melton, Gay B.

Koocher, Gerald P. & O'Malley, John E. The Damocles Syndrome: Psychosocial Consequences of Surviving Childhood Cancer. 1981. 19.95 (ISBN 0-07-035340-9). McGraw.

Koocher, Gerald P., ed. Children's Rights & the Mental Health Professions. LC 76-16062. (Personality Processes Ser.). 259p. 1976. 35.00 (ISBN 0-471-01736-1, Pub. by Wiley-Interscience). Wiley.

Kooijmans, jt. auth. see Kapteyn.

Kooiker, Leonie. The Magic Stone. Winston, Richard & Winston, Clara, trs. from Dutch. (Illus.). (gr. 3-7). 1978. 9.75 (ISBN 0-688-22143-2); PLB 9.36 (ISBN 0-688-32143-7). Morrow.

Kooker, Earl W. & Robb, George P. Introduction to Descriptive Statistics. (Illus.). 176p. 1982. pap. 18.75x spiral (ISBN 0-398-04564-X). C C Thomas.

Koolish, Ruth K., ed. see Information Sources, Inc.

Koomans, jt. auth. see Kapteyn.

Koon, Helene & Switzer, Richard. Eugene Scribe. (World Authors Ser.). 1980. lib. bdg. 15.95 (ISBN 0-8057-6390-2, Twayne). G K Hall.

Koon, Helene W., ed. Death of a Salesman: A Collection of Critical Essays. 115p. 1983. 10.95 (ISBN 0-13-198135-8); pap. 4.95 (ISBN 0-13-198127-7). P-H.

Koontz, Dean. Night Chills. 320p. 1983. pap. 2.95 (ISBN 0-425-05852-2). Berkley Pub.

--The Vision. LC 77-7079. 1977. 8.95 o.p. (ISBN 0-399-12063-7). Putnam Pub Group.

Koontz, Dean R. Phantoms. 320p. 1983. 15.95 (ISBN 0-399-12655-4). Putnam Pub Group.

--Whispers. LC 79-22858. 1980. 12.95 o.p. (ISBN 0-399-12351-2). Putnam Pub Group.

Koontz, Elizabeth. Best Kept Secret of the Past Five Thousand: Women Are Ready for Leadership in Education. LC 76-190069. (Fastback Ser.: No. 2). (Orig.). 1972. pap. 0.75 o.p. (ISBN 0-87367-002-7). Phi Delta Kappa.

Koontz, H., et al. Essentials of Management. 3rd ed. (Management Ser.). 1982. 18.95x (ISBN 0-07-035419-7); info. instructor's manual & test file 14.00 (ISBN 0-07-035420-0). McGraw.

Koontz, Harold. Board of Directors & Effective Management. 2nd ed. 286p. 1981. lib. bdg. cancelled o.p. (ISBN 0-89874-188-2). Krieger.

Koontz, Harold & O'Donnell, Cyril. Essentials of Management. 2nd ed. Davis, Keith, ed. (Management Ser.). (Illus.). 1977. pap. text ed. 18.95 (ISBN 0-07-035372-7, C); instructor's manual 25.00 (ISBN 0-07-035373-5). McGraw.

Koontz, Harold, et al. Management. 7th, rev. ed. (Illus.). 1980. text ed. 29.95 (ISBN 0-07-035377-8); instructor's manual 25.00 (ISBN 0-07-035378-6); study guide 8.95 (ISBN 0-07-035379-4). McGraw.

Koontz, Harold D. Appraising Managers As Managers. 1971. 19.75 o.p. (ISBN 0-07-035315-8, P&RB). McGraw.

Koontz, Harold D. & O'Donnell, Cyril. Management: A Book of Readings. 4th ed. 1976. text ed. 15.50 o.p. (ISBN 0-07-035353-0, C); pap. text ed. 10.95 o.p. (ISBN 0-07-035352-2). McGraw.

Koonz, Claudia, jt. auth. see Bridenthal, Renate.

Koop, Albert J. & Inada, Hogitaro. Japanese Names & How to Read Them: A Manual for Art-Collectors & Students. 1972. 75.00 o.p. (ISBN 0-7100-1707-3). Routledge & Kegan.

Koop, C. Everett. The Right to Live: the Right to Die. 1976. pap. 3.95 (ISBN 0-8423-5593-6). Tyndale.

Koop, Gordon, et al. The Deni of Western Brazil. (Museum of Anthropology Ser.: No. 7). 79p. 1980. pap. 5.95x (ISBN 0-88312-156-5); microfiche 1.50x (ISBN 0-88312-243-X). Summer Inst Ling.

Koopman, Leroy. Beauty Care for the Ears. 1980. pap. 2.50 o.p. (ISBN 0-310-26872-9). Zondervan.

--Beauty Care for the Tongue. (Illus.). 96p. (Orig.). 1974. pap. 2.50 (ISBN 0-310-26842-7). Zondervan.

Koopmans, T. C. Three Essays on the State of Economic Science. 1968. pap. text ed. 13.95 (ISBN 0-07-035335-2, C). McGraw.

Koopowitz, Harold & Kaye, Hilary. Plant Extinction: A Global Crisis. LC 82-62894. 256p. 1983. 16.95 (ISBN 0-913276-44-8). Stone Wall Pr.

Koos, Leonard V. Junior-College Movement. Repr. of 1925 ed. lib. bdg. 19.75x (ISBN 0-8371-3973-2, KOJM). Greenwood.

Kooser, Ted, jt. auth. see Kloefkorn, William.

Koosis, P. J. Introduction to Hp Spaces. LC 80-65175. (London Mathematical Society Lecture Note Ser.: No. 40). (Illus.). 380p. (Orig.). 1980. pap. 25.95 (ISBN 0-521-23159-0). Cambridge U Pr.

Kootstra, G. & Jorning, P. J. Access Surgery. 350p. 1982. text ed. 60.00 (ISBN 0-85200-453-2, Pub. by MTP Pr England). Kluwer Boston.

Kooymans, jt. auth. see Kapteyn.

Kopaczynski, Germain. Linguistic Ramifications of the Essence-Existence Debate. LC 79-5373. 1979. pap. text ed. 10.50 (ISBN 0-8191-0865-0). U Pr of Amer.

Kopal, Z. & Rahe, J. Binary & Multiple Stars as Tracers of Stellar Evolution. 1982. 67.50 (ISBN 90-277-1436-3, Pub. by Reidel Holland). Kluwer Boston.

Kopal, Zdenek. Man & His Universe. (Illus.). 320p. 1972. pap. 3.95 o.p. (ISBN 0-688-05014-X). Morrow.

--The Solar System. (Illus.). 1973. pap. text ed. 4.95x o.p. (ISBN 0-19-888061-8). Oxford U Pr.

Kopal, Zdenek, ed. Physics & Astronomy of the Moon. 2nd ed. 1971. 53.50 (ISBN 0-12-419340-4). Acad Pr.

Kopan, jt. auth. see Kowtaluk.

Kopech, Gertrude, jt. ed. see Murray, Margaret R.

Kopecky, J., jt. auth. see Deyl, Z.

Kopecky, Lilli. In the Shadow of the Flames: Six Lectures on the Holocaust. LC 82-72377. (Witness to the Holocaust Ser.: No. 4). 1982. pap. 6.75 (ISBN 0-89937-034-9). Ctr Res Soc Chg.

Kopelev, Lev. The Education of a True Believer. Kern, Gary, tr. from Rus. LC 79-3397. 16.30i (ISBN 0-06-012476-8, HarpT). Har-Row.

Kopelev, Lev Z. I Sotvoril Sebe Kumir. 1978. 15.00 o.p. (ISBN 0-88233-311-9); pap. 8.50 (ISBN 0-88233-312-7). Ardis Pubs.

Kopell, Sandra. Spelling Mazes. (Basic Activity Bks.). (Illus.). 64p. (gr. 1-5). 1975. pap. 1.25 (ISBN 0-448-11962-5, G&D). Putnam Pub Group.

Koperwas, Sam. Easy Money. LC 82-14399. 297p. 1983. 13.95 (ISBN 0-688-01550-6). Morrow.

Kopf, Alfred W., et al. Malignant Melanoma. LC 78-71687. (Illus.). 256p. 1979. 66.25x (ISBN 0-89352-040-3). Masson Pub.

Kopf, David. British Orientalism & the Bengal Renaissance: The Dynamics of Indian Modernization, 1773-1835. LC 69-13135. 1969. 30.00x (ISBN 0-520-00665-8). U of Cal Pr.

Kopf, David & Bishop, C. James. The Indian World. LC 77-81185. (World of Asia Ser.). (Illus., Orig.). 1977. pap. text ed. 4.25x (ISBN 0-88273-503-9). Forum Pr IL.

Kopf, Ebs Dumm. How to Seduce Married Women. Fonyam, John, ed. (Illus.). 415p. 1983. 25.00 (ISBN 0-910253-00-5). Backwards & Backwards.

Kopff, E. Christian, ed. see Otis, Brooks.

Kopin, I. J., jt. auth. see Rall, J. E.

Kopin, Irwin J., ed. Neurotransmitters. LC 72-75942. (ARNMD Research Publications Ser: Vol. 50). 565p. 1972. 38.00 (ISBN 0-683-00244-9). Raven.

Kopin, Irwin J., jt. ed. see Ehrenpreis, Seymour.

Kopland, Rutger. An Empty Place to Stay & Other Selected Poems. Leigh-Loohuizen, Ria, tr. from Dutch. 74p. 1980. pap. text ed. 4.00 (ISBN 0-918786-22-3). Lost Roads.

Kopmeyer, M. R. Here's Help. LC 73-87471. 336p. 1974. 12.95x (ISBN 0-913200-03-4). Success Found.

--How to Get Whatever You Want. LC 72-84127. 336p. 1972. 12.95x (ISBN 0-913200-02-6). Success Found.

--How You Can Get Richer Quicker. LC 74-22549. 336p. 1975. 12.95x (ISBN 0-913200-04-2). Success Found.

--Thoughts to Build On. LC 72-122340. 336p. 1970. 12.95x (ISBN 0-913200-01-8). Success Found.

Kopp, Bea. Eye Level. LC 80-27908. (Illus., Orig.). 1981. pap. 12.95 o.p. (ISBN 0-89865-130-1). Donning Co.

Kopp, Claire B. & Krakow, Joanne B. The Child: Development in a Social Context. (Illus.). 640p. 1982. text ed. 23.95 (ISBN 0-201-10590-X); write for info. (ISBN 0-201-10591-8); write for info. (ISBN 0-201-10592-6). A-W.

Kopp, Ernestine, et al. Designing Apparel Through the Flat Pattern. 4th ed. LC 73-132040. 1971. 13.50 o.p. (ISBN 0-87005-094-X). Fairchild.

Kopp, Frederick. Something Like This Happens Every War. LC 81-81947. 181p. 1983. 11.95 (ISBN 0-86666-042-9). GWP.

Kopp, O. W., jt. auth. see Allman, S. Andean.

Kopp, Richard D. & Fraser, Theodore P. Readings in French Literature. 1975. pap. text ed. 12.50 (ISBN 0-395-13638-5). HM.

Kopp, Richard L. & Fraser, Theodore P. The Moralist Tradition in France. LC 81-69245. 287p. (Orig.). 1982. text ed. 18.50x (ISBN 0-86733-017-1). Assoc Faculty Pr.

Kopp, Sheldon. Back to One: A Practical Guide for Psychotherapists. LC 77-608269. 1977. 8.95 (ISBN 0-8314-0055-2). Sci & Behavior.

Kopp, Sheldon B. Guru: Metaphors from a Psychotherapist. LC 71-142730. 1971. 6.95 (ISBN 0-8314-0025-0). Sci & Behavior.

--The Hanged Man. LC 74-79081. 1975. 7.95 (ISBN 0-8314-0036-6). Sci & Behavior.

--If You Meet the Buddha on the Road, Kill Him! LC 77-188144. 220p. 1972. 7.95 (ISBN 0-8314-0032-3). Sci & Behavior.

--If You Meet the Buddha on the Road, Kill Him! 3.50 o.p. (ISBN 0-686-92363-4, 6474). Hazelden.

Kopp, W. LaMarr. German Literature in the United States, 1945-1960. (Studies in Comparative Literature Ser.: No. 42). xvii, 230p. 1968. 13.50x o.p. (ISBN 0-8078-7042-0). U of NC Pr.

Koppel, L. B., jt. auth. see Coughanowr, Donald R.

Koppel, Ted, jt. auth. see Kalb, Marvin.

Koppelman, Lee E., et al. The Urban Sea: Long Island Sound. LC 74-3161. (Illus.). 1976. text ed. 31.95 o.p. (ISBN 0-275-09010-8). Praeger.

Koppenaal, Dave, jt. auth. see Robl, Tom.

Koppenhaver, April M., ed. see Frompovich, Catherine J.

Kopper, Edward A., Jr. John Milligan Synge: A Reference Guide. 1979. lib. bdg. 27.00 (ISBN 0-8161-8119-5, Hall Reference). G K Hall.

Kopper, Edward J., Jr. Lady Isabella Persse Gregory. (English Authors Ser). 1976. lib. bdg. 13.95 (ISBN 0-8057-6658-8, Twayne). G K Hall.

Kopper, Philip. The National Museum of Natural History. 496p. 1982. 60.00 (ISBN 0-8109-1359-3). Abrams.

Kopper, Philip, ed. & intro. by. A Christmas Testament. LC 82-5843. (Illus.). 144p. 1982. 25.00 (ISBN 0-941434-23-0, 8010). Stewart Tabori & Chang.

Koppett, Leonard. Forty-Niner Fever! (Illus.). 256p. 1982. pap. 3.95 (ISBN 0-86576-044-6). W Kaufmann.

Koppisch, Michael S. The Dissolution of Character: Changing Perspectives in La Bruyere's Caracteres. LC 80-70808. (French Forum Monographs: No.24). 127p. (Orig.). 1981. pap. 9.50x (ISBN 0-917058-23-2). French Forum.

Kopple, Robert C. & Stiglitz, Bruce M. Taxation of the Motion Picture Industry. 290p. 1978. 35.00 o.p. (ISBN 0-87179-267-2). BNA.

Koppman, Lionel, jt. auth. see Postal, Bernard.

Koprowski, Hilary, jt. ed. see Maramorosch, Karl.

Koprulu, Mehmet Fuat. Les Origines De L'empire Ottoman. LC 78-2453. (Studies in Islamic History: No. 8). 146p. Repr. of 1935 ed. lib. bdg. 17.50x (ISBN 0-87991-457-2). Porcupine Pr.

Kops, L. & Ramalingham, R., eds. On the Art of Cutting Metals: Seventy Five Years Later. (PED Ser.: Vol. 7). 1982. 40.00 (H00251). ASME.

Kopycinski, Joseph V., ed. Textile Industry Information Sources. LC 64-25644. (Management Information Guide Ser.: No. 4). 1964. 42.00x (ISBN 0-8103-0804-5). Gale.

Korach. Manual of Radiographic Techniques of the Skull. LC 80-29002. 1981. 28.50x (ISBN 0-89352-098-5). Masson Pub.

Korah, V. Competition Law of Britain & the Common Market. 1982. lib. bdg. 59.00 (ISBN 0-686-37430-4, Pub. by Martinus Nijhoff Netherlands). Kluwer Boston.

Koran, Al. How to Bring Out the Magic in Your Mind. 272p. 1976. pap. 4.95 (ISBN 0-8119-0377-X). Fell.

Koran, Dennis. Vacancies. (A Mother's Hen Book). 1975. pap. 4.50 (ISBN 0-915572-45-1). Panjandrum.

Koran, Dennis, ed. Panjandrum V: An Anthology of Poetry. (Panjandrum Poetry Journal: No. 5). (Illus.). 1977. pap. 4.95 (ISBN 0-915572-15-X). Panjandrum.

Koran, Dennis & Guss, David, eds. Talking Leaves: Panjandrum No. 4. 1975. pap. 4.95 (ISBN 0-915572-33-8). Panjandrum.

Korb, Johann G. Diary of an Austrian Secretary of Legation at the Court of Czar Peter the Great, 2 Vols. (Russia Through European Eyes Ser). 1968. Repr. of 1863 ed. Set. lib. bdg. 75.00 (ISBN 0-686-85845-X). Da Capo.

Korb, Lawrence J. The Fall & Rise of the Pentagon: American Defense Policies in the 1970s. LC 78-73795. (Contributions in Political Science: No. 27). (Illus.). 1979. lib. bdg. 25.00 (ISBN 0-313-21087-X, KFR/). Greenwood.

Korczak, Janusz. Ghetto Diary. LC 77-91911. (Illus.). 1978. 8.95 (ISBN 0-8052-5004-2, Pub by Holocaust Library); pap. 4.95. Schocken.

--Ghetto Diary. 192p. 8.95 (ISBN 0-686-95064-X); pap. 4.95 (ISBN 0-686-99456-6). ADL.

--King Matt the First. Lourie, Richard, tr. (Illus.). 160p. (Orig.). (gr. k up). 1983. 12.95 (ISBN 0-374-34139-7). FS&G.

--The Warsaw Ghetto Memoirs of Janusz Korczak. Kulawiec, Edwin P., tr. from Polish. LC 78-63065. 1978. pap. text ed. 9.00 (ISBN 0-8191-0611-9). U Pr of Amer.

Kord, Catherine. Richard Artschwager, Chuck Close, Joe Zucker. (Illus.). 28p. 1976. 2.00x (ISBN 0-686-99810-3). La Jolla Mus Contemp Art.

Korda, Michael. Worldly Goods. 1982. 14.95 (ISBN 0-394-51251-0). Random.

--Worldly Goods. (General Ser.). 1983. lib. bdg. 17.95 (ISBN 0-8161-3503-7, Large Print Bks). G K Hall.

Kordel, Lelord. The Easy, Low-Cost Way to Total Beauty. LC 78-15816. (Illus.). 1979. 10.00 (ISBN 0-399-11914-0). Putnam Pub Group.

--Lelord Kordel's Natural Folk Remedies. LC 73-78591. 320p. 1974. 7.95 o.p. (ISBN 0-399-11205-7). Putnam Pub Group.

--You're Younger Than You Think: The Mature Person's Guide to Vibrant Health. LC 75-43930. 1976. 8.95 o.p. (ISBN 0-399-11566-8). Putnam Pub Group.

Korea Development Institute. Long-Term Prospect for Economic & Social Development of Korea, 1977-1991. 310p. 1979. pap. text ed. 10.00x (ISBN 0-8248-0641-7, Korea Devel Inst). UH Pr.

Korean Traders Association. Korean Trade Directory, 1982-83. 23rd ed. LC 60-45910. 905p. 1982. 35.00x (ISBN 0-8002-3039-6). Intl Pubns Serv.

Korein, Julius, ed. Brain Death: Interrelated Medical & Social Issues, Vol. 315. (Annals of the New York Academy of Sciences). 454p. 1978. pap. 61.00x (ISBN 0-89072-073-8). NY Acad Sci.

Korelitz, Burton I., ed. Inflammatory Bowel Diseases. (Illus.). 248p. 1982. 34.00 (ISBN 0-88416-310-5). Wright-PSG.

Koren. Macrophage-Mediated Antibody... (Immunology Ser.). 384p. 1983. price not set (ISBN 0-8247-7011-0). Dekker.

Koren, Henry J. To the Ends of the Earth: A General History of the Congregation of the Holy Ghost. 656p. 1982. text ed. 18.50x (ISBN 0-8207-0157-2). Duquesne.

Koren, Henry J., jt. auth. see Luijpen, William A.

Koren, Herman. Environmental Health & Safety. LC 72-11634. 338p. 1974. text ed. 26.00 o.p. (ISBN 0-08-017077-3); pap. text ed. 14.50 o.p. (ISBN 0-08-017623-2). Pergamon.

--Handbook of Environmental Health & Safety: Principles & Practices, 2 pts. (Illus.). 750p. 1980. pap. 27.00 ea. Pt. I (ISBN 0-08-025080-7). Pt. II (ISBN 0-08-025081-5). Pergamon.

Koreneva, Ye. V. see Alexandrov, Eugene.

Korenman. Endocrine Aspects of Aging. (Current Endocrinology Ser.: Vol. 6). 1982. 39.95 (ISBN 0-444-00681-8). Elsevier.

Korenman, Stanley G., et al. Practical Diagnosis: Endocrine Diseases. (Illus.). 1978. pap. 26.00 (ISBN 0-471-09486-2, Pub. by Wiley Med). Wiley.

Korenyi-Both, Andras L. Muscle Pathology in Neuromuscular Disease. (Illus.). 528p. 1983. 74.50x (ISBN 0-398-04690-5). C C Thomas.

Koretz, R. see Schwartz, B., et al.

Koretz, Ronald L., ed. Practical Gastroenterology. LC 81-3373. (Family Practice Today: A Comprehensive Postgraduate Library). 395p. 1982. 35.00 (ISBN 0-471-09513-3, Pub. by Wiley Med). Wiley.

Korff, Serge A. Electron & Nuclear Counters: Theory & Use. Repr. of 1955 ed. lib. bdg. 18.00x (ISBN 0-8371-2395-X, KONC). Greenwood.

Korfhage, R. R. Logic & Algorithms with Applications to the Computer & Information Sciences. LC 66-25225. 194p. 1966. 29.95x (ISBN 0-471-50365-7). Wiley.

Korfhage, Robert R., ed. Computer Networks & Communication. (The Information Technology Ser.: Vol. IV). 150p. 1977. pap. 23.00 (ISBN 0-88283-017-1). AFIPS Pr.

Korfhage, Robert R., ed. see National Computer Conference, 1977.

Korg, Jacob. Dylan Thomas. (English Authors Ser.). 1964. lib. bdg. 12.95 (ISBN 0-8057-1548-7, Twayne). G K Hall.

Korg, Jacob, ed. Twentieth Century Interpretations of Bleak House. LC 69-11357. 1968. pap. text ed. 1.25 o.p. (ISBN 0-13-077610-6, Spec). P-H.

Korg, Jacob, ed. see Gissing, George.

Korin, Basil P. Statisical Concepts for the Social Sciences. 1975. text ed. 17.95 (ISBN 0-316-50174-3); wkbk. 7.95 (ISBN 0-316-50175-1); ans. key free (ISBN 0-316-50177-8). Little.

Korite, J. C. & Sick, H. Atlas of Sectional Human Anatomy: Frontal, Sagittal & Horizontal Planes, 2 vols. Incl. Vol. 1. Head, Neck, Thorax. 175p (ISBN 0-8067-1031-4); Vol. 2. Abdomen, Pelvis. 172p (ISBN 0-8067-1032-2). (Illus.). 1982. text ed. 89.50 ea.; Set. text ed. 165.00 (ISBN 0-8067-1030-6). Urban & S.

Korkina, M. Psychiatric Ward Practice. 168p. 1981. pap. 5.00 (ISBN 0-8285-2110-7, Pub. by Mir Pubs USSR). Imported Pubns.

Korkisch, J. Modern Methods for the Separation of Rarer Metal Ions. 1969. text ed. 65.00 o.p. (ISBN 0-08-012921-8). Pergamon.

Korling, Torkel & Petty, Robert O. Wild Plants in Flower: Eastern Deciduous Forest. LC 78-59759. (Illus.). 1978. 6.95 o.p. (ISBN 0-930404-01-7). Chicago Review.

Korman, Abraham. Organizational Behavior. (Illus.). 1977. 23.95 (ISBN 0-13-640938-5). P-H.

Korman, Abraham & Korman, Rhoda. Career Success-Personal Failure. 150p. 1980. text ed. 15.95 (ISBN 0-13-114777-3). P-H.

Korman, Abraham K. The Psychology of Motivation. (Experimental Psychology Ser.). (Illus.). 288p. 1974. 23.95 (ISBN 0-13-733279-3). P-H.

Korman, Avery. Kramer Versus Kramer (Movie Edition) (RL 6). 1979. pap. 3.50 (ISBN 0-451-12322-0, AE2322, Sig). NAL.

Korman, Keith. Archangel. 320p. 1983. 17.75 (ISBN 0-670-13063-X). Viking Pr.

Korman, Rhoda, jt. auth. see Korman, Abraham.

Korman, Richard I., compiled by. An Annotated Guide to National Bibliographies. (Government Documents Bibliographies Ser.). 1983. 75.00x (ISBN 0-930466-40-3). Meckler Pub.

--Guide to Presidential Advisory Commissions, 1973-1981. (Government Documents Bibliographies Ser.). 1982. 75.00x (ISBN 0-930466-39-X). Meckler Pub.

Kormondy, Edward, jt. auth. see Essenfeld, Bernice.

Kormondy, Edward J. Concepts of Ecology. 2nd ed. 256p. 1976. 14.95 o.p. (ISBN 0-13-166470-0); pap. 13.95 (ISBN 0-13-166462-X). P-H.

Kormos, Zsofia, tr. see Lukacs, Lajos.

Kormoss, I. B., ed. see Clarendon Press, Cartographic Dept.

Korn, Alfons L. Victorian Visitors. 1958. 14.95 (ISBN 0-87022-421-2). UH Pr.

Korn, Alfons L., ed. News from Molokai: Letters Between Peter Kaeo & Queen Emma, 1873-1876. LC 76-16823. 448p. 1976. 15.95 (ISBN 0-8248-0399-X). UH Pr.

Korn, Alfons L., jt. ed. see Pukui, Mary K.

Korn, Alfons L., tr. see De Varigny, Charles.

Korn, Alfons L., jt. tr. see Pukui, Mary K.

Korn, Alfons L., tr. see Pukui, Mary K. & Korn, Alfons L.

Korn, Bernhard C. The Story of Bay View. LC 80-83069. (Illus.). 136p. (gr. 6-12). 1980. 6.95 (ISBN 0-938076-05-1). Milwaukee County.

Korn, Charlotte. A Real Estate Agent's Guide to Successful Sales & Listings. (Illus.). 1976. 13.95 (ISBN 0-87909-711-6). Reston.

Korn, Donald H., jt. auth. see Bradley, James W.

Korn, Ellen, ed. Teach Yourself Calligraphy: For Beginners from Eight to Eighty. (Illus.). 96p. (gr. 8 up). pap. 6.95 comb binding (ISBN 0-688-01487-9). Morrow.

Korn, Errol R. & Johnson, Karen. Visualization: The Uses of Imagery in the Health Professions. LC 82-73617. (The Dorsey Professional Ser.). 300p. 1983. 27.95 (ISBN 0-87094-403-7). Dow Jones-Irwin.

Korn, Francis. Elementary Structures Reconsidered: Levi-Strauss on Kinship. LC 73-78212. 1973. 27.50x (ISBN 0-520-02476-1). U of Cal Pr.

Korn, Granino A. Microprocessors & Small Digital Computer Systems: For Engineers & Scientists. LC 77-492. 1977. 43.50 o.p. (ISBN 0-07-035367-0, P&RB). McGraw.

Korn, Granino A. & Korn, Theresa M. Mathematical Handbook for Scientists & Engineers. 2nd ed. 1968. 64.50 (ISBN 0-07-035370-0, P&RB). McGraw.

Korn, Granino A. & Wait, John V. Digital Continuous System Simulation. (Illus.). 1978. ref. ed. 28.95 (ISBN 0-13-212274-X). P-H.

Korn, Henri, jt. ed. see Faber, Donald.

Korn, Henry R. & Liberi, Albert W. An Elementary Approach to Functions. (Illus.). 1977. text ed. 24.50 (ISBN 0-07-035401-4, C); info instructor's manual 4.95 (ISBN 0-07-035402-2); student guide 9.95 (ISBN 0-07-035403-0). McGraw.

Korn, Larry, ed. see Tilth.

Korn, Richard. Union & Its Retired Workers: A Case Study of the UAW. (Key Issues Ser.: No. 21). 60p. 1976. pap. 3.00 (ISBN 0-87546-230-8). ILR Pr.

Korn, S. Winton & Boyd, Thomas. Accounting for Decision Makers. 2nd ed. (Professional Development Programs). 320p. 1983. text ed. 55.95x (ISBN 0-471-87246-6). Wiley.

--Managerial Accounting: A Short Course for Non-Financial Managers. LC 74-31816. (Business Administration Ser). 295p. 1975. text ed. 49.95x o.p. (ISBN 0-471-50390-8). Wiley.

Korn, Theresa M., jt. auth. see Korn, Granino A.

Kornai. Anti-Equilibrium. LC 75-134644. 1971. 59.75 (ISBN 0-444-10122-5, North-Holland); pap. 22.00 (ISBN 0-444-10342-2). Elsevier.

Kornai, J. Economics of Shortage, 2 vols. (Contributions to Economic Analysis Ser.: Vol. 13). 1981. Set. 81.00 (ISBN 0-444-86059-2); Vol. 1. 47.00 (ISBN 0-444-85426-6); Vol. 2. 47.00 (ISBN 0-444-86058-4). Elsevier.

Kornai, J. & Martos, B., eds. Non-Price Control: Contributions to Economic Analysis Ser. (Vol. 133). 1981. 47.00 (ISBN 0-444-85486-X). Elsevier.

Kornai, Janos. Growth, Shortage & Efficiency: A Macrodynamic Model of the Socialist Economy. 142p. 1983. text ed. 19.50x (ISBN 0-520-04901-2). U of Cal Pr.

--Mathematical Planning of Structural Decisions. 2nd ed. (Contributions to Economic Analysis Ser.). 644p. 1975. 64.00 (ISBN 0-444-10734-7, North-Holland). Elsevier.

Kornberg, Allan & Clarke, Harold D., eds. Political Support in Canada: The Crisis Years. Duke University Center for Commonwealth & Comparative Studies. 375p. 1983. 27.50x (ISBN 0-8223-0546-1). Duke.

Kornberg, Patti. But It Is in Brevard. Stewart, Sally A. & Hellmich, Nanci, eds. (Illus.). 216p. (Orig.). Date not set. pap. 4.95 (ISBN 0-686-82539-X). P Kornberg.

Kornbluh, Elain, ed. Barron's Regents Exams & Answers Bookkeeping. rev. ed. LC 58-32560. 250p. (gr. 9-12). 1982. pap. text ed. 4.50 (ISBN 0-8120-3130-X). Barron.

Kornbluh, Elaine, ed. Barron's Regents Exams & Answers Business Mathematics. rev. ed. LC 60-19236. 250p. (gr. 10-12). 1982. pap. text ed. 4.50 (ISBN 0-8120-3187-3). Barron.

Kornbluh, Elaine, jt. ed. see Neinstein, Murray.

Kornblum, Allan. Threshold. LC 76-21744. 13p. 1976. pap. 1.50 o.p. (ISBN 0-915124-18-1). Toothpaste.

Kornbluth, Jesse, jt. auth. see Osborn, Jack R.

Kornegay, Francis A., jt. ed. see El-Khawas, Mohamed A.

Korneitchouk, Ursula, tr. see Goddad, Don.

Korneitchouk, Ursula, tr. see Kunkel, Reinhard.

Kornèr, Bruno. Fluency Drills in German. pap. 7.50x (ISBN 0-392-08376-0, SpS). Sportshelf.

Korner, Eva, intro. by. Gyula Derkovits. Hoch, Elizabeth, tr. (Illus.). 238p. 1980. 55.00 (ISBN 0-89893-153-3). CDP.

Korner, S., et al, eds. see Robinson.

Korner, Stephan, ed. Philosophy of Logic. LC 76-6020. 1976. 37.50x (ISBN 0-520-03235-7). U of Cal Pr.

Kornetsky, Conan. Pharmacology: Drugs Affecting Behavior. LC 76-6062. 275p. 1976. 28.95 o.p. (ISBN 0-471-50410-6, Pub. by Wiley-Interscience). Wiley.

--Pharmacology: Drugs Affecting Behavior. LC 76-6062. 288p. Repr. of 1976 ed. text ed. 28.95 (ISBN 0-471-50410-6). Krieger.

Kornfeld, Anita C. Vintage. 614p. 1982. pap. 3.95 (ISBN 0-553-20103-4). Bantam.

Kornfeld, Lewis. To Catch a Mouse, Make a Noise Like a Cheese. LC 82-13320. 1982. 15.00 (ISBN 0-13-922930-2, Busn). P-H.

Kornfield, Jack. Living Buddhist Masters. (Illus.). 334p. 1983. pap. 10.00 (ISBN 0-87773-768-1). Great Eastern.

Kornhaber, Bruce & Stanicek, Frank. Making It Happen: The Art of Relating Humanly. 1978. pap. text ed. 9.95x o.p. (ISBN 0-917974-26-3). Waveland Pr.

Kornhauser, Arthur. Detroit As the People See It: A Survey of Attitudes in an Industrial City. LC 76-46362. 1977. Repr. of 1952 ed. lib. bdg. 18.50x (ISBN 0-8371-9299-4, KODE). Greenwood.

Kornhuber, H. H. & Deecke, L., eds. Motivation, Motor & Sensory Processes of the Brain: Electrical Potentials Behavior & Clinical Use. (Progress in Brain Research Ser.: Vol. 54). 150.00 (ISBN 0-444-80196-0). Elsevier.

Kornicker, Louis S., ed. see Park, Taisoo.

Kornstein, Daniel. The Music of the Laws. (Illus.). 192p. 1982. 10.00 (ISBN 0-89696-185-0, An Everest House Book). Dodd.

Kornup, A. & Wanscher, J. H. Methuen Handbook of Colour. 3rd ed. (Illus.). 1978. 33.00x (ISBN 0-413-33400-7). Methuen Inc.

Kornweibel, Theodore, jt. auth. see Detweiler, Robert.

Kornweibel, Theodore, Jr. No Crystal Stair: Black Life & the Messenger, 1917-1928. LC 75-16967. (Contributions in Afro-American & African Studies: No. 20). 306p. 1975. lib. bdg. 29.95 (ISBN 0-8371-8284-0, KCS/). Greenwood.

Korobkin, Rowena & Guilleminault, Christian. Progress in Perinatal Neurology, Vol. 1. (Illus.). 256p. 1981. lib. bdg. 35.00 (ISBN 0-683-04751-5). Williams & Wilkins.

Korolenko, V. Selected Stories. 391p. 1978. 5.45 (ISBN 0-686-98354-8, Pub. by Progress Pubs USSR). Imported Pubns.

Korolenko, Vladimir. In a Strange Land. Zilboorg, Gregory, tr. LC 74-14354. 214p. 1975. Repr. of 1925 ed. lib. bdg. 15.75x (ISBN 0-8371-7801-0, KOSL). Greenwood.

Korolkovas, Andrejus. Essentials of Molecular Pharmacology: Background for Drug Design. LC 74-112849. 1970. 29.95 o.p. (ISBN 0-471-50418-1, Pub. by Wiley-Interscience). Wiley.

Korolkovas, Andrejus & Burckhalter, Joseph H. Essentials of Medicinal Chemistry. LC 75-37801. 697p. 1976. 49.50x (ISBN 0-471-12325-0, Pub. by Wiley-Interscience). Wiley.

Korologos, Tom. Washingtonspeak: A User's Guide to Access & Influence. 160p. 1983. pap. 5.95 (ISBN 0-201-14935-4). A-W.

Korones, Sheldon B. High Risk Newborn Infants: The Basis for Intensive Nursing Care. 3rd ed. LC 81-963. (Illus.). 399p. 1981. text ed. 22.95 (ISBN 0-8016-2738-9). Mosby.

--Neonatal Decision Making. 350p. 1983. text ed. 30.00 (ISBN 0-941158-15-2, D2734-6). Mosby.

Koropeckyj, I. S. & Schroeder, Gertrude E., eds. Economics of Soviet Regions. 476p. 1981. 37.95 o.p. (ISBN 0-03-059702-1). Praeger.

Korpi, Walter. The Democratic Class Struggle. 300p. 1983. 27.95 (ISBN 0-7100-9436-1). Routledge & Kegan.

Korr, Charles P. Cromwell & the New Model Foreign Policy. 1975. 29.75x (ISBN 0-520-02281-5). U of Cal Pr.

Korr, David. Cookie Monster & the Cookie Tree. LC 79-10796. (Big Picture Bks.). (Illus.). (ps-k). 1979. 1.95 (ISBN 0-307-10821-X, Golden Pr); PLB 7.62 (ISBN 0-307-60821-2); PLB 2.95 Little Golden Reader (ISBN 0-307-60159-5). Western Pub.

Korringa, P. Farming Cupped Oysters of the Genus Crassostrea. (Developments in Aquaculture & Fisheries Science Ser.: Vol. 2). 1976. 47.00 (ISBN 0-444-41333-2). Elsevier.

--Farming Marine Organisms Low in the Food Chain. (Developments in Aquaculture & Fisheries Science: Vol. 1). 1976. 47.00 (ISBN 0-444-41332-4). Elsevier.

--Farming the Flat Oyster of the Genus Ostrea. (Developments in Aquaculture & Fisheries Science Ser.: Vol. 3). 1976. 47.00 (ISBN 0-444-41334-0). Elsevier.

Korrol, Virginia E. Sanchez see Sanchez Korrol, Virginia E.

Korschelt, O. Theory & Practice of Go. Leckie, George & King, Samuel P., trs. LC 65-22637. (Illus.). 1965. 8.95 (ISBN 0-8048-0572-5). C E Tuttle.

Korschunow, Irina. A Night in Distant Motion. LC 81-47325. 159p. 1983. 10.00 (ISBN 0-87923-399-0). Godine.

--Who Killed Christopher? Mayer, Eva, tr. from Ger. LC 79-11432. 156p. (gr. 7-12). 1980. 8.95 (ISBN 0-529-05523-6, Philomel). Putnam Pub Group.

Korst, J. K. Pirprofen in the Treatment of Pain & Inflammation. (Illus.). 92p. (Orig.). 1982. pap. text ed. 14.00 (ISBN 3-456-81207-8, Pub by Hans Huber Switzerland). J K Burgess.

Kort, Carol, jt. ed. see Friedland, Ronnie.

Kort, Wesley A. Narrative Elements & Religious Meaning. LC 75-15257. 128p. 1975. pap. 0.50 (ISBN 0-8006-1433-X). Fortress.

Kort, Wolfgang. Alfred Doblin. LC 73-16222. (World Author Ser.). 1974. lib. bdg. 15.95 (ISBN 0-8057-2266-1, Twayne). G K Hall.

Korte, B., ed. Modern Applied Mathematics: Optimization & Operations Research. 675p. 1982. 119.25 (ISBN 0-444-86134-3). Elsevier.

Korten, David C. & Alfonso, Felipe B., eds. Bureaucracy & the Poor: Closing the Gap. LC 82-83847. (Library of Management for Development). xiv, 258p. (Orig.). 1983. pap. write for info. (ISBN 0-931816-30-0). Kumarian Pr.

Korteweg, Pieter. Exchange-Rate Policy, Monetary Policy, & Real Exchange-Rate Variability. LC 80-39553. (Essays in International Finance Ser.: No. 140). 1980. pap. text ed. 2.50x (ISBN 0-88165-047-1). Princeton U Int Finan Econ.

Korth, Bob, ed. see Courtney, Dayle.

Korth, Bob, ed. see Foster, Lewis & Stedman, Jon.

Korth, Russ, jt. auth. see Schneider, Henry.

Korting, G. W. Geriatric Dermatology. (Illus.). 194p. 1981. text ed. 26.00 (ISBN 0-7216-5495-9). Saunders.

Korting, G. W., et al. Diseases of the Skin in Children & Adolescents. 3rd. ed. LC 77-24000. (Illus.). 1979. text ed. 32.00 (ISBN 0-7216-5491-6). Saunders.

Korting, Gunter W. The Skin & Eye: A Dermatologic Correlation of Diseases of the Periolital Region. Curth, William, et al, trs. LC 76-108370. (Illus.). 1974. 12.00 (ISBN 0-7216-5492-4). Saunders.

Korting, Gunter W. & Denk, R. Differential Diagnosis in Dermatology. Curth, Helen O. & Curth, William, trs. LC 74-9434. (Illus.). 765p. 1976. 105.00 o.p. (ISBN 0-7216-5488-6). Saunders.

Kortum, Gustav. Treatise on Electrochemistry. 2nd rev. ed. 1965. 93.75 (ISBN 0-444-40338-8). Elsevier.

Kortvelyessy, Eniko, tr. see Vanbery, Armin.

Korty, John, jt. auth. see Hall, Avery.

Korty, Margaret B. Audio-Visual Materials in the Church Library: How to Select, Catalog, Process, Store, Circulate & Promote. LC 77-74780. (Illus.). 1977. spiral bdg. 4.95 (ISBN 0-9603060-0-5). Church Lib.

Korvetz, Elliot, jt. auth. see Nankin, Michael.

Korwin-Rodziszewski, Audrey, tr. see Konwicki, Tadeusz.

Korwin-Rodziszewski, George, tr. see Konwicki, Tadeusz.

Koryta, J. Ion Selective Electrodes. LC 75-9090. (Cambridge Physical Chemistry Monographs). (Illus.). 250p. 1975. 45.00 (ISBN 0-521-20569-7). Cambridge U Pr.

Koryta, Jiri. Ions, Electrodes & Membranes. 197p. 1982. 39.95x (ISBN 0-471-10007-2, Pub. by Wiley-Interscience); pap. 18.95x (ISBN 0-471-10008-0, Pub. by Wiley-Interscience). Wiley.

Korzenlowsky, Carole, jt. auth. see Corsaro, Maria.

Korzybski, Alfred. General Semantics Bulletin: Official Annual Journal of the Institute of General Semantics. Pula, Robert, ed. 25.00 (ISBN 0-910780-00-5). Inst Gen Semantics.

Kos, Leon, jt. auth. see Sani, Guelfo.

Kosakai, N., ed. Quality Control. (International Congress Ser.: Vol. 483). 1980. 84.75 (ISBN 0-444-90085-3). Elsevier.

Kosakai, Nozomu, ed. see Suzuki, Shoichiro & Ueno, Kazue.

Kosambi, Damodar D. Indian Numismatics. (Illus.). 159p. 1981. text ed. 25.00x (ISBN 0-86131-018-7, Pub. by Orient Longman Ltd India). Apt Bks.

Kosberg, Jordan I. Abuse & Maltreatment of the Elderly. (Illus.). 480p. 1983. text ed. 32.50 (ISBN 0-7236-7025-0). Wright PSG.

--Attitudes Toward the Elderly: Do We Honor & Respect Our Senior Citizens? (Vital Issues, Vol. XXIX 1979-80). 0.50 (ISBN 0-686-81611-0). Ctr Info Am.

Kosberg, Jordan I., ed. Working with & for the Aged. LC 79-88366. (NASW Reprint Collection Ser.). 1979. pap. 12.95 (ISBN 0-87101-101-8, CAB-101-C). Natl Assn Soc Wkrs.

Kosecoff, Jacqueline & Fink, Arlene. Do-It-Yourself Evaluation: A Practitioner's Guide. (Illus.). 280p. 1982. 29.95 (ISBN 0-8039-1896-8); pap. 14.95 (ISBN 0-8039-1897-6). Sage.

Koshel, Jeffrey. Deinstitutionalization - Delinquent Children. 1973. pap. 3.50 o.p. (ISBN 0-87766-108-1). Urban Inst.

Koshel, Patrica P., jt. auth. see Gramlich, Edward M.

Koshland, Daniel E., Jr. Bacterial Chemotaxis As a Model Behavioral System. (Distinguished Lecture Series of the Society of General Physiologists: Vol. 2). 210p. 1980. text ed. 21.50 (ISBN 0-89004-468-6). Raven.

Koshy, Thomas. An Elementary Approach to Mathematics. LC 75-11271. 512p. 1976. text ed. 18.95x (ISBN 0-673-16232-X). Scott F.

--Finite Mathematics & Calculus. 1979. text ed. 22.50x (ISBN 0-673-16234-6). Scott F.

Kosicki, George W. & Farrell, Gerald J. The Spirit & the Bride Say, "Come!". Mary's Role in the New Pentecost. 112p. pap. 3.25 (ISBN 0-911988-41-6). AMI Pr.

Kosinski, Jerzy. Blind Date. 1977. 8.95 o.p. (ISBN 0-395-25781-6). HM.

--The Devil Tree. rev. ed. 224p. 1981. 12.95 (ISBN 0-312-19794-2). St Martin.

--Painted Bird. 2nd ed. LC 82-42869. 1982. Repr. 6.95 (ISBN 0-394-60433-4). Modern Lib.

Kosinski, Jerzy N. Steps. LC 68-28544. 1968. 6.95 (ISBN 0-394-60209-9). Random.

Kosinski, L. A., ed. People on the Move. Prothero, R. M. 393p. 1975. 39.95x (ISBN 0-416-78410-0); pap. 18.95x (ISBN 0-416-83000-5). Methuen Inc.

Kosinski, Leszek A., ed. Demographic Developments in Eastern Europe. LC 76-12858. (Special Studies). 1977. 37.95 o.p. (ISBN 0-275-56180-1). Praeger.

Koske, R. E. Cookbook Statistics for Plant Pathology & Mycology. 65p. (Orig.). 1982. pap. text ed. 7.50x (ISBN 0-934454-94-9). Lubrecht & Cramer.

Koski, Vernon, jt. auth. see Whyte, Malcolm.

Koslow, Irving, jt. ed. see Cummings, William W.

Koslow, Stephen, jt. ed. see Hanin, Israel.

Kosnar, Carl J. How to Sell Your Home Without a Real Estate Broker. 208p. 1975. 32.95 (ISBN 0-07-035364-6, P&RB). McGraw.

Kosnioswski, Czes, ed. A First Course in Algebraic Topology. LC 79-41682. 280p. 1980. 49.50 (ISBN 0-521-23195-7); pap. 17.95 (ISBN 0-521-29864-4). Cambridge U Pr.

Kosniowski, C. Actions of Finite Abelian Groups. (Research Notes in Mathematics: No. 18). 230p. (Orig.). 1978. pap. text ed. 21.95 (ISBN 0-273-08405-4). Pitman Pub MA.

Kosniowski, Czes, ed. Transformation Groups. LC 76-40837. (London Mathematical Society Lecture Notes Ser.: No. 26). 1977. limp bdg. 21.95 (ISBN 0-521-21509-9). Cambridge U Pr.

Kosof, Anna. Runaways. (gr. 7 up). 1977. PLB 8.90 (ISBN 0-531-01293-X). Watts.

Kosoff, A. United States Dimes. 2nd ed. (Illus.). 1982. softcover 6.00 o.p. (ISBN 0-915262-88-6). S J Durst.

Kosoff, A., jt. ed. see Bressett, Ken.

Kosolapoff, G. M. & Maier, L. Organic Phosphorus Compounds, Vol. 6. 1983. Repr. of 1973 ed. lib. bdg. write for info. (ISBN 0-88275-802-0). Krieger.

Kosow, Irving L. Control of Electric Machines. LC 72-5631. (Electronic Technology Ser). (Illus.). 368p. 1973. ref. ed. 24.95 (ISBN 0-13-171785-5). P-H.

Kosowicz, Jerzy. Atlas of Endocrine Diseases. (Illus.). 360p. 1978. text ed. 26.00 o.p. (ISBN 0-913486-86-8). Charles.

Koss, Gerhard. Names of Germany. (International Library of Names). 250p. 1983. text ed. 24.50x (ISBN 0-8290-1285-0). Irvington.

Koss, Leopold G. Diagnostic Cytology, 2 vols. 3rd ed. LC 78-24140. 1979. Set. text ed. 137.50x o.p. (ISBN 0-397-50402-0, Lippincott Nursing). Lippincott.

Koss, Margo, jt. auth. see Schainblatt, Al.

Koss, Stephen. Asquith. LC 76-20200. (British Political Biography Ser.). 1976. text ed. 20.00 (ISBN 0-312-05740-7). St Martin.

Kossen, Stan. Human Side of Organizations. 2nd ed. 1978. text ed. 22.95 scp o.p. (ISBN 0-06-384719-1, HarpC); instr's. manual avail. o.p. (ISBN 0-06-373618-7); scp wkbk. 8.50 o.p. (ISBN 0-06-384724-8). Har-Row.

--The Human Side of Organizations. 3rd ed. 544p. 1983. text ed. 23.50 scp (ISBN 0-06-043775-8, HarpC); instr's. manual avail. (ISBN 0-06-363711-1); learning guide 8.50 (ISBN 0-06-043776-6). Har-Row.

Kossen, Stan, jt. auth. see Straub, Joseph T.

Kosser, Michael. Those Bold & Beautiful Country Girls. LC 79-52515. (Illus.). 1979. pap. 6.95 (ISBN 0-686-59392-8). Delilah Bks.

Kossler, Richard. Sozialverischerungspringzip und Staatszuschusse In der Gesetzlichen Rentenversicherung. 241p. (Ger.). 1982. write for info. (ISBN 3-8204-5749-6). P Lang Pubs.

Kosslyn, Stephen M. Ghosts in the Mind's Machine: How We Create & Use Pictures in Our Brains. (Illus.). 1983. 20.00 (ISBN 0-393-95257-6). Norton.

--Imaging. 1983. write for info o.p. (ISBN 0-393-95257-6). Norton.

Kossmann, E. H. & Mellink, A. F., eds. Texts Concerning the Revolt of the Netherlands. LC 73-83103. (Studies in the History & Theory of Politics). 320p. 1975. 37.50 (ISBN 0-521-20014-8). Cambridge U Pr.

Kostanick, Huey. Population & Migration Trends in Eastern Europe. LC 77-1905. (Westview Special Studies on the Soviet Union & Eastern Europe). 1978. lib. bdg. 22.00 (ISBN 0-89158-147-2). Westview.

Kostanoski, John, jt. auth. see Bottom, Norman R.

Koste, Virginia. The Wonderful Wizard of Oz. 60p. (gr. 3-7). 1982. saddle stitch 2.50x (ISBN 0-88020-106-1). Coach Hse.

Kostecki, M. M. East-West Trade & the GATT System. 1979. 30.00x (ISBN 0-312-22500-8). St Martin.

Kostelanetz, Richard. Arenas, Fields, Turfs, Pitches. 72p. (Orig.). 1982. pap. 4.50 (ISBN 0-933532-42-3). BkMk.

--Autobiographies. LC 79-87601. (Erasmus Editions Ser.). 288p. (Orig.). 1980. pap. 8.00 (ISBN 0-930012-42-9); 15.00 o.p. (ISBN 0-930012-41-0). Bandanna Bks.

--Constructs Two. 1978. pap. 3.00 (ISBN 0-87924-041-5). Membrane Pr.

--In Youth. 1978. pap. 20.00 (ISBN 0-932360-15-7). RK Edns.

--The Old Poetries & the New. LC 80-16318. (Poets on Poetry Ser.). 336p. 1981. pap. 7.95 (ISBN 0-472-06319-7). U of Mich Pr.

--Reincarnations. 1981. pap. 5.00 (ISBN 0-686-84602-8); signed 50.00 (ISBN 0-686-84603-6). Future Pr.

--Symmetries. 1983. pap. 12.00 (ISBN 0-918406-24-2); signed 100.00 (ISBN 0-686-84605-2). Future Pr.

Kostelanetz, Richard, ed. Beyond Left & Right. LC 68-22431. 1978. pap. 10.00 o.p. (ISBN 0-932360-07-6). RK Edns.

--Esthetics Contemporary. LC 77-73848. 444p. 1978. 19.95 (ISBN 0-87975-105-3); pap. 12.95 (ISBN 0-87975-094-4). Prometheus Bks.

--John Cage. LC 70-12174. (Illus.). 1978. 15.00 (ISBN 0-932360-09-2); pap. 10.00 (ISBN 0-932360-10-6). RK Edns.

--Moholy-Nagy. LC 70-12175. (Illus.). 1978. 12.50 o.p. (ISBN 0-932360-12-2); pap. 20.00 (ISBN 0-932360-11-4). RK Edns.

--On Contemporary Literature. 1st ed. LC 72-156674. 1978. 50.00 (ISBN 0-932360-01-7); pap. 20.00 (ISBN 0-932360-00-9). RK Edns.

--Twenties in the Sixties: Previously Uncollected Critical Essays. LC 78-20012. 1979. lib. bdg. 29.95 (ISBN 0-313-21205-8, KTW/). Greenwood.

Kostelnik, Marjorie J. & Phenice, Lillian A., eds. Child Nurturance, Vol. 2: Patterns of Supplementary Parenting. 332p. 1982. 32.50x (ISBN 0-306-41175-X, Plenum Pr). Plenum Pub.

Kostenuk, Samuel & Griffin, John. RCAF Squadron Histories & Aircraft: 1924-1968. (Illus.). 1977. 24.95 o.p. (ISBN 0-88866-577-6). Samuel Stevens.

Koster, Donald N. Transcendentalism in America. (World Leaders Ser.). 1975. lib. bdg. 12.95 (ISBN 0-8057-3727-8, Twayne). G K Hall.

Koster, Donald N., ed. American Literature & Language: A Guide to Information Sources. LC 73-17565. (American Studies Information Guide Ser.: Vol. 13). 300p. 1982. 42.00x (ISBN 0-8103-1258-1). Gale.

Koster, Jan, jt. ed. see May, Robert.

Koster, John, jt. auth. see Keogh, James.

Koster, M. D. The Peshitta of Exodus, the Development of Its Text in the Course of Fifteen Centuries. (Studia Semitica Neerlandica: No. 19). 1977. text ed. 116.85x o.p. (ISBN 90-232-1503-6). Humanities.

Koster, R. M. The Dissertation. LC 80-20066. 438p. 1981. pap. 7.95 (ISBN 0-688-00043-6). Quill NY.

--The Prince. LC 78-155996. 1979. pap. 5.95 (ISBN 0-688-05108-1). Quill NY.

Kosterlitz, H., ed. Opiates & Endogenous Opioid Peptides. 1976. 149.00 (ISBN 0-7204-0599-8, North-Holland). Elsevier.

Kostich, Dragos. The Land & People of the Balkans. rev. ed. LC 73-7709. (Portraits of the Nations Series). (Illus.). 1973. 10.53i (ISBN 0-397-31397-7, JBL-J). Har-Row.

Kostick, Marilyn G., ed. see Murphy, Margaret D.

Kostiner, Edward & Rea, Jesse R. Fundamentals of Chemistry. 480p. 1979. text ed. 22.95 (ISBN 0-15-529430-X, HC); instructor's manual avail. (ISBN 0-15-529431-8); study guide. pap. 8.95 (ISBN 0-15-529433-4); lab manual 7.95 (ISBN 0-15-529432-6). HarBraceJ.

Kostiuk, Hryhoriy, ed. see Khvylovy, Mykola.

Kostka, Dorothy. The Best of "Freedom After Fifty" 1976. pap. text ed. 4.50x (ISBN 0-87315-065-1). Golden Bell.

Kostka, Stefan M. A Bibliography of Computer Applications in Music. (Music Indexes & Bibliographies: No. 7). 1974. pap. 5.00 (ISBN 0-913574-07-4). Eur-Am Music.

Kostman, Samuel, ed. Barron's Regents Exams & Answers Comprehensive English (3 & 4 Years) rev. ed. LC 56-35602. 300p. (gr. 9-12). 1982. pap. text ed. 4.50 (ISBN 0-8120-3145-8). Barron.

Kostopoulos, George K. Digital Engineering. LC 74-13427. 508p. 1975. 47.50 o.p. (ISBN 0-471-50460-2, Pub. by Wiley-Interscience). Wiley.

Kostrich, Leslie J., jt. auth. see Tannenbaum, Percy H.

Kostrikin, A. I. Introduction to Algebra. (Universitext Ser.). 575p. 1982. 28.00 (ISBN 0-387-90711-4). Springer-Verlag.

Kostrov, Konstantin A., tr. see Rastyannikov, V. G.

Kostynuik, Doreen. Songs of the Desert. 1979. 4.95 o.p. (ISBN 0-533-03552-X). Vantage.

Kostyu, Frank A. The Time of Your Life Is Now. 1977. 1.00 (ISBN 0-8164-0375-9). Seabury.

Koszarowski, Tadeusz. Cancer Surgery. LC 78-27389. (Illus.). 1983. text ed. 18.50 (ISBN 0-8067-1021-7). Urban & S.

Koszarski, Richard. The Astoria Studio & Its Fabulous Films: A Picture History with 225 Stills & Photographs. (Illus.). 144p. (Orig.). (gr. 7 up). 1983. pap. 9.95 (ISBN 0-486-24475-X). Dover.

--The Man You Loved to Hate: Erich von Stroheim & Hollywood. (Illus.). 364p. 1983. 29.95 (ISBN 0-19-503239-X). Oxford U Pr.

Koszarski, Richard, ed. Hollywood Directors: 1914-1940. LC 76-9262. (Illus.). 1976. 25.00x (ISBN 0-19-502085-5). Oxford U Pr.

--Hollywood Directors, 1941-1976. LC 76-51716. (Illus.). 1977. 27.50x (ISBN 0-19-502217-3). Oxford U Pr.

--Hollywood Directors, 1941-1976. LC 76-51716. (Illus.). 1977. pap. 8.95 (ISBN 0-19-502218-1, GB 509, GB). Oxford U Pr.

Koszarski, Richard, ed. & intro. by. Mystery of the Wax Museum. LC 78-53296. (Wisconsin-Warner Bros. Screenplay Ser.). (Illus.). 164p. 1979. 17.50 (ISBN 0-299-07670-9); pap. 6.95t (ISBN 0-299-07674-1). U of Wis Pr.

Kotani, Masao, ed. Advances in Biophysics, Vol. 14. 280p. 1981. text ed. 39.50 o.p. (ISBN 0-8391-0111-2). Univ Park.

Kotarba, Joseph A. Chronic Pain. (Sociological Observations Ser.: Vol. 13). 256p. 1982. 25.00 (ISBN 0-8039-1880-1); pap. 12.50 (ISBN 0-8039-1881-X). Sage.

Kotchen, Jane M., jt. auth. see Kotchen, Theodore A.

Kotchen, Theodore A. & Kotchen, Jane M. High Blood Pressure in the Young. 1983. text ed. 34.50 (ISBN 0-7236-7032-3). Wright-PSG.

Koteliansky, S. S., tr. see Rozanov, Vasilii V.

Koteskey, Ronald L. General Psychology for Christian Counselors. 308p. (Orig.). 1983. pap. 10.95 (ISBN 0-687-14044-7). Abingdon.

Kotey, Paul F. Directions in Ghanaian Linguistics: A Brief Survey. LC 71-630646. (Papers in International Studies: Africa: No. 2). 1969. pap. 3.25x (ISBN 0-89680-036-9, Ohio U Ctr Intl). Ohio U Pr.

Kothandaraman, C. P. & Subramanyan, S. Heat & Mass Transfer Data Book. 3rd ed. 149p. 1977. 15.95x o.s.i. (ISBN 0-470-99078-3). Halsted Pr.

Kothari, C. R. An Introduction to Operational Research. 250p. 1982. text ed. 30.00x (ISBN 0-7069-1749-9, Pub by Vikas India). Advent NY.

Kothari, Raj. To Tell the World. (Illus.). 208p. Date not set. pap. cancelled (ISBN 0-7224-0220-1). Robinson & Wat.

Kothman, Thomas H., ed. see Davis, Keith.

Kotkin, Joel. The Valley. (Orig.). Date not set. cancelled o.p. (ISBN 0-88496-185-0); pap. 8.95 o.p. (ISBN 0-88496-189-3). Capra Pr.

Kotkin, Joel & Grabowicz, Paul. California Inc. 336p. 1983. pap. 3.95 (ISBN 0-380-62398-6, Discus). Avon.

Kotlar, Barbara, jt. auth. see Silva, Tony.

Kotler, Milton, jt. auth. see Cunningham, James V.

Kotler, Philip. Marketing Management: Analysis, Planning & Control. 4th ed. 1980. text ed. 27.95 (ISBN 0-13-557975-9). P-H.

--Marketing Management: Analysis, Planning & Control. 4th ed. 722p. 1980. 26.00 (ISBN 0-686-98042-5). Telecom Lib.

Kotler, Philip & Cox, Keith. Marketing Management & Strategy: A Reader. rev. ed. (Illus.). 1980. pap. text ed. 16.95 (ISBN 0-13-558122-2). P-H.

Kotliar, B. C. X. Neutral Mechanism of Conditioning. LC 80-25451. 205p. 1983. 11.00 (ISBN 0-08-026334-8). Pergamon.

Kotov, A. & Yudovich, M. The Soviet School of Chess. Stoklitsky, L., tr. 1958. pap. 6.50 (ISBN 0-486-20026-4). Dover.

Kotschevar, L. H. & McWilliams, Margaret. Understanding Food. LC 69-19238. 684p. 1969. pap. 25.95x (ISBN 0-471-50530-7). Wiley.

Kotschevar, Lendal H. Quantity Food Purchasing. 2nd ed. LC 74-17407. 684p. 1975. text ed. 35.95x (ISBN 0-471-50524-2). Wiley.

Kotschevar, Lendal H. & Terrell, Margaret E. Food Service Planning: Layout & Equipment. 2nd ed. LC 76-28763. 601p. 1977. 34.95x (ISBN 0-471-50491-2). Wiley.

Kott, Jan. Shakespeare Our Contemporary. 400p. 1974. pap. 6.95 (ISBN 0-393-00736-7, Norton Lib). Norton.

Kott, P., ed. Antarctic Ascidiacea. LC 77-601086. (Antarctic Research Ser.: Vol. 13). 1969. 18.00 (ISBN 0-87590-113-1). Am Geophysical.

Kottak, Conrad. Anthropology: The Exploration of Human Diversity. 3rd ed. 584p. 1982. text ed. 21.00 (ISBN 0-394-32867-1). Random.

Kottak, Conrad P. Cultural Anthropology. 2nd ed. LC 78-15704. (Illus.). 1978. pap. text ed. 13.95x o.p. (ISBN 0-394-32221-5). Random.

Kotter, John P. The General Managers. (Illus.). 1982. 15.95 (ISBN 0-02-918000-7, 91800). Free Pr.

Kottke, Frank. The Promotion of Price Competition Where Sellers Are Few. LC 77-18328. (Illus.). 240p. 1978. 22.95 (ISBN 0-669-02094-X). Lexington Bks.

Kottler, Jeffrey A. Pragmatic Group Leadership. LC 82-17895. (Counseling Ser.). 400p. 1982. text ed. 21.95 (ISBN 0-534-01254-X). Brooks-Cole.

Kottmeyer, William. Our Constitution & What It Means. 5th ed. 1975. 4.40 (ISBN 0-07-033640-7, W); tests 6.56 (ISBN 0-07-033641-5). McGraw.

Kottmeyer, William & Claus, Audrey. Basic Goals in Reading, Level 6. (Basic Goals in Reading Ser). (Illus.). 1978. pap. text ed. 5.88 pupil's ed. (ISBN 0-07-035146-5, W); tchr's ed. 10.60 (ISBN 0-07-035156-2). McGraw.

--Basic Goals in Reading: Level 4. (Basic Goals in Reading Ser.). (Illus.). (gr. 4). 1977. pap. text ed. 5.88 pupil's ed. (ISBN 0-07-035144-9, W); tchr's. ed. 10.60 (ISBN 0-07-035154-6). McGraw.

--Basic Goals in Reading: Level 5. (Illus.). 1978. pap. text ed. 5.88 pupil's ed. (ISBN 0-07-035145-7, W); tchr's. ed. 10.60 (ISBN 0-07-035155-4). McGraw.

--Basic Goals in Spelling, 4 Levels. 7th ed. Incl. Level 1. 160p. pap. text ed. 4.64 (ISBN 0-07-034651-8, W); tchr's. ed. 16.60 (ISBN 0-07-034661-5, W); Level 2. 192p. text ed. 9.32 (ISBN 0-07-034632-1, W); pap. text ed. 4.64 (ISBN 0-07-034652-6, W); tchr's. ed. 16.60 (ISBN 0-07-034662-3); Level 3. 192p. text ed. 9.32 (ISBN 0-07-034633-X, W); pap. text ed. 4.64 (ISBN 0-07-034653-4, W); tchr's. ed. 16.60 (ISBN 0-07-034663-1); Level 4. 192p. text ed. 9.32 (ISBN 0-07-034634-8, W); pap. text ed. 4.76 (ISBN 0-07-034654-2, W); tchr's. ed. 17.20 (ISBN 0-07-034664-X). (Illus.). Date not set. McGraw.

--Basic Goals in Spelling, Levels 7-8. (gr. 7-8). 1975. Level 7. text ed. 9.96 (ISBN 0-07-034307-1, W); Level 8. text ed. 9.96 (ISBN 0-07-034308-X); Level 7. tchr's ed. 15.28 (ISBN 0-07-034317-9); Level 8. tchr's ed. 15.28 (ISBN 0-07-034318-7); wkbks. 5.00 ea.; tchr's. eds. wkbk. 14.64 ea. McGraw.

Kottmeyer, William, ed. Ivanhoe. (Everyreader Ser). (gr. 4 up). 1962. pap. 5.20 o.p. (ISBN 0-07-033741-1, W). McGraw.

Kottmeyer, William, et al. Fables & Folktales, Level A. (Plus Ten Vocabulary Booster Ser.). (Illus.). 256p. (gr. 4). 1972. text ed. 8.72 (ISBN 0-07-033974-0, W). McGraw.

Kottmeyer, William A. Decoding & Meaning: A Modest Proposal. 1974. text ed. 14.76 (ISBN 0-07-033705-5, W). McGraw.

--Doctor Spello. 2nd ed. 1968. text ed. 4.24 o.p. (ISBN 0-07-033548-6, W); tchr's ed. 6.12 o.p. (ISBN 0-07-033549-4). McGraw.

--Juarez: Hero of Mexico. 1962. pap. 5.20 o.p. (ISBN 0-07-033743-8, W). McGraw.

--Modern American Spelling. (gr. 9-12). 1971. text ed. 6.64 o.p. (ISBN 0-07-033942-2, W). McGraw.

--Silver Skates. 1972. text ed. 5.76 o.p. (ISBN 0-07-034019-6, W). McGraw.

--Teacher's Guide for Remedial Reading. 1959. text ed. 13.32 (ISBN 0-07-033704-7, W). McGraw.

Kottmeyer, William A. & Claus, Audrey. Basic Goals in Reading, Level. 2. (Illus.). (gr. 2). 1977. pap. text ed. 5.32 pupil's ed. (ISBN 0-07-035142-2, W); tchr's. ed. 10.60 (ISBN 0-07-035152-X). McGraw.

--Basic Goals in Reading, Level 3. (Illus.). (gr. 3). 1977. pap. text ed. 5.60 pupil's ed. (ISBN 0-07-035143-0, W); tchr's. ed. 10.60 (ISBN 0-07-035153-8). McGraw.

--Basic Goals in Spelling, Levels 2-6. 5th ed. (Level 1 o.p.). 1975. Texts Levels 2-6. 9.96 (ISBN 0-686-66127-3, W); tchr's. eds. levels 2-6 15.28 ea.; wkbks. levels 2-3 4.88 (ISBN 0-07-034321-7). wkbks. levels 4-6 5.00 ea.; tchr's. eds. wkbks. levels 2-6 14.64 ea.; Webstermasters 39.56 ea. McGraw.

Kottmeyer, William A. & Ware, Kay. Conquests in Reading. 1963. wkbk. 4.36 (ISBN 0-07-033765-9, W); tchr's ed. 9.32 (ISBN 0-07-033764-0). McGraw.

Kottmeyer, William A., ed. Bob: Son of Battle. 1962. pap. 5.76 o.p. (ISBN 0-07-033730-6, W). McGraw.

--Kidnapped. 1972. text ed. 5.76 o.p. (ISBN 0-07-034021-8, W). McGraw.

--Treasure Island. 1972. text ed. 5.76 o.p. (ISBN 0-07-034020-X, W). McGraw.

--Trojan War. 1962. pap. 5.96 o.p. (ISBN 0-07-033733-0, W). McGraw.

Kottmeyer, William A., et al. Greek & Roman Myths. 1962. pap. 5.76 o.p. (ISBN 0-07-033738-1, W). McGraw.

--Indian Paint. 1970. pap. 5.76 (ISBN 0-07-009287-7, W). McGraw.

Kottmeyer, William A., et al, eds. Cases of Sherlock Holmes. (Everyreader Ser). (gr. 4 up). 1962. pap. 5.76 o.p. (ISBN 0-07-033734-9, W). McGraw.

--Robin Hood Stories. (Everyreader Ser). 1962. pap. 5.76 o.p. (ISBN 0-07-033731-4, W). McGraw.

Kottmeyer, William A., et al, eds. see Seton, Ernest T.

Kottowski, H. M., ed. Safety Problems Related to Socium Handling in LFBR & Large Test Facilities. (Ispra Courses on Nuclear Engineering & Technology). 258p. 1982. 38.00 (ISBN 3-7186-0087-0). Harwood Academic.

Kotwal, Firoze M. & Boyd, James W. A Guide to the Zoroastrian Religion: A Nineteenth Century Catechism with Modern Commentary. LC 82-3236. (Harvard University - Center for the Study of World Religions Ser.). 1982. 18.75 (ISBN 0-89130-573-4, 03-00-03); pap. 12.50 (ISBN 0-89130-574-2). Scholars Pr CA.

Kotz, David M. Bank Control of Large Corporations in the United States. LC 76-24585. 1978. 19.50x (ISBN 0-520-03321-3); pap. 3.95 (ISBN 0-520-03937-8). U of Cal Pr.

Kotz, Mary L., jt. auth. see Bayh, Marvella.

Kotz, Samuel & Johnson, Norman L. Encyclopedia of Statistical Sciences, 2 vols. LC 81-10353. (Encyclopedia of Statistical Sciences Ser.). 1982. Vol. 1, Circular Probable Error, 480p. 75.00x (ISBN 0-471-05546-8, Pub. by Wiley-Interscience); Vol. 2. text ed. 75.00x (ISBN 0-471-05547-6, Pub. by Wiley-Interscience). Wiley.

Kotz, Samuel, jt. auth. see Johnson, Norman.

Kotze, D. A. African Politics in South Africa: Parties & Issues. LC 75-6050. 350p. 1975. 32.50 (ISBN 0-312-01015-X). St Martin.

Kotzwinkle, William. Christmas at Fontaine's. (Illus.). 1982. 11.95 (ISBN 0-399-12737-2). Putnam Pub Group.

--E. T. The Extra-Terrestrial. 1982. 12.95 (ISBN 0-399-12730-5). Putnam Pub Group.

--The Extra Terrestrial Storybook. 1982. 6.95 (ISBN 0-399-20936-0). Putnam Pub Group.

--Jack in the Box. 1980. 10.95 (ISBN 0-399-12502-7). Putnam Pub Group.

--The Leopard's Tooth. 96p. 1983. pap. 2.95 (ISBN 0-380-62869-4, 62869, Bard). Avon.

--The Nap Master. LC 78-12178. (Illus.). (gr. k-3). 1979. pap. 2.50 (ISBN 0-15-665325-7, VoyB). HarBraceJ.

--Superman III. 240p. 1983. pap. 2.95 (ISBN 0-446-30699-1). Warner Bks.

--Swimmer in the Secret Sea. 1975. pap. 2.25 (ISBN 0-380-00342-2, 55228). Avon.

Koukou-Lehman & Lehman, eds. Functional States of the Brain: Their Determinants. 1980. 57.50 (ISBN 0-444-80258-4). Elsevier.

Koulack, David, jt. auth. see Gatley, Richard.

Koullis, L., jt. ed. see Brookes, N.

Koumouledes, John T., jt. ed. see Hoover, Dwight W.

Koumoulides, John T., ed. Hellenic Perspectives: Essays in the History of Greece. LC 80-5475. 398p. 1980. lib. bdg. 23.25 (ISBN 0-8191-1107-4); pap. text ed. 14.25 (ISBN 0-8191-1108-2). U Pr of Amer.

Koung, Stephen, tr. see Nee, Watchman.

Kounovsky, Nicholas. Instant Fitness: How to Stay Fit & Healthy in Six Minutes a Day. LC 79-14727. (Illus.). 1979. pap. 4.95 (ISBN 0-399-50400-1, Perige). Putnam Pub Group.

Kourdakov, Sergei. Persecutor. (Illus.). 256p. 1974. Repr. pap. 2.95 (ISBN 0-8007-8177-5, Spire Bks). Revell.

Kourganoff, Vladimir. Introduction a la Theorie Generale Du Transfer les Particules. (Cours & Documents de Mathematiques & de Physique Ser.). 216p. (Orig.). 1967. 50.00x (ISBN 0-677-50050-5). Gordon.

--Introduction to the General Theory of Particle Transfer. (Documents on Modern Physics Ser.). 230p. 1969. 38.00x (ISBN 0-677-30050-6). Gordon.

Kouri, Fred, et al. The Elusive Peace in the Middle East. Kerr, Malcolm H., ed. LC 75-15581. 350p. 1975. 34.50x (ISBN 0-87395-305-3); pap. 10.95x (ISBN 0-87395-306-1). State U NY Pr.

Kourvetaris, George A. & Dobratz, Betty A. Society & Politics: An Overview & Reappraisal of Political Sociology. 176p. 1980. pap. text ed. 9.95 (ISBN 0-8403-2238-0). Kendall-Hunt.

Koushiafes, Nicholas J. God. LC 81-90329. (Illus.). 300p. 1982. 25.00 (ISBN 0-9607228-0-7). Gods Universe.

Koustrup, Soren. Ireland in Flight. Christianson, John & Christianson, Birgitta, trs. from Danish. (Dream of America Ser.). Orig. Title: Irland pa flugt. (Illus.). 102p. (gr. 7-12). 1982. lib. bdg. 59.50 (ISBN 0-87191-711-4). Creative Ed.

--Shattered Dreams: Joe Hill. Christianson, John & Christianson, Birgitta, trs. from Danish. (Dream of America Ser.). Orig. Title: Joe Hill--en svensker i USA. (Illus.). 72p. (gr. 7-12). 1982. lib. bdg. 59.50 (ISBN 0-87191-710-6). Creative Ed.

Koutnik, Paul G., jt. auth. see Andersen, Hans O.

Koutsoyiannis, A. Modern Microeconomics. 2nd ed. (Illus.). 1979. 19.95x o.p. (ISBN 0-312-54103-1). St Martin.

Kouwenhoven, John A. Arts in Modern American Civilization. Orig. Title: Made in America. (Illus.). 1967. pap. 6.95 (ISBN 0-393-00404-X, Norton Lib). Norton.

--Half A Truth is Better Than None: Some Unsystematic Conjectures about Art, Disorder, & American Experience. LC 81-24051. 1982. 17.95 (ISBN 0-226-45155-0). U of Chicago Pr.

Kouymjian, Angele, jt. ed. see Kouymjian, Dickran.

Kouymjian, Dickran & Kouymjian, Angele, eds. The Splendor of Egypt. LC 75-2270. (Illus.). 230p. 1977. deluxe ed. 400.00x (ISBN 0-88206-008-2). Caravan Bks.

Kovac, Alexander. Guide to Diagnostic Imaging: The Liver & Spleen, Vol. 1. 1982. text ed. 33.00 (ISBN 0-87488-417-9). Med Exam.

Kovac, Alexander & Kozarek, Richard. Guide to Diagnostic Imaging: Vol. III - The Pancreas. 1983. write for info. (ISBN 0-87488-415-2). Med Exam.

Kovac, Alexander & Sanowski, Robert A. Guide to Diagnostic Imaging: Gallbladder & Biliary System, Vol. 2. 1983. text ed. write for info (ISBN 0-87488-414-4). Med Exam.

Kovach, E. G., ed. Technology of Efficient Energy Utilization: Report, Nato Science Committee Conference, les Arcs, France, Oct. 1973. LC 74-19839. 82p. 1974. pap. text ed. 10.75 (ISBN 0-08-018314-X). Pergamon.

Kovach, Joseph K., jt. auth. see Murphy, Gardner.

Kovach, Kenneth A. Organization Size, Job Satisfaction, Absenteeism & Turnover. 148p. 1977. pap. text ed. 8.75 (ISBN 0-8191-0242-3). U Pr of Amer.

--Readings & Cases in Contemporary Labor Relations 1980. LC 80-1429. 359p. 1981. pap. text ed. 13.50 (ISBN 0-8191-1362-X). U Pr of Amer.

--Readings & Cases in Contemporary Personnel Management. LC 81-40882. 420p. (Orig.). 1982. lib. bdg. 26.25 (ISBN 0-8191-2106-1); pap. text ed. 15.00 (ISBN 0-8191-2107-X). U Pr of Amer.

Kovach, Ladis D. Advanced Engineering Mathematics. LC 81-14936. (Mathematics Ser.). (Illus.). 1000p. 1982. text ed. 30.95 (ISBN 0-201-10340-0). A-W.

Kovacic, Michael L. Calculus: A Tool for Analysis & Decision. 1977. text ed. write for info. (ISBN 0-87150-233-X, PWS 1871). Prindle.

Kovacs, D., jt. auth. see Pickett, B.

Kovacs, David. Andromache of Euripides: An Interpretation. LC 80-11220. write for info. (ISBN 0-89130-389-8, 40-04-06); lib. bdg. 10.50x (ISBN 0-89130-390-1). Scholars Pr CA.

Kovacs, F. High-Frequency Application of Semiconductor Devices. (Studies in Electrical & Electronic Engineering: Vol. 5). Date not set. 74.50 (ISBN 0-444-99756-3). Elsevier.

Kovacs, F., ed. High-Frequency Application of Semiconductor Devices. 1981. 74.50 (ISBN 0-444-99756-3). Elsevier.

Kovacs, G. Seepage Hydraulics. (Developments in Water Science Ser.: Vol. 10). 1981. 117.00 (ISBN 0-444-99755-5). Elsevier.

Kovacs, I. Rotational Structure of the Spectra of Diatomic Molecules. 1970. 27.95 o.p. (ISBN 0-444-19672-2). Elsevier.

Kovacs, Klara L. Collected Poems of Klara L. Kovacs: Eszmeles. (Rainbow Bks.: No. 1). (Illus.). 1980. 6.50 (ISBN 0-936398-01-9). Framo Pub.

Kovacs, L. G., ed. see International Conference on the Theory of Groups, 1969.

Kovacs, William D. & Holtz, Robert D. An Introduction to Geotechnical Engineering. (Illus.). 720p. 1981. text ed. 33.95 (ISBN 0-13-484394-0). P-H.

Kovaleff, Theodore P. Business & Government During the Eisenhower Administration: A Study of the Antitrust Policy of the Antitrust Division of the Justice Department. LC 79-25590. x, 313p. 1980. 19.95x (ISBN 0-8214-0416-4, 82-83079). Ohio U Pr.

Kovalic, Joan. Clean Water Act. 162p. 1982. pap. text ed. 5.00 (ISBN 0-943244-40-4). Water Pollution.

Kovar, J., jt. auth. see Bohdanecky, M.

Kovarik, Tom, et al. Wind Energy. LC 78-24721. (Illus.). 1979. 12.50 o.p. (ISBN 0-89196-034-1, Domus Bks); pap. 6.95 o.p. (ISBN 0-89196-032-5). Quality Bks IL.

Kovats, Alexandra. Prayer: A Discovery of Life. (Nazareth Bks). 120p. 1983. pap. 3.95 (ISBN 0-86683-714-0). Winston Pr.

Kovda, Viktor. Land Aridization & Drought Control. (Westview Special Studies in Natural Resources & Energy Management). 1980. lib. bdg. 32.00 (ISBN 0-89158-259-2). Westview.

Kovel, Ralph & Kovel, Terry. American Country Furniture 1780-1875. (Illus.). 256p. 1980. 15.95 (ISBN 0-517-09737-0); pap. write for info (ISBN 0-517-54668-X). Crown.

--A Directory of American Silver. (Illus.). 352p. 1961. 9.95 (ISBN 0-686-36477-5). Md Hist.

--The Kovel Collector's Guide to Limited Editions. (Illus.). 160p. 1974. 9.95 o.p. (ISBN 0-517-51508-3). Crown.

--Kovels' Antique & Collectibles Price List. 15th ed. (Illus.). 800p. 1982. 10.95 (ISBN 0-517-54761-9). Crown.

--The Kovels' Collectors' Source Book. 1983. 25.50 (ISBN 0-517-54846-1); pap. 13.95 (ISBN 0-517-54791-0). Crown.

--The Kovels' Illustrated Price Guide to Depression Glass & American Dinnerware. (Illus.). 1983. pap. 10.95 (ISBN 0-517-54974-3). Crown.

Kovel, Ralph M. & Kovel, Terry H. Dictionary of Marks: Pottery & Porcelain. 1953. 8.95 (ISBN 0-517-00141-1). Crown.

--Kovel's Collector's Guide to American Art Pottery. (Illus.). 320p. 1974. 17.95 (ISBN 0-517-51676-4); pap. 9.95 (ISBN 0-517-54980-8). Crown.

Kovel, Terry, jt. auth. see Kovel, Ralph.

Kovel, Terry H., jt. auth. see Kovel, Ralph M.

Kovenock, David M., et al. Explaining the Vote: Presidential Choices in the Nation & the States, 1968. Incl. Pt. 1. The Theoretical Approach. 92p. pap. text ed. 2.50 (ISBN 0-89143-001-6); Pt. 2. Presidential Choices in Individual States. 601p. pap. text ed. 10.00 (ISBN 0-89143-002-4). (Comparative State Elections Project Monograph Ser.). 1973. pap. U NC Inst Res Soc Sci.

Kovic, Ron. Born on the Fourth of July. LC 76-7508. 204p. 1976. 8.95 o.p. (ISBN 0-07-035359-X, GB). McGraw.

Kovner, Abba. A Canopy in the Desert: Selected Poems. Kaufman, Shirley, tr. (Pitt Poetry Ser). 1973. 10.95 o.p. (ISBN 0-8229-3260-1); pap. 4.95 o.p. (ISBN 0-8229-5232-7). U of Pittsburgh Pr.

Kovner, Anthony R. & Martin, Samuel P., eds. Community Health & Medical Care. 496p. 1978. 44.50 o.p. (ISBN 0-8089-1046-9). Grune.

Kowal, Dennis, Jr. & Meilach, Dona Z. Sculpture Casting. LC 72-84319. (Arts & Crafts Ser). (Illus.). 224p. 1972. 9.95 o.p. (ISBN 0-517-50059-0). Crown.

Kowalewski. Transnational Corporations & Caribbean Inequalities. 252p. 1982. 27.95 (ISBN 0-03-062001-5). Praeger.

Kowalewski, Gerhard. Determinantentheorie. 3rd ed. LC 49-22682. (Ger). 18.50 (ISBN 0-8284-0039-3). Chelsea Pub.

Kowalewski, Victor, jt. auth. see Farmer, Richard.

Kowalik, Z., jt. auth. see Ramming, H. G.

Kowaliski, Paul. Applied Photographic Theory. LC 72-613. (Ser. on Photographic Sciences & Technology & Graphic Arts). 672p. 1972. 84.50 o.p. (ISBN 0-471-50600-1, Pub. by Wiley-Interscience). Wiley.

Kowalski, Casimir & Cangemi, Joseph P. Participative Management: A Practical Approach. 1983. 12.50 (ISBN 0-8022-2422-9). Philos Lib.

Kowalski, Casimir, jt. auth. see Cangemi, Joseph.

Kowalski, Theodore J. & Nelson, Norbert. Solving Educational Facility Problems. 300p. 1983. pap. text ed. price not set (ISBN 0-915202-36-0). Accel Devel.

Kowal-Wolk, Tatjana. Die Sowjetische Staatsburgerschaft. 199p. (Ger.). 1982. write for info. (ISBN 3-8204-7132-4). P Lang Pubs.

Kowan, Theodor. Agatha. 80p. 1983. 7.95 (ISBN 0-89962-317-4). Todd & Honeywell.

Kowet, Don. Franco Harris. LC 77-7508. (Illus.). 1977. 7.95 o.p. (ISBN 0-698-10778-0, Coward). Putnam Pub Group.

--The Jet Set Jet Lag Book: How to Rest Your Mind & Body & Beat the Fatigue & Confusion of Jet Lag. 1983. pap. 4.95 (ISBN 0-517-54895-X). Crown.

Kowet, Donald. Vida Blue: Coming up Again. (Putnam Sports Shelf). 128p. (gr. 5 up). 1974. PLB 6.29 o.p. (ISBN 0-399-60890-7). Putnam Pub Group.

Kowit, Steve. Lurid Confessions. LC 82-12915. 96p. (Orig.). 1983. pap. 5.95 (ISBN 0-914140-12-4). Carpenter Pr.

Kownslar, A. Teaching State Government. 1980. 8.00 (ISBN 0-07-035411-1). McGraw.

Kownslar, Allan O. & Smart, Terry L. American Government. 2nd ed. Nirkind, Bob, ed. (Illus.). 640p. (gr. 11-12). 1983. text ed. 19.84 (ISBN 0-07-035438-3, W); tchr's. resource guide 13.32 (ISBN 0-07-035439-1). McGraw.

--Civics: Citizens & Society. 2nd ed. Nirkind, Bob, ed. (Illus.). 576p. (gr. 7-8). 1983. text ed. 17.36 (ISBN 0-07-035433-2, W); tchr's. resource guide 14.24 (ISBN 0-07-035434-0); wkbk. 4.72 (ISBN 0-07-035435-9). McGraw.

Kownslar, Allan O., et al. American Government. (Illus.). (gr. 9-12). 1980. text ed. 20.52x (ISBN 0-07-035406-5); instr.'s manual 14.56x (ISBN 0-07-035407-3). McGraw.

Kowtaluk. Discovering Food. (gr. 7-9). 1982. text ed. 9.88 (ISBN 0-87002-369-1). Bennett IL.

Kowtaluk & Kopan. Food for Today. rev. ed. (gr. 9-12). 1982. text ed. 19.48 (ISBN 0-87002-334-9); student guide 3.96 (ISBN 0-87002-359-4); 17.28 (ISBN 0-87002-354-3). Bennett IL.

Kowtaluk, Helen. The Cook's Problem Solver. 296p. (Orig.). 1983. pap. 8.95 (ISBN 0-910469-00-8). IAM Ent.

--Discovering Food. (gr. 9-12). 1978. 9.28 o.p. (ISBN 0-87002-270-9); pap. 7.92 (ISBN 0-87002-272-5); student guide 3.96 (ISBN 0-87002-278-4); tchr's. guide 1982 ed. 13.28 (ISBN 0-87002-375-6). Bennett IL.

--Discovering Nutrition. 1980. text ed. 11.40 (ISBN 0-87002-310-1); tchr's guide 7.96 (ISBN 0-87002-318-7); student guide 3.68 (ISBN 0-87002-317-9). Bennett IL.

Koyama, Kosuke. Fifty Meditations. LC 77-7026. (Illus.). 191p. (Orig.). 1979. pap. 6.95 (ISBN 0-88344-134-9). Orbis Bks.

Koykka, Arthur S. Project Remember: A National Index of Grave Sites of Notable Americans. Irvine, Keith, ed. 550p. 1983. 49.95 (ISBN 0-917256-22-0). Ref Pubns.

Koyna, Allan. Design Primer for Hot Climates. (Illus.). 132p. 1980. 19.95 (ISBN 0-8230-7148-0, Whitney Lib). Watson-Guptill.

Koza, Russell C., jt. auth. see Hinkle, Charles L.

Kozai, T. & Goudriaan, J. Light Transmission & Phitisynthesis in Greenhouses. 105p. 1978. pap. 13.25 (ISBN 0-686-93165-3, PDC104, Pudoc). Unipub.

Kozak, George P. Clinical Diabetes Mellitus. (Illus.). 541p. 1982. 65.00 (ISBN 0-7216-5502-5). Saunders.

Kozarek, Richard, jt. auth. see Kovac, Alexander.

Kozarich, J. W., jt. auth. see Dannies, P.

Kozhevnikov, A. V. Electron-Ion Exchangers: A New Group of Redoxites. Pick, A., ed. Kondor, R., tr. from Rus. LC 74-32247. 129p. 1975. 34.95 o.p. (ISBN 0-470-50626-1). Halsted Pr.

Kozhina, Elena, intro. by. The Hermitage: Western European Painting of the 13th to 18th Centuries. 1979. 19.95 (ISBN 0-89893-002-2). CDP.

Koziakin, Vladimir. Color Designs Three: Optical Illusions. (Illus.). 64p. pap. 2.95 (ISBN 0-671-42658-3). Wanderer Bks.

--Mazes. (Illus.). 1971. pap. 2.50 o.p. (ISBN 0-448-01836-5, G&D). Putnam Pub Group.

--Mazes, No. 2. (Illus.). 64p. 1972. pap. 2.50 (ISBN 0-448-01829-2, G&D). Putnam Pub Group.

--Mazes, No. 3. (Illus.). 96p. 1973. pap. 2.50 (ISBN 0-448-02064-5, G&D). Putnam Pub Group.

--Mazes, No. 4. 96p. 1974. pap. 2.50 (ISBN 0-448-11655-3, G&D). Putnam Pub Group.

--Mazes, No. 5. (Illus.). 96p. 1975. pap. 2.50 (ISBN 0-448-11877-7, G&D). Putnam Pub Group.

--Mazes, No. 6. 96p. 1976. pap. 2.50 o.s.i. (ISBN 0-448-12155-7, G&D). Putnam Pub Group.

--Mazes for Fun, Nos. 1-4. (Basic Activity Bks.). 64p. (gr. 2-5). 1973. pap. 1.50 ea. (G&D); No. 1. (ISBN 0-448-03800-5); No. 2. (ISBN 0-448-03801-3); No. 3. (ISBN 0-448-11734-7); No. 4. (ISBN 0-448-11735-5). Putnam Pub Group.

--Mazes for Fun, No. 5. (Elephant Bks.). (Illus.). 64p. (gr. 2-5). 1976. pap. 1.50 (ISBN 0-448-12515-3, G&D). Putnam Pub Group.

--Mazes: No. 7. 1977. pap. 2.50 (ISBN 0-448-12896-9, G&D). Putnam Pub Group.

--Mazewarps. 1983. pap. 2.50 (ISBN 0-517-54965-4, C N Potter Bks). Crown.

--Three D Mazes. Schneider, Meg, ed. (Illus.). 64p. (Orig.). (gr. 8-12). Date not set. pap. 2.50 (ISBN 0-671-43448-9). Wanderer Bks. Postponed.

--Travel Mazes. (Basic Activity Bks.). 64p. (gr. 2-6). 1976. pap. 1.25 (ISBN 0-448-12139-5, G&D). Putnam Pub Group.

Kozicki, Richard J., ed. International Relations of South Asia, 1947 to 1980: A Guide to Information Sources. LC 73-17510. (International Relations Information Guide Ser.: Vol. 10). 225p. 1981. 42.00x (ISBN 0-8103-1329-4). Gale.

Kozier, Barbara & Erb, Glenora. Fundamentals of Nursing. 2nd ed. 1983. 22.95 (ISBN 0-201-11711-8, Med-Nurse); instr's guide avail. (ISBN 0-201-11712-6); wkbk 10.95 (ISBN 0-201-11714-2). A-W.

Kozier, Barbara & Glenora, Erb. Fundamentals of Nursing: Concepts & Procedures. 1979. transparency resource kit 50.00 (ISBN 0-201-03918-4, Med-Nurse). A-W.

Kozier, Barbara B. & Erb, Glenora L. Fundamentals of Nursing: Concepts & Procedures. LC 78-7776. 1979. 28.95 o.p. (ISBN 0-201-03904-4, Med-Nurse); instr's guide 3.95 o.p. (ISBN 0-201-03905-2). A-W.

Kozik, T. J., ed. Risers-Arctic Design Criteria-Equipment Reliability In Hydrocarbon Processing: A Workbook for Engineers. 242p. 1981. 30.00 (I00144). ASME.

Kozintzev, Grigori. King Lear: the Space of Tragedy: The Diary of a Film Director. Mackintosh, Mary, tr. LC 76-50248. (Illus.). 1977. 21.50x (ISBN 0-520-03392-2). U of Cal Pr.

Kozlak, Chet, illus. Dakota Indians Coloring Book. Cavender, Elsie & Prescott, Evelyn, trs. 32p. (Eng. & Eastern Dakota.). 1979. pap. 2.00 (ISBN 0-87351-149-2). Minn Hist.

--A Great Lakes Fur Trade Coloring Book. Belanger, Jean-Pierre, tr. 32p. (Eng. & Fr.). 1981. pap. 2.00 (ISBN 0-87351-154-9). Minn Hist.

Kozloff, Eugene. Seashore Life of the Northern Pacific Coast: An Illustrated Guide to the Common Marine Organisms of Northern California, Oregon, Washington & British Columbia. 1983. write for info. U of Wash Pr.

Kozloff, M. Educating Children with Learning & Behavior Problems. LC 74-11304. 459p. 1974. 37.50x (ISBN 0-471-50630-3, Pub. by Wiley-Interscience). Wiley.

Kozloff, Martin A. A Program for Families of Children with Learning & Behavior Problems. LC 78-26578. 450p. 1979. 37.95x (ISBN 0-471-04434-2, Pub. by Wiley-Interscience). Wiley.

Kozloff, Max. Renderings: Critical Essays on a Century of Modern Art. 1968. pap. 2.95 o.p. (ISBN 0-671-20248-0, Touchstone Bks). S&S.

Kozlovsky, Daniel G., ed. An Ecological & Evolutionary Ethic. (Illus.). 128p. 1974. pap. 12.95 (ISBN 0-13-222935-8). P-H.

Kozlowski, T. K., jt. ed. see Tibbitts, T.

Kozlowski, T. T., jt. auth. see Kramer, Paul J.

Kozlowski, T. T. & Riker, A. J., eds. Water Deficits & Plant Growth: Additional Woody Crop Plants. (Vol. 7). Date not set. price not set (ISBN 0-12-424157-3). Acad Pr.

Kozlowski, Theodore T., ed. Tree Growth. (Illus.). 442p. 1962. 29.95x (ISBN 0-471-06836-5, Pub. by Wiley-Interscience). Wiley.

Kozma, Ferenc. Economy Integration & Economic Strategy. 1982. lib. bdg. 48.00 (ISBN 90-247-2649-2, Pub. by Martinus Nijhoff Netherlands). Kluwer Boston.

Kozma, Pal, ed. Control of the Nutrition of Cultivated Plants-Controle De L'Alimentation Des Plantes Cultivees, 2 Vols. (Third Colloque Europeen et Meditarrneen, Budapest, Universite d'Horticulture, 1972). (Illus.). 1975. 67.50 (ISBN 963-05-0911-3). Intl Pubns Serv.

Kozo, T., jt. auth. see Seiyama, S.

Kozub, Jacques. Portugal: Agricultural Sector Survey. v, 323p. 1978. pap. 20.00 (ISBN 0-686-36117-2, RC-7803). World Bank.

Kozuki, Russell. Junior Karate. LC 71-167665. (Illus.). (gr. 3 up). 1971. 8.95 (ISBN 0-8069-4446-3); PLB 10.99 (ISBN 0-8069-4447-1). Sterling.

--Karate for Young People. LC 73-93590. (Athletic Institute Ser.). (Illus.). 128p. (gr. 3 up). 1974. 8.95 (ISBN 0-8069-4074-3); PLB 10.99 (ISBN 0-8069-4075-1). Sterling.

--Karate for Young People. LC 73-93590. (Illus.). 128p. (gr. 5 up). 1982. pap. 4.95 (ISBN 0-8069-7560-1). Sterling.

--Power Karate. LC 82-19321. (Illus.). 144p. (Orig.). 1983. pap. 5.95 (ISBN 0-8069-7720-5). Sterling.

Kozuki, Russell & Lee, Douglas. Kung Fu for Young People: The Ving Tsun System. LC 75-14504. (Illus.). 128p. (gr. 8 up). 1982. pap. 4.95 (ISBN 0-8069-7656-X). Sterling.

Kozuszek, Jane E. Hygiene. (First Bks.). (Illus.). (gr. 4 up). 1978. PLB 8.90 s&l (ISBN 0-531-01410-X). Watts.

Kpomassie, Tete-Michel. An African in Greenland. Kirkup, James, tr. (Illus.). 224p. 14.95 (ISBN 0-15-105589-0). HarBraceJ.

Kra, Siegfried J. Basic M-Mode Echocardiography. 1982. 37.50 (ISBN 0-87488-978-2). Med Exam.

Krabbe, E. C., jt. ed. see Barth, E. M.

Krabbenhoft, Kenneth, tr. see Trias, Eugenio.

Krabs, W. Optimization & Approximation. LC 78-10448. 220p. 1979. 47.95x (ISBN 0-471-99741-2, Pub. by Wiley-Interscience). Wiley.

Kracauer, Siegfried. Theory of Film: The Redemption of Physical Reality. (Illus.). 1965. pap. 8.95 (ISBN 0-19-500721-2, GB). Oxford U Pr.

Kracker, Deitz. The Good Morning Grump. LC 81-22876. 32p. (gr. k-3). 1982. 10.95g (ISBN 0-687-15520-7). Abingdon.

Kracum, Vincent D. Respiratory Therapy Examination Review Book, Vol. 1. 3rd ed. 1975. spiral bdg. 12.75 (ISBN 0-87488-471-3). Med Exam.

Kraegel, Janet M., ed. Organization-Environment Relationships. 233p. 1980. pap. 19.95 (ISBN 0-913654-58-2). Aspen Systems.

Kraehenbuehl, David. Jazz & Blues. Clark, Frances & Goss, Louise, eds. Incl. Book 1. pap. text ed.; Book 2. pap. text ed. 3.40 op (ISBN 0-87487-112-3); Books 5 & 6. 1974. pap. text ed. 5.00 (ISBN 0-87487-113-1). (Frances Clark Library for Piano Students Ser.). 1963. Summy.

Kraehenbuehl, David, et al. Keyboard Theory, 6 books. Incl. Book 1. 1965. pap. text ed. 5.95 (ISBN 0-87487-115-8); Book 2. 1965. pap. text ed. 6.45 (ISBN 0-87487-116-6); Book 3. 1965. pap. text ed. 5.95 (ISBN 0-87487-117-4); Book 4. 1965. pap. text ed. 6.45 (ISBN 0-87487-118-2); Books 5 & 6. pap. text ed. 7.95 (ISBN 0-87487-119-0). (Frances Clark Library for Piano Students). Summy.

Kraeling, Emil G. I Have Kept the Faith: The Life of the Apostle Paul. LC 65-15357. (Illus.). 1979. pap. 4.95 o.p. (ISBN 0-528-88015-2). Rand.

Kraemer, Eric, jt. auth. see Leinfellner, Werner.

Kraemer, Joel L., ed. Jerusalem: Problems & Prospects. 245p. pap. 9.95 (ISBN 0-686-95162-X). ADL.

Kraemer, Kenneth L., jt. auth. see Perry, James L.

Kraemer, Kenneth L. & King, John L., eds. Computers & Local Government: A Manager's Guide, Vol. 1. LC 77-23886. (Praeger Special Studies). 1977. 25.95 o.p. (ISBN 0-03-040846-6). Praeger.

Kraemer, Kenneth L., jt. ed. see Perry, James L.

Kraemer, Richard & Newell, Charldean. Essentials of Texas Politics. 2nd ed. (Illus.). 225p. pap. text ed. 11.95 (ISBN 0-314-69659-8); tchrs.' manual avail. (ISBN 0-314-71104-X). West Pub.

--Texas Politics. (Illus.). 1979. pap. text ed. 12.95 o.s.i. (ISBN 0-8299-0286-4); instrs.' manual avail. o.s.i. (ISBN 0-8299-0499-9). West Pub.

Kraemer, Richard, et al. American Democracy: The Third Century. (Illus.). 1978. pap. text ed. 16.95 (ISBN 0-8299-0160-4); instrs.' manual avail. (ISBN 0-8299-0498-0). West Pub.

Kraemer, Richard H., et al. Politics in Texas. abridged ed. LC 75-19338. (Illus.). 200p. 1975. pap. text ed. 9.50 (ISBN 0-8299-0022-5). West Pub.

--Understanding Texas Politics. LC 75-4719. (Illus.). 560p. 1975. pap. text ed. 11.50 (ISBN 0-8299-0045-4). West Pub.

Kraenzlin, F. W. Orchidacearum Genera et Species. (Plant Monograph Reprint Ser.: No. 6). (Illus.). 1969. Repr. of 1904 ed. 80.00 (ISBN 3-7682-0649-1). Lubrecht & Cramer.

Kraenzlin, R. Monographie von Masdevallia Ruiz et Pavon Lothiana Kraenz: Scaphosepalum Pfitzer, Cryptophoranthus Bearb, Rodr., Pseudostomeria Kraenzl. (Feddes Repertorium: Beiheft 34). 240p. (Ger.). 1980. Repr. of 1925 ed. lib. bdg. 36.80x (ISBN 3-87429-184-7). Lubrecht & Cramer.

Krafft-Ebbing, Richard Von. An Experimental Study in the Domain of Hypnotism. (Hypnosis & Altered States of Consciousness Ser.). 129p. 1982. Repr. of 1893 ed. lib. bdg. 19.50 (ISBN 0-306-76162-9). Da Capo.

Kraft & Casey. Roles in Off-Campus Student Teaching. 1967. 8.00x (ISBN 0-87563-016-2); pap. 5.90x o.p. (ISBN 0-686-96897-2). Stipes.

Kraft, Amy L., jt. auth. see Lager, Lance.

Kraft, Anthony D. The Fantastic Four: The Secret Story of Marvel's Cosmic Quartet. LC 81-10019. (Secret Stories of the Sensational Super Heroes). (Illus.). 64p. (gr. 3 up). 1981. PLB 9.25 (ISBN 0-516-02412-4). Childrens.

Kraft, Barbara S. The Money Management Workbook. (Illus., Orig.). Date not set. pap. 5.95 (ISBN 0-89104-308-X, A & W Visual Library). A & W Pubs. Postponed.

Kraft, Betsy H. Coal. rev. ed. LC 80-54726. (First Bks.). (Illus.). 72p. (gr. 4 up). 1982. PLB 8.90 (ISBN 0-531-00336-1). Watts.

--Oil & Natural Gas. (First Bks). (Illus.). (gr. 4 up). 1978. PLB 8.90 (ISBN 0-531-01411-8). Watts.

Kraft, Carlotte, jt. auth. see Allen, Robert F.

Kraft, Charles H. Communication Theory for Christian Witness. 256p. (Orig.). 1983. pap. 11.95 (ISBN 0-687-09224-8). Abingdon.

Kraft, Charles H. & Kraft, Marguerite G. Introductory Hausa. LC 70-161997. 1974. 27.50x (ISBN 0-520-01988-1). U of Cal Pr.

Kraft, Charlotte, jt. auth. see Allen, Robert F.

Kraft, David A. Captain America: The Secret Story of Marvel's Star-Spangled Super Hero. LC 81-10020. (Secret Stories of the Sensational Super Heroes Ser). (Illus.). 64p. (gr. 3 up). 1981. PLB 9.25 (ISBN 0-516-02411-6). Childrens.

--The Incredible Hulk: The Secret Story of Marvel's Gamma-Powered Goliath. LC 81-10021. (Secret Stories of the Sensational Super Heroes). (Illus.). 64p. (gr. 3 up). 1981. PLB 9.25 (ISBN 0-516-02413-2). Childrens.

Kraft, Dean. Portrait of a Psychic Healer. 192p. 1981. 11.95 (ISBN 0-399-12517-5). Putnam Pub Group.

--Portrait of a Psychic Healer. 192p. 1982. pap. 2.50 (ISBN 0-425-05664-3). Berkley Pub.

Kraft, Eric. My Mother Takes a Tumble. (The Portable Peter Leroy Ser.: Vol. 1). 96p. 1982. pap. 4.95 (ISBN 0-686-82274-9). Apple Wood.

Kraft, Eva, ed. Japanese Institutions. 611p. (Japanese & Eng.). 1972. text ed. 42.00x (ISBN 3-7940-5041-X, Pub. by K G Saur). Gale.

Kraft, Eve. The Tennis Workbook-Unit I. (Illus.). 64p. 1980. 2.95 (ISBN 0-686-37475-4). USTA.

Kraft, Eve & Conroy, John. The Tennis Teacher's Guide: Group Instruction & Team Coaching. (Illus.). 96p. 1980. 4.50 (ISBN 0-686-37474-6). USTA.

--The Tennis Workbook-Unit II. (Illus.). 72p. 1982. 3.50 (ISBN 0-686-37476-2). USTA.

Kraft Foods. Complete Cheese Cookbook. LC 77-160673. 6.95 (ISBN 0-87502-018-6); pap. 1.95 (ISBN 0-87502-093-3). Benjamin Co.

Kraft, George D. & Toy, Wing N. Microprogrammed Control & Reliable Design of Small Computers. (Illus.). 248p. 1981. text ed. 29.95 (ISBN 0-13-581140-6). P-H.

Kraft, James, ed. see Bynner, Wittter.

Kraft, John & Osterbind, Carter C., eds. Older People in Florida, Nineteen Eighty to Nineteen Eighty-One: A Statistical Abstract. 264p. (Orig.). 1981. pap. 11.50 (ISBN 0-8130-0703-8). U Presses Fla.

Kraft, Leo. Gradus-An Integrated Approach to Harmony, Counterpoint, & Analysis: Gradus One (Text & Anthology) Incl. Gradus One (Text & Anthology) 360p. pap. text ed. 5.50x (ISBN 0-393-09180-5); Anthology. pap. text ed. 5.50x (ISBN 0-393-09185-6). 1976. Vol. 1. 19.95x set (ISBN 0-393-09154-6); Vol. 2. 19.95x (ISBN 0-393-09148-1). Norton.

--New Approach to Ear Training. (Orig., Prog. Bk.). 1967. 8.95x (ISBN 0-393-09764-1, NortonC); tapes 185.00 (ISBN 0-393-09916-4); tchrs. manual free (ISBN 0-393-09788-9). Norton.

Kraft, Marguerite G., jt. auth. see Kraft, Charles H.

Kraft, Michael & Schneider, Mark, eds. Population Policy. new ed. 1977. pap. 6.00 (ISBN 0-918592-23-2). Policy Studies.

Kraft, Michael E. & Schneider, Mark, eds. Population Policy Analysis: Issues in American Politics. LC 77-221. (Policy Studies Organization Ser.). 224p. 1978. 19.95 (ISBN 0-669-01456-7, Dist. by Transaction Bks). Lexington Bks.

Kraft, Steven, ed. Tennis Drills for Self-Improvement. (Illus.). 83p. 1978. 2.95 o.p. (ISBN 0-686-37480-0). USTA.

Kraft, Virginia. Tennis Instruction for Fun & Competition. LC 73-18527. (Illus.). 192p. 1976. 5.95 (ISBN 0-448-11698-7, G&D); pap. 2.95 (ISBN 0-448-12201-4). Putnam Pub Group.

Kraft, William F. The Search for the Holy. LC 72-152336. 1971. pap. 4.95 (ISBN 0-664-24923-X). Westminster.

Kraft, Wolfgang S. Deutsch: Aktuell 1. LC 78-11445. 1979. 10.95 (ISBN 0-88436-539-5); pap. 7.50 (ISBN 0-88436-537-9). EMC.

--Deutsch: Aktuell 2. LC 79-12315. (Illus.). 1980. 11.70 (ISBN 0-88436-542-5); pap. 7.95 (ISBN 0-88436-540-9, 45251). EMC.

Kraftds, Melvin D. Using Experts in Civil Cases. 2nd ed. 356p. 1982. text ed. 45.00 (ISBN 0-686-81879-2, H3-2965). PLI.

Kragelsky, I. V. & Alisin, V. V., eds. Friction, Wear & Lubrication: A Complete Handbook of Tribology, 3 Vols. (Illus.). 800p. 120.00 (ISBN 0-08-027591-5, A115); firm 60.00 (ISBN 0-686-97493-X). Pergamon.

Kragelsky, I. V., et al. Friction & Wear: Calculation Methods. LC 80-41669. (Illus.). 450p. 1982. 100.00 (ISBN 0-08-025461-6); pap. 60.00 o.p. (ISBN 0-08-027320-3). Pergamon.

Krahenmann, Heidi. Das Gegensatzliche In Heinrich Federers Leben und Werk. 318p. (Ger.). 1982. write for info. (ISBN 3-261-05012-8). P Lang Pubs.

Krahn, Fernando. April Fools. LC 73-16279. (Illus.). 32p. (ps-2). 1974. 8.95 (ISBN 0-525-25825-6, 0869-260). Dutton.

--Here Comes Alex Pumpernickel. (Illus.). 32p. (ps up). 1981. 6.95 (ISBN 0-316-50311-8, Atlantic). Little.

--How Santa Claus Had a Long & Difficult Journey Delivering His Presents. LC 72-122769. (Illus.). (ps-3). 1970. PLB 7.45 o.s.i. (ISBN 0-440-03887-1, Sey Lawr); 7.95 o.s.i. (ISBN 0-440-03886-3). Delacorte.
--How Santa Claus Had a Long & Difficult Journey Delivering His Presents. LC 72-122769. 32p. (gr. k-2). 1977. pap. 2.50 o.s.i. (ISBN 0-440-03725-5, Sey Lawr). Delacorte.
--Sebastian & the Mushroom. LC 75-32918. 24p. (ps). 1976. 4.95 o.s.i. (ISBN 0-440-07694-3, Sey Lawr); PLB 4.58 o.s.i. (ISBN 0-440-07695-1). Delacorte.
--The Secret in the Dungeon. (Illus.). 32p. (gr. 2). 1983. 9.95 (ISBN 0-89919-148-7, Clarion). HM.
--The Self-Made Snowman. LC 74-551. (gr. 1-3). 1974. PLB 9.89 (ISBN 0-397-31472-8, JBL-J). Har-Row.
--Sleep Tight, Alex Pumpernickel. 32p. (ps up). 1982. 7.95 (ISBN 0-316-50312-6, Pub. by Atlantic Monthly Pr). Little.
Krailsheimer, A. Conversion. (Student Christian Movement Press). (Orig.). 1980. pap. 7.95x (ISBN 0-19-520326-7). Oxford U Pr.
Krailsheimer, A. J., tr. see Flaubert, Gustave.
Krainin, Harold L. What You Should Know About Operating Your Business As a Corporation. LC 66-30351. (Business Almanac Ser.: No. 7). 1967. 5.95 o.p. (ISBN 0-379-11207-8). Oceana.
Krajewski, Lee J. & Thompson, Howard E., eds. Management Science: Quantitative Methods in Context. LC 80-17103. (Management Ser.). 544p. 1981. text ed. 32.95 (ISBN 0-471-06109-3); tchr's. manual 13.75 (ISBN 0-471-09115-4). Wiley.
Krajicek, M. & Tearney, A., eds. Detection of Developmental Problems in Children. (Illus.). 224p. 1976. pap. text ed. 14.95 (ISBN 0-8391-0949-0). Univ Park.
Krakauer, L. J. Year Book of Sports Medicine 1983. 1983. 40.00 (ISBN 0-8151-5157-8). Year Bk Med.
Krakauer, Lewis J. Year Book of Sports Medicine, 1982. Anderson, James L., et al, eds. (Illus.). 400p. 1982. 39.95 (ISBN 0-8151-5156-X). Year Bk Med.
Krakel, Dean, II. Season of the Elk. LC 75-42982. (Illus.). 128p. 1980. 22.95 (ISBN 0-913504-28-9); pap. 14.95 (ISBN 0-913504-29-7). Lowell Pr.
Krakiwsky, E. J., jt. auth. see Vanicek, P.
Krakow, Joanne B., jt. auth. see Kopp, Claire B.
Krakowski, A. J. & Kimball, C. P., eds. Psychosomatic Medicine in a Changing World: Theoretical, Clinical & Transcultural Aspects. (Journal of Psychotherapy & Psychosomatics: Vol. 38, No. 1-4). (Illus.). 310p. 1982. pap. 79.25 (ISBN 3-8055-3544-9). S Karger.
Krakowski, Shmuel. The War of the Doomed: Jewish Armed Resistance in Poland, 1942-1944. 250p. 1983. text ed. 35.00x (ISBN 0-8419-0851-6); pap. text ed. 18.50x (ISBN 0-8419-0852-4). Holmes & Meier.
Krall. World Book of Practical Diabetes. Date not set. price not set (ISBN 0-444-90286-4). Elsevier.
Krall, A. M. Linear Methods of Applied Analysis. 1973. 19.50 (ISBN 0-201-03902-8); pap. 19.50 (ISBN 0-201-03903-6). A-W.
Krall, Nicholas A. & Trivelpiece, Alvin W. Principles of Plasma Physics. (International Ser. in Pure & Applied Physics). (Illus.). 704p. 1972. text ed. 46.00 o.p. (ISBN 0-07-035346-8, C). McGraw.
Kram, Shirley W. & Frank, Neil A. The Law of Child Custody: Development of the Substantive Law. LC 79-7717. 192p. 1982. 19.95x (ISBN 0-669-03183-6). Lexington Bks.
Kramarae, Cheris, ed. The Voices & Words of Women & Men. 195p. 1981. 38.00 (ISBN 0-08-026106-X). Pergamon.
Kramer, A. D. Fundamentals of Technical Mathematics. 1982. 20.95x (ISBN 0-07-035427-8). McGraw.
Kramer, Aaron. In Wicked Times. Strahan, Bradley R., ed. (Black Buzzard Illustrated Poetry Chapbook Ser.). (Illus.). 40p. 1983. pap. text ed. 3.50 (ISBN 0-938872-05-2). Black Buzzard.
Kramer, Aaron, tr. see Rilke, Rainer M.
Kramer, Alan H., ed. Gifted Children: Challenging their Potential. 331p. (Orig.). 1981. pap. 14.00 (ISBN 0-89824-027-1). Trillium Pr.
Kramer, Alex, jt. auth. see Stark, Paul.
Kramer, Anneliese. The Languages of Linguistic Theory: Aesthetic Dimensions of a Scientific Discipline. (The Language & Being Ser.). 1983. write for info. (ISBN 0-89391-112-7). Ablex Pub.
Kramer, Arthur, jt. auth. see Burke, Ronald.
Kramer, Carol. Village Ethnoarchaeology: Rural Iran in Archaeological Perspective. (Studies in Archaeology). 302p. 1982. 34.50 (ISBN 0-12-425020-3). Acad Pr.
Kramer, Charles H. Becoming a Family Therapist: Developing an Integrated Approach to Working with Families. LC 80-11322. 322p. 1980. text ed. 29.95 (ISBN 0-87705-470-3). Human Sci Pr.
Kramer, D., et al. Exact Solutions of Einstein's Field Equations. (Cambridge Monographs on Mathematical Physics). 400p. 1981. 75.00 (ISBN 0-521-23041-1). Cambridge U Pr.
Kramer, Dale. Charles Robert Maturin. (English Authors Ser.). 1973. lib. bdg. 14.95 (ISBN 0-8057-1382-4, Twayne). G K Hall.
Kramer, Dean C. Medical Practice Management. 288p. 1982. pap. 15.95 (ISBN 0-316-50322-3). Little.
Kramer, Edith. Art Therapy in a Children's Community. LC 77-75292. (Illus.). 1978. pap. 8.95 o.p. (ISBN 0-8052-0574-8). Schocken.
Kramer, Fred, tr. see Chemnitz, Martin.
Kramer, Fred A. Contemporary Approaches to Public Budgeting. (Orig.). 1979. pap. text ed. 9.95 (ISBN 0-316-50316-9). Little.
--Dynamics of Public Bureaucracy: An Introduction to Public Management. 2nd ed. 1981. text ed. 18.95 (ISBN 0-316-50318-5). Little.
Kramer, J. Travels with the Celestial Dog. 1977. 10.00 o.p. (ISBN 0-7045-0146-5). State Mutual Bk.
Kramer, J. K. & Saver, F. D., eds. High & Low Erucic Acid Rapeseed Oils: Production, Usage, Chemistry & Toxilogical Evaluation. LC 82-13805. Date not set. price not set (ISBN 0-12-425080-7). Acad Pr.
Kramer, Jack. Cacti & Other Succulents. LC 77-5881. (Illus.). 1978. pap. 7.95 (ISBN 0-8109-2096-4). Abrams.
--The Everest House Complete Book of Gardening. LC 79-51198. (Illus.). 384p. 1982. 29.95 (ISBN 0-89696-041-2, An Everest House Book). Dodd.
--Finishing Touches. LC 77-17924. 1978. 15.95 o.p. (ISBN 0-07-035393-X, GB). McGraw.
--Gift Plants: House Plant Beauty All Year Long. (Illus.). 1976. 8.95 o.p. (ISBN 0-399-11715-6). Putnam Pub Group.
--Indoor Trees. 1980. 25.00x o.p. (ISBN 0-232-51399-6, Pub. by Darton-Longman-Todd England). State Mutual Bk.
--The Log House Book. (Illus., Orig.). 1979. pap. 6.95 (ISBN 0-452-25379-9, Z5379, Plume). NAL.
--Once-a-Week Indoor Gardening Guide. (Orig.). pap. 1.75 o.s.i. (ISBN 0-515-04475-X). Jove Pubns.
--One Thousand Beautiful Garden Plants & How to Grow Them. LC 76-984. (Illus.). 1979. pap. 6.95 o.p. (ISBN 0-688-08025-1). Morrow.
--Plant Hobbies: A Beginner's Book of Gardening Projects, Principles & Pleasures. LC 77-25336. (Illus.). (gr. 4 up). 1978. 7.95 o.p. (ISBN 0-529-05341-1, Philomel). Putnam Pub Group.
--Plant Sculptures: Making Miniature Indoor Topiaries. (Illus.). (gr. 3-12). 1978. 8.75 (ISBN 0-688-22144-0); PLB 8.40 (ISBN 0-688-32144-5). Morrow.
--Queen's Tears & Elephant's Ears: A Guide to Growing Unusual House Plants. LC 77-3258. (Illus.). (gr. 4 up). 1977. 5.95 o.p. (ISBN 0-529-05330-6, A4656, Philomel). Putnam Pub Group.
Kramer, Jack & Deford, Frank. The Game: My Forty Years in Tennis. LC 78-31299. (Illus.). 1979. 11.95 o.p. (ISBN 0-399-12336-9). Putnam Pub Group.
Kramer, Janice. Donkey Daniel in Bethlehem. (Arch Bks: Set 7). (Illus., Orig.). (ps-4). 1970. pap. 0.89 (ISBN 0-570-06053-2, 59-1169). Concordia.
--Princess & the Baby. (Arch Bks: Set 6). 1969. laminated bdg 0.89 (ISBN 0-570-06043-5, 59-1158). Concordia.
--Simeon's Secret. (Arch Bks: Set 6). (ps-3). 1969. laminated bdg. 0.89 (ISBN 0-570-06045-1, 59-1160). Concordia.
--Sir Abner & His Grape Pickers. (Arch Bks.: Set 7). (Illus., Orig.). (ps-4). 1970. pap. 0.89 (ISBN 0-570-06051-6, 59-1167). Concordia.
--Unforgiving Servant. (Arch Bks: Set 5). (Illus.). (gr. 5). 1968. laminated bdg. 0.89 (ISBN 0-570-06035-4, 59-1148): Concordia.
Kramer, Janice & Mathews. Good Samaritan. LC 63-23369. (Arch Bks: Set 1). (Illus.). 1964. laminated bdg 0.89 (ISBN 0-570-06000-1, 59-1102). Concordia.
--Rich Fool. LC 64-16984. (Arch Bks: Set 1). (Illus.). (gr. 1-3). 1964. 0.89 (ISBN 0-570-06004-4, 59-1109). Concordia.
Kramer, M., jt. auth. see Hilsen, R.
Kramer, Marc B., ed. Forensic Audiology. (Perspectives in Audiology Ser.). 376p. 1982. text ed. 44.95 (ISBN 0-8391-1613-6). Univ Park.
Kramer, Marlene. Reality Shock: Why Nurses Leave Nursing. LC 73-22243. (Illus.). 250p. 1974. pap. text ed. 13.95 o.p. (ISBN 0-8016-2741-9). Mosby.
Kramer, Marlene & Schmalenberg, Claudia. Path to Biculturalism. LC 77-7202. 315p. 1977. pap. 16.50 (ISBN 0-913654-30-2). Aspen Systems.
Kramer, Marlene, jt. auth. see Carl, Mary K.
Kramer, Melinda G. & Rigg, Donald C. Prentice-Hall Workbook for Writers. 3rd ed. 320p. 1983. pap. 8.95 (ISBN 0-13-695981-4). P-H.
Kramer, Michael S., jt. auth. see Levy, Mark R.
Kramer, P. J., jt. auth. see Turner, N. C.
Kramer, Paul J. & Kozlowski, T. T. Physiology of Trees. (Botanical Sciences Ser.). 1960. text ed. 42.50 (ISBN 0-07-035351-4, C). McGraw.
Kramer, Paul J., jt. auth. see Raper, C. David.
Kramer, Paul J., ed. Water Relations of Plants. 428p. 1983. price not set (ISBN 0-12-425040-8). Acad Pr.
Kramer, Ralph M. Community Development in Israel & the Netherlands: A Comparative Analysis. LC 70-632526. (Research Ser.: No. 14). 1970. pap. 2.50x o.p. (ISBN 0-87725-114-2). U of Cal Intl St.
Kramer, Ralph M. & Specht, Harry, eds. Readings in Community Organization Practice. 2nd ed. (Illus.). 432p. 1975. pap. text ed. 18.95 (ISBN 0-13-755769-8). P-H.
Kramer, Rita. In Defense of the Family: Raising Children in America Today. 1983. 15.50 (ISBN 0-465-03215-X). Basic.
Kramer, Rita W. Marriage Happens to the Nicest People. (Illus.). 128p. 1983. 6.00 (ISBN 0-682-49949-8). Exposition.
--Peanut Butter on My Pillow. LC 80-12777. 144p. 1980. pap. 4.95 (ISBN 0-8407-5724-7). Nelson.
Kramer, Samuel N. Cradle of Civilization. LC 67-29528. (Great Ages of Man). (Illus.). (gr. 6 up). 1967. PLB 19.96 (ISBN 0-8094-0378-1, Pub. by Time-Life). Silver.
--From the Poetry of Sumer: Creation, Glorification, Adoration. LC 78-57321. 1979. 17.50x (ISBN 0-520-03703-0). U of Cal Pr.
--Sumerians: Their History, Culture & Character. LC 63-11398. (Illus.). 1971. pap. 8.95 (ISBN 0-226-45238-7, P422, Phoen). U of Chicago Pr.
Kramer, Samuel N., jt. auth. see Wolkstein, Diane.
Kramer, Sidney. A History of Stone & Kimball & Herbert S. Stone & Company: With a Bibliography of Their Publications, 1893-1905. 1940. limited, boxed & signed 100.00x (ISBN 0-686-17403-8). R S Barnes.
Kramer, T., jt. ed. see Spiertz, J. H.
Kramer, Victor A. James Agee. LC 74-23882. (U. S. Authors Ser.: No. 252). 1975. lib. bdg. 9.95 o.p. (ISBN 0-8057-0006-4, Twayne). G K Hall.
Kramer, Victor A. & Bailey, Patricia A. Andrew Lytle, Walker Percy, Peter Taylor: A Reference Guide. 1983. lib. bdg. 39.00 (ISBN 0-8161-8399-6, Hall Reference). G K Hall.
Kramer, William. Hans Burkhardt: Artist & Patron of the Arts. (Santa Susana Pr California Masters Ser.: No. 6). (Illus.). 1983. 150.00 (ISBN 0-937048-34-8). CSUN.
Kramer, Wolfgang. Tortula Hedw. Sect. Rurales De Not. Pottiaceae, Musci in der Oestlichen Holarktis. (Bryophytorum Bibliotheca: 21). 250p. (Ger.). 1980. lib. bdg. 24.00x (ISBN 3-7682-1266-1). Lubrecht & Cramer.
Kramerae, Cheris. Women & Men Speaking. (Orig.). 1981. pap. text ed. 13.95 (ISBN 0-88377-179-9). Newbury Hse.
Kramer-Lampher, A. H. Baby Born in a Stable. LC 65-15145. (Arch Bks: Set. 2). 1965. pap. 0.89 (ISBN 0-570-06013-3, 59-1118). Concordia.
Kramers. Dutch-English, English-Dutch Dictionary, 2 vols. 36th, rev., enl. ed. 1978. 35.00 (ISBN 9-0100-2541-1). Heinman.
Kramlinger, Thomas, jt. auth. see Zemke, Ron.
Krammer, Arnold. Nazi Prisoners of War in America. LC 78-24155. (Illus.). 1979. 21.95 (ISBN 0-8128-2571-3). Stein & Day.
Krammer, Kurt. Valve Morphology in the Genus Cymbella: C. A. Agardh. Helmcke, J. G. & Krammer, Kurt, eds. (Micromorphology of Datom Valves Ser.). (Illus.). 300p. (Orig.). 1982. lib. bdg. 67.50x (ISBN 3-7682-1333-1). Lubrecht & Cramer.
Krammer, Kurt, ed. see Krammer, Kurt.
Kramnick, Isaac & Watkins, Frederick. Age of Ideology: Political Thought 1750 to the Present. 2nd ed. (Foundations of Modern Political Science Ser.). 1979. pap. 9.95 ref. ed. (ISBN 0-13-018499-3). P-H.
Kramnick, Miriam, ed. see Wollstonecraft, Mary.
Kramp, Harry & Sullivan, George. Swimming. LC 70-125024. (All-Star Sports Bks). (Illus.). (gr. 5 up). 1971. 3.95 o.s.i. (ISBN 0-695-40187-4); lib. ed. 5.97 o.s.i. (ISBN 0-685-00936-X). Follett.
Krampen, Martin. Meaning in the Urban Environment. (Research in Planning & Design Ser.). 365p. 1979. 33.00x (ISBN 0-85086-067-9, Pub. by Pion England). Methuen Inc.
Krampitz, Sydney D., jt. auth. see Manfreda, Marguerite L.
Krane, Ronald E. International Labor Migration in Europe. LC 78-19746. (Praeger Special Studies). 1979. 28.95 (ISBN 0-03-022361-X). Praeger.
Krane, Stephen M., jt. ed. see Avioli, Louis V.
Krane, Susan. The Paintings of Joe Zucker Nineteen Sixty-Nine to Nineteen Eighty-Two. LC 82-72220. (Illus.). 1982. pap. 12.00 (ISBN 0-914782-45-2). Buffalo Acad.
Kranendonk, Jan Van see Van Kranendonk, Jan.
Kranendonk, Van see Van Kranendonk.
Kranes, Judith E. The Hidden Handicap. 1980. 10.95 o.p. (ISBN 0-671-24242-3). S&S.
Kranich, Roger, jt. auth. see Messec, Jerry.
Kranich, Roger E. & Messec, Jerry L. Visual Data. 1979. pap. 2.75 (ISBN 0-88323-153-0, 243); answer key 1.00x (ISBN 0-88323-157-3). Richards Pub.
Kranich, Robert E. & Messec, Jerry L. Learning to Use Maps. (Illus.). 1978. text ed. write for info. (ISBN 0-88323-149-2, 236); 2.75x (ISBN 0-88323-150-6); teacher's answer key free (239). Richards Pub.
Krannich, Caryl R., et al. Interview with Success. 1981. write for info. (ISBN 0-940010-02-X). Impact VA.
Krannich, Ronald L. Cutback Management: Improving the Productivity of Scarce Resources. 200p. (Orig.). 1983. pap. 14.95 (ISBN 0-942710-03-7). Impact VA.
--Mayors & Managers in Thailand: The Struggle for Political Life in Administrative Settings. LC 78-13452. (Papers in International Studies: South Asia: No. 51). (Illus.). 1978. pap. 9.00x (ISBN 0-89680-073-3, Ohio U Ctr Intl). Ohio U Pr.
--Re-Careering in Turbulent Times: Skills & Strategies for Success in Today's Job Market. LC 82-82720. 200p. (Orig.). 1983. pap. 7.95 (ISBN 0-942710-02-9). Impact Va.
Krannich, Ronald L. & Banis, William J. High Impact Resumes & Letters. (Illus.). 146p. (Orig.). 1982. pap. 7.95 (ISBN 0-942710-04-5). Impact VA.
--Job Targeting for the Public Service: The Guide to Federal, State, & Local Government Employment. 1981. write for info. (ISBN 0-940010-05-4). Impact VA.
--Re-Careering in Turbulent Times: The Guide to Career Management & Change for the 80's. 1981. write for info. (ISBN 0-940010-04-6). Impact VA.
Krannich, Ronald L. & Bants, William J. Moving Out of Education: The Educator's Guide To Career Management & Change. 264p. 1981. 14.95 (ISBN 0-940010-00-3). Impact VA.
Krannich, Ronald L., jt. auth. see Banis, William J.
Krans, J. M., jt. ed. see Hessel, L. W.
Krant, Melvin J. Dying & Dignity: The Meaning & Control of a Personal Death. 164p. 1974. photocopy ed. spiral 16.75x (ISBN 0-398-02995-4); pap. 8.50 (ISBN 0-398-02996-2). C C Thomas.
Krantz, David S. & Baum, Andrew. Handbook of Psychology & Health: Cardiovascular Disorders & Behavior, No.3. 400p. 1983. text ed. write for info. (ISBN 0-89859-185-6). L Erlbaum Assocs.
Krantz, Judith. Princess Daisy. 480p. 1980. 12.95 o.p. (ISBN 0-517-53606-4). Crown.
Krantz, Les. The Texas Art Review. 1982. 35.00 (ISBN 0-87201-018-X). Gulf Pub.
Krantz, Les, ed. The New York Art Review: An Art Explorer's Guide. LC 82-73113. (Illus.). 192p. 1983. 25.95 (ISBN 0-02-566630-4); pap. 12.95 (ISBN 0-02-000700-0). Macmillan.
Krantz, Lucretia, jt. auth. see Zim, Herbert S.
Krantz, Sheldon, jt. auth. see Bittner, Egon.
Krantz, Sheldon, et al. Right to Counsel in Criminal Cases: The Mandate of Argersinger V Hamlin. LC 75-14111. 1976. prof ref 35.00x (ISBN 0-88410-213-0). Ballinger Pub.
Krantz, Steve. Skycastle. 304p. 1981. 13.95x (ISBN 0-02-566690-8). Macmillan.
--Skycastle. 1983. pap. 3.50 (ISBN 0-440-17601-8). Dell.
Krantz, Steven G. Function Theory of Several Complex Variables: Pure & Applied Mathematics. LC 81-10447. (Pure & Applied Mathematics: A W-I Ser. of Texts, Monographs, Tracts). 437p. 1982. 39.95x (ISBN 0-471-09324-6, Pub. by Wiley-Interscience). Wiley.
Krantzler, Mel. Creative Divorce. 1975. pap. 2.95 (ISBN 0-451-11239-3, AE1239, Sig). NAL.
Kranz, Henry, ed. Open Stock. 1980. 3.00 (ISBN 0-942582-02-0). Erie St Pr.
Kranz, Henry, ed. see Lohman, Lou & Saffar, Ruth E.
Kranz, J., et al, eds. Diseases, Pests & Weeds in Tropical Crops. LC 78-6212. 666p. 1978. 95.95x (ISBN 0-471-99667-X, Pub. by Wiley-Interscience). Wiley.
Kranz, Kurt. Early Form Sequences: 1927-1932. LC 75-27384. 1975. 50.00 (ISBN 0-262-11060-1). MIT Pr.
Kranz, Sheldon, et al. Personal & Impersonal: Six Aesthetic Realists. LC 59-10629. (Orig.). 1959. 3.00 o.p. (ISBN 0-910492-06-9); pap. 1.45 (ISBN 0-910492-21-2). Definition.
--The H Persuasion: How Persons Have Permanently Changed from Homosexuality Through the Study of Aesthetic Realism with Eli Siegel. LC 70-161981. 1971. 4.95 o.p. (ISBN 0-910492-14-X); pap. 2.50 (ISBN 0-910492-26-3). Definition.
Kranzberg, Melvin. Technology & Culture. (Orig.). 1975. pap. 4.95 o.p. (ISBN 0-452-00426-8, F426, Mer). NAL.
Kranzberg, Melvin & Gies, Joseph. By the Sweat of Thy Brow: Work in the Western World. 224p. 1975. 6.95 o.p. (ISBN 0-399-11312-6). Putnam Pub Group.
Kranzberg, Melvin, ed. Ethics in an Age of Pervasive Technology. 220p. 1980. lib. bdg. 27.00 (ISBN 0-89158-686-5); text ed. 15.00. Westview.
Kranzberg, Melvin & Pursell, Carroll W., Jr., eds. Technology in Western Civilization, 2 vols. Incl. Vol. 1. The Emergence of Modern Industrial Society: Earliest Times to 1900. text ed. 22.50x (ISBN 0-19-500938-X); study guide 0.75x (ISBN 0-685-24431-8); Vol. 2. Technology in the Twentieth Century. text ed. 22.50x (ISBN 0-19-500939-8); study guide free (ISBN 0-19-501028-0). (YA) (gr. 9up). 1967. Oxford U Pr.
Kranzberg, Melvin, et al, eds. Energy & the Way We Live. LC 79-25054. (Illus.). 520p. 1980. lib. bdg. 16.00x (ISBN 0-87835-092-6); pap. text ed. 10.95x (ISBN 0-87835-084-5); study guide 3.95x (ISBN 0-87835-089-6); pap. text bd. with study guide 14.95x (ISBN 0-87835-090-X); article bk. 4.95x (ISBN 0-686-96683-X); source bk. 4.95x (ISBN 0-87835-091-8). Boyd & Fraser.
Krapf, Norbert. Lines Drawn from Durer. 48p. 1981. 25.00x (ISBN 0-915408-27-9); pap. 4.95 (ISBN 0-686-96650-3). Ally Pr.
Krapin, Louis. The Poetry of Life. LC 78-65996. 1979. 4.95 o.p. (ISBN 0-533-04134-1). Vantage.
Krappe, A. Haggerty. Raymond Foulche-Delbosc. (Illus.). 1930. 0.25 (ISBN 0-87535-026-7). Hispanic Soc.
Krappe, Alexander H., tr. see Grimm Brothers.

Krar, S. F. & Oswald, J. W. Drilling Technology. LC 73-13486. 1977. pap. text ed. 9.60 (ISBN 0-8273-0210-X). Delmar.
--Grinding Technology. LC 72-7935. 1974. pap. text ed. 14.20 (ISBN 0-8273-0208-8); instructor's guide 3.25 (ISBN 0-8273-0209-6). Delmar.
--Machine Tool Operations Visutext. 208p. 1983. text ed. write for info. (ISBN 0-07-035431-6). McGraw.
--Turning Technology: Engine & Turret Lathes. LC 78-153723. 1971. pap. text ed. 14.20 (ISBN 0-8273-0206-1); instructor's guide 3.25 (ISBN 0-8273-0207-X). Delmar.
Krar, S. F., et al. Entrenamiento En el Taller Mecanico. 1974. 9.95 o.p. (ISBN 0-07-091612-8, G). McGraw.
Krar, Stephen F., et al. Technology of Machine Tools. 2nd ed. LC 77-3663. (Illus.). 1977. text ed. 24.95 (ISBN 0-07-035383-2, G); answer key to workbook 4.50 (ISBN 0-07-035384-0). McGraw.
Krar, Steve F. Machine Tool Operations. LC 81-185871. (Illus.). 400p. (gr. 9-12). 1983. 18.95x (ISBN 0-07-035430-8); instr.'s manual 4.00 (ISBN 0-07-035432-4). McGraw.
Krasavina, L. K., jt. auth. see Gollerbach, M.
Krase, Jerome. Self & Community in the City. LC 81-1430. (Illus.). 232p. (Orig.). 1982. lib. bdg. 23.00 (ISBN 0-8191-2283-1); pap. text ed. 10.75 (ISBN 0-8191-2284-X). U Pr of Amer.
Krashen, Stephen D., jt. ed. see Scarcella, Robin C.
Krashen, Stephen D., et al, eds. Child-Adult Differences in Second Language Acquisition. (Issues in Second Language Research Ser.). 336p. 1982. pap. text ed. 17.95 (ISBN 0-88377-206-X). Newbury Hse.
Krasilovsky, M. William, jt. auth. see Shemel, Sidney.
Krasilovsky, Phyllis. Man Who Didn't Wash His Dishes. (Illus.). (gr. k-3). 1950. pap. 1.95 o.p. (ISBN 0-385-13343-X, Zephyr). Doubleday.
--The Man Who Entered a Contest. LC 79-3112. (Reading-on-My-Own Ser.). (Illus.). 64p. (gr. 2). 1980. 6.95a o.p. (ISBN 0-385-13351-0); PLB 6.95a (ISBN 0-385-13352-9). Doubleday.
--Very Little Boy. LC 62-7276. (gr. k-1). pap. 7.95 o.p. (ISBN 0-385-02756-7). Doubleday.
--Very Little Boy. LC 62-7276. (gr. k-1). pap. 1.95 o.p. (ISBN 0-385-00947-X, Zephyr). Doubleday.
Krasinski, Zygmunt. Iridion. Noyes, George R., ed. Noyes, Florence, tr. from Pol. LC 74-30841. 281p. 1975. Repr. of 1927 ed. lib. bdg. 18.25x (ISBN 0-8371-7937-8, KRIR). Greenwood.
Kraske, Robert. America the Beautiful: Stories of Patriotic Songs. LC 73-183845. (American Democracy Ser.). (Illus.). 96p. (gr. 3-6). 1972. PLB 7.12 (ISBN 0-8116-6506-2). Garrard.
Krasner, Lee, intro. by. Lee Krasner, Solstice. (Illus.). 24p. (Orig.). 1981. pap. 9.00 (ISBN 0-938608-02-9). Pace Gallery Pubns.
Krasner, Leonard, jt. auth. see Ullmann, Leonard.
Krasner, Stephen, ed. see Young, Oran R.
Krasner, Stephen D., ed. International Regimes. (Political Economy Ser.). 384p. 1983. text ed. 29.95x (ISBN 0-8014-1550-0); pap. text ed. 9.95x (ISBN 0-8014-9250-5). Cornell U Pr.
Krasnoselskiy, M. A., et al. Plane Vector Fields. 1966. 41.50 (ISBN 0-12-425950-2). Acad Pr.
Krasnov. Aerodynamics of Bodies of Revolution: A Rand Corporation Research Study. 1970. 17.50 (ISBN 0-444-00076-3). Elsevier.
Krasnov, Mikhail M. Microsurgery of the Glaucomas. LC 78-26221. (Illus.). 184p. 1979. text ed. 44.50 o.p. (ISBN 0-8016-2743-5). Mosby.
Krasnow, Erwin G. & Longley, Lawrence D. The Politics of Broadcast Regulation. 3rd ed. LC 81-51850. 304p. 1982. text ed. 16.95 (ISBN 0-312-62653-3); pap. text ed. 8.95 (ISBN 0-312-62654-1). St Martin.
Kraszewski, Andreej. Microwave Gas Discharge Devices. Benson, F. A., ed. (Illus.). 1969. 21.25x o.p. (ISBN 0-592-02780-5). Transatlantic.
Krat, Siegfried J. & Boltax, Robert S. Is Surgery Necessary? 1982. pap. 3.50 (ISBN 0-451-11741-7, AE1741, Sig). NAL.
Kratchman, Stanley H., jt. auth. see Benjamin, James J.
Kratcoski, L., jt. auth. see Kratcoski, P.
Kratcoski, P. & Kratcoski, L. Juvenile Delinquency. 1979. 21.95 (ISBN 0-13-514281-4). P-H.
Kratcoski, Peter C. & Walker, Donald B. Criminal Justice in America: Process & Issues. 1978. text ed. 18.95x o.p. (ISBN 0-673-15051-8). Scott F.
Kratins, Ojars. The Dream of Chivalry: A Study of Chretien De Troyee's Yvan & Hartmann Von Aue's Iwein. LC 81-43669. 252p. (Orig.). 1982. lib. bdg. 23.25 (ISBN 0-8191-2520-2); pap. text ed. 10.75 (ISBN 0-8191-2521-0). U Pr of Amer.
Kratochwil, Friedrich V. International Order & Foreign Policy: A Theoretical Sketch of Post-War Internaional Politics. LC 77-94107. (Westview Replica Edition Ser.). 1978. lib. bdg. 32.50 o.p. (ISBN 0-89158-065-4). Westview.
Kratochwil, Friedrich V., jt. ed. see Falk, Richard.
Kratochwill, A., jt. ed. see Kurjak, A.
Kratochwill, Thomas R., jt. auth. see Morris, Richard J.
Kratochwill, Thomas R., ed. Advances in School Psychology, Vol.3. 400p. 1983. text ed. write for info. (ISBN 0-89859-280-1). L Erlbaum Assocs.
Kratochwill, Thomas R., jt. ed. see Morris, Richard J.
Kratovil, Robert & Werner, Raymond J. Real Estate Law. 8th ed. 640p. 1983. 31.95 (ISBN 0-13-763292-4); student ed. 24.95 (ISBN 0-686-82022-3). P-H.
Kratzig, Guillermo, tr. see Greenway, Rogelio S.
Kratzig, Guillermo, tr. see Haney, David.
Kratzig, Guillermo, tr. see Neighbour, Ralph.
Kratzmann, G. Anglo-Scottish Literary Relations: Fourteen Thirty to Fifteen Fifty. LC 78-74537. 1980. 37.50 (ISBN 0-521-22665-1). Cambridge U Pr.
Kratzsch, H. Mining Subsidence Engineering. Fleming, R. F., tr. from Ger. (Illus.). 580p. 1983. 59.00 (ISBN 0-387-11930-2). Springer-Verlag.
Kraulis, J. A., ed. Canada: A Landscape Portrait. 128p. 1983. 27.50 (ISBN 0-295-96004-3, Pub. by Hurtig Pubs). U of Wash Pr.
Kraus & Rollain. Exploring Electricity & Electronics with the Electrical Team. LC 76-3947. (Illus.). 1979. pap. 12.40 (ISBN 0-8273-1166-4); research manual 4.80 (ISBN 0-8273-1167-2); instructor's guide 3.25 (ISBN 0-8273-1168-0). Delmar.
Kraus, Alan. Basic College Issues. 1968. pap. text ed. 4.95 (ISBN 0-685-77201-2). Phila Bk Co.
Kraus, Barbara. Barbara Kraus Calories & Carbohydrates. 1979. pap. 6.95 (ISBN 0-452-25388-8, Z5388, Plume). NAL.
--Barbara Kraus Guide to Calories: 1981 Edition. (Orig.). 1981. pap. 1.75 o.p. (ISBN 0-451-09580-4, E9580, Sig). NAL.
--Barbara Kraus Guide to Calories: 1982 Edition. (Orig.). 1982. pap. 1.95 o.p. (ISBN 0-451-11287-3, AJ1287, Sig). NAL.
--Barbara Kraus Guide to Carbohydrates: 1982 Edition. (Orig.). 1982. pap. 1.95 o.p. (ISBN 0-451-11288-1, AJ1288, Sig). NAL.
--Barbara Kraus Guide to Carbohydrates: 1981 Edition. (Orig.). 1981. pap. 1.75 o.p. (ISBN 0-451-09581-2, E9581, Sig). NAL.
--Barbara Kraus Guide to Fiber in Food. (Orig.). 1975. pap. 1.75 o.p. (ISBN 0-451-07857-8, E7857, Sig). NAL.
--Barbara Kraus Guide to Fibers in Foods. 1980. 7.95 o.p. (ISBN 0-453-00368-0, H368). NAL.
--Barbara Kraus 1980 Calorie Guide to Brand Names & Basic Foods. (Orig.). 1980. pap. 1.50 o.p. (ISBN 0-451-09032-2, W9032, Sig). NAL.
--Barbara Kraus 1980 Carbohydrate Guide to Brand Names & Basic Foods. (Orig.). 1980. pap. 1.50 o.p. (ISBN 0-451-09033-0, W9033, Sig). NAL.
--The Basic Food & Brand-Name Calorie Counter. 128p. 1974. pap. 2.95 (ISBN 0-448-11684-7, G&D). Putnam Pub Group.
--The Basic Food & Brand-Name Carbohydrate Counter. 128p. 1974. pap. 2.95 (ISBN 0-448-11685-5, G&D). Putnam Pub Group.
--Calories & Carbohydrates. 4th, rev. ed. 1981. pap. 6.95 (ISBN 0-452-25388-6, Z5388, Plume). NAL.
--Calories & Carbohydrates: A Dictionary of 7500 Brand Names & Basic Foods with Their Caloric & Carbohydrate Count. rev. ed. 384p. 1975. pap. 3.50 (ISBN 0-451-08544-2, E9774, Sig). NAL.
--Dictionary of Sodium, Fats & Cholesterol. LC 72-90848. (Illus.). 256p. 1974. 9.95 o.p. (ISBN 0-448-01371-1); pap. 3.95 o.p. (ISBN 0-448-12298-7, G&D). Putnam Pub Group.
--The Dictionary of Sodium, Fats, & Cholesterol. (Illus.). 384p. Date not set. pap. price not set (ISBN 0-448-12298-7, G&D). Putnam Pub Group.
Kraus, Charles & Kraus, Linda. Charles the Clown's Guide to Children's Parties. LC 82-83062. 300p. (Orig.). 1983. pap. 9.95 (ISBN 0-915190-37-0). Jalmar Pr.
Kraus, Edward H. & Slawson, Chester B. Gems & Gem Materials. 5th ed. (Illus.). 1947. text ed. 34.00 o.p. (ISBN 0-07-035361-1, C). McGraw.
Kraus, Ernest A. Pathways Back to the Community. LC 71-100099. 1970. Set. pap. 18.00 (ISBN 0-8261-1093-2); 3.95 (ISBN 0-686-66539-2). Springer Pub.
Kraus, Frederick T. & Friedrich, Ernst. Vulval Diseases. LC 77-6108. (Illus.). 1978. text ed. 80.00 text & slides (ISBN 0-89189-032-7, 15-1-024-00). Am Soc Clinical.
Kraus, H. P. A Rare Book Saga: The Autobiography of H. P. Kraus. LC 77-28643. (Illus.). 1978. 15.00 o.p. (ISBN 0-399-12064-5). Putnam Pub Group.
Kraus, John D. Antennas. (Electrical & Electronic Engineering Ser.). 1950. text ed. 42.50 (ISBN 0-07-035410-3, C). McGraw.
--Electromagnetics. 2nd ed. (Electrical & Electronic Engineering Ser.). (Illus.). 848p. 1973. text ed. 35.00 (ISBN 0-07-035396-4, C); instructor's manual 25.00 (ISBN 0-07-035397-2). McGraw.
Kraus, Linda, jt. auth. see Kraus, Charles.
Kraus, M. B. Development Without Aid: Growth, Poverty & Government. 256p. 1982. 17.95 (ISBN 0-07-035468-5). McGraw.
Kraus, Michael. The Atlantic Civilization: Eighteenth Century Origins. 345p. 1966. pap. 6.95x (ISBN 0-686-92637-4). Cornell U Pr.
Kraus, Milton N., ed. see Chemical Engineering Magazine.
Kraus, Oskar, ed. see Brentano, Franz.
Kraus, Philip E. Yesterday's Children: A Longitudinal Study of Children from Kindergarten into the Adult Years. LC 81-4751. 208p. 1981. Repr. of 1973 ed. lib. bdg. write for info. o.p. (ISBN 0-89874-311-7). Krieger.
Kraus, Richard. A Cotton & Cotton Goods in China. LC 78-22779. (The Modern Chinese Economy Ser.). 500p. 1980. lib. bdg. 50.00 o.s.i. (ISBN 0-8240-4276-X). Garland Pub.
--Recreation & Leisure in Modern Society. 2nd ed. LC 77-20705. 1978. text ed. 21.95x (ISBN 0-673-16200-1). Scott F.
Kraus, Richard & Charman, Sarah. A History of the Dance in Art & Education. 2nd ed. (Illus.). 432p. 1981. text ed. 20.95 (ISBN 0-13-390021-5). P-H.
Kraus, Richard & Scanlin, Margery. Introduction to Camp Counseling. (Illus.). 352p. 1983. 20.95 (ISBN 0-13-479188-6). P-H.
Kraus, Richard G. Recreation Leader's Handbook. (Health Education, Physical Education & Recreation Ser.). 1955. text ed. 22.00 o.p. (ISBN 0-07-035405-7, C). McGraw.
--Recreation Today: Program Planning & Leadership. 2d ed. LC 76-49059. (Illus.). 1977. text ed. 21.95x (ISBN 0-673-16201-X). Scott F.
Kraus, Richard G. & Curtis, Joseph E. Creative Management in Recreation & Parks. 3rd ed. LC 81-14099. (Illus.). 397p. 1982. pap. text ed. 19.95 (ISBN 0-8016-2745-1). Mosby.
Kraus, Robert. Animal Families. LC 80-51360. (Windmill Board Bks.). (Illus.). 16p. (ps). 1980. board book 3.50 o.p. (ISBN 0-671-41532-8, Pub. by Windmill). S&S.
--Bunya the Witch. LC 80-13252. (Illus.). 32p. (ps-2). 1980. pap. 3.95 o.p. (ISBN 0-671-96038-5, Pub. by Windmill). S&S.
--The Christmas Cookie Sprinkle Snitcher. LC 80-13641. (Illus.). 32p. (gr. k-3). 1980. pap. 4.50 o.p. (ISBN 0-671-41199-3, Pub. by Windmill). S&S.
--Daddy Long Ears. (Illus.). 32p. (ps-2). 1982. pap. 3.95 (ISBN 0-671-42582-X, Pub. by Windmill). S&S.
--The First Robin. (Illus.). 48p. (ps up). 1982. Repr. 3.95 (ISBN 0-671-44565-0). Windmill Bks.
--Good Night Little One. (Good Night Bks.). (Illus.). 32p. (ps-2). 1981. paper over board 3.50 o.p. (ISBN 0-671-41091-1, Pub. by Windmill). S&S.
--Good Night Richard Rabbit. (Illus.). 32p. (ps-2). 1981. paper over board 3.50 o.p. (ISBN 0-671-41090-3, Pub. by Windmill). S&S.
--Herby Is a Careless Driver. (Early Bloomer Bks.). (Illus.). 48p. (gr. 1-3). 1982. pap. 4.95 o.s.i. (ISBN 0-671-44570-7, Pub. by Windmill). S&S.
--Herman the Helper. LC 73-9319. (Illus.). 30p. (gr. 1 up). 1974. 3.95. Windmill Bks.
--Ivor the Biter. (Early Bloomer Bks.). (Illus.). 48p. (gr. 1-3). 1982. pap. 4.95 o.s.i. (ISBN 0-671-44470-0, Pub. by Windmill). S&S.
--Leo the Late Bloomer. abr. ed. LC 80-51357. (Windmill Board Bks.). (Illus.). 16p. (ps). 1980. board book 3.95 (Pub. by Windmill). S&S.
--Leo the Late Bloomer Bakes a Cake. LC 81-51112. (Puppet Pals Ser.). (Illus.). 14p. (ps up). pap. 4.95 o.p. (ISBN 0-671-43085-8). Windmill Bks.
--Milton the Early Riser. 2nd, abr. ed. LC 80-51358. (Windmill Board Bks.). (Illus.). 16p. (ps). 1980. 3.95 (ISBN 0-671-41203-5, Pub. by Windmill). S&S.
--Milton the Early Riser Takes a Trip. LC 81-51111. (Puppet Pals Ser.). (Illus.). 14p. (ps up). pap. 4.95 o.p. (ISBN 0-671-43088-2). Windmill Bks.
--Owliver the Actor Takes a Bow. LC 81-51110. (Puppet Pals Ser.). (Illus.). 14p. (ps up). pap. 4.95 o.p. (ISBN 0-671-43087-4). Windmill Bks.
--The Rabbit Brothers. (Illus.). 34p. 0.35 (ISBN 0-686-74883-2); discussion guide incl.; filmstrip 8.00 (ISBN 0-686-74884-0). ADL.
--Screamy Mimi. (Early Bloomer Bks.). (Illus.). 48p. (gr. 1-3). 1982. pap. 4.95 o.s.i. (ISBN 0-671-44471-9, Pub. by Windmill). S&S.
--See the Moon: A Glow-in-the-Dark Book. LC 80-51361. (Windmill Board Bks.). (Illus.). 8p. (ps). 1980. 3.95 o.p. (ISBN 0-671-41206-X, Pub. by Windmill). S&S.
--Shaggy Fur Face. (Illus.). 32p. (ps-3). pap. 3.95 o.p. (ISBN 0-671-41358-9). Windmill Bks.
--Temper Tantrum Pam. (Early Bloomer Bks.). (Illus.). 48p. (gr. 1-3). 1982. pap. 4.95 (ISBN 0-671-42303-7, Pub. by Windmill). S&S.
Kraus, Robert, ed. see Smith, Dennis.
Kraus, Robert, ed. see Smith, Wendy.
Kraus, Robert, et al. Another Mouse to Feed. LC 78-21259. (Illus.). 32p. (gr. k-4). 1980. PLB 8.95 o.p. (ISBN 0-671-96076-8). Windmill Bks.
Kraus, Ronnie. Goofy Visits the Hospital. LC 79-91868. (Illus.). 48p. (gr. 1-3). 1981. 4.95 (ISBN 0-448-16583-X, G&D); PLB 9.30 (ISBN 0-448-13642-2). Putnam Pub Group.
Kraus, Sidney & Davis, Dennis. The Effects of Mass Communication on Political Behavior. LC 76-3480. (Illus.). 1976. 19.50x (ISBN 0-271-01226-9); pap. 9.95x (ISBN 0-271-00501-7). Pa St U Pr.
Kraus, William. Let the People Decide. Jennings, Mary L., ed. LC 82-73285. 224p. 1983. 13.95 (ISBN 0-89803-119-2). Caroline Hse.
Kraus, William A. Collaboration in Organizations: Alternatives to Hierarchy. LC 80-11291. 274p. 1980. text ed. 29.95 (ISBN 0-87705-491-6). Human Sci Pr.
Krause, Chester L. Guidebook of Franklin Mint Issues: 1980. (Illus.). 304p. 1980. pap. 11.50 o.s.i. (ISBN 0-87341-053-X). Krause Pubns.
Krause, Chester L. & Lemke, Robert F. Standard Catalog of United States Paper Money. LC 81-81876. (Illus.). 208p. (Orig.). 1981. pap. 14.50 o.s.i. (ISBN 0-87341-064-5). Krause Pubns.
--Standard Catalog of United States Paper Money. 2nd ed. LC 81-81976. (Illus.). 1982. pap. 14.50 (ISBN 0-87341-074-2). Krause Pubns.
Krause, Claire S. Genealogy: Your Past Revisited. Smith, Linda H., ed. 1980. pap. 4.95 (ISBN 0-936386-08-8). Creative Learning.
Krause, Corinne. How to up Your Potassium. 5.95 o.p. (ISBN 0-9604104-0-6). Green Hill.
Krause, D., jt. ed. see Kaufmann, W.
Krause, Daniel R. Home Bittersweet Home: Old Age Institutions in America. (Illus.). 168p. 1983. 14.95x (ISBN 0-398-04749-9). C C Thomas.
Krause, E., ed. Eighth International Conference on Numerical Methods in Fluid Dynamics, Aachen, FRG, 1982: Proceedings. (Lecture Notes in Physics Ser.: Vol. 170). 569p. 1983. pap. 27.20 (ISBN 0-387-11948-5). Springer-Verlag.
Krause, E., jt. ed. see Fernholz, H.
Krause, Elliot A. Power & Illness: The Political Sociology of Health & Medical Care. LC 77-317. 1977. text ed. 22.00 (ISBN 0-444-99037-2); pap. 13.50 (ISBN 0-444-99056-9). Elsevier.
Krause, Emil. Book of Cons. LC 80-68663. (Illus.). 96p. (Orig.). 1980. pap. 4.95 o.p. (ISBN 0-89708-029-7). And Bks.
Krause, Engelbert. Die Gegenseitigen Unterhalltsanspruche Zwichen Eltern und Kindern In der Deutschen Privatrechtsgeschichte. vi, 237p. (Ger.). 1982. write for info. (ISBN 3-8204-7123-5). P Lang Pubs.
Krause, Eugene, jt. auth. see Brumfiel, Charles.
Krause, Eugene F. Mathematics for Elementary Teachers. (Illus.). 1978. text ed. 23.95 (ISBN 0-13-562702-8). P-H.
Krause, Frank, jt. auth. see Dimick, Kenneth.
Krause, Laurence, jt. ed. see Nast, Lenora H.
Krause, Laurence B., jt. ed. see Hong, Wontack.
Krause, Lawrence B. Sequel to Bretton Woods: A Proposal to Reform the World Monetary System. 50p. 1971. pap. 3.95 (ISBN 0-8157-5035-8). Brookings.
--U. S. Economic Policy toward the Association of Southeast Asian Nations: Meeting the Japaneses Challenge. LC 82-9656. 1982. 12.95 (ISBN 0-8157-5026-9); pap. 5.95 (ISBN 0-8157-5025-0). Brookings.
Krause, Lawrence B. & Salant, Walter S., eds. Worldwide Inflation: Theory & Recent Experience. LC 76-51580. 1976. 28.95 (ISBN 0-8157-5030-7); pap. 14.95 (ISBN 0-8157-5029-3). Brookings.
Krause, Lawrence B. & Sekiguchi, Sueo, eds. Economic Interaction in the Pacific Basin. 1980. 16.95 (ISBN 0-8157-5028-5); pap. 6.95 (ISBN 0-8157-5027-7). Brookings.
Krause, Lawrence B., jt. ed. see Bergsten, A. Fred.
Krause, Lawrence B., jt. ed. see Caves, Richard E.
Krause, Marie V. & Mahan, Kathleen L. Food, Nutrition & Diet Therapy. 6th ed. LC 77-11341. 1979. text ed. 24.50 (ISBN 0-7216-5513-0). Saunders.
Krause, Martin F., Jr. Master Drawings & Watercolors From the Collection of the Indianapolis Museum of Art. LC 82-84037. (Centennial Catalogue Ser.). (Illus.). 256p. (Orig.). 1983. 30.00x (ISBN 0-936260-06-8); pap. 20.00x (ISBN 0-936260-07-6). Ind Mus Art.
Krause, Peter & Shull, Henry. Complete Guide to Cibachrome Printing, Vol. 14. 160p. 1982. pap. 14.95 (ISBN 0-89586-176-3). H P Bks.
Krause, Richard M., jt. ed. see Haber, Edgar.
Krause, Steven A. Wine from the Wilds: Using Wild Trees, Herbs, & Flowers in Home Winemaking. LC 81-16685. (Illus.). 192p. 1982. 9.95 (ISBN 0-686-97298-8). Stackpole.
Krause, Sydney, ed. see Brown, Charles B.
Krause, Tina. I Am As Dark As Your Smile November. Fleming, Farold, ed. (Black Willow Poetry Chapbook Ser.). (Orig.). 1982. pap. 3.00 (ISBN 0-910047-01-4). Black Willow.
Krause, William J. & Cutts, J. Harry. Concise Text of Histology. (Illus.). 412p. 1981. soft cover 19.50 (ISBN 0-683-04784-1, 4784-1). Williams & Wilkins.
Kraushaar, James M., jt. auth. see Sebesta, Robert W.
Krauskopf, Joan M. Advocacy for the Aging. LC 82-23729. (Handbook Ser.). 603p. 1983. text ed. write for info. (ISBN 0-314-72235-1). West Pub.
Krauskopf, K. B., jt. auth. see Maurer, Robert.
Krauskopf, Konrad B. Introduction to Geochemistry. (Illus.). 1967. text ed. 23.00 o.p. (ISBN 0-07-035443-X, C). McGraw.
--Introduction to Geochemistry. 2nd ed. (International Earth & Planetary Sciences Ser.). (Illus.). 1979. text ed. 38.50 (ISBN 0-07-035447-2, C). McGraw.
Krauskopf, Konrad B. & Beiser, Arthur. Fundamentals of Physical Science. 6th ed. LC 76-152006. (Illus.). 1971. text ed. 26.95 (ISBN 0-07-035440-5, C); instructor's manual 15.00 (ISBN 0-07-035441-3); study guide by Beiser 12.95 (ISBN 0-07-004342-6). McGraw.

--The Physical Universe. 3rd ed. 736p. 1973. text ed. 16.50 o.p. (ISBN 0-07-035459-6, C); study guide 7.50 o.p. (ISBN 0-07-004353-1); 1.50 o.p. instructor's manual (ISBN 0-07-004358-2). McGraw.
--The Physical Universe. 4th ed. (Illus.). 1979. text ed. 27.00 (ISBN 0-07-035460-X, C); instr.'s manual 15.00 (ISBN 0-07-035464-2). McGraw.
Krauskopf, Konrad B., jt. auth. see Beiser, Arthur.
Kraus-Machiw, Ellen & O'Connor, G. Richard. Uveitis-Pathophysiology & Therapy. (Illus.). 144p. 1983. write for info. (ISBN 0-86577-073-5). Thieme-Stratton.
Krauss, Bob, jt. ed. see McGrath, Edward.
Krauss, Ellis S. Japanese Radicals Revisited: Student Protest in Postwar Japan. LC 73-78546. 1974. 29.75x (ISBN 0-520-02467-2). U of Cal Pr.
Krauss, George. Principles of Heat Treatment of Steel. 1980. 62.00 (ISBN 0-87170-100-6). ASM.
Krauss, H. L. & Bostian, C. W. Solid State Radio Engineering. 534p. 1980. 33.95 (ISBN 0-471-03018-X). Wiley.
Krauss, Henning & Wolff, Reinhold. Psychoanalytische Literaturwissenschaft und Literatursoziologie. 253p. (Ger.). 1982. write for info. (ISBN 3-8204-6211-2). P Lang Pubs.
Krauss, Leonard I. & MacGahar, Aileen. Computer Fraud & Countermeasures. (Illus.). 1979. ref. ed. 38.95 (ISBN 0-13-164772-5). P-H.
Krauss, Robert M., jt. auth. see Deutsch, Morton.
Krauss, Robert M., intro. by see Heider, Fritz.
Krauss, Ronnie. Donald & His Nephews Visit the Doctor. (Illus.). 48p. 1980. 4.95 (ISBN 0-448-16584-8, G&D); PLB 9.30 (ISBN 0-448-13641-4). Putnam Pub Group.
--Mickey Visits the Dentist. (Illus.). 48p. (gr. k-4). 1980. PLB 9.30 (ISBN 0-448-13640-6, G&D); text ed. 4.95 (ISBN 0-448-16582-1). Putnam Pub Group.
--Mickey's Question & Answer Book. LC 79-50667. (Illus.). 1979. 5.95 (ISBN 0-448-16565-1, G&D). Putnam Pub Group.
--Visit to the Dentist. LC 79-55010. (Illus.). (gr. k-4). 1980. pap. cancelled (ISBN 0-448-16582-1, G&D). Putnam Pub Group.
Krauss, Rosalind E. Terminal Iron Works: The Sculpture of David Smith. (Illus.). 1972. 17.50x (ISBN 0-262-11057-1); pap. 8.95 (ISBN 0-262-61032-9). MIT Pr.
Krauss, Ruth. Birthday Party. (Illus.). (gr. k-3). 1957. 7.64i (ISBN 0-06-023329-X, HarpJ); PLB 8.89 (ISBN 0-06-023330-3). Har-Row.
--Charlotte & the White Horse. LC 55-8819. (gr. k-3). 1955. 2.95 o.p. (ISBN 0-06-023360-5, HarpJ); PLB 7.89 (ISBN 0-06-023361-3). Har-Row.
--Growing Story. LC 47-30688. (Illus.). (gr. k-3). 1947. 8.95 (ISBN 0-06-023380-X, HarpJ); PLB 9.89 o.p. (ISBN 0-06-023381-8). Har-Row.
--The Happy Egg. LC 72-186887. (A Lead-off Bk). (Illus.). 32p. (ps-1). 1972. cancelled 1.95 o.p. (ISBN 0-87955-101-1); PLB 1.99 o.p. (ISBN 0-87955-701-X). O'Hara.
--I Want to Paint My Bathroom Blue. LC 56-8141. (gr. k-3). 1956. PLB 9.89 o.p. (ISBN 0-06-023425-3, HarpJ). Har-Row.
--I'll Be You & You Be Me. LC 54-9214. (Illus.). (gr. k-3). 1954. 8.95 (ISBN 0-06-023430-X, HarpJ); PLB 9.89 (ISBN 0-06-023431-8). Har-Row.
--Re-Examination of Freedom. (Illus.). 12p. 1981. pap. 20.00 o.p. (ISBN 0-915124-49-1). Toothpaste.
--Somebody Else's Nut Tree & Other Tales From Children. (Illus.). 48p. 1983. Repr. of 1958 ed. 6.50 (ISBN 0-913660-19-1). Magic Circle Pr.
--Very Special House. LC 53-7115. (Illus.). (ps-1). 1953. 9.95 o.p. (ISBN 0-06-023455-5, HarpJ); PLB 9.89 (ISBN 0-06-023456-3). Har-Row.
--When I Walk I Change the Earth. (Burning Deck Poetry Ser). 1978. pap. 3.00 (ISBN 0-930900-50-2); signed ed 20.00x (ISBN 0-930900-51-0). Burning Deck.
Krauss, S., et al. Encyclopedia of Medical Psychology. LC 75-33106. 1976. 29.95 (ISBN 0-407-00044-5). Butterworth.
Krausz, A. S. & Eyring, H. Deformation Kinetics. LC 75-12554. 398p. 1975. 49.95x (ISBN 0-471-24983-1, Pub. by Wiley-Interscience). Wiley.
Krausz, Ernest, ed. Sociology of the Kibbutz. (Studies of Israeli Society: Vol. II). 423p. 1983. 29.95 (ISBN 0-87855-455-6); pap. 9.95 (ISBN 0-87855-902-7). Transaction Bks.
Kraut, Alan M. The Huddled Masses: The Immigrant in American Society, 1880-1921. (The American History Ser.). (Illus.). 256p. (Orig.). 1982. pap. text ed. 8.95x (ISBN 0-88295-810-0). Harlan Davidson.
Kraut, Edgar A. Fundamentals of Mathematical Physics. LC 79-4467. 480p. 1979. Repr. of 1967 ed. lib. bdg. 23.50 (ISBN 0-88275-918-3). Krieger.
Krauth, Harald. Artistic Photography: Methods & Techniques. LC 75-42771. (Illus.). 1976. pap. 7.95 o.p. (ISBN 0-8174-2402-4, Amphoto). Watson-Guptill.
Krauth, Nigel. New Guinea Images in Australian Literature. LC 82-2812. (Portable Australian Authors Ser.). 279p. 1982. text ed. 22.50 (ISBN 0-7022-1960-6, AACR2); pap. 10.95 (ISBN 0-7022-1970-3). U of Queensland Pr.
Krautheimer, Richard. Three Christian Capitals: Topography & Politics. (A Volume in Una's Lectures). 168p. 27.50 (ISBN 0-520-04541-6). U of Cal Pr.
Krautkraemer, H., jt. auth. see Krautkraemer, J.
Krautkraemer, J. & Krautkraemer, H. Ultrasonic Testing of Materials. 3rd, rev. ed. Zenzinger, B. W., tr. from Ger. (Illus.). 79.50 (ISBN 0-387-11733-4). Springer-Verlag.
Kravette, Steve. Complete Relaxation. (Illus., Orig.). 1979. pap. 9.95 (ISBN 0-914918-14-1). Para Res.
Kravig, Jane. Mem Kha's Love Story. (Daybreak Ser.). 122p. Date not set. pap. 3.95 (ISBN 0-8163-0480-7). Pacific Pr Pub Assn.
Kravis, Thomas C. & Warner, Carmen G. Emergency Medicine: A Comprehensive Review. LC 82-11505. 1200p. 1982. 110.00 (ISBN 0-89443-365-2). Aspen Systems.
Kravitt, Gregory I. & Grossman, Jeffrey E. How to Prepare & Present a Business Plan. LC 82-73630. 250p. 1983. 27.50 (ISBN 0-87094-380-4). Dow Jones-Irwin.
Kravitz, David. Who's Who in Greek & Roman Mythology. 1977. 10.00 (ISBN 0-517-52746-4, C N Potter Bks); pap. 3.95 (ISBN 0-517-52747-2). Crown.
Kravitz, Linda, jt. auth. see Dunbar, Tony.
Kravitz, Nathaniel. Three Thousand Years of Hebrew Literature: From the Earliest Time Through the 20th Century. LC 82-72478. 586p. 1971. 20.00 (ISBN 0-8040-0505-2); limited ed. 50.00 (ISBN 0-8040-0728-4). Swallow.
Kravitz, Wallace. Bookkeeping the Easy Way. (Easy Way Ser.). 272p. (gr. 11-12). 1983. pap. write for info. (ISBN 0-8120-2622-5). Barron.
Kravontka, Stanley J. Communications for Fire Fighting & Evaluation. 1976. 3.25 (ISBN 0-686-17607-3, TR 76-5). Society Fire Protect.
--Elevator Use During Fires in Megastructures. Date not set. 2.50 (ISBN 0-686-22737-9, TR-76-1). Society Fire Protect.
Krawiec, F. Industrial Biomass Market Assessment. (Progress in Solar Energy Ser.: Suppl.). 250p. 1983. pap. text ed. 21.50x (ISBN 0-89553-102-X). Am Solar Energy.
Krawitt, Laura P. & Weinberger, Emily K. Practical Low Protein Cookery. (Illus.). 128p. 1971. spiral 10.50x (ISBN 0-398-01049-8). C C Thomas.
Krawitz, Klein. Royal American Symphonic Theatre. 211p. 1975. 8.95 o.p. (ISBN 0-02-566700-9). Macmillan.
Krawitz, Ruth, jt. auth. see Finkel, Lawrence S.
Krawltz, Ruth, jt. auth. see Finkel, Lawrence S.
Krawzya, L., jt. ed. see Van Stijgeren, E.
Kraybill, Donald B. Facing Nuclear War. LC 82-11765. 320p. (Orig.). 1982. pap. 8.95 (ISBN 0-8361-3312-9). Herald Pr.
Kraybill, H. F., et al, eds. Aquatic Pollutants & Biologic Effects with Emphasis on Neoplasia, Vol. 298. (Annals of the New York Academy of Sciences). 604p. 1977. 54.00x (ISBN 0-89072-044-4). NY Acad Sci.
Krayenbuehl, H. Cerebral Angiography in Clinic & Practice. (Illus.). 603p. 1982. 85.00 (ISBN 0-86577-067-0). Thieme-Stratton.
Krayenbuehl, H., et al, eds. Advances & Technical Standards in Neurosurgery, Vol.9. (Illus.). 177p. 1983. 37.00 (ISBN 0-387-81718-2). Springer-Verlag.
--Cranicocerebral Trauma. (Progress in Neurological Surgery Ser.: Vol. 10). (Illus.). xiv, 402p. 1981. 178.50 (ISBN 3-8055-0134-X). S Karger.
Kraytman, M. The Complete Patient History. 1979. 16.95 (ISBN 0-07-035421-9). McGraw.
Kraytman, Maurice. Guide to Clinical Reasoning. 560p. 1981. pap. text ed. 16.95 (ISBN 0-07-035451-0, HP). McGraw.
Krazer, Adolph. Lehrbuch der Thetafunktionen. LC 75-113132. (Ger). 1970. Repr. of 1903 ed. 25.00 (ISBN 0-8284-0244-2). Chelsea Pub.
Krcma. Manual of Nonwovens. 2nd ed. 1971. 42.00x (ISBN 0-87245-171-2). Textile Bk.
Kreager, Paul S. Practical Aspects of Data Communications. (Illus.). 224p. 1983. 29.95 (ISBN 0-07-035429-4, P&RB). McGraw.
Krebs, Al H., jt. auth. see Crunkilton, John R.
Krebs, Alfred H. Agriculture in Our Lives. 4th ed. LC 78-51664. (Illus.). 1978. text ed. 16.50x (ISBN 0-8134-2024-5, 2024). Interstate.
Krebs, B. P., et al, eds. Clinical Application of Carcinoembryonic Antigen Assay. (International Congress Ser.: No. 439). 1978. 19.75 (ISBN 0-444-90028-4). Elsevier.
Krebs, Carl. Dittersdorfiana. LC 72-166092. (Music Ser.). 1972. Repr. of 1900 ed. lib. bdg. 22.50 (ISBN 0-306-70259-2). Da Capo.
Krebs, John E. To Rome & Beyond. LC 81-83372. (Illus.). 224p. 1981. 15.00 (ISBN 0-9607026-0-1). J E Krebs.
Krebs, R., jt. ed. see Puech, P.
Krebs, R. D. & Walker, R. D. Highway Materials. 1971. text ed. 36.50 (ISBN 0-07-035465-0, C). McGraw.
Krech, David, jt. ed. see Bruner, Jerome S.
Krech, Shepard, III. Praise the Bridge That Carries You Over: The Life of Joseph L. Sutton. 1981. lib. bdg. 18.50 (ISBN 0-8161-9038-0, Univ Bks). G K Hall.
Kredenser, Gail. One Dancing Drum. LC 79-146845. (Illus.). (gr. k-3). 1971. 10.95 (ISBN 0-87599-178-5). S G Phillips.
Kreeft, Peter J. Everything You Ever Wanted to Know About Heaven--But Never Dreamed of Asking. LC 82-47747. 160p. (Orig.). 1982. pap. 6.68i (ISBN 0-06-064777-9, HarpR). Har-Row.
Kreeger, Lionel, ed. The Large Group: Dynamics & Therapy. 344p. 1975. text ed. 14.95 (ISBN 0-87581-182-5). Peacock Pubs.
Kreel, L. Computerized Tomography. 2nd ed. (incl. 400 slides). 1978. pap. 532.00 (ISBN 0-444-90053-5). Elsevier.
Krefeld, R., jt. ed. see Betteridge, W.
Krefetz, Gerald. Jews & Money: The Myths & the Reality. LC 82-5639. 280p. 1982. 13.95 (ISBN 0-89919-129-0). Ticknor & Fields.
Kregel-Javaux, M. P., tr. see Abraham-Frois, Gilbert & Berrebi, E.
Kreh, Lefty. Fly Fishing in Salt Water. LC 73-82957. (Sportsmen's Classic Ser). 252p. 1974. 12.95 o.p. (ISBN 0-517-50613-0). Crown.
--Fly Fishing in Salt Water. write for info. N Lyons Bks.
Kreh, Lefty & Sosin, Mark. Practical Fishing Knots. write for info. N Lyons Bks.
Kreh, Lefty, jt. auth. see Sosin, Mark.
Kreh, Richard. Masonry Skills. 2nd ed. LC 80-70701. (Masonry Trades Ser.). 328p. 1982. text ed. 18.00 (ISBN 0-8273-2153-8); pap. text ed. 13.80 (ISBN 0-8273-1957-6); instr's. guide 4.25 (ISBN 0-8273-1768-9). Delmar.
Kreh, Richard T. Safety for Masons. LC 78-53663. 1979. pap. text ed. 7.00 (ISBN 0-8273-1668-2); instructor's guide 2.00 (ISBN 0-8273-1669-0). Delmar.
Kreh, Richard T., Sr. Advanced Masonry Skills. 2nd ed. LC 82-70523. (Illus.). 368p. 1983. pap. text ed. 17.00 (ISBN 0-8273-2148-1); instr's guide 4.75. Delmar.
Krehbiel, Henry. Chapters of Opera. (Music Reprint Ser.). (Illus.). xvii, 435p. 1980. Repr. of 1909 ed. lib. bdg. 42.50 (ISBN 0-306-76036-3). Da Capo.
Krehbiel, Henry E. More Chapters of Opera: Being Historical & Critical Observations & Records Concerning the Lyric Drama in New York from 1908-1918. LC 78-66910. (Encore Music Editions Ser.). 1981. Repr. of 1919 ed. 45.00 (ISBN 0-88355-749-5). Hyperion Conn.
--Music & Manners in the Classical Period. 286p. 1983. pap. 6.75 (ISBN 0-686-38399-0). Tanager Bks.
--The Pianoforte & It's Music. 324p. 1983. pap. 6.75x (ISBN 0-88072-007-7). Tanager Bks.
Krehbiel, Henry E., tr. see Kerst, Friedrich.
Kreider, Barbara A. Index to Children's Plays in Collections. 2nd ed. LC 76-49666. 1977. 12.50 o.p. (ISBN 0-8108-0992-3). Scarecrow.
Kreider, Jan & Kreith, Frank. Solar Heating & Cooling: Active & Passive Design. 2nd ed. 496p. 1982. 34.50x (ISBN 0-07-035486-3). McGraw.
Kreider, Jan F. The Solar Heating Design Process: Active & Passive. (Illus.). 432p. 1982. 31.50x (ISBN 0-07-035478-2). McGraw.
Kreider, Jan F., jt. auth. see Kreith, Frank.
Kreider, Jan F. & Kreith, Frank, eds. Solar Energy Handbook. (Illus.). 1099p. 1981. 56.00 (ISBN 0-07-035474-X). McGraw.
Kreidl, John. Jean-Luc Godard. (Filmmakers Ser.). 1980. lib. bdg. 12.95 (ISBN 0-8057-9270-8, Twayne). G K Hall.
Kreidl, John F. Alain Resnais. (Filmmakers Ser.). 1978. 12.95 (ISBN 0-8057-9256-2, Twayne). G K Hall.
--Nicholas Ray. (Filmmakers Ser.). 1977. lib. bdg. 12.95 (ISBN 0-8057-9250-3, Twayne). G K Hall.
Kreidl, N. J., jt. ed. see Uhlmann, D. R.
Kreier, Julius P., jt. ed. see Ristic, Miodrag.
Kreigh, Helen Z. & Perko, Joanne E. Psychiatric & Mental Health Nursing: Commitment to Care & Concern. (Illus.). 1979. text ed. 18.95 (ISBN 0-8359-5711-X); instrs'. manual o.p. avail. (ISBN 0-8359-5712-8). Reston.
Kreimer, E., jt. auth. see Mallas, J. H.
Krein, S. G. Linear Equations in Banach Spaces. 128p. Date not set. text ed. 14.95x (ISBN 3-7643-3101-1). Birkhauser.
Kreinin, Mordechai. Economics: An Introductory Text. (Illus.). 544p. 1983. pap. text ed. 19.95 (ISBN 0-13-224261-3). P-H.
Kreis, Bernadine & Pattie, Alice. Up from Grief: Patterns of Recovery. 160p. 1982. pap. 5.95 (ISBN 0-8164-2364-4). Seabury.
Kreisberg, Louis, ed. Research in Social Movements, Conflicts & Change, Vol. 4. 300p. 1981. 45.00 (ISBN 0-89232-201-2). Jai Pr.
Kreischer, Lois. String Art Pattern Book I. 1976. pap. 3.95 o.p. (ISBN 0-517-52396-5). Crown.
--String Art: Symmography. (Arts & Crafts Ser). (Illus.). 62p. 1971. 4.95 (ISBN 0-517-50274-7, N04901); pap. 3.95 o.p. (ISBN 0-517-54310-9). Crown.
Kreisel, H. Die Phytopathogehen Grosspilze Deutschlands (Basidiomycetes mit Ausschluss der Rost-und Brandpilze) (Illus.). 1979. Repr. of 1961 ed. lib. bdg. 20.00x (ISBN 3-7682-1228-9). Lubrecht & Cramer.
--Taxonomisch-Pflanzengeographische Monographie der Gattung Bovista. 1967. pap. 40.00 (ISBN 3-7682-5425-9). Lubrecht & Cramer.
Kreisel, Hans. Grundzuege Eines Natuerlichen Systems der Pilze. (Illus.). 1969. pap. 16.00 (ISBN 3-7682-0630-0). Lubrecht & Cramer.
--Die Lycoperdaceae Der DDR. 1973. Repr. of 1962 ed. 12.00 (ISBN 3-7682-0852-4). Lubrecht & Cramer.
Kreisler, Max Von see Von Kreisler, Max.
Kreissman, C. J., jt. ed. see Wolfe, R.
Kreith, Frank & Kreider, Jan F. Principles of Solar Engineering. LC 77-27861. (McGraw-Hill - Hemisphere Thermal & Fluids Engineering Ser). (Illus.). 1978. pap. 34.95 (ISBN 0-07-035476-6, C); instr.'s manual 10.00 (ISBN 0-07-035477-4). McGraw.
Kreith, Frank & Wrenn, Catherine B. The Nuclear Impact: A Case Study of the Plowshare Program to Produce Natural Gas by Underground Nuclear Stimulation in the Rocky Mountains. LC 75-31708. (Special Studies on Technology, Natural Resources & the Environment). 250p. 1976. softcover 20.00 o.p. (ISBN 0-89158-005-0). Westview.
Kreith, Frank, jt. auth. see Kreider, Jan.
Kreith, Frank, jt. ed. see Kreider, Jan F.
Kreitman, N., jt. ed. see Sainsbury, P.
Kreitman, Norman, ed. Parasuicide. LC 76-30355. 1977. 42.00 o.p. (ISBN 0-471-99472-3, Pub by Wiley-Interscience). Wiley.
Kreitner, Robert. Management. 2nd ed. LC 82-83364. 656p. 1982. text ed. 24.94 (ISBN 0-395-32620-6). HM.
--Management: A Problem-Solving Process. LC 79-88719. (Illus.). 1980. text ed. 23.95 (ISBN 0-395-28490-2); instr's. manual 1.90 (ISBN 0-395-28491-0); tests bank 6.45 (ISBN 0-395-31768-1). HM.
Kreitner, Robert & Sova, Margaret. Understanding Management: Study Guide to Management: A Problem-Solving Process. LC 79-88719. (Illus.). pap. 8.95 (ISBN 0-395-28492-9). HM.
Kreitner, Robert, jt. auth. see Luthans, Fred.
Kreitz, Helmut. Wir Lernen Deutsch: German for the First Year. 1974. text ed. 13.95x o.p. (ISBN 0-673-05276-1). Scott F.
Krejci, Jaroslav. Social Structure in Divided Germany: A Contribution to the Comparative Analysis of Social Systems. LC 76-1338. 192p. 1976. 25.00 (ISBN 0-312-73535-9). St Martin.
Krekule, Ivan, jt. auth. see Bures, Jan.
Krell, David, tr. see Heidegger, Martin.
Krell, I. E., ed. Handbook of Laboratory Distillation: With an Introduction into the Pilot Plant Distillation. 2nd ed. (Techniques & Instrumentation in Analytical Chemistry Ser.: Vol. 2). 1982. 95.75 (ISBN 0-444-99723-7). Elsevier.
Kremenak, Nellie W., jt. auth. see Huyck, Peter.
Krementz, Jill. How it Feels to be Adopted. LC 82-48012. (YA) 1982. 11.95 (ISBN 0-394-52851-4). Knopf.
--How It Feels When a Parent Dies. LC 80-8808. (Illus.). 128p. 1981. 11.95 (ISBN 0-394-51911-6). Knopf.
--A Very Young Dancer. LC 76-13700. (YA) 1976. 10.95 (ISBN 0-394-40885-3). Knopf.
Kremer, Bruce. Mental Health in the Schools. 2nd ed. 340p. 1981. lib. bdg. 22.25 (ISBN 0-8191-1572-X); pap. text ed. 12.25 (ISBN 0-8191-1573-8). U Pr of Amer.
Kremer, Karl, jt. auth. see Grewe, Horst-Eberhard.
Kremer, Ron. Coloring Puzzles, Bk. 1. (gr. 1-4). 1978. pap. 6.50 (ISBN 0-88488-111-3). Creative Pubns.
--Coloring Puzzles, Bk. 2. (gr. 2-6). 1978. pap. 6.50 (ISBN 0-88488-112-1). Creative Pubns.
Kreml, Patricia B. Slim for Him. 1978. pap. 4.95 (ISBN 0-88270-300-5, Pub. by Logos). Bridge Pub.
Kremmer, T. & Boross, L. Gel Chromatography. LC 77-24994. 299p. 1980. 71.95x (ISBN 0-471-99548-7, Pub. by Wiley-Interscience). Wiley.
Krempel, D., jt. auth. see Clay, James H.
Kren, George & Rappoport, Leon, eds. Varieties of Psychohistory. LC 76-225. 1976. text ed. 23.95 (ISBN 0-8261-1940-9); pap. text ed. 15.95 (ISBN 0-8261-1941-7). Springer Pub.
Krenek, Ernst. Horizons Circled: Reflections on My Music. LC 72-89790. (Illus.). 1975. 21.50x (ISBN 0-520-02338-2). U of Cal Pr.
Krenek, Harry. The Power Vested. (Illus.). 1980. 12.75 o.s.i. (ISBN 0-935978-00-3); pap. text ed. 8.75 o.s.i. (ISBN 0-686-61000-8); collectors special 40.00 (ISBN 0-686-61001-6). Presidial.
Krens, Thomas. The Drawings of Robert Morris. LC 80-8703. (Icon Editors Ser.). (Illus.). 288p. 1982. price not set (ISBN 0-06-434021-X, IN-111, HarpT); pap. write for info (ISBN 0-06-430111-7, HarpT). Har-Row.
Krensky, Stephen. The Dragon Circle. LC 77-2002. (Illus.). (gr. 4-6). 1977. 6.95 o.p. (ISBN 0-689-30588-5). Atheneum.
--The Lion Upstairs. LC 82-13761. (Illus.). 40p. (ps-2). 1982. write for info. (ISBN 0-689-30969-4). Atheneum.
--The Wilder Plot. LC 82-1828. 168p. (gr. 6-9). 1982. 10.95 (ISBN 0-689-30927-9). Atheneum.
Krentz, Edgar. The Historical-Critical Method. LC 74-26345. (Guides to Biblical Scholarship: Old Testament Ser.). 96p. 1975. pap. 3.25 (ISBN 0-8006-0460-1, 1-460). Fortress.
Krentz, Edgar, ed. see Hahn, Ferdinand.
Krentz, Klaus. Integrated Atlas of Gastric Diseases. LC 75-16099. (Illus.). 212p. 1976. 25.00 o.p. (ISBN 0-88416-058-0). Wright-PSG.
Krentz, Peter. The Thirty at Athens. LC 81-70697. (Illus.). 168p. 1982. 17.50x (ISBN 0-8014-1450-4). Cornell U Pr.

Krentzman, et al. Techniques & Strategies for Effective Small Business Management. 1981. pap. 10.00 (ISBN 0-8359-7542-8, Reward Edn); text ed. 16.00 (ISBN 0-8359-7543-6). Reston.
Krenz, Nancy, jt. auth. see Byrnes, Patricia.
Krenzel, Kathleen & Heckendorf, Robyn. The Sporting Life Gourmet. (Illus.). 74p. (Orig.). 1980. 9.95x (ISBN 0-9605410-0-4). R Louis Pub.
Kreps, Georgian, tr. see Imbo, M.
Kreps, Juanita M. Women & the American Economy: A Look to the 1980's. LC 76-4105. (American Assembly Ser.). (Illus.). 192p. 1976. pap. 4.00 o.p. (ISBN 0-13-962316-7, Spec). P-H.
Kreps, Karen & Smith, Richard. The Sixty Day Diet Diary. (Orig.). 1983. pap. 3.95 (ISBN 0-440-57946-5, Dell Trade Pbks). Dell.
Kresh, Joseph, tr. see Kafka, Franz.
Kress, Gunther, ed. see Halliday, M. A. K.
Kress, Jack M. Prescripton for Justice: The Theory & Practice of Sentencing Guidelines. 384p. 1980. prof ref 27.50x (ISBN 0-88410-792-2). Ballinger Pub.
Kress, Rainer, jt. auth. see Colton, David.
Kress, Robert. A Rahner Handbook. LC 81-85333. 118p. 1982. pap. 9.95 (ISBN 0-8042-0652-X). John Knox.
Kressel, H., ed. Characterization of Epitaxial Semiconductor Films. (Methods & Phenomena Ser.: Vol. 2). 1976. 51.00 (ISBN 0-444-41438-X). Elsevier.
Kressen, David C. Teach Your Computer to Think in BASIC. Jacobs, Russell, ed. (Illus.). 88p. (YA) (gr. 5-12). 1983. pap. text ed. 7.50 (ISBN 0-918272-10-6). Jacobs.
Kresta, Jiri E. Reaction Injection Molding & Fast Polymerization Reactions. (Polymer Science & Technology Ser.: Vol. 18). 310p. 1982. 42.50x (ISBN 0-306-41120-2, Plenum Pr). Plenum Pub.
Kreta, Eleanor, jt. auth. see Brown, Charles.
Kretchmer & Brasel. Biomedical & Social Bases of Pediatrics. LC 80-39874. 220p. 1981. 51.50x (ISBN 0-89352-093-4). Masson Pub.
Kretchmer, Norman & Hasselmeyer, Eileen G. Horizons in Perinatal Research. LC 73-14803. 211p. 1974. 16.50 o.p. (ISBN 0-471-50723-7, Pub. by Wiley). Krieger.
Kretchmer, Norman see Walcher, Dwain N., et al.
Kretchmer, Norman, jt. ed. see Quilligan, E. J.
Kretchmer, Norman, jt. ed. see Walcher, Dwain N.
Kreter, D. M. de see De Kreter, D. M., et al.
Kreter, L. Sight & Sound: A Manual of Aural Musicianship, 2 vols. 1976. Vol. 1. pap. 15.95 (ISBN 0-13-809905-7); Vol. 2. pap. 14.95 (ISBN 0-13-809913-8); Tapes Vols. 1 & 2. 175.00 (ISBN 0-13-809921-9). P-H.
Kretlow, William, jt. auth. see Moyer, Charles R.
Kretsch, Robert W. Images et Reflets Litteraires. 1967. text ed. 16.95 (ISBN 0-07-035491-X, C). McGraw.
Kretschmer, K. Peter. The Intestinal Stoma: Indications, Operative Methods, Care, Rehabilitation. LC 78-52733. (Major Problems in Clinical Surgery Ser.: Vol. 24). (Illus.). 1979. text ed. 14.00 (ISBN 0-7216-5535-1). Saunders.
Kretz, Sandra E., jt. auth. see Wallack, Stanley S.
Kretzmann, Norman, tr. see Shirwood, William.
Kretzmann, Norman, tr. see William Of Ockham.
Kretzmann, O. P. & Oldsen, A. C. Voices of the Passion: Meditations for Lent & Easter. rev. ed. LC 77-84080. 1977. pap. 3.50 o.p. (ISBN 0-8066-1605-9, 10-6860). Augsburg.
Kreuder, Manfred, jt. auth. see Mentwig, Joachim.
Kreuder, Manfred, jt. auth. see Nentwig, Joachim.
Kreutker, C. W. & Collins, E. W. Geology & Geohydrology of the East Texas Basin: A Report on the Progress of Nuclear Waste Isolation Feasibility Studies. (Geological Circular Ser. of Nuclear Waste Isolation Feasibility Studies: 81-7). (Illus.). 207p. 1980. 5.00 (ISBN 0-686-36595-X). Bur Econ Geology.
Kreutler, Patricia. Nutrition in Perspective. (Illus.). 1980. text ed. 25.95 (ISBN 0-13-627752-7); wkbk. 9.95 (ISBN 0-13-627778-0). P-H.
Kreutzberg, G. W., ed. Physiology & Pathology of Dendrites. LC 74-14474. (Advances in Neurology Ser: Vol. 12). 523p. 1975. 48.00 (ISBN 0-911216-99-5). Raven.
Kreutzberger, Max, ed. see Baeck.
Kreuziger, Frederick. Apocalypse & Science Fiction: A Dialectic of Religious & Secular Soteriologies. LC 81-21482. (AAR Academy Ser.). 1981. 13.50 (ISBN 0-89130-562-9, 01-01-40). Scholars Pr CA.
Krevelan, D. W. Van see Van Krevelen, D. W.
Krevolin, Nathan. Communication Systems & Procedures for the Modern Office. (Illus.). 464p. 1983. 21.95 (ISBN 0-13-153668-0). P-H.
Krevolin, R., jt. auth. see Lloyd, Alan C.
Krey, Isabelle A. & Metzler, Bernadette V. Principles & Techniques of Effective Business Communication: A Text-Workbook. (Illus.). 532p. 1976. pap. text ed. 12.95 o.p. (ISBN 0-15-571310-8, HC); instructor's manual avail. o.p. (ISBN 0-15-571311-6). HarBraceJ.
Kreyche, Gerald F. Thirteen Thinkers: A Sampler of Great Philosophers. 1976. pap. text ed. 5.75 (ISBN 0-8191-0067-6). U Pr of Amer.
Kreydt, James, ed. Dance Magazine Annual 1983. 340p. 1982. pap. 20.00 (ISBN 0-930036-07-7). Dance Mag Inc.
Kreyszig, E. Advanced Engineering Mathematics. 4th ed. LC 78-5073. 1032p. 1979. text ed. 36.95 (ISBN 0-471-02140-7). Wiley.
Kreyszig, Erwin. Advanced Engineering Mathematics. 5th ed. 1100p. 1983. text ed. 36.95 (ISBN 0-471-86251-7); tchrs.' manual avail. (ISBN 0-471-89855-4). Wiley.
--Introductory Mathematical Statistics: Principles & Methods. LC 70-107583. 470p. 1970. 33.95x (ISBN 0-471-50730-X). Wiley.
Kribbs, Jayne K. An Annotated Bibliography of American Literary Periodicals, 1741-1850. 1977. lib. bdg. 41.00 (ISBN 0-8161-7970-0, Hall Reference). G K Hall.
Krich, A. M. Sweethearts: A Novel. 1983. 14.95 (ISBN 0-517-54744-9). Crown.
Krichbaum, Jorg & Zondergeld, Rein. Dictionary of Fantastic Art. (Pocket Art Ser.). (Illus.). 1983. pap. 5.95 (ISBN 0-8120-2110-X). Barron.
Krick, Edward V. Introduction to Engineering: Methods, Concepts & Issues. LC 75-41432. 358p. 1976. text ed. 23.95x (ISBN 0-471-50750-4); instructor's manual 4.00x (ISBN 0-471-01912-7). Wiley.
--Methods Engineering. LC 62-8775. (Illus.). 530p. 1962. text ed. 39.50x o.s.i. (ISBN 0-471-50754-7); tchr's. manual 4.00x (ISBN 0-471-50756-3). Wiley.
--Modern Engineering: A Short Course for Professionals. LC 76-1702. (Wiley Professional Development Programs Ser.). 356p. 1977. Set. 39.95x (ISBN 0-471-01702-7). Wiley.
Krickel, Edward. John Ciardi. (United States Authors Ser.). 1980. lib. bdg. 11.95 (ISBN 0-8057-7306-1, Twayne). G K Hall.
Krickus, Richard. Pursuing the American Dream: White Ethnics & the New Populism. LC 75-21336. 448p. 1976. 12.50x o.p. (ISBN 0-253-34727-0). Ind U Pr.
Krider, J. L. & Carroll, W. E. Swine Production. 4th ed. 1971. text ed. 34.95 (ISBN 0-07-035502-9, C). McGraw.
Krider, J. L., et al. Swine Production. 5th ed. (Agricultural Science Ser.). 688p. 1982. 32.50x (ISBN 0-07-035503-7). McGraw.
Kriechbaum, Casimer, Jr. & Dillon, Jacquelyn. How to Design & Teach a Successful School String & Orchestra Program. LC 78-54217. 1978. pap. text ed. 16.95 (ISBN 0-8497-5400-3, WS5, Pub. by Kjos West). Kjos.
Kriedler, William. Classroom Management. 1983. pap. text ed. 9.95 (ISBN 0-673-15642-7). Scott F.
Krieg, Carl E. What to Believe? The Questions of Christian Faith. LC 74-80415. 128p. (Orig.). 1974. pap. 1.00 o.p. (ISBN 0-8006-1085-7, 1-1085). Fortress.
Kriegel, H. P., jt. ed. see Cremers, A. B.
Kriegel, Harriet, ed. Women in Drama: An Anthology. (Orig.). 1975. pap. 4.95 (ISBN 0-451-62147-6, ME2147, Ment). NAL.
Kriegel, John. Houston Home & Garden's Complete Guide to Houston Gardening. 425p. 1983. 24.95 (ISBN 0-940672-08-1). Shearer Pub.
Kriegel, Leonard & Lass, Abraham. Stories of the American Experience. 1973. pap. 3.50 (ISBN 0-451-62022-4, ME2022, Ment). NAL.
Krieger, Dorothy T., ed. Endocrine Rhythms: Comprehensive Endocrinology. LC 77-75655. 344p. 1979. 38.00 (ISBN 0-89004-234-9). Raven.
Krieger, Dorothy T. & Bardin, C. Wayne, eds. Current Therapy in Endocrinology. 420p. 1983. 44.00 (ISBN 0-941158-04-7, D2755-9). Mosby.
Krieger, Henry A. Measure-Theoretic Probability. LC 80-1431. 394p. 1980. lib. bdg. 23.25 (ISBN 0-8191-1228-3); pap. text ed. 13.75 (ISBN 0-8191-1229-1). U Pr of Amer.
Krieger, Joel, jt. auth. see Douglass, David.
Krieger, John A., jt. auth. see Hale, Ralph W.
Krieger, M., jt. auth. see Hancock, L.
Krieger, Martin H. Advice & Planning. 256p. 1981. 27.95 (ISBN 0-87722-217-7). Temple U Pr.
Krieger, Morris. Homeowner's Encyclopedia of House Construction. (Illus.). 1978. 27.50 (ISBN 0-07-035497-9, P&RB). McGraw.
Krieger, Murray. Arts on the Level: The Fall of the Elite Object. LC 80-25401. (The Hodges Lectures). (Illus.). 84p. 1981. text ed. 7.50x (ISBN 0-87049-256-X). U of Tenn Pr.
--The New Apologists for Poetry. LC 77-21933. 1977. Repr. of 1956 ed. lib. bdg. 20.00x (ISBN 0-8371-9787-2, KRNA). Greenwood.
Krieger, Murray, jt. auth. see Corbman, Bernard P.
Krieger, Murray & Dembo, L. S., eds. Directions for Criticism: Structuralism & Its Alternatives. 1977. 25.00 (ISBN 0-299-07390-4, 7395); pap. text ed. 8.95 (ISBN 0-299-07394-7). U of Wis Pr.
Krieger, Robin, ed. see Crowe, Steve.
Krieger, Susan. The Mirror Dance: Identity in a Women's Community. 1983. write for info. (ISBN 0-87722-304-1). Temple U Pr.
Krieger, W. & Gerloff, J. Die Gattung Cosmarium. Fasc.1-4(1962-69) 48.00 (ISBN 3-7682-0130-9). Lubrecht & Cramer.
Krieger, W., jt. auth. see Helmcke, J. G.
Kriegman, George, et al, eds. American Psychiatry: Past, Present, & Future. LC 75-8962. 200p. 1975. 13.95x (ISBN 0-8139-0571-0). U Pr of Va.
Kriegsman, Sali Ann. Modern Dance in America: The Bennington Years. 1981. lib. bdg. 85.00 (ISBN 0-8161-8528-X, Hall Reference). G K Hall.
Kriegsmann, Klaus-Peter & Neu, Axel D. Globale Regionale und Sektorale Wettbewerbsfahigkeit der Deutschen Wirtschaft. x, 295p. (Ger.). 1982. write for info. (ISBN 3-8204-5809-3). P Lang Pubs.
Krier, James E. & Ursin, Edmund. Pollution & Policy: A Case Essay on California & Federal Experience with Motor Vehicle Air Pollution, 1940-1975. LC 76-3881. 1978. 22.50x (ISBN 0-520-03204-7). U of Cal Pr.
Krier, James E., jt. auth. see Dukeminier, Jesse.
Krier, James E., jt. auth. see Stewart, Richard B.
Krier, Rob. Rob Krier on Architecture. (Academy Architecture Ser.). (Illus.). 96p. 1982. 25.00 (ISBN 0-312-68541-6); pap. 19.95 (ISBN 0-312-68542-4). St Martin.
Kriesberg, Louis. Social Conflicts. 2nd ed. (Prentice Hall Ser. in Sociology). (Illus.). 352p. 1982. pap. text ed. 16.95 (ISBN 0-13-815589-5). P-H.
--Social Inequality. (P-H Ser. in Sociology). (Illus.). 1979. ref. ed. 22.95 (ISBN 0-13-815860-6). P-H.
Kriesberg, Louis, ed. Research in Social Movements, Conflicts & Change: An Annual Compilation of Research, Vol. 1. 1978. lib. bdg. 40.00 (ISBN 0-89232-027-3). Jai Pr.
Kriesburg, Louis, ed. Research in Social Movements, Conflicts & Change, Vol. 2. 293p. 1979. 40.00 (ISBN 0-89232-108-3). Jai Pr.
Krigbaum, W. R., jt. ed. see Ciferri, A.
Krige, D. G. Lognormal: De Wijsian Geostatistics for Ore Evaluation. 50p. 1980. 30.00x (ISBN 0-620-03006-2, Pub. by Mining Journal England). State Mutual Bk.
Kriin, Vera, ed. Sheraton World Cookbook. 304p. (Orig.). 1983. pap. 9.95 (ISBN 0-672-52761-8). Bobbs.
Krikler, Dennis M. & Goodwin, John F., eds. Cardiac Arrhythmias. LC 75-11582. (Illus.). 255p. 1975. text ed. 12.00 (ISBN 0-7216-5516-5). Saunders.
Krill, Richard M. Forty Fabulous Fables of Aesop. 90p. (gr. 3-6). 1982. 7.95 (ISBN 0-942624-00-9). Promethean Arts.
Kriloff, Lou. Letterpower in Action, 12 vols. Set. pap. 16.80 boxed o.p. (ISBN 0-911744-53-3). Career Inst.
Krimm, Irwinn F. Your Happiness Here & Hereafter. 1977. pap. 5.95 o.p. (ISBN 0-9606402-2-3). Happy Health.
Kriney, Marilyn, jt. auth. see Gustafson, Anita.
Krinsky, Carol. Rockefeller Center. (Illus.). 1978. 25.00x (ISBN 0-19-502317-X). Oxford U Pr.
Kripalani, Krishna, tr. see Tagore, Rabindranath.
Kripalvandji, Swami Shri. Pilgrimage of Love, Bk. II. 416p. (Orig.). 1982. pap. 7.95 (ISBN 0-940258-05-6). Kripalu Pubns.
Kripke, Dorothy K. Let's Talk About the Jewish Holidays. LC 75-104328. (Illus.). (gr. k-4). 1970. 5.95 o.p. (ISBN 0-8246-0106-8). Jonathan David.
Krippner, Stanley. Advances in Parapsychological Research, Vol. 3. 352p. 1982. 32.50x (ISBN 0-306-40944-5, Plenum Pr). Plenum Pub.
Krippner, Stanley & Villoldo, Alberto. The Realms of Healing. LC 75-7858. 1976. pap. 7.95 o.p. (ISBN 0-89087-112-4). Celestial Arts.
Krisberg, Barry & Austin, James, eds. The Children of Ishmael: Critical Perspectives on Juvenile Justice. LC 77-89919. 586p. 1978. text ed. 8.95 o.p. (ISBN 0-87484-388-X); pap. text ed. 14.95 (ISBN 0-87484-387-1). Mayfield Pub.
Krisch, K., ed. Schilddruesentumoren. (Beitraege zur Onkologie. Contributions to Oncology Ser.: Vol. 16). (Illus.). vi, 74p. 1983. pap. 24.95 (ISBN 3-8055-3695-X). S Karger.
Krishan Rao, V. S. Dictionary of Bharatnatya. 1981. 15.00x (ISBN 0-8364-0698-2, Orient Longman). South Asia Bks.
Krishef, Curtis H. An Introduction to Mental Retardation. (Illus.). 352p. 1983. 19.75x (ISBN 0-398-04748-0); instructor's manual, spiral 7.50x (ISBN 0-686-83145-4). C C Thomas.
Krishef, Robert K. Daytona Five Hundred. LC 74-33527. (Superwheels & Thrill Sports Bks.). (Illus.). 56p. (gr. 5-10). 1976. PLB 7.95g (ISBN 0-8225-0411-1). Lerner Pubns.
--Grand Ole Opry. LC 77-90151. (Country Music Bks.). (Illus.). 1978. PLB 5.95g (ISBN 0-8225-1405-2). Lerner Pubns.
--Hank Williams. LC 77-90157. (Country Music Bks.). (Illus.). (gr. 5 up). 1978. PLB 5.95g (ISBN 0-8225-1402-8). Lerner Pubns.
--Indianapolis Five Hundred. LC 73-22152. (Superwheels & Thrill Sports Bks.). (Illus.). 52p. (gr. 5-10). 1974. PLB 7.95g (ISBN 0-8225-0412-X). Lerner Pubns.
--Introducing Country Music. LC 77-90148. (Country Music Books). (Illus.). (gr. 5 up). 1979. PLB 5.95g (ISBN 0-8225-1408-7). Lerner Pubns.
--Jimmie Rodgers. LC 77-90156. (Country Music Bks.). (Illus.). (gr. 5 up). 1978. PLB 5.95g (ISBN 0-8225-1404-4). Lerner Pubns.
--Loretta Lynn. LC 77-90155. (Country Music Bks.). (Illus.). 64p. (gr. 5 up). 1978. 5.95g (ISBN 0-8225-1401-X). Lerner Pubns.
--The New Breed. LC 77-90153. (Country Music Bks.). (Illus.). (gr. 5 up). 1978. PLB 5.95g (ISBN 0-8225-1406-0). Lerner Pubns.
--Our Remarkable Feet. LC 67-30693. (Medical Bks for Children). (Illus.). (gr. 3-9). 1968. PLB 3.95g (ISBN 0-8225-0018-3). Lerner Pubns.
--Playback: The Story of Recording Devices. rev. ed. LC 62-18817. (Musical Books for Young People Ser). (gr. 5-11). 1974. PLB 3.95g (ISBN 0-8225-0056-6). Lerner Pubns.
Krishef, Robert K., jt. auth. see Harris, Stacy.
Krishna, Jai & Chandrasekaran, A. R. Elements of Earthquake Engineering. 260p. Date not set. 12.95 (ISBN 0-9605004-2-1, Pub. by Sarita Prakashan India). Eng Pubns.
Krishna, P. Cable-Suspended Roofs. 1978. 36.50 (ISBN 0-07-035504-5). McGraw.
Krishna, Raj & Raychaudhuri, G. S. Some Aspects of Wheat & Rice Price Policy in India. (Working Paper: No. 381). 62p. 1980. 5.00 (ISBN 0-686-36078-8, WP-0381). World Bank.
Krishna, Valerie. The Alliterative Morte Arthure: A New Verse Translation. LC 82-24838. 144p. (Orig.). 1983. lib. bdg. 19.75 (ISBN 0-8191-3035-4); pap. text ed. 8.25 (ISBN 0-8191-3036-2). U Pr of Amer.
Krishna, Valerie see Hamalian, Leo & Volpe, Edmond.
Krishnaiah. Multivariate Analysis: Proceedings of Third International Symposium. 1973. 72.00 (ISBN 0-12-426653-3). Acad Pr.
Krishnaiah, P. R. Analysis of Variance. (Handbook of Statistics: Vol. I). 1981. 117.00 (ISBN 0-444-85335-9). Elsevier.
--Applications of Statistics. 1977. 78.75 (ISBN 0-444-85034-1). Elsevier.
--Multivariate Analysis 5. 1980. 85.00 (ISBN 0-444-85321-9). Elsevier.
Krishnaiah, P. R. & Kanal, L. Classification Pattern Recognition & Reduction of Dimension. (Handbook of Statistics: Vol. 2). Date not set. 117.00 (ISBN 0-444-86217-X). Elsevier.
Krishnaiah, P. R., jt. auth. see International Symposium, Fourth, Wright State University, June, 1975.
Krishnaiah, P. R., ed. Developments in Statistics, Vol. 4. Date not set. 62.00 (ISBN 0-12-426604-5). Acad Pr.
Krishna Kumar Sugandhi. Thyristors Theory & Applications. LC 80-28159. 240p. 1981. 24.95x o.p. (ISBN 0-470-27134-5). Halsted Pr.
Krishnamachar, P., jt. auth. see Manohar, M.
Krishnamurthy, K., tr. see Panikkar, K. M.
Krishnamurthy, R. The Saints of the Cauvery Delta. 1979. text ed. 10.50x (ISBN 0-391-01844-2). Humanities.
Krishnamurti, J. Talks & Dialogues of J. Krishnamurti. 1976. pap. 2.25 o.p. (ISBN 0-380-01573-0, 38133). Avon.
--Truth & Actuality: Conversations on Science & Consciousness. LC 77-20450. 176p. 1980. pap. 6.95i (ISBN 0-06-064875-9, RD 334, HarpR). Har-Row.
Krishnamurti, J. see Alcyone, pseud.
Krishnamurti, Jiddu. Beyond Violence. LC 72-9875. 176p. 1973. pap. 5.95i (ISBN 0-06-064839-2, RD 61, HarpR). Har-Row.
--The First & Last Freedom. LC 74-25687. 228p. 1975. pap. 6.95i (ISBN 0-06-064831-7, RD 91, HarpR). Har-Row.
--Flight of the Eagle. LC 74-146005. (Orig.). 1971. pap. 1.95i o.p. (ISBN 0-06-064835-X, RD-38, HarpR). Har-Row.
--Freedom from the Known. LC 69-17013. 128p. 1975. pap. 5.95i (ISBN 0-06-064808-2, RD 90, HarpR). Har-Row.
--You Are the World. 160p. 1973. pap. 3.37i (ISBN 0-06-080303-7, P303, PL). Har-Row.
Krishnan, M. Nights & Days in the Indian Wilderness: A Naturalist Photographer's Diary. 200p. 1982. 51.00x (ISBN 0-686-94074-1, Pub. by Garlandfold England). State Mutual Bk.
Krishnan-Kutty, G. Money & Banking. 1979. text ed. 9.75x (ISBN 0-391-01815-9). Humanities.
Krishnaswamy, S., jt. auth. see Barnouw, Erik.
Krislovsky, M. William, jt. auth. see Shemel, Sidney.
Krispyn, Egbert. Gunter Eich. (World Authors Ser.: No. 148). 12.95 (ISBN 0-8057-2292-0, Twayne). G K Hall.
Krispyn, Egbert, ed. Modern Stories from Holland & Flanders. (International Studies & Translations Ser). lib. bdg. 9.95 o.p. (ISBN 0-8057-3449-X, Twayne). G K Hall.
Krispyn, Egbert, ed. see Streuvels, Stijn.
Kristal, Leonard, ed. The ABC of Psychology. 256p. 1982. 14.95x (ISBN 0-87196-678-6). Facts on File.
Kristein, Marvin M. Corporation Finance. 2nd ed. LC 75-10813. (Illus.). 256p. (Orig.). 1975. pap. 5.50 (ISBN 0-06-460161-7, CO 161, COS). B&N NY.
Kristek, Vladimir. Theory of Box Girders. LC 78-8637. 371p. 1980. 51.95x (ISBN 0-471-99678-5, Pub. by Wiley-Interscience). Wiley.
Kristeller, Paul O. Renaissance Thought: The Classic, Scholastic & Humanistic Strains, Vol. 1. 10.00 (ISBN 0-8446-2405-5). Peter Smith.
Kristensen. Development in Rich & Poor Countries. 2nd ed. 152p. 1982. 20.95 (ISBN 0-03-059053-1). Praeger.
Kristensen, jt. auth. see Holm.
Kristensen, F. & Antczak, D. F. Advances in Veterinary Immunology: 1981. (Developments in Animal & Veterinary Science: Vol. 9). 1982. 56.00 (ISBN 0-444-42051-7). Elsevier.

Kristensen, Thorkil, et al. The Economic World Balance. LC 73-19571. (Illus.). 377p. 1974. Repr. of 1960 ed. lib. bdg. 21.00x (ISBN 0-8371-7295-0, KREW). Greenwood.

Kristiansen, M., jt. auth. see Hagler, M. O.

Kristjansson, Jonas. Icelandic Sagas & Manuscripts. rev. & updated ed. (Illus.). 1980. 22.50 (ISBN 0-686-91768-5). Heinman.

Kristo, Janice V. & Heath, Phillip A., eds. Today's Curriculum: An Integrative Approach. LC 81-43666. 90p. (Orig.). 1982. pap. text ed. 7.00 (ISBN 0-8191-2149-5). U Pr of Amer.

Kristol, Irving. Two Cheers for Capitalism. 1979. pap. 2.95 (ISBN 0-451-62046-1, ME2046, Ment). NAL.

Kristol, Irving, jt. ed. see Bell, Daniel.

Kristol, Irving, ed. see Commission on Critical Choices.

Krisvoy, Juel. The Good Apple Puppet Book. 9.95 (ISBN 0-86653-033-9, GA 261). Good Apple.

--Paper Crafts to Make You Smile. (ps-3). 1981. 6.95 (ISBN 0-86653-032-0, GA 260). Good Apple.

Kritchevsky, David & Gibney, Michael J., eds. Animal & Vegetable Proteins in Lipid Metabolism & Atherosclerosis. LC 82-23961. (Current Topics in Nutrition & Disease Ser.: Vol. 8). 200p. 1983. write for info. (ISBN 0-8451-1607-X). A R Liss.

Kritchevsky, David, jt. ed. see Paoletti, Rodolfo.

Kritsch, Erna & Schlimbach, Alice, eds. Moderne Erzahlungen Fur Die Unter - Und Mittelstufe. (Illus., Orig., Ger.). 1964. pap. text ed. 11.95 (ISBN 0-13-594291-8). P-H.

Kritz, Mary, ed. U. S. Immigration & Refugee Policy. LC 82-47513. 448p. 1982. 23.95xc (ISBN 0-669-05543-3). Lexington Bks.

Kritz, Mary M., et al, eds. Global Trends in Migration: Theory & Research in International Population Movements. LC 80-68399. 532p. 1981. 14.95x (ISBN 0-913256-54-4, Dist. by Ozer); pap. text ed. 9.95x (ISBN 0-686-85840-9, Dist. by Ozer). Ctr Migration.

Kritzeck, James, ed. Anthology of Islamic Literature: From the Rise of Islam to Modern Times. 1975. pap. 9.95 (ISBN 0-452-00628-7, F628, Mer). NAL.

Kritzman, Lawrence D. Destruction-Decouverte: Le Fontionnement de la Rhetorique dans les Essais de Montaigne. LC 80-66329. (French Forum Monographs: No. 21). 187p. (Orig.). 1980. pap. 12.50x (ISBN 0-917058-20-8). French Forum.

Krivanek, Jara A. Drug Problems, People Problems: Causes, Treatment & Prevention. 256p. 1983. text ed. 28.50x (ISBN 0-86861-364-9); pap. 10.95 (ISBN 0-86861-372-X). Allen Unwin.

Krivchenkov, V. D., jt. auth. see Goldman, I.

Kriyananda, Swami. The Art of Creative Leadership. 16p. 1980. pap. 2.95 (ISBN 0-916124-20-7). Ananda.

--How to use Money for Your Own Highest Good. 48p. 1981. pap. write for info. (ISBN 0-916124-22-3). Ananda.

--Letters from India. 1973. pap. 2.95 (ISBN 0-916124-06-1). Ananda.

--Yours - the Universe! 2nd ed. (Illus.). 96p. 1970. pap. 2.95 (ISBN 0-916124-10-X). Ananda.

Kriz, Joseph & Duggan, Curt. Your Dynamic World of Business. (Illus.). 448p. 1973. text ed. 15.95 o.p. (ISBN 0-07-035505-3, C); 4.95 o.p. instructor's manual (ISBN 0-07-035508-8). McGraw.

Kriz, Thomas, et al. Thermal Energy Storage for Process Heat & Building Applications. (Progress in Solar Enery Ser.: Suppl.). 200p. 1983. pap. text ed. 16.50 (ISBN 0-89553-138-0). Am Solar Energy.

Kriz, Wilhelm, jt. auth. see Jamison, Rex L.

Kroack, Lou. Collecting & Building Model Trucks. (Modern Automotive Ser.). 1980. 14.95 (ISBN 0-8306-9720-9); pap. 9.95 o.p. (ISBN 0-8306-2057-5, 2057). TAB Bks.

Krobloch, E. & Cerna-Heyrovska, J. Fodder Biofactors: Their Methods of Determination. LC 78-25777. 318p. 1980. 61.75 (ISBN 0-444-99783-0). Elsevier.

Kroc Foundation Conference, Oct. 12-16, 1981. Alzheimer's Disease, Down's Syndrome, & Aging: Proceedings, Vol. 396. Sinex, F. Marott & Merril, Carl R., eds. 199p. 1982. 35.00 (ISBN 0-89766-182-6); pap. write for info. (ISBN 0-89766-183-4). NY Acad Sci.

Krockover, Gerald H., jt. auth. see DeVito, Alfred.

Krodel, Gerhard, ed. see Fuller, Reginald H., et al.

Kroeber, A. L. Franz Boaz: Eighteen Fifty-Eight to Nineteen Forty-Two. LC 44-1376. 1943. pap. 12.00 (ISBN 0-527-00560-6). Kraus Repr.

--Handbook of the Indians of California. LC 76-19514. (Illus.). 1976. lib. bdg. 21.00x (ISBN 0-88307-585-7). Gannon.

Kroeber, A. L., jt. auth. see Dorsey, G. A.

Kroeber, Alfred L. Anthropology: Biology & Race. LC 63-12159. 1963. pap. 2.65 (ISBN 0-15-607804-X, Harv). HarBraceJ.

--Anthropology: Culture Patterns & Processes. LC 63-12160. 1963. pap. 3.45 (ISBN 0-15-607805-8, Harv). HarBraceJ.

--Mohave Indians. Horr, David A., ed. (American Indian Ethnohistory Ser.). 1978. lib. bdg. 42.00 o.s.i. (ISBN 0-8240-0738-7). Garland Pub.

--Style & Civilizations. LC 73-8560. 191p. 1973. Repr. of 1957 ed. lib. bdg. 15.75x (ISBN 0-8371-6966-6, KRSC). Greenwood.

--Walapai Ethnography. LC 35-6835. 1935. pap. 34.00 (ISBN 0-527-00541-X). Kraus Repr.

Kroeber, Donald & LaForge, R. Lawrence. The Manager's Guide to Statistics & Quantitative Methods. (Illus.). 1980. 23.95 (ISBN 0-07-035520-7). McGraw.

Kroeber, Donald W. Management Information Systems: A Handbook for Modern Managers. (Illus.). 288p. 1982. 17.95 (ISBN 0-686-94150-0). Free Pr.

Kroeber, Karl. Romantic Landscape Vision: Constable & Wordsworth. LC 74-5905. (Illus.). 156p. 1975. 25.00 (ISBN 0-299-06710-6). U of Wis Pr.

Kroeber, Theodora. Ishi in Two Worlds: A Biography of the Last Wild Indian in North America. LC 61-7530. (Illus.). 1961. 14.95 (ISBN 0-520-00674-7); pap. 4.95 (ISBN 0-520-00675-5, CAL94). U of Cal Pr.

Kroeger, Axel & Barbira-Freedman, Francois. Cultural Change & Health: The Case of South American Rainforest Indians. 73p. 1982. write for info. (ISBN 3-8204-6277-5). P Lang Pubs.

Kroeker, N. J. First Mennonite Villages in Russia 1789-1943: Khortistsa-Rosental. LC 82-167271. (Illus.). 279p. 1981. 20.00 (ISBN 0-88925-294-7). N J Kroeker.

Kroenke, David H. Database: A Professional's Primer. LC 78-6080. 323p. 1978. 29.95 o.s.i. (ISBN 0-574-21210-8, 13-4210). Sci Res Assoc Coll.

Kroenke, David M. Business Computer Systems: An Introduction. LC 80-84140. (Illus.). 576p. 1981. 19.95 (ISBN 0-938188-00-3). Mitchell Pub.

--Database Processing: Fundamentals, Design, Implementation. 2nd ed. 448p. 1982. text ed. write for info. (ISBN 0-574-21320-1, 13-4320); write for info. instr's. guide (ISBN 0-574-21321-X, 13-4321). SRA.

Kroes, Rob. Soldiers & Students. 1975. 16.50x o.p. (ISBN 0-7100-8089-1); pap. 10.00 (ISBN 0-7100-8090-5). Routledge & Kegan.

Kroeze, J. H., ed. see European Chemoreception Research Organisation, Symposium, Netherlands, 1979.

Kroff, A. Y., jt. auth. see Bree, G.

Krogdahl, Wasley S. Tensor Analysis: Fundamentals & Applications. LC 78-62755. 1978. pap. text ed. 20.50 (ISBN 0-8191-0594-5). U Pr of Amer.

Kroger, Catharine, tr. see Vivien, Renee.

Kroger, F. A. The Chemistry of Imperfect Crystals, Vol. 1. 313p. 1974. 61.75 (ISBN 0-444-10561-1, North-Holland). Elsevier.

--The Chemistry of Imperfect Crystals, Vol. 2. 2nd rev. ed. 988p. 1974. 170.25 (ISBN 0-444-10562-X, North-Holland). Elsevier.

--The Chemistry of Imperfect Crystals, Vol. 3. 1975. 61.75 (ISBN 0-444-10563-8, North-Holland); Vols. 1-3. 272.00 (ISBN 0-686-85932-4). Elsevier.

Kroger, William S. Childbirth with Hypnosis. (Illus.). pap. 5.00 (ISBN 0-87980-021-6). Wilshire.

--Clinical & Experimental Hypnosis: In Medicine, Dentistry & Psychology. 2nd ed. LC 77-10320. 1977. 32.50 (ISBN 0-397-50377-6, Lippincott Medical). Lippincott.

Krogh, August. Anatomy & Physiology of Capillaries. 1929. 75.00x (ISBN 0-685-89734-6). Elliots Bks.

Krogh, Daniel & McCarty, John. The Amazing Herschell Gordon Lewis & His World of Exploitation Films. (Illus.). 240p. (Orig.). 1983. pap. 14.95x (ISBN 0-938782-03-7). Fantaco.

Krogh, Peter F., jt. auth. see Herz, Martin F.

Krogh, Suzanne, jt. auth. see Schuncke, George.

Krogman, Dane & Holelson, Doug. Skeleton Boy: The Nuclear Hero. (Illus.). 80p. 1982. 8.95 (ISBN 0-910519-00-5). Daneco Pubns.

Krogman, David W. The Biochemistry of Green Plants. LC 73-7637. (Foundatons of Modern Biochemistry Ser). (Illus.). 224p. 1973. pap. 13.95 ref. ed. o.p. (ISBN 0-13-076455-8). P-H.

Krohn, Ernst C. The History of Music. LC 65-23398. (Music Reprint Ser.). 1973. Repr. of 1958 ed. lib. bdg. 32.50 (ISBN 0-306-70595-8). Da Capo.

--Missouri Music. LC 65-23398. (Music Ser.). xlvi, 380p. 1971. Repr. of 1924 ed. lib. bdg. 39.50 (ISBN 0-306-70932-5). Da Capo.

Krohn, Robert, jt. auth. see English Language Institute.

Krohn, Roger G. Social Shaping of Science: Institutions, Ideology, & Careers in Science. LC 75-90792. (Contributions in Sociology: No. 4). (Illus.). 1971. lib. bdg. 29.95 (ISBN 0-8371-1852-2, KRS/). Greenwood.

Krohn, Val F. Hawaii Dye Plants & Dye Recipes. LC 79-27162. (Illus.). 136p. 1980. pap. 8.95 (ISBN 0-8248-0698-0). UH Pr.

Krohne, H. W. Achievement, Stress & Anxiety. 1981. 34.50 (ISBN 0-07-035521-5). McGraw.

Krois, John M., tr. see Grassi, Ernesto.

Kroitor, Harry P., jt. auth. see Martin, Lee J.

Krol, B. & Tinbergen, B. J., eds. Proceedings of the International Symposium on Nitrite in Meat Products. 266p. 1974. pap. 36.00 o.p. (ISBN 90-220-0463-5, Pub. by PUDOC). Unipub.

Kroll, Arthur M., et al. Career Development: Growth & Crisis. LC 81-19342. 272p. 1983. Repr. of 1970 ed. lib. bdg. cancelled o.p. (ISBN 0-89874-398-2). Krieger.

--Career Development: Growth & Crisis. LC 79-96048. 262p. 1970. 23.50 o.p. (ISBN 0-471-50850-0, Pub. by Wiley-Interscience). Wiley.

Kroll, Jarrett & Kroll, Stanley. Cruising the Inland Waterways of Europe. LC 78-2151. 1979. 21.10i (ISBN 0-06-012456-3, HarpT). Har-Row.

Kroll, Larry J. & Silverman, Manuel S. Opiate Addiction: Theory & Process. LC 80-8283. 199p. 1980. lib. bdg. 19.75 (ISBN 0-8191-1324-7); pap. text ed. 9.75 (ISBN 0-8191-1325-5). U Pr of Amer.

Kroll, Paul W. Meng Hao-Jan. (World Authors Ser.). 1981. lib. bdg. 15.95 (ISBN 0-8057-6470-4, Twayne). G K Hall.

Kroll, Stanley. The Professional Commodity Trader: Look Over My Shoulder. LC 74-1827. 192p. 1974. 18.22i (ISBN 0-06-012468-7, HarpT). Har-Row.

Kroll, Stanley, jt. auth. see Kroll, Jarrett.

Kroll, Steven. Amanda & the Giggling Ghost. LC 79-28379. (Illus.). 40p. (ps-3). 1980. PLB 9.95 (ISBN 0-8234-0408-0). Holiday.

--Big Bunny & the Easter Eggs. LC 81-11613. (Illus.). 32p. (ps-3). 1982. PLB 11.95 (ISBN 0-8234-0436-6). Holiday.

--The Candy Witch. LC 79-10141. (Illus.). 32p. (gr. k-3). 1979. PLB 9.95 (ISBN 0-8234-0359-9). Holiday.

--Friday the Thirteenth. LC 80-28769. (Illus.). 32p. (gr. k-3). 1981. PLB 9.95 (ISBN 0-8234-0392-0). Holiday.

--The Goat Parade. (Illus.). 48p. (ps-3). 1983. 5.50 (ISBN 0-8193-1099-9); PLB 5.95 (ISBN 0-8193-1100-6). Parents.

--Is Milton Missing? LC 75-4586. (Illus.). 32p. (ps-3). 1975. PLB 8.95 (ISBN 0-8234-0261-4). Holiday.

--One Tough Turkey. LC 82-2925. (Illus.). 32p. (ps-3). 1982. Reinforced bdg. 10.95 (ISBN 0-8234-0457-9). Holiday.

--Otto. (Illus.). 48p. (ps-3). 1983. 5.50 (ISBN 0-8193-1105-7); PLB 5.95 (ISBN 0-8193-1106-5). Parents.

--Santa's Crash-Bang Christmas. LC 77-3025. (Illus.). (gr. k-3). 1977. PLB 9.95 (ISBN 0-8234-0302-5). Holiday.

--T. J. Folger. Thief. LC 77-24575. (Illus.). (gr. 1-3). 1978. PLB 5.95 (ISBN 0-8234-0313-0). Holiday.

--Toot! Toot! LC 82-9356. (Illus.). 32p. (ps-3). 1983. reinforced binding 12.95 (ISBN 0-8234-0471-4). Holiday.

--The Tyrannosaurus Game. LC 75-37078. (Illus.). 40p. (ps-3). 1976. PLB 8.95 (ISBN 0-8234-0275-4). Holiday.

--Woof, Woof! LC 82-9776. (Illus.). 32p. (ps-3). 1983. lib. bdg. 10.95 (ISBN 0-8037-9653-6, 01063-320); 10.89 (ISBN 0-8037-9651-X). Dial Bks Young.

Kroll, Walter P. Graduate Study & Research in Physical Education. Rev. ed. LC 82-81057. 361p. 1982. text ed. 19.95x (ISBN 0-931250-31-5). Human Kinetics.

Kroll, Woodrow M. Bible Country. LC 81-60782. (Accent Imperials Ser.). (Illus.). 64p. (Orig.). 1982. gift book 29.95 (ISBN 0-89636-060-1); pap. 19.95 softcover (ISBN 0-89636-098-9). Accent Bks.

Krom, Charles, jt. auth. see Fulsher, Keith.

Kroman, Henry S. & Bender, Sheldon R., eds. Theory & Application of Gas Chromatography in Industry & Medicine. (Illus.). 320p. 1968. 74.00 o.p. (ISBN 0-8089-0248-2). Grune.

Kroman, Vera. How to Raise & Train a Samoyed. (Orig.). pap. 2.95 (ISBN 0-87666-378-1, DS1113). TFH Pubns.

Kromdijk, G. Two-Hundred House Plants in Color. (Illus.). 1972. 15.95 o.p. (ISBN 0-07-073280-9, GB). McGraw.

Kromer, Helen. Communes & Communitarians in America. (Jackdaw Ser: No. A4). (Illus.). 1972. 6.95 o.p. (ISBN 0-670-23305-6, Grossman). Viking Pr.

Kromholz, Susan F. The Bronze Age Necropolis at Ayia Paraskevi (Nicosia) Unpublished Tombs in the Cyprus Museum. (Studies in Mediterranean Archaeology: No. 17). 360p. 1982. pap. text ed. 34.50x (ISBN 91-86098-01-2, Pub. by Astroms Sweden). Humanities.

Krommenhoek, W. Biological Structure. 144p. 1979. text ed. 19.95 (ISBN 0-8391-1402-8). Univ Park.

Krommer-Benz, Magdalena. World Guide to Terminological Activities. (Infoterm Ser.: Vol. 4). 311p. 1977. pap. text ed. 45.00x (ISBN 3-7940-5504-7, Pub. by K G Saur). Gale.

Kromschlies, C., jt. auth. see Mrachek, L.

Kron, Joan & Slesin, Suzanne. High-Tech: The Industrial-Style Source Book for the Home. (Illus.). 1978. 29.95 (ISBN 0-517-53262-X, C N Potter Bks). Crown.

Kron, Thora. The Management of Patient Care: Putting Leadership Skill to Work. 4th ed. LC 75-38153. (Illus.). 1976. pap. text ed. 9.95 o.p. (ISBN 0-7216-5528-9). Saunders.

Kronberger, Helge F., tr. see Sechrist, Elsie.

Krone, Robert. Systems Analysis & Policy Sciences. LC 80-13335. (Systems Engineering & Analysis Ser.). 216p. 1980. 29.95x (ISBN 0-471-05864-5, Pub. by Wiley-Interscience). Wiley.

Kronecker, L., ed. see Lejeune-Dirichlet, P. G.

Kronecker, Leopold. Werke, 5 vols. LC 66-20394. 1969. Repr. Set. 125.00 (ISBN 0-8284-0224-8). Chelsea Pub.

Kronemeyer, Robert, et al. Overcoming Homosexuality. LC 79-23644. 160p. 1980. 11.95 (ISBN 0-02-566850-1). Macmillan.

Kronenberg, Philip, jt. ed. see Lovell, John.

Kronenfeld, Jennie J., jt. ed. see Charles, Edgar D.

Kroner, A., ed. Precambrian Plate Tectonics: Developments in Precambrian Geology Ser. (Vol. 4). 1981. 161.75 (ISBN 0-444-41910-1). Elsevier.

Kronick, Doreen, et al. What about Me? The LD Adolescent. LC 74-29558. 1975. pap. 7.00x (ISBN 0-87879-095-0). Acad Therapy.

Kronk, Gary W. Comets: A Descriptive Catalog. LC 82-20971. 256p. 1983. pap. text ed. 19.95x (ISBN 0-89490-071-4); 29.95 (ISBN 0-89490-094-3). Enslow Pubs.

--Meteor Showers: A Descriptive Catalog. (Illus.). 128p. 1983. pap. text ed. 11.95x (ISBN 0-89490-072-2). Enslow Pubs.

Kronman, Anthony T. Max Weber. LC 82-80923. (Jurists, Profiles in Legal Theory). 224p. 1983. 18.50x (ISBN 0-8047-1140-2). Stanford U Pr.

Kronsjo, L. Algorithms: Their Complexity & Efficiency. 361p. 1979. 62.95x (ISBN 0-471-99752-8). Wiley.

Kronstein, Heinrich D., et al. Major American Antitrust Laws: A Guide to Their Domestic & Foreign Application. LC 65-14218. 442p. 1965. 25.00 (ISBN 0-379-11604-9). Oceana.

Kronus, Sidney. Black Middle Class. LC 79-148247. 1971. pap. text ed. 3.95x o.p. (ISBN 0-675-09218-3). Merrill.

Kroodsma, Donald, et al, eds. Accoustic Communication in Birds: Vol. 1: Sounds Production, Perception & Design Features of Sounds. (Communication & Behavior Ser.). 318p. 1983. 36.00 (ISBN 0-12-426801-3). Acad Pr.

--Accoustic Communication in Birds: Vol. 2: Song Learning & Its Consequences. (Communication & Behavior Ser.). 318p. 1983. 39.00 (ISBN 0-12-426802-1). Acad Pr.

Kroon, A. M. & Saccone, C. Organization & Expression of the Mithcondrial Genome, Vol. 2. (Proceedings). 1980. 81.00 (ISBN 0-444-80276-2). Elsevier.

Krooss, Herman E. & Gilbert, Charles. American Business History. 352p. 1972. pap. 14.95 ref ed. (ISBN 0-13-024083-4). P-H.

Krooss, Herman E., jt. auth. see Blyn, Martin R.

Kropf, William, jt. auth. see Houben, Milton.

Kropotkin, Igor, jt. auth. see Kropotkin, Marjorie.

Kropotkin, Marjorie & Kropotkin, Igor. The Inn Cookbook: New England. 288p. 1983. 18.45 (ISBN 0-316-50473-4); pap. 9.70i (ISBN 0-316-50474-2). Little.

Kropotkin, Peter. In Russian & French Prisons. LC 70-163332. (Studies in the Libertarian & Utopian Tradition). 1971. 9.00x o.p. (ISBN 0-8052-3422-5); pap. 4.95 (ISBN 0-8052-0318-4). Schocken.

--Kropotkin's Revolutionary Pamphlets. Baldwin, Roger, ed. 9.25 (ISBN 0-8446-0748-7). Peter Smith.

--Memoirs of a Revolutionist. 1970. pap. 6.00 o.s.i. (ISBN 0-486-22485-6). Dover.

--Mutual Aid. (Extending Horizons Ser). 1976. pap. 6.95 (ISBN 0-87558-024-6). Porter Sargent.

Kropotkin, Petr A. Fields, Factories & Workshops or Industry Combined with Agriculture & Brain Work with Manual Work. LC 68-28589. (Illus.). 1968. Repr. of 1901 ed. lib. bdg. 16.25x (ISBN 0-8371-0135-2, KRBM). Greenwood.

Kropp, Paul. Baby, Baby. LC 82-12931. (Encounter Ser.). (Illus.). 96p. 1982. pap. text ed. 3.95 (ISBN 0-88436-962-5); wkbk. 1.20 (ISBN 0-88436-966-8). EMC.

--Burn Out. LC 81-5357. (Encounters Ser.). (Illus.). 96p. (gr. 7-12). 1982. pap. 3.95 (ISBN 0-88436-815-7, 35271); wkbk. 1.20 (ISBN 0-88436-924-2, 35684). EMC.

--Dead On. LC 81-7871. (Encounters Ser.). (Illus.). 96p. (gr. 7-12). 1982. pap. text ed. 3.95 (ISBN 0-88436-816-5, 35267); wkbk. 1.20 (ISBN 0-88436-925-0, 35680). EMC.

--Dirt Bike. LC 81-5367. (Encounters Ser.). (Illus.). 96p. (gr. 7-12). 1982. pap. text ed. 3.95 (ISBN 0-88436-817-3, 35268); wkbk. 1.20 (ISBN 0-88436-926-9, 35681). EMC.

--Dope Deal. LC 81-9766. (Encounters Ser.). (Illus.). 96p. (gr. 7-12). 1982. pap. 3.95 (ISBN 0-88436-818-1, 35272); wkbk. 1.20 (ISBN 0-88436-927-7, 35685). EMC.

--Fair Play. LC 81-5366. (Encounters Ser.). (Illus.). 96p. (gr. 7-12). 1982. pap. text ed. 3.95 (ISBN 0-88436-819-X, 35274); wkbk. 1.20 (ISBN 0-88436-928-5, 35687). EMC.

--Gang War. LC 82-12928. (Encounter Ser.). (Illus.). 96p. 1982. pap. text ed. 3.95 (ISBN 0-88436-963-3); wkbk. 1.20 (ISBN 0-88436-967-6). EMC.

--Hot Cars. LC 81-5358. (Encounters Ser.). (Illus.). 96p. (gr. 7-12). 1981. pap. text ed. 3.95 (ISBN 0-88436-820-3, 35270); wkbk. 1.20 (ISBN 0-88436-929-3, 35683). EMC.

--No Way. LC 81-5557. (Encounters Ser.). (Illus.). 96p. (gr. 7-12). 1982. pap. text ed. 3.95 (ISBN 0-88436-821-1, 35269); wkbk. 1.20 (ISBN 0-88436-930-7, 35682). EMC.

--Runaway. LC 81-5356. (Encounters Ser.). (Illus.). 96p. (gr. 7-12). 1982. pap. 3.95 (ISBN 0-88436-822-X, 35273); wkbk. 1.20 (ISBN 0-88436-931-5, 35686). EMC.

--Snow Ghost. LC 82-12930. (Encounters Ser.). (Illus.). 96p. 1982. pap. text ed. 3.95 (ISBN 0-88436-964-1); wkbk. 1.20 (ISBN 0-88436-968-4). EMC.

--Wild One. LC 82-12929. (Encounters Ser.). 96p. 1982. pap. text ed. 3.95 (ISBN 0-88436-965-X); wkbk. 1.20 (ISBN 0-88436-969-2). EMC.

--Wilted: A Novel. LC 79-4592. (gr. 6-10). 1980. 7.95 (ISBN 0-698-20493-X, Coward). Putnam Pub Group.
Kropt, Wilbur D. Jewelry & the Wedding Band. 1969. 1.00 (ISBN 0-686-30766-6). Rod & Staff.
Krosby, H. Peter. Finland, Germany & the Soviet Union, 1940-1941: The Petsamo Dispute. (Illus.). 294p. 1968. 27.50x (ISBN 0-299-05140-4). U of Wis Pr.
Kroschwitz, Jacqueline I. & Winokur, Melvin. Chemistry: A First Course. (Illus.). 1980. text ed. 23.95x (ISBN 0-07-035531-2); lab. manual 14.95x (ISBN 0-07-035534-7); study guide 11.95x (ISBN 0-07-035533-9); instr's manual 12.00x (ISBN 0-07-035532-0). McGraw.
Kross, Jessica. The Evolution of an American Town: Newtown, New York, 1642-1775. 277p. 1982. text ed. 29.95 (ISBN 0-87722-277-0). Temple U Pr.
Kroth, Jerome A. Child Sexual Abuse: Analysis of a Family Therapy Approach. (Illus.). 216p. 1979. photocopy ed. spiral 21.75x (ISBN 0-398-03906-2). C C Thomas.
Krotkoff, Georg. A Neo-Aramaic Dialect of Kurdistan. (American Oriental Ser.: Vol. 64). 1982. 21.00 (ISBN 0-940490-64-1). Am Orient Soc.
Krotkov, Yuri. The Nobel Prize. 1980. 12.95 o.p. (ISBN 0-671-24255-5, 24255). S&S.
Kroto, H. W. Molecular Rotation Spectra. LC 73-14381. 346p. 1975. 50.00 o.p. (ISBN 0-471-50853-5, Pub. by Wiley-Interscience). Wiley.
Krouse, Charles. A Fool's Bubbles. 1976. pap. 1.50 (ISBN 0-686-17459-3). Windmill Pr.
--Spider Bite & Other Poems. 60p. 1976. pap. 2.95 (ISBN 0-686-15618-8). Windmill Pr.
Krout, John A. & Rice, Arnold S. United States Since 1865. LC 76-18396. (Illus.). 310p. (Orig.). 1977. pap. 4.95 (ISBN 0-06-460168-4, COS CO 168). B&N NY.
Krout, John S. Annals of American Sport. 1929. text ed. 22.50x (ISBN 0-686-83470-4). Elliots Bks.
Krstulovic, Ante M. & Brown, Phyllis R. Reversed-Phase High Performance Liquid Chromatography: Theory, Practice, & Biomedical Applications. LC 81-15944. 296p. 1982. 39.50x (ISBN 0-471-05369-4, Pub. by Wiley Interscience). Wiley.
Kruberg, Galina. A Handbook for Translating from English into Russian. 172p. 1982. pap. text ed. 13.95x (ISBN 0-8020-2473-4). U of Toronto Pr.
Kruchko, John G. Birth of a Union Local: The History of UAW Local 674, Norwood, Ohio, 1933-1940. LC 72-619603. 80p. 1972. pap. 3.50 (ISBN 0-87546-046-1). ILR Pr.
Krudy, E S & Shiers, D, eds. Mycoplasma: A Bibliography. 180p. 24.00 (ISBN 0-904147-06-1). IRL Pr.
Krudy, E S, et al, eds. Time: A Bibliograpy. 207p. 24.00 (ISBN 0-904147-05-3). IRL Pr.
Krueckeberg, Donald A. The American Planner. 1983. 29.95x (ISBN 0-416-33360-5). Methuen Inc.
Kruegar, Janelle C. & Nelson, Allen H. Nursing Research: Development, Collaboration & Utilization. LC 78-26215. 324p. 1979. text ed. 34.50 (ISBN 0-89443-082-3). Aspen Systems.
Krueger. The Hypodermic Injection: A Programmed Unit. pap. text ed. 7.50 (ISBN 0-686-97976-1, Lippincott Nursing). Lippincott.
Krueger, Anne O. Exchange Rate Determination. LC 82-14649. (Cambridge Surveys of Economic Literature Ser.). (Illus.). 240p. Date not set. price not set (ISBN 0-521-25304-7); pap. price not set (ISBN 0-521-27301-3). Cambridge U Pr.
--Foreign Trade Regimes & Economic Development: Liberalization Attempts & Consequences. LC 77-14401. (Foreign Trade Regimes & Economic Development Ser.: Vol. 10). 336p. 1978. prof ref 25.00x (ISBN 0-88410-483-4, Pub for the National Bureau of Economic Research). Ballinger Pub.
--Foreign Trade Regimes & Economic Development: Liberalization Attempts & Consequences. (Studies in International Economic Relations; Special Conference Ser. on Foreign Trade Regimes & Economic Development: No. 9; No. 10). 1978. prof ref 18.50x (ISBN 0-88410-483-4). Ballinger Pub.
--Trade & Employment in Developing Countries: Synthesis & Conclusions, Vol. 3. LC 80-15826. (National Bureau of Economic Research - Monograph). 232p. 1983. 25.00x (ISBN 0-226-45494-0). U of Chicago Pr.
Krueger, Anne O. & Tuncer, Baran. Estimating Total Factor Productivity Growth in a Developing Country. (Working Paper: No. 422). 64p. 1980. 3.00 (ISBN 0-686-36182-2, WP-0422). World Bank.
Krueger, Anne O., jt. ed. see Hong, Wontack.
Krueger, Catherine M. Mother Was a Bachelor. 1983. 10.00 (ISBN 0-533-05496-6). Vantage.
Krueger, Dottie M. Dottie's Poems. 1983. 6.95 (ISBN 0-686-42944-3). Carlton.
Krueger, Glee F. A Gallery of American Samplers: The Theodore Kapnek Collection. 1978. 19.95 o.p. (ISBN 0-525-11130-1); pap. 10.95 o.p. (ISBN 0-525-47515-X). Dutton.
Krueger, Janelle, jt. auth. see Luke, Roice D.
Krueger, John R. Mongolian Epigraphical Dictionary in reverse Listing. LC 67-63757. (Uralic & Altaic Ser: Vol. 88). (Orig., Mongolian). 1967. pap. text ed. 6.00x o.p. (ISBN 0-87750-078-9). Res Ctr Lang Semiotic.
Krueger, John R., ed. Cheremis-Chuvash Lexical Relationships. (Uralic & Altaic Ser: Vol. 94). 1968. pap. text ed. 8.00x o.p. (ISBN 0-87750-039-8). Res Ctr Lang Semiotic.
--Turkic Peoples: Selected Russian Entries from the Great Soviet Encyclopedia with an Index in English. LC 63-64306. (Uralic & Altaic Ser: Vol. 32). (Orig.). 1963. pap. text ed. 12.00x o.p. (ISBN 0-87750-057-6). Res Ctr Lang Semiotic.
Krueger, John R., jt. ed. see Gronbech, Kaare.
Krueger, Marlis & Silvert, Frieda. Dissent Denied. LC 75-8273. 1975. 16.95 (ISBN 0-444-99005-4, North Holland). Elsevier.
Krueger, Myron W. Artificial Reality. LC 82-3897. (Illus.). 312p. 1983. pap. 10.95 (ISBN 0-201-04765-9). A-W.
Krueger, Robert, ed. see Davies, John.
Krug, C. A. & De Poerck, R. A. World Coffee Survey. (Agricultural Study: No. 76). (Illus., Orig.). 1969. pap. 26.25 (ISBN 0-685-20811-7, F505, FAO). Unipub.
Krug, Edward A. Shaping of the American High School, Vol. 1, 1880-1920. LC 64-12801. 504p. 1969. pap. text ed. 12.50 (ISBN 0-299-05165-X). U of Wis Pr.
Krug, Mark M., ed. What Will Be Taught: The Next Decade. LC 77-174167. 1972. pap. text ed. 8.50 (ISBN 0-87581-117-5). Peacock Pubs.
Krug, Samuel E. Interpreting 16 PF Profile Patterns. LC 81-7012. 1981. pap. 14.95 (ISBN 0-918296-16-1). Inst Personality & Ability.
Krugar, A. N., jt. auth. see Manicas, Peter T.
Kruger, A. N. Modern Debate: Its Logic & Strategy. (Speech Ser.). 1960. text ed. 14.95 o.p. (ISBN 0-07-035545-2, C); 0.75 o.p. instructor's manual (ISBN 0-07-035547-9). McGraw.
Kruger, Barbara. No Progress in Pleasure. (Illus.). 16p. (Orig.). 1982. pap. 4.00 (ISBN 0-939784-02-5). CEPA Gall.
Kruger, C. H., jt. auth. see Vincenti, W. G.
Kruger, Daniel H. & Schmidt, Charles T., Jr. Collective Bargaining in the Public Service. 1969. pap. text ed. 4.95x (ISBN 0-685-30608-9). Phila Bk Co.
Kruger, F. J., et al, eds. Mediterranean-Type Ecosystems: The Role of Nutrients. (Ecological Studies: Vol. 43). (Illus.). 530p. 1983. 39.50 (ISBN 0-387-12158-7). Springer-Verlag.
Kruger, Gustav O. Textbook of Oral & Maxillofacial Surgery. 5th ed. LC 78-26118. (Illus.). 174p. 1979. 39.95 (ISBN 0-8016-2792-3). Mosby.
Kruger, Horst. A Crack in the Wall. Hein, Ruth, tr. from Ger. LC 81-22180. Orig. Title: Das Zerbrochene Haus. 250p. 1982. 13.95 (ISBN 0-88064-000-6). Fromm Intl Pub.
Kruger, James E., ed. see International Symposium on Pre-Harvest Sprouting in Cereals.
Kruger, L. Die Hamburgische Musikorganisation Im XVII. (Sammlung Mw. Abh. Ser.). viii, 276p. 35.00 o.s.i. (ISBN 90-6027-286-2, Pub. by Frits Knuf Netherlands). Pendragon NY.
Kruger, Mollee. Daughters of Chutzpah: Humorous Verse on the Jewish Woman. LC 82-71394. (Illus.). 110p. (Orig.). 1983. pap. 5.50x (ISBN 0-9602036-7-2). Biblio NY.
Kruger, Paul & Otte, Carel, eds. Geothermal Energy: Resources, Production, Stimulation. LC 72-85700. (Illus.). xii, 356p. 1973. 22.50x (ISBN 0-8047-0822-3). Stanford U Pr.
Krugers, J. & Keulemans, A. I., eds. Practical Instrumental Analysis. 1965. 25.75 (ISBN 0-444-40342-6). Elsevier.
Kruglak & Moore. Basic Mathematics for the Physical Sciences. 1963. pap. 9.95 o.p. (ISBN 0-07-035550-9, C). McGraw.
Kruglak, Gregory T. The Politics of United States Decision-Making in United Nations Specialized Agencies: The Case of the International Labor Organization. LC 80-5318. 300p. 1980. lib. bdg. 19.75 (ISBN 0-8191-1075-2); pap. text ed. 11.75 (ISBN 0-8191-1076-0). U Pr of Amer.
Kruglak, Haym & Moore, J. T. Basic Mathematics with Applications. (Schaum Outline Ser.). 1973. text ed. 5.95 (ISBN 0-07-035551-7, SP). McGraw.
Kruglinski, David. Data Base Management Systems: A Guide to Microcomputer Software. 272p. (Orig.). 1982. pap. 16.95 (ISBN 0-931988-84-5). Osborne-McGraw.
Krugman, Saul & Gocke, David J. Viral Hepatitis. LC 77-16974. (Major Problems in Internal Medicine Ser.: Vol. 15). (Illus.). 1978. text ed. 22.00 o.p. (ISBN 0-7216-5538-6). Saunders.
Krugman, Saul & Katz, Samuel L. Infectious Diseases of Children. 7th ed. LC 80-24696. (Illus.). 607p. 1980. text ed. 45.50 (ISBN 0-8016-2796-6). Mosby.
Kruif, Paul De see De Kruif, Paul.
Kruk, Leonard, jt. auth. see Kleinschrod, Walter.
Kruk, Z. L., jt. auth. see D'Mello, A.
Kruk, Zygmunt L. Neurotransmitters & Drugs. 176p. 1979. pap. text ed. 12.95 (ISBN 0-8391-1483-4). Univ Park.
Krulik, Stephen, et al. The Civil Service Examination Handbook. rev ed. (RL 8). 1979. pap. 3.95 (ISBN 0-451-11166-4, AE1166, Sig). NAL.
Krull, Kathleen, jt. auth. see Allington, Richard L.
Krull, Kathleen, ed. see Allington, Richard L. & Krull, Kathleen.
Kruman, Marc W. Parties & Politics in North Carolina, 1836 to 1865. LC 82-20364. 384p. 1983. text ed. 37.50x (ISBN 0-8071-1041-8); pap. text ed. 14.95x (ISBN 0-8071-1061-2). La State U Pr.
Krumbein, William C. & Graybill, F. A. Introduction to Statistical Models in Geology. (International Ser.in the Earth & Planetary Sciences). 1965. text ed. 21.95 o.p. (ISBN 0-07-035555-X, C). McGraw.
Krumbein, Wolfgang E., ed. Environmental Biogeochemistry & Geomicrobiology, 3 vols. LC 77-84416. 1978. Vol. 1. 40.00 (ISBN 0-250-40218-1); Vol. 2. 50.00 (ISBN 0-250-40219-X); Vol. 3. 50.00 (ISBN 0-250-40220-3). Ann Arbor Science.
Krumboltz, Helen, jt. auth. see Krumboltz, John D.
Krumboltz, John D. & Hamel, Daniel A. Assessing Career Development. LC 81-84697. 296p. 1982. 22.95 (ISBN 0-87484-552-1). Mayfield Pub.
Krumboltz, John D. & Krumboltz, Helen. Changing Children's Behavior. (Counseling & Guidance Ser). 1972. 21.95 (ISBN 0-13-127951-3); pap. text ed. 15.95 (ISBN 0-13-127944-0). P-H.
Krummel, D. W., ed. see Newberry Library.
Krummel, Don W., ed. see International Association of Music Libraries.
Krummes, Daniel & Kleiber, Michael. Recent Transportation Literature for Planning & Engineering Librarians. (Public Administration Ser.: Bibliography P 1077). 49p. 1982. pap. 7.50 (ISBN 0-88066-267-0). Vance Biblios.
--Recent Transportation Literature for Planning & Engineering Librarians. (Public Administration Ser.). 51p. 1983. pap. 7.50 (ISBN 0-88066-348-0, P 1118). Vance Biblios.
Krump, John. What a Modern Catholic Believes About Eucharist. 96p. (Orig.). 1974. pap. 5.95 o.p. (ISBN 0-88347-040-3). Thomas More.
Krumphanzl, V., et al, eds. Overproduction of Microbial Products. 1982. 75.00 (ISBN 0-12-426920-6). Acad Pr.
Krumwiede, Heinrich, jt. auth. see Grabendorff, Wolf.
Krupa, Gene. Situational Writing. 272p. 1982. pap. text ed. 8.95x (ISBN 0-534-01082-2). Wadsworth Pub.
Krupa, S. V., ed. Ecology of Root Pathogens. Dommergues, Y. R., tr. (Developments in Agricultural & Managed-Forest Ecology: Vol. 5). 1979. 81.00 (ISBN 0-444-41639-0). Elsevier.
Krupat, Edward. Psychology Is Social: Readings & Conversations in Social Psychology. 2nd ed. 1982. pap. text ed. 13.50x (ISBN 0-673-15382-7). Scott F.
Krupin, Theodore, jt. auth. see Waltman, Stephen R.
Krupinski, Jerzy & Stoller, Alan. The Family in Australia: Social, Demographic & Psychological Aspects. 273p. 1974. text ed. 28.00 o.p. (ISBN 0-08-017374-8). Pergamon.
--The Family in Australia: Social, Demographic & Psychological Aspects. 2nd ed. 1978. text ed. 20.00 (ISBN 0-08-022260-9); pap. text ed. 13.50 (ISBN 0-08-022259-5). Pergamon.
Krupp, E. C. Echoes of the Ancient Skies: The Astronomy of Lost Civilization. LC 82-48121. (Illus.). 352p. 1983. 19.18i (ISBN 0-06-015101-3, HarpT). Har-Row.
Krupp, E. C., ed. Archaeoastronomy & the Roots of Science. (AAAS Selected Symposium Ser.: No. 71). 400p. 1983. price not set (ISBN 0-86531-406-3). Westview.
--In Search of Ancient Astronomies: Stonehenge to von Daniken: Archaeoastronomy Discovers Our Sophisticated Ancestors. (Illus.). 1979. pap. 5.95 (ISBN 0-07-035556-8, SP). McGraw.
Krupp, Marcus A. & Chatton, Milton J., eds. Current Medical Diagnosis & Treatment. rev. ed. LC 74-641062. 1130p. 1983. lexotone cover 24.00 (ISBN 0-87041-253-1). Lange.
Kruppa, Thomas. Die Bankenhaftung Bei der Sanierung Einter Kapitalgesellschaft Im Insolvenzfall. lxiii, 310p. (Ger.). 1982. write for info. (ISBN 3-8204-7115-4). P Lang Pubs.
Krupski, AnnMarie. Inside the Adolescent Alcoholic. 4.95 (ISBN 0-89486-159-X). Hazelden.
Kruschke, Earl R. An Introduction to the Constitution of the United States. 250p. 1968. pap. 8.50 (ISBN 0-442-33130-4, Pub. by Van Nos Reinhold). Krieger.
Kruse, Arthur H. Localization & Iteration of Axiomatic Set Theory. LC 68-29739. 1969. 15.95x o.p. (ISBN 0-8143-1354-X). Wayne St U Pr.
Kruse, Christine G. Patient Centered Audit. (Illus.). 180p. (Orig.). 1983. 19.75 (ISBN 0-87527-247-9). Green.
Kruse, Douglas C. Monetary Integration in Western Europe. LC 80-40980. (Butterworths European Studies Ser.). (Illus.). 256p. 1980. text ed. 39.95 (ISBN 0-408-10666-2). Butterworth.
Kruse, E. G. & Burdick, C. R., eds. Environmentally Sound Water & Soil Management. LC 82-72213. 544p. 1982. pap. text ed. 42.50 (ISBN 0-87262-312-2). Am Soc Civil Eng.
Kruse, Gunther O., jt. ed. see Pritchard, Mary H.
Kruse, John. Red Omega. LC 81-40230. 384p. 1981. 14.50 (ISBN 0-394-52141-2). Random.
--Red Omega. 1983. pap. 3.50 (ISBN 0-686-43297-5). PB.
Kruse, John A. Subsistence & the North Slope Imprint: The Effects of Energy Development. (ISER Report Ser.: No. 56). 45p. 1982. pap. 6.50 (ISBN 0-88353-034-1). U Alaska Inst Res.
Kruse, Olan E. General Physics Demonstration Manual. 1973. Repr. pap. 5.50x wkbk. (ISBN 0-934786-06-2). G Davis.
Kruse, Olan E., et al. Technical Physics Laboratory Manual. 1971. Repr. workbook 6.45x (ISBN 0-934786-07-0). G Davis.
Krusell, Cynthia H., jt. auth. see Coons, Quentin.
Krusentierna, Sten von see Von Krusenstierna, Sten.
Krushchov, N. Problems of Developmental Biology. 207p. 1981. pap. 6.95 (ISBN 0-8285-2444-0, Pub. by Mir Pubs USSR). Imported Pubns.
Krussman, Gerd. A Pocket Guide to Choosing Woody Ornamentals. Epp, Michael, tr. from Ger. Orig. Title: Taschenbuch Der Geholzverwendung. (Illus.). 140p. 1982. pap. 14.95 (ISBN 0-917304-24-1). Timber.
Krussmann, Gerd. The Complete Book of Roses. LC 81-16611. (Illus.). 436p. 1981. 50.00 (ISBN 0-917304-64-0). Timber.
Krustrup, Erik V. Gateway to America: New York City. Christianson, John & Christianson, Birgitta, trs. from Danish. (Dream of America Ser.). Orig. Title: Porten til Amerika: New York City. (Illus.). 72p. (gr. 7-12). 1982. lib. bdg. 59.50 (ISBN 0-87191-709-2). Creative Ed.
Kruszewski, Z. Anthony & Hough, Richard L., eds. Politics & Society in the Southwest: Ethnicity & Chicano Pluralism. (Replicia Edition Ser.). 245p. 1982. softcover 21.50 (ISBN 0-86531-908-1). Westview.
Krutch, John. Experiments in Artificial Intelligence for Small Computers. 1981. pap. 8.95 (ISBN 0-672-21785-6). Sams.
Krutch, Joseph W. Five Masters: A Study in the Mutations of the Novel. 8.50 (ISBN 0-8446-0750-9). Peter Smith.
--Henry David Thoreau. LC 72-9589. (Illus.). 298p. 1973. Repr. of 1948 ed. lib. bdg. 19.25x (ISBN 0-8371-6587-3, KRHT). Greenwood.
--Herbal. LC 65-20676. (Illus.). 256p. 1976. Repr. of 1966 ed. 40.00x (ISBN 0-87923-171-8); pap. 10.00 o.p. (ISBN 0-87923-165-3). Godine.
--Human Nature & the Human Condition. LC 78-12131. 1979. Repr. of 1959 ed. lib. bdg. 19.75x (ISBN 0-313-21010-1, KRHN). Greenwood.
--A Krutch Omnibus: Forty Years of Social & Literary Criticism. LC 80-14794. 342p. 1980. 6.95 (ISBN 0-688-00389-3). Quill NY.
--Modern Temper: A Study & a Confession. LC 29-8012. 1956. pap. 3.95 (ISBN 0-15-661757-9, Harv). HarBraceJ.
Krutch, Joseph W., jt. auth. see Thoreau, Henry D.
Krutchkoff, R. G. Probability & Statistical Inference. 306p. 1970. 52.00 (ISBN 0-677-02530-0). Gordon.
Krutz, Ronald L. Microprocessors & Logic Design. LC 79-17874. 467p. 1980. text ed. 34.95x (ISBN 0-471-02083-4). Wiley.
Krutza, William J. & Dicicco, Philip P. Facing the Issues, No. 3. (Contemporary Discussion Ser.). (Orig.). 1970. pap. 3.50 (ISBN 0-8010-5300-5). Baker Bk.
Krutzch, William C., jt. auth. see Karassik, Igor J.
Kruys, M. H. Verzameling Van Disposities der Verschillende Orgels in Nederland. 2nd. ed. (Bibliotheca Organologica: Vol. 1). 1972. 35.00 o.s.i. (ISBN 90-6027-285-4, Pub. by Frits Knuf Netherlands); wrappers 22.50 o.s.i. (ISBN 90-6027-148-3). Pendragon NY.
Kruzas, Anthony T., ed. Health Services Directory: A Guide to Clinics, Treatment Centers, Rehabilitation Facilities, Care Programs Counseling-Diagnostic Resources & Related Human Services Institutions, Agencies & Associations. 620p. 1981. 78.00x (ISBN 0-8103-0272-1). Gale.
--Medical & Health Information Directory: A Guide to Professional & Nonprofit Organizations, Government Agencies, Educational Institutions, Grant Award Sources, Health Care Insurers, Journals, Newsletters, Review Serials, Etc. 2nd ed. LC 77-82802. 1980. 145.00x (ISBN 0-8103-0267-5). Gale.
--Social Service Organizations & Agencies Directory. 525p. 1982. 68.00x (ISBN 0-8103-0329-9). Gale.
Kruzas, Anthony T. & Gill, Kay, eds. Government Research Centers Directory: A Descriptive Guide to Government & Government-Related Research & Development Centers, Institutes, Laboratories, Test Stations Bureaus, Offices & Other Related Facilities. 2nd ed. 500p. 1982. 200.00x (ISBN 0-8103-0461-9). Gale.
--International Research Centers Directory: A Guide to University-Related, Independent, & Government Research Organizations Established on a Permanent Basis & Carrying on Continuing Research Programs. 400p. 1981. 145.00x (ISBN 0-8103-0465-1). Gale.
--New Government Research Centers Directory. 2nd ed. 434p. 1982. 150.00x (ISBN 0-8103-0462-7). Gale.
--Research Activities & Funding Pogrrams. (The Encyclopedia of Associations Ser.: Vol. 5). Date not set. pap. 150.00 (ISBN 0-8103-0149-0). Gale.
Kruzas, Anthony T. & Schmittroth, John, Jr., eds. New Information Systems & Systems: Supplement to Encyclopedia of Information Systems & Services. 4th ed. 180p. 1981. 170.00 o.p. (ISBN 0-8103-0941-6). Gale.

Kruzas, Anthony T. & Thomas, Robert C., eds. Business Organizations & Agencies Directory. LC 80-32. 1980. 150.00x (ISBN 0-8103-1135-6). Gale.

Kruzas, Anthony T., jt. ed. see Schmittroth, John, Jr.

Kryger, Joanne. Going on: Selected Poems, Nineteen Fifty-Eight to Nineteen Eighty. 80p. 1983. 12.50 (ISBN 0-525-24171-X, 01214-360); pap. 5.95 (ISBN 0-525-48055-2, 0577-180). Dutton.

Kryger, Meir H. Pathophysiology of Respiration. LC 81-2113. (Wiley Ser. in Pathophysiology). 352p. 1981. 19.50x (ISBN 0-471-05923-4, Pub. by Wiley Med). Wiley.

Krygier, Martin, jt. ed. see Kamenka, Eugene.

Krylov. The Soviet Economy: How It Really Works. LC 78-22286. (Illus.). 272p. 1979. 21.95x (ISBN 0-669-02743-X). Lexington Bks.

Krylov, N. M. Introduction to Nonlinear Mechanics. Repr. of 1943 ed. pap. 12.00 (ISBN 0-527-02727-8). Kraus Repr.

Krynine, Dimitri P. & Judd, William R. Principles of Engineering Geology & Geotechnics. (Soil Mechanics & Foundations Library). (Illus.). 1957. text ed. 42.50 (ISBN 0-07-035560-6, C). McGraw.

Krypton, Constantine. Northern Sea Route & the Economy of the Soviet North. LC 76-9087. (Studies of the Research Program on the U.S.S.R: No.14). (Illus.). 1976. Repr. of 1956 ed. lib. bdg. 17.25x (ISBN 0-8371-8886-5, KRNS). Greenwood.

Kryskill, William. Check Out. 6.95 (ISBN 0-8062-1878-9). Carlton.

Kryston, Leonard J. Endocrine Disorders: Focus on Clinical Diagnosis. 1981. pap. text ed. 22.00 (ISBN 0-87488-824-7). Med Exam.

Kryt, D. Dictionary of Chemical Terminology. (Eng. & Ger. & Fr. & Pol. & Rus.). 1980. 83.00 (ISBN 0-444-99788-1). Elsevier.

Krythe, Maymie R. What So Proudly We Hail: All About Our American Flag, Monuments & Symbols. LC 68-15993. (YA) 1968. 9.95 o.p. (ISBN 0-06-003157-3, HarpT); lib. bdg. 9.97 (ISBN 0-06-012464-4). Har-Row.

Krzisnik, Zoran, intro. by. Lines: Janez Bernik. (Illus.). 214p. 1980. 30.00 (ISBN 0-89893-113-4). CDP.

Krzisnik, Zoran, ed. Rihard Jakopic. Jereb, Elza & Mackinnon, Alasdair, trs. (Illus.). 230p. 1981. 50.00 (ISBN 0-89893-170-3). CDP.

Krzys & Litton. World Librarianship: A Comparative Study. (Books in Library & Information Ser.). 232p. 1983. 38.50 (ISBN 0-8247-1731-7). Dekker.

Krzyz, J. G. Problems in Complex Variable Theory. (Modern Analytic & Computational Methods in Science & Mathematics: Vol. 36). 1972. 31.95 (ISBN 0-444-00098-4, North Holland). Elsevier.

Krzyzanowski, Jerzy. Wladyslaw Stanislaw Reymont. (World Authors Ser.). lib. bdg. 15.95 (ISBN 0-8057-2758-2, Twayne). G K Hall.

Krzyzanowski, Ludwik, jt. ed. see Gillon, Adam.

Kschessinska, Mathilde. Dancing in Petersburg: The Memoirs of Kschessinska. Haskell, Arnold, tr. LC 77-7719. (Series in Dance). (Illus.). 1977. Repr. of 1961 ed. lib. bdg. 27.50 (ISBN 0-306-77433-X). Da Capo.

Kselman, Thomas A. Miracles & Prophecies in Nineteenth-Century France. (Illus.). 312p. 1983. 27.50 (ISBN 0-8135-0963-7). Rutgers U Pr.

Kshirsagar. A Course in Linear Models. (Statistics: Textbooks & Monographs). 488p. 1983. write for info. (ISBN 0-8247-1585-3). Dekker.

Ku, Chieh-Kang. The Autobiography of a Chinese Historian. Hummel, Arthur W., ed. (Perspectives in Asian History Ser: No. 12). Repr. of 1931 ed. lib. bdg. 19.50x (ISBN 0-87991-077-1). Porcupine Pr.

Kuan Chu, Wen, tr. see Huai-Chen, Nan.

Kubal, John, ed. Fifty Years of Movie Posters. (Illus.). 168p. 1974. spiral bdg. 9.95 o.p. (ISBN 0-517-51386-2). Crown.

Kubala, T. S. Circuit Concepts: Direct & Alternating Current. LC 75-19521. 1976. pap. 10.00 (ISBN 0-8273-1169-9); instructor's guide 2.75 (ISBN 0-8273-1170-2). Delmar.

Kubala, Thomas S. Electricity One: Devices, Circuits, Materials. LC 79-93322. (Electrical Trades Ser.). 134p. 1981. pap. text ed. 7.00 (ISBN 0-8273-1357-8); instr's. manual 2.50 (ISBN 0-8273-1358-6). Delmar.

--Electricity Two: Devices, Circuits, Materials. LC 79-93323. (Electrical Trades Ser.). 116p. 1981. pap. text ed. 7.00 (ISBN 0-8273-1359-4); instr's. guide 2.50 (ISBN 0-8273-1360-8). Delmar.

Kuballa. Seeing the Real Moscow. 1983. pap. cancelled (ISBN 0-8120-2180-0). Barron.

Kube, Alfred N., intro. by. Italian Majolica XV-XVIII Centuries. Kolokolov, G. S., tr. (Illus.). 299p. 1980. 50.00 (ISBN 0-89893-037-5). CDP.

Kubeck, James J. & Doran, Thomas J., Jr. The Results Kit: How to Hire, Reward & Promote the Winners. LC 81-65592. (Illus.). 110p. 1981. 99.00 (ISBN 0-939550-00-8). DK Halcyon.

Kubeczka, K. H., jt. auth. see Formacek, V.

Kubek, Anthony. Arthur's Faith. Clinkscales, C. C., III, ed. LC 82-73312. 355p. (Orig.). 1982. 9.95 (ISBN 0-9605724-1-4); pap. 7.95 (ISBN 0-9605724-0-6). C & L Pub Co.

Kubie, Nora B. Israel. 2nd rev. ed. (First Bks.). (Illus.). (gr. 4-6). 1978. PLB 8.90 s&l (ISBN 0-531-02239-0). Watts.

Kubiena, Walter L. Micromorphological Features of Soil Geography. 1971. 35.00x o.p. (ISBN 0-8135-0671-9). Rutgers U Pr.

Kubin, Alfred. Kubin's Dance of Death & Other Drawings. LC 72-81285. Orig. Title: Die Blatter Mit Dem Tod. (Illus.). 1973. pap. 3.00 o.p. (ISBN 0-486-22884-3). Dover.

Kubitzki, Klaus & Renner, Susanne. Lauraceae I (Aniba & Aiouea) (Flora Neotropica Ser.: No. 31). (Illus.). 1982. pap. 22.50 (ISBN 0-89327-244-2). NY Botanical.

Kubler, George. Art & Architecture of Ancient America. 1982. pap. 16.95x (ISBN 0-14-056121-8, Pelican). Penguin.

Kubler, Hans. Wood As Building & Hobby Material: How to Use Lumber & Wood-Base Panels & Round Wood Wisely in Construction, for Furniture, & As Fuel. LC 80-13380. 256p. 1980. 24.95x (ISBN 0-471-05390-2, Pub. by Wiley-Interscience); pap. 13.95x (ISBN 0-471-09848-5). Wiley.

Kubler, Rolf. Light in the Aquarium. Ahrens, Christa, tr. from Ger. 1973. pap. 4.95 (ISBN 0-87666-096-0, PS-301). TFH Pubns.

Kubler-Ross, Elisabeth. Living with Death & Dying. (Illus.). 192p. 1981. 10.95 (ISBN 0-02-567140-5). Macmillan.

--Questions & Answers on Death & Dying. LC 73-19046. 177p. 1974. 6.95 o.p. (ISBN 0-02-567120-0). Macmillan.

Kubler-Ross, Elisabeth & Warshaw, M. To Live Until We Say Good-Bye. LC 78-10301. 1978. 12.95 (ISBN 0-13-922955-8); pap. 5.95 (ISBN 0-13-922948-5). P-H.

Kubler-Ross, Elisabeth, ed. see Ewens, Jim & Herrington, Pat.

Kubly, Vincent. The Louisiana Capitol: Its Art & Architecture. LC 76-49889. (Illus.). 1977. 22.50 (ISBN 0-88289-082-4). Pelican.

Kubo, R. Statistical Mechanics. 1965. text ed. 49.00 (ISBN 0-444-10224-8, North-Holland). Elsevier.

--Thermodynamics. 1968. 42.75 (ISBN 0-444-10225-6, North-Holland). Elsevier.

Kubo, Sakae. A Beginner's New Testament Greek Grammar. LC 79-64247. 1979. pap. text ed. 10.25 (ISBN 0-8191-0761-1). U Pr of Amer.

Kubo, Sakae & Specht, Walter. So Many Versions? 320p. 1983. pap. 9.95 (ISBN 0-310-45691-6). Zondervan.

Kubota, Takayuki. Fighting Karate Gosoku Ryu. LC 80-53036. (Illus.). 160p. (Orig.). 1980. pap. 6.95 (ISBN 0-86568-010-8). Unique Pubns.

--Weapons Kumite: Fighting with Traditional Weapons. Gierman, James, ed. (Illus.). 200p. (Orig.). 1983. pap. 7.95 (ISBN 0-86568-042-6, 307). Unique Pubns.

Kubovy, Michael & Pomerantz, James, eds. Perceptual Organization. LC 81-786. 608p. 1981. text ed. 36.00 (ISBN 0-89859-056-6). L Erlbaum Assocs.

Kuc, M. Bryogeography of Expedition Area, Axelberg Heiberg Island, N. W. T. Canada. 1973. 20.00 (ISBN 3-7682-0912-1). Lubrecht & Cramer.

Kucera, Clair L. The Challenge of Ecology. 2nd ed. LC 77-14596. (Illus.). 326p. 1978. pap. text ed. 13.95 o.p. (ISBN 0-8016-2802-4). Mosby.

Kucera, M., ed. see Summer School, Babylon, Czechoslovakia, Sept. 1971.

Kucera, Vladimir. Discrete Linear Control: The Polynomial Equation Approach. LC 78-12956. 206p. 1980. 52.95x (ISBN 0-471-99726-9, Pub. by Wiley-Interscience). Wiley.

Kuch, Peter, ed. Writings on Art & Literature. (Collected Edition of the Writing of G. W. Russell Ser.: No. 4). Date not set. text ed. price not set (ISBN 0-391-01188-X). Humanities.

Kucharek, Casimar. Our Faith. De Vinck, Jose M., ed. LC 82-73784. 350p. 1983. 15.75 (ISBN 0-911726-43-8). Alleluia Pr.

Kuchel, Otto, jt. auth. see Genest, Jacques.

Kuchiba, Masuo, et al, eds. Three Malay Villages: A Sociology of Paddy Growers in West Malaysia. LC 79-573. (Monographs of the Center for Southeast Asian Studies, Kyoto University). 1979. text ed. 22.00x (ISBN 0-8248-0665-4); pap. text ed. 13.00x (ISBN 0-8248-0666-2). UH Pr.

Ku Chieh-Kang. Marriage & Funerals of Su-Chow. Bd. with Marriage & Funerals of Canton. Liu Wan-Chang. (Folklore Series of National Sun Yat-Sen University: No. 21). (Chinese.). 15.00 (ISBN 0-89986-065-6). Oriental Bk Store.

Kuchler, A. W. Vegetation Mapping. (Illus.). 472p. 1967. 30.95x (ISBN 0-471-06812-8, Pub. by Wiley-Interscience). Wiley.

Kuchowicz, B. Bibliography of the Neutrino. 446p. 1967. 103.00x (ISBN 0-677-11490-7). Gordon.

--Nuclear & Relativistic Astrophysics & Nuclidic Cosmochemistry: 1963-1967, 4 vols. 1976. Vol. 1, 380p. 76.00 (ISBN 0-677-02760-5); Vol. 2, 304p. microform 43.00 (ISBN 0-677-02770-2); Vol. 3, 200p. microform 39.00 (ISBN 0-677-02780-X); Vol. 4, 212p. write for info. (ISBN 0-677-02790-7). Gordon.

Kuck, David J. The Structure of Computers & Computations, Vol. 1. LC 78-5412. 1978. text ed. 35.95x (ISBN 0-471-02716-2); tchr's manual 10.00x (ISBN 0-471-05294-9). Wiley.

Kuck, J. A., ed. Methods in Microanalysis. Incl. Vol. 5. The Determination of Oxygen, Selenium, Chromium, & Tungsten. 522p. 1977. 107.00x (ISBN 0-677-20920-7); Vol. 6. The Determination of Sulfur. 466p. 1978. 92.00 (ISBN 0-677-20770-0). Gordon.

--Methods in Microanalysis, Vols. 1-4. Incl. Vol. 1. Simultaneous Rapid Combustion. 576p. 1964. 131.00 (ISBN 0-677-10220-8); Vol. 2. Wet Combustion & Catalytic Methods in Microanalysis. 432p. 1965. 103.00 (ISBN 0-677-10230-5); Vol. 3. The Determination of Carbon & Hydrogen & the Use of New Combustion Catalysts. 602p. 1968. 138.00 (ISBN 0-677-20620-8); Vol. 4. The Determination of Carbon & Hydrogen in the Presence of Other Elements or Simultaneously with Them. 532p. 1969. 115.00x (ISBN 0-677-20630-5). LC 64-18800. Gordon.

Kuczkowski, jt. auth. see Gersting, Judith L.

Kuczynski, Jurgen. Germany: Economic & Labour Conditions Under Fascism. LC 68-30824. (Illus.). 1968. Repr. of 1945 ed. lib. bdg. 17.25x (ISBN 0-8371-0519-6, KUGE). Greenwood.

--The Rise of the Working Class. (Illus., Orig.). 1968. pap. 3.95 o.p. (ISBN 0-07-035580-0, SP). McGraw.

Kudlick, Michael D. Assembly Language Programming for the IBM Systems 360 & 370 for OS-DOS. 2nd ed. 560p. 1983. pap. text ed. write for info. (ISBN 0-697-08166-4); solutions manual avail. (ISBN 0-697-08184-2). Wm C Brown.

Kudlick, Michael D. & Ledin, George, Jr. The COBOL Programmer's Book of Rules. (Computer Technology Ser.). (Illus.). 224p. pap. 14.95 (ISBN 0-534-97923-8). Lifetime Learn.

Kudrle, Robert T. Agricultural Tractors: A World Industry Study. LC 75-20444. 304p. 1976. prof ref 20.00x (ISBN 0-88410-034-0). Ballinger Pub.

Kudrle, Robert T. & Meskin, Lawrence, eds. Reducing the Cost of Dental Care. 240p. 1982. 25.00x (ISBN 0-8166-1118-1). U of Minn Pr.

Kudrow, Lee. Cluster Headache: Mechanisms & Management. (Illus.). 1981. 32.50x (ISBN 0-19-261169-0). Oxford U Pr.

Kuebler, Roy R., Jr. & Smith, Harry, Jr. Statistics: A Beginning. LC 75-35719. 320p. 1976. text ed. 24.95x (ISBN 0-471-50928-0); instructor's manual 7.00x (ISBN 0-471-01541-5); wkbk. 11.95x (ISBN 0-471-02638-7); answers 8.00x (ISBN 0-471-02757-X). Wiley.

Kueck, H. -U. Struktur und Funktionen Mitochondrialer Dna Bei Pilzen. (No. 84, Bibliotheca Mycologica Ser.). (Illus.). 148p. (German.). pap. text ed. 16.80x (ISBN 3-7682-1323-4). Lubrecht & Cramer.

Kuecken, John A. Handbook of Microprocessor Applications. (Illus.). 308p. (Orig.). 1980. 14.95 o.p. (ISBN 0-8306-9935-X); pap. 8.95 (ISBN 0-8306-1203-3). Tab Bks.

--Talking Computers & Telecommunications. 256p. 1982. text ed. 26.50 (ISBN 0-442-24721-4). Van Nos Reinhold.

Kuehl. A Taxonomy of Critical Tasks for Evaluating Student Teaching. 1979. 2.50 (ISBN 0-686-38070-3). Assn Tchr Ed.

Kuehl, John. The Apprentice Fiction of F. Scott Fitzgerald, 1909-1917. (Orig.). 1974. pap. 4.95 (ISBN 0-8135-0790-1). Rutgers U Pr.

--John Hawkes & the Craft of Conflict. 1975. 16.50 (ISBN 0-8135-0802-9). Rutgers U Pr.

Kuehn, Dick & RAK Associates. Interconnect: Why & How. 75p. 1982. 15.00 (ISBN 0-686-98038-7). Telecom Lib.

Kuehn, K., et al, eds. New Trends in Basement Membrane Research. (Tenth Workshop-Conference Hoechst Ser.). 285p. 1982. text ed. 63.00 (ISBN 0-89004-774-X). Raven.

Kuehn, Lowell L., jt. auth. see Kernes, Steven T.

Kuehn, Martin H. Mathematics for Electricians. 3rd ed. 1949. text ed. 23.95 (ISBN 0-07-035599-1, G). McGraw.

Kuehnemund, Terry M., ed. Treasure House: Museums of the Empire State. LC 79-53226. (Illus.). 1979. pap. 10.00 (ISBN 0-89062-042-3, Pub by Roberson Center). Pub Ctr Cult Res.

Kuehner, R. & Romagnesi, H. Complements a la "Flore Analytique". (Bibliotheca Mycologica Ser.: No. 56). (Illus.). 1977. Repr. of 1954 ed. lib. bdg. 40.00x (ISBN 3-7682-1131-2). Lubrecht & Cramer.

Kuehni, Rolf G. Computer Colorant Formulation. 144p. 1975. 20.95x (ISBN 0-669-03335-9). Lexington Bks.

Kuemmerle. Antimicrobial Chemotherapy. 1983. price not set (ISBN 0-86577-082-4). Thieme-Stratton.

--Clinical Pharmacology in Pregnancy. 1983. price not set (ISBN 0-86577-074-3). Thieme-Stratton.

--Fundamentals of Chemotherapy. Date not set. price not set (ISBN 0-86577-066-2). Thieme-Stratton.

Kuemmerle, H. P., et al, eds. Problems of Clinical Pharmacology in Therapeutic Research: Phase I. LC 77-12627. (Advances in Clinical Pharmacology: Vol. 13). (Illus.). 433p. 1977. pap. text ed. 28.50 o.p. (ISBN 0-8067-0113-7). Urban & S.

Kuemmerle, Helmut P. Fundamentals: Clinical Chemotherapy, Vol. 1. (Illus.). 440p. 1983. price not set (ISBN 0-86577-075-1). Thieme-Stratton.

Kuenne, Horst. Laubwaldgesellschaften der Frankenalb. (Illus.). 1969. 12.00 (ISBN 3-7682-0610-6). Lubrecht & Cramer.

Kuenzlen, Martin. Playing Urban Games: The Systems Approach to Planning. LC 75-189032. 1978. 10.00x (ISBN 0-262-11069-5); pap. 4.95x (ISBN 0-262-61028-0). MIT Pr.

Kueppers, B. O. Molecular Theory of Evolution: Outline of a Physico-Chemical Theory of the Origin of Life. (Illus.). 321p. 1983. 32.00 (ISBN 0-387-12080-7). Springer-Verlag.

Kuerti, G. see Von Mises, Richard & Von Karman, Theodore.

Kueshana, Eklal. The Ultimate Frontier. rev., expanded ed. (Illus., Twenty percent discount on 1-4 copies, forty percent on 5-23 copies, fifty on 24 or more). 1982. pap. 5.95 (ISBN 0-9600308-1-6). Stelle.

Kuester & Mize. Optimization Techniques with FORTRAN. 256p. 1973. text ed. 27.50 (ISBN 0-07-035606-8, C). McGraw.

Kuethe, Arnold M. & Chow, Chuen-Yen. Foundations of Aerodynamics: Bases of Aerodynamic Design. 3rd ed. LC 76-20761. 527p. 1976. text ed. 39.95x (ISBN 0-471-50953-1). Wiley.

Kuetzing, F. T. Tabulae Phycologicae, 20 vols. in four. (Bibliotheca Phycologica Ser.: No. 32). 1977. Repr. lib. bdg. 600.00x (ISBN 3-7682-1143-6). Lubrecht & Cramer.

Kuffel & Abdullah, M. High Voltage Engineering. 1970. text ed. 30.00 o.p. (ISBN 0-08-006383-7); pap. text ed. 15.00 (ISBN 0-08-006382-9). Pergamon.

Kufner, A. & Kadlec, J. Fourier Series. 372p. 1971. 22.95 (ISBN 0-592-03944-7). Butterworth.

Kufner, A., jt. auth. see Fucik, S.

Kugel, Yerachmiel & Cohen, Neal P. Government Regulation of Business Ethics: U. S. International Payoffs, 3 vols. LC 77-25901. 1978. Vol. 1-3. looseleaf 85.00 ea. (ISBN 0-379-10258-7); Set. 255.00 (ISBN 0-686-77307-1); Rel. 1. 75.00; Rel. 2. 60.00. Oceana.

Kugelmann, Robert. The Windows of Soul. LC 81-70032. 220p. 1983. 24.50 (ISBN 0-8387-5035-4). Bucknell U Pr.

Kugelmass, I. Newton. Mastering Adolescence in a Dangerous World. LC 77-81795. 264p. 1983. 22.50 (ISBN 0-87527-167-7). Green.

Kugler, Paul. The Alchemy of Discourse: An Archetypal Approach to Language. 144p. 1982. 21.50 (ISBN 0-8387-5020-6). Bucknell U Pr.

Kuh, E. S., jt. auth. see Desoer, C. A.

Kuhfittig, Peter. Technical Calculus with Analytic Geometry. LC 82-9714. (Mathematics Ser.). 512p. 1982. text ed. 22.95 (ISBN 0-534-01191-8). Brooks-Cole.

Kuhl, D. E., ed. Principles of Radionuclide Emission Imaging. 318p. 1983. 25.00 (ISBN 0-08-027093-X). Pergamon.

Kuhlenbeck, H. The World of Philosophy. Gerlach, J., ed. (Limited Volume Series: The Human Brain & Its Universe: Vol. 3). xiv, 508p. 1982. 178.00 (ISBN 3-8055-3419-1). S Karger.

Kuhler, W. J. Computer Assisted Tomography. (International Congress Ser.: No. 419). 1977. pap. 28.50 (ISBN 0-444-15274-1). Elsevier.

Kuhlman, Augustus F. Guide to Material on Crime & Criminal Justice. LC 69-16240. (Criminology, Law Enforcement, & Social Problems Ser.: No. 98). (Added author index prepared by Dorothy C. Culver). 1969. Repr. of 1929 ed. 30.00x (ISBN 0-87585-098-7). Patterson Smith.

Kuhlman, Kathryn. I Believe in Miracles. 1969. pap. 2.25 (ISBN 0-515-04684-1). Jove Pubns.

Kuhlmann, Caspar. Frieden: Kein Thema Europaischer Schulgeschichtsbucher? 298p. (Ger.). 1982. write for info. (ISBN 3-8204-7028-X). P Lang Pubs.

Kuhlthau, Carol. School Librarian's Grade-by-Grade Activities Program. 1981. 23.50x (ISBN 0-87628-744-5). Ctr Appl Res.

Kuhn, A., ed. Industrial Electrochemical Processes. LC 70-118254. (Illus.). 655p. 1971. 98.00 (ISBN 0-444-40885-1). Elsevier.

Kuhn, Alfred & Beam, Robert D. The Logic of Organization: A System-Based Social Science Framework for Organization. LC 82-48059. (Social & Behavioral Science Ser.). 1982. text ed. 22.95x (ISBN 0-87589-529-8). Jossey Bass.

Kuhn, Bob. The Animal Art of Bob Kuhn: A Lifetime of Drawing & Painting. 1982. pap. 15.95 (ISBN 0-89134-050-5). North Light Pub.

Kuhn, D. & Meacham, J. A., eds. On the Development of Developmental Psychology. (Contributions to Human Development: Vol. 8). (Illus.). xii, 160p. 1982. pap. 29.50 (ISBN 3-8055-3568-6). S Karger.

Kuhn, G. & Weiss, D. Guide to Illinois Real Estate License Preparation. 1979. pap. 21.95 (ISBN 0-13-370254-5). P-H.

Kuhn, Gerald W., jt. auth. see Dasso, Jerome.

Kuhn, Helmut. Encounter with Nothingness: An Essay on Existentialism. LC 74-29635. 168p. 1976. Repr. of 1949 ed. lib. bdg. 16.00x (ISBN 0-8371-7982-3, KUEN). Greenwood.

Kuhn, Isobel. Second-Mile People. 1982. pap. 3.50 (ISBN 0-85363-145-X). OMF Bks.

Kuhn, J. W., jt. auth. see Chamberlain, Neil W.

Kuhn, Joaquin & Kuhn, Maura. Rats Live on No Evil Star. 224p. (Orig.). 1981. pap. 7.95 (ISBN 0-89696-122-2, An Everest House Book). Dodd.

Kuhn, Karl F. Basic Physics. LC 78-23384. (Self Teaching Guides Ser.). 326p. 1979. pap. text ed. 8.95 (ISBN 0-471-03011-2). Wiley.

Kuhn, Ludwig. The Milky Way: The Structure & Development of Our Star System. LC 82-2820. 151p. 1982. 31.95x (ISBN 0-471-10277-6, Pub. by Wiley-Interscience). Wiley.

Kuhn, M., et al. The Radiation Budget at Plateau Station, Antarctica: Paper 5 in Meteorological Studies at Plateau Station, Antarctica. Businger, Joost A., ed. (Antarctic Research Ser.: Vol. 25). 1977. pap. 16.90 (ISBN 0-87590-139-5). Am Geophysical.

Kuhn, Martin C., ed. Process & Fundamental Considerations of Selected Hydrometallurgical Systems. LC 79-57685. (Orig.). 1981. pap. text ed. 22.00x (ISBN 0-89520-282-4). Soc Mining Eng.

Kuhn, Mary S. The Joy of Tatting. (Illus.). pap. 4.95 (ISBN 0-87069-333-6, 99030). Wallace-Homestead.

Kuhn, Maura, jt. auth. see Kuhn, Joaquin.

Kuhn, Reinhard. Corruption in Paradise: The Child in Western Literature. LC 81-43693. 280p. 1982. text ed. 20.00x (ISBN 0-87451-235-2). U Pr of New Eng.

Kuhn, Reinhard, ed. L' Espirit Moderne Dans la Litterature Francaise. (Fr.). 1972. pap. 10.95x (ISBN 0-19-501529-0). Oxford U Pr.

Kuhn, Sarah. Computer Manufacturing in New England. (Illus.). 187p. 1982. pap. 12.00 (ISBN 0-943142-03-2). Joint Cen Urban.

Kuhn, Thomas S. The Essential Tension: Selected Studies in Scientific Tradition & Change. LC 77-78069. (Illus.). 1979. lib. bdg. 20.00x (ISBN 0-226-45805-9); pap. 8.95 (ISBN 0-226-45806-7, P831, Phoen). U of Chicago Pr.

--Structure of Scientific Revolutions. 2nd ed. LC 70-107472. (Foundations of the Unity of Science Ser: Vol. 2, No. 2). 1970. pap. 4.95 (ISBN 0-226-45804-0, P411, Phoen). U of Chicago Pr.

Kuhn, Tillo E. Public Enterprise: Economics & Transport Problems. LC 76-5904. (Illus.). 243p. 1976. Repr. of 1962 ed. lib. bdg. 19.00x (ISBN 0-8371-8798-2, KUPE). Greenwood.

Kuhn, W., jt. auth. see Graeff, H.

Kuhn, W. D., jt. auth. see Cook, W. D.

Kuhne, Gary W. La Dinamica de Adiestrar Discipulos. 160p. Date not set. 2.50 (ISBN 0-88113-040-0). Edit Betania.

Kuhne, Karl. Economics & Marxism, 2 vols. Shaw, Robert, tr. Incl. Vol. 1. The Renaissance of the Marxian System (ISBN 0-312-23436-8); Vol. 2. The Dynamics of the Marxian System (ISBN 0-312-23437-6). 1979. Set. 27.50x ea. (ISBN 0-686-52171-4). St Martin.

Kuhne, Walter G. The Liassic Therapsid Oligokyphus. (Illus.). iii, 150p. 1956. 21.50x (ISBN 0-565-00115-9, Pub. by British Mus Nat Hist England). Sabbot-Natural Hist Bks.

Kuhnen, F. Agriculture & Beginning Industrialization: West Pakistan. 1968. 11.00x o.p. (ISBN 3-8100-0104-X). Intl Pubns Serv.

Kuhner, David & Rizzo, Tania, eds. Biblioteca De Re Metallica: The Herbert Clark Hoover Collection of Mining & Metallurgy. LC 80-82055. (Illus.). 219p. 1980. 125.00 (ISBN 0-937368-00-8). Honnold Lib.

Kuhnert-Brandstatter, M. Thermomicroscopy in the Analysis of Pharmaceuticals. 424p. 1971. 77.00 (ISBN 0-08-006990-8). Pergamon.

Kuhnreuther, H. & Ley, E. V., eds. Risk Analysis Controversy-An Institutional Perspective, Laxenburg, Austria: Proceedings, 1981. (Illus.). 236p. 1983. 24.00. Springer-Verlag.

Kuhns, Eileen & Martorana, S. V., eds. Qualitative Methods for Institutional Decision Making. LC 81-48574. 1982. 7.95x (ISBN 0-87589-904-8, IR-34). Jossey-Bass.

Kuhns, Oscar. German & Swiss Settlements of Colonial Pennsylvania: A Study of the So-Called Pennsylvania Dutch. 268p. 1979. Repr. of 1901 ed. 30.00x (ISBN 0-686-80391-4). Gale.

Kuhre, Bruce E., jt. ed. see Ergood, Bruce.

Kuijt, Job. The Biology of Parasitic Flowering Plants. LC 68-9722. (Illus.). 1969. 52.50x (ISBN 0-520-01490-1). U of Cal Pr.

Kuiper, F. B., ed. see Irwin, John.

Kuiper, P. J., jt. ed. see Wintermans, J. F.

Kuiper, R. B. The Bible Tells Us So: Twelve Short Chapters on Major Themes of the Bible. 1978. pap. 3.45 (ISBN 0-85151-001-9). Banner of Truth.

Kuipers, J. F. World's Truck Catalogue: International Listings. (Illus.). Date not set. pap. 16.95 cancelled (ISBN 0-89404-013-8). Aztex. Postponed.

Kuipers, L. & Niederreiter, H. Uniform Distribution of Sequences. LC 73-20497. (Pure & Applied Mathematics Ser.). 390p. 1974. 45.95x (ISBN 0-471-51045-9, Pub. by Wiley-Interscience). Wiley.

Kuipers, S. K. & Lanjouw, G. J. Prospects of Economic Growth. 1980. 51.00 (ISBN 0-444-85535-3). Elsevier.

Kuisel, Richard F. Capitalism & the State in Modern France: Renovation & Economic Management in the Twentieth Century. 352p. 1981. 39.50 (ISBN 0-521-23474-3). Cambridge U Pr.

--Capitalism & the State in Modern France: Renovation & Economic Management in the Twentieth Century. LC 81-616. (Cambridge Paperback Library Ser.). 344p. Date not set. pap. 14.95 (ISBN 0-521-27378-1). Cambridge U Pr.

Kuist, Howard T. Jeremiah, Lamentations. LC 59-10454. (Layman's Bible Commentary Ser: Vol. 12). 1960. pap. 3.95 (ISBN 0-8042-3072-2). John Knox.

Kujawa, Duane. International Dimensions of Industrial Relations. Ricks, David A., ed. (International Dimensions of Business Ser.). 200p. 1983. text ed. write for info. (ISBN 0-534-01391-0). Kent Pub Co.

Kujoth, Jean S., ed. Teacher & School Discipline. LC 75-9770. 1970. 11.00 o.p. (ISBN 0-8108-0300-3). Scarecrow.

Kukacka, Lawrence E., ed. Applications of Polymer Concrete. LC 81-67492. (SP-69). 228p. (Orig.). 1981. pap. 32.25 (ISBN 0-686-95240-5). ACI.

Kukin, Arthur S., jt. ed. see Simmons, David J.

Kuklick, Bruce, ed. see James, William.

Kuklick, Henrika, jt. ed. see Jones, Robert A.

Kuklin, R. Learn to Invest & Trade on Wall Street. 2nd ed. LC 79-64472. 240p. 1982. pap. 7.95 (ISBN 0-9606504-5-8). Dill Ent.

Kuklin, R. M. Learn to Invest & Trade on Wall Street: A Basic Book for the Beginner & Those Who Wish to Increase Their Stock Market Profits. LC 79-64472. 219p. 1979. 12.95 o.s.i. (ISBN 0-933962-00-2); pap. 6.95 o.s.i. (ISBN 0-933962-01-0). Dill Ent.

Kuklinski, James H., jt. auth. see Knoke, David.

Kula, Eric & Weiss, Volker, eds. Residual Stress & Stress Relaxation, Vol.28. (Sagamore Army Materials Research Conference Proceedings). 540p. 1982. 72.50x (ISBN 0-306-41102-4, Plenum Pr). Plenum Pub.

Kula, Witold. An Economic Theory of the Feudal System. (Illus.). 1976. 14.50 (ISBN 0-8052-7022-1, Pub. by NLB). Schocken.

Kulaev, I. S. The Biochemistry of Inorganic Polyphosphates. LC 78-31627. 255p. 1980. 74.95x (ISBN 0-471-27574-3, Pub. by Wiley-Interscience). Wiley.

Kulas, Jim. Let's Count All the Animals. (A Tell-a-Tale Reader Ser.). (Illus.). (gr. k-3). 1979. PLB 5.00 (ISBN 0-307-68407-5, Golden Pr). Western Pub.

Kulawiec, Edwin P., tr. see Korczak, Janusz.

Kulb, Nancy, jt. auth. see Buckley, Kathleen.

Kulbertus, Henri E., jt. ed. see Wellens, Hein J.

Kulczyckyj, John. I Caught Detroit's Express. 1980. 5.95 (ISBN 0-8062-1529-1). Carlton.

Kuldau, John M., ed. Treatment for Psychosomatic Problems. LC 81-48484. 1982. 7.95x (ISBN 0-87589-909-9, MHS-15). Jossey-Bass.

Kulhanek, O. Introduction to Digital Filtering in Geophysics. (Developments in Solid Earth Geophysics Ser.: Vol. 8). 1976. 51.00 (ISBN 0-444-41331-6). Elsevier.

Kulick, Florence & Matthews, Florence. The Hamptons Health Spa Diet Cookbook. 224p. (Orig.). 1983. pap. 8.95 (ISBN 0-932966-28-4). Permanent Pr.

Kulik, William R. & Omans, Glen A. Faces of Authority. 1972. pap. 7.95x (ISBN 0-673-07689-X). Scott F.

Kulikowski, Casimir A. & Weiss, Sholom M. A Practical Guide to Building Expert Systems. 220p. 1983. text ed. 24.95x (ISBN 0-86598-108-6). Allanheld.

Kulikowski, J. L., ed. Discrete Mathematics. (Banach Center Publications: Vol. 7). (Illus.). 224p. 1982. 40.00x (ISBN 83-01-01494-6). Intl Pubns Serv.

Kulin, Agnes. Hilda. 1983. 10.00 (ISBN 0-533-05608-X). Vantage.

Kulk, W. Van Der see Schouten, Jan A. & Van Der Kulk, W.

Kulkarni, H. B. Stephen Spender: An Annotated Bibliography of His Works & Criticism. LC 75-24090. (Reference Library of the Humanities: Vol. 43). 200p. 1975. lib. bdg. 31.00 o.s.i. (ISBN 0-8240-9960-5). Garland Pub.

Kulkin, Mary E. Her Way: Biographies of Women for Young People. LC 76-25861. (gr. 6-9). 1976. 30.00 (ISBN 0-8389-0221-9). ALA.

Kullak, Adolf. The Aesthetics of Pianoforte-Playing. LC 69-16652. (Music Reprint Ser.). 340p. 1972. Repr. of 1893 ed. lib. bdg. 32.50 (ISBN 0-306-71095-1). Da Capo.

Kullak, Franz. Beethoven's Piano-Playing: With an Essay on the Execution of the Trill. LC 72-14059. 101p. 1973. Repr. of 1901 ed. lib. bdg. 16.95 (ISBN 0-306-70564-8). Da Capo.

Kullman, Harry. The Battle Horse. Blecher, George & Blecher, Lone T., trs. from Swedish. LC 81-2192. Orig. Title: Stridshasten. 204p. (gr. 6-9). 1981. 9.95 (ISBN 0-02-751240-1). Bradbury Pr.

Kulman, Charles. Massacre Survivor! The Story of Frank Finkel. A Trooper with Custer. (Illus.). 1972. pap. 2.00 (ISBN 0-88342-200-X). Old Army.

Kulp, C. A. & Hall, J. W. Casualty Insurance. 4th ed. 1072p. 1968. 44.95x (ISBN 0-471-06568-4). Wiley.

Kulp, G. & Holcomb, M. C. Transportation Energy Data Book. 6th ed. LC 82-14135. (Illus.). 205p. 1982. 36.00 (ISBN 0-8155-0919-7). Noyes.

Kulshrestha, Chirantan. Saul Bellow: The Problem of Affirmation. 1979. text ed. 10.50x o.p. (ISBN 0-685-99601-8). Humanities.

Kulshrestha, V. V. Experimental Physiology. 1977. 8.95x o.p. (ISBN 0-7069-0551-2, Pub. by Vikas India). Advent NY.

Kulski, Wladyslaw W. De Gaulle & the World: The Foreign Policy of the Fifth French Republic. LC 66-28137. 1966. 18.95x (ISBN 0-8156-0052-6). Syracuse U Pr.

Kulund, Daniel N. The Injured Athlete. (Illus.). 526p. 1982. text ed. 42.50 (ISBN 0-397-50449-7, Lippincott Medical). Lippincott.

Kumagai, Kenji. The Sushi Handbook. (Illus., Orig.). 1983. pap. 8.95 (ISBN 0-89346-211-X). Heian Intl.

Kumakhov, M. & Komarov, F. Energy Losses & Ion Ranges in Solids. 296p. 1981. 94.00 (ISBN 0-677-21220-8). Gordon.

Kuman, Alexandra, jt. ed. see DuBane, Janet.

Kumar, Dharma. India & the European Economic Community. 1967. 8.50x o.p. (ISBN 0-210-27182-5). Asia.

Kumar, Frederick L. The Philosophy of Saivism: An Existential Analysis of its Underlying Experiences. LC 79-56036. xii, 125p. 1980. 10.95 (ISBN 0-89386-001-8). Acorn NC.

Kumar, Krishan. Library Manual. 300p. 1982. text ed. 32.50x (ISBN 0-7069-1751-0, Pub. by Vikas India). Advent NY.

Kumar, Krishna, ed. Bonds Without Bondage: Explorations in Transcultural Interactions. LC 78-31546. 1979. pap. text ed. 10.75x (ISBN 0-8248-0636-0, Eastwest Ctr). UH Pr.

--Transnational Enterprises: Their Impact on Third World Secieties & Cultures. (Westview Special Studies in International Business & Economics). (Illus.). 400p. 1980. lib. bdg. 29.50 o.p. (ISBN 0-89158-852-3); pap. 12.95 o.p. (ISBN 0-86531-409-8). Westview.

Kumar, Krishna & McLeod, Maxwell G., eds. Multinationals from Developing Countries. LC 80-8531. 204p. 1981. 24.95 (ISBN 0-669-04113-0). Lexington Bks.

Kumar, Mahendra. Violence & Nonviolence in International Relations. 256p. 1976. text ed. 13.00x (ISBN 0-391-00622-3). Humanities.

Kumar, R., jt. ed. see Brockington, I. F.

Kumar, Raj. Annie Besant's Rise to Power in Indian Politics, 1914-1917. 190p. 1982. text ed. 15.75x (ISBN 0-391-02492-2, Pub. by Concept India). Humanities.

Kumar, Ravinder & Panigrahi, D. N., eds. Selected Works of Motilal Nehru, Vol. 1. 400p. 1983. text ed. 45.00x (ISBN 0-7069-1885-1, Pub. by Vikas India). Advent NY.

Kumar, Ray. Insect Pest Control: With Special Reference to African Agriculture. 288p. 1983. pap. text ed. price not set (ISBN 0-7131-8083-8). E Arnold.

Kumar, S., jt. auth. see Rathi, M. L.

Kumar, Shiv K. Bergson & the Stream of Consciousness Novel. LC 78-26162. 1979. Repr. of 1963 ed. lib. bdg. 19.25x (ISBN 0-313-20806-9, KUBE). Greenwood.

Kumar, Sushil & Venkataraman, K. State-Panchayati Raj Relations. 148p. 1974. lib. bdg. 8.95x (ISBN 0-210-40503-1). Asia.

Kumar, Vinay. Experimental Techniques in Quantitative Chemical Analysis. LC 80-69043. 183p. (Orig.). 1981. pap. text ed. 10.50 (ISBN 0-8191-1509-6). U Pr of Amer.

Kumarappa, Bharatan, ed. see Gandhi, Mohandas K.

Kume, Genichi. Picture Play: Kintaro's Adventures. LC 64-20366. (Illus.). 5.50 (ISBN 0-8048-0342-0). C E Tuttle.

Kumin, Maxine. Our Ground Time Here Will Be Brief: New & Selected Poems. LC 81-69995. 256p. 1982. 16.95 (ISBN 0-670-53108-1); pap. 7.95 o.p. (ISBN 0-14-042298-6). Viking Pr.

--To Make a Prairie: Essays on Poets, Poetry, & Country Living. LC 79-13289. (Poets on Poetry Ser.). 1979. pap. 7.95 (ISBN 0-472-06306-5). U of Mich Pr.

--What Color Is Caesar. (ps-3). 1978. 8.95 (ISBN 0-07-035638-6, GB). McGraw.

Kumin, Maxine & Sexton, Ann. The Wizard's Tears. LC 75-8822. (Illus.). 48p. (Orig.). (gr. 4-6). 1975. 6.95 o.p. (ISBN 0-07-035636-X, GB); PLB 7.95 o.p. (ISBN 0-07-035637-8). McGraw.

Kumin, Maxine & Sexton, Anne. Joey & the Birthday Present. (Illus.). (gr. 1-4). 1971. PLB 4.95 o.p. (ISBN 0-07-035635-1, GB). McGraw.

Kumin, Maxine W. Beach Before Breakfast. (Illus.). (gr. 2-4). 1964. PLB 5.49 o.p. (ISBN 0-399-60048-5). Putnam Pub Group.

--Mittens in May. (See & Read Storybooks). (Illus.). (gr. k-3). 1962. PLB 4.29 o.p. (ISBN 0-399-60467-7). Putnam Pub Group.

--Spring Things. (See & Read Storybooks in Verse). (Illus.). (gr. k-3). 1961. PLB 4.89 o.p. (ISBN 0-399-60604-1). Putnam Pub Group.

Kumler, Kipton, photos by. Plant Leaves. LC 78-58508. (Illus., Text by Hilton Kramer). 1980. pap. 5.95 (ISBN 0-87923-258-7). Godine.

Kumli, Karl F. Introductory Chemistry: A Survey of General, Organic, & Biological Chemistry. (Illus.). 608p. 1974. text ed. 24.95 o.p. (ISBN 0-13-501668-1); study guide pap. 8.95 o.p. (ISBN 0-13-501684-3). P-H.

Kumm, Alan, jt. auth. see Evans, Hazel.

Kummel, W. G. Promise & Fulfillment: The Eschatological Message of Jesus. 3rd ed. Barton, Dorothea M., ed. (Student Christian Movement Press Ser.). (Orig.). 1957. text ed. 10.95x (ISBN 0-19-520327-5). Oxford U Pr.

Kummerly & Frey. Europe Road Atlas. 9.95 (ISBN 0-528-85774-6); vinyl cover 10.95 (ISBN 0-528-85769-X); indexed 13.95 (ISBN 0-528-85762-2). Rand.

Kummings, Donald D. Walt Whitman, 1940-1975: A Reference Guide. 330p. 1982. lib. bdg. 45.00 (ISBN 0-8161-7802-X, Hall Reference). G K Hall.

Kump, Peter. Breakthrough Rapid Reading. 256p. 1980. 14.95 o.p. (ISBN 0-13-081562-4, Reward); pap. 5.95 o.p. (ISBN 0-13-081554-3). P-H.

--Quiche & Pate. LC 82-47862. (Great American Cooking Schools Ser.). (Illus.). 84p. 1982. 8.61i (ISBN 0-06-015067-X, HarpT). Har-Row.

Kun, N. De see De Kun, N.

Kunberger, William, jt. auth. see Bearman, Toni C.

Kunc, Norman. Ready, Willing & Disabled. 112p. 1981. 7.95 (ISBN 0-920510-56-6, Pub. by Personal Lib). Dodd.

Kundell, James E. & White, Fred C. Prime Farmland in Georgia. 49p. 1982. pap. 6.50 (ISBN 0-89854-081-X). U of GA Inst Govt.

Kundera, Milan. The Joke. Heim, Michael H., tr. from Czech. LC 81-48055. 320p. 1982. 14.37i (ISBN 0-06-014987-6, HarpT). Har-Row.

Kundsin, Ruth B., ed. see New York Academy of Sciences, Nov. 7-9, 1979.

Kunen, K. Set Theory: An Introduction to Independence Proofs. (Studies in Logic: Vol. 102). 1981. 40.50 (ISBN 0-444-85401-0). Elsevier.

Kunene, Mazisi. Zulu Poems. LC 70-136492. 1970. 12.75x (ISBN 0-8419-0061-2, Africana); pap. 7.50x (ISBN 0-8419-0064-7, Africana). Holmes & Meier.

Kunetka, James W. Oppenheimer: The Years of Risk. 336p. 1982. 15.95 (ISBN 0-13-638007-7). P-H.

Kung, David. Contemporary Artist in Japan. (Illus.). 1966. 20.00 (ISBN 0-8248-0056-7, Eastwest Ctr). UH Pr.

Kung, Hans. The Christian Challenge. Quinn, Edward, tr. LC 78-22815. (Illus.). 1979. 9.95 o.p. (ISBN 0-385-15266-3). Doubleday.

--The Church. 600p. 1976. pap. 6.95 (ISBN 0-385-11367-6, Im). Doubleday.

--Future of Ecumenism. LC 71-84552. (Concilium Ser.: Vol. 44). 191p. 6.95 o.p. (ISBN 0-8091-0050-9). Paulist Pr.

--Infallible? An Inquiry. LC 82-45641. 288p. 1983. pap. 10.95 (ISBN 0-385-18483-2). Doubleday.

Kung, Hans & Moltmann, Jurgen. Mary in the Churches. (Concilium 1983: Vol. 168). 128p. (Orig.). 1983. pap. 6.95 (ISBN 0-8164-2448-9). Seabury.

Kung, Hans & Moltmann, Jurgen, eds. Conflicting Ways of Interpreting the Bible. (Concilium Ser.: Vol. 138). 128p. (Orig.). 1980. pap. 5.95 (ISBN 0-8164-2280-X). Seabury.

Kung, Hans & Schillebeeckx, Edward, eds. Concilium: Religion in the Eighties, 10 Vols. (Concilium Ser.: Vols. 141-150). 128p. (Orig.). 1981. pap. 62.55 (ISBN 0-8164-2352-0). Seabury.

--Concilium: Religion in the Eighties. (Concilium Ser.: Vols. 151-160). 128p. (Orig.). 1982. pap. 62.55 (ISBN 0-8164-2392-X). Seabury.

Kung, Hans & Schillebeeckz, Edward, eds. Concilium: Religion in the Eighties. (Concilium Ser.: Vols. 131-140). 128p. (Orig.). 1980. pap. 53.55 (ISBN 0-8164-2283-4). Seabury.

Kung, Hans, et al, eds. Council Speeches of Vatican Two. LC 64-18548. 288p. (Orig.). 1964. pap. 2.95 o.p. (ISBN 0-8091-1530-1, Deus). Paulist Pr.

K'ung, Shang-Jen. The Peach Blossom Fan. Chen, S. H., et al, trs. from Chinese. LC 74-27294. 350p. (Eng.). 1976. 26.50x (ISBN 0-520-02928-3); pap. 3.95 (ISBN 0-520-03201-2). U of Cal Pr.

Kunhappa, Murkot. Three Bags of Gold & Other Indian Folktales. 1964. 5.00x o.p. (ISBN 0-210-34077-0). Asia.

Kunhardt, Erich E. & Luessen, Lawrence H., eds. Electrical Breakdown & Discharges in Gases, Pt. A: Fundamental Processes & Breakdown. (NATO ASI Series B, Physics: Vol. 89a). 475p. 1983. 65.00x (ISBN 0-306-41194-6, Plenum Pr). Plenum Pub.

--Electrical Breakdown & Discharges in Gases, Pt. B: Macroscopic Processes & Discharges. (NATO ASI Series B, Physics: Vol. 89b). 469p. 1983. 65.00x (ISBN 0-306-41195-4, Plenum Pr). Plenum Pub.

Kuniansky, Harry R. & Marsh, William H. New Cases in Managerial Finance. 1979. pap. text ed. 11.95 scp o.p. (ISBN 0-06-043819-3, HarpC); inst. manual avail. o.p. (ISBN 0-06-362357-9). Har-Row.

Kuniczak, W. S. The March. LC 78-22598. 1979. 17.95 o.p. (ISBN 0-385-00204-1). Doubleday.

Kuniholm, Whitney. Galatians, Ephesians, Philippians, & Colossians: A Daily Dialogue with God. (Personal Bible Studyguides). 144p. 1983. pap. 4.95 (ISBN 0-87788-292-4). Shaw Pubs.

Kunii, Daizo & Levenspiel, Octave. Fluidization Engineering. LC 77-2885. (Illus.). 556p. 1977. Repr. of 1969 ed. lib. bdg. 32.50 (ISBN 0-88275-542-0). Krieger.

Kunii, T. L., jt. ed. see Fu, K. S.

Kunin. Mega Nutrition. 1980. 12.95 (ISBN 0-07-035639-4). McGraw.

Kunin, Arthur S. & Simons, David J., eds. Skeletal Research: An Experimental Approach, Vol. 2. Date not set. price not set (ISBN 0-12-429002-7). Acad Pr.

Kunin, I. A. Elastic Media with Microstructure II: Three Dimensional Models. (Springer Ser. in Solid-State Physics: Vol. 44). (Illus.). 290p. 1983. 39.50 (ISBN 0-387-12078-5). Springer-Verlag.

Kunin, Madeleine & Stout, Marilyn. The Big Green Book: A Four-Season Guide to Vermont. (Illus.). 352p. 1976. pap. 6.95 o.p. (ISBN 0-517-52517-8). Crown.

Kunin, R. A. Mega-Nutrition for Women. 224p. 1983. 14.95 (ISBN 0-07-035642-4, GB). McGraw.

Kunin, Richard A. Mega-Nutrition: The New Prescription for Maximum Health, Energy & Longevity. 1981. pap. 6.95 (ISBN 0-452-25344-6, Z5344, Plume). NAL.

--Mega-Nutrition: The New Prescription for Maximum Health, Energy & Longevity. LC 81-220. (Medical Library). 312p. 1982. pap. 6.95 (ISBN 0-686-84853-5, 2808-3). Mosby.

Kunin, Robert. Elements of Ion Exchange. LC 60-8970. 194p. 1971. Repr. of 1960 ed. 10.50 (ISBN 0-88275-036-4). Krieger.

Kunio, Yoshihara. Sogo Shosha: The Vanguard of Japanese Economy. (Illus.). 376p. 1982. 24.95x (ISBN 0-19-582534-9). Oxford U Pr.

Kunitskaya-Peterson, Christina. International Dictionary of Obscenities: A Guide to Dirty Words & Indecent Expressions in Spanish, Italian, French, German, & Russian. 93p. (Orig.). 1981. pap. 5.95 (ISBN 0-933884-18-4). Berkeley Slavic.

Kunitz, Stanley. The Wellfleet Whale & Other Poems of Cape Cod. (Illus.). 32p. 1983. 25.00 o.p. (ISBN 0-935296-37-9); pap. 5.95 o.p. (ISBN 0-935296-36-0). Sheep Meadow.

Kunitz, Stanley J. & Colby, Vineta, eds. European Authors, One Thousand to Nineteen Hundred. (Illus.). 1016p. 1967. 33.00 (ISBN 0-8242-0013-6). Wilson.

Kunitz, Stanley J. & Haycraft, Howard, eds. American Authors: Sixteen Hundred-Nineteen Hundred. 8th, 1971 ed. (Illus.). 1977. 23.00 (ISBN 0-8242-0001-2). Wilson.

--British Authors Before Eighteen Hundred. (Illus.). 584p. 1952. 20.00 (ISBN 0-8242-0006-3). Wilson.

--British Authors of the Nineteenth Century. (Illus.). 677p. 1936. 23.00 (ISBN 0-8242-0007-1). Wilson.

--Junior Book of Authors. 2nd rev. ed. (Illus.). 309p. 1951. 14.00 (ISBN 0-8242-0028-4). Wilson.

--Twentieth Century Authors. (Illus.). 1123p. 1942. 42.00 (ISBN 0-8242-0049-7); 1st suppl. 1955. 33.00 (ISBN 0-8242-0050-0). Wilson.

Kunkel, Bill, jt. auth. see Katz, Arnie.

Kunkel, G. The Vegetation of Hormoz, Queshm & Neighbouring Islands (Southern Persian Gulf Area, No. 6. (Flora et Vegetatio Mundi Ser.). (Illus.). 186p. 1977. text ed. 24.00x (ISBN 3-7682-1120-7). Lubrecht & Cramer.

Kunkel, Henry & Dixon, Frank, eds. Advances in Immunology, Vol. 33. 367p. 1982. 45.00 (ISBN 0-12-022433-X). Acad Pr.

Kunkel, Henry G. see Taliaferro, W. H. & Humphrey, J. H.

Kunkel, John, jt. ed. see Hamblin, Robert L.

Kunkel, Reinhard. Elephants. Korneitchouk, Ursula, tr. from Ger. LC 81-15020. (Illus.). 256p. 1982. 50.00 (ISBN 0-8109-0863-8). Abrams.

Kunkel, Wolfgang. An Introduction to Roman Legal & Constitutional History. 2nd ed. Kelly, J. M., tr. 1973. 32.50x (ISBN 0-19-825317-6). Oxford U Pr.

Kunkel, Wulf B. Plasma Physics in Theory & Application. 1966. text ed. 26.95 o.p. (ISBN 0-07-035629-7, C). McGraw.

Kunnas, Mauri. Santa Claus & His Elves. (gr. 2-6). PLB 13.00 (ISBN 0-382-06678-2). Silver.

Kunne-Ibsch, Elrud, jt. auth. see Fokkema, D. W.

Kunos, George. Adrenoceptors & Catecholamine Action. LC 81-10431. (Neurotransmitter Receptors Ser.: Vol. 1, Pt. A). 343p. 1981. 56.50x (ISBN 0-471-05725-8, Pub. by Wiley-Interscience). Wiley.

--Adrenoceptors & Catecholamine Action: Part B. (Neurotransmitter Receptors Ser.). 336p. 1983. 75.00 (ISBN 0-471-05726-6, Pub. by Wiley-Interscience). Wiley.

Kunos, Ignacz & Munkacsi, Bernat, eds. Keleti Szemle - Revue Orientale, 21 vols. Incl. Vol. 1. 1966 (ISBN 0-87750-089-4); Vol. 2. 1966 (ISBN 0-87750-090-8); Vol. 3. 1966 (ISBN 0-87750-091-6); Vol. 4. 1966 (ISBN 0-87750-092-4); Vol. 5. 1966 (ISBN 0-87750-093-2); Vol. 6. 1966 (ISBN 0-87750-094-0); Vol. 7. 1967 (ISBN 0-87750-095-9); Vol. 8. 1966 (ISBN 0-87750-096-7); Vol. 9. 1968 (ISBN 0-87750-097-5); Vol. 10. 1968 (ISBN 0-87750-098-3); Vol. 11. 1968 (ISBN 0-87750-099-1); Vol. 12. 1968 (ISBN 0-87750-100-9); Vol. 13. 1969 (ISBN 0-87750-101-7); Vol. 14. 1969 (ISBN 0-87750-102-5); Vol. 15. 1969 (ISBN 0-87750-103-3); Vol. 16. 1969 (ISBN 0-87750-104-1); Vol. 17. 1969 (ISBN 0-87750-105-X); Vol. 18. 1969 (ISBN 0-87750-106-8); Vol. 19. 1969 (ISBN 0-87750-107-6); Vol. 20. 1969 (ISBN 0-87750-108-4); Vol. 21. 1969 (ISBN 0-87750-109-2). LC 66-63014. (Uralic & Altaic Ser.: Vol. 66.1-66.21). (Ger, Fr & Hung.). pap. text ed. 10.00 ea. o.p. Res Ctr Lang Semiotic.

Kunreuther, Howard. Disaster Insurance Protection: Public Policy Lessons. LC 77-179. 400p. 1978. 55.95x (ISBN 0-471-03259-X, Pub. by Wiley-Interscience). Wiley.

Kuns, Ray F. Automotive Essentials. rev ed. 1962. 6.96 o.p. (ISBN 0-02-820040-3). Glencoe.

Kunstadt, Leonard, jt. auth. see Charters, Samuel B.

Kunstadter, Peter, et al, eds. Farmers in the Forest: Economic Development & Marginal Agriculture in Northern Thailand. LC 77-27263. 1978. text ed. 26.00x (ISBN 0-8248-0366-3, Eastwest Ctr). UH Pr.

Kunstler, James H. A Clown in the Moonlight. 256p. 1981. 10.95 o.p. (ISBN 0-312-14495-4). St Martin.

--The Life of Byron Jaynes: A Novel. 1983. 16.50 (ISBN 0-393-01721-4); pap. 7.95 (ISBN 0-393-30116-8). Norton.

Kunstler, William M. Beyond a Reasonable Doubt? The Original Trial of Caryl Chessman. LC 73-8155. (Illus.). 304p. 1973. Repr. of 1961 ed. lib. bdg. 20.75x (ISBN 0-8371-6951-8, CHBR). Greenwood.

--First Degree. LC 60-14789. (Orig.). 1960. 6.00 o.p. (ISBN 0-379-00068-7). Oceana.

--The Hall-Mills Murder Case: The Minister & the Choir Singer. 350p. 1983. pap. 9.95 (ISBN 0-8135-0912-2). Rutgers U Pr.

Kunt, I. M. The Sultan's Servants: The Transformation of Ottoman Provincial Government, 1550-1650. 200p. 1983. text ed. 25.00x (ISBN 0-231-05578-1). Columbia U Pr.

Kunt, M. & De Coulon, F., eds. Signal Processing: Theories & Applications. 1980. 95.75 (ISBN 0-444-86050-9). Elsevier.

Kunth, C. S. Nova Genera & Species Plantarum Quas in Peregrinatione Orbis Collegerunt: 1815-25, 7 vols. in 3. 1963. 480.00 (ISBN 3-7682-0165-1). Lubrecht & Cramer.

Kuntscher, Gerhard. Practice of Intramedullary Nailing. (Illus.). 388p. 1967. photocopy ed. spiral 35.75x (ISBN 0-398-01067-6). C C Thomas.

Kuntz, Arnold G. Serving God Always. 1966. pap. text ed. 2.75 (ISBN 0-570-06645-X, 22-2014); pap. 5.85 manual (ISBN 0-570-06646-8, 22-2015). Concordia.

Kuntz, Eugene. Curing Land Titles. 1982. 45.00 (ISBN 0-89419-198-5). Inst Energy.

--How to Keep the Oil & Gas Lease Alive Through Operations. 1982. 40.00 (ISBN 0-89419-182-9). Inst Energy.

--Kansas Law of Oil & Gas. 1982. 38.00 (ISBN 0-89419-239-6). Inst Energy.

--Oklahoma Law of Oil & Gas. 1982. 38.00 (ISBN 0-89419-190-X). Inst Energy.

--Texas Law of Oil & Gas. 1981. 38.00 (ISBN 0-89419-234-5). Inst Energy.

Kuntz, Eugene, ed. Pooling & Utilization in Oklahoma. 1982. 39.00 (ISBN 0-89419-219-1). Inst Energy.

Kuntz, Joseph M., jt. auth. see Martinez, Nancy C.

Kuntze, H. Iron Clogging in Soils & Pipes. (Water Resources Engineering Ser.). 140p. 1982. pap. text ed. 32.95 (ISBN 0-273-08561-1). Pitman Pub MA.

Kuntzlemann, Charles T., ed. see Consumers Guide Editors.

Kunz, Barbara, jt. auth. see Kunz, Kevin.

Kunz, E. Ebene Geometrie: Grundlagen der Geometrie. (Mathematik Grundkurs Ser.). 147p. (Ger.). 1976. pap. 8.00x (ISBN 0-686-62182-4). Birkhauser.

--Introduction to Commutative Algebra & Algebraic Geometry. Date not set. text ed. price not set (ISBN 3-7643-3065-1). Birkhauser.

Kunz, Josef L. Latin-American Philosophy of Law in the Twentieth Century. viii, 120p. 1981. Repr. of 1950 ed. lib. bdg. 29.00x (ISBN 0-8377-0736-6). Rothman.

Kunz, Kevin & Kunz, Barbara. The Complete Guide To Foot Reflexology. Shoemaker, Ken, ed. 150p. 1982. 16.95 (ISBN 0-686-97525-1, Reward); pap. 8.95 (ISBN 0-13-160580-1, Reward). P-H.

Kunz, M. & Schell, C. Amos (Neighborhood Bible Study) pap. 2.50 (ISBN 0-8423-0067-8). Tyndale.

Kunz, Marilyn. Patterns for Living with God. pap. 2.25 (ISBN 0-87784-409-7). Inter-Varsity.

Kunz, Marilyn & Schell, Catherine. Acts, Neighborhood Bible Study. pap. 2.50 (ISBN 0-8423-0030-9). Tyndale.

--Choose Life. (Neighborhood Bible Studies). 1970. pap. 1.95 (ISBN 0-8423-0460-6). Tyndale.

--Ephesians & Philemon. (Neighborhood Bible Studies). 1965. pap. 2.50 (ISBN 0-8423-0695-1). Tyndale.

--Four Men of God, Neighborhood Bible Study. pap. 2.50 (ISBN 0-8423-0900-4). Tyndale.

--Hebrews, Neighborhood Bible Study. pap. 2.50 (ISBN 0-8423-1410-5). Tyndale.

--John, One, & James, Neighborhood Bible Study. pap. 2.50 (ISBN 0-8423-1930-1). Tyndale.

--Luke. (Neighborhood Bible Studies). 1973. pap. 2.50 (ISBN 0-8423-3880-2). Tyndale.

--Mark, Neighborhood Bible Study. pap. 2.50 (ISBN 0-8423-4101-3). Tyndale.

--Philippians & Colossians. (Neighborhood Bible Studies). 1972. pap. 2.50 (ISBN 0-8423-4825-5). Tyndale.

--Psalms & Proverbs, Neighborhood Bible Study. pap. 2.50 (ISBN 0-8423-4991-X). Tyndale.

--Romans, Neighborhood Bible Study. pap. 2.50 (ISBN 0-8423-5701-7). Tyndale.

Kunz, Robert, jt. auth. see Weissbach, Herbert.

Kunz, Thomas H., ed. Ecology of Bats. 450p. 1982. 49.50x (ISBN 0-306-40950-X, Plenum Pr). Plenum Pub.

Kunze, Linda A., ed. see Educational Research Council of America.

Kunze, Linda J., ed. see Educational Research Council of America.

Kunze, Ray, jt. auth. see Hoffman, Kenneth.

Kunzelmann, Harold P., et al, eds. Precision Teaching: An Initial Training Sequencer. LC 75-134774. (Illus., Orig.). 1970. pap. 9.00x o.p. (ISBN 0-87562-025-6). Spec Child.

Kunzer, Ruth G., jt. auth. see Bahr, Ehrhard.

Kunzli, Naude, tr. see Hahnemann, Samuel.

Kuo, Benjamin C. Automatic Control System. 4th ed. (Illus.). 720p. 1982. 31.95 (ISBN 0-13-054817-0). P-H.

Kuo, Benjamin C., ed. Theory & Applications of Step Motors. LC 74-4508. 576p. 1974. text ed. 44.95 (ISBN 0-8299-0015-2). West Pub.

Kuo, C. Computer Applications in Ship Technology. 1977. 42.95 (ISBN 0-471-25840-7, Pub. by Wiley Heyden). Wiley.

Kuo, C., et al, eds. see IFIP-IFAC International Conference, 3rd, Univ. of Strathclyde, Scotland, June 1979.

Kuo, F., jt. ed. see Abramson, N.

Kuo, Franklin F. Network Analysis & Synthesis. 2nd ed. LC 66-16127. 515p. 1966. 35.95x (ISBN 0-471-51118-8). Wiley.

Kuo, Ping-Chia. China: New Age & New Outlook. LC 74-30084. (China in the 20th Century Ser). xix, 231p. 1975. Repr. of 1956 ed. lib. bdg. 27.50 (ISBN 0-306-70679-2). Da Capo.

Kuo, Shan S. Computer Applications of Numerical Methods. LC 78-164654. 1972. text ed. 25.95 (ISBN 0-201-03956-7). A-W.

Kuo, Shirley W. Y. The Taiwan Economy in Transition. 370p. 1983. lib. bdg. 22.00x (ISBN 0-86531-611-2). Westview.

Kuo, T. T., jt. ed. see Huang, P. C.

Kuo, William. Teaching Grammar of Thai. LC 82-13519. (Illus.). 500p. 1983. lib. bdg. 29.25 (ISBN 0-8191-2678-0); pap. text ed. 17.25 (ISBN 0-8191-2679-9). U Pr of Amer.

Kuo-c'Hing Tu. Li Ho. (World Authors Ser.). 1979. lib. bdg. 15.95 (ISBN 0-8057-6379-1, Twayne). G K Hall.

Kuong, J. F. Controls for Advanced On-line Data Base Systems, 2 pts. 1982. Pt. 1. 49.00 (ISBN 0-686-34562-2); Pt. 2. 50.00 (ISBN 0-686-35702-7). Management Advisory Pubns.

Kuong, J. F., ed. Checklists & Guidelines for Reviewing Computer Security & Installations (Map-4) Updated & Complete Edition 1976. (Illus.). 1976. prepaid manual form, 3-ring binder 55.00 (ISBN 0-686-16682-5, MAP-4). Management Advisory Pubns.

Kuong, Javier F. Applied Nomography, Vol. 1. 130p. 1965. 16.95x (ISBN 0-87201-585-8). Gulf Pub.

--Applied Nomography, Vol. 2. 116p. 1968. 16.95x (ISBN 0-87201-586-6). Gulf Pub.

--Applied Nomography, Vol. 3. 135p. 1969. 16.95x (ISBN 0-87201-587-4). Gulf Pub.

--EDP Auditability: Approaches & Techniques, MAP-17. 1983. 65.00 (ISBN 0-686-30598-1). Management Advisory Pubns.

Kuong, Javier F., jt. auth. see Perry, William E.

Kup, A. P. Sierra Leone: A Concise History. LC 74-31820. 272p. 1975. 18.95 o.p. (ISBN 0-312-72415-2). St Martin.

Kup, Karl. Christmas Story in Medieval & Renaissance Manuscripts from the Spencer Collection, the New York Public Library. LC 70-98680. (Illus.). 1969. 12.00 o.s.i. (ISBN 0-87104-052-2); pap. 10.00 (ISBN 0-87104-053-0). NY Pub Lib.

Kup, Peter. Story of Sierra Leone. 1964. 3.95 (ISBN 0-521-05499-0). Cambridge U Pr.

Kupelnick, Bruce S., ed. see Gassner, John & Nicholas, Dudley.

Kupelnick, Bruce S., ed. see Marion, Frances.

Kupelnick, Bruce S., ed. see Pasolini, Pier P.

Kupelnick, Bruce S., ed. see Patterson, Frances.

Kupelnick, Bruce S., ed. see Pirandello, Luigi.

Kuper, Adam. Anthropology & Anthropologists: The Modern British School. Rev. ed. 220p. 1983. pap. price not set. Routledge & Kegan.

--Changing Jamaica. 160p. 1975. 18.50x o.p. (ISBN 0-7100-8241-X). Routledge & Kegan.

--Kalahari Village Politics: An African Democracy. LC 70-112470. (Studies in Social Anthropology). (Illus.). 1970. 27.95 (ISBN 0-521-07863-6). Cambridge U Pr.

Kuper, Adam, jt. ed. see Richards, A. I.

Kuper, Hilda. Indian People in Natal. LC 73-21261. (Illus.). 305p. 1974. Repr. of 1960 ed. lib. bdg. 20.50x (ISBN 0-8371-6096-0, KUIP). Greenwood.

Kuper, Hilda, jt. auth. see Kuper, Leo.

Kuper, Hilda & California University at Los Angeles African Studies Center, eds. Urbanization & Migration in West Africa. LC 76-51201. (Illus.). 1977. Repr. of 1965 ed. lib. bdg. 18.75x (ISBN 0-8371-8762-1, KUUM). Greenwood.

Kuper, Jack. Child of the Holocaust. 1980. pap. 2.50 (ISBN 0-451-11248-2, AE1248, Sig). NAL.

Kuper, Jessica, ed. The Anthropologists' Cookbook. (Illus.). 208p. 14.95 (ISBN 0-7100-8583-4). Routledge & Kegan.

Kuper, Leo & Kuper, Hilda. South Africa, 2 Pts. Incl. Pt. 1 - Human Rights & Genocide; Pt. 2 - Biography as Interpretation. (Hans Wolff Memorial Lecture Ser.). 63p. (Orig.). 1981. pap. text ed. 5.00 (ISBN 0-941934-33-0). Ind U Afro-Amer Arts.

Kupferberg, Herbert. Opera. LC 74-83891. (World of Culture Ser.). (Illus.). 192p. 1975. 7.95 (ISBN 0-88225-117-1). Newsweek.

Kupferberg, Tuli & Topp, Sylvia. First Glance. Brady, Frank, ed. (Illus., Orig.). 1978. 12.95 (ISBN 0-8437-3403-5); pap. 7.95 (ISBN 0-8437-3402-7). Hammond Inc.

Kupferle, Mary L. God Never Fails. 141p. 1983. pap. 4.50 (ISBN 0-87516-513-3). De Vorss.

Kupferman, Martin. Slowth: The Changing Economy & How You Can Successfully Cope. Levi, Maurice D., ed. LC 80-18863. 250p. 1980. 18.95 (ISBN 0-471-08090-X). Wiley.

Kupferschmid, Gene S. Y Tu...Que Dices? 256p. (Span.). pap. text ed. 10.95 (ISBN 0-669-03694-3). Heath.

Kupka, I. & Wilsing, N. Conversational Languages. LC 80-40120. (Computing Ser.). 117p. 1980. text ed. 32.95x (ISBN 0-471-27778-9, Pub. by Wiley-Interscience). Wiley.

Kupper, Lawrence L., jt. auth. see Kleinbaum, David G.

Kupperman, Joel J. The Foundations of Morality. (Unwin Education Bks.). 176p. 1983. text ed. 25.00x (ISBN 0-04-370124-8); pap. text ed. 9.95x (ISBN 0-04-370125-6). Allen Unwin.

Kupperman, Phyllis P. Summer Speech Book. (Illus.). 1968. pap. text ed. 0.60x (ISBN 0-8134-0976-4, 976). Interstate.

Kupperstein, Lenore, et al, eds. Drugs & Social Policy. LC 74-84800. (Annals Ser: No. 417). 250p. 1975. 15.00 (ISBN 0-87761-184-X); pap. 7.95 (ISBN 0-87761-185-8). Am Acad Pol Soc Sci.

Kuppuswamy, Gowri & Hariharan, H. Teaching of Music. 88p. 1980. 9.95 (ISBN 0-940500-57-4, Pub. by Sterling India). Asia Bk Corp.

Kuppuswamy, Gowry. Indian Dance & Music Literature: A Select Bibliography. 1982. 12.00x (ISBN 0-8364-0903-5, Pub. by Biblia Impex). South Asia Bks.

Kuppuswany, B., et al, eds. Population Education: A Panel Discussion. 1971. 8.00x o.p. (ISBN 0-210-22336-7). Asia.

Kuprin, A. Garnet Bracelet. 379p. 1982. pap. 4.00 (ISBN 0-8285-2288-X, Pub. by Progress Pubs USSR). Imported Pubns.

Kuprin, Aleksandr I. The Duel. LC 76-23881. (Classics of Russian Literature). 1977. 13.50 (ISBN 0-88355-491-7); pap. 4.95 o.p. (ISBN 0-88355-492-5). Hyperion Conn.

Kupris, Bronnie. The Dell Smart Shopping with Coupons & Refunds Book. (Orig.). 1980. pap. 1.75 o.s.i. (ISBN 0-440-11429-2). Dell.

Kupsh, Joyce. Duplicating: Machine Operation & Decision Making. 1972. pap. text ed. 5.25x o.p. (ISBN 0-02-476100-1, 47610). Glencoe.

Kupsh, Joyce, et al. Machine Transcription & Dictation. LC 77-15790. (Wiley Word Processing Ser.). 246p. 1978. 17.95x (ISBN 0-471-02734-0); tchr's. manual 4.00x (ISBN 0-471-04211-0). Wiley.

Kurata, Mamoru. Numerical Analysis for Semiconductor Devices. LC 80-8374. 288p. 1981. 29.95x (ISBN 0-669-04043-6). Lexington Bks.

Kurata, Michio. Thermodynamics of Polymer Solutions. Fujita, Hiroshi, tr. from Jap. (MMI Press Polymer Monographs: Vol. 1). 310p. Date not set. write for info. (ISBN 3-7186-0023-4). Harwood Academic.

Kurath, Hans. Phonology & Prosody of Modern English. LC 64-13467. 1949. 10.00x o.p. (ISBN 0-472-08530-1). U of Mich Pr.

Kurath, Hans & McDavid, Raven I., Jr. The Pronunciation of English in the Atlantic States: Based Upon the Collections of the Linguistic Atlas of the Eastern United States. LC 60-5671. (Illus.). 384p. 1983. pap. text ed. 25.00 (ISBN 0-8173-0129-1). U of Ala Pr.

Kuratowski, K. & Mostawski, A. Set Theory. 2nd ed. LC 74-83731. (Studies in Logic and the Foundations of Mathematics: Vol. 86). 1976. 68.00 (ISBN 0-7204-0470-3, North-Holland). Elsevier.

Kuratowski, Kazimierz. Topology, 2 vols. Incl. Vol. 1. 1966. 54.00 (ISBN 0-12-429201-1); Vol. 2. 1969. 63.50 (ISBN 0-12-429202-X). Acad Pr.

Kurganov, B. I. Allosteric Enzymes: Kinetic Behaviour. 400p. 1982. 64.95 (ISBN 0-471-10195-8, Pub. by Wiley-Interscience). Wiley.

Kurian, George, ed. Cross-Cultural Perspectives of Mate-Selection & Marriage. LC 78-19306. (Contributions in Family Studies: No. 3). 1979. lib. bdg. 29.95 (ISBN 0-313-20624-4, KCC/). Greenwood.

Kurian, Rachel. Women Workers in the Sri Lanka Plantation Sector: An Historical & Contemporary Analysis. International Labour Office, ed. (Women, Work & Development Ser.: No. 5). xiv, 138p. (Orig.). 1982. pap. 11.40 (ISBN 92-2-102992-1). Intl Labour Office.

Kuriloff, A. & Hemphill, J. How to Start Your Own Business & Succeed. Rev. ed. 1981. 21.95 (ISBN 0-07-035650-5). McGraw.

Kuriloff, Arthur & Hemphill, John, Jr. Starting & Managing the Small Business. (Illus.). 608p. 1983. text ed. 22.95x (ISBN 0-07-035662-9, C); instr's manual 10.95 (ISBN 0-07-035663-7). McGraw.

Kuriloff, Arthur, jt. auth. see Schollhammer, Hans.

Kuriloff, Arthur H. & Hemphill, John M. How to Start Your Own Business & Succeed. 1978. 3-ring binder 48.00 (ISBN 0-07-035648-3, C). McGraw.

Kurita, Valerie. The Second Big Book of Afghans. 168p. 1982. 16.95 (ISBN 0-442-24863-6). Van Nos Reinhold.

Kuritsky, Joel, jt. auth. see Schapiro, Melvin.

Kuritz, Paul. Playing: An Introduction to Acting. 250p. 1982. 18.95 (ISBN 0-13-682906-6). P-H.

Kuriyama, Kurt Y. Humanists & Technocrats: Political Conflict in Contemporary China. LC 79-66648. 1979. pap. text ed. 10.50 (ISBN 0-8191-0846-4). U Pr of Amer.

Kurjak, ed. Current Status of EPH Gestosis. (International Congress Ser.: Vol. 534). 1981. 98.75 (ISBN 0-444-90171-X). Elsevier.

Kurjak, A., ed. Progress in Medical Ultrasound: Reviews & Comments, Vol. 1: 1980. 1980. 61.75 (ISBN 0-444-90144-2). Elsevier.

--Progress in Medical Ultrasound, Volume 3: Reviews & Comments. 376p. 1982. 67.50 (ISBN 0-444-90242-2, Excerpta Medica). Elsevier.

--Recent Advances in Ultrasound Diagnosis, Vol. 1. (Proceedings). 1978. 72.00 (ISBN 0-444-90022-5). Elsevier.

--Recent Advances in Ultrasound Diagnosis, Vol. 2. (International Congress Ser.: Vol. 498). 1980. 105.75 (ISBN 0-444-90125-6). Elsevier.

Kurjak, A. & Kratochwill, A., eds. Recent Advances in Ultrasound Diagnosis, Vol. 3. (International Congress Ser.: No. 553). 1981. 92.00 (ISBN 0-444-40963-7). Elsevier.

Kurjam. Progress in Medical Ultrasound, Vol. 2. Date not set. 58.25 (ISBN 0-444-90208-2). Elsevier.

Kurland, Gerald. American History, One (to 1865) (College Outlines Ser.). pap. 4.95 o.p. (ISBN 0-671-08046-6). Monarch Pr.

--The Creation of Bangla Desh. (Events of Our Times Ser.: No. 12). 32p. (Orig.). (gr. 7-12). 1973. lib. bdg. 2.95 incl. catalog cards (ISBN 0-87157-213-3); pap. 1.95 vinyl laminated covers (ISBN 0-87157-713-5). SamHar Pr.

--The Czechoslovakian Crisis of 1968. (Events of Our Times: No. 15). 32p. (Orig.). (gr. 7-12). lib. bdg. 2.95 incl. catalog cards (ISBN 0-87157-716-X); pap. 1.95 vinyl laminated covers (ISBN 0-87157-216-8). SamHar Pr.

--The Growth of Presidential Power. Rahmas, D. Steve, ed. (Topics of Our Times Ser.: No. 12). 32p. (gr. 7-12). lib. bdg. 2.95 incl. catalog cards (ISBN 0-87157-813-1); pap. 1.95 vinyl laminated covers (ISBN 0-87157-313-X). SamHar Pr.

--The Gulf of Tonkin Incidents. new ed. Rahmas, D. Steve, ed. (Events of Our Times Ser.). 32p. 1975. lib. bdg. 2.95 incl. catalog cards (ISBN 0-87157-222-2); pap. 1.95 vinyl laminated covers (ISBN 0-87157-722-4). SamHar Pr.

--The Hiroshima Atomic Bomb Blast. Rahmas, D. Steve, ed. LC 73-78401. (Events of Our Times Ser: No. 7). 32p. (Orig.). (gr. 7-12). 1973. lib. bdg. 2.95 incl. catalog cards (ISBN 0-87157-709-7); pap. 1.95 vinyl laminated covers (ISBN 0-87157-209-5). SamHar Pr.

--The Hungarian Rebellion of 1956. (Events of Our Times Ser.: No. 17). 32p. (Orig.). (gr. 7-12). 1974. lib. bdg. 2.95 incl. catalog cards (ISBN 0-87157-718-6); pap. 1.95 vinyl laminated covers (ISBN 0-87157-218-4). SamHar Pr.

--The Korean War. (Events of Our Times Ser.: No. 13). 32p. lib. bdg. 2.95 incl. catalog cards (ISBN 0-686-07222-7); pap. 1.95 vinyl laminated covers (ISBN 0-686-07223-5). SamHar Pr.

--Lindbergh Flies the Atlantic. new ed. Rahmas, D. Steve, ed. (Events of Our Time Ser.). 32p. 1975. lib. bdg. 2.95 incl. catalog cards (ISBN 0-686-11243-1); pap. 1.95 vinyl laminated covers (ISBN 0-686-11244-X). SamHar Pr.

--The Political Machine: What It Is, How It Works. (Topics of Our Times Ser.: No. 9). 32p. lib. bdg. 2.95 incl. catalog cards (ISBN 0-87157-810-7); pap. 1.95 vinyl laminated covers (ISBN 0-87157-310-5). SamHar Pr.

--Suez Crisis, Nineteen Fifty-Six. Rahmas, D. Steve, ed. LC 73-78400. (Events of Our Times Ser: No. 9). 32p. (Orig.). (gr. 7-12). 1973. lib. bdg. 2.95 incl. catalog cards (ISBN 0-87157-711-9); pap. 1.95 vinyl laminated covers (ISBN 0-87157-211-7). SamHar Pr.

--Thomas Edison, Father of Electricity & Master Inventor of Our Modern Age. Rahmas, D. Steve, ed. LC 72-89210. (Outstanding Personalities Ser.: No. 46). 32p. 1972. lib. bdg. 2.95 incl. catalog cards (ISBN 0-87157-542-6); pap. 1.95 vinyl laminated covers (ISBN 0-87157-042-4). SamHar Pr.

--The United States: Policeman of the World. (Topics of Our Times Ser.: No. 10). 32p. lib. bdg. 2.95 incl. catalog cards (ISBN 0-87157-811-5); pap. 1.95 vinyl laminated covers (ISBN 0-87157-311-3). SamHar Pr.

--Western Civilization, No. 1,(to 1500) (Monarch College Outlines). pap. 4.95 o.p. (ISBN 0-671-08045-8). Monarch Pr.

--Western Civilization, No. 2,(from 1500) (Monarch College Outlines). pap. 4.95 o.p. (ISBN 0-671-08050-4). Monarch Pr.

Kurland, Gerald, jt. auth. see Fredman, Lionel E.

Kurland, Gerald, ed. Origins of the Cold War. (Controversial Issues in U. S. History). 176p. (gr. 12). 1975. pap. 2.95 o.p. (ISBN 0-671-18736-8). Monarch Pr.

--The United States in Vietnam. (Controversial Issues on U. S. History Ser.). 216p. (gr. 12). 1975. pap. 2.95 o.p. (ISBN 0-671-18733-3). Monarch Pr.

Kurland, Gerald, ed. see Mushkat, Jerome.

Kurland, Gerald R. Communism & the Red Scare: Topics of Our Times Ser. Rahmas, Sigurd C., ed. (No. 18). 32p. (Orig.). 1982. 2.95x (ISBN 0-87157-819-0); pap. text ed. 1.95 (ISBN 0-87157-319-9). SamHar Pr.

--Creation of the Common Market. Rahmas, Sigurd C., ed. (Topics of Our Times Ser.: No. 16). 32p. (Orig.). 1982. 2.95x (ISBN 0-87157-817-4); pap. text ed. 1.95 (ISBN 0-87157-317-2). SamHar Pr.

Kurland, Howard D. Back Pains: Quick Relief Without Drugs. (Illus.). 192p. 1983. pap. 7.95 (ISBN 0-671-41380-5, Fireside). S&S.

Kurland, L. T., jt. ed. see Kuroiwa, Y.

Kurland, Michael. Death by Gaslight. 1982. pap. 3.50 (ISBN 0-451-11915-0, AE1915, Sig). NAL.

--The Infernal Device. (Orig.). 1979. pap. 1.95 o.p. (ISBN 0-451-08492-6, J8492, Sig). NAL.

--PSI Hunt. 1980. pap. 2.25 o.p. (ISBN 0-425-04664-8). Berkley Pub.

Kurland, Michael & Barton, S. W. The Last President. LC 79-29751. (A Bernard Geis Assoc. Bk.). 384p. 1980. 11.95 o.p. (ISBN 0-688-03610-4). Morrow.

Kurland, Philip B. & Casper, Gerhard, eds. The Supreme Court Review, 1982. 2nd ed. LC 60-14353. (The Supreme Court Review Ser.). 432p. 1983. lib. bdg. 30.00x (ISBN 0-226-46435-0). U of Chicago Pr.

Kurlbaum-Siebert, Margarete. Mary Queen of Scots. Hamilton, Mary A., tr. 504p. 1982. Repr. of 1929 ed. lib. bdg. 40.00 (ISBN 0-8495-3137-3). Arden Lib.

Kurmann, J. & Rasic, J. Bifidobacteria & Their Use. (Experientia Supplementum: Vol. 39). 304p. Date not set. text ed. price not set (ISBN 3-7643-1214-9). Birkhauser.

Kurnitz, Julie, jt. auth. see Eaton, John P.

Kuroda, Yasumasa. Reed Town, Japan: A Study in Community Power Structure & Political Change. LC 73-85580. 320p. 1974. text ed. 15.00x (ISBN 0-8248-0292-6). UH Pr.

Kuroiwa, Y. & Kurland, L. T., eds. Multiple Sclerosis East & West. (Illus.). vi, 398p. 1983. 118.75 (ISBN 3-8055-3674-7). S Karger.

Kurokawa, K. & Tanner, R., eds. Recent Advances in Renal Metabolism. (Mineral Electrolyte Metabolism Ser.: Vol. 9: No. 4-5). (Illus.). 140p. 1983. pap. price not set (ISBN 3-8055-3652-6). S Karger.

Kurokawa, S. A Monograph of the Genus Anaptychia. 1962. pap. 16.00 (ISBN 3-7682-5406-2). Lubrecht & Cramer.

Kurosawa, Akira. Seven Samurai. (Film Scripts-Modern Ser). 1970. pap. 3.45 o.p. (ISBN 0-671-20619-2, Touchstone Bks). S&S.

--Something Like an Autobiography. Bock, Audie E., tr. from Japanese. LC 82-48900. 240p. 1983. pap. 6.95 (ISBN 0-394-71439-3, Vin). Random.

Kurosh, Alexander G. Group Theory, Vol. 1. LC 60-8965. 1979. text ed. 14.95 (ISBN 0-8284-0107-1). Chelsea Pub.

--Group Theory, Vol. 2. 2nd ed. LC 60-8965. 1979. text ed. 14.95 (ISBN 0-8284-0109-8). Chelsea Pub.

Kurpius, DeWayne, ed. Consultation I & Consultation II. 107p. Repr. of 1978 ed. 5.25 (ISBN 0-686-36422-8, 72135); 6.75 (ISBN 0-686-37313-8). Am Personnel.

Kurpius, DeWayne J., et al, eds. Supervision of Applied Training: A Comparative Review. LC 76-28640. 1977. lib. bdg. 29.95 (ISBN 0-8371-9288-9, KSA/). Greenwood.

Kurpkawa, Minako, ed. Minority Responses. LC 81-40764. 384p. 1981. pap. text ed. 12.25 (ISBN 0-8191-1818-4). U Pr of Amer.

Kursh, Harry. The United States Office of Education: A Century of Service. LC 76-2509. (Illus.). 1977. Repr. of 1965 ed. lib. bdg. 15.75x (ISBN 0-8371-8341-3, KUUS). Greenwood.

Kursham, Barbara, jt. auth. see Weinman, David.

Kurstak. Invertebrate Systems In Vitro. 1980. 133.25 (ISBN 0-444-80181-2). Elsevier.

Kurstak, C., jt. ed. see Kurstak, E.

Kurstak, Christine, jt. auth. see Kurstak, E.

Kurstak, E. & Kurstak, Christine. Comparative Diagnosis of Viral Diseases: Human & Related Viruses, Vol. 1 A. 1978. 75.00 (ISBN 0-12-429701-3); by subscription 65.00 (ISBN 0-12-429701-3). Acad Pr.

--Comparative Diagnosis of [illegible]ral Diseases, Vol. 2 B. 1977. 58.50 (ISBN 0-12-4[illegible]9702-1); by subscription 49.50 (ISBN 0-12-42970[illegible]1). Acad Pr.

Kurstak, E., ed. Handbook [illegible] Plant Virus Infections Comparative Diagnosis. 1981. 181.75 (ISBN 0-444-80309-2). Elsevier.

Kurstak, E. & Kurstak, C., eds. Comparative Diagnosis of Viral Diseases, Vol. 3: Vertebrate Animal & Related Viruses, DNA Viruses, Vol. 3 Part A. LC 81-7951. 1981. 54.00 (ISBN 0-12-429703-X); subscription 46.00 (ISBN 0-686-85518-3). Acad Pr.

--Comparative Diagnosis of Viral Diseases, Vol. 4: Vertebrate Animal & Related Viruses, Part B-BNA Viruses, Vol. 4, Part B. LC 81-7951. 1981. subscription 67.00 79.00 (ISBN 0-12-429704-8). Acad Pr.

Kursunglu, Behram N. & Perlmutter, Arnold, eds. Energy for Developed & Developing Countries. LC 81-48092. 224p. 1983. 28.95x (ISBN 0-669-05274-4). Lexington Bks.

Kursunoglu, Behram & Perlmutter, Arnold, eds. Directions in Energy Policy: A Comprehensive Approach to Energy Resource Decision-Making. LC 79-21524. 544p. prof ref 40.00x (ISBN 0-88410-089-8). Ballinger Pub.

Kursunoglu, Behram, et al, eds. A Global View of Energy. LC 81-47525. 352p. 1982. 36.95x (ISBN 0-669-04647-7). Lexington Bks.

Kurten, Bjorn. Age of the Dinosaurs. (Illus., Orig.). 1968. pap. 3.95 o.p. (ISBN 0-07-035660-2, SP). McGraw.

--The Ice Age. (Illus.). 1972. 16.95 o.p. (ISBN 0-399-11010-0). Putnam Pub Group.

Kurten, Nancy N. Needlepoint in Minature. (Illus.). 160p. 1983. pap. 10.95 (ISBN 0-686-83786-X, ScribT). Scribner.

Kurth, Ann. Prescription: Murder. (Illus.). 1981. pap. 2.95 (ISBN 0-451-12026-4, AE2026, Sig). NAL.

Kurth, Geneste, jt. auth. see Kurth, Heinz.

Kurth, Heinz & Kurth, Geneste. Barbecue. (Illus.). 1980. pap. 4.95 (ISBN 0-8256-3181-5, Quick Fox). Putnam Pub Group.

Kurth, Peter. Anastasia: The Life of Anna Anderson. (Illus.). 384p. 1983. 17.95i (ISBN 0-316-50716-4). Little.

Kurth, Rudolf. Remarks About Academic Matters. LC 81-40177. 124p. (Orig.). 1982. lib. bdg. 19.00 (ISBN 0-8191-1855-9); pap. text ed. 8.25 (ISBN 0-8191-1856-7). U Pr of Amer.

Kurth-Scherer, S., tr. see Fuhrmann, W. & Vogel, F.

Kurti, N. The Selected Works of Louis Neel. 615p. 1982. write for info. (ISBN 0-677-30980-5). Gordon.

Kurtin, Stephen B., jt. auth. see Imber, Gerald.

Kurtinitis, Sandra. A Brief & Lively No-Nonsense Guide to Writing. 1981. pap. text ed. 9.95x (ISBN 0-673-15240-5). Scott F.

Kurtsin, I. T. Theoretical Principles of Psychosomatic Medicine. Kaner, N., tr. from Rus. LC 75-5587. 257p. 1976. 76.95x o.p. (ISBN 0-470-51100-1). Halsted Pr.

Kurtz, jt. auth. see Boone.

Kurtz, Benjamin P., ed. see Mills, Gayley C. & Young, C. C.

Kurtz, Carol S. Designing for Weaving: A Study Guide for Weavers. (Illus.). 96p. 1981. 18.95 (ISBN 0-8038-1579-4). Hastings.

Kurtz, David L. & Boone, Louis E. Principles of Management. Incl. Student Mastery Guide. Baird, James, et al. 265p. wkbk. 10.00 (ISBN 0-394-32697-0). 624p. 1981. pap. text ed. 24.95 (ISBN 0-394-32246-0). Random.

Kurtz, David L., jt. auth. see Boone, Louis E.

Kurtz, Donna & Sparkes, Brian, eds. The Eye of Greece: Studies in the Art of Athens. LC 81-21672. (Illus.). 256p. 1982. 59.50 (ISBN 0-521-23726-2). Cambridge U Pr.

Kurtz, E. Shame & Guilt: An Historical Perspective for Professionals. 1981. 3.50 o.p. (ISBN 0-89486-132-8). Hazelden.

Kurtz, Edwin B. The Lineman's & Cableman's Handbook. 5th ed. 864p. 1976. 42.50 (ISBN 0-07-035652-1, P&RB). McGraw.

Kurtz, Ernest. Not-God: A History of Alcoholics Anonymous. 1979. 12.95 (ISBN 0-89486-065-8). Hazelden.

--Shame & Guilt: Characteristics of the Dependency Cycle. 3.95 (ISBN 0-89486-132-8, 1940A). Hazelden.

Kurtz, Howard A. The Beaten Victim. LC 82-50373. 125p. (Orig.). 1983. pap. 9.95 (ISBN 0-88247-684-X). R & E Res Assoc.

Kurtz, John H. Sacrificial Worship of the Old Testament. 1979. 16.50 (ISBN 0-86524-012-4, 8703). Klock & Klock.

Kurtz, John W. John Frederick Oberlin. rev. ed. LC 76-25211. 1977. lib. bdg. 24.50 o.p. (ISBN 0-89158-118-9). Westview.

Kurtz, Larry, jt. auth. see Hollstein, Milton.

Kurtz, M., et al. Ten Thousand Legal Words. 1971. 6.56 (ISBN 0-07-035669-6, G). McGraw.

Kurtz, Margaret, jt. auth. see Adams, Dorothy.

Kurtz, Max. Comprehensive Structural Design Guide. LC 68-29913. (Illus.). 1969. 27.50 o.p. (ISBN 0-07-035658-0, P&RB). McGraw.

--Engineering Economics for Professional Engineers' Examinations. 2nd ed. (Illus.). 288p. 1975. 32.50 (ISBN 0-07-035675-0, P&RB). McGraw.

--Structural Engineering for Professional Engineer's Examination. 3rd ed. (Illus.). 1978. 24.50 (ISBN 0-07-035657-2, P&RB); pap. 13.95 (ISBN 0-07-035674-2). McGraw.

Kurtz, Norman R. Introduction to Social Statistics. (Illus.). 416p. 1983. text ed. 22.95x (ISBN 0-07-035676-9, C); write for info. instr's manual (ISBN 0-07-035677-7). McGraw.

Kurtz, P. David, jt. auth. see Marshall, Eldon K.

Kurtz, Paul. The Fullness of Life. LC 74-11176. 216p. 1974. pap. 6.95 (ISBN 0-87975-205-X). Prometheus Bks.

Kurtz, Ray, jt. auth. see Albracht, James.

Kurtz, Sheldon F. Problems, Cases & Other Materials on Family Estate Planning. LC 82-21920. (American Casebook Ser.). 853p. 1982. text ed. 23.95 (ISBN 0-314-69313-0); tchrs.' manual avail. (ISBN 0-314-72900-3). West Pub.

Kurtz, Susanne M., jt. auth. see Riccardi, Vincent M.

Kurtz, Thomas E., jt. auth. see Kemeny, John G.

Kurtz, V. Ray. Teaching Metric Awareness. LC 75-22174. (Illus.). 84p. 1976. pap. text ed. 7.00 o.p. (ISBN 0-8016-2811-3). Mosby.

Kurtzman, Joel, jt. ed. see Laszlo, Ervin.

Kurylo, Friedrich & Susskind, Charles. Ferdinand Braun: A Life of the Nobel Prize Winner & Inventor of the Cathode-Ray Oscilloscope. (Illus.). 304p. 1981. 35.00x (ISBN 0-262-11077-6). MIT Pr.

Kurz, Albert L. Disciple-Maker Workbook. 1981. pap. 9.95 o.p. (ISBN 0-8024-2217-9). Moody.

Kurz, William S. & Karris, Robert J. The Acts of the Apostles, No. 5. LC 82-20872. (Collegeville Bible Commentary Ser.). (Illus.). 112p. 1983. pap. 2.50 (ISBN 0-8146-1305-5). Liturgical Pr.

Kurzawa, Werner. Analytische Aspekte der Literarischen Wertung. 254p. (Ger.). 1982. write for info. P Lang Pubs.

Kurzban, Stan & Rosen, Mel. The Compleat Cruciverbalist. (Illus.). 192p. 1982. pap. 4.76i (ISBN 0-06-463544-9, EH 544, EH). B&N NY.

Kurzban, Stanley A., et al. Operating Systems Principles. LC 75-2400. 480p. (Orig.). 1975. 18.95 o.p. (ISBN 0-88405-294-X). Krieger.

Kurzig, Carol M. Foundation Fundamentals: A Guide for Grantseekers. rev. ed. LC 80-67501. (Illus.). 148p. (Orig.). 1981. pap. 6.50 (ISBN 0-87954-049-4). Foundation Ctr.

Kurzman, Dan. Ben-Gurion: Prophet of Fire. 1983. price not set (ISBN 0-671-23094-8). S&S.

--The Bravest Battle. 1980. pap. 2.50 o.p. (ISBN 0-523-40182-5). Pinnacle Bks.

--Bravest Battle: The Twenty Eight Days of the Warsaw Ghetto Uprising. LC 76-2694. (Illus.). 1976. 10.00 o.p. (ISBN 0-399-11692-3). Putnam Pub Group.

--The Miracle of November: Madrid's Epic Stand, Nineteen Thirty-Six. LC 79-12555. (Illus.). 1980. 14.95 o.p. (ISBN 0-399-12271-0). Putnam Pub Group.

--The Race for Rome. 1977. pap. 2.50 o.p. (ISBN 0-523-40013-6). Pinnacle Bks.

Kurzman, Paul, jt. auth. see Akabas, Sheila H.

Kurzman, Robert G. & Gilbert, Rita K. Paralegals & Successful Law Practice. LC 81-13157. 401p. 1981. 49.50 (ISBN 0-87624-426-6). Inst Busn Plan.

Kurzman-Seppala, Tersa. A Primer on the Prevention of Chemical Use Problems. 1979. 1.95 (ISBN 0-89486-041-0). Hazelden.

Kurzweil, Edith & Phillips, William, eds. Writers & Politics: A Partisan Review Reader. 352p. 1983. pap. 11.95 (ISBN 0-7100-9316-0). Routledge & Kegan.

Kuschner, David S., jt. auth. see Forman, George E.

Kuse, James & Luedtke, Ralph D., eds. Once Upon a Rhyme. (ps). 1978. pap. 3.95 o.p. (ISBN 0-89542-055-4). Ideals.

Kush, S. S. The End Befallen Edgar Allen Poe. 28p. 1982. pap. 2.00x (ISBN 0-686-38373-7). Singing Horse.

Kushi, Michio. The Book of Macrobiotics: The Universal Way of Health & Happiness. LC 76-29341. (Illus.). 176p. (Orig.). 1977. pap. 11.95 (ISBN 0-87040-381-8). Japan Pubns.

--Macrobiotic Approach to Cancer. 1981. 6.95x (ISBN 0-89529-209-2). Cancer Control Soc.

--The Macrobiotic Diet & Exercise Book. 176p. 1983. pap. 7.95 (ISBN 0-686-43184-7). Avery Pub.

--Natural Healing Through Macrobiotics. LC 79-1959. (Illus.). 1979. pap. 11.95 (ISBN 0-87040-457-1). Japan Pubns.

--Your Face Never Lies: An Introduction to Oriental Diagnosis. (The Macrobiotic Home Library). 144p. 1983. pap. 7.95 (ISBN 0-89529-214-9). Avery Pub.

Kushi, Michio & East-West Foundation. The Macrobiotic Approach to Cancer. 2nd ed. (Macrobiotic Home Library Ser.). 128p. (Orig.). 1982. pap. 6.95 (ISBN 0-686-43109-X). Avery Pub.

Kushi, Michio & Jack, Alex. The Cancer-Prevention Diet. 1983. 13.95 (ISBN 0-312-11837-6). St Martin.

Kushins, Milton, jt. auth. see Gold, Faye.

Kushma, John J. & Maizlish, Steven E., eds. Essays on American Antebellum Politics, 1840-1860. LC 82-40314. (Walter Prescott Webb Memorial Lectures Ser.: No. 16). 240p. 1982. 19.50x (ISBN 0-89096-136-0). Tex A&M Univ Pr.

Kushner, Bill, jt. auth. see Tatum, Jack.

Kushner, Eva, tr. see Mehl, Roger.

Kushner, Gilbert, jt. ed. see Castile, George P.

Kushner, Harold S. When Bad Things Happen to Good People. 160p. 1983. pap. 3.50 (ISBN 0-380-60392-6, 60392-6). Avon.

--When Bad Things Happen to Good People. (General Ser.). 1982. lib. bdg. 11.95 (ISBN 0-8161-3465-0, Large Print Bks). G K Hall.

--When Children Ask About God. LC 76-9140. 1976. pap. 4.95 (ISBN 0-8052-0549-7). Schocken.

Kushner, Harvey W. & De Maio, Gerald. Understanding Basic Statistics. LC 78-54195. 1980. text ed. 20.95x (ISBN 0-8162-4874-5); sol. manual 6.00x (ISBN 0-686-76791-8, 0-8162-8475). Holden-Day.

Kushner, Howard I. Conflict on the Northwest Coast: American-Russian Rivalry in the Pacific Northwest, 1790-1867. LC 75-67. (Contributions in American History: No. 41). (Illus.). 1975. lib. bdg. 27.50 (ISBN 0-8371-7873-8, KCN/). Greenwood.

Kushner, Howard I. & Sherrill, Anne H. John Milton Hay. (World Leaders Ser.). 1977. lib. bdg. 13.95 (ISBN 0-8057-7719-9, Twayne). G K Hall.

Kushner, James A. Apartheid in America: An Historical & Legal Analysis of Contemporary Racial Residential Segregation in the United States. LC 80-67048. (Scholarly Monographs). 135p. 1980. pap. 12.00 o.p. (ISBN 0-8408-0509-8). Carrollton Pr.

Kushner, M. & Zucker, C. RPG: Language & Techniques. LC 73-8644. 482p. 1974. pap. 26.95x o.p. (ISBN 0-471-51117-X). Wiley.

Kushner, Maureen. The Every Excuse in the Book Book. Schneider, Meg, ed. (Funnybones Ser.). (Illus.). 64p. (gr. 3-7). 1983. pap. 1.95 (ISBN 0-671-44446-8). Wanderer Bks.

Kushner, Rose. Why Me? What Every Woman Should Know About Breast Cancer to Save Her Life. Orig. Title: Breast Cancer. 1977. pap. 2.50 o.p. (ISBN 0-451-07692-3, E7692, Sig). NAL.

Kushner, Thomasine. The Anatomy of Art. 300p. 1983. 27.50 (ISBN 0-87527-248-7). Green.

Kushnirsky, Fyodor I. Soviet Economic Planning, Nineteen Sixty-Five to Nineteen Eighty. 150p. 1982. softcover 16.50 (ISBN 0-86531-928-6). Westview.

Kusin, V. From Dubcek to Charter Seventy-Seven. LC 78-60995. 1978. 25.00x (ISBN 0-312-30717-9). St Martin.

Kuska, George & Linse, Barbara. The California Missions Through Children's Eyes. 140p. 1983. 8.95 (ISBN 0-9607458-1-5). Arts Bks.

Kuske, A. & Robertson, G. Photoelastic Stress Analysis. LC 73-2788. 519p. 1974. 92.00x (ISBN 0-471-51101-3, Pub. by Wiley-Interscience). Wiley.

Kuskin, Karla. Dogs & Dragons, Trees & Dreams: A Collection of Poems. LC 79-2814. (Illus.). 96p. (gr. 1-6). 1980. 9.57i o.p. (ISBN 0-06-023543-8, HarpJ); PLB 9.89 (ISBN 0-06-023544-6). Har-Row.

--James & the Rain. LC 57-6851. (Illus.). (ps-3). 1957. PLB 9.89 o.p. (ISBN 0-06-023601-9, HarpJ). Har-Row.

--Sand & Snow. LC 65-11456. (Illus.). (gr. k-3). 1965. PLB 7.89 o.p. (ISBN 0-06-023646-9, HarpJ). Har-Row.

--Which Horse Is William. LC 59-8974. (Illus.). (ps-1). 1959. 8.95i o.p. (ISBN 0-06-023660-4, HarpJ); PLB 8.79 o.p. (ISBN 0-06-023661-2). Har-Row.

Kusko, Alexander. Solid-State DC Motor Drives. 1969. 20.00x (ISBN 0-262-11031-8). MIT Pr.

Kuslan, Louis I., see Weaver, Glenn.

Kusler, Jon A. Regulating Sensitive Lands. 264p. 1980. prof ref 30.00x (ISBN 0-88410-095-2). Ballinger Pub.

Kusnet, Jack, et al. Real Estate Law Digest, 2 vols. 2nd ed. 1981. Set. 75.00 (ISBN 0-88262-591-8). Warren.

Kusnetz, Len. Your Child Can Be a Super Reader. LC 79-84790. 128p. 1980. pap. 4.95 (ISBN 0-9602730-0-X). Liberty Pub.

--Your Child Can Be a Super-Reader: A Fun & Easy Approach to Reading Improvement. LC 79-84790. (Illus.). 132p. (Orig.). 1982. pap. 4.95 o.p. (ISBN 0-9602730-0-X, Dist. by Liberty Pub. Co). Learning Hse.

--Your Child Can Be a Super-Reader: A Fun & Easy Approach to Reading Improvement. LC 79-84790. (Illus.). 132p. 1982. 4.95 (ISBN 0-686-84883-7, Dist. by Liberty Pub. Co). Learning Hse.

Kuspira, John & Walker, G. W. Genetics: Questions & Problems. 1973. pap. text ed. 20.00 (ISBN 0-07-035672-6, C). McGraw.

Kuspit, Donald, ed. see Buckley, Harry E.

Kuspit, Donald, ed. see Buettner, Stewart.

Kuspit, Donald, ed. see Plank, William G.

Kuspit, Donald, ed. see Zemel, Carol M.

Kuspit, Donald B. Clement Greenberg, Art Critic. LC 79-3967. 232p. 1979. 19.50 (ISBN 0-299-07900-7). U of Wis Pr.

Kuspit, Donald B., ed. see Flanary, David A.

Kuspit, Donald B., ed. see Gelber, Lynne L.

Kuss, Rene & Murphy, Gerald P., eds. Renal Tumors: Proceedings of the International Symposium on Kidney Tumors, 1st. LC 82-14008. (Progress in Clinical & Biological Research Ser.: Vol. 100). 692p. 1982. 72.00 (ISBN 0-8451-0100-5). A R Liss.

Kussi, Peter see Liehm, Antonin.

Kussi, Peter, jt. ed. see Liehm, Antonin.

Kussmaul, A. Stochastic Integration & Genaralized Martingales. (Research Notes in Mathematics Ser.: No. 11). 163p. (Orig.). 1977. pap. text ed. 19.95 (ISBN 0-273-01030-1). Pitman Pub MA.

Kust, Matthew. Man & Horse in History. (Illus.). 159p. 1983. 15.95x (ISBN 0-89891-005-6, Plutarch Pr). Advent NY.

Kuster, Gustavo G. Hepatic Support in Acute Liver Failure. (Illus.). 320p. 1976. 31.75x o.p. (ISBN 0-398-03539-3). C C Thomas.

Kustra, Mary E., jt. ed. see Elliott, Norman F.

Kuswa, Webster. Big Paybacks from Small Budget Advertising. 1982. 87.50 (ISBN 0-85013-128-6). Dartnell Corp.

Kut & Hare. Applied Solar Energy. 2nd ed. 1983. text ed. 34.95 (ISBN 0-408-01244-7). Butterworth.

Kut, David. Dictionary of Applied Conservation. 208p. 1982. 32.00 o.p. (ISBN 0-686-98385-8). Nichols Pub.

--Dictionary of Applied Energy Conservation: An Illustrated Dictionary of Terms. (Illus.). 300p. 1983. 32.00 (ISBN 0-89397-131-6). Nichols Pub.

Kut, Gunay, jt. ed. see Chambers, Richard L.

Kutac, Edward A. & Caran, S. Christopher. A Bird Finding & Naturalist's Guide for the Austin, Texas Area. Simmons, Roger & Diercks, Char, trs. LC 76-5316. (Illus.). 1976. pap. 4.00 o.p. (ISBN 0-916378-04-7). Oasis Pr CA.

Kutash, Irwin L., et al. Handbook on Stress & Anxiety: Contemporary Knowledge, Theory, & Treatment. LC 80-8014. (Social & Behavioral Science Ser.). 1980. text ed. 29.95x (ISBN 0-87589-478-X). Jossey-Bass.

Kutcher, Arthur. New Jerusalem: Planning & Politics. 1975. 16.00x o.p. (ISBN 0-262-11058-X); pap. 7.95x (ISBN 0-262-61020-5). MIT Pr.

Kutie, Rita & Huffman, Virginia. The Wiley Office Handbook. 460p. 1981. 12.95 (ISBN 0-686-98092-1). Telecom Lib.

--The WP Book. LC 79-18274. 1980. pap. text ed. 12.95x (ISBN 0-471-03881-4); study guide 7.95x (ISBN 0-471-07863-8). Wiley.

Kutie, Rita C. & Rhodes, Joan. Secretarial Procedures for the Electronic Office. LC 82-11047. 371p. 1983. text ed. 17.95x (ISBN 0-471-86156-1); tchrs.' manual avail. Wiley.

Kutler, Stanley I. The American Inquisition: Justice & Injustice in the Cold War. 290p. 1982. 16.50 (ISBN 0-8090-2475-6). Hill & Wang.

Kutner, Marc L., jt. auth. see Pasachoff, Jay M.

Kutner, Mark A., jt. ed. see Sherman, Joel D.

Kutnick, Richard W., ed. see Shannon, Doug.

Kutrth & Ver Hoef. Creative Teachers. (gr. 1-3). pap. text ed. 4.77 (ISBN 0-8372-4247-9); tchr's handbk. 4.77 (ISBN 0-8372-4248-7); tapes avail. Bowmar-Noble.

Kutscher, Austin, et al, eds. Hospice U. S. A. (Foundation of Thanatology Ser.). 304p. 1983. text ed. 22.50 (ISBN 0-231-05082-8). Columbia U Pr.

Kutscher, Austin H., et al, eds. Pharmacology for the Dental Hygienist. 2nd ed. LC 81-19395. (Illus.). 389p. 1982. text ed. 19.50 (ISBN 0-8121-0802-7). Lea & Febiger.

Kutscher, C. & Barlow, R. Dynamic Performance of Packed Bed Dehumidifiers: Experimental Results from the SERI Desiccant Test Loop. (Progress in Solar Energy Supplements SERI Ser.). 75p. 1983. pap. text ed. 9.00x (ISBN 0-89553-085-6). Am Solar Energy.

Kutscher, C., et al. Design Approaches for Solar Industrial Process Heat Systems. (Progress in Solar Energy Supplements SERI Ser.). 500p. 1983. pap. text ed. 45.00x (ISBN 0-89553-083-X). Am Solar Energy.

Kutscher, Charles F. & Davenport, R. L. Design Approaches for Solar Industrial Process Heat Systems: Nontracking & Line Focus Collector Technologies. (Progress in Solar Energy Ser.). 452p. 1983. pap. text ed. 31.50 (ISBN 0-89553-113-5). Am Solar Energy.

Kutscher, Lillian G., jt. auth. see Austin, H.

Kutt, Henn, jt. ed. see Solomon, Gail E.

Kuttin & Baum, eds. Human & Animal Mycology. (International Congress Ser.: Vol. 480). 1980. 61.00 (ISBN 0-444-90099-3). Elsevier.

Kuttner, Henry. Murder of a Wife. Barzun, J. & Taylor, W. H., eds. LC 81-47403. (Crime Fiction 1950-1975 Ser.). 182p. 1982. lib. bdg. 14.95 (ISBN 0-8240-4971-3). Garland Pub.

Kuttner, Henry, jt. auth. see Moore, C. L.

Kuttner, Monroe S. Managing the Paperwork Pipeline. LC 77-15041. 244p. 1978. 33.95x (ISBN 0-471-03154-2, Pub. by Wiley-Interscience). Wiley.

Kuttner, Paul, tr. see Paraquin, Charles H.

Kuttner, Paul, tr. see Strose, Susanne.

Kuttner, Robert. Revolt of the Haves: Tax Rebellions & Hard Times. 1980. 13.95 o.p. (ISBN 0-671-25099-X). S&S.

Kuttruff, H. Room Acoustics. LC 73-16149. (Illus.). 298p. 1973. 54.95 o.s.i. (ISBN 0-470-51105-2). Halsted Pr.

Kuttruff, K. H. Room Acoustics. 2nd ed. (Illus.). 1979. 51.25x (ISBN 0-85334-813-8, Pub. by Applied Sci England). Elsevier.

Kuuser, Ted. The Blizzard Voices. 1983. price not set; pap. price not set. Bieler.

Kuusi, Juha. Host State & the Transnational Corporation. 1980. text ed. 31.50 (ISBN 0-566-00249-3). Gower Pub Ltd.

Kuvas, J., ed. Boss Nineteen Seventy-Six: Proceedings of an International Conference on the Behavior of off-Shore Structures, Norwegian Institute of Technology, Trondheim, 2-5 August 1976. LC 77-75338. 1977. text ed. write for info. o.p. (ISBN 0-08-021739-7). Pergamon.

Kuvshinoff, B. W., et al, eds. Fire Sciences Dictionary. LC 77-3489. 439p. 1977. 23.50x (ISBN 0-471-51113-7, Pub. by Wiley-Interscience). Wiley.

Kuwana, Ted & Osa, Tetsuo, eds. Physical Methods in Modern Chemical Analysis, Vol. 1. 1978. 41.00 (ISBN 0-12-430801-5); by subscription 41.00 (ISBN 0-12-430801-5). Acad Pr.

Kuwana, Theodore, ed. Physical Methods in Modern Chemical Analysis, Vol. 2. LC 77-92242. 1980. 45.00 (ISBN 0-12-430802-3); subscription 45.00 (ISBN 0-12-430802-3). Acad Pr.

Kuwayama, George. Far Eastern Lacquer. Einzig, Barbara, ed. (Illus.). 128p. (Orig.). 1982. pap. 15.95 (ISBN 0-87587-108-9). LA Co Art Mus.

Kuyk, Dirk, Jr. Threads Cable-Strong. LC 81-72030. 192p. 1982. 22.50 (ISBN 0-8387-5037-0). Bucknell U Pr.

Kuykendall, Bill, jt. auth. see Hampton, Veita J.

Kuykendall, John W., jt. auth. see Lingle, Walter L.

Kuykendall, Karen. Art & Design in Papier-Mache. LC 68-8519. (Illus.). 1968. 8.95 (ISBN 0-8208-0301-4). Hearthside.

Kuykendall, Ralph S. The Hawaiian Kingdom, 3 vols. Incl. Vol. 1. 1778-1854, Foundation & Transformation. 462p. 1938. 16.95 (ISBN 0-87022-431-X); Vol. 2. 1854-1874, Twenty Critical Years. 320p. 1953. 14.95 (ISBN 0-87022-432-8); Vol. 3. 1874-1893, the Kalakaua Dynasty. 776p. 1967. 19.95 ea. (ISBN 0-87022-433-6). (Illus.). UH Pr.

Kuykendall, William J. A Subject of Innocence. LC 80-52887. 53p. 1982. 6.95 (ISBN 0-533-04794-3). Vantage.

Kuypers, H. G. Descending Pathways to the Spinal Cord. Martin, G. F., ed. (Progress in Brain Research Ser.: Vol. 57). 428p. 1982. 93.00 (ISBN 0-444-80413-7). Elsevier.

Kuzma, Kay. Filling Your Love Cup. 90p. (Orig.). 1982. 9.95x (ISBN 0-910529-01-9); pap. 5.95 (ISBN 0-910529-00-0). Parent Scene.

Kuzma, Kay, ed. Working Mothers. 2nd ed. LC 81-51822. 1981. 14.95 (ISBN 0-936906-08-1). Stratford Pr.

Kuzmanovic, A. Cermanovic see Cermanovic-Kuzmanovic, A.

Kuzmin, Mikhail. Chudesnaia Zhizn' Iosifa Bal'Zamo, Grafa Kaliostro. 250p. (Rus.). 1982. pap. 9.95 (ISBN 0-89830-037-1). Russica Pubs.

--Travellers by Land & Sea. Barnstead, John, tr. from Rus. 140p. 1983. 15.00 (ISBN 0-88233-810-2); pap. 5.00 (ISBN 0-88233-811-0). Ardis Pubs.

Kuz'mina, G. V., jt. auth. see Steklov Institute of Mathematics.

Kuz'Minskii, A. S., ed. Ageing & Stabilisation of Polymers. Leyland, B. N., tr. from Russian. (Illus.). 1971. text ed. 48.50x (ISBN 0-444-20076-2, Pub. by Applied Sci England). Burgess Intl Ideas.

Kuzmits, Frank E. Exercises in Personnel Management. 1982. pap. text ed. 8.95 (ISBN 0-675-09791-6). Additional supplements may be obtained from publisher. Merrill.

Kuznetsov, S. I. The Microflora of Lakes & Its Geochemical Activity. Oppenheimer, Carl H., ed. LC 73-21215. (Illus.). 503p. 1975. 27.50x (ISBN 0-292-75010-2). U of Tex Pr.

Kuznetsov, Yury & Linnik, Irene. Dutch Painting in Soviet Museums. LC 80-66702. (Illus.). 523p. 1982. 45.00 (ISBN 0-8109-0803-4). Abrams.

Kuzvart, M. & Bohmer, M. Prospecting & Exploration for Mineral Deposits. 1978. 78.00 (ISBN 0-444-99876-4). Elsevier.

Kvale, O., jt. ed. see Hoyem, T.

Kvalseth. Ergonomics in Action. 1983. text ed. write for info. (ISBN 0-86103-061-3). Butterworth.

Kvam, Wayne E. Hemingway in Germany. LC 79-181689. x, 214p. 1973. 12.95x (ISBN 0-8214-0126-2, 82-81297). Ohio U Pr.

Kvande, Carol, jt. auth. see Fideler, Raymond.

Kvaraceus, William C. Prevention & Control of Delinquency: The School Counselor's Role. (Guidance Monograph). 1970. pap. 2.40 o.p. (ISBN 0-395-09950-1, 9-78850). HM.

Kvart, Igal. A Theory of Counterfactuals. 272p. 1983. text ed. 30.00 (ISBN 0-915145-63-4). Hackett Pub.

Kvasnicka, Robert M., jt. ed. see Smith, Jane F.

Kvasnicker, Ted, et al. Bicentennial Wagon Train Pilgrimage. Sherman, Bill & Matolek, Marmie, eds. LC 77-90957. (Illus.). 1977. 36.50 (ISBN 0-685-86987-3). Jem Pubs.

Kvenvolden, Keith A., ed. Geochemistry of Organic Molecules. LC 79-18201. (Benchmark Papers in Geology Ser.: Vol. 52). 357p. 1980. 44.50 (ISBN 0-87933-353-7). Hutchinson Ross.

Kvetnansky, jt. auth. see Usdin.

Kwak, N. K. Mathematical Programming with Business Applications. (Illus.). 384p. 1972. text ed. 23.50 o.p. (ISBN 0-07-035717-X, C); instructor's manual 4.95 o.p. (ISBN 0-07-035718-8). McGraw.

Kwak, N. K. & Schniederjans, Marc J. Managerial Applications of Operations Research. LC 81-40623. (Illus.). 452p. (Orig.). 1982. lib. bdg. 31.50 (ISBN 0-8191-2227-0); pap. text ed. 18.50 (ISBN 0-8191-2228-9). U Pr of Amer.

Kwak, Tai-Hwan & Chay, John, eds. U. S. - Korean Relations, 1882-1982. 433p. 1983. lib. bdg. 25.00x (ISBN 0-86531-608-2). Westview.

Kwakernaak, Huibert & Sivan, Raphael. Linear Optimal Control Systems. LC 72-3576. 544p. 1972. 55.95x (ISBN 0-471-51110-2, Pub. by Wiley-Interscience). Wiley.

Kwamena, Poh, et al. African History in Maps. LC 81-675343. (Illus.). 80p. (Orig.). 1982. pap. text ed. 4.95x (ISBN 0-582-60331-5). Longman.

Kwami, Thomas, jt. ed. see Djoleto, Amu.

Kwancho, C. K. Underground Notebooks on Intellects. 193p. (Orig.). 1982. pap. 8.50x (ISBN 0-9609544-0-6, Aletheia Bks). U Pubns Amer.

Kwang-Ching, Lui, jt. auth. see Fairbank, John K.

Kwan Ha Yim, ed. China & the U. S., Vol. 1: 1955-63. LC 72-80832. 187p. 1973. lib. bdg. 17.50x o.p. (ISBN 0-87196-206-3). Facts on File.

--China & the U. S., Vol. 2: 1964-72. LC 72-80832. 270p. 1975. lib. bdg. 17.50x o.p. (ISBN 0-87196-207-1). Facts on File.

Kwasa, Shadrack O., jt. auth. see Gilmore, Theopolis L.

Kwiatkowski, Alexsander. Swedish Film Classics: A Pictorial Study or Twenty-Five Films from 1913-1957. (Illus.). 144p. 1983. pap. 7.95 (ISBN 0-486-24304-4). Dover.

Kwiatkowski, Joan, jt. auth. see Shriberg, Lawrence D.

Kwitny, Jonathan. The Mullendore Murder Case. LC 74-14650. (Illus.). 336p. 1974. 11.95 o.p. (ISBN 0-374-21599-5). FS&G.

--Shakedown. LC 76-51436. 1977. 7.95 o.p. (ISBN 0-399-11915-9). Putnam Pub Group.

Kwitz, Mary. Rabbits' Search for a Little House. LC 76-45432. (gr. k-2). 1977. reinforced lib. bdg. 6.95 o.p. (ISBN 0-517-52867-3). Crown.

Kwock, C. H. & McHugh, Vincent, trs. Old Friend from Far Away: One Hundred Fifty Chinese Poems from the Great Dynasties. LC 80-18321. 224p. 1980. 16.50 (ISBN 0-86547-017-0); pap. 6.50 (ISBN 0-86547-018-9). N Point Pr.

Kwock, Laureen. Samantha. 224p. (Orig.). 1983. pap. 2.25 (ISBN 0-449-20217-8, Crest). Fawcett.

Kwong, Yat-Sang. On Reductions & Livelocks in Asynchronous Parallel Computation. Stone, Harold, ed. LC 82-6888. (Computer Science: Systems Programming Ser.: No. 7). 120p. (gr. k-6). 1982. 34.95 (ISBN 0-8357-1342-3). Univ Microfilms.

Kwong Ki Chaou. Dictionary of English Phrases with Illustrative Sentences. LC 74-136559. (Illus.). 1971. Repr. of 1881 ed. 63.00 (ISBN 0-8103-3386-4). Gale.

Kwun Sup Chung, et al. Modernization & Its Impact Upon Korean Law. (Korea Research Monographs: No. 3). 150p. 1981. pap. 12.50x o.p. (ISBN 0-686-69422-8). IEAS.

Kyasht, Lydia. Romantic Recollections. Beale, Erica, ed. (Series in Dance). (Illus.). 1978. Repr. of 1929 ed. lib. bdg. 22.50 (ISBN 0-306-77572-7). Da Capo.

Kyber, M. Among Animals. 10.00 o.p. (ISBN 0-87556-142-X). Saifer.

Kyber, Manfred. Among Animals. Fishwick, Olive, tr. (gr. 3 up). 1968. 7.50 o.s.i. (ISBN 0-8283-1152-8). Branden.

Kybett, Harry. Electronics. LC 78-16821. (Wiley Self-Teaching Guides Ser.). 260p. 1979. 8.95x (ISBN 0-471-01748-5). Wiley.

Kyburg, Henry E. & Smokler, Howard E. Studies in Subjective Probability. 2nd ed. LC 79-16294. 272p. 1980. pap. 11.50 (ISBN 0-88275-296-0). Krieger.

Kyburg, Henry E., Jr. Epistemology & Inference. (Illus.). 400p. 1983. 39.50x (ISBN 0-8166-1149-1); pap. 15.95x (ISBN 0-8166-1150-5). U of Minn Pr.

Kyd, Thomas. The First Part of Hieronimo. Cairncross, Andrew S., ed. Bd. with The Spanish Tragedy. LC 66-20826. (Regents Renaissance Drama Ser.). xxxiv, 186p. 1967. 14.50x o.p. (ISBN 0-8032-0267-9); pap. 5.50x o.p. (ISBN 0-8032-5267-6, BB 221, Bison). U of Nebr Pr.

--The Spanish Tragedy. Prouty, Charles T., ed. LC 52-409. (Crofts Classics Ser.). 1951. pap. text ed. 3.50x (ISBN 0-88295-051-7). Harlan Davidson.

Kydd, Rachael. Long Distance Riding Explained. LC 78-8998. (Horseman's Handbook Ser.). (Illus.). 1979. 7.95 o.p. (ISBN 0-668-04579-5); pap. 3.95 (ISBN 0-668-04583-3). Arco.

Kydd, Sam. For You, the War Is Over. 1974. 9.50 o.p. (ISBN 0-85974-005-6). Transatlantic.

Kyed, James M. & Matarazzo, James H., eds. Scientific, Engineering & Medical Societies Publications in Print 1978-1979. 3rd ed. LC 79-17264. 1979. 35.00 o.p. (ISBN 0-8352-1212-2). Bowker.

Kyger, Joanne. The Wonderful Focus of You. rev. ed. (Orig.). 1980. pap. 5.00 (ISBN 0-915990-22-9). Z Pr.

Kyker, Rex, compiled by. I Am Born Again. (Undenominational Christianity Ser.: Vol. 2). 94p. (Orig.). 1983. pap. 2.95 (ISBN 0-88027-110-8). Firm Foun Pub.

Kyker, Rex, compiled by see Lemmons, Reuel & Bannister, John.

Kyle, David A. Lensman from Rigel. 224p. 1982. pap. 2.50 (ISBN 0-553-20499-8). Bantam.

Kyle, J., ed. Pye's Surgical Handicraft. 20th ed. 756p. 1977. text ed. 26.50 (ISBN 0-7236-0432-0). Wright-PSG.

Kyle, Jim & Woll, Bencie, eds. Language in Sign: An International Perspective on Sign Language. 320p. 1983. pap. text ed. 19.50x (ISBN 0-7099-1528-4, Pub by Croom Helm Ltd England). Biblio Dist.

Kyle, Peggy. My Heart Must Sing. LC 76-151723. 1971. 4.00 (ISBN 0-911838-11-2). Windy Row.

Kyle, R. A. & Shampo, M. A. Medicine & Stamps, 2 vols. LC 79-26733. 528p. 1980. Vol. 1. lib. bdg. 12.50 (ISBN 0-89874-085-1); Vol. 2. lib. bdg. 15.50 (ISBN 0-89874-072-X); Set. lib. bdg. 24.00 (ISBN 0-89874-234-X). Krieger.

Kyle, Robert C. & Kennehan, Ann. Property Management. 1979. pap. 18.75 o.s.i. (ISBN 0-695-81244-0). Follett.

Kylstra, F. J., ed. Performance, 1981: Proceedings of International Symposium on Computer Performance Modelling, Measurement. 545p. 1982. 74.50 (ISBN 0-444-86330-3). Elsevier.

Kynaston, Trent & Ricci, Robert. Jazz Improvisation. LC 77-28290. (Illus.). 1978. 15.95 (ISBN 0-13-509315-5, Spec); pap. 10.95 (ISBN 0-13-509307-4). P-H.

Kynoch, P. A., jt. ed. see Lehmann, H.

Kyper, Frank & Rainey, Lee. East Broad Top Railroad. (Illus.). 224p. 36.95 (ISBN 0-87095-078-9). Golden West.

Kyrala, A. Applied Functions of a Complex Variable. LC 74-176285. 374p. 1972. 36.50 o.p. (ISBN 0-471-51129-3, Pub. by Wiley-Interscience). Wiley.

Kyriacou, Demetrios. Basics of Electrooranic Synthesis. 230p. 1980. 29.95x (ISBN 0-471-07975-8, Pub. by Wiley-Interscience). Wiley.

Kyriakopoulos, Irene, jt. auth. see Binkin, Martin.

Kysar, Ardis & McLinn, Dianne. New Faces, New Spaces: Helping Children Cope with Change. 67p. (Orig.). 1980. pap. 8.95 (ISBN 0-934140-03-0). Toys N Things.

Kysar, Ardis & Overstad, Elizabeth, eds. Helping Young Children Cope with Crisis: A Guide for Training Child Care Workers. 69p. (Orig.). pap. text ed. 8.95 (ISBN 0-934140-12-X). Toys N Things.

Kysar, Robert. John, the Maverick Gospel. LC 76-12393. (Biblical Foundations Ser.). 1976. pap. 6.50 (ISBN 0-8042-0302-4). John Knox.

Kysela, Z., jt. auth. see Myslivec, A.

Kyselka, Will & Lanterman, Ray. Maui: How It Came to Be. LC 80-10743. (Illus.). 128p. (gr. 5-10). 1980. pap. 5.95 (ISBN 0-8248-0530-5). UH Pr.

--North Star to Southern Cross. LC 75-37655. (Illus.). 160p. 1976. 10.00x (ISBN 0-8248-0411-2); pap. 4.95 (ISBN 0-8248-0419-8). UH Pr.

Kyte, Barbara & Greenberg, Kathy. Cooking for One or Two. Reynolds, Maureen, ed. LC 80-81246. (Illus.). 192p. 1980. pap. 5.95 (ISBN 0-911954-71-6). Nitty Gritty.

Kyte, Kathy S. In Charge: A Complete Handbook for Kids with Working Parents. LC 82-17927. (Illus.). 96p. (gr. 4 up). 1983. 5.95 (ISBN 0-394-85408-X); lib. bdg. 8.99 (ISBN 0-394-95408-4). Knopf.

Kytle, Calvin. Gandhi: Soldier of Nonviolence. LC 82-10633. (Illus.). 208p. 1983. 13.95 (ISBN 0-932020-18-6); pap. 8.95 (ISBN 0-932020-19-4). Seven Locks Pr.

Kytle, Elizabeth. Home on the Canal. LC 82-19416. (Illus.). 304p. 1983. 19.95 (ISBN 0-932020-13-5). Seven Locks Pr.

Kytle, Ray. Concepts in Context: Aspects of the Writer's Craft. 1974. pap. text ed. 13.95x (ISBN 0-673-15687-7). Scott F.

Kytle, Ray, Jr. Composition: Discovery & Communication. 1970. pap. text ed. 4.75x (ISBN 0-394-30334-2). Phila Bk Co.

--Pre-Writing: Strategies for Exploration & Discovery. 1972. pap. text ed. 1.95x (ISBN 0-685-55626-3, 31542). Phila Bk Co.

--The Wrought Response: Reading & Writing About Literature. 2nd ed. 1976. pap. text ed. 9.95x o.p. (ISBN 0-8221-0183-1). Dickenson.

Kytle, Ray, Jr., ed. Confrontation, Issues of the 70's. 1971. pap. text ed. 5.95x (ISBN 0-394-31013-6). Phila Bk Co.

Kyuma, Kazutake, jt. auth. see Kawaguchi, Keizaburo.

Kyvig, David & Marty, Myron A. Your Family History: A Handbook for Research & Writing. LC 77-86030. 1978. pap. text ed. 4.50x (ISBN 0-88295-774-0). Harlan Davidson.

Kyvig, David E. & Marty, Myron A. Nearby History: Exploring the Past Around You. LC 82-6855. (Illus.). 300p. 1982. 15.95 (ISBN 0-910050-59-7). AASLH.

L

L. L. Bean Staff, jt. auth. see Riviere, William.

Laak, Rein. Wastewater Engineering Design for Unsewered Areas. LC 80-65509. (Illus.). 172p. 1980. 29.95 (ISBN 0-250-40373-0). Ann Arbor Science.

Laakso, Elia, ed. see Central Statistical Office of Finland.

LaAlt, Paul. A Changing America: Conservatives View the 80's from the U. S. Senate. LC 80-80290. 1980. 10.95 (ISBN 0-89526-676-8). Regnery-Gateway.

La-Anyane, Seth. Economics of Agricultural Development in Tropical Africa. 150p. 1983. write for info. (ISBN 0-471-90034-6, Pub. by Wiley-Interscience). Wiley.

LaArta, Moulton. Nature's Medicine Chest, Set 4. 96p. 1975. 5.50 (ISBN 0-935596-07-0). Gluten Co.

Laatsch, R. Basic Algebraic Systems: An Introduction to Abstract Algebra. LC 68-12266. 1968. text ed. 17.95 o.p. (ISBN 0-07-035721-8, C). McGraw.

Laban, Rudolf. Life for Dance. LC 74-32538. (Illus.). 1975. 10.95 o.p. (ISBN 0-87830-073-2). Theatre Arts.

Laban, Rudolph & Lawrence, F. C. Effort. 112p. 1979. 30.00x (ISBN 0-7121-0534-4, Pub. by Macdonald & Evans). State Mutual Bk.

Labanyi, Peter, tr. see Henze, Hans W.

La Barba, Richard. Foundations of Developmental Psychology. LC 80-615. 1980. 25.00 (ISBN 0-12-432350-2); instr's. manual 3.50 (ISBN 0-12-432355-3). Acad Pr.

LaBare, Martha. Shooting Star & Other Poems. 64p. (Orig.). 1982. pap. 4.50 (ISBN 0-9609090-2-8). Swollen Magpie.

Labaree, Benjamin W. The Boston Tea Party. LC 79-5423. (Illus.). 347p. 1979. pap. text ed. 9.95x (ISBN 0-930350-05-7). NE U Pr.

--Colonial Massachusetts: A History. LC 79-33. (A History of the American Colonies Ser.). 1979. lib. bdg. 30.00 (ISBN 0-527-18714-3). Kraus Intl.

Labarge, Margaret W. Medieval Travellers. (Illus.). 1983. 17.50 (ISBN 0-393-01739-7). Norton.

--Simon De Montfort. LC 75-22643. (Illus.). 312p. 1976. Repr. of 1963 ed. lib. bdg. 19.25x (ISBN 0-8371-8359-6, LASM). Greenwood.

LaBarr, Dorothy F. & Singer, J. David. The Study of International Politics: A Guide to the Sources for the Student, Teacher, & Researcher. LC 76-12545. 211p. 1976. text ed. 21.75 o.p. (ISBN 0-87436-233-4). ABC-Clio.

LaBarre & Mitchell. College Typewriting: Advanced. 1982. 13.95 (ISBN 0-686-97512-X); Working Papers 7.95 (ISBN 0-686-97513-8). SRA.

La Barre, George. Collecting Stocks & Bonds, Vol. 1. 1980. 5.00 (ISBN 0-913702-42-0). Heart Am Pr.

--Collecting Stocks & Bonds, Vol. 2. 1981. 5.00 (ISBN 0-913902-43-8). Heart Am Pr.

--Collecting Stocks & Bonds, Vol. 3. 1981. 5.00 (ISBN 0-913902-44-6). Heart Am Pr.

La Barre, W. Aymare Indians of the Lake Titicaca Plateau, Bolivia. LC 48-5985. 1948. pap. 26.00 (ISBN 0-527-00567-3). Kraus Repr.

La Barre, Weston. Ghost Dance. 1972. pap. 4.95 o.s.i. (ISBN 0-440-52842-9, Delta). Dell.

--The Peyote Cult. 4th ed. LC 75-10608. (Illus.). 1976. pap. 5.95 (ISBN 0-8052-0493-8). Schocken.

--They Shall Take up Serpents: Psychology of the Southern Snake-Handling Cult. LC 71-91547. (Illus.). 1974. pap. 3.45 o.p. (ISBN 0-8052-0435-0). Schocken.

LaBastille, Anne. Women & Wilderness. LC 80-14369. (Illus.). 320p. 1980. 12.95 (ISBN 0-87156-234-0). Sierra.

--Woodswoman. LC 75-34071. 1976. 10.95 (ISBN 0-525-23715-1, 0558-170); pap. 5.75 (ISBN 0-525-47504-4). Dutton.

Labat, Jean-Baptiste. Relation Historique de l'Ethiopie Occidentale, 5 vols. (Bibliotheque Africaine Ser.). (Fr.). 1974. Repr. of 1732 ed. Set. lib. bdg. 619.00x o.p. (ISBN 0-8287-0474-0). Clearwater Pub.

Labat, Joseph, et al, eds. La France en Mutation. 1979. pap. text ed. 12.95 o.p. (ISBN 0-88377-160-8). Newbury Hse.

L'Abate, Bess, jt. auth. see L'Abate, Luciano.

Labate, Christina, jt. auth. see Platt, Jerome.

L'Abate, Luciano. Family Psychology: Theory, Therapy, & Training. LC 82-20255. 328p. (Orig.). 1983. lib. bdg. 25.75 (ISBN 0-8191-2883-X); pap. text ed. 13.75 (ISBN 0-8191-2884-8). U Pr of Amer.

L'Abate, Luciano & L'Abate, Bess. How to Avoid Divorce. LC 76-12389. 1976. pap. 4.95 o.p. (ISBN 0-8042-1118-3). John Knox.

L'Abate, Luciano, jt. auth. see Weeks, Gerald R.

L'Abate, Luciano & McHenry, Sherry, eds. Methods of Marital Intervention. Date not set. price not set (ISBN 0-8089-1502-9). Grune.

L'Abate, Lucinano, jt. auth. see Hansen, James.

Labe, Louise. Louise Labe: Sonnets. Martin, Graham D., tr. (Edinburgh Bilingual Library: No. 7). 119p. 1972. 7.95x (ISBN 0-292-74603-2); pap. 3.95x (ISBN 0-292-74602-4). U of Tex Pr.

La Beau, Dennis, ed. Author Biographies Master Index, 2 vols. LC 76-27212. (Gale Biographical Index: No. 3). 1978. Set. 140.00x (ISBN 0-8103-1085-6). Gale.

LaBeau, Dennis, ed. Women's Biographical Dictionaries Master Index. (Gale Biographical Index Ser.). Date not set. 48.00x (ISBN 0-8103-1087-2). Gale. Postponed.

Labedz, Leopold, jt. ed. see Hayward, Max.

LaBelle, Judith L., jt. auth. see Waugh, Carol W.

LaBelle, Susan. Flopsy, Mopsy & Cottontail: A Little Book of Paper Dolls in Full Color. (Toy Bks., Paper Dolls). (Illus.). 48p. (gr. 1 up). 1983. pap. 2.00 (ISBN 0-486-24376-1). Dover.

Laber, Jeri, ed. Woman's Day Cooking for One. (Illus.). 1978. 10.95 (ISBN 0-394-41209-5). Random.

LaBerge, Armand J., jt. auth. see Fryklund, Verne C.

Laberge, David & Samuels, Jay S., eds. Basic Processes in Reading: Perception & Comprehension. 370p. 1977. 19.95x o.p. (ISBN 0-470-99354-5). Halsted Pr.

LaBerge, Donald E., ed. see International Symposium on Pre-Harvest Sprouting in Cereals.

Labes, M. M., ed. see Sixth International Liquid Crystals Conference, Kyoto, Japan, June 30-July 4, 1980.

La Billardiere, J. De & Stafleu, F. A. Novae Hollandiae Plantarum Specimen: 1894-06, 2 vols. in 1. 1966. 96.00 (ISBN 3-7682-0344-1). Lubrecht & Cramer.

La Billardiere, J. J. Icones Plantarum Syriae Rariorum: Descriptionibus & Observationibus Illustratar 1791-1812. (Illus.). 1968. 40.00 (ISBN 3-7682-0540-1). Lubrecht & Cramer.

La Billardiere, J. J. De see De La Billardiere, J. J.

Labine, Clem, ed. The Old-House Journal Compendium. LC 78-4360. (Illus.). 400p. 1980. 25.00 (ISBN 0-87951-080-3). Overlook Pr.

Labinowicz, Edward P. The Piaget Primer. (gr. k-12). 1980. pap. text ed. 16.90 (ISBN 0-201-04090-5, Sch Div). A-W.

Labonne, M., jt. auth. see Mondot-Bernard, J.

Labonville, J., jt. auth. see Block, J.

Labor, Brian. Dublin: Ninety Drawings by Brian Labor. 1983. pap. 11.95 (ISBN 0-7100-9497-3). Routledge & Kegan.

Labor, Earle. Jack London. (United States Authors Ser.). 1974. lib. bdg. 11.95 (ISBN 0-8057-0455-8, Twayne). G K Hall.

Labor, Earle, ed. see London, Jack.

Labor Law Group. Arbitration & Conflict Resolution: Unit Six Labor Relations & Social Problems: A Course Book. Teple, Edwin R. & Moberly, Robert B., eds. LC 79-16839. 614p. 1979. 20.00 (ISBN 0-87179-308-3). BNA.

--Cases & Materials on Negotiation: Unit 5, Labor Relations & Social Problems, a Course Book. 2nd ed. Peck, Cornelius J., ed. 280p. 1980. text ed. 12.00 (ISBN 0-87179-335-0). BNA.

--Collective Bargaining in Private Employment: Labor Relations & Social Problems, a Course Book, Unit One. Sherman, Herbert L., Jr., et al, eds. LC 78-606151. 840p. 1978. 24.00 (ISBN 0-87179-281-8). BNA.

Labor Law Group, ed. Labor Relations & Social Problems: A Course Book. Incl. Unit 1: Collective Bargaining in Private Employment. Atleson, James B., et al, eds. 820p. with 1982 Suppl. 24.00 (ISBN 0-87179-281-8); Unit 2: Legislation Protecting the Individual Employee. Covington, Robert N. & Goldman, Alvin L., eds. 814p. 1982. 22.50 (ISBN 0-87179-377-6); Unit 3: Discrimination in Employment. 4th ed. Getman, Julius, et al, eds. 870p. 1979. with 1982 Suppl. 24.00 (ISBN 0-87179-397-0); Unit 4: Collective Bargaining in Public Employment. 3rd ed. Grodin, Joseph R., et al, eds. 430p. 1979. 15.00 (ISBN 0-87179-310-5); Unit 5: Cases & Materials on Negotiation. 2nd ed. 280p. 1980. 12.00 (ISBN 0-87179-335-0); Unit 6: Arbitration & Conflict Resolution. Teple, Edwin R. & Moberly, Robert B., eds. 614p. 1979. 20.00 (ISBN 0-87179-308-3); Unit Reference Supplement. 5th ed. Aaron, Benjamin, ed. 210p. 1981. 6.00 (ISBN 0-87179-345-8); Unit R-2: Reference Supplement -- Discrimination in Employment. Jones, James E., **Jr., ed. 304p. 1979. 6.00 (ISBN 0-87179-311-3). BNA.**

Laborde, Genie S. Influencing with Integrity. 1983. 19.95 (ISBN 0-686-43050-6). Sci & Behavior.

Laborit, Henri. Decoding the Human Message. LC 76-53312. 1977. text ed. 17.95x o.p. (ISBN 0-312-19022-0). St Martin.

LaBossiere, Eileen. Histological Processing for the Neural Sciences. (Illus.). 100p. 1976. spiral 10.75x (ISBN 0-398-03516-4). C C Thomas.

Laboulaye, Charles. Les Droits des Ouvries: Etude sur l'Ordre dans l'Industrie. (Conditions of the 19th Century French Working Class Ser.). 117p. (Fr.). 1974. Repr. of 1873 ed. lib. bdg. 39.00x o.p. (ISBN 0-8287-0476-7, 1121). Clearwater Pub.

Labov, W. & Fanshell, D. Therapeutic Discourse: Psychotherapy As Conversation. 1977. 18.50 (ISBN 0-12-432050-3). Acad Pr.

Labov, William. The Social Stratification of English in New York City. 2nd ed. 1982. 29.95x (ISBN 0-87281-177-8); pap. 12.50 (ISBN 0-87281-149-2). Ctr Appl Ling.

Labovitz, M. L., jt. ed. see Craig, R. G.

Labovitz, Sanford I. & Hagedorn, Robert B. Introduction to Social Research. 3rd ed. 1981. 10.95 (ISBN 0-07-035777-3). McGraw.

--Introduction to Social Research. 2nd ed. 176p. 1975. text ed. 14.00 o.p. (ISBN 0-07-035776-5, C); pap. text ed. 7.95 o.p. (ISBN 0-07-035775-7). McGraw.

Labowitz, L. C. & Arents, J. S. Physical Chemistry Problems & Solutions. 1969. text ed. 15.25 o.s.i. (ISBN 0-12-432150-X). Acad Pr.

Labowitz, Leonard. Chemistry, One. (Monarch College Outlines). pap. 4.95 o.p. (ISBN 0-671-08042-3). Monarch Pr.

La Brant, Lou L. We Teach English. LC 70-104229. viii, 342p. Repr. of 1951 ed. lib. bdg. 16.25x (ISBN 0-8371-3339-4, LATE). Greenwood.

Labrary, Michael. Sextuplets of Loqmaria. 9.50 (ISBN 0-392-04537-0, SpS). Sportshelf.

LaBrecque, S. V., jt. auth. see Nies, J. I.

Labrie, Roger, et al, eds. U. S. Arms Sales Policy: Background & Issues. 1982. pap. 4.95 (ISBN 0-8447-3491-8). Am Enterprise.

Labrie, Ross. The Art of Thomas Merton. LC 79-1341. 1979. 11.00 o.p. (ISBN 0-912646-48-9); pap. 9.95x (ISBN 0-912646-55-1). Tex Christian.

--Howard Nemerov. (United States Authors Series). 1980. lib. bdg. 12.95 (ISBN 0-8057-7298-7, Twayne). G K Hall.

--James Merrill. (United States Authors Ser.). 1982. lib. bdg. 15.95 (ISBN 0-8057-7361-4, Twayne). G K Hall.

Labriola, Antonio. Essays on the Materialistic Conception of History. Kerr, Charles H., tr. LC 82-73433. 246p. Repr. of 1908 ed. lib. bdg. 18.50x (ISBN 0-88116-006-7). Brenner Bks.

LaBrucherie, Roger A. A Barbados Journey. (Illus.). 112p. 1982. 16.95 (ISBN 0-939302-06-3); deluxe ed. 21.00 (ISBN 0-939302-07-1). Imagenes.

--Imagenes De Santo Domingo: A Reminiscence of the Dominican Republic. bilingual ed. Espinosa, Mayra C., tr. (Illus.). 112p. (Orig.). 1978. pap. 10.95 (ISBN 0-939302-00-4). Imagenes.

--Images of Barbados. 2nd ed. (Illus.). 112p. 1979. 12.00 (ISBN 0-939302-05-5); pap. 10.95 (ISBN 0-939302-01-2). Imagenes.

--Images of Bermuda. 2nd ed. (Illus.). 112p. 1981. deluxe ed. 21.00 (ISBN 0-939302-04-7); 17.00 (ISBN 0-939302-02-0). Imagenes.

--A Jamaica Journey. (Illus.). 112p. 1983. 16.95 (ISBN 0-939302-08-X, Pub. by Imagenes Pr). C E Tuttle.

Labs, Kenneth, jt. auth. see Watson, Donald.

Labuta, J. Guide to Accountability in Music Instruction. 1973. 11.95 o.p. (ISBN 0-13-367953-5, Parker). P-H.

Labuta, Joseph A. Basic Conducting Techniques. (Illus.). 224p. 1982. pap. 16.95 (ISBN 0-13-058305-7). P-H.

Labuz, Ronald. Interfacing in the Eighties: How to Set up Communications Between Word Processors & Phototypesetters. 1983. pap. 3.95 (ISBN 0-86610-125-X). Meridian Pub.

Labuza, Theodore P. Food & Your Well-Being. (Illus.). 1977. pap. text ed. 14.95 (ISBN 0-8299-0129-9); instrs.' manual & study guide 5.95 (ISBN 0-8299-0162-0). West Pub.

--The Nutrition Crisis: A Reader. LC 75-20459. (Illus.). 512p. 1975. pap. text ed. 13.95 (ISBN 0-8299-0063-2). West Pub.

Labys, Walter & Granger, Clive W. Speculation, Hedging, & Commodity Price Forecasts. 352p. 1971. 22.95x (ISBN 0-669-61051-8). Lexington Bks.

Labys, Walter C. Market Structure, Bargaining Power, & Resource Price Formation. LC 78-19541. 256p. 1980. 25.95x (ISBN 0-669-02511-9). Lexington Bks.

Labys, Walter C., et al, eds. Commodity Markets & Latin American Development: A Modeling Approach. LC 79-16533. 296p. 1980. prof ref 27.50x (ISBN 0-88410-481-8). Ballinger Pub.

Lacan, J. Feminine Sexuality. Mitchell, J. & Rose, J., eds. 1982. 40.00x (ISBN 0-686-42938-9, Pub. by Macmillan England). State Mutual Bk.

Lacan, Jacques & Ecole Freudienne. Feminine Sexuality. Mitchell, Juliet, ed. Rose, Jacqueline, tr. from Fr. (Eng.). 1983. text ed. 18.95 (ISBN 0-393-01633-1, Co-pub. by Pantheon Bks.). Norton.

LaCarrubba, Joseph & Zimmer, Louis. How to Buy, Install & Maintain Your Own Telephone Equipment. 50p. 1978. 3.50 (ISBN 0-686-98105-7). Telecom Lib.

Lacasse, Walter J., jt. auth. see Carpenter, Stanley J.

LaCasse, William. Rid Maine of Out-of-Staters: The Dickey-Lincoln Project. LC 78-65170. 1979. 6.95 o.p. (ISBN 0-533-04063-9). Vantage.

LaCava, Jerry J., jt. auth. see Richards, Larry E.

Lacayo, Carmela G. National Study to Assess the Service Needs of the Hispanic Elderly. Smith, Margaret, ed. 502p. Date not set. 45.00; pap. text ed. price not set. Assn Personas Mayores.

--A Research, Bibliographic, & Resource Guide on the Hispanic Elderly. Lacayo, Carmela G., ed. 421p. 1981. 20.00; pap. text ed. write for info. Assn Personas Mayores.

--Serving the Hispanic Elderly of the United States: A National Community Service Directory. 234p. 1982. write for info. Assn Personas Mayores.

Lacaze, Andre. The Tunnel at Loibl Pass. 608p. 1982. pap. 3.95 (ISBN 0-553-22584-7). Bantam.

Lace, Vivian & Carlsen, Fran, eds. Harris Ohio Marketers Industrial Directory, 1983. (Illus.). 1000p. 1982. 78.00 (ISBN 0-916512-58-4). Harris Pub.

Lace, Vivian, jt. ed. see Harris, Beatrice.

La Ceppede, Jean de see De La Ceppede, Jean.

LaCerra, Charles, Jr. Looking at the American Government: Past & Present. LC 78-61390. 1978. pap. text ed. 9.50 (ISBN 0-8191-0602-X). U Pr of Amer.

Lacey, C. Hightown Grammar. 1970. pap. 7.00 (ISBN 0-7190-0485-3). Manchester.

Lacey, Colin. Socialization of Teachers. 1977. pap. 7.50x (ISBN 0-416-56240-X). Methuen Inc.

Lacey, Colin & Lawton, Denis, eds. Issues in Evaluation & Accountability. 1982. 24.00x (ISBN 0-416-74740-X); pap. 10.95x (ISBN 0-416-74750-7). Methuen Inc.

Lacey, E. A., tr. see Caminha, Adolfo.

Lacey, E. A., tr. see Zapata, Luis.

Lacey, James, jt. auth. see Carothers, Gibson.

Lacey, Kenneth. Profit Measurement & Price Changes. LC 82-48370. (Accountancy in Transition Ser.). 148p. 1982. lib. bdg. 20.00 (ISBN 0-8240-5323-0). Garland Pub.

Lacey, Robert. The Kingdom. 656p. 1983. pap. 4.95 (ISBN 0-380-61762-5). Avon.

--The Life & Times of Henry VIII. Fraser, Antonio, ed. (Kings & Queens of England Ser.). (Illus.). 224p. 1972. text ed. 17.50x (ISBN 0-297-99434-4, Pub. by Weidenfeld & Nicolson England). Biblio Dist.

--Majesty. 1978. pap. 3.95 (ISBN 0-380-01842-X, 62976-3). Avon.

Lach, C. S. How to Help Cases of Distress. 152p. 1977. 30.00x (ISBN 0-7121-0814-9, Pub. by Macdonald & Evans). State Mutual Bk.

LaChance, Paul R. Appalachian Maryland & the World. LC 81-40627. 302p. 1981. lib. bdg. 22.75 (ISBN 0-8191-1994-6); pap. text ed. 12.25 (ISBN 0-8191-1995-4). U Pr of Amer.

La Chapelle, Edward R. ABC of Avalanche Safety. 1978. pap. 2.50 (ISBN 0-916890-68-6). Mountaineers.

Lachapelle, Rejean & Henripin, Jacques. The Demolinuistic Situation in Canada: Past Trends & Future Prospects. 387p. 1982. pap. text ed. 24.95x (ISBN 0-920380-42-5, Pub. by Inst Res Pub Canada). Renouf.

LaChappelle, Nancy, jt. auth. see Abbate, Marcia.

La Charite, Raymond C. Recreation, Reflection & Re-Creation: Perspectives on Rabelais's Pantagruel. LC 79-53402. (French Forum Monographs: No. 19). 140p. 1980. pap. 9.50x (ISBN 0-917058-18-6). French Forum.

La Charite, Raymond C., ed. & tr. see Des Periers, Bonaventure.

La Charite, Virginia A. Henri Michaux. (World Authors Ser.). 1977. lib. bdg. 15.95 (ISBN 0-8057-6302-3, Twayne). G K Hall.

La Chavignerie, Emile B. De see De La Chavignerie, Emile B. & Auvray, Louis.

Lachenbruch, David. Video Cassette Recorders: The Complete Home Guide. LC 78-72182. (Illus.). 1979. pap. 6.95 (ISBN 0-89696-016-1, An Everest House Book). Dodd.

Lachenbruch, David & Norback, Craig. The Complete Book of Adult Toys. LC 82-47663. (Illus.). 240p. Date not set. price not set (ISBN 0-15-120642-2, Harv). HarBraceJ. Postponed.

--The Complete Book of Adult Toys. (Illus.). 168p. pap. 12.95 (ISBN 0-15-620946-2, Harv). HarBraceJ.

Lacher, Mortimer J., ed. Hodgkin's Disease. LC 75-25644. 464p. 1976. 50.50 o.p. (ISBN 0-471-51149-8, Pub. by Wiley Medical). Wiley.

Lachman, Seymour P., ed. see Groisser, Philip L.

Lachman, Vicki D. Stress Management: A Manual for Nurses. write for info (ISBN 0-8089-1554-1). Grune.

Lachmann, L. M. The Legacy of Max Weber. 149p. 1971. 16.00x o.p. (ISBN 0-87835-106-X). Boyd & Fraser.

Lachnit-Fixson, jt. auth. see Hammerstein.

Lachs, John. Intermediate Man. LC 81-4806. 152p. 1981. 19.50 (ISBN 0-915145-12-X); pap. text ed. 9.95 (ISBN 0-915145-13-8). Hackett Pub.

Lachs, John, ed. see Fichte, J. G.

Lachs, John, tr. see Fichte, J. G.

Lachs, Manfred. The Teacher in International Law. 1982. lib. bdg. 47.50 (ISBN 90-247-2566-6, Pub. by Martinus Nijhoff Netherlands). Kluwer Boston.

Lachuk, John. The Gun Digest Book of the .22 Rimfire. 1978. pap. 6.95 o.s.i. (ISBN 0-695-81197-5). Follett.

Lack, David. Darwin's Finches. Boag, P. & Ratcliffe, L., eds. LC 82-19856. (Cambridge Science Classics). (Illus.). 240p. Date not set. price not set (ISBN 0-521-25243-1); pap. price not set (ISBN 0-521-27242-4). Cambridge U Pr.

--Surfts in a Tower. 2nd ed. (Illus.). 1979. 14.95x o.p. (ISBN 0-412-21870-4, Pub. by Chapman & Hall). Methuen Inc.

Lackey, Louana M. The Pottery of Acatlan: A Changing Mexican Tradition. LC 81-40280. (Illus.). 208p. 1981. 25.00 (ISBN 0-8061-1811-3). U of Okla Pr.

Lackmann, Ron. Remember Television. (Illus.). 1971. 7.95 o.p. (ISBN 0-399-10687-1). Putnam Pub Group.

Lackner, Bede K., jt. ed. see Stark, Gary D.

Lackner, Marie & Paterno, Cynthia. Practice RCT Reading Exam, No. 1. 1982. of 10 9.95 set (ISBN 0-937820-34-2). Westsea Pub.

--Practice RCT Reading Exam, No. 2. of 10 9.95 set (ISBN 0-937820-35-0). Westsea Pub.

La Clair, Earl E. Wood & the Wool. 1966. 3.00 o.p. (ISBN 0-8233-0055-2). Golden Quill.

Laclau, Ernesto. Politics & Ideology in Marxist Theory: Capitalism - Fascism - Populism. 1979. 12.50x (ISBN 0-8052-7030-2); pap. 5.75 (ISBN 0-8052-7060-4, Pub. by NLB). Schocken.

LaClotte, Michel. The Louvre. LC 79-57409. (Abbeville Library of Art: No. 3). (Illus.). 112p. 1980. pap. 4.95 o.p. (ISBN 0-89659-097-6). Abbeville Pr.

Laclotte, Michel & Cuzin, Jean-Pierre. The Louvre: French & Other European Paintings. (Illus.). 264p. 1983. text ed. 29.95x (ISBN 0-85667-147-9, Pub. by Sotheby Pubns England). Biblio Dist.

Laclotte-Cuzin. The Louvre. 29.95 (ISBN 0-935748-49-0). ScalaBooks.

Lacocque, Andre. The Book of Daniel. LC 78-2036. 1978. 19.95 (ISBN 0-8042-0090-4). John Knox.

Lacombe, J., jt. auth. see Cleary, J. B.

Lacombe, J. M., jt. auth. see Cleary, J. B.

Laconte, M. Pierre & Lambert, Richard D., eds. Changing Cities: A Challenge to Planning. LC 80-66619. (The Annals of the American Academy of Political & Social Science Ser.: No. 451). 250p. 1980. 15.00 (ISBN 0-87761-254-4); pap. text ed. 7.95 (ISBN 0-87761-255-2). Am Acad Pol Soc Sci.

LaConte, P. & Gibson, J. E. Human & Energy Factors: Factors in Urban Planning; A Systems Approach. 1982. 50.00 (ISBN 90-247-2688-3, Pub. by Martinus Nijhoff Netherlands). Kluwer Boston.

LaConte, P. & Haines, Y. Y. Water Resources & Land-Use Planning: A Systems Approach. 1982. lib. bdg. 57.50 (ISBN 90-247-2726-X, Pub. by Martinus Nijhoff Netherlands). Kluwer Boston.

Lacoste, Auguste. Henri Arnaud und die Waldenser. (Basler und Berner Studien zur historischen und systematischen: Vol. 47). 213p. 1982. write for info. (ISBN 3-261-04890-5). P Lang Pubs.

Lacoste, Michel C. Kandinsky. (Crown QLP Ser.). (Illus.). 1979. 7.95 (ISBN 0-517-53884-9). Crown.

LaCour, L. F., jt. auth. see Darlington, C. D.

LaCour, Pierre. Manufacture of Liquers, Wines, & Cordials Without the Aid of Distillation. (Illus.). 1982. Repr. of 1853 ed. lib. bdg. 25.00 o.p. (ISBN 0-915262-52-5). S J Durst.

Lacour-Gayet, Robert. Everyday Life in the United States before the Civil War, 1830-1860. Ilford, Mary, tr. from French. LC 70-81571. 310p. 1983. pap. 7.95 (ISBN 0-8044-6376-X). Ungar.

Lacouture, Jean. Leon Blum. Holoch, George, tr. from Fr. LC 81-20083. 571p. 1982. text ed. 39.50x (ISBN 0-8419-0775-7); pap. text ed. 24.50x (ISBN 0-8419-0776-5). Holmes & Meier.

Lacret-Subirat, Fabian. Lacret Mathematics Basic Concepts & Skills: Grade 9-12. 2nd ed. (Illus.). 518p. 1983. 12.85 (ISBN 0-686-43020-4); s.p. 8.00 (ISBN 0-686-43021-2). Lacret Pub.

--Lacret Plane Geometry: Grade 9-12. 2nd ed. (Illus.). 478p. 1983. 13.75 (ISBN 0-686-43022-0); s.p. 8.00 (ISBN 0-943144-05-1). Lacret Pub.

La Croix. Relation Universelle de l'Afrique Ancienne et Muderne, 4 vols. (Bibliotheque Africaine Ser.). (Fr.). 1974. Repr. of 1688 ed. lib. bdg. 652.50x o.p. (ISBN 0-8287-0480-5, 72-2164). Clearwater Pub.

La Croix, Don, jt. ed. see Kaufman, Peter B.

LaCroix, Flora. Concepts of Imagination Development. 1983. lib. bdg. price not set (ISBN 0-89874-594-2). Krieger.

La Croix, Grethe. Beads Plus Macrame: Applying Knotting Techniques to Beadcraft. LC 78-151710. (Little Craft Book Ser). (Illus.). (gr. 8 up). 1971. 5.95 (ISBN 0-8069-5168-0); PLB 8.99 (ISBN 0-8069-5169-9). Sterling.

La Croix, Horst De see Cohen, Kathleen & Croix, Horst de la.

LaCroix, W. L. Meaning & Reason in Ethics. rev. ed. LC 79-52963. 1979. pap. text ed. 8.25 (ISBN 0-8191-0786-7). U Pr of Amer.

Lacue, Juan J., tr. see Francisco, C. T.

Lacy, Alan, tr. see Paul, Gunter.

Lacy, Allen, jt. tr. see Kerrigan, Anthony.

Lacy, Barbara, tr. see Paul, Gunter.

Lacy, Dan. White Use of Blacks in America. LC 77-175286. 1972. 7.95 o.p. (ISBN 0-689-10476-6). Atheneum.

Lacy, Dan, jt. auth. see Stage, John L.

Lacy, G. H. Introduccion a la Teologia Sistematica. 417p. (Span.). 1979. pap. 6.95 (ISBN 0-311-09032-X). Casa Bautista.

Lacy, George, jt. auth. see Mount, Mark S.

Lacy, George, jt. ed. see Mount, M. S.

Lacy, Madison S. & Morgan, Don. Hollywood Cheesecake. 288p. 1983. pap. 9.95 (ISBN 0-686-82477-6). Citadel Pr.

Lacy, Norris J., ed. L' Istoyre de Jehan Coqualt: A Literary Forgery. 12.00 (ISBN 0-917786-29-7). French Lit.

Lacy, Norris J. & Nash, Jerry C., eds. Essays in Early French Literature, Presented to Barbara M. Craig. 17.00 (ISBN 0-917786-28-9). French Lit.

Lacy, Susana, tr. see Ortlund, Raymond C.

Lacy, Susana B., tr. see Cho, Paul Y.

Lacy, Willard C., ed. Mineral Exploration. LC 82-969. (Benchmark Papers in Geology Ser.: Vol. 70). 448p. 1983. 52.00 (ISBN 0-87933-425-8). Hutchinson Ross.

--Mining Geology. LC 82-968. (Benchmark Papers in Geology: Vol. 69). 480p. 1983. 58.00 (ISBN 0-87933-426-6). Hutchinson Ross.

Lacy, William B., jt. auth. see Busch, Lawerence.

Laczniak, Gene R., jt. auth. see Udell, Jon G.

Ladany, S. P., ed. Management Science Applications to Leisure-Time Operations. (Studies in Management Science & Systems: Vol. 4). 1975. 56.00 (ISBN 0-444-10960-9, North-Holland). Elsevier.

Ladany, S. P. & Machol, R. E., eds. Optimal Strategies in Sports. (Studies in Management Science & Systems: Vol. 5). 1977. 34.00 (ISBN 0-7204-0528-9, North-Holland). Elsevier.

Ladas, A. S., jt. auth. see Ma, Tis.

Ladas, Gerasimbs E., jt. auth. see Grove, Edward A.

Ladas, Gerasimons, jt. auth. see Finizio, Norman.

Ladbury, Ann. The Dressmaker's Dictionary. LC 82-8725. (Illus.). 360p. 1983. 19.95 (ISBN 0-668-05653-3, 5653). Arco.

Ladd, Cathryn. Centennial Summer. (Adventures in Love Ser.: No. 23). 1982. pap. 1.75 (ISBN 0-451-11524-4, Sig). NAL.

--Island Autumn. (Adventures in Love Ser.: No. 30). 1982. pap. 1.75 (ISBN 0-451-11747-6, AE1747, Sig). NAL.

--Tapestry of Love. (Adventures in Love Ser.: No. 32). 1982. pap. 1.75 (ISBN 0-451-11786-7, AE1786, Sig). NAL.

Ladd, D. Robert, tr. see Pascu, Stefan.

Ladd, Doris F. The Irish. 640p. (Orig.). 1983. pap. 3.95 (ISBN 0-440-04845-1, Banbury). Dell.

Ladd, Doris M. The Mexican Nobility at Independence, 1780-1826. LC 75-720106. (Latin American Monographs: No. 40). 332p. 1976. 15.95x o.p. (ISBN 0-292-75026-9); pap. 9.95x o.p. (ISBN 0-292-75027-7). U of Tex Pr.

Ladd, Everett C., Jr. American Political Parties. LC 78-116124. 1970. pap. 9.95x (ISBN 0-393-09964-4). Norton.

--Where Have All the Voters Gone? The Fracturing of America's Political Parties. 2nd ed. 144p. 1982. 14.95x (ISBN 0-393-01574-2); pap. text ed. 4.95x (ISBN 0-393-95225-8). Norton.

Ladd, Fred, jt. auth. see Benson, Murray.

Ladd, George T. Knowledge, Life & Reality. 1918. 36.50x (ISBN 0-685-69836-X). Elliots Bks.

Ladd, George T., jt. auth. see Brown, George D.

Ladd, George T., jt. auth. see Brown, George D., Jr.

Ladd, Helen F., jt. auth. see Schafer, Robert.

Ladd, J. D. Assault from the Sea 1939-1945: The Craft, the Landings, the Men. LC 75-3746. (Illus.). 240p. 1976. 12.50 o.p. (ISBN 0-88254-392-X). Hippocrene Bks.

Ladd, J. D., jt. auth. see Fletcher, N. E.

Ladd, John, ed. Ethical Issues Relating to Life & Death. 1979. text ed. 13.95x o.p. (ISBN 0-19-502543-1); pap. text ed. 9.95x (ISBN 0-19-502544-X). Oxford U Pr.

Ladd, Paul R. Early American Fireplaces. (Illus.). 1977. 16.95 o.s.i. (ISBN 0-8038-1930-7). Hastings.

Ladd, William. An Essay on a Congress of Nations for the Adjustment of International Disputes Without Resort to Arms. LC 72-137550. (Peace Movement in America Ser). 1162p. 1972. Repr. of 1916 ed. lib. bdg. 13.95x (ISBN 0-89198-078-4). Ozer.

Laddha, G. S. & Degaleesan, T. E. Transport Phenomena in Liquid Extraction. LC 77-20848. 1979. text ed. 19.00x o.p. (ISBN 0-07-096688-5, C). McGraw.

Lade, John, ed. see Headington, Christopher.

Ladebat De, Monique P. see De Ladebat, Monique P.

Ladefoged, Peter. Preliminaries to Linguistic Phonetics. pap. 6.00 (ISBN 0-226-46787-2). U of Chicago Pr.

--Three Areas of Experimental Phonetics. (Language & Language Learning Ser.). (Orig.). 1967. pap. 6.00x o.p. (ISBN 0-19-437025-9). Oxford U Pr.

Ladenson, Robert F. A Philosophy of Free Expression & Its Constitutional Applications. LC 82-18106. (Philosophy & Society Ser.). 224p. 1983. text ed. 34.50x (ISBN 0-8476-6761-8). Rowman.

Lader, Lawrence. The Bold Brahmins: New England's War Against Slavery, 1831-1863. LC 73-11624. (Illus.). 318p. 1973. Repr. of 1961 ed. lib. bdg. 17.25x (ISBN 0-8371-7081-8, LABB). Greenwood.

--Power on the Left: American Radical Movements Since 1946. (Illus.). 1979. 19.95 (ISBN 0-393-01258-1); pap. 6.95 cancelled (ISBN 0-393-30029-3). Norton.

Lader, M., jt. ed. see Clare, A. W.

Lader, Malcolm. Priorities in Psychiatric Research. LC 80-40583. 231p. 1980. 44.95x (ISBN 0-471-27833-5, Pub. by Wiley-Interscience). Wiley.

Ladewig, D. & Hobi, V. Drogen unter uns. 4th ed. Dubacher, H. & Faust, V., eds. (Illus.). 108p. 1983. pap. 5.25 (ISBN 3-8055-3608-9). S Karger.

Ladewig, D., ed. Drogen und Alkohol 2. viii, 172p. 1982. pap. 23.50 (ISBN 3-8055-3599-6). S Karger.

Ladis, Andrew. Taddeo Gaddi: A Critical Reappraisal & Catalogue Raisonne, 1320-1366. (Illus.). 288p. 1983. 70.00 (ISBN 0-8262-0382-5). U of Mo Pr.

La Dixmerie, Nicolas B. Le Sauvage de Taiti aux Francais avec un Envoi au Philosophe Ami des Sauvages. (Utopias in the Enlightenment Ser.). 168p. (Fr.). 1974. Repr. of 1770 ed. lib. bdg. 50.00x o.p. (ISBN 0-8287-0481-3, 044). Clearwater Pub.

Ladley, Barbara & Wilford, Jane. Money & Finance: Sources of Print & Nonprint Materials. (Neal-Schuman Sourcebook Ser.). 208p. 1980. 24.95 (ISBN 0-918212-23-5). Neal-Schuman.

Ladley, Betty A. & Patt, Jerry. Office Procedures for the Dental Team. LC 77-23557. 1977. pap. text ed. 20.95 (ISBN 0-8016-2815-6). Mosby.

Ladman, Jerry R., ed. Modern Day Bolivia: The Legacy of the Past & Prospects for the Future. Date not set. write for info. (ISBN 0-87918-052-8). ASU Lat Am St. Postponed.

Ladman, Jerry R., et al, eds. U. S. - Mexican Energy Relationships: Realities & Prospects. LC 80-8878. 256p. 1981. 25.95x (ISBN 0-669-04398-2). Lexington Bks.

Ladner, Joyce A. Tomorrow's Tomorrow. LC 78-139038. 320p. 1972. pap. 2.95 (ISBN 0-385-00941-0, Anch). Doubleday.

Lado, Maria D. Las Guerras Carlistas y el Reinado Isabelino en la Obra de Ramon del Valle-Inclan. LC 65-29106. (U of Fla. Humanities Monographs: No. 18). 1966. pap. 2.75 (ISBN 0-8130-0139-0). U Presses Fla.

Lado, R., et al. Tesoro Hispanico. 2nd ed. 1982. 22.20 (ISBN 0-07-035756-0); instr's manual 2.48 (ISBN 0-07-035757-9). McGraw.

Lado, Robert. Lado English Series, Bk. 2. 1978. pap. text ed. 3.95 (ISBN 0-88345-329-0); tchr's manual 5.50 (ISBN 0-88345-341-X); wkbk. 2.75 (ISBN 0-88345-335-5); cassettes 80.00 (ISBN 0-686-59595-5); 20.00 o.p. testbook (ISBN 0-88345-382-7). Regents Pub.

--Lado English Series, Bk. 5. (Illus.). 198p. (gr. 7-12). 1980. pap. text ed. 4.25 (ISBN 0-88345-332-0, 18749); tchr's manual 5.50 (ISBN 0-88345-344-4); wkbk., 132 pp. 2.75 (ISBN 0-88345-338-X, 18755). Regents Pub.

--Language Teaching, a Scientific Approach. 1964. pap. text ed. 15.75 (ISBN 0-07-035740-4, C). McGraw.

--Language Testing: The Construction & Use of Foreign Language Tests. 1964. text ed. 11.95 o.p. (ISBN 0-07-035750-1, C). McGraw.

--Linguistics Across Cultures: Applied Linguistics for Language Teachers. 1957. pap. 8.50x (ISBN 0-472-08542-5). U of Mich Pr.

Lado, Robert & Blansitt, E. Contemporary Spanish: Espanol. (Illus.). 1967. text ed. 16.95 o.p. (ISBN 0-07-035761-7, C); instructor's manual 3.95 o.p. (ISBN 0-07-035762-5). McGraw.

Lado, Robert & Woodward, P. E. Espanol: Lengua y Letras. (gr. 10-12). 1970. text ed. 15.95 o. p (ISBN 0-07-035763-3, C); instructor's manual 3.95 (ISBN 0-07-035764-1); excercises 13.95 (ISBN 0-07-035768-4); tests 65.00 (ISBN 0-07-035770-6). McGraw.

Lado, Robert, et al. Galeria Hispanica. (gr. 9-12). 1965. text ed. 15.60 o.p. (ISBN 0-07-035741-2, W); tchrs' ed. 9.60 o.p. (ISBN 0-07-035742-0); tapes 199.95 o.p. (ISBN 0-07-098535-9). McGraw.

--Galeria Hispanica. 2nd ed. (Level 3 or 4). 1971. text ed. 20.92 o.p. (ISBN 0-07-035747-1, W); instructor's manual 3.48 o.p. (ISBN 0-07-035748-X); tests 85.56 o.p. (ISBN 0-07-035749-8); tapes 497.96 o.p. (ISBN 0-07-098590-1). McGraw.

--Tesoro Hispanico. LC 68-13093. (Span). (gr. 9-12). 1968. text ed. 22.40 o.p. (ISBN 0-07-035743-9, W); instructors' manual. 2.60 o.p. (ISBN 0-07-035746-3); tapes 200.00 o.p. (ISBN 0-07-098350-X). McGraw.

LaDou, Joseph & Likens, James D. Medicine & Money: Physicians As Businessmen. LC 77-2332. 200p. 1977. prof ref 20.00x (ISBN 0-88410-145-2). Ballinger Pub.

Ladouceur, Andre. An Intellectual Approach Toward the Scientific Conjugations in the English Language. 1983. 7.95 (ISBN 0-533-05406-0). Vantage.

LaDu, Bert, et al, eds. Fundamentals of Drug Metabolism & Drug Disposition. LC 78-26155. 634p. 1979. Repr. of 1971 ed. lib. bdg. 33.00 (ISBN 0-88275-799-7). Krieger.

Ladurie, Emmanuel L. Love, Death & Money in the Pays D'oc. Sheridan, Alan, tr. from Fr. LC 82-9422. 597p. 1982. 30.00 (ISBN 0-8076-1038-0). Braziller.

Lady Allen Of Hurtwood. Planning for Play. LC 69-16908. 144p. 1969. pap. 6.95x (ISBN 0-262-51013-8). MIT Pr.

Ladzik, Kathleen, jt. auth. see Hayes, Stephanie.

Lael, Richard L. The Yamashita Precedent: War Crimes & Command Responsibility. LC 82-17024. 165p. 1982. lib. bdg. 19.95 (ISBN 0-8420-2202-3). Scholarly Res Inc.

Laemmlen, Ann, jt. auth. see Owen, Jackie.

Laetsch, Theodore. Minor Prophets. 1956. 13.95 (ISBN 0-570-03249-0, 15-1719). Concordia.

Laetsch, Watson M. Plants: Basic Concepts in Botany. 1979. text ed. 20.95 (ISBN 0-316-51186-2); tchrs' manual avail. (ISBN 0-316-51185-4). Little.

Laeuchli, Samuel. Power & Sexuality: The Emergence of Canon Law at the Synod of Elvira. LC 72-83671. 143p. 1972. 9.95 (ISBN 0-87722-015-8). Temple U Pr.

Laevastu, Taivo, jt. auth. see Hela, Ilmo.

Laf. Deviled Eggbert. Date not set. pap. price not set (ISBN 0-671-82191-1, Wallaby). PB.

La Farelle, F. F. De see De La Farelle, F. F.

LaFarge, Henry A, ed. see Carcow Museum Curatorial Staff.

La Farge, Henry A., ed. see Pischel, Gina, et al.

La Farge, John. Artist's Letters from Japan. LC 74-130311. (Library of American Art Ser.). (Illus.). 1970. Repr. of 1897 ed. lib. bdg. 37.50 (ISBN 0-306-70064-6). Da Capo.

--Considerations on Painting. LC 70-9611. (Library of American Art Ser). 1969. Repr. of 1895 ed. lib. bdg. 35.00 (ISBN 0-306-71824-3). Da Capo.

La Farge, Oliver. Behind the Mountains. LC 74-81915. xii, 180p. 1974. Repr. of 1956 ed. 15.00 (ISBN 0-88307-511-3); pap. 6.95 (ISBN 0-88307-527-X). Gannon.

--Laughing Boy. (RL 10). 1971. pap. 2.50 (ISBN 0-451-51769-5, CE1769, Sig Classics). NAL.

LaFarge, Oliver. The Mother Ditch. Ortego, Pedro R., tr. (Illus.). 78p. (Eng. & Span.). (gr. 1-8). 1983. pap. 8.95 (ISBN 0-86534-009-9). Sunstone Pr.

La Farge, Oliver. A Pictorial History of the American Indian. rev. ed. (Illus.). 288p. 1974. 17.95 o.p. (ISBN 0-517-51476-1). Crown.

La Farge, Sheila. Golden Butter. (Illus.). (gr. k-4). 1969. 3.95 o.s.i. (ISBN 0-8037-2968-5). Dial.

La Farge, Sheila, tr. see Beskow, Elsa.

La Farge, Sheila, tr. see Bodker, Cecil.

La Farge, Sheila, tr. see Gripe, Maria.

Lafargue, Fernand. Le Goli: Contribution a l'Etude des Masques Baoule. (Black Africa Ser.). 33p. (Fr.). 1974. Repr. of 1970 ed. 25.50 o.p. (ISBN 0-8287-0483-X, 71-2023). Clearwater Pub.
--Le Komyen Chez les Baoule. (Black Africa Ser.). 33p. (Fr.). 1974. Repr. of 1970 ed. 25.50x o.p. (ISBN 0-8287-1382-0, 71-2022). Clearwater Pub.
--La Religion Traditionnelle des Abidji. (Black Africa Ser.). 290p. (Fr.). 1974. Repr. of 1968 ed. lib. bdg. 77.50x o.p. (ISBN 0-8287-0484-8, 71-2017). Clearwater Pub.
Lafargue, Valerie. Fievre A Malte. (Collection Colombine Ser.). 192p. 1983. pap. 1.95 (ISBN 0-373-48065-2). Harlequin Bks.
La Faso, John, jt. auth. see Flynn, Elizabeth.
LaFaso, John F., jt. auth. see Flynn, Elizabeth W.
La Faso, John F., jt. auth. see Flynn, Elizabeth W.
La Fauci, H. M. & Richter, P. Team Teaching at the College Level. LC 73-88573. 1971. 17.75 (ISBN 0-08-006946-0). Pergamon.
La Fauci, Nunzio, jt. ed. see Guillet, Alain.
La Fave, L. J., et al. Problem Solving: The Computer Approach. LC 72-10018. (Illus.). 176p. 1973. text ed. 14.96 o.p. (ISBN 0-07-035785-4, G); tchr's. suppl. 12.95 o.p. (ISBN 0-07-035786-2); resource bk. avail. o.p. (ISBN 0-07-077476-5). McGraw.
LaFave, Wayne, jt. auth. see Kamisar, Yale.
LaFave, Wayne R. Arrest: The Decision to Take a Suspect into Custody. 1965. pap. 7.95 (ISBN 0-316-51193-5). Little.
--Principles of Criminal Law. (Criminal Justice Ser.). 1978. text ed. 22.50 (ISBN 0-8299-0215-5); instrs. manual avail. (ISBN 0-8299-0595-2). West Pub.
Lafayette, Marie. The Princess of Cleves. LC 77-22941. 1977. Repr. of 1951 ed. lib. bdg. 19.25x (ISBN 0-8371-9729-5, LAFPC). Greenwood.
LaFeber, Walter. The Panama Canal: The Crisis in Historical Perspective. 1978. 15.95x (ISBN 0-19-502360-9). Oxford U Pr.
LaFeber, Walter & Polenberg, Richard. The American Century: A History of the United States Since the 1890's. 2nd ed. LC 79-12000. 546p. 1979. pap. text ed. 19.95x (ISBN 0-471-05135-7); tchrs. manual 6.00x (ISBN 0-471-05133-0). Wiley.
LaFeber, Walter, ed. America in the Cold War: Twenty Years of Revolution & Response, 1947-1967. LC 70-78475. 232p. 1969. text ed. 9.50 o.p. (ISBN 0-471-51132-3, Pub. by Wiley). Krieger.
LaFetra, W. How to Clip & Groom Your Poodle. 1969. 7.95 (ISBN 0-87666-356-0, H926). TFH Pubns.
Lafever, Minard. Beauties of Modern Architecture. 2nd ed. LC 68-29602. (Architecture & Decorative Art Ser.: Vol. 18). (Illus.). 1968. Repr. of 1835 ed. lib. bdg. 29.50 (ISBN 0-306-71040-4). Da Capo.
LaFever, Walter F., jt. auth. see Gardner, Lloyd C.
LaFevor, C. S., jt. auth. see Hendrix, T. G.
Laffer, Arthur B. & Miles, Marc A. International Economics in an Integrated World. 1982. text ed. 24.50x (ISBN 0-673-16020-3). Scott F.
Lafferty, J. M., jt. auth. see Dushman, S.
Lafferty, Maude W. Lure of Kentucky: A Historical Guide Book. LC 71-153018. (Illus.). 1971. Repr. of 1939 ed. 34.00x (ISBN 0-8103-3344-9). Gale.
Lafferty, R. A. Aurelia. Stine, Hank, ed. LC 82-5011. (Illus., Orig.). 1982. pap. 5.95 (ISBN 0-89865-194-8, AACR2, Starblaze). Donning Co.
--The Devil Is Dead. (Science Fiction: No.3). 1977. Repr. of 1971 ed. lib. bdg. 11.00 o.p. (ISBN 0-8398-2364-9, Gregg). G K Hall.
--More Than Melchisedech. Stine, Hank, ed. LC 82-12870. (Illus.). 380p. (Orig.). 1983. pap. 5.95 (ISBN 0-89865-254-5). Donning Co.
Lafferty, Sarah R. Selections: Six in Ohio. (Illus.). 1982. write for info. (ISBN 0-917562-24-0). Contemp Arts.
Laffon, Rafael. Seville. (Spanish Guide Ser). (Illus.). 1964. 4.50x o.p. (ISBN 0-8002-1927-9). Intl Pubns Serv.
Laffont, J. J., ed. Aggregation & Revelation of Preferences. (Studies in Public Economics: Vol. 2). 1979. 64.00 (ISBN 0-444-85326-X, North Holland). Elsevier.
Lafitte, Lucette. Eau Trouble. 1963. text ed. 3.95x (ISBN 0-521-05506-7). Cambridge U Pr.
LaFleur, James K. Tax Sheltered Financing Through the R&D Limited Partnership. (Professional Banking & Finance Ser.). 528p. 1983. 65.00x (ISBN 0-471-87066-8, Pub. by Wiley-Interscience). Wiley.
LaFleur, William R. The Karma of Words: Buddhism & the Literary Arts in Medieval Japan. LC 82-45909. 232p. 1983. text ed. 25.00x (ISBN 0-520-04600-5). U of Cal Pr.
LaFollette, Hugh, jt. auth. see Aiken, William.
La Follette, P., jt. auth. see Hunter, W. F.
Lafontaine, Henry C. De see De Lafontaine, Henry C.
La Fontaine, J. S. City Politics: A Study of Leopoldville, 1962-63. (African Studies). (Illus.). 1970. 29.50 (ISBN 0-521-07627-7). Cambridge U Pr.
La Fontaine, Jean de. La Fontaine: Selected Fables. Mitchie, James, tr. from Fr. 1982. pap. 3.95 (ISBN 0-14-044376-2). Penguin.
LaForce, Beatrice. Devil's Cuspidor. 1981. pap. 1.50 (ISBN 0-686-37157-7). Eldridge Pub.
Laforet, Claude. La Vie Musicale Au Temps Romantique. LC 77-4153. (Music Reprint Ser., 1977). 1977. Repr. of 1929 ed. lib. bdg. 22.50 (ISBN 0-306-70890-6). Da Capo.
La Forge, P. G. Counseling & Culture in Second Language Acquisition. (Language Teaching Methodology Ser.). 128p. 1983. pap. 111.90 (ISBN 0-08-029477-4). Pergamon.
LaForge, R. Lawrence, jt. auth. see Kroeber, Donald.
Laforteza, Purificacion G. Creative Kindergarten Teaching. 127p. (Orig.). 1982. pap. 8.00 (ISBN 0-686-37576-9, Pub. by New Day Philippines). Cellar.
LaFountain, William. Setting Limits: Parents, Kids & Drugs. 1.75 (ISBN 0-89486-145-X). Hazelden.
La Fountaine, George. Flashpoint. LC 76-3622. 256p. 1976. 6.95 o.p. (ISBN 0-698-10742-X, Coward). Putnam Pub Group.
--The Scott-Dunlap Ring. LC 77-20112. 1978. 8.95 o.p. (ISBN 0-698-10871-X, Pub. by Coward). Putnam Pub Group.
--Two Minute Warning. LC 74-16642. 256p. 1975. 6.95 o.p. (ISBN 0-698-10633-4, Coward). Putnam Pub Group.
Lafourcade, Bernard, jt. auth. see Morrow, Bradford.
Lafourcade, Bernard, ed. see Lewis, Wyndham.
LaFrance, Marston. Reading of Stephen Crane. 1971. 15.00x (ISBN 0-19-812011-7). Oxford U Pr.
LaFray, J., ed. see Baldwin, Barbie.
LaFreniere, Joan G. The Low Back Patient. LC 78-61474. (Illus.). 208p. 1979. 23.75x (ISBN 0-89352-033-0). Masson Pub.
La Fuente, R. De see World Congress of Psychiatry 5th, Mexico, D. F. Nov. 25 - Dec. 4, 1971.
Lagadec, P. Major Technological Risk: An Assessment of Industrial Disasters. (Illus.). 536p. 1982. 60.00 (ISBN 0-08-028913-4). Pergamon.
Lagal, Roy. Detector Owner's Field Manual. rev. ed. Nelson, Bettye, ed. LC 75-44706. (Illus.). 236p. (Orig.). 1982. pap. 7.95 (ISBN 0-915920-43-3). Ram Pub.
--Gold Panning Is Easy. rev. ed. Nelson, Bettye, ed. LC 76-11382. (Guidebook Ser.). (Illus.). 112p. (Orig.). 1982. pap. 4.95 (ISBN 0-915920-45-X). Ram Pub.
Lagarde, A. & Michard, L. Collection Litteraire, 6 vols. Incl. Vol. 1. Moyen Age. 11.75 (ISBN 0-685-58371-6); Vol. 2. Seizieme Siecle. 11.75 (ISBN 0-685-58372-4); Vol. 3. Dix-Septieme Siecle. 13.95 (ISBN 0-685-58373-2); Vol. 4. Dix-Huitieme Siecle. 13.95 (ISBN 0-685-58374-0); Vol. 5. Dix-Neuvieme Siecle. 16.25 (ISBN 0-685-58375-9); Vol. 6. Vingtieme Siecle. 17.50 (ISBN 0-685-58376-7). (Fr.). Schoenhof.
Lagassa, George K., jt. auth. see Daneke, Gregory A.
Lagauskas, Valerie. Parades: How to Plan, Promote & Stage Them. LC 81-85038. (Illus.). 160p. 1982. 16.95 (ISBN 0-8069-0236-1); lib. bdg. 19.99 (ISBN 0-8069-0237-X). Sterling.
Lage, Ida De see DeLage, Ida.
Lagemann, Ellen. Nursing History: New Perspectives, New Possibilities. 1983. pap. text ed. write for info. Tchrs Coll.
Lagemann, Ellen C. Private Power for the Public Good: A History of the Carnegie Foundation for the Advancement of Teaching. 272p. 1982. 17.95 (ISBN 0-8195-5085-X). Wesleyan U Pr.
Lager, Eric & Zwerling, Isreal. Psychotherapy in the Community. Gardner, Alvjn F., ed. (Allied Health Professions Monograph Ser.). 1983. write for info. (ISBN 0-87527-315-7). Green.
Lager, Lance & Kraft, Amy L. Mental Judo: How to Communicate for Success in Business, Professional, Social or Family Life. 192p. 1981. 9.95 o.p. (ISBN 0-517-54315-X). Crown.
Lagerberg, Kees. West Irian & Jakarat Imperialism. LC 79-11232. 1979. 22.50x (ISBN 0-312-86322-5). St Martin.
Lagerkvist, Par. Barabbas. Blair, Alain, tr. 1955. pap. 2.95 (ISBN 0-394-70134-8, Vin). Random.
--The Dwarf. Dick, Alexandra, tr. 228p. (Orig.). 1958. pap. 5.25 (ISBN 0-8090-1303-7). Hill & Wang.
--The Eternal Smile. Mesterton, Erik & O'Gorman, David, trs. from Sw. LC 78-145810. 206p. 1971. pap. 5.95 o.p. (ISBN 0-8090-1358-4). Hill & Wang.
--Sibyl. Walford, Naomi, tr. 1963. pap. 2.95 (ISBN 0-394-70240-9, Vin). Random.
Lagerlof, Selma. Marbacka. Howard, Velma S., tr. LC 70-167024. (Illus.). viii, 288p. 1974. Repr. of 1926 ed. 34.00x (ISBN 0-8103-4031-3). Gale.
Lagerlof, Selma O. Jerusalem. Brochner, Jessie, tr. Repr. of 1903 ed. lib. bdg. 18.50x (ISBN 0-8371-3120-0, LAJE). Greenwood.
Lagerquist, Sally. Addison-Wesley's Nursing Examination. 2nd ed. 1982. soft bdg. 19.95 (ISBN 0-201-14190-6, Med-Nurse). A-W.
Lagerwerff, Ellen B. & Perlroth, Karen A. Mensendieck Your Posture, Encountering Gravity the Correct & Beautiful Way. Rev. ed. LC 72-97093. (Illus.). 1982. pap. 10.00 (ISBN 0-686-84332-0). Aries Pr.
Lagler, Karl F., et al. Ichthyology. 2nd ed. LC 76-50114. 506p. 1977. text ed. 29.95 (ISBN 0-471-51166-8). Wiley.
Lagnado, J. R., tr. see Youdim, M. B. & Lovenberg, W.
Lago, G. & Benningfield, L. M. Circuit & System Theory. LC 79-10878. 575p. 1979. text ed. 40.95x (ISBN 0-471-04927-1). Wiley.
Lago, Mary, tr. see Tagore, Rabindranath.
Lago, Mary M. Rabindranath Tagore. (World Authors Ser.). 1976. lib. bdg. 13.95 (ISBN 0-8057-6242-6, Twayne). G K Hall.
Lagos, Jorge C. Seizures, Epilepsy, & Your Child: A Handbook for Parents, Teachers, & Epileptics of All Ages. LC 74-5792. (Illus.). 256p. 1974. 12.45i (ISBN 0-06-012504-7, HarpT). Har-Row.
Lagowski, Joseph J., jt. auth. see Sorum, Henry.
Lagoy, Stephen P., ed. New Perspectives on Urban Crime. 112p. 1982. softcover 8.95 (ISBN 0-932930-44-1). Pilgrimage Inc.
LaGrange, Joseph-Louis. Lecons Sur le Calcul Des Fonctions. Repr. of 1806 ed. 138.00 o.p. (ISBN 0-8287-0485-6). Clearwater Pub.
--Mecanique Analytique. Repr. of 1788 ed. 140.00 o.p. (ISBN 0-8287-0486-4). Clearwater Pub.
--Theorie Des Fonctions Analytiques Contenant les Principes Du Calcul Differentiel. 81.00 o.p. (ISBN 0-8287-0487-2). Clearwater Pub.
Lagroye, Jacques & Wright, Vincent, eds. Local Government in Britain & France: Problems & Progress. (New Local Government Ser.: No. 18). (Illus.). 1979. text ed. 27.50x (ISBN 0-04-352081-2). Allen Unwin.
Laguardia Community College, Social Science Faculty. Work & Society: An Introduction to the Social Sciences. 1982. text ed. 13.95 (ISBN 0-8403-2821-4, 40282101). Kendall-Hunt.
Laguerre, E. Oeuvres, 2 Vols. LC 70-125075. (Fr). 1971. Repr. of 1905 ed. text ed. 49.50 (ISBN 0-8284-0263-9). Chelsea Pub.
Laguerre, Michael S. Urban Life in the Caribbean. 256p. 1983. 16.95 (ISBN 0-87073-734-1); pap. 8.95 (ISBN 0-87073-735-X). Schenkman.
Laguerre, Michel. The Complete Haitiana: A Bibliographic Guide to the Scholarly Literature, 1900 to 1980, 2 vols. LC 81-17190. 1982. lib. bdg. 270.00 (ISBN 0-527-54040-4). Kraus Intl.
La Guma, A. In the Fog of the Season's End. LC 72-93381. 1973. 8.95 o.p. (ISBN 0-89388-058-2). Okpaku Communications.
Lagumina, Salvatore J., jt. auth. see Cavaioli, Frank J.
Lagundimao, Clemente, Jr., jt. auth. see Golt, Rick.
Laha, R. G. & Rohatgi, V. K. Probability Theory. LC 78-24431. (Probability & Mathematical Statistics Ser.). 557p. 1979. 54.95x (ISBN 0-471-03262-X, Pub. by Wiley-Interscience). Wiley.
LaHaye, Berverly & LaHaye, Tim. La Familia Sujeta al Espiritu. 208p. Date not set. 2.95 (ISBN 0-88113-085-0). Edit Betania.
LaHaye, Beverly. Como Desarrollar el Temperamento de Su Hijo. 182p. Date not set. 2.95 (ISBN 0-88113-036-2). Edit Betania.
--How to Develop Your Child's Temperament. LC 77-73633. 1976. pap. 2.50 o.p. (ISBN 0-89081-272-1, 2251). Harvest Hse.
La Haye, Beverly. I Am a Woman by God's Design. 160p. 1980. 9.95 (ISBN 0-8007-1131-9); pap. 5.95 (ISBN 0-8007-5100-0, Power Bks); study guide 3.95 (ISBN 0-8007-1294-3). Revell.
LaHaye, Beverly. La Mujer Sujeta al Espiritu. 208p. Date not set. 2.75 (ISBN 0-88113-210-1). Edit Betania.
LaHaye, Beverly, jt. auth. see LaHaye, Tim.
LaHaye, Tim. The Battle for the Family. 256p. 1983. pap. 6.95 (ISBN 0-8007-5117-5). Revell.
--The Battle for the Mind. 224p. 1980. 8.95 o.p. (ISBN 0-8007-1112-2); pap. 5.95 (ISBN 0-8007-5043-8, Power Bks). Revell.
--The Battle for the Public Schools. (Illus.). 1982. 11.95 (ISBN 0-8007-1320-6, Power Bks); pap. 6.95 (ISBN 0-8007-5091-8). Revell.
--Beginning of the End. pap. 5.95 (ISBN 0-8423-0106-2). Tyndale.
--Como Estudiar la Biblia por Si Mismo. 192p. Date not set. 2.95 (ISBN 0-88113-042-7); 2.95 (ISBN 0-88113-033-8). Edit Betania.
--How to Be Happy Though Married. 5.95 (ISBN 0-8423-1500-4); pap. 4.95 (ISBN 0-8423-1501-2). Tyndale.
--Six Keys to a Happy Marriage. 1978. pap. 1.75 (ISBN 0-8423-5895-1). Tyndale.
--Spirit Controlled Temperament: Discussion Guide. pap. 1.25 (ISBN 0-8423-6402-1). Tyndale.
--Transformed Temperaments. pap. 4.95 (ISBN 0-8423-7306-3). Tyndale.
--El Varon y Su Temperamento. 217p. Date not set. 3.25 (ISBN 0-88113-340-X). Edit Betania.
LaHaye, Tim & LaHaye, Beverly. The Act of Marriage. 1976. pap. 6.95 (ISBN 0-686-96928-6); pap. 3.95 (ISBN 0-310-27062-6). Zondervan.
--Spirit Controlled Family Living. 1978. pap. 6.95 (ISBN 0-8007-5026-8, Power Bks). Revell.
LaHaye, Tim & Phillips, Bob. Anger Is a Choice. 160p. (Orig.). 1982. pap. 5.95 (ISBN 0-310-27071-5). Zondervan.
LaHaye, Tim, jt. auth. see LaHaye, Berverly.
Lahde, James A. Planning for Change: A Course of Study in Ecological Planning. 1982. text ed. 13.95x (ISBN 0-8077-2685-0); tchrs. manual 1.95x (ISBN 0-8077-2698-2); Activities Manual 5.95x (ISBN 0-8077-2693-1). Tchrs Coll.
Lahee, Frederick H. Field Geology. 6th ed. 1961. text ed. 43.50 (ISBN 0-07-035808-7, C). McGraw.
Lahey, Benjamin B. Psychology: An Introduction. 640p. 1983. text ed. write for info. (ISBN 0-697-06560-X); instrs' manual avail. (ISBN 0-697-06562-6); study guide avail. (ISBN 0-697-06561-8). Wm C Brown.
Lahey, Benjamin B. & Ciminero, Anthony R. Maladaptive Behavior: An Introduction to Abnormal Psychology. 1980. text ed. 23.50x (ISBN 0-673-15151-4). Scott F.
Lahey, Benjamin B. & Johnson, Martha S. Psychology & Instruction: A Practical Approach to Educational Psychology. 1978. pap. 16.50x (ISBN 0-673-15040-2). Scott F.
Lahey, Benjamin B., ed. Behavior Therapy with Hyperactive & Learning Disabled Children. (Illus.). 1979. text ed. 17.95x (ISBN 0-19-502478-8); pap. text ed. 12.50x (ISBN 0-19-502479-6). Oxford U Pr.
Lahey, Benjamin B. & Kazdin, Alan, eds. Advances in Clinical Child Psychology, Vol. 5. 375p. 1982. 35.00x (ISBN 0-306-41043-5, Plenum Pr). Plenum Pub.
Lahey, Ciminero. Maladaptive Behavior: Study Guide. 1980. pap. text ed. 7.95x (ISBN 0-673-15152-2). Scott F.
Lahey, G. Gerard Manley Hopkins. LC 72-95435. (Studies in Poetry, No. 38). 1969. Repr. of 1930 ed. lib. bdg. 29.95x (ISBN 0-8383-0986-0). Haskell.
Lahey, Margaret, jt. auth. see Bloom, Lois.
Lahey, Margaret, ed. Readings in Childhood Language Disorders. LC 77-21408. (Communications Disorders Ser.). 426p. 1978. text ed. 28.95 (ISBN 0-471-51167-6). Wiley.
Lahiff. Hard-to-Help Families. 9.95 (ISBN 0-471-25842-3, Pub. by Wiley Heyden). Wiley.
Lahiri, R. K. Family Farming in a Developing Economy. 1979. pap. text ed. 8.50x (ISBN 0-391-01851-5). Humanities.
Lahirl, K. The Econometrics of Inflationary Expectations. (Studies in Monetary Economics: Vol. 7). 1981. 34.00 (ISBN 0-444-86208-0). Elsevier.
Lahr, Georgiana L. A Medley of Songs. 1983. 7.95 (ISBN 0-686-84438-6). Vantage.
--Songs of Many Colors. 1980. 5.95 o.p. (ISBN 0-533-04406-5). Vantage.
Lahr, Jane & Tabori, Lena, eds. Love: A Celebration in Art & Literature. LC 82-5680. (Illus.). 240p. 1982. 35.00 (ISBN 0-941434-20-6, 8007). Stewart Tabori & Chang.
Lahr, John. Noel Coward. pap. cancelled (ISBN 0-686-98289-4, E829, Ever). Grove.
Lai, T. C. A Chinese Book of Friendship. (Illus.). 88p. 9.95 (ISBN 0-86519-025-9). Lee Pubs Group.
--Chinese Couplets. 13p. 1983. pap. 6.95 (ISBN 0-686-43000-X, Swindon Hong Kong). Hippocrene Bks.
--Chinese Decorated Letter Papers. (Illus.). 138p. 12.95 (ISBN 0-86519-098-4). Lee Pubs Group.
--Chinese Food for Thought. (Illus.). 96p. 9.95 (ISBN 0-86519-094-1). Lee Pubs Group.
--Chinese Proverbs. (Illus.). 96p. 5.95 (ISBN 0-86519-022-4). Lee Pubs Group.
--The Eight Immortals. (Illus.). 90p. 8.95 (ISBN 0-86519-097-6). Lee Pubs Group.
--Kweilin. (Illus.). 96p. 8.95 (ISBN 0-86519-023-2). LEE PUBS GROUP.
--More Chinese Sayings. 86p. 1983. 6.95 (ISBN 0-686-42996-6, Swindon Hong Kong). Hippocrene Bks.
--Selected Chinese Sayings. 198p. 1983. pap. 4.95 (ISBN 0-686-42995-8, Swindon Hong Kong). Hippocrene Bks.
--Things Chinese. (Illus.). 213p. 12.95 (ISBN 0-86519-096-8). Lee Pubs Group.
--Treasures of a Chinese Studio. (Illus.). 152p. 12.95 (ISBN 0-86519-095-X). Lee Pubs Group.
--Understanding Chinese Painting. (Illus.). 240p. 16.95 (ISBN 0-86519-021-6). Lee Pubs Group.
--Visiting China: A Cultured Guide. 248p. 1983. 12.95 (ISBN 0-686-42997-4, Swindon Hong Kong). Hippocrene Bks.
Lai, Whalen, jt. ed. see Lancaster, Lewis.
Laible, Roy C. Ballistic Materials & Penetration Mechanics. (Methods & Phenomena Ser.: Vol. 5). 1980. 64.00 (ISBN 0-444-41928-4). Elsevier.
Laidlaw, A. F. Training & Extension in the Co-operative Movement. (FAO Economic & Social Development Ser.: No. 11). 78p. 1962. pap. 4.75 (ISBN 0-686-92712-5, F480, FAO). Unipub.
Laidlaw, G. Norman. Elysian Encounter: Diderot & Gide. LC 63-19193. 1963. 15.95x (ISBN 0-8156-2054-3). Syracuse U Pr.
Laidlaw, R. A., jt. auth. see Edman, V. E.
Laidlaw-Dickson, D. J. Radio Control Model Cars Manual. (Illus.). 128p. (Orig.). 1979. pap. 10.00x o.p. (ISBN 0-906958-00-8). Intl Pubns Serv.
Laidler & Meiser. Physical Chemistry. 1982. 29.95 (ISBN 0-8053-5682-7, 35682); solns. manual 7.95 (ISBN 0-8053-5683-5). Benjamin-Cummings.
Laidler, ed. see International Congress of Pure & Applied Chemistry 28th, Vancouver, BC, Canada, 16-22 August 1981.
Laidler, David. Monetarist Perspectives. 224p. 1983. text ed. 20.00x (ISBN 0-674-58240-3). Harvard U Pr.
Laidler, Harry W. & Thomas, Norman. The Socialism of Our Times: A Symposium, Prelude to Depression. LC 76-27725. 1976. Repr. of 1929 ed. lib. bdg. 45.00 (ISBN 0-306-70850-7). Da Capo.
Laidler, Keith L. Chemical Kinetics. 2nd ed. 1965. text ed. 23.50 o.p. (ISBN 0-07-035831-1, C). McGraw.

Laidman, Hugh. Figures-Faces: A Sketcher's Handbook. (Illus.). 1979. 14.95 o.p. (ISBN 0-670-31319-X, Studio). Viking Pr.

Laiken, D. S., jt. auth. see Rowan, Lilian.

Laiken, Deidre. Beautiful Body Building. (Illus.). 1979. pap. 2.50 (ISBN 0-451-11368-3, AE1368, Sig). NAL.

--The First Kiss: A Teenager's Guide to the Gentle Art of Kissing. (Illus.). 32p. 1982. pap. 1.95 (ISBN 0-399-50618-7, Perige); pap. 46.80 24-copy counterpack (ISBN 0-399-50627-6). Putnam Pub Group.

Laiken, Deidre S. Mind - Body - Spirit: The Martial Arts & Oriental Medicine. LC 77-29101. (Illus.). 192p. (gr. 7 up). 1978. PLB 7.79 o.p. (ISBN 0-671-32894-8). Messner.

--Pain-Free, Drug-Free Menstruation Exercises for a Carefree Month. (Illus.). 32p. 1982. pap. 1.95 (ISBN 0-399-50576-8, Perige). Putnam Pub Group.

Laimons, Juris G. Garskis Oasis. LC 77-86554. 1982. write for info. o.p. (ISBN 0-9600288-4-6). Poet Papers.

Laine, Aarne. The Thrill of Burgundy. 50p. 1983. 5.95 (ISBN 0-533-03873-1). Vantage.

Laine, I., jt. auth. see Laine, S.

Laine, Michael. Bibliography of Works on John Stuart Mill. 176p. 1982. 35.00x (ISBN 0-8020-2414-9). U of Toronto Pr.

Laine, Pascal. Tender Cousins. LC 82-50002. (Illus.). 112p. (Orig.). 1982. pap. 12.95 (ISBN 0-688-01462-3). Quill NY.

Laine, S. & Laine, I. Promotion in Food Service. 1972. 13.95 (ISBN 0-07-035843-5, G); instructor's manual 3.50 (ISBN 0-07-035844-3). McGraw.

Laing, E. M., jt. auth. see Hulse, J. H.

Laing, E. W. Plasma Physics. 30.00x (ISBN 0-686-97016-0, Pub. by Scottish Academic Pr Scotland). State Mutual Bk.

Laing, Frederick. Tales from Scandinavia. LC 78-56060. (The World Folktale Library). (Illus.). 1979. PLB 12.68 (ISBN 0-382-03355-8). Silver.

Laing, Jennifer. The Greek & Roman Gods: A Pocket Guide. (Illus.). 64p. 1982. 8.95 (ISBN 0-7153-8292-6). David & Charles.

Laing, Lloyd. The Archaeology of Late Celtic Britain & Ireland, c.400-1200 A.D. 512p. 1975. 55.00x (ISBN 0-416-65970-5); pap. 20.00x (ISBN 0-416-82360-2). Methuen Inc.

Laing, M. E. D., ed. see Hartel, Herbert & Yaldiz, Marianne.

Laing, Malcolm. Preliminary Dissertation on the Participation of Mary, Queen of Scots, in the Murder of Darnley, 2 Vols. 371p. 1982. Repr. of 1804 ed. Set. lib. bdg. 200.00 (ISBN 0-89987-549-1). Darby Bks.

Laing, Margaret. Edward Heath: Prime Minister. LC 72-95089. 258p. 1973. 10.00 o.s.i. (ISBN 0-89388-086-8). Okpaku Communications.

Lainoff, Seymour. Ludwig Lewisohn. (United States Authors Ser.). 1982. lib. bdg. 15.95 (ISBN 0-8057-7375-4, Twayne). G K Hall.

Lainoff, Seymour, jt. ed. see Braun, Sidney D.

Laiou-Thomadakis, Angeliki, ed. Charanis Studies: Essays in Honor of Peter Charanis. (Illus.). 1980. 25.00 (ISBN 0-8135-0875-4). Rutgers U Pr.

Lai Po, Kan. Ancient Chinese. LC 80-53847. (Peoples of the Past Ser.). PLB 12.68 (ISBN 0-382-06446-1). Silver.

Lair, Jacqueline C. & Lechler, Walther H. I Exist, I Need, I'm Entitled: A Story of Love, Courage & Survival. LC 79-8011. 240p. 1980. 8.95 o.p. (ISBN 0-385-15632-4). Doubleday.

Lair, Jacqueline C., jt. auth. see Lair, Jess.

Lair, Jess. Ain't I a Wonder... & Ain't You a Wonder, Too! 2.50 o.p. (ISBN 0-686-92281-6, 6304). Hazelden.

--I Ain't Much, Baby-But I'm All I've Got. 2.50 o.p. (ISBN 0-686-92357-X, 6469). Hazelden.

--I Ain't Well-But I Sure Am Better. 2.50 o.p. (ISBN 0-686-92361-8, 6470). Hazelden.

--I Don't Know Where I'm Going, but I Sure Ain't Lost. LC 78-22795. 192p. 1981. pap. 6.95 (ISBN 0-385-13392-8). Doubleday.

--I Don't Know Where I'm Going, but I Sure Ain't Lost. 256p. 1983. pap. 2.75 (ISBN 0-449-20056-6, Crest). Fawcett.

--Sex-If I Didn't Laugh I'd Cry. LC 77-27678. 1979. pap. 5.95 (ISBN 0-385-13391-X). Doubleday.

Lair, Jess & Lair, Jacqueline C. Hey God, What Should I Do Now? 2.50 o.p. (ISBN 0-686-92340-5, 6460). Hazelden.

Laird. The Alphabet Zoo. LC 74-190264. (ps-2). 1972. PLB 6.75x (ISBN 0-87783-053-3); pap. 2.95x deluxe ed. (ISBN 0-87783-079-7). Oddo.

Laird, Becky. Portraits of People in Places Not Like Home. 1982. pap. 2.95 (ISBN 0-8341-0802-X). Beacon Hill.

Laird, Betty A., jt. auth. see Francisco, Ronald A.

Laird, Charles. Webster's New World Thesaurus. 544p. 1982. pap. 2.25 (ISBN 0-446-31053-0). Warner Bks.

Laird, Charles, et al. Modern English Reader. 2nd ed. (Illus.). 416p. 1977. pap. text ed. 12.95 (ISBN 0-13-594176-8). P-H.

Laird, Charlton. The Word: A Look at the Vocabulary of English. 1981. 14.95 o.p. (ISBN 0-671-42185-9). S&S.

Laird, Charlton, jt. auth. see Gorrell, Robert.

Laird, Charlton, jt. auth. see Gorrell, Robert M.

Laird, Charlton, ed. Webster's New World Thesaurus. pap. 8.95 (ISBN 0-452-00627-9, F627, Mer). NAL.

Laird, Donald & Laird, Eleanor. The New Psychology for Leadership, Based on Researches in Group Dynamics & Human Relations. LC 75-26763. (Illus.). 226p. 1975. Repr. of 1956 ed. lib. bdg. 15.75x (ISBN 0-8371-8370-7, LANP). Greenwood.

Laird, Donald A. & Laird, Eleanor C. Sizing up People. 1961. pap. 3.95 o.p. (ISBN 0-07-036006-5, SP). McGraw.

--Techniques for Efficient Remembering. 1960. 5.95 (ISBN 0-07-036075-8, GB); pap. 3.95 (ISBN 0-07-036076-6). McGraw.

Laird, Donald A., et al. Psychology: Human Relations & Motivation. 5th ed. Stoner, G. O., ed. (Illus.). 448p. 1975. text ed. 20.05 (ISBN 0-07-036015-4, G); teacher's manual & key 2.65 (ISBN 0-07-036017-0). McGraw.

--Psychology: Human Relations & Motivation. 6th ed. LC 82-217. 416p. 1982. text ed. 20.95 (ISBN 0-07-036018-9); instr's manual 2.30 (ISBN 0-07-036019-7). McGraw.

Laird, Donivee M. Wil Wai Kula & the Three Mongooses. (Illus.). 44p. (gr. k-3). 1983. 6.95 (ISBN 0-940350-04-1). Barnaby Bks.

Laird, Eleanor, jt. auth. see Laird, Donald.

Laird, Eleanor C., jt. auth. see Laird, Donald A.

Laird, James R. The Cheyenne Saddle. (Illus.). 100p. (Orig.). 1982. pap. write for info. (ISBN 0-9609648-0-0). Cheyenne Cor.

Laird, M. A., ed. Bishop Heber in Northern India: Selections from Heber's Journal. LC 70-123673. (European Understanding of India Ser). (Illus.). 1971. 34.50 (ISBN 0-521-07873-3). Cambridge U Pr.

Laird, Melvin R. Energy-A Crisis in Public Policy. 1977. pap. 2.25 (ISBN 0-8447-3255-9). Am Enterprise.

Laishley, Jennie. Working with Young Children. 160p. 1983. pap. text ed. price not set (ISBN 0-7131-3479-8). E Arnold.

Laistner, M. L. The Greater Roman Historians. (Sather Classical Lectures Ser: Vol. 21). 1947. 17.50x (ISBN 0-520-03365-5). U of Cal Pr.

Laita, Luis M. Cortina-Grosset Basic Spanish Dictionary. Berberi, Dilaver & Berberi, Edel A., eds. LC 73-18525. 384p. 1975. 3.95 (ISBN 0-448-11559-X, G&D). Putnam Pub Group.

Laita, Luis M., ed. Cortina-Grosset Basic Spanish Dictionary. 1977. pap. 3.50 (ISBN 0-448-14032-2, G&D). Putnam Pub Group.

Laithwaite, E. R., ed. Transport Without Wheels. LC 76-53107. (Illus.). 1977. lib. bdg. 51.25 o.p. (ISBN 0-89158-724-1). Westview.

Laithwaite, L. & Freris, T. Electrical Energy: Its Generation, Transmission & Use. 365p. 1982. 20.95 (ISBN 0-07-084109-8). McGraw.

Laitinen, Herbert A. & Harris, Walter E. Chemical Analysis. 2nd ed. (Advanced Chemistry Ser.). (Illus.). 611p. 1975. text ed. 42.50 (ISBN 0-07-036086-3, C). McGraw.

Laitinen, K. Theory of the Multi-Product Firm. (Studies in Mathematical & Managerial Economics Ser.: Vol. 28). 1981. 40.50 (ISBN 0-686-95530-7). Elsevier.

Laitos, Jan G. A Legal-Economic History of Air Pollution Controls. LC 80-67046. (Scholarly Monograph Ser.). 350p. 1980. pap. 27.50 o.p. (ISBN 0-8408-0507-1). Carrollton Pr.

Lajolo, Davide. An Absurd Vice: A Biography of Cesare Pavese. Pietralunga, Mario, tr. Pietralunga, Mark. LC 82-14482. 288p. (Ital.). 1983. 18.50 (ISBN 0-8112-0850-8); pap. 9.25 (ISBN 0-8112-0851-6, NDP545). New Directions.

Lajtha, A. & Ford, Donald H., eds. Brain Barrier Systems. (Progress in Brain Research: Vol. 29). 1968. 138.75 (ISBN 0-444-40352-3, North Holland). Elsevier.

Lajtha, A., jt. ed. see Roberts, S.

Lajtha, Abel, ed. Handbook of Neurochemistry: Vol. 2, Experimental Neurochemistry. 2nd ed. 450p. 1982. 59.50x (ISBN 0-306-40972-0, Plenum Pr). Plenum Pub.

Lakatos, Imre. Philosophical Papers: Mathematics, Science & Epistemology, Vol. 2. Worrall, J. & Currie, G., eds. LC 77-14374. 295p. 1980. pap. 13.95 (ISBN 0-521-28030-3). Cambridge U Pr.

--Philosophical Papers: Mathematics, Science & Epistemology, Vol. 2. Worrall, J. & Currie, G., eds. LC 77-71415. 1978. 39.50 (ISBN 0-521-21769-5). Cambridge U Pr.

--Philosophical Papers: The Methodology of Scientific Research Programmes, Vol. 1. Worrall, J. & Currie, G., eds. LC 77-71415. 258p. 1980. pap. 12.95 (ISBN 0-521-28031-1). Cambridge U Pr.

--Philosophical Papers: The Methodology of Scientific Research Programmes, Vol. 1. Worrall, J. & Currie, G., eds. LC 77-71415. 1978. 37.50 (ISBN 0-521-21644-3). Cambridge U Pr.

Lakatos, Imre & Musgrave, A. E., eds. Criticism & the Growth of Knowledge. LC 78-105496. 1970. 42.50 (ISBN 0-521-07826-1); pap. 11.95 (ISBN 0-521-09623-5). Cambridge U Pr.

Lake. Environmental Regulation. 160p. 1982. 20.95 (ISBN 0-03-062761-3). Praeger.

Lake, Bonnie. Western Stars of Country Music. LC 77-90149. (Country Music Books). (Illus.). (gr. 5 up). 1978. PLB 5.95g (ISBN 0-8225-1407-9). Lerner Pubns.

Lake, Dale. Perceiving & Behaving. LC 72-77891. (Illus.). 1970. text ed. 11.95x (ISBN 0-8077-1658-8). Tchrs Coll.

Lake, Dale G., et al, eds. Measuring Human Behavior: Tools for the Assessment of Social Functioning. LC 72-82083. 1973. pap. text ed. 12.95x (ISBN 0-8077-1648-0). Tchrs Coll.

Lake, Elizabeth, et al. Who Pays for Clean Water? (A Westview Replica Edition Ser.). (An Urban systems research report). 1979. lib. bdg. 27.50 (ISBN 0-89158-586-9). Westview.

Lake, Frances, jt. auth. see Newmark, Joseph.

Lake, H. S., tr. see Van Eeden, Frederik.

Lake, Hank. How to Win at Atlantic City, Las Vegas & Caribbean Gaming. (Illus.). 71p. 1982. pap. 3.95 (ISBN 0-938512-05-6). Brigadoon.

Lake, Henry B. How to Win at Atlantic City, Las Vegas & Caribbean Gaming. (Illus.). 50p. (Orig.). 1981. pap. 3.50 programmed bk o.p. (ISBN 0-938512-01-3). Brigadoon.

Lake, Nan, ed. Bountiful: A Poetry Digest. (Anthology Poetry Ser.). 1982. pap. 4.95 (ISBN 0-938512-04-8). Brigadoon.

Lake, Patricia. Moment of Madness. (Harlequin Presents Ser.). 192p. 1983. pap. 1.95 (ISBN 0-373-10593-2). Harlequin Bks.

--The Silver Casket. (Harlequin Presents Ser.). 192p. 1983. pap. 1.95 (ISBN 0-373-10578-9). Harlequin Bks.

--A Step Backwards. (Harlequin Presents Ser.). 192p. 1983. pap. 1.75 (ISBN 0-373-10570-3). Harlequin Bks.

Lake, Sara, ed. Drug Abuse. (Special Interest Resource Guides in Education Ser.). 1980. pap. text ed. 15.00 (ISBN 0-912700-72-6). Oryx Pr.

Lake, Tony & Hills, A. Affairs: How to Cope with Extra-Marital Relationships. 224p. 1981. 10.95 (ISBN 0-13-018671-6, Spec); pap. 5.95 (ISBN 0-13-018663-5). P-H.

Lakebrink, Joan M. Children's Success in School. (Illus.). 260p. 1983. 19.75x (ISBN 0-398-04776-6). C C Thomas.

Lakein, Alan. How to Get Control of Your Time & Your Life. 160p. 1974. pap. 2.50 (ISBN 0-451-09587-1, E9587, Sig). NAL.

--How to Get Control of Your Time & Your Life. 2.50 o.p. (ISBN 0-686-92349-9, 6464). Hazelden.

Lakela, Olga & Long, Robert W. Ferns of Florida. LC 76-18950. (Illus.). 1976. 12.50 (ISBN 0-916224-03-1). Banyan Bks.

Lakela, Olga & Wunderlin, Richard P. Trees of Central Florida. LC 80-12797. (Illus.). 208p. 14.95 (ISBN 0-686-84243-X). Banyan Bks.

Laken, William D. & Sanchez, David A. Topics in Ordinary Differential Equations. 160p. 1982. pap. 4.00 (ISBN 0-486-61606-1). Dover.

Laker, K., jt. auth. see Ghausi, M.

Laker, Rosalind. Banners of Silk. 1982. pap. 3.50 (ISBN 0-451-11545-7, AE1545, Sig). NAL.

--Gilded Splendour. (General Ser.). 1982. lib. bdg. 17.95 (ISBN 0-8161-3476-6, Large Print Bks). G K Hall.

--Jewelled Path. LC 82-45264. (Illus.). 384p. 1983. 15.95 (ISBN 0-385-18089-6). Doubleday.

Lakey, Berit. Meeting Faciliation: The No Magic Method. 10p. 1975. pap. 0.50 stapleback bdg. (ISBN 0-86571-013-9). New Soc Pubs.

Lakhanpal, T. N. & Mukerji, K. G. Taxonomy of the Indian Myxomycetes. (Bibliotheca Mycologica: No. 78). (Illus.). 532p. 1981. lib. bdg. 46.00x (ISBN 3-7682-1287-4). Lubrecht & Cramer.

Lakin, jt. auth. see Meyers.

Lakin, Leonard & Beane, Leona. Materials in the Law of Business Contracts. 352p. 1982. pap. text ed. 9.50 (ISBN 0-8403-2825-7). Kendall-Hunt.

Lakin, Martin. Interpersonal Encounter Theory & Practice in Sensitivity Training. (Psychology Ser.). (Illus.). 320p. 1971. text ed. 17.50 o.p. (ISBN 0-07-036065-0, C). McGraw.

Laklan, C. Golden Women. 1983. 10.95 (ISBN 0-07-036079-0). McGraw.

Laklan, Carli. Golden Girls: True Stories of Olympic Women Stars. LC 79-24052. (Illus.). (gr. 7-10). 1980. 9.95 (ISBN 0-07-036074-X). McGraw.

--Ski Bum. new ed. LC 73-6664. 160p. (gr. 9-12). 1973. PLB 6.95 o.p. (ISBN 0-07-035891-5, GB). McGraw.

Lakoff, George & Johnson, Mark. Metaphors We Live by. LC 80-10783. xiv, 242p. 1981. 6.95 (ISBN 0-226-46801-1, Phoen). U of Chicago Pr.

Lakoff, George, ed. see Borkin, Ann.

Lakoff, Sanford A. & Rich, Daniel. Private Government: Introductory Readings. 1972. pap. 8.95x (ISBN 0-673-07612-1). Scott F.

Lakoff, Sanford A., ed. Science & Ethical Responsibility. 1980. pap. text ed. 19.50 (ISBN 0-201-03993-1). A-W.

Lakovaara, Seppo, ed. Advances in Genetics, Development & Evolution of Drosophila. LC 82-9154. 480p. 1982. 57.50x (ISBN 0-306-41106-7, Plenum Pr). Plenum Pub.

Lakritz, Joyce. Verbal Workbook for the ACT. LC 82-11644. 192p. 1983. pap. 6.00 (ISBN 0-668-05348-8, 5348). Arco.

Lakshin, Vladimir. Solzhenitsyn, Tvardovsky & Novy Mir. Glenny, Michael, tr. from Rus. 208p. 1980. 12.50 (ISBN 0-262-12086-0); pap. 5.95 (ISBN 0-262-62039-1). MIT Pr.

Lakshmikantham, V., jt. auth. see Bernfeld, Stephen R.

Lakshmikantham, V., ed. Nonlinear Phenomena in Mathematical Science: (Symposium) LC 82-20734. 1982. 94.50 (ISBN 0-12-434170-5). Acad Pr.

Lal, jt. auth. see Sachchidananda.

Lal, Chaman. India: Cradle of Cultures. (Illus.). 346p. 1980. text ed. 31.50x (ISBN 0-391-01872-8). Humanities.

Lal, D. Early Solar Systems Processes & the Present Solar System. (Enrico Fermi Summer School Ser.: Vol. 73). 1980. 53.25 (ISBN 0-444-85458-4). Elsevier.

Lal, Deepak. A Liberal International Economic Order: The International Monetary System & Economic Development. LC 80-22523. (Essays in International Finance Ser.: No. 139). 1980. pap. text ed. 2.50x (ISBN 0-88165-046-3). Princeton U Int Finan Econ.

Lal, Deepak, jt. auth. see Collier, Paul.

Lal, Kundan, jt. auth. see Agrawal, A. N.

Lal, Nand. From Collective Security to Peacekeeping: A Study of India's Contribution to the UN Emergency Force, 1956-67. LC 76-900622. 1976. 10.00x o.p. (ISBN 0-88386-537-8). South Asia Bks.

Lal, P., jt. auth. see Devi, Shyamasree.

Lal, P., tr. from Sanskrit. The Bhagavad Gita. 71p. 1973. 8.00 (ISBN 0-88253-304-5); flexible bdg. o.s.i. 4.80 (ISBN 0-89253-542-3). Ind-US Inc.

Lal, P., tr. Mahabharata, 114 vols. 1973. 4.00 ea. Ind-US Inc.

Lal, P., tr. see Tagore, Rabindranath.

Lal, R. & Greenland, D. J., eds. Soil Physical Properties & Crop Production in the Tropics. LC 79-40583. 551p. 1979. 119.95x (ISBN 0-471-99757-9, Pub. by Wiley-Interscience). Wiley.

Lal, R. & Russell, E. W., eds. Tropical Agricultural Hydrology: Watershed Management & Land Use. LC 80-41590. 448p. 1981. 62.95x (ISBN 0-471-27931-5, Pub. by Wiley-Interscience). Wiley.

Lal, R., jt. ed. see Greenland, D. J.

Lalande, Jerome. Memoire Sur l'Interieur De l'Afrique. (Bibliotheque Africaine Ser.). 40p. (Fr.). 1974. Repr. lib. bdg. 22.00x o.p. (ISBN 0-8287-0493-7, 72-2103). Clearwater Pub.

Lalane, Henry, et al. Grammar for the Professional Writer. 1979. pap. text ed. 10.95 (ISBN 0-8403-2081-7). Kendall-Hunt.

Lall, Bernard M., jt. auth. see Lall, Geeta R.

Lall, Geeta R. & Lall, Bernard M. Comparative Early Childhood Education. 168p. 1983. 16.75x (ISBN 0-398-04777-4). C C Thomas.

--Ways Children Learn: What Do Experts Say? 80p. 1983. 11.75x (ISBN 0-398-04754-5). C C Thomas.

Lall, K. B. & Chopra, H. S., eds. EEC & The Third World. 500p. 1980. text ed. 33.00x (ISBN 0-391-02004-8). Humanities.

Lall, Rama Rani. Satiric Fable in English. 1980. text ed. 12.50x (ISBN 0-391-01732-2). Humanities.

Lall, Sanjaya. Developing Countries as Exporters of Technology & Capital Goods. 134p. 1982. text ed. 31.50x (ISBN 0-333-28844-0, 50921, Pub. by Macmillan England). Humanities.

Lallemand, Leon. La Question des Enfants Abandonnes et Delaisses au 19th Siecle. (Conditions of the 19th Century French Working Class Ser.). 238p. (Fr.). 1974. Repr. of 1885 ed. lib. bdg. 66.00x o.p. (ISBN 0-8287-0494-5, 1064). Clearwater Pub.

Lallement, Gerard. Semigroups & Combinatorial Applications. LC 78-23561. (Pure & Applied Mathematics Ser.). 400p. 1979. 45.00x (ISBN 0-471-04379-6, Pub. by Wiley-Interscience). Wiley.

Lall Nigam, B. M. Banking Law & Practice. 3rd rev. ed. 500p. 1983. text ed. 40.00x (ISBN 0-7069-1103-2, Pub. by Vikas India). Advent NY.

Lally, James, jt. auth. see Baldock, Cora V.

Lally, Michael. Just let me do it: Love Poems 1967-77. 88p. 1978. 20.00 (ISBN 0-931428-05-X); pap. 3.50 o.p. (ISBN 0-931428-04-1). Vehicle Edns.

Lally, Michael, ed. None of the Above. LC 76-27647. (The Crossing Press Contemporary Anthologies Ser.). (Illus.). 200p. 1976. 16.95 (ISBN 0-912278-75-7); pap. 6.95 (ISBN 0-912278-76-5). Crossing Pr.

LaLonde, W. S. Professional Engineers Examination Questions & Answers. 4th ed. 544p. 1983. 35.00 (ISBN 0-07-036099-5, P&RB). McGraw.

LaLonde, William S. & Stack-Staikidis, William. Professional Engineer's Examination Questions & Answers. 3rd ed. 1976. 32.50 (ISBN 0-07-036093-6, P&RB); pap. 17.95 (ISBN 0-07-036095-2). McGraw.

La Lone, Mary. Gabrielino Indians of Southern California: An Annotated Ethnohistoric Bibliography. (Occasional Papers: No. 6). 72p. 1980. pap. 5.00 (ISBN 0-917956-15-X). UCLA Arch.

Lalor, et al. Mathematics: Back to Basics. 1977. 8.95x (ISBN 0-916060-03-9). Math Alternatives.

Lalor, John J., tr. see Nohl, Louis.

Laloy, J. R., jt. auth. see Dany, M.

Lam, Chan. Techniques for the Analysis & Modeling of Enzyme Kinetic Mechanisms. (Medical Computing Ser.). 396p. 1981. 55.00 (ISBN 0-471-09981-3, Pub. by Res Stud Pr). Wiley.

Lam, Roger. The Cuckoo Clock Adventure. Gibb, George, ed. LC 82-99848. (Illus., Orig.). (gr. 5-12). 1983. pap. 2.25 (ISBN 0-943310-01-6). Six Pr.

Lam, Rosalind. Getting Together: Study of Members of PHAB Clubs. (NFER General Ser.). 163p. 1982. pap. text ed. 10.50x (ISBN 0-85633-244-5, NFER). Humanities.

Lam, W. Perception & Lighting As Formgivers for Architecture. 1977. 49.00 (ISBN 0-07-036094-4, P&RB). McGraw.

Lama A., intro. by see Winkler, Kenneth D.

Lama Chimpa, Alaka Chattopadhyaya, tr. see Taranatha, Lama.

Lamadrid, Enrique E., et al. Communicating in Spanish, Level I. 800p. (Sp.). 1974. text ed. 21.95 (ISBN 0-395-27062-6); instr's. manual 13.25 (ISBN 0-395-17530-5); wkbk. 8.95 (ISBN 0-395-17531-3); tapes 230.00 (ISBN 0-395-17534-8). HM.

Lamagna, Joseph. Wild Game Cookbook for Beginner & Expert: Outdoor Cook's Almanac. (Illus.). spiral bdg. 6.95 (ISBN 0-9610464-0-6). J Lamagna.

Lamanna, Mary A. & Riedmann, Agnes. Marriages & Families. 640p. 1981. text ed. 21.95x (ISBN 0-534-00953-0); wkbk. 7.95x (ISBN 0-534-00956-5). Wadsworth Pub.

Lamantia, Philip. Becoming Visible. (Pocket Poet Ser.: No. 39). 88p. 1981. 10.95 (ISBN 0-87286-124-4); pap. 3.95 (ISBN 0-87286-129-5). City Lights.

Lamar, Kristena A. Divorce Guide for Oregon. 2nd ed. (Illus.). 120p. 1982. pap. 8.95 (ISBN 0-88908-813-6). Self Counsel Pr.

Lamar, Nedra N. How to Speak the Written Word: A Guide to Effective Public Reading. rev. ed. 192p. 10.95 (ISBN 0-8007-0143-7). Revell.

LaMar, Virginia, ed. see Shakespeare, William.

LaMar, Virginia A., ed. see Shakespeare, William.

La Mar, Virginia A., ed. see Shakespeare, William.

LaMarche, Bob. Tennis Basics. (Illus.). 48p. (gr. 3-7). 1983. 8.95 (ISBN 0-13-903237-1). P-H.

Lamarck, J. B. Philosophie Zoologique, 2 vols. in 1. 1960. Repr. of 1809 ed. 48.00 (ISBN 3-7682-0028-0). Lubrecht & Cramer.

Lamarck, Jean-Baptiste. Systeme Analytique Des Connaissances Positives De L'homme Restreintes a Celles Qui Proviennent Directement De L'observation. Repr. of 1830 ed. 130.00 o.p. (ISBN 0-8287-0495-3). Clearwater Pub.

Lamare, James W. Texas Politics: Economics, Power, & Policy. 267p. 1981. pap. text ed. 10.95 (ISBN 0-8299-0390-9). West Pub.

Lamarra, Vincent A. see Adams, V. Dean.

Lamarsh, J. R. Introduction to Nuclear Reactor Theory. 1966. 34.95 (ISBN 0-201-04120-0). A-W.

Lamarsh, John R. Introduction to Nuclear Engineering. 2nd ed. LC 82-8678. (AW-Nuclear Science & Engineering Ser.). (Illus.). 652p. Date not set. text ed. price not set (ISBN 0-201-14200-7). A-W.

Lamartine, Alphonse de. A Pilgrimage to the Holy Land. LC 78-14368. 1978. Repr. of 1838 ed. 55.00x (ISBN 0-8201-1323-9). Schol Facsimiles.

Lamartine, De see De Lamartine.

LaMay, Jack D. Shelley & the Animals. 1983. 4.50 (ISBN 0-686-84432-7). Vantage.

Lamb, Berton L., ed. Water Quality Administration: A Focus on Section 208. LC 79-55144. 1980. 39.95 (ISBN 0-250-40292-0). Ann Arbor Science.

Lamb, Caroline. Glenarvon, 3 vols. in 1. LC 71-161933. 272p. 1972. Repr. of 1816 ed. 40.00x (ISBN 0-8201-1093-0). Schol Facsimiles.

Lamb, Charles. Essays of Elia. Bd. with Last Essays of Elia. 1978. Repr. of 1906 ed. 9.95x (ISBN 0-460-00014-4, Evman). Biblio Dist.

--The Portable Charles Lamb. Brown, John M., ed. (Viking Portable Library). 43p. 1980. pap. 6.95 (ISBN 0-14-015043-9). Penguin.

Lamb, Charles & Lamb, Mary. Tales from Shakespeare. 1981. 9.95x (ISBN 0-460-00008-X, Evman); pap. 2.95x (ISBN 0-460-01008-5, Evman). Biblio Dist.

--Tales from Shakespeare. (Childrens Illustrated Classics Ser). (Illus.). 200p. 1983. Repr. of 1957 ed. text ed. 11.95 o.p. (ISBN 0-460-05039-7, Pub. by J. M. Dent England). Biblio Dist.

Lamb, Charles see Eyre, A. G.

Lamb, Charles see Fenwick, Eliza.

Lamb, Charles E., jt. auth. see Lamberg, Walter J.

Lamb, Charles M., jt. auth. see Bullock, Charles S., III.

Lamb, Charles W., Jr. Marketing: Cases for Analysis. LC 82-81740. 512p. 1982. pap. 13.95 (ISBN 0-395-32636-2); write for info. instr's manual (ISBN 0-395-32637-0). HM.

Lamb, Charlotte. Betrayal. (Harlequin Presents Ser.). 192p. 1983. pap. 1.95 (ISBN 0-373-10585-1). Harlequin Bks.

--Pour Oublier un Reve. (Collection Harlequin). 192p. 1983. pap. 1.95 (ISBN 0-373-49321-5). Harlequin Bks.

--Quand L'Amour est une Guerre. (Harlequin Romantique Ser.). 192p. 1983. pap. 1.95 (ISBN 0-373-41177-4). Harlequin Bks.

Lamb, Curt. Homestyles. LC 78-21201. (Illus.). 1979. 14.95 (ISBN 0-312-38899-3); pap. 8.95 o.p. (ISBN 0-312-38900-0). St Martin.

--Political Power in Poor Neighborhoods. LC 75-19435. 315p. 1976. 21.50x o.p. (ISBN 0-470-51196-6); pap. 9.50x o.p. (ISBN 0-470-51197-4). Halsted Pr.

Lamb, D. Language & Perception in Hegel & Wittgenstein. 1979. 45.00x o.p. (ISBN 0-86127-101-7, Pub. by Avebury Pub England). State Mutual Bk.

Lamb, D. & Easton, S. The Philosophy of Scientific Development: A Study of Multiple Discoveries. 1981. 60.00x o.p. (ISBN 0-686-75435-2, Pub. by Avebury Pub England). State Mutual Bk.

Lamb, David. The Africans. LC 81-48271. (Illus.). 384p. 1983. 17.95 (ISBN 0-394-51887-X). Random.

--Language & Perception in Hegel & Wittgenstein. LC 80-505. 135p. 1980. 25.00 (ISBN 0-312-46612-9). St Martin.

Lamb, David R. Physiology of Exercise: Responses & Adaptations. (Illus.). 1978. text ed. 21.95x (ISBN 0-02-367200-5). Macmillan.

--Physiology of Exercises: Responses & Adaptations. 2nd ed. 464p. 1983. text ed. 20.95 (ISBN 0-02-367210-2); lab manual 9.95 (ISBN 0-02-367220-X). Macmillan.

Lamb, G. F. True Book About the South Pole. (Illus.). (gr. 7 up). 12.75x (ISBN 0-392-05204-0, LTB). Sportshelf.

Lamb, G. M. Computers in the Public Service. 260p. 1973. 40.00x (ISBN 0-04-363003-0, Pub by Royal Inst Pub Anmin England). State Mutual Bk.

Lamb, Geoff. Peasant Politics: Conflict & Development in Murang'a. LC 74-77270. 172p. 1974. 20.00 (ISBN 0-312-59990-0). St Martin.

Lamb, Geoffrey. Magic, Witchcraft & the Occult. (Illus.). 176p. 1982. Repr. of 1977 ed. pap. 9.95 (ISBN 0-88254-705-4). Hippocrene Bks.

--Wheaton Book of Magic Stories. (Illus.). (gr. 9-12). 8.90 o.p. (ISBN 0-686-77946-0). Putnam Pub Group.

Lamb, George, tr. see Nuttin, Jozef.

Lamb, George L. Elements of Solition Theory. LC 80-13373. (Pure & Applied Mathematics: Texts & Monographs). 289p. 1980. 33.95x (ISBN 0-471-04559-4, Pub. by Wiley-Interscience). Wiley.

Lamb, H. H. Climate: Present, Past & Future, Vol. 2. 835p. 1977. 140.00x (ISBN 0-416-11540-3). Methuen Inc.

Lamb, H. Richard. Treating the Long-Term Mentally Ill: Beyond Deinstitutionalization. LC 82-48391. (Social & Behavioral Science Ser.). 1982. text ed. 17.95x (ISBN 0-87589-553-0). Jossey Bass.

Lamb, H. Richard, et al. Rehabilitation in Community Mental Health. LC 76-168989. (Social & Behavioral Science Ser.). 1971. 17.95x (ISBN 0-87589-107-1). Jossey-Bass.

Lamb, Harold. Charlemagne: The Legend & the Man. LC 54-5368. 1954. 4.95 (ISBN 0-385-04066-0). Doubleday.

Lamb, Helen B. Vietnam's Will to Live: Resistance to Foreign Aggression from Early Times Through the Nineteenth Century. LC 68-59046. (Illus.). 352p. 1973. pap. 3.95 (ISBN 0-85345-286-5, PB-2865). Monthly Rev.

Lamb, Helen B. & Lamont, Corliss. Studies on India & Vietnam. LC 76-1668. 288p. 1976. 16.50 (ISBN 0-85345-384-5, CL3845). Monthly Rev.

Lamb, Howard. The Fatbook. 133p. 1982. loose-leaf 39.95 (ISBN 0-9609150-0-1). H Lamb.

Lamb, I. Mackenzie & Zimmerman, Martin H. Benthic Marine Algae of the Antarctic Peninsula: Paper 3 in Biology of the Antarctic Seas V. Pawson, David L., ed. (Antarctic Research Ser: Vol. 23). 1977. pap. 25.00 (ISBN 0-87590-127-1). Am Geophysical.

Lamb, Karl A. The Guardians: Leadership Values & the American Tradition. 1983. 18.95 (ISBN 0-393-01575-0); pap. 5.95x (ISBN 0-393-95226-6). Norton.

Lamb, Karl A., jt. auth. see Thomas, Norman C.

Lamb, M. W. & Harden, M. L. Meaning of Human Nutrition. 1975. text ed. 20.00 (ISBN 0-08-017078-1); pap. text ed. 10.25 (ISBN 0-08-017079-X). Pergamon.

Lamb, Margaret. Colorado High Country. LC 82-70357. (Illus., Orig.). 1965. pap. 3.25 (ISBN 0-8040-0053-0, SB). Swallow.

--Nationalism. (History Monographs: Bk. 8). 1974. pap. text ed. 4.50x o.p. (ISBN 0-435-31530-7). Heinemann Ed.

Lamb, Mary see Eyre, A. G.

Lamb, Mary, jt. auth. see Lamb, Charles.

Lamb, Matthew L. History, Method, & Theology: A Dialectical Comparison of Wilhelm Dilthey's Critique of Historical Reason & Bernard Lonergan's Meta-Methodology. LC 78-18707. 1978. 13.95 (ISBN 0-89130-238-7, 01-01-25). Scholars Pr Ca.

Lamb, Matthew L., ed. Creativity & Method: Studies in Honor of Rev. Bernard Lonergan, S.J. 600p. 1981. 29.95 (ISBN 0-87462-533-5). Marquette.

Lamb, Michael E. The Role of the Father in Child Development. 2nd ed. LC 81-13063. (Wiley Series on Personality Process). 582p. 1981. 32.50x (ISBN 0-471-07739-9, Pub. by Wiley-Interscience). Wiley.

--The Role of the Father in Child Development. LC 76-21778. (Personality Processes Ser.). 407p. 1976. 25.95 o.p. (ISBN 0-471-51172-2, Pub. by Wiley-Interscience). Wiley.

Lamb, Michael E. & Brown, Ann L., eds. Advances in Developmental Psychology, Vol. 2. 224p. 1982. text ed. 24.95X (ISBN 0-89859-244-5). L Erlbaum Assocs.

Lamb, Michael E. & Sagi, Abraham, eds. Fatherhood & Family Policy. 288p. 1983. text ed. 24.95 (ISBN 0-89859-190-2). L Erlbaum Assocs.

Lamb, Michael E., et al, eds. Social Interaction Analysis: Methodological Issues. LC 78-53287. (Illus.). 336p. 1979. 27.50 (ISBN 0-299-07590-7). U of Wis Pr.

Lamb, Norman. Guide to Teaching Strings. 4th ed. (College Instrumental Technique Ser.). 190p. 1983. text ed. write for info. (ISBN 0-697-03539-5). Wm C Brown.

Lamb, Patricia F. & Hohlwein, Kathryn J. Touchstones: Letters Between Two Women, 1953-1964. LC 81-47662. 288p. 1983. 14.37i (ISBN 0-06-014942-6, HarpT). Har-Row.

Lamb, Peter J., jt. auth. see Hastenrath, Stefan.

Lamb, Pose & Arnold, Richard. Teaching Reading: Foundations & Strategies. 2nd ed. 432p. 1980. text ed. 21.95x (ISBN 0-534-00847-X). Wadsworth Pub.

Lamb, Robert & Rappaport, Stephen. Municipal Bonds: The Comprehensive Review of Tax-Exempt Securities & Municipal Finance. (Illus.). 384p. 1980. 22.00 (ISBN 0-07-036082-0, P&RB). McGraw.

Lamb, Russell, photos by. The Cascades. Beckey, Fred. LC 81-86041. (Illus.). 128p. 1982. 29.50 (ISBN 0-912856-78-5). Graphic Arts Ctr.

--Wyoming. LC 78-51215. (Belding Imprint Ser.). (Illus.). 128p. (Text by Archie Satterfield). 1978. 28.50 (ISBN 0-912856-41-6). Graphic Arts Ctr.

Lamb, Ruth S., ed. see Taylor, Barbara H.

Lamb, Samuel, jt. auth. see Miller, Howard.

Lamb, Samuel H. Native Trees & Shrubs of the Hawaii Islands. Engestrom, Melissa, ed. LC 80-19715. 160p. 1981. pap. 14.95 (ISBN 0-913270-91-1). Sunstone Pr.

--Woody Plants of the Southwest. LC 76-357696. (Illus.). 1977. pap. 12.95 (ISBN 0-913270-50-4). Sunstone Pr.

Lamb, Tony & Duffy, Dave. Retirement Threat. 177p. 1977. text ed. 13.95 (ISBN 0-686-91718-9). Learning Concepts.

Lamb, Walter. Always Begin Where You Are: Themes in Poetry & Song. LC 78-32108. (Illus.). 1979. pap. text ed. 7.96 (ISBN 0-07-035921-0, W); tchrs' manual 2.00 (ISBN 0-07-035922-9). McGraw.

Lambard, Neil. Pocket Dictionary of Banjo Chords. pap. 1.50 (ISBN 0-934286-19-1). Kenyon.

Lambdin, Thomas O. Introduction to Sahidic Coptic. 240p. 1983. 27.95x (ISBN 0-86554-048-9). Mercer Univ Pr.

Lambdin, William. Doublespeak Dictionary. (Orig.). 1979. pap. 6.95 o.p. (ISBN 0-523-40626-6). Pinnacle Bks.

Lambe, T. William. Soil Testing for Engineers. (Soil Engineering Ser.). 165p. 1951. pap. text ed. 30.95x (ISBN 0-471-51183-8). Wiley.

Lambe, T. William & Whitman, Robert V. Soil Mechanics. LC 68-30915. (Soil Engineering Ser). 553p. 1969. 40.95x (ISBN 0-471-51192-7). Wiley.

--Soil Mechanics, SI Version. LC 77-14210. (Geotechnical Engineering Ser.). 553p. 1979. text ed. 40.95x (ISBN 0-471-02491-0). Wiley.

Lambeck. Hydraulic Pumps & Motors. (Mechanical Engineering Ser.). 240p. 1983. price not set. Dekker.

Lambeck, K. The Earth's Variable Rotation. LC 79-7653. (Cambridge Monographs on Mechanics & Applied Mathematics). (Illus.). 400p. 1980. 99.50 (ISBN 0-521-22769-0). Cambridge U Pr.

Lamberg, Walter J. & Lamb, Charles E. Reading Instruction in the Content Areas. 21.95 (ISBN 0-395-30648-5); Instr's. manual 2.00 (ISBN 0-395-30649-3). HM.

Lamberson, L. K., jt. auth. see Kapur, K. C.

Lambert, Adelard. L' Innocente Victime. (Novels by Franco-Americans in New England 1850-1940 Ser.). 82p. (Fr.). (gr. 10 up). 1980. pap. 4.50x (ISBN 0-911409-16-5). Natl Mat Dev.

Lambert, Byron C., ed. The Essential Paul Elmer More: A Selection of His Writings. 1972. 12.95 o.p. (ISBN 0-87000-162-0, Arlington Hse). Crown.

Lambert, Charles J. Sweet Waters, a Chilean Farm. LC 75-14091. (Illus.). 212p. 1975. Repr. of 1952 ed. lib. bdg. 18.50x (ISBN 0-8371-8201-8, LASWA). Greenwood.

Lambert, Clark. Field Selling Skills. LC 81-7526. 271p. 1981. 24.95x (ISBN 0-471-08012-8, Pub. by Ronald Pr). Wiley.

Lambert, Clinton E., Jr., jt. auth. see Lambert, Vickie A.

Lambert, David. The Active Earth. (Illus.). (gr. 3-7). 1982. 8.50 (ISBN 0-688-00924-7). Morrow.

Lambert, David & Halstead, L. B. Dinosaurs. (Easy-Read Fact Bks). (Illus.). 32p. (gr. 2-4). 1982. PLB 8.60 (ISBN 0-531-04371-1). Watts.

Lambert, David & Salt, J. Earthquakes. (Easy-Read Fact Bks). (Illus.). 32p. (gr. 2-4). 1982. PLB 8.60 o.p. (ISBN 0-531-04372-X). Watts.

Lambert, Derek. The Red Dove. LC 82-42837. 270p. 1983. 14.95 (ISBN 0-8128-2913-1). Stein & Day.

Lambert, Douglas M. The Distribution Channels Decision. 197p. pap. 14.95 (ISBN 0-86641-037-6, 78100). Natl Assn Accts.

Lambert, E. N. & Mohammed, M. J. Comprehensive Qualitative Analysis for Advanced Level Chemistry. 1978. pap. text ed. 5.95x o.p. (ISBN 0-435-65537-X). Heinemann Ed.

Lambert, F. W. Graphics-Britain. 1972. 25.00 o.p. (ISBN 0-7137-0554-X). Transatlantic.

Lambert, Frederick. Letter Forms: 110 Complete Alphabets. Menten, Theodore, ed. (Illus.). 9.50 (ISBN 0-8446-4567-2). Peter Smith.

Lambert, Gavin. Running Time. (Illus.). 352p. 1983. 15.95 (ISBN 0-02-567680-6). Macmillan.

Lambert, Hazel. As the Colors Change. 64p. 1972. 4.00 (ISBN 0-911838-24-4). Windy Row.

Lambert, Herbert G., ed. see Plywood Clinic, 3rd, Portland, Mar.1975.

Lambert, Herbert G., ed. see Sawmill Clinic, 4th, New Orleans, Nov. 1974.

Lambert, Hugh K., jt. auth. see Parker, Watson.

Lambert, J. & Muir, T. A. Practical Chemistry. 1973. text ed. 14.50x o.p. (ISBN 0-435-65536-1). Heinemann Ed.

Lambert, J. D. Computational Methods in Ordinary Differential Equations. LC 72-5718. (Introductory Mathematics for Scientists & Engineers Ser.). 278p. 1973. text ed. 41.94x (ISBN 0-471-51194-3, Pub. by Wiley-Interscience). Wiley.

Lambert, Jean, ed. Bibliography of Museum & Art Gallery Publications & Audio Visual Aids in Great Britain & Ireland, 1977. 1978. lib. bdg. 56.00x (ISBN 0-85964-097-3). Somerset Hse.

Lambert, Jean-Henri. Essais D'hygrometrie. Repr. of 1769 ed. 32.00 o.p. (ISBN 0-8287-0496-1). Clearwater Pub.

Lambert, John W. The Long Campaign: History of the 15th Fighter Group in WW 2. 1982. 35.00 (ISBN 0-686-96389-X). MA-AH Pub.

--The Long Campaign: The History of the 15th Fighter Group in WW II. 1982. 35.00x (ISBN 0-89745-032-9). Sunflower U Pr.

Lambert, Joseph B., et al. Organic Structural Analysis. (Illus.). 640p. 1976. text ed. 29.95x (ISBN 0-02-367290-0). Macmillan.

Lambert, Karel & Brittan, Gordon G., Jr. An Introduction to the Philosophy of Science. rev. 2nd ed. 1979. lib. bdg. 24.00 (ISBN 0-917930-37-1); pap. text ed. 8.50x (ISBN 0-917930-17-7). Ridgeview.

Lambert, Karel & Ulrich, William. The Nature of Argument. (Illus.). 1980. text ed. 19.95x (ISBN 0-02-367280-3). Macmillan.

Lambert, Marcus. Pennsylvania German Dictionary. (Illus.). 188p. pap. 15.00 (ISBN 0-916838-07-2). Schiffer.

Lambert, Marcus B. A Dictionary of Non-English Words of the Pennsylvania German Dialect. 1977. 15.00 (ISBN 0-686-79892-9); pap. 8.50 o.p. (ISBN 0-686-79893-7). Penn German Soc.

Lambert, Mark. Fifty Facts About Dinosaurs. (Fifty Facts About Ser.). (Illus.). 32p. (gr. 4-6). 1983. PLB 8.90 (ISBN 0-531-09209-7). Watts.

--Fifty Facts About Space. (Fifty Facts About Ser.). (Illus.). 32p. (gr. 4-6). 1983. PLB 8.90 (ISBN 0-531-09210-0). Watts.

--Rainbow Encyclopedia of Prehistoric Life. (Illus.). 144p. (gr. 4 up). 1982. 9.95 (ISBN 0-528-82388-4). Rand.

--Transport Through the Ages. LC 80-50336. (World of Knowledge Ser.). PLB 16.72 (ISBN 0-382-06410-0). Silver.

Lambert, Michael & Lauper, Lorraine. Behavior Change Research: A Bibliography. 500p. 1980. pap. 8.95 (ISBN 0-932930-26-3). Pilgrimage Inc.

Lambert, Michael J. The Effects of Psychotherapy. Horrobin, D. F., ed. (Annual Research Reviews: Vol. II). 304p. 1982. 24.95 (ISBN 0-89885-099-1). Human Sci Pr.

Lambert, Michael J. & Christensen, Edwin R. The Assessment of Psychotherapy Outcome. (Personality Processes Ser.). 600p. 1983. 39.95 (ISBN 0-471-08383-6, Pub. by Wiley-Interscience). Wiley.

Lambert, Michael J., ed. Psychotherapy & Patient Relationships. LC 82-71876. (Dorsey Professional Ser.). 400p. 1982. 29.95 (ISBN 0-87094-249-2). Dow Jones-Irwin.

Lambert, P. M. & Roger, E. H. Hospital Statistics in Europe. Date not set. 34.00 (ISBN 0-444-86383-4). Elsevier.

Lambert, Paul F., jt. auth. see Franks, Kenny A.

Lambert, R. M., jt. auth. see Thomas, J. M.

Lambert, Regina. Every Woman Has a Ministry. LC 79-84321. 1979. pap. 2.50 (ISBN 0-89221-062-1). New Leaf.

--Valerie's Adventure at Crystal Lake. LC 23-892. 128p. (gr. 6-9). 1980. pap. 2.95 (ISBN 0-8024-3937-3). Moody.

--Valerie's Adventure at the Last Chance Mine. LC 82-2107. 128p. 1982. pap. 2.95 (ISBN 0-8024-3938-1). Moody.

--Valerie's Wilderness Adventure. LC 78-9027. 1978. 2.95 (ISBN 0-8024-3936-5). Moody.

Lambert, Richard D., jt. auth. see Lyons, Gene M.

Lambert, Richard D., ed. America's Most Challenging Objectives. LC 76-160739. (Annals Ser.: 396). 1971. 15.00 (ISBN 0-87761-140-8); pap. 7.95 (ISBN 0-87761-139-4). Am Acad Pol Soc Sci.

--China in the World Today. LC 72-78295. (Annals Ser.: 402). 300p. 1972. pap. 7.95 (ISBN 0-87761-150-5). Am Acad Pol Soc Sci.

--New Directions in International Education. LC 80-65243. (The Annals of the American Academy of Political & Social Science: No. 449). 1980. 15.00 (ISBN 0-87761-250-1); pap. text ed. 7.95 (ISBN 0-87761-251-X). Am Acad Pol Soc.

Lambert, Richard D. & Hoselitz, Bert F., eds. The Role of Savings & Wealth in Southern Asia & the West. 432p. 1963. pap. 9.50 (ISBN 0-686-94180-2, U945, UNESCO). Unipub.

Lambert, Richard D., jt. ed. see Alexander, Herbert E.

Lambert, Richard D., jt. ed. see Altbach, Philip G.

Lambert, Richard D., ed. see American Academy of Political & Social Science Annual Meeting, 82nd.

Lambert, Richard D., ed. see American Academy of Political & Social Science, 78th.

Lambert, Richard D., ed. see American Academy of Political & Social Science, 79th.

Lambert, Richard D., jt. ed. see Barber, Bernard.

Lambert, Richard D., jt. ed. see Blake, David H.

Lambert, Richard D., ed. see Bradway, John S.

Lambert, Richard D., jt. ed. see Bressler, Marvin.

Lambert, Richard D., ed. see Charlesworth, James C.

Lambert, Richard D., jt. ed. see Charlesworth, James C.

Lambert, Richard D., jt. ed. see Clemente, Frank.

Lambert, Richard D., jt. ed. see Cook, Philip J.

Lambert, Richard D., ed. see Ferman, Louis A.

Lambert, Richard D., jt. ed. see Fox, Renee C.

Lambert, Richard D., jt. ed. see Fox, William T.

Lambert, Richard D., jt. ed. see Galnoor, Itzhal.

Lambert, Richard D., jt. ed. see Gordon, Milton M.

Lambert, Richard D., jt. ed. see Greenberg, Jack.

Lambert, Richard D., jt. ed. see Gross, Bertram M.

Lambert, Richard D., ed. see Hart, Parker T.

Lambert, Richard D., jt. ed. see Heisler, Martin O.

Lambert, Richard D., jt. ed. see Holland, Kenneth.

Lambert, Richard D., jt. ed. see Hollingsworth, J. Rogers.

Lambert, Richard D., jt. ed. see Laconte, M. Pierre.

Lambert, Richard D., jt. ed. see Lamberton, Donald M.

Lambert, Richard D., jt. ed. see Martin, L. John.

Lambert, Richard D., jt. ed. see Mott, George F.

Lambert, Richard D., jt. ed. see Ornstein, Norman J.

Lambert, Richard D., jt. ed. see Park, Richard L.

Lambert, Richard D., jt. ed. see Sherman, Lawrence W.

Lambert, Richard D., ed. see Shur, Irene G. & Littell, Franklin H.

Lambert, Richard D., jt. ed. see Taeuber, Conrad.

Lambert, Richard D., jt. ed. see Weintraub, Sidney.

Lambert, Richard D., ed. see Wilcox, Wayne.

Lambert, Richard D., jt. ed. see Windmuller, John P.

Lambert, Richard D., jt. ed. see Wolfgang, Marvin E.

Lambert, Richard D., jt. ed. see Yarmolinsky, Adam.

Lambert, Rosemary. The Twentieth Century. LC 80-40456. (Cambridge Introduction to the History of Art: No. 7). (Illus.). 90p. 1981. 19.95 (ISBN 0-521-22715-1); pap. 7.50 (ISBN 0-521-29622-6). Cambridge U Pr.

Lambert, Stephen. Channel Four: Television with a Difference. 152p. 1982. 22.00 (ISBN 0-85170-141-8); pap. 10.95 (ISBN 0-85170-124-8). NY Zoetrope.

Lambert, Susan, jt. auth. see Schniedman, Rose.

Lambert, Vickie A. & Lambert, Clinton E., Jr. The Impact of Physical Illness & Related Mental Health Concepts. (Illus.). 1979. pap. 16.95 ref. ed. (ISBN 0-13-451732-6). P-H.

Lambert, Wallace E., jt. auth. see Lambert, William W.

Lambert, Wallace E., et al. Child Rearing Values: A Cross National Study. LC 78-19747. 1979. 33.95 o.p. (ISBN 0-03-049086-3). Praeger.

Lambert, Wilfred G. Babylonian Wisdom Literature. (Illus.). 1960. 49.95x (ISBN 0-19-815424-0). Oxford U Pr.

Lambert, Willa. Love's Golden Spell. (Superromances Ser.). 384p. 1983. pap. 2.95 (ISBN 0-373-70059-8, Pub. by Worldwide). Harlequin Bks.

Lambert, William W. & Lambert, Wallace E. Social Psychology. 2nd ed. (Foundations of Modern Psychology Ser.). (Illus.). 192p. (Reference eds.). 1973. ref. ed. op 16.95 (ISBN 0-13-818021-0); pap. 10.95 (ISBN 0-13-818013-X). P-H.

Lambert, Yvon & Barthes, Roland. Cy Twombly: A Catologue Raisome. (Illus.). 222p. 1983. 95.00 (ISBN 0-8390-0305-6). Allanheld & Schram.

Lamberth, John. Social Psychology. (Illus.). 1980. text ed. 22.95x (ISBN 0-02-367310-9). Macmillan.

Lambertini, Adrain, jt. auth. see Choe, Boum Jone.

Lambert-Legace, Louise. Feeding Your Child: From Infancy to Six Years Old. LC 82-12889. 233p. 1983. pap. 9.95 (ISBN 0-8253-0119-X). Beaufort Bks NY.

Lamberton, Donald M. & Lambert, Richard D., eds. The Information Revolution. LC 73-89781. (The Annals of the American Academy of Political & Social Science: No. 412). 300p. 1974. pap. 7.95 (ISBN 0-87761-175-0). Am Acad Pol Soc Sci.

Lamberton, Robert, tr. Cave of Nymphs: Porphry. 64p. (Orig.). 1983. 10.00 (ISBN 0-930794-71-0); pap. 4.95 (ISBN 0-930794-72-9). Station Hill Pr.

Lamberts, J. J. A Short Introduction to English Usage. LC 80-28499. 400p. 1981. Repr. lib. bdg. 18.00 (ISBN 0-89874-328-1). Krieger.

--Short Introduction to English Usage. 1971. text ed. 13.95 o.p. (ISBN 0-07-036083-9, C). McGraw.

Lamberts, Steven W. & MacLeod, Robert M. Physiological & Pathological Aspects of Prolactin Secretion, Vol. 1. Horrobin, David F., ed. (Annual Research Reviews Ser.). 1978. 19.20 (ISBN 0-88831-034-X). Eden Pr.

Lambeth, Ida M., ed. Directory of Texas Manufacturers, 1983, 2 Vols. LC 34-27861. 1200p. Date not set. Set. pap. 85.00 (ISBN 0-686-83437-2). U of Tex Busn Res.

Lambeth, Joseph. Lambeth Method of Cake Decoration & Practical Pastries. (Illus.). 1980. 55.00x (ISBN 0-911202-24-2). Radio City.

Lambeth, M. Strawcraft. 72p. 1974. 9.95 o.p. (ISBN 0-212-97010-0). Transatlantic.

Lambie, Beatrice R. The Mackenzie: River to the Top of the World. LC 67-10040. (Rivers of the World Ser.). (Illus.). (gr. 4-7). 1967. PLB 3.98 (ISBN 0-8116-6369-8). Garrard.

Lamblin, Simone. The World We Live In. Wald, Susan, tr. (Illus.). (gr. 9-12). 9.95 (ISBN 0-686-94009-1). Larousse.

Lamborn, E. A. Poetic Values: A Guide to the Appreciation of the Golden Treasury. 226p. 1982. Repr. of 1928 ed. lib. bdg. 25.00 (ISBN 0-89984-805-2). Century Bookbindery.

Lamborn, F., tr. see Lindgren, Astrid.

Lamborn, Kathleen R., jt. auth. see Tashman, Leonard J.

Lambourne, Lionel. Ernest Griset: Fantasies of a Victorian Illustrator. (Illus.). 1979. pap. 8.95 o.p. (ISBN 0-500-27160-7). Thames Hudson.

--Introduction to Caricature. (The Victoria & Albert Museum Introductions to the Decorative Arts). (Illus.). 48p. 1983. 9.95 (ISBN 0-88045-018-5). Stemmer Hse.

--Introduction to Victorian Genre Painting. (The Victoria & Albert Museum Introductions to the Decorative Arts Ser.). (Illus.). 48p. 1982. 9.95 (ISBN 0-88045-009-6). Stemmer Hse.

--Utopian Craftsmen. 232p. 1982. pap. 14.95 (ISBN 0-442-25977-8). Van Nos Reinhold.

Lambrecht, Richard M. & Morcos, Nabil, eds. Nuclear & Radiochemistry Applications. LC 82-9111. (Illus.). 592p. 1982. 85.00 (ISBN 0-08-027544-3, E125); 68.00 (ISBN 0-08-029389-1). Pergamon.

Lambright, W. Henry, et al. Technology Transfer to Cities: Process of Choice at the Local Level. (Special Studies in Public Policy & Public Systems Management). 1979. lib. bdg. 24.00 (ISBN 0-89158-366-1). Westview.

Lambro, Donald. The Conscience of a Young Conservative. 1976. 6.95 o.p. (ISBN 0-87000-344-5, Arlington Hse). Crown.

--Fat City: How Washington Wastes Your Taxes. LC 79-66498. 336p. 1980. 12.95 (ISBN 0-89526-680-6). Regnery-Gateway.

Lambton, Ann K. Persian Vocabulary. 1954-1962. pap. 24.95x (ISBN 0-521-09154-3). Cambridge U Pr.

Lambuth, David, et al. The Golden Book of Writing. (Handbooks Ser). 1976. pap. 2.95 (ISBN 0-14-046263-5). Penguin.

Lamdin, Louis S., ed. see Demarest, David P.

Lameijer, J., jt. auth. see Cockroft, A. N.

Lameijer, J. N., jt. auth. see Cockroft, A. N.

Lamennais, Hughes F. Words of a Believer & the Past & Future of the People. vi, 208p. 1972. Repr. of 1891 ed. 15.00 o.p. (ISBN 0-86527-212-3). Fertig.

Lamerton, Richard. Care of the Dying. 1981. pap. 4.50 o.p. (ISBN 0-14-022275-8). Penguin.

La Mettrie, Julien O. Man a Machine. 216p. (Fr. & Eng.). 16.00 (ISBN 0-87548-040-3); pap. 6.00 (ISBN 0-87548-041-1). Open Court.

La Mettrie, Julien O. De see La Mettrie, Julien O.

Lamey, C. A. Metallic & Industrial Mineral Deposits. 1966. text ed. 28.00 o.p. (ISBN 0-07-036091-X, C). McGraw.

Lamie, Edward L. PL One Programming. 352p. 1981. pap. text ed. 18.95x (ISBN 0-534-01067-9). Wadsworth Pub.

Laming, D. J., jt. auth. see Durrance, E. M.

Lamiral, D. H. Memoire sur le Senegal. (Bibliotheque Africaine Ser.). 52p. (Fr.). 1974. Repr. of 1791 ed. lib. bdg. 24.00x o.p. (ISBN 0-8287-0497-X, 72-2107). Clearwater Pub.

Lamiral, Dominique-Harcourt. L' Afrique et le Peuple Africain Consideres sous Tous Leurs Rapports avec Notre Commerce et Nos Colonies. (Bibliotheque Africaine Ser. & Slave Trade in France, 1744-1848, Ser.). 412p. (Fr.). 1974. Repr. of 1789 ed. lib. bdg. 104.50 o.p. (ISBN 0-8287-0498-8, 72-2126). Clearwater Pub.

Lamit, Gary. Descriptive Geometry. (Illus.). 464p. 1983. 21.95 (ISBN 0-13-199802-1); pap. 14.95 (ISBN 0-13-199828-5). P-H.

--Industrial Model Building. (Illus.). 528p. 1981. text ed. 30.95 (ISBN 0-13-461566-2). P-H.

Lamkin, Selma. Do It Right the First Time: Guide to Computer Installation. Date not set. 6.00 (ISBN 0-686-37906-3). Nikmal Pub.

Lamley, Harry J., ed. East Asian Occasional Papers, 2 Vols. Incl. Vol. 1. (Asian Studies at Hawaii: No. 3). 180p. 1969. o.p. (ISBN 0-87022-443-3); Vol. 2. (Asian Studies at Hawaii: No. 4). 176p. 1970 (ISBN 0-87022-444-1). pap. 5.50x ea. UH Pr.

Lamm, Joanne. The Quarter of Six Cookbook. 96p. 1982. 4.95 (ISBN 0-932128-03-3). Lamm Morada.

Lamm, Maurice. Jewish Way in Death & Mourning. rev. ed. LC 69-11684. 1972. pap. 6.95 (ISBN 0-8246-0126-2). Jonathan David.

--The Jewish Way in Love & Marriage. LC 79-1760. 1980. 14.95i o.p. (ISBN 0-06-064916-X, HarpR). Har-Row.

Lamm, Robert P., jt. auth. see Schaefer, Richard T.

Lamm, Stanley S., et al. Learning Disabilities Explained: The Lamm Institute's Guide to Diagnosis, Remediation, & Help for Your Learning Disabled Child. LC 82-45232. 288p. 1982. 16.95 (ISBN 0-385-15781-9). Doubleday.

Lamm, Ursula, tr. see Bauer, Arnold.

Lamm, Vanda, jt. ed. see Peteri, Zoltan.

Lamm, Zvi. Conflicting Theories of Instruction: Conceptual Dimensions. LC 76-9238. 1976. 21.75x (ISBN 0-8211-1112-4); text ed. 19.50x (ISBN 0-685-73826-4). McCutchan.

Lammarque, J. L. & Bruel, J. M. Abdominal Computerized Tomography. (International Congress Ser.: No. 463). 1980. 101.00 (ISBN 0-444-90083-7). Elsevier.

Lamme, Linda L., et al. Raising Readers: A Guide to Sharing Literature with Young Children. 192p. 1980. 11.95 (ISBN 0-8027-0654-1). Walker & Co.

Lammers, Bernard. The Teaching of Legislative Drafting & Process in U.S. Law Schools. 1977. pap. 5.00 o.p. (ISBN 0-910058-87-3). Am Bar Foun.

Lammers, Herbert B., jt. auth. see Woodruff, Everett B.

Lammers, Stanton M. The Last Gunsmoke. 1979. 7.95 o.p. (ISBN 0-533-04252-6). Vantage.

Lammers, William. Public Policy & the Aging. 250p. 1983. pap. 7.95 (ISBN 0-87187-246-3). Congr Quarterly.

Lammich, G. & Kadow, H. Warm up for Soccer. LC 74-31697. (Illus.). 128p. (gr. 5 up). 1975. 9.95 (ISBN 0-8069-4090-5); PLB 12.49 (ISBN 0-8069-4091-3). Sterling.

Lamming, George. Season of Adventure. 368p. 14.95 (ISBN 0-8052-8012-X, Pub. by Allison & Busby England); pap. 6.95 (ISBN 0-8052-8035-9). Schocken.

Lamnin, Marlene. Quality Assurance in Hospital Pharmacy: Strategies & Techniques. LC 82-18167. 224p. 1982. 25.00 (ISBN 0-89443-925-1). Aspen Systems.

Lamoitier, J. P. BASIC Exercises for the Atari. 250p. 1983. pap. 12.95 (ISBN 0-89588-101-2); pap. text ed. 12.95. Sybex.

--Basic Exercises for the IBM Personal Computer. LC 82-60234. (Illus.). 252p. (Orig.). 1982. pap. text ed. 13.95 (ISBN 0-89588-088-1). Sybex.

LaMond, Annette M. Competition in the General-Freight Motor-Carrier Industry. LC 79-3048. 128p. 1980. 19.95x (ISBN 0-669-03308-1). Lexington Bks.

LaMond, Annette M., jt. ed. see Wallace, Phyllis A.

La Monica, Elaine. Nursing Leadership & Management: An Experiential Approach. 300p. 1983. text ed. 22.95 (ISBN 0-534-01337-6). Brooks-Cole.

Lamont, Corliss. Freedom Is As Freedom Does. LC 74-171384. (Civil Liberties in American History Ser.). 1972. Repr. of 1956 ed. lib. bdg. 42.50 (ISBN 0-306-70497-8). Da Capo.

--Humanist Funeral Service. LC 77-76001. 48p. 1977. 7.95o.p. (ISBN 0-87975-093-6); pap. 4.95 (ISBN 0-87975-090-1). Prometheus Bks.

Lamont, Corliss, jt. auth. see Lamb, Helen B.

Lamont, Douglas F. Foreign State Enterprises: A Threat to American Business. LC 78-19818. 1979. 12.95x o.s.i. (ISBN 0-465-02482-3). Basic.

LaMont, M. Dean. A Safe House Electronically. radio shack ed. (Illus.). 128p. 1979. 1.75 o.p. (ISBN 0-89512-036-4). Tex Instr Inc.

La Mont, M. Dean. Understanding Electronic Security Systems. LC 82-50800. (Understanding Ser.). (Illus.). 128p. 1982. pap. 6.95 (ISBN 0-686-84790-3, 7201). Tex Instr Inc.

Lamont, Marianne. Nine Moons Wasted. LC 76-43147. 1976. 8.95 o.p. (ISBN 0-399-11848-9). Putnam Pub Group.

Lamont, W. D. Law & the Moral Order. 150p. 1981. 22.00 (ISBN 0-08-025742-9); pap. 12.00 (ISBN 0-08-025746-1). Pergamon.

Lamont, William & Oldfield, Sybil, eds. Politics, Religion & Literature in the Seventeenth Century. (Rowman & Littlefield University Library). 248p. 1975. 13.75 o.p. (ISBN 0-87471-575-X); pap. 7.00x (ISBN 0-87471-576-8). Rowman.

Lamont, William D. The Value Judgement. LC 72-11738. 335p. 1974. Repr. of 1955 ed. lib. bdg. 17.50x (ISBN 0-8371-6709-4, LAVJ). Greenwood.

Lamorisse, Albert. Red Balloon. LC 57-9229. (Illus.). (gr. 3-5). 10.95 (ISBN 0-385-00343-9). Doubleday.

L'Amorosa, Ero. The Madrigal Collection L'amorosa Ero (Brescia, 1588) Lincoln, Harry B., ed. LC 66-64728. 1968. 22.50x (ISBN 0-87395-030-5). State U NY Pr.

La Morte, Michael W. School Law: Cases & Concepts. (Illus.). 448p. 1982. 25.95 (ISBN 0-13-793695-8). P-H.

Lamot, Clare, ed. see Scott, Walter.

Lamott, Anne. Hard Laughter. 1981. pap. 2.95 o.p. (ISBN 0-451-11072-2, AE1072, Sig). NAL.

Lamour, Dorothy. Dorothy Lamour: My Side of the Road. LC 79-26300. (Illus.). 300p. 1980. 12.95 o.p. (ISBN 0-13-218594-6). P-H.

L'Amour, Lewis. Bowdrie. 1983. pap. 2.95. Bantam.

L'Amour, Louis. The Cherokee Trail. 1982. 12.95 (ISBN 0-553-05029-X); pap. 2.95 (ISBN 0-553-20846-2). Bantam.

--The Cherokee Trail. (General Ser.). 1983. lib. bdg. 12.95 (ISBN 0-8161-3464-2, Large Print Bks). G K Hall.

--Complete L'Amour, 9 bks. Incl. To Tame a Land; Heller With a Gun; The Tall Stranger; Last Stand at Papago Wells; Hondo; Kilkenny; Showdown at Yellow Butte; Utah Blaine; Crossfire Trail. (Western Fiction Ser.). 1981. Repr. of 1978 ed. Set. lib. bdg. 74.50 (ISBN 0-8398-2662-1, Gregg). G K Hall.

--Conagher. Date not set. pap. 2.50 (ISBN 0-553-22843-9). Bantam.

--Crossfire Trail. 1980. lib. bdg. 9.95 (ISBN 0-8398-2691-5, Gregg). G K Hall.

--Heller With a Gun. 1981. lib. bdg. 11.95 (ISBN 0-8398-2696-6, Gregg). G K Hall.

--Hondo. 1978. lib. bdg. 10.95 (ISBN 0-8398-2452-1, Gregg). G K Hall.

--Iron Marshall. (gr. 7-12). 1979. lib. bdg. 12.95 o.p. (ISBN 0-8161-3015-9, Large Print Bks). G K Hall.

--Kilkenny. 1980. lib. bdg. 9.95 (ISBN 0-8398-2692-3, Gregg). G K Hall.

--L'Amour Westerns, 4 bks. Incl. To Tame a Land; Heller With a Gun; The Tall Stranger; Last Stand at Papago Wells. (Western Fiction Ser.). 1981. Set. lib. bdg. 40.00 (ISBN 0-8398-2661-3, Gregg). G K Hall.

--Last Stand at Papago Wells. 1981. lib. bdg. 10.95 (ISBN 0-8398-2694-X, Gregg). G K Hall.

--Lonely on the Mountain. (General Ser.). 1981. lib. bdg. 11.95 (ISBN 0-8161-3247-X, Large Print Bks). G K Hall.

--The Lonesome Gods. 464p. 1983. 14.95 (ISBN 0-553-05014-1). Bantam.

--The Mountain Valley War. 208p. 1982. pap. 2.50 (ISBN 0-553-23219-3). Bantam.

--Reilly's Luck. 224p. (Orig.). 1982. pap. 2.50 (ISBN 0-553-22674-6, Y13589-9). Bantam.

--The Shadow Riders. 192p. 1982. pap. 2.95 (ISBN 0-553-23132-4). Bantam.

--Showdown at Yellow Butte. 1980. lib. bdg. 9.95 (ISBN 0-8398-2690-7, Gregg). G K Hall.

--Sitka. 1983. pap. 2.50 (ISBN 0-553-20725-3). Bantam.

--Taggart. 160p. 1982. pap. 2.50 (ISBN 0-553-22799-8, 13372-1). Bantam.

--The Tall Stranger. 1981. lib. bdg. 10.95 (ISBN 0-8398-2695-8, Gregg). G K Hall.

--To Tame a Land. 1981. lib. bdg. 11.95 (ISBN 0-8398-2697-4, Gregg). G K Hall.

--Utah Blaine. 1980. lib. bdg. 9.95 (ISBN 0-8398-2693-1, Gregg). G K Hall.

Lamparski, Richard. Whatever Became of....? (Eighth Ser.). (Illus.). 320p. 1982. 17.95 (ISBN 0-517-54346-X); pap. 8.95 (ISBN 0-517-54855-0). Crown.

Lampe, Geoffrey W. Explorations in Theology. (Student Christian Movement Press Ser.). (Orig.). 1981. pap. 11.95x (ISBN 0-19-520353-4). Oxford U Pr.

Lampe, Gerald N., jt. auth. see Mannheimer, Jeffrey S.

Lampert, Lyndon J., jt. auth. see McLeod, Robert W.

Lamphear, John. The Traditional History of the Jie of Uganda. (Oxford Studies in African Affairs). (Illus.). 1976. 42.50x (ISBN 0-19-821692-0). Oxford U Pr.

Lamphere, Louise, jt. ed. see Rosaldo, Michelle Z.

Lamphier, Timothy A. Guidelines for Medical & Surgical Emergencies. (Illus.). 700p. 1983. lib. bdg. write for info (ISBN 0-89352-173-6). Masson Pub.

Lamping, Ed. The Awareness Book. (Illus.). 40p. (gr. 3-6). 1982. 5.00 (ISBN 0-940444-15-1). Kabyn.

Lamplugh, B. Trans-Siberia by Rail. (Illus.). 155p. 1979. pap. 7.95 (ISBN 0-903909-07-3). Bradt Ent.

Lamplugh, Barbara. Kathmandu by Truck. (Illus.). 1976. pap. 6.95 (ISBN 0-903909-03-0, Roger Lascelles). Bradt Ent.

Lampman, Archibald. The Poems of Archibald Lampman. Incl. At the Long Sault. LC 73-92517. (Literature of Canada Ser.). 1974. 25.00x o.p. (ISBN 0-8020-2074-7). U of Toronto Pr.

Lampman, Ben H. Coming of the Pond Fishes. 12.50 (ISBN 0-8323-0341-0). Binford.

--A Leaf from French Eddy: On Fish, Anglers & Fisherman. LC 78-15836. (Illus.). 1979. 7.95i o.p. (ISBN 0-06-250500-9, HarpR). Har-Row.

Lampman, Linda & Sterling, Julie. The Portland Guidebook. LC 78-17274. (Illus.). 1978. pap. 4.95 (ISBN 0-916076-42-3). Writing.

Lampo, Hubert. The Coming of Joachim Stiller. (International Studies & Translations Ser.). 1974. lib. bdg. 9.95 o.p. (ISBN 0-8057-3416-3, Twayne). G K Hall.

Lamport, F. J. Lessing & the Drama. 1981. text ed. 36.00x (ISBN 0-19-815767-3). Oxford U Pr.

Lamport, Felicia & Gorey, Edward. Light Metres. (Illus.). 128p. 1982. 10.95 (ISBN 0-89696-090-0, An Everest House Book); limited ed. 60.00 (ISBN 0-89696-168-0). Dodd.

Lamprecht, Hartmut, jt. auth. see Frobish, Dieter.

Lamprecht, Sterling P., ed. see Hobbes, Thomas.

Lamprey, Hugh F. The Distribution of Protected Areas in Relation to the Needs of Biotic Community Conservation in Eastern Africa. (Illus.). 1975. pap. 9.00 (ISBN 2-88032-038-0, IUCN4, IUCN). Unipub.

Lamprey, Louise. Children of Ancient Gaul. LC 60-16708. (Illus.). (gr. 7-11). 8.00x (ISBN 0-8196-0109-8). Biblo.

--Children of Ancient Rome. LC 61-12876. (Illus.). (gr. 7-11). 8.00x (ISBN 0-8196-0114-4). Biblo.

Lampson, Judith. Sparks of Light. LC 81-81943. 144p. 1983. pap. 6.95 (ISBN 0-86666-028-3). GWP.

Lampton. Black Holes & Other Secrets of the Universe. (gr. 7 up). 1980. PLB 8.90 (ISBN 0-531-02284-6). Watts.

--Meterology. 1981. 8.90 (ISBN 0-531-04260-X). Watts.

Lampton, Christopher. Dinosaurs & the Age of Reptiles. (First Bk.). (Illus.). 96p. (gr. 4 up). 1983. PLB 8.90 (ISBN 0-531-04526-9). Watts.

--Fusion: The Eternal Flame. LC 82-4828. (Illus.). 96p. (gr. 7 up). 1982. PLB 8.90 (ISBN 0-531-04485-8). Watts.

--Planet Earth. (First Bks). (Illus.). 72p. (gr. 4 up). 1982. PLB 8.90 (ISBN 0-531-04387-8). Watts.

--Space Sciences. (A Reference First Bk.). (Illus.). 96p. (gr. 4 up). 1983. PLB 8.90 (ISBN 0-531-04539-0). Watts.

--The Sun. (First Bks). (Illus.). 72p. (gr. 4 up). 1982. PLB 8.90 (ISBN 0-531-04390-8). Watts.

Lampugnani, Vittorio M. Architecture of the Twentieth Century in Drawings. LC 82-42534. (Illus.). 192p. 1982. 35.00 (ISBN 0-8478-0464-X). Rizzoli Intl.

Lamsa, George M. Holy Bible from the Peshitta. 16.95 (ISBN 0-87981-026-2); lea. bndg. 35.95 (ISBN 0-87981-084-X). Holman.

--Idioms in the Bible Explained: A Key to the Holy Scriptures. 1978. pap. 2.50 (ISBN 0-87981-095-5). Holman.

--New Testament. 5.95 o.s.i. (ISBN 0-87981-085-8); pap. 5.95 (ISBN 0-686-66452-3). Holman.

--New Testament Commentary: Acts to Revelation. 11.95 (ISBN 0-87981-049-1). Holman.

--Pearls of Wisdom. 1978. pap. 2.50 o.p. (ISBN 0-87516-270-3). De Vorss.

Lamson-Scribner, Frank H., Jr. Industrial Project Analysis: Case Studies. xiii, 211p. 1977. pap. 5.00 (ISBN 0-686-36184-9). World Bank.

Lamson-Scribner, Frank H., Jr. & Huang, John, eds. Municipal Water Supply Project Analysis: Case Studies. ix, 520p. 1977. pap. 8.50 (ISBN 0-686-36158-X). World Bank.

Lamstein, Joel, jt. auth. see Hirschnorn, Nobert.

Lamstein, Joel, jt. auth. see Hirschhorn, Norbert.

Lamy, A. Enquete sur le Francais des Eleves de Sixieme. (Black Africa Ser.). 79p. (Fr.). 1974. Repr. of 1970 ed. lib. bdg. 30.50x o.p. (ISBN 0-8287-0499-6, 71-2005). Clearwater Pub.

Lamy, A. & Berthet, P. Cours et Exercices Pour les Stages de Recyclage des Moniteurs. (Black Africa Ser.). 153p. (Fr.). 1974. Repr. of 1970 ed. lib. bdg. 47.00 o.p. (ISBN 0-8287-0500-3, 71-2006). Clearwater Pub.

--L' Expression du Temps. (Black Africa Ser.). 89p. (Fr.). 1974. Repr. of 1970 ed. lib. bdg. 35.00x o.p. (ISBN 0-8287-0501-1, 71-2007). Clearwater Pub.

Lamy, A. & Duponchel, L. Exercices Structuraux: Quatre Lecons Radiodiffusees. (Black Africa Ser.). 30p. (Fr.). 1974. Repr. of 1971 ed. lib. bdg. 19.00x o.p. (ISBN 0-8287-1373-1, 71-2010). Clearwater Pub.

Lamy, B. De l'Art de Parler. (Linguistics 13th-18th Centuries Ser.). 288p. (Fr.). 1974. Repr. of 1675 ed. lib. bdg. 77.00x o.p. (ISBN 0-8287-0502-X, 71-5016). Clearwater Pub.

Lan, David. Sergeant Ola & His Followers. 1981. pap. 5.95 (ISBN 0-413-47590-5). Methuen Inc.

Lana, R. E. The Foundations of Psychological Theory. LC 76-13446. 177p. 1976. 14.95x o.s.i. (ISBN 0-470-15122-6). Halsted Pr.

Lana, Robert, ed. see Goldstein, Jeffrey H.

Lancashire, Douglas. Li Po-Yuan. (World Authors Ser.). 1981. lib. bdg. 15.95 (ISBN 0-8057-6449-6, Twayne). G K Hall.

Lancashire, Ian. Dramatic Texts & Records of Britain: A Chronological Topography to 1558. (Studies in Early English Drama). 320p. 1983. 50.00x (ISBN 0-686-79615-2). U of Toronto Pr.

Lancaster, Bob & Hall, B. C. Judgement Day. LC 80-80381. 224p. 1982. 12.95 (ISBN 0-87223-797-4). Playboy.

Lancaster, Bruce. Trumpet to Arms. 1976. pap. 1.75 o.p. (ISBN 0-523-00887-2). Pinnacle Bks.

Lancaster, Bruce & Plumb, John H. American Heritage Book of the Revolution. 1965. pap. 2.25 (ISBN 0-440-90114-6, LE). Dell.

Lancaster, Clay. The American Bungalow: 1880 to 1920's. (Illus.). 224p. 1983. 29.95 (ISBN 0-89659-340-1). Abbeville Pr.

--East Hampton's Heritage: An Illustrated Architectural Record. 1982. 25.00 (ISBN 0-393-01572-6); pap. 12.95 (ISBN 0-393-30058-7). Norton.

--The Japanese Influence in America. LC 82-22650. (Illus.). 314p. 1983. Repr. of 1963 ed. 39.95 (ISBN 0-89659-342-8). Abbeville Pr.

--Nantucket in the Nineteenth Century. LC 77-75512. (Illus.). 1979. pap. 7.95 (ISBN 0-486-23747-8). Dover.

Lancaster, Clay & Grow, Lawrence, eds. Waiting for Five O Five: Terminal, Station, & Depot in America. LC 76-56632. (Illus.). 1977. 12.50x (ISBN 0-87663-283-5, Main Street); pap. 6.95 (ISBN 0-87663-957-0). Universe.

Lancaster, F. W. Information Retrieval Systems: Characteristics, Testing & Evaluation. 2nd ed. LC 78-11078. (Information Sciences Ser.). 381p. 1979. 36.95x (ISBN 0-471-04673-6, Pub. by Wiley-Interscience). Wiley.

--Libraries & Librarians in on Age of Electronics. LC 82-81403. (Illus.). ix, 229p. 1982. text ed. 22.50 (ISBN 0-87815-040-4). Info Resources.

Lancaster, F. W. & Fayen, E. G. Information Retrieval On-Line. LC 73-9697. (Information Sciences Ser.). 597p. 1973. 32.95 o.p. (ISBN 0-471-51235-4, Pub. by Wiley-Interscience). Wiley.

Lancaster, F. W., ed. see Library Applications of Data Processing Clinic, 1979.

Lancaster, Fidelity. The Bedouin. LC 78-2679. (Civilization Library). (Illus.). (gr. 5 up). 1978. PLB 9.40 s&l (ISBN 0-531-01447-9, Warwick Pr). Watts.

Lancaster, H. O. An Introduction to Medical Statistics. LC 73-11323. (Ser. in Probability & Mathematical Statistics). 305p. 1974. 36.00 o.p. (ISBN 0-471-51250-8, Pub. by Wiley-Interscience). Wiley.

Lancaster, J. F. Metallurgy of Welding. 3rd ed. (Illus.). 272p. 1980. text ed. 45.00x (ISBN 0-04-669008-5); pap. text ed. 22.95x (ISBN 0-04-669009-3). Allen Unwin.

Lancaster, Jan, et al, eds. see Phillips, Marjorie.

Lancaster, Janet & Gaunt, Joan. Developments in Early Childhood Education. (Changing Classroom). 1976. text ed. 11.75x o.p. (ISBN 0-7291-0027-8); pap. text ed. 4.75x o.p. (ISBN 0-7291-0022-7). Humanities.

Lancaster, Jeanette. Adult Psychiatric Nursing. (Current Clinical Nursing Ser.). 1979. 25.00 (ISBN 0-87488-599-X); pap. 18.00 (ISBN 0-87488-577-9). Med Exam.

Lancaster, Jeanette & Lancaster, Wade. Concepts for Advanced Nursing Practice: The Nurse As a Change Agent. 1st ed. LC 81-14061. (Illus.). 476p. 1981. pap. text ed. 14.95 (ISBN 0-8016-2832-6). Mosby.

Lancaster, John. Lettering Techniques. LC 82-82920. (Illus.). 120p. 1983. pap. 7.95 (ISBN 0-668-05716-5, 5716). Arco.

Lancaster, Kathleen L., ed. International Telecommunications: User Requirements & Supplier Strategies. LC 81-48462. (An Arthur D. Little Bk.). 208p. 1982. 24.95x (ISBN 0-669-05368-6). Lexington Bks.

Lancaster, Larry E. The Patient with End Stage Renal Disease. LC 78-23659. 349p. 1979. 26.00x (ISBN 0-471-03564-5, Pub. by Wiley Medical). Wiley.

Lancaster, Lewis & Lai, Whalen, eds. Early Ch'an in China & Tibet. 1983. 25.00 (ISBN 0-89581-152-9). Lancaster-Miller.

Lancaster, Lewis, jt. ed. see Conze, Edward.

Lancaster, Lewis R., ed. The Korean Buddhist Canon: A Descriptive Catalogue. LC 75-40662. 1980. 50.00x (ISBN 0-520-03159-8). U of Cal Pr.

Lancaster, Lydia. Desire & Dreams of Glory. (Orig.). 1979. pap. 2.50 o.s.i. (ISBN 0-446-81549-7). Warner Bks.

--Heaven's Horizon. 464p. 1983. pap. 3.50 (ISBN 0-446-90581-X). Warner Bks.

--Stolen Rapture. (Orig.). 1978. pap. 2.50 o.p. (ISBN 0-446-81777-5). Warner Bks.

Lancaster, Osbert. A Cartoon History of Architecture. LC 75-19929. (Illus.). 1975. 11.95 (ISBN 0-87645-092-3). Gambit.

Lancaster, Osbert, jt. auth. see Scott-James, Anne.

Lancaster, Roy. Plant Hunting in Nepal. (Illus.). 194p. 1981. 19.00x o.p. (ISBN 0-7099-1606-X, Pub. by Croom Helm Ltd England). Biblio Dist.

--Plant Hunting in Nepal. (Illus.). 194p. 1982. 19.95 (ISBN 0-7099-1606-X). Timber.

Lancaster, Sheila. Dark Sweet Wanton. (Historical Romance Ser.). 256p. (Orig.). 1981. pap. 2.50 o.s.i. (ISBN 0-515-05759-2). Jove Pubns.

Lancaster, Wade, jt. auth. see Lancaster, Jeanette.

Lancaster, William. The Rwala Bedouin Today. (Changing Cultures Ser.). (Illus.). 192p. 1981. 37.50 (ISBN 0-521-23877-3); pap. 12.95 (ISBN 0-521-28275-6). Cambridge U Pr.

Lancaster-Gaye, Derek, ed. Personal Relationships, the Handicapped & the Community: Some European Thoughts & Solutions. (Illus.). 156p. 1972. 12.00 o.p. (ISBN 0-7100-7478-6). Routledge & Kegan.

Lancaster-Smith, jt. auth. see Williams, Fry.

Lancaster-Smith, Michael J., jt. auth. see Williams, Kenneth G.

Lance, Algie L. Introduction to Microwave Theory & Measurements. 1964. text ed. 22.95 (ISBN 0-07-036104-5, G); answer key 0.25 (ISBN 0-07-036105-3). McGraw.

Lance, J. G. & McLeod, J. G. A Physiological Approach to Clinical Neurology. 2nd ed. LC 80-49872. 1975. 32.95 o.p. (ISBN 0-407-00022-4). Butterworth.

Lance, James W. Mechanisms & Management of Headache. 4th ed. 264p. 1982. text ed. 39.95 (ISBN 0-407-26458-2). Butterworth.

Lance, Kathryn. Running for Health & Beauty. LC 76-45576. (Illus.). 1977. 8.95 o.p. (ISBN 0-672-52252-7). Bobbs.

--A Woman's Guide to Spectator Sports. LC 79-23448. (Illus.). 352p. 1980. 12.95 o.s.i. (ISBN 0-89104-183-4, A & W Visual Library); pap. 7.95 o.s.i. (ISBN 0-89104-182-6). A & W Pubs.

Lance, Robert. Directory of CSIRO Research Programs 1982. 496p. 1983. pap. 18.95 (ISBN 0-686-84838-1, Pub. by CSIRO Australia). Intl Schol Bk Serv.

Lancelot, G. & Arnauld, A. Grammaire Generale et Raisonnee. (Linguistics 13th-18th Centuries Ser.). 226p. (Fr.). 1974. Repr. of 1754 ed. lib. bdg. 63.00x o.p. (ISBN 0-8287-0503-8, 71-5017). Clearwater Pub.

Lancelot-Harrington, Katherine. America--Past & Present: Challenge. (America--Past & Present Ser.: Vol II). 160p. 1982. pap. text ed. 9.95 (ISBN 0-88377-255-8). Newbury Hse.

--America Past & Present: Discovery, Vol. 1. 192p. 1981. pap. text ed. 9.95 (ISBN 0-88377-235-3). Newbury Hse.

Lanchester, Elsa. Elsa Lanchester, Herself. (Illus.). 416p. 1983. 17.95 (ISBN 0-312-24376-6). St Martin.

Lanchner, Carolyn & Rosenstock, Laura. Four Modern Masters: De Chirico, Ernst, Magritte, & Miro. (Illus.). 122p. 1982. pap. 14.95 (ISBN 0-686-83914-5, 28738-6). U of Chicago Pr.

Lanciaux, D. Operating Systems: Theory & Practice. 1979. 64.00 (ISBN 0-444-85300-6, North Holland). Elsevier.

Lancour, jt. auth. see Kent.

Lancour, Harold & Wolfe, Richard J., eds. Bibliography of Ship Passenger Lists, Fifteen Thirty-Eight to Eighteen Twenty-Five: A Guide to Published Lists of Early Immigrants to North America. 3rd ed. rev ed. LC 63-18141. 1978. 10.00 o.p. (ISBN 0-87104-023-9). NY Pub Lib.

Lancourt, Joan E. Confront or Concede: The Alinsky Citizen-Action Organizations. (Illus.). 208p. 1979. 21.95x (ISBN 0-669-02715-4). Lexington Bks.

Lancy, David. Cross-Cultural Studies in Cognition & Mathematics. (Developmental Psychology Ser.). 220p. 1982. 24.50 (ISBN 0-12-435620-6). Acad Pr.

Land, A. E., ed. The Expedition Handbook. 2nd ed. (Illus.). 1978. 19.95 (ISBN 0-408-71308-9). Butterworth.

Land, A. H. & Powell, S. Fortran Codes for Mathematical Programming: Linear, Quadratic & Discrete. LC 73-2789. 249p. 1973. 45.95x (ISBN 0-471-51270-2, Pub. by Wiley-Interscience). Wiley.

Land, Aubrey C. Colonial Maryland: A History. LC 80-21732. (A History of the American Colonies Ser.). 1981. lib. bdg. 30.00 (ISBN 0-527-18713-5). Kraus Intl.

Land, Brian. Directory of Associations in Canada. 4th ed. 317p. pap. 60.00x (ISBN 0-88892-342-2, Pub. by Micromedia Ltd). Gale.

Land, D. G. & Nursten, H. E., eds. Progress in Flavour Research. (Illus.). 1979. 63.75 (ISBN 0-85334-818-9, Pub. by Applied Sci England). Elsevier.

Land, George T. Grow or Die. 1974. pap. 4.95 o.s.i. (ISBN 0-440-53267-1, Delta). Dell.

Land, Hugh C. Birds of Guatemala. LC 70-88371. (Illus.). 1970. 15.00 o.p. (ISBN 0-915180-10-3). Harrowood Bks.

Land, Kenneth C. & Rogers, Andrei, eds. Multidimensional Mathematical Demography. LC 82-6821. (Studies in Population). 602p. 1982. 24.50 (ISBN 0-12-435640-0). Acad Pr.

Land, Kenneth C. & Spilerman, Seymour, eds. Social Indicator Models. LC 74-79447. 412p. 1975. 15.95x (ISBN 0-87154-505-5). Russell Sage.

Land, Myrick. The Fine Art of Literary Mayhem: A Lively Account of Famous Writers & Their Feuds. 2nd, Rev. ed. 272p. Date not set. pap. 8.95 (ISBN 0-938530-11-9, 11-9). Lexikos.

Land Study Bureau, Univ. of Hawaii. Compensible Regulations: Their Potential for Land Use & Development Control in Hawaii. (Land Study Bureau Report: No. 7). 55p. 1968. pap. 3.00x (ISBN 0-8248-0316-7). UH Pr.

--Detailed Land Classification. Incl. Island of Hawaii. (No. 6). 763p. 1965. pap. 38.00 o.p. (ISBN 0-8248-0311-6); Island of Kauai. (No. 9). 151p. 1967. pap. 9.00x o.p. (ISBN 0-8248-0309-4); Island of Lanai. (No. 8). (Illus.). 60p. 1967. pap. 3.00x (ISBN 0-8248-0310-8); Island of Maui. (No. 7). (Illus.). 167p. 1967. pap. 9.50x (ISBN 0-8248-0312-4); Island of Molokai. (No. 10). (Illus.). 95p. 1968. pap. 5.00x (ISBN 0-8248-0308-6); Island of Oahu. rev. ed. (No. 11). 320p. 1973. pap. 17.00x o.p. (ISBN 0-8248-0320-5). (Land Study Bureau Bulletin Ser.). pap. UH Pr.

--Kauai Lands Classified by Physical Qualities for Urban Usage. (Land Study Bureau Circular: No. 17). (Illus.). 38p. 1973. pap. 15.00x (ISBN 0-8248-0348-5). UH Pr.

--Land Use & Productivity Data, State of Hawaii, 1968. (Land Study Bureau Circular: No. 15). 95p. 1969. pap. 5.00x (ISBN 0-8248-0314-0). UH Pr.

--Land Use Classification & Determination of Highest & Best Use of Hawaii's Agricultural Lands. (Land Study Bureau Report: No. 10). (Illus.). 26p. 1972. pap. 3.00x (ISBN 0-8248-0315-9). UH Pr.

--Maui Lands Classified by Physical Qualities for Urban Usage. (Land Study Bureau Circular Ser.: No. 16). (Illus.). 52p. 1970. pap. 18.00x o.p. (ISBN 0-8248-0317-5). UH Pr.

--Molokai: Present & Potential Land Use. (Land Study Bureau Bulletin: No. 1). (Illus.). 90p. 1960. pap. 5.00x o.p. (ISBN 0-8248-0313-2). UH Pr.

Landa, Diego De see De Landa, Diego.

Landaner. Dieters Workshop Success Diet: Health, Nutrition, & Well-Being. 10.00 o.p. (ISBN 0-448-14540-5, G&D). Putnam Pub Group.

Landau see Weyl, Hermann, et al.

Landau, ed. see Menashe Har-El.

Landau, et al. Quantum Electrodynamics. 2nd ed. (Course of Theoretical Physics Ser.: Vol. 4). (Illus.). 550p. 1982. 69.00 (ISBN 0-08-026503-0); pap. 29.50 (ISBN 0-08-026504-9). Pergamon.

Landau, Anneliese. The Lied: The Unfolding of Its Style. LC 79-6725. 1980. text ed. 17.50 (ISBN 0-8191-0935-5); pap. text ed. 8.50 (ISBN 0-8191-0936-3). U Pr of Amer.

Landau, Barbara R. Essential Human Anatomy & Physiology. 2nd ed. 1980. text ed. 26.50x (ISBN 0-673-15249-9). Scott F.

Landau, E. D., et al. The Teaching Experience: An Introduction to Education Through Literature. (Illus.). 496p. 1976. pap. text ed. 18.95 (ISBN 0-13-892539-9). P-H.

Landau, Edmund. Algebraische Zahlen. 2nd ed. (Ger). 9.95 (ISBN 0-8284-0062-8). Chelsea Pub.

--Differential & Integral Calculus. LC 65-4331. 372p. 1981. text ed. 17.95x (ISBN 0-8284-0078-4). Chelsea Pub.

--Elementare Zahlentheorie. LC 49-235. (Ger). 12.00 (ISBN 0-8284-0026-1). Chelsea Pub.

--Elementary Number Theory. 2nd ed. LC 57-8494. 13.95 (ISBN 0-8284-0125-X). Chelsea Pub.

--Foundations of Analysis. 2nd ed. LC 60-15580. (gr. 9 up). 1960. text ed. 10.95 (ISBN 0-8284-0079-2). Chelsea Pub.

--Grundlagen der Analysis: With Complete German-English Vocabulary. 4th ed. LC 60-7485. (Ger). o. p. 6.95 (ISBN 0-8284-0024-5); pap. 4.95 (ISBN 0-8284-0141-1). Chelsea Pub.

--Vorlesungen Ueber Zahlentheorie, 3 Vols. in One. LC 49-235. (Ger). 39.95 (ISBN 0-8284-0032-6). Chelsea Pub.

Landau, Elaine. Death: Everyone's Heritage. LC 76-18094. 128p. (gr. 7 up). 1976. PLB 7.29 o.p. (ISBN 0-671-32807-7). Messner.

--Occult Visions: A Mystical Gaze into the Future. LC 79-16873. (Illus.). 160p. (gr. 7 up). 1979. PLB 7.79 o.p. (ISBN 0-671-32930-8). Messner.

--Why Are They Starving Themselves? Understanding Anorexia Nervosa & Bulimia. 128p. (gr. 9-12). 1983. PLB 9.29 (ISBN 0-671-45582-6). Messner.

--Yoga for You. LC 77-22053. (Illus.). 128p. (gr. 7 up). 1977. PLB 7.29 o.p. (ISBN 0-671-32859-X). Messner.

Landau, Eli, jt. auth. see Aricha, Amos.

Landau, Elliot, et al. The Exceptional Child Through Literature. (Illus.). 1978. ref. ed. 16.95 (ISBN 0-13-293860-X). P-H.

Landau, Elliott, et al. Child Development Through Literature. 1972. pap. text ed. 18.95 (ISBN 0-13-130674-X). P-H.

Landau, Jacob M. Arabs in Israel: A Political Study. (Royal Institute of International Affairs Ser.). 1969. 14.50x o.p. (ISBN 0-19-214977-6). Oxford U Pr.

Landau, Luis. Dominican Republic: Its Main Economic Development Problems. xv, 468p. 1978. pap. 20.00 (ISBN 0-686-36104-0, RC-7805). World Bank.

Landau, Martin. Political Theory & Political Science. 1979. text ed. 12.50x (ISBN 0-391-01050-6); pap. text ed. 6.95x (ISBN 0-391-01237-1). Humanities.

Landau, Michael, ed. Accountant-Auditor. 8th ed. LC 82-11428. 192p. 1983. pap. 10.00 (ISBN 0-668-05544-8, 5544). Arco.

Landau, Robert M., ed. see ASIS Workshop on Computer Composition.

Landau, Robert M., et al, eds. Emerging Office Systems. (Communication & Information Science Ser.). 250p. 1982. 29.50x (ISBN 0-89391-075-9). Ablex Pub.

Landau, Sarah B. P. B. Wight: Architect, Contractor, & Critic, 1838-1925. (Illus.). 108p. 1981. pap. 14.95 (ISBN 0-86559-051-6). Art Inst Chi.

Landau, Sidney & Bogus, Donald. Webster Illustrated Contemporary Dictionary. LC 82-45499. 1024p. 1982. 12.95 (ISBN 0-385-18306-2). Doubleday.

Landau, Sidney & Bogus, Ronald, eds. Doubleday Dictionary: For Home, School & Office. LC 74-3543. 936p. 1975. 9.95 (ISBN 0-385-04099-7); thumb-indexed 10.95 (ISBN 0-385-03368-0). Doubleday.

--Doubleday Roget's Thesaurus in Dictionary Form. LC 76-7696. 564p. 1977. 9.95 (ISBN 0-385-01236-5); thumb-indexed 11.95 (ISBN 0-385-12379-5). Doubleday.

Landau, Simha F. & Sebba, Leslie. Criminology in Perspective: Essays in Honor of Israel Drapkin. LC 76-50437. 272p. 1978. 22.95x (ISBN 0-669-01281-5). Lexington Bks.

Landau, Suzanne & Bailey, Geoffrey. The Landau Strategy: How Working Women Win Top Jobs. 192p. 1980. 9.95 o.p. (ISBN 0-517-54045-2, C N Potter Bks). Crown.

Landau, Yehuda H., et al, eds. Rural Communities: Inter-Cooperation & Development. LC 75-19779. (Special Studies). (Illus.). 192p. 1976. 25.95 o.p. (ISBN 0-275-55700-6). Praeger.

Landauer, Thomas K. Psychology: A Brief Overview. (Illus.). 416p. 1972. text ed. 16.95 o.p. (ISBN 0-07-036113-4, C); instructor's manual 2.95 o.p. (ISBN 0-07-036117-7); wkbk. & study guide 6.50 o.p. (ISBN 0-07-043625-8). McGraw.

Landcaster, Gerald, jt. auth. see Weisberger, Bernard A.

Lande, Nathaniel. Cricket. 1982. pap. write for info. o.p. (ISBN 0-451-11397-7, AE1397, Sig). NAL.

Lande, Paul S., jt. ed. see Bell, Michael E.

Landeira, Ricardo. Ramiro de Maeztu. (World Authors Ser.). 1978. lib. bdg. 15.95 (ISBN 0-8057-6325-2, Twayne). G K Hall.

Landekich, Stephen, jt. auth. see Caplan, Edwin H.

Landell-Mills, Pierre. The Comoros: Problems & Prospects of a Small, Island Economy. vii, 177p. 1979. pap. 15.00 (ISBN 0-686-36103-2, RC-7907). World Bank.

Lander, Ernest M., Jr. The Calhoun Family & Thomas Green Clemson: The Decline of a Southern Patriarch. LC 82-13568. 221p. 1983. 17.95 (ISBN 0-87249-413-6). U of SC Pr.

Lander, Gerald H., jt. auth. see Holmes, James R.

Lander, J. R. Conflict & Stability in Fifteenth Century England. 3rd ed. 1977. pap. 8.50x (ISBN 0-09-095741-5, Hutchinson U Lib). Humanities.

Lander, Jack R. How to Get Hired Faster, for More Money, Whether You Are Presently Working or Not. LC 79-56038. (Illus.). 80p. 1980. 10.95 o.p. (ISBN 0-935722-01-7); pap. 5.95 (ISBN 0-935722-00-9). Exponent.

Lander, Jeannette. Ezra Pound. LC 71-134828. (Literature and Life Ser.). 1971. 11.95 (ISBN 0-8044-2486-1); pap. 4.95 (ISBN 0-8044-6380-8). Ungar.

Lander, L., tr. see Brocker, T. H.

Lander, Patricia S. In the Shadow of the Factory: Social Change in a Finnish Community. LC 75-37634. 198p. 1976. text ed. 12.50x o.p. (ISBN 0-470-01379-6); pap. text ed. 5.95 o.p. (ISBN 0-470-01380-X). Halsted Pr.

Landerman, Peter. Vocabulario Quechua del Pastaza. (Peruvian Linguistic Ser.: No. 8). 165p. 1973. pap. 2.50x (ISBN 0-88312-664-8); microfiche 2.25 (ISBN 0-88312-366-5). Summer Inst Ling.

Landers, Ann. The Ann Landers Encyclopedia, A-Z: Improve Your Life Emotionally, Medically, Sexually, Spiritually. LC 77-25601. 1978. 19.95 (ISBN 0-385-12951-3). Doubleday.

--Ann Landers Says...Truth Is Stranger. 222p. 1982. pap. 5.95 (ISBN 0-13-036889-X). P-H.

--Since You Asked Me. 206p. 1983. pap. 5.95 (ISBN 0-13-810531-6). P-H.

Landers, Jack M. Construction. LC 75-4032. (Illus.). 480p. 1976. text ed. 12.80 (ISBN 0-87006-202-6); lab manual 3.80 (ISBN 0-87006-291-3). Goodheart.

Landers, Jonathan M. & Martin, James A. Basic Civil Procedure: Cases & Materials. 1196p. 1981. 26.00 (ISBN 0-316-51355-5). Little.

Landers, Jonathan M., jt. auth. see Epstein, David G.

Landers, Jonathon & Martin, James A. Civil Procedure, 1982 Supplememt. 1982. pap. 8.50 (ISBN 0-316-51357-1). Little.

Landes, Alison & Landes, Sonia. Pariswalks. LC 75-8699. (Illus.). 208p. 1975. pap. 4.50 (ISBN 0-915220-02-4, 23049). New Republic.

Landes, Daniel, jt. ed. see Grobman, Alex.

Landes, David S. Unbound Prometheus: Technological Change & Industrial Development in Western Europe from 1750 to the Present. 49.50 (ISBN 0-521-07200-X); pap. 11.95 (ISBN 0-521-09418-6). Cambridge U Pr.

Landes, David S., ed. see Commission on Critical Choices.

Landes, George M., ed. Report on Archaeological Work at Suwannet eth-Thaniya, Tananir, & Khirbet Minha. LC 75-30540. (American Schools of Oriental Research, Supplement Ser.: Vol. 21). 117p. text ed. 9.00x (ISBN 0-89757-317-X, Am Sch Orient Res); pap. text ed. 6.00x (ISBN 0-89757-321-8). Eisenbrauns.

Landes, Kenneth K. Petroleum Geology. 2nd ed. LC 74-26700. 458p. 1975. Repr. of 1959 ed. 24.00 (ISBN 0-88275-226-X). Krieger.

--Petroleum Geology of the United States. LC 77-101975. 571p. 1970. 69.95x (ISBN 0-471-51335-0, Pub. by Wiley-Interscience). Wiley.

Landes, Margaret W., ed. see Burthogge, Richard.

Landes, Paula F. Augustine on Romans: Propositions From the Epistle to the Romans & Unfinished Commentary on the Epistle to the Romans. LC 82-10259. (Society of Biblical Literature, Texts & Translations Ser.). 124p. 1982. pap. 12.75 (ISBN 0-89130-583-1, 06-02-23). Scholars Pr CA.

Landes, Ronald G. A Handbook for Hospital Nights: Vol. 2: the Rational & Irrational Elements of Hospital Healing. 1982. 11.95 (ISBN 0-941432-00-9); pap. 5.95x (ISBN 0-941432-02-5). Silvergirl Bks.

Landes, Sonia, jt. auth. see Landes, Alison.

Landesman, Fran. Ballad of the Sad Young Men. LC 81-85724. 1982. 5.95 (ISBN 0-932966-18-7). Permanent Pr.

Landess, Thomas H. Julia Peterkin. (United States Authors Ser.). 1976. lib. bdg. 12.95 (ISBN 0-8057-7173-5, Twayne). G K Hall.

Landey, Dora & Klein, Elinor. Triptych. 1983. 16.95 (ISBN 0-395-33126-9). HM.

Landey, Dora, jt. auth. see Klein, Elinor.

Landgrebe, Gary. Tofu Goes West. LC 78-67462. (Illus.). 114p. (Orig.). 1978. pap. 5.95 (ISBN 0-9601398-2-6). Fresh Pr.

Landgrebe, John A. Theory & Practice in the Organic Laboratory. 3rd ed. 576p. 1982. pap. text ed. 23.95 (ISBN 0-669-04494-6). Heath.

--Theory & Practice in the Organic Laboratory. 2nd ed. 1976. pap. text ed. 17.95x o.p. (ISBN 0-669-99937-7). Heath.

Landgrebe, Ludwig. Major Problems in Contemporary European Philosophy: From Dilthey to Heidegger. Reinhardt, Kurt F., tr. LC 64-25558. 12.50 (ISBN 0-8044-5604-6). Ungar.

Landham, Sonny. The Total Man. LC 79-11128. 1981. 13.95 (ISBN 0-87949-157-4). Ashley Bks.

Landin, Judy. The Well Dressed Salad. (Illus.). 32p. (Orig.). 1981. pap. 2.00 (ISBN 0-9609266-0-7). GNK Pr.

Landingham, S. L. Van see Van Landingham, S. L.

Landis. Building a Successful Marriage. 7th ed. 1977. 22.95 (ISBN 0-13-087007-2). P-H.

Landis, Arthur A. Camelot in Orbit. (Science Fiction Ser.). (Orig.). 1978. pap. 2.35 (ISBN 0-87997-782-5, UE1782). DAW Bks.

Landis, Arthur H. Home-to-Avalon. 1982. pap. 2.50 (ISBN 0-87997-778-7, UE1778). Daw Bks.

Landis, Beth & Carder, Polly. Eclectic Curriculum in American Music Education: Contributions of Dalcroze, Kodaly, & Orff. LC 72-83395. (Illus.). 147p. 1972. pap. 8.00x (ISBN 0-940796-03-1, 1013). Music Ed.

Landis, Beth, jt. auth. see Gary, Charles L.

Landis, Brook I. Value Judgments in Arbitration: A Case Study of Saul Wallen. LC 77-8131. (Cornell Studies in Industrial & Labor Relations: No. 19). 200p. 1977. 10.00 (ISBN 0-87546-063-1). ILR Pr.

Landis, Carolyn R., jt. ed. see Hamblen, John W.

Landis, Dan, ed. Handbook of Intercultural Training: Issues in Theory & Design, Vol. 1. (Pergamon General Psychology Ser.: No. 116). (Illus.). 300p. 1983. 40.00 (ISBN 0-08-027533-8). Pergamon.

Landis, Dan & Brislin, Richard W., eds. Handbook of Intercultural Training: Area Studies in Intercultural Training, Vol. III. (General Psychology Ser.: No. 116). 325p. 1983. 40.00 (ISBN 0-08-027535-4); Set. before 4/83 85.00 (ISBN 0-08-027537-0). Pergamon.

--Handbook of Intercultural Training: Issues in Training Methodology, Vol. II. (Pergamon General Psychology Ser.: No. 116). (Illus.). 400p. 1983. 40.00 (ISBN 0-08-027534-6). Pergamon.

Landis, Dennis C., jt. auth. see Alden, John.

Landis, J. Richard & Eklund, Stephen A. A Statistical Methodology for Analyzing Data from a Complex Survey: The First National Health & Nutrition Examination Survey. Cox, Klaudia, ed. (No. 92). 50p. 1982. pap. 1.75 (ISBN 0-686-81990-X). Natl Ctr Health Stats.

Landis, James, ed. see Silverstein, Charles.

Landis, James M. The Administrative Process. LC 73-17952. 160p. 1974. Repr. lib. bdg. 20.50x (ISBN 0-8371-7284-5, LAAP). Greenwood.

Landis, Judson R. Sociology: Concepts & Characteristics. 4th ed. 416p. 1979. pap. text ed. 16.95x (ISBN 0-534-00784-8). Wadsworth Pub.

Landis, Mary. Bettys Geheimnis. (Ger.). pap. 2.90 (ISBN 0-686-32318-1). Rod & Staff.

--Die Truhe im Dachgeschoss. (Ger.). pap. 2.90 (ISBN 0-686-32322-X). Rod & Staff.

Landis, Mary M. The Coon Tree Summer: Merry Brook Farm Story. 1978. 6.55 (ISBN 0-686-22987-8). Rod & Staff.

--David & Susan at the Little Green House. 1975. 6.00 (ISBN 0-686-11146-X). Rod & Staff.

--David & Susan at Wild Rose Cottage. 1979. 6.45 (ISBN 0-686-22988-6). Rod & Staff.

--Dear Princess. 6.95 (ISBN 0-686-05602-7). Rod & Staff.

--Health for the Glory of God. (gr. 4-5). 1976. write for info. (ISBN 0-686-15484-3); avail.tchrs's ed. (ISBN 0-686-15485-1). Rod & Staff.

--Ice Slide Winter: Merry Brook Farm Story. 1981. 6.50 (ISBN 0-686-30772-0). Rod & Staff.

--The Missing Popcorn & Other Stories. (gr. 3-6). 1976. 6.00 (ISBN 0-686-15480-0). Rod & Staff.

--Summer Days with the Treelo Triplets. 192p. (YA) 1971. 6.15 (ISBN 0-686-05591-8). Rod & Staff.

--Trouble at Windy Acres. (gr. 5-10). 1976. 6.30 (ISBN 0-686-15486-X). Rod & Staff.

Landis, Michael & Moholt, Ray. Patios & Decks: How to Plan, Build & Enjoy. (Illus.). 193p. 1983. pap. 9.95 (ISBN 0-89586-162-3). H P Bks.

Landis, Paul H. Making the Most of Marriage. 5th ed. 624p. 1975. text ed. 22.95 (ISBN 0-13-547968-1). P-H.

--Your Dating Days: Looking Forward to Successful Marriage. 2nd ed. (gr. 7 up). 1971. PLB 6.95 o.p. (ISBN 0-07-036128-2, GB). McGraw.

--Your Marriage & Family Living. 3rd ed. (American Home & Family Ser.). 1969. text ed. 19.84 (ISBN 0-07-036185-1, W); tchrs' manual 1.72 (ISBN 0-07-036186-X). McGraw.

--Your Marriage & Family Living. 4th ed. (Illus.). (gr. 10-12). 1976. text ed. 19.32 (ISBN 0-07-036187-8, W). McGraw.

Landis, Paul M. Purity in the Christian Home. 1978. 1.00 (ISBN 0-686-25260-8). Rod & Staff.

Landis, Robin C. OPEC: Policy Implications for the United States. Klass, Michael W., ed. LC 78-19457. (Praeger Special Studies). (Illus.). 304p. 1980. 33.95 o.p. (ISBN 0-03-044361-X). Praeger.

Landman, David, jt. ed. see Fairchild, Johnson E.

Landmark, ed. see Bouwsma, O. K.

Landmark, ed. see Woodress, James.

Landolt, A. M., ed. Complications in Neurosurgery I. (Progress in Neurological Surgery Ser.: Vol. 11). (Illus.). viii, 130p. 1983. 58.75 (ISBN 3-8055-3691-7). S Karger.

Landon, Charles. Classic Moments of Athletics. 144p. 1982. 35.00x (ISBN 0-86190-053-7, Pub. by Moorland). State Mutual Bk.

--Classic Moments of Wimbledon. 144p. 1982. 35.00x (ISBN 0-86190-052-9, Pub. by Moorland). State Mutual Bk.

Landon, D. H., ed. The Peripheral Nerve. 1976. 86.00x (ISBN 0-412-11740-1, Pub. by Chapman & Hall). Methuen Inc.

Landon, Grelun, jt. auth. see Stambler, Irwin.

Landon, H. C. Mozart & the Masons: New Light Shed on the Lodge "Crowned Hope". (Illus.). 1983. 10.95 (ISBN 0-500-55014-X). Thames Hudson.

Landon, H. C., et al. The Haydn Yearbook, Vol. XIII. LC 63-3879. 256p. 1983. pap. 25.00x (ISBN 0-253-37113-9). Ind U Pr.

Landon, Joseph W. How to Write Learning Activity Packages for Music Education. (Contemporary Music Education Ser.). 109p. 1973. pap. 6.95x (ISBN 0-930424-01-8). Music Educ Pubns.

--Leadership for Learning in Music Education. LC 75-305303. (Contemporary Music Eduction Ser.). 306p. (Orig.). 1975. pap. 9.95x (ISBN 0-943988-02-0). Music Educ Pubns.

--Music Lab. (Mini-Modular Series in Music Education). (Illus.). 182p. (Orig.). (gr. 3-8). 1982. pap. 10.95x (ISBN 0-943988-00-4). Music Educ Pubns.

Landon, Richard G. Book Selling & Book Buying: Aspects of the Nineteenth-Century British & North American Book Trade, No. 40. LC 78-31812. (ACRL Publication in Librarianship Ser.). 1979. pap. 15.00 (ISBN 0-8389-3224-X). ALA.

Landon, Robbins H. & Chapman, Roger. Studies in Eighteenth Century Music: A Tribute to Karl Geiringer on His 70th Birthday. (Music Reprint Ser.). 1979. Repr. of 1970 ed. lib. bdg. 39.50 (ISBN 0-306-79519-1). Da Capo.

Landor, S. R., ed. The Chemistry of the Allenes: Vol. 2, Reactions of Allenes. 1982. 86.00 (ISBN 0-12-436102-1). Acad Pr.

Landor, Stephen, ed. The Chemistry of the Allenes: Vol. 3, Stereochemical, Spectroscopic & Special Aspects. 1982. 86.00 (ISBN 0-12-436103-X). Acad Pr.

Landor, Walter S. Selected Poetry & Prose. Hanley, Keith, ed. LC 79-91173. 224p. 1981. 20.00 o.p. (ISBN 0-89255-045-7). Persea Bks.

Landorf, Joyce. Changepoints. 192p. 1981. 9.95 (ISBN 0-8007-1257-9). Revell.

--Fragrance of Beauty. LC 74-76813. 1973. pap. 4.50 (ISBN 0-88207-231-5). Victor Bks.

--I Came to Love You Late. 1981. pap. 2.50 o.p. (ISBN 0-451-09897-8, E9897, Sig). NAL.

--Irregular People. 1982. 8.95 (ISBN 0-8499-0291-6). Word Pub.

--Joyce, I Feel Like I Know You. 1976. pap. 3.95 (ISBN 0-88207-742-2). Victor Bks.

--Mix Butter with Love. LC 74-18857. 1974. gift ed. 6.95 (ISBN 0-89081-035-4, 0354). Harvest Hse.

--Mourning Song. 192p. 1974. 9.95 (ISBN 0-8007-0680-3). Revell.

--Tough & Tender. rev. ed. 160p. 1981. 8.95 (ISBN 0-8007-1283-8). Revell.

Landovitz, Leon, jt. auth. see Schwartz, Edmund.

Landovitz, Leon F., jt. auth. see Schwartz, Edmund I.

Landow, George P., jt. auth. see Johnson, Diana L.

Landow, George P., ed. Approaches to Victorian Autobiography. LC 77-91505. xlvi, 354p. 1979. 22.95x (ISBN 0-8214-0400-8, 82-82931). Ohio U Pr.

Landow, R. K. Herpes in Focus. (Illus.). 288p. 1983. 17.95 (ISBN 0-8065-0837-X). Citadel Pr. Postponed.

Landreth, Garry L. Play Therapy: Dynamics of the Process of Counseling with Children. 460p. 1982. 29.75x (ISBN 0-398-04716-2). C C Thomas.

Landreth, Harry H. History of Economic Theory: Scope, Method & Content. LC 75-31003. (Illus.). 512p. 1976. text ed. 26.95 (ISBN 0-395-19234-X). HM.

Landrum, Eli, Jr. More Than Symbol. LC 81-86669. (Orig.). 1983. pap. 3.95 (ISBN 0-8054-2304-4). Broadman.

Landrum, Larry N., ed. American Popular Culture: A Guide to Information Sources. LC 73-17554. (American Studies Information Guide). 350p. 1982. 42.00x (ISBN 0-8103-1260-3). Gale.

Landrum, Leslie R. Myrceugenia (Myrtaceae) (Flora Neotropica Monograph: No. 29). (Illus.). 1981. pap. 20.00 (ISBN 0-89327-236-1). NY Botanical.

Landrum, Phil, jt. auth. see Brandt, Henry.

Landrum, Roger. A Daydream I Had at Night: Teaching Children How to Make Their Own Readers. rev. ed. 124p. (Orig.). 1974. pap. 5.00 (ISBN 0-915924-01-3). Tchrs & Writers Coll.

--National Service & the General Welfare: Has the Time for it Come? (Vital Issues, Vol. XXX 1980-81: No. 9). 0.60 (ISBN 0-686-81604-8). Ctr Info Am.

Landry, David M. & Parker, Joseph B. Mississippi Government & Politics in Transition. LC 76-13763. (Government Ser.). 1976. pap. text ed. 7.95 (ISBN 0-8403-1482-5). Kendall-Hunt.

Landry, Hilton. Interpretations in Shakespeare's Sonnets. LC 76-1901. (Perspectives in Criticism Ser.: No. 14). (Illus.). 185p. 1976. Repr. of 1963 ed. lib. bdg. 18.50x (ISBN 0-8371-8749-4, LAIS). Greenwood.

Landry, Judith, tr. see Benevolo, Leonardo.

Landry, Monica & Olivier, Julien. Tantine: l'Histoire de Lucille Landry Augustine Gabrielle. Anderson, Penny & Granger, Mary, trs. (Oral History Ser.). (Illus.). 45p. (Fr.). (gr. 9). 1981. pap. 2.00x (ISBN 0-911409-05-X). Natl Mat Dev.

Lands, William, jt. ed. see Colowick, S. P.

Landsberg, G., jt. auth. see Hensel, Kurt.

Landsberg, H. E. General Climatology, Vol. 1. Date not set. price not set (ISBN 0-444-40734-0). Elsevier.

Landsberg, H. E., ed. Advances in Geophysics, 19 vols. Incl. Vol. 1. 1952 (ISBN 0-12-018801-5); Vol. 2. 1955 (ISBN 0-12-018802-3); Vol. 3. 1956 (ISBN 0-12-018803-1); Vol. 4. Landsberg, H. E. & Van Mieghen, J., eds. 1958 (ISBN 0-12-018804-X); Vol. 5. 1958 (ISBN 0-12-018805-8); Vol. 6. Atmospheric Diffusion & Air Pollution: Proceedings. Frenkiel, F. N. & Sheppard, P. A., eds. 1959 (ISBN 0-12-018806-6); Vol. 7. 1961 (ISBN 0-12-018807-4); Vol. 8. 1961 (ISBN 0-12-018808-2); Vol. 9. 1962 (ISBN 0-12-018809-0); Vol. 10. 1964 (ISBN 0-12-018810-4); Vol. 11. 1965 (ISBN 0-12-018811-2); Vol. 12. 1967 (ISBN 0-12-018812-0); Vol. 13. 1969 (ISBN 0-12-018813-9); Vol. 14. 1970 (ISBN 0-12-018814-7); Vol. 15. 1971 (ISBN 0-12-018815-5); Suppl. 1. Biometeorological Methods. Munn, R. E. 1966. 40.00 (ISBN 0-12-018861-9); Vol. 16. 1973 (ISBN 0-12-018816-3); Vol. 17. 1974 (ISBN 0-12-018817-1); Vol. 18A. 1974. 33.00 (ISBN 0-12-018818-X); Vol. 19. 1976. 63.00 (ISBN 0-12-018819-8). Vols. 1-17. 68.00 ea. Acad Pr.

--General Climatology, Vol. 3. (World Survey of Climatology). 1981. 106.50 (ISBN 0-444-41776-1). Elsevier.

Landsberg, H. E. & Wallen, C. C., eds. Climates of Central & Southern Europe. (World Survey of Climatology: Vol. 6). 1977. 98.00 (ISBN 0-444-41336-7). Elsevier.

Landsberg, Hans, ed. Energy: The Next Twenty Years. LC 79-5226. 656p. 1979. prof ref 32.50x (ISBN 0-88410-092-8); pap. 15.00 (ISBN 0-88410-094-4). Ballinger Pub.

--Selected Studies on Energy: Background Papers for Energy, The Next Twenty Years. LC 79-24800. 464p. 1980. prof ref 39.50x (ISBN 0-88410-093-6). Ballinger Pub.

Landsberg, P. T. & Willoughby, A. F, eds. Recombination in Semiconductors: Selected Proceedings of the International Conference Held at the University of Southampton, England. 30 August - 1st September 1978. 1979. 52.00 (ISBN 0-08-024226-X). Pergamon.

Landsberger, B. The Conceptual Autonomy of the Babylonian World (1926) Jacobsen, T., tr. (Monographs on the Ancient Near East). 16p. Repr. of 1976 ed. pap. 3.00 o.p. (ISBN 0-686-33119-2). Undena Pubns.

Landsberger, Frank R., jt. ed. see Scanu, Angelo M.

Landsberger, Henry. Hawthorne Revisited: Management & the Worker, Its Critics & Developments in Human Relations in Industry. LC 58-63022. (Cornell Studies Ser: No. 9). 1957. pap. 1.75 o.s.i. (ISBN 0-87546-003-8); pap. 4.75 special hard bdg. o.s.i. (ISBN 0-87546-264-2). ILR Pr.

Landsburg, Alan. In Search of... LC 78-58809. 1978. 8.95 o.p. (ISBN 0-89696-013-7, An Everest House Book). Dodd.

Landscape Architecture Magazine. Home Landscape, 1980. (Illus.). 1980. pap. 5.95 o.p. (ISBN 0-07-036192-4). McGraw.

--Landscapes for Living. (Illus.). 1980. 24.95 (ISBN 0-07-036191-6). McGraw.

--Water & Landscape. (Illus.). 1979. 32.50 (ISBN 0-07-036190-8, P&RB). McGraw.

Landshoff, P. V. & Metherell, A. J. Simple Quantum Physics. LC 78-73244. (Illus.). 1980. 32.50 (ISBN 0-521-22498-5); pap. 10.95 (ISBN 0-521-29538-6). Cambridge U Pr.

Landsman, Michael. Doubling your Ability through God. 58p. 1982. pap. 1.95 (ISBN 0-89274-266-6). Harrison Hse.

Landsman, Ted, jt. auth. see Jourard, Sidney M.

Landwehr, Gotz. Studien Zu Den Germanischen Volksrechten Gedachtnisschrift Fur Wilhelm Ebel. 217p. (Ger.). 1982. write for info. (ISBN 3-8204-6412-3). P Lang Pubs.

Landwehr, Richard. Lions of Flanders Flemish Volunteers of the Waffen-SS 1941-1945. (Illus.). 224p. 1982. 14.95 (ISBN 0-918184-04-5). Bibliophile.

--Narva Nineteen Forty-Four: The Waffen-SS & the Battle for Europe. (Illus.). 184p. 1981. pap. 6.95 (ISBN 0-918184-02-9). Bibliophile.

Landwehr, Sheldon, ed. see Sheldon Landwehr & Associates.

Landwehr, Stephana J., jt. auth. see Brayton, Abbott A.

Landy, David. Culture, Disease, & Healing: Studies in Medical Anthropology. (Illus.). 1977. 23.95x (ISBN 0-02-367390-7). Macmillan.

Landy, Eugene E. The Underground Dictionary. 1971. pap. 3.95 o.p. (ISBN 0-671-20803-9, Touchstone Bks). S&S.

Landy, Francis. Paradoxes & Paradise: Identity & Difference in the Song of Songs. (Bible & Literature Ser.: No. 6). 1983. text ed. 29.95x (ISBN 0-907459-16-1, Pub. by Almond Pr England); pap. text ed. 15.95x (ISBN 0-907459-17-X, Pub. by Almond Pr England). Eisenbrauns.

Landy, Harold M. How to Avoid Intercourse with Your Unfriendly Car Mechanic. LC 76-13309. 1977. 7.95 (ISBN 0-87949-080-2). Ashley Bks.
Landy, Maurice & Braun, W., eds. Immunological Tolerance. (Perspectives in Immunology Ser). 1969. 38.50 (ISBN 0-12-435650-8). Acad Pr.
Landy, Maurice, jt. ed. see Smith, Richard T.
Landy, Maurice, jt. ed. see Uhr, Jonathan W.
Lane, jt. ed. see Baruth.
Lane, et al. Worldwide. (gr. k-3). pupil's material 9.15 (ISBN 0-8372-4228-2); tchr's handbk. 4.29 (ISBN 0-8372-4229-0); tapes & dupl. masters avail. Bowmar-Noble.
Lane, Alaine, ed. Abnormal Psychology: The Problems of Disordered Emotional & Behavioral Mental Development. (Special Education Ser.). (Illus., Orig.). 1979. pap. text ed. 15.00 (ISBN 0-89568-109-9). Spec Learn Corp.
Lane, Alexander. Functional Human Anatomy: The Regional Approach. 3rd ed. 1981. pap. text ed. 16.95 (ISBN 0-8403-2340-9). Kendall-Hunt.
Lane, Alfred H. Gifts & Exchange Manual. LC 79-7590. 1980. lib. bdg. 19.95 (ISBN 0-313-21389-5, LGE/). Greenwood.
Lane, Allison. Revelations. 352p. (Orig.). 1981. pap. 2.75 o.s.i. (ISBN 0-515-05665-0). Jove Pubns.
Lane, Anne J., ed. see Beard, Mary R.
Lane, Arthur. Dancing in the Dark. LC 76-51658. (Illus.). 1977. text ed. 15.00x (ISBN 0-918298-01-6); pap. text ed. 6.50x (ISBN 0-918298-00-8). Kenmore.
--French Faience. 2nd ed. 151p. 1970. 19.95 o.p. (ISBN 0-571-04638-X). Faber & Faber.
--Handing Over. (Illus.). 38p. 1981. 15.00 (ISBN 0-918298-07-5). Kenmore.
Lane, Billy & Graham, Colin. Billy Lanes Encyclopaedia of Float Fishing. (Illus.). 1971. 9.50 o.p. (ISBN 0-7207-0514-2). Transatlantic.
Lane, Calvin W. Evelyn Waugh. (English Authors Ser.). 1981. lib. bdg. 11.95 (ISBN 0-8057-6793-2, Twayne). G K Hall.
Lane, Charles. A Voluntary Political Government: Letters from Charles Lane. 104p. (Orig.). 1982. pap. 5.95 (ISBN 0-9602574-3-8). M E Coughlin.
Lane, Christel. Christian Religion in the Soviet Union: A Sociological Study. LC 77-801. 1978. 44.50x (ISBN 0-87395-327-4). State U NY Pr.
--The Rites of Rulers: Ritual in Industrial Society-the Soviet Case. LC 80-41747. (Illus.). 338p. 1981. 49.50 (ISBN 0-521-22608-2); pap. 14.95 (ISBN 0-521-28347-7). Cambridge U Pr.
Lane, Christy. All That Jazz & More: The Complete Book of Jazz Dancing. LC 82-83944. (Illus.). 400p. (Orig.). 1983. pap. 19.95 (ISBN 0-88011-124-0). Leisure Pr.
Lane, David. Leninism: A Sociological Interpretation. (Themes in the Social Sciences Ser.). (Illus.). 176p. 1981. 32.50 (ISBN 0-521-23855-2); pap. 9.95 (ISBN 0-521-28259-4). Cambridge U Pr.
--The Roots of Russian Communism: A Social and Historical Study of Russian Social Democracy 1898-1907. LC 74-15196. 1975. pap. text ed. 10.00x (ISBN 0-271-01178-5). Pa St U Pr.
--The Socialist Industrial State: Toward a Political Sociology of State Socialism. LC 75-33036. 220p. 1976. 27.50 o.p. (ISBN 0-89158-523-0). Westview.
Lane, David & O'Dell, Felicity. The Soviet Industrial Worker: Social Class, Education & Control. LC 78-60509. 1978. 20.00 (ISBN 0-312-74841-8). St Martin.
Lane, Denis. God's Powerful Weapon. 1977. pap. 1.25 (ISBN 0-85363-117-4). OMF Bks.
--Keeping Body & Soul Together. 1982. pap. 2.75 (ISBN 0-85363-144-1). OMF Bks.
Lane, Donald & Storr, Anthony. Asthma: The Facts. (Illus.). 1980. text ed. 12.95x (ISBN 0-19-261175-5). Oxford U Pr.
Lane, Donna M. Target Practice. 150p. (Orig.). 1983. pap. 7.95 (ISBN 0-939140-01-2). Continuing SAGA.
Lane, Earle, jt. auth. see Davis, Mikol.
Lane, Elizabeth. China Song. (The China Ser.: No. 1). (Orig.). 1983. pap. 3.50 (ISBN 0-440-01493-X). Dell.
Lane, Frederic C. Venetian Ships & Shipbuilders of the Renaissance. LC 74-14356. (Illus.). 285p. 1975. Repr. of 1934 ed. lib. bdg. 17.25x (ISBN 0-8371-7800-2, LAVS). Greenwood.
Lane, Frederick S., ed. Managing State & Local Government: Cases & Readings. 509p. (Orig.). 1980. text ed. 18.95x (ISBN 0-312-51241-4); pap. text ed. 11.95x (ISBN 0-312-51242-2); instructor's manual available (ISBN 0-312-51243-0). St Martin.
Lane, G. B. The Trombone in the Middle Ages & the Renaissance. LC 82-47639. 240p. 1982. 25.00X (ISBN 0-253-36091-9). Ind U Pr.
Lane, Hana, ed. The World Almanac Consumer Survival Kit. 62p. (Orig.). 1983. pap. 1.50 (ISBN 0-911818-37-5). World Almanac.
Lane, Hana U., ed. The World Almanac & Book of Facts Nineteen Eighty-One. 976p. 1980. 8.95 o.p. (ISBN 0-911818-17-0); pap. 4.50 o.p. (ISBN 0-911818-09-X). World Almanac.
Lane, Hana U., ed. see Newspaper Enterprise Assn.
Lane, Harlan, tr. see De Condillac, Etienne Bonnot.
Lane, Helen, tr. see Barincou, Edmond.
Lane, Helen, tr. see Orieux, Jean.
Lane, Helen R., tr. see Durand, Loup.
Lane, Helen R., tr. see Sullerot, Evelyn.
Lane, Helen R., tr. see Vargas-Llosa, Mario.
Lane, Henry W., et al. Managing Large Research & Development Programs. LC 81-849. 250p. 44.50x (ISBN 0-87395-473-4); pap. 14.95x (ISBN 0-87395-474-2). State U NY Pr.
Lane, Howard A. Shall Children, Too, Be Free? 33p. 0.50 o.p. (ISBN 0-686-74886-7). ADL.
Lane, J., jt. auth. see Miller, Madeleine S.
Lane, J. E. Microprocessors & Information Handling. (Computing in the Eighties Ser.). 67p. 1981. pap. 15.00x (ISBN 0-85012-334-8). Intl Pubns Serv.
Lane, J. G. Diagnosis & Treatment of Ear & Oral Surgery of the Dog & Cat: Veterinary Practitioner Handbook. 1982. text ed. 24.50 (ISBN 0-7236-0659-5). Wright-PSG.
Lane, Jack C. Armed Progressive: General Leonard Wood. LC 76-58763. (Illus.). 1978. 16.95 o.p. (ISBN 0-89141-009-0). Presidio Pr.
Lane, Jack C., ed. America's Military Past: A Guide to Information Sources. LC 74-11517. (The American Government & History Information Guide Ser.: Vol. 7). 1980. 42.00x (ISBN 0-8103-1205-0). Gale.
Lane, Jane & Lane, John. How to Make Play Places & Secret Hidy Holes. (Illus.). 1979. 7.95 (ISBN 0-385-13048-1); PLB o.p. (ISBN 0-385-13056-2). Doubleday.
Lane, John, jt. auth. see Lane, Jane.
Lane, John E. Choosing Programs for Microcomputers. LC 80-142911. 138p. (Orig.). 1980. pap. 22.50x o.p. (ISBN 0-85012-255-4). Intl Pubns Serv.
Lane, Joseph F., jt. auth. see Sullivan, Daniel J.
Lane, Maggie. Gold & Silver Needlepoint. (Illus.). 168p. 1983. 19.95 (ISBN 0-686-83805-X, ScribT). Scribner.
Lane, Marc. Taxation for Small Manufacturers. (Small Business Management Ser.). 163p. 1980. 31.50 (ISBN 0-471-05709-6). Ronald Pr.
--Taxation for the Computer Industry. (Small Business Management Ser.). 165p. 1980. 31.50 (ISBN 0-471-05710-X). Ronald Pr.
Lane, Marc J. Taxation for the Computer Industry. 165p. 1980. 31.50 o.p. (ISBN 0-471-05710-X). Wiley.
Lane, Margaret. The Beaver. (Illus.). 32p. 1983. pap. 3.50 (ISBN 0-8037-0637-5, 0340-100). Dial Bks Young.
--Bronte Story. LC 75-108394. (Illus.). 1971. Repr. of 1953 ed. lib. bdg. 17.75x (ISBN 0-8371-3817-5, LABS). Greenwood.
--The Fish: The Story of the Stickleback. (Illus.). 32p. (gr. k-4). 1983. pap. 3.50 (ISBN 0-8037-2603-1, 0340-100). Dial Bks Young.
--The Frog. (Pied Piper Bks.). (Illus.). 32p. (gr. k-3). 1982. pap. 3.25 (ISBN 0-8037-2748-8). Dial.
--The Squirrel. (Pied Piper Bks.). (Illus.). 32p. (gr. k-3). 1982. pap. 3.50 (ISBN 0-8037-8330-2). Dial.
Lane, Mary E. Mizora: A Prophecy. (Science Fiction Ser). 328p. 1975. Repr. of 1890 ed. lib. bdg. 14.00 o.p. (ISBN 0-8398-2306-1, Gregg). G K Hall.
Lane, Max, tr. see Rendra, Willibordus S.
Lane, Michael. Books & Publishers: Commerce Against Culture in Postwar Britain. LC 79-3135. 160p. 1980. 19.95x (ISBN 0-669-03383-9). Lexington Bks.
Lane, N. Gary. Life of the Past. 1978. pap. text ed. 16.95 (ISBN 0-675-08411-3). Merrill.
Lane, Nancy. How to Keep Your Face Looking Young. 224p. (Orig.). 1980. pap. 2.25 o.p. (ISBN 0-523-40926-5). Pinnacle Bks.
Lane, Patrick. Poems New & Selected. 1980. pap. 5.95 o.p. (ISBN 0-19-540296-0). Oxford U Pr.
Lane, Paul. Dow Jones-Irwin Guide to College Financial Planning. LC 81-67120. 285p. 1981. 16.95 (ISBN 0-87094-267-0). Dow Jones-Irwin.
Lane, Paul H. & Rossman, Antonio. Owens Valley Groundwater Conflict. Smith, Genny, ed. 1978. pap. 2.50 (ISBN 0-931378-03-6, Dist. by W. Kaufmann Inc.). Genny Smith Bks.
Lane, Peter. Europe in the Twentieth Century. (Twentieth Century World History Ser.). 1978. 14.95 o.p. (ISBN 0-7134-0984-3, Pub. by Batsford England). David & Charles.
--The U. S. A. in the Twentieth Century. 1978. 14.95 o.p. (ISBN 0-7134-0975-4, Pub. by Batsford England). David & Charles.
Lane, Richard. Images from the Floating World: The Japanese Print, Including an Illustrated Dictionary of Ukiyo-e. LC 78-53445. (Illus.). 1978. 60.00 (ISBN 0-399-12193-5). Putnam Pub Group.
--Lane's English As a Second Language. LC 79-90621. (English As a Second Language Ser.: Bk. 5). (Illus.). 95p. pap. text ed. 4.95 (ISBN 0-935606-01-7). Lane Pr.
--Lane's English As a Second Language. (English As a Second Language Ser.: Bk. 2). (Illus.). 83p. 1981. pap. text ed. 4.95 (ISBN 0-686-83956-0). Lane Pr.
--Lane's English As a Second Language. (English As a Second Language Ser.: Bk. 3). (Illus.). 82p. 1981. pap. text ed. 4.95 (ISBN 0-686-83957-9). Lane Pr.
--Lane's English As a Second Language. (Language As a Second Language Ser.: Bk. 4). (Illus.). 84p. 1981. pap. text ed. 4.95 (ISBN 0-686-83959-5). Lane Pr.
--Lane's English As a Second Language. (English Language Ser.: Bk. 6). (Illus.). 105p. 1981. pap. text ed. 4.95 (ISBN 0-686-83961-7). Lane Pr.
--Lane's English Pronunciation Guide. LC 79-90622. (Illus.). 64p. 1979. pap. text ed. 4.95 (ISBN 0-686-83962-5). Lane Pr.
Lane, Robert, et al. Analytical Transport Planning. LC 72-11852. 283p. 1973. 33.95x o.p. (ISBN 0-470-51440-X). Halsted Pr.
Lane, Robert S., jt. auth. see Middlekauff, Woodrow W.
Lane, Roger & Turner, John J., Jr., eds. Riot, Rout, & Tumult: Readings in American Social & Political Violence. LC 77-84752. (Contributions in American History: No. 69). 1978. lib. bdg. 29.95x (ISBN 0-8371-9845-3, LRR/). Greenwood.
Lane, Rose W. Woman's Day Book of American Needlework. Woman's Day Editors, ed. 1977. pap. 8.95 o.p. (ISBN 0-671-22786-6, Fireside). S&S.
--Young Pioneers. LC 75-46559. (YA) 1976. 10.95 (ISBN 0-07-036205-X, GB). McGraw.
Lane, Rose W. & Boylston, Helen D. Travels with Zenobia: Paris to Albania by Model T Ford. Holtz, William, ed. LC 82-13554. 128p. 1983. text ed. 13.00x (ISBN 0-8262-0390-6). U of Mo Pr.
Lane, Rose W. & MacBride, Roger L. Rose Wilder Lane: Her Story. LC 77-12072. 238p. 1980. pap. 7.95 (ISBN 0-8128-6077-2). Stein & Day.
Lane, S., jt. auth. see Jackson, S. M.
Lane, S., jt. auth. see Phillips, E. B.
Lane, Sylvia, jt. ed. see Phillips, E. Bryant.
Lane, Tamar. What's Wrong with the Movies? LC 78-160237. (Moving Pictures Ser). 254p. 1971. Repr. of 1923 ed. lib. bdg. 13.95x (ISBN 0-89198-038-5). Ozer.
Lane, William G. Richard Harris Barham. LC 67-15811. 287p. 1967. 16.00x (ISBN 0-8262-0070-2). U of Mo Pr.
Lane, Wm. An Arabic-English Lexicon, 8 Vols. Set. 295.00x (ISBN 0-86685-087-2). Intl Bk Ctr.
Lanegran, David & Palm, Risa. An Invitation to Geography. (Geography Ser.). (Illus.). 1977. pap. text ed. 14.95 (ISBN 0-07-036216-5, C). McGraw.
Lanegran, David, jt. auth. see Martin, Judith A.
Lane-Poole, S. History of Egypt in the Middle Ages. LC 68-25246. (World History Ser., No. 48). 1969. Repr. of 1901 ed. lib. bdg. 33.95x (ISBN 0-8383-0210-6). Haskell.
Laney, J. Carl. Ezra & Nehemiah. (Everyman's Bible Commentary Ser.). (Orig.). 1982. pap. 4.50 (ISBN 0-8024-2014-1). Moody.
--First & Second Samuel. (Everyman's Bible Commentary Ser.). 1982. pap. 4.50 (ISBN 0-8024-2010-9). Moody.
--Marching Orders. 168p. 1983. pap. 4.95 (ISBN 0-88207-398-2). Victor Bks.
Laney, William R. & Gibilisco, Joseph A., eds. Diagnosis & Treatment in Prosthodontics. LC 82-15171. (Illus.). 561p. 1983. text ed. write for info (ISBN 0-8121-0275-4). Lea & Febiger.
Lanez, Manual M. The Wandering Unicorn: A Novel. Fitton, Mary, tr. from Span. LC 82-19598. 1983. 16.95 (ISBN 0-8008-8041-2). Taplinger.
Lanford, Sondra G. Red Bird of Ireland. LC 82-13897. 192p. (gr. 4-7). 1983. 10.95 (ISBN 0-689-50270-2, McElderry Bk). Atheneum.
Lang, Andrew. The Arabian Nights Entertainments. 9.50 (ISBN 0-8446-0752-5). Peter Smith.
--The Book of Dreams & Ghosts. LC 80-19690. 301p. 1980. Repr. of 1972 ed. lib. bdg. 12.95x (ISBN 0-89370-610-8). Borgo Pr.
--Book of Dreams & Ghosts. 1972. pap. 4.95 o.p. (ISBN 0-87877-010-0, P-10). Newcastle Pub.
--The Crimson Fairy Book. 9.00 (ISBN 0-8446-0753-3). Peter Smith.
--Favorite Andrew Lang Fairy Tale Books in Many Colors: Red, Green & Blue Fairy Tale Books. (Illus.). 1979. pap. 15.95 boxed set (ISBN 0-486-23407-X). Dover.
--John Knox & the Reformation. LC 66-25923. Repr. of 1905 ed. 13.50 o.p. (ISBN 0-8046-0258-1). Kennikat.
--The Orange Fairy Book. 9.00 (ISBN 0-8446-4770-5). Peter Smith.
--Pink Fairy Book. (Illus.). (gr. 4-6). 1966. pap. 5.00 (ISBN 0-486-21792-2). Dover.
--Prince Prigio, Repr. Of 1889 Ed. Bd. with Prince Ricardo of Pantouflia. Repr. of 1893 ed. LC 75-32195. (Classics of Children's Literature, 1621-1932: Vol. 57). (Illus.). 1976. PLB 38.00 o.s.i. (ISBN 0-8240-2306-4). Garland Pub.
Lang, Andrew, ed. Crimson Fairy Book. (Illus.). (gr. 4-6). 1966. pap. 5.00 (ISBN 0-486-21799-X). Dover.
--The Green Fairy Book. (Illus.). 9.00 (ISBN 0-8446-5056-0). Peter Smith.
--King Arthur: Tales of the Round Table. LC 67-26996. (Illus.). (gr. 5 up). 1968. pap. 3.95 (ISBN 0-8052-0196-3). Schocken.
--Olive Fairy Book. (Illus.). (gr. 4-6). 1966. pap. 4.50 (ISBN 0-486-21908-9). Dover.
Lang, Anne, jt. ed. see Gassen, Hans G.
Lang, Anton, ed. see Society for the Study of Experimental Biology - 28th Symposium, 1969.
Lang, Berel. F A C E S... & Other Ironies of Writing & Reading. 100p. 1983. 9.75 (ISBN 0-915145-49-9). Hackett Pub.
--Philosophy & the Art of Writing: Studies in Philosophical & Literary Style. LC 81-65865. 248p. 1982. 28.50 (ISBN 0-8387-5030-3). Bucknell U Pr.
Lang, Cecil Y., ed. see Swinburne, Algernon C.
Lang, David, tr. & intro. by see Mepisashvili, Rusudan & Tsintsadze, Vakhtang.
Lang, David M. A Modern History of Soviet Georgia. LC 75-11426. (Illus.). 298p. 1975. Repr. of 1962 ed. lib. bdg. 20.00x (ISBN 0-8371-8183-6, LASG). Greenwood.
Lang, David M., tr. The Balavariani (Barlaam & Josaphat): A Tale from the Christian East. (Near Eastern Center, UCLA). 1966. 27.50x (ISBN 0-520-00697-6). U of Cal Pr.
Lang, Doe. The Secret of Charisma. 1982. 7.50 (ISBN 0-87223-790-7). Wideview Bks.
Lang, Elizabeth E., jt. auth. see Tighe, Mary Ann.
Lang, George. Lang's Compendium of Culinary Nonsense & Trivia. (Illus.). 1980. 10.00 (ISBN 0-517-54148-3, C N Potter Bks). Crown.
Lang, Gladys E. The Battle for Public Opinion: The President, the Press & the Polls During Watergate. Lang, Kurt, ed. 360p. 1983. 32.00x (ISBN 0-231-05548-X); pap. 12.50x (ISBN 0-231-05549-8). Columbia U Pr.
Lang, Grace. Love a Hostage. (YA) 1970. 6.95 (ISBN 0-685-07445-5, Avalon). Bouregy.
Lang, H. Jack. Letters in American History: Words to Remember. (Illus.). 144p. 1982. 12.95 (ISBN 0-517-54795-3, Harmony); pap. 6.95 (ISBN 0-517-54796-1). Crown.
Lang, Iain. Jazz in Perspective. LC 76-6985. (Roots of Jazz Ser.). 1976. lib. bdg. 19.50 (ISBN 0-306-70814-0). Da Capo.
Lang, J. Clinical Anatomy of the Head: Neurocranium, Orbita, Craniocervical Regions. (Illus.). 489p. 1983. 490.00 (ISBN 0-387-11014-3). Springer-Verlag.
Lang, J., et al, eds. Designing for Human Behavior: Architecture & the Behavioral Sciences. (Community Development Ser.: Vol. 6). 353p. 1974. pap. text ed. 19.50 (ISBN 0-87933-217-4). Hutchinson Ross.
Lang, Jochen von see Von Lang, Jochen & Sibyll, Claus.
Lang, Jochen von see Von Lang, Jochen.
Lang, Josephine. Selected Songs. (Women Composers Ser.: No. 11). 1982. Repr. of 1871 ed. lib. bdg. 22.50 (ISBN 0-306-76097-5). Da Capo.
Lang, June & Carl, Angela. Twenty-Six Children's Church Programs: Getting to Know Jesus. (Illus.). 112p. 1983. pap. 6.95 (ISBN 0-87239-608-8, 3378). Standard Pub.
Lang, K. Monographie der Harpacticiden. (Illus.). 1682p. (Ger.). 1975. Repr. of 1948 ed. lib. bdg. 192.00 (ISBN 3-87429-089-1). Lubrecht & Cramer.
Lang, K. R. Astrophysical Formulae: A Compendium for the Physicist & Astrophysicist. (Springer Study Edition). (Illus.). 1979. pap. 53.00 (ISBN 0-387-09933-6). Springer-Verlag.
Lang, Kurt, ed. see Lang, Gladys E.
Lang, L., ed. Absorption Spectra in the Ultraviolet & Visible Region. Incl. Vols. 3-4. 1962-63. 72.00 ea. Vol. 3 (ISBN 0-12-436303-2). Vol. 4 (ISBN 0-12-436304-0); Vol. 5. 1965. 72.00 (ISBN 0-12-436305-9); Vols. 6-12. 1966-73. 72.00 ea. Vol. 6 (ISBN 0-12-436306-7). Vol. 7 (ISBN 0-12-436307-5). Vol. 8 (ISBN 0-12-436308-3). Vol. 9 (ISBN 0-12-436309-1). Vol. 10 (ISBN 0-12-436310-5). Vol. 11. (ISBN 0-12-436311-3); Vol. 12. (ISBN 0-12-436312-1); Index to Volumes. 1969. 36.00 (ISBN 0-12-436356-3); Vols. 13-15. 1970. 72.00 ea. Vol. 13 (ISBN 0-12-436313-X). Vol. 14 (ISBN 0-12-436314-8). Vol. 15 (ISBN 0-12-436315-6); Index to Volumes 11-15. 1971. 36.00 (ISBN 0-12-436357-1); Vols. 16-17. 1972-73. 71.00 ea. Vol. 17 (ISBN 0-12-436317-2). Acad Pr.
--Absorption Spectra in the Ultraviolet & Visible Region, Vol. 24. 420p. 1980. lib. bdg. 46.50 o.p. (ISBN 0-89874-093-2). Krieger.
Lang, Larry. Strategy for Personal Finance. 2nd ed. 1981. text ed. 22.95 (ISBN 0-07-036281-5, C) (ISBN 0-07-036283-1). wkbk. 8.95 (ISBN 0-07-036282-3). McGraw.
Lang, Larry & Gillespie, Thomas. Strategy for Personal Finance. (Illus.). 1976. text ed. 16.00 o.p. (ISBN 0-07-036247-5, C); instructor's manual 5.95 o.p. (ISBN 0-07-036249-1); wkbk. 6.50 o.p. (ISBN 0-07-036248-3); transparency masters 4.95 o.p. (ISBN 0-07-074713-X). McGraw.
Lang, Laszlo. The Poor Rich. LC 82-141712. (Studies on Developing Countries: No. 108). 130p. (Orig.). 1981. pap. 13.50x (ISBN 963-301-081-0). Intl Pubns Serv.
Lang, Maud. The Moon Tree. LC 77-10071. 1978. 9.95 o.p. (ISBN 0-698-10861-2, Coward). Putnam Pub Group.
--Summer Station. LC 75-38763. 288p. 1976. 8.95 o.p. (ISBN 0-698-10732-2, Coward). Putnam Pub Group.
Lang, Michael. Gentrification Amid Urban Decline. 168p. 1982. prof ref 22.50x (ISBN 0-88410-697-7). Ballinger Pub.
Lang, Othmar F. If You Are Silenced, I Will Speak for You. Mayer, Eva, tr. from Ger. LC 78-59819. (gr. 6 up). 1978. 6.95 o.p. (ISBN 0-529-05432-9, Philomel). Putnam Pub Group.
Lang, Paul H., ed. Creative World of Mozart. (Illus.). 1963. pap. 5.95 (ISBN 0-393-00218-7, Norton Lib). Norton.
--Haydn Commemorative Issue of "The Musical Quarterly". (Music Reprint Ser.). 1983. Repr. of 1932 ed. lib. bdg. 25.00 (ISBN 0-306-76156-4). Da Capo.
Lang, R., jt. auth. see Whitcomb, Helen.

Lang, Regine. A Century of Health Care Ministry: A History of St. Francis Medical Center. (Illus.). 224p. 1982. text ed. 24.95 (ISBN 0-88136-011-2). Jostens.

Lang, Robert E., jt. auth. see Ma, T. S.

Lang, Rosalind, jt. auth. see Whitcomb, Helen.

Lang, Serge. Calculus of Several Variables. 2nd ed. LC 78-55822. (Mathematics Ser.). (Illus.). 1979. text ed. 28.95 (ISBN 0-201-04299-1). A-W.

--Elliptic Functions. LC 72-1767. 350p. 1973. text ed. 29.50 (ISBN 0-201-04162-6, Adv Bk Prog). A-W.

--First Course in Calculus. 4th ed. LC 77-76193. (Mathematics Ser.). (Illus.). 1978. text ed. 25.95 (ISBN 0-201-04149-9). A-W.

--Introduction to Algebraic & Abelian Functions. LC 72-1765. 1972. text ed. 19.95 (ISBN 0-201-04163-4, Adv Bk Prog). A-W.

Lang, Serge & Murrow, Gene. Geometry. (Illus.). 464p. 1982. pap. text ed. 24.00 (ISBN 0-387-90727-0). Springer-Verlag.

Lang, Serge A. Introduction to Algebraic Geometry. 3rd ed. 1958. 19.95 (ISBN 0-201-04164-2, Adv Bk Prog). A-W.

--SL-Two(R) 1975. text ed. 29.50 (ISBN 0-201-04248-7). A-W.

Lang, Steven & Spectre, Peter. On the Hawser: A Tugboat Album. LC 79-67416. (Illus.). 522p. 1980. 30.00 (ISBN 0-89272-071-9, PIC436). Down East.

Lang, Susanna, tr. see Bonnefoy, Yves.

Lang, Thomas A., jt. auth. see Reed-Flora, Rosalind.

Lang, V. Paul. Heating & Cooling Safety. LC 76-24983. (gr. 9-12). 1977. pap. 7.00 (ISBN 0-8273-1011-0); instructor's guide 2.00 (ISBN 0-8273-1012-9). Delmar.

--Principles of Air Conditioning. LC 77-78900. (Air Conditioning, Refrigeration Ser.). 1979. text ed. cancelled (ISBN 0-8273-1001-3); pap. text ed. 14.60 (ISBN 0-8273-1009-9); instructor's guide 2.00 (ISBN 0-8273-1002-1). Delmar.

Langacker, Ronald. An Overview of Utoaztecan Grammar: Studies in Uto-Aztecan Grammer, I. (Publications in Linguistics & Related Fields Ser.: No. 56). 199p. 1977. 9.00x (ISBN 0-88312-070-4); microfiche 3.00 (ISBN 0-88312-469-6). Summer Inst Ling.

Langacker, Ronald, ed. Modern Aztec Grammatical Sketches: Studies in Uto-Aztecan Grammar II. (Publications in Linguistics & Related Fields: No. 56 Vol. II). 380p. 1979. pap. 13.50x (ISBN 0-88312-069-0); microfiche 3.75 (ISBN 0-88312-072-0). Summer Inst Ling.

Langacker, Ronald W., jt. auth. see Kalectaca, Milo.

Langacker, Ronald W., ed. see Tuggy, David H. & Brockway, Earl.

Langan, J. Reading & Study Skills. 2nd ed. 464p. 1982. 12.95x (ISBN 0-07-036263-7); instr's manual 10.00 (ISBN 0-07-036264-5). McGraw.

--Sentence Skills. 2nd ed. 336p. 1983. text ed. 11.95x (ISBN 0-07-036267-X); write for info instr's manual (ISBN 0-07-036268-8). McGraw.

Langan, John. English Skills. 2nd ed. (Illus.). 416p. 1980. text ed. 13.95x (ISBN 0-07-036265-3, C); instructor's manual 15.00x (ISBN 0-07-036266-1). McGraw.

--English Skills. (Illus.). 1977. pap. text ed. 9.95 o.p. (ISBN 0-07-036253-X, C); instructor's manual 3.95 o.p. (ISBN 0-07-036254-8). McGraw.

--Reading & Study Skills. (Illus.). (gr. 8-12). 1978. pap. text ed. 10.95 (ISBN 0-07-036257-2, C); instr's. manual 4.95 (ISBN 0-07-036258-0). McGraw.

--Sentence Skills: A Workbook for Writers. 1979. pap. 12.95 (ISBN 0-07-036255-6, C); instructors manual 18.00 (ISBN 0-07-036256-4). McGraw.

Langan, John & Nadell, Judith. Doing Well in College: A Concise Guide to Reading, Writing & Study Skills. Talkington, William A., ed. (Illus.). 208p. (Orig.). 1980. pap. text ed. 9.95 (ISBN 0-07-036262-9). McGraw.

Langan, John & Clapp, Jeremy, eds. Ligand Assay: Analysis of International Developments on Isotopic & Nonisotopic Immunoassay. LC 80-39663. (Illus.). 304p. 1980. 43.50x (ISBN 0-89352-094-2). Masson Pub.

Langbaum, Robert, ed. see Shakespeare, William.

Langbein, Laura I. Discovering Whether Programs Work. 1980. pap. text ed. 10.95x (ISBN 0-673-16260-5). Scott F.

Langdale, John V., jt. ed. see Cardew, Richard V.

Langdon, Dolly, jt. auth. see Bell, Sally C.

Langdon, Helen J., jt. auth. see Langdon, Lawrence.

Langdon, Larry. Creating Peace: A Positve Handbook. LC 82-13021. 64p. 1982. pap. 3.95 (ISBN 0-943726-00-X). Langdon Pubns.

Langdon, Lawrence & Langdon, Helen J. Initiating Occupational Therapy Programs Within the Public School System: A Guide for Occupational Therapists & Public School Administrators. LC 82-60925. 112p. Date not set. 14.50 (ISBN 0-913590-91-6). Slack Inc.

Langdon, S. Sumerian Grammatical Texts. (Publications of the Babylonian Section: Vol. 12). (Illus.). 44p. bound 7.00xsoft o.p. (ISBN 0-686-11925-8). Univ Mus of U PA.

Lange & Hora. Collins Guide to Mushrooms & Toadstools. 29.95 (ISBN 0-686-42766-1, Collins Pub England). Greene.

Lange, Arthur J., jt. auth. see Jakubowski, Patricia.

Lange, Brian M. & Entwistle, Beverly M. Dental Management of the Handicapped & Approaches for Dental Auxiliaries. (Illus.). 150p. 1982. text ed. write for info. (ISBN 0-8121-0884-1). Lea & Febiger.

Lange, Catherine, ed. see Ragan Report Workshop.

Lange, Charles H. Cochiti: New Mexico Pueblo, Past & Present. LC 58-10852. (Arcturus Books Paperbacks). (Illus.). 642p. pap. 11.95 o.p. (ISBN 0-8093-0296-9). S Ill U Pr.

Lange, Crystal M. Identification of Learning Styles. 32p. 1979. 3.50 (ISBN 0-686-38264-1, 23-1793). Natl League Nurse.

Lange, Crystal M., jt. auth. see Robischon, Paulette.

Lange, Debbie, jt. ed. see Harris, Beatrice.

Lange, Ed. Elysium Experience: Fun in the Sun. 32p. (Orig.). 1983. pap. write for info. (ISBN 0-910550-20-4). Elysium.

Lange, Frances, ed. see Grass, Gunter.

Lange, Francois-Joseph. Plaintes et Representations. (Fr.). 1977. lib. bdg. 13.75x o.p. (ISBN 0-8287-0506-2); pap. text ed. 3.75x o.p. (ISBN 0-685-77006-0). Clearwater Pub.

Lange, Johannes. Crime & Destiny. Haldane, Charlotte, tr. from Ger. (Historical Foundations of Forensic Psychiatry & Psychology Ser.). 250p. 1983. Repr. of 1930 ed. lib. bdg. 25.00 (ISBN 0-306-76209-9). Da Capo.

Lange, Joseph & Cushing, Anthony. Freedom & Healing. LC 75-40648. (Living Christian Community Ser.). 114p. 1976. pap. 4.95 o.p. (ISBN 0-8091-1920-X). Paulist Pr.

Lange, Julian E. & Mills, Daniel Q., eds. The Construction Industry: Balance Wheel of the Economy. LC 79-1562. 256p. 1979. 21.95x (ISBN 0-669-02913-0). Lexington Bks.

Lange, Max. The Chess Genius of Paul Morphy. Falkbeer, Ernest, tr. LC 73-83322. (Chess Classics Ser.). (Illus.). 356p. 1974. Repr. 15.95. Hippocrene Bks.

Lange, Monique. Piaf. 252p. 1983. 11.95 (ISBN 0-394-62428-9). Seaver Bks.

Lange, Muriel W. Geometry in Modules A-D, Bks. 1-4. (gr. 10-12). 1975. pap. text ed. 5.16 ea. (Sch Div); No. 1. pap. text ed. (ISBN 0-201-04125-1). No. 2 (ISBN 0-201-04126-X). No. 3 (ISBN 0-201-04127-8). No. 4 (ISBN 0-201-04128-6). tchr's commentary 15.52 (ISBN 0-201-04129-4). A-W.

Lange, O. H. see Ordway, Frederick I., 3rd.

Lange, O. L., et al, eds. Physiological Plant Ecology III: Responses to the Chemical & Biological Environment. (Encyclopedia of Plant Physiology Ser.: Vol. 12C). (Illus.). 850p. 1983. 120.00 (ISBN 0-387-10907-2). Springer-Verlag.

Lange, Oskar. On Political Economy & Econometrics. 1966. 60.00 (ISBN 0-08-011588-8). Pergamon.

Lange, Oskar & Taylor, Fred M. On the Economic Theory of Socialism. 1956. pap. 3.95 (ISBN 0-07-036259-9, SP). McGraw.

Lange, Peter & Ross, George. Unions, Change & Crisis: French & Italian Union Strategy & the Political Economy 1945-1980. 280p. 1983. text ed. 35.00x (ISBN 0-04-331088-5). Allen Unwin.

Lange, Roland A. Two Hundred & One Japanese Verbs Fully Conjugated in All the Forms. LC 76-140634. (Orig.). 1971. pap. text ed. 5.95 (ISBN 0-8120-0391-8). Barron.

Lange, Suzanne. The Year. LC 78-120787. (gr. 8 up). 1970. 10.95 (ISBN 0-87599-173-4). S G Phillips.

Lange, Victor. Classical Age of German Literature, 1740-1815. 256p. (Orig.). 1983. text ed. 26.00x (ISBN 0-8419-0853-2); pap. text ed. 17.50x (ISBN 0-8419-0854-0). Holmes & Meier.

Lange, Victor, ed. see Grass, Gunter.

Langen, Dietrich. Speaking of: Sleeping Problems. (Geneal Ser.). 1980. lib. bdg. 8.95 (ISBN 0-8161-6765-6, Large Print Bks). G K Hall.

Langenbach, Robert & Nesnow, Stephen, eds. Organ & Species Specificity in Chemical Carcinogenesis. 704p. 1983. 79.50x (ISBN 0-306-41184-9, Plenum Pr). Plenum Pub.

Langenheim, Jean H. & Thimann, Kenneth V. Botany: Plant Biology & Its Relation to Human Affairs. LC 81-7466. 624p. 1982. text ed. 28.50x (ISBN 0-471-85880-3). Wiley.

Langenkamp, R. D. Handbook of Oil Industry Terms & Phrases. 3rd ed. 250p. 1981. 23.95x (ISBN 0-87814-171-5). Pennwell Books Division.

--Handbook of Oil Industry Terms & Phrases. 2nd ed. LC 74-80034. 208p. 1977. 23.95x o.p. (ISBN 0-87814-034-4). Pennwell Pub.

Langenkamp, Robert & Gerolde, Steven. The Illustrated Petroleum Reference Dictionary. 580p. 1980. 45.95x (ISBN 0-87814-099-9). Pennwell Book Division.

Langenkamp, Robert D. Oil Business Fundamentals. 152p. 1982. 25.00x (ISBN 0-87814-198-7). Pennwell Books Division.

Langenkamp, Robert D., ed. Illustrated Petroleum: Reference Dictionary. 2nd ed. (Illus.). 584p. 1982. 45.95x (ISBN 0-87814-160-X). Pennwell Book Division.

Langer, Ellen J. & Dweck, Carol S. Personal Politics: The Psychology of Making It. (Illus.). 192p. 1973. pap. text ed. 11.95 (ISBN 0-13-657247-2). P-H.

Langer, Herbert. Thirty Years War. Orig. Title: Horticus Bellicus. (Illus.). 260p. 1980. 35.00 o.p. (ISBN 0-88254-497-7). Hippocrene Bks.

Langer, Jiri. Nine Gates: To the Chasidic Mysteries. Jolly, Stephen, tr. 295p. 1961. 17.50 (ISBN 0-227-67552-5). Attic Pr.

Langer, Maria. The Endocrine & the Liver: Proceedings of the Serono Symposia, No. 51. 64.00 (ISBN 0-12-436580-9). Acad Pr.

Langer, Marshall J. & Povell, Roy A. Foreign Tax Planning 1981: A Course Handbook. 767p. 1981. pap. 25.00 o.p. (ISBN 0-686-96137-4, J4-3483). PLI.

Langer, Nola. By the Light of the Silvery Moon. LC 82-12726. (Illus.). 32p. (gr. 1-3). 1983. 9.00 (ISBN 0-688-01661-8); PLB 8.59 (ISBN 0-688-01663-4). Lothrop.

Langer, Paul, jt. auth. see Swearingen, A. Rodger.

Langer, R. H., ed. Pastures & Pasture Plants. (Illus.). 1973. pap. 19.50 o.p. (ISBN 0-589-01039-5, Pub. by Reed Books Australia). C E Tuttle.

Langer, Robert. Seizure of Territory, the Stimson Doctrine & Related Principles in Legal Theory & Diplomatic Practice. Repr. of 1947 ed. lib. bdg. 20.75x (ISBN 0-8371-0907-8, LASD). Greenwood.

Langer, S. Z., et al, eds. see Official Satellite Symposium, International Congress of Pharmacology, Nagasaki, Japan, 8th 30-31 July 1982.

Langer, Sidney. Scared Straight: Fear in the Deterrence of Delinquency. LC 80-5859. 141p. 1981. lib. bdg. 15.50 o.p. (ISBN 0-8191-1494-4); pap. text ed. 6.75 o.p. (ISBN 0-8191-1495-2). U Pr of Amer.

Langer, Steven. Compensation of Industrial Engineers. 5th ed. 1980. pap. 50.00 o.p. (ISBN 0-916506-50-9). Abbott Langer Assocs.

--Income in Sales-Marketing Management. 1981. pap. 85.00 o.p. (ISBN 0-916506-58-4). Abbott Langer Assocs.

--Inter-City Wage & Salary Differentials 1980. 3rd ed. 1980. pap. 50.00 o.p. (ISBN 0-916506-36-3). Abbott Langer Assocs.

--The Personnel-Industrial Relations Report, Pt. III: Departmental Budgets & Staffing Ratios. 1980. pap. 85.00 o.p. (ISBN 0-916506-35-5). Abbott Langer Assocs.

--The Personnel-Industrial Relations Report, Pt. II: Income by Type & Size of Employer. 1980. pap. 85.00 o.p. (ISBN 0-916506-53-3). Abbott Langer Assocs.

--Salaries & Related Matters in the Service Department 1980. 1980. pap. 60.00 o.p. (ISBN 0-916506-38-X). Abbott Langer Assocs.

Langer, Steven, jt. auth. see Serebriakoff, Victor.

Langer, Steven, ed. The Accounting-Financial Report, 2 pts. Incl. Pt. 1. Public Accounting Firms (ISBN 0-916506-48-7); Pt. 2. Industry, Government, Education, Non-Profit (ISBN 0-916506-49-5). 1980. pap. 60.00 ea. o.p. Abbott Langer Assocs.

--Accounting-Financial Report. 3rd ed. 1982. pap. 85.00 ea. Pt. I: Public Accounting Firms (ISBN 0-916506-71-1). Pt. II: Industry, Government, & Education, Non-Profit (ISBN 0-916506-72-X). Abbott Langer Assocs.

--The Accounting-Financial Report: Industry-Government-Education-Non-Profit, Pt. II. 2nd ed. 1981. pap. 75.00 o.p. (ISBN 0-916506-61-4). Abbott Langer Assocs.

--The Accounting-Financial Report: Public Accounting Firms, Pt. I. 2nd ed. 1981. pap. 75.00 o.p. (ISBN 0-916506-60-6). Abbott Langer Assocs.

--Available Pay Survey Reports: An Annotated Bibliography, 3 pts. 2nd ed. 1980. Pt. I. pap. 95.00 (ISBN 0-916506-44-4); Pt. II. pap. 40.00 (ISBN 0-916506-45-2); Pt. III. pap. 45.00 (ISBN 0-916506-46-0). Abbott Langer Assocs.

--College Recruiting Report: 1980. pap. 75.00 o.p. (ISBN 0-916506-57-6). Abbott Langer Assocs.

--College Recruiting Report, 1982. 1982. pap. 95.00 (ISBN 0-686-84830-6). Abbott Langer Assocs.

--Compensation in Human Resource Development. 1981. pap. 75.00 o.p. (ISBN 0-916506-59-2). Abbott Langer Assocs.

--Compensation in Manufacturing: Engineers & Managers. 3rd ed. 1980. pap. 75.00 o.p. (ISBN 0-916506-56-8). Abbott Langer Assocs.

--Compensation in Manufacturing: Engineers & Managers. 4th ed. 1982. pap. 95.00 (ISBN 0-916506-74-6). Abbott Langer Assocs.

--Compensation in Training & Development. 2nd ed. 1982. pap. 95.00 (ISBN 0-686-84833-0). Abbott Langer Assocs.

--Compensation of Attorneys: Non-Law Firms. 4th ed. 1982. pap. 110.00 (ISBN 0-686-84834-9). Abbott Langer Assocs.

--Compensation of Attorneys, Pt. I: Non-Law Firms. 2nd ed. 1980. pap. 50.00 o.p. (ISBN 0-916506-51-7). Abbott Langer Assocs.

--Compensation of Attorneys: Pt. II, Law Firms. 1978. pap. 50.00 o.p. (ISBN 0-916506-26-6). Abbott Langer Assocs.

--Compensation of Industrial Engineering. 6th ed. 1981. 60.00 o.p. (ISBN 0-916506-63-0). Abbott Langer Assocs.

--Compensation of Industrial Engineers. 7th ed. 1982. pap. 75.00 (ISBN 0-916506-75-4). Abbott Langer Assocs.

--Compensation of MBA's. 2nd ed. 1978. pap. 50.00 o.p. (ISBN 0-916506-28-2). Abbott Langer Assocs.

--Income in Sales-Marketing Management. 3rd ed. 1982. pap. 95.00 (ISBN 0-686-84835-7). Abbott Langer Assocs.

--Industrial Recreation Report - 1977. 1977. pap. 60.00 o.p. (ISBN 0-916506-18-5). Abbott Langer Assocs.

--Inter-City Wage & Salary Differentials, 1981. 1981. pap. 75.00 o.p. (ISBN 0-916506-62-2). Abbott Langer Assocs.

--Inter-City Wage & Salary Differentials. 3rd ed. 1982. pap. 85.00 (ISBN 0-686-84836-5). Abbott Langer Assocs.

--Personnel-Industrial Relations Report, Pt. I: Income by Individual Variables. 1980. pap. 85.00 o.p. (ISBN 0-916506-54-1). Abbott Langer Assocs.

--Salaries & Bonuses in Personnel-Industrial Relations Functions. 4th ed. 1982. pap. 150.00 (ISBN 0-686-84837-3). Abbott Langer Assocs.

--Salaries & Fringe Benefits in the Kitchen Cabinet Industry. 1977. pap. 125.00 o.p. (ISBN 0-916506-16-9). Abbott Langer Assocs.

--Salaries & Related Matters in the Service Department, 1981. 1981. pap. 85.00 o.p. (ISBN 0-686-69467-8). Abbott Langer Assocs.

--Salaries & Related Matters in the Service Department, 1982. 1982. pap. 95.00 (ISBN 0-686-84839-X). Abbott Langer Assocs.

--The Security Report. 1978. pap. 60.00 o.p. (ISBN 0-916506-32-0). Abbott Langer Assocs.

--The Security Report. 2nd ed. 1982. pap. 85.00 (ISBN 0-916506-70-3). Abbott Langer Assocs.

Langer, Steven & Lutz, Carl F., eds. Municipal Personnel Report. 1979. pap. 75.00 o.p. (ISBN 0-916506-42-8). Abbott Langer Assocs.

Langer, Susanne K. Philosophy in a New Key: A Study in the Symbolism of Reason, Rite & Art. 3rd ed. LC 57-1386. 1957. 17.50x (ISBN 0-674-66500-7); pap. 6.95 (ISBN 0-674-66503-1). Harvard U Pr.

Langer, Thomas E. Christian Marriage: A Guide for Young People. rev. ed. 1967. pap. 2.96 o.p. (ISBN 0-02-820180-9). Glencoe.

Langer, Walter. The Mind of Adolf Hitler. 1978. pap. 3.50 (ISBN 0-451-62106-9, ME2040, Ment). NAL.

Langer, William L., et al. Western Civilization, 2 vols. 2nd ed. Incl. Vol. 1. Prehistory to the Peace of Utrecht. 526p (ISBN 0-06-043844-4); Vol. 2. The Expansion of Empire to Europe in the Modern World. 485p (ISBN 0-06-043846-0). 1975. pap. text ed. 18.50 ea. scp (ISBN 0-686-67088-4, HarpC); test item to accompany vol. 1 avail. (ISBN 0-06-363843-6); test item to accompany vol. 2 avail. (ISBN 0-06-363844-4). Har-Row.

Langerfield, Eugene V. The Two Major Enemies of Mankind. (The Great Currents of History Library Book). (Illus.). 139p. 1983. 81.65 (ISBN 0-86722-018-X). Inst Econ Pol.

Langevin, R. Sexual Strands: Understanding & Treating Sexual Anomalies in Men. (Illus.). 560p. 1982. text ed. 49.95 (ISBN 0-89859-205-4). L Erlbaum Assocs.

Langewiesche, Wolfgang. Stick & Rudder. (Illus.). 1944. 15.95 (ISBN 0-07-036240-8, GB). McGraw.

Langfield, Paul. Chess. LC 80-50947. (Whizz Kids Ser.). 8.00 (ISBN 0-382-06440-2). Silver.

--A Picture Guide to Chess. LC 75-46637. 1977. 9.57 (ISBN 0-397-31681-X, JBL-J); pap. 2.95 (ISBN 0-397-31682-8). Har-Row.

Langfitt, Dot E. Critical Care: Certification Practice Exams. (Illus.). 224p. 1983. pap. text ed. 12.95 (ISBN 0-89303-246-8). R J Brady.

--Critical Care: Certification Preparation & Review. (Illus.). 640p. 1983. text ed. 27.95 (ISBN 0-89303-245-X). R J Brady.

Langfitt, Dot E., jt. auth. see Barber, Triphy.

Langford, Bill. Spaces. 39p. 1982. pap. 2.50 (ISBN 0-943504-00-7). B Langford.

Langford, D. A. Direct Labour Organizations in the Construction Industry. 135p. 1982. text ed. 35.50x (ISBN 0-566-00542-5). Gower Pub Ltd.

Langford, David. War in Two Thousand Eighty: The Future of Military Technology. (Illus.). 232p. 1983. Repr. of 1979 ed. 16.50 (ISBN 0-7153-7661-6). David & Charles.

Langford, David, jt. auth. see Nicholls, Peter.

Langford, Herbert G. & Watson, Robert. Preventing Hypertension. 280p. 1983. 22.50 (ISBN 0-87527-185-5). Green.

Langford, J. O. & Gipson, Fred. Big Bend: A Homesteader's Story. (Illus.). 191p. 1981. pap. 7.95 (ISBN 0-292-70734-7). U of Tex Pr.

Langford, Jerome J. Galileo, Science & the Church. rev. ed. 1971. pap. 5.95x (ISBN 0-472-06173-9, 173, AA). U of Mich Pr.

Langford, Jim. The Game Is Never Over: An Appreciative History of the Chicago Cubs. 2nd, rev. ed. (Illus.). 288p. 1982. pap. 7.95 (ISBN 0-89651-266-5). Icarus.

Langford, Michael. Basic Photography. new, rev., 4th ed. (Illus.). 1977. 29.95 (ISBN 0-240-50954-4); pap. text ed. 18.95 (ISBN 0-240-50955-2). Focal Pr.

--Better Photography. (Illus.). 1978. 10.95 (ISBN 0-686-34365-4); pap. 7.95 o.p. (ISBN 0-240-50983-8). Focal Pr.

--Michael Langford's 35 MM Handbook. LC 82-48555. 1983. 16.95 (ISBN 0-394-53129-9); pap. 9.95 (ISBN 0-394-71369-9). Knopf.

--Starting Photography. 1976. 10.95 o.p. (ISBN 0-240-51099-2); pap. 7.95 (ISBN 0-240-50903-X). Focal Pr.

--The Step-by-Step Guide to Photography. LC 78-54894. (Illus.). 1978. 19.95 (ISBN 0-394-41604-X). Knopf.

Langford, Paul. Eighteenth Century, Sixteen Eighty-Eight to Eighteen Fifteen. LC 76-8805. (Modern British Foreign Policy Ser.). 1976. 17.95x o.p. (ISBN 0-312-24010-4). St Martin.

Langford, T. E. Electricity Generation & the Ecology of Natural Waters. 376p. 1982. 90.00x (ISBN 0-85323-334-9, Pub. by Liverpool Univ England). State Mutual Bk.

Langford, Teddy. Managing & Being Managed: Preparation for Professional Nursing Practice. (Illus.). 304p. 1981. text ed. 19.95 (ISBN 0-13-550525-9); pap. text ed. 15.95 (ISBN 0-13-550517-8). P-H.

Langford, Thomas, jt. auth. see Isard, Walter.

Langford, Thomas A. Practical Divinity: Theology in the Wesleyan Tradition. 304p. (Orig.). 1983. pap. 9.95 (ISBN 0-687-33326-1). Abingdon.

Langford, Thomas A., jt. ed. see Abernethy, George L.

Langford, W. J., ed. see Neville, Eric H.

Langhaar, Henry L. Energy Methods in Applied Mechanics. LC 62-10925. 350p. 1962. 34.95x (ISBN 0-471-51711-9, Pub. by Wiley-Interscience). Wiley.

Langham, Ian G., jt. auth. see Oldroyd, David R.

Langham, James M. Planetary Effects on Commodity Prices. (Illus.). 153p. 1982. 195.45 (ISBN 0-86654-028-8). Inst Econ Finan.

Langham, M. J., jt. auth. see Hussey, David.

Langham, Thomas A. Border Trials: Ricardo Flores Magon & the Mexican Liberals. (Southwestern Studies Ser.: No. 65). 1981. pap. 3.00x (ISBN 0-87404-123-6). Tex Western.

Langham, Tony, tr. see Hammacher, A. M.

Langhans, Edward A. Restoration Promptbooks. LC 80-15626. 704p. 1981. 90.00x (ISBN 0-8093-0855-X). S Ill U Pr.

Langhorne, Richard. The Collapse of the Concert of Europe Eighteen Ninety to Nineteen Fourteen. 1981. 22.50 (ISBN 0-312-14723-6). St Martin.

Langlais, Robert, jt. auth. see Kasle, Myron J.

Langland, Elizabeth & Gove, Walter, eds. A Feminist Perspective in the Academy: The Difference It Makes. LC 82-17520. 168p. 1981. pap. 5.95 (ISBN 0-226-46875-5). U of Chicago Pr.

Langland, William. Piers Plowman: An Edition of the C-Text. Pearsall, Derek, ed. LC 78-64463. (York Medieval Texts: Ser. 2). 1979. 44.00x (ISBN 0-520-03793-6). U of Cal Pr.

--Vision of William Concerning Piers the Plowman, in Three Parallel Texts, Together with Richard the Redeless, 2 Vols. Skeat, W. W., ed. 1886. 77.00x (ISBN 0-19-811366-8). Oxford U Pr.

Langley, Andrew. Explorers on the Nile. LC 81-86275. (In Profile Ser.). PLB 12.68 (ISBN 0-382-06637-5). Silver.

Langley, Bill. Basic Refrigeration. 416p. 1982. text ed. 23.95 (ISBN 0-8359-0417-2); solutions manual free (ISBN 0-8359-0418-0). Reston.

Langley, Billy. Air Conditioning & Refrigeration Trouble-Shooting Handbook. (Illus.). 650p. 1980. text ed. 31.95 (ISBN 0-8359-0204-8). Reston.

Langley, Billy C. Comfort Heating. 2nd ed. (Illus.). 1978. ref. 20.95 (ISBN 0-87909-091-X); instrs' manual avail. (ISBN 0-87909-092-8). Reston.

--Electric Controls for Refrigeration & Air Conditioning. 1974. 22.95 (ISBN 0-13-247072-1); pap. 16.95 ref. ed. (ISBN 0-13-247064-0). P-H.

Langley, Dorothy. Swamp Angel. 237p. 1982. 14.95 (ISBN 0-89733-060-9); pap. 5.95 (ISBN 0-89733-061-7). Academy Chi Ltd.

Langley, Elizabeth. Mission Thailand. 1977. 4.95 o.p. (ISBN 0-533-02806-X). Vantage.

Langley, H. D., jt. ed. see Loewenheim, F. L.

Langley, Harold D., ed. To Utah with the Dragoons; & Glimpses of Life in Arizona & California, 1858-1859. LC 73-80998. (University of Utah Publications in the American West: Vol. 11). (Illus.). 220p. 1974. 20.00 o.p. (ISBN 0-87480-087-0). U of Utah Pr.

Langley, Joan & Langley, Wright. Key West Images of the Past. LC 81-71478. (Illus.). 132p. 1982. 19.95 (ISBN 0-9609272-1-2); pap. 9.95 (ISBN 0-9609272-0-4). Images Key.

Langley, L. L., ed. Contraception. LC 73-4256. (Benchmark Papers in Human Physiology: Vol. 2). 500p. 1973. text ed. 55.00 (ISBN 0-87933-025-2). Hutchinson Ross.

Langley, L. L., et al. Dynamic Anatomy & Physiology. 4th ed. (Illus.). 1974. text ed. 18.95 o.p. (ISBN 0-07-036274-2). McGraw.

--Dynamic Anatomy & Physiology. 5th ed. (Illus.). 1980. text ed. 28.95 (ISBN 0-07-036275-0); instructor's manual 10.95 (ISBN 0-07-036284-X); study guide 13.95 (ISBN 0-07-036277-7). McGraw.

Langley, Lester D. U. S., Cuba & the Cold War: American Failure or Communist Conspiracy. (Problems in American Civilization Ser). 1970. pap. text ed. 5.50 o.p. (ISBN 0-669-51839-5). Heath.

Langley, Michael. Protection of Minority Political Participation Abadoned in Supreme Court's Ruling on Mobile Elections. 1980. 1.00 (ISBN 0-686-38004-5). Voter Ed Proj.

--State of Florida's Procurement Policies & Minority Business Enterprises. 1980. 1.00 (ISBN 0-686-38006-1). Voter Ed Proj.

--State of North Carolina's Procurement Policies & Minority Business Enterprises. 1980. 1.00 (ISBN 0-686-38008-8). Voter Ed Proj.

--Supreme Court Says Minority Enterprises Must be Given a Piece of the Action. 1980. 1.00 (ISBN 0-686-38005-3). Voter Ed Proj.

Langley, Myrtle S. The Nandi of Kenya: Life Crisis Rituals in a Period of Change. LC 78-31186. 1979. 26.00x (ISBN 0-312-55884-8). St Martin.

Langley, Nadine. Your Favorite Recipes. 225p. (Orig.). 1982. pap. 5.00 (ISBN 0-932970-32-X). Prinit Pr.

Langley, Stephen. Theatre Management in America; Principle & Practice: Producing for the Commercial Stock, Resident, College, & Community Theatre. rev. ed. LC 79-26028. (Illus.). 512p. 1980. text ed. 19.95x (ISBN 0-89676-024-3). Drama Bk.

Langley, Wright, jt. auth. see Langley, Joan.

Langley, Wright, jt. auth. see Windhorn, Stan.

Langley-Price, Pat, jt. auth. see Ouvry, Phil.

Langlois, Marc H. The Art & Life of Jean-Francois Millet. (Illus.). 121p. 1980. 49.75 (ISBN 0-930582-76-4). Gloucester Art.

Langlois, Richard N., jt. ed. see Fusfeld, Herbert I.

Langlois, Vincent W. Keynes & the Economic Bankruptcy of the Modern State. (Illus.). 139p. 1982. 78.45 (ISBN 0-86654-031-8). Inst Econ Finan.

Langman, Jan. Medical Embryology. 4th ed. 392p. 1981. 22.00 (ISBN 0-686-77742-5, 4858-9). Williams & Wilkins.

Langman, Jan & Woerdeman, M. W. Atlas of Medical Anatomy. LC 81-51356. 523p. 1981. pap. 14.95 (ISBN 0-7216-5622-6). Saunders.

Langman, Jan & Woerdman, M. W. Atlas of Medical Anatomy. LC 75-22735. (Illus.). 1978. text ed. 16.95 (ISBN 0-7216-5626-9). Saunders.

Langmeier, J. & Matejcek, Z. Psychological Deprivation in Childhood. 3rd ed. LC 75-16185. 496p. 1975. 34.95x o.s.i. (ISBN 0-470-51718-2). Halsted Pr.

--Psychological Deprivation in Childhood. 3rd ed. LC 75-16185. 496p. 1975. 23.50 (ISBN 0-470-51718-2, Pub. by Wiley). Krieger.

Langnas, I., ed. Twelve Hundred Russian Proverbs. 1960. pap. 1.50 (ISBN 0-8022-0925-4). Philos Lib.

Langner, Nola. Dusty. LC 76-15216. (Break-of-Day Bk.). (Illus.). (gr. k-3). 1976. PLB 6.99 (ISBN 0-698-30634-1, Coward). Putnam Pub Group.

Langness, L. L., ed. see Eastman, Carol M.

Langness, L. L., ed. see Kearney, Michael.

Lango, John. Whitehead's Ontology. LC 78-171184. 1972. 21.50x (ISBN 0-87395-093-3). State U NY Pr.

Langone, John. Bombed, Buzzed, Smashed, or... Sober: A Book About Alcohol. 7.95 o.p. (ISBN 0-686-92240-9, 5007). Hazelden.

--Death Is a Noun: A View of the End of Life. 240p. (gr. 7 up). 1972. 8.95 (ISBN 0-316-51420-9). Little.

--Human Engineering: Marvel or Menace? (gr. 7 up). 1978. 7.95 (ISBN 0-316-51427-6). Little.

--Life at the Bottom: The People of Antarctica. 1977. 8.95 o.p. (ISBN 0-316-51426-8). Little.

--Long Life: What We Know & Are Learning About the Aging Process. LC 78-17349. 1978. 9.95 o.p. (ISBN 0-316-51428-4). Little.

--Vital Signs: The Way We Die in America. LC 74-929. 420p. 1974. pap. 4.95 o.p. (ISBN 0-316-51423-3). Little.

Langone, John, jt. ed. see Colowick, S.

Langouche, F. & Roekaerts, D. Functional Integration & Semiclassical Expansions. 1982. 39.50 (ISBN 90-277-1472-X, Pub. by Reidel Holland). Kluwer Boston.

Langridge, D. W. Classification & Indexing in the Humanities. 224p. 1976. 13.95 o.p. (ISBN 0-408-70777-1). Butterworth.

Langrish, J., et al. Wealth from Knowledge. 477p. 1972. 29.95x o.s.i. (ISBN 0-470-51721-2). Halsted Pr.

Langrod, Jerzy S. International Civil Service. LC 63-22349. 358p. 1963. 25.00 (ISBN 0-379-00216-7). Oceana.

Langs, Robert. International Journal of Psychoanalytic Psychotherapy, Vol 7. LC 75-648853. 1979. 30.00x o.s.i. (ISBN 0-87668-265-4). Aronson.

--The Psychotherapeutic Conspiracy. LC 81-20601. 324p. 1982. 20.00 (ISBN 0-87668-488-6). Aronson.

--Psychotherapy: A Basic Text. LC 81-17663. 771p. 1982. 40.00 (ISBN 0-87668-466-5). Aronson.

--Unconscious Communication in Everyday Life. LC 82-1669. 224p. 1983. 17.50 (ISBN 0-87668-492-4). Aronson.

Langs, Robert, ed. International Journal of Psychoanalytic Psychotherapy, No. 6. LC 75-648853. 498p. 1977. 25.00 o.s.i. (ISBN 0-87668-282-4). Aronson.

--International Journal of Psychoanalytic Psychotherapy: 1982-1983, Vol. 9. Editorial Board. LC 75-648853. 832p. 1982. 35.00 (ISBN 0-87668-491-6). Aronson.

Langseth-Christensen, Lillian. The Instant Epicure Cookbook. 320p. 1975. pap. 3.00 o.p. (ISBN 0-486-23128-3). Dover.

Langsner, Drew. Country Woodcraft. LC 78-780. 1978. 15.95 (ISBN 0-87857-200-7); pap. 10.95 o.p. (ISBN 0-87857-201-5). Rodale Pr Inc.

Langstaff, Eleanor D. Andrew Lang. (English Authors Ser.). 1978. 12.95 (ISBN 0-8057-6719-3, Twayne). G K Hall.

Langstaff, Eleanor DeS. Panama. (World Bibliographical Ser.: No. 14). 197p. 1982. 28.00 (ISBN 0-903450-26-7). ABC-Clio.

Langstaff, John & Rojankovsky, Feodor. Over in the Meadow. LC 57-8587. (Illus.). 32p. (ps-3). 1973. pap. 2.25 (ISBN 0-15-670500-1, VoyB). HarBraceJ.

Langston, A. Leon, ed. see Leavitt, Guy P.

Langston, Charles S. & Squire, Lucy F. The Emergency Patient: Exercises in Diagnostic Radiology, Vol. 7. LC 74-113034. (Illus.). 255p. 1975. pap. text ed. 11.95 (ISBN 0-7216-5627-7). Saunders.

Langston, Charles S. see Squire, Lucy F., et al.

Langston, Deborah P. Living with Herpes. LC 82-45627. (Illus.). 216p. 1983. pap. 7.95 (ISBN 0-385-18410-7, Dolp). Doubleday.

Langston, Eugene, tr. see Niwano, Nikkyo.

Langston, Jack M. Lexigrow: A New & Easy Gardening Concept. LC 82-90041. (Illus.). 160p. (Orig.). 1982. pap. 8.95 (ISBN 0-910387-00-1). Lexigrow Intl.

Langstroth, Lorenzo L. Langstroth on the Hive & the Honey-Bee. (Illus.). 1977. Repr. of 1914 ed. text ed. 10.95 (ISBN 0-686-23279-8). A I Root.

Langton, J. Geographical Change & Industrial Revolution. LC 78-67428. (Cambridge Geographical Studies: No. 11). (Illus.). 1980. 59.50 (ISBN 0-521-22490-X). Cambridge U Pr.

Langton, Jane. Astonishing Stereoscope. LC 74-157894. (Illus.). (gr. 5 up). 1971. PLB 10.89 (ISBN 0-06-023683-3, HarpJ). Har-Row.

--The Astonishing Stereoscope. LC 74-157894. (A Trophy Bk.). (Illus.). 256p. (gr. 5 up). 1983. pap. 3.13i (ISBN 0-06-440133-2, Trophy). Har-Row.

--Diamond in the Window. LC 62-7312. (Illus.). (gr. 5 up). 1962. PLB 10.89 (ISBN 0-06-023681-7, HarpJ). Har-Row.

--Fledgling. LC 79-2008. (Ursula Nordstrom Bk.). 192p. (gr. 5 up). 1980. 9.57i (ISBN 0-06-023678-7, HarpJ); PLB 9.89 (ISBN 0-06-023679-5). Har-Row.

--Paper Chains. LC 76-41520. (gr. 7 up). 1977. 8.95 o.p. (ISBN 0-06-023688-4, HarpJ); PLB 10.89 (ISBN 0-06-023689-2). Har-Row.

--Swing in the Summerhouse. LC 67-4193. (Illus.). (gr. 5 up). 1967. PLB 9.89 o.p. (ISBN 0-06-023693-0, HarpJ). Har-Row.

Langton, Jane, ed. see Dickinson, Emily.

Langton, Kenneth P. Political Socialization. (Behavioral Political Science Studies). 1969. pap. 5.95x o.p. (ISBN 0-19-500945-2). Oxford U Pr.

Langton, Stuart, ed. Citizen Participation in America: Essays on the State of the Art. LC 78-19913. 1978. 16.95x (ISBN 0-669-02651-4); pap. 10.95 (ISBN 0-669-02465-1). Lexington Bks.

Language & Orientation Resource Center. Indochinese Students in U.S. Schools: A Guide for Administrators. LC 81-15554. (Language in Education Ser.: No. 42). 1981. 14.95x (ISBN 0-87281-297-9); pap. 7.00 (ISBN 0-686-96697-X). Ctr Appl Ling.

Language Center, Inc., tr. see Calin, Andrei & Calabro, John J.

Langwill, L. G. An Index of Musical Wind-Instrument Makers, Vol. 28. 6th, rev. & enl. ed. (Illus.). 1980. 125.00 (ISBN 90-247-2599-2). Heinman.

Langworthy, Franklin. Scenery of the Plains, Mountains & Mines. LC 76-87645. (American Scene Ser). (Illus.). 292p. 1972. Repr. of 1932 ed. lib. bdg. 39.50 (ISBN 0-306-71785-9). Da Capo.

Langworthy, J. Lamont & McNeil, Katherine. Hillside Homes. LC 82-82433. (Illus.). 128p. (Orig.). 1983. pap. 10.00 (ISBN 0-9609334-0-9). IO.

Langworthy, Orthello R. The Sensory Control of Posture & Movement. LC 79-125297. 129p. 1970. 12.00 (ISBN 0-683-04872-4). Krieger.

Lanham, Edwin M. Murder on My Street. LC 58-5472. 1958. 3.50 o.p. (ISBN 0-15-163551-X). HarBraceJ.

Lanham, Hedy G. Cooking for Company. 1983. 12.95 (ISBN 0-8120-5437-7). Barron.

Lanham, Jan, jt. auth. see Paul, Cecil.

Lanham, Richard A. A Handlist of Rhetorical Terms: A Guide for Students of English Literature. LC 68-31636. 1968. pap. 5.95x (ISBN 0-520-01414-6). U of Cal Pr.

--The Motives of Eloquence: Literary Rhetoric in the Renaissance. LC 75-43323. (Illus.). 1976. 18.00x o.p. (ISBN 0-300-02002-3, Y-453); pap. text ed. 7.95x (ISBN 0-300-02985-3). Yale U Pr.

--Tristram Shandy: The Games of Pleasure. LC 70-174461. 1973. 26.50x (ISBN 0-520-02144-4). U of Cal Pr.

Lanier, Alison R. Update--Bahrain-Qatar. LC 80-83911. (Country Orientation Ser.). 104p. 1978. pap. text ed. 27.50 (ISBN 0-933662-43-2). Intercult Pr.

--Update--Belgium. LC 80-83924. (Country Orientation Ser.). 73p. 1978. pap. text ed. 27.50 (ISBN 0-933662-28-9). Intercult Pr.

--Update--Brazil. LC 80-83916. (Country Orientation Ser.). 146p. 1982. pap. text ed. 27.50 (ISBN 0-933662-36-X). Intercult Pr.

--Update--Hong Kong. LC 80-83914. (Country Orientation Ser.). 1982. pap. 27.50 (ISBN 0-933662-38-6). Intercult Pr.

--Update--Indonesia. LC 80-83915. (Counry Orientation Ser.). 1982. pap. text ed. 27.50 (ISBN 0-933662-37-8). Intercult Pr.

--Update-Egypt. LC 80-83920. (Country Orientation Ser.). 94p. 1982. pap. text ed. 27.50 (ISBN 0-933662-32-7). Intercult Pr.

--Update-United Arab Emirates. LC 80-83911. (Country Orientation Ser.). 103p. 1978. pap. text ed. 27.50 (ISBN 0-933662-42-4). Intercult Pr.

Lanier, Emilia. Poems of Shakespeare's Dark Lady. 1979. 10.00 o.p. (ISBN 0-517-53745-1, C N Potter Bks). Crown.

Lanier, Jean. The Awakening of Adam. 1973. pap. 2.25 (ISBN 0-913456-63-2). Transbooks.

--The Evolution of Eve. 2nd ed. 96p. 1973. pap. 2.25 (ISBN 0-913456-62-4). Transbooks.

--Paraphrases for Pilgrims. 1977. pap. 1.75 (ISBN 0-89192-187-7). Transbooks.

Lanier, Linda K., ed. see Lovelace, Alice.

Lanier, Lyle H. & Andersen, Charles J. Study of the Financial Conditions of Colleges & Universities: 1972-75. 1975. pap. 4.00 o.p. (ISBN 0-685-84001-8). ACE.

Lanier, Sidney, ed. see Mallory, Thomas.

Lanier, Sterling E. Hiero's Journey. 352p. 1983. pap. 2.95 (ISBN 0-345-30841-7, Del Rey). Ballantine.

--The Unforsaken Hiero. LC 82-20793. 224p. 1983. 11.95 (ISBN 0-345-31048-9, Del Rey). Ballantine.

Lanigan, Anne. The Yogurt Cookbook. (Illus.). 1978. 10.95 (ISBN 0-8256-3140-8, Quick Fox); pap. 5.95 (ISBN 0-8256-3129-7). Putnam Pub Group.

Lanigan, Catherine. Admit Desire. (Avon Romance Ser.). 352p. 1983. pap. 2.95 (ISBN 0-380-81810-8, 81810-8). Avon.

Laning. Perspective for Artists. (Pitman Art Ser.: Vol. 22). pap. 1.95 o.p. (ISBN 0-448-00531-X, G&D). Putnam Pub Group.

Laning, Edward. Act of Drawing. (Illus.). 1971. 12.50 o.p. (ISBN 0-07-036349-8, GB). McGraw.

--Mural Paintings of Edward Laning in the New York Public Library. (Illus.). 1963. Repr. of 1951 ed. pap. 2.00 o.p. (ISBN 0-87104-123-5). NY Pub Lib.

Lanjouw, G. J., jt. auth. see Kuipers, S. K.

Lank, Edith. Selling Your Home with an Agent. 1982. pap. 9.95 (ISBN 0-8359-6986-X); text ed. 14.95 (ISBN 0-686-82959-X). Reston.

Lankevich, George. Atlanta: A Chronological & Documentary History, 1813-1978. LC 77-25048. (American Cities Chronology Ser.). 154p. 1978. 8.50 (ISBN 0-379-00618-9). Oceana.

--Gerald R. Ford, 1913-... Chronology, Documents, Bibliographical Aids. LC 77-8429. (Presidential Chronology Ser.). 1977. 15.00 (ISBN 0-379-12084-4). Oceana.

Lankevich, George J. Ethnic America Nineteen Seventy-Eight to Nineteen Eighty. LC 81-11207. 434p. 1981. lib. bdg. 25.00 (ISBN 0-379-00711-8). Oceana.

--James E. Carter (1924-) Chronology, Documents, Bibliographical Aids. LC 81-4007. (Presidential Chronology Ser.). 153p. 1981. lib. bdg. 12.50 (ISBN 0-379-12086-0). Oceana.

Lankford, T. Randall. Integrated Science for Health Students. 2nd ed. (Illus.). 1979. text ed. 21.95 (ISBN 0-8359-3103-X); pap. 9.95 lab manual (ISBN 0-8359-3105-6); instrs' manual avail. (ISBN 0-8359-3104-8). Reston.

Lankton, Carol H., jt. auth. see Lankton, Stephen R.

Lankton, Stephen R. & Lankton, Carol H. The Answer Within: A Clinical Framework of Ericksonian Hypnotherapy. 400p. 1983. 35.00 (ISBN 0-87630-320-3). Brunner-Mazel.

Lanman, Charles. Biographical Annals of the Civil Government of the United States. LC 68-30626. 1976. Repr. of 1876 ed. 68.00x (ISBN 0-8103-4300-2). Gale.

Lanmon, Dwight P., jt. auth. see Hollister, Paul.

Lannestock, Gustaf, tr. see Sandemose, Aksel.

Lannie, Vincent P. Henry Barnard: American Educator. LC 74-4827. 1974. text ed. 10.00 (ISBN 0-8077-2441-6); pap. text ed. 5.00 (ISBN 0-8077-2443-2). Tchrs Coll.

Lannon, John M. Technical Writing. 2nd ed. 1982. pap. text ed. 15.95 (ISBN 0-316-51435-7); tchrs' manual avail. (ISBN 0-316-51436-5). Little.

Lannoy, Richard. Speaking Tree: A Study of Indian Culture & Society. 1971. 29.95x (ISBN 0-19-501469-3). Oxford U Pr.

Lano, R. J. A Technique for Software & Systems Design. (TRW Ser. on Software Technology: Vol. 3). 1979. 38.50 (ISBN 0-444-85354-5, North Holland). Elsevier.

LaNoue, George R. Educational Vouchers: Concepts & Controversies. LC 78-187726. (Illus.). 1972. text ed. 11.95x (ISBN 0-8077-1660-X); pap. text ed. 6.95x (ISBN 0-8077-1661-8). Tchrs Coll.

Lanoux, Armand. Chateaux of the Loire. 260p. 1981. 60.00 (ISBN 0-686-98221-5). Edns Vilo.

Lanros. Assessment Intervention in Emergency Nursing. LC 78-9832. 21.95 o.p. (ISBN 0-87618-990-7). R J Brady.

Lanros, Nedell E. Assessment & Intervention in Emergency Nursing. 2nd ed. 624p. 1982. text ed. 27.95 (ISBN 0-89303-114-3). R J Brady.

--Review Manual for Certification: Emergency Nursing. 1982. pap. text ed. 13.95 (ISBN 0-89303-244-1). R J Brady.

Lansberg, H. E., ed. see Orvig, S.

Lansdell, Gwen, jt. auth. see King, Anny.

Lansdorp, Robert & Cubbedge, Robert. The Making of a Champion: Robert Ladsdorp's Unique Strategies for Winning Tennis. (Illus.). 192p. 1982. cancelled (ISBN 0-87131-387-1). M Evans.

Lansford, Josh. Make Friends with Your Tax Return. 1979. pap. 4.95 (ISBN 0-936562-00-5). Landown Hse.

--Real Estate Rules of Thumb & Memory Aids. LC 70-80838. 1969. pap. 3.00 (ISBN 0-686-74337-7). Landown Hse.

Lansing, Adrienne & Goldsmith, Alice. Summer Camps & Programs: Over 250 of the Best for Children Ages 8 to 18. Levy, Laurie, ed. 1983. 14.95 (ISBN 0-517-54960-3, Harmony); pap. 8.95 (ISBN 0-517-54832-1). Crown.

Lansing, Alfred, jt. auth. see Modell, Walter.

Lansing, John B. & Morgan, James N. Economic Survey Methods. LC 71-633672. 448p. 1971. cloth 20.00x (ISBN 0-87944-009-0); pap. 14.00x (ISBN 0-87944-008-2). Inst Soc Res.

Lansing, John B., et al. New Homes & Poor People: A Study of Chains of Moves. LC 67-65325. 136p. 1969. pap. 7.00x (ISBN 0-87944-064-3). Inst Soc Res.

--Planned Residential Environments. LC 76-632967. 283p. 1970. 20.00x (ISBN 0-87944-088-0). Inst Soc Res.

Lansing, John S. Evil in the Morning of the World: Phenomenological Approaches to a Balinese Community. LC 74-620023. (Michigan Papers on South & Southeast Asia No. 6). (Illus.). x, 104p. (Orig.). 1974. pap. 6.50x (ISBN 0-89148-006-4). Ctr S&SE Asian.

Lansing, Robert. Peace Negotiations: A Personal Narrative. LC 74-110852. (Illus.). 1971. Repr. of 1921 ed. lib. bdg. 16.00x (ISBN 0-8371-4519-8, LAPN). Greenwood.

Lansky, Bruce. The Incomplete Runner. (Illus.). 1978. pap. 2.95 o.p. (ISBN 0-932672-00-0). Lansky & Assoc.

--Make Your Own Crazy Animals. (Creative Kids Stencil Bks.). (Illus.). 12p. (Orig.). (ps-8). 1982. spiral bdg. 4.95 o.p. (ISBN 0-915658-63-1). Meadowbrook Pr.

Lansky, Vicki. Dear Babysitter: Sitter's Handbook & Notepad. Ring, Kathryn, ed. (Illus.). 98p. 1982. 7.95 (ISBN 0-915658-60-7). Meadowbrook Pr.

--Feed Me! I'm Yours. 1974. spiral bdg 4.95 (ISBN 0-915658-01-1); 10.95 (ISBN 0-915658-00-3). Meadowbrook Pr.

--Taming of the Candy Monster. LC 78-102315. 1978. 10.95 (ISBN 0-915658-09-7); pap. 4.95 (ISBN 0-915658-08-9). Meadowbrook Pr.

--Vicky Lansky's Practical Parenting Tips. rev. ed. Ring, Kathryn, ed. LC 80-18646. (Illus.). 168p. 1982. 10.95 (ISBN 0-915658-70-4); pap. 4.95 (ISBN 0-915658-69-0). Meadowbrook Pr.

Lanterman, Ray, jt. auth. see Kyselka, Will.

Lantz, Kenneth. Nikolay Leskov. (World Authors Ser.). 1979. lib. bdg. 15.95 (ISBN 0-8057-6364-3, Twayne). G K Hall.

Lantz, Louise K. Old American Kitchenware: Seventeen Twenty-Five to Nineteen Twenty-Five. (Illus.). 15.00 (ISBN 0-8407-4317-3). Wallace-Homestead.

--Old American Kitchenware, Seventeen Twenty-Five to Nineteen Twenty-Five. (Illus.). 290p. 1970. 15.00 (ISBN 0-686-36479-1). Md Hist.

Lanyi, Marton, jt. auth. see Hoeffken, Walther.

Lanyon, Andrew. A St. Ives Album. 72p. 1980. 10.00x o.p. (ISBN 0-906720-00-1, Pub. by Hodge England). State Mutual Bk.

Lanyon, Richard I. & Goodstein, Leonard D. Personality Assessment. 2nd ed. LC 81-23081. 311p. 1982. 23.95x (ISBN 0-471-04087-8, Pub. by Wiley-Interscience). Wiley.

Lanyon, Richard I., jt. auth. see Goodstein, Leonard D.

Lanyon, Walter. The Temple Not Made with Hands. 1981. 25.00x o.p. (ISBN 0-7224-0049-7, Pub. by Watkins England). State Mutual Bk.

Lanyon, Wesley E. The Comparative Biology of the Meadowlarks (Sturnella) in Wisconsin. (Illus.). 66p. 1957. cloth bdg. 6.00 (ISBN 0-686-35784-1); pap. 4.00 (ISBN 0-686-37167-4). Nuttall Ornithological.

Lanyun, Liu. Golden Millet Dream & Other Stories. Fanqin, Yu & Mingjie, Wang, trs. from Span. (The Chinese-English Readers). (Illus.). 296p. (Orig.). 1982. pap. 4.95 (ISBN 0-8351-1102-4). China Bks.

Lanz, Henry. Physical Basis of Rime: An Essay on the Aesthetics of Sound. LC 69-10115. (Illus.). 1969. Repr. of 1931 ed. lib. bdg. 20.75x (ISBN 0-8371-0136-0, LABR). Greenwood.

Lanz, Kurt. Around the World with Chemistry. LC 79-21209. Orig. Title: Weltreisender in Chemie. 1979. Repr. of 1978 ed. 14.95 o.p. (ISBN 0-07-036356-0). McGraw.

Lanz, Sally J. An Introduction to the Profession of Dietetics. LC 82-18683. (Illus.). 160p. 1983. pap. price not set (ISBN 0-8121-0883-3). Lea & Febiger.

Lanzano, Paolo, ed. Deformations of an Elastic Earth. (International Geophysics Ser.). 268p. 1982. 44.00 (ISBN 0-12-436620-1). Acad Pr.

Lanzendorf, Peter. The Video Taping Handbook: The Newest Systems, Cameras, & Techniques. 1983. 16.95 (ISBN 0-517-54952-2, Harmony); pap. 7.95 (ISBN 0-517-54953-0). Crown.

Lanzendorfer, Frank. The Climb Back. (Illus.). 144p. 1983. 9.95 (ISBN 0-89962-313-1). Todd & Honeywell.

Lanzerotti, L. J. & Park, C., eds. Upper Atmosphere Research in Antarctica. 1977. 50.00 (ISBN 0-87590-141-7). Am Geophysical.

Lanzkowsky, Philip. Pediatric Hematology-Oncology: A Treatise for the Clinician. (Illus.). 1979. 33.00 (ISBN 0-07-036340-4, HP). McGraw.

Lao Tzu. Way of Life: Tao Te Ching. Blakney, R. B., tr. 1955. pap. 2.50 (ISBN 0-451-62152-2, ME2152, Ment). NAL.

Lao She. Beneath the Red Banner. Cohn, Don J., tr. from Chinese. (Panda Ser.). 215p. (Orig.). 1982. pap. 3.95 (ISBN 0-8351-1026-5). China Bks.

--Rickshaw. James, Jean M., tr. from Chinese. LC 79-10658. Orig. Title: Lo-to Hsiang Tzu. 1979. text ed. 12.00x (ISBN 0-8248-0616-6); pap. text ed. 4.95x (ISBN 0-8248-0655-7). UH Pr.

Lao Tsu. Tao Te Ching. 1972. 9.95 (ISBN 0-394-71833-X). Knopf.

Lao-Tze. The Canon of Reason & Virtue. Carus, Paul, ed. LC 73-21701. 209p. 1973. 16.00 (ISBN 0-87548-063-2); pap. 6.00 (ISBN 0-87548-064-0). Open Court.

Lao Tze. Treatise on Response & Retribution. Carus, Paul & Suzuki, D. T., trs. from Chin. LC 6-28775. (Illus.). 139p. 1973. 9.95 o.p. (ISBN 0-87548-071-3); pap. 5.00 (ISBN 0-87548-244-9). Open Court.

LaPalombara, Joseph G. The Italian Labor Movement: Problems & Prospects. LC 82-11885. 192p. 1982. Repr. of 1957 ed. lib. bdg. 27.50x (ISBN 0-313-23553-8, LAIT). Greenwood.

LaPalombara, Lyda E. An Introduction to English Grammar: Traditional, Structural, Transformational. 1976. text ed. 14.95 (ISBN 0-316-51445-4). Little.

LaPalombra, Joseph. Politics Within Nations. (Contemporary Comparative Politics Ser.). 608p. 1974. text ed. 22.95 (ISBN 0-13-687814-8). P-H.

Lapan, Stephen D., jt. auth. see House, Ernest R.

Lapanje, Savo. Physicochemical Aspects of Protein Denaturation. LC 78-1919. 331p. 1978. 40.50 o.p. (ISBN 0-471-03409-6, Pub. by Wiley-Interscience). Wiley.

--Physicochemical Aspects of Protein Denaturation. LC 78-1919. 346p. Repr. of 1978 ed. text ed. 40.50 (ISBN 0-471-03409-6). Krieger.

Lapati, Americo D. John Henry Newman. (English Authors Ser.: No. 140). lib. bdg. 10.95 o.p. (ISBN 0-8057-1416-2, Twayne). G K Hall.

Lapatine, Sol. Electronics in Communications. LC 77-17573. (Electronic Technology Ser.). 1978. text ed. 25.95x (ISBN 0-471-01842-2); solutions manual 3.00 (ISBN 0-471-03713-3). Wiley.

LaPatra, Jack. Healing: The Coming Revolution in Holistic Medicine. 1978. 9.95 o.p. (ISBN 0-07-036359-5, GB). McGraw.

Lapatra, Jack, jt. auth. see Temes, Gabor.

Lapchick, Richard E. The Politics of Race & International Sport: The Case of South Africa. LC 74-11705. (Studies in Human Rights: No. 1). 268p. 1975. lib. bdg. 29.95 (ISBN 0-8371-7691-3, LPR/). Greenwood.

La Pelle, Rolland R. Practical Vacuum Systems. (Illus.). 288p. 1972. 41.95 (ISBN 0-07-036355-2, P&RB). McGraw.

Lapena-Bonifacio, Amelia. Sepang Loca & Others. 296p. 1982. text ed. 13.50x (ISBN 0-8248-0768-5, Pub by U of Philippines Pr); pap. text ed. 9.50x (ISBN 0-8248-0769-3). UH Pr.

Lapenna, Ivo. Soviet Penal Policy. LC 80-15755. (Background Bk.). 148p. 1980. Repr. of 1968 ed. lib. bdg. 19.25x (ISBN 0-313-22570-2, LASP). Greenwood.

Lapenna, Ivo, et al. Esperanto en Perspektivo. Lapenna, Ivo, ed. (Illus., Esperanto.). 1974. 40.00x (ISBN 0-685-71606-6, 1709). Esperanto League North Am.

LaPenta, Anthony V., Jr. The Sniper. LC 75-16563. 1976. 6.95 (ISBN 0-87949-042-X). Ashley Bks.

La Perouse, Comte De. Voyages & Adventures of La Perouse. Gassner, Julius S., tr. (Illus.). 1969. 12.00 (ISBN 0-87022-445-X). UH Pr.

La Perriere, Guillaume de. Le Theatre Des Bons Engins, 1539. LC 63-7783. 1963. Repr. of 1539 ed. 30.00x (ISBN 0-8201-1036-1). Schol Facsimiles.

Lapham, William B. History of Bethel, Maine. 1981. Repr. of 1891 ed. 125.00x (ISBN 0-89725-023-0). NH Pub Co.

La Piana, Angelina. Dante's American Pilgrimage: A Historical Survey of Dante Studies in the United States, Eighteen Hundred to Nineteen Forty-Four. 1948. 49.50x (ISBN 0-686-51368-1). Elliots Bks.

Lapidge, Michael, jt. ed. see Dumville, David.

Lapidoth, R. The Red Sea & the Gulf of Aden. 1982. lib. bdg. 65.00 (ISBN 90-247-2501-1, Pub. by Martinus Nijhoff Netherlands). Kluwer Boston.

Lapidus, Gail W. Women in Soviet Society: Equality, Development, & Social Change. LC 74-16710. 1978. 30.00x o.p. (ISBN 0-520-02868-6); pap. 5.95 (ISBN 0-520-03938-6). U of Cal Pr.

Lapidus, Ira M., ed. Middle Eastern Cities: A Symposium on Ancient, Islamic, & Contemporary Middle Eastern Urbanism. LC 72-81939. (Library Reprint Ser.: No. 99). 1979. Repr. of 1969 ed. 27.50x (ISBN 0-520-03850-9). U of Cal Pr.

Lapidus, Jacqueline. Ready to Survive. LC 75-9593. 24p. 1975. pap. 2.50 (ISBN 0-914610-04-X). Hanging Loose.

Lapidus, Leon & Pinder, George F. Numerical Solution of Partial Differential Equations in Science & Engineering. LC 81-16491. 677p. 1982. 44.95x (ISBN 0-471-09866-3, Pub. by Wiley-Interscience). Wiley.

LaPiere, Richard T. The Freudian Ethic. LC 74-6710. 299p. 1974. Repr. of 1959 ed. lib. bdg. 15.75x o.p. (ISBN 0-8371-7543-7, LAFE). Greenwood.

Lapierre, Dominique, jt. auth. see Collins, Larry.

La Pierre, Dominique, jt. auth. see Collins, Larry.

Lapierre, Dominique, jt. auth. see Collins, Larry.

LaPietra, Mary. A Tomahawk for Christmas. LC 76-11478. (gr. 5 up). 1976. pap. 1.50 o.p. (ISBN 0-89191-052-2). Cook.

Lapin, Jackie, jt. auth. see Parkhouse, Bonnie L.

Lapin, Lawrence. Quantitative Methods for Business Decisions. 774p. 1981. text ed. 25.95 (ISBN 0-15-574319-8, HC); instructor's manual avail. (ISBN 0-15-574320-1). HarbraceJ.

Lapin, Lawrence L. Management Science for Business Decisions. 613p. 1980. text ed. 25.95 (ISBN 0-15-554690-2, HC); instructor's manual avail. HarBraceJ.

--Statistics: Meaning & Method. 2nd ed. 543p. 1980. text ed. 22.95 (ISBN 0-15-583769-9, HC); study guide 7.95 (ISBN 0-15-583770-2); instrs. manual avail. 4.50 (ISBN 0-15-583778-8). HarBraceJ.

Lapina, Ronald P. Estimating Centifugal Compressor Performance. (Process Compressor Technology Ser.: Vol. 1). 1982. 39.95 (ISBN 0-87201-101-1). Gulf Pub.

--TI-Fifty-Nine Manual for Estimating Centrifugal Compressor Performance. (Process Compressor Technology Ser.). 1983. text ed. 42.95x (ISBN 0-87201-100-3). Gulf Pub.

Lapine, James. Table Settings: A Contemporary Comedy. LC 82-80614. 106p. 1982. pap. 4.95 (ISBN 0-933826-32-X). Performing Arts.

--Twelve Dreams. LC 82-81974. 55p. 1982. pap. 3.95 (ISBN 0-933826-33-8). Performing Arts.

Laping, Francis & Knight, Hans. Remember Hungary 1956: A Pictorial History of the Hungarian Revolution in 1956. 300p. (YA) 1975. 35.00 (ISBN 0-912404-01-9). Alpha Pubns.

Lapis, K. & Johannessen, J. V. Liver Carcinogenesis. 1979. 35.00 (ISBN 0-07-036368-4). McGraw.

LaPlace, John. Health. 3rd ed. (Illus.). 1980. text ed. 18.95 (ISBN 0-13-385393-4); cloth 18.95 (ISBN 0-13-385427-2). P-H.

Laplace, Pierre S. Celestial Mechanics, Vols. 1-4. LC 69-11316. Set. text ed. 195.00 (ISBN 0-8284-0194-2). Chelsea Pub.

--Celestial Mechanics, Vol. 5. LC 63-11316. (Mecanique Celeste, Tome V, Fr). 1969. Repr. of 1832 ed. text ed. 27.50 (ISBN 0-8284-0214-0). Chelsea Pub.

Laplante, A. & Samake, F. Family Planning in Mali. 12p. 1975. pap. 5.00 (ISBN 0-88936-056-1, IDRC45, IDRC). Unipub.

Laplante, Jerry C. Plastic Furniture for the Home Craftsman. LC 77-87474. (Illus.). 1978. pap. 5.95 o.p. (ISBN 0-8069-8566-6). Sterling.

LaPlante, Sr. Mary C. Come to the Holy Table. LC 73-82653. (gr. 1-2). 1973. 2.95 o.p. (ISBN 0-87973-824-3). Our Sunday Visitor.

La Plantz, Shereen. Plaited Basketry: The Woven Form. LC 82-90066. 1982. pap. 17.95 (ISBN 0-942002-00-8). Press Plantz.

Lapointe, Francois H., compiled by. Ludwig Wittgenstein: A Comprehensive Bibliography. LC 79-6565. 1980. lib. bdg. 35.00 (ISBN 0-313-22127-8, LAW/). Greenwood.

Lapointe, Juliet G., tr. see Bosquet, Alain.

La Pointe, Ken. Hey Joe! The Portrait of a Wisconsin Woodsman. 1979. 7.50 o.p. (ISBN 0-682-49452-6). Exposition.

Lapomarda, Vincent A. The Knights of Columbus in Massachusetts. 158p. (Orig.). 1982. 12.00 (ISBN 0-9608258-0-0); pap. 10.00 (ISBN 0-9608258-1-9). Mass State.

Laporte, Leo F. Ancient Environments. 2nd ed. (Foundations of the Earth Ser.). (Illus.). 1979. ref. 15.95 (ISBN 0-13-036392-8); pap. 10.95 ref. (ISBN 0-13-036384-7). P-H.

La Porte, Robert. Power & Privilege: Influence & Decision-Making in Pakistan. LC 74-79765. 250p. 1976. 32.50x (ISBN 0-520-02783-3). U of Cal Pr.

LaPorte, Valerie, jt. ed. see Rubin, Jeffrey.

Lapp, Carolyn. Dentists' Tools. LC 61-13574. (Medical Bks. for Children). (Illus.). (gr. 3-9). 1961. PLB 3.95g (ISBN 0-8225-0010-8). Lerner Pubns.

Lapp, Diane & Flood, James. Teaching Reading to Every Child. (Illus.). 1978. text ed. 22.95x (ISBN 0-02-367610-8). Macmillan.

Lapp, Diane, jt. auth. see Anderson, Paul S.

Lapp, Diane, jt. auth. see Flood, James E.

Lapp, Elaenor. The Blueberry Bears. Fay, Ann, ed. (Just for Fun Bks.). (Illus.). 32p. (ps-2). 1983. PLB 7.50 (ISBN 0-8075-0796-2). A Whitman.

Lapp, John C. Esthetics of Negligence: La Fontaine's Contes. LC 72-142130. 1971. 44.50 (ISBN 0-521-08067-3). Cambridge U Pr.

Lapp, N. LeRoy, ed. Medical Examination Review: Pulmonary Diseases, Vol. 24. 3rd ed. 1983. pap. text ed. 23.00 (ISBN 0-87488-143-9). Med Exam.

Lapp, Nancy L., jt. ed. see Lapp, Paul W.

Lapp, Paul W. & Lapp, Nancy L., eds. Discoveries in the Wadi ed-Daliyeh. (American Schools of Oriental Research Ser.: Vol. 41). (Illus.). 106p. 1974. text ed. 10.50x (ISBN 0-89757-041-3, Am Sch Orient Res). Eisenbrauns.

Lapp, Rudolph M. Afro-Americans in California. Hundley, Norris, Jr. & Shutz, John A., eds. LC 79-17918. (Golden State Ser.). (Illus.). 80p. 1979. pap. text ed. 5.95x (ISBN 0-87835-094-2). Boyd & Fraser.

Lappa, Ellen, ed. see Himes, Gary K., et al.

Lappe & Collins. Food First: Beyond the Myth of Scarcity. pap. 2.95 (ISBN 0-686-95396-7). Am Fr Serv Comm.

Lappe, Frances M. & Collins, Joseph. Now We Can Speak: A Journey Through the New Nicaragua. 128p. (Orig.). 1982. pap. 4.95 (ISBN 0-935028-14-5). Inst Food & Develop.

Lappe, Francis M. & Collins, Joseph. Food First: Beyond the Myth of Scarcity. 1977. 11.95 o.s.i. (ISBN 0-395-25347-0). HM.

Lappe, Marc. Genetic Politics. 1979. 9.95 o.p. (ISBN 0-671-22546-4). S&S.

Lappe, Marc & Morison, Robert S., eds. Ethical & Scientific Issues Posed by Human Uses of Molecular Genetics, Vol. 265. (Annals of the New York Academy of Sciences). 208p. 1976. 26.00x (ISBN 0-89072-019-3). NY Acad Sci.

Lappen, Lee E. & Card, Maura. HeartBeat for God (The Elmer Lappen Story) LC 79-90719. 1980. 6.95 o.p. (ISBN 0-918956-53-6). Campus Crusade.

Lappin, Alvin R. Plastics - Projects & Techniques. (gr. 9 up). 1965. text ed. 14.64 (ISBN 0-87345-159-7). McKnight.

Lappin, Peter. Give Me Souls! Life of Don Bosco. LC 77-10350. 1977. 9.95 o.p. (ISBN 0-87973-749-2, 749). Our Sunday Visitor.

Lappo-Danilevskii, J. A. Systemes Des Equations Differentielles, 3 Vols. in 1. LC 53-7110. (Fr). 27.50 (ISBN 0-8284-0094-6). Chelsea Pub.

Laprade, William T. Public Opinion & Politics in Eighteenth Century England to the Fall of Walpole. LC 70-114538. 1971. Repr. of 1936 ed. lib. bdg. 21.00x (ISBN 0-8371-4806-5, LAPO). Greenwood.

Lapsley, Susan. I Am Adopted. (Illus.). 28p. (ps-2). 1983. bds. 3.95 (ISBN 0-370-02032-4, Pub by The Bodley Head). Merrimack Bk Serv.

Lapuente, F. A., jt. auth. see Rogers, P. P.

Lapuz, Lourdes V. Filipino Marriages in Crisis. 1977. wrps. 5.75x (ISBN 0-686-09466-2). Cellar.

Lapwood, E. R. & Usami, T. Free Oscillations of the Earth. (Cambridge Monographs on Mechanics & Applied Mathematics). (Illus.). 168p. 1981. 54.50 (ISBN 0-521-23536-7). Cambridge U Pr.

Laquatra, Idamarie, et al. Helping Skills II: Life Development Intervention. pap. text ed. 9.95 (ISBN 0-89885-145-9); wkbk. 9.95 (ISBN 0-89885-146-7); both 14.95 (ISBN 0-89885-158-0). Human Sci Pr.

LaQue, Francis L. Marine Corrosion: Causes & Prevention. LC 75-16307. (Corrosion Monograph Ser). 332p. 1975. 39.50x (ISBN 0-471-51745-3, Pub. by Wiley-Interscience). Wiley.

Laqueur, Walter. America, Europe, & the Soviet Union: Selected Essays. 1983. 22.95 (ISBN 0-87855-362-2). Transaction Bks.

--A Continent Astray: Europe, 1970-1978. 1979. 22.50x (ISBN 0-19-502510-5). Oxford U Pr.

--Europe Since Hitler: The Rebirth of Europe. rev. ed. 580p. 1982. pap. 6.95 (ISBN 0-14-021411-9, Pelican). Penguin.

--A History of Zionism. LC 75-36491. (Illus.). 1976. pap. 8.95 (ISBN 0-8052-0523-3). Schocken.

--Out of the Ruins of Europe. 534p. 27.50 (ISBN 0-912050-01-2, Library Press). Open Court.

--Weimar: A Cultural History. LC 74-16605. (Illus.). 295p. 1976. 4.95 (ISBN 0-399-50346-3, Perigee). Putnam Pub Group.

Laqueur, Walter, ed. Fascism-A Readers' Guide: Analysis, Interpretations, Bibliography. LC 75-13158. 1977. 40.00x (ISBN 0-520-03033-8); pap. 6.95 (ISBN 0-520-03642-5). U of Cal Pr.

--The Guerrilla Reader: A Historical Anthology. LC 76-47429. 256p. 1977. 29.95 (ISBN 0-87722-095-6). Temple U Pr.

--The Terrorism Reader: A Historical Anthology. LC 77-87449. 301p. 1978. 24.95 (ISBN 0-87722-119-7). Temple U Pr.

Laqueur, Walter & Rubin, Barry, eds. The Human Rights Reader. 384p. 1979. 27.95 (ISBN 0-87722-170-7). Temple U Pr.

Laquian, Aprodicio A. Slums Are for People. rev. ed. (Illus.). 1971. 14.00x (ISBN 0-8248-0098-2, Eastwest Ctr). UH Pr.

Lara-Braud, Dorothy. Good Food Kids Love. (Illus.). 128p. 1980. pap. 6.95 (ISBN 0-8256-3199-8, Quick Fox). Putnam Pub Group.

Laracy, Hugh. Marists & Melanesians: A History of Catholic Missions in the Solomon Islands. 256p. 1976. text ed. 14.00x (ISBN 0-8248-0361-2). UH Pr.

La Ramee, Louise De see De La Ramee, Louise.

LaRaus, Roger & Remy, Richard. Citizenship Decision Making. (gr. 10-12). 1978. pap. text ed. 14.55 (ISBN 0-201-04088-3). A-W.

Larbalestrier, Deborah E. Paralegal Training Manual. LC 81-5054. 270p. 1981. 19.95 (ISBN 0-13-648626-6, Busn). P-H.

Larcher, Jean. Op Art Coloring Book. (Dover Coloring Bk Ser.). (Illus.). 32p. (Orig.). 1975. pap. 1.95 (ISBN 0-486-23172-0). Dover.
--Ready to Use News Announcements. 1981. pap. 2.75 (ISBN 0-486-24173-4). Dover.
--Three-D Alphabet Coloring Book. (Illus.). 1978. pap. 1.75 (ISBN 0-486-23632-3). Dover.
Larcher, W. Physiological Plant Ecology. Biederman-Thorson, M. A., tr. from Ger. LC 75-16488. (Illus.). 250p. 1975. 24.00 o.p. (ISBN 0-387-07336-1). Springer-Verlag.
Larcombe, Claudia, jt. ed. see Weigle, Marta.
Lardner, R. W., jt. auth. see Arya, J. C.
Lardner, Rex. Complete Beginner's Guide to Tennis. LC 67-17265. (YA) (gr. 9 up). 1967. 9.95a o.p. (ISBN 0-385-04101-2); PLB 9.95a (ISBN 0-385-07546-4). Doubleday.
--The Great Golfers. LC 76-113510. (Putnam Sports Shelf). (gr. 5 up). 1970. PLB 4.97 o.p. (ISBN 0-399-60211-9). Putnam Pub Group.
Lardner, Robin W., jt. auth. see Arya, Jagdish C.
Lardo, Vince. China House. 180p. (Orig.). 1983. pap. 4.95 (ISBN 0-932870-30-9). Alyson Pubns.
Lardy, N. Economic Growth & Distribution in China. (Illus.). 1978. 37.50 (ISBN 0-521-21904-3). Cambridge U Pr.
Lardy, Nicholas R. & Lieberthal, Kenneth, eds. Chen Yun's Strategy for China's Development. LC 82-16776. 250p. 1983. 25.00 (ISBN 0-87332-225-8). M E Sharpe.
Laredo, Victor. New York City: A Photographic Portrait. (Illus.). 188p. 1972. pap. text ed. 5.95 (ISBN 0-486-22852-5). Dover.
Larew, Hiram & Capizzi, Joseph. Common Insect & Mite Galls of the Pacific Northwest. (Oregon State Monographs; Studies in Entomology: No. 5). (Illus.). 80p. (Orig.). 1983. pap. 4.95 (ISBN 0-87071-055-9). Oreg St U Pr.
Largay, James A. & Livingstone, J. L. Accounting for Changing Prices: Replacement Cost & General Price Level Adjustments. LC 76-7491. (Accounting, Management & Information Systems Ser.). 303p. 1976. text ed. 35.95x (ISBN 0-471-54210-5); solutions manual 9.00 (ISBN 0-471-02139-3). Wiley.
Large, George E. & Chen, T. Y. Reinforced Concrete Design. 3rd ed. LC 69-14677. (Illus.). 1969. 31.95 (ISBN 0-471-06667-2). Wiley.
Largen, Velda L. Guide to Good Food. (Illus.). 640p. 1981. 17.28 (ISBN 0-87006-272-7); wkbk. 3.52 (ISBN 0-87006-419-3). Goodheart.
Largent, D. L. Leptonia & Related Genera of the West Coast. 1976. 32.00 (ISBN 3-7682-1114-2). Lubrecht & Cramer.
Largent, Jill A., jt. auth. see Urizar, Rodrigo E.
Largo, Gerald A. Community & Liturgy: An Historical Overview. LC 80-1434. 151p. 1980. lib. bdg. 18.50 (ISBN 0-8191-1302-6); pap. text ed. 8.50 (ISBN 0-8191-1303-4). U Pr of Amer.
Larid, Marshall & Miles, James W., eds. Integrated Mosquito Control Methodologies, Vol. 1. Date not set. price not set (ISBN 0-12-434001-6). Acad Pr.
Larimore, John. The Creator of This World & the Universe. LC 78-54161. 1979. 12.95 (ISBN 0-87949-115-9). Ashley Bks.
Lariviere, Susan & Schiffman, Ted. Amphoto Guide to Backpacking Photography. (Illus.). 168p. 1981. 12.95 o.p. (ISBN 0-8174-3520-4, Amphoto); pap. 7.95 (ISBN 0-8174-3519-0). Watson-Guptill.
Larke, T. A. Index to Liechtenstein, 1 Vol. 1982. pap. text ed. 14.95 (ISBN 0-9608460-4-2, FL1). Answer-Bk.
Larken, H. W. Compositors Work in Painting. 3rd ed. 382p. 1969. 29.00x (ISBN 0-905418-08-5, Pub. by Gresham England). State Mutual Bk.
Lark-Horovitz, Betty, et al. Understanding Children's Art for Better Teaching. 2nd ed. LC 73-81970. 1973. text ed. 19.95 (ISBN 0-675-08927-1). Merrill.
Larkin, Bruce D. China & Africa, Nineteen Forty-Nine to Nineteen Seventy: The Foreign Policy of the People's Republic of China. LC 78-123624. (Center for Chinese Studies, UC Berkeley). (Illus.). 1971. 27.50x (ISBN 0-520-01761-7); pap. 4.95x (ISBN 0-520-02357-9, CAMPUS87). U of Cal Pr.
Larkin, Bryant. Larkin's Dulcimer Book. (Illus.). 103p. 1982. pap. 6.95 (ISBN 0-943644-00-3); cassette 6.95; Set. 12.95. Ivory Pal.
Larkin, Elinor. Twice Bought Bride. (Orig.). 1980. pap. 1.50 o.s.i. (ISBN 0-440-18607-2). Dell.
Larkin, J. Practical Problems in Mathematics for Mechanical Drafting. LC 77-78236. 1979. pap. 7.80 (ISBN 0-8273-1670-4); instructor's guide 3.25 (ISBN 0-8273-1671-2). Delmar.
Larkin, James F., ed. Stuart Royal Proclamations: Volume II: Royal Proclamations of King Charles I, 1625-46. 1144p. 1983. 154.00 (ISBN 0-19-822466-4). Oxford U Pr.
Larkin, Joan, jt. ed. see Bulkin, Elly.
Larkin, John A. The Pampangans: Colonial Society in a Philippine Province. LC 74-165232. (Center for South & Southeast Asia Studies, Uc Berkeley). (Illus.). 300p. 1972. 35.00x (ISBN 0-520-02076-6). U of Cal Pr.
Larkin, John A., ed. Perspectives on Philipine Historigraphy: A Symposium. iv, 74p. 1970. pap. 8.00 (ISBN 0-686-38045-2). Yale U SE Asia.
Larkin, Joy. Strangers No More: The Diary of a Schizo. 1978. 7.95 o.p. (ISBN 0-533-03362-4). Vantage.
Larkin, Larry. Full Speed Ahead. LC 72-80818. (Illus.). 146p. Repr. of 1972 ed. 12.00 (ISBN 0-686-36269-1). Larkin.
Larkin, Margaret, ed. Singing Cowboy. LC 78-31779. (Music Reprint Ser.). 176p. 1979. Repr. of 1931 ed. 22.50 (ISBN 0-306-79555-8). Da Capo.
Larkin, Patricia & Backer, Barbara. Problem-Oriented Nursing Assessment. 1977. pap. text ed. 11.95 (ISBN 0-07-036450-8, HP). McGraw.
Larkin, Philip. High Windows. LC 74-9800. 42p. 1974. pap. 6.95 (ISBN 0-374-51212-4). FS&G.
Larkin, Philip, ed. The Oxford Book of Twentieth Century English Verse. 1973. 25.00x (ISBN 0-19-812137-7). Oxford U Pr.
Larkin, Regina & Davis, Julie. Thirty Days to a Better Bust. 1982. pap. 2.95 (ISBN 0-553-01488-9). Bantam.
Larkin, Robert P., jt. auth. see Peters, Gary L.
Larkin, Robert P., et al. People, Environment & Place: An Introduction to Human Geography. (Illus.). 368p. 1981. text ed. 25.95 (ISBN 0-675-08085-1). Additional supplements may be obtained from publisher. Merrill.
Larkin, Rochelle. Glitterball. (Orig.). 1980. pap. 2.50 o.p. (ISBN 0-451-09525-1, E9525, Sig). NAL.
--Harvest of Desire. 1977. pap. 2.25 o.p. (ISBN 0-451-08771-2, E8771, Sig). NAL.
Larkin, Sarah. Mountain in the Field. 159p. 1972. 5.95 o.p. (ISBN 0-911660-12-7). Yankee Peddler.
--Old Master-Other Tails. (Illus.). 1968. 4.95 o.p. (ISBN 0-911660-07-0). Yankee Peddler.
--Vignettes of a Life. 1982. 8.95 (ISBN 0-686-97605-3). Vantage.
Larkins, A. Guy, jt. auth. see Shaver, James P.
Larkman, Simon, jt. auth. see Meadows, Eric G.
Larlham, Hattie. Dear Children. 152p. 1983. 9.95 (ISBN 0-8361-3325-0). Herald Pr.
Larmer, Oscar, jt. auth. see Tomasch, E. J.
Larned, Joseph N. Life & Work of William Pryor Letchworth, Student & Minister of Public Benevolence. LC 71-172592. (Criminology, Law Enforcement & Social Problems Ser.: No. 182). (Illus.). 1974. Repr. of 1912 ed. 15.00x (ISBN 0-87585-182-7). Patterson Smith.
La Rocca, Eugenio, jt. auth. see Boardman, John.
Laroche, Lucienne. The Middle East. Nannicini, Giuliana & Bowman, John, eds. Mondadori, tr. from Ital. LC 72-79616. (Monuments of Civilization Ser.). (Illus.). 192p. 1974. 25.00 (ISBN 0-448-02021-1, G&D). Putnam Pub Group.
LaRoche, Nancy & Urdang, Laurence, eds. Picturesque Expressions: A Thematic Dictionary. LC 80-22705. 300p. 1980. 50.00x (ISBN 0-8103-1122-4). Gale.
La Rochelle, Pierre Drieu. The Man on Horseback. Hines, Thomas M., tr. 14.00 (ISBN 0-917786-07-6). French Lit.
Larock, Bruce E., jt. auth. see Newnan, Donald G.
Laron, Z. & Butenandt, O., eds. Evaluation of Growth Hormone Secretion. (Pediatric & Adolescent Endocrinology: Vol. 12). 200p. 1983. 58.75 (ISBN 3-8055-3623-2). S Karger.
Laron, Z. & Galatzer, A., eds. Psychological Aspects of Diabetes in Children & Adolescents. (Pediatric & Adolescent Endocrinology: Vol. 10). xvi, 248p. 1983. 110.25 (ISBN 3-8055-3575-9). S Karger.
--Recent Progress in Medico-Social Problems in Juvenile Diabetics, Pt. II. (Pediatric & Adolescent Endocrinology Ser.: Vol. 11). (Illus.). x, 210p. 1983. 91.75 (ISBN 3-8055-3594-5). S Karger.
LaRondelle, Hans K. The Israel of God in Prophecy: Principles of Prophetic Interpretation. LC 82-74358. (Andrews University Monographs, Studies in Religion: Vol.13). 1983. 13.95 (ISBN 0-943872-13-8); pap. 10.95 (ISBN 0-943872-14-6). Andrews Univ Pr.
Laronne, Jonathan & Mosley, M. Paul, eds. Erosion & Sediment Yield. LC 81-6456. (Benchmark Papers in Geology: Vol. 63). 400p. 1982. 47.00 (ISBN 0-87933-409-6). Hutchinson Ross.
La Rosa, Mathilde, tr. see Boni, Ada.
La Rosa, Michael M. de see Kolin, Michael J. & De La Rosa, Denise M.
Larousse. Larousse De Poche. 505p. (Orig.). pap. 4.95 (ISBN 0-671-43484-5). WSP.
--Larousse Encyclopedia of Archaeology. Charles-Picard, Gilbert, ed. (Illus.). 1972. 25.00 o.p. (ISBN 0-399-10997-8). Putnam Pub Group.
--Nouveau Petit Larousse. 39.95 (ISBN 0-685-20242-9). Schoenhof.
Larousse & Co. Dictionnaire du francais contemporain. (Fr). 27.50 o.p. (ISBN 0-685-13872-0, 3745). Larousse.
Larousse And Co. Larousse de poche, francais-allemand et allemand-francais. pap. 6.95 (ISBN 0-685-13959-X). Larousse.
--Larousse de poche, francais-italien et italien-francais. (Fr. & It.). pap. 6.95 (ISBN 0-685-13960-3, 1012). Larousse.
--Larousse de poche French-English & English-French. (Fr. & Eng.). pap. 6.95 (ISBN 2-03-029203-6, 1009). Larousse.
--Ma Premiere Encyclopedie. (Illus., Fr.). 22.95x (3797). Larousse.
Larousse, Pierre, jt. auth. see Clement, Felix.
Larrabee, Graydon B., jt. auth. see Kane, Philip F.
Larrabee, Harold A. Reliable Knowledge: Scientific Methods in the Social Studies. rev. ed. LC 81-40150. 415p. 1981. pap. text ed. 14.25 (ISBN 0-8191-1627-0). U Pr of Amer.
Larrabee, John W., jt. auth. see Hansman, Robert J.
Larrain, Michael. Promises Kept in Sleep. 1981. 1.00 (ISBN 0-686-38918-2). Wilderness Poetry Press.
Larranaga, Robert D. Famous Crimefighters. LC 78-84413. (Pull Ahead Books Ser). (Illus.). (gr. 5-11). 1970. PLB 4.95g (ISBN 0-8225-0459-6). Lerner Pubns.
Larrauri, A. Dictionary of Oto-Rhino-Laryngology in Five Languages: English-French-Spanish-German-Italian. LC 71-501781. 1008p. 1971. 65.00x (ISBN 0-8002-0197-3). Intl Pubns Serv.
Larrea, Gabriel P., tr. see Gaunt, Leonard.
Larrea, Jean-Jacques. The Diary of a Paper Boy. (Illus.). (gr. 5-9). 1972. 5.50 o.p. (ISBN 0-399-20255-2). Putnam Pub Group.
Larreche, Jean-C & Gatignon, Hubert. Markstrat: A Marketing Strategy Game. LC 77-89287. 1977. pap. 13.75x (ISBN 0-89426-010-3); teaching notes 13.75x (ISBN 0-89426-011-1). Scientific Pr.
Larrick, jt. auth. see Melcher, Daniel.
Larrick, Nancy. A Parent's Guide to Children's Reading. Rev., 5th ed. LC 82-24702. (Illus.). 288p. 1983. write for info. (ISBN 0-664-32705-2). Westminster.
--Rain, Hail, Sleet & Snow. LC 61-5488. (Junior Science Books Ser). (gr. 2-5). 1961. PLB 6.69 (ISBN 0-8116-6157-1). Garrard.
Larrick, Nancy, ed. More Poetry for Holidays. LC 73-6806. (Poetry Ser.). (Illus.). 96p. (gr. 2-5). 1973. PLB 6.69 (ISBN 0-8116-4116-3). Garrard.
--Piping Down the Valleys Wild. (gr. k-6). 1982. pap. 2.95 (ISBN 0-440-46952-X, YB). Dell.
--Poetry for Holidays. LC 66-10724. (Poetry Ser.). (gr. 2-5). 1966. PLB 6.69 (ISBN 0-8116-4100-7). Garrard.
--Somebody Turned on a Tap in These Kids: Poetry & Young People Today. LC 76-135380. 1971. 5.95 o.s.i. (ISBN 0-440-08112-2). Delacorte.
Larrieu, Jean-Claude. Montastruc: Seen by its Cooking. (Illus.). 128p. 1983. 27.50 (ISBN 0-937950-05-X). Xavier-Moreau.
Larrison, Earl J., jt. auth. see Christensen, James R.
Larrowe, Charles P. Harry Bridges: The Rise & Fall of Radical Labor in the United States. rev. ed. LC 72-78321. 416p. 1977. pap. 9.95 (ISBN 0-88208-001-6). Lawrence Hill.
--Shape-Up & Hiring Hall. LC 75-46614. (Illus.). 250p. 1976. Repr. of 1955 ed. lib. bdg. 17.00x (ISBN 0-8371-8750-8, LASU). Greenwood.
Larsen, Arthur. Next Year Will be Better. 175p. write for info (ISBN 0-931170-22-2). Ctr Western Studies.
Larsen, Arthur, jt. auth. see Snyder, John.
Larsen, Chris, jt. auth. see Kolbrek, Loyal.
Larsen, Dale, jt. auth. see Larsen, Sandy.
Larsen, David, jt. auth. see Titus, Jonathan.
Larsen, David C. Who Gets It When You Go? 1982. 10.50 (ISBN 0-394-52426-8); pap. 4.95 (ISBN 0-394-70658-7). Random.
--Who Gets It When You Go? Wills, Probate & Inheritance Taxes for the Hawaii Resident. LC 79-25776. (Illus.). 128p. 1980. pap. 4.95 (ISBN 0-8248-0695-6). UH Pr.
Larsen, David C., ed. Thermal Conductivity Sixteen. 625p. 1982. 79.50x (ISBN 0-306-41032-X, Plenum Pr). Plenum Pub.
--Thermal Expansion Seven. 225p. 1982. 45.00x (ISBN 0-306-41031-1, Plenum Pr). Plenum Pub.
Larsen, E. A., jt. auth. see Mosich, A. N.
Larsen, E. J., jt. auth. see Mosich, A. N.
Larsen, Earnest. Body of Christ. LC 76-6703. (Illus.). 1976. pap. 1.75 o.p. (ISBN 0-8189-1134-4, Pub. by Alba Bks). Alba.
--Jesus Christ: The Gate of Power. LC 76-21589. (Illus.). 1977. pap. 1.75 o.p. (ISBN 0-8189-1136-0, Pub. by Alba Bks). Alba.
--Week of Fire. 7.50 o.p. (ISBN 0-8091-8755-8). Paulist Pr.
--Whatever Happened to Good Old Plastic Jesus? 144p. 1978. pap. 3.95 (ISBN 0-697-01696-X). Wm C Brown.
Larsen, Elaine. Israel. (Batsford Countries Ser.). 1976. 10.95 o.p. (ISBN 0-8038-3400-4). Hastings.
Larsen, Ellouise B. American Historical Views on Staffordshire China. LC 74-22896. (Illus.). 343p. 1975. 17.50 (ISBN 0-486-23088-0); pap. 10.00 (ISBN 0-486-23055-4). Dover.
Larsen, G. & Chilingar, G. V., eds. Diagenesis in Sediments & Sedimentary Rocks. (Developments in Sedimentology: Vol. 25A). 1979. 74.50 (ISBN 0-444-41657-9). Elsevier.
Larsen, Gaylord. Trouble Crossing the Pyrenees. 1983. pap. 6.95 (ISBN 0-8307-0880-4). Regal.
Larsen, Gerald H., jt. auth. see Bernacchi, Richard L.
Larsen, Hanna A., tr. see Jacobsen, J. P.
Larsen, J. A. Representative Government in Greek & Roman History. (Sather Classical Lectures Ser.: No. 28). 1976. 26.50x (ISBN 0-520-03240-3). U of Cal Pr.
Larsen, Jackie. Beyond This Colored Glass. LC 77-83904. (Illus.). 1970. prepub. 4.95x softcover (ISBN 0-9602474-2-4). J Larsen.
Larsen, James B. & Billings, Jeffrey D. Laboratory Manual for Human Physiology. 128p. 1982. pap. text ed. 8.95 (ISBN 0-8403-2782-X). Kendall-Hunt.
Larsen, Jeanne. James Cook in Search of Terra Incognita. (Virginia Commonwealth University Series for Contemporary Poetry). 81p. 1980. text ed. 8.95x (ISBN 0-8139-0849-3). U Pr of Va.
Larsen, Jens P. & Feder, Georg. The New Grove Haydn. (New Grove Composer Biography Ser.). (Illus.). 1983. 15.95 (ISBN 0-393-01681-1); pap. 7.95 (ISBN 0-393-30085-4). Norton.
Larsen, Jo, jt. auth. see Nordhoff, Nancy S.
Larsen, John, jt. auth. see Mosich, A. N.
Larsen, Lawrence H. & Cottrell, Barbara J. The Gate City: A History of Omaha. (Western Urban History: Vol IV.). (Illus.). 300p. 1982. 16.50 (ISBN 0-87108-603-4). Pruett.
Larsen, Max D., jt. auth. see Boisen, Monte B., Jr.
Larsen, Norma C. His Everlasting Love, Vol. 2. LC 81-80956. 150p. Date not set. 7.95 (ISBN 0-88290-182-6, 1062). Horizon Utah. Postponed.
Larsen, Norma S. Pot in a Pillow Cooking. Smith, Elizabeth, ed. (Illus.). 1982. pap. write for info. Hen's Pub.
Larsen, Phyllis. Ghirardelli Original Chocolate Cookbook. 2nd ed. Allen, Vera, ed. (Orig.). 4.95 (ISBN 0-9610218-0-2). Ghirardelli Choc.
Larsen, R. & Marx, M. Introduction to Mathematical Statistics & Its Applications. 1981. 28.95 (ISBN 0-13-487744-6). P-H.
Larsen, Richard J. Statistics for the Allied Health Sciences. 320p. 1975. text ed. 23.95 (ISBN 0-675-08782-1). Merrill.
Larsen, Richard J. & Stroup, Donna F. Statistics in the Real World: A Book of Examples. (Illus.). 224p. 1976. pap. text ed. 12.95x (ISBN 0-02-367720-1). Macmillan.
Larsen, Richard W. Bundy: The Deliberate Stranger. LC 80-15795. 1980. 10.95 o.p. (ISBN 0-13-089185-1). P-H.
Larsen, Sally G. Computers for Kids: Apple II Plus Edition. LC 80-68961. (Illus.). 75p. (Orig.). (gr. 4-10). 1981. pap. 4.95 (ISBN 0-916688-21-6). Creative Comp.
--Computers for Kids: Atari Edition. LC 81-66614. (Illus.). 85p. (Orig.). (gr. 4-10). 1981. pap. 4.95 (ISBN 0-916688-22-4). Creative Comp.
--Computers for Kids: Commodore VIC-20 Edition. (Illus.). 88p. (gr. 4-10). 1983. pap. 4.95 (ISBN 0-916688-42-9). Creative Comp.
--Computers for Kids: TRS-80 Edition. LC 80-68962. (Illus.). 53p. (Orig.). (gr. 4-10). 1980. pap. 4.95 (ISBN 0-916688-20-8). Creative Comp.
Larsen, Sandy & Larsen, Dale. Choices: Picking Your Way Through the Ethical Jungle. (Young Fisherman Bible Studyguides). (Illus.). 80p. (Orig.). (gr. 2-12). 1983. saddle-stitched student ed. 2.95 (ISBN 0-87788-113-8); tchr's. ed. 3.95 (ISBN 0-87788-114-6). Shaw Pubs.
--Galatians: Free at Last. (Young Fisherman Bible Studyguides). (Illus.). 80p. (gr. 7-12). 1982. tchr's ed. 3.95 (ISBN 0-87788-294-0); saddle-stitched student ed. 2.95 (ISBN 0-87788-293-2). Shaw Pubs.
--Mark: Good News for Today. (Carpenter Studyguides Ser.). 80p. 1983. member's handbook 1.95 (ISBN 0-87788-540-0); saddle-stitched leader's handbook 2.95 (ISBN 0-87788-541-9). Shaw Pubs.
Larsen, Wanda. Rem Recycling. 1978. 10.00 o.p. (ISBN 0-533-03575-9). Vantage.
Larsen, Wendy U., jt. auth. see Siemon, Charles L.
Larsen-Freeman, Diane, ed. Discourse Analysis in Second Language Research. 283p. (Orig.). 1981. pap. text ed. 13.95 (ISBN 0-88377-163-2). Newbury Hse.
Larsgaard, Mary. Map Librarianship: An Introduction. LC 77-28821. (Library Science Text Ser.). 330p. 1978. 25.00x o.p. (ISBN 0-87287-182-7). Libs Unl.
--World Planimetric & Contour Mapping. 550p. 1983. text ed. 37.50 (ISBN 0-87287-276-9). Libs Unl.
Larson, Arthur, jt. auth. see Whitton, John B.
Larson, Arthur, ed. Warless World. 1963. 4.95 o.p. (ISBN 0-07-036493-1, GB). McGraw.
Larson, Arthur D., ed. National Security Affairs: A Guide to Information Sources. LC 70-184013. (Management Information Guide Ser.: No. 27). 350p. 1973. 42.00x (ISBN 0-8103-0827-4). Gale.
Larson, Bob. Larson's Book of Cults. 1982. 7.95 (ISBN 0-8423-2104-7). Tyndale.
--Rock. 1980. pap. 4.95 (ISBN 0-8423-5685-1). Tyndale.
Larson, Boyd. Power Control Electronics. 2nd ed. (Illus.). 176p. 1982. text ed. 21.95 (ISBN 0-13-687186-0). P-H.
Larson, Bruce. The Communicator's Commentary-Luke, Vol. 3. Ogilvie, Lloyd J., ed. (The Communicator's Commentary Ser.). 1983. 14.95 (ISBN 0-8499-0156-1). Word Pub.
--The One & Only You. (Orig.). 1976. pap. 1.50 o.s.i. (ISBN 0-89129-135-0). Jove Pubns.
Larson, Bruce L. & Smith, Vearl R., eds. Lactation: A Comprehensive Treatise. Incl. Vol. 1, 1974. Development, Lactogenesis. 63.50 (ISBN 0-12-436701-1); subscription 63.50 (ISBN 0-12-436701-1); Vol. 2. 1974. by subscription 56.00 56.00 (ISBN 0-12-436702-X); Vol. 3. Milk, Nutrition & Maintenance. 1974. 56.00, by subscription 56.00 (ISBN 0-12-436703-8); Vol. 4. 1978. 66.50, by subscription 66.50 (ISBN 0-12-436704-6). Acad Pr.
Larson, Carl, jt. auth. see Goldberg, Alvin.
Larson, Carroll B. & Gould, Marjorie. Orthopedic Nursing. 9th ed. LC 77-3429. (Illus.). 496p. 1978. text ed. 24.95 (ISBN 0-8016-2866-0). Mosby.

Larson, Charles. Fulke Greville. (English Authors Ser.). 1980. lib. bdg. 14.95 (ISBN 0-8057-6794-0, Twayne). G K Hall.

Larson, Charles, jt. auth. see Nyland, Ralph.

Larson, Charles R. Arthur Dimmesdale. 228p. 1983. 16.95 (ISBN 0-89479-115-X). A & W Pubs.

Larson, David L. United States Foreign Policy Toward Yugoslavia, 1943-1963. LC 78-71369. 1979. pap. 12.25 o.p. (ISBN 0-8191-0669-0). U Pr of Amer.

Larson, David U. What's Happening: Europe. Date not set. 3.00 (ISBN 0-686-02400-1). Larson.

Larson, E. Great Ideas in Engineering. inquire for price o.p. (ISBN 0-08-007078-7). Pergamon.

Larson, E. Richard. Sue Your Boss. 1981. 19.95 (ISBN 0-374-27161-5); pap. 9.95 (ISBN 0-374-51608-1). FS&G.

Larson, Esther E. Swedish Commentators on America 1638-1865: An Annotated List of Selected Manuscript & Printed Materials. LC 63-14658. (Orig.). 1963. pap. 7.50 o.p. (ISBN 0-87104-174-X). NY Pub Lib.

Larson, G. J. Classical Sankhya. 1979. 16.95 o.p. (ISBN 0-89684-058-1, Dist. by Motilal Banarsidass India). Orient Bk Dist.

Larson, Gary O. The Reluctant Patron: The United States Government & the Arts, 1943-1965. LC 82-40492. (Illus.). 320p. (Orig.). 1983. 30.00x (ISBN 0-8122-7876-3); pap. 12.95 (ISBN 0-8122-1144-8). U of Pa Pr.

Larson, Gena. Fact-Book on Better Food for Better Babies & Their Families. LC 72-83519. (Pivot Original Health Book). 128p. 1972. pap. 2.25 (ISBN 0-87983-023-9). Keats.

Larson, Gene F. The Unforgettable. rev. ed. 1978. 10.00 (ISBN 0-686-68574-1, 1491). Healthcare Fin Man Assn.

Larson, Gerald J., et al, eds. Myth & Indo-European Antiquity. LC 72-93522. 1974. 30.00x (ISBN 0-520-02378-1). U of Cal Pr.

Larson, Glen A. & Thurston, Robert. The Battlestar Galactica Story Book. Mercer, Charles, adapted by. LC 79-198. (Illus.). 1979. 4.95 (ISBN 0-399-20683-3). Putnam Pub Group.

Larson, Harold J. Introduction to Probability Theory & Statistical Inference. 3rd ed. 637p. 1982. text ed. 30.50 (ISBN 0-471-05909-9); pap. text ed. 9.00x solutions manual (ISBN 0-471-09919-8). Wiley.

--Introduction to Probability Theory & Statistical Inference. 2nd ed. LC 73-19852. (Ser. in Probability & Mathematical Statistics). 430p. 1974. 26.50x o.p. (ISBN 0-471-51781-X). Wiley.

Larson, Harold J. & Shubert, Bruno O. Probabilistic Models in Engineering Sciences, 2 vols. Incl. Vol. 1. Random Variables & Stochastic Processes. text ed. 40.50x (ISBN 0-471-01751-5); solutions manual 8.95x (ISBN 0-471-05759-2); Vol. 2. Random Noise Signals & Dynamic Systems. text ed. 38.95x (ISBN 0-471-05179-9); solutions manual 10.95x (ISBN 0-471-05760-6). LC 79-755. 544p. 1979. Wiley.

Larson, James. Ecology of the Northern Lowland Bogs & Conifer Forests. 307p. 1982. 34.00 (ISBN 0-12-436860-3). Acad Pr.

Larson, James A. Database Management System Anatomy. (Illus.). 208p. 1981. 24.95x (ISBN 0-669-04544-6). Lexington Bks.

Larson, James L. Reason & Experience: The Representation of Natural Order in the Work of Carl von Linne. LC 70-632164. 1971. 24.50x (ISBN 0-520-01834-6). U of Cal Pr.

Larson, Jean R. The Glass Mountain & Other Arabian Tales. (Illus.). 112p. (gr. 4 up). 1972. 6.25 (ISBN 0-8255-5190-0); PLB 5.97 (ISBN 0-8255-5191-9). Macrae.

Larson, John A., et al. Lying & Its Detection: A Study of Deception & Deception Tests. LC 69-16241. (Criminology, Law Enforcement & Social Problems Ser.: No. 78). 1969. Repr. of 1932 ed. 20.00x (ISBN 0-87585-078-2). Patterson Smith.

Larson, Joyce E., ed. New Foundations for Asian & Pacific Security. 300p. 1980. text ed. 24.95 (ISBN 0-87855-413-0); pap. text ed. 7.95 (ISBN 0-686-71728-7). Transaction Bk.

Larson, Judith. Guide to Rapid Reading. 1970. pap. text ed. 7.00 (ISBN 0-394-30361-X). Knopf.

Larson, Kenneth H., jt. auth. see Hays, Joyce S.

Larson, Lane & Larson, Peggy. Caving: The Sierra Club Guide to Spelunking. LC 80-23110. (Sierra Club Outdoor Activities Guides Ser.). (Illus.). 320p. (Orig.). 1982. pap. 10.95 (ISBN 0-87156-246-4). Sierra.

Larson, Linda L. Protocols for Advanced Emergency Care. 288p. 1981. pap. text ed. 17.95 (ISBN 0-87619-993-7). R J Brady.

Larson, Magali S. The Rise of Professionalism: A Sociological Analysis. LC 74-30533. 1977. 28.50x (ISBN 0-520-02938-0); pap. 10.95x (ISBN 0-520-03950-5). U of Cal Pr.

Larson, Margaret A., jt. auth. see Fitch, Grace E.

Larson, Martin A. IRS vs. Middle Class. 1983. 12.95 (ISBN 0-8159-5824-2); pap. 5.95 (ISBN 0-8159-5827-7). Devin.

Larson, Martin A. & Stanley, Lowell C. The Religious Empire. LC 75-27270. 1976. pap. 10.00 o.p. (ISBN 0-88331-082-1). Luce.

Larson, Maurice A., jt. auth. see Randolph, Alan D.

Larson, Mildred. Studies in Peruvian Indian Languages One. (Publications in Linguistics & Related Fields Ser.: No. 9). 220p. 1963. pap. 1.50x (ISBN 0-88312-009-7); microfiche 3.00x (ISBN 0-88312-409-2). Summer Inst Ling.

Larson, Mildred L. The Functions of Reported Speech in Discourse. (Publications in Linguistics & Related Fields: No. 59). 421p. 1978. pap. 13.50x (ISBN 0-88312-073-9); microfiche 4.50x (ISBN 0-88312-472-6). Summer Inst Ling.

--Vocabulario Aguaruna de Amazonas. (Peruvian Linguistic Ser: No. 3). 211p. 1966. pap. 3.00x (ISBN 0-88312-653-2). Summer Inst Ling.

Larson, Mildred L., ed. Bilingual Education: An Experience in Peruvian Amazonia. Davis, Patricia M. 417p. 1981. pap. 10.40x (ISBN 0-88312-918-3); microfiche 4.50 (ISBN 0-88312-596-X). Summer Inst Ling.

Larson, Milton E. Teaching Related Subjects in Trade & Industrial & Technical Education. LC 72-80235. 1972. text ed. 21.50 (ISBN 0-675-09073-3). Merrill.

Larson, Norita D. Langston Hughes, Poet of Harlem. Redpath, Ann, ed. (People to Remember Ser.). (Illus.). 32p. (gr. 5-9). 1981. PLB 7.95 (ISBN 0-87191-798-X). Creative Ed.

Larson, P. S. & Silvette, H. Tobacco: Experimental & Clinical Studies. 38.00 ea.; Supplement 1, 1968 816p. 42.00 ea. (ISBN 0-683-04877-5); 38.00 (ISBN 0-683-04898-8). Supplement 3, 1975 798p (Pub. by W&W). Krieger.

Larson, Peggy, jt. auth. see Larson, Lane.

Larson, Philip M., Jr. Vital Church Management. LC 76-12394. 1977. 3.99 (ISBN 0-8042-1883-8). John Knox.

Larson, R. & Odoni, A. Urban Operations Research. 1981. 34.00 (ISBN 0-13-939447-8). P-H.

Larson, R. A. Of Wind, a Hawk & Kiona. 1978. pap. 2.50 o.p. (ISBN 0-917652-16-9). Confluence Pr.

Larson, Randall D. A Survey of Film Music in the Fantastic Cinema. 1982. pap. 3.50 ltd. ed. cancelled (ISBN 0-9607178-0-3). Fandom Unltd.

Larson, Raymond, ed. & tr. The Symposium & the Phaedo: Plato. LC 79-55931. (Crofts Classics Ser.). (Orig.). 1980. text ed. 11.95x (ISBN 0-88295-119-X); pap. text ed. 3.75x (ISBN 0-88295-122-X). Harlan Davidson.

Larson, Raymond, ed. & tr. see Plato.

Larson, Richard C. Innovative Resource Planning in Urban Public Safety Systems: Police Deployment: New Tools for Planners. LC 77-9135. (IRP Ser.: Vol. 1). (Illus.). 272p. 1978. 25.95x (ISBN 0-669-01783-3). Lexington Bks.

--Innovative Resource Planning in Urban Public Safety Systems: Police Accountability: Performance Measures & Unionism. LC 77-9136. (IRP Ser.: Vol. 2). 240p. 1977. 24.95x (ISBN 0-669-01785-X). Lexington Bks.

--Urban Police Patrol Analysis. 256p. 1972. 20.00x (ISBN 0-262-12052-6). MIT Pr.

Larson, Richard C., jt. ed. see Willemain, Thomas R.

Larson, Richard F., jt. auth. see Ott, Lyman.

Larson, Richard L., ed. Children & Writing in the Elementary School: Theories & Techniques. (Illus.). 1975. pap. text ed. 9.95x (ISBN 0-19-501914-8). Oxford U Pr.

Larson, Robert W. New Mexico Populism: A Study of Radical Protest in a Western Territory. LC 73-89256. 1974. 13.50x (ISBN 0-87081-054-5). Colo Assoc.

Larson, Roger R. Puritan Five. 1983. 14.95 (ISBN 0-87949-220-1). Ashley Bks.

Larson, Roland E. & Hostetler, Robert P. Brief Calculus with Applications. 736p. Date not set. text ed. 23.95 (ISBN 0-669-04803-8). Heath.

--Calculus with Analytic Geometry. 1979. text ed. 31.95 o.p. (ISBN 0-669-01301-3); solution manuals 7.95 ea. o.p. Vol. 1 (ISBN 0-669-03187-9). Vol. 2 (ISBN 0-669-03188-7). Vol. 3 (ISBN 0-669-03189-5). differential equations suppl. 1.95 o.p. (ISBN 0-669-03204-2); student manual 8.95 o.p. (ISBN 0-669-01705-1); appendix d 1.95 o.p. (ISBN 0-669-03190-9); instructor's manual to adopters 1.95 o.p. (ISBN 0-669-01302-1). Heath.

Larson, Roland S. Greet Those at Home. (Illus.). 64p. (Orig.). 1982. pap. 8.95 (ISBN 0-86683-684-5). Winston Pr.

Larson, Ronald A. & Hostetler, Robert P. Calculus. 2nd ed. 1120p. 1981. text ed. 31.95 (ISBN 0-669-04530-6); solutions guide 8.95 (ISBN 0-669-04533-0); avail instr's guide (ISBN 0-669-04532-2); Vol. I. 8.95 (ISBN 0-669-05248-5); Vol. II. 8.95 (ISBN 0-669-05250-7); Vol. III. 8.95 (ISBN 0-669-05251-5). Heath.

Larson, Russ, ed. N Scale Model Railroad Track Plans. LC 71-107073. (Illus.). 44p. 1969. pap. 4.00 (ISBN 0-89024-509-6). Kalmbach.

Larson, Steven M., jt. auth. see Thorell, Jan I.

Larson, T. A., ed. see Nye, Bill.

Larson, Vicki L., jt. auth. see Boyce, Nancy L.

Larson, W. C., jt. ed. see Schlitt, W. J.

Larson, William E. & Walsh, Leo M, eds. Soil & Water Resources: Reasearch Priorities for the Nation-Proceedings. 229p. 1981. 12.00 (ISBN 0-89118-768-5). Soil Sci Soc Am.

Larsson, Carl, jt. auth. see Rudstrom, Lennart.

Larsson, Carl, illus. The World of Carl Larsson. Koster, Hans-Curt, ed. Rice, Alan, tr. (Illus.). 220p. 1982. 29.95 o.p. (ISBN 0-914676-93-8, Star & Eleph Bks). Green Tiger Pr.

Larsson, L. H. Advances in Elasto-Plastic Fracture Mechanics. 1980. 45.00 (ISBN 0-85334-889-8, Pub. by Applied Sci England). Elsevier.

Lartigue, Jacques-Henri & Metral, Yvette. My Photography Book. Bernard, J. F., tr. from Fr. LC 79-18486. (gr. k-12). Date not set. cancelled (ISBN 0-8120-5339-7). Barron.

Larue, Brandy. Ecstasy Reclaimed. (Second Chance at Love Ser.: No. 97). 192p. 1983. pap. 1.75 (ISBN 0-515-06861-6). Jove Pubns.

LaRue, Charlotte, tr. see Petersen, Carol.

Larue, Gerald. Human Sexuality & the Bible. 212p. 1983. 17.95 (ISBN 0-87975-206-8); pap. 8.95 (ISBN 0-87975-213-0). Prometheus Bks.

Larue, Gerald A. Ancient Myth & Modern Man. LC 74-9527. 320p. (Orig.). 1975. 16.95 o.p. (ISBN 0-13-035493-7); pap. 14.95 (ISBN 0-13-035485-6). P-H.

LaRue, Jaine, ed. see McGinty, Patricia.

Larwood, Laurie & Wood, Marion M. Women in Management. LC 76-27033. 1977. 20.95x (ISBN 0-669-00973-3). Lexington Bks.

Lary, Hal B., et al. The United States in the World Economy. LC 75-26859. (Economic Series: No. 23). 216p. 1975. Repr. of 1943 ed. lib. bdg. 29.75x (ISBN 0-8371-8257-3, LAUS). Greenwood.

Larzelere, Bob. The Harmony of Love. LC 81-3189. 144p. (Orig.). 1982. pap. 7.95 (ISBN 0-932654-03-7). Context Pubns.

Lasaga, Manuel. The Copper Industry in the Chilean Economy: An Econometric Analysis. LC 81-47025. (The Wharton Econometric Studies). (Illus.). 224p. 1981. 23.95x (ISBN 0-669-04543-8). Lexington Bks.

Lasagna, Louis. The VD Epidemic: How It Started, Where It's Going, & What to Do About It. LC 74-29475. 184p. 1975. 24.95 (ISBN 0-87722-041-7). Temple U Pr.

Lasagna, Louis, ed. Controversies in Therapeutics. LC 77-86015. (Illus.). 603p. 1980. text ed. 32.00 (ISBN 0-7216-5653-6). Saunders.

Lasagna, Michele, jt. auth. see Faber, Gail.

LaSalle, J. P. The Stability of Dynamical Systems. (CBMS Regional Conference Ser.: Vol. 25). v, 76p. (Orig.). 1976. pap. text ed. 12.50 (ISBN 0-89871-022-7). Soc Indus-Appl Math.

La Sasso, Wilma R. Regional Italian Cooking: From the Alps to the Mediterranean. (Illus.). 268p. 1975. pap. 1.95 o.p. (ISBN 0-02-009780-8, Collier). Macmillan.

Las Brozas, F. Sanchez de see Sanchez de Las Brozas, F.

Lascar, D., jt. ed. see Van Dalen, D.

Lascari, Andre. Hematologic Aspects of Systemic Disease of Children. (Masson Monographs in Pediatric Hematology-Oncology: Vol. 5). (Illus.). 352p. 1983. cancelled (ISBN 0-89352-176-0). Masson Pub.

Lascelles, Mary, ed. see Johnson, Samuel.

Laschever, Barnett D. Getting to Know Hawaii. (Getting to Know Ser.). (Illus.). (gr. 3-5). 1959. PLB 3.97 o.p. (ISBN 0-698-30122-6, Coward). Putnam Pub Group.

Lasdon, Gail S. Improving Ambulatory Health Care Delivery: Multidisciplinary Applications. LC 77-75659. (Ambulatory Care Systems Ser.). 1977. 22.95x (ISBN 0-669-01514-8). Lexington Bks.

Lasdon, Leon S. Optimization Theory for Large Systems. (Illus.). 1970. 25.95x (ISBN 0-02-367800-3). Macmillan.

Laseelles. Motoring Holidays in Spain. 11.50x (ISBN 0-392-15957-0, SpS). Sportshelf.

Lasegue, A. Musee Botanique de M. Benjamin Delessert. 1970. Repr. of 1845 ed. 40.00 (ISBN 3-7682-0686-6). Lubrecht & Cramer.

Lash, James & Burger, Max M., eds. Cell & Tissue Interactions. LC 77-83689. (Society of General Physiologists Ser: Vol. 32). 331p. 1977. 32.50 (ISBN 0-89004-180-6). Raven.

Lash, Joseph P. Dag Hamarskjold, Custodian of the Brushfire Peace. LC 73-22637. 304p. 1974. Repr. of 1961 ed. lib. bdg. 17.00x (ISBN 0-8371-6995-X, LADJ). Greenwood.

--Eleanor & Franklin. (RL 10). 1973. pap. 4.95 (ISBN 0-451-11231-8, AE1231, Sig). NAL.

--Eleanor: The Years Alone. Pitkin, Walter, ed. (Illus.). (RL 10). 1973. pap. 3.95 (ISBN 0-451-11293-8, AE1293, Sig). NAL.

--Helen & Teacher: The Story of Helen Keller & Anne Sullivan Macy. 1980. 17.95 o.s.i. (ISBN 0-440-03654-2). Delacorte.

Lash, MaryAnn, jt. auth. see Brackett, Babette.

Lash, Nicholas. Acts of the Apostles. (Scripture Discussion Outlines Ser). 1968. pap. 0.75 o.p. (ISBN 0-685-07606-7, 80390). Glencoe.

Lash, Nicholas, jt. auth. see Tracy, David.

Lashner, Robert T., jt. ed. see Massey, E. Wayne.

Lashomb, James & Casagrande, Richard, eds. Advances in Potato Pest Management. LC 81-6442. 304p. 1982. 22.00 (ISBN 0-87933-407-X). Hutchinson Ross.

Lasjaunias, Pierre. Craniofacial & Upper Cervical Arteries: Collateral Circulation & Angiographic Protocols. 300p. 1983. lib. bdg. write for info. (ISBN 0-683-04898-8). Williams & Wilkins.

--Craniofacial & Upper Cervical Arteries: Functional, Clinical & Angiographic Aspects. (Illus.). 211p. 1981. lib. bdg. 75.00 (ISBN 0-683-04898-8). Williams & Wilkins.

Lask, I. M., tr. see Agnon, S. Y.

Laska, Eugene M., et al, eds. Information Support to Mental Health Programs: An International Perspective. 240p. 1983. 29.95 (ISBN 0-89885-083-5). Human Sci Pr.

Laska, John A. Schooling & Education: Basic Concepts & Problems. 1976. pap. 6.50x (ISBN 0-442-24622-6). Van Nos Reinhold.

Laska, Vera. Women in the Resistance & in the Holocaust: The Voices of Eyewitnesses. LC 82-12018. (Contributions in Women Studies: No. 37). 352p. 1983. lib. bdg. 29.95 (ISBN 0-313-23457-4, LWH/). Greenwood.

Lasker, Anabel C., jt. auth. see Wheeler, Esther.

Lasker, Bruno. Race Attitudes in Children. Repr. of 1929 ed. lib. bdg. 20.00x (ISBN 0-8371-0340-1, LARA). Greenwood.

Lasker, Daniel J. Jewish Philosophical Polemics Against Christianity in the Middle Ages. 320p. 15.00 (ISBN 0-686-95177-8). ADL.

Lasker, Edward. Chess Secrets I Learned From the Masters. (Illus.). 1969. pap. 4.95 o.p. (ISBN 0-486-22266-7). Dover.

Lasker, Emanuel. Lasker's How to Play Chess. 1970. 2.98 o.p. (ISBN 0-517-02965-0). Crown.

Lasker, Michael & Simmons, Richard A. The Gangster Chronicles: TV Tie-in. 224p. (Orig.). 1981. pap. 2.50 o.s.i. (ISBN 0-515-05808-4). Jove Pubns.

Lasker-Schuler, Else. The Blossoms of My Body. Wolf, Joan, tr. LC 82-81351. 1983. 10.00 (ISBN 0-930100-13-1); pap. 4.00 (ISBN 0-930100-12-3). Holy Cow.

--Your Diamond Dreams Cut Open My Arteries. Newton, Robert P., tr. LC 82-2656. (Studies in the Germanic Languages & Literatures: No. 100). x, 317p. 1983. 20.00 (ISBN 0-8078-8100-7). U of NC Pr.

Laskevich, Leonarda A., jt. auth. see Kane, Michael T.

Laski, Harold. The American Presidency. LC 80-50104. (The Social Science Classics Ser.). 278p. 1980. 29.95 (ISBN 0-87855-390-8); pap. 6.95 (ISBN 0-87855-821-7). Transaction Bks.

Laski, Harold J. American Democracy. LC 74-122066. Repr. of 1948 ed. 35.00x (ISBN 0-678-03165-7). Kelley.

--The American Presidency, an Interpretation. LC 79-138120. 278p. 1972. Repr. of 1940 ed. lib. bdg. 17.50x (ISBN 0-8371-5696-3, LAPR). Greenwood.

--Communism. LC 68-56057. Repr. of 1927 ed. 23.50x o.p. (ISBN 0-678-05061-9). Kelley.

--Studies in Law & Politics. LC 68-57616. (Illus.). 1969. Repr. of 1932 ed. lib. bdg. 15.50x (ISBN 0-8371-0528-5, LALP). Greenwood.

Laskin. Spasibo za Vnimanie. (Easy Reader, B). pap. 3.95 (ISBN 0-88436-052-0, 65251). EMC.

Laskin, Allen, ed. Advances in Applied Microbiology, Vol. 28. (Serial Publication). 304p. 1982. 35.00 (ISBN 0-12-002628-7). Acad Pr.

Laskin, Allen I., jt. ed. see Hollaender, Alexander.

Laskin, Daniel M. Oral & Maxillofacial Surgery: The Biomedical & Clinical Basis for Surgical Practice, Vol. 1. 6th. ed. LC 79-18723. 736p. 1979. text ed. 79.50 (ISBN 0-8016-2822-9). Mosby.

Laskin, S., et al. Benzine Toxicity: A Critical Evaluation. LC 77-17128. (Illus.). 1978. text ed. 23.00 o.p. (ISBN 0-07-036507-5, HP). McGraw.

Laskowski, J., ed. Mineral Processing: Developments in Mineral Processing, 2 Vols. (Vol. 2). 1981. Set. 234.00 (ISBN 0-444-99775-X). Elsevier.

Laskowski, Lester, jt. auth. see Tocci, Ronald.

Laskowski, Lester P., jt. auth. see Tocci, Ronald J.

Lasky, Elaine Z. & Katz, Jack, eds. Central Auditory Processing Disorders: Problems of Speech, Language & Learning. (Illus.). 1983. 29.95 (ISBN 0-8391-1802-3, 18368). Univ Park.

Lasky, Katherine. Sugaring Time. LC 82-23928. (Illus.). 68p. (gr. 4-7). 1983. 10.95 (ISBN 0-02-751680-6). Macmillan.

Lasky, Kathryn. Beyond the Divide. LC 82-22867. (Illus.). 276p. (gr. 7 up). 1983. 11.95 (ISBN 0-02-751670-9). Macmillan.

Lasky, Michael. The Complete Junk Food Book. LC 77-9367. 1977. o. p 10.95 (ISBN 0-07-036501-6, GB); pap. 7.95 (ISBN 0-07-036502-4). McGraw.

Lasky, Richard. Evaluation of Criminal Responsibility in Multiple Personality & the Related Dissociative Disorders: A Psychoanalytic Consideration. 238p. 1982. 20.75x (ISBN 0-398-04673-5). C C Thomas.

Lasky, Victor. Jimmy Carter: The Man & the Myth. LC 79-625. 1979. 12.50 o.p. (ISBN 0-399-90042-X, Marek). Putnam Pub Group.

--Never Complain, Never Explain: The Story of Henry Ford. 420p. 1981. 13.95 (ISBN 0-399-90104-3, Marek). Putnam Pub Group.

--Never Complain, Never Explain: The Story of Henry Ford II. 288p. Date not set. pap. 3.50 (ISBN 0-425-05750-X). Berkley Pub. Postponed.

--Richard Nixon. 1983. write for info (Coward). Putnam Pub Group.

Lasl, F. T., et al. Biology of Trees. (Tertiary Level Biology Ser.). 1982. 45.00x (ISBN 0-412-00041-5, Pub. by Chapman & Hall England); pap. 18.95x (ISBN 0-412-00051-2). Methuen Inc.

Laslett, P. & Wall, R., eds. Household & Family in Past Time. LC 77-190420. 608p. 1972. 59.50 (ISBN 0-521-08473-3); pap. 18.95 (ISBN 0-521-09901-3). Cambridge U Pr.

Laslett, Peter. Family Life & Illicit Love in Earlier Generations. 1977. 54.50 (ISBN 0-521-21408-4); pap. 14.95 (ISBN 0-521-29221-2). Cambridge U Pr.

Laslett, Peter, ed. see Locke, John.

Lasley, J. Beef Cattle Production. 1981. 23.95 (ISBN 0-13-072629-X). P-H.

Lasley, John F. Genetics of Livestock Improvement. 3rd ed. LC 77-22807. (Illus.). 1978. ref. ed. 28.95 (ISBN 0-13-351106-5). P-H.

Lasley, John F., jt. auth. see Campbell, John R.

Lasnik, Robert S. A Parent's Guide to Adoption. LC 78-56845. 192p. 1980. pap. 7.95 (ISBN 0-8069-8956-4). Sterling.

--A Parent's Guide to Adoption. LC 78-56895. 1979. 12.95 o.p. (ISBN 0-8069-8830-4); PLB 10.79 o.p. (ISBN 0-8069-8831-2). Sterling.

Lasocki, David, jt. auth. see Mather, Betty Bang.

LaSor, William S. Handbook of Biblical Hebrew, 3 vols. Set. 14.95x (ISBN 0-8028-2379-3). Eerdmans.

--The Truth About Armageddon: What the Bible Says about the End of Times. LC 82-47748. 160p. (Orig.). 1982. pap. 6.68i (ISBN 0-06-064919-4, HarpR). Har-Row.

Lass, A., jt. ed. see Goldstone, Richard.

Lass, A. H. Business Spelling & Word Power. 7th ed. 1961. pap. text ed. 9.95 (ISBN 0-672-96012-5); tchr's key (2nd ed.) 6.67 (ISBN 0-672-96014-1); tchr's manual (2nd ed.) 6.67 (ISBN 0-672-96013-3); test pkg. 3.95 (ISBN 0-672-96015-X). Bobbs.

Lass, A. H., jt. auth. see Flesch, Rudolf.

Lass, Abraham, jt. auth. see Kriegel, Leonard.

Lass, Abraham & Tasman, Norma, eds. Secret Sharer & Other Great Stories. (Orig.). 1969. pap. 2.25 (ISBN 0-451-62084-4, ME2084, Ment). NAL.

--Twenty-One Great Stories. (Orig.). 1969. pap. 2.25 (ISBN 0-451-62066-6, ME2066, Ment). NAL.

Lass, Abraham H. & Levin, Milton, eds. A Students's Guide to Fifty American Plays. 316p. 1978. pap. 2.50 o.s.i. (ISBN 0-671-48907-0). WSP.

Lass, Harry. Vector & Tensor Analysis. (International Ser. in Pure & Applied Mathematics). 1950. text ed. 19.95 o.p. (ISBN 0-07-036520-2, C). McGraw.

Lass, Norman. Speech & Language: Advances in Basic Research & Practice, Vol. 7. (Serial Publication Ser.). 1982. 44.00 (ISBN 0-12-608607-9). Acad Pr.

Lass, Norman J., ed. Speech & Language: Advances in Basic Research & Practice. (Serial Publication: Vol. 9). Date not set. price not set (ISBN 0-12-608609-5). Acad Pr.

--Speech & Language: Advances in Basic Research & Practice, Vol. 1. (Serial Publication). 1979. 34.50 (ISBN 0-12-608601-X). Acad Pr.

--Speech & Language: Advances in Basic Research & Practice, Vol. 6. (Serial Publication). 496p. 1982. 55.00 (ISBN 0-12-608606-0). Acad Pr.

--Speech & Language: Advances in Basic Research & Practice, Vol. 8. (Serial Publication Ser.). 1982. 45.00 (ISBN 0-12-608608-7). Acad Pr.

Lass, Norman J., et al. Speech, Language & Hearing: Normal Processes & Clinical Disorders. LC 77-77198. (Illus.). 1000p. 1982. text ed. 69.00 (ISBN 0-7216-5634-X). Saunders.

Lass, R., tr. see Wunderlich, D.

Lass, Roger. On Explaining Language Change. LC 79-51825. (Studies in Linguistics Ser.: No. 27). (Illus.). 1980. 32.50 (ISBN 0-521-22836-0). Cambridge U Pr.

Lassaigne, Jack. El Greco. (Illus.). 264p. 1974. 28.00 o.p. (ISBN 0-500-18142-X); pap. 11.50 o.p. (ISBN 0-500-20136-6). Transatlantic.

Lassaletta, Manuel, tr. see Nee, Watchman.

Lassalle, H. M. Enomiya: Zen Meditation for Christians. Maraldo, John C., tr. 187p. 15.50 (ISBN 0-87548-151-5). Open Court.

Lassay, Armand-Leon. Relation du Royaume des Feliciens. (Utopias in the Enlightenment Ser.). 148p. (Fr.). 1974. Repr. of 1756 ed. lib. bdg. 46.00x o.p. (ISBN 0-8287-1411-8, 048). Clearwater Pub.

Lassen, Niels A. & Perl, William. Tracer Kinetic Methods in Medical Physiology. LC 75-43198. 199p. 1979. text ed. 28.50 (ISBN 0-89004-114-8). Raven.

Lasser. Professional Edition of Your Income Tax, 1975. 1981. 20.95 o.s.i. (ISBN 0-671-41230-2). S&S.

Lasser, A. Jay. Everyone's Income Tax Guide, 1980. LC 58-3391. 1980. pap. 2.95 (ISBN 0-399-50402-8, Perige). Putnam Pub Group.

Lasser Institute. J. K. Lasser's Managing Your Family Finances. 1976. 14.95 (ISBN 0-671-22306-2). S&S.

Lasser, Jacob K. Business Management Handbook. 3rd ed. 1968. 49.95 (ISBN 0-07-036555-5, P&RB). McGraw.

--Handbook of Successful Tax Procedures. 1956. 4.95 o.p. (ISBN 0-671-29650-7). S&S.

--How to Run a Small Business. 4th ed. 306p. 1974. 24.95 (ISBN 0-07-036565-2, P&RB). McGraw.

Lasser, S. J. Everyone's Income Tax Guide, 1983. 200p. 1982. 5.95 (ISBN 0-937782-02-5). Hilltop Pubns.

Lassey, jt. auth. see Carlson.

Lassey, William R. Planning in Rural Environments. (McGraw-Hill Publications in the Agricultural Sciences). 1977. text ed. 28.00 (ISBN 0-07-036580-6, C). McGraw.

Lassiter, Barbara B. American Wilderness: The Hudson River School of Painting. LC 73-13089. (gr. 7 up). 1978. 8.95 (ISBN 0-385-08192-8); PLB 8.95 o.p. (ISBN 0-385-04376-7). Doubleday.

Lassiter, J. W. & Edwards, Hardy M. Animal Nutrition. 1982. text ed. 20.95 (ISBN 0-8359-0222-6); instr's. manual free (ISBN 0-8359-0223-4). Reston.

Lassiter, Luther. Billiards for Everyone. (Illus.). 1965. pap. 2.95 o.p. (ISBN 0-448-01519-6, G&D). Putnam Pub Group.

Lassiter, Robert A., et al. Vocational Evaluation, Work Adjustment, & Independent Living for Severely Disabled People. (Illus.). 436p. 1983. 37.50x (ISBN 0-398-04695-6). C C Thomas.

Lassman, L. P., jt. auth. see James, C. C. M.

Lasson, Frans, ed. see Svendsen, Clara.

Lasson, Kenneth & Public Citizen Litigation Group. Representing Yourself: What You Can do Without a Lawyer. 1983. 16.50 (ISBN 0-374-24943-1); pap. text ed. 8.25 (ISBN 0-374-51726-6). FS&G.

Lasson, Kenneth, jt. auth. see Cohen, William S.

Lasson, Nelson B. History & Development of the Fourth Amendment to the United States Constitution. LC 75-87389. (American Constitutional & Legal History Ser.). 1970. Repr. of 1937 ed. lib. bdg. 27.50 (ISBN 0-306-71532-5). Da Capo.

Lassus, Orlandus. Ten Madrigals. Arnold, Denis, ed. 11.95 (ISBN 0-19-343668-X). Oxford U Pr.

Lasswell, H. D. A Pre-View of Policy Sciences. (Policy Sciences Ser.). 1971. text ed. 19.95 (ISBN 0-444-00112-3, North Holland). Elsevier.

Lasswell, Harold, et al, eds. Propaganda & Communication in World History: The Symbolic Instrument in Early Times, Vol. 1. LC 78-23964. (Propaganda & Communication in World History Ser.). 1979. text ed. 27.50x (ISBN 0-8248-0496-1, Eastwest Ctr). UH Pr.

Lasswell, Harold D. National Security & Individual Freedom. LC 71-139193. (Civil Liberty in American History Ser.). 1971. Repr. of 1950 ed. lib. bdg. 32.50 (ISBN 0-306-70085-9). Da Capo.

--Power & Personality. LC 75-22644. 262p. 1976. Repr. of 1948 ed. lib. bdg. 20.25x (ISBN 0-8371-8374-X, LAPOP). Greenwood.

--Propaganda Technique in World War I. 1971. pap. 4.95 (ISBN 0-262-62018-9). MIT Pr.

--World Revolutionary Propaganda. LC 71-110854. (Illus.). xii, 393p. Repr. of 1939 ed. lib. bdg. 17.75x o.p. (ISBN 0-8371-4521-X, LAWR). Greenwood.

Lasswell, Harold D., jt. auth. see Chen, Lung-Chu.

Lasswell, Harold D., et al. Language of Politics: Studies in Quantitative Semantics. 1965. pap. 4.95 o.p. (ISBN 0-262-62009-X). MIT Pr.

Lasswell, Harold D., et al, eds. Propaganda & Communication in World History: A Pluralizing World in Formation, Vol. 3. LC 78-23964. (Propaganda & Communication in World History Ser.). 1980. text ed. 27.50x (ISBN 0-8248-0507-0, Eastwest Ctr). UH Pr.

--Propaganda & Communication in World History: Emergence of Public Opinion in the West, Vol. 2. LC 78-23964. (Propaganda & Communication in World History Ser.). 1979. text ed. 27.50x (ISBN 0-8248-0504-6, Eastwest Ctr). UH Pr.

--Values & Development: Appraising Asian Experience. 1977. text ed. 25.00x (ISBN 0-262-12074-7). MIT Pr.

Lasswell, Marcia & Lobsenz, Norman. Equal Time: The New Way of Living, Loving, & Working Together. LC 82-45254. 240p. 1983. 15.95 (ISBN 0-385-17473-X). Doubleday.

Lasswell, Marcia, jt. auth. see Lasswell, Thomas E.

Lasswell, Marcia E., jt. auth. see Lasswell, Thomas E.

Lasswell, Thomas E. & Lasswell, Marcia E. Love-Marriage-Family: A Developmental Approach. 1973. pap. 10.95x o.p. (ISBN 0-673-07523-0). Scott F.

Lasswell, Thomas E. & Lasswell, Marcia. Marriage & the Family. 544p. 1982. text ed. 20.95 (ISBN 0-669-04373-7); study guide 4.95 (ISBN 0-669-04372-9); instr's guide 1.95 (ISBN 0-669-04371-0). Heath.

Lasswell, Thomas E., et al. Life in Society: Readings in Sociology. rev. ed. 1970. pap. 9.95x o.p. (ISBN 0-673-05935-9). Scott F.

Lass-Woodfin, Mary J., ed. Books on American Indians & Eskimos. LC 77-17271. 1977. text ed. 25.00 (ISBN 0-8389-0241-3). ALA.

Last, Arthur, jt. auth. see Rayner-Canham, Geoffrey.

Last, Murray. Sokoto Caliphate. LC 67-16974. (Ibadan History Ser.). (Illus.). 1967. pap. text ed. 8.00x o.p. (ISBN 0-582-64504-2). Humanities.

Last, Rex W. German Dadaist Literature. (World Authors Ser.). 1973. lib. bdg. 13.95 (ISBN 0-8057-2361-7, Twayne). G K Hall.

Laster, James, compiled by. Catalogue of Choral Music Arranged in Biblical Order. LC 82-16745. 269p. 1983. 22.50 (ISBN 0-8108-1592-3). Scarecrow.

Lastigzon, J. World Fertilizer Progress in to the 1980's. (Technical Bulletin Ser.: T-22). (Illus.). 64p. (Orig.). 1981. pap. 4.00 (ISBN 0-88090-021-0). Intl Fertilizer.

Lastrucci, Carlo. Scientific Approach. 272p. 1967. 6.50 o.p. (ISBN 0-87073-042-8). Schenkman.

Laszlo, E. Human Values & the Mind of Man: Current Topics of Contemporary Thought. 184p. 1971. 35.00 (ISBN 0-677-14590-X). Gordon.

--Systems Science & World Order: Selected Studies. (Systems Science & World Order Library). 278p. 1982. 35.00 (ISBN 0-08-028924-X). Pergamon.

Laszlo, Ernest. Goals for Mankind: A Report to the Club of Rome on the New Horizons of Global Community. rev ed. (Club of Rome Ser: No. 4). 1978. pap. 2.50 o.p. (ISBN 0-451-08023-8, E8023, Sig). NAL.

Laszlo, Ervin & Kurtzman, Joel, eds. Eastern Europe & the New International Economic Order: A Review of Four Representative Samples of Socialist Perspectives. LC 79-20028. (Pergamon Policy Studies). 110p. 1980. 20.00 (ISBN 0-08-025115-3). Pergamon.

Laszlo, Ervin, ed. see Conference On Value Inquiry - 1st & 2nd.

Laszlo, Ervin, ed. see Conference On Value Inquiry - 3rd.

Laszlo, Ervin, jt. ed. see Gotesky, Rubin.

Laszlo, Ervin, jt. ed. see Nicol, Davidson.

Laszlo, John. Antiemetics & Cancer Chemotherapy. (Illus.). 200p. 1982. pap. 19.95 (ISBN 0-683-04899-6). Williams & Wilkins.

Laszlo, Orszagh. English-Hungarian Dictionary. 10th ed. LC 70-250364. 1973. 5.00x o.p. (ISBN 0-8002-1399-8). Intl Pubns Serv.

Latapi, F., ed. Leprosy. (International Congress Ser.: Vol. 466). 1980. 95.50 (ISBN 0-444-90092-6). Elsevier.

Latchem, Colin. Looking at Nigeria. LC 75-15967. (Looking at Other Countries Ser.). (gr. 4-7). 1976. 10.53i (ISBN 0-397-31652-6, JBL-J). Har-Row.

Lateef, Noel V. Crisis in the Sahel. (Special Studies in Social, Political, & Economic Development). (Illus.). 285p. 1980. lib. bdg. 28.50 (ISBN 0-89158-991-0). Westview.

La Terreur, Marc see Halpenny, Francess.

Latham, jt. auth. see Burgess.

Latham, Agnes, ed. see Shakespeare, William.

Latham, Bryan. Victorian Staffordshire Portrait Figures. (Illus.). 5.95 o.s.i. (ISBN 0-85670-073-8). Transatlantic.

Latham, Donald C., jt. auth. see Martin, Thomas L., Jr.

Latham, Earl. The Declaration of Independence & the Constitution. 3rd ed. (Problems in American Civilization). 1976. pap. 6.95x (ISBN 0-669-94888-8). Heath.

--J. F. Kennedy & Presidential Power. 1973. pap. text ed. 6.95x (ISBN 0-669-82099-7). Heath.

Latham, Earl, ed. Meaning of McCarthyism. 2nd ed. (Problems in American Civilization Ser.). 1972. pap. text ed. 5.95 (ISBN 0-669-81851-8). Heath.

Latham, Edward. Dictionary of Names, Nicknames, & Surnames. LC 66-22674. 1966. Repr. of 1904 ed. 37.00x (ISBN 0-8103-0157-1). Gale.

--Famous Sayings & Their Authors: A Collection of Historical Sayings in English, French, German, Greek, Italian, & Latin. LC 68-26582. 1970. Repr. of 1904 ed. 34.00x (ISBN 0-8103-3141-1). Gale.

Latham, Gary, jt. auth. see Wexley, Kenneth.

Latham, Jean L. The Columbia: Powerhouse of North America. LC 67-10022. (Rivers of the World). (Illus.). (gr. 4-7). 1967. PLB 3.98 (ISBN 0-8116-6367-1). Garrard.

--Elizabeth Blackwell: Pioneer Woman Doctor. LC 75-4808. (Discovery Books Ser.). (Illus.). 80p. (gr. 2-5). 1975. PLB 6.69 (ISBN 0-8116-6319-1). Garrard.

--Rachel Carson: Who Loved the Sea. LC 72-11475. (Discovery Ser.). (Illus.). 80p. (gr. 2-5). 1973. PLB 6.69 (ISBN 0-8116-6312-4). Garrard.

--Story of Eli Whitney. LC 62-16413. (Illus.). (gr. 5 up). 1962. PLB 8.79 o.p. (ISBN 0-06-023735-X, HarpJ). Har-Row.

--Who Lives Here? LC 73-22080. (Easy Venture Ser). (Illus.). 32p. (gr. k-2). 1974. PLB 6.69 (ISBN 0-8116-6063-X). Garrard.

Latham, Marcia L., tr. see Descartes, Rene.

Latham, P. R. & Linkl, E. J., eds. Marine Affairs Journal, No. 2. 123p. 1974. 1.00 (ISBN 0-686-36972-6, P368). URI Mas.

Latham, Robert, ed. Catalogue of the Pepys Library at Magdalene College Cambridge: Volume 5, Part 2: Modern Manuscripts, Vol. V - Pt. 2. 302p. 1981. 135.00x (ISBN 0-8476-7050-3). Rowman.

--The Illustrated Pepys: Extracts from the Diary. 240p. 1982. 30.00x (ISBN 0-686-82321-4, Pub. by Bell & Hyman England). State Mutual Bk.

Latham, Robert, ed. see Pepys, Samuel.

Latham, Robert, compiled by see Pepys, Samuel.

Latham, Robert, ed. see Pepys, Samuel.

Latham, Robert, et al, eds. see Pepys, Samuel.

Latham, Ronald, tr. see Polo, Marco.

Latham, Sidney. Filter Guide. (Illus.). 1977. pap. 2.95 o.p. (ISBN 0-8174-0229-2, Amphoto). Watson-Guptill.

Lathem, Edward. Robert Frost One Hundred. LC 74-15258. 1974. 10.00 (ISBN 0-87923-111-4); pap. 4.50 o.p. (ISBN 0-87923-112-2). Godine.

Lathen, Emma. Green Grow the Dollars. 1982. 12.95 (ISBN 0-671-44130-2). S&S.

Lathi, Bhagwandas P. Signals, Systems & Communication. 1965. 39.95 (ISBN 0-471-51835-2); tchr's. manual 6.00x (ISBN 0-471-51836-0). Wiley.

Lathi, Bhagwandas P. Communication Systems. 431p. 1968. 39.50 (ISBN 0-471-51832-8). Wiley.

Lathrap, Donald W. The Upper Amazon. (Illus.). 1979. 15.95 (ISBN 0-500-02067-1). Thames Hudson.

Lathrop, Irving T., jt. auth. see Lindbeck, John R.

Lathrop, J. W., ed. see International Workshop, IIASA, Laxenburg, Austria, 28-31 January 1980.

Lathrop, T. A. Espanol! Lengua y cultura de Hoy. 1974. 20.95 (ISBN 0-02-367940-9). Macmillan.

Latif, S. A. The Mind Al-Quran Builds. 7.50 (ISBN 0-686-18510-2). Kazi Pubns.

Latil, M. Enhanced Oil Recovery. 170p. 1980. 27.95x (ISBN 0-87201-775-3). Gulf Pub.

Latimer & Sayer. Teach Yourself Indoor Aquaria. 8.50x (ISBN 0-392-08328-0, SpS). Sportshelf.

Latimer, Heather. Louis Wain: King of The Cat Artists: A Dramatized Biography (Born 1860 Died 1939) LC 82-82032. (Illus.). 172p. 1982. 50.00 (ISBN 0-943698-00-6). Papyrus Pubs.

Latimer, Henry. Production Planning & Repro Mechanicals for Offset Printing. (Illus.). 1980. 31.00 (ISBN 0-07-036621-7). McGraw.

Latimer, Henry C. Preparing Art & Camera Copy for Printing: A Contemporary Procedures Techniques for Mechanicals & Related Copy. 1977. 34.95 (ISBN 0-07-036620-9, P&RB). McGraw.

Latimer, Hugh. Seven Sermons Before Edward VI Fifteen Forty-Nine. Arber, Edward, ed. Date not set. pap. 17.50. Saifer.

Latimer, Jonathan. Headed for a Hearse. 1980. lib. bdg. 12.95 (ISBN 0-8398-2652-4, Gregg). G K Hall.

Latimer, Margery. The Guardian Angel & Other Stories. 224p. 1983. 16.95 (ISBN 0-935312-12-9); pap. 7.95 (ISBN 0-935312-13-7). Feminist Pr.

Latimer, Paul R. A Behavioral Medicine Approach: Functional Gastrointestinal Disorders. 176p. 1983. text ed. 23.95 (ISBN 0-8261-4310-5). Springer Pub.

Latimer, Wedall M. & Powell, R. E. Laboratory Course in General Chemistry. 1964. pap. text ed. 8.95x (ISBN 0-02-367960-3). Macmillan.

Latin American Collection, Yale University. The Allende Years: A List of Chilean Imprints in Selected U.S. Libraries, 1970-1973. 1977. lib. bdg. 24.00 (ISBN 0-8161-7972-7, Hall Reference). G K Hall.

Latin School of Physics, 14th Caracas, Venezuela July 10-28, 1972. Selected Topics in Physics: Astrophysic & Biophysics, Proceedings. Abecassis De Laredo, E. & Jurisic, N. K., eds. LC 73-83563. 420p. 1973. lib. bdg. 71.00 (ISBN 90-277-0367-1, Pub. by Reidel Holland). Kluwer Boston.

Latin, V. Ultrasonics in Medicine: Abstracts. (International Congress Ser.: Vol. 547). 1981. 24.00 (ISBN 0-444-90200-7). Elsevier.

Latman, Alan. The Copyright Law: Howell's Copyright Law Revised & the 1976 Act. 5th & rev. ed. LC 78-606114. 578p. 1979. 32.50 (ISBN 0-87179-276-1). BNA.

Latman, Alan & Gorman, Robert A. Copyright for the Eighties. (Contemporary Legal Education Ser.). 622p. 1981. text ed. 26.50 (ISBN 0-87215-403-3). Michie-Bobbs.

Latman, Alan & Lightstone, James F., eds. Kaminstein Legislative History Project: A Compendium & Analytical Index of Materials Leading to the Copyright Act of 1976, Vol. II; Sections 109-114. LC 81-5953. xxxviii, 490p. 1982. text ed. 95.00x (ISBN 0-8377-0732-3). Rothman.

Latner, A. L. & Schwartz, M. K., eds. Advances in Clinical Chemistry, Vol. 22. (Serial Publication). 1981. 38.00 (ISBN 0-12-010322-2); lib. ed. 49.50 (ISBN 0-12-010384-2); microfiche 26.50 (ISBN 0-12-010385-0). Acad Pr.

Latner, A. L. see Sobotka, Harry & Stewart, C. P.

Latner, Joel. The Gestalt Therapy Book. LC 73-82442. 224p. 1974. 6.95 o.p. (ISBN 0-517-52762-6). Crown.

Latombe, J. C., ed. Artificial Intelligence & Pattern Recognition in Computer Aided Design: Proceedings of the IFIP Working Conference, Grenoble, France, March 17-19, 1978. 1979. 76.75 (ISBN 0-444-85229-8, North Holland). Elsevier.

Latorre, Dolores L., jt. auth. see Latorre, Felipe A.

Latorre, Felipe A. & Latorre, Dolores L. The Mexican Kickapoo Indians. LC 75-11654. (Texas Pan American Ser). (Illus.). 421p. 1976. 22.50x (ISBN 0-292-75023-4). U of Tex Pr.

Latorre, G., jt. auth. see Ewer, J. R.

Latorre, Guillermo, jt. auth. see Garfinkel, Alan.

Latortue, Regine & Adams, Gleason R., trs. Les Cenelles: A Collection of Poems by Creole Writers of the Early Nineteenth Century. 1979. lib. bdg. 22.00 (ISBN 0-8161-8325-2, Hall Reference). G K Hall.

Latouche, G., jt. ed. see Louchard, G.

LaTouche, Robert. The Birth of Western Economy: Economic Aspects of the Dark Ages. Wilkinson, E. M., tr. 368p. 1981. 44.00x (ISBN 0-416-32090-2). Methuen Inc.

LaTouche, Rose. John Ruskin & Rose la Touche: New Unpublished Diaries of 1861 & 1867. Burd, Van Akin, ed. (Illus.). 212p. 1979. text ed. 22.50x (ISBN 0-19-812633-6). Oxford U Pr.

Latourelle, Rene & O'Collins, Gerald. Problems & Perspectives of Fundamental Theology. 416p. 1982. pap. 12.95 (ISBN 0-8091-2466-1). Paulist Pr.

Latourette, Jane & Mathews. Daniel in the Lions' Den. (Arch Bks: Set 3). 1966. laminated bdg. 0.89 (ISBN 0-570-06018-4, 59-1127). Concordia.

--House on the Rock. (Arch Bks: Set 3). 1966. laminated bdg. 0.89 (ISBN 0-570-06019-2, 59-1128). Concordia.

--Story of Noah's Ark. LC 63-23144. (Arch Bks: Set 2). 1965. laminated bdg. 0.89 (ISBN 0-570-06009-5, 59-1110). Concordia.

Latourette, Jane & Wind, Betty. Jon & the Little Lost Lamb. LC 65-15145. (Arch Bks: Set 2). 1965. pap. 0.89 (ISBN 0-570-06008-7, 59-1106). Concordia.

Latourette, Kenneth S. Christianity in a Revolutionary Age: A History of Christianity in the Nineteenth & Twentieth Centuries, 5 vols. Incl. Vol. 1, the 19th Century in Europe - Background & the Roman Catholic Phase (ISBN 0-310-27301-3); Vol. 2, the 19th Century in Europe - the Protestant & Eastern Churches (ISBN 0-310-27311-0); Vol. 3, the 19th Century Outside Europe - the Americas, the Pacific, Asia & Africa. o.p. (ISBN 0-310-27321-8); Vol. 4, the 20th Century in Europe - the Roman Catholic, Protestant & Eastern Churches. o.p. (ISBN 0-310-27331-5); Vol. 5, Twentieth Century Outside Europe (ISBN 0-310-27341-2). kivar 5.95 ea. o.p.; Set. slipcased kivar 28.75 o.p. (ISBN 0-310-27358-7). Zondervan.

--Historia del Cristianismo, Toma II. Quarles, Jaime C. & Quarles, Lemuel C., trs. (Desde el Siglo XVI Hasta el Siglo XX). Orig. Title: A History of the Expansion of Christianity. 968p. 1980. pap. 13.75 (ISBN 0-311-15012-8). Casa Bautista.

--Historia del Cristianismo, Tomo I. Quarles, Jaime C. & Quarles, Lemuel C., trs. from Eng. (Illus.). 819p. 1959. pap. 13.75 (ISBN 0-311-15010-1). Casa Bautista.

--A History of the Expansion of Christianity, 7 vols. Incl. Vol. 1, the First Five Centuries (to 500 A.D. (ISBN 0-310-27361-7); Vol. 2, the Thousand Years of Uncertainty (500 A.D. to 1500 A.D. (ISBN 0-310-27371-4); Vol. 3, Three Centuries of Advance (1500 A.D. to 1800 A.D. (ISBN 0-310-27381-1); Vol. 4, the Great Century - Europe & the United States (1800 A.D. to 1914 A.D. (ISBN 0-310-27391-9); Vol. 5, the Great Century - the Americas, Australia, & Africa (1800 A.D. to 1914 A.D. (ISBN 0-310-27401-X); Vol. 6, the Great Century - North Africa & Asia (1800 A.D. to 1914 A.D. (ISBN 0-310-27411-7); Vol. 7, Advance Through Storm (A.D. 1914 & After with Concluding Generalizations (ISBN 0-310-27421-4). kivar 8.95 ea. o.p.; Set. slipcased kivar 59.95 o.p. (ISBN 0-310-27438-9). Zondervan.

La Tourette, Jacqueline. Shadows in Umbria. LC 78-23798. 1979. 9.95 o.p. (ISBN 0-399-12182-X). Putnam Pub Group.

Latsis, Spiro J., ed. Method & Appraisal in Economics. LC 75-44581. 230p. 1981. pap. 14.95 (ISBN 0-521-28050-8). Cambridge U Pr.

--Method & Appraisal in Economics. LC 75-44581. 220p. 1976. 44.50 (ISBN 0-521-21076-3). Cambridge U Pr.

Latta, Geoffrey W. Profit Sharing, Employee Stock Ownership, Savings, & Asset Formation Plans in the Western World. LC 79-5162. (Multinational Industrial Relations Ser.: No. 5). 192p. 1979. pap. 15.00 (ISBN 0-89546-015-7). Indus Res Unit-Wharton.

Latta, Gordon, jt. auth. see Polya, George.

Latta, John. Rubbing Torsos. LC 79-465. 93p. 1979. 4.50 (ISBN 0-87886-101-7). Ithaca Hse.

Lattimer, John K., et al. Urology & Psychosocial Aspects of Chronic, Critical & Terminal Illness. 256p. 1983. 19.75x (ISBN 0-398-04729-4). C C Thomas.

Lattimore, Dan, jt. auth. see Shook, Frederick.

Lattimore, Eleanor F. Adam's Key. LC 76-13013. (Illus.). (gr. 2-5). 1976. PLB 8.59 (ISBN 0-688-32089-9). Morrow.

--Bird Song. LC 68-19034. (Illus.). (gr. 2-5). 1968. 8.50 (ISBN 0-688-21097-X); PLB 6.48 o.s.i. (ISBN 0-688-31097-4). Morrow.

--The Bus Trip. (Illus.). (gr. 2-5). 1965. 8.95 (ISBN 0-688-21133-X). Morrow.

--Little Pear. LC 31-22069. (Illus.). (gr. k-3). 1968. pap. 2.95 (ISBN 0-15-652799-5, VoyB). HarBraceJ.

--Proudfoot's Way. LC 77-20057. (Illus.). (gr. 2-5). 1978. 9.75 (ISBN 0-688-22145-9); PLB 9.36 (ISBN 0-688-32145-3). Morrow.

--The Three Firecrackers. (Illus.). (gr. 2-5). 1970. 8.50 (ISBN 0-688-21691-9). Morrow.

Lattimore, Owen. Gold Tribe Fishskin Tatars of the Lower Sungari. LC 34-3704. 1933. pap. 12.00 (ISBN 0-527-00539-8). Kraus Repr.

Lattimore, Richard, ed. see Euripides.

Lattimore, Richmond, ed. see Sophocles.

Lattimore, Richmond, tr. from Greek. Acts & Letters of the Apostles. 1982. 16.50 (ISBN 0-374-10082-9). FS&G.

--The Four Gospels & Revelation. 320p. 1979. 14.95 (ISBN 0-374-15801-0). FS&G.

Lattimore, Richmond, tr. The Iliad of Homer. 63p. pap. 4.95 (ISBN 0-226-46940-9). U of Chicago Pr.

Lattimore, Richmond, tr. & intro. by see Aeschylus.

Lattimore, Richmond, tr. see Euripides.

Lattimore, Steven. The Marine Thiasos in Greek Sculpture. LC 76-18609. (Monumenta Archaeologica: 3). (Illus.). 81p. 1977. 12.50 (ISBN 0-917956-02-8). UCLA Arch.

Lattman, Eaton, jt. ed. see Love, Warner.

Lattman, Laurence H., jt. auth. see Zillman, Donald N.

Latzko, D. G., ed. Post-Yield Fracture Mechanics. (Illus.). 1979. 78.00 (ISBN 0-85334-775-1, Pub. by Applied Sci England). Elsevier.

Lau, Alan C., jt. ed. see Tsutakawa, Mayumi.

Lau, Barbara, jt. auth. see Edwards, Ted L., Jr.

Lau, Charlie. Art of Hitting Three Hundred. 1980. 15.95 (ISBN 0-8015-0364-7, Hawthorn); pap. 9.25 (ISBN 0-8015-0365-5, 0898-270, Hawthorn). Dutton.

Lau, D. C., tr. see Confucius.

Lau, Edwin J. Performance Improvement of Virtual Memory Systems. Stone, Harold, ed. LC 82-13393. (Computer Science: Systems Programming Ser.: No. 17). 228p. 1982. 44.95 (ISBN 0-8357-1366-0, Pub. by UMI Res Pr). Univ Microfilms.

Lau, L. Wang. Elements of Nuclear Reactor Engineering. new ed. LC 77-156083. 256p. 1974. 60.00x (ISBN 0-677-02270-0). Gordon.

Lau, Lillian, ed. see American Micro Systems.

Lau, Theodora. The Handbook of Chinese Horoscopes. LC 77-11814. (Illus.). 1980. pap. 6.68i (ISBN 0-06-090752-5, CN 752, CN). Har-Row.

Laub, Donald R., ed. see Vistnes, Lars M., et al.

Laub, Richard J. & Pecsok, Robert L. Physiochemical Applications of Gas Chromatography. LC 78-5493. 300p. 1978. 41.50 o.p. (ISBN 0-471-51838-7, Pub. by Wiley-Interscience). Wiley.

Laubach, Frank, jt. auth. see Brother Lawerance.

Laubenfels, Jean M. The Gifted Student: An Annotated Bibliography. (Contemporary Problems of Childhood: No. 1). 1977. lib. bdg. 25.00 (ISBN 0-8371-9760-0, LGC/). Greenwood.

Lauber. The Politics of Economic Policy. 128p. 1983. write for info. Praeger.

Lauber, John. Sir Walter Scott. (English Authors Ser.). 1966. lib. bdg. 12.95 (ISBN 0-8057-1476-6, Twayne). G K Hall.

Lauber, K. Chemie im Laboratorium. 4th ed. (Illus.). viii, 372p. 1983. softcover 42.00 (ISBN 3-8055-3547-3). S Karger.

Lauber, Patricia. Clarence & the Burglar. (Break-of-Day Bk.). (Illus.). 48p. (gr. 1-3). 1973. PLB 4.99 o.p. (ISBN 0-698-30489-6, Coward). Putnam Pub Group.

--Clarence & the Cat. LC 77-1276. (Break-of-Day Ser.). (Illus.). (gr. k-4). 1977. PLB 6.99 o.p. (ISBN 0-698-30667-8, Coward). Putnam Pub Group.

--The Congo: River into Central Africa. LC 64-10111. (Rivers of the World Ser.). (Illus.). (gr. 4-7). 1964. PLB 3.98 (ISBN 0-8116-6358-2). Garrard.

--Earthworms: Underground Farmers. LC 75-25820. (Good Earth Ser.). (Illus.). 64p. (gr. 2-6). 1976. PLB 6.57 o.p. (ISBN 0-8116-6104-0). Garrard.

--Great Whales. LC 74-28231. (Good Earth Ser). (Illus.). 64p. (gr. 2-6). 1975. PLB 7.22 (ISBN 0-8116-6103-2). Garrard.

--Home at Last: A Young Cat's Tale. (Illus.). 48p. (gr. 3-5). 1980. 6.95 (ISBN 0-698-20507-3, Coward). Putnam Pub Group.

--Icebergs & Glaciers. LC 61-9738. (Junior Science Ser.). (gr. 2-5). 1961. PLB 6.69 (ISBN 0-8116-6158-X). Garrard.

--Look-It-Up Book of Stars and Planets. (Look-It-up Bks.). (Illus.). (gr. 1-6). 1967. 4.95 o.p. (ISBN 0-394-81683-8, BYR); PLB 5.99 (ISBN 0-394-91683-2). Random.

--Mystery Monsters of Loch Ness. LC 77-13913. (Good Earth Ser.). (Illus.). (gr. 2-6). 1978. PLB 7.22 (ISBN 0-8116-6109-1). Garrard.

--Sea Otters & Seaweed. LC 76-17796. (Good Earth Bks). (Illus.). 64p. (gr. 2-6). 1976. lib. bdg. 7.22 (ISBN 0-8116-6106-7). Garrard.

--Tapping Earth's Heat. LC 78-6283. (Good Earth Ser.). (Illus.). (gr. 2-6). 1978. PLB 7.22 (ISBN 0-8116-6110-5). Garrard.

--Too Much Garbage. LC 74-8455. (Good Earth Bks). (Illus.). 64p. (gr. 2-6). 1974. PLB 7.22 (ISBN 0-8116-6102-4). Garrard.

--Who Needs Alligators? LC 73-22102. (Good Earth Bks). (Illus.). 64p. (gr. 2-6). 1974. PLB 7.22 (ISBN 0-8116-6100-8). Garrard.

--Your Body & How It Works. (Gateway Ser.: No. 25). (Illus.). (gr. 3-5). 1962. 2.95 (ISBN 0-394-80125-3, BYR); PLB 5.99 (ISBN 0-394-90125-8). Random.

Laubich, Arnold & Spencer, Ray. Art Tatum: A Guide to His Recorded Music. LC 82-10752. (Studies in Jazz: No. 2). 359p. 1982. 17.50 (ISBN 0-8108-1582-6). Scarecrow.

Laubin, Gladys, jt. auth. see Laubin, Reginald.

Laubin, Reginald & Laubin, Gladys. American Indian Archery. LC 78-58108. (Civil. of the American Indian Ser.: Vol. 154). (Illus.). 1980. 16.50 (ISBN 0-8061-1467-3). U of Okla Pr.

Laubscher, B. J. Where Mystery Dwells: A Psychiatrist Studies Psychical Phenomena. 272p. 1972. 10.95 (ISBN 0-227-67801-X). Attic Pr.

Laubscher, G. G. Syntactical Causes of Case Reduction in Old French. (Elliott Monographs: Vol. 7). 1921. pap. 15.00 (ISBN 0-527-02611-5). Kraus Repr.

Laudan, Larry. Progress & Its Problems: Towards a Theory of Scientific Growth. LC 76-24586. 1977. 21.00x (ISBN 0-520-03330-2); pap. 6.95x (ISBN 0-520-03721-9). U of Cal Pr.

Laude, Theresita & Russo, Raymond M. Dermatologic Disorders in Dark-Skinned Children & Adolescents. 1983. text ed. price not set (ISBN 0-87488-409-8). Med Exam.

Lauder, Phyllis. The Siamese Cat. 1978. 19.95 o.p. (ISBN 0-7134-1733-1, Pub. by Batsford England). David & Charles.

Lauder, Robert E. Loneliness Is for Loving. LC 77-94033. (Illus.). 144p. 1978. pap. 2.95 (ISBN 0-87793-147-X). Ave Maria.

--The Love Explosion: Human Experience & the Christian Mystery. (Orig.). 1979. pap. 2.95 (ISBN 0-914544-22-5). Living Flame Pr.

Lauderdale, Beverly & Shelgren, Margaret. Ten Women & God. LC 78-75316. (Illus.). write for info. (ISBN 0-498-02329-X). A S Barnes.

Lauderdale, William B. Progressive Education: Lessons from Three Schools. LC 81-82472. (Fastback Ser.: No. 166). 50p. 1981. pap. 0.75 (ISBN 0-87367-166-X). Phi Delta Kappa.

Laudin, Harvey. Victims of Culture. LC 73-75408. 1973. pap. text ed. 7.95 (ISBN 0-675-08938-7). Merrill.

Laudon, Kenneth C. Communications Technology & Democratic Participation. LC 77-7471. (Special Studies). 1977. 22.95 o.p. (ISBN 0-03-021836-5). Praeger.

Laue, Max Von see Von Laue, Max.

Lauer, Gary. Principles & Practices of the College-Based Radiography Program. Gardner, Alvin F., ed. (Allied Health Professions Monograph). 1983. write for info. (ISBN 0-87527-310-6). Green.

Lauer, Hans E. Aggression & Repression in the Individual & Society. Castelliz, K. & Davies, Saunders, trs. from Ger. 111p. 1981. pap. 7.95 (ISBN 0-85440-359-0, Pub. by Steinerbooks). Anthroposophic.

Lauer, Quentin. Hegel's Concept of God. 432p. 1982. 33.50x (ISBN 0-87395-597-8); pap. 10.95x (ISBN 0-686-79524-5). State U NY Pr.

--Hegel's Idea of Philosophy. rev. ed. LC 74-152244. 1974. pap. 6.00 (ISBN 0-8232-0926-1). Fordham.

Lauer, R. M. & Shekelle, R. B., eds. Childhood Prevention of Atherosclerosis. 502p. 1979. 53.50 (ISBN 0-89004-381-7). Raven.

Lauer, Robert H. & Handel, Warren H. Social Psychology: The Theory & Application of Symbolic Interactionism. LC 76-10895. 512p. 1977. text ed. 20.95 o.p. (ISBN 0-395-24333-5); instr's. manual 1.35 o.p. (ISBN 0-395-24334-3). HM.

--Social Psychology: The Theory & Application of Symbolic Interactionism, 2nd ed. 400p. 1983. 21.95 (ISBN 0-13-817841-0). P-H.

Lauerhass, Ludwig, Jr. & Haugse, Vera L. Education in Latin America: A Bibliography. lib. bdg. 55.00 (ISBN 0-8161-8516-6, Hall Reference). G K Hall.

Lauersen, Neils H. & Hochberg, Howard. Clinical Perinatal Biochemical Monitoring. 320p. 1981. 36.00 (ISBN 0-683-04901-1, 4901-1). Williams & Wilkins.

Lauersen, Niels & Stukane, Eileen. Listen to Your Body: A Gynecologist Answers Women's Most Intimate Questions. LC 82-16989. 513p. (Orig.). 1981. pap. 9.95 (ISBN 0-671-43648-1, Fireside). S&S.

Lauersen, Niels & Whitney, Steven. It's Your Body: A Woman's Guide to Gynecology. (Illus.). 576p. Date not set. pap. price not set (ISBN 0-448-16525-2, G&D). Putnam Pub Group.

Lauf, Detlef I. Secret Doctrines of the Tibetan Books of the Dead. Parkes, Graham, tr. from Ger. LC 76-53363. (Illus.). 1977. pap. 5.95 o.p. (ISBN 0-394-73351-7). Shambhala Pubns.

Laufer, B. Notes on Turquois in the East. Bd. with Chinese Clay Figures. 1914. 1913. pap. 45.00 (ISBN 0-527-01873-2). Kraus Repr.

Laufer, Berthold. Chinese Baskets. LC 28-1443. (Illus.). 1925. 50.00x (ISBN 0-686-25961-0). J G Stanoff.

--Historical Jottings on Amber in Asia. LC 8-11467. 1906. pap. 8.00 (ISBN 0-527-00502-9). Kraus Repr.

--Reindeer & Its Domestication. LC 18-12075. 1917. pap. 8.00 (ISBN 0-527-00517-7). Kraus Repr.

Laufer, Miguel, jt. ed. see Drujan, Boris D.

Laufer, Robert, jt. ed. see Altbach, Philip G.

Laufer, William S. & Day, James M, eds. Personality Theory, Moral Development, & Criminal Behavior. LC 82-47684. 1983. write for info. (ISBN 0-669-05556-5). Lexington Bks.

Lauffer, A., jt. auth. see Ecklein, J. L.

Lauffer, Armand. Assessment Tools: For Practitioners, Managers & Trainers. (Sage Human Services Guides: Vol. 30). 172p. 1982. pap. 8.50 (ISBN 0-8039-1007-X). Sage.

--Getting the Resources You Need. (Sage Human Services Guides Ser.: Vol. 26). (Illus.). 160p. 1982. pap. 8.00 (ISBN 0-8039-0788-5). Sage.

--Practice of Continuing Education in the Human Services. (Illus.). 1977. text ed. 17.95 (ISBN 0-07-036625-X, C). McGraw.

--Social Planning at the Community Level. (P-H Ser. in Social Work Practice). (Illus.). 1978. 22.95 (ISBN 0-13-817189-0). P-H.

Lauffer, Armand & Sturdevant, Celeste. Doing Continuing Education & Staff Development. (Illus.). 1978. pap. text ed. 17.95 (ISBN 0-07-036624-1, C). McGraw.

Lauffer, Barbara, jt. auth. see Yasko, Joyce.

Lauffer, M. A., ed. Advances in Virus Research, Vol. 27. (Serial Publication Ser.). 334p. 1982. 45.00 (ISBN 0-12-039827-3). Acad Pr.

Laufman, Alan K. The Law of Medical Malpractice in Texas: A Primer for the Medical Community. LC 77-420. (Illus.). 136p. 1977. 10.00x (ISBN 0-292-74620-2). U of Tex Pr.

Laufman, Dudley. Okay, Let's Try a Contra: Men on the Right, Ladies on the Left, Up & Down the Hall, or Blow Away the Morning Dew & Other Country Dances. (Illus.). 1973. pap. 3.00 (ISBN 0-917024-02-8). Country Dance & Song.

Lauger, E. Eurocron Eighty-Two Reliability in Electrical & Electronic Components & Systems. 1982. 106.50 (ISBN 0-444-86419-9). Elsevier.

Laughlin. Roe's Laboratory Guide in Chemistry. 7th ed. (Illus.). 238p. 1976. pap. text ed. 9.00 o.p. (ISBN 0-8016-1473-2). Mosby.

Laughlin, Alice. Roe's Principles of Chemistry. 12th ed. LC 75-37565. (Illus.). 400p. 1976. text ed. 16.95 o.p. (ISBN 0-8016-1470-8). Mosby.

Laughlin, Clarence J. Ghosts Along The Mississippi: The Magic of Old Houses of Louisiana. 1981. 12.98 (ISBN 0-517-00608-1). Crown.

Laughlin, H. P. The Neuroses. 1088p. 1967. 35.95 o.p. (ISBN 0-407-99992-2). Butterworth.

Laughlin, J. & Glassgold, Peter, eds. New Directions Forty-Six. LC 37-1751. 192p. 1983. 17.25 (ISBN 0-8112-0865-6); pap. 8.75 (ISBN 0-8112-0866-4, NDP553). New Directions.

--New Directions In Prose & Poetry, No. 45. LC 37-1751. (New Directions In Prose Poetry Ser.). 192p. 1982. 16.95 (ISBN 0-8112-0844-3); pap. 6.95 (ISBN 0-8112-0845-1, NDP541). New Directions.

Laughlin, J., et al, eds. New Directions 40. LC 37-1751. (New Directions in Prose & Poetry Ser.). 1980. 15.95 (ISBN 0-8112-0762-5); pap. 5.95 (ISBN 0-8112-0763-3, NDP500). New Directions.

Laughlin, James, ed. New Directions in Prose & Poetry, No. 41. 15.95 (ISBN 0-8112-0770-6); pap. 5.95 (ISBN 0-8112-0771-4). New Directions.

Laughlin, Mildred. Reading for Young People: The Great Plains. LC 78-27242. 1979. pap. 11.00 (ISBN 0-8389-0265-0). ALA.

Laugier, Odile, jt. auth. see McQuown, Judith H.

Laumann, E. O. & Pappi, F. U. Networks of Collective Action: A Perspective on Community Influence Systems. 1976. 36.50 (ISBN 0-12-437850-1). Acad Pr.

Laumann, Edward O. & Heinz, John P. Chicago Lawyers: The Professions of the Bar. 1983. 27.50 (ISBN 0-87154-378-8). Basic.

Laumann, Edward O., jt. auth. see Heinz, John P.

Laumer, Helmut & Ziegler, Maria, eds. International Research on Business Cycle Surveys: Papers Presented at the 15th Conference Proceedings, Athens, 1981. 499p. 1982. text ed. 63.00x (ISBN 0-566-00439-9). Gower Pub Ltd.

Laumer, Keith. Dinosaur Beach. (Science Fiction Ser). pap. 1.75 o.p. (ISBN 0-87997-332-3, UW1332). DAW Bks.

--Retief & the Warlords. 1978. pap. 1.95 o.p. (ISBN 0-671-81864-3, Timescape). PB.

--Retief & the Warlords. 176p. 1982. pap. 2.50 (ISBN 0-671-46321-7, Timescape). PB.

--Retief to the Rescue. 256p. 1983. 14.95 (Timescape). PB.

--Star Colony. 1983. pap. 2.95 (ISBN 0-441-78035-0, Pub. by Ace Science Fiction). Ace Bks.

Launay, Robert. Traders Without Trade: Responses to Change in Two Dyula Communities. LC 82-4500. (Cambridge Studies in Social Anthropology: No. 42). 196p. 1983. 34.50 (ISBN 0-521-24179-0). Cambridge U Pr.

Launchbury. Nature Photography. (Photographer's Library). (Illus.). 1983. pap. 12.95x (ISBN 0-240-51193-X). Focal Pr.

Launder, B. E., ed. Studies in Convection: Theory Measurement & Applications, Vol. 2. 1978. 35.50 (ISBN 0-12-438002-6). Acad Pr.

Launder, John. Office Management for Co-operatives. 103p. (Orig.). 1980. pap. 6.95x (ISBN 0-903031-73-6, Pub. by Intermediate Tech England). Intermediate Tech.

Laundergan, J. Clark & Spicer, Jerry. Are Court Referrals Effective? 2.50 (ISBN 0-89486-079-8, 1933B). Hazelden.

Launer, Deborah J., jt. auth. see Selbst, Paul L.

Launey, Andre. Morrocco. 1976. 19.95 o.p. (ISBN 0-7134-3182-2, Pub. by Batsford England). David & Charles.

Launie, J. J. & Lee, J. Finley. Principles of Property & Liability Underwriting. 2nd ed. LC 77-81988. 562p. 1981. text ed. 18.00 (ISBN 0-89462-002-9). IIA.

Launie, J. J., jt. auth. see Hollingsworth, E. P., Jr.

Launie, J. J., jt. auth. see Webb, Bernard L.

Lauper, Lorraine, jt. auth. see Lambert, Michael.

Laura, Martin. American Wildflowers: Fact & Folklore. 1983. 14.95 (ISBN 0-932298-36-2). Copple Hse.

Laurance, Alice, jt. ed. see Asimov, Isaac.

Laurance, Mike. The Canon Guide. (Illus.). 1979. 11.95 o.p. (ISBN 0-8174-2473-3, Amphoto); pap. 6.95 o.p. (ISBN 0-8174-2148-3). Watson-Guptill.

Laureano, Alban. Autumn's Legacy. LC 82-6455. 77p. 1982. 18.95 (ISBN 0-686-84427-0); pap. 10.95 (ISBN 0-8214-0696-5). Swallow.

Laurel Editions Editors. Six Great Modern Plays. Incl. Three Sisters. Chekhov, Anton; Master Builder. Ibsen, Henrik; Mrs. Warren's Profession. Shaw, George B; Red Roses for Me. O'Casey, Sean; Glass Menagerie. Williams, Tennessee; All My Sons. Miller, Arthur. 1964. pap. 3.95 (ISBN 0-440-37984-9, LE). Dell.

Laurell, C. B. Electrophoretic & Electro-Immuno-Chemical Analysis of Proteins. (Illus.). 1977. 34.50 o.p. (ISBN 0-8391-0990-3). Univ Park.

Lauren, Paul, jt. auth. see Geffner, Saul.

Laurence, jt. auth. see Rocker.

Laurence, D. R. & Bacharach, A. L., eds. Evaluation of Drug Activities: Pharmacometrics, 2 Vols. 1965. Vol. 1. o.s. 68.00 (ISBN 0-12-438301-7); Vol. 2. 68.00 (ISBN 0-12-438302-5). Acad Pr.

Laurence, Dan H. Bernard Shaw: A Bibliography, 2 vols. (Illus.). 1024p. 1982. Set. 98.00 (ISBN 0-19-818179-5). Oxford U Pr.

Laurence, John. The History of Capital Punishment. (Illus.). 230p. 1983. pap. 4.95 (ISBN 0-8065-0840-X). Citadel Pr.

Laurence, Lance T. Couple Constancy: Conversations with Today's Happily Married People. Nathan, Peter, ed. LC 82-13682. (Research in Clinical Psychology Ser.: No. 1). 182p. 1982. 34.95 (ISBN 0-8357-1373-3, Pub. by UMI Res Pr). Univ Microfilms.

Laurence, Margaret. The Diviners. 480p. 1982. pap. 3.95 (ISBN 0-553-22604-5, Windstone). Bantam.

Laurence, Michael, jt. auth. see Foxworth, Thomas.

Laurence Press Staff. Low-Cost Word Processing: Microcomputer Bks.-Executive. 244p. 1982. pap. 10.95 (ISBN 0-201-05735-2). A-W.

Laurence, Theodor. The Parker Lifetime Treasury of Mystic & Occult Powers. (Illus.). 1978. 14.95 o.p. (ISBN 0-13-650754-9, Parker). P-H.

--The Sexual Key to the Tarot. 1973. pap. 2.50 (ISBN 0-451-11962-2, AE1962, Sig). NAL.

Laurence Urdang Associates Under the Editorial Supervision of the Longman Dictionary Department. Longman Dictionary of English Idioms. (Illus.). 404p. 1979. 18.95 (ISBN 0-582-55524-8). Longman.

Laurence, William L. Dawn Over Zero: The Story of the Atomic Bomb. LC 71-153156. (Illus.). 289p. 1972. Repr. of 1946 ed. lib. bdg. 17.50x (ISBN 0-8371-6064-2, LADZ). Greenwood.

Laurenson, Diana T. & Swingewood, Alan. The Sociology of Literature. LC 72-79743. 281p. 1972. 12.00x o.p. (ISBN 0-8052-3457-8). Schocken.

Laurenson, R. M. & Yuceoglu, U., eds. Advances In Aerospace Structures & Materials, 1982. (AD-03). 1982. 30.00 (H00240). ASME.

Laurent, G. Dizionario Italiano-Francese, Francese-Italiano. 413p. (Fr. & Ital.). 1979. leatherette 5.95 (ISBN 0-686-97341-0, M-9173). French & Eur.

Laurent, Laurence L., jt. auth. see Gotshall, Daniel W.

Laurent, Pierre-Henri & Ginsberg, Ralph B., eds. The European Community After Twenty Years. LC 78-62596. (Annals: No. 440). 1978. 7.50 o.p. (ISBN 0-87761-232-3); pap. 7.95 (ISBN 0-87761-233-1). Am Acad Pol Soc Sci.

Laurent'ev, M., et al, eds. Problems of Hydrodynamics & Continuum Mechanics. (Illus.). xi, 815p. 1969. text ed. 49.50 (ISBN 0-89871-039-1). Soc Indus-Appl Math.

Laurenti, Joseph see Siracusa, Joseph.

Laurenti, Joseph L. & Poqueras-Mayo, A. The Spanish Golden Age (1472-1700) A Catalog of Rare Books Held in the Library of the University of Illinois & in Selected North American Libraries. 1979. lib. bdg. 55.00 (ISBN 0-8161-8286-8, Hall Reference). G K Hall.

Laurenti, Luigi. Property Values & Race: Studies in Seven Cities. LC 76-5437. (Illus.). 256p. 1976. Repr. of 1961 ed. lib. bdg. 18.25x (ISBN 0-8371-8795-8, LAPV). Greenwood.

Laurentian Hormone Conferences. Recent Progress in Hormone Research: Proceedings. Pincus, Gregory, ed. Incl. Vols. 1-5. 1947-50. Set. Vol. 1. 54.50 (ISBN 0-12-571101-8); Vol. 2. 54.50 (ISBN 0-12-571102-6); Vol. 3. 55.50 (ISBN 0-12-571103-4); Vol. 4. 55.50 (ISBN 0-12-571104-2); Vol. 5. 59.50 (ISBN 0-12-571105-0); Vols. 6-11. 1951-55. Vol. 6. 55.50 (ISBN 0-12-571106-9); Vol. 7. 59.50 (ISBN 0-12-571107-7); Vol. 8. 59.50 (ISBN 0-12-571108-5); Vol. 9. 55.50 (ISBN 0-12-571109-3); Vol. 10. 59.50 (ISBN 0-12-571110-7). Vol. 11 (ISBN 0-12-571111-5); Vol. 12. 1956. 55.50 (ISBN 0-12-571112-3); Vol. 13. 1957. 59.50 (ISBN 0-12-571113-1); Vols. 14-15. 1958-59. 59.50 ea. Vol. 14 (ISBN 0-12-571114-X). Vol. 15 (ISBN 0-12-571115-8); Vol. 16. 1960. 64.00 (ISBN 0-12-571116-6); Vols. 17-18. 1961-62. 59.50 ea. Vol. 17 (ISBN 0-12-571117-4). Vol. 18 (ISBN 0-12-571118-2); Vol. 19. 1963. 68.50 (ISBN 0-12-571119-0); Vol. 20. 1964. 68.50 (ISBN 0-12-571120-4); Vol. 21. 1965. 68.50 (ISBN 0-12-571121-2); Vol. 22. 1966. 68.50 (ISBN 0-12-**571122-0); Vol. 23. 1967. 77.50 (ISBN 0-12-571123-9); Vol. 24. Astwood, E. B., ed. 1968. 77.50 (ISBN 0-12-571124-7); Vol. 25. 1969. 77.50 (ISBN 0-12-571125-5); Vols. 26-27. 1970-71. 77.50 ea. Vol. 26 (ISBN 0-12-571126-3). Vol. 27 (ISBN 0-12-571127-1); Vol. 28. 1972. 77.50 (ISBN 0-12-571128-X); Vol. 29. 1973. 77.50 (ISBN 0-12-571129-8); Vol. 32. Greep, Roy O., ed. 1976. 77.50 (ISBN 0-12-571132-8); Vol. 33. Greep, Roy O., ed. 1977. 67.50 (ISBN 0-12-571133-6); Vol. 34. Greep, Roy O., ed. 1978. 66.00 (ISBN 0-12-571134-4). Acad Pr.**

Lauria, Marie. How to Be a Good Secretary. pap. 3.50 o.p. (ISBN 0-06-463334-9, EH 334, EH). B&N NY.

Laurie, Alex, et al. Commercial Flower Forcing. 7th ed. 1968. text ed. 19.00 o.p. (ISBN 0-07-036632-2, C). McGraw.

--Commercial Flower Forcing. 8th ed. (Illus.). 1979. text ed. 32.50x (ISBN 0-07-036633-0, C). McGraw.

Laurie, Arthur P. Painter's Methods & Materials. (Illus.). 1967. pap. 5.00 (ISBN 0-486-21868-6). Dover.

Laurie, Bruce. Working People of Philadelphia, Eighteen Hundred to Eighteen Fifty. 264p. 1980. pap. 29.95 (ISBN 0-87722-168-5). Temple U Pr.

Laurie, Bruce, jt. ed. see Cantor, Milton.

Laurie, Greg. God's Design for Christian Dating. 2nd ed. LC 82-83836. 96p. (YA) (gr. 10-12). 1983. pap. 1.95 (ISBN 0-89081-373-6). Harvest Hse.

--Occupy Till I Come. LC 82-81919. 176p. (Orig.). 1982. pap. 3.95 (ISBN 0-686-97204-X). Harvest Hse.

Laurie, Ian C., ed. Nature in Cities: The Natural Environment in the Design & Development of Urban Green Space. LC 77-20987. 428p. 1979. 71.95 (ISBN 0-471-99605-X, Pub. by Wiley-Interscience). Wiley.

Laurie, R. Developments in Meat Science, Vols. 1 & 2. 1980-81. Vol. 1. 43.00 (ISBN 0-85334-866-9, Pub. by Applied Sci England); Vol. 2. 65.75 (ISBN 0-85334-986-X). Elsevier.

Laurikietis, Rae, jt. auth. see Adams, Carol.

Laurila, Simo H. Electronic Surveying & Navigation. LC 75-41461. 545p. 1976. 49.95 (ISBN 0-471-51865-4, Pub. by Wiley-Interscience). Wiley.

--Electronic Surveying in Practice. 325p. 1983. 29.95 (ISBN 0-471-09021-2, Pub. by Wiley-Interscience). Wiley.

Laurin, Anne. Perfect Crane. LC 80-7912. (Illus.). 32p. (gr. 1-4). 1981. 8.95 (ISBN 0-06-023743-0, HarpJ); PLB 8.79g (ISBN 0-06-023744-9). Har-Row.

Laurina, Vera & Pushkariov, Vasily, eds. Novgorod Icons 12th-17th Century. Cook, Kathleen, et al, trs. (Illus.). 348p. 1981. 45.00 (ISBN 0-89893-077-4). CDP.

Laurins, Alex, jt. auth. see Schneider, Jerome.

Laurita, Raymond E. Reading, Writing & Creativity. LC 72-75225. (Orig.). 1973. pap. 7.50x o.p. (ISBN 0-87562-038-8). Spec Child.

Lauritzen, Ornulf & Norsk Polarinstitiutt. Investigations of Carboniferous & Permian Sediments in Svalbard. (Norsk Polarinstitutt Skrifter Ser.: No. 176). 44p. (Orig.). 1982. pap. 8.00 (ISBN 82-00-29196-0). Universitet.

Lauritzen, Tryntje. Painted Rock Creatures. LC 76-13069. (Early Craft Books). (gr. k-3). 1977. PLB 3.95g (ISBN 0-8225-0878-8). Lerner Pubns.

Laurmann, John A. see Von Mises, Richard & Von Karman, Theodore.

Laursen, Finn. Toward a New International Marine Order. 1982. lib. bdg. 39.00 (ISBN 90-247-2597-6, Pub. by Martinus Nijhoff Netherlands). Kluwer Boston.

Laursen, Harold I. Structural Analysis. 2nd ed. (Illus.). 1977. text ed. 34.50x (ISBN 0-07-036643-8, C); solutions manual 19.00 (ISBN 0-07-036644-6). McGraw.

Lausch, Hans & Nobauer, Wilfried. Algebra of Polynomials. LC 72-88283. (Mathematical Library: Vol. 5). 256p. 1974. 32.75 (ISBN 0-444-10441-0, North-Holland). Elsevier.

Laut, A. C. Lords of the North. 442p. 1982. Repr. of 1900 ed. lib. bdg. 45.00 (ISBN 0-89760-514-4). Telegraph Bks.

Laut, Phil, jt. auth. see Leonard, Jim.

Lauter, Leah & Jacks, Elaine B. You & Your Aging Parent. 1978. pap. 4.00 (ISBN 0-88461-005-5). Adelphi Univ.

Lauterbach, C. A., jt. auth. see Schumann, K. M.

Lauterbach, Wolf. Soviet Psychotherapy. 1984. 24.01 (ISBN 0-08-024291-X). Pergamon.

Lauterpacht, Elihu & Collier, John G. Individual Rights & the State in Foreign Affairs: An International Compendium. LC 77-8010. (Praeger Special Studies). 1977. 59.95 o.p. (ISBN 0-275-24350-8). Praeger.

Lauterpacht, Hersch. Function of Law in the International Community. LC 79-147755. (Library of War & Peace; International Law). lib. bdg. 38.00 o.s.i. (ISBN 0-8240-0493-0). Garland Pub.

--International Law & Human Rights. LC 72-147756. (Library of War & Peace; International Law). lib. bdg. 38.00 o.s.i. (ISBN 0-8240-0494-9). Garland Pub.

Lautreamont. Poesies: & Complete Miscellanea. bilingual ed. Lykiard, Alexis, tr. from Fr. 152p. 1980. 9.95 (ISBN 0-8052-8035-9, Pub. by Allison & Busby England); pap. 5.95 (ISBN 0-8052-8034-0, Pub. by Allison & Busby England). Schocken.

Lautt, W. Wayne, ed. Hepatic Circulation in Health & Disease. 392p. 1981. text ed. 43.00 (ISBN 0-89004-617-4). Raven.

Lauwerier, H. A., ed. see Renyi, A.

Lauwerys, Joseph & Tayar, Graham, eds. Education at Home & Abroad. (Students Library of Education). 144p. 1973. 14.95x (ISBN 0-7100-7567-7). Routledge & Kegan.

Lauwerys, Roberts R. Industrial Chemical Exposure: Guidelines for Biological Monitoring. LC 82-70668. (Illus.). 150p. 1983. text ed. 22.50 (ISBN 0-931890-10-1). Biomed Pubns.

Laux. In First Gear. 251p. 1982. 50.00x (ISBN 0-85323-213-X, Pub. by Liverpool Univ England). State Mutual Bk.

Laux, James M., ed. see Kafker, Frank A.

Laux, Patricia. The Modernized Metric System... Explained. LC 75-2632. (8ors). (Illus.). 1976. pap. 0.50 (ISBN 0-934674-34-5). J J Keller.

Laux, Patricia, ed. Metric Yearbook: Metrication in the United States--Progress in Industry, Education & Government During 1980. LC 76-4217. (10gss). 1981. pap. 25.00 (ISBN 0-934674-31-0). J J Keller.

--Private Fleet Management Guide. LC 82-84709. 350p. 1983. loose-leaf 65.00 (ISBN 0-934674-47-7). J J Keller.

Laux, Patricia, et al, eds. see Keller, John J.

La Valle, Maria T., et al, trs. see Grant, Wilson W.

LaValle, Teresa, tr. see Ralph, Margaret.

Lavan, George, ed. see Cannon, James P.

Lavater, J. C. Aphorisms on Man. LC 79-23298. 1980. Repr. of 1788 ed. 35.00x (ISBN 0-8201-1336-0). Schol Facsimiles.

Lavater, John c. The Science of Physiognomy. (The Most Meaningful Classics in World Culture Ser.). (Illus.). 156p. 1983. Repr. of 1810 ed. 115.00 (ISBN 0-89901-100-4). Found Class Reprints.

Lave, Lester B. & Omenn, Gilbert S. Clearing the Air: Reforming the Clean Air Act. LC 81-70469. (Regulation of Economic Activity). 65p. 1981. pap. 5.95 (ISBN 0-8157-5159-1). Brookings.

Lave, Lester B., ed. Quantitative Risk Assessment for Health Regulation. LC 82-22603. (Studies in the Regulation of Economic Activity). 1983. 26.95 (ISBN 0-8157-5164-8); pap. 10.95 (ISBN 0-8157-5163-X). Brookings.

Lavelle, Doris. Latin & American Dances. (gr. 7 up). 1979. text ed. 22.50x (ISBN 0-273-41640-5, LTB). Sportshelf.

LaVelle, Mike. Crazy for Love. (Illus., Orig.). 1983. pap. 4.95 (ISBN 0-440-50926-2, Dell Trade Pbks). Dell.

Lavely, Joe & Ruckman, Paul. Simultaneous Compounding & Discounting Tables & Uses. 736p. 1979. 41.95x (ISBN 0-669-02810-X). Lexington Bks.

Lavenberg, Stephen, ed. Computer Performance Modeling Handbook. (Notes & Reports in Computer Science & Applied Mathematics Ser.: No. 3). 1982. 45.00 (ISBN 0-12-438720-9). Acad Pr.

Lavenda, B. H. Thermodynamics of Irreversible Processes. LC 76-22604. 182p. 1978. 49.95x o.s.i. (ISBN 0-470-98898-3). Halsted Pr.

Lavender, Abraham D., ed. A Coat of Many Colors: Jewish Subcommunities in the United States. LC 77-71865. (Contributions in Family Studies: No. 1). 1977. lib. bdg. 29.95 (ISBN 0-8371-9539-X, LCM/). Greenwood.

Lavender, David. The Overland Migrations. 113p. 1981. pap. 6.00 (ISBN 0-686-95731-8). Jefferson Natl.

--The Southwest. LC 78-69622. (Regions of America Ser.). (Illus.). 1980. 16.30i (ISBN 0-06-012519-5, HarpT). Har-Row.

--Westward Vision: The Story of the Oregon Trail. (American Trails Library Ser.). 1963. 9.95 o.p. (ISBN 0-07-036675-6, GB); pap. 3.50 o.p. (ISBN 0-07-036676-4). McGraw.

Lavender, J. Peter, ed. Clinical & Experimental Applications of Krypton-81m. 1978. 50.00x (ISBN 0-686-99802-2, Pub. by Brit Inst Radiology England). State Mutual Bk.

Lavender, John A. Beat the Blues. 1982. pap. 5.95 (ISBN 0-8423-0128-3). Tyndale.

--Marriage at Its Best. LC 82-71375. 160p. (Orig.). 1982. pap. 4.95 (ISBN 0-89636-091-1). Accent Bks.

Lavender, Lucille. They Cry, Too. 1979. pap. 5.95 (ISBN 0-8423-7070-6). Tyndale.

Laver. The Significance of Computing. 1979. 11.95 (ISBN 0-471-25845-8, Wiley Heyden). Wiley.

Laver, J. The Phonetic Description of Voice Quality. LC 77-82501. (Cambridge Studies in Linguistics: No. 31). (Illus.). 225p. 1980. 38.50 (ISBN 0-521-23176-0). Cambridge U Pr.

Laver, James. A Concise History of Costume. (World of Art Ser.). (Illus.). 1982. pap. 9.95 o.p. (ISBN 0-19-520379-8). Oxford U Pr.

--Costume & Fashion: A Concise History. rev. ed. (World of Art Ser.). (Illus.). 322p. 1983. pap. 9.95 (ISBN 0-19-520390-9, GB). Oxford U Pr.

Laver, John. Voice Quality: A Classified Research Bibliography. (Library & Information Sources in Linguistics Ser.). viii, 225p. 1979. 25.00 (ISBN 90-272-0996-0, 5). Benjamins North Am.

Laver, Murray. Computers & Social Change. (Cambridge Computer Science Texts Ser.: No. 10). 128p. 1980. 21.95 (ISBN 0-521-23027-6); pap. 8.95x (ISBN 0-521-29771-0). Cambridge U Pr.

--An Introduction to the Uses of Computers. LC 75-23535. (Cambridge Computer Science Texts Ser.: No. 5). (Illus.). 187p. 1976. 12.95x (ISBN 0-521-29035-X). Cambridge U Pr.

Laver, Rod. Two Hundred & Twenty-Eight Tennis Tips by Rod Laver. (Illus.). 1977. pap. 3.95 o.s.i. (ISBN 0-695-80716-1). Follett.

Laverdant, Gabriel-Desire. Socialisme Catholique. (Nineteenth Century Russia Ser.). 424p. (Fr.). 1974. Repr. of 1851 ed. lib. bdg. 107.00 o.p. (ISBN 0-8287-0512-7, R29). Clearwater Pub.

LaVerdiere, Eugene. When We Pray: Meditation on the Lord's Prayer. LC 82-73512. 176p. 1983. pap. 4.95 (ISBN 0-87793-263-8). Ave Maria.

Lavergne, Real P., ed. The Political Economy of U. S. Tariffs: An Empirical Analysis. (Economic Theory, Econometrics, Mathematical Economics Ser.). Date not set. price not set (ISBN 0-12-438740-3). Acad Pr.

Lavers, Annette. Roland Barthes: Structuralism & After. LC 81-13447. 320p. 1982. text ed. 25.00x (ISBN 0-674-77721-2). Harvard U Pr.

Lavers, J., jt. auth. see Myers, T. F.

Lavers, Norman. Jerzy Kosinski. (United States Authors Ser.). 1982. lib. bdg. 11.95 (ISBN 0-8057-7352-5, Twayne). G K Hall.

--Mark Harris. (United States Authors Ser.). 1978. lib. bdg. 13.95 (ISBN 0-8057-7209-X, Twayne). G K Hall.

LaVey, Anton S. The Satanic Rituals. 1972. pap. 3.95 (ISBN 0-380-01392-4, 83634-3). Avon.

La Via, Mariano F., jt. ed. see Hill, Rol la B.

Lavier, J. Chinese Micro-Massage: Acupuncture Without Needles. (Illus.). 96p. (Orig.). 1983. pap. 5.95 (ISBN 0-7225-0362-8, Pub. by Thorsons Pubs England). Sterling.

La Villa Hauelin, Jim. What the Diamond Does Is Hold It All In. 1978. 1.50 o.p. (ISBN 0-934834-18-0). White Pine.

Lavin, David E., et al. Right Versus Privilege: The Open Admissions Experiment at the City University of New York. LC 80-69571. (Illus.). 1981. 19.95 (ISBN 0-02-918080-5). Free Pr.

Lavin, Margaret M. Charlie. LC 67-31203. 1967. 4.00 o.p. (ISBN 0-8233-0058-7). Golden Quill.

--Landscape with Figures. 1961. 3.00 o.p. (ISBN 0-8233-0057-9). Golden Quill.

Lavin, Mary. The Becker Wives. pap. 3.50 o.p. (ISBN 0-452-25048-X, Z5048, Plume). NAL.

Lavin, Mary A., jt. auth. see Hamilton, William P.

Lavin, Mary A., jt. ed. see Gebbie, Kristine M.

Lavine, Emanuel H. The Third Degree: A Detailed Account of Police Brutality. LC 74-676. (Civil Liberties in American History Ser.). 248p. 1974. Repr. of 1930 ed. lib. bdg. 32.50 (ISBN 0-306-70601-6). Da Capo.

Lavine, Irvin, jt. auth. see Zimmerman, O. T.

LaVine, Lance. Five Degrees of Conservation: A Graphic Analysis of Energy Alternatives for a Northern Climate. (Illus.). 72p. 1982. 19.50x (ISBN 0-943352-00-2); pap. 10.95 (ISBN 0-943352-01-0). Univ Minn Sch.

Lavine, Robert A. Neurophysiology: The Fundamentals. LC 80-2611. 192p. 1982. 13.95 (ISBN 0-669-04343-5). Heath.

Lavine, Sigmund. Wonders of Rhinos. LC 82-45387. (Wonders Ser.). (Illus.). 80p. (gr. 4 up). 1982. PLB 8.95 (ISBN 0-396-08094-4). Dodd.

Lavine, Sigmund A. & Casey, Brigid. Wonders of Draft Horses. LC 82-46002. (Wonders Ser.). (Illus.). 80p. (gr. 4 up). 1983. PLB 9.95 (ISBN 0-396-08138-X). Dodd.

Lavine, Sigmund A. & Scuro, Vincent. Wonders of Sheep. LC 82-46001. (Wonder Ser.). (Illus.). 80p. (gr. 4 up). 1983. PLB 9.95 (ISBN 0-396-08137-1). Dodd.

La Vine, W. Robert. In a Glamorous Fashion: The Fabulous Years of Hollywood Costume Design. (Illus.). 272p. 1982. pap. 12.95 (ISBN 0-684-17661-0, ScribT). Scribner.

Lavington, S. H., ed. Information Processing Eighty. 1980. 89.50 (ISBN 0-444-86034-7). Elsevier.

Lavipour, Farid G., jt. ed. see Sauvant, Karl P.

Lavitt, jt. auth. see McDowell.

Lavitt, Edward & McDowell, Robert. In the Beginning Creation Stories. new ed. 156p. (gr. 6-12). 1973. 6.95 o.p. (ISBN 0-89388-096-5). Okpaku Communications.

Lavoie, Don C. National Economic Planning: What Is Left? 175p. 1983. pap. 6.95 (ISBN 0-932790-35-6). Cato Inst.

Lavoie, Don C., ed. Solidarnosc z Wolnoscia: Solidarity with Liberty. 253p. 1983. pap. 9.95 (ISBN 0-932790-33-X). Cato Inst.

LaVor, Marty. Ceramics for Any Hands. (Illus.). 104p. 1975. 6.00 (ISBN 0-686-36023-0); pap. o.p. (ISBN 0-686-37268-9). Scott Pubns MI.

Lavosier, Antoine-Laurent. Oeuvres, 1864-1893. 1322.00 o.p. (ISBN 0-8287-0513-5). Clearwater Pub.

Lavrentjev, Alexander. Rodchenko Photograph. LC 82-60031. (Illus.). 140p. 1982. 25.00 (ISBN 0-8478-0459-3). Rizzoli Intl.

Lavrin, Asuncion, ed. Latin American Women: Historical Perspectives. LC 77-94758. (Contributions in Women's Studies: No. 3). 1978. lib. bdg. 29.95x (ISBN 0-313-20309-1, LLA/). Greenwood.

Lavrin, Janko. Lermontov. 1959. pap. text ed. 6.00x (ISBN 0-391-02003-X). Humanities.

Lavrin, Janko, ed. A First Series of Representative Russian Stories, Pushkin to Gorky. LC 74-114539. (Illus.). 239p. 1975. Repr. of 1946 ed. lib. bdg. 15.50x (ISBN 0-8371-4740-9, LARS). Greenwood.

Lavroff, Ellen C. & Wishard, Armin, eds. Mas Cuentos Y Juegos. rev. ed. (Illus.). 1982. pap. text ed. 5.95x (ISBN 0-393-95108-1). Norton.

Lavrov, Peter. Historical Letters. Scanlan, James P., tr. LC 67-18900. 1967. 35.00x (ISBN 0-520-01136-8). U of Cal Pr.

Law, jt. auth. see Ireland.

Law & Economics Center of Emory University. Supreme Court Economic Review, Vol. I. Aranson, Peter H., ed. 1983. 29.95X (ISBN 0-02-918160-7). Macmillan.

Law & Economics Center, University of Miami School of Law. The Attack on Corporate America: The Corporate Issues Sourcebook. (Illus.). 1978. 24.95 (ISBN 0-07-036693-4, P&RB). McGraw.

Law, Averill M. & Kelton, David. Simulation Modeling & Analysis. (Illus.). 416p. 1982. text ed. 25.90x (ISBN 0-07-036696-9); solns. manual 15.00 (ISBN 0-07-036697-7). McGraw.

Law, Carol R. Overture to Love. 384p. (Orig.). 1981. pap. 2.50 o.p. (ISBN 0-523-40615-0). Pinnacle Bks.

Law, David B., et al. Atlas of Pedodontics. LC 69-17820. (Illus.). 1969. 27.50 o.p. (ISBN 0-7216-5655-2). Saunders.

Law, Donald. Starting Mountaineering & Rockclimbing. 1977. 10.50 o.p. (ISBN 0-7153-7322-6). David & Charles.

Law, Elmo A. A Workbook for the Life Sciences. 1980. pap. text ed. 7.95 (ISBN 0-8403-2122-8). Kendall-Hunt.

Law, Emma, jt. auth. see DeBolt, Margaret W.

Law Enforcement. National Crime Surveys: National Sample, 1973-71979. LC 78-71979. 1979. write for info. code bk. o.p. (ISBN 0-89138-991-1). ICPSR.

Law Enforcement Assistance Administration. Public Image of Courts, 1977: General Public Data. LC 79-91248. 1980. write for info. (ISBN 0-89138-962-8). ICPSR.

Law, Henry. Construction of Common Roads Circa 1855. 12.50 (ISBN 0-87556-146-2). Saifer.

Law, J. & Oliver, H. J. Glossary of Histopathological Terms. (Illus.). 128p. 1972. text ed. 13.95 (ISBN 0-407-72730-2). Butterworth.

Law, Kathryn. Tales from the Bitterfoot Valley. (Indian Culture Ser.). (gr. 1-4). 1971. 1.95 o.p. (ISBN 0-89992-014-4). MT Coun Indian.

Law of the Sea Institute, 10th Annual Conference. Law of the Sea: Conference Outcomes & Problems of Implementation: Proceedings. Miles, Edward L. & Gamble, John K., Jr., eds. LC 77-1544. 448p. 1977. prof ref 22.50x (ISBN 0-88410-051-0). Ballinger Pub.

Law of the Sea Institute 11th. Annual Conference. Regionalization in the Law of the Sea: Proceedings. Johnston, Douglas, ed. LC 78-15357. 1978. prof ref 28.00x (ISBN 0-88410-075-8). Ballinger Pub.

Law, Preston. Shipboard Antennas. (Artech Radar Library). (Illus.). 400p. 1982. 50.00 (ISBN 0-89006-123-8). Artech Hse.

Law, R., jt. auth. see Blaikie, W. G.

Law, Robert. Tests of Life. 3rd ed. (Thornapple Commentary Ser.). 1978. pap. 11.95 (ISBN 0-8010-5501-6). Baker Bk.

Law, Robin. The Oyo Empire: A West African Imperialism in the Era of the Atlantic Slave Trade. (Oxford Studies in African Matters). (Illus.). 1977. 49.00x o.p. (ISBN 0-19-822709-4). Oxford U Pr.

Law, Ruth. Dim Sum: Fast & Festive Chinese Cooking. (Illus.). 256p. 1982. pap. 9.95 (ISBN 0-8092-5881-1). Contemp Bks.

Law, Victor J. ANSI FORTRAN 77: An Introduction to Software Design. 400p. 1983. pap. text ed. write for info (ISBN 0-697-08167-2); instr's manual avail. (ISBN 0-697-08175-3); wkbk. avail. (ISBN 0-697-08176-1). Wm C Brown.

Law, Vivien. The Insular Latin Grammarians. (Studies in Celtic History: No. III). 128p. 1983. text ed. 49.50x (ISBN 0-85115-147-7, Pub. by Boydell & Brewer). Biblio Dist.

Law, William. A Serious Call to a Devout & Holy Life. LC 82-80470. (Treasures from the Spiritual Classics Ser.). 64p. 1982. pap. 2.95 (ISBN 0-8192-1306-3). Morehouse.

Lawall, David B. Asher Brown Durand: His Art & Art Theory in Relations to His Times. LC 76-23635. (Outstanding Dissertations in the Fine Arts Ser.). 1978. lib. bdg. 97.00x o.s.i. (ISBN 0-8240-2704-3). Garland Pub.

Lawall, Gilbert, ed. Petronius: Selections from the Satiricon. (Bolchazy-Carducci Textbook). 260p. (Orig.). 1981. pap. text ed. 11.50x (ISBN 0-86516-006-6). Bolchazy-Carducci.

Lawall, Gilbert & Quinn, Betty N., eds. Plautus' Menaechmi. (Bolchazy-Carducci Textbooks). (Illus.). 200p. (Orig.). 1981. pap. 10.50x (ISBN 0-86516-007-4). Bolchazy-Carducci.

Lawani, S. M. & Alluri, F. M. Farming Systems in Africa: A Working Bibliography, 1930-1978. 1979. lib. bdg. 32.00 (ISBN 0-8161-8293-0, Hall Reference). G K Hall.

Lawden, D. F. Analytical Mechanics. (Problem Solvers). (Illus.). 1972. text ed. 9.50x o.p. (ISBN 0-04-531004-1); pap. text ed. 3.95x o.p. (ISBN 0-04-531005-X). Allen Unwin.

--An Introduction to Tensor Calculus, Relativity & Cosmology. 3rd ed. 208p. 1982. pap. 16.95x (ISBN 0-471-10096-X, Pub. by Wiley-Interscience). Wiley.

Lawden, Derek F. Introduction to Tensor Calculus & Relativity. 2nd ed. 1967. pap. 10.95x (ISBN 0-412-20370-7, Pub. by Chapman & Hall). Methuen Inc.

Lawder, et al. A Followup Study of Adoptions: Postplacement Functioning of Adoption Families, Vol. 1. LC 71-89863. 232p. 1970. pap. 6.90 (ISBN 0-87868-016-0, A-32). Child Welfare.

Lawder, Elizabeth A., et al. Five Models of Foster Family Group Homes. LC 74-75756. (Orig.). 1974. pap. 6.60 (ISBN 0-87868-122-1, GH-13). Child Welfare.

Lawes, Lewis E. Man's Judgment of Death: An Analysis of the Operation & Effect of Capital Punishment Based on Facts, Not On Sentiment. LC 69-14938. (Criminology, Law Enforcement, & Social Problems Ser.: No. 62). 1969. Repr. of 1924 ed. 8.00x (ISBN 0-87585-062-6). Patterson Smith.

Lawford, James. Wellington's Peninsular Army. LC 73-83323. (Men-at-Arms Ser.). (Illus.). 40p. 1973. pap. 7.95 o.p. (ISBN 0-88254-170-6). Hippocrene Bks.

Lawhead, Stephen R. In the Hall of the Dragon King. 348p. (gr. 7-12). 1982. pap. 7.95 (ISBN 0-89107-257-8, Crossway Bks). Good News.

--The Warlords of Nin. 396p. 1983. pap. 7.95 (ISBN 0-89107-278-0, Crossway Bks). Good News.

Lawhead, Steve, jt. auth. see Yancey, Philip.

Lawing, Betty S. Solving Mathematical Word Problems. LC 81-68876. (General Mathematics Ser.). (Illus.). 128p. (Orig.). 1983. pap. text ed. 8.80 (ISBN 0-8273-1587-2); pap. text ed. 7.80 combined edition with solutions & tests, 224p. (ISBN 0-8273-1589-9). Delmar.

Lawler, Donald L. Approaches to Science Fiction. LC 77-77995. (Illus.). 1978. pap. text ed. 13.95 (ISBN 0-395-25496-5); instr's. manual 0.75 (ISBN 0-395-25497-3). HM.

Lawler, Donald L., jt. auth. see Klinkowitz, Jerome.

Lawler, E. Pay & Organizational Effectiveness: A Psychological View. (Psychology Ser.). 1971. text ed. 32.50 (ISBN 0-07-036700-0, C). McGraw.

Lawler, Edward, jt. auth. see Seashore, Stanley E.

Lawler, Edward E. & Rhode, John G. Information & Control in Organizations. LC 75-20582. (Goodyear Series in Management & Organizations). (Illus.). 208p. 1976. text ed. 13.95 (ISBN 0-87620-424-8); pap. text ed. 12.95x (ISBN 0-673-16088-2). Scott F.

Lawler, Edward E., et al. Organizational Assessment: Perspectives on the Measurement of Organizational Behavior & the Quality of Working Life. (Wiley Series on Organizational Assessment & Change). 669p. 1980. 39.95x (ISBN 0-471-04836-4, Pub. by Wiley-Interscience). Wiley.

Lawler, James H. Patterns of Civilizations. LC 77-18670. 1978. pap. text ed. 6.50 (ISBN 0-8191-0431-0). U Pr of Amer.

Lawler, James R. The Poet As Analyst: Essays on Paul Valery. LC 73-76114. 1974. 33.00x (ISBN 0-520-02450-8). U of Cal Pr.

Lawler, James R., ed. Anthology of French Poetry. 3rd ed. 1969. pap. 6.95x (ISBN 0-19-500342-X). Oxford U Pr.

Lawler, John. Book Auctions in England in the Seventeenth Century. LC 68-30614. 1968. Repr. of 1898 ed. 30.00x (ISBN 0-8103-3310-4). Gale.

Lawler, Justus G. Celestial Pantomime: Poetic Structures of Transcendence. LC 78-21964. 1979. 25.00x (ISBN 0-300-02323-5). Yale U Pr.

Lawler, L. J., jt. auth. see Lawler, Sylvia.

Lawler, Michael G. Raid on the Inarticulate: An Invitation to Adult Religion. LC 80-1438. 168p. 1980. pap. text ed. 8.25 (ISBN 0-8191-1186-4). U Pr of Amer.

Lawler, Peter A., ed. American Political Rhetoric: A Reader. LC 81-43468. 182p. 1983. pap. text ed. 9.25 (ISBN 0-8191-2705-1). U Pr of Amer.

Lawler, Ronald. Philosophical Analysis & Ethics. (Horizons in Philosophy Ser). 1968. pap. 2.95x o.p. (ISBN 0-02-820280-5). Glencoe.

Lawler, Sylvia & Lawler, L. J. Human Blood Groups & Inheritance. 3rd ed. LC 79-183395. 1972. 20.00 (ISBN 0-312-39830-1). St Martin.

Lawler, Thomas C. The Letters of St. Cyprian of Carthage, Vol. 1. Clarke, G. W. & Burghardt, Walter J., eds. (Ancient Christian Writers Ser.: No. 43). 416p. 1983. 24.95 (ISBN 0-8091-0341-9) Paulist Pr.

--The Letters of St. Cyprian of Carthage, Vol. 2. Clarke, G. W. & Burghardt, Walter J., eds. (Ancient Christian Writers Ser.: No. 44). 352p. 1983. 22.95 (ISBN 0-8091-0342-7). Paulist Pr.

Lawless, David J. Organizational Behavior: The Psychology of Effective Management. 2nd ed. (Illus.). 1979. text ed. 23.95 (ISBN 0-13-640706-4). P-H.

Lawless, J. F. Statistical Models & Methods for Lifetime Data. LC 81-11446. (Wiley Ser. in Probability & Mathematical Statistics). 580p. 1980. 36.95x (ISBN 0-471-08544-8, Pub. by Wiley-Interscience). Wiley.

Lawless, Ken. Dissolving Rubik's Cube: The Ultimate Solution. (Illus.). 96p. 1982. pap. 1.95 (ISBN 0-399-50639-X, Perige); pap. 23.40 12-copy counterpack (ISBN 0-399-50640-3). Putnam Pub Group.

--Real Extraterrestrials Don't Phone. (Illus.). 96p. 1982. pap. 3.95 (ISBN 0-943392-11-X). Tribeca Comm.

Lawless, Richard I. Algeria. (World Bibliographical Ser.: No. 19). 215p. 1980. 34.50 (ISBN 0-903450-32-1). ABC-Clio.

Lawless, Robert & Sutlive, Vinson H., Jr., eds. Fieldwork: The Human Experience. (Library of Anthropology). 132p. 1983. 29.50 (ISBN 0-677-16460-2). Gordon.

Lawley, Francis E. The Growth of Collective Economy, 2 vols. LC 80-20904. (Studies in International Economics: No. 1). Repr. of 1938 ed. Set. lib. bdg. 65.00x (ISBN 0-87991-850-0). Porcupine Pr.

Lawley, K., ed. Potential Energy Surfaces. (Advances in Chemical Physics: Vol. 42). 610p. 1980. 115.00x (ISBN 0-471-27633-2, Pub. by Wiley-Interscience). Wiley.

Lawley, K. P. Dynamics of the Excited State, Vol. 50. (Advances in Chemical Physics Ser.). 656p. 1982. 83.00 (ISBN 0-471-10059-5, Pub. by Wiley-Interscience). Wiley.

Lawley, K. P., ed. Molecular Scattering: Physical & Chemical Applications. LC 74-23667. (Advances in Chemical Physics Ser.). 541p. 1975. 118.95 (ISBN 0-471-51900-6, Pub. by Wiley-Interscience). Wiley.

Lawlis, G. Frank, jt. auth. see Achterberg, Jeanne.

Lawliss, Chuck. Country Inns: The Mississippi. 96p. 1983. pap. 10.95 (ISBN 0-03-062212-3). HR&W.

Lawlor, Deborah, tr. from French see Schwaller de Lubicz, R. A.

Lawlor, John, ed. Essays & Studies-1973. (Essays & Studies: Vol. 26). 112p. 1973. text ed. 12.50x (ISBN 0-391-00279-1). Humanities.

Lawman, Anthony. A Private Truce. 1981. 12.95 o.p. (ISBN 0-671-25408-1). S&S.

Lawn, B. R. & Wilshaw, T. R. Fracture of Brittle Solids. LC 74-12970. (Cambridge Solid State Science Ser.). (Illus.). 160p. 1975. 47.00 (ISBN 0-521-20654-5); pap. 18.95x (ISBN 0-521-09952-8). Cambridge U Pr.

Lawn, Martin. Rethinking Curriculum Studies: A Radical Approach. 253p. 1981. 27.95x o.p. (ISBN 0-470-27097-7). Halsted Pr.

Lawrence. Growth in Animals. LC 79-41574. (SAFS). 1980. 62.95 (ISBN 0-408-10638-7). Butterworth.

--Practice of the Presence of God. pap. 2.50 (ISBN 0-8007-8034-5, Spire Bks). Revell.

--The Prince Still Smiled. 1979. pap. 2.95 (ISBN 0-8423-8209-7). Tyndale.

Lawrence, tr. see Gascar, Pierre.

Lawrence, A. Architectural Acoustics. 1970. 35.00 (ISBN 0-444-20059-2). Elsevier.

Lawrence, Alan, ed. China's Foreign Relations Since Nineteen Forty-Nine. (World Studies). 1975. 22.50x (ISBN 0-7100-8092-1). Routledge & Kegan.

Lawrence, Alexander A. James Moore Wayne, Southern Unionist. LC 75-135511. (Illus.). xiv, 250p. Repr. of 1943 ed. lib. bdg. 15.00x o.p. (ISBN 0-8371-5177-5, LAJW). Greenwood.

Lawrence, Andrew. Tennis: Great Stars, Great Moments. LC 76-11008. (Putnam Sports Shelf). (gr. 5 up). 1976. PLB 5.49 o.p. (ISBN 0-399-61029-4). Putnam Pub Group.

Lawrence, Arthur. Sir Arthur Sullivan. (Music Reprint 1980 Ser.). (Illus.). 340p. 1980. Repr. of 1900 ed. lib. bdg. 29.50 (ISBN 0-306-76029-0). Da Capo.

Lawrence, Barbara. Fisherman's Wharf Cookbook. LC 79-30867. (Illus., Orig.). 1971. pap. 5.95 (ISBN 0-911954-73-2). Nitty Gritty.

Lawrence, Betsy, ed. see Cooper, Sandi.

Lawrence, Bro. Practice of the Presence of God. Attwater, Donald, tr. 1981. 6.95 (ISBN 0-87243-104-5). Templegate.

Lawrence, Brother. Practice of the Presence of God. LC 78-61665. (Spiritual Masters Ser.). 128p. 1978. pap. 2.95 o.p. (ISBN 0-8091-2137-9). Paulist Pr.

Lawrence, C. C., jt. auth. see Hackett, L. C.

Lawrence, C. W. Cellular Radiobiology. (Studies in Biology: No. 30). 64p. 1971. pap. text ed. 8.95 (ISBN 0-7131-2336-2). E Arnold.

Lawrence, Christopher W. Induced Mutagenesis: Molecular Mechanisms & Thier Implications for Enviornmental Protection. (Basic Life Sciences Ser.). 434p. 1982. 55.00x (ISBN 0-306-41163-6, Plenum Pr). Plenum Pub.

Lawrence Country Day School Cookbook. The Cookbook That Counts. LC 72-89450. 242p. 1972. spiral bdg. 6.50 (ISBN 0-9601046-1-5). E Diemar.

Lawrence, D. Black Migrants, White Natives. LC 73-89005. 256p. 1974. 31.95 o.p. (ISBN 0-521-20353-8); pap. 10.95 (ISBN 0-521-09847-5). Cambridge U Pr.

Lawrence, D. Baloti & Harrison, Lewis. Massageworks: A Practical Encyclopedia of Massage Techniques. LC 82-82309. 256p. (Orig.). 1982. pap. 8.95 (ISBN 0-448-07355-2, G&D). Putnam Pub Group.

Lawrence, D. H. Apocalypse. LC 82-70233. 192p. 1982. 20.00 (ISBN 0-670-12952-6). Viking Pr.

--Collected Letters, 2 vols. 1962. Set. 40.00 (ISBN 0-670-22773-0). Viking Pr.

--D. H. Lawrence & New Mexico. Sagar, Keith, ed. (Illus.). 250p. 1982. 9.95 (ISBN 0-87905-122-1); pap. 7.95 o.p. (ISBN 0-686-96848-4). Peregrine Smith.

--Kangaroo. 1980. pap. 4.95 (ISBN 0-14-000751-2). Penguin.

--Lady Chatterley's Lover. Durrell, Lawrence, ed. (Bantam Classics Ser.). 360p. 1983. pap. 2.95 (ISBN 0-553-21097-1). Bantam.

--The Lost Girl. LC 82-70234. 432p. 1982. 22.95 (ISBN 0-670-44101-5). Viking Pr.

--Mornings in Mexico. (Illus.). 224p. 1982. avail. (ISBN 0-87905-123-X); pap. 6.95 (ISBN 0-686-96849-2). Peregrine Smith.

--Movements in European History. 2nd ed. (Illus.). 1981. pap. 6.95 (ISBN 0-19-285113-6). Oxford U Pr.

--The Prussian Officer. (Creative's Classics Ser.). 56p. (gr. 1-7). 1982. lib. bdg. 6.95 (ISBN 0-87191-892-7). Creative Ed.

--The Rainbow. 6.95 (ISBN 0-394-60491-1). Modern Lib.

--The Rocking Horse Winner. (Creative's Classics Ser.). 40p. (gr. 1-7). 1982. lib. bdg. 6.95 (ISBN 0-87191-893-5). Creative Ed.

--Sea & Sardinia. 1981. pap. 3.95 (ISBN 0-14-000465-3). Penguin.

--Selected Letters. 1978. pap. 5.95 (ISBN 0-14-000759-8). Penguin.

--Selected Poems. (Poets Ser.). 1980. pap. 3.95 (ISBN 0-14-042281-1). Penguin.

--Sons & Lovers: A Facsimile of the Manuscript. Schorer, Mark, ed. LC 75-46037. 1978. 150.00x (ISBN 0-520-03190-3). U of Cal Pr.

--Sons & Lovers: T. V. edition. 1983. pap. 3.95 (ISBN 0-14-006682-9). Penguin.

--Studies in Classic American Literature. 1977. pap. 3.95 (ISBN 0-14-003300-9). Penguin.

--The Trespasser. Mansfield, Elizabeth, ed. (Cambridge Edition Ser.). 256p. 1983. 17.75 (ISBN 0-670-72991-4). Viking Pr.

--Women in Love. 6.95 (ISBN 0-394-60442-3). Modern Lib.

--You Touched Me. (Creative's Classics Ser.). 48p. (gr. 1-7). 1982. lib. bdg. 6.95 (ISBN 0-87191-894-3). Creative Ed.

Lawrence, D. H., tr. see Verga, Giovanni.

Lawrence, David E. The Wheels of Heaven. LC 81-66612. 1981. pap. 4.95 (ISBN 0-89107-218-7, Crossway Bks). Good News.

Lawrence, David H. Lady Chatterley's Lover. 2nd ed. LC 82-42866. 1982. 7.95 (ISBN 0-394-60430-X). Modern Lib.

--Saint Mawr. Bd. with The Man Who Died. 1959. pap. 3.95 (ISBN 0-394-70071-6, Vin). Random.

--Sons & Lovers. 1962. 6.95 (ISBN 0-394-60452-0). Modern Lib.

Lawrence, Deborah & Villanueva, Aggie. Chase the Wind. 256p. 1983. pap. 5.95 (ISBN 0-8407-5840-5). Nelson.

Lawrence, Edgar D. Focus on Deafness: Selected Readings on Deafness for Paraprofessionals. 1978. pap. text ed. 10.50 o.p. (ISBN 0-8191-0389-6). U Pr of Amer.

Lawrence, Emeric. Believe the Good News: Daily Meditations on the Lenten Masses. LC 82-97. 144p. 1982. pap. 5.75 (ISBN 0-8146-1256-3). Liturgical Pr.

--Jesus Present & Coming: Daily Meditations on the Advent & Christmas Masses. LC 82-20380. 128p. 1982. pap. 7.95 (ISBN 0-8146-1284-9). Liturgical Pr.

Lawrence, Emeric A. The Ministry of Believers. 24p. (Orig.). 1982. pap. text ed. 1.00 (ISBN 0-8146-1276-8). Liturgical Pr.

Lawrence, F. C., jt. auth. see Laban, Rudolph.

Lawrence, Faye B., jt. auth. see Mason, William H.

Lawrence, G., et al. Catalogue of the Strandell Collection at the Hunt Institute for Botanical Documentation. 1000p. Date not set. 180.00 (ISBN 0-913196-21-5). Hunt Inst Botanical. Postponed.

Lawrence, G. R. Cartographic Methods. 2nd ed. (Illus.). xvi, 154p. 1979. 19.95x (ISBN 0-416-71640-7); pap. 10.95x (ISBN 0-416-71650-4). Methuen Inc.

Lawrence, George H. Introduction to Plant Taxonomy. (Illus.). 1955. text ed. 20.95x (ISBN 0-02-368120-9). Macmillan.
--Taxonomy of Vascular Plants. (Illus.). 1951. text ed. 32.95x (ISBN 0-02-368190-X). Macmillan.
Lawrence, Grace. Aqua-Fitness for Women. (Illus.). 1981. pap. 8.95 (ISBN 0-920510-54-X, Pub. by Personal Lib). Dodd.
Lawrence, Henry W. The Not-Quite Puritans: Some Genial Follies & Peculiar Frailities of Our Revered New England Ancestors. (Illus.). 1975. Repr. of 1928 ed. 34.00x (ISBN 0-8103-3993-5). Gale.
Lawrence, James. Trace Analysis, Vol. 2. (Serial Publication Ser.). 35.00 (ISBN 0-12-682102-X). Acad Pr.
Lawrence, James C. Your Fortune in Futures: A Guide to Commodity Futures Trading. 1976. 3.98 o.p. (ISBN 0-312-89810-X). St Martin.
Lawrence, James H. Empire of the Nairs: Or, the Rights of Women, 4 vols. in 1. LC 76-21346. 1050p. 1976. Repr. of 1811 ed. 90.00x (ISBN 0-8201-1270-4). Schol Facsimiles.
Lawrence, Jim, jt. auth. see Morrow, Gray.
Lawrence, John. A History of Russia. rev. ed. 1978. pap. 6.95 (ISBN 0-452-00608-2, F608, Mer). NAL.
Lawrence, John H. & Hamilton, J. G., eds. Advances in Biological & Medical Physics, 17 vols. Incl. Vol. 1. 1948 (ISBN 0-12-005201-6); Vol. 2. 1951 (ISBN 0-12-005202-4); Vol. 3. Lawrence, John H. & Tobias, Cornelius, eds. 1953 (ISBN 0-12-005203-2); Vol. 4. 1956 (ISBN 0-12-005204-0); Vol. 5. 1957 (ISBN 0-12-005205-9); Vol. 6. Tobias, Cornelius A. & Lawrence, John H., eds. 1958 (ISBN 0-12-005206-7); Vol. 7. 1960 (ISBN 0-12-005207-5); Vol. 8. 1962 (ISBN 0-12-005208-3); Vol. 9. Lawrence, John H. & Gofman, John W., eds. (ISBN 0-12-005209-1); Vol. 10. 1965 (ISBN 0-12-005210-5); Vol. 11. 1967. o.s.i (ISBN 0-12-005211-3); Vol. 12. 1968 (ISBN 0-12-005212-1); Vol. 13. 1971 (ISBN 0-12-005213-X); Vol. 14. 1973 (ISBN 0-12-005214-8); Vol. 15. 1974 (ISBN 0-12-005215-6); Vol. 16. 1978. 63.50 (ISBN 0-12-005216-4); lib. ed. 78.00 (ISBN 0-12-005274-1); microfiche 46.00 (ISBN 0-12-005275-X); Vol. 17. 1980. 59.00 (ISBN 0-12-005217-2); lib. ed. 75.00 (ISBN 0-12-005276-8); microfiche 42.50 (ISBN 0-12-005277-6). Vols. 1-16. 64.00 ea. Acad Pr.
Lawrence, John H. see Lawrence, John H. & Hamilton, J. G.
Lawrence, John S. & Timberg, Bernard, eds. Fair Use & Free Inquiry: Copyright Law & the New Media. (Communication & Information Science Ser.). 1980. 34.00x (ISBN 0-89391-028-7). Ablex Pub.
Lawrence, John T. History of Russia. 2nd ed. 1962. pap. 1.50 o.p. (ISBN 0-451-61318-X, MW1318, Ment). NAL.
Lawrence, Judith. Goat for Carlo. LC 79-161028. (Venture Ser). (Illus.). (gr. 1). 1971. PLB 6.69 (ISBN 0-8116-6709-X). Garrard.
Lawrence, Judy M. Common Cent: The Complete Money Management Workbook. 57p. (Orig.). 1981. pap. 5.95 (ISBN 0-9607096-0-6). JML Ent.
Lawrence, K., jt. auth. see Strojan, C.
Lawrence, Kenneth. Health Care Executive's Appointment Book, 1983. 256p. 1982. 28.50 (ISBN 0-89443-848-4). Aspen Systems.
Lawrence, Kenneth & Rowland, Howard, eds. The National Nursing Directory. LC 82-11345. 424p. 1982. 34.50 (ISBN 0-89443-805-0). Aspen Systems.
Lawrence, Lee & Vaizey, Marina. Stained Glass. 1976. 39.95 o.p. (ISBN 0-517-52728-6). Crown.
Lawrence, Leslie, ed. see Bizer, Linda & Nathan, Beverly.
Lawrence, Leslie, ed. see Heath, Mary L.
Lawrence, Leslie, ed. see Kinsman, Barbara.
Lawrence, Leslie, ed. see Oppenheim, Joanne.
Lawrence, Leslie, ed. see Taylor, Jane.
Lawrence, Louise. Cat Call. LC 78-22476. 224p. (gr. 7 up). 1980. 9.89x (ISBN 0-06-023753-8, HarpJ); PLB 8.79 (ISBN 0-06-023754-6). Har-Row.
--Star Lord. LC 77-25674. (gr. 7 up). 1978. 8.95i (ISBN 0-06-023776-7, HarpJ); PLB 10.89 (ISBN 0-06-023777-5). Har-Row.
Lawrence, Louise D. Another Winter, Another Spring: A Love Remembered. LC 76-19094. 1977. 8.95 o.p. (ISBN 0-07-036722-1, GB). McGraw.
Lawrence, Lynn. The Familiar Touch, No. 85. 1982. pap. 1.75. Jove Pubns.
Lawrence, M. Hand Analysis. 1972. pap. 4.95 (ISBN 0-13-372466-2, Reward). P-H.
Lawrence, M. J. & Mason, K. L. Key to Advanced Spanish Course. LC 78-122008. 1970. 4.80 o.s.i. (ISBN 0-08-016084-0); pap. 3.85 (ISBN 0-08-016083-2). Pergamon.
Lawrence, M. Therese. Toward a New Christendom. LC 81-84244. (Illus.). 80p. 1982. pap. 5.95 write for info. (ISBN 0-938034-05-7). PAL Pr.
Lawrence, Mary, compiled by. Lovers: One Hundred Works Of Art Celebrating Romantic Love, with Commentaries by the Distinguished & the Great. (Illus.). 220p. 1982. 40.00 (ISBN 0-89479-116-8). A & W Pubs.
Lawrence, Mary S. Reading, Thinking, Writing: A Text for Students of English As a Second Language. 1975. 7.95x (ISBN 0-472-08548-4); s.p. tchrs' manual 1.00, net (ISBN 0-472-08549-2). U of Mich Pr.
--Writing As a Thinking Process. LC 78-185153. (Illus.). 1972. pap. text ed. 7.50x (ISBN 0-472-08550-6); s.p. tchrs.' manual 1.95, net (ISBN 0-472-08551-4). U of Mich Pr.
Lawrence, Michael. Working with Wood. LC 78-65631. (Illus.). 1979. 11.95i o.p. (ISBN 0-690-01810-X); pap. 5.95i (ISBN 0-690-01820-7, TYC-T). T Y Crowell.
Lawrence, Mike. The Complete Book on Hand Evaluation in Contract Bridge. 1983. pap. 8.95 (ISBN 0-939460-28-9). M Hardy.
--Judgement at Bridge. 1976. pap. 5.95 o.p. (ISBN 0-939460-02-5). M Hardy.
--Judgement at Bridge. LC 80-123381. 151p. 1976. pap. 6.95 (ISBN 0-939460-02-5). M Hardy.
Lawrence, Mildred. Peachtree Island. LC 48-9018. (Illus.). (gr. 3-6). 1966. pap. 2.95 (ISBN 0-15-671560-0, VoyB). HarBraceJ.
Lawrence, Nathaniel. Whitehead's Philosophical Development. LC 68-23306. 1968. Repr. of 1956 ed. lib. bdg. 20.75x (ISBN 0-8371-0139-5, LAWD). Greenwood.
Lawrence, Nelda R. & Tebeaux, Elizabeth. Writing Communications in Business & Industry. 3rd ed. (Illus.). 272p. 1982. 16.95 (ISBN 0-13-970467-1). P-H.
Lawrence, P. & Meggitt, M. J., eds. Gods, Ghosts & Men in Melanesia. 1965. pap. 14.95x (ISBN 0-19-550147-0). Oxford U Pr.
Lawrence, P. A. Insect Development. LC 76-8196. (Royal Entomological Society of London Symposium Ser.). 230p. 1976. 38.95x o.s.i. (ISBN 0-470-15098-X). Halsted Pr.
Lawrence, Patty, jt. auth. see Hyman, Jane.
Lawrence, Paul, jt. auth. see Brown, Robert M.
Lawrence, Paul A. Lomi-Lomi Hawaiian Massage. 3rd ed. LC 80-83756. (Positive Health Ser.). (Illus.). 80p. (YA) 1981. 12.95 o.p. (ISBN 0-938034-01-4); pap. 5.95 o.p. (ISBN 0-938034-02-2). PAL Pr.
Lawrence, Paul R. & Dyer, Davis. Renewing American Industry. LC 82-72096. 400p. 1983. 25.00 (ISBN 0-02-918170-4). Free Pr.
Lawrence, Paul R. & Lorsch, Jay W. Organization & Environment: Managing Differentiation & Integration. LC 67-30338. 1967. 15.00x (ISBN 0-87584-064-7). Harvard Busn.
Lawrence, Paul R., jt. auth. see Ronken, Harriet O.
Lawrence, Peter. A Kid's New York. 1982. pap. 6.95 (ISBN 0-380-81315-7, 81315). Avon.
--Managers & Management in West Germany. LC 79-23970. 220p. 1980. 30.00 (ISBN 0-312-51237-6). St Martin.
Lawrence, R. D. The Ghost Walker. LC 82-12111. 264p. 1982. 15.95 (ISBN 0-03-061594-1). HR&W.
Lawrence, Ralph R. & Richards, H. E. Principles of Alternating-Current Machinery. 4th ed. 1953. text ed. 17.95 o.p. (ISBN 0-07-036709-4, C). McGraw.
Lawrence, Richard D. & Record, Jeffrey. U. S. Force Structure in NATO: An Alternative. (Studies in Defense Policy). 136p. 1974. pap. 4.95 (ISBN 0-8157-5171-0). Brookings.
Lawrence, Richard M., jt. auth. see Ault, Frederick K.
Lawrence, Robert. New Dimensions to Energy Policy. LC 78-389. (Policy Studies Organization Ser.). 256p. 1979. 24.95x (ISBN 0-669-02172-5). Lexington Bks.
--The World of Opera. LC 77-2268. (Illus.). 1977. Repr. of 1956 ed. lib. bdg. 19.75x (ISBN 0-8371-9551-9, LAWO). Greenwood.
Lawrence, Robert, ed. Energy Policy Issues. 1978. pap. 6.00 (ISBN 0-918592-28-3). Policy Studies.
Lawrence, Robert M. Magic of the Horseshoe. LC 68-22034. 1968. Repr. of 1898 ed. 34.00x (ISBN 0-8103-3452-6). Gale.
Lawrence, Robert M. & Heisler, Martin O., eds. International Energy Policy. LC 79-4748. (A Policy Studies Organization Book). 240p. 1980. 25.95x (ISBN 0-669-02929-7). Lexington Bks.
Lawrence, Ronald M. & Rosenberg, Stanley. Pain Relief with Osteomassage. LC 82-13451. (Illus.). 128p. (Orig.). 1982. pap. 4.95 (ISBN 0-912800-27-5). Woodbridge Pr.
Lawrence, Roy T. The Two Basic Psychological Forces Prompting Men to Action & How to Utilize Them Effectively. (Essential Knowledge Library Bk.). (Illus.). 1979. 26.00 (ISBN 0-89266-158-5). Am Classical Coll Pr.
Lawrence, Seymour, ed. Big Rock Candy Mountain: Resources for Our Education. 192p. 1972. pap. 4.00 o.s.i. (ISBN 0-440-50705-7, Delta). Dell.
Lawrence, T. E. Evolution of a Revolt: Early Postwar Writings of T. E. Lawrence. Weintraub, Stanley & Weintraub, Rodelle, eds. LC 67-27112. 1967. 14.95x (ISBN 0-271-73133-8). Pa St U Pr.
--Seven Pillars of Wisdom. (Illus.). 1976. pap. 7.95 (ISBN 0-14-001696-1). Penguin.
Lawrence, V. B. & LoCicero, J. L., eds. Tutorials in Modern Communications. 1983. text ed. 33.95 (ISBN 0-914894-48-X). Computer Sci.
Lawrence, Vera B., ed. see Joplin, Scott.
Lawrence, Vera Brodsky, ed. see Joplin, Scott.
Lawrence, W. Gordon. Exploring Individual & Organizational Boundaries: A Tavistock Open Systems Approach. LC 78-8603. (Individuals, Groups & Organizations Ser.). 256p. 1979. 42.95 (ISBN 0-471-99679-3, Pub. by Wiley-Interscience). Wiley.
Lawrence, William H. see Minan, John H.
Lawrence, William J. Plant Breeding. (Studies in Biology: No. 12). 64p. 1968. pap. text ed. 8.95 (ISBN 0-7131-2205-6). E Arnold.
Lawrie, D., jt. auth. see Macfarlane, P. W.
Lawrie, R. A. Meat Science. 2nd ed. 1973. text ed. 30.00 o.p. (ISBN 0-08-017133-8); pap. text ed. 17.05 o.p. (ISBN 0-08-017811-1). Pergamon.
Lawrie, Ralston, ed. Developments in Meat Science, Vol. 2. (Illus.). xii, 295p. 1981. 67.75 (ISBN 0-85334-986-X, Pub. by Applied Sci England). Elsevier.
Lawry, John D. Guide to the History of Psychology. (Littlefield, Adams Quality Paperback Ser.: No. 361). 128p. 1981. pap. text ed. 3.95 (ISBN 0-8226-0361-6). Littlefield.
Lawry, Robert P., jt. auth. see Davies, Jack.
Laws, Edward A. Aquatic Pollution. LC 80-23311. (Environmental Science & Technology Ser.). 504p. 1981. 41.95 (ISBN 0-471-05797-5, Pub. by Wiley-Interscience). Wiley.
Laws, Judith L. & Schwartz, Pepper. Sexual Scripts. LC 80-6313. 256p. 1982. lib. bdg. 22.75 (ISBN 0-8191-1859-1); pap. text ed. 11.50 (ISBN 0-8191-1860-5). U Pr of Amer.
Laws, K. G., jt. auth. see Jones, R. J.
Laws, Phe. International Gourmet Cooking with Microwave. LC 76-12163. 288p. 1981. spiral bdg. 6.95 (ISBN 0-686-82945-X, Hidden Hse). Music Sales.
--Vegetable Cookery. 256p. 1980. pap. 6.95 (ISBN 0-8256-3828-3, Quick Fox). Putnam Pub Group.
Laws, Priscilla W. Medical & Dental X-Rays: A Consumer's Guide to Avoiding Unnecessary Radiation Exposure. 73p. 1982. 3.25 (ISBN 0-686-96287-7). Pub Citizen Health.
Laws, Priscilla W. & Public Citizen Health Research Group. The X-Ray Information Book: A Consumer's Guide to Avoiding Unnecessary Medical & Dental X-Rays. 1983. 16.50 (ISBN 0-374-29342-2); pap. 7.25 (ISBN 0-374-51730-4). FS&G.
Laws, Robert J. Solar Cells: What You Always Wanted to Know. LC 82-1510. (Illus.). 128p. 1983. 9.95 (ISBN 0-89490-069-2). Enslow Pubs.
Lawshe, Charles H. & Balma, M. J. Principles of Personnel Testing. 2nd ed. 1966. text ed. 17.95 o.p. (ISBN 0-07-036761-2, C). McGraw.
Lawson, Agnes M. Hints to Bible Study. 1973. 7.95 (ISBN 0-686-24358-7); pap. 4.50 (ISBN 0-686-24359-5). Divine Sci Fed.
Lawson, Audrey & Lawson, Herbert. Man Who Freed the Slaves: The Story of William Wilberforce. (gr. 7 up). 4.95 o.p. (ISBN 0-571-05061-1). Transatlantic.
Lawson, Charles L. & Hanson, Richard J. Solving Least Squares Problems. (Illus.). 384p. 1974. 29.95 (ISBN 0-13-822585-0). P-H.
Lawson, David H. & Richards, R. Michael. Clinical Pharmacy. 1982. 39.95x (ISBN 0-412-22760-6, Pub. by Chapman & Hall). Methuen Inc.
Lawson, Don. An Album of World War II Home Fronts. LC 79-23583. (Picture Albums Ser.). (Illus.). (gr. 5 up). 1980. 9.60 (ISBN 0-531-01504-1). Watts.
--American Revolution: America's First War for Independence. LC 73-18545. (Young People's History of America's Wars Ser.). (Illus.). 160p. (gr. 7-12). 1974. 10.95 o.p. (ISBN 0-200-00131-0, AbS-J). Har-Row.
--The Changing Face of the Constitution. LC 78-11570. (gr. 7 up). 1979. PLB 8.40 s&l (ISBN 0-531-02923-9). Watts.
--Libya & Qaddafi. (Impact Bks.). (Illus.). 96p. (gr. 7 up). 1982. PLB 8.90 (ISBN 0-531-04492-0). Watts.
--The Long March: Red China under Chairman Mao. LC 82-45580. (Illus.). 160p. (YA) (gr. 7 up). 1983. 10.10i (ISBN 0-690-04271-X, TYC-J); PLB 10.89g (ISBN 0-690-04272-8). Har-Row.
--The Secret World War II. (Illus.). (gr. 7 up). 1978. PLB 8.90 s&l (ISBN 0-531-01459-2). Watts.
--The War in Vietnam. (First Bks.). (Illus.). 96p. (gr. 4 up). 1981. lib. bdg. 8.90 (ISBN 0-531-04331-2). Watts.
Lawson, Donna. Kid's Clothes for Under Five Dollars. LC 77-93715. 1978. 9.95 (ISBN 0-8256-3118-1, Quick Fox); pap. 3.95 (ISBN 0-8256-3051-7). Putnam Pub Group.
Lawson, Douglas E. Wisdom & Education. LC 61-11660. 168p. 1961. 4.75x (ISBN 0-8093-0048-6). S Ill U Pr.
Lawson, F. H. The Comparison: Selected Essays, Vol. 2. (European Studies in Law: Vol. 5). 1978. 61.75 (ISBN 0-7204-0760-5, North-Holland). Elsevier.
--Roman Law Reader. LC 69-15388. 1969. text ed. 7.50 o.p. (ISBN 0-379-11317-1); pap. 2.50 o.p. (ISBN 0-379-11300-7). Oceana.
Lawson, F. H. & Markesinis, B. S. Tortious Liability for Unintentional Harm in the Common Law & the Civil Law, 2 vols. LC 81-102302. (Cambridge Studies in International & Comparative Law). (280p ea.). 1982. Vol. 1: Texts. text ed. 49.50 (ISBN 0-521-23585-5); pap. 24.95 (ISBN 0-521-27209-2); Vol. 2: Materials. text ed. 49.50 (ISBN 0-521-23586-3); pap. 24.95 (ISBN 0-521-27210-6). Cambridge U Pr.
Lawson, Frederick H. A Common Lawyer Looks at the Civil Law: Five Lectures Delivered at the University of Michigan, November 16, 17, 18, 19, and 20, 1953. LC 77-23760. (Thomas M. Cooley Lecture Ser.). 1977. Repr. of 1953 ed. lib. bdg. 28.75x (ISBN 0-8371-9778-3, LACO). Greenwood.
--Introduction to the Law of Property. (Clarendon Law Ser.). 1958. pap. 9.95x o.p. (ISBN 0-19-876064-7). Oxford U Pr.
Lawson, Frederick H. & Rudden, Bernard. The Law of Property. 2nd ed. (Clarendon Law Ser.). (Illus.). 258p. 1982. text ed. 34.95x (ISBN 0-19-876128-7); pap. text ed. 15.95x (ISBN 0-19-876129-5). Oxford U Pr.
Lawson, G. W. & John, D. M. The Marine Algae & Coastal Environment of Tropical West Africa. (Nova Hedwigia Beiheft Ser.: No. 70). (Illus.). 450p. 1982. lib. bdg. 80.00x (ISBN 3-7682-5470-4). Lubrecht & Cramer.
Lawson, Gary & Peterson, James. Alcoholism & the Family: A Guide to Treatment & Prevention. 300p. 1983. write for info. (ISBN 0-89443-674-0). Aspen Systems.
Lawson, Greg, photos by. Beauty Spot-Santa Barbara. Builder, Janine & Mendenhall, Matthew, trs. LC 81-68211. (Illus.). 56p. (Span., Fr., Ger., Eng.,). 1982. 14.95 (ISBN 0-9606704-0-8); pap. 8.95 (ISBN 0-9606704-1-6). First Choice.
--Colorado. (Illus.). 72p. (Orig., Eng., Span., Fr., Ger.). 1983. pap. 8.95 (ISBN 0-9606704-5-9). First Choice.
--Western Oregon. LC 81-71871. (Illus.). 64p. (Eng., Sp., Fr., Ger., Japanese.). Date not set. price not set (ISBN 0-9606704-2-4); pap. 8.95 (ISBN 0-9606704-4-0). First Choice.
Lawson, H. W., et al. Large Scale Integration: Technology, Applications, & Impacts. (Proceedings). 1979. 64.00 (ISBN 0-444-85249-2). Elsevier.
Lawson, Harold. Understanding Computer Systems. (gr. 10-12). 1982. pap. text ed. 11.95x (ISBN 0-914894-31-5); suppl. materials avail. Computer Sci.
Lawson, Harry O., et al. Personnel Administration in the Courts. (A Westview Special Study). 1979. lib. bdg. 38.50 (ISBN 0-89158-588-5). Westview.
Lawson, Herbert, jt. auth. see Lawson, Audrey.
Lawson, James. The Girl Watcher. LC 76-10613. 1976. 7.95 o.p. (ISBN 0-399-11814-4). Putnam Pub Group.
Lawson, James G., compiled by. The Best-Loved Religious Poems. 256p. 1981. 9.95 (ISBN 0-8007-0019-8). Revell.
--The Best-Loved Religious Poems. cancelled (ISBN 0-8007-5086-1, Power Bks). Revell.
Lawson, Jo. Curado Do Cancer. (Port.). 1980. pap. 1.40 (ISBN 0-8297-1049-3). Life Pubs Intl.
Lawson, Joan. More Soviet Dances. (Illus., Orig.). pap. 8.00x (ISBN 0-392-03999-0, SpS). Sportshelf.
Lawson, John & Silver, Harold. A Social History of Education in England. (Illus.). 1979. 25.95x o.p. (ISBN 0-416-08670-5); pap. 14.95x (ISBN 0-416-08680-2). Methuen Inc.
Lawson, Jonathan. Robert Bloomfield. (English Authors Ser.). 1980. lib. bdg. 14.95 (ISBN 0-8057-6802-5, Twayne). G K Hall.
Lawson, Jonathan N., ed. & intro. by see Bloomfield, Robert.
Lawson, L. L. & Rushforth, S. R. The Diatom Flora of the Provo River, Utah (USA) 1975. 20.00 (ISBN 3-7682-0955-5). Lubrecht & Cramer.
Lawson, LeRoy. Cracking the Code. LC 76-57045. 1977. pap. 1.95 (ISBN 0-87239-125-6, 40042). Standard Pub.
--Lord of Promises: Adult Course. LC 82-17034. 112p. 1983. pap. 2.50 (ISBN 0-87239-611-8). Standard Pub.
--Lord of Promises (Student) Adult Course. 96p. 1983. pap. 2.25 (ISBN 0-87239-612-6). SRA.
--The New Testament Church Then & Now Workbook. 48p. 1983. pap. 1.75 (ISBN 0-87239-609-6, 88586). Standard Pub.
Lawson, Leslie G., et al. Lead On! The Complete Handbook for Group Leaders. LC 82-15553. (Orig.). 1982. pap. 5.95 (ISBN 0-915166-27-5). Impact Pubs Cal.
Lawson, Maron. Maggie Flying Bird. LC 74-6551. (Illus.). 160p. (gr. 7 up). 1974. 7.50 o.s.i. (ISBN 0-688-21825-3); PLB 8.59 (ISBN 0-688-31825-8). Morrow.
Lawson, Merlin P., et al. Climatic Atlas of Nebraska. LC 77-6643. (Nebraska Atlas Project Ser.). (Illus.). xiv, 88p. 1977. 15.95x (ISBN 0-8032-0924-X). U of Nebr Pr.
Lawson, Murray B. Fur: A Study in English Mercantilism Seventeen Hundred to Seventeen Seventy-Five. (Illus.). Repr. of 1943 ed. lib. bdg. 17.50x (ISBN 0-87991-813-6). Porcupine Pr.
Lawson, P. H. Many Laws: Selected Essays, Vol. 1. (European Studies in Law: Vol. 4). 1978. 53.25 (ISBN 0-7204-0759-1, North-Holland). Elsevier.
Lawson, Paul E. Solving Somebody Else's Blues: A Study of Police Mediation Activities. LC 81-40881. (Illus.). 246p. (Orig.). 1982. lib. bdg. 22.00 (ISBN 0-8191-2173-8); pap. text ed. 10.75 (ISBN 0-8191-2174-6). U Pr of Amer.
Lawson, R. G. Advertising & Labelling Laws in the Common Market. 1975. looseleaf bdg. 67.50x o.p. (ISBN 0-85308-040-2); 1978 supplement o.p. Rothman.

--Advertising Law. 400p. 1978. 60.00x (ISBN 0-7121-1239-1, Pub. by Macdonald & Evans). State Mutual Bk.

Lawson, Richard H. Edith Wharton. LC 77-40. (Literature and Life Ser.). 1977. 11.95 (ISBN 0-8044-2496-9). Ungar.

Lawson, Robert. Ben & Me. (Illus.). (gr. 7-10). 1939. 9.95 (ISBN 0-316-51732-1). Little.

--Principles & Methods of Social Psychology. 3rd ed. (Illus.). 1975. text ed. 13.95x o.p. (ISBN 0-19-501850-8). Oxford U Pr.

--Robbut: A Tale of Tails. 1981. lib. bdg. 7.95 (ISBN 0-8398-2728-8, Gregg). G K Hall.

Lawson, Robert F. & Schnell, R. L., eds. Education Studies: Foundations of Policy. LC 82-21924. 468p. (Orig.). 1983. lib. bdg. 29.75 (ISBN 0-8191-2919-4); pap. text ed. 17.25 (ISBN 0-8191-2920-8). U Pr of Amer.

Lawson, Robert W., tr. see Einstein, Albert.

Lawson, S. J., tr. see Benda, Julien.

Lawson, T. V. Wind Effects on Buildings, Vols. 1 & 2. 1980. Vol. 1: Design Applications. 53.50 (ISBN 0-85334-887-1, Pub. by Applied Sci England); Vol. 2: Statistics & Meteorology. 30.75 (ISBN 0-85334-893-6). Elsevier.

Lawson, V. Practical Experience of Machine Translation. 1982. 42.75 (ISBN 0-444-86381-8). Elsevier.

Lawson, William. The Western Scar: The Theme of the Been-to in West African Literature. LC 82-6372. x, 150p. 1982. lib. bdg. 18.95 (ISBN 0-8214-0649-3, 82-84184); pap. text ed. 11.95 (ISBN 0-8214-0695-7, 82-84648). Ohio U Pr.

Lawson, William M., jt. auth. see Friedland, Seymour.

Lawson-Wood, D., jt. auth. see Lawson-Wood, J.

Lawson-Wood, Denis & Joyce. The Incredible Healing Needles: A Layman's Guide to Chinese Acupuncture. 1974. pap. 1.25 (ISBN 0-87728-298-6). Weiser.

Lawson-Wood, J. & Lawson-Wood, D. Acupuncture Handbook. 141p. 1973. 7.95x o.p. (ISBN 0-8464-0989-5). Beekman Pubs.

Lawther, John D. The Learning & Performance of Physical Skills. 2nd ed. (Illus.). 1977. text ed. 15.95 (ISBN 0-13-527325-0). P-H.

Lawton, David A., ed. Middle English Alliterative Poetry & Its Literary Background. 224p. 1983. text ed. 49.50x (ISBN 0-85991-097-0, Pub. by Boydell & Brewer). Biblio Dist.

Lawton, Denis. Class, Culture & the Curriculum. (Students Library of Education). 1975. 12.75x o.s.i. (ISBN 0-7100-8053-0); pap. 7.00 o.p. (ISBN 0-7100-8054-9). Routledge & Kegan.

--Social Class, Language & Education. (International Library of Sociology). 192p. 1968. pap. 8.95 (ISBN 0-7100-6895-6). Routledge & Kegan.

Lawton, Denis, jt. ed. see Lacey, Colin.

Lawton, Lynna. Under Crimson Sails. 352p. 1982. pap. 3.25 o.p. (ISBN 0-505-51852-X). Tower Bks.

--Under Crimson Sails. 352p. 1983. pap. 3.50 (ISBN 0-8439-2002-5, Leisure Bks). Dorchester Pub Co.

Lawton, M. Murray, et al. Lawton's & Foy's Textbook for Medical Assistants. 4th ed. LC 80-15524. (Illus.). 456p. 1980. text ed. 22.95 (ISBN 0-8016-2893-8). Mosby.

Lawton, M. Powell. Planning & Managing Housing for the Elderly. LC 74-28099. 304p. 1975. 44.95 (ISBN 0-471-51894-8, Pub. by Wiley-Interscience). Wiley.

Lawton, M. Powell, et al. Community Planning for an Aging Society: Designing Services & Facilities. LC 75-45302. (Community Development Ser.: Vol. 20). 1978. 25.00 o.p. (ISBN 0-87933-195-X). Hutchinson Ross.

Lawton, Mary, jt. auth. see Paderewski, Jan I.

Lawton, Susan. Hysterical Fugue. 66p. (Orig.). 1982. pap. 5.00 (ISBN 0-937998-07-9). Cumberland.

--Hysterical Fugue. 1983. pap. 5.00 (ISBN 0-937998-07-9). Devin.

Lawton, Thomas. Chinese Art of the Warring States Period: Change & Continuity, 480-222 B.C. LC 82-600184. (Illus.). 204p. (Orig.). 1983. 35.00x (ISBN 0-934686-39-4); pap. 20.00x (ISBN 0-934686-50-5). Freer.

Lax, Howard L. Political Risk in the International Oil & Gas Industry. LC 82-83329. (Illus.). 212p. 1983. text ed. 28.00 (ISBN 0-934634-20-3). Intl Human Res.

Lax, Howard L., jt. auth. see Prast, William G.

Lax, Melvin. Symmetry Principles in Solid State & Molecular Physics. LC 74-1215. 499p. 1974. 26.95 o.p. (ISBN 0-471-51903-0, Pub. by Wiley-Interscience); pap. 29.95x (ISBN 0-471-51904-9). Wiley.

Lax, P. D. Hyperbolic Systems of Conservation Laws & the Mathematical Theory of Shock Waves. (CBMS-NSF Regional Conference Ser.: No. 11). v, 48p. 1973. pap. 7.00 (ISBN 0-89871-177-0). Soc Indus-Appl Math.

Lax, Roger, jt. auth. see Carvainis, Maria.

Laxalt, Paul. A Changing America: A View from the United States Senate. LC 80-80290. 156p. 1980. pap. 2.95 (ISBN 0-89526-892-2). Regnery-Gateway.

Laxen, D. P., jt. auth. see Harrison, R. M.

Laxness, Halldor. The Atom Station. LC 81-85725. 208p. 1982. 16.95 (ISBN 0-933256-31-0, Dist. by Watts); pap. 8.95 (ISBN 0-531-07348-3). Second Chance.

--Salka Valka. 1963. 8.95 o.p. (ISBN 0-04-823030-8). Allen Unwin.

Lay, D., jt. auth. see Taylor, A.

Lay, David, jt. auth. see Goldstein, Larry J.

Lay, Elery A. Trek to the King's Mountain. LC 76-46777. 1976. 8.95 (ISBN 0-87716-077-5, Pub. by Moore Pub Co). F Apple.

Lay, N., jt. auth. see Fassler, D.

Lay, Richard A. Measuring the Metric Way. (Illus.). 1975. pap. text ed. 2.75x (ISBN 0-88323-123-9, 211). Richards Pub.

Lay, Steven R. Convex Sets & Their Applications. (Pure & Applied Mathematics Ser.: Texts, Monographs & Tracts). 244p. 1982. 29.50x (ISBN 0-471-09584-2, Pub. by Wiley-Interscience). Wiley.

Laya, Jean H. Voltaire Aux Francais, Sur Leur Constitution. Repr. of 1789 ed. 28.00 o.p. (ISBN 0-8287-0514-3). Clearwater Pub.

Layamon. Brut, Vol. 1. Brook, George L. & Leslie, R. F., eds. (Early English Text Society Ser.). 1963. 29.95x (ISBN 0-19-722250-1); 29.50x (ISBN 0-19-722279-X, VOL. 2, 1978). Oxford U Pr.

Layamon, jt. auth. see Wace, Robert.

Layard, et al. Images of the Untouched. Thomas, Gail & Stroud, Joanne, eds. LC 81-84496. 201p. (Orig.). 1982. pap. text ed. 13.50 (ISBN 0-88214-317-4). Spring Pubns.

Layard, Richard, et al. Microeconomic Theory. (Illus.). 1978. text ed. 26.95 (ISBN 0-07-036786-8, C). McGraw.

Laybourne, Gerry B., jt. auth. see Gaffney, Maureen.

Laybourne, Kit. The Animation Book. 1978. 15.95 (ISBN 0-517-53389-8); pap. 10.95 (ISBN 0-517-52946-7). Crown.

Laycock, A. L. Adolescence & Social Work. (Library of Social Work). 1970. 12.95x (ISBN 0-7100-6781-X); pap. 5.95 (ISBN 0-7100-6782-8). Routledge & Kegan.

Laycock, Ellen, jt. auth. see Laycock, George.

Laycock, Frank. Gifted Children. 1979. pap. text ed. 10.95x (ISBN 0-673-15142-5). Scott F.

Laycock, George. The Birdwatcher's Bible. LC 74-2532. 192p. 1976. pap. 4.50 (ISBN 0-385-09611-9). Doubleday.

--Complete Beginner's Guide to Photography. (Illus.). 1979. PLB 9.95 (ISBN 0-385-13265-4). Doubleday.

--Deer Hunter's Bible. rev. ed. LC 76-50875. 1971. softbound 4.95 (ISBN 0-385-12896-7). Doubleday.

--Does Your Pet Have a Sixth Sense. LC 79-7689. (Illus.). 1980. PLB 7.95a o.p. (ISBN 0-385-14998-0). Doubleday.

--How to Buy & Enjoy a Small Farm: Your Comprehensive Guide to the Country Life. (Illus.). 1978. pap. 5.95 o.p. (ISBN 0-679-50865-1). McKay.

--Shotgunner's Bible. LC 69-15216. 1969. pap. 4.95 (ISBN 0-385-00978-X). Doubleday.

--Strange Monsters & Great Searches. LC 72-76185. 120p. (gr. 4-7). 1973. 7.95 o.p. (ISBN 0-385-03818-6). Doubleday.

Laycock, George & Laycock, Ellen. The Ohio Valley Guide to America's Heartland. LC 81-43579. (Illus.). 400p. 1983. pap. 10.95 (ISBN 0-385-17591-4, Dolp). Doubleday.

Laycock, Mary, jt. auth. see Stokes, William T.

Laycock, Mary, ed. see Bureloff, Morris.

Layden, Milton. Escaping the Hostility Trap: The One Sure Way to Deal with Impossible People. LC 76-54672. 1977. pap. 3.95 (ISBN 0-13-283606-8); 7.95 (ISBN 0-13-283580-0). P-H.

Lay-Dopyera, Margaret Z. & Dopyera, John E. Becoming a Teacher of Young Children. 2nd ed. 576p. 1982. text ed. 18.95 (ISBN 0-669-03357-X); instr's guide 1.95 (ISBN 0-669-03625-0). Heath.

Laye, Camara. The Dark Child. Kirkup, James, et al, trs. from Fr. 188p. 1954. 5.95 o.p. (ISBN 0-374-13472-3); pap. 4.95 (ISBN 0-374-50768-6, N365). FS&G.

--Enfant Noir. Hutchinson, Joyce A., ed. 1966. pap. text ed. 6.50x (ISBN 0-521-05357-9). Cambridge U Pr.

Layer & Vegh. Turkish Rugs. 1982. 95.00x (ISBN 0-903580-20-9, Pub. by Element Bks). State Mutual Bk.

Layhe, Robert, jt. ed. see Andrews, Peter P.

Layish, Aharon. Marriage, Divorce & Succession in the Druz Family: A Study Based on Decisions of Druz Arbitrators & Religious Courts in Israel & the Golan Heights. (Social, Economic & Political Studies of the Middle East Ser.: Vol. 31). (Illus.). xxv, 474p. 1982. pap. write for info. (ISBN 90-04-06412-5). E J Brill.

Layman, Dale P. The Terminology of Anatomy & Physiology: A Programmed Approach. LC 82-13448. 293p. 1983. pap. 10.95 (ISBN 0-471-86262-2, Pub. by Wiley Med). Wiley.

Layman, Donald, ed. see Levin, Paul.

Layman, N. Kathryn & Renner, Adrienne G. Word Processors: A Programmed Training Guide with Practical Applications. (Illus.). 352p. 1981. text ed. 22.95 (ISBN 0-13-963520-3). P-H.

Layman, Richard, jt. ed. see Bruccoli, Matthew J.

Laymon, Charles M., jt. ed. see Weaver, Horace R.

Laymon, Richard. Out Are the Lights. 224p. (Orig.) 1983. pap. 2.75 (ISBN 0-446-90519-4). Warner Bks.

Layne, Ken, ed. Tune-up Service Manual. (Illus.). 1978. pap. 4.95 o.p. (ISBN 0-913040-44-4, Gousha Chek-Chart); pap. text ed. 7.80 o.p. (ISBN 0-913040-29-0). H M Gousha.

Layne, Ken & Clark, Gordon, eds. Car Service. (Illus.). 1979. pap. text ed. 8.00 o.p. (ISBN 0-913040-53-3, Gousha Chek-Chart). H M Gousha.

Layng, Anthony. The Carib Reserve: Identity & Security in the West Indies. LC 82-21739. (Illus.). 200p. (Orig.). 1983. lib. bdg. 20.75 (ISBN 0-8191-2808-2); pap. text ed. 9.75 (ISBN 0-8191-2809-0). U Pr of Amer.

Layton, C. W. Dictionary of Nautical Words & Terms. 2nd, rev. ed. 395p. 1982. text ed. 32.50x (ISBN 0-85174-422-2). Sheridan.

Layton, Gustave. The Dreamy, Romantic & Symbolic Art by Fantin-Latour. (Art Library of the Great Masters). (Illus.). 133p. 1983. 59.85 (ISBN 0-86650-057-X). Gloucester Art.

Layton, J. M. Multivariable Control Theory. (IEE Control Engineering Ser.: No. 1). (Illus.). 247p. 1976. casebound 39.00 (ISBN 0-901223-89-1). Inst Elect Eng.

Layton, Monique, tr. see Levi-Strauss, Claude.

Layton, R. C., jt. auth. see Marr, G. W.

Layton, W. I. Essential Business Mathematics. LC 77-24766. 312p. 1977. Repr. of 1965 ed. lib. bdg. 15.50 (ISBN 0-88275-596-X). Krieger.

Layton-Henry, Zig, ed. Conservative Politics in Western Europe. LC 81-710. 320p. 1982. 25.00x (ISBN 0-312-16418-1). St Martin.

Laz, Medard. Learning to Live Again. 1983. pap. 1.50 (ISBN 0-89243-176-8). Liguori Pubns.

--Lift up My Spirit, Lord. (Emmuas Book Ser.). 1977. pap. 1.95 o.p. (ISBN 0-8091-1991-9). Paulist Pr.

Lazar, jt. auth. see Cedeno.

Lazar, Irving. As the Twig Is Bent: Lasting Effects of Early Education. (Consortium for Longitudinal Studies). 469p. 1983. text ed. write for info. (ISBN 0-89859-271-2). L Erlbaum Assocs.

Lazar, Irwin. Electrical Systems Analysis & Design for Industrial Plants. (Illus.). 1980. 27.00 (ISBN 0-07-036789-2). McGraw.

Lazar, Leonard. Transnational Economic & Monetary Law Transactions & Contracts, 7 vols. LC 77-8398. 1977. Binders 1-3. looseleaf 85.00 ea. (ISBN 0-379-10215-3); 595.00 set (ISBN 0-686-77298-9); Rel. 1-2. 170.00 ea.; Rel. 3. 85.00. Oceana.

Lazar, Marlene & Lazar, Stephen H. Financial Aid for College-Bound Athletes. 288p. 1982. 14.95 (ISBN 0-668-05499-9); pap. 8.95 (ISBN 0-668-05500-6). Arco.

Lazar, Maslu, ed. Play Durrenmatt. (Interplay Ser.: Vol. 3). 200p. 1983. pap. price not set (ISBN 0-89003-129-0, 82-50986); price not set (ISBN 0-89003-130-4). Undena Pubns.

Lazar, Moshe, ed. The Anxious Subject: Nightmares & Daymares in Literature, Art & Film. LC 82-70791. (Interplay Ser.: Vol. 2). 208p. 1982. 20.00x (ISBN 0-89003-117-7); pap. 15.50x (ISBN 0-89003-116-9). Undena Pubns.

--The Dream & the Play: Ionesco's Theatrical Quest. LC 81-71734. (Interplay Ser.: Vol. 1). 184p. (Orig.). 1982. 20.50x (ISBN 0-89003-109-6); pap. 15.50x (ISBN 0-89003-108-8). Undena Pubns.

Lazar, Stephen H., jt. auth. see Lazar, Marlene.

Lazar, Wendy P. Jewish Holiday Book. LC 76-42342. (gr. 6-12). 1977. 12.95a o.p. (ISBN 0-385-11426-5); PLB (ISBN 0-385-11427-3). Doubleday.

Lazard, Naomi. The Moonlit Upper Deckerina. LC 76-57519. 65p. 1977. pap. 3.95 (ISBN 0-8180-1540-3). Sheep Meadow.

Lazare, jt. auth. see Burgess, A. W.

Lazare, Aaron, jt. auth. see Burgess, Ann W.

Lazarev, Viktor N., compiled by. Pages from the History of Novgorodian Painting. Strelkova, G. V., tr. 1980. 12.50 (ISBN 0-89893-042-1). CDP.

Lazarides, M. The Tropical Grasses of Southeast Asia: Excluding Bamboos. 350p. 1980. lib. bdg. 32.00 (ISBN 3-7682-1255-6). Lubrecht & Cramer.

Lazarnick, George. Netsuke & Inro Artists, & How to Read Their Signatures, 2 vols. LC 81-51945. (Illus.). 1376p. 1982. Set. 475.00 (ISBN 0-917064-02-X); Vol. 1. (ISBN 0-917064-03-8); Vol. 2. (ISBN 0-917064-04-6); Set. signed leather bd. 950.00 (ISBN 0-686-79507-5). Reed Pubs HI.

Lazaro, Timothy. Urban Hydrology: A Multidisciplinary Perspective. LC 79-55149. 1979. 29.95 (ISBN 0-250-40330-7). Ann Arbor Science.

Lazarsfeld, Patricia K., ed. The Varied Sociology of Paul Lazarsfeld. 400p. 1982. 35.00x (ISBN 0-231-05122-0, 81-24205); pap. 17.50 (ISBN 0-231-05123-9). Columbia U Pr.

Lazarus, Arnold. Multimodal Behavior Therapy. LC 76-4464. (Behavior Modification Ser.: Vol. 1). 1976. text ed. 18.95 (ISBN 0-8261-2160-8). Springer Pub.

Lazarus, Arnold & Fay, Allen. I Can If I Want to. 1977. pap. 2.95 (ISBN 0-446-30734-3). Warner Bks.

Lazarus, Arnold A. Behavior Therapy & Beyond. (Psychology Ser.). (Illus.). 300p. 1971. text ed. 29.00 (ISBN 0-07-036800-7, C). McGraw.

--In the Mind's Eye. 6.95 (ISBN 0-686-36767-7). Inst Rat Liv.

--The Practical of Multimodal Therapy. 18.95 (ISBN 0-686-36778-2). Inst Rat Liv.

--The Practice of Multimodal Therapy. (Illus.). 256p. 1980. 19.95 (ISBN 0-07-036813-9, P&RB). McGraw.

Lazarus, Harold, jt. auth. see Tomeski, Edward.

Lazarus, Lois. Country Is My Music! LC 79-27868. (Illus.). 192p. (gr. 7 up). 1980. PLB 8.29 o.p. (ISBN 0-671-32953-7). Messner.

Lazarus, Mitchell. Educating the Handicapped: Where We've Been, Where We're Going. 1980. pap. 11.95 o.p. (ISBN 0-87545-019-9). Natl Sch PR.

Lazarus, Pat. Keep Your Pet Healthy the Natural Way. 224p. 1983. 12.95 (ISBN 0-672-52726-X). Bobbs.

Lazarus, Richard. Patterns of Adjustment. 3rd ed. (Illus.). 448p. 1976. text ed. 27.50 (ISBN 0-07-036802-3, C); instructor's manual 7.95 (ISBN 0-07-036803-1). McGraw.

Lazarus, Richard S. & Monat, Alan. Personality. 3rd ed. (Foundations of Modern Psychology Ser.). (Illus.). 1979. text ed. 19.95 (ISBN 0-13-657916-7); pap. text ed. 14.95 (ISBN 0-13-657908-6). P-H.

Lazarus, S. The Parenthood Handbook. 1980. pap. 13.25 (ISBN 0-201-04370-X). A-W.

Lazarus, Stephen M. Self-Assessment of Current Knowledge in Urology. 2nd ed. 1974. spiral bdg. 15.50 (ISBN 0-87488-251-6). Med Exam.

Lazarus, Stephen M., ed. Urology. 4th ed. (Medical Examination Review Bk.: Vol. 14). 1977. pap. 23.00 (ISBN 0-87488-114-5). Med Exam.

Lazarus-Yafeh, Hava. Some Religious Aspects of Islam: A Collection of Articles. xii, 181p. 1981. text ed. 25.75x (ISBN 90-04-06329-3, Pub. by E J Brill Holland). Humanities.

LaZebnik, Edith. Such a Life. LC 78-759. 1978. 8.95 o.p. (ISBN 0-688-03280-X). Morrow.

Lazell, Barry, jt. auth. see Rees, Dafydd.

Lazenby, David & Phillips, Paul. Cutting for Construction: A Handbook of Methods & Applications of Hard Cutting & Breaking on Site. LC 78-40610. 116p. 1978. 29.95x o.s.i. (ISBN 0-470-26437-3). Halsted Pr.

Lazenby, Walter. Arthur Wing Pinero. (English Authors Ser.: No. 150). lib. bdg. 10.95 o.p. (ISBN 0-8057-1444-8, Twayne). G K Hall.

Lazer & Culley. Marketing Management: Foundations & Practices. 1983. text ed. 28.95 (ISBN 0-686-84533-1, BS28); instr's. manual avail. HM.

Lazer, Ellen A., ed. The Teleconferencing Handbook: A Guide to Cost-Effective Communication. Elton, Martin C., et al. LC 82-18739. (Communications Library). 200p. 1983. text ed. 34.95 (ISBN 0-86729-022-6). Knowledge Indus.

Lazer, Harriet L., jt. auth. see Walker, James W.

Lazer, William & Culley, James. Marketing Management: Foundations & Practices. LC 82-84160. 820p. 1983. 26.95 (ISBN 0-395-32716-4); write for info. instr's. manual (ISBN 0-395-33178-1). HM.

Lazerowitz, Morris, jt. ed. see Ambrose, Alice.

Lazerson, Marvin & Grubb, W. Norton. Broken Promises: How Americans Fail Their Children. 1982. 20.75 (ISBN 0-465-00774-0). Basic.

Lazerson, Marvin & Grubb, W. Norton, eds. American Education & Vocationalism: A Documentary History 1870-1970. LC 73-87511. 1974. text ed. 10.00x (ISBN 0-8077-2413-0); pap. text ed. 5.00x (ISBN 0-8077-2414-9). Tchrs Coll.

Lazes, Peter, ed. The Handbook of Health Education. LC 79-50. 456p. 1979. 39.50 (ISBN 0-89443-085-8). Aspen Systems.

Laznicka, M. Physics of Solid Surfaces. (Studies in Surface Science & Catalysts: Vol. 9). 1982. 66.00 (ISBN 0-444-99716-4). Elsevier.

Lazo-Margain, A., ed. see Ramirez-Vazquez, P.

Lazreg, Marnia. The Emergence of Classes in Algeria: Colonialism & Socio-Political Change. LC 76-7955. (Westview Special Studies on Social Political, & Economic Development Ser). 250p. 1976. 32.50 o.p. (ISBN 0-89158-107-3). Westview.

Lazzarino, Alex A., jt. auth. see Hayes, E. Kent.

Lazzarino, Graziana, et al. Prego! An Invitation to Italian. 544p. 1980. text ed. 21.00 (ISBN 0-394-32376-9); wkbk. 8.00 (ISBN 0-394-32538-9); lab manual 8.00 (ISBN 0-394-32539-7); tape program 200.00 (ISBN 0-394-32541-9). Random.

Lazzaro. Experiences Pour Servir a L'histoire de la Generation des Animaux et des Plantes Avec une Ebauche de L'histoire des Etres Organises Avant Leur Fecondation. Repr. of 1785 ed. 127.00 o.p. (ISBN 0-8287-1374-X). Clearwater Pub.

Lazzaro, Victor. Systems & Procedures: A Handbook for Business & Industry. 2nd ed. 1968. text ed. 29.95 (ISBN 0-13-881425-2). P-H.

Lazzerini, Edward J., jt. auth. see Yang, Richard.

LBJ School of Public Affairs. The Supply of Physicians & Physicians' Incomes Alternative Projections of the Future. (Occasional Paper Ser.: No. 1). 2.50 o.p. (ISBN 0-686-10606-7). LBJ Sch Public Affairs.

Le Corbusier. City of Tomorrow. (Illus.). 1971. pap. 8.95x (ISBN 0-262-62017-0). MIT Pr.

Lea, Elizabeth E. A Quaker Woman's Cookbook: The Domestic Cookery of Elizabeth Ellicott Lea. Weaver, William W., ed. LC 82-60260. 402p. 1982. 20.00 (ISBN 0-8122-7848-8). U of Pa Pr.

Lea, F. Shelley & the Romantic Revolution. LC 71-164028. (Studies in Shelley, No. 25). 1971. Repr. of 1945 ed. lib. bdg. 52.95x (ISBN 0-8383-1328-0). Haskell.

Lea, Henry C. Superstition & Force. 2nd rev. ed. LC 68-19288. xii, 480p. Repr. of 1870 ed. lib. bdg. 19.25x (ISBN 0-8371-0142-5, LESF). Greenwood.

Lea, John P., jt. auth. see Murison, Hamish S.

Lea, Robert N., jt. auth. see Miller, Daniel J.
Lea, Tom. The Wonderful Country. 1979. lib. bdg. 9.95 (ISBN 0-8398-2587-0, Gregg). G K Hall.
Lea, W. Trends in Speech Recognition. 1980. text ed. 36.00 (ISBN 0-13-930768-0). P-H.
Lea, Wayne A. Selecting, Designing, & Using Speech Recognizers. (Speech Technology Ser.). (Illus.). 400p. 1982. 74.00 (ISBN 0-686-37644-7); Student Ed. 49.00 (ISBN 0-686-37645-5). Speech Science.
Leab, Daniel J., jt. ed. see Leab, Katherine K.
Leab, Katherine, ed. American Book Prices. 1982. Vol. 87. o. p. 87.00 (ISBN 0-914022-37-7); Vol. 88. 88.95 (ISBN 0-914022-39-3). Am Bk Prices.
--American Book Prices Current Index, 1975-1979, 2 Vols. 1980. 250.00 (ISBN 0-686-98176-6). Am Bk Prices.
Leab, Katherine K. & Leab, Daniel J., eds. American Book Prices Current, Vol. 87. 1050p. 1982. 87.95 o.p. (ISBN 0-914022-12-1). Bancroft Parkman.
Leach. Intergovernmental Relations in the 1980's. (Annuals of Public Administration Ser.). 128p. 1983. 19.75 (ISBN 0-8247-1742-2). Dekker.
Leach, Alison. The Amazing Fact Book of Weapons, Vol. 12. LC 80-65594. (Illus.). 32p. (Orig.). (gr. 4 up). 1980. 5.95 (ISBN 0-86550-022-3); PLB 8.95 (ISBN 0-686-96987-1); pap. 2.95 (ISBN 0-86550-023-1). A & P Bks.
Leach, Bernard. Potter's Book. (gr. 9-12). o. p. 20.00 (ISBN 0-693-01117-3); pap. 10.00 (ISBN 0-693-01157-2). Transatlantic.
Leach, C. Introduction to Statistics: A Nonparametric Approach for the Social Sciences. 339p. 1979. 64.95 (ISBN 0-471-99743-9, Pub. by Wiley-Interscience); pap. 21.95 (ISBN 0-471-99742-0). Wiley.
Leach, Christopher. The Great Book Raid. LC 79-14137. (gr. 5-7). 1979. 7.95 o.p. (ISBN 0-7232-6174-1). Warne.
--Letter to a Younger Son. 1982. pap. 2.25 (ISBN 0-451-11920-7, AE1920, Sig). NAL.
--Meeting Miss Hannah. LC 79-21818. (gr. 5-9). 1980. 7.95g o.p. (ISBN 0-7232-6178-4). Warne.
--Rosalinda. LC 77-15923. (gr. 5 up). 1978. 6.95 o.p. (ISBN 0-7232-6153-9). Warne.
--Texas Station. 256p. 15.95 (ISBN 0-15-188762-4). HarBraceJ.
Leach, D. Mathematics for Electronics. 1979. 21.95 (ISBN 0-8359-4277-5); students manual avail. (ISBN 0-8359-4278-3). Reston.
Leach, D. J. & Raybould, E. C. Learning & Behaviour Difficulties in School. (Psychology & Education Ser.). 1977. text ed. 11.75x o.p. (ISBN 0-7291-0076-6); pap. text ed. 5.25x o.p. (ISBN 0-7291-0071-5). Humanities.
Leach, Donald, jt. auth. see Malvino, A. P.
Leach, Donald, jt. auth. see Malvino, Albert P.
Leach, Donald P. Basic Electric Circuits. 2nd ed. LC 75-35751. 637p. 1976. text ed. 29.95 (ISBN 0-471-52003-9); solution manual 4.00x (ISBN 0-471-01713-2). Wiley.
--Experiments in Digital Principles. (Illus.). 128p. 1976. text ed. 18.95 (ISBN 0-07-036915-1, G). McGraw.
--Experiments in Digital Principles. 2nd ed. (Illus.). 176p. 1980. 18.95x (ISBN 0-07-036916-X, G); instr's guide 2.50 (ISBN 0-07-036917-8); instr's guide 2.50. McGraw.
Leach, Donald P., jt. auth. see Malvino, Albert P.
Leach, Douglas E. The Northern Colonial Frontier, 1607-1763. LC 66-10083. (Histories of the American Frontier Ser.). (Illus.). 282p. 1966. pap. 9.95x (ISBN 0-8263-0337-4). U of NM Pr.
Leach, E. R. Rethinking Anthropology. (Monographs on Social Anthropology Ser: No. 22). 1971. text ed. 24.25x (ISBN 0-391-02078-1, Athlone Pr); pap. text ed. 12.50x (ISBN 0-391-00146-9). Humanities.
Leach, Edmund, ed. Structural Study of Myth & Totemism. (Orig.). 1968. pap. 10.95 (ISBN 0-422-72530-7, Pub by Tavistock England). Methuen Inc.
Leach, Edmund R. Aspects of Caste in South India, Ceylon & North West Pakistan. (Cambridge Papers in Social Anthropology: No. 2). (Illus.). 1971. 17.95 o.p. (ISBN 0-521-07729-X); pap. 9.95x (ISBN 0-521-09664-2). Cambridge U Pr.
--Culture & Communication. LC 75-30439. (Themes in the Social Sciences Ser.). (Illus.). 120p. 1976. 18.95 (ISBN 0-521-21131-X); pap. 7.95x (ISBN 0-521-29052-X). Cambridge U Pr.
--Dialectic in Practical Religion. (Cambridge Papers in Social Anthropology: No. 5). 27.95 (ISBN 0-521-05525-3). Cambridge U Pr.
--Pul Eliya: A Village in Ceylon. 1961. 29.95 (ISBN 0-521-05524-5). Cambridge U Pr.
Leach, Edmund R. & Mukherjee, Soumyendra N. Elites in South Asia. (Illus.). 1970. 32.50 (ISBN 0-521-07710-9). Cambridge U Pr.
Leach, George. Hope for Healing. LC 78-70231. 160p. 1978. pap. 6.95 o.p. (ISBN 0-8091-2178-6). Paulist Pr.
Leach, H. W., jt. auth. see Beakley, George C.
Leach, Ilo M. Vocabulario Ocaina. (Peruvian Linguistic Ser: No. 4). 176p. 1969. pap. 2.50x (ISBN 0-88312-662-1); microfiche 2.25 (ISBN 0-88312-364-9). Summer Inst Ling.
Leach, K. G. The Physical Aspects of Radioisotopic Organ Imaging. 1976. 25.00x (ISBN 0-686-99803-0, Pub. by Brit Inst Radiology England). State Mutual Bk.
Leach, M. Logic & Boolean Algebra. (Finite Math Text Ser.). write for info. (ISBN 0-685-84475-7). J W Wills.
--Statistics: An Introduction. (Finite Math Text Ser.). write for info. (ISBN 0-685-84476-5). J W Wills.
Leach, Maria. The Lion Sneezed: Folktales & Myths of the Cat. LC 77-3665. (gr. 3-5). 1977. 9.57i (ISBN 0-690-01364-7, TYC-J). Har-Row.
--Noodles, Nitwits & Numskulls. LC 61-14112. (Illus.). (gr. 3-5). 1961. PLB 6.99 o.s.i. (ISBN 0-529-03662-2, Philomel). Putnam Pub Group.
--Riddle Me, Riddle Me, Ree. 144p. (gr. 3 up). 1977. pap. 1.50 o.p. (ISBN 0-14-030960-8, Puffin). Penguin.
--The Thing at the Foot of My Bed. (gr. 4-5). 1977. pap. 2.25 (ISBN 0-440-48773-0, YB). Dell.
--Thing at the Foot of the Bed. LC 59-6658. (Illus.). (gr. 3-5). 1959. PLB 7.99 o.p. (ISBN 0-399-61207-6, Philomel). Putnam Pub Group.
--Whistle in the Graveyard: Folktales to Chill Your Bones. (Illus.). (gr. 3-7). 1982. pap. 3.50 (ISBN 0-14-031529-2, Puffin). Penguin.
Leach, Mark, ed. Italian Masters of the Seventeenth Century, Vols. 44,45. (Illus.). 1982. 120.00 (ISBN 0-89835-041-7). Abaris Bks.
Leach, Michael. Don't Call Me Orphan! LC 78-26928. 1979. 8.95 (ISBN 0-664-32645-5). Westminster.
Leach, Penelope. Babyhood. 2nd, Enl. ed. LC 82-48881. 1983. 17.95 (ISBN 0-394-53092-6); pap. 9.95 (ISBN 0-394-71436-9). Knopf.
--Your Baby & Child: From Birth to Age Five. pap. 11.95 (ISBN 0-394-73509-9). Knopf.
Leach, Peter, ed. Archaeology in Kent to AD 1500. (CBA Research Report: No. 48). 144p. 1982. pap. text ed. 31.50x (ISBN 0-906780-18-7, 50019, Pub. by Coun Brit Archaeology England). Humanities.
Leach, R. & Palmer, R., eds. Folk Music in School. LC 77-71416. (Resources of Music Ser.). 1978. 18.95 (ISBN 0-521-21595-1); pap. 8.95 (ISBN 0-521-29206-9). Cambridge U Pr.
Leach, R. M., jt. auth. see Milton, J. H.
Leach, Richard H., jt. auth. see Mason, Alpheus T.
Leach, Robert E. & Hoaglund, Franklin T. Controversies in Orthopaedic Surgery. (Illus.). 516p. 1982. 49.50 (ISBN 0-7216-5657-9). Saunders.
Leach, S. A., ed. Dental Plaque & Surface Interactions in the Oral Cavity: Proceedings. (Illus.). 340p. 1980. 40.00 o.p. (ISBN 0-904147-15-0); pap. 23.00 (ISBN 0-904147-16-9). IRL Pr.
Leach, S. A., jt. ed. see Frank, R. M.
Leach, Sid D. Techniques of Interior Design Rendering & Presentation. 1978. 34.50 (ISBN 0-07-036805-8, P&RB). McGraw.
--Techniques of Interior Rendering & Design Presentation. (Illus.). 200p. 1983. 29.95 (ISBN 0-07-036806-6, P&RB). McGraw.
Leach, Virgil. Attitudes I. 1979. pap. 3.55 (ISBN 0-89137-803-0). Quality Pubns.
Leach, W. Barton, jt. auth. see Casner, A. James.
Leacock, Eleanor B. & Lee, Richard B., eds. Politics & History in Band Societies. (Illus.). 368p. 1982. 44.50 (ISBN 0-521-24063-8); pap. 17.95 (ISBN 0-521-28412-0). Cambridge U Pr.
Leacock, Stephen. Mark Twain. LC 73-21633. (Mark Twain Ser., No. 76). 1974. lib. bdg. 49.95x o.p. (ISBN 0-8383-1789-8). Haskell.
Leadbetter, M. R., et al. Extremes & Related Properties of Random Sequences & Processes. (Springer Series in Statistics). (Illus.). 368p. 1982. 36.00 (ISBN 0-387-90731-9). Springer-Verlag.
Leader, Elliot & Predazzi, Enrico. An Introduction to Gauge Theories & the "New Physics". LC 81-3860. (Illus.). 400p. 1982. 65.00 (ISBN 0-521-23375-5); pap. 27.50 (ISBN 0-521-29937-3). Cambridge U Pr.
Leader, John P., jt. ed. see Macknight, Anthony D.
Leader, Mary. The Pact. (Fic). 1977. 8.95 o.p. (ISBN 0-698-10724-1, Coward). Putnam Pub Group.
--Salem's Children. LC 78-24115. 1979. 10.95 o.p. (ISBN 0-698-10724-1, Coward). Putnam Pub Group.
Leadley-Brown, Alison. Ecology of Fresh Water. LC 75-156140. (Illus.). 1971. 7.95x o.p. (ISBN 0-674-22447-7). Harvard U Pr.
Leaf, Alexander & Cotran, Ramzi. Renal Pathophysiology. 2nd ed. (Illus.). 1980. text ed. 24.95x (ISBN 0-19-502688-8); pap. text ed. 15.95x (ISBN 0-19-502689-6). Oxford U Pr.
Leaf, Alexander, et al, eds. Renal Pathophysiology - Recent Advances. 293p. 1980. text ed. 39.00 (ISBN 0-89004-399-X). Raven.
Leaf, Carol A., jt. auth. see Fordham, Sheldon L.
Leaf, David. The Beach Boys & the California Myth. LC 77-88432. (Illus.). 1978. 14.95 o.p. (ISBN 0-448-14625-8, D&G); pap. 7.95 o.p. (ISBN 0-448-14626-6, Today Press). Putnam Pub Group.
Leaf, David, ed. see Gibb, Robin, et al.
Leaf, Hayim, jt. ed. see Ben-Asher, Naomi.
Leaf, Munro. Manners Can Be Fun. rev. ed. LC 58-5611. (Illus.). (gr. k-3). 1958. 7.95 o.p. (ISBN 0-686-96735-6, JBL-J); PLB 10.89 (ISBN 0-397-31603-8). Har-Row.
--Metric Can Be Fun. LC 75-29223. (gr. 1-3). 1976. 10.89 (ISBN 0-397-31679-8, JBL-J); pap. 1.95 (ISBN 0-397-31680-1). Har-Row.
--Safety Can Be Fun. rev. ed. LC 61-14579. (Illus.). (gr. k-3). 1961. 10.89 (ISBN 0-397-31593-7, JBL-J). Har-Row.
Leaf, Murray J. Information & Behavior in a Sikh Village: Social Organization Reconsidered. LC 78-172390. (Illus.). 300p. 1972. 30.00x (ISBN 0-520-02115-0). U of Cal Pr.
Leaf, Russell C., ed. see Barron, Frank.
Leaf, Ruth. Intaglio Printmaking Techniques. (Illus., Orig.). 1976. 25.00 o.p. (ISBN 0-8230-2554-3). Watson-Guptill.
Leafe, Margaret. Secretarial Duties: Revision Notes & Exercises. (Illus.). 96p. 1981. pap. 7.50 (ISBN 0-7131-0553-4). Intl Ideas.
League of Nations. Taxation of Foreign & National Enterprises, 5 vols. in 4. 1933. 100.00 o.s.i. (ISBN 0-379-20875-X). Oceana.
League of Woman Voters of New York State. The Judicial System in New York State. rev. ed. Anderson, Claire, ed. (Illus.). 39p. 1982. pap. 2.75 (ISBN 0-938588-04-4). LWV NYS.
League of Women Voters Education Fund. Choosing the President. LC 79-47989. 108p. 1980. pap. 1.95 o.p. (ISBN 0-8407-5726-3). Nelson.
--Energy Dilemmas: An Overview of U. S. Energy Problems & Issues. (Illus.). 39p. 1977. pap. 1.00 o.p. (ISBN 0-89959-102-7, 688); pap. 0.80 ea. 5-9 copies, .70 ea. 10-49 copies, 0.60 ea. 50 or more copies o.p. LWV US.
--Energy Options: Examining Sources & Defining Government's Role. (Illus.). 1977. pap. 1.00 o.p. (ISBN 0-89959-103-5, 628); pap. 0.80 ea. 5-9 copies, .70 ea. 10-49 copies, .60 ea. 50 copies or more o.p. LWV US.
--Know Your Community. 1972. pap. 0.75 o.p. (ISBN 0-89959-056-X, 288). LWV US.
--A Nuclear Power Primer: Issues for Citizens. 50p. 1981. pap. 5.95 (ISBN 0-89959-290-2, 575). LWV US.
--A Nuclear Waste Primer. (Illus.). 64p. 1982. pap. 5.95 (ISBN 0-89959-253-8, 391). LWV US.
--School Finance Reform in the Nineteen Eighties: Social Needs & the New Federalism. 64p. 1982. pap. 3.50 (ISBN 0-89959-327-5, 523). LWV US.
League of Women Voters Education Fund, ed. School Finance Reform in the Nineteen Eighties. 64p. 1982. 3.50 o.p. (ISBN 0-89959-315-1, 640). LWV US.
League of Women Voters of Minnesota. How Will We Pay for Our Schools? Financing Public Education in Minnesota (K-12) (Illus.). 59p. (Orig.). 1982. pap. text ed. 5.00 (ISBN 0-939816-02-4). LWV MN.
League of Women Voters of New Jersey. New Jersey: Spotlight on Government. 1978. 25.00x o.p. (ISBN 0-8135-0854-1); pap. 12.50x o.p. (ISBN 0-8135-0860-6). Rutgers U Pr.
League of Women Voters Staff. North Carolina: Our State Government. (Illus.). 116p. 1982. lib. bdg. 12.95 (ISBN 0-89089-029-3). Carolina Acad.
Leahey, Thomas H. A History of Psychology. (Illus.). 1980. text ed. 23.95 (ISBN 0-13-391755-X). P-H.
Leahy, Christopher W. The Birdwatcher's Companion: An Encyclopedic Handbook of North American Birdlife. (Illus.). 900p. 1982. 29.50 (ISBN 0-8090-3036-5). Hill & Wang.
Leahy, Irene M., et al. The Nurse & Radiotherapy: A Manual for Daily Care. LC 78-12296. 172p. 1978. pap. text ed. 11.95 o.p. (ISBN 0-8016-2896-2). Mosby.
Leahy, K., et al. Community Health Nursing. 4th ed. 432p. 1982. 19.95x (ISBN 0-07-036834-1). McGraw.
Leahy, Kathleen M., et al. Community Health Nursing. 3rd ed. (Illus.). 1977. text ed. 17.95 (ISBN 0-07-036832-5, HP). McGraw.
Leahy, Syrell R. Circle of Love. 1980. 10.95 (ISBN 0-399-12475-6). Putnam Pub Group.
--Circle of Love. 240p. 1982. 2.50 (ISBN 0-553-20029-1). Bantam.
--Family Ties. 448p. 1982. 14.95 (ISBN 0-399-12741-0). Putnam Pub Group.
Leahy, William F. Microprocesor Architecture & Programming. LC 77-1552. 252p. Repr. of 1977 ed. text ed. 29.95 (ISBN 0-471-01889-9). Krieger.
--Microprocessor Architecture & Programming. LC 77-1552. 237p. 1977. 29.95 o.p. (ISBN 0-471-01889-9, Pub. by Wiley-Interscience). Wiley.
Leak, J. India: A Practical Guide. 240p. (Orig.). 1982. pap. 11.95 (ISBN 0-933982-29-1, Lascelles). Bradt Ent.
Leake, B. E., jt. auth. see Bowes, D. R.
Leake, Chauncey D. Percival's Medical Ethics: With Supplemental Material. LC 76-8603. 352p. 1975. Repr. of 1927 ed. 17.00 (ISBN 0-88275-176-X). Krieger.
Leake, I. Q. Memoir of the Life & Times of General John Lamb. LC 72-152230. (Era of the American Revolution Ser). 1971. Repr. of 1850 ed. lib. bdg. 59.50 (ISBN 0-306-70122-7). Da Capo.
Leake, John B., jt. auth. see Holmes, Neal J.
Leakey, L. S. Adam's Ancestors: The Evolution of Man & His Culture. pap. 2.95xi o.p. (ISBN 0-06-131019-0, TB1019, Torch). Har-Row.
Leakey, L. S. & Bestor, William S., eds. Adam or Ape: A Sourcebook of Discoveries About Early Man. 540p. 1983. 18.95x (ISBN 0-87073-700-7); pap. text ed. 9.95x (ISBN 0-87073-701-5). Schenkman.
Leakey, L. S. & Tobias, P. V., eds. Olduvai Gorge, Vol. 1 & 2: Nineteen Fifty-One To Nineteen Sixty-One. 1965. Vol. 1. 70.00 (ISBN 0-521-05527-X); Vol. 2. 89.50 (ISBN 0-521-06901-7). Cambridge U Pr.
Leakey, M. D., ed. Olduvai Gorge, Vol. 3: Nineteen Sixty - Nineteen Sixty-Three. 1972. 120.00 (ISBN 0-521-07723-0). Cambridge U Pr.
Leakey, Richard & Lewin, Roger. Origins: What New Discoveries Reveal About the Emergence of Our Species & Its Possible Future. 1977. 17.95 (ISBN 0-525-17194-0); pap. 6.95 (ISBN 0-525-48013-7, 0674-210). Dutton.
Leakey, Richard E. Human Origins. (Illus.). 96p. (YA) 1982. 14.95 (ISBN 0-525-66784-9, 01451-440). Lodestar Bks.
Leaky, Syrell R. A Book of Ruth. 272p. 1982. pap. 2.95 (ISBN 0-553-22582-0). Bantam.
Leal, A. R. Retailing. 160p. 1982. pap. cancelled (ISBN 0-7131-1851-2). Intl Ideas.
Leal, Luis. Breve Historia De la Literatura Hispanoamerica. text ed. 6.00x (ISBN 0-685-55627-1, 31015). Phila Bk Co.
--Mexico: Civilizaciones y Culturas. rev. ed. (Illus.). 1971. pap. text ed. 10.50 (ISBN 0-395-12744-0, 3-32161). HM.
Leal, Magdalena Leon de, jt. auth. see Deere, Carmen.
Leal, Robert B. Drieu la Rochelle. (Twayne's World Authors Ser.). 1982. lib. bdg. 17.95 (ISBN 0-8057-6510-7, Twayne). G K Hall.
Leal, V. N. Coronelismo. Henfrey, J., tr. LC 76-46044. (Cambridge Latin American Studies: No. 28). 1977. 32.50 (ISBN 0-521-21488-2). Cambridge U Pr.
Leamer, Edward E. Specification Searches: Ad Hoc Inference with Nonexperimental Data. LC 77-26855. (Probability & Mathematical Statistics: Applied Probability & Statistics Ser.). 370p. 1978. 43.95x (ISBN 0-471-01520-2, Pub. by Wiley-Interscience). Wiley.
Leamer, Laurence. Ascent: The Spiritual & Physical Quest of Willi Unsoeld. 1982. 16.95 (ISBN 0-671-41734-7). S&S.
--Make-Believe. LC 82-48123. (Illus.). 288p. 1983. 13.41i (ISBN 0-06-015102-1, HarpT). Har-Row.
--Paper Revolutionaries. 1972. pap. 2.95 o.p. (ISBN 0-671-21144-7, Touchstone Bks). S&S.
Leaming, Barbara. Grigori Kozintsev. (Theatrical Arts Ser.). 1980. lib. bdg. 14.95 (ISBN 0-8057-9276-7, Twayne). G K Hall.
--Polanski. 1983. pap. price not set (ISBN 0-671-24986-X, Touchstone Bks). S&S.
--Polanski: A Biography, the Filmaker as Voyeur. 1982. 14.95 (ISBN 0-671-24985-1). S&S.
Leamy & Pile. Grain Boundaries in Semiconductors. (Materials Research Society Symposia Proceedings Ser.: Vol. 5). 1982. 65.00 (ISBN 0-444-00697-4). Elsevier.
Leamy, H. J. see Gilman, J. J.
Lean, Garth. Strangely Warmed. 1979. pap. 4.95 (ISBN 0-8423-6662-8). Tyndale.
Lean, Lim Lin, jt. auth. see Cheok, Cheong Kee.
Lean, Vincent S. Lean's Collectanea, 5 vols. LC 68-26583. 1969. Repr. of 1902 ed. Set. 191.00x (ISBN 0-8103-3203-5). Gale.
Leap, William L., jt. ed. see St. Clair, Robert N.
Leapman, Michael. Companion Guide to New York. (Illus.). 352p. 1983. 15.95 (ISBN 0-13-154682-1); pap. 7.95 (ISBN 0-13-154674-0). P-H.
--More Signs of the Times: A Further Selection of Comic Signs from "the Times Diary". 1976. pap. 2.95 o.p. (ISBN 0-241-89296-1). Transatlantic.
Lear, Edward. A Book of Nonsense. (Illus.). 56p. (gr. 4 up). 1980. 9.95 (ISBN 0-670-18011-4, Studio). Viking Pr.
--The Book of Nonsense, Repr. Of 1846 Ed. Bd. with The English Struwwelpeter. Hoffman, Heinrich. Repr. of 1848 ed; The Fairy Library. Cruikshank, George. Repr. of 1864 ed. LC 75-32161. (Classics of Children's Literature, 1621-1932: Vol. 26). 1976. PLB 38.00 o.s.i. (ISBN 0-8240-2275-0). Garland Pub.
--The Complete Nonsense of Edward Lear. Jackson, Holdrook, ed. (Illus.). 9.00 (ISBN 0-8446-0722-3). Peter Smith.
--An Edward Lear Alphabet. LC 82-10037. (Illus.). 32p. (gr. k-3). 1983. 9.50 (ISBN 0-688-00964-6); PLB 9.12 (ISBN 0-688-00965-4). Lothrop.
--The Owl & the Pussy Cat. LC 77-77869. (gr. k-4). 1977. 6.95 o.p. (ISBN 0-689-30609-1). Atheneum.
--The Owl & the Pussycat. LC 82-12092. (Illus.). 32p. (ps-3). 1983. reinforced binding 12.95 (ISBN 0-8234-0474-9). Holiday.
Lear, Edward, et al. A Book of Nonsense. 1975. 6.95x (ISBN 0-460-00806-4, Evman); pap. 1.95x (ISBN 0-460-01806-X, Evman). Biblio Dist.
Lear, George, jt. auth. see Mosher, Lynn S.
Lear, John. The Powerlifters Manual. (Illus.). 64p. (Orig.). 1982. pap. 4.95 (ISBN 0-686-97935-4, Pub. by EP Publishing England). Sterling.
Lear, Jonathan. Aristotle & Logical Theory. LC 79-20273. (Illus.). 1980. 22.95 (ISBN 0-521-23031-4). Cambridge U Pr.
Lear, Pat. The New Carbohydrate Diet Counter. 64p. 1982. pap. 2.00 (ISBN 0-941990-00-1). Lear.
Lear, Pat, ed. see Rajneesh, Bhagwan S.
Lear, Peter. Spider Girl. 300p. 1980. 10.95 o.p. (ISBN 0-670-66274-7). Viking Pr.

Learmouth, John. Soccer Fundamentals: Basic Techniques & Training for Beginning Players. LC 78-19415. (Illus.). 1979. 8.95 (ISBN 0-312-73132-9); pap. 3.95 (ISBN 0-312-73133-7). St Martin.

Learn, C. R. Bowhunter's Digest. (DBI Bks). 1974. pap. 6.95 o.s.i. (ISBN 0-695-80451-0). Follett.

--The Digest Book of Backpacking. (Sports & Leisure Library). (Illus.). 1979. pap. 2.95 o.s.i. (ISBN 0-695-81282-3). Follett.

Learn, C. R. & Lewis, Jack, eds. Backpacker's Digest. 2nd. rev. ed. (DBI Bks). 288p. (Orig.). 1976. pap. 7.95 o.s.i. (ISBN 0-695-80645-9). Follett.

Learned, M. D., ed. Guide to Manuscript Materials Relating to American History in the German State Archives. 1912. pap. 32.00 (ISBN 0-527-00691-2). Kraus Repr.

Learner, Richard. Astronomy through the Telescope: The 500-year Story of the Instruments, the Inventors & their Discoveries. 224p. 1982. 59.00x (ISBN 0-686-81700-1, Pub. by Evans Bros). State Mutual Bk.

Learning Achievement Corp. Decimals, Percent & Money: Measurement & Transportation. Zak, Therese A., ed. (MATCH Ser.: Bk. 4). (Illus.). 144p. 1981. text ed. 5.80 (ISBN 0-07-037114-8, G). McGraw.

Learning Achievement Corporation. Fractions & Food: Fractions, Decimals & Electronic Communications. Zak, Therese A., ed. (MATCH Ser.: Bk. 3). (Illus.). 144p. 1981. text ed. 5.80 (ISBN 0-07-037113-X, G). McGraw.

--Geometry & Design & Maintenance: Ratio, Proportion, Reading Graphs & Data. Zak, Therese A., ed. (MATCH Ser.: Bk. 5). (Illus.). 128p. 1981. text ed. 5.80 (ISBN 0-07-037115-6, G); tchr's manual for series 3.30 (ISBN 0-07-037116-4). McGraw.

--Multiplication & Energy & Construction: Division & Medicine. Zak, Therese A., ed. (MATCH Ser.: Bk. 2). (Illus.). 144p. 1981. text ed. 5.80 (ISBN 0-07-037112-1, G). McGraw.

--Number Systems, Addition & Personal Communication; Subtraction & Recreation. (MATCH Bks.: Bk. 1). (Illus.). 128p. 1981. 5.80 (ISBN 0-07-037111-3). McGraw.

Learning Institute of North Carolina. Who Cares for Children? A Survey of Child Care Services in North Carolina. 1974. pap. 3.00 (ISBN 0-686-10550-8). Learning Inst NC.

Learning Technology Inc, ed. Library Skills: A Program for Self-Instruction. 1970. text ed. 13.50 (ISBN 0-07-051376-7). McGraw.

--Writing Skills Two: A Program for Self-Instruction. 1970. text ed. 11.95 (ISBN 0-07-051398-8). McGraw.

Learning Technology Inc & Barett, B., eds. Paragraph Patterns: A Program for Self-Instruction. 1970. text ed. 11.95 o.p. (ISBN 0-07-051399-6). McGraw.

Learning Technology Incorporated. Basic Spelling Skills. 2nd ed. Raygor, Alton L., ed. (Basic Skills Ser.). 1979. pap. text ed. 13.50x (ISBN 0-07-044415-3); cassette tapes & transcripts 50.00 (ISBN 0-07-044416-1). McGraw.

Learoyd, Stan. Conservation & Restoration of Antique Furniture. (Illus.). 140p. (Orig.). 1983. pap. 9.95 (ISBN 0-8069-7682-9). Sterling.

Learsi, Rufus. Prince of Judah & Other Stories of a Great Journey. 1962 ed. LC 62-21985. (Illus.). (gr. 5-9). 4.95 (ISBN 0-88400-031-1). Shengold.

LeArta, Moulton. Nature's Medicine Chest, 6 bks. Set. 32.00 (ISBN 0-935596-10-0). Gluten Co.

--Nature's Medicine Chest, Set 2. 96p. 1975. 5.00 (ISBN 0-935596-05-4). Gluten Co.

--Nature's Medicine Chest, Set 3. 96p. 1976. 5.50 (ISBN 0-935596-06-2). Gluten Co.

--Nature's Medicine Chest, Set 5. 96p. 1976. 5.50 (ISBN 0-935596-08-9). Gluten Co.

--Nature's Medicine Chest, Set 6. 96p. 1977. 5.50 (ISBN 0-935596-09-7). Gluten Co.

Leary, Daniel. Macbeth. (Parallel Text Ser.). 1975. pap. 2.95 o.p. (ISBN 0-671-18741-4). Monarch Pr.

Leary, Daniel, ed. Macbeth. (Parallel-Text Shakespeare Ser.). 1975. pap. 2.95 o.p. (ISBN 0-671-18741-4). S&S.

Leary, Daniel J. Shaw's Plays in Performance. LC 82-644184. (Shaw: The Annual of Bernard Shaw Studies: Vol. 3). 268p. 1983. 16.95 (ISBN 0-271-00346-4). Pa St U Pr.

--Voices of Convergence. 1969. 4.95 o.p. (ISBN 0-685-07673-3, 80394). Glencoe.

Leary, Lewis. American Literature: A Study & Research Guide. LC 75-38017. 150p. 1976. text ed. 12.95x o.p. (ISBN 0-312-02520-3); pap. text ed. 5.95x (ISBN 0-312-02555-6). St Martin.

--John Greenleaf Whittier. (United States Authors Ser.). lib. bdg. 10.95 (ISBN 0-8057-0796-4, Twayne). G K Hall.

--Ralph Waldo Emerson: An Interpretive Essay. (United States Authors Ser.). 1980. lib. bdg. 13.95 (ISBN 0-8057-9012-8, Twayne). G K Hall.

Leary, Lewis, intro. by. American Literature to Nineteen Hundred. 1981. pap. 8.95 o.p. (ISBN 0-312-02876-8). St Martin.

Leary, Lewis, ed. see Thoreau, Henry D.

Leary, Lewis, ed. see Twain, Mark.

Leary, Lewis G., ed. Bible When You Want It. Date not set. 1.95 (ISBN 0-8096-1023-X). Follett.

Leary, Susan L. Not Just a Housewife. (Illus.). 64p. 1982. 6.95 (ISBN 0-89962-288-7). Todd & Honeywell.

Leary, T. Interpersonal Diagnosis of Personality: A Functional Theory & Methodology for Personality Evaluation. 518p. 1957. 35.95 (ISBN 0-471-06915-9). Wiley.

Leary, Timothy. Interpersonal Diagnosis of Personality: A Functional Theory & Methodology for Personality Evaluation. (Illus.). 1957. 35.95 (ISBN 0-471-06915-9). Ronald Pr.

--Jail Notes. 1973. pap. 1.50 o.s.i. (ISBN 0-394-17815-7, B367, BC). Grove.

Leary, Virginia. International Labour & National Law. 1981. lib. bdg. 52.50 (ISBN 90-247-2551-8, Pub. by Martinus Nijhoff Netherlands). Kluwer Boston.

Leary, William M., Jr. & Link, Arthur S., eds. The Progressive Era & the Great War: 1896-1920. 2nd ed. LC 78-70030. (Goldentree Bibliographies in American History). 1978. text ed. 22.50x (ISBN 0-88295-574-8); pap. text ed. 13.95x (ISBN 0-88295-575-6). Harlan Davidson.

Leas, Lyle S. Amish Country Cookbook. LC 81-14972. (Illus.). 1983. 16.95 (ISBN 0-87949-200-7). Ashley Bks.

Leasher, Evelyn, compiled by. Oregon Women: A Bio-Bibliography. (Bibliographic Ser.: No. 18). 64p. 1981. pap. 5.00 (ISBN 0-87071-138-5). Oreg St U Pr.

Leaska, Mitchell A., ed. see Woolf, Virginia.

Leason, Barney. Rodeo Drive. 416p. (Orig.). 1981. pap. 3.75 (ISBN 0-523-42054-4). Pinnacle Bks.

Leasor, James. The Red Fort: The Story of the Indian Mutiny of 1857. (Illus.). 384p. 1982. pap. 8.95 (ISBN 0-02-034200-4). Macmillan.

Least Heat Moon, William. Blue Highways: A Journey into America. 1983. 17.00i (ISBN 0-316-35395-7). Little.

Leasure, Jan. Big Bucks for Kids. 128p. (gr. 4-7). 1983. pap. 5.95 (ISBN 0-8362-4211-4). Andrews & McMeel.

Leatham, Aubrey. An Introduction to the Examination of the Cardiovascular System. 2nd ed. (Illus.). 1980. pap. text ed. 7.95x (ISBN 0-19-261194-1). Oxford U Pr.

Leathart, Scott. Trees of the World. LC 76-52282. (Illus.). 1977. 19.95 o.s.i. (ISBN 0-89479-000-5). A & W Pubs.

Leather, Edwin. The Duveen Letter. 224p. 1981. pap. 2.25 o.p. (ISBN 0-523-41542-7). Pinnacle Bks.

Leather, John. The Big Class Racing Yachts. (Illus.). 190p. 1982. 27.50 (ISBN 0-540-07417-9). Sheridan.

--Gaff Rig. LC 70-187291. (Illus.). 1971. 27.50 (ISBN 0-87742-023-8). Intl Marine.

--Sail & Oar. LC 82-48098. (Illus.). 144p. 1982. 20.00 (ISBN 0-87742-161-7). Intl Marine.

Leatherbarrow, David, jt. ed. see Powell, Helen.

Leatherbarrow, William J. Feodor Dostoevsky. (World Authors Ser.). 12.95 (ISBN 0-8057-6480-1, Twayne). G K Hall.

Leatherdale, Clive. Britain & Saudi Arabia 1925-1939: An Imperial Oasis. 200p. 1983. text ed. 37.50x (ISBN 0-7146-3220-1, F Cass Co). Biblio Dist.

Leatherman, Stephen P., ed. Overwash Processes. LC 80-28753. (Benchmark Papers in Geology Ser.: Vol. 58). 400p. 1981. 45.00 (ISBN 0-87933-375-8). Hutchinson Ross.

Leathers. Orientations to Researching Communication. Applbaum, Ronald & Hart, Roderick, eds. LC 77-20988. (MODCOM - Modules in Speech Communication). 1978. pap. text ed. 2.75 (ISBN 0-574-22535-8, 13-5535). SRA.

Leatherwood, Stephen, et al. Marine Mammals of the World, 2 vols. Date not set. 90.00 set (ISBN 0-525-10474-7). Dutton.

Leaton, Gwen, jt. auth. see Kinney, Jean.

Leatz, Christine A. Unwinding: How to Turn Stress into Positive Energy. 182p. 1981. 11.95 o.p. (ISBN 0-13-937888-X); pap. 4.95 o.p. (ISBN 0-13-937870-7). P-H.

Leatzow, Nancy & Neuhauser, Carol. Creating Discipline in the Early Childhood Classroom. (Illus., Orig.). 1983. pap. text ed. 8.95 (ISBN 0-8425-2112-7). BYU Clark Law.

Leavell, L. P., jt. auth. see Bunyan, Juan.

Leavell, Landrum P. The Harvest of the Spirit. LC 76-4373. 96p. 1976. pap. 2.95 o.p. (ISBN 0-8054-1937-3). Broadman.

Leavell, Marta B. Hacia un Hogar Cristiano. Quarles, J. C., tr. from Eng. Orig. Title: Building a Christian Home. 157p. 1981. Repr. of 1978 ed. pap. 2.25 (ISBN 0-311-46007-0). Casa Bautista.

Leavenworth, C., jt. auth. see Hendricks, C.

Leavenworth, Carol. Love & Commitment: You Don't Have to Settle for Less. (Illus.). 174p. 1981. 11.95t (ISBN 0-13-540971-3, Spec); pap. 5.95 (ISBN 0-13-540963-2). P-H.

Leavenworth, Richard, jt. auth. see Grant, Eugene L.

Leaverton. Environmental Epidemiology. 192p. 1982. 23.50 (ISBN 0-03-061716-2). Praeger.

Leavis, F. R. The Critic as Anti-Philosopher. Singh, G., ed. Bd. with Essays & Papers. LC 82-13580. 208p. 1983. text ed. 16.00x (ISBN 0-8203-0656-8). U of Ga Pr.

--Determinations: Critical Essays. LC 70-119085. (English Literature Ser., No. 33). 1970. Repr. of 1934 ed. lib. bdg. 36.95x (ISBN 0-8383-1081-8). Haskell.

Leavis, F. R., ed. see Mill, J. S.

Leavis, Frank R. Education & the University. 1979. 24.95 (ISBN 0-521-22610-4); pap. 7.95 (ISBN 0-521-29573-4). Cambridge U Pr.

--English Literature in Our Time & the University. LC 78-73128. 1979. 27.95 (ISBN 0-521-22609-0); pap. 7.95 (ISBN 0-521-29574-2). Cambridge U Pr.

Leavitt, Fred. Drugs & Behavior. 2nd ed. LC 81-16320. (Wiley Series on Personality Processes). 515p. 1982. 39.95x (ISBN 0-471-08226-0, Pub. by Wiley-Interscience). Wiley.

Leavitt, G. S. Oral-Aural Communications (OAC) A Teacher's Manual. (Illus.). 136p. 1974. 11.75x (ISBN 0-398-03061-8); pap. 8.25x (ISBN 0-398-03063-4). C C Thomas.

Leavitt, Guy P. Superintend with Success. rev. ed. Langston, A. Leon, ed. LC 79-66658. (Illus.). 144p. 1980. pap. 6.95 (ISBN 0-87239-377-1, 3203). Standard Pub.

--Teach with Success. rev. ed. Daniel, Eleanor, rev. by. LC 78-63285. (Illus.). 160p. (Orig.). 1978. pap. 6.95 (ISBN 0-87239-231-7, 3232). Standard Pub.

Leavitt, Harold, et al, eds. Organizations of the Future: Interaction with the External Environment. LC 74-1733. (Special Studies). (Illus.). 220p. 1974. 28.95 o.p. (ISBN 0-275-28864-1). Praeger.

Leavitt, Judith A., ed. Women in Management: An Annotated Bibliography & Sourcelist. LC 82-2190. 216p. 1982. lib. bdg. 25.00 (ISBN 0-89774-026-2). Oryx Pr.

Leavitt, Mel. A Short History of New Orleans. (Illus.). 160p. (Orig.). 1982. pap. 8.95 (ISBN 0-938530-03-8). Lexikos.

Leavitt, Richard F. The World of Tennessee Williams. LC 76-28473. (Illus.). 1978. 20.00 o.p. (ISBN 0-399-11773-3). Putnam Pub Group.

Leavitt, Ruth, ed. Artist & Computer. (Illus.). 1976. 4.95 o.p. (ISBN 0-517-52787-1, Dist. by Crown); pap. 4.95 o.p. (ISBN 0-517-52735-9). Crown.

Leavitt, Teddy C. Limits & Continuity. 1967. pap. text ed. 7.95 o.p. (ISBN 0-07-036960-7, C). McGraw.

Leavitt, Thomas. Karel Appel, West Coast Exhibition 1961-1962. (Illus.). 23p. 1962. 3.00x (ISBN 0-686-99844-8). La Jolla Mus Contemp Art.

Leavy, Morton L., jt. auth. see Baumgarten, Paul A.

Lebacqz, Karen. Genetics, Ethics & Parenthood. 128p. (Orig.). 1983. pap. 7.95 (ISBN 0-8298-0671-7). Pilgrim NY.

Le-Ba-Khanh, jt. ed. see Le-Ba-Kong.

Le-Ba-Kong & Le-Ba-Khanh, eds. Vietnamese-English, English Vietnamese Dictionary. 25.00 (ISBN 0-8044-0310-4). Ungar.

Lebano, Edoardo A. & Baldini, Pier R. Buon Giorno a Tutti: First-Year Italian. 512p. 1983. text ed. 20.95 (ISBN 0-471-04308-7); tchrs.' avail. (ISBN 0-471-05793-2); wkbk. avail. (ISBN 0-471-04309-5). Wiley.

LeBar, Frank M. & Suddard, Adrienne, eds. Laos. LC 60-7381. (Area & County Surveys Ser.). 312p. (YA) (gr. 10 up). 1967. 18.00x (ISBN 0-87536-915-4). HRAFP.

Lebar, Lois & Berg, Miguel. Llamados a Ensenar. Blanch, Jose M., tr. from Eng. LC 77-5183. (Illus.). 160p. (Span.). 1970. pap. 3.75 (ISBN 0-89922-006-1). Edit Caribe.

LeBar, Mary. How God Gives Us Apples. (A Happy Day Book). (Illus.). 24p. (gr. k-5). 1979. 1.29 (ISBN 0-87239-357-7, 3627). Standard Pub.

--How God Gives Us Bread. (A Happy Day Book). (Illus.). 24p. (gr. k-5). 1979. 1.29 (ISBN 0-87239-359-3, 3629). Standard Pub.

--How God Gives Us Ice Cream. (A Happy Day Book). (Illus.). 24p. (gr. k-5). 1979. 1.29 (ISBN 0-87239-358-5, 3628). Standard Pub.

--How God Gives Us Peanut Butter. (A Happy Day Book). (Illus.). 24p. (gr. k-5). 1979. 1.29 (ISBN 0-87239-356-9, 3626). Standard Pub.

LeBaron, Charles. Gentle Vengeance. 1981. 12.95 o.s.i. (ISBN 0-399-90112-4, Marek). Putnam Pub Group.

Lebaron, Homer M. & Gressel, Jonathan. Herbicide Resistance in Plants. LC 81-16381. 416p. 1982. 47.50 o.s.i. (ISBN 0-471-08701-7, Pub. by Wiley-Interscience). Wiley.

Lebaron, John. Making Television: A Video Production Guide for Teachers. LC 81-703. (Orig.). 1981. pap. text ed. 17.95x (ISBN 0-8077-2636-2). Tchrs Coll.

LeBarre, James, et al. Machine Calculation of Business Problems. 233p. 1981. pap. 8.95 (ISBN 0-911744-75-4). Intl Educ Systems.

Lebart, L., jt. ed. see Diday, E.

Lebas, Elizabeth, tr. see Castells, Manuel.

Le Bas, M. J. Carbonatite-Nephelinite Volcanism: An African Case History. 1977. 99.95 (ISBN 0-471-99422-7, Pub. by Wiley-Interscience). Wiley.

Lebauer, R. S., ed. Reading Skills for the Future: An Intermediate Workbook for Reading Comprehension. (Materials for Language Practice Ser.). (Illus.). 128p. 1983. pap. 6.95 (ISBN 0-08-028619-4). Pergamon.

Lebaye, Pierre. Le Symbolisme De Morike. 339p. (Fr.). 1982. write for info. (ISBN 3-261-04970-7). P Lang Pubs.

LeBeau, Roy. Rifle River. (Buckskin Ser.: No. 1). 240p. (Orig.). 1982. pap. (ISBN 0-505-51801-5). Tower Bks.

--Rifle River. (Buckskin Ser.: No. 1). 240p. (Orig.). 1982. pap. 2.25 o.s.i. (ISBN 0-8439-1158-1, Leisure Bks). Nordon Pubns.

Lebeaux, Charles N., jt. auth. see Wilensky, Harold L.

Lebeaux, Richard. Young Man Thoreau. 1978. pap. 3.95i o.p. (ISBN 0-06-090614-6, CN 614, CN). Har-Row.

Lebeck, Robert. The Kiss. (Illus.). 176p. 1981. pap. 6.95 o.p. (ISBN 0-312-45687-5). St Martin.

--Playgirls of Yesteryear. (Illus.). 176p. 1981. pap. 6.95 o.p. (ISBN 0-312-61553-1). St Martin.

Lebedev, N. A., jt. auth. see Smirnov, Vladimir I.

Lebedev, N. N., et al. Worked Problems in Applied Mathematics. LC 78-67857. 1979. pap. text ed. 7.00 (ISBN 0-486-63730-1). Dover.

Lebedoff, David. The New Elite: The Death of Democracy. 208p. 1983. pap. 8.95 (ISBN 0-8092-5617-7). Contemp Bks.

Le Bendig, Michael & Diamond, Elliot. Podiatric Resource Guide for Preventive & Rehabilitative Foot & Leg Care. LC 75-45780. 156p. 1976. monograph 18.25 (ISBN 0-87993-080-2). Futura Pub.

Lebensohn, J. E., ed. An Anthology of Ophthamolic Classes. LC 76-94010. 424p. 1969. 24.00 (ISBN 0-683-04905-4, Pub. by Williams & Wilkins). Krieger.

Lebenthal, Emanuel, ed. Textbook of Gastroenterology & Nutrition in Infancy, 2 vols. (Illus.). 1198p. 1981. Set. text ed. 110.00 (ISBN 0-686-77542-2). Vol. 1: Gastrointestinal Development & Perinatal Nutrition (ISBN 0-89004-526-7). Vol. 2: Gastrointestinal Disease & Nutritional Inadequacies (ISBN 0-89004-533-X). Raven.

Leber, Max. The Corner Drugstore: What You Should Know about Everything Pharmacies Sell. 288p. 1983. pap. 6.95 (ISBN 0-446-97989-9). Warner Bks.

Leber, Philip, jt. ed. see Jones, Peter W.

Lebergott, Stanley G. The Americans: An Economic Record. 1983. pap. text ed. write for info (ISBN 0-393-95311-4). Norton.

Lebesgue, Henri. Lecons Sur L'integration et la Recherche des Fonctions Primitives. 3rd ed. LC 73-921. 340p. (Fr.). (gr. 12 up). 1973. text ed. 13.95 (ISBN 0-8284-0267-1). Chelsea Pub.

Lebesque, Jacques. L'URSS et la Revolution Cubaine. (Travaux et Recherches Ser: No. 42). (Fr.). 1977. lib. bdg. 28.75x o.p. (ISBN 2-7246-0350-8, Pub by Presses De la Fondation Nationale Des Sciences Politiques); pap. text ed. 18.75x o.p. (ISBN 2-7246-0344-3). Clearwater Pub.

Le Beux, P., jt. ed. see Richter, L.

Leblanc, C. L' Infrastructure Scolaire En Cote d'Ivoire. (Black Africa Ser.). 95p. (Fr.). 1974. Repr. lib. bdg. 34.00x o.p. (ISBN 0-8287-0515-1, 71-2011). Clearwater Pub.

Leblanc, Georgette. Souvenirs, Eighteen Ninety-five to Nineteen Eighteen: My Life with Maeterlinck. Flanner, Janet, tr. from Fr. 352p. 1976. Repr. of 1932 ed. lib. bdg. 32.50 (ISBN 0-306-70841-8). Da Capo.

Le Blanc, L. Little Frog Learns to Sing. LC 68-16394. (Illus.). (ps-2). 1967. PLB 6.75x (ISBN 0-87783-022-3). cassette 5.95x (ISBN 0-87783-191-2). Oddo.

LeBlanc, Lanie. Reading Competencies. 1983. pap. text ed. 9.95 (ISBN 0-673-15801-2). Scott F.

LeBlanc, Richard. The Fangs of the Vampire. LC 78-65867. 1979. 7.95 o.p. (ISBN 0-533-04117-1). Vantage.

LeBlanc, Steven A. The Mimbres People: Ancient Pueblo Painters of the American Southwest. (New Aspects of Antiquity Ser.). (Illus.). 1983. 29.95 (ISBN 0-500-39017-7). Thames Hudson.

Le Blon, J. C. Coloritto. 98p. 1980. 12.50 o.p. (ISBN 0-442-24723-0). Van Nos Reinhold.

Leblon, Jean M., tr. see Zola, Emile.

LeBoeuf, C., jt. auth. see Schell, D.

LeBoeuf, M. The Productivity Challenge: How to Make it Work for America & You. 256p. 1982. 12.95 (ISBN 0-07-036970-4). McGraw.

Lebon, G., jt. ed. see Vazquez, J. C.

LeBon, Gustave. The French Revolution & the Psychology of Revolution. LC 78-62691. (Social Science Classics Ser.). 337p. 1980. 29.95 (ISBN 0-87855-310-X); pap. 6.95 (ISBN 0-87855-697-4). Transaction Bks.

Le Bon, Gustave. The Psychology of Revolution. 1968. Repr. of 1913 ed. flexible cover 10.00 (ISBN 0-87034-026-3). Fraser Pub Co.

LeBond, P. H. & Mysak, L. A. Waves in the Ocean. (Elsevier Oceanography Ser.: Vol. 20). 1981. 47.00 (ISBN 0-444-41926-8). Elsevier.

Lebour, M. V. The Planktonic Diatoms of Northern Seas. (Ray Society Publication Ser.: No. 116). (Illus.). 244p. 1978. Repr. of 1930 ed. lib. bdg. 24.00x (ISBN 3-87429-147-2). Lubrecht & Cramer.

LeBoutillier, John. Harvard Hates America. LC 78-60229. 1978. 7.95 (ISBN 0-89526-688-1). Regnery-Gateway.

Lebovici, Elisabeth, jt. auth. see Bracco, Patrick.

Lebovitz, jt. auth. see Fritz.

LeBow, Gustave. The Crowd. LC 26-6009. 1969. pap. 4.95 (ISBN 0-910220-16-6). Berg.

Lebow, Jared. All About Soccer. Berger, Kathleen, ed. LC 77-99208. 1978. 13.95 o.p. (ISBN 0-88225-257-7). Newsweek.

LeBow, Michael D., ed. Weight Control: The Behavioural Strategies. LC 79-41728. 346p. 1981. 39.95 (ISBN 0-471-27745-2, Pub. by Wiley-Interscience). Wiley.

Lebowitz, Carl R., jt. auth. see Edwards, Charles M., Jr.

Lebowitz, Fran. Social Studies. 1982. pap. 3.25 (ISBN 0-671-45047-6). PB.

Lebowitz, J. L., jt. ed. see Montroll, E. W.

Lebowitz, Joel L., et al, eds. International Conference on Collective Phenomena, 3rd. new ed. LC 80-17323. (Annals of the New York Academy of Sciences: Vol. 337). 41.00x (ISBN 0-89766-074-9); pap. 41.00x (ISBN 0-89766-075-7). NY Acad Sci.

Lebowitz, Milton M., ed. Practice Issues in Social Welfare Administration, Policy & Planning. LC 82-6269. (Administration in Social Work Ser.: Vol. 6, Nos. 2-3). 167p. 1982. text ed. 30.00 (ISBN 0-86656-142-0, B142); pap. text ed. 14.95 (ISBN 0-86656-166-8, B166). Haworth Pr.

Lebowitz, Philip W. & Newberg, Leslie A. Clinical Anesthesia Procedures of the Massachusetts General Hospital. 2nd ed. 1982. pap. text ed. 14.95 (ISBN 0-316-51867-0). Little.

Lebowitz, Philip W., ed. see Massachusetts General Hospital.

Leboyer, Frederick. Loving Hands: The Traditional Indian Art of Baby Massaging. 1976. 14.95 (ISBN 0-394-40469-6). Knopf.

Lebra, Joyce, et al, eds. Women in Changing Japan. LC 75-33663. (Special Studies on China & East Asia Ser.). 250p. 1976. 31.00 o.p. (ISBN 0-89158-019-0). Westview.

Lebra, Takie S. Japanese Patterns of Behavior. LC 76-110392. 1976. pap. text ed. 5.95x (ISBN 0-8248-0460-0, Eastwest Ctr). UH Pr.

Lebra, Takie S. & Lebra, William P., eds. Japanese Culture & Behavior: Selected Readings. LC 73-78978. 494p. (Orig.). 1974. pap. text ed. 6.95x (ISBN 0-8248-0276-4, Eastwest Ctr). UH Pr.

Lebra, William P. Okinawan Religion: Belief, Ritual, & Social Structure. LC 66-16506. (Illus., Orig.). 1966. pap. text ed. 6.00x o.p. (ISBN 0-87022-450-6). UH Pr.

--Youth, Socialization, & Mental Health. LC 73-85581. (Mental Health Research in Asia & the Pacific Ser: Vol. 3). 320p. 1974. text ed. 17.50x (ISBN 0-8248-0293-4, Eastwest Ctr). UH Pr.

Lebra, William P., ed. Culture-Bound Syndromes, Ethno-Psychiatry, & Alternate Therapies. LC 74-78860. (Mental Health Research in Asia & the Pacific Ser.: Vol. 4). 384p. 1976. text ed. 16.00x o.p. (ISBN 0-8248-0339-6, Eastwest Ctr). UH Pr.

--Transcultural Research in Mental Health. (Mental Health Research in Asia & the Pacific Ser: Vol. 2). 480p. 1972. 20.00x (ISBN 0-8248-0105-9, Eastwest Ctr). UH Pr.

Lebra, William P., jt. ed. see Lebra, Takie S.

Lebrecht, Norman. Discord. LC 82-21872. (Illus.). 272p. 1983. 25.00 (ISBN 0-87663-389-0). Universe.

Lebredo, Raquel, jt. auth. see Jarvis, Ana C.

Lebrun, Claude. Little Brown Bear Eats His Egg. (Little Brown Bear Ser.). 14p. (gr. k-3). 1983. 2.95 (ISBN 0-8120-5504-7). Barron.

--Little Brown Bear is Angry at His Mama. (Little Brown Bear Ser.). (Illus.). 14p. (gr. k-3). 1983. 2.95 (ISBN 0-8120-5498-9). Barron.

--Little Brown Bear Is Not Hungry. (Little Brown Bear Ser.). (Illus.). 14p. (gr. k-3). 1983. 2.95 (ISBN 0-8120-5496-2). Barron.

--Little Brown Bear Rides a Tricycle. (Little Brown Bear Ser.). (Illus.). 14p. (gr. k-3). 1983. 2.95 (ISBN 0-8120-5494-6). Barron.

--Little Brown Bear Takes a Bath. (Little Brown Bear Ser.). 14p. (gr. k-3). 1982. 2.95 (ISBN 0-8120-5505-5). Barron.

--Little Brown Bear Wants to Hear Stories. (Little Brown Bear Ser.). (Illus.). 14p. (gr. k-3). 1983. 2.95 (ISBN 0-8120-5497-0). Barron.

Lebrun, Rico. Rico Lebrun Drawings. LC 60-16562. 1961. 33.00x (ISBN 0-520-00717-4). U of Cal Pr.

Lebrun-Tossa. Voltaire, Juge Par les Faits. Repr. of 1817 ed. 30.00 o.p. (ISBN 0-8287-0516-X). Clearwater Pub.

Lebsock, Suzanne. Gender, Wealth & Power in the Old South. 1983. write for info (ISBN 0-393-95264-9). Norton.

Le Cain, Errol. The White Cat. LC 73-94115. (Illus.). 32p. (ps-2). 1975. 6.95 o.p. (ISBN 0-87888-071-2). Bradbury Pr.

Le Cain, George, jt. auth. see Donaldson, Cyril.

Le Cam, L. & Neyman, J., eds. Probability Models & Cancer: Proceedings of an Interdisciplinary Cancer Study Conference. 310p. 1983. 51.00 (ISBN 0-444-86514-4, North Holland). Elsevier.

Le Cam, Lucien, et al, eds. see Berkeley Symposia on Mathematical Statistics & Probability, 6th.

Lecar, Harold, jt. ed. see Marton, Clare.

Lecarme, O., ed. see IFIP World Conference, 2nd.

Le Carre, John. The Little Drummer Girl. LC 82-48733. 448p. 1983. 15.95 (ISBN 0-394-53015-2). Knopf.

--The Looking Glass War. 1965. 5.95 o.p. (ISBN 0-698-10218-5, Coward). Putnam Pub Group.

LeCarre, John. The Quest for Karla. LC 82-47961. 1982. 10.95 (ISBN 0-394-52848-4). Knopf.

Le Carre, John. Smileys People. 400p. 1982. pap. 3.95 (ISBN 0-553-23149-9). Bantam.

--The Spy Who Came in from the Cold. 1978. 9.95 (ISBN 0-698-10916-3, Coward). Putnam Pub Group.

Le Carre, John see Eyre, A. G.

Lecca, Pedro J., jt. auth. see Tharp, C. Patrick.

Lecca, Pedro J., jt. ed. see Callicutt, James W.

Lechleitner, Hans, jt. auth. see Breuer, Reinhard.

Lechler, Walther H., jt. auth. see Lair, Jacqueline C.

Lechner. EEG & Clinical Neurophysiology. (International Congress Ser.: Vol. 526). 1980. 153.25 (ISBN 0-444-90172-8). Elsevier.

Lechner, Alan. Street Games: Inside Stories of the Wall Street Hustle. LC 79-2627. (Illus.). 1980. 10.53i (ISBN 0-06-012553-5, HarpT). Har-Row.

Lechner, Jack. The Ivy League Rock Quiz Book. (Illus.). 144p. (Orig.). 1983. pap. 6.95 (ISBN 0-933328-62-1). Delilah Bks.

Lechner, Sr. Joan M. Renaissance Concepts of the Commonplaces. LC 74-6153. 268p. 1974. Repr. of 1962 ed. lib. bdg. 16.25x (ISBN 0-8371-7491-0, LERC). Greenwood.

Lecht, Charles P. The Waves of Change. 2nd ed. 1979. pap. 10.95 (ISBN 0-07-036967-4). McGraw.

Lechtman, Max D., jt. auth. see Wistreich, George A.

Lechtman, Max D., et al. The Games Cells Play. LC 78-57373. 1979. text ed. 11.95 (ISBN 0-8053-6094-8). Benjamin-Cummings.

Leckart, Bruce & Weinberger, Lilla G. Up from Boredom, Down from Fear. 1980. 10.95 o.p. (ISBN 0-399-90046-2, Marek). Putnam Pub Group.

Lecker, Robert & David, Jack. The Annotated Bibliography to Canada's Major Authors: Vol. 4-A. J. M. Smith, Earle Birney, Dorothy Livesay & F. R. Scott. 1983. lib. bdg. 42.50 (ISBN 0-8161-8638-3, Hall Reference). G K Hall.

Lecker, Robert & David, Jack, eds. Annotated Bibliography of Canada's Major Authors, Vol. I: Margaret Atwood, Margaret Laurence, Hugh Maclennan, Mordecai Richler, Gabrielle Roy. 1980. lib. bdg. 25.00 o.p. (ISBN 0-8161-8491-7, Hall Reference). G K Hall.

--The Annotated Bibliography of Canada's Major Authors, Vol. 3: Ernest Buckler, Robertson Davies, Raymond Knister, W. O. Mitchell, & Sinclair Ross. 1982. lib. bdg. 35.00 (ISBN 0-8161-8617-0, Hall Reference). G K Hall.

Lecker, Sidney. The Natural Way to Successful Stress Control. LC 77-87787. 1978. 8.95 o.p. (ISBN 0-448-14539-1, G&D). Putnam Pub Group.

Leckie, George, tr. see Korschelt, O.

Leckie, Robert. Americans at War. 1981. pap. 2.95 o.p. (ISBN 0-686-72178-0, Sig). NAL.

--Battle for Iwo Jima. (gr. 5-9). 1967. 2.95 o.p. (ISBN 0-394-80418-X, BYR); PLB 5.99 (ISBN 0-394-90418-4). Random.

--The Bloodborn. (Americans at War Ser.: No. 1). (Orig.). 1981. pap. 2.95 o.p. (ISBN 0-451-09801-3, E9801, Sig). NAL.

--Forged in Blood. (Americans at War Ser.: No. 2). (Orig.). 1982. pap. 2.95 (ISBN 0-451-11337-3, AE1337, Sig). NAL.

--The War Nobody Won: 1812. LC 74-76358. (Illus.). 192p. (gr. 6 up). 1974. 5.95 o.p. (ISBN 0-399-20406-7). Putnam Pub Group.

--The World Turned Upside Down: The Story of the American Revolution. (Illus.). 256p. (gr. 6 up). 1973. 6.95 o.p. (ISBN 0-399-20312-5). Putnam Pub Group.

Lecky, Prescott. Self-Consistency: A Theory of Personality. 2nd ed. v, 275p. 1973. Repr. of 1951 ed. 13.50 o.p. (ISBN 0-208-00542-0, Archon). Shoe String.

Lecky, william E. Leaders of Public Opinion in Ireland, 2 vols. LC 76-159800. (Europe 1815-1945 Ser.). 720p. 1973. Repr. of 1903 ed. Set. lib. bdg. 79.50 (ISBN 0-306-70574-5). Da Capo.

LeClair, Thomas & McCaffery, Larry, eds. Anything Can Happen: Interviews with Contemporary American Novelists. LC 82-2867. (Illus.). 320p. 1983. 15.95 (ISBN 0-252-00970-3). U of Ill Pr.

Leclaire, Lucien. A General Analytical Bibliography of the Regional Novelists of the British Isles: 1800-1950. 399p. 1983. Repr. of 1954 ed. lib. bdg. 100.00 (ISBN 0-89984-811-7). Century Bookbindery.

Lecler, D., jt. auth. see Thureau, P.

Lecler, Rene. The Three Hundred Best Hotels in the World. LC 82-10778. (Illus.). 240p. 1983. pap. 9.95 (ISBN 0-89919-160-6). Ticknor & Fields.

Leclerc, Eloi. Francis of Assisi: Return to the Gospel. Arnandez, Richard, tr. 1983. 9.50 (ISBN 0-8199-0854-1). Franciscan Herald.

Leclerc, J. C. & Cornu, A. Neutron Activation Analysis Tables. 1974. 76.00 o.p. (ISBN 0-471-25846-6, Wiley Heyden). Wiley.

Leclercq, Dom H. & Marron, Henri. Dictionnaire d'Archeologie Chretienne et de Liturgie, 28 vols. (Fr.). 1903. Set. 1995.00 (ISBN 0-686-57001-4, M-6342). French & Eur.

Le Clercq, Jacques, tr. see Goncourt, Edmond L.

Leclercq, Jean. Love of Learning & Desire for God: A Study of Monastic Culture. 3rd ed. LC 60-53004. 1982. pap. 10.00 (ISBN 0-8232-0407-3). Fordham.

LeClercq, Jean, et al. A History of Christian Spirituality, 3 vols. 1982. Set. pap. 37.50 slip-cased (ISBN 0-8164-2369-5). Seabury.

Lecomber, Brian. Talk Down. LC 78-5794. 1978. 8.95 o.p. (ISBN 0-698-10937-6, Coward). Putnam Pub Group.

Le Corbusier, pseud. Complete Works, 8 vols. Incl. Vol. 1. 1910-29. Boesiger, Willy & Stonorov, eds. 52.50x o.s.i. (ISBN 0-685-22831-2); Vol. 2. 1929-34. Boesiger, Willy, ed. 52.50x o.s.i. (ISBN 0-685-22832-0); Vol. 3. 1934-38. Max, Bill, ed. 52.50x o.s.i. (ISBN 0-685-22833-9); Vol. 4. 1938-46. Boesiger, Willy, ed. 52.50x o.s.i. (ISBN 0-685-22834-7); Vol. 5. 1946-52. Boesiger, Willy, ed. 52.50x o.s.i. (ISBN 0-685-22835-5); Vol. 6. 1952-57. Boesiger, Willy, ed. 52.50x o.s.i. (ISBN 0-685-22836-3); Vol. 7. 1957-65. Boesiger, Willy, ed. 52.50x o.s.i. (ISBN 0-685-22837-1); Vol. 8. The Last Works. Boesiger, Wlly, ed. 52.50x o.s.i. (ISBN 0-685-22838-X). (Illus., Eng., Fr. & Ger.). Museum Bks.

Le Corbusier, see Jeanneret, Charles E., pseud.

Le Corbusier, jt. ed. see Ozenfant, Amadee.

Le Cordeur, Basil A. The Politics of Eastern Cape Separatism, 1820-1854. (Illus.). 328p. 1981. 39.00x (ISBN 0-19-570196-8). Oxford U Pr.

Le Cour Grand Maison. Rapport Preliminaire D'Enquete des Zones d'Extension des Secteurs Pilotes Diabo-Brobo. (Black Africa Ser.). 98p. (Fr.). 1974. Repr. of 1969 ed. lib. bdg. 35.00x o.p. (ISBN 0-8287-1404-5, 71-2046). Clearwater Pub.

Lecourt, Dominique. Proletarian Science? The Case of Lysenko. 1978. 14.00 (ISBN 0-8052-7006-X, Pub by NLB). Schocken.

LeCron, Leslie M. The Complete Guide to Hypnosis. 240p. 1976. pap. 3.50 (ISBN 0-06-465069-3, BN 5069, BN). B&N NY.

--Magic Mind Power: Make it work for You! 2nd ed. 176p. pap. 4.95 (ISBN 0-87516-496-X). De Vorss.

--Self Hypnotism: The Technique & Its Use in Daily Living. 1970. pap. 2.95 (ISBN 0-451-12097-3, AE2097, Sig). NAL.

LeCroy, Craig W., ed. Social Skills Training for Children & Youth. (Child & Youth Services Ser.: Vol. 5, No. 3 & 4). 184p. 1983. text ed. 19.95 (ISBN 0-86656-184-6, B184). Haworth Pr.

Le Cunff, Madeleine see Cunff, Madeleine Le.

Leczinski, Stanislas. Entretien d'un Europeen avec un Insulaire du Royaume de Dumocala. (Utopias in the Enlightenment Ser.). 204p. (Fr.). 1974. Repr. of 1752 ed. lib. bdg. 58.00x o.p. (ISBN 0-8287-0518-6, 045). Clearwater Pub.

Ledbetter, Bonnie, jt. auth. see Ainslie, Tom.

Ledbetter, Carl S. & Nering, Evar D. The Cubemaster's Sourcebook. (Orig.). 1982. pap. 6.95 o.p. (ISBN 0-932238-15-7). Avant Bks.

Ledbetter, Elaine & Young, Jay. Keys to Chemistry: Metric. 2nd ed. (gr. 11-12). 1977. text ed. 18.64 (ISBN 0-201-04361-0, Sch Div). lab man. 6.92 (ISBN 0-201-04363-7). A-W.

Ledbetter-Hancock, Betsy. School Social Work. (Prentice Hall Series in Social Work Practice). 336p. 1982. 22.95 (ISBN 0-13-794453-5). P-H.

Ledd, Paul. Shelter, No. 1: Prisoner of Revenge. 224p. (Orig.). 1980. pap. 1.95 (ISBN 0-89083-598-5). Zebra.

--Shelter, No. 10: Massacre Mountain. (Orig.). 1982. pap. 2.25 (ISBN 0-89083-972-7). Zebra.

--Shelter, No. 11: Rio Rampage. 1983. pap. 2.25 (ISBN 0-8217-1141-5). Zebra.

--Shelter, No. 2: Hanging Moon. 256p. (Orig.). 1980. pap. 1.95 (ISBN 0-89083-637-X). Zebra.

--Shelter, No. 3: Chain Gang Kill. 256p. (Orig.). 1980. pap. 1.95 (ISBN 0-89083-658-2). Zebra.

--Shelter, No. 4: China Doll. 1980. pap. 1.95 (ISBN 0-89083-682-5). Zebra.

--Shelter, No. 5: The Lazarus Guns. 256p. (Orig.). 1980. pap. 1.95 (ISBN 0-89083-694-9). Zebra.

--Shelter, No. 6: Circus of Death. (Orig.). 1981. pap. 1.95 (ISBN 0-89083-723-6). Zebra.

--Shelter, No. 7: Lookout Mountain. 1981. pap. 1.95 (ISBN 0-89083-756-2). Zebra.

--Shelter, No. 8: The Bandit Queen. (Orig.). 1981. pap. 2.25 (ISBN 0-89083-869-0). Zebra.

--Shelter, No. 9: Apache Trail. (Orig.). 1982. pap. 2.25 (ISBN 0-89083-956-5). Zebra.

Leddy, Tracy. Allison's Shadow. LC 82-61020. 124p. (Orig.). 1982. pap. 12.00 (ISBN 0-89142-040-1). Sant Bani Ash.

Ledebour, K. F. Icones Plantarum Novarum Vel Imperfecte Cognitarum Floram Rossicam, 5vols. in 1. 1968. 304.00 (ISBN 3-7682-0567-3). Lubrecht & Cramer.

Leder, Robert H., ed. CISP International Studies Funding Book. 3rd ed. 1982. Repr. looseleaf 50.00 (ISBN 0-939288-00-1). CISP.

Lederberg, Joshua, jt. ed. see Epstein, Samuel.

Lederer, C. Michael & Shirley, V. S. Table of Isotopes. 7th ed. LC 78-14938. 1978. 63.95x (ISBN 0-471-04179-3); pap. 41.50 (ISBN 0-471-04180-7, Pub. by Wiley-Interscience). Wiley.

Lederer, Katherine. Lillian Hellman. (United States Authors Ser.). 1979. 11.95 (ISBN 0-8057-7275-8, Twayne). G K Hall.

Lederer, Laura, ed. Take Back the Night: Women on Pornography. LC 80-23701. 352p. (Orig.). 1980. pap. 7.95 (ISBN 0-688-08728-0). Quill NY.

Lederer, Muriel. Blue-Collar Jobs for Women. 1979. 12.95 (ISBN 0-87690-311-1); pap. 8.95 (ISBN 0-87690-319-7, 0869-280). Dutton.

Lederer, Paul. Tecumseh. 1982. pap. 2.95 (ISBN 0-451-11410-8, AE1410, Sig). NAL.

Lederer, Paul J. Manitou's Daughter. (Indian Heritage Ser.: No. 1). 1982. pap. 2.95 (ISBN 0-451-11767-0, AE1767, Sig). NAL.

Lederer, William H. & Fensterheim, Robert J., eds. Arsenic: Industrial, Biomedical, Enviornmental Perspectives. 464p. 1982. text ed. 42.00 (ISBN 0-442-21496-0). Van Nos Reinhold.

Lederer, William J. A Happy Book of Happy Stories. 96p. 1981. 5.95 (ISBN 0-393-01414-2). Norton.

--A Nation of Sheep. (gr. 10 up). 1961. 6.95 o.p. (ISBN 0-393-05288-5). Norton.

Lederer, William J. & Burdick, Eugene. Ugly American. (gr. 9 up). 1958. 7.95 o.p. (ISBN 0-393-08461-2, Norton Lib); pap. 5.95 (ISBN 0-393-00305-1). Norton.

Lederer, Wolfgang. Fear of Women. LC 68-16305. (Illus.). 1970. pap. 4.95 o.p. (ISBN 0-15-630419-8, HB184, Harv). HarBraceJ.

Lederer, Zdenek. Ghetto Theresienstadt. Weisskopf, K., tr. 275p. 1983. Repr. of 1953 ed. 23.50x (ISBN 0-86527-341-3). Fertig.

Lederman, D., tr. see Dukhin, S. S. & Shilov, V. N.

Lederman, D., tr. see Sedunov, Yu. S.

Lederman, E. K. Existential Neurosis. (Illus.). 150p. 1972. 10.60 o.p. (ISBN 0-407-17040-5). Butterworth.

Lederman, L., jt. ed. see Weneser, J.

Lederman, Linda C. New Dimensions: An Introduction to Human Communication. 414p. 1977. pap. text ed. write for info. (ISBN 0-697-04118-2); instr's manual avail. (ISBN 0-697-04236-7). Wm C Brown.

Lederman, Minna, ed. Stravinsky in the Theatre. LC 74-34377. (Music Reprint Ser.). (Illus.). 228p. 1975. Repr. of 1949 ed. lib. bdg. 25.00 (ISBN 0-306-70665-2); pap. 5.95 (ISBN 0-306-80022-5). Da Capo.

Lederman, Walter & Vajda, Steven. Handbook of Applicable Mathematics: Vol. IV, Analysis. (Handbook of Applicable Mathematic Ser.). 865p. 1982. 85.00 (ISBN 0-471-10141-9, Pub. by Wiley-Interscience). Wiley.

Ledermann. Handbook of Applicable Mathematics: Probability, Vol. 2. LC 79-42724. (Handbook of Applicable Mathematics Ser.). 450p. 1981. 85.00x (ISBN 0-471-27821-1, Pub. by Wiley-Interscience). Wiley.

Ledermann, W. Introduction to Group Characters. LC 76-46858. (Illus.). 1977. 47.00 (ISBN 0-521-21486-6); pap. 13.95 (ISBN 0-521-29170-4). Cambridge U Pr.

Ledermann, Walter. Handbook of Applicable Mathematics: Vol. 3: Numerical Methods. LC 79-42724. (Handbook of Applicable Mathematics Ser.). 592p. 1981. 85.00x (ISBN 0-471-27947-1, Pub. by Wiley-Interscience). Wiley.

Ledet, David, jt. auth. see Sprenkle, Robert.

Ledgard, Henry & Singer, Andrew. Elementary BASIC. 384p. 1982. pap. text ed. 13.95 (ISBN 0-574-21385-6, 13-4385). SRA.

--Elementary BASIC. 1982. 20.00 (ISBN 0-394-52423-3). Random.

--Elementary PASCAL. 1982. 20.00 (ISBN 0-394-52424-1). Random.

Ledgister, Elgeta O. Musings of Life. 1982. 5.95 (ISBN 0-533-05474-5). Vantage.

Ledieu, Alcius. Les Villains dans les Oeuvres des Trouveres. 114p. (Fr.). 1982. Repr. of 1890 ed. lib. bdg. 55.00 (ISBN 0-8287-1771-0). Clearwater Pub.

Ledin, George, jt. auth. see Louden, Robert K.

Ledin, George, Jr PASCAL. (Illus.). 281p. 1982. pap. text ed. 14.95 (ISBN 0-88284-173-4); avail. instructor's manual. Alfred Pub.

--A Structured Approach to Essential Basic. LC 79-26549. 176p. 1979. pap. text ed. 8.95x (ISBN 0-87835-077-2). Boyd & Fraser.

Ledin, George, Jr. & Ledin, Victor. The Programmer's Book of Rules. LC 79-13746. 1979. pap. 11.95 (ISBN 0-534-97993-9). Lifetime Learn.

Ledin, George, Jr., jt. auth. see Kudlick, Michael D.

Ledin, Victor, jt. auth. see Ledin, George, Jr.

Ledley, Robert S., et al. Cross Sectional Anatomy: An Atlas for Computerized Tomography. (Illus.). 347p. 1977. 19.95 (ISBN 0-683-04920-8). Williams & Wilkins.

Lednicer, Daniel. Central Analgetics. LC 82-8567. (Chemistry & Pharmacology of Drugs Monographs). 219p. 1982. 47.50 (ISBN 0-471-08314-3, Pub. by Wiley-Interscience). Wiley.

Lednicer, Daniel & Mitscher, Lester A. Organic Chemistry of Drug Synthesis, 2 vols. LC 76-28387. Vol. 1, 1977. 37.95x (ISBN 0-471-52141-8, Pub. by Wiley-Interscience); Vol. 2, 1980. 36.50x (ISBN 0-471-04392-3). Wiley.

Lednicer, Daniel, jt. auth. see Bindra, Jasjit S.

Lednicki, Waclaw, ed. Adam Mickiewicz in World Literature: A Symposium. LC 76-2017. 626p. 1976. Repr. of 1956 ed. lib. bdg. 35.25x o.p. (ISBN 0-8371-8765-6, LEAM). Greenwood.

Le-Douarin, Nicole. The Neural Crest. LC 82-1183. (Developmental & Cell Biology Ser.: No. 12). (Illus.). 200p. 1983. 65.00 (ISBN 0-521-24770-5). Cambridge U Pr.

LeDuc, Don R. Cable Television & the FCC: A Crisis in Media Control. LC 72-95885. 299p. 1973. 24.95 (ISBN 0-87722-062-X). Temple U Pr.

Leduc, Lucien P. Behavior Modification Comes to Camelot. (Scholarly Monograph). 140p. 1980. pap. 9.00 o.p. (ISBN 0-686-77613-5). Carrollton Pr.

Ledwidge, Bernard. De Gaulle. (Illus.). 448p. 1983. 17.95 (ISBN 0-312-19127-8). St Martin.

--Frontiers. LC 79-5037. 1979. 10.00 o.p. (ISBN 0-312-30910-4). St Martin.

Ledwith, A. & North, A. M., eds. Molecular Behavior & the Development of Polymer Materials. 1975. 65.00x (ISBN 0-412-12400-9, Pub. by Chapman & Hall). Methuen Inc.

Lee. Crohn's Workshop: A Global Assessment of Crohn's Disease, No. 1. 42.95x (ISBN 0-471-25847-4, Pub. by Wiley Heyden). Wiley.

--The Hidden Events: Incredible Life & Behavior of Insects. 1983. cancelled (ISBN 0-8120-5340-0). Barron.

--Japanese Management. 318p. 1982. 30.95 (ISBN 0-03-061773-1). Praeger.

--Management by Japanese Systems. 576p. 1982. 31.95 (ISBN 0-03-062051-1). Praeger.

Lee, jt. auth. see BUncel.

Lee, jt. auth. see James, L. D.

Lee, jt. auth. see Tyrer.

Lee, jt. auth. see Way.

Lee, et al. Guided Weapons. (Brassey's Battlefield Weapons Systems & Technology: Vol. 8). 160p. 1983. 26.01 (ISBN 0-08-028336-5); pap. 13.01 (ISBN 0-08-028337-3). Pergamon.

Lee, A. G., ed. see Ovid.

Lee, A. J. & Albrektsson, T. Clinical Applications of Biomaterials, Vol. 4. (Advances in Biomaterials Ser.). 356p. 1982. 63.95 (ISBN 0-471-10403-5, Pub. by Wiley-Interscience). Wiley.

Lee, A. Robert, ed. Ernest Hemingway: New Critical Essays. (Critical Studies Ser.). 224p. 1983. text ed. 27.50x (ISBN 0-389-20284-3). B&N Imports.

Lee, Albert. Thrilling Escapes by Night. 296p. 6.95 (ISBN 0-686-05596-9). Rod & Staff.

--Weather Wisdom: A Practical Guide to the Facts & Folklore of Natural Weather. LC 75-40733. (Illus.). 168p. 1976. 12.95 (ISBN 0-385-11016-2). Doubleday.

Lee, Alec M. Applied Queueing Theory. (Illus.). 1966. 14.00 o.p. (ISBN 0-312-04620-0). St Martin.

Lee, Alfred M. Electronic-Message Transfer & its Implications. LC 82-47683. 224p. 1983. 23.95x (ISBN 0-669-05555-7). Lexington Bks.

--Sociology for Whom? 1978. 14.95x (ISBN 0-19-502336-6); pap. 4.95x (ISBN 0-19-502335-8). Oxford U Pr.

Lee, Alfred T. Handbook for the Executive as a Witness. 2nd ed. 53p. 1974. pap. 5.00 (ISBN 0-686-36822-3). US Trademark.

Lee, Allan W. One Great Fellowship Travels of a Global Minister. 1974. pap. 2.50 o.p. (ISBN 0-682-48095-9, Banner). Exposition.

Lee, Alvin A. James Reany. (World Authors Ser.: No. 119). 15.95 (ISBN 0-8057-2750-7, Twayne). G K Hall.

Lee, Andrea. Russian Journal. LC 81-40214. 1981. 13.50 (ISBN 0-394-51891-8). Random.

Lee, Audrey E., jt. auth. see Lee, Calvin B.

Lee, Barbara. The Woman's Guide to the Stockmarket. 224p. 1982. 11.95 (ISBN 0-517-54622-1, Harmony). Crown.

Lee, Barbara & Rudman, Masha K. Mind over Media: New Ways to Improve Your Child's Reading & Writing Skills. LC 81-84522. 260p. 1982. 12.95 (ISBN 0-87223-776-1). Seaview Bks.

Lee, Barry. Introducing Systems Analysis & Design, Vol. 1. LC 79-301329. (Illus.). 1978. pap. 30.00x (ISBN 0-85012-206-6). Intl Pubns Serv.

--Introducing Systems Analysis & Design, Vol. 2. (Illus., Orig.). 1979. pap. 42.00x (ISBN 0-85012-207-4). Intl Pubns Serv.

Lee, Benjamin. Psychosocial Theories of the Self. (Path in Psychology). 230p. 1982. 27.50x (ISBN 0-306-41117-2, Plenum Pr). Plenum Pub.

Lee, Betsy. Miracle in the Making. LC 82-72647. 128p. (Orig.). 1983. pap. 4.95 (ISBN 0-8066-1954-6, 10-4451). Augsburg.

Lee, Beverly. Easy Way to Chinese Cooking. 1971. pap. 2.25 (ISBN 0-451-11299-7, AE1299, Sig). NAL.

Lee, Bob, jt. auth. see Arnold, Henri.

Lee, Bob, jt. ed. see Arnold, Henri.

Lee, Brian. The Novels of Henry James: A Study of Culture & Consciousness. LC 78-16902. 1979. 19.95 (ISBN 0-312-57969-1). St Martin.

Lee, Brian, ed. Byron-Don Juan (1819) 192p. 1969. 15.00x (ISBN 0-686-81912-8, Pub. by Macdonald & Evans). State Mutual Bk.

Lee, Briant H. & Wedwick, Daryl M. Corrugated Scenery. LC 82-81244. (Illus.). 96p. 1982. pap. 10.50 (ISBN 0-88127-004-0). Oracle Pr LA.

Lee, Byung I., jt. auth. see Edmister, Wayne C.

Lee, Byung S. & Huang, Lien-Fu. Fundamental Statistics in Business & Economics. LC 78-68690. 1979. pap. text ed. 19.25 (ISBN 0-8191-0701-8). U Pr of Amer.

Lee, C. C., jt. ed. see Buncel, E.

Lee, C. H. The Quantitative Approach to Economic History. LC 77-77354. 1977. 18.95 (ISBN 0-312-65818-4). St Martin.

Lee, C. K., ed. Developments in Food Carbohydrate--Three. (Illus.). xii, 216p. 1982. 53.50 (ISBN 0-85334-996-7, Pub. by Applied Sci England). Elsevier.

Lee, C. K., et al, eds. Developments in Food Carbohydrates, Vols. 1 & 2. Vol. 1, 1977. 41.00 (ISBN 0-85334-733-6, Pub. by Applied Sci England); Vol. 2, 1980. 74.00 (ISBN 0-85334-857-X). Elsevier.

Lee, C. M. & Inglis, J. K. Science for Hairdressing Students. 3rd ed. (Illus.). 200p. 1983. 40.00 (ISBN 0-08-027440-4); 15.00 (ISBN 0-08-027439-0). Pergamon.

Lee, C. P., et al. Membrane Bioenergetics: Volume Honoring Professor Efriam Racker. Schatz, G. & Ernster, L., eds. (Illus.). 650p. 1980. pap. text ed. 28.50 (ISBN 0-201-03999-0). A W.

Lee, C. Y. Madame Goldenflower. LC 75-2697. 310p. 1975. Repr. of 1960 ed. lib. bdg. 18.25x (ISBN 0-8371-8030-9, LIMG). Greenwood.

Lee, Calvin B. & Lee, Audrey E. The Gourmet Chinese Regional Cookbook. LC 75-45095. 1976. 10.95 o.p. (ISBN 0-399-11673-7). Putnam Pub Group.

Lee, Charles R., Jr. The Confederate Constitutions. LC 73-16628. 225p. 1974. Repr. of 1963 ed. lib. bdg. 25.00x (ISBN 0-8371-7201-2, LECC). Greenwood.

Lee, Charlotte I. Oral Reading of the Scriptures. 1974. text ed. 16.50 o.p. (ISBN 0-395-18940-3). HM.

Lee, Charlotte I. & Gura, Timothy. Oral Interpretations. 6th ed. LC 76-13095. (Illus.). 1982. text ed. 18.95 (ISBN 0-395-31705-3). HM.

Lee, Chauncey. The American Accompant. LC 82-48375. (Accountancy in Transition Ser.). 318p. 1982. lib. bdg. 30.00 (ISBN 0-8240-5324-9). Garland Pub.

Lee, Chip. On Edge: The Life & Climbs of Henry Barber. (Illus.). 240p. (Orig.). 1982. 14.95 (ISBN 0-910146-35-7). Appalach Mtn.

Lee, Chong. Advanced Explosive Kicks. LC 78-61152. (Ser. 133). (Illus.). 1978. pap. 6.95 (ISBN 0-89750-060-1). Ohara Pubns.

--Kicks for Competition. LC 82-61733. (Illus.). 124p. (Orig.). 1982. pap. 6.50 (ISBN 0-89750-083-0, 420). Ohara Pubns.

Lee, Clarence L., ed. see Carpenter, H. J.

Lee, Clarence L., ed. see Jones, A. H.

Lee, D., jt. auth. see Leggett, G.

Lee, D. E. & Brower, W. A. Secretarial Office Procedures. 3rd ed. 1976. text ed. 19.10 (ISBN 0-07-037035-4, G); instructor's manual 8.45 (ISBN 0-07-037036-2). McGraw.

Lee, David & Doerr, Paul, eds. The Complete Guide to Freedom & Survival, Vol. III. 150p. (Orig.). 1982. write for info. Live Free.

Lee, David D. Tennessee in Turmoil: Politics in the Volunteer State, 1920-1932. LC 79-9264. 1979. 15.00x o.p. (ISBN 0-87870-048-X). Memphis St Univ.

Lee, David G. The Complete Guide to Freedom & Survival. (Illus.). 1980. pap. text ed. 8.95 (ISBN 0-686-28071-7). Live Free.

Lee, Deemer. Esther's Town. 190p. 1980. 10.95 (ISBN 0-8138-0460-4). Iowa St U Pr.

Lee, Delene W. & Lee, Jasper S. Agribusiness Procedures & Practices. (Career Preparation for Agriculture-Agribusiness Ser.). (Illus.). 1980. pap. text ed. 6.95 (ISBN 0-07-036737-X, G); tchr's manual & key 3.00 (ISBN 0-07-036739-6); activity guide 4.96 (ISBN 0-07-036738-8). McGraw.

Lee, Derek. Control of the Economy. (Studies in the British Economy). 1974. pap. text ed. 4.00x o.p. (ISBN 0-435-84542-X). Heinemann Ed.

--Regional Planning & Location of Industry. 3rd ed. (Studies in the British Economy). 1980. pap. text ed. 7.50x o.p. (ISBN 0-435-84577-2). Heinemann Ed.

Lee, Don Y. An Annotated Bibliography on Inner Asia. 1983. 25.50x (ISBN 0-939758-04-0). Eastern Pr.

Lee, Donald G. Oxidation of Organic Compounds by Permanganate Ion & Hexavalent Chromium. 176p. 1980. 30.00 (ISBN 0-87548-351-8). Open Court.

Lee, Dorothy E. & Brower, Walter A. Secretarial Office Procedures. 2nd, rev. ed. (Illus.). 416p. 1981. pap. text ed. 16.40 (ISBN 0-07-037037-0, G); instr's manual & key 7.25 (ISBN 0-07-037038-9); instr's manual & key 7.25 (ISBN 0-07-037038-9). McGraw.

Lee, Dorris & Rubin, Joseph B. Children & Language. 1979. text ed. 19.95x o.p. (ISBN 0-534-00686-8). Wadsworth Pub.

Lee, Dorris M. & Allen, Richard V. Learning to Read Through Experience. 2nd ed. (Illus.). (YA) (gr. 9-12). 1966. pap. text ed. 15.95 (ISBN 0-13-527523-7). P-H.

Lee, Douglas, jt. auth. see Kozuki, Russell.

Lee, Douglas H., jt. auth. see Selikoff, Irving.

Lee, Douglas H., ed. Environmental Factors in Respiratory Disease. (Environmental Science Ser.). 1972. 29.50 o.p. (ISBN 0-12-440655-6). Acad Pr.

Lee, Dwight. The Outbreak of the First World War. 4th ed. (Problems in European Civilization Ser.). 168p. 1975. pap. text ed. 5.50 (ISBN 0-669-94706-7). Heath.

Lee, Dwight R. & McNown, Robert F. Economics in Our Time: Concepts & Issues. LC 74-18924. 224p. 1975. pap. text ed. 7.95 (ISBN 0-574-18222-5, 13-2220); instr's guide avail. (ISBN 0-574-18221-7, 13-2221). SRA.

--Economics in Our Time: Concepts & Issues. 2nd ed. 224p. 1983. pap. text ed. write for info. (ISBN 0-574-19435-5, 13-2435); write for info. instr's. guide (ISBN 0-574-19436-3). SRA.

Lee, Dwight R., jt. auth. see Glahe, Fred R.

Lee, Dwight R., jt. auth. see McNown, Robert F.

Lee, E. B. & Markus, L. Foundations of Optimal Control Theory. LC 67-22414. (SIAM Series in Applied Mathematics). 1967. 59.95x (ISBN 0-471-52263-5, Pub. by Wiley-Interscience). Wiley.

Lee, E. Stanley, jt. ed. see Wen, C. Y.

Lee, Ed, jt. ed. see Vulliamy, Graham.

Lee, Edward. Folksong & Music Hall. (Routledge Popular Music Ser.). (Illus.). 128p. 1982. 12.95 (ISBN 0-7100-0902-X). Routledge & Kegan.

Lee, Elisa T. Statistical Methods for Survival Data Analysis. LC 80-24720. 557p. 1980. 28.95 (ISBN 0-534-97987-4); solutions manual 4.95. Lifetime Learn.

Lee, Ellen W. & Smith, Tracy E. The Aura of Neo-Impressionism: The W. J. Holliday Collection of the Indianapolis Museum of Art. LC 82-84036. (Centennial Catalogue Series). (Illus.). 296p. (Orig.). 1983. 45.00x (ISBN 0-936260-04-1); pap. 25.00x (ISBN 0-936260-05-X). Ind Mus Art.

Lee, Ernest M. Story of Opera. LC 69-16803. (Music Story Ser). 1968. Repr. of 1909 ed. 30.00x (ISBN 0-8103-3359-7). Gale.

--Story of Symphony. LC 69-16804. (Illus.). 1968. Repr. of 1916 ed. 38.00x (ISBN 0-8103-3568-9). Gale.

Lee, Essie. Careers in the Health Field. rev. ed. LC 74-9681. (Career Bks.). (Illus.). 192p. (gr. 7 up). 1974. PLB 7.29 o.p. (ISBN 0-671-32513-2). Messner.

Lee, Essie E. Marriage & Families. LC 77-26962. 224p. (gr. 7 up). 1978. PLB 7.79 o.p. (ISBN 0-671-32854-9). Messner.

Lee, Francis G. Neither Conservative nor Liberal: The Burger Court on Civil Rights & Civil Liberties. LC 82-120. (Orig.). 1983. pap. text ed. 6.50 (ISBN 0-89874-425-3). Krieger.

Lee, Frank. Bedtime Stories of the Saints, Bk. 1. rev ed. (Illus.). 96p. (ps-5). 1974. saddle stitch 1.75 (ISBN 0-89243-003-6, 27227). Liguori Pubns.

Lee, Frank A. Basic Food Chemistry. (Illus.). 1975. pap. text ed. 22.00 o.p. (ISBN 0-87055-289-9). AVI.

--Basic Food Chemistry. 2nd ed. (Illus.). 1983. pap. text ed. 22.00 (ISBN 0-87055-416-6). AVI.

Lee, Frank E. Central Office Plant, Vol. III. 1976. 6.75 (ISBN 0-686-98059-X). Telecom Lib.

--Station Installation & Maintenance, Vol. II. 1976. 6.75 (ISBN 0-686-98058-1). Telecom Lib.

--Telephone Theory, Principles & Practice, Vol. I. 1976. 6.95 (ISBN 0-686-98057-3). Telecom Lib.

Lee, Frank K. Outside Plant: Engineering & Practice, Vol. IV. 1977. 6.50 (ISBN 0-686-98060-3). Telecom Lib.

Lee, Frederick G. A Glossary of Liturgical & Ecclesiastical Terms. LC 76-174069. (Tower Bks). (Illus.). xl, 452p. 1972. Repr. of 1877 ed. 38.00x (ISBN 0-8103-3949-8). Gale.

Lee, G. From Hardware to Software: An Introduction to Computers. 1982. 40.00x (ISBN 0-333-24363-3, Pub. by Macmillan England). State Mutual Bk.

Lee, Gary. Chinese Vegetarian Cookbook. LC 72-194449. (Illus.). 192p. (Orig.). 1972. pap. 4.95 o.p. (ISBN 0-911954-20-1). Nitty Gritty.

--Wok Appetizers & Light Snacks. (Illus.). 182p. (Orig.). 1982. pap. 5.95 (ISBN 0-911954-67-8). Nitty Gritty.

Lee, Gary R. Family Structure & Interaction: A Comparative Analysis. 2nd ed. LC 82-4844. 352p. 1982. 19.95x (ISBN 0-8166-1091-6). U of Minn Pr.

Lee, Georgia. The Portable Cosmos: Effigies, Ornaments & Incised Stone from the Chumash Area. (Ballena Press Anthropological Papers: No. 21). (Illus.). 114p. (Orig.). 1981. pap. 6.95 o.p. (ISBN 0-87919-093-0). Ballena Pr.

Lee, Gloria L. Who Gets to the Top? 160p. 1981. text ed. 33.00x (ISBN 0-566-00497-6). Gower Pub Ltd.

Lee, Gordon, ed. see Goldstein, Stephen R.

Lee, Gordon C., ed. Crusade Against Ignorance: Thomas Jefferson on Education. LC 61-10961. (Orig.). 1961. text ed. 10.00 (ISBN 0-8077-1671-5); pap. text ed. 5.00x (ISBN 0-8077-1668-5). Tchrs Coll.

Lee, H. Alton. Seven Feet Four & Growing. LC 77-13923. 1978. 8.95 (ISBN 0-664-32623-4). Westminster.

Lee, H. D., tr. see Plato.

Lee, H. L. & Neville, K. O. Handbook of Epoxy Resins. 1966. 55.00 o.p. (ISBN 0-07-036997-6, P&RB). McGraw.

Lee, Hahn-Been. Korea: Time, Change & Administration. LC 67-28036. (Illus.). 1968. 14.00x (ISBN 0-8248-0072-9, Eastwest Ctr). UH Pr.

Lee, Hans, jt. auth. see Cohen, Bernard P.

Lee, Harper. To Kill a Mockingbird. LC 60-7847. 1960. 13.41i (ISBN 0-397-00151-7). Har-Row.

--To Kill a Mockingbird. 284p. 1982. pap. 3.50 (ISBN 0-446-31049-2). Warner Bks.

Lee, Harry O. & LeForestier, Wilford A. Review & Reduction of Real Property Assessments in New York. 2nd ed. LC 77-14270. 1978. 50.00 (ISBN 0-87632-214-3); 1981 supplement incl. Boardman.

Lee, Helen. This Is My Home, Lord. 128p. 1983. pap. 4.95 (ISBN 0-86683-683-7). Winston Pr.

Lee, Hermione, ed. see Smith, Stevie.

Lee, Hor M., tr. see Anhui Medical School Hospital.

Lee, Howard W. Eye Care: What You Need to Know before You See the Eye Doctor. 250p. 1982. pap. 6.95 (ISBN 0-914091-16-6). Chicago Review.

Lee, Ian. The Third Word War. (Illus.). 128p. 1978. pap. 4.95 o.s.i. (ISBN 0-89104-115-X, A & W Visual Library). A & W Pubs.

Lee, Isaiah. Medical Care in a Mexican American Community. LC 76-4706. (Illus.). 186p. 1976. pap. text ed. 5.95 o.p. (ISBN 0-89260-024-1). Hwong Pub.

Lee, Iva H. Data Entry: Concepts & Exercises. LC 81-11403. 355p. 1982. text ed. 19.95x (ISBN 0-471-08605-3); tchrs' manual 25.00x (ISBN 0-471-86584-2). Wiley.

Lee, J. Finley, jt. auth. see Launie, J. J.

Lee, J. M. & Petter, Martin. The Colonial Office: War & Development Policy. 1981. 60.00x (ISBN 0-686-82395-8, Pub. by M Temple Smith). State Mutual Bk.

Lee, J. S. Introduction to Geomechanics. 2nd ed. 140p. 1983. 58.75 (ISBN 0-677-31070-6). Gordon.

Lee, J. S. & Rom. Legal & Ethical Dilemmas in Occupational Health. LC 81-71827. 450p. 1982. 39.95 (ISBN 0-250-40479-6). Ann Arbor Science.

Lee, J. S., jt. ed. see Klein, F. J.

Lee, James, jt. auth. see Falk, Nicholas.

Lee, James, et al. Radio Frequency Testers. Cole, Sandy & Force, Rich, eds. (Seventy-Three Test Equipment Library: Vol. 3). 112p. pap. text ed. 4.95 o.p. (ISBN 0-88006-012-3, LB 7361). Green Pub Inc.

Lee, James A. The Gold & the Garbage in Management Theories & Prescriptions. LC 80-12758. (Illus.). x, 480p. 1980. 22.95x (ISBN 0-8214-0436-9, 82-83228); pap. 11.95 (ISBN 0-8214-0578-0, 82-83236). Ohio U Pr.

Lee, James B., ed. Renal Prostaglandins, Vol. 1. (Annual Research Reviews Ser.). 1979. 28.80 (ISBN 0-88831-037-4). Eden Pr.

Lee, James Michael. The Flow of Religious Instruction: A Social-Science Approach. LC 74-29824. (Illus.). 379p. (Orig.). 1973. lib. bdg. 12.95 (ISBN 0-89135-001-2); pap. 8.95 o.p. (ISBN 0-89135-003-9). Religious Educ.

--The Shape of Religious Instruction: A Social-Science Approach. LC 74-29823. 330p. (Orig.). 1971. lib. bdg. 12.95 (ISBN 0-89135-000-4); pap. 9.95 (ISBN 0-89135-002-0). Religious Educ.

Lee, James W. John Braine. (English Authors Ser.). 13.95 (ISBN 0-8057-1056-6, Twayne). G K Hall.

Lee, Jasper S. Commercial Catfish Farming. 2nd ed. (Illus.). 1981. 13.95 (ISBN 0-8134-2156-X, 2156). Interstate.

--Working in Agricultural Industry. (Illus.). (gr. 9-10). 1978. pap. text ed. 7.96 (ISBN 0-07-000831-0, G). McGraw.

--Working in Agricultural Industry: Activity Guide. Amberson, Max L., ed. (gr. 9-10). 1978. pap. 4.96 (ISBN 0-07-000832-9, G); tchr's manual 3.50 (ISBN 0-07-000833-7). McGraw.

Lee, Jasper S., jt. auth. see Lee, Delene W.

Lee, Jasper S., jt. auth. see McGuire, James E.

Lee, Jasper S., ed. see Brown, Ronald & Oren, John W.

Lee, Jasper S., ed. see Dillon, Roy.

Lee, Jasper S., ed. see Long, Don L., et al.

Lee, Jasper S., ed. see Miller, Larry.

Lee, Jeanne. Legend of the Li River. (Illus.). 32p. (gr. k-3). 1983. 11.95 (ISBN 0-03-063523-3). HR&W.

Lee, Joanna. I Want to Keep My Baby. (Orig.). (RL 10). 1977. pap. 1.75 (ISBN 0-451-09884-6, E9884, Sig). NAL.

Lee, Joe. Bankruptcy. LC 79-92367. 1981. 72.50 (ISBN 0-686-35938-0). Lawyers Co-Op.

Lee, John. Lago. 1981. pap. 2.95 o.s.i. (ISBN 0-440-14788-3). Dell.

--Lago. LC 78-60293. (Illus.). 1980. 11.95 o.p. (ISBN 0-385-12993-9). Doubleday.

--The Ninth Man. 1979. pap. 2.25 o.s.i. (ISBN 0-440-16425-7). Dell.

--The Thirteenth Hour. LC 77-82768. 1978. 12.95 o.p. (ISBN 0-385-12992-0). Doubleday.

Lee, John A. The Anatomy of a Compiler. 2nd ed. (Computer Science Ser). 1974. text ed. 17.95 (ISBN 0-442-24733-8); pap. 12.95 (ISBN 0-442-24734-6). Van Nos Reinhold.

Lee, John J. Microbiology. (Illus.). 352p. (Orig.). 1982. pap. 5.72i (COS CO 183). B&N NY.

Lee, Joseph J. Wang Ch'ang-Ling. (World Authors Ser.). 1982. lib. bdg. 16.95 (ISBN 0-8057-6465-8, Twayne). G K Hall.

Lee, Joyce. The Best Laid Schemes. (Orig.). 1980. pap. 1.50 o.s.i. (ISBN 0-440-11011-4). Dell.

--Oh, What a Tangled Web. (Candlelight Romance Ser.). (Orig.). 1981. pap. 1.50 o.s.i. (ISBN 0-440-16821-X). Dell.

Lee, Juanita E., jt. auth. see Shortridge, Lillie M.

Lee, Jung Y. A Child Sacrifice in the Public School. (Cross-Cultural Studies). (Orig.). 1978. 7.95 (ISBN 0-918972-01-9); pap. 3.95 (ISBN 0-918972-02-7). Far Eastern Cult.

--Death Overcome: Towards a Convergence of Eastern & Western Views. LC 82-20192. 98p. (Orig.). 1983. lib. bdg. 17.25 (ISBN 0-8191-2902-X); pap. text ed. 7.25 (ISBN 0-8191-2901-1). U Pr of Amer.

Lee, K. A New Logical Basis for Moral Philosophy. 1981. 60.00x o.p. (ISBN 0-86127-108-4, Pub. by Avebury Pub England). State Mutual Bk.

Lee, K. J. Essential Otolaryngology. 3rd ed. 1982. pap. 23.50 (ISBN 0-87488-313-X). Med Exam.

Lee, K. S., jt. ed. see Whelan, A.

Lee, K. S., ed. see Whelan, A.

Lee, K. Wayne. Equality Without Regimentation: An Introduction to Mutualism. LC 82-62539. 240p. 1983. pap. 9.50 (ISBN 0-88100-020-5). New Tide.

Lee, Karen & Friedman, Aileen R. Chinese Cooking for the American Kitchen. LC 76-11858. (Illus.). 1980. pap. 8.95 (ISBN 0-689-70596-4, 256); o. p 12.95 (ISBN 0-689-10751-X). Atheneum.

Lee, Karen, ed. see Angel, Velma.

Lee, Kay & Lee, Marshall. America's Favorites. (Illus.). 160p. 1980. 17.95 o.p. (ISBN 0-399-12514-0). Putnam Pub Group.

--The Illuminated Book of Days. LC 79-87621. (Illus.). 1979. 14.95 o.p. (ISBN 0-399-12406-3). Putnam Pub Group.

Lee, Kay, jt. auth. see Clark, Linda.

Lee, Keat-Jin, ed. Essential Otolaryngology: A Board Preparation & Concise Reference. 2nd ed. 1977. spiral bdg. 23.50 o.p. (ISBN 0-87488-313-X). Med Exam.

Lee, Kee-Dong. Kusaiean-English Dictionary. (PALI Language Texts-Micronesia). 336p. 1976. pap. text ed. 12.00x (ISBN 0-8248-0413-9). UH Pr.

--Kusaiean Reference Grammar. LC 75-6863. (PALI Language Texts: Micronesia). 554p. 1975. pap. text ed. 14.50x (ISBN 0-8248-0355-8). UH Pr.

Lee, Ki-Baik. A New History of Korea. Wagner, Edward W. & Schultz, Edward J., trs. from Korean. (Harvard-Yenching Institute Ser.). (Illus.). 472p. 1983. text ed. 25.00x (ISBN 0-674-61575-1). Harvard U Pr.

Lee, Kyung-Shik, tr. see Han, Woo-Keun.

Lee, L. L. Vladimir Nabokov. (United states Authors Ser.). 1976. lib. bdg. 12.95 (ISBN 0-8057-7166-2, Twayne). G K Hall.

Lee, Lamar, Jr. & Dobler, Donald W. Purchasing & Materials Management. 3rd ed. 1976. 28.95 (ISBN 0-07-037027-3, C); instructor's manual 25.00 (ISBN 0-07-037028-1). McGraw.

Lee, Lauri F. Foundations. (Gateway to English Program). (Illus.). 128p. (Orig.). 1981. cancelled o.p. (ISBN 0-88377-176-4); student wkbk 1.95 o.p. (ISBN 0-88377-177-2). Newbury Hse.

Lee, Laurie. Laurie Lee. (Pocket Poet Ser.). 1961. pap. 1.25 (ISBN 0-8023-9045-5). Dufour.

Lee, Lawrence. The American As Faust. (Orig.). 1965. 2.95 o.p. (ISBN 0-910286-46-9); pap. 1.95 o.p. (ISBN 0-910286-15-9). Boxwood.

--Cockcrow at Night, the Heroic Journey, & 18 Other Stories. (Illus.). 250p. (Orig.). 1973. 6.00 o.p. (ISBN 0-910286-35-3); pap. 4.50 o.p. (ISBN 0-910286-30-2). Boxwood.

--Horse of Selene. 1977. pap. 4.95 o.p. (ISBN 0-910286-64-7). Boxwood.

--Voice of the Furies. (Orig.). 1969. pap. 1.95 o.p. (ISBN 0-910286-08-6). Boxwood.

Lee, Lawrence, jt. auth. see Gifford, Barry.

Lee, Lawrence B. Reclaiming the American West: An Historiography & Guide. LC 79-20007. 131p. 1980. text ed. 16.50 (ISBN 0-87436-298-9). ABC-Clio.

Lee, Leonard S., jt. auth. see Kalthoff, Robert J.

Lee, Leslie W. & Schmidt, L. M. Elementary Principles of Laboratory Instruments. 5th ed. (Illus.). 416p. 1983. text ed. 19.95 (ISBN 0-8016-2918-7). Mosby.

Lee, Linda. Out of Wedlock: A Love Story. (Illus.). 320p. 1982. 15.50 (ISBN 0-316-51951-0). Little.

Lee, Lynn. Don Marquis. (United States Authors Ser.). 1981. lib. bdg. 13.95 (ISBN 0-8057-7282-0, Twayne). G K Hall.

Lee, M. A. The Droplet Size Distribution of Oils Emulsified in Sea Water by Concentrate Dispersants, 1980. 1981. 30.00x (ISBN 0-686-97064-0, Pub. by W Spring England). State Mutual Bk.

--Investigation of the Demulsification of Water-in-Oil Emulsions for Med When Crude Oil or Fuel Oil is Spilt on the Sea, 1980. 1981. 40.00x (ISBN 0-686-97090-X, Pub. by W Spring England). State Mutual Bk.

Lee, M. D., ed. see Bayle, Pierre.

Lee, M. J. The United Nations & World Realities. 1966. 24.00 o.p. (ISBN 0-08-011350-8); pap. 10.75 o.p. (ISBN 0-08-011349-4). Pergamon.

Lee, M. J., jt. auth. see Bunting, G. R.

Lee, M. O. Fathers & Sons in Virgil's Aeneid: Tum Genitor Natum. 1979. 34.50x (ISBN 0-87395-402-5); pap. 11.95x (ISBN 0-87395-451-3). State U NY Pr.

Lee, M. P. Chinese Cookery. (Illus.). 1943. 2.50 o.p. (ISBN 0-571-06217-2). Transatlantic.

Lee, M. R. Renin & Hypertension: A Modern Synthesis. 234p. 1969. 12.50 o.p. (ISBN 0-685-72299-6, Pub. by Williams & Wilkins). Krieger.

Lee, Mabel. History of Physical Education & Sports in the U. S. A. 384p. 1983. text ed. 16.95 (ISBN 0-471-86315-7). Wiley.

--Memories Beyond Bloomers. 476p. 1978. 9.95 (ISBN 0-88314-129-9, 240-26218). AAHPERD.

--Memories of a Bloomer Girl. 368p. 1977. 9.95 (ISBN 0-88314-130-2, 240-25974). AAHPERD.

Lee, Mabel & Wagner, Miriam M. Fundamentals of Body Mechanics & Conditioning: An Illustrated Teaching Manual. Repr. of 1949 ed. lib. bdg. 17.75x (ISBN 0-8371-2417-4). Greenwood.

Lee, Marian. Solve a Mystery: Book One, from the Casebook of J.P. Landers, Master Detective. LC 82-9712. (Illus.). (gr. 4 up). 1982. PLB 8.60g (ISBN 0-516-01991-0). Childrens.

--Solve a Mystery: Book Three, from the Casebook of J.P. Landers, Master Detective. LC 82-9712. (Illus.). (gr. 4 up). 1982. PLB 8.60g (ISBN 0-516-01993-7). Childrens.

--Solve a Mystery: Book Two, from the Casebook of J.P. Landers, Master Detective. LC 82-9712. (Illus.). (gr. 4 up). 1982. PLB 8.60g (ISBN 0-516-01992-9). Childrens.

Lee, Mark W. How to Have a Good Marriage. LC 78-56794. 1981. pap. 5.95 (ISBN 0-915684-89-6). Chr Pubns.

--Time Bombs in Marriage. LC 81-65727. 192p. 1981. pap. 5.95 o.p. (ISBN 0-915684-92-6). Christian Herald.

Lee, Marshall, jt. auth. see Lee, Kay.

Lee, Maurice. Government by Pen: The Scotland of James VI & I. LC 79-16830. 224p. 1980. 16.00 o.p. (ISBN 0-252-00765-4). U of Ill Pr.

--James Stewart, Earl of Moray: A Political Study of the Reformation in Scotland. LC 73-104251. 1971. Repr. of 1953 ed. lib. bdg. 17.00x (ISBN 0-8371-3975-9, LEJS). Greenwood.

Lee, Mildred. Fog. 240p. 1974. pap. 1.25 o.p. (ISBN 0-440-93133-9, LFL). Dell.

--People Therein. 1982. pap. 1.95 (ISBN 0-451-11355-1, Sig Vista). NAL.

--Sycamore Year. 160p. (RL 6). Date not set. pap. 1.75 (ISBN 0-451-11357-8, AE1357, Sig). NAL.

--Sycamore Year. 1982. pap. 1.75 (ISBN 0-451-11357-8, AE1357, Vista). NAL.

Lee, Molly K., ed. East Asian Economies: A Guide to Information Sources. LC 78-13114. (Economics Information Guide Ser.: Vol. 1). 1979. 42.00x (ISBN 0-8103-1427-4). Gale.

Lee, N., jt. auth. see Wood, C. M.

Lee, Nancy. Targeting the Top: Everything a Woman Needs to Know to Develop a Successful Career in Business Year After Year. LC 78-22736. 408p. 1980. 11.95 o.p. (ISBN 0-385-13244-1). Doubleday.

Lee, Norman. Teaching Economics. 1975. text ed. 21.50x o.p. (ISBN 0-435-84523-3); pap. text ed. 16.50 (ISBN 0-435-84524-1). Heinemann Ed.

Lee, Owen. Skin Diver's Bible. LC 67-11191. 1963. pap. 4.50 (ISBN 0-385-03737-6). Doubleday.

Lee, Pao-Chen. Read About China. 4.95 (ISBN 0-686-09946-X); tapes avail. (ISBN 0-686-09947-8). Far Eastern Pubns.

Lee, Pat, jt. auth. see Wilson, Ron.

Lee, Patrick. Six-Gun Warrior, No. 7: Prairie Caesar. 208p. (Orig.). 1983. pap. 2.25. Pinnacle Bks.

Lee, Peter H., ed. Anthology of Korean Literature: From Early Times to the Nineteenth Century. LC 81-69567. 448p. 1981. lib. bdg. 24.00x (ISBN 0-8248-0739-1); pap. text ed. 12.00x (ISBN 0-8248-0756-1). UH Pr.

--Flowers of Fire: Twentieth Century Korean Stories. LC 73-90853. 336p. 1974. 14.00x (ISBN 0-8248-0302-7, Eastwest Ctr). UH Pr.

Lee, Peter H., ed. & tr. from Korean. Poems from Korea: A Historical Anthology. rev. ed. LC 73-80209. 196p. 1974. 8.50x o.p. (ISBN 0-8248-0263-2, Eastwest Ctr). UH Pr.

Lee, Peter H., ed. The Silence of Love: Twentieth-Century Korean Poetry. LC 80-21999. 368p. 1980. text ed. 17.95x (ISBN 0-8248-0711-1); pap. 8.95 (ISBN 0-8248-0732-4). UH Pr.

Lee, Philip R., jt. auth. see Silverman, Milton.

Lee, Phillip R., et al. Primary Care in a Specialized World. LC 76-10222. 256p. 1976. prof ref 22.50x (ISBN 0-88410-139-8). Ballinger Pub.

Lee, Pong K. & Ryu, Chi Sik. Easy Way to Korean Conversation. 2nd, rev. ed. (Illus.). 77p. 1983. 14.95 (ISBN 0-930878-30-2); cassette incl. Hollym Intl.

Lee, R. Public Personnel Systems. 254p. 1979. text ed. 22.50 (ISBN 0-8391-1452-4). Univ Park.

Lee, R. D. & Johnson, R. W., eds. Public Budgeting Systems. 2nd ed. 392p. 1977. text ed. 22.50 (ISBN 0-8391-0988-1). Univ Park.

Lee, R. K., jt. auth. see Hodder, B. K.

Lee, R. M. A Short Course in Basic FORTRAN IV Programming: Based on the IBM System,360-370. 2nd, rev. ed. 1972. 21.95 (ISBN 0-07-036998-4, C). McGraw.

Lee, Rachel G. Learning Centers for Better Christian Education. 80p. 1982. pap. 7.95 (ISBN 0-8170-0959-2). Judson.

Lee, Ralph. Modern Caravanning. (Illus.). 5.50x (ISBN 0-392-03968-0, SpS). Sportshelf.

Lee, Richard B. The Kung San: Men, Women, & Work in a Foraging Society. LC 78-29504. (Illus.). 1979. 47.50 (ISBN 0-521-22578-7); pap. 12.95x (ISBN 0-521-29561-0). Cambridge U Pr.

Lee, Richard B., jt. ed. see Leacock, Eleanor B.

Lee, Robert. China Journal: Glimpses of a Nation in Transition. LC 80-52783. (Illus., Orig.). 1980. 9.25 (ISBN 0-934788-00-6); pap. 5.25 (ISBN 0-686-96708-9). E-W Pub Co.

Lee, Robert & Misiorowski, Robert. Script Models: A Handbook for the Media Writer. 1978. 9.50 o.p. (ISBN 0-8038-6755-7); pap. 5.95 (ISBN 0-8038-6754-9). Hastings.

Lee, Robert A. Alistair MacLean: The Key Is Fear. LC 76-29047. (The Milford Ser.: Popular Writers of Today Vol. 2). 1976. lib. bdg. 9.95x (ISBN 0-89370-103-3); pap. 3.95x (ISBN 0-89370-203-X). Borgo Pr.

Lee, Robert C. It's a Mile from Here to Glory. (gr. 5 up). 1972. 7.95 (ISBN 0-316-51949-9). Little.

--Timequake. LC 82-13567. (gr. 5-9). 9.95 (ISBN 0-664-32698-6). Westminster.

Lee, Robert D., Jr. Public Budgeting Systems. 3rd ed. 392p. 1982. text ed. 19.95 (ISBN 0-8391-1736-1). Univ Park.

Lee, Robert E. North Carolina Family Law, 4 vols. 4th ed. 1979-81. 140.00 (ISBN 0-87215-473-4). Michie-Bobbs.

--Phycology. LC 79-25402. (Illus.). 450p. 1980. 59.50 (ISBN 0-521-22530-2); pap. 18.95 (ISBN 0-521-29541-6). Cambridge U Pr.

Lee, Ronald R. Clergy & Clients: The Practice of Pastoral Psychotherapy. 1980. 10.95 (ISBN 0-8164-0115-2). Seabury.

Lee, Roy F. Setting for Black Business Development: A Study in Sociology & Political Economy. LC 72-619630. 272p. 1973. pap. 7.00 (ISBN 0-87546-039-9); pap. 10.00 special hard bdg (ISBN 0-87546-275-8). ILR Pr.

Lee, Ruth W. Antique Fakes & Reproductions. rev. ed. (Illus.). 15.00 (ISBN 0-910872-07-4). Lee Pubns.

--Current Values of Antique Glass. rev. ed. 8.95 (ISBN 0-910872-08-2). Lee Pubns.

--Early American Pressed Glass. rev. ed. (Illus.). 25.00 (ISBN 0-910872-00-7). Lee Pubns.

--Handbook of Early American Pressed Glass Patterns. (Illus.). 6.95 (ISBN 0-910872-01-5). Lee Pubns.

--A History of Valentines. (Illus.). 1962. 15.00 (ISBN 0-910872-10-4). Lee Pubns.

--Nineteenth Century Art Glass. (Illus.). Date not set. 7.95 (ISBN 0-910872-19-8). Lee Pubns.

--Price Guide to Pattern Glass. rev. ed. 8.95 (ISBN 0-910872-09-0). Lee Pubns.

--Sandwich Glass. rev. ed. (Illus.). 25.00 (ISBN 0-910872-04-X). Lee Pubns.

--Sandwich Glass Handbook. (Illus.). 6.95 (ISBN 0-910872-05-8). Lee Pubns.

--Victorian Glass. (Illus.). 25.00 (ISBN 0-910872-02-3). Lee Pubns.

--Victorian Glass Handbook. (Illus.). 6.95 (ISBN 0-910872-03-1). Lee Pubns.

Lee, Ruth W. & Rose, James H. American Glass Cup Plates. (Illus.). 445p. 1971. 35.00 (ISBN 0-910872-18-X). Lee Pubns.

Lee, Ruth W., ed. Boston & Sandwich Glass Co. Factory Catalogue. 6.95 (ISBN 0-910872-06-6). Lee Pubns.

Lee, S. C. Auburn-Alabama Joke Book. LC 74-21104. 1974. 2.95 (ISBN 0-87397-059-4). Strode.

--Full Time Football Player. LC 72-77597. (Super Star Ser.). (Illus.). 128p. (gr. 3-8). 1973. 4.95 (ISBN 0-87397-018-7). Strode.

--Georgia-Georgia Tech Joke Book. 104p. pap. 2.95 (ISBN 0-87397-083-7). Strode.

--Little League Baseball Leader. LC 74-77738. (Super Star Ser.). 1974. 4.95 (ISBN 0-87397-046-2). Strode.

--Michigan-Michigan State Joke Book. 1975. 1.98 (ISBN 0-87397-088-8). Strode.

--Texas-Texas A & M Joke Book. LC 75-15218. 1975. 2.95 (ISBN 0-87397-084-5). Strode.

Lee, S. D. & Mudd, J. Brian. Assessing Toxic Effects of Environmental Pollutants. LC 78-71430. 1979. 49.95 (ISBN 0-250-40266-1). Ann Arbor Science.

Lee, S. D., ed. Biochemical Effects of Environmental Pollutants. LC 76-46022. 1977. 39.95 o.p. (ISBN 0-250-40143-6). Ann Arbor Science.

--Nitrogen Oxides & Their Effects on Health. LC 79-53421. 1980. 49.95 (ISBN 0-250-40289-0). Ann Arbor Science.

Lee, S. E. Recollections of Country Joe. LC 75-31650. (Illus.). 128p. 1976. 6.95 (ISBN 0-88289-040-9). Pelican.

Lee, S. K., jt. auth. see Jasentuliyana, Nandasiri.

Lee, S. Y. Financial Structures & Monetary Policy. 300p. 1982. 49.00x (ISBN 0-333-28617-0, Pub. by Macmillan England). State Mutual Bk.

Lee, Samuel C. Digital Circuits & Logic Design. (Illus.). 1976. 32.95 (ISBN 0-13-212225-1). P-H.

--Modern Switching Theory & Digital Design. 1978. ref. 32.95 (ISBN 0-13-598680-X). P-H.

Lee, Samuel S., jt. ed. see Sengupta, Subrata.

Lee, Sang Hyun, jt. ed. see Kim, Byong-suh.

Lee, Sang M. Goal Programming Methods for Multiple Objective Integer Programs. 1979. pap. text ed. 14.00 (ISBN 0-89806-001-X, 125); pap. text ed. 7.00 members. Inst Indus Eng.

--Introduction to Management Science. 736p. 1983. text ed. 28.95 (ISBN 0-686-38856-9). Dryden Pr.

Lee, Sang M. & Van Horn, James C. Academic Administration: Planning, Budgeting, & Decision Making with Multiple Objectives. LC 81-24061. xii, 257p. 1983. 29.95x (ISBN 0-8032-2856-2). U of Nebr Pr.

Lee, Sheila. From Beginning to Beginning. LC 77-82837. (Illus.). 1977. 9.95 (ISBN 0-930554-02-7). Victory Day.

--In My Solitude. LC 77-82840. (Illus.). 1977. 7.95 (ISBN 0-930554-06-X). Victory Day.

--Kinds of Love. LC 77-82846. (Illus.). 1977. 7.95 (ISBN 0-930554-04-3). Victory Day.

--Life Is Eternal. LC 77-82845. (Illus.). 1977. 6.95 (ISBN 0-930554-03-5). Victory Day.

--Lovers. LC 77-82843. (Illus.). 1977. 6.95 (ISBN 0-930554-01-9). Victory Day.

--Prayers in Poetry. LC 77-82844. (Illus.). 1977. 6.95 (ISBN 0-930554-07-8). Victory Day.

--Thoughts One Afternoon. LC 77-82841. (Illus.). 1977. 6.95 (ISBN 0-930554-05-1). Victory Day.

Lee, Sherman E. Asian Art: Selections from the Collection of Mr. & Mrs. John D. Rockefeller, 3rd. (Illus.). 1970. pap. text ed. 35.00 (ISBN 0-89192-278-4); 31 35mm color slides, paper, notes 25.00. Interbk Inc.

--History of Far Eastern Art. rev. ed. LC 73-2670. 1974. 40.00 o.p. (ISBN 0-8109-0113-7). Abrams.

--Past, Present, East & West. Saissenlin, Remy & Goodman, Nelson, eds. (Illus.). 1983. 25.00 (ISBN 0-8076-1064-X). Braziller.

Lee, Sherman E. & Cunningham, Michael R. Reflections of Reality in Japanese Art. LC 82-45940. (Illus.). 350p. 1983. price not set (ISBN 0-910386-70-6, Pub. by Cleveland Mus Art). Ind U Pr.

Lee, Sherman E., ed. On Understanding Art Museums. 1975. 9.95 o.p. (ISBN 0-13-936286-X); pap. 2.95 (ISBN 0-13-936278-9). Am Assembly.

Lee, Sherry, et al. Chromosomes & Genes: An Interracial Anthology. 54p. (Orig.). 1982. pap. 3.50 (ISBN 0-940248-12-3). Guild Pr.

Lee, Sidney, ed. see Herbert, Edward H.

Lee, Stan. The Best of the Worst. LC 79-1671. (Illus.). 1979. pap. 4.95i o.p. (ISBN 0-06-090728-2, CN 728, CN). Har-Row.

--Dr. Strange. 1979. 12.95 (ISBN 0-671-25206-2, Fireside); pap. 3.95 o.p. (ISBN 0-671-24814-6). S&S.

Lee, Stan & Buscema, John. How to Draw Comics the Marvel Way. (Illus.). 1977. 13.50 (ISBN 0-671-22548-0). S&S.

Lee, Stanley M., jt. auth. see Ogden, david A.

Lee, Stephen J. Aspects of European History, 1494-1789. (Illus.). 1978. 29.95x (ISBN 0-416-70930-3); pap. 11.95x (ISBN 0-416-70940-0). Methuen Inc.

--Aspects of European History: 1789-1980. 1982. 25.00x (ISBN 0-416-73170-8); pap. 11.95x (ISBN 0-416-73180-5). Methuen Inc.

Lee, Steven J. & Hassay, Karen A. Women's Handbook of Independent Financial Management. 1979. 12.95 o.p. (ISBN 0-442-26154-3). Van Nos Reinhold.

Lee, Sung Jin. The Value of Children: a Cross-National Study: Korea, Vol. 7. LC 75-8934. 1979. pap. text ed. 3.00x o.p. (ISBN 0-8248-0388-4, Eastwest Ctr). UH Pr.

Lee, Susan & Robinson, Sondra T. Dear John. 320p. 1980. 11.95 (ISBN 0-399-90091-8, Marek). Putnam Pub Group.

--Dear John. 1981. pap. 2.75 o.p. (ISBN 0-451-11016-1, AE1016, Sig). NAL.

Lee, T. A. Income & Value Measurement. 2nd ed. 216p. 1980. pap. text ed. 18.50 (ISBN 0-8391-4129-7). Univ Park.

Lee, T. D. Statistical Mechanics. (Concepts in Contemporary Physics Ser.). 550p. Date not set. lib. bdg. write for info. (ISBN 3-7186-0052-8); pap. write for info. (ISBN 3-7186-0053-6). Harwood Academic.

Lee, T. D., ed. Particle Physics & Introduction to Field Theory. (Concepts in Contemporary Physics Ser.: Vol. 1). 750p. 1981. 60.00 (ISBN 3-7186-0032-3); pap. 20.00 (ISBN 3-7186-0033-1). Harwood Academic.

Lee, Tanith. The Birthgrave. (Science Fiction Ser). 1975. pap. 3.50 (ISBN 0-87997-776-0, UE1776). DAW Bks.

--Companions on the Road. LC 76-62780. 1977. 8.95 o.p. (ISBN 0-312-15312-0). St Martin.

--Cyrion. 304p. 1982. pap. 2.95 o.p. (ISBN 0-87997-765-5). DAW Bks.

--Death's Master. (Science Fiction Ser). 1979. pap. 2.95 (ISBN 0-87997-741-8, UE1806). DAW Bks.

--Don't Bite the Sun. (Science Fiction Ser.). 1976. pap. 1.75 (ISBN 0-87997-486-9, UE1486). DAW Bks.

--Drinking Sapphire Wine. (Science Fiction Ser.). 1977. pap. 1.75 o.p. (ISBN 0-87997-565-2, VE1565). DAW Bks.

--Red as Blood. 208p. 1983. pap. 2.50. NAL.

--The Silver Metal Lover. 1982. pap. 2.75 (ISBN 0-87997-721-3, UE1721). Daw Bks.

Lee, Thomas F. The Seaweed Handbook: An Illustrated Guide to Seaweeds from North Carolina to the Arctic. LC 77-6966. (Illus.). 1977. case 20.00x (ISBN 0-913352-04-7). Mariners Boston.

Lee, Tong H., et al. Regional & Interregional Intersectoral Flow Analysis: The Method & an Application to the Tennessee Economy. LC 72-187360. 168p. 1973. 12.50x (ISBN 0-87049-139-3). U of Tenn Pr.

Lee, Vera G., ed. see Ionesco, Eugene.

Lee, Vernon. Miss Brown. Fletcher, Ian & Stokes, John, eds. LC 76-20088. (Decadent Consciousness Ser.). 1978. lib. bdg. 38.00 o.s.i. (ISBN 0-8240-2766-3). Garland Pub.

Lee, Vernon & Paget, Violet. Studies of the Eighteenth Century in Italy. LC 77-17466. (Music Reprint Ser.: 1978). 1978. Repr. of 1887 ed. lib. bdg. 29.50 (ISBN 0-306-77517-4). Da Capo.

Lee, Virginia, jt. auth. see Claiborne, Craig.

Lee, W. I., jt. ed. see Satelle, D. B.

Lee, W. Melville. History of Police in England. LC 70-108236. (Criminology, Law Enforcement, & Social Problems Ser.: No. 119). (With intro. added). 1970. Repr. of 1901 ed. 15.00x (ISBN 0-87585-119-3). Patterson Smith.

Lee, W. R. European Demography & Economic Growth. LC 77-26118. 1979. 30.00 (ISBN 0-312-26935-8). St Martin.

Lee, W. R., jt. auth. see Haycraft, Brita.

Lee, Wayne C. Putnam's Ranch War. 1982. pap. 6.95 (Avalon). Bouregy.

--Skirmish at Fort Phil Kearny. (YA) 1977. 6.95 (ISBN 0-685-74268-7, Avalon). Bouregy.

Lee, William. Raw Fruit & Vegetable Juices & Drinks. LC 82-82323. 32p. (Orig.). 1982. pap. 2.95 (ISBN 0-87983-306-8). Keats.

Lee, William F. Stan Kenton: Artistry in Rhythm. (Illus.). 832p. 29.95 (ISBN 0-686-72145-4). Creative Pr.

Lee, William R. Language Teaching Games & Contests. 2nd ed. 1979. pap. text ed. 6.95x (ISBN 0-19-432716-7). Oxford U Pr.

Lee, William R., et al, eds. Kelp & Other Supplements from the Sea. (Good Health Guide Ser.). 1983. pap. text ed. 1.45 (ISBN 0-87983-313-0). Keats.

Lee, William T. The Estimation of Soviet Defense Expenditures, 1955-75: An Unconventional Approach. LC 76-24357. (Special Studies). 1977. 41.95 o.p. (ISBN 0-275-56900-4). Praeger.

Lee, William W. L. Decisions in Marine Mining: The Role of Preferences & Tradeoffs. LC 79-648. 240p. 1979. prof ref 20.00x (ISBN 0-88410-369-2). Ballinger Pub.

Lee, Yur-Bok. Diplomatic Relations Between the United States & Korea 1866-1887. 1970. text ed. 15.00x (ISBN 0-391-00084-5). Humanities.

Leebaert, ed. European Security: Prospects for the 1980's. (Illus.). 320p. 1979. 17.95x (ISBN 0-669-02518-6). Lexington Bks.

Leebaert, Derek, jt. ed. see Zeckhauser, Richard F.

Leebron, Elizabeth, jt. auth. see Lynn, Gartley.

Leech, C. John Webster. LC 78-143481. (English Biography Ser.: No. 31). 1969. Repr. of 1951 ed. lib. bdg. 26.95x (ISBN 0-8383-0690-X). Haskell.

Leech, C., ed. Marlowe: A Collection of Critical Essays. 1964. 12.95 o.p. (ISBN 0-13-558353-5, Spec). P-H.

Leech, Clifford. Twelfth Night & Shakespearian Comedy. LC 65-9768. 1965. pap. 3.00 o.p. (ISBN 0-8020-6080-3). U of Toronto Pr.

Leech, Clifford see Henderson, Philip.

Leech, D. J. Economics & Financial Studies for Engineers. 260p. 1982. 49.95x (ISBN 0-470-27351-8); pap. 23.95x (ISBN 0-470-27352-6). Halsted Pr.

Leech, J. W. Classical Mechanics. 1965. pap. 5.95x (ISBN 0-412-20070-8, Pub. by Chapman & Hall England). Methuen Inc.

Leech, J. W. & Newman, D. J. How to Use Groups. 1969. pap. 10.95x o.p. (ISBN 0-412-20660-9, Pub. by Chapman & Hall). Methuen Inc.

Leech, Jane K., jt. auth. see Brown, Marion M.

Leech, Jay & Spencer, Zane. Moon of the Big-Dog. LC 79-7893. (Illus.). 64p. (gr. 2-6). 1980. 6.95i o.p. (ISBN 0-690-04001-6, TYC-J); PLB 8.89 (ISBN 0-690-04002-4). Har-Row.

Leech, John & Wing, John. Helping Destitute Men. 1980. 21.00x (ISBN 0-422-76760-3, Pub. by Tavistock England). Methuen Inc.

Leech, Joseph. Rural Rides of the Bristol Churchgoer. 348p. 1982. text ed. 20.25x (ISBN 0-904387-50-X, Pub. by Sutton England); pap. text ed. 11.25x (ISBN 0-904387-68-2). Humanities.

Leech, Julia & Nettle, Gillian. Read, Write & Spell, 4 stages. Incl. Stage 1. wkbk 3.00x o.p. (ISBN 0-435-01500-1); flashcards 6.50x o.p. (ISBN 0-435-01504-4); Stage 2. wkbk 3.00x o.p. (ISBN 0-435-01501-X); flashcards 10.50x o.p. (ISBN 0-435-01505-2); Stage 3. wkbk 3.00x o.p. (ISBN 0-435-01502-8); flashcards 8.50x o.p. (ISBN 0-435-01506-0); Stage 4. wkbk 3.00x o.p. (ISBN 0-435-01503-6); flashcards 6.50x o.p. (ISBN 0-435-01507-9). (Illus.). 1977. Heinemann Ed.

Leech, Michael. Italy. LC 75-44863. (Macdonald Countries Ser.). (Illus.). (gr. 6 up). 1976. PLB 12.68 (ISBN 0-382-06107-1, Pub. by Macdonald Ed). Silver.

Leech, Rachel M., jt. auth. see Reid, Robert A.

Leech, Richard W. & Shuman, Robert M. Neuropathology: A Summary for Students. (Illus.). 352p. 1982. text ed. 15.75x (ISBN 0-06-141526-X, Harper Medical). Lippincott.

Leech, Thomas F. How to Prepare, Stage & Deliver Winning Presentations. 416p. 1982. 39.95 (ISBN 0-8144-5613-8). Am Mgmt.

Leed, Lawrence, ed. Cathedral Poets II: New Poetry. Dunham, Mildred. 1976. pap. 4.95 o.p. (ISBN 0-910286-57-4). Boxwood.

Leed, Richard L., tr. see Illich-Svitych, Vladislav M.

Leeder, M R. Sedimentology: Process & Product. (Illus.). 528p. 1982. text ed. 50.00x (ISBN 0-04-551053-9); pap. text ed. 24.95x (ISBN 0-04-551054-7). Allen Unwin.

Leedham-Green, E. S. Guide to the Archives of the Cambridge University Press 1696-1902. (Archives of British Publishers on Microfilm). 36p. (Orig.). 1974. pap. 6.00x (ISBN 0-914146-14-9). Somerset Hse.

Leeds, Barry H. Ken Kesey. LC 81-40466. (Literature and Life Ser.). 146p. 1981. 11.95 (ISBN 0-8044-2497-7). Ungar.

Leedy, Jack J., ed. Compensation in Psychiatric Disability & Rehabilitation. (Illus.). 384p. 1971. photocopy ed. spiral 38.75x (ISBN 0-398-02186-4). C C Thomas.

--Poetry Therapy: The Use of Poetry in the Treatment of Emotional Disorders. LC 67-15033. 1969. 12.75i (ISBN 0-397-59040-7). Har-Row.

Leedy, Paul D. How to Read Research & Understand It. 1981. write for info. (ISBN 0-02-369250-2). Macmillan.

--Practical Research: Planning & Design. 2nd ed. (Illus.). 1980. pap. text ed. 11.95x (ISBN 0-02-369230-8). Macmillan.

--Read with Speed & Precision. 1963. pap. 12.95 (ISBN 0-07-037011-7, C). McGraw.

Leefeldt, Ed. In Search of the Paper Children. 1982. 6.00 (ISBN 0-686-82891-7). Ctr Analysis Public Issues.

Leege, David C. & Francis, Wayne L. Political Research: Design Measurement & Analysis. LC 73-82232. 1974. text ed. 15.00x o.s.i. (ISBN 0-465-05937-6). Basic.

Leek, Margaret. We Must Have a Trial. (Raven House Mysteries Ser.). 224p. 1983. pap. cancelled (ISBN 0-373-63050-6, Pub. by Worldwide). Harlequin Bks.

Leek, Stephen, jt. auth. see Leek, Sybil.

Leek, Sybil. The Complete Art of Witchcraft. (Illus.). 208p. 1973. pap. 2.25 (ISBN 0-451-11008-0, AE1008, Sig). NAL.

--Diary of a Witch. 1972. pap. 1.25 o.p. (ISBN 0-451-07319-3, Y7319, Sig). NAL.

--Mr. Hotfoot Jackson, Story of a Jackdaw. 8.50 (ISBN 0-392-09415-0, SpS). Sportshelf.

--Sybil Leek's Book of Herbs. LC 73-10205. (Illus.). 160p. 1973. 7.95 o.p. (ISBN 0-525-66304-5). Lodestar Bks.

Leek, Sybil & Leek, Stephen. Ring of Magic Islands. (Illus.). 1976. 11.95 o.p. (ISBN 0-8174-0587-9, Amphoto). Watson-Guptill.

Leeker, Robert, ed. The Annotated Bibliography of Canada's Major Authors, Vol. 2: Margaret Atwood, Leonard Cohen, Archibald Lampman, E. J. Pratt, & Al Purdy. 1981. 26.00 (ISBN 0-8161-8552-2, Hall Reference). G K Hall.

Leekley, John, jt. auth. see Leekley, Sheryle.

Leekley, Sheryle & Leekley, John. Moments: The Pulitzer Prize Photographs 1942-1982. Enl. Rev. ed. (Illus.). 160p. 1982. 25.00 (ISBN 0-517-54736-8). Crown.

Leeman, Wayne A. Centralized & Decentralized Economic Systems. 1977. 22.95 (ISBN 0-395-30659-0). HM.

Leemhuis, Roger P. James L. Orr & the Sectional Conflict. LC 78-65850. 1979. pap. text ed. 10.25 o.p. (ISBN 0-8191-0679-8). U Pr of Amer.

Leeming, D. W., jt. auth. see Farrar, C. L.

Leeming, David. Mythology. LC 75-2276. (World of Culture Ser.). (Illus.). 192p. 1976. 7.95 (ISBN 0-88225-135-X). Newsweek.

Leeming, Donald, jt. auth. see Tidy, Michael.

Leeming, G. & Trussler, S. The Plays of Arnold Wesker: An Assessment. (Studies of Major New English Dramatists: No. 2). 222p. 1974. text ed. 6.50x o.p. (ISBN 0-575-00724-9). Humanities.

Leeming, Glenda. Wesker: A Study of His Plays. 1982. 14.95 (ISBN 0-413-49230-3); pap. 9.95 (ISBN 0-413-49240-0). Methuen Inc.

Leeming, Glenda & Trussler, Simon. The Plays of Arnold Wesker. 1971. 16.50 (ISBN 0-575-00724-9, Pub. by Gollancz England). David & Charles.

Leeming, Joseph. Fun with Pencil & Paper. (Illus.). (gr. 4-6). 1955. 10.53i o.p. (ISBN 0-397-30300-9, JBL-J). Har-Row.

Leemon, Thomas A. The Rites of Passage in a Student Culture. LC 72-81190. 1972. pap. text ed. 9.95x (ISBN 0-8077-1673-1). Tchrs Coll.

Leen, Edie & Bertling, Ed. The Bodybuilder's Training Diary. 160p. 1983. spiral bdg. 6.95 (ISBN 0-89037-258-6). Anderson World.

Leenhardt, Franz J., jt. auth. see Cullmann, Oscar.

Leeper, John & Tomassoni, Mark, eds. Coal Exports & Port Development. LC 81-71245. (Illus.). 112p. 1982. pap. text ed. 10.00x (ISBN 0-87033-286-4). Cornell Maritime.

Leeper, N. C., jt. auth. see Canning, R. G.

Leeper, Sarah H., et al. Good Schools for Young Children. 4th ed. (Illus.). 1979. text ed. 22.95x (ISBN 0-02-369260-X). Macmillan.

Leer, J. Arthur, jt. auth. see Horngren, Charles T.

Lees, et al. Freedom, or Free for All. 2.50 o.p. (ISBN 0-255-69531-4). Transatlantic.

Lees, Alfred W. & Heyn, Ernest V. Popular Science Leisure Homes: A Selection of Fifty-Six Unique Houses with Interiors & Floorplans. (Popular Science Bks.). 320p. 1980. 18.95 o.p. (ISBN 0-442-21263-1). Van Nos Reinhold.

Lees, Andrew & Lees, Lynn. Urbanization of European Society in the Nineteenth Century. (Problems in European Civilization). 1976. pap. text ed. 5.95 (ISBN 0-669-95992-8). Heath.

Lees, Beatrice. How to Prepare for the Graduate Record Examination - Mathematics. 1979. pap. 5.95 o.p. (ISBN 0-07-037045-1, SP). McGraw.

Lees, David H. & Singer, Albert. Color Atlas of Gynecological Surgery, Vol. 6: Surgery of Conditions Complicating Pregnancy. (Illus.). 1983. 70.00t (ISBN 0-8151-5356-2). Year Bk Med.

Lees, Dennis & Shaw, Stella. Impairment, Disability & Handicap. 1974. text ed. 19.00x (ISBN 0-435-82530-5). Heinemann Ed.

Lees, Francis & Brooks, Hugh C. The Economic & Political Development of the Sudan. LC 77-5252. (Illus.). 1978. lib. bdg. 30.00 o.p. (ISBN 0-89158-816-7). Westview.

Lees, Frank P. Loss Prevention in the Process Industry, 2 vols. new ed. 1980. 199.00 set (ISBN 0-408-10604-2); Vol. 1. 110.00 (ISBN 0-408-10697-2); Vol. 2. 110.00 (ISBN 0-408-10698-0). Butterworth.

Lees, Frank P., jt. auth. see Edwards, Elwyn.

Lees, Herbert & Lovell, Mary. The New Iris Syrett Cookery Book. (Illus.). 392p. 1978. 12.95 o.p. (ISBN 0-571-09613-1); pap. 7.95 o.p. (ISBN 0-571-11227-7). Faber & Faber.

Lees, J. D. & Maidment, R. A. American Politics Today. 160p. 1982. 15.00 (ISBN 0-7190-0867-0). Manchester.

Lees, John D. The Political System of the United States. rev. ed. LC 82-24190. 424p. 1983. pap. 12.95 (ISBN 0-571-18068-X). Faber & Faber.

Lees, Lynn, jt. auth. see Lees, Andrew.

Lees, Mary W., jt. auth. see Powers, Edward A.

Lees, R. & Jackson, B. Sugar Confectionery & Chocolate Manufacture. 1973. 34.00 o.p. (ISBN 0-8206-0241-8). Chem Pub.

Lees, R. & Smith, G. Action-Research in Community Development. 1975. 14.95x (ISBN 0-7100-8310-6). Routledge & Kegan.

Lees, Ray. Politics & Social Work. (Library of Social Work). 130p. 1972. 12.50x o.p. (ISBN 0-7100-7398-4); pap. 3.95 O.P. o.p. (ISBN 0-7100-7417-4). Routledge & Kegan.

--Research Strategies for Social Welfare. (Library of Social Work). 128p. 1975. 14.00x (ISBN 0-7100-8253-3); pap. 6.00 (ISBN 0-7100-8254-1). Routledge & Kegan.

Lees, Shirley. Drunk Before Dawn. 1979. pap. 3.50 (ISBN 0-85363-128-X). OMF Bks.

Leese, Elizabeth. Costume Design in the Movies. LC 77-2442. (Ungar Film Library). (Illus.). 1977. 22.00 (ISBN 0-8044-3143-4); pap. 11.95 (ISBN 0-8044-6395-6). Ungar.

Leeser, Ilse R., et al. Community Health Nursing. (Nursing Outline Ser.). 1975. 12.75 (ISBN 0-87488-382-2). Med Exam.

Lees-Haley, Paul R. The Questionnaire Design Handbook. LC 80-82969. 150p. (Orig.). 1980. pap. 9.95 (ISBN 0-938124-00-5). P R Lees-Haley.

Leeson, C. Roland & Leeson, Thomas S. Histology. 3rd ed. LC 74-14783. (Illus.). 605p. 1976. text ed. 19.50 o.p. (ISBN 0-7216-5708-7). Saunders.

--Practical Histology: A Self-Instructional Laboratory Manual in Filmstrip. 1973. pap. 7.50 o.p. (ISBN 0-7216-9831-X); with 4 full-color filmstrips 45.00 o.p. (ISBN 0-7216-9838-7). Saunders.

Leeson, Edward, ed. see Hardy, Thomas.

Leeson, J. & Gray, J. Women & Medicine. (Women at Work Ser.). 245p. 1979. 25.00x (ISBN 0-422-76020-X, Pub. by Tavistock England); pap. 9.95x (ISBN 0-422-76030-7). Methuen Inc.

Leeson, Marjorie. Delta Products Case Study. 112p. 1980. pap. text ed. 7.95 (ISBN 0-574-21288-4, 13-4288); solutions manual avail. (ISBN 0-574-21289-2, 13-4289). SRA.

--Systems Analysis & Design. 464p. 1980. text ed. 17.95 (ISBN 0-574-21279-5, 13-4285); instr's. guide avail. (ISBN 0-574-21286-8, 13-4286); write for info. transparency masters (ISBN 0-574-21287-6, 13-4287). SRA.

Leeson, Marjorie M. Programming Logic. 320p. 1983. pap. text ed. write for info. (ISBN 0-574-21420-8, 13-4420); write for info. instr's. guide (ISBN 0-574-21421-6, 13-4421). SRA.

Leeson, R. Voyage a Paris. (Illus., Fr.). (gr. 7-10). 1969. pap. 7.95 o.p. (ISBN 0-312-85260-6). St Martin.

Leeson, Robert. Silver's Revenge. LC 78-26952. (gr. 5 up). 1979. 7.95 o.p. (ISBN 0-529-05530-9, Philomel). Putnam Pub Group.

Leeson, Thomas S., jt. auth. see Leeson, C. Roland.

Lees-Smith, Hastings B., ed. The Encyclopaedia of the Labour Movement, 3 vols. 7th ed. LC 73-167033. xxv, 1132p. 1972. Repr. of 1928 ed. Set. 163.00x (ISBN 0-8103-3028-8). Gale.

Leestma, Sanford, jt. auth. see Nyhoff, Larry.

Leet, Don R. & Shaw, John A. Economics: Concepts, Themes & Applications. 464p. 1980. pap. text ed. 18.95x (ISBN 0-534-00793-7); wkbk. 7.95x (ISBN 0-534-00826-7). Wadsworth Pub.

Leet, Kenneth. Reinforced Concrete Design. (Illus.). 544p. 1982. 32.00x (ISBN 0-07-037024-9). McGraw.

Leet, Lewis D. Vibrations from Blasting Rock. LC 60-10037. 1960. 8.95x o.p. (ISBN 0-674-93526-8). Harvard U Pr.

Leete, Burt A. Business Law: Text & Cases. 2nd ed. 1982. text ed. 26.95x (ISBN 0-02-369360-6). Macmillan.

Leeuw, Cateau De see De Leeuw, Cateau.

Leeuw, Frank de, et al. The Web of Urban Housing. 240p. 1975. 10.00 (ISBN 0-87766-151-0, 12900); pap. 4.95 (ISBN 0-686-96914-6, 12700). Urban Inst.

Leeuw, Gerardus Van Der see Van Der Leeuw, Gerardus.

Leeuw, J. H. De see Von Mises, Richard & Von Karman, Theodore.

Leeuw, S. De see Southworth, R. & De Leeuw, S.

Leeuwen, Jean Van see Van Leeuwen, Jean.

Leeuwen, Mary S. van see Van Leeuwen, Mary S.

Leeuwenberg, E. L. & Buffart, H. F. Formal Theories of Visual Perception. LC 77-12441. 1978. 68.95 (ISBN 0-471-99586-X, Pub. by Wiley-Interscience). Wiley.

Leeuwen Boomkamp, C. Van see Van Leeuwen Bookmkamp, C. & Van der Meer, J. H.

Leewen, Eva C. van see Van Leewen, Eva C.

Le Fanu, Mark, ed. see James, Henry.

LeFanu, Sheridan. The Rose & the Key. (Mystery Ser.). 448p. 1983. pap. 6.95 (ISBN 0-486-24377-X). Dover.

Lefcoe, George. A Conference on Land Policy & Housing Development. (Lincoln Institute Monograph Ser. No. 81-5). 335p. 1981. pap. text ed. 7.00 (ISBN 0-686-35842-2). Lincoln Inst Land.

--An Introduction to American Land Law: Cases & Materials. LC 74-2945. (Contemporary Legal Education Ser). 1974. text ed. 18.00 o.p. (ISBN 0-672-81893-0, Bobbs-Merrill Law). Michie-Bobbs.

--Land Finance Law. (Contemporary Legal Education Ser). 1969. 18.00 o.p. (ISBN 0-672-80999-0, Bobbs-Merrill Law). Michie-Bobbs.

Lefcoe, George, ed. Urban Land Policy for the Reagan Years: The Message for State & Local Governments. LC 82-48492. (A Lincoln Institute of Land Policy Bk.). 240p. 1983. 28.95x (ISBN 0-669-06157-3). Lexington Bks.

Lefcourt, Herbert M. Locus of Control: Current Trends in Theory & Research. 2nd ed. 288p. 1982. text ed. 24.95 (ISBN 0-89859-222-4). L Erlbaum Assocs.

Lefcowitz. Writer's Handbook. 1976. text ed. 13.95 (ISBN 0-13-969923-6); pap. text ed. 8.95 wkbk. (ISBN 0-13-969907-4); pap. text ed. 12.00 net,diagnostic test (ISBN 0-13-970012-9). P-H.

Lefebre, Adrian. The New Frontiers of Interior Decoration. (Illus.). 127p. 1982. 57.85 (ISBN 0-86650-031-6). Gloucester Art.

Lefebver, Henri. The Survival of Capitalism: The Re-Production of the Relations of Production. LC 75-32932. 208p. 1976. 20.00 (ISBN 0-312-77910-0). St Martin.

Lefebvre, Adrian. The New Frontiers of Interior Decoration. (Illus.). 1980. deluxe ed. 57.85 (ISBN 0-930582-60-8). Gloucester Art.

Lefebvre, Arthur H. Gas Turbine Combustion. (In Energy, Combustion, & Environment Ser.). (Illus.). 416p. 1983. text ed. 37.50 (ISBN 0-07-037029-X, C). McGraw.

Lefebvre, Claire. Syntaxe de l'Haitien. Magloire-Holly, Helene & Piou, Nanie, eds. xiv, 251p. (Fr.). 1982. pap. 15.00 (ISBN 0-89720-055-1). Karoma.

Lefebvre, G. G. & Vahey, Esther J. Using Your Food Processor. (Audio Cassette Cooking School Library). (Illus., Orig.). 1982. pap. 12.95 (ISBN 0-910327-03-3). Cuisine Con.

Lefebvre, G. Godchaux. Wok Cooking, Vol. 1. (Audio Cassette Cooking School Library). 16p. 1982. pap. text ed. 12.95x (ISBN 0-910327-01-7). Cuisine Con.

Lefebvre, Georges. Simplicity: The Heart of Prayer. Livingston, Dinah, tr. from Fr. 80p. 1975. pap. 2.95 o.p. (ISBN 0-8091-1881-5). Paulist Pr.

Lefebvre, Henri. The Explosion: Marxism & the French Upheaval. Ehrenfeld, Alfred, tr. from Fr. LC 69-19790. 1969. 5.95 o.p. (ISBN 0-85345-083-8). Monthly Rev.

Lefebvre, Jacques. Clinical Practice in Pediatric Radiology: The Heart & Great Vessels, Vol. I. Kaufmann, Herbert J., ed. LC 79-83739. (Great Pediatric Radiology Ser.). Orig. Title: Radiopediatrie. 1979. 39.00x (ISBN 0-89352-015-2). Masson Pub.

--Clinical Practice in Pediatric Radiology: The Respiratory System, Vol. II. Kaufman, Herbert J., ed. LC 79-83739. 448p. 1979. 43.00x (ISBN 0-89352-066-7). Masson Pub.

Lefer, Allan M. & Schumer, William, eds. Molecular & Cellular Aspects of Shock & Trauma. LC 82-25875. (Progress in Clinical & Biological Research Ser.: Vol. 111). 354p. 1983. 60.00 (ISBN 0-686-42967-2). A R Liss.

Lefever, Ernest W. Nuclear Arms in the Third World: U. S. Policy Dilemma. 1979. 11.95 o.p. (ISBN 0-8157-5202-4); pap. 4.95 o.p. (ISBN 0-8157-5201-6). Brookings.

Lefever, Ernest W. & English, Raymond. Scholars, Dollars & Public Policy: New Frontiers in Corporate Giving. LC 82-25126. 62p. (Orig.). 1983. pap. 4.00 (ISBN 0-89633-065-6). Ethics & Public Policy.

Lefever, Ernest W. & Hunt, E. Stephen, eds. The Apocalyptic Premise: Nuclear Arms Debated. LC 82-18315. 429p. (Orig.). 1982. 14.00 (ISBN 0-89633-062-1); pap. 9.00 (ISBN 0-89633-063-X). Ethics & Public Policy.

Lefever, R. & Goldbeter, A., eds. Molecular Movements & Chemical Reactivity As Conditioned by Membranes, Enzymes & Other Macromolecules. LC 58-9935. (Advances in Chemical Physics Ser.: Vol. 39). 1978. 72.00x (ISBN 0-471-03541-6, Pub. by Wiley-Interscience). Wiley.

Lefever, R., jt. ed. see Nicolis, G.

Lefevere, A. Translating Poetry. (Translation Studies: No. 1). 136p. 1975. text ed. 17.25x o.p. (ISBN 90-232-1263-0). Humanities.

Lefevre, Carl A. Linguistics, English & the Language Arts. LC 73-15655. 371p. 1974. Repr. of 1970 ed. text ed. 9.50x (ISBN 0-8077-2428-9). Tchrs Coll.

Lefevre, Edwin. Reminiscences of a Stock Operator. 1982. Repr. of 1923 ed. text ed. 20.00 (ISBN 0-87034-065-4). Fraser Pub Co.

Lefevre, Enrique. Panama Scandal: Why They Hate Us. 1979. 6.95 o.p. (ISBN 0-533-04128-7). Vantage.

Lefevre, Felicite. Cock, the Mouse & the Little Red Hen. (Illus.). (gr. 1-3). 1947. PLB 6.47 (ISBN 0-8255-5276-1). Macrae.

Lefevre, Helen E., et al. Oral-Written Practice. 1970. pap. text ed. 5.95 (ISBN 0-394-30338-5). Random.

Lefevre, Henri. The Sociology of Marx. 218p. 1982. 25.00 (ISBN 0-231-05580-3, Pub. by Morningside); pap. 7.95 (ISBN 0-231-05581-1). Columbia U Pr.

Lefevre, J. Central Asian Carpets. 1982. 50.00x (ISBN 0-903580-40-3, Pub. by Element Bks). State Mutual Bk.

Lefevre, M. J., ed. First Aid Manual for Chemical Accidents: For Use with Nonpharmaceutical Chemicals. Solvay American Corporation & Becker, Ernest I., trs. from Fr. LC 80-17518. 218p. 1980. pap. 16.50 (ISBN 0-87933-395-2). Hutchinson Ross.

LeFevre, Perry. Understandings of Man. LC 66-10432. 1966. pap. 4.95 (ISBN 0-664-24678-8). Westminster.

LeFevre, Robert. Nature of Man & His Government. LC 59-5901. 1959. pap. 3.95 (ISBN 0-87004-086-3). Caxton.

Leff, Edward, jt. auth. see Emanuel, Pericles.

Leff, G. Paris & Oxford Universities in the 13th & 14th Centuries: An Institutional & Intellectual History. LC 75-12725. 344p. 1975. Repr. of 1968 ed. 16.50 (ISBN 0-88275-297-9). Krieger.

Leff, J. P. & Isaacs, A. D. Psychiatric Examination in Clinical Practice. 2nd ed. (Illus.). 144p. 1981. pap. text ed. 15.50 (ISBN 0-632-00818-0, B 2920-9). Mosby.

Leff, J. P., jt. auth. see Hirsch, S. R.

Leff, Joy, jt. auth. see Left, Ruth.

Leff, Nathaniel H. Underdevelopment & Development in Brazil. 1982. Vol. I: Economic Structure & Change, 1822-1947 280 pgs. text ed. 29.50x (ISBN 0-04-330325-0); Vol. II: Reassessing the Obstacles to Economic Development. text ed. 24.00x (ISBN 0-04-330324-2). Allen Unwin.

Leffert, H. L., ed. Growth Regulation by Ion Fluxes. LC 80-13986. (Annals of the New York Academy of Sciences: Vol. 339). 335p. 62.00x (ISBN 0-89766-049-8). NY Acad Sci.

Lefferts, Robert. The Basic Handbook of Grants Management. 300p. 1983. 20.95 (ISBN 0-465-00600-0). Basic.

Leffingwell, Elsie, jt. auth. see Brendel, LeRoy A.

Leffkowitz, M. & Steinitz, H., eds. Ninth Congress of Life Assurance Medicine, Tel Aviv, March 1967: Proceedings. vi, 368p. 1968. pap. 68.50 (ISBN 3-8055-0910-3). S Karger.

Leffland, Ella. Rumors of Peace. LC 78-20209. 1979. 12.45i (ISBN 0-06-012572-1, HarpT). Har-Row.

Leffler, G. L. & Farwell, L. C. The Stock Market. 3rd ed. (Illus.). 1963. 24.95 o.p. (ISBN 0-471-06571-4). Ronald Pr.

--The Stock Market. 3rd ed. 654p. 1963. 24.95x o.p. (ISBN 0-471-06571-4). Wiley.

--The Stock Market. 4th ed. 654p. 24.95x (ISBN 0-471-08588-X). Wiley.

Leffler, John F. Short Course in Modern Organic Chemistry. Smith, James, ed. 366p. 1973. text ed. 23.95x (ISBN 0-02-369320-7). Macmillan.

Leffler, William L. Petroleum Refining for the Non-Technical Person. 150p. 1979. 33.95x (ISBN 0-87814-106-5). Pennwell Pub.

Leffler, William L., jt. auth. see Burdick, Donald L.

Lefft, Elizabeth, jt. auth. see Gethers, Judith.

Lefkovits, I., jt. ed. see Steinberg, C. M.

Lefkovitz, Ivan & Waldmann, Hermann. Limiting Dilution Analysis of Cells in the Immune System. LC 77-82502. (Illus.). 1980. 47.50 (ISBN 0-521-22771-2). Cambridge U Pr.

Lefkowitz, Bonnie. Health Planning: Lessons for the Future. LC 82-18491. 206p. 1982. 23.50 (ISBN 0-89443-927-8). Aspen Systems.

Lefkowitz, I., jt. auth. see International Conference on Low Lying Lattice Vibrational Modes & Their Relationship to Superconductivity & Ferroelectricity, Puerto Rico, 1975.

Lefkowitz, Lester. The Manual of Close-up Photography. (Illus.). 1979. 19.95 (ISBN 0-8174-2456-3, Amphoto); pap. 12.95 (ISBN 0-8174-2130-0). Watson-Guptill.

Lefkowitz, R. J., jt. auth. see Bendick, Jeanne.

Lefkowitz, R. J., ed. Receptor Regulation. LC 80-41408. (Receptors & Recognition Ser. B: Vol. 13). (Illus.). 320p. 1981. 45.00x (ISBN 0-412-15930-9, Pub by Chapman & Hall England). Methuen Inc.

Lefkowitz, Robert J., jt. auth. see Williams, Lewis T.

Leflar, Robert B. & Lillie, Helen. Cataracts: A Consumer's Guide to Choosing the Best Treatment. 116p. 1982. 3.50 (ISBN 0-686-96277-X). Pub Citizen Health.

Leflar, Robert B., jt. auth. see Amchin, Jess.

Lefler, Hugh T. & Powell, William S. Colonial North Carolina: A History. LC 73-5188. (A History of the American Colonies Ser.). 1973. lib. bdg. 30.00 (ISBN 0-527-18718-6). Kraus Intl.

Lefler, Hugh T., ed. see Clark, Walter.

Le Flore, Ron & Hawkins, Jim. Breakout: From Prison to the Big League. LC 77-3759. (Associated Features Bk.). (Illus.). 1978. 11.49i (ISBN 0-06-012552-7, HarpT). Har-Row.

Le Fontaine, J. R. Write Yourself a Fortune: Write, Publish & Sell Information. 106p. 1982. 19.95 (ISBN 0-686-37027-9); pap. 14.95 (ISBN 0-686-37028-7). Pegasus Van Nuys.

LeForestier, Wilford A., jt. auth. see Lee, Harry O.

LeFort, David, tr. see Rein, Gerhard.

Lefort, G. Algebra & Analysis. 1966. 44.00 (ISBN 0-7204-2016-4). Elsevier.

Lefort, Joseph. Etudes sur la Moralisation et le Bien-Etre des Classes Ouvrieres. (Conditions of the 19th Century French Working Class Ser.). 362p. (Fr.). 1974. Repr. of 1875 ed. lib. bdg. 94.00x o.p. (ISBN 0-8287-0519-4, 1164). Clearwater Pub.

Lefort, Rafael. The Teachers of Gurdjieff. LC 66-68145. 157p. 1973. pap. 2.45 (ISBN 0-87728-283-8). Weiser.

Lefrancois, Guy R. Adolescents. 2nd ed. 432p. 1980. text ed. 22.95x (ISBN 0-534-00857-7). Wadsworth Pub.

--Of Children: An Introduction to Child Development. 3rd ed. 560p. 1979. text ed. 22.95x (ISBN 0-534-00806-2); study guide 7.95x (ISBN 0-534-00840-2). Wadsworth Pub.

--Psychological Theories of Human Learning. 2nd ed. LC 81-15511. (Psychology Ser.). 483p. 1982. text ed. 20.95 (ISBN 0-8185-0501-X). Brooks-Cole.

--Psychology for Teaching: A Bear Rarely Faces the Front. 4th ed. 448p. 1981. pap. text ed. 19.95x (ISBN 0-534-01019-9). Wadsworth Pub.

Lefschetz, S. Applications of Algebraictopology, Graphs & Networks: The Picard-Lefschetz Theory & Feynman Integrals. LC 75-6924. (Applied Mathematical Sciences Ser.: Vol. 16). (Illus.). 200p. 1975. pap. 23.00 (ISBN 0-387-90137-X). Springer-Verlag.

--Contributions to the Theory of Nonlinear Oscillations, Vols. 1-3 & 5, 1950-1960. (Annals of Mathematics Studies) Vol. 1. 26.00 (ISBN 0-527-02736-7); Vol. 2. 12.00 (ISBN 0-527-02745-6); Vol. 3. 23.00 (ISBN 0-527-02753-7); Vol. 5. 23.00 (ISBN 0-527-02761-8). Kraus Repr.

--Lectures on Differential Equations. 1946. pap. 16.00 (ISBN 0-527-02730-8). Kraus Repr.

--Topics in Topology. 1942. pap. 12.00 (ISBN 0-527-02726-X). Kraus Repr.

Lefschetz, Solomon. Selected Papers. LC 73-113137. 1971. text ed. 32.50 (ISBN 0-8284-0234-5). Chelsea Pub.

--Topology. 2nd ed. LC 56-11513. 15.95 (ISBN 0-8284-0116-0). Chelsea Pub.

Lefson, Edward. All the Happiness... 1982. pap. write for info. (ISBN 0-937922-04-8). SAA Pub.

Lefson, Edward, ed. see Hubbard, L. Ron.

Left, Ruth & Leff, Joy. Use Your Senses. 1979. 35.00 (ISBN 0-88450-787-4, 3091-B). Communication Skill.

Lefton, Mark, jt. auth. see Rosengren, William.

Lefton, Phillip, ed. Barron's Regents Exams & Answers Comprehensive Social Studies (Grade 11) American Studies. rev. ed. LC 74-146833. 300p. (gr. 9-12). 1982. pap. text ed. 4.50 (ISBN 0-8120-3157-1). Barron.

Lefton, Robert, et al. Improving Productivity Through People Skills: Dimensional Management Studies. 520p. 1981. prof ref 22.50x (ISBN 0-88410-498-2). Ballinger Pub.

Leftschatz, William. The Fall of Heaven. LC 82-83494. (Orig.). pap. 6.95 (ISBN 0-86666-122-0). GWP.

Legal Forms Committee State Bar of Texas, ed. Legal Form Manual for Real Estate Transactions: 1982 Supplement. Rev. ed. 101p. 1982. loose-leaf 20.00 (ISBN 0-938160-29-X, 2436). State Bar TX.

Le Gal, M. Recherches Sur les Ornementations Sporales Des Discomycetes Opercules. 1970. Repr. of 1947 ed. 16.00 (ISBN 3-7682-0694-7). Lubrecht & Cramer.

LeGalley, Donald P. Space Physics. 1979. Repr. of 1964 ed. lib. bdg. write for info. o.p. (ISBN 0-88275-795-4). Krieger.

Legalley, Donald P., ed. Ballistic Missile & Space Technology: Proceedings of a Symposium, 4 vols. Incl. Vol. 1 o.p. Bioastronautics & Electronics & Invited Addresses. 1961 (ISBN 0-12-440901-6); Vol. 2. Propulsion & Auxiliary Power Systems. 1960 (ISBN 0-12-440902-4); Vol. 3. Guidance, Navigation, Tracking & Space Physics. 1960 (ISBN 0-12-440903-2); Vol. 4. Re-Entry & Vehicle Design. 1960 (ISBN 0-12-440904-0). 1960. 54.00 ea. Acad Pr.

LeGallienne, Eva. With a Quiet Heart: An Autobiography. LC 74-3745. (Illus.). 311p. 1974. Repr. of 1953 ed. lib. bdg. 19.00x (ISBN 0-8371-7470-8, LEQH). Greenwood.

Le Gallienne, Eva, tr. see Andersen, Hans C.

Le Gallienne, Eva, tr. see Ibsen, Henrik.

Le Gallienne, Richard. The Highway to Happiness. 154p. 1982. Repr. of 1913 ed. lib. bdg. 30.00 (ISBN 0-89987-317-0). Darby Bks.

Legare, H. S. Writings of Hugh Swinton Legare. Bullen, Mary S. L., ed. LC 70-107413. (American Public Figures Ser). 1970. Repr. of 1846 ed. lib. bdg. 145.00 (ISBN 0-306-71885-5). Da Capo.

Legat, Michael. Dear Author: Letters from a Working Publisher to Authors - Prospective & Practised. 160p. 1972. 7.50 o.p. (ISBN 0-7207-0558-4). Transatlantic.

Legates, J. E., jt. auth. see Warwick, E. J.

Legator & Hollaender. Occupational Monitoring for Genetic Hazards, Vol. 269. 1975. 17.00 (ISBN 0-89072-023-1). NY Acad Sci.

Legator, Marvin, jt. auth. see Epstein, Samuel.

Leger, Jack-Alain. Monsignore. (Orig.). 1982. pap. 3.50 (ISBN 0-440-15752-8). Dell.

Leger, Robert G. & Stratton, John R. The Sociology of Corrections: A Book of Readings. LC 76-51462. 1977. text ed. 21.95x (ISBN 0-471-01680-2). Wiley.

Legere, Thomas E. Thoughts on the Run: Glimpses of Wholistic Spirituality. 144p. 1983. pap. 7.95 (ISBN 0-86683-698-5). Winston Pr.

Leger-Gordon, Ruth. The Witchcraft & Folklore of Dartmoor. 192p. 1982. pap. text ed. 8.25x (ISBN 0-86299-021-1, 51426, Pub. by Sutton England). Humanities.

LeGette, Bernard. LeGette's Calorie Encyclopedia. 448p. 1983. pap. 3.50 (ISBN 0-446-90919-X, 97-919-8). Warner Bks.

Legeza, Laslo, jt. auth. see Rawson, Philip.

Legg, Larry. Biological Science: Lab-Lecture Guide Biology, No. 115. (Illus.). 384p. 19.95x (ISBN 0-88136-000-7). Jostens.

Leggatt, Alexander. Ben Johnson: His Vision & His Art. 1981. 35.00x (ISBN 0-416-74660-8). Methuen Inc.

--Shakespeare's Comedy of Love. 1974. pap. 10.95x (ISBN 0-416-79130-1). Methuen Inc.

Legge, Dormer H. Penny Kangaroo of Australia, 1913. 11.95 (ISBN 0-85259-071-7). StanGib Ltd.

Legge, J., tr. Texts of Taoism: The Sacred Books of China, 2 Vols. (Sacred Books of the East Ser). 10.00 ea. (ISBN 0-8446-3059-4). Peter Smith.

Legge, James. I Ching: Book of Changes. 449p. 1983. pap. 7.95 (ISBN 0-8065-0458-7). Citadel Pr.

--The Sacred Books of China. (Sacred Bks. of the East: Vols. 3, 16, 27, 28, 39, 40). 6 vols. 66.00 (ISBN 0-686-97476-X); 11.00 ea. Lancaster-Miller.

Legge, James, ed. see Mencius.

Legge, James, tr. see I Ching.

Legge, James, tr. see Mencius.

Legge, K. & Mugford, E. Designing Organisations for Satisfaction & Efficiency. 160p. 1978. text ed. 29.00x (ISBN 0-566-02102-1). Gower Pub Ltd.

Legget, Robert & Karrow, Paul F. Handbook of Geology in Civil Engineering. 3rd ed. (Illus.). 1184p. 1982. 69.95 (ISBN 0-07-037061-3). McGraw.

Legget, Robert F. Geology & Engineering. 2nd ed. (International Ser. in Earth & Planetary Sciences). (Illus.). 1962. 49.95 (ISBN 0-07-037059-1, P&RB). McGraw.

Leggett, B. J. Housman's Land of Lost Content: A Critical Study of "A Shropshire Lad". LC 71-100407. 172p. 1970. 12.50x (ISBN 0-87049-106-7). U of Tenn Pr.

Leggett, G. & Lee, D. Writers Workbook A: Form D. 1967. pap. 8.95 o.p. (ISBN 0-13-970087-0). P-H.

Leggett, Gerene C. How to Raise & Train a Bouvier Des Flandres. (Orig.). 1965. pap. 2.50 o.p. (ISBN 0-87666-252-1, DS1061). TFH Pubns.

Leggett, John. Gulliver House. 1979. 10.95 o.s.i. (ISBN 0-395-27759-0). HM.

Leggett, Les. The Philosophy of Coaching. (Illus.). 256p. 1983. text ed. 19.75 (ISBN 0-398-04784-7). C C Thomas.

Leggett, S., et al. Planning Flexible Learning Places. 1977. 27.50 (ISBN 0-07-037060-5, P&RB). McGraw.

Leggett, Trevor. Encounters in Yoga & Zen. 1982. pap. 8.95 (ISBN 0-7100-9241-5). Routledge & Kegan.

--The Tiger's Cave: Translations of Japanese Zen Texts. (Illus.). 1977. pap. 6.95 o.p. (ISBN 0-7100-8636-9). Routledge & Kegan.

Leggett, Trevor P. Shogi: Japan's Game of Strategy. LC 66-11011. (Illus.). 1966. 12.95 (ISBN 0-8048-0526-1). C E Tuttle.

Leggewie, Robert, jt. ed. see Clouard, Henri.

Leggon, Cheryl, jt. ed. see Marett, Cora B.

Leggon, Cheryl B., jt. ed. see Marett, Cora B.

Legislative Wives Club. Around the Spiral Staircase. Brown, Virginia P., ed. LC 77-14842. 1978. 8.95 o.p. (ISBN 0-87397-131-0). Strode.

Legman, G. No Laughing Matter: An Analysis of Sexual Humor, 2 vols. Incl. Vol. I. 816p (ISBN 0-253-34775-0); Vol. II. 992p (ISBN 0-253-34776-9). LC 81-48469. 1982. Repr. of 1968 ed. 75.00x set (ISBN 0-253-34777-7); 37.50 ea. Ind U Pr.

--No Laughing Matter: Rationale of the Dirty Joke. 1976. 18.00 o.p. (ISBN 0-517-52568-2). Crown.

Legmann, P., jt. auth. see Burstein, M.

Le Gourieres, D. Wind Power Plants: Theory & Design. 300p. 1982. 50.00 (ISBN 0-08-029967-9); pap. 25.00 (ISBN 0-08-029966-0). Pergamon.

Legouve, Ernest. Edith de Falsen: L'Education d'un Pere. 325p. (Fr.). 1982. Repr. of 1860 ed. lib. bdg. 125.00 (ISBN 0-8287-1772-9). Clearwater Pub.

Legrain, L. Terra-Cottas from Nippur. (Publications of the Babylonian Section: Vol. 16). (Illus.). 52p. 1930. with folio of plates 25.00xbound (ISBN 0-686-11926-6). Univ Mus of U PA.

LeGrand, Julian & Robinson, Ray. The Economics of Social Problems. 200p. 1980. pap. text ed. 9.95 (ISBN 0-15-518910-7, HC). HarBraceJ.

Legrand, Marc-Antoine. Le Roi de Cocagne. (Utopias in the Enlightenment Ser.). 79p. (Fr.). 1974. Repr. of 1719 ed. 23.50x o.p. (ISBN 0-8287-0523-2, 039). Clearwater Pub.

Le Grand, Rupert. Manufacturing Engineer's Manual: American Machinist Reference Book Sheets. 1971. 26.50 o.p. (ISBN 0-07-037066-4, P&RB). McGraw.

LeGrande, James L. The Basic Processes of Criminal Justice. LC 72-85759. (Criminal Justice Ser.). 288p. 1973. text ed. 9.95x o.p. (ISBN 0-02-476090-0). Glencoe.

Legras, R., jt. auth. see Mercier, J. P.

LeGrice, E. B. Rose Growing for Everyone. LC 79-393987. (Illus.). 1969. 5.25x o.p. (ISBN 0-571-08682-9). Intl Pubns Serv.

LeGrice, Malcolm. Abstract Film & Beyond. 1977. 13.95 (ISBN 0-262-12077-1); pap. 5.95 (ISBN 0-262-62038-3). MIT Pr.

Leguat, Francois. Voyage et Aventures de Fr. Leguat en Deux Isles Desertes des Indes Orientales, 2 vols. (Bibliotheque Africaine Ser.). 472p. (Fr.). 1974. Repr. of 1708 ed. lib. bdg. 130.00x o.p. (ISBN 0-8287-0524-0, 72-2114). Clearwater Pub.

Le Guin, Ursula. The Dispossessed. 1975. pap. 2.95 (ISBN 0-380-00382-1, 62091). Avon.

Le Guin, Ursula K. The Altered I: Ursula K. Le Guin's Science Fiction Writing Workshop. Harding, Lee, ed. 1978. pap. 7.50 (ISBN 0-425-03849-1). Ultramarine Pub.

--The Compass Rose. LC 81-48158. 224p. 1982. 14.37i (ISBN 0-06-014988-4, HarpT). Har-Row.

--The Dispossessed. LC 73-18667. 352p. (YA) 1974. 11.49i (ISBN 0-06-012563-2, HarpT). Har-Row.

--The Eye of the Heron. LC 82-48146. 176p. 1983. 11.49i (ISBN 0-06-015086-6, HarpT). Har-Row.

--The Language of the Night. Wood, Susan, ed. LC 78-24350. 270p. 1979. 12.50 (ISBN 0-399-12325-3). Ultramarine Pub.

Leguin, Ursula K. The Language of the Night: Essays on Fantasy & Science Fiction. Wood, Susan, intro. by. 1979. 9.95 o.p. (ISBN 0-399-12325-3). Berkley Pub.

Le Guin, Ursula K. The Language of the Night: Essays on Fantasy & Science Fiction. LC 78-24350. 1979. 9.95 (ISBN 0-399-12325-3). Putnam Pub Group.

--The Language of the Night: Essays on Fantasy & Science Fiction. 270p. 1980. pap. 4.95 (ISBN 0-399-50482-6, Perige). Putnam Pub Group.

--The Lathe of Heaven. LC 81-18093. 192p. 1982. Repr. of 1971 ed. 12.50x (ISBN 0-8376-0464-8). Bentley.

--The Left Hand of Darkness. LC 79-2652. (Harper Science Fiction Ser.). 208p. 1980. 12.45i (ISBN 0-06-012574-8, HarpT). Har-Row.

--Malafrena. LC 79-11042. 1979. 9.95 (ISBN 0-399-12410-1). Putnam Pub Group.

--Planet of Exile. (Orig.). 1983. pap. 1.95 (ISBN 0-441-66957-3, Pub. by Ace Science Fiction). Ace Bks.

--Planet of Exile. Del Ray, Lester, ed. LC 75-418. (Library of Science Fiction). 1975. lib. bdg. 17.50 o.s.i. (ISBN 0-8240-1423-5). Garland Pub.

LeGuin, Ursula K. Rocannon's World. LC 76-47250. 1977. Repr. of 1966 ed. 11.49i (ISBN 0-06-012568-3, HarpT). Har-Row.

Le Guin, Ursula K. Solomon Leviathan's Nine Hundred & Thirty-First Trip Around the World. rev. ed. (Adventures in Kroy Ser.: No. 2). (Illus.). 32p. 1983. Repr. of 1976 ed. 75.00 (ISBN 0-941826-03-1). Cheap St.

Leguizamon, Martha, tr. see Tobin, William J.

Legum, Colin. Africa Contemporary Record, Vol. 12. LC 70-7957. 1400p. 1981. text ed. 159.50x (ISBN 0-8419-0550-9, Africana). Holmes & Meier.

--Africa: The Year of the Students. (Current Affairs Ser.). 28p. 1972. pap. 3.50 (ISBN 0-8419-0101-5). Holmes & Meier.

Legum, Colin, ed. Africa Contemporary Record, Vol. 9. LC 70-7957. (Illus.). 1977. 159.50x (ISBN 0-8419-0158-9, Africana). Holmes & Meier.

--Africa Contemporary Record, Vol. 10. LC 70-7957. 1979. 159.50x (ISBN 0-8419-0159-7, Africana). Holmes & Meier.

--Africa Contemporary Record, Vol. 11. LC 70-7957. 1980. 159.50x (ISBN 0-8419-0160-0, Africana). Holmes & Meier.

--Africa Contemporary Record: Annual Survey & Documents. Incl. Vol. 1. 1968-69. 904p (ISBN 0-8419-0150-3); Vol. 2. 1969-70. 1213p (ISBN 0-8419-0151-1); Vol. 3. 1970-71. 1065p (ISBN 0-8419-0152-X); Vol. 4. 1971-1972. 1100p (ISBN 0-8419-0153-8); Vol. 5. 1972-73. Legum, Colin, ed (ISBN 0-8419-0154-6). LC 70-7957. 159.50x ea. (Africana). Holmes & Meier.

--Africa Contemporary Record: Annual Survey & Documents 1975-76, Vol. 8. LC 70-7957. (Illus.). 1976. text ed. 159.50x (ISBN 0-8419-0157-0, Africana). Holmes & Meier.

--Africa Contemporary Record: 1973-74, Vol. 6. LC 70-7957. (Illus.). 1200p. 1974. 159.50x (ISBN 0-8419-0155-4, Africana). Holmes & Meier.

--Africa Contemporary Record: 1974-75, Vol. 7. LC 70-7957. (Illus.). 1100p. 1975. 159.50x (ISBN 0-8419-0156-2, Africana). Holmes & Meier.

--Africa Contemporary Record 1981-82, Vol. 14. 1200p. 1983. text ed. 159.50x (ISBN 0-8419-0551-7). Holmes & Meier.

Legum, Colin & Shaked, Haim, eds. Middle East Contemporary Survey, Vol. 2. LC 78-648245. (Illus.). 1979. 140.00x (ISBN 0-8419-0398-0). Holmes & Meier.

--Middle East Contemporary Survey: 1978-1979, Vol. 3. LC 78-648245. (Illus.). 1980. text ed. 140.00x (ISBN 0-8419-0514-2). Holmes & Meier.

--Middle East Contemporary Survey 1980-81, Vol. V. 1000p. 1983. text ed. 140.00x (ISBN 0-8419-0825-7). Holmes & Meier.

Legum, Colin, et al, eds. Crisis & Conflicts in the Middle East-The Changing Strategy: From Iran to Afghanistan. LC 81-84135. 180p. (Orig.). 1982. pap. 12.50x (ISBN 0-8419-0784-6). Holmes & Meier.

Lehan, Edward A. Simplified Governmental Budgeting. LC 81-82463. (Illus.). 86p. 1981. nonmemeber 30.00 (ISBN 0-686-84272-3); member 25.00 (ISBN 0-686-84273-1). Municipal.

Lehan, Richard D. F. Scott Fitzgerald & the Craft of Fiction. LC 66-5059. (Crosscurrents-Modern Critiques Ser.). 221p. 1966. 13.95 o.p. (ISBN 0-8093-0216-0). S Ill U Pr.

Lehane, B. Dublin. (The Great Cities Ser.). (Illus.). 1978. lib. bdg. 12.00 (ISBN 0-8094-2344-8). Silver.

Lehane, Brendan. The Northwest Passage. LC 80-27723. (Seafarers Ser.). lib. bdg. 19.92 (ISBN 0-8094-2731-1). Silver.

Lehane, Stephen. The Creative Child: How to Encourage the Natural Creativity of Your Pre-Schooler. (Illus.). 1980. 11.95 (ISBN 0-13-189118-9, Spec); pap. 5.95 (ISBN 0-13-189100-6, Spec). P-H.

Lehane, Stephen, ed. see Goldman, Richard, et al.

Le Harpe, J. F. Commentaire Sur le Theatre De Voltaire. Repr. of 1814 ed. 143.00 o.p. (ISBN 0-8287-1347-2). Clearwater Pub.

Lehemberg, Stanford E. Sir Thomas Elyot, Tudor Humanist. Repr. of 1960 ed. lib. bdg. 15.50x (ISBN 0-8371-2123-X, LETE). Greenwood.

Leheny, James, ed. see Addison, Joseph.

Lehiste, Ilse. Consonant Quantity & Phonological Units in Estonian. (Uralic & Altaic Ser.: Vol. 65). 1966. pap. text ed. 5.50x o.p. (ISBN 0-87750-022-3). Res Ctr Lang Semiotic.

--Suprasegmentals. 1970. 17.50x (ISBN 0-262-12023-2). MIT Pr.

Lehiste, Ilse, jt. auth. see Jeffers, Robert J.

Lehiste, Ilse, ed. Readings in Acoustic Phonetics. 1967. 22.50x o.p. (ISBN 0-262-12025-9). MIT Pr.

Lehman, jt. ed. see Koukou-Lehman.

Lehman, Anita J., jt. auth. see Holmes, Paul C.

Lehman, Dennis, jt. auth. see Sackheim, George.

Lehman, Ernest. Screening Sickness: And Other Tales of Tinsel Town. 208p. 1982. 5.95 (ISBN 0-399-50683-7, Perige). Putnam Pub Group.

Lehman, James. The Old Brethren. (Orig.). 1976. pap. write for info (ISBN 0-515-09623-7). Jove Pubns.

Lehman, Jane, jt. auth. see Kolzow, Lee.

Lehman, Jerry D. Three Approaches to Classroom Management: Views From a Psychological Perspective. LC 81-43843. 130p. (Orig.). 1982. lib. bdg. 19.00 (ISBN 0-8191-2572-5); pap. 8.25 (ISBN 0-8191-2573-3). U Pr of Amer.

Lehman, John. The Executive, Congress, & Foreign Policy: Studies of the Nixon Administration. LC 76-13835. (Special Studies). 1976. 27.95 o.p. (ISBN 0-275-56490-8). Praeger.

Lehman, Peter & Luhr, William. Blake Edwards. LC 80-28440. (Illus.). xiv, 288p. 1981. 18.95x (ISBN 0-8214-0605-1, 82-83905); pap. 8.95 (ISBN 0-8214-0616-7, 82-83913). Ohio U Pr.

Lehman, Peter, jt. auth. see Luhr, William.

Lehman, S. C. Nutrition & Food Preparation & Preventive Care & Maintenance. (Lifeworks Ser.). 1981. text ed. 5.80 (ISBN 0-07-037094-X). McGraw.

Lehman, Scott C. Government Structures & Citizen Rights & Duties. Zak, Therese A., ed. (Lifeworks Ser.). (Illus.). 144p. 1981. 5.80 (ISBN 0-07-037095-8). McGraw.

Lehmann, Christian. Interaction of Radiation with Solids & Elementary Defect Production. (Defects in Crystalline Solids Ser.: Vol. 10). 1977. 68.00 (ISBN 0-7204-0416-9, North-Holland). Elsevier.

--Der Relativsatz: Typologie seiner Strukturen, Theorie seiner Funktionen, Kompendium seiner Grammatik. (Language Universal Ser.: 4). 1983. write for info (ISBN 3-87808-982-1). Benjamins North Am.

Lehmann, David, ed. Ecology & Exchange in the Andes. LC 81-21776. (Cambridge Studies in Social Anthropology: No. 41). 280p. 1982. 39.50 (ISBN 0-521-23950-8). Cambridge U Pr.

Lehmann, E. L. Nonparametrics: Statistical Methods Based on Ranks. LC 72-93538. 1975. text ed. 33.50x (ISBN 0-8162-4994-6). Holden-Day.

Lehmann, E. L., jt. auth. see Hodges, J. L., Jr.

Lehmann, Erich L. Testing Statistical Hypotheses. LC 59-11803. (Illus.). 1959. 33.95 (ISBN 0-471-52470-0). Wiley.

--Theory of Point Estimation. (Wiley Series in Probability & Mathematical Statistics Ser.). 525p. 1983. 45.00x (ISBN 0-471-05849-1, Pub. by Wiley-Interscience). Wiley.

Lehmann, F. G., ed. Carcino-Embryonic Proteins: Chemistry, Biology, Clinical Application, 2 vols. 1979. Set. 183.00 (ISBN 0-444-80097-2, North Holland); Vol. 1. 135.75 (ISBN 0-444-80095-6); Vol. 2. 135.75 (ISBN 0-444-80096-4). Elsevier.

Lehmann, H. & Kynoch, P. A., eds. Human Hemoglobin Variants & Their Characteristics. 1976. 55.50 (ISBN 0-7204-0585-8, North-Holland). Elsevier.

Lehmann, H. L., tr. see Heckner, Fritz.

Lehmann, Jean-Pierre. The Roots of Modern Japan. LC 82-743. 372p. 1982. 26.00x (ISBN 0-312-69310-9). St Martin.

Lehmann, Johannes. Rabbi J. LC 70-163348. 176p. 1982. pap. 7.95 (ISBN 0-8128-6172-8). Stein & Day.

Lehmann, Justus F. & Basmajian, John V. Therapeutic Heat & Cold. 3rd ed. (Rehabilitation Medicine Library). (Illus.). 650p. 1982. lib. bdg. 46.00 (ISBN 0-683-04907-0). Williams & Wilkins.

Lehmann, Linwood, tr. see Jefferson, Thomas.

Lehmann, Peter, ed. see Heckner, Fritz.

Lehmann, W. P., jt. ed. see Heffner, Roe-Merrill S.

Lehmann, Winfred P. & Malkiel, Yakov. Perspectives on Historical Linguistics. 500p. 50.00 (ISBN 90-272-3516-3). Benjamins North Am.

Lehmann, Winifred P. Descriptive Linguistics: An Introduction. 2nd ed. 288p. 1976. text ed. 12.00 (ISBN 0-394-30265-6, RanC); wkbk. 5.50 (ISBN 0-394-31177-9). Random.

Lehmann-Haupt, Hellmut. The Life of the Book. LC 75-17193. (Illus.). 240p. 1975. Repr. of 1957 ed. lib. bdg. 17.00x (ISBN 0-8371-8293-X, LELB). Greenwood.

Lehmberg, S. E. The Later Parliaments of Henry VIII, 1536-1547. LC 76-7804. 1977. 54.50 (ISBN 0-521-21256-1). Cambridge U Pr.

Lehmbruch, Gerhard & Schmitter, Philippe C., eds. Patterns of Corporatist Policy-Making. LC 82-80178. (Sage Modern Politics Ser.: Vol. 7). (Illus.). 296p. 1982. 25.00 (ISBN 0-686-91805-3); pap. 12.50 (ISBN 0-686-98299-1). Sage.

Lehmer, Isabel. Keyboard Harmony. LC 66-24048. 1967. pap. 9.95 (ISBN 0-935058-00-1). Donato Music.

Lehmkuhl, Donald & Smith, Laura, eds. Brunnstrom's Clinical Kinesiology. 4th ed. (Illus.). 385p. 1983. text ed. 24.95 (ISBN 0-8036-5529-0). Davis Co.

Lehmkuhl, Donald, et al. The Flights of Icarus. (Illus.). 160p. 1978 (A & W Visual Library). pap. 12.50 o.s.i. (ISBN 0-89104-117-6). A & W Pubs.

Lehn, Cornelia. God Keeps His Promise. LC 76-90377. (gr. k). 1970. cancelled 9.95 o.p. (ISBN 0-8361-1615-1). Herald Pr.

--The Sun & the Wind. (Illus.). 32p. 1983. 11.95 (ISBN 0-87303-072-9). Faith & Life.

Lehn, J. M. Preparative Organic Photochemistry. (Topics in Current Chemistry Ser.: Vol. 103). (Illus.). 94p. 1982. 21.00 (ISBN 0-387-11388-6). Springer-Verlag.

Lehnartz, Klaus. New York in the Sixties. LC 78-53190. (Illus.). 1978. pap. 6.00 (ISBN 0-486-23674-9). Dover.

Lehnen, Robert G., jt. auth. see Forthofer, Ronald N.

Lehner, Lois. Complete Book of American Kitchen & Dinner Wares. (Illus.). pap. 12.95 (ISBN 0-87069-320-4). Wallace-Homestead.

Lehner, Mark. The Egyptian Heritage: Based on the Edgar Cayce Readings. 136p. 1974. pap. 3.95 (ISBN 0-87604-071-7). ARE Pr.

Lehnert, Bruce E. & Schachter, E. Neil. The Pharmacology of Respiratory Care. LC 79-28446. (Illus.). 334p. 1980. pap. text ed. 19.95 (ISBN 0-8016-2921-7). Mosby.

Lehnert, Joseph. Introduction to Telegraph Engineering. 1977. 31.00 (ISBN 0-471-25848-2, Wiley Heyden). Wiley.

Lehninger, Albert L. Biochemistry: The Molecular Bases of All Structure & Function. 2nd ed. LC 75-11082. 1975. text ed. 37.95x (ISBN 0-87901-047-9). Worth.

--Bioenergetics: The Molecular Basis of Biological Energy Transformations. 2nd ed. (Biology Teaching Monograph). 1971. pap. text ed. 15.95 (ISBN 0-8053-6103-0). Benjamin-Cummings.

--Principles of Biochemistry. (Illus.). 1011p. 1982. text ed. 33.95x (ISBN 0-87901-136-X). Worth.

--A Short Course in Biochemistry. LC 72-93199. (Illus.). 400p. 1973. text ed. 26.95x (ISBN 0-87901-024-X). Worth.

Lehnus, Donald J. Book Numbers: Their History, Principles, and Application. LC 80-23100. 158p. 1980. pap. 8.00 (ISBN 0-8389-0316-9). ALA.

Lehodey, Dom V. The Ways of Mental Prayer. 408p. 1924. pap. 6.00 (ISBN 0-686-81633-1). TAN Bks Pubs.

Lehr, Jay H., et al. Domestic Water Conditioning. (Illus.). 1979. 21.95 (ISBN 0-07-037068-0, P&RB). McGraw.

Lehrer, Adrienne. Wine & Conversation. LC 82-48538. 256p. 1983. 25.00x (ISBN 0-253-36550-3). Ind U Pr.

--Wine & Conversation. LC 82-48538. (Midland Bks.). 256p. (Orig.). 1983. pap. 17.50x (ISBN 0-253-20308-2). Ind U Pr.

Lehrer, Keith, ed. see Reid, Thomas.

Lehrer, Robert N. Participative Productivity & Quality of Work Life. (Illus.). 1981. 21.95 (ISBN 0-13-651398-0). P-H.

--White Collar Productivity. LC 82-118. (Illus.). 384p. 1982. 24.95 (ISBN 0-07-037078-8, P&RB); pap. 19.95 (ISBN 0-07-037077-X). McGraw.

Lehrer, Stanley, jt. auth. see Brickman, William W.

Lehrman, Albert M. The Complete Book of Wills & Trusts. LC 78-61133. (IEstate Planning & Administration Ser.). 592p. 59.00 (ISBN 0-87624-100-3). Inst Busn Plan.

Lehrman, Lewis E. Real Money: The Case for the Gold Standard. 1982. 13.50 (ISBN 0-394-51904-3). Random.

Lehrman, Steve. Your Career in Harness Racing. LC 75-38343. (YA) (gr. 9 up). 1976. 6.95 o.p. (ISBN 0-689-10714-5). Atheneum.

Lehrman, Walter D. & Sarafinski, Dolores J. The Plays of Ben Jonson: A Reference Guide. 1980. lib. bdg. 36.00 (ISBN 0-8161-8112-8, Hall Reference). G K Hall.

Lehrmann, Winfred P. Linguistische Theorien der Moderne. 173p. (Ger.). 1981. write for info. (ISBN 3-261-04889-1). P Lang Pubs.

Le Huede, Henri. Great Recipes from Le France. McAdoo, Dale, tr. from Fr. 264p. 1981. 17.95 o.p. (ISBN 0-86565-013-6). Vendome.

Le Huray, Peter. Music & the Reformation in England: Fifteen Forty-Nine to Sixteen Sixty. LC 77-87383. (Cambridge Studies in Music). (Illus.). 1978. 69.50 (ISBN 0-521-21958-2); pap. 19.95x (ISBN 0-521-29418-5). Cambridge U Pr.

Le Huray, Peter, ed. The Treasury of English Church Music 1545-1650. 250p. 1982. 39.50 (ISBN 0-521-24889-2); pap. 17.50 (ISBN 0-521-28405-8). Cambridge U Pr.

Leib, Amos P. & Day, A. Grove. Hawaiian Legends in English: An Annotated Bibliography. rev., 2nd ed. LC 79-16156. 1979. text ed. 10.00x (ISBN 0-8248-0671-9). UH Pr.

Leib, Hans-Heinrich. Intergrational Linguistics: Volume 5, Morphology & Morphosemant-Tics. (Current Issues in Linguistic Theory Ser.: No. 17). 250p. 1981. text ed. 28.50x o.p. (ISBN 90-272-3508-2). Benjamins North Am.

Leibel, Rudolph, jt. ed. see Pollitt, Ernesto.

Leibenguth, Charla, jt. ed. see Ebershoff-Coles, Susan.

Leibenstein, Harvey. Beyond Economic Man: A New Approach to Micro-Economic Theory. (Illus.). 288p. 1976. 17.50x (ISBN 0-674-06891-2); pap. 7.95x (ISBN 0-674-06892-0). Harvard U Pr.

--Theory of Economic-Demographic Development. Repr. of 1954 ed. lib. bdg. 19.25x (ISBN 0-8371-1046-7, LEED). Greenwood.

Leiber, Fritz. The Big Time. 1976. Repr. of 1961 ed. lib. bdg. 10.95 (ISBN 0-8398-2334-7, Gregg). G K Hall.

--The Book of Fritz Leiber. (Science Fiction Ser.). pap. 1.25 o.p. (ISBN 0-87997-269-6, UY1269). DAW Bks.

--The Book of Fritz Leiber, Vols. I & II. 1980. lib. bdg. 19.95 (ISBN 0-8398-2638-9, Gregg). G K Hall.

--The Change War. 15.00 (ISBN 0-8398-2493-9, Gregg). G K Hall.

--Changewar. 1983. pap. 2.50 (ISBN 0-441-10259-X, Pub. by Ace Science Fiction). Ace Bks.

--Conjure Wife. 1977. Repr. of 1953 ed. lib. bdg. 10.95 o.p. (ISBN 0-8398-2377-0, Gregg). G K Hall.

--The Fafhrd & the Gray Mouser Saga. (Science Fiction Ser.). 1977. 50.00 o.p. (ISBN 4-4444-7010-0, Gregg). G K Hall.

--Gather, Darkness! 1980. lib. bdg. 14.95 (ISBN 0-8398-2639-7, Gregg). G K Hall.

--The Green Millennium. 1980. lib. bdg. 14.95 (ISBN 0-8398-2641-9, Gregg). G K Hall.

--In the Beginning. (Illus.). 32p. 1983. Repr. signed, casebound 65.00 (ISBN 0-941826-01-5); deluxe ed. avail. (ISBN 0-941826-02-3). Cheap St.

--Night's Black Agents. 1980. lib. bdg. 15.00 (ISBN 0-8398-2640-0, Gregg). G K Hall.

--The Sinful Ones. 1980. lib. bdg. 13.95 (ISBN 0-8398-2643-5, Gregg). G K Hall.

--Swords Against Death. (Science Fiction Ser.). 1977. lib. bdg. 9.95 o.p. (ISBN 0-8398-2399-1, Gregg). G K Hall.

--Swords Against Wizardry. (Science Fiction Ser.). 1977. lib. bdg. 9.95 o.p. (ISBN 0-8398-2401-7, Gregg). G K Hall.

--Swords & Deviltry. (The Fafhrd & the Gray Mouser Saga of Fritz Leiber). 1977. lib. bdg. 9.95 o.p. (ISBN 0-8398-2398-3, Gregg). G K Hall.

--Swords & Ice Magic. 1977. lib. bdg. 9.95 (ISBN 0-8398-2403-3, Gregg). G K Hall.

--Swords in the Mist. (Science Fiction Ser.). 1977. lib. bdg. 9.95 o.p. (ISBN 0-8398-2400-9, Gregg). G K Hall.

--The Swords of Lankhmar. 1977. lib. bdg. 9.95 (ISBN 0-8398-2402-5, Gregg). G K Hall.

--The Wanderer. 1980. lib. bdg. 15.95 (ISBN 0-8398-2642-7, Gregg). G K Hall.

--The Worlds of Fritz Leiber. 1979. lib. bdg. 15.00 (ISBN 0-8398-2477-7, Gregg). G K Hall.

Leiber, Justin. Structuralism. (World Leaders Ser.). 1978. lib. bdg. 12.95 (ISBN 0-8057-7721-0, Twayne). G K Hall.

Leiberman, Norman P. Process Design in Practice. 1983. text ed. 38.95 (ISBN 0-87201-747-8). Gulf Pub.

Leibholz, Stephhen W., ed. see Hoeber, Francis P.

Leiblum, Sandra R. & Pervin, Lawrence A., eds. Principles & Practice of Sex Therapy. LC 80-20062. (Illus.). 410p. 1980. 25.00 (ISBN 0-89862-600-5). Guilford Pr.

Leibniz. The Leibniz-Clarke Correspondence. Alexander, H. G., ed. 200p. 1977. 15.00x o.p. (ISBN 0-7190-0669-4, Pub. by Manchester U Pr England). State Mutual Bk.

Leibniz, G. W. New Essays on Human Understanding. abr. ed. Remnant, Peter & Bennett, Jonathan, eds. Remnant, Peter & Bennett, Jonathan, trs. LC 82-1334. 280p. 1982. 10.95 (ISBN 0-521-28539-9). Cambridge U Pr.

Leibniz, Gottfried W. Discourse on Metaphysics. 2nd ed. Montgomery, George R., tr. from Fr. Bd. with Correspondence with Arnauld; Monadology. LC 51-45405. xxiii, 295p. 1973. 18.00 (ISBN 0-87548-029-2); pap. 8.50 (ISBN 0-87548-030-6). Open Court.

--Discourse on the Natural Theology of the Chinese. Rosemont, Henry, Jr. & Cook, Daniel J., trs. from Ger. LC 77-24111. (Society for Asian & Comparative Philosophy: No. 4). 208p. (Orig.). 1977. pap. text ed. 6.00x (ISBN 0-8248-0542-9). UH Pr.

Leibositz, S. & Hughes, A. C. Immunology of the Nervous System. (Current Topics in Immunology Ser.). 320p. 1983. text ed. price not set (ISBN 0-7131-4300-2). E Arnold.

Leibowitz, Alan. The Record Collector's Handbook. LC 78-72181. (Illus.). 284p. 1980. pap. 9.95 o.p. (ISBN 0-89696-015-3, An Everest House Book). Dodd.

Leibowitz, Arnold H. Bilingual Education Act: A Legislative Analysis. LC 80-80121. 80p. (Orig.). 1980. pap. 6.25 (ISBN 0-89763-022-X). Natl Clearinghse Bilingual Ed.

--Colonial Emancipation in the Pacific & the Caribbean: A Legal & Political Analysis. LC 75-19801. (Prae Ger Special Studies Ser.). 240p. 1976. 27.95 o.p. (ISBN 0-275-56000-7). Praeger.

--Federal Recognition of Minority Language Groups in the United States. LC 81-82492. 224p. (Orig.). 1982. pap. 20.00 (ISBN 0-89763-068-8). Natl Clearinghse Bilingual Ed.

Leibowitz, Herbert A., ed. see Rosenfeld, Paul.

Leibowitz, J. O. & Marcus, Shlomo, eds. Moses Maimonides on the Causes of Symptoms. LC 71-187873. 1974. 20.00x o.p. (ISBN 0-520-02224-6). U of Cal Pr.

Leibowitz, Rene. Schoenberg & His School: The Contemporary Stage of the Language of Music. Newlin, Dika, tr. from Fr. LC 75-115338. (Music Ser). 1970. Repr. of 1949 ed. lib. bdg. 29.50 (ISBN 0-306-71930-4). Da Capo.

Leicester, Chas. Bloodstock Breeding: Theory & Practice. 35.00x o.p. (ISBN 0-87556-148-9). Saifer.

Leicester Conference, 1976. Public Understanding of Science & Technology: Proceedings Leicester Conference, 1976. 160p. 1980. pap. 21.00x (ISBN 0-942776-00-3, Pub by I.C.P.). Pub Ctr Cult Res.

Leich, Christopher M., jt. ed. see Holtzman, Steven H.

Leichter, H. M. The Comparative Study of Public Policy. LC 79-50625. (Illus.). 1979. 34.50 (ISBN 0-521-22648-1); pap. 10.95x (ISBN 0-521-29601-3). Cambridge U Pr.

Leichter, Hope J. & Mitchell, William E. Kinship & Casework. LC 66-24898. 344p. 1967. 11.00x (ISBN 0-87154-522-5). Russell Sage.

--Kinship & Casework. rev. ed. LC 78-15482. 1978. pap. text ed. 13.50x (ISBN 0-8077-2530-7). Tchrs Coll.

Leichter, Hope J., ed. The Family As Educator. LC 75-16252. 1975. pap. 6.50x (ISBN 0-8077-2496-3). Tchrs Coll.

Leichter, Howard M. Political Regime & Public Policy in the Philippines: A Comparison of Bacolod & Iloilo Cities. (Special Report Ser.: No. 11). 1975. wrps. 4.00 (ISBN 0-686-09458-1). Cellar.

Leichtman, Robert R. Arthur Ford Returns. (From Heaven to Earth Ser.). (Illus.). 88p. (Orig.). 1979. pap. 3.00 (ISBN 0-89804-058-2). Ariel OH.

--Cheiro Returns. (From Heaven to Earth Ser.). (Illus.). 78p. (Orig.). 1979. pap. 3.00 (ISBN 0-89804-053-1). Ariel OH.

--Churchill Returns. LC 81-66847. (From Heaven to Earth Ser.). (Illus.). 96p. (Orig.). 1981. pap. 3.00 (ISBN 0-89804-065-5). Ariel OH.

--Edgar Cayce Returns. (From Heaven to Earth Ser.). (Illus.). 112p. (Orig.). 1978. pap. 3.00 (ISBN 0-89804-051-5). Ariel OH.

--Eileen Garrett Returns. (From Heaven to Earth Ser.). 96p. (Orig.). 1980. pap. 3.00 (ISBN 0-89804-061-2). Ariel OH.

--Einstein Returns. LC 81-69184. (From Heaven to Earth Ser.). (Illus.). 112p. (Orig.). 1982. pap. 3.00 (ISBN 0-89804-068-X). Ariel OH.

--Franklin Returns. LC 81-69138. (From Heaven to Earth Ser.). 96p. (Orig.). 1982. pap. 3.00 (ISBN 0-89804-069-8). Ariel OH.

--H. P. Blatavsky Returns. (From Heaven to Earth Ser.). 95p. (Orig.). 1980. pap. 3.00 (ISBN 0-89804-059-0). Ariel OH.

--Jefferson Returns. (From Heaven to Earth Ser.). 64p. (Orig.). 1979. pap. 3.00 (ISBN 0-89804-057-4). Ariel OH.

--Jung & Freud Return. (From Heaven to Earth Ser.). 102p. (Orig.). 1979. pap. 3.00 (ISBN 0-89804-054-X). Ariel OH.

--Leadbeater Returns. (From Heaven to Earth Ser.). (Illus.). 96p. (Orig.). 1979. pap. 3.00 (ISBN 0-89804-055-8). Ariel OH.
--Mark Twain Returns. LC 81-69185. (From Heaven to Earth Ser.). 80p. (Orig.). 1982. pap. 3.00 (ISBN 0-89804-067-1). Ariel OH.
--Nikola Tesla Returns. (From Heaven to Earth Ser.). (Illus.). 104p. (Orig.). 1980. pap. 3.00 (ISBN 0-89804-060-4). Ariel OH.
--Rembrandt Returns. (From Heavens to Earth Ser.). (Illus.). 96p. (Orig.). 1981. pap. 3.00 (ISBN 0-89804-089-2). Ariel OH.
--Shakespeare Returns. (From Heaven to Earth Ser.). (Illus.). 70p. (Orig.). 1978. pap. 3.00 (ISBN 0-89804-052-3). Ariel OH.
--Sir Oliver Lodge Returns. (From Heaven to Earth Ser.). (Illus.). 96p. (Orig.). 1979. pap. 3.00 (ISBN 0-89804-056-6). Ariel OH.
--Stewart White Returns. (From Heaven to Earth Ser.). (Illus.). 96p. (Orig.). 1980. pap. 3.00 (ISBN 0-89804-062-0). Ariel OH.
--Sweitzer Returns. (From Heaven to Earth Ser.). 104p. (Orig.). 1980. pap. 3.00 (ISBN 0-89804-063-9). Ariel OH.
Leichtman, Robert R. & Japikse, Carl. Active Meditation: The Western Tradition. LC 82-72785. 512p. 1983. 24.50 (ISBN 0-89804-040-X). Ariel OH.
--The Art of Living, Vol. I. 242p. 1979. pap. 6.00 (ISBN 0-89804-032-9). Ariel OH.
--The Art of Living, Vol. II. (Illus.). 249p. (Orig.). 1980. pap. 6.00 (ISBN 0-89804-033-7). Ariel OH.
--The Art of Living, Vol. III. LC 81-69186. (Illus.). 250p. (Orig.). 1982. pap. 5.00 (ISBN 0-89804-034-5). Ariel OH.
--The Way to Health. (Art of Living Ser.). 90p. 1979. pap. 3.00 (ISBN 0-89804-037-X). Ariel OH.
Leiden, Carl, jt. auth. see Bill, James A.
Leider, Frida. Playing My Part. Osborne, Charles, tr. LC 77-26171. (Music Reprint Ser., 1978). (Illus.). 1978. Repr. of 1959 ed. lib. bdg. 25.00 (ISBN 0-306-77535-2). Da Capo.
Leider, Robert. College Grants from Uncle Sam: Am I Eligible & for How Much 1983-84. rev., 2nd ed. 1982. pap. 1.25 (ISBN 0-917760-32-8). Octameron Assocs.
--College Loans from Uncle Sam: The Borrower's Guide That Explains It All-From Locating Lenders to Loan Forgiveness, 1882-1984. rev., 2nd ed. 1982. pap. 1.25 (ISBN 0-917760-33-6). Octameron Assocs.
--Your Own Financial Aid Factory: The Guide to Locating College Money. 184p. 1982. pap. 6.95 (ISBN 0-686-82955-7). Petersons Guides.
Leifer, Glora. Principles & Techniques in Pediatric Nursing. 3rd ed. (Illus.). 1977. text ed. 8.95 o.p. (ISBN 0-7216-5713-3); pap. text ed. 10.95 o.p. (ISBN 0-7216-5719-2). Saunders.
Leifer, P. This Sonata. 1977. 10.95 (ISBN 0-931338-01-8). Arum Pr.
Leiff, Jonathan D. & Brown, Richard. A Handbook of Geropsychiatric Programs. 1983. price not set prof ref (ISBN 0-88410-742-6). Ballinger Pub.
Leigh, C. H., jt. auth. see Aiken, S. R.
Leigh, D. A. & Robinson, O. P. Augmentin: Clavulanate-Potenciated Amoxycillin. (International Congress Ser.: Vol. 590). 1982. 47.00 (ISBN 0-444-90271-6). Elsevier.
Leigh, D. C. Nonlinear Continuum Mechanics. (Mechanical Engineering Ser.). 1968. text ed. 22.50 o.p. (ISBN 0-07-037085-0, C). McGraw.
Leigh, Egbert G., Jr., et al, eds. The Ecology of a Tropical Forest: Seasonal Rhythms & Long Term Changes. (Illus.). 480p. 1982. pap. text ed. 22.50x (ISBN 0-87474-601-9). Smithsonian.
Leigh, J. R. Applied Control Theory. (IEE Control Engineering Ser.: No. 18). 192p. 1982. 56.00 (ISBN 0-906048-72-9). Inst Elect Eng.
Leigh, James. The Ludi Victor. 320p. 1980. 11.95 (ISBN 0-698-11038-2, Coward). Putnam Pub Group.
--The Ludi Victor. 1981. pap. 2.75 o.p. (ISBN 0-451-11111-7, AE1111, Sig). NAL.
Leigh, James H. & Martin, Claude R., Jr., eds. Current Issues & Research in Advertising, 1982. 180p. (Orig.). 1983. pap. 6.50 (ISBN 0-87712-225-3). U Mich Busn Div Res.
Leigh, L. H. Economic Crime in Europe. 1980. 25.00 (ISBN 0-312-22788-4). St Martin.
Leigh, Michael. Mobilizing Consent: Public Opinion & American Foreign Policy, 1937-1947. LC 75-44656. 256p. 1976. lib. bdg. 25.00 (ISBN 0-8371-8772-9, LMC/). Greenwood.
Leigh, R. John & Zee, David S. The Neurology of Eye Movement. LC 82-12710. (Contemporary Neurology Ser.: No. 23). 1983. 40.00x (ISBN 0-8036-5524-X). Davis Co.
Leigh, Robert. First & Last Murder. 256p. 1983. 10.95 (ISBN 0-312-29222-8). St Martin.
--Index to Song Books. LC 72-8344. (Music Ser). 242p. 1973. Repr. of 1964 ed. lib. bdg. 22.50 (ISBN 0-306-70553-2). Da Capo.
Leigh, Robert D. A Free & Responsible Press, a General Report on Mass Communication: Newspapers, Radio, Motion Pictures, Magazines & Books. Commission on Freedom of the Press, ed. LC 46-13. (Midway Reprint Ser.). 139p. 1947. pap. text ed. 5.00x (ISBN 0-226-47135-7). U of Chicago Pr.
Leigh, Roberta. Love Match. 352p. 1983. pap. 2.25 (ISBN 0-373-97003-X, Pub. by Worldwide). Harlequin Bks.
Leigh, Susannah. Winter Fire. (Orig.). 1978. pap. 2.50 o.p. (ISBN 0-451-08680-5, E8680, Sig). NAL.
--Yesterday's Tears. 1982. pap. 3.50 (ISBN 0-451-11764-6, AE1764, Sig). NAL.
Leigh, Wendy. What Makes a Man G.I.B. (Good in Bed) (Orig.). 1979. pap. 2.50 o.p. (ISBN 0-451-08927-8, E8927, Sig). NAL.
Leigh, Wilhelmina A. Shelter Affordability for Blacks: Crisis or Clamor? 90p. (Orig.). 1982. pap. 5.95x (ISBN 0-87855-901-9). Transaction Bks.
Leighbody, G. B., jt. auth. see Kidd, D. M.
Leigh-Loohuizen, Ria, tr. see Kopland, Rutger.
Leighly, John, ed. see Sauer, Carl O.
Leight, Warren D. The I Hate New York Guidebook. (Orig.). 1983. pap. price not set (ISBN 0-440-53609-X, Dell Trade Pbks). Dell.
Leighton, Alexander. Commonwealth Tracts 1625-1650: A Shorte Treatise Against Stage-Playes. Bd. with The Stage Players Complaint; Declaration...Also an Ordinance of Both Houses, for the Supression of Stage Playes; The Actors Remonstrance; Two Ordinances; An Ordinance for the Utter Suppression & Abolishing of All Stage-Playes & Interludes; The Dagonizing of Bartholomew Fayre; The Humble Petition of Diverse Poor & Distressed Men, Heretofore the Actors of Blackfriers & the Cock-Pit. LC 71-170417. (The English Stage Ser.: Vol. 14). lib. bdg. 50.00 o.s.i. (ISBN 0-8240-0597-X). Garland Pub.
Leighton, D. S., jt. ed. see Thompson, D. N.
Leighton, Frances S., jt. auth. see Allyson, June.
Leighton, Frances S., jt. auth. see Dahlinger, John D.
Leighton, Frances S., jt. auth. see Szostak, John M.
Leighton, Isabel. Aspirin Age: 1919-1941. 1963. pap. 9.50 (ISBN 0-671-20062-3, Touchstone Bks). S&S.
Leighton, Jack R. Fitness, Body Development, & Sports Conditioning Through Weight Training. 2nd ed. (Illus.). 234p. 1983. 24.50x (ISBN 0-398-04761-8). C C Thomas.
Leighton, Lauren G. Alexander Bestuzhev-Marlinsky. (World Authors Ser.: No. 344). 15.95 o.p. (ISBN 0-8057-2149-5, Twayne). G K Hall.
Leighton, Lauren G., jt. ed. see Gutsche, George J.
Leighton, Neil & Stalley, Richard. Rights & Responsibilities. (Community Care Practice Handbooks Ser.). vii, 62p. (Orig.). 1982. pap. text ed. 7.95x (ISBN 0-435-82515-1). Heinemann Ed.
Leighton, Ralph & Feynman, Carl. How to Count Sheep Without Falling Asleep. LC 76-10237. (Illus.). (gr. 1-4). 1976. PLB 5.95 o.p. (ISBN 0-13-404459-2). P-H.
Leighton, Robert B. Principles of Modern Physics. (International Ser. in Pure & Applied Physics). 1959. text ed. 36.00 o.p. (ISBN 0-07-037130-X, C). McGraw.
Leih. Portrait of a Fulfilled Woman. 1979. pap. 3.95 (ISBN 0-8423-4860-3). Tyndale.
Leijonhufvud, Axel. Information & Coordination: Essays in Macroeconomic Theory. (Illus.). 400p. 1981. text ed. 22.50x (ISBN 0-19-502814-7); pap. text ed. 12.95x (ISBN 0-19-502815-5). Oxford U Pr.
--On Keynesian Economics & the Economics of Keynes: A Study in Monetary Theory. 1968. text ed. 16.95x (ISBN 0-19-500948-7). Oxford U Pr.
Leik, Robert K. & Meeker, Barbara F. Mathematical Sociology. LC 74-22271. (Methods of Social Science Ser.). (Illus.). 272p. 1975. 21.95 o.p. (ISBN 0-13-562108-9). P-H.
Leiken, Robert S. Soviet Strategy & Latin America. (Washington Papers: No. 93). 144p. 1982. 6.95 (ISBN 0-03-062017-1). Praeger.
Leiman, Arnold L., jt. auth. see Rosenzweig, Mark R.
Leiman, M., jt. auth. see Romano, R.
Leimas, Brooke. The Intruder. (Orig.). 1980. pap. 2.50 o.p. (ISBN 0-451-09524-3, E9524, Sig). NAL.
Leimbach, Patricia P. All My Meadows. LC 77-24352. (Illus.). 1977. 12.95 (ISBN 0-13-022525-8). P-H.
Leimberg, Stephen, jt. auth. see Plotnick, Charles.
Leimburg, jt. auth. see Parker.
Leimer, Karl, jt. auth. see Gieseking, Walter.
Leimus, Brooke. The Summer Visitors. (Orig.). (YA) 1980. pap. 1.95 o.p. (ISBN 0-451-09247-3, J9247, Sig). NAL.
Lein, Laura & Sussman, Marvin B., eds. The Ties That Bind: Men's & Women's Social Networks. LC 82-23230. (Marriage & Family Review Ser.: Vol. 5, No. 4). 128p. 1983. text ed. 19.95 (ISBN 0-86656-161-7, B161). Haworth Pr.
Leinbach, L. Carl. Calculus with the Computer: A Laboratory Manual. (Illus.). 208p. 1974. pap. text ed. 10.95x o.p. (ISBN 0-13-111518-9). P-H.
Leiner, Jacqueline. Imaginaire-Language-Identite Culterelle-Negritude. (Etudes Litteraires Francaises Ser.: No. 10). 167p. (Orig.). 1980. pap. 19.80 (ISBN 3-87808-889-2, Pub. by G. N. Verlag Germany). Benjamins North Am.
Leinfellner, Werner & Kraemer, Eric. Language & Ontology. (Sprachen und Ontologie.). 1982. lib. bdg. 78.00 (ISBN 90-277-9080-9, Pub. by Reidel Holland). Kluwer Boston.
Leininger, G., ed. Computer Aided Design of Multivariate Technological Systems: Proceedings of the IFAC Symposium, Indiana, USA, 15-17 September 1982. (IFAC Proceedings Ser.). 600p. 1983. 150.00 (ISBN 0-08-029357-3). Pergamon.
Leininger, Joseph E. & Gilchrist, Bruce, eds. Computers, Society & Law: The Role of Legal Education. LC 73-93427. (Illus.). 264p. 1973. pap. 12.00 (ISBN 0-88283-001-5). AFIPS Pr.
Leininger, Madeleine. Transcultural Nursing: Concepts, Theories & Practices. LC 77-28250. 1977. text ed. 35.00x (ISBN 0-471-52608-8, Pub by Wiley Medical). Wiley.
Leininger, Madeline, ed. Transcultural Nursing, 1979. LC 79-66888. (Illus.). 742p. 1979. text ed. 37.50 (ISBN 0-89352-079-9). Masson Pub.
Leininger, Sheryl, ed. Internal Theft: Investigation & Control. LC 75-17137. 256p. (Anthology). 1975. 18.95 (ISBN 0-913708-21-6). Butterworth.
Leininger, Steve. The Official Country & Western Joke Book. 1983. pap. 1.95 (ISBN 0-523-41913-9). Pinnacle Bks.
--The Official Iranian Joke Book. 192p. 1981. pap. 2.25 (ISBN 0-523-41839-6). Pinnacle Bks.
Leininger, Wayne E. Quantitative Methods in Accounting. LC 79-66015. 353p. 1980. text ed. 23.95x (ISBN 0-442-80503-9). Kent Pub Co.
Leininger, Wayne E., jt. auth. see Hicks, James O., Jr.
Leino, Lily, tr. see Tuominen, Arvo P.
Leinsdorf, Erich. The Composer's Advocate: A Radical Orthodoxy for Musicians. LC 80-17614. (Illus.). 232p. 1981. 16.95x (ISBN 0-300-02427-4, Y-437); pap. 7.95 (ISBN 0-300-02887-3). Yale U Pr.
Leinster, Murray. Doctor to the Stars. 1977. pap. 1.50 o.p. (ISBN 0-515-04482-2). Jove Pubns.
--The Med Series. 1983. pap. 2.95 (ISBN 0-441-52360-9, Pub. by Ace Science Fiction). Ace Bks.
Leinwand, Gerald. Teaching of World History. LC 77-95099. (Bulletin Ser.: No. 54). (Illus.). 1978. pap. 6.95 (ISBN 0-87986-019-7, 498-15268). Coun Soc Studies.
Leinwoll, Stanley. The Book of Pets. LC 80-17598. (Illus.). 128p. (gr. 7 up). 1980. PLB 8.79 o.p. (ISBN 0-671-33071-3). Messner.
Leipholz, H. H., ed. Structural Control. 1980. 85.00 (ISBN 0-444-85485-1). Elsevier.
Leipnitz, Walter, ed. Petroleum Refining & Petrochemistry Four-Language Dictionary. 228p. 1980. 24.95x (ISBN 0-87201-673-0). Gulf Pub.
Leipold, L. E. Come Along to Saudi Arabia. (Illus.). (gr. 5 up). 1974. PLB 3.50 o.p. (ISBN 0-513-01249-4). Denison.
Leipziger, Danny M. & Mudge, James L. Seabed Mineral Resources: The Economic Interests of Developing Countries. LC 76-19076. 1976. prof ref 27.50x (ISBN 0-88410-049-9). Ballinger Pub.
Leiris, Michel. Race & Culture. 1965. pap. 2.50 o.p. (ISBN 92-3-100435-2, U506, UNESCO). Unipub.
Leiser, Burton M. Liberty, Justice, & Morals: Contemporary Value Conflicts. 2nd ed. (Illus.). 1979. text ed. 14.95x (ISBN 0-02-369510-2). Macmillan.
--Values in Conflict: Life, Liberty & the Rule of Law. 1980. pap. text ed. 14.95x (ISBN 0-02-369520-X). Macmillan.
Leiser, Clara. Jean De Reszke & the Great Days of the Opera. Repr. of 1934 ed. lib. bdg. 18.75x (ISBN 0-8371-4256-3, LEJR). Greenwood.
Leiser, Eric. Fly-Tying Materials. 224p. 1973. 10.00 o.p. (ISBN 0-517-50350-6). Crown.
Leiserson, Avery. Administrative Regulation, a Study in Representation of Interests. rev. ed. LC 74-12761. 292p. 1975. Repr. of 1942 ed. lib. bdg. 18.75x (ISBN 0-8371-7744-8, LEAR). Greenwood.
Leiserson, Mark. Indonesia: Employment & Income Distribution in Indonesia. xii, 187p. 1980. pap. 15.00 (ISBN 0-686-36109-1, RC-8008). World Bank.
Leiserson, Mark, jt. auth. see Anderson, Dennis.
Leiserson, W. M; see Bernard, William S.
Leish, Kenneth. Cinema. LC 73-89395. (World of Culture Ser.). (Illus.). 12.95 o.p. (ISBN 0-88225-109-0). Newsweek.
Leishman, J. B., tr. see Rilke, Rainer M.
Leishman, Thomas L. The Continuity of the Bible: Prophetic Writings, Vol. 3. 1973. 4.50 (ISBN 0-87510-086-4). Chr Science.
Leisner, Tony. The Official Guide to Country Dance Steps. LC 79-67001. (Illus.). 96p. 1980. 5.98 o.p. (ISBN 0-89196-062-7, Domus Bks). Quality Bks IL.
Leiss, Ernst L. Principles of Data Security. (Foundations of Computer Science Ser.). 200p. 1982. 25.00x (ISBN 0-306-41098-2, Plenum Pr). Plenum Pub.
Leissner, Aryeh. Street Club Work in Tel Aviv & New York. (Studies in Child Development). (Illus., Orig.). 1969. pap. text ed. 9.50x (ISBN 0-582-32444-0). Humanities.
Leistner, Otto. Internationale Titelabkurzungen Von Zeitschriften, Zeitungen, Wichtingen Handbuchern, Worterbuchern, Gesetzen, & C. in Allen Sprachen. 2nd ed. 903p. 1970. 212.50x o.p. (ISBN 3-7648-1092-0). Intl Pubns Serv.
Leistritz, F. Larry & Murdock, Steven H. The Socioeconomic Impact of Resource Development: Methods for Assessment. (Social Impact Assessment Ser.: No. 6). 250p. 1981. lib. bdg. 24.50 (ISBN 0-89158-978-3). Westview.
Leistritz, F. Larry, jt. auth. see Murdock, Steve H.
Leisy, James. Calories in - Calories Out: The Energy Budget Way to Fitness & Weight Control. 128p. 1980. 10.95 o.s.i. (ISBN 0-8289-0413-8); pap. 6.95 o.s.i. (ISBN 0-8289-0414-6). Greene.
Leitch, Carol, jt. auth. see Clack, Alice.
Leitch, D. B. Engine Pass: New Zealand's Railways. 15.00x (ISBN 0-392-15554-0, ABC). Sportshelf.
Leitch, J. M. Food Science & Technology, 5 vols. 3456p. 1969. Set. 736.00x (ISBN 0-677-10290-9). Gordon.
Leitch, J. M., ed. see International Congress of Food & Science Technology-1st-London, 1962.
Leitch, Robert A. & Davis, K. Roscoe. Accounting Information Systems. (Illus.). 720p. 1983. 29.95 (ISBN 0-13-002949-1). P-H.
Leitch, Vincent B. Deconstructive Criticism: An Advanced Introduction & Survey. LC 82-120. 256p. 1982. text ed. 25.00x (ISBN 0-231-05472-6); pap. 8.95 (ISBN 0-231-05473-4). Columbia U Pr.
Leitch, William C. Hand Hewn. LC 82-1279. (Illus.). 160p. 1982. pap. 7.95 (ISBN 0-87701-265-2). Chronicle Bks.
--South America: A Field Guide to the National Parks. (Illus.). 144p. (Orig.). 1984. pap. 10.95 (ISBN 0-686-98029-8). Bradt Ent. Postponed.
Leite, Daliel. Don't Scratch! The Book About Poison-Oak. LC 82-70943. (Illus.). 64p. 1982. pap. 3.95 (ISBN 0-943246-01-6). Weathervane CA.
Leite, Elizabeth. C Eighty-Three a Park Bear. LC 82-60289. (Illus.). 72p. 1983. pap. 3.95 (ISBN 0-943246-02-4). Weathervane CA.
--Simply Beautiful: Living with the Earth in Mind. 3.95 (ISBN 0-686-95903-5). Alternatives.
Leiteizen, C., ed. see Lenin, Vladimir I.
Leitenberg, Milton, jt. auth. see Burns, Richard D.
Leitenberg, Milton & Ball, Nicole, eds. The Structure of the Defense Industry: An International Survey. LC 82-42565. 1982. 27.50x (ISBN 0-312-76757-9). St Martin.
Leiter, Elliot, jt. ed. see Whitehead, E. Douglas.
Leiter, Kelly, jt. auth. see Harriss, Julian.
Leiter, Louis, jt. auth. see Clerc, Charles.
Leiter, Louis H., jt. auth. see Clerc, Charles.
Leiter, Michael P. & Webb, Mark. Developing Human Service Networks: Community & Organizatonal Relations. 279p. 1983. text ed. 19.50x (ISBN 0-8290-1262-1). Irvington.
Leiter, Samuel. From Belasco to Brook: Great Stage Directors of the Twentieth Century. Date not set. 19.95 (ISBN 0-89676-057-X). Drama Bk. Postponed.
Leiter, Samuel L. The Art of Kabuki: Famous Plays in Performance. LC 77-83107. 1979. 18.95 (ISBN 0-520-03555-0). U of Cal Pr.
--Kabuki Encyclopedia: An English-Language Adaptation of Kabuki Jiten. LC 78-73801. (Illus.). 1979. lib. bdg. 45.00 (ISBN 0-313-20654-6, LKE). Greenwood.
Leiter, Sharon. Akhmatova's Petersburg. LC 82-40491. 224p. 1983. 20.00 (ISBN 0-8122-7864-X). U of Pa Pr.
Leites, N. & Marvick, Elizabeth W. Psychopolitical Analysis: Selected Writings of Nathan Leites. LC 77-2972. 384p. 1977. 21.95x o.p. (ISBN 0-470-99058-9). Halsted Pr.
Leites, Nathan. Depression & Masochism: An Account of Mechanisms. 1979. 19.95x o.p. (ISBN 0-393-01247-6). Norton.
Leitgeb, Grete, tr. see Saint-Exupery, Antoine De.
Leitgeb, H. Utersuchungen Ueber Die Lebermoose. 1970. 80.00 (ISBN 3-7682-7187-0). Lubrecht & Cramer.
Leitgeb, Josef, tr. see Saint-Exupery, Antoine De.
Leith, Dick. A Social History of English. (Language & Society Ser.). 224p. 1983. 19.95 (ISBN 0-7100-9260-1); pap. 9.95 (ISBN 0-7100-9261-X). Routledge & Kegan.
Leith, J. Clark, jt. auth. see Ellsworth, Paul T.
Leith, John H. Assembly at Westminster: Reformed Theology in the Making. LC 72-11162. 128p. (Orig.). 1973. pap. 4.75 (ISBN 0-8042-0885-9). John Knox.
--The Church, a Believing Fellowship. LC 80-82192. 192p. 1981. pap. 3.49 (ISBN 0-8042-0518-3). John Knox.
--Introduction to the Reformed Tradition: A Way of Being the Christian Community. rev. ed. LC 81-5968. (Illus.). 253p. 1981. pap. 9.95 (ISBN 0-8042-0479-9). John Knox.
Leith, Prudence & Waldegrave, Caroline. Leith's Cookery Course: A Guide to Perfect Cooking. (Illus.). 1982. 24.95 (ISBN 0-233-97153-X, Pub. by Salem Hse Ltd). Merrimack Bk Serv.
Leithauser, Brad. Hundreds of Fireflies. 71p. 11.50 (ISBN 0-394-51949-3); pap. 5.95 (ISBN 0-394-74896-4). Knopf.
Leithe-Jasper, Manfred & Distelberger, Rudolf. The Kunsthistorische Museum Vienna. (Illus.). 136p. 1982. pap. 12.50 (ISBN 0-85667-137-1, Pub. by Sotheby Pubns England). Biblio Dist.
Leithold, Louis. El Calculo. 4th ed. 1350p. (Span.). 1982. pap. text ed. 15.00 (ISBN 0-06-315013-1, Pub. by HarLA Mexico). Har-Row.
--Calculo. (Span.). 1973. pap. 17.50 o.p. (ISBN 0-06-315010-7, IntlDept). Har-Row.

--The Calculus with Analytic Geometry, 2 vols. 4th ed. Incl. Vol. I. Functions of One Variable, Plane Analytic Geometry, & Infinite Series. 819p. text ed. 25.95 scp (ISBN 0-06-043936-X); Vol. II. Infinite Series, Vectors, & Functions of Several Variables. 410p. text ed. 25.95 scp (ISBN 0-06-043937-8). 1981. Set, 2 vols. in 1. text ed. 36.50 scp (ISBN 0-06-043935-1, HarpC); scp sol. manual 16.50 (ISBN 0-06-043938-6); ans. key avail. (ISBN 0-06-363958-0); outline to accompany text, Vol. I 10.95 (ISBN 0-06-043938-6); outline to accompany text, Vol. II 10.95 (ISBN 0-06-044544-0); outline to accompany text, Vol. III 10.95 (ISBN 0-06-044545-9). Har-Row.

--The Calculus with Analytic Geometry: Infinite Series, Vectors, & Functions of Several Variables, No. 2. 4th. ed. 410p. 1980. text ed. 20.95 scp o.p. (ISBN 0-06-043937-8, HarpC). Har-Row.

--College Algebra. 2nd ed. (Illus.). 1980. text ed. 23.95x (ISBN 0-02-369580-3). Macmillan.

--Intermediate Algebra for College Students. 2nd ed. 1979. text ed. 22.95x (ISBN 0-02-369640-0). Macmillan.

Leitner, Irving A., ed. see Leitner, Isabella.

Leitner, Isabella. Fragments of Isabella: A Memoir of Auschwitz. Leitner, Irving A., ed. LC 78-4766. 1978. 11.49 (ISBN 0-690-01779-0). T Y Crowell.

Leitz, Pierr M., jt. auth. see Edge, Nellie.

Leitz, Robert C., et al, eds. The Selected Letters of W. D. Howells: Volume 3: 1882-1891. (Critical Editions Program). 1980. lib. bdg. 27.50 (ISBN 0-8057-8529-9, Twayne). G K Hall.

Leiva, Erasmo, tr. see Von Balthasar, Hans.

Leix, Alfred. Turkestan & Its Textile Craft. 1982. 40.00x (ISBN 0-903580-10-1, Pub. by Element Bks). State Mutual Bk.

Lejeune, Yves. Recueil Des Accords International Conclus Par les Cantons Suisses. 500p. (Fr.). 1982. write for info. (ISBN 3-261-04736-4). P Lang Pubs.

Lejeune-Dirichlet, P. G. Werke, 2 Vols. in 1. Kronecker, L., ed. LC 68-54716. (Ger). 1969. Repr. 49.50 (ISBN 0-8284-0225-6). Chelsea Pub.

Lejeune-Dirichlet, P. G. & Dedekind, R. Zahlentheorie. 4th ed. LC 68-54716. (Ger). 1969. text ed. 39.50 (ISBN 0-8284-0213-2). Chelsea Pub.

Lekachman, Robert. Economists at Bay: Why the Experts Will Never Solve Your Problems. 1976. 8.95 (ISBN 0-07-037153-9, GB); pap. 4.95 (ISBN 0-07-037158-X, GB). McGraw.

--A History of Economic Ideas. 1976. pap. 6.95 (ISBN 0-07-037155-5, SP). McGraw.

Leki, Ilona. Alain Robbe-Grillet. (World Authors Ser.). 200p. 1983. lib. bdg. 16.95 (ISBN 0-8057-6529-8, Twayne). G K Hall.

Lekkerkerker, C. J., jt. ed. see Kaper, H. G.

Lekovic, Zdravko & Bjelica, Mihalo. Communication Policies in Yugoslavia. 66p. 1977. pap. 4.75 o.p. (ISBN 92-3-101409-9, U88, UNESCO). Unipub.

Leland, Caryn. The Art Law Primer. 32p. 1981. pap. 5.00x (ISBN 0-933032-03-X). FCA Bks.

Leland Centennial Committee. Milestones Along the Way: Leland, Iowa. 227p. 1982. pap. 20.00 (ISBN 0-89279-047-4). Graphic Pub.

Leland, Charles G. Algonquin Legends of New England. LC 68-31217. 1968. Repr. of 1884 ed. 40.00x (ISBN 0-8103-3468-2). Gale.

--English Gypsies & Their Language. LC 68-22035. 1969. Repr. of 1874 ed. 40.00x (ISBN 0-8103-3883-1). Gale.

--Legends of Florence, 2 Vols. LC 68-27173. 1969. Repr. of 1895 ed. 30.00x ea. Vol. 1, First Ser (ISBN 0-8103-3843-2). Vol. 2, Second Ser. (ISBN 0-8103-3844-0); Set. write for info. (ISBN 0-8103-3899-8). Gale.

--Memoirs. LC 68-22036. 1968. Repr. of 1893 ed. 37.00x (ISBN 0-8103-3533-6). Gale.

--Sunshine in Thought. LC 59-6526. 1959. 21.00x o.p. (ISBN 0-8201-1055-8). Schol Facsimiles.

Leland, Charles G., ed. see Barrere, Albert.

Leland, David, jt. auth. see Sharma, C. H.

Leland, G. Waldo & Mereness, Newton D. Introduction to the American Official Sources for the Economic & Social History of the World War. LC 74-75248. (The United States in World War 1 Ser). xlvii, 532p. 1974. Repr. of 1926 ed. lib. bdg. 27.95x (ISBN 0-89198-109-8). Ozer.

Leland, Henry & Deutsch, Marilyn W., eds. Abnormal Behavior: A Guide to Information Sources. LC 80-65. (The Psychology Information Guide Ser.: Vol. 5). 261p. 1980. 42.00x (ISBN 0-8103-1416-9). Gale.

Leland, Louis S. Kiwi: Yankee Dictionary. 115p. 1980. pap. 5.95 (ISBN 0-86868-001-X). Bradt Ent.

Leland, Tom W., jt. auth. see Kim, Daeshik.

Leland, W. G. Guide to Materials for American History in the Libraries & Archives of Paris, 2 Vols. 1932-1943. Set. pap. 100.00 (ISBN 0-527-00692-0). Kraus Repr.

Leland, W. G., jt. auth. see Van Tyne, C. H.

Lelchuk, Alan. American Mischief. 480p. 1974. pap. 2.25 o.p. (ISBN 0-451-06185-3, E6185, Sig). NAL.

--Miriam at Thirty-Four. 1975. pap. 2.50 (ISBN 0-451-11330-6, AE1330, Sig). NAL.

--Shrinking. 1979. pap. 2.95 o.p. (ISBN 0-451-08653-8, E8653, Sig). NAL.

Lelchuk, Alan & Shaked, Gerson, eds. Eight Great Hebrew Short Stories. 1983. pap. 7.95 (ISBN 0-452-00605-8, Mer). NAL.

Le Letty, L. see IFAC.

Leliavsky, S. Dams. (Design Textbooks in Civil Engineering Ser.: Vol. 6). (Illus.). 250p. 1981. 35.00x (ISBN 0-412-22550-6, 6596). Methuen Inc.

--Design Textbooks in Civil Engineering, Vol. 3: Design of Dams for Percolation & Erosion. 1965. 35.00x (ISBN 0-412-07340-4, Pub. by Chapman & Hall). Methuen Inc.

--Design Textbooks in Civil Engineering, Vol. 4: River & Canal Hydraulics. 240p. 1965. 35.00x (ISBN 0-412-07350-1, Pub. by Chapman & Hall England). Methuen Inc.

LeLieuvre, Robert B., jt. auth. see Powell, Judith W.

Lellis, Geore, jt. auth. see Wead, George.

Lellis, George. Bertolt Brecht "Cahiers du Cinema " & Contemporary Film Theory. Kirkpatrick, Diane, ed. LC 82-2051. (Studies in Cinema: No. 13). 208p. 1982. 39.95 (ISBN 0-8357-1300-8, Pub. by UMI Res Pr). Univ Microfilms.

Lellis, George, jt. ed. see Wead, George.

Lelouche, Claude. Man & A Woman. (Film Scripts-Modern Ser.). 1971. pap. 2.25 o.p. (ISBN 0-671-20963-9, Touchstone Bks). S&S.

LeLoup, Lance T. The Fiscal Congress: Legislative Control of the Budget. LC 79-6823. (Contributions in Political Science: No. 47). (Illus.). xii, 227p. 1980. lib. bdg. 27.50 (ISBN 0-313-22009-3, LFC/). Greenwood.

Lely, James A. Aquarius. (Sun Signs Ser.). (Illus.). (gr. 4-12). 1978. PLB 6.95 (ISBN 0-87191-651-7); pap. 3.25 (ISBN 0-89812-080-2). Creative Ed.

--Libra. (Sun Signs Ser.). (Illus.). (gr. 4-12). 1978. PLB 6.95 (ISBN 0-87191-647-9); pap. 3.25 (ISBN 0-685-86522-3). Creative Ed.

--Virgo. (Sun Signs Ser.). (Illus.). (gr. 4-12). 1978. PLB 6.95 (ISBN 0-87191-646-0); pap. 3.25 (ISBN 0-89812-076-4). Creative Ed.

Lem, Stanislaw. The Chain of Chance. 1979. pap. 1.75 o.s.i. (ISBN 0-515-05138-1). Jove Pubns.

--The Futurological Congress. 1976. pap. 2.75 (ISBN 0-380-00584-0, 58289, Bard). Avon.

--His Master's Voice. Kandel, Michael, tr. LC 82-47668. (A Helen & Kurt Wolff Bk.). 228p. 1983. 12.95 (ISBN 0-15-140360-0). HarBraceJ.

--The Investigation. 1976. pap. 1.50 o.p. (ISBN 0-380-00665-0, 29314). Avon.

--Memoirs of a Space Traveler: Further Reminiscences of Ijon Tichy. Stern, Joel & Swiecicka-Ziemianek, Maria, trs. LC 81-47310. (Helen & Kurt Wolff Bk.). 156p. 1982. 9.95 (ISBN 0-15-158856-2). HarBraceJ.

--Memoirs of A Space Traveler: Further Reminiscences of Ijon Tichy. Stern, Joel & Swiecicka-Ziemianek, Maria, trs. 156p. pap. 3.95 (ISBN 0-15-658635-5, Harv). HarBraceJ.

--A Perfect Vacuum. Kandel, Michael, tr. 240p. pap. 3.95 (ISBN 0-15-671686-0, Harv). HarBraceJ.

--Return from the Stars. Marszal, Barbara & Simpson, Frank, trs. LC 79-3358. (Helen & Kurt Wolff Bk.). 312p. 1980. 8.95 (ISBN 0-15-177082-4). HarBraceJ.

LeMagnen, J., ed. see International Symposium on Olfaction & Taste, 6th, Gif Sur Yvette, France, 1977.

LeMaire, H. Paul. Personal Decisions. LC 81-43668. 220p. (Orig.). 1982. lib. bdg. 22.25 (ISBN 0-8191-2329-3); pap. text ed. 10.25 (ISBN 0-8191-2330-7). U Pr of Amer.

Le Maire, Jacques. Les Voyages du Sieur Le Maire aux Iles Canaries, Cap-Vert, Senegal et Gambie. (Bibliotheque Africaine Ser.). 240p. (Fr.). 1974. Repr. of 1695 ed. lib. bdg. 66.00x o.p. (ISBN 0-8287-0528-3, 72-2119). Clearwater Pub.

LeMaire, T. R. Stones from the Stars: The Unsolved Mysteries of Meteorites. LC 79-21158. 204p. 1980. 9.95 o.p. (ISBN 0-13-846881-8). P-H.

Le Maitre, R. W. Numerical Petrology. (Developments in Petrology Ser.: No. 8). 282p. 1982. 57.50 (ISBN 0-444-42098-3). Elsevier.

Leman, Bonnie. Quick & Easy Quilting. (Illus.). 192p. 1972. lib. bdg. 7.95 (ISBN 0-8208-0343-X). Hearthside.

Leman, Christopher. The Collapse of Welfare Reform: Political Institutions, Policy & the Poor in Canada & the United States. (Illus.). 1980. text ed. 22.50x (ISBN 0-262-12081-X). MIT Pr.

Leman, Kevin. Parenthood Without Hassles - Well Almost. LC 78-65621. 1979. pap. 3.95 o.p. (ISBN 0-89081-183-0, 1830). Harvest Hse.

--Smart Girls Don't: And Guys Don't Either. 1982. 8.95 (ISBN 0-8307-0824-3, 5109808). Regal.

Lemann, Bernard, jt. auth. see Wilson, Samuel, Jr.

Lemarchand, Elizabeth. Change for the Worse. 185p. 1983. pap. 2.95 (ISBN 0-8027-3028-0). Walker & Co.

--Step in the Dark. 173p. 1983. pap. 2.95 (ISBN 0-8027-3027-2). Walker & Co.

--Unhappy Returns. 175p. 1983. pap. 2.95 (ISBN 0-8027-3007-8). Walker & Co.

Lemarchand, Rene, ed. American Policy in Southern Africa: The Stakes & the Stance. 2nd ed. LC 80-6222. 513p. 1981. lib. bdg. 24.25 (ISBN 0-8191-1436-7); pap. text ed. 13.25 (ISBN 0-8191-1437-5). U Pr of Amer.

Lemaster, A. James, ed. see Grubbs, Robert L. & Ober, B. Scot.

LeMaster, J. R. Jesse Stuart: A Reference Guide. 1979. lib. bdg. 26.00 (ISBN 0-8161-8041-5, Hall Reference). G K Hall.

--Jesse Stuart: Kentucky's Chronicler-Poet. LC 79-28224. 1980. 14.95x o.p. (ISBN 0-87870-049-8). Memphis St Univ.

Le Master, Richard. Wildlife in Wood. 1978. 35.00 (ISBN 0-8092-7336-5, Pub. by Model Tech). Contemp Bks.

LeMasters, Karen, jt. auth. see Zaltman, Gerald.

Le May, Alan. The Searchers. 1978. lib. bdg. 9.95 (ISBN 0-8398-2464-5, Gregg). G K Hall.

LeMay, Alan. The Searchers. 352p. 1982. pap. 2.95 (ISBN 0-441-75693-X, Pub. by Charter Bks). Ace Bks.

Le May, Alan. The Unforgiven. 1978. lib. bdg. 9.95 (ISBN 0-8398-2465-3, Gregg). G K Hall.

Le May, Eugene, jt. auth. see Brown, Theodore.

Le May, G. H. The Victorian Constitution. 1979. 26.00x (ISBN 0-312-84145-0). St Martin.

LeMay, H. Eugene, jt. auth. see Brown, Theodore L.

LeMay, Iain & Schetky, L. McDonald. Copper in Iron & Steel. LC 82-17615. 423p. 1982. 59.50 (ISBN 0-471-05913-7, Pub. by Wiley-Interscience). Wiley.

Lemay, Nita K., jt. auth. see Newman, Matt.

Lemberger, L. & Rubin, A. Physiologic Disposition of Drugs of Abuse. LC 76-13. (Monographs in Pharmacology & Physiology). 401p. 1976. 29.50x o.s.i. (ISBN 0-470-15021-1). Halsted Pr.

Lembke, Janet. Bronze & Iron: Old Latin Poetry from Its Beginning to 100 B. C. 1973. 24.50x (ISBN 0-520-02164-9). U of Cal Pr.

Lembo, John w., ed. How to Cope with Your Fears & Frustrations. 6.95 (ISBN 0-686-36751-0). Inst Rat Liv.

Le Mercier De La Riviere. L' Heureuse Nation, 2 vols. (Utopias in the Enlightenment Ser.). 898p. (Fr.). 1974. Repr. of 1792 ed. lib. bdg. 225.00x set o.p. (ISBN 0-8287-0532-1). Vol. 1 (016). Vol. 2 (017). Clearwater Pub.

Lemerle, Paul. Le Monde De Byzance: Histoire et Institutions. 450p. 1978. 60.00x (ISBN 0-686-97609-6, Pub. by Variorum). State Mutual Bk.

Lemert, Charles C. Sociology & the Twilight of Man: Homocentrism & Discourse in Sociological Theory. LC 78-17146. 276p. 1980. pap. 9.95 (ISBN 0-8093-0975-0). S Ill U Pr.

Lemeshow, Stanley, jt. auth. see Levy, Paul S.

Lemesurier, Peter. The Great Pyramid Decoded. 1982. 30.00x (ISBN 0-85955-015-X, Pub. by Element Bks). State Mutual Bk.

Lemieux, Joanne H. Diet Signs: Follow Your Horoscope to a Slimmer You. 1982. pap. 6.95 (ISBN 0-87491-495-7). Acropolis.

Lemin, Brian. First Line Nursing Management. (Illus.). 1977. 15.95x o.p. (ISBN 0-8464-0415-X). Beekman Pubs.

Lemire, Deacon H., jt. auth. see Kleiber, Kenneth.

Lemire, Ronald J., et al. Anencephaly. LC 77-83688. 270p. 1977. 31.00 (ISBN 0-89004-179-2). Raven.

Lemius, J. B. Catechism of Modernism. 160p. pap. 2.00 (ISBN 0-686-81624-2). TAN Bks Pubs.

Lemkau, Paul V., jt. ed. see Wagenfeld, Morton O

Lemke, Bob, jt. auth. see Wilhite, Bob.

Lemke, Elmer & Wiersma, William. Principles of Psychological Measurement. LC 80-80803. 380p. 1976. text ed. 24.50 (ISBN 0-395-30821-6). HM.

Lemke, Horst, illus. Places & Faces. LC 78-160446. (Illus.). 32p. (ps-k). 5.95 (ISBN 0-87592-041-1). Scroll Pr.

Lemke, Kenneth W., jt. ed. see Sterling, Robert R.

Lemke, Robert F., jt. auth. see Krause, Chester L.

Lemke, Steve. Joy in Christ: Studies in Philippians. 36p. 1982. pap. 3.50 (ISBN 0-939298-10-4). J M Prods.

--Living Hope: Studies in 1 Peter. 32p. (Orig.). 1982. pap. 3.50 (ISBN 0-939298-12-0, 120). J M Prods.

Lemlech, Johanna K. Handbook for Successful Urban Teaching. 1977. pap. text ed. 13.50 scp o.p. (ISBN 0-06-043944-0, HarpC). Har-Row.

Lemmel, Maurice. Gambling Nevada Style. LC 64-16205. 1964. pap. 2.95 (ISBN 0-385-07257-0, Dolp). Doubleday.

Lemmerz, A. H. & Schmidt, R. R. Auswertung und Deutung des EKG 11. Auflage. (Illus.). 1976. pap. 34.75 (ISBN 3-8055-0548-5). S Karger.

Lemmon, E. J. & Schumm, George. Beginning Logic: Teaching Companion. 100p. (Orig.). 1979. pap. text ed. 3.95x (ISBN 0-915144-65-4). Hackett Pub.

Lemmon, Robert S. All About Moths & Butterflies. (gr. 4-6). 1956. 2.95 (ISBN 0-394-80215-2, BYR); PLB 4.39 (ISBN 0-394-90215-7). Random.

--All About Strange Beasts of the Present. (Allabout Ser.: No. 19). (Illus.). (gr. 4-6). 1957. 5.39 (ISBN 0-394-90219-X, BYR). Random.

Lemmons, Reuel & Bannister, John. Unto Us a Child is Born. Kyker, Rex, compiled by. 126p. (Orig.). 1982. pap. 2.95 (ISBN 0-88027-109-4). Firm Foun Pub.

Lemmons, Reuel, ed. Hymns of Praise. 1978. 4.25x (ISBN 0-88027-055-1). Firm Foun Pub.

Lemmons, Reuel G., et al, eds. see Smith, William.

Lemoine, Francoise, jt. auth. see Sokoloff, Georges.

Lemoine, J., jt. auth. see Crane, A.

LeMoine, Suzanne & Vandermyn, Gaye. Dieting Out in Seattle: Restaurant Feasts, Facts & Tips for the Slender Gourmet. LC 79-14031. 1979. pap. 5.95 o.p. (ISBN 0-916076-32-6). Writing.

Lemon, Edgar R. Co2 & Plants. 350p. 1983. lib. bdg. 25.00x (ISBN 0-86531-597-3). Westview.

Lemon, Nigel. Attitudes & Their Measurement. 1973. 33.00 o.p. (ISBN 0-7134-0983-5, Pub. by Batsford England). David & Charles.

Lemon, Richard. Troubled American. LC 73-130481. 1971. pap. 2.95 o.p. (ISBN 0-671-21065-3, Touchstone Bks). S&S.

Lemond, Alan & Shaw, Grace. Bravo Baryshnikov. (Illus.). 1978. 12.95 o.p. (ISBN 0-448-16386-1, Today Pr); pap. 5.95 o.p. (ISBN 0-448-16388-8, G&D). Putnam PubGroup.

Lemons, Wayne & Price, Bill. How to Repair Home & Auto Air Conditioners. LC 74-120384. 1970. pap. 5.95 o.p. (ISBN 0-8306-9520-6, 520). TAB Bks.

Lemordant, Jean-Julien. Jean-Juliem Lemordant: Ensemble of the Decorative Works of the Painter. (Illus.). 1919. pap. 42.50x (ISBN 0-686-51409-2). Elliots Bks.

Lemos, Pan J. Mediterranean Songs. 1979. 5.95 o.p. (ISBN 0-533-03423-X). Vantage.

Lempert, Richard O. & Saltzburg, Stephen A. A Modern Approach to Evidence: Text, Problems, Transcripts, & Cases. 2nd ed. LC 82-13578. (American Casebook Ser.). 1296p. 1982. text ed. 27.95 (ISBN 0-314-67594-9). West Pub.

Lempriere, Raoul. Portrait of the Channel Islands. LC 70-515033. (Portrait Bks.). (Illus.). 1979. 11.50x o.p. (ISBN 0-7091-7624-4). Intl Pubns Serv.

Lemuel, A., jt. ed. see Johnson.

Lenahan, Sheila, ed. & illus. see Toy, Gerald.

Lenard, Yvone. Parole et Pensee: Introduction Au Francais D'aujourd'hui. 4th ed. 655p. 1982. text ed. 23.50 scp (ISBN 0-06-043962-9, HarpC); scp lab manual 8.50 (ISBN 0-06-043965-3); tchr's guide avail. (ISBN 0-06-363967-X); scp reel to reel tapes 295.00 (ISBN 0-06-047496-3); scp cassette tapes 295.00 (ISBN 0-06-047439-4). Har-Row.

Lenard, Yvone & Hester, Ralph. L' Art De la Conversation. 1967. text ed. 18.95 scp (ISBN 0-06-043966-1, HarpC); scp tapes 195.00 (ISBN 0-06-047460-2); texte de bande sohores avail. (ISBN 0-06-363966-1). Har-Row.

Lenardon, Robert J., jt. auth. see Morford, Mark P.

Lenaz, Mamie W. Treasury of the Heart. 1983. 6.95 (ISBN 0-533-05675-6). Vantage.

Lenburg, Jeff. Dudley Moore: An Informal Biography. (Illus.). 144p. (Orig.). 1982. pap. 9.95 (ISBN 0-933328-56-7). Delilah Bks.

--The Encyclopedia of Animated Cartoon Series. (Quality Paperbacks Ser.). (Illus.). 192p. 1983. pap. 14.95 (ISBN 0-306-80191-4). Da Capo.

--The Great Cartoon Directors. LC 82-23923. (Illus.). 1983. lib. bdg. price not set (ISBN 0-89950-036-6). McFarland & Co.

Lenburg, Jeff & Maurer, Joan H. The Three Stooges Scrapbook. 256p. 1982. 18.95 (ISBN 0-8065-0803-5). Citadel Pr.

Lenburg, Len. Dustin Hoffman: Hollywood's Anti-Hero. (Illus.). 192p. 1983. 10.95 (ISBN 0-312-22268-8). St Martin.

Lencek, Rado L. The Structure & History of the Slovene Language. (Illus.). 365p. 1982. 19.95 (ISBN 0-89357-099-0). Slavica.

Lencek, Rado L. & Cooper, Henry R., Jr., eds. Papers in Slavic Philology: To Honor Jernej Kopitar, No. 2. 1982. pap. 7.00 (ISBN 0-930042-46-8). Mich Slavic Pubns.

Lenczner, D. Movement in Buildings. LC 73-4253. 108p. 1973. text ed. 13.25 o.p. (ISBN 0-08-017136-2). Pergamon.

Lender, Mark E. & Martin, James K. Drinking in America: A History. (Illus.). 1982. 19.95 (ISBN 0-02-918530-0). Macmillan.

--Drinking in America: A History. (Illus.). 256p. 1982. 19.95 (ISBN 0-02-918530-0). Free Pr.

Lender, Mark E., jt. auth. see Martin, James K.

Lenderink, R. S. & Siebrand, J. C. A Disequalibrium of the Labour Market. 1979. text ed. 19.00x (ISBN 90-237-2277-9). Gower Pub Ltd.

Lendon, Alan. Australian Parrots in Field & Aviary. (Illus.). 344p. 1979. 32.95 (ISBN 0-207-12424-8). Avian Pubns.

Lendvai, Paul. The Bureaucracy of Truth. 350p. 1981. lib. bdg. 28.00 (ISBN 0-86531-142-0). Westview.

Lenf, John D. Handbook of Simplified Solid State Circuit Design. 2nd ed. LC 77-23555. (Illus.). 1978. ref. 21.95 (ISBN 0-13-381715-6); pap. 7.95 (ISBN 0-13-381707-5). P-H.

Leng, Shao-Chuan, ed. Post-Mao China & U. S. China Trade. LC 77-20811. 1978. 12.95x (ISBN 0-8139-0733-0). U Pr of Va.

Lenga, Rosalind. The Amazing Fact Book of Birds, Vol. 9. LC 80-80668. (Illus.). 32p. (Orig.). (gr. 4 up). 1980. 5.95 (ISBN 0-86550-016-9); PLB 8.95 (ISBN 0-686-96981-2); pap. 2.95 (ISBN 0-86550-017-7). A & P Bks.

--The Amazing Fact Book of Fish, Vol. 2. LC 80-80620. (Illus.). 32p. (Orig.). (gr. 4 up). 1980. 5.95 (ISBN 0-86550-002-9); lib. bdg. 8.95 (ISBN 0-686-96963-4); pap. 2.95 (ISBN 0-86550-003-7). A & P Bks.

--The Amazing Fact Book of Planes, Vol. 4. LC 80-80619. (Illus.). 32p. (Orig.). (gr. 4 up). 1980. 5.95 (ISBN 0-86550-006-1); lib. bdg. 8.95 (ISBN 0-686-96967-7); pap. 2.95 (ISBN 0-86550-007-X). A & P Bks.

Lengacher, Cecile A., jt. auth. see Curran, Connie L.

Lengel, Nancy. Handbook of Nursing Diagnosis. 208p. 1982. pap. text ed. 9.95 (ISBN 0-89303-057-0). R J Brady.

Lengel, Olga. Five Chimneys: The Story of Auschwitz. Coch, Clifford, tr. LC 81-20260. 213p. (Fr.). 1983. Repr. of 1947 ed. 13.50x (ISBN 0-86527-343-X). Fertig.

Lengenfelder, Helga, ed. International Bibliography of Directories. 6th rev. ed. 1978. 72.00x (ISBN 0-89664-002-7, Pub. by K G Saur). Gale.

Lengermann. Definitions of Sociology: Historical Approach. 1974. text ed. 9.95 o.p. (ISBN 0-675-08896-8). Merrill.

L'Engle, Madeleine. And Both Were Young. (Young Love Romance Ser.). (Orig.). (YA) (gr. 7-12). 1983. pap. 2.50 (ISBN 0-440-90229-0, LFL). Dell.
--And Both Were Young. LC 82-72751. 240p. (YA) (gr. 7 up). 1983. 13.95 (ISBN 0-686-38332-X). Delacorte.
--And It Was Good. 1983. 9.95; pap. 5.95 (ISBN 0-87788-046-8). Shaw Pubs.
--A Circle of Quiet. 246p. 1972. 12.50 (ISBN 0-374-12374-8). FS&G.
--A Circle of Quiet. (The Crosswicks Journal Trilogy). 246p. 1977. pap. 6.95 (ISBN 0-8164-2260-5); Three Volume Set. 19.95 (ISBN 0-8164-2617-1). Seabury.
--Dance in the Desert. LC 68-29465. (Illus.). (gr. 4 up). 1969. 10.95 (ISBN 0-374-31684-8). FS&G.
--Everyday Prayers. (Illus.). (ps-3). 1974. 1.35 o.p. (ISBN 0-8192-1154-0). Morehouse.
--The Irrational Season. (The Crosswicks Journal Trilogy). 224p. 1977. 10.95 (ISBN 0-8164-0324-4); pap. 6.95 (ISBN 0-8164-2261-3); Three Volume Set 19.95 (ISBN 0-8164-2617-1). Seabury.
--The Love Letters. (Epiphany Ser.). 384p. 1983. pap. 2.95 (ISBN 0-345-30617-1). Ballantine.
--Meet the Austins. (YA) (gr. 7-12). 1981. pap. 2.25 (ISBN 0-440-95777-X, LE). Dell.
--Prelude. LC 68-56600. (gr. 7 up). 6.95 o.s.i. (ISBN 0-8149-0351-7). Vanguard.
--A Ring of Endless Light. LC 79-27679. 356p. (gr. 4 up). 1980. 10.95 (ISBN 0-374-36299-8). FS&G.
--A Severed Wasp. 1983. 15.50 (ISBN 0-374-26131-8). FS&G.
--The Summer of the Great Grandmother. LC 74-13157. (Illus.). 245p. 1974. 10.95 (ISBN 0-374-27174-7). FS&G.
--The Summer of the Great Grandmother. (The Crosswicks Journal Trilogy). 1980. 6.95 (ISBN 0-8164-2259-1). Seabury.
--A Swiftly Tilting Planet. (YA) 1980. pap. 2.25 (ISBN 0-440-90158-8, LFL). Dell.
--A Swiftly Tilting Planet. LC 78-9648. 288p. (gr. 4 up). 1978. 9.95 (ISBN 0-374-37362-0). FS&G.
--The Time Trilogy: A Wrinkle in Time; A Wind in the Door; A Swiftly Tilting Planet, 3 vols. (gr. 4 up). 1979. Boxed Set. 29.85 (ISBN 0-374-37592-5). FS&G.
--Walking on Water: Reflections on Faith & Art. LC 80-21066. (Wheaton Literary Ser.). 200p. 1980. 8.95 (ISBN 0-87788-918-X); pap. 4.95 (ISBN 0-87788-919-8). Shaw Pubs.
--The Weather of the Heart. LC 78-62202. (Wheaton Literary Ser.). 1978. 7.95 (ISBN 0-87788-685-7). Shaw Pubs.
--A Wind in the Door. (gr. 7 up). 1974. pap. 2.50 (ISBN 0-440-48761-7, YB). Dell.
--A Wind in the Door. LC 73-75176. 224p. (gr. 7 up). 1973. 9.95 (ISBN 0-374-38443-6). FS&G.
--A Wrinkle in Time. (gr. 5-8). 1973. pap. 2.50 (ISBN 0-440-49805-8, YB). Dell.
--Wrinkle in Time. LC 62-7203. (Illus.). 224p. (gr. 7 up). 1962. 9.95 (ISBN 0-374-38613-7). FS&G.

L'Engle, Madeline. The Arm of the Starfish. (YA) (gr. 7-12). 1979. pap. 2.25 (ISBN 0-440-90183-9, LFL). Dell.
--Arm of the Starfish. LC 65-10919. 256p. (gr. 7 up). 1965. 11.95 (ISBN 0-374-30396-7). FS&G.
--A Swiftly Tilting Planet. (gr. 7 up). 1981. pap. 2.50 (ISBN 0-440-40158-5, YB). Dell.
--Walking on Water. 208p. 1982. 2.50 (ISBN 0-553-20938-8). Bantam.

Lenglyel, Olga. Five Chimneys. 222p. 1982. pap. 4.95 (ISBN 0-583-12139-X, Pub. by Granada England). Academy Chi Ltd.

Leng Shao-Chuan & Palmer, Norman D. Sun Yat-Sen & Communism. LC 75-27683. (Foreign Policy Research Institute Ser: No. 10). 234p. 1976. Repr. of 1961 ed. lib. bdg. 18.50x (ISBN 0-8371-8455-X, LESY). Greenwood.

Lengstrand, Rolf. Horse Astray in Stockholm. LC 65-25945. (Foreign Lands Bks). (Illus.). (gr. k-5). 1965. PLB 3.95g (ISBN 0-8225-0354-9). Lerner Pubns.

Lengstrand, Rolf & Rolen, Pierre L. Have Fun with Your Horse. 1978. 9.95 (ISBN 0-8120-5208-0). Barron.

Lengyel, Bela A. Lasers. 2nd ed. LC 77-139279. (Ser. in Pure & Applied Optics). 1971. 47.50x (ISBN 0-471-52620-7, Pub. by Wiley-Interscience). Wiley.

Lengyel, Cornel. The Case of Benedict Arnold. LC 79-56427. (New Poetic Drama Ser.: No. 2). 1982. pap. 3.50 (ISBN 0-934218-20-X). Dragons Teeth.

Lengyel, Emil. Americans from Hungary. LC 72-12628. 319p. 1975. Repr. of 1948 ed. lib. bdg. 17.00x (ISBN 0-8371-6678-0, LEAH). Greenwood.
--Dan. (First Bks.). (Illus.). (gr. 4-6). 1981. PLB 7.90 s & l (ISBN 0-686-75378-X). Watts.
--Iran. LC 78-18857. (Middle East Bks.). (gr. 4-6). 1981. PLB 8.90 (ISBN 0-531-02242-0). Watts.
--Modern Egypt. rev. ed. (First Bks). (Illus.). (gr. 5-7). 1978. PLB 8.90 s&l (ISBN 0-531-02240-4). Watts.

Lenham, B. J., jt. auth. see Titow, W. V.

Lenhardt, G., tr. see Adorno, T. W.

Lenhert, Donald H., jt. auth. see Swaay, Maarten V.

Lenhoff, Howard M. & Muscatine, Leonard, eds. Experimental Coelenterate Biology. LC 73-127331. 1971. text ed. 14.00x (ISBN 0-87022-454-9). UH Pr.

Lenier, Minette & Maker, Janet. Key to a Powerful Vocabulary: Level Two. (Illus.). 224p. 1983. pap. text ed. 10.95 (ISBN 0-13-514992-4). P-H.

Lenier, Minnette & Maker, Janet. Keys to College Success: Reading & Study Improvement. (Illus.). 1980. pap. text ed. 12.95 (ISBN 0-13-514885-5). P-H.

Lenier, Minnette, jt. auth. see Maker, Janet.

Lenihan, J. M. & Thomson, S. J., eds. Advances in Activation Analysis, Vols. 1-2. Vol. 1. 1969. 36.00 (ISBN 0-12-000401-1); Vol 2. 1972. 56.00 o.s.i. (ISBN 0-12-000402-X). Acad Pr.

Lenihan, John & Fletcher, William W. Measuring & Monitoring the Environment. 132p. 1978. 70.00x (ISBN 0-216-90135-9, Pub. by Blackie Pub Scotland); Limp 35.00x (ISBN 0-686-97094-2). State Mutual Bk.

Lenihan, John & Fletcher, William, eds. Environment & Man: Vol. 8, the Built Environment. 1979. 26.50 (ISBN 0-12-443508-4); 19.50 set (ISBN 0-12-443508-4). Acad Pr.

Lenihan, John & Fletcher, William W., eds. Economics of the Environment. 194p. 1979. cased 70.00x (ISBN 0-216-90752-7, Pub. by Blackie Pub Scotland); limp 35.00x (ISBN 0-216-90751-9). State Mutual Bk.

Lenin, V. I. Imperialism & the Split in Socialism. 22p. 1979. pap. 0.50 (ISBN 0-8285-0131-9, Pub. by Progress Pubs USSR). Imported Pubns.
--Marx-Engels-Marxism. 176p. 1977. pap. 1.40 (ISBN 0-8285-2194-8, Pub. by Progress Pubs USSR). Imported Pubns.
--Marxism on the State. 134p. 1978. pap. 0.50 (ISBN 0-8285-2263-4, Pub. by Progress Pubs USSR). Imported Pubns.

Lenin, Vladimir I. Lenin on the United States. Leiteizen, C. & Allen, J. S., eds. LC 70-111375. 1970. pap. 3.65 o.p. (ISBN 0-7178-0262-0). Intl Pub Co.

Lenk, John D. Handbook for Transistors. (Illus.). 320p. 1976. 21.95 (ISBN 0-13-382259-1); pap. 7.95 (ISBN 0-13-382267-2). P-H.
--Handbook of Advanced Troubleshooting. (Illus.). 352p. 1983. text ed. 22.95 (ISBN 0-13-372391-7). P-H.
--Handbook of Controls & Instrumentation. (Illus.). 1980. text ed. 22.95 (ISBN 0-13-377069-9). P-H.
--Handbook of Digital Electronics. (Illus.). 384p. 1981. text ed. 22.95 (ISBN 0-13-377184-9). P-H.
--Handbook of Electronic Components & Circuits. LC 73-11038. (Illus.). 224p. 1973. ref. ed. 21.95x (ISBN 0-13-377283-7). P-H.
--Handbook of Electronic Meters: Theory & Application. rev. & enlarged ed. 1981. 20.95 (ISBN 0-13-377333-7). P-H.
--Handbook of Electronic Test Procedures. (Illus.). 320p. 1982. 22.95 (ISBN 0-13-377457-0). P-H.
--Handbook of Modern Solid State Amplifiers. (Illus.). 400p. 1974. ref. ed 24.95 (ISBN 0-13-380394-5); pap. 7.95 (ISBN 0-13-380386-4). P-H.
--Handbook of Oscilloscopes: Theory & Application. rev., enl. ed. (Illus.). 320p. 1982. 20.95 (ISBN 0-13-380576-X). P-H.
--Handbook of Practical Solid State Troubleshooting. (Illus.). 1971. ref. ed. 21.95 (ISBN 0-13-380642-1); pap. 10.95 (ISBN 0-13-380725-8). P-H.
--Logic Designer's Manual. (Illus.). 512p. 1977. text ed. 22.95 (ISBN 0-87909-450-8). Reston.
--Understanding Electronic Schematics. (Illus.). 304p. 1981. text ed. 22.95 (ISBN 0-13-935908-7). P-H.

Lenk, R. Brownian Motion & Spin Relaxation. 1977. 47.00 (ISBN 0-444-41592-0). Elsevier.

Lenk, R. S. Polymer Rheology. (Illus.). 1978. 69.75 (ISBN 0-85334-765-4, Pub. by Applied Sci England). Elsevier.

Lenkerd, Barbara, jt. ed. see Reining, Priscilla.

Lenn, Dorothy, tr. see Steiner, Rudolf.

Lenna, Harry R., jt. auth. see Woodman, Natalie J.

Lennard, Erica. Classic Gardens. LC 83-80908. (Illus.). 128p. 1982. 27.95 (ISBN 0-912810-38-6). Lustrum Pr.

Lenneberg, Edith & Rowbotham, John L. The Ileostomy Patient. (Illus.). 228p. 1970. 22.50x o.p. (ISBN 0-398-01095-1). C C Thomas.

Lenneberg, Eric H. Biological Foundations of Language. LC 66-28746. 1967. 39.95 (ISBN 0-471-52626-6). Wiley.

Lenner, L. Thomas Hardy's "The Mayor of Casterbridge". Tragedy or Social History? 17.00x (ISBN 0-686-97027-6, Pub. by Scottish Academic Pr Scotland). State Mutual Bk.

Lennette, David A. Diagnosis of Viral Infections. 272p. 1979. text ed. 29.95 (ISBN 0-686-72903-X). Univ Park.
--A User's Guide to the Diagnostic Virology Laboratory. 128p. 1980. pap. text ed. 12.95 (ISBN 0-8391-1623-3). Univ Park.

Lennie, Delia & Grego, M. Italian for You. 3rd ed. (Illus.). 1966. pap. text ed. 6.25x (ISBN 0-582-36407-8). Longman.

Lennon. Biochemistry of Metabolic Processes. Date not set. 75.00 (ISBN 0-444-00727-X). Elsevier.

Lennon, jt. auth. see Rolfe.

Lennon, Colm. Richard Stanihurst the Dubliner, 1547-1618: A Biography with a Stanihurst Text on Ireland's Past. 186p. 1981. 27.50x (ISBN 0-7165-0069-8, Pub. by Irish Academic Pr Ireland). Biblio Dist.

Lennon, John. The Writings of John Lennon: In His Own Write & A Spaniard in the Works. 1981. 10.95 o.p. (ISBN 0-671-43257-5). S&S.

Lennon, John, et al. The Last Lennon Tapes. (Fred Jordan Bks.). 1983. pap. 7.95 (ISBN 0-440-04903-2, Dell Trade Pbks). Dell.

Lennon, Nigey. Mark Twain in California. LC 82-4184. (Illus.). 96p. 1982. pap. 5.95 (ISBN 0-87701-198-2). Chronicle Bks.

Lennon, Nigey, jt. auth. see Rolfe, Lionel.

Lennon, Tom, ed. The Thirteenth, Fourteenth, & Fifteenth Publication Design Annual. (Illus.). 700p. 1982. 39.95 (ISBN 0-937414-24-7). R Silver.

Lennox, Art. Banking, Budgeting & Employment. 1977. pap. text ed. 2.75x (ISBN 0-88323-128-X, 217); key to text free (ISBN 0-88323-131-X). Richards Pub.

Lennox, Charlotte. Henrietta, 2 vols. in 1. (The Flowering of the Novel Ser, 1740-1775: Vol. 50). 1974. Repr. of 1758 ed. lib. bdg. 50.00 o.s.i. (ISBN 0-8240-1149-X). Garland Pub.
--Sophia, 2 vols. in 1. Shugrue, Michael F., ed. (The Flowering of the Novel, 1740-1775 Ser: Vol. 61). 1974. Repr. of 1762 ed. lib. bdg. 50.00 o.s.i. (ISBN 0-8240-1160-0). Garland Pub.

Lennox-Kerr, P. Carpet Surfaces. Pointon, ed. 1975. 20.00 o.p. (ISBN 0-87245-549-1). Textile Bk.

Lennox-Kerr, Peter. Flexible Textile Composites. 13.50x (ISBN 0-87245-513-0). Textile Bk.
--Needle-Felted Fabrics. 13.50x (ISBN 0-87245-514-9). Textile Bk.
--Nonwovens, '71. 28.95x (ISBN 0-87245-515-7). Textile Bk.
--World Fibres Book. 16.95x (ISBN 0-87245-516-5). Textile Bk.

Lenoir, Ruth. When the Last Trumpet Is Sounded. 1978. 8.95 o.p. (ISBN 0-87604-103-9). ARE Pr.

Lenoir, Timothy. The Strategy of Life. 1982. 59.00 (ISBN 90-277-1363-4, Pub. by Reidel Holland). Kluwer Boston.

Lenon, Robert, jt. auth. see Young, Otis E., Jr.

Lenormand, Rene & Carner, Mosco. A Study of Twentieth-Century Harmony: Harmony in France to 1914 & Contemporary Harmony, 2 vols. in 1. LC 76-40058. (Music Reprint Ser). 1975. Repr. of 1940 ed. lib. bdg. 25.00 (ISBN 0-306-70717-9). Da Capo.

Lenormant, Charles F. J. J. Rousseau Aristocrate. (Rousseauism, 1788-1797). 1978. Repr. lib. bdg. 37.00x o.p. (ISBN 0-8287-0534-8). Clearwater Pub.

LeNotre, Gaston. LeNotre's Book of Desserts & Pastries. Hyman, Philip & Hyman, Mary, trs. from Fr. LC 77-13231. 1977. 19.95 (ISBN 0-8120-5137-8). Barron.
--Lenotre's Ice Cream & Candies. Hyman, Philip & Hyman, Mary, trs. LC 79-17809. (Illus.). 1979. 19.95 (ISBN 0-8120-5334-6). Barron.

Lenowitz, Harris, jt. auth. see Rothenberg, Jerome.

Lenroot-Ernt, Lois, ed. Directory of Special Libraries & Information Centers: Geographic & Personnel Indexes, Vol. 2. 7th ed. 824p. 1982. 210.00x (ISBN 0-8103-0262-4). Gale.
--Directory of Special Libraries & Information Centers: Special Libraries in the U. S. & Canada, Vol. 1. 7th ed. 1512p. 1982. 240.00x (ISBN 0-8103-0261-6). Gale.
--Subject Directory of Special Libraries: Business & Law Libraries, Including Military & Transportation Libraries, Vol. 1. 7th ed. 1982. 100.00x (ISBN 0-8103-0655-7). Gale.
--Subject Directory of Special Libraries: Education & Information Science Libraries, Including Picture, Audiovisual, Publishing, Rare Book, & Recreational Libraries, Vol. 2. 7th ed. 1982. 100.00x (ISBN 0-686-94166-7). Gale.
--Subject Directory of Special Libraries: Health Sciences Libraries, Including All Aspects of Basic & Applied Medical Sciences, Vol. 3. 7th ed. 1982. 100.00x (ISBN 0-8103-0657-3). Gale.
--Subject Directory of Special Libraries: Science & Technology Libraries, Including Agricultural, Energy, Environmental-Conservation, & Food Science Libraries, Vol. 5. 7th ed. 1982. 100.00x (ISBN 0-8103-0659-X). Gale.
--Subject Directory of Special Libraries: Social Sciences & Humanities Libraries, Including Area-Ethnic, Art, Geography-Map, History, Music, Religion-Theology, Theatre, & Urban-Regional Planning Libraries, Vol. 4. 7th ed. 1982. 100.00x (ISBN 0-8103-0658-1). Gale.

Lenrow, Elbert, ed. & tr. The Letters of Richard Wagner to Anton Pusinelli. LC 72-93825. 293p. Date not set. Repr. of 1932 ed. price not set. Vienna Hse.

Lens, Sidney. Africa: Awakening Giant. (Illus.). (gr. 5-7). 1962. 5.95 o.p. (ISBN 0-399-20003-7). Putnam Pub Group.
--The Maginot Line Syndrome: America's Hopeless Foreign Policy. 204p. 1982. prof ref 14.50 (ISBN 0-88410-842-2). Ballinger Pub.

Lensen, George A. Russia's Japan Expedition of Eighteen Eighty-Five. LC 82-9156. (Illus.). xxviii, 208p. 1982. Repr. lib. bdg. 29.75 (ISBN 0-313-23621-6, LERJ). Greenwood.

Lenski, G. & Lenski, J. Human Societies: An Introduction to Macrosociology. 4th ed. 1982. 24.50x (ISBN 0-07-037176-8); instructor's manual 8.95 (ISBN 0-07-037177-6). McGraw.

Lenski, Gerhard E. Power & Privilege: A Theory of Social Stratification. (Sociology Ser.). 1966. text ed. 30.50 (ISBN 0-07-037165-2, C). McGraw.

Lenski, Gerhard E. & Lenski, Jean. Human Societies: An Introduction to Macrosociology. 3rd ed. (Illus.). 1977. text ed. 21.95 (ISBN 0-07-037174-1, C); instrs'. manual 3.95 (ISBN 0-07-037175-X). McGraw.

Lenski, J., jt. auth. see Lenski, G.

Lenski, Jean, jt. auth. see Lenski, Gerhard E.

Lenski, Lois. Indian Captive: The Story of Mary Jemison. LC 41-51956. (Illus.). (gr. 7-9). 1941. 12.95 (ISBN 0-397-30072-7, JBL-J). Har-Row.
--Judy's Journey. LC 47-4504. (Regional Stories Ser). (Illus.). (gr. 4-6). 1947. 11.84 (ISBN 0-397-30131-6, JBL-J). Har-Row.
--More Mister Small. (ps-3). 1979. 9.95 (ISBN 0-8098-6300-6, Walk). McKay.
--Prairie School. LC 51-11169. (Illus.). 204p. 1951. 11.89 (ISBN 0-397-30194-4, JBL-J). Har-Row.

Lensner, Gordon, jt. ed. see Keronode, Dale.

Lent, Deane. Analysis & Design of Mechanisms. 2nd ed. (Technology Ser). 1970. text ed. 23.95 (ISBN 0-13-032797-2). P-H.

Lent, Henry B. Men at Work in New England. rev. ed. (Men at Work Series). (Illus.). (gr. 4-6). 1967. 4.40 o.p. (ISBN 0-399-20166-1). Putnam Pub Group.
--Men at Work in the South. rev. ed. (Men at Work Ser.). (Illus.). (gr. 4-6). 1970. 4.40 o.p. (ISBN 0-399-20167-X). Putnam Pub Group.
--The X Cars: Detroit's One-Of-A-Kind Autos. (Illus.). (gr. 5 up). 1971. PLB 5.69 o.p. (ISBN 0-399-60690-4). Putnam Pub Group.

Lent, James & Willians, Judy. Rolling Your Hair. (Project MORE Daily Living Skill Ser.). 60p. 1979. pap. text ed. 8.50 (ISBN 0-8331-1247-3). Hubbard Sci.

Lent, James, jt. auth. see Ferneti, Casper.

Lent, John A., ed. Broadcasting in Asia & the Pacific: A Continental Survey of Radio & Television. LC 75-44708. (International & Comparative Broadcasting Ser.). 449p. 1978. 34.95 (ISBN 0-87722-068-9). Temple U Pr.

Lenthall, Ben, jt. auth. see Friedhoff, Herman.

Lenthall, Patricia R. Carlotta & the Scientist. 2nd ed. LC 76-20841. 47p. (gr. k-4). 1976. 6.50 (ISBN 0-914996-14-2); pap. 3.00 (ISBN 0-914996-12-6). Lollipop Power.

Lentner, Howard H. Foreign Policy Analysis: A Comparative & Conceptual Analysis. LC 73-85554. 1974. text ed. 13.95x (ISBN 0-675-08884-4). Merrill.

Lento, Robert. Woodworking: Tools, Fabrication, Design, & Manufacturing. (Illus.). 1979. ref. 21.95 (ISBN 0-13-962514-3); students' ed. 18.95 (ISBN 0-686-96838-7). P-H.

Lento, Robert, jt. auth. see Hayward, Charles.

Lenton & Colledge. British Warship Losses of World War Two. pap. 4.00x05687676x (ISBN 0-392-09107-0, SpS). Sportshelf.

Lenton, Roberto L., jt. auth. see Major, David C.

Lentvorsky, Marie G. Read Before Kickoff: Building the High School Football Player. 1978. 6.50 o.p. (ISBN 0-533-03630-5). Vantage.

Lentz. Cell Biology of Hydra. 1967. 12.95 (ISBN 0-444-10231-0). Elsevier.

Lentz, Gloria. The Embattled Parent. 1979. 10.95 o.p. (ISBN 0-87000-440-9, Arlington Hse). Crown.

Lentz, Harris M., III. Science Fiction, Horror, Fantasy Film & Television Credits, 2 Vols. LC 82-23956. 1000p. 1983. lib. bdg. 49.95 set (ISBN 0-89950-071-4); Vol. 1. lib. bdg. price not set (ISBN 0-89950-069-2); Vol. 2. lib. bdg. price not set (ISBN 0-89950-070-6). McFarland & Co.

Lentz, M. M., et al. French in the Office. 2nd ed. 1978. pap. text ed. 5.25x (ISBN 0-582-35153-7). Longman.

Le Ny, J. F. & Kintsch, W. Language & Comprehension. Date not set. 51.00 (ISBN 0-444-86538-1). Elsevier.

Lenz. Lotte soll nicht sterben. (Easy Reader, A). pap. 2.95 (ISBN 0-88436-039-3, 45260). EMC.

Lenz, Bernie. The Complete Book of Fashion Modeling. (Illus.). 320p. 1969. 8.95 o.p. (ISBN 0-517-50193-7). Crown.

Lenz, E. Creating & Marketing Programs in Continuing Education. 1980. 18.95 (ISBN 0-07-037190-3). McGraw.

Lenz, Elinor. Once My Child, Now My Friend. 252p. (Orig.). 1982. pap. 2.95 (ISBN 0-446-51224-9); pap. 2.95 (ISBN 0-446-90560-7). Warner Bks.

Lenz, Frederick. Lifetimes: True Accounts of Reincarnation. LC 78-11209. 1979. 10.00 o.p. (ISBN 0-672-52490-2). Bobbs.

Lenz, Frederick, jt. ed. see Atmananda.

Lenz, Gary L. Fixed Asset Accounting & Reporting. (Illus.). 432p. 1980. pap. 27.50 nonmember (ISBN 0-686-84265-0); pap. 25.00 member (ISBN 0-686-84266-9). Municipal.

Lenz, Heinz & Murray, John L. Fit for Life: The Annapolis Way. (Illus.). 354p. 1983. 11.95 (ISBN 0-88011-032-5). Leisure Pr.

Lenz, John W., ed. see Hume, David.

Lenz, Marjorie & Shaevitz, Marjorie. So You Want to Go Back to School. (Illus.). 1977. pap. 9.95 (ISBN 0-07-037178-4, C). McGraw.

Lenz, Martin. Aussensteurrecht und Organisationsstruktur. 502p. (Ger.). 1982. write for info. (ISBN 3-8204-5829-8). P Lang Pubs.

Lenz, Robert W. Organic Chemistry of Synthetic High Polymers. LC 66-22057. 1967. 47.95x (ISBN 0-470-52630-0, Pub. by Wiley-Interscience). Wiley.

Lenz, Siegfried. Das Feuerschiff. (Easy Readers, B. Ser.). 88p. 1976. pap. text ed. 3.95 (ISBN 0-88436-276-0). EMC.

--Das Rock & Other Stories. Russ, C. A., ed. 168p. (Orig.). 1967. pap. text ed. 4.50x (ISBN 0-435-38536-4). Heinemann Ed.

Lenz, W., jt. ed. see Suendermann, J.

Lenzen. Diamonds & Diamond Grading. 1983. text ed. 59.95 (ISBN 0-408-00547-5). Butterworth.

Lenzen, V. F. Benjamin Peirce & the U.S. Coast Survey. LC 68-56135. (History of Technology Monographs). (Illus.). 1968. 5.00 (ISBN 0-911302-06-9). San Francisco Pr.

Leo, Joseph Di see Di Leo, Joseph.

Leo, Miriam & Forlini, Gary. The S.A.T. Home Study Kit. Gruber, Michael, ed. (Home Study Ser.). 1982. 69.50 (ISBN 0-686-82415-6); workbook-audio-tape kit avail. (ISBN 0-910859-01-9). Pinebrook Pr.

Leogrande, Ernest, jt. auth. see Alpert, George.

Leokum, Arkady. Another Tell Me Why. LC 77-71529. (gr. k-6). 1977. 7.95 (ISBN 0-448-12954-X, G&D); PLB 6.99 o.p. (ISBN 0-448-13419-5). Putnam Pub Group.

--The Curious Book. 1978. pap. 2.25 (ISBN 0-451-11944-4, AE1944, Sig). NAL.

--Lots More Tell Me Why. (Illus.). 480p. (gr. k-6). 1972. 7.95 (ISBN 0-448-02463-2, G&D). Putnam Pub Group.

--More Tell Me Why. (gr. k-6). 1967. 7.95 (ISBN 0-448-04442-0, G&D). Putnam Pub Group.

--Quizzes, Tricks, Stunts, Puzzles & Brain Teasers from Tell Me Why. (Illus.). 80p. (gr. 1-7). Date not set. price not set (G&D). Putnam Pub Group.

--Still More Tell Me Why. (Illus.). (gr. k-6). 1968. 7.95 (ISBN 0-448-04458-7, G&D). Putnam Pub Group.

--Tell Me Why. (Illus.). (gr. k-6). 1969. 7.95 (ISBN 0-448-04430-7, G&D). Putnam Pub Group.

Leon, Daniel De see Bebel, August.

Leon, Dennis. Paul Harris. LC 75-1480. (Modern Artist Ser.). 1975. 12.50 o.p. (ISBN 0-8109-4427-8). Abrams.

Leon, Dorothy. One Eye, Two Eyes, Three Eyes, Four... The Many Ways Animals See. LC 80-15468. (Illus.). 64p. (gr. 4-6). 1980. PLB 7.29 o.p. (ISBN 0-671-34001-8). Messner.

Leon, Fray L. de see De Leon, Fray L.

Leon, H. & Alain, Hermano. Flora de Cuba, 2 vols. (Illus.). 2317p. (Span., Lat.). 1979. Repr. of 1946 ed. lib. bdg. 208.00 five parts bound in 2 vols. (ISBN 3-87429-077-8). Lubrecht & Cramer.

Leon, Jorge A. Psicologia Pastoral de la Iglesia. LC 77-43121. 192p. (Orig., Span.). 1978. pap. 4.95 o.s.i. (ISBN 0-89922-113-0). Edit Caribe.

Leon, Joseph J., jt. ed. see Cretser, Gary A.

Leon, Joseph M. Worldly Philosophers Notes. (Orig.). 1974. pap. 2.75 (ISBN 0-8220-1385-1). Cliffs.

Leon, Loretta T., ed. Readings in Autism. rev. ed. (Special Education Ser.). (Illus.). 224p. 1981. pap. text ed. 15.00 (ISBN 0-686-77779-4). Spec Learn Corp.

Leon, Philip W., compiled by. William Styron: An Annotated Bibliography of Criticism. LC 78-60256. 1978. lib. bdg. 25.00 (ISBN 0-313-20558-2, LWS/). Greenwood.

Leon, Steven J. Linear Algebra with Applications. (Illus.). 1980. text ed. 22.95x (ISBN 0-02-369870-5). Macmillan.

Leon, Vicki & Haag, Michael. The Moneywise Guide to North America. (Illus.). 400p. (Orig.). 1983. pap. 9.95 (ISBN 0-89141-172-0). Presidio Pr.

Leonard, jt. auth. see Humphreys.

Leonard, Albert, Jr., jt. auth. see Coulson, William D.

Leonard, Anne & Terrell, John. Patterns of Paradise. Bushman, Tanisse, ed. LC 80-65125. (Illus.). 76p. 1980. pap. 9.95 (ISBN 0-914868-05-5). Field Mus.

Leonard, B., jt. auth. see Redland, A.

Leonard, Charles B., Jr. Concentrations of Solutions. 120p. 1971. spiral bdg. 8.00 o.p. (ISBN 0-87488-602-3). Med Exam.

Leonard, Chien-Fu-Wu, jt. ed. see Box, G. E.

Leonard, Cliff R. License to Steal: Secrets of Acquiring Distress Property in Florida. McCarthy, Patricia, ed. 200p. 1982. pap. 55.00 over-sized (ISBN 0-9603818-2-1, Dist. by Creative Pubns). C R Leonard & D Coleman.

Leonard, Cliff R. & Greene, Bill. Distress Property Workbook: How to Buy it in Florida. 300p. (Orig.). 1982. 55.00x (ISBN 0-9603818-1-3, Dist. by Creative Pubns). C R Leonard & D Coleman.

Leonard, Constance. Stowaway. LC 82-45996. 160p. (gr. 7 up). 1983. PLB 9.95 (ISBN 0-396-08144-4). Dodd.

Leonard, David C. & McGuire, Peter J. Readings in Technical Writing. 304p. 1983. pap. text ed. 11.95 (ISBN 0-02-369840-3). Macmillan.

Leonard, David K. & Marshall, Dale R., eds. Institutions of Rural Development for the Poor: Decentralization & Organizational Linkages. LC 82-15651. (Research Ser.: No. 49). xii, 237p. 1982. pap. 11.50x (ISBN 0-87725-149-5). U of Cal Intl St.

Leonard, Diana. Sex & Generation. 1980. 29.95x (ISBN 0-422-77170-8, Pub. by Tavistock England); pap. 11.95x (ISBN 0-422-78220-3). Methuen Inc.

Leonard, Donald J. Shurter's Communication in Business. 4th ed. (Illus.). 1979. text ed. 23.95 (ISBN 0-07-037183-0, C); instructor's manual 14.50 (ISBN 0-07-037184-9). McGraw.

Leonard, Edward C. Vinyl & Diene Monomers. (High Polymer Ser.: Vol. 24, Pt. 2). 1971. 61.00 (ISBN 0-471-39329-0, Pub. by Wiley). Krieger.

Leonard, Edward F., jt. ed. see Vroman, Leo.

Leonard, Ellen M., ed. Wood Burning for Power Production. 135p. pap. 17.95x (ISBN 0-89934-048-2, B048-PP). Solar Energy Info.

Leonard, Ellis P. Fundamentals of Small Animal Surgery. LC 68-10402. (Illus.). 1968. 22.00 o.p. (ISBN 0-7216-5725-7). Saunders.

Leonard, Elmore. Split Images. 288p. pap. 2.95 (ISBN 0-380-63107-5). Avon.

--Stick. LC 82-72073. 1983. 14.25 (ISBN 0-87795-436-4). Arbor Hse.

Leonard, Frances M., ed. see Hardison, O. B., Jr. & Greer, Germaine.

Leonard, Fred H., jt. auth. see Chalmers, James A.

Leonard, George. The End of Sex. 240p. 1983. 12.95 (ISBN 0-87477-178-1). J P Tarcher.

--Man & Woman Thing & Other Provocations. 1971. pap. 2.25 o.s.i. (ISBN 0-440-55280-X, Delta). Dell.

--The Silent Pulse: A Search for the Perfect Rhythm That Exists in Each of Us. 1978. 10.95 o.p. (ISBN 0-525-20450-4). Dutton.

Leonard, George B. Education & Ecstasy. 1969. pap. text ed. 3.95 o.s.i. (ISBN 0-440-52247-1, Delta). Dell.

Leonard, Irving A. Colonial Travelers in Latin America. (Borzoi Latin American Ser). 1972. pap. text ed. 3.95x (ISBN 0-394-31063-2). Phila Bk Co.

Leonard, J. Edson. The Essential Fly Tier. LC 76-9043. (Illus.). 1976. 12.95 o.p. (ISBN 0-13-286120-8). P-H.

Leonard, J. W., jt. auth. see Allen, Shirley W.

Leonard, Jane K. Wie Yuan & China's Rediscovery of the Maritime World. (Duke Press Policy Studies). 250p. 1983. 35.00 (ISBN 0-8223-0549-6). Duke.

Leonard, Jim & Laut, Phil. Rebirthing: The Science of Enjoying all of Your Life. 90p. (Orig.). 1983. pap. 5.00 (ISBN 0-686-84663-X). Trinity Pubns.

Leonard, Joe H., Jr. Living with the Handicapped. (Christian Living Ser). 16p. 1976. pap. 0.30 o.p. (ISBN 0-8170-0726-1). Judson.

Leonard, Joe, Jr. Planning Family Ministry: A Guide for the Teaching Church. 64p. 1982. pap. 3.95 (ISBN 0-8170-0971-X). Judson.

Leonard, John & Warner, Blaine. Beginning Mathematics for College Students. (Illus.). 416p. 1971. text ed. 19.95 (ISBN 0-13-074013-6). P-H.

Leonard, Jon & Taylor, Elaine. The Live Longer Now Cookbook. LC 76-47997. 1979. Repr. 12.95 o.p. (ISBN 0-448-14337-2, G&D); pap. 6.95 (ISBN 0-448-16802-2). Putnam Pub Group.

Leonard, Jon L. The Live Longer Now Quick Weight-Loss Program. LC 79-87440. 1980. 12.95 (ISBN 0-448-14337-2, G&D). Putnam Pub Group.

Leonard, Jon N., et al. Live Longer Now: The First One Hundred Years of Your Life. 256p. 1976. pap. 4.95 (ISBN 0-448-12262-6, G&D). Putnam Pub Group.

--Live Longer Now. (Illus.). 256p. Date not set. pap. price not set (ISBN 0-448-12262-6, G&D). Putnam Pub Group.

--Live Longer Now: The First 100 Years of Your Life. LC 73-11398. (Illus.). 256p. 1974. 7.95 o.p. (ISBN 0-448-11504-2, G&D). Putnam Pub Group.

Leonard, Jonathan. Ancient America. LC 67-15619. (Great Ages of Man Ser.). (Illus.). (gr. 6 up). 1967. PLB 19.96 (ISBN 0-8094-0374-9, Pub. by Time-Life). Silver.

--Atlantic Beaches. LC 72-79775. (American Wilderness Ser). (Illus.). (gr. 6 up). 1972. lib. bdg. 15.96 (ISBN 0-8094-1157-1, Pub. by Time-Life). Silver.

Leonard, Jonathan N. American Cooking: New England. LC 70-133841. (Foods of the World Ser.). (Illus.). (gr. 6 up). 1970. lib. bdg. 17.28 (ISBN 0-8094-0076-6, Pub. by Time-Life). Silver.

--American Cooking: The Great West. LC 76-156273. (Foods of the World Ser.). (Illus.). (gr. 6 up). 1971. 17.28 (ISBN 0-8094-0080-4, Pub. by Time-Life). Silver.

--Early Japan. LC 68-27297. (Great Ages of Man). (Illus.). (gr. 6 up). 1968. PLB 19.96 (ISBN 0-8094-0382-X, Pub. by Time-Life). Silver.

--Latin American Cooking. LC 68-58451. (Foods of the World Ser). (Illus.). (gr. 6 up). 1968. PLB 17.28 (ISBN 0-8094-0063-4, Pub. by Time-Life). Silver.

--World of Gainsborough. LC 73-84574. (Library of Art Ser.). (Illus.). (gr. 6 up). 1969. 19.92 (ISBN 0-8094-0282-3, Pub. by Time-Life). Silver.

Leonard, Joseph W., ed. Coal Preperation. 4th ed. LC 79-52245. (Illus.). 1204p. 1979. text ed. 46.00x (ISBN 0-89520-258-1). Soc Mining Eng.

Leonard, Karen I. Social History of an Indian Caste: The Kayasths of Hyderabad. LC 76-52031. (Center for South & Southeast Asian Studies). 1978. 28.50x (ISBN 0-520-03431-7). U of Cal Pr.

Leonard, Lawrence L. Self Mastery, Bk. I. LC 82-72723. 70p. (Orig.). 1982. pap. 3.50 (ISBN 0-931494-28-1). Brunswick Pub.

Leonard, Leah W. Jewish Cookery. (International Cook Book Ser.). 1949. 9.95 (ISBN 0-517-09758-3). Crown.

Leonard, Linda S. The Wounded Woman: Healing the Father-Daughter Relationship. LC 82-75414. xx, 186p. 1982. 17.95 (ISBN 0-8040-0397-1). Swallow.

Leonard, Merton C., jt. auth. see Wait, Minnie W.

Leonard, Mimi, jt. auth. see Rubin, Jerry.

Leonard, Peter, jt. auth. see Corrigan, Paul.

Leonard, Phyllis. Mariposa. (Orig.). 1983. pap. 3.95 (ISBN 0-440-16071-5). Dell.

--Tarnished Angel. LC 79-20795. 1980. 10.95 (ISBN 0-698-10999-6, Coward). Putnam Pub Group.

--Warrior's Woman. LC 77-4822. 1977. 8.95 o.p. (ISBN 0-698-10843-4, Coward). Putnam Pub Group.

--Warrior's Woman. 1978. pap. 2.25 o.s.i. (ISBN 0-515-04620-5). Jove Pubns.

Leonard, R. M., jt. auth. see Jerrold, Walter C.

Leonard, Richard W. South Africa at War. 256p. (Orig.). 1983. 16.95 (ISBN 0-88208-108-X); pap. 8.95 (ISBN 0-88208-109-8). Lawrence Hill.

Leonard, Robert C., jt. auth. see Wooldridge, Powhatan.

Leonard, Robert J. & De Beer, Peter H. Composition Practice Book: Survival Kit Individual Student Workbooks. 96p. 1982. pap. 2.95x (ISBN 0-87628-778-X). Ctr Appl Res.

--A Survival Kit for Teachers of Composition: Skill-by-Skill Writing Improvement Program. 1982. comb-bound 19.95x (ISBN 0-87628-777-1). Ctr Appl Res.

Leonard, V. A. Fundamentals of Law Enforcement: Problems & Issues. (Criminal Jusice Ser.). (Illus.). 350p. 1980. text ed. 19.50 (ISBN 0-8299-0222-8); instrs.' manual avail. (ISBN 0-8299-0596-0). West Pub.

--Police Detective Function. 124p. 1970. photocopy ed. spiral 14.75x (ISBN 0-398-01099-4). C C Thomas.

--Police Enterprise: Its Organization & Management. (Illus.). 104p. 1969. photocopy ed. spiral 10.75x (ISBN 0-398-01100-1). C C Thomas.

--Police Personnel Administration. 144p. 1970. photocopy ed. spiral 15.75x (ISBN 0-398-01103-6). C C Thomas.

--Police Pre-Disaster Preparation. (Illus.). 344p. 1973. photocopy ed. spiral 34.50x (ISBN 0-398-02693-9). C C Thomas.

--Police Traffic Control. 176p. 1971. photocopy ed. spiral 17.75x (ISBN 0-398-01107-9). C C Thomas.

Leonard, Warren H. & Martin, John H. Cereal Crops. 1963. text ed. 25.95x (ISBN 0-02-369830-6). Macmillan.

Leonard, Wilbert. Basic Social Statistics. LC 75-38772. (Illus.). 375p. 1976. text ed. 22.95 (ISBN 0-8299-0072-1). West Pub.

Leonard, Wilbert M., 2nd. A Sociological Perspective of Sport. LC 79-54688. (Orig.). 1980. 14.95x (ISBN 0-8087-1296-9). Burgess.

Leonard, William E. Aesop & Hyssop. 158p. 1921. 16.00 (ISBN 0-87548-252-X); pap. 5.00 (ISBN 0-87548-253-8). Open Court.

Leonard, William E., ed. see Lucretius.

Leonard, William E., tr. from Gr. & see Empedocles.

Leonard, William L., ed. Radiologic Technology Examination Review Book, Vol. 1. 4th ed. 1979. pap. 12.75 (ISBN 0-87488-441-1). Med Exam.

Leonardo Da Vinci. Notebooks of Leonardo Da Vinci. Richter, Jean P., ed. (Illus.). 1970. pap. 9.95 ea.; Vol. 1. pap. (ISBN 0-486-22572-0); Vol. 2. pap. (ISBN 0-486-22573-9). Dover.

Leonards, G. A., ed. Foundation Engineering. (Civil Engineering Ser.). 1962. 65.00 (ISBN 0-07-037198-9, P&RB). McGraw.

Leonbardt, Barbara A. & Berzoa, Morton, eds. Insect Pheromone Technology: Chemistry & Applications. (ACS Symposium Ser.: No. 190). 1982. write for info. (ISBN 0-8412-0724-0). Am Chemical.

Leon de Leal, Magdalena see Deere, Carmen & Leal, Magdalena Leon de.

Leondes, C. T., ed. Advances in Control & Dynamic Systems, Vol. 19. (Serial Publication). Date not set. price not set (ISBN 0-12-012719-9). Acad Pr.

--Advances in Control & Dynamic Systems: Series Publication, Vol. 20. Date not set. price not set (ISBN 0-12-012720-2). Acad Pr.

Leon-Dufour, Xavier, ed. Dictionary of Biblical Theology. new ed. Cahill, P. Joseph, tr. from Fr. LC 73-6437. 710p. 1973. Repr. 27.50 (ISBN 0-8164-1146-8). Seabury.

Leone, Bruno. Maria Montessori: Knight of the Child. Bender, David L. & McCuen, Gary E., eds. (Focus on Famous Women Ser.). (Illus.). (gr. 3 up). 1978. 8.95 (ISBN 0-912616-47-4); read along cassette 9.95 (ISBN 0-89908-246-7). Greenhaven.

Leone, Bruno, ed. Capitalism: Opposing Viewpoints. (ISMS Ser.). (Illus.). (gr. 9-12). 1978. 10.95 (ISBN 0-912616-51-2); pap. 5.95 (ISBN 0-912616-50-4). Greenhaven.

--Communism: Opposing Viewpoints. (ISMS Ser.). (Illus.). (gr. 9-12). 1978. 10.95 (ISBN 0-912616-53-9); pap. 5.95 (ISBN 0-912616-52-0). Greenhaven.

--Internationalism: Opposing Viewpoints. (ISMS Ser.). (Illus.). (gr. 9-12). 1978. 10.95 (ISBN 0-912616-59-8); pap. 5.95 (ISBN 0-912616-58-X). Greenhaven.

--Nationalism: Opposing Viewpoints. (ISMS Ser.). (Illus.). (gr. 9-12). 1978. 10.95 (ISBN 0-912616-57-1); pap. 5.95 (ISBN 0-912616-56-3). Greenhaven.

--Racism: Opposing Viewpoints. (ISMS Ser.). (Illus.). (gr. 9-12). 1978. 10.95 (ISBN 0-912616-61-X); pap. 5.95 (ISBN 0-912616-60-1). Greenhaven.

--Socialism: Opposing Viewpoints. (ISMS Ser.). (Illus.). (gr. 9-12). 1978. 10.95 (ISBN 0-912616-55-5); pap. 5.95 (ISBN 0-912616-54-7). Greenhaven.

Leone, Diana. Investments. 120p. 1982. pap. 11.95 (ISBN 0-942786-02-5). Leone Pubns.

--The Sampler Quilt. 6th ed. (Illus.). 68p. pap. text ed. 8.95x (ISBN 0-942786-01-7). Leone Pubns.

Leone, Gene. Leone's Italian Cookbook. (Illus.). 1967. 13.41i (ISBN 0-06-111012-4, HarpT). Har-Row.

Leong, Basil K. J. Inhalation Toxicology & Technology. LC 81-67510. (Illus.). 313p. 1981. 39.95 (ISBN 0-250-40414-1). Ann Arbor Science.

Leong, Che Kan, jt. auth. see Downing, John.

Leong, James. The Low Calorie Chinese Gourmet Cookbook. (Illus.). 142p. 1980. pap. 5.95 o.p. (ISBN 0-89474-020-2). Pinnacle Bks.

Leong, Lucille. Acupuncture: A Layman's View. pap. 1.50 o.p. (ISBN 0-451-05852-6, W5852, Sig). NAL.

Leong, Lucille A. Acupuncture: A Layman's View. 1975. pap. 1.50 (ISBN 0-685-57127-0, Pub. by NAL). Formur Intl.

Leong, Sow-Theng. Sino-Soviet Diplomatic Relations, 1917-1926. LC 76-4960. 384p. 1976. text ed. 17.50x (ISBN 0-8248-0401-5). UH Pr.

Leong-Hong, Belkis W. & Plagman, Bernard K. Data Dictionary-Directory Systems: Administration Implementation & Usage. LC 81-21875. 328p. 1982. 27.95x (ISBN 0-471-05164-0, Pub. by Wiley-Interscience). Wiley.

Leonhard, Charles & House, Robert W. Foundations & Principles of Music Education. 2nd ed. 448p. 1971. text ed. 24.50 (ISBN 0-07-037199-7, C). McGraw.

Leonhardt, F. Prestressed Concrete Design & Construction. 2nd rev. ed. (Illus.). 1964. 60.00 (ISBN 0-685-12040-6). Heinman.

Leonhardy, Adele. Introductory College Mathematics. 2nd ed. LC 63-12284. 1963. text ed. 26.50 (ISBN 0-471-52736-X). Wiley.

Leoni, Bruno. Freedom & the Law. (Humane Studies). 204p. 1980. text ed. 7.50x (ISBN 0-8402-1215-1); pap. text ed. 4.95x. Humanities.

Leoni, Edgar. Nostradamus: Life & Literature. 1982. 16.00 (ISBN 0-517-38809-X). Nosbooks.

Leonida, G. Handbook of Printed Circuit Design Manufacture, Components & Assembly. 700p. 1980. 150.00 (ISBN 0-901150-08-8, Pub. by Electrochemical Scotland). State Mutual Bk.

Leonidas. Secrets of Stage Hypnotism. LC 80-19741. 149p. 1980. Repr. of 1975 ed. lib. bdg. 11.95x (ISBN 0-89370-629-9). Borgo Pr.

Leonidas, Professor. Secrets of Stage Hypnotism. new ed. LC 74-23500. Orig. Title: Stage Hypnotism. 149p. 1975. pap. 3.95 o.p. (ISBN 0-87877-029-1, P-29). Newcastle Pub.

Leonor, M. D. & Richards, P. J., eds. Target Setting for Basic Needs: The Operation of Selected Government Services. 220p. 1982. 14.25 (ISBN 92-2-102946-8). Intl Labour Office.

Leonov, Leonid M. Skutarevsky. Brown, Alec, tr. LC 76-135250. 1971. Repr. of 1936 ed. lib. bdg. 20.25x (ISBN 0-8371-5170-8, LESK). Greenwood.

Leon-Portilla, Miguel. Aztec Thought & Culture: A Study of the Ancient Nahuatl Mind. Davis, Jack E., tr. (Civilization of the American Indian Ser.: Vol. 67). (Illus.). 1978. Repr. of 1963 ed. 16.95 (ISBN 0-8061-0569-0). U of Okla Pr.

Leons, Madeline B. & Rothstein, Frances, eds. New Directions in Political Economy: An Approach from Anthropology. LC 78-4290. (Contributions in Economics & Economic History: No. 22). xxviii, 350p. lib. bdg. 29.95 (ISBN 0-313-20414-4, LND/). Greenwood.

Leontief, Wassily. Essays in Economics: Theories & Theorizing, Vol. 1. LC 76-21999. 1976. 22.50 (ISBN 0-87332-091-3). M E Sharpe.

--Essays in Economics: Theories, Facts & Policies, Vol. 2. LC 77-79062. 1978. 22.50 (ISBN 0-87332-092-1). M E Sharpe.

Leontief, Wassily & Duchin, Faye. Military Spending: Facts & Figures, Worldwide Implications, & Future Outlook. (Illus.). 160p. 1983. 19.95 (ISBN 0-19-503191-1). Oxford U Pr.

Leontief, Wassily W. Input-Output Economics. 1966. 25.00x (ISBN 0-19-500616-X). Oxford U Pr.

--The Structure of American Economy, 1919-1939: An Empirical Application of Equilibrium Analysis. 2nd enlarged ed. LC 76-17415. 1976. Repr. of 1951 ed. 35.00 (ISBN 0-87332-087-5). M E Sharpe.

--Studies in Structure of American Economy: Theoretical & Empirical Explorations in Input-Output Analysis. LC 76-16433. 1976. Repr. of 1953 ed. 45.00 (ISBN 0-87332-086-7). M E Sharpe.

Leopard, Donald D. World War II: A Concise History. (Illus.). 155p. 1982. pap. 7.95x (ISBN 0-686-43048-4). Waveland Pr.

Leopardi, Giacomo. Operette Morali: Essays & Dialogues. Cecchetti, Giovanni del, tr. from Ital. LC 82-2627. (Biblioteca Italiana Ser.). 672p. 1982. 28.00x (ISBN 0-520-04704-4). U of Cal Pr.

Leopold, A., et al. Plant Growth & Development. rev. ed. 1975. 37.95 (ISBN 0-07-037200-4, C). McGraw.

Leopold, A. Starker. The Desert. (Young Readers Library). (Illus.). 1977. PLB 6.80 (ISBN 0-8094-1360-4). Silver.

Leopold, A. Starker & Gutierrez, Ralph J. North American Game Birds & Mammals. (Illus.). 208p. 1983. pap. 10.95 (ISBN 0-686-83783-5, ScribT). Scribner.

Leopold, Aldo. A Sand County Almanac, & Sketches Here & There. (Illus.). 1949. pap. 5.95 (ISBN 0-19-500777-8, GB). Oxford U Pr.

--Sand County Almanac: With Other Essays on Conservation from Round River. (Illus.). 1966. 17.95 (ISBN 0-19-500619-4). Oxford U Pr.

Leopold, George R. & Asher, W. Michael. Fundamentals of Abdominal & Pelvic Ultrasonography. LC 74-6688. (Monographs in Clinical Radiology: Vol. 6). (Illus.). 250p. 1975. text ed. 28.00 o.p. (ISBN 0-7216-5731-1). Saunders.

Leopold, I. H. Cases in Diagnostic Ultrasound. 206p. 1980. 40.00 (ISBN 0-471-08731-9, Pub. by Wiley Med). Wiley.

Leopold, Irving H. & Burns, Robert P., eds. Symposium on Ocular Therapy, Vol. 8. LC 66-22972. 92p. (Orig.). 24.00 (ISBN 0-471-52771-8). Krieger.

--Symposium on Ocular Therapy: Proceedings, Vol. 8. LC 66-22972. 92p. 1976. 24.00 (ISBN 0-471-52771-8, Pub. by Wiley). Krieger.

--Symposium on Ocular Therapy: Proceedings, Vol. 9. LC 66-22972. 162p. 1976. 24.00 (ISBN 0-471-01717-5). Krieger.

Leopold, Jay, jt. auth. see McMahon, Bob.

Leopold, Joan. The Letter Liveth: The Life Work & Library of August Friedrick Pott (1802-1887) (Library & Information Sources in Linguistics (LISL): 9). 500p. 1983. 50.00 (ISBN 90-272-3733-6). Benjamins North Am.

Leopold, Luna, jt. auth. see Davis, Kenneth S.

Leopold, Richard W. Elihu Root & the Conservative Tradition. (The Library of American Biography). 222p. 1965. pap. text ed. 5.95 (ISBN 0-316-52114-0). Little.

Leo Thirteenth, Pope, et al. Seven Great Encyclicals. (Orig.). 1969. pap. 4.95 o.p. (ISBN 0-8091-1680-4). Paulist Pr.

Leotta, G. G., jt. ed. see Gormezano, C.

Lep, Annette. Crocheting Baby Blankets & Carriage Covers. (Illus.). 48p. (Orig.). 1983. pap. 2.25 (ISBN 0-486-24480-6). Dover.

Lepa, E., tr. see Scharf, W.

Lepage, Henri. Tomorrow, Capitalism: The Economics of Economic Freedom. Ogilvie, Sheilagh C., tr. from Fr. LC 82-2291. 256p. 1982. 14.95 (ISBN 0-87548-367-4). Open Court.

Le Page, R. B., jt. ed. see Cassidy, Frederick G.

LePage, Wilbur, jt. auth. see Balabanian, Norman.

LePak, Roy C. A Theology of Christian Mystical Experience. 1977. pap. text ed. 12.00 o.p. (ISBN 0-8191-0148-6). U Pr of Amer.

Lepan, E. M. Vie Politique, Litteraire et Morale De Voltaire. Repr. of 1817 ed. 98.00 o.p. (ISBN 0-8287-0535-6). Clearwater Pub.

Le Patourel, John. The Norman Empire. (Illus.). 1977. 57.00x (ISBN 0-19-822525-3). Oxford U Pr.

Le Peau, Andrew T. Paths of Leadership. 132p. (Orig.). 1983. pap. 3.95 (ISBN 0-87784-806-8). Inter-Varsity.

Le Pichon, Yann. Henri Rousseau. LC 82-2047. (Illus.). 286p. 1982. 75.00 (ISBN 0-670-36691-9, Studio). Viking Pr.

Le Play, Frederic. On Family, Work, & Social Change. Silver, Catherine, ed. LC 81-23125. (Heritage of Sociology Ser.). 1982. lib. bdg. 30.00x (ISBN 0-226-47266-3). U of Chicago Pr.

--Les Ouvriers Europeens, 6 vols. (Conditions of the 19th Century French Working Class Ser.). (Fr.). 1974. lib. bdg. 967.00 o.p. (ISBN 0-8287-0536-4, 1067-72). Clearwater Pub.

Lepley, M., jt. auth. see Jones, D. A.

Leplin, Jarrett. Propositional Logic. LC 79-63560. 1979. pap. text ed. 7.75 o.p. (ISBN 0-8191-0728-X). U Pr of Amer.

Lepman, Jella. Bridge of Children's Books. McCormick, Edith, tr. LC 68-54215. 1969. 5.00 o.p. (ISBN 0-8389-0070-4). ALA.

Leporati, Ezio. The Assessment of Structural Safety. (Structural Engineering Research Ser.). 133p. 1980. pap. 26.95 (ISBN 0-471-27886-6). Res Stud Pr.

Leporqti, E. The Assessment of Structural Safety: A Comparative Statistical Study of the Evolution & Use of Levels 1, 2, & 3, Vol. 1. 1979 ed. 133p. pap. 26.95 (ISBN 0-471-27886-6, Pub. by Research Studies Pr). Wiley.

Lepp, H. Dynamic Earth: An Introduction to Earth Sciences. 1973. text ed. 17.50 o.p. (ISBN 0-07-037204-7, C); instructors' manual 1.50 o.p. (ISBN 0-07-037205-5). McGraw.

Lepp, Ignace. Death & Its Mysteries. 1968. 5.95 o.p. (ISBN 0-02-570260-2); pap. 1.95 o.p. (ISBN 0-02-086660-7). Macmillan.

Lepp, N. W., ed. Effect of Heavy Metal Pollution on Plants: Vol. 1, Effects of Trace Metals on Plant Function. (Pollution Monitoring Ser.). (Illus.). 352p. 1981. 57.50 (ISBN 0-85334-959-2, Pub. by Applied Sci England). Elsevier.

--Effect of Heavy Metal Pollution on Plants: Vol. 2, Metals in the Environment. (Pollution Monitoring Ser.). (Illus.). 257p. 1981. 47.25 (ISBN 0-85334-923-1, Pub. by Applied Sci England). Elsevier.

Leppanen, George C. The Intelligence Quotient. 1978. 6.50 o.p. (ISBN 0-533-03787-5). Vantage.

Leppard, Lois. Mandie & the Cherokee Legend. (Mandie Ser.). 144p. (Orig.). (gr. 4-7). 1983. pap. 2.95 (ISBN 0-87123-321-5). Bethany Hse.

Leppard, Lois G. Mandie & the Secret Tunnel. (Mandie Ser.: No. 1). 144p. (Orig.). (gr. 4-7). 1983. pap. 2.95 (ISBN 0-87123-320-7). Bethany Hse.

Leppzer, Robert. Voices from Three-Mile Island: The People Speak Out. LC 80-20933. (Illus.). 1980. 12.95 (ISBN 0-89594-041-8); pap. 3.95 (ISBN 0-89594-042-6). Crossing Pr.

Leps, A. Arvo, jt. auth. see Wood, Donald N.

Lepthien, Emilie U. Australia, Enchantment of the World. LC 82-4541. (Illus.). (gr. 5-9). 1982. PLB 13.25g (ISBN 0-516-02751-4). Childrens.

Leptich, Anne & Evans, Jacque. Calligrapher's Reference Book. pap. 7.00 (ISBN 0-87980-386-X). Wilshire.

Lequime. Prevention & Treatment of Coronary Heart Disease. (International Congress Ser.: Vol. 530). 1980. 42.25 (ISBN 0-444-90162-0). Elsevier.

Leray, Jean. Lagrangian Analysis & Quantum Mechanics: A Mathematical Structure Related to Asymptotic Expansions & the Maslov Index. Schroeder, Carolyn, tr. 1982. 35.00 (ISBN 0-262-12087-9). MIT Pr.

Lerbinger, Otto, jt. auth. see Sperber, Nathaniel N.

Lerch, Constance & Bliss, Jane. Maternity Nursing: A Self Study Guide. 4th ed. (Illus.). 220p. 1978. pap. text ed. 10.50 o.p. (ISBN 0-8016-2959-4). Mosby.

Lerch, Constance & Bliss, Virginia. Maternity Nursing. 3rd ed. LC 77-13983. (Illus.). 578p. 1978. text ed. 18.95 o.p. (ISBN 0-8016-2961-6). Mosby.

Lerch, Harold A., jt. auth. see Welch, Paula D.

Lerch, Harold H. Active Learning Experiences for Teaching Elementary School Mathematics. (Illus.). 592p. 1981. pap. text ed. 12.95 (ISBN 0-395-29764-8). HM.

--Teaching Elementary School Mathematics: An Active Learning Approach. (Illus.). 416p. 1981. text ed. 18.50 (ISBN 0-395-29762-1); instr's. manual 0.85 (ISBN 0-395-29763-X). HM.

Lerche, Charles O., Jr. America in World Affairs. LC 79-26759. (Foundations of American Government and Political Science). (Illus.). 118p. 1980. Repr. of 1967 ed. lib. bdg. 16.25x (ISBN 0-313-22315-7, LEAMW). Greenwood.

Lerche, Charles Q., jt. auth. see Said, Abdul A.

Lerche, Hans-Werner. Luftwaffe Test Pilot. (Illus.). 158p. 1981. 19.95 (ISBN 0-86720-583-0). Sci Bks Intl.

Lerdahl, Fred & Jackendoff, Ray. A Generative Theory of Tonal Music. (Cognitive Theory & Mental Representation Ser.). (Illus.). 434p. 1983. write for info. MIT Pr.

LeResche, Robert E., jt. auth. see Ainley, David G.

LeRiche, W. Harding. A Chemical Feast. 192p. 1982. 13.95 (ISBN 0-87196-643-3). Facts on File.

Lerici, Carlo M., jt. auth. see Rainey, Froelich G.

Lerin, Alfredo, compiled by. Quinientas Ilustraciones. 324p. (Span.). 1980. pap. 5.75 (ISBN 0-311-42037-0). Casa Bautista.

Lerin, Alfredo, tr. see Summers, Ray.

Lerin, Olivia de see Crane, J. D.

Lerin, Olivia S. D. de see Sutton, Joan L. & Watson de Barros, Leda.

Lerin, Olivia S. de see De Lerin, Olivia S.

Lerin, Olivia Y Alfredo, tr. see Brown, Raymond B.

Lerin, S. D. de, tr. see Stowell, Gordon.

Lerin, S. D. De, tr. see Stowell, Gordon.

Lerin, S. D. de, tr. see Stowell, Gordon.

Lerman, A. Geochemical Processes: Water & Sediment Environments. LC 78-15039. 1979. 41.95 (ISBN 0-471-03263-8, Pub. by Wiley-Interscience). Wiley.

Lerman, Arthur J. Taiwan's Politics: The Provincial Assemblyman's World. LC 78-64524. 1978. pap. text ed. 12.50 (ISBN 0-8191-0632-1). U Pr of Amer.

Lerman, Paul. Deinstitutionalization & the Welfare State. (Illus.). 264p. 1982. 26.00 (ISBN 0-8135-0934-3). Rutgers U Pr.

Lermonton, Mihail see Bond, Otto F., et al.

Lermontov. A Hero of Our Time. Foote, Paul, tr. (Classics Ser). 1966. pap. 3.95 (ISBN 0-14-044176-X). Penguin.

Lermontov, M. Y. Bela. Domb, J. & Shoenberg, Z., trs. from Rus. (Harrap's Bilingual Ser.). 126p. Date not set. 5.00 (ISBN 0-911268-53-7); pocket size 5.00 (ISBN 0-686-84536-6). Rogers Bk.

Lermontov, Mihail. A Hero of Our Time. Nabokov, Vladimir & Nabokov, Dmitri, trs. from Rus. (Anchor Literary Library). 1982. pap. 4.95 (ISBN 0-385-09344-6, Anch). Doubleday.

Lermontov, Mihail L. see Bond, Otto F., et al.

Lermontov, Mikhail. Vadim. Goscilo, Helena, ed. & tr. from Rus. 100p. 1983. 15.00 (ISBN 0-88233-682-7). Ardis Pubs.

Lerner, A. B., jt. auth. see Luce, Marnie.

Lerner, Aaron B. Einstein & Newton: A Comparison of the Two Greatest Scientists. LC 72-7653. (Adult & Young Adult Bks.). (Illus.). (gr. 9 up). 1973. PLB 8.95g (ISBN 0-8225-0752-8). Lerner Pubns.

Lerner, Abba & Colander, David. MAP: A Market Anti-Inflation Plan. 128p. 1980. pap. text ed. 8.95 (ISBN 0-15-555060-8, HC). HarBraceJ.

Lerner, Abba P. & Ben-Shahar, Haim. The Economics of Efficiency & Growth: Lessons from Israel & the West Bank. LC 74-32140. 208p. 1975. prof ref 22.00x (ISBN 0-88410-276-9). Ballinger Pub.

Lerner, Alan J. My Fair Lady. (RL 9). pap. 2.50 (ISBN 0-451-11900-2, AE1900, Sig). NAL.

Lerner, Alan J., jt. auth. see Shaw, G. B.

Lerner, Anne L. Passing the Love of Women: A Study of Gide's Saul & Its Biblical Roots. LC 80-5477. 148p. 1980. lib. bdg. 18.00 (ISBN 0-8191-1109-0); pap. text ed. 8.25 (ISBN 0-8191-1110-4). U Pr of Amer.

Lerner, Carol. Flowers of a Woodland Spring. LC 78-32154. (Illus.). 32p. (gr. k-3). 1979. 9.75 (ISBN 0-688-22190-4); PLB 9.36 (ISBN 0-688-32190-9). Morrow.

--On the Forest Edge. (Illus.). (gr. k-3). 1978. 7.75 o.s.i. (ISBN 0-688-22162-9); PLB 8.40 (ISBN 0-688-32162-3). Morrow.

--Seasons of the Tallgrass Prairie. LC 80-13078. (Illus.). 48p. (gr. k-3). 1980. 9.75 (ISBN 0-688-22245-5); PLB 9.36 (ISBN 0-688-32245-X). Morrow.

Lerner, Craig A. The Grants Register, 1983-1985. 825p. 1982. 35.00x o.p. (ISBN 0-312-34408-2). St Martin.

Lerner, Craig A., ed. Grants Register, 1981 to 1983. 7th ed. LC 77-12055. 782p. 32.50 o.p. (ISBN 0-686-75646-0). St Martin.

Lerner, D. E. & Sommers, P. D., eds. Complex Manifold Techniques in Theoretical Physics. (Research Notes in Mathematics Ser.: No. 32). 320p. (Orig.). 1979. pap. text ed. 26.50 (ISBN 0-273-08437-2). Pitman Pub MA.

Lerner, Daniel & Gorden, Morton. Euratlantica: Changing Perspectives of the European Elites. 1969. 20.00x (ISBN 0-262-12029-1). MIT Pr.

Lerner, Daniel & Nelson, Lyle M., eds. Communication Research: A Half-Century Appraisal. LC 77-89616. 1977. text ed. 16.00x o.p. (ISBN 0-8248-0566-6, Eastwest Ctr). UH Pr.

Lerner, Daniel, jt. ed. see Schramm, Wilbur.

Lerner, Edward R. Study Scores of Musical Styles. 1968. pap. text ed. 26.50 (ISBN 0-07-037211-X, C). McGraw.

Lerner, Elaine & Abbott, C. B. The Way to Go: A Woman's Guide to Careers in Travel. 208p. 1982. pap. 6.95 (ISBN 0-446-37022-3). Warner Bks.

Lerner, Eric. Journey of Insight Meditation: A Personal Experience of the Buddha's Way. LC 76-49726. 1978. 8.95x (ISBN 0-8052-3648-1); pap. 4.95 (ISBN 0-8052-0593-4). Schocken.

Lerner, Eugene M., jt. auth. see Rappaport, Alfred.

Lerner, Gerda. The Grimke Sisters from South Carolina: Pioneers for Women's Rights & Abolition. LC 67-25218. (Studies in the Life of Women). 1971. pap. 7.95 (ISBN 0-8052-0321-4). Schocken.

Lerner, J. W. & List, L. K. Reading & Learning Disabilities. Date not set. price not set (ISBN 0-07-037220-9). McGraw.

Lerner, Janet W. Children with Learning Disabilities. 2nd ed. LC 75-26085. (Illus.). 448p. 1976. text ed. 17.95 o.p. (ISBN 0-395-20474-7); inst. manual 1.25 o.p. (ISBN 0-395-20473-9). HM.

--Learning Disabilities: Theories, Diagnosis, & Teaching Strategies. 3rd ed. LC 80-82975. (Illus.). 560p. 1981. text ed. 22.95 (ISBN 0-395-29710-9); study guide 9.50 (ISBN 0-395-30371-0); instr's manual 1.00 (ISBN 0-395-29711-7). HM.

Lerner, Janet W., et al. Cases in Learning & Behavior Problems. LC 79-88101. 1980. pap. text ed. 12.95 (ISBN 0-395-28493-7); instr's. manual 0.50 (ISBN 0-395-28494-5). HM.

--Special Education for the Early Childhood Years. 416p. 1981. text ed. 23.95 (ISBN 0-13-826461-9). P-H.

Lerner, Jean, tr. see Mendras, Henri.

Lerner, Joel. Schaum's Outline of Theory & Problems of Bookeeping. 1978. pap. 6.95 (ISBN 0-07-037221-7, SP). McGraw.

Lerner, Joel J., jt. auth. see Cashin, James A.

Lerner, Joel V. & Baker, H. A. Introduction to Business. (Schaum's Outline Ser). 160p. (Orig.). 1976. pap. 5.95 (ISBN 0-07-003345-5, SP). McGraw.

Lerner, Judith & Khan, Zafar. Mosby's Manual of Urologic Nursing. LC 81-18948. (Illus.). 721p. 1982. pap. text ed. 29.50 (ISBN 0-8016-2947-0). Mosby.

Lerner, Laurence. A.R.T.H.U.R. & M.A.R.T.H.A. Loves of the Computer. 1980. pap. 7.50 (ISBN 0-436-24440-3, Pub by Secker & Warburg). David & Charles.

--Love & Marriage: Literature & Its Social Context. 1979. 27.50x (ISBN 0-312-49938-8). St Martin.

Lerner, Lawrence S., jt. auth. see Eisberg, Robert M.

Lerner, Leila, ed. Women & Individuation: Emerging Views. 160p. 9.95 (ISBN 0-89885-134-3). Human Sci Pr.

Lerner, Marguerite R. Color & People: The Story of Pigmentation. LC 70-128800. (Real World: Crisis & Conflict Ser). (Illus.). (gr. 5-11). 1971. PLB 5.95g (ISBN 0-8225-0625-4). Lerner Pubns.

--Dear Little Mumps Child. LC 59-15145. (Medical Bks. for Children). (Illus.). (gr. k-5). 1959. PLB 3.95g (ISBN 0-8225-0003-5). Lerner Pubns.

--Doctors' Tools. LC 59-15484. (Medical Bks. for Children). (Illus.). (gr. k-6). 1960. PLB 3.95g (ISBN 0-8225-0004-3). Lerner Pubns.

--Fur, Feathers, Hair. LC 62-16851. (Medical Books for Children). (Illus.). (gr. 3-9). 1962. PLB 3.95g (ISBN 0-8225-0014-0). Lerner Pubns.

--Horns, Hoofs, Nails. LC 65-29040. (Medical Bks for Children). (Illus.). (gr. 3-9). 1965. PLB 3.95g (ISBN 0-8225-0015-9). Lerner Pubns.

--Lefty: The Story of Left-Handedness. LC 60-14007. (Medical Bks for Children). (Illus.). (gr. k-5). 1960. PLB 3.95g (ISBN 0-8225-0005-1). Lerner Pubns.

--Peter Gets the Chickenpox. LC 59-15144. (Medical Bks for Children). (Illus.). (gr. k-5). 1959. PLB 3.95g (ISBN 0-8225-0002-7). Lerner Pubns.

--Red Man, White Man, African Chief: The Story of Skin Color. LC 60-14005. (Medical Books for Children). (Illus.). (gr. k-9). 1960. PLB 3.95g (ISBN 0-8225-0007-8). Lerner Pubns.

--Twins: The Story of Twins. LC 61-13577. (Medical Bks. for Children). (Illus.). (gr. k-6). 1961. PLB 3.95g (ISBN 0-8225-0009-4). Lerner Pubns.

--Where Do You Come From: The Story of Evolution. LC 67-15706. (Medical Bks for Children). (Illus.). (gr. 5 up). 1967. PLB 3.95g (ISBN 0-8225-0019-1). Lerner Pubns.

Lerner, Mark. Bowling Is for Me. LC 81-12433. (Sports for Me Bks.). (Illus.). 48p. (gr. 2-5). 1981. PLB 6.95g (ISBN 0-8225-1099-5). Lerner Pubns.

--Careers in a Restaurant. LC 77-27435. (Early Career Bks.). (Illus.). (gr. 2-5). 1979. PLB 5.95g (ISBN 0-8225-0336-0). Lerner Pubns.

--Careers in a Supermarket. LC 77-72424. (Early Career Bks.). (Illus.). (gr. 2-5). 1977. PLB 5.95g (ISBN 0-8225-0332-8). Lerner Pubns.

--Careers in Auto Racing. LC 80-12047. (Early Career Bks.). (Illus.). (gr. 2-5). 1980. PLB 5.95g (ISBN 0-8225-0343-3). Lerner Pubns.

--Careers in Basketball. LC 82-17265. (Early Career Bks.). (Illus.). 36p. (gr. 2-5). 1983. PLB 5.95g (ISBN 0-8225-0311-5). Lerner Pubns.

--Careers in Beauty & Grooming. LC 77-72419. (Early Career Bks.). (Illus.). (gr. 2-5). 1977. PLB 5.95g (ISBN 0-8225-0328-X). Lerner Pubns.

--Careers in Hotels & Motels. LC 78-21171. (Early Career Bks.). (Illus.). (gr. 2-5). 1979. PLB 5.95g (ISBN 0-8225-0335-2). Lerner Pubns.

--Careers with a Newspaper. LC 77-72422. (Early Career Bks.). (Illus.). (gr. 2-5). 1977. PLB 5.95g (ISBN 0-8225-0330-1). Lerner Pubns.

--Careers with a Radio Station. LC 82-20349. (Early Career Bks.). (Illus.). 36p. (gr. 2-5). 1983. PLB 5.95g (ISBN 0-8225-0312-3). Lerner Pubns.

--Quarter-Midget Racing Is for Me. LC 81-41. (Sports for Me Bks.). (Illus.). (gr. 2-5). 1981. PLB 6.95g (ISBN 0-8225-1125-8). Lerner Pubns.

Lerner, Max. America As a Civilization, 2 vols. Incl. Vol. 1. Culture & Personality. 1967 (ISBN 0-671-20161-1); Vol. 2. The Basic Frame (ISBN 0-671-20162-X). 1967. pap. 6.95 ea o.s.i. (Touchstone Bks). S&S.

Lerner, Michael G. Pierre Loti. (World Authors Ser.). 1974. lib. bdg. 15.95 (ISBN 0-8057-2546-6, Twayne). G K Hall.

Lerner, Morris W. The Analysis of Elemental Boron. LC 74-607964. (AEC Critical Review Ser.). 125p. 1970. pap. 11.25 (ISBN 0-87079-134-6, TID-25190); microfiche 4.50 (ISBN 0-87079-135-4, TID-25190). DOE.

Lerner, N., jt. auth. see Brownstein, I.

Lerner, Norbert, jt. auth. see Sobel, Max A.

Lerner, Norbert, jt. auth. see Sobel, Max A.

Lerner, Peter M. Famous Chess Players. LC 72-3593. (Pull Ahead Bks.). (Illus.). 96p. (gr. 6-11). 1973. PLB 4.95g (ISBN 0-8225-0466-9). Lerner Pubns.

Lerner, Richard M. Concepts & Theories of Human Development. LC 75-12098. 1976. text ed. 20.95 (ISBN 0-201-04342-4). A-W.

Lerner, Richard M. & Hultsch, David F. Human Development: A Life-Span Perspective. (Illus.). 688p. 1983. text ed. 24.95x (ISBN 0-07-037216-0, C); instructor's manual 16.95 (ISBN 0-07-037217-9). McGraw.

Lerner, Richard M. & Spanier, Graham B. Adolescent Development. (Illus.). 1980. text ed. 23.00 (ISBN 0-07-037186-5); instructor's manual 21.95 (ISBN 0-07-037187-3). McGraw.

Lerner, Richard M., ed. Developmental Psychology: Historical & Philosophical Perspectives. 288p. 1983. text ed. 24.95 (ISBN 0-89859-247-X). L Erlbaum Assocs.

Lerner, Robert E. The Heresy of the Free Spirit in the Later Middle Ages. LC 78-145790. 1972. 36.50x (ISBN 0-520-01908-3). U of Cal Pr.

--The Powers of Prophecy: The Cedar of Lebanon Vision from the Mongol Onslaught to the Dawn of the Enlightenment. LC 82-4824. 256p. 1983. text ed. 32.50x (ISBN 0-520-04461-4). U of Cal Pr.

Lerner, Sharon. I Found a Leaf. LC 64-25679. (Nature Bks for Young Readers). (Illus.). (gr. k-5). 1967. PLB 4.95g (ISBN 0-8225-0251-8). Lerner Pubns.
--I Like Vegetables. LC 67-15698. (Nature Bks for Young Readers). (Illus.). (gr. k-5). 1967. PLB 4.95g (ISBN 0-8225-0260-7). Lerner Pubns.
--I Picked a Flower. LC 67-15699. (Nature Bks for Young Readers). (Illus.). (gr. k-5). 1967. PLB 4.95g (ISBN 0-8225-0261-5). Lerner Pubns.
--Making Jewelry. LC 76-13066. (Early Craft Bks.). (gr. k-3). 1977. PLB 3.95g (ISBN 0-8225-0862-1). Lerner Pubns.
--Places of Musical Fame. LC 62-20803. (Musical Books for Young People Ser.). (gr. 5-11). 1962. PLB 3.95g (ISBN 0-8225-0055-8). Lerner Pubns.
--Self-Portrait in Art. LC 64-8202. (Fine Art Books). (Illus.). (gr. 5-11). 1965. PLB 4.95g (ISBN 0-8225-0154-6). Lerner Pubns.
--Who Will Wake up Spring? LC 67-15700. (General Juvenile Bks). (Illus.). (gr. k-3). 1967. PLB 3.95g (ISBN 0-8225-0262-3). Lerner Pubns.
Lerner, Warren. A History of Socialism & Communism in Modern Times: Theorists, Activities & Humanists. 400p. (Orig.). 1982. pap. 12.95 reference (ISBN 0-13-392183-2). P-H.
Leroe, Ellen. Single Bed Blues. Fitzgerald, Elisa B., ed. 72p. 1982. pap. 5.95 o.p. (ISBN 0-913024-12-0). Tandem Pr.
LeRoi, David. The Aquarium. 6.50x (ISBN 0-392-06613-0, LTB). Sportshelf.
--Budgerigars, Canaries & Other Cage Birds. Date not set. 6.50x o.p. (ISBN 0-392-13917-0, SpS). Sportshelf.
Leroi-Gourhan, Andre. The Dawn of European Art: An Introduction to Palaeolithic Cave Painting. LC 81-21715. (The Imprint of Man Ser.). (Illus.). 144p. 1982. 19.95 (ISBN 0-521-24459-5). Cambridge U Pr.
Le Roux, J. H., jt. ed. see Coetzer, P. W.
Leroux, Michele, jt. auth. see Logan, Gerald E.
Le Roy. Evangelismo En Accion. Pierson, Carlos C., tr. 144p. 1979. 4.95 (ISBN 0-311-13831-4). Casa Bautista.
Le Roy, Bruce, ed. see Chittenden, Hiram Martin.
LeRoy, Gen. Billy's Shoes. Higginbottom, J. Winslow, tr. (Illus.). (gr. 1-3). 1981. 9.95 (ISBN 0-07-037201-2). McGraw.
--Hotheads. LC 76-41519. (gr. 5 up). 1977. 6.95 o.p. (ISBN 0-06-023786-4, HarpJ); PLB 9.89 o.p. (ISBN 0-06-023787-2). Har-Row.
--Lucky Stiff! (Illus.). 48p. (gr. 1-3). 1981. 9.95 (ISBN 0-07-037203-9). McGraw.
LeRoy, Lauren, et al. Deliberations & Compromise: The Health Professions Educational Assistance Act of 1976. LC 77-8966. 1977. prof ref 25.00 (ISBN 0-88410-149-5). Ballinger Pub.
Leroy, Maurice. Main Trends in Modern Linguistics. Price, Glanville, tr. from Fr. LC 81-20302. xi, 155p. 1982. Repr. of 1967 ed. lib. bdg. 19.25x (ISBN 0-313-23407-8, LEMAT). Greenwood.
Leroy, Pierre. Letters from My Friend Teilhard De Chardin. Lucas, Mary, tr. from Fr. LC 80-81883. (Illus.). 224p. 1980. 10.95; pap. 6.95 (ISBN 0-8091-2292-8). Paulist Pr.
Leroy-Beaulieu, P. La Travail des Femmes au Nineteenth Siecle. (Conditions of the 19th Century French Working Class Ser.). 464p. (Fr.). 1974. Repr. of 1873 ed. lib. bdg. 116.00 o.p. (ISBN 0-8287-0538-0, 1099). Clearwater Pub.
Le Roy-Ladurie, Emmanuel. The Mind & Method of the Historian. Reynolds, Sian & Reynolds, Ben, trs. LC 81-449. 224p. 1981. 21.00 (ISBN 0-226-47326-0). U of Chicago Pr.
--The Territory of the Historian. LC 78-31362. 1979. Repr. of 1973 ed. lib. bdg. 21.00 (ISBN 0-226-47327-9). U of Chicago Pr.
Le Sage, Alain R. The History & Adventures of Gil Blas of Santillane. LC 74-170537. (Foundations of the Novel Ser.: Vol. 27). Part 1. lib. bdg. 50.00 o.s.i. (ISBN 0-8240-0539-2). Garland Pub.
--The History & Adventures of Gil Blas of Santillane. LC 71-170539. (Foundations of the Novel Ser.: Vol. 28). Part 2. lib. bdg. 50.00 o.s.i. (ISBN 0-8240-0540-6). Garland Pub.
Lesage, Julia. Jean-Luc Godard: A Guide to References & Resources. 1979. lib. bdg. 45.00 (ISBN 0-8161-7925-5, Hall Reference). G K Hall.
LeSage, Laurent & Yon, Andre. Dictionnaire Des Critiques Litteraires: Guide De la Critique De la Vingtieme Siecle. LC 68-8181. (Fr.). 1969. 17.50x (ISBN 0-271-00081-3). Pa St U Pr.
Lesavoy, Malcolm A. Reconstruction of the Head & Neck. (Illus.). 334p. 1983. 47.00 (ISBN 0-683-04949-6). Williams & Wilkins.
Lesberg, Sandy. The Master Chef's Cookbook. 1981. 14.95 o.p. (ISBN 0-07-037333-7). McGraw.
--The Master Chefs Institute Guide to Dining Out in America. 1982. pap. 9.95 (ISBN 0-452-25378-0, Z5378, Plume). NAL.
Lesberg, Sandy, ed. The Master Chefs of America Recipe Book. (Illus.). 192p. 1982. 24.95 (ISBN 0-89696-141-9, An Everest House Book). Dodd.
Lesbian & Gay Media Advocates. Talk Back: The Gay Person's Guide to Media Action. 120p. 1982. pap. 3.95 (ISBN 0-932870-10-4). Alyson Pubns.
Lesburg, Sandy. Sandy Lesburg's One Hundred Great Restaurants of America. Michaelman, Herbert, ed. (Illus.). 1981. 12.95 o.p. (ISBN 0-517-53988-8, Michaelman Books). Crown.
Lesch, Michael, intro. by. Current Concepts in Cardiology. (Illus.). 121p. (Orig.). 1979. pap. text ed. 6.00 (ISBN 0-910133-03-4). MA Med Soc.
Lesch, Mosely. Political Perceptions of the Palestinians on the West Bank & Gaza. pap. 3.00 (ISBN 0-686-95357-6). Am Fr Serv Comm.
Leschonski, K. & Carter, F. T., eds. Elsevier's Dictionary of Particle Technology. (Ger. & Eng.). 1978. 68.00 (ISBN 0-444-41746-X). Elsevier.
Lesconvel, Pierre De. Relation du Prince de Montmeraud dans l'Ile de Naudely. (Utopias in the Enlightenment Ser.). 351p. (Fr.). 1974. Repr. of 1706 ed. lib. bdg. 91.00x o.p. (ISBN 0-8287-0539-9, 001). Clearwater Pub.
LeShan, Eda. On Living Your Life. 1982. 11.49i (ISBN 0-06-014958-2). Har-Row.
--What Makes Me Feel This Way: Growing up with Human Emotions. LC 71-165573. (Illus.). 128p. (gr. 3-6). 1974. pap. 2.95 (ISBN 0-02-044340-4, Collier). Macmillan.
Leshan, Eda J. Natural Parenthood. 1970. pap. 1.95 (ISBN 0-451-11192-3, Pub. by NAL). Formur Intl.
LeShan, Lawrence. How to Meditate: Guide to Self-Discovery. 2.95 o.p. (ISBN 0-686-92352-9, 6467). Hazelden.
--You Can Fight for Your Life. 1978. pap. 1.95 o.s.i. (ISBN 0-515-04502-0). Jove Pubns.
Lesher, Stephen, jt. auth. see Schwartz, Bernard.
Leshin, Geraldine. Equal Employment Opportunity & Affirmative Action in Labor-Management Relations: A Primer (Consolidated Edition) 557p. 1979. pap. text ed. 20.00 (ISBN 0-89215-107-2). U Cal LA Indus Rel.
--Report on Equal Employment Opportunity & Affirmative Action, 1980: The Roots Grow Deeper. 526p. 1980. pap. text ed. 20.00 (ISBN 0-89215-110-2). U Cal LA Indus Rel.
Leshing, Sophia, jt. auth. see Mattson, Marylu.
Leshner, Alan I. Introduction to Behavioral Endocrinology. (Illus.). 1978. text ed. 19.95x (ISBN 0-19-502266-1); pap. text ed. 9.95x (ISBN 0-19-502267-X). Oxford U Pr.
Le Sieg, Theodore. Come Over to My House. LC 66-10686. (Illus.). (gr. k-3). 1966. 3.95 o.p. (ISBN 0-394-80044-3); PLB 5.99 (ISBN 0-394-90044-8). Beginner.
--I Wish I Had Duck Feet. LC 65-21211. (Illus.). (gr. k-3). 1965. 4.95 (ISBN 0-394-80040-0); PLB 5.99 (ISBN 0-394-90040-5). Beginner.
Lesikar, Raymond V. How to Write a Report Your Boss Will Read & Remember. LC 74-10902. 216p. 1974. 12.95 (ISBN 0-87094-078-3). Dow Jones-Irwin.
--How to Write a Report Your Boss Will Read & Remember. 212p. 1983. pap. 6.95 (ISBN 0-87094-414-2). Dow Jones-Irwin.
Lesk, Arthur. Introduction to Physical Chemistry. (Illus.). 784p. 1982. text ed. 30.95 (ISBN 0-13-492710-9). P-H.
--Introduction to Physical Chemistry: Solutions manual. 100p. 1983. pap. 11.95 (ISBN 0-13-492728-1). P-H.
Lesko, Leonard H. The Ancient Egyptian Book of Two Ways. (California Library Reprint Ser.). 1978. 23.00x (ISBN 0-520-03514-3). U of Cal Pr.
Lesko, Leonard H., ed. Dictionary of Late Egyptian, Vol. 1 of 3 Vols. 1982. lib. bdg. 35.00x (ISBN 0-930548-03-5); pap. text ed. 20.00x (ISBN 0-930548-04-3). B C Scribe.
Lesko, Matthew. How to Get Free Tax Help. 192p. 1983. pap. 2.95 (ISBN 0-553-22936-2). Bantam.
--Information U. S. A. 1224p. 1983. pap. 19.95 (ISBN 0-14-046564-2). Penguin.
--Information U. S. A. 1983. 41.75 (ISBN 0-670-39823-3). Viking Pr.
Leskov, Nikolai S. The Cathedral Folk. Hapgood, Isabel F., tr. from Rus. LC 75-110855. 439p. Repr. of 1924 ed. lib. bdg. 19.75x (ISBN 0-8371-4522-8, LECF). Greenwood.
--The Enchanted Pilgrim & Other Stories. Magarshack, David, tr. from Rus. LC 76-23886. (Classics of Russian Literature). 1977. 12.50 (ISBN 0-88355-497-6); pap. o.p. (ISBN 0-88355-498-4). Hyperion Conn.
Lesky, Albin. Greek Tragic Poetry. LC 82-1886. 528p. 1983. text ed. 50.00x (ISBN 0-300-02647-1). Yale U Pr.
--History of Greek Literature. LC 65-25033. 1966. 22.07i (ISBN 0-690-38372-X). T Y Crowell.
Leslie, A. & Willson, Jeanne, eds. A Tribute to Hermann Weigand. 144p. 1982. pap. 9.95 (ISBN 0-911173-00-5). Dimension Pr.
Leslie, Charles, ed. Asian Medical Systems: A Comparative Study. LC 73-91674. 1976. 30.00x (ISBN 0-520-02680-2); pap. 10.95x (ISBN 0-520-03511-9). U of Cal Pr.
Leslie, Charles, ed. see Rodwin, Victor G.
Leslie, Charles M. Now We Are Civilized: A Study of the World View of the Zapotec Indians of Mitla, Oaxaca. LC 81-14. (Illus.). xi, 108p. 1981. Repr. of 1960 ed. lib. bdg. 20.00x (ISBN 0-313-22847-7, LENW). Greenwood.
Leslie, D. C. Developments in the Theory of Turbulence. (Illus.). 388p. 1983. pap. 27.50 (ISBN 0-19-856161-X). Oxford u Pr.
Leslie, Elizabeth M., jt. auth. see Leslie, Gerald R.
Leslie, Gerald R. & Leslie, Elizabeth M. Marriage in a Changing World. 2nd ed. LC 79-16195. 1980. text ed. 21.95x (ISBN 0-471-05593-X). study guide 8.95 (ISBN 0-471-06104-2); tchrs' manual 9.95 (ISBN 0-471-06271-5). Wiley.
Leslie, Gerald R., jt. auth. see Horton, Paul B.
Leslie, John F., et al. Core Mathematics. 2nd ed. 1980. pap. text ed. 14.50x (ISBN 0-673-15320-7). Scott F.
Leslie, John K. Spanish for Conversation. 4th ed. LC 75-3774. 1976. text ed. 21.95 (ISBN 0-471-52810-2); tchrs' manual 7.00x (ISBN 0-471-01417-6); wkbk. 9.50x (ISBN 0-471-52811-0); tapes o.s.i. 3.00 (ISBN 0-471-01841-4). Wiley.
Leslie, Julian C., jt. auth. see Millenson, J. R.
Leslie, Kathy, ed. Special Education. rev. ed. (Special Education Ser.). (Illus.). 1979. pap. text ed. 15.00 (ISBN 0-89568-120-X). Spec Learn Corp.
Leslie, L. A. & Zoubek, C. E. Gregg Shorthand1, Series 90: A Gregg Text-Kit in Continuing Education. 1983. 18.95x (ISBN 0-07-037769-3, G). McGraw.
--Gregg Shorthand2, Series 90: A Gregg Text-Kit in Continuing Education. 1983. 18.95x (ISBN 0-07-037770-7, G). McGraw.
Leslie, L. Et Al & Zoubek, C. Gregg Shorthand for Colleges, Transcription. 2nd ed. LC 79-11916. (Series 90). (Illus.). 448p. 1980. text ed. 19.60 (ISBN 0-07-037760-X, G); instructor's manual 6.50 (ISBN 0-07-037764-2); wkbk. 7.85 (ISBN 0-07-037762-6); key to wkbk. 4.15 (ISBN 0-07-037763-4); student's trans. 6.45 (ISBN 0-07-037761-8). McGraw.
Leslie, Louis A. Twenty Thousand Words. 7th ed. LC 77-71178. 1977. 6.95 (ISBN 0-07-037392-2, G); text ed. 5.48 (ISBN 0-07-037393-0). McGraw.
Leslie, Louis A. & Coffin, Kenneth B. Handbook for the Legal Secretary: Diamond Jubilee Series. 1968. 22.00 (ISBN 0-07-037277-2, G); pap. 4.95 (ISBN 0-07-037279-9). McGraw.
Leslie, Louis A. & Zoubek, Charles E. Dictation for Mailable Transcripts. 1950. 19.85 (ISBN 0-07-037236-5, G). McGraw.
--Dictation for Transcription. (Diamond Jubilee Ser). 1963. 18.60 (ISBN 0-07-037315-9, G). McGraw.
--Dictation for Transcription. 2nd ed. (Diamond Jubilee Ser). 1972. 18.60 (ISBN 0-07-037248-9, G). McGraw.
--Gregg Shorthand: A Gregg Text-Kit in Continuing Education, 2 bks. (Diamond Jubilee Ser.). 1965. Bk. 1. 16.50 (ISBN 0-07-037225-X, G); Bk. 2. 17.05 (ISBN 0-07-037227-6). McGraw.
--Gregg Shorthand, Functional Method. (Diamond Jubilee Ser). 1963. text ed. 14.92 (ISBN 0-07-037310-8, G); wkbk. 6.12 (ISBN 0-07-037308-6). McGraw.
--Gregg Shorthand Functional Method. 2nd ed. (Diamond Jubilee Ser). 1971. text ed. 14.32 (ISBN 0-07-037255-1, G); instr's handbk. 5.50 (ISBN 0-07-037256-X); wkbk. 6.12 (ISBN 0-07-037250-0); key to wkbk. 3.90 (ISBN 0-07-037251-9). McGraw.
--Gregg Shorthand Theory Presentation Booklet. (Diamond Jubilee Ser). 1971. 6.40 (ISBN 0-07-037247-0, G). McGraw.
--Gregg Transcription. 2nd ed. (Diamond Jubilee Ser). 1971. 14.52 (ISBN 0-07-037262-4, G); instructor's handbk 5.25 (ISBN 0-07-037263-2); wkbk. 6.32 (ISBN 0-07-037265-9); key to wkbk. 5.65 (ISBN 0-07-037266-7); student's transcript 5.52 (ISBN 0-07-037264-0). McGraw.
--Transcription Dictation. 1956. 19.60 (ISBN 0-07-037276-4, G). McGraw.
Leslie, Louis A. Twenty-Thousand Words. 282p. 1972. 3.95 o.p. (ISBN 0-07-037340-X, GB). McGraw.
Leslie, Louis A., et al. Gregg Dictation & Transcription: Individual Progress Method. (Diamond Jubilee Ser, Kit 2). 1974. 26.75 (ISBN 0-07-037249-7, G). McGraw.
--Gregg Dictation: Diamond Jubilee Series. 1963. text ed. 13.96 (ISBN 0-07-037305-1, G); instructor's handbk 4.85 (ISBN 0-07-037307-8); student transcript 5.32 (ISBN 0-07-037306-X); wkbk. 6.12 (ISBN 0-07-037309-4) (ISBN 0-07-037312-4). McGraw.
--Gregg Dictation: Diamond Jubilee Series. 2nd ed. 1970. text ed. 14.32 (ISBN 0-07-037257-8, G); instructor's handbk 5.50 (ISBN 0-07-037258-6); student transcript 5.32 (ISBN 0-07-037259-4); wkbk 6.12 (ISBN 0-07-037260-8); key to wkbk 4.05 (ISBN 0-07-037261-6); tapes avail. McGraw.
--Gregg Notehand. 2nd ed. 1968. text ed. 15.44 (ISBN 0-07-037331-0, G); instructor's guide 6.05 (ISBN 0-07-037338-8); exercises 7.28 (ISBN 0-07-037343-4); inst. key to exercises 6.05 (ISBN 0-07-037344-2). McGraw.
--Gregg Shorthand for Colleges, Transcription. (Diamond Jubilee Ser). 21.80 (ISBN 0-07-037425-2, G); instructor's handbk. 6.45 (ISBN 0-07-037429-5); wkbk. 7.85 (ISBN 0-07-037427-9); key to wkbk. 4.60 (ISBN 0-07-037428-7); student transcript 7.15 (ISBN 0-07-037426-0). McGraw.
--Gregg Shorthand, Individual Progress Method. (Diamond Jubilee Ser Kit 1). 1972, 26.75 (ISBN 0-07-037233-0, G). McGraw.
--College Dictation for Transcription. (Diamond Jubilee Ser). 384p. 1974. 18.00 (ISBN 0-07-037430-9, G). McGraw.
--Gregg Shorthand for Colleges, Vol. 1. 2nd ed. (Diamond Jubilee Ser.). (Illus.). 352p. 1973. text ed. 21.80 (ISBN 0-07-037401-5, G); instructor's handbk. 5.25 (ISBN 0-07-037404-X); wkbk. 7.85 (ISBN 0-07-037403-1); key to wkbk. 4.60 (ISBN 0-07-037405-8); student transcript 7.15 (ISBN 0-07-037402-3). McGraw.
--Gregg Shorthand for Colleges, Vol. 1. (Series 90). 1980. text ed. 21.80 (ISBN 0-07-037749-9, G); tchr ed 6.50 (ISBN 0-07-037753-7); wkbk 7.85 (ISBN 0-07-037751-0); key 4.70 (ISBN 0-07-037752-9); transcript 7.15 (ISBN 0-07-037750-2). McGraw.
--Gregg Shorthand for Colleges, Vol. 2. 2nd ed. (Diamond Jubilee Ser.). (Illus.). 448p. 1973. text ed. 21.80 (ISBN 0-07-037406-6, G); instr's. handbk. 6.25 (ISBN 0-07-037409-0); wkbk. 7.85 (ISBN 0-07-037408-2); key to wkbk. 4.50 (ISBN 0-07-037410-4); o.p. tapes (ISBN 0-07-086345-8); student transcript 7.15 (ISBN 0-07-037407-4); o.p. cassettes (ISBN 0-07-087615-0). McGraw.
--Gregg Shorthand for Colleges, Vol. 2. (Series 90). 1980. text ed. 21.80 (ISBN 0-07-037754-5, G); instructor's handbook 6.50 (ISBN 0-07-037758-8); wkbk 7.85 (ISBN 0-07-037756-1); key to wkbk. 4.70 (ISBN 0-07-037757-X); transcript 7.15 (ISBN 0-07-037755-3); self checks 5.00 (ISBN 0-07-037775-8). McGraw.
--Gregg Speed Building. (Series 90). 1979. text ed. 14.92 (ISBN 0-07-024476-6, G); instructor's handbook 5.75 (ISBN 0-07-024480-4); wkbk. 6.32 (ISBN 0-07-024478-2); student's transcript 5.64 (ISBN 0-07-024477-4); key to wkbk. 5.70 (ISBN 0-07-024479-0). McGraw.
--Gregg Transcription. (Series 90). 1979. text ed. 14.92 (ISBN 0-07-037740-5, G); instructor's handbook 5.30 (ISBN 0-07-037744-8); wkbk. 6.48 (ISBN 0-07-037742-1); student's transcript 5.52 (ISBN 0-07-037741-3); key to wkbk. 5.72 (ISBN 0-07-037743-X). McGraw.
Leslie, Louise. Tazewell County. LC 81-69331. 768p. 1982. 35.00 (ISBN 0-89227-043-8). Commonwealth Pr.
Leslie, R. F. History of Poland Since Eighteen Sixty-Three. LC 78-73246. (Soviet & East European Studies). 528p. 1980. 54.50 (ISBN 0-521-22645-7). Cambridge U Pr.
Leslie, R. F., ed. The Wanderer. (Old & Middle English Text Ser.). 1966. pap. 5.00 (ISBN 0-7190-0120-X). Manchester.
Leslie, R. F., ed. see Layamon.
Leslie, Robert F. In the Shadow of a Rainbow: The True Story of a Friendship Between Man & Wolf. (RL 7). 1975. pap. 1.75 o.p. (ISBN 0-451-09110-8, E9110, Sig). NAL.
Leslie, Rochelle. Tears of Passion, Tears of Shame. 384p. (Orig.). 1980. pap. 2.25 o.s.i. (ISBN 0-515-05445-3). Jove Pubns.
Leslie, Serge. A Bibliography of the Dance Collection of Doris Niles & Serge Leslie: A-Z, Pt. 4. 283p. 1981. 28.50 (ISBN 0-903102-56-0). Princeton Bk Co.
Leslie, Stuart W. Boss Kettering. (Illus.). 416p. 1983. 19.95 (ISBN 0-231-05600-1). Columbia U Pr.
Leslie, William C. The Physical Metallurgy of Steels. (M-H Materials Science & Engineering Ser.). 368p. 1981. text ed. 36.50 (ISBN 0-07-037780-4). McGraw.
Leslie-Melville, Betty, jt. auth. see Leslie-Melville, Jock.
Leslie-Melville, Jock & Leslie-Melville, Betty. Bagamoyo. 384p. 1983. 14.95 (ISBN 0-688-00814-3). Morrow.
Lesly, Philip. Lesly's Public Relations Handbook. 3rd ed. 557p. 1978. 29.95 (ISBN 0-13-530741-4, Busn). P-H.
Lesner, Patricia A. Pediatric Nursing. LC 81-82910. (Illus.). 544p. (Orig.). 1982. pap. text ed. 19.80 (ISBN 0-8273-1932-0); 2.00 (ISBN 0-8273-1933-9). Delmar.
Lesniak, Rose. Throwing Spitballs at the Nuns. (Illus.). 12p. (Orig.). 1982. pap. 7.50 o.p. (ISBN 0-915124-54-8). Toothpaste.
Lesnikowski, W. Rationalism & Romanticism in Architecture: A Selected Inquiry into the Nature of Both Trends. 1982. write for info. (ISBN 0-07-037417-1); pap. 19.95 (ISBN 0-07-037416-3). McGraw.
Lesnoff-Caravaglia, Gari, ed. Perspectives on Aging. 141p. 1977. pap. text ed. 7.95x (ISBN 0-686-84084-4). Irvington.
--The World of the Older Woman. (Frontiers in Aging Ser.: Vol. III). 176p. 1983. 19.95 (ISBN 0-89885-089-4). Human Sci Pr.
Lesnoff-Caravaglia, Gari, ed. see Pitskhelauri, G. Z.
Le Sourd, Leonard, jt. auth. see Marshall, Catherine.
LeSourd, Leonard, jt. auth. see Marshall, Catherine.
Lesourne. Cost Benefit Analysis & Economic Theory. LC 74-84213. (Studies in Mathematical & Managerial Economics: Vol. 19). 521p. 1975. pap. 53.75 (ISBN 0-444-10804-1, North Holland); cloth 57.50 (ISBN 0-7204-3097-6). Elsevier.
Lesowitz, Robert I. Rules for Raising Kids. (Illus.). 200p. 1974. pap. 19.75x spiral (ISBN 0-398-03146-0). C C Thomas.
Less, Menaham & Colverd, Edward C. Hand Controls & Assistive Devices For The Physically Disabled Driver. (Illus.). 60p. 1977. 5.00 (ISBN 0-686-38804-6). Human Res Ctr.

Less, Menahem & Colverd, Edward C. Evaluating Driving Potential of Persons With Physical Disabilities. LC 78-62052. (Illus.). 36p. 1978. 4.25 (ISBN 0-686-38803-8). Human Res Ctr.

Less, Menahem, jt. auth. see Colverd, Edward C.

Lessa, W. A. Appraisal of Constitutional Typologies. LC 44-4905. 1943. pap. 10.00 (ISBN 0-527-00561-4). Kraus Repr.

Lessa, William A. Drake's Island of Thieves: Ethnological Sleuthing. LC 74-81140. (Illus.). 320p. 1975. 14.00x (ISBN 0-8248-0333-7). UH Pr.

--More Tales from Ulithi Atoll. (U. C. Publications in Folklore & Mythology Studies: Vol. 32). 1980. pap. 16.50x (ISBN 0-520-09615-0). U of Cal Pr.

Lessac, Arthur. Body Wisdom: The Use & Training of the Human Body. 342p. (Orig.). 1981. text ed. 16.95x (ISBN 0-89676-070-7); pap. text ed. 12.50 (ISBN 0-89676-031-6). Drama Bk.

--Use & Training of the Human Voice: A Practical Approach to Speech & Voice Dynamics. LC 67-28352. (Illus.). 320p. 1967. pap. text ed. 12.50x (ISBN 0-89676-072-3). Drama Bk.

Lessard, Donald, ed. International Financial Management Theory & Application. LC 79-501. 626p. 1979. pap. text ed. 13.95 o.p. (ISBN 0-88262-344-3). Warren.

Lessard, Donald R. International Financial Management: Theory & Application. LC 79-501. 626p. 1982. text ed. 18.95 (ISBN 0-471-87747-6). Wiley.

Lessard, Victoria C., jt. auth. see Hall, Jack.

Lessard-Bissonette, Camille. Canuck. (Novels by Franco-Americans in New England 1850-1940 Ser.). 119p. (Fr.). (gr. 10 up). 1980. pap. 4.50x (ISBN 0-911409-19-X). Natl Mat Dev.

Lessel. Neuro-Ophthalmology: Annual 1 (1980) 1980. 81.00 (ISBN 0-444-90143-4). Elsevier.

Lessell, S. & Van Dalen, J. T., eds. Neuro-Ophthalmology, 1982, Annual 2. 430p. 1982. 81.00 (ISBN 0-444-90210-4). Elsevier.

Lessem, Don. Aerphobics: The Scientific Way to Stop Exercising. LC 80-13489. (Illus.). 128p. 1980. 8.95 o.p. (ISBN 0-688-03663-5, Quill); pap. 3.95 o.p. (ISBN 0-688-08663-2, Quill). Morrow.

Lesser, Alexander. The Pawnee Ghost Dance Hand Game: A Study of Cultural Change. LC 79-82340. (Illus.). 368p. 1978. 22.50 (ISBN 0-299-07480-3); pap. 8.95 (ISBN 0-299-07484-6). U of Wis Pr.

Lesser, M. X. Jonathan Edwards: A Reference Guide. 1981. lib. bdg. 35.00 (ISBN 0-8161-7837-2, Hall Reference). G K Hall.

Lesser, M. X. & Morris, J. N. Modern Short Stories: The Fiction of Experience. 1962. pap. 16.50 (ISBN 0-07-037336-1, C); teacher's manual 20.00 (ISBN 0-07-037334-5). McGraw.

Lesser, Rika. Etruscan Things. LC 82-12824. (Braziller Series of Poetry). (Illus.). 96p. 1983. 10.95 (ISBN 0-8076-1059-3); pap. 4.95. Braziller.

Lesser, Rika, tr. see Ekelof, Gunnar.

Lesser, Rika, tr. see Hesse, Hermann.

Lesser, Stephen, jt. ed. see Morsberger, Robert.

Lessin, Roy. Como Criar Hijos Felices y Obedientes. 160p. Date not set. 2.25 (ISBN 0-88113-037-0). Edit Betania.

--Como Disciplinar a Tus Hijos. 96p. Date not set. 1.75 (ISBN 0-88113-032-X). Edit Betania.

--How to Be Parents of Happy Obedient Children. 1978. 8.95 (ISBN 0-89728-003-2, 702120); pap. 4.95 (ISBN 0-686-67298-4). Omega Pubns OR.

Lessing, Doris. Briefing for a Descent into Hell. 1971. 2.95 (ISBN 0-394-74662-7). Knopf.

--Documents Relating to the Sentimental Agents in the Volyen Empire. LC 82-48744. 1983. 12.95 (ISBN 0-394-52968-5). Knopf.

--Golden Notebook. 1962. 19.95 o.p. (ISBN 0-671-28770-2). S&S.

--The Grass Is Singing. 1976. pap. 4.95 (ISBN 0-452-25347-0, Z5347, Plume). NAL.

--Habit of Loving. 320p. 1974. Repr. of 1957 ed. 10.53i (ISBN 0-690-00501-6). T Y Crowell.

--The Making of the Representative for Planet Eight: Canopus in Argos: Archives. LC 82-40422. (Canopus Ser.). 160p. 1983. pap. 4.95 (ISBN 0-394-71377-X, Vin). Random.

--Martha Quest: A Complete Novel from Doris Lessing's Masterwork, Children of Violence. 1970. pap. 4.95 (ISBN 0-452-25353-5, Z5353, Plume). NAL.

--Re: Colonized Planet 5-Shikasta. LC 81-40194. 384p. 1981. pap. 5.95 (ISBN 0-394-74977-4, Vin). Random.

--The Summer Before Dark. LC 82-40421. 256p. 1983. pap. 3.95 (ISBN 0-394-71095-9, Vin). Random.

Lessing, F. D. Mongolian-English Dictionary. LC 60-14517. 1220p. 1982. Repr. of 1960 ed. 55.00x (ISBN 0-910980-40-3). Mongolia.

Lessiter, Frank D. Horsepower. LC 76-45044. 1977. 9.95 (ISBN 0-89821-018-6). Reiman Assocs.

Lessof, M. H. Clinical Reations to Food. 1983. 17.50 (ISBN 0-471-10436-1, Pub. by Wiley Med). Wiley.

LesStrong, Jacques. Seaway. LC 76-2471. (Illus.). 1976. 14.95 o.p. (ISBN 0-87564-216-0). Superior Pub.

Lester & Levy. Jacob Epstein. LC 78-50724. Date not set. price not set casebound o.s.i. (ISBN 0-916526-05-4). Maran Pub.

Lester, Andrew D. Coping with Your Anger: A Christian Guide. LC 82-24730. 120p. 1983. pap. 5.95 (ISBN 0-664-24471-8). Westminster.

Lester, Barry M., jt. ed. see Fitzgerald, Hiram E.

Lester, Charles E. Artists of America: A Series of Biographical Sketches of American Artists. LC 68-8689. (American Art Ser). (Illus.). 1969. Repr. of 1846 ed. lib. bdg. 32.50 (ISBN 0-306-71169-9). Da Capo.

Lester, Colin, ed. The International Science Fiction Yearbook. (Illus.). 1978. pap. 7.95 o.p. (ISBN 0-8256-3121-1, Quick Fox). Putnam Pub Group.

Lester, David. A Physiological Basis for Personality Traits: A New Theory of Personality. (Illus.). 138p. 1974. photocopy ed. spiral 13.75x (ISBN 0-398-03078-2). C C Thomas.

--Quarrying & Rockbreaking: The Operation & Maintenance of Mobile Processing Plants. (Illus.). 117p. 1981. 13.50x (ISBN 0-903031-80-9, Pub. by Intermediate Tech England). Intermediate Tech.

--The Structure of the Mind: An Analysis of Intrapsychic Theories of Personality. LC 81-40936. 190p. (Orig.). 1982. lib. bdg. 22.00 (ISBN 0-8191-2217-3); pap. text ed. 10.00 (ISBN 0-8191-2218-1). U Pr of Amer.

--Why People Kill Themselves: A 1980's Summary of Research Findings on Suicidal Behavior. 110p. 1983. text ed. price not set (ISBN 0-398-04826-6). C C Thomas.

Lester, David, jt. auth. see Murrell, Mary.

Lester, David, et al, eds. Suicide: A Guide to Information Sources. LC 80-71. (Social Issues & Social Problems Information Guide Ser.: Vol. 3). 42.00x (ISBN 0-8103-1415-0). Gale.

Lester, Elenore. Wallenberg-The Man in the Iron Web. LC 81-21161. 183p. 1982. 12.95 (ISBN 0-13-944322-3). P-H.

Lester, Helen. The Wizard, the Fairy & the Magic Chicken. LC 82-21302. (Illus.). 32p. (gr. k-3). 1983. pap. text ed. 9.95 (ISBN 0-395-33885-9). HM.

Lester, J. C. & Wilson, D. L. Ku Klux Klan. LC 71-114758. (Civil Liberties in Amer. History Ser.). (Illus.). 208p. 1973. Repr. of 1905 ed. lib. bdg. 29.50 (ISBN 0-306-71927-4). Da Capo.

Lester, James D. Writing Research Papers: A Complete Guide. 3rd ed. 1980. pap. text ed. 5.50x (ISBN 0-673-15327-4). Scott F.

Lester, James P. & Bowman, Ann, eds. The Responsible Management of Hazardous Waste. (Duke Press Policy Studies). 300p. (Orig.). Date not set. text ed. 30.00 (ISBN 0-8223-0507-0); pap. text ed. 10.00 (ISBN 0-8223-0523-2). Duke.

Lester, Julius. Look Out Whitey! Black Power's Gon Get Your Mama! 1969. pap. 1.95 o.s.i. (ISBN 0-394-17139-X, B197, BC). Grove.

Lester, Katherine, et al. Historic Costume. rev. ed. (gr. 10-12). 1977. text ed. 15.88 (ISBN 0-87002-174-5). Bennett IL.

Lester, Lane P. & Hefley, James C. Cloning: Miracle or Menace. pap. 4.95 (ISBN 0-8423-0294-8). Tyndale.

Lester, Richard. Anti-Bias Regulations of Universities. 168p. Repr. 5.95 o.p. (ISBN 0-686-95016-X). ADL.

Lester, Robert C. Theravada Buddhism in Southeast Asia. LC 71-185154. 1973. 5.95 (ISBN 0-472-06184-4). U of Mich Pr.

Lester, Samantha. The Duke's Ward. (Orig.). 1980. pap. 1.50 o.s.i. (ISBN 0-440-11925-1). Dell.

Lester, Teri, jt. auth. see Nichols, Pamela.

Lester-Massman, Gordon. Worker's Lament. 16p. 1982. pap. 1.00 (ISBN 0-686-37940-3). Samisdat.

LeStourgeon, Diana E. Rosamond Lehmann. (English Authors Ser.). 14.95 (ISBN 0-8057-1324-7, Twayne). G K Hall.

LeStrange, Guy. Baghdad during the Abbasid Caliphate: From Contemporary Arabic & Persian Sources. LC 82-25143. xxxi, 381p. 1983. Repr. of 1942 ed. lib. bdg. 65.00x (ISBN 0-313-23198-2, LEBC). Greenwood.

Le Strange, Richard. Complete Descriptive Guide to British Monumental Brasses. 1972. 7.50 o.p. (ISBN 0-500-27018-X). Transatlantic.

--A History of Herbal Plants. LC 77-3366. 1977. 15.00 o.p. (ISBN 0-668-04247-8, 4247). Arco.

Lestz, Gerald S. Baer's Agricultural Almanac, 1980. (Illus.). 1979. pap. 1.25 o.p. (ISBN 0-448-16399-3, G&D). Putnam Pub Group.

Le Sueur, Meridel. The Girl. LC 82-20021. 159p. 1982. 14.95x (ISBN 0-930656-27-X); pap. 4.50 (ISBN 0-930656-28-8). MEP Pubns.

--Harvest & Song For My Time. LC 77-14856. (Illus.). 1982. pap. 4.50 (ISBN 0-931122-27-9). West End.

--Harvest & Song for My Time. LC 82-20060. 135p. 1982. 14.95x (ISBN 0-930656-29-6); pap. 4.50 (ISBN 0-930656-30-X). MEP Pubns.

--River Road: A Story of Abraham Lincoln. (Illus.). (gr. 5 up). 1954. PLB 5.39 o.p. (ISBN 0-394-91551-8). Knopf.

Le Sueur, Meridel & Crawford, John. Worker Writers. (Worker Writer Ser.: No. 4). 32p. (Orig.). 1982. pap. 2.00 (ISBN 0-931122-07-4). West End.

Le Sueur, Sadie. Recipes, Party Plans, & Garnishes. rev. ed. 1970. 7.95 (ISBN 0-8208-0224-7). Hearthside.

Lesur. Histoire des Kosaques, 2 vols. (Nineteenth Century Russia Ser.). 842p. (Fr.). 1974. Repr. of 1814 ed. Set. lib. bdg. 212.50x o.p. (ISBN 0-8287-0541-0). Vol. 1 (R74). Vol. 2 (R75). Clearwater Pub.

--Des Progres De la Puissance Russe Depuis Son Origine Jusqu'au Commencement Du Dix-Neuvieme Siecle. (Nineteenth Century Russia Ser.). 514p. (Fr.). 1974. Repr. of 1812 ed. lib. bdg. 127.00x o.p. (ISBN 0-8287-0540-2, R73). Clearwater Pub.

Lesur, Rosalynde, jt. auth. see Putterman, Jaydie.

Lesznai, Lajos. Bartok. (Master Musicians Ser). (Illus.). 224p. 1973. 11.00x o.p. (ISBN 0-460-03136-8, Pub. by J. M. Dent England). Biblio Dist.

LeTan, Pierre. Visit to the North Pole. 1982. 7.95 (ISBN 0-517-54893-3, C N Potter). Crown.

Le-Tan, Pierre. Visit to the North Pole. (Illus.). 32p. 1983. 7.95 (ISBN 0-686-84346-0). Crown.

LeTan, Pierre. Visit with a Mermaid. 1982. 7.95 (ISBN 0-517-54894-1, C N Potter). Crown.

Le-Tan, Pierre. Visit With a Mermaid. (Illus.). 32p. 1983. 7.95 (ISBN 0-686-84347-9). Crown.

Letarouilly, Paul M. Edifices de Rome Moderne. (Illus.). 368p. 1982. Repr. of 1840 ed. 55.00 (ISBN 0-910413-00-2). Princeton Arch.

LeTarte, Clyde, jt. auth. see Minzey, Jack.

Letchworth, Beverly J. Pax & the Mutt. Schroeder, Howard, ed. LC 81-3302. (Roundup Ser.). (Illus.). 48p. (Orig.). (gr. 3 up). 1981. PLB 7.95 (ISBN 0-89686-153-8); pap. text ed. 3.95 (ISBN 0-89686-161-9). Crestwood Hse.

Letendre, Lorin, jt. auth. see Clowers, Myles L.

Leteurtre, J. & Quere, Y. Irradiation Effects in Fissile Materials. (Defects in Crystalline Solids Ser.: Vol. 6). 1972. 21.50 (ISBN 0-444-10382-1, North-Holland). Elsevier.

Leth, Pamela C. & Leth, Steven A. Public Communications. Brooks, W. D. & Vogel, R. A., eds. LC 76-44139. (Series in Speech Communication). 1977. pap. text ed. 9.95 (ISBN 0-8465-7604-X); instr's guide 4.95 (ISBN 0-8465-7607-4). Benjamin-Cummings.

Leth, Steven A., jt. auth. see Leth, Pamela C.

Letham, D. S., jt. ed. see Stewart, P. R.

Letham, D. S., et al, eds. Phytohormones & Related Compounds: A Comprehensive Treatise, 2 vols. 1979. Set. 170.25 (ISBN 0-686-96711-9, Biomedical Pr); 128.50 ea. Vol. 1: Biochemistry of Phytohormones (ISBN 0-444-80053-0). Vol. 2: Phytohormones & Development of Higher Plants (ISBN 0-444-80054-9). Elsevier.

Lethbridge, T. C. Ghost & Ghoul. 1967. pap. 4.95 o.p. (ISBN 0-7100-6191-9). Routledge & Kegan.

--The Legend of the Sons of God: A Fantasy? (Illus.). 1972. 12.00 o.p. (ISBN 0-7100-7159-0). Routledge & Kegan.

--The Legend of the Sons of God: A Fantasy? (Illus.). 128p. 1983. pap. 5.95 (ISBN 0-7100-9500-7). Routledge & Kegan.

--The Monkey's Tail: A Study in Evolution & Parapsychology. (Illus.). 1969. 12.00 o.p. (ISBN 0-7100-6598-1). Routledge & Kegan.

--The Power of the Pendulum. (Illus.). 160p. 1983. pap. 5.95 (ISBN 0-7100-9499-X). Routledge & Kegan.

Letheby, Sam. Moving Along. (Illus.). 100p. 1983. 9.95 (ISBN 0-939644-06-1). Media Prods & Mktg.

Lethem, Francis J., jt. auth. see Perrett, Heli.

Le Tirant, Pierre. Seabed Reconnaissance & Offshore Soil Mechanics for the Installation of Petroleum Structures. (Illus.). 508p. 1980. 95.00 (ISBN 0-87201-794-X). Gulf Pub.

Letman, Sloan T. Criminal Justice: The Main Issues. Bracey, Dorothy H., intro. by. LC 82-23928. 1983. lib. bdg. 15.95x (ISBN 0-89950-039-0). McFarland & Co.

--Issues in the Law of Criminal Corrections, Vol. I. 72p. 1979. softcover 6.95 o.p. (ISBN 0-932930-11-5). Pilgrimage Inc.

Letman, Sloan T., jt. auth. see Edwards, Dan W.

Letman, Sloan T., et al. Contemporary Issues in Corrections. 101p. 1981. 8.95 (ISBN 0-932930-43-3). Pilgrimage Inc.

Letolle, R., jt. ed. see Back, W.

LeTourneau, R. G. Mover of Men & Mountains: The Autobiography of R. G. LeTourneau. LC 60-8319. 1967. pap. 4.95 (ISBN 0-8024-3818-0). Moody.

Lett, John T., et al, eds. Advances in Radiation Biology. Incl. Vol. 5. 1975. 57.00 (ISBN 0-12-035405-5); lib. ed 74.00 (ISBN 0-12-035474-8); microfiche 40.00 (ISBN 0-12-035475-6); Vol. 6. 1976. 55.00 (ISBN 0-12-035406-3); lib. ed 65.00 (ISBN 0-12-035476-4); microfiche 40.00 (ISBN 0-12-035477-2). (Serial Publication). Acad Pr.

Lett, Monica. Rent Control: Concepts, Realities & Mechanisms. LC 76-18791. 1976. 17.95 o.p. (ISBN 0-88285-034-2). Ctr Urban Pol Res.

Lettau, H., et al. Air Temperature & Two-Dimensional Wind Profiles in the Lowest 32 Meters As a Function of Bulk Stability, Stability Related Wind Spiraling in the Lowest 32 Meters, & Variations of Temperature & Air Motion in the 0 to 32m Layer at Plateau Station, Antartica: Papers 6, 7, & 8 in Meteorological Studies at Plateau Station, Antarctica. Businer, Joost A., ed. (Antarctic Research Ser.: Vol. 25). 1977. pap. 13.50 (ISBN 0-87590-140-9). Am Geophysical.

Lettau, Reinhard & Ferlinghetti, Lawrence, eds. Love Poems of Karl Marx. LC 76-8200. pap. 2.00 o.s.i. (ISBN 0-87286-087-6). City Lights.

Letter, Richard. Mountain Men of Wyoming. (Wyoming Frontier Ser.). 64p. 1982. pap. 3.95 (ISBN 0-686-97819-6). Johnson Bks.

Letterman, Lester D. The Major Contemporary Political Forces & the Political Future of the World. (Illus.). 131p. 1982. 69.85 (ISBN 0-686-83072-5). Inst Econ Pol.

Letton, Francis, jt. auth. see Letton, Jennette.

Letton, Jeannette. The Robsart Affair. 268p. 1976. Repr. of 1956 ed. lib. bdg. 16.95x (ISBN 0-89244-015-5). Queens Hse.

Letton, Jennette & Letton, Francis. The Young Elizabeth. 1976. Repr. of 1953 ed. lib. bdg. 16.95x (ISBN 0-89244-014-7). Queens Hse.

Letts, Mary. Al Capone. LC 75-7633. (Illus.). 95p. (gr. 5-9). 1975. 6.95 o.p. (ISBN 0-312-01645-X). St Martin.

Lettvin, Maggie. Maggie's Woman's Book: Her Personal Plan for Health & Fitness for Women of Every Age. (Illus.). 256p. 1980. 12.95 (ISBN 0-395-29472-X); pap. 7.95 (ISBN 0-395-29758-3). HM.

Letty, L. le, ed. see IFAC.

Letwin, William. The Origins of Scientific Economics. LC 75-8721. 1975. Repr. of 1963 ed. lib. bdg. 25.00x (ISBN 0-8371-8038-4, LEOS). Greenwood.

Leuba, Walter. George Saintsbury. (English Authors Ser.: No. 56). 14.95 o.p. (ISBN 0-8057-1474-X, Twayne). G K Hall.

Leuchtenburg, William. Franklin D. Roosevelt & the New Deal, 1932-1940. (New American Nation Ser.). (Illus.). pap. 5.95xi o.p. (ISBN 0-06-133025-6, TB3025, Torch). Har-Row.

Leuchtenburg, William E. Age of Change, from Nineteen Forty-Five. LC 63-8572. (Life History of the United States). (Illus.). (gr. 5 up). 1974. lib. bdg. 10.60 (ISBN 0-8094-0522-9, Pub. by Time-Life). Silver.

--Flood Control Politics: The Connecticut River Valley Problem, 1927-1950. LC 73-38834. (FDR & the Era of the New Deal Ser.). (Illus.). 1972. Repr. of 1953 ed. lib. bdg. 39.50 (ISBN 0-306-70446-3). Da Capo.

--Franklin D. Roosevelt & the New Deal, 1932-1940. (New American Nation Ser.). (Illus.). 1963. 17.26xi (ISBN 0-06-010541-0, HarpT). Har-Row.

--New Deal & War, 1933-1945. LC 63-8572. (Life History of the United States). (Illus.). (gr. 5 up). 1974. PLB 10.60 (ISBN 0-8094-0560-1, Pub. by Time-Life). Silver.

--Perils of Prosperity: Nineteen Fourteen - Thirty Two. LC 58-5680. (Chicago History of America Civilization Ser). pap. 6.50 (ISBN 0-226-47369-4, CHAC12). U of Chicago Pr.

Leuchtenburg, William E., ed. The Unfinished Century: America Since 1900. 984p. 1973. pap. 13.95 o.p. (ISBN 0-316-52184-1). Little.

Leuchtenburg, William E., ed. see Tucker, Nancy B.

Leuchtmann, H., ed. Dictionary of Musical Terms in Seven Languages. 2nd ed. (Illus., Eng. Ger. Fr. Ital. Span. Hungarian. Russ.). 1980. 120.00 (ISBN 0-686-77981-9). Heinman.

Leuchtmann, Horst, ed. see International Association of Music Libraries & International Musicological Society.

Leukart, R. H., jt. auth. see Otis, Jay L.

Leukel, Francis P., ed. Issues in Physiological Psychology. LC 73-12703. 340p. 1974. text ed. 8.95 o.p. (ISBN 0-8016-2970-5). Mosby.

Leuner, H. D. When Compassion Was a Crime: Germany's Silent Heroes, 1933-1945. 1978. pap. text ed. 10.00x o.p. (ISBN 0-85496-138-0). Humanities.

Leung, Albert Y. Encyclopedia of Common Natural Ingredients Used in Foods, Drugs, Cosmetics & Medicine. LC 79-25998. 1980. 60.00 (ISBN 0-471-04954-9, Pub. by Wiley-Interscience). Wiley.

Leung, G. K., tr. see Chen, James.

Leung, Mai. Mai Leung's Dim Sum & other Chinese Street Food. 1982. pap. 6.68 (ISBN 0-06-090919-6, HarpT, CN-919). Har-Row.

Leung, Mariano. Dionysius "Home Sweet Home" 1983. 10.95 (ISBN 0-533-05318-8). Vantage.

Leunig, Mary. There's No Place Like Home: Drawings. 1983. pap. 6.95 (ISBN 0-14-006443-5). Penguin.

Leunig, Michael. The Penguin Leunig. (Illus.). 1983. pap. 4.95 (ISBN 0-14-004019-6). Penguin.

Leupold, Herbert C. Exposition of Zechariah. 1965. 9.95 (ISBN 0-8010-5512-1). Baker Bk.

Leuschner, J. Germany in the Late Middle Ages. (Europe in the Middle Ages: Selected Studies: Vol. 17). 250p. 1979. 51.00 (ISBN 0-444-85135-6, North Holland). Elsevier.

Leusen, Isadore, jt. ed. see Vanhoutte, Paul M.

Leute, George, jt. auth. see Keefe, John.

Leuthner, Stuart. The Railroaders. LC 81-40236. (Illus.). 160p. 1982. 19.95 (ISBN 0-394-51861-6). Random.

Leutscher, Alfred. Dinosaurs & Other Ancient Reptiles & Mammals. LC 73-154875. (Illus.). 86p. (gr. 3-7). 1975. Repr. 3.95 o.s.i. (ISBN 0-448-00365-1, G&D). Putnam Pub Group.

Leuv, John H. Van de see American College of Emergency Physicians.

Leuven, Edwin P. Van see Van Leuven, Edwin P.

Leuzzi, J. P., jt. ed. see Knauth, Christopher R.

Leuzzi, Lawrence, jt. auth. see Liang, Tung.

Lev, Baruch. Financial Statement Analysis: A New Approach. (Contemporary Topics in Accounting Ser: Foundations of Finance). (Illus.). 288p. 1974. pap. text ed. 12.95 (ISBN 0-13-316364-4). P-H.

Lev, Daniel S. Islamic Courts in Indonesia: A Study in the Political Bases of Legal Institutions. LC 78-182281. 304p. 1972. 32.50x (ISBN 0-520-02173-8). U of Cal Pr.

Lev, Maurice, jt. auth. see Bharati, Saroja.

Lev, Peter. Claude Lelouch, Film Director. LC 81-72036. (Illus.). 184p. 1982. 24.50 (ISBN 0-8386-3114-2). Fairleigh Dickinson.

Leval, Gaston. Collectives in the Spanish Revolution. Richards, Vernon, tr. from Fr. 368p. 1975. pap. 6.50 (ISBN 0-900384-10-7). Left Bank.

Levande & Koch. Marriage & the Family. 1983. 19.95 (ISBN 0-686-84655-9); supplementary materials avail. HM.

Levande, Diane I. & Koch, Joanne B. Marriage & the Family. LC 82-81562. 496p. 1982. pap. text ed. 20.95 (ISBN 0-395-32577-3); instrs.' manual avail. (ISBN 0-395-32578-1). HM.

Levander, O. A., ed. see New York Academy of Sciences, Feb 20-22, 1980.

Levandowsky, M. & Hunter, S. H., eds. Biochemistry & Physiology of Protozoa, Vol. 4. 2nd ed. 1980. 58.00 (ISBN 0-12-444604-3); subscription price 49.50 (ISBN 0-12-444604-3). Acad Pr.

Levandowsky, Michael & Hutner, S. H., eds. Biochemistry & Physiology of Protozoa, Vol. 2. 2nd ed. 1979. 55.00 (ISBN 0-12-444602-7); subscription 48.00 (ISBN 0-12-444602-7). Acad Pr.

Levangie, Pamela, jt. auth. see Norkin, Cynthia.

Levanon, Yosef. The Jewish Travellers in the Twelfth Century. LC 80-5521. 431p. 1980. lib. bdg. 24.25 (ISBN 0-8191-1122-8); pap. text ed. 15.00 (ISBN 0-8191-1123-6). U Pr of Amer.

Levanthal, Lance. Assembly Language Programming: Z Eighty. (Orig.). 1979. pap. text ed. 16.99 (ISBN 0-931988-21-7). Osborne-McGraw.

--Microcomputer Experimentation with the Synertek SYM-1. (Illus.). 512p. 1983. text ed. 19.95 (ISBN 0-13-580910-X). P-H.

Levanway, Russell W. Advanced General Psychology. LC 70-145878. 1972. 24.50x (ISBN 0-88295-206-4). Harlan Davidson.

Levarie, Norma. Art & History of Books. LC 67-11681. (Illus.). 1968. 25.00 o.p. (ISBN 0-685-11946-7). Heineman.

--The Art & History of Books. (Quality Paperbacks Ser.). (Illus.). 315p. 1982. pap. 18.95 (ISBN 0-306-80181-7). Da Capo.

Levarie, Siegmund. Guillaume De Machaut. LC 70-98309. (Music Ser). 1969. Repr. of 1954 ed. lib. bdg. 16.50 (ISBN 0-306-71831-6). Da Capo.

--Mozart's Le Nozze Di Figaro. LC 77-5150. (Music Reprint Ser.). 1977. Repr. of 1952 ed. lib. bdg. 29.50 (ISBN 0-306-70897-3). Da Capo.

--Musical Italy Revisited. LC 73-7196. (Illus.). 212p. 1973. Repr. of 1963 ed. lib. bdg. 15.50x (ISBN 0-8371-6916-X, LEMU). Greenwood.

Levarie, Siegmund & Levy, Ernst. Musical Morphology: A Discourse & a Dictionary. LC 82-21274. (Illus.). 376p. 1983. 29.50X (ISBN 0-87338-286-2). Kent St U Pr.

Levarie, Siegmund, tr. see Dahlhaus, Carl.

Levatino, Anthony J. The Black Market Soldiers. (Orig.). 1983. pap. 3.25 (ISBN 0-440-10968-X). Dell.

Le Vay, David, tr. see Roth, Joseph.

Levchev, Lyubomir. The Mysterious Man. Phillipov, Vladimir, tr. LC 80-83426. (International Poetry: Vol. 4). 30p. 1981. 11.95x (ISBN 0-8214-0594-2, 82-83822); pap. 6.95 (ISBN 0-8214-0595-0, 82-83830). Ohio U Pr.

Levcik, Friedrich & Stankovsky, Jan. Industrial Cooperation Between East & West. LC 78-73222. 1979. 30.00 (ISBN 0-87332-126-X). M E Sharpe.

Leve, Chuck, jt. auth. see Shay, Arthur.

Leve, Mort & Lewis, Fred. Percentage Handball. LC 82-83942. 160p. (Orig.). 1983. pap. 7.95 (ISBN 0-88011-111-9). Leisure Pr.

LeVeau, Barney, jt. auth. see Singleton, Mary C.

Levelt, A. H., jt. auth. see Van Den Essen, A. R.

Levelt, W. J. & D'Arcais, G. B. Studies in the Perception of Language. LC 78-2548. 1978. 58.95 (ISBN 0-471-99633-5, Pub. by Wiley-Interscience). Wiley.

Levelt, W. J., jt. ed. see Flores D'Arcais, G. B.

Leven, Charles L., et al. Analytical Framework for Regional Development Policy. 1970. 20.00x (ISBN 0-262-12036-4). MIT Pr.

Leven, Deborah, jt. auth. see Parker, Carolyn.

Leven, Jeremy. Creator. 1980. 11.95 (ISBN 0-698-11012-9, Coward). Putnam Pub Group.

--Satan. 576p. 1983. pap. 3.95 (ISBN 0-345-30265-6). Ballantine.

Levenbach, Hans & Brelsford, William M. Statlib Primer: The Forecasting Process Through Statistical Computing. (Research Methods Ser.). (Illus.). 250p. pap. 16.95 (ISBN 0-534-97936-X). Lifetime Learn.

Levenbach, Hans & Cleary, James P. The Beginning Forecaster: The Forecasting Process Through Data Analysis. (Illus.). 350p. 1981. 31.50 (ISBN 0-534-97975-0). Lifetime Learn.

Levenbach, Hans, jt. auth. see Cleary, James P.

Levendosky, Charles. Nocturnes. (Illus.). 24p. 1982. pap. 6.00 (ISBN 0-937160-07-5). Dooryard.

Levene. Clinical Refraction & Visual Science. 575p. 1977. 39.95x o.p. (ISBN 0-407-00043-7). Butterworth.

Levene, John R., jt. auth. see Gerstman, Daniel R.

Levenkron, David J. Sand & Rubble: The Salton City Story. LC 81-83733. (Illus.). 319p. (Orig.). 1982. pap. 9.95x (ISBN 0-941348-00-8, 825). Justice Pubs.

Levenkron, Stephen. Treating & Overcoming Anorexia Nervosa. 224p. 1983. pap. 3.50 (ISBN 0-446-90982-3). Warner Bks.

Levens. Problems in Mechanical Drawing. 5th ed. 1980. text ed. 14.25 (ISBN 0-07-037440-6). McGraw.

Levens, A. S. & Edstrom, A. E. Problems in Mechanical Drawing. 4th ed. 1974. 15.80 (ISBN 0-07-037349-3, W); answer key 1.80 (ISBN 0-07-037355-8). McGraw.

Levens, Alexander & Chalk, William. Graphics in Engineering Design. 3rd ed. LC 79-17291. 1980. text ed. 33.95x (ISBN 0-471-01478-8). wkbk. 1A 14.95x (ISBN 0-471-03133-X); wkbk. 2A 14.95x (ISBN 0-471-03214-X); wkbk. 3A 9.50x (ISBN 0-471-07749-6); solution wkbk. graph 3A 22.50x (ISBN 0-471-08518-9); wkbk. graphics 3A 11.95x (ISBN 0-471-03215-8); solutions wkbk. graph 3A 9.50x (ISBN 0-471-08104-3). Wiley.

Levenson, Alvin, ed. The Neuropsychiatric Side Effects of Drugs in the Elderly. LC 78-55806. (Aging Ser.: Vol. 9). 252p. 1979. 26.50 (ISBN 0-89004-285-3). Raven.

Levenson, Alvin J. Basic Psychopharmacology for Health Professionals. 1981. text ed. o.p. (ISBN 0-8261-2680-4); pap. text ed. 13.95 (ISBN 0-8261-2681-2). Springer Pub.

--Geriatric Psychopharmacotherapy: Optimal Technique. (Illus.). 160p. 1982. 24.75x (ISBN 0-398-04666-2). C C Thomas.

Levenson, Alvin J. & Hall, Richard C., eds. Neuropsychiatric Manifestations of Physical Disease in the Elderly. (Aging Ser.: Vol. 14). 168p. 1981. text ed. 20.50 (ISBN 0-89004-493-7). Raven.

Levenson, Christopher, et al, trs. see Hamburger, Michael.

Levenson, Dorothy. The First Book of the Civil War. rev. ed. LC 77-7153. (First Bks.). (Illus.). (gr. 4-7). 1977. lib. bdg. 7.90 s&l (ISBN 0-531-01291-3). Watts.

Levenson, Edward R., jt. ed. see Elwell, Ellen S.

Levenson, Eleanore, jt. auth. see Goldberg, Louis P.

Levenson, Goldie. Use of Patient Statistics for Program Planning. 33p. 1979. 3.95 (ISBN 0-686-38176-9, 21-1794). Natl League Nurse.

Levenson, J. C., ed. see Adams, Henry.

Levenson, Jordan. Retail Fruit Species: Your Shopper's Guide to Their Best Varieties. 2nd ed. LC 79-369. (Illus.). 1980. pap. 9.87x o.p. (ISBN 0-914442-06-6). Levenson Pr.

Levenson, Joseph R. Confucian China & Its Modern Fate: A Trilogy. 1968. 32.50x (ISBN 0-520-00736-0); pap. 10.95x (ISBN 0-520-00737-9, CAMPUS12). U of Cal Pr.

--Revolution & Cosmopolitanism: The Western Stage & the Chinese Stages. LC 73-121188. (Illus.). 1971. 18.95x (ISBN 0-520-01737-4). U of Cal Pr.

Levenson, L. L., ed. see Conference on Surface Properties of Materials, Held at the University of Missouri, Rolla, June 24-27, 1974.

Levenspiel, Octave. Chemical Reaction Engineering. 2nd ed. LC 72-178146. 1972. text ed. 37.95 (ISBN 0-471-53016-6). Wiley.

Levenspiel, Octave, jt. auth. see Kunii, Daizo.

Levenstein, Harvey A. Labor Organization in the United States & Mexico: A History of Their Relations. LC 79-133498. 240p. 1971. lib. bdg. 27.50 (ISBN 0-8371-5151-1, LLO/). Greenwood.

Levenston, Edward A., jt. auth. see Sivan, Reuven.

Levenston, Edward A. & Sivan, Reuban, eds. The Megiddo Modern Dictionary: English-Hebrew, Hebrew-English, 3 Vols. 1983. 75.00 (ISBN 0-686-43009-3, Carta Maps & Guides Pub Isreal). Hippocrene Bks.

Leventhal, Lance. Assembly Language Programming: Sixty-Eight Hundred Nine. 530p. 1980. pap. text ed. 16.99 (ISBN 0-931988-35-7). Osborne-McGraw.

Leventhal, Lance, et al. Assembly Language Programming: Z Eight Thousand. 930p. (Orig.). 1980. pap. text ed. 19.99 (ISBN 0-931988-36-5). Osborne-McGraw.

Leventhal, Lance A. Assembly Language Programming: Eighty-Eighty A-Eighty-Eighty-Five. (Eighty-Eighty A - Eighty-Eighty-Five). (Orig.). 1978. pap. text ed. 15.99 (ISBN 0-931988-10-1). Osborne-McGraw.

--Assembly Language Programming: Sixty-Eight Hundred. 480p. (Orig.). 1978. pap. text ed. 15.99 (ISBN 0-931988-12-8). Osborne-McGraw.

--Introduction to Microprocessors: Software, Hardware, Programming. LC 78-7800. (Illus.). 1978. ref. ed. 32.95 (ISBN 0-13-487868-X). P-H.

--Microcomputer Experimentation with the MOS Technology KIM-1. (Illus.). 480p. 1982. 18.95 (ISBN 0-13-580779-4). P-H.

Leventhal, Lance A. & Sayville, Winthrop. Z Eighty Assembly Language Subroutines. 550p. (Orig.). 1983. pap. 15.95 (ISBN 0-931988-91-8). Osborne-McGraw.

Leventhal, Lance A. & Stafford, Irving. Why Do You Need a Personal Computer. LC 80-2391. (Self-Teaching Guide Ser.). 320p. 1981. pap. text ed. 9.95 (ISBN 0-471-04784-8). Wiley.

Leventhal, Lance A., ed. Modeling & Simulation on Microcomputers, 1982. 119p. 1982. pap. 20.00 (ISBN 0-686-36686-7). Soc Computer Sim.

Leventhal, Lawrence A., et al. The New Hobby Computers. Force, Rich, ed. (Illus.). 96p. 1977. pap. 4.95 o.p. (ISBN 0-88006-022-0, BK 7340). Green Pub Inc.

LeVeque, W. J., ed. Studies in Number Theory. LC 75-76868. (MAA Studies: No. 6). 212p. 1969. 16.50 o.s.i. (ISBN 0-88385-106-7). Math Assn.

Lever, A. B. & Gray, H. B., eds. Iron Porphyrins. (Physical Bioinorganic Chemistry Ser.). 256p. 1982. Pt. 1. write for info. (ISBN 0-201-05816-2); Pt. 2. 37.95 (ISBN 0-201-05817-0). A-W.

Lever, B., ed. see Parker, John L.

Lever, Henry, jt. ed. see Hellmann, Ellen.

Lever, Janet. Soccer Madness. 200p. 1983. 17.50 (ISBN 0-226-47382-1). U of Chicago Pr.

Lever, Jill. Architects' Design for Furniture. LC 82-50499. (RIBA Ser.). (Illus.). 160p. 1982. 25.00 (ISBN 0-8478-0442-9); pap. 15.00 (ISBN 0-8478-0443-7). Rizzoli Intl.

Lever, Jill & Richardson, Margaret. Great Drawings from the Royal Institute of British Architects. (Illus.). 124p. 1983. pap. 15.00 (ISBN 0-8478-0481-X). Rizzoli Intl.

Lever, Judy. TV Studio. LC 78-61232. (Careers Ser.). (Illus.). 1979. PLB 12.68 (ISBN 0-382-06198-5). Silver.

Lever, Judy & Brush, Michael G. Pre-Menstrual Tension. 128p. 1982. 2.95 (ISBN 0-553-20939-6). Bantam.

Lever, Thomas. Sermons. 143p. pap. 15.00 (ISBN 0-87556-200-0). Saifer.

Lever, Walter F. & Schaumberg-Lever, Gundula. Histopathology of the Skin. 6th ed. (Illus.). 900p. 1983. text ed. 82.50 (ISBN 0-397-52095-6, Lippincott Medical). Lippincott.

Levere, Trevor H. Poetry Realized in Nature: Samuel Taylor Coleridge & Early Nineteenth-Century Science. LC 81-1930. 272p. 1981. 44.50 (ISBN 0-521-23920-6). Cambridge U Pr.

Leverenz, John. Rand McNally Road Atlas, 1982. 1982. pap. 5.95 o.p. (ISBN 0-686-93286-2). Rand.

Leverett, James, ed. Information for Playwrights: Nineteen Eighty to Eighty-One. 24p. (Orig.). 1980. pap. 4.00x o.p. (ISBN 0-930452-16-X). Theatre Comm.

Leverett, James & Izakowitz, David, eds. Dramatists Sourcebook Nineteen Eighty-One to Eighty-Two: Translators, Librettists, Lyricists & Composers. rev. ed. (Orig.). 1981. pap. 6.95 o.p. (ISBN 0-930452-18-6). Theatre Comm.

Leverich, Kathleen & Cricket Magazine Editors. Cricket's Expeditions: Outdoor & Indoor Activities. LC 77-3231. (Illus.). (gr. 1-6). 1977. 2.95 o.p. (ISBN 0-394-83543-3, BYR); PLB 3.99 o.p. (ISBN 0-394-93543-8). Random.

Levering, Ralph B. The Cold War, Nineteen Forty-Five to Nineteen Seventy-Two. (American History Ser.). 184p. (Orig.). 1982. pap. text ed. 7.95x (ISBN 0-88295-811-9). Harlan Davidson.

Levernier, James & Cohen, Hennig, eds. The Indians & Their Captives. LC 76-57831. (Contributions in American Studies: No. 31). 1977. lib. bdg. 29.95 (ISBN 0-8371-9535-7, CIC/). Greenwood.

Levernier, James A., ed. Sermons & Cannonballs. LC 81-13594. (The Sermon in America Series, 1620-1800). 1982. Repr. 55.00x (ISBN 0-8201-1370-0). Schol Facsimiles.

--Souldiery Spiritualized: Seven Sermons Preached Before the Artillery Companies of New England, 1674-1774. LC 79-9727. 1979. 60.00x (ISBN 0-8201-1325-5). Schol Facsimiles.

Levers, Joan, ed. see McQueen, Iris.

Levertov, Denise. Candles in Babylon. 144p. 1982. 12.95 (ISBN 0-8112-0830-3); pap. 5.95 (ISBN 0-8112-0831-1, NDP533). New Directions.

--Jacob's Ladder. LC 61-17868. (Orig.). 1961. pap. 3.25 o.p. (ISBN 0-8112-0083-3, NDP112). New Directions.

--Life in the Forest. LC 78-9356. 1978. 8.00 (ISBN 0-8112-0692-0); pap. 4.95 (ISBN 0-8112-0693-9, NDP461). New Directions.

--Modulations for Solo Voice. (Illus.). 1977. cancelled (ISBN 0-686-20976-1); ltd. ed. signed 75.00x (ISBN 0-686-20977-X). Five Trees.

--O Taste & See. LC 64-16820. (Orig.). 1964. pap. 3.95 o.p. (ISBN 0-8112-0084-1, NDP149). New Directions.

--Poems Nineteen Sixty to Nineteen Sixty-Seven: Including Jacob's Ladder, O Taste & See, & The Sorrow Dance. 256p. 1983. 14.50X (ISBN 0-8112-0858-3); pap. 6.25X (ISBN 0-8112-0859-1, NDP549). New Directions.

--Sorrow Dance. LC 67-14561. (Orig.). 1967. pap. 3.95 o.p. (ISBN 0-8112-0086-8, NDP222). New Directions.

Leveson, David J. A Sense of the Earth. LC 82-11437. (Illus.). 176p. 18.00 (ISBN 0-404-19149-5). AMS Pr.

Leveson, Irving. Economic Future of the United States. (Hudson Institute Studies on the Prospects for Mankind). 300p. 1982. lib. bdg. 28.75 cancelled (ISBN 0-86531-097-1). Westview.

Leveson, Irving & Wheeler, Jimmy W., eds. Western Economies in Transition: Structural Change & Adjustment Policies in Industrial Countries. LC 79-16548. (Hudson Institute Studies for the Prospects of Mankind). 1979. lib. bdg. 33.50 (ISBN 0-89158-589-3). Westview.

Levesque, Albert. Contribution to the National Bibliography of Rwanda: 1965-1970. 1979. lib. bdg. 45.00 (ISBN 0-8161-8296-5, Hall Reference). G K Hall.

Levesque, Alston. The Alstonics of Mellow. 1983. 7.95 (ISBN 0-533-05630-6). Vantage.

Levesque, Jacques. The U. S. S. R. & the Cuban Revolution: Soviet Ideological & Strategical Perspectives, 1959-77. LC 78-16188. (Special Studies). 1978. 27.95 o.p. (ISBN 0-03-042261-2). Praeger.

Levett, Carl. Crossings: A Transpersonal Approach. (God Ser.). 1976. No. 401. 8.50 (ISBN 0-89007-401-1); No. 402. pap. 4.50 (ISBN 0-89007-402-X). C Stark.

Levett, John, ed. Jane's Urban Transport Systems, 1982. (Jane's Yearbooks). (Illus.). 500p. 1982. 110.00 (ISBN 0-86720-612-8). Sci Bks Intl.

--Jane's Urban Transport Systems 1983. 2nd ed. (Jane's Yearbooks). (Illus.). 500p. 1983. 125.00 (ISBN 0-86720-645-4). Sci Bks Intl.

Levey, A. B., jt. auth. see Martin, I.

Levey, Joseph. The Jazz Experience: A Guide to Appreciation. (Illus.). 144p. 1983. 13.95 (ISBN 0-13-510248-0); pap. 6.95 (ISBN 0-13-510230-8). P-H.

Levey, Marc B., et al. Photography: Buying. Choosing. Using. (Illus.). 1979. 14.95 o.p. (ISBN 0-8174-2459-8, Amphoto); pap. 9.95 o.p. (ISBN 0-8174-2133-5). Watson-Guptill.

--Photography: Composition, Color, Display. (Illus.). 1979. 12.95 o.p. (ISBN 0-8174-2460-1, Amphoto); pap. 6.95 o.p. (ISBN 0-8174-2134-3). Watson-Guptill.

Levey, Martin. Medical Ethics of Medieval Islam with Special Reference to Al Ruhawi's "Practical Ethics of the Phyician". LC 67-22797. (Transactions Ser.: Vol. 57, Pt. 3). 1967. pap. 1.00 o.p. (ISBN 0-87169-573-1). Am Philos.

Levey, Martin & Petruck, Marvin, eds. Kushyar ibn Labban: "Principles of Hindu Reckoning". (Medieval Science Pubns., No. 8). 128p. 1965. 25.00 (ISBN 0-299-03610-3). U of Wis Pr.

Levey, Martin, tr. see Al-Kindi.

Levey, Michael. Tempting Fate. 224p. 1983. 16.95 (ISBN 0-241-10801-2, Pub. by Hamish Hamilton England). David & Charles.

Levi, Albert W., jt. auth. see Frye, Albert M.

Levi, Arrigo. Journey Among the Economists. LC 73-83218. 284p. 1974. 18.50x (ISBN 0-912050-12-8, Library Pr). Open Court.

Levi, Donald R. Real Estate Law. (Illus.). 1980. text ed. 20.95 (ISBN 0-8359-6536-8). Reston.

Levi, Eliphas. The Key of the Mysteries. 1980. pap. 6.95 o.p. (ISBN 0-87728-078-9). Weiser.

--Transcendental Magic. Waite, A. E., tr. from Fr. LC 72-16629. (Illus.). 1980. pap. 8.95 (ISBN 0-87728-079-7). Weiser.

Levi, Enrico & Panzer, Marvin. Electromechanical Power Conversion: Low-Frequency, Low-Velocity Conversion Processes. LC 82-45. 662p. 1982. Repr. of 1974 ed. 33.50 (ISBN 0-89874-436-9). Krieger.

Levi, Isaac. The Enterprise of Knowledge: An Essay on Knowledge, Credal Probability, & Chance. 1980. text ed. 35.00x (ISBN 0-262-12082-8). MIT Pr.

Levi, Isaac & Parsons, Charles, eds. How Many Questions? Essays in Honor of Sidney Morgenbesser. 448p. 30.00 (ISBN 0-686-83521-2); pap. text ed. 12.50 (ISBN 0-915145-58-8). Hackett Pub.

Levi, L. Applied Optics: A Guide to Optical Systems Design, 2 vols. LC 67-29942. (Pure & Applied Optics Ser.). Vol. 1, 1968. 51.95x (ISBN 0-471-53110-3, Pub. by Wiley-Interscience); Vol. 2, 1980. 95.95x (ISBN 0-471-05054-7). Wiley.

Levi, Lennart. Society, Stress, & Disease: The Productive & Reproductive Age-Male-Female Roles & Relationships, Vol. 3. (Illus.). 1978. 75.00x (ISBN 0-19-261306-5). Oxford U Pr.

Levi, Lennart, ed. Emotions: Their Parameters & Measurement. LC 74-80539. 814p. 1975. 51.00 (ISBN 0-89004-019-2). Raven.

--Society, Stress, & Disease: Childhood & Adolescence, Vol. 2. (Illus.). 1976. 75.00x (ISBN 0-19-264418-1). Oxford U Pr.

Levi, Leone. The History of British Commerce & of the Economic Progress of the British Nation, 1763-1878. (The Development of Industrial Society Ser.). 600p. 1971. Repr. of 1880 ed. text ed. 29.00x (ISBN 0-7165-1586-5, Pub. by Irish Academic Pr England). Biblio Dist.

Levi, Lernnart. Preventing Work Stress. 1981. 7.00 (ISBN 0-201-04317-3). A-W.

Levi, M., tr. see Vinnichenko, N. K. & Gorelik, A. G.

Levi, Maurice. Economics Deciphered: A Layman's Survival Guide. 1982. pap. 6.95 (ISBN 0-465-01795-9). Basic.

Levi, Maurice D., ed. see Kupferman, Martin.

Levi, Peter. Atlas of Greek World. 239p. 1981. 35.00 (ISBN 0-87196-448-1). Facts on File.

Levi, Peter, tr. see Papadiamantis, Alexandros.

Levi, S., ed. Ultrasound & Cancer: Invited Papers & Selected Free Communications Presented at the First International Symposium, Brussels, Belgium, July 23-24, 1982. (International Congress Ser.: No. 587). 384p. 1982. 88.25 (ISBN 0-444-90270-8, Excerpta Medica). Elsevier.

Levi, S. Gershon, tr. see Hazaz, Haim.

Levi, Shonie B. & Kaplan, Sylvia R. Guide for the Jewish Homemaker. 2nd ed. LC 59-12039. (Illus.). 1965. pap. 6.95 (ISBN 0-8052-0087-8). Schocken.

Levi, Steven C. The Committee of Vigilance of Nineteen Sixteen: A Case Study in Official Hysteria. (Illus.). 128p. 1983. lib. bdg. 15.95x (ISBN 0-89950-058-7). McFarland & Co.

Levi, Sylvain. The Theatre of India, Vol. 1. 2nd ed. Mukherji, Narayan, tr. from Fr. Orig. Title: Le Theatre Indien. (Illus.). 282p. 1978. Repr. of 1890 ed. 20.00 (ISBN 0-86578-045-5); flexible bdg. 12.00 (ISBN 0-86578-044-7). Ind-US Inc.

--The Theatre of India, Vol. 2. 2nd ed. Mukherji, Narayan, tr. from Fr. Orig. Title: Le Theatre Indien. (Illus.). 162p. 1978. Repr. of 1890 ed. 20.00 (ISBN 0-86578-047-1); flexible bdg. 12.00 (ISBN 0-86578-046-3). Ind-US Inc.

Levi, Vicki G. & Eisenberg, Lee. Atlantic City: 125 Years of Ocean Madness. (Illus.). 1979. 15.95 (ISBN 0-517-53603-X, C N Potter Bks); pap. 8.95 (ISBN 0-517-53604-8, C N Potter). Crown.

Levi, Vicki G., jt. auth. see Shepard, Ricahrd F.

Levi, Werner. Contemporary International Law: A Concise Introduction. 1978. lib. bdg. 32.50 (ISBN 0-89158-184-7); pap. 12.50 (ISBN 0-89158-187-1). Westview.

Levich, Richard M. The International Money Market. Altman, Edward I. & Walter, Ingo, eds. LC 78-13841. (Contemporary Studies in Economic & Financial Analysis: Vol. 22). 178p. 1979. 36.00 (ISBN 0-89232-109-1). Jai Pr.

Levich, Richard M. & Wihlborg, Clas G., eds. Exchange Risk & Exposure: Current Developments in International Financial Management. LC 79-5181. (Illus.). 224p. 1980. 25.95x (ISBN 0-669-03246-8). Lexington Bks.

Levich, V. Physiochemical Hydrodynamics. 1962. ref. ed. 47.95 (ISBN 0-13-674440-0). P-H.

Levidow, Les & Young, Bob, eds. Science, Technology & the Labour Process. (Marxist Studies: Vol. 1). 203p. 1981. text ed. 30.00x (ISBN 0-906336-20-1, Pub. by CSE Bks England); pap. text ed. 15.00x (ISBN 0-906336-21-X, Pub. by CSE Bks England). Humanities.

Levie, H. S. When Battle Rages How Can Law Protect? Carey, John, ed. LC 78-123998. (Hammarskjold Forum Ser.: No. 14). 115p. 1971. 10.00 (ISBN 0-379-11814-9). Oceana.

Levie, Howard S. Protection of War Victims: Protocol One to the Nineteen Forty-Nine Geneva Conventions, 4 vols. LC 79-16960. 1979. 45.00 ea. (ISBN 0-379-00786-X). Oceana.

Levien, Michael, ed. Naval Surgeon: The Voyages of Dr. Edward H. Cree, Royal Navy, as Related to his private journals, 1837-1856. (Illus.). 276p. 1982. 24.75 (ISBN 0-525-24121-3, 02403-720). Dutton.

Levieux, Eleanor, tr. see Duby, Georges.

Levieux, Eleanor, tr. see Memmi, Albert.

Levi-Montalcini, R. Nerve Cells, Transmitters & Behavior. 1980. 119.75 (ISBN 0-444-80243-6). Elsevier.

Levin & Christensen. Apple Orchard Cookbook. LC 78-60319. (Orig.). 1978. pap. 5.95 (ISBN 0-912944-49-8). Berkshire Traveller.

Levin, A. Leo, ed. The American Judiciary: Critical Issues. Wheeler, Russell R. (The Annals of the American Academy of Political & Social Science: Vol. 462). 224p. 1982. 15.00 (ISBN 0-8039-1852-6); pap. 7.95 (ISBN 0-8039-1853-4). Sage.

Levin, Alex see Green, Alex, pseud.

Levin, Alexander A. Solid State Quantum Chemistry: The Chemical Bond & Energy Bands in Tetrahedral Semiconductors. 1977. text ed. 32.95x (ISBN 0-07-037435-X, C). McGraw.

Levin, Arthur, ed. Health Services: The Local Perspective. LC 77-73219. (Praeger Special Studies). 1977. 29.95 o.p. (ISBN 0-03-039731-6). Praeger.

Levin, Bella & Whelan, Dan. City Guide, 1983: San Francisco Bay Area & Northern California. (Illus.). 312p. (Orig.). 1982. pap. 4.95 (ISBN 0-940562-10-3). Danella Pubns.

--Cityguide, Southern California: 1982-83. (Illus.). 208p. (Orig.). 1982. pap. 4.95 (ISBN 0-940562-05-7). Belldan Pubns.

Levin, Bernard. Speaking up. 267p. 1983. 16.95 (ISBN 0-686-38946-8, Pub by Jonathan Cape). Merrimack Bk Serv.

--Taking Sides. 200p. 1983. 16.95 (ISBN 0-686-38945-X, Pub by Jonathan Cape). Merrimack Bk Serv.

Levin, Betty. The Zoo Conspiracy. (Illus.). (gr. 3-7). 1979. pap. 1.50 o.p. (ISBN 0-380-43265-X, 43265, Camelot). Avon.

Levin, Daniel L., et al. A Practical Guide to Pediatric Intensive Care. LC 79-13793. (Illus.). 494p. 1979. pap. text ed. 29.95 (ISBN 0-8016-3011-8). Mosby.

Levin, David, jt. auth. see Gross, Theodore L.

Levin, David, ed. see Parkman, Francis.

Levin, David, ed. see Parkman, Francis, Jr.

Levin, Deana. Nikolai Lives in Moscow. (Children Everywhere Ser.: No. 5). (gr. 2-4). 1968. PLB 4.95 o.p. (ISBN 0-8038-5007-7). Hastings.

Levin, Dick. Buy Low, Sell High, Collect Early & Pay Late: The Manager's Guide to Financial Survival. (Illus.). 224p. 1983. 15.95 (ISBN 0-13-109439-4). P-H.

Levin, Donald A., ed. Hybridization: An Evolutionary Perspective. LC 78-10947. (Benchmark Papers in Genetics: Vol. 11). 321p. 1979. 36.50 (ISBN 0-87933-341-3). Hutchinson Ross.

Levin, Dov. Lithuanian Jewry's Armed Resistance to the Nazis. 224p. 1983. text ed. 35.00x (ISBN 0-8419-0831-1). Holmes & Meier.

Levin, Edward. Negotiating Tactics: Bargain Your Way to Winning. Date not set. pap. 6.95 (ISBN 0-449-90074-6, Columbine). Fawcett.

Levin, Edward & De Santis, Daniel V. Mediation: An Annotated Bibliography. LC 78-18359. (Industrial & Labor Relations Bibliography Ser.: No. 15). 32p. 1978. pap. 3.25 (ISBN 0-87546-069-0). ILR Pr.

Levin, Gerald. Prose Models. 5th ed. 372p. 1981. pap. text ed. 9.95 (ISBN 0-15-572280-8, HC); instructor's manual avail. 1.50 (ISBN 0-15-572281-6). HarBraceJ.

--Sigmund Freud. LC 74-31135. (World Authors Ser.: Austria: No. 357). 1975. lib. bdg. 12.50 o.p. (ISBN 0-8057-2330-7, Twayne). G K Hall.

--Writing & Logic. 276p. 1982. pap. text ed. 8.95 (ISBN 0-15-597788-1, HC). HarBraceJ.

--Writing & Logic. 256p. (Orig.). 1982. pap. text ed. 8.95 (ISBN 0-15-597788-1); instructor's manual 3.95 (ISBN 0-15-597789-X). HarBraceJ.

Levin, Gerald R. Child Psychology. LC 82-9691. (Psychology Ser.). 576p. 1982. text ed. 22.95 (ISBN 0-534-01229-9). Brooks-Cole.

Levin, Gilbert, et al. The Dynamics of Human Service Delivery. LC 75-46547. 280p. 1976. prof ref 22.00x (ISBN 0-88410-132-0). Ballinger Pub.

Levin, H., ed. see Hawthorne, Nathaniel.

Levin, Harold L., jt. auth. see Brice, James C.

Levin, Harry. The House of the Seven Gables. (gr. 9-12). 1969. pap. text ed. 1.95x o.p. (ISBN 0-675-09470-4). Merrill.

--Memories of the Moderns. LC 80-36827. 256p. 1982. 15.95 (ISBN 0-8112-0733-1); pap. 7.95 (ISBN 0-8112-0842-7, NDP539). New Directions.

--Myth of the Golden Age in the Renaissance. 1972. pap. 6.95 (ISBN 0-19-501602-5, GB). Oxford U Pr.

--The Portable James Joyce. 1966. 14.95 (ISBN 0-670-40998-7). Viking Pr.

--The Power of Blackness: Hawthorne, Poe, Melville. LC 80-83221. xxii, 263p. 1980. pap. 6.95x (ISBN 0-8214-0581-0, 82-83699). Ohio U Pr.

--Question of Hamlet. 1959. 15.75 (ISBN 0-19-500621-6). Oxford U Pr.

--Question of Hamlet. LC 59-5784. 1970. pap. 5.95 (ISBN 0-19-500808-1, 318, GB). Oxford U Pr.

--Shakespeare & the Revolution of the Times: Perspectives & Commentaries. 1978. pap. 8.95 (ISBN 0-19-502362-5, GB528, GB). Oxford U Pr.

Levin, Harry & Addis, Ann B. The Eye-Voice Span. (Illus.). 1979. text ed. 17.50x (ISBN 0-262-12076-3). MIT Pr.

Levin, Harry, jt. auth. see Gibson, Eleanor J.

Levin, Harry, ed. see Shakespeare, William.

Levin, Harvey J. Fact & Fancy in Television Regulation: An Economic Study of Policy Alternatives. LC 79-90148. 544p. 1980. 20.00x (ISBN 0-87154-531-4). Russell Sage.

Levin, Henry M., ed. Community Control of Schools. 1970. pap. 2.95 o.p. (ISBN 0-671-20784-9, Touchstone Bks). S&S.

Levin, Herman, jt. auth. see Axinn, June.

Levin, I., tr. see Ginsberg, Lev.

Levin, Ilya, tr. see Schmidt, Paul.

Levin, Ira. The Boys from Brazil. 1978. pap. 3.25 (ISBN 0-440-10760-1). Dell.

--A Kiss Before Dying. 304p. 1981. pap. 2.95 (ISBN 0-515-07143-9). Jove Pubns.

--This Perfect Day. 1970. 7.95 (ISBN 0-394-44858-8). Random.

Levin, J., jt. auth. see Ferman, G. S.

Levin, Jack. Elementary Statistics in Social Research. 2nd ed. 1977. text ed. 20.95 scp o.p. (ISBN 0-06-043985-8, HarpC); scp wkbk. 8.95 o.p. (ISBN 0-06-043993-9); solutions manual avail. o.p. (ISBN 0-06-363984-X). Har-Row.

--Elementary Statistics in Social Research. 3rd ed. 336p. 1983. pap. text ed. 19.50 scp (ISBN 0-06-044071-6, HarpC); scp wkbk. 6.50 (ISBN 0-06-043934-3); sol. manual avail. (ISBN 0-06-363985-8). Har-Row.

--Estadistica en Investigacion. (Span.). 1979. pap. text ed. 12.00 o.p. (ISBN 0-06-315012-3, Pub. by HarLA Mexico). Har-Row.

Levin, Jack, jt. auth. see Bourne, Richard.

Levin, Jack, jt. auth. see Zieve, Philip D.

Levin, Jack, jt. ed. see Watson, Stanley W.

Levin, Jenifer. Water Dancer. 361p. 1982. 15.95 (ISBN 0-671-44764-5, Poseidon). PB.

Levin, Joel R., jt. auth. see Marascuilo, Leonard A.

Levin, Jules F., et al. Reading Modern Russian. (Illus.). vi, 321p. 1979. pap. text ed. 12.95 (ISBN 0-89357-059-1). Slavica.

Levin, Kim, jt. auth. see Crary, Jonathan.

Levin, Lowell & Idler, Ellen. The Hidden Health Care System: Mediating Structures & Medicine. 288p. 1981. prof ref 19.00x (ISBN 0-88410-822-8). Ballinger Pub.

Levin, Malinda. Psychology: A Biographical Approach. (Illus.). 1978. text ed. 26.00 (ISBN 0-07-037387-6, C); instr's manual 13.00 (ISBN 0-07-037388-4); test file 17.00 (ISBN 0-07-037394-9). McGraw.

Levin, Marvin E. & O'Neal, Lawrence W. The Diabetic Foot. 3rd ed. LC 82-3456. (Illus.). 397p. 1982. text ed. 44.50 (ISBN 0-8016-2991-8). Mosby.

--The Diabetic Foot. 2nd ed. LC 77-7909. (Illus.). 290p. 1977. text ed. 37.50 (ISBN 0-8016-2984-5). Mosby.

Levin, Melvin R. & Shank, Alan, eds. Educational Investment in an Urban Society: Costs, Benefits, & Public Policy. LC 70-110397. (Illus.). 1970. pap. text ed. 14.95x (ISBN 0-8077-1684-7). Tchrs Coll.

Levin, Meyer. The Architect. 1982. 15.50 o.s.i. (ISBN 0-671-24892-8). S&S.

--Classic Hassidic Tales. (Illus.). 6.50 o.p. (ISBN 0-8446-5216-4). Peter Smith.

--The Harvest. 1978. 11.95 o.p. (ISBN 0-671-22550-2). S&S.

Levin, Milton. Noel Coward. (English Authors Ser.). 1969. lib. bdg. 12.95 (ISBN 0-8057-1120-1, Twayne). G K Hall.

Levin, Milton, jt. ed. see Lass, Abraham H.

Levin, Morris A., et al. Applied Genetic Engineering: Future Trends & Problems. LC 82-14401. (Illus.). 191p. 1983. 24.00 (ISBN 0-8155-0925-1). Noyes.

Levin, Murray B. & Repak, T. A. Edward Kennedy: The Myth of Leadership. 1980. 10.95 o.s.i. (ISBN 0-395-29249-2). HM.

Levin, N. Gordon, Jr. Woodrow Wilson & the Paris Peace Conference. 2nd ed. (Problems in American Civilization Ser.). 1972. pap. text ed. 3.95x o.p. (ISBN 0-669-83915-9). Heath.

--Woodrow Wilson & World Politics: America's Response to War & Revolution. LC 68-15893. 1970. pap. 8.95x (ISBN 0-19-500803-0). Oxford U Pr.

Levin, Noel A. & Brossman, Mark E. Social Investing for Pension Funds: For Love or Money. 113p. (Orig.). 1982. pap. 16.00 (ISBN 0-89154-183-7). Intl Found Employ.

Levin, Noel A. & Aksen, Gerald, eds. Arbitrating Labor Cases. 1974. text ed. 20.00 o.p. (ISBN 0-685-85362-4, B3-1206). PLI.

Levin, Paul. Claims & Changes: Handbook for Construction Contract Management. Kidd, Dusty & Baumgarner, James, eds. (Illus.). 222p. 23.50 (ISBN 0-686-36279-9). Constr Ind Pr.

--Construction Computer Applications Directory. 2nd ed. Layman, Donald & Steinman, Laura, eds. 530p. 95.00 o.p. (ISBN 0-9605442-0-8). Constr Ind Pr.

--Construction Computer Applications Directory. 3rd ed. Layman, Donald & Young, Nancy A., eds. 600p. 135.00 (ISBN 0-686-42716-5). Constr Ind Pr.

Levin, R. & Rubin, D. Applied Elementary Statistics. 1980. 25.95 (ISBN 0-13-040113-7); pap. 8.95 study guide (ISBN 0-13-040105-6). P-H.

Levin, R. I. & Kirkpatrick, C. A. Quantitative Approaches to Management. 5th ed. 798p. 1982. 27.95x (ISBN 0-07-037436-8); instr's manual 12.50 (ISBN 0-07-037437-6); wkbk. 9.95 (ISBN 0-07-037438-4). McGraw.

Levin, Rich, jt. auth. see Goodrich, Gail.

Levin, Richard, jt. auth. see Johnson, Earvin.

Levin, Richard I. Statistics for Management. 2nd ed. (Illus.). 800p. 1981. text ed. 25.95 (ISBN 0-13-845255-5). P-H.

--Statistics for Management. (Illus.). 1978. text ed. 22.95 o.p. (ISBN 0-13-845305-5); wkbk. 7.95 o.p. (ISBN 0-13-845321-7). P-H.

Levin, Richard I. & Kirkpatrick, C. A. Planning & Control with PERT-CPM. 1966. 20.95 o.p. (ISBN 0-07-037364-7, C); pap. 12.95 o.p. (ISBN 0-07-037365-5). McGraw.

Levin, Richard I. & Kirkpatrick, Charles A. Quantitative Approaches to Management. 4th ed. (Illus.). 1978. text ed. 23.95 o.p. (ISBN 0-07-037423-6, C); instructor's manual 7.95 o.p. (ISBN 0-07-037424-4); student wkbk. 9.95 o.p. (ISBN 0-07-037434-1). McGraw.

Levin, Richard I. & Rubin, David. Elementary Statistics. text ed. 17.95 o.p. (ISBN 0-13-260059-5). P-H.

Levin, Richard I., et al. Production-Operations Management. (Management Ser). (Illus.). 416p. 1972. text ed. 30.95 (ISBN 0-07-037369-8, C); instructors' manual 7.95 (ISBN 0-07-037372-8). McGraw.

Levin, Sheila. Simple Truths. LC 81-22217. 288p. 1982. 12.95 (ISBN 0-517-54718-X). Crown.

Levin, Simon, ed. Studies in Mathematical Biology Part 1: Cellular Behavior & Development of Pattern. LC 78-53425. (Studies in Mathematics: Vol. 15). 1979. 21.00 (ISBN 0-88385-115-6). Math Assn.

Levin, Simon A., jt. ed. see Whittaker, Robert H.

Levine. Cancer in the Young. LC 81-15751. (Illus.). 762p. 1982. 99.75x (ISBN 0-89352-052-7). Masson Pub.

--Realtors' Liability. LC 79-4133. (Real Estate for Professional Practitioners Ser.). 1979. 33.95 (ISBN 0-471-05208-6). Ronald Pr.

Levine, jt. auth. see Bergson.

Levine, Alan H. The Rights of Students. 1977. pap. 2.50 o.p. (ISBN 0-380-00945-5, 53702, Discus). Avon.

Levine, Arnold J., jt. ed. see Varmus, Harold.

Levine, Arthur. Handbook on Undergraduate Curriculum: Prepared for the Carnegie Council on Policy Studies in Higher Education. LC 78-50893. (Carnegie Council Ser.). (Illus.). 1978. text ed. 25.95x (ISBN 0-87589-376-7). Jossey-Bass.

--Why Innovation Fails: The Institutionalization & Termination of Innovation in Higher Education. LC 80-14950. 182p. 1980. 40.50x (ISBN 0-87395-412-2); pap. 14.95x (ISBN 0-87395-421-1). State U NY Pr.

LeVine, B. B., jt. auth. see LeVine, Robert A.

Levine, Baroch. Group Psychotherapy: Practice & Development. 1979. 23.95 (ISBN 0-13-365296-3). P-H.

Levine, Barry B. Benjy Lopez: A Picaresque Tale of Emigration & Return. LC 79-2749. 202p. 1980. 12.95 o.s.i. (ISBN 0-465-00653-1). Basic.

--The New Cuban Presence in the Caribbean. (Special Studies on Latin America & theCaribbean). 250p. 1983. lib. bdg. price not set (ISBN 0-86531-538-8); pap. text ed. price not set (ISBN 0-86531-567-1). Westview.

Levine, Beverly. Fifty Grand Picnics in the San Francisco Bay Area. LC 82-1280. (Illus.). 120p. 1982. pap. 6.95 (ISBN 0-87701-189-3). Chronicle Bks.

Levine, Brian. Cities of Gold: History of the Victor-Cripple Creek Mining District. (Illus.). pap. 6.95 (ISBN 0-937080-09-8). Century One.

--Lowell Thomas' Victor. (Illus., Orig.). 1982. pap. 6.95 (ISBN 0-937080-07-1). Century One.

Levine, Carol & Veatch, Robert M., eds. Cases in Bioethics from the Hastings Center Report. LC 82-81217. 124p. 1982. pap. 7.95 (ISBN 0-916558-17-7). Inst Soc Ethics.

Levine, Caroline A. The Silly Kid Joke Book. LC 82-17727. (Illus.). 64p. (gr. 1-3). 1983. 9.95 (ISBN 0-525-44039-9, 0966-290). Dutton.

Levine, D., jt. auth. see Berenson, M.

Levine, D., ed. Family Formation in an Age of Nascent Capitalism. 1977. 22.50 (ISBN 0-12-445050-4). Acad Pr.

Levine, Daniel. Varieties of Reform Thought. LC 79-28658. xiii, 149p. 1980. Repr. of 1964 ed. lib. bdg. 17.50x (ISBN 0-313-22345-9, LEVR). Greenwood.

Levine, Daniel U., jt. auth. see Ornstein, Allan C.

Levine, Daniel V. & Havighurst, Robert J., eds. The Future of Big-City Schools: Desegregation Policies & Magnet Alternatives. LC 76-62900. 1977. 21.75x (ISBN 0-8211-1113-2); text ed. 19.50x 10 or more copies (ISBN 0-685-75000-0). McCutchan.

Levine, David. No Known Survivors: David Levine's Political Plank. LC 77-118213. (Illus.). 1970. 10.95 (ISBN 0-87645-030-3); signed limited ed. 25.00 (ISBN 0-87645-106-7). Gambit.

--Pens and Needles: Literary Caricatures Introduced & Selected by John Updike. LC 70-98143. (Illus.). 1969. 10.95 (ISBN 0-87645-006-0). Gambit.

--The Watercolors of David Levine. LC 81-127264. (Illus.). 24p. 1981. pap. 9.00 (ISBN 0-295-95817-0, Phillips). U of Wash Pr.

Levine, David, jt. auth. see Wrightson, Keith.

Levine, David, ed. & illus. The Fables of Aesop. LC 72-96878. (Illus.). (gr. 5 up). 1975. 10.95 (ISBN 0-87645-074-5). Gambit.

Levine, David A. Internal Combustion: The Races in Detroit 1915-1926. LC 75-35347. 224p. 1976. lib. bdg. 27.50 (ISBN 0-8371-8588-2, LIC/). Greenwood.

Levine, David M., jt. auth. see Berenson, Mark L.

Levine, Deena & Adelman, Mara B. Beyond Language: Intercultural Communication for ESL. (Illus.). 200p. 1982. pap. 10.95 (ISBN 0-13-076000-5). P-H.

Levine, Edna S., ed. The Preparation of Psychological Service Providers to the Deaf. (Monograph: No. 4). 1977. pap. text ed. 4.00 (ISBN 0-914494-05-8). Am Deaf & Rehab.

Levine, Elaine S. & Padilla, Amado M. Crossing Cultures in Therapy: Pluralistic Counseling for the Hispanic. LC 79-9504. (Orig.). 1979. pap. text ed. 13.95 (ISBN 0-8185-0337-8). Brooks-Cole.

Levine, Erwin L. & Wexler, Elizabeth. PL Ninety-Four - One Forty-Two: An Act of Congress. 128p. 1981. pap. text ed. 10.95 (ISBN 0-02-370270-2). Macmillan.

Levine, Etan. Exile: Insights Into the Jewish Condition. LC 82-6723. 350p. Date not set. 20.00 (ISBN 0-87668-601-3). Aronson.

Levine, Eugene, jt. auth. see Abdella, Fay G.

Levine, Faye. Solomon & Sheba. LC 79-24671. 1981. 10.95 (ISBN 0-399-90069-1, Marek). Putnam Pub Group.

--Splendor & Misery: A Novel of Harvard. 288p. 1983. 13.95 (ISBN 0-312-75269-5). St Martin.

Levine, Gemma & Meir, Golda. Israel: Faces & Places. LC 78-53457. (Illus.). 1978. 17.50 o.p. (ISBN 0-399-12195-1). Putnam Pub Group.

Levine, George. The Realistic Imagination: English Fiction from Frankenstein to Lady Chatterley. LC 80-17444. 358p. 1981. pap. 10.95 (ISBN 0-226-47551-4). U of Chicago Pr.

Levine, George & Madden, William. Art of Victorian Prose. 1968. pap. 7.95x o.p. (ISBN 0-19-500953-3). Oxford U Pr.

Levine, George & Knoepflmacher, U. C., eds. The Endurance of Frankenstein: Essays on Mary Shelley's Novel. LC 77-20325. 1979. 17.95x (ISBN 0-520-03612-3). U of Cal Pr.

Levine, H. Unidirectional Wave Motion. (North-Holland Ser. in Applied Mathematics & Mechanics: Vol. 23). 1978. 89.50 (ISBN 0-444-85043-0, North-Holland). Elsevier.

Levine, H. B. & Levine, Marlene. Urbanization in Papua New Guinea. LC 78-58795. (Urbanization in Developing Countries Ser.). 1979. 29.95 (ISBN 0-521-22230-3); pap. 11.95 (ISBN 0-521-29410-X). Cambridge U Pr.

Levine, Harold. English Alive Workbook: Complete Edition. (Orig.). (gr. 8-11). 1981. 7.08 (ISBN 0-87720-429-2). AMSCO Sch.

--English Alive Workbook: Grammar. (Orig.). (gr. 8-11). 1981. 5.00 (ISBN 0-87720-426-8). AMSCO Sch.

--Vocabulary for the College-Bound Student. (Orig.). (gr. 9-12). 1964. text ed. 10.92 (ISBN 0-87720-367-9); pap. text ed. 5.83 (ISBN 0-87720-366-0); wkbk. o.p. 6.58 (ISBN 0-87720-312-1); with answers 4.20 (ISBN 0-87720-313-X). AMSCO Sch.

--Vocabulary for the High School Student. (Orig.). (gr. 9-12). 1967. text ed. 10.92 (ISBN 0-87720-365-2); pap. text ed. 5.83 (ISBN 0-87720-364-4); wkbk. o.p. 6.58 (ISBN 0-87720-310-5); with answers 4.20 (ISBN 0-87720-311-3). AMSCO Sch.

--Vocabulary for the High School Student. 2nd ed. (gr. 10-12). 1982. wkbk. 7.00 (ISBN 0-87720-437-3). AMSCO Sch.

Levine, Herbert M. How the System Really Works: Readings in American Government. 1982. pap. text ed. 12.50x (ISBN 0-673-15509-9). Scott F.

--Point-Counterpoint: Readings in American Government. 1979. pap. text ed. 12.50x (ISBN 0-673-15297-9). Scott F.

--Point-Counterpoint: Readings in American Government. 2nd ed. 1983. pap. text ed. 12.95x (ISBN 0-673-15625-7). Scott F.

--Political Issues Debated: An Introduction to Politics. (Illus.). 352p. 1982. pap. 14.95 (ISBN 0-13-685032-4). P-H.

--World Politics Debated. 1st ed. 384p. 1983. pap. text ed. 14.95x (ISBN 0-07-037433-3, C). McGraw.

Levine, Hermon M. The Naked Emperor. 171p. 1977. pap. 5.00 o.p. (ISBN 0-686-96154-4). Am Atheist.

Levine, Howard, jt. auth. see Rheingold, Howard.

Levine, Ira N. Molecular Spectroscopy. LC 74-30477. 480p. 1975. 39.50x (ISBN 0-471-53128-6, Pub. by Wiley-Interscience). Wiley.

--Physical Chemistry. (Illus.). 1978. text ed. 28.95 (ISBN 0-07-037418-X, C); solutions manual 12.95 (ISBN 0-07-037419-8). McGraw.

--Physical Chemistry. 2nd ed. (Illus.). 992p. 1983. text ed. 32.95 (ISBN 0-07-037421-X, C); solutions manual 12.95 (ISBN 0-07-037422-8). McGraw.

Levine, Jack. The Complete Graphic Work of Jack Levine. (Fine Art Ser.). (Illus.). 112p. (Orig.). 1983. pap. 6.00 (ISBN 0-486-24481-4). Dover.

Levine, James P., et al. Criminal Justice: A Public Policy Approach. 591p. 1980. text ed. 20.95 (ISBN 0-15-516094-X, HC); test bklt. avail. (ISBN 0-15-516095-8). HarBraceJ.

Levine, Jerome, ed. Contemporary Standards for the Pharmacotherapy of Mental Disorders. new ed. LC 76-27215. (Principles & Techniques of Human Research & Therapeutics: Vol. 12). 1978. 16.00 o.p. (ISBN 0-87993-084-5); monograph 16.00 o.p. (ISBN 0-685-71485-3). Futura Pub.

Levine, Jerome, et al, eds. Psychopharmacological Agents. LC 74-21395. (Principles & Techniques of Human Research & Therapeutics Ser.: Vol. 8). (Illus.). 272p. 1975. 17.00 o.p. (ISBN 0-87993-052-7). Futura Pub.

Levine, Jonathan, jt. auth. see Greenberg, Sidney.

Levine, Joseph, jt. auth. see Pine, Tillie S.

Levine, Joseph M. Dr. Woodward's Shield: History, Science, & Satire in Augustan England. 1977. 36.50x (ISBN 0-520-03132-6). U of Cal Pr.

Levine, Lawrence J. Black Culture & Black Consciousness: Afro-American Folk Thought from Slavery to Freedom. 1977. 25.00x (ISBN 0-19-502088-X). Oxford U Pr.

Levine, Lawrence W. Black Culture & Black Consciousness: Afro-American Folk Thought from Slavery to Freedom. LC 76-9223. 1978. pap. 9.95 (ISBN 0-19-502374-9, GB530, GB). Oxford U Pr.

Levine, Lee I., ed. The Jerusalem Cathedra: Studies in the History, Archaeology, Geography, & Ethnography of the Land of Israel, Vol. 1. (Illus.). 368p. 1982. 25.00 (ISBN 0-8143-1691-3). Wayne St U Pr.

--The Jerusalem Cathedral, Vol. 2. (Studies in the History, Archaeology, Geography & Ethnography of the Land of Israel). 300p. 1982. 25.00 (ISBN 0-8143-1715-4). Wayne St U Pr.

Levine, Lenore, jt. ed. see New, Maria.

Levine, Leon. Methods for Solving Engineering Problems: Using Analog Computers. (Information Processing & Computers Ser.). 1964. text ed. 32.50 o.p. (ISBN 0-07-037373-6, P&RB). McGraw.

Levine, Lois, jt. auth. see Burros, Marian.

Levine, Louis. Biology for a Modern Society. LC 76-46318. (Illus.). 452p. 1977. pap. 12.95 o.p. (ISBN 0-8016-2990-X). Mosby.

--Biology of the Gene. 3rd ed. LC 80-10730. (Illus.). 542p. 1980. pap. text ed. 23.95 (ISBN 0-8016-2988-8). Mosby.

Levine, Louis D. & Young, T. Cuyler, Jr., eds. Mountains & Lowlands: Essays in the Archaeology of Greater Mesopotamia. LC 77-75777. (Bibliotheca Mesopotamica: Vol. 7). (Illus.). 405p. 1977. text ed. 21.00 o.p. (ISBN 0-89003-053-7); pap. 16.50 o.p. (ISBN 0-89003-052-9). Undena Pubns.

Levine, M. Digital Theory & Experimentation Using Integrated Circuits. LC 73-12863. 1974. pap. 16.95 ref. ed. (ISBN 0-13-212258-8). P-H.

Levine, Madeline G. Contemporary Polish Poetry, Nineteen Twenty-Five to Nineteen Seventy-Five. (World Authors Ser.). 1981. lib. bdg. 15.95 (ISBN 0-8057-6428-3, Twayne). G K Hall.

Levine, Mark D. see Craig, Paul P.

Levine, Mark L. Real Estate Tax-Shelter Desk Book. 2nd ed. LC 77-90141. 1978. 59.50 o.p. (ISBN 0-87624-502-5). Inst Busn Plan.

--Real Estate Tax Shelter Desk Book. 3rd ed. LC 81-22569. 463p. 1982. text ed. 49.50 (ISBN 0-87624-489-4). Inst Busn Plan.

Levine, Marlene, jt. auth. see Levine, H. B.

Levine, Marvin. A Cognitive Theory of Learning: Research on Hypothesis Testing. LC 75-5561. 313p. 1975. 18.00 (ISBN 0-470-53126-6, Pub. by Wiley). Krieger.

Levine, Marvin A. Personnel Management for Public Sector Employees. (Illus.). 500p. 1983. text ed. 24.95x (ISBN 0-89832-023-2). Brighton Pub Co.

Levine, Marvin J. & Hagburg, Eugene C. Public Sector Labor Relations. 1979. text ed. 20.50 (ISBN 0-8299-0184-1). West Pub.

Levine, Marvin J., jt. auth. see Hagburg, Eugene C.

Levine, Melvin D., et al. Pediatric Approach to Learning Disorders. LC 79-21839. 1980. 30.00x (ISBN 0-471-04736-8, Pub. by Wiley-Medical). Wiley.

Levine, Michael W. & Shefner, Jeremy M. Fundamentals of Sensation & Perception. (Psychology Ser.). (Illus.). 480p. 1981. text ed. 23.95 (ISBN 0-201-04339-4). A-W.

Levine, Morris E. Digital Theory & Experimentation Using Integrated Circuits. rev. & enl. ed. (Illus.). 272p. 1982. 16.95 (ISBN 0-13-212688-5). P-H.

--Digital Theory & Practice Using Integrated Circuits. 1978. ref. 23.95 (ISBN 0-13-212613-3). P-H.

Levine, Mortimer, ed. Bibliographical Handbook on Tudor England: 1485-1603. (Bibliographical Handbooks of the Conference on British Studies). 1968. 17.95 (ISBN 0-521-05543-1). Cambridge U Pr.

Levine, Murray. From State Hospital to Psychiatric Center: The Implementation of Planned Organizational Charge. 160p. 1980. 18.95x (ISBN 0-669-03810-5). Lexington Bks.

Levine, Nathan. Teach Yourself Typing. (Illus.). 96p. 1982. pap. 3.95 (ISBN 0-668-05455-7, 5455). Arco.

Levine, Norman D., ed. see Naumov, N. P.

Levine, Norman G. How to build a One Hundred Million Dollar Agency in 5 years or Less. LC 79-54234. 1979. 11.95 (ISBN 0-87863-203-4). Farnsworth Pub.

Levine, Philip. Don't Ask. LC 80-24992. (Poets on Poetry Ser.). 192p. 1981. pap. 7.95 (ISBN 0-472-06327-8). U of Mich Pr.

Levine, R. D. & Jortner, J. Molecular Energy Transfer. LC 75-37726. 1976. 54.95 o.s.i. (ISBN 0-470-15205-2). Halsted Pr.

--Molecular Energy Transfer. LC 75-37726. 310p. (Orig.). 40.25 o.p. (ISBN 0-470-15205-2). Krieger.

Levine, Rachmiel & Luft, Rolf, eds. Advances in Metabolic Disorders, Vol. 10. Date not set. price not set (ISBN 0-12-027310-1); price not set lib. ed. (ISBN 0-12-027388-8); price not set microfiche (ISBN 0-12-027389-6). Acad Pr.

Levine, Raphael D. & Tribus, Myron, eds. The Maximum Entropy Formalism. 1979. text ed. 30.00x (ISBN 0-262-12080-1). MIT Pr.

Levine, Richard A. The Victorian Experience: The Novelists. LC 75-15338. 272p. 1983. pap. 10.95 (ISBN 0-8214-0747-3, 82-85165). Ohio U Pr.

Levine, Richard A., ed. The Victorian Experience: The Novelists. LC 75-15338. 273p. 1976. 15.95x (ISBN 0-8214-0190-4, 82-81933). Ohio U Pr.

Levine, Richard A., intro. by. The Victorian Experience: The Poets. LC 81-4020. 202p. 1982. text ed. 19.95x (ISBN 0-8214-0447-4, 82-83392). Ohio U Pr.

Levine, Richard A., ed. The Victorian Experience: The Poets. LC 81-4020. x, 202p. 1983. pap. 10.95 (ISBN 0-8214-0748-1, 82-85173). Ohio U Pr.

--The Victorian Experience: The Prose Writers. LC 81-22493. 239p. 1982. lib. bdg. 20.95x (ISBN 0-8214-0446-6, 82-83384). Ohio U Pr.

--The Victorian Experience: The Prose Writers. LC 81-22492. 239p. 1983. pap. 10.95 (ISBN 0-8214-0707-4, 82-84762). Ohio U Pr.

Levine, Robert. Ethics & Regulation of Clinical Research. LC 81-11399. 317p. 1981. text ed. 35.00 (ISBN 0-8067-1111-6). Urban & S.

LeVine, Robert A. Dreams & Deeds: Achievement Motivation in Nigeria. LC 66-20580. (Midway Reprint Ser.). 123p. Date not set. pap. write for info. (ISBN 0-226-47572-7). U of Chicago Pr.

LeVine, Robert A. & LeVine, B. B. Nyansongo: A Gusii Community in Kenya. LC 76-52994. 240p. 1977. pap. 7.50 (ISBN 0-88275-514-5). Krieger.

Levine, Samuel. You Take Jesus, I'll Take God. LC 80-82731. 134p. (Orig.). 1980. pap. 4.95 o.p. (ISBN 0-9604754-1-9); pap. 4.95 o.p. (ISBN 0-9604754-1-9). Hamoroh Pr.

Levine, Shlomo D. The Singular Problems of the Single Jewish Parent. 39p. (Orig.). 1981. pap. text ed. 1.25 (ISBN 0-8381-2115-2). United Synagogue.

Levine, Sol. Your Future in NASA. LC 69-11498. (Careers in Depth Ser). (gr. 7 up). 1969. PLB 7.97 o.p. (ISBN 0-8239-0055-X). Rosen Pr.

--Your Future in NASA: National Aeronautic & Space Administration. LC 78-114111. (Career Guidance Ser). 1971. pap. 4.50 (ISBN 0-668-02255-8). Arco.

Levine, Sol, jt. auth. see Croog, Sydney H.

Levine, Steve. A Blue Tongue. LC 76-41297. 20p. 1976. pap. 3.00 o.p. (ISBN 0-915124-19-X). Toothpaste.

Levine, Steven Z. Monet & His Critics. LC 75-23800. (Outstanding Dissertations in the Fine Arts - 19th Century). (Illus.). 1976. lib. bdg. 45.00 o.s.i. (ISBN 0-8240-1995-4). Garland Pub.

Levine, Summer N., ed. Financial Analyst's Handbook. Incl. Vol. 1. Portfolio Management. 1492p. 45.00 (ISBN 0-87094-082-1); Vol. 2. Analysis by Industry. 1032p. o.p. (ISBN 0-87094-083-X). LC 74-81386. 1975. Dow Jones-Irwin.

Levine, Sumner N., ed. Investment Manager's Handbook. LC 79-53965. 1037p. 1980. 45.00 (ISBN 0-87094-207-7). Dow Jones-Irwin.

Levine, Susan P. & Sharow, Nancy. Recreation Experiences for the Severly Impaired or Nonambulatory Child. (Illus.). 96p. 1983. pap. 11.75x (ISBN 0-398-04783-9). C C Thomas.

Levine, Suzanne, et al. The Decade of Women: A Ms. History of the Seventies in Words & Pictures. 17.95 o.p. (ISBN 0-399-12490-X). Putnam Pub Group.

Levine, Suzanne J., jt. auth. see Monegal, Emir R.

Levine, Suzanne J., tr. see Puig, Manuel.

Levine, Talya. Chronic Cholecystitis: Its Pathology & the Role of Vascular Factors in Its Pathogenesis. LC 75-6842. 1975. 49.95 o.s.i. (ISBN 0-470-53122-3). Halsted Pr.

Le Vine, Victor T. Cameroon Federal Republic. Carter, Gwendolen M., ed. LC 70-148025. (Africa in the Modern World Ser). 1971. 24.95x (ISBN 0-8014-0637-4); pap. 5.95x o.p. (ISBN 0-8014-9121-5, CP121). Cornell U Pr.

Levine, Victor T. & Luke, Timothy W. The Arab-African Connection: Political & Economic Realities. (Special Studies on Africa & the Middle East). 1979. lib. bdg. 18.50 (ISBN 0-89158-398-X). Westview.

Levin-Epstein, Michael, jt. auth. see Anderson, Howard J.

Levinger, Elma E. Great Jews Since Bible Times. (Illus.). (gr. 1-4). 2.50x o.p. (ISBN 0-87441-053-3). Behrman.

Levins, Hoag. Arab Reach: The Secret War Against Israel. LC 82-45255. 336p. 1983. 17.95 (ISBN 0-385-18057-8). Doubleday.

Levinson, A. A. & Taylor, Ross. Moon Rocks & Minerals. 240p. 1972. text ed. 33.00 (ISBN 0-08-016669-5). Pergamon.

Levinson, A. A., ed. Apollo Eleven Lunar Science Conference, Jan., 1970: Proceedings, 3 vols. Incl. Vol. 1. Minerology & Petrology; Vol. 2. Chemical & Isotope Analysis; Vol. 3. Physical Properties. LC 72-119485. c, 2000p. 1971. Set. 275.00 (ISBN 0-08-016392-0). Pergamon.

Levinson, Abraham. The Mentally Retarded Child. rev. & enl. ed. LC 77-25884. (Illus.). 1978. Repr. of 1965 ed. lib. bdg. 21.00x (ISBN 0-313-20123-4, LEMR). Greenwood.

Levinson, Andre. Marie Taglioni (1804-1884) Beaumont, Cyril W., tr. from Fre. (Illus.). 111p. 1977. pap. 6.95 (ISBN 0-903102-33-1). Princeton Bk Co.

Levinson, Daniel R. Personal Liability of Managers & Supervisors for Corporate EEO Policies & Decisions. LC 82-84264. (EEAC Monograph Ser.). 52p. (Orig.). 1982. pap. 6.95 (ISBN 0-937856-06-1). Equal Employ.

Levinson, David, ed. A Guide to Alcoholism Treatment Research: Vol I Behavioral Medicine - Behavior Modification. LC 82-82466. (Theoretical Information Control Guides Ser.). 525p. (Orig.). 1981. pap. 60.00 (ISBN 0-87536-736-4). HRAFP.

Levinson, E. D. Architectural Rendering. 240p. 1983. 18.95x (ISBN 0-07-037413-9). McGraw.

Levinson, Harold M. Collective Bargaining & Technological Change in American Transportation. 723p. 1971. 9.00 (ISBN 0-686-94027-X, Trans). Northwestern U Pr.

Levinson, Harry. Casebook for Psychological Man. LC 82-8955. 208p. 1982. pap. 6.95 (ISBN 0-916516-04-0); 6.95 (ISBN 0-916516-05-9). Levinson Inst.

--Emotional Health in the World of Work. rev ed. LC 63-20323. 298p. 1964. pap. 7.95 (ISBN 0-916516-03-2). Levinson Inst.

--Executive. rev. ed. LC 80-26107. 382p. 18.50 (ISBN 0-674-27395-8); pap. 7.95 (ISBN 0-674-27396-6). Harvard U Pr.

--Psychological Man. LC 76-2583. 147p. (Orig.). 1976. pap. text ed. 5.95 (ISBN 0-916516-02-4). Levinson Inst.

Levinson, Henry S. Science, Metaphysics, & the Chance of Salvation: An Interpretation of the Thought of William James. LC 78-7383. 1978. pap. 9.95 (ISBN 0-89130-234-4, 01-01-24). Scholars Pr Ca.

Levinson, Irving J. Introduction to Mechanics. 2nd ed. 1968. text ed. 22.95 (ISBN 0-13-487660-1). P-H.

--Mechanics of Materials. 2nd ed. 1970. text ed. 22.95 (ISBN 0-13-571380-3). P-H.

--Preparing for the Engineer-In-Training Examination. LC 82-18251. 242p. 1983. pap. 12.95 (ISBN 0-910554-40-4). Eng Pr.

--Statics & Strength of Materials. 1970. 23.95 (ISBN 0-13-844506-0). P-H.

Levinson, Leah. With Wooden Sword. (Illus.). 350p. 1983. 22.95X (ISBN 0-930350-42-1). NE U Pr.

Levinson, Louis, jt. ed. see Singer, Richard B.

Levinson, Michael see Wruble, Lawrence D., et al.

Levinson, N., jt. auth. see Coddington, Earl A.

Levinson, Nancy S. The First Women Who Spoke Out. Hopkins, Terry, ed. (Contributions of Women Ser.). (Illus.). 112p. (gr. 6 up). 1983. PLB 8.95 (ISBN 0-87518-235-6). Dillon.

--Silent Fear. Schroeder, Howard, ed. LC 81-3301. (Roundup Ser.). (Illus.). 48p. (gr. 3 up). 1981. PLB 7.95 (ISBN 0-89686-154-6); pap. text ed. 3.95 (ISBN 0-89686-162-7). Crestwood Hse.

Levinson, Norman & Redheffer, Raymond. Complex Variables. LC 76-113833. (Illus.). 1970. text ed. 26.95x (ISBN 0-8162-5104-5); sol. man. 6.00 (ISBN 0-8162-5114-2). Holden-Day.

Levinson, Paul, ed. In Pursuit of Truth: Essays on the Philosophy of Karl Popper on the Occasion of His 80th Birthday. 304p. 1982. text ed. 25.00x (ISBN 0-391-02609-7, Pub. by Harvester England). Humanities.

Levinson, Robert. The Jews in the California Gold Rush. 20.00 (ISBN 0-87068-436-1). Ktav.

Levinson, Robert E. The Decentralized Company: Making the Most of Entrepreneurial Management. 192p. 1982. 15.95 (ISBN 0-8144-5674-X). Am Mgmt.

Levinthal, Charles F. Introduction to Physiological Psychology. 2nd ed. (Illus.). 528p. 1983. prof. ref. 25.95 (ISBN 0-13-493056-8). P-H.

--The Physiological Approach in Psychology. (Illus.). 1979. 24.95 (ISBN 0-13-674796-5). P-H.

Levinthal, Lance & Kane, Gerry. Assembly Language Programming: Sixty-Eight Thousand. 600p. 1981. pap. 16.99 (ISBN 0-931988-62-4). Osborne-McGraw.

Levis, Allen. General Merchandise in Food Stores. 1981. 21.95 (ISBN 0-86730-313-1). Lebhar Friedman.

Levis, Larry. The Dollmaker's Ghost. 1981. 10.25 (ISBN 0-525-09450-4, 0995-300); pap. 6.25 (ISBN 0-525-47662-8, 0607-180). Dutton.

Levison, Andrew. The Full Employment Alternative. LC 79-17768. 1980. 10.95 o.p. (ISBN 0-698-10814-0, Coward). Putnam Pub Group.

--The Working Class Majority. LC 73-78756. 320p. 1975. 8.95 o.p. (ISBN 0-698-10553-2, Coward). Putnam Pub Group.

--The Working Class Majority. 1975. pap. 3.95 o.p. (ISBN 0-14-004084-6). Penguin.

Levison, Matthew E. Pneumonia: A Clinical Approach to Infectious Diseases of the Lower Respiratory Tract. (Illus.). 480p. 1983. text ed. 45.00 (ISBN 0-7236-7020-X). Wright PSG.

Levison, Peter, ed. Substance Abuse, Habitual Behavior & Self-Control. cancelled (ISBN 0-86531-034-3). Westview.

Levison, Peter K. & Gerstein, Dean R., eds. Commonalities in Substance Abuse & Habitual Behavior. LC 82-48537. 384p. 1983. 33.95x (ISBN 0-669-06293-6). Lexington Bks.

Levi-Strauss, Claude. From Honey to Ashes: Introduction to a Science of Mythology, Vol. 2. Weightman, John & Weightman, Doreen, trs. LC 82-15965. 512p. 1973. pap. 10.95 (ISBN 0-226-47489-5). U of Chicago Pr.

--Myth & Meaning. LC 78-25833. 1979. 8.95x (ISBN 0-8052-3710-0); pap. 3.95 (ISBN 0-8052-0622-1). Schocken.

--The Naked Man. LC 79-3399. (Illus.). 747p. 1983. pap. 8.61i (ISBN 0-06-090892-0, CN 892, CN). Har-Row.

--The Raw & the Cooked: Introduction to a Science of Mythology, Vol. 1. Weightman, John & Weightman, Doreen, trs. LC 82-15895. (Illus.). xiv, 388p. 1969. pap. 8.95 (ISBN 0-226-47487-9). U of Chicago Pr.

--Structural Anthropology, Vol. 1. LC 63-17344. 1963. o.s. 14.00x (ISBN 0-465-08228-9); pap. 7.95x (ISBN 0-465-09516-X, TB5017). Basic.

--Structural Anthropology, Vol. 2. Layton, Monique, tr. LC 63-17344. 416p. 1976. 19.00x o.s.i. (ISBN 0-465-08230-0). Basic.

--Structural Anthropology, Vol. 2. Layton, Monique, tr. LC 82-16115. xvi, 384p. 1976. pap. 10.95 (ISBN 0-226-47491-7). U of Chicago Pr.

--The Way of the Masks. Modelski, Sylvia, tr. from Fr. LC 82-2723. (Illus.). 276p. 1982. 18.95 (ISBN 0-295-95929-0). U of Wash Pr.

Levitan, B. M. & Zhikov, V. V. Almost Periodic Functions & Differential Equations. Longdon, L. V., tr. LC 82-4352. 150p. 1983. 34.50 (ISBN 0-521-24407-2). Cambridge U Pr.

Levitan, E. L. Alphabetical Guide to Motion Picture, Television & Videotape Production. 1970. 16.25 o.p. (ISBN 0-07-037384-1, P&RB). McGraw.

Levitan, Max & Montagu, Ashley. Textbook of Human Genetics. 2nd ed. (Illus.). 1977. text ed. 29.95x (ISBN 0-19-502101-0). Oxford U Pr.

Levitan, S. A. Big Brother's Indian Programs: With Reservations. 1971. 12.95 (ISBN 0-07-037391-4, P&RB). McGraw.

Levitas, G. B., ed. The World of Psychology, 2 Vols. 17.50, boxed set o.s.i. (ISBN 0-8076-0208-6). Braziller.

Levith, Murray. Musical Masterpieces in Prose. (Illus.). 220p. 1981. 12.95 (ISBN 0-87666-585-7, Z-55). Paganiniana Pubns.

Levith, Murray J., ed. Fiddlers in Fiction. (Illus.). 220p. 1979. 12.95 (ISBN 0-87666-616-0, Z-27). Paganiniana Pubns.

Levitin, Sonia. Nobody Stole the Pie. LC 79-90032. (Illus.). 32p. (gr. k-4). 1980. pap. 3.50 (ISBN 0-15-665959-X, VoyB). HarBraceJ.

Levitin, Yevgeny, intro. by. Rembrandt Etchings. Baratt, Andrew, tr. (Illus.). 1979. 100.00 (ISBN 0-89893-000-6). CDP.

Levitine, George. The Dawn of Bohemianism: The Barbu Rebellion & Primitivism in Neoclassical France. LC 77-13892. (Illus.). 1978. 23.95x (ISBN 0-271-00527-0). Pa St U Pr.

Leviton, A. E., jt. auth. see Kockelman, W. J.

Leviton, A. E. & Rodda, P. U., eds. Frontiers of Geological Exploration of Western North America. 248p. (Orig.). 1982. 16.95 (ISBN 0-934394-03-2). AAASPD.

Leviton, Roberta. The Jewish Low Cholesterol Cookbook. 1979. pap. 2.50 o.p. (ISBN 0-451-08623-6, E8623, Sig). NAL.

Levitsky, Abraham, ed. see Simkin, James S.

Levitt & Guralnick. Cancer Reference Book. 256p. 1983. pap. text ed. 15.50 (ISBN 0-06-318230-0, Pub. by Har-Row Ltd England). Har-Row.

Levitt & Pickett. Sensory Aids for the Hearing Impaired. LC 76-28875. 566p. 1980. 51.95 (ISBN 0-471-08436-0, Pub. by Wiley-Interscience); pap. 33.95x (ISBN 0-471-08437-9). Wiley.

Levitt, Annette S., jt. ed. see Bertholf, Robert J.

Levitt, Arthur, Jr. How to Make Your Money Make Money. LC 80-70617. 220p. 1981. 17.50 o.p. (ISBN 0-87094-236-0). Dow Jones-Irwin.

Levitt, Barbara, jt. auth. see Levitt, Leonard S.

Levitt, Benjamin. Oils, Detergents & Maintenance Specialties, 2 Vols. 1967. 25.00 ea. o.p. Vol. 1 (ISBN 0-8206-0232-9). Vol. 2 (ISBN 0-8206-0258-2). Chem Pub.

Levitt, Dulcie. Plants & People: Aboriginal Uses of Plants on Groote Eylandt. (Australian Institute of Aborigianl Studies). 1981. text ed. 28.00x (ISBN 0-391-02195-8); pap. text ed. 22.50x. Humanities.

Levitt, Eleanor. Natural Food Cookery. (Illus.). 9.00 (ISBN 0-8446-5900-2). Peter Smith.

--Wonderful World of Natural Foods. LC 77-151462. (Illus.). 1971. 7.95 (ISBN 0-8208-0227-1). Hearthside.

Levitt, Eugene E. The Psychology of Anxiety. 2nd ed. LC 80-107. 188p. 1980. text ed. 16.50 (ISBN 0-89859-040-X). L Erlbaum Assocs.

Levitt, Eugene E. & Lubin, Bernard. Depression: Concepts, Controversies & Some New Facts. 2nd ed. 208p. 1983. text ed. write for info. (ISBN 0-89859-278-X). L Erlbaum Assocs.

Levitt, H., et al, eds. Sensory Aids for the Hearing Impaired. LC 76-28875. 1980. 51.95 (ISBN 0-87942-087-1). Inst Electrical.

Levitt, James H. For Want of Trade: Shipping & the New Jersey Ports, 1680-1783, Vol. 17. 224p. 1981. 19.95 (ISBN 0-911020-03-9). NJ Hist Soc.

Levitt, John, jt. auth. see Davies, Stella.

Levitt, Kari. Silent Surrender: The Multinational Corporation in Canada. 1970. 17.95 o.p. (ISBN 0-312-72450-0). St Martin.

Levitt, Leonard S. & Levitt, Barbara. Comprehensive Solved Problems in Organic Chemistry. LC 78-54189. Date not set. pap. text ed. 12.95x (ISBN 0-8162-5151-7). Holden-Day. Postponed.

Levitt, M., ed. Precast Concrete: Materials, Manufacture, Properties & Usage. (Illus.). ix, 233p. 1982. 49.25 (ISBN 0-85334-994-0, Pub. by Applied Sci England). Elsevier.

Levitt, Michael, jt. auth. see Levitt, Morton.

Levitt, Morris J. & Feldbaum, Eleanor G. Of, by & for the People: State & Local Governments & Politics. 300p. 1980. lib. bdg. 29.50x (ISBN 0-89158-591-5); pap. text ed. 12.00 (ISBN 0-89158-896-5). Westview.

Levitt, Morton & Levitt, Michael. A Tissue of Lies: Nixon vs. Hiss. 1979. 14.95 o.p. (ISBN 0-07-037397-3, GB). McGraw.

Levitt, Paul, et al. Cancer Reference Book. (Orig.). 1980. pap. 4.95 o.s.i. (ISBN 0-440-51353-7, Delta). Dell.

Levitt, Raymond E., jt. auth. see Bourdon, Clinton C.

Levitt, Sophie. Physiotherapy in Cerebral Palsy: A Handbook. (Illus.). 148p. 1962. photocopy ed. spiral 14.75x (ISBN 0-398-04337-X). C C Thomas.

Levitt, Theodore. Innovation in Marketing: New Perspectives for Profit & Growth. (Marketing & Advertising Ser.). 1962. text ed. 27.95 (ISBN 0-07-037377-9, P&RB); pap. text ed. 7.95 o.p. (ISBN 0-07-037378-7). McGraw.

--Marketing for Business Growth. Orig. Title: The Marketing Mode. (Illus.). 288p. 1974. 29.95 (ISBN 0-07-037415-5, P&RB). McGraw.

Levitt, Zola. Creation: A Scientist's Choice. 1981. pap. 4.95 (ISBN 0-89051-074-1). CLP Pubs.

--An Israeli Love Story. LC 77-27611. 1977. pap. 2.95 (ISBN 0-8024-4181-5). Moody.

Levitt, Zola, jt. auth. see McCall, Thomas.

Levitt, Zola, jt. auth. see McCall, Thomas S.

Levitt, Zola, jt. auth. see Weldon, John.

LeVitte, Dorrit, intro. by. Artists from Israel. (Illus.). 13p. 1979. pap. 3.00 (ISBN 0-89062-129-2, Pub by A.I.R. Gallery). Pub Ctr Cult Res.

Levitzki, A., jt. auth. see Schulster, D.

Levitzky, M. G. Pulmonary Physiology. 1982. 12.95 (ISBN 0-07-037431-7). McGraw.

Levkov, Jerome S., jt. auth. see Califana, Anthony.

Le Vot, Andre. F. Scott Fitzgerald. Byron, William, tr. from Fr. LC 80-2420. (Illus.). 408p. 1983. 19.95 (ISBN 0-385-17175-7). Doubleday.

Levoy, Myron. Penny Tunes & Princesses. LC 72-76517. (Illus.). 32p. (gr. k up). 1972. PLB 10.89 (ISBN 0-06-023798-8, HarpJ). Har-Row.

--A Shadow Like a Leopard. 1982. pap. 2.25 (ISBN 0-451-11796-4, AE1796, Sig). NAL.

Levstik, Frank R., compiled by. A Directory of State Archives in the United States. 66p. 1980. pap. 8.00 o.p. (ISBN 0-931828-26-0). Soc Am Archivists.

Levton, Sharon C., jt. auth. see Greenstone, James L.

Levy, jt. auth. see Lester.

Levy, Alan. Ezra Pound: The Voice of Silence. LC 82-83126. 128p. 1982. 9.95 (ISBN 0-932966-25-X). Permanent Pr.

--Good Men Still Live! ('I Am the Other Karel Capek') The Odyssey of a Professional Prisoner. LC 73-4746. 320p. 1974. 10.00 (ISBN 0-87955-308-1). O'Hara.

--W. H. Auden: In the Autumn of the Age of Anxiety. LC 82-84008. (Illus.). 128p. 1983. pap. 9.95 (ISBN 0-932966-31-4). Permanent Pr.

Levy, Alan H. Musical Nationalism: American Composers' Search for Identity. LC 82-12168. (Contributions in American Studies: No. 66). 208p. 1983. lib. bdg. 27.95 (ISBN 0-313-23709-3, LMN/). Greenwood.

Levy, Alex & Frankel, M. Television Servicing. 1959. text ed. 14.95 o.p. (ISBN 0-07-037380-9, G). McGraw.

Levy, Alex, jt. auth. see Marcus, William.

Levy, Armand. La Russie sur la Danube. (Nineteenth Century Russia Ser.). 45p. (Fr.). 1974. Repr. of 1853 ed. 26.00x o.p. (ISBN 0-8287-0545-3, R31). Clearwater Pub.

Levy, B., jt. ed. see Hirschowitz, R. G.

Levy, Babette M. Cotton Mather. (United States Authors Ser.). 1979. lib. bdg. 11.95 (ISBN 0-8057-7261-8, Twayne). G K Hall.

Levy, Barry S. & Wegman, David H., eds. Occupational Health: Recognizing & Preventing Work-Related Diseases. 1982. pap. text ed. 19.95 (ISBN 0-316-52234-1). Little.

Levy, Charles. Biology: Human Perspectives. LC 78-21136. 1979. text ed. 25.50x (ISBN 0-673-16244-3). Scott F.

Levy, Charles K. Elements of Biology. 3rd ed. LC 81-17556. (Biology Ser.). (Illus.). 550p. 1982. text ed. 25.95 (ISBN 0-201-04564-8). A-W.

--Elements of Biology. 3rd ed. 204p. 1982. pap. text ed. write for info. Instrs' Manual (ISBN 0-201-04565-6). A-W.

--A Guide to Dangerous Animals of North America: Including Central America. (Illus.). 192p. 1983. pap. 9.95 (ISBN 0-8289-0503-7). Greene.

Levy, Charles S. Guide to Ethical Decisions & Actions for Social Service Administrators. LC 81-13511. (Administration in Social Work, Monographic Ser.: Vol. 6). 172p. 1982. text ed. 25.00 (ISBN 0-86656-106-4, B106). Haworth Pr.

Levy, D. A., et al. Zen Concrete & Etc. (Illus.). 60p. 1983. pap. 5.00 (ISBN 0-941160-04-1). Ghost Pony Pr.

Levy, D. N. One b-Four: Sokolsky Opening. (Chess Player Ser.). 1977. pap. 6.95 o.p. (ISBN 0-900928-97-2, H-128). Hippocrene Bks.

Levy, D. N., jt. auth. see Keene, R. D.

Levy, Dana & Sneider, Lea. Kanban: Shop Signs of Japan. (Illus.). 168p. 1983. 29.95 (ISBN 0-8348-0180-9). Weatherhill.

Levy, David. Benko Counter Gambit. 1978. 15.95 o.p. (ISBN 0-7134-1058-2, Pub. by Batsford England). David & Charles.

Levy, David & Newborn, Monroe. More Chess & Computers. 1982. pap. 19.95 (ISBN 0-914894-74-9). Computer Sci.

Levy, David & O'Connell, Kevin. How to Play the Sicilian Defence. 144p. 1981. 19.95 (ISBN 0-7134-0757-3, Pub. by Batsford England). David & Charles.

Levy, David, jt. auth. see Levy, S. Jay.

Levy, Diane W. Ironic Techniques in Anatole France's "Les Sept Femmes de la Barbe-Bleue". LC 78-18827. (Studies in the Romance Languages & Literatures: No. 201). 160p. 1978. pap. 12.00x (ISBN 0-8078-9201-7). U of NC Pr.

Levy, Donald, jt. auth. see Goldsmith, Donald.

Levy, Donald L., tr. see Haggai, J. E.

Levy, E., ed. see Triennial World Congress World Association of Societies of Pathology (Anatomic & Clinical) Laboratory Medicine, Jerusalem, Israel, XIth, 20-25 Sept. 1981.

Levy, Edward. Came a Spider. 1980. pap. 2.50 o.p. (ISBN 0-425-04481-5). Berkley Pub.

Levy, Elizabeth. Dracula Is a Pain in the Neck. LC 82-47707. (Illus.). 80p. (gr. 2-6). 1983. 9.57i (ISBN 0-06-023822-4, HarpJ); PLB 9.89g (ISBN 0-06-023823-2). Har-Row.

--Lizzie Lies a Lot. (gr. 3-5). 1977. pap. 1.75 (ISBN 0-440-44714-3, YB). Dell.

--The Runt. (Orig.). (gr. k-6). 1981. pap. 1.95 o.p. (ISBN 0-440-47538-4, YB). Dell.

--Something Queer at the Ballpark. LC 74-16332. (gr. 1-3). 1979. pap. 2.75 o.s.i. (ISBN 0-440-08287-0). Delacorte.

--Something Queer at the Haunted School. (gr. k-6). 1983. pap. 1.75 (ISBN 0-440-48461-8, YB). Dell.

--Something Queer at the Lemonade Stand. (gr. k-6). 1983. pap. 1.75 (ISBN 0-440-48495-2, YB). Dell.

--Something Queer at the Library. LC 76-49906. (Illus.). (gr. 1-3). 1977. 6.95 o.p. (ISBN 0-440-08127-0); PLB 10.89 o.s.i. (ISBN 0-440-08128-9). Delacorte.

--Something Queer at the Library. LC 76-49906. (Illus.). (gr. 1-3). 1979. pap. 2.75 o.s.i. (ISBN 0-440-08288-9). Delacorte.

--Something Queer Is Going on. LC 72-7959. (ps-3). 1978. pap. 2.75 o.s.i. (ISBN 0-440-08141-6). Delacorte.

Levy, Elizabeth, adapted by. Father Murphy's First Miracle. (Illus.). 128p. (gr. 4-8). 1983. pap. 1.95 (ISBN 0-394-85810-7). Random.

Levy, Ernst, jt. auth. see Levarie, Siegmund.

Levy, Esther. Jewish Cookery Book. (Jewish Cookery Classics Ser.). (Illus.). 10.95; pap. 8.95 (ISBN 0-910231-00-1). Pholiota.

Levy, Ezra C. New Table of Laplace Transformation Pairs. 3rd ed. 1982. pap. 5.95 (ISBN 0-910266-11-5). Bk Page.

Levy, Ferdinand K., jt. auth. see Wiest, Jerome D.

Levy, Frank S., et al. Urban Outcomes: Schools, Streets, & Libraries. (The Oakland Project). 1974. 30.00x (ISBN 0-520-02546-6); pap. 8.50x (ISBN 0-520-03045-1). U of Cal Pr.

Levy, Fred D. Chile: An Economy in Transition. viii, 584p. 1980. pap. 20.00 (ISBN 0-686-36102-4, RC-8001). World Bank.

Levy, George C. Topics in Carbon-13 NMR Spectroscopy, Vol. 3. LC 74-10529. (Topics in Carbon-13 NMR Spectroscopy Ser.). 1979. 55.95x (ISBN 0-471-02873-8, Pub. by Wiley-Interscience). Wiley.

Levy, George C. & Lichter, Robert L. Nitrogen-Fifteen Nuclear Magnetic Resonance Spectroscopy. LC 78-4016. 1979. 26.50x (ISBN 0-471-02954-8, Pub by Wiley-Interscience). Wiley.

Levy, George C. & Terpstra, Dan. Computer Networks in the Chemical Laboratory. LC 81-599. 221p. 1981. 30.95x (ISBN 0-471-08471-9, Pub. by Wiley-Interscience). Wiley.

Levy, Gertrude R. The Sword from the Rock: An Investigation into the Origins of Epic Literature & the Development of the Hero. LC 76-47642. (Illus.). 1977. Repr. of 1953 ed. lib. bdg. 20.50x (ISBN 0-8371-9300-1, LESFR). Greenwood.

Levy, Haim, jt. auth. see Ben-Horim, Moshe.

Levy, Haim, ed. Research in Finance, Vol. 1. 1979. lib. bdg. 38.50 (ISBN 0-89232-043-5). Jai Pr.

--Research in Finance, Vol. 2. 250p. (Orig.). 1980. lib. bdg. 38.50 (ISBN 0-89232-043-5). Jai Pr.

--Research in Finance, Vol. 3. 225p. 1981. 38.50 (ISBN 0-89232-218-7). Jai Pr.

Levy, Henry M. Capability-Based Computer Systems. 200p. 1983. 25.00 (ISBN 0-932376-22-3). Digital Pr.

Levy, Herbert M. How to Handle an Appeal. 569p. 1982. 35.00 o.p. (ISBN 0-686-96185-4, H1-2963). PLI.

Levy, Howard S. Harem Favorites of an Illustrious Celestial. 1957. 15.00 (ISBN 0-686-00724-7, Pub. by Langstaff-Levy). Oriental Bk Store.

--Japan's Poetress of Love: Izumi Shikibu (Flourished 990-1020), 300 Poems. (East Asian Poetry in Translation Ser.: No. 16-18). 1981. pap. 16.00 (ISBN 0-686-37538-6). Oriental Bk Store.

--Oriental Sex Manners. 1978. text ed. 15.00 (ISBN 0-685-67212-3, Pub. by Langstaff-Levy). Oriental Bk Store.

Levy, Howard S., jt. auth. see Ishihara, Akira.

Levy, Howard S., tr. from Chinese. China's Dirtiest Trickster: Folklore About Hsu Wen-ch'ang (1521-1593) (Sino-Japanese Folklore Translations Ser.: No. 1). (Illus.). 68p. 1974. 15.00 (ISBN 0-686-05428-8, Pub. by Langstaff-Levy). Oriental BK Store.

Levy, Howard S., tr. Fujiwara No Teika: One Hundred Selections. (East Asian Poetry in Translation Ser.: No. 19). 1981. pap. 8.00 (ISBN 0-686-37539-4). Oriental Bk Store.

--Japanese Sex Jokes in Traditional Times: 207 Stories. 1973. pap. 10.00 (ISBN 0-686-05007-X, Pub. by Langstaff-Levy). Oriental Bk Store.

--Korean Sex Jokes in Traditional Times: 206 Stories. 1972. pap. 15.00 (ISBN 0-686-01302-6, Pub. by Langstaff-Levy). Oriental Bk Store.

--Minamoto No Sanetomo (1192-1219) As a Love Poet (Japanese Love Poems 501-600) (East Asian Poetry in Translation Ser.: No. 14). 1980. pap. 8.00 (ISBN 0-686-37536-X). Oriental Bk Store.

--One Hundred Selections from Kokinshu, Vol. 3. 1976. pap. 8.00 (ISBN 0-89986-259-4). Oriental Bk Store.

--Po Chu-i: Lament Everlasting. 1962. pap. 7.00 (ISBN 0-686-00726-3, Pub. by Langstaff-Levy). Oriental Bk Store.

--Saigyo: More Love Poems (101-200) (East Asian Poetry in Translation Ser.: No. 15). 1981. pap. 8.00 (ISBN 0-686-37537-8). Oriental Bk Store.

--Saigyo (1112-1190) As a Love Poet: One Hundred More Selections (210-300), Japanese Love Poems (1001-1100) (East Asian Poetry in Translation Ser.: No. 20). 1981. pap. 8.00 (ISBN 0-686-37540-8). Oriental Bk Store.

--Saigyo (1118-1190) As a Love Poet (Japanese Love Poems, 401-500) (East Asian Poetry in Translation Ser.: No. 12). 1980. pap. 8.00 (ISBN 0-686-37534-3). Oriental Bk Store.

--Saigyo (1118-1190) the Poet of Reflective Being & Natural Scene. (East Asian Poetry in Translation Ser.: No. 13). 1980. pap. 8.00 (ISBN 0-686-37535-1). Oriental Bk Store.

Levy, Howard S. & Kawatani, Michiko, trs. Japan's Dirty Old Man: Sex Adventures of Hirota Kicchomu. 1979. 15.00 (ISBN 0-686-37541-6). Oriental Bk Store.

Levy, Howard S. & Ohsawa, Junko, trs. Japanese Love Poems (301-400) (East Asian Poetry in Translation Ser.: No. 11). 1980. pap. 8.00 (ISBN 0-686-37533-5). Oriental Bk Store.

--Senryu Selections. (East Asian Poetry in Translation Ser.: No. 10). 1979. pap. 8.00 (ISBN 0-686-37532-7). Oriental Bk Store.

Levy, Howard S., tr. see Chang, Ching-sheng.

Levy, Howard S., tr. see Chang Wen-Ch'eng.

Levy, Howard S., tr. see Yu, Huai.

Levy, J. Literary Translation As an Art Form. Flatauer, S., tr. (Approaches to Translation Studies: No. 6). Date not set. pap. text ed. price not set (ISBN 0-391-01196-0). Humanities.

Levy, Jonathan. Marco Polo & Other Plays for Children. LC 81-9830. (Illus.). 1983. pap. 12.00 (ISBN 0-89676-067-7). Drama Bk.

Levy, Joseph. Play Behavior. LC 77-12504. 1978. pap. text ed. 24.95x o.p. (ISBN 0-471-01712-4). Wiley.

--Punched Card Data Processing. 1967. text ed. 24.95 (ISBN 0-07-037386-8, C). McGraw.

Levy, Judy. Patchwork Pillows. LC 76-47804. (Dover Needlework Ser.). (Illus.). 1977. pap. 2.95 (ISBN 0-486-23473-8). Dover.

Levy, Julien. Memoir of an Art Gallery. LC 76-24793. (Illus.). 1977. 8.95 o.p. (ISBN 0-399-11847-0). Putnam Pub Group.

Levy, Karen D. Jacques Riviere. (World Authors Ser.). 1982. lib. bdg. 17.95 (ISBN 0-8057-6476-3, Twayne). G K Hall.

Levy, Kenneth. Music: A Listener's Introduction. 640p. 1983. text ed. 20.50 scp (ISBN 0-06-043978-5, HarpC); instr's. manual avail. (ISBN 0-06-364005-8); scp study guide 8.95 (ISBN 0-06-044072-4); Record program 40.50 (ISBN 0-06-043933-5). Har-Row.

Levy, Kurt L. Tomas Carrasquilla. (World Authors Ser.). 1980. lib. bdg. 15.95 (ISBN 0-8057-6389-9, Twayne). G K Hall.

Levy, Laurie, ed. see Lansing, Adrienne & Goldsmith, Alice.

Levy, Leon S. Discrete Structures of Computer Science. LC 79-11218. 1980. text ed. 25.95x (ISBN 0-471-03208-5). Wiley.

Levy, Leonard. Blasphemy in Massachusetts: Freedom of Conscience & the Abner Kneeland Case. LC 70-16634. 592p. 1973. lib. bdg. 65.00 (ISBN 0-306-70221-5). Da Capo.

Levy, Leonard W. Origins of the Fifth Amendment: The Right Against Self-Incrimination. 1971. pap. 7.95 o.p. (ISBN 0-19-501356-5, GB34, GB). Oxford U Pr.

Levy, Leonard W. & Jones, Douglas L., eds. Jim Crow in Boston: The Origin of the "Separate but Equal Doctrine". LC 73-39622. (Civil Liberties in American History Ser). 1974. lib. bdg. 35.00 (ISBN 0-306-70157-X). Da Capo.

Levy, Lester S. Picture the Songs: Lithographs from the Sheet Music of Nineteenth Century America. (Illus.). 213p. 1976. 25.00 (ISBN 0-686-36480-5). Md Hist.

Levy, M., jt. auth. see Salvadori, Mario.

Levy, Marc. Photography Textbook. (Illus.). 208p. 1980. 25.00 o.p. (ISBN 0-8174-5514-0, Amphoto); pap. 14.95 o.p. (ISBN 0-8174-5515-9). Watson-Guptill.

Levy, Mark R. & Kramer, Michael S. The Ethnic Factor: How America's Minorities Decide Elections. 1973. pap. 3.95 o.p. (ISBN 0-671-21527-2, Touchstone Bks). S&S.

Levy, Matthew N. & Vassalle, Mario. Excitation & Neural Control of the Heart. (Illus.). 312p. 1982. 33.50 (ISBN 0-686-36137-7). Longman.

Levy, Matthew N., jt. auth. see Berne, Robert M.

Levy, Norman. The Foundations of the South African Cheap Labour System. (International Library of Sociology). 300p. 1982. 32.50 (ISBN 0-7100-0909-7). Routledge & Kegan.

Levy, Norman B., jt. ed. see Solomon, Kenneth.

Levy, Norman S., jt. auth. see Schachar, Ronald A.

Levy, Norman S., jt. auth. see Schacher, Ronald A.

Levy, Oscar, ed. see Nietzsche, Friedrich.

Levy, Paul, ed. see Strachey, Lytton.

Levy, Paul S. & Lemeshow, Stanley. Sampling for Health Professionals. LC 80-14733. 320p. 1980. pap. 26.00 (ISBN 0-534-97986-6); solutions manual 3.95. Lifetime Learn.

Levy, Penny A. & George, Levy. The Complete Book of Fearless Flying. 208p. 1982. pap. 2.95 (ISBN 0-936750-04-9). Wetherall.

Levy, Reuben. A Baghdad Chronicle. LC 77-10580. (Studies in Islamic History: No. 17). (Illus.). Repr. of 1929 ed. lib. bdg. 22.50x (ISBN 0-87991-466-1). Porcupine Pr.

--Social Structure of Islam. 1957. 59.50 (ISBN 0-521-05544-X). Cambridge U Pr.

Levy, Robert I., et al, eds. Nutrition, Lipids & Coronary Heart Disease. LC 78-67020. (Nutrition in Health & Disease Ser.: Vol. 1). 576p. 1979. 57.00 (ISBN 0-89004-181-4). Raven.

Levy, Robert J., jt. auth. see Feld, Barry.

Levy, Ronald. The New Language of Psychiatry: Learning & Using DSM-III. 384p. 1981. text ed. 24.95 (ISBN 0-316-52236-8). Little.

Levy, S. J. Managing the Drugs in Your Life: A Personal & Family Guide. 352p. 1983. 16.95 (ISBN 0-07-037411-2, GB). McGraw.

Levy, S. Jay & Levy, David. Profits & the Future of American Society. LC 81-47663. 224p. 1983. write for info (ISBN 0-06-014943-4, HarpT). Har-Row.

Levy, Salomon see Heat Transfer & Fluid Mechanics Institute.

Levy, Samuel & Wilkinson, John P. D. Component Element Method in Dynamics. 1976. 49.50 (ISBN 0-07-037398-1, P&RB). McGraw.

Levy, Seymour. Improving Performance through Performance Review: A Guide to the Employee. 1970. 4.94 (ISBN 0-935198-02-4). M M Bruce.

Levy, Sidney J., jt. auth. see Boyd, Harper W., Jr.

Levy, Sydney. The Play of the Text: Max Jacob's "Le Cornet a Des". LC 80-52298. 174p. 1981. 22.50 (ISBN 0-299-08510-4). U of Wis Pr.

Levy, Valerie, jt. auth. see Glotzer, Arline.

Levy, Valerie, ed. A Guide to Shakespeare's Best Works. 608p. 1982. pap. 9.95 (ISBN 0-671-45871-X). Monarch Pr.

Levy, Valerie, ed. see Cornelius, Hal & Lewis, William.

Levy, Valerie, ed. see Lovejoy.

Levy, Valerie, ed. see Munzert, Alfred.

Levy, Valerie, ed. see Rosenberg, Richard.

Levy, William S. Skin Problems of the Amputee. LC 78-50196. (Illus.). 320p. 1983. 49.75 (ISBN 0-87527-181-2). Green.

Levytsky, Borys, compiled by. The Stalinist Terror in the Thirties: Documentation from the Soviet Press. LC 72-137404. (Publications Ser.: No. 126). (Illus.). 521p. 1974. 16.95x o.p. (ISBN 0-8179-6261-1). Hoover Inst Pr.

Lew, Gordon, tr. see Lim, Genny.

Lew, J. Art of Stretching & Kicking. 1977. 4.95x (ISBN 0-685-83170-1). Wehman.

Lew, James. The Art of Stretching & Kicking. LC 80-106144. (Illus.). 104p. 1977. pap. 4.95 (ISBN 0-86568-007-8). Unique Pubns.

Lew, Jennifer & Proctor, Richard. Surface Design for Fabric. 1983. write for info. U of Wash Pr.

Lew, Marvin I. Hospital Pharmacy Journal Articles. 3rd ed. 1977. spiral bdg. 15.50 o.p. (ISBN 0-87488-799-2). Med Exam.

Lewald, H. Ernest. Eduardo Mallea. (World Authors Ser.). 1977. lib. bdg. 15.95 (ISBN 0-8057-6273-6, Twayne). G K Hall.

--Latin America: Sus Culturas y Sociedades. (Illus.). 384p. 1973. text ed. 27.50 (ISBN 0-07-037420-1, C). McGraw.

Lewald, H. Ernest & Yates, Donald A. El Espiritu de la Juventad: A Spanish American Reader. 128p. 1981. pap. text ed. 9.95 (ISBN 0-13-246983-9). P-H.

Lewald, H. Ernest, ed. The Web: Feminist Stories by Argentine Women. LC 81-51646. 135p. 1983. 16.00 (ISBN 0-89410-295-8); pap. 8.00 (ISBN 0-89410-296-6). Three Continents.

Lewandowski, A. Response Time Testing on Concentrating Collectors. (Progress in Solar Energy Supplements SERI Ser.). 1983. pap. text ed. 7.50x (ISBN 0-89553-090-2). Am Solar Energy.

Lewandowski, Stephen. Inside & Out. LC 78-17776. 1979. 10.95 (ISBN 0-89594-023-X); pap. 3.95 (ISBN 0-89594-012-4). Crossing Pr.

Lewandowski, Stephen, ed. Farmer's & Housekeepers's Cyclopaedia of 1888. LC 77-23827. 1978. 18.95 (ISBN 0-912278-91-9); pap. 10.95 (ISBN 0-686-71761-9). Crossing Pr.

Lewanski, Richard C. Bibliography of Slavic Dictionaries: Belorussian, Bulgarian, Czech, Kashubian, Lusatian, Old Church Slavic,Macedonian, Polabian, Serbocroation, Slovak, Slovenian, Ukrainian, Vol. 2. LC 62-18516. (Orig.). 1963. pap. 7.50 o.p. (ISBN 0-87104-025-5). NY Pub Lib.

--Bibliography of Slavic Dictionaries: Polish, Vol.1. LC 59-10238. Orig. Title: Bibliography of Polish Dictionaries. (Orig.). 1965. pap. 3.00 o.p. (ISBN 0-87104-024-7). NY Pub Lib.

--Bibliography of Slavic Dictionaries: Russian, Vol. 3. LC 62-18516. (Orig.). 1963. pap. 8.50 o.p. (ISBN 0-87104-026-3). NY Pub Lib.

Lewanski, Richard C., compiled by. A Bibliography of Slavic Dictionaries, 4 vols. (Vols. 1-3, 2nd. & enl. ed.). 1973. Set. 137.00 o.p. (ISBN 3-262-00812-5). Benjamins North Am.

Lewanski, Richard C., ed. Eastern Europe & Russia-Soviet Union: A Handbook of West European Archival & Library Resources. LC 79-19520. 317p. 1980. 75.00x (ISBN 3-598-40015-2). Gale.

Lewanski, Robert T. & Zuraw, Robert A. Health Force. 2nd, rev. ed. (Illus.). 252p. 1982. 24.95 (ISBN 0-9608030-0-9). Taoist Pubs.

Lewart, Cass. Science & Engineering for the IBM-PC. (Illus.). 150p. 1983. 18.95 (ISBN 0-13-794925-1); pap. 12.95 (ISBN 0-13-794917-0). P-H.

--Science & Engineering Sourcebook. LC 82-80269. (Illus.). 96p. (Orig.). 1982. pap. 9.95 (ISBN 0-942412-02-8); Pre-recorded cass. 8.95 (ISBN 0-686-98227-4). Micro Text Pubs.

--Science & Engineering Sourcebook. 96p. 1982. 17.95 (ISBN 0-13-795229-5); pap. 9.95 (ISBN 0-13-795211-2). P-H.

Lewbin, Hyman J. Rebirth of Jewish Art: The Unfolding of Jewish Art in the Nineteenth Century. LC 74-76483. (Illus.). 1974. 8.95 (ISBN 0-88400-007-9). Shengold.

Lewellen, John. Moon, Sun & Stars. LC 81-7749. (The New True Bks.). (Illus.). 48p. (gr. k-4). 1981. PLB 9.25 (ISBN 0-516-01637-7). Childrens.

Lewellen, Ted C. Political Anthropology: An Introduction. (Illus.). 192p. 1983. text ed. 22.95x (ISBN 0-89789-028-0); pap. text ed. 10.95x (ISBN 0-89789-029-9). J F Bergin.

Lewellen, Theodore C. Peasants in Transition: The Changing Economy of the Peruvian Aymara: a General Systems Approach. LC 78-343. (A Westview Replica Edition Ser.). 1978. lib. bdg. 26.50 o.p. (ISBN 0-89158-076-X). Westview.

Lewenhak, Sheila. Women & Work. LC 80-16906. 1980. 25.00 (ISBN 0-312-88778-7). St Martin.

Lewery, A. J. Narrow Boat Painting: A History & Description of the English Narrow Boats' Traditional Paintwork. LC 74-81074. 1975. 17.50 (ISBN 0-7153-6771-4). David & Charles.

Lewes, George H. Ranthorpe. Smalley, Barbara, ed. LC 74-82496. lvii, 369p. 1974. 12.00x (ISBN 0-8214-0167-X, 82-81669); pap. 4.25 (ISBN 0-8214-0168-8, 82-81677). Ohio U Pr.

Lewi, Bee. Fritz, the Too-Long Dog. LC 79-18361. (For Real Ser.). (Illus.). 40p. (gr. 1-5). 1980. PLB 6.69 (ISBN 0-8116-4314-X). Garrard.

--A Holiday for August. LC 77-13775. (Imagination Ser.). (Illus.). (gr. 1-5). 1978. PLB 6.69 (ISBN 0-8116-4408-1). Garrard.

--We Like Noise. LC 73-22081. (Easy Venture Ser). (Illus.). 32p. (gr. k-2). 1974. PLB 6.69 (ISBN 0-8116-6061-3). Garrard.

Lewi, J. see Tiberghien, J. & Carlstedt, G.

Lewi, J., et al, eds. A Programming Methodology in Compiler Construction: Concepts, 2 pts. Pt. 1: Concepts, 1979. 40.50 (ISBN 0-444-85288-3, North Holland); Pt. 2 Implementation. 53.25 (ISBN 0-444-86339-7). Elsevier.

Lewi, P. J. & Marsboom, R. P., eds. Toxicology Reference Data-Wistar Rat. (Janssen Research Foundations Ser.: Vol. 4). 1981. 59.75 (ISBN 0-444-80342-4). Elsevier.

Lewi, Paul J. Multivariate Data Analysis in Industrial Practice. LC 82-6906. (Chemometrics Research Studies Ser.). 244p. 1982. 31.95 (ISBN 0-471-10466-3, Pub. by Res Stud Pr). Wiley.

Lewicki, T. West African Food in the Middle Ages. LC 72-88615. 288p. 1974. 42.50 (ISBN 0-521-08673-6). Cambridge U Pr.

Lewick-Wallace, M. Grammar & Sentence Structure. (Communications Skills Ser.). 240p. 1983. text ed. 11.95 (ISBN 0-07-067904-5). McGraw.

--Punctuation & Mechanics. 240p. 1982. 11.95x (ISBN 0-07-067903-7). McGraw.

Lewick-Wallace, Mary. Vocabulary Building & Word Study. Raygor, Alton, ed. (Communication Skills Ser.). 240p. (Orig.). 1981. pap. text ed. 11.95 (ISBN 0-07-067902-9, C). McGraw.

Lewin, A. C. Housing Cooperatives in Developing Countries: A Manual for Self-Help in Low Cost Housing Schemes. LC 80-40500. 170p. 1981. 39.95 (ISBN 0-471-27820-3, Pub. by Wiley-Intrscience). Wiley.

Lewin, Albert E., jt. auth. see Panama, Norman.

Lewin, Benjamin. Gene Expression: Eucaryotic Chromosomes, 1 of 3 vols, Vol. 2. 2nd ed. LC 80-10849. 1160p. 1980. 54.95x (ISBN 0-471-01977-1, Pub. by Wiley-Interscience); pap. 30.95x (ISBN 0-471-01976-3, Pub. by Wiley-Interscience). Wiley.

--Gene Expression, Vol. 1: Bacterial Genomes. LC 73-14382. (Illus.). 688p. 1974. 57.75 o.p. (ISBN 0-471-53167-7, Pub. by Wiley-Interscience); pap. 25.95 (ISBN 0-471-53168-5). Wiley.

--Gene Expression, Vol. 3: Plasmids & Phages. LC 73-14382. 1977. 48.95x (ISBN 0-471-53170-7, Pub. by Wiley-Interscience); pap. 27.95 (ISBN 0-471-02715-4). Wiley.

--Genes. 800p. 1983. text ed. 31.95 (ISBN 0-471-09316-5); lab. manual avail. (ISBN 0-471-89851-1). Wiley.

Lewin, Douglas. Logical Design of Switching Circuits. 2nd ed. 1974. 18.95 (ISBN 0-444-19546-7). Elsevier.

Lewin, Elyse, jt. auth. see Salomon, Allyn.

Lewin, Hugh. Jafta. LC 82-12847. (Illus.). 24p. (ps-3). 1983. PLB 7.95g (ISBN 0-87614-207-2). Carolrhoda Bks.

--Jafta & the Wedding. LC 82-12836. (Illus.). 24p. (ps-3). 1983. PLB 7.95g (ISBN 0-87614-210-2). Carolrhoda Bks.

--Jafta's Father. LC 82-12837. (Illus.). 24p. (ps-3). 1983. PLB 7.95g (ISBN 0-87614-209-9). Carolrhoda Bks.

--Jafta's Mother. LC 82-12863. (Illus.). 24p. (ps-3). 1983. PLB 7.95g (ISBN 0-87614-208-0). Carolrhoda Bks.

Lewin, John, ed. British Rivers. (Illus.). 228p. 1981. text ed. 60.00x (ISBN 0-04-551047-4). Allen Unwin.

Lewin, Karl K. Heritage of Illusions. LC 76-528. 192p. 1977. 12.50 (ISBN 0-87527-157-X). Green.

Lewin, Kurt. Dynamic Theory of Personality. 1955. pap. 3.95 o.p. (ISBN 0-07-037451-1, SP). McGraw.

Lewin, Larry, jt. auth. see Knight, Tanis.

Lewin, Leonard C. Report from Iron Mountain. 1969. pap. 2.45 o.s.i. (ISBN 0-440-57366-1, Delta). Dell.

Lewin, M., ed. Fiber Science: JAPS Symposium, No. 31. 1977. 33.95x (ISBN 0-471-04563-2, Pub. by Wiley-Interscience). Wiley.

Lewin, Michael. The Silent Salesman. 1980. pap. 2.25 o.p. (ISBN 0-425-04031-3). Berkley Pub.

Lewin, Michael Z. Hard Line. 1982. 11.45 (ISBN 0-688-01335-X). Morrow.

Lewin, Miriam. Understanding Psychological Research: The Student Researcher's Handbook. LC 78-27842. 1979. text ed. 27.95x (ISBN 0-471-65837-5); tchrs. manual 5.50 (ISBN 0-471-05037-7). Wiley.

Lewin, Moshe. Lenin's Last Struggle. LC 78-59693. 1978. pap. 5.95 (ISBN 0-85345-473-6, PB-4736). Monthly Rev.

Lewin, Ralph A. The Biology of Algae & Other Verses. LC 81-40015. 112p. 1981. pap. text ed. 7.00 (ISBN 0-8191-1689-0). U Pr of Amer.

Lewin, Roger. Darwin's Forgotten World. LC 78-51057. (Illus.). 1978. 9.98 (ISBN 0-89169-513-3). Reed Bks.

--Thread of Life: The Smithsonian Looks at Evolution. LC 82-16834. (Illus.). 256p. 1982. 27.50 (ISBN 0-89599-010-5). Smithsonian Bks.

Lewin, Roger, jt. auth. see Leakey, Richard.

Lewin, Roland. The American Magic: Codes, Ciphers & the Defeat of Japan. 1983. pap. 5.95 (ISBN 0-14-006471-0). Penguin.

Lewin, Ronald. Ultra Goes to War. 1978. 12.95 o.p. (ISBN 0-07-037453-8, GB). McGraw.

Lewin, Susan Grant, jt. auth. see Tigerman, Stanley.

Lewine, Harris, jt. auth. see Driggs, Frank.

LeWinn, Edward B. Human Neurological Organization. (Illus.). 244p. 1977. 14.75x (ISBN 0-398-01122-2). C C Thomas.

Lewis. Criminal Procedure: The Supreme Court's View - Cases. (Criminal Justice Ser.). 131p. 1980. pap. text ed. 8.50 (ISBN 0-8299-0321-6); 1980 Supplement avail. West Pub.

--Problem-Solving Principles for ADA Programmers: Applied Logic, Psychology, & Grit. Date not set. 9.95 (ISBN 0-686-82005-3, 5211). Hayden.

Lewis & Lyman. Essential English. 1981. pap. text ed. 10.95x (ISBN 0-673-16218-4). Scott F.

Lewis, jt. auth. see Ray.

Lewis, et al. How to Choose, Change, Advance Your Career. 1983. pap. 4.95 (ISBN 0-8120-2245-9). Barron.

Lewis, A. S., ed. see Romen, A. S.

Lewis, Adele. How to Write Better Resumes. rev. ed. LC 77-14. 1983. pap. 4.95 (ISBN 0-8120-2372-2). Barron.

Lewis, Adele & Marks, Edith. Job Hunting for the Disabled. 1983. pap. 7.95 (ISBN 0-8120-2487-7). Barron.

Lewis, Alan. The Psychology of Taxation. LC 82-10656. 224p. 1982. 25.00x (ISBN 0-312-65330-1). St Martin.

--Selenium: The Facts about This Essential Element. 2.50x (ISBN 0-7225-0734-8). Cancer Control Soc.

Lewis, Albert B. Melanesian Shell Money in Field Museum Collections. 1929. pap. 10.00 (ISBN 0-527-01879-1). Kraus Repr.

Lewis, Alfred J. Using American Law Books. 136p. 1983. pap. text ed. 7.95 (ISBN 0-8403-2869-9). Kendall-Hunt.

--Using Law Books. LC 75-35385. 1977. perfect bdg. 5.95 (ISBN 0-686-86238-4, 40133206). Kendall-Hunt.

Lewis, Allan. American Plays & Playwrights of the Contemporary Theatre. rev. ed. 1970. 6.95 o.p. (ISBN 0-517-50947-4). Crown.

--Ionesco. (World Authors Ser.). lib. bdg. 12.95 (ISBN 0-8057-2452-4, Twayne). G K Hall.

Lewis, Anne G. Making Rugs. LC 76-13067. (Early Craft Bks.). (Illus.). (gr. k-3). 1976. PLB 3.95g (ISBN 0-8225-0876-1). Lerner Pubns.

Lewis, Anthony. Gideon's Trumpet. 1964. 2.95 (ISBN 0-394-74410-1). Random.

Lewis, Arnold. American Country Houses of the Gilded Age: Sheldon's "Artistic Country-Seats". (Illus.). 128p. 1983. pap. 7.95 (ISBN 0-486-24301-X). Dover.

Lewis, Arnold & Morgan, Keith, eds. American Victorian Architecture. LC 73-92261. Orig. Title: L' Architecture American. (Illus.). 160p. 1975. pap. 7.95 (ISBN 0-486-23177-1). Dover.

Lewis, Arthur. Judges, Ruth. (Every Man's Bible Commentary Ser.). 1979. pap. 4.50 (ISBN 0-8024-2007-9). Moody.

Lewis, Arthur, jt. auth. see Darrow, Clarence.

Lewis, Arthur M., jt. auth. see Darrow, Clarence S.

Lewis, Aubrey. The Later Papers of Sir Aubrey Lewis. 1979. text ed. 37.50x o.p. (ISBN 0-19-712150-0). Oxford U Pr.

Lewis, Aubrey, ed. see Maudsley, Henry.

Lewis, B., ed. Bioacoustics: A Comparative Approach. (Illus.). Date not set. price not set (ISBN 0-12-446550-1). Acad Pr.

Lewis, B. T. & Marron, J. P. Facilities & Plant Engineering Handbook. 1974. 55.00 (ISBN 0-07-037560-7, P&RB). McGraw.

Lewis, Barbara. Fernand Leger: The Paintings. LC 79-91826. (Illus.). 40p. Date not set. lib. bdg. price not set (ISBN 0-87817-256-4). Hacker.

Lewis, Benjamin. Riding. 1958. 7.95 (ISBN 0-448-01299-5, G&D). Putnam Pub Group.

Lewis, Benjamin & Wilkin, Leon O., Jr. Veterinary Drug Index. LC 78-64717. 600p. 1981. text ed. write for info. o.p. (ISBN 0-7216-5764-8). Saunders.

Lewis, Bernard. Islam in History. LC 72-6284. 350p. 1972. 21.00x (ISBN 0-912050-35-7, Library Pr). Open Court.

Lewis, Bernard & Von Elbe, Guenther. Combustion, Flames, & Explosions of Gases. 2nd ed. 1961. 76.00 (ISBN 0-12-446750-4). Acad Pr.

Lewis, Bernard, ed. & tr. Diwan: Poems in Arabic, Persian, Turkish & Hebrew Eighth to Eighteenth Centuries. 150p. 1983. 21.50 (ISBN 0-8419-0458-8). Holmes & Meier.

Lewis, Bernard, ed. Islam, from the Prophet Muhammad to the Capture of Constantinople Vol. 1: Politics & War. (Documentary History of Western Civilization Ser.). 1973. pap. 6.95xi o.p. (ISBN 0-06-131749-7, TB1749, Torch). Har-Row.

--Islam, from the Prophet Muhammad to the Capture of Constantinople, Vol. 2: Religion & Society. 1973. pap. 5.95xi o.p. (ISBN 0-06-131750-0, TB1750, Torch). Har-Row.

Lewis, Bernard, jt. ed. see Braude, Benjamin.

Lewis, Bernard T. Management Handbook for Plant Engineers. LC 82-89. 1983. Repr. of 1977 ed. (ISBN 0-89874-413-X). Krieger.

--Management Handbook for Plant Engineers. 1976. 36.50 o.p. (ISBN 0-07-037530-5, P&RB). McGraw.

Lewis, Bruce. What Is a Laser? LC 78-11100. (Skylight Bks.). (Illus.). (gr. 2-5). 1979. 6.95 (ISBN 0-396-07646-7). Dodd.

Lewis, Bruce R. & Ford, Richard K. Basic Statistics Using SAS. 200p. 1983. pap. text ed. 7.95 (ISBN 0-314-70619-4). West Pub.

Lewis, Byron A. & Pucelik, R. Frank. Magic Demystified: A Pragmatic Guide to Communication & Change. (Illus.). 164p. 1982. pap. 12.95 (ISBN 0-943920-00-0). Metamorphous Pr.

Lewis, C. D. The Otterbury Incident. (Illus.). 160p. (gr. 5 up). bds. 7.95 (ISBN 0-370-01002-7, Pub by The Bodley Head). Merrimack Bk Serv.

Lewis, C. L. & Ott, L. Analytical Chemistry of Nickel. 1970. inquire for price o.p. (ISBN 0-08-015876-5). Pergamon.

Lewis, C. S. Abolition of Man. 1962. pap. 2.95 (ISBN 0-02-066230-0, Collier). Macmillan.

--Chronicles of Narnia, 7 bks. 1970. Set. pap. 14.95 boxed (ISBN 0-685-38343-1). Macmillan.

--Cristianismo...y Nada Mas. Orozco, Julio, tr. from Eng. LC 77-85609. 216p. (Span.). 1977. pap. 3.50 o.s.i. (ISBN 0-89922-096-7). Edit Caribe.

--God in the Dock. Hooper, Walter, ed. 1970. pap. 6.95 (ISBN 0-8028-1456-5). Eerdmans.

--The Grand Miracle. (Epiphany Ser.). 176p. 1983. pap. 2.95 (ISBN 0-345-30539-6). Ballantine.

--Grief Observed. 1963. 6.95 (ISBN 0-8164-0137-3). Seabury.

--Horse & His Boy. (gr. 5 up). 1970. pap. 2.25 (ISBN 0-02-044200-9, Collier). Macmillan.

--The Joyful Christian: One Hundred Readings from the Works of C. S. Lewis. LC 77-21685. 1977. 10.95 (ISBN 0-02-570900-3). Macmillan.

--Last Battle. (gr. 5 up). 1970. pap. 2.95 (ISBN 0-02-044210-6, Collier). Macmillan.

--Magician's Nephew. (gr. 5 up). 1970. pap. 2.25 (ISBN 0-02-044230-0, Collier). Macmillan.

--Mere Christianity. 1964. 9.95 (ISBN 0-02-570610-1); pap. 2.95 (ISBN 0-02-086810-3). Macmillan.

--Out of the Silent Planet. 1965. pap. 2.95 (ISBN 0-02-086880-4, Collier). Macmillan.

--The Screwtape Letters. Bd. with Screwtape Proposes a Toast. 1964-67. 9.95 (ISBN 0-02-571240-3, 57124); large print ed. 9.95 (ISBN 0-02-489410-9, 48941); pap. 2.95 (ISBN 0-685-22912-2). Macmillan.

--The Screwtape Letters. (Illus.). 1978. pap. 1.95 (ISBN 0-8007-8336-0, Spire Bks); pap. 4.95 (ISBN 0-8007-5014-4, Power Bks, Power Bks). Revell.

--Silver Chair. (gr. 5 up). 1970. pap. 2.25 (ISBN 0-02-044250-5, Collier). Macmillan.
--Six by Lewis. 1978. pap. 14.95 (ISBN 0-02-086770-0). Macmillan.
--Space Trilogy. Incl. Out of the Silent Planet; Perelandra; That Hideous Strength. 768p. 1975. pap. 8.95 boxed set (ISBN 0-02-022350-1). Macmillan.
--Voyage of the Dawn Treader. (gr. 5 up). 1970. pap. 2.95 (ISBN 0-02-044260-2, Collier). Macmillan.
Lewis, Cecil. Sagittarius Rising. 1983. 17.95 (ISBN 0-434-80600-5, Pub. by Heinemann England). David & Charles.
Lewis, Charles, et al. A Right to Health: The Problem of Access to Primary Medical Care. LC 76-18129. (Health, Medicine, & Society Ser.). 416p. 1976. 30.95 o.p. (ISBN 0-471-01494-X, Pub. by Wiley-Interscience). Wiley.
Lewis, Charles E. & Fein, Rashi. A Right to Health: The Problem of Access to Primary Medical Care. LC 76-181829. 380p. Repr. of 1976 ed. text ed. 29.50 (ISBN 0-471-01494-X). Krieger.
Lewis, Charles F., ed. see Christiansen, M. N.
Lewis, Charles L. Books of the Sea: An Introduction to Nautical Literature. LC 77-113059. 318p. 1972. Repr. of 1943 ed. lib. bdg. 19.25x (ISBN 0-8371-4700-X, LEBS). Greenwood.
Lewis, Chris. Biological Fuels. (Studies in Biology: No. 153). 64p. 1982. pap. text ed. 8.95 (ISBN 0-7131-2864-X). E Arnold.
Lewis, Chris, jt. auth. see Slesser, Malcolm.
Lewis, Clara M. Nutrition & Diet Therapy. (Illus.). 750p. 1982. cancelled 22.00 (ISBN 0-8036-5627-0). Davis Co.
--Nutrition: Proteins Carbohydrates & Lipids. LC 75-43830. (Illus.). 170p. 1978. pap. text ed. 7.00x o.p. (ISBN 0-8036-5621-1). Davis Co.
Lewis, Clara M., jt. auth. see Bailey, Carolyn S.
Lewis, Clarence I. Analysis of Knowledge & Valuation. LC 47-20878. (Paul Carus Lecture Ser.). xxi, 610p. 1971. 30.00 (ISBN 0-87548-093-4); pap. 12.00 (ISBN 0-87548-094-2). Open Court.
Lewis, Claudia. A Big Bite of the World: Children's Creative Writing. (Illus.). 1979. text ed. 14.95 o.p. (ISBN 0-13-076273-3, Spec); pap. text ed. 6.95 o.p. (ISBN 0-13-076265-2). P-H.
Lewis, Clive S. Discarded Image. LC 64-21555. (Orig.). 1968. 29.95 (ISBN 0-521-05551-2); pap. 8.50 (ISBN 0-521-09450-X). Cambridge U Pr.
--Experiment in Criticism. 1961. 24.95 (ISBN 0-521-05553-9); pap. 7.95 (ISBN 0-521-09350-3). Cambridge U Pr.
--Preface to Paradise Lost. 1942. pap. 5.95x (ISBN 0-686-76896-5). Oxford U Pr.
--Spenser's Images of Life. Fowler, A., ed. 1967. 29.95 (ISBN 0-521-05546-6); pap. 7.95, 1978 (ISBN 0-521-29284-0). Cambridge U Pr.
--Studies in Medieval & Renaissance Literature. 1980. 29.95 (ISBN 0-521-05545-8); pap. 8.95 (ISBN 0-521-29701-X). Cambridge U Pr.
--Studies in Words. 2nd ed. 1960. 34.50 (ISBN 0-521-05547-4); pap. 11.95 (ISBN 0-521-09371-6). Cambridge U Pr.
Lewis, Colleen. Nurse at Lookout Rock. 1982. pap. 6.95 (ISBN 0-686-84709-1, Avalon). Bouregy.
--Tracy Sterling, M.D. 1981. pap. 6.95 (ISBN 0-686-84673-7, Avalon). Bouregy.
Lewis, Cris W., jt. auth. see Prescott, James R.
Lewis, D. Urban Structure. LC 68-57502. 283p. (Orig.). 21.50 (ISBN 0-471-53375-0). Krieger.
Lewis, D., jt. auth. see Bartenieff, I.
Lewis, D., jt. auth. see Lowe, J.
Lewis, D. G., jt. auth. see Oades, J. M.
Lewis, D. Sclater. Royal Victoria Hospital Eighteen Eighty-Seven to Nineteen Forty-Seven. 352p. 1969. 10.00 o.p. (ISBN 0-7735-9073-0). McGill-Queens U Pr.
Lewis, Dan, jt. auth. see Reginald, R.
Lewis, Daniel, jt. auth. see Helberg, Kristen.
Lewis, Darrell R. & Becker, William E., eds. Academic Rewards in Higher Education. LC 79-11692. 368p. 1979. prof ref 25.00x (ISBN 0-88410-189-4). Ballinger Pub.
Lewis, David. Growth of Cities. LC 70-171916. 1971. 41.95x o.s.i. (ISBN 0-471-53198-7). Halsted Pr.
--Philosophical Papers, Vol. 1. 320p. 1983. 29.95 (ISBN 0-19-503203-9); pap. 9.95 (ISBN 0-19-503204-7). Oxford U Pr.
--We, the Navigators: The Ancient Art of Landfinding in the Pacific. LC 72-82139. (Illus.). 368p. 1975. pap. 5.95 (ISBN 0-8248-0394-9). UH Pr.
Lewis, David, jt. auth. see Green, James.
Lewis, David, ed. see Coleman, Kenneth.
Lewis, David L. King: A Biography. 2nd ed. (Blacks in the New World Ser.). 1978. 17.50 o.p. (ISBN 0-252-00679-8); pap. 5.95 (ISBN 0-252-00680-1). U of Ill Pr.
Lewis, David Maybury see Maybury-Lewis, David.
Lewis, E. E. Nuclear Power Reactor Safety. LC 77-21360. 1977. 55.95x (ISBN 0-471-53335-1, Pub. by Wiley-Interscience). Wiley.
Lewis, E. R. Life & Teaching of Jesus Christ: According to the Synoptic Gospels. (London Divinity Ser.). 170p. 1977. pap. 4.95 (ISBN 0-227-67519-3). Attic Pr.
Lewis, E. Ridley. Acts of the Apostles & the Letters of St. Paul. (London Divinity Ser.). 160p. 1964. Repr. of 1960 ed. 4.95 (ISBN 0-227-67401-4). Attic Pr.
--Johannine Writings & Other Epistles. (London Divinity Ser). 144p. 1961. 4.95 (ISBN 0-227-67663-7). Attic Pr.
Lewis, E. S. see Weissberger, A.
Lewis, E. St. Elmo. Efficient Cost Keeping: A Study of the Most Effective Applications of Cost Keeping Principles to Certain Types of Management. 3rd rev. ed. (Management History Ser.: No. 83). (Illus.). 256p. 1980. Repr. of 1914 ed. lib. bdg. 20.00 o.p. (ISBN 0-87960-104-3). Hive Pub.
Lewis, Edith. Willa Cather Living: A Personal Record. LC 76-17551. 1976. pap. 2.95 o.p. (ISBN 0-8032-5849-6, BB 623, Bison). U of Nebr Pr.
Lewis, Edward S., ed. Investigation of Rates & Mechanisms of Reactions, Vol. 6, Pt.1. 3d ed. LC 74-8850. (Techniques of Chemistry Ser.). 852p. Repr. of 1974 ed. text ed. 67.50 (ISBN 0-686-84487-4). Krieger.
Lewis, Edwin H. Marketing Channels: Structure & Strategy. 1968. pap. text ed. 6.95 o.p. (ISBN 0-07-037520-8, C). McGraw.
Lewis, Eleanor, ed. Darkroom. (Illus.). 1979. pap. 17.50 o.p. (ISBN 0-912810-19-X, Amphoto). Watson-Guptill.
--Darkroom. LC 76-57201. (Illus.). 184p. (Orig.). 1979. pap. 17.50 (ISBN 0-912810-19-X). Lustrum Pr.
Lewis, Elliot. Dirty Linen. (Bennett Ser.: No. 2). 192p. (Orig.). 1980. pap. 1.75 o.p. (ISBN 0-523-40653-3). Pinnacle Bks.
Lewis, Eloise R. & Maszkiewicz, Ruth C. Developing the Functional Role in Master's Education in Nursing. 63p. 1980. 5.50 (ISBN 0-686-38263-3, 15-1840). Natl League Nurse.
Lewis, Ernest L., jt. auth. see Beggs, Donald L.
Lewis, Ervin, jt. ed. see Bain, Mildred.
Lewis, Evelyn L. Housing Decisions. LC 80-19068. 1980. text ed. 14.64 (ISBN 0-87006-302-2). Goodheart.
Lewis, Felice F., jt. ed. see Gertz, Elmer.
Lewis, Ferris E. Michigan Yesterday & Today. 9th ed. (Illus.). 591p. (gr. 10-12). 1980. text ed. 19.68x (ISBN 0-910726-52-3); tchr's guide 3.00x (ISBN 0-910726-51-5). Hillsdale Educ.
Lewis, Ferris E. & McConell, David B. Our Own State, Michigan. rev. 15th ed. (Illus.). (gr. 7-10). 1982. pap. text ed. 5.50x (ISBN 0-910726-22-1); tchr's guide 3.00x (ISBN 0-910726-24-8); questions & ans. for teachers. 8.00x (ISBN 0-910726-23-X). Hillsdale Educ.
Lewis, Finlay. Mondale: Portrait of an American Politician. LC 79-1672. 1980. 13.41i (ISBN 0-06-012599-3, HarpT). Har-Row.
Lewis, Frank. Best Design Versus Best Seller. 26.95x (ISBN 0-87245-180-1). Textile Bk.
--Best Design Versus Best Seller: In Relation to Textiles & Wallpapers. (Illus.). 1965. text ed. 15.00x (ISBN 0-85317-910-7, Pub. by A & C Black England). Humanities.
--Flower Arrangements. 22.50x (ISBN 0-87245-181-X). Textile Bk.
Lewis, Frank R., Jr., jt. ed. see Trunkey, Donald T.
Lewis, Fred, jt. auth. see Leve, Mort.
Lewis, Frederick P. The Dilemma in the Congressional Power to Enforce the Fourteenth Amendment. 110p. 1980. text ed. 17.75 (ISBN 0-8191-1045-0); pap. text ed. 8.25 (ISBN 0-8191-1046-9). U Pr of Amer.
Lewis, G. P. & Ginsburg, M, eds. Mechanisms of Steroid Action: Biological Council Symposia on Drug Action. 288p. 1981. 90.00x (ISBN 0-333-32455-2, Pub. by Macmillan England). State Mutual Bk.
Lewis, Gaspar. Cabinetmaking, Patternmaking & Millwork. LC 79-50917. (Carpentry-Cabinetmaking Ser.). 438p. 1981. text ed. 18.00 (ISBN 0-8273-1814-6); instructor's guide 4.75 (ISBN 0-8273-1815-4). Delmar.
--Safety for Carpenters & Woodworkers. LC 80-66859. (Carpentry-Cabinetmaking Ser.). 1981. pap. text ed. 7.00 (ISBN 0-8273-1869-3); instructor's guide 2.00 (ISBN 0-8273-1870-7). Delmar.
Lewis, Geoffrey, tr. The Book of Dede Korkut. (Penguin Classic Ser.). 1982. pap. 4.95 (ISBN 0-14-044298-7). Penguin.
Lewis, Georgina K. John Greenleaf Whittier: His Life & Work. LC 70-160767. 1971. Repr. of 1913 ed. 12.50 o.p. (ISBN 0-8046-1589-6). Kennikat.
Lewis, Gerald E. My Big Buck: Outdoor Stories of Maine. LC 78-26185. (Illus.). 1978. lib. bdg. 9.50 o.p. (ISBN 0-89621-021-9); pap. 4.95 o.p. (ISBN 0-89621-020-0). Thorndike Pr.
Lewis, Geroge K., jt. auth. see Cozen, Michalel P.
Lewis, Gilbert. Day of Shining Red. LC 78-68354. (Studies in Social Anthropology: No. 27). 1980. 29.95 (ISBN 0-521-22278-8). Cambridge U Pr.
Lewis, Glenn, jt. auth. see Harper, Ann.
Lewis, Gloria, jt. auth. see Pisano, Beverly.
Lewis, Gogo, jt. auth. see Manley, Seon.
Lewis, Gogo, jt. ed. see Manley, Seon.
Lewis, Gordon R. Testing Christianity's Truth Claims. LC 75-38501. 350p. 1976. pap. 8.95 (ISBN 0-8024-8595-2). Moody.
Lewis, Greg. Photographing Your Family. (Illus.). 160p. 1981. 21.95 o.p. (ISBN 0-8174-5473-X, Amphoto); pap. 12.95 (ISBN 0-8174-5474-8). Watson-Guptill.
--Wedding Photography for Today. (Illus.). 136p. 1980. 19.95 o.p. (ISBN 0-8174-6410-7, Amphoto); pap. 9.95 (ISBN 0-8174-6411-5). Watson-Guptill.
Lewis, Gwynne. Life in Revolutionary France. (European Life Ser). (Illus.). 192p. 1972. 6.75 o.p. (ISBN 0-399-20256-0). Putnam Pub Group.
Lewis, H., jt. auth. see Rosenberg, R. Robert.
Lewis, H. D. The Elusive Self. 1982. 50.00x (ISBN 0-686-42924-9, Pub. by Macmillan England). State Mutual Bk.
Lewis, H. G. The Businessman's Guide to Advertising & Sales Promotion. new ed. (Illus.). 224p. (Orig.). 1974. pap. text ed. 14.50 (ISBN 0-07-037526-7, G); tchr's manual & key 4.50 (ISBN 0-07-037527-5). McGraw.
Lewis, H. H. The Lawyers' Round Table of Baltimore & Its Charter Members. 86p. 1978. 7.50 (ISBN 0-686-36496-1). Md Hist.
Lewis, H. H. Walker. Without Fear or Favor. 556p. 1965. 7.50 (ISBN 0-686-36715-4). Md Hist.
Lewis, H. R., tr. see Pauli, Wolfgang.
Lewis, H. T., jt. ed. see Armstrong, R. W.
Lewis, Hal M. Arthur Frommer's Guide to Philadelphia, 1983-84. (Illus.). 224p. Date not set. pap. 3.95 (ISBN 0-671-45414-5). Frommer-Pasmantier.
Lewis, Harriet. The Last Garage Sale. 56p. (Orig.). 1982. pap. 6.95 (ISBN 0-933294-02-6). Backroads.
Lewis, Harry. Elementary Algebra Skills for College. (Orig.). 1980. pap. text ed. 14.95 (ISBN 0-442-20396-9). Van Nos Reinhold.
--Intermediate Algebra Skills for College. (Orig.). Date not set. pap. text ed. price not set o.s.i. (ISBN 0-442-23163-6); price not set instr's. manual o.s.i. (ISBN 0-442-28663-5). Van Nos Reinhold.
--An Introduction to Computer Programming & Data Structures Using MACRO-11. 188p. 1981. text ed. 19.95 (ISBN 0-8359-3143-9); soln. manual avail. (ISBN 0-8359-3144-7). Reston.
--Mathematics for Business. LC 81-70341. (Illus.). 528p. 1983. pap. text ed. 19.80 (ISBN 0-8273-1913-4); instr's. guide 4.25 (ISBN 0-8273-1914-2). Delmar.
Lewis, Harry R. Unsolvable Classes of Quantificational Formulas. LC 79-17573. 1979. pap. text ed. 19.50 (ISBN 0-201-04069-7). A-W.
Lewis, Harry R & Papadimitriou, Christos H. Elements of the Theory of Computation. (Software Ser.). (Illus.). 496p. 1981. text ed. 26.95 (ISBN 0-13-273417-6). P-H.
Lewis, Helen C. All About Families: The Second Time Around. Reynolds, Amy, ed. LC 79-26694. (Illus.). 1980. 7.95 o.p. (ISBN 0-931948-06-1). Peachtree Pubs.
Lewis, Hilda. Ship That Flew. LC 58-5903. (Illus.). (gr. 3-7). 1958. 10.95 (ISBN 0-87599-067-3). S G Phillips.
Lewis, Hilda S. Deprived Children: The Mersham Experiment; a Social & Clinical Study. LC 77-27491. 1978. Repr. of 1954 ed. lib. bdg. 17.00x (ISBN 0-8371-9070-3, LEDC). Greenwood.
Lewis, Hunter & Allison, Donald. The Real World War. 256p. 1982. 14.95 (ISBN 0-698-11122-2, Coward). Putnam Pub Group.
Lewis, Irving J. & Sheps, Cecil G. The Sick Citadel: The American Academic Medical Center & the Public Interest. 224p. 1983. text ed. 25.00 (ISBN 0-89946-173-5). Oelgeschlager.
Lewis, J. Architectural Draftsman's Reference Handbook. 1982. 27.00 (ISBN 0-13-044164-3). P-H.
Lewis, J. G. The Biology of Centipedes. (Illus.). 350p. 1981. 75.00 (ISBN 0-521-23413-1). Cambridge U Pr.
Lewis, J. R. Cases for Discussion. 1966. 14.75 o.p. (ISBN 0-08-011352-4); pap. 6.25 o.p. (ISBN 0-08-011351-6). Pergamon.
Lewis, J. W., ed. Party Leadership & Revolutionary Power in China. (Publications of the Contemporary China Institute Ser). 1970. 49.50 (ISBN 0-521-07792-3); pap. 13.95x (ISBN 0-521-09614-6). Cambridge U Pr.
Lewis, Jack. Black Powder Gun Digest. 3rd ed. (Illus.). 256p. 1982. pap. 9.95 (ISBN 0-910676-41-0). DBI.
--The Digest Book of Horse Care. (The Sports & Leisure Library). (Illus.). 96p. 1979. pap. 2.95 o.s.i. (ISBN 0-695-81325-0). Follett.
--The Gun Digest Book of Modern Gun Values. (Illus.). 1978. pap. 7.95 o.s.i. (ISBN 0-695-81196-7). Follett.
--Gun Digest Book of Modern Gun Values. 288p. 1976. pap. 7.95 o.s.i. (ISBN 0-695-80620-3). Follett.
--Law Enforcement Handgun Digest. 3rd ed. 288p. 1980. pap. 8.95 o.s.i. (ISBN 0-695-81413-3). Follett.
Lewis, Jack & Hughes, B. R. Gun Digest Book of Folding Knives. (DBI Ser.). 1977. pap. 7.95 o.s.i. (ISBN 0-695-80839-7). Follett.
Lewis, Jack, jt. auth. see Fanta, Ladd.
Lewis, Jack, ed. Archer's Digest. 2nd ed. (DBI Bks). (Illus.). 1977. pap. 7.95 o.s.i. (ISBN 0-695-80718-8). Follett.
Lewis, Jack & Springer, Robert, eds. Black Powder Gun Digest. 2nd ed. (DBI Bks). (Illus.). 1977. pap. 7.95 o.s.i. (ISBN 0-695-80714-5). Follett.
Lewis, Jack, jt. ed. see Learn, C. R.
Lewis, Jack R. Architects & Engineers Office Practice Guide. (Illus.). 1978. ref. ed. 19.95 (ISBN 0-13-044669-6). P-H.
--Basic Construction Estimating. (Illus.). 176p. 1983. text ed. 19.95 (ISBN 0-13-058313-8). P-H.
--Construction Specifications. 352p. 1975. ref. ed. 25.95 (ISBN 0-13-169375-1). P-H.
Lewis, James. West Virginia Pilgrim. 228p. 1976. 1.50 (ISBN 0-8164-0297-3). Seabury.
Lewis, James A., jt. auth. see Carlsen, Robert D.
Lewis, James C. The World of the Wild Turkey. LC 72-2923. (Living World Bks.). (Illus.). (YA) 1973. 11.49i (ISBN 0-397-00788-4). Har-Row.
Lewis, Jane, ed. Women's Welfare, Women's Rights. 224p. 1983. text ed. 29.25 (ISBN 0-7099-1610-8, Pub. by Croom Helm Ltd England). Biblio Dist.
Lewis, Janet. Ghost of Monsieur Scarron. LC 82-70506. 378p. 1959. 20.00 (ISBN 0-8040-0076-X); pap. 8.95 (ISBN 0-8040-0133-2). Swallow.
--Invasion: A Narrative of Events Concerning the Johnston Family of St. Mary's. LC 82-71066. 356p. 1964. 10.95 (ISBN 0-8040-0166-9); pap. 6.95 (ISBN 0-8040-0167-7). Swallow.
--Poems Old & New: 1918-1978. LC 82-75190. xvi, 112p. 1981. 15.95x (ISBN 0-8040-0371-8); pap. 9.95 (ISBN 0-8040-0372-6). Swallow.
--Trial of Soren Qvist. LC 82-72114. 256p. 1959. pap. 5.95 (ISBN 0-8040-0297-5). Swallow.
--Wife of Martin Guerre. LC 82-70548. 109p. 1967. 5.00 o.s.i. (ISBN 0-8040-0079-4); pap. 4.95 (ISBN 0-8040-0321-1). Swallow.
Lewis, Jeffery. Dreamscapes: The Landscape of Dreams: an Orientation. 1982. 1.50x (ISBN 0-939878-05-4). Dreams Unltd.
Lewis, Jeffrey D., jt. auth. see Stern, Joseph J.
Lewis, Jerry M., jt. auth. see Hensley, Thomas R.
Lewis, Jerry M. & Usdin, Gene, eds. Treatment Planning in Psychiatry. LC 82-3985. (Illus.). 433p. 1982. 27.50 (ISBN 0-89042-045-9, 42-045-9). Am Psychiatric.
Lewis, Jerry M., jt. ed. see Usdin, Gene.
Lewis, Jerry M., jt. auth. see Gossett, John T.
Lewis, Jim. Spiritual Gospel. LC 82-51231. 145p. (Orig.). 1982. pap. write for info. (ISBN 0-942482-05-0). Unity Church Denver.
--The Upward Path. LC 82-60277. 150p. (Orig.). 1982. pap. 4.95 (ISBN 0-942482-04-2). Unity Church Denver.
Lewis, John. The Chinese Word for Horse: And Other Stories. LC 79-25679. (Illus.). 96p. (Orig.). 1980. 9.95x o.p. (ISBN 0-8052-3736-4); pap. 5.95 o.p. (ISBN 0-8052-0640-X). Schocken.
--Election Law Changes in Cities & Counties in Georgia. 1976. 1.00 (ISBN 0-686-38002-9). Voter Ed Proj.
Lewis, John & Towers, Bernard. Naked Ape or Homo Sapiens: A Reply to Desmond Morris. 2nd ed. (Teilhard Study Library). 1972. text ed. 10.00x (ISBN 0-900391-21-9). Humanities.
Lewis, John E. The Bulletproof Sheriff. 1981. pap. 6.95 (ISBN 0-686-84708-3, Avalon). Bouregy.
--Escape to Fort Bridger. (YA) 1980. 6.95 (ISBN 0-686-73919-1, Avalon). Bouregy.
--The Fallen Badge. 1982. pap. 6.95 (ISBN 0-686-84740-7, Avalon). Bouregy.
--The Guns of Tombstone. (YA) 1981. 6.95 (ISBN 0-686-73947-7, Avalon). Bouregy.
--Railway Guns. 1983. 6.95 (ISBN 0-686-84193-X, Avalon). Bouregy.
--Silver Mine Trail. (YA) 1979. 6.95 (ISBN 0-686-59802-4, Avalon). Bouregy.
--Six-Gun Mission. 1982. 6.95 (Avalon). Bouregy.
--Utah Vengeance. (YA) 1981. 6.95 (ISBN 0-686-73961-2, Avalon). Bouregy.
Lewis, John P. Quiet Crisis in India: Economic Development & American Policy. LC 73-16742. 350p. 1974. Repr. of 1962 ed. lib. bdg. 19.00x (ISBN 0-8371-7225-X, LEQC). Greenwood.
Lewis, John P. & Turner, R. C. Business Conditions Analysis. 2nd ed. 1967. 29.95 (ISBN 0-07-037600-X, C). McGraw.
Lewis, John R. First Year College Chemistry. 9th ed. (Illus., Orig.). 1971. pap. 4.95 (ISBN 0-06-460005-X, CO 5, COS). B&N NY.
--Uncertain Judgment: A Bibliography of War Crimes Trials. Burns, Richard D., ed. LC 78-27904. (War-Peace Bibliography Ser.: No. 8). 251p. 1979. text ed. 26.50 (ISBN 0-87436-288-1). ABC-Clio.
Lewis, Joseph. In the Name of Humanity. 154p. 1949. 8.00 (ISBN 0-686-96142-0). Am Atheist.
--The Ten Commandments. 644p. 1982. 42.50 (ISBN 0-686-83180-2). Am Atheist.
Lewis, Judith A. & Lewis, Michael D. Community Counseling: A Human Services Approach. LC 76-15274. (Wiley Series in Counseling & Human Development). 1977. text ed. 24.95x (ISBN 0-471-53203-7). Wiley.
--Management of Human Service Programs. LC 82-14684. (Counseling Ser.). 320p. 1982. text ed. 18.95 (ISBN 0-534-01335-X). Brooks-Cole.
Lewis, Kay O. The Christian Wedding Handbook. 1981. 9.95 (ISBN 0-8007-1259-5). Revell.
Lewis, Keith P., jt. auth. see Knobf, Mary K.
Lewis, Kenneth, jt. auth. see John, Bernard.
Lewis, L. M. Footprints on the Sands of Time. (Orig.). 1975. pap. 1.50 o.p. (ISBN 0-451-06722-3, W6722, Sig). NAL.
Lewis, Larry L. Organize to Evangelize. 1980. pap. 4.50 (ISBN 0-88207-219-6). Victor Bks.

Lewis, Laurie, photos by. The Concerts. LC 79-50588. (Illus.). 120p. (Orig.). 1979. pap. 12.50 o.s.i. (ISBN 0-89104-143-5, A & W Visual Library); 27.50 o.s.i. (ISBN 0-89104-142-7, A & W Visual Library). A & W Pubs.

Lewis, Leslie L., jt. auth. see Altenbernd, Lynn.

Lewis, Lou C. Be Restored to Health: How to Manage Stress, Heal Your Self & Be Whole Again. 224p. 1982. 11.95 (ISBN 0-920510-67-1, Pub. by Personal Lib). Dodd.

Lewis, LuVerne W. Lippincott's State Board Examination Review for Nurses. LC 77-27368. 1978. pap. text ed. 15.75 (ISBN 0-397-54214-3, Lippincott Nursing). Lippincott.

--Lippincott's State Board Examination Review for Registered Nurses. (Illus.). 768p. 1982. pap. text ed. 15.75 (ISBN 0-397-54363-8, Lippincott Nursing). Lippincott.

Lewis, M. & Rosenblum, L. A. Origins of Behavior, 4 vols. Incl. Vol. 1. The Effect of the Infant on Its Caregiver. 1974. 36.95 (ISBN 0-471-53202-9); Vol. 3. Structure & Transformation: Developmental & Historical Aspects. Riegel, K. F. & Rosenwald, G. C., eds. LC 75-15659. 1975. 27.95 (ISBN 0-471-72140-9); Vol. 4. Friendship & Peer Relations. LC 75-20181. 1975. 40.50 (ISBN 0-471-53345-9). LC 73-12804 (Pub. by Wiley-Interscience). Wiley.

Lewis, M. F., ed. Current Research in Marijuana. 1972. 27.50 (ISBN 0-12-447050-5). Acad Pr.

Lewis, M. H., jt. auth. see Chapman, M. A.

Lewis, M. K. The Hollywood Actor's Survival Handbook: How to Break into Movies. 1983. 10.95 o.p. (ISBN 0-517-54911-5). Crown.

Lewis, M. K. & Lewis, Rosemary. Your Film Acting Career: How to Break into the Movies & TV & Survive in Hollywood. (Illus.). 1983. 10.95 (ISBN 0-517-54911-5); pap. 6.95 (ISBN 0-517-54912-3). Crown.

Lewis, M. M., jt. ed. see Clarke, A. D.

Lewis, Marjorie. The Boy Who Would be a Hero. LC 81-15147. (Illus.). 32p. 1982. 9.95 (ISBN 0-698-20546-4, Coward). Putnam Pub Group.

--Ernie & the Mile-Long Muffler. (Illus.). 40p. (gr. 6-9). 1982. 9.95 (ISBN 0-698-20557-X, Coward). Putnam Pub Group.

Lewis, Marti & Warden, Carol D. Law & Ethics in the Medical Office Including Bioethical Issues. LC 82-9993. 227p. 1982. pap. text ed. 12.95 (ISBN 0-8036-5616-5). Davis Co.

Lewis, Mary. Midsummer Bride. 192p. (Orig.). 1980. pap. 1.50 (ISBN 0-671-57007-2, Pub. by Silhouette Bks). S&S.

Lewis, Matthew. The Monk. Anderson, Howard, ed. (World's Classics Ser.). 1982. pap. 4.95 (ISBN 0-19-281524-5). Oxford U Pr.

Lewis, Mel. How to Make Money from Antiques. (Illus.). 160p. 1981. 12.50 o.p. (ISBN 0-7137-1084-5, Pub. by Blandford Pr England). Sterling.

Lewis, Meriwether & Clark, William. Journals of Lewis & Clark: A New Selection. Bakeless, John, ed. (Orig.). 1964. pap. 2.95 (ISBN 0-451-62088-7, ME2088, Ment). NAL.

Lewis, Merlin, et al. An Introduction to the Courts & Judicial Process. LC 77-13100. (P-H Ser. in Criminal Justice). (Illus.). 1978. ref. ed. 20.95 (ISBN 0-13-481333-2). P-H.

Lewis, Mervyn. British Tax Law. 704p. 1979. 79.00x (ISBN 0-686-81905-5, Pub. by McDonald & Evans). State Mutual Bk.

Lewis, Michael. The Culture of Inequality. 1979. pap. 5.95 (ISBN 0-452-00572-8, F572, Mer). NAL.

Lewis, Michael & Rosenblum, Leonard A. Interaction, Conversation & the Development of Language. LC 82-21225. 344p. 1983. Repr. of 1977 ed. lib. bdg. write for info. (ISBN 0-89874-588-8). Krieger.

Lewis, Michael, ed. Research in Social Problems & Public Policy, Vol. 1. (Orig.). 1979. lib. bdg. 40.00 (ISBN 0-89232-068-0). Jai Pr.

--Research in Social Problems & Public Policy, Vol. 2. 250p. 1981. 40.00 (ISBN 0-89232-195-4). Jai Pr.

Lewis, Michael & Rosenblum, Leonard, eds. Interaction, Conversation, & the Development of Language. LC 76-49037. (Origins of Behavior: Vol. 5). 1977. 34.95x o.p. (ISBN 0-471-02526-7, Pub. by Wiley-Interscience). Wiley.

Lewis, Michael D., jt. auth. see Lewis, Judith A.

Lewis, Mumford. The Golden Day: A Study in American Literature & Culture. LC 82-24199. xxx, 144p. 1983. Repr. of 1957 ed. lib. bdg. 22.50x (ISBN 0-313-23845-6, MUGO). Greenwood.

Lewis, Myra & Silver, Murray. Great Balls of Fire: The Uncensored Story of Jerry Lee Lewis. LC 82-9085. (Illus.). 332p. 1982. pap. 7.50 (ISBN 0-688-01480-1). Quill NY.

Lewis, Myrna I., jt. auth. see Butler, Robert N.

Lewis, Myron see Wruble, Lawrence D., et al.

Lewis, Myron, jt. auth. see Wruble, Lawrence D.

Lewis, Nancy, ed. My Roots Be Coming Back. (Illus.). 24p. 1973. pap. 3.50 (ISBN 0-89062-034-2, Pub. by Touchstone). Pub Ctr Cult Res.

--Out of My Body. (Illus.). 20p. 1974. pap. 3.00 (ISBN 0-89062-035-0, Pub. by Touchtone). Pub Ctr Cult Res.

Lewis, Naomi, jt. auth. see Thompson, Janice.

Lewis, Naomi, adapted by see Andersen, Hans C.

Lewis, Naphtali & Reinhold, Meyer, eds. Roman Civilization: Sourcebook 1-The Republic, Sourcebook 2-The Empire. Bk. 1. pap. 8.50xi (ISBN 0-06-131231-2, TB1231, Torch); Bk. 2. pap. 7.50xi (ISBN 0-06-131232-0, TB1232, Torch). Har-Row.

Lewis, Nigel. Paperchase: Mozart, Beethoven, Bach...The Search for their Lost Music. 246p. 1982. 19.95 (ISBN 0-241-10235-9, Pub. by Hamish Hamilton England). David & Charles.

Lewis, Norman. Better English. 1981. pap. 2.50 o.p. (ISBN 0-440-30548-9, LE). Dell.

--Cuban Passage. 1983. pap. 2.95 (ISBN 0-394-71420-2). Pantheon.

--How to Read Better & Faster. 4th rev. ed. LC 78-3307. 1978. 13.95i (ISBN 0-690-01528-3). T Y Crowell.

--Instant Word Power. 1982. pap. 3.50 (ISBN 0-451-11791-3, AE1791, Sig). NAL.

--The New Roget's Thesaurus in Dictionary Form. rev. ed. LC 77-24457. 552p. 8.95 (ISBN 0-399-12678-3); Thumb-indexed ed. 9.95 (ISBN 0-399-12679-1). Putnam Pub Group.

--Rapid Vocabulary Builder. 1958. pap. 2.50 o.p. (ISBN 0-448-01505-6, G&D). Putnam Pub Group.

--RSVP, Bk. 1. Rev. ed. (gr. 10-12). 1982. wkbk. 7.50 (ISBN 0-87720-440-3). AMSCO Sch.

--RSVP, Bk 2. rev. ed. (Orig.). (gr. 10-12). 1983. text ed. write for info (ISBN 0-87720-443-8). AMSCO Sch.

Lewis, Norman, jt. auth. see Funk, Wilfred.

Lewis, Orlando F. Development of American Prisons & Prisons Customs, 1776-1845. LC 67-5252. (Criminology, Law Enforcement, & Social Problems Ser.: No. 1). (With intro. added). 1967. Repr. of 1922 ed. 15.00x (ISBN 0-87585-001-4). Patterson Smith.

Lewis, Oscar. Death in the Sanchez Family. LC 75-85569. 1970. pap. 3.95 (ISBN 0-394-70860-1, V634, Vin). Random.

--High Sierra Country. LC 77-883. 1977. Repr. of 1955 ed. lib. bdg. 19.75x o.p. (ISBN 0-8371-9462-8, LEHS). Greenwood.

--A Study in Slum Culture. pap. text ed. 7.95x (ISBN 0-394-30367-9). Phila Bk Co.

Lewis, P. Enterprise Sandwich Shops: A Market Simulation Apple II Plus (on Apple with Applesoft) Version. 1982. 99.00 (ISBN 0-07-037536-4, G). McGraw.

Lewis, P. A., jt. auth. see Cox, D. R.

Lewis, P. J. Essential Clinical Pharmacology. (Illus.). 1983. pap. text ed. 12.50 (ISBN 0-85200-372-2, Pub. by MTP Pr England). Kluwer Boston.

Lewis, P. R. & Knight, D. P. Staining Methods for Sectioned Material. (Practical Methods in Electron Microscopy: Vol. 5, Pt. 1). 1977. 25.75 (ISBN 0-7204-0606-4, North-Holland). Elsevier.

Lewis, P. S. Later Medieval France: The Polity. 1968. 22.50 (ISBN 0-312-47250-1). St Martin.

Lewis, Patricia & Ferneti, Casper. Using Deodorant. (Project MORE Daily Living Skills Ser.). 32p. 1979. Repr. of 1975 ed. pap. text ed. 5.95 (ISBN 0-8331-1242-2). Hubbard Sci.

--Washing Your Hair. (Project MORE Daily Living Skills Ser.). 32p. 1978. Repr. of 1975 ed. pap. text ed. 5.95 (ISBN 0-8331-1244-9). Hubbard Sci.

Lewis, Patricia A. Of Other Realms: A Journey of the Soul. LC 82-60760. (Illus.). 112p. (Orig.). 1982. pap. 5.50 (ISBN 0-935834-08-7). Rainbow Betty.

Lewis, Paul D., jt. auth. see Pallis, Christopher A.

Lewis, Peirce F. New Orleans: The Making of an Urban Landscape. LC 76-4797. (Contemporary Metropolitan Analysis Ser.). (Illus.). 136p. 1976. pap. 8.95x prof ref (ISBN 0-88410-433-8). Ballinger Pub.

Lewis, Peter, jt. auth. see Wright, Jack.

Lewis, Peter J. & O'Grady, John M., eds. Clinical Pharmacology of Prostacyclin. 274p. 1981. 32.50 (ISBN 0-89004-591-7). Raven.

Lewis, Peter W. Criminal Procedure: The Supreme Court's View Cases. (Criminal Justice Ser.). (Illus.). 1979. pap. text ed. 19.50 (ISBN 0-8299-0236-8); resource manual avail. (ISBN 0-8299-0597-9). West Pub.

Lewis, Philip, jt. auth. see Dingwall, Robert.

Lewis, Philip M., 2nd, et al. Compiler Design Theory. LC 75-9012. (Illus.). 672p. 1976. text ed. 29.95 (ISBN 0-201-14455-7). A-W.

Lewis, Philip V. & Baker, William H. Business Report Writing. 2nd ed. LC 82-15436. (Grid Series in Business Communications). 350p. 1983. text ed. 25.95 (ISBN 0-88244-257-0). Grid Pub.

Lewis, Phillip V. Managing Human Relations. 512p. 1983. text ed. 22.95x (ISBN 0-534-01428-3). Kent Pub Co.

Lewis, R. Everyday Life in Ottoman Turkey. (Everyday Life Ser). (Illus.). (gr. 10 up). 1971. 6.75 o.p. (ISBN 0-399-20067-3). Putnam Pub Group.

Lewis, R. & Pendrill, D. Advanced Financial Accounting. 528p. 1981. 50.00x (ISBN 0-273-01640-7, Pub. by Pitman Bks England). State Mutual Bk.

Lewis, R., ed. Involving Micros in Education: Proceedings of the IFIP TC 3 & University of Lancaster Joint Working Conference, Lancaster, England, March 24-26, 1982. 240p. 1982. 36.25 (ISBN 0-444-86459-8). Elsevier.

Lewis, R. & Tagg, E. D., eds. Computers in Education. 1982. 95.75 (ISBN 0-444-86255-2). Elsevier.

Lewis, R., ed. see IFIP World Conference, 2nd.

Lewis, R. T., jt. ed. see Knowles, E. W.

Lewis, R. W. & Morgan, K. Numerical Methods in Heat Transfer. Zienkiewicz, O. C., ed. LC 80-49973. (Numerical Methods in Engineering Ser.). 536p. 1981. 83.95 (ISBN 0-471-27803-3, Pub. by Wiley-Interscience). Wiley.

Lewis, R. W., ed. Paper Coating Additives Test Procedures by Functional Properties. 102p. 1976. soft cover 19.95 (ISBN 0-686-98478-1, 01-01-R063). TAPPI.

Lewis, Raphael O. Current Constitutional Controversies. 1977. pap. text ed. 8.00 o.p. (ISBN 0-8191-0192-3). U Pr of Amer.

Lewis, Reggie. The Case For Food Supplements. 1973. 2.00x (ISBN 0-686-36339-6). Cancer Control Soc.

Lewis, Rena, jt. auth. see McLoughlin, James.

Lewis, Rena B. & Doorlag, Donald H. Teaching Special Students in the Mainstream. 1983. text ed. 17.95 (ISBN 0-675-20011-3). Additional supplements may be obtained from publisher. Merrill.

Lewis, Richard. The Park. LC 68-28917. (Illus.). (ps-3). 1968. 3.95 o.p. (ISBN 0-671-65028-9, Juveniles). S&S.

--Reading for Adults. (English As a Second Language Bk.). (Illus.). 1977. Bk. 1: Pre-Intermediate. pap. text ed. 5.75x (ISBN 0-582-52790-2); Bk. 2: Intermediate. pap. text ed. 5.75x (ISBN 0-582-52791-0); Bk. 3: High-Intermediate. pap. text ed. 5.75x (ISBN 0-582-52792-9). Longman.

Lewis, Richard A. Edwin Chadwick & the Public Health Movement 1832-1854. LC 52-14559. Repr. of 1952 ed. lib. bdg. 27.50x (ISBN 0-678-08038-0). Kelley.

Lewis, Richard B., jt. ed. see Brown, James W.

Lewis, Richard B., jt. auth. see Brown, James W.

Lewis, Richard S. The Coming of the Ice Age. 1979. 10.00 o.p. (ISBN 0-399-12374-1). Putnam Pub Group.

Lewis, Richard W. American Adam. LC 55-5133. 1955. pap. 6.95 (ISBN 0-226-47681-2, P38, Phoen). U of Chicago Pr.

Lewis, Robert. Advice to the Players. LC 79-3291. (Illus.). 1980. 12.45i (ISBN 0-06-012615-9, HarpT). Har-Row.

--Science & Industrialization in U. S. S. R. LC 79-1380. 1979. text ed. 34.50x (ISBN 0-8419-0494-4). Holmes & Meier.

Lewis, Robert T. Taking Chances: The Psychology of Losing & How to Profit from It. 1979. 7.95 o.s.i. (ISBN 0-395-27606-3). HM.

Lewis, Roger. The Carbon Gang. 64p. 1983. pap. 4.00x (ISBN 0-916156-64-8). Cherry Valley.

--Color & the Edgar Cayce Readings. 48p. 1973. pap. 3.50 (ISBN 0-87604-068-7). Are Pr.

Lewis, Ronald L. see Foner, Philip S.

Lewis, Ronald L., jt. ed. see Foner, Philip S.

Lewis, Rose. Mademoiselle. 192p. (Orig.). 1981. pap. 1.95 o.p. (ISBN 0-523-40962-1). Pinnacle Bks.

Lewis, Rosemary, jt. auth. see Lewis, M. K.

Lewis, Roth. Principles of Epidemiology: A Self Teaching Guide. 1982. 24.50 (ISBN 0-12-593180-8). Acad Pr.

Lewis, Roy. Dwell in Danger. 192p. 1982. 10.95 (ISBN 0-312-22286-6). St Martin.

Lewis, Roy Harley. A Pension for Death: A Matthew Coll Mystery. 192p. 1983. 12.95 (ISBN 0-686-42923-0). St Martin.

Lewis, Russell. Margaret Thatcher: A Personal & Political Biography. (Illus.). 200p. 1975. 13.33 o.p. (ISBN 0-7100-8283-5). Routledge & Kegan.

Lewis, Ruth P., jt. ed. see Browning, Mary H.

Lewis, S. & Collier, I. Medical Surgical Nursing: Assessment & Management of Clinical Problems. 1888p. 1983. text ed. 45.95x (ISBN 0-07-037561-5). McGraw.

Lewis, S. M. & Coster, J., eds. Quality Control in Haematology. 1976. 36.50 (ISBN 0-12-446850-0). Acad Pr.

Lewis, Samuel L. Spiritual Dancing: Yesterday, Today & Tomorrow. Klotz, Saadi, ed. 120p. (Orig.). 1983. pap. 9.50x (ISBN 0-915424-11-8). Sufi Islamia-Prophecy.

--Sufi Vision & Initiation: Meetings with Remarkable Beings. Klotz, Saadi, ed. (Bismillah Bks.: No. 4). (Illus.). 175p. (Orig.). 1984. pap. 5.50 (ISBN 0-915424-10-X). Sufi Islamia-Prophecy.

--Talks of an American Sufi: Life Before Birth, Life After Death, Life Now, Vol. II. Klotz, Saadi, ed. (Bismillah Bks.: No. 4). (Illus.). 112p. (Orig.). 1984. pap. 5.50 (ISBN 0-915424-09-6). Sufi Islamia-Prophecy.

Lewis, Sandra. Providing for the Older Adult: A Gerontological Handbook. 1982. pap. 14.50 (ISBN 0-913590-82-7). Slack Inc.

Lewis, Shari & Oppenheimer, Lillian. Folding Paper Puppets. LC 62-20094. 1977. pap. 5.95 (ISBN 0-8128-1950-0). Stein & Day.

--Folding Paper Toys. LC 63-20060. 1977. pap. 5.95 (ISBN 0-8128-1953-5). Stein & Day.

Lewis, Shari & Reinach, Jacquelyn. Headstart Book of Looking & Listening. (Young Pioneer Bks.). (ps). 1966. 4.95 o.p. (ISBN 0-07-078001-3, GB). McGraw.

Lewis, Shelby, ed. see Hudlin, Richard A.

Lewis, Shelby, jt. auth. see Hudlin, Richard A.

Lewis, Sherwood A. The Illustrated Book of American Gardens. (An American Culture Library Book). (Illus.). 117p. 1983. 67.85 (ISBN 0-86650-050-2). Gloucester Art.

Lewis, Sinclair. Arrowsmith. pap. 2.50 (ISBN 0-451-51671-0, CE1671, Sig Classics). NAL.

--Babbitt. LC 22-14419. (Modern Classic Ser.). 1949. 14.95 (ISBN 0-15-110421-2). HarBraceJ.

--Babbitt. pap. 2.50 (ISBN 0-451-51703-2, CE1703, Sig Classics). NAL.

--Dodsworth. 1971. pap. 3.50 (ISBN 0-451-51704-0, CE1704, Sig Classics). NAL.

--Elmer Gantry. 1971. pap. 2.95 (ISBN 0-451-51653-2, CE1653, Sig Classics). NAL.

--Main Street. LC 20-18934. (Modern Classic Ser.). (gr. 10 up). 1950. 14.95 (ISBN 0-15-155547-8). HarBraceJ.

--Main Street. 1974. pap. 3.50 (ISBN 0-451-51712-1, CE1712, Sig Classics). NAL.

Lewis, Stephen. Beach House. 384p. (Orig.). 1980. pap. 2.25 o.p. (ISBN 0-523-40967-2). Pinnacle Bks.

--The Best Sellers. 320p. 1981. pap. 2.50 (ISBN 0-8439-0960-9, Leisure Bks). Nordon Pubns.

Lewis, Stephen C. & Forte, M. Cecile. Writing Through Reading. (Illus.). 372p. 1983. pap. text ed. 11.95 (ISBN 0-13-971630-0). P-H.

Lewis, Stephen R., Jr. Economic Policy & Industrial Growth in Pakistan. 1969. 17.50x (ISBN 0-262-12031-3). MIT Pr.

Lewis, Sylvan R. Slim Hips, Slim Thighs, Slim Bunns. (Illus.). 128p. 1981. pap. text ed. 1.95 (ISBN 0-936320-06-0). Compact Pubns.

Lewis, T. Using the Osbourne-1 Computer. 1982. 19.95 (ISBN 0-8359-8142-8); pap. 14.95 (ISBN 0-8359-8141-X). Reston.

Lewis, T. G. Using the IBM Personal Computer. 1982. text ed. 18.95 (ISBN 0-8359-8140-1); pap. text ed. 14.95 (ISBN 0-8359-8138-X). Reston.

Lewis, T. G. & Smith, M. Z. Applying Data Structures. 2nd ed. LC 81-83273. 1982. 26.95 (ISBN 0-395-31706-1). HM.

Lewis, T. L., jt. auth. see Clayton, Stanley.

Lewis, Ted. Boldt. (Orig.). pap. 2.25 o.s.i. (ISBN 0-515-05640-5). Jove Pubns.

--Grievous Bodily Harm. (Orig.). pap. 2.25 o.s.i. (ISBN 0-686-29452-1). Jove Pubns.

--Microbook: Database Management for the Apple II Computer. 190p. (Orig.). 1982. pap. 19.95 (ISBN 0-88056-072-X); diskette (includes book) 34.95 (ISBN 0-686-82898-4). Dilithium Pr.

--Thirty Two Visicalc Worksheets. Rev. ed. 150p. 1982. pap. 19.95 (ISBN 0-88056-085-1). Dilithium Pr.

Lewis, Theodore G. Distribution Sampling for Computer Simulation. LC 74-25058. 176p. 1975. 22.95x (ISBN 0-669-97139-1). Lexington Bks.

--PASCAL Programming for the Apple. 224p. 1981. 19.95 (ISBN 0-8359-5455-2); pap. 14.95 (ISBN 0-8359-5454-4). Reston.

Lewis, Theodore G. & Smith, Brian J. Computer Principles of Modeling & Simulation. LC 78-69604. (Illus.). 1979. text ed. 29.95 (ISBN 0-395-27143-6); instr's. manual 1.00 (ISBN 0-395-27144-4). HM.

Lewis, Thomas M. & Kneberg, Madeline. Tribes That Slumber: Indians of the Tennessee Region. LC 58-12085. (Illus.). 1958. pap. 8.95 (ISBN 0-87049-021-4). U of Tenn Pr.

Lewis, Thomas P. Hill of Fire. LC 70-121802. (I Can Read History Books). (Illus.). (gr. k-3). 1971. 7.64i (ISBN 0-06-023803-8, HarpJ); PLB 8.89 (ISBN 0-06-023804-6). Har-Row.

Lewis, Thomas R. Near the Long Tidal River: Readings in the Historical Geography of Central Connecticut. LC 80-6181. 156p. 1981. lib. bdg. 19.50 (ISBN 0-8191-1464-2); pap. text ed. 9.50 (ISBN 0-8191-1465-0). U Pr of Amer.

Lewis, Toby, jt. auth. see Barnett, Vic.

Lewis, Tom. Rooftops. 1982. pap. 2.95 (ISBN 0-451-11735-2, AE1735, Sig). NAL.

Lewis, Ursula. Chart Your Own Horoscope. (Illus.). 1979. pap. 2.95 (ISBN 0-523-40651-7). Pinnacle Bks.

--Chart Your Own Horoscope. (Illus.). 192p. Date not set. pap. price not set (ISBN 0-448-12114-X, G&D). Putnam Pub Group.

Lewis, W. Engine Service. 256p. 1980. pap. 13.95 (ISBN 0-13-277236-1). P-H.

Lewis, W. Bennett, jt. ed. see Chayes, Abraham.

Lewis, W. M., ed. Developments in Water Treatment, Vols. 1 & 2. 1980. Vol. 1. 43.00 (ISBN 0-85334-902-9, Pub. by Applied Sci England); Vol. 2. 43.00 (ISBN 0-85334-903-7). Elsevier.

Lewis, W. M., Jr. Zooplankton Community Analysis Studies on a Tropical System. (Illus.). 1979. 28.00 (ISBN 0-387-90434-4). Springer-Verlag.

Lewis, W. S., ed. see Walpole, Horace.

Lewis, Walter H. & Elvin-Lewis, P. F. Medical Botany: Plants Affecting Man's Health. LC 76-44376. 1977. 43.50x (ISBN 0-471-53320-3, Pub by Wiley-Interscience). Wiley.

Lewis, Warren H. Brothers & Friends: The Diaries of Major Warren Hamilton Lewis. Kilby, Clyde S. & Mead, Majorie L., eds. LC 80-7756. (Illus.). 320p. 1982. 15.95i (ISBN 0-06-064575-X, HarpT). Har-Row.

Lewis, William. Son of Sato. 1978. 25.00x (ISBN 0-918824-10-9); pap. 3.00 (ISBN 0-918824-09-5). Turkey Pr.

Lewis, William, jt. auth. see Cornelius, Hal.
Lewis, William J. Interpreting for Park Visitors. (Illus.). 160p. 1981. pap. 1.95 (ISBN 0-915992-11-6). Eastern Acorn.
Lewis, William J., ed. see Institute for Policy Analysis.
Lewis, Wilmarth. Collector's Progress. LC 73-16738. (Illus.). 253p. 1974. Repr. of 1951 ed. lib. bdg. 18.25x (ISBN 0-8371-7219-5, LECP). Greenwood.
Lewis, Wilmarth S. Horace Walpole. LC 61-7449. (Illus.). 13.00 o.p. (ISBN 0-691-09790-9). Natl Gallery Art.
Lewis, Wyndham. Blasting & Bombardiering. 2nd rev. ed. 1967. 32.50x (ISBN 0-520-00742-5). U of Cal Pr.
--Collected Poems & Plays. Munton, Alan, ed. (Poetry Ser.). 229p. 1979. 14.95 o.p. (ISBN 0-85635-171-7, Pub. by Carcanet New Pr England). Humanities.
--The Complete Wild Body. Lafourcade, Bernard, ed. (Illus.). 418p. 1982. 20.00 (ISBN 0-87685-552-4); deluxe ed. 30.00 (ISBN 0-87685-553-2); pap. 12.50 (ISBN 0-87685-551-6). Black Sparrow.
--Journey into Barbary. Fox, C. J., ed. (Illus.). 400p. (Orig.). 1983. 20.00 (ISBN 0-87685-519-2); pap. 12.50 (ISBN 0-87685-518-4); signed ed. 30.00 (ISBN 0-87685-520-6). Black Sparrow.
--Self Condemned. 420p. 1983. 20.00 (ISBN 0-87685-576-1); deluxe ed. 30.00 (ISBN 0-87685-577-X); pap. 12.50 (ISBN 0-87685-575-3). Black Sparrow.
--Tarr. 1983. pap. 5.95 (ISBN 0-14-006289-0). Penguin.
--The Writer & the Absolute. LC 75-7240. 202p. 1975. Repr. of 1952 ed. lib. bdg. 19.75x (ISBN 0-8371-8098-8, LEWR). Greenwood.
Lewisohn, Ludwig. Anniversary. LC 74-156199. 304p. 1972. Repr. of 1948 ed. lib. bdg. 15.50x (ISBN 0-8371-5974-1, LEAN). Greenwood.
--A Modern Book of Criticism. 210p. 1982. Repr. of 1919 ed. lib. bdg. 25.00 (ISBN 0-89760-515-2). Telegraph Bks.
Lewison, Dale & DeLozier, M. Wayne. Retailing: Cases & Applications. 1981. text ed. 24.95 (ISBN 0-675-09920-X); Additional Supplements May Be Obtained from the Publisher. casebook 10.95 (ISBN 0-675-09853-X); study guide 9.95 (ISBN 0-675-09852-1). Merrill.
Lewison, Edward F. & Montague, Albert C. Diagnosis & Treatment of Breast Cancer: International Clinical Congress. (Illus.). 336p. 1981. 45.00 (ISBN 0-683-04945-3, 4954-2). Williams & Wilkins.
Lewit, Jane & Epstein, Ellen R. The Bar-Bat Mitzvah Planbook. LC 81-48459. (Illus.). 176p. 1982. 18.95 (ISBN 0-8128-2861-5). Stein & Day.
Lewit, S., ed. Abortion Techniques & Services. 1972. 29.50 (ISBN 90-219-0194-3). Elsevier.
--Advances in Planned Parenthood, Vol. 8. (International Congress Ser.: No. 271). 1973. pap. 28.00 (ISBN 0-444-15023-4). Elsevier.
LeWitt, Joe. Isometric Drawings. 1981. pap. 10.00 (ISBN 0-686-43403-X). J Weber Gall.
LeWitt, Sol. On the Walls of the Lower East Side. LC 80-70532. (Illus.). 76p. (Orig.). Date not set. pap. cancelled o.p. (ISBN 0-9601068-8-X). Agrinde Pubns. Postponed.
Lewitt, Suzanne M. Physician Recruitment: Strategies That Work. LC 82-4088. 222p. 1982. 27.50 (ISBN 0-89443-693-7). Aspen Systems.
Lewty, Marjorie. De L'Autre Cote Des Recifs. (Collection Harlequin Ser.). 192p. 1983. pap. 1.95 (ISBN 0-373-49335-5). Harlequin Bks.
--Makeshift Marriage. (Harlequin Romances Ser.). 192p. 1983. pap. 1.75 (ISBN 0-373-02546-7). Harlequin Bks.
Lewus, William, tr. see Zlotin, R. I. & Khodashova, K. S.
Lewy, C., jt. auth. see Broad, C. D.
Lewy, C., ed. see Broad, O. D.
Lewy, Guenter. America in Vietnam. LC 77-26204. (Illus.). 1978. 25.00x (ISBN 0-19-502391-9). Oxford U Pr.
--False Consciousness: An Essay on Mystification. 192p. 1982. 19.95 (ISBN 0-87855-451-3). Transaction Bks.
Lewy, Hans, et al, eds. Three Jewish Philosophers: Philo, Saadya, Gaon, Jehuda, Halevi. LC 60-9081. 1969. pap. text ed. 7.95x (ISBN 0-689-70126-8, T6). Atheneum.
Lewytzki, Borys. The Soviet Union: Figures - Facts - Data. 614p. 1979. 85.00x (ISBN 0-89664-010-8, Pub. by K G Saur). Gale.
Lewytzkyi, Borys & Stroynowski, Julius. Who's Who in the Socialist Countries. new ed. 736p. 1978. 140.00x (ISBN 0-89664-011-6, Pub. by K G Saur). Gale.
Lexau, Joan. The Spider Makes a Web. (Illus.). (ps-3). 1979. 6.95g o.s.i. (ISBN 0-8038-6766-2). Hastings.
Lexau, Joan M. Crocodile & Hen. LC 70-85017. (Illus.). (ps-1). 1969. PLB 9.89 o.p. (ISBN 0-06-023867-4, HarpJ). Har-Row.
--T for Tommy. LC 74-161032. (Venture Ser). (Illus.). (gr. 1). 1971. PLB 6.69 (ISBN 0-8116-6719-7). Garrard.
--That's Just Fine & Who-O-O Did It. LC 70-155568. (Venture Ser.). (Illus.). (gr. 1). 1971. PLB 6.69 (ISBN 0-685-00127-X). Garrard.
Lexus. The French Travelmate. LC 82-83997. 128p. 1983. pap. 1.95 (ISBN 0-307-46602-7, Golden Pr). Western Pub.
--The German Travelmate. LC 82-83996. 128p. 1983. pap. 1.95 (ISBN 0-307-46603-5, Golden Pr). Western Pr.
--The Greek Travelmate. LC 82-83993. 128p. 1983. pap. 1.95 (ISBN 0-307-46605-1, Golden Pr). Western Pub.
--The Italian Travelmate. LC 82-83994. (Illus.). 128p. 1983. pap. 1.95 (ISBN 0-307-46604-3, Golden Pr). Western Pub.
--The Mexican-Spanish Travelmate. 128p. 1983. pap. 1.95 (ISBN 0-307-46607-8, Golden Pr). Western Pub.
--The Portuguese Travelmate. LC 82-83992. 128p. 1983. pap. 1.95 (ISBN 0-307-46606-X, Golden Pr). Western Pub.
--The Spanish Travelmate. LC 82-83995. (Illus.). 128p. 1983. pap. 1.95 (ISBN 0-307-46601-9, Golden Pr). Western Pub.
Ley, C. J., jt. auth. see Anderson, E. P.
Ley, David. A Social Geography of the City. 528p. 1983. pap. text ed. 17.50 scp (ISBN 0-06-384875-9, HarpC). Har-Row.
Ley, David & Samuels, M. Humanistic Geography. 1978. 18.95x (ISBN 0-416-60101-4). Methuen Inc.
Ley, David & Samuels, Marwyn S., eds. Humanistic Geography: Prospects & Problems. LC 78-52408. (Illus.). 1978. text ed. 14.95x (ISBN 0-88425-013-X). Maaroufa Pr.
Ley, E. V., jt. ed. see Kuhnreuther, H.
Ley, Rosamond, tr. see Busoni, Ferruccio.
Ley, Willy. The Poles. rev. ed. LC 80-52604. (Life Nature Library). PLB 13.40 (ISBN 0-8094-3923-9). Silver.
Leyburn, Ellen D. Satiric Allegory: Mirror of Man. LC 78-5886. (Yale Studies in English Ser.: Vol. 130). 1978. Repr. of 1956 ed. lib. bdg. 16.25x (ISBN 0-313-20457-8, LESM). Greenwood.
Leyburn, James G. Scotch-Irish. LC 68-14360. 1962. 17.95 (ISBN 0-8078-0843-1). U of NC Pr.
Leyda, Jay. Dianying - Electric Shadows: An Account of Films & the Film Audience in China. 272p. 1972. 17.50x (ISBN 0-262-12046-1); pap. 5.95 (ISBN 0-262-62030-8). MIT Pr.
--The Portable Melville. 1957. 14.95 (ISBN 0-670-46710-3). Viking Pr.
Leyda, Jay & Voynow, Zina. Eisenstein at Work. 1982. 30.00 (ISBN 0-394-41262-1); pap. 15.00 (ISBN 0-394-74812-3). Pantheon.
Leyda, Jay, jt. auth. see Bertensson, Sergei.
Leyda, Jay & Bertensson, Sergei, eds. Mussorgsky Reader: A Life of Modeste Petrovich Mussorgsky in Letters & Documents. LC 70-87393. (Music Ser). (Illus.). 1970. Repr. of 1947 ed. lib. bdg. 35.00 (ISBN 0-306-71534-1). Da Capo.
Leyda, Jay, ed. see Melville, Herman.
Leyden, D. E. & Cox, R. H. Analytical Applications of NMR. LC 77-1229. (Chemical Analysis Ser: Vol. 48). 1977. 58.50 (ISBN 0-471-53403-X, Pub. by Wiley-Interscience). Wiley.
Leyden, James L., jt. ed. see Kligman, Albert M.
Leyden, Michael, jt. auth. see Barr, Bonnie.
Leyden, Michael B. & Peterson, Maria P. Career Education & Physical Sciences. (Guidance Monograph). 1975. pap. 2.60 o.p. (ISBN 0-395-20187-X). HM.
Leyden, W. von see Von Leyden, W.
Leydenfrost, Robert. The Funny Farm. LC 82-83125. 128p. 1982. pap. 4.95 (ISBN 0-932966-24-1). Permanent Pr.
--The Snake That Sneezed. (Illus.). (gr. 3-6). 1970. PLB 5.29 o.p. (ISBN 0-399-60587-8). Putnam Pub Group.
Leyel, C. F. THe Truth About Herbs. 106p. 4.50 (ISBN 0-686-38236-6). Sun Bks.
Leyel, Mrs. C. F., ed. see Grieve, M.
Leyerle, Anne L. & Leyerle, William D., eds. French Diction Songs. 130p. 1983. pap. text ed. 8.95 (ISBN 0-9602296-2-0). W D Leyerle.
Leyerle, William D., jt. ed. see Leyerle, Anne L.
Leyhausen, Paul. Cat Behavior: The Predatory & Social Behavior of Domestic & Wild Cats. new ed. (LC 77-087165). 1980. text ed. 32.50x o.s.i. (ISBN 0-8240-7017-8, Garland STPM Pr). Garland Pub.
Leyland, B. N., tr. see Kuz'Minskii, A. S.
Leyland, Eric. Dogs. 6.50x (ISBN 0-392-06353-0, SpS). Sportshelf.
--Oil Man. (Illus.). 9.50x (ISBN 0-392-04084-0, SpS). Sportshelf.
--Scotland Yard Detective. 8.50 (ISBN 0-392-08491-0, SpS). Sportshelf.
--Ship's Captain. 8.50 (ISBN 0-392-04568-0, SpS). Sportshelf.
Leyland, Winston, ed. Gay Sunshine Interviews, Vol. 2. (Illus.). 288p. (Orig.). 1982. 20.00 (ISBN 0-917342-62-3); pap. 10.00 (ISBN 0-917342-63-1). Gay Sunshine.
Leyland, Winston, jt. ed. see McDonald, Boyd.
Leyman, Juliellen. The Complete Guide to Thailand. (The Complete Asian Guide Ser.). 108p. (Orig.). 1981. pap. 6.95 (ISBN 962-7031-04-6, Pub. by CFW Pubns Hong Kong). C E Tuttle.
Leymarie, Jean, intro. by. The Jerusalem Windows of Marc Chagall. LC 62-18146. (Illus.). 120p. 1975. 15.00 o.s.i. (ISBN 0-8076-0423-2); pap. 9.95 o.s.i. (ISBN 0-8076-0807-6). Braziller.
Leyner, Mark. I Smell Esther Williams & Other Stories. LC 82-83107. 1983. 11.95 (ISBN 0-914590-76-6); pap. 5.95 (ISBN 0-914590-77-4). Fiction Coll.
Leynse, James P. Freedom's Gateway. (Orig.). pap. 3.00 (ISBN 0-685-08699-2). Creative Pr.
--Twain Shall Meet. (Orig.). pap. 2.50 (ISBN 0-685-08707-7). Creative Pr.
Leypoldt, Martha M. Forty Ways to Teach in Groups. (Orig.). 1967. pap. text ed. 4.95 (ISBN 0-8170-0376-2). Judson.
Leys, Colin. Underdevelopment in Kenya: The Political Economy of Neo-Colonialism, 1964-71. LC 74-76387. 1975. 26.50x (ISBN 0-520-02731-0); pap. 7.95x (ISBN 0-520-02770-1). U of Cal Pr.
Leys, Simon. Broken Images: Essays on Chinese Culture & Politics. LC 79-15198. 1979. 20.00 (ISBN 0-312-10594-0). St Martin.
--The Chairman's New Clothes: Mao & the Cultural Revolution. LC 77-12772. 1978. 22.50 (ISBN 0-312-12791-X). St Martin.
Leys, Wayne A. Ethics for Policy Decisions: The Art of Asking Deliberate Questions. LC 69-10118. (Illus.). 1968. Repr. of 1952 ed. lib. bdg. 20.75x (ISBN 0-8371-0146-8, LEPD). Greenwood.
Leyshon, Glynn. Programmed Functional Anatomy. LC 73-22279. 1974. pap. text ed. 10.00 o.p. (ISBN 0-8016-2999-3). Mosby.
Leytman, Igor. Kontury Luchshikh Vremen: The Outline Of Better Times. 128p. 1982. pap. 7.00 (ISBN 0-938920-13-8). Hermitage MI.
Lezak, Muriel D. Neuropsychological Assessment. 2nd ed. (Illus.). 1976. text ed. 29.50x (ISBN 0-19-503039-7). Oxford U Pr.
Lezhnev, Abram. Pushkin's Prose. Reeder, Roberta, tr. from Rus. Orig. Title: Proza Pushkina. 300p. 1983. 22.95 (ISBN 0-88233-627-4). Ardis Pubs.
Lhalungpa, Lobsang. Tibet: The Sacred Realm, Photographs 1860-1950. (Illus.). 160p. 1983. 30.00 (ISBN 0-89381-109-2). Aperture.
L'Hermite, P. & Handtschutter, J., eds. Copper in Animal Wastes & Sewage Sludge. 1981. 42.00 (ISBN 0-686-36959-9, Pub. by Reidel Holland). Kluwer Boston.
Lhertier, Michel, et al. Histoire Du Depotisme Eclaire. (Perspectives in European History Ser.: No. 13). 376p. Repr. of 1937 ed. lib. bdg. 35.00x (ISBN 0-87991-620-6). Porcupine Pr.
L'Heureux, Conrad E. In & Out of Paradise: From Adam & Eve to the Tower of Babel. LC 82-62415. 1983. pap. 4.95 (ISBN 0-8091-2530-7). Paulist Pr.
L'Heureux, Maurice. Into the Back Country. 160p. 1983. pap. 2.75 (ISBN 0-380-81588-5). Avon.
Lhevinne, Josef. Basic Principles in Pianoforte Playing. LC 74-157433. Orig. Title: The Etude. 1972. pap. 1.95 (ISBN 0-486-22820-7). Dover.
L'Hospital, J. E. Apologie De Voltaire. Repr. of 1786 ed. 68.00 o.p. (ISBN 0-8287-0452-X). Clearwater Pub.
Lhote, Henri. The Search for the Tassili Frescoes: The Story of the Prehistoric Rock-Paintings of the Sahara. 2nd rev. ed. 1973. text ed. 15.50x o.p. (ISBN 0-09-112380-1). Humanities.
Lhuyd, Edward. Archaeologia Britannica: An Account of the Languages, Histories & Customs of the Original Inhabitants of Great Britain from Collections: Glossography, Vol. I. 484p. 1971. Repr. of 1707 ed. text ed. 48.00x (ISBN 0-7165-0031-0, Pub. by Irish Academic Pr England). Biblio Dist.
Li. Cost Accounting for Management Application. 1966. text ed. 20.95x (ISBN 0-675-09883-1). Additional supplements may be obtained from publisher. Merrill.
Li, Charles N., ed. see Symposium, University of California, Santa Barbara, Mar. 1975.
Li, Ching Chun. Analysis of Unbalanced Data: A Pre-Program Introduction. LC 82-4253. (Illus.). 160p. 1983. 19.95 (ISBN 0-521-24749-7). Cambridge U Pr.
Li, David H. Accounting-Computers-Management Information Systems. LC 68-20720. (Accounting Ser.). 1968. text ed. 17.95 o.p. (ISBN 0-07-037703-0, C); 2.50 o.p. instructor's manual (ISBN 0-07-037704-9). McGraw.
Li, Dun J. Essence of Chinese Civilization. 1967. pap. text ed. 7.95x (ISBN 0-442-04788-6). Van Nos Reinhold.
Li, Fang-Kuei. A Handbook of Comparative Tai. (Oceanic Linguistics Special Publication: No. 15). (Orig.). 1977. pap. text ed. 12.00x (ISBN 0-8248-0540-2). UH Pr.
Li, Jenny. Learning Chinese with Fun. (Illus., Orig.). 1967. pap. 3.75x (ISBN 0-910286-24-8). Boxwood.
--Sanmau, the Second Grader. (Illus., Orig., Chinese). (gr. 6-10). 1968. text ed. 4.50 (ISBN 0-910286-26-4); pap. text ed. 2.75 (ISBN 0-910286-00-0). Boxwood.
Li, Ju-chen. Flowers in the Mirror. Tai-yi Lin, ed. & tr. 1965. 30.00x (ISBN 0-520-00747-6). U of Cal Pr.
Li, Jui. The Early Revolutionary Activities of Comrade Mao Tse-Tung. Hsiung, James C., ed. Sariti, Anthony W., tr. from Chinese. LC 74-24422. (The China Book Project Ser.). 1977. 32.50 (ISBN 0-87332-070-0). M E Sharpe.
Li, P. H. & Sakai, A., eds. Plant Cold Hardiness & Freezing Stress: Vol. 2: Mechanisms & Crop Implications. LC 78-7038. (Symposium). 1982. 39.50 (ISBN 0-12-447602-3). Acad Pr.
Li, Peter. T'seng P'u. (World Authors Ser.). 1980. lib. bdg. 15.95 (ISBN 0-8057-6418-6, Twayne). G K Hall.
Li, Peter, jt. ed. see Yang, Winston L.
Li, Sun. Lotus Greek & Other Stories. 123p. (Orig.). 1982. pap. 2.95 (ISBN 0-8351-0972-0). China Bks.
--Stormy Years. Yang, Gladys, tr. from Chinese. 437p. 1982. pap. 6.96 (ISBN 0-686-84097-6). China Bks.
Li, Ta M., intro. by. Mineral Resources of the Pacific Rim. LC 82-71990. (Illus.). 229p. (Orig.). 1982. pap. 30.00x (ISBN 0-89520-299-9, 299-9). Soc Mining Eng.
Li, Tien-Yi, ed. Chinese Newspaper Manual. rev. ed. 5.95 (ISBN 0-686-09983-4). Far Eastern Pubns.
Li, Victor C., ed. The Future of Taiwan. LC 80-50142. 1980. text ed. 22.50 (ISBN 0-87332-173-1). M E Sharpe.
Li, Victor H. Law Without Lawyers: A Comparative View of Law in the United States & China. LC 78-568. 1978. lib. bdg. 21.50 o.p. (ISBN 0-89158-160-X); pap. text ed. 8.00 o.p. (ISBN 0-89158-161-8). Westview.
Li, Wen-Hsiung, ed. Stochastic Models in Population Genetics. (Benchmark Papers in Genetics: Vol. 7). 1977. 53.50 (ISBN 0-12-786955-7). Acad Pr.
Li, Yao T., ed. see MIT Students' System Project.
Liad, Woody M. & Boockholdt, James L. Cost Accounting: Managerial Planning, Decision Making, & Control. LC 81-69691. 606p. 1983. text ed. 27.95x (ISBN 0-931920-34-5). Dame Pubns.
Lial, Margaret A. & Miller, Charles D. Intermediate Algebra: Study Guide. 3rd ed. 1981. pap. text ed. 8.95x (ISBN 0-673-15480-7). Scott F.
Lial, Margaret L. & Miller, Charles D. Algebra & Trigonometry. 2nd ed. 1980. text ed. 24.50x (ISBN 0-673-15272-3). Scott F.
--Algebra & Trigonometry. 3rd ed. 1983. text ed. 20.95x (ISBN 0-673-15794-6). Scott F.
--Beginning Algebra. 3rd ed. 1980. text ed. 21.95x (ISBN 0-673-15330-4). Scott F.
--College Algebra. 3rd ed. 1981. text ed. 23.95x (ISBN 0-673-15407-6); pap. text ed. 8.95x study guide (ISBN 0-673-15477-7). Scott F.
--Essential Calculus with Applications. 2nd ed. 1980. text ed. 24.50x (ISBN 0-673-15248-0). Scott F.
--Finite Mathematics. 2nd ed. 1981. pap. text ed. 21.95x (ISBN 0-673-15536-6). Scott F.
--Fundamentals of College Algebra. 1982. text ed. 21.95x (ISBN 0-673-15613-3). Scott F.
--Intermediate Algebra. 1976. 15.95x (ISBN 0-673-15271-5). Scott F.
--Intermediate Algebra. 3rd ed. 1981. text ed. 23.50x (ISBN 0-673-15406-8). Scott F.
--Mathematics: With Applications in the Management, Natural, & Social Sciences. 2nd ed. 1979. text ed. 25.50x (ISBN 0-673-15185-9); study guide 7.95x (ISBN 0-673-15187-5). Scott F.
--Mathematics with Applications in the Management, Natural, & Social Sciences. 3rd ed. 1982. text ed. 25.95x (ISBN 0-673-15793-8). Scott F.
--Trigonometry. 2nd ed. 1981. text ed. 21.95x (ISBN 0-673-15432-7). Scott F.
Lial, Margaret L., jt. auth. see Helton, Floyd F.
Lial, Margaret L., jt. auth. see Miller, Charles D.
Liang, Cecilia. Chinese Folk Poetry. 108p. Date not set. pap. 4.00 (ISBN 0-686-37600-5). Beyond Baroque.
Liang, Ch'ing. Flower Adornment Sutra Prologue, Vol. 1. Ch'an, Master Hua, commentary by. Bhikshuni Heng Hsien, et al, trs. from Chinese. (Illus.). 252p. (Orig.). 1981. pap. 10.00 (ISBN 0-917512-66-9). Buddhist Text.
Liang, Ernest P. China: Railways & Agricultural Development, Eighteen Seventy-Five to Nineteen Thirty-Five. LC 82-4749. (Research Paper Ser.: No. 203). 186p. 1982. pap. 8.00 (ISBN 0-89065-109-4). U Chicago Dept Geog.
Liang, Hsi-huey. The Berlin Police Force in the Weimar Republic, 1918-1933. LC 74-85452. (Illus.). 1970. 30.00x (ISBN 0-520-01603-3). U of Cal Pr.
Liang, James. Pronunciation Exercises for Beginning Chinese. 1.50 (ISBN 0-686-38041-X). Far Eastern Pubns.
Liang, James C. & DeFrancis, John. Varieties of Spoken Standard Chinese, Vol. I: A Speaker from Tianjin. 120p. 1982. pap. 14.00x (ISBN 0-686-37586-6). Foris Pubns.
Liang, Lucille. Chinese Regional Cooking: Authentic Recipies of the Liang School. LC 79-65067. (Illus.). 1979. 13.95 (ISBN 0-8069-0148-9); lib. bdg. 16.79 (ISBN 0-8069-0149-7). Sterling.
--Chinese Regional Cooking: Authentic Recipes of the Liang School. LC 79-65067. (Illus.). 212p. 1979. pap. 8.95 (ISBN 0-8069-7574-1). Sterling.
Liang, Ssu Y. New Stone Age Pottery from the Prehistoric Site at Hsi-Yin-Tsun, Shansi China. LC 30-7774. 1930. pap. 16.00 (ISBN 0-527-00536-3). Kraus Repr.
Liang, Tung & Leuzzi, Lawrence. An Integrated Approach to Resource Planning: A Computer Model for the Minimization of Resource Shortage in a Dynamic Economy. 1978. pap. text ed. 12.00x o.p. (ISBN 0-8248-0610-7). UH Pr.
Liao, S. Microwave Devices & Circuits. 1980. 36.00 (ISBN 0-13-581207-0). P-H.
Liao, Shu S., jt. auth. see Fremgen, James M.
Liao, Wen Kwei. The Individual & the Community: A Historical Analysis of the Motivating Factors of Social Conduct. 313p. 1982. Repr. of 1933 ed. text ed. 50.00 (ISBN 0-8495-3266-3). Arden Lib.

Liao Wen-Kuei. The Individual & the Community. LC 73-14035. (International Library of Psychology, Philosophy & Scientific Method Ser). 314p. 1974. Repr. of 1933 ed. lib. bdg. 17.75x (ISBN 0-8371-7142-3, LIIN). Greenwood.

Liapounoff, M. A. Probleme General De la Stabilite Du Mouvement. 1947. pap. 23.00 (ISBN 0-527-02733-2). Kraus Repr.

Lias, Ed. Income from Your Home Computer: Thirty Ways to Make Extra Money. 1982. text ed. 17.95 (ISBN 0-8359-3047-5); pap. text ed. 12.95 (ISBN 0-8359-3046-7). Reston.

Lias, Edward J. Future Mind: The Computer-New Medium, New Mental Environment. 1982. text ed. 18.95 (ISBN 0-316-52421-2); pap. 10.95 (ISBN 0-316-52422-0). Little.

Lias, Geoffrey. With Garibaldi in Italy. (Illus.). (gr. 7 up). 12.75x (ISBN 0-392-01881-0, LTB). Sportshelf.

Lias, John J. First Epistle of John. 1982. lib. bdg. 15.75 (ISBN 0-86524-092-2, 6201). Klock & Klock.

Libaire, George, tr. see Caulaincourt, Armand.

Libbey, Elizabeth. Songs of a Returning Soul. LC 81-71587. 1981. pap. 4.95 (ISBN 0-915604-67-1). Carnegie-Mellon.

Libby, Bill. A. J. Foyt: Racing Champion. LC 78-767. (Sports Shelf Ser.). (Illus.). (gr. 6-8). 1978. PLB 6.99 o.p. (ISBN 0-399-61123-1). Putnam Pub Group.

--Baseball's Greatest Sluggers. (Major League Baseball Library: No. 19). (Illus.). (gr. 5 up). 1973. 2.50 o.p. (ISBN 0-394-82538-1, BYR); PLB 3.69 o.p. (ISBN 0-394-92538-6). Random.

--Bud Harrelson: Super Shortstop. (Putnam Sport Shelf). (gr. 5-8). 1974. PLB 6.29 o.p. (ISBN 0-399-60901-6). Putnam Pub Group.

--Ernie Banks: Mr. Cub. (Putnam Sports Shelf). (gr. 5 up). 1971. PLB 5.49 o.p. (ISBN 0-399-60156-2). Putnam Pub Group.

--Fred Lynn: Young Star. LC 77-4278. (Putnam Sports Shelf). (Illus.). (gr. 6-8). 1977. PLB 6.29 o.p. (ISBN 0-399-61102-9). Putnam Pub Group.

--Great Stanley Cup Playoffs. (Pro Hockey Library: No. 4). (Illus.). (gr. 5 up). 1972. 2.50 o.p. (ISBN 0-394-82404-0, BYR); PLB 3.69 o.p. (ISBN 0-394-92404-5). Random.

--Johnny Bench: The Little General. new ed. (Putnam Sports Shelf). 160p. (gr. 5 up). 1973. PLB 5.29 o.p. (ISBN 0-399-60860-5). Putnam Pub Group.

--Ken Stabler: Southpaw Passer. new ed. LC 76-23468. (Putnam Sport Shelf). (Illus.). (gr. 6-8). 1977. PLB 5.29 o.p. (ISBN 0-399-61056-1). Putnam Pub Group.

--Nolan Ryan: Fireballer. LC 75-10437. (Putnam Sports Shelf). 160p. (gr. 5 up). 1975. PLB 5.29 o.p. (ISBN 0-399-60951-2). Putnam Pub Group.

--Nolan Ryan: Fireballer. (Putnam's Sports Shelf Ser.). (Illus.). (gr. 6-8). 1975. PLB 6.29 o.p. (ISBN 0-399-60951-2). Putnam Pub Group.

--O. J. The Story of Football's Fabulous O. J. Simpson. new ed. LC 73-88519. (Putnam Sports Shelf). 160p. (gr. 5 up). 1974. PLB 6.29 o.p. (ISBN 0-399-60874-5). Putnam Pub Group.

--Pete Rose: They Call Him Charlie Hustle. (Putnam Sports Shelf). (gr. 5 up). 1972. PLB 4.97 o.p. (ISBN 0-399-60749-8). Putnam Pub Group.

--Phil Esposito: Hockey's Greatest Scorer. new ed. (Putnam Sports Shelf). 160p. (gr. 5 up). 1975. 5.95 o.p. (ISBN 0-399-20475-X). Putnam Pub Group.

--Rod Carew: Master Hitter. new ed. LC 76-933. (Putnam Sports Shelf). 128p. (gr. 5 up). 1976. PLB 5.29 o.p. (ISBN 0-399-60996-2). Putnam Pub Group.

--Star Running Backs of the NFL. (NFL Punt, Pass & Kick Library: No. 15). (Illus.). (gr. 5-9). 1971. 2.50 o.p. (ISBN 0-394-82285-4, BYR); PLB 3.69 (ISBN 0-394-92285-9). Random.

--Superdrivers: Three Auto Racing Champions. LC 76-47475. (Sports Library). (Illus.). (gr. 3-6). 1977. lib. bdg. 7.12 (ISBN 0-8116-6681-6). Garrard.

--They Didn't Win the Oscars. (Illus.). 256p. 1980. 18.95 o.p. (ISBN 0-87000-455-7, Arlington Hse). Crown.

--Thurman Munson: Pressure Player. LC 78-2843. (Putnam Sports Shelf Biography Ser.). (Illus.). (gr. 6-8). 1978. PLB 6.99 (ISBN 0-399-61124-X). Putnam Pub Group.

--The Walton Gang. LC 73-78769. (Illus.). 256p. 1974. 8.95 o.p. (ISBN 0-698-10565-6, Coward). Putnam Pub Group.

--Willie Stargell: Baseball Slugger. new ed. (Putnam Sports Shelf). 160p. (gr. 5 up). 1973. PLB 6.29 o.p. (ISBN 0-399-60823-0). Putnam Pub Group.

--The Young Swimmer. LC 82-17289. (Illus.). 160p. (gr. 4 up). 1983. 10.00 (ISBN 0-688-01992-7). Lothrop.

Libby, Bill, jt. auth. see Forrest, Helen.

Libby, Bill, jt. auth. see Roseboro, John.

Libby, Charles T; see Wakefield, Robert S.

Libby, Leona M. Past Climates: Tree Thermometers, Commodities & People. 157p. 1983. text ed. 25.00x (ISBN 0-292-73019-5). U of Tex Pr.

Libby, Leona M. & Bergle, Rainer, eds. Life Work of Noble Laureate Willard Frank Libby, 7 vols. 1982. Set. pap. 15.00 (ISBN 0-941054-00-4); Vol. I, 640p. pap. 15.00 (ISBN 0-941054-01-2); Vol. II, 540p. pap. 15.00 (ISBN 0-941054-02-0); Vol. III, 500p. pap. 15.00 (ISBN 0-941054-03-9); Vol. IV, 400p. pap. 15.00 (ISBN 0-941054-04-7); Vol. V, 500p. pap. 15.00 (ISBN 0-941054-05-5); Vol. VI, 550p. pap. 15.00 (ISBN 0-941054-06-3); Vol. VII, 600p. pap. 15.00 (ISBN 0-941054-07-1). GeoScience Anal.

Libby, O. G., ed. The Arikara Narrative of the Campaign Against the Hostile Dakotas, June 1876: The Custer Battle at the Little Big Horn. LC 76-49533. (Beautiful Rio Grande Classics Ser.). 1976. lib. bdg. 12.50 o.p. (ISBN 0-87380-118-0). Rio Grande.

Libby, Paul A., et al see Heat Transfer & Fluid Mechanics Institute.

Libby, Roger W. & Whitehurst, Robert N. Marriage & Alternatives: Exploring Intimate Relationships. 1977. pap. 11.95x o.p. (ISBN 0-673-15050-X). Scott F.

Libecap, Gary. Locking up the Range: Federal Land Controls & Grazing. (Pacific Institute for Public Policy Research Ser.). 128p. 1981. prof ref 16.50x (ISBN 0-88410-382-X). Ballinger Pub.

Liben, Lynn, ed. Piaget & the Foundations of Knowledge. 288p. 1983. text ed. write for info. (ISBN 0-89859-248-8). L Erlbaum Assocs.

Liberace. The Things I Love. 1.95 (ISBN 0-448-12718-0, G&D). Putnam Pub Group.

Liberatore, Karen. The Complete Guide to the Golden Gate National Recreation Area. LC 82-4241. (Illus.). 120p. 1982. pap. 7.95 (ISBN 0-87701-259-8). Chronicle Bks.

Liberi, Albert W., jt. auth. see Korn, Henry R.

Liberia, Republic of. Liberia Supreme Court Reports, 27 vols. Incl. Vol. 1. January Term, 1861-January Term 1907. 556p (ISBN 0-8014-0466-5); Vol. 2. January Term, 1908-November Term, 1926. (Illus.). xvi, 687p. Repr (ISBN 0-8014-0261-1); Vol. 3. November Term, 1927-November Term, 1932. xii, 479p (ISBN 0-8014-0262-X); Vol. 4. November Term, 1933-April Term, 1935. ix, 444p (ISBN 0-8014-0263-8); Vol. 5. November Term, 1935-November Term, 1936. rev ed. ix, 474p (ISBN 0-8014-0264-6); Vol. 6. April Term, 1937-November Term, 1938. viii, 345p (ISBN 0-8014-0265-4); Vol. 7. April Term, 1939-November Term, 1941. ix, 423p (ISBN 0-8014-0266-2); Vol. 8. April Term, 1942-October Term, 1944. x, 500p (ISBN 0-8014-0267-0); Vol. 9. March Term, 1945-October Term, 1947. ix, 476p (ISBN 0-8014-0268-9); Vol. 10. April Term, 1948-October Term, 1950. ix, 478p (ISBN 0-8014-0269-7); Vol. 11. March Term, 1951-October Term, 1953. ix, 509p (ISBN 0-8014-0270-0); Vol. 12. March Term, 1954-October Term, 1956. x, 491p (ISBN 0-8014-0271-9); **Vol. 13. March Term, 1957-October Term, 1959. xii, 730p (ISBN 0-8014-0272-7); Vol. 14. March Term, 1960-October Term, 1961. x, 642p (ISBN 0-8014-0273-5); Vol. 15. March Term, 1962-October Term, 1963. 732p (ISBN 0-8014-0274-3); Vol. 16. March Term, 1964-October Term, 1964. 413p (ISBN 0-8014-0275-1); Vol. 17. March Term, 1965-October Term, 1966. 776p (ISBN 0-8014-0646-3); Vol. 18. March Term, 1967 - October Term, 1967. 384p (ISBN 0-8014-0755-9); Vol. 19. March Term, 1968 - October Term, 1969. 571p (ISBN 0-8014-0781-8); Cumulative Index & Table of Cases. 163p (ISBN 0-8014-0503-3). 1959-66. 50.00x ea.; index 40.00x (ISBN 0-686-66590-2). Cornell U Pr.**

Liberman, R. P. A Guide to Behavioral Analysis & Therapy. 368p. 1974. text ed. 18.50 (ISBN 0-08-016645-8); pap. text ed. 9.25 (ISBN 0-08-016786-1). Pergamon.

Libertino, John A. & Zinman, Leonard. Pediatric & Adult Reconstructive Urologic Surgery. 380p. 1977. 46.00 (ISBN 0-683-04978-X). Williams & Wilkins.

Liberty, Margot, jt. auth. see Stands In Timber, John.

Liberty, Margot, ed. see American Ethnological Society.

Libes, Sol & Garetz, Mark. Interfacing to S-100 IEEE 696 Microcomputers. (Orig.). 1981. pap. text ed. 15.00 (ISBN 0-931988-37-3). Osborne-McGraw.

Libes, Sol, ed. Programmer's Guide to CP MR. 200p. 1983. pap. 12.95 (ISBN 0-916688-37-2). Creative Comp.

Libey, Donald R., jt. ed. see Lipscomb, H. A.

Libman, Valentina A., jt. ed. see Gohdes, Clarence.

Libo, Ken, jt. auth. see Howe, Irving.

Liboff, Richard L. Introductory Quantum Mechanics. LC 78-54197. 1980. text ed. 30.00x (ISBN 0-8162-5172-X). Holden-Day.

Libow, Leslie S. & Sherman, Fredrick T. The Core of Geriatric Medicine: A Guide for Students & Practitioners. LC 80-24704. (Illus.). 354p. 1980. text ed. 25.95 (ISBN 0-8016-3096-7). Mosby.

Librach, Hank. Pocket Computer Primer. 96p. 1982. 17.95 (ISBN 0-13-683862-6); pap. 9.95 (ISBN 0-13-683854-5). P-H.

Library Applications of Data Processing Clinic, 1979. Role of the Library in an Electronic Society: Proceedings. Lancaster, F. W., ed. LC 79-19449. 200p. 1980. 9.00 (ISBN 0-87845-053-X). U of Ill Lib Info Sci.

Library Associaion, London. Report of the Commission on the Supply of & Demand for Qualified Librarians. 72p. (Orig.). 1977. pap. text ed. 10.50x o.p. (ISBN 0-85365-870-6, Pub. by Lib Assn England). Oryx Pr.

Library Association, ed. British Humanities Index 1977. LC 63-24940. 1978. 175.00x o.p. (ISBN 0-85365-940-0). Intl Pubns Serv.

Library Association, London. Adult Education in Public Libraries in the Nineteen Eighties. 96p. 1980. pap. text ed. 16.00x (ISBN 0-85365-662-2, Pub by Lib Assn England). Oryx Pr.

--Conference Proceedings: Nottingham 1979. (Orig.). 1979. pap. text ed. 10.35 (ISBN 0-85365-503-0, Pub. by Lib Assn England). Oryx Pr.

Library Association (London), ed. British Humanities Index 1978. LC 63-24940. 802p. 1979. 175.00x o.p. (ISBN 0-85365-901-X). Intl Pubns Serv.

Library Association of Australia, Special Libraries Section. Directory of Special Libraries in Australia. 5th ed. 425p. 1982. 65.00x (ISBN 0-909915-93-8). Intl Pubns Serv.

Library Buildings Institute And Alta Workshop - Detroit - 1965. Libraries: Building for the Future: Proceedings. Shaw, Robert J., ed. LC 67-23001. (Illus.). 1967. pap. 6.00 o.p. (ISBN 0-8389-0035-6). ALA.

Library Buildings Institute, San Francisco, June, 1967. Library Buildings, Innovation for Changing Needs: Proceedings. LC 73-39011. (Illus.). 302p. 1972. pap. 12.00 (ISBN 0-8389-3132-4). ALA.

Library Equipment Institute, New York, July 7-9, 1966. Procurement of Library Furnishings: Specifications, Bid Documents, & Evaluation: Proceedings. Poole, Frazer G. & Trezza, Alphonse E., eds. LC 70-77274. (Orig.). 1969. pap. 9.00 (ISBN 0-8389-3093-X). ALA.

Library for Contemporary History - World War Library, Stuttgart. Catalog from the Library for Contemporary History - World War Library, 2 pts. Incl. Pt. 1. Alphabetical Catalog, 11 vols. 1968. Set. 860.00 (ISBN 0-8161-0798-X); Pt. 2. Classified Catalog, 20 vols. 1968. Set. 1590.00 (ISBN 0-8161-0175-2). Hall Library). G K Hall.

Library of Congress. Bibliography of the Catholic Church. LC 72-46748. 576p. 1970. 72.00 o.p. (ISBN 0-7201-0134-4, Pub. by Mansell England). Wilson.

--Catalog of Brazilian Acquisitions of the Library of Congress, 1964-1974. 1977. 95.00 (ISBN 0-8161-0033-0, Hall Library). G K Hall.

--United States Catalog of Census Publications: 1946-1972. LC 75-15961. 591p. 1975. Repr. of 1974 ed. lib. bdg. 30.00x (ISBN 0-8371-8242-5, USCQ). Greenwood.

Library of Congress, jt. auth. see Research Libraries of New York Public Library.

Library of Congress, jt. auth. see Research Libraries of the New York Public Libraries.

Library of Congress, jt. auth. see Research Libraries of the New York Public Library.

Library of Congress, jt. auth. see Research Libraries of the New york Public Library.

Library of Congress, jt. auth. see Research Libraries of the New York Public Library.

Library of Congress, Geography & Map Division (Washington, D. C.) The Bibliography of Cartography, First Supplement. 1979. lib. bdg. 250.00 (ISBN 0-8161-0259-7, Hall Library). G K Hall.

Library of Congress Geography & Map Division Staff. Fire Insurance Maps in the Library of Congress. LC 80-607938. (Illus.). x, 773p. 1981. 32.00 (ISBN 0-8444-0337-7). Lib Congress.

Library of Congress, Washington, D. C. Africa South of the Sahara: Index to Periodical Literature, First Supplement. 1973. lib. bdg. 105.00 (ISBN 0-8161-1048-4, Hall Library). G K Hall.

--Africa South of the Sahara: Index to Periodical Literature, 1900-1970, 4 vols. 1971. Set. 380.00 (ISBN 0-8161-0892-7, Hall Library). G K Hall.

--Catalog of Broadsides in the Rare Book Division, 4 vols. 1972. Set. lib. bdg. 425.00 (ISBN 0-8161-0990-7, Hall Library). G K Hall.

--Far Eastern Languages Catalog, 22 vols. 1972. Set. lib. bdg. 2175.00 (ISBN 0-8161-0980-X, Hall Library). G K Hall.

--Index to Latin American Legislation, First Supplement, 1961-1965, 2 vols. 1970. Set. lib bdg. 210.00 (ISBN 0-8161-0875-7, Hall Library). G K Hall.

--Index to Latin American Legislation, Second Supplement, 2 vols. 1973. Set. lib. bdg. 115.00 (ISBN 0-8161-1020-4, Hall Library). G K Hall.

--Index to Latin American Legislation, 1950-1960, 2 Vols. 1961. Set. 190.00 (ISBN 0-8161-0594-4, Hall Library). G K Hall.

--Southeast Asia Subject Catalog, 6 vols. 1972. Set. lib. bdg. 570.00 (ISBN 0-8161-0857-9, Hall Library). G K Hall.

Library of Congress, Washington, D.C. Geography & Map Division. The Bibliography of Cartography, 5 vols. 1973. Set. lib. bdg. 535.00 (ISBN 0-8161-1008-5, Hall Library). G K Hall.

LiBrotto, Ellen V., ed. New Directions for Young Adult Services. 256p. 1983. 24.95 (ISBN 0-8352-1684-5). Bowker.

Licata, Salvatore J. & Petersen, Robert P., eds. Historical Perspectives on Homosexuality. LC 80-6262. (Research on Homosexuality Ser.: No. 2). 235p. 1982. text ed. 17.95 (ISBN 0-917724-27-5, B27). Haworth Pr.

Liccardi, Millicent & Grimes, Joseph. Entonacion y Fonemas del Itonama. (Notas Linguisticas De Bolivia Ser.: No. 3). 30p. (Span. & Eng.). 1961. pap. 0.75 o.p. (ISBN 0-88312-755-5); 1.50 o.p. Summer Inst Ling.

Lich, Glen E. & Reeves, Dona B., eds. German Culture in Texas. (Immigrant Heritage of American Ser.). 1980. lib. bdg. 16.00 (ISBN 0-8057-8415-2, Twayne). G K Hall.

Lichardus, R., et al, eds. Hormonal Regulation of Sodium Excretion. (Developments in Endocrinology Ser.: Vol. 10). 1981. 63.00 (ISBN 0-444-80289-4). Elsevier.

Lichfield, N., et al. Evaluation in the Planning Process. 336p. 1975. text ed. 39.00 (ISBN 0-08-017843-X); pap. text ed. 19.50 (ISBN 0-08-018243-7). Pergamon.

Lichine, Alexis. Alexis Lichine's New Encyclopedia of Wines & Spirits. 3rd ed. LC 80-22385. (Illus.). 736p. 1981. 29.95 (ISBN 0-394-51781-4). Knopf.

Lichstein, Herman C., ed. Bacterial Nutrition. LC 82-11720. (Benchmark Papers in Microbiology: Vol. 19). 400p. 1982. 47.00 (ISBN 0-87933-439-8). Hutchinson Ross.

Licht, Fred. Canova. LC 82-16309. (Illus.). 280p. 1983. 85.00 (ISBN 0-89659-327-4). Abbeville Pr.

--Goya: The Origins of the Modern Temper in Art. LC 78-54780. (Illus.). 288p. 1979. 16.50x (ISBN 0-87663-294-0). Universe.

--Goya: The Origins of the Modern Temper in Art. (Icon Edition). (Illus.). 288p. 1983. pap. 11.49i (ISBN 0-06-430123-0, IN-123, HarpT). Har-Row.

Licht, Sidney, ed. Arthritis & Physical Medicine. LC 74-76392. 522p. 1969. 26.50 (ISBN 0-686-65364-5, Pub. by Williams & Wilkins). Krieger.

--Massage, Manipulation & Traction. LC 76-7959. 292p. 1976. Repr. of 1960 ed. 16.00 (ISBN 0-88275-415-7). Krieger.

--Medical Climatology. LC 78-7672. 774p. 1978. Repr. of 1964 ed. lib. bdg. 24.50 (ISBN 0-88275-685-0). Krieger.

--Therapeutic Electricity & Ultraviolet Radiation. 2nd ed. LC 67-14433. 434p. 1967. 22.00 (ISBN 0-686-65365-3, Pub. by Williams & Wilkins). Krieger.

--Therapeutic Heat & Cold. 2nd ed. (Physical Medicine Library: Vol. 2). 1965. 12.00 o.p. (ISBN 0-683-05003-6). Williams & Wilkins.

Licht, W. Air Pollution Control Engineering. (Pollution Engineering & Technology Ser.: Vol. 10). 1980. 34.25 (ISBN 0-8247-6846-9). Dekker.

Licht, Walter. Working for the Railroad: The Organization of Work in the Nineteenth Century. LC 82-61372. (Illus.). 352p. 1983. 27.50x (ISBN 0-691-04700-6). Princeton U Pr.

Lichtblau, Myron I. Manuel Galvez. (World Authors Ser.). lib. bdg. 15.95 (ISBN 0-8057-2340-4, Twayne). G K Hall.

Lichten, Frances. Folk Art Motifs of Pennsylvania. LC 75-28849. (Pictorial Archive Ser.). (Illus.). 96p. 1976. pap. 4.50 (ISBN 0-486-23303-0). Dover.

--Folk Art Motifs of Pennsylvania. (Illus.). 9.00 (ISBN 0-8446-5466-3). Peter Smith.

Lichten, William. Physics. (Orig.). (gr. 7-12). 1973. 7.04 (ISBN 0-201-04242-8, Sch Div); tchr's manual 3.48 (ISBN 0-201-04243-6). A-W.

Lichtenberg, A. J. & Lieberman, M. A. Regular & Stochastic Motion. (Applied Mathematical Sciences Ser.: Vol. 38). (Illus.). 499p. 1983. 36.00 (ISBN 0-387-90707-6). Springer-Verlag.

Lichtenberg, Betty K., jt. auth. see Troutman, Andria P.

Lichtenberg, D. B. Meson & Baryon Spectroscopy. rev. ed. (Illus.). 1965. pap. 9.00 o.p. (ISBN 0-387-90000-4). Springer-Verlag.

Lichtenberg, Jacqueline. Mahogany Trinrose. LC 79-8563. (Double D Science Fiction Ser.). 224p. 1981. 11.95 o.p. (ISBN 0-385-15476-3). Doubleday.

Lichtenberg, Joseph D. Psychoanalysis & Infant Research. 176p. 1983. text ed. price not set (ISBN 0-88163-002-0). L Erlbaum Assocs.

Lichtenberg, Joseph D. & Kaplan, Samuel. Reflections on Self Psychology. 1983. write for info (ISBN 0-8236-5790-6). Intl Univs Pr.

Lichtenberg, Joseph D., ed. Empathy. 1983. write for info (ISBN 0-8236-1670-3). Intl Univs Pr.

Lichtenberg, Joseph D. & Kaplan, Samuel, eds. Reflections on Self Psychology. 1983. text ed. write for info. (ISBN 0-88163-001-2). L Erlbaum Assocs.

Lichtenberk, Frantisek. A Grammar of Manam. LC 81-11362. (Oceanic Linguistics Special Publications Ser.: No. 18). 652p. 1983. pap. text ed. 25.00x (ISBN 0-8248-0764-2). UH Pr.

Lichtendorf, Susan S. Eve's Journey: The Physical Experience of Being Female. 304p. 1982. 16.95 (ISBN 0-399-12712-7). Putnam Pub Group.

--Eve's Journey: The Physical Experience of Being Female. 368p. 1983. pap. 3.95 (ISBN 0-425-05868-9). Berkley Pub.

Lichtenstadter, Ilse. Introduction to Classical Arabic Literature. (International Studies & Translations). 1974. lib. bdg. 10.95 o.p. (ISBN 0-8057-3111-3, Twayne). G K Hall.

Lichtensteiger, W., jt. ed. see Schlumpf, M.

Lichtenstein, Edward. Psychotherapy: Approaches & Applications. LC 79-25036. 1980. text ed. 19.95 (ISBN 0-8185-0381-5). Brooks-Cole.

Lichtenstein, Lawrence M. & Fauci, Anthony S. Current Therapy in Allergy & Immunology. 400p. 1983. 44.00 (ISBN 0-941158-07-1, D3002-9). Mosby.

Lichtenstein, Louis. Diseases of Bone & Joints. 2nd ed. LC 74-14781. (Illus.). 314p. 1975. 42.50 o.p. (ISBN 0-8016-3007-X). Mosby.

Lichtenstein, Nelson. Labor's War at Home: The CIO in World War II. LC 82-4349. 304p. 1983. 29.95 (ISBN 0-521-23472-7). Cambridge U Pr.

Lichtenstein, Peter M. An Introduction to Post-Keynesian & Marxian Theories of Value & Price. 1983. 15.95 (ISBN 0-87332-214-2). M E Sharpe.

Lichtenwanger, William, ed. Oscar Sonneck & American Music. LC 82-13670. 280p. 1983. 22.50 (ISBN 0-252-01021-3). U of Ill Pr.

Lichter, Linda & Lichter, S. Robert. Prime Time Crime: Criminals & Law Enforcers in TV Entertainment. Media Institute, ed. LC 82-73726. (Illus.). 76p. (Orig.). 1983. pap. 5.00 (ISBN 0-937790-14-1). Media Inst.

Lichter, Robert L., jt. auth. see Levy, George C.

Lichter, S. Robert, jt. auth. see Lichter, Linda.

Lichtheim, George. Marxism: A Historical & Critical Study. rev. ed. 432p. 1964. pap. 10.00 (ISBN 0-7100-4645-6). Routledge & Kegan.

Lichtiger, Joshua. The Odyssey of a Jew. 1978. 7.95 o.p. (ISBN 0-533-03686-0). Vantage.

Lichtlen, P. R. Coronary Angiography & Angina Pectoris. LC 76-9263. (Illus.). 402p. 1976. 34.00 o.p. (ISBN 0-88416-086-6). Wright-PSG.

Lichtlen, P. R. & Kimura, E., eds. International ADALAT Panel Discussion. (International Congress Ser.: vol. 474). 1980. 30.75 (ISBN 0-444-90082-9). Elsevier.

Lichtman, Ronnie, jt. auth. see Mahoney, Marnie.

Lichtman, Wendy. The Boy Who Wanted a Baby. (Illus.). 96p. (gr. 4 up). 1982. text ed. 8.95 (ISBN 0-935312-10-2). Feminist Pr.

Lichtner, Schomer. Alphabet Drawings. (Illus.). 88p. (Orig.). (gr. k up). 1973. pap. 4.50 (ISBN 0-686-97176-0). Lichtner.

Lichty, Lester. Combustion Engine Processes. 7th ed. (Mechanical Engineering Ser.). 1967. text ed. 40.50 o.p. (ISBN 0-07-037720-0, C). McGraw.

Lick, Rainer F. Color Atlas of Surgical Diagnosis. LC 78-54518. (Illus.). 530p. 1980. text ed. 40.00 (ISBN 0-7216-5767-2). Saunders.

Lickley, W. A. Malachi: Lessons for Today. pap. 1.95 (ISBN 0-88172-114-X). Believers Bkshelf.

Licklider, J. C. Libraries of the Future. 1965. 15.00x (ISBN 0-262-12016-X). MIT Pr.

Licklider, Patricia. At Your Command: A Basic English Workbook. 404p. 1980. pap. text ed. 10.95 (ISBN 0-316-52426-3); instructor's manual avail. (ISBN 0-316-52427-1). Little.

--Building a College Vocabulary. 256p. (Orig.). 1981. pap. text ed. 8.95 (ISBN 0-316-52424-7); tchrs'. manual avail. (ISBN 0-316-52425-5). Little.

Lickorish, J. R., jt. auth. see Howells, John G.

Licther, Robert S., jt. auth. see Rothman, Stanley.

Lid, R. W. Ford Madox Ford: The Essence of His Art. 1964. 26.00x (ISBN 0-520-00748-4). U of Cal Pr.

Liddell, Howard S. Emotional Hazards in Animals & Man. 116p. 1956. photocopy ed. spiral 11.75x (ISBN 0-398-04339-6). C C Thomas.

Liddell, Louise A. Clothes & Your Appearance. rev. ed. LC 80-25167. (Illus.). 352p. 1981. text ed. 14.64 (ISBN 0-87006-311-1). Goodheart.

Liddell, Robert. The Novels of George Eliot. LC 77-71671. 1977. 22.50x (ISBN 0-312-57968-3). St Martin.

Liddell, Roger, tr. see Hoveyda, Fereydoun.

Liddell, Viola G. A Place of Springs. LC 78-31572. vii, 177p. 1982. 10.95 o.p. (ISBN 0-8173-5318-6); pap. 6.95 (ISBN 0-8173-0121-6). U of Ala Pr.

--With a Southern Accent. LC 82-10893. 272p. 1982. pap. 8.95 (ISBN 0-8173-0130-5). U of Ala Pr.

Liddell Hart, B. H. History of the Second World War. (Illus.). 1971. 17.50 o.p. (ISBN 0-399-10414-3). Putnam Pub Group.

--History of the Second World War. LC 79-136796. (Illus.). 1980. pap. 8.95 (ISBN 0-399-50445-1, Perigre). Putnam Pub Group.

Liddell Hart, Basil H. Defence of the West. LC 79-113062. x, 335p. Repr. of 1950 ed. lib. bdg. 16.25x (ISBN 0-8371-4701-8, LIDW). Greenwood.

--The Revolution in Warfare. LC 79-22632. 1980. Repr. of 1947 ed. lib. bdg. 18.50x (ISBN 0-313-22173-1, LHRW). Greenwood.

Lidden, H. P. & Orr, J. The Birth of Christ. 1980. 15.25 (ISBN 0-86524-058-2, 9502). Klock & Klock.

Liddiard, Jean. Isaac Rosenberg: The Half Used Life. LC 75-331140. 1975. 17.50x o.p. (ISBN 0-575-01834-8). Intl Pubns Serv.

Liddington, Jill & Norris, Jill. One Hand Tied Behind Us: The Rise of the Women's Suffrage Movement. (Illus.). 304p. 1983. pap. 7.95 (ISBN 0-86068-008-8, Virago Pr). Merrimack Bk Serv.

Liddle. Ears. (gr. k-3). pap. 2.28 response bk. (ISBN 0-8372-4235-5); tchr's handbk. 2.28 (ISBN 0-8372-4236-3); tape set avail. Bowmar-Noble.

Liddle, R. William, et al, eds. Political Participation in Modern Indonesia. LC 73-89521. (Monograph Ser.: No. 19). (Illus.). 206p. 1973. 9.50x (ISBN 0-686-30900-6). Yale U SE Asia.

--Political Participation in Modern Indonesia. (Illus.). x, 206p. pap. 9.50 (ISBN 0-686-38046-0). Yale U SE Asia.

Liddle, William. Reading for Concept Bks: Bks. A-H. 2nd ed. (Illus.). (gr. 3-9). 1977. Bk. A. pap. text ed. 6.04 (ISBN 0-07-037661-1, W); Bk. B. pap. text ed. 6.04 (ISBN 0-07-037662-X); Bk. C. pap. text ed. 6.04 (ISBN 0-07-037663-8); Bk. D. pap. text ed. 6.04 (ISBN 0-07-037664-6); Bk. E. pap. text ed. 6.04 (ISBN 0-07-037665-4); Bk. F. pap. text ed. 6.52 (ISBN 0-07-037666-2); Bk. G. pap. text ed. 6.52 (ISBN 0-07-037667-0); Bk. H. pap. text ed. 6.52 (ISBN 0-07-037668-9); tchr's guide 3.64 (ISBN 0-07-037669-7). McGraw.

Liddon, Henry P. The Divinity of Our Lord. 1978. 20.50 (ISBN 0-86524-130-9, 9801). Klock & Klock.

--The First Epistle to Timothy. 1978. 6.00 (ISBN 0-86524-109-0, 5401). Klock & Klock.

Liddy, G. Gordon. Will: The Autobiography of G. Gordon Liddy. 1980. 13.95 o.p. (ISBN 0-312-88014-6). St Martin.

Liddy, James, ed. This Was Arena. 115p. 1982. pap. text ed. 9.25x (ISBN 0-905261-10-0, 51037, Pub. by Malton Pr Ireland). Humanities.

Liden, Kathie, jt. auth. see Anson, Elva.

Lider, Julian. Military Police. 1980. text ed. 44.50x (ISBN 0-566-00296-5). Gower Pub Ltd.

--On the Nature of War. 420p. 1977. text ed. 40.00x (ISBN 0-566-00178-0). Gower Pub Ltd.

--The Political & Military Laws of War. 1979. text ed. 32.75x (ISBN 0-566-00231-0). Gower Pub Ltd.

Lider, Julien. Military Theory: Concept, Structure, Problems. LC 82-734. 426p. 1982. 35.00x (ISBN 0-312-53240-7). St Martin.

Lidgett, John S. The Biblical Doctrine of the Atonement. 522p. 1983. 19.50 (ISBN 0-86524-145-7). Klock & Klock.

Lidicker, W. Z., Jr. & Caldwell, R. L., eds. Dispersal & Migration. LC 82-9326. (Benchmark Papers in Ecology: Vol. 11). 320p. 1982. 39.50 (ISBN 0-87933-435-5). Hutchinson Ross.

Lidin, Harold J. History of the Puerto Rican Independence Movement: Vol. I, 19th Century. 212p. (Orig.). 1982. pap. 10.00 (ISBN 0-943862-00-0). Waterfront NJ.

--History of the Puerto Rican Independence Movement: Vol. II, 20th Century. 250p. 1983. 18.95 (ISBN 0-943862-01-9); pap. 10.00 (ISBN 0-943862-02-7). Waterfront NJ.

Lidoff, Joan. Christina Stead. LC 82-40283. 200p. 1982. 14.50x (ISBN 0-8044-2520-5); pap. 6.95 (ISBN 0-8044-6413-8). Ungar.

Lidstone, Herrick K., ed. A Tax Guide for Artists & Arts Organizations. LC 76-53905. (Illus.). 1979. 25.95x (ISBN 0-669-01294-7); pap. 11.95x (ISBN 0-669-01295-5). Lexington Bks.

Lidstone, John. Motivating Your Sales Force. 1978. text ed. 30.25 (ISBN 0-566-02082-3). Gower Pub Ltd.

--Recruiting & Selecting Salesmen. 1979. text ed. 33.50x (ISBN 0-566-02153-6). Gower Pub Ltd.

Lidz, Jane. One of a Kind. (Illus.). 32p. 1982. 5.95 (ISBN 0-89479-095-1). A & W Pubs.

--Rolling Homes: Handmade Houses on Wheels. LC 78-72506. (Illus.). 96p. 1979. 14.95 o.s.i. (ISBN 0-89104-128-1, A & W Visual Library); pap. 7.95 o.s.i. (ISBN 0-89104-129-X). A & W Pubs.

Lidz, Richard. Many Kinds of Courage: An Oral History of World War II. LC 79-1031. 267p. (gr. 7-12). 1980. 10.95 (ISBN 0-399-20690-6). Putnam Pub Group.

Lidz, Theodore. The Person: His & Her Development Throughout the Life Cycle. 615p. 1983. pap. 13.50 (ISBN 0-465-05541-9). Basic.

Lie, Sophus. Differentialgleichungen. LC 66-12880. (Ger). 25.00 (ISBN 0-8284-0206-X). Chelsea Pub.

--Transformationsgruppen, 3 Vols. 2nd ed. LC 76-113135. (Ger). 1970. 99.50 set (ISBN 0-8284-0232-9). Chelsea Pub.

--Vorlesungen Uber Continuierliche Gruppen Mit Geometrischen und Anderen Anwendungen. 2nd ed. LC 66-12879. (Ger). 1971. text ed. 39.95 (ISBN 0-8284-0199-3). Chelsea Pub.

Lieb, Frederick G. Baseball As I Have Known It. LC 77-5309. (Illus.). 1977. 9.95 o.p. (ISBN 0-698-10815-9, Coward). Putnam Pub Group.

Lieb, Hans H. Intergrational Linguistics, 6 vols. (Current Issues in Linguistics Theory: 17). 1410p. 1983. Set 130.00 (ISBN 90-272-3508-2). Vol. 1, General Outline (ISBN 0-686-36248-9). Vol. 2, A Theory of Grammar (ISBN 0-686-37279-4). Vol. 4, Syntax & Symantics (ISBN 0-686-37280-8). Vol. 5., Mophology & Morphosemantics (ISBN 0-686-37281-6). Vol. 6, Lexical Semantics (ISBN 0-686-37282-4). Vol. 3, Concept of Language Universal (ISBN 0-686-37791-5). Benjamins North Am.

Lieb, Julian & Slaby, Andrew E. Integrated Psychiatric Treatment. 1975. pap. text ed. 15.50x o.p. (ISBN 0-06-141539-1, Harper Medical). Lippincott.

Lieb, Michael. The Dialectics of Creation: Patterns of Birth & Regeneration in "Paradise Lost". LC 71-76047. 1970. 14.50x (ISBN 0-87023-049-2). U of Mass Pr.

Lieb, Robert. Transportation: The Domestic System. 2nd ed. 1980. text ed. 21.95 (ISBN 0-8359-7826-5); instrs' manual avail. Reston.

Lieb, Thom. Everybody's Book of Bicycle Riding. McCullagh, Chuck, ed. (Illus.). 336p. 1981. 14.95 (ISBN 0-87857-322-4); pap. 10.95 (ISBN 0-87857-323-2). Rodale Pr Inc.

Liebegott, Jeanne M. Learning Is Out the Door. (gr. k-6). 1981. 8.95 (ISBN 0-86653-026-6, GA 277). Good Apple.

Liebenow, J. Gus. Agriculture, Education, & Rural Transformation: With Particular Reference to East Africa. (African Humanities Ser.). 31p. (Orig.). 1969. pap. text ed. 2.00 (ISBN 0-941934-00-4). Ind U Afro-Amer Arts.

Liebenstein-Kurtz, Ruth F. von see Von Liebenstein-Kurtz, Ruth F.

Lieber, Charles S., ed. Recent Advances in the Biology of Alcoholism. LC 82-1033. (Advances in Alcohol & Substance Abuse Ser.: Vol. 1, No. 2). 132p. 1982. text ed. 25.00 (ISBN 0-86656-104-8, B104). Haworth Pr.

Lieber, Francis. Lieber's Code & the Law of War. Hartigan, Richard S., ed. 1983. 14.95 (ISBN 0-913750-25-5). Precedent Pub.

--On Civil Liberty & Self Government. LC 76-169655. (Civil Liberties in American History Ser). 1972. Repr. of 1877 ed. lib. bdg. 75.00 (ISBN 0-306-70284-3). Da Capo.

Lieber, Harvey. Federalism & Clean Waters: The 1972 Water Pollution Control Act. LC 74-33980. (Illus.). 304p. 1975. 24.95x (ISBN 0-669-99150-3). Lexington Bks.

Lieber, Hugh G. & Lieber, Lillian R. The Education of T. C. Mits. (Illus.). 1944, o.s.i. 7.95 (ISBN 0-393-06278-3); pap. 5.95 1978 (ISBN 0-393-00906-8). Norton.

Lieber, Justin. Noam Chomsky: A Philosophic Overview. (World Leaders Ser: No. 36). 1975. lib. bdg. 9.95 o.p. (ISBN 0-8057-3661-1, Twayne). G K Hall.

Lieber, Lillian R., jt. auth. see Lieber, Hugh G.

Lieber, Michael. Street Life: Afro-American Culture in Urban Trinidad. 1981. lib. bdg. 15.95 (ISBN 0-8161-9033-X, Univ Bks). G K Hall.

Lieber, Michael D. & Dikepa, Kalio H. Kapingamarangi Lexicon. LC 73-90855. (Pali Language Texts: Polynesia). 380p. (Orig.). 1974. pap. text ed. 14.00x (ISBN 0-8248-0304-3). UH Pr.

Lieber, Michael D., ed. Exiles & Migrants in Oceania. LC 77-10756. (Association for Social Anthropology in Oceania, Monograph No. 5). (Illus.). 1978. text ed. 17.50x (ISBN 0-8248-0557-7). UH Pr.

Lieber, Nancy, ed. Eurosocialism & America: Political Economy for the 1980s. 250p. 1982. 22.95 (ISBN 0-87722-273-8). Temple U Pr.

Lieber, Robert J. British Politics & European Unity: Parties, Elites & Pressure Groups. LC 70-104104. 1970. 30.00x (ISBN 0-520-01675-0). U of Cal Pr.

--Theory of World Politics. 1977. text ed. 11.95 (ISBN 0-316-52499-9); pap. text ed. 8.95 (ISBN 0-316-52500-6). Little.

Lieberman & Schimmel. Typing the Easy Way. 1982. pap. 6.95 (ISBN 0-8120-2284-X). Barron.

Lieberman, Ann & Miller, Lynn. Staff Development: New Demands, New Realities, New Perspectives. LC 78-27453. 1979. 11.95x (ISBN 0-8077-2512-9). Tchrs Coll.

Lieberman, Arnold. Case Capsules: The Droll, Directing, Devilish, Definitely Different. (Illus.). 356p. 1964. photocopy ed. spiral 29.75x (ISBN 0-398-01127-3). C C Thomas.

Lieberman, Arthur. College Mathematics for Business & the Social Sciences. LC 81-17976. (Mathematics Ser.). 618p. 1982. text ed. 25.95 (ISBN 0-8185-0474-9). Brooks-Cole.

Lieberman, Bernhardt, ed. Contemporary Problems in Statistics: A Book of Readings for the Behavioral Sciences. (Orig.). 1971. pap. text ed. 11.50x (ISBN 0-19-501231-3). Oxford U Pr.

Lieberman, Bonnie, ed. see Reynolds, Lloyd G.

Lieberman, Chaim. The Grave Concern. LC 68-58650. 202p. 1968. 4.95 o.p. (ISBN 0-88400-016-8). Shengold.

Lieberman, David E., ed. Computer Methods: The Fundamentals of Digital Nuclear Medicine. LC 77-10999. (Illus.). 226p. 1977. pap. 20.00 (ISBN 0-8016-3009-6). Mosby.

Lieberman, E. J. & Peck, Ellen. Sex & Birth Control: A Guide for the Young. rev. ed. LC 79-7094. (Illus.). 320p. 1981. 13.41i (ISBN 0-690-01837-1, HarpT). Har-Row.

Lieberman, E. James & Peck, Ellen. Sex & Birth Control: A Guide for the Young. LC 73-7806. 224p. 1973. 13.44i (ISBN 0-690-01837-1). T Y Crowell.

Lieberman, E. James, ed. Mental Health: The Public Health Challenge. LC 74-34564. 300p. 1975. pap. 7.50x (ISBN 0-87553-075-3, 021). Am Pub Health.

Lieberman, Ellin, ed. Clinical Pediatric Nephrology. LC 75-40110. (Illus.). 589p. 1976. 49.00 (ISBN 0-397-50318-0, Lippincott Medical). Lippincott.

Lieberman, Fredric. Chinese Music: An Annotated Bibliography. 2nd ed. LC 76-24755. (Reference Library of the Humanities Ser.: Vol. 75). 1976. lib. bdg. 35.00 o.s.i. (ISBN 0-8240-9922-2). Garland Pub.

Lieberman, Gerald, jt. auth. see Bowker, Albert.

Lieberman, Gerald F. Three Thousand Five Hundred Good Quotes for Speakers. LC 81-43552. 480p. 1983. 17.95 (ISBN 0-385-17766-6). Doubleday.

Lieberman, Gerald J., jt. auth. see Hillier, Frederick S.

Lieberman, Herbert. Night Call From a Distant Time Zone. 1983. pap. 3.50 (ISBN 0-686-42962-1, Sig). NAL.

Lieberman, Jerry. Three Thousand Five Hundred Good Jokes for Speakers. LC 74-29354. 480p. 1975. pap. 5.95 (ISBN 0-385-00545-8, Dolp). Doubleday.

Lieberman, Jethro K. & Rhodes, Neil S. The Complete Nineteen Eighty CB Handbook. 1980. pap. 2.95 o.p. (ISBN 0-380-48587-7, 48587). Avon.

Lieberman, Laurence. Eros at the World Kite Pageant: Poems 1979-1982. 144p. 1983. 15.75 (ISBN 0-02-571860-6); pap. 8.95 (ISBN 0-02-069810-0). Macmillan.

Lieberman, Leo. What Can I Be? A Guide to 525 Liberal Arts & Business Careers. LC 75-26001. 1976. 14.24 (ISBN 0-935198-03-2). M M Bruce.

Lieberman, Leo & Beringause, Arthur. Classics of Jewish Literature. 1983. 20.00 (ISBN 0-8022-2092-4). Philos Lib.

Lieberman, M. & Sano, T., eds. Developmental & Physiological Correlates of Cardiac Muscle: Perspectives in Cardiovascular Research, Vol. 1. LC 74-21979. 336p. 1976. 38.00 (ISBN 0-89004-027-3). Raven.

Lieberman, M. A., jt. auth. see Lichtenberg, A. J.

Lieberman, Mark A., et al. Office Automation: A Manager's Guide for Improved Productivity. LC 81-23114. 331p. 1982. 27.95x (ISBN 0-471-07983-9, Pub. by Wiley-Interscience). Wiley.

Lieberman, Maurice. Ear Training & Sight Singing. 1959. 9.95x (ISBN 0-393-09519-3, NortonC). Norton.

Lieberman, Morton & Tobin, Sheldon. The Experience of Old Age: Stress, Coping, & Survival. 400p. 1983. 25.00 (ISBN 0-465-02532-2). Basic.

Lieberman, Myron. Public-Sector Bargaining: A Policy Reappraisal. LC 80-8426. 1980. 21.95x (ISBN 0-669-04110-6). Lexington Bks.

Lieberman, Norman P. Troubleshooting Refinery Processes. 408p. 1981. 43.95x (ISBN 0-87814-157-X). Pennwell Book Division.

Lieberman, Philip. Intonation, Perception, & Language. LC 67-13392. (Press Research Monographs: No. 38). 1967. 17.50x o.p. (ISBN 0-262-12024-0); pap. 4.95x o.p. (ISBN 0-262-62031-6). MIT Pr.

--On the Origin of Languages: An Introduction to the Evolution of Human Language. 1975. pap. 14.95x (ISBN 0-02-370690-2). Macmillan.

--Speech Physiology & Acoustic Phonetics. (Illus.). 1977. text ed. 21.95x (ISBN 0-02-370620-1). Macmillan.

Lieberman, Ralph. Renaissance Architecture in Venice: 1450-1540. LC 82-22606. (Illus.). 144p. 1982. 37.50 (ISBN 0-89659-310-X). Abbeville Pr.

Lieberman, Robert. Baby. 352p. 1981. 12.95 o.p. (ISBN 0-517-54488-1). Crown.

Lieberman, Ronald. Keystone Tercentenary. 1983. 10.00 (ISBN 0-934630-12-7); lib. bdg. 10.00 (ISBN 0-934630-13-5); pap. 6.00 (ISBN 0-934630-14-3). Family Album.

Lieberman, William. Images. 1982. signed limited ed. 15.00 (ISBN 0-934630-15-1); 7.50 (ISBN 0-934630-11-9). Family Album.

Liebermann, Jeremiah, ed. see Garvy, John W., Jr.

Liebermann-Meffert, D., et al, eds. Greater Omentum: Anatomy, Physiology, Pathology, Surgery. (Illus.). 361p. 1983. 166.00 (ISBN 0-387-11882-9). Springer-Verlag.

Liebers, Arthur. The Complete Book of Cross Country Skiing & Ski Touring. LC 73-78759. (Illus.). 320p. 1974. 8.95 o.p. (ISBN 0-698-10533-8, Coward). Putnam Pub Group.

--Housebreak & Train Your Dog. (Orig.). 1958. pap. 2.95 (ISBN 0-87666-318-8, DS1020). TFH Pubns.

--How to Raise & Train a Dalmatian. (Illus.). pap. 2.95 (ISBN 0-87666-279-3, DS1012). TFH Pubns.

--How to Raise & Train a German Short-Haired Pointer. pap. 2.95 (ISBN 0-87666-301-3, DS1016). TFH Pubns.

--How to Raise & Train a Maltese. pap. 2.95 (ISBN 0-87666-335-8, DS1025). TFH Pubns.

--How to Raise & Train an English Springer Spaniel. pap. 2.95 (ISBN 0-87666-398-6, DS1034). TFH Pubns.

--Liebers' Guide. LC 76-30709. 1977. 7.95 o.p. (ISBN 0-688-03175-7). Morrow.

Liebers, Arthur & Jeffries, Paul. How to Raise & Train a Weimaraner. pap. 2.95 (ISBN 0-87666-405-2, DS1035). TFH Pubns.

Liebers, Arthur & Miller, Dana. How to Raise & Train a Yorkshire Terrier. (Illus.). pap. 2.95 (ISBN 0-87666-410-9, DS1037). TFH Pubns.

Liebers, Arthur & Sheppard, Georgie M. How to Raise & Train a Pomeranian. (Illus.). pap. 2.95 (ISBN 0-87666-352-8, DS1029). TFH Pubns.

Liebert, Burt & Liebert, Marjorie. A Schoolwide Secondary Reading Program: Here's How. LC 78-10904. 1979. text ed. 25.95x (ISBN 0-471-03549-1). Wiley.

Liebert, Marjorie, jt. auth. see Liebert, Burt.

Liebert, R. M., et al. The Early Window: The Effect of Television on Children & Youth. 1973. 21.00 (ISBN 0-08-017091-9); pap. 8.75 (ISBN 0-08-017780-8). Pergamon.

Liebert, Robert M. & Neale, John M. Psychology. LC 76-54530. 1977. text ed. 27.95x (ISBN 0-471-53431-5); Set. 21.40x (ISBN 0-686-86905-2); study guide 12.50 (ISBN 0-471-01776-0); test 3.00x (ISBN 0-471-01775-2); 8.00x (ISBN 0-471-03403-7); tchrs' manual 3.00x (ISBN 0-471-01777-9). Wiley.

Liebert, Robert M. & Pelson, Wickes. Developmental Psychology. 3rd ed. (Illus.). 640p. 1981. text ed. 24.95 (ISBN 0-13-208256-X). P-H.

Liebert, Robert M., jt. auth. see Neale, John M.

Liebert, Robert S. Michelangelo: A Psychoanalytic Study of His Life & Images. LC 82-7042. (Illus.). 480p. 1983. text ed. 29.95x (ISBN 0-300-02793-1). Yale U Pr.

Lieberthal, E. A., jt. auth. see Gurau, Peter K.

Lieberthal, Edwin M. The Complete Book of Fingermath. (Illus.). 1979. 25.60 (ISBN 0-07-037680-8, W). McGraw.

Lieberthal, Edwin M., jt. auth. see Gurau, Peter K.

Lieberthal, Kenneth, jt. ed. see Lardy, Nicholas R.

Lieberthal, Moilton M., jt. auth. see Conn, Harold.

Liebesny, F. Mainly on Patents. 1972. 15.95 o.p. (ISBN 0-408-70368-7). Butterworth.

Liebetrau, Preben. Oriental Rugs in Color. 1963. 10.95 (ISBN 0-02-571840-1). Macmillan.

Liebhafsky, H. A., et al. X-Rays, Electrons, & Analytical Chemistry: Spectrochemical Analysis with X-Rays. 566p. 1972. 55.50x o.p. (ISBN 0-471-53428-5). Wiley.

Liebich, Andre, ed. Selected Writings of August Cieszkowski. LC 77-94371. (Studies in the History & Theory of Politics). 1979. 29.95 (ISBN 0-521-21986-8). Cambridge U Pr.

Liebing, Ralph W. Systematic Construction Inspection. 119p. 1982. 27.95x (ISBN 0-471-08065-9, Pub. by Wiley-Interscience). Wiley.

Liebing, Ralph W. & Paul, Mimi F. Architectural Working Drawings. LC 76-48154. 1977. 28.00x (ISBN 0-471-53432-3, Pub. by Wiley-Interscience). Wiley.

--Architectural Working Drawings. 2nd ed. 352p. 1982. 25.00 (ISBN 0-471-86649-0, Pub. by Wiley-Interscience). Wiley.

Liebknecht, Karl. Militarism & Anti-Militarism. Sirnis, A., tr. 192p. 1972. pap. 2.00 o.p. (ISBN 0-486-22840-1). Dover.

--Militarism & Antimilitarism: With Special Regard to the International Young Socialist Movement. Lock, Grahame, tr. from Ger. 162p. 1974. text ed. 10.00x o.p. (ISBN 0-9502495-7-2); pap. text ed. 4.00x o.p. (ISBN 0-9502495-8-0). Humanities.

Liebler, Joan G. Managing Health Records: Administrative Principles. LC 79-22455. 306p. 1980. text ed. 30.50 (ISBN 0-89443-168-4). Aspen Systems.

Lieblich, Garnet M., ed. Qualified Products List & Sources. 62nd ed. 315p. 1983. lib. bdg. 57.50 (ISBN 0-912702-20-6). Global Eng.

Lieblich, Jerome H. Dimensioning & Tolerancing: An Interpretation of ANSI Y14.5M, 1982. 97p. 1983. lib. bdg. 6.50x (ISBN 0-912702-19-2). Global Eng.

--Drawing Requirements Manual. 5th ed. 719p. 1983. perfect bdg. 29.95 (ISBN 0-912702-18-4); loose leaf 44.95 (ISBN 0-912702-17-6). Global Eng.

Liebling, A. J. The Sweet Science. 1956. 14.95 (ISBN 0-670-68653-0). Viking Pr.

Liebling, Jerome. Jerome Liebling Photographs. LC 82-6919. (Illus.). 108p. 1982. 25.00 (ISBN 0-87023-371-8). U of Mass Pr.

Liebman, Arthur. Jews & the Left. LC 78-20871. (Contemporary Religious Movements Ser.). 1979. 24.95 (ISBN 0-471-53433-1, Pub. by Wiley-Interscience). Wiley.

Liebman, Bonnie, jt. auth. see Jackson, Michael M.

Liebman, Charles S. & Don-Yehiya, Eliezer. Civil Religion in Israel: Traditional Judaism & Political Culture in the Jewish State. LC 82-17427. 270p. 1983. 19.95x (ISBN 0-520-04817-2). U of Cal Pr.

Liebman, Ellen. California Farmland: A History of Large Agricultural Landholdings. LC 82-20759. 280p. 1983. text ed. 25.95x (ISBN 0-86598-107-8). Allanheld.

Liebman, Jerome, et al. Pediatric Electrocardiography. (Illus.). 348p. 1982. lib. bdg. 55.00 (ISBN 0-683-05030-3). Williams & Wilkins.

Liebman, Joshua L. Peace of Mind. 8.95 o.p. (ISBN 0-671-56010-7); large type ed. avail. o.p. S&S.

Liebman, Lance, jt. auth. see Haar, Charles M.

Liebman, Michael. Neuroanatomy Made Easy & Understandable. 112p. 1979. pap. text ed. 12.95 (ISBN 0-8391-1513-X). Univ Park.

Liebman, Seymour. The Enlightened. 1967. pap. 6.95 (ISBN 0-87024-311-X). U of Miami Pr.

Liebmann-Smith, Richard, jt. auth. see Glass, Lillian.

Liebow, Elliot. Tally's Corners. 1967. 7.95 (ISBN 0-316-52513-8); pap. 3.95 (ISBN 0-316-52514-6). Little.

Liebowitz, Harold. The Oriental Institute Excavations at Selenkahiye, Syria, Fascicle 3: Terra-Cotta Figurines & Model Vehicles. Van Loon, M., ed. LC 81-71738. (Bibliotheca Mesopotamica Ser.). 1983. write for info. (ISBN 0-89003-104-5); pap. write for info. (ISBN 0-89003-105-3). Undena Pubns.

Liebowitz, M., jt. auth. see Johnston, P. M.

Liebowitz, Michael R. The Chemistry of Love. 1983. 15.50i (ISBN 0-316-52430-1). Little.

Liebowitz, Murray, jt. auth. see Johnston, Philip M.

Liebrenz, Noelle, jt. auth. see Hargrove, Penny.

Liebson, Philip R., jt. ed. see Shakibi, Jami G.

Liechty, Richard D. & Soper, Robert T. Synopsis of Surgery. 4th ed. LC 80-12884. (Illus.). 716p. 1980. pap. text ed. 29.95 (ISBN 0-8016-3012-6). Mosby.

Liederbach, Robert J., ed. see Ryan, Abram.

Liederman, David & Urvater, Michele. Cooking the Nouvelle Cuisine in America. LC 79-64785. (Illus.). 480p. 1979. 14.95 o.s.i. (ISBN 0-89480-111-2); pap. 9.95 (ISBN 0-89480-215-1). Workman Pub.

Liederman, Judith. The Moneyman. 1979. 10.95 o.s.i. (ISBN 0-395-27099-5). HM.

--The Moneyman. 1980. pap. 2.75 o.p. (ISBN 0-451-09164-7, E9164, Sig). NAL.

--The Pleasure Dome. 1983. pap. 3.75 (ISBN 0-8217-1134-2). Zebra.

Liedloff, jt. auth. see Moeller.

Liedloff, Helmut. Ohne Muhe! LC 79-84596. (German Sequential Readers Ser.). (Illus.). (gr. 9-10). 1980. text ed. 3.24 (ISBN 0-395-27931-3). HM.

Liedloff, Helmut, jt. auth. see Moeller, Jack R.

Lief, Harold I. & Karlen, Arno, eds. Sex Education in Medicine. LC 76-44. 1976. 12.95x o.s.i. (ISBN 0-470-15023-8). Halsted Pr.

Lief, Nina. First Year of Life: A Guide for Parenting. pap. 8.95 (ISBN 0-8215-9895-3). Sadlier.

Lief, Nina R. The First Year of Life: A Curriculum for Parenting Information. 362p. 19.95 (ISBN 0-686-86720-3). Sadlier.

--The Second Year of Life: Curriculum Edition. 1983. write for info. o.p. (ISBN 0-8215-9899-6). Sadlier.

Lief, Philip. Cat's Revenge. 1981. pap. 3.95 o.s.i. (ISBN 0-686-78810-9). S&S.

Lieff, Jonathan D. How to Buy A Personal Computer Without Anxiety. LC 82-11673. 128p. 1982. 16.50x (ISBN 0-88410-920-8); pap. 9.95 (ISBN 0-88410-743-4). Ballinger Pub.

Liehm, Antonin, ed. The Writing on the Wall: An Anthology of Czechoslovak Literature Today. Kussi, Peter. 256p. 1983. 25.95 (ISBN 0-918294-19-3). Karz-Cohl Pub.

Liehm, Antonin & Kussi, Peter, eds. The Writing on the Wall: An Anthology of Contemporary Czech Literature. 256p. 1983. 29.95 (ISBN 0-943828-53-8); pap. 12.95 (ISBN 0-943828-54-6). Karz-Cohl Pub.

Liehm, Antonin J. Closely Watched Films: The Czechoslovak Experience. Polackova, Kaca, tr. LC 72-94987. (Illus.). 1974. 22.50 (ISBN 0-87332-036-0). M E Sharpe.

--The Milos Forman Stories. LC 73-92806. 191p. 1975. 22.50 (ISBN 0-87332-051-4). M E Sharpe.

Liehr, H. & Grun, M., eds. Reticuloendothelial System & Pathogenesis of Liver Disease. 1980. 70.00 (ISBN 0-444-80240-1). Elsevier.

Liem, Nguyen Dang. Vietnamese Pronunciation. LC 70-128082. (PALI Language Texts: SE Asia). (Orig.). 1970. pap. text ed. 7.00x (ISBN 0-87022-462-X). UH Pr.

Lien, David A. Controlling the World with Your TRS-80. Gunzel, David, ed. (CompuSoft Learning Ser.). (Illus.). 600p. (Orig.). 1983. pap. price not set (ISBN 0-932760-03-1). CompuSoft.

--Learning Disk BASIC & TRS DOS. Gunzel, David, ed. LC 82-71959. (CompuSoft Learning Ser.). (Illus.). 400p. (gr. 7 up). 1983. pap. write for info. (ISBN 0-932760-02-3). CompuSoft.

--Learning IBM BASIC for the Personal Computer: CompuSoft Learning Ser. LC 82-73471. (Illus.). 448p. (Orig.). 1982. pap. 19.95 (ISBN 0-932760-13-9). CompuSoft.

--Learning Timex Sinclair BASIC for the Timex Sinclair 1000 & the ZX81. LC 82-73469. (CompuSoft Learning Ser.). (Illus.). 350p. (Orig.). 1983. pap. 14.95 (ISBN 0-932760-15-5). CompuSoft.

Lien, David A., jt. auth. see English, W. E.

Lien Ch'in & Ch'an Master Hua, eds. Essentials of the Shramanera Vinaya & Rules of Deportment: A General Explanation. Bhiksuni Heng Yin, tr. from Chinese. (Illus.). 112p. (Orig., Eng.). 1975. pap. 4.00 (ISBN 0-917512-04-9). Buddhist Text.

Lienhard, John. A Heat Transfer Textbook. (Illus.). 480p. 1981. text ed. 31.95 (ISBN 0-13-385112-5). P-H.

Lienhard, John H., jt. auth. see Tien, Chang-Lim.

Lienhardt, Godfrey. Social Anthropology. 2nd ed. 1966. pap. text ed. 5.95x (ISBN 0-19-888015-4). Oxford U Pr.

Lientz, Bennett, jt. auth. see Allen, Joe.

Lientz, Bennett P., jt. auth. see Allen, R. J.

Liepmann, Hans W. & Roshko, A. Elements of Gasdynamics. LC 56-9823. 1957. text ed. 39.95 (ISBN 0-471-53460-9). Wiley.

Liepmann, Kate K. The Journey to Work. LC 73-13403. (Illus.). 199p. 1974. Repr. of 1944 ed. lib. bdg. 17.50x (ISBN 0-8371-7051-6, LIJW). Greenwood.

Lier, H. N. van see Van Lier, H. N.

Lierman, Deonna. Pocketful of Promises. (Illus.). 24p. 1983. pap. 0.45 (ISBN 0-87239-650-9, 2120). Standard Pub.

Liesener, James W. Systematic Process for Planning Media Programs. LC 76-3507. 1976. pap. text ed. 9.00 (ISBN 0-8389-0176-X). ALA.

Liesenfeld, Vincent J. & Backscheider, P. R., eds. The Stage & the Licensing Act, 1729-1739. LC 78-66661. (Eighteenth Century English Drama Ser.). lib. bdg. 50.00 (ISBN 0-8240-3576-3). Garland Pub.

Liesting, G. T. Sacrament of the Eucharist. 7.50 o.p. (ISBN 0-8091-0129-7). Paulist Pr.

Liestol, Knut. The Origin of the Icelandic Family Sagas. LC 73-17630. 261p. 1974. Repr. of 1930 ed. lib. bdg. 17.50x (ISBN 0-8371-7253-5, LIIF). Greenwood.

Lieth, H., jt. ed. see Gollery, F. B.

Lieth, Helmut F., ed. Patterns of Primary Production in the Biosphere. LC 78-18691. (Benchmark Papers in Ecology: Vol. 8). 342p. 1978. 46.00 (ISBN 0-87933-327-8). Hutchinson Ross.

Lietz, Gerald S. Bacteria. LC 64-10067. (Junior Science Books Ser.). (gr. 2-5). 1964. PLB 6.69 (ISBN 0-8116-6167-9). Garrard.

Lietz, Gerald S., jt. auth. see White, Anne T.

Lietz, Jeremy J. & Towle, Maxine. The Elementary Principal's Role in Special Education. (Illus.). 188p. 1982. 19.75x (ISBN 0-398-04677-8). C C Thomas.

Lievano, Francisco, tr. see Getz, Gene.

Lievano, Francisco, tr. see Johnson, James L.

Lievense, W. De Familie Mozart Op Bezoek in Nederland: Een Reisverslag. 1965. 22.50 o.p. (ISBN 90-6027-019-3, Pub. by Frits Knuf Netherlands). Pendragon NY.

Liew, Kit S. Struggle for Democracy: Sung Chiao-Jen & the 1911 Revolution. LC 74-123623. 1971. 26.50x o.s.i. (ISBN 0-520-01760-9). U of Cal Pr.

Lifar, Serge. Serge Diaghilev: His Life, His Work, His Legend. LC 76-25041. (Series in Dance). 1976. Repr. of 1940 ed. lib. bdg. 25.00 (ISBN 0-306-70839-6). Da Capo.

Lifchez, Aaron S., jt. auth. see Fenton, Judith A.

Life Office Management Associates, ed. Teaching Part 1: Principles of Life Insurance. (FLMI Insurance Education Program Ser.). 167p. 1972. pap. 8.00 (ISBN 0-915322-02-1). LOMA.

Life Office Management Association, ed. Life Company Operations. LC 74-83846. (FLMI Insurance Education Program Ser.). 540p. 1974. pap. text ed. 12.00 (ISBN 0-915322-10-2); 4.50 o.p. student guide (ISBN 0-915322-11-0); Teaching Part 2, 1975. 8.00 o.p. (ISBN 0-915322-09-9). LOMA.

--Life Insurance Investments: Readings. (FLMI Insurance Education Program Ser.). 186p. 1982. pap. text ed. 10.00 (ISBN 0-915322-48-X). LOMA.

--Pension Planning: Readings. (FLMI Insurance Education Program Ser.). 177p. 1982. pap. text ed. 10.00 (ISBN 0-915322-49-8). LOMA.

--Readings for the Group Insurance Specialty. (FLMI Insurance Education Program Ser.). 45p. (Orig.). 1980. pap. text ed. 4.00 (ISBN 0-915322-40-4). Loma.

--Readings for the Information Systems Specialty. (FLMI Insurance Education Program Ser.). (Illus.). 186p. (Orig.). 1980. pap. text ed. 10.00 (ISBN 0-915322-39-0). LOMA.

--Readings for the Life Insurance Investments Specialty, II. (FLMI Insurance Education Program Ser.). 204p. 1980. pap. text ed. 9.50 o.p. (ISBN 0-915322-35-8). LOMA.

--Readings for the Pension Planning Specialty. (FLMI Insurance Education Program Ser.). 132p. 1980. pap. 7.50 o.p. (ISBN 0-915322-33-1). LOMA.

--Readings for the Personnel Administration Specialty. (FLMI Insurance Education Program Ser.). 95p. (Orig.). 1980. pap. text ed. 6.00 (ISBN 0-915322-41-2). LOMA.

--Readings for the Selection of Risks Specialty. (FLMI Insurance Education Program Ser.). 94p. 1980. pap. text ed. 7.00 (ISBN 0-915322-34-X). LOMA.

--Readings in Management Principles. (FLMI Insurance Education Program Ser.). 68p. (Orig.). 1980. pap. text ed. 5.00 (ISBN 0-915322-37-4). LOMA.

--Student Guide for Canadian, Pt. 3. (FLMI Insurance Education Program Ser.). 1976. pap. 8.00 workbook (ISBN 0-915322-20-X). LOMA.

Life Office Management Association. Student Guide for Management Principles. 3rd ed. (FLMI Insurance Education Program Ser.). 200p. 1981. pap. 4.00 workbook (ISBN 0-915322-43-9). LOMA.

Life Office Management Association, ed. Student Guide for Systems & Data Processing in Insurance Companies. 1977. 4.00 o.p. (ISBN 0-915322-27-7). LOMA.

--Student Guide to Accounting for Life Insurance Companies. (FLMI Insurance Education Program Ser.). 94p. (Orig.). 1980. pap. 4.00 workbook (ISBN 0-915322-42-0). LOMA.

Liff, Alvin. Color & Black & White Television Theory & Servicing. (Illus.). 1979. text ed. 26.95 (ISBN 0-13-151209-9). P-H.

Liffick, Blaise, ed. Program Design. LC 78-8649. 1978. pap. 8.95 (ISBN 0-07-037825-8, BYTE Bks). McGraw.

--Simulation: Programming Techniques. LC 78-8649. 1979. pap. 8.95 (ISBN 0-07-037826-6, BYTE Bks). McGraw.

Lifflander, Matthew. Final Treatment: The File on Dr. X. 1979. 11.95 (ISBN 0-393-08833-2). Norton.

Liffring-Zug, Joan. Seven Amana Villages: Recipes, Crafts, Folk Arts. 36p. pap. 2.75 (ISBN 0-9603858-7-8). Penfield.

Liffring-Zug, Joan & Zug, John. The Amana Colonies. 48p. pap. 4.75 (ISBN 0-9603858-9-4). Penfield.

Liffring-Zug, Joan, compiled by. The Amanas Yesterday: A Religious Communal Society. 48p. pap. 4.85 (ISBN 0-9603858-8-6). Penfield.

--The American Gothic Cookbook. 72p. pap. 4.75 (ISBN 0-9603858-0-0). Penfield.

--Recipes from Our Annual Fourth of July Potluck Picnic for Friends & Relations. 36p. pap. 2.45 (ISBN 0-9603858-1-9). Penfield.

--This is Grant Wood Country. 2nd ed. (Illus.). 64p. pap. 9.00 (ISBN 0-9603858-2-7). Penfield.

Liffring-Zug, Joan, photos by. Women Nineteen Fifty-Seven to Nineteen Seventy-Five. (Illus.). 72p. 20.50 (ISBN 0-9603858-5-1); pap. 10.50 (ISBN 0-9603858-4-3). Penfield.

Lifland, William T., jt. auth. see Van Cise, Jerrold G.

Lifschultz, Larry. Bangladesh: The Unfinished Revolution. 212p. (Orig.). 1979. pap. 8.50 (ISBN 0-905762-07-X, Pub. by Zed Pr England). Lawrence Hill.

Lifshin, Lyn. Doctors & Doctors of English. LC 80-83209. 56p. (Orig.). Date not set. pap. 7.00 (ISBN 0-930012-28-3). Mudborn.

--Madonna Who Shifts For Herself. 64p. 1983. pap. 4.95 (ISBN 0-930090-18-7); 10.00 (ISBN 0-930090-19-5). Applezaba.

--Upstate Madonna: Poems 1970-1974. new ed. LC 75-11946. (Selected Poets Ser.). 128p. (Orig.). 1975. 13.95 (ISBN 0-912278-58-7); pap. 5.95 (ISBN 0-912278-59-5). Crossing Pr.

Lifshin, Lyn, ed. Ariadne's Thread: A Collection of Contemporary Women's Journals. LC 81-48042. 288p. 1982. 17.26i (ISBN 0-06-014989-2, HarpT); pap. 6.68i (ISBN 0-06-090941-2, CN-914). Har-Row.

Lifshitz, Baruch, jt. auth. see Schwabe, Moshe.

Lifshitz, Fima, ed. Pediatric Nutrition: Infant Feedings-Deficiencies-Diseases. (Clinical Disorders in Pediatric Nutrition Ser.: Vol. 2). 608p. 1982. 55.00 (ISBN 0-8247-1430-X). Dekker.

Lifshitz, Mikhail. Philosophy of Art of Karl Marx. 118p. 1980. Repr. of 1933 ed. 10.00 (ISBN 0-686-91964-5). Pluto Pr.

Lifson, Melvin W. & Shaifer, Edward F. Decision & Risk Analysis for Construction Management. LC 81-15942. (Construction Management & Engineering Ser.). 222p. 1982. 32.95 (ISBN 0-471-03167-4, Pub. by Wiley-Interscience). Wiley.

Lifton, Betty J. Twice Born: Memoirs of an Adopted Daughter. 1977. pap. 3.95 (ISBN 0-14-004404-3). Penguin.

Lifton, James & Hardy, Owen B. Site Selection for Health Care Facilities. LC 82-13745. 64p. (Orig.). 1982. pap. 18.75 (ISBN 0-87258-382-1, AHA-127200). Am Hospital.

Lifton, Robert J. America & the Asian Revolutions. 2nd ed. 178p. 1973. 9.95 (ISBN 0-87855-065-8); pap. text ed. 3.95x (ISBN 0-87855-562-5). Transaction Bks.

--Broken Connection. 1979. 15.95 o.p. (ISBN 0-671-22561-8). S&S.

--Death in Life: Survivors of Hiroshima. LC 67-22658. 1982. 18.75 (ISBN 0-686-98006-9); pap. 10.50 (ISBN 0-686-98007-7). Basic.

--Home from the War: Vietnam Veterans: Neither Victims nor Executioners. 1974. pap. 3.95 o.p. (ISBN 0-671-21727-5, Touchstone Bks). S&S.

Lifton, Robert J. & Falk, Richard. Indefensible Weapons: The Political & Psychological Case Against Nuclearism. LC 82-7000850. 1982. 15.50 (ISBN 0-465-03236-2); pap. 6.95 (ISBN 0-465-03237-0). Basic.

Lifton, Robert J. & Olson, Eric, eds. Explorations in Psychohistory: The Wellfleet Papers of Erik Erikson, Robert Jay Lifton & Kenneth Kenniston. LC 74-13758. 1975. 9.95 o.p. (ISBN 0-671-21848-4); pap. 3.95 o.p. (ISBN 0-671-21849-2). S&S.

Lifton, Walter. Groups: Facilitating Individual Growth & Societal Change. LC 72-566. 1972. 23.50 (ISBN 0-471-53491-9). Wiley.

Lifton, Walter M. & Bernier, Joseph E., eds. Family Counseling & Changing Values. 1982. 2.50 (ISBN 0-686-36368-X); 3.00 (ISBN 0-686-37292-1). Am Personnel.

Ligare, Kathleen M. Illinois Women's Directory: A Comprehensive Guide to Women's Organizations & Programs Throughout Illinois and Northwestern Indiana. LC 82-74870. (Illus.). 168p. 1978. pap. 5.95 (ISBN 0-8040-0802-7). Swallow.

Ligeti, Sandor. Selective Credit Policy in the Developing Countries. LC 82-177319. (Studies on Developing Countries: No. 109). 78p. (Orig.). 1981. pap. 7.50x (ISBN 963-301-082-9). Intl Pubns Serv.

Liggett, J. A. & Liu, Philip L. The Boundary Integral Equation Method for Porous Media Flow. 272p. 1982. text ed. 35.00x (ISBN 0-04-620011-8). Allen Unwin.

Light. Light's Manual: Intertidal Invertebrates of the Central California Coast. 3rd ed. Smith, Ralph I. & Carlton, James T., eds. 1975. 26.50x o.p. (ISBN 0-520-02113-4). U of Cal Pr.

Light, jt. auth. see Preece.

Light, Donald, Jr., jt. auth. see Henslin, James M.

Light, Ivan H. Ethnic Enterprise in America: Business & Welfare Among Chinese, Japanese, & Blacks. 1972. 23.75x (ISBN 0-520-01738-2); pap. 7.25x (ISBN 0-520-02485-0). U of Cal Pr.

Light, James F. John William De Forest. (United States Authors Ser.). 13.95 (ISBN 0-8057-0192-3, Twayne). G K Hall.

Light, Marilyn. Hypoglycemia. Passwater, Richard A. & Mindell, Earl, eds. (Good Health Guide Ser.). (Orig.). 1983. pap. 1.45 (ISBN 0-87983-302-5). Keats.

Light, Richard W. Pleural Diseases. (Illus.). 300p. 1982. text ed. write for info. (ISBN 0-8121-0886-8). Lea & Febiger.

Lightbown, Ronald. Sandro Botticelli, 2 vols. Incl. Vol. 1. Life & Work (ISBN 0-520-03372-8); Vol. 2. Complete Catalogue (ISBN 0-520-03574-7). (Illus.). 1978. boxed set 145.00x (ISBN 0-685-85680-1). U of Cal Pr.

Lightbown, Ronald W. Donatello & Michelozzo: An Artistic Partnership & Its Patrons in the Early Renaissance, 2 vols. (Illus.). 460p. 1980. 74.00x (ISBN 0-19-921024-1). Oxford U Pr.

Lighter, Frederick J., jt. auth. see Reese, Ernst S.

Lightfoot, Albert. Urban Education in Social Perspectives. 1978. pap. 15.95 (ISBN 0-395-30660-4). HM.

Lightfoot, D. W. Principles of Diachronic Syntax. LC 78-54717. (Cambridge Studies in Linguistics Monograph: No. 23). (Illus.). 1979. 69.50 (ISBN 0-521-22082-3); pap. 22.95x (ISBN 0-521-29350-2). Cambridge U Pr.

Lightfoot, David. The Language Lottery: Toward a Biology of Grammars. 192p. 1983. 17.50 (ISBN 0-262-12096-8). MIT Pr.

Lightfoot, Gordon. The Pony Man. LC 71-184374. (Illus.). 32p. (YA) 1972. 6.95 o.p. (ISBN 0-06-126325-7); lib. bdg. 10.89i (ISBN 0-06-126326-5). Har-Row.

Lightfoot, Keith. Philippines. (Nations of the Modern World). 1977. lib. bdg. 19.75x o.p. (ISBN 0-89158-735-7). Westview.

Lightfoot, Neil R. Jesus Christ Today. LC 76-42590. 360p. 1976. pap. 8.95 (ISBN 0-8010-5604-7). Baker Bk.

Lightfoot, Paul. The Mekong. LC 80-53606. (Rivers of the World Ser.). PLB 12.68 (ISBN 0-382-06520-4). Silver.

Lighthill, J. Mathematical Biofluid Dynamics. (CBMS-NSF Regional Conference Ser.: No. 17). ix, 281p. 1975. 31.00 (ISBN 0-89871-014-6). Soc Indus-Appl Math.

Lighthill, James. Waves in Fluids. LC 77-8174. (Illus.). 1978. 61.50 (ISBN 0-521-21689-3); pap. 24.95x (ISBN 0-521-29233-6). Cambridge U Pr.

Lighthill, M. J. Introduction to Fourier Analysis & Generalized Functions. (Cambridge Monographs on Mechanics & Applied Mathematics). 19.95 (ISBN 0-521-05556-3); pap. text ed. 9.95 (ISBN 0-521-09128-4). Cambridge U Pr.

Lightle, R. Paul. Blueprint Reading & Sketching. (gr. 9-10). 1965. pap. 5.28 (ISBN 0-87345-053-1). McKnight.

Lightman, Alan P., jt. auth. see Rybicki, George B.

Lightman, Bernard, jt. auth. see Eisen, Sydney.

Lightman, Marjorie & Zeisel, William, eds. Outside Academe: New Ways of Working in the Humanities. LC 81-13463. 83p. (Orig.). 1982. pap. text ed. 12.00 (ISBN 0-86656-132-3, B132). Haworth Pr.

Lightman, Sidney, ed. The Jewish Travel Guide 1983. (Illus.). 290p. (Orig.). 1983. pap. 8.95 (ISBN 0-900498-84-6). Hermon.

Lightner, Ted. Introduction to English Derivational Morophology. 533p. 1983. 55.00 (ISBN 90-272-3116-8). Benjamins North Am.

Lightstone, James F., jt. ed. see Latman, Alan.

Lightwood, John M. The Nature of Positive Law. xiv, 419p. 1982. Repr. of 1883 ed. lib. bdg. 35.00x (ISBN 0-8377-0814-1). Rothman.

Lightwood, Martha B., ed. Public & Business Planning in the United States: A Bibliography. LC 79-165488. (Management Information Guide Ser.: No. 26). 1972. 42.00x (ISBN 0-8103-0826-6). Gale.

Ligon, Mary G. & McDaniel, Sarah W. Teachers Role in Counseling. (Foundations of Secondary Education Ser). 1970. pap. 15.95 ref. ed. (ISBN 0-13-891119-3). P-H.

Liguori, Alphonse. The Blessed Virgin Mary. 96p. pap. 3.00 (ISBN 0-686-81623-4). TAN Bks Pubs.

Liguori, Alphonsus. Preparation for Death. pap. 4.00 (ISBN 0-686-81628-5). TAN Bks Pubs.

Liguori, F., ed. Automatic Test Equipment: Hardware, Software, & Management. LC 74-18892. (IEEE Press Selected Reprint Ser). 253p. 1974. 21.95x (ISBN 0-471-53536-2, Pub. by Wiley-Interscience); pap. 8.95x o.p. (ISBN 0-471-53537-0). Wiley.

Liguori, Fred, ed. Automatic Test Equipment: Hardware, Software & Management. LC 74-18892. (Illus.). 1974. 21.95 (ISBN 0-87942-049-9). Inst Electrical.

Lihani, John. Bartolome de Torres Naharro. (World Authors Ser.). 1979. lib. bdg. 15.95 (ISBN 0-8057-6363-5, Twayne). G K Hall.

--Lucas Fernandez. (World Authors Ser.). 1971. lib. bdg. 15.95 (ISBN 0-8057-2290-4, Twayne). G K Hall.

Liholiho, Alexander. Journal of Prince Alexander Liholiho: Voyages Made to the United States, England, & France in 1849-50. Adler, Jacob, ed. LC 67-27052. (Personal Diary, Photos, Index, Notes, 188p). 1967. 10.00 (ISBN 0-87022-009-8). UH Pr.

Lijegren, Sten. Studies in Milton. LC 67-30816. (Studies in Milton, No. 22). 1969. Repr. of 1918 ed. lib. bdg. 49.95x (ISBN 0-8383-0718-3). Haskell.

Lijphart, Arend. The Politics of Accommodation: Pluralism & Democracy in the Netherlands. new ed. 1976. 30.00x (ISBN 0-520-02918-6); pap. 7.95x (ISBN 0-520-02900-3). U of Cal Pr.

Likens, Gene E. Some Perpectives of the Major Biochemical Cycles Scope 17: The Scientific Committee on Problems of the Environment. LC 80-42017. 192p. 1981. 29.95 (ISBN 0-471-27989-7, Pub. by Wiley-Interscience). Wiley.

Likens, James D., jt. auth. see LaDou, Joseph.

Likert, Jane G., jt. auth. see Likert, Rensis.

Likert, Rensis. Human Organization: Its Management & Value. (Illus.). 1967. 28.95 (ISBN 0-07-037851-7, C). McGraw.

--New Patterns of Management. 1961. 27.00 o.p. (ISBN 0-07-037850-9, C). McGraw.

Likert, Rensis & Likert, Jane G. New Ways of Managing Conflict. 1976. 29.95 (ISBN 0-07-037842-8, P&RB). McGraw.

Likes, Robert C. & Day, Glenn R. From This Mountain-Cerro Gordo. LC 75-44236. (Illus.). 86p. 1975. 7.95 (ISBN 0-912494-16-6); pap. 4.95 (ISBN 0-912494-15-8). Chalfant Pr.

Likhanov, Albert. Shadows Across the Sun. Lourie, Richard, tr. from Rus. LC 80-8440. 128p. (YA) (gr. 7 up). 1983. 10.10i (ISBN 0-06-023868-2, HarpJ); PLB 10.89g (ISBN 0-06-023869-0). Har-Row.

Likoff, William, jt. auth. see Segal, Bernard L.

Likoff, William & Moyer, John H., eds. Coronary Heart Disease. LC 62-19444. (The Seventh Hahnemann Symposium). (Illus.). 496p. 1963. 68.00 o.p. (ISBN 0-8089-0264-4). Grune.

Liles, B. Basic Grammar of Modern English. 1979. 17.95 (ISBN 0-13-061853-5). P-H.

Liles, Bruce L. An Introduction to Linguistics. 368p. 1975. ref. ed. o.p. 14.50 (ISBN 0-13-486134-5); pap. text ed. 14.95 (ISBN 0-13-486126-4). P-H.

--Introductory Transformational Grammar. LC 70-122388. (Illus.). 1971. pap. text ed. 10.95 (ISBN 0-13-502286-X). P-H.

Liles, Parker, et al. Typing Mailable Letters. 3rd ed. Rubin, Audrey, ed. (Illus.). (gr. 9-12). 1978. pap. 6.56 (ISBN 0-07-037855-X, G); solutions manual 4.00 (ISBN 0-07-037856-8). McGraw.

Liley, P. E., ed. see Symposium on Thermophysical Properties, 6th.

Lilge, Frederic, tr. see Bernfeld, Siegfried.

Lilien, Gary L., jt. auth. see Choffray, Jean-Marie.

Lilienfeld, Abraham M. & Lilienfeld, David E. Foundations of Epidemiology. 2nd ed. (Illus.). 384p. 1980. text ed. 24.95x (ISBN 0-19-502722-1); pap. text ed. 14.95x (ISBN 0-19-502723-X). Oxford U Pr.

Lilienfeld, David E., jt. auth. see Lilienfeld, Abraham M.

Lilienfeld, Robert. Learning to Read Music. 136p. 1979. pap. 4.50 (ISBN 0-06-463495-7, EH 495, EH). B&N NY.

--The Rise of Systems Theory: An Ideological Analysis. LC 77-12609. 1978. 39.50 (ISBN 0-471-53533-8, Pub. by Wiley-Interscience). Wiley.

Lilienthal, Alfred M. The Zionist Connection II: What Price Peace? Rev. ed. 904p. 1982. Repr. of 1978 ed. 11.95 (ISBN 0-686-43256-8); pap. 9.95. North American Inc.

Lilienthal, David E. Atomic Energy: A New Start. LC 79-3668. 160p. 1980. 10.53i (ISBN 0-06-012617-5, HarpT). Har-Row.

--The Journals of David E. Lilienthal, 6 vols. Incl. Vol. 2. The Atomic Energy Years, 1945-50. 1964. o.p. (ISBN 0-06-012611-6); Vol. 3. Venturesome Years, 1950-55. 1966 (ISBN 0-06-012612-4); Vol. 4. The Road to Change, 1955-59. 1969 (ISBN 0-06-012613-2); Vol. 5. The Harvest Years, 1959-63. 1971 (ISBN 0-06-012614-0); Vol. 6. Creativity & Conflict, 1964-1967. 1976. o.p. (ISBN 0-06-012619-1). LC 64-18056. (Illus.). 20.00 ea. (ISBN 0-06-012610-8, HarpT). Har-Row.

Lilius, Irmelin S. Gold Crown Lane. Helweg, Marianne, tr. from Swedish. LC 79-2103. (gr. 5 up). 1980. 7.95 o.s.i. (ISBN 0-440-04231-3, Sey Lawr); PLB 7.45 o.s.i. (ISBN 0-440-04232-1). Delacorte.

--The Goldmaker's House. Helweg, Marianne, tr. from Swedish. LC 79-2104. (gr. 5 up). 1980. 7.95 o.s.i. (ISBN 0-440-04200-3, Sey Lawr); PLB 7.45 o.s.i. (ISBN 0-440-04201-1). Delacorte.

--Horses of the Night. Tate, Joan, tr. from Swedish. LC 79-2105. (gr. 5 up). 1980. 7.95 o.s.i. (ISBN 0-440-04450-2, Sey Lawr); PLB 7.45 o.s.i. (ISBN 0-440-04451-0). Delacorte.

Lilja, Saara. The Roman Elegists' Attitude Towards Women. Commager, Steele, ed. LC 77-70836. (Latin Poetry Ser.: Vol. 25). 1979. Repr. of 1965 ed. lib. bdg. 31.00 o.s.i. (ISBN 0-8240-2974-7). Garland Pub.

Liljegren, S. B. Revolt Against Romanticism in American Literature as Evidenced in the Work of S. L. Clemens. 59p. pap. 12.50 (ISBN 0-87556-576-X). Saifer.

Liljegren, Sten. American & European in the Works of Henry James. LC 71-119080. (Studies in Henry James, No. 17). 1970. Repr. of 1919 ed. lib. bdg. 32.95x (ISBN 0-8383-1076-1). Haskell.

--Revolt Against Romanticism in American Literature: As Evidenced in the Works of S. L. Clemens. LC 65-15896. (Studies in Fiction: No. 34). 1969. Repr. of 1945 ed. lib. bdg. 22.95x (ISBN 0-8383-0583-0). Haskell.

Liljegren, Sten B. Essence & Attitudes in English Romanticism. (Studies in Comparative Literature: No. 10). Repr. of 1945 ed. lib. bdg. 19.50x (ISBN 0-87991-513-7). Porcupine Pr.

Liljergren, S. B., ed. see Marilla, E. L.

Liljestrand, G., jt. ed. see Holmstedt, Bo.

Lilker, Shalom. Kibbutz Judaism: A New Tradition in the Making. (Kibbutz, Cooperative Society, & Alternative Social Policy Ser.: Vol. 7). 264p. 1982. lib. bdg. 14.95 (ISBN 0-8482-4876-7). Norwood Edns.

Lillard, Paula P. Montessori: A Modern Approach. LC 78-163334. (Illus.). 1973. 8.95x (ISBN 0-8052-3423-3); pap. 3.95 (ISBN 0-8052-0394-X). Schocken.

Lillard, Richard G. The Great Forest. LC 72-8129. (Illus.). 452p. 1973. Repr. of 1947 ed. lib. bdg. 49.50 (ISBN 0-306-70534-6). Da Capo.

Lillegraven, Jason A., et al, eds. Mesozoic Mammals: The First Two-Thirds of Mammalian History. 1980. 47.50x (ISBN 0-520-03582-8); pap. 12.95x (ISBN 0-520-03951-3, CAMPUS NO. 234). U of Cal Pr.

Lillesand, Thomas M. & Kiefer, Ralph W. Remote Sensing & Image Interpretation. LC 78-27846. 1979. text ed. 32.95x (ISBN 0-471-02609-3). Wiley.

Lilley. Information Sources in Agriculture & Food Science. (Butterworths Guides to Information Sources Ser.). 1981. text ed. 69.95 (ISBN 0-408-10612-3). Butterworth.

Lilley, A. E. & Midgley, W. A Book of Studies in Plant Form: With Some Suggestions for Their Application to Design. LC 70-89276. (Tower Bks). (Illus.). xvi, 131p. 1972. Repr. of 1896 ed. 30.00x (ISBN 0-8103-3947-1). Gale.

Lilley, David G., jt. auth. see Croft, David R.

Lilley, Dorothy B. & Badough, Rose M., eds. Library & Information Sciences: A Guide to Information Sources. (Bks., Libraries, & Publishing Information Guide Ser.: Vol. 5). 200p. 1981. 42.00x (ISBN 0-8103-1501-7). Gale.

Lilley, Peter, jt. auth. see Brittan, Samuel.

Lillibridge, G. D. Images of American Society: A History of the United States, 2 vols. LC 75-31017. (Illus.). 736p. 1976. pap. text ed. 14.50 ea.; Vol. 1. pap. text ed. (ISBN 0-395-21873-X); Vol. 2. pap. text ed. (ISBN 0-395-21874-8); instr's. manual 2.45 (ISBN 0-395-20371-6). HM.

Lillich, Richard B. International Aspects of Criminal Law: Enforcing United States Law in the World Community. 215p. 1981. 19.50 (ISBN 0-87215-388-6). Michie-Bobbs.

--International Law of State Responsibility for Injuries to Aliens. LC 82-13697. (Virginia Legal Studies). 1982. write for info. (ISBN 0-8139-0961-9). U Pr of Va.

Lillich, Richard B., ed. The Family in International Law: Some Emerging Problems. 160p. 1981. 17.50 (ISBN 0-87215-355-X). Michie-Bobbs.

--Transnational Terrorism: Conventions & Commentary. 282p. 1982. 25.00 (ISBN 0-87215-494-7). Michie-Bobbs.

Lillich, Richard B. & Weston, Burns H., eds. International Claims: Contemporary European Practice. LC 81-21957. (Procedural Aspects of International Law Ser.). 224p. 1982. 25.00x (ISBN 0-8139-0927-9). U Pr of Va.

Lillich, Thomas T., jt. auth. see Calmes, Robert B.

Lillie, Arthur. India in Primitive Christianity. 2nd ed. 299p. 1981. Repr. of 1893 ed. text ed. 23.50x (ISBN 0-391-02335-7, Pub. by Concept India). Humanities.

Lillie, David L. Early Childhood Education: An Individualized Approach to Developmental Instruction. LC 74-29042. (Illus.). 256p. 1975. text ed. 15.95 (ISBN 0-574-18602-6, 13-6020). SRA.

Lillie, David L. & Place, Patricia A. Partners: A Guide for Parents of Children with Special Needs. 1981. pap. 8.95x (ISBN 0-673-16036-X). Scott F.

Lillie, Helen, jt. auth. see Leflar, Robert B.

Lillie, John. Lectures on the First & Second Epistles of Peter. 1978. 19.75 (ISBN 0-86524-116-3, 7102). Klock & Klock.

Lillie, Mary P. A Decade of Dreams. LC 79-53015. (Living Poets' Library Ser.: Vol. 23). 1979. pap. 3.50 (ISBN 0-686-81663-3). Dragons Teeth.

Lillie, Ralph D & Fullmer, Hareld M. Histopathologic Technic & Practical Histochemistry. 4th ed. 1976. 48.00 o.p. (ISBN 0-07-037862-2, HP). McGraw.

Lillington, Glen A. & Jamplis, R. W. Diagnostic Approach to Chest Diseases. 2nd ed. (Illus.). 549p. 57.00 o.p. (ISBN 0-683-05037-0). Williams & Wilkins.

Lillington, Glen A. & Jamplis, Robert W. A Diagnostic Approach to Chest Diseases. 3rd ed. 1983. write for info (ISBN 0-683-05038-9). Williams & Wilkins.

Lillis, Carol. Brady's Introduction to Medical Terminology. 2nd ed. (Illus.). 224p. 1983. pap. text ed. 10.95 (ISBN 0-89303-234-4). R J Brady.

Lilly, Anthony D. A Few Observations on the Natural History of the Sperm Whale. 1981. 40.00x (ISBN 0-686-97092-6, Pub. by Corner Place England). State Mutual Bk.

Lilly, Claude C. III, jt. auth. see Wood, Glenn L.

Lilly, John C. The Deep Self. 336p. 1978. pap. 2.95 o.p. (ISBN 0-446-33023-X). Warner Bks.

--Lilly on Dolphins-Humans of the Sea. LC 75-2854. (Illus.). 520p. 1975. pap. 7.95 (ISBN 0-385-11037-5, Anch). Doubleday.

--Programming & Metaprogramming in the Human Biocomputer. LC 73-79777. 190p. 1972. 8.00 o.p. (ISBN 0-517-52757-X); pap. 4.95 o.p. (ISBN 0-517-52758-8). Crown.

--Simulations of God. LC 75-1039. 1975. 9.95 o.p. (ISBN 0-671-21981-2). S&S.

Lilly, Susan C., tr. see Megged, Aharon.

Lillyquist, Michael J. Understanding & Changing Criminal Behavior. (Ser. in Criminal Justice). 1980. text ed. 21.95 (ISBN 0-13-935528-6). P-H.

Lillywhite, Fred & Marlar, Robin. English Cricketers Trip to Canada & the U. S. A. 1859. 1980. 12.50 (ISBN 0-437-08930-4, Pub. by World's Work). David & Charles.

Lillywhite, Herold S., jt. auth. see Weiss, Curtis E.

Lillywhite, Herolds, jt. auth. see Weiss, Curtis E.

Lilow, Ira. Making a Dress. (Illus.). 3.95 (ISBN 0-8208-0314-6). Hearthside.

Lily, William. A Shorte Introduction of Grammar. LC 45-4059. 1977. Repr. of 1567 ed. 30.00x (ISBN 0-8201-1208-9). Schol Facsimiles.

Lim, Arthur & Constable, Ian J. Colour Atlas of Ophthalmology. (Illus.). 1979. 24.95 (ISBN 0-471-09487-0, Pub. by Wiley Med). Wiley.

Lim, B. P., et al. Environmental Factors in the Design of Building Fenestration. (Illus.). 1979. 47.25x (ISBN 0-85334-807-3, Pub. by Applied Sci England). Elsevier.

Lim, E. R. & Shilling, John. Thailand: Toward a Development Strategy of Full Participation. xiv, 232p. 1980. pap. 15.00 (ISBN 0-686-36122-9, RC-8002). World Bank.

Lim, Edward. Excited States, Vol. 5. (Serial Publication Ser.). 220p. 1982. 49.50 (ISBN 0-12-227205-6); lib. ed 64.50 (ISBN 0-12-227280-3); microfiche 35.00 (ISBN 0-12-227281-1). Acad Pr.

Lim, Edward, ed. Excited States, Vol. 6. 216p. 1982. 48.00 (ISBN 0-12-227206-4). Acad Pr.

Lim, Edward C., ed. Excited States, Vol. 4. (Serial Publication). 1980. 52.50 (ISBN 0-12-227204-8); lib. ed. 67.00 (ISBN 0-12-227278-1); microfiche 37.50 (ISBN 0-12-227279-X). Acad Pr.

Lim, Genny. Wings for Lai Ho. Lew, Gordon, tr. (Illus.). 48p. (Orig.). (gr. 5-8). 1982. pap. 5.95 (ISBN 0-934788-01-4). E-W Pub Co.

Lim, Gill C., ed. Regional Planning: Evolution, Crisis & Prospects. LC 82-13839. 198p. 1983. text ed. 15.95x (ISBN 0-86598-097-7). Allanheld.

Lim, H. C., jt. auth. see Harper, W. M.

Lim, Jae S. Speech Enhancement. (Illus.). 384p. 1983. 34.95 (ISBN 0-13-829705-3). P-H.

Lim, Paul S. Some Arrivals, but Mostly Departures. 136p. pap. 7.50 (ISBN 0-686-37573-4, Pub. by New Day Philippines). Cellar.

Lim, R. K., ed. Pharmacology of Pain: Proceedings Vol. 9. 1968. inquire for price o.p. (ISBN 0-08-012374-0). Pergamon.

Lim, Sing. West Coast Chinese Boy. (Illus.). 64p. (gr. 6-12). 1979. 12.95 (ISBN 0-88776-121-6). Tundra Bks.

Lim, Thomas P. Physiology of the Lung. (Illus.). 200p. 1983. pap. 16.75x spiral (ISBN 0-398-04727-8). C C Thomas.

Lim, Youngil. Government Policy & Private Enterprise: Korean Experience in Industrialization. LC 81-84218. (Korea Research Monographs: No. 6). 1981. pap. 8.00x (ISBN 0-912966-36-X). IEAS.

Limardo, Miguel. Luces Encendidas Para Cada Dia. 376p. 1981. Repr. of 1978 ed. 4.95 (ISBN 0-311-40038-8). Casa Bautista.

Limb, Sue & Cordingley, Patrick. Captain Oates: Soldier & Explorer. (Illus.). 176p. 1982. 31.50 (ISBN 0-7134-2693-4, Pub. by Batsford England). David & Charles.

Limbacher, James L., ed. Feature Films on Eight Millimeter & Sixteen Millimeter & Videotape. 6th ed. 1979. 26.25 o.p. (ISBN 0-8352-1112-6). Bowker.

Limbrunner, Alfred, jt. auth. see Pforr, Manfred.

Limbrunner, Alfred, jt. auth. see Prorr, Manfred.

Limbrunner, George F., jt. auth. see Spiegel, Leonard.

Limburg, James. Old Testament Stories for a New Time. LC 82-49019. 127p. 1983. pap. 7.95 (ISBN 0-8042-0148-X). John Knox.

Limburg, Peter. The Story of Your Heart. LC 78-24308. (Health Bk.). (Illus.). (gr. 3-7). 1979. PLB 6.99 (ISBN 0-698-30705-4, Coward). Putnam Pub Group.

--What's in the Names of Birds. (What's Behind the Word Ser.). (Illus.). 160p. (gr. 6-8). 1975. PLB 5.89 o.p. (ISBN 0-698-30515-9, Coward). Putnam Pub Group.

--What's in the Names of Flowers. LC 73-88535. (What's Behind the Word Ser.). (Illus.). 160p. (gr. 6-8). 1974. PLB 4.64 o.p. (ISBN 0-698-30537-X, Coward). Putnam Pub Group.

--What's in the Names of Fruit. (What's Behind the Word Ser.). (Illus.). 128p. (gr. 5-10). 1972. PLB 4.64 o.p. (ISBN 0-698-30441-1, Coward). Putnam Pub Group.

--What's in the Names of Stars & Constellations. LC 76-13637. (What's Behind the Word Ser.). (Illus.). (gr. 6-8). 1976. PLB 5.99 o.p. (ISBN 0-698-30611-2, Coward). Putnam Pub Group.

--What's in the Names of Wild Animals. (What's Behind the Word Ser.). (Illus.). 208p. (gr. 6-8). 1977. PLB 5.99 o.p. (ISBN 0-698-30661-9, Coward). Putnam Pub Group.

Limburg, Peter R. Watch Out, It's Poison Ivy. LC 72-11964. (Illus.). 96p. (gr. 3-6). 1973. PLB 5.79 o.p. (ISBN 0-671-32564-7). Messner.

Limce, Alison de see Silk, Gerald & De Limce, Alison.

Limebeer, Dora E. The Greeks & the Romans. 2nd ed. 1949. pap. text ed. 5.95x (ISBN 0-521-05558-X). Cambridge U Pr.

Limmer, Ruth, ed. see Bogan, Louise.

Limochel, F. La France Demandant ses Colonies. (Slave Trade in France, 1744-1848, Ser.). 112p. (Fr.). 1974. Repr. of 1797 ed. lib. bdg. 38.00x o.p. (ISBN 0-8287-0546-1, TN118). Clearwater Pub.

Limouze, Cary, jt. ed. see Williamson, Cecile.

Limouzy, Pierre & Bourgeacq, Jacques A. Manuel De Composition Francaise. (Fr). 1970. text ed. 14.00 (ISBN 0-394-30363-6, RanC); o.p. tchr's. ed. (ISBN 0-394-30695-3). Random.

Limpert, Rudolf. Vehicle System Components: Design & Safety. LC 81-23061. 160p. 1982. 32.95x (ISBN 0-471-08133-7, Pub. by Wiley-Interscience). Wiley.

Lin, et al. Dawn Over Chungking. LC 74-31239. (China in the 20th Century Ser). 240p. 1975. Repr. of 1941 ed. lib. bdg. 29.50 (ISBN 0-306-70692-X). Da Capo.

Lin, Adet, tr. see Hsieh Pingying.

Lin, Anor, tr. see Hsieh Pingying.

Lin, C. C. & Segel, L. A. Mathematics Applied to Deterministic Problems in the Natural Sciences. (Illus.). 640p. 1974. text ed. 29.95x (ISBN 0-02-370720-8). Macmillan.

Lin, Florence. Florence Lin's Chinese Vegetarian Cookbook. LC 75-28686. 1977. pap. 4.95 o.p. (ISBN 0-8015-2677-9, Hawthorn). Dutton.

Lin, N. Conducting Social Research. 1976. text ed. 12.00 o.p. (ISBN 0-07-037868-1, C). McGraw.

--Foundations of Social Research. 1976. text ed. 30.00 (ISBN 0-07-037867-3, C); inst's manual 3.95 (ISBN 0-07-037873-8). McGraw.

Lin, Nan, jt. auth. see Marsden, Peter V.

Lin, Nancy T., ed. In Quest. (Illus.). 51p. 1979. pap. 1.95 o.p. (ISBN 0-686-74336-9). Lancaster-Miller.

Lin, P., jt. auth. see Chua, L.

Lin, Paul, jt. auth. see Harter, Jim.

Lin, Paul M. Posterior Lumbar Interbody Fusion. (Illus.). 392p. 1982. 44.50x (ISBN 0-398-04709-X). C C Thomas.

Lin, Robert H. The Taiping Revolution: A Failure of Two Missions. 1979. pap. text ed. 9.50 (ISBN 0-8191-0734-4). U Pr of Amer.

Lin, Shu. Introduction to Error-Correcting Codes. LC 76-124417. 1970. ref. ed. 32.00 (ISBN 0-13-482810-0). P-H.

Lin, T. Y. & Burns, Ned H. Design of Prestressed Concrete Structures. 3rd ed. LC 80-20619. 752p. 1981. text ed. 37.95 (ISBN 0-471-01898-8); tchrs' ed. 33.95 (ISBN 0-471-08788-2). Wiley.

Lin, Y. K. Probabilistic Theory of Structural Dynamics. LC 75-42154. 380p. 1976. Repr. of 1967 ed. 22.50 (ISBN 0-88275-377-0). Krieger.

Lin, Yi. Me Hizo Pasas for las Aguas. Carrodeguas, Andy & Marosi, Esteban, eds. Riddering, David, tr. 144p. (Span.). 1982. pap. 2.00 (ISBN 0-8297-1323-9). Life Pubs Intl.

Lin, Yu-Sheng. The Crisis of Chinese Consciousness: Radical Antitraditionalism in the May Fourth Era. LC 77-91057. 216p. 1978. 27.50 (ISBN 0-299-07410-2). U of Wis Pr.

Lin, Yu-Sheng see Lin, Yu-Sheng.

Linaker, Michael R. Scorpion. 1981. pap. 1.95 o.p. (ISBN 0-451-09606-1, J9606, Sig). NAL.

Linakis, Steven. Diva: The Life & Death of Maria Callas. LC 80-18919. 1980. 10.95 o.p. (ISBN 0-13-216572-4). P-H.

Linares, Enrique. A Scientific Approach to the Metaphysics of Astrology. Robertson, Arlene, ed. 170p. (Orig.). 1982. pap. 7.95 (ISBN 0-930706-10-2). Seek-It Pubns.

Linchevsky, B. Methods of Metallurgical Experiment. 296p. 1982. 7.00 (ISBN 0-8285-2283-9, Pub. by Mir Pubs USSR). Imported Pubns.

Lincicome, David R., ed. International Review of Tropical Medicine. Incl. Vol. 1. 1960 (ISBN 0-12-367501-4); Vol. 2 o.p. 1963 (ISBN 0-12-367502-2); Vol. 3. 1969 (ISBN 0-12-367503-0); Vol. 4. Lincicome, David R. & Woodruff, A. W., eds. 1971 (ISBN 0-12-367504-9). 50.00 ea. Acad Pr.

Lincoln. The Ancient Adirondacks. LC 74-75617. (American Wilderness). (Illus.). (gr. 6 up). 1974. PLB 15.96 (ISBN 0-8094-1234-9, Pub. by Time-Life). Silver.

Lincoln, Abraham & Douglas, Stephen. Lincoln-Douglas Debates of Eighteen Fifty-Eight. Johannsen, Robert W., ed. (Orig.). 1965. pap. 7.95x (ISBN 0-19-500921-5). Oxford U Pr.

Lincoln, Andrew T. Paradise Now & Not Yet. LC 80-41024. (Society for the New Testament Studies Monographs: No. 43). 240p. 1981. 37.50 (ISBN 0-521-22944-8). Cambridge U Pr.

Lincoln, C. I., jt. auth. see Chalofsky, N.

Lincoln, E. Catalog of Papal Medals. updated ed. 1983. Repr. of 1898 ed. softcover 10.00 (ISBN 0-915262-83-5). S J Durst.

Lincoln, Eleanor T. Through the Grecourt Gates. (Illus.). 118p. 1978. pap. 3.50 (ISBN 0-87391-025-7). Smith Coll.

Lincoln, Francis G. Mining Districts & Mineral Resources of Nevada. (Illus.). 1982. 12.95 (ISBN 0-913814-48-2). Nevada Pubns.

Lincoln, George. The History of the Town of Hingham, MA: The Genealogy, Vol. II & III. 924p. 1982. Repr. of 1893 ed. 55.00 (ISBN 0-89725-029-X). New England Hist.

Lincoln, Harry B., ed. see L'Amorosa, Ero.

Lincoln, Jennie I., jt. ed. see Ferris, Elizabeth G.

Lincoln, John E., jt. auth. see Heffernan, James A.

Lincoln, John R., jt. auth. see Heffernan, James A. W.

Lincoln, R. J. & Boxshall, G. A. A Dictionary of Ecology, Evolution & Systematics. LC 81-18013. 350p. 1982. 47.50 (ISBN 0-521-23957-5). Cambridge U Pr.

Lincoln, R. J. & Sheals, J. G. Collecting Invertebrate Animals. LC 79-14530. (Illus.). 1980. 27.50 (ISBN 0-521-22851-4); pap. 9.95 (ISBN 0-521-29677-3). Cambridge U Pr.

Lincoln, W. Bruce. In the Vanguard of Reform: Russia's Enlightened Bureaucrats, 1825-1861. LC 82-6509. (Illus.). 325p. 1982. 23.00 (ISBN 0-87580-084-X). N Ill U Pr.

--In War's Dark Shadow: The Russians Before the Great War. (Illus.). 1983. 19.95 (ISBN 0-686-43198-7). Dial.

Lincoln, Warren B., et al. Be Liked. Nye, Richard C., intro. by. (Guidebooks: No. 1). 68p. (Orig.). 1982. pap. text ed. 1.95 (ISBN 0-910031-00-2). Ahday Pubs.

--Stay Cheerful. Wilson, Pat, intro. by. (Guidebooks: No. 2). 67p. (Orig.). 1982. pap. text ed. 1.95 (ISBN 0-910031-01-0). Ahday Pubs.

Lind, Andrew W. Hawaii's People. rev. ed. LC 80-10764. 1980. pap. text ed. 5.00x (ISBN 0-8248-0704-9). UH Pr.

--Nanyang Perspective: Chinese Students in Multiracial Singapore. LC 74-75816. (Asian Studies at Hawaii Ser.: No. 13). 1974. pap. text ed. 9.00x (ISBN 0-8248-0330-2). UH Pr.

Lind, Carolyn P., pseud. One Hundred Four Ideas for Improving Your Young Child's Language Skills. (Illus.). 80p. (Orig.). 1980. pap. 5.00 (ISBN 0-9604940-0-6). Lindell Pubs.

Lind, H., jt. auth. see Tetsmann, A.

Lind, Ingrid. Astrologically Speaking. 276p. 1982. 34.00x (ISBN 0-686-82394-X, Pub. by L N Fowler). State Mutual Bk.

Lind, Jakov. The Stove. 110p. 1983. 13.95 (ISBN 0-935296-26-3); pap. 7.95 (ISBN 0-935296-27-1). Sheep Meadow.

Lind, John, jt. auth. see Yao, Alice C.

Lind, L. F. & Nelson, J. C. Analysis & Design of Sequential Digital Systems. LC 76-49959. 1977. 34.95 o.p. (ISBN 0-470-99021-X). Halsted Pr.

Lind, L. R., tr. from Fr. Andre Chenier: Elegies & Camille. Bilingual ed. LC 77-18578. 1978. pap. text ed. 8.50 (ISBN 0-8191-0412-4). U Pr of Amer.

Lindamood, Suzanne & Hanna, Sherman D. Housing, Society & Consumers: An Introduction. (Illus.). 1979. text ed. 23.50 (ISBN 0-8299-0230-9). West Pub.

Lindars, B. & Smalley, S. S. Christ & Spirit in the New Testament. LC 72-91367. 300p. 1974. 67.50 (ISBN 0-521-20148-9). Cambridge U Pr.

Lindars, Barnabas, jt. ed. see Ackroyd, Peter R.

Lindbeck. Metric Practices in Drafting. 1979. pap. 5.28 (ISBN 0-87002-298-9). Bennett IL.

Lindbeck, jt. auth. see Feirer.

Lindbeck, et al. Basic Crafts. (gr. 7-12). 1979. text ed. 14.60 (ISBN 0-87002-275-X); student guide 3.68 (ISBN 0-87002-296-2). Bennett IL.

Lindbeck, A., ed. Inflation & Employment in Open Economies: Essays by Members of the Institute for International Economic Studies, Univ. of Stockholm, Sweden. (Studies in International Economics: Vol. 5). 1979. 59.75 (ISBN 0-444-85227-1, North Holland). Elsevier.

Lindbeck, Assar. Swedish Economic Policy. 1973. 28.50x (ISBN 0-520-02422-2). U of Cal Pr.

Lindbeck, George A. Infallibility. (Pere Marquette Theology Lectures). 1972. 7.95 (ISBN 0-87462-504-1). Marquette.

Lindbeck, John R. Designing Today's Manufactured Products. LC 72-79110. 225p. (gr. 10-12). 1972. text ed. 21.28 (ISBN 0-87345-440-5). McKnight.

--Metrics in Career Education. 120p. (gr. 7-12). 1975. pap. text ed. 6.60 (ISBN 0-87002-082-X). Bennett IL.

Lindbeck, John R. & Lathrop, Irving T. General Industry. (Illus.). (gr. 7-9). 1977. 17.96 (ISBN 0-87002-185-0). student guide 5.28 (ISBN 0-87002-196-6). answer sheet free. Bennett IL.

Lindbeck, John R., jt. auth. see Feirer, John L.

Lindberg, jt. auth. see Simms.

Lindberg, Charles A., ed. see Bozza, Linda.

Lindberg, D. A. & Kaihara, S. Medinfo Eighty, 2 vols. 1981. Set. 149.00 (ISBN 0-444-86029-0). Elsevier.

Lindberg, David C. Theories of Vision from Al-Kindi to Kepler. LC 75-19504. (Chicago History of Science & Medicine Ser). 448p. 1976. lib. bdg. 22.50x o.p. (ISBN 0-226-48234-0). U of Chicago Pr.

Lindberg, Donald A. The Growth of Medical Information Systems in the United States. LC 79-1555. 208p. 1979. 23.95x (ISBN 0-669-02911-4). Lexington Bks.

Lindberg, Gary. The Confidence Man in American Literature. LC 80-29233. 1982. 19.95x (ISBN 0-19-502939-9). Oxford U Pr.

Lindberg, Jana H. Counted Cross-Stitch Designs for All Seasons. (Illus.). 96p. 1983. 15.95 (ISBN 0-686-83666-9, ScribT). Scribner.

Lindberg, John. Routines for Research: A Handbook of Basic Library Skills. LC 82-15962. 172p. 1983. lib. bdg. 20.75 (ISBN 0-8191-2750-7); pap. text ed. 10.00 (ISBN 0-8191-2751-5). U Pr of Amer.

--Three Steps to the Essay: An Expository Handbook. LC 80-69031. 320p. 1981. pap. text ed. 12.25 (ISBN 0-8191-1714-5). U Pr of Amer.

Lindberg Pr. Charted Christmas Designs for Counted Cross-Stitch & Other Needlecrafts: From the Archives of the Lindberg Press. (Needlework Ser.). (Illus.). 42p. (Orig.). 1982. pap. 1.95 (ISBN 0-486-24356-7). Dover.

Lindberg, Richard. Who's on Third? The Chicago White Sox Story. (Illus.). 1983. 13.95 (ISBN 0-89651-901-5). Icarus.

Lindberg, Roy, jt. auth. see Cohn, Theodore.

Lindberg, Stanley W. & Walsh, J. Martyn. Van Nostrand's Plain English Handbook. rev. ed. 202p. 1980. text ed. 6.95 (ISBN 0-442-26355-4). Van Nos Reinhold.

Lindbergh, Anne. The People in Pineapple Place. (gr. 4-6). 1982. 10.95 (ISBN 0-15-260517-7, HJ). HarBraceJ.

Lindbergh, Anne M. Bring Me a Unicorn. 240p. (RL 10). 1974. pap. 1.75 o.p. (ISBN 0-451-08447-0, E8447, Sig). NAL.

--The Flower & the Nettle: Diaries & Letters of Anne Morrow Lindbergh 1936-1939. LC 75-25708. (A Helen & Kurt Wolff Bk). (Illus.). 605p. 1976. 12.95 o.p. (ISBN 0-15-131501-9). HarBraceJ.

--Gift from the Sea. LC 55-5065. 1955. 7.95 (ISBN 0-394-41255-9); pap. 5.00 o.p. (ISBN 0-686-36901-7). Pantheon.

--Hour of Gold, Hour of Lead. 288p. (RL 10). 1974. pap. 1.75 o.p. (ISBN 0-451-05825-9, E5825, Sig). NAL.

--North to the Orient. LC 35-27279. 1966. pap. 3.95 (ISBN 0-15-667140-9, Harv). HarBraceJ.

Lindbergh, Charles A. Radio Speeches of Charles A. Lindbergh: 1939-1940. 1982. lib. bdg. 69.95 (ISBN 0-87700-455-2). Revisionist Pr.

--We. (Illus.). 1927. 7.95 o.s.i. (ISBN 0-399-10856-4). Putnam Pub Group.

Lindblad, Ishrat. Pamela Hansford Johnson. (English Author Ser.). 1982. lib. bdg. 14.95 (ISBN 0-8057-6762-2, Twayne). G K Hall.

Lindblad, Lois. Learning to Swim. 1977. 2.50 (ISBN 0-918116-02-3). Jawbone Pr.

Lindblom, C. Policy Making Process. 2nd ed. 1980. pap. 9.95 (ISBN 0-13-686543-7). P-H.

Lindblom, U. E. & Gnirk, P. F. Nuclear Waste Disposal: Can We Rely on Bedrock? 80p. 1981. 45.00 (ISBN 0-08-027608-3); pap. 18.00 (ISBN 0-08-027595-8). Pergamon.

Linde, Charlotte. The Creation of Coherence in Life Stories. (The Language & Being Ser.). 1983. write for info. (ISBN 0-89391-056-2). Ablex Pub.

Linde, Richard M., jt. auth. see Wakita, Osamu A.

Linde, Shirley. Wholehealth Catalogue. 6.95x o.p. (ISBN 0-89256-012-6). Cancer Control Soc.

Linde, Shirley M. & Savary, Louis M. The Joy of Sleep: Facts, Fantasy, & Folklore Relating to the Mystery of Sleep with 22 Remedies for Insomniacs. LC 73-7066. 192p. 1980. pap. 4.95i o.p. (ISBN 0-06-250515-7, BN 3002, HarpR). Har-Row.

Lindeberger, Herbert. Georg Trakl. (World Authors Ser.: Austria: No. 171). lib. bdg. 12.95 (ISBN 0-8057-2886-4, Twayne). G K Hall.

Lindeburg, F. A. Teaching Physical Education in the Secondary School. 237p. 1978. 24.95 (ISBN 0-471-03452-5). Wiley.

Lindeburg, Michael R. Civil Engineering Review Manual. 3rd ed. LC 81-81682. (Engineering Review Manual Ser.). (Illus.). 784p. (Orig.). 1981. pap. 33.50 (ISBN 0-932276-28-8); wkbk. o.p. 4.00 (ISBN 0-932276-17-2). Prof Engine.

--Engineer-in-Training Review Manual. 6th ed. LC 81-84850. (Engineering Review Manual Ser.). (Illus.). 760p. 1982. pap. 33.50 (ISBN 0-932276-31-8); wkbk. o.p. 7.00 (ISBN 0-932276-16-4); 35.50. Prof Engine.

--Mechanical Engineering Review Manual. 6th ed. LC 80-83176. (Engineering Review Manual Ser.). (Illus.). 800p. 1980. pap. 30.50 (ISBN 0-932276-29-6); wkbk. o.p. 7.00 (ISBN 0-932276-23-7). Prof Engine.

--Seismic Design for the Professional Engineering Examination. 3rd ed. LC 80-81796. (Engineering Review Manual Ser.). (Illus.). 104p. 1980. pap. 12.50 (ISBN 0-932276-32-6). Prof Engine.

Lindeke, W. Four-Language Technical Dictionary of Heating, Ventilation & Sanitary Engineering. English, German, French, Russian. LC 79-81248. 1970. 54.00 (ISBN 0-08-006426-4). Pergamon.

Lindell, Anne. Intensive English for Communication, Bk. 2. (Illus.). 294p. 1980. pap. text ed. 7.95x (ISBN 0-472-08572-7). U of Mich Pr.

Lindell, Anne & Hagiwara, M. Peter. Intensive English for Communication, Bk. 1. LC 78-58152. (Illus.). 1979. pap. text ed. 7.95x (ISBN 0-472-08570-0, 08570); pap. text ed. 5.95x wkbk. (ISBN 0-472-08571-9). U of Mich Pr.

Lindell, Arthur G. School Section Sixteen. 1983. 12.95 (ISBN 0-533-05293-9). Vantage.

Lindell, K., et al. The Kammu Year: Its Lore & Music. (Studies on Asian Topics: No. 4). 191p. 1982. pap. text ed. 10.50x (ISBN 0-7007-0151-6, Pub by Curzon Pr England). Humanities.

Lindell, Kristina. The Student Lovers. DeFrancis, John, ed. LC 70-189615. (Pali Language Texts - Chinese). (Illus.). 40p. (Orig.). 1975. pap. text ed. 1.95x (ISBN 0-8248-0225-X). UH Pr.

Lindell, Paul J. The Mystery of Pain. LC 74-77676. 80p. (Orig.). 1974. pap. 1.75 o.p. (ISBN 0-8066-1424-2, 10-4639). Augsburg.

Lindelof, E. T. Cobra: The Computer-Designed Bidding System. (Master Bridge Ser.). 320p. 1983. 34.00 (ISBN 0-575-02987-0, Pub. by Gollancz England). David & Charles.

Lindeman, Bruce. Real Estate Brokerage. 450p. 1981. text ed. 19.95 (ISBN 0-8359-6517-1); instr's. manual free (ISBN 0-8359-6518-X). Reston.

Lindeman, Fredrik O. The Triple Representation of Schwa in Greek & Some Related Problems of Indo-European Phonology. 90p. 1982. 15.00 (ISBN 82-00-09533-9). Universitet.

Lindeman, Ralph D. Norman Douglas. (English Authors Ser.). 14.95 (ISBN 0-8057-1160-0, Twayne). G K Hall.

Lindeman, Richard, et al. Introduction to Bivariate & Multivariate Statistics. 1980. text ed. 24.50x (ISBN 0-673-15099-2). Scott F.

Lindeman, Richard H. & Merenda, Peter F. Educational Measurement. 2nd ed. 1979. pap. text ed. 12.50x (ISBN 0-673-15096-8). Scott F.

Lindemann, Albert S. A History of European Socialism. LC 82-40167. 416p. 1983. text ed. 25.00x (ISBN 0-300-02797-4). Yale U Pr.

--A History of European Socialism. 25.00 (ISBN 0-686-42815-3). Yale U Pr.

--The Red Years: European Socialism Versus Bolshevism, 1919-1921. LC 73-80834. 1975. 30.00x o.p. (ISBN 0-520-02511-3). U of Cal Pr.

Lindemann, Fred. Sermon & the Propers, 4 Vols. 10.95 ea. (ISBN 0-570-03283-0); o. p 37.50 set (ISBN 0-570-03250-4, 15-1840); Vol. 1. 10.95 (15-1822). Vol. 2 (15-1823 O. P). Vol. 3. 10.95 (15-1830); Vol. 4. 10.95 (15-1831). Concordia.

Lindemann, Herbert, ed. Daily Office. LC 65-26201. 1965. red vinyl o.p. 16.95 o.p. (ISBN 0-570-03060-9, 6-1086); red mor leather 29.95 o.p. (ISBN 0-570-03061-7, 6-1087). Concordia.

Lindemann, J. W. Old English Preverbal GE, Its Meaning. LC 79-130689. 88p. 1970. 7.50x o.p. (ISBN 0-8139-0319-X); pap. 5.00x o.p. (ISBN 0-8139-0320-3). U Pr of Va.

Lindemann, Kelvin. The Red Umbrellas. LC 74-30367. 214p. 1975. Repr. of 1955 ed. lib. bdg. 15.50x (ISBN 0-8371-7521-6, LIRU). Greenwood.

Linden, Catherine. The Baron's Woman. 272p. 2.75 (ISBN 0-380-82982-7). Avon.

--Kiss... but Never Tell. 192p. 1980. pap. 1.95 o.p. (ISBN 0-523-40862-5). Pinnacle Bks.

Linden, D. Handbook of Batteries & Fuel Cells. 1024p. 1983. 49.50 (ISBN 0-07-037874-6, P&RB). McGraw.

Linden, Eugene, jt. auth. see Patterson, Francine.

Linden, Ian. Emirs & Evangelicals. 1983. 29.50x (ISBN 0-7146-3146-9, F Cass Co). Biblio Dist.

Linden, Ian & Linden, Jane. Catholics, Peasants & Chewa Resistance in Nyasaland, 1889-1939. 1974. 33.00x (ISBN 0-520-02500-8). U of Cal Pr.

Linden, James D. & Linden, Kathryn W. Tests on Trial. (Guidance Monograph). 1968. pap. 2.60 o.p. (ISBN 0-395-09930-7, 9-78830). HM.

Linden, James D., jt. auth. see Linden, Kathryn W.

Linden, James D., jt. auth. see Shertzer, Bruce.

Linden, Jane, jt. auth. see Linden, Ian.

Linden, Kathryn W. & Linden, James D. Modern Mental Measurement: A Historical Perspective. (Guidance Monograph). 1968. pap. 2.60 o.p. (ISBN 0-395-09924-2, 9-78823). HM.

Linden, Kathryn W., jt. auth. see Linden, James D.

Linden, W. Psychologishe Perspektiven des Bluthodrucks. (Illus.). vi, 130p. 1983. 47.50 (ISBN 3-8055-3642-9). S Karger.

Linden, Wilhelm Zur. A Child is Born: Pregnancy, Birth, Early Childhood. Collis, J., ed. & tr. from Ger. 223p. 1980. pap. 6.95 (ISBN 0-85440-357-4, Pub.by Steinerbooks). Anthroposophic.

Lindenauer, Nancy, jt. auth. see Selman, Edythea G.

Lindenberg, Marc & Crosby, Benjamin. Managing Development: The Political Dimension. LC 80-83345. 200p. 1981. text ed. 19.95 o.p. (ISBN 0-931816-49-1); pap. text ed. 9.95 o.p. (ISBN 0-931816-27-0). Transaction Bk.

Lindenberg, Steven P. Group Psychotherapy with People who Are Dying. (Illus.). 400p. 1983. text ed. 24.75x (ISBN 0-398-04814-2). C C Thomas.
Lindenberger, Herbert S. On Wordsworth's Prelude. LC 75-25493. 316p. 1976. Repr. of 1963 ed. lib. bdg. 17.75x (ISBN 0-8371-8417-7, LIOW). Greenwood.
Lindencrone-Hegermann, L. De see De Hegermann-Lindencrone, L.
Lindenfeld, Frank & Rothschild-Whitt, Joyce, eds. Workplace Democracy & Social Change. LC 82-80137. 456p. 1982. 20.00 (ISBN 0-87558-101-3, Pub. by Extending Hor Bks); pap. 12.00 (ISBN 0-87558-102-1). Porter Sargent.
Lindenfeld, J., jt. auth. see Dostert, L.
Lindenmann, jt. auth. see Edelhart.
Lindenmann, Walter K. Attitude & Opinion Research. 2nd ed. 83p. 1981. 14.50 (ISBN 0-89964-196-2). CASE.
Lindenov, Christopher. First Triple Alliance: Letters of Christopher Lindenov, Danish Envoy to London, 1668-1672. Westergaard, Waldemar, ed. 1947. text ed. 49.50x (ISBN 0-686-83551-4). Elliots Bks.
Linder, Bill R. How to Trace Your Family History: A Basic Guide to Genealogy. LC 78-57418. 1978. 7.95 (ISBN 0-89696-022-6, An Everest House Book). Dodd.
Linder, Elisha & Raban, Avner. Introducing Underwater Archaeology. LC 72-10801. (Lerner Archaeology Ser.: Digging up the Past). (gr. 5 up). 1976. PLB 7.95g (ISBN 0-8225-0834-6). Lerner Pubns.
Linder, Erik. Hjalmar Bergman. (World Authors Ser.). 1975. lib. bdg. 15.95 (ISBN 0-8057-2147-9, Twayne). G K Hall.
Linder, Frank Van Der see Van Der Linder, Frank.
Linder, Robert. The Fifty-Minute Hour: A Collection of True Psychoanalytic Tales. LC 82-6765. 294p. 1982. 14.50 (ISBN 0-87668-608-0). Aronson.
Linder, Toni W. Early Childhood Special Education: Program Development & Administration. LC 82-4496. (Illus.). 308p. (Orig.). 1983. pap. text ed. 15.95 (ISBN 0-933716-28-1). P H Brookes.
Linderman, Charles R. See it Now. LC 82-73246. 210p. 1982. pap. 12.50 (ISBN 0-941216-02-0). Cay-Bel.
Linderman, Eark W. & Linderman, Marlene M. Arts & Crafts in the Classroom. 450p. 1984. text ed. 18.95 (ISBN 0-02-370860-3). Macmillan.
Linderman, Marlene M., jt. auth. see Linderman, Eark W.
Lindert, Peter H. Prices, Jobs & Growth: An Introduction to Macroeconomics. (Series in Economics). 1976. text ed. 10.95 (ISBN 0-316-52630-4); instr's manual avail. (ISBN 0-316-52631-2). Little.
Lindey, A., jt. auth. see Ernst, M. L.
Lindfors, Bernth. Folklore in Nigerian Literature. LC 72-91804. 200p. 1974. text ed. 24.50x (ISBN 0-8419-0134-1, Africana). Holmes & Meier.
--Mazungumzo: Interviews with East African Writers, Publishers, Editors & Scholars. LC 80-25684. (Africa Ser., Ohio University Papers in International Studies: No. 41). 179p. 1981. pap. 13.00 (ISBN 0-89680-108-X, Ohio U Ctr Intl). Ohio U Pr.
Lindfors, Bernth & Owomoyela, Oyekan. Yoruba Proverbs: Translation & Annotation. LC 73-620032. (African Ser.). 1973. pap. 4.00x o.s.i. (ISBN 0-89680-050-4, Ohio U Ctr Intl). Ohio U Pr.
Lindfors, Bernth, ed. Black African Literature in English: A Guide to Information Sources. LC 73-16983. (American Literature, English Literature, & World Literatures in English Information Guide Ser.: Vol. 23). 1979. 42.00x (ISBN 0-8103-1206-9). Gale.
Lindfors, Berth. Early Nigerian Literature. 180p. 1983. text ed. 32.50x (ISBN 0-8419-0740-4). Holmes & Meier.
Lindfors, Eula A., ed. Guild Musicianship. 64p. (gr. 3-12). 1974. pap. text ed. 8.40 (ISBN 0-87487-638-9). Summy.
Lindfors, Judith W., jt. auth. see Campbell, Russell N.
Lindfors, Viveca. Viveca: An Actress, a Woman, a Life. 320p. 1981. 13.95 (ISBN 0-686-30958-8, An Everest House Book). Dodd.
Lindgren, Alvin J. & Shawchuck, Norman. Let My People Go: Empowering Laity for Ministry. LC 80-16035. 144p. (Orig.). 1982. pap. 6.95 (ISBN 0-687-21377-0). Abingdon.
Lindgren, Astrid. Children of Noisy Village. Lamborn, F., tr. (Illus.). (gr. 1-5). 1962. PLB 9.95 (ISBN 0-670-21674-7). Viking Pr.
--Christmas in the Stable. (Illus.). (gr. 1-3). 1962. PLB 5.99 (ISBN 0-698-30042-4, Coward). Putnam Pub Group.
--Christmas in the Stable. new ed. LC 62-14449. (Illus.). (gr. k-2). 1979. pap. text ed. 3.95 (ISBN 0-698-20489-1, Coward). Putnam Pub Group.
--Emil & the Piggy Beast. Heron, Michael, tr. LC 72-91228. 128p. (gr. 2-6). 1973. 5.95 o.s.i. (ISBN 0-695-80356-5, T0356). Follett.
--Emil in the Soup Tureen. LC 79-93795. (Illus.). (gr. 2-6). 1970. 5.95 o.s.i. (ISBN 0-695-82210-1). Follett.
--Emil's Pranks. (gr. 1-3). PLB 5.97 o.s.i. (ISBN 0-695-40158-0). Follett.
--Of Course Polly Can Do Almost Everything. (Illus.). 1978. 6.95 o.s.i. (ISBN 0-695-80967-9); lib. bdg. 6.99 o.s.i. (ISBN 0-695-40967-0). Follett.
--Of Course Polly Can Ride a Bike. (Picture Bk). (Illus.). 32p. (gr. k-3). 1972. 6.95 o.s.i. (ISBN 0-695-40349-4). Follett.
--Ronia, the Robber's Daughter. 192p. (gr. 4-8). 1983. 12.50 (ISBN 0-670-60640-5). Viking Pr.
--The Tomten. (Illus.). (gr. 1-3). 1961. 6.95 (ISBN 0-698-20147-7, Coward); gb 5.99 (ISBN 0-698-30370-9). Putnam Pub Group.
--The Tomten. LC 61-10658. (Illus.). (ps-2). 1979. pap. 3.95 (ISBN 0-698-20487-5, Coward). Putnam PubGroup.
--The Tomten & the Fox. (Illus.). (gr. k-3). 1965. PLB 5.99 (ISBN 0-698-30371-7, Coward). Putnam Pub Group.
--The Tomten & the Fox. LC 65-25501. (Illus.). (ps-2). 1979. pap. 3.95 (ISBN 0-698-20488-3, Coward). Putnam Pub Group.
Lindgren, Barbro. The Wild Baby Goes to Sea. Prelutsky, Jack, tr. LC 82-15623. (Illus.). 24p. (gr. k-3). 1983. 9.00 (ISBN 0-688-01960-9); PLB 8.59 (ISBN 0-688-01961-7). Greenwillow.
Lindgren, Bernard & Berry, Donald. Elementary Statistics. 1981. text ed. 22.95x (ISBN 0-02-370790-9). Macmillan.
Lindgren, Bernard W. Statistical Theory. 3rd ed. (Illus.). 576p. 1976. text ed. 29.95x (ISBN 0-02-370830-1). Macmillan.
Lindgren, Bernard W. & McElrath, G. Introduction to Probability & Statistics. 4th ed. 1978. text ed. 22.95x (ISBN 0-02-370900-6, 37090). Macmillan.
Lindgren, Henry C. Educational Psychology in the Classroom. 6th ed. (Illus.). 1980. pap. text ed. 19.95x (ISBN 0-19-502617-9); 5.95x (ISBN 0-19-502663-2); instructor's manual free (ISBN 0-19-502662-4). Oxford U Pr.
--Leadership, Authority & Powersharing. LC 81-18644. 186p. (Orig.). 1982. lib. bdg. 11.50 (ISBN 0-89874-251-X). Krieger.
Lindgren, Henry C. & Byrne, Donn. Psychology: An Introduction to a Behavioral Science. 4th ed. LC 74-23293. 448p. 1975. text ed. 26.50 (ISBN 0-471-53603-2); tchrs' manual 8.00x (ISBN 0-471-53641-5). Wiley.
Lindgren, Henry C. & Fisk, Leonard W., Jr. Psychology of Personal Development. 3rd ed. LC 75-34926. 1976. 29.95 (ISBN 0-471-53769-1); tchrs' manual 6.00x (ISBN 0-471-01472-9). Wiley.
Lindgren, Henry C. & Harvey, John H. An Introduction to Social Psychology. 3rd ed. LC 80-39897. (Illus.). 583p. 1981. text ed. 24.95 (ISBN 0-8016-3038-X). Mosby.
Lindgren, Henry C., jt. auth. see Fisk, Loretta Z.
Lindgren, Henry C., jt. auth. see Fisk, Lori.
Lindgren, Henry C., jt. auth. see Watson, Robert I.
Lindgrenson, Sonja, tr. see Hallberg, Peter.
Lindh, Gunnar, jt. auth. see Falkenmark, Malin.
Lindhe, Linda. The Purge of the Splatter. 1979. 6.50 o.p. (ISBN 0-533-03830-8). Vantage.
Lindhe, Richard & Grossman, Steven D. Accounting Information Systems. 500p. 1980. text ed. 28.95x (ISBN 0-931920-23-X). Dame Pubns.
Lindheim, Nancy. The Structure of Sidney's Arcadia. 232p. 1982. 30.00x (ISBN 0-8020-2374-6). U of Toronto Pr.
Lindheimer, Marshall D., ed. see National Institutes of Health, the Chicago Heart Association & the University of Chicago, et al.
Lindholm, Richard, ed. Land Value Taxation: The "Progress & Poverty" Centenary. LC 80-52299. (Taxation, Resources & Economic Development (TRED) Ser.: No. 11). 260p. 1982. text ed. 20.00 (ISBN 0-299-08520-1). U of Wis Pr.
Lindholm, Richard W. The Economics of VAT: Preserving Efficiency, Capitalism & Social Progress. LC 80-8428. 208p. 1980. 22.95x (ISBN 0-669-04111-4). Lexington Bks.
Lindholm, Richard W. & Wignjowijoto, Hortojo. Financing & Managing State & Local Government. LC 78-19227. (Illus.). 464p. 1979. 32.95x (ISBN 0-669-02434-1). Lexington Bks.
Lindholm, Richard W., ed. Property Taxation & the Finance of Education. LC 73-2046. (TRED Ser.). (Illus.). 346p. 1974. 30.00 (ISBN 0-299-06440-9). U of Wis Pr.
--Property Taxation, USA: Proceedings. (Committee on Taxation, Resources and Economic Development Ser. No. 2). (Illus.). 332p. 1967. pap. 12.50 (ISBN 0-299-04544-7). U of Wis Pr.
Lindholm, Richard W. & Lynn, Arthur D., Jr., eds. Land Value Taxation: The Progress & Poverty Centenary. 248p. 1982. 20.00 (ISBN 0-299-08520-1). Schalkenbach.
Lindholm, U. S., ed. see Symposium on Mechanical Behavior of Materials Under Dynamic Loads, San Antonio, 1967.
Lindley, Betty & Lindley, E. K. A New Deal for Youth: The Story of the National Youth Adminsistration. LC 72-172687. (FDR & the Era of the New Deal Ser.). (Illus.). 316p. 1972. Repr. of 1938 ed. lib. bdg. 39.50 (ISBN 0-306-70382-3). Da Capo.
Lindley, Craig A. & McCarthy, Nan. The TRS Eighty & Z-Eighty Assembly Language Library. (Illus.). 1983. pap. write for info. LooseleafBinder (ISBN 0-88006-060-3). Green.
Lindley, D. V. Bayesian Statistics, a Review: Proceedings. (CBMS Regional Conference Ser.: No. 2). (Illus.). 83p. (Orig.). 1972. pap. text ed. 9.00 (ISBN 0-89871-002-2). Soc Indus-Appl Math.
--Making Decisions. LC 75-143798. 1971. 21.95 (ISBN 0-471-53785-3, Pub. by Wiley Interscience). Wiley.
Lindley, Dennis V. Introduction to Probability & Statistics from a Bayesian Viewpoint: Pt. 1 Probability. (Illus.). 270p. 1980. text ed. 42.50x (ISBN 0-521-05562-8); pap. 16.95x (ISBN 0-521-29867-9). Cambridge U Pr.
--Introduction to Probability & Statistics from a Bayesian Viewpoint: Pt. 2: Inference. (Illus.). 300p. 1980. text ed. 44.50x (ISBN 0-521-05563-6); pap. 16.95x (ISBN 0-521-29866-0). Cambridge U Pr.
Lindley, Dennis V. & Miller, Jeffrey C. Cambridge Elementary Statistical Tables. 1953. text ed. 4.95x (ISBN 0-521-05564-4). Cambridge U Pr.
Lindley, Denver, tr. see Hesse, Hermann.
Lindley, E. K. Franklin Delano Roosevelt: A Career in Progressive Democracy. rev. ed. LC 73-21771. (FDR & the Era of the New Deal Ser.). 366p. 1974. Repr. of 1933 ed. lib. bdg. 39.50 (ISBN 0-306-70634-2). Da Capo.
Lindley, E. K., jt. auth. see Lindley, Betty.
Lindley, Erica. Belladona. (Orig.). 1978. pap. 1.95 o.p. (ISBN 0-451-08387-3, J8387, Sig). NAL.
--Devil in Crystal. 1977. pap. 1.95 o.p. (ISBN 0-451-07643-5, E7643, Sig). NAL.
--Harvest of Destiny. (Orig.). 1979. pap. 1.95 o.p. (ISBN 0-451-08919-7, J8919, Sig). NAL.
Lindley, Ernest K. Half Way with Roosevelt. LC 75-8789. (FDR & the Era of the New Deal Ser.). x, 449p. 1975. Repr. of 1937 ed. lib. bdg. 49.50 (ISBN 0-306-70706-3). Da Capo.
--The Roosevelt Revolution, First Phase. LC 74-637. (FDR & the Era of the New Deal Ser.). 328p. 1974. Repr. of 1933 ed. lib. bdg. 39.50 (ISBN 0-306-70651-2). Da Capo.
Lindley, Kenneth. Graves & Graveyards. (Local Search Ser.). (Illus.). 1972. text ed. 8.95 (ISBN 0-7100-7234-1). Routledge & Kegan.
--Town Time & People. (Illus.). 10.00 (ISBN 0-392-05042-0, SpS). Sportshelf.
Lindley, Richard B. Haciendas & Economic Development: Guadalajara Mexico at Independence. (Latin American Monographs: No. 58). 156p. 1983. text ed. 19.95x (ISBN 0-292-72042-4). U of Tex Pr.
Lindman, Maj. Flicka, Ricka, Dicka & the New Dotted Dresses. (Illus.). (gr. k-2). 5.75g o.p. (ISBN 0-8075-2482-4). A Whitman.
--Flicka, Ricka, Dicka & Their New Skates. (Illus.). (gr. k-2). 1950. 5.75g o.p. (ISBN 0-8075-2488-3). A Whitman.
--Snipp, Snapp, Snurr Learn to Swim. LC 54-9945. (Illus.). (gr. k-2). 1954. 5.75g o.p. (ISBN 0-8075-7506-2). A Whitman.
Lindman, N., jt. ed. see Chadwick, M. J.
Lindmayer, Joseph, et al. Fundamentals of Semiconductor Devices. LC 76-16765. 506p. 1979. Repr. of 1965 ed. 31.00 (ISBN 0-88275-424-6). Krieger.
Lindner, Arthur E., jt. auth. see Marshak, Richard H.
Lindner, C. C. & Rosa, A. Topics on Steiner Systems. (Annals of Discrete Mathematics Ser.). 1980. 68.00 (ISBN 0-444-85484-3). Elsevier.
Lindner, R., jt. auth. see Muller, W.
Lindner, R., ed. see International Conference, 5th, Baden-Baden, Sep. 10-13, 1975.
Lindner, Robert. Prescription for Rebellion. 305p. 1975. Repr. of 1952 ed. lib. bdg. 19.25x (ISBN 0-8371-8016-3, LIPRE). Greenwood.
Lindner, Vicki, ed. see Ohashi, Watari.
Lindon, Edmund. Cuba. LC 79-24010. (gr. 4 up). 1980. PLB 8.90 (ISBN 0-531-04101-8). Watts.
Lindop, Greves, ed. see Chatterton, Thomas.
Lindow, Ch. W. Historic Organs in France. Blanchard, Homer D., tr. LC 80-138201. (The Little Organ Books Ser.: No. 1). (Illus.). 1980. pap. 21.00 o.p. (ISBN 0-930112-03-2). Praestant.
Lindquist, Claude S. Active Network Design. LC 76-14238. 1977. 28.95 (ISBN 0-917144-01-5). Steward & Sons.
Lindquist, Donald. The Red Gods. 1981. 11.95 o.s.i. (ISBN 0-440-07349-9). Delacorte.
Lindquist, Hal, ed. see Groneman, Chris H.
Lindquist, Hal, ed. see Helsel, Jay & Urbanick, Byron.
Lindquist, John A., jt. auth. see Deibel, Robert H.
Lindquist, Linnea. Teaching Tips for Cosmetology. 28p. 1981. pap. text ed. 4.50 (ISBN 0-314-63395-2). West Pub.
Lindquist, Linnea M. West's Comprehensive Cosmetology Outline. 216p. 1982. pap. text ed. 14.95 (ISBN 0-314-68253-8). West Pub.
Lindquist, Mary M., ed. Selected Issues in Mathematics Education. LC 80-82903. (National Society for the Education Series on Contemporary Education Issues). 250p. 1981. text ed. 19.50 (ISBN 0-8211-1114-0); text ed. 18.50 (ISBN 0-686-77731-X). McCutchan.
--Selected Issues in Mathematics Education. LC 80-82903. 268p. 1981. pap. 15.00 o.p. (ISBN 0-8211-1114-0). NCTM.
Lindreas, D. Brown Adipose Tissue. 1970. 29.50 (ISBN 0-444-00080-1). Elsevier.
Lindroos, Maria. Me & My Life. 1980. 7.50 o.p. (ISBN 0-682-49558-1). Exposition.
Lindroth, Stan, et al. Linnaeus: The Man & His Work. Frangsmyr, Tore, ed. Srigley, Michael & Vowles, Bernard, trs. from Swedish. LC 82-2044. (Illus.). 288p. 1983. text ed. 25.00x (ISBN 0-520-04568-8). U of Cal Pr.
Lindsay, A. D., tr. see Plato.
Lindsay, Alexander D. The Essentials of Democracy. 2nd ed. LC 80-12414. (William J. Cooper Foundation Lectures, Swarthmore College, 1929). 74p. 1980. Repr. of 1935 ed. lib. bdg. 15.50x (ISBN 0-313-22386-6, LIED). Greenwood.
--Kant. LC 76-109970. Repr. of 1934 ed. lib. bdg. 15.75x (ISBN 0-8371-4473-6, LIKA). Greenwood.
Lindsay, Charles, Jr. Music Blank Book. 112p. 1981. pap. 4.95 (ISBN 0-8256-3254-4, Quick Fox). Putnam Pub Group.
Lindsay, Cotton M., ed. New Directions in Public Health Care: A Prescription for the 1980s. 3rd ed. LC 79-92868. 290p. 1980. text ed. 18.95 (ISBN 0-87855-394-0); pap. text ed. 6.95 (ISBN 0-917616-37-5). ICS Pr.
--Pharmaceutical Industry: Economics, Performance & Government Regulation. LC 77-27062. 1978. 23.50 o.p. (ISBN 0-471-04077-0, Pub. by Wiley Medical). Wiley.
Lindsay, D. B., jt. auth. see Buttery, P. J.
Lindsay, David. A Voyage to Arcturus. 1977. Repr. of 1920 ed. lib. bdg. 15.00 o.p. (ISBN 0-8398-2375-4, Gregg). G K Hall.
Lindsay, Donald & Price, Mary R. Authority & Challenge: A Portrait of Europe 1300-1600. (A Portrait of Europe Ser). (Illus.). 1975. 16.00x o.p. (ISBN 0-19-913118-X); pap. 9.95x o.p. (ISBN 0-19-913220-8). Oxford U Pr.
Lindsay, Franklin A. New Techniques for Management Decision Making. 1963. pap. 2.95 o.p. (ISBN 0-07-037893-2, SP). McGraw.
Lindsay, Gordon. Apostles, Prophets & Governments. 1.25 (ISBN 0-89985-121-5). Christ Nations.
--Death & Resurrection of Christ. (Life of Christ Ser.: Vol. 3). (Span.). 1.50 (ISBN 0-89985-983-6). Christ Nations.
--The Death Cheaters. (Sorcery & Spirit World Ser.). 1.25 (ISBN 0-89985-081-2). Christ Nations.
--Demons & the Occult. (Sorcery & Spirit World Ser.: Vol. 6). 1.25 (ISBN 0-89985-089-8). Christ Nations.
--Did Politics Influence Jesus? 2.50 (ISBN 0-89985-113-4). Christ Nations.
--Flying Saucers. pap. 0.95 o.p. (ISBN 0-89985-199-1). Christ Nations.
--God's Twentieth Century Barnabus. pap. 3.95 o.p. (ISBN 0-89985-002-2). Christ Nations.
--Hades-Abode of the Unrighteous Dead. (Sorcery & Spirit World Ser.). 1.25 (ISBN 0-89985-082-0). Christ Nations.
--How to Find the Perfect Will of God. 1.25 (ISBN 0-89985-003-0). Christ Nations.
--Israel: Prophetic Signs. 1.95 (ISBN 0-89985-189-4). Christ Nations.
--It's Sooner Than You Think. (Prophecy Ser.). 1.25 (ISBN 0-89985-057-X). Christ Nations.
--The Key to Israel's Future-The Forgotten Covenant. 1.95 (ISBN 0-89985-191-6). Christ Nations.
--Life & Teachings of Christ, Vol. 1. (Life of Christ & Parable Ser.). pap. 5.00 (ISBN 0-89985-967-4). Christ Nations.
--Life & Teachings of Christ, Vol. 2. (Life of Christ & Parable Ser.). pap. 5.00 (ISBN 0-89985-968-2). Christ Nations.
--Life & Teachings of Christ, Vol. 3. (Life of Christ & Parable Ser.). pap. 5.75 (ISBN 0-89985-969-0). Christ Nations.
--Ministry of Angels. 1.25 (ISBN 0-89985-018-9). Christ Nations.
--Ministry of Casting Out Demons, Vol. 7. (Sorcery & Spirit World Ser.). 1.25 (ISBN 0-89985-090-1). Christ Nations.
--Miracles of Christ, 2 parts, Vols. 2 & 3. (Miracles in the Bible Ser.). 0.95 ea. Vol. 2 (ISBN 0-89985-960-7). Vol. 3 (ISBN 0-89985-960-7). Christ Nations.
--One Body, One Spirit, One Lord. pap. 3.95 (ISBN 0-89985-991-7). Christ Nations.
--The Real Reason Why Christians Are Sick. (Divine Healing & Health Ser.). 2.50 (ISBN 0-89985-029-4). Christ Nations.
--Satan, Rebellion & Fall, 3 vols. (Sorcery & Spirit World Ser.: Vol. 3). 1.25 ea. (ISBN 0-89985-953-4). Christ Nations.
--The Sermons of John Alexander Dowie. (Champion of the Faith Ser.). 2.50 (ISBN 0-89985-193-2). Christ Nations.
--Sorcery in America Series. (Sorcery & Spirit World Ser.: Vol. 2). 0.95 ea. (ISBN 0-89985-951-8). Christ Nations.
--Will the Antichrist Come Out of Russia? (Prophecy Ser.). 1.25 (ISBN 0-89985-066-9). Christ Nations.
--The Worlds Best Loved Christian Poems, 2 vols. 1.00 ea. o.p. Christ Nations.
Lindsay, J. William Blake: Creative Will & the Poetic Image. LC 70-118005. (Studies in Blake, No. 3). 1970. Repr. of 1929 ed. lib. bdg. 27.95x (ISBN 0-8383-1061-3). Haskell.
Lindsay, J. V., et al. Urban Crisis: A Symposium. LC 71-146555. (Symposia on Law & Society Ser). 1971. Repr. of 1969 ed. lib. bdg. 19.50 (ISBN 0-306-70115-4). Da Capo.

Lindsay, Jack. Ancient Egyptian Alchemy. O'Quinn, John, ed. 44p. 1981. pap. text ed. 5.95 (ISBN 0-9609802-4-5). Life Science.

--The Monster City: Defoe's London, 1688-1730. LC 78-58316. 1978. 22.50x (ISBN 0-312-54612-2). St Martin.

Lindsay, Jack, ed. & tr. from Rus. Russian Poetry, Nineteen Seventeen to Nineteen Fifty-Five. LC 77-13747. 1978. Repr. of 1957 ed. lib. bdg. 16.00x (ISBN 0-313-20000-9, LIRP). Greenwood.

Lindsay, Jack, tr. see Bruno, Giordano.

Lindsay, Jeanne W. Parenting Preschoolers. LC 78-62011. (Illus.). 1978. Curriculum Help & Study Guides. 7.95 o.p. (ISBN 0-930934-03-2); Study Guides For Child Care Books (for Students) 3.95 o.p. (ISBN 0-930934-02-4). Morning Glory.

--Pregnant Too Soon: Adoption Is an Option. LC 79-93356. (Illus.). (gr. 7-12). 1980. pap. text ed. 6.95 (ISBN 0-88436-778-9); tchr's ed. avail. (ISBN 0-88436-780-0); wkbk. 1.95 (ISBN 0-88436-779-7). EMC.

Lindsay, Joan. Picnic at Hanging Rock. 1977. pap. 3.50 (ISBN 0-14-003149-9). Penguin.

Lindsay, Kennedy. The British Intelligence Services in Action. (Illus.). 288p. (Orig.). 1980. pap. 12.50 o.p. (ISBN 0-86202-112-X, Pub. by Dunrod England). Facsimile Bk.

Lindsay, Kenneth C., ed. see Kandinsky, Wassily.

Lindsay, Len. Comal Handbook. 1982. pap. text ed. 18.95 (ISBN 0-8359-0878-X). Reston.

Lindsay, Len, jt. auth. see Kohl, Herb.

Lindsay, Maurice. The Eye Is Delighted: Some Romantic Travellers in Scotland. 1972. 10.00 o.p. (ISBN 0-584-10082-5). Transatlantic.

Lindsay, Maurice, ed. Modern Scottish Poetry: An Anthology of the Scottish Renaissance 1925-1975. 248p. 1976. pap. text ed. write for info. (ISBN 0-85635-160-1, Pub. by Carcanet New Pr England). Humanities.

Lindsay, Merrill. The Lure of Antique Arms. (Illus.). 1978. pap. 5.95 o.s.i. (ISBN 0-695-80928-8). Follett.

Lindsay, Michael, et al. Notes on Educational Problems in Communist China, 1941-47. LC 77-10962. 1977. Repr. of 1950 ed. lib. bdg. 18.25x (ISBN 0-8371-9815-1, LINE). Greenwood.

Lindsay, Noel, tr. see Marczewski, Jan.

Lindsay, P. A. Introduction to Quantum Electronics. LC 75-15696. 202p. 1975. 36.95x o.s.i. (ISBN 0-470-53891-0). Halsted Pr.

Lindsay, Peter H. & Norman, Donald A. Human Information Processing: An Introduction to Psychology. 2nd ed. 1977. 23.00 (ISBN 0-12-450960-6); test bklet. 3.50 (ISBN 0-12-450963-0); student guide 7.70 (ISBN 0-12-450962-2). Acad Pr.

Lindsay, R. Bruce. The Control of Energy. (Benchmark Papers in Energy Ser.: Vol. 6). 1977. 52.50 (ISBN 0-12-786962-X). Acad Pr.

Lindsay, R. Bruce, ed. Energy: Historical Development of the Concept. LC 75-30719. (Benchmark Papers on Energy Ser.: Vol 1). 369p. 1975. 55.50 (ISBN 0-12-786963-8). Acad Pr.

Lindsay, R. K., et al. Applications of Artificial Intelligence for Organic Chemistry: The Dendral Project. (Artificial Intelligence Ser.). (Illus.). 208p. 1981. text ed. 42.00 (ISBN 0-07-037895-9, C). McGraw.

Lindsay, Rae. The Left-Handed Book. (gr. 4 up). 1980. PLB 8.90 (ISBN 0-531-02258-7). Watts.

Lindsay, Rae & Rowe, Diane. How to Be A Perfect Bitch. 1983. pap. 4.95 (ISBN 0-8329-0258-6). New Century.

Lindsay, Ray, jt. auth. see Michael, George.

Lindsay, Richard, jt. ed. see Bhateja, Chander.

Lindsay, Robert, ed. Early Concepts in Energy in Atomic Physics. LC 78-23311. 402p. 1979. 50.00 (ISBN 0-87933-340-5). Hutchinson Ross.

Lindsay, Robert B. The Role of Science in Civilization. LC 73-3234. (Illus.). 318p. 1973. Repr. of 1963 ed. lib. bdg. 20.50x (ISBN 0-8371-6837-6, LIRS). Greenwood.

Lindsay, Stephen. Lover's Choice. (Illus.). Date not set. pap. write for info. (ISBN 0-917982-15-0). Cougar Bks.

Lindsay, T. F. & Harrington, Michael. The Conservative Party: Nineteen Eighteen to Nineteen Seventy. LC 73-88672. 300p. 1974. 22.50 (ISBN 0-312-16415-7). St Martin.

Lindsay, Thomas. Plant Names. LC 75-16423. viii, 93p. 1976. Repr. of 1923 ed. 30.00x (ISBN 0-8103-4160-3). Gale.

Lindsay, Vachel. Collected Poems, Vol. 1. Camp, Dennis, ed. 320p. 1983. 24.95 (ISBN 0-933180-45-4). Spoon Riv Poetry.

Lindsay, Willard L. Chemical Equilibria in Soils. LC 79-12151. 1979. 32.50x (ISBN 0-471-02704-9, Pub. by Wiley-Interscience). Wiley.

Lindsell, Harold. The Charismatic Christian. 256p. 1983. 11.95 (ISBN 0-8407-5279-2). Nelson.

--Free Enterprise: A Judeo-Christian Defense. 1982. pap. 5.95 (ISBN 0-8423-0922-5). Tyndale.

Lindsell, Sheryl L. The Secretary's Quick Reference Manual. LC 82-8888. 288p. (Orig.). 1983. pap. 2.95 (ISBN 0-668-05595-2, 5595). Arco.

Lindsey, Almont. Pullman Strike. LC 64-32413. 1964. pap. 8.95 (ISBN 0-226-48383-5, P165, Phoen). U of Chicago Pr.

Lindsey, Bonnie J. The Administrative Medical Assistant. 184p. 1979. pap. text ed. 11.95 (ISBN 0-87619-435-8). R J Brady.

Lindsey, C. H. & Vander Meulen, S. V. Informal Introduction to Algol 68. 2nd ed. 1977. text ed. 47.00 (ISBN 0-7204-0504-1, North-Holland); pap. text ed. 27.75 (ISBN 0-7204-0726-5). Elsevier.

Lindsey, Darry. The Design & Drafting of Printed Circuits. 2nd ed. (Illus.). 400p. 1983. 45.95 (ISBN 0-07-037844-4, P&RB). McGraw.

Lindsey, David. Americans in Conflict: The Civil War & Reconstruction. 208p. 1974. pap. text ed. 10.50 (ISBN 0-395-14068-4, 3-33320). HM.

--Black Gold, Red Death. 280p. 1983. pap. 2.75 (ISBN 0-449-12434-7, GM). Fawcett.

Lindsey, Hal. Compte a Rebours D'Harmaguedon. Cosson, Annie, ed. Remoussin, Philippe, tr. from Eng. Orig. Title: The 1980's, Countdown to Armageddon. 192p. (Fr.). 1982. pap. 2.25 (ISBN 0-8297-1327-1). Life Pubs Intl.

--La Liberacion del Planeta Tierra. (Span.). 1982. pap. 3.95 (ISBN 0-311-13023-2). Casa Bautista.

--The Nineteen Eighties Countdown to Armageddon. 1982. pap. 2.95 (ISBN 0-553-20102-6). Bantam.

--The Promise. LC 74-18859. 224p. 1982. pap. 3.25 (ISBN 0-89081-351-5). Harvest Hse.

Lindsey, J. P. & Gilbertson, R. L. Basidiomycetes That Decay Aspen in North America. (Bibliotheca Mycologica Ser.: No. 63). 1978. lib. bdg. 48.00 (ISBN 3-7682-1193-2). Lubrecht & Cramer.

Lindsey, Johanna. Captive Bride. 1977. pap. 3.50 (ISBN 0-380-01697-4, 81901-5). Avon.

--Fires of Winter. 368p. 1980. pap. 3.50 (ISBN 0-380-75747-8, 82909-6). Avon.

--A Pirate's Love. 1978. pap. 3.50 (ISBN 0-380-40048-0, 81638-5). Avon.

--So Speaks the Heart. 368p. 1983. pap. 3.95 (ISBN 0-380-81471-4). Avon.

Lindsey, Karen. Friends As Family. LC 80-70360. 294p. 1982. pap. 8.61 (ISBN 0-8070-2725-1, BP640). Beacon Pr.

Lindsey, Leslie. Photocraft. (Orig.). 1980. pap. 7.95 o.s.i. (ISBN 0-440-56812-9, Delta). Dell.

Lindsey, Linda, jt. auth. see Davis, Norah D.

Lindsey, Margaret. Training Teachers of the Gifted & Talented. Tannenbaum, Abraham J., ed. LC 80-11867. (Perspectives on Gifted & Talented Education Ser.). (Orig.). 1980. pap. text ed. 5.95x (ISBN 0-8077-2590-0). Tchrs Coll.

Lindsey, Margaret, et al. Inquiry into Teaching Behavior of Supervisors in Teacher Education Laboratories. LC 79-106358. (Illus.). 1969. pap. 5.95x (ISBN 0-8077-1693-6). Tchrs Coll.

Lindsey, Robert. The Falcon & the Snowman. 1979. 12.95 o.p. (ISBN 0-671-24560-0). S&S.

Lindsey, Ruth, et al. Body Mechanics: Posture, Figure, Fitness. 4th ed. 165p. 1979. pap. text ed. write for info. o.p. (ISBN 0-697-07162-6); avail. instr's manual o.p. Wm C Brown.

--Fitness for Health, Figure, Physique, Posture. 5th ed. 135p. 1983. pap. text ed. write for info. (ISBN 0-697-07267-3); instr's manual avail. (ISBN 0-697-07268-1). Wm C Brown.

Lindsey, W. C. & Simon, M. K. Phase Locked Loops & Their Applications. (IEEE Press Reprint Ser.). 1977. 36.95 (ISBN 0-471-04175-0); pap. 23.95 (ISBN 0-471-04176-9, Pub. by Wiley-Interscience). Wiley.

Lindsey, William C. & Simon, Marvin K. Telecommunication Systems Engineering. (Illus.). 672p. 1972. ref. ed. 39.95 (ISBN 0-13-902429-8). P-H.

Lindsey, William C. & Simon, Mark K., eds. Phase-Locked Loops & Their Application. LC 77-73101. 1978. 36.95 (ISBN 0-87942-101-0). Inst Electrical.

Lindskog, Robert, jt. auth. see Raphael, Coleman.

Lindskold, Svern, jt. auth. see Tedeschi, James T.

Lindskoog, Carrie, jt. auth. see Lindskoog, John.

Lindskoog, John & Lindskoog, Carrie. Vocabulario Cayapa. (Vocabularios Indigenas Ser.: No. 9). 129p. 1964. pap. 2.50 o. p. (ISBN 0-88312-654-0); microfiche 2.25 (ISBN 0-88312-316-9). Summer Inst Ling.

Lindstrom, Aletha J. Sojourner Truth: Slave, Abolitionist, Fighter for Women's Rights. LC 79-25576. (Illus.). 128p. (gr. 4-6). 1980. PLB 8.79 o.p. (ISBN 0-671-32988-X). Messner.

Lindstrom, Mauritz. Conodonts. 1964. 56.00 (ISBN 0-444-40372-8). Elsevier.

Lindstrom, Thais S. Nikolay Gogol. (World Authors Ser.: Russia: No. 299). 1974. lib. bdg. 12.50 o.p. (ISBN 0-8057-2377-3, Twayne). G K Hall.

Lindstrom, William J., jt. auth. see Zikmund, William.

Lindvall, C. M., ed. Defining Educational Objectives. 1964. pap. 3.95x o.p. (ISBN 0-8229-6072-9). U of Pittsburgh Pr.

Lindvall, Ella K. Read-Aloud Bible Stories, Vol. 1. LC 82-2114. 160p. (ps). 1982. 15.95 (ISBN 0-8024-7163-3). Moody.

Lindwall, Ted. Poder Espiritual. Repr. of 1977 ed. (ISBN 0-311-46068-2). Casa Bautista.

Lindzey, Gardner & Aronson, E. Handbook of Social Psychology, 5 vols. 2nd ed. Incl. Vol. 1. Systematic Positions (ISBN 0-201-04262-2); Vol. 2. Research Methods (ISBN 0-201-04263-0); Vol. 3. The Individual in a Social Context (ISBN 0-201-04264-9); Vol. 4. Group Psychology & Phenomena of Interaction (ISBN 0-201-04265-7); Vol. 5. Applied Social Psychology (ISBN 0-201-04266-5). 1968. 21.95 ea. A-W.

Lindzey, Gardner, jt. auth. see Hall, Calvin S.

Lindzey, Gardner, et al. Psychology. 2nd ed. LC 77-86622. (Illus.). 1978. 22.95x (ISBN 0-87901-089-4); study guide 7.95x (ISBN 0-87901-090-8). Worth.

Lindzey, Gardner, et al, eds. Theories of Personality: Primary Sources & Research. 2nd ed. LC 72-6983. 512p. 1973. pap. text ed. 24.95 (ISBN 0-471-53901-5). Wiley.

Line, David. Soldier & Me. LC 65-21018. (gr. 5-9). 1965. PLB 9.89 (ISBN 0-06-023906-9, HarpJ). Har-Row.

Line, Les & Reiger, George. The World Book Library of Wildlife Ser. LC 81-52955. (The World Book Library of Wildlife Ser.). (Illus.). 96p. (gr. 4-12). 1981. PLB write for info. (ISBN 0-7166-2302-1). World Bk.

Line, Les & Ricciuti, Edward. The World Book of Big Cats & Other Predators. LC 81-52956. (The World Book Library of Wildlife Ser.). (Illus.). 96p. (gr. 4-12). 1981. PLB write for info. (ISBN 0-7166-2301-3). World Bk.

--The World Book of Elephants, Zebras & Other Plant Eaters. LC 81-52954. (The World Book Library of Wildlife Ser.). (Illus.). 96p. (gr. 4-12). 1981. write for info. (ISBN 0-7166-2303-X). World Bk.

Line, Maurice B. & Vickers, Stephen. Universal Availability of Publications. (IFLA Publications: No. 25). 200p. 1983. price not set (ISBN 3-598-20387-X, Pub. by K G Saur). Shoe String.

Lineaweaver, Thomas H., 3rd & Backus, Richard H. Natural History of Sharks. LC 75-109174. (Illus.). 1970. 11.49i (ISBN 0-397-00660-8). Har-Row.

Lineback, Neal G. Laboratory Manual in Physical Geography. 2nd ed. 1976. pap. text ed. 8.95 (ISBN 0-8403-1089-7). Kendall-Hunt.

Linebarger, J. M. John Berryman. (United States Authors Ser.: No. 244). 1974. lib. bdg. 10.95 o.p. (ISBN 0-8057-0054-4, Twayne). G K Hall.

Linebarger, Paul. The Political Doctrines of Sun Yat-Sen. LC 73-3926. 278p. 1973. Repr. of 1937 ed. lib. bdg. 16.25x (ISBN 0-8371-6855-4, LISY). Greenwood.

Lineberry, Robert & Masotti, Louis, eds. Urban Policy Problems. 1975. pap. 6.00 (ISBN 0-918592-11-9). Policy Studies.

Lineberry, Robert L. Government in America: People, Politics, & Policy. (Illus.). 601p. 1980. text ed. 21.95 (ISBN 0-316-52671-1); instructor's manual avail. (ISBN 0-316-52666-5); student study guide 7.95 (ISBN 0-316-52667-3); test bank avail. (ISBN 0-316-52668-1). Little.

Lineberry, Robert L., jt. ed. see Masotti, Louis H.

Linecar, Howard. Beginner's Guide to Coin Collecting. 9.95 o.p. (ISBN 0-7207-0015-9). Transatlantic.

Linecar, Howard A. The Commemorative Medal: Its Appreciation & Collection. LC 72-12989. (Illus.). 250p. 1974. 24.00x (ISBN 0-8103-2012-6). Gale.

Linedecker, Clifford L. Children in Chains. LC 80-28492. 352p. 1981. 15.95 (ISBN 0-89696-088-9, An Everest House Book). Dodd.

--The Swastika & the Eagle: Neo-Nazism in America Today. (Illus.). 448p. Date not set. 17.95 (ISBN 0-89479-100-1). A & W Pubs. Postponed.

Linehan, James, ed. see Gibson, Grace L. & Bayes, Ronald H.

Linehan, Jean, jt. ed. see Linehan, John.

Linehan, John & Linehan, Jean, eds. Concerns of the Nation: Series A, 5 bks. Incl. Are We Neglecting the Elderly; Can We Stop Slaughter on Our Highways; Is Black Bitterness Justified; Is Space Exploration Worth the Cost; Should Everybody Have the Right to Own a Gun. (gr. 8-12). pap. text ed. 0.68 ea. o.p.; Set. pap. text ed. 2.40 o.p. (ISBN 0-685-25921-8); tchrs' guide 0.80 o.p. (ISBN 0-685-25922-6). Bobbs.

Linehan, Peter. Spanish Church & the Papacy in the Thirteenth Century. LC 75-154505. (Studies in Medieval Life & Thought, Third Ser: No. 4). (Illus.). 1971. 49.50 (ISBN 0-521-08039-8). Cambridge U Pr.

Linell, Per. Psychological Reality in Phonology. LC 78-67429. (Cambridge Studies in Linguistics: No. 25). (Illus.). 1979. 49.50 (ISBN 0-521-22234-6). Cambridge U Pr.

Lineman, Rose & Popelka, Jan. The Compendium of Astrology. 1982. pap. 24.95 (ISBN 0-914918-43-5). Para Res.

Linenthal, Edward T. Changing Images of the Warrior Hero in America: A History of Popular Symbolism. (Studies in American Religion: Vol. 6). 296p. 1983. 39.95 (ISBN 0-88946-921-0). E Mellen.

Liner, Tom, jt. auth. see Kirby, Dan.

Lines, James. Beyond the Balance Sheet: Evaluating Profit Potential. LC 74-5512. 1974. 23.95x o.s.i. (ISBN 0-470-53906-2). Halsted Pr.

Lines, Kathleen, ed. Faber Book of Greek Legends. 268p. 1973. 12.95 (ISBN 0-571-09830-4). Faber & Faber.

--Faber Storybook. (gr. k-3). 1967. 8.95 o.p. (ISBN 0-571-04359-3). Transatlantic.

Lines, Kathleen, ed. see Uttley, Alison.

Lines, Kathleen, selected by see Uttley, Alison.

Linesberry, Robert L. & Masotti, Louis H., eds. Urban Problems & Public Policy. (Policy Studies Organization Ser.). 240p. 1975. 19.95x (ISBN 0-669-00017-5, Dist. by Transaction Bks). Lexington Bks.

Linet, Beverly, jt. auth. see Stacy, Pat.

Linfield, Trudy. English Spoken Here. (English Spoken Here (ESL) Ser.). Date not set. tchrs. manual 13.20 (ISBN 0-8428-0862-0). Cambridge Bk.

Ling, et al. Private Capital for New Towns. (Institute of Economic Affairs, Occasional Papers Ser.: No. 28). pap. 2.50 o.p. (ISBN 0-255-69645-0). Transatlantic.

Ling, Daniel. Speech & the Hearing Impaired Child: Theory & Practice. LC 76-21920. (Illus.). 1976. text ed. 15.50 (ISBN 0-88200-074-8, A0669). Alexander Graham.

Ling, Dwight L. Morocco & Tunisia: A Comparative History. LC 79-5364. 1979. pap. text ed. 10.75 (ISBN 0-8191-0873-1). U Pr of Amer.

Ling, Evelyn R. Archives in the Church or Synagogue Library. (Guide Ser.: No. 10). 1981. pap. 4.50 (ISBN 0-915324-18-0). CSLA.

Ling, N. R. & Kay, J. E., eds. Lymphocyte Stimulation. rev. 2nd ed. LC 74-83274. 397p. 1975. 119.25x (ISBN 0-444-10701-0, North-Holland). Elsevier.

Ling, Roger, jt. auth. see Davey, Norman.

Ling, S. C., jt. auth. see Chua, J. E.

Ling, Teresa. Calculus: Study Guide. 1980. 10.95 (ISBN 0-8053-6933-3). Benjamin Cummings.

Ling, Trevor. Buddha, Marx & God: Some Aspects of Religion in the Modern World. 2nd ed. 1979. 26.00 (ISBN 0-312-10679-3). St Martin.

--Buddhist Revival in India: Aspects of the Sociology of Buddhism. LC 79-20167. 1980. 25.00 (ISBN 0-312-10681-5). St Martin.

Lingard, Joan. The Reunion. LC 78-2793. (gr. 7 up). 1978. 7.95 o.p. (ISBN 0-525-66592-7). Lodestar Bks.

Lingat, Robert. The Classical Law of India. Derrett, J. Duncan, tr. from Fr. LC 76-81798. Orig. Title: Sources Du Droit Dans le Systeme Traditionnel De L'inde. 1973. 37.50 (ISBN 0-520-01898-2). U of Cal Pr.

Linge, G. J., jt. auth. see Hamilton, F. E.

Linge, G. J., jt. ed. see Hamilton, F. E.

Lingeman, C. H., ed. Carcinogenic Hormones. (Recent Results in Cancer Research Ser.: Vol. 66). (Illus.). 1979. 45.10 o.p. (ISBN 0-387-08995-0). Springer-Verlag.

Lingeman, Richard. Small Town America: A Narrative History, 1620-the Present. 1980. 15.95 (ISBN 0-399-11988-4). Putnam Pub Group.

Lingeman, Richard R. Drugs from A to Z: A Dictionary. 2nd ed. (McGraw-Hill Paperbacks). 320p. (Orig.). 1974. text ed. 9.95 (ISBN 0-07-037913-0, SP); pap. 5.95 (ISBN 0-07-037912-2). McGraw.

--Drugs from A to Z: A Dictionary. 2nd ed. 4.95 o.p. (ISBN 0-686-92196-8, 4260). Hazeldden.

Lingenberg, Rolf. Metric Planes & Metric Vector Spaces. LC 78-21906. (Pure & Applied Mathematics: Texts, Monographs & Tracts). 1979. 33.95 o.p. (ISBN 0-471-04901-8, Pub. by Wiley-Interscience). Wiley.

--Metric Planes & Metric Vector Spaces. LC 78-21906. 274p. Repr. of 1979 ed. text ed. 28.50 (ISBN 0-686-84493-9). Krieger.

Lingenfelter, Richard E. The Hardrock Miners: A History of the Mining Labor Movement in the American West, 1863-1893. 1981. 18.95 (ISBN 0-520-02468-0, CAL 529); pap. 9.95 (ISBN 0-520-04512-2). U of Cal Pr.

Lingenfelter, Richard E. & Dwyer, Richard A., eds. Songs of the American West. (Illus.). 1968. 35.00 (ISBN 0-520-00753-0). U of Cal Pr.

Lingenfelter, Sherwood G. YAP: Political Leadership & Culture Change in an Island Society. 256p. 1975. text ed. 16.00x (ISBN 0-8248-0301-9). UH Pr.

Linger, R. C., et al. Structured Programming: Theory & Practice. LC 78-18641. 1979. text ed. 26.95 (ISBN 0-201-14461-1). A-W.

Lingerman, Hal A. Healing Energies of Music. LC 82-42706. 198p. (Orig.). 1983. pap. 6.50 (ISBN 0-8356-0570-1, Quest). Theos Pub Hse.

Lingle, Walter L. & Kuykendall, John W. Presbyterians: Their History & Beliefs. LC 77-15750. 1978. pap. 4.95 (ISBN 0-8042-0985-5). John Knox.

Lingleb, Al H., jt. auth. see Meiners, Roger E.

Lingo, T. D. First Workbook into Brain. 50p. (Orig.). 1981. pap. 11.00 looseleaf o.p. (ISBN 0-686-31344-5). Dormant Brain Res.

--Self Transcendence Workbook. 55p. (Orig.). 1982. pap. 11.00 (ISBN 0-686-37712-5). Dormant Brain Res.

Lingren, Wesley E. Inorganic Nomenclature: A Programmed Approach. (Illus.). 1980. pap. text ed. 11.95 (ISBN 0-13-466607-0). P-H.

Lings, Martin. Muhammad. 349p. 1983. 24.95 (ISBN 0-89281-046-7). Inner Tradit.
--A Sufi Saint of the Twentieth Century: Shaikh Ahmad al-'Alawi, His Spiritual Heritage & Legacy. (Illus.). 242p. 1972. 27.50x (ISBN 0-520-02174-6); pap. 4.95 (ISBN 0-520-02486-9). U of Cal Pr.

Lingua Press. Lingua Press Collection One Catalogue. Gaburo, Kenneth, ed. (Vol. 1). (Illus.). 44p. 1976. saddle stitched 1.50 (ISBN 0-939044-00-5). Lingua Pr.

Linguet, Simon. Examen Des Ouvrages De M. De Voltaire. Repr. of 1788 ed. 63.00 o.p. (ISBN 0-8287-0548-8). Clearwater Pub.

Linguistic Association of Canada & the U. S. Eighth LACUS Forum: Proceedings. Gutwinski, Waldemar & Jolly, Grace, eds. 1981. pap. text ed. 10.95 (ISBN 0-917496-22-1). Hornbeam Pr.

Linguistic Association of Canada & the U.S. The Fourth LACUS Forum: Proceedings. Paradis, Michel, ed. 1977. pap. text ed. 10.95 (ISBN 0-917496-09-4). Hornbeam Pr.
--The Second LACUS Forum: Proceedings. Reich, Peter A., ed. 1975. pap. text ed. 15.00 (ISBN 0-917496-05-1). Hornbeam Pr.
--Seventh Lacus Forum: Proceedings. Copeland, J. E. & Davis, P. W., eds. 1980. pap. text ed. 10.95 (ISBN 0-917496-19-1). Hornbeam Pr.

Linguistic Circle of Saigon & Summer Institute of Linguistics. Mon-Khmer Studies, No. 1-4. Incl. No. 1. Banker, John, et al. 163p. 1964. microfiche 2.25x (ISBN 0-88312-541-2); pap. 2.00; No. 2. Thomas, David, et al, eds. 111p. 1966. microfiche 2.25x (ISBN 0-88312-542-0); No. 3. Burton, Eva, et al. 147p. 1969. microfiche 2.25x (ISBN 0-685-41028-5); No. 4. Thomas, David D. & Hoa, Nguyen D. 1973. pap. 3.50x (ISBN 0-685-41029-3); microfiche 2.25x (ISBN 0-88312-357-6). Summer Inst Ling.

Linhart, J. F., ed. Plasma Physics: Proceedings of the EUR-CNEN Association Meeting, 1969. 1975. pap. text ed. 16.25 o.p. (ISBN 0-08-020450-3). Pergamon.

Linhart, Joseph W. & Joyner, Claude. Diagnostic Echocardiography. LC 81-14075. (Illus.). 373p. 1981. text ed. 54.50 (ISBN 0-8016-3042-8). Mosby.

Linhart, Robert. The Assembly Line. Crosland, Margaret, tr. from Fr. LC 81-1703. Orig. Title: L'Etabli. 160p. (Orig.). 1981. pap. text ed. 7.50x (ISBN 0-87023-322-X). U of Mass Pr.

Lininger, Charles A., jt. auth. see Warwick, Donald P.

Link, Arthur S. The Papers of Woodrow Wilson, June 25-August 20,1917. LC 66-10880. (Vol. 43). (Illus.). 552p. 1983. 32.50x (ISBN 0-691-04701-4). Princeton U Pr.
--Woodrow Wilson & the Progressive Era, 1910-1917. (New American Nation Ser.). 1954. 16.30xi (ISBN 0-06-012650-7, HarpT). Har-Row.
--Woodrow Wilson & the Progressive Era: 1910-1917. (New American Nation Ser.). (Illus.). pap. 8.50xi (ISBN 0-06-133023-X, TB3023, Torch). Har-Row.

Link, Arthur S. & Catton, William B. American Epoch, 2 vols. 5th ed. 1980. pap. text ed. 12.00 ea. Vol. 1, 640p (ISBN 0-394-32357-2). Vol. 2, 496p (ISBN 0-394-32358-0). Knopf.

Link, Arthur S. & Coben, Stanley. The Democratic Heritage: A History of the United States. LC 69-11030. 688p. (Orig.). 16.50 (ISBN 0-686-81279-4). Krieger.

Link, Arthur S. & Link, William A. The Twentieth Century: An American History. LC 82-22080. (Illus.). 384p. 1983. text ed. 27.50 (ISBN 0-88295-815-1); pap. text ed. 16.95 (ISBN 0-88295-816-X). Harlan Davidson.

Link, Arthur S. & McCormick, Richard L. Progressivism. LC 82-15857. (American History Ser.). 164p. 1983. pap. text ed. 6.95 (ISBN 0-88295-814-3). Harlan Davidson.

Link, Arthur S. & Hirst, David W., eds. November Twentieth, 1916 to November Twenty-Third, 1917. LC 66-10880. (The Papers of Woodrow Wilson Ser.: Vol. 40). (Illus.). 600p. 1982. 30.00x (ISBN 0-691-04690-5). Princeton U Pr.

Link, Arthur S., jt. ed. see Leary, William M., Jr.

Link, Arthur S., et al. The American People: A History. (Illus.). 1208p. 1981. text ed. 26.00x (ISBN 0-88295-804-6); Vol. I. pap. text ed. 13.95x (ISBN 0-88295-805-4); Vol. II. pap. text ed. 13.95x (ISBN 0-88295-806-2). Harlan Davidson.

Link, Carolyn W. Waters Under the Earth. 1968. 4.00 o.p. (ISBN 0-8233-0059-5). Golden Quill.

Link, Frederick. Aphra Behn. (English Authors Ser.). 14.95 (ISBN 0-8057-1040-X, Twayne). G K Hall.

Link, Frederick M., ed. English Drama, Sixteen Sixty-Eighteen Hundred: A Guide to Information Sources. LC 73-16984. (American Literature English Literature & World Literatures in English Information Guide Ser.: Vol.9). 360p. 1976. 42.00x (ISBN 0-8103-1224-7). Gale.

Link House Mag., Croydon Ltd., ed. Pro-Audio Yearbook Nineteen Eighty One. 1981. 49.50x (ISBN 0-686-97110-8, Pub. by Link Hse Mag England). State Mutual Bk.

Link, Howard A., et al. Primitve Ukiyo-E: From the James A. Michener Collection in the Honolulu Academy of Arts. LC 79-6397. (Illus.). 384p. 1980. 55.00 (ISBN 0-8248-0483-X). UH Pr.

Link, Irene, jt. auth. see Farnham, Rebecca.

Link, Perry, ed. Stubborn Weeds: Chinese Literature after the Cultural Revolution. LC 82-48268. 320p. 1983. 22.50x (ISBN 0-253-35512-5). Ind U Pr.

Link, Phoebe F. Small? Tall? Not at All! (Early Childhood Bk.). (Illus.). (ps-2). PLB 4.95 o.p. (ISBN 0-513-01297-4). Denison.

Link, William A., jt. auth. see Link, Arthur S.

Linke, Frances, psend. Space Patrol Memories, by Tonga. Wahle, Ted, ed. (Space Patrol Ser.: No. 1). (Illus.). 173p. (Orig.). 1976. 25.00 (ISBN 0-933276-00-1); lib. bdg. 30.00x (ISBN 0-933276-01-X); pap. 20.00 (ISBN 0-933276-03-6). Nin-Ra Ent.

Linke, Hawley K., jt. auth. see Fareed, George C.

Linkens, D. A., jt. ed. see Bennett, S.

Linkert, Lo. Lo Linkert's Golftoons. 3rd ed. (Illus.). 1980. 4.95 (ISBN 0-89149-037-X). Jolex.

Linkhart, Luther. The Trinity Alps: A Hiking & Backpacking Guide. Winnett, Thomas, ed. (Illus.). 192p. 1983. pap. 9.95 (ISBN 0-89997-024-9). Wilderness Pr.

Linkl, E. J., jt. ed. see Latham, P. R.

Linklater & Sunday Times of London Insight Team. War in the Falklands: The Full Story. LC 82-48612. (Illus.). 320p. 1982. 14.95 (ISBN 0-06-015082-3, HarpT). Har-Row.

Linklater, Kristin. Freeing the Natural Voice. LC 75-28172. (Illus.). 224p. 1976. pap. text ed. 12.50x (ISBN 0-89676-071-5). Drama Bk.

Linklater, Magnus. Massacre: The Story of Glencoe. (Illus.). 160p. 1983. 24.95 (ISBN 0-00-435669-1, Collins Pub England). Greene.

Linklater, R. Bruce. Internal Control of Hospital Finances: A Guide for Management. (Financial Management Ser.). (Illus.). 96p. 1983. 32.50 (ISBN 0-87258-398-8, AHA-061150). Am Hospital.

Linkletter, Art. Linkletter on Dynamic Selling. 210p. 1982. 5.95 (ISBN 0-13-537050-7). P-H.
--Public Speaking for Private People. LC 80-691. 300p. 1980. 11.95 o.p. (ISBN 0-672-52652-2). Bobbs.
--Yes, You Can. (General Ser.). 1980. lib. bdg. 12.95 (ISBN 0-8161-6763-X, Large Print Bks). G K Hall.
--Yes, You Can! 1979. 9.95 o.p. (ISBN 0-671-24025-0). S&S.
--Yes, You Can! 224p. 1982. pap. 2.95 (ISBN 0-515-06442-4). Jove Pubns.

Linko, P. Food Processing Engineering, 2 Vols. 1980. Vol. 1: Food Processing Systems. 203.00 (ISBN 0-85334-896-0, Pub. by Applied Sci England); Vol. 2: Enzyme Engineering in Food Processing. 74.00 (ISBN 0-85334-897-9). Elsevier.

Linkow, Leonard I. Dental Implants. (Illus.). 1983. 17.50 (ISBN 0-8315-0162-6). Speller.

Links, J. G. Canaletto. LC 82-70752. (Illus.). 240p. 1982. 48.50x (ISBN 0-8014-1532-2). Cornell U Pr.

Links, J. G., ed. see Constable, W. G.

Links, Sara, jt. auth. see Lobo, Ben.

Link-Salinger, Ruth. Jewish Law in Our Time. 22.50x (ISBN 0-8197-0486-5); pap. 12.95x (ISBN 0-8197-0487-3). Bloch.

Linkugel, Wil A., et al. Contemporary American Speeches. 5th ed. LC 77-20387. 1981. pap. text ed. 10.95 (ISBN 0-8403-2616-5, 40261601). Kendall-Hunt.

Linman, J. W. Principles of Hematology. 1966. text ed. 57.50 (ISBN 0-02-370940-5). Macmillan.

Linn, Charles F. Probability. LC 79-171006. (Young Math Ser.). (Illus.). 40p. (gr. 1-4). 1972. PLB 10.89 (ISBN 0-690-65602-5, TYC-J). Har-Row.

Linn, Dennis & Linn, Matthew. Healing Life's Hurts. LC 77-14794. 264p. 1978. pap. 4.95 (ISBN 0-8091-2059-3). Paulist Pr.

Linn, Dennis, jt. auth. see Linn, Matthew.

Linn, Don. Harrier in Action. (Illus.). 50p. 1982. 4.95 (ISBN 0-89747-139-3). Squad Sig Pubns.

Linn, Ed, jt. auth. see Papanek, Ernst.

Linn, Harriet. Figures from Wonderland. 1982. pap. 2.50 (ISBN 0-9604740-2-1). Ampersand RI.

Linn, Sr. Mary J., et al. Healing the Dying. LC 79-53111. 128p. 1979. pap. 3.95 (ISBN 0-8091-2212-X). Paulist Pr.

Linn, Matthew & Linn, Dennis. Prayer Course for Healing Life's Hurts. 128p. 1983. pap. 5.95 (ISBN 0-8091-2522-6). Paulist Pr.

Linn, Matthew, jt. auth. see Linn, Dennis.

Linn, Robert. Staying Thin. 1980. 10.95 (ISBN 0-399-12449-7). Putnam Pub Group.

Linn, S., jt. ed. see Roberts, R.

Linnaeus, C. Genera Plantarum. 1960. Repr. of 1754 ed. 60.00 (ISBN 3-7682-0014-0). Lubrecht & Cramer.
--Hortus Cliffortianus. (Illus.). 1968. Repr. of 1737 ed. 96.00 (ISBN 3-7682-0543-6). Lubrecht & Cramer.
--Mantissa Plantarum: 1767-71, 2vols. in 1. 1960. 48.00 (ISBN 3-7682-0037-X). Lubrecht & Cramer.
--Philosophia Botanica. (Illus.). 1966. Repr. of 1751 ed. 60.00 (ISBN 3-7682-0350-6). Lubrecht & Cramer.
--Systema Naturae: Tomus II, Vegetabilia. 10th ed. 1964. Repr. of 1759 ed. 60.00 (ISBN 3-7682-0219-4). Lubrecht & Cramer.

Linnaeus, C., ed. see Artedi, P.

Linnaeus, Carl. Caroli Linnaei, Systema Naturae: A Photographic Facsimile of the First Volume of the Tenth Edition (1758) Regnum Animale. 824p. 1978. Repr. of 1956 ed. 30.00x (ISBN 0-565-00103-5, Pub. by Brit Mus Nat Hist England). Sabbot-Natural Hist Bks.

Linnear, Angus. Sit, Walk, Stand. 1977. pap. 2.50 (ISBN 0-8423-5893-5). Tyndale.

Linnebach, Karl, ed. see Von Scharnhorst, Gerhard J.

Linnegar, S., jt. auth. see Cassidy, G. E.

Linnell, Robert. Dollars & Scholars. Clark, Henry B. & Dillon, Kristine E., eds. (Orig.). 1982. 12.00 (ISBN 0-88474-106-0); pap. 8.00 (ISBN 0-686-82258-7). U of S Cal Pr.

Linneman, R. Shirt Sleeve Approach to Long Range Planning for the Smaller Growing Corporation. 1980. 19.95 (ISBN 0-13-808972-8). P-H.

Linneman, William R. Richard Hovey. (United States Authors Ser.). 1976. lib. bdg. 13.95 (ISBN 0-8057-7162-X, Twayne). G K Hall.

Linnemann, Russell J., ed. Alain Locke: Reflections on a Modern Renaissance Man. 176p. 1982. text ed. 15.95x (ISBN 0-8071-1036-1). La State U Pr.

Linner, Sven. Starets Zomima in the Brothers Karamazov: A Study in the Mimesis of Virtue. (Stockholm-Studies in Russian Literature: No. 4). 1976. pap. text ed. 17.50x (ISBN 0-686-86111-6). Humanities.

Linnert, G. E. Metallurgy, Welding, Carbon & Alloy Steels: Fundamentals, Vol. 1. 3rd ed. 474p. 1965. 25.00 (ISBN 0-686-95602-8, WM1). Am Welding.
--Metallurgy, Welding, Carbon & Alloy Steels: Technology, Vol. 2. 3rd ed. 674p. 1967. 30.00 (ISBN 0-686-95605-2, WM2). Am Welding.
--Welding Metallurgy, 2 vols. Vol. 1-fundamentals. 15.00 o.p. (ISBN 0-685-65961-5); Vol. 2-technology. 20.00 o.p. (ISBN 0-685-65962-3). Am Welding.

Linney. Management of Multiple Birth. 1981. write for info. (ISBN 0-471-25849-0). Wiley.

Linnhoff, B., et al. Process Integration & Energy Efficiency: A User's Guide. 1983. text ed. 39.95 (ISBN 0-87201-250-6). Gulf Pub.

Linnik, I., compiled by. The Hermitage: Western European Painting. Pamfilov, Yu. & Nemetsky, Yu., trs. 1979. 24.95 (ISBN 0-89893-001-4). CDP.

Linnik, Irene, jt. auth. see Kuznetsov, Yury.

Linowes, R. Robert & Allensworth, Don T. The States & Land-Use Control. LC 75-3624. (Special Studies). (Illus.). 262p. 1975. 31.95 o.p. (ISBN 0-275-05210-9). Praeger.

Lins, David A., jt. auth. see Penson, John B., Jr.

Lins, Osman. Avalovara. Rabassa, Gregoy, tr. from Portuguese. LC 79-1214. 1980. 12.95 o.p. (ISBN 0-394-49851-8). Knopf.

Linschoten, J. H. Van. Histoire de la Navigation de J. H. de Linscot et Son Voyage des Indes Orientales. (Bibliotheque Africaine Ser.). 300p. (Fr.). 1974. Repr. of 1610 ed. lib. bdg. 79.50x o.p. (ISBN 0-8287-0851-7, 72-2158). Clearwater Pub.

Linse, Barbara, jt. auth. see Kuska, George.

Linsell, Tony. Mr. Ferdinand Fisk, Cat Detective. LC 79-12422. (Illus.). (gr. k-3). 1979. 6.95 (ISBN 0-07-037950-5). McGraw.

Linsenmaier, Walter. Wonders of Nature. LC 78-62133. (Picturebacks Ser.). (Illus.). 32p. (ps-3). 1980. PLB 4.99 (ISBN 0-394-94091-1, BYR); pap. 1.50 (ISBN 0-394-84091-7). Random.

Linsk, Joseph A. & Franzen, Sixten, eds. Clinical Aspiration Cytology. (Illus.). 386p. 1983. text ed. 59.00 (ISBN 0-397-50504-3, Lippincott Medical). Lippincott.

Linskill, Mary. Cleveden. 35.00x (ISBN 0-686-98235-5, Pub. by Caedmon of Whitby). State Mutual Bk.

Linsky, B., ed. see Chicago Association of Commerce & Industry, Committee of Investigation on Smoke Abatement.

Linsky, Benjamin, ed. see Chicago Association of Commerce & Industry, Committee of Investigation on Smoke Abatement.

Linsky, E. G., jt. auth. see Chemsak, John A.

Linsky, L., ed. Reference & Modality. (Readings in Philosophy Ser). (Orig.). 1971. pap. text ed. 8.95x (ISBN 0-19-875017-X). Oxford U Pr.

Linsley, E. G. & MacSwain, J. W. Nesting Biology & Associates of Melitoma (Hymenoptera, Anthrophoridae) (U. C. Publications in Entomology: Vol. 90). 1980. pap. 10.50x (ISBN 0-520-09618-5). U of Cal Pr.

Linsley, E. Gorton. The Cerambycidae of North America. Incl. Pt. I. Introduction. (U. C. Publ. in Entomology: Vol. 18). 1961. pap. o.p. (ISBN 0-520-09079-9); Pt. II. Taxonomy & Classification of the Parandrinae, Prioninae, Spondylinae, & Aseminae. (U. C. Publ. in Entomology: Vol. 19). 1962. pap. o.p. (ISBN 0-520-09080-2); Pt. III. Taxonomy & Classification of the Subfamily Cerambycinae, Tribes Opsimini Through Megaderini. (U. C. Publ. in Entomology: Vol. 20). 1962. pap. 11.00x (ISBN 0-520-09081-0); Pt. IV. Taxonomy & Classification of the Subfamily Cerambycinae, Tribes Elaphidionini Through Rhinotragini. (U. C. Publ. in Entomology: Vol. 21). 1963. pap. 3.50x o.p. (ISBN 0-520-09082-9); Pt. V. Taxonomy & Classification of the Subfamily Cerambycinae, Tribes Callichromini Through Ancylocerini. (U. C. Publ. in Entomology: Vol. 22). 1964. pap. 11.50x (ISBN 0-520-09083-7). pap. U of Cal Pr.

Linsley, Frank. Electrical Drawing for Technicians, 1. (TEC Ser.). (Illus.). 1979. pap. 11.95 (ISBN 0-408-00417-7). Butterworth.

Linsley, Joy L., jt. ed. see Wasserman, Julian N.

Linsley, Leslie. Army Navy Surplus: A Unique Source of Decorating Ideas. 1979. pap. 7.95 o.s.i. (ISBN 0-440-50480-5, Delta). Dell.
--The Great Bazaar. (Illus.). 1981. 17.95 o.s.i. (ISBN 0-440-03077-3). Delacorte.
--Leslie Linsley's Christmas Ornaments & Stockings. (Illus.). 160p. 1982. 17.95 (ISBN 0-312-48131-4). St Martin.
--Making It Personal: With Monograms, Initials & Names. (Illus.). 184p. 1981. 17.95 (ISBN 0-399-90125-6, Marek). Putnam Pub Group.
--Scrimshaw. 1979. pap. 13.95 (ISBN 0-8015-6609-6, 01354-410, Hawthorn). Dutton.
--Scrimshaw: A Traditional Folk Art, a Contemporary Craft. (Illus.). 1979. pap. 13.95 (ISBN 0-8015-6609-6, 01354-410, Hawthorn). Dutton.

Linsley, Leslie & Aron, Jon. Air Crafts: Playthings to Make & Fly. (Illus.). 32p. (gr. 3-5). 1982. 8.95 (ISBN 0-525-66766-0, 0869-260). Lodestar Bks.
--Photocraft. (Illus.). 176p. 1980. 15.95 o.s.i. (ISBN 0-440-06802-9). Delacorte.

Linsley, Ray K. & Franzini, Joseph. Water Resources Engineering. 3rd ed. (Water Resources & Environmental Engineering Ser.). (Illus.). 1979. text ed. 34.50 (ISBN 0-07-037965-3); solutions manual 25.00 (ISBN 0-07-037966-1). McGraw.

Linsley, Ray K., et al. Hydrology for Engineers. 2nd ed. (Environmental Engineering & Water Resources Ser.). 1974. text ed. 36.50 (ISBN 0-07-037967-X, C); solutions manual 7.95 (ISBN 0-07-037969-6). McGraw.
--Hydrology for Engineers. 3rd ed. (Water Resources & Environmental Engineering Ser.). (Illus.). 496p. 1982. 32.50 (ISBN 0-07-037956-4); solutions manual 10.00 (ISBN 0-07-037957-2). McGraw.

Linson, Corwin K. My Stephen Crane. LC 58-9279. (Illus.). 1958. 11.95x o.p. (ISBN 0-8156-0012-7). Syracuse U Pr.

Linssen, John. Tabitha Fffoulkes. LC 78-57319. 1978. 8.95 (ISBN 0-87795-192-6). Arbor Hse.

Linstone, Harold A. & Simmonds, W. H., eds. Futures Research: New Directions. 1977. text ed. 28.50 (ISBN 0-201-04096-4, Adv Bk Prog). A-W.

Linstone, Harold A. & Turoff, Murray, eds. Delphi Method: Techniques & Applications. LC 75-25650. 672p. 1975. text ed. 38.50 (ISBN 0-201-04294-0, Adv Bk Prog); pap. text ed. 26.50 (ISBN 0-201-04293-2, Adv Bk Prog). A-W.

Linstromberg, Walter W. & Baumgarten, Henry E. Organic Chemistry: A Brief Course. 4th ed. 1978. text ed. 23.95x (ISBN 0-669-00637-8); study guide with problems & solutions manual 8.95x (ISBN 0-669-00640-8). Heath.
--Organic Chemistry: A Brief Course. 5th ed. 448p. lib. bdg. 23.95 (ISBN 0-669-05525-5); pap. text ed. 8.95 Problems & Solutions Guide (ISBN 0-669-05526-3); pap. text ed. 10.95 Organic Experiments (ISBN 0-669-05524-7). Heath.

Linstromberg, Walter W. & Baumgarten, Henry F. Organic Experiments. 4th rev. ed. 1980. pap. text ed. 12.95 (ISBN 0-669-02902-5). Heath.

Lint, J. H. Van see Cameron, P. J. & Van Lint, J. H.

Lint, V. A. Van see Van Lint, V. A., et al.

Linthorst, Ann T. A Gift of Love: Marriage As a Spiritual Journey. LC 79-53953. 180p. 1979. 9.95 (ISBN 0-8091-0299-4). Paulist Pr.

Lintner, Jay, jt. auth. see Cory, Carol.

Linton, Alan H., jt. ed. see Hawker, Lilian A.

Linton, Eliza L. The Autobiography of Christopher Kirkland, 1885. Wolff, Robert L., ed. LC 75-1532. (Victorian Fiction Ser.). 1975. lib. bdg. 66.00 o.s.i. (ISBN 0-8240-1604-1). Garland Pub.

Linton, George E. The Modern Textile & Apparel Dictionary. rev. 4th ed. Orig. Title: The Modern Textile Dictionary. 1973. 20.00x (ISBN 0-87245-500-9). Textile Bk.
--The Modern Textile & Apparel Dictionary. 4th, rev. enlarged ed. 89.00x (ISBN 0-686-97037-3, Pub. by Meadowfield Pr England). State Mutual Bk.

Linton, Irwin. A Lawyer Examines the Bible. pap. 5.95 (ISBN 0-89051-033-4). CLP Pubs.

Linton, Irwin H. A Lawyer Examines the Bible: A Defense of the Faith. 1977. pap. 4.50 o.p. (ISBN 0-8010-5565-2). Baker Bk.

Linton, Marigold & Gallo, Phillip S., Jr. The Practical Statistician: Simplified Handbook of Statistics. LC 73-91423. (Illus.). 1975. pap. text ed. 14.95 (ISBN 0-8185-0127-8). Brooks-Cole.

Linton, Ralph. The Cultural Background of Personality. LC 80-29240. xix, 157p. 1981. Repr. of 1945 ed. lib. bdg. 19.25x (ISBN 0-313-22783-7, LICU). Greenwood.

Linton, Stanley. Conducting Fundamentals. (Illus.). 256p. 1982. text ed. 18.95 (ISBN 0-13-167320-3). P-H.

Lintz, Joseph, Jr. & Simonett, David S., eds. Remote Sensing of Environment. LC 76-47661. (Illus.). 1976. text ed. 39.50 (ISBN 0-201-04245-2, Adv Bk Prog). A-W.

Linver, Sandy. Speak & Get Results: Complete Guide to Presentations & Speeches That Work in Any Business Situation. 256p. 1983. 13.95 (ISBN 0-671-44204-X). Summit Bks.

Lin Yen Tung & Stotesbury, Sidney D. Structural Concepts & Systems for Architects & Engineers. LC 79-23458. 608p. 1981. text ed. 39.95 (ISBN 0-471-05186-1). Wiley.

Linz, Cathie. Wild Fire. (Candlelight Ecstasy Ser.: No. 157). (Orig.). 1983. pap. 1.95 (ISBN 0-440-18953-5). Dell.

Linz, Peter. Programming Concepts & Problem Solving. 1982. 24.95 (ISBN 0-8053-5710-6, 35710). Benjamin-Cummings.

--Theoretical Numerical Analysis: An Introduction to Advanced Techniques. LC 78-15178. (Pure & Applied Mathematics: Texts, Monographs & Tracts). 1979. 32.50x (ISBN 0-471-04561-6, Pub. by Wiley-Interscience). Wiley.

Linzell, J. L., jt. auth. see Peaker, M.

Linzey, Donald W. Snakes of Alabama. (Illus.). 136p. 1979. 9.95 (ISBN 0-87397-091-8). Strode.

Linzey, Stanford E. Why I Believe in the Baptism with the Holy Spirit. 1962. pap. 0.75 (ISBN 0-88243-764-X, 02-0764). Gospel Pub.

Lion, Edgar. Building Renovation & Recycling. LC 81-19464. 132p. 1982. 27.95 (ISBN 0-471-86444-7, Pub. by Wiley-Interscience). Wiley.

--Shopping Centers: Planning, Development & Administration. LC 75-33374. 1976. 32.50 (ISBN 0-471-54020-X, Pub. by Wiley-Interscience). Wiley.

Lion, Elizabeth M. Human Sexuality in Nursing Process. LC 81-16201. 496p. 1982. 15.95 (ISBN 0-471-03869-5, Pub. by Wiley Med). Wiley.

Lion, Eugene & Ball, David, eds. Guthrie New Theatre, Vol. 1. Incl. Afternoon Tea. Perr, Harvey; Cold. Casale, Michael; The Future Pit. McKillop, Menzies; Glutt. Schrock, Gladden; Swellfoot's Tears. Katz, Leon; Taps. Schrock, Gladden; Waterman. Ford, Frank B. 1976. pap. 4.95 o.s.i. (ISBN 0-394-17907-2, E668, Ever). Grove.

Lion, J. R., jt. ed. see Madden, D. J.

Lion, John R. Personality Disorders: Diagnosis & Management. 2nd. ed. 588p. 1981. lib. bdg. 36.00 (ISBN 0-683-05044-3). Williams & Wilkins.

Lion, John R. & Reid, William H. Assalts Within Psychiatric Facilities. write for info (ISBN 0-8089-1559-2). Grune.

Lionberger, Herbert F. & Gwin, Paul. Communication Strategies: A Guide for Agricultural Change Agents. 1982. text ed. 8.95x (ISBN 0-8134-2236-1). Interstate.

Lionel, Frederic. The Magic Tarot: Vehicle of Eternal Wisdom. Gadzuk, Marilyn W., tr. (Illus.). 160p. 1982. 17.95 (ISBN 0-7100-9416-7). Routledge & Kegan.

Lionni, Leo. Cornelius. LC 82-6442. (Illus.). 40p. (ps-2). 1983. 9.95 (ISBN 0-394-85419-5); PLB 9.99 (ISBN 0-394-95419-X). Pantheon.

Lionni, Paolo, jt. auth. see Klass, Lance J.

Lions, jt. ed. see Glowinski.

Lions, J. L. Some Aspects of the Optimal Control of Distributed Parameter Systems: Proceedings. (CBMS Regional Conference Ser.: Vol. 6). (Illus.). vi, 92p. (Orig.). 1972. pap. text ed. 9.50 (ISBN 0-89871-004-9). Soc Indus-Appl Math.

Lions, J. L., jt. auth. see Bensoussan, A.

Lions, J. L., jt. auth. see Brezis, H.

Lions, J. L. see Cottle, R. W., et al.

Lions, J. L., jt. ed. see Bensoussan, A.

Lions, J. L., jt. ed. see Brezis, H.

Lions, J. L., jt. ed. see Glowinski, R.

Lions, P. L. Generalized Solutions of Hamilton-Jacobi Equations. (Research Notes In Mathematics: No. 69). 230p. 1982. pap. text ed. 27.50 (ISBN 0-273-08556-5). Pitman Pub MA.

Liotti, G., jt. auth. see Guidano, V. F.

Lioy, Paul J., jt. ed. see Kneip, Theo J.

Lipatov, Yu. S & Sergeeva, L. M. Absorption of Polymers. Slutzkin, D., ed. Kondor, R., tr. from Rus. LC 74-12194. 177p. 1974. 35.95 o.s.i. (ISBN 0-470-54040-0). Halsted Pr.

Lipay, Raymond J. Accounting Services for Your Small Business: A Guide for Evaluating Company Performance, Obtaining Financing & Selling Your Business. LC 82-13647. 258p. 1983. 29.50x (ISBN 0-471-09160-X). Ronald Pr.

Lipe, Bob & Lipe, Karen. Boats Canvas from Cover to Cover. (Illus.). 192p. 1978. 11.95 (ISBN 0-915160-21-8). Seven Seas.

Lipe, Dewey, jt. auth. see Wolff, Jurgen M.

Lipe, Karen, jt. auth. see Lipe, Bob.

Lipetz, Marcia J., jt. auth. see Ellis, Robert L.

Lipham, James M. & Hoeh, James A., Jr. The Principalship: Foundations & Functions. 1974. text ed. 26.50 scp o.p. (ISBN 0-06-044032-5, HarpC). Har-Row.

Lipinski, Andrew J., jt. auth. see Amara, Roy C.

Lipke, Jean. Marriage. LC 70-104896. (Being Together Books). Orig. Title: Sex Outside of Marriage. (gr. 5-11). 1971. PLB 4.95g (ISBN 0-8225-0598-3). Lerner Pubns.

Lipke, Jean C. Conception & Contraception. LC 73-104889. (Being Together Books). (Illus.). (gr. 5-11). 1971. PLB 4.95g (ISBN 0-8225-0594-0). Lerner Pubns.

--Heredity. LC 78-104892. (Being Together Books). (Illus.). (gr. 5-11). 1971. PLB 4.95g (ISBN 0-8225-0597-5). Lerner Pubns.

--Loving. LC 72-104894. (Being Together Books). Orig. Title: Getting Ready for Marriage. (gr. 5-11). 1971. PLB 4.95g (ISBN 0-8225-0593-2). Lerner Pubns.

--Puberty & Adolescence. LC 70-104888. (Being Together Books). (Illus.). (gr. 5-11). 1971. PLB 4.95g (ISBN 0-8225-0591-6). Lerner Pubns.

--Sex Outside of Marriage. LC 76-104895. (Being Together Books). (gr. 5-11). 1971. PLB 4.95g (ISBN 0-8225-0599-1). Lerner Pubns.

Lipke, William C. & Grime, Philip N., eds. Vermont Landscape Images, Seventeen Seventy-Six to Nineteen Seventy-Six. (Illus.). 119p. (Orig.). 1976. pap. 12.50 (ISBN 0-87451-991-8). U Pr of New Eng.

Lipke, William C., jt. ed. see Kebabian, Paul B.

Lipkin. Psychosocial Factors Affecting Health. 396p. 1982. 37.95 (ISBN 0-03-061964-5). Praeger.

Lipkin, Gladys B., jt. auth. see Cohen, Roberta G.

Lipkin, Gladys B., jt. auth. see Hoffman, Claire P.

Lipkin, H. J. Beta Decay for Pedestrians. 1962. 15.00 (ISBN 0-444-10235-3, North-Holland). Elsevier.

Lipkin, Warren. The Appelations. (Illus.). 36p. 1983. pap. 4.00 o.p. (ISBN 0-9603950-6-7). Somrie Pr.

Lipking, Lawrence I., jt. ed. see Litz, Walton A., Jr.

Lipkowitz, Marcel. French Royal & Administrative Acts, Twelve Fifty-Six to Seventeen Ninety-Four: A Subject Guide to the New York Public Library Collection of Sixteen Thousand Pamphlets Now on Microfilm. LC 78-8497. 206p. 1978. 65.00 (ISBN 0-89235-011-3). Res Pubns Conn.

Lipman, Burton E. The Executive Job Search Program. LC 82-90123. (Illus.). 187p. (Orig.). 1982. 29.95x (ISBN 0-943064-00-7); pap. 19.95 (ISBN 0-943064-01-5). Bell Pub.

--How to Become a Vice President in Two Weeks (More or Less) (Illus.). 180p. 1983. pap. 24.95x (ISBN 0-943064-04-X). Bell Pub.

--How to Control & Reduce Inventory. rev. ed. LC 72-4485. (Illus.). 197p. 1983. pap. 36.50x (ISBN 0-943064-02-3). Bell Pub.

--Successful Cost Reduction & Control. rev. ed. 267p. 1983. pap. 39.50 (ISBN 0-943064-03-1). Bell Pub.

--Successful Cost Reduction & Control: The Probe Systematics Approach. 320p. 1978. 39.50 o.p. (ISBN 0-13-860460-6, Busn). P-H.

Lipman, David. Joe Namath: A Football Legend. (Putnam Sports Shelf). (Illus.). (gr. 5 up). 1968. PLB 5.29 o.p. (ISBN 0-399-60317-4). Putnam Pub Group.

Lipman, David & Lipnan, Marilyn. Jim Hart: Underrated Quaterback. new ed. (Putnam Sports Shelf). (Illus.). (gr. 6-8). 1977. PLB 5.29 o.p. (ISBN 0-399-61057-X). Putnam Pub Group.

Lipman, David & Wilks, Ed. Bob Gibson: Pitching Ace. LC 73-93755. (Putnam Sports Shelf). 192p. (gr. 5 up). 1974. PLB 6.29 o.p. (ISBN 0-399-60896-6). Putnam Pub Group.

--The Speed King: Bob Hayes of the Dallas Cowboys. (Putnam Sports Shelf). (gr. 5 up). 1971. PLB 6.29 o.p. (ISBN 0-399-60597-5). Putnam Pub Group.

Lipman, Ed. No Capital Crime. 1975. pap. 2.00x (ISBN 0-915016-04-4). Second Coming.

Lipman, Eugene, tr. see Lipman, Eugene J.

Lipman, Eugene J., compiled by. The Mishnah: Oral Teachings of Judaism. Lipman, Eugene, tr. LC 72-12621. 318p. 1974. pap. 7.95 (ISBN 0-8052-0441-5). Schocken.

Lipman, J. see Zariski, Oscar.

Lipman, Jean. American Folk Art in Wood, Metal & Stone. pap. 6.50 (ISBN 0-486-22816-9). Dover.

--American Primitive Painting. LC 79-184124. (Illus.). 158p. 1972. pap. 6.95 (ISBN 0-486-22815-0). Dover.

--Rufus Porter Rediscovered. LC 79-28517. 202p. (Orig.). 1980. pap. 10.00 (ISBN 0-517-54116-5, Pub. by Hudson River Mus). Pub Ctr Cult Res.

Lipman, Jean & Armstrong, Tom. American Folk Art Address Book. 144p. 1981. 14.95 (ISBN 0-517-54556-X, C N Potter Bks). Crown.

Lipman, Jean & Mevlendyke, Eve. American Folk Decoration. (Illus.). xii, 163p. 1972. pap. 6.50 (ISBN 0-486-22217-9). Dover.

Lipman, Matthew. Harry Stottlemeier's Discovery. rev. ed. 96p. (gr. 5-6). 1982. pap. 6.50 (ISBN 0-916834-06-9, TX516-633). Inst Adv Philo.

--Kio & Gus. LC 79-9315. (Philosophy for Children Ser.). 77p. (gr. k-4). 1982. pap. 6.50 (ISBN 0-916834-19-0). Inst Adv Philo.

Lipman, Matthew & Sharp, A. M. Looking for Meaning: Instructional Manual to Accompany Pixie. 390p. 1982. tchrs. ed. 30.00 (ISBN 0-916834-18-2). Inst Adv Philo.

Lipman, Matthew & Sharp, Ann M. Philosophy in the Classroom. 2nd ed. 248p. 1980. 29.95 (ISBN 0-87722-177-4); pap. 12.95 (ISBN 0-87722-183-9). Temple U Pr.

--Wondering at the World: Instructional Manual to Accompany KIO & GUS. (Philosophy for Children Ser.). 400p. 1983. 40.00 (ISBN 0-916834-20-4). Inst Adv Philo.

Lipman, Matthew & Sharp, Ann M., eds. Growing Up with Philosophy. LC 77-93451. 416p. 1978. 29.95 (ISBN 0-87722-118-9). Temple U Pr.

Lipman, Michael & Joyner, Russell. How to Write Clearly: Guidelines & Exercises for Clear Writing. 1983. pap. 1.60 (ISBN 0-686-84057-7). Intl Gen Semantics.

Lipman, Samuel. Music After Modernism. LC 78-73768. 1979. 12.95 o.s.i. (ISBN 0-465-04740-8). Basic.

Lipnack, Jessica & Stamps, Jeffrey. Networking: The First Report & Directory. LC 81-43292. 416p. 1982. 24.95 (ISBN 0-385-18121-3); pap. 15.95 (ISBN 0-385-17772-0, Dolphin). Doubleday.

Lipnan, Marilyn, jt. auth. see Lipman, David.

Lipner, Harry, jt. auth. see Frieden, Earl.

Lipovski, Gerald J. Microcomputer Interfacing: Principles & Practice. LC 79-9683. 448p. 1980. 26.95x (ISBN 0-669-03619-6). Lexington Bks.

Lipowski, Z. J., et al, eds. Psychosomatic Medicine: Current Trends & Clinical Applications. (Illus.). 1977. text ed. 29.50x (ISBN 0-19-502169-X). Oxford U Pr.

Lipp, Solomon. Leopoldo Zea: From Mexicanidad to a Philosophy of History. 146p. 1980. text ed. 10.50x (ISBN 0-88920-079-3, Pub. by Wilfrid Laurier U Pr Canada). Humanities.

Lipp, Solomon, tr. see Frondizi, Risieri.

Lippa, Erik A. Mathematics for Freshman in the Life Sciences. (Illus.). 319p. (Orig.). 1977. pap. text ed. 25.00 (ISBN 0-9607980-0-5). EA Lippa.

Lippard, Lucy R. Changing: Essays in Art Criticism. (Illus.). 1971. pap. 4.95 o.p. (ISBN 0-525-47243-6). Dutton.

--From the Center: Feminist Essays on Women's Art. 1976. pap. 9.50 (ISBN 0-525-47427-7, 0922-280). Dutton.

--Get the Message? Activist Essays on Art & Politics. (Illus.). 288p. 1983. pap. 10.95 (ISBN 0-525-48037-4, 01064-310). Dutton.

Lippard, Stephen J. Progress in Inorganic Chemistry, Vol. 30. (Progress in Inorganic Chemistry Ser.). 382p. 1983. 45.00 (ISBN 0-471-87022-6, Pub. by Wiley-Interscience). Wiley.

Lippard, Stephen J., ed. Progress in Inorganic Chemistry. (Progress in Inorganic Chemistry Ser.). Vol. 12, 1970. 38.50 o.p. (ISBN 0-471-54082-X); Vol. 15, 1972. 32.50 o.p. (ISBN 0-471-54085-4); Vol. 18, 1973. 45.50 o.p. (ISBN 0-471-54088-9); Vol. 20, 1976. o.p.; Vol. 21, 1976. o. p. 38.00 (ISBN 0-471-54091-9); Vol. 22, 1976. o. p. 43.50 (ISBN 0-471-54092-7); Vol. 23, 1977. o. p. 46.00 (ISBN 0-471-02186-5); Vol. 24, 1978. 49.50 (ISBN 0-471-03874-1); Vol. 25, 1979. 48.95x (ISBN 0-471-04943-3). Wiley.

--Progress in Inorganic Chemistry, Vols. 11, 14, 16. Vol. 11, 1970. 29.50 (ISBN 0-471-54081-1); Vol. 14, 1971. 36.00 (ISBN 0-471-54084-6); Vol. 16, 1972. 27.50 (ISBN 0-471-54086-2, Pub. by Wiley). Krieger.

--Progress in Inorganic Chemistry, Vol. 19. 376p. 1983. Repr. of 1975 ed. lib. bdg. write for info. (ISBN 0-89874-208-0). Krieger.

--Progress in Inorganic Chemistry, Vols. 26-28. Vol. 26. 54.95x (ISBN 0-471-04944-1); Vol. 27. 57.50 (ISBN 0-471-06000-3); Vol. 28. 49.50 (ISBN 0-471-08310-0). Wiley.

--Progress in Inorganic Chemistry, Vol. 29. LC 59-13035. (Progress in Inorganic Chemistry Ser.). 401p. 1982. 49.50 (ISBN 0-471-09370-X, Pub. by Wiley-Interscience). Wiley.

Lippe, Aschwin De see De Lippe, Aschwin.

Lippert, Frederick G., III & Farmer, James. Psychomotor Skills in Orthopaedic Surgery. (Illus.). 171p. Date not set. lib. bdg. price not set (ISBN 0-683-05051-6). Williams & Wilkins.

Lippett, Peter. Estate Planning after the Reagan Tax Cut. 1982. text ed. 15.95 (ISBN 0-8359-1779-7). Reston.

Lippincott, David. The Blood of October. 1977. pap. 1.95 o.p. (ISBN 0-451-06874-2, J7785, Sig). NAL.

--The Nursery. (Orig.). 1983. pap. 3.50 (ISBN 0-440-16474-5). Dell.

--Salt Mine. 1980. pap. 2.25 o.p. (ISBN 0-451-09158-2, E9158, Sig). NAL.

--Savage Ransom. 1979. pap. 2.25 o.p. (ISBN 0-451-08749-6, E8749, Sig). NAL.

Lippincott, Joseph W. Striped Coat, the Skunk. rev. ed. (Illus.). (gr. 4-6). 1954. 8.95i (ISBN 0-397-30283-5, JBL-J). Har-Row.

Lippincott, Sarah L., jt. auth. see Joseph, Joseph M.

Lippincott, W. T. Chemistry, A Study of Matter. 3rd ed. 1977. 30.95x (ISBN 0-471-29246-X); study guide 9.50 (ISBN 0-471-02221-7); tchrs. manual 5.00 (ISBN 0-471-02689-1). Wiley.

Lippis, John. The Challenge to Be Pro Life. 2nd, rev. ed. (Illus.). 28p. (gr. 8-12). 1982. pap. write for info. (ISBN 0-9609902-0-8). Santa Barb Pro.

Lippit, Noriko & Selden, Kyoko, eds. Stories by Contemporary Japanese Women Writers. 400p. 1982. 25.00 (ISBN 0-87332-193-6); pap. 12.95 (ISBN 0-87332-223-1). M E Sharpe.

Lippit, Victor D. Land Reform & Economic Development in China: A Study of Institutional Change & Development Finance. LC 74-15391. 172p. 1975. 25.00 (ISBN 0-87332-064-6). M E Sharpe.

Lippitt, Gordon & Lippitt, Ronald. The Consulting Process in Action. LC 77-15681. 130p. 1978. pap. 15.00 (ISBN 0-88390-141-2). Univ Assocs.

Lippitt, Gordon L. Visualizing Change: Model Building & the Change Process. LC 73-81361. (Illus.). 370p. 1973. pap. 14.50 o.p. (ISBN 0-88390-125-0). Univ Assocs.

Lippitt, Gordon L., jt. auth. see Ford, George A.

Lippitt, Peggy, et al. Cross-Age Helping Package. rev. ed. LC 78-164709. 244p. 1972. pap. 8.00x (ISBN 0-87944-108-9). Inst Soc Res.

Lippitt, Ronald, jt. auth. see Lippitt, Gordon.

Lippitt, Ronald, jt. auth. see Schindler-Rainman, Eva.

Lippitt, Vernon G. The National Economic Environment. (Illus.). 576p. 1975. text ed. 26.95 (ISBN 0-07-037972-6, C); instructors' manual 3.50 (ISBN 0-07-037973-4). McGraw.

Lippman, Edward A. Musical Thought in Ancient Greece. LC 74-23415. (Music Reprint Ser.). 1975. Repr. of 1964 ed. lib. bdg. 25.00 (ISBN 0-306-70669-5). Da Capo.

Lippman, Leopold & Goldberg, I. Ignacy. Right to Education: Anatomy of the Pennsylvania Case & Its Implications for Exceptional Children. LC 73-78038. 1973. text ed. 10.95x (ISBN 0-8077-2401-7); pap. text ed. 6.50x o.p. (ISBN 0-8077-2406-8). Tchrs Coll.

Lippman, Peter. Mix or Match Mysteries: Carstairs Cat Solves Millions of Cases! LC 82-61988. (Illus.). 9p. (ps-3). 1983. spiral plastic 3.50 (ISBN 0-394-85809-3). Random.

Lippman, S. A. & McCall, J. J., eds. Studies of the Economics of Search. (Contributions to Economic Analysis Ser.: Vol. 123). 1979. 40.50 (ISBN 0-444-85222-0, North Holland). Elsevier.

Lippman, Thomas W. Understanding Islam: An Introduction to the Moslem World. LC 81-85142. 196p. 1982. pap. 2.95 (ISBN 0-451-62079-8, ME2079, Ment). NAL.

Lippman, Walter. U.S. War Aims. LC 76-16079. 235p. 1976. Repr. of 1944 ed. lib. bdg. 29.50 (ISBN 0-306-70773-X). Da Capo.

Lippmann, Margrit. Cat Training. rev. ed. 1975. pap. 4.95 (ISBN 0-87666-778-7, HS1200). TFH Pubns.

Lippmann, Morton & Schlesinger, Richard B. Chemical Contamination in the Human Environment. (Illus.). 1979. text ed. 30.00x (ISBN 0-19-502441-9); pap. text ed. 16.95x (ISBN 0-19-502442-7). Oxford U Pr.

Lippmann, Morton, jt. ed. see Kneip, T. J.

Lippmann, Walter. Drift & Mastery: An Attempt to Diagnose the Current Unrest. LC 77-13882. 1978. Repr. of 1961 ed. lib. bdg. 20.50x (ISBN 0-313-20004-1, LIDM). Greenwood.

--An Inquiry into the Principles of the Good Society. LC 72-7871. 402p. 1973. Repr. of 1943 ed. lib. bdg. 29.75x (ISBN 0-8371-6522-9, LIGS). Greenwood.

--Public Philosophy. pap. 1.50 o.p. (ISBN 0-451-61866-1, MW1866, Ment). NAL.

Lipps, Jere H., jt. auth. see Cowen, Richard.

Lippson, Alice J. The Chesapeake Bay in Maryland. (Illus.). 1974. pap. 5.95 (ISBN 0-686-36758-8). Md Hist.

Lipscher, Betty S., ed. Forensic Services Directory, 1982-1983: The National Register of Forensic Experts,Litigation Consultants & Legal Support Specialists. 3rd ed. 1982. 69.50 (ISBN 0-9602962-1-2). Natl Forensic.

Lipschutz, Martin. Differential Geometry. (Schaum's Outline Ser). 1969. pap. 6.95 (ISBN 0-07-037985-8, SP). McGraw.

Lipschutz, Martin & Lipschutz, Seymour. Schaum's Outline of Data Processing. (Schaum's Outline Ser.). (Illus.). 224p. (Orig.). 1981. pap. 6.95 (ISBN 0-07-037983-1, SP). McGraw.

Lipschutz, Ronnie. Radioactive Waste: Politics, Technology & Risk. LC 79-19649. 272p. 1980. prof ref 22.50x (ISBN 0-88410-621-7). Ballinger Pub.

Lipschutz, Seymour. Finite Mathematics. 1966. pap. 6.95 (ISBN 0-07-037987-4, SP). McGraw.

--General Topology. (Orig.). 1965. pap. 7.95 (ISBN 0-07-037988-2, SP). McGraw.

--Linear Algebra. (Schaum's Outline Ser). (Orig.). 1968. pap. 6.95 (ISBN 0-07-037989-0, SP). McGraw.

--Outline of Discrete Mathematics. (Schaum's Outline Ser.). (Illus.). 1976. pap. 6.95 (ISBN 0-07-037981-5, SP). McGraw.

--Probability. (Schaum's Outline Ser). 1968. pap. 5.95 (ISBN 0-07-037982-3, SP). McGraw.

--Set Theory & Related Topics. (Orig.). 1964. pap. 5.95 (ISBN 0-07-037986-6, SP). McGraw.

Lipschutz, Seymour & Poe, Arthur. Schaum's Outline of Programming with FORTRAN IV. (Schaum's Outline Ser.). 1978. pap. 7.95 (ISBN 0-07-037984-X, SP). McGraw.

Lipschutz, Seymour, jt. auth. see Lipschutz, Martin.

Lipscomb, David see Gospel Advocate.

Lipscomb, David M., ed. Noise & Audiology. (Perspectives in Audiology). 488p. 1978. text ed. 29.95 (ISBN 0-8391-1203-3). Univ Park.

Lipscomb, H. A. & Libey, Donald R., eds. On Gold. LC 82-61848. 464p. (Orig.). 1982. pap. 24.00 (ISBN 0-938912-00-3). Waterleaf Pr.

Lipscomb, J. F. Those Days Before Yesterday. 1978. 5.95 o.p. (ISBN 0-533-03435-3). Vantage.

Lipscomb, Susan D. & Zuanich, Margaret A. BASIC Fun: Computer Games, Puzzles & Problems Children Can Write. 128p. (gr. k-7). 1982. 2.25 (ISBN 0-380-80606-1, 80606, Camelot). Avon.

Lipset, Seymour L. & Schneider, William. The Confidence Gap: Business, Labor & Government in the Public Mind. (Illus.). 496p. 1983. text ed. 29.95 (ISBN 0-02-919230-7). Free Pr.

Lipset, Seymour M. & Raab, Earl. The Politics of Unreason: Right-Wing Extremism in America, 1790-1970. (Patterns of American Prejudice Ser.). 420p. 12.50 (ISBN 0-686-95046-1); pap. 7.95 (ISBN 0-686-99454-X). ADL.

Lipset, Seymour M. & Rokkan, S. Party Systems & Voter Alignments. LC 67-25332. 1967. 17.95 (ISBN 0-02-919150-5). Free Pr.

Lipset, Seymour M., jt. auth. see Horowitz, Irving L.

Lipset, Seymour M., ed. Party Coalitions in the Nineteen Eighties. LC 81-83095. 480p. (Orig.). 1981. text ed. 19.95 (ISBN 0-917616-45-6); pap. text ed. 8.95 (ISBN 0-917616-43-X). ICS Pr.

--The Third Century: America As a Post-Industrial Society. LC 78-70400. (Publications Ser.: No. 203). 468p. 1979. 16.95 o.p. (ISBN 0-8179-7031-2). Hoover Inst Pr.

Lipset, Seymour M., jt. ed. see Hofstadter, Richard.

Lipset, Seymour M., et al. Emerging Coalitions in American Politics. Lipset, Seymour M., ed. LC 78-53414. 1978. pap. 6.95 o.p. (ISBN 0-917616-22-7). ICS Pr.

Lipsett, Suzanne, jt. auth. see Ogden, Paul W.

Lipsey, Richard G., et al. Economics. 4th ed. 992p. 1982. text ed. 28.50 scp (ISBN 0-06-044075-9, HarpC); scp study guide 12.50 (ISBN 0-06-044053-8); instr' manual avail. (ISBN 0-06-364014-7); test bank avail. (ISBN 0-06-364013-9). Har-Row.

Lipsey, Robert, jt. auth. see Cagan, Phillip.

Lipsey, Sally I. Mathematics for Nursing Science: A Programmed Text. 2nd ed. LC 76-44843. 1977. text ed. 12.00x (ISBN 0-471-01798-1, Pub. by Wiley-Medical). Wiley.

Lipsitt, L. P. & Spiker, C. C., eds. Advances in Child Development, Vol. 17. 318p. 1982. 32.00 (ISBN 0-12-009717-6); lib ed. 42.00 (ISBN 0-12-009788-5); microfiche 22.50 (ISBN 0-12-009789-3). Acad Pr.

Lipsitt, Lewis P. Child Development. 1979. pap. text ed. 9.95x (ISBN 0-673-05009-2). Scott F.

Lipsitt, Lewis P., ed. Advances in Infancy Research, Vol. 1. Rovee-Collier, Carolyn E. 300p. 1981. 32.50x (ISBN 0-89391-045-7). Ablex Pub.

--Advances in Infancy Research, Vol. 2. Rovee-Collier, Carolyn. (Advances in Infancy Research Ser.). 1983. 32.50x (ISBN 0-89391-113-5). Ablex Pub.

--Developmental Psychobiology: The Significance of Infancy. LC 76-14775. 160p. 1976. text ed. 14.95 (ISBN 0-89859-134-1). L Erlbaum Assocs.

Lipsitt, Lewis P. & Field, Tiffany M., eds. Perinatal Risk & Newborn Behavior. 208p. 1982. text ed. 19.95x (ISBN 0-89391-123-2). Ablex Pub.

Lipsitt, Lewis P., ed. see Moerk, Ernst L.

Lipsitt, Lewis P., ed. see Plooij, Frans X.

Lipsitt, Lewis P. see Reese, Hayne.

Lipsitt, Lewis P see Reese, Hayne.

Lipsitt, Lewis P., jt. ed. see Reese, Hayne W.

Lipsitz, Joan. Growing up Forgotten: A Review of Research & Programs Concerning Early Adolescence. LC 76-28621. 288p. 1976. 21.95x (ISBN 0-669-00975-X). Lexington Bks.

Lipske, Michael & Center for Science in the Public Interest Staff. Chemical Additives in Booze. Jacobson, Michael, ed. 133p. (Orig.). 1983. pap. 4.95 (ISBN 0-89329-098-X). Ctr Sci Public.

Lipsky, David B., jt. ed. see Siegel, Abraham J.

Lipsky, Louis. Tales of the Yiddish Rialto: Reminiscences of Playwrights & Players in New York's Jewish Theatre in the Early 1900's. LC 77-7895. 1977. Repr. of 1962 ed. lib. bdg. 19.25x (ISBN 0-8371-9681-7, LITY). Greenwood.

Lipsky, Michael. Street-Level Bureaucracy: Dilemmas of the Individual in Public Services. LC 79-7350. 244p. 1980. 10.95x (ISBN 0-87154-524-1). Russell Sage.

Lipsky, Michael, ed. Law & Order: Police Encounters. LC 72-91468. 144p. 1970. pap. text ed. 3.95 (ISBN 0-87855-563-3). Transaction Bks.

Lipsky, Richard. How We Play the Game: Why Sports Dominate American Life. LC 80-66074. (Illus.). 256p. 1980. 12.98 (ISBN 0-8070-3224-7). Beacon Pr.

Lipsman, Samuel L., jt. auth. see Doyle, Edward G.

Lipson, Alexander. A Russian Course, Pt. 3. (Illus.). iv, 105p. (Orig.). 1981. pap. text ed. 8.95 (ISBN 0-89357-082-6); tchr's. manual pap. 9.95 (ISBN 0-89357-083-4). Slavica.

Lipson, Charles & Sheth, N. J. Statistical Design & Analysis of Engineering Experiments. (Illus.). 544p. 1972. text ed. 35.50 (ISBN 0-07-037991-2, C). McGraw.

Lipson, Greta & Bolkosky, Sidney. Mighty Myth. (gr. 5-12). 1982. 9.95 (ISBN 0-86653-064-9, GA 419). Good Apple.

Lipson, Greta & Greenberg, Bernice. Extra! Extra! Read All About It. (gr. 4-8). 1981. 9.95 (ISBN 0-86653-006-1, GA 234). Good Apple.

Lipson, Greta & Romantowski, Jane. Calliope. (gr. 4-8). 1981. 9.95 (ISBN 0-86653-025-8, GA230). Good Apple.

Lipson, H., jt. auth. see Lipson, S. G.

Lipson, Harry A. & Darling, John R. Marketing Fundamentals: Text & Cases. LC 80-12441. 590p. 1980. Repr. of 1974 ed. lib. bdg. 24.50 (ISBN 0-89874-166-1). Krieger.

Lipson, Leslie. American Governor from Figurehead to Leader. (Illus.). 1969. Repr. of 1939 ed. lib. bdg. 15.75x (ISBN 0-8371-0540-4, LIAG). Greenwood.

--The Great Issues of Politics. 6th ed. (Illus.). 448p. 1981. text ed. 21.95 (ISBN 0-13-363903-7). P-H.

Lipson, S. G. & Lipson, H. Optical Physics. 2nd ed. LC 79-8963. (Illus.). 496p. 1981. 57.50 (ISBN 0-521-22630-9); pap. 23.95 (ISBN 0-521-29584-X). Cambridge U Pr.

Lipson, Shelley. It's Basic: The ABC's of Computer Programming. LC 81-20027. (Illus.). 48p. (gr. 2-6). 1982. 8.70 (ISBN 0-03-061592-5). HR&W.

Lipson, Stephen H. & Hensel, Mary D. Hospital Manpower Budget Preparation Manual. 200p. 1975. 12.00 (ISBN 0-686-68583-0, 14917). Healthcare Fin Man Assn.

Lipsyte, Marjorie. Hot Type. LC 79-8502. 1980. 9.95 o.p. (ISBN 0-385-15798-3). Doubleday.

Lipsyte, Robert. The Contender. LC 67-19623. 1967. PLB 10.89 (ISBN 0-06-023920-4, HarpJ). Har Row.

--One Fat Summer. LC 76-49746. (gr. 7 up). 1977. 8.95 o.p. (ISBN 0-06-023895-X, HarpJ); PLB 8.79 o.p. (ISBN 0-06-023896-8). Har-Row.

Liptak, Bela G., ed. Instrument Engineer's Handbook: Process Measurement. 2nd rev. ed. LC 81-70914. 1600p. 1982. 65.00 (ISBN 0-8019-6971-9). Chilton.

Liptak, David Q. Biblical Lenten Homilies for Preaching & Meditation. 9.95 (ISBN 0-941850-05-6). Sunday Pubn.

--Questions about Faith, Bk. IV. pap. 3.95 (ISBN 0-941850-09-9). Sunday Pubn.

Liptay, G. Atlas of Thermoanalytical Curves, 5 Vols. Incl. Vol. 1. 50p. 1971. 59.95 (ISBN 0-471-87718-2); Vol. 2. 75p. 1973. 59.95 (ISBN 0-471-87719-0); Vol. 4. 75p. 1975. 59.95 (ISBN 0-471-87720-4). 1976. Set 380.00 (ISBN 0-471-25853-9, Pub. by Wiley Heyden). Wiley.

Liptay, G., ed. Atlas of Thermoanalytical Curves, 5 vols. Set. 380.00 (ISBN 0-471-25853-9, Wiley Heyden). Wiley.

Liptay, Lynne, jt. auth. see Mueser, Anne.

Lipton, Barbara. Survival: Life & Art of the Alaskan Eskimo. LC 76-53613. 1977. 7.95 (ISBN 0-932828-04-3). Newark Mus.

Lipton, Gladys. French Bilingual Dictionary: A Beginner's Guide in Words & Pictures. rev. ed. LC 72-84411. (gr. 4-12). 1984. pap. text ed. 4.50 (ISBN 0-8120-2330-7). Barron.

--French Bilingual Dictionary: Compact Ed. rev. ed. LC 78-20788. (Illus.). (gr. 7-12). 1979. pap. 3.25 (ISBN 0-8120-2007-3). Barron.

Lipton, Gladys & Munoz, Olivia. Spanish Bilingual Dictionary: Compact Guide. rev. ed. LC 78-27770. (Illus.). (gr. 7-12). 1979. pap. 3.95 (ISBN 0-8120-2540-7). Barron.

Lipton, James M., ed. Fever. 275p. 1980. text ed. 38.00 (ISBN 0-89004-451-1). Raven.

Lipton, June, jt. auth. see O'Donnell, Asta.

Lipton, Martin, jt. ed. see Fleischer, Arthur, Jr.

Lipton, Robert J. The Life of the Self. 1976. pap. 4.95 o.p. (ISBN 0-671-22425-5, Touchstone Bks). S&S.

Liroff, Richard A. Protecting Open Space: Land Use Control in the Adirondack Park. (Environmental Law Institute Book). 320p. 1981. prof ref 32.50x (ISBN 0-88410-643-8). Ballinger Pub.

Lisann, Maury. Broadcasting to the Soviet Union: International Politics & Radio. LC 74-14046. (Illus.). 224p. 1975. 27.95 o.p. (ISBN 0-275-05590-6). Praeger.

Lisch, W. Hereditary Vitreoretinal Degeneration. (Developments in Opthalmology Ser.: Vol. 8). (Illus.). 100p. 1983. 36.00 (ISBN 3-8055-3615-1). S Karger.

Lisciandro, Frank. Jim Morrison: An Hour for Magic. LC 81-71007. (Illus.). 60p. 1982. pap. 9.95 (ISBN 0-933328-22-2). Delilah Bks.

Liscom, W., ed. The Energy Decade: 1970-1980. (World Energy Industry Information Services Ser.). (Illus.). 1982. 125.00 (ISBN 0-686-83190-X). Busn Info.

Lish, Gordon. Dear Mr. Capote. LC 82-15543. 264p. 1983. 15.95 (ISBN 0-03-061477-5). HR&W.

Lish, Kenneth C. Nuclear Power Plant Systems & Equipment. new ed. LC 77-185989. (Illus.). 160p. 1972. 24.50 o.p. (ISBN 0-8311-1078-3). Indus Pr.

Lisi, Patrick J. My Time in Hell. LC 76-9013. 1977. 9.95 o.p. (ISBN 0-87949-070-5). Ashley Bks.

Lisieski, W., jt. auth. see Scherf, W.

Lisitsyn, G. M. & Cafferty, B. First Book of Chess Strategy. 1978. pap. 9.95 o.p. (ISBN 0-7134-1423-5, Pub. by Batsford England). David & Charles.

--The Strategy of Chess. (Clubplayers Library). (Illus.). 160p. (Orig.). 1980. pap. 13.95 o.p. (ISBN 0-7134-3330-2, Pub. by Batsford England). David & Charles.

Lisitzin, E. Sea Level Changes. (Oceanography Ser.: Vol. 8). 1974. 59.75 (ISBN 0-444-41157-7). Elsevier.

Liska, Ken. Drugs & the Human Body. 1981. pap. text ed. 12.95x (ISBN 0-02-370960-X). Macmillan.

Liske, C., et al. Comparative Public Policy: Issues, Theories & Methods. LC 73-91354. (Comparative Political Economies & Public Policy Ser.). 1975. 20.00x o.p. (ISBN 0-470-54116-4). Halsted Pr.

Liske, C. T., jt. ed. see Raichur, S.

Lisker, Sonia O. I Am. (Illus.). (gr. 6-9). 1974. PLB 4.95 o.p. (ISBN 0-8038-3387-3). Hastings.

Lisker, Tom. First to the Top of the World: Admiral Peary at the North Pole. LC 78-14924. (Famous Firsts Ser.). (Illus.). 1978. PLB 10.76 (ISBN 0-89547-047-0). Silver.

--Mysterious Castle Builders. LC 78-21886. (Unsolved Mysteries of the World Ser.). PLB 11.96 (ISBN 0-89547-074-8). Silver.

--The Mystery of Robin Hood. LC 79-18396. (Unsolved Mysteries of the World Ser.). PLB 11.96 (ISBN 0-89547-079-9). Silver.

Liskov, B. CLU Reference Manual. (Lecture Notes in Computer Science Ser.: Vol. 114). 190p. 1981. pap. 9.00 (ISBN 0-387-10836-X). Springer-Verlag.

Lisowski, Gabriel. Roncalli's Magnificent Circus. LC 79-8430. (Illus.). 32p. (gr. 2). 1980. 9.95a o.p. (ISBN 0-385-14856-9); PLB 9.95a (ISBN 0-385-14857-7). Doubleday.

Liss, Bonnie. Cruising at Thirty-Thousand Feet. 192p. 1983. 12.50 (ISBN 0-02-572980-2). Macmillan.

Liss, Douglas, jt. auth. see Aderton, Mimi.

Liss, Howard. Bobby Orr: Lightning on Ice. LC 75-2423. (Sports Ser.). (Illus.). 96p. (gr. 3-6). 1975. PLB 7.12 (ISBN 0-8116-6672-7). Garrard.

--The Boston Red Sox. 1982. 13.50 (ISBN 0-671-42058-5). S&S.

--Fishing Talk for Beginners. LC 77-25258. (Illus.). 96p. (gr. 3 up). 1978. PLB 8.79 o.p. (ISBN 0-671-32882-4). Messner.

--Football Talk. (Illus.). (gr. 4-6). 1973. pap. 1.75 (ISBN 0-671-43472-1). Archway.

--Football Talk for Beginners. LC 76-102184. (Illus.). 96p. (gr. 4 up). 1970. PLB 7.29 o.p. (ISBN 0-671-32241-9). Messner.

--Friction. (Science Is What & Why Ser). (gr. k-4). 1968. PLB 4.49 o.p. (ISBN 0-698-30095-5, Coward). Putnam Pub Group.

--The Giant Book of More Strange but True Sports Stories. LC 82-13236. (Illus.). 160p. (gr. 5-10). 1983. PLB 5.99 (ISBN 0-394-95633-8); pap. 4.95 (ISBN 0-394-85633-3). Random.

--The Giant Book of Strange but True Sports Stories. LC 76-8132. (Illus.). (gr. 5-9). 1976. 4.95 (ISBN 0-394-83287-6, BYR); PLB 6.99 (ISBN 0-394-93287-0). Random.

--The Great Game of Soccer. LC 78-9842. (Illus.). (gr. 5 up). 1979. 8.95 o.p. (ISBN 0-399-20644-2). Putnam Pub Group.

--Heat. (Science Is What & Why Ser). (Illus.). (gr. k-4). 1965. PLB 4.49 o.p. (ISBN 0-698-30186-2, Coward). Putnam Pub Group.

--Strange but True Basketball Stories. LC 82-13138. (Random House Sports Library). (Illus.). 144p. (gr. 5-10). 1983. pap. 1.95 (ISBN 0-394-85631-7). Random.

--Strange but True Hockey Stories. (Illus.). (gr. 5 up). 1972. 2.95 o.p. (ISBN 0-394-82463-6, BYR); PLB 4.39 (ISBN 0-394-92463-0). Random.

--A Treasury of Golf Humor. (Illus.). 256p. 1983. 12.95 (ISBN 0-87396-090-4). Stravon.

Liss, P., et al. Environmental Chemistry. LC 80-12132. (Resource & Environmental Science Ser.). 184p. 1980. pap. text ed. 16.95x o.p. (ISBN 0-470-26968-5). Halsted Pr.

Lissagaray, P. O. History of the Commune of 1871. Aveling, Eleanor M., tr. LC 82-73427. 500p. Repr. of 1898 ed. lib. bdg. 37.50x (ISBN 0-88116-007-5). Brenner Bks.

Lissant. Demulsification. (Surfactant Science Ser.). 176p. 1983. 37.50 (ISBN 0-8247-1802-X). Dekker.

Lissfelt, J. Fred. Kaffeeklatsch. (Orig.). 1955. pap. 2.50 o.p. (ISBN 0-910286-23-X). Boxwood.

Lissim, Simon, et al. Dreams in the Theatre: Designs of Simon Lissim. LC 75-31917. (Illus.). 40p. (Orig.). 1975. pap. 6.00 o.p. (ISBN 0-87104-261-4). NY Pub Lib.

Lissitzyn, Oliver J. International Air Transport & National Policy. (Airlines History Project Ser.). Date not set. write for info. (ISBN 0-404-19327-7). AMS Pr.

Lisska. Philosophy Matters. 1977. 14.95 (ISBN 0-675-08592-6). Merrill.

Lissner, H. R., jt. auth. see Perry, C. C.

List, George. Music & Poetry in a Colombian Village: A Tri-Cultural Heritage. LC 82-48534. (Illus.). 640p. 1983. 35.00x (ISBN 0-253-33951-0). Ind U Pr.

List, H., jt. auth. see Schmidt, Alois X.

List, Ilka. Grandma's Beach Surprise. new ed. (Illus.). 48p. (gr. k-3). 1975. PLB 5.29 o.p. (ISBN 0-399-60958-X). Putnam Pub Group.

List, L. K., jt. auth. see Lerner, J. W.

List, Lynne K. Music Art & Drama Activities for the Elementary Classroom. LC 81-14575. (Orig.). 1982. pap. text ed. 16.50x (ISBN 0-8077-2696-6). Tchrs Coll.

List, Robert N. Dedalus in Harlem: The Joyce-Ellison Connection. LC 81-43837. 330p. (Orig.). 1982. lib. bdg. 24.00 (ISBN 0-8191-2630-6); pap. text ed. 12.75 (ISBN 0-8191-2631-4). U Pr of Amer.

Liste, Peter C., jt. auth. see Clarke, Ronald O.

Lister, Eugene C. Electric Circuits & Machines. 5th ed. (Illus.). 448p. 1975. text ed. 24.95 (ISBN 0-07-038026-0, G); answers to even-numbered problems 1.50 (ISBN 0-07-038027-9). McGraw.

--Electrical Circuits & Machines. 4th ed. LC 68-13519. 1968. text ed. 23.05 o.p. (ISBN 0-07-038024-4, G). McGraw.

Lister, Florence C., jt. auth. see Lister, Robert H.

Lister, Louis & Lister, Rebecca. The Religious School Board: A Manual. 1978. pap. 5.00 o.p. (ISBN 0-8074-0014-9, 243870). UAHC.

Lister, Priscilla, jt. ed. see Ferguson, Larry.

Lister, Rebecca, jt. auth. see Lister, Louis.

Lister, Robert H. & Lister, Florence C. Those Who Came Before: Southwestern Archeology in the National Park System. Houk, Rose & Priehs, T. J., eds. 1983. pap. price not set (ISBN 0-911408-62-2). SW Pks Mnmts.

Lister-Kaye, Charles. Welsh Corgi. 4th ed. LC 62-16144. 1970. 8.95 o.p. (ISBN 0-668-00944-6). Arco.

Listerman, Mary S. Angel Maria De Lera. (Twayne's World Authors Ser.). 1982. lib. bdg. 17.95 (ISBN 0-8057-6495-X, Twayne). G K Hall.

Listokin, David. Historic Preservation & the Property Tax. (Center for Urban Policy Research Bk.). 166p. 1982. pap. 20.00 (ISBN 0-88285-077-6). Transaction Bks.

Listokin, David & Casey, Stephen. Mortgage Lending & Race: Conceptual & Analytical Perspectives of the Urban Financing Problem. LC 79-12209. 1980. text ed. 20.00 (ISBN 0-88285-060-1). Ctr Urban Pol Res.

Liston, Mary D., jt. ed. see Stapp, William B.

Liston, R. A., jt. auth. see Crosby, R. M.

Liston, Robert. We the People: Congressional Power. 160p. (gr. 9-12). 1975. PLB 7.95 (ISBN 0-07-038067-8, GB). McGraw.

Liston, Robert A. By These Faiths: Religions for Today. LC 77-23324. 192p. (gr. 7 up). 1977. PLB 7.79 o.p. (ISBN 0-671-32836-0). Messner.

--The Great Teams-Why They Win All the Time. LC 78-20081. (Illus.). 1979. 8.95a o.p. (ISBN 0-385-03590-X); PLB 8.95a (ISBN 0-385-03620-5). Doubleday.

--Promise or Peril? The Role of Technology in Society. LC 76-148. 144p. (gr. 7 up). 1976. 7.95 o.p. (ISBN 0-525-66478-5). Lodestar Bks.

Listro, John P. Accounting for Nonprofit Organizations. 112p. 1983. pap. text ed. 9.95 (ISBN 0-8403-2912-1). Kendall-Hunt.

Litchblau, Myron, tr. see Mallea, Eduardo.

Litchfield, Carolyn, jt. auth. see Vorndran, Barbara S.

Litchfield, Jack. The Canadian Jazz Discography. 945p. 1982. 75.00x (ISBN 0-8020-2448-3). U of Toronto Pr.

Litchfield, Michael W. Renovation: A Complete Guide. LC 82-7100. 571p. 1983. text ed. 29.95 (ISBN 0-471-04903-4). Wiley.

Litchfield, Thorndike, jt. auth. see Ward, Sol A.

Literary Services Agency, Inc., ed. see Lopez, Jesus.

Litfin, Duane & Robinson, Haddon, eds. Recent Homiletical Thought: A Bibliography, 1966-1979. LC 82-72135. 296p. 1982. 11.95 (ISBN 0-8010-5613-6). Baker Bk.

Litherland, Janet. Clown Ministry Handbook. Meyer, Sheila & Zapel, Arthur L., eds. LC 82-61091. (Illus.). 80p. (Orig.). 1982. pap. text ed. 6.95 (ISBN 0-916260-20-8). Meriwether Pub.

Lithgow, Daphne, jt. auth. see Lithgow, David.

Lithgow, David & Lithgow, Daphne. Muyuw Dictionary. 1974. pap. 2.50x o. p. (ISBN 0-7263-0205-8); microfiche 2.25 (ISBN 0-88312-332-0). Summer Inst Ling.

Litka, Michael P. Business Law. 2nd ed. Sutton, L., ed. LC 76-2999. (Law Ser.). 1977. text ed. 29.50x (ISBN 0-471-87011-0); study 11.95x (ISBN 0-471-87013-7); tchrs.' manual 13.00x (ISBN 0-471-87012-9). Wiley.

Litka, Michael P. & Inman, James E. Legal Environment of Business: Public & Private Laws. 3rd ed. 1983. text ed. 25.95 (ISBN 0-471-87455-8); study guide 11.95 (ISBN 0-471-89869-4). Wiley.

--Legal Environment of Business: Text Cases & Readings. 2nd ed. Sutton, L., ed. LC 79-16507. (Grid Ser. in Law). 544p. 1980. text ed. 29.95x (ISBN 0-471-87008-0); tchr's manual avail.; student study guide 8.95 (ISBN 0-471-87010-2). Wiley.

Litle, William A. Reliability of Shell Buckling Predictions. (Press Research Monographs: No. 25). 1964. 22.50x (ISBN 0-262-12013-5). MIT Pr.

Litoff, Carol, jt. auth. see Roman-Lopez, Carmen.

Litoff, Judy B. American Midwives: 1860 to the Present. LC 77-83893. (Contributions in Medical History: No. 1). 1978. lib. bdg. 25.00 (ISBN 0-8371-9824-0, LAM/). Greenwood.

Litowinsky, Olga & Willoughby, Bebe. The Dream Book. LC 77-22922. (Illus.). (gr. 6-8). 1978. 8.95 (ISBN 0-698-20427-1, Coward). Putnam Pub Group.

Litsky, Frank. The Complete Book of Boxing. LC 79-6836. 1981. 14.95 o.p. (ISBN 0-672-52641-7). Bobbs.

--The Complete Book of Indoor Sports. LC 79-9634. 1981. 14.95 o.p. (ISBN 0-672-52646-8). Bobbs.

--The Complete Book of Outdoor Sports. LC 79-6848. 1981. 14.95 o.p. (ISBN 0-672-52645-X). Bobbs.

--The Winter Olympics. (First Bks.). (Illus.). (gr. 4 up). 1979. PLB 8.90 s&l (ISBN 0-531-02946-8). Watts.

Litsky, Warren, jt. auth. see Miller, Brimtom M.

Litt, D., jt. auth. see Harris, Errol E.

Litt, Edgar. Political Cultures of Massachusetts. 1965. 20.00x (ISBN 0-262-12021-6). MIT Pr.

Litt, Edgar & Parkinson, Michael. U. S. & U. K. Education Policy: A Decade of Reform. LC 78-19759. (Praeger Special Studies). 1979. 26.95 o.p. (ISBN 0-03-046706-3). Praeger.

Littauer, Florence. After Every Wedding Comes a Marriage. LC 81-80023. 208p. (Orig.). 1981. pap. 4.95 (ISBN 0-89081-289-6); write for info. wkbk. (ISBN 0-89081-294-2); write for info. cassette pack (ISBN 0-89081-361-2). Harvest Hse.

--Christian Leader's & Speaker's Seminar. 100p. 1983. lab manual 69.95 (ISBN 0-89081-369-8). Harvest Hse.

--Personality Plus. (Illus.). 192p. 1982. pap. 9.95 o.p. (ISBN 0-8007-1323-0). Revell.

--Personality Plus. (Illus.). 192p. 1982. 9.95 o.p. (ISBN 0-8007-1323-0). Messner.

Littauer, Florence, jt. auth. see Littauer, Marita.

Littauer, Marita & Littauer, Florence. Shades of Beauty. LC 82-81086. 184p. (Orig.). 1982. pap. 9.95 (ISBN 0-89081-315-9, 3159). Harvest Hse.

Littauer, U. Z., jt. auth. see Weizman Institute of Science, Rehovot, Israel, Feb. 1980.

Littauer, Vladimir S. Schooling Your Horse. (Illus.). 196p. 1982. pap. 6.95 (ISBN 0-668-05556-1, 5556). Arco.

Littell, Franklin H. A Pilgrim's Interfaith Guide to the Holy Land. (Illus.). 84p. 1982. 7.95 (ISBN 0-686-43011-5, Carta Maps & Guides Pub Isreal). Hippocrene Bks.

Littell, Franklin H., jt. auth. see Shur, Irene G.

Littell, Norman M. Trails of the Sea. 1983. 12.95 (ISBN 0-533-05304-8). Vantage.

Littell, Robert. The Debriefing. LC 78-22442. 1979. 10.53i (ISBN 0-06-012656-6, HarpT). Har-Row.

Litterer, J. Organizations: Structure & Behavior. 3rd ed. LC 80-15645. (Wiley Series in Management). 625p. 1980. pap. 21.95x (ISBN 0-471-07786-0). Wiley.

Litterer, Joseph A. The Analysis of Organizations. 2nd ed. LC 72-8586. (Management & Administration Ser.). (Illus.). 640p. 1973. text ed. 33.95 (ISBN 0-471-54106-0). Wiley.

--An Introduction to Management. LC 77-23820. (Ser. in Management & Administration). 1978. text ed. 24.95 o.s.i. (ISBN 0-471-54100-1). Wiley.

Little & Carnevali. Nursing Care Planning. 2nd ed. pap. text ed. 10.75 (ISBN 0-686-97989-3, Lippincott Nursing). Lippincott.

Little, Allan S. Scotland's Garden. 1982. 55.00 (ISBN 0-686-92016-3, SpurBooks Scotland). State Mutual Bk.

Little, Anthony J. Deceleration in the Eighteenth-Century British Economy. 111p. 1976. 16.50x o.p. (ISBN 0-87471-928-3). Rowman.

Little, Arthur D. International Competition in Pulp, Paper & Paperboard: The Future North American Position & Its Implications. (Illus.). 138p. 1982. Miller Freeman.

Little, Bill, jt. auth. see Evans, Wilbur.

Little, Billie. Recipes for Allergies. 304p. 1983. pap. 3.95. Bantam.

--Recipes for Diabetics. rev. ed. LC 80-84944. 288p. 1981. pap. 7.95 (ISBN 0-448-14620-7, G&D). Putnam Pub Group.

Little, Billie & Thorup, Penny L. Recipes for Diabetics. LC 74-120420. 224p. 1972. 7.95 o.p. (ISBN 0-448-02456-X, G&D). Putnam Pub Group.

Little Brothers & Sisters of Jesus. Cry the Gospel With Your Life. 6.95 (ISBN 0-87193-152-4). Dimension Bks.

Little, Brown Editors, jt. auth. see Fowler, H. Ramsey.

Little, Bryan. Church Treasures in Bristol. 40p. 1982. 25.00x (ISBN 0-905459-12-1, Pub. by Redcliffe England). State Mutual Bk.

--Churches in Bristol. 40p. 1982. 25.00x (ISBN 0-905459-06-7, Pub. by Redcliffe England). State Mutual Bk.

Little, Charles E. Cyclopedia of Classified Dates, with Exhaustive Index. LC 66-27839. 1967. Repr. of 1900 ed. 87.00x (ISBN 0-8103-3334-1). Gale.

--Historical Lights, 2 vols. 3rd ed. LC 68-27175. 1968. Repr. of 1886 ed. Set. 44.00x (ISBN 0-8103-3186-1). Gale.

Little, Craig B. Understanding Deviance. LC 82-61588. 256p. 1983. pap. text ed. 10.95 (ISBN 0-87581-289-9). Peacock Pubs.

Little, Craig B., jt. ed. see Traub, Stuart H.

Little, Dennis L., et al, eds. Renewable Natural Resources: A Management Handbook for the Eighties. (Special Studies in Natural Resources & Energy Management). 375p. (Orig.). 1982. 26.25 (ISBN 0-89158-665-2); pap. text ed. 12.50 (ISBN 0-86531-221-4). Westview.

Little, Elbert L., Jr. Audubon Field Guide to North American Trees. western ed. 1980. 12.00 (ISBN 0-394-50761-4). Knopf.

Little, Geraldine. Hakugai: Poems from a Concentration Camp. Taylor, R. D. & Sheppard, Ann, eds. 150p. 1983. 9.95 (ISBN 0-931604-16-8); pap. 4.95 (ISBN 0-931604-17-6). Curbstone Pub NY TX.

Little, Geraldine C. Contrasting in Keening: Ireland. 50p. (Orig.). 1982. pap. 2.50 (ISBN 0-943710-00-6). Silver App Pr.

Little, Gilbert. Nervous Christians. 1956. pap. 2.95 (ISBN 0-8024-5878-5). Moody.

--Tension Nerviosa. Orig. Title: Nervous Christians. (Span). 1956. pap. 1.95 o.p. (ISBN 0-8024-8400-X). Moody.

Little, Hunter & Jack, Robert L. Diabetic Retinopathy: Pathogenesis & Treatment. (Illus.). 568p. 1983. write for info. (ISBN 0-86577-076-X). Thieme-Stratton.

Little, Ian M. Economic Development: Theory, Policy, & International Relations. LC 82-71366. 1982. 22.95 (ISBN 0-465-01787-8). Basic.

Little, J. C., et al. Psychiatry in a General Hospital. 1974. 7.95 o.p. (ISBN 0-407-36690-3). Butterworth.

Little, James W. & Falace. Dental Management of the Medically Compromised Patient. LC 80-15164. (Illus.). 248p. 1980. pap. text ed. 18.95 (ISBN 0-8016-3045-2). Mosby.

Little, Jean. From Anna. LC 72-76505. (Illus.). 203p. (gr. 4-6). 1972. 10.89 (ISBN 0-06-023912-3, HarpJ). Har-Row.

--Kate. LC 70-148419. (gr. 5-7). 1971. PLB 10.89 (ISBN 0-06-023914-X, HarpJ). Har-Row.

--Listen for the Singing. (gr. 5-7). 1977. 9.95 o.p. (ISBN 0-525-33705-9). Dutton.

--Look Through My Window. LC 71-105470. (Illus.). (gr. 4-6). 1970. PLB 10.89 (ISBN 0-06-023924-7, HarpJ). Har-Row.

--Mine for Keeps. (Illus.). (gr. 4-6). 1974. pap. 1.95 (ISBN 0-671-42455-6). Archway.

--Spring Begins in March. (Illus.). (gr. 4-6). 1966. 7.95 (ISBN 0-316-52785-8). Little.

Little, Jeffrey B. Forecasting Stock Prices. (Illus.). 192p. 1983. pap. 9.95 (ISBN 0-89709-042-X). Liberty Pub.

Little, Jeffrey B. & Rhodes, Lucien. Understanding Wall Street. LC 78-54787. (Illus.). 220p. 1982. pap. 7.95 o.p. (ISBN 0-89709-010-1). Liberty Pub.

Little, Julia, jt. auth. see Macdonald, Eleanor.

Little, Karen E. Monkey Match. (ps-1). 1981. 4.50 (ISBN 0-686-38125-4). Moonlight FL.

--Penguin Partners. (Illus.). (gr. 2 up). 1981. 4.50 (ISBN 0-686-38124-6). Moonlight FL.

Little, Kenneth. African Women in Towns. LC 73-77175. 238p. 1974. 32.50 (ISBN 0-521-20237-X); 9.95x (ISBN 0-521-09819-X). Cambridge U Pr.

--West African Urbanization: Voluntary Associations in Social Change. (Orig.). o. p. 19.95 (ISBN 0-521-05565-2); pap. 8.95x (ISBN 0-521-09263-9). Cambridge U Pr.

Little, Lessie J., jt. auth. see Greenfield, Eloise.

Little, Lester K., ed. see Chenu, M. D.

Little, Lester K., tr. see Chenu, M. D.

Little, Marilyn. Family Breakup: Understanding Marital Patterns & the Mediating of Child Custody Decisions. LC 82-48068. (Social & Behavioral Science Ser.). 1982. text ed. 15.95x (ISBN 0-87589-552-2). Jossey Bass.

Little, Mary E. One, Two, Three for the Library. LC 74-75564. (Illus.). 32p. (ps-1). 1974. 5.95 o.p. (ISBN 0-689-30411-0). Atheneum.

Little, Michael A., jt. auth. see Dyson-Hudson, Rada.

Little, Mildred J. Camper's Guide to Texas Parks, Lakes & Forests. LC 77-73561. (Illus.). 144p. 1978. pap. 7.95 (ISBN 0-88415-097-6). Pacesetter Pr.

Little, Nina F. Neat & Tidy: Boxes in Early American Homes. (Illus.). 1980. pap. 10.95 (ISBN 0-525-47641-5). Dutton.

--Paintings by New England Provincial Artists, 1775-1800. (Illus.). 176p. 1976. pap. 8.95 (ISBN 0-87846-100-0). Mus Fine Arts Boston.

Little, Paul E. Como Compartir Su Fe. 144p. 1979. Repr. of 1978 ed. pap. 3.75 (ISBN 0-311-13025-9). Casa Bautista.

--Know What You Believe. LC 76-105667. 192p. 1970. pap. 4.50 (ISBN 0-88207-024-X). Victor Bks.

--Know Why You Believe. LC 67-12231. 1967. pap. 4.50 (ISBN 0-88207-022-3). Victor Bks.

--Paul Little's Why & What Book. 240p. 1980. text ed. 9.95 (ISBN 0-88207-814-3). Victor Bks.

Little, Richard L. Metalworking Technology. (Illus.). 1976. text ed. 24.95 (ISBN 0-07-038097-X, G). McGraw.

--Welding & Welding Technology. 1972. text ed. 24.95 (ISBN 0-07-038095-3, G); instructor's manual 3.50 (ISBN 0-07-038096-1). McGraw.

Little, Roger W., ed. Selective Service & American Society. LC 68-54411. 220p. 1969. 9.95x (ISBN 0-87154-548-9). Russell Sage.

Little, Sara. Language of the Christian Community. (Illus., Orig.). (gr. 11-12). 1965. pap. 3.45 o.p. (ISBN 0-8042-9240-X); tchrs' guide pap. 4.50 o.p. (ISBN 0-686-76882-5). John Knox.

--Learning Together in the Christian Fellowship. LC 56-9220. (Orig.). 1956. pap. 2.25 (ISBN 0-8042-1320-8). John Knox.

--To Set One's Heart: Belief & Teaching in the Church. LC 82-49020. 160p. 1983. pap. 7.50 (ISBN 0-8042-1442-5). John Knox.

Little, T. E. The Fantasts: Studies of J. R. R. Tolkien, Lewis Carroll, Mervyn Peake, Nikolay Gogol & Kenneth Grahame. 1981. 50.00x o.p. (ISBN 0-86127-212-9, Pub. by Avebury Pub England). State Mutual Bk.

Little, Thomas. Agriculture Experimentation: Design & Analysis. Hills, F. Jackson, ed. LC 77-26745. 350p. 1978. text ed. 24.95 o.s.i. (ISBN 0-471-02352-3). Wiley.

Little, Vera. Tears in My Eyes. 1978. 4.95 o.p. (ISBN 0-533-03311-X). Vantage.

Little, William A. Gottfried August Burger. (World Authors Ser.: Germany: No. 270). 1974. lib. bdg. 15.95 (ISBN 0-8057-2185-1, Twayne). G K Hall.

Littlebird, Harold. On Mountain's Breath. 72p. (Orig.). 1982. pap. 6.00 (ISBN 0-940510-03-0). Tooth of Time.

Littlefield, Daniel F., Jr. Africans & Creeks: From the Colonial Period to the Civil War. LC 78-75238. (Contributions in Afro-American & African Studies: No. 47). (Illus.). 1979. lib. bdg. 27.50 (ISBN 0-313-20703-8, LAF/). Greenwood.

--Africans & Seminoles: From Removal to Emancipation. LC 77-86. (Contributions in Afro-American & African Studies: No. 32). 1977. lib. bdg. 27.50x (ISBN 0-8371-9529-2, LAS/). Greenwood.

--The Cherokee Freedmen: From Emancipation to American Citizenship. LC 78-53659. (Contributions in Afro-American & African Studies: No. 40). 1978. lib. bdg. 27.50 (ISBN 0-313-20413-6, LCH/). Greenwood.

--The Chickasaw Freedmen: A People Without a Country. LC 79-6192. (Contributions in Afro-American and African Studies: No. 54). xii, 248p. 1980. lib. bdg. 27.50 (ISBN 0-313-22313-0, LCF/). Greenwood.

Littlefield, J. W., et al. Birth Defects. (Proceedings). 1978. 113.75 (ISBN 0-444-90024-1). Elsevier.

Littlefield, James E. Readings in Advertising. 450p. 1975. pap. text ed. 11.50 (ISBN 0-8299-0030-6). West Pub.

Littlefield, Mark G. A Bibliographic Index to Romance Philology, Vols. 1-25. 1974. 50.00x (ISBN 0-520-02455-9). U of Cal Pr.

Littlefield, Roy E., III. William Randolph Hearst: His Role in American Progressivism. LC 80-5729. 405p. 1980. lib. bdg. 25.50 (ISBN 0-8191-1320-4); pap. text ed. 15.00 (ISBN 0-8191-1321-2). U Pr of Amer.

Littlefield, Thomson, ed. see Robbins, Daniel.

Littlefield, W., ed. Birth Defects. 1977. 28.50 (ISBN 0-444-15275-X). Elsevier.

Littlejohn, David. Foreign Legions of the Third Reich, Vol. 1. (Illus.). 208p. 1979. 17.95 (ISBN 0-912138-17-3). Bender Pub CA.

--Going to California. 456p. 1981. 13.95 (ISBN 0-698-11042-0, Coward). Putnam Pub Group.

Littlejohn, G. N., jt. auth. see Freebairen-Smith, S. J.

Littlejohn, G. N., jt. auth. see Freebairn-Smith, S. J.

Littlejohn, Gary, et al, eds. Power & the State. Smart, Barry & Wakeford, John. LC 77-25197. 1978. 21.50 o.p. (ISBN 0-312-63378-5). St Martin.

Littlejohn, Patricia & Stokes, Susan. Nutritious Nibbles for Kids & Others. (Illus.). 79p. (Orig.). 1981. pap. 6.95 (ISBN 0-9607374-0-5). Palasam Pub.

Littlejohn, Stephen, jt. auth. see Jabusch, David M.

Littlejohns, J., jt. auth. see Richmond, Leonard.

Little Pigeon, pseud. Children of the Ancient Ones. 1982. pap. 12.00 (ISBN 0-8309-0344-5). Herald Hse.

Little Pigeon, jt. auth. see Grey Owl.

Littler, D. J., ed. Thermal Stresses & Thermal Fatigue. 586p. 1972. 49.50 o.p. (ISBN 0-408-70128-5). Butterworth.

Littleton, Jesse T. & Durizch, Mary L., eds. Sectional Imaging Methods: A Comparison. (Illus.). 1983. 65.00 (ISBN 0-8391-1783-3, 18597). Univ Park.

Littleton, Taylor, jt. auth. see Benson, Carl.

Littlewood, Barbara, jt. auth. see Hansjurgen Press.

Littlewood, Ian. The Writings of Evelyn Waugh. LC 82-18513. 256p. 1983. text ed. 24.50x (ISBN 0-389-20350-5). B&N Imports.

Littlewood, William. Communicative Language Teaching: An Introduction. LC 80-41563. (Cambridge English Language Learning Ser.). (Illus.). 128p. 1981. pap. 8.95 (ISBN 0-521-28154-7). Cambridge U Pr.

Littman, Connie. Practical Problems in Mathematics for Consumers. LC 74-24811. 1975. pap. 7.00 (ISBN 0-8273-0266-5); instructor's guide 2.50 (ISBN 0-8273-0267-3). Delmar.

Littman, Robert J. The Greek Experiment: Imperialism & Social Conflict, 800-400 B.C. (Library of European Civilization Ser.). (Illus.). 180p. 1974. 8.75 o.p. (ISBN 0-500-32030-6). Transatlantic.

Littman, Walter, ed. Studies in Partial Differential Equations. (MAA Studies in Mathematics Ser.: No. 23). 200p. Date not set. price not set (ISBN 0-88385-125-3). Math Assn.

Littmann, David. Textbook of Electrocardiography. (Illus.). 1972. 30.00 (ISBN 0-06-141544-8, Harper Medical). Lippincott.

Littmark, U. & Ziegler, J. F. Handbook of Range Distributions for Energetic Ions in All Elements. LC 79-27825. (The Stopping & Ranges of Ions in Matter Ser.: Vol. 6). 490p. 1980. 77.00 (ISBN 0-08-023879-3). Pergamon.

Littner, Ner. Five More. LC 80-80866. (Orig.). 1980. pap. text ed. 3.95 (ISBN 0-87868-189-2, CW-33). Child Welfare.

Litton, jt. auth. see Krzys.

Littrup, Leif. Subbureaucratic Government in China Ming Times: A Study of Shandong Province in the Sixteenth Century. 224p. 1982. 23.00 (ISBN 82-00-09531-2). Universitet.

Litvack, Frances. Le Droigt du Seigneur in Eurpoean & American Literature. 18.00. French Lit.

Litvack, James M., jt. auth. see Branson, William H.

Litvag, Irving. The Master of Sunnybank: A Biography of Albert Payson Terhune. LC 76-10071. (Illus.). 1977. 12.45i (ISBN 0-06-126345-1, HarpT). Har-Row.

Litvak, James, jt. auth. see Branson, William H.

Litvak, Lawrence, et al. South Africa: Foreign Investment & Apartheid. Hopps, Helen, ed. 100p. 1979. pap. 4.95 (ISBN 0-89758-009-5). Inst Policy Stud.

Litvak, Stuart. Seeking Wisdom: The Sufi Path. 128p. (Orig.). Date not set. pap. write for info. Weiser.

Litvinoff, Barnet. The Essential Chaim Weizmann: The Man, The Statesman, The Scientist. 1983. text ed. 27.50x (ISBN 0-8419-0823-0). Holmes & Meier.

--Weizmann: Last of the Patriarchs. LC 76-22549. (Illus.). 1976. 10.00 o.p. (ISBN 0-399-11718-0). Putnam Pub Group.

Litwack, B. H. The Last Shiksa. LC 77-23900. 1978. 9.95 o.p. (ISBN 0-399-12065-3). Putnam Pub Group.

Litwack, Georgia, jt. auth. see Avery, Mary E.

Litwack, Gerald, ed. Biochemical Actions of Hormones, Vol. 10. LC 70-107567. 374p. 1982. 42.00 (ISBN 0-12-452809-0). Acad Pr.

Litwack, Lawrence L. & Forbes, Elizabeth. The Challenge of Clinical Evaluation. 42p. 1979. 4.50 (ISBN 0-686-38284-6, 16-1763). Natl League Nurse.

Litwak, Robert. Sources of Inter-State Conflict. LC 80-28448. (Security in the Persian Gulf Ser.: Vol. 2). 100p. 1981. pap. text ed. 10.00x (ISBN 0-86598-045-4). Allanheld.

Litwin, W., jt. ed. see Delobel, C.

Litz, A. Walton. James Joyce. (English Authors Ser.). 1966. lib. bdg. 11.95 (ISBN 0-8057-1300-X, Twayne). G K Hall.

Litz, Walton A. Introspective Voyager: The Poetic Development of Wallace Stevens. 1972. 19.95x (ISBN 0-19-501518-5). Oxford U Pr.

Litz, Walton A., Jr. & Lipking, Lawrence I., eds. Modern Literary Criticism: 1900-1970. LC 71-152045. 1972. pap. text ed. 12.95 o.p. (ISBN 0-689-10419-7). Atheneum.

Litzel, Otto. Darkroom Magic. 2nd ed. (Illus.). 160p. 1975. 11.95 o.p. (ISBN 0-8174-0509-7, Amphoto). Watson-Guptill.

--Litzel on Photographic Composition. (Illus.). 160p. 1974. 13.95 o.p. (ISBN 0-8174-0572-0, Amphoto). Watson-Guptill.

Litzinger, Boyd. The Heath Reader. 1982. pap. 9.95 (ISBN 0-669-05416-X); pap. 1.95 instr. manual (ISBN 0-669-05417-8). Heath.

--Watch It, Dr. Adrian. LC 77-4312. 1977. 8.95 o.p. (ISBN 0-399-12015-7). Putnam Pub Group.

Litzman, Berthold, ed. Letters of Clara Schumann & Johannes Brahms, 2 vols. LC 77-163792. Date not set. Repr. of 1927 ed. price not set. Vienna Hse.

Litzmann, Berthold. Clara Schumann: An Artist's Life, 2 vols. (Music Reprint Ser.). 1979. Repr. of 1913 ed. Set. lib. bdg. 75.00 (ISBN 0-306-79582-5). Da Capo.

Litzmann, Berthold, ed. Clara Schumann: An Artist's Life from Diaries & Letters, 2 vols. Hadow, Grace E., tr. LC 70-163793. Date not set. Repr. of 1913 ed. price not set. Vienna Hse.

Liu, Alan J. American Sporting Collector's Handbook. (Stoeger Bks). 1977. pap. 5.95 o.s.i. (ISBN 0-695-80852-4). Follett.

Liu, Alan P. Communications & National Integration in Communist China. (Center for Chinese Studies, Univ. of Michigan). 1971. 34.50x (ISBN 0-520-01882-6); pap. 8.50x (ISBN 0-520-02901-1). U of Cal Pr.

--Political Culture & Group Conflict in Communist China. LC 74-14195. (Studies in International & Comparative Politics: No. 4). 205p. 1976. text ed. 22.50 o.p. (ISBN 0-87436-196-6); pap. text ed. 9.85 o.p. (ISBN 0-87436-197-4). ABC-Clio.

Liu, B. Y. H., jt. ed. see Marple, V. A.

Liu, Bede, jt. auth. see Peled, Abraham.

Liu, C. L., jt. auth. see Belford, G.

Liu, Cheng. Soils & Foundations for Engineering Technology. Evett, Jack B., tr. (Illus.). 320p. 1981. text ed. 19.95 (ISBN 0-13-822239-8). P-H.

Liu, Chung L. Elements of Discrete Mathematics. (Computer Science Ser.). 1977. text ed. 31.95 o.p. (ISBN 0-07-038131-3, C); instructor's manual 25.00 o.p. (ISBN 0-07-038132-1). McGraw.

--Introduction to Applied Combinatorial Mathematics. 1968. text ed. 36.95 (ISBN 0-07-038124-0, C). McGraw.

Liu, Chung L. & Liu, J. W. Linear Systems Analysis. (Illus.). 416p. 1975. text ed. 34.50 (ISBN 0-07-038120-8, C). McGraw.

Liu, Da. Taoist Health Exercise Book. (Illus.). 136p. 1981. pap. 4.95 (ISBN 0-8256-3029-0, Quick Fox). Putnam Pub Group.

Liu, H. Mei. Biology & Pathology of Nerve Growth. LC 81-3630. 1981. 35.00 (ISBN 0-12-452960-7). Acad Pr.

Liu, Henry. Travel Aid to China. 110p. 1982. 10.00 (ISBN 0-533-04985-7). Vantage.

Liu, J. W., jt. auth. see Liu, Chung L.

Liu, James J. Y. The Art of Chinese Poetry. LC 62-7475. (Midway Reprint Ser.). xii, 164p. 1962. pap. write for info. (ISBN 0-226-48685-0). U of Chicago Pr.

Liu, Jin-An. Sino-American Juvenile Justice System. LC 80-67051. (Scholarly Monographs). 340p. 1980. pap. 27.50 o.p. (ISBN 0-8408-0512-8). Carrollton Pr.

Liu, Joseph W., jt. auth. see George, Alan.

Liu, K. C., ed. see I. S. S. C. T. Congress, 13th, Taiwan, 1968.

Liu, Leonard Y., ed. see National Computer Conference, 1978.

Liu, Philip L., jt. auth. see Liggett, J. A.

Liu, Shao. Study of Human Abilities. 1937. pap. 20.00 (ISBN 0-527-02685-9). Kraus Repr.

Liu, Stephen S. N. Dream Journeys to China. (Illus.). 182p. (Engl. & Chinese.). 1982. pap. 4.95 (ISBN 0-8351-1113-X). China Bks.

Liu, T. Y., et al, eds. Chemical Synthesis & Sequencing of Peptides & Proteins. (Developments in Biochemistry Ser.: Vol. 17). 1981. 55.00 (ISBN 0-444-00623-0). Elsevier.

Liu, William T. & Pallone, Nathaniel J. Catholics U. S. A: Perspectives on Social Change. LC 72-93299. 1970. 10.95 o.p. (ISBN 0-471-54149-4, Pub. by Wiley). Krieger.

Liu, William T., ed. Methodological Problems in Minority Research. LC 80-21325. (Occasional Paper Ser.: No. 7). ix, 118p. (Orig.). 1982. pap. 5.00 (ISBN 0-934584-09-5). Pacific-Asian.

Liu, Wu-Chi & Lo, Irving Yucheng, eds. Sunflower Splendor: Three Thousand Years of Chinese Poetry. LC 74-25136. 696p. 1975. 6.95 o.p. (ISBN 0-385-09716-6, Anch). Doubleday.

Liu, Yu-Cheng, jt. auth. see Gibson, Glenn A.

Liu Da. Ta'i Chi Chu'uan & I Ching: A Choreography of Body & Mind. LC 79-183640. (Illus.). 1972. pap. 1.95i o.p. (ISBN 0-06-061667-9, RD-46, HarpR). Har-Row.

Liu Qian. Panda Bear Goes Visiting. (Illus.). 22p. (gr. 3-5). 1982. pap. 3.95 (ISBN 0-8351-1108-3). China Bks.

Liu Wan-Chang see Ku Chieh-Kang.

Liuzzi, A., jt. auth. see Chiodini, P. G.

Liv, C. H., jt. auth. see Yeh, K. C.

Live, Anna H. Yesterday & Today in the U.S.A. Intermediate ESL Reader. 1977. pap. text ed. 11.95 (ISBN 0-13-972273-4). P-H.

Live, Anna H. & Sandkowsky, Suzanne H. American Mosaic: Intermediate-Advanced ESL Reader. LC 79-16352. 1980. pap. text ed. 12.95 (ISBN 0-13-028126-3). P-H.

Lively, C. E. & Taeuber, Conrad. Rural Migration in the United States. LC 71-165601. (Research Monograph Ser.: Vol. 19). 1971. Repr. of 1939 ed. pap. 25.00 (ISBN 0-306-70351-3). Da Capo.

Lively, Jack. Democracy. LC 74-22665. 160p. 1975. text ed. 16.95 o.p. (ISBN 0-312-19215-0). St Martin.

Lively, Jack, ed. see De Maistre, Joseph.

Lively, Penelope. The Whispering Knights. (Illus.). 160p. (gr. 5-6). 1976. 7.95 o.p. (ISBN 0-525-42635-3). Dutton.

Liveright, James. Simple Methods for Detecting Buying & Selling Points in Securities. 1968. Repr. of 1926 ed. flexible cover 4.00 (ISBN 0-87034-028-X). Fraser Pub Co.

Livermore Arms Control Conference. Arms Control in Transition: Proceedings. Heckrotte, Warren & Smith, George C., eds. (Special Study in National Security & Defense Policy). 215p. 1982. lib. bdg. 16.50 (ISBN 0-86531-496-9). Westview.

Livermore, Elaine. Find the Cat. LC 75-5401. (Illus.). 48p. (ps-2). 1973. reinforced bdg. 7.95 (ISBN 0-395-14756-5). HM.

Livermore, Harold U. New History of Portugal. 2nd ed. (Illus.). 1977. 54.50 (ISBN 0-521-21320-7); pap. 15.95x (ISBN 0-521-29103-8). Cambridge U Pr.

Livermore, Jesse. Smart Livermore's Tricks for Stock Market Success. (The Recondite Sources of Stock Market Action Library). (Illus.). 132p. 1983. 47.85 (ISBN 0-86654-045-8). Inst Econ Finan.

Livermore, Mary A., jt. auth. see Willard, Frances E.

Livermore, Putnam, jt. auth. see Barrett, Thomas S.

Livernash, E. Robert, jt. auth. see Foulkes, Fred K.

Liverpool, Charles J. Collection of All the Treaties of Peace, Alliance & Commerce Between Great Britain & Other Powers, 3 Vols. LC 69-16554. Repr. of 1785 ed. 75.00x (ISBN 0-678-00486-2). Kelley.

Liversidge, Joan. Everyday Life in the Roman Empire. LC 76-13350. (Everyday Life Ser.). (gr. 6-8). 1977. 7.50 o.p. (ISBN 0-399-20554-3). Putnam Pub Group.

--Roman Britain. Reeves, Marjorie, ed. (Then & There Ser.). (Illus.). 90p. (Orig.). (gr. 7-12). 1958. pap. text ed. 3.10 (ISBN 0-582-20384-8). Longman.

Livesay, Harold. Andrew Carnegie & the Rise of Big Business. (Library of American Biography). 240p. 1975. pap. text ed. 5.95 (ISBN 0-316-52870-6). Little.

--Samuel Gompers & Organized Labor in America. (Library of American Biography). 1978. 9.95 (ISBN 0-316-52873-0); pap. text ed. 5.95 (ISBN 0-316-52872-2). Little.

Livesay, John. Bible Beasts. (YA) 1976. 8.00 (ISBN 0-686-57854-6). Ind Pr MO.

Liveseu, Herbert. Second Chance: How to Change Your Career in Mid-Life. 1979. pap. 2.25 o.p. (ISBN 0-451-08469-1, E8469, Sig). NAL.

Livesey, Frank. Distributive Trades. (Studies in the British Economy). (Orig.). 1979. pap. text ed. 6.50x o.p. (ISBN 0-435-84553-5). Heinemann Ed.

Livesey, Herbert B., jt. auth. see Doughty, Harold.

Livesey, W. A. Motor Trade Handbook. new ed. 256p. Date not set. pap. text ed. price not set (ISBN 0-408-01135-1). Butterworth.

Livesley, W. J. & Bromley, D. B. Person Perception in Childhood & Adolescence. LC 72-8606. 320p. 1973. 52.95 (ISBN 0-471-54160-5, Pub. by Wiley-Interscience). Wiley.

Liveson, Jay A. & Ma, Dong M. Nerve Conduction Handbook. (Illus.). 380p. 1983. pap. text ed. 22.50 (ISBN 0-8036-5646-7, 5646-7). Davis Co.

Livezey, William E. Mahan on Sea Power. rev. ed. LC 79-6720. (Illus.). 389p. 1981. 19.95 (ISBN 0-8061-1569-6). U of Okla Pr.

Livezey, William E., jt. auth. see Grunder, Garel A.

Livgren, Kerry & Boa, Kenneth. Seeds of Change. 180p. 1983. pap. 7.95 (ISBN 0-89107-265-9, Crossway Bks). Good News.

Livingood, J. J., jt. auth. see Harnwell, G. P.

Livingood, John J. Optics of Dipole Magnets. 1969. 53.00 o.p. (ISBN 0-12-453050-8). Acad Pr.

Livingston, A. D. Advanced Poker Strategy & Winning Play. 1975. pap. 5.00 (ISBN 0-87980-296-0). Wilshire.

Livingston, Arthur, tr. see Scheffer, Paul.

Livingston, Beverly, tr. see Tristan, Flora.

Livingston, Booth, ed. Directory of Grant-Making Trusts: Great Britain. 5th ed. LC 74-188784. 1976. 40.00x o.p. (ISBN 0-904757-00-5). Intl Pubns Serv.

Livingston, Carole. Why Was I Adopted. 1978. text ed. 12.00 (ISBN 0-8184-0257-1). Lyle Stuart.

Livingston, Carole & Ciliotta, Claire. Why Am I Going to the Hospital? 1981. 12.00 (ISBN 0-8184-0316-0). Lyle Stuart.

Livingston, Dinah, tr. see Lefebvre, Georges.

Livingston, E. A., ed. see International Congress on Biblical Studies.

Livingston, Edward. Complete Works on Criminal Jurisprudence: Consisting of Systems of Penal Law for the State of Louisiana & for the United States of America, with Introductory Reports to the Same, 2 vols. LC 68-55775. (Criminology, Law Enforcement, & Social Problems Ser.: No. 7). (With an intro. by Salmon P. Chase). 1968. Repr. of 1873 ed. Set. 40.00x (ISBN 0-87585-007-3). Patterson Smith.

Livingston, Elizabeth & Starbuck, Carol. Miami for Kids: A Family Guide to Greater Miami Including Everglades National Park & the Florida Keys. LC 81-65980. 80p. Date not set. pap. 4.95 (ISBN 0-686-84246-4). Banyan Bks.

Livingston, Elizabeth J. The Hideout. 100p. (Orig.). 1983. pap. 2.95 (ISBN 0-8024-3532-7). Moody.

Livingston, Hazel. Officer on the Witness Stand. 1967. pap. text ed. 1.50x o.p. (ISBN 0-910874-16-6). Legal Bk Co.

Livingston, Mrs. J. B. Love Yourself. 1.95 (ISBN 0-89137-421-3). Quality Pubns.

Livingston, James A. & Poland, Michael D. Accountability & Objectives for Music Education. (Contemporary Music Education Ser.). (Orig.). 1972. pap. 4.95x (ISBN 0-930424-00-X). Music Educ Pubns.

Livingston, James C. Modern Christian Thought: From the Enlightenment to Vatican Two. 1971. text ed. 22.95x (ISBN 0-02-371420-4). Macmillan.

Livingston, Jane. M. Alvarez Bravo. LC 78-67204. (Illus.). 1980. 40.00 (ISBN 0-87923-266-8). Godine.

Livingston, Jane & Beardsley, John. Black Folk Art in America, 1930-1980. LC 81-24072. (Illus.). 176p. (Orig.). 1982. pap. 20.00 (ISBN 0-87805-158-9). U Pr of Miss.

Livingston, Lida, jt. auth. see Fillian, Barbia.

Livingston, M. Jay. The Prodigy. LC 78-17370. 1978. 8.95 o.p. (ISBN 0-698-10926-0, Coward). Putnam Pub Group.

Livingston, Martha, jt. auth. see Lowinger, Paul.

Livingston, Michael M. Back Aid. (Illus.). 180p. 10.95 (ISBN 0-89313-063-X). G F Stickley.

Livingston, Myra C. A Lollygag of Limericks. LC 77-18060. (Illus.). 48p. (gr. 5 up). 1978. 9.95 (ISBN 0-689-50104-8, McElderry Bk). Atheneum.

--When You Are Alone It Keeps You Capone: An Approach to Creative Writing with Children. LC 73-80758. 256p. 1973. 7.95 o.p. (ISBN 0-689-10579-7). Atheneum.

Livingston, Myra C., ed. How Pleasant to Know Mr. Lear! LC 82-80822. (Illus.). 96p. 1982. 10.95 (ISBN 0-8234-0462-5). Holiday.

--What a Wonderful Bird the Frog Are: An Assortment of Humorous Poetry-Verse. LC 72-88171. (gr. 5-9). 1973. 5.25 o.p. (ISBN 0-15-295400-7, HJ). HarBraceJ.

--Why Am I Grown So Cold: Poems of the Unknowable. LC 82-6646. 264p. 1982. 12.95 (ISBN 0-689-50242-7, McElderry Bk). Atheneum.

Livingston, Myra C., compiled by see Carroll, Lewis.

Livingston, Peter, et al. The Complete Book to Country Swing & Western Dance. 1981. pap. 10.95 o.p. (ISBN 0-385-17601-5, Dolp). Doubleday.

Livingston, Robert A. How to Legally Reduce Your Taxes: For the Complete Idiot. 1982. 10.00 (ISBN 0-9607558-3-7). GLGLC Music.

--Livingston's Complete Music Industry Business & Law Reference Book. 340p. 1981. 26.00 (ISBN 0-9607558-0-2); pap. 19.95 (ISBN 0-9607558-1-0). GLGLC Music.

--The Music Information & Education Guide. 1983. 10.00 (ISBN 0-9607558-2-9). GLGLC Music.

--The Tax Deduction Checklist: Songwriters, Musicians, Performers. 1982. 6.95 (ISBN 0-9607558-4-5). GLGLC Music.

Livingston, Robert B. Sensory Processing, Perception, & Behavior. LC 76-19854. 120p. 1978. soft cover 11.50 (ISBN 0-89004-134-2). Raven.

Livingston, Virginia. Cancer: A New Breakthrough. 7.00 (ISBN 0-686-29786-5). Cancer Control Soc.

--Office Administration of Oil & Gas Leases. 1982. 30.00 (ISBN 0-89419-208-6). Inst Energy.

--Physician's Handbook to Microbiology of Cancer. 1977. 2.00x (ISBN 0-918816-06-8). Cancer Control Soc.

Livingstone, Dinah, tr. see Voillaume, Rene.

Livingstone, E. A., ed. Studia Patristica XVII, 3 Vols. 1520p. 1982. Set. 180.00 (ISBN 0-08-025779-8). Pergamon.

Livingstone, E. A., ed. see International Congress on Biblical Studies, 6th, Oxford, 3-7 April,1978.

Livingstone, Elizabeth A., jt. auth. see Cross, F. L.

Livingstone, I., jt. auth. see Hazlewood, A.

Livingstone, I., et al, eds. The Teaching of Economics in Africa. Report of a Conference Held in April 1969 in Dares Salaam, United Republic of Tanzania. 30.00x (ISBN 0-686-97025-X, Pub. by Scottish Academic Pr Scotland). State Mutual Bk.

Livingstone, J. L. & Kerrigan, H. D. Modern Accounting Systems. 4th ed. 1975. 49.95 (ISBN 0-471-06539-0, Pub. by Wiley-Interscience). Wiley.

Livingstone, J. L., jt. auth. see Largay, James A.

Livingstone, James V. The British Economy in Theory & Practice. LC 74-13513. 240p. 1975. 22.50 (ISBN 0-312-10080-9). St Martin.

Livingstone, Myra C. A Circle of Seasons. LC 81-20305. (Illus.). 32p. (ps-3). 1982. Reinforced bdg. 12.95 (ISBN 0-8234-0452-8). Holiday.

Livingstone, Neil C. The War Against Terrorism. LC 81-48331. 304p. 1982. 29.95x (ISBN 0-669-05333-3). Lexington Bks.

Livingstone, Richard, ed. see Thucydides.

Livingstone, Richard W. Greek Ideals & Modern Life. LC 72-82814. 1969. Repr. of 1935 ed. 10.00x (ISBN 0-8196-0245-0). Biblo.

Livingstone, Richard W., ed. The Mission of Greece: Some Views of Life in the Roman World. LC 75-17473. (Illus.). 1976. Repr. of 1928 ed. lib. bdg. 21.00x (ISBN 0-8371-8312-X, LIMGR). Greenwood.

Livingstone, Richard W., tr. see Plato.

Livingstone, Rodney, ed. see Lukacs, Georg.

Livingstone, Rodney, tr. see Lukacs, Georg.

Livingstone, Rodney, tr. see Marx, Karl & Engels, Frederick.

Livingstone-Learmonth, John & Master, Melvyn C. The Wines of the Rhone. 2nd ed. LC 82-24207. (Books on Wine). 255p. 1983. 24.95 (ISBN 0-571-18075-2); pap. 9.95 (ISBN 0-571-13055-0). Faber & Faber.

Livoni, Cathy. Element of Time. LC 82-48761. 192p. (gr. 12 up). 12.95 (ISBN 0-15-225369-6, HJ). HarBraceJ.

Livsey, Clara. The Manson Women: A "Family" Portrait. LC 79-26454. 1980. 10.95 (ISBN 0-399-90073-X, Marek). Putnam Pub Group.

Livy. Ab Urbe Condita, Bk. 1. Gould, Howard E. & Whiteley, Joseph L., eds. (Modern School Classics Ser). (Lat). 1952. 12.95 (ISBN 0-312-49280-4). St Martin.

--Ab Urbe Condita, Bk. 30. Whiteley, Joseph L., ed. (Modern School Classics Ser.). (Lat). 5.95 o.p. (ISBN 0-312-49315-0). St Martin.

--Ab Urbe Condita: Selections, Bks. 21-23. Bd. with Hannibal Triumphant; Hannibal. Nepos. (Illus.). 124p. (Lat.). 1946. 3.95x o.p. (ISBN 0-312-36085-1). St Martin.

Li Wan Po, A. Non-Prescription Drugs. (Illus.). 488p. 1982. pap. text ed. 49.95 (ISBN 0-632-00857-1, B2969-1). Mosby.

Lizarralde, German, jt. auth. see Colwell, John A.

Ljungberg, G., ed. see Conference on Instruments & Measurements.

Ljungmark, Lars. Swedish Exodus. Westerberg, Kermit B., tr. from Swedish. LC 79-10498. 192p. 1979. 14.95 (ISBN 0-8093-0905-X). S Ill U Pr.

Llamzon, Benjamin S. Reason, Experience & the Moral Life. LC 78-58444. 1978. pap. text ed. 11.25 (ISBN 0-8191-0534-1). U Pr of Amer.

--The Self Beyond: Toward Life's Meaning. LC 82-16073. 198p. 1983. pap. text ed. 10.75 (ISBN 0-8191-2741-8). U Pr of Amer.

Llanas, A., jt. auth. see Adams, L.

Llano, George A., ed. Antarctic Terrestrial Biology. LC 72-92709. (Antarctic Research Ser.: Vol. 20). (Illus.). 1972. 39.00 (ISBN 0-87590-120-4). Am Geophysical.

--Biology of the Antarctic Seas Two. LC 64-60030. (Antarctic Research Ser.: Vol. 5). 1965. 15.00 (ISBN 0-87590-105-0). Am Geophysical.

Llano, George A. & Schmitt, Waldo L., eds. Biology of the Antarctic Seas Three. LC 64-60030. (Antarctic Research Ser.: Vol. 11). 1967. 17.00 (ISBN 0-87590-111-5). Am Geophysical.

Llano, George A. & Wallen, I. Eugene, eds. Biology of the Antarctic Seas Four. LC 64-60030. (Antarctic Research Ser.: Vol. 17). (Illus.). 1971. 39.00 (ISBN 0-87590-117-4). Am Geophysical.

Llewellyn, Alexander. Decade of Reform: English Politics and Opinion in the 1830's. LC 71-182187. 1972. text ed. 17.95 o.p. (ISBN 0-312-18970-2). St Martin.

Llewellyn, D., et al. Case Studies in International Economics. Maunder, Peter, ed. (Case Studies in Economic Analysis). 1977. 5.00x o.p. (ISBN 0-435-84471-7); tchr's. ed. 8.50x o.p. (ISBN 0-435-84472-5). Heinemann Ed.

Llewellyn, David T. International Financial Integration: The Limits of Sovereignty. LC 80-11699. (Problems of Economic Integration Ser.). 215p. 1981. 36.95 (ISBN 0-470-26960-X). Halsted Pr.

Llewellyn, Edward. The Bright Companion. (Science Fiction Ser.). 1980. pap. 1.75 o.p. (ISBN 0-87997-511-3, UE1511). DAW Bks.

--The Douglas Convolution. (Daw Science Fiction Ser.). 1979. pap. 1.75 o.p. (ISBN 0-87997-495-8, UE1495). Daw Bks.

--Prelude to Chaos. 256p. 1983. pap. 2.75 (ISBN 0-686-84672-9). DAW Bks.

Llewellyn, Jack H. & Blucher, Judy. Psychology of Coaching: Theory & Application. (Illus.). 200p. 1982. 14.95x (ISBN 0-8087-1243-8). Burgess.

Llewellyn, Megan. The Eagle of Gwernabwy: Tales from Wales. 1971. pap. 1.90 (ISBN 0-08-015698-3). Pergamon.

Llewellyn, Michael J., jt. auth. see Brafield, Alan E.

Llewellyn, P. J., jt. auth. see Ratcliffe, N. A.

Llewellyn, Robert, photos by. The Academic Village: Thomas Jefferson University. (Illus.). 80p. 1982. 22.50 (ISBN 0-934738-03-3). Thomasson-Grant.

Llewellyn, Robert W. Information Systems. LC 75-40223. (Illus.). 368p. 1976. 21.95x (ISBN 0-13-464487-5). P-H.

Llewellyn-Jones, Derek. Breast Feeding-How to Succeed: Questions & Answers for Mothers. LC 82-21051. (Illus.). 192p. 1983. 14.95 (ISBN 0-571-13003-8); pap. 5.95 (ISBN 0-571-13004-6). Faber & Faber.

--Fundamental of Obstetrics & Gynaecology, Vol. I: Obstetrics. rev. 2nd ed. (Illus.). 472p. 1977. 32.00 o.p. (ISBN 0-571-04913-3); pap. 25.00 o.p. (ISBN 0-571-04914-1). Faber & Faber.

--Fundamentals of Obstetrics & Gynecology, Vol. 2: Gynecology. (Illus.). 296p. 1978. 29.00 o.p. (ISBN 0-571-04929-X); pap. 18.00 o.p. (ISBN 0-571-04958-3). Faber & Faber.

--People Populating. 384p. 1976. 18.00 o.p. (ISBN 0-571-09943-2). Transatlantic.

Llewelyn, J. J., jt. auth. see Froud, Brian.

Llewelyn-Jones, Derek. Every Body: A Nutritional Guide to Life. (Illus.). 1980. 17.95x (ISBN 0-19-217691-9). Oxford U Pr.

Llewllyn, P. J., jt. auth. see Ratcliffe, N. A.

Llimona, Mercedes, illus. The Seasons with Strawberry Shortcake (A Strawberry Shortcake Bk.) LC 80-50180. (Board Books). (Illus.). 14p. (ps). 1980. bds. 3.50 (ISBN 0-394-84569-2). Random.

--Strawberry Shortcake's Favorite Mother Goose Rhymes. LC 82-5204. (Illus.). 48p. (ps-1). 1983. PLB 6.99 (ISBN 0-394-95431-9); pap. 5.95 (ISBN 0-394-85431-4). Random.

Lloyd, jt. auth. see Rawson.

Lloyd, et al. Proofguides for Gregg Typing for Colleges: Lessons 1-75. (Gregg College Typing: Ser. 4). 48p. 1978. pap. text ed. 3.95 o.p. (ISBN 0-07-038260-3, G). McGraw.

Lloyd, A., et al. Typing Skill Drives. 2nd ed. 1974. 7.96 (ISBN 0-07-038161-5, G). McGraw.

--Series Seven Typing Complete Course, Gregg Typing. 496p. (gr. 11-12). 1982. 18.60 (ISBN 0-07-038280-8, G). learning guides & working papers. 4 sets 3.12 (ISBN 0-686-86312-7). Lessons 1-75 (ISBN 0-07-038283-2). Lessons 76-150. learning guides & working papers 3.96 (ISBN 0-07-038284-0); Lessons 151-225. learning guides & working papers 5.20 (ISBN 0-07-038285-9); Lessons 226-300. learning guides & working papers 5.40 (ISBN 0-07-038286-7). McGraw.

Lloyd, A. C., jt. auth. see Condon, Arnold.

Lloyd, A. C., et al. Gregg Typing for Colleges: Intensive Course. (Gregg College Typing Ser.: Series 4). 1978. pap. text ed. 15.00 (ISBN 0-07-038252-2, G); instructor's manual 20.00 (ISBN 0-07-038259-X); proofguide for lessons 3.95 (ISBN 0-07-038261-1); 3 wkguides for lessons 8.55 ea. McGraw.

--Gregg College Typing, Series Five, Typing 75, Basic Kit. 320p. 1983. pap. 14.50x (includes text, guide, proofguide & easel) (ISBN 0-07-038322-7, Gregg). McGraw.

Lloyd, A. C., et al, eds. Typing Seventy Five: Advanced. (Gregg College Typing: Ser. 4). 1979. pap. text ed. 14.20 (ISBN 0-07-038257-3, G). McGraw.

--Typing Seventy Five: Basic. (Gregg College Typing, Ser. Four). 1978. pap. text ed. 14.20 (ISBN 0-07-038256-5, G). McGraw.

--Typing Seventy Five: Expert. 4th ed. (Gregg College Typing Ser.: Series 4). 1978. pap. text ed. 14.20 (ISBN 0-07-038258-1, G). McGraw.

Lloyd, A. R. Kine. 256p. 1983. 11.95 (ISBN 0-686-83434-8). St Martin.

Lloyd, Alan. Alive in the Last Days of Pompeii. 1979. pap. 2.50 o.p. (ISBN 0-523-40612-6). Pinnacle Bks.

--The Gliders: The Story of the Wooden Chariots of World War II. (Airborne Ser.: No. 17). (Illus.). 196p. 1982. 16.95x (ISBN 0-89839-066-4). Battery Pr.

--The Great Prize Fight. 1977. 8.95 o.p. (ISBN 0-698-10829-9, Coward). Putnam Pub Group.

--Trade Imperial. LC 78-26239. 1979. 10.95 o.s.i. (ISBN 0-698-10970-8, Coward). Putnam Pub Group.

Lloyd, Alan C. & Hosler, R. J. Personal Typing. 3rd ed. 1967. text ed. 10.68 o.p. (ISBN 0-07-038187-9, G). McGraw.

Lloyd, Alan C. & Hosler, Russell J. Personal Typing. 4th ed. (Illus.). 1978. text ed. 12.00 (ISBN 0-07-038208-5, G); tchr's manual & key 5.00 (ISBN 0-07-038209-3). McGraw.

Lloyd, Alan C. & Krevolin, R. You Learn to Type. 1966. 15.24 (ISBN 0-07-038160-7, W); records 441.60 (ISBN 0-07-089690-9). McGraw.

Lloyd, Alan C., et al. Typing Power Drills. 2nd ed. 1965. text ed. 8.48 (ISBN 0-07-038171-2, G). McGraw.

--Gregg Typewriting for Colleges Intensive Course. 2nd ed. Incl. Basic Course. text ed. 8.25 o.p. (ISBN 0-07-038193-3); Complete Course. text ed. 12.80 o.p. (ISBN 0-07-038199-2). 1964. instructor's manual 6.47 o.p. (ISBN 0-07-038188-7, G); wkbks 5.55 ea. o.p. McGraw.

--Typing One: General Course. (Illus.). (gr. 9-12). 1976. text ed. 13.32x (ISBN 0-07-038241-7, G); course management manual 15.95 (ISBN 0-07-038247-6); wkbks. 3.96x ea. (ISBN 0-07-038247-6); learning guide 1 3.96 (ISBN 0-07-038243-3); learning guide 2 3.24 (ISBN 0-07-038242-5). McGraw.

--Typing One: General Course Gregg Typing. LC 81-15629. (Gregg Typing, Ser. 7). (Illus.). 288p. 1982. text ed. 13.80 (ISBN 0-07-038281-6, G). McGraw.

--Typing Two, Advanced Course. (Illus.). (gr. 9-12). 1977. text ed. 10.72 (ISBN 0-07-038244-1, G); wkbks. 5.40 ea.; tchrs manual & key 15.95 (ISBN 0-07-038247-6). McGraw.

--Typing Two: Advanced Course Gregg Typing. LC 81-15629. (Gregg Typing, Ser. 7). (Illus.). 288p. 1982. text ed. 13.80 (ISBN 0-07-038282-4, G). McGraw.

Lloyd, Albert. Deutsch und Deutschland Heute. 2nd ed. 1981. text ed. write for info. (ISBN 0-442-24461-4). Van Nos Reinhold.

Lloyd, Albert L. Anatomy of the Verb: The Gothic Verb As a Model for a Unified Theory of Aspect, Actional Types, & Verbal Velocity. (Studies in Language Companion Ser.). x, 351p. 1979. 32.00 (ISBN 90-272-3003-X, 4). Benjamins North Am.

Lloyd, Alexander. The Foundling. (gr. k-6). 1982. pap. 1.95 (ISBN 0-440-42536-0, YB). Dell.

Lloyd, Barbara & Gay, John, eds. Universals of Human Thought: Some African Evidence. LC 79-41471. (Illus.). 300p. 1981. 49.50 (ISBN 0-521-22953-7); pap. 14.95 (ISBN 0-521-29818-0). Cambridge U Pr.

LLoyd, C. & Ress, D. A., eds. Cellular Controls in Differentiation. LC 81-6783. 336p. 1982. 25.50 (ISBN 0-12-453580-1). Acad Pr.

Lloyd, C. H. Durer to Cezanne: Northern European Drawings from the Ashmolean. 152p. 49.00x (ISBN 0-900090-89-8, Pub. by Ashmolean Mus Oxford). State Mutual Bk.

Lloyd, Charles. Desultory Thoughts in London; Titus & Gisippus; with Other Poems. 1821. Reiman, Donald H., ed. LC 75-31227. (Romantic Context Ser.: Poetry 1789-1830). 1978. lib. bdg. 47.00 o.s.i. (ISBN 0-8240-2177-0). Garland Pub.

--Nugae Canorae: Poems. 1819. Reiman, Donald H., ed. LC 75-31226. (Romantic Context Ser.: Poetry 1789-1830). 1978. lib. bdg. 47.00 o.s.i. (ISBN 0-8240-2176-2). Garland Pub.

Lloyd, Christopher. Atlas of Maritime History. LC 74-32634. (Illus.). 1975. Repr. 35.00 o.p. (ISBN 0-668-03779-2). Arco.

--Nation & the Navy. LC 74-383. (Illus.). 314p. 1974. Repr. of 1961 ed. lib. bdg. 18.50x (ISBN 0-8371-7379-5, LLNN). Greenwood.

Lloyd, Christopher, ed. Social Theory & Political Practice. (Wolfson College Lectures Ser.). 190p. 1983. 24.95 (ISBN 0-19-827447-5); pap. 12.95 (ISBN 0-19-827448-3). Oxford U Pr.

Lloyd, David. Air. LC 82-9440. (Illus.). 32p. (ps-4). 1983. 9.95 (ISBN 0-8037-0141-1). Dial Bks Young.

Lloyd, David, ed. Workmen's Compensation Law Review, 5 vols. LC 73-93978. 1974-80. Set. lib. bdg. write for info (ISBN 0-930342-54-2); Vol. 1, 1974. lib. bdg. 35.00 (ISBN 0-930342-27-5); Vol. 2, 1975. lib. bdg. 35.00 (ISBN 0-930342-28-3); Vol. 3, 1976. lib. bdg. 35.00 (ISBN 0-930342-53-4); Vol. 4, 1977-8. lib. bdg. 35.00 (ISBN 0-930342-59-3); Vol. 5, 1979-80. lib. bdg. 37.50 (ISBN 0-89941-102-9). W S Hein.

Lloyd, E. Keith, ed. see Tomescu, Ioan.

Lloyd, Errol. Nandy's Bedtime. (Illus.). 32p. (ps). 1982. bds. 6.95 (ISBN 0-370-30395-4, Pub by The Bodley Head). Merrimack Bk Serv.

Lloyd, G. A. Radiology of the Orbit. (Monographs in Clinical Radiology: Vol. 7). (Illus.). 250p. 1975. text ed. 16.00 (ISBN 0-7216-5792-3). Saunders.

Lloyd, G. E. Early Greek Science: Thales to Aristotle. Finley, M. I., ed. (Ancient Culture & Society Ser). (Illus.). 1971. 6.00x o.p. (ISBN 0-393-04340-1); pap. 4.95x (ISBN 0-393-00583-6). Norton.

Lloyd, G. E., ed. Hippocratic Writings. (Classics Ser.). 1978. pap. 4.95 o.p. (ISBN 0-14-040031-1, Pelican). Penguin.

Lloyd, Geoffrey E. Aristotle: Growth & Structure of His Thought. LC 68-21195. (Orig.). 1968. 39.50 (ISBN 0-521-07049-X); pap. 10.95x (ISBN 0-521-09456-9). Cambridge U Pr.

Lloyd, Geoffrey E. & Owen, G. E., eds. Aristotle on Mind & the Senses. LC 77-9389. (Classical Studies). 1978. 39.50 (ISBN 0-521-21669-9). Cambridge U Pr.

Lloyd, Gordon B. Don't Call It "Dirt"! Improving Your Garden Soil. (Illus.). 128p. 1976. 6.95 (ISBN 0-916302-12-1); pap. 3.95 (ISBN 0-916302-02-4). Bookworm NY.

Lloyd, H. G. The Red Fox. (Illus.). 320p. 1980. 40.00 (ISBN 0-7134-1190-2, Pub. by Batsford England). David & Charles.

Lloyd, Henry D., ed. Wealth Against Commonwealth. LC 76-7. 184p. 1976. Repr. of 1963 ed. lib. bdg. 18.00x (ISBN 0-8371-8726-5, LLWA). Greenwood.

Lloyd, Howell. The State, France, & the Sixteenth Century. (Early Modern Europe Today Ser.). 256p. 1983. text ed. 25.00x (ISBN 0-04-940066-5). Allen Unwin.

Lloyd, J. Guth de see Guth de Lloyd, J.

Lloyd, J. H. Operational Research on Preventive Control of the Red Locust (Nomadacris Septemfasciata Serville) 1959. 35.00x (ISBN 0-85135-020-8, Pub. by Centre Overseas Research). State Mutual Bk.

Lloyd, Jack I. Don't Fall off Your Boat. 1980. 12.00x o.p. (ISBN 0-900093-61-7, Pub. by Roundwood). State Mutual Bk.

Lloyd, Janet, tr. see Agulhon, Maurice.

Lloyd, Janet, tr. see De Heusch, Luc.

Lloyd, Janet, tr. see Garlan, Yvon.

Lloyd, Janice, jt. auth. see Marzollo, Jean.

Lloyd, Jean, et al. Sociology & Social Life. 6th ed. 1979. text ed. 13.95 (ISBN 0-442-23373-6); instructor's manual pap 1.50x (ISBN 0-442-23232-2). Van Nos Reinhold.

Lloyd, Joan. Guatemala, Land of the Mayas. LC 74-2557. (Illus.). 175p. 1974. Repr. of 1963 ed. lib. bdg. 15.50x (ISBN 0-8371-7415-5, LLGU). Greenwood.

Lloyd, John, jt. auth. see Benson, Ian.

Lloyd, John U. Etidorpha or the End of Earth. 386p. 1974. pap. 15.00 (ISBN 0-89540-004-9). Sun Pub.

Lloyd, Lewis E. Tariffs: The Case for Protectionism. 6.50 (ISBN 0-8159-6902-3). Devin.

Lloyd, Lyle L. & Kaplan, Harriet. Audiometric Interpretation: A Manual of Basic Audiometry. 236p. 1978. pap. text ed. 24.95 (ISBN 0-8391-0759-5). Univ Park.

Lloyd, Lyle L., ed. Communication Assessment & Intervention Strategies. (Illus.). 928p. 1976. text ed. 19.95 (ISBN 0-8391-0758-7). Univ Park.

Lloyd, Lyle L., jt. ed. see Minifie, Fred D.

Lloyd, N. G. Degree Theory. LC 77-3205. (Tracts in Mathematics Ser.: No. 73). (Illus.). 1978. 38.50 (ISBN 0-521-21614-1). Cambridge U Pr.

Lloyd, Norman, jt. auth. see Boni, Margaret.

Lloyd, P. The Young Towns of Lima. LC 79-51826. (Urbanization in Developing Countries Ser.). (Orig.). 1980. 37.50 (ISBN 0-521-22871-9); pap. 10.95 (ISBN 0-521-29688-9). Cambridge U Pr.

Lloyd, P. C., ed. The New Elites of Tropical Africa. 1978. pap. 19.50x o.p. (ISBN 0-19-724203-0). Oxford U Pr.

Lloyd, Paul M. Desarrollando Destrezas en Preparacion Para el Examen de Equivalencia de Escuela Superior en Espanol: El Escribir. (Span.). (gr. 9-12). Date not set. pap. text ed. 3.75 (ISBN 0-8120-0559-7). Barron.

Lloyd, Peter, jt. auth. see Dicken, Peter.

Lloyd, Peter C. Slums of Hope? Shanty Towns of the Third World. LC 78-24770. 1979. 20.00x (ISBN 0-312-72963-4). St Martin.

Lloyd, Rawson. The Easter-Story. (Children's Picture Bible). (gr. 4-6). 1981. 6.95 (ISBN 0-86020-515-0, Usborne-Hayes); PLB 9.95 (ISBN 0-88110-096-X); pap. 3.95 (ISBN 0-86020-520-7). EDC.

--Stories Jesus Told. (Children's Picture Bible Ser.). (gr. 4-6). 1982. 6.95 (ISBN 0-86020-516-9, Usborne-Hayes); PLB 9.95 (ISBN 0-88110-097-8); pap. 3.95 (ISBN 0-86020-521-5). EDC.

Lloyd, Richard & Thomas, Antony. Frank Terpil: Portrait of a Dangerous Man. 256p. 1983. 14.95 (ISBN 0-86579-023-X). Seaver Bks.

Lloyd, Richard & Alabaster, J. S., eds. Water Quality Criteria for Fresh Water Fish. LC 79-41350. 1980. text ed. 52.50 o.p. (ISBN 0-408-10673-5). Butterworth.

Lloyd, Richard, jt. ed. see Davidson, Joan.

Lloyd, Robert A. Everything You Wanted to Know About Venereal Disease but Were Afraid to Ask. (Studies in Health: Vol. 3). (Illus.). 185p. (Orig.). 1983. 16.95 (ISBN 0-86663-654-4); pap. 9.95 (ISBN 0-86663-655-2). Ide Hse.

Lloyd, Rosemary H. Baudelaire et Hoffmann. LC 78-58796. (Fr.). 1979. 41.50 (ISBN 0-521-22459-4). Cambridge U Pr.

Lloyd, Selwyn. Mr. Speaker, Sir. 1977. 12.50 o.s.i. (ISBN 0-224-01318-1). Transatlantic.

Lloyd, T. H. The English Wool Trade in the Middle Ages. LC 76-11086. (Illus.). 1977. 59.50 (ISBN 0-521-21239-1). Cambridge U Pr.

Lloyd, William B., Jr. Waging Peace: The Swiss Experience. LC 80-15577. (Illus.). xii, 101p. 1980. Repr. of 1958 ed. lib. bdg. 18.50x (ISBN 0-313-22506-0, LLWP). Greenwood.

Lloyd-Bostock, Sally M. & Clifford, Brian R. Evaluating Witness Evidence: Recent Psychological Research & New Perspectives. 350p. 1983. 43.95 (ISBN 0-471-10463-9, Pub. by Wiley-Interscience). Wiley.

Lloyd George, David. Memoirs of the Peace Conference, 2 vols. 1939. Set. 75.00x o.p. (ISBN 0-686-51415-7). Elliots Bks.

Lloyd-Hart. Health in the Vale of Aylesbury. 19.95 (ISBN 0-471-25859-8, Pub. by Wiley Heyden). Wiley.

LLoyd Hart, V. E. John Wilkes & the Founding Hospital at Aylesbury 1759-1768. 80p. 1980. text ed. 19.95x (ISBN 0-471-25860-1, Pub. by Wiley-Interscience). Wiley.

Lloyd-Jones, D. Martyn. Christian Unity: An Exposition of Ephesians 4: 1-16. 280p. 1981. 10.95 (ISBN 0-8010-5607-1). Baker Bk.

--Darkness & Light: An Exposition of Ephesians 4 17-5 17. 408p. 1983. Repr. of 1965 ed. 10.95 (ISBN 0-8010-5617-9). Baker Bk.

--First Book of Daily Readings. 1970. pap. 6.95 (ISBN 0-8028-1354-2). Eerdmans.

--Lloyd-Jones Expositions of Ephesians, 8 Vols. 1983. 79.95 (ISBN 0-8010-5623-3). Baker Bk.

Lloyd Jones, Hilary. Pets & Pet Care. LC 77-10262. (Illus.). 1978. 14.95 o.p. (ISBN 0-399-12092-0). Putnam Pub Group.

Lloyd-Jones, Hugh. The Justice of Zeus. (Sather Classical Lectures: No. 41). 1971. 28.50x (ISBN 0-520-01739-0); pap. 3.45x o.p. (ISBN 0-520-02359-5). U of Cal Pr.

--The Justice of Zeus. 2nd ed. 290p. 1983. pap. 7.95 (ISBN 0-520-04688-9, CAL 567). U of Cal Pr.

--Myths of the Zodiac. LC 78-69955. 1978. 20.00x (ISBN 0-312-55870-8). St Martin.

Lloyd-Jones, Hugh & Pearl, Valerie, eds. History & Imagination: Essays in Honor of H. R. Trevor-Roper. 386p. 1982. 45.00 (ISBN 0-8419-0782-X). Holmes & Meier.

Lloyd-Still, J. D. Malnutrition & Intellectual Development. LC 76-17432. (Illus.). 202p. 1976. 19.50 o.p. (ISBN 0-88416-181-1). Wright-PSG.

Lluis, E., jt. ed. see Auslander, M.

Llywelyn, Morgan. The Wind From Hastings. 368p. 1982. pap. 2.95 (ISBN 0-446-30522-7). Warner Bks.

Lo, Benjamin P., et al. The Essence of T'ai Chi Ch'uan: The Literary Tradition. Inn, Martin & Amacker, Robert, eds. 1979. 15.00; pap. 5.95 (ISBN 0-913028-63-0). North Atlantic.

Lo, Irving Yucheng, jt. ed. see Liu, Wu-Chi.

Lo, S. Y. The Development Performance of West Malaysia, Nineteen Fifty-Five to Nineteen Sixty-Seven. 1972. pap. text ed. 7.50x o.p. (ISBN 0-686-60348-6, 00110). Heinemann Ed.

Lo, Sara De Mundo see De Mundo Lo, Sara.

Lo, Teh C., et al. Handbook of Solvent Extraction. 992p. 1983. 125.00 (ISBN 0-471-04164-5, Pub. by Wiley-Interscience). Wiley.

Loach, Alan. Anesthesia of Orthopedic Patients. 1983. text ed. price not set (ISBN 0-7131-4419-X). E Arnold.

Loader, Anne, compiled by. Pregnancy & Parenthood. (Illus.). 1980. 16.95x o.p. (ISBN 0-19-217684-6); pap. 8.95x o.p. (ISBN 0-19-286006-2). Oxford U Pr.

Loades, Ann see Eaton, Jeffrey C.

Loades, D. M. Politics & the Nation, Fourteen Fifty-Sixteen Sixty: Obedience, Resistance & Public Order. Elton, Y. R., ed. (Fontana Library of English History). 484p. 1974. text ed. 22.25x o.p. (ISBN 0-901759-34-1). Humanities.

--The Reign of Mary Tudor: Politics, Government & Religions in England Fifteen Fifty-Three to Fifteen Fifty-Eight. LC 79-16479. 1979. 27.50x (ISBN 0-312-67029-X). St Martin.

Loam, Jayson, ed. Family Naturism in Europe. (Fun in the Sun Ser.). 100p. 1983. pap. 14.95 (ISBN 0-910550-20-4). Elysium.

Loane, Marcus L. Godliness & Contentment: Studies in The Three Pastoral Epistles. (Canterbury Bks.). 128p. (Orig.). 1982. pap. 5.95 (ISBN 0-8010-5619-5). Baker Bk.

Loannides, C., jt. ed. see Gibson, G. G.

Loasby, B. J. Choice, Complexity & Ignorance. LC 75-22558. 1976. 42.50 (ISBN 0-521-21065-8). Cambridge U Pr.

Lobanov-Rostovsky, Andrei A. Russia & Asia. 1951. 4.95x o.s.i. (ISBN 0-685-21802-3). Wahr.

--Russia & Europe Eighteen Twenty-Five to Eighteen Seventy-Eight. 1954. 6.00x (ISBN 0-685-21803-1). Wahr.

Lobb, Charlotte. Exploring Careers Through Part-Time & Summer Employment. rev. ed. (gr. 7-12). 1982. PLB 7.97 o.p. (ISBN 0-8239-0371-0). Rosen Pr.

--Exploring Vocational School Careers. rev. ed. (Careers in Depth Ser.). (Illus.). (gr. 7-12). 1982. PLB 7.97 o.p. (ISBN 0-8239-0468-7). Rosen Pr.

Lobb, Nancy. Basic Health, Bk. 1. 1979. pap. 2.75x (ISBN 0-88323-155-7, 244). Richards Pub.

--Everyday First Aid Skills. 1979. pap. 2.75x (ISBN 0-88323-148-4, 235). Richards Pub.

Lobdell, Jared, ed. A Tolkien Compass. LC 74-20681. 1975. 18.50 (ISBN 0-87548-316-X); pap. 6.50 (ISBN 0-87548-303-8). Open Court.

Lobe, Mira, jt. auth. see Opgenoorth, Winfried.

Lobeck, A. K. Geomorphology. (Illus.). 1939. text ed. 23.50 o.p. (ISBN 0-07-038210-7, C). McGraw.

Lobel, Adrianne. A Small Sheep in a Pear Tree. LC 76-58721. (gr. k-3). 1977. 7.64i (ISBN 0-06-023952-2, HarpJ); PLB 8.89 (ISBN 0-06-023953-0). Har-Row.

Lobel, Anita. The Pancake. LC 77-24970. (Greenwillow Read-Alone Bks.). (Illus.). 48p. (gr. 1-4). 1978. 5.95 (ISBN 0-688-80125-0); PLB 5.71 (ISBN 0-688-84125-2). Greenwillow.

--Potatoes, Potatoes. LC 67-16231. (Illus.). (gr. k-3). 1967. PLB 7.89 o.p. (ISBN 0-06-023927-1, HarpJ). Har-Row.

--The Straw Maid: A Greenwillow Read-ALone Book. LC 81-6325. (Illus.). 48p. (gr. 1-3). 1983. 9.00 (ISBN 0-688-00344-3); lib. bdg. 8.59 (ISBN 0-688-00330-3). Greenwillow.

Lobel, Arnold. The Book of Pigericks. LC 82-47730. (Illus.). 48p. (gr. k-3). 1983. 9.57i (ISBN 0-06-023982-4, HarpJ); PLB 9.89g (ISBN 0-06-023983-2). Har-Row.

--How the Rooster Saved the Day. LC 76-17602. (Illus.). 32p. (gr. k-3). 1977. 10.00 (ISBN 0-688-80063-7); PLB 7.92 o.p. (ISBN 0-688-84063-9). Greenwillow.

--The Man Who Took the Indoors Out. LC 74-2618. (Illus.). 32p. (gr. k-3). 1974. 10.53i (ISBN 0-06-023946-8, HarpJ); PLB 10.89 o.p. (ISBN 0-06-023947-6). Har-Row.

--Ming Lo Moves the Mountain. (Illus.). (ps-3). 1982. 9.50 (ISBN 0-688-00610-8); PLB 8.59 (ISBN 0-688-00611-6). Morrow.

--Mouse Soup. LC 76-41517. (I Can Read Bk.). (Illus.). (gr. k-3). 1977. 7.64i (ISBN 0-06-023967-0, HarpJ); PLB 8.89 (ISBN 0-06-023968-9). Har-Row.

--Uncle Elephant. LC 80-8944. (An I Can Read Bk.). (Illus.). 64p. (gr. k-3). 1981. 7.64i (ISBN 0-06-023979-4, HarpJ); PLB 8.89g (ISBN 0-06-023980-8). Har-Row.

Lobel, Brana. The Revenant. 1980. pap. 2.25 o.p. (ISBN 0-451-09451-4, E9451, Sig). NAL.

Lobel, Leon & Lobel, Stanley. Meat. LC 78-5939. 1978. pap. 3.95 (ISBN 0-15-658549-9, Harv). HarBraceJ.

Lobel, Stanley, jt. auth. see Lobel, Leon.

Lobell, John. Between Silence & Light: Spirit in the Architecture of Louis I. Kahn. LC 78-65437. (Illus.). 1979. pap. 10.95 (ISBN 0-394-73687-7). Shambhala Pubns.

Lober, Arnold, jt. auth. see Viorst, Judith.

Loblay, R. H. & Tiller, D. J. Fluid, Electrolyte & Acid-Base Disturbances: A Practical Guide for Interns. 144p. 1976. text ed. 14.95 (ISBN 0-471-25861-X, Pub. by Wiley Med). Wiley.

Lobo, Ben & Links, Sara. Side of the Road: A Hitchhiker's Guide to the United States. LC 71-175046. 1972. pap. 1.95 o.p. (ISBN 0-671-21236-2, Fireside). S&S.

Lobo, Jerome. Relation Historique d'Abissinie traduite du Portugais. (Bibliotheque Africaine Ser.). 550p. (Fr.). 1974. Repr. of 1728 ed. lib. bdg. 135.00x o.p. (ISBN 0-8287-0550-X, 72-2144). Clearwater Pub.

Lobsenz, Norman, jt. auth. see Lasswell, Marcia.

Lobsenz, Norman, jt. auth. see Weisinger, Hendrie.

Lobsenz, Norman M., jt. auth. see Weisinger, Hendrie.

LoBue, Joseph & Gordon, Albert S., eds. Humoral Control of Growth & Differentiation, 2 vols. Incl. Vol. 1. Vertebrate Regulatory Factors. 1973. 60.00 (ISBN 0-12-453801-0); Vol. 2. Nonvertebrate Neuroendocrinology & Ageing. 1974. 51.50 (ISBN 0-12-453802-9). Set. 90.50 (ISBN 0-686-85524-8). Acad Pr.

Lochak, Michele & Mangin, Marie-France. Suzette & Nicholas & the Sunijudi Circus. (Illus.). 32p. (gr. 4-8). 1981. 7.95 (ISBN 0-399-20750-3, Philomel); lib. bdg. 7.99 (ISBN 0-399-61160-6). Putnam Pub Group.

Locher, Carl & Dobler, J. Die Orgel-Register und Ihre Klangfarben: Ein Nachschlagewerk Fur Organisten, Physiker und Physiologen. (Bibliotheca Organologica: Vol. 12). 1971. 37.50 o.s.i. (ISBN 90-6027-290-0, Pub. by Frits Knuf Netherlands); wrappers 22.50 o.s.i. (ISBN 90-6027-151-3). Pendragon NY.

Locher, Frances, ed. Contemporary Authors, Vol. 106. (Contemporary Authors Ser.). 600p. 1982. 74.00x (ISBN 0-8103-1906-3). Gale.

--Contemporary Authors: A Bio-Bibliographical Guide to Current Writers in Fiction, General Non-Fiction, Poetry, Journalism, Drama, Motion Pictures, Television, & Other Fields. LC 62-52046. (Contemporary Authors Ser.: Vol. 103). 850p. 1981. 74.00x (ISBN 0-8103-1903-9). Gale.

--Contemporary Authors: A Bio-Bibliographical Guide to Current Writers in Fiction, General Non-Fiction, Poetry, Journalism, Drama, Motion Pictures, Television & Other Fields, Vol. 102. LC 62-52046. (Contemporary Authors Ser.). 900p. 1981. 74.00x (ISBN 0-8103-1902-0). Gale.

--Contemporary Authors: A Bio-Bibliographical Guide to Current Writers in Fiction, General Nonfiction, Poetry, Journalism, Drama, Motion Pictures, Television & Other Fields, Vol. 104. LC 62-52046. (Contemporary Authors Ser.). 800p. 1982. 74.00 (ISBN 0-8103-1904-7). Gale.

Locher, Frances C., ed. Contemporary Authors, Vol. 105. (Contemporary Authors Ser.). 600p. 1982. 74.00x (ISBN 0-8103-1905-5). Gale.

Locher, Frances C. & Evory, Ann, eds. Contemporary Authors: A Bibliographical Guide to Current Writers in Fiction, General Nonfiction, Poetry, Journalism, Drama, Motion Pictures, Television, & Other Fields. Incl. Vols. 1-4. rev. ed. 1967. (ISBN 0-8103-0000-1); Vols. 5-8. rev. ed. 1969. (ISBN 0-8103-0001-X); Vols. 9-12. rev. ed. 1974. (ISBN 0-8103-0002-8); Vols. 13-16. rev. ed. 1975. (ISBN 0-8103-0027-3); Vol. 17-20. rev. ed. 1976. (ISBN 0-8103-0032-X); Vols. 21-24. rev. ed. 1976. (ISBN 0-8103-0033-8); Vols. 25-28. rev. ed. 1977. (ISBN 0-8103-0034-6); Vols. 29-32. rev. ed. 1978. (ISBN 0-685-59670-2); Vols. 33-36. rev. ed. 1978. (ISBN 0-8103-0014-1); Vols. 37-40. rev. ed. 1979. (ISBN 0-8103-0016-8); Vols. 41-44. rev. ed. 1979. (ISBN 0-8103-0041-9); Vols. 45-48. 1974. (ISBN 0-8103-0020-6); Vols. 49-52. 1974. (ISBN 0-8103-0024-9); Vols. 53-56. 1975. (ISBN 0-8103-0022-2); Vols. 57-60. 1976. (ISBN 0-8103-0026-5); Vols. 61-64. 1976. (ISBN 0-8103-0028-1); Vols. 69-72. 1978. (ISBN 0-8103-0030-3); Vols. 73-76. (ISBN 0-8103-0031-1); **Vol. 77-80. 1978 (ISBN 0-8103-0039-7); Vols. 81-84. 1979 (ISBN 0-8103-0046-X); Vols. 85-88. 1979 (ISBN 0-8103-0047-8); Vols. 89-92. 1980 (ISBN 0-8103-0048-6); Vols. 93-96. 1980 (ISBN 0-8103-0049-4). LC 62-52046. sold in 4 vol. units 74.00x ea. Gale.**

Locher, J. C., jt. auth. see Escher, M. C.

Lochhead, Jack, jt. auth. see Whimbey, Arthur.

Lochhead, Marion. Renaissance of Wonder: The Fantasy Worlds of J. R. Tolkein, C. S. Lewis, George MacDonald, E. Nesbit, & Others. LC 80-7753. 192p. 1980. 8.95i (ISBN 0-06-250520-3, HarpR). Har-Row.

Lochner, Louis P. Kreisler. enl. ed. (Illus.). 455p. 1981. Repr. of 1950 ed. 25.00 (ISBN 0-87666-575-X, Z-46). Paganiniana Pubns.

Lochovsky, F. H., jt. auth. see Tsichritzis, Dennis C.

Lochte-Holtgreven, W., ed. Plasma Diagnostics. 1968. 97.75 (ISBN 0-444-10237-X, North-Holland). Elsevier.

LoCicero, J. L., jt. ed. see Lawrence, V. B.

LoCigno, Joseph P., jt. ed. see Marcoux, Paul.

Lock, D. S. Engineers' Metric Manual & Buyers' Guide. 1974. text ed. 245.00 (ISBN 0-08-018220-8). Pergamon.

Lock, F. P. Susanna Centlivre. (English Authors Ser.). 1979. lib. bdg. 14.95 (ISBN 0-8057-6744-4, Twayne). G K Hall.

Lock, Grahame, tr. see Liebknecht, Karl.

Lock, Margaret M. East Asian Medicine in Urban Japan: Varieties of Medical Experience. 1980. 30.00x (ISBN 0-520-03820-7). U of Cal Pr.

Lock, R. N. Library Administration. 3rd ed. 200p. 1973. 10.95x o.p. (ISBN 0-8464-0566-0). Beekman Pubs.

Lockard, Duane. Perverted Priorities of American Politics. 2nd ed. 1976. 14.95x (ISBN 0-02-371590-1, 37159). Macmillan.

Lockard, Duane & Murphy, Walter L. Basic Cases in Constitutional Law. 1980. pap. text ed. 13.95x (ISBN 0-02-371510-3). Macmillan.

Lockard, Dunne. The Politics of State & Local Government. 3rd ed. 288p. 1983. pap. text ed. 20.95 (ISBN 0-02-371530-8). Macmillan.

Lockard, Joan S. & Ward, Arthur A., Jr., eds. Epilepsy: A Window to Brain Mechanisms. 296p. 1980. text ed. 36.00 (ISBN 0-89004-499-6). Raven.

Lockard, Peggy Hamilton. This Is Tucson: Guidebook to the Old Pueblo. (Illus.). 260p. 1982. pap. 8.00 (ISBN 0-914468-08-1). Pepper Pub.

Lockard, Thaddeus, jt. auth. see Ware, Porter.

Lockard, William K. Drawing As a Means to Architecture. rev. ed. LC 76-47137. (Illus.). 1977. pap. 15.00x (ISBN 0-914468-04-9). Pepper Pub.

Locke, Don, jt. auth. see Weinreich-Haste, Helen.

Locke, Flora M. College Mathematics for Business. 2nd ed. LC 73-10090. 384p. 1974. text ed. 21.95 (ISBN 0-471-54321-7); tchrs' manual 6.25x (ISBN 0-471-54320-9). Wiley.

--Electronic Calculators for Business Use. LC 78-1852. 1978. pap. text ed. 21.95x (ISBN 0-471-03579-3); pap. text ed. 5.00 (ISBN 0-471-03766-4). Wiley.

Locke, Harvey J. Predicting Adjustment in Marriage: A Comparison of a Divorced & a Happily Married Group. LC 68-54424. (Illus.). 1968. Repr. of 1951 ed. lib. bdg. 19.25x (ISBN 0-8371-0541-2, LOMA). Greenwood.

Locke, John. The Correspondence of John Locke, 2 vols. De Beer, E. S., ed. Incl. Letters 1-461, Covering the Years 1650-1679. Vol. 1. 98.00x (ISBN 0-19-824396-0); Letters - 462-848 Covering the Years 1679-1686. Vol. 2. 110.00x (ISBN 0-19-824559-9). 1976. Oxford U Pr.

--The Correspondence of John Locke, Vol. 4. De Beer, E. S., ed. (Clarendon Edition of the Works of John Locke). 1979. 110.00x (ISBN 0-19-824561-0). Oxford U Pr.

--The Correspondence of John Locke: Vol. 5, Letters 1702-2198 Covering the Years 1694-1697. DeBeer, E. S., ed. 1979. text ed. 110.00x (ISBN 0-19-824562-9). Oxford U Pr.

--The Correspondence of John Locke, Vol. 6: Letters 2199 to 2664. De Beer, E. S., ed. 806p. 1981. text ed. 119.00x (ISBN 0-19-824563-7). Oxford U Pr.

--The Correspondence of John Locke: Volume 3, Letters 849-1241. De Beer, Gavin R., ed. (Clarendon Edition of the Works of John Locke). 1978. 110.00x (ISBN 0-19-824560-2). Oxford U Pr.

--Essay Concerning Human Understanding. Woozley, A. O., ed. pap. 6.95 (ISBN 0-452-00579-5, F579, Mer). NAL.

--An Essay Concerning Human Understanding. Nidditch, Peter H., ed. (Clarendon Edition of the Works of John Locke Ser). 1975. 62.00x (ISBN 0-19-824386-3). Oxford U Pr.

--Essay Concerning Human Understanding, 2 Vols. Fraser, Alexander C., ed. Set. 26.00 (ISBN 0-8446-2478-0). Peter Smith.

--A Letter Concerning Toleration. Tully, James, ed. (HPC Philosophical Classics Ser.). 96p. 1983. pap. text ed. 3.95 (ISBN 0-915145-60-X). Hackett Pub.

--Locke's Essay Concerning Human Understanding, Bks. II & IV. 405p. 1962. Repr. of 1905 ed. 24.50 (ISBN 0-87548-033-0). Open Court.

--Of Civil Government, 2nd Essay. 224p. 1955. pap. 5.95 (ISBN 0-89526-921-X). Regnery-Gateway.

--Second Treatise of Government. Macpherson, C. B., ed. (Philosophical Classsics Ser.). 138p. 1980. lib. bdg. 12.50 (ISBN 0-915144-93-X); pap. text ed. 2.95 (ISBN 0-915144-86-7). Hackett Pub.

--Several Papers Relating to Money, Interest & Trade, Etc. LC 67-29701. Repr. of 1696 ed. 35.00x (ISBN 0-678-00334-3). Kelley.

--Two Tracts on Government. Abrams, Philip, ed. 1967. 37.50 (ISBN 0-521-05583-0). Cambridge U Pr.

--Two Treatises of Government. Laslett, Peter, ed. 1960. 49.50 (ISBN 0-521-06903-3). Cambridge U Pr.

--Two Treatises of Government. pap. 4.95 (ISBN 0-451-62020-8, ME2303, Ment). NAL.

Locke, John F., tr. see Maquet, J. P.

Locke, Lawrence F. & Wyrick-Spirduso, Waneen. Proposals That Work: A Guide for Planning Research. LC 76-4965. 1976. pap. 9.50x (ISBN 0-8077-2495-5). Tchrs Coll.

Locke, M., ed. see Society for the Study of Development & Growth - Symposium.

Locke, M., ed. see Society For The Study Of Developmental Biology - 24th Symposium.

Locke, Michael. Power & Politics in the School System: A Guidebook. 192p. 1974. 18.95x (ISBN 0-7100-7732-7); pap. 8.95 (ISBN 0-7100-7733-5). Routledge & Kegan.

Locke, Michael & Locke, Michael, eds. Cellular Membranes in Development. 1964. 53.50 (ISBN 0-12-454168-2). Acad Pr.

Locke, N., ed. see Society For The Study Of Developmental Biology - 27th Symposium.

Locke, Richard A. The Moon Hoax. (Science Fiction Ser). 120p. 1975. Repr. of 1854 ed. lib. bdg. 9.95 o.p. (ISBN 0-8398-2308-8, Gregg). G K Hall.

Locke, Robert, ed. Hollywood Reporter Studio Blu-Book. 280p. 1983. pap. 25.00 (ISBN 0-941140-01-6). Verdugo Pr.

Locke, Steven & Hornig-Rohan, Mady. Mind & Immunity: Behavioral Immunology (1976-1982)--an Annotated Bibliography. 240p. (Orig.). 1983. 35.00 (ISBN 0-910903-01-8); pap. 22.50 (ISBN 0-910903-02-6). Elliot Pr.

Locke, William N. & Booth, E. Donald, eds. Machine Translation of Languages: Fourteen Essays. LC 75-29339. 243p. 1976. Repr. of 1955 ed. lib. bdg. 17.00x (ISBN 0-8371-8434-7, LOMT). Greenwood.

Lockemann, P. C., ed. Systems for Large Data Bases. 1977. 32.75 (ISBN 0-7204-0546-7, North-Holland). Elsevier.

Locker, Kitty O., jt. auth. see Weeks, Francis W.

Lockerbie, Jeanette. A Cup of Sugar, Neighbor. (Quiet Time Bks.). 128p. 1974. pap. text ed. 2.95 (ISBN 0-8024-1681-0). Moody.

--Living on the Plus Side. 1980. 5.95 (ISBN 0-8024-9819-1). Moody.

--More Salt in My Kitchen. LC 80-12357. (Moody Quiet Time Ser.). 1980. pap. 2.95 (ISBN 0-8024-5668-5). Moody.

Lockerbie, Jeanette, jt. auth. see Graham, Franklinn.

Lockery, Shirley, jt. ed. see Stanford, E. P.

Lockett, Betty A. Aging, Politics & Research: Setting the Federal Agenda for Research on Aging. 1983. text ed. price not set (ISBN 0-8261-4430-6). Springer Pub.

Lockett, Clay, jt. auth. see Perceval, Don.

Lockett, David. Getting New Business Leads: A Guide for Advertising Agencies. LC 80-70204. 1981. 9.95 (ISBN 0-87251-062-X). Crain Bks.

Lockett, T. A. Davenport Pottery & Porcelain: 1794-1887. 1973. 10.00 o.p. (ISBN 0-8048-1079-6). C E Tuttle.

Lockhart, B. B., jt. auth. see Antonacci, R. J.

Lockhart, Bill C., jt. auth. see Beitler, Ethel J.

Lockhart, Carol A. & Werther, William B., eds. Labor Relations in Nursing. LC 79-90382. 176p. 1980. pap. text ed. 19.95 (ISBN 0-913654-63-9). Aspen Systems.

Lockhart, Ian M., jt. auth. see Ellis, Gwynn P.

Lockhart, J. & Otte, E. Letters & People of the Spanish Indies. LC 75-6007. (Cambridge Latin American Studies: No. 22). 322p. 1976. 37.50 (ISBN 0-521-20883-1); pap. 10.95x (ISBN 0-521-09990-0). Cambridge U Pr.

Lockhart, J. A. & Wiseman, A. J. Introduction to Crop Husbandry. 5th ed. (Illus.). 300p. 1983. 40.00 (ISBN 0-08-029793-5); pap. 16.00 (ISBN 0-08-029792-7). Pergamon.

Lockhart, J. C. Redistribution Reactions. 1970. 37.50 (ISBN 0-12-454450-9). Acad Pr.

Lockhart, J. Stewart. The Lockhart Collection of Chinese Copper Coins. LC 74-27610. (Illus.). 240p. 1975. Repr. 35.00x o.s.i. (ISBN 0-88000-056-2). Quarterman.

Lockhart, James. Spanish Peru, Fifteen Thirty-Two to Fifteen Sixty: A Colonial Society. LC 68-14032. (Illus.). 298p. 1968. 25.00 (ISBN 0-299-04660-5); pap. 9.95 (ISBN 0-299-04664-8). U of Wis Pr.

Lockhart, John G. Curses, Lucks & Talismans. LC 70-132016. (Illus.). 1971. Repr. of 1938 ed. 34.00 o.p. (ISBN 0-8103-3376-7). Gale.

--Life of Sir Walter Scott. 1969. Repr. of 1906 ed. 8.95x (ISBN 0-460-00039-X, Evman). Biblio Dist.

Lockhart, Saul. The Complete Guide to Phillippines. (The Complete Asian Guide Ser.). (Illus., Orig.). 1981. pap. 6.95 (ISBN 962-7031-06-2). C E Tuttle.

--Manila by Night. Maitland, Derek, ed. (Asia by Night Ser.). (Illus., Orig.). 1981. pap. 4.95 (ISBN 962-7031-08-9, Pub. by CFW Pubns. Hong Kong). C E Tuttle.

Lockhart, William B., et al. Cases & Materials on Constitutional Rights & Liberties. 5th ed. LC 80-54541. (American Casebook Ser.). 1290p. 1981. text ed. 26.95 (ISBN 0-8299-2135-4). West Pub.

Lockhead, Jack, jt. auth. see Whimbey, Arthur.

Locklear, Edmond, Jr. Your Future in Accounting. LC 73-114134. (Career Guidance Ser). 1971. pap. 4.50 (ISBN 0-668-02232-9). Arco.

Lockler, et al. Historias y Cuentos le Todos los Tiempos. (Illus.). (gr. 3). 1977. text ed. 10.48 tchr's manual (ISBN 0-87443-014-3). Benson.

Lockley, Fred. The Lockley Files, Vol. 3: Visionaries, Mountain Men, & Empire Builders. LC 81-50845. 385p. 1982. pap. 9.95 (ISBN 0-931742-10-2). Rainy Day Oreg.

--The Lockley Files, Vol. 4: A Bit of Verse: Poems from the Lockley Files. Helm, Mike, ed. & intro. by. LC 81-50845. 150p. (Orig.). 1982. pap. 9.95x (ISBN 0-931742-13-7). Rainy Day Oreg.

Lockley, R. M. Britain in Colour. 1976. 10.95 o.p. (ISBN 0-7134-0016-1, Pub. by Batsford England). David & Charles.

Lockley, Ronald. New Zealand Birds. (Illus.). 179p. 1983. 45.00 (ISBN 0-686-83935-8, Pub. by Heinemann Pub New Zealand). Intl Schol Bk Serv.

--Orielton-the Human & Natural History of a Welsh Manor. (Illus.). 1978. 15.00 o.s.i. (ISBN 0-233-96928-4). Transatlantic.

Lockley, Ronald, jt. auth. see Adams, Richard.

Lockley, Ronald M. Flight of the Storm Petrel. LC 82-18361. (Illus.). 192p. 1983. 16.95 (ISBN 0-8397-2312-1). Eriksson.

Locklin, Gerald. Two for the Seesaw, One for the Road. LC 80-80783. 1980. 13.50 (ISBN 0-89002-155-4); pap. 5.00 (ISBN 0-89002-154-6). Northwoods Pr.

Lockmiller, David A. Enoch H. Crowder: Soldier, Lawyer & Statesman. LC 55-62560. 286p. 1955. 18.00x (ISBN 0-8262-0538-0). U of Mo Pr.

Lockridge, Frances, jt. auth. see Lockridge, Richard.

Lockridge, Kenneth A. Settlement & Unsettlement in Early America: The Crisis of Political Legitimacy Before the Revolution. LC 80-25658. (Illus.). 96p. 1981. 12.95 (ISBN 0-521-23707-6). Cambridge U Pr.

Lockridge, Richard. The Old Die Young. LC 80-7775. 224p. 1980. 11.49i (ISBN 0-690-01948-3). Har-Row.

--One Lady, Two Cats. LC 67-13302. 1967. 6.68i (ISBN 0-397-00492-3). Har-Row.

Lockridge, Richard & Lockridge, Frances. Death Takes a Bow. (Mr. & Mrs. North Ser.: No. 4). 240p. 1982. pap. 2.95 (ISBN 0-671-44337-2). PB.

--Murder in a Hurry. 1982. pap. 2.95 (ISBN 0-686-83088-1). PB.

--Murder Within Murder. (Mr. & Mrs. North Mystery Ser.). 1982. pap. 2.95 (ISBN 0-671-44334-8). PB.

Lockshin, R., jt. auth. see Bowen, I.

Locksley, G., jt. auth. see Shackleton, J. R.

Locksley, Gareth, jt. auth. see Shackleton, J. R.

Locksley, N. Applied Linear Algebra: An Introduction. (Finite Math Text Ser.). write for info. (ISBN 0-685-84477-3). J W Wills.

Lockspeiser, E. Debussy: His Life & Mind. LC 78-51668. (Illus.). 1979. Vol. 1. 44.50 (ISBN 0-521-22053-X); pap. 12.95 (ISBN 0-521-29341-3); Vol. 2. 54.50 (ISBN 0-521-22054-8); pap. 14.95 (ISBN 0-521-29342-1). Cambridge U Pr.

Lockspeiser, Edward, jt. auth. see Blunt, Anthony.

Lockspeiser, Edward, tr. & ed. see Prunieres, Henry.

Lockwood. The Membranes of Animal Cells. 2nd ed. (Studies in Biology: No. 27). 1979. 5.95 o.p. (ISBN 0-8391-0155-4). Univ Park.

--Prison Sexual Violence. 1979. 16.95 (ISBN 0-444-99067-4). Elsevier.

Lockwood, A. P., jt. auth. see Hempleman, H. V.

Lockwood, A. P., ed. Effects of Pollutants on Aquatic Organisms. LC 75-32448. (Society for Experimental Biology Seminar Ser.: No. 2). 180p. 1976. 42.50 (ISBN 0-521-21103-4); pap. 16.95x (ISBN 0-521-29044-9). Cambridge U Pr.

Lockwood, Albert. Notes on the Literature of the Piano. LC 67-30400. (Music Ser). 1968. Repr. of 1940 ed. lib. bdg. 25.00 (ISBN 0-306-70983-X). Da Capo.

Lockwood, Barbara, jt. auth. see Sheldon, Margaret.

Lockwood, Dean P. Survey of Classical Roman Literature, 2 Vols. LC 34-40316. 1962. Vol. 1. pap. 7.50x (ISBN 0-226-48962-0); Vol. 2. pap. 12.00x (ISBN 0-226-48963-9, Midway Reprint). U of Chicago Pr.

Lockwood, Deborah, compiled by. Library Instruction: A Bibliography. LC 78-20011. 1979. lib. bdg. 22.50 (ISBN 0-313-20720-8, LL1/). Greenwood.

Lockwood, DeLauna, ed. Cumulative Index to Nursing & Allied Health Literature, Vol. 25. LC 78-643434. 1980. 80.00 (ISBN 0-910478-16-3). Glendale Advent Med.

--Cumulative Index to Nursing & Allied Health Literature, Vol. 26. LC 78-643434. 1981. 90.00 (ISBN 0-910478-17-1). Glendale Advent Med.

--Cumulative Index to Nursing & Allied Health Literature, Vol. 27. LC 78-643434. 110p. 1982. write for info. (ISBN 0-910478-18-X). Glendale Advent Med.

Lockwood, Edward H. & Macmillan, R. H. Geometric Symmetry. LC 77-77713. (Illus.). 1978. 37.50 (ISBN 0-521-21685-0). Cambridge U Pr.

Lockwood, Edward H. & Prag, A. Book of Curves. 1961. 36.50 (ISBN 0-521-05585-7). Cambridge U Pr.

Lockwood, J. G. World Climatology: An Environmental Approach. LC 73-91113. (Illus.). 352p. 1974. 29.95 o.p. (ISBN 0-312-89110-5). St Martin.

Lockwood, Jonathan S. The Soviet View of U. S. Strategic Doctrine: Implications for Decisionmaking. (Illus.). 175p. 1983. 19.95 (ISBN 0-87855-467-X). Transaction Bks.

Lockwood, Loni, tr. see Steiner, Rudolf.

Lockwood, Luke V. Furniture Collector's Glossary. LC 67-27460. (Architecture & Decorative Art Ser). 1967. Repr. of 1940 ed. lib. bdg. 15.00 (ISBN 0-306-70968-6). Da Capo.

Lockwood, Luke V., jt. auth. see Barber, Edward A.

Lockwood, Robert S. & Hillier, Carol M. Legislative Analysis: With Emphasis on National Security Affairs. LC 81-67633. 112p. 1981. 17.50 (ISBN 0-89089-185-0); pap. 8.95 (ISBN 0-89089-186-9). Carolina Acad Pr.

Lockwood, Samuel, tr. see Steiner, Rudolf.

Lockwood, W. B. Languages of the British Isles, Past & Present. (Andre Deutsch Language Library). 1977. lib. bdg. 30.75 o.p. (ISBN 0-233-96666-8). Westview.

Lockwood, W. D. A Panorama of Indo-European Languages. 1972. text ed. 14.50x o.p. (ISBN 0-09-111020-3, Hutchinson U Lib); pap. text ed. 10.00x o.p. (ISBN 0-09-111021-1, Hutchinson U Lib). Humanities.

Lockyer, Herbert. The All Series, Bks. 1-14. Incl. Bk. 1. All the Apostles of the Bible. 13.95 (ISBN 0-310-28010-9); Bk. 2. All the Books & Chapters of the Bible. 13.95 (ISBN 0-310-28020-6); Bk. 3. All the Doctrines of the Bible. 13.95 (ISBN 0-310-28050-8); Bks. 2 & 3 Set. 21.90 o.p. (ISBN 0-310-28168-7); Bk. 4. All the Children of the Bible. 12.95 (ISBN 0-310-28030-3); Bk. 5. All the Holy Days & Holidays. 13.95 (ISBN 0-310-28060-5); Bk. 6. All the Kings & Queens of the Bible. 13.95 (ISBN 0-310-28070-2); Bks. 5 & 6 Set. 21.90 o.p. (ISBN 0-310-28178-4); Bk. 7. All the Men of the Bible. 14.95 (ISBN 0-310-28080-X); Bk. 8. All the Women of the Bible. 12.95 (ISBN 0-310-28150-4); Bks. 7 & 8 Set. 20.90 o.p. (ISBN 0-310-28188-1); Bk. 9. All the Miracles of the Bible. 12.95 (ISBN 0-310-28100-8); Bk. 10. All the Parables of the Bible. 14.95 (ISBN 0-310-28110-5); Bks. 9 & 10 Set. 21.90 o.p. (ISBN 0-310-28198-9); Bk. 11. All the Prayers of the Bible. 12.95 (ISBN 0-310-28120-2); Bk. 12. All the Promises **of the Bible. 14.95 (ISBN 0-310-28130-X); Bks. 11 & 12 Set. 24.90 o.p. (ISBN 0-310-28208-X); Bk. 13. All the Trades & Occupations of the Bible. 13.95 (ISBN 0-310-28140-7); Bk. 14. All the Messianic Prophecies of the Bible. 14.95 (ISBN 0-310-28090-7). Zondervan.**

--Portraits of the Savior. 144p. 1983. 9.95 (ISBN 0-8407-5288-1); pap. 4.95 (ISBN 0-8407-5838-3). Nelson.

Lockyer, Herbert, Sr. Apocalipsis: El Drama de los Siglos. Carrodeguas, Andy, ed. Calderon, Wilfredo, tr. from Eng. Orig. Title: Revelation: The Drama of the Ages. 274p. (Span.). 1982. pap. 4.00 (ISBN 0-8297-1292-5). Life Pubs Intl.

Lockyer, W. John. Essentials of ABO-Rh Grouping & Compatibility Testing: Theoretical Aspects & Practical Application. (Illus.). 152p. 1982. text ed. 16.50 (ISBN 0-7236-0635-8). Wright-PSG.

Locquin. Handbook of Microscopy. 1982. text ed. 119.95 (ISBN 0-408-10679-4). Butterworth.

Lodder, J. Yeasts: A Taxonomic Study. 2nd ed. Date not set. 181.50 (ISBN 0-444-80421-8). Elsevier.

Loddy, Edmund J., Jr., jt. auth. see Roach, Don.

Lodewick, L. & Gunn, A. D. The Physical Examination. 270p. 1982. text ed. 35.00 (ISBN 0-85200-395-1, Pub. by MTP Pr England). Kluwer Boston.

Lodge, Ann, ed. Creation Sings. 1980. pap. 1.25 (ISBN 0-664-10091-0). Westminster.

Lodge, David. Souls & Bodies. LC 82-61673. 252p. 1983. Repr. pap. 5.95 (ISBN 0-688-01594-8). Quill NY.

Lodge, David, ed. see Eliot, George.

Lodge, Edith. Journey Through Noon. 64p. 1974. 4.00 (ISBN 0-911838-39-2). Windy Row.

Lodge, H. C. & Redmond, C. F., eds. Selections from the Correspondence of Theodore Roosevelt & Henry Cabot Lodge, 1884-1918, 2 Vols. LC 72-146156. (American Public Figures Ser). 1971. Repr. of 1925 ed. Set. lib. bdg. 125.00 (ISBN 0-306-70129-4). Da Capo.

Lodge, Henry C., ed. see Cabot, George.

Lodge, James P., Jr., ed. The Smoke of London: Two Prophecies. Incl. Fumifugium or, The Inconvience of the Aer-Smoake of London Dissipated. Evelyn, John; The Doom of London. Barr, Robert. 7.50 o.p. (ISBN 0-08-022309-5). Pergamon.

Lodge, Jim, tr. see Denaerde, Stefan & Stevens, Wendelle C.

Lodge, Juliet. Institutions & Policies of the European Community. LC 81-23271. 320p. 1982. 32.50 (ISBN 0-312-41887-6). St Martin.

--Terrorism: A Challenge to the State. 256p. 1981. 26.00x (ISBN 0-312-79230-1). St Martin.

Lodge, Juliet, jt. auth. see Herman, Valentine.

Lodge, Milton. Soviet Elite Attitudes Since Stalin. LC 73-86335. 1969. pap. text ed. 4.50 (ISBN 0-675-09435-6). Merrill.

Lodge, Paul & Blackstone, Tessa. Educational Policy & Educational Inequality. 270p. 1983. text ed. 19.95x (ISBN 0-85520-192-4, Pub. by Martin Robertson England). Biblio Dist.

Lodge, Richard. Studies in Eighteenth-Century Diplomacy, 1740-1748. Repr. of 1930 ed. lib. bdg. 19.75x (ISBN 0-8371-4261-X, LODI). Greenwood.

Lodge, Rupert. Great Thinkers. LC 68-26212. Repr. of 1949 ed. 13.50 o.p. (ISBN 0-8046-0276-X). Kennikat.

Lodge, Thomas see Gosson, Stephen.

Lodi, Else. Color Treasury of Aquarium Fish. (Bounty Bk. Ser.). (Illus.). 64p. 1974. pap. 1.98 o.p. (ISBN 0-517-51430-3). Crown.

Lodo, Venerable L. Bardo Teachings: The Way of Death & Rebirth. Clark, Nancy & Parke, Caroline M., eds. (Illus.). 76p. 1982. pap. text ed. 5.95 (ISBN 0-910165-00-9). KDK Pubns.

Lods, Adolphe. Israel, from Its Beginning to the Middle of the Eighth Century. Hooke, S. H., tr. LC 75-41180. 1948. 24.75 (ISBN 0-404-14569-8). AMS PR.

Lodwick, Gwilym S. The Bones & Joints. (Atlas of Tumor Radiology Ser.). (Illus.). 1971. 49.50 o.p. (ISBN 0-8151-5625-1). Year Bk Med.

Lodwig, Robert R. Career English. LC 80-24831. 200p. (Orig.). 1981. pap. text ed. 7.25x (ISBN 0-686-84386-X). Boynton Cook Pubs.

Loe, Kelley, jt. auth. see Neuberger, Richard L.

Loeb, Arthur L. Space Structures: Their Harmony & Counterpoint. 192p. 1976. text ed. 26.50 (ISBN 0-201-04650-4); pap. text ed. 19.50 (ISBN 0-201-04651-2). A-W.

Loeb, Benjamin S., jt. auth. see Seaborg, Glenn T.

Loeb, Edwin M. Blood Sacrifice Complex. LC 24-4020. 1924. pap. 8.00 (ISBN 0-527-00529-0). Kraus Repr.

Loeb, Gerald M. The Battle for Investment Survival. rev. ed. 9.95 o.p. (ISBN 0-671-21303-2). S&S.

Loeb, Jo & Loeb, Paul. Cathletics: Ways to Amuse & Exercise Your Cat. LC 80-39813. (Illus.). 96p. 1981. pap. 4.50 (ISBN 0-13-121004-1). P-H.

--You Can Train Your Cat. 1977. 9.95 o.p. (ISBN 0-671-22578-2). S&S.

Loeb, Marcia. Art Deco Designs & Motifs. (Dover Pictorial Archives Ser). (Illus.). 96p. (Orig.). 1972. pap. 4.00 (ISBN 0-486-22826-6). Dover.

--Art Deco Designs & Motifs. (Illus.). 8.00 (ISBN 0-8446-4575-3). Peter Smith.

Loeb, Millie, jt. auth. see Houston, Jean.

Loeb, Paul, jt. auth. see Loeb, Jo.

Loeb, Robert. Crime & Capital Punishment. LC 78-23890. (Impact Books Ser.). (Illus.). (gr. 7 up). 1978. PLB 8.90 s&l (ISBN 0-531-01453-3). Watts.

--Your Legal Rights As a Minor. rev. ed. LC 78-7856. 1978. lib. bdg. 8.90 s&l o.p. (ISBN 0-531-02231-5). Watts.

Loeb, Robert H., Jr. New England Village: Everyday Life in 1810. LC 76-2791. (gr. 4-5). 1976. PLB 8.95a o.p. (ISBN 0-385-11489-3). Doubleday.

Loeb, Stephen E. Ethics in the Accounting Profession. LC 77-16081. (Ser. in Accounting & Information Systems). 1978. pap. text ed. 31.95x (ISBN 0-471-54331-4); solutions manual 4.00x (ISBN 0-471-04348-6). Wiley.

Loebbecke, James K., jt. auth. see Arens, Alvin A.

Loebe, Paul. Nuclear Culture: Living & Working in the Worlds Largest Atomic Complex. LC 81-3194. 320p. 1982. 13.95 (ISBN 0-698-11104-4, Coward). Putnam Pub Group.

Loebel. Programmed Problem Solving for First Year Chemistry. 1983. text ed. 12.95 (ISBN 0-686-84542-0). HM.

Loebel, Arnold. Programmed Problem Solving for First Year Chemistry. LC 82-83359. 512p. pap. text ed. 13.95 (ISBN 0-395-32626-5). HM.

Loebel, JoAnn, jt. auth. see Cramblit, Joella.

Loeber, Dietrich A. East-West & Intersocialist Trade: A Source Book on the International Economic Relations of Soviet Countries, 5 Vols. LC 76-1017. 1976. text ed. 45.00 ea. Vol. 1 (ISBN 0-379-00485-2). Vol. 2 (ISBN 0-379-00486-0). Vol. 3 (ISBN 0-379-00487-9). Vol. 4 (ISBN 0-379-00488-7). Set. Oceana.

Loebl, Suzanne. Conception, Contraception: A New Look. LC 73-8018. (Illus.). 144p. (gr. 9 up). 1974. PLB 7.95 o.p. (ISBN 0-07-038340-5, GB). McGraw.

Loechel, William E. Atlas of Anatomy for Attorneys. (Illus.). 264p. 1983. spiral 26.50x (ISBN 0-398-04735-9). C C Thomas.

--Pictorial Medical Terminology. 126p. 1981. pap. 14.75x spiral (ISBN 0-398-04581-X). C C Thomas.

Loeckx, J. Computability & Decidability. LC 72-82761. (Lecture Notes in Economics & Mathematical Systems: Vol. 68). (Illus.). 82p. 1972. pap. 6.30 o.p. (ISBN 0-387-05869-9). Springer-Verlag.

Loeffler, F. J. & Proctor, C. R., eds. Unit & Bulk Materials Handling. 289p. 1980. 60.00 (ISBN 0-686-69864-9, H00163). ASME.

Loeffler, M., ed. Adolphe Appia: Staging Wagnerian Drama. 96p. Date not set. pap. 4.95 (ISBN 3-7643-1363-3). Birkhauser.

Loehr, Franklin. Diary After Death. 1976. pap. write for info (ISBN 0-515-09568-0). Jove Pubns.

Loehr, James E. & Van Der Meer, Dennis. Mind over Tennis. (Illus.). 192p. cancelled (ISBN 0-914178-52-0, 45026). Golf Digest.

Loehr, Max. The Great Painters of China. LC 79-6030. (Icon Editions). (Illus.). 336p. 1980. 29.95i (ISBN 0-06-435326-5, HarpT); pap. 16.95 (ISBN 0-06-430105-2, IN-105). Har-Row.

Loehr, Raymond C., ed. Phosphorus Management Strategies for Lakes. LC 79-55150. (Illus.). 1980. 59.95 (ISBN 0-250-40332-3). Ann Arbor Science.

Loehr, Raymond C., ed. see Cornell University Agricultural Waste Management Conference, 10th, 1978.

Loehr, Raymond C., ed. see Cornell Waste Management Conference, 8th.

Loehr, Raymond C., ed. see Cornell Waste Management Conference, 9th.

Loehr, Raymond C., et al. Land Application of Wastes, 2 vols. LC 78-27646. 1979. Vol. 1, 332p. 24.50 (ISBN 0-442-21705-6); Vol. 2, 456p. 26.50 (ISBN 0-442-21707-2); Set. 42.50 (ISBN 0-686-92641-2). Krieger.

Loehr, William & Powelson, John P. The Economics of Development & Distribution. 436p. 1981. text ed. 23.95 (ISBN 0-15-518905-0, HC). HarBraceJ.

--Threat to Development: Pitfalls of the NIE. (Special Study in Social, Political, & Economic Developmen). 160p. 1982. lib. bdg. 22.00X (ISBN 0-86531-128-5); pap. text ed. 10.00 (ISBN 0-86531-129-3). Westview.

Loehr, Wm. & Powelson, J. Economic Development, Poverty & Income Distribution. LC 77-23270. 1977. lib. bdg. 29.50 o.p. (ISBN 0-89158-248-7). Westview.

Loeks, Mary Foxwell. Object Lessons for Children's Worship. (Object Lesson Ser). 1979. pap. 3.50 (ISBN 0-8010-5584-9). Baker Bk.

Loellgen, H., ed. Oberrheinisches Kardiologen-Symposium, Freiburg, May 1982: Journal: Cardiology, Vol. 70, Suppl. 1, 1983. (Illus.). vi, 118p. 1983. pap. price not set (ISBN 3-8055-3688-7). S Karger.

Loelling, Carol. Whose House Is This? (Surprise Bk). (ps-4). 1978. 4.95 (ISBN 0-8431-0444-9). Price Stern.

Loen, R. O. Manage More by Doing Less. 1970. 26.95 (ISBN 0-07-038370-7, P&RB). McGraw.

Loeper, John J. The House on Spruce Street. LC 82-1821. (Illus.). 96p. (gr. 4-6). 1982. 9.95 (ISBN 0-689-30929-5). Atheneum.

Loesche, Walter J. Dental Caries: A Treatable Infection. (Illus.). 576p. 1982. spiral 29.75x (ISBN 0-398-04767-7). C C Thomas.

Loeschen, John R. Wrestling with Luther. LC 75-33815. 232p. 1976. 11.50 (ISBN 0-570-03256-3, 15-2164). Concordia.

Loeschen, R., jt. auth. see Bauer, R.

Loesser, Arthur. Humor in American Song. LC 79-181804. (Illus.). 317p. 1975. Repr. of 1942 ed. 34.00x (ISBN 0-8103-4040-2). Gale.

Loetscher, Lefferts A. The Broadening Church: A Study of Theological Issues in the Presbyterian Church Since 1869. LC 54-7110. 195p. text ed. 9.00 (ISBN 0-686-98359-9). Brown Bk.

--Facing the Enlightenment & Pietism: Archibald Alexander & the Founding of Princeton Theological Seminary. LC 82-11995. (Contributions to the Study of Religion Ser.: No. 8). 352p. 1983. lib. bdg. 35.00 (ISBN 0-313-23677-1, LOE/). Greenwood.

--Problem of Christian Unity in Early 19th Century America. Wolf, Richard C., ed. LC 69-14622. (Facet Bks.). 1969. pap. 1.00 o.p. (ISBN 0-8006-3053-X, 1-3053). Fortress.

Loeve, M. Probability Theory II. (Graduate Texts in Mathematics: Vol. 46). 1977. 29.80 (ISBN 0-387-90262-7). Springer-Verlag.

Loew, Clemens, jt. ed. see Grayson, Henry.

Loewe, L. Basil Henriques: A Portrait. 1976. 16.95 o.p. (ISBN 0-7100-8439-0). Routledge & Kegan.

Loewe, Ralph E. A Reader for College Writers: Models..Methods..Mirrors. (Illus.). 1980. pap. text ed. 12.95 (ISBN 0-13-753582-1). P-H.

--The Writing Clinic. 2nd ed. LC 77-17542. (Illus.). 1978. pap. text ed. 12.95 (ISBN 0-13-970434-5). P-H.

Loewenberg, Bert J. Darwinism Comes to America: 1859-1900. Wolf, Richard C., ed. LC 79-84546. (Facet Bks.). (Orig.). 1969. pap. 1.00 o.p. (ISBN 0-8006-3055-6, 1-3055). Fortress.

Loewenberg, Frank & Dolgoff, Ralph. Ethical Decisions for Social Work Practice. LC 81-82888. 126p. 1982. pap. text ed. 8.50 (ISBN 0-87581-273-2). Peacock Pubs.

Loewenberg, Gerhard & Patterson, Samuel C. Comparing Legislatures. (Little, Brown Analytic Studies). 1979. pap. text ed. 10.95 (ISBN 0-316-53078-6). Little.

Loewenberg, J. Hegel's Phenomenology: Dialogues on the Life of Mind. LC 65-15621. xv, 392p. 1965. 24.50 (ISBN 0-87548-022-5). Open Court.

Loewenberg, Jacob. Reason & the Nature of Things. LC 58-6818. (Paul Carus Lecture Ser.). xiv, 399p. 1959. 23.50x (ISBN 0-87548-105-1). Open Court.

Loewenberg, Peter. Decoding the Past: The Psychohistorical Approach. LC 82-47796. 1983. 20.00 (ISBN 0-394-48152-6). Knopf.

Loewenfeld, Hans. Leonhard Kleber und Sein Orgeltabulaturbuch Als Beitrag Zur Geschicte der Orgelmusik Im Beginnenden XVI. (Bibliotheca Organologica: Vol. 19). 1968. Repr. of 1897 ed. 20.00 o.s.i. (ISBN 90-6027-050-9, Pub. by Frits Knuf Netherlands). Pendragon NY.

Loewenheim, F. L. & Langley, H. D., eds. The Politics of Integrity: The Diaries of Henry L. Stimson. LC 75-12711. Date not set. cancelled (ISBN 0-07-038410-X). McGraw.

Loewenstein, Rudolph M. Practice & Precept in Psychoanalytic Technique: Selected Papers of Rudolph M. Loewenstein. LC 81-21859. 248p. 1982. 22.50x (ISBN 0-300-02531-9). Yale U Pr.

Loewenthal, H. J. Guide for the Perplexed Organic Expermentalist. 1978. 19.95 (ISBN 0-471-25862-8, Pub. by Wiley Heyden). Wiley.

Loewenthal, Norman H. & Burby, Raymond J., 3rd, eds. Health Care in New Communities. LC 76-27978. (New Communities Research Ser.). 1976. prof ref 17.50x (ISBN 0-88410-463-X). Ballinger Pub.

Loewenthal, R. E. & Marais, G. V. Carbonate Chemistry of Aquatic Systems, Vol. 2. 600p. 1983. 37.50 (ISBN 0-250-40150-9). Ann Arbor Science.

--Carbonate Chemistry of Aquatic Systems: Theory & Application, Vol. 1. LC 76-24963. 1976. 37.50 (ISBN 0-250-40141-X). Ann Arbor Science.

Loewer, H. Peter. Bringing the Outdoors In. Date not set. pap. 4.95 (ISBN 0-449-08464-7, Columbine). Fawcett.

Loewinsohn, Ron. The Leaves. 50p. (Orig.). 1973. pap. 2.00 o.p. (ISBN 0-87685-146-4). Black Sparrow.

--Magnetic Field(s) LC 82-48879. 1983. 12.95 (ISBN 0-394-53105-1). Knopf.

Loewner, Charles, et al. Charles Loewner: Theory of Continuous Groups. (Mathematicians of Our Time Ser). 1971. 20.00x (ISBN 0-262-06041-8). MIT Pr.

Loewy, Raymond. Industrial Design. LC 79-15104. (Illus.). 250p. 1979. 60.00 (ISBN 0-87951-098-6); deluxe ed. 275.00 signed, ltd. ed. (ISBN 0-87951-102-8). Overlook Pr.

Lofchie, Michael F., ed. The State of the Nations: Constraints on Development in Independent Africa. (African Studies Center, UCLA). 1971. 30.00x (ISBN 0-520-01740-4). U of Cal Pr.

Loffler, E. Geomorphology of Papua New Guinea. 1982. 65.00x (ISBN 0-686-97911-7, Pub. by CSIRO Australia). State Mutual Bk.

Loffler, Fritz. Otto Dix: Life & Work. Hollingdale, R. J., tr. from Ger. LC 81-2947. (Illus.). 424p. 1983. text ed. 95.00x (ISBN 0-8419-0578-9). Holmes & Meier.

Lofgren, Ulf. The Boy Who Ate More Than the Giant, & Other Swedish Folktales. LC 78-8653. (Unicef Storycraft Bks.). (Illus.). (ps-3). 1978. 6.95 o.s.i. (ISBN 0-529-05450-7, Philomel); PLB 6.99 o.s.i. (ISBN 0-529-05451-5). Putnam Pub Group.

--Swedish Toys, Dolls, & Gifts You Can Make Yourself: Traditional Swedish Handicrafts. LC 78-8619. (Unicef Storycraft Bks.). (Illus.). (ps-3). 1978. 6.95 o.s.i. (ISBN 0-529-05448-5, Philomel); PLB 6.99 o.s.i. (ISBN 0-529-05449-3). Putnam Pub Group.

Lofland, John. Analyzing Social Settings. 1971. pap. 9.95x (ISBN 0-534-00631-0). Wadsworth Pub.

--Deviance & Identity. 1969. pap. text ed. 15.95 (ISBN 0-13-208413-9). P-H.

Lofland, John & Fink, Michael. Symbolic Sit-Ins: Protest Occupations at the California Capitol. LC 81-40725. 128p. (Orig.). 1982. PLB 19.75 (ISBN 0-8191-2503-2); pap. text ed. 8.00 (ISBN 0-8191-2504-0). U Pr of Amer.

Lofstedt, Einar. Roman Literary Portraits. Fraser, P. M., tr. LC 78-5638. 1978. Repr. of 1958 ed. lib. bdg. 19.00x (ISBN 0-313-20455-1, LORL). Greenwood.

Lofthouse, Peter, jt. auth. see Carroll, Jean.

Lofthouse, Peter, jt. auth. see Carroll, Joan.

Lofthus, Myrna. A Spiritual Approach to Astrology: A Complete Textbook of Astrology. LC 78-62936. (Illus.). 428p. 1983. 12.50 (ISBN 0-916360-10-5). CRCS Pubns NV.

Loftin, Richard, ed. Databook of Venture Capital Sources for High-Technology Companies. (Illus.). 576p. (Orig.). 1981. pap. 89.50 (ISBN 0-940758-00-8). Finan Data Corp.

--Sell Your Software! 400p. (Orig.). 1983. pap. 24.95 (ISBN 0-940758-25-3). Finan Data Corp.

--Venture Capital for Computer Software. 64p. 1983. pap. 18.95 o.p. (ISBN 0-940758-01-6). Finan Data Corp.

Loftin, Tee, tr. see Zarambouka, Sofia.

Lofting, Hugh. Doctor Dolittle & the Pirates. Perkins, Al, ed. LC 68-14483. (ps-3). 1968. 3.95 o.p. (ISBN 0-394-80049-4); PLB 5.99 (ISBN 0-394-90049-9). Beginner.

--Doctor Dolittle's Birthday Book. LC 68-8923. (Illus.). (gr. 4-6). 1968. 9.57i o.p. (ISBN 0-397-30996-1, JBL-J). Har-Row.

Loftis, J., et al, eds. The Revels History of Drama in English, Vol. 5: 1660-1750. 335p. 1976. text ed. 53.00x (ISBN 0-416-13060-7); pap. 18.95x (ISBN 0-416-81370-4). Methuen Inc.

Loftis, John see Dryden, John.

Loftis, John, et al see Dryden, John.

Loftis, Norman. From Barbarism to Decadence & Other Essays. 150p. (Orig.). 1982. 10.95 (ISBN 0-938764-05-5); pap. 5.95 (ISBN 0-938764-06-3). Alpha-Omega Bks.

--Life Force. Orig. Title: Signs of Life. 200p. 1982. 10.95 (ISBN 0-938764-01-2). Alpha-Omega Bks.

Loftness, Robert L. Energy Handbook. 1978. text ed. 52.50 o.p. (ISBN 0-442-24836-9). Van Nos Reinhold.

Lofts, Norah. Anne Boleyn. LC 79-10526. (Illus.). 1979. 15.95 (ISBN 0-698-11005-6, Coward). Putnam Pub Group.

--Bless This House. 1977. Repr. of 1954 ed. lib. bdg. 15.95x (ISBN 0-89244-048-1). Queens Hse.

--Day of the Butterfly. LC 79-7566. 1980. 10.00 o.p. (ISBN 0-385-15285-X). Doubleday.

--Emma Hamilton. LC 77-26868. (Illus.). 1978. 14.95 o.p. (ISBN 0-698-10912-0, Coward). Putnam Pub Group.

--Madselin. LC 81-43769. 216p. 1983. 13.95 (ISBN 0-385-18103-5). Doubleday.

--The Old Priory. pap. 3.50 (ISBN 0-380-62380-3). Avon.

--Out of the Dark. LC 71-180087. 364p. 1972. 13.95 (ISBN 0-385-01948-3). Doubleday.

--Requiem for Idols - You're Best Alone. LC 78-22817. 1981. 13.95 (ISBN 0-385-01768-5). Doubleday.

--A Wayside Tavern. LC 80-954. 384p. 1980. 13.95 (ISBN 0-385-17201-X). Doubleday.

Loftsgaarden, Don O., jt. auth. see Reinhardt, Howard E.

Loftus, Elizabeth & Wortman, Camille. Psychology. 672p. 1981. text ed. 22.00 (ISBN 0-394-32428-5); wkbk. 8.00 (ISBN 0-394-32730-6). Knopf.

Loftus, Elizabeth, et al. Cognitive Processes. LC 78-16953. (P-H Ser. in Experimental Psychology). 1979. ref. ed. 23.95 (ISBN 0-13-139634-X). P-H.

Loftus, Elizabeth F., jt. auth. see Loftus, Geoffrey R.

Loftus, Geoffrey R. & Loftus, Elizabeth F. Essence of Statistics. LC 81-12312. (Statistics Ser.). 950p. 1982. text ed. 26.95 (ISBN 0-8185-0475-7). Brooks-Cole.

--Human Memory: The Processing of Information. 192p. 1976. pap. text ed. 6.95 (ISBN 0-89859-135-X). L Erlbaum Assocs.

Loftus, Mick. Disguises & Make-Up. LC 80-53612. (Whizz Kids Ser.). PLB 8.00 (ISBN 0-382-06462-3). Silver.

--How to Be a Detective. LC 80-50945. (Whizz Kids Ser.). 8.00 (ISBN 0-382-06437-2). Silver.

Loftus, P., jt. auth. see Abraham, R. J.

Lofty, J. R., jt. auth. see Edwards, C. A.

Lo Fu-Chen & Salih, K., eds. Growth Pole Strategy & Regional Development Policy: Asian Experiences & Alternative Approaches. (Illus.). 1978. text ed. 55.00 o.p. (ISBN 0-08-021984-5). Pergamon.

Logan, Ben. The Empty Meadow. (Illus.). 232p. 1983. 14.95 (ISBN 0-88361-087-6). Stanton & Lee.

--The Land Remembers. 1976. pap. 1.75 o.p. (ISBN 0-380-00663-4, 27714). Avon.

--The Land Remembers: The Story of a Farm & Its People. LC 74-6565. 320p. 1975. 11.95 o.p. (ISBN 0-670-41761-0). Viking Pr.

Logan, Ben & Moody, Kate, eds. Television Awareness Training: Viewers Guide. 1983. 16.00 (ISBN 0-686-84065-8). Intl Gen Semantics.

Logan County Heritage Foundation, ed. History of Logan County, Illinois, Nineteen Eighty-Two. (Illus.). 700p. 1982. write for info. Logan County.

Logan, Dan P., Sr. Do You Want Me to Do All That & Plow Too? 1978. 7.50 o.p. (ISBN 0-682-49146-2). Exposition.

Logan, F. Donald. The Vikings in History. (Illus.). 224p. 1983. text ed. 23.50x (ISBN 0-389-20384-X). B&N Imports.

Logan, Frank A. Incentive: How the Conditions of Reinforcement Affect the Performance of Rats. 1960. 49.50x (ISBN 0-686-51403-3). Elliots Bks.

Logan, Frank A. & Ferraro, Douglas P. Systematic Analyses of Learning & Motivation. LC 78-6870. 1978. text ed. 24.95x o.s.i. (ISBN 0-471-04130-0). Wiley.

Logan, Frank A., et al. Behavior Theory & Social Science. LC 77-22402. 1977. Repr. of 1955 ed. lib. bdg. 16.25x (ISBN 0-8371-9734-1, LOBT). Greenwood.

Logan, G. & Bals, H. Spanish Conversational Practice. 1976. pap. text ed. 6.95 students bk. (ISBN 0-88377-048-2); teacher's guide 5.95 (ISBN 0-88377-049-0). Newbury Hse.

Logan, George M. The Meaning of More's Utopia. LC 82-16147. (Illus.). 320p. 1983. 27.50x (ISBN 0-691-06557-8). Princeton U Pr.

Logan, Gerald E. German Conversational Practice. 1974. pap. text ed. 6.95 students bk (ISBN 0-88377-012-1); tchr's bk 5.95 (ISBN 0-88377-015-6). Newbury Hse.

Logan, Gerald E. & Banks, Caroline. Italian Conversational Practice. 1977. pap. text ed. 4.95 o.p. (ISBN 0-88377-073-3); tchrs.' guide 5.95 o.p. (ISBN 0-88377-084-9). Newbury Hse.

Logan, Gerald E. & Leroux, Michele. French Conversational Practice. 1975. tchr's bk 5.95 (ISBN 0-88377-046-6); student's bk 6.95 (ISBN 0-88377-045-8). Newbury Hse.

Logan, Ian, illus. Lost Glory. (Illus.). 1977. pap. 4.95 o.p. (ISBN 0-517-53096-1, Harmony). Crown.

Logan, Jake. Across the Rio Grande. LC 75-23640. 208p. 1982. pap. 2.25 (ISBN 0-86721-216-0). Playboy Pbks.

--The Jackson Hole Trouble. 224p. (Orig.). 1983. pap. 2.25 (ISBN 0-425-06139-6). Berkley Pub.

--Law Comes to Cold Rain. LC 82-60686. (Jake Logan Western Ser.). 1983. pap. 2.25 (ISBN 0-86721-243-8). Playboy Pbks.

--Silver City Shootout. 224p. (Orig.). 1983. pap. 2.25 (ISBN 0-425-06132-9). Berkley Pub.

--Slocum & the Law. 224p. (Orig.). 1983. pap. 2.25 (ISBN 0-425-06153-1). Berkley Pub.

--Slocum's Drive. 224p. (Orig.). 1983. pap. 2.25 (ISBN 0-425-05998-7). Berkley Pub.

Logan, John. Poem in Progress. (Illus.). 1975. pap. 6.50 (ISBN 0-931848-09-1). Dryad Pr.

Logan, John A. No Transfer: An American Security Principle. 1961. 49.50x (ISBN 0-685-69838-6). Elliots Bks.

Logan, John, Jr. A Ballet for the Ear: Interviews, Essays, & Reviews. Poulin, A., ed. (Poets on Poetry Ser.). 304p. 1983. pap. 7.95 (ISBN 0-472-06336-7). U of Mich Pr.

Logan, Joshua. Movie Stars, Real People, & Me. 1978. 11.95 o.s.i. (ISBN 0-440-06258-6). Delacorte.

Logan, L., et al. Creative Communication: Teaching the Language Arts. 1972. text ed. 15.95 o.p. (ISBN 0-07-092672-7, C). McGraw.

Logan, Margaret. Happy Endings. 1979. 7.95 o.s.i. (ISBN 0-395-27591-1). HM.

Logan, Mark. The Captain's Woman. 1977. pap. 1.95 o.p. (ISBN 0-451-07488-2, J7488, Sig). NAL.

--December Passion. 1979. pap. 1.95 o.p. (ISBN 0-451-08551-5, J8551, Sig). NAL.

--French Kiss. Orig. Title: Guillotine. 1978. pap. 1.95 o.p. (ISBN 0-451-07876-4, J7876, Sig). NAL.

Logan, Marvin. Make More Money: One Hundred Thirty-Six Places to Apply for a Job. LC 81-90489. 1982. 7.95 (ISBN 0-533-05202-5). Vantage.

Logan, Patrick. Irish Country Cures. (Illus.). 192p. 1982. 12.95x (ISBN 0-904651-80-0, Pub. by Appletree Ireland); pap. 6.95 (ISBN 0-904651-81-9). State Mutual Bk.

--The Old Gods: The Facts about Irish Fairies. 152p. 1982. 12.95 (ISBN 0-904651-82-7, Pub. by Salem Hse Ltd.); pap. 6.95 (ISBN 0-904651-83-5, Pub. by Salem Hse Ltd.). Merrimack Bk Serv.

Logan, Rayford W. & Cohen, Irving S. American Negro: Old World Background & New World Experience. rev. ed. Anderson, Howard R., ed. (Illus.). (gr. 7-12). 1970. 7.68 (ISBN 0-395-03158-3, 2-33570); pap. 4.56 o.p. (ISBN 0-395-03157-5). HM.

Logan, Rayford W. & Winston, Michael R., eds. Dictionary of American Negro Biography. LC 81-9629. 1983. 49.50 (ISBN 0-393-01513-0). Norton.

Logan, Robert. The Bulls & Chicago: A Stormy Affair. (Illus.). 256p. 1975. 7.95 o.s.i. (ISBN 0-695-80619-X). Follett.

--Instructional Systems Development: An International View of Theory & Practice. (Educational Technology Ser.). 304p. 1982. 32.50 (ISBN 0-12-455450-4). Acad Pr.

Logan, Wende W. & Muntz, E. Phillip. Reduced Dose Mammography. LC 79-63202. (Illus.). 576p. 1979. 47.75x (ISBN 0-89352-060-8). Masson Pub.

Logan, William. Mathematics in Marketing. 2nd ed. Dorr, Eugene L., ed. (Occupational Manuals & Projects in Marketing Ser.). (Illus.). (gr. 11-12). 1978. pap. text ed. 7.32 (ISBN 0-07-038462-2, G); tchrs manual & key 4.95 (ISBN 0-07-038463-0). McGraw.

--Sad-Faced Men. LC 80-83947. (Poetry Chapbook, Fourth Ser.). 40p. 1981. 8.95 (ISBN 0-87923-365-6). Godine.

Logan, William & Petras, Herman. Handbook of the Martial Arts. LC 82-48832. (Illus.). 284p. 1983. pap. 7.95 (ISBN 0-06-464064-7, BN 4064). B&N NY.

Logan, William B. & Freeman, M. Herbert. Merchandising Mathematics. (Illus.). 160p. 1973. pap. text ed. 12.35 (ISBN 0-07-038470-3, G); tchr's ed. 5.50 (ISBN 0-07-038471-1). McGraw.

Logan, William B., et al. Mathematics in Marketing. 1970. text ed. 5.96 o.p. (ISBN 0-07-038460-6, G); tchr's manual 3.50 o.p. (ISBN 0-07-038461-4). McGraw.

Logan, William H. Pedlar's Pack of Ballads & Songs. LC 67-23929. 1968. Repr. of 1869 ed. 38.00x (ISBN 0-8103-3534-4). Gale.

Logan-Edwards, R. Manual of Laparoscopy & Culdoscopy. new ed. 160p. 1983. text ed. write for info. (ISBN 0-407-00195-6). Butterworth.

LoGatto, A. F. The Italians in America 1492-1972: A Chronology & Factbook. LC 72-7427. (Ethnic Chronology Ser.: No. 4). 149p. 1972. 8.50 (ISBN 0-379-00503-4). Oceana.

Loge, Marc, tr. see Steinilber-Oberlin, Emile.

Logeman, Henri. Commentary, Critical, & Explanatory, on the Norwegian Text of Henrik Ibsen's Peer Gynt: Its Language, Literary Association & Folklore. Repr. of 1917 ed. lib. bdg. 19.75x (ISBN 0-8371-3027-1, LOIP). Greenwood.

Loges, Werner. Turkoman Tribal Rugs. (Illus.). 1980. text ed. 75.00x (ISBN 0-391-01736-5). Humanities.

Loggins, Vernon. Hawthornes: The Story of Seven Generations of an American Family. LC 69-10121. (Illus.). 1968. Repr. of 1951 ed. lib. bdg. 19.00x (ISBN 0-8371-0149-2, LOH). Greenwood.

--Where the Word Ends: The Life of Louis Moreau Gottschalk. LC 58-7553. (Illus.). xii, 273p. 1958. 25.00x (ISBN 0-8071-0607-0); pap. 7.95 (ISBN 0-8071-0373-X). La State U Pr.

Logie, G. Glossary of Employment & Industry. (International Planning Glossaries Ser.: Vol. 3). 1982. 57.50 (ISBN 0-444-42064-9). Elsevier.

--Glossary of Transport. (International Planning Glossaries Ser.: Vol. 2). (in 6 languages). 1980. 53.25 (ISBN 0-444-41888-1). Elsevier.

Logier, Johann B. Logier's Comprehensive Course in Music, Harmony & Practical Composition. LC 76-15186. (Music Reprint Ser.). 1976. Repr. of 1888 ed. lib. bdg. 35.00 (ISBN 0-306-70794-2). Da Capo.

--A System of the Science of Music & Practical Composition: Incidentally Comprising What Is Usually Understood by the Term Through Bass. LC 76-20715. (Music Reprint Ser). 1976. Repr. of 1897 ed. lib. bdg. 35.00 (ISBN 0-306-70793-4). Da Capo.

Logsdon. How to Cope with Computers. 1983. pap. 10.95 (ISBN 0-686-82003-7, 5193). Hayden.

Logsdon, Gene. Wildlife in Your Garden: Or Dealing with Deer, Rabbits, Raccoons, Moles, Crows, Sparrows, & Other of Nature's Creatures in Ways That Keep Them Around but Away from Your Fruits & Vegetables. Wallace, Dan, ed. (Illus.). 416p. 1983. 16.95 (ISBN 0-87857-454-9, 01-028-0). Rodale Pr Inc.

Logsdon, Jim, jt. auth. see Campbell, Sid.

Logsdon, Joseph. Horace White, Nineteenth Century Liberal. LC 77-105982. (Contributions in American History: No. 10). (Illus.). 1971. lib. bdg. 29.95 (ISBN 0-8371-3309-2, LHW/). Greenwood.

Logsdon, Thomas. Computers & Social Controversy. LC 79-24611. (Illus.). 1980. text ed. 23.95 (ISBN 0-914894-14-5). Computer Sci.

Logue, Calvin, ed. see McGill, Ralph.

Logue, Calvin M. Ralph McGill, Editor & Publisher, 2 vols. Incl. Vol. 1. Biography. 256p. 10.95 (ISBN 0-87716-013-9); Vol. 2. Famous Speeches. 517p. 12.95 (ISBN 0-87716-014-7). LC 71-97784. 1969 (Pub. by Moore Pub Co). F Apple.

Logue, Christopher. Ode to the Dodo: Poems 1953-1978. 176p. 1983. 13.95 (ISBN 0-224-01892-2, Pub by Jonathan Cape); pap. 8.95 (ISBN 0-224-01893-0). Merrimack Bk Serv.

--War Music: An Account of Books Sixteen to Nineteen of Homer's Iliad. 86p. 1983. 9.95 (ISBN 0-224-01534-6, Pub by Jonathan Cape). Merrimack Bk Serv.

Logue, Christopher, ed. London in Verse. 96p. 1983. 13.95 (ISBN 0-436-25675-4, Pub. by Secker & Warburg). David & Charles.

Logue, H. E. & Simms, John D. Auburn: A Pictorial History. LC 80-20868. (Illus.). 192p. 1980. pap. 12.95 o.p. (ISBN 0-89865-049-6). Donning Co.

Logue, John. Follow the Leader. 224p. 1983. pap. 2.50 (ISBN 0-686-84486-6). Ballantine.

Logue, John, jt. auth. see Einhorn, Eric.

Logue, William. From Philosophy to Sociology: The Evolution of French Liberalism, 1870-1914. 270p. 1983. write for info (ISBN 0-87580-088-2). N Ill U Pr.

Loh, I. & Nida, E. A. Translator's Handbook on Paul's Letter to the Philippians. (Helps for Translators Ser.). 1979. Repr. of 1977 ed. soft cover 2.70x (ISBN 0-8267-0144-2, 08528). United Bible.

Loh, Pai Ye. The Chinese Connection. 1978. pap. 4.95 o.p. (ISBN 0-8007-5063-2, Power Bks). Revell.

Loh, W. H. Jet, Rocket, Nuclear, Ion & Electric Propulsion. LC 68-26005. (Applied Physics & Engineering Ser.: Vol. 7). 1968. 70.00 o.p. (ISBN 0-387-04053-6). Springer-Verlag.

Lohafer, Susan. Coming to Terms with the Short Story. LC 82-20366. 200p. 1983. text ed. 18.95X (ISBN 0-8071-1086-8). La State U Pr.

Lohan, Frank J. Pen & Ink Techniques. 1978. 11.95 o.p. (ISBN 0-8092-7439-6); pap. 7.95 (ISBN 0-8092-7438-8). Contemp Bks.

Lohan, Robert, ed. Christmas Tales for Reading Aloud. 3rd enl. ed. LC 66-10811. (gr. 1-5). 12.95 (ISBN 0-8044-2534-5, Pub. by Stephen Daye Pr). Ungar.

Lohf, Kenneth A., jt. auth. see Sheehy, Eugene P.

Lohf, Kenneth A., intro. by. Columbia University Libraries, The History of Printing from Its Beginnings to 1930: The Subject Catalogue of the American Type Founders Company Library in the Columbia University Libraries, 4 vols. LC 80-13377. 1980. Set. lib. bdg. 355.00 (ISBN 0-527-18763-1). Kraus Intl.

Lohman, Joseph D. Cultural Patterns in Urban Schools: A Manual for Teachers, Counselors, & Administrators. 1967. pap. 7.50x o.p. (ISBN 0-520-01424-3, CAMPUS24). U of Cal Pr.

Lohman, Lou & Saffar, Ruth E. Kettlestrings. Kranz, Henry, ed. 1976. 1.50 (ISBN 0-942582-00-4). Erie St Pr.

Lohmann, Christopher K., jt. auth. see Fischer, William C.

Lohmann, G. P., jt. auth. see Tjalsma, R. C.

Lohmann, Jeanne. Where the Field Goes. (Illus.). 1976. pap. 3.00 o.p. (ISBN 0-9607688-0-7). J A Lohmann.

Lohmann, Roger. Breaking Even: Financial Management in Human Service Organizations. 336p. 1980. 29.95 (ISBN 0-87722-166-9). Temple U Pr.

Lohmann, Roger A. Breaking Even: Financial Management in Human Service Organizations. 316p. 1981. pap. text ed. 14.95 (ISBN 0-87722-247-9). Temple U Pr.

Lohner, Edgar & Hannum, H. G. Modern German Drama. LC 66-3026. 1966. text ed. 25.95 o.p. (ISBN 0-395-04808-7, 3-33585). HM.

Lohner, Edgar, jt. ed. see Foulkes, A. Peter.

Lohnes, Paul R., jt. auth. see Ackerman, Winona B.

Lohnes, Paul R., jt. auth. see Cooley, William W.

Lohnes, Walter F. & Strothmann, F. W. German: A Structural Approach. 3rd ed. 1980. text ed. 15.95x (ISBN 0-393-95059-X); tchrs'. manual avail. (ISBN 0-393-95068-9); study guide 4.95x (ISBN 0-393-95064-6). Norton.

Lohnes, Walter F. & Hopkins, Edwin A., eds. The Contrastive Grammar of English & German. xx, 231p. 1982. pap. 19.50 (ISBN 0-89720-052-7). Karoma.

Lohr, Charles H. St. Thomas Aquinas: Scriptum Super Sententiis: An Index of Authorities Cited. viii, 391p. 1980. text ed. 45.00x o.p. (ISBN 0-8232-0103-1). Fordham.

Lohr, Gordon, jt. auth. see Melchor, Jim.

Lohr, Thelma, jt. auth. see Hudak, Carolyn.

Lohren, Carl & Dennis, Larry. One Move to Better Golf. 1976. pap. 2.25 (E9390, Sig). NAL.

Lohse, Eduard. Colossians & Philemon. Koester, Helmut, ed. Poehlman, William R. & Karris, Robert J., trs. from Ger. LC 76-157550. (Hermeneia: A Critical & Historical Commentary on the Bible Ser). 256p. 1971. 19.95 (ISBN 0-8006-6001-3, 20-6001). Fortress.

--The First Christians: Their Beginnings, Writings, & Beliefs. LC 82-7454. 128p. (Orig.). 1983. pap. 6.95 (ISBN 0-8006-1646-4). Fortress.

Lohse, Friedrich, jt. auth. see Batzer, Hans.

Lo Hui-Min, ed. The Correspondence of G. E. Morrison, 2 vols. LC 74-31805. 825p. 1976. Vol. 1, 1895-1912. 130.00 (ISBN 0-521-20486-0); Vol. 2, 1912-1920. 150.00 (ISBN 0-521-21561-7); Set. 265.00 (ISBN 0-521-08779-1). Cambridge U Pr.

Loiry, William S. The Impact of Youth: Pt. 1, The Past. (Illus.). 300p. (gr. 7-12). 1983. pap. price not set (ISBN 0-9607654-1-7). Loiry Pubs Hse.

--Winning with Science: The Complete Guide to Science Research & Programs for Students. (Illus.). 350p. (Orig.). (gr. 7-12). 1983. pap. 7.95 (ISBN 0-9607654-3-3). Loiry Pubs Hse.

Loiseau, Maurice, jt. auth. see Miller, J. Dale.

Lois Mei Chan, ed. Marlowe Criticism: A Bibliography. 1978. lib. bdg. 29.00 (ISBN 0-8161-7835-6, Hall Reference). G K Hall.

Loisy, Alfred F. My Duel with the Vatican: The Autobiography of a Catholic Modernist. Boynton, Richard W., tr. 1968. Repr. of 1924 ed. lib. bdg. 16.25x (ISBN 0-8371-0148-4, LODV). Greenwood.

Loizos, Peter. The Greek Gift: Politics & Solidarity in a Cypriot Village. LC 74-83246. (Illus.). 352p. 1975. 30.00 (ISBN 0-312-34790-1). St Martin.

--The Heart Grown Bitter: A Chronicle of Cypriot War Refugees. LC 81-10037. (Illus.). 252p. 1982. 37.50 (ISBN 0-521-24230-4); pap. 10.95 (ISBN 0-521-28546-1). Cambridge U Pr.

Loke, M., jt. auth. see Roes, Carol.

Loke, Y. W. Immunology & Immunopathology of the Human Foetal-Maternal Interaction. 1978. 87.25 (ISBN 0-444-80055-7, Biomedical Pr). Elsevier.

Loken, Newton C. Gymnastics. LC 66-16202. (Athletic Institute Ser). (Illus.). (gr. 9-12). 1969. 8.95 (ISBN 0-8069-4314-9); PLB 10.99 (ISBN 0-8069-4315-7). Sterling.

Loken, Newton C. & Willoughby, Robert J. The Complete Book of Gymnastics. 3rd ed. (Illus.). 256p. 1977. text ed. 20.95 (ISBN 0-13-157172-9). P-H.

Loken, Newton C., jt. auth. see Wachtel, Erna.

Lokich, Jacob J. Primer of Cancer Management. 1978. lib. bdg. 25.00 (ISBN 0-8161-2102-8, Pub. by Hall Medical). G K Hall.

Lolley, R. N., jt. ed. see Bazan, N. G.

Lolley, W. Randall & McEachern, Alton H. Bold Preaching About Christ. LC 78-19964. 1978. 3.95 o.p. (ISBN 0-8054-1949-7). Broadman.

Lolli, F., jt. auth. see Bosco, F. J.

Lom, W. L. & Williams, A. F. Substitute Natural Gas: Manufacture & Properties. 1976. 54.95x o.p. (ISBN 0-470-15018-1). Halsted Pr.

Lom, W. L., jt. auth. see Williams, A. F.

Lom, Walter L. Lifquefied Natural Gas. (Illus.). viii, 178p. 1974. 39.00 (ISBN 0-85334-583-X, Pub. by Applied Sci England). Elsevier.

Loman, Anna. Looking at Holland. LC 66-10905. (Illus.). 64p. 1966. 9.57i o.p. (ISBN 0-397-30893-0, JBL-J). Har-Row.

Loman, L. Anthony, jt. auth. see Siegel, Gary L.

Lomas, Charles W. & Taylor, Michael, eds. Rhetoric of the British Peace Movement. (Issues & Spokeman Ser). (Orig.). 1971. pap. text ed. 2.50x (ISBN 0-685-04768-7). Phila Bk Co.

Lomas, Peter. The Case for a Personal Psychotherapy. 1982. 19.95x (ISBN 0-19-217680-3). Oxford U Pr.

Lomask, Martha. Low, Slow, Delicious: Recipes for Casseroles & Electric Slow-Cooking Pots. (Illus.). 160p. 1981. 20.95 (ISBN 0-571-11384-2). Faber & Faber.

Lomask, Milton. Aaron Burr: The Conspiracy & Years of Exile, 1804-1836. (Illus.). 1982. 22.50 (ISBN 0-374-10017-9). FS&G.

--Beauty & the Traitor: The Story of Mrs. Benedict Arnold. (gr. 7-10). 1967. 6.25 (ISBN 0-8255-5400-4). Macrae.

Lomasney, Eileen. Timmy Greenthumb. LC 82-72646. 32p. (Orig.). 1983. pap. 3.50 (ISBN 0-8066-1953-8, 10-6487). Augsburg.

Lomax, Alan. The Folk Songs of North America. LC 60-2043. (Illus.). 656p. 1960. pap. 12.95 (ISBN 0-385-03772-4, Dolp). Doubleday.

Lomax, Alan, jt. auth. see Lomax, John.

Lomax, D. E., jt. ed. see Butcher, H. J.

Lomax, Deane R. Pine Ridge Poems. LC 75-4488. 1975. 7.95 (ISBN 0-87716-059-7, Pub. by Moore Pub Co). F Apple.

Lomax, J. D. Documentation of Software Products. (Illus.). 1977. pap. 32.50x (ISBN 0-85012-166-3). Intl Pubns Serv.

Lomax, John & Lomax, Alan. Folk Song U. S. A. (RL 6). 1975. pap. 6.95 (ISBN 0-452-25307-1, Z5307, Plume). NAL.

Lomax, Louis E. When the Word Is Given... A Report on Elijah Muhammad, Malcolm X, & the Black Muslim World. LC 78-14002. (Illus.). 1979. Repr. of 1964 ed. lib. bdg. 19.25x (ISBN 0-313-21002-0, LOWW). Greenwood.

Lomax, P. & Schoenbaum, E. Enivironment, Drugs & Thermoregulation: International Symposium on the Pharmacology of Thermoregulation, 5th, Saint-Paul-de-Vence, November 1982. (Illus.). xii, 224p. 1983. 47.50 (ISBN 3-8055-3654-2). S Karger.

Lombard, Avima D. Success Begins at Home: Educational Foundations for Preschoolers. LC 81-47740. 176p. 1981. 18.95x (ISBN 0-669-04798-8). Lexington Bks.

Lombard, Charles M. Joseph de Maistre. (World Authors Ser). 1976. lib. bdg. 15.95 (ISBN 0-8057-6247-7, Twayne). G K Hall.

--Lamartine. (World Authors Ser.). 1973. lib. bdg. 13.95 (ISBN 0-8057-2510-5, Twayne). G K Hall.

--Thomas Choley Chivers. (United States Authors Ser.). 1979. lib. bdg. 10.95 (ISBN 0-8057-7258-8, Twayne). G K Hall.

--Thomas Holley Chivers. (United States Authors Ser.). 1979. lib. bdg. 13.95 (ISBN 0-8057-7258-8, Twayne). G K Hall.

--Xavier de Maistre. (World Authors Ser.). 1977. lib. bdg. 15.95 (ISBN 0-8057-6284-1, Twayne). G K Hall.

Lombard, Eric. By Lust Possessed. 1980. pap. 1.95 o.p. (ISBN 0-451-09084-5, J9084, Sig). NAL.

Lombard, Francois J. The Foreign Investment Screening Process in L.D.C.'s: The Case of Columbia, 1967-1975. (Replica Edition Ser.). 171p. 1979. softcover 25.00x (ISBN 0-89158-399-8). Westview.

Lombard, George F., ed. see Roethlisberger, Fritz J.

Lombard, R. S. American-Venezuelan Private International Law. LC 65-20284. (Bilateral Studies in Private International Law: No. 14). 125p. 1965. 15.00 (ISBN 0-379-11414-3). Oceana.

Lombardi, Felipe R. A to Z No-Cook Cookbook. LC 72-79753. 1975. 5.95 o.p. (ISBN 0-910294-12-7). Brown Bk.

Lombardi, Frances G., jt. auth. see Lombardi, Gerald S.

Lombardi, Gerald S. & Lombardi, Frances G. The Circle Without End: A Sourcebook of American Indian Ethics. (Illus.). 224p. 1982. lib. bdg. 11.95 (ISBN 0-87961-114-6); pap. 6.95 (ISBN 0-87961-115-4). Naturegraph.

Lombardi, John V. Decline & Abolition of Negro Slavery in Venezuela, 1820-1854. (Contributions in Afro-American & African Studies: No. 1). (Illus.). 1971. lib. bdg. 27.50 (ISBN 0-8371-3303-3, LOD/). Greenwood.

--Venezuelan History: A Comprehensive Bibliography. 1977. lib. bdg. 25.00 (ISBN 0-8161-7876-3, Hall Reference). G K Hall.

Lombardi, Ronald P. & De Peters, Amalia B. Modern Spoken Spanish: An Interdisciplinary Perspective. LC 80-1442. 507p. (Orig.). 1981. pap. text ed. 17.75 (ISBN 0-8191-1513-4). U Pr of Amer.

Lombardi, Vince & Heinz, W. C. Run to Daylight. (Illus.). 304p. 1982. pap. 8.95 (ISBN 0-13-783845-X). P-H.

Lombardi, Vincent L. Crisis in Marriage: Efforts Toward Spiritual Transformation. LC 81-40531. 96p. 1982. lib. bdg. 18.50 (ISBN 0-8191-1892-3); pap. text ed. 7.00 (ISBN 0-8191-1893-1). U Pr of Amer.

Lombardo, Edith F., jt. auth. see Lombardo, Victor S.

Lombardo, Josef V. Engineering Drawing. (College Outline Ser.). pap. 5.50 (ISBN 0-06-460086-6, CO 86, COS). B&N NY.

Lombardo, Michael, et al. Looking Glass: An Organizational Simulation. 1983. pap. text ed. 18.95x (ISBN 0-673-15862-4). Scott F.

Lombardo, Victor S. & Lombardo, Edith F. Developing & Administering Early Childhood Programs. (Illus.). 224p. 1983. 23.50x (ISBN 0-398-04773-1). C C Thomas.

Lombra, Raymond & Witte, Willard E. The Political Economy of Domestic & International Monetary Relations. (Illus.). 376p. 1982. pap. text ed. 15.95x (ISBN 0-8138-1372-7). Iowa St U Pr.

Lombra, Raymond E., et al. Money & the Financial System: Theory, Institutions & Policy. (Illus.). 1980. text ed. 23.95x (ISBN 0-07-038607-2); instructor's manual 15.95 (ISBN 0-07-038608-0). McGraw.

Lombroso, Cesare. Crime, Its Causes & Remedies. Horton, Henry P., tr. LC 68-55776. (Criminology, Law Enforcement, & Social Problems Ser.: No. 14). 1968. Repr. of 1911 ed. 22.50x (ISBN 0-87585-014-6). Patterson Smith.

Lombroso-Ferrero, Gina & Savitz, Leonard D. Criminal Man: According to the Classification of Cesare Lombroso. LC 70-129338. (Criminology, Law Enforcement, & Social Problems Ser.: No. 134). (Illus.). 395p. (With intro. added). 1972. lib. bdg. 17.00xx (ISBN 0-87585-134-7); pap. 7.00x (ISBN 0-87585-915-1). Patterson-Smith.

Lomner, Norman, ed. Perek "Hamafkid". pap. text ed. 3.25 (ISBN 0-686-33054-4, A51). Torah Umesorah.

Lomnitz, C. Global Tectonics & Earthquake Risk. LC 72-87960. (Developments in Geotectonics Ser.: Vol. 5). 330p. 1974. 78.75 (ISBN 0-444-41076-7). Elsevier.

Lomnitz, C. & Rosenblueth, E. Seismic Risk & Engineering Decisions. (Developments in Geotechnical Engineering Ser.: Vol. 15). 1976. 78.75 (ISBN 0-444-41494-0). Elsevier.

Lompscher, jt. auth. see Glaser.

Londenberg, K. Papier & Form: Paper & Form. (Illus., Ger.). 1972. pap. 25.00x o.s.i. (ISBN 0-685-41587-2). Museum Bks.

Londgren, Richard E. Communication by Objectives: A Guide to Productive & Cost-Effective Public Relations & Marketing. (Illus.). 208p. 1983. 16.95 (ISBN 0-13-153650-8); pap. 7.95 (ISBN 0-13-153643-5). P-H.

Londo, Richard J. Common Sense in Business Writing. 1982. text ed. 15.95x (ISBN 0-02-371740-8). Macmillan.

London, A. L., jt. auth. see Kays, William M.

London, A. L., jt. auth. see Shah, Ramesh.

London, Anne. American-International Encyclopedia Cookbook. (Illus.). 1972. 23.99i (ISBN 0-690-07236-8). T Y Crowell.

London, Ephraim, ed. Law As Literature. 1965. pap. 8.95 o.p. (ISBN 0-671-41060-1, Touchstone Bks). S&S.

--World of Law, 2 Vols. 1960. Set. 25.00 o.p. (ISBN 0-671-82936-X). S&S.

London, Harvey & Exner, John E., Jr. Dimensions of Personality. LC 77-25328. (Wiley Series on Personality Processes). 1978. 37.95 (ISBN 0-471-54392-6, Pub. by Wiley-Interscience). Wiley.

London, Herbert. The Seventies: Counterfeit Decade. LC 79-65632. 1979. pap. text ed. 9.25 (ISBN 0-8191-0788-3). U Pr of Amer.

London, Herbert I. & Weeks, Albert. Myths That Rule America. LC 80-5866. 176p. 1981. lib. bdg. 14.50 (ISBN 0-8191-1446-4); pap. text ed. 7.25 (ISBN 0-8191-1447-2). U Pr of Amer.

London, Howard B. The Culture of a Community College. LC 78-8697. (Praeger Special Studies). 1978. 25.95 o.p. (ISBN 0-03-044701-1). Praeger.

London, Jack. The Assassination Bureau, Ltd. (Crime Ser). 1978. pap. 3.95 (ISBN 0-14-004688-7). Penguin.

--Best Short Stories of Jack London. LC 45-3830. 1953. 10.95 (ISBN 0-385-00021-9). Doubleday.

--To Build a Fire. (Creative's Classics Ser.). (Illus.). 48p. (gr. 4-9). 1980. PLB 7.95 (ISBN 0-87191-769-6). Creative Ed.

--The Call of the Wild. Bd. with White Fang. (Bantam Classics Ser.). 293p. (gr. 7-12). 1981. pap. 1.75 (ISBN 0-553-21005-X). Bantam.

--The Call of the Wild. (Childrens Illustrated Classics Ser). (Illus.). 119p. 1974. Repr. of 1968 ed. 9.00x o.p. (ISBN 0-460-05077-X, Pub. by J. M. Dent. England). Biblio Dist.

--The Call of the Wild. Bd. with White Fang. pap. 1.75 (ISBN 0-671-42070-4). WSP.

--The Call of the Wild. 1983. pap. 1.95 (ISBN 0-14-035000-4, Puffin). Penguin.

--Call of the Wild & Other Stories. (Illus.). (gr. 4-9). il. jr. lib. 5.95 (ISBN 0-448-05827-8, G&D); Companion Lib. ed. 2.95 (ISBN 0-448-05458-2); deluxe ed. 8.95 (ISBN 0-448-06027-2). Putnam Pub Group.

--The Cruise of the Dazzler. (Illus.). 250p. 1981. pap. 5.95 (ISBN 0-932458-06-8). Star Rover.

--Diable, a Dog. Pauk, Walter & Harris, Raymond, eds. (Jamestown Classics Ser.). (Illus.). 39p. (gr. 5). 1976. pap. text ed. 2.00x (ISBN 0-89061-046-0, 513); tchrs. ed. 3.00 (ISBN 0-89061-047-9, 515). Jamestown Pubs.

--Great Short Works of Jack London: Call of the Wild, White Fang & Six Stories. Labor, Earle, ed. pap. 2.84i (ISBN 0-06-083041-7, P3041, PL). Har-Row.

--Jack London Stories. (gr. 3 up). Date not set. price not set (ISBN 0-448-41103-2, G&D). Putnam Pub Group.

--Jack London's Klondike Tales. 224p. (Orig.). Date not set. pap. price not set o.p. (ISBN 0-505-51797-3). Tower Bks.

--Jack London's Tales of Hawaii. LC 81-23492. 80p. 1982. pap. 4.95 o.p. (ISBN 0-916630-25-0). Pr Pacifica.

--Jack London's Yukon Women. 224p. Date not set. pap. price not set o.p. (ISBN 0-505-51807-4). Tower Bks.

--The Law of Life. Pauk, Walter & Harris, Raymond, eds. (Jamestown Classics Ser.). (Illus.). 35p. (gr. 6-12). 1976. pap. text ed. 2.00x (ISBN 0-89061-040-1, 501); tchrs. ed. 3.00 (ISBN 0-89061-041-X, 503). Jamestown Pubs.

--The Man with the Gash. (Illus.). 299p. 1981. pap. 5.95 (ISBN 0-932458-04-1). Star Rover.

--The Marriage of Lit-Lit. Pauk, Walter & Harris, Raymond, eds. (Jamestown Classics Ser.). (Illus.). 39p. (gr. 6-12). 1976. pap. text ed. 2.00x (ISBN 0-89061-044-4, 509); tchrs. ed. 3.00 (ISBN 0-89061-045-2, 511). Jamestown Pubs.

--Nam Bok. (Illus.). 250p. (Orig.). pap. 5.95 (ISBN 0-932458-03-3). Star Rover.

--Nam-Bok, the Liar. Pauk, Walter & Harris, Raymond, eds. (Jamestown Classics Ser.). (Illus.). 43p. (gr. 6-12). 1976. pap. text ed. 2.00x (ISBN 0-89061-042-8, 505); tchrs. ed. 3.00 (ISBN 0-89061-043-6, 507). Jamestown Pubs.

--Novels & Social Writings. Pizer, Donald, ed. LC 82-6940. 1192p. 1982. 27.50 (ISBN 0-940450-06-2). Literary Classics.

--Novels & Stories. Pizer, Donald, ed. LC 82-249. 1026p. 1982. 27.50 (ISBN 0-940450-05-4). Literary Classics.

--The People of the Abyss. (Illus.). 319p. 1982. pap. 6.95 (ISBN 0-932458-08-4). Star Rover.

--The Science Fiction of Jack London: An Anthology 1901-1918. 1975. Repr. lib. bdg. 15.00 (ISBN 0-8398-2307-X, Gregg). G K Hall.

--The Sea Wolf. (Bantam Classics Ser.). 252p. (gr. 7-12). 1981. pap. 1.50 (ISBN 0-553-21006-8). Bantam.

--Sea-Wolf. 1937. 15.95 (ISBN 0-02-574630-8); large print ed. o.p. 7.95 (ISBN 0-02-489420-6). Macmillan.

--Sea Wolf & Selected Stories. (RL 8). pap. 1.50 (ISBN 0-451-51552-8, CW1552, Sig Classics). NAL.

--Son of the Wolf. (Illus.). 250p. 1980. pap. 5.95 (ISBN 0-932458-02-5). Star Rover.

--Tales of the Fish Patrol. (Illus.). 243p. 1982. pap. 5.95 (ISBN 0-932458-07-6). Star Rover.

--White Fang. (gr. 7 up). 1935. 13.95 (ISBN 0-02-574750-9). Macmillan.

London, Jack see Swan, D. K.

London, K. The People Side of Systems. 1976. 23.95 o.p. (ISBN 0-07-084463-1, P&RB). McGraw.

London, Kurt. Seven Soviet Arts. Repr. of 1937 ed. lib. bdg. 20.25x (ISBN 0-8371-4263-6, LOSA). Greenwood.

London, Kurt, ed. The Soviet Union in World Politics. LC 79-19503. 380p. 1980. 31.50 (ISBN 0-89158-263-0); pap. 12.95 (ISBN 0-86531-147-1). Westview.

London, Kurt L., ed. The Soviet Impact on World Politics. 312p. 1982. text ed. 29.50x (ISBN 0-8290-0983-3); pap. text ed. 12.95x (ISBN 0-8290-0992-2). Irvington.

London, Laura. Love's a Stage. (Orig.). 1980. pap. 1.50 o.s.i. (ISBN 0-440-15387-5). Dell.

--Moonlight Mist. 1979. pap. 1.50 o.s.i. (ISBN 0-685-65931-3). Dell.

London Mathematical Society Committee, ed. see Hardy, Godfrey H.

London, P., jt. auth. see Heilbroner, R. L.

London, P. S. Accident Surgery. 3rd ed. Rob, Charles, ed. Smith, Rodney. (Operative Surgery Ser.). (Illus.). 1978. text ed. 160.00 o.p. (ISBN 0-407-00640-0). Butterworth.

--Modern Trends in Accident Surgery & Medicine-2. 1970. 17.95 o.p. (ISBN 0-407-28001-4). Butterworth.

London, P. S., jt. auth. see Tubbs, N.

London Stationers' Company. An Analytical Index to the Ballad-Entries (1557-1709) in the Registers of the Company of Stationers of London. LC 67-1586. xviii, 324p. Repr. of 1967 ed. 30.00x (ISBN 0-8103-5019-X). Gale.

London Times Editors, ed. Signs of the Times: A Selection of Comic Signs from the "The Times Diary". (Illus.). 1975. pap. 2.95 o.p. (ISBN 0-241-89162-0). Transatlantic.

Londos, Eutychia G. AV Health: Current Publications of the United States Government. LC 82-10366. 240p. 1982. 17.50 (ISBN 0-8108-1571-0). Scarecrow.

Londre, Felicia H. Tennessee Williams. LC 79-4830. (Literature and Life Ser.). 1980. 11.95 (ISBN 0-8044-2539-6). Ungar.

--Tom Stoppard. 1981. 11.95 (ISBN 0-8044-2538-8). Ungar.

Lone, Mary La see La Lone, Mary.

Lonergan, Bernard. Doctrinal Pluralism. (Pere Marquette Theology Lectures). 1971. 7.95 (ISBN 0-87462-503-3). Marquette.

--Insight. 1957. pap. 14.95 (ISBN 0-8022-0994-7). Philos Lib.

--Subject. LC 68-22238. (Aquinas Lectures Ser). 1968. 7.95 (ISBN 0-87462-133-X). Marquette.

Lonergan, Bernard J. Insight: A Study of Human Understanding. LC 77-20441. 1977. pap. 14.95xi (ISBN 0-06-065269-1, RD 251, HarpR). Har-Row.

Lonergan, Elaine C. Group Intervention: How to Begin & Maintain Groups in Medical & Psychiatric Settings. LC 81-66759. 381p. 1982. 25.00 (ISBN 0-686-82859-3). Aronson.

Loney, Glenn, ed. California Gold-Rush Plays. Orig. Title: American Pioneer Drama. 1983. 19.95 (ISBN 0-933826-34-6); pap. 7.95 (ISBN 0-933826-35-4). Performing Arts.

Loney, Glenn M., jt. ed. see Corrigan, Robert W.

Loney, Jan, jt. ed. see Gadow, Kenneth D.

Long, jt. auth. see Williams.

Long, tr. see Kierkegaard, Soren.

Long, A. A. Hellenistic Philosophy: Stoics, Epicureans, Sceptics. (Classical Life & Letters Ser.). 262p. 1974. 40.50x o.p. (ISBN 0-7156-0667-0, 298, Pub. by Duckworth England). Biblio Dist.

Long, A. F. & Mercer, G. Manpower Planning in the National Health Service. 184p. 1981. text ed. 36.00x (ISBN 0-566-00425-9). Gower Pub Ltd.

Long, Amos M., Jr. Pennsylvania German Family Farm, Vol. VI. LC 72-87149. 1972. 20.00 (ISBN 0-911122-28-1). Penn German Soc.

Long, B., et al. Group Performance of Literature. (Illus.). 1977. pap. text ed. 17.95 (ISBN 0-13-365346-3). P-H.

Long, Barbara, jt. auth. see Long, E. B.

Long, Barbara C., jt. auth. see Phipps, Wilma J.

Long, Beverly & Hopkins, Mary F. Performing Literature: An Introduction to Oral Interpretation. (Illus.). 550p. 1982. text ed. 20.95 (ISBN 0-13-657171-9). P-H.

Long, Chalmers G., Jr., jt. auth. see Dubin, Fred S.

Long, Charles A. & Killingley, Carl A. The Badgers of the World. (Illus.). 504p. 1983. 39.75x (ISBN 0-398-04741-3). C C Thomas.

Long, Charles H. Alpha: The Myths of Creation. LC 82-21532. (AAR-SP Classics in Religious Studies). 320p. 1982. Repr. of 1963 ed. 13.50x (ISBN 0-89130-604-8, 00-05-04). Scholars Pr CA.

Long, Charles H., ed. Anglican Cycle of Prayer: Partners in Prayer, 1984. (A Cycle of Prayer Ser.). (Illus.). 128p. (Orig.). 1983. pap. price not set (ISBN 0-88028-024-7). Forward Movement.

Long, Claudia. Albert's Story. LC 77-72614. (gr. k-2). 1978. 6.95 o.s.i. (ISBN 0-440-00079-3); PLB 6.46 o.s.i. (ISBN 0-440-00080-7). Delacorte.

Long, D. A. Raman Spectroscopy. 1977. text ed. 42.50x (ISBN 0-07-038675-7, C). McGraw.

Long, D. T., jt. ed. see Angino, E. D.

Long, Dale D. Physics Around You. 608p. 1980. text ed. 21.95x (ISBN 0-534-00770-8). Wadsworth Pub.

Long, David E. The Persian Gulf: An Introduction to Its Peoples, Politics, & Economics. rev. ed. LC 76-6531. (Westview Special Studies on the Middle East Ser.). (Illus.). 1978. softcover 15.00 o.p. (ISBN 0-89158-826-4). Westview.

Long, David E. & Reich, Bernard, eds. The Government & Politics of the Middle East & North Africa. 465p. 1980. lib. bdg. 33.00 (ISBN 0-89158-593-1); pap. 13.50 (ISBN 0-89158-871-X). Westview.

Long, David F. A Documentary History of U. S. Foreign Relations: From Seventeen Sixty to the Mid-Eighteen Nineties, Selections from Ruhl J. Bartlett's "The Record of American Diplomacy", Vol. I. LC 79-5349. 132p. 1980. pap. text ed. 8.00 (ISBN 0-8191-1038-8). U Pr of Amer.

--Sailor-Diplomat: A Biography of Commander James Biddle, 1783-1848. (Illus.). 350p. 1983. 22.95 (ISBN 0-930350-39-1). NE U Pr.

Long, David F., ed. A Documentary History of U. S. Foreign Relations: The Mid-1890's to 1979; Selections from & Additions to Ruhl J. Bartlett's the Record of American Diplomacy. LC 79-5349. 1979. pap. text ed. 9.00 (ISBN 0-8191-0866-9). U Pr of Amer.

Long, Dolores A. The Chicago Trivia Book. (Illus.). 128p. 1982. pap. 4.95 (ISBN 0-8092-5690-8). Contemp Bks.

Long, Don L., et al. Introduction to Agribusiness Management. Lee, Jasper S., ed. (Careeer Preparation for Agriculture-Agribusiness). 1979. pap. text ed. 6.96x (ISBN 0-07-038665-X, G); activity guide 4.96x (ISBN 0-07-038666-8); tchrs manual & key 3.00x (ISBN 0-07-038667-6). McGraw.

Long, Donlin M., jt. ed. see Hopkins, Leo N.

Long, Doug, jt. auth. see Mayhew, Vic.

Long, E. B. & Long, Barbara. Civil War Day by Day: An Almanac 1861-1865. LC 73-163653. (Illus.). 1971. 19.95 (ISBN 0-385-01264-0). Doubleday.

Long, Edward L., Jr. Survey of Christian Ethics. 1967. text ed. 13.95x o.p. (ISBN 0-19-500955-X). Oxford U Pr.

--A Survey of Christian Ethics. 1967. pap. 12.95 (ISBN 0-19-503242-X). Oxford U Pr.

--A Survey of Recent Christian Ethics. 1982. 12.95x (ISBN 0-19-503159-8); pap. 7.95x (ISBN 0-19-503160-1). Oxford U Pr.

Long, Frank W. Lapidary Carving: Design & Techniques. 144p. 1982. 24.95 (ISBN 0-442-24882-2). Van Nos Reinhold.

Long, Franklin A. & Oleson, Sandy. Appropriate Technology & Social Values: A Critical Appraisal. LC 79-18528. (American Academy of Arts & Sciences Ser.). 304p. 1980. prof ref 25.00x (ISBN 0-88410-373-0). Ballinger Pub.

Long, George. Folklore Calendar. LC 76-78191. 1970. Repr. of 1930 ed. 33.00x (ISBN 0-8103-3367-8). Gale.

Long, George, tr. see Aurelius, Marcus.

Long, Harold & Wheeler, Allen. Dynamics of Isshinryu Karate Orange Belt, Bk. 1. Condry, Steve, ed. (Isshinryu Karate Ser.). (Illus.). 1978. pap. 3.95 (ISBN 0-89826-002-7). Natl Paperback.

--Who's Who in Karate. 110p. (Orig.). 1981. pap. 3.95 (ISBN 0-89826-007-8). Natl Paperback.

Long, Harry A. Personal & Family Names. LC 68-26584. 1968. Repr. of 1883 ed. 42.00x (ISBN 0-8103-3128-4). Gale.

Long, Huey B. Adult Learning: Research & Practice. 304p. Date not set. 19.95 (ISBN 0-695-81666-7). Follett.

Long, Huey P. My First Days in the White House. LC 70-171695. (FDR & the Era of the New Deal Ser). (Illus.). 146p. 1972. Repr. of 1935 ed. lib. bdg. 19.50 (ISBN 0-306-70383-1). Da Capo.

Long, Hugh W., jt. auth. see Bourdeaux, Kenneth J.

Long, I. L., jt. auth. see Honeybone, R. C.

Long, J. B., ed. Judaism & the Christian Seminary Curriculum. 166p. pap. 2.95 (ISBN 0-686-95180-8). ADL.

Long, James. The German-Russians: A Bibliography. LC 78-19071. 136p. 1978. text ed. 17.50 o.p. (ISBN 0-87436-282-2). ABC-Clio.

--Life: Jesus-Style. 1978. pap. 3.95 (ISBN 0-88207-575-6). Victor Bks.

--Life Letter. 144p. 1982. pap. 4.50 (ISBN 0-88207-590-X). Victor Bks.

--Living in Sunshine! 1980. pap. 3.95 (ISBN 0-88207-576-4). Victor Bks.

Long, James see McReynolds, Paul.

Long, James D. & Williams, Robert L. SOS for Teachers: Strategies of Self-Improvement. LC 81-84078. (Illus.). 252p. 1982. pap. text ed. 9.95 (ISBN 0-916622-23-1). Princeton Bk Co.

Long, James D., jt. auth. see Williams, Robert L.

Long, James W. The Essential Guide to Prescription Drugs: What You Need to Know for Safe Drug Use. rev. ed. LC 78-20218. (Illus.). 1980. 25.00i o.p. (ISBN 0-06-012674-4, HarpT); pap. 8.95i o.p. (ISBN 0-06-090715-0, CN 715). Har-Row.

Long, Jean. How to Paint the Chinese Way. (Illus.). 128p. 1983. pap. 7.50 (ISBN 0-7137-1343-7, Pub. by Blandford Pr England). Sterling.

Long, Jennie D. Album of Candy Containers. (Illus.). pap. 10.50 (ISBN 0-87069-334-4, 99003). Wallace-Homestead. *

Long, Jeremy, jt. auth. see Rogers, Jane.

Long, Jerry & Tenzer, Jeff. The Cambridge Program for the High School Equivalency Examination. Schenk, Brian, ed. (GED Preparation Ser.). (Illus.). 816p. (Orig.). 1981. pap. text ed. 8.80 (ISBN 0-8428-9385-7); Supplementary Writing Skills Exercises, 64pgs. supple. 1.66 (ISBN 0-8428-9392-X). Cambridge Bk.

Long, John, et al, eds. Menus of the Valley's Finest Restaurants: Nineteen Eighty-Two Edition. 176p. 1981. pap. 5.95 o.p. (ISBN 0-930380-13-4, 0148-4133). Quail Run.

Long, John D., ed. Issues in Insurance, 2 vols. 1978. write for info. o.p. (CPCU 10). IIA.

--Issues in Insurance, 2 vols. 2nd ed. LC 81-66116. 852p. 1981. text ed. 18.00 ea. Vol. (ISBN 0-89463-034-2). Am Inst Property.

Long, John H. Shakespeare's Use of Music: A Study of the Music & Its Performance in the Original Production of Seven Comedies. LC 77-5643. (Music Reprint Ser.). 1977. Repr. of 1955 ed. lib. bdg. 25.00 (ISBN 0-306-77423-2). Da Capo.

--Shakespeare's Use of Music: The Final Comedies. LC 77-5644. (Music Reprint Ser.). 1977. Repr. of 1961 ed. lib. bdg. 22.50 (ISBN 0-306-77424-0). Da Capo.

Long, John V., jt. auth. see Green, Samuel.

Long, Joseph. Psyche Versus Soma: Traditional Healing Choices in Jamaica. (Traditional Healing Ser.). 300p. 1983. 25.75 (ISBN 0-932426-20-4); pap. 9.95 (ISBN 0-932426-21-2). Conch Mag.

--Psyche Versus Soma: Traditional Healing Choices in Jamaica. (Traditional Healing Ser.). 250p. 1983. 25.75 (ISBN 0-932426-20-4); pap. text ed. 15.00 (ISBN 0-932426-21-2). Trado-Medic.

Long, Kenneth. Introduction to Economics. (Illus.). Date not set. text ed. price not set o.s.i. (ISBN 0-442-23894-0). Van Nos Reinhold.

Long, Larry. Managers Guide to Computers & Information Systems. (Illus.). 400p. 1983. text ed. 25.00 (ISBN 0-13-549394-3). P-H.

Long, Larry W., jt. auth. see Cummings, H. Wayland.

Long, Leon E. Geology. (Illus.). 544p. 1974. text ed. 29.00 (ISBN 0-07-038672-2, C). McGraw.

--Geology. (Illus.). 526p. 1982. pap. text ed. 18.95x (ISBN 0-89641-110-9). American Pr.

Long, Lynette & Long, Thomas. The Handbook for Latchkey Children & Their Parents: A Complete Guide for Latchkey Kids & Their Working Parents. 1983. 16.95 (ISBN 0-87795-506-9, Pub. by Priam); pap. 7.95 (ISBN 0-87795-507-7). Arbor Hse.

Long, Lynette & Prophit, Penny. Understanding Responding: A Communication Manual for Nurses. 1980. pap. text ed. 11.95 (ISBN 0-87872-284-X). Brooks-Cole.

Long, Lynette, et al. Questioning: Skills for the Helping Process. LC 80-24385. (Orig.). 1980. pap. text ed. 11.95 (ISBN 0-8185-0371-8). Brooks-Cole.

Long, M. The Unnatural Scene: A Study of Shakespearian Tragedy. 262p. 1976. 19.95x (ISBN 0-416-82140-5). Methuen Inc.

Long, M. J. & White, J. H. Fundamental Chemistry. 1977. pap. text ed. 6.50x o.p. (ISBN 0-435-64520-X). Heinemann Ed.

Long, Mark & Keating, Jeffrey. The World of Satellite Television. McClure, Matthew, ed. (Illus.). 224p. 1983. 15.95 (ISBN 0-913990-46-9); pap. 8.95 (ISBN 0-913990-45-0). Book Pub Co.

Long, Max F. Growing into Light. 1955. pap. 4.95 (ISBN 0-87516-043-3). De Vorss.

--Secret Science at Work. 1953. pap. 6.50 (ISBN 0-87516-046-8). De Vorss.

--Secret Science Behind Miracles. 1948. pap. 6.95 (ISBN 0-87516-047-6). De Vorss.

Long, Michael, et al. Reading English for Academic Study. (Illus.). 160p. (Orig.). 1980. pap. text ed. 8.95 (ISBN 0-88377-108-X). Newbury Hse.

Long, Michael H., jt. auth. see Bailey, Kathleen M.

Long, Michael H., jt. ed. see Seliger, Herbert W.

Long, Nguyen & Kendall, Harry H. After Saigon Fell: Daily Life Under the Vietnamese Communists. LC 81-85304. (Research Papers & Policy Studies: RPPS, No. 4). (Orig.). 1981. pap. 8.00x (ISBN 0-912966-46-7). IEAS.

Long, Norman. An Introduction to the Sociology of Rural Development. (Illus.). 221p. (Orig.). 1982. pap. text ed. 12.95 (ISBN 0-422-74490-5). Westview.

Long, Patricia J. & Shannon, Barbara. Focus on Nutrition. (Illus.). 336p. 1983. pap. 13.95 (ISBN 0-13-322800-2). P H.

--Nutrition: An Inquiry into the Issues. (Illus.). 608p. 1983. pap. text ed. 23.95 (ISBN 0-13-627802-7). P-H.

Long, Patrick D. De see De Long, Patrick D.

Long, Paul E. Introduction to General Topography. LC 71-138370. 1971. text ed. 21.95 (ISBN 0-675-09253-1). Merrill.

Long, Peter L., ed. The Biology of the Coccidia. 512p. 1982. text ed. 74.50 (ISBN 0-8391-1680-2). Univ Park.

Long, R. A., jt. auth. see Jackman, E. R.

Long, R. E., tr. see Chekhov, Anton.

Long, R. G., jt. auth. see Bloom, Stephen R.

Long, Richard. Tawfiq Al Hakim: Playwright of Egypt. (Illus.). 235p. 1979. 22.00x o.s.i. (ISBN 0-903729-35-0). Three Continents.

Long, Robert. What It Is. 28p. 1981. pap. 3.00 (ISBN 0-935252-30-4); pap. 10.00 op (ISBN 0-686-86778-5). Street Pr.

Long, Robert E. The Great Succession: Henry James & the Legacy of Hawthorne. LC 79-922. (Critical Essays in Modern Literature Ser.). 1979. 14.95 (ISBN 0-8229-3398-5). U of Pittsburgh Pr.

--Henry James: The Early Novels. (United States Authors Ser.). 225p. 1983. lib. bdg. 13.95 (ISBN 0-8057-7379-7, Twayne). G K Hall.

Long, Robert L. & O'Brien, Paul, eds. Fast Burst Reactors: Proceedings. LC 73-603552. (AEC Symposium Ser.). 646p. 1969. pap. 24.25 (ISBN 0-87079-208-3, CONF-690102); microfiche 4.00 (ISBN 0-87079-209-1, CONF-690102). DOE.

Long, Robert W., jt. auth. see Lakela, Olga.

Long, Rose-Carol. Kandinsky: The Development of an Abstract Style. (Studies in the History of Art & Architecture). (Illus.). 1980. 98.00x o.p. (ISBN 0-19-817311-3). Oxford U Pr.

Long, Rosemary. Systematic Nursing Care. (Illus.). 96p. 1981. 21.00 (ISBN 0-571-11616-7); pap. 7.95 (ISBN 0-686-82940-9). Faber & Faber.

Long, Ruth Y. Nutrition & Cancer Update. 1980. 3.00 (ISBN 0-686-32617-2). Cancer Control Soc.

Long, Sandra M. Using the Census as a Creative Teaching Resource. LC 82-60804. (Fastback Ser.: No. 184). 50p. 1982. pap. 0.75 (ISBN 0-87367-184-8). Phi Delta Kappa.

Long, Terry L. Granville Hicks. (United States Authors Ser.: No. 387). 1981. lib. bdg. 12.95 (ISBN 0-8057-7319-3, Twayne). G K Hall.

Long, Theodore E., jt. ed. see Hadden, Jeffrey K.

Long, Thomas, jt. auth. see Long, Lynette.

Long, Tic. Resource Directory for Youth Workers, 1983. 1983. pap. 8.95 spiral bdg. (ISBN 0-687-36165-6). Abingdon.

Long, Valentine. Upon this Rock. 1983. 8.00 (ISBN 0-8199-0834-7). Franciscan Herald.

Long, W. E. & Evans, P. L. Electronic Principles & Circuits: An Introduction to Electronics for the Technicians. LC 73-11096. 432p. 1974. 30.95 (ISBN 0-471-54455-8); pap. text ed. 5.00x tchrs' manual (ISBN 0-471-54454-X). Wiley.

Long, William A. & Seo, K. K. Management in Japan & India: With Reference to the United States. LC 77-7824. (Praeger Special Studies). 1977. 39.95 o.p. (ISBN 0-03-022651-1). Praeger.

Long, William E., jt. auth. see Coffron, James W.

Longacre, Paul. Fund-Rasing Projects with a World Hunger Emphasis. 1.95 (ISBN 0-686-95919-1). Alternatives.

Longacre, R. E. Discourse Grammars: Studies in Indigenous Languages of Columbia, Panama & Equador, 3 vols. (SIL Ser: No. 52). 1977. Vol. I. pap. 7.50x, 445p. (ISBN 0-88312-063-1); Vol. II. pap. 5.50x, 299p. (ISBN 0-88312-064-X); Vol. III. pap. 7.00x, 377p. (ISBN 0-88312-065-8); Set. pap. 18.00x (ISBN 0-88312-062-3); microfiche vol. 1 4.50x (ISBN 0-88312-463-7); microfiche vol. 2 3.75x (ISBN 0-88312-464-5); microfiche vol. 3 3.75x (ISBN 0-88312-465-3); microfiche set 12.00x (ISBN 0-88312-447-5). Summer Inst Ling.

Longacre, Robert E. Philippine Languages: Discourse, Paragraph & Sentence Structure. (Publications in Linguistics & Related Fields Ser.: No. 21). 456p. 1968. pap. 6.50x (ISBN 0-88312-023-2); microfiche 5.25x (ISBN 0-88312-423-8). Summer Inst Ling.

Longacre, Robert E. & Jones, Linda K., eds. Discourse Studies in Meso American Languages, 2 vols. (SIL Publications in Linguistics No. 58). 1979. Set. 20.00x (ISBN 0-88312-080-1); Vol. 1. 379p. 11.50x (ISBN 0-88312-078-X); Vol. 2. 223p. 8.50x (ISBN 0-88312-079-8); microfiche vol. 1 3.75x (ISBN 0-88312-479-3); microfiche vol. 2 3.00x (ISBN 0-88312-480-7); microfiche set 6.75x (ISBN 0-88312-478-5). Summer Inst Ling.

Longacre, William A. & Holbrook, Sally J., eds. Multidisciplinary Research at Grasshopper Pueblo, Arizona. (Anthropological Papers: No. 40). 150p. 1982. pap. 12.95x monograph (ISBN 0-8165-0425-3). U of Ariz Pr.

Longair, Malcolm S. High Energy Astrophysics: An Informal Introduction for Students of Physics & Astronomy. LC 81-7702. (Illus.). 300p. 1981. 52.50 (ISBN 0-521-23513-8); pap. 19.95 (ISBN 0-521-28013-3). Cambridge U Pr.

Longaker, Jon D. Art, Style & History: A Selective History of Art. 1970. pap. 10.95x (ISBN 0-673-05998-7). Scott F.

Longberg-Holm, K., et al, eds. Virus Receptors, 2 pts. (Receptors & Recognition Ser. B: Vols. 7 & 8). Set. 80.00x (ISBN 0-686-80429-5, Pub. by Chapman & Hall England); Pt. 1: Bacterial Viruses. 43.00 (ISBN 0-412-16410-8); Pt. 2: Animal Viruses. 43.00x (ISBN 0-412-15660-1). Methuen Inc.

Longbottom, Roy. Computer System Reliability. LC 79-40649. (Wiley Ser. in Computing). 1980. 49.95 (ISBN 0-471-27634-0, Pub. by Wiley-Interscience). Wiley.

Longbrake, David B. & Nichols, Woodrow W., Jr. Sunshine & Shadows in Metropolitan Miami. LC 76-4792. (Contemporary Metropolitan Analysis Ser.). (Illus.). 80p. 1976. pap. 8.95x prof ref (ISBN 0-88410-443-5). Ballinger Pub.

Longchamp, S. G. & Wagniere, J. L. Memoires Sur Voltaire et Sur Ses Ouvrages Par Longchamp et Wagniere. Repr. of 1826 ed. 283.00 o.p. (ISBN 0-8287-0552-6). Clearwater Pub.

Longchamps, Joanne de see De Longchamps, Joanne.

Longdon, L. V., tr. see Levitan, B. M. & Zhikov, V. V.

Longenecker, Justin G. Essentials of Management: A Behavioral Approach. 1977. text ed. 15.95 (ISBN 0-675-08552-7). Additional supplements may be obtained from publisher. Merrill.

--Principles of Management & Organizational Behavior. 4th ed. 1977. text ed. 19.95 (ISBN 0-675-08556-X). Additional supplements may be obtained from publisher. Merrill.

Longenecker, Justin G. & Pringle, Charles D. Management. 5th ed. (Illus.). 544p. 1981. text ed. 23.95 (ISBN 0-675-08061-4); study guide 4.95 (ISBN 0-675-09995-1). Additional supplements may be obtained from publisher. Merrill.

Longerich, Mary C. Manual for the Aphasia Patient. 1958. text ed. 14.95x (ISBN 0-02-371620-7). Macmillan.

Longest, Beafort B., Jr. Management Practices for the Health Professional. 2nd ed. (Illus.). 1980. text ed. 18.50 (ISBN 0-8359-4224-4). Reston.

Longest, Beaufort B., Jr. Principles of Hospital Business Office Management. 1975. 11.75 (ISBN 0-930228-02-2); instr's manual 23.50 (ISBN 0-686-77078-1, 1448). Healthcare Fin Man Assn.

Longest, George C., ed. Three Virginia Writers: A Reference Guide. 1978. lib. bdg. 27.00 (ISBN 0-8161-7841-0, Hall Reference). G K Hall.

Longfellow, Henry W. Children's Own Longfellow. (Illus.). (gr. 4-6). 1908. 9.95 (ISBN 0-395-06889-4). HM.

--Evangeline & Selected Tales & Poems. Gregory, Horace, ed. pap. 2.95 (ISBN 0-451-51724-5, CE1724, Sig Classics). NAL.

--The Letters of Henry Wadsworth Longfellow: Vols. 5 & 6, 1866-1882. Hilen, Andrew, ed. (Illus.). 1696p. 1983. Set. text ed. 80.00 (ISBN 0-686-97213-9). Vol. V, 1866-1875. Vol. VI, 1875-1882. Harvard U pr.

--The Letters of Henry Wadsworth Longfellow, 4 vols. Hilen, Andrew R., ed. Incl. Vols. 1-2. 1814-36; 1837-43. 1967; Vols. 3-4. 1844-1856; 1857-1865. 1972. Set. 50.00x (ISBN 0-674-52728-3). LC 66-18248. Set. 55.00x (Belknap Pr). Harvard U Pr.

--Poems. 1932. 3.95 o.s.i. (ISBN 0-394-60056-8, M56). Modern Lib.

--Poetical Works. (Oxford Standard Authors Ser.). 1904. 35.00x (ISBN 0-19-254133-1). Oxford U Pr.

--The Poetical Works of Longfellow. rev. new ed. Monteiro, George, intro. by. (Cambridge Editions Ser.). 1975. 19.95 (ISBN 0-395-18487-8). HM.

--Song of Hiawatha. facs. ed. (Bounty Bks.). (Illus.). 1969. 5.98 o.p. (ISBN 0-517-00197-7). Crown.

Longfield, Diane M. Passage to ESL Literacy Instructor's Guide. 432p. (Orig.). 1981. pap. text ed. 14.95 (ISBN 0-937354-03-1). Delta Systems.

--Passage to ESL Literacy Student Workbook. 224p. (Orig.). 1981. pap. text ed. 4.50 (ISBN 0-937354-01-5). Delta Systems.

Longford, Lord. Abraham Lincoln. LC 74-19870. (Illus.). 1975. 12.95 o.p. (ISBN 0-399-11473-4). Putnam Pub Group.

--Pope John Paul II: An Authorized Biography. LC 82-8001. (Illus.). 208p. 1982. 20.50 (ISBN 0-688-01393-7). Morrow.

Longgood, William. The Darkening Land. 1972. 9.95 o.p. (ISBN 0-671-21217-6). S&S.

Longhetts, A. Atmospheric Planetary Boundary Layer Physics: Proceedings, Vol. 11. (Developments in Atmospheric Science Ser.). 1980. 68.00 (ISBN 0-444-41885-7). Elsevier.

Longhorn. Psychiatric Care. 2nd ed. 1981. write for info. (ISBN 0-471-25863-6, Wiley Heyden). Wiley.

Longhurst, Jean, jt. auth. see Singlemann, Jay.

Longinus, Cassius. Longinus on the Sublime. Prickard, A. O., tr. LC 78-6552. 1978. Repr. of 1926 ed. lib. bdg. 16.25x (ISBN 0-313-20479-9, LOSD). Greenwood.

--Longinus on the Sublime: The Peri Hupsous in Translations by Nicolas Boileau-Despreaux (1674) & William Smith (1739) LC 75-8892. 390p. 1975. lib. bdg. 50.00x (ISBN 0-8201-1153-8). Schol Facsimiles.

Longley, D., jt. auth. see Shain, M.

Longley, Dennis & Shain, Michael. Dictionary of Information Technology. 450p. 1983. 34.95 (ISBN 0-471-89574-1, Pub. by Wiley-Interscience). Wiley.

Longley, Edna, ed. Edward Thomas: Poems & Last Poems. 432p. 1978. 29.00x (ISBN 0-7121-0146-2, Pub. by Macdonald & Evans). State Mutual Bk.

Longley, Lawrence D., jt. auth. see Krasnow, Erwin G.

Longley, Peter. Contemporary Logic. LC 80-1443. 178p. (Orig.). 1981. pap. text ed. 9.50 (ISBN 0-8191-1458-8). U Pr of Amer.

Longley, W. R., et al. Analytic Geometry & Calculus. 1960. 27.50x o.p. (ISBN 0-471-00344-1). Wiley.

Longley-Cook, Laurence H. Statistical Problems. LC 76-126340. (Illus., Orig.). 1971. pap. 5.50 (ISBN 0-06-460009-2, CO 9, COS). B&N NY.

Longman, Harold. What's Behind the Word? (Illus.). (gr. 6-9). 1968. PLB 4.99 o.p. (ISBN 0-698-30397-0, Coward). Putnam Pub Group.

Longman, W. Tokens of the Eighteenth Century, Connected with Booksellers & Bookmakers (Authors, Printers, Publishers, Engravers, & Paper Makers) LC 70-78192. (Illus.). 90p. 1970. Repr. of 1916 ed. 30.00x (ISBN 0-8103-3368-6). Gale.

Longmate, Elizabeth & Reeves, Marjorie. Children at Work, 1830-1885. (Then & There Ser.). (Illus.). 96p. (Orig.). (gr. 7-12). 1981. pap. text ed. 3.10 (ISBN 0-582-22294-X). Longman.

Longmore, Donald. Heart. LC 74-104743. (Illus., Orig.). 1971. pap. 2.45 o.p. (ISBN 0-07-038678-1, SP). McGraw.

Longmore, Donald B. Towards Safer Cardiac Surgery. 1981. lib. bdg. 39.95 (ISBN 0-8161-2232-6, Hall Medical). G K Hall.

Longo, Frederick R. Porphyrin Chemistry Advances. LC 77-85094. 1979. 37.50 o.p. (ISBN 0-250-40229-7). Ann Arbor Science.

Longo, Gianni, jt. auth. see Brambilla, Robert.

Longo, Gianni, jt. auth. see Brambilla, Roberto.

Longo, Giovanni E., jt. auth. see Beltramo, Mario.

Longo, Lucas. O. Henry, Short Story Writer. Rahmas, Sigurd C., ed. (Outstanding Personalities Ser.: No. 88). 32p. (gr. 9-12). 1982. 2.95 (ISBN 0-87157-588-4); pap. text ed. 1.95 (ISBN 0-87157-088-2). SamHar Pr.

Longo, Michael. Fundamentals of Elementary Particle Physics. (M-H Ser. in Funds. of Physics). (Illus.). 192p. 1972. text ed. 21.95 o.p. (ISBN 0-07-038689-7, C). McGraw.

Longree, Karla. Quantity Food Sanitation. 3rd ed. LC 80-11551. 1980. 35.50 (ISBN 0-471-06424-6, Pub. by Wiley Interscience). Wiley.

--Sanitary Techniques in Food Service. 2nd ed. LC 81-3047. 271p. 1982. text ed. 18.95x (ISBN 0-471-08820-X). Wiley.

Longrigg, Roger. The History of Foxhunting. (Illus.). 272p. 1975. 29.95 o.p. (ISBN 0-517-52003-6, C N Potter Bks). Crown.

--Outcross. LC 82-6283. 375p. 1982. 14.95 (ISBN 0-688-01334-1). Morrow.

Longrigg, Stephen. Four Centuries of Modern Iraq. (Arab Background Ser.). 18.00x o.s.i. (ISBN 0-86685-019-8). Intl Bk Ctr.

Longrigg, Stephen H. A Short History of Eritrea. LC 74-9274. (Illus.). 188p. 1975. Repr. of 1945 ed. lib. bdg. 15.50x (ISBN 0-8371-7636-0, LOSH). Greenwood.

Longstaff, R. W., jt. ed. see Orchard, D. B.

Longstreet, Stephen. Ambassador. 1978. pap. 1.95 o.s.i. (ISBN 0-380-00938-2, 31997). Avon.

--The Bank. LC 75-40494. 1976. 8.95 o.p. (ISBN 0-399-11658-3). Putnam Pub Group.

--The Canvas Falcons. (War Library). 416p. 1983. pap. 3.95 (ISBN 0-345-30891-3). Ballantine.

--The Pembroke Colors. 320p. 1981. 12.95 o.p. (ISBN 0-399-12582-5). Putnam Pub Group.

--Storm Watch. LC 79-1293. 1979. 10.95 o.p. (ISBN 0-399-12330-X). Putnam Pub Group.

--Straw Boss. LC 78-5258. 1978. 10.95 o.p. (ISBN 0-399-12196-X). Putnam Pub Group.

--Strike the Bell Boldly. 1977. 8.95 o.p. (ISBN 0-399-11916-7). Putnam Pub Group.

Longstreet, Stephen, jt. auth. see Carmichael, Hoagy.

Longstreet, Wilma. Aspects of Ethnicity: Understanding Differences in Pluralistic Classrooms. LC 78-16631. (Orig.). 1978. pap. text ed. 10.95x (ISBN 0-8077-2529-3). Tchrs Coll.

Longstreth, Billie J., et al. Tangled Emotions. LC 82-80742. 357p. 1983. 10.95 (ISBN 0-9608142-0-5); pap. 2.95 (ISBN 0-9608142-1-3). Shamrock Pubns.

Longstreth, Richard W., jt. auth. see Teitelman, Edward.

Longsworth, Polly. Emily Dickinson: Her Letter to the World. LC 65-14902. (gr. 7 up). 1965. 10.53i (ISBN 0-690-25945-X, TYC-J). Har-Row.

--I, Charlotte Forten, Black & Free. LC 79-109901. (gr. 5-8). 1970. 12.45i (ISBN 0-690-42869-3, TYC-J). Har-Row.

Longsworth, Robert. The Desigh of Drama. new ed. Buell, Lawrence, ed. LC 73-75453. 78p. (Orig.). (gr. 7-12). 1973. pap. text ed. 1.45 o.p. (ISBN 0-88301-081-X). Pendulum Pr.

Longtin, Ray C. Three Writers of the Far West: A Reference Guide. 1980. lib. bdg. 35.00 (ISBN 0-8161-7832-1, Hall Reference). G K Hall.

Longtree, Warren T. Dark Angel Riding. (Ruff Justice Ser.: No. 7). 1982. pap. 2.50 (ISBN 0-451-11882-0, AE1882, Sig). NAL.

--Ruff Justice, No. 6: The Spirit Woman War. 1982. pap. 2.50 (ISBN 0-451-11783-2, AE1783, Sig). NAL.

--Valley of Golden Tombs. (Ruff Justice Ser.: No. 5). Date not set. pap. 2.50 (ISBN 0-451-11563-5, AE1563, Sig). NAL.

--Widow Creek. (Ruff Justice Ser.: No. 4). 1982. pap. 2.50 (ISBN 0-451-11422-1, AE1422, Sig). NAL.

Longworth, G. Standards in Programming. (Illus.). 206p. 1981. text ed. 110.00x (ISBN 0-85012-341-0). Intl Pubns Serv.

Longyear, Marie. The McGraw-Hill Style Manual: Concise Guide for Writers & Editors. LC 82-195. (Illus.). 256p. 1982. 24.95 (ISBN 0-07-038676-5). McGraw.

Longyear, Rey M., ed. The Northern Italian Symphony 1800-1840. (The Symphony 1720-1840 Series A: Vol. 6). 1982. lib. bdg. 90.00 (ISBN 0-8240-3819-3). Garland Pub.

Lonning, Per. The Dilemma of Contemporary Theology: Prefigured in Luther, Pascal, Kierkegaard, Nietzsche. LC 78-16470. 1978. Repr. of 1962 ed. lib. bdg. 20.00x (ISBN 0-313-20596-5, LODC). Greenwood.

Lonnroth, Lars. Njals Saga: A Critical Approach. LC 73-94437. 400p. 1976. 34.50x (ISBN 0-520-02708-6). U. of Cal Pr.

Lonnroth, Mans, jt. auth. see Walker, William.

Lono, Luz P., ed. see Ozaeta, Pablo.

Lonsdale, Anne. Merchant Adventurers in the East. Reeves, Marjorie, ed. (Then & There Ser.). (Illus.). 96p. (Orig.). (gr. 7-12). 1980. pap. text ed. 3.10 (ISBN 0-582-21723-7). Longman.

Lonsdale, Richard E., ed. Economic Atlas of Nebraska. LC 76-30887. (Nebraska Atlas Project). (Illus.). xviii, 165p. 1977. 17.95x (ISBN 0-8032-0911-8). U. of Nebr Pr.

Loo, Shirley, ed. Managememt by Design: Library Management, Vol. 2. 1982. pap. 13.00 (ISBN 0-87111-301-5). SLA.

Loo, Yew C. & Cusens, Anthony R. The Finite-Strip Method in Bridge Engineering. (Viewpoint Publication Ser.). (Illus.). 1979. pap. text ed. 25.00x (ISBN 0-7210-1041-5). Scholium Intl.

Loofbourow, Leon. He Shall Be Like a Tree: An Interpretation of the Seguoias. (Illus.). 1968. pap. 1.50 o.s.i. (ISBN 0-918634-27-X). D M Chase.

Loofs-Wissowa, H. H. E., ed. The Diffusion of Material Culture. (Asian & Pacific Archaeology Ser.: No.9). (Illus.). 393p. (Orig.). 1980. pap. 10.00x (ISBN 0-8248-0744-8). UH Pr.

Loogen, F. & Seipel, L., eds. Detection of Ischaemic Myocardium with Exercise: Symposium. (Illus.). 191p. 1982. pap. 28.50 (ISBN 0-387-11237-5). Springer-Verlag.

Look, Al. Bits of Colorado History. 1976. pap. 5.50x (ISBN 0-87315-063-5). Golden Bell.

--No Advertising. (Illus.). 1968. 1.75x (ISBN 0-87315-028-7). Golden Bell.

Look, Dwight C., Jr. & Sauer, Harry, Jr. Thermodynamics. (Engineering Ser.). 565p. 1982. text ed. 31.95 (ISBN 0-8185-0491-9). Brooks-Cole.

Look Magazine & the American Federation of the Arts. Look at America. (Illus.). 14p. 1957. 1.00x (ISBN 0-686-99845-6). La Jolla Mus Comtemp Art.

Look, Mrs. Travis, jt. auth. see McCarty, Diane.

Loomba, N. Paul. Linear Programming. 2nd ed. (Illus.). 1976. text ed. 25.95x (ISBN 0-02-371630-4). Macmillan.

Loomba, N. Paul & Holsinger, Alden O., Jr. Management: A Quantative Perspective. (Illus.). 1978. text ed. 24.95x (ISBN 0-02-371640-1); study guide 6.95 (ISBN 0-02-371670-3). Macmillan.

Loomes, Brian. The White Dial Clock. LC 74-13515. (Illus.). 172p. 1975. 10.95 o.p. (ISBN 0-8069-8772-3). Sterling.

Loomis, Albertine. For Whom Are the Stars? LC 76-16778. 256p. 1976. 10.95 (ISBN 0-8248-0416-3). UH Pr.

Loomis, Andrew. Figure Drawing for All It's Worth. (Illus.). (YA) (gr. 9 up). 1943. 18.95 (ISBN 0-670-31255-X). Viking Pr.

Loomis, Burdett, jt. auth. see Cigler, Allan.

Loomis, Darlene. Growing Together With Guys, Gals & Animal Pals. (Illus., Orig.). 1977. pap. 2.00 (ISBN 0-686-36276-4). Drain Enterprise.

--He Touched Me. (Illus.). 62p. (Orig.). 1977. pap. 3.00 (ISBN 0-686-36275-6). Drain Enterprise.

--Joint Heirs in Christ. (Illus., Orig.). 1977. pap. 2.00 (ISBN 0-686-36277-2). Drain Enterprise.

--Joint Heirs in Christ. (Illus.). 80p. 1983. 6.95 (ISBN 0-89962-330-1). Todd & Honeywell.

--Those Who Won't & Those Who Will. (Illus.). 12p. (Orig.). 1977. pap. 1.00 (ISBN 0-686-36278-0). Drain Enterprise.

Loomis, Edward. The Charcoal Horse. LC 82-70233. 124p. 1959. 4.50 (ISBN 0-8040-0035-2). Swallow.

--On Fiction: Critical Essays & Notes. LC 82-71587. 71p. 1966. 3.25 (ISBN 0-8040-0231-2). Swallow.

--Vedettes: A Collection of Stories. LC 82-72171. 112p. (Orig.). 1964. 6.50 (ISBN 0-8040-0309-2); pap. 3.50 (ISBN 0-8040-0310-6). Swallow.

Loomis, Kristin S. & Spaeth, Steven E., eds. National Directory of Addresses & Telephone Numbers: 1983 Edition. LC 81-52822. 1982. pap. 24.95 (ISBN 0-940994-25-9). Concord Ref Bks.

Loomis, Kristin S., et al, eds. National Directory of Addresses & Telephone Numbers. LC 81-52822. 1981. pap. 19.95 o.p. (ISBN 0-940994-00-3). Concord Ref Bks.

--National Directory of Addresses & Telephone Numbers: 1982 Edition. rev. ed. LC 81-52822. 1982. pap. 19.95 o.p. (ISBN 0-940994-03-8). Concord Ref Bks.

Loomis, Laura H. & Loomis, Roger S., eds. Medieval Romances. 1965. pap. 3.25 (ISBN 0-394-30970-7, 30970, Mod LibC). Modern Lib.

Loomis, Lynn H. Calculus. 3rd ed. LC 81-14937. (Mathematics Ser.). (Illus.). 1000p. 1982. text ed. 33.95 (ISBN 0-201-05045-5); student supplement 9.95 (ISBN 0-201-05046-3); write for info. solutions manual (ISBN 0-201-05047-1). A-W.

Loomis, Mary E. Data Communications. (Illus.). 256p. 1983. text ed. 24.95 (ISBN 0-13-196469-0). P-H.

--Data Management & File Processing. (Software Ser.). (Illus.). 544p. 1983. 28.95 (ISBN 0-13-196477-1). P-H.

Loomis, Mary W. Custom Make Your Own Shoes & Handbags. (Illus.). 1978. pap. 4.95 o.p. (ISBN 0-517-53139-9). Crown.

Loomis, Noel M. & Nasatir, Abraham P. Pedro Vial & the Roads to Santa Fe. (American Exploration & Travel Ser.: Vol. 49). (Illus.). 1967. 25.00 (ISBN 0-8061-0730-8); pap. 12.95 (ISBN 0-8061-1110-0). U of Okla Pr.

Loomis, Roger S., ed. Arthurian Literature in the Middle Ages: A Collaborative History. 1959. 63.00x (ISBN 0-19-811588-1). Oxford U Pr.

Loomis, Roger S., jt. ed. see Loomis, Laura H.

Loomis, William, ed. The Development of Dictyostelium Disoideum. 522p. 1982. 74.50 (ISBN 0-12-455620-5). Acad Pr.

Loon, Antonia Van see Van Loon, Antonia.

Loon, J. H. van see Van Loon, J. H. & Staudt, F. J.

Loon, M. N. Van see Van Loon, M. N.

Loon, M. Van see Liebowitz, Harold.

Looney. Development Alternatives of Mexico. 286p. 1982. 25.95 (ISBN 0-03-060242-4). Praeger.

Looney, Gerald, jt. auth. see Newton, Kathleen.

Looney, J. W., jt. auth. see Uchtmann, Donald L.

Looney, John G., jt. ed. see Feinstein, Sherman C.

Looney, Ralph. Haunted Highways: The Ghost Towns of New Mexico. (Illus.). 1979. pap. 9.95 (ISBN 0-8263-0506-7). U of NM Pr.

Looney, Robert E. A Development Strategy for Iran Through the 1980's. LC 75-44936. (Praeger Special Studies). 1977. text ed. 23.95 (ISBN 0-03-021956-6). Praeger.

--The Economic Consequences of World Inflation on Semi-Dependent Countries. LC 78-65351. 1978. pap. text ed. 12.75 (ISBN 0-8191-0654-2). U Pr of Amer.

--The Economic Development of Panama: The Impact of World Inflation on an Open Economy. LC 74-33038. (Illus.). 1976. 35.95 o.p. (ISBN 0-275-05390-3). Praeger.

--Mexican Development Strategies: The Limits of Oil-Based Growth. (Duke Press Policy Studies). 250p. Date not set. text ed. 27.50 (ISBN 0-8223-0557-7). Duke.

--Saudi Arabia's Development Potential: Application of an Islamic Growth/Model. LC 79-2274. 384p. 1981. 34.95x (ISBN 0-669-03083-X). Lexington Bks.

Looper, C. Eugene. Banker's Guide to Personnel Administration. LC 82-24400. 360p. 1983. 39.00 (ISBN 0-87267-041-4). Bankers.

Loor, F. & Roelants, G. E., eds. B & T Cells in Immune Recognition. LC 76-26913. 1977. 85.00 (ISBN 0-471-99438-3, Pub. by Wiley-Interscience). Wiley.

Loor, G. P. De see De Loor, G. P.

Loos. Cast of Thousands. 1977. 8.95 (ISBN 0-448-12264-2, G&D). Putnam Pub Group.

Loos, Amandus W., tr. see Brunner, Emil.

Loos, Anita. Gentlemen Prefer Blondes But Gentlemen Marry Brunettes. LC 82-48893. 256p. 1983. pap. 3.95 (ISBN 0-686-43024-7, Vin). Random.

Loos, Bob. The Way Grampa Tells Stories. (Illus.). 32p. 1982. 5.75 (ISBN 0-682-49850-5). Exposition.

Loos, Eugene. Estudios Panos V: Verbos Performativos. (Serie Linguistica Peruana: No. 14). 221p. 1976. pap. 3.00x o.s.i. (ISBN 0-685-51592-3); microfiche 3.00x (ISBN 0-88312-345-2). Summer Inst Ling.

Loos, Eugene, ed. Materiales Para Estudios Fonologicos, 2 vols. (Documentos Del Trabajo (Peru) Ser.: No. 9). Set. pap. 18.00x (ISBN 0-88312-787-3); microfiche 6.00x (ISBN 0-88312-355-X). Summer Inst Ling.

Loos, Eugene E. Phonology of Capanahua & Its Grammatical Basis. (Publications in Linguistics & Related Fields Ser.: No. 20). 233p. 1969. pap. 3.50x (ISBN 0-88312-022-4); microfiche 3.00x (ISBN 0-88312-422-X). Summer Inst Ling.

Loos, Madge. Puppet Without Worlds. LC 69-19406. 1969. 4.00 o.p. (ISBN 0-8233-0130-3). Golden Quill.

Loose, Frances F. Bonus Points: Teacher's Handbook. 55p. 1976. 3.50 (ISBN 0-89039-174-2). Ann Arbor Pubs.

--Decimals & Percentages. (Illus.). 96p. (gr. 4-6). 1977. 7.00 (ISBN 0-89039-200-5); answer key incl. Ann Arbor Pubs.

--Fractions, Book 1: Reusable Edition. (gr. 4). 1973. wkbk. 7.00 (ISBN 0-89039-064-9). Ann Arbor Pubs.

--Fractions, Book 2: Reusable Edition. (gr. 4-6). 1973. wkbk. 7.50 (ISBN 0-89039-066-5). Ann Arbor Pubs.

Loose, Gerhard. Ernst Junger. (World Authors Ser.). 1974. lib. bdg. 15.95 (ISBN 0-8057-2479-6, Twayne). G K Hall.

Loose Leaf Reference Service. Clinical Ophthalmology, 5 vols. & index. Duane, Thomas, ed. (Illus.). Set. looseleaf 400.00 (ISBN 0-06-148007-X, Harper Medical); annual revision pages. 55.00 (ISBN 0-685-71848-4). Lippincott.

Loose Leaf Reference Services. Baker's Clinical Neurology, 3 vols. Baker, Abe B., et al, eds. loose leaf bdg. 300.00 (ISBN 0-06-148006-1, Harper Medical); annual revision pages 40.00 (ISBN 0-686-86013-6). Lippincott.

--Otolaryngology, 5 vols. English, Gerald, ed. loose leaf bdg. 375.00 (ISBN 0-06-148010-X, Harper Medical); revision pages 55.00 (ISBN 0-686-86019-5). Lippincott.

--Practice of Pediatrics, 10 vols. Kelley, Vicent C., ed. looseleaf bdg. 300.00 (ISBN 0-06-148011-8, Harper Medical); revision pages 95.00 (ISBN 0-685-57886-0). Lippincott.

Loose Leaf References Services. Laboratory Medicine, 4 vols. Race, George J., ed. loose leaf bdg. 325.00 (ISBN 0-06-148009-6, Harper Medical); revision pages 95.00 (ISBN 0-685-57897-6). Lippincott.

Loose, S. & Ramb, R. Southeast Asia Handbook: Singapore, Burma, Brunei, Borneo, Malaysia, Thailand. (Illus.). 550p. 1983. pap. 13.95 (ISBN 3-922025-07-2). Bradt Ent.

Loosli, J. K. & McDonald, I. Nonprotein Nitrogen in the Nutrition of Ruminants. (FAO Agricultural Studies: No. 75). 94p. 1968. pap. 13.25 (ISBN 0-686-92774-5, F299, FAO). Unipub.

Loosli, J. K., jt. auth. see Maynard, Leonard A.

Lootens, J. Ghislain. Lootens on Photographic Enlarging & Print Quality. 8th ed. Bogen, Lester, ed. (Illus.). 256p. 1975. 13.95 o.p. (ISBN 0-8174-0467-8, Amphoto). Watson-Guptill.

Lopach, James, et al. We the People of Montana. 320p. 1983. 19.95 (ISBN 0-87842-154-8); pap. 10.95 (ISBN 0-87842-159-9). Mountain Pr.

Lopata, Helen Z. Polish Americans: Status Competition in an Ethnic Community. (Ethnic Groups in American Life Ser). (Illus.). 224p. 1976. pap. text ed. 10.95 (ISBN 0-13-686436-8). P-H.

Lopata, Helena. Marriages & Families. (Transaction Ser.). 1973. pap. text ed. 9.95x (ISBN 0-442-24888-1). Van Nos Reinhold.

Lopata, Helena Z. & Brehm, Henry P. Widowhood. LC 78-19789. 200p. 1983. 23.95 (ISBN 0-03-046109-X). Praeger.

Lopata, Helena Z., ed. Research in the Interweave of Social Roles, Vol. 1. (Orig.). 1980. lib. bdg. 42.50 (ISBN 0-89232-066-4). Jai Pr.

Lopata, Helena Z. & Maines, David R., eds. Research in the Interweave of Social Roles, Vol. 2. 325p. 1981. 42.50 (ISBN 0-89232-191-1). Jai Pr.

Lopate, Philip. Confessions of Summer. LC 78-19715. 1979. 9.95 o.p. (ISBN 0-385-12619-0). Doubleday.

Lopate, Phillip. Bachelorhood: Tales of the Metropolis. 1981. 13.95 (ISBN 0-316-53198-7). Little.

--Confessions of Summer. LC 78-19715. 330p. 1979. 6.00 (ISBN 0-385-12619-0). SUN.

--The Daily Round: New Poems. LC 76-7709. 1976. 10.00 (ISBN 0-915342-15-4); pap. 5.00 (ISBN 0-915342-14-6). SUN.

Lope De Vega, Carpio. Caballero de Olmedo. Macdonald, I. T., ed. text ed. 7.95x (ISBN 0-521-06676-X). Cambridge U Pr.

Loper. Direct Current Fundamentals. 2nd ed. LC 70-153729. 352p. 1978. 16.60 (ISBN 0-8273-1143-5); pap. 12.60 (ISBN 0-8273-1147-8); instructor's guide 3.75 (ISBN 0-8273-1145-1). Delmar.

Loper, Marvin, jt. auth. see Reeser, Clayton.

Loper, Orla, et al. Introduction to Electricity & Electronics. LC 77-78174. 1979. text ed. 18.40 (ISBN 0-8273-1160-5); 4.75 (ISBN 0-8273-1162-1). Delmar.

Lopes, Maria Luisa. A Portugese Colonial in America: Belmira Nunes Lopes: The Autobiography of a Cape Verdean-American. Miller, Yvette E., ed. 215p. 1982. pap. 11.95 (ISBN 0-935480-07-2); 25.00 (ISBN 0-935480-08-0). Lat Am Lit Rev Pr.

Lopez, Adalberto & Petras, James, eds. Puerto Rico & the Puerto Ricans: Studies in History & Society. 500p. 1974. 16.95x o.p. (ISBN 0-87073-807-0); pap. 8.95 o.p. (ISBN 0-686-77092-7). Schenkman.

Lopez, Albert C., tr. see Ray, C. A.

Lopez, Alberto, tr. see Edge, Findley B.

Lopez, Antonio, jt. auth. see Louie, Elaine.

Lopez, Claude-Anne & Herbert, Eugenia W. The Private Franklin: The Man & His Family. (Illus.). 361p. 1975. 11.95 o.p. (ISBN 0-393-07496-X). Norton.

Lopez, Enrique Campos & Anderson, Robert J., eds. Natural Resources & Development in Arid & Semi-Arid Regions. 350p. 1982. lib. bdg. 25.00 (ISBN 0-86531-418-7). Westview.

Lopez, Felix M. Personnel Interviewing: The Working Woman's Resourse Book. 2nd ed. (Illus.). 384p. 1975. 34.95 (ISBN 0-07-038726-5, P&RB). McGraw.

Lopez, George A., jt. auth. see Garrigan, Timothy B.

Lopez, Jadwiga, ed. see Ross, Corinne.

Lopez, Jesus. Of Human Dignity. Literary Services Agency, Inc., ed. 485p. 1982. pap. 3.95 (ISBN 0-917188-20-9). Nationwide Pr.

Lopez, Juan E. & Cabat, Louis. Barron's How to Prepare for the College Board Achievement Tests-Spanish. rev. ed. (gr. 11-12). 1982. pap. 8.95 (ISBN 0-8120-0978-9). Barron.

Lopez, Martita A. & Feldman, Howard. Developmental Psychology for the Health Care Professions: Young Adult Through Late Aging, Pt. II. (Behavioral Sciences for Health Care Professionals Ser.). 128p. (Orig.). 1982. lib. bdg. 17.50 (ISBN 0-86531-012-2); pap. 8.95 (ISBN 0-86531-013-0). Westview.

Lopez, Martita A. & Hoyer, William J. Behavioral Gerontology. 225p. 1983. 25.00 (ISBN 0-08-028040-4); pap. 12.95 (ISBN 0-08-028039-0). Pergamon.

Lopez, N. C. King Pancho & the First Clock. LC 63-16396. (Illus.). (gr. 2-7). 1967. PLB 6.75x (ISBN 0-87783-020-7); pap. 2.95x deluxe ed. (ISBN 0-87783-098-3); cassette 5.95x (ISBN 0-87783-188-2). Oddo.

Lopez, Nancy & Schwed, Peter. The Education of a Woman Golfer. 1979. 9.95 o.p. (ISBN 0-671-24756-5). S&S.

Lopez, Norbert. Cuento Del Rey Pancho y el Primer Reloj. LC 70-108730. (Illus., Span). (gr. 2-7). 1970. PLB 6.75x (ISBN 0-87783-010-X); pap. 2.95x deluxe ed. (ISBN 0-87783-104-1); cassette 5.95x (ISBN 0-87783-188-2). Oddo.

Lopez, R. S. The Commercial Revolution of the Middle Ages, 950-1350. LC 75-35453. (Illus.). 204p. 1976. 29.95 (ISBN 0-521-21111-5); pap. 9.95x (ISBN 0-521-29046-5). Cambridge U Pr.

Lopez, Robert S. & Raymond, Irving W., eds. Medieval Trade in the Mediterranean World: Illustrative Documents. (Columbia University Records of Civilization Series). 1967. pap. 5.95x o.p. (ISBN 0-393-09720-X, NortonC). Norton.

Lopez, Ulises M. & Warrin, George E. Electronic Drawing & Technology. LC 77-16452. (Electronic Technology Ser.). 1978. text ed. 28.95 (ISBN 0-471-02377-9); solutions manual 4.00 (ISBN 0-471-03715-X). Wiley.

Lopez, Violeta B. The Mangyans of Mindoro: An Ethnohistory. (Illus.). 1976. text ed. 10.65x (ISBN 0-8248-0472-4). UH Pr.

Lopez-Baralt, Mercedes. Mito Taino. (Coleccion semilla). 111p. 1977. pap. 2.10 o.p. (ISBN 0-940238-27-6). Ediciones Huracan.

Lopez-Morillas, J. The Krausist Movement & Ideological Change in Spain: 1854-1874. (Iberian & Latin American Studies). 180p. 1981. 39.50 (ISBN 0-521-23256-2). Cambridge U Pr.

Lopez-Morillas, Juan. New Spanish Self-Taught. 340p. (Span.). 1982. pap. text ed. 4.76i (ISBN 0-06-463617-8, EH 617, EH). B&N NY.

Lopez-Pedraza, Rafael. Hermes & His Children. 2nd ed. (Seminar Ser.: No. 13). (Illus.). 134p. (Orig.). 1983. pap. 8.00 (ISBN 0-88214-113-9). Spring Pubns.

Lopinot, Neal H. & Hutto, M. Denise. Archaeological Investigations at the Kingfish Site, St. Clair County, Illinois. LC 82-50285. (Research Paper Ser.: No. 25). Date not set. price not set (ISBN 0-88104-001-0). S Ill U Pr.

Lopo, Ana, jt. auth. see Murphy, Bruce.

LoPreato, Joseph, jt. auth. see Jackson, Eugene.

Lopreato, Sally C., jt. auth. see Cunningham, William H.

Lops, R. L. H. La Bible de Mace de la Charite Vol. VII: Apocalypse. (Leidse Romanistische Reeks Ser.: Vol. 10). (Illus.). xiii, 263p. 1982. pap. write for info (ISBN 90-04-06758-2). E J Brill.

Lopshire, Robert. The Beginner Book of Things to Make. LC 64-22011. (Beginner Bk: No. 37). (Illus.). (gr. k-3). 1977. 4.95 (ISBN 0-394-83493-7); PLB 5.99 o.p. (ISBN 0-394-93493-8). Beginner.

Lora, G. A History of the Bolivian Labour Movement 1848-1971. Whitehead, L., ed. Whitehead, Christine, tr. LC 76-22988. (Latin American Studies: No. 27). 1977. 54.50 (ISBN 0-521-21400-9). Cambridge U Pr.

Lora, Ronald, ed. America in the Sixties: Cultural Authorities in Transition. LC 73-22224. 1974. pap. text ed. 15.95 (ISBN 0-471-54611-9). Wiley.

Lorain. Tableau de l'Instruction Primaire en France. (Conditions of the 19th Century French Working Class Ser.). 410p. 1974. Repr. of 1837 ed. lib. bdg. 104.00 o.p. (ISBN 0-8287-0553-4, 1124). Clearwater Pub.

Lorain, Pierre. Clandestine Operations: The Arms & Techniques of the Resistance, 1941-1944. (Illus.). 192p. 1983. 19.95 (ISBN 0-02-575200-6). Macmillan.

Loraine, J. A., ed. Understanding Homosexuality. 217p. 1974. 22.95 (ISBN 0-444-19519-X). Elsevier.

Loraine, Michael. Prosody & Rhyme in Classical Arabic & Persian. 1983. write for info. U of Wash Pr.

Loraine, Philip. Sea-Change. 192p. 1983. 10.95 (ISBN 0-312-70811-4). St Martin.

Loram, Ian & Phelps, Leland, eds. Aus Unserer Zeit. 3rd. ed. LC 78-141590. 423p. (Ger.). 1972. pap. text ed. 9.95x (ISBN 0-393-09389-1). Norton.

Loran, Erle. Cezanne's Composition: Analysis of His Form with Diagrams & Photographs of His Motifs. 3rd ed. (Illus.). 1963. 25.00 (ISBN 0-520-00768-9). U of Cal Pr.

Lorange, Peter. Corporate Planning: An Executive Viewpoint. (Illus.). 1980. text ed. 24.95 (ISBN 0-13-174755-X). P-H.

--Implementation of Strategic Planning. (Illus.). 288p. 1982. text ed. 23.95 (ISBN 0-13-451815-2). P-H.

Lorange, Peter & Vancil, Richard F. Strategic Planning Systems. (Illus.). 1977. ref. ed. 23.95 (ISBN 0-13-851006-7). P-H.

Lorant, Tessa. The Batsford Book of Hand & Machine Knitted Laces. (Illus.). 144p. 1982. 27.50 (ISBN 0-7134-3920-3, Pub. by Batsford England). David & Charles.

Loranth, Alice N., ed. Catalog of Folklore, Folklife & Folk Songs, 3 vols. 2nd ed. 1978. Set. lib. bdg. 245.00 (ISBN 0-8161-0249-X, Hall Library). G K Hall.

Lorayne, Harry. The Magic Book: The Complete Beginner's Guide to Anytime, Anywhere, Sleight-of-Hand Magic. LC 77-1080. (Illus.). 1977. 8.95 o.p. (ISBN 0-399-11956-6). Putnam Pub Group.

--Secrets of Mind Power. 1975. pap. 2.25 (ISBN 0-451-11501-5, AE1501, Sig.). NAL.

Lorber, Lawrence C., et al, eds. Equal Employment Practice Guide--1981, 2 vols. Set. 60.00 o.p. (ISBN 0-686-77574-0). BNA.

Lorber, Michael A. & Pierce, Walter D. Objectives, Methods & Evaluation for Secondary Teaching. (Illus.). 272p. 1983. prof. ref. 20.95 (ISBN 0-13-629014-0). P-H.

Lorca, Federico G. The New York Poems. Belitt, Ben, ed. LC 82-47987. 288p. (Orig.). pap. cancelled (ISBN 0-394-62413-0, E815, Ever). Grove.

Lorca, Federico Garcia. Five Plays: Comedies & Tragicomedies. O'Connell, Richard L. & Graham-Lujan, James, trs. Incl. Shoemaker's Prodigious Wife; Don Perlimplin; Dona Rosita the Spinster; Billy-Club Puppets; Butterfly's Evil Spell. LC 63-13642. 1964. pap. 6.95 (ISBN 0-8112-0090-6, NDP232). New Directions.

--Selected Poems. Allen, Donald M., ed. LC 54-9872. (Span. & Eng., Cloth 1955; pap 1968). pap. 4.95 (ISBN 0-8112-0091-4, NDP114). New Directions.

Lorca, Federico Garcia see Garcia Lorca, Federico.

Lorch, Carlos. Lopez: Hawaiian Surf Legend. (Illus.). 84p. 1982. pap. 8.95 (ISBN 0-911449-01-9). Mntn & Sea.

Lorch, Robert S. Democratic Process & Administrative Law. rev. ed. LC 69-10420. (Waynebooks Ser: No. 39). 1973. 11.50 (ISBN 0-8143-1362-0); pap. 6.50x (ISBN 0-686-83009-1). Wayne St U Pr.

--Public Administration. 1977. pap. text ed. 13.50 (ISBN 0-8299-0144-2). West Pub.

--State & Local Politics: The Great Entanglement. (Illus.). 432p. 1983. text ed. 22.95 (ISBN 0-13-843482-4). P-H.

Lorch, Sue. Basic Writing: A Practical Approach. (Orig.). 1981. pap. text ed. 8.95 (ISBN 0-316-53275-4); tchr's ed. avail. (ISBN 0-316-53276-2). Little.

Lord, A. R., jt. ed. see Banner, F. T.

Lord, Alexandra. A Harmless Ruse. (Orig.). 1981. pap. 1.50 o.s.i. (ISBN 0-440-13582-6). Dell.

Lord, B. I. & Potten, C. S., eds. Stem Cells & Tissue Homeostasis. LC 77-80844. (British Society for Cell Biology Symposium Ser.). (Illus.). 1978. 75.00 (ISBN 0-521-21799-7). Cambridge U Pr.

Lord, Beman. The Perfect Pitch. 1981. PLB 7.95 (ISBN 0-8398-2724-5, Gregg). G K Hall.

Lord, Bette B. Spring Moon. 1982. pap. 3.95 (ISBN 0-380-59923-6, 59923). Avon.

Lord, Carnes, tr. see Tasso, Torquato.

Lord, Clifford, ed. see Tucker, Louis L.

Lord, George D. Homeric Renaissance: The Odyssey of George Chapman. 1956. text ed. 14.50x (ISBN 0-686-83567-0). Elliots Bks.

--Trials of the Self: Heroic Ordeals in the Epic Tradition. 1983. 27.50 (ISBN 0-208-02013-6, Archon). Shoe String.

Lord, George D., ed. Andrew Marvell: Complete Poetry. pap. text ed. 3.65x (ISBN 0-394-30865-4). Phila Bk Co.

Lord, George D., jt. ed. see Mack, Maynard.

Lord, Harold W., et al. Noise Control for Engineers. (Illus.). 448p. 1979. text ed. 32.95x (ISBN 0-07-038738-9). McGraw.

Lord, Harvey G. Car Care for Kids...& Former Kids. LC 82-13778. (Illus.). 160p. (gr. 4 up). 1983. 11.95 (ISBN 0-689-30975-9); pap. 7.95 (ISBN 0-689-70648-0). Atheneum.

Lord, James. A Giacometti Portrait. (Illus.). 117p. 1980. 10.95 (ISBN 0-374-16199-2); pap. 7.95 (ISBN 0-374-51573-5). FS&G.

Lord, Jeffrey. Blade, No. 12: King of Zunga. 224p. 1975. pap. 1.50 o.p. (ISBN 0-523-40441-7). Pinnacle Bks.

--Blade, No. 18: Warlords of Gaikon. 192p. 1976. pap. 1.75 o.p. (ISBN 0-523-40791-2). Pinnacle Bks.

--Blade No. 23: Empire of Blood. 1977. pap. 2.25 (ISBN 0-523-41723-3). Pinnacle Bks.

--Blade No. 24: The Dragons of Englor. 192p. (Orig.). 1977. pap. 1.50 o.p. (ISBN 0-523-40260-0). Pinnacle Bks.

--Blade No. 31: Gladiators of Hapanu. 1979. pap. 1.50 o.p. (ISBN 0-523-40648-7). Pinnacle Bks.

--The Bronze Axe: Blade No. 1. (Richard Blade Ser., No. 1). 192p. 1973. pap. 1.75 o.p. (ISBN 0-523-40774-2). Pinnacle Bks.

--Champion of the Gods. (Richard Balde Ser: No.21). 1976. pap. 1.50 o.p. (ISBN 0-523-40257-0). Pinnacle Bks.

--The Crystal Seas. (Blade Ser.: No. 16). 192p. 1975. pap. 1.75 o.p. (ISBN 0-523-40789-0). Pinnacle Bks.

--The Jade Warrior. (Richard Blade Ser.: No. 2). 224p. 1973. pap. 1.75 o.p. (ISBN 0-523-40775-0). Pinnacle Bks.

--Jewel of Tharn. new ed. (Blade Ser., No. 3). 224p. (Orig.). 1973. pap. 1.50 o.p. (ISBN 0-523-40433-6). Pinnacle Bks.

--Looters of Tharn. (Blade Ser.: No. 19). 192p. 1976. pap. 1.25 o.p. (ISBN 0-523-22855-4). Pinnacle Bks.

--Pearl of Patmos: Blade. (Blade Ser. No. 7). 192p. 1973. pap. 1.50 o.p. (ISBN 0-523-40437-9). Pinnacle Bks.

--Pirates of Gohar. (Blade Ser.: No. 32). 1979. pap. 2.25 (ISBN 0-523-41724-1). Pinnacle Bks.

--Quardians Coral Throne. (Blade Ser.: No.20). (Orig.). 1976. pap. 1.75 o.p. (ISBN 0-523-40793-9). Pinnacle Bks.

--Return to Kaldak. (Blade Ser.: No. 36). 224p. (Orig.). 1983. pap. 2.25 (ISBN 0-523-41210-X). Pinnacle Bks.

--Slave of Sarma. (Blade Ser., No. 4). 192p. 1973. pap. 2.25 (ISBN 0-523-41721-7). Pinnacle Bks.

--The Technical Substance of Stock Market Action & Its Impact upon the Current & the Ultimate Direction of the Market. (The Recondite Sources of Stock Market Action Library). (Illus.). 141p. 1983. 49.75 (ISBN 0-86654-055-5). Inst Econ Finan.

--The Torian Pearls. (Blade Ser: No. 25). 1977. pap. 1.50 o.p. (ISBN 0-523-40444-1). Pinnacle Bks.

--The Towers of Melnon. (Blade Ser. No. 15). 192p. 1975. pap. 2.25 (ISBN 0-523-41722-5). Pinnacle Bks.

--Treasure of the Stars. (Blade Ser.: No. 29). 1978. pap. 1.50 o.p. (ISBN 0-523-40207-4). Pinnacle Bks.

--Wizard of Rentoro. (Blade: No. 28). 1978. pap. 1.50 o.p. (ISBN 0-523-40206-6). Pinnacle Bks.

Lord, M. G. Mean Sheets: Political Cartoons. 1982. 14.95 (ISBN 0-316-53279-7); pap. 7.95 (ISBN 0-316-53280-0). Little.

Lord, Moira. Calendar of Sinners. (Orig.). 1980. pap. 1.95 o.p. (ISBN 0-451-09021-7, J9021, Sig). NAL.

Lord, N. W., et al. Heat Pump Technology. LC 79-56112. (Electrotechnology Ser.: Vol. 4). (Illus.). 1980. 39.95 (ISBN 0-250-40341-2). Ann Arbor Science.

Lord, Norman W. Advances in Electric Heat Treatment of Metals. LC 77-85093. (Electrotechnology Ser.: Vol. 7). 1981. text ed. 39.95 (ISBN 0-250-40481-8). Ann Arbor Science.

--Coal-Oil Mixture Technology. LC 81-69551. 148p. 1982. 29.95 (ISBN 0-250-40495-8). Ann Arbor Science.

Lord, Norman W. & Giragosian, Paul A. Advanced Computers: Parallel & Biochip Processors. (Illus.). 170p. 29.50 (ISBN 0-686-84668-0). Ann Arbor Science.

Lord, P. R. Spinning in the Seventies. 1970. 26.50x (ISBN 0-87245-517-3). Textile Bk.

--Weaving: Conversion of Yarn to Fabric. 1975. 22.50x (ISBN 0-87245-552-1). Textile Bk.

Lord, Richard A. Complete Preparation for the Multi-State Bar Examination. LC 81-13029. (Illus.). 336p. 1982. 14.95 (ISBN 0-668-05158-2); pap. 7.95 (ISBN 0-668-05160-4). Arco.

Lord, Russell. Behold Our Land. LC 74-2395. (FDR & the Era of the New Deal Ser.). 309p. 1974. Repr. of 1938 ed. lib. bdg. 39.50 (ISBN 0-306-70593-1). Da Capo.

--The Henry Wallaces of Iowa. LC 76-167843. (FDR & the Era of the New Deal Ser.). (Illus.). 615p. 1971. Repr. of 1947 ed. lib. bdg. 69.50 (ISBN 0-306-70325-4). Da Capo.

--To Hold This Soil. LC 78-171385. (FDR & the Era of the New Deal Ser). (Illus.). 124p. 1972. Repr. of 1938 ed. lib. bdg. 22.50 (ISBN 0-306-70384-X). Da Capo.

Lord, Sydney N. A Tale of Two Pities. 1978. 5.95 o.p. (ISBN 0-533-03051-X). Vantage.

Lord, Walter. A Time to Stand. LC 78-8708. (Illus.). 271p. 1978. pap. 5.95 (ISBN 0-8032-7902-7, BB 678, Bison). U of Nebr Pr.

Lord, William J., Jr., jt. auth. see Dawe, Jessamon.

Lord Byron, see Byron.

Lorde, Audre. Zami: A New Spelling of My Name. LC 82-15086. 264p. (Orig.). 1982. pap. 7.95 (ISBN 0-930436-15-6). Persephone.

Lord Kinross. The Ottoman Centuries: The Rise & Fall of the Turkish Empire. LC 76-28498. (Illus.). 1979. pap. 7.95 (ISBN 0-688-08093-6). Quill NY.

Lord Raglan. The Hero. 1979. pap. 4.95 o.p. (ISBN 0-452-00507-8, F507, Mer). NAL.

Lord Walston. Dealing with Hunger. 1977. 10.00 o.p. (ISBN 0-370-10464-1). Transatlantic.

Lore, Elana, ed. Alfred Hitchcock's Fatal Attractions. 348p. 1983. 12.95 (ISBN 0-385-27914-0). Davis Pubns.

Lore, Segal, tr. see Grimm, Jacob & Grimm, Wilhelm.

Lore, Wallace, tr. see Huber, Bruno & Huber, Louise.

Loren, Amii. Morning Rose, Evening Savage. (Orig.). 1980. pap. 1.50 o.s.i. (ISBN 0-440-15568-1). Dell.

Lorena, Hickok, jt. auth. see Gould, Jean.

Lorente De No, Raphael, ed. The Primary Acoustic Nuclei. Orig. Title: The Cochlear Nuclei. (Illus.). 189p. 1981. text ed. 35.00 (ISBN 0-89004-318-3). Raven.

Lorentz, Pare, jt. auth. see Ernst, Morris.

Lorentzen, Karin. Lanky Longlegs. Tate, Joan, tr. from Norwegian. LC 82-72246. (Illus.). (gr. 3-7). 1983. 9.95 (ISBN 0-689-50260-5, McElderry Bk). Atheneum.

Lorenz, Clarissa M. Lorelei Two: My Life with Conrad Aiken. LC 82-17347. (Illus.). 248p. 1983. 19.95 (ISBN 0-8203-0661-4). U of Ga Pr.

Lorenz, J. D. Jerry Brown: Man on the White Horse. 1978. 8.95 o.s.i. (ISBN 0-395-25767-0). HM.

Lorenz, Konrad. The Foundations of Ethology. 1983. pap. 9.95 (ISBN 0-671-44573-1, Touchstone Bks). S&S.

--King Solomon's Ring. (RL 7). pap. 2.25 (ISBN 0-451-11372-1, AE1372, Sig). NAL.

--On Aggression. Wilson, Marjorie K., tr. from Ger. LC 74-5306. (Helen & Kurt Wolff Bk). (Illus.). 306p. 1974. pap. 4.95 (ISBN 0-15-668741-0, Harv). HarBraceJ.

Lorenz, Konrad Z. King Solomon's Ring. LC 52-7373. (Illus.). 1979. pap. 4.95xi (ISBN 0-06-131976-7, TB 1976, Torch). Har-Row.

Lorenz, Lee. The Feathered Ogre. (Illus.). 48p. (gr. 1-4). 1981. 9.95 (ISBN 0-13-308304-7). P-H.

--Hugo & the Space Dog. (Illus.). 32p. (ps-3). 1983. 9.95 (ISBN 0-13-444497-3). P-H.

--Pinchpenny John. 32p. 1981. 9.95x o.p. (ISBN 0-686-73244-8). P-H.

--Pinchpenny John. (Illus.). 48p. (gr. 1-4). 1981. 9.95 (ISBN 0-13-676254-9). P-H.

Lorenz, Marian B. Patterns of American English: A Guide for Speakers of Other Languages. rev. ed. LC 75-34457. 201p. 1976. pap. text ed. 7.50 (ISBN 0-379-00806-8). Oceana.

Lorenz, R., ed. see Vollrath, H. K.

Lorenz, R., ed. see Wood, S. R. & Nichols, H. E.

Lorenz, Richard. Landscape Images: Recent Photographs by Linda Connor, Judy Fiskin & Ruth Thorne-Thomsen. (Illus.). 40p. 1980. pap. 4.70x (ISBN 0-934418-08-X). La Jolla Mus Contemp Art.

Lorenzen, Betty Jo. Examination Review for Dental Assistants. LC 79-53191. (Dental Assisting Ser.). 1981. 8.80 (ISBN 0-8273-1672-0). Delmar.

Lorenzen, David N. The Kapalikas & Kalamukhas: Two Lost Saivite Sects. LC 70-138509. (Center for South & Southeast Asia Studies, UC Berkeley). 1972. 30.00x (ISBN 0-520-01842-7). U of Cal Pr.

Lorenzen, Ernest G. The Conflict of Laws Relating to Bills & Notes. 1919. 65.00x (ISBN 0-686-51359-2). Elliots Bks.

Lorenzen, Lilly. Of Swedish Ways. (Illus.). 1978. pap. 4.95 (ISBN 0-06-464021-3, BN 4021, BN). B&N NY.

--Of Swedish Ways. (Heritage Bks.). (Illus.). 1964. 11.95 (ISBN 0-87518-002-7). Dillon.

Lorenzen, Violette A. How to Type Practically Anything Easily. 52p. 1977. pap. text ed. 7.00 (ISBN 0-686-38824-0). V A Lorenzen.

Lorenzi, Peter, jt. auth. see Herbert, Theodore T.

Lorenzo. Chasin' the Blues Away: An Anti-Depression, Anti-Anxiety Emergency Kit. (Illus.). 176p. 1982. pap. write for info. Prema Bks.

Lorenzo, Carol L. The White Sand Road. LC 77-11837. 1978. 6.95i o.p. (ISBN 0-06-024011-3, HarpJ); PLB 6.79 o.p. (ISBN 0-06-024012-1). Har-Row.

Lorenzo, O. A. & Maynard, D. N. Knots' Handbook for Vegetable Growers. 2nd ed. 390p. 1980. pap. 18.95x (ISBN 0-471-05322-8, Pub. by Wiley-Interscience). Wiley.

Lorenzo, Thomas, ed. see Grant, Ruthie.

Lorenzoni, A. B., jt. auth. see Clark, F. D.

Loret, Pierre. The Story of the Mass: From the Last Supper to the Present Day. 144p. 1982. pap. 3.50 (ISBN 0-89243-171-7). Liguori Pubns.

Loretan, Joseph O. Teaching the Disadvantaged: New Curriculum Approaches. LC 66-15325. (Illus.). 1966. text ed. 9.50 o.p. (ISBN 0-8077-1713-4). Tchrs Coll.

Loretto, M. H. & Smallman, R. E. Defect Analysis in Electron Microscopy. 1976. 31.95x o.p. (ISBN 0-412-13760-7, Pub. by Chapman & Hall). Methuen Inc.

Lorhan, Paul H. Anesthesia for the Aged. 168p. 1971. photocopy ed. spiral 17.00x (ISBN 0-398-01143-5). C C Thomas.

--Geriatric Anesthesia. 104p. 1955. photocopy ed. spiral 10.50x (ISBN 0-398-01144-3). C C Thomas.

Lorian, Victor. Significance of Medical Microbiology in the Care of Patients. 2nd ed. (Illus.). 488p. 1982. lib. bdg. 60.00 (ISBN 0-683-05165-2). Williams & Wilkins.

Lorie & Brealy. Modern Development in Investment Management. 2nd ed. 1978. pap. 15.95 (ISBN 0-03-040716-8). Dryden Pr.

Loriferne, Bernard. Analog-Digital & Digital-Analog Conversion. 195p. 1982. 29.95 (ISBN 0-471-26219-6, Pub. by Wiley Heyden). Wiley.

Lorillard, Didi. Buy the Best: The Ultimate Guide to Art & Antiques in Manhattan. 320p. 1983. pap. 8.95 (ISBN 0-525-93231-3, 0869-260). Dutton.

Lorimar, Donald & Bull, Deborah. Up the Nile: A Photographic Excursion, Egypt 1839-1898. 1979. 25.00 o.p. (ISBN 0-517-53512-2, C N Potter Bks). Crown.

Lorimer, E. O., tr. see Carcopino, Jerome.

Lorimer, James J. & Perlet, Harry F., Jr. The Legal Environment of Insurance, 2 Vols. LC 81-66114. 823p. 1981. Vol. 1. text ed. 18.00 (ISBN 0-89463-026-1); Vol. 2. text ed. 18.00 (ISBN 0-686-82668-X). Am Inst Property.

Lorimer, Janet. The Biggest Bubble in the World. (Easy-Read Story Bks). (Illus.). 32p. (gr. k-3). 1982. 3.95 (ISBN 0-531-03551-4); PLB 8.60 (ISBN 0-531-04378-9). Watts.

Lorimer, L. T. Secrets. 192p. 1982. pap. 2.25 (ISBN 0-441-05691-1, Pub. by Tempo). Ace Bks.

Lorimer, Lawrence T. & Devaney, John. The Football Book. LC 77-74461. (Illus.). (gr. 5 up). 1977. PLB 7.99 (ISBN 0-394-93574-8, BYR); pap. 4.95 (ISBN 0-394-83574-3). Random.

Lorimer, Lawrence T., retold by. Noah's Ark. LC 77-92377. (Picturebacks Ser.). (Illus.). (ps-2). 1978. PLB 4.99 (ISBN 0-394-93861-5, BYR); pap. 1.50 (ISBN 0-394-83861-0). Random.

Lorin, Harold. Aspects of Distributed Computer Systems. LC 80-16689. 286p. 1980. 32.50 (ISBN 0-471-08114-0, Pub. by Wiley-Interscience). Wiley.

--Introduction to Computer Architecture & Organization. LC 82-8640. 311p. 1982. 25.00 (ISBN 0-471-86679-2, Pub. by Wiley-Interscience). Wiley.

--Parallelism in Hardware & Software: Real & Apparent Concurrency. (Automatic Computation Ser). (Illus.). 1972. ref. ed. 28.95 (ISBN 0-13-648634-7). P-H.

--Sorting & Sort Systems. (Illus.). 480p. 1975. 25.95 (ISBN 0-201-14453-0). A-W.

Lorin, Harold & Deitel, Harvey. Operating Systems. LC 80-10625. (Computer Science: Systems Programming (IBM) Ser.). (Illus.). 480p. 1981. text ed. 25.95 (ISBN 0-201-14464-6). A-W.

Lorin, Harold, jt. auth. see Goldberg, Robert.

Lorin, Harold, jt. ed. see Goldberg, Robert.

Lorin, Martin I. The Febrile Child: Clinical Management of Fever & Other Types of Pyrexia. LC 82-8550. 246p. 1982. 25.95 (ISBN 0-471-08329-1, Pub. by Wiley Med). Wiley.

Lorinczy, Gyorgy. Sopron. (Illus.). 116p. 1971. 7.50x (ISBN 0-686-43339-4). Intl Pubns Serv.

Loring, Andrew. Rhymers' Lexicon. 2nd. ed. LC 78-156926. 1971. Repr. of 1905 ed. 45.00x (ISBN 0-8103-3341-4). Gale.

Loring, Emilie. There is Always Love. (General Ser.). 1983. lib. bdg. 14.50 (ISBN 0-8161-3518-5, Large Print Bks). G K Hall.

Loring, J. M. & Loring, Louise. Pictographs & Petroglyphs of the Oregon Country: Columbia River & Northern Oregon, Pt. 1. (Monograph XXI). (Illus.). pap. 18.50 (ISBN 0-917956-35-4). UCLA Arch.

Loring, Louise, jt. auth. see Loring, J. M.

Loring, Lynne. The Snow Kiss. 1982. 6.95 (ISBN 0-686-84173-5, Avalon). Bouregy.

Loring, Marion. A Christian View of Economics. 80p. 1982. 5.50 (ISBN 0-682-49903-X). Exposition.

Loring, Murray & Glasofer, Seymour. Animal Laffs. LC 82-9985. (Illus.). 96p. 1982. pap. 3.95 (ISBN 0-8246-0287-0). Jonathan David.

Loring, Murray, jt. ed. see Favre, David S.

Loring, Rosalind K. & Otto, Herbert A. New Life Options. 1976. 18.95 (ISBN 0-07-038742-7, C). McGraw.

Loring, Ruth, jt. auth. see Thomas, James L.

Lorion, Raymond P., tr. see De Ajuriaguerra, J.

Lorkovic, Tanja, jt. auth. see Whitby, Thomas.

Lorr, Maurice. Cluster Analysis for Social Scientists: Techniques for Analyzing & Simplifying Complex Blocks of Data. LC 82-49283. (Social & Behavioral Science Ser.). 1983. text ed. price not set (ISBN 0-87589-566-2). Jossey-Bass.

Lorraine, Marian. The Ardent Suitor. 1980. pap. 1.50 o.s.i. (ISBN 0-440-10256-1). Dell.

--The Enterprising Minx. (Orig.). 1981. pap. 1.50 o.s.i. (ISBN 0-440-12270-8). Dell.

--The Mischievous Spinster. 192p. 1983. 11.95 (ISBN 0-8027-0726-2). Walker & Co.

Lorrance, Arleen. Buddha from Brooklyn. LC 75-28258. (Illus.). 221p. (Orig.). 1975. pap. 4.00 o.p. (ISBN 0-916192-00-8). L P Pubns.

Lorrance, Arleen, jt. auth. see Pike, Diane K.

Lorre, C. de see De Lorre, C. & Willis, A.

Lorrimer, James, et al. The Legal Environment of Insurance, 2 vols. 1978. write for info. o.p. (CPCU 6). IIA.

Lorris, Guillaume De see De Lorris, Guillaume & De Meun, Jean.

Lorsch, Jay W. & Allen, Stephen A., 3rd. Managing Diversity & Interdependence: An Organizational Study of Multidivisional Firms. LC 72-97571. (Illus.). 288p. 1973. 15.00x (ISBN 0-87584-103-1). Harvard Busn.

Lorsch, Jay W., jt. auth. see Lawrence, Paul R.

Lorthe, Gabriel A. De. Eloge De J. J. Rousseau Mis Au Concours De 1790. (Rousseauism: 1788-1797). (Fr.). 1978. Repr. of 1790 ed. lib. bdg. 33.50x o.p. (ISBN 0-8287-0554-2). Clearwater Pub.

Lortie, Pierre. Economic Integration & the Law of Gatt. LC 75-3626. (Special Studies). (Illus.). 202p. 1975. 29.95 o.p. (ISBN 0-275-05230-3). Praeger.

Lorton, P., jt. auth. see Muscat, E.

Lortz, Richard. Bereavements. LC 80-65001. 215p. 1983. pap. 8.95 (ISBN 0-932966-32-2). Permanent Pr.

--Lovers Living, Lovers Dead. LC 77-89086. 1977. 7.95 o.p. (ISBN 0-399-12066-1). Putnam Pub Group.

--Lovers Living, Lovers Dead. LC 81-80896. 223p. 1982. 16.95 (ISBN 0-933256-28-0); pap. 8.95 (ISBN 0-933256-29-9). Second Chance.

Lorus, J. & Milne, Margery. The Mountains. rev. ed. LC 80-52605. (Life Nature Library). 13.40 (ISBN 0-8094-3875-5). Silver.

Lory, Hillis. Japan's Military Masters: The Army in Japanese Life. LC 72-9367. 256p. 1973. Repr. of 1943 ed. lib. bdg. 17.75x (ISBN 0-8371-6581-4, LOMM). Greenwood.

Los Angeles Police Department. Daily Training Bulletin of the Los Angeles Police Department: Consisting of Bulletins from Vols. II, III, IV. Parker, W. H., ed. (Illus.). 304p. 1958. photocopy ed. spiral 30.50x (ISBN 0-398-04346-9). C C Thomas.

Los Angeles Public Library. Catalog of the Police Library of the Los Angeles Public Library, 2 vols. 1972. Set. lib. bdg. 190.00 (ISBN 0-8161-0964-8, Hall Library). G K Hall.

--Catalog of the Police Library of the Los Angeles Public Library, First Supplement. (Library Catalogs). 1980. lib. bdg. 220.00 (ISBN 0-8161-0328-3, Hall Library). G K Hall.

--Index to the Stories of Guy de Maupassant. 1960. lib. bdg. 65.00 (ISBN 0-8161-0513-8, Hall Library). G K Hall.

Los Angeles Unified School District. Drafting. LC 77-73291. 64p. (gr. 7-9). 1978. pap. text ed. 3.00 (ISBN 0-02-820410-7). Glencoe.

--Electricity. LC 77-73243. 96p. (gr. 7-9). 1978. pap. text ed. 4.00 (ISBN 0-02-820440-9). Glencoe.

Los Angeles Unified School District, et al. FORE Language. Rev. ed. Bagai, Eric & Bagai, Judith, eds. (System FORE Ser.: Vol. 2). (Illus.). 452p. 1977. wkbk 20.00x (ISBN 0-943292-02-6). Foreworks.

--FORE Mathematics. Rev. ed. Bagai, Eric & Bagai, Judith, eds. (System FORE Ser.: Vol. 4). (Illus.). 232p. 1977. 13.00x (ISBN 0-943292-04-2). Foreworks.

Los Angeles Unified School District. General Industrial Education. LC 77-73280. 552p. (gr. 7-9). 1978. text ed. 13.17 (ISBN 0-02-820350-X). Glencoe.

--Graphic Arts. LC 77-73302. 128p. (gr. 7-9). 1978. pap. text ed. 3.60 (ISBN 0-02-820430-1). Glencoe.

--Metalworking. LC 77-73297. 96p. (gr. 7-9). 1978. pap. text ed. 3.60 (ISBN 0-02-820420-4). Glencoe.

--Woodworking. LC 77-73286. 96p. (gr. 7-9). 1978. pap. text ed. 3.60 (ISBN 0-02-820400-X). Glencoe.

Loschetter, Richard F. RPG for IBM Systems-360, 370 & System 3. (Illus.). 448p. 1975. ref. ed. 27.95 (ISBN 0-13-773713-0). P-H.

Losey, Eugene see Chang, Raymond.

Loshak, Lionel, jt. auth. see Frishman, Bernard L.

Losoncy, Lewis. Think Your Way to Success. Date not set. pap. 5.00 (ISBN 0-87980-396-7). Wilshire.

Losos, G. & Chouinard, A., eds. Pathogenicity of Trypanosomes: Proceedings of a Workshop held in Nairobi, Kenya, 20-30 November 1978. 216p. 1979. pap. 11.00 (ISBN 0-88936-214-9, IDRC132, IDRC). Unipub.

Los Rios Magrina, Emilios De see De Los Rios Magrina, Emilios.

Loss, Eugene, ed. Estudios Panos I. (Peruvian Linguistic Ser.: No. 10). 211p. 1973. pap. 3.75x (ISBN 0-88312-759-8); microfiche 3.00x (ISBN 0-88312-342-8). Summer Inst Ling.

Loss, Louis. Commentaries on the Uniform Securities Act. 1976. text ed. 40.00 (ISBN 0-316-53326-2). Little.

--Securities Regulation: Student Edition. 2nd ed. 1234p. 1961. 20.00 o.p. (ISBN 0-316-53313-0). Little.

Loss, Richard, ed. see Gentz, Friedrich Von.

Losseau, Leon. De la Reparation des Accidents de Travail. (Conditions of the 19th Century French Working Class Ser.). 376p. (Fr.). 1974. Repr. of 1897 ed. lib. bdg. 97.00x o.p. (ISBN 0-8287-0555-0, 1091). Clearwater Pub.

Lossing, Benson J. Harper's Encyclopaedia of United States History, from 458 A. D. to 1905: With Special Contributions Covering Every Phase of American History & Development by Eminent Authorities, 10 vols. new ed. LC 73-22093. (Illus.). 1974. Repr. of 1915 ed. Set. 360.00x (ISBN 0-8103-3954-4). Gale.

--The Life & Times of Philip Schuyler, 2 vols. LC 78-167944. (Era of the American Revolution Ser). 1052p. 1973. Repr. of 1873 ed. Set. lib. bdg. 95.00 (ISBN 0-306-70533-8). Da Capo.

--The Pictorial Field-Book of the War of 1812. LC 73-76395. 1096p. 1976. Repr. of 1868 ed. 45.00 (ISBN 0-912274-31-X). NH Pub Co.

--Seventeen Seventy-Six: Or, the War of Independence. LC 74-99070. (Illus.). 1970. Repr. of 1847 ed. 37.00x (ISBN 0-8103-3584-0). Gale.

Lossky, Vladimir. Mystical Theology of the Eastern Church. 252p. 1973. Repr. of 1957 ed. 17.00 (ISBN 0-227-67536-3). Attic Pr.

Lot, Ferdinand. L' Impot Foncier et la Capitation Personnelle Sous le Bas-Empire et a l'Epoque Franque. LC 80-2018. Date not set. Repr. of 1928 ed. 21.50 (ISBN 0-404-18576-2). AMS Pr.

Loth, David. The Brownings: A Victorian Idyll. 289p. 1982. lib. bdg. 35.00 (ISBN 0-89760-517-9). Telegraph Bks.

Loth, David & Ernst, Morris L. The Taming of Technology. 1972. 6.95 o.p. (ISBN 0-671-21199-4). S&S.

Loth, David G. Chief Justice: John Marshall & the Growth of the Republic. Repr. of 1949 ed. lib. bdg. 20.75x (ISBN 0-8371-2450-6, LOJM). Greenwood.

--Public Plunder: A History of Graft in America. Repr. of 1938 ed. lib. bdg. 19.25x (ISBN 0-8371-3838-8, LOPP). Greenwood.

Lothe, J., jt. auth. see Hirth, John P.

Lothe, Jens, jt. auth. see Hirth, John P.

Lothers, John E. Design in Structural Steel. 3rd ed. LC 71-160254. (Civil Engineering & Engineering Mechanics Ser). (Illus.). 1972. 34.95 (ISBN 0-13-201921-3). P-H.

Lothian, J. M., ed. see Shakespeare, William.

Lothrop, Eaton S., Jr. Century of Cameras. 2nd ed. (Illus.). 192p. 1982. pap. 19.95 (ISBN 0-87100-163-2). Morgan.

Loti, Pierre. The Marriage of Loti. Frierson, Wright & Frierson, Eleanor, trs. from Fr. LC 75-37685. 256p. 1976. 10.95x (ISBN 0-8248-0395-7). UH Pr.

Lotman, Lydia M. Afanasy Fet. (World Author Ser.). 1976. lib. bdg. 15.95 (ISBN 0-8057-2309-9, Twayne). G K Hall.

Lotskar, Elaine, jt. auth. see Gregorakis, Karen.

Lotspeich, William D. Metabolic Aspects of Renal Function. (Illus.). 228p. 1959. photocopy ed. spiral 22.75x (ISBN 0-398-01147-8). C C Thomas.

Lott, Clarinda. The Bone Tree. (New Poet Ser.: Vol. 2). 1972. pap. 1.95 o.s.i. (ISBN 0-685-52487-6). New Poets.

Lott, Clarinda H. Domestic Animals. (Fanfare Ser.). 1982. pap. 2.00 multifolded broadsheet (ISBN 0-686-82297-8). New Poets.

Lott, George & Bairstow, Jeffrey. How to Play Winning Doubles. LC 77-92904. (Illus.). 1979. 10.95 o.s.i. (ISBN 0-914178-20-2, 24923, Pub. by Tennis Mag); pap. 6.95 (ISBN 0-914178-30-X). Golf Digest.

Lott, Johnny & Brainard, Kathy. The Complete Book of Foosball. (Illus.). 1980. 9.95 o.p. (ISBN 0-8092-5999-0); pap. 5.95 o.p. (ISBN 0-8092-5998-2). Contemp Bks.

Lott, K. A., jt. auth. see Bell, C. F.

Lott, Milton. The Last Hunt. 1979. lib. bdg. 12.95 (ISBN 0-8398-2581-1, Gregg). G K Hall.

Lott, Richard W. Basic with Business Applications. 2nd ed. LC 81-16447. 320p. 1982. text ed. 18.50 (ISBN 0-471-08560-X); 10.00x (ISBN 0-471-87480-9). Wiley.

Lottinville, Savoie, ed. see Hyde, George E.

Lottman, Eileen. All Night Long. 192p. (Orig.). 1981. pap. 2.50 o.s.i. (ISBN 0-515-06000-3). Jove Pubns.

Lotz, Klaus. Normbegrundung Als Legitimation Fur Padagogisches Argumentieren und Entscheiden. 274p. (Ger.). 1982. write for info. (ISBN 3-8204-5819-0). P Lang Pubs.

Lotz, Wolfgang. A Handbook for Spies. LC 79-2628. 1980. 10.53i (ISBN 0-06-012707-4, HarpT). Harper Row.

--Studies in Italian Renaissance Architecture. LC 76-44833. (Illus.). 256p. 1977. 25.00x (ISBN 0-262-12073-9); pap. 7.95 (ISBN 0-262-62036-7). MIT Pr.

Lotz, Wolfgang, jt. auth. see Heydenreich, Ludwig.

Lotze, Dieter. Imre Madach. (World Authors Ser.). 1981. lib. bdg. 15.95 (ISBN 0-8057-6459-3, Twayne). G K Hall.

Lotze, Dieter P. Wilhelm Busch. (World Authors Ser.). 1979. lib. bdg. 15.95 (ISBN 0-8057-6365-1, Twayne). G K Hall.

Lou, Hans C. Developmental Neurology. 301p. 1982. text ed. 32.50 (ISBN 0-89004-700-6). Raven.

Louchard, G. & Latouche, G., eds. Probability Theory & Computer Science. (International Lecture Series in Computer Science). 27.50 (ISBN 0-12-455820-8). Acad Pr.

Louck, J. D., jt. auth. see Biedenharn, L. C.

Loucks, Daniel P., et al. Water Resources Systems Planning & Analysis. (Illus.). 560p. 1981. text ed. 33.95 (ISBN 0-13-945923-5). P-H.

Loucks, R. G. & Richmann, D. L. Factors Controlling Reservoir Quality in Tertiary Sandstones & Their Significance to Geopressured Geothermal Production. (Report of Investigations Ser.: No. 111). (Illus.). 41p. 1.50 (ISBN 0-686-36590-9). Bur Econ Geology.

--Report of Investigations No. One Hundred Eleven: Factors Controlling Reservoir Quality in Tertiary Sandstones & Their Significance to Geopressured Geothermal Production, No. 111. (Illus.). 41p. 1981. 1.50 (ISBN 0-686-36599-2). Bur Econ Geology.

Loucks, R. G., jt. auth. see Budd, D. A.

Louda, Jiri & Maclagan, Michael. Heraldry of the Royal Families of Europe. (Illus.). 344p. 1981. pap. 30.00 (ISBN 0-517-54558-6, C N Potter Bks). Crown.

Louden, Louise & Boye, Fred. Beating & Refining. LC 82-80231. (Bibliography Ser.: No. 291). 1982. pap. 58.00 (ISBN 0-87010-064-5). Inst Paper Chem.

Louden, Robert K. & Ledin, George. Programming the IBM 1130. 2nd ed. (Illus.). 448p. 1972. pap. 21.95 ref. ed. (ISBN 0-13-730275-4). P-H.

Louderback, Joseph G. & Dominiak, Geraldine F. Managerial Accounting. 3rd ed. 784p. 1982. text ed. 24.95x (ISBN 0-534-01113-6); study guide avail. (ISBN 0-534-01114-4). Kent Pub Co.

Louderback, Joseph G., jt. auth. see Hirsch, Maurice L., Jr.

Louderback, Joseph G., jt. auth. see Manners, George E., Jr.

Louderback, Joseph G., 3rd & Dominiak, Geraldine F. Managerial Accounting. 2nd ed. 1978. text ed. 22.95x o.p. (ISBN 0-534-00556-X); study guide 7.95x o.p. (ISBN 0-534-00603-5). Wadsworth Pub.

Loudon, David L. Consumer Behavior: Concepts & Applications. (Marketing). (Illus.). 1979. text ed. 24.95 (ISBN 0-07-038753-2, C); instructor's manual 19.00 (ISBN 0-07-038754-0). McGraw.

Loudon, G. Marc. Organic Chemistry. (Chemistry Ser.). 1200p. 1984. text ed. 34.95 (ISBN 0-201-14438-7). A-W.

Loudon, Rodney, jt. auth. see Hayes, William.

Louf, Andre. Teach Us to Pray: Learning a Little About God. LC 76-49322. 1977. pap. 2.95 o.p. (ISBN 0-8091-2001-1). Paulist Pr.

Lough, John. The Encyclopedie in Eighteenth-Century England: And Other Studies. 1970. 16.50x o.p. (ISBN 0-85362-078-4, Oriel). Routledge & Kegan.

--Philosophies & Post-Revolutionary France. 1982. 52.00x (ISBN 0-19-821921-0). Oxford U Pr.

Loughary, John W. & Hopson, Barrie. Producing Workshops, Seminars, & Short Courses: A Trainer's Manual. 192p. 1979. 15.95 (ISBN 0-695-81214-9, T1214). Follett.

Loughary, John W. & Ripley, Theresa M. Career & Life Planning Guide: How to Choose Your Job, How to Change Your Career, How to Manage Your Life. (Illus.). 204p. 1976. pap. 5.95 (ISBN 0-695-80678-5, Dist. by Caroline Hse). Follett.

--Helping Others Help Themselves: A Guide to Counseling Skills. (Illus.). 218p. 1979. pap. text ed. 13.95x (ISBN 0-07-038756-7, C); instructor's manual 10.50 (ISBN 0-07-038757-5). McGraw.

Lougheed, A. L., jt. auth. see Kenwood, A. G.

Lougheed, Joyce & Meyers, eds. In Services of Youth: New Roles in the Governance of Teacher Education. 1980. 4.50 (ISBN 0-686-38074-6). Assn Tchr Ed.

Loughheed, A. L., jt. auth. see Kenwood, A. G.

Loughlin, Catherine E. & Suina, Joseph H. The Learning Environment: An Instructional Strategy. LC 81-23353. (Illus.). 1982. pap. text ed. 14.95x (ISBN 0-8077-2714-8). Tchrs Coll.

Lougy, Robert E., intro. by see Gordon, Mary & Swinburne, Algernon C.

Louie, Al-Ling. Yeh Shen: A Cinderella Story from China. (Illus.). 32p. 1982. 10.95 (ISBN 0-399-20900-X, Philomel). Putnam Pub Group.

Louie, Elaine & Lopez, Antonio. Working Style: Successful Women Show You How to Create a Working Wardrobe with Style. 1982. 19.95 o.p. (ISBN 0-686-91675-1); pap. 12.95 o.p. (ISBN 0-686-97624-X). Little.

Louie, Kamm. Critiques of Confucius in Contemporary China. LC 80-214. 210p. 1980. 25.00 (ISBN 0-312-17645-7). St Martin.

Louis, Arthur. The Tycoons. 1981. 13.95 o.p. (ISBN 0-671-24974-6). S&S.

Louis, Dorothy. My Father, the Chef. (Illus.). 148p. (Orig.). 1978. pap. 6.00 (ISBN 0-9609624-0-9). Bookworm NY.

Louis, J. C. & Yazijian, Harvey. The Cola Wars. LC 79-51190. 512p. 1980. 15.95 (ISBN 0-89696-052-8, An Everest House Book). Dodd.

Louis, Jennifer, jt. auth. see Louis, Victor.

Louis, Kenneth R., et al, eds. Literary Interpretations of Biblical Narratives. LC 74-12400. (The Bible in Literature Courses). 352p. (Orig.). 1974. pap. 6.95 o.p. (ISBN 0-687-22131-5). Abingdon.

Louis, Louise. The Dervish Dance. 40p. 1971. Repr. of 1958 ed. text ed. 5.95 (ISBN 0-941242-00-5). Pen-Art.

--Peopled Parables: Anthology. (New York Poetry Forum First Anthology). (Illus.). 100p. text ed. 5.50 (ISBN 0-941242-04-8). Pen-Art.

--Perennial Promise: First Lillibook Anthology. 48p. 1979. pap. 3.50 o.p. (ISBN 0-941242-14-5). Pen-Art.

Louis, R. Surgery of the Spine: Surgical Anatomy & Operative Approaches. (Illus.). 328p. 1983. 124.00 (ISBN 0-387-11412-2). Springer-Verlag.

Louis, Victor & Louis, Jennifer. The Complete Guide to the Soviet Union. LC 76-16686. (Illus.). 1977. 17.95 o.p. (ISBN 0-312-15750-9). St Martin.

Louis, William R. Imperialism at Bay: The United States & the Decolonization of the British Empire, 1941-1945. 1978. 29.95x (ISBN 0-19-821125-2). Oxford U Pr.

Louis, William R., jt. ed. see Gifford, Prosser.

Louisell, William H. Quantum Statistical Properties of Radiation. LC 73-547. (Pure & Applied Optics Ser.). 640p. 1973. 64.95 (ISBN 0-471-54785-9, Pub. by Wiley-Interscience). Wiley.

Lounds, Morris, Jr. Israel's Black Hebrews: Black Americans in Search of Identity. LC 80-5651. 231p. 1981. lib. bdg. 20.75 (ISBN 0-8191-1400-6); pap. text ed. 10.75 (ISBN 0-8191-1401-4). U Pr of Amer.

Lounsbury, John F. A Workbook for Weather & Climate. 3rd ed. 144p. 1973. write for info. wire coil o.p. (ISBN 0-697-05253-2); tchr's manual avail. o.p. Wm C Brown.

Lounsbury, John F., jt. auth. see Haring, Lloyd.

Lounsbury, Thomas R. The Early Literary Career of Robert Browning. 205p. 1982. Repr. of 1911 ed. lib. bdg. 40.00 (ISBN 0-89984-802-8). Century Bookbindery.

--English Spelling & Spelling Reform. Repr. of 1909 ed. lib. bdg. 17.50x (ISBN 0-8371-4264-4, LOES). Greenwood.

--James Fenimore Cooper. LC 67-23882. 1968. Repr. of 1882 ed. 29.00x (ISBN 0-8103-3037-7). Gale.

--Shakespeare & Voltaire. 463p. 1982. Repr. of 1902 ed. lib. bdg. 40.00 (ISBN 0-89987-523-8). Darby Bks.

Lourie, J. A. Medical Eponyms: Who Was Coude? 224p. 1982. pap. text ed. 19.95 (ISBN 0-272-79643-3). Pitman Pub MA.

Lourie, Margaret & Conklin, Nancy. A Host of Tongues. 272p. 1983. write for info. (ISBN 0-02-906390-6); pap. text ed. write for info. (ISBN 0-02-906500-3). Free Pr.

Lourie, Richard, tr. see Konwicki, Taducz.

Lourie, Richard, tr. see Korczak, Janusz.

Lourie, Richard, tr. see Likhanov, Albert.

Lourie, Richard, tr. see Milosz, Czeslaw.

Lourie, Richard, tr. see Sevela, Efraim.

Lourie, Richard, tr. see Voinovich, Vladimir.

Louros, N., ed. see International College of Surgeons, Biennial World Congress.

Louscher, David J., jt. auth. see Hammon, Paul Y.

Lousley, J. E. Flora of the Isles of Scilly. (Flora Ser.). (Illus.). 320p. 1972. 7.50 o.p. (ISBN 0-7153-5465-5). David & Charles.

Louthan, William C. The Politics of Managerial Morality: A Value-Critical Approach to Political Corruption & Ethics Policy. LC 81-40366. (Illus.). 126p. (Orig.). 1981. lib. bdg. 19.00 (ISBN 0-8191-1841-9); pap. text ed. 8.25 (ISBN 0-8191-1842-7). U Pr of Amer.

Louw, J. P. Semantics of New Testament Greek. (Semeia Studies). 12.95 (ISBN 0-686-96226-5, 06 06 11). Scholars Pr CA.

Louw, Michael, jt. ed. see Barrat, John.

Loux, Michael J., ed. Universals & Particulars: Readings in Ontology. LC 76-745. 359p. 1976. text ed. 7.95 (ISBN 0-268-01908-8); pap. 5.95x o.p. (ISBN 0-268-01909-6). U of Notre Dame Pr.

Lovaas, Ivar & Bucker, Bradley. Perspectives in Behavior Modification with Deviant Children. LC 7-18357. (Illus.). 512p. 1974. 29.95 (ISBN 0-13-657130-1). P-H.

Lovaas, O. Ivar. The Autistic Child: Language Development Through Behavior Modification. LC 76-5890. 1977. 15.95x o.p. (ISBN 0-470-15065-3). Halsted Pr.

Lovasik, Lawrence. Meditations on the Rosary. LC 82-72204. (Living Meditation & Prayerbook Ser.). (Illus.). 270p. (Orig.). 1983. pap. text ed. 6.00 (ISBN 0-932406-09-2). AFC.

Lovasy, L. Combinatorial Problems & Exercises. LC 78-12133. 450p. 1979. 64.00 (ISBN 0-444-85242-5, North Holland); pap. 36.25 (ISBN 0-444-85219-0, North Holland). Elsevier.

Lovasz, L., ed. Algebraic Methods in Graph Theory, 2 vols. (Colloquia Mathematica: Vol. 25). 1981. Set. 134.00 (ISBN 0-444-85442-8). Elsevier.

Lovato, Charles. Life Under the Sun. Hausman, Gerald, ed. (Illus.). 48p. 1982. 35.00 (ISBN 0-86534-010-2). Sunstone Pr.

Love. Love. 100p. 1982. pap. 4.75 (ISBN 0-9608692-0-4). Love.

Love, A. Cytotaxonimical Atlas of the Pteridophyta, Vol. 3. (Cytotaxonomical Atlases Ser.: Vol. 3). 1977. 60.00 (ISBN 3-7682-1103-7). Lubrecht & Cramer.

Love, A. & Love, D. Cytotaxonomical Atlas of the Arctic Flora. (Cytotaxonomical Atlases: Vol. 2). (Illus.). 598p. 1975. lib. bdg. 80.00x (ISBN 3-7682-0976-8). Lubrecht & Cramer.

--Cytotaxonomical Atlas of the Slovenian Flora. (Cytotaxonimcal Atlases: Vol. 1). (Illus.). 1242p. 1974. lib. bdg. 80.00x (ISBN 3-7682-0932-6). Lubrecht & Cramer.

--Plant Chromosomes. 1975. 14.40 (ISBN 3-7682-0966-0). Lubrecht & Cramer.

Love, A. W., ed. Electromagnetic Horn Antennas. LC 75-44649. 1976. 34.95 (ISBN 0-87942-075-8). Inst Electrical.

--Reflector Antennas. LC 77-94519. 1978. 43.95 (ISBN 0-87942-103-7). Inst Electrical.

Love, Brian. Play the Game: A Collection from the Golden Age of Board Games. LC 78-51056. (Illus.). 1978. 19.95 (ISBN 0-89169-515-X). Reed Bks.

Love, C. & Tinervia, J. Commercial Correspondence: For Students of English as a Second Language. 2nd ed. 1980. text ed. 7.25 (ISBN 0-07-038785-0). McGraw.

Love, D., jt. auth. see Love, A.

Love, Doris, tr. see Aleksandrova, V. D.

Love, Edmund G. Set up. LC 78-22737. 288p. 1980. 10.00 o.p. (ISBN 0-385-02729-X). Doubleday.

Love, Frank. Mining Camps & Ghost Towns: Along the Lower Colorado in Arizona & California. LC 73-86960. (Great West & Indian Ser.: Vol. 42). (Illus.). 240p. 8.95 (ISBN 0-87026-031-6). Westernlore.

Love, G. B., jt. ed. see Irwin, Walter.

Love, Harold. Congreve. (Plays & Playwrights Ser.). 131p. 1975. 12.50x o.p. (ISBN 0-87471-623-3). Rowman.

Love, Harriet. Harriet Love's Guide to Vintage Chic. (Illus.). 1982. 21.50 (ISBN 0-03-056238-4); pap. 12.50 (ISBN 0-03-056239-2, Owl Bks). HR&W.

Love, Jean O. Virginia Woolf: Sources of Madness & Art. LC 76-48808. 1978. 22.50x (ISBN 0-520-03358-2). U of Cal Pr.

Love, John & Hodgkins, John. Chess Battle Strategies. LC 79-65066. (Illus.). 1979. 10.95 (ISBN 0-8069-4952-X); lib. bdg. 13.29 (ISBN 0-8069-4953-8). Sterling.

Love, Julian P. First John-Revelation. LC 59-10454. (Layman's Bible Commentary, Vol. 25). pap. 3.95 (ISBN 0-8042-3085-4). John Knox.

Love, L. Carl. Welding: Procedures & Applications. (Illus.). 256p. 1975. pap. 12.95 (ISBN 0-13-948034-X). P-H.

Love, Lenore R. & Kaswan, Jaques W. Troubled Children: Their Families, Schools & Treatments. LC 74-12232. 314p. (Orig.). 1974. 16.50 (ISBN 0-471-54788-3). Krieger.

Love, Milton & Cailliet, Gregor M., eds. Readings in Ichthyology. LC 78-16654. (Illus.). 1979. pap. 19.95x (ISBN 0-673-16249-4). Scott F.

Love, Paula M. Will Rogers Book. 1972. 9.95 (ISBN 0-87244-030-3); soft cover 5.25 (ISBN 0-87244-031-1). Texian.

Love, Richard H. Cassatt: The Independent. LC 80-84838. (Illus.). 270p. 1980. 38.00 (ISBN 0-940114-13-5). R H Love Gall.

--Drawings by Isabel Bishop. LC 76-41120. (Illus.). 17p. (Orig.). 1976. pap. 2.50 (ISBN 0-940114-04-6). R H Love Gall.

--Feminine Subjects in Nineteenth Century Paintings. LC 75-21715. (Illus.). 26p. (Orig.). 1975. pap. 2.00 (ISBN 0-940114-00-3). R H Love Gall.

--Harriet Randall Lumis (1870-1953) An American Impressionist. LC 77-90984. (Illus.). 64p. (Orig.). 1977. 12.00 (ISBN 0-940114-07-0); pap. 6.00 (ISBN 0-940114-06-2). R H Love Gall.

--John Barber: The Artist, the Man. Huntley, G. Haydn & Babusis, Vytautas, eds. LC 81-82250. (Illus.). 208p. 1981. 25.00 (ISBN 0-940114-14-3). Haase-Mumm Pub Co.

--Theodore Earl Butler (Eighteen Sixty to Nineteen Thirty-Six) LC 75-42998. (Illus.). 30p. (Orig.). 1976. pap. 5.00 o.p. (ISBN 0-940114-02-X). R H Love Gall.

--Walter & Eliot Clark: A Tradition in American Painting. LC 80-82915. (Illus.). 70p. (Orig.). 1980. pap. 6.50 (ISBN 0-940114-12-7). R H Love Gall.

--Walter Griffin: American Impressionist (1861-1935) (Illus.). 25p. 1975. pap. 5.00 (ISBN 0-940114-01-1). R H Love Gall.

--William Chadwick (Eighteen Seventy-Nine to Nineteen Sixty-Two) An American Impressionist. LC 78-61711. (Illus.). 110p. (Orig.). 1978. 15.00 (ISBN 0-940114-09-7); pap. 7.50 (ISBN 0-940114-08-9). R H Love Gall.

Love, Sandra. Dive for the Sun. (gr. 7 up). 1982. PLB 10.95 (ISBN 0-395-32864-0); 10.45. HM.

Love, Stephen. Inventory Control. (Industrial Engineering & Management Science Ser.). (Illus.). 1979. text ed. 22.50 (ISBN 0-07-038782-6, C); solutions manual 12.95 (ISBN 0-07-038783-4). McGraw.

Love, Sydney F. Planning & Creating Successful Engineered Designs. 269p. 1980. text ed. 19.95 o.p. (ISBN 0-442-20272-5). Van Nos Reinhold.

Love, T. W. Construction Manual: Rough Carpentry. LC 76-21704. (Illus.). 220p. 1976. pap. 12.25 (ISBN 0-910460-18-3). Craftsman.

Love, W. W. Disposal Systems. (Mud Equipment Manual Ser.: No. 11). 1982. pap. 10.75x (ISBN 0-87201-623-4). Gulf Pub.

Love, W. W. & Brandt, Louis. Shale Shakers. (Mud Equipment Manual Ser.: No. 3). 1982. pap. text ed. 10.75 (ISBN 0-87201-615-3). Gulf Pub.

Love, Warner & Lattman, Eaton, eds. Biophysical Applications of Crystallographic Techniques. pap. 7.50 (ISBN 0-686-60380-X). Polycrystal Bk Serv.

Loveday, Alexander. Reflections on International Administration. LC 74-9168. 334p. 1974. Repr. of 1956 ed. lib. bdg. 19.00x (ISBN 0-8371-7618-2, LOIA). Greenwood.

Loveday, George. Electronic Testing & Troubleshooting. LC 81-12948. 293p. 1982. text ed. 21.95 (ISBN 0-471-08718-1). Wiley.

Loveday, George C. & Seidman, Arthur H. Troubleshooting Solid State Circuits. LC 80-21954. 110p. 1981. pap. text ed. 10.95 (ISBN 0-471-08371-2). Wiley.

Loveday, P. & Jaensch, D. NAC Election in the Northern Territory 1981. (North Australia Research Unit Monograph). 67p. (Orig.). 1982. pap. text ed. 9.95 (ISBN 0-86784-120-6, 1232). Bks Australia.

Loveday, P., ed. Service Delivery to Outstations. new ed. (North Ausralia Research Unit Monograph: No. 2). 97p. (Orig.). 1982. pap. text ed. 9.95 (ISBN 0-86784-160-5, 1257, Pub. by ANUP Australia). Bks Australia.

Loveday, Robert. First Course in Statistics. text ed. 7.95x (ISBN 0-521-05601-2). Cambridge U Pr.

--Practical Statistics & Probability. 256p. 1974. pap. text ed. 7.95x (ISBN 0-521-20291-4). Cambridge U Pr.

--Statistical Mathematics. 1973. text ed. 6.95x (ISBN 0-521-08643-4). Cambridge U Pr.

--Statistics: A Second Course in Statistics. 2nd ed. LC 74-96095. (Illus.). 1969. text ed. 11.95x (ISBN 0-521-07234-4). Cambridge U Pr.

Lovejoy. Lovejoy's College Guide. Levy, Valerie, ed. (Orig.). 1983. pap. 12.95 (ISBN 0-671-47170-8). Monarch Pr.

Lovejoy, Arthur O. Great Chain of Being: A Study of the History of an Idea. LC 36-14264. (William James Lectures Ser.). 1936. 18.50x (ISBN 0-674-36150-4); pap. 8.95 (ISBN 0-674-36153-9). Harvard U Pr.

--Revolt Against Dualism. 2nd ed. (Paul Carus Lecture Ser.). 420p. 1960. 23.50x (ISBN 0-87548-106-X); pap. 10.00x (ISBN 0-87548-107-8). Open Court.

Lovejoy, Bahija, jt. auth. see Cohen, Barbara.

Lovejoy, Clarence E. Lovejoy's Career & Vocational School Guide. 5th ed. 1978. 9.95 (ISBN 0-671-24022-6); pap. 5.95 (ISBN 0-671-24021-8). S&S.

--Lovejoy's College Guide. 15th ed. 1981. 15.95 (ISBN 0-671-41233-7); pap. 8.95 (ISBN 0-671-41234-5). S&S.

--Lovejoy's College Guide. 14th ed. 1979. 15.95 (ISBN 0-671-24392-6); pap. 8.95 (ISBN 0-671-24563-5). S&S.

Lovejoy, Paul. Transformations in Slavery: A History of Slavery in Africa. LC 82-1284. (African Studies: No. 36). (Illus.). 352p. Date not set. price not set (ISBN 0-521-24369-6); pap. price not set (ISBN 0-521-28646-8). Cambridge U Pr.

Lovejoy, W., jt. auth. see Garfield, Paul.

Lovelace, Alice. The Kitchen Survival Almanac. Johnson, Sylvia L. & Lanier, Linda K., eds. (Illus.). 500p. (Orig.). Date not set. pap. 9.95 (ISBN 0-942050-04-5). Southern-Lite.

Lovelace, Betty I. Little Snoop. LC 82-90020. 219p. 1982. 11.95 (ISBN 0-533-05213-0). Vantage.

--My Gentle Macho. 1983. 12.95 (ISBN 0-533-05671-3). Vantage.

Lovelace, Earl. The Dragon Can't Dance. 240p. (Orig.). 1981. 10.00x o.s.i. (ISBN 0-89410-178-1); pap. 5.00x o.s.i. (ISBN 0-89410-179-X). Three Continents.

Lovelace, Jane. The Eccentric Lady. 192p. 1983. 11.95 (ISBN 0-8027-0727-0). Walker & Co.

Lovelace, M. May. My Childhood Experience: Tears & Laughter. 1979. 4.95 o.p. (ISBN 0-533-03811-1). Vantage.

Lovelace, Maud H. Betsy & Tacy Go Over the Big Hill. LC 42-23557. (Illus.). (gr. 3-7). 1942. 12.45i (ISBN 0-690-13521-1, TYC-J); PLB 10.89 (ISBN 0-686-82912-3). Har-Row.

--Betsy & the Great World. LC 52-8657. (Illus.). (gr. 5-11). 1952. 14.38i (ISBN 0-690-13591-2, TYC-J). Har-Row.

--Betsy in Spite of Herself. LC 46-11995. (Illus.). (gr. 5-11). 1946. 12.45i (ISBN 0-690-13662-5, TYC-J). Har-Row.

Loveland, D. W. Automated Theorem Proving: A Logical Basis. (Fundamental Studies in Computer Science: Vol. 6). 1978. 68.00 (ISBN 0-7204-0499-1, North-Holland). Elsevier.

Loveland, D. W., ed. Automated Deduction New York 1982, Sixth Conference: Proceedings. (Lecture Notes in Computer Science Ser.: Vol. 138). 389p. 1982. pap. 17.60 (ISBN 0-387-11558-7). Springer-Verlag.

Loveland, Lilly A. Johan Stal-John Steel: From Smaland Farmer Lad to Idaho Prune King. (Illus.). 1.50 o.p. (ISBN 0-8338-0041-8). M Jones.

Loveland, W., jt. auth. see Seaborg, G. T.

Loveless, Anthony. Genetic & Allied Effects of Alkylating Agents. LC 66-24944. (Illus.). 1966. 24.50x (ISBN 0-271-00047-3). Pa St U Pr.

Loveless, Cheri, jt. auth. see Salsbury, Barbara.

Loveless, E. E., jt. auth. see Davis, Jack.

Lovell, B. Astronomy. 1970. 71.75 (ISBN 0-444-20102-5). Elsevier.

Lovell, Bernard. Emerging Cosmology. Anshen, Ruth N., ed. LC 79-50416. (Crossing the Frontiers Ser.). 1980. 10.00 o.p. (ISBN 0-448-15517-6, G&D). Putnam Pub Group.

--In the Center of Immensities. Anshen, Ruth N., ed. LC 76-26241. (World Perspectives Ser.: Vol. 53). 1978. 13.41i (ISBN 0-06-012716-3, HarpT). Har-Row.

Lovell, John & Kronenberg, Philip, eds. New Civil Military Relations. LC 72-94547. (Social Policy Ser). 352p. 1974. pap. 5.95 (ISBN 0-87855-571-4); 14.95 (ISBN 0-87855-075-5). Transaction Bks.

Lovell, John C. Stevedores & Dockers: A Study of Trade Unionism in the Port of London, 1870-1914. LC 74-99263. (Illus.). 1969. 19.50x (ISBN 0-678-07003-2). Kelley.

Lovell, John T., jt. auth. see Wiles, Kimball.

Lovell, K. & Elkind, David. An Introduction to Human Development. 1971. pap. 7.95x (ISBN 0-673-07583-4). Scott F.

Lovell, M. Your Growing Child. 1976. 12.95 o.p. (ISBN 0-7100-8431-5). Routledge & Kegan.

Lovell, M. C. & Avery, A. J. Physical Properties of Materials. LC 75-35836. 316p. (Orig.). 1976. Repr. of 1977 ed. 29.50 (ISBN 0-442-30096-4); o. p 13.10 (ISBN 0-442-30097-2). Krieger.

Lovell, Marc. Apple Spy in the Sky. LC 82-45453. (Crime Club Ser.). 192p. 1983. 11.95 (ISBN 0-385-18308-9). Doubleday.

--Apple to the Core. LC 82-48708. (Crime Club Ser.). 192p. 1983. 11.95 (ISBN 0-385-18749-1). Doubleday.

--The Spy Game. LC 80-499. (Crime Club Ser.). 192p. 1980. 10.95 o.p. (ISBN 0-385-17073-4). Doubleday.

--Spy on the Run. LC 81-43778. (Crime Club Ser.). 192p. 1982. 10.95 (ISBN 0-385-18095-0). Doubleday.

Lovell, Mark. How Children Grow: From Conception to Two. (Illus.). 1975. 6.95 (ISBN 0-7100-8093-X); pap. 4.00 o.p. (ISBN 0-7100-8094-8). Routledge & Kegan.

Lovell, Mary, jt. auth. see Lees, Herbert.

Lovell, R. Bernard. Adult Learning. Hills, P. J., ed. (New Patterns of Learning Ser.). 170p. 1980. 25.95x o.p. (ISBN 0-470-26935-9). Halsted Pr.

--Adult Learning. (New Patterns of Learning Ser.). 170p. 1982. 14.95 (ISBN 0-470-27368-2). Halsted Pr.

Lovell, Robert E., jt. auth. see Beakley, George C.

Lovell, Ronald P. Reporting Public Affairs: Problems & Solutions. 432p. 1982. text ed. 18.95X (ISBN 0-534-01126-8). Wadsworth Pub.

Lovell, S. An Introduction to Radiation Dosimetry. LC 78-67261. (Techniques of Measurement in Medicine Ser.: No. 4). (Illus.). 1979. 24.95 (ISBN 0-521-22436-5); pap. 7.95x (ISBN 0-521-29497-5). Cambridge U Pr.

Lovelock, Christopher & Weinberg, Charles. Cases in Public & Nonprofit Marketing. LC 77-87274. 1977. pap. 17.50x (ISBN 0-89426-015-4); teaching notes 17.50 (ISBN 0-89426-016-2). Scientific Pr.

Lovelock, Christopher H. Services Marketing: Texts, Cases & Readings. (Illus.). 624p. 1983. 27.95 (ISBN 0-13-806786-4). P-H.

Lovelock, Christopher H. & Weinberg, Charles B. Marketing for Public & Non-Profit Managers. 400p. 1983. text ed. write for info. (ISBN 0-471-03722-2). Wiley.

--Readings in Public & Nonprofit Marketing. LC 78-59621. 1978. pap. 17.50x (ISBN 0-89426-019-7). Scientific Pr.

Lovelock, J. E. Gala: A New Look at Life on Earth. (Illus.). 1979. 14.95 (ISBN 0-19-217665-X). Oxford U Pr.

Lovelock, James, jt. auth. see Allaby, Michael.

Lovelock, Julian, jt. ed. see Dyson, A. E.

Loveman, Brian. Chile: The Legacy of Hispanic Capitalism. LC 78-13965. (Latin American Histories Ser.). (Illus.). 1979. 18.95x (ISBN 0-19-502518-0); pap. text ed. 7.95x (ISBN 0-19-502520-2). Oxford U Pr.

Lovenberg, W., jt. ed. see Youdim, M. B.

Lover, Stanley. Association Football (Soccer) Laws Illustrated. 1977. 14.00 o.p. (ISBN 0-7207-0879-6). Transatlantic.

--Association Football(Soccer) Match Control: An Illustrated Handbook for the Football(Soccer) Referee. 1978. 22.50 o.s.i. (ISBN 0-7207-1035-9). Transatlantic.

Loveridge, Mark. Laurence Sterne & the Argument about Design. 375p. 1981. 49.00x (ISBN 0-333-29401-7, Pub. by Macmillan England). State Mutual Bk.

Lovering, David G., ed. Molten Salt Technology. 550p. 1982. 65.00x (ISBN 0-306-41076-1, Plenum Pr). Plenum Pub.

Lovering, Joseph. Gerald Warner Brace. (Twayne's United States Authors Ser.). 1981. 13.95 (ISBN 0-8057-7318-5, Twayne). G K Hall.

Lovesey, John & Mason, Nicholas. Sunday Times Sports Book. 1979. 19.95 (ISBN 0-437-15445-9, Pub. by World's Work). David & Charles.

Lovesey, Peter. The False Inspector Dew. (Nightingale Series Paperbacks). 1983. pap. 9.95 (ISBN 0-8161-3481-2, Large Print Bks). G K Hall.

--The False Inspector Dew. 1983. pap. 2.95 (ISBN 0-394-71338-9). Pantheon.

--Five Kings of Distance. (Illus.). 197p. 1981. 10.95 o.p. (ISBN 0-312-29484-0). St Martin.

Lovett, D. R., jt. auth. see Ballentyne, D. W.

Lovett, Donald B. When I but Think of You. LC 79-66653. (Illus.). 1979. pap. 3.95 (ISBN 0-9603328-0-4). D B Lovett.

Lovett, Gabriel. The Duke of Rivas. (World Authors Ser.). 1977. lib. bdg. 15.95 (ISBN 0-8057-6289-2, Twayne). G K Hall.

Lovett, Robert M., jt. auth. see Moody, William V.

Lovett, Robert W., ed. American Economic & Business History Information Sources. LC 78-137573. (Management Information Guide Ser.: No. 23). 1971. 42.00x (ISBN 0-8103-0823-1). Gale.

Lovett, William & Collins, John. Chartism: A New Organization of the People. (Victorian Library). 1969. Repr. of 1840 ed. text ed. 15.00x (ISBN 0-7185-5006-4, Leicester). Humanities.

Lovett, William A. Inflation & Politics: Fiscal, Monetary & Wage-Price Discipline. LC 81-47982. 288p. 1982. 28.95x (ISBN 0-669-05211-6). Lexington Bks.

Lovgren, Sven. The Genesis of Modernism. LC 81-81720. (Illus.). xvi, 184p. 1983. Repr. of 1971 ed. lib. bdg. 40.00 (ISBN 0-87817-280-7). Hacker.

Lovin, Roger. Apostle. Freas, Polly & Freas, Kelly, eds. LC 78-15252. (Illus.). 1978. pap. 4.95 o.p. (ISBN 0-915442-61-2, Starblaze). Donning Co.

Loving, Jerome. Emerson, Whitman, & the American Muse. LC 82-1868. xii, 220p. 1982. 22.00 (ISBN 0-8078-1523-3). U of NC Pr.

Loving, Waldon, jt. auth. see Bowling, W Kerby.

Lovinggood, Penman. Famous Modern Negro Musicians. LC 77-22215. (Music Reprint Ser.). (Illus.). 1978. Repr. lib. bdg. 16.50 (ISBN 0-306-77523-9). Da Capo.

Lovins, Amory & Lovins, Hunter. Brittle Power: Energy Strategy for National Security. 512p. 1983. pap. 8.95 (ISBN 0-931790-49-2). Brick Hse Pub.

Lovins, Amory, et al. Least-Cost Energy: Solving the Carbon Dioxide Problem. 192p. 1982. 21.95 (ISBN 0-471-88645-9, Pub. by Brick Hse Pub.). Wiley.

Lovins, Amory B. World Energy Strategies, Facts, Issues, & Options. LC 75-2010. 1975. text ed. 18.00 (ISBN 0-88410-600-4); pap. 8.95x prof ref (ISBN 0-88410-601-2). Ballinger Pub.

--World Energy Strategies: Facts, Issues, & Options. LC 75-2010. 1980. pap. 2.95i o.p. (ISBN 0-06-090778-9, CN778, CN). Har-Row.

Lovins, Amory B. & Price, John H. Non-Nuclear Futures: The Case for an Ethical Energy Strategy. LC 75-20260. 1980. pap. 3.95i o.p. (ISBN 0-06-090777-0, CN777, CN). Har-Row.

Lovins, Hunter, jt. auth. see Lovins, Amory.

Lovisone, Carter. The Disco Hustle. LC 79-63090. (Illus.). 96p. 1979. pap. 3.95 o.p. (ISBN 0-8069-8838-X). Sterling.

Lovitt, Thomas C. Because of My Persistance, I've Learned from Children: Comments on Issues in Special Education. 244p. 1982. pap. text ed. 12.95 (ISBN 0-675-09825-4). Merrill.

--In Spite of My Resistance, I've Learned from Children. (Special Education Ser.). 1977. pap. text ed. 12.95 (ISBN 0-675-08528-4). Merrill.

Lovitt, William, tr. see Heidegger, Martin.

Lovoos, Janice. Frederic Whitaker. LC 77-188290. (Illus.). 168p. 1972. 17.50 o.p. (ISBN 0-87358-094-X). Northland.

Lovrinic, Jean H., jt. auth. see Durrant, John H.

Lovtrup, Soren. Epigenetics: A Treatise on Theoretical Biology. LC 72-5719. 550p. 1974. 91.75x o.s.i. (ISBN 0-471-54900-2, Pub. by Wiley-Interscience). Wiley.

--The Phylogeny of Vertebrata. LC 76-18707. 1977. 71.95 (ISBN 0-471-99412-X, Pub. by Wiley-Interscience). Wiley.

Low, A. W. Encyclopedia of Black America. 1978. 55.50 (ISBN 0-07-038834-2, P&RB). McGraw.

Low, Alice. Herbert's Treasure. (Illus.). (gr. 1-3). 1971. PLB 3.97 o.p. (ISBN 0-399-60239-9). Putnam Pub Group.

--Summer. LC 63-15628. (Illus.). (gr. 2-3). 1963. PLB 5.99 (ISBN 0-394-90032-4). Beginner.

Low, Anthony. Augustine Baker. (English Authors Ser.). lib. bdg. 14.95 (ISBN 0-8057-1020-5, Twayne). G K Hall.

Low, Anthony, ed. Congress & the Raj. 1977. 24.00x (ISBN 0-8364-0007-0). South Asia Bks.

Low, Barbara, tr. see Freud, Anna.

Low, D. A. Buganda in Modern History. LC 73-10019. (Illus.). 1971. 34.50x (ISBN 0-520-01640-8). U of Cal Pr.

Low, D. A., et al. Government Archives in South Asia. LC 69-16283. 1969. 44.50 (ISBN 0-521-07507-6). Cambridge U Pr.

Low, David. Europe Since Versailles: A History in One Hundred Cartoons with a Narrative Text. LC 72-147685. (Library of War & Peace; Artists on War). lib. bdg. 38.00 o.s.i. (ISBN 0-8240-0442-6). Garland Pub.

Low, Donald A., ed. Critical Essay on Robert Burns. 1975. 18.95 (ISBN 0-7100-8109-X). Routledge & Kegan.

Low, George & Barkow, Al. The Master of Putting. LC 82-73018. 160p. 1983. 12.95 (ISBN 0-689-11355-2). Atheneum.

Low, J. D. & Warner, William L. Social System of the Modern Factory: The Strike, a Social Analysis. 1947. text ed. 15.50x (ISBN 0-686-83772-X). Elliots Bks.

Low, J. O., jt. auth. see Warner, William L.

Low, Jackson Mac see Mac Low, Jackson.

Low, Jennie. Chopsticks, Cleaver & Wok - Vol. 1: Homestyle Chinese Cooking. Tien, Doong, ed. (Illus.). 187p. (Orig.). 1974. pap. 5.95 (ISBN 0-9602820-0-9). J Low.

--Jennie Low's Szechuan Cookbook: Szechuan, Mandarin, & Dim Sum. (Illus., Orig.). 1982. pap. 7.95 (ISBN 0-89141-165-8). Presidio Pr.

Low, Jennie, jt. auth. see St. Pierre, Brian.

Low, Joseph. Beastly, Buggy, Fishy, Flighty Riddles. 48p. (gr. 1-3). 1983. 8.95 (ISBN 0-686-82194-7). Macmillan.

--The Devil Himself. (Illus.). (ps-3). 1978. 7.95 o.p. (ISBN 0-07-038795-8, GB). McGraw.

--Don't Drag Your Feet. LC 82-13898. (Illus.). 32p. (ps-4). 1983. 9.95 (ISBN 0-689-50271-0, McElderry Bk). Atheneum.

--Little Though I Be. (Illus.). 40p. (ps-3). 1976. 8.95 (ISBN 0-07-038842-3, GB); PLB 6.95 (ISBN 0-07-038843-1). McGraw.

--Trust Reba. new ed. LC 73-17418. (Illus.). 40p. (gr. 1-4). 1974. PLB 5.72 o.p. (ISBN 0-07-038839-3, GB). McGraw.

Low, Lyman. Hard Times Tokens. updated ed. (Illus.). 1983. Repr. of 1900 ed. lib. bdg. 18.00 (ISBN 0-915262-16-9). S J Durst.

Low, Rosemary. Beginner's Guide to Birdkeeping. (Illus.). 217p. 1975. 14.95 o.p. (ISBN 0-7207-0673-4). Transatlantic.

--How to Keep Parrots, Cockatiels & Macaws in Cage or Aviary. (Illus.). 96p. 1980. 3.95 (ISBN 0-7028-1029-0). Avian Pubns.

--Lories & Lorikeets. (Illus.). 1979. pap. 14.95 (ISBN 0-87666-980-1, PS-773). TFH Pubns.

--Mynah Birds. (Illus.). 93p. 3.95 (ISBN 0-7028-1002-9). Avian Pubns.

Low, Shirley P., jt. auth. see Alderson, William T.

Low, Victor N., ed. African History & Societies to 1914: A Critical Survey of Relevant Books with Special References to West Africa, 2 vols. Incl. Vol. 1. Africa at Large; Vol. 2. West Africa Region by Region. 1700p. 1983. 225.00x set (ISBN 0-7146-3056-X, F Cass Co). Biblio Dist.

--From "West Africa". A Social, Political & Economic Record 1917-1977, 4 vols. 1983. Set. 250.00x (ISBN 0-7146-3055-1, F Cass Co). Biblio Dist.

Low, Werner. Low Wit. LC 81-69718. 79p. (Orig.). 1982. pap. 3.95 (ISBN 0-917976-15-0). White Ewe.

Low-Beer, J. R. Protest & Participation. LC 77-8084. (American Sociological Association Rose Monograph: No. 4). (Illus.). 1978. 24.95 (ISBN 0-521-21782-2); pap. 8.95x (ISBN 0-521-29277-8). Cambridge U Pr.

Lowbury, E. J., et al, eds. Control of Hospital Infection: A Practical Handbook. 2nd ed. (Illus.). 325p. 1981. text ed. 27.50 (ISBN 0-397-58280-3, Lippincott Medical). Lippincott.

Lowden. Transformer Design Manual. 1983. write for info. (ISBN 0-07-038841-5). McGraw.

Lowden, J. Alexander, jt. ed. see Callahan, John W.

Lowder, Hughston E. & Scott, Jack. Batfish: The Champion "Submarine-Killer" Submarine of World War II. LC 80-12155. (Illus.). 300p. 1980. 10.95 o.p. (ISBN 0-13-066563-0). P-H.

Lowder, Richard E. Cribbage Is the Name of the Game. (Everday Handbook Ser.). (Illus.). 96p. 1975. pap. 2.50 o.p. (ISBN 0-06-463402-7, EH 402, EH). B&N NY.

Lowdermilk, Walter C. Palestine: Land of Promise. rev. ed. LC 68-23308. (Illus.). 1968. Repr. of 1944 ed. lib. bdg. 15.50x (ISBN 0-8371-2616-9, LOPL). Greenwood.

Lowdin, P. O. Complex Scaling in the Spectral Theory of the Hamiltonian: Proceedings of the 1978 Sanibel Workshop. (International Journal of Quantum Chemistry Ser.: Vol. XIII, No. 4). 1978. pap. 53.95 (ISBN 0-471-05774-6, Pub. by Wiley-Interscience). Wiley.

Lowdin, P. O. & Ohrn, Y. Proceedings. (International Journal of Quantum Chemistry-Quantum Chemistry Symposium: No. 12). 550p. 1978. 62.95 (ISBN 0-471-05633-2). Wiley.

Lowdin, P. O., ed. see International Journal of Quantum Chemisty-Symposium, 15th.

Lowdin, Per-Olav, ed. see International Symposium on Quantum Biology & Quantum Pharmacology.

Lowdin, Per-Olov, ed. Advances in Quantum Chemistry, Vols. 1-11. Incl. Vol. 1. 1964. 61.00 (ISBN 0-12-034801-2); Vol. 2. Vol. 2, 1966. 61.00 (ISBN 0-12-034802-0); Vol. 3. 1967. 61.00 (ISBN 0-12-034803-9); Vol. 4. 1968. 61.00 (ISBN 0-12-034804-7); Vol. 5. 1970. 61.00 (ISBN 0-12-034805-5); Vol. 6. 1972. 61.00 (ISBN 0-12-034806-3); Vol. 7. Vol. 7, 1973. 61.00 o.p. (ISBN 0-12-034807-1); Vol. 8. 1974. 61.00 (ISBN 0-12-034808-X); Vol. 9. 1975. 67.00 (ISBN 0-12-034809-8); Vol. 10. 1977. 62.00 (ISBN 0-12-034810-1); Vol. 11. 1979. 63.00 (ISBN 0-12-034811-X). Acad Pr.

--Advances in Quantum Chemistry, Vol. 12. LC 64-8029. 1980. 55.00 (ISBN 0-12-034812-8). Acad Pr.

--Advances in Quantum Chemistry, 2 vols, Vols. 13 & 14. (Serial Publication Ser.). 1981. Vol. 13. 42.00 (ISBN 0-12-034813-6); Vol. 14. 46.00 (ISBN 0-12-034814-4). Acad Pr.

--Advances in Quantum Chemistry, Vol. 15. 312p. 1982. 54.00 (ISBN 0-12-034815-2). Acad Pr.

--Advances in Quantum Chemsitry, Vol. 16. 318p. 1982. 56.00 (ISBN 0-12-034816-0). Acad Pr.

Lowdin, Per-Olov, et al. Chemical Physics of Surfaces, Catalysis & Membranes. (International Journal of Quantum Chemistry Ser.: Supplement 2). 1978. pap. 36.95 (ISBN 0-471-05247-7, Pub. by Wiley-Interscience). Wiley.

--Quantum Chemistry: A Scientific Melting Pot. (International Journal of Quantum Chemistry Ser.: Vol. 12, Suppl.). 1978. 59.95 (ISBN 0-471-05248-5, Pub. by Wiley-Interscience). Wiley.

Lowe, A. The Path of Economic Growth. LC 75-38186. (Illus.). 1976. 49.50 (ISBN 0-521-20888-2). Cambridge U Pr.

Lowe, Benjamin. The Beauty of Sport: A Cross-Disciplinary Inquiry. (Illus.). 1977. 19.95 (ISBN 0-13-066589-4). P-H.

Lowe, Brian. Hunting the Clean Boot: The Working Bloodhound. (Illus.). 240p. 1981. 22.50 o.p. (ISBN 0-7137-0950-2, Pub. by Blandford Pr England). Sterling.

Lowe, C. J. & Dockrill, M. L. The Mirage of Power, British Foreign Policy. Incl. Vol. 1. 1902-1914. 15.95x (ISBN 0-7100-7092-6); Vol. 2. 1914-1922. 19.95x (ISBN 0-7100-7093-4); Vol. 3. The Documents. 25.00x (ISBN 0-7100-7094-2). (Foreign Policies of the Great Powers Ser). 1972. Set. 50.00 (ISBN 0-685-25614-6). Routledge & Kegan.

Lowe, C. Marshall. Value Orientations in Counseling & Psychotherapy: The Meanings of Mental Health. 2nd ed. LC 76-25957. 1976. pap. text ed. 10.50x (ISBN 0-910328-09-9). Carroll Pr.

Lowe, C. R. An Introduction to Affinity Chromatography. (Laboratory Techniques in Biochemistry & Molecular Biology: Vol. 7, Pt. II). 1979. 28.00 (ISBN 0-7204-4223-0, North Holland). Elsevier.

Lowe, Carl & Nechas, Jim. Body Healing. (Illus.). 440p. 1983. 21.95 (ISBN 0-87857-441-7, 05-024-0). Rodale Pr Inc.

Lowe, Cecilia, jt. auth. see Nowlan, Robert A.

Lowe, Charles R. & Lwanga, S. K., eds. Health Statistics: A Manual for Teachers of Medical Students. (Illus.). 1978. pap. text ed. 14.95x (ISBN 0-19-261134-8). Oxford U Pr.

Lowe, David, jt. auth. see Nugent, Neill.

Lowe, David, ed. Turgenev Letters. 1983. 50.00 (ISBN 0-686-43065-4). Ardis Pubs.

Lowe, David, tr. see Varlamova, Inna.

Lowe, Don & Lowe, Roberta. Eighty Northern Colorado Hiking Trails. LC 73-80046. 1973. pap. 10.95 (ISBN 0-911518-20-7). Touchstone Pr Ore.

--The John Muir Trail. LC 75-28572. (Illus., Orig.). 1982. pap. 7.95 (ISBN 0-87004-251-3). Caxton.

Lowe, Donald M. History of Bourgeois Perception. LC 81-7529. (Illus.). x, 226p. 1982. pap. 6.95 (ISBN 0-226-49429-2). U of Chicago Pr.

Lowe, Doug. OS Utilities. Eckols, Steve & Taylor, Judy, eds. LC 80-84103. (Illus.). 185p. (Orig.). 1981. pap. text ed. 15.00 (ISBN 0-911625-11-9). M Murach & Assoc.

--VSAM for the COBOL Programmer. Murach, Mike, ed. (Illus.). 150p. 1982. pap. text ed. 15.00 (ISBN 0-911625-12-7). M Murach & Assoc.

Lowe, E. Fundamentals of Molecular Spectroscopy. 3rd ed. 192p. 1983. 8.50 (ISBN 0-07-084139-X). McGraw.

--Successful Retailing through Advertising. 192p. 1983. 7.95 (ISBN 0-07-084588-3, P&RB). McGraw.

Lowe, E. A., ed. Codices Latini Antiquiores, Pt. 2: Great Britain - Ireland. 2nd ed. (Illus.). 1972. 58.00x o.p. (ISBN 0-19-818222-8). Oxford U Pr.

Lowe, E. Nobles & Shargel, Harry D. Legal & Other Aspects of Terrorism. LC 79-52885. (Corporate Law & Practice Course Handbook Ser.: 1978-1979). 1979. pap. text ed. 20.00 o.p. (ISBN 0-686-59551-3, B4-6506). PLI.

Lowe, H., jt. auth. see McDonald, A. C.

Lowe, Harry J. & Ernst, Edward A. The Quantitative Practice of Anesthesia: Use of Closed Circuit. (Illus.). 238p. 1981. 37.00 (ISBN 0-686-77739-5, 5200-4). Williams & Wilkins.

Lowe, J. & Lewis, D. Total Environmental Control: The Economics of Cross-Media Pollution Transfers. LC 82-9827. (Illus.). 134p. 1982. 21.50 (ISBN 0-08-026276-7). Pergamon.

Lowe, James N. & Ingraham, Lloyd L. An Introduction to Biochemical Reaction Mechanisms. (Foundations of Modern Biochemistry Ser). (Illus.). 160p. 1974. ref. ed. 17.95 o.p. (ISBN 0-13-478545-2). P-H.

Lowe, James T. Geopolitics & War: Mackinder's Philosophy of Power. LC 81-4862. (Illus.). 732p. (Orig.). 1981. lib. bdg. 30.50 (ISBN 0-8191-1542-8); pap. text ed. 20.75 (ISBN 0-8191-1543-6). U Pr of Amer.

Lowe, John. Quantum Chemistry: Student Edition. 1979. 22.50 (ISBN 0-12-457552-8). Acad Pr.

Lowe, John, ed. Fundamentals of Petroleum Land Titles. 1982. 46.00 (ISBN 0-89931-034-6). Inst Energy.

Lowe, John C. & Moryadas, S. Spatial Interaction: The Geography of Movement. 1975. text ed. 28.95 (ISBN 0-395-18584-X). HM.

Lowe, John S. Basic Principles of Oil & Gas Law & Taxation. 1982. 50.00 (ISBN 0-89419-187-X). Inst Energy.

--Colorado Oil & Gas Law & Land Practices. 1982. cancelled 42.00 (ISBN 0-89419-252-3). Inst Energy.

--Delay Rentals & Lease Adminstration. 1981. 42.00 (ISBN 0-89419-238-8). Inst Energy.

--Fundamentals of Gas Contracts. 1982. 40.00 (ISBN 0-89419-192-6). Inst Energy.

--Gas Contracts. 1981. 50.00 (ISBN 0-89419-236-1). Inst Energy.

Lowe, John S., ed. Fundamentals of Oil & Gas Leasing. 1982. 48.00 (ISBN 0-89931-030-3). Inst Energy.

--Oil & Gas Law for Attorneys. 1982. 58.00 (ISBN 0-89419-199-3). Inst Energy.

--Oil & Gas of the Williston Basin. 1982. 55.00 (ISBN 0-89419-224-8). Inst Energy.

Lowe, Joseph D., compiled by. Catalog of the Official Gazetteers of China in the University of Washington. LC 70-476883. 79p. 1966. 15.00x o.p. (ISBN 0-8002-1241-X). Intl Pubns Serv.

Lowe, Kenneth S., ed. see Petersen, Eugene T.

Lowe, Michael J., jt. auth. see Pierre, Donald A.

Lowe, N. Lancashire Textile Industry in the Sixteenth Century. 1972. 19.00 (ISBN 0-7190-1156-6). Manchester.

Lowe, P. G. Basic Principles of Plate Theory. (Illus.). 180p. 1982. 48.00x (ISBN 0-903384-26-4); pap. text ed. 24.00x (ISBN 0-903384-25-6). Intl Ideas.

Lowe, Peter. Great Britain & Japan Nineteen Eleven to Nineteen Fifteen: A Study of British Far Eastern Policy. (Illus.). 1969. 29.00 (ISBN 0-312-34510-0). St Martin.

--Great Britain & the Origins of the Pacific War: A Study of British Policy in East Asia, 1937 to 1941. (Illus.). 1977. text ed. 45.00x (ISBN 0-19-822427-3). Oxford U Pr.

Lowe, Peter G. Classical Theory of Structures. (Illus.). 1971. 42.50 (ISBN 0-521-08089-4). Cambridge U Pr.

Lowe, Philip & Goyder, Jane. Environmental Groups in Politics. (Resource Management Ser.: No. 6). (Illus.). 240p. 1983. text ed. 30.00x (ISBN 0-04-329043-4); pap. text ed. 13.95x (ISBN 0-04-329044-2). Allen Unwin.

Lowe, Robert. Build & Fly Your Own Plane. 220p. 1980. 16.95 o.p. (ISBN 0-442-21936-9). Van Nos Reinhold.

Lowe, Robert C. State Public Welfare Legislation. LC 75-165602. (Research Monograph Ser.: Vol. 20). 1971. Repr. of 1939 ed. lib. bdg. 49.50 (ISBN 0-306-70352-1). Da Capo.

Lowe, Robert W. Bibliographical Account of English Theatrical Literature. LC 66-27665. 1966. Repr. of 1888 ed. 40.00x (ISBN 0-8103-3216-7). Gale.

Lowe, Roberta, jt. auth. see Lowe, Don.

Lowe, Sue D. Stieglitz: A Memoir-Biography. (Illus.). 1982. 25.50 (ISBN 0-374-15006-0). FS&G.

--Stieglitz: A Memoir-Biography. (Illus.). 450p. 1983. 22.50 (ISBN 0-374-26990-4). FS&G.

Lowe, Sue D., et al. Ten Minutes Ahead of the Rest of the World. LC 81-51534. (Illus.). 250p. 1982. 25.00 (ISBN 0-9607742-0-3). Milford Hist Soc.

Lowe, W. D. & Freeman, C. E., eds. Rome & Her Kings: Extracts from Livy I. (Bolchazy-Carduci Textbooks). 110p. 1981. pap. text ed. 7.00 (ISBN 0-86516-000-7). Bolchazy-Carducci.

Lowe, W. H., tr. see Andreyev, L. N.

Lowe, Walter, Jr., jt. auth. see Jacobson, Walter.

Lowell, Abbott L. At War with Academic Traditions in America. LC 79-108395. (Illus.). xiv, 357p. Repr. of 1934 ed. lib. bdg. 17.50x (ISBN 0-8371-3818-3, LOAT). Greenwood.

Lowell, Amy. Poetry & Poets. LC 77-162298. 1971. Repr. of 1930 ed. 10.00x (ISBN 0-8196-0274-4). Biblo.

Lowell, Elaine. This Time Forever. 256p. (YA) 1972. 6.95 (ISBN 0-685-27367-9, Avalon). Bouregy.

Lowell, Fred R. Profits in Soybeans. 1966. 11.95 o.p. (ISBN 0-686-00671-2). Keltner.

--Wheat Market. 1968. 12.95 o.p. (ISBN 0-686-00672-0). Keltner.

Lowell Historical Society. Cotton Was King: A History of Lowell, Mass. Eno, Arthur L., Jr., ed. LC 76-11304. (Illus.). 1976. pap. 6.95 o.p. (ISBN 0-912274-61-1). NH Pub Co.

Lowell, James R. Uncollected Poems. Smith, Thelma, ed. 1976. Repr. of 1950 ed. lib. bdg. 20.75x (ISBN 0-8371-8852-0, LOUP). Greenwood.

Lowell, R. P., jt. auth. see Rona, P. A.

Lowell, Robert & Lowell, Robert, trs. from Fr. Racine's Phaedre. 213p. 1961. pap. 4.95 o.p. (ISBN 0-374-50911-5, N403). FS&G.

Lowell, S. Introduction to Powder Surface Area. LC 79-15878. 1979. 33.95 (ISBN 0-471-04771-6, Pub. by Wiley-Interscience). Wiley.

Lowell, jt. auth. see Buechner, Katy.

Lowe-McConnell, R. H. Ecology of Fishes. (Studies in Biology: No. 76). 68p. 1977. pap. text ed. 8.95 (ISBN 0-7131-2595-0). E Arnold.

Lowen, Alexander. Pleasure: A Creative Approach to Life. 1975. pap. 3.95 (ISBN 0-14-004033-1). Penguin.

Lowen, Walter. Dichotomies of the Mind: A Systems Science Model of the Mind & Personality. 360p. 1982. 28.50 (ISBN 0-471-08331-3, Pub. by Wiley-Interscience). Wiley.

Lowenberg, Bert J. American History in American Thought. 1973. pap. 5.95 o.p. (ISBN 0-671-20857-8, Touchstone Bks). S&S.

Lowenberg, Edwin C. Electronic Circuits. (Schaum's Outline Ser). (Orig.). 1967. pap. 6.95 (ISBN 0-07-038835-0, SP). McGraw.

Lowenberg, J. & Moskow, M. Collective Bargaining in Government: Readings & Cases. (Illus.). 1972. pap. text ed. 14.95 (ISBN 0-13-140483-0). P-H.

Lowenberg, Miriam E., et al. Food & People. 3rd ed. LC 78-19172. 1979. text ed. 25.95x (ISBN 0-471-02690-5). Wiley.

Lowenbraun, Sheila, et al. Teaching the Hearing Impaired. (Special Education Ser.). 224p. 1980. text ed. 19.95 (ISBN 0-675-08199-8). Merrill.

Lowenfeld, Viktor & Brittain, W. Lambert. Creative & Mental Growth. 7th ed. 1982. text ed. 21.95x (ISBN 0-02-372080-8). Macmillan.

Lowenfels, Walter. The Tenderest Lover: Walt Whitman's Love Poems. 1972. pap. 2.95 o.s.i. (ISBN 0-440-58606-2, Delta). Dell.

Lowengrub, M. & Stampfli, J. G. Topics in Calculus. 2nd ed. LC 7-78064. 400p. 1975. text ed. 27.95 (ISBN 0-471-01088-X). Wiley.

Lowenhardt, John. The Soviet Politburo. LC 81-8759. 192p. 1982. 20.00x (ISBN 0-312-74843-4). St Martin.

Lowenheim, Frederick A. Electroplating: Fundamentals of Surface Finishing. (Illus.). 1977. 33.95 (ISBN 0-07-038836-9, P&RB). McGraw.

Lowenheim, Frederick A. & Moran, Margaerite K. Faith, Keyes, & Clark's Industrial Chemicals. 4th ed. LC 75-17951. 904p. 1975. 105.00 (ISBN 0-471-54964-9, Pub. by Wiley-Interscience). Wiley.

Lowenridge, Matthew R. Mastering the Art of Oriental, German & British Pottery. (Promotion of the Arts Library). (Illus.). 121p. 1982. 67.85 (ISBN 0-86650-038-3). Gloucester Art.

Lowens, Irving, pref. by. Lectures on the History & Art of Music: The Louis Charles Elson Memorial Lectures at the Library of Congress 1946-1965. LC 68-55319. (Music Ser.). 1968. Repr. of 1963 ed. lib. bdg. 25.00 (ISBN 0-306-71193-1). Da Capo.

Lowenstam, Heinz A. Biostratigraphic Studies of the Niagaran Inter-Reef Formations of Northeastern Illinois. (Scientific Papers Ser.: Vol. IV). (Illus.). 146p. 1948. 3.00 (ISBN 0-89792-093-7); pap. 2.00 (ISBN 0-89792-005-8). Ill St Museum.

Lowenstein, Bertrand E. & Preger, Paul D., Jr. Diabetes: New Look at an Old Problem. LC 75-6346. 298p. 1976. 13.41i (ISBN 0-06-012718-X, HarpT). Har-Row.

Lowenstein, Douglas, jt. ed. see Stone, Gregory.

Lowenstein, Janet & Taylor, Mary L., eds. Study in the American Republics Area, Vol. 2. LC 76-22817. (Handbook on International Study for U.S. Nationals Ser.). (Orig.). 1976. 13.95 (ISBN 0-87206-080-2); pap. 9.95 (ISBN 0-87206-104-3). Inst Intl Educ.

Lowenstein, Leah M., jt. ed. see Shapiro, Eileen C.

Lowenstein, O., ed. Advances in Comparative Physiology, Vol. 8. 368p. 1982. 49.50 (ISBN 0-12-011508-5); lib. bdg. 64.50 lib ed. (ISBN 0-12-011578-6); microfiche 35.00 (ISBN 0-12-011579-4). Acad Pr.

--Advances in Comparative Physiology & Biochemistry, Vol. 7. 1978. 48.50 (ISBN 0-12-011507-7); lib. ed. 62.00 (ISBN 0-12-001576-5); microfiche 35.50 (ISBN 0-12-011577-8). Acad Pr.

Lowenthal, A. Agar Gel Electrophoresis in Neurology. 1964. 18.00 (ISBN 0-444-40377-9). Elsevier.

Lowenthal, A. & Mori, A., eds. Urea Cycle Diseases. (Advances in Experimental Medicine & Biology). 516p. 1982. 62.50x (ISBN 0-306-41037-0, Plenum Pr). Plenum Pub.

Lowenthal, Abraham F., jt. ed. see McClintock, Cynthia.

Lowenthal, David & Binney, Marcus, eds. Our Past Before Us: Why Do We Save It? 1981. 33.00x (ISBN 0-85117-219-9, Pub. by M Temple Smith). State Mutual Bk.

Lowenthal, David T., jt. auth. see Jenis, Edwin H.

Lowenthal, F. & Cordier, J., eds. Language & Language Acquisition. 373p. 1982. 42.50 (ISBN 0-306-41128-8, Plenum Pr). Plenum Pub.

Lowenthal, Larry. Iron Mine Railroads of New Jersey. (Illus.). 145p. 1981. 17.95 (ISBN 0-686-36238-1); pap. 12.95 (ISBN 0-686-99308-X). Tri-State Rail.

Lowenthal, Marvin. The Autobiography of Michel De Montaigne. 348p. 1982. Repr. of 1935 ed. lib. bdg. 25.00 (ISBN 0-89760-516-0). Telegraph Bks.

--Henrietta Szold: Life & Letters. LC 72-595. (Illus.). 350p. 1975. Repr. of 1942 ed. lib. bdg. 16.00x (ISBN 0-8371-5998-9, LOHS). Greenwood.

Lowenthal, Richard. Model or Ally? The Communist Powers & the Developing Countries. 1976. 22.50x (ISBN 0-19-502105-3). Oxford U Pr.

Lowenthal, Werner. Pharmaceutical Calculations: A Self-Instructional Text. rev. ed. LC 74-9564. 460p. 1978. pap. 12.50 (ISBN 0-88275-573-0). Krieger.

Lowe-Porter, H. T., tr. see Mann, Thomas.

Lower, A. R., jt. ed. see Innis, Harold A.

Lower, Arthur R. North American Assault on the Canadian Forest: A History of the Lumber Trade Between Canada & the United States. LC 68-57620. (Illus.). 1969. Repr. of 1938 ed. lib. bdg. 20.00x (ISBN 0-8371-0543-9, LOLT). Greenwood.

Lower, Mark A. English Surnames, 2 Vols. 4th ed. LC 68-22037. 1968. Repr. of 1875 ed. Set. 37.00x (ISBN 0-8103-3129-2). Gale.

Lowerre, George F. & Scandure, Alice M. Critical Reading: Workbook A Reusable Edition. (gr. 3-8). 1973. 4.50x (ISBN 0-89039-070-3); tchrs' manual 2.00 (ISBN 0-89039-077-0). Ann Arbor Pubs.

Lowers, James K. Hamlet Notes. (Orig.). 1971. pap. 2.95 (ISBN 0-8220-0018-0). Cliffs.

--King Henry Fourth, Pt. 1 Notes. (Orig.). 1971. pap. 2.95 (ISBN 0-8220-0023-7). Cliffs.

--King Lear Notes. (Orig.). 1968. pap. 2.95 (ISBN 0-8220-0041-5). Cliffs.

--Richard Third Notes. (Orig.). 1966. pap. 2.95 (ISBN 0-8220-0071-7). Cliffs.

--Shaw's Plays: Man & Superman Notes & Caesar & Cleopatra Notes. (Orig.). 1982. pap. 2.95 (ISBN 0-8220-0808-4). Cliffs.

Lowerson, J. R., ed. Southern History: A Review of History of Southern England, Vol. 3. 256p. 1981. text ed. 28.25x (ISBN 0-391-02316-0, Pub. by Sutton England); pap. text ed. 17.00x (ISBN 0-904387-66-6). Humanities.

--Southern History, 1982, Vol. 4. 320p. 1983. text ed. 28.25x (ISBN 0-904387-93-3, Pub. by Sutton England); pap. text ed. 17.00x (ISBN 0-904387-94-1). Humanities.

Lowery, Daniel. Following Christ: A Handbook of Catholic Moral Teaching. 160p. 1983. pap. 3.50 (ISBN 0-89243-173-3). Liguori Pubns.

Lowery, Fred. Whistling in the Dark. McDonnell, John, as told to. 416p. 1983. 15.95 (ISBN 0-88289-298-3). Pelican.

Lowery, James L., Jr. Peers, Tents, & Owls: Some Solutions to Problems of the Clergy Today. 160p. (Orig.). 1973. pap. 3.95 o.p. (ISBN 0-8192-1155-9). Morehouse.

Lowery, James L., Jr., ed. Case Histories of Tentmakers. 1976. pap. 3.50 o.p. (ISBN 0-8192-1216-4). Morehouse.

Lowery, Joan, jt. auth. see Nixon, Hershell H.

Lowery, Marilyn. The Reluctant Duke. (Orig.). 1981. pap. 1.50 o.s.i. (ISBN 0-440-17234-9). Dell.

Lowery, Robert, ed. O'Casey Annual. (Literary Annuals: No. 2). 240p. 1983. text ed. 42.00x (ISBN 0-333-32458-7, 40972, Pub. by Macmillan England). Humanities.

Lowery, Robert G., ed. Essays on Sean O'Casey's Autobiographies. 268p. 1981. text ed. 22.50x (ISBN 0-389-20180-4). B&N Imports.

Lowery, Robert G., ed. see Atkinson, Brooks.

Lowery, Shearon, jt. auth. see DeFleur, Melvin.

Lowery, William R., et al. College Admissions Counseling: A Handbook for the Profession. LC 82-48086. (Higher Education Ser.). 1982. text ed. 25.95x (ISBN 0-87589-549-2). Jossey Bass.

Lowes, Ruth, jt. auth. see Bates, Enid.

Lowey, Warren G. An Indian Tale of Old Long Island. 64p. (gr. 3-8). 1957. pap. 2.00 (ISBN 0-912954-00-0). Edmond Pub Co.

--Little Fox, Indian Boy. (Illus.). (gr. 3-9). 1972. 3.95 (ISBN 0-912954-02-7). Edmond Pub Co.

Lowey, Warren G., ed. The Golden Ours. 144p. 1972. 2.00 (ISBN 0-912954-06-X). Edmond Pub Co.

--Sea Green Eyes. 64p. 1971. lib. bdg. 2.00 (ISBN 0-912954-04-3). Edmond Pub Co.

Lowic, Lawrence. The Architectural Heritage of St. Louis 1803-1891. 160p. 1982. pap. 10.00 (ISBN 0-936316-02-0). Wash U Gallery.

Lowie, Robert H. The Crow Indians. (Illus.). xxii, 350p. 1983. pap. 8.95 (ISBN 0-8032-7909-4, BB836, Bison). U of Nebr Pr.

--Robert H. Lowie, Ethnologist: A Personal Record. (Illus.). 1959. 32.50x (ISBN 0-520-00775-1). U of Cal Pr.

Lowinger, Paul & Livingston, Martha. The Minds of the Chinese People. 256p. 1983. 16.95 (ISBN 0-13-583294-2). P-H.

Lowinsky, Edward E., ed. Josquin Des Prez. (Illus.). 1977. incl. 3 seven inch discs 79.00x (ISBN 0-19-315229-0). Oxford U Pr.

Lowinson, Joyce & Ruiz, Pedro. Substance Abuse. (Illus.). 896p. 1981. 65.00 (ISBN 0-686-77749-2, 5210-1). Williams & Wilkins.

Lowitt, Richard, jt. ed. see Burke, Robert E.

Lowitz, A., jt. auth. see Lowitz, S.

Lowitz, Anson, jt. auth. see Lowitz, Sadybeth.

Lowitz, Anson, jt. auth. see Lowitz, Sadyebeth.

Lowitz, S. & Lowitz, A. Mr. Key's Song: The Star-Spangled Banner. 60p. 1971. 3.00 (ISBN 0-686-36838-X). Md Hist.

Lowitz, Sadybeth & Lowitz, Anson. Mr. Kay's Song. (Really Truly Stories Ser.). (Illus.). 60p. (gr. 2-5). 1967. PLB 3.95g (ISBN 0-8225-0137-6). Lerner Pubns.

Lowitz, Sadyebeth & Lowitz, Anson. Barefoot Abe. LC 67-29824. (Illus.). 56p. (gr. 2-5). 1967. PLB 3.95g (ISBN 0-8225-0135-X). Lerner Pubns.

--The Cruise of Mr. Christopher Columbus. LC 64-13676. (Really Truly Stories Ser.). (Illus.). 80p. (gr. 2-5). 1967. PLB 3.95g (ISBN 0-8225-0131-7). Lerner Pubns.

--General George the Great. (Really True Stories Ser.). (Illus.). 60p. (gr. 2-5). 1967. PLB 3.95g (ISBN 0-8225-0131-7). Lerner Pubns.

--The Magic Fountain. (Really Truly Stories Ser.). (Illus.). 60p. (gr. 2-5). 1967. PLB 3.95g (ISBN 0-8225-0134-1). Lerner Pubns.

--The Pilgrims' Party. LC 64-13677. (Really Truly Stories Ser.). 76p. (gr. 2 up). 1967. PLB 3.95g (ISBN 0-8225-0133-3). Lerner Pubns.

--Tom Edison Finds Out. 1979. pap. 0.95 o.p. (ISBN 0-440-48384-0, YB). Dell.

--Tom Edison Finds Out. (Really Truly Stories Ser.). (Illus.). 48p. (gr. 2-5). 1967. PLB 3.95g (ISBN 0-8225-0136-8). Lerner Pubns.

Lowman, Charles E. Magnetic Recording. (Illus.). 320p. 1972. 38.50 o.p. (ISBN 0-07-038845-8, P&RB). McGraw.

Lowman, Kathleen D., jt. ed. see Benjamin, Ludy T.

Lowman, Kaye & Kaszonyi, Kay. Especially for You. (Illus.). 1978. 9.50 (ISBN 0-912500-07-7). La Leche.

Lowman, Robert & Hall, Virginia. APA Guide to Research Support. (Orig.). 1981. pap. 16.00x o.p. (ISBN 0-686-73732-6). Am Psychol.

Lowman, Robert G. & Reeves, Perry B. Experimental Introductory Chemistry. 195p. 1981. pap. text ed. 4.95x (ISBN 0-89641-096-X). American Pr.

Lown, Elizabeth M., jt. ed. see Strausz, Otto P.

Lowndes, George A. The British Educational Systems. 1977. Repr. of 1955 ed. lib. bdg. 16.25x (ISBN 0-8371-9592-6, LOBE). Greenwood.

Lowndes, William T. Bibliographer's Manual of English Literature, 8 Vols. LC 66-28042. 1967. Repr. of 1864 ed. 196.00x (ISBN 0-8103-3217-5). Gale.

Lownes, Victor. The Day the Bunny Died. (Illus.). 224p. 1983. 14.95 (ISBN 0-8184-0340-3). Lyle Stuart.

Lowrey, Janette S. Six Silver Spoons. LC 77-105469. (I Can Read History Books). (Illus.). (ps-2). 1971. PLB 8.89 (ISBN 0-06-024037-7, HarpJ). Har-Row.

Lowrie, Donald A. Rebellious Prophet: A Life of Nicolai Berdgaev. LC 73-11867. (Illus.). 310p. 1974. Repr. of 1960 ed. lib. bdg. 17.25x (ISBN 0-8371-7095-8, LORP). Greenwood.

Lowrie, R. S., ed. see Jones, C. E.

Lowrie, Walter. The Classical Cemeteries As Works of Art. (Illus.). 137p. 1982. 47.85 (ISBN 0-86650-030-8). Gloucester Art.

Lowry, Albert J. How to Become Financially Independent by Investing in Real Estate. (Illus.). 1977. 16.50 (ISBN 0-671-22693-2). S&S.

--How You Can Become Financially Independent by Investing in Real Estate. 1982. 16.50 (ISBN 0-671-44959-1). S&S.

Lowry, Anna M., jt. auth. see Case, Project N.

Lowry, Bates. Visual Experience: An Introduction to Art. (Illus.). 1961. 20.00 o.p. (ISBN 0-8109-0530-2). Abrams.

Lowry, Charles W. William Temple: An Archbishop for All Seasons. LC 81-43869. 170p. (Orig.). 1982. lib. bdg. 17.75 (ISBN 0-8191-2355-2); pap. text ed. 6.50 (ISBN 0-8191-2356-0). U Pr of Amer.

Lowry, Eugene. The Homiletical Plot: The Sermon As Narrative Art Form. LC 79-92074. 100p. (Orig.). 1980. pap. 4.95 (ISBN 0-8042-1652-5). John Knox.

Lowry, H. F., ed. see Arnold, Matthew.

Lowry, H. H. The Chemistry of Coal Utilization, Vols. 1 & 2. LC 45-5498. 1945. Set. 95.00 (ISBN 0-471-02494-5, Pub. by Wiley-Interscience); suppl. vol. (1963) 107.00x (ISBN 0-471-55158-9); 4 vols. set 354.00x (ISBN 0-471-07816-6). Wiley.

Lowry, Isabel B., ed. County Court Houses of the United States, Vol. 1: Alabama-Louisiana. (Visual Documentation Program of American Art Ser.). 1981. 275.00x (ISBN 0-89481-007-3). Dunlap Soc.

Lowry, James K. Soft Bottom Macrobenthic Community of Arthur Harbor, Antarctica: Paper 1 in Biology of the Antarctic Seas V. Pawson, David L., ed. LC 75-22056. (Antarctic Research Ser: Vol. 23). (Illus.). 1975. pap. 5.20 (ISBN 0-87590-123-9). Am Geophysical.

Lowry, Lois. Anastasia Again! (Illus.). (gr. 3-6). 1981. 9.95 (ISBN 0-395-31147-0). HM.

--Anastasia Again! (gr. 4-7). 1982. pap. 1.95 (ISBN 0-440-40009-0, LFL). Dell.

--Anastasia at Your Service. (gr. 3-6). 1982. PLB 9.95 (ISBN 0-395-32865-9); 9.70. HM.

--Taking Care of Terrific. LC 82-15769. 160p. (gr. 5 up). 1983. 8.95. HM.

Lowry, Malcolm. Selected Poems. (Orig.). 1963. pap. 2.00 (ISBN 0-87286-030-2, PP17). City Lights.

--Under the Volcano. LC 65-11640. 1965. 14.37i (ISBN 0-397-00402-8). Har-Row.

Lowry, Marjorie, ed. Malcolm Lowry: Psalms & Songs. (Orig.). 1975. pap. 5.95 o.p. (ISBN 0-452-25110-9, Z5110, Plume). NAL.

Lowry, Michael R. Preventing Mental Depression. 300p. 1983. 22.50 (ISBN 0-87527-186-3). Green.

Lowry, Ritchie P. Social Problems: A Critical Analysis of Theories & Public Policy. 1974. pap. text ed. 12.95 (ISBN 0-669-85332-1). Heath.

Lowry, Ritchie P. & Rankin, Robert P. Sociology: Social Science & Social Concerns. 3rd ed. 1977. text ed. 22.95x (ISBN 0-669-99648-3); instr's manual 1.95 (ISBN 0-669-03186-0); study guide 7.95x (ISBN 0-669-00339-5). Heath.

Lowry, S. M., et al. Time & Motion Study & Formulas for Wage Incentives. 3rd ed. LC 80-12407. 446p. 1981. Repr. of 1940 ed. write for info. o.p. (ISBN 0-89874-174-2). Krieger.

Lowry, Terry. The Battle of Scary Creek Military Operations in the Kanawha Valley, April - July 1861. LC 82-81716. (Illus.). 192p. (Orig.). Date not set. pap. 7.95 (ISBN 0-933126-22-0). Pictorial Hist.

Lowry, W. McNeil, ed. The Performing Arts in American Society. LC 78-1404. (American Assembly Ser.). 1978. 10.95 (ISBN 0-13-657155-7, Spec); pap. 4.95 o.p. (ISBN 0-13-657148-4, Spec). P-H.

Lowry, William P. Weather & Life: An Introduction to Biometeorology. 1969. text ed. 20.75 (ISBN 0-12-457750-4); ans. bklet. o.s. 3.50 (ISBN 0-12-457756-3). Acad Pr.

Lowth, Robert. A Short Introduction to English Grammar. LC 79-4675. (Amer. Linguistics Ser.). 1979. Repr. of 1775 ed. lib. bdg. 30.00x (ISBN 0-8201-1332-8). Schol Facsimiles.

Lowther, Gerald, jt. auth. see Bier, Norman.

Lowther, Kevin & Lucas, C. Payne. Keeping Kennedy's Promise: The Peace Corps: Unmet Hope of the New Frontier. LC 77-21187. 1978. lib. bdg. 20.00 o.p. (ISBN 0-89158-422-6). Westview.

Lowy, Louis. Social Policies & Programs on Aging: What Is & What Should Be in the Later Years. LC 78-55355. 288p. 1980. 23.95x (ISBN 0-669-02342-6). Lexington Bks.

--Social Work with the Aging: The Challenge & Promise of the Later Years. (Boehm Ser.). 1979. text ed. 17.95 scp o.p. (ISBN 0-06-044085-6, HarpC). Har-Row.

Lowy, Michael. Georg Lukacs: From Romanticism to Bolshevism. 220p. 1980. 24.75 (ISBN 0-8052-7077-9, Pub. by NLB). Schocken.

Lowy, Samuel. Should You Be Psychoanalyzed. LC 62-18542. 1963. 6.00 o.p. (ISBN 0-8022-1003-1). Philos Lib.

Lox, Ginger. Sense You. 2nd ed. (Illus.). 42p. (Orig.). 1981. pap. 3.50 (ISBN 0-9604178-0-X). G Rose Pr.

Loxton, John. Practical Map Production. LC 80-40118. 137p. 1980. 29.95 (ISBN 0-471-27782-7, Pub. by Wiley-Interscience); pap. 16.95 (ISBN 0-471-27783-5). Wiley.

Loy, John W., et al. Sport & Social Systems. (Social Significance of Sport Ser.). (Illus.). 1978. text ed. 20.95 (ISBN 0-201-04143-X). A-W.

Loy, Mina. The Last Lunar Baedeker: The Poems of Mina Loy. 1982. 25.00 (ISBN 0-912330-46-5, Dist by Inland Bk). Jargon Soc.

Loyd, Marianne. Journey to a Western Island. 28p. (Orig.). 1981. pap. 4.50 (ISBN 0-918092-28-0); signed ed. 10.00 (ISBN 0-918092-27-2). Tamarack Edns.

Loyd, Mary, tr. see Waliszewski, Kazimierz.

Loyd, Richard B. & Mundy, Bernard K. Lynchburg: A Pictorial History. LC 75-20230. (Illus.). 1975. 13.95 o.p. (ISBN 0-915442-06-X). Donning Co.

Loyd, Sam. More Mathematical Puzzles of Sam Loyd. pap. 3.00 (ISBN 0-486-20709-9). Dover.

Loye, David. The Knowable Future: A Psychology of Forecasting & Prophecy. LC 77-26713. 1978. 24.95 (ISBN 0-471-03566-1, Pub. by Wiley-Interscience). Wiley.

Loyer, Godefroy. Relation du Voyage du Royaume d'Issigny, Cote d'Or, Pays de Guinee, en Afrique. (Bibliotheque Africaine Ser.). 318p. (Fr.). 1974. Repr. of 1714 ed. lib. bdg. 84.00x o.p. (ISBN 0-8287-0556-9, 72-2121). Clearwater Pub.

Loyn, H. R. The Vikings in Britain. LC 77-73918. (Illus.). 1977. 15.95x o.p. (ISBN 0-312-84671-1). St Martin.

Loyn, H. R. & Peroival, J., eds. The Reign of Charlemagne: Documents on Carolingian Government & Administration. LC 75-32935. (Documents of Medieval History Ser.). 256p. 1976. 25.00 (ISBN 0-312-66990-9). St Martin.

Loyola College, Pastoral & Counseling Faculty. Pastoral Counseling. (Illus.). 352p. 1982. 21.95 (ISBN 0-13-652867-8). P-H.

Loyola, Gloria, jt. ed. see Wilson, Rex.

Lozano, Francisco & Sturtevant, Jane. Life Styles: An Intermediate American English Series, 3 bks. Incl. Bk. 1. student bk. (ISBN 0-582-79754-3); tchr's manual (ISBN 0-582-79755-1); wkbk. (ISBN 0-582-79756-X); cassette (ISBN 0-582-78311-9); Bk. 2. student bk. (ISBN 0-582-79757-8); tchr's manual (ISBN 0-582-79758-6); wkbk. (ISBN 0-582-79759-4); cassette (ISBN 0-582-78312-7); Bk. 3. student bk. (ISBN 0-582-79760-8); tchr's manual (ISBN 0-582-79761-6); wkbk. (ISBN 0-582-79762-4); cassette (ISBN 0-582-78313-5). (English As a Second Lanugage Bk.). 1981-82. student bks. 4.65x ea.; tchr's manuals 5.50x ea.; wkbks. 2.75x ea.; cassettes 22.95x ea. Longman.

Lozano, M., jt. auth. see Madurga, G.

Lozano, Wendy. Sweet Abandon. 272p. 1980. pap. 2.25 o.p. (ISBN 0-380-75416-9, 75416). Avon.

Lozanov, G. Suggestology & Outlines of Suggestopedy. (Psychic Studies). 386p. 1978. 21.00 (ISBN 0-677-30940-6). Gordon.

Lozier, M. Wayne De see Lewison, Dale & DeLozier, M. Wayne.

Lozina-Lozinskii, L. K. Studies in Cryobiology. Harry, P., tr. from Rus. LC 74-8277. (Illus.). 259p. 1974. 54.95 o.p. (ISBN 0-470-54347-7). Halsted Pr.

Lozovsky, A. see Dridzo, Solomon A.

Lozoya, Jorge A., ed. International Trade, Industrialization & the New International Economic Order. (Pergamon Policy Studies). 1981. 22.00 (ISBN 0-08-025120-X). Pergamon.

Lozynsky, Artem, jt. ed. see Francis, Gloria A.

LRH Personal Compilations Bureau, ed. see Medicus & Hubbard, L. Ron.

Lu, David J. Sources of Japanese History, 2 vols. 696p. 1974. Vol. 1. 20.00 o.p. (ISBN 0-07-038902-0, C); Vol. 2. 20.00 o.p. (ISBN 0-07-038903-9); Vol. 1. pap. text ed. 17.00 o.p. (ISBN 0-07-038904-7); Vol. 2. pap. text ed. 9.95 o.p. (ISBN 0-07-038905-5). McGraw.

Lu, Gwei-Djen & Needham, J. Celestial Lancets: History & Rationale of Acupuncture & Moxa. LC 79-41734. (Illus.). 400p. 1980. 99.00 (ISBN 0-521-21513-7). Cambridge U Pr.

Lu, Hsien, ed. Major Topics & Issues in Psychology: Scientific Studies in Behavioral Development. 97p. 1972. 14.95x (ISBN 0-8422-0165-3). Irvington.

Lu, P. Introduction to the Mechanics of Viscous Fluids. LC 77-3428. (Thermal & Fluids Engineering Ser.). (Illus.). 1977. Repr. of 1973 ed. text ed. 29.95 (ISBN 0-07-038907-1, C). McGraw.

Luard, D. E., jt. auth. see Hughes, Trevor J.

Luard, Evan. International Agencies: The Emerging Framework of Interdependence. LC 76-15414. 1977. lib. bdg. 40.00 (ISBN 0-379-00686-3). Oceana.

--Socialism Without the State. LC 78-10608. 1979. 25.00x (ISBN 0-312-73718-1). St Martin.

--The United Nations: How It Works & What It Does. 1979. 26.00x (ISBN 0-312-83310-5). St Martin.

Luard, Nicholas. The Last Wilderness: A Journey Across the Great Kalahari Desert. 1981. 14.95 o.p. (ISBN 0-671-41264-7). S&S.

Lubac, Henri De. The Motherhood of the Church. Englund, Sr. Sergia, tr. from Fr. LC 81-83857. 275p. (Orig.). 1983. pap. 10.95 (ISBN 0-89870-014-0). Ignatius Pr.

Lubac, Henri De see De Lubac, Henri.

Lubachko, Ivan S. Belorussia Under Soviet Rule, Nineteen Seventeen to Nineteen Fifty-Seven. LC 79-160047. (Illus.). 240p. 1972. 13.00x (ISBN 0-8131-1263-X). U Pr of Ky.

Lubar, Steven D., jt. ed. see Folsom, Michael B.

Lubbock, Basil. The Best of Sail. LC 74-7554. (Illus.). 192p. 1975. 17.95 o.p. (ISBN 0-448-11840-8, G&D). Putnam Pub Group.

Lubbock, Percy. Earlham. LC 74-11936. (Illus.). 254p. 1974. Repr. of 1922 ed. lib. bdg. 17.25x (ISBN 0-8371-7722-7, LUEA). Greenwood.

--Percy Lubbock Reader. Harkness, Marjory G., ed. LC 57-12349. 1957. 9.95 (ISBN 0-87027-058-3). Cumberland Pr.

Lubec, G. Noninvasive Diagnosis of Kidney Disease. (Karger Continuing Education Ser.: Vol. 3). (Illus.). xii, 368p. 1983. 58.75 (ISBN 3-8055-3051-X). S Karger.

--Renal Immunology. (Contributions to Nephrology Ser.: Vol. 35). (Illus.). vi, 194p. 1983. pap. 58.25 (ISBN 3-8055-3587-2). S Karger.

Lubelfeld, J., jt. auth. see Houpis, C. H.

Luber, Raymond F. & Anderson, Carol, eds. Family Intervention with Psychiatric Patients. 160p. 1982. 18.95 (ISBN 0-89885-031-2). Human Sci Pr.

Lubetski, Edith & Lubetski, Meir. Building a Judaica Library Collection. 260p. Date not set. lib. bdg. 27.50 (ISBN 0-87287-375-7). Libs Unl.

Lubetski, Meir, jt. auth. see Lubetski, Edith.

Lubian, Rafael & Arias, M. M. Marti en los Campos de Cuba Libre. (Illus.). 186p. (Span.). 1982. pap. 9.95 (ISBN 0-89729-319-3). Ediciones.

Lubic, Lowell G. & Palkovitz, Harry. Stroke: Contemporary Patient Management. 2nd ed. (Contemporary Patient Management Ser.). 1983. text ed. 13.00 not set (ISBN 0-87488-893-X). Med Exam.

Lubic, Lowell G. & Palkovitz, Harry P. Stroke. (Discussions in Patient Management Ser.). 1979. pap. 13.00 o.p. (ISBN 0-87488-893-X). Med Exam.

Lubin. Medical Management of the Surgical Patient. 1982. 69.95 (ISBN 0-409-95011-4). Butterworth.

Lubin, Bernard, jt. auth. see Levitt, Eugene E.

Lubin, Bertram, ed. see New York Academy of Sciences Annals, Nov. 11-13, 1981.

Lubitz, Wolfgang. Lev Davydovic Trockj. 512p. 1983. cancelled (ISBN 3-598-10469-3, Pub. by K G Saur). Shoe String.

Lubitz, Wolfgang, ed. Trotsky Bibiliography: List of Separately Published Titles in Collections Treating L. D. Trotsky & Trotskyism. 458p. 1982. 65.00x (ISBN 3-598-10469-3). Gale.

Lubke, Kraus, jt. ed. see Schroder, Eberhard.

Lubkemann, Ernest C., Jr. Carving Twigs & Branches. LC 81-50980. (Illus.). 96p. (Orig.). (YA) (gr. 10 up). 1981. pap. 6.95 (ISBN 0-8069-7532-6). Sterling.

Lubker, Robert. Von der Syntax Des Englischen Verbs In Seinen Finiten Formen. 430p. (Ger.). 1982. write for info. (ISBN 3-8204-6158-2). P Lang Pubs.

Lubkin. Cohomology of Completions. (Mathematics Study Ser.: Vol. 42). 1980. 74.50 (ISBN 0-444-86042-8, North Holland). Elsevier.

Lubliner, Jerry & Bednarski, Mary W. An Introduction to Medical Malpractice. (Learning Packages in Policy Issues Ser.: No. 1). 52p. 1976. pap. text ed. 1.50x (ISBN 0-936826-10-X). Pol Stud Assocs.

Lublinskaya, Alexandra D. French Absolutism: The Crucial Phase, 1620-1629. (Illus.). 1968. 49.50 (ISBN 0-521-07117-8). Cambridge U Pr.

Lubman, Stanley B., jt. auth. see Murray, Douglas P.

Lubove, Roy. The Progressives & the Slums. LC 74-4843. (Illus.). 284p. 1974. Repr. of 1962 ed. lib. bdg. 32.25 (ISBN 0-8371-7487-2, LUPS). Greenwood.

--Twentieth Century Pittsburgh: Government, Business & Environmental Change. LC 69-19234. (New-Dimensions Historical Cities Ser). (Illus.). 1969. pap. text ed. 14.95 (ISBN 0-471-55251-8). Wiley.

Lubrano, Linda L. & Solomon, Susan G., eds. The Social Context of Soviet Science. (Special Studies on the Soviet Union & Eastern Europe). 1980. lib. bdg. 30.00 (ISBN 0-89158-450-1). Westview.

Lubs, Herbert & Cruz, Felix de la, eds. Genetic Counseling. LC 76-52601. 616p. 1977. 41.50 (ISBN 0-89004-150-4). Raven.

Luby, Sue. Hatha Yoga for Total Health: Handbook of Practical Programs. (Illus.). 1977. pap. 14.95 (ISBN 0-13-384123-5). P-H.

Luca, Hector F. De see De Luca, Hector F. & Frost, H. M.

Lucafo, Rosemarie, jt. auth. see Hoemann, Harry.

Lucaire, Ed, jt. auth. see Embery, Joan.

Lucantoni, D. M. Algorithmic Analysis of a Communication Model with Retransmission of Fluid Messages. (Research Notes in Mathematics Ser.). 154p. 1983. pap. text ed. 18.95 (ISBN 0-273-08571-9). Pitman Pub MA.

Lucarelli. Fetal Liver Transplantation. (International Congress Ser.: Vol. 514). 1980. 66.50 (ISBN 0-444-90180-9). Elsevier.

Lucas, Alec. Peter McArthur. (World Authors Ser.). 1975. lib. bdg. 15.95 (ISBN 0-8057-6214-0, Twayne). G K Hall.

Lucas, Angela. Women in the Middle Ages. LC 82-42578. 1982. 25.00x (ISBN 0-312-88743-4). St Martin.

Lucas, Bob, jt. auth. see Carcione, Joe.

Lucas, C. Payne, jt. auth. see Lowther, Kevin.

Lucas, Cristopher J. Our Western Educational Heritage. 608p. 1972. text ed. 22.95x (ISBN 0-02-372200-2). Macmillan.

Lucas, DeWitt B. God Tells the World. 1964. pap. 2.00 (ISBN 0-910140-08-1). Anthony.

--Secret Bible Prophecies. 1965. pap. 2.00 (ISBN 0-910140-10-3). Anthony.

--Visions of the New Life. 1963. pap. 2.00 (ISBN 0-910140-11-1). Anthony.

Lucas, Elissa. Chinese Medical Modernization: Comparative Policy Continuity from 1930-1980. 190p. 1982. 25.95 (ISBN 0-03-059454-5). Praeger.

Lucas, Elizabeth H., ed. Calligraphy, An Affair of the Heart: Italic Letterforms. 1982. write for info. E H Lucas.

Lucas, Georges. Transfer Theory for Trapped Electromagnetic Energy. 74p. 1982. 16.95x (ISBN 0-471-10500-7, Pub. by Wiley-Interscience). Wiley.

Lucas, H. C. Information Systems Concepts for Management. 2nd ed. 1982. 28.95 (ISBN 0-07-038924-1); instr's manual 10.00 (ISBN 0-07-038925-X). McGraw.

Lucas, H. C., ed. Information Systems Environment. 1980. 40.50 (ISBN 0-444-86036-3). Elsevier.

Lucas, Harold. Computers in Management & Business Studies. 272p. 1979. 35.00x (ISBN 0-7121-0390-2, Pub. by Macdonald & Evans). State Mutual Bk.

Lucas, Henry. The Management of Information Systems. (Management Information Systems Ser.). 1978. text ed. 23.95 o.p. (ISBN 0-07-038922-5, C); inst. manual 9.00 o.p. (ISBN 0-07-038923-3). McGraw.

Lucas, Henry & Gibson, Cyrusf. Casebook for Management Information Systems. 2nd ed. (Management Information Systems Ser.). (Illus.). 480p. 1980. pap. text ed. 13.95 (ISBN 0-07-038939-X, C); instructor's guide 4.95 (ISBN 0-07-038941-1). McGraw.

Lucas, Henry C. The Analysis, Design & Implementation of Information Systems. rev. ed. (Management Information Systems Ser.). (Illus.). 416p. 1980. text ed. 31.95 (ISBN 0-07-038927-6, C); instructor's manual 9.95 (ISBN 0-07-038928-4). McGraw.

--Computer-Based Information Systems in Organizations. LC 72-92561. (Illus.). 292p. 1973. text ed. 19.95 (ISBN 0-574-18590-9, 13-1590); instr's guide avail. (ISBN 0-574-18591-7, 13-1591). SRA.

--Coping with Computers: A Manager's Guide to Controlling Information Processing. (Illus.). 192p. 1982. 14.95 (ISBN 0-02-919310-9). Free Pr.

Lucas, Henry C., Jr. Coping with Computers: A Manager's Guide to Controlling Information Processing. 160p. 1982. 14.95 (ISBN 0-686-83160-8). Macmillan.

--Implementation of Computer-Based Models. 94p. 1976. 7.95 (ISBN 0-86641-046-5, 7682). Natl Assn Accts.

Lucas, Jack A. & Park, Michael A. Workbook in General Anthropology. 1979. pap. text ed. 9.95 (ISBN 0-8403-1950-9, 40195001). Kendall-Hunt.

Lucas, James. Alpine Elite. (Illus.). 226p. 1981. 19.95 (ISBN 0-86720-586-5). Sci Bks Intl.

Lucas, James L. The Religious Dimension of Twentieth-Century British & American Literature: A Textbook in the Analysis of Types. LC 81-40605. (Illus.). 306p. (Orig.). 1982. lib. bdg. 24.00 (ISBN 0-8191-2108-8); pap. text ed. 12.75 (ISBN 0-8191-2109-6). U Pr of Amer.

Lucas, Jay P. & Adams, Russell E., eds. Personal Computing: Proceedings. (Illus.). viii, 439p. 1979. pap. 9.50 (ISBN 0-88283-020-1). AFIPS Pr.

Lucas, John. Romantic to Modern Literature: Essays & Ideas of Culture 1750-1900. LC 82-6842. 240p. 1982. text ed. 26.50x (ISBN 0-389-20311-4). B&N Imports.

Lucas, John, jt. auth. see Dickinson, Colin.

Lucas, Linda & Karrenbrock, Marilyn H. The Disabled Child in the Library. 1983. lib. bdg. 22.50 (ISBN 0-87287-355-2). Libs Unl.

Lucas, Lois. Plants of Old Hawaii. (Illus.). 112p. (Orig.). 1982. pap. 4.95 (ISBN 0-935848-11-8). Bess Pr.

Lucas, Martin, jt. auth. see Dixon, Terence.

Lucas, Mary, tr. see Leroy, Pierre.

Lucas, N. J., ed. Local Energy Centres. (Illus.). 1978. text ed. 41.00 (ISBN 0-85334-782-4, Pub. by Applied Sci England). Elsevier.

Lucas, Nanci D., jt. auth. see Ahern, John F.

Lucas, Pat, ed. see Barth & Deal.

Lucas, Richard. Common & Uncommon Uses of Herbs for Healthful Living. LC 74-128898. 1970. pap. 2.50 (ISBN 0-668-02396-1). Arco.

Lucas, Robert E., Jr. Studies in Business Cycle Theory. 256p. 1981. text ed. 19.50x (ISBN 0-262-12089-5). MIT Pr.

--Studies in Business-Cycle Theory. 312p. 1983. pap. 9.95x (ISBN 0-262-62044-8). MIT Pr.

Lucas, St. John & Jones, P. M., eds. Oxford Book of French Verse, Thirteenth Century to Twentieth Century. 2nd ed. (Fr). 1957. 27.50x (ISBN 0-19-812109-1). Oxford U Pr.

Lucas, Stephen E. Portents of Rebellion: Rhetoric & Revolution in Philadelphia, 1765-1776. LC 75-30281. 355p. 1976. 22.95 (ISBN 0-87722-087-5). Temple U Pr.

Lucas, T. S. Understanding Inflation Accounting. 1981. 7.95 (ISBN 0-07-020830-1). McGraw.

Lucas, Ted & Riess, Fred. How to Convert to an Electric Car. (Illus.). 192p. 1980. pap. 5.95 (ISBN 0-517-53990-X). Crown.

Lucas, Thomas E. Elder Olson. (United States Authors Ser.). lib. bdg. 14.95 (ISBN 0-8057-0568-6, Twayne). G K Hall.

Lucas, Virginia H., jt. auth. see Barbe, Walter B.

Lucas, Virginia H., et al. Problem Solving Activities for Teaching Daily Living Skills: A Curriculum Handbook. LC 81-71180. 220p. 1982. pap. text ed. 19.00 (ISBN 0-936326-01-8). Cedars Pr.

Lucas, W. F., ed. Modules in Applied Mathematics: Differential Equation Models, Vol. 1. (Illus.). 400p. 1982. 28.00 (ISBN 0-387-90695-9). Springer-Verlag.

--Modules in Applied Mathematics, Vol. 2: Political & Related Models. (Illus.). 396p. 1983. 28.00 (ISBN 0-387-90696-7). Springer-Verlag.

--Modules in Applied Mathematics, Vol. 4: Life Science Models. (Illus.). 416p. 1983. 28.00 (ISBN 0-387-90739-4). Springer-Verlag.

Lucas, W. F., et al, eds. Modules in Applied Mathematics, Vol. 3: Discrete & System Models. (Illus.). 416p. 1983. 28.00 (ISBN 0-387-90724-6). Springer-Verlag.

Lucas, W. J., jt. auth. see Spanswick, R. M.

Lucas, Warren J. Protection Made Easy. Clinkscales, C. C., III, ed. LC 80-69587. (Illus.). 162p. (Orig.). 1981. 7.95 (ISBN 0-9605724-0-6); pap. 5.95 (ISBN 0-9605724-1-4). C & L Pub Co.

Lucas, William M., Jr., jt. auth. see Willems, Nicholas.

Lucas-Dubreton, J. The Fourth Musketeer: The Life of Alexander Dumas. Darnton, Maida C., tr. 276p. Repr. of 1928 ed. lib. bdg. 35.00 (ISBN 0-89984-812-5). Century Bookbindery.

--Louis XVIII. Lyon, F. H., tr. 303p. 1982. Repr. of 1927 ed. lib. bdg. 40.00 (ISBN 0-8495-3268-X). Arden Lib.

Luc-Barbier, Jean, tr. see Rodriguez, Cookie.

Luc-Barbier, Jean, tr. see Taylor, Thomas.

Lucchelli, P. E., jt. auth. see Torsoli, A.

Lucchi, Lorna De, tr. Anthology of Italian Poems, 13th-19th Century. LC 66-30496. (Eng. & Ital.). 1922. 10.00x (ISBN 0-8196-0198-5). Biblo.

Luce, Arthur A. Life of George Berkeley, Bishop of Cloyne. LC 68-23309. 1968. Repr. of 1949 ed. lib. bdg. 17.50x (ISBN 0-8371-0153-0, LULB). Greenwood.

Luce, Celia, jt. auth. see Luce, Willard.

Luce, Clare B., jt. auth. see Mabardi, Georges.

Luce, G. H. Phases of Pre-Pagan Burma: Languages & History, Vols. I & II. (Illus.). 1982. 188.00x (ISBN 0-19-713595-1). Oxford U Pr.

Luce, Gary. Your Second Life. 1980. pap. 6.95 o.s.i. (ISBN 0-440-59852-4, Delta). Dell.

Luce, Gay G. Your Second Life: Vitality in Middle & Later Age. 1979. 10.95 o.s.i. (ISBN 0-440-09864-5, Sey Lawr). Delacorte.

Luce, Gay G. & Segal, Julius. Sleep. 1966. 7.95 o.p. (ISBN 0-698-10343-2, Coward). Putnam Pub Group.

Luce, Gordon H. Old Burma-Early Pagan, 3 Vols. 1969. 120.00 set (ISBN 0-686-92654-4). J J Augustin.

Luce, James S., ed. The Kondratieff Theory & the Explosion of the Third World War. (Illus.). 152p. 1982. 98.75 (ISBN 0-86722-005-8). Inst Econ Pol.

Luce, John, jt. auth. see Smith, David E.

Luce, Marnie. Measurement: How Much? How Many? How Far? LC 68-56707. (Math Concept Bks). (gr. 3-6). 1969. PLB 3.95g (ISBN 0-8225-0578-9). Lerner Pubns.

--Points, Lines, & Planes. LC 68-56704. (Math Concept Bks). (gr. 3-6). 1969. PLB 3.95g (ISBN 0-8225-0575-4). Lerner Pubns.

--Polygons: Points in a Plane. LC 68-56705. (Math Concept Bks). (Illus.). (gr. 3-6). 1969. PLB 3.95g (ISBN 0-8225-0576-2). Lerner Pubns.

--Polyhedrons: Intersecting Planes. LC 68-56706. (Math Concept Bks.). (Illus.). (gr. 3-6). 1969. PLB 3.95g (ISBN 0-8225-0577-0). Lerner Pubns.

--Primes Are Builders. LC 68-56702. (Math Concept Bks). (Illus.). (gr. 3-6). 1969. PLB 3.95g (ISBN 0-8225-0573-8). Lerner Pubns.

--Sets: What Are They? LC 68-56703. (Math Concept Bks). (Illus.). (gr. 3-6). 1969. PLB 3.95g (ISBN 0-8225-0574-6). Lerner Pubns.

--Ten: Why Is It Important? LC 68-56709. (Math Concept Bks). (Illus.). (gr. 3-6). 1969. PLB 3.95g (ISBN 0-8225-0580-0). Lerner Pubns.

--Zero Is Something. LC 68-28034. (Math Concept Bks). (Illus.). (gr. 3-6). 1969. PLB 3.95g (ISBN 0-8225-0571-1). Lerner Pubns.

Luce, Marnie & Lerner, A. B. Infinity: What Is It? LC 68-56711. (Math Concept Bks). (gr. 3-6). 1969. PLB 3.95g (ISBN 0-8225-0582-7). Lerner Pubns.

Luce, Robert. Legislative Assemblies. LC 73-5617. (American Constitutional & Legal History Ser.). 692p. 1974. Repr. of 1924 ed. lib. bdg. 75.00 (ISBN 0-306-70583-4). Da Capo.

--Legislative Principles. LC 77-148083. (American Constitutional & Legal History Ser). 1971. Repr. of 1930 ed. lib. bdg. 69.50 (ISBN 0-306-70144-8). Da Capo.

--Legislative Problems. LC 76-152834. (American Constitutional & Legal History Ser). 1971. Repr. of 1935 ed. lib. bdg. 75.00 (ISBN 0-306-70153-7). Da Capo.

--Legislative Procedure. LC 72-6113. (American Constitutional & Legal History Ser). 640p. 1973. Repr. of 1922 ed. lib. bdg. 69.50 (ISBN 0-306-70522-2). Da Capo.

Luce, Robert D. Individual Choice Behavior: A Theoretical Analysis. LC 78-25881. (Illus.). 1979. Repr. of 1959 ed. lib. bdg. 18.25x (ISBN 0-313-20778-X, LUIC). Greenwood.

Luce, Robert D. & Raiffa, H. Games & Decisions: Introduction & Critical Survey. LC 57-12295. 1957. 32.95 (ISBN 0-471-55341-7). Wiley.

Luce, T. James, ed. Ancient Writers: Greece & Rome, 2 Vols. LC 82-50612. (YA) 1982. lib. bdg. 110.00 (ISBN 0-684-16595-3). Scribner.

Luce, Willard & Luce, Celia. Lou Gehrig: Iron Man of Baseball. LC 78-103956. (Americans All Ser). (Illus.). (gr. 3-6). 1970. PLB 6.48 o.p. (ISBN 0-8116-4559-2). Garrard.

--Utah. rev. ed. LC 75-24986. (Illus.). (gr. 4). 1980. text ed. 13.00x (ISBN 0-87905-036-5). Peregrine Smith.

Luce, William. Belle of Amherst. (Paperback Ser.). 1978. pap. 4.95 (ISBN 0-395-26253-4). HM.

Lucero. Little Indians' ABC. LC 73-87800. (Illus.). (gr. k-2). 1974. PLB 6.75x (ISBN 0-87783-129-7); pap. 2.95x deluxe ed. (ISBN 0-87783-130-0). Oddo.

Lucey, Dan & Lucey, Rose. Living, Loving Generation. LC 69-17322. (Illus., Orig.). 1969. pap. 1.95 o.p. (ISBN 0-685-07651-2, 80410). Glencoe.

Lucey, Kenneth & Machan, Tibor, eds. Recent Work in Philosophy. LC 82-3741. (APQ Library of Philosophy). 336p. 1983. text ed. 36.95x (ISBN 0-8476-7103-8). Rowman.

Lucey, Rose, jt. auth. see Lucey, Dan.

Lucey, T. Quantitative Techniques: An Instructional Manual. 589p. 1982. pap. text ed. 12.00x (ISBN 0-905435-27-3). Verry.

Luchet, Jean-Pierre-Louis. La Reine de Benni. (Utopias in the Enlightenment Ser.). 114p. (Fr.). 1974. Repr. of 1766 ed. lib. bdg. 38.00x o.p. (ISBN 0-8287-0559-3, 041). Clearwater Pub.

Luchins, Abraham S. & Luchins, Edith H. Revisting Wertheimer's Seminars, 2 vols. Incl. Vol. 1. Value, Social Influence, & Power (ISBN 0-8387-1227-4); Vol. 2. Problems in Social Psychology (ISBN 0-8387-1570-2). LC 72-3525. 1046p. 1978. Set. 65.00 (ISBN 0-686-96685-6); 45.00 ea. Bucknell U Pr.

Luchins, Edith H., jt. auth. see Luchins, Abraham S.

Luchner, Adolf. Crystal-Glass Mosaic. (Illus.). 80p. 1975. 4.75 o.p. (ISBN 0-263-70141-7). Transatlantic.

Luchs, Esther-Martina. Yoga for Children. pap. 4.95 o.p. (ISBN 0-8091-2023-2). Paulist Pr.

Luchsinger, Arlene E., jt. auth. see Jones, Samuel.

Lucia, Nancy, jt. auth. see Abate, Susan.

Lucia, Victor O. Modern Gnathological Concepts. (Illus.). 1983. text ed. 160.00 (ISBN 0-86715-105-6). Quint Pub Co.

Lucian. True History & Lucius or the Ass. Turner, Paul, tr. LC 58-8065. (Midland Bks.: No. 176). (Illus.). 120p. 1958. 5.95x (ISBN 0-253-36090-0); pap. 1.95x o.p. (ISBN 0-253-20176-4). Ind U Pr.

Luciano, Dorothy S. & Vander, Arthur J. Human Anatomy & Physiology: Structure & Function. 2nd ed. (Illus.). 1983. text ed. 28.95 (ISBN 0-07-038962-4, C); instr's. manual 8.00 (ISBN 0-07-038963-2); study guide 9.95 (ISBN 0-07-038964-0). McGraw.

Luciano, Dorothy S., et al. Human Function & Structure. (Illus.). 1978. text ed. 28.95 (ISBN 0-07-038942-X, C); study guide 13.95 (ISBN 0-07-038944-6); inst's manual 14.95 (ISBN 0-07-038943-8). McGraw.

Luciano, Ron & Fisher, David. The Umpire Strikes Back. 1982. 12.95 (ISBN 0-553-05010-9). Bantam.

Lucier, R. J., jt. auth. see Markel, Michael H.

Lucie-Smith, Edward. The Body: Images of the Nude in Art. (Illus.). 1981. 14.98 (ISBN 0-500-23339-X). Thames Hudson.

Lucie-Smith, Edward, intro. by. Masterpieces from the Pompidou Center. (Orig.). 1983. pap. 14.95 (ISBN 0-500-27282-4). Thames Hudson.

Lucie-Smith, Edward, ed. see Browning, Robert.

Lucie-Smith, Edward, jt. ed. see Taylor, Simon W.

Lucio, William H. & McNeil, John D. Supervision: A Synthesis of Thought & Action. 2nd ed. LC 68-30560. (Supervision Curriculum & Methods Ser). (Illus.). 1968. text ed. 14.95 o.p. (ISBN 0-07-038951-9, C). McGraw.

--Supervision in Thought & Action. 3rd ed. (Illus.). 1979. text ed. 22.95 (ISBN 0-07-038952-7, C). McGraw.

Luck, David J. & Ferrell, O. C. Marketing Strategy & Plans. (Illus.). 1979. ref. ed. 26.95 (ISBN 0-13-558254-7). P-H.

Luck, David J., et al. Experiential Exercises in Marketing Research. (Illus.). 192p. 1980. pap. text ed. 12.95 (ISBN 0-13-295220-3). P-H.

Luck, G. Coleman. Bible Book by Book. (Orig.). 1955. pap. 3.95 (ISBN 0-8024-0045-0). Moody.

--Daniel. rev. ed. (Everyman's Bible Commentary Ser). (Orig.). 1969. pap. 4.50 (ISBN 0-8024-2027-3). Moody.

--Ezra & Nehemiah. (Everyman's Bible Commentary Ser.). 1970. pap. 3.95 o.p. (ISBN 0-8024-2015-X). Moody.

--First Corinthians. (Everyman's Bible Commentary). 1967. pap. 4.50 (ISBN 0-8024-2046-X). Moody.

--James, Faith in Action. (Everyman's Bible Commentary Ser.). Orig. Title: James: Christian Faith in Action. 1967. pap. 4.50 (ISBN 0-8024-2059-1). Moody.

--Luke. (Everyman's Bible Commentary Ser.). 1969. pap. 4.50 (ISBN 0-8024-2042-7). Moody.

--Second Corinthians. (Everyman's Bible Commentary Ser). 1968. pap. 4.50 (ISBN 0-8024-2047-8). Moody.

--Zechariah. (Everyman's Bible Commentary Ser.). 1969. pap. 4.50 (ISBN 0-8024-2038-9). Moody.

Luck, James T. Creative Music for the Classroom Teacher. 1970. pap. text ed. 6.95x (ISBN 0-394-30369-5). Phila Bk Co.

Luckenbill, David F. & Best, Joel. Organizing Deviance. (Illus.). 272p. 1982. pap. 14.95 (ISBN 0-13-641605-5). P-H.

Luckert, Karl W. A Navajo Bringing-Home Ceremony: The Claus Chee Sonny Version of Deerway Ajilee. LC 78-59701. (Illus.). xiv, 224p. 1978. pap. 14.95x (ISBN 0-89734-027-2). Mus Northern Ariz.

--Navajo Mountain & Rainbow Bridge Religion. (Illus.). vii, 157p. 1980. pap. 9.95x o.p. (ISBN 0-89734-025-6). Mus Northern Ariz.

Luckett, D. Money & Banking Supplement. 2nd ed. 1981. 2.95 (ISBN 0-07-038958-6). McGraw.

Luckettt, Dudley. Money & Banking. 2nd rev. ed. (Illus.). 1980. text ed. 23.95 (ISBN 0-07-038956-X); instrs' manual 25.00 (ISBN 0-07-038957-8). McGraw.

Luckey, Camilla. You Can Live on Half Your Income. 192p. (Orig.). 1982. mass market pb 3.95 (ISBN 0-310-45582-0). Zondervan.

Luckey, Carl. Old Fishing Lures & Tackle: A Collectors Identification & Value Guide. (Illus.). pap. 14.95 (ISBN 0-89689-018-X). Wallace-Homestead.

Luckey, Carl F. Collecting Antique American Bird Decoys: Identification & Value Guide. (Illus.). 208p. 1983. pap. 14.95 (ISBN 0-89689-043-0). Bks Americana.

--Collector Prints Old & New: Identification & Value Guide. (Illus.). 400p. 1981. pap. 14.95 o.p. (ISBN 0-517-54406-7, Americana). Crown.

--Hummel Figurines & Plates. 4th ed. (Illus.). 300p. 1981. pap. 9.95 o.p. (ISBN 0-517-54405-9, Americana). Crown.

--Hummel Figurines & Plates. 3rd ed. (Illus.). 304p. 1980. pap. 9.95 o.p. (ISBN 0-517-54111-4, Americana). Crown.

--Hummel Figurines & Plates. 2nd ed. (Illus., Orig.). 1979. pap. 8.95 o.p. (ISBN 0-517-53954-3, Americana). Crown.

Luckham, R., ed. Studies of Law in Social Change & Development: Law & Social Enquiry-Case Studies of Research. 20.00 (ISBN 0-686-35903-8); pap. 12.00 (ISBN 0-686-37206-9). Intl Ctr Law.

Luckham, R., jt. ed. see Ghai, Y.

Luckham, R., jt. ed. see Dias, C. J.

Luckham, Robin. Nigerian Military: A Sociological Analysis of Authority & Revolt, 1960-67. (African Studies: No. 4). (Illus.). 1971. 47.50 (ISBN 0-521-08129-7); pap. 14.95x (ISBN 0-521-09882-3). Cambridge U Pr.

Luckhardt, C. G., tr. see Wittgenstein, Ludwig.

Luckiesh, Matthew. Visual Illusions: Their Causes, Characteristics & Applications. (Illus.). 1965. pap. 4.50 (ISBN 0-486-21530-X). Dover.

Lucking, Richard C. Mathematics for Management. LC 80-40127. 1980. 62.95 (ISBN 0-471-27779-7, Pub. by Wiley-Interscience); pap. write for info. (ISBN 0-471-27781-9). Wiley.

Luckingham, Bradford. The Urban Southwest: A Profile History of Albuquerque, El Paso, Phoenix, Tucson. (Illus.). 196p. 1982. 15.00x (ISBN 0-87404-067-1); pap. 10.00x (ISBN 0-87404-068-X). Tex Western.

Luckman, A. Dick, ed. see Sloan, Tod.

Luckmann, Joan & Sorensen, Karen C. Medical-Surgical Nursing: A Psychophysiologic Approach. 2nd ed. LC 77-16973. (Illus.). 2276p. 1980. text ed. 45.00 (ISBN 0-7216-5806-7). Saunders.

Luckmann, Joan, jt. auth. see Sorensen, Karen C.

Luckmann, William H., jt. auth. see Metcalf, Robert L.

Luckock. Simon de Montfort: Reformer & Rebel. 3.38 o.p. (ISBN 0-08-008757-4). Pergamon.

Luckraft, Dorothy, ed. Black Awareness: Implications for Black Patient Care. LC 75-25301. 43p. 1976. pap. text ed. write for info. (ISBN 0-937126-78-0). Am Journal Nur.

Luckwill, Leonard C. Growth Regulators in Group Production. (Studies in Biology: No. 129). 64p. 1980. pap. text ed. 8.95 (ISBN 0-7131-2816-X). E Arnold.

Lucky, Carl F. Depression: Era Glassware. (Identification & Value Guide Ser.). (Illus.). 200p. 1983. pap. 9.95 (ISBN 0-89689-040-6). Bks Americana.

--Hummel Figurines & Plates: A Collectors Identification & Value Guide. 5th ed. (Illus.). 370p. 1983. pap. 9.95 (ISBN 0-89689-042-2). Bks Americana.

Lucky, Luretha F. & Miller, Nancy O. Engineering Learning Through Creativity: Recycling Instructional Resources. 1979. pap. text ed. 10.50 (ISBN 0-8191-0779-4). U Pr of Amer.

Lucky, R. W. & Salz, J. Principles of Data Communication. LC 82-14857. 1983. Repr. of 1968 ed. lib. bdg. p.n.s. (ISBN 0-89874-550-0). Krieger.

Lucky, R. W., jt. ed. see Green, P. E.

Luckyj, George S., ed. & tr. from Ukrainian. Modern Ukrainian Short Stories. LC 72-95387. 228p. 1973. lib. bdg. 8.50 o.p. (ISBN 0-87287-061-8). Ukrainian Acad.

Lucofsky, G., jt. ed. see Cohen, M.

Lucow, Ben. James Shirley. (English Authors Ser.). 1981. lib. bdg. 13.95 (ISBN 0-8057-6716-9, Twayne). G K Hall.

Lucretius. De Rerum Natura. Kenney, Ed, ed. (Cambridge Greek & Latin Classics Ser.: Bk. 3). 42.00 (ISBN 0-521-08142-4); pap. 12.95x (ISBN 0-521-29177-1). Cambridge U Pr.

--De Rerum Natura, Bk. 5. Duff, James D., ed. text ed. 4.95x (ISBN 0-521-05610-1). Cambridge U Pr.

--De Rerum Natura: The Latin Text of Lucretius. Leonard, William E. & Smith, Stanley B., eds. (Illus.). 896p. 1942. text ed. 22.50 (ISBN 0-299-00362-0). U of Wis Pr.

--The Poem on Nature. Sisson, C. H., tr. 210p. 1976. text ed. 14.75x (ISBN 0-85635-115-6, Pub. by Carcanet New Pr England). Humanities.

Ludanyi, Andrew, jt. ed. see Cadzow, John F.

Luddington, John. Antique Silver: A Guide for Would Be Connoisseurs. 1973. 10.00 o.p. (ISBN 0-7207-0497-9). Transatlantic.

Ludeke, John, jt. ed. see Boyd, W. Harland.

Ludford, G. S. S., jt. auth. see Buckmaster, J. D.

Ludig, Sandra G. Between the Lines: Ladies & Letters at the Clark. (Illus.). 39p. 1982. pap. 4.00 (ISBN 0-686-37428-2). S & F Clark.

Ludlam, James E. Informed Consent. LC 78-24495. 96p. (Orig.). 1978. 8.75 o.p. (ISBN 0-87258-243-4, 118153). Am Hospital.

Ludle, Jacqueline. Margaret Mead. (Impact Biography Ser.). (Illus.). (gr. 7 up). 1983. PLB 8.90 (ISBN 0-531-04590-0). Watts.

Ludlow. The Making of the European Monetary System. 1982. text ed. 29.95 (ISBN 0-408-10728-6). Butterworth.

Ludlow, Cynthia B. Historic Easton. (Illus.). 112p. 1979. 17.50 (ISBN 0-686-36701-4). Md Hist.

Ludlow, Daniel H. Companion to Your Study of the Four Gospels. 454p. 1982. pap. 9.95 (ISBN 0-87747-945-3). Deseret Bk.

Ludlow, Fitz H. The Hasheesh Eater: Being Passages from the Life of a Pythagorean. LC 79-12049. pap. 6.95 (ISBN 0-87286-131-7). City Lights.

Ludlow, Margaret. The Trouble with Timothy. (Illus.). 40p. (ps-3). 1983. 5.95 (ISBN 0-910313-00-8). Parker Bro.

Ludlow, Norman H., Jr. Clip Book Number Eight: Kids & Grown-Ups Doing Things. (Illus.). 1982. pap. 12.95x o.p. (ISBN 0-916706-26-5). N H Ludlow.

--Clip Book Number Seven: Family & Small Group Activities. (Illus.). 1982. pap. 12.95x o.p. (ISBN 0-916706-25-7). N H Ludlow.

--Clip Book Number Six of Program & Activity Artwork. (Illus.). 1982. pap. 11.95x o.p. (ISBN 0-916706-27-3). N H Ludlow.

--The Potpourri Clip Book of Line Artwork. (Illus.). 1979. pap. 9.95x (ISBN 0-916706-17-6). N H Ludlow.

Ludlow, Norman, Jr. Potpourri: Number Two Clipbook of Line Artwork. (Illus.). 1982. pap. 10.95 (ISBN 0-916706-28-1). N H Ludlow.

Ludlum, David M. The New Jersey Weather Book. 250p. Date not set. 24.95 (ISBN 0-8135-0915-7); pap. 14.95 (ISBN 0-8135-0940-8). Rutgers U Pr.

Ludlum, Robert. The Bourne Identity. LC 79-23638. 1980. 12.95 o.s.i. (ISBN 0-399-90070-5, Marek). Putnam Pub Group.

--The Gemini Contenders. 1977. pap. 3.95 (ISBN 0-440-12859-5). Dell.

--The Holcroft Covenant. 512p. 1982. pap. 3.95 (ISBN 0-553-20783-0). Bantam.

--The Holcroft Covenant. LC 77-95295. 1978. 10.95 o.s.i. (ISBN 0-399-90001-2, Marek). Putnam Pub Group.

--The Matarese Circle. LC 78-31673. 1979. 12.50 o.s.i. (ISBN 0-399-90043-8, Marek). Putnam Pub Group.

--The Matlock Paper. 384p. 1974. pap. 3.95 (ISBN 0-440-15538-X). Dell.

--The Parsifal Mosaic. 1982. 15.95 (ISBN 0-394-52111-0). Random.

--The Parsifal Mosaic. 1983. pap. 4.50 (ISBN 0-686-43046-8). Bantam.

--The Road to Gandolfo. (General Ser.). 1983. lib. bdg. 15.95 (ISBN 0-8161-3506-1, Large Print Bks). G K Hall.

Ludman, Allan, ed. Guidebook for Field Trips in Southeastern Maine & South Western New Brunswick. (Geological Bulletins). pap. text ed. 2.50 o.p. (ISBN 0-930146-05-0). Queens Coll Pr.

Ludman, Allan, et al. Physical Geology. (Illus.). 576p. 1982. text ed. 27.95x (ISBN 0-07-011510-9). McGraw.

Ludman, Joan, jt. auth. see Mason, Lauris.

Ludman, Joan, jt. ed. see Mason, Lauris.

Ludolf, H. Nouvelle Histoire d'Abissinie ou d'Ethiope. (Bibliotheque Africaine Ser.). 324p. (Fr.). 1974. Repr. of 1684 ed. lib. bdg. 85.00x o.p. (ISBN 0-8287-0560-7, 72-2139). Clearwater Pub.

Ludolphy, Ingetraut. From Luther to Fifteen Eighty: A Pictorial Account. (Illus.). 1977. 15.95 (ISBN 0-570-03264-4, 15-2710). Concordia.

Ludovici, A. Nietzsche & Art. LC 72-148824. (Studies in German Literature, No. 13). 1971. Repr. lib. bdg. 38.95x (ISBN 0-8383-1229-2). Haskell.

Ludovici, Laurence J. The Origins of Language. (Science Survey Ser.). (Illus.). (gr. 5-9). 1965. PLB 5.29 o.p. (ISBN 0-399-60500-2). Putnam Pub Group.

Ludowyk, Evelyn F. Understanding Shakespeare. 1962. 34.50 (ISBN 0-521-05611-X); pap. 11.95 (ISBN 0-521-09242-6). Cambridge U Pr.

Ludvigsen, Karl. Guide to Corvette Speed. 1969. pap. 3.95 o.p. (ISBN 0-8306-2010-9, 2010). TAB Bks.

Ludvigsen, Karl, jt. auth. see Christy, Joe.

Ludwig & Bernal. California Story & Coloring Book. (Illus.). 32p. (Orig.). pap. 2.95 (ISBN 0-930504-01-1). Polaris Pr.

Ludwig, Charles. At the Cross. 1975. pap. 1.25 o.p. (ISBN 0-89129-070-2). Jove Pubns.

Ludwig, Charles H., jt. auth. see Sarkanen, K. V.

Ludwig, D., ed. see SIMS Conference on Epidemiology, Alta, UT, July 8-12, 1974.

Ludwig, Emil. Genius & Character: Shakespeare, Voltaire, Goethe, Balzac. 330p. 1982. Repr. of 1927 ed. lib. bdg. 35.00 (ISBN 0-8495-3267-1). Arden Lib.

Ludwig, Ernest. Applied Process Design for Chemical & Petrochemical Plants, 3 vols. Vol. 1. 1977, 2nd Ed. 42.95x (ISBN 0-87201-755-9); Vol. 2. 1979, 2nd Ed. 42.95x (ISBN 0-87201-753-2); Vol. 3. 42.95 (ISBN 0-87201-754-0). Gulf Pub.

Ludwig, G. Foundations of Quantum Mechanics I. (Texts & Monographs in Physics). (Illus.). 426p. 1983. 48.00 (ISBN 0-387-11683-4). Springer-Verlag.

Ludwig, H., jt. ed. see Steffen, C.

Ludwig, Jan K., ed. Philosophy & Parapsychology. LC 77-91852. 454p. 1978. 16.95 (ISBN 0-87975-075-8); pap. 10.95 (ISBN 0-87975-076-6). Prometheus Bks.

Ludwig, Jurgen. Current Methods of Autopsy Practice. 2nd ed. LC 77-2100. (Illus.). 1979. text ed. 65.00 o.p. (ISBN 0-7216-5804-0). Saunders.

Ludwig, Lyndell. The Shoemaker's Gift. LC 82-73196. (Children's Ser.). (Illus.). 50p. 1983. pap. 4.95 (ISBN 0-916870-53-7). Creative Arts Bk.

--Ts'ao Chung Weighs an Elephant. LC 82-73197. (Children's Ser.). (Illus.). 50p. (Orig.). 1983. pap. 4.95 (ISBN 0-916870-52-9). Creative Arts Bk.

Ludwig, Oswald A. & McCarthy, Willard J. Metalwork Technology & Practice. rev. & 7th ed. (Illus.). (gr. 11-12). 1982. text ed. 20.64 (ISBN 0-87345-104-X); instr's guide 5.28; study guide 6.00. McKnight.

Ludwig, Stephen, jt. auth. see Fleisher, Gary.

Ludwigson, Kathryn R. Edward Dowden. (English Authors Ser.). lib. bdg. 14.95 (ISBN 0-8057-1164-3, Twayne). G K Hall.

Ludy, Andrew. Condominium Ownership: A Buyer's Guide. (Illus.). 128p. 1982. pap. 7.95 (ISBN 0-943912-00-8). Landing Pr.

Ludz, Peter C., ed. Changing Party Elite in East Germany. 1972. 19.95x o.p. (ISBN 0-262-12053-4). MIT Pr.

Ludz, Peter C., et al. Dilemmas of the Atlantic Alliance: Two Germanys, Scandinavia, Canada, Nato & the EEC. LC 75-25737. (Atlantic Institute Studies: No. 1). 1975. 29.95 o.p. (ISBN 0-275-01490-8). Praeger.

Luebbert, William F. The Guide to What's Where in the Apple. 1982. 9.95 (ISBN 0-938222-10-4). Micro Ink.

--What's Where in the Apple? An Atlas to the Apple Computer. 128p. 1981. 14.95 o.p. (ISBN 0-938222-07-4). Micro Ink.

--What's Where in the Apple...Plus...the All New Guide to What's Where. 1982. 24.95 (ISBN 0-938222-09-0). Micro Ink.

Luecke, Gerald, jt. auth. see Cannon, Don L.

Luecke, Jack, et al. Semiconductor Memory Design & Application. (Texas Instruments Electronics Ser.). (Illus.). 352p. 1973. 36.50 o.p. (ISBN 0-07-038975-6, P&RB). McGraw.

Lueder, D. R. Aerial Photographic Interpretation. (Civil Engineering Ser.). 1959. 44.50 o.p. (ISBN 0-07-038990-X, P&RB). McGraw.

Lueders, Edward. The Clam Lake Papers: A Winter in the North Woods. LC 77-7845. 1977. 7.95i o.p. (ISBN 0-06-065312-4, HarpR). Har-Row.

Lueders, Hermine, jt. auth. see Cho, Emily.

Luedke, Ralph D., jt. ed. see Moon, Clarice.

Luedke, Ralph D., jt. ed. see Wright, Gertrude.

Luedtke, Julie. Dare to Love. 1982. 6.95 (ISBN 0-686-84163-8, Avalon). Bouregy.

--Therapy of Love. 1981. pap. 6.95 (ISBN 0-686-84695-8, Avalon). Bouregy.

Luedtke, Peter & Luedtke, Rainer. Your First Business Computer. 250p. 1983. 22.00 (ISBN 0-932376-26-6); pap. 15.00 (ISBN 0-932376-27-4). Digital Pr.

Luedtke, Rainer, jt. auth. see Luedtke, Peter.

Luedtke, Ralph D., jt. ed. see Kuse, James.

Luehrmann, A. & Peckham, H. Hands On BASIC: For the Atari 400 & 800 Computer. 448p. 1983. 22.95 (ISBN 0-07-049177-1). McGraw.

--Hands-On Pascal: For the IBM Personal Computer. 448p. 1983. 22.95 (ISBN 0-07-049176-3). McGraw.

Luehrmann, Arthur & Peckham, Herbert. Apple-Pascal: A Hands-on Approach. (Programming Language Ser.). (Illus.). 384p. 1981. spiral bdg. 18.95 (ISBN 0-07-049171-2, C). McGraw.

Luenberger, David G. Introduction to Dynamic Systems: Theory, Models & Applications. LC 78-12366. 1979. 36.95 (ISBN 0-471-02594-1); solutions manual 6.95x (ISBN 0-471-06081-X). Wiley.

--Introduction to Linear & Nonlinear Programming. LC 72-186209. 1973. text ed. 24.95 (ISBN 0-201-04347-5). A-W.

Luening, R. A. & Mortenson, W. P. Farm Management Handbook. 6th ed. (Illus.). (gr. 9-12). 1979. 19.00 (ISBN 0-8134-2082-2, 2082); text ed. 14.25x. Interstate.

Luessen, Lawrence H., jt. ed. see Kunhardt, Erich E.

Luetje, C., jt. auth. see House.

Luetscher, George D. Early Political Machinery in the United States. LC 70-155356. (Studies in American History & Government Ser.). 1971. Repr. of 1903 ed. lib. bdg. 27.50 (ISBN 0-306-70187-1). Da Capo.

Luey, Beth, tr. see De Rougemont, Denis.

Luff, N. A. D. M. S. Working Atlas of Infrared Spectroscopy. 1972. text ed. 43.50 o.p. (ISBN 0-407-69999-6). Butterworth.

Luffberry, Henry B. A New Manual for Vestrymen. LC 72-75651. 96p. (Orig.). 1972. pap. 1.00 o.p. (ISBN 0-8006-0122-X, 1-122). Fortress.

Luffe, Heinz C. Zur Textkonstitution Afro-Amerikanischer Initiationsliterature. 194p. (Ger.). 1982. write for info. (ISBN 3-8204-5956-1). P Lang Pubs.

Lufkin, Milton T. Henry, a Man of Aroostook: Pioneer in Northern Maine. LC 76-8088. (Illus.). 1976. 10.00 o.p. (ISBN 0-87027-173-3). Cumberland Pr.

Luft, David S. Robert Musil & the Crisis of European Culture, 1880-1942. LC 78-66008. 336p. 1980. 27.50x (ISBN 0-520-03852-5). U of Cal Pr.

Luft, Harold S. Poverty & Health: Economic Causes & Consequences of Health Problems. 288p. 1978. prof ref 22.50x (ISBN 0-88410-515-6). Ballinger Pub.

Luft, Rolf, jt. ed. see Levine, Rachmiel.

Luftig, Milton. Computer Programmer Analyst Trainee. 5th ed. LC 82-4110. 256p. (Orig.). 1982. pap. 8.00 (ISBN 0-668-05310-0, 5310). Arco.

Lug, Sieglinde. Poetic Techniques & Conceptual Elements in Ibn Zaydun's Love Poetry. LC 81-43813. 184p. (Orig.). 1982. lib. bdg. 23.00 (ISBN 0-8191-2515-6); pap. text ed. 10.00 (ISBN 0-8191-2516-4). U Pr of Amer.

Luger, Jack, ed. Kill the Bastards. 1982. 14.95 o.p. (ISBN 0-936062-13-4). MBB Pub.

Luggr, J., jt. ed. see Elbert, R.

Lught, Hans J. Vortex Flow in Nature & Technology. 600p. 1983. 70.00 (ISBN 0-471-86925-2, Pub. by Wiley-Interscience). Wiley.

Lugo, Felix A. Auxiliar De la Taguigrafia Gregg. 1977. 10.00 (ISBN 0-07-039000-2, G). McGraw.

Lugo, James O. & Hershey, Gerald L. Living Psychology. 3rd ed. 564p. 1981. text ed. 22.95 (ISBN 0-02-372250-9). Macmillan.

Lugones, Noevia, tr. see Horowitz, Irving L.

Lugton, Robert C. American Topics: A Reading Vocabulary Text for Speakers of ESL. (Illus.). 1978. pap. text ed. 11.95 (ISBN 0-13-029561-2). P-H.

Luhan, Mabel D. Winter in Taos. (Illus.). 264p. Repr. of 1935 ed. pap. 14.95 (ISBN 0-686-38775-9). Las Palomas.

Luhman, Reid A. The Sociological Outlook. 528p. 1982. pap. text ed. 16.95x (ISBN 0-534-01060-1). Wadsworth Pub.

Luhmann, M. Trust & Power. 228p. 1982. 41.00x o.p. (ISBN 0-913844-14-4, Pub. by Wiley-Interscience); pap. 6.95 o.p. (ISBN 0-913844-12-8). Wiley.

Luhr, William. Raymond Chandler & Film. LC 81-70115. (Illus.). 300p. 1982. 14.95 (ISBN 0-8044-2556-6); pap. text ed. 7.95 (ISBN 0-8044-6447-2). Ungar.

Luhr, William & Lehman, Peter. Authorship & Narrative in the Cinema: Issues in Contemporary Aesthetics & Criticism. LC 76-13887. (Illus.). 1977. 8.95 o.p. (ISBN 0-399-11785-7). Putnam Pub Group.

Luhr, William, jt. auth. see Lehman, Peter.

Lu Hsun. Selected Stories of Lu Hsun. Yang Hsien-Yi & Yang, Gladys, trs. 1977. pap. 4.95 (ISBN 0-393-00848-7, Norton Lib). Norton.

Luick, John F. & Ziegler, William L. Sales Promotion & Modern Merchandising. 1968. pap. text ed. 11.95 (ISBN 0-07-038998-5, C). McGraw.

Luigia La Penta, Barbara, tr. see Ciucci, Giorgio, et al.

Luijpen, W. A. Existential Phenomenology. rev. ed. (Philosophical Ser.: No. 12). 1969. pap. text ed. 10.50x (ISBN 0-391-00705-X). Duquesne.

Luijpen, William A. & Koren, Henry J. Religion & Atheism. LC 73-143295. 1971. text ed. 10.95x (ISBN 0-8207-0133-5). Duquesne.

Luis, Edward San see San Luis, Edward.

Luizzi, Vincent. A Naturalist Theory of Justice: Critical Commentary on, & Selected Readings from, C. I. Lewis' Ethics. LC 80-69055. 120p. (Orig.). 1981. lib. bdg. 19.50 (ISBN 0-8191-1732-3); pap. text ed. 9.00 (ISBN 0-8191-1733-1). U Pr of Amer.

Luk, Charles, pseud. Practical Buddhism. LC 72-91124. 177p. 1973. 5.95 o.p. (ISBN 0-8356-0212-5). Theos Pub Hse.

Luk, Charles. Secrets of Chinese Meditation. (Illus.). 1980. pap. 4.95 (ISBN 0-87728-066-5). Weiser.

Lukach, Joan. Hilla Rebay: In Search of the Spirit in Art. (Illus.). 1983. 30.00 (ISBN 0-8076-1067-4). Braziller.

Lukacs, Eugene. Probability & Mathematical Statistics: An Introduction. 1972. text ed. 23.00 (ISBN 0-12-459850-1). Acad Pr.

Lukacs, Georg. Essays on Realism. Livingstone, Rodney, ed. Fernbach, David, tr. from Ger. 256p. 1981. 22.50x (ISBN 0-262-12088-7). MIT Pr.

--Essays on Thomas Mann. Mitchell, S., tr. from Ger. 169p. Date not set. text ed. price not set (ISBN 0-85036-070-6); pap. text ed. 5.00x (ISBN 0-85036-238-5). Humanities.

--History & Class Consciousness. Livingstone, Rodney, tr. from Ger. 1971. pap. 6.95 (ISBN 0-262-62020-0). MIT Pr.

--The Meaning of Contemporary Realism. 137p. 1980. text ed. 9.50x (ISBN 0-85036-069-2); pap. text ed. 5.25x (ISBN 0-85036-250-4). Humanities.

--Theory of the Novel. Bostock, Anna, tr. from Ger. 1971. pap. 5.95 (ISBN 0-262-62027-8). MIT Pr.

Lukacs, Georg & Pinkus, Theo. Conversations with Lukacs. LC 74-34021. 1975. 9.95x o.p. (ISBN 0-262-16062-5); pap. 4.95 (ISBN 0-262-66044-X). MIT Pr.

Lukacs, John. Philadelphia: Patricians & Philistines, 1900 to 1950. LC 81-15754. (Illus.). 360p. 1982. pap. 9.50 (ISBN 0-89727-044-4). Inst Study Human.

Lukacs, Lajos. The Vatican & Hungary 1846-1878: Reports & Correspondence on Hungary of the Apostolic Nuncios in Vienna. Kormos, Zsofia, tr. 795p. 1981. text ed. 55.00x (ISBN 963-05-2446-5, 41422, Pub. by Kultura Pr Hungary). Humanities.

Lukacs, Laszlo, tr. see Roman, Zoltan.

Lukacs, Paul & Rubens, Jeff. Test Your Play As Declarer. 192p. (Orig.). 1977. pap. 4.95 o.s.i. (ISBN 0-89104-251-2). A & W Pubs.

Lukacs, Paul, jt. auth. see Darvas, Robert.

Lukas, Johannes. Study of the Kanuri Language. LC 68-87331. (African Languages & Linguistics Ser). 1967. 11.25x o.p. (ISBN 0-7129-0146-9). Intl Pubns Serv.

Lukas, P., jt. auth. see Klesnil, M.

Lukas, Richard C. The Strange Allies: The United States & Poland, 1941-1945. LC 77-8585. 1978. 16.50x (ISBN 0-87049-229-2). U of Tenn Pr.

Lukas, Susan. Morgana's Fault. 228p. 1981. 10.95 o.p. (ISBN 0-399-12584-1). Putnam Pub Group.

Lukash, William M. & Johnson, Raymond B., eds. The Systemic Manifestations of Inflammatory Bowel Disease. (Illus.). 368p. 1975. 21.75x o.p. (ISBN 0-398-03242-4). C C Thomas.

Lukashok, Alvin. Communications Satellites: How They Work. (How It Works Ser). (Illus.). (gr. 5-8). 1967. PLB 4.29 o.p. (ISBN 0-399-60102-3). Putnam Pub Group.

Lukasiewicz, J. Elements of Mathematical Logic. 2nd ed. (International Series in Pure & Applied Mathematics: Vol. 31). 1964. 12.10 o.p. (ISBN 0-08-010393-6); pap. inquire for price o.p. (ISBN 0-08-013695-8). Pergamon.

Lukatsky, Debbie, jt. auth. see Tobak, Sandy B.

Luke, jt. auth. see Arnold.

Luke, Ann W., jt. ed. see Cuadra, Carlos.

Luke, Ann W., jt. ed. see Cuadra, Carlos A.

Luke, Ann W., ed. see Cuadra, Carlos A.

Luke, David, tr. see Grimm, Jacob & Grimm, Wilhelm.

Luke, Hugh D. Automation for Productivity. LC 72-5441. 298p. 1972. 18.00 (ISBN 0-471-55400-6, Pub. by Wiley). Krieger.

Luke, Larry S., jt. ed. see Barber, Thomas K.

Luke, Mary M. Gloriana: The Years of Elizabeth I. (Illus.). 788p. 1973. 12.50 o.p. (ISBN 0-698-10543-5, Pub. by Coward). Putnam Pub Group.

--The Nonsuch Lure. LC 76-12605. 288p. 1976. 9.95 (ISBN 0-698-10750-0, Coward). Putnam Pub Group.

Luke, Roice D. & Bauer, Jeffrey C. Issues in Health Economics. LC 81-20674. 624p. 1982. text ed. 34.95 (ISBN 0-89443-381-4). Aspen Systems.

Luke, Roice D. & Krueger, Janelle. Quality Assurance. 400p. 1983. write for info. (ISBN 0-89443-930-8). Aspen Systems.

Luke, Timothy W., jt. auth. see Levine, Victor T.

Lukeman, Tim. Koren. LC 79-7692. (Science Fiction Ser.). 192p. 1981. 10.95 o.p. (ISBN 0-385-15239-6). Doubleday.

--Rajan. 192p. 1982. pap. 2.25 (ISBN 0-441-70801-3, Pub. by Ace Science Fiction). Ace Bks.

Luken, Ralph A. Preservation vs. Development: An Economic Analysis of San Francisco Bay Wetlands. LC 76-2907. (Special Studies). (Illus.). 176p. 1976. 27.95 o.p. (ISBN 0-275-56590-4). Praeger.

Lukenbill, W. Bernard & Adams, Elaine P., eds. Media & the Young Adult: A Selected Bibliography, 1973-1977. LC 81-7977. 344p. 1981. pap. 10.00 (ISBN 0-8389-3264-9). ALA.

Lukens, Rebecca J. A Critical Handbook of Children's Literature. 2nd ed. 1981. pap. text ed. 9.95x (ISBN 0-673-15504-8). Scott F.

Luker, A. J. & Luker, H. S. Laboratory Exercises in Zoology. 268p. 1971. 9.95 o.p. (ISBN 0-408-57850-5). Butterworth.

Luker, Genevo Jo W., jt. auth. see Luker, William A.

Luker, H. S., jt. auth. see Luker, A. J.

Luker, Nicholas J. Alexander Kuprin. (World Authors Ser.). 1978. lib. bdg. 15.95 (ISBN 0-8057-6322-8, Twayne). G K Hall.

Luker, William A. & Luker, Genevo Jo W. Hard Choices: The Economics of the American Free Enterprise System. 2nd ed. (Illus.). 388p. (gr. 10-12). 1981. 17.95 (ISBN 0-88408-143-5); school price 14.98 (ISBN 0-88408-142-7). Sterling Swift.

Lukes, Dahlard L. Differential Equation: Classical to Controlled. (Mathematics in Science and Engineering Ser.). 1982. 37.50 (ISBN 0-12-459980-X). Acad Pr.

Lukes, S. Development of the Sociology of Knowledge. (Studies in Sociology). Date not set. pap. text ed. price not set (ISBN 0-391-01130-8). Humanities.

Lukes, Steven. Power: A Radical View. (Studies in Sociology). 64p. 1975. pap. 5.75x (ISBN 0-333-16672-8). Humanities.

Lukes, Steven, ed. see Durkheim, Emile.

Lukes, Steven, jt. ed. see Hollis, Martin.

Lukevics, E. & Skorova, A. E. Thiophene Derivatives of Group IV B Elements. (Sulpher Reports: Vol. 2, No. 5). 38p. 1982. 24.50 (ISBN 3-7186-0133-8). Harwood Academic.

Lukman, Mphahlele K. The Critical Issues of Skin Colour: A Treatise on the Sociological, Economic & Political Reality of Blacks in a White Society. 300p. 1982. text ed. 15.95 (ISBN 0-9602660-0-3). M Lukman.

Lukoff, Fred. An Introductory Course in Korean. 518p. (Orig.). 1983. pap. text ed. 20.00 (ISBN 0-295-95948-7). U of Wash Pr.

Lukovich, I. Electric Foil Fencing. (Illus.). 1978. 14.00 (ISBN 0-912728-95-7). Newbury Bks.

Lukovich, Istvan. Electric Foil Fencing. (Illus.). 1971. 22.50x (ISBN 0-392-05526-0, SpS). Sportshelf.

Lukowski, Susan, ed. see Shosteck, Robert.

Luks, Allan. Will America Sober Up? LC 82-73964. 192p. 1983. 13.41 (ISBN 0-8070-2154-7). Beacon Pr.

Lu K'Uan Yu, see Luk, Charles, pseud.

Luling, Virginia. Indians of the North American Plains. LC 79-65843. (Surviving Peoples Ser.). PLB 12.68 (ISBN 0-382-06303-1). Silver.

Lulow, JoAnn. Your Career in the Fashion Industry. LC 78-12724. (Arco Career Guidance Ser.). 1979. lib. bdg. 7.95 (ISBN 0-668-04613-9); pap. 4.50 (ISBN 0-668-04620-1). Arco.

Lum, Doman & Zuniga-Martinez, Maria. Ethnic Minority Social Work Practice: Individual, Family & Community Dimensions. 1983. pap. text ed. price not set (ISBN 0-8391-1787-6, 19585). Univ Park.

Lum, L. F., jt. ed. see Gould, R. G.

Lum, Peter. Growth of Civilization in East Asia. LC 73-77311. (Illus.). (gr. 8 up). 1969. 12.95 (ISBN 0-87599-144-0). S G Phillips.

--Six Centuries in East Asia: China, Japan & Korea from the 14th Century to 1912. LC 72-12582. (Illus.). 288p. 1973. 12.95 (ISBN 0-87599-183-1). S G Phillips.

Lumb, Fred A. What Every Woman Should Know About Finances. 1979. pap. 2.25 o.p. (ISBN 0-425-04132-8). Berkley Pub.

Lumb, Mitchell & Mitchell, Dobbie. Handbook of Surgical Diathermy. 2nd ed. 142p. 1978. 25.00 (ISBN 0-7236-0449-5). Wright-PSG.

Lumbra, Elaine, ed. More Hoosier Cooking. LC 82-47959. 256p. 1982. 12.95 (ISBN 0-253-15430-8). Ind U Pr.

Lumbreras, Luis G. The Peoples & Cultures of Ancient Peru. LC 74-2104. (Illus.). 248p. 1974. 19.95 o.p. (ISBN 0-87474-146-7); pap. 12.50x (ISBN 0-87474-151-3). Smithsonian.

Lumely, James E. Real Estate Psychology: The Dynamics of Successful Selling. LC 81-10473. (Real Estate for Professional Practioners Ser.). 221p. 1981. 17.95 (ISBN 0-471-09610-5, Pub. by Wiley-Interscience). Wiley.

Lumiansky, R. M. & Mills, David. The Chester Mystery Cycle: Essays & Documents. LC 82-1838. vii, 321p. 1982. 40.00x (ISBN 0-8078-1522-5). U of NC Pr.

Lumiere, Cornel & World Tennis Magazine Editors. Book of Tennis: How to Play the Game. (Illus.). 1970. pap. 3.95 (ISBN 0-448-01948-5, G&D). Putnam Pub Group.

Lumiere, Richard, jt. auth. see Cook, Stephani.

Lumisden, Andrew. A Collection of Some of the Rarest & Most Valuable Engravings of the Antiquites & Ruins of Rome. (Illus.). 103p. 1983. 257.85 (ISBN 0-86650-062-6). Gloucester Art.

Lumley, Benjamin. Reminiscences of the Opera. LC 76-15185. (Music Reprint Ser.). 448p. 1976. Repr. of 1864 ed. 39.50 (ISBN 0-306-70842-6). Da Capo.

Lumley, Brian. In the Moons of Borea. (Orig.). 1979. pap. 1.75 o.s.i. (ISBN 0-515-05125-X). Jove Pubns.

--Khai of Ancient Khem. 1980. pap. 1.95 o.p. (ISBN 0-425-04528-5). Berkley Pub.

Lumley, J. S. Surgical Review, No. 1. 407p. pap. text ed. 29.95 o.p. (ISBN 0-272-79525-9). Univ Park.

Lumley, John L., jt. auth. see Tennekes, Hendrik.

Lumley, John L., ed. see Monin, A. S. & Yaglom, A. M.

Lumley, Kathryn W. Monkeys & Apes. LC 82-12779. (New True Bks.). (Illus.). (gr. k-4). 1982. PLB 9.25g (ISBN 0-516-01633-4). Childrens.

Lummis, Charles F. My Friend Will. 1972. 3.50 (ISBN 0-87516-161-8). De Vorss.

Lumpkin, Katharine D. The Making of a Southerner. LC 70-135602. 247p. Repr. of 1947 ed. lib. bdg. 15.00 o.p. (ISBN 0-8371-5194-5, LUMS). Greenwood.

Lumpkin, Kirk D. Co-Hearing. 64p. 1983. pap. 3.50 (ISBN 0-9608438-0-9). ZYGA.

Lumpkin, Thomas A. & Plucknett, Donald L. Azolla As an Aquatic Green Manure: Use & Management in Crop Production. (Tropical Agriculture Ser.: No. 15). 1982. lib. bdg. 20.00 (ISBN 0-89158-451-X). Westview.

Lumpkin, William L. A Chronicle of Christian Heritage: Dover Baptist Association, 1783-1983. 145p. (Orig.). 1983. pap. text ed. 7.95 (ISBN 0-931804-11-6). Skipworth Pr.

Lumpp, D., jt. auth. see Kolb, R.

Lumpuy, Luis B., jt. auth. see Munoz, Lopez A.

Lumsden, Charles J. & Wilson, Edward O. Promethean Fire: Reflections on the Origin of Mind. (Illus.). 256p. 1983. 17.50 (ISBN 0-674-71445-8). Harvard U Pr.

Lumsden, D. Barry, ed. The Older Adult as Learner: Aspects of Educational Gerontology. (Illus.). 400p. Date not set. text ed. 24.50 (ISBN 0-89116-291-7). Hemisphere Pub.

Lumsden, George J. How to Succeed in Middle Management. 208p. 1983. 14.95 (ISBN 0-8144-5757-6). Am Mgmt.

Lumsden, W. H., et al, eds. Advances in Parasitology, Vol. 19. (Serial Publication). 224p. 1982. 39.50 (ISBN 0-12-031719-2). Acad Pr.

--Advances in Parasitology, Vol. 20. (Serial Publication). 1982. 58.50 (ISBN 0-12-031720-6). Acad Pr.

Luna. Aquarius Woman, 1981. 96p. (Orig.). 1980. pap. 1.50 o.p. (ISBN 0-523-41045-X). Pinnacle Bks.

--Aries Woman, 1981. 96p. (Orig.). 1980. pap. 1.50 o.p. (ISBN 0-523-41035-2). Pinnacle Bks.

--Cancer Woman, 1981. 96p. (Orig.). 1980. pap. 1.50 o.p. (ISBN 0-523-41038-7). Pinnacle Bks.

--Capricorn Woman, 1981. 96p. (Orig.). 1980. pap. 1.50 o.p. (ISBN 0-523-41044-1). Pinnacle Bks.

--Gemini Woman, 1981. 96p. (Orig.). 1980. pap. 1.50 o.p. (ISBN 0-523-41037-9). Pinnacle Bks.

--Leo Woman, 1981. 96p. (Orig.). 1980. pap. 1.50 o.p. (ISBN 0-523-41039-5). Pinnacle Bks.

--Libra Woman, 1981. 96p. (Orig.). 1980. pap. 1.50 o.p. (ISBN 0-523-41041-7). Pinnacle Bks.

--Pisces Woman, 1981. 96p. (Orig.). 1980. pap. 1.50 o.p. (ISBN 0-523-41046-8). Pinnacle Bks.

--Sagittarius Woman, 1981. 96p. (Orig.). 1980. pap. 1.50 o.p. (ISBN 0-523-41043-3). Pinnacle Bks.

--Scorpio Woman, 1981. 96p. (Orig.). 1980. pap. 1.50 o.p. (ISBN 0-523-41042-5). Pinnacle Bks.

--Taurus Woman, 1981. 96p. (Orig.). 1980. pap. 1.50 o.p. (ISBN 0-523-41036-0). Pinnacle Bks.

--Virgo Woman, 1981. 96p. (Orig.). 1980. pap. 1.50 o.p. (ISBN 0-523-41040-9). Pinnacle Bks.

Luna, Lee G., jt. auth. see Thompson, Samuel W.

Lunar Science Symposium on Planetary Cratering Mechanics, Flagstaff, Ariz., 1976. Impact & Explosion Cratering, Planetary & Terrestrial Implications: Proceedings. Roddy, D. J., et al, eds. LC 77-24753. 900p. 1978. 150.00 (ISBN 0-08-022050-9). Pergamon.

Lunati, Rinaldo. Book Selection: Principles & Practice. Marulli, Luciana, tr. LC 75-2349. 1975. 10.00 (ISBN 0-8108-0846-3). Scarecrow.

Lunch, Lydia & Cervenka, Exene. Adulterers Anonymous. LC 82-48019. 96p. 1982. pap. 6.95 (ISBN 0-394-62412-2, E826, Ever). Grove.

Lunch, Richard L., jt. ed. see Lynch, R. L.

Lund, C. & Anderson, E. Computer Graphing Experiments One: Algebra One & Algebra Two. (Computer Graphing Experiments Ser.). (gr. 9-12). 1982. Binder & Diskettes 72.00 (ISBN 0-201-23465-3, Sch Div). A-W.

--Computer Graphing Experiments Three: Conic Sections. (Computer Graphing Experiments Ser.). (gr. 10-12). 1982. binder, worksheets & diskettes 72.00 (ISBN 0-201-23475-0, Sch Div); tchr's ed. 3.32 (ISBN 0-201-42670-6). A-W.

Lund, Candida. Coming of Age. 1982. 12.95 (ISBN 0-88347-146-9). Thomas More.

Lund, Charles. Computer Math Games. (Computer Math Games Ser.). (gr. 1-9). 1982. Vol. 1. 72.00 (ISBN 0-201-23561-7, Sch Div); Vol. 2. 72.00 (ISBN 0-201-23562-5); Vol. 3. 72.00 (ISBN 0-201-23563-3); Vol. 4. 72.00 (ISBN 0-201-23564-1); Vol. 5. 52.00 (ISBN 0-201-23565-X); Vol. 6. 72.00 (ISBN 0-201-23566-8); Vol. 7. 60.00 (ISBN 0-201-23567-6). A-W.

Lund, Charles & Anderson, E. Computer Graphing Experiments: Trigonometric Functions. (Computer Graphing Experiments Ser.). (gr. 10-12). 1982. Binder, worsheets & diskettes 72.00 (ISBN 0-201-23470-X, Sch Div). A-W.

Lund, Dale. All About Tarantulas. (Illus.). 1977. 9.95 (ISBN 0-87666-909-7, PS-749). TFH Pubns.

Lund, Doris. Eric. LC 74-7061. 1974. 13.41i (ISBN 0-397-01046-X). Har-Row.

--Patchwork Clan. 1983. pap. 3.50 (ISBN 0-440-17035-4). Dell.

Lund, Duane R. Nature's Bounty for Your Take. 1982. 6.95 (ISBN 0-934860-20-3). Adventure Pubns.

Lund, H. F. Industrial Pollution Control Handbook. 1971. 65.95 (ISBN 0-07-039095-9, P&RB). McGraw.

Lund, Judy. Pearl That Changes a Life. (Arch Bks: Set 7). (Illus., Orig.). (ps-4). 1970. pap. 0.89 (ISBN 0-570-06049-4, 591165). Concordia.

Lund, Marsha M. Indian Jewelry: Fact & Fantasy. LC 76-5401. (Illus.). 1976. pap. 6.95 (ISBN 0-87364-052-7, Paladin Press). Paladin Pr.

Lund, Morten. Eastward in Five Sounds: Cruising from New York to Nantucket. 1971. 10.00 o.s.i. (ISBN 0-8027-0338-0). Walker & Co.

--The Skier's Bible: A Complete Guide to the Sport of Skiing-Eastern & Western. rev. ed. LC 77-164722. 176p. 1972. pap. 4.95 (ISBN 0-385-04733-9). Doubleday.

Lund, Morten & Gillen, Bob. The Ski Book. LC 82-72066. (Illus.). 1982. 22.95 (ISBN 0-87795-430-5). Arbor Hse.

Lund, Morten & Williams, Bea. The Snowmobiler's Bible. LC 73-18519. (Illus.). 192p. 1974. pap. 4.50 (ISBN 0-385-06799-2). Doubleday.

Lund, Nancy J. & Duchan, Judith F. Assessing Children's Language in Naturalistic Contexts. 368p. 1983. 21.95 (ISBN 0-13-049668-5). P-H.

Lund, Philip R. Sales Reports, Records & Systems. 97p. 1979. text ed. 26.00x (ISBN 0-566-02125-0). Gower Pub Ltd.

Lund, Preben. Generation of Precision Artwork for Printed Circuit Boards. LC 77-12388. 1978. 64.95 (ISBN 0-471-99587-8, Pub. by Wiley-Interscience). Wiley.

Lund, Ragnar, ed. Scandinavian Adult Education: Denmark, Finland, Norway, Sweden. Repr. of 1949 ed. lib. bdg. 17.75x (ISBN 0-8371-3979-1, LUSA). Greenwood.

Lund, Raymond D. Development & Plasticity of the Brain: An Introduction. (Illus.). 1978. text ed. 24.95x (ISBN 0-19-502307-2); pap. text ed. 14.95x (ISBN 0-19-502308-0). Oxford U Pr.

Lund, Steven. James Joyce: Letters, Manuscripts & Photographs at Southern Illinois University. LC 82-50414. 170p. 1983. 18.50 (ISBN 0-87875-253-6). Whitston Pub.

Lundahl, Mats. Peasants & Poverty. LC 78-11918. 1979. 37.50x o.p. (ISBN 0-312-59994-3). St Martin.

Lundberg, Ferdinand. Imperial Hearst: A Social Biography. Repr. of 1936 ed. lib. bdg. 17.00x (ISBN 0-8371-2963-X, LUIH). Greenwood.

--The Treason of the People. LC 73-19114. 370p. 1974. Repr. of 1954 ed. lib. bdg. 19.00x (ISBN 0-8371-7307-8, LUTP). Greenwood.

Lundberg, George A. Foundations of Sociology. LC 79-9742. (Illus.). 1979. Repr. of 1964 ed. lib. bdg. 17.75x (ISBN 0-313-21264-3, LUFS). Greenwood.

Lundberg, George D. Using the Clinical Laboratory in Medical Decision Making. 1983. text ed. 30.00 (ISBN 0-89189-164-1, 45-9-013-00). Am Soc Clinical.

Lundberg, Knud. The Olympic Hope. 9.95 o.p. (ISBN 0-392-15344-0, SpS). Sportshelf.

Lundberg, Margaret J. The Incomplete Adult. LC 74-67. (Illus.). 245p. 1974. lib. bdg. 27.50 (ISBN 0-8371-7362-0, LUA/). Greenwood.

Lundbergh, Holger, tr. from Swedish. Great Swedish Fairy Tales. LC 73-132364. (Illus.). 224p. (gr. 4-6). 1973. 14.95 o.p. (ISBN 0-440-03043-9, Sey Lawr); pap. 10.95 (ISBN 0-440-03041-2). Delacorte.

Lundblad, R. L., et al, eds. The Chemistry & Biology of Heparin. (Developments in Biochemistry Ser.: Vol. 12). 1981. 91.50 (ISBN 0-444-00445-9). Elsevier.

--Chemistry & Biology of Thrombin. LC 77-76907. 1977. 49.95 (ISBN 0-250-40160-6). Ann Arbor Science.

Lunde, Erik S. Horace Greeley. (United States Authors Ser.). 1981. lib. bdg. 10.95 (ISBN 0-8057-7343-6, Twayne). G K Hall.

Lunde, Peter J. Solar Thermal Engineering: Space Heating & Hot Water Systems. LC 79-15389. 1980. deluxe ed. 37.95 (ISBN 0-471-03085-6). Wiley.

Lundeen, Gerald W., jt. auth. see Davis, Charles H.

Lundeen, Richard. Hunter's Orange. 208p. 1982. pap. 1.75 (ISBN 0-910937-02-8). Laranmark.

Lundegren, Herberta M., jt. auth. see Farrell, Patricia.

Lundell, Laila. The Complete Book of Weaving. (Illus.). 1983. 30.00 (ISBN 0-8038-1280-9). Hastings.

Lundell, Torborg. Lars Ahlin. LC 76-40314. (World Authors Ser.). 1977. lib. bdg. 15.95 (ISBN 0-8057-6270-1, Twayne). G K Hall.

Lundgaard, Kris, jt. auth. see Bailey, T. E.

Lundgren, Charles, ed. see Duroska, Lud.

Lundgren, Earl F., et al. Supervision. 178p. 1978. text ed. 14.95 (ISBN 0-471-87704-2); tchr's ed. 4.00 (ISBN 0-471-87705-0). Wiley.

Lundgren, Hal. Earl Campbell: The Texas Tornado, Sports Stars. LC 81-6137. (Illus.). 48p. (gr. 2-8). 1981. PLB 7.95 (ISBN 0-516-04316-1); pap. 2.50 (ISBN 0-516-44316-X). Childrens.

Lundgren, R. F. Lundgren's Handbook on California Arrest, Search & Seizure Rules. 2nd ed. LC 81-836893. 1982. 8.00x (ISBN 0-910874-53-0). Legal Bk Co.

Lundgren, Sheila, jt. auth. see Muyskens, Judith A.

Lundin, Frank E., jt. ed. see Chiazze, Leonard, Jr.

Lundin, Robert W. An Objective Psychology of Music. 2nd ed. 1967. 22.95 (ISBN 0-471-07027-0). Wiley.

--Personality: A Behavioral Analysis. 2nd ed. (Illus.). 480p. 1974. text ed. 26.95x (ISBN 0-02-372670-9). Macmillan.

--Theories & Systems of Psychology. 2nd ed. 1979. text ed. 19.95x (ISBN 0-669-01915-1). Heath.

Lundkvist, Artur. Agadir. Smith, William Jay & Sjoberg, Leif, trs. from Swedish. LC 80-15978. (International Poetry Ser.: Vol. 2). (Illus.). xiii, 57p. 1979. 12.95x (ISBN 0-8214-0444-X, 82-83343); pap. 7.95 (ISBN 0-8214-0561-6, 82-83350). Ohio U Pr.

--The Talking Tree: Poems in Prose. Wormuth, Diana, tr. 240p. 1982. 9.95 (ISBN 0-686-83165-9); pap. 5.95 (ISBN 0-8425-2103-8). Brigham.

Lundquist, James. Chester Himes. LC 75-42864. (Literature & Life Ser.). 170p. 1976. 11.95 (ISBN 0-8044-2561-2). Ungar.

--J. D. Salinger. LC 78-4301. (Literature and Life Ser.). 1978. 11.95 (ISBN 0-8044-2560-4); pap. 4.95 (ISBN 0-8044-6452-9). Ungar.

--Kurt Vonnegut. LC 76-15654. (Literature and Life Ser.). 1977. 11.95 (ISBN 0-8044-2564-7); pap. 4.95 (ISBN 0-8044-6458-8). Ungar.

--Sinclair Lewis. LC 72-76774. (Literature and Life Ser.). 11.95 (ISBN 0-8044-2562-0). Ungar.

--Theodore Dreiser. LC 73-84600. (Literature & Life Ser.). 150p. 1974. 11.95 (ISBN 0-8044-2563-9). Ungar.

Lundquist, Lennart. The Party & the Masses. LC 82-8505. 336p. 1982. lib. bdg. 29.50 (ISBN 0-941320-03-0). Transnatl Pubs.

Lundquist, M. Thimble Treasury. 1975. 9.95 (ISBN 0-87069-123-6). Wallace-Homestead.

Lundsgaarde, Henry P. Murder in Space City: A Cultural Analysis of Houston Homicide Patterns. (Illus.). 1977. pap. text ed. 7.95x (ISBN 0-19-502984-4). Oxford U Pr.

Lundsgaarde, Henry P., ed. Land Tenure in Oceania. LC 73-90854. (Association for Social Anthropology in Oceania Monographs: No. 2). 320p. 1974. text ed. 15.00x (ISBN 0-8248-0321-3). UH Pr.

Lundsted, Betty. Transits: The Time of Your Life. 1980. pap. 7.95 (ISBN 0-87728-503-9). Weiser.

Lundstedt, Sven B. & Colglazier, E. William, eds. Managing Innovation: The Social Dimensions of Creativity, Invention & Technology. 260p. 29.50 (ISBN 0-686-84788-1). Work in Amer.

Lundsteen, S. Children Learn to Communicate: Language Arts Through Creative Problem Solving. (Illus.). 1976. ref. ed. 24.95 (ISBN 0-13-131888-8); Ideas Into Practice companion guide 12.95 (ISBN 0-13-449231-5). P-H.

Lundsteen, Sara & Bernstein-Tarrow, Norma. Guiding Young Children's Learning. (Illus.). 528p. 1981. text ed. 22.50 (ISBN 0-07-039105-X, C). Activities & Resources 13.95 (ISBN 0-07-039108-4). McGraw.

Lundsteen, Sara W., jt. auth. see Tarrow, Norma B.

Lundstrom, ed. Pediatric Echocardiography: Cross Sectional, M-Mode & Doppler. 1980. 68.00 (ISBN 0-444-80262-2). Elsevier.

Lundstrom, G., et al, eds. Industrial Robots: A Survey Details of Construction, Performance, Prices & Applications. (Illus.). 176p. 1972. pap. text ed. 52.20x o.p. (ISBN 0-685-40729-2). Scholium Intl.

Lundstrom, John B. The First South Pacific Campaign: Pacific Fleet Strategy, December 1941-June 1942. LC 76-23507. 1976. 14.50 o.p. (ISBN 0-87021-185-4). Naval Inst Pr.

Lunduist, Par. Color Graphics. (Illus.). 188p. 1980. 29.95 (ISBN 0-240-51046-1). Focal Pr.

Lundy, Carl P., jt. auth. see Keir, Jack.

Lundy, Carl P., jt. auth. see Keir, Jack C.

Lundy, Eileen, jt. auth. see Howard, C. Jeriel.

Lundy, Kathryn R. Women View Librarianship: Nine Perspectives. LC 80-23611. (ACRL Publications in Librarianship: No. 41). 108p. 1980. pap. 8.00 (ISBN 0-8389-3251-7). ALA.

Lungberg, Madeleine. Scandinavian Cooking. (Illus.). 1976. pap. 4.95 o.p. (ISBN 0-517-52619-0). Crown.

Lungina, Tatiana. Wolf Messing-Chelovek-Zagadka: Wolf Messing-A Mystery-Man. (Illus.). 270p. (Rus.). 1982. pap. 12.00 (ISBN 0-938920-12-X). Hermitage MI.

Lunin, Lois F., ed. Health Sciences & Services: A Guide to Information Sources. LC 77-80614. (Management Information Guide Ser.: No. 36). 1979. 42.00x (ISBN 0-8103-0836-3). Gale.

Lunin, Lois F., et al, eds. see American Society for Information Science, 44th, 1981.

Lunk, William A. The Rough-Winged Swallow Stelgidopteryx Ruficollis (Viellot) A Study Based on Its Breeding Biology in Michigan. (Illus.). 155p. 1962. 6.00 (ISBN 0-686-35790-6). Nuttall Ornithological.

Lunn, Arnold. Spanish Rehearsal: An Eye Witness Account of the Spanish Civil War. LC 72-85731. 1975. 8.95 (ISBN 0-8159-6819-1). Devin.

Lunn, Eugene. Prophet of Community: The Romantic Socialism of Gustav Landauer. LC 70-186105. 1973. 37.50x (ISBN 0-520-02207-6). U of Cal Pr.

Lunn, Janet. The Root Cellar. 256p. (gr. 5-7). 1983. 12.95 (ISBN 0-684-17855-9). Scribner.

Lunn, Kenneth, ed. Hosts, Immigrants & Minorities: Historical Responses to Newcomers in British Society 1870-1914. 1980. 26.00 (ISBN 0-312-39238-9). St Martin.

Lunn, Kenneth & Thurlow, Richard C., eds. British Fascism: Essays on the Radical Right in Inter-War Britain. LC 79-21249. 1980. 26.00 (ISBN 0-312-10130-9). St Martin.

Lunneborg & Abbott. Applications of Basic Structure. Date not set. price not set (ISBN 0-444-00753-9). Elsevier.

Lunny, Robert M. Early Maps of North America. (Illus.). 48p. 1961. pap. 4.00 (ISBN 0-686-81821-0). NJ Hist Soc.

Lunt, Paul S., jt. auth. see Warner, W. Lloyd.

Lunt, Peter. Udo Fahrt Nach Koln. LC 73-20464. (Ger). 1971. pap. text ed. 6.72 (ISBN 0-395-11058-0, 2-34500). HM.

Lunt, R. M. Handbook of Ultrasonic B-Scanning in Medicine. LC 77-22257. (Techniques of Measurement in Medicine Ser.: No. 1). (Illus.). 1978. 34.95 (ISBN 0-521-21753-9); pap. 11.95x (ISBN 0-521-29264-6). Cambridge U Pr.

Lunt, W. E. Financial Relations of the Papacy with England to 1327. 1967. Repr. of 1939 ed. 20.00X (ISBN 0-910956-13-8). Medieval Acad.

--Financial Relations of the Papacy with England, 1327-1534. 1962. 25.00X (ISBN 0-910956-48-0). Medieval Acad.

Lunz, Mary E. Organization & Communication in Health Care. 420p. 1983. text ed. write for info (ISBN 0-914904-69-8). Health Admin Pr.

Luoma, Gary A. Accounting Information in Managerial Decision-Making for Small & Medium Manufacturers. 87p. 7.95 (ISBN 0-86641-032-5, 6742). Natl Assn Accts.

Luomala, Katherine. Hula Ki'i: Hawaiian Puppetry. 1983. 12.95 (ISBN 0-939154-30-7); pap. 7.95 (ISBN 0-939154-31-5). Inst Polynesian.

Luongo, C. Paul. America's Best One Hundred. LC 79-91375. (Illus.). 256p. 1980. 10.95 o.p. (ISBN 0-8069-0178-0); lib. bdg. 9.29 o.p. (ISBN 0-8069-0179-9). Sterling.

Lupatelli, Anthony. Lupatelli's Favorite Nursery Tales. LC 77-73192. (Illus.). (gr. k-6). 1977. 4.95 o.p. (ISBN 0-448-14300-3, G&D); PLB 5.94 o.p. (ISBN 0-448-13065-3). Putnam Pub Group.

--One Hundred One Favorite Nursery Rhymes. LC 76-6816. 64p. (gr. 1-5). 1976. 4.95 o.p. (ISBN 0-448-12578-1, G&D). Putnam Pub Group.

Luper, Albert T., jt. auth. see Helm, Eugene.

Luper, Harold L. & Mulder, Robert L. Stuttering: Therapy for Children. 1964. text ed. 17.95 (ISBN 0-13-858985-2). P-H.

Lupis, C. H. Chemical Thermodynamics of Materials. 608p. 1982. 75.00 (ISBN 0-444-00713-X, North Holland). Elsevier.

Lupoff, Richard. Buck Rogers in the Twenty Fifth Century. 1978. pap. 1.95 o.s.i. (ISBN 0-440-10843-8). Dell.

--Stroka Prospekt. Disch, Thomas M., ed. LC 82-19269. (Singularities Ser.). (Illus.). 48p. (Orig.). 1982. 35.00 (ISBN 0-915124-72-6); pap. 10.00 (ISBN 0-915124-73-4). Toothpaste.

Lupoff, Richard A. Space War Blues. 15.00 (ISBN 0-8398-2596-X, Gregg). G K Hall.

Lupton, Kenneth. Mungo Park: The African Traveler. (Illus.). 1979. 32.50x (ISBN 0-19-211749-1). Oxford U Pr.

Lupton, Martha. They Tell a Story. LC 74-167052. vi, 553p. 1972. Repr. of 1940 ed. 37.00x (ISBN 0-8103-3112-8). Gale.

Lupton, Mary. Fantasy at Midnight. 1982. 6.95 (ISBN 0-686-84165-4, Avalon). Bouregy.

--Night Glow. 1982. pap. 6.95 (ISBN 0-686-84745-8, Avalon). Bouregy.

Lupus, Peter & Homola, Samuel. Peter Lupus' Guide to Radiant Health & Beauty: Mission Possible for Women. (Illus.). 1977. 14.95 o.p. (ISBN 0-13-661884-7, Parker). P-H.

Lurcat, Jean, et al. The Book of Tapestry: History & Technique. (Illus.). 1978. 40.00 (ISBN 0-670-18015-7, The Vendome Pr.). Viking Pr.

Lurch, Norman E. Fundamentals of Electronics. 3rd ed. LC 79-18696. 601p. 1981. text ed. 27.95 (ISBN 0-471-03494-0); solution manual 8.00 (ISBN 0-471-03716-8). Wiley.

Luria, A. R. The Mind of a Mnemonist: A Little Book About a Vast Memory. Solotaroff, Lynn, tr. from Rus. LC 76-11237. 1976. pap. 3.95 o.p. (ISBN 0-8092-8007-8). Contemp Bks.

Luria, Alexander R. Language & Cognition. LC 81-70188. 264p. 1982. 23.50x (ISBN 0-471-09302-5, Pub. by Wiley-Interscience). Wiley.

Luria, Gina, ed. see Brunton, Mary.

Luria, Gina, ed. see Du Bois, Edward.

Luria, Gina, ed. see Hamilton, Elizabeth.

Luria, Gina, ed. see Smith, Charlotte.

Luria, Gina, ed. see West, Jane.

Luria, Maxwell S., jt. ed. see Hoffman, Richard L.

Luria, S. E., et al. General Virology. 3rd ed. LC 77-9498. 1978. text ed. 36.50 (ISBN 0-471-55640-8). Wiley.

Luria, Salvador E., et al. A View of Life. 1981. 29.95 (ISBN 0-8053-6648-2). Benjamin-Cummings.

Luria, Zella & Rose, Mitchel D. The Psychology of Human Sexuality. LC 78-8716. 1979. text ed. 23.95 (ISBN 0-471-55635-1); study guide 10.95 (ISBN 0-471-06328-2); tchr's manual 9.50 (ISBN 0-471-08299-6); test 6.00 (ISBN 0-471-04217-X). Wiley.

Lurie, Abraham & Rosenberg, Gary, eds. Social Work With Groups in Health Settings. LC 82-18151. 124p. 1982. pap. 7.95 (ISBN 0-88202-137-0). N Watson.

Lurie, Adolph. Business Segments: A Guide for Managers & Accountants. (Illus.). 1979. 22.50 (ISBN 0-07-039113-0). McGraw.

Lurie, Alison. The Language of Clothes. LC 81-40220. (Illus.). 256p. 1981. 20.00 (ISBN 0-394-51302-9). Random.

--Nowhere City. 1976. pap. 1.65 o.p. (ISBN 0-380-00230-2, 23754). Avon.

--Only Children. (General Ser.). 1980. lib. bdg. 13.95 (ISBN 0-8161-3021-3, Large Print Bks). G K Hall.

Lurie, Alison, ed. see Ballantyne, Robert.

Lurie, Alison, ed. see Boreman, Thomas.

Lurie, Alison, ed. see Charlesworth, Maria L.

Lurie, Alison, ed. see D'Aulnoy, Marie C.

Lurie, Alison, ed. see Finley, Martha.

Lurie, Alison, ed. see Harris, Benjamin.

Lurie, Alison, ed. see Newbery, F.

Lurie, Alison, ed. see Wilde, Oscar.

Lurie, Ann T., et al. European Paintings Sixteenth, Seventeenth, & Eighteenth Centuries: The Cleveland Museum of Art Catalogue of Paintings. LC 81-3961. (Part 3). (Illus.). 576p. 1982. 75.00x o.p. (ISBN 0-910386-66-8, Pub. by Cleveland Mus Art). Ind U Pr.

Lurie, Charles N. Everyday Sayings: Their Meanings Explained, Their Origins Given. LC 68-28334. 1968. Repr. of 1928 ed. 42.00x (ISBN 0-8103-0158-X). Gale.

Lurie, Hugh J. Practical Management of Emotional Problems in Medicine. 2nd ed. 385p. 1982. text ed. 20.00 (ISBN 0-89004-707-3); pap. 15.00 (ISBN 0-89004-849-5). Raven.

Lurie, Morris. Dirty Friends: Stories. 1983. pap. 4.95 (ISBN 0-14-005825-7). Penguin.

Lurie, Nancy O., ed. Mountain Wolf Woman, Sister of Crashing Thunder: The Autobiography of a Winnebago Indian. (Illus.). 1961. pap. 4.95 (ISBN 0-472-06109-7, 109, AA). U of Mich Pr.

Lurie, Ranan. Lurie's Almanac. 160p. 1983. 12.95 (ISBN 0-8362-1252-5); pap. 6.95 (ISBN 0-8362-1253-3). Andrews & McMeel.

Lurie, Ranan R. Lurie's Worlds, 1970-1980. LC 80-15526. (Illus.). 452p. 1980. 45.00 (ISBN 0-8248-0731-6); pap. 14.95 (ISBN 0-8248-0723-5). UH Pr.

Lurie, Robert & Neugebauer, Roger, eds. Caring for Infants & Toddlers: What Works, What Doesn't, Vol. II. 182p. (Orig.). pap. 10.00 (ISBN 0-942702-01-8). Child Care.

Lurio, David. Special Recipes for Special People. LC 82-60769. (Illus.). 70p. (gr. 1-3). 1982. 9.95 (ISBN 0-910423-00-8). Skylight.

Lurker, Manfred. The Gods & Symbols of Ancient Egypt: An Illustrated Dictionary. Clayton, Peter A., rev. by. (Illus.). 144p. 1980. 18.95 (ISBN 0-500-11018-2, Quest). Thames Hudson.

Lurkis, Alexander. The Power Brink. (Illus.). 207p. (Orig.). 1982. 13.95x (ISBN 0-9609492-1-6); pap. 9.95x (ISBN 0-9609492-0-8). Icare Pr.

Lury, D. A., jt. auth. see Casley, D. J.

Lusar, Rudolph. German Weapons of the Second World War. 1959. 10.00 o.p. (ISBN 0-8022-1005-8). Philos Lib.

Lusch, R. F., jt. ed. see Darden, W. R.

Luschen, Gunther. The Cross-Cultural Analysis of Sport & Games. 1970. pap. 5.80x (ISBN 0-87563-038-3). Stipes.

Luscher, Kurt K., et al. Early Child Care in Switzerland. (International Monograph Series on Early Child Care). (Illus.). 134p. 1973. 24.00x (ISBN 0-677-04930-7). Gordon.

Luscher, Max. Personality Signs. (Orig.). 1981. pap. 2.50 o.s.i. (ISBN 0-446-81317-6). Warner Bks.

Luscher, Rolf. Enige Versuche In Grundlosem. 151p. (Ger.). 1982. write for info. (ISBN 3-261-05020-9). P Lang Pubs.

Luscome, William, ed. Care & Maintenance of Sports Equipment. 6.00x o.p. (ISBN 0-392-06904-0, SpS). Sportshelf.

Lusher, Jeanne M. & Barnhardt, Marion I. Acquired Bleeding Disorders in Children: Abnormalities of Hemostasis. LC 81-2780. (Monographs in Pediatric Hematology-Oncology: Vol. 3). 152p. 1981. 25.50x (ISBN 0-89352-127-2). Masson Pub.

Lusher, Jeanne M. & Barnhart, Marion I., eds. Acquired Bleeding Disorders in Children: Platelet Abnormalities & Laboratory Methods. LC 81-2780. (Mason Monographs in Pediatric Hemotology Oncology: Vol. 4). 208p. 1981. 31.75x (ISBN 0-89352-141-8). Masson Pub.

Lushington, H. N. Libraries Designed for Users. 1979. 22.50 o.p. (ISBN 0-915794-29-2, 6559). Gaylord Prof Pubns.

Lusigi, W. Planning Human Activities on Protected Natural Ecosystems. (Dissertationes Botanica: No. 48). (Illus.). 1979. pap. 16.00x (ISBN 3-7682-1214-9). Lubrecht & Cramer.

Lusin, Nicolas. Lecons Sur les Ensembles Analytiques. LC 74-144043. xv, 328p. (Fr.). 1972. Repr. of 1930 ed. text ed. 15.95 (ISBN 0-8284-0250-7). Chelsea Pub.

Lusk, David T. Within the Halls of Pilate. write for info. (ISBN 0-89137-538-4). Quality Pubns.

Lusk, Edward J. & Lusk, Janice G. Financial & Managerial Control: A Health Care Perspective. LC 78-10606. 564p. 1979. text ed. 51.50 o.p. (ISBN 0-89443-036-X). Aspen Systems.

Lusk, Graham. The Elements of the Science of Nutrition. (Nutrition Foundations Reprint Ser.). 844p. 1982. 38.50 (ISBN 0-12-460460-9). Acad Pr.

--The Fundamental Basis of Nutrition. 1923. 19.50x (ISBN 0-686-51390-8). Elliots Bks.

Lusk, Janice G., jt. auth. see Lusk, Edward J.

Lusky, W., jt. auth. see Fuchssteiner, B.

Luso-Brazilian Council see Canning House Library.

Lussato, Bruno. A Critical Introduction to Organisation Theory. 1976. text ed. 20.00x o.s.i. (ISBN 0-8419-5019-9). Holmes & Meier.

Lussier, Ernest. Getting to Know the Eucharist. new ed. LC 74-3236. 192p. 1974. 4.95 o.p. (ISBN 0-8189-0289-2). Alba.

Lussier, Virginia L., jt. ed. see Wheeler, Kenneth W.

Lustbader, Eric Van. Black Heart. 544p. 1982. 16.95 (ISBN 0-87131-395-2). M Evans.

Lustbader, Eric Van see Van Lustbader, Eric.

Lustgarten, Edgar. One More Unfortunate. 1980. lib. bdg. 11.95 (ISBN 0-8398-2651-6, Gregg). G K Hall.

Lustick, Sheldon I., jt. ed. see Aspey, Wayne P.

Lustig, Arnold. Darkness Casts No Shadow. 1978. pap. 1.75 o.p. (ISBN 0-380-01952-3, 38323). Avon.

Lustig, Arnost. Dita Saxova. LC 78-69505. 1979. 11.49 (ISBN 0-06-012712-0, HarpT). Har-Row.

Lustig, R. J. Corporate Liberalism: The Origins of Modern American Political Theory, 1890-1920. LC 81-16376. 350p. 1982. 25.00 (ISBN 0-520-04387-1). U of Cal Pr.

Luszki, Walter A. Winning Tennis Through Mental Toughness. (Illus.). 96p. (Orig.). 1982. pap. 7.95 (ISBN 0-89696-150-8, An Everest House Book). Dodd.

Luter, James G., jt. auth. see Modisett, Noah F.

Lutgens, Fred, jt. auth. see Tarbuck, Edward.

Lutgens, Frederick K. & Tarbuck, Edward J. The Atmosphere: An Introduction to Meteorology. (Illus.). 496p. 1982. text ed. 26.95 (ISBN 0-13-050120-4). P-H.

--Essentials of Geology. 352p. 1982. pap. text ed. 16.95 (ISBN 0-675-09845-9). Merrill.

Lutgens, Frederick K., jt. auth. see Tarbuck, Edward J.

Luthans, Fred. Introduction to Management: A Contingency Approach. 1975. text ed. 25.95x (ISBN 0-07-039125-4, C); instructor's manual 15.95 (ISBN 0-07-039126-2). McGraw.

--Organizational Behavior. 3rd ed. (Illus.). 1981. text ed. 24.95 (ISBN 0-07-039144-0, C); instructor's manual 18.95 (ISBN 0-07-039145-9). McGraw.

Luthans, Fred & Kreitner, Robert. Organizational Behavior Modification. 192p. 1975. pap. 10.95x (ISBN 0-673-07966-X). Scott F.

Luthans, Fred & Martinko, Mark. The Practice of Supervision & Management. (Illus.). 1979. text ed. 23.95 (ISBN 0-07-039123-8, C); instructor's manual 20.00 (ISBN 0-07-039124-6). McGraw.

Luthans, Fred & Thompson, Kenneth R. Contemporary Readings in Organizational Behavior. 3rd ed. (Management Ser.). (Illus.). 528p. 1981. text ed. 14.95 (ISBN 0-07-039148-3). McGraw.

Luthans, Fred, jt. auth. see Wortmen, Max S., Jr.

Luthans, Fred, et al. Social Issues in Business. 3rd ed. (Illus.). 1980. text ed. 22.95x (ISBN 0-02-372920-1). Macmillan.

Luthe, Wolfgang. Creativity Mobilization Technique. LC 75-20214. (Illus.). 296p. 1976. 55.50 (ISBN 0-8089-0903-7). Grune.

Luther, Frederic. Microfilm: A History, 1839 to 1900. 1983. Repr. of 1959 ed. 25.00x (ISBN 0-913672-34-3). Microform Rev.

Luther, Leslie L. A Complete Name Index to the History of Cayuga Co., NY of Eighteen Seventy-Nine. 1978. 10.00x (ISBN 0-932334-07-5); pap. 5.00x (ISBN 0-932334-08-3). Heart of the Lakes.

Luther, Martin. The Bondage of the Will. Packer, J. I. & Johnston, O. R., trs. from Ger. 323p. 1973. Repr. of 1957 ed. 15.95 (ISBN 0-227-67417-0). Attic Pr.

--Commentary on Epistles of Peter & Jude. 1982. 12.95 (ISBN 0-8254-3125-5). Kregel.

--Devotions & Prayers of Martin Luther: 52 One-Page Meditations & Prayers on the Psalms. 1978. pap. 2.45 (ISBN 0-8010-5582-2). Baker Bk.

Luthin, jt. auth. see Marino, M. A.

Luthman, Shirley & Kirschenbaum, Martin. The Dynamic Family. LC 74-84560. 1975. 9.95 (ISBN 0-8314-0037-4). Sci & Behavior.

Luthman, Shirley G. Energy & Personal Power. (Orig.). 1982. pap. 10.95 (ISBN 0-686-98386-6). Mehetabel & Co.

Luthuli, Albert. Let My People Go. 1969. pap. 3.95 o.p. (ISBN 0-452-00404-7, F404, Mer). NAL.

Luthy, W. Mozart und Die Tonarten-Characteristik. (Sammlung Mw.Abh. Ser.). iv, 94p. 24.50 o.s.i. (ISBN 90-6027-291-9, Pub. by Frits Knuf Netherlands). Pendragon NY.

Lutin, Michael. Two Year Horoscopes 1977-1978. Incl. Aries (ISBN 0-448-12071-2); Taurus (ISBN 0-448-12072-0); Gemini (ISBN 0-448-12073-9); Cancer (ISBN 0-448-12074-7); Leo (ISBN 0-448-12075-5); Virgo (ISBN 0-448-12076-3); Libra (ISBN 0-448-12077-1); Scorpio (ISBN 0-448-12078-X); Sagittarius (ISBN 0-448-12079-8); Capricorn (ISBN 0-448-12080-1); Aquarius (ISBN 0-448-12081-X); Pisces (ISBN 0-448-12082-8). 384p. 1976. pap. 2.95 ea. o.p. (G&D). Putnam Pub Group.

Lutkus, Anthony, jt. ed. see Baird, John C.

Lutman, M. E. & Haggard, M. P., eds. Hearing Science & Hearing Disorders. Date not set. 28.00 (ISBN 0-12-460440-4). Acad Pr.

Luton, Mildred. Little Chicks' Mothers: And All the Others. (Illus.). 32p. (ps-3). 1983. 11.50 (ISBN 0-670-43113-3). Viking Pr.

Lutrin, Carl E. & Settle, Allen K. American Public Administration: Concepts & Cases. 2nd ed. LC 78-89922. (Illus.). 430p. 1980. text ed. 18.95 (ISBN 0-87484-450-9). Mayfield Pub.

Lutsenburg Maas, Jacob van & Criel, Geert. Primary School Participation & Its Internal Distribution in Eastern Africa. LC 82-10839. (World Bank Staff Working Papers: No. 511). (Orig.). 1982. pap. text ed. 5.00 (ISBN 0-8213-0055-5). World Bank.

Luttbeg, Norman R., jt. auth. see Hilll, David B.

Luttrell, E. S. Taxonomy of the Pyrenomycetes. 1967. Repr. 16.00 (ISBN 3-7682-0513-4). Lubrecht & Cramer.

Luttwak, Edward N. Strategy & Politics: Collected Essays. LC 79-65224. 328p. 1980. pap. 9.95 (ISBN 0-87855-904-3). Transaction Bks.

Luttwak, Edward N. & Horowitz, Daniel. The Israeli Army; 1948 to 1973, Vol. 1. 1983. text ed. 25.00 (ISBN 0-686-84857-8). Abt Bks.

Lutyens, Mary. Krishnamurti: The Years of Fulfillment. 1983. 15.50 (ISBN 0-374-18224-8). FS&G.

Lutz, Carl F., jt. ed. see Langer, Steven.

Lutz, Ernst, jt. auth. see Sapir, Andre.

Lutz, Frank E. Field Book of Insects of the U. S. & Canada. rev. ed. (Putnam's Nature Field Bks.). (gr. 7 up). 1948. 5.95 o.p. (ISBN 0-399-10289-2). Putnam Pub Group.

Lutz, Frank W. & Iannaccone, Laurence, eds. Public Participation in Local School Districts. LC 77-260. (Politics of Education Ser.). 160p. 1978. 17.95x (ISBN 0-669-01466-4). Lexington Bks.

Lutz, Giles. The Feud. 208p. 1983. pap. 2.25 (ISBN 0-345-30255-9). Ballantine.

Lutz, Giles A. The Great Railroad War. LC 80-1851. (Double D Western Ser.). 192p. 1981. 10.95 o.p. (ISBN 0-385-17348-2). Doubleday.

--The Tangled Web. LC 82-45614. (D. D. Western Ser.). 192p. 1983. 11.95 (ISBN 0-385-18433-6). Doubleday.

Lutz, James, jt. auth. see Green, Robert T.

Lutz, Jesse G. & El-Shakhs, Salah S. Tradition & Modernity: The Role of Traditionalism in the Modernization Process. LC 81-43464. 234p. 1982. lib. bdg. 23.00 (ISBN 0-8191-2326-9); pap. text ed. 10.75 (ISBN 0-8191-2327-7). U Pr of Amer.

Lutz, John. Bonegrinder. LC 77-3312. 1977. 7.95 o.p. (ISBN 0-399-11990-6). Putnam Pub Group.

--Buyer Beware. LC 76-14787. 1976. 6.95 o.p. (ISBN 0-399-11811-X). Putnam Pub Group.

--Jericho Man. 224p. 1981. pap. 2.50 o.p. (ISBN 0-425-05003-3). Berkley Pub.

--Lazarus Man. 1980. pap. 2.50 o.p. (ISBN 0-425-04544-7). Berkley Pub.

Lutz, Nancie A. The Doll Directory: Including Miniatures. (Illus.). 180p. (Orig.). lib. bdg. 29.00 (ISBN 0-940070-17-0); pap. 9.50 (ISBN 0-940070-16-2). Doll Works.

Lutz, R. A. Mussel Culture & Harvest: A North American Perspective. (Developments in Acquaculture & Fisheries Science Ser.: Vol. 7). 1980. 64.00 (ISBN 0-444-41866-0). Elsevier.

Lutz, Richard J. Contemporary Perspectives in Consumer Research. (Business Ser.). 466p. 1981. pap. text ed. 12.95x (ISBN 0-534-00942-5). Kent Pub Co.

Lutz, Vera. Italy, a Study in Economic Development. LC 75-3738. (Illus.). 342p. 1975. Repr. of 1962 ed. lib. bdg. 20.75x (ISBN 0-8371-8055-4, LUIT). Greenwood.

Lutz, William, jt. auth. see Brent, Harry.

Lutze, W. Scientific Basis for Nuclear Waste Management. (Materials Research Society Ser.: Vol. 11). 1982. 95.00 (ISBN 0-444-00725-3). Elsevier.

Lutzenkirchen, Hans P. Optimale Fuhrparkbestandsplanung. 316p. (Ger.). 1982. write for info. (ISBN 3-8204-5802-6). P Lang Pubs.

Lutzer, Erwin. Failure: The Back Door to Success. LC 75-16177. 1977. pap. 2.95 (ISBN 0-8024-2516-X). Moody.

--How in This World Can I Be Holy? pap. 7.95 study ed (ISBN 0-8024-3591-2). Moody.

--Managing Your Emotions. 180p. 1983. pap. 4.95 (ISBN 0-88207-386-9). Victor Bks.

Lutzer, Erwin & Orr, Bill. If I Could Change My Mom & Dad. 128p. 1983. pap. 3.50 (ISBN 0-8024-0174-0). Moody.

Lutzer, Erwin W. How in This World Can I Be Holy? Leader's Guide. (Leader's Guide Ser.). (Illus.). 1978. pap. 3.95 o.p. (ISBN 0-8024-3592-0). Moody.

--How to Say No to a Stubborn Habit. 1979. pap. 4.50 (ISBN 0-88207-787-2). Victor Bks.

--You're Richer Than You Think! 1978. pap. 3.95 (ISBN 0-88207-777-5). Victor Bks.

Lutzin, Sidney G., ed. Managing Municipal Leisure Services. LC 80-17378. (Municipal Management). 1980. pap. text ed. 19.50 (ISBN 0-87326-023-6). Intl City Mgt.

Lutzker, John & Martin, Jerry. Behavior Change. LC 80-20798. 400p. 1980. text ed. 19.95 (ISBN 0-8185-0420-X). Brooks-Cole.

Lutzker, John R., et al. Behavioral Pediatrics. 1983. prof ref 25.00x (ISBN 0-88410-732-9). Ballinger Pub.

Luvaas, Jay, ed. Dear Miss Em: General Eichelberger's War in the Pacific, 1942-1945. LC 71-176429. (Contributions in Military History: No. 2). 1972. lib. bdg. 29.95 (ISBN 0-8371-6278-5, LDM/). Greenwood.

Luvera, Paul N., Jr. Attorney's Guidebook of Trial Forms & Techniques for Successful Handling of Personal Injury Cases. 1979. 89.50 (ISBN 0-13-050294-4). Exec Reports.

Lux, Don. Introduction to Construction Careers. (gr. 7-10). 1975. pap. text ed. 7.33 activity ed. (ISBN 0-87345-187-2). McKnight.

Lux, Donald G., et al. The World of Construction. (gr. 7-9). 1982. text ed. 17.28 (ISBN 0-87345-406-5); tchrs' guide 34.64 (ISBN 0-87345-465-0); lab. manual no. 1 6.00 (ISBN 0-87345-463-4); lab. manual no. 2 5.00 (ISBN 0-686-34415-4); filmstrip set 481.00 (ISBN 0-686-35697-7); transparency set 160.00 (ISBN 0-686-36900-9). McKnight.

Lux, H. D. & Aldenhoff, J. B., eds. Basic Mechanisms in the Action of Lithium: Proceedings of a Symposium at Schloss Ringberg, Bavaria, Germany, October 4-6,1981. (International Congress Ser.: No. 572). 272p. 1982. 74.50 (ISBN 0-444-90249-X, Excerpta Medica). Elsevier.

Lux, J. Scott. How to Help Your Teenagers Become Themselves. 140p. 1982. pap. 7.95 (ISBN 0-9609324-0-2). Family Friends.

Lux, P. Fairy Tales from the Barbary Coast. (gr. 1-4). 1971. 7.95 o.p. (ISBN 0-584-62366-6). Transatlantic.

Luxem, Phyllis. Blue Harbor. (YA) 1966. 6.95 (ISBN 0-685-07425-0, Avalon). Bouregy.

Luxemburg & Zaanen. Riesz Spaces. (Mathematical Library: Vol. 1). 85.00 (ISBN 0-444-10129-2, North-Holland). Elsevier.

Luxemburg, Rosa. Comrade & Lover: Rosa Luxemburg's Letters to Leo Jogiches. Ettinger, Elzbieta, ed. 1979. 16.50x (ISBN 0-262-05021-8); pap. 4.95 (ISBN 0-262-62037-5). MIT Pr.

--The Crisis in German Social Democracy. 1918. 17.50x (ISBN 0-86527-037-6). Fertig.
--The National Question: Selected Writings. Davis, Horace B., ed. & tr. from Pol. LC 74-2148. 320p. 1976. 16.50 (ISBN 0-85345-355-1, CL3551). Monthly Rev.
--The Russian Revolution, & Leninism or Marxism? LC 80-24374. (Ann Arbor Ser. for the Study of Communism & Marxism). 109p. 1981. Repr. of 1961 ed. lib. bdg. 20.75x (ISBN 0-313-22429-3, LURR). Greenwood.
Luxemburg, Rosa & Bukharin, Nikolai. The Accumulation of Capital--An Anti-Critique: Imperialism & the Accumulation of Capital. Tarbuck, Kenneth J., ed. Wichmann, Rudolf, tr. from Ger. LC 72-81768. 368p. 1972. 9.50 (ISBN 0-85345-265-2, CL2652); pap. 5.95 (ISBN 0-85345-291-1, PB2911). Monthly Rev.
Luxemburg, Rosa & Howard, Dick. Selected Political Writings. LC 75-142991. 1971. 11.50 o.p. (ISBN 0-85345-142-7, CL-1427); pap. 8.50 (ISBN 0-85345-197-4, PB-1974). Monthly Rev.
Luxon, James T., jt. auth. see Till, William C.
Luxon, Norval N. Niles' Weekly Register, News Magazine of the Nineteenth Century. LC 72-90550. (Illus.). viii, 337p. Repr. of 1947 ed. lib. bdg. 15.75x (ISBN 0-8371-3045-X, LUNR). Greenwood.
Luxon, S. G., jt. auth. see Collings, A. J.
Luxton, Richard. The Mystery of the Mayan Hieroglyphs: The Vision of an Ancient Tradition. Balam, Pablo, ed. LC 81-48211. 247p. (Orig.). 1982. pap. 7.64i (ISBN 0-06-065315-9, CN 4035, HarpR). Har-Row.
Lu Xun. A Brief History of Chinese Fiction. (Illus.). 452p. 1982. 13.95x (ISBN 0-8044-2555-8). Ungar.
--Lu Xun: Selected Poems. Jenner, W. J. F., tr. from Chinese. 160p. 1982. pap. 4.95 (ISBN 0-8351-1002-8). China Bks.
Luyben, W. L. Process Modeling, Simulation, & Control for Chemical Engineers. (Civil Engineering Ser.). (Illus.). 500p. 1972. text ed. 34.95 (ISBN 0-07-039157-2, C). McGraw.
Luyendijk. Cerebral Circulation. (Progress in Brain Research Ser.: Vol. 30). 1968. 53.75 (ISBN 0-444-40691-3). Elsevier.
Luzadder, Warren J. Fundamentals of Engineering Drawing. 1981. 28.95 (ISBN 0-13-338350-4). P-H.
Luzuriaga, Carlos & Zuvekas, Clarence, Jr. Income Distribution & Poverty in Rural Ecuador: A Survey of the Literature, Nineteen Fifty to Nineteen Seventy-Nine. 1983. write for info (ISBN 0-87918-054-4). ASU Lat Am St.
Luzzalto, Gino. Economic History of Italy: From the Fall of the Roman Empire to the Beginning of the 16th Century. Jones, Philip, tr. 1961. 8.25 o.p. (ISBN 0-7100-1767-7). Routledge & Kegan.
Luzzato, Paola C. Long Ago When the Earth Was Flat: Three Tales from Africa. LC 79-14426. (Illus.). (ps-4). 1979. 8.95 o.s.i. (ISBN 0-529-05541-4, Philomel); PLB 8.99 o.s.i. (ISBN 0-529-05542-2). Putnam Pub Group.
Luzzatti, G. & Salvadori, B. Xermammography. 1980. 157.50 (ISBN 0-444-90167-1). Elsevier.
L'Vov, B. U. Atomic Absorption: Spectrochemical Analysis. 1971. 65.00 (ISBN 0-444-19618-8). Elsevier.
L'Vovich, M. I. World Water Resources & Their Future. LC 79-67029. 416p. 1979. 34.00 (ISBN 0-87590-224-3). Am Geophysical.
Lwanga, S. K., jt. ed. see Lowe, Charles R.
Lyall, Archibald. Companion Guide to the South of France. (Illus.). 288p. 1983. 15.95 (ISBN 0-13-154641-4); pap. 7.95 (ISBN 0-13-154633-3). P-H.
Lyall, Gavin. The Conduct of Major Maxim. 264p. 1983. 14.95 (ISBN 0-670-23711-6). Viking Pr.
Lyall, Katharine C., jt. auth. see Rossi, Peter H.
Lyall, Leslie. Three of China's Mighty Men. pap. 3.95 (ISBN 0-340-25561-7). OMF Bks.
Lyas, Colin, ed. Philosophy and Linguistics. 1971. text ed. 16.95 o.p. (ISBN 0-312-60655-9). St Martin.
Lybrand, jt. auth. see Coopers.
Lybyer, J. M. David Copperfield Notes. (Orig.). 1980. pap. 2.75 (ISBN 0-8220-0364-3). Cliffs.
--Jane Eyre Notes. (Orig.). 1977. pap. 2.95 (ISBN 0-8220-0672-3). Cliffs.
--Lord Jim Notes. (Orig.). 1962. pap. 2.95 (ISBN 0-8220-0762-2). Cliffs.
--Red Badge of Courage Notes. (Orig.). 1964. pap. 2.50 (ISBN 0-8220-1120-4). Cliffs.
Lyda, Harold. Motel-Hotel Management Directory. 1977. looseleaf 29.95 o.p. (ISBN 0-915260-06-9). Atcom.
Lyday, Leon F., jt. auth. see Dauster, Frank.
Lyday, Leon F. & Woodyard, George W., eds. Dramatists in Revolt: The New Latin American Theater. (Texas Pan American Ser.). 291p. 1976. 20.00x o.p. (ISBN 0-292-71510-2). U of Tex Pr.
Lydecker, Beatrice. What the Animals Tell Me. 1979. pap. 1.95 o.p. (ISBN 0-451-08704-6, J8704, Sig). NAL.
Lyden, Fremont J. & Miller, Ernest G. Public Budgeting. 3rd ed. 1978. pap. 14.95 o.p. (ISBN 0-395-30661-2). HM.
--Public Budgeting: Program Planning & Implementation. 4th ed. (Illus.). 384p. 1982. 15.95 (ISBN 0-13-737403-8). P-H.
Lyden, Kathryn C. The Struggle to Become a Butterfly. (Illus.). 87p. (Orig.). 1982. pap. 2.50 spiral bound (ISBN 0-9609152-0-6). K C Lyden.
Lydenberg, Harry M., ed. Archibald Robertson, Lieutenant General Royal Engineers: His Diaries & Sketches in America, 1762-1780. LC 70-140879. (Illus.). 1971. Repr. of 1930 ed. 12.00x o.p. (ISBN 0-87104-513-3). NY Pub Lib.
Lydersen, Aksel L. Fluid Flow & Heat Transfer. LC 78-18467. 1979. 69.95 (ISBN 0-471-99697-1); pap. 26.95 (ISBN 0-471-99696-3, Pub. by Wiley-Interscience). Wiley.
--Mass Transfer in Engineering Practice. 300p. 1983. 39.95 (ISBN 0-471-10437-X, Pub. by Wiley-Interscience). Wiley.
Lydolph, P. Geography of the U.S.S.R. 3rd ed. 1977. 33.95x (ISBN 0-471-55724-2). Wiley.
Lydolph, P. E. Climates of the Soviet Union. (World Survey of Climatology: Vol. 7). 1977. 110.75 (ISBN 0-444-41516-5). Elsevier.
Lydon, F. D. Concrete Mix Design. 2nd ed. (Illus.). xii, 196p. 1983. 45.00 (ISBN 0-85334-162-1, Pub. by Applied Sci England). Elsevier.
--Developments in Concrete Technology, Vol. 1. 1979. 53.50 (ISBN 0-85334-855-3, Pub. by Applied Sci England). Elsevier.
Lydon, Michael. Rock Folk. 1973. pap. 2.45 o.s.i. (ISBN 0-440-57402-1, Delta). Dell.
Lye, Keith. Take a Trip to India. (Take a Trip to Ser.). 32p. (gr. 1-3). 1982. PLB 8.41 (ISBN 0-531-04347-9). Watts.
--Take a Trip to Mexico. LC 82-50061. (Take a Trip to Ser.). 32p. (gr. 1-3). 1982. PLB 8.40 (ISBN 0-531-04471-8). Watts.
--Take a Trip to Russia. LC 82-50062. (Take a Trip to Ser.). (gr. 1-3). 1982. PLB 8.40 (ISBN 0-531-04472-6). Watts.
Lye, Keith & Moore, Linda. All About our Earth. (Full Color Fact Books). (Illus.). 32p. (gr. 4-12). 1982. PLB 7.95 (ISBN 0-8219-0013-7, 35546). EMC.
Lyell, Charles. Principles of Geology, 3 vols. (Illus.). 1970. Repr. of 1833 ed. Set. text ed. 104.00 (ISBN 3-7682-0685-8). Lubrecht & Cramer.
Lyell, William A., Jr. Lu Hsun's Vision of Reality. LC 74-30527. 1976. 32.50x (ISBN 0-520-02940-2). U of Cal Pr.
Lyfick, Warren. Fish Stories. LC 81-80077. (Illus.). 32p. Date not set. PLB 5.89 (ISBN 0-933258-03-8). Riverhouse Pubns.
Lyford, Joseph P. The Berkeley Archipelago. LC 81-52138. 288p. 1982. 15.95 (ISBN 0-89526-669-5); pap. 9.95 (ISBN 0-89526-874-4). Regnery Gateway.
Lygin, V. I., jt. auth. see Kiselev, A. V.
Lyke, J., et al. Keyboard Musicianship: Group Piano for Adults, Vol. 2. 1980. spiral bdg. 10.80x (ISBN 0-87563-183-5). Stipes.
--Keyboard Musicianship: Group Piano for Adults, 1. 1983. spiral bdg. 9.80x (ISBN 0-87563-230-0). Stipes.
Lykiard, Alexis, tr. see Lautreamont.
Lykken, David T. A Tremor in the Blood: Uses & Abuses of the Lie Detector. LC 80-10697. 320p. 1980. 17.95 (ISBN 0-07-039210-2). McGraw.
Lyko, James J., jt. auth. see Sweeney, Dennis M.
Lykos, Peter. Personal Computers in Chemistry. LC 80-25445. 262p. 1981. 30.95x (ISBN 0-471-08508-1, Pub. by Wiley-Interscience). Wiley.
Lykos, Peter & Shavitt, Isaiah, eds. Supercomputers in Chemistry. (ACS Symposium Ser.: No. 173). 1981. write for info. (ISBN 0-8412-0666-X). Am Chemical.
Lyle & Brinkley. Contemporary Clothing. 1983. text ed. write for info. (ISBN 0-87002-381-0). Bennett Il.
Lyle, Dorothy S. Performance of Textiles. LC 76-54110. 1977. 34.95x (ISBN 0-471-01418-4). Wiley.
Lyle, Guy R. Administration of the College Library. 4th ed. 320p. 1974. 12.00 (ISBN 0-8242-0552-9). Wilson.
Lyle, Guy R. & Guinagh, Kevin, eds. I Am Happy to Present: A Book of Introductions. 2nd ed. LC 68-17133. 251p. 1968. 10.00 (ISBN 0-8242-0020-9). Wilson.
Lyle, Katie. Dark but Full of Diamonds. (gr. 12 up). 1981. 9.95 (ISBN 0-698-20517-0, Coward). Putnam Pub Group.
Lyle, Katie L. Finders Weepers. 224p. 1982. 11.95 (ISBN 0-698-20556-1, Coward). Putnam Pub Group.
--The Golden Shores of Heaven. LC 75-34627. (gr. 7 up). 1976. 10.53i (ISBN 0-397-31625-9, JBL-J). Har-Row.
--I Will Go Barefoot All Summer for You. LC 72-13700. (gr. 7 up). 1973. 10.53i (ISBN 0-397-31445-0, JBL-J). Har-Row.
Lyle, Rob. Mistral. 1953. 29.50x (ISBN 0-686-50050-4). Elliots Bks.
Lyle, Sparky & Golenbock, Peter. The Bronx Zoo. 1979. 8.95 o.p. (ISBN 0-517-53726-5). Crown.
Lyly, John. Complete Works, 3 Vols. Bond, R. Warwick, ed. 1902. 110.00x (ISBN 0-19-811472-9). Oxford U Pr.
Lym, Glenn R. A Psychology of Building: How We Shape & Experience Our Structured Spaces. (Patterns of Social Behavior Ser.). (Illus.). 1980. 12.95 o.p. (ISBN 0-13-735225-5, Spec); pap. 4.95 o.p. (ISBN 0-13-735217-4). P-H.
Lyman, jt. auth. see Lewis.
Lyman, Charles, et al. Hibernation & Torpor in Mammals & Birds. (Physiological Ecology Ser.). 317p. 1982. 37.50 (ISBN 0-12-460420-X). Acad Pr.
Lyman, Clara, ed. see Women of Christ Church Cathedral.
Lyman, Edna, pseud. Story Telling: What to Tell & How to Tell It. 3rd ed. LC 74-167166. 1971. Repr. of 1911 ed. 40.00x (ISBN 0-8103-3403-8). Gale.
Lyman, Hal, jt. auth. see Woolner, Frank.
Lyman, Helen H. Library Materials in Service to the Adult New Reader. LC 72-11668. 1973. pap. 13.00 (ISBN 0-8389-0147-6). ALA.
--Literacy & the Nations's Libraries. LC 77-4450. 1977. 15.00 o.p. (ISBN 0-8389-0244-8). ALA.
Lyman, Howard B. Intelligence, Aptitude & Achievement Testing. (Guidance Monograph). 1968. pap. 2.40 o.p. (ISBN 0-395-09928-5, 9-78827). HM.
--Test Scores & What They Mean. 3rd ed. (Illus.). 1978. ref. ed. o. p. 14.95 (ISBN 0-13-903823-X); pap. 15.95 ref. ed. (ISBN 0-13-903815-9). P-H.
Lyman, John, adapted by see Biggs, J. B.
Lyman, Kennie, ed. see Bigon, Mario & Regazzoni, Guido.
Lyman, Richard see Seabury, Paul, et al.
Lyman, Robert D., jt. ed. see Roberts, Michael C.
Lyman, Robert H., ed. The World Almanac & Book of Facts for 1929. rev. 2nd ed. LC 71-437810. (Illus.). 1971. pap. 3.95 o.p. (ISBN 0-911818-14-6). World Almanac.
Lyman, S. M., jt. ed. see Brown, R. H.
Lyman, Stanford. Chinese Americans. (Rose Ser: Ethnic Groups in Comparative Perspective). 1974. pap. text ed. 7.00 (ISBN 0-394-31157-4). Random.
Lyman, Stanford M. The Asian in North America. LC 77-9095. 299p. 1977. text ed. 17.50 o.p. (ISBN 0-87436-254-7). ABC-Clio.
Lyman, Theodore R., jt. auth. see Gardiner, John A.
Lyn, Edita Van Der see Van Der Lyn, Edita.
Lyn, Klug, jt. auth. see Klug, Ron.
Lynall, Leonard D., tr. see Confucius.
Lynch, A. J. Mineral Crushing & Grinding Circuits: Their Simulation, Design & Control. (Developments in Mineral Processing: Vol. 1). 1977. 59.75 (ISBN 0-444-41528-9). Elsevier.
Lynch, A. J., et al. Mineral & Coal Flotation Circuits: Their Simulation & Control. (Developments in Mineral Processing Ser.: Vol. 3). 1981. 66.00 (ISBN 0-444-41919-5). Elsevier.
Lynch, Alfred F., jt. auth. see Newman, Pamela.
Lynch, Annette. Redesigning School Health Services. LC 82-12178. (Illus.). 272p. 1983. 29.95x (ISBN 0-89885-102-5). Human Sci Pr.
Lynch, B. Max Beerbohm in Perspective. LC 73-21682. (English Biography Ser., No. 31). 1974. lib. bdg. 53.95x (ISBN 0-8383-1788-X). Haskell.
Lynch, B. & Smith, J. Dispersants for Oil Spill Clean-Up Operations at Sea, on Coastal Waters & Beaches, 1979. 1981. 40.00 (ISBN 0-686-97062-4, Pub. by W Spring England). State Mutual Bk.
Lynch, B., rev. by see Nichols, J. A.
Lynch, B. W., jt. auth. see Martinelli, F. N.
Lynch, Beverly P., jt. ed. see Galvin, Thomas J.
Lynch, Bohun. A History of Caricature. LC 74-6414. (Illus.). 126p. 1975. Repr. of 1927 ed. 30.00x (ISBN 0-8103-4044-5). Gale.
--Max Beerbohm in Perspective. LC 74-13999. (Illus.). xx, 185p. 1975. Repr. of 1922 ed. 34.00x (ISBN 0-8103-4065-8). Gale.
Lynch, D. O., ed. Studies of Law in Social Change & Development: Legal Roles in Columbia, No. 4. 14.00 (ISBN 0-686-35900-3); pap. 7.00 (ISBN 0-686-37204-2). Intl Ctr Law.
Lynch, David. Focalguide to Color. (Focalguide Ser.). (Illus.). 200p. 1976. pap. 7.95 (ISBN 0-240-50921-8). Focal Pr.
Lynch, Donald F., jt. auth. see Pearson, Roger W.
Lynch, Dudley. Duke of Durval. 1976. 8.50 o.p. (ISBN 0-87244-044-3); pap. 5.95 o.p. (ISBN 0-87244-050-8). Texian.
Lynch, Eleanor A. Evaluation: Principles & Processes. 32p. 1978. 3.50 (ISBN 0-686-38295-1, 23-1721). Natl League Nurse.
--A Historical Survey of the Test Services of the NLN. 76p. 1980. 4.95 (ISBN 0-686-38314-1, 17-1777). Natl League Nurse.
Lynch, Eleanor A. & Torres, Gertrude J. Curriculum Evaluation. (Faculty-Curriculum Development Ser.: Pt. II). 52p. 1974. 4.50 (ISBN 0-686-38266-8, 15-1530). Natl League Nurse.
Lynch, Eleanor A., jt. auth. see Torres, Gertrude.
Lynch, Frances. In the House of Dark Music. 352p. 1983. pap. 2.75 (ISBN 0-446-30544-8). Warner Bks.
Lynch, George. Canaries in Colour. 1971. 4.95 (ISBN 0-7137-0540-X). Palmetto Pub.
Lynch, Gloria E., ed. see Thibodaux Service League Members.
Lynch, Hollis R., ed. The Selected Letters of Edward Wilmot Blyden. LC 76-56887. (African Diaspora Ser.). 1978. 40.00 (ISBN 0-527-58890-3). Kraus Intl.
Lynch, James. Multicultural Curriculum. 160p. 1983. pap. 17.50 (ISBN 0-7134-4510-6, Pub. by Batsford England). David & Charles.
Lynch, James J. The Broken Heart: The Medical Consequences of Loneliness. LC 77-2173. 1979. 12.95 o.s.i. (ISBN 0-465-00772-4); pap. 5.95 o.s.i. (ISBN 0-465-00771-6). Basic.
Lynch, Jane S. & Smith, Sara L. The Women's Guide to Legal Rights. 1979. 12.95 o.p. (ISBN 0-8092-7368-3); pap. 5.95 o.p. (ISBN 0-8092-7367-5). Contemp Bks.
Lynch, John D., jt. auth. see Ballinger, Royce E.
Lynch, John G., tr. see Ganoczy, Alexander.
Lynch, K., jt. auth. see Willigan, Dennis J.
Lynch, Kathleen M. Jacob Tonson, Kit-Cat Publisher. LC 77-111046. (Illus.). 256p. 1971. 17.50x (ISBN 0-87049-122-9). U of Tenn Pr.
Lynch, Kevin. Image of the City. (Illus.). 1960. 17.50x (ISBN 0-262-12004-6); pap. 5.95x (ISBN 0-262-62001-4, 11). MIT Pr.
--Site Planning. 2nd rev. ed. 1971. 16.95x (ISBN 0-262-12050-X). MIT Pr.
--A Theory of Good City Form. (Illus.). 514p. 1981. 25.00 (ISBN 0-262-12085-2). MIT Pr.
Lynch, Kevin, ed. Growing up in Cities. LC 77-6789. 1977. 17.50x (ISBN 0-262-12078-X). MIT Pr.
Lynch, Kevin A. Managing the Sense of a Region. 152p. 1976. text ed. 19.00x (ISBN 0-262-12072-0); pap. 5.95x (ISBN 0-262-62035-9). MIT Pr.
Lynch, Kevin W. A Woman's Guide to Cleveland Men. 224p. 1982. pap. 5.95 (ISBN 0-911671-00-5). Lynch Group Pub.
Lynch, L. R. Educational Approaches to High Level Wellness: An Annotated Bibliography. 1982. pap. 4.95 (ISBN 0-935872-01-9). R Bernard.
Lynch, Lawrence W. Eighteenth Century French Novelists & the Novel. 17.00 (ISBN 0-917786-16-5). French Lit.
Lynch, M. & Roberts, J. C. The Consequences of Child Abuse. 23.50 (ISBN 0-12-460570-2). Acad Pr.
Lynch, M. F. Computer Handling of Chemical Structure Information. (Computer Monograph Ser: Vol. 13). 1972. 16.95 o.p. (ISBN 0-444-19586-6). Elsevier.
Lynch, Mary Jo & Myers, Margaret. ALA Survey of Librarian Salaries. LC 82-11537. 112p. 1982. pap. text ed. 40.00 (ISBN 0-8389-3275-4). ALA.
Lynch, Mervin D., et al. Self Concept: Advances in Theory & Research. Gergen, Kenneth & Norem-Hebeison, Ardyth A., eds. 392p. 1981. prof ref 32.50x (ISBN 0-88410-376-5). Ballinger Pub.
Lynch, Miriam. Spellbound. 1979. pap. 1.75 o.p. (ISBN 0-523-40170-1). Pinnacle Bks.
Lynch, Norman E. From Rehoboam to Joash; Jonah; Amos the Prophet. LC 80-17529. (Bible Story Cartoons Ser.). (Illus.). 1977. pap. 0.89 o.s.i. (ISBN 0-87239-293-7, 7976). Standard Pub.
Lynch, Paul Robert. The Farm Boy's Adventure in the Mines. 88p. Date not set. 7.95 (ISBN 0-8059-2857-X). Dorrance.
Lynch, Peter J. Dermatology for the House Officer: Problem Oriented Approach. (House Officer Ser.). 288p. 1982. soft cover 9.95 (ISBN 0-683-05250-0). Williams & Wilkins.
Lynch, Peter J. & Epstein, Stephan B. Burckhardt's Atlas & Manual of Dermatology & Venereology. 3rd ed. (Illus.). 288p. 1977. 21.00 (ISBN 0-683-01134-0). Williams & Wilkins.
Lynch, Philip F. Downhole Operations. (Primer in Drilling & Production Equipment Ser.: Vol. 3). (Illus.). 120p. (Orig.). 1981. pap. 16.95x (ISBN 0-87201-201-8). Gulf Pub.
--The Powertrain. (A Primer in Drilling & Production Equipment Ser.: Vol. 1). (Illus.). 165p. (Orig.). 1980. pap. 16.95x (ISBN 0-87201-198-4). Gulf Pub.
Lynch, R., jt. auth. see Bia, Fred.
Lynch, R. L. & Lunch, Richard L., eds. Food Marketing. (Career Competencies in Marketing Ser.). (Illus.). 1979. pap. text ed. 7.32 (ISBN 0-07-051483-6, G); teacher's manual & key 4.50 (ISBN 0-07-051484-4). McGraw.
Lynch, R. M. & Williamson, R. W. Accounting for Management. 3rd ed. 576p. 1983. 25.00x (ISBN 0-07-039221-8, C); Supplementary materials avail. solutions manual 15.00 (ISBN 0-07-039222-6). McGraw.
Lynch, R. V., et al. Calculus with Computer Applications. 1973. text ed. 33.95 (ISBN 0-471-00909-1). Wiley.
Lynch, Ransom V. & Ostberg, Donald R. Calculus: A First Course. 1970. text ed. 30.50 (ISBN 0-471-00350-6); answers o.s.i. avail. (ISBN 0-471-00351-4). Wiley.
--Calculus: A First Course. 704p. 1983. Repr. of 1970 ed. text ed. 32.50 (ISBN 0-89874-597-7). Krieger.
Lynch, Richard. Health & Spiritual Healing. 140p. 5.50 (ISBN 0-686-38221-8). Sun Bks.
Lynch, Richard & Williamson, Robert. Accounting for Management: Planning & Control. 2nd ed. 1975. 25.00 (ISBN 0-07-039217-X, C); wkbk. 8.00 (ISBN 0-07-039219-6). McGraw.
Lynch, Richard, jt. auth. see Crawford, Lucy.
Lynch, Richard & Rae, Helen, eds. Signal Fire 1982. (Signal Fire Ser.). (Illus.). 104p. (Orig.). 1982. pap. 3.95 (ISBN 0-941588-13-0). Creative Assoc.
Lynch, Richard, ed. see Mathisen, Marilyn.
Lynch, Richard, ed. see Smith, William O.
Lynch, Richard, ed. see Vorndran, Barbara S. & Litchfield, Carolyn.
Lynch, Richard, ed. see Wray, Ralph.

Lynch, Richard L. Getting the Job. Herr, Edwin L., ed. (Cooperative Work Experience Education for Careers Program). (Illus.). (gr. 11-12). 1976. pap. text ed. 7.96 (ISBN 0-07-028335-4, G); tchr's manual & key 3.50 (ISBN 0-07-028336-2). McGraw.

Lynch, Robert E. & Swanzey, Thomas B. The Example of Science: An Anthology for College Composition. 320p. 1981. pap. text ed. 11.95 (ISBN 0-686-69275-6). P-H.

Lynch, Robert N., jt. ed. see Poggie, John J., Jr.

Lynch, Terry. The Railroads of Kansas City. 1983. price not set (ISBN 0-87108-637-9). Pruett.

Lynch, Thomas D. Exercises in Public Budgeting. (Illus.). 176p. 1983. pap. 12.95 (ISBN 0-13-294082-5, Busn). P-H.

--Public Budgeting in America. (Illus.). 1979. ref. 23.95 (ISBN 0-13-737346-5). P-H.

Lynchburg College Faculty, ed. Education: Ends & Means-Series One, Volume II. LC 82-45157. (Classical Selections on Great Issues, Symposium Readings Ser.). 534p. (Orig.). 1982. lib. bdg. 18.75 (ISBN 0-8191-2464-8); pap. text ed. 8.50 (ISBN 0-8191-2465-6). U Pr of Amer.

--Faith & Morals. LC 81-71948. (Classical Selections on Great Issues, Symposium Readings Ser.: Vol. 4). 472p. 1982. lib. bdg. 18.75 (ISBN 0-8191-2301-3); pap. text ed. 8.50 (ISBN 0-8191-2302-1). U Pr of Amer.

--Man & Society. LC 81-71467. (Classical Selections on Great Issues, Symposium Readings: Series 2, Vol. 5). 490p. 1982. lib. bdg. 18.75 (ISBN 0-8191-2296-3); pap. text ed. 8.50 (ISBN 0-8191-2253-X). U Pr of Amer.

--Man & the Imagination. LC 81-43905. (Classical Selections on Great Issues, Symposium Readings: Series 2, Vol. 3). 466p. 1982. lib. bdg. 18.75 (ISBN 0-8191-2299-8); pap. text ed. 8.50 (ISBN 0-8191-2300-5). U Pr of Amer.

--Man & the Universe. LC 81-71466. (Classical Selections on Great Issues, Symposium Readings: Series 2, Vol. 1). 386p. 1982. lib. bdg. 18.75 (ISBN 0-8191-2295-5); pap. text ed. 8.50 (ISBN 0-8191-2252-1). U Pr of Amer.

--Science, Technology & Society. LC 81-71947. (Classical Selections on Great Issues, Symposium Readings: Series 2, Vol. 2). 468p. 1982. lib. bdg. 18.50 (ISBN 0-8191-2297-1); pap. text ed. 8.50 (ISBN 0-8191-2298-X). U Pr of Amer.

--War & Peace: Series One, Volume V. LC 82-45154. (Classical Selections on Great Issues, Symposium Readings). 648p. (Orig.). 1982. lib. bdg. 18.75 (ISBN 0-8191-2470-2); pap. text ed. 8.50 (ISBN 0-8191-2471-0). U Pr of Amer.

Lynch-Watson, Janet. The Shadow Puppet Book. LC 79-65069. (Illus.). (gr. 3 up). 1979. 10.95 (ISBN 0-8069-7030-8); PLB 13.29 (ISBN 0-8069-7031-6). Sterling.

Lynd, R. Dr. Johnson & Company. LC 73-21749. (English Biography Ser., No. 31). 1974. lib. bdg. 49.95x (ISBN 0-8383-1836-3). Haskell.

Lynd, Staughton. Fight Against Shutdowns: Youngstown's Fight Against Steelmill Closings. LC 82-60169. 256p. (Orig.). 1982. pap. 9.95 (ISBN 0-917300-14-9). Miles & Weir.

Lynden-Bell, D., jt. ed. see Fall, S. M.

Lyndon, Donlyn. The City Observed: Boston. 1982. 18.50 (ISBN 0-394-50475-5); pap. 7.95 (ISBN 0-394-74894-8). Random.

Lyne, P., jt. auth. see Collins, C. H.

Lyne, R. O., ed. see Catullus.

Lyne, R. O., ed. see Virgil.

Lyneis, James M. Corporate Planning & Policy Design: A System Dynamics Approach. (Illus.). 520p. 1980. 32.50x (ISBN 0-262-12083-6). MIT Pr.

Lynes, Alice. How to Organize a Local Collection. 128p. 1974. 15.00 (ISBN 0-233-96452-5, 05804-1, Pub. by Gower Pub Co England). Lexington Bks.

Lynes, J. A. & Pritchard, D. C., eds. Developments in Lighting, Vols. 1 & 2. Vol. 1, 1978. 47.25 (ISBN 0-85334-774-3, Pub. by Applied Sci England); Vol. 2, 1982. 51.25 (ISBN 0-85334-985-1). Elsevier.

Lynes, Russell. The Art Makers: An Informal History of Painting, Sculpture, & Architecture in 19th Century America. (Illus.). xii, 514p. 1982. pap. 9.95 (ISBN 0-486-24239-0). Dover.

--A Surfeit of Honey. LC 74-6779. 140p. 1974. Repr. of 1957 ed. lib. bdg. 15.00 o.p. (ISBN 0-8371-7572-0, LYSH). Greenwood.

--The Tastemakers. LC 82-25116. (Illus.). xiv, 362p. 1983. Repr. of 1955 ed. lib. bdg. 45.00x (ISBN 0-313-23843-X, LYTA). Greenwood.

Lyng, Merwin J., et al. Applied Technical Mathematics. LC 77-76423. (Illus.). 1976. text ed. 21.95 (ISBN 0-395-25429-9); instr's. manual 1.00 (ISBN 0-395-25428-0). HM.

Lyngstad, Alexandra & Lyngstad, Sverre. Ivan Goncharov. (World Authors Ser.). lib. bdg. 14.95 (ISBN 0-8057-2380-3, Twayne). G K Hall.

Lyngstad, Sverre. Jonas Lie. (World Authors Ser.). 1977. lib. bdg. 15.95 (ISBN 0-8057-6274-4, Twayne). G K Hall.

Lyngstad, Sverre, jt. auth. see Lyngstad, Alexandra.

Lynn, Arthur D., Jr., ed. see Committee on Taxation, Resources, & Economic Development.

Lynn, Arthur D., Jr., jt. ed. see Lindholm, Richard W.

Lynn, E. Russell, Jr. The Mters-Briggs Type Indicator: The Dignity of Difference. (Illus.). 1983. write for info. (ISBN 0-935652-10-8). Ctr Applications Psych.

Lynn, Edward S. & Freeman, Robert J. Fund Accounting: Theory & Practice. 1974. ref. ed. 27.95 (ISBN 0-13-332379-X). P-H.

--Fund Accounting: Theory & Practice. 2nd ed. (Illus.). 896p. 1983. text ed. 29.95 (ISBN 0-13-332411-7). P-H.

Lynn, Elizabeth A. The Northern Girl. 1980. 13.95 o.p. (ISBN 0-399-12409-8). Putnam Pub Group.

--The Sardonyx Net. (Orig.). 1982. pap. 2.95 (ISBN 0-425-06127-2). Berkley Pub.

--The Sardonyx Net. 252p. 1981. 15.95 (ISBN 0-399-12588-4). Putnam Pub Group.

--Watchtower. LC 78-12602. 1979. 9.95 o.p. (ISBN 0-399-12272-9, Pub. by Berkley). Putnam Pub Group.

Lynn, Gartley & Leebron, Elizabeth. Walt Disney: A Guide to References & Resources. 1979. lib. bdg. 30.00 (ISBN 0-8161-8004-0, Hall Reference). G K Hall.

Lynn, Jack. The Kennedy Connection. LC 82-48837. 320p. 1983. 13.41i (ISBN 0-06-015162-5, HarpT). Har-Row.

--The Professor. 1971. 7.95 o.p. (ISBN 0-916988-03-1). Pendragon Hse.

Lynn, James J., jt. auth. see Weagraff, Patrick J.

Lynn, Karen. Dual Destiny. LC 82-45204. (Starlight Romance Ser.). 192p. 1983. 11.95 (ISBN 0-385-18219-8). Doubleday.

Lynn, Kenneth S. The Air-Line to Seattle: Studies in Literary & Historical Writing about America. 240p. 1983. lib. bdg. 17.50x (ISBN 0-226-49832-8). U of Chicago Pr.

--A Divided People. LC 76-25779. (Contributions in American Studies: No. 30). 1977. lib. bdg. 25.00 (ISBN 0-8371-9271-4, LYD/). Greenwood.

--Mark Twain & Southwestern Humor. LC 70-176135. (Illus.). 300p. 1972. Repr. of 1960 ed. lib. bdg. 20.25 (ISBN 0-8371-6270-X, LYMT); pap. 5.95 (ISBN 0-8371-8942-X). Greenwood.

--Visions of America: Eleven Literary Historical Essays. (Contributions in American Studies: No. 6). 205p. 1973. lib. bdg. 25.00 (ISBN 0-8371-6386-2, LYV/). Greenwood.

Lynn, Kenneth S., ed. Comic Tradition in America: An Anthology of American Humor. 1968. pap. 8.95 (ISBN 0-393-00447-3, Norton Lib). Norton.

--Huckleberry Finn: Text, Sources & Criticism. (Orig.). 1961. pap. text ed. 9.95 (ISBN 0-15-539490-8, HC). HarBraceJ.

Lynn, Laurence E., Jr. The State & Human Services: Organizational Change in a Political Context. 1980. text ed. 17.50x (ISBN 0-262-12084-4). MIT Pr.

Lynn, Laurence E., Jr. & Whitman, David def. The President As Policymaker: Jimmy Carter & Welfare Reform. 351p. 1981. 29.95 (ISBN 0-87722-223-1); pap. 9.95x (ISBN 0-87722-238-X). Temple U Pr.

Lynn, Lawrence E. Designing Public Policy: A Case Book on the Role of Policy Analysis. 1980. 23.50x (ISBN 0-673-16258-3). Scott F.

Lynn, Loretta & Vecsey, George. Coal Miner's Daughter. Orig. Title: Loretta Lynn: Coal Miner's Daughter. (Illus.). 1977. pap. 3.50 (ISBN 0-446-30248-1). Warner Bks.

Lynn, Melvyn & Solotorovsky, Morris, eds. Chemotherapeutic Agents for Bacterial Infections. LC 80-13504. (Benchmark Papers in Microbiology Ser.: No. 14). 432p. 1981. 45.00 (ISBN 0-87933-374-X). Hutchinson Ross.

Lynn, Paul P., jt. auth. see Boresi, Arthur P.

Lynn, R. Personality & National Character. 1971. write for info. (ISBN 0-08-016516-8). Pergamon.

Lynn, Richard J. Kuan Yun-Shih. (World Authors Ser.). 1980. lib. bdg. 15.95 (ISBN 0-8057-6404-6, Twayne). G K Hall.

Lynn, Robert. Basic Economic Principles. rev. ed. (Illus.). 1980. text ed. 20.95 (ISBN 0-07-039264-1); instructor's manual 15.95 (ISBN 0-07-039265-X). McGraw.

Lynn, Robert A. Basic Economic Principles. 3rd ed. (Illus.). 416p. 1974. text ed. 14.95 o.p. (ISBN 0-07-039262-5, C); inst manual 4.95 o.p. (ISBN 0-07-039263-3). McGraw.

Lynn, Robert A. & O'Grady, James P. Elements of Business. LC 77-75881. (Illus.). 1977. text ed. 22.95 (ISBN 0-395-25107-9); inst. resource guide 1.50 (ISBN 0-395-25106-0); study guide 8.50 (ISBN 0-395-25108-7). HM.

Lynn, Robert H. All the King's Men Notes. (Orig.). 1982. pap. 2.25 (ISBN 0-8220-0146-2). Cliffs.

Lynn, Robert J. The Pension Crisis. LC 82-48795. 192p. 1983. 21.95x (ISBN 0-669-06374-6). Lexington Bks.

Lynn, T. S. & Goldberg, Harry F. Real Estate Limited Partnership: 1979 Suppplement. LC 79-88895. 1979. pap. 19.95 (ISBN 0-471-05284-1, Pub. by Wiley-Interscience). Wiley.

Lynn, Theodore S. & Goldberg, Harry F. Real Estate Limited Partnerships. 2nd ed. 480p. 1983. 44.95x (ISBN 0-471-09082-4, Pub. by Wiley-Interscience). Wiley.

Lynne, James B. Jet Race. LC 77-25752. 1978. 9.95 o.p. (ISBN 0-399-11917-5). Putnam Pub Group.

Lynton, Ernest, jt. auth. see Ford Foundation.

Lynton, Harriet R. & Rajan, Mohini. The Days of the Beloved. 1974. 24.50x (ISBN 0-520-02442-7); pap. 5.95 (ISBN 0-520-03939-4). U of Cal Pr.

Lynton, Norbert. The Story of Modern Art. 382p. 1983. 30.00 (ISBN 0-686-84546-3); pap. text ed. 14.95 (ISBN 0-686-84547-1). P-H.

Lyon, Bruce & Rowen, Herbert H. A History of the Western World, 3 vols. 2nd ed. 1974. pap. 13.95 ea.; Vol. I (ISBN 0-395-30662-0); Vol. II (ISBN 0-395-30663-9); Vol. III (ISBN 0-395-30664-7); Instr's. manual 0.75 (ISBN 0-395-30665-5). HM.

Lyon, Danny, ed. Pictures from the New World. (Illus.). 144p. 1983. pap. 17.95 (ISBN 0-89381-108-4). Aperture.

Lyon, Edward, et al. Earth Science Manual. 4th ed. 224p. 1976. write for info. wire coil (ISBN 0-697-05079-3); tchr's manual avail. (ISBN 0-697-05059-9). Wm C Brown.

Lyon, Edward E., jt. auth. see Dillon, Lowell I.

Lyon, Eugene. The Enterprise of Florida: Pedro Menendez de Aviles & the Spanish Conquest of 1565-1568. LC 76-29612. (Illus.). 1976. 10.00 o.p. (ISBN 0-8130-0533-7). U Presses Fla.

Lyon, F. H., tr. see Lucas-Dubreton, J.

Lyon, G., jt. auth. see Adams, R. D.

Lyon, Herbert L., jt. auth. see Ivancevich, John M.

Lyon, Hugh. An Illustrated Guide to Modern Warships. LC 80-65166. (Illustrated Military Guides Ser.). (Illus.). 160p. 1980. 8.95 (ISBN 0-668-04966-9, 4966-9). Arco.

Lyon, James. Urania: A Choice Collection of Psalm-Tunes, Anthems & Hymns. LC 69-11667. (Music Reprint Ser.). 198p. 1974. Repr. of 1761 ed. lib. bdg. 29.50 (ISBN 0-306-71198-2). Da Capo.

Lyon, John K. The Database Administrator. LC 75-42442. (Business Data Processing Ser). 240p. 1976. 35.95 (ISBN 0-471-55741-2, Pub. by Wiley-Interscience). Wiley.

Lyon, Laurie A. Guidelines for High School Students on Conducting Research in the Sciences. 1980. 1.25 (ISBN 0-87716-114-3, Pub. by Moore Pub Co). F Apple.

Lyon, Leverett, et al. The National Recovery Administration. LC 71-171386. (FDR & the Era of the New Deal Ser.). 1972. Repr. of 1935 ed. lib. bdg. 95.00 (ISBN 0-306-70385-8). Da Capo.

Lyon, Ninette. Meat at Any Price. Benton, Peggie, tr. 5.75 o.p. (ISBN 0-571-06944-4). Transatlantic.

Lyon, Richard H. Statistical Energy Analysis of Dynamical Systems: Theory & Applications. LC 75-19074. 400p. 1975. text ed. 32.50x (ISBN 0-262-12071-2). MIT Pr.

Lyon, Roy B. Bosquejos Utiles para Laicos. (Illus.). 96p. (Span.). 1980. pap. 1.95 (ISBN 0-311-42401-5). Casa Bautista.

Lyon, Thomas E. Juan Godoy. (World Authors Ser.). lib. bdg. 15.95 (ISBN 0-8057-2376-5, Twayne). G K Hall.

Lyon, Thomas J. Frank Waters. (United States Authors Ser.). 1973. lib. bdg. 13.95 (ISBN 0-8057-0775-1, Twayne). G K Hall.

--Revision Notes on English Law. 1973. pap. 1.95 o.p. (ISBN 0-7195-1831-8). Transatlantic.

Lyon, W. S. Trace Element Measurements at the Coal-Fired Steam Plant. LC 77-435. 146p. Repr. of 1977 ed. text ed. 44.50 (ISBN 0-8493-5118-9). Krieger.

Lyon, W. S., ed. Progress & Problems in Radioelement Analysis. LC 79-55145. 1980. 29.95 o.p. (ISBN 0-250-40343-9). Ann Arbor Science.

Lyon, W. S., ed. see Analytical Chemistry in Energy Technology.

Lyon, William & Duke, Bill. Introduction to Human Services. (Illus.). 320p. 1981. pap. text ed. 16.95 (ISBN 0-8359-3216-8). Reston.

Lyon, William F., jt. auth. see Davidson, Ralph.

Lyon, William F., jt. auth. see Davidson, Ralph H.

Lyon, William S., Jr., ed. Guide to Activation Analysis. LC 64-23964. 206p. 1972. Repr. of 1964 ed. 12.00 o.p. (ISBN 0-88275-040-2). Krieger.

Lyone, Stanley. Management Guide to Modern Industrial Lighting. 2nd ed. 176p. 1983. text ed. write for info. (ISBN 0-408-01147-5). Butterworth.

Lyonga, S. N., jt. auth. see Miege, J.

Lyon-Jenness, Cheryl, compiled by. From the Homestead Kitchen. (Illus.). 233p. 1982. pap. 10.00 (ISBN 0-939294-12-5). Beech Leaf.

Lyons. The Biology of Helminth Parasites. (Studies in Biology: No. 102). 1979. 5.95 o.p. (ISBN 0-8391-0252-6). Univ Park.

--Handbook of Industrial Lighting. 1981. text ed. 38.95 (ISBN 0-408-00525-4). Butterworth.

Lyons, Arthur. At the Hands of Another. LC 82-21315. (A Rinehart Suspense Novel). 240p. 1983. 13.50 (ISBN 0-03-059616-5). HR&W.

Lyons, Augusta W. Murder at Prospect, Kentucky. LC 77-24462. 1977. 7.95 o.p. (ISBN 0-399-12067-X). Putnam Pub Group.

Lyons, Bernard. Voices from the Back Pew. 1970. 5.95 o.p. (ISBN 0-685-07672-5, 80416). Glencoe.

Lyons, Bridget G. Voices of Melancholy. (Ideas & Forms in English Literature). 1971. 17.95x (ISBN 0-7100-7001-2). Routledge & Kegan.

Lyons, C. G., et al. Concise Textbook of Organic Chemistry. 1965. 14.50 o.p. (ISBN 0-08-010657-9); pap. 6.25 o.p. (ISBN 0-08-010656-0). Pergamon.

Lyons, Charles. Samuel Beckett. (Grove Press Modern Dramatists Ser.). (Illus.). 196p. 1983. pap. 11.95 (ISBN 0-394-62411-4, Ever). Grove.

Lyons, Charles H. To Wash an Aethiop White: British Ideas About Black Educability, 1530-1960. LC 74-23396. 1975. text ed. 11.95x (ISBN 0-8077-2464-5). Tchrs Coll.

Lyons, Daniel S. J. Is There a Population Explosion? 12p. pap. 0.50 (ISBN 0-686-81639-0). TAN Bks Pubs.

Lyons, Dorothy. Blue Smoke. LC 53-7867. (Illus.). (gr. 6 up). 1968. pap. 1.95 (ISBN 0-15-613275-3, VoyB). HarBraceJ.

--Dark Sunshine. LC 51-11741. 1965. pap. 1.95 (ISBN 0-15-623936-1, VoyB). HarBraceJ.

Lyons, Eugene. Life & Death of Sacco & Vanzetti. LC 74-107414. (Civil Liberties in American History Ser). 1970. Repr. of 1927 ed. lib. bdg. 27.50 (ISBN 0-306-71888-X). Da Capo.

Lyons, Eugene, ed. Six Soviet Plays. Repr. of 1934 ed. lib. bdg. 20.75x (ISBN 0-8371-0154-9, LYSP). Greenwood.

Lyons, Francis S. The Irish Parliamentary Party, 1890-1910. LC 74-12646. 284p. 1975. Repr. of 1951 ed. lib. bdg. 17.25x (ISBN 0-8371-7734-0, LYIP). Greenwood.

Lyons, Gene M. The Uneasy Partnership: Social Science & the Federal Government in the Twentieth Century. LC 72-93761. 394p. 1969. 10.50x (ISBN 0-87154-561-6). Russell Sage.

Lyons, Gene M. & Lambert, Richard D. Social Science & the Federal Government. LC 76-148005. (Annals of the American Academy of Political & Social Science: No. 394). 1971. 15.00 (ISBN 0-87761-137-8); pap. 7.95 (ISBN 0-87761-136-X). Am Acad Pol Soc Sci.

Lyons, Gene M. & Masland, John W. Education & Military Leadership: A Study of the R.O.T.C. LC 75-18401. (Illus.). 283p. 1975. Repr. of 1959 ed. lib. bdg. 18.75x (ISBN 0-8371-8335-9, LYED). Greenwood.

Lyons, Gene M., ed. The Role of Ideas in American Foreign Policy. LC 78-155480. (An Orvil E. Dryfoos Conference Report). 67p. 1971. pap. text ed. 4.50x o.s.i. (ISBN 0-87451-055-4). U Pr of New Eng.

Lyons, Grant. The Creek Indians. LC 77-29255. (Illus.). 96p. (gr. 4 up). 1978. PLB 7.29 o.p. (ISBN 0-671-32895-6). Messner.

--Pacific Coast Indians of North America. (Illus.). 96p. (gr. 4-6). 1983. PLB 8.29 (ISBN 0-671-45801-9). Messner.

--Tales the People Tell in Mexico. LC 72-1424. (Illus.). 96p. (gr. 3-6). 1972. PLB 6.64 o.p. (ISBN 0-671-32534-5). Messner.

Lyons, Ivan, jt. auth. see Lyons, Nan.

Lyons, J. A. The Cosmic Christ in Origin & Teilhard de Chardin. Wiles, Maurice, ed. (Theological Monographs). 248p. 1982. 33.50x (ISBN 0-19-826721-5). Oxford U Pr.

Lyons, J. B. Brief Lives of Irish Doctors, Sixteen Hundred to Nineteen Sixty-Five. 1981. 40.00 (ISBN 0-686-96952-9, Pub. by Blackwater Pr Ireland). State Mutual Bk.

Lyons, James, jt. auth. see Howard, John T.

Lyons, Jeanne Marie, tr. see Bigo, Pierre.

Lyons, John. Introduction to Theoretical Linguistics. (Illus., Orig.). 1968. 54.50 (ISBN 0-521-05617-9); pap. text ed. 15.95x (ISBN 0-521-09510-7). Cambridge U Pr.

--Language & Linguistics. LC 80-42002. (Illus.). 280p. 1981. 27.95 (ISBN 0-521-23034-9); pap. 9.95 (ISBN 0-521-29775-3). Cambridge U Pr.

--Semantics One. LC 76-40838. (Illus.). 1977. 49.50 (ISBN 0-521-21473-4); pap. 13.95 (ISBN 0-521-29165-8). Cambridge U Pr.

--Semantics Two. LC 76-40838. (Illus.). 1977. 59.50 (ISBN 0-521-21560-9); pap. 15.95x (ISBN 0-521-29186-0). Cambridge U Pr.

Lyons, John D. The Listening Voice: An Essay on the Rhetoric of Saint-Amant. LC 82-82429. (French Forum Monographs: No. 40). 138p. (Orig.). 1982. pap. 10.00x (ISBN 0-917058-39-9). French Forum.

--A Theatre of Disguise: Studies in French Baroque Drama (1630-1660) 14.00 (ISBN 0-917786-25-4). French Lit.

Lyons, John M. & Brown, Elsa L. Analyzing the Cost of Baccalaureate Nursing Education. 32p. 1982. 4.95 (ISBN 0-686-38138-6, 15-1880). Natl League Nurse.

Lyons, John W. Chemistry & Uses of Fire Retardants. LC 71-112595. 1970. 64.00 o.s.i. (ISBN 0-471-55740-4, Pub. by Wiley-Interscience). Wiley.

Lyons, Ken. Complete Guide to Winning Slot-I Football. 240p. 1982. 15.95 (ISBN 0-13-160697-2, Parker). P-H.

Lyons, L. J., ed. see Craighead, J. J. & Sumner, J. S.

Lyons, Lawrence, jt. auth. see Gutmann, Felix.

Lyons, Len. The Great Jazz Pianists: Speaking of Their Lives & Music. (Illus.). 224p. 1983. 12.95 (ISBN 0-688-01920-X). Morrow.

--The Great Jazz Pianists: Speaking of Their Lives & Music. (Illus.). 224p. 1983. pap. 6.95 (ISBN 0-688-01921-8). Quill NY.

--The One Hundred One Best Jazz Albums: A History of Jazz on Records. 1980. 17.95 (ISBN 0-688-03720-8). Morrow.

--The One Hundred One Best Jazz Albums: A History of Jazz on Records. 1980. pap. 9.95 (ISBN 0-688-08720-5). Quill NY.

Lyons, M. France under the Directory. (Illus.). 256p. 1975. 39.50 (ISBN 0-521-20785-1); pap. 12.95x (ISBN 0-521-09950-1). Cambridge U Pr.

Lyons, Maggie. Bayou Passions. (Orig.). 1979. pap. 1.95 o.s.i. (ISBN 0-515-04740-6, 04740-6). Jove Pubns.

--Flame of Savannah. (Orig.). 1980. pap. 2.25 o.s.i. (ISBN 0-515-04745-7). Jove Pubns.

Lyons, Malcom C. & Jackson, D. E. Saladin: The Politics of the Holy War. LC 79-13078. (Cambridge University Oriental Publications Ser.: No. 30). (Illus.). 400p. 1982. 39.50 (ISBN 0-521-22358-X). Cambridge U Pr.

Lyons, Nan & Lyons, Ivan. Sold! 1982. 12.95 (ISBN 0-698-11148-6, Coward). Putnam Pub Group.

Lyons, Nick. Locked Jaws. 1979. 7.95 o.p. (ISBN 0-517-53855-5). Crown.

--The Sony Vision. (Illus.). 1976. 7.95 o.p. (ISBN 0-517-52739-1). Crown.

Lyons, Nick, jt. auth. see Tanzer, Herbert.

Lyons, Nick, ed. Art Flick's Master Fly-Tying Guide. write for info. N Lyons Bks.

--Art Flick's New Streamside Guide. write for info. N Lyons Bks.

Lyons, Nick, ed. see Jennings, Preston.

Lyons, Paul. Philadelphia Communists, 1936-1956. 244p. 1982. 25.95 (ISBN 0-87722-259-2). Temple U Pr.

--Real Estate Investor's Tax & Profit Planner. 1981. case 18.95 (ISBN 0-8359-6530-9); pap. 12.95 (ISBN 0-8359-6529-5). Reston.

Lyons, Richard. Scanning the Land, Poems in North Dakota. (Illus.). 157p. 1980. 11.75 (ISBN 0-911042-23-7). N Dak Inst.

Lyons, S. L. Exterior Lighting for Industry & Security. 1980. 49.25 (ISBN 0-85334-879-0, Pub. by Applied Sci England). Elsevier.

Lyons, Vincent, jt. ed. see Battle, Vincent M.

Lyons, W. James. Impact Phenomena in Textiles. (Press Research Monographs: No. 19). 1963. 15.00x (ISBN 0-262-12008-9). MIT Pr.

Lyons, William, ed. see Elder, Crawford.

Lys, Claudia De see Batchelor, Julie F. & De Lys, Claudia.

Lysaught, Jerome P. Action in Affirmation: Towards an Unambiguous Profession of Nursing. (Illus.). 224p. 1981. pap. text ed. 18.50 (ISBN 0-07-039271-4, HP). McGraw.

Lysaught, Jerome P., ed. A Luther Christman Anthology. LC 78-53078. 90p. 1978. pap. 12.95 (ISBN 0-913654-45-0). Aspen Systems.

Lysek, G., jt. auth. see Kloidt, M.

Lysons, C. K. Purchasing. 224p. 1981. 29.00 (ISBN 0-7121-1752-0, Pub. by Macdonald & Evans). State Mutual Bk.

Lystad, Mary. At Home in America: As Seen Through Its Books for Children. 256p. 1983. 16.95 (ISBN 0-87073-378-8); pap. 11.25 (ISBN 0-87073-379-6). Schenkman.

--The Halloween Parade. (Illus.). 32p. (ps-3). 1973. PLB 4.99 o.p. (ISBN 0-399-60847-8). Putnam Pub Group.

--James the Jaguar. (Illus.). (gr. k-3). 1972. PLB 4.49 o.p. (ISBN 0-399-60750-1). Putnam Pub Group.

Lyster, Alan F., jt. auth. see Grosse, Lloyd T.

Lyston, Lord see Swan, D. K.

Lystra, Helen P., ed. Kitchen Sampler, a Heritage Cookbook. (Illus.). 192p. (Orig.). 1982. pap. 6.95 (ISBN 0-9608642-0-2). UMCD.

Lyte, Charles. The Thames. LC 80-50936. (Rivers of the World Ser.). PLB 12.68 (ISBN 0-382-06369-4). Silver.

Lythe, S. G. Economy of Scotland in Its European Setting: 1550-1625. LC 75-31475. 1976. Repr. of 1960 ed. lib. bdg. 20.50x (ISBN 0-8371-8533-5, LYES). Greenwood.

Lythgoe, Dennis L. Let'em Holler: A Political Biography of J. Bracken Lee. LC 82-60039. (Illus.). xii, 343p. 1982. 17.50 (ISBN 0-913738-33-6). Utah St Hist Soc.

Lytle, B. J., et al. Tunnel & Other Stories. Elwood, Roger, ed. LC 73-21483. (Science Fiction Bks). 48p. (gr. 4-8). 1974. PLB 3.95g (ISBN 0-8225-0952-0). Lerner Pubns.

Lytle, Howard H. The Lytles: Their Life on the Farm. 1978. 6.95 o.p. (ISBN 0-533-03364-0). Vantage.

Lytle, L. D., jt. ed. see Jacoby, J. H.

Lytle, R. J. American Metric Handbook. 1981. 19.95 (ISBN 0-07-039277-3). McGraw.

--Farm Builder's Handbook. 3rd ed. 1981. 27.50 (ISBN 0-07-039276-5). McGraw.

Lytle, R. J. & Reschke, R. C. Component & Modular Techniques: A Builder's Handbook. 2nd ed. 1981. 27.50 (ISBN 0-07-039274-9). McGraw.

Lytle, Richard H., ed. Management of Archives & Manuscript Collections for Librarians. LC 79-92650. 124p. 1980. Repr. of 1975 ed. 8.00 (ISBN 0-931828-27-9). Soc Am Archivists.

Lyttelton, Humphrey. The Best of Jazz I: Basin Street to Harlem, 1917-1930. LC 81-21418. (Illus.). 214p. 1982. pap. 5.95 (ISBN 0-8008-0729-4, Crescendo). Taplinger.

Lyttle, Richard B. The Complete Beginner's Guide to Physical Fitness. LC 77-80896. (gr. 1 up). 1978. 9.95a o.p. (ISBN 0-385-12773-1); PLB 9.95a (ISBN 0-385-12774-X). Doubleday.

--The Complete Beginners Guide to Skiing. LC 77-25602. (gr. 1 up). 1978. 9.95a o.p. (ISBN 0-385-09717-4); PLB 9.95a (ISBN 0-385-09719-0). Doubleday.

--The Games They Played. LC 82-1749. (Illus.). 160p. (gr. 6 up). 1982. 10.95 (ISBN 0-689-30928-7). Atheneum.

--Getting into Pro Basketball. (Getting into the Pros Ser.). (Illus.). (gr. 6 up). 1979. PLB 8.40 s&l (ISBN 0-531-01451-7). Watts.

--Jogging & Running. (Concise Guides Ser.). (gr. 5 up). 1979. PLB 8.90 s&l (ISBN 0-531-02949-2). Watts.

--Nazi Hunting. (Triumph Bks). (Illus.). 112p. (gr. 7 up). 1982. lib. bdg. 8.90 (ISBN 0-531-04410-6). Watts.

--The Official Baseball Scorecard Book. (Illus.). 64p. (Orig.). (gr. 3 up). 1982. pap. 7.25 (ISBN 0-671-44423-9). Wanderer Bks.

--Shale Oil & Tar Sands: The Promises & Pitfalls. LC 82-6913. (Impact Bks.). (Illus.). 96p. (gr. 7 up). 1982. PLB 8.90 (ISBN 0-531-04489-0). Watts.

Lyttle, Richard B., jt. auth. see Dolan, Edward F., Jr.

Lyttleton, Humphrey. The Best of Jazz II: Enter the Giants, 1931-1944. LC 81-21418. (Illus.). 239p. 1983. pap. 6.95 (ISBN 0-8008-0731-6, Crescendo). Taplinger.

--Humphrey Lyttelton's Jazz & Big Band Quiz. 1979. 12.95 o.p. (ISBN 0-7134-2011-1, Pub. by Batsford England). David & Charles.

Lyttleton, R. A. The Earth & Its Mountains. 206p. 1982. 38.95 (ISBN 0-471-10530-9, Pub. by Wiley-Interscience). Wiley.

Lytton, Edward B. Vril: The Power of the Coming Race. 2nd ed. LC 71-183054. 256p. 1982. Repr. of 1972 ed. 11.00 (ISBN 0-89345-406-0, Spirit Fiction). Garber Comm.

Lyvely & Farmer. Abortion Eve. (On Abortion Ser.). (Illus.). 1973. 1.25 (ISBN 0-918440-01-7). Nanny Goat.

--Pandora's Box. (Women's Humor Ser.). (Illus.). 1973. 1.25 (ISBN 0-918440-02-5). Nanny Goat.

Lyvely, jt. auth. see Farmer.

Lyzell, Richard, ed. The Artist's Directory. Wadell, Heather. (Art Guide Ser.). (Illus.). 250p. (Orig.). 1982. pap. 12.00 (ISBN 0-686-95009-7, Pub. By Art Guide England). Morgan.

M

M, pseud. The Condensed Gospel of Sri Ramakrishna. 1979. 10.50x o.s.i. (ISBN 0-87481-488-X); pap. 4.95 o.s.i. (ISBN 0-87481-489-8). Vedanta Pr.

M. D. Anderson Hospital & Tumor Institute, ed. see Annual Clinical Conference on Cancer, 22nd.

M. D. Anderson Symposia on Fundamental Cancer Research, 33rd. Genes, Chromosomes, & Neoplasia. Arrighi, Frances E., et al, eds. 550p. 1981. 67.50 (ISBN 0-89004-532-1). Raven.

M. Radetzki & S. Zorn Mining Journals Books Ltd. Financing Mining Projects in Developing Countries. 200p. 1980. 23.00x o.p. (ISBN 0-900117-17-6, Pub. by Mining Journal England); soft cover 17.00x o.p. (ISBN 0-686-64743-2). State Mutual Bk.

Ma, Cynthia, jt. auth. see Seeborg, Irmtraud.

Ma, Dong M., jt. auth. see Liveson, Jay A.

Ma, Laurence J. & Hanten, Edward W., eds. Urban Development in Modern China. (Special Studies on China & East Asia). 250p. 1981. lib. bdg. 20.00 (ISBN 0-86531-120-X). Westview.

Ma, Laurence J. C., jt. auth. see Pannell, Clifton W.

Ma, Mark T. Theory & Application of Antenna Arrays. LC 73-15615. 416p. 1974. 49.95x o.s.i. (ISBN 0-471-55795-1, Pub. by Wiley-Interscience). Wiley.

Ma, Nancy C. Mrs. Ma's Japanese Cooking. LC 79-1964. (Illus.). 1980. 13.50 (ISBN 0-87040-463-6). Japan Pubns.

Ma, T. S. & Horak, V. Microscale Manipulations in Chemistry. LC 75-20093. (Chemical Analysis Ser: Vol. 44). 480p. 1976. 66.00 (ISBN 0-471-55799-4, Pub. by Wiley-Interscience). Wiley.

Ma, T. S. & Lang, Robert E. Quantitative Analysis of Organic Mixtures: Part 1, General Principles. LC 78-23202. 1979. 46.00 (ISBN 0-471-55800-1, Pub. by Wiley-Interscience). Wiley.

Ma, Tis & Ladas, A. S. Organic Functional Group Analysis by Gas Chromatography. (Analyses of Organic Materials Ser.). 1976. 36.50 o.s.i. (ISBN 0-12-462850-8). Acad Pr.

Ma, Wendy Y., jt. ed. see Edgar, Neal L.

MAA Committee on Advisement & Personnel. Professional Opportunities in Mathematics. 11th ed. 1983. pap. 1.50 (ISBN 0-88385-440-6). Math Assn.

Maaloe, Ole, jt. auth. see Ingraham, John L.

Maanen, John Van see Van Maanen, John.

Maar, Len, jt. auth. see Doty, Roy.

Maaranen, Steven A., jt. ed. see Taylor, William J., Jr.

Maarse, H. & Belz, R. Isolation, Separation & Identification of Volatile Compounds in Aroma Research. 1982. lib. bdg. 54.50 (ISBN 90-277-1432-0, Pub. by Reidel Holland). Kluwer Boston.

Maas, Henry. The Letters of A. E. Housman. 488p. 1980. text ed. 14.50x o.p. (ISBN 0-246-64007-3). Humanities.

Maas, Henry S., ed. Social Service Research: Reviews of Studies. LC 78-65077. (NASW Research Ser.). 232p. 1978. pap. 12.95 (ISBN 0-685-46002-9, CBO-618-C). Natl Assn Soc Wrks.

Maas, J., ed. Medicinal Chemistry, Proceedings, Vol. IV. 350p. 1975. 66.00 (ISBN 0-444-41296-4). Elsevier.

Maas, James W., ed. MHPG (3-Methoxy 4-Hydroxyphenethyle Neglycol) Basic Mechansims & Psychopathology. LC 82-11640. (Behavioral Biology Ser.). Date not set. price not set (ISBN 0-12-462920-2). Acad Pr.

Maas, James W., jt. ed. see Davis, John M.

Maas, Peter. The Valachi Papers. (Illus.). 1968. 7.95 o.p. (ISBN 0-399-10832-7). Putnam Pub Group.

Maass, Arthur. Muddy Waters: The Army Engineers & the Nation's Rivers. LC 73-20238. (FDR & the Era of the New Deal Ser). 306p. 1974. Repr. of 1951 ed. lib. bdg. 39.50 (ISBN 0-306-70607-5). Da Capo.

Maass, Arthur & Anderson, Raymond L. And the Desert Shall Rejoice: Conflict, Growth, & Justice in Arid Environments. LC 77-17866. 1978. 27.50x (ISBN 0-262-13134-X). MIT Pr.

Maass, Joachim. Kleist: A Biography. Manheim, Ralph, tr. from Ger. 320p. 1983. 17.95 (ISBN 0-374-18162-4). FS&G.

Mabardi, Georges & Luce, Clare B. Vanity Fair's Backgammon to Win. 1974. 5.95 o.p. (ISBN 0-671-21766-6). S&S.

Mabbott, J. D. State & the Citizen: An Introduction to Political Philosophy. 2nd ed. 1967. pap. text ed. 6.50x o.p. (ISBN 0-391-02081-1, Hutchinson U Lib). Humanities.

Mabbott, T. O., ed. see Poe, Edgar Allan.

Mabbott, Thomas O., ed. see Poe, Edgar Allan.

Mabbutt, J. A. Desert Landforms. 1977. 22.00x (ISBN 0-262-13131-5). MIT Pr.

Mabbutt, J. A. & Floret, C., eds. Case Studies on Desertification. (Natural Resources Research Ser.: No. 18). (Illus.). 280p. 1981. pap. 44.75 (ISBN 92-3-101820-5, U1103, UNESCO). Unipub.

Mabert, Vincent A. An Introduction to Short Term Forecasting Using the Box-Jenkins Methodology. 1975. pap. text ed. 14.00 (ISBN 0-89806-023-0, 53); pap. text ed. 7.00 members. Inst Indus Eng.

Mabert, Vincent A. & Moodie, Colin L., eds. Production Planning, Scheduling, & Inventory Control: Concepts, Techniques, & Systems. 2nd ed. 1982. 21.00 (ISBN 0-89806-032-X); members 12.00. Inst Indus Eng.

Mabey, Richard. Oak & Company. LC 82-15618. (Illus.). 28p. (gr. 1-3). 1983. 9.00 (ISBN 0-688-01993-5). Greenwillow.

Mabey, Richard, jt. auth. see Jeffries.

Mabie, C. W. Behold I Show You a Mystery. LC 80-82229. 150p. (Orig.). 1980. pap. 3.95 (ISBN 0-9601416-5-0). J C Print.

Mabie, Hamilton H. & Ocvirk, Fred W. Mechanisms & Dynamics of Machinery. 3rd ed. LC 74-30405. 616p. 1975. text ed. 39.95 (ISBN 0-471-55935-0); solutions 10.00 (ISBN 0-471-55938-5). Wiley.

--Mechanisms & Dynamics of Machinery, SI Version. 3rd ed. LC 78-1382. 1978. text ed. 40.95x (ISBN 0-471-02380-9); solutions 17.50 (ISBN 0-471-04134-3). Wiley.

Mabie, Hamilton W., ed. Folk Tales Every Child Should Know. (Illus.). 215p. 1983. Repr. of 1914 ed. lib. bdg. 30.00 (ISBN 0-89760-572-1). Telegraph Bks.

Mabogunje, A. L., et al. Shelter Provision in Developing Countries: Scope Report 11. Jackson, Ian, ed. LC 77-14301. (Scientific Comittee on Problems of the Environment). 1978. 16.95 (ISBN 0-471-99581-9, Pub. by Wiley-Interscience). Wiley.

Mabott, T. O., ed. see Poe, Edgar Allan.

Mabro, Robert. The Egyptian Economy 1952-1972. (Economies of the World Ser). 368p. 1974. text ed. 24.00x o.p. (ISBN 0-19-877030-8). Oxford U Pr.

Mabry, C. Charlton, et al. Recent Advances in Pediatric Clinical Pathology. LC 68-13195. 256p. 1968. 57.00 o.p. (ISBN 0-8089-0275-X). Grune.

Mabry, Edward & Barnes, Richard. The Dynamics of Small Group Communication. LC 78-69597. (Illus.). 1979. text ed. 10.95 o.p. (ISBN 0-395-26713-7); inst. manual write for info. o.p. (ISBN 0-395-26714-5). HM.

Mabry, Edward A. & Barnes, Richard E. The Dynamics of Small Group Communication. (Illus.). 1980. text ed. 21.95 (ISBN 0-13-222000-8). P-H.

Mabry, T. J., et al, eds. Creosote Bush. LC 76-58381. (US-IBP Synthesis Ser.). 1977. 46.00 (ISBN 0-12-787010-5). Acad Pr.

McAally, Mary, ed. We Sing Our Struggle: A Tribute to Us All. (Illus.). 82p. (Orig.). 1982. pap. 5.00 (ISBN 0-943594-03-0). Cardinal Pr.

Macadam, Alta. Venice. (Blue Guide Ser.). 1982. 24.95 (ISBN 0-393-01555-6); pap. 13.95 (ISBN 0-393-30007-2). Norton.

MacAdam, David L., ed. Sources of Color Science. LC 77-110231. 1970. pap. 5.95 o.p. (ISBN 0-262-63064-8). MIT Pr.

McAdam, Doug. Political Process & the Development of Black Insurgency, 1930 to 1970. LC 82-2712. (Illus.). 1982. lib. bdg. 25.00x (ISBN 0-226-55551-8). U of Chicago Pr.

McAdam, E. L., Jr., ed. see Johnson, Samuel.

McAdam, E. L., Jr., et al, eds. see Johnson, Samuel.

McAdam, Edward, ed. see Johnson, Samuel.

Macadam, I., ed. Annual Register of World Events, 10 vols. Incl. Vol. 1. 1961. 600p. o.p. (ISBN 0-685-23140-2); Vol. 3. 1965. 582p. o.p. (ISBN 0-685-23141-0); Vol. 4. 1966. 574p. o.p. (ISBN 0-685-23142-9); Vol. 5. 1967. 562p. 25.00x o.p. (ISBN 0-685-23143-7); Vol. 6. 1968. 600p. o.p. (ISBN 0-312-03920-4); Vol. 7. 1969. 600p. o.p. (ISBN 0-312-03955-7). (Vol. 2, 1962). St Martin.

McAdam, Pat & Snider, Sandra. Arcadia: Where Ranch & City Meet. (Illus.). 180p. 1981. 30.00 o.p. (ISBN 0-686-31780-7). Friends Arcadia.

McAdam, Robert E., et al. Research & Project Funding for the Uninitiated. (Illus.). 82p. 1982. spiral 17.75x (ISBN 0-398-04635-2). C C Thomas.

McAdam, Stephen J., jt. auth. see Armendariz, Efraim P.

MacAdams, Cynthia. Rising Goddess. Morgan, Jennifer, ed. (Illus.). 128p. (Orig.). 1982. pap. 18.95 (ISBN 0-87100-186-1). Morgan.

McAdams, Phyllis J. The Parent in the Shadows. 1972. pap. 0.50 (ISBN 0-87868-103-5, FP-1). Child Welfare.

McAdams, William H. Heat Transmission. 3rd ed. (Chemical Engineering Ser.). (Illus.). 1954. text ed. 38.95 (ISBN 0-07-044799-3, C); answers 3.00 (ISBN 0-07-044800-0). McGraw.

McAdoo, Dale, tr. see Le Huede, Henri.

McAdoo, Eleanor Wilson, ed. see Wilson, Woodrow & Wilson, Ellen Axson.

McAdoo, Henry R. The Unity of Anglicanism: Catholic & Reformed. 48p. 1983. pap. write for info. (ISBN 0-8192-1324-1). Morehouse.

McAdow, Berl. From Crested Peaks: The Story of Adams State College of Colorado. LC 82-72395. 103p. 1961. 3.95 (ISBN 0-8040-0335-1). Swallow.

McAfee, John P., et al. Vietnam Heroes II: The Tears of a Generation. Poems & Prose on the Consequences of War. Topham, J., ed. LC 82-11465. 40p. (Orig.). 1982. pap. text ed. 3.95 (ISBN 0-933486-38-3). Am Poetry Pr.

Macafee, Norman, tr. see Pasolini, Pier P.

McAfee, R. Bruce, jt. auth. see Maier, Ernest L.

McAfee, Ward. California's Railroad Era Eighteen-Fifty to-Nineteen Eleven. LC 73-18280. (Illus.). 296p. 14.95 (ISBN 0-87095-048-7). Golden West.

McAleavey, David. The Forty Days. 40p. 1975. 3.50 (ISBN 0-87886-071-1). Ithaca Hse.

--Shrine, Shelter, Cave. LC 80-19572. 72p. 1980. 4.00 (ISBN 0-87886-110-6). Ithaca Hse.

McAleavvy, David. Sterling Four-O-Three. 1971. 2.95 o.p. (ISBN 0-87886-012-6). Ithaca Hse.

McAleer, Edward C. The Brownings of Casa Guidi. (Illus.). 15.75x (ISBN 0-685-99384-1, Pub. by Browning Inst); pap. 8.45x o.p. (ISBN 0-930252-04-7). Pub Ctr Cult Res.

McAleer, Edward C., ed. see Browning, Robert.

McAleer, John & Dickson, Billy. Unit Pride. 1982. pap. 2.95 (ISBN 0-553-20904-3). Bantam.

McAleese, Ray, jt. ed. see Unwin, Derick.

McAlester, A. Earth: An Introduction to the Geological & Geophysical Sciences. 1973. 26.95 (ISBN 0-13-222422-4); instr. res. bk. 1.95 (ISBN 0-13-222695-2); study guide 5.95 (ISBN 0-13-222380-5). P-H.

McAlester, A. Lee. The History of Life. 2nd ed. (Illus.). 1977. 11.95 (ISBN 0-13-390146-7); pap. text ed. 8.95 (ISBN 0-13-390120-3). P-H.

McAlester, A. Lee & Hay, Edward A. Physical Geology: Principles & Perspectives. (Illus.). 448p. 1975. 25.95 (ISBN 0-13-669523-X); study guide 5.95 (ISBN 0-13-669531-0). P-H.

McAlester, Lee, jt. auth. see Eicher, Don.

McAlexander, Aaron. Hands-On Applied Physics. LC 79-356. 1979. text ed. 19.95 (ISBN 0-8053-7030-7). Benjamin-Cummings.

McAlister, Joan. Radionuclide Techniques in Medicine. LC 78-68348. (Techniques of Measurement in Medicine: No. 3). 1980. 45.00 (ISBN 0-521-22402-0); pap. 13.95x (ISBN 0-521-29474-6). Cambridge U Pr.

McAlister, Linda. The Development of Franz Brentano's Ethics. 170p. 1982. pap. text ed. 16.25x (ISBN 0-391-01954-6). Humanities.

McAlister, Linda, tr. see Brentano, Franz.

McAlister, Linda L., tr. see Wittgenstein, Ludwig.

McAlister, Marcia. With House in Hand. Steich, Marianne, ed. (Illus.). 30p. 1982. pap. 11.95 (ISBN 0-939114-80-1). Wimmer Bks.

McAlister, Pam, ed. Reweaving the Web of Life: Feminism & Nonviolence. LC 82-81879. 440p. 1982. 19.95 (ISBN 0-86571-017-1); pap. 8.95 (ISBN 0-86571-016-3). New Soc Pubs.

McAllister, David F., jt. auth. see Stanat, Donald F.

McAllister, David W. The Reconstruction of Gianbattista Vico's Theory of the Cycles of History with Applications to Contemporary Historical Experience. (The Essential Library of the Great Philosophers). (Illus.). 149p. 1983. 47.75 (ISBN 0-89266-396-0). Am Classical Coll Pr.

McAllister, Donald. Evaluation in Environmental Planning: Assessing Environmental, Social, Economic & Political Tradeoffs. 1980. 27.50x o.p. (ISBN 0-262-13146-3); pap. 9.95x (ISBN 0-262-63087-7). MIT Pr.

McAllister, Eugene J., ed. Agenda for Progress. 1981. pap. cancelled o.p. (ISBN 0-89195-029-X). Caroline Hse.

McAllister, Ian. Regional Development & the European Economic Community: A Canadian Perspective. 243p. 1982. pap. 13.95x (ISBN 0-920380-59-X, Pub. by Inst Res Pub Canada). Renouf.

McAllister, Ian, jt. auth. see Rose, Richard.

McAlpin, Heller. Nostalgia. 272p. 1982. 12.95 (ISBN 0-684-17768-4, ScribT). Scribner.

McAlpin, Michelle B. Subject to Famine: Food Crisis & Economic Change in Western India, 1860-1920. LC 82-61376. 320p. 1983. 35.00x (ISBN 0-691-05385-5). Princeton U Pr.

McAlpine, Helen & McAlpine, William. Japanese Tales & Legends. (Oxford Myths & Legends Ser.). (Illus.). (gr. 3-12). 1980. 14.95 (ISBN 0-19-274125-X). Oxford U Pr.

Macalpine, Ida, jt. auth. see Hunter, Richard.

McAlpine, William, jt. auth. see McAlpine, Helen.

MacAmhlaigh, Donall. An Irish Navvy: The Diary of an Exile. Iremonger, Valentin, tr. 1964. pap. 5.95 o.p. (ISBN 0-7100-2854-7). Routledge & Kegan.

McAnally, David R. Irish Wonders: The Ghosts, Giants, Pookas, Demons, Leprechauns, Banshees, Fairies, Witches, Widows, Old Maids, & Other Marvels of the Emerald Isle. Popular Tales As Told by the People. LC 79-175738. (Illus.). xii, 218p. 1971. Repr. of 1888 ed. 40.00x (ISBN 0-8103-3818-1). Gale.

McAnany, Patrick D., jt. ed. see Gerber, Rudolph J.

McAnarney, Elizabeth. Premature Adolescent Pregnancy & Parenthood. Date not set. price not set (ISBN 0-8089-1518-5). Grune.

McAnarney, Elizabeth R., jt. auth. see Aten, Marilyn J.

MacAndrew, Andrew, tr. see Dostoyevsky, Fedor.

MacAndrew, Andrew R., tr. see Dostoevsky, Fyodor.

MacAndrew, Andrew R., tr. see Dostoyevsky, Fyodor.

Macandrew, Hugh. Catalogue of the Italian Drawings in the Museum of Fine Arts, Boston. (Illus.). 128p. 1983. 17.50x (ISBN 0-87846-228-7). Mus Fine Arts Boston.

McAndrew, John. Venetian Architecture of the Early Renaissance. (Illus.). 672p. 1980. 45.00 (ISBN 0-262-13157-9). MIT Pr.

MacAndrews, C., jt. auth. see Chia, L. S.

MacAndrews, Colin & Sien, Chia Lin, eds. Too Rapid Rural Development: Perceptions & Perspectives from Southeast Asia. LC 82-60405. xiv, 370p. 1982. lib. bdg. 19.95x (ISBN 0-8214-0668-X, 82-84366); pap. 10.95 (ISBN 0-8214-0669-8, 82-84374). Ohio U Pr.

Macaraya, Batua A., jt. auth. see McKaughan, Howard P.

McArdle, Alma deC. & McArdle, Deirdred B. Carpenter Gothic: Nineteenth Century Ornamented Houses of New England. (Illus.). 160p. 1983. pap. 14.95 (ISBN 0-8230-7101-4, Whitney Lib). Watson-Guptill.

McArdle, Deirdred B., jt. auth. see McArdle, Alma deC.

Macardle, Dorothy. The Uninvited. 342p. 1976. Repr. of 1942 ed. lib. bdg. 17.95x (ISBN 0-89244-068-6). Queens Hse.

McArdle, Frank. Altopascio: A Study in Tuscan Rural Society, 1587-1784. LC 76-53261. (Cambridge Studies in Early Modern History). (Illus.). 1978. 37.50 (ISBN 0-521-21619-2). Cambridge U Pr.

McArdle, H. & Suggitt, G. Per Saecula. 1974. Pt. 1. pap. text ed. 4.00x (ISBN 0-05-002171-0); Pt. 2. pap. text ed. 4.00x (ISBN 0-05-002684-4); Pt. 3. pap. text ed. 4.00x (ISBN 0-05-002685-2). Longman.

McArdle, William D., jt. auth. see Katch, Frank I.

Macaree, David & Macaree, Mary. One Hundred & Nine Walks In B.C.'s Lower Mainland. 2nd ed. (Illus.). 192p. 1983. pap. 7.95 (ISBN 0-89886-068-7). Mountaineers.

--One Hundred Nine Walks in B.C.'s Lower Mainland. LC 76-19472. (Illus.). 192p. (Orig.). 1976. pap. 6.95 o.p. (ISBN 0-916890-42-2). Mountaineers.

Macaree, Mary, jt. auth. see Macaree, David.

Maca-Roueche, Suanne & Patterson, Dorothy. Awareness: Exercises in Basic Composition Skills. 2nd ed. LC 77-20918. 1978. pap. text ed. 15.50x (ISBN 0-673-15689-3). Scott F.

MacArthur, Catherine. George's Women. LC 79-3991. 1979. 8.95 o.p. (ISBN 0-312-32461-8). St Martin.

McArthur, Colin, ed. Scotch Reels. (Illus.). 96p. 1982. pap. 9.95 (ISBN 0-85170-121-3). NY Zoetrope.

McArthur, D. G. Les Constructions Verbales du Francais Contemporain. 1971. 12.00 (ISBN 0-7190-1250-3). Manchester.

McArthur, Edwin. Flagstad: A Personal Memoir. (Music Reprint Ser.: 1980). (Illus.). 1980. Repr. of 1965 ed. lib. bdg. 29.50 (ISBN 0-306-76028-2). Da Capo.

McArthur, Harvey K. Understanding the Sermon on the Mount. LC 78-16404. 1978. Repr. of 1960 ed. lib. bdg. 20.75 (ISBN 0-313-20569-8, MCUS). Greenwood.

MacArthur, John. Giving God's Way. 1978. pap. 2.50 pocket paper (ISBN 0-8423-1034-7). Tyndale.

MacArthur, John F., Jr. Keys to Spiritual Growth. 1976. pap. 4.95 (ISBN 0-8007-5013-6, Power Bks). Revell.

MacArthur, John, Jr. Beware the Pretenders. 94p. 1980. pap. 1.95 o.p. (ISBN 0-88207-798-8). Victor Bks.

--Jesus' Pattern of Prayer. LC 81-3947. 200p. 1981. 8.95 (ISBN 0-8024-4961-1). Moody.

--Kingdom Living Here & Now. LC 79-25326. 1980. pap. 5.95 (ISBN 0-8024-4562-4). Moody.

--The Ultimate Priority. 1983. pap. 4.95 (ISBN 0-8024-0186-4). Moody.

--Why I Trust the Bible. 120p. 1983. pap. 3.95 (ISBN 0-88207-389-3). Victor Bks.

McArthur, Lewis A. Oregon Geographic Names. 5th, rev. ed. McArthur, Lewis L., rev. by. 864p. 1982. 21.95 (ISBN 0-87595-113-9, Western Imprints); pap. 14.95 (ISBN 0-87595-114-7, Western Imprints). Oreg Hist Soc.

McArthur, Lewis L., rev. by see McArthur, Lewis A.

McArthur, Norma. Island Populations of the Pacific. LC 82-24169. (Illus.). xvi, 381p. 1983. Repr. of 1967 ed. lib. bdg. 45.00x (ISBN 0-313-22914-7, MCIPP). Greenwood.

MacArthur, William J. Knoxville: Crossroads of the New South. Silvey, Kitty & Alexander, Lynn, eds. LC 82-71491. (The American Portrait Ser.). (Illus.). 240p. 1982. 29.95 (ISBN 0-932986-32-3). Continent Herit.

MacArthur, William J., Jr., ed. Old Knoxville Postcards. LC 81-14805. (Illus.). 16p. 1982. pap. 3.95 (ISBN 0-87049-337-X). U of Tenn Pr.

Macartney, C. A., tr. see Shestov, Lev.

Macartney-Filgate, Terence, jt. auth. see Whitehead, William.

MacAulay, Barbara D., jt. ed. see Sloane, Howard N., Jr.

Macaulay, Catharine. Letters on Education, with Observations on Religious & Metaphysical Subjects. (The Feminist Controversy in England, 1788-1810 Ser.). 1974. lib. bdg. 50.00 o.s.i. (ISBN 0-8240-0872-3). Garland Pub.

Macaulay, David. Castle. LC 77-7159. (Illus.). (gr. 1 up). 1977. 13.95 (ISBN 0-395-25784-0). HM.

--Underground. (Illus.). 112p. 1983. 5.95 (ISBN 0-395-34065-9). HM.

Macaulay, J. C. Behold Your King. LC 81-22580. 256p. 1982. pap. 7.95 (ISBN 0-8024-2417-1). Moody.

--Expository Commentary on Acts. 1978. 9.95 o.p. (ISBN 0-8024-2421-X). Moody.

--Expository Commentary on Hebrews. 1978. 9.95 o.p. (ISBN 0-8024-2422-8). Moody.

--Expository Commentary on John. 1978. 9.95 o.p. (ISBN 0-8024-2420-1). Moody.

--Life in Spirit. LC 77-27455. 1978. pap. 2.95 (ISBN 0-8024-4784-8). Moody.

Macaulay, Janet, jt. auth. see Cox, Barbara G.

Macaulay, Ranald & Barrs, Jerram. Being Human: The Nature of Spiritual Experience. LC 77-11365. 1978. pap. 6.95 (ISBN 0-87784-796-7). Inter-Varsity.

Macaulay, Ronald. Generally Speaking: How Children Learn Language. (Orig.). 1980. pap. text ed. 9.95 (ISBN 0-88377-162-4). Newbury Hse.

McAulay, Sara. In Search of the Petroglyph. LC 78-9290. (Illus.). (gr. 6-8). 1978. 7.95 o.p. (ISBN 0-698-20470-0, Coward). Putnam Pub Group.

Macaulay, Stewart. Law & the Balance of Power: The Automobile Manufacturers & Their Dealers. LC 66-26503. 224p. 1966. 8.50x (ISBN 0-87154-574-8). Russell Sage.

Macaulay, Thomas. Critical & Historical Essays, Vol. 1. 1966. Repr. of 1907 ed. 9.95x (ISBN 0-460-00225-2, Evman). Biblio Dist.

--The History of England. Trevor-Roper, Hugh, ed. (English Library Ser.). 1979. pap. 5.95 (ISBN 0-14-043133-0). Penguin.

Macaulay, Thomas B. Critical & Historical Essays, Vol. 2. 9.95x (ISBN 0-460-00226-0, Evman). Biblio Dist.

--History of England, Vol. 2. 1976. 14.95x (ISBN 0-460-00035-7, Evman). Biblio Dist.

--History of England, Vol. 3. 1976. 14.95x (ISBN 0-460-00036-5, Evman). Biblio Dist.

--History of England, Vol. 4. 1976. 14.95x (ISBN 0-460-00037-3, Evman). Biblio Dist.

--History of England: From the Accession of James II, Vol. 1. 1976. 14.95x (ISBN 0-460-00034-9, Evman). Biblio Dist.

--Selected Writings. Clive, John & Pinney, Thomas, eds. LC 78-171350. (Classics of British Historical Literature Ser). 544p. 1972. 25.00x o.s.i. (ISBN 0-226-49996-0); pap. write for info. U of Chicago Pr.

--Speeches by Lord Macaulay, with His Minute on Indian Education. Young, G. M., ed. LC 76-29441. 1935. 28.00 (ISBN 0-404-15348-8). AMS Pr.

McAuley, Alastair. Economic Welfare in the Soviet Union: Poverty, Living Standards, & Inequality. LC 78-53290. 400p. 1979. 35.00 (ISBN 0-299-07640-7). U of Wis Pr.

Macauley, Hugh, Jr. & Yandle, Bruce, Jr. Environmental Use & the Market. LC 77-91. 160p. 1977. 19.95x (ISBN 0-669-01431-1). Lexington Bks.

McAuley, James. Versification: A Short Introduction. viii, 83p. 1966. 3.00 o.p. (ISBN 0-87013-096-X). Mich St U Pr.

McAuley, James, ed. A Map of Australian Verse: The Twentieth Century. 1976. pap. 18.95x (ISBN 0-19-550474-7). Oxford U Pr.

McAuley, James J. Exile's Book of Hours: A Sequence. 1982. pap. 4.00 (ISBN 0-917652-29-0). Confluence Pr.

McAuley, Milt. Hiking Trails of Malibu Creek State Park (Santa Monica Mountains) LC 82-74274. (Illus.). 112p. 1983. pap. 5.95 (ISBN 0-942568-04-4). Canyon Pub Co.

Macauley, Ted. The Yamaha Legend. 248p. 1980. 15.95 o.p. (ISBN 0-312-89609-3). St Martin.

Macauley, Thomas B. The Letters of Thomas Babington Macaulay. Pinney, T., ed. LC 73-75860. 1977. Vol. 1. 72.00 (ISBN 0-521-20201-9); Vol. 2. 72.00 (ISBN 0-521-20202-7); Vol. 3. 72.00 (ISBN 0-521-21125-5); Vol. 4. 72.00 (ISBN 0-521-21126-3); Vol. 5. 95.00 (ISBN 0-521-22749-6); Vol. 6. 95.00 (ISBN 0-521-22750-X). Cambridge U Pr.

McAuliffe, Charles A. Hydrogen & Energy. 112p. 1980. 12.95 (ISBN 0-87201-372-3). Gulf Pub.

McAuliffe, Conn. Re-Action. LC 74-141218. (Illus.). 1971. pap. cancelled o.p. (ISBN 0-87835-014-4). Boyd & Fraser.

McAuliffe, Kathleen, jt. auth. see McAuliffe, Sharon.

McAuliffe, Sharon & McAuliffe, Kathleen. Life for Sale. 288p. 1981. 12.95 (ISBN 0-698-11098-6, Coward). Putnam Pub Group.

McAuslan, J. P., jt. ed. see Kanyeihamba, G. W.

MacAvoy, Paul W. Crude Oil Prices: As Determined by OPEC & Market Fundamentals. 224p. 1982. prof ref 26.50x (ISBN 0-88410-870-8). Ballinger Pub.

--Economic Strategy for Developing Nuclear Breeder Reactors. 1969. 25.00x (ISBN 0-262-13054-8). MIT Pr.

--Energy Policy: An Economic Analysis. (Illus.). 1983. 17.50 (ISBN 0-393-01723-0). Norton.

--Energy Policy: An Economic Analysis. pap. text ed. 4.95x (ISBN 0-393-95321-1). Norton.

MacAvoy, Paul W., jt. auth. see Breyer, Stephen G.

Macavoy, Paul W., ed. Unsettled Questions on Regulatory Reform. 1978. pap. 3.25 (ISBN 0-8447-3328-8). Am Enterprise.

Macavoy, Paul W. & Snow, John W., eds. Regulation of Passenger Fares & Competition Among Airlines. 1977. pap. 7.25 (ISBN 0-8447-3256-7). Am Enterprise.

McAvoy, Thomas T. Formation of the American Catholic Minority, 1820-1860. Wolf, Richard C., ed. LC 67-22985. (Facet Bks). 1967. pap. 0.50 o.p. (ISBN 0-8006-3042-4, 1-3042). Fortress.

McAvoy, William C. Dramatic Tragedy. (Patterns in Literary Art Ser.). 1971. 9.16 (ISBN 0-07-044790-X, W). McGraw.

McBain, Ed. Beauty & the Beast. LC 82-11896. 228p. 1983. 13.50 (ISBN 0-03-062198-4). HR&W.

--Blood Relatives. 1982. pap. 2.50 (ISBN 0-451-11854-5, AE1854, Sig). NAL.

--Bread. 1982. pap. 2.25 (ISBN 0-451-11279-2, AE1279, Sig). NAL.

--The Empty Hours. 1982. pap. 2.25 (ISBN 0-451-11835-9, AE1835, Sig). NAL.

--Even the Wicked. 1982. pap. 2.25 (ISBN 0-451-11872-3, AE1872, Sig). NAL.

--Fuzz. pap. 1.75 o.p. (ISBN 0-451-08399-7, E8399, Sig). NAL.

--Ghosts. (Large Print Bks.). 1980. lib. bdg. 12.95 o.p. (ISBN 0-8161-3128-7). G K Hall.

--Heat. 208p. 1983. pap. 2.50 (ISBN 0-345-30673-2). Ballantine.

--The Heckler. 1982. pap. 2.25 (ISBN 0-451-11421-3, AE1421, Sig). NAL.

--Ice. 305p. 1983. 15.50 (ISBN 0-87795-468-2). Arbor Hse.

--Lady, Lady, I Did It. 1982. pap. 2.25 (ISBN 0-451-11779-4, AE1779, Sig). NAL.

--Like Love. 1982. pap. 2.25 (ISBN 0-451-11628-3, AE1628, Sig). NAL.

--Long Time No See: Eighty-Seventh Precinct Mystery. 1982. pap. 2.50 (ISBN 0-553-23130-8). Bantam.

--Ten Plus One. 1982. pap. 2.25 (ISBN 0-451-11923-1, AE1923, Sig). NAL.

--Vanishing Ladies. 1982. pap. 2.25 (ISBN 0-451-11463-9, AE1463, Sig). NAL.

McBain, Laurie. Chance the Winds of Fortune. 416p. 1980. pap. 3.95 (ISBN 0-380-75796-6, 82545-7). Avon.

--Devil's Desire. 1975. pap. 3.50 (ISBN 0-380-00295-7, 81802-7). Avon.

--Moonstruck Madness. 408p. 1977. pap. 3.95 (ISBN 0-380-00871-8, 82552). Avon.

MacBean, Alasdair & Balasubramanyam, V. N. Meeting the Third World Challenge. LC 76-16702. (World Economic Issues Ser.). 1976. 23.00 (ISBN 0-312-52850-7). St Martin.

McBean, Eleanor. Answers for the Worried Smoker. 3.00x (ISBN 0-686-29801-2). Cancer Control Soc.

--Vaccination Condemned. 1981. 12.50 (ISBN 0-686-37948-9). Cancer Control Soc.

McBeath, Gerald A. & Morehouse, Thomas A. The Dynamics of Alaska Native Self-Government. LC 80-8166. 141p. 1980. lib. bdg. 18.75 (ISBN 0-8191-1171-6); pap. text ed. 8.25 (ISBN 0-8191-1172-4). U Pr of Amer.

McBeath, Ron & Sleeman, Phillip, eds. Trends & Practices. (Instructional Media & Technology Ser.: Vol. 1). 210p. (Orig.). 1983. pap. text ed. 11.50 (ISBN 0-89503-041-1). Baywood Pub.

McBeath, Ronald J., ed. see Finn, James D.

McBee, Robert & Burgess, Tom, eds. Coaches' Guide to Championship Baseball Drills & Fundamentals. LC 82-45643. 250p. 1982. pap. write for info. (ISBN 0-9609500-0-1). McBee Sports.

MacBeth, Brian, tr. see Da Silva, Raul, et al.

MacBeth, George. The Katana. 1982. 13.95 (ISBN 0-671-43245-1). S&S.

--The Katana. 240p. 1983. pap. 2.95 (ISBN 0-425-05823-9). Berkley Pub.

--Night of Stones. LC 69-15506. 1968. pap. 2.45 o.p. (ISBN 0-689-10173-2). Atheneum.

--Poems from Oby. LC 82-73012. 72p. (Orig.). 1983. 10.95 (ISBN 0-689-11373-0); pap. 6.95 (ISBN 0-689-11374-9). Atheneum.

--The Samurai. LC 75-2234. 240p. 1975. 6.95 o.p. (ISBN 0-15-179270-4). HarBraceJ.

--The Samurai. 1976. pap. 1.95 o.p. (ISBN 0-451-07021-6, J7021, Sig). NAL.

McBeth, Leon. Hombres Claves En las Misiones. Orig. Title: Men Who Made Missions. 128p. 1980. pap. 3.75 (ISBN 0-311-01070-9). Casa Bautista.

McBeth, Leon H. History of Baptists. 1983. 17.95 (ISBN 0-8054-6569-3). Broadman.

Macbeth, Norman. Darwin Retried: An Appeal to Reason. LC 73-160418. 1979. pap. 5.95 (ISBN 0-87645-105-9). Gambit.

McBeth, Sally J. Ethnic Identity & the Boarding School Experience of West-Central Oklahoma American Indians. LC 82-21983. (Illus.). 184p. (Orig.). 1983. lib. bdg. 21.75 (ISBN 0-8191-2895-3); pap. text ed. 10.00 (ISBN 0-8191-2896-1). U Pr of Amer.

McBirney, A. R. Igneous Petrology. 1983. write for info. (ISBN 0-87735-323-9). Freeman C.

McBirney, Alexander R., jt. auth. see Williams, Howel.

McBirnie, S. C. & Fox, W. J. Marine Steam Engines & Turbines. 4th ed. (Illus.). 672p. 1980. text ed. 49.95 (ISBN 0-408-00387-1). Butterworth.

McBirnie, William. Search for the Early Church. 1978. pap. 3.95 (ISBN 0-8423-5834-X). Tyndale.

--Seven Sins of Jonah. 1981. pap. 2.25 (ISBN 0-8423-5876-5). Tyndale.

McBirnie, William S. How to Motivate Your Child Toward Success. 1979. pap. 3.95 (ISBN 0-8423-1528-4). Tyndale.

M'Bow, Amadou-Mahtar. The Spirit of Nairobi. 190p. 1978. pap. 7.00 o.p. (ISBN 0-686-94173-X, UNESCO). Unipub.

M'Bow, Amadou-Mahtar & Vercoutter, Jean. The Image of the Black in Western Art, Vol. I: From the Pharaohs to the Fall of the Roman Empire. Bugner, Ladislas, ed. (Illus.). 352p. 1983. 65.00 (ISBN 0-939594-01-3). Menil Found.

McBoyle, Geoffrey. Climate in Review. LC 72-3536. 1973. pap. text ed. 14.95 (ISBN 0-395-16007-3). HM.

McBriar, A. M. Fabian Socialism & English Politics, Eighteen Eighty-Four - Nineteen Eighteen. 1962. pap. 16.95x (ISBN 0-521-09351-1). Cambridge U Pr.

McBride, A. Human Dimension of Catechetics. 1969. pap. 2.95 o.p. (ISBN 0-685-43926-7, 80454). Glencoe.

McBride, Adam C. Fractional Calculus & Integral Transforms of Generalized Functions. (Research in Mathematics Ser.: No. 31). 179p. (Orig.). 1979. pap. text ed. 20.95 (ISBN 0-273-08415-1). Pitman Pub MA.

McBride, Alfred. Catechetics: A Theology of Proclamation. (Orig.). 1966. pap. 2.25 o.p. (ISBN 0-685-07616-4, 80450). Glencoe.

--Death Shall Have No Dominion. 208p. 1979. pap. 4.60 (ISBN 0-697-01700-1); tchr's manual 3.75 (ISBN 0-697-01707-9); pap. text ed. write for info. Wm C Brown.

--Saints Are People: Church History Through the Saints. 144p. (Orig.). 1981. pap. 4.50 (ISBN 0-697-01783-4). Wm C Brown.

--Year of the Lord: Reflections on the Sunday Readings. cycle A 6.95 (ISBN 0-697-01847-4); cycle B 6.95 (ISBN 0-697-01848-2). Wm C Brown.

McBride, Angela B. Living with Contradictions: A Married Feminist. 1977. pap. 4.95i o.p. (ISBN 0-06-090556-5, CN 556, CN). Har-Row.

Mcbride, Davil. Evaders. LC 81-86159. 233p. 1983. pap. 5.95 (ISBN 0-86666-063-1). GWP.

McBride, Dick. Cometh with Clouds, (Memory: Allen Ginsberg) 64p. 1982. 12.00x (ISBN 0-916156-54-0); pap. 5.00x (ISBN 0-916156-51-6). Cherry Valley.

McBride, Joseph. Orson Welles. 1972. pap. 8.95 (ISBN 0-436-09927-6, Pub by Secker & Warburg). David & Charles.

McBride, Joseph & Wilmington, Michael. John Ford. LC 75-19281. (Theatre, Film & the Performing Arts Ser.). (Illus.). 234p. 1975. lib. bdg. 22.50 (ISBN 0-306-70750-0); pap. 6.95 (ISBN 0-306-80016-0). Da Capo.

McBride, Mekeel. No Ordinary World. LC 79-51606. (Poetry Ser.). 1979. 8.95 (ISBN 0-915604-29-9); pap. 4.95 (ISBN 0-915604-30-2). Carnegie-Mellon.

McBride, Neal. Adult Class: Caring for Each Other. 1978. pap. 1.50 (ISBN 0-8307-0507-4, 99-703-04). Regal.

McBride, Richard. Lonely the Autumn Bird: Two Novels. LC 82-71231. 93p. (Orig.). 1963. pap. 3.75 (ISBN 0-8040-0189-8). Swallow.

--Memoirs of a Natural-Born Expatriate. LC 82-71348. 115p. 1966. 5.95 (ISBN 0-8040-0201-0); pap. 3.25 (ISBN 0-8040-0202-9). Swallow.

McBride, Richard, jt. ed. see Crabbe, David.

McBride, Robert L. Art of Instructing the Jury with 1978 Supplement. 545p. 1969. text ed. 47.50 (ISBN 0-87084-553-5). Anderson Pub Co.

MacBride, Roger L., jt. auth. see Lane, Rose W.
McBride, William G., jt. auth. see Cline, Ruth K.
McBride, William L. The Philosophy of Marx. LC 77-74774. 1977. 17.95x (ISBN 0-312-60675-3). St Martin.
Macbridge, Angus, ed. Way They Lived. 8.50 (ISBN 0-392-16638-0, SpS). Sportshelf.
McBryde, I. M., ed. Records of Time Past: Ethnohistorical Essays on the Culture & Ecology of the New England Tribes. (AIAS Ethnohistory: No. 3). 1978. pap. text ed. 21.75x (ISBN 0-85575-067-7). Humanities.
McBryde, Isabel, ed. Myall Creek Massacre. Date not set. pap. text ed. price not set (ISBN 0-391-01197-9). Humanities.
McBurney, Bill. Star People. (Illus.). 64p. 1983. pap. 2.95 (ISBN 0-943392-08-X). Tribeca Comm.
McBurney, C. B. Haua Fteah & the Stone Age of the South-East Mediterranean. 1968. 110.00 (ISBN 0-521-06915-7). Cambridge U Pr.
McBurney, D. & Collings. Introduction to Sensation-Perception. (Experimental Psychology Ser.). 1977. 23.95 (ISBN 0-13-496000-9). P-H.
McBurney, James H. Discussions in Human Affairs. LC 75-109296. 1971. Repr. of 1950 ed. lib. bdg. 19.75x (ISBN 0-8371-3839-6, MCHA). Greenwood.
M'buyinga, Elenga. Pan Africanism or Neo-Colonialism: The Bankruptcy of the OAU. 242p. 1982. 25.00 (ISBN 0-86232-076-3, Pub. by Zed Pr England); pap. 9.50 (ISBN 0-86232-013-5, Pub. by Zed Pr England). Lawrence Hill.
McCaa, Robert. Marriage & Fertility in Chile: Demographic Turning Points in the Petorca Valley, 1840-1976. (Dellplain Latin American Studies: No. 14). 250p. 1982. softcover 20.00x (ISBN 0-86531-532-9). Westview.
McCabe, Bernard, ed. see Educational Research Council of America.
McCabe, C. Kevin. Forth Fundamentals, Vol. 1. Barry, Tim, ed. 301p. 1983. pap. 15.95 (ISBN 0-88056-091-6). Dilithium Pr.
--Forth Fundamentals, Vol. 2. Barry, Tim, ed. 246p. 1983. pap. price not set (ISBN 0-88056-092-4). Dilithium Pr.
McCabe, Cameron. The Face on the Cutting Room Floor. 1981. 14.95 (ISBN 0-8398-2738-5, Gregg). G K Hall.
MacCabe, Colin. The Talking Cure: Essays in Psychoanalysis. 1981. 26.00 (ISBN 0-312-78474-0). St Martin.
MacCabe, Colin, ed. James Joyce: New Perspectives. LC 82-47941. 212p. 1982. 19.50 (ISBN 0-253-33176-5). Ind U Pr.
McCabe, Eugene. Cancer. (Adaptations Ser.). pap. 2.95x (ISBN 0-912262-68-0). Proscenium.
--King of the Castle. signed 7.50 (ISBN 0-912262-49-4); pap. 2.95x (ISBN 0-912262-50-8). Proscenium.
McCabe, James, jt. auth. see Hallak, Jacques.
McCabe, James P. A Critical Guide to Catholic Reference Books. 2nd ed. LC 80-16209. (Research Studies in Library Science: No. 2). 1980. lib. bdg. 27.50 (ISBN 0-87287-203-3). Libs Unl.
McCabe, John. Mr. Laurel & Mr. Hardy. (RL 9). pap. 1.50 o.p. (ISBN 0-451-07313-4, W7313, Sig). NAL.
McCabe, Joseph. The Church Defies Modern Life. 31p. 1942. pap. write for info. Am Atheist.
--The Church, the Enemy of the Workers. 32p. 1942. write for info. Am Atheist.
--Fascist Romanism Defies Civilization. 32p. pap. 3.00 (ISBN 0-686-95319-3). Am Atheist.
--The History & Meaning of the Catholic Index of Forbidden Books. 107p. pap. 4.00 (ISBN 0-686-95323-1). Am Atheist.
--History of Free Masonry. 331p. pap. 3.00 (ISBN 0-686-95310-X). Am Atheist.
--How the Faith is Protected. 31p. pap. 3.00 (ISBN 0-686-95328-2). Am Atheist.
--Is the Position of Atheism Growing Stronger. 30p. pap. 3.00 (ISBN 0-686-95330-4). Am Atheist.
--The Pope & the Italian Jackal. 31p. pap. 3.00 (ISBN 0-686-95336-3). Am Atheist.
--The Pope Helps Hitler to World Power. 30p. pap. 3.00 (ISBN 0-686-95335-5). Am Atheist.
--Rationalist Encyclopaedia: A Book of Reference on Religion, Philosophy, Ethics, & Science. LC 79-164054. 1971. Repr. of 1948 ed. 45.00x (ISBN 0-8103-3754-1). Gale.
--The Totalitarian Church of Rome. 32p. pap. 3.00 (ISBN 0-686-95343-6). Am Atheist.
--The Tyranny of the Clerical Gestapo. 32p. pap. 3.00 (ISBN 0-686-95345-2). Am Atheist.
--Vice in German Monasteries. 30p. pap. 3.00 (ISBN 0-686-95346-0). Am Atheist.
McCabe, Joseph E. Handel's Messiah: A Devotional Commentary. LC 77-25860. 1978. softcover 5.95 (ISBN 0-664-24192-1). Westminster.
McCabe, R. & Mines, R. Man & Environment, Vols. 1-2. 1973-74. Vol. 1. pap. 15.95 (ISBN 0-13-548230-5); Vol. 2. pap. 14.95 (ISBN 0-13-547984-3). P-H.
McCabe, Thomas. McCabe Reading Program, 4 vols. level 1, lessons 1-75 18.90x (ISBN 0-87628-579-5); duplicating masters 18.90x (ISBN 0-87628-580-9); level 2, lessons 76-123 18.90x (ISBN 0-87628-581-7); duplicating masters 18.90x (ISBN 0-87628-582-5). Ctr Appl Res.
--Victims No More. LC 77-94792. (Orig.). 1978. pap. 5.95 (ISBN 0-89486-049-6). Hazelden.
McCabe, Warren & Smith, Julian C. Unit Operations in Chemical Engineering. 3rd ed. (Engineering Ser.). 1975. text ed. 37.00 (ISBN 0-07-044825-6, C); solutions manual 25.00 (ISBN 0-07-044827-2). McGraw.
McCabe, William R., jt. ed. see Finland, Maxwell.
McCadden, Joseph F. The Flight from Women in the Fiction of Saul Bellow. LC 80-5641. 299p. 1980. lib. bdg. 21.25 (ISBN 0-8191-1308-5); pap. text ed. 11.50 (ISBN 0-8191-1309-3). U Pr of Amer.
McCaeeree, Sharon. Now & Forever. (American Romance Ser.). 192p. 1983. pap. 2.25 (ISBN 0-373-16004-6). Harlequin Bks.
McCaffery. Nursing Management of the Patient with Pain. 1983. pap. text ed. 15.50 (ISBN 0-06-318239-4, Pub. by Har-Row Ltd England). Har-Row.
McCaffery, Edward L. Laboratory Preparation for Macromolecular Chemistry. LC 77-90014. 1970. text ed. 36.50 (ISBN 0-07-044813-2, C). McGraw.
McCaffery, Jerry & Mikesell, John, eds. Urban Finance & Administration: A Guide to Information Sources. (Urban Studies Information Guide: Vol. 12). 200p. 1980. 42.00x (ISBN 0-8103-1464-9). Gale.
McCaffery, John K. Ernest Hemingway: The Man & His Work. LC 69-17516. Repr. of 1950 ed. 18.50x o.p. (ISBN 0-8154-0277-5). Cooper Sq.
McCaffery, Larry. The Metafictional Muse: The Work of Robert Coover, Donald Barthelme, & William H. Gass. LC 82-1872. (Critical Essays in Modern Literature Ser.). xi, 300p. 1982. 22.95 (ISBN 0-8229-3462-0). U of Pittsburgh Pr.
McCaffery, Larry, jt. ed. see LeClair, Thomas.
McCaffery, Robert M. Managing the Employee Benefits Program. rev. ed. 256p. 1983. 29.95 (ISBN 0-8144-5760-6). Am Mgmt Assns.
McCaffrey, Anne. The Coelura. 100p. 1983. 11.95 (ISBN 0-686-82271-4). Underwood-Miller.
--Dragonquest, Vol. 2. 1979. 8.95 (ISBN 0-686-96669-4, Del Rey). Ballantine.
--The White Dragon. 1981. 12.50 (ISBN 0-345-27567-5). Ultramarine Pub.
McCaffrey, David P. OSHA & the Politics of Health Regulation. LC 82-11201. 200p. 1982. 24.50x (ISBN 0-306-41050-8, Plenum Pr). Plenum Pub.
McCaffrey, Lawrence J. Ireland: From Colony to Nation State. 1979. 17.95 (ISBN 0-13-506196-2); pap. 15.95 (ISBN 0-13-506188-1). P-H.
McCaffrey, Mary. My Brother Ange. LC 81-43887. (Illus.). 96p. (gr. 3-6). 1982. 9.13 (ISBN 0-690-04194-2, TYC-J); PLB 9.89 (ISBN 0-690-04195-0). Har-Row.
McCaffrey, Mike & Derloshon, Jerry. Personal Marketing Strategies: How to Sell Yourself, Your Ideas & Your Services. (Illus.). 240p. 1983. 21.95 (ISBN 0-13-657452-1); pap. 11.95 (ISBN 0-13-657114-X). P-H.
McCagg, William O. & Silver, Brian D., eds. Soviet Asian Ethnic Frontiers. LC 77-11796. (Pergamon Policy Studies). (Illus.). 1979. 39.00 (ISBN 0-08-024637-0). Pergamon.
McCaghy, Charles H. Crime in American Society. (Illus.). 1980. text ed. 21.95x (ISBN 0-02-378420-2). Macmillan.
--Deviant Behavior: Crime, Conflict & Interest Groups. 400p. 1976. pap. text ed. 14.95x (ISBN 0-02-378400-8). Macmillan.
McCague, James. FBI: Democracy's Guardian. LC 73-9790. (American Democracy Ser). (Illus.). 96p. (gr. 3-6). 1974. PLB 7.12 (ISBN 0-8116-6508-9). Garrard.
--The Long Bondage: 1441-1815. LC 74-151988. (Toward Freedom Ser.). (Illus.). (gr. 5-9). 1972. PLB 3.98 (ISBN 0-8116-4800-1). Garrard.
--The Office of President. LC 75-9937. (American Democracy Ser.). (Illus.). 96p. (gr. 3-6). 1975. PLB 7.12 (ISBN 0-8116-6510-0). Garrard.
--The Road to Freedom: 1815-1900. LC 72-75074. (Toward Freedom Ser.). (gr. 5-9). 1972. PLB 3.98 (ISBN 0-8116-4803-6). Garrard.
--Tecumseh: Shawnee Warrior-Statesman. LC 73-83167. (Indians Ser). (Illus.). (gr. 2-5). 1970. PLB 6.69 (ISBN 0-8116-6607-7). Garrard.
McCahill, Thomas W. & Meyer, Linda C. The Aftermath of Rape. LC 79-1952. (Illus.). 288p. 1979. 24.95x (ISBN 0-669-03018-X). Lexington Bks.
McCaig, M. Permanent Magnets in Theory & Practice. LC 77-23949. 1977. 49.95x (ISBN 0-470-99269-7). Halsted Pr.
McCain, Mic. Inflation: Its Real Causes, Its Gross Effects & How It Pertains to the United States. LC 82-90210. 124p. (Orig.). 1982. pap. 6.95 (ISBN 0-686-36936-X). Adams Pr.
McCain, R. Markets, Decisions & Organizations: Intermediate Microeconomic Theory. 1980. 24.95 (ISBN 0-13-557884-1). P-H.
McCain, W. Calvin. Pieces of Peace. LC 74-25235. 80p. Date not set. pap. text ed. 5.00 (ISBN 0-931680-01-8). Dunbar Pub.
--Soul in the Opera House. 80p. 1982. pap. 5.00 (ISBN 0-931680-02-6). Dunbar Pub.
McCain, William D., Jr. Properties of Petroleum Fluids. LC 73-78008. 350p. 1974. 43.95x (ISBN 0-87814-021-2). Pennwell Pub.
McCalden, David. Exiles from History. (Illus.). 40p. (Orig.). 1982. pap. 5.00 (ISBN 0-910607-00-1). D McCalden.
McCaleb, Robert B. Small Business Computer Primer. 200p. 1982. pap. 14.95 (ISBN 0-88056-067-3). Dilithium Pr.
McCaleb, Walter F. The Aaron Burr Conspiracy. Bd. with A New Light on Aaron Burr. 1963. 476p. 1966. Repr. of 1903 ed. 17.50 (ISBN 0-87266-021-4). Argosy.
McCall, Andrew. The Medieval Underworld. (Illus.). 329p. 1979. 22.00 o.p. (ISBN 0-241-10018-6, Pub. by Hamish Hamilton England). David & Charles.
McCall, Bruce. Zany Afternoons. LC 82-47835. 1982. 25.00 (ISBN 0-394-42683-5); pap. 14.95 (ISBN 0-394-73504-8). Knopf.
McCall, Chester H., Jr. Sampling & Statistics Handbook for Research. (Illus.). 366p. 1982. pap. text ed. 25.95x (ISBN 0-8138-1628-9). Iowa St U Pr.
McCall, Chester H., Sr. Action Guide to Sure-Sale Real Estate Listings. 1979. 49.50 (ISBN 0-13-003111-9). Exec Reports.
McCall, Connie, jt. auth. see McCall, Sherwood.
McCall, Dan. Bluebird Canyon. 384p. 1983. 14.95 (ISBN 0-312-92057-1). Congdon & Weed.
McCall, Daniel F. Africa in Time Perspective: A Discussion of Historical Reconstruction from Unwritten Sources. (Illus.). 1969. pap. text ed. 6.95x (ISBN 0-19-500352-7). Oxford U Pr.
--Wolf Courts Girl: The Equivalence of Hunting & Mating in Bushman Thought. LC 79-631803. (Papers in International Studies: Africa: No. 7). 1970. pap. 3.25 (ISBN 0-89680-040-7, Ohio U Ctr Intl). Ohio U Pr.
McCall, G. J. Meteorites & Their Origins. 352p. 1973. 16.00 (ISBN 0-7153-5560-0, Pub. by Wiley). Krieger.
McCall, G. J., ed. Astroblemes-Cryptoexplosion Structures. LC 79-10991. (Benchmark Papers in Geology: Vol. 50). 437p. 1979. 55.00 (ISBN 0-87933-342-1). Hutchinson Ross.
--Ophiolitic & Related Melanges. (Benchmark Papers in Geology Ser.: Vol. 66). 1982. cancelled (ISBN 0-12-787027-X). Acad Pr.
--Ophiolitic & Related Melanges. LC 81-13490. (Benchmark Papers in Geology Ser.: Vol. 66). 464p. 1983. 56.00 (ISBN 0-87933-421-5, Pub. by Van Nos Reinhold). Hutchinson Ross.
McCall, Grant. Rapanui: Tradition & Survival on Easter Island. LC 80-54833. 176p. 1981. text ed. 16.95x (ISBN 0-8248-0746-4). UH Pr.
McCall, Grant, ed. see Young Nations Conference, Sydney, 1976.
McCall, J. J., jt. ed. see Lippman, S. A.
McCall, John. How to Write Themes & Essays. 1976. pap. 2.95 (ISBN 0-671-18754-6). Monarch Pr.
--William Shakespeare: Spacious in the Possession of Dirt. 1978. pap. text ed. 12.00 o.p. (ISBN 0-8191-0378-0). U Pr of Amer.
McCall, John P. Chaucer Among the Gods: The Poetics of Classical Myth. LC 78-50003. 1979. text ed. 15.25x (ISBN 0-271-00201-8). Pa St U Pr.
McCall, P. L. & Tevesz, M. J. S., eds. Animal-Sediment Relations, Vol.2. LC 82-16523. (Topics in GeoBiology). 352p. 1982. 42.50x (ISBN 0-306-41078-8, Plenum Pr). Plenum Pub.
McCall, Raymond J. Basic Logic: The Fundamental Principles of Formal Deductive Reasoning. 2nd ed. 1962. pap. 4.95 (ISBN 0-06-460052-1, CO 52, COS). B&N NY.
McCall, Sherwood & McCall, Connie. The Art of Picture Framing. LC 80-2734. 1981. pap. 10.95 (ISBN 0-672-52390-6). Bobbs.
McCall, Thomas & Levitt, Zola. El Anticristo y el Santuario. (Editorial Moody-Spanish Publications). 1977. pap. 2.95 (ISBN 0-8024-0291-7). Moody.
McCall, Thomas S. & Levitt, Zola. The Coming Russian Invasion of Israel. 96p. 1976. pap. 4.95 (ISBN 0-8024-1607-1). Moody.
McCall, Virginia N. Civil Service Careers. LC 77-6794. (Career Concise Guides Ser.). (Illus.). (gr. 7 up). 1977. PLB 8.90 s&l (ISBN 0-531-01302-2). Watts.
McCall, William A. & Harby, Mary L. Test Lessons in Primary Reading. 2nd ed. 1980. pap. text ed. 3.25 (ISBN 0-8077-5965-1); manual 1.00 (ISBN 0-8077-5966-X). Tchrs Coll.
McCall, William A. & Schroeder, Lelah Crabbs. McCall-Crabbs Standard Test Lessons in Reading, Books A-F. 4th ed. 1979. Kit & Manual. pap. text ed. 17.15 (ISBN 0-8077-5554-0). Tchrs Coll.
McCall, Yvonne. Happiest Search. (Arch Bks: Set 8). (Illus., Orig.). (ps-4). 1971. pap. 0.89 (ISBN 0-570-06061-3, 59-1178). Concordia.
--Man Who Won Without Fighting: Gideon. (Arch Bks: Set 8). (Illus., Orig.). (ps-4). 1971. pap. 0.89 (ISBN 0-570-06060-5, 059-1177). Concordia.
--The Prince & the Promise. (Arch Bk Ser.: No. 15). (Illus.). (gr. k-3). 1978. 0.89 (ISBN 0-570-06117-2, 59-1235). Concordia.
--Samir's Midnight Friend: How God Answers Prayer. (Arch Bks: Set 8). (Illus., Orig.). (ps-4). 1971. pap. 0.89 (ISBN 0-570-06059-1, 59-1176). Concordia.
--The Wicked Trick. (Arch Bks. No. 9). (Illus.). 32p. (ps-4). 1972. pap. 0.89 (ISBN 0-570-06068-0, 59-1186). Concordia.
McCall, Yvonne H. The Angry King. (Arch Books Series Fourteen). (gr. k-2). 1977. pap. 0.89 (ISBN 0-570-06110-5, 59-1228). Concordia.
--The Man Who Didn't Have Time. (Arch Bks.: Set 14). 1977. pap. 0.89 (ISBN 0-570-06112-1, 59-1231). Concordia.
McCalla, Douglas B., ed. see Federico, Pat A., et al.
McCalla, Thomas R. Introduction to Numerical Methods & FORTRAN Programming. LC 66-28745. 1967. 27.95 (ISBN 0-471-58125-9, Pub. by Wiley-Interscience). Wiley.
McCalley, John W. Nantucket, Yesterday & Today. 13.50 (ISBN 0-8446-5902-9). Peter Smith.
McCall's Food Staff. McCall's Superb Dessert Cookbook. Eckley, Mary, ed. 1978. 13.50 (ISBN 0-394-41279-6). Random.
--The New McCall's Cook Book. (Illus.). 1973. 12.95 ea. o.p.; green bdg. o.p. (ISBN 0-394-48785-0); red bdg. o.p. (ISBN 0-394-48518-1); yellow bdg. o.p. (ISBN 0-394-48783-4); blue bdg. o.p. (ISBN 0-394-48784-2). Random.
McCall's Magazine Editors. McCall's Sewing for Your Home. 1977. 12.50 o.p. (ISBN 0-671-22372-0). S&S.
McCall's Needlework, ed. The McCall's Book of Afghans. 1976. 9.95 o.p. (ISBN 0-671-22224-4, 22224). S&S.
McCall's Needlework & Crafts Editors. The McCall's Crochet Treasury. 1977. 17.50 o.p. (ISBN 0-671-22317-8). S&S.
McCall's Publishing Company. The McCall's Needlework Treasury. 1977. pap. 9.95 o.p. (ISBN 0-394-73399-1). Random.
McCallum, Andrew. Fun with Stagecraft. LC 80-27686. (Illus.). 96p. 1982. 9.95 (ISBN 0-89490-008-0). Enslow Pubs.
MacCallum, Elizabeth P. The Nationalist Crusade in Syria. LC 79-2873. (Illus.). 299p. 1981. Repr. of 1928 ed. 24.00 (ISBN 0-8305-0043-X). Hyperion Conn.
McCallum, Geo, ed. see Stockton, Frank.
McCallum, Geo. P., adapted by. Six Stories for Acting. 1976. pap. 3.75 (ISBN 0-89318-031-9); cassettes 29.50 (ISBN 0-89318-034-3). ELS Intl.
McCallum, George P. Idiom Drills: For Students of English as a Second Language. 2nd ed. 160p. 1982. pap. text ed. 8.50 scp (ISBN 0-06-044322-7, HarpC). Har-Row.
--One Hundred & One Word Games. 1980. pap. text ed. 6.50x (ISBN 0-19-502742-6). Oxford U Pr.
--Visitor from Another Planet & Other Plays. 158p. 1982. 4.95x (ISBN 0-19-502743-4); tchr's. ed. 5.95x (ISBN 0-19-503167-9). Oxford U Pr.
--Words People Use: Passive-Active Vocabulary Skills for Students of ESL. 317p. 1982. pap. text ed. 8.50 scp (ISBN 0-06-044321-9, HarpC). Har-Row.
McCallum, George P., adapted by. Seven Plays from American Literature. rev. ed. 1977. pap. 3.75 (ISBN 0-87789-062-5); cassette tapes 39.50 (ISBN 0-87789-126-5). Eng Language.
McCallum, Jack, jt. auth. see Sciacchetano, Larry.
McCallum, James D., ed. Letters of Eleazar Wheelock's Indians. LC 32-6653. (Dartmouth College Manuscript Ser.: No. 1). (Illus.). 327p. 1932. text ed. 10.00x (ISBN 0-87451-003-1). U Pr of New Eng.
McCallum, John D. Getting into Pro Football. (Getting into the Pros Ser.). (Illus.). (gr. 6 up). 1979. PLB 8.40 s&l (ISBN 0-531-02279-X). Watts.
--Pac-Ten Football: The Rose Bowl Conference. (Illus.). 352p. 1982. 24.95 (ISBN 0-916076-52-0); pap. text ed. 14.95 (ISBN 0-916076-56-3). Writing.
McCallum, Pamela. Literature & Method: Towards a Critique of I. A. Richards, T. S. Eliot & F. R. Leavis. (Literature & Society Ser.). 288p. 1982. text ed. 42.00x (ISBN 0-391-02795-6). Humanities.
MacCallum, Spencer H., ed. see Riegel, E. C.
McCalpin, James P. Quaternary Geology & Neotectonics of the West Flank of the Northern Sangre de Cristo Mountains, South-Central Colorado. Raese, Jon Wl & Goldberg, J. H., eds. (Colorado School of Mines Quarterly: Vol. 77, No. 3). 100p. 1982. pap. text ed. 12.00 (ISBN 0-686-82132-7). Colo Sch Mines.
MacCameron, Robert. Bananas, Labor, & Politics in Honduras: 1954-1963. (Foreign & Comparative Studies Program, Latin American Ser.: No. 5). (Orig.). 1982. pap. text ed. write for info. (ISBN 0-915984-96-2). Syracuse U Foreign Comp.
McCamisch, M., jt. ed. see Frigerio, A.
McCammon, Robert. Mystery Walk. LC 82-15419. 396p. 1983. 13.95 (ISBN 0-03-061832-0). HR&W.
MacCampbell, Donald. The Writing Business. 1978. 6.95 (ISBN 0-517-53277-8); pap. 3.95 (ISBN 0-517-54227-7). Crown.
McCamy, John & Presley, James. Human Life Styling. 1977. pap. 4.95i (ISBN 0-06-090540-9, CN 540, CN). Har-Row.
Mac Cana, Proinsias. Literature in Irish. (Aspects of Ireland Ser.: Vol. 8). (Illus.). 69p. 1981. pap. 6.95 (ISBN 0-906404-08-8, Pub. by Dept Foreign Ireland). Irish Bks Media.
McCance. Preventing Aging. 1983. write for info. (ISBN 0-87527-223-1). Green.
McCance, M. E., jt. ed. see Harrigan, W. F.
McCandless, C. A. Urban Government & Politics. (Political Science Ser.). 1970. 15.95 o.p. (ISBN 0-07-044814-0, C). McGraw.
McCanles, Michael. Dialectical Criticism & Renaissance Literature. 1975. 33.00x (ISBN 0-520-02694-2). U of Cal Pr.

McCanliss, Irene. Weight on the Thoroughbred Racehorse. 1967. lib. bdg. 7.50 o.p. (ISBN 0-686-28404-6). Blood-Horse.

McCann, Brian, jt. ed. see Menolascino, Frank J.

MacCann, Donnarae & Richard, Olga. The Child's First Books. 135p. 1973. 15.00 (ISBN 0-8242-0501-4). Wilson.

McCann, Lee. Nostradamus: The Man Who Saw Through Time. 1982. 23.50 (ISBN 0-374-22317-3); pap. 7.95 (ISBN 0-374-51754-1). FS&G.

McCann, Michael. Health Hazards Manual for Artists. rev. ed. LC 78-70898. (Illus.). 48p. 1978. pap. 3.50x (ISBN 0-933032-00-5). FCA Bks.

McCann, Richard. A Dream of the Traveler. 68p. 1976. 3.50 (ISBN 0-87886-070-3). Ithaca Hse.

MacCann, Richard D. Hollywood in Transition. LC 77-5314. 1977. Repr. of 1962 ed. lib. bdg. 18.50x (ISBN 0-8371-9616-7, MAHT). Greenwood.

MacCann, Richard D., ed. Film: A Montage of Theories. pap. 6.25 (ISBN 0-525-47181-2, 0607-180). Dutton.

McCann, Roger C. Introduction to Ordinary Differential Equations. 448p. 1982. text ed. 24.95 (ISBN 0-15-543485-3, HC); answer manual 4.95 (ISBN 0-15-543486-1). HarBraceJ.

McCann, Timothy J. West Sussex Probate Inventories, 1521-1834. 1981. 95.00x (ISBN 0-86260-005-7). State Mutual Bk.

McCann, W. P., jt. auth. see Stewart, W. A.

McCann, W. P., jt. auth. see Young, F. A.

MacCannell, Dean. The Tourist: A New Theory of the Leisure Class. LC 75-7770. 224p. 1976. pap. 6.95 (ISBN 0-8052-0529-2). Schocken.

McCannon, Dinga. Peaches. (YA) 1977. pap. 1.25 o.p. (ISBN 0-440-96832-1, LFL). Dell.

McCannon, Dingda. Wilhemina Jones, Future Star. LC 79-53602. (YA) (gr. 8-12). 1980. 8.95 o.s.i. (ISBN 0-440-09857-2). Delacorte.

McCardell, John. The Idea of a Southern Nation: Southern Nationalists & Southern Nationalism, 1830-1860. 432p. 1981. pap. text ed. 6.95x (ISBN 0-686-86518-9). Norton.

McCarr & Wisser. Curriculum Material Useful for the Hearing Impaired. 204p. 1980. 9.95 (ISBN 0-86575-131-5). Dormac.

McCarren, Vincent P. Michigan Papyri XIV. (American Studies in Papyrology: No. 22). 22.50 (ISBN 0-89130-295-6, 21-00-22). Scholars Pr CA.

McCarrick, Earlean M., ed. United States Constitution: A Guide to Information Sources. LC 74-15403. (American Government & History Information Guide Ser.: Vol. 4). 1980. 42.00x (ISBN 0-8103-1203-4). Gale.

McCarroll, H. Relton, Jr., jt. auth. see Jewett, Don L.

McCarroll, Tolbert. Exploring the Inner World: A Guidebook for Personal Growth & Renewal. (RL 10). 1976. pap. 1.50 o.p. (ISBN 0-451-07028-3, W7028, Sig). NAL.

McCarry, Charles. The Last Supper. 384p. 1983. 15.95 (ISBN 0-525-24173-6, 01549-460). Dutton.

McCarter, Neely D. Hear the Word of the Lord. (Illus., Orig.). (gr. 11-12). 1964. pap. 3.95 tchrs' guide (ISBN 0-8042-9210-8). John Knox.

McCarter, P. Kyle, Jr. Samuel One: Volume Eight, a New Translation with Introduction & Commentary. LC 79-7201. (Anchor Bible Ser.). 1980. 18.00 (ISBN 0-385-06760-7). Doubleday.

McCarter, Pender M., jt. ed. see Nyborg, Philip S.

McCarter, Phyllis M. A Legacy of Love. 1983. 5.95 (ISBN 0-533-05571-7). Vantage.

McCarthy, Albert, jt. auth. see Hentoff, Nat.

McCarthy, Albert J., ed. see Hentoff, Nat.

McCarthy, B. Eugene. William Wycherley: A Biography. LC 79-9210. (Illus.). xii, 255p. 1980. 17.95x (ISBN 0-8214-0410-5, 82-82998). Ohio U Pr.

McCarthy, Belinda R. Easy Time: The Experiences of Female Inmates on Temporary Release. LC 78-13819. 240p. 1979. 24.95x (ISBN 0-669-02669-7). Lexington Bks.

McCarthy, Bernice. The FourMat System: Teaching to Learning Styles with Right-Left Mode Techniques. LC 80-70421. 1980. 22.95 (ISBN 0-686-32594-X). Excel.

McCarthy, Carlton. Detailed Minutiae of Soldier Life. (Collector's Library of the Civil War). 1982. 26.60 (ISBN 0-8094-4245-0). Silver.

McCarthy, Charlene. Set My People Free. 1st ed. 1976. pap. 3.50 o.p. (ISBN 0-02-655500-X, 65550). Glencoe.

McCarthy, Charlotte. The Fair Moralist; or, Love & Virtue, 1745. Shugrue, Michael F., ed. Bd. with The Case of John Nelson, Written by Himself, 1745. Nelson, John. (The Flowering of the Novel, 1740-1775 Ser: Vol. 16). 1974. lib. bdg. 50.00 o.s.i. (ISBN 0-8240-1115-5). Garland Pub.

McCarthy, Claire, jt. auth. see Peterson, Craig A.

McCarthy, David. Essentials of Soil Mechanics & Foundations. 2nd ed. 640p. 1982. text ed. 22.95 (ISBN 0-8359-1781-9); solutions manual free (ISBN 0-8359-1782-7). Reston.

McCarthy, Dennis. The Afghan Hound. 1977. pap. 2.50 (ISBN 0-7028-1054-1). Palmetto Pub.

McCarthy, Dennis J. Kings & Prophets. (Contemporary College Theology Ser). 1968. pap. 3.95x o.p. (ISBN 0-02-820480-8). Glencoe.

MacCarthy, Desmond. Theatre. LC 76-49881. 1977. Repr. of 1954 ed. lib. bdg. 16.00x (ISBN 0-8371-9333-8, MATHE). Greenwood.

McCarthy, Dorothea. The Language Development of the Preschool Child. LC 74-141549. (Univ. of Minnesota Institute of Child Welfare Monographs: No. 4). (Illus.). 174p. 1975. Repr. of 1930 ed. lib. bdg. 29.75 (ISBN 0-8371-5896-6, CWML). Greenwood.

McCarthy, F. D. Rock Art of the Cobar Pediplain in Central Western New South Wales. (Aias Research & Regional Studies: No. 7). 1976. text ed. 15.50x (ISBN 0-85575-049-9). Humanities.

McCarthy, G. D. & Healy, R. E. Valuing a Company: Practices & Procedures. 521p. 1971. 55.95x (ISBN 0-471-06542-0). Ronald Pr.

McCarthy, Gary. Mustang Fever. LC 79-7501. (Double D Western Ser.). 1980. 10.95 o.p. (ISBN 0-385-15472-0). Doubleday.

McCarthy, Gerald. War Story: Vietnam War Poems by an Ex-Marine. LC 77-23320. 1977. 13.95 (ISBN 0-912278-87-0); pap. 4.95 (ISBN 0-912278-86-2). Crossing Pr.

McCarthy, Ginny, jt. ed. see Crow, Ruth.

McCarthy, Henry & Smart, Lana. Affirmative Action in Action: Strategies for Enchancing Employment Prospects of Qualified Handicapped Individuals. LC 79-90291. 40p. 1979. 3.75 (ISBN 0-686-38808-9). Human Res Ctr.

McCarthy, I. E. Introduction to Nuclear Theory. LC 68-19781. 555p. 1968. text ed. 21.50 (ISBN 0-471-58140-2, Pub. by Wiley). Krieger.

McCarthy, Jane. Listen to the Skylark. 192p. (YA) 1975. 6.95 (ISBN 0-685-52912-6, Avalon). Bouregy.

McCarthy, Jeanne M., jt. auth. see Kirk, Samuel A.

McCarthy, Joe. Papal Bulls & English Muffins: Meditations for Everyday in Lent. LC 73-91372. 128p. 1974. pap. 2.45 o.p. (ISBN 0-8091-1812-2). Paulist Pr.

McCarthy, John, ed. Home Book of Irish Humor. LC 68-15417. 1968. 10.95 (ISBN 0-396-05673-3). Dodd.

McCarthy, John A. Christoph Martin Wieland. (World Authors Ser.). 1979. lib. bdg. 15.95 (ISBN 0-8057-6369-4, Twayne). G K Hall.

McCarthy, John D., jt. auth. see Zald, Mayer N.

McCarthy, John J. John J. McCarthy's Secrets of Super Selling. LC 82-9533. 320p. 1982. 50.00 (ISBN 0-932648-25-8). Boardroom.

McCarthy, John J., jt. ed. see Baker, C. L.

McCarthy, Joseph. America's Retreat from Victory. 1955. 6.95 (ISBN 0-8159-5004-7). Devin.

McCarthy, Joseph M., ed. see Fenwick, Benedict J.

McCarthy, Justin. The Arab World, Turkey, & the Balkans 1878-1914: A Handbook of Historical Statistics. 1982. lib. bdg. 75.00 (ISBN 0-8161-8164-0, Hall Reference). G K Hall.

McCarthy, Kenneth G., Jr., ed. Hattiesburg: A Pictorial History. LC 82-10868. (Illus.). 240p. 1982. 25.00 (ISBN 0-87805-169-4). U Pr of Miss.

McCarthy, Kevin. Grammar & Usage: A Rapid Review. 199p. 1980. pap. text ed. 9.95 (ISBN 0-15-529680-9, HC); instructor's manual avail. (ISBN 0-15-529681-7). HarBraceJ.

McCarthy, Martha M. & Deigan, Paul T. What Legally Constitues an Adequate Public Education? LC 82-81596. 125p. 1982. pap. 5.00 (ISBN 0-87367-781-1). Phi Delta Kappa.

McCarthy, Mary. Birds of America. LC 75-147230. 1971. 11.95 (ISBN 0-15-112770-0). HarBraceJ.

--Birds of America. 1972. pap. 1.50 o.p. (ISBN 0-451-05001-0, W5001, Sig). NAL.

--A Charmed Life. LC 55-10153. 1955. 15.95 (ISBN 0-15-116907-1). HarBraceJ.

--The Group. 1972. pap. 1.95 o.p. (ISBN 0-451-08446-2, J8446, Sig). NAL.

--Groves of Academe. Date not set. pap. 3.95 o.p. (ISBN 0-452-25084-6, 25084, Plume). NAL.

--Medina. LC 72-79919. 88p. 1972. pap. 2.45 (ISBN 0-15-158530-X, Harv). HarBraceJ.

--Memories of a Catholic Girlhood. LC 57-8842. (Illus.). 1957. 12.95 (ISBN 0-15-158859-7). HarBraceJ.

McCarthy, Mary F., tr. see Ciria, Alberto.

McCarthy, Mary S. Balzac & His Reader: A Study of the Creation of Meaning in La Comedie Humaine. LC 82-2667. 176p. 1983. 18.00 (ISBN 0-8262-0378-7). U of MO Pr.

McCarthy, Melodie A. & Houston, John P. Fundamentals of Early Childhood Education. 1979. text ed. 17.95 (ISBN 0-316-37442-3). Little.

McCarthy, Muriel Q. David R. Williams: Pioneer Architect. (Illus.). 300p. 1983. 25.00 (ISBN 0-87074-182-9). SMU Press.

McCarthy, Nan, jt. auth. see Lindley, Craig A.

McCarthy, Nan, ed. see Ramella, Richard.

McCarthy, Nancy M. & Tuggle, Joyce. Now Where? Places in Oregon to Go with Kids. 1977. pap. 3.45 o.s.i. (ISBN 0-917304-06-3). Timber.

McCarthy, Oliver J. MOS Design Guide. LC 81-14645. (Wiley Ser. in Computing). 261p. 1982. 46.95x (ISBN 0-471-10026-9, Pub. by Wiley-Interscience). Wiley.

McCarthy, P., jt. auth. see Shklar, G.

McCarthy, Patricia, ed. see Leonard, Cliff R.

McCarthy, Patrick A. Olaf Stapledon. (English Author Ser.). 1982. lib. bdg. 13.95 (ISBN 0-8057-6826-2, Twayne). G K Hall.

McCarthy, Paul. John Steinbeck. LC 78-20929. (Literature & Life Ser.). 1980. 11.95 (ISBN 0-8044-2606-6). Ungar.

McCarthy, Paul J. Algebraic Extensions of Fields. 2nd ed. LC 75-41499. ix, 166p. 1976. 12.00 (ISBN 0-8284-1284-7). Chelsea Pub.

McCarthy, Paul J., ed. see Nakamoto, Kazno.

McCarthy, Philip J. Introduction to Statistical Reasoning. LC 78-1044. 416p. 1978. Repr. of 1957 ed. lib. bdg. 21.00 (ISBN 0-88275-661-3). Krieger.

McCarthy, Richard J. Freedom & Fulfillment. Al-Ghazali, tr. (International Studies & Translations Program). 1980. lib. bdg. 27.00 (ISBN 0-8057-8167-6, Twayne). G K Hall.

McCarthy, Rockne & Skillen, James. Disestablishment a Second Time. 204p. (Orig.). 1982. pap. 5.95 (ISBN 0-8028-1931-1). Eerdmans.

McCarthy, Shawna, ed. Isaac Asimov's Aliens & Outworlders. 288p. 1983. 12.95 (ISBN 0-385-27912-4). Davis Pubns.

McCarthy, Shawna, jt. ed. see Moloney, Kathleen.

McCarthy, Thomas. The Critical Theory of Jurgen Habermas. 1978. 25.00x (ISBN 0-262-13138-2); pap. 12.50 (ISBN 0-262-63073-7). MIT Pr.

McCarthy, Timothy. Marx & the Proletariat: A Study in Social Theory. LC 78-4025. (Contributions in Political Science: No. 18). 1978. lib. bdg. 25.00 (ISBN 0-313-20412-8, MPL/). Greenwood.

McCarthy, Willard J. & Repp, Victor. Machine Tool Technology. (Illus.). (gr. 11-12). 1979. text ed. 21.97 (ISBN 0-87345-143-0); Study Guide 1. 4.67 (ISBN 0-87345-144-9); Study Guide 2. 4.67 (ISBN 0-87345-145-7); ans. key avail. McKnight.

McCarthy, Willard J., jt. auth. see Ludwig, Oswald A.

McCartney, Brenna. Passion's Blossom. 1982. pap. 3.50 (ISBN 0-8217-1109-1). Zebra.

McCartney, Earl J. Optics of the Atmosphere: Scattering by Molecules & Particles. LC 76-10941. (Pure & Applied Optics Ser). 1976. 58.50 (ISBN 0-471-01526-1, Pub. by Wiley-Interscience). Wiley.

McCartney, Eugene S., ed. see Campbell, Oscar J., et al.

McCartney, Kevin & Ford, Brian. Practical Solar Hot Water: A Home Owner's Guide. 138p. 1983. 8.95 (ISBN 0-442-26471-2). Van Nos Reinhold.

McCartney, Linda. Photographs. 1982. 29.95 (ISBN 0-671-45985-6); pap. 12.95 (ISBN 0-671-45986-4). S&S.

McCartney, Mike. The Macs: The McCartney Family Album. LC 81-67645. (Illus.). 192p. 1981. pap. 8.95 (ISBN 0-933328-05-2). Delilah Bks.

McCarty, Clifford. Film Composers in America: A Checklist of Their Work. LC 72-4448. (Music Ser.). 196p. 1972. Repr. of 1953 ed. lib. bdg. 22.50 (ISBN 0-306-70495-1). Da Capo.

McCarty, Diane. Great Danes. (Illus.). 125p. 1980. 4.95 (ISBN 0-87666-693-4, KW-082). TFH Pubns.

--Labrador Retrievers. (Illus.). 1979. 4.95 (ISBN 0-87666-689-6, KW-040-). TFH Pubns.

--Lhasa Apsos. (Illus.). 125p. 1979. 4.95 (ISBN 0-87666-681-0, KW-076). TFH Pubns.

McCarty, Diane & Henneberry, Mrs. Janet. English Springer Spaniels. (Illus.). 1980. 4.95 (ISBN 0-87666-687-X, KW-081). TFH Pubns.

McCarty, Diane & Kattell, Ted. Collies. (Illus.). 128p. 1980. 4.95 (ISBN 0-87666-684-5, KW-078). TFH Pubns.

McCarty, Diane & Look, Mrs. Travis. Basset Hounds. (Illus.). 125p. 1979. 4.95 (ISBN 0-87666-679-9, KW-069). TFH Pubns.

McCarty, Diane, ed. German Shorthaired Pointers. (Illus.). 128p. 1980. 4.95 (ISBN 0-87666-700-0, KW-086). TFH Pubns.

McCarty, Donald J. & Ramsey, Charles E. The School Managers: Power & Conflict in American Public Education. LC 70-105975. (Illus.). 281p. 1971. lib. bdg. 29.95 (ISBN 0-8371-3299-1, MSM/). Greenwood.

McCarty, Dwight G. Psychology for the Lawyer. (Historical Foundations of Forensic Psychiatry & Psychology Ser.). 1980. lib. bdg. 59.50 (ISBN 0-306-76068-1). Da Capo.

McCarty, George S. Topology: An Introduction with Application to Topological Groups. (International Series in Pure & Applied Mathematics). (Illus.). 1967. text ed. 12.95 o.p. (ISBN 0-07-044815-9, C). McGraw.

McCarty, James A. & Elkins, Don. The RA Material: An Ancient Astronaut Speaks. Stine, Hank, ed. LC 82-12967. 192p. (Orig.). 1983. pap. 6.95 (ISBN 0-89865-260-X). Donning Co.

McCarty, John. Splatter Movies Two: Breaking the Last Taboo. rev. ed. (Illus.). 250p. 1983. pap. 14.95x (ISBN 0-938782-04-5). Fantaco.

--Video Screams. 1983 ed. (Illus.). 250p. (Orig.). 1983. pap. 7.95x (ISBN 0-938782-02-9). Fantaco.

McCarty, John, jt. auth. see Krogh, Daniel.

McCarty, Kenneth, jt. ed. see Padilla, George.

McCarty, Mari, jt. ed. see Eisinger, Erica M.

McCarty, Marilu. Dollars & Sense: Introduction to Economics. 3rd ed. 1982. pap. text ed. 16.50x (ISBN 0-673-15603-6). Scott F.

McCarty, Marilu, jt. auth. see Chisholm, Roger.

McCarty, Marilu H. Money & Banking: Financial Institutions & Economic Policy. (Economics Ser.). (Illus.). 544p. 1982. text ed. 22.95 (ISBN 0-201-05098-6); instr's manual 1.50 (ISBN 0-201-05099-4). A-W.

McCarty, Michele. Becoming. 1983. pap. write for info. (ISBN 0-697-01856-3); program manual avail. (ISBN 0-697-01857-1). Wm C Brown.

--Believing. 160p. 1980. pap. text ed. 5.00 (ISBN 0-697-01753-2); tchr's manual 5.00 (ISBN 0-697-01754-0). Wm C Brown.

--Deciding. (Orig.). (gr. 11-12). 1981. pap. text ed. 5.00 (ISBN 0-697-01778-8); tchr's manual 6.00 (ISBN 0-697-01779-6); casebk. 7.95 (ISBN 0-697-01780-X). Wm C Brown.

--Loving. 256p. (Orig.). (gr. 11-12). 1982. pap. text ed. 6.50 (ISBN 0-697-01808-3); tchrs. manual 7.00 (ISBN 0-697-01809-1). Wm C Brown.

--Relating. 128p. (Orig.). (gr. 11-12). 1979. pap. text ed. 4.25 (ISBN 0-697-01710-9); tchr's manual 5.00 (ISBN 0-697-01711-7). Wm C Brown.

McCarty, Nan, jt. auth. see Sinclair, Ian R.

McCarty, Perry L., jt. auth. see Sawyer, Clair.

McCarty, Toni. The Skull in the Snow & Other Folktales. LC 80-68730. (Illus.). 128p. (gr. 4-8). 1981. 7.95 o.s.i. (ISBN 0-440-08028-2); PLB 7.45 o.s.i. (ISBN 0-440-08030-4). Delacorte.

McCarus, Ernest, et al. First Lessons in Literary Arabic. (Orig.). (gr. 7-12). pap. text ed. 4.00x (ISBN 0-916798-08-9, Pub. by Mich Dept Near East Stud). Eisenbrauns.

McCary, Ben C. Indians in Seventhteenth Century Virginia. (Illus.). 93p. 1980. pap. 2.95 (ISBN 0-8139-0142-1). U Pr of Va.

--John Smith's Map of Virginia: With a Brief Account of Its History. (Illus.). 1957. pap. 2.95 (ISBN 0-8139-0127-8). U Pr of Va.

McCary, James L. Freedom & Growth in Marriage. 2nd ed. LC 79-17199. 1980. text ed. 21.95 (ISBN 0-471-05341-4); tchrs' manual 5.00 (ISBN 0-471-07845-X). Wiley.

--Human Sexuality. 3rd ed. (Illus.). 1978. text ed. 16.95 (ISBN 0-442-25237-4); instructors' manual 3.50x (ISBN 0-442-25241-2); study guide 4.95x (ISBN 0-442-25244-7). Van Nos Reinhold.

--Human Sexuality. brief ed. 1979. pap. text ed. 9.95 (ISBN 0-442-25236-6). Van Nos Reinhold.

--McCary's Human Sexuality. 3rd ed. 1978. 20.00 o.p. (ISBN 0-442-25240-4). Van Nos Reinhold.

--Sexual Myths & Fallacies. LC 77-159148. 222p. (YA) 1973. pap. 2.95 o.p. (ISBN 0-8052-0382-6). Schocken.

McCary, James L. & McCary, Stephen P. McCary's Human Sexuality. 4th ed. 688p. 1981. text ed. 20.95x (ISBN 0-534-01108-X); student self-study guide 7.95x (ISBN 0-534-01109-8). Wadsworth Pub.

McCary, Stephen P., jt. auth. see McCary, James L.

MacCary, W. T. Childlike Achilles: Ontogeny & Phylogeny in the Iliad. LC 82-4458. 304p. 1982. text ed. 25.00 (ISBN 0-686-82113-0). Columbia U Pr.

Maccary, W. T., ed. see Plautus.

McCash, William B. Thomas R. R. Cobb: The Making of a Southern Nationalist. 208p. Date not set. text ed. 14.95x (ISBN 0-86554-049-7). Mercer Univ Pr.

McCaskey, Mary J., ed. see Pierce, Eleanor B.

McCaskey, Michael. The Executive Challenge: Managing Change & Ambiguity. LC 82-628. (Pitman Series in Business Management & Organizational Behavior). 256p. 1982. text ed. 18.95 (ISBN 0-273-01846-9). Pitman Pub MA.

MacCasKey, Michael. Lawns & Ground Covers: How to Select, Grow & Enjoy. 160p. (Orig.). 1982. pap. 7.95 (ISBN 0-89586-099-6). H P Bks.

MacCaskey, Michael & Stebbins, Robert L. Pruning: How to Guide for Gardeners. 160p. 1982. pap. 7.95 (ISBN 0-89586-188-7). H P Bks.

McCaskill, Lance. Unspoiled South Island. (Illus.). 1976. 13.35 o.p. (ISBN 0-589-00961-3, Pub. by Reed Books Australia). C E Tuttle.

McCaskill, Mizzy, jt. auth. see Gilliam, Dona.

McCasland, Dave. The Culture Trap. (gr. 9-12). 1982. pap. 3.95 (ISBN 0-88207-191-2). Victor Bks.

McCasland, David C. Open to Change. 144p. 1981. pap. 4.50 (ISBN 0-88207-258-7). Victor Bks.

McCaslin, Nellie. Act Now: Plays & Ways to Make Them. LC 75-25557. (Illus.). 134p. (gr. 4-7). 1975. 10.95 (ISBN 0-87599-216-1). S G Phillips.

McCaslin, Rosemary W. The Older Person as a Mental Health Worker. (Adult & Aging Ser.: Vol. 12). 1983. text ed. 21.95 (ISBN 0-8261-4290-7). Springer Pub.

McCaughrean, Geraldine, tr. One Thousand One Arabian Nights. (Illus.). 256p. 1982. 14.95 (ISBN 0-19-274530-1, Pub. by Oxford U Pr Childrens). Merrimack Bk Serv.

McCaul, Earles. TRS-80 Assembly Language Made Simple. 1981. pap. 12.95 (ISBN 0-672-21851-8). Sams.

MacCauley, Billy R. Cinderella. (Illus.). 1976p. pap. 9.95 (ISBN 0-916378-07-1). PSI Res.

--Cinderella: An Original Version. (Illus.). 1976. pap. 7.95 o.p. (ISBN 0-916378-07-1). Oasis Pr CA.

McCauley, George. The Unfinished Image. 1983. 10.95 (ISBN 0-8215-9903-8). Sadlier.

McCauley, Michael F. In the Name of the Father. 1983. 12.95 (ISBN 0-88347-147-7). Thomas More.

McCauley, Rosemarie. Mini Sims Temporaries: Modern Office Simulations 2. 232p. (Orig.). 1979. pap. text ed. 11.50 (ISBN 0-672-97424-X); Tchr's Ed. 6.67 (ISBN 0-672-97168-2). Bobbs.

McCauley, Rosemarie & Slocum, Keith. Business Spelling & Word Power. 2nd ed. 336p. 1983. pap. text ed. 10.95 (ISBN 0-672-97975-6); instr's. guide 3.33 (ISBN 0-672-97976-4). Bobbs.

McCausland, Bob & Rudow, Martin. Hairbreadth Husky. LC 82-14060. (Illus.). 96p. (Orig.). 1982. pap. 5.95 (ISBN 0-914842-95-1). Madrona Pubs.
McCausland, Elizabeth. Eyewitness: The Growth of Photography. Peters, Susan D., ed. (Illus.). 250p. 1983. 22.50 (ISBN 0-8180-1421-0). Horizon.
--Life & Work of Edward Lamson Henry N. A. LC 74-100614. (Library of American Art Ser.). (Illus.). 1970. Repr. of 1945 ed. lib. bdg. 42.50 (ISBN 0-306-71866-9). Da Capo.
McCausland, M. A., jt. auth. see Calvert, J. M.
McCavitt, William E. Radio & Television: A Selected, Annotated Bibliography Supplement One: 1977-1981. LC 82-5743. 167p. 1982. 12.00 (ISBN 0-8108-1556-7). Scarecrow.
McCavitt, William E., ed. see Fugate, Howard.
McCaw, Mabel N. What God Can Do. LC 81-70865. (gr. k-3). 1982. 5.95 (ISBN 0-8054-4290-1). Broadman.
McCawley, Chris. The First Thing in the Field. LC 82-12061. (Kestrel Chapbks.). 32p. (Orig.). 1982. pap. 3.00 (ISBN 0-914974-33-5). Holmgangers.
McCawley, Peter, jt. ed. see Booth, Anne.
McCay, Jeanette B. Create with Cones. (Nature Crafts for Leisure Years). (Illus.). 32p. (Orig.). 1972. pap. 1.95 o.p. (ISBN 0-8200-0506-1). Great Outdoors.
McCay, Winsor. Little Nemo. 264p. 1975. 24.95 o.p. (ISBN 0-517-52191-1). Crown.
McCcane, Kenneth A. These Halves Are Whole. Fleming, Harold, ed. (Black Willow Poetry Chapbook Ser.). 24p. (Orig.). 1983. pap. 3.00 (ISBN 0-910047-03-0). Black Willow.
McCgracken, Daiel D. A Guide to NOMAD for Applications Development. (Computer Science Ser.). (10/1981). pap. text ed. 18.95 (ISBN 0-201-04624-5). A-W.
McCgwire, Michael & McDonnell, John, eds. Soviet Naval Influence: Domestic & Foreign Dimensions. LC 75-23982. (Special Studies). 1977. text ed. 57.95 (ISBN 0-275-56290-5). Praeger.
McCGwire, Michael, et al, eds. Soviet Naval Policy: Objectives & Constraints. LC 74-11923. (Illus.). 692p. 1975. 49.95 o.p. (ISBN 0-275-09720-X). Praeger.
McChesney, et al. Guide to Language & Study Skills, for College Students of English As a Second Language. 1977. pap. text ed. 11.95 (ISBN 0-13-370452-1). P-H.
Macchesney, J. Packaging of Cosmetics & Toiletries. 1974. text ed. 16.95 o.p. (ISBN 0-408-00125-9). Butterworth.
M'Cheyne, Robert M. Comfort in Sickness & Death. (Summit Books). Orig. Title: Bethany. 1976. pap. 1.65 o.p. (ISBN 0-8010-6034-6). Baker Bk.
Maccia, E. S., et al, eds. Women & Education. 396p. 1975. photocopy spiral ed. 39.75x (ISBN 0-398-02914-8); pap. 14.00o.p. (ISBN 0-398-03223-8). C C Thomas.
McClain, Bebe F. Super Eight Filmaking from Scratch. (Illus.). 1978. ref. 16.95 (ISBN 0-13-876128-0); pap. 9.95 (ISBN 0-13-876110-8). P-H.
MacClain, George, jt. auth. see Ames, Lee.
McClanahan, Ed. The Natural Man. 1983. 11.95 (ISBN 0-374-21969-9). FS&G.
McClanathan, Richard. Brandywine Heritage: Howard Pyle, N. C. Wyeth, Andrew Wyeth, James Wyeth. LC 78-164689. (Illus.). 1971. 15.95 o.p. (ISBN 0-912416-01-7, Pub. by Brandywine Mus). NYGS.
McClane, A. J. The Practical Fly Fisherman. (Illus.). 1978. pap. 6.95 o.s.i. (ISBN 0-695-80929-6). Follett.
--The Practical Fly Fisherman. (Illus.). 292p. pap. 6.95 o.p. (ISBN 0-686-97181-7). Stoeger Pub Co.
--The Practical Fly Fisherman. 288p. 1983. pap. 7.95 (ISBN 0-13-689380-5, Reward). P-H.
McClane, Kenneth A. Moons & Low Times. LC 78-1951. 67p. 1978. 3.50 (ISBN 0-87886-093-2). Ithaca Hse.
--Out Beyond the Bay. 70p. 1975. 3.50 (ISBN 0-87886-059-2). Ithaca Hse.
McClarin, Judith A., jt. auth. see Brown, William H.
McClary, George O. Interpreting Guidance Programs to Pupils. (Guidance Monograph). 1968. pap. 2.40 o.p. (ISBN 0-395-09912-9, 9-78810). HM.
McClaskey, Marilyn J., jt. auth. see Simonton, Wesley.
McClave, James T. & Benson, P. George. A First Course in Business Statistics. 2nd ed. (Illus.). 1983. text ed. 24.95 (ISBN 0-89517-043-4). Dellen Pub.
McClave, James T. & Dietrich, Frank H., II. A First Course in Statistics. (Illus.). 1983. text ed. 24.95 (ISBN 0-89517-050-7). Dellen Pub.
McClean, J. D., jt. auth. see Bottoms, A. E.
McClean, Lenora J., jt. ed. see Anderson, Dorothy B.
McCleary, Elliott, ed. see Ferguson, Charles W., et al.
McClellan, Albert, compiled by. Meet Southern Baptists. LC 78-52960. (Illus.). 1978. pap. 5.95 (ISBN 0-8054-6534-0). Broadman.
McClellan, David. Young Hegelians & Karl Marx. 1918. Repr. of 1964 ed. text ed. 10.00x (ISBN 0-333-08788-7). Humanities.
McClellan, Edwin, tr. see Soseki, Natsume.
McClellan, G. B., jt. auth. see Marcy, Randolph B.
McClellan, Henry B. I Rode with Jeb Stuart: The Life & Campaigns of Major General J. E. B. Stuart. LC 58-12208. (Indiana University Civil War Centennial Ser). (Illus.). 1968. Repr. of 1958 ed. 40.00 (ISBN 0-527-59100-9). Kraus Repr.
McClellan, J. Mac. Pilot's Guide to Preventive Aircraft Maintenance. LC 80-2865. (Illus.). 192p. 1982. 14.95 (ISBN 0-385-15105-5). Doubleday.
McClellan, James, jt. auth. see Redden, Kenneth R.
McClellan, James E. Philosophy of Education. (Foundation of Philosophy Ser). 192p. 1976. ref. ed. o.p. 12.50x (ISBN 0-13-663302-1); pap. text ed. 10.95 (ISBN 0-13-663294-7). P-H.
McClellan, Mary Elizabeth. Felt-Silk-Straw Handmade Hats: Tools & Processes, Vol. III. (Illus.). 1978. pap. 3.50 (ISBN 0-910302-04-9). Bucks Co Hist.
McClellan, Val J. This Is Our Land, Vol. 1. LC 77-151749. (Illus.). 1977. 12.50x (ISBN 0-533-02248-7). Western Pubs FL.
--This Is Our Land, Vol. 2. LC 77-151749. (Illus.). 1979. 13.95x (ISBN 0-9602218-0-8). Western Pubs FL.
McClelland. The Origins of the Romantic Movement in Spain. 414p. 1982. 30.00x (ISBN 0-686-81800-8, Pub. by Liverpool Univ England). State Mutual Bk.
--Spanish Drama of Pathos 1750-1808, Vols. I & II. 663p. 1982. Set. 60.00x (ISBN 0-686-81793-1, Pub. by Liverpool Univ England). State Mutual Bk.
McClelland, B. J. Statistical Thermodynamics. (Studies in Chemical Physics). (Illus.). 1973. 26.95x o.p. (ISBN 0-412-10350-8, Pub. by Chapman & Hall); pap. 19.95x (ISBN 0-412-20780-X). Methuen Inc.
McClelland, Charles. State, Society & University in Germany, Seventeen Hundred to Nineteen Fourteen. LC 79-13575. 1980. 42.50 (ISBN 0-521-22742-9). Cambridge U Pr.
McClelland, Charles E. German Historians & England: A Study in Nineteenth Century Views. LC 79-154514. 1971. 44.50 (ISBN 0-521-08063-0). Cambridge U Pr.
McClelland, David C. The Achieving Society. LC 75-34465. (Social Relation Ser.). 1976. 17.95x o.p. (ISBN 0-470-01397-4). Halsted Pr.
McClelland, Doug. Hollywood on Ronald Reagan: Friends & Enemies Discuss Our President, the Actor. (Illus.). 125p. (Orig.). 1983. pap. 10.95 (ISBN 0-571-12522-0). Faber & Faber.
McClelland, Herbert L. Secret Flower of Rantan. LC 82-71949. (Rantan Stories: No. 1). (Illus.). 60p. (gr. k-5). 1982. pap. 2.95x (ISBN 0-943864-10-0). Davenport.
McClelland, I. L. Diego De Torres Villarroel. (World Authos Ser.). 1976. lib. bdg. 15.95 (ISBN 0-8057-6237-X, Twayne). G K Hall.
McClelland, Ivy L. Ignacio de Luzan. (World Authors Ser.). lib. bdg. 15.95 (ISBN 0-8057-2552-0, Twayne). G K Hall.
McClelland, James N., jt. auth. see Bradley, Jack I.
McClelland, L. & Hale, P. English Grammar Through Guided Writing: Verbs. 1979. pap. 9.95 (ISBN 0-13-281097-2). P-H.
--English Grammar Through Guided Writing: Parts of Speech. 1979. pap. 9.95 (ISBN 0-13-281089-1). P-H.
McClelland, L., et al. English Sounds & Spelling. 1979. pap. 9.95 (ISBN 0-13-282954-1). P-H.
McClelland, Nina, ed. Individual Onsite Wastewater Systems, Vol. 1. LC 76-50983. 1982. 30.00 o.p. (ISBN 0-250-40208-4). Ann Arbor Science.
--Individual Onsite Wastewater Systems, Vol.2. LC 76-50983. 1977. 30.00 o.p. (ISBN 0-250-40209-2). Ann Arbor Science.
--Individual Onsite Wastewater Systems, Vol. 3. LC 76-50983. 1978. 30.00 o.p. (ISBN 0-250-40156-8). Ann Arbor Science.
McClelland, Nina I., ed. Individual Onsite Wastewater Systems, Vol. 4. LC 76-50983. 1978. 30.00 o.p. (ISBN 0-250-40210-6). Ann Arbor Science.
--Individual Onsite Wastewater Systems, Vol. 5. LC 76-50983. (Illus.). 1979. 30.00 o.p. (ISBN 0-250-40277-7). Ann Arbor Science.
--Individual Onsite Wastewater Systems, Vol. 6. LC 76-50983. (Individual Onsite Waste Water Systems Ser.: Vol. 6). (Illus.). 1980. 39.95 (ISBN 0-250-40345-5). Ann Arbor Science.
McClelland, Peter D. & Zeckhauser, Richard J. Demographic Dimensions of the New Republic: American Interregional Migration, Vital Statistics, & Manumissions, 1800-1860. (Illus.). 220p. p.n.s. (ISBN 0-521-24309-2). Cambridge U Pr.
McClelland, Peter D., ed. Introductory Macroeconomics, 1982-83: Readings on Contemporary Issues. LC 77-6193. (Illus.). 224p. 1982. pap. 9.95x (ISBN 0-8014-9879-1). Cornell U Pr.
McClements, Leslie. The Economics of Social Security. LC 79-305864. (Studies in Social Policy & Welfare). 1978. text ed. 17.00x (ISBN 0-435-82598-4); pap. text ed. 10.00x (ISBN 0-435-82599-2). Heinemann Ed.
McClenathan, Louise. My Mother Sends Her Wisdom. LC 79-164. (Illus.). 32p. (gr. k-3). 1979. 9.75 (ISBN 0-688-22193-9); PLB 9.36 (ISBN 0-688-32193-3). Morrow.
McClendon, Ruth A., jt. auth. see Kadis, Leslie B.
McClintic, J. Robert. Basic Anatomy & Physiology of the Human Body. 2nd ed. LC 79-14295. 1980. text ed. 30.95x (ISBN 0-471-03876-8); experiments 12.95x (ISBN 0-471-05118-7). Wiley.
--Human Anatomy. (Illus.). 544p. 1983. pap. text ed. 28.95 (ISBN 0-8016-3225-0). Mosby.
--Physiology of the Human Body. 2nd ed. LC 77-27066. 1978. text ed. 30.95x (ISBN 0-471-02664-6). Wiley.
McClintic, Miranda, jt. auth. see Fry, Edward F.
McClintic, Robert J., jt. auth. see Crouch, James E.
McClintick, David. Indecent Exposure: A True Story of Hollywood & Wall Street. LC 82-3574. (Illus.). 560p. 1982. 17.50 (ISBN 0-688-01349-X). Morrow.
--Stealing from the Rich: The Story of the Swindle of the Century. 348p. 1983. pap. 6.95 (ISBN 0-688-01967-6). Quill NY.
McClintock & Fitter. Collins Pocket Guide to Wild Flowers. 27.95 (ISBN 0-686-42769-6, Collins Pub England). Greene.
McClintock, Cynthia & Lowenthal, Abraham F., eds. The Peruvian Experiment Reconsidered. LC 82-61377. 484p. 1983. 45.00x (ISBN 0-691-07648-0); pap. 11.95 (ISBN 0-691-02214-3). Princeton U Pr.
McClintock, David W. U. S. Food: Making the Most of a Global Resource. 1979. lib. bdg. 20.00 (ISBN 0-89158-183-9). Westview.
McClintock, Elizabeth, et al. An Annotated Checklist of Ornamental Plants of Coastal Southern California. 272p. (Orig.). 1982. pap. text ed. 9.00x (ISBN 0-931876-58-3, 3276). Ag Sci Pubns.
McClintock, F. A. & Argon, A. S. Mechanical Behavior of Materials. 1966. 34.95 (ISBN 0-201-04545-1). A-W.
McClintock, H. F. Handbook on the Traditional Old Irish Dress. (Illus.). 9.95 o.p. (ISBN 0-85221-034-5). Dufour.
McClintock, Jack. The Book of Darts. 1977. 8.95 (ISBN 0-394-40805-5); pap. 4.95 (ISBN 0-394-73370-3). Random.
MacClintock, Lander, tr. see Offenbach, Jacques.
McClintock, Marian, jt. auth. see Bracy, Jane.
McClintock, Michael C. NLRB General Counsel: Unreviewable Power to Refuse to Issue an Unfair Labor Practice Complaint. LC 80-67049. (Scholarly Monographs). 180p. 1980. pap. 15.00 o.p. (ISBN 0-8408-0510-1). Carrollton Pr.
McClintock, Mike. David & the Giant. LC 60-11196. (I Can Read Books). (Illus.). (gr. k-3). 1960. PLB 7.89 o.p. (ISBN 0-06-024126-8, HarpJ). Har-Row.
--Stop That Ball. LC 59-9741. (Illus.). (gr. 1-2). 1959. 4.95 o.p. (ISBN 0-394-80010-9); PLB 5.99 (ISBN 0-394-90010-3). Beginner.
McClintock, Robert. Man & His Circumstances: Ortega As Educator. LC 76-149404. 1971. text ed. 22.95x (ISBN 0-8077-1726-6). Tchrs Coll.
McClinton, Katharine M. The Chromolithographs of Louis Prang. (Illus.). 256p. 1973. 15.00 o.p. (ISBN 0-517-50411-1). Crown.
McClinton, Katherine M. Art Deco: A Guide for Collectors. (Illus.). 288p. 1972. 17.95 (ISBN 0-517-50076-0, C N Potter Bks). Crown.
McClory, Robert. The Man Who Beat Clout City. LC 82-742762. (Illus.). 224p. 1977. 12.95 (ISBN 0-8040-0777-2). Swallow.
McCloskey, Burr. He Will Stay till You Come. LC 78-59114. 1978. 10.95 (ISBN 0-87716-090-2, Pub. by Moore Pub Co). F Apple.
McCloskey, Donald N. The Applied Theory of Price. 1982. text ed. 24.95x (ISBN 0-02-379420-8). Macmillan.
McCloskey, Esther. This Is the Collie. 1963. 12.95 (ISBN 0-87666-273-4, PS619). TFH Pubns.
McCloskey, Gordon. With Love & Anger. 1979. 4.95 o.p. (ISBN 0-533-03967-3). Vantage.
McCloskey, H. J. Ecological Ethics & Politics. LC 82-3840. (Philosophy & Society Ser.). 176p. 1983. text ed. 27.50x (ISBN 0-8476-7111-9). Rowman.
McCloskey, Joanne C., et al. Current Issues in Nursing. (Illus.). 816p. (Orig.). 1981. pap. text ed. 22.50 (ISBN 0-86542-005-X). Blackwell Sci.
McCloskey, Mark, tr. see Herbert, George.
McCloskey, Marsha. Wall Quilts. (Illus.). 48p. 1983. 6.00 (ISBN 0-943574-22-6). That Patchwork.
McCloskey, Marsha R. Small Quilts. (Illus.). 48p. 1982. pap. 6.00 (ISBN 0-943574-15-3). That Patchwork.
McCloskey, Richard V. Self-Assessment of Current Knowledge in Infectious Diseases. 2nd ed. 1974. spiral bdg. 15.00 o.p. (ISBN 0-87488-263-X). Med Exam.
McClosky, Herbert & Brill, Alida. Dimensions of Tolerance: What Americans Believe about Civil Liberties. LC 82-72959. 450p. 1983. 27.50x (ISBN 0-87154-591-8). Russell Sage.
McClowry, Dan P., et al, eds. Infant Communication: Development Assessment & Intervention. Date not set. price not set (ISBN 0-8089-1533-9). Grune.
McCloy, Helen. Burn This. LC 80-26053. 287p. 1980. Repr. of 1980 ed. large print ed. 10.95x o.p. (ISBN 0-89621-261-0). Thorndike Pr.
McCloy, Shelby T. Government Assistance in Eighteenth Century France. LC 77-23743. (Perspectives in European History Ser.: No. 14). xi, 496p. Repr. of 1946 ed. lib. bdg. 27.50x (ISBN 0-87991-621-4). Porcupine Pr.
McCluggage, Denise. The Centered Skier. 1978. pap. 2.50 o.p. (ISBN 0-446-91061-9). Warner Bks.
McCluney, Daniel C., jt. auth. see Kauf, Robert.
McClung. The Anaerobic Bacteria. 1982. Set. 990.00 (ISBN 0-686-97208-2); Pt. 1, Vol. 1. (ISBN 0-8247-1202-1); Pt. 2, Vol. 1. (ISBN 0-8247-1207-2); Pt. 1, Vol. 3. (ISBN 0-8247-1204-8); Pt. 1, Vol. 4. (ISBN 0-8247-1205-6); Pt. 2, Vol. 2. (ISBN 0-8247-1208-0). Dekker.
McClung, Robert. Hunted Mammals of the Sea. (Illus.). (gr. 7 up). 1978. 10.75 (ISBN 0-688-22146-7); PLB 10.32 (ISBN 0-688-32146-1). Morrow.
McClung, Robert M. All About Animals & Their Young. (Allabout Ser.: No. 25). (Illus.). (gr. 4-6). 1958. PLB 5.39 o.p. (ISBN 0-394-90225-4, BYR); pap. 2.95 (ISBN 0-394-80225-X). Random.
--America's Endangered Birds: Programs & People Working to Save Them. LC 79-9241. (Illus.). 160p. (gr. 7-9). 1979. 9.75 (ISBN 0-688-22208-0); PLB 9.36 (ISBN 0-688-32208-5). Morrow.
--Bees, Wasps, & Hornets. LC 73-151942. (Illus.). (gr. 3-7). PLB 7.95 o.s.i. (ISBN 0-688-21075-9); PLB 8.59 (ISBN 0-688-31075-3). Morrow.
--Black Jack: Last of the Big Alligators. (Illus.). (gr. 3-7). 1967. PLB 8.59 (ISBN 0-688-31103-2). Morrow.
--Green Darner: The Story of Dragonfly. LC 79-18922. (Illus.). 32p. (gr. k-3). 1980. 8.75 (ISBN 0-688-22216-1); PLB 7.44 o.p. (ISBN 0-688-32216-6). Morrow.
--Gypsy Moth: Its History in America. LC 74-6245. (Illus.). (gr. 5-9). 1974. PLB 6.96 o.p. (ISBN 0-688-20124-5); PLB 8.59 (ISBN 0-688-30124-X). Morrow.
--Lost Wild Worlds: The Story of Extinct & Vanishing Wildlife of the Eastern Hemisphere. (Illus.). 256p. (gr. 7 up). 1976. 11.25 (ISBN 0-688-22090-8). Morrow.
--Mice, Moose & Men: How Their Populations Rise & Fall. LC 73-4926. (Illus.). 64p. (gr. 3-7). 1973. 8.95 (ISBN 0-688-20087-7); PLB 8.59 (ISBN 0-688-30087-1). Morrow.
--Mysteries of Migration. LC 82-15740. (Illus.). 64p. (gr. 4-6). 1983. PLB write for info. (ISBN 0-8116-2950-3). Garrard.
--Peeper, First Voice of Spring. LC 77-2410. (Illus.). (gr. 1-5). 1977. PLB 8.59 (ISBN 0-688-32116-X). Morrow.
--Possum. (gr. 1-5). 1963. PLB 9.12 (ISBN 0-688-31508-9). Morrow.
--Rajpur: Last of the Bengal Tigers. LC 82-3478. (Illus.). 96p. (gr. 4-6). 1982. 9.00 (ISBN 0-688-01495-X). Morrow.
--Ruby Throat: The Story of a Hummingbird. (Illus.). (gr. 1-5). 1950. PLB 8.59 (ISBN 0-688-31538-0); pap. 3.80 pkg. of 4 (ISBN 0-688-35012-7); pap. 9.75 pkg. of 4 with cassette (ISBN 0-688-35011-9). Morrow.
--Samson, Last of the California Grizzlies. (Illus.). 96p. (gr. 3-7). 1973. 6.25 o.p. (ISBN 0-688-21935-7); PLB 8.16 (ISBN 0-688-31935-1). Morrow.
--Sea Star. LC 75-2247. (Illus.). 48p. (gr. k-3). 1975. PLB 8.59 (ISBN 0-688-32034-1). Morrow.
--Snakes: Their Place in the Sun. LC 79-10238. (Good Earth Books). (Illus.). (gr. 2-6). 1979. PLB 7.22 (ISBN 0-8116-6112-1). Garrard.
--Sphinx: The Story of a Caterpillar. rev. ed. LC 80-27362. (Illus.). 32p. (gr. k-3). 1981. 7.95 (ISBN 0-688-00464-4); PLB 7.63 (ISBN 0-688-00465-2). Morrow.
--Vanishing Wildlife of Latin America. LC 80-25639. (Illus.). 160p. (gr. 7-9). 1981. 9.95 (ISBN 0-688-00378-8); PLB 9.55 (ISBN 0-688-00379-6). Morrow.
McClung, William A. The Architecture of Paradise: Survivals of Eden & Jerusalem. LC 81-24071. (Illus.). 172p. 1983. text ed. 22.50x (ISBN 0-520-04587-4). U of Cal Pr.
--The Country House in English Renaissance Poetry. 1977. 27.50x (ISBN 0-520-03137-7). U of Cal Pr.
McClure, Arthur F. Research Guide to Film History. LC 81-86010. 125p. (Orig.). 1983. pap. 15.95 (ISBN 0-88247-689-0). R & E Res Assoc.
--William Inge: A Bibliography. 1981. lib. bdg. 18.00 o.s.i. (ISBN 0-8240-9486-7). Garland Pub.
McClure, Charles R. Information for Academic Library Decision Making: The Case for Organizational Information Management. LC 79-8412. (Contributions in Librarianship & Information Science: No. 31). (Illus.). xvi, 227p. 1980. lib. bdg. 27.50 (ISBN 0-313-21398-4, MCA/). Greenwood.
McClure, Charles R. & Samuels, Alan R. Strategies for Library Administration: Concepts & Approaches. LC 81-12408. 451p. 1982. lib. bdg. 28.50 (ISBN 0-87287-265-3). Libs Unl.
McClure, Charles R., ed. Planning for Library Services: A Guide to Utilizing Planning Methods for Library Management. LC 82-896. (Journal of Library Administration Ser.: Vol. 2, Nos. 2-4). 1982. 29.95 (ISBN 0-917724-84-4, B85); pap. text ed. 14.95 (ISBN 0-917724-85-2). Haworth Pr.
McClure, Charlotte S. Gertrude Atherton. (United States Ser.). 1979. lib. bdg. 9.95 (ISBN 0-8057-7216-2, Twayne). G K Hall.
McClure, Jesse F., ed. Managing Human Services. LC 79-66853. (Dialogue Bks). 232p. (Orig.). 1979. pap. 9.75 (ISBN 0-89881-006-X). Intl Dialogue Pr.
McClure, Judith S., jt. auth. see Stock, Claudette.
McClure, Mark S., jt. ed. see Denno, Robert F.
McClure, Matthew, ed. see Long, Mark & Keating, Jeffrey.

McClure, Michael. Fragments of Perseus. 1983. pap. 6.25 (ISBN 0-8112-0867-2, NDP554). New Directions.

--Scratching the Beat Surface. LC 81-86249. (Illus.). 176p. 1982. 17.50 (ISBN 0-86547-073-1). N Point Pr.

McClure, Robert D., jt. auth. see Patterson, Thomas E.

McClure, Ruth K., ed. see Walpole, Horace.

McClure, Susan H., ed. Health Care, 1980: A Bibliographic Guide to the Documents Update. 30p. 1982. 25.00 (ISBN 0-667-00635-4). Microfilming Corp.

McClure, Wayne. Keno Winning Ways. Rev. ed. LC 82-83487. (Illus.). 234p. 1983. pap. 8.95 (ISBN 0-89650-780-7). Gamblers.

McCluskey, Kathleen, jt. ed. see Callahan, Edward J.

McCluskey, Neil G., ed. Catholic Education in America: A Documentary History. LC 64-23904. (Orig.). 1964. text ed. 10.00 o.p. (ISBN 0-8077-1731-2); pap. text ed. 5.50x (ISBN 0-8077-1728-2). Tchrs Coll.

McCluskey, Neil Gerard. Public Schools & Moral Education. LC 74-12848. 315p. 1975. Repr. of 1958 ed. lib. bdg. 19.25x (ISBN 0-8371-7762-6, MCPS). Greenwood.

McClusky, Mary. Bel-Air. 256p. (Orig.). 1981. pap. 2.50 o.p. (ISBN 0-523-41158-8). Pinnacle Bks.

McClusky, Pamela. African Masks & Muses: Selections of African Art in the Seattle Art Museum. LC 77-93881. (Illus.). 50p. (Orig.). 1983. pap. 8.95 (ISBN 0-295-96000-0, Pub. by Seattle Art Museum). U of Wash Pr.

McClymer, John F. War & Welfare: Social Engineering in America, 1890-1925. LC 79-54060. (Contributions in American History: No. 84). xvi, 248p. 1980. lib. bdg. 27.50 (ISBN 0-313-21129-9, MWW/). Greenwood.

Maccoby, Hyam. The Sacred Executioner: Human Sacrifice & the Legacy of Guilt. LC 82-80492. (Illus.). 208p. 1983. 19.95 (ISBN 0-500-01281-4). Thames Hudson.

Maccoby, Michael. The Leader: A New Face for American Management. 288p. 1983. pap. 6.95 (ISBN 0-345-30856-5). Ballantine.

McCoin, John M. Adult Foster Homes: Their Managers & Residents. LC 82-6083. 272p. 1983. 26.95 (ISBN 0-89885-087-8). Human Sci Pr.

McColgan, Kristian P. Henry James, 1917-1959: A Reference Guide. 1979. lib. bdg. 32.00 (ISBN 0-8161-7851-8, Hall Reference). G K Hall.

MacColl, Ewan & Seeger, Peggy. Travellers' Songs from England & Scotland. LC 76-2854. 1977. 25.00x (ISBN 0-87049-191-1). U of Tenn Pr.

MacCollam, Joel A. Carnival of Souls: Religious Cults & Young People. 1979. 10.95 (ISBN 0-8164-0436-4); pap. 5.95 (ISBN 0-8164-2211-7). Seabury.

McColley, Diane K. Milton's Eve. (Illus.). 1983. 17.50 (ISBN 0-252-00980-0). U of Ill Pr.

McCollister, J. Philosophy of Flight. 170p. 1980. pap. 10.95 (ISBN 0-686-43358-0, Pub. by JSB Enterprises). Aviation.

McCollough, Albert. The Complete Book of Buddy "L" Toys: A Greenberg Guide. (Illus.). 160p. 1982. 29.95 (ISBN 0-89778-009-4). Greenberg Pub Co.

McCollough, C. R., jt. ed. see Faulkner, Charles H.

McCollough, Celeste. Introduction to Statistical Analysis: A Semiprogrammed Approach. (Illus.). 400p. (Prog. Bk.). 1974. text ed. 19.95 (ISBN 0-07-044805-1, C); pap. text ed. 16.95 (ISBN 0-07-044804-3). McGraw.

McCollum, Bill, ed. Selected Letters of Don Marquis. 1982. 16.95 (ISBN 0-89002-195-3); pap. 9.95 (ISBN 0-89002-194-5). Northwoods Pr.

McCollum, J. P., jt. auth. see Ware, George W.

McCollum, John. Ah-Hah! LC 77-17137. (Illus.). 1978. text ed. 13.95x (ISBN 0-673-16340-7); pap. text ed. 11.95x (ISBN 0-673-16341-5). Scott F.

McCollum, John I., ed. The Restoration Stage. LC 72-7812. 240p. Repr. of 1961 ed. lib. bdg. 18.25x (ISBN 0-8371-6532-6, MCRS). Greenwood.

McColvin, Lionel R. Public Library Services for Children. (Unesco Manuals for Libraries: No. 9). 103p. 1957. pap. 4.75 (ISBN 0-686-94171-3, U503, UNESCO). Unipub.

McComas, A. J., jt. auth. see Kiloh, L. G.

McComas, Alan. Neuromuscular Functions & Disorders. 1977. 79.95 (ISBN 0-407-00058-5). Butterworth.

McComas, Donna C., jt. auth. see Husinger, Margorie.

McComb, Bettie, ed. Family Counseling. 1982. 3.00 (ISBN 0-686-36362-0); nonmembers 3.50 (ISBN 0-686-37290-5). Am Personnel.

McComb, F. Wilson. MGB: MGB Roadster & GT, MGC, MGB V8. (AutoHistory Ser.). (Illus.). 136p. 1982. 14.95 (ISBN 0-85045-455-7, Pub. by Osprey England). Motorbooks Intl.

McComb, H. G., jt. ed. see Noor, A. K.

McComber, W. E. Holy God-Holy People. 1982. pap. 3.95 (ISBN 0-8341-0779-1). Beacon Hill.

McCombs, Don & Worth, Fred L. World War II Superfacts. 672p. (Orig.). 1983. pap. 3.95 (ISBN 0-446-30157-4). Warner Bks.

McCombs, L. & Rosa, N. What's Ecology? Rev. ed. (gr. 6). 1978. pap. text ed. 8.76 (ISBN 0-201-04541-9, Sch Div); tchr's guide 3.28 (ISBN 0-201-04542-7). A-W.

McCombs, Maxwell, et al. Handbook of Reporting Methods. LC 75-31009. (Illus.). 1976. text ed. 18.95 (ISBN 0-395-18958-6); instr's. manual 1.10 (ISBN 0-395-18957-8). HM.

McCombs, Maxwell E. & Becker, Lee. Using Mass Communication Theory. (Topics in Mass Communications). 1979. pap. 10.95 ref. ed. (ISBN 0-13-939702-7). P-H.

McConahay, John B., jt. auth. see Ashmore, Richard.

McConahay, John B., jt. auth. see Sears, David O.

MacConaill, M. A., jt. auth. see Basmajian, J. V.

McConatha, Douglas, jt. ed. see Boyd, Rosamonde R.

McConell, David B., jt. auth. see Lewis, Ferris E.

McConkey, Gladys, jt. ed. see Prock, Alfred.

McConkey, James. Court of Memory. 356p. 1983. 14.95 (ISBN 0-525-24147-7, 01451-440). Dutton.

McConkey, James H. El Triple Secreto Del Espiritu Santo. Agostini, Beatrice, tr. from Eng. Orig. Title: The Three Fold Secret of the Holy Spirit. 112p. (Span.). 1980. pap. 2.00 (ISBN 0-311-09090-7). Casa Bautista.

McConkey, Lee, jt. auth. see Klinge, Peter.

McConn, Rita, ed. The Role of Chemical Mediators in the Pathophysiology of Acute Illness & Injury. 400p. 1982. text ed. 58.00 (ISBN 0-89004-682-4). Raven.

McConnaughey, Bayard H. & Zottoli, Robert. Introduction to Marine Biology. 4th ed. 660p. 1983. text ed. 27.95 (ISBN 0-8016-3259-5). Mosby.

McConnell, Adeline P. & Anderson, Beverly. Single After Fifty: How to Have the Time of Your Life. 1978. 10.95 (ISBN 0-07-044873-6, GB). McGraw.

McConnell, Campbell R. Economic Issues: A Book of Readings. 5th ed. (Illus.). 400p. 1975. pap. text ed. 16.95 (ISBN 0-07-044908-2, C). McGraw.

--Economics: Principles, Problems & Policies. 8th, rev. ed. (Illus.). 992p. 1980. text ed. 24.95x (ISBN 0-07-044930-9, C); instructor's manual 20.95 (ISBN 0-07-044931-7); study guide 9.95x (ISBN 0-07-044932-5); economics concepts 12.95x (ISBN 0-07-044936-8); transparency masters 30.00 (ISBN 0-07-044934-1). McGraw.

McConnell, Charles R. The Effective Health Care Supervisor. LC 81-19058. 317p. 1982. text ed. 28.50 (ISBN 0-89443-390-3). Aspen Systems.

--The Health Care Supervisor's Casebook. LC 82-8875. 198p. 1982. 22.50 (ISBN 0-89443-699-6). Aspen Systems.

McConnell, David, jt. auth. see Parker, Lois.

McConnell, David B. Discover Michigan. LC 81-6722. (Illus.). 144p. (gr. 4). 1981. text ed. 11.80x (ISBN 0-910726-07-8); tchrs. guide 3.00x (ISBN 0-910726-08-6); cancelled student wkbk. (ISBN 0-910726-09-4). Hillsdale Educ.

--A Puzzle Book for Young Michiganians. (Illus.). 24p. (Orig.). (gr. 3-6). 1982. pap. 2.95 (ISBN 0-910726-17-5). Hillsdale Educ.

McConnell, Edwina A. Burnout in the Nursing Profession: Coping Strategies, Causes, & Costs. LC 81-18776. (Illus.). 299p. 1982. pap. text ed. 12.50 (ISBN 0-8016-3223-4). Mosby.

McConnell, Edwina A. & Zimmerman, Mary F. Care of Patients with Urologic Problems. (Illus.). 309p. 1982. pap. text ed. 16.50 (ISBN 0-397-54402-2, Lippincott Nursing). Lippincott.

McConnell, Frank. The Science Fiction of H. G. Wells. (Science Fiction Writers Ser.: No. 622). (Illus.). 250p. 1981. pap. 6.95 (ISBN 0-19-502812-0, GB). Oxford U Pr.

--Storytelling & Mythmaking: Images from Film & Literature. LC 78-27538. (Illus.). 1979. 16.95 o.p. (ISBN 0-19-502572-5). Oxford U Pr.

McConnell, Jeff, jt. auth. see Kelly, John.

McConnell, Joan & McConnell, Teena. Ballet As Body Language: The Anatomy of Ballet for Student & Dance Lover. 1977. 14.37i (ISBN 0-06-012957-3, HarpT); pap. 7.95 o.p. (ISBN 0-06-012964-6, TD-289, HarpT). Har-Row.

McConnell, Josephine. The Fairy Tale Writer: Hans Christian Andersen. 42p. (Orig.). 1982. pap. 3.95 (ISBN 0-931494-35-4). Brunswick Pub.

McConnell, Keith. The SeAlphabet Encyclopedia. (The NaturAlphabet Ser.). (Illus.). 48p. (gr. 4 up). 1982. pap. 2.95 (ISBN 0-88045-016-9). Stemmer Hse.

McConnell, Lorraine. Machu Picchu: Mystery City of the Incas. LC 78-22058. (Unsolved Mysteries of the World Ser.). 11.96 (ISBN 0-89547-069-1). Silver.

--Mysterious Sunken Treasures. LC 79-16807. (Unsolved Mysteries of the World Ser.). PLB 11.96 (ISBN 0-89547-082-9). Silver.

MacConnell, Margaret. Open Then the Door. 1968. 5.95 o.p. (ISBN 0-685-20609-2). Transatlantic.

McConnell, P. S. & Boer, H. J. Adaptive Capabilities of the Nervous System. (Progress in Brain Research Ser.: Vol. 53). 1980. 95.50 (ISBN 0-444-80207-X). Elsevier.

McConnell, R. A. Introduction to Parapsychology in the Context of Science. LC 82-99945. (Illus.). 352p. Date not set. pap. 11.00 (ISBN 0-686-37890-3). R A McConnell.

McConnell, R. A., jt. auth. see Schmeidler, Gertrude R.

McConnell, R. A., ed. Encounters with Parapsychology. LC 81-90032. (Illus.). ix, 235p. 1982. pap. 9.00 (ISBN 0-686-37892-X). R A McConnell.

--Parapsychology & Self-Deception in Science. LC 81-90464. (Illus.). vii, 150p. Date not set. pap. 7.00 (ISBN 0-686-37891-1). R A McConnell.

McConnell, Rosemary. The Amazon. LC 78-62990. (Rivers of the World Ser.). (Illus.). 1978. PLB 12.68 (ISBN 0-382-06201-9). Silver.

McConnell, Scott, jt. auth. see Walker, Hill M.

McConnell, Teena, jt. auth. see McConnell, Joan.

McConnell, William T. The Gift of Time. 132p. (Orig.). 1983. pap. 3.95 (ISBN 0-87784-838-6). Inter-Varsity.

McConochie, Jean, jt. auth. see Osman, Alice H.

MacConomy, Alma D., ed. see Borland, Hal.

MacConomy, Alma D., ed. see Peterson, Roger T., et al.

McConoughey, Jana. Bald Eagle. Schroeder, Howard, ed. (Wildlife Habits & Habitat Ser.). (Illus.). 48p. (gr. 4-5). 1983. lib. bdg. 8.95 (ISBN 0-89686-218-6). Crestwood Hse.

--The Squirrels. Schroeder, Howard, ed. (Wildlife Habits & Habitat). (Illus.). 48p. (gr. 4-5). 1983. lib. bdg. 8.95 (ISBN 0-89686-223-2). Crestwood Hse.

--The Wolves. Schroeder, Howard, ed. (Wildlife Habits & Habitat Ser.). (Illus.). 48p. (gr. 4-5). 1983. lib. bdg. 8.95 (ISBN 0-89686-225-9). Crestwood Hse.

McConville, Michael, jt. auth. see Baldwin, John.

McConville, Michael J., jt. auth. see Baldwin, John.

McConville, Robert. History of Board Games. 1974. pap. text ed. 7.50 (ISBN 0-88488-009-5). Creative Pubns.

McConville, S. The Use of Imprisonment: Essays in the Changing State of English Penal Policy. (Direct Edition Ser.). (Orig.). 1975. pap. 8.25 o.p. (ISBN 0-7100-8309-2). Routledge & Kegan.

McCook, Barbara. The Office: Procedures with Simulated Practice. 1972. pap. text ed. 5.95x o.p. (ISBN 0-685-02784-8, 47633). Glencoe.

McCool, Barbara P., jt. auth. see Brown, Montague.

McCool, Gerald A. Catholic Theology in the Nineteenth Century: The Quest for a Unitary Method. 312p. 1977. 14.95 (ISBN 0-8164-0339-2). Seabury.

McCooll, Colin. Cricket is a Game. 10.50x (ISBN 0-392-10743-0, SpS). Sportshelf.

McCord, Clinton D., Jr. Oculoplastic Surgery. 388p. 1981. 57.50 (ISBN 0-89004-633-6). Raven.

McCord, David. About Boston: Sight, Sound, Flavor & Inflection. (Illus.). 1973. pap. 4.95 o.p. (ISBN 0-316-55512-6). Little.

--Every Time I Climb a Tree. (Illus.). (gr. k-3). 1967. 8.95g o.p. (ISBN 0-316-55514-2); PLB (ISBN 0-316-55495-2). Little.

--A Loser, a Winner, & a Wise Guy-Saul, David & Solomon. Root, Orrin, ed. LC 79-67438. 96p. 1980. pap. 1.95 (ISBN 0-87239-380-1, 40084). Standard Pub.

McCord, Howard. The Great Toad Hunt & Other Expeditions. LC 79-23842. 1980. 12.95 (ISBN 0-89594-015-9); pap. 5.95 (ISBN 0-89594-014-0). Crossing Pr.

--The Selected Poems of Howard McCord, 1955-1971. LC 75-5701. (Crossing Press Ser of Selected Poets). 128p. 1975. 13.95 (ISBN 0-912278-56-0); pap. 5.95 (ISBN 0-912278-57-9). Crossing Pr.

McCord, Jean. Bitter is the Hawk's Path. LC 71-154756. 1972. 4.50 (ISBN 0-689-20682-8). Atheneum.

McCord, Joan & McCord, William. Origins of Crime: A New Evaluation of the Cambridge-Sommerville Youth Study. LC 69-14939. (Criminology, Law Enforcement, & Social Problems Ser.: No. 49). 1969. 15.00x (ISBN 0-87585-049-9); pap. 7.50x (ISBN 0-87585-908-9). Patterson Smith.

McCord, John H., jt. auth. see O'Byrne, John C.

McCord, Norman. Strikes. 1980. 26.00 (ISBN 0-312-76640-8). St Martin.

McCord, William, jt. auth. see McCord, Joan.

McCord, William J., ed. Psychopathology & Milieu Therapy: A Longitudinal Study. 296p. 1982. 29.50 (ISBN 0-12-482180-4). Acad Pr.

McCorkle, Chester O., Jr. & Archibald, Sandra O. Management & Leadership in Higher Education: Applying Modern Techniques of Planning, Resource Management & Evaluation. LC 82-48073. (Higher Education Ser.). 1982. text ed. 16.95x (ISBN 0-87589-532-8). Jossey Bass.

McCorkle, James E., et al. Basic Telecommunications for Emergency Medical Services. LC 77-27303. 176p. 1978. prof ref 19.50x (ISBN 0-88410-703-5). Ballinger Pub.

McCorkle, Ruth M. & Dingus, S. D. Rapid Reading. (Quality Paperback: No. 21). (Orig.). 1978. pap. 3.50 (ISBN 0-8226-0021-8). Littlefield.

McCormac. Analisis Estructural. 3rd ed. 680p. (Span.). 1983. pap. text ed. write for info (ISBN 0-06-315551-6, Pub. by HarLA Mexico). Har-Row.

--Diseno De Concreto Reforzado. 1983. pap. text ed. price not set (ISBN 0-06-315550-8, Pub. by HarLA Mexico). Har-Row.

McCormac, Billy M., ed. Solar-Terrestrial Influences on Weather & Climate. 1983. 19.50x (ISBN 0-87081-138-X). Colo Assoc.

McCormac, Jack C. Structural Analysis. 3rd ed. 600p. 1975. text ed. 37.50 scp (ISBN 0-7002-2473-4, HarpC); solution struct. anal. avail. (ISBN 0-7002-2476-9). Har-Row.

--Structural Steel Design. 3rd ed. (Illus.). 661p. 1981. text ed. 35.50 scp (ISBN 0-06-044344-8, HarpC); sol. manual avail. (ISBN 0-06-364115-1). Har-Row.

McCormac, Jack S. Surveying. (Illus.). 288p. 1976. 18.95 (ISBN 0-13-879064-7). P-H.

McCormack, Allison, jt. auth. see Davis, William S.

MacCormack, Carol & Strathern, Marilyn, eds. Nature, Culture & Gender. (Illus.). 1980. 29.95 (ISBN 0-521-23491-3); pap. 9.95 (ISBN 0-521-28001-X). Cambridge U Pr.

McCormack, Erliss. How to Raise & Train a Cairn Terrier. pap. 2.95 (ISBN 0-87666-262-9, DS1068). TFH Pubns.

McCormack, James E. & Chalmers, Amanda J. Early Cognitive Instruction for the Moderately & Severely Handicapped. LC 78-62903. (Illus.). 1978. loose-leaf & program guide 46.95 (ISBN 0-87822-188-3, 1882). Res Press.

McCormack, Lily. I Hear You Calling Me. LC 75-20980. (Illus.). 201p. 1976. Repr. of 1949 ed. lib. bdg. 17.00x (ISBN 0-8371-8350-2, MCIH). Greenwood.

McCormack, Michael K., ed. Prevention of Mental Retardation & Other Developlmental Disabilities. (Pediatric Habilitation Ser.: Vol. 1). (Illus.). 680p. 1980. 49.75 (ISBN 0-8247-6950-3). Dekker.

McCormack, P. D. & Crane, Lawrence. Physical Fluid Dynamics. 1973. 43.50 (ISBN 0-12-482250-9). Acad Pr.

McCormack, R. M. & Watson, J. Plastic Surgery: Operative Surgery Ser. 3rd ed. LC 79-40787. (Illus.). 1979. 149.95 (ISBN 0-407-00637-0). Butterworth.

McCormack, T. J., tr. see Mach, Ernst.

McCormack, Thelma, ed. Studies in Communications, Vol. 1. 200p. 1980. lib. bdg. 38.50 (ISBN 0-89232-146-6). Jai Pr.

McCormack, Thomas J., ed. see Berkeley, George.

McCormack, Thomas J., ed. & pref. by see Berkeley, George.

McCormack, Thomas J., ed. see Hume, David.

McCormack, Tom, ed. see Hanzak, Jan & Veselovsky, Zdenek.

McCormack, William M. Diagnosis & Treatment of Sexually Transmitted Diseases. LC 82-8386. 272p. 1982. text ed. 29.50 (ISBN 0-7236-7021-8). Wright-PSG.

McCormally, Kevin, jt. auth. see Mezvinsky, Edward.

McCormick & Co. Spices of the World Cookbook. rev. ed. 1979. 16.95 (ISBN 0-07-044871-X, GB). McGraw.

McCormick, Barnes W. Aerodynamics, Aeronautics, & Flight Mechanics. LC 79-11073. 1979. text ed. 39.95x (ISBN 0-471-03032-5). Wiley.

McCormick, E. A., jt. auth. see Ryder, F. G.

McCormick, E. H. Omai, Pacific Envoy. (Illus.). 382p. 1977. 33.00x (ISBN 0-19-647952-5). Oxford U Pr.

--Portrait of Frances Hodgkins. (Illus.). 1981. 29.95x o.p. (ISBN 0-19-647991-6). Oxford U Pr.

McCormick, E. J. Human Factors in Engineering & Design. 4th ed. 1975. text ed. 33.50 (ISBN 0-07-044886-8, C). McGraw.

McCormick, E. J. & Sanders, M. S. Human Factors in Engineering & Design. 5th ed. 1982. 34.50 (ISBN 0-07-044902-3). McGraw.

McCormick, Edith, tr. see Lepman, Jella.

McCormick, Edith, tr. see Winterfeld, Henry.

McCormick, Ernest J. & Ilgan, Daniel R. Industrial Psychology. 7th ed. (Illus.). 1980. text ed. 23.95 (ISBN 0-13-463117-X). P-H.

McCormick, Garth. Nonlinear Programming: Theory, Algorithms, & Applications. 550p. 1983. 44.95 (ISBN 0-471-09309-2, Pub. by Wiley Interscience). Wiley.

McCormick, Harvey L. Social Security Claims & Procedures. 3rd ed. LC 82-51096. 1300p. 1982. pap. text ed. write for info. (ISBN 0-314-71743-9). West Pub.

McCormick, J. Life of the Forest. (Our Living World of Nature Ser.). 1966. 14.95 (ISBN 0-07-044875-2, P&RB); by subscription 12.95 (ISBN 0-07-046001-9). McGraw.

McCormick, Jo M. Etti-Cat, the Courtesy Cat. (Illus.). (ps-3). 1965. 5.95g o.p. (ISBN 0-8038-1886-6). Hastings.

McCormick, John & Davis, W. Grayburn. The Management of Medical Practice. LC 78-2383. 416p. 1978. prof ref 28.00x (ISBN 0-88410-512-1). Ballinger Pub.

McCormick, John F. Saint Thomas & the Life of Learning. (Aquinas Lecture). 1937. 7.95 (ISBN 0-87462-101-1). Marquette.

McCormick, Maurice D. An Invitation to Grow. 135p. 1977. pap. text ed. 7.00 (ISBN 0-8191-0034-X). U Pr of Amer.

McCormick, Michael E. Ocean Engineering Wave Mechanics. LC 72-12756. (Ocean Engineering Ser.). 192p. 1973. 42.50 (ISBN 0-471-58177-1, Pub. by Wiley-Interscience). Wiley.

--Ocean Wave Energy Conversion. LC 81-494. (Alternate Energy Ser.). 233p. 1981. 42.50 (ISBN 0-471-08543-X, Pub. by Wiley-Interscience). Wiley.

McCormick, Michael E., ed. Anchoring Systems. 1979. text ed. 30.00 (ISBN 0-08-022694-9). Pergamon.

McCormick, Naomi, jt. ed. see Allgeier, Elizabeth.

MacCormick, Neil. Legal Reasoning & Legal Theory. (Clarendon Law Ser.). 1979. 19.95x (ISBN 0-19-876080-9). Oxford U Pr.

--Legal Right & Social Democracy: Essays in Legal & Political Philosophy. 1982. 39.95 (ISBN 0-19-825385-0). Oxford U Pr.

McCormick, Pat. Success Training for Children. (Illus.). 1981. 3.95 o.s.i. (ISBN 0-913290-33-5). Camaro Pub.

McCormick, Richard, jt. auth. see Curran, Charles E.

McCormick, Richard A. Notes on Moral Theology. LC 80-5682. 902p. 1981. lib. bdg. 26.25 (ISBN 0-8191-1439-1); pap. text ed. 15.75 (ISBN 0-8191-1440-5). U Pr of Amer.

McCormick, Richard L., jt. auth. see Link, Arthur S.

McCormick, Richard P. & Schlatter, Richard, eds. The Selected Speeches of Mason Gross. 160p. 1980. 14.95 (ISBN 0-87855-388-6). Transaction Bks.

McCormick, Robert, ed. Calling Education to Account. (Open University Ser.). 376p. (Orig.). 1972. pap. text ed. 19.50x (ISBN 0-686-98156-1). Heinemann Ed.

McCormick, Thomas & Fish, Sharon. Meditation: A Practical Guide to a Spiritual Discipline. 132p. (Orig.). 1983. pap. 3.95 (ISBN 0-87784-844-0). Inter-Varsity.

McCormick, Thomas C. Comparative Study of Rural Relief & Non-Relief Households. LC 70-165684. (Research Monograph Ser.: Vol. 2). 1971. Repr. of 1935 ed. lib. bdg. 22.50 (ISBN 0-306-70334-3). Da Capo.

McCormick, William, jt. auth. see Bell, William E.

McCormick, William F. & Schochet, Sidney S. Atlas of Cerebrovascular Disease. LC 75-10387. (Illus.). 370p. 1976. text ed. 29.75 o.p. (ISBN 0-7216-5896-2). Saunders.

McCormick, William F., jt. auth. see Schochet, Sydney S., Jr.

McCormmach, Russell. Night Thoughts of a Classical Physicist. 240p. 1983. pap. 5.95 (ISBN 0-380-56283-9, 56283-9). Avon.

MacCorqvodale, Patricia, jt. auth. see DeLamater, John.

McCorry, Jesse J. Marcus Foster & the Oakland Public Schools: Leadership in an Urban Bureaucracy. LC 76-55567. 1978. 15.95 (ISBN 0-520-03397-3). U of Cal Pr.

McCorry, Jesse J., Jr., jt. auth. see Barker, Lucius J.

McCort, James. Abdominal Radiology. (Illus.). 360p. 1981. lib. bdg. 49.50 (ISBN 0-683-05751-0). Williams & Wilkins.

McCosh, Andrew M. & Scott-Morton, Michael S. Management Decision Support Systems. LC 77-13305. 1978. 29.95x (ISBN 0-470-99326-X). Halsted Pr.

McCoubrey, John W., ed. American Art, Seventeen Hundred to Nineteen Sixty: Sources & Documents. (Orig.). 1965. pap. 13.95x ref. ed. (ISBN 0-13-024521-6). P-H.

McCourtney, Lorena. Legacy of the Heart. (Orig.). 1980. pap. 1.25 o.s.i. (ISBN 0-440-15645-9). Dell.

--Shadows of the Heart. (Orig.). 1980. pap. 1.50 o.s.i. (ISBN 0-440-17998-X). Dell.

McCowen, Alec. Young Gemini. LC 79-1991. 1979. 7.95 o.p. (ISBN 0-689-11004-9). Atheneum.

McCown, E., jt. auth. see Isaac, G.

McCown, Wayne & Massey, James, eds. An Inquiry into Hermeneutics, Vol. II. 1982. 14.95 (ISBN 0-87162-257-2, WP#4851). Warner Pr.

McCoy, Alfred W. The Politics of Heroin in Southeast Asia. 325p. 1973. pap. 7.95xi o.p. (ISBN 0-06-131942-2, TB 1942, Torch). Har-Row.

McCoy, Alfred W., ed. Southeast Asia Under Japanese Occupation: Transition & Transformation. LC 80-121. (Monograph: No. 22, Yale University Southeast Studies). (Illus.). 302p. 1980. pap. 12.00x (ISBN 0-686-27179-3). Yale U SE Asia.

McCoy, Alfred W. & De Jesus, Ed. C., eds. Philippine Social History: Global Trade & Local Transformations. 488p. 1982. pap. text ed. 9.50x (ISBN 0-8248-0803-7). UH Pr.

McCoy, Alfred W., et al, eds. Southeast Asia Under Japanese Occupation. (Illus.). v, 302p. 1980. pap. 12.00 (ISBN 0-686-38044-4). Yale U SE Asia.

McCoy, Drew R. The Elusive Rebublic: Political Economy in Jeffersonian America. 288p. 1983. pap. 5.95x (ISBN 0-393-95239-8). Norton.

McCoy, Esther & Goldstein, Barbara. Guide to U. S. Architecture: Nineteen Forty to Nineteen Eighty. (Illus., Orig.). 1982. pap. 9.95 (ISBN 0-931228-06-9). Arts & Arch.

McCoy, F. N. Researching & Writing in History: A Practical Handbook for Student. 1974. 14.95x o.p. (ISBN 0-520-02447-8); pap. 4.95x (ISBN 0-520-02621-7, CAMPUS 274). U of Cal Pr.

--Robert Baillie & the Second Scots Reformation. 1974. 30.00x (ISBN 0-520-02385-4). U of Cal Pr.

McCoy, Frederick J., ed. Year Book of Plastic & Reconstructive Surgery 1983. 1983. 45.00 (ISBN 0-686-83767-3). Year Bk Med.

McCoy, George F., jt. auth. see Clarizio, Harvey F.

McCoy, George F., jt. auth. see Clarizo, Harvey F.

McCoy, Ingeborg & Ginsburg, Harvey. Bilingualism & Reversible Thought. St. Clair, Robert N., ed. (Language & Literacy Monograph Ser.). 1983. pap. text ed. 14.95 (ISBN 0-88499-602-6). Inst Mod Lang.

McCoy, J. J. The Complete Book of Cat Health & Care. (Illus.). 256p. 1982. pap. 5.95 (ISBN 0-399-50623-3, Perige). Putnam Pub Group.

--A Sea of Troubles. LC 74-22474. (Illus.). 192p. (gr. 6 up). 1975. 7.95 (ISBN 0-395-28916-5, Clarion). HM.

McCoy, James L. Rooted in Slavery. 12.95 (ISBN 0-686-37036-8); pap. 10.95 (ISBN 0-686-37037-6). Del Casa Educ.

McCoy, James W. Chemical Treatment of Cooling Water. (Illus.). 1974. 28.50 o.p. (ISBN 0-8206-0211-6). Chem Pub.

--Chemical Treatment of Cooling Water. 2nd ed. (Illus.). 1983. 40.00 (ISBN 0-8206-0298-1). Chem Pub.

--Industrial Chemical Cleaning. (Illus.). 1983. 40.00 (ISBN 0-8206-0305-8). Chem Pub.

McCoy, K. Landscape Planning for a New Australian Town. (Developments in Landscape Management & Urban Planning: Vol. 3). 1976. 38.50 (ISBN 0-444-41340-5). Elsevier.

McCoy, Kathleen. Coping with Teenage Depression: A Parent's Guide. 352p. 1982. 14.95 (ISBN 0-453-00415-6, H415). NAL.

McCoy, Lowell E., jt. ed. see Walz, Daniel A.

McCoy, Malachy. Steve McQueen. Date not set. pap. 2.50 o.p. (ISBN 0-451-09930-3, E9930, Sig). NAL.

McCoy, N. H. Rings & Ideals. (Carus Monograph: No. 8). 216p. 1948. 16.50 (ISBN 0-88385-008-7). Math Assn.

McCoy, Neal H. The Theory of Rings. LC 72-11558. xxi, 161p. 1972. Repr. of 1964 ed. text ed. 9.50 (ISBN 0-8284-0266-3). Chelsea Pub.

McCoy, Robert A. Practical Photography. rev ed. (Illus.). (gr. 10-12). 1972. text ed. 17.28 (ISBN 0-87345-431-6). McKnight.

McCoy, T. L., ed. Dynamics of Population Policy in Latin America. LC 73-16353. 448p. 1974. prof ref 20.00x (ISBN 0-88410-350-1). Ballinger Pub.

McCoy, W. S., ed. see Deming, H. G.

McCoy, William R., jt. auth. see Warren, James R.

McCrachen, Betsy. Farm Journal's Homemade Pickles & Relishes. LC 76-14048. 128p. (Orig.). 1976. pap. 3.95 (ISBN 0-89795-018-6). Farm Journal.

McCracken, Alexander W. & Cawson, Broderick A. Clinical & Oral Microbiology. (Illus.). 1982. text ed. 32.00 (ISBN 0-07-010296-1, C). McGraw.

McCracken, Alexander W., jt. auth. see Cawson, Roderick A.

MacCracken, Calvin D. A Handbook for Inventors. (Illus.). 224p. 1983. 14.95 (ISBN 0-686-83660-X, ScribT). Scribner.

McCracken, Charles J. Malebranche & British Philosophy. (Illus.). 1982. 58.00x (ISBN 0-19-824664-1). Oxford U Pr.

McCracken, D. D. & Garbassi, U. A Guide to COBOL Programming. 2nd ed. 1970. 17.50 o.p. (ISBN 0-471-58244-1); pap. 19.50 (ISBN 0-471-58243-3). Wiley.

McCracken, Daniel. A Simplified Guide to Fortran Programming. LC 74-876. 288p. 1974. text ed. 19.95 (ISBN 0-471-58292-1); tchr's manual avail. Wiley.

--A Simplified Guide to Structured COBOL Programming. LC 75-44339. 400p. 1976. text ed. 20.95 (ISBN 0-471-58284-0). Wiley.

McCracken, Daniel D. Fortran with Engineering Applications. LC 67-17343. (Illus.). 1967. pap. 22.50 (ISBN 0-471-58236-0, Pub. by Wiley-Interscience). Wiley.

--Guide to Algol Programming. LC 62-17464. 1962. pap. 16.95 (ISBN 0-471-58234-4, Pub. by Wiley-Interscience). Wiley.

--A Guide to Fortran IV Programming. 2nd ed. LC 72-4745. (Illus.). 256p. 1972. pap. 20.95 (ISBN 0-471-58281-6); tchr's manual avail. Wiley.

--Guide to Fortran Programming. LC 61-16618. 1961. pap. 14.50 (ISBN 0-471-58212-3, Pub. by Wiley-Interscience). Wiley.

McCracken, Daniel D., jt. auth. see Dorn, William S.

McCracken, Daniel D., jt. auth. see Gruenberger, Fred J.

McCracken, Daniel D., jt. ed. see Dorn, William S.

McCracken, David. Junius & Philip Francis. (English Authors Ser.). 1979. lib. bdg. 14.95 (ISBN 0-8057-6753-3, Twayne). G K Hall.

McCracken, G. M., et al, eds. Plasma Surface Interactions in Controlled Fusion Devices: Proceedings of the Third Int'l. Conference, U. K., 1978. 1978. 149.00 (ISBN 0-444-85212-3, North Holland). Elsevier.

McCracken, George H. & Nelson, John D., eds. Antimicrobial Therapy for Newborns: Practical Application. write for info (ISBN 0-8089-1565-7). Grune.

MacCracken, H. N. & Pierce, F. E. An Introduction to Shakespeare. 222p. 1982. Repr. of 1929 ed. lib. bdg. 35.00 (ISBN 0-89987-589-0). Darby Bks.

McCracken, J. Politics & Christianity in Malawi 1875-1940. LC 76-27905. (Cambridge Commonwealth Ser.). (Illus.). 1977. 47.50 (ISBN 0-521-21444-0). Cambridge U Pr.

MacCracken, Mary. Lovey: A Very Special Child. LC 76-15389. 1976. 12.45i (ISBN 0-397-01129-6). Har-Row.

--Lovey: A Very Special Child. (RL 9). 1977. pap. 2.75 (ISBN 0-451-11950-9, AE1950, Sig). NAL.

McCracken, May Lou. The Deep South Natural Foods Cookbook. 1977. pap. 1.75 o.s.i. (ISBN 0-515-03661-7). Jove Pubns.

McCracken, Samuel. The War Against the Atom. 1982. 18.50 (ISBN 0-465-09062-1). Basic.

McCrae, W. Basic Organic Reactions. 1973. 38.00 (ISBN 0-471-25870-9, Pub. by Wiley Heyden); pap. 29.95 (ISBN 0-471-25869-5). Wiley.

McCraken, J. L. Representative Government in Ireland: A Study of Dail Eireann, 1919-48. LC 75-31470. (Illus.). 1976. Repr. of 1958 ed. lib. bdg. 17.75x (ISBN 0-8371-8534-3, MCRG). Greenwood.

MacCrakin, Mark. A Winning Position. (gr. 5 up). 1982. pap. 1.75 (ISBN 0-440-99483-7, LFL). Dell.

McCrank, Lawrence J., ed. Automating the Archives: Issues & Problems in Computer Applications. LC 81-11732. (American Society for Information Science). 363p. 1980. text ed. 34.50 (ISBN 0-914236-95-4); pap. text ed. 27.50x (ISBN 0-914236-86-5). Knowledge Indus.

McCrary, Blanche. The Redneck Way of Knowledge. 1983. pap. 4.95 (ISBN 0-14-006725-6). Penguin.

MacCrate, Robert & Hopkins, James D. Appelate Justice in New York. LC 82-72701. (Orig.). 1982. pap. 6.95 (ISBN 0-938870-27-0, 8571). Am Judicature.

McCrath, H. Marie, jt. auth. see Jacobson, Sharol F.

McCray, A. W. Petroleum Evaluations & Economic Decision. (Illus.). 544p. 1975. 37.95 (ISBN 0-13-662213-5). P-H.

McCray, Walter A. How to Stick Together During Times of Tension: Directives for Christian Black Unity. 76p. (Orig.). 1982. pap. 5.50 (ISBN 0-933176-03-1). Black Light Fellow.

McCrea, Joan. Texas Labor Laws. 3rd ed. 100p. 1978. pap. 6.95 (ISBN 0-87201-414-2). Gulf Pub.

McCreadie, R. G. Rehabilitation in Psychiatric Practice. 228p. 1982. pap. text ed. 33.50 (ISBN 0-272-79647-6). Pitman Pub MA.

McCready, Albert L. Railroads in the Days of Steam. LC 60-8812. (American Heritage Junior Library). 154p. (YA) (gr. 7 up). 1960. PLB 14.89 o.p. (ISBN 0-06-024151-9, HarpJ). Har-Row.

McCready, Richard R. Business Mathematics. 4th ed. 1978. pap. text ed. 18.95x (ISBN 0-534-01075-X). Kent Pub Co.

--Learning Business Math with Electronic Calculators. 2nd ed. 297p. 1980. 17.95x (ISBN 0-534-00741-4); solutions manaual avail. Kent Pub Co.

--Office Machines: Electronic Calculators. 6th ed. 248p. 1983. pap. 16.95x (ISBN 0-534-01285-X). Kent Pub Co.

--Solving Business Problems with Calculators. 5th ed. 1977. 16.95x (ISBN 0-534-00495-4). Kent Pub Co.

McCready, V. Ralph, jt. auth. see Cosgrove, David O.

McCready, William C., ed. Culture, Ethnicity, & Identity: Current Issues in Research. LC 82-22651. Date not set. price not set (ISBN 0-12-482920-1). Acad Pr.

McCreary, Paul. Perceptual Activities Level 1 Primary: A Multitude of Perceptual Activities. rev. ed. 62p. (gr. 2-4). 1976. 4.00 (ISBN 0-89039-048-7). Ann Arbor Pubs.

--Perceptual Activities Level 2-Advanced: A Multitude of Reusable Perceptual Activities. rev. ed. (Perceptual Activities Ser.). (Illus.). (gr. 2-4). 1976. 5.00 (ISBN 0-89039-047-9). Ann Arbor Pubs.

--Remedial Reading Program. 1975. text ed. 9.95x (ISBN 0-8134-1702-3). Interstate.

McCreary, Susan A. Strawberry Patchwork. (Illus.). 104p. 1977. pap. 4.00 (ISBN 0-9608428-1-0). Straw Patch.

McCreary, Susan A., ed. Strawberry Sportcake. (Illus.). 96p. 1982. pap. 4.00 (ISBN 0-686-37646-3). Strawberry Works.

McCreary, W. Burgess. One Thousand Bible Drill Questions. 1975. pap. 1.75 (ISBN 0-87162-263-7, WP#D5899). Warner Pr.

McCredie, John, ed. Campus Computing Strategies. 320p. 1983. 21.00 (ISBN 0-932376-20-7). Digital Pr.

McCredie, Kenneth B., ed. Diagnosis & the Management of the Leukemias. (M. D. Anderson Ser. on the Diagnosis & Management of Cancer). Date not set. price not set (ISBN 0-89004-323-X, 472). Raven.

McCree, Marcia. Flea Market America: The Bargain Hunter's Passport to Fleadom. (Illus.). 128p. 1983. pap. 7.50 (ISBN 0-912528-31-1). John Muir.

McCreedy, James, jt. auth. see Mandell, Barbara.

McCreerdy, David. Development & the State in Reforma Guatemala, 1871-1885. (Latin American Series, Ohio University Papers in International Studies). (Illus.). 93p. (Orig.). 1982. pap. text ed. 13.00 (ISBN 0-89680-113-6, Ohio U Ctr Intl). Ohio U Pr.

McCreery, David. Development & the State in Reform Guatemala. 150p. 1982. pap. 13.00 (ISBN 0-686-94075-X, Ohio U Ctr Intl). Ohio U Pr.

McCreight, Ruby E. Horses. (Illus.). 32p. (gr. k-4). 1981. 6.75 o.p. (ISBN 0-525-66743-1, 0655-200). Lodestar Bks.

McCreight, Ruby E. & Frame, Paul. Horses. LC 81-2242. (Illus.). 32p. (gr. k-4). 1982. 6.75. Dandelion Pr.

McCreless, Patrick P. Wagner's Siegfried: Its Drama, History, & Music. Buelow, George, ed. LC 82-11184. (Studies in Musicology: No. 59). 262p. 1982. 44.95 (ISBN 0-8357-1361-X, Pub. by UMI Res Pr). Univ Microfilms.

McCrickard, Eleanor F., ed. Alessandro Stradella's "Esule dalle sfere". Cantata for the Souls of Purgatory. Scaglione, Aldo, tr. from Ital. LC 82-17544. (Early Musical Masterworks). 152p. 1983. 27.00x (ISBN 0-8078-1536-5). U of NC Pr.

McCrie, Robert, ed. Security Letter Sourcebook, 1983. 250p. (Orig.). 1983. prepub. 49.95 (ISBN 0-9609820-0-0); pap. 75.00. Security Let.

McCrimmon, James M. Teaching with a Purpose. instr's manual 1.35 (ISBN 0-395-28254-3). HM.

McCrimmon, James M., et al. Writing with a Purpose. 7th ed. LC 79-88599. 1980. text ed. 14.95 (ISBN 0-395-28253-5). HM.

--Writing with a Purpose: Short Edition. LC 79-90088. 1980. pap. text ed. 13.95 (ISBN 0-395-28939-4). HM.

McCrone, Carole N. & Rose-Hancock, Marga, eds. Fresh, Fast, & Fabulous. 190p. 1982. pap. 8.95 (ISBN 0-89716-122-X). Peanut Butter.

McCrone, David, jt. auth. see Elliott, Brian.

McCrone, Walter C. The Asbestos Particle Atlas. LC 80-66474. (Illus.). 128p. 1980. 47.50 (ISBN 0-250-40372-2). Ann Arbor Science.

--The Particle Atlas: Electron-Optical Atlas & Techniques, Vol. 6. LC 72-90881. (Illus.). 1980. 67.50 (ISBN 0-250-40196-7). Ann Arbor Science.

McCrone, Walter C., et al. Polarized Light Microscopy. LC 78-61047. (Illus.). 1979. 39.50 (ISBN 0-250-40262-9). Ann Arbor Science.

McCrory, G. Jacobs. Baseball Rules in Pictures. pap. 3.95 (ISBN 0-448-11555-7, G&D). Putnam Pub Group.

--Softball Rules in Pictures. (Illus.). (gr. 4 up). 1974. pap. 3.95 (ISBN 0-448-11554-9, G&D). Putnam Pub Group.

McCrory, Margaret D. A Woman Lawyer Talks about Divorce. LC 79-53926. 117p. 1981. 10.95 (ISBN 0-934256-02-0); pap. 6.50 (ISBN 0-934256-01-2). Dean Co WA.

McCroskey, James C. & Richmond, Virginia P. The Quiet Ones: Communication Apprehension & Shyness. (Comm Comp Ser.). 39p. 1982. pap. text ed. 2.95x (ISBN 0-89787-313-0). Gorsuch Scarisbrick.

McCroskey, James C., et al. Introduction to Interpersonal Communication. LC 71-126966. 1971. text ed. 18.95x (ISBN 0-13-485425-X). P-H.

McCrossan, T. J. Bodily Healing & the Atonement. 1982. pap. 3.50 (ISBN 0-89276-505-4). Hagin Ministry.

--Speaking with Other Tongues. 53p. 0.75 (ISBN 0-87509-132-6). Chr Pubns.

McCrum, Robert. In the Secret State. 1980. 10.95 o.p. (ISBN 0-671-25282-8, 25282). S&S.

Maccuaig, R. D. & Yeates, M. N. Theoretical Studies on the Efficiency of Insecticidal Sprays for the Control of Flying Locust Swarms. 35.00x (ISBN 0-85135-057-7, Pub. by Centre Overseas Research). State Mutual Bk.

McCubbin, Hamilton I. & Figley, Charles R., eds. Stress & the Family: Coping with Normative Transitions, Vol. I. 300p. 1983. price not set (ISBN 0-87630-321-1). Brunner-Mazel.

McCubbin, Hamilton I. & Sussman, Marvin B., eds. Social Stress & the Family: Advances & Developments in Family Stress Therapy & Research. (Marriage & Family Review Ser.: Vol. 6, No. 1 & 2). 136p. 1983. text ed. 28.00 (ISBN 0-86656-163-3). Haworth Pr.

McCubbin, Hamilton I., jt. ed. see Figley, Charles R.

McCubbin, Hamilton I., et al. Family Stress, Coping, & Social Support. (Illus.). 294p. 1982. 22.50x (ISBN 0-398-04692-1). C C Thomas.

McCue, C. F., et al, eds. Performance Testing of Lubricants for Automotive Engines & Transmissions. (Illus.). 1974. 53.50 (ISBN 0-85334-468-X, Pub. by Applied Sci England). Elsevier.

McCue, George, ed. Music in American Society 1776-1976. LC 76-24527. (Illus.). 201p. 1976. text ed. 14.95 (ISBN 0-87855-209-X); pap. text ed. 3.95 (ISBN 0-87855-634-6). Transaction Bks.

McCue, Marion. How to Pick the Right Name for Your Baby. 1977. pap. 2.95 (ISBN 0-448-12977-9, G&D). Putnam Pub Group.

McCue, Noelle B. The Joining Stone. (Loveswept Ser.: No. 3). 1983. pap. 1.95 (ISBN 0-686-43204-5). Bantam.

McCuen & Winkler. Exposition. 1982. 9.95 o.p. (ISBN 0-574-22070-4); instr's. guide 2.00 o.p. (ISBN 0-574-22071-2). SRA.

McCuen, Gary E., ed. American Justice: Is America a Just Society? (Opposing Viewpoints Ser.: Vol. 9). (Illus.). 1975. lib. bdg. 10.95 (ISBN 0-912616-34-2); pap. text ed. 5.95 (ISBN 0-912616-15-6). Greenhaven.

--The Racist Reader: Analyzing Primary Source Readings by American Race Supremacists. (Illus.). 1974. lib. bdg. 14.95 (ISBN 0-912616-33-4); pap. text ed. 7.95 (ISBN 0-912616-14-8). Greenhaven.

McCuen, Gary E., jt. ed. see Bender, David L.

Mc Cuen, Gary E., ed. see Church, Carol B.

McCuen, Gary E., ed. see Church, Carol B.

Mc Cuen, Gary E., ed. see Church, Carol B.

McCuen, Gary E., ed. see Leone, Bruno.

McCuen, Jo R., jt. auth. see Winkler, Anthony C.

McCuen, Jo Ray, jt. auth. see Winkler, Anthony.

McCuen, JoRay & Winkler, Anthony C. From Idea to Essay. 2nd ed. 1980. pap. text ed. 10.95 (ISBN 0-574-22055-0, 13-5055); instr's guide avail. (ISBN 0-574-22056-9, 13-5056). SRA.
--From Idea to Essay: A Rhetoric, Reader & Handbook. 3rd ed. 432p. 1982. pap. text ed. write for info. (ISBN 0-574-22085-2, 13-5085); write for info. answer bk (ISBN 0-574-22086-0, 13-5086). SRA.
McCuen, R. Fortran Programming for Civil Engineers. 1975. pap. 23.95 (ISBN 0-13-329417-X). P-H.
McCuen, Richard H. A Guide to Hydrologic Analysis Using SCS Methods. (Illus.). 160p. 1982. 27.95 (ISBN 0-13-370205-7). P-H.
McCullagh, Chuck, ed. see Lieb, Thom.
McCullagh, James C., ed. Ways to Play: Alternate Forms of Recreation. LC 77-29228. 1978. pap. 7.95 o.p. (ISBN 0-87857-226-0). Rodale Pr Inc.
McCullagh, M. J., jt. ed. see Davis, J. C.
McCullagh, P. S., jt. auth. see Hammond, R.
McCullagh, Suzanne Folds, tr. see Goguel, Catherine M. & Viatte, Francoise.
McCullers, Carson. Square Root of Wonderful. LC 58-6501. 1971. 9.95 (ISBN 0-910220-32-8). Berg.
McCullers, Levis D. & Schroeder, Richard G. Accounting Theory: Text & Readings. 2nd ed. LC 81-14729. (Wiley Series in Accounting & Information Systems). 590p. 1980. text ed. 29.95x (ISBN 0-471-06029-1). Wiley.
McCulloch, A., jt. auth. see Abrams, P.
McCulloch, Frank. Eagle in the Sky. (Illus.). 1975. pap. 4.95 (ISBN 0-913270-74-1). Sunstone Pr.
McCulloch, Hugh. Men & Measures of Half a Century. LC 77-87404. (American Scene Ser.). 1969. Repr. of 1888 ed. lib. bdg. 65.00 (ISBN 0-306-71548-1). Da Capo.
McCulloch, J. In the Twilight of the Revolution: The Political Theory of Amilcar Cabral. 200p. (Orig.). 1982. pap. write for info. (ISBN 0-7100-9411-6). Routledge & Kegan.
McCulloch, J. H. Money & Inflation: A Monetarist Approach. 2nd ed. 1981. 8.00 (ISBN 0-686-83746-0). Acad Pr.
McCulloch, J. P., tr. see Propertius, Sextus.
McCulloch, J. W. & Philip, A. E. Suicidal Behavior. LC 72-188140. 133p. 1972. text ed. 23.00 (ISBN 0-08-016855-8). Pergamon.
McCulloch, Jock. Black Soul White Artifact: Fanon's Clinical Psychology & Social Theory. LC 82-14605. 240p. Date not set. price not set (ISBN 0-521-24700-4). Cambridge U Pr.
MacCulloch, John A. Celtic Mythology & Slavic Mythology. Bd. with Machal, Jan. LC 63-19088. (Mythology of All Races Ser.: Vol. 3). (Illus.). 477p. Repr. of 1964 ed. 27.50x (ISBN 0-8154-0142-6). Cooper Sq.
--Childhood of Fiction. LC 74-78208. 1971. Repr. of 1905 ed. 38.00x (ISBN 0-8103-3628-6). Gale.
McCulloch, John R., ed. Select Collection of Scarce & Valuable Economical Tracts. LC 65-16988. Repr. of 1859 ed. 37.50x (ISBN 0-678-00145-6). Kelley.
McCulloch, K. Selecting Employees Safely Under the Law. 1981. 24.95 (ISBN 0-13-802959-8). P-H.
McCulloch, Lou W. Children's Books of the Nineteenth Century. (Illus.). 1978. 9.95 (ISBN 0-87069-239-9). Wallace-Homestead.
MacCulloch, M., jt. auth. see Feldman, P.
McCulloch, Peter B., jt. auth. see Brain, Michael C.
McCulloch, Walter F. Woods Words. 219p. 1958. pap. 19.95 (ISBN 0-686-86360-7, Pub. by Oregon Historical Society & Champorg Press). Miller Freeman.
McCulloch, Winifred. A Short History of the American Teilhard Association. 1979. pap. 2.00 (ISBN 0-89012-013-7). Anima Pubns.
McCulloh, James H. Researches on America: Being an Attempt to Settle Some Points Relative to the Aboriginess of America. 220p. 1982. pap. 7.95 (ISBN 0-912526-32-7). Lib Res.
McCulloh, Walter. Conservation of Water. (Illus.). 1913. 65.00x (ISBN 0-686-51362-2). Elliots Bks.
McCullough, Bonnie & Cooper, Bev. Seventy-Six Ways to Get Organized for Christmas & Make it Special, Too. (Illus.). 96p. 1982. pap. 3.95 (ISBN 0-312-71327-4); pap. 39.50 ppk. of 10. St Martin.
McCullough, Coleen. Tim. 255p. 1982. pap. 3.50 (ISBN 0-446-31047-6). Warner Bks.
McCullough, Colleen. An Indecent Obsession. 1982. pap. 3.95 (ISBN 0-380-60376-4, 60376). Avon.
--The Thorn Birds. 1978. pap. 3.95 (ISBN 0-380-01817-9, 61564-9). Avon.
McCullough, Colleen & Easthope, Jean. Cooking with Colleen McCullough & Jean Easthope. LC 82-47528. (Illus.). 208p. 1982. 14.37i (ISBN 0-06-015039-4, HarpT). Har-Row.
McCullough, Constance M., jt. auth. see Tinker, Miles A.
McCullough, D. R. The Tule Elk: Its History, Behavior & Ecology. (California Library Reprint Series: No. 16). 1971. 32.00x (ISBN 0-520-01921-0); pap. 10.50x o.p. (ISBN 0-520-09345-3). U of Cal Pr.
McCullough, David. The Great Bridge. 1983. pap. 9.95 (ISBN 0-671-45711-X, Touchstone Bks). S&S.
--Mornings on Horseback. 1982. pap. 9.50 (ISBN 0-671-44754-8, Touchstone Bks). S&S.
--Mornings on Horseback: The Story of an Extraordinary Family, a Vanquished Way of Life, & the Unique Child Who Became Theodore Roosevelt. 1981. 17.95 o.s.i. (ISBN 0-671-22711-4). S&S.
--The Path Between the Seas: The Creation the Panama Canal 1870-1914. (Illus.). 1978. pap. 11.50 (ISBN 0-671-24409-4, Touchstone Bks). S&S.
McCullough, David G., ed. see Sulzberger, C. L.
McCullough, Edo. Washington Sideshow. (Illus.). 1982. 10.00 (ISBN 0-686-98360-2). M Jones.
McCullough, Frances, ed. Love Is Like the Lion's Tooth. LC 77-25659. 124p. (YA) (gr. 7 up). 1983. 9.13i (ISBN 0-06-024138-1, HarpJ); PLB 8.89g (ISBN 0-06-024139-X). Har-Row. Postponed.
McCullough, Frances M., ed. Earth, Air, Fire & Water. (gr. 6-8). 1971. 5.95 o.p. (ISBN 0-698-20037-3, Coward). Putnam Pub Group.
McCullough, Jerry, jt. auth. see Bleich, Arthur H.
McCullough, Joseph B. Hamlin Garland. (United States Authors Ser.). 1978. lib. bdg. 11.95 (ISBN 0-8057-7203-0, Twayne). G K Hall.
McCullough, Lorene. Clay Flowers Technique Book I. (Illus.). 155p. 1982. 10.00 (ISBN 0-686-36019-2); pap. o.p. (ISBN 0-686-37264-6). Scott Pubns MI.
McCullough, W., jt. auth. see Munro, A.
McCullough, W. Stewart. A Short History of Syriac Christianity to the Rise of Islam. LC 80-29297. (Scholars Press Polebridge Bks.). 1981. 21.95 (ISBN 0-89130-454-1, 00-03-04). Scholars Pr CA.
McCullougl, Jeff, ed. The Biology & Function of the Major Histocompatibility Complex. 79p. 1980. 11.00 (ISBN 0-914404-62-8). Am Assn Blood.
McCullum, Anne, ed. World Hotel Directory 1981-1982. 7th ed. 887p. 1981. 47.50x (ISBN 0-582-90308-4). Intl Pubns Serv.
McCully, H., ed. see Von Marx, Bomer.
McCully, Helen. The Waste Not Want Not Cookbook: A Cookbook of Delicious Foods from Leftovers. 1975. 8.95 o.p. (ISBN 0-394-49549-7). Random.
McCumber, W. E. The Good News. 184p. 1982. pap. 4.95 (ISBN 0-8341-0699-X). Beacon Hill.
McCumber, William E., et al. Beacon Bible Expositions: Vol. 1, Matthew. (Beacon Bible Expositions Ser.). 1975. 6.95 (ISBN 0-8341-0312-5). Beacon Hill.
McCune, D. L., ed. IFDC Annual Report 1975. (Circular Ser.: No. S-3). (Illus.). 64p. (Orig.). 1979. pap. 5.00 (ISBN 0-88090-029-6). Intl Fertilizer.
--IFDC Annual Report, 1978. (Circular Ser.: No. S-2). (Illus.). 24p. (Orig.). 1979. pap. 5.00 (ISBN 0-88090-028-8). Intl Fertilizer.
--IFDC Progress Report 1975-1976. (Circular Ser.: S-0). (Illus.). 30p. (Orig.). 1977. pap. 4.00 (ISBN 0-88090-026-1). Intl Fertilizer.
--IFDC Progress Report 1977. (Circular Ser.: S-1). 40p. (Orig.). 1978. pap. 4.00 (ISBN 0-88090-027-X). Intl Fertilizer.
McCune, D. L., intro. by see Chaung, Y. H. & Hill, J. M.
McCune, D. L., intro. by see Von Breman, L., et al.
McCune, Donald L. Fertilizers for Tropical & Subtropical Agriculture. Thompson, Marie K., ed. LC 82-11908. (Special Publication Ser.: Sp-2). (Illus.). 26p. (Orig.). pap. text ed. 4.00 (ISBN 0-88090-040-7). Intl Fertilizer.
McCune, George M. Korea Today. LC 82-20290. xxi, 372p. 1982. Repr. of 1950 ed. lib. bdg. 45.00x (ISBN 0-313-23446-9, MCKT). Greenwood.
McCune, Wesley. Farm Bloc. LC 68-8065. (Illus.). 1968. Repr. of 1943 ed. lib. bdg. 15.50x (ISBN 0-8371-0178-6, MCFB). Greenwood.
McCunn, Ruthanne L. Thousand Pieces of Gold: A Biographical Novel. 1983. pap. 3.95 (ISBN 0-440-38883-X, LE). Dell.
MacCurdy, C. Grant. Jorge Guillen. (World Author Ser.). 1981. lib. bdg. 15.95 (ISBN 0-8057-6485-2, Twayne). G K Hall.
McCurdy, David W., jt. auth. see Spradley, James P.
McCurdy, Doug & Tully, Shawn. Sports Illustrated Tennis. (Illus.). 194p. 1980. 8.95 o.p. (ISBN 0-690-01901-7); pap. 5.95i (ISBN 0-690-01900-9). T Y Crowell.
MacCurdy, G. G. Human Skulls from Gazelle Peninsula. (Anthropological Publications Ser.: Vol. 6). (Illus.). 1914. 2.00x (ISBN 0-686-24089-8). Univ Mus of U.
Mc Curdy, Harold G. Personality of Shakespeare: A Venture in Psychological Method. 1953. text ed. 12.50x (ISBN 0-686-83695-2). Elliots Bks.
McCurdy, John A., Jr. The Complete Guide to Your Sinuses, Allergies, & Nasal Problems. LC 81-383. (Illus.). 256p. 1982. text ed. write for info (ISBN 0-8119-0429-6). Fell.
McCurdy, Lyle B. & McHenry, Albert L. Digital Logic Design & Applications: An Experimental Approach. (Illus.). 144p. 1981. pap. text ed. 14.95 (ISBN 0-13-212381-9). P-H.
MacCurdy, Raymond R. & De Rojas Zorrilla, Francisco, eds. Lucrecia y Tarquino. LC 62-18560. 1963. 5.95x o.p. (ISBN 0-8263-0072-3). U of NM Pr.
McCurley, Foster, tr. see Wolff, Hans W.
McCurley, Foster R. Ancient Myths & Biblical Faith. LC 82-48589. 208p. 1983. pap. 11.95 (ISBN 0-8006-1696-0, 1-1696). Fortress.
McCurry, Don M., ed. The Gospel & Islam: A Nineteen Seventy-Eight Compendium. 1979. pap. 6.50 (ISBN 0-912552-26-3). MARC.
Mac Curtain, Margaret & O'Corrain, Donncha, eds. Women in Irish Society: The Historical Dimension. LC 79-964. (Contributions in Women's Studies: No. 11). 1979. lib. bdg. 19.95 (ISBN 0-313-21254-6, MWI/). Greenwood.
McCurtin, Peter. Battle Pay. (Soldier of Fortune Ser.: No. 9). 192p. 1982. pap. 2.25 o.p. (ISBN 0-505-51841-4). Tower Bks.
--Drumfire. (Sundance Ser.: No. 38). 192p. 1982. pap. 1.95 o.s.i. (ISBN 0-8439-0976-5, Leisure Bks). Nordon Pubns.
--Iron Men. (Sundance: No. 37). 192p. 1981. pap. 1.95 (ISBN 0-8439-0977-3, Leisure Bks). Nordon Pubns.
--Summer Friends. 384p. (Orig.). 1983. pap. 3.50 (ISBN 0-8439-1167-0, Leisure Bks). Dorchester Pub Co.
McCusker, J. How to Measure & Evaluate Community Health. 2nd ed. 1982. 29.00x (ISBN 0-333-31680-0, Pub. by Macmillan Bk). State Mutual Bk.
McCutchan, Nell. Focus on Reading. (English As a Second Language Ser.). (Illus.). 1980. pap. text ed. 11.95 (ISBN 0-13-322776-6). P-H.
McCutchan, Philip. Cameron in the Gap. 160p. 1983. 9.95 (ISBN 0-312-11448-6). St Martin.
--Great Yachts. (Illus.). 1979. 14.95 o.p. (ISBN 0-517-53915-2). Crown.
--Halfhyde & the Flag Captain. LC 80-29075. 183p. 1981. 9.95 o.p. (ISBN 0-312-35684-6). St Martin.
--Halfhyde on Zanatu. 176p. 1982. 10.95 (ISBN 0-312-35688-9). St Martin.
--Halfhyde Ordered South. 1980. 9.95 o.p. (ISBN 0-312-35689-7). St Martin.
McCutcheon, James M. China & America: A Bibliography of Interactions, Foreign & Domestic. LC 74-190449. (East-West Bibliographic Ser.: No. 1). 88p. (Orig.). 1973. pap. text ed. 7.50x (ISBN 0-8248-0230-6). UH Pr.
McCutcheon, Lynn E. Rhythm & Blues. (Illus.). 1971. 8.95 (ISBN 0-87948-028-9); pap. 5.95 (ISBN 0-686-96672-4). Beatty.
McCutcheon, Robert. Limits of a Modern World. (Science in a Social Context Ser.). 1979. pap. text ed. 3.95 o.p. (ISBN 0-408-71310-0). Butterworth.
McDanel, Ralph C. The Virginia Constitutional Convention of 1901-1902. LC 75-146556. (American Constitutional & Legal History Ser.). 1972. Repr. of 1928 ed. lib. bdg. 24.50 (ISBN 0-306-70204-5). Da Capo.
McDaniel, Audrey. Greatest of These Is Love. LC 64-23538. (Illus.). 1972. boxed 5.50 (ISBN 0-8378-1713-7). Gibson.
--Love's Promise: Favorite Selections from the Inspirational Works of Audrey McDaniel. LC 79-8935. (Illus.). 96p. 1980. 6.95 o.p. (ISBN 0-385-15607-3). Doubleday.
McDaniel, Carl see Gitman, Lawrence J.
McDaniel, Carl, Jr. Marketing: An Integrated Approach. 2nd ed. 768p. 1982. text ed. 24.50 scp (ISBN 0-06-044359-6, HarpC); study guide scp 8.50 (ISBN 0-06-041549-5); inst man. avail. (ISBN 0-06-364243-3); test bank avail. (ISBN 0-06-364237-9); transparencies avail. (ISBN 0-06-364244-1); scp dynamics marketing 9.50 (ISBN 0-06-042848-1). Har-Row.
McDaniel, D. H., jt. auth. see Douglas, Bodie E.
McDaniel, Earl, jt. ed. see Massey, H. S.
McDaniel, Edwin B., ed. Second Asian Regional Workshop on Injectable Contraceptives. (Illus.). 93p. 1982. pap. 5.00 (ISBN 0-942716-04-3). World Neigh.
McDaniel, G. Floral Design & Arrangement. 250p. 1981. text ed. 18.95 (ISBN 0-8359-2072-0); instr's. manual o.p. free (ISBN 0-8359-2073-9). Reston.
McDaniel, Gary. Ornamental Horticulture. 2nd ed. 1982. text ed. 19.95 (ISBN 0-8359-5348-3); instrs'. manual avail. (ISBN 0-8359-5349-1). Reston.
McDaniel, George W. Hearth & Home: Preserving a People's Culture. (American Civilization Ser.). (Illus.). 297p. 1982. 29.95 (ISBN 0-87722-233-9). Temple U Pr.
McDaniel, Herman. Personal Records Directory. 1979. text ed. 8.95 (ISBN 0-89433-088-8); pap. 7.50 (ISBN 0-89433-089-6). Petrocelli.
McDaniel, James W. Physical Disability & Human Behavior. 2nd ed. 232p. 1976. text ed. 17.25 o.p. (ISBN 0-08-019722-1); pap. text ed. 9.25 o.p. (ISBN 0-08-019721-3). Pergamon.
McDaniel, Kindig. Bones, Joints & Muscles of the Human Body. 1970. 5.95 o.p. (ISBN 0-685-88883-5). Slack Inc.
McDaniel, Lucy V., et al. Selected Neurological Disabilities. LC 74-78553. (Prog. Bk.). 1974. pap. text ed. 5.95x o.p. (ISBN 0-913590-19-3); wkbk 1.50x o.p. (ISBN 0-913590-20-7); plate 1.95 o.p. (ISBN 0-685-50191-4). Slack Inc.
--Selected Orthopedic Disabilities. LC 73-79321. 156p. 1974. text ed. 5.95x o.p. (ISBN 0-913590-12-6); plate 1.95x o.p. (ISBN 0-685-40633-4). Slack Inc.
--Selected Medical Disabilities. LC 73-79322. 102p. 1973. text ed. 5.95x o.p. (ISBN 0-913590-10-X); plate 1.95x o.p. (ISBN 0-685-40632-6). Slack Inc.
McDaniel, Sarah W., jt. auth. see Ligon, Mary G.
McDaniel, Stephen W., jt. auth. see McNeal, James U
McDaniel, Thomas R. The Teacher's Dilemma: Essays of School Law & School Discipline. LC 82-21743. (Illus.). 158p. (Orig.). 1983. lib. bdg. 19.75 (ISBN 0-8191-2944-5); pap. text ed. 9.75 (ISBN 0-8191-2945-3). U Pr of Amer.
--The Teacher's Profession: Essays on Becoming an Educator. LC 82-10949. 192p. (Orig.). 1982. lib. bdg. 22.00 (ISBN 0-8191-2619-5); pap. text ed. 10.00 (ISBN 0-8191-2620-9). U Pr of Amer.
McDaniel, Wilma E. Flowers in a Tin Can. 40p. 1982. pap. 2.00 (ISBN 0-935390-07-3). Wormwood Rev.
McDaniels, David K. The Sun: Our Future Energy Source. 271p. 1980. text ed. 23.95 (ISBN 0-471-08213-9). Wiley.
McDannel, Kathleen H. & Putnam, Margaret. Advanced Series. (Hedman Stenotype System Ser.). (Illus.). 153p. 1980. text ed. 16.00x (ISBN 0-939056-02-X). Hedman Steno.
McDarrah, Fred W. Museums in New York. 1978. pap. 5.95 (ISBN 0-8256-3112-2, Quick Fox). Putnam Pub Group.
McDavid, John W. & Garwood, S. Gray. Understanding Children: Promoting Human Growth. 1978. text ed. 20.95 (ISBN 0-669-93088-1). Heath.
McDavid, Raven I., Jr., jt. auth. see Kurath, Hans.
McDavid, Raven I., Jr., jt. ed. see Blair, Walter.
McDavid, Virginia & Creswell, Thomas J. Today's English: Keys to Basic Writing. 464p. 1983. pap. text ed. 10.95 scp (ISBN 0-06-044351-0, HarpC); instr's manual avail. (ISBN 0-06-361410-3). Har-Row.
Macdermat & Clinker. History of the Great Western Railway 1863-1921. 22.50x (ISBN 0-392-07891-0, SpS). Sportshelf.
McDermid, Patt C. Mountainhouse: A Novella. 137p. (Orig.). 8.25 o.s.i. (ISBN 0-912288-18-3); pap. 5.25 (ISBN 0-686-96851-4). Perivale Pr.
McDermid, Susie, tr. see Postma, Minnie.
McDermott, A. Cytogenetics of Man & Other Animals. (Outline Studies in Biology). 1975. pap. 6.50x (ISBN 0-412-13910-3, Pub. by Chapman & Hall). Methuen Inc.
McDermott, A. Charlene. Godfrey of Fontaine's Abridgement of Boethius of Dacia's Modi Significandi Sive Questiones Super Priscianum Maiorem. (Studies in History of Linguistics Ser.: No. 22). viii, 237p. 1980. 30.00 (ISBN 90-272-4503-7, SIHOL 22). Benjamins North Am.
McDermott, Alice. A Bigamist's Daughter. 1982. 13.50 (ISBN 0-394-52202-8). Random.
MacDermott, Alice. A Bigamist's Daughter. 256p. 1983. pap. 3.50 (ISBN 0-449-20105-8, Crest). Fawcett.
McDermott, Beatrice S. & Coleman, Freada A., eds. Government Regulation of Business Including Antitrust Information Sources. LC 67-25294. (Management Information Guide Ser.: No. 11). 229p. 1967. 42.00x (ISBN 0-8103-0810-X). Gale.
Mc Dermott, Irene E. & Nicholas, Jeanne L. Homemaking for Teenagers, Bk. 1. new ed. (gr. 7-12). 1975. Bk 1. 19.96 (ISBN 0-87002-070-6). Bennett IL.
McDermott, Irene E. & Norris, Jeanne L. Opportunities in Clothing. rev. ed. (Illus.). (gr. 9-12). 1972. text ed. 18.64 (ISBN 0-87002-140-0). Bennett IL.
McDermott, John E., ed. Indeterminacy in Education. LC 76-2987. 1976. 20.75x o.p. (ISBN 0-8211-1251-1); text ed. 18.95x o.p. (ISBN 0-685-71411-X). McCutchan.
McDermott, John F., ed. Research Opportunities in American Cultural History. LC 77-22111. 1977. Repr. of 1961 ed. lib. bdg. 18.00x (ISBN 0-8371-9754-6, MCRO). Greenwood.
McDermott, John F., Jr., et al, eds. People & Cultures of Hawaii: A Psychocultural Profile. LC 80-11959. 242p. 1980. pap. 7.50 (ISBN 0-8248-0706-5). UH Pr.
McDermott, John J., ed. see James, William.
McDermott, John W. How to Get Lost & Found in Australia. 1980. 9.95 (ISBN 0-686-37615-3). Orafa Pub Co.
--How to Get Lost & Found in California & Other Lovely Places. 1982. 9.95 (ISBN 0-686-37621-8). Orafa Pub Co.
--How to Get Lost & Found in Fiji. 3rd ed. 1981. 9.95 (ISBN 0-686-37616-1). Orafa Pub Co.
--How to Get Lost & Found in New Zealand. 4th ed. 1981. 9.95 (ISBN 0-686-37617-X). Orafa Pub Co.
--How to Get Lost & Found in Tahiti. 1979. 9.95 (ISBN 0-686-37618-8). Orafa Pub Co.
--How to Get Lost & Found in the Cook Islands. 1979. 9.95 (ISBN 0-686-37619-6). Orafa Pub Co.
McDermott, Phillip & Taylor, Michael. Industrial Organisation & Location. LC 81-21586. (Cambridge Geographical Studies: No. 16). 248p. 1982. 44.50 (ISBN 0-521-24671-7). Cambridge U Pr.
McDermott, Robert, ed. see Aurobindo, Sri.
McDermott, Thomas J. Ohio Real Property Law & Practice: 1980 Supplements. 1982. write for info. A Smith Co.
McDermott, Vern & Fisher, Diana. Learning BASIC: Step by Step. (gr. 10-12). 1982. teachers guide 17.95 (ISBN 0-914894-33-1); student ed. 15.95 (ISBN 0-686-82885-2). Computer Sci.

McDermott, William V., Jr., ed. Atlas of Standard Surgical Procedures. LC 82-12714. (Illus.). 250p. 1983. text ed. write for info. (ISBN 0-8121-0842-6). Lea & Febiger.

McDermottt, Irene, et al. Homemaking for Teen-Agers, Bk. 2. rev. ed. (gr. 9-12). 1976. text ed. 21.20 (ISBN 0-87002-171-0). Bennett IL.

McDevitt, David, ed. Cell Biology of the Eye. (Cell Biology Ser.). 1982. 67.50 (ISBN 0-12-483180-X). Acad Pr.

McDevitt, Matthew. Joseph McKenna. LC 73-21874. (American Constitutional & Legal History Ser.). 250p. 1974. Repr. of 1946 ed. lib. bdg. 32.50 (ISBN 0-306-70632-6). Da Capo.

McDevitt, Robert see Weaver, Glenn.

Mac Diarmid, A. G. Inorganic Syntheses, Vol. 17. 1977. 32.50 (ISBN 0-07-044327-0). McGraw.

MacDiarmid, Hugh. The Hugh MacDiarmid Anthology: Poems in Scots & English. Grieve, Michael & Scott, Alexander, eds. (The Scottish Ser). 1972. 20.00 (ISBN 0-7100-7432-8). Routledge & Kegan.

--Lucky Poet: A Self-Study in Literature & Political Ideas Being the Autobiography of Hugh Macdiarmid. LC 76-138287. 1972. 26.50x o.p. (ISBN 0-520-01852-4). U of Cal Pr.

--More Collected Poems. LC 82-71462. 108p. 1970. 8.95 (ISBN 0-8040-0213-4). Swallow.

--Selected Essays of Hugh MacDiarmid. Glen, Duncan, ed. & intro. by. LC 76-99506. 1970. 16.95x o.p. (ISBN 0-520-01618-1). U of Cal Pr.

--Selected Poems of Robert Burns. 64p. 1982. Repr. of 1949 ed. lib. bdg. 15.00 (ISBN 0-89987-592-0). Darby Bks.

MacDiarmid, Hugh, ed. Henryson: Selected Poems. (Poets Ser.). 1973. pap. 1.65 o.p. (ISBN 0-14-042152-1). Penguin.

McDiarmid, Norma J., et al. Loving & Learning: Interacting with Your Child from Birth to Three. LC 76-40330. 1977. pap. 7.95 (ISBN 0-15-654200-5, Harv). HarBraceJ.

McDicken, W. N. Diagnostic Ultrasonics: Principles & Use of Instruments. 2nd ed. LC 80-20750. 381p. 1981. 44.00x (ISBN 0-471-05740-1, Pub. by Wiley Med). Wiley.

McDill, Wayne. Making Friends for Christ. LC 79-55290. 1980. pap. 4.95 (ISBN 0-8054-6224-4). Broadman.

McDole, Brad & Jerome, Chris. Kit Houses by Mail. LC 79-51121. (Illus.). 1979. 14.95 o.p. (ISBN 0-448-15705-5, G&D). Putnam Pub Group.

McDole, Robert E., jt. auth. see Barker, Raymond J.

McDonagh, tr. see Camara, Dom H.

McDonagh, Don. Dance Fever. LC 78-21812. (Illus.). 1979. 12.95 o.p. (ISBN 0-394-50410-0); pap. 5.95 o.p. (ISBN 0-394-73667-2). Random.

--How to Enjoy Ballet. LC 77-82958. 1978. 12.95 o.p. (ISBN 0-385-12690-5). Doubleday.

--How to Enjoy Ballet. LC 77-82958. (Illus.). 1980. pap. 7.95 o.p. (ISBN 0-385-12691-3, Dolp). Doubleday.

Macdonagh, Donagh & Robinson, Lennox, eds. Oxford Book of Irish Verse Seventeenth to Twentieth Century. 1958. 25.95x (ISBN 0-19-812115-6). Oxford U Pr.

McDonagh, Enda. Social Ethics & the Christian: Towards Freedom in Communion. 89p. 1979. pap. 7.50x o.p. (ISBN 0-8476-2405-6). Rowman.

McDonagh, Francis, tr. see Camara, Dom H.

McDonagh, Francis, tr. see Theissen, Gerd.

McDonagh, I., et al. Engineering Science for Technicians, Vol. 1. 2nd ed. (Illus.). 256p. 1982. pap. text ed. 13.95x (ISBN 0-686-83107-1). Intl Ideas.

MacDonald. Dictionary of Canadian Artists, 6 Vols. 1977. 100.00 (ISBN 0-686-43129-4). Apollo.

McDonald & Smith. Spearfishing in Britain. (Illus.). 12.50 (ISBN 0-392-04702-0, SpS). Sportshelf.

Macdonald, jt. auth. see Bohm.

Macdonald, jt. auth. see Mudie.

McDonald, A. C. & Lowe, H. Feedback & Control Systems. 1981. text ed. 24.95 (ISBN 0-8359-1898-X); instrs' manual avail. Reston.

Macdonald, A. G. Physiological Aspects of Deep Sea Biology. LC 73-90652. (Physiological Society Monographs: No. 31). (Illus.). 440p. 1975. 99.00 (ISBN 0-521-20397-X). Cambridge U Pr.

MacDonald, A. G. & Priede, J. G., eds. Experimental Biology at Sea. Date not set. price not set (ISBN 0-12-464160-1). Acad Pr.

McDonald, Agnes, jt. auth. see Blackburn, Kate.

McDonald, Alan T., jt. auth. see Fox, Robert W.

MacDonald, Alastair, tr. see Malraux, Andre.

Macdonald, Allan H. Richard Hovey, Man & Craftsman. LC 68-29745. (Illus.). 1968. Repr. of 1957 ed. lib. bdg. 16.00x o.p. (ISBN 0-8371-0157-3, MARH). Greenwood.

Macdonald, Angus. Middle Ground. 1971. 17.50 (ISBN 0-262-13073-4). MIT Pr.

MacDonald, Angus J. Power: Mechanics of Energy Control. (gr. 9-12). 1970. text ed. 15.96 (ISBN 0-87345-486-3); mechanical control man. 7.32 (ISBN 0-87345-484-7); fluid control man. 7.32 (ISBN 0-87345-488-X); electric control man. 7.32 (ISBN 0-87345-487-1); optional experiments 7.32 (ISBN 0-87345-489-8); wkbk. & tests 4.67 (ISBN 0-87345-498-7); tchr's guide 46.67 (ISBN 0-87345-497-9); lab manual set 28.00 (ISBN 0-685-04238-3). McKnight.

McDonald, Angus W., Jr. The Urban Origins of Rural Revolution: Elites & the Masses in Hunan Province, China, 1911-1927. LC 76-7764. 1978. 30.00x (ISBN 0-520-03228-4). U of Cal Pr.

McDonald, Anne & Markowitz, Grace. Sources of Insurance Statistics. 1983. write for info. SLA.

McDonald, Archie P. The Old Stone Fort. 1981. pap. 1.95 (ISBN 0-87611-057-X). Tex St Hist Assn.

--Republic of Texas. Rosenbaum, Robert J., ed. (Texas History Ser.). (Illus.). 40p. 1981. pap. 1.95 (ISBN 0-89641-073-0). American Pr.

MacDonald, Arley L. Managers View Information. 104p. 1983. write for info (ISBN 0-87111-283-3). SLA.

Macdonald, Barrie. Cinderellas of the Empire. LC 81-68450. 335p. (Orig.). 1982. pap. text ed. 29.95 (ISBN 0-7081-1616-7, 1183, Pub. by ANUP Australia). Bks Australia.

Macdonald, Bernice. How to Use Reference Materials. (gr. 7 up). 1980. PLB 8.90 (ISBN 0-531-04134-4). Watts.

MacDonald, Betty. Egg & I. LC 45-336. 1963. 12.45i (ISBN 0-397-00279-3). Har-Row.

McDonald, Boyd & Leyland, Winston, eds. Sex: True Homosexual Experiences from STH Writers, Vol.3. (Illus.). 192p. (Orig.). 1982. pap. 12.00 (ISBN 0-917342-98-4). Gay Sunshine.

McDonald, Bruce & Orsinsi, Leslie. Basic Language Skills Through Film: An Instructional Program for Secondary Students. 300p. 1983. lib. bdg. 22.50 (ISBN 0-87287-368-4). Libs Unl.

MacDonald, C. A. The United States, Britain & Appeasement 1936-1939. LC 79-27121. 224p. 1980. 26.00 (ISBN 0-312-83313-X). St Martin.

MacDonald, Charles B., jt. auth. see Brown, Anthony C.

Macdonald, Charles R. MBO Can Work! How to Manage by Contract. (Illus.). 224p. 1982. 18.95 (ISBN 0-07-044331-9). McGraw.

--Twenty-Four Ways to Greater Business Productivity: Master Checklists for Marketing Advertising, Sales Distribution & Customer Service. LC 81-7096. 446p. 1981. 79.50 (ISBN 0-87624-203-4). Inst Busn Plan.

MacDonald, D. F. Age of Transition: Britain in the Nineteenth Twentieth Centuries. 1967. 16.95 o.p. (ISBN 0-312-01330-2). St Martin.

MacDonald, Dan, jt. auth. see Rubright, Bob.

McDonald, Daniel. The Language of Argument. 4th ed. 352p. 1982. pap. text ed. 10.95 scp (ISBN 0-06-044361-8, HarpC). Har-Row.

MacDonald, David W. Rabies & Wildlife: A Biologist's Perspective. (Illus.). 1980. text ed. 38.00x o.p. (ISBN 0-686-77773-5); pap. 11.95x (ISBN 0-19-857576-9). Oxford U Pr.

MacDonald, Dennis Ronald. The Legend & the Apostle: The Battle for Paul in Story & Canon. LC 82-21953. 144p. (Orig.). 1983. pap. 9.95 (ISBN 0-664-24464-5). Westminster.

Macdonald, Donald. Lewis: A History of the Island. (Illus.). 1978. 19.95x o.p. (ISBN 0-8464-0564-4). Beekman Pubs.

MacDonald, Donald, jt. auth. see Dunlop, Stewart.

Macdonald, Donald, jt. auth. see Dunlop, Stewart.

MacDonald, Donald L. Corporate Risk Control. 1966. 34.50 (ISBN 0-471-06572-2). Wiley.

McDonald, Douglas. The Price of Punishment: Public Spending for Corrections in New York. (A Westview Special Study). 150p. 1980. lib. bdg. 18.00 (ISBN 0-89158-912-0). Westview.

--Virginia City & the Silver Region of the Comstock Lode. (Illus.). 1982. 8.95 (ISBN 0-913814-50-4). Nevada Pubns.

MacDonald, Douglass, jt. auth. see Edwards, James.

MacDonald, Duncan A. Federal Banking Laws. 4th. ed. 496p. 1979. 54.00 (ISBN 0-88262-350-8, 79-0816). Warren.

McDonald, Durstan, et al. Scripture Today. LC 80-81100. 102p. (Orig.). 1981. pap. 4.95 (ISBN 0-8192-1271-7). Morehouse.

McDonald, Durstan R., et al, eds. The Myth: Truth of God Incarnate. Nineham, Dennis & Sano, Roy. LC 79-91091. 122p. (Orig.). 1979. pap. 4.95 (ISBN 0-8192-1266-0). Morehouse.

MacDonald, Edgar E., jt. ed. see Inge, M. Thomas.

Macdonald, Eleanor & Little, Julia. The Successful Secretary. 176p. 1980. 26.00x (ISBN 0-7121-1976-0, Pub. by Macdonald & Evans). State Mutual Bk.

Macdonald, Eleanor J. & Heinze, Evelyn B. Epidemiology of Cancer in Texas: Incidence Analyzed by Type, Ethnic Group, & Geographic Location. LC 77-85516. 669p. 1978. 61.50 (ISBN 0-89004-203-9). Raven.

MacDonald, Elisabeth. Watch for the Morning. 1979. pap. 2.25 o.p. (ISBN 0-451-08550-7, E8550, Sig). NAL.

McDonald, Ellen E., jt. auth. see Karve, D. D.

McDonald, Elvin. Easy Gardens. 1981. 8.95 o.p. (ISBN 0-916752-20-8). Green Hill.

McDonald, Eugene T. & Chance, B., Jr. Cerebral Palsy. 1964. ref. ed. 16.95 (ISBN 0-13-122812-9). P-H.

Macdonald, Fergus. The Catholic Church & the Secret Societies in the United States. LC 46-8049. (Monograph Ser.: No. 22). 1946. 12.50x (ISBN 0-930060-04-0). US Cath Hist.

McDonald, Forrest. Alexander Hamilton: A Biography. LC 78-26554. 1979. 19.95 o.p. (ISBN 0-393-01218-2). Norton.

McDonald, Forrest, jt. auth. see Genovese, Eugene D.

McDonald, Frank B., jt. ed. see Fichtel, Carl E.

MacDonald, George. The Baronet's Song. Rev. & abr. ed. Phillips, Michael, ed. 192p. 1983. pap. 4.95 (ISBN 0-686-42981-8). Bethany Hse.

--The Complete Fairy Tales of George MacDonald. LC 77-80272. (Illus.). (gr. 3-9). 1979. PLB 10.95 (ISBN 0-8052-3700-3); pap. 5.95 (ISBN 0-8052-0579-9). Schocken.

--Diary of an Old Soul. LC 65-12143. 132p. 1965. pap. 4.50 (ISBN 0-8066-1503-6, 10-1895). Augsburg.

--Flight of the Shadow. 288p. 1983. pap. 6.95 (ISBN 0-06-250563-7, CN-4055, HarpT). Har-Row.

--The Marquis' Secret: Sequel to The Fisherman's Lady. Phillips, Mike, ed. 228p. 1982. pap. 4.95 (ISBN 0-87123-324-X, 210324). Bethany Hse.

--Princess & the Goblin. (Classics Ser). (gr. 3 up). 1967. pap. 1.50 (ISBN 0-8049-0156-2, CL-156). Airmont.

--The Princess & the Goblin. (Illus.). (gr. 4 up). 1983. 12.95 (ISBN 0-89191-557-5, 55574). Cook.

--Princess & the Goblin. (gr. 1-4). 1964. pap. 2.50 (ISBN 0-14-030220-4, Puffin). Penguin.

--Sir Gibbie. Yates, Elizabeth, ed. LC 79-64123. (gr. 7-12). 1979. lib. bdg. 9.95x (ISBN 0-8052-3730-5); pap. 5.95 (ISBN 0-8052-0637-X). Schocken.

--The Son of the Day & the Daughter of the Night. pap. 8.95 (ISBN 0-914676-45-8). Green Tiger Pr.

--Thumbscrew & Rack. (Illus.). 25p. 1982. pap. 3.00 (ISBN 0-686-83181-0). Am Atheist.

--The Wise Woman, or the Lost Princess. LC 75-32187. (Classics of Children's Literature, 1621-1932: Vol. 50). (Illus.). 1976. Repr. of 1882 ed. PLB 38.00 o.s.i. (ISBN 0-8240-2299-8). Garland Pub.

MacDonald, Gerald, ed. Vocabulario De Romance En Latin: Antonio De Nebrija. LC 72-96003. 214p. (Lat. & Sp.). 1973. 19.95 (ISBN 0-87722-018-2). Temple U Pr.

McDonald, Gerald W., jt. auth. see Nass, Gilbert D.

MacDonald, Golden. Red Light Green Light. (gr. k-2). 1944. 5.95 o.p. (ISBN 0-385-07651-7). Doubleday.

MacDonald, Gordon. The Effective Father. 1977. pap. 6.95 (ISBN 0-8423-0680-3). Tyndale.

--Magnificent Marriage. 1976. pap. 6.95 (ISBN 0-8423-3890-X). Tyndale.

Macdonald, Gordon & Macdonald, Kyselka. Anatomy of an Island: A Geological History of Oahu. (Special Publication Ser.: No. 55). (Illus.). 37p. 1967. pap. 3.25 (ISBN 0-910240-14-0). Bishop Mus.

MacDonald, Gordon, ed. The Long Term Impacts of Increasing Atmospheric Levels of Carbon Dioxide. 280p. 1982. prof ref 35.00x (ISBN 0-88410-902-X). Ballinger Pub.

Macdonald, Gordon A. Volcanoes. 1972. 35.95 (ISBN 0-13-942219-6). P-H.

Macdonald, Gordon A. & Abbott, Agatin T. Volcanoes in the Sea: The Geology of Hawaii. (Illus.). 1970. 20.00 (ISBN 0-87022-495-6). UH Pr.

Macdonald, Gregory. Fletch & the Widow Bradley. 288p. (Orig.). 1982. pap. 2.95 o.p. (ISBN 0-446-90922-X). Warner Bks.

McDonald, Gregory. Fletch's Moxie. 288p. (Orig.). 1982. pap. 3.25 (ISBN 0-446-90923-8). Warner Bks.

--Who Took Toby Rinaldi? LC 79-24295. 1980. 9.95 o.s.i. (ISBN 0-399-12344-X). Putnam Pub Group.

MacDonald, Gus. Camera: Victorian Eyewitness; A History of Photography, 1826-1913. LC 79-5296. (Illus.). 1980. 17.95 o.p. (ISBN 0-670-20056-5, Studio). Viking Pr.

McDonald, Hamish. Suharto's Indonesia. 277p. 1981. pap. text ed. 5.95x (ISBN 0-8248-0781-2). UH Pr.

McDonald, Hope. Descubramos Como Orar. Coleman, F. G., tr. from Eng. 128p. (Span.). 1980. pap. 3.20 (ISBN 0-311-40040-X). Casa Bautista.

MacDonald, Hope. When Angels Appear. 128p. (Orig.). 1982. pap. 4.95 (ISBN 0-310-28531-3). Zondervan.

Macdonald, Hugh. Berlioz. (The Master Musicians Ser.). 272p. 1982. text ed. 17.95x (ISBN 0-460-03156-2, Pub. by J. M. Dent England). Biblio Dist.

--Portraits in Prose: A Collection of Characters. 1946. 19.50x (ISBN 0-685-89772-9). Elliots Bks.

MacDonald, Hugh, ed. see Marvell, Andrew.

McDonald, I., jt. auth. see Loosli, J. K.

MacDonald, I. G. Symmetric Functions & Hall Polynomials. (Oxford Mathematical Monographs). 1980. 39.95x (ISBN 0-19-853530-9). Oxford U Pr.

Macdonald, I. T., ed. see Lope De Vega, Carpio.

MacDonald, Ian. Get to Know Germany. 1975. pap. text ed. 5.00x o.p. (ISBN 0-435-38560-7). Heinemann Ed.

MacDonald, J. A. Handbook of Construction Resources & Support Services. 595p. 1979. pap. 55.95x (ISBN 0-471-09354-8, Pub. by Wiley-Interscience). Wiley.

MacDonald, J. Fred. Blacks & White TV: Afro-Americans in Television Since 1948. (Illus.). 288p. 1983. text ed. 23.95X (ISBN 0-8304-1020-1); pap. 11.95X (ISBN 0-88229-816-X). Nelson-Hall.

Macdonald, J. Ransay, ed. Women in the Printing Trades: A Sociological Study. LC 79-56961. (The English Working Class Ser.). 1980. lib. bdg. 18.00 o.s.i. (ISBN 0-8240-0114-1). Garland Pub.

MacDonald, Jack. Handbook of Radio Publicity & Promotion. LC 73-114020. 1970. 34.95 (ISBN 0-8306-0213-5, 213A). TAB Bks.

McDonald, Jack, jt. auth. see McDonald, Nancy.

McDonald, Jack R. & Dean, Alan H. Electrostatic Precipitator Manual. LC 82-3449. (Pollution Tech. Ser., Rev. 91). (Illus.). 484p. 1982. 48.00 (ISBN 0-8155-0895-6). Noyes.

Macdonald, James, ed. see Herrick, Virgil E.

MacDonald, James M. Ecclesiastes. 1982. lib. bdg. 15.50 (ISBN 0-86524-091-4, 2101). Klock & Klock.

MacDonald, Janet & Francis, Valerie. Riding Side Saddle. (Pelham Horsemaster Ser.). (Illus.). 1979. 14.00 o.s.i. (ISBN 0-7207-1100-2). Transatlantic.

MacDonald, John. Cinnamon Skin. 1983. pap. 3.50 (ISBN 0-449-12505-X). Fawcett.

McDonald, John. The Magic Story: Message of a Master. pap. 2.00 (ISBN 0-910140-23-5). Anthony.

Macdonald, John. The Theology of the Samaritans. LC 65-10060. (New Testament Library). 1964. text ed. 22.50x (ISBN 0-8401-1464-8). Allenson-Breckinridge.

McDonald, John A. & Gardner, G. H. Seismic Studies in Physical Modeling: Physical Modeling. LC 82-81374. (Illus.). 354p. 1982. text ed. 34.00 (ISBN 0-934634-39-4); pap. text ed. 24.00 (ISBN 0-934634-47-5). Intl Human Res.

McDonald, John C. & Rohr, Michael S. Transplantation of the Human Kidney & Other Organs. 1983. price not set (ISBN 0-686-83003-2). Urban & S.

MacDonald, John D. Cinnamon Skin. (General Ser.). 1983. lib. bdg. 14.95 (ISBN 0-8161-3504-5, Large Print Bks). G K Hall.

--Cinnamon Skin: The Twentieth Adventure of Travis McGee. LC 81-48159. 288p. 1982. 13.41i (ISBN 0-06-014990-6, HarpT). Har-Row.

--The Empty Copper Sea. 1979. lib. bdg. 13.50 o.p. (ISBN 0-8161-6702-8, Large Print Bks). G K Hall.

--The Empty Copper Sea. (Travis McGee Mystery Ser). 1978. 11.49i (ISBN 0-397-01220-9). Har-Row.

--Free Fall in Crimson. LC 80-7871. 224p. 1981. 12.45i (ISBN 0-06-014833-0, HarpT). Har-Row.

--The Good Old Stuff. LC 82-47540. 384p. 1982. 14.37i (ISBN 0-06-015038-6, HarpT). Har-Row.

--The Green Ripper. LC 79-12063. 1979. 11.49i (ISBN 0-397-01362-0). Har-Row.

--Nightmare in Pink. LC 75-31753. (Travis McGee Mystery Ser.). 1976. 11.49 (ISBN 0-397-01116-4). Har-Row.

--A Purple Place for Dying. LC 76-4096. 1976. 11.49i (ISBN 0-397-01166-0). Har-Row.

--The Quick Red Fox. LC 73-16074. 1974. 11.49i (ISBN 0-397-01015-X). Har-Row.

McDonald, John W. The North-South Dialogue & the United Nations. LC 82-1039. 24p. 1982. 1.25 (ISBN 0-934742-16-2, Inst Study Diplomacy). Geo U Sch For Serv.

McDonald, Julie. The Sailing Out. 168p. 1982. 10.95 (ISBN 0-8138-1624-6). Iowa St U Pr.

McDonald, Julie J. Delectably Danish: Recipes & Reflections. 64p. pap. 5.75 (ISBN 0-941016-04-8). Penfield.

--Pathways to the Present in Fifty Iowa & Illinois Communities. LC 77-153937. (Illus.). 310p. 1981. pap. 15.50x (ISBN 0-9608464-0-9). Boyar.

Macdonald, Kathleen. When Writers Write. (Illus.). 320p. 1983. pap. text ed. 10.95 (ISBN 0-13-956490-X). P-H.

McDonald, Kay L. The Brightwood Expedition. 342p. 1976. 8.95 o.s.i. (ISBN 0-87140-605-5). Liveright.

--The Vision is Fulfilled. 300p. 1983. 13.95 (ISBN 0-8027-4019-7). Walker & Co.

MacDonald, Kenneth & Throckmorton, Tom. Drink Thy Wine with a Merry Heart: A Guide to Enjoying Wine. 136p. 1983. pap. 7.50 (ISBN 0-8138-0476-0). Iowa St U Pr.

Macdonald, Kyselka, jt. auth. see Macdonald, Gordon.

McDonald, L., et al, eds. Very Early Recognition of Coronary Heart Disease. (International Congress Ser.: No. 435). 1978. 45.00 (ISBN 0-444-90007-1). Elsevier.

McDonald, Larry. We Hold These Truths. LC 78-57969. (gr. 12). 1979. pap. 3.95 o.p. (ISBN 0-89245-013-4). Seventy-Six.

McDonald, Lawrence P. We Hold These Truths. LC 76-14010. (YA) 1976. 8.95 o.p. (ISBN 0-89245-005-3). Seventy Six.

McDonald, Lee C. Human Rights & Educational Responsibility. LC 79-22051. 269p. 1979. pap. text ed. 9.85 (ISBN 0-87436-257-1). ABC-Clio.

McDonald, Lillie B. Programmed: An Introduction of Concept of a Language Arts Unit for Advanced Educatable Mentally Retarded. LC 79-89926. 1979. pap. text ed. 5.75 (ISBN 0-8191-0853-7). U Pr of Amer.

Macdonald, Lynn. Bordeaux & Aquitane. 1976. 19.95 (ISBN 0-7134-3183-0, Pub by Batsford, England). David & Charles.

McDonald, Lynn. The Sociology of Law & Order. LC 76-9753. 330p. 1976. lib. bdg. 32.50 o.p. (ISBN 0-89158-614-8); text ed. 15.00 o.p. (ISBN 0-686-67421-9). Westview.

Macdonald, Malcolm. Abigail. LC 79-392. (Illus.). 1979. 11.95 o.p. (ISBN 0-394-50492-5). Knopf.

--Goldeneye. 1982. pap. 3.95 (ISBN 0-451-11546-5, AE1546, Sig). NAL.

--The Rich Are with You Always. 1977. pap. 2.25 o.p. (ISBN 0-451-07682-6, E7682, Sig). NAL.

--The World from Rough Stones. 1976. pap. 2.95 (ISBN 0-451-09639-8, E9639, Sig). NAL.

MacDonald, Margaret. Whistler's Mother's Cookbook. LC 79-84553. 1979. 7.95 o.p. (ISBN 0-399-12402-0). Putnam Pub Group.

MacDonald, Margaret R., ed. Storyteller's Sourcebook. (A Neal Schuman Book). 750p. 1982. 64.00x (ISBN 0-8103-0471-6). Gale.

MacDonald, Michael. Mystical Bedlam: Madness, Anxiety, & Healing in Seventeenth Century England. LC 80-25787. (Cambridge Monographs on the History of Medicine). (Illus.). 323p. Date not set. pap. 14.95 (ISBN 0-521-27382-X). Cambridge U Pr.

McDonald, Michael J. & Muldowny, John. TVA & the Dispossessed: The Resettlement of Population in the Norris Dam Area. LC 81-16333. (Illus.). 352p. 1982. 28.50x (ISBN 0-87049-345-0). U of Tenn Pr.

McDonald, Nancy & McDonald, Jack. This Is America's Story. 1975. pap. 3.50 o.p. (ISBN 0-671-18715-5). Monarch Pr.

--This Is America's Story. (Illus.). 256p. (gr. 4-5). 1973. pap. 3.50 o.p. (ISBN 0-671-18715-5). Monarch Pr.

MacDonald, Oliver. Polish August: Documents from the Beginnings of the Polish Workers' Rebellion. (Illus.). 177p. 1982. pap. 6.00 (ISBN 0-939306-02-6). Left Bank.

MacDonald, Patricia J. Stranger in the House. (Orig.). 1983. pap. 3.50 (ISBN 0-440-18455-X). Dell.

MacDonald, Philip. The Rasp. 1979. pap. 4.50 (ISBN 0-486-23864-4). Dover.

MacDonald, R. D., jt. auth. see Clow, C. A.

MacDonald, R. P. see Reiner, Miriam, et al.

McDonald, Ralph E. & Avery, David R. Dentistry for the Child & Adolescent. 4th ed. (Illus.). 852p. 1983. text ed. 38.50 (ISBN 0-8016-3277-3). Mosby.

McDonald, Robert. Artist Quilts. (Illus.). 32p. 1981. 9.50x (ISBN 0-686-99806-5). La Jolla Mus Contemp Art.

--The Carolyn & Jack Farris Collection: Selected Contemporary Works. LC 82-81520. (Illus.). 68p. 1982. 13.50 (ISBN 0-934418-13-6). La Jolla Mus Contemp Art.

--A Contemporary Collection on Loan from the Rothschild Bank AG, Zurich. (Illus.). 1983. write for info. (ISBN 0-934418-16-0). La Jolla Mus Contemp Art.

--Craig Kauffman: A Comprehensive Survey 1957-1980. LC 80-70807. (Illus.). 96p. 1981. pap. 12.00x (ISBN 0-934418-09-8). La Jolla Mus Contemp Art.

--Jewelry by Svetozar Radokovich. (Illus.). 14p. 1980. pap. 2.50x (ISBN 0-934418-07-1). La Jolla Mus Contemp Art.

McDonald, Robert & Rabkin, Leo. Leo Rabkin Works. LC 81-83642. (Illus.). 74p. (Orig.). 1981. pap. 15.00x (ISBN 0-934418-11-X). La Jolla Mus Contemp Art.

MacDonald, Robert D. Chinchilla. (Phoenix Theatre Ser.). pap. 2.95x (ISBN 0-912262-73-7). Proscenium.

MacDonald, Roger. Britain Versus Europe. 15.00 (ISBN 0-392-15070-0, SpS). Sportshelf.

McDonald, Roger. Slipstream. 1983. 15.00i (ISBN 0-316-55553-3). Little.

MacDonald, Ross. The Blue Hammer. 1976. Repr. lib. bdg. 13.50 o.p. (ISBN 0-8161-6431-2, Large Print Bks). G K Hall.

--A Collection of Reviews. 80p. 1980. limited, signed ed. 50.00 (ISBN 0-935716-06-8). Lord John.

--The Dark Tunnel. 1980. lib. bdg. 12.95 (ISBN 0-8398-2657-5, Gregg). G K Hall.

--The Drowning Pool. LC 75-44990. (Crime Fiction Ser). 1976. Repr. of 1950 ed. lib. bdg. 17.50 o.s.i. (ISBN 0-8240-2382-X). Garland Pub.

--Far Side of the Dollar. 1982. pap. 125.00 ltd. manuscript ed. (ISBN 0-89723-037-X). Bruccoli.

--The Moving Target. 1979. lib. bdg. 9.95 (ISBN 0-8398-2538-2, Gregg). G K Hall.

--Self-Portrait: Ceaselessly into the Past. Sipper, Ralph, ed. LC 81-10258. 144p. (Orig.). 1981. 15.00 (ISBN 0-88496-170-2); pap. 6.95 (ISBN 0-88496-169-9); signed ltd. ed. 75.00 (ISBN 0-88496-171-0). Capra Pr.

Macdonald, Ross & Troike, Rudpolph. Improving Techniques in Teaching English for the Job. LC 82-225216. 160p. (Orig.). 1982. pap. 5.75 (ISBN 0-89763-069-6). Natl Clearinghse Bilingual Ed.

MacDonald, Scott. Critical Essays on Erskine Caldwell. (Critical Essays on American Literature). 1981. lib. bdg. 25.00 (ISBN 0-8161-8299-X, Twayne). G K Hall.

Macdonald, Shelagh. Five from Me, Five from You. LC 80-2695. 192p. (gr. 6 up). 1981. 8.95 (ISBN 0-233-96554-8). Andre Deutsch.

Macdonald, Stuart, jt. auth. see Braun, Ernest.

MacDonald, Susan. Dangerous As Daughters. (Illus., Orig.). pap. 3.00 (ISBN 0-686-23232-1). Five Trees.

--A Smart Dithyramb. (Flowering Quince Poetry Ser.: No. 3). 28p. (Orig.). 1979. pap. 4.00 (ISBN 0-940592-04-5). Heyeck Pr.

--Your Career in the Beauty Industry. LC 78-17138. (Arco Career Guidance Ser.). 1979. lib. bdg. 7.95 (ISBN 0-668-04612-0); pap. 4.50 (ISBN 0-668-04623-6). Arco.

McDonald, Susan, jt. auth. see Mottram, Maxine.

McDonald, T. Marll. Mathematical Methods for Social & Management Scientists. 544p. 1974. text ed. 26.50 (ISBN 0-395-17089-3); instr's. manual 2.45 (ISBN 0-395-17858-4). HM.

MacDonald, Violet M., tr. see Vollard, Ambroise.

McDonald, W. F. Notes on the Problems of Cargo Ventilation. (Technical Note Ser.). 1968. pap. 7.00 (ISBN 0-685-22329-9, W11, WMO). Unipub.

MacDonald, W. S., jt. ed. see Donald, L.

McDonald, Walter. Burning the Fence. LC 80-54792. 58p. (Orig.). 1981. 7.95 (ISBN 0-89672-088-8); pap. 4.95 (ISBN 0-89672-087-X). Tex Tech Pr.

MacDonald, William. Acts: Studies in Dynamic Christianity. 4.95 (ISBN 0-937396-01-X). Walterick Pubs.

--Enjoying the Proverbs. 1982. pap. 3.50 (ISBN 0-937396-23-0). Walterick Pubs.

--Enjoying the Psalms, 2 vols. 1977. pap. 7.00 ea. Vol. 1 (ISBN 0-937396-34-6). Vol. 2 (ISBN 0-937396-35-4). Walterick Pubs.

--Grasping for Shadows. pap. 1.00 (ISBN 0-937396-19-2). Walterick Pubs.

--Here's the Difference. pap. 2.50 (ISBN 0-937396-55-9). Walterick Pubs.

--I Peter: Faith Tested, Future Triumphant. LC 72-94099. (Cornerstone Commentaries Ser.). 112p. 1972. kivar 2.95 (ISBN 0-87788-675-X). Shaw Pubs.

--II Peter & Jude: The Christian & Apostasy. LC 72-94373. (Cornerstone Commentaries Ser.). 96p. 1972. kivar 2.95 (ISBN 0-87788-676-8). Shaw Pubs.

McDonald, William. Letters to the Thessalonians. rev. ed. 1982. pap. 3.50 (ISBN 0-937396-43-5). Walterick Pubs.

MacDonald, William. Winning Souls the Bible Way. pap. 2.50 (ISBN 0-937396-56-7). Walterick Pubs.

McDonald, William A. & Coulson, William D., eds. Excavations at Nichoria in Southwest Greece, Vol. III: The Dark Age & Byzantine Occupation. LC 78-3198. (Illus.). 544p. 1983. 49.50x (ISBN 0-8166-1144-0). U of Minn Pr.

McDonald, William F. & Cramer, James A., eds. Plea Bargaining. LC 78-2102. 224p. 1980. 23.95x (ISBN 0-669-02363-9). Lexington Bks.

McDonald, William J., ed. The General Council: Special Studies in Doctrinal & Historical Background. LC 78-10099. 1979. Repr. of 1962 ed. lib. bdg. 17.50x (ISBN 0-313-20753-4, MCGC). Greenwood.

MacDonald, William W., et al, eds. European Traditions in the Twentieth Century. LC 79-52456. 1979. pap. text ed. 10.95x (ISBN 0-88273-375-3). Forum Pr IL.

Macdonell, A. A. Vedic Grammar for Students. 1977. pap. 12.50 (ISBN 0-686-51865-9). Orient Bk Dist.

McDonnell. The Use of Hand Woodworking Tools. LC 76-48504. 301p. 1978. pap. 9.80 (ISBN 0-8273-1098-6); instr.'s guide 2.75 (ISBN 0-8273-1099-4). Delmar.

--The Use of Portable Power Tools. LC 77-85761. 1979. pap. 11.00 (ISBN 0-8273-1100-1); instructor's guide 2.75 (ISBN 0-685-93221-4). Delmar.

McDonnell, J. A., ed. Cosmic Dust. LC 77-2895. 1978. text ed. 154.95 (ISBN 0-471-99512-6, Pub. by Wiley-Interscience). Wiley.

Macdonnell, John & Manson, Edward, eds. Great Jurists of the World, from Gaius to Von Ihering. (Continental Legal History Ser: Vol. 2). (Illus.). xxxii, 608p. 1968. Repr. of 1914 ed. 22.50x o.p. (ISBN 0-8377-2425-2). Rothman.

McDonnell, John, as told to see Lowery, Fred.

McDonnell, John, jt. ed. see McGwire, Michael.

McDonnell, John F., tr. see Hauret, Charles.

McDonnell, Julian B., jt. auth. see Frankel, Lionel H.

McDonnell, Kilian. Charismatic Renewal & Ecumenism. pap. 4.95 o.p. (ISBN 0-8091-2124-7). Paulist Pr.

McDonnell, Kilian, ed. Presence, Power, Praise: Documents on Charismatic Renewal: National Documents, Vol. 1. LC 79-26080. 696p. 1980. 35.00 (ISBN 0-8146-1066-8). Liturgical Pr.

McDonnell, Leo & Ball, John. Blueprint Reading & Sketching for Carpenters: Residential. 3rd ed. LC 80-66027. (Blueprint Reading Ser.). (Illus.). 151p. 1981. pap. text ed. 11.80 (ISBN 0-8273-1354-3); instructor's guide 3.75 (ISBN 0-8273-1355-1). Delmar.

McDonnell, Thomas. Listening to the Lord in Literature: The Sister's Life Revisited. LC 77-88108. (Orig.). 1978. pap. 1.85 o.p. (ISBN 0-8189-1154-9, 154, Pub. by Alba Bks). Alba.

McDonnell, Unity, jt. ed. see Edwardss, Marcia.

McDonough, B. T. Nietzsche & Kazantzakis. LC 78-61302. 1978. pap. text ed. 8.00 (ISBN 0-8191-0607-0). U Pr of Amer.

McDonough, James L. Stones River: Bloody Winter in Tennessee. LC 80-11580. 272p. 1980. 14.95 (ISBN 0-87049-301-9); pap. 7.95 (ISBN 0-87049-373-6). U of Tenn Pr.

McDonough, John J., jt. auth. see Culbert, Samuel A.

McDonough, Kathleen, jt. auth. see Fox, Micheal.

McDonough, Marian. Wagon Wheels to Denver. (Illus.). (gr. 4-9). 1960. 3.50x (ISBN 0-87315-044-9). Golden Bell.

McDonough, Mary. Divine Life. Date not set. pap. 5.95 (ISBN 0-940232-10-3). Christian Bks.

McDonough, Michael. Assistant Accountant. 3rd ed. LC 82-18439. 160p. 1983. pap. text ed. 8.00 (ISBN 0-668-05613-4, 5613). Arco.

McDonough, Nancy. Garden Sass: A Catalog of Arkansas Folkways. LC 74-16633. (Illus.). 320p. 1975. 8.95 o.p. (ISBN 0-698-10640-7, Coward); pap. 4.95 o.p. (ISBN 0-698-10644-X). Putnam Pub Group.

McDorman, Ted L. & Beauchamp, Kenneth P. Maritime Boundary Delimitation: An Annotated Bibliography. 224p. 1983. 24.95x (ISBN 0-669-06146-8). Lexington Bks.

McDougal, Luther L., jt. auth. see McDougal, Myers S.

McDougal, Marianne, jt. auth. see Dowling, Barbara T.

McDougal, Myers S. & McDougal, Luther L. Property, Wealth, Land. 2nd ed. 1981. 28.00 (ISBN 0-672-84349-8). Michie-Bobbs.

McDougal, Stan. World's Greatest Golf Jokes. 1983. pap. 4.95 (ISBN 0-8065-0831-0). Citadel Pr.

McDougal, W. Scott & Persky, Lester. Traumatic Injuries of the Genitourinary System, Vol. I. (Illus.). 148p. 1980. 26.95 (ISBN 0-683-05768-5, 5768-5). Williams & Wilkins.

McDougald. Handbook of Poultry Parasites. 250p. 1983. 29.50 (ISBN 0-03-062489-4). Praeger.

MacDougall, Allan R., ed. Letters of Edna St. Vincent Millay. 384p. pap. 7.95 (ISBN 0-89272-152-9). Down East.

MacDougall, Arthur, Jr. Dud Dean, Maine Guide: Tales of Hunting & Fishing. 1976. pap. 3.95 (ISBN 0-87027-178-4). Cumberland Pr.

MacDougall, Curtis. Hoaxes. 2nd ed. 1982. pap. 4.50 (ISBN 0-486-20465-0). Dover.

MacDougall, Curtis D. Interpretative Reporting. 8th ed. 1982. text ed. 18.95x (ISBN 0-02-373120-6). Macmillan.

--Superstition & the Press. 600p. 1983. 29.95 (ISBN 0-87975-211-4); pap. 12.95 (ISBN 0-87975-212-2). Prometheus Bks.

MacDougall, Donald. Studies in Political Economy, 2 vols. Incl. Vol. 1. The Interwar Years & the 1940s. 288p (ISBN 0-8448-0894-6); Vol. 2. International Trade & Domestic Economic Policy. 276p (ISBN 0-8448-0895-4). 1975. 27.50x ea. o.s.i. Crane-Russak Co.

McDougall, Duncan & Quirk, James. Economics. 800p. 1981. text ed. 22.95 (ISBN 0-574-19405-3, 13-2405); instr's. guide avail. (ISBN 0-574-19406-1, 13-2406); study guide 7.95 (ISBN 0-574-19407-X, 13-2407). SRA.

McDougall, Duncan & Quirk, James P. Macroeconomics. 1981. pap. text ed. 14.95 (ISBN 0-574-19415-0, 13-2415); instr's guide avail. (ISBN 0-574-19416-9, 13-2416). SRA.

McDougall, Duncan, jt. auth. see Dernburg, Thomas.

McDougall, Duncan, jt. auth. see Dernburg, Thomas F.

McDougall, Duncan, jt. auth. see Quirk, James P.

McDougall, G., jt. ed. see Healey, P.

MacDougall, Hamilton C. Early New England Psalmody: An Historical Appreciation, 1620-1820. LC 79-87398. (Music Reprint Ser). 1969. Repr. of 1940 ed. lib. bdg. 22.50 (ISBN 0-306-71542-2). Da Capo.

MacDougall, Hugh A. Racial Myth in English History: Trojans, Teutons, & Anglo-Saxons. LC 81-69941. 160p. 1982. text ed. 15.00x (ISBN 0-87451-228-X). U Pr of New Eng.

--Racial Myth in English History: Trojans, Teutons, & Anglo-Saxons. LC 81-69941. 160p. 1983. pap. text ed. 6.50x (ISBN 0-87451-229-8). U Pr of New Eng.

MacDougall, James. Highland Fairy Legends. Calder, George, ed. (Illus.). 117p. 1978. Repr. of 1910 ed. 11.50x o.p. (ISBN 0-8476-6041-9). Rowman.

MacDougall, James K. Death & the Maiden. LC 78-51084. 1978. 8.95 o.p. (ISBN 0-672-52512-7). Bobbs.

MacDougall, John A., jt. auth. see Foon, Chew S.

MacDougall, Malcolm. The Kingmaker. 1978. 8.95 o.p. (ISBN 0-517-53232-8, C N Potter Bks). Crown.

McDougall, Mary L. The Working Class in Modern Europe. (Problems in European Civilization Ser.). 1975. pap. 5.95x (ISBN 0-669-92833-X). Heath.

Macdougall, Norman. James III: A Political Study. 323p. 1982. text ed. 38.00x (ISBN 0-85976-078-2, Pub. by Donald Scotland). Humanities.

McDougall, T. W., jt. auth. see MacNaughton, E. G.

MacDougall, Trudie. Beyond Dreamtime: The Life & Lore of the Aboriginal Australian. LC 77-13944. (Illus.). (gr. 2-6). 1978. PLB 5.64 o.p. (ISBN 0-698-30688-0, Coward). Putnam Pub Group.

McDougall, W. B. Seed Plants of Wupatki & Sunset Crater National Monuments. (MNA Bulletin Ser.: No. 37). 1962. pap. 1.80 o.p. (ISBN 0-685-76474-5). Mus Northern Ariz.

McDougall, W. B. & Haskell, H. S. Seed Plants of Montezuma Castle National Monument, with Keys for the Identification of Species. (MNA Bulletin Ser.: No. 35). 1960. pap. 1.80 (ISBN 0-685-76473-7). Mus Northern Ariz.

McDougall, William. Body & Mind. LC 73-13025. (Illus.). 384p. 1974. Repr. of 1911 ed. lib. bdg. 20.75x (ISBN 0-8371-7107-5, MCBM). Greenwood.

MacDougall, William L. American Revolutionary: A Biography of General Alexander McDougall. LC 76-15324. (Contributions in American History: No. 57). (Illus.). 1977. lib. bdg. 25.00 (ISBN 0-8371-9035-5, MAR/). Greenwood.

McDowall, Josh. More Evidence That Demands a Verdict. 1975. pap. 7.95 o.p. (ISBN 0-918956-25-0). Campus Crusade.

McDowall, R. W. Recording Old Houses: A Guide. 36p. 1980. pap. text ed. 5.95x (ISBN 0-906780-03-9, Pub. by Coun Brit Archaeology). Humanities.

McDowell & Lavitt. Third World Voices for Children. 1981. 7.95 o.s.i. (ISBN 0-686-70399-5). Okpaku Communications.

McDowell, Charles A., ed. Mass Spectrometry. 1963. text ed. 33.50 o.p. (ISBN 0-07-044940-6, P&RB). McGraw.

MacDowell, D. M. Athenian Homicide Law in the Age of the Orators. 1963. 14.50 (ISBN 0-7190-1212-0). Manchester.

MacDowell, Edward. Critical & Historical Essays. 2nd ed. LC 69-11289. 1969. Repr. of 1912 ed. lib. bdg. 29.50 (ISBN 0-306-71098-6). Da Capo.

--Piano Pieces, (Opus 51, 55, 61, 62) LC 70-170391. (Earlier American Music Ser.: No. 8). 144p. 1972. Repr. lib. bdg. 25.00 (ISBN 0-306-77308-2). Da Capo.

--Songs (Opus 40, 47, 56, 58, 60) LC 73-170392. (Earlier American Music Ser.: No. 7). 1972. Repr. lib. bdg. 18.50 (ISBN 0-686-85851-4). Da Capo.

McDowell, Ernest R. Boeing B-17 Flying Fortress. LC 71-113951. (Arco-Aircam Aviation Ser. 17). 1970. pap. 3.95 (ISBN 0-668-02296-5). Arco.

--Republic F RF-84F Thunderflash Thunderstreak. LC 78-113950. (Arco-Aircam Aviation Ser. 16). 1970. pap. 2.95 o.p. (ISBN 0-668-02294-9). Arco.

McDowell, Ernest R., jt. auth. see Ward, Richard.

McDowell, F., ed. see Canadian-American Conference on Parkinson's Disease, 2nd.

McDowell, Frank, ed. The Honolulu Index: 1971 A.D. to 1976 A.D. (McDowell Indexes of Plastic Surgical Literature: Vol. 5). 849p. 1977. 90.00 o.p. (ISBN 0-683-05764-2). Williams & Wilkins.

--The Source Book of Plastic & Reconstruction Surgery. (Illus.). 532p. 1977. 49.95 (ISBN 0-683-05766-9). Williams & Wilkins.

McDowell, Frederick P. E. M. Forster. rev. ed. (English Author Ser.). 1982. lib. bdg. 11.95 (ISBN 0-8057-6817-3, Twayne). G K Hall.

--E. M. Forster. (English Authors Ser.: No. 89). lib. bdg. 10.95 o.p. (ISBN 0-8057-1208-9, Twayne). G K Hall.

McDowell, George, ed. Interstate Commerce Guide (30g) LC 81-86201. 400p. 1982. 3-ring binder 95.00 (ISBN 0-934674-45-0). J J Keller.

McDowell, George B., ed. Hazardous Materials Guide: Shipping, Materials Handling & Transportation. rev. ed. LC 76-40627. (20g). 1981. looseleaf 95.00 (ISBN 0-934674-10-8). J J Keller.

McDowell, George B., ed. see Keller, J. J., & Assocs., Inc.

McDowell, George B., et al, eds. see Keller, John J.

McDowell, Jack, jt. auth. see Ketels, Hank.

McDowell, John, ed. see Evans, Gareth.

McDowell, Josh. Bien Plus Qu'un Charpentier. Cosson, Annie, ed. Flammanc, Solveng, tr. Orig. Title: More Than a Carpenter. 128p. 1982. pap. 1.75 (ISBN 0-8297-1248-8). Life Pubs Intl.

--Evidence That Demands a Verdict Study Guide. 1979. pap. 1.95 o.p. (ISBN 0-918956-51-X). Campus Crusade.

--Guide To Understanding Your Bible. 1982. pap. 4.95 (ISBN 0-686-37703-6). Here's Life.

--Mas Que un Carpintero. 137p. Date not set. not set 2.25e (ISBN 0-88113-203-9). Edit Betania.

--More Than a Carpenter. 1977. pap. 2.25 (ISBN 0-8423-4550-7). Tyndale.

McDowell, Josh & Stewart, Don. Understanding Secular Religions: A Handbook of Today's Religions. 160p. 1982. pap. 5.95 (ISBN 0-86605-093-0). Here's Life.

MacDowell, Laurel S. Remember Kirkland Lake: The Gold-Miners' Strike of 1941-42. (The State & Economic Life Ser.). 308p. 1983. 30.00x (ISBN 0-8020-5585-0); pap. 12.50 (ISBN 0-8020-6457-4). U of Toronto Pr.

McDowell, Margaret B. Carson McCullers. (United States Authors Ser.). 1980. lib. bdg. 10.95 (ISBN 0-8057-7297-9, Twayne). G K Hall.

--Edith Wharton. (U. S. Authors Ser.: No. 265). 1976. lib. bdg. 10.95 (ISBN 0-8057-7164-6, Twayne). G K Hall.

McDowell, Mary. Never Too Late. 2nd ed. LC 82-82811. 160p. 1983. pap. 4.95 (ISBN 0-89081-365-5). Harvest Hse.

McDowell, Michael. Blackwater, I: The Flood. 1983. pap. 2.50 (ISBN 0-380-81489-7, 81489-7). Avon.

--Blackwater, II: The Levee. 1983. pap. 2.50 (ISBN 0-380-82206-7, 82206-7). Avon.

--Blackwater, III: The House. 176p. (Orig.). 1983. pap. 2.50 (ISBN 0-380-82594-5, 82594-5). Avon.

--Blackwater, IV: The War. 192p. 1983. pap. 2.50 (ISBN 0-380-82776-X). Avon.

--Blackwater: Rain. 1983. pap. 2.50 (ISBN 0-380-82792-1, 82792-1). Avon.

--Blackwater, V: The Fortune. 176p. 1983. pap. 2.50 (ISBN 0-380-82784-0). Avon.

--Katie. 1982. pap. 3.50 (ISBN 0-380-80184-1, 80184). Avon.

McDowell, Mildred. With an Open Heart. LC 77-14821. 1978. pap. 2.45 o.p. (ISBN 0-8091-2075-5). Paulist Pr.

McDowell, R. B. Church of Ireland. (Studies in Irish History). 1975. 16.95x (ISBN 0-7100-8072-7). Routledge & Kegan.

--Public Opinion & Government Policy in Ireland, 1801-1846. LC 74-31010. 303p. 1975. Repr. of 1952 ed. lib. bdg. 18.75x (ISBN 0-8371-7915-7, MCPO). Greenwood.

McDowell, R. B. & Webb, D. A. Trinity College Dublin, 1592-1952: An Academic History. LC 81-12262. (Illus.). 678p. 1982. 74.50 (ISBN 0-521-23931-1). Cambridge U Pr.

McDowell, R. B., jt. auth. see Stanford, W. B.

McDowell, Richard L., jt. auth. see Wagonseller, Bill R.

McDowell, Robert, jt. auth. see Lavitt, Edward.

McDowell, Robert B. Irish Public Opinion, 1750-1800. LC 70-114543. 306p. 1975. Repr. of 1944 ed. lib. bdg. 16.25x (ISBN 0-8371-4742-5, MCIP). Greenwood.

McDowell, Robert H., jt. auth. see Gillman, Leonard.

McDowell, Virginia. Re-Creating: The Experience of Life-Change & Religion. LC 77-75443. 1978. 10.10 (ISBN 0-8070-2732-4); pap. 5.95 (ISBN 0-8070-2733-2, BP593). Beacon Pr.

McDowell, William W. Granddaddy Longwheels. LC 81-85706. 80p. 1983. pap. 3.95 (ISBN 0-686-42878-1). GWP.

MacDuffee, Cyrus C. Theory of Matrices. 2nd ed. LC 49-2197. 10.95 (ISBN 0-8284-0028-8). Chelsea Pub.

Mace, A. C., jt. auth. see Carter, Howard.

Mace, Charles D. The Spirit of America: An Epic in Four Parts. 1979. 4.95 o.p. (ISBN 0-533-02925-2). Vantage.

Mace, David. Sexual Difficulties in Marriage. Julme, William E., ed. LC 72-75652. (Pocket Counsel Bks.). 64p. (Orig.). 1972. pap. 1.75 o.p. (ISBN 0-8006-1108-X, 1-1108). Fortress.

Mace, David & Mace, Vera. How to Have a Happy Marriage. 1983. pap. 2.95 (ISBN 0-687-17831-2, Festival). Abingdon.

--Men, Women, & God. 1976. pap. 4.75 (ISBN 0-8042-8076-2). John Knox.

Mace, David R. A los Que Dios Ha Juntado En Matrimonio. 96p. 1978. pap. 2.25 (ISBN 0-311-40036-1, Edit Mundo). Casa Bautista.

--Christian Response to the Sexual Revolution. (Orig.). 1970. pap. 5.95 (ISBN 0-687-07570-X). Abingdon.

--Close Companions: The Marriage Enrichment Handbook. 224p. 1982. 17.50 (ISBN 0-8264-0206-2). Continuum.

--Success in Marriage. (Festival Ser.). 160p. 1980. pap. 1.95 (ISBN 0-687-40555-6). Abingdon.

Mace, Gertrude. Elusive Memory. (YA) 1978. 6.95 (ISBN 0-685-85777-8, Avalon). Bouregy.

--Follow Your Dream. (YA) 1979. 6.95 (ISBN 0-685-59934-5, Avalon). Bouregy.

Mace, Varian, jt. auth. see Moen, Ann.

Mace, Vera, jt. auth. see Mace, David.

McEachern, Alton H. From the Mountain. LC 82-82948. (Orig.). 1983. pap. 4.95 (ISBN 0-8054-1529-7). Broadman.

McEachern, Alton H., jt. auth. see Lolley, W. Randall.

McEachern, D. A Class Against Itself. 245p. 1980. 32.50 (ISBN 0-521-22985-5); pap. cancelled (ISBN 0-521-28054-0). Cambridge U Pr.

McEathron, Margaret & Holmes, Fenwicke. I Am Two Men. LC 80-15442. (YA) 1983. pap. 9.95 (ISBN 0-87949-190-6). Ashley Bks.

McEathron, Margaret, jt. auth. see Holmes, Fenwicke.

Macebuh, Stanley. The Tyranny of Things: An Inquiry into the Foundations of African Aesthetics. LC 75-506. (Library of Criticism Ser., No. 3). 208p. 1977. cancelled (ISBN 0-89388-199-6). Okpaku Communications.

Macedo, Helder & De Melo e Castro, E. M., eds. Contemporary Portuguese Poetry: An Anthology in English. Brook-Smith, John, et al, trs. from Port. (Translation Ser.). 270p. 1979. 10.95 o.p. (ISBN 0-85635-244-6, Pub. by Carcanet New Pr England). Humanities.

Macedo, Manuel C., Jr., et al. Value Management for Construction. LC 78-6255. (Construction Management & Engineering Ser.). 1978. 41.95 (ISBN 0-471-03166-6, Pub. by Wiley-Interscience). Wiley.

Macedo, Suzette, tr. see Prado, Caio, Jr.

Macek, K. Bibliography of Paper & Thin Layer Tography, 1966-69, Vol. 2. (Journal of Chromatography Suppl. Ser.). 1972. 85.00 (ISBN 0-444-40953-X). Elsevier.

--Pharmaceutical Applications of Thin-Layer & Paper Chromatography. 1972. 117.00 (ISBN 0-444-40923-8). Elsevier.

Macek, K., et al. Bibliography of Paper & Thin-Layer Chromatography, 1970-1973 & Survey of Applications. (Journal of Chromatography Supplement: Vol. 5). 1976. 85.00 (ISBN 0-444-41299-9). Elsevier.

Macek, Vladko. In the Struggle for Freedom. LC 68-8182. (Illus.). 1968. 18.95x (ISBN 0-271-00069-4). Pa St U Pr.

McElderry, B. R., Jr., ed. see Shelley, Percy B.

McElderry, Bruce R., Jr. Henry James. (United States Authors Ser.). 1965. lib. bdg. 10.95 (ISBN 0-8057-0404-3, Twayne). G K Hall.

--Thomas Wolfe. (United States Authors Ser.). 1963. lib. bdg. 11.95 (ISBN 0-8057-0833-2, Twayne). G K Hall.

McElfresh, Beth. Chuck Wagon Cookbook. LC 82-70282. 72p. 1960. pap. 4.95 (ISBN 0-8040-0042-5, SB). Swallow.

McElhanon, K. A. Selepet Grammar, Pt. 1. (Pacific Linguistics, Ser. B: No. 21). 116p. 1972. pap. 4.25x o. s. i. (ISBN 0-88312-643-5); microfiche 2.25 (ISBN 0-88312-495-5). Summer Inst Ling.

McElhanon, K. A. & McElhanon, N. A. Selepet-English Dictionary. (Pacific Linguistics, Ser. C: No. 15). xxi, 151p. 1970. pap. 6.00x o.s.i. (ISBN 0-88312-642-7); microfiche 2.25 o.s.i. (ISBN 0-88312-494-7). Summer Inst Ling.

McElhanon, K. A., ed. Legends of Papua New Guinea. 237p. 1974. pap. 7.00x (ISBN 0-7263-0274-0); 3.00 (ISBN 0-88312-325-8). Summer Inst Ling.

McElhanon, N. A., jt. auth. see McElhanon, K. A.

McElheny, Kenneth R., jt. ed. see Moffett, James.

McElhiney, Paul T., jt. auth. see Farris, Martin T.

McElhinney, M. W. Palaeomagnetism & Plate Tectonics. LC 72-80590. (Earth Science Ser). (Illus.). 368p. 1973. 72.50 (ISBN 0-521-08707-4); pap. 21.95x (ISBN 0-521-29753-2). Cambridge U Pr.

McEliece, R. J. The Theory of Information & Coding: A Mathematical Framework for Communication. (Encyclopedia of Mathematics & Its Applications: Vol. 3). 1977. text ed. 28.95 (ISBN 0-201-13502-7, Adv Bk Prog). A-W.

McElligott, T. J. Secondary Education in Ireland 1870-1921. 200p. 1981. 35.00x (ISBN 0-7165-0074-4, Pub. by Irish Academic Pr England). Biblio Dist.

McElmurry, Mary Anne. Caring. (gr. 4-8). 1981. 5.95 (ISBN 0-86653-052-5, GA275). Good Apple.

--Feelings. (gr. 3-8). 1981. 6.95 (ISBN 0-86653-027-4, GA 276). Good Apple.

McElrath, G., jt. auth. see Lindgren, Bernard W.

McElrath, Joseph. Walden Notes. (Orig.). 1971. pap. 2.50 (ISBN 0-8220-1358-4). Cliffs.

McElrath, Joseph R., Jr., jt. auth. see Crisler, Jesse E.

McElrath, Joseph R., Jr. & Robb, Allan P., eds. The Complete Works of Anne Bradstreet. (Critical Editions Program Ser.). 1981. lib. bdg. 35.00 (ISBN 0-8057-8533-7, Twayne). G K Hall.

McElreath, Jesse, jt. auth. see Robinson, Ras.

McElroy, Donald L. Handbook of Oral Diagnosis & Treatment Planning. LC 69-14460. 230p. 1974. Repr. of 1969 ed. 11.50 (ISBN 0-88275-126-3). Krieger.

McElroy, Elam E. Applied Business Statistics: An Elementary Approach. 2nd ed. 1979. text ed. 21.95x (ISBN 0-8162-5535-0); inst. manual 6.00x (ISBN 0-8162-5537-7); wkbk. 7.95x (ISBN 0-8162-5536-9). Holden-Day.

McElroy, H. B., jt. auth. see Evans, Wilbur.

McElroy, John, ed. The Life & Voyages of Christopher Columbus: The Complete Works of W. Irving. (Critical Editions Program). 1981. lib. bdg. 60.00 (ISBN 0-8057-8516-7, Twayne). G K Hall.

McElroy, Lee. Eyes of the Hawk. large type ed. LC 82-10542. 299p. 1982. Repr. of 1982 ed. 9.95 (ISBN 0-89621-384-6). Thorndike Pr.

McElroy, Samuel R. The Handbook on the Psychology of Hemoglobin-S: A Perspicacious View of Sickle Cell Disease. LC 80-8170. 133p. 1980. pap. text ed. 8.25 (ISBN 0-8191-1132-5). U Pr of Amer.

McElroy, Wendy, ed. Freedom, Feminism, & the State. 357p. 1982. pap. 7.95 (ISBN 0-932790-32-1). Cato Inst.

McElroy, William D. Cell Physiology & Biochemistry. 3rd ed. (Foundations of Modern Biology Ser). (Illus.). 1971. ref. ed. 12.95 (ISBN 0-13-122168-X). P-H.

McElvaine, Robert S., ed. Down & Out in the Great Depression: Letters from the "Forgotten Man". LC 82-7022. (Illus.). xvii, 251p. 1983. 23.00x (ISBN 0-8078-1534-9); pap. 8.95 (ISBN 0-8078-4099-8). U of NC Pr.

McElwee, William. The Wisest Fool in Christendom. LC 74-7449. (Illus.). 296p. 1974. Repr. of 1958 ed. lib. bdg. 17.75x (ISBN 0-8371-7522-4, MCWF). Greenwood.

McEntee, Howard C. Radio Control Handbook. 4th, rev. ed. (Illus.). 1979. pap. 12.95 (ISBN 0-8306-9772-1, 1093). TAB Bks.

McEntee, Howard G. The Model Aircraft Handbook. rev. ed. LC 68-27317. (Funk & W Bk.). (Illus.). 240p. 1968. 8.95i (ISBN 0-690-54632-7, F109, TYC-T). T Y Crowell.

McEntire, Patricia. Zap-Ping the Food Demons: Resolving Your Child's Behavior Problems. (Orig.). Date not set. pap. 7.95 (ISBN 0-917982-22-3). Cougar Bks. Postponed.

McEntyre, John G. Land Survey Systems. LC 78-8551. 1978. text ed. 38.95 (ISBN 0-471-02492-9). Wiley.

McEntyre, Robert L. Practical Guide to the Care of the Surgical Patient. LC 79-16116. 268p. 1979. pap. 12.95 (ISBN 0-8016-3056-8). Mosby.

McE Stiles, H., et al, eds. Microbial Aspects of Dental Caries: Proceedings, 3 Vols. LC 76-22950. 1976. Repr. Set. 40.00 (ISBN 0-917000-01-3). IRL Pr.

McEuen, Caroline K., ed. see Gittinger, Mattiebelle.

McEvedy, Colin. The Penguin Atlas of Recent History: Europe since 1815. 1982. pap. 5.95 (ISBN 0-14-070834-0). Penguin.

McEvers, Joan, jt. auth. see March, Marion.

McEvily, A. J., jt. auth. see Tetelman, A. S.

McEvoy, H. K. Knife-Throwing. 3.95x (ISBN 0-685-63762-X). Wehman.

McEvoy, James. The Philosophy of Robert Grosseteste. 576p. 1982. 74.00x (ISBN 0-19-824645-5). Oxford U Pr.

McEvoy, Marjorie. Calabrian Summer. LC 79-6540. (Romantic Suspense). 192p. 1980. 10.95 o.p. (ISBN 0-385-15939-0). Doubleday.

MacEwan, Arthur. Revolution & Economic Development in Cuba: Moving Towards Socialism. LC 80-11130. 240p. 1981. 25.00 (ISBN 0-312-67980-7). St Martin.

McEwan, Gilbert J., ed. Texts from Hellenistic Babylonia in the Ashmolean Museum. (Oxford Editions of Cuneiform Texts Ser.). (Illus.). 1982. pap. 48.00 (ISBN 0-19-815457-7). Oxford U Pr.

McEwan, Graham J. Sea Serpents, Sailors & Sceptics. (Illus.). 1978. 14.00 (ISBN 0-7100-8931-7). Routledge & Kegan.

McEwan, Ian. The Comfort of Strangers. 1981. 9.95 o.p. (ISBN 0-671-42850-0). S&S.

--First Love, Last Rites. 1980. pap. 2.25 o.p. (ISBN 0-425-04501-3). Berkley Pub.

--In Between the Sheets. 1980. pap. 2.25 o.p. (ISBN 0-425-04719-9). Berkley Pub.

MacEwan, Malcolm, jt. auth. see MacEwen, Ann.

McEwan, P. J., ed. Second Special Conference Issue. 144p. 1982. 19.85 (ISBN 0-08-027937-6). Pergamon.

--Twentieth-Century Africa. (Illus., Orig.). 1968. pap. 8.95x o.p. (ISBN 0-19-501250-X). Oxford U Pr.

McEwan, Peter J., ed. International Conference on Social Science & Medicine, 6th, Amsterdam, 1979: Second Special Conference Issue. 80p. 1981. pap. 14.40 (ISBN 0-08-026763-7). Pergamon.

MacEwen, Ann & MacEwan, Malcolm. National Parks: Conservation or Cosmetics. (The Resource Management Ser.). 1982. text ed. 35.00x (ISBN 0-04-719003-5); pap. text ed. 19.95x (ISBN 0-04-719004-3). Allen Unwin.

McEwen, Bruce S., jt. ed. see Goy, Robert W.

McEwen, Craig A. Designing Correctional Organizations for Youth: Dilemmas & Possibilities in Directing Subcultural Development. LC 77-27488. 248p. 1978. prof ref 18.00x (ISBN 0-88410-789-2). Ballinger Pub.

McEwen, F. L. & Stephenson, G. R. The Use & Significance of Pesticides in the Environment. LC 78-23368. 1979. 40.95 (ISBN 0-471-03903-9, Pub. by Wiley-Interscience). Wiley.

MacEwen, Glenn H. Introduction to Computer Systems Using the PDP-Eleven & Pascal. (Computer Science Ser.). (Illus.). 400p. 1980. text ed. 31.95 (ISBN 0-07-044350-5, C). McGraw.

McEwen, Phyllis. Hystery, & Other Tools for Women. (Herland Ser.: No. 2). (Illus.). 35p. (Orig.). 1983. pap. 4.00 (ISBN 0-934996-20-2). Am Stud Pr.

McEwen, Robert B., ed. see William T. Pecora Memorial Symposium, 2nd. Annual.

McEwen, Todd. Fisher's Hornpipe. LC 82-48684. 224p. 1983. 12.45 (ISBN 0-06-015164-1, HarpT). Har-Row.

Macey, Robert I. Human Physiology. 2nd ed. (Illus.). 224p. 1975. pap. 13.95 ref. ed. (ISBN 0-13-445288-7). P-H.

McFadden, Carol H., jt. auth. see Keeton, William T.

McFadden, Cyra. The Serial. 1978. pap. 2.50 (ISBN 0-451-09267-8, E9267, Sig). NAL.

McFadden, D. & Fuss, M. Production Economics: A Dual Approach to Theory & Applications, 2 Vols. (Contributions to Economic Analysis: Vols. 110 & 111). 1978. Vol. 1. 74.50 (ISBN 0-444-85012-0, North-Holland); Vol. 2. 51.00 (ISBN 0-444-85013-9); Set. 110.75 (ISBN 0-444-85014-7). Elsevier.

McFadden, Daniel, jt. ed. see Manski, Charles F.

McFadden, David. English, American, & Continental Silver in the Minneapolis Institute of Arts. (Illus.). 1983. write for info. (ISBN 0-912964-14-6); pap. write for info. (ISBN 0-912964-13-8). Minneapolis Inst Arts.

McFadden, David, jt. auth. see Phillips, Calvin.

McFadden, David, ed. Scandinavian Modern Design: Eighteen Eighty to Nineteen Eighty. LC 82-8899. (Illus.). 288p. 1982. 45.00 (ISBN 0-8109-1643-6). Abrams.

McFadden, Fred, jt. auth. see Couger, Dan.

McFadden, Fred R., jt. auth. see Couger, J. Daniel.

McFadden, Jim. The Fear Factor: Everyone Has it, You Can Master It. (Living As a Christian Ser.). (Orig.). 1983. pap. write for info. (ISBN 0-89283-159-6). Servant.

McFadden, Margaret, jt. auth. see Gerber, Leslie E.

McFadden, S. Michele, ed. see Abraham, Samuel V.

McFadden, S. Michele, ed. see Agee, Roy.

McFadden, S. Michele, et al, eds. see Stockton, Elizabeth.

McFadden, W. H. Techniques of Combined Gas Chromatography - Mass Spectrometry: Applications in Organic Analysis. LC 73-6916. 463p. 1973. 46.50 (ISBN 0-471-58388-X, Pub. by Wiley-Interscience). Wiley.

McFaddon, Carol H., jt. auth. see Keeton, William T.

MacFadyen, Dugald. Sir Ebenezer Howard & the Town Planning Movement. 1970. 20.00x (ISBN 0-262-13066-1). MIT Pr.

McFadzean, Frank, ed. Towards an Open World Economy. LC 72-91277. 264p. 1979. 22.50 (ISBN 0-312-81060-1). St Martin.

McFague, Sallie. Metaphorical Theology: Models of God in Religious Language. LC 82-7246. 240p. 1982. pap. 11.95 (ISBN 0-8006-1687-1, 1-1687). Fortress.

McFall, Leslie. The Enigma of the Hebrew Verbal System: Solutions from Ewald to the Present Day. (Historic Texts & Interpreters in Biblical Scholarship Ser.: No. 2). 272p. 1983. text ed. 29.95x (ISBN 0-907459-20-X, Pub. by Almond Pr England); pap. 16.95 (ISBN 0-907459-21-8). Eisenbrauns.

MacFall, Russell P. Gem Hunter's Guide. rev. 5th ed. LC 74-19469. (Illus.). 336p. 1975. 13.41i (ISBN 0-690-00656-X); pap. 5.95i (ISBN 0-690-01221-7, TYC-T). T Y Crowell.

--Rock Hunter's Guide. LC 78-22457. (Illus.). 1980. 13.41i (ISBN 0-690-01812-6). T Y Crowell.

McFalls, Joseph A. & Tolnay, Stewart E. Black Fertility in the U. S. A Social Demographic History. 400p. Date not set. text ed. 40.00 (ISBN 0-8223-0560-7). Duke.

Macfarlan, Allan A. Boy's Book of Biking. (gr. 4-6). 1970. pap. 1.25 o.p. (ISBN 0-671-29739-2). Archway.

McFarlan, F. Warren & McKenney, James L. Corporate Information Systems Management: The Issues Facing Senior Executives. LC 82-73926. 180p. 1982. 17.95 (ISBN 0-87094-347-2). Dow Jones-Irwin.

McFarlan, F. Warren, et al. Information Systems Administration. LC 81-40920. (Illus.). 608p. 1982. pap. text ed. 20.75 (ISBN 0-8191-2158-4). U Pr of Amer.

McFarland, C. K. Readings in Intellectual History. LC 70-107429. 473p. 1970. pap. 11.50 (ISBN 0-03-081298-4, Pub. by HR&W). Krieger.

--Roosevelt, Lewis & the New Deal: 1933-1940. LC 73-98123. (History & Culture Monograph Ser., No.7). 1970. 6.00x (ISBN 0-912646-06-3). Tex Christian.

McFarland, Carl, jt. auth. see Cummings, Homer.

McFarland, Carl L. Oil & Gas Exploration in Washington: 1900-1981. (Information Circular Ser.: No. 67R). (Illus.). 119p. 1979. 2.50 (ISBN 0-686-34740-4). Geologic Pubns.

McFarland, Dalton E. Management & Society: An Institutional Framework. (Illus.). 512p. 1982. text ed. 23.95 (ISBN 0-13-549147-9). P-H.

--Management: Foundations & Practices. 5th ed. 1979. text ed. 24.95x (ISBN 0-02-378890-9); instrs'. manual avail. Macmillan.

McFarland, David D., ed. see Wiggins, Lee M.

McFarland, Dorothy T. Flannery O'Connor. LC 74-78443. (Literature and Life Ser.). 140p. 1976. 11.95 (ISBN 0-8044-2609-0). Ungar.

--Simone Weil. (Literature & Life Ser.). 220p. 1983. 11.95 (ISBN 0-8044-2604-X). Ungar.

--Willa Cather. LC 74-190351. (Literature & Life Ser.). 1972. 11.95 (ISBN 0-8044-2610-4). Ungar.

McFarland, E. M. The Cripple Creek Road: A Midland Terminal Guide & Data Book. (Illus.). 1983. price not set (ISBN 0-87108-647-6). Pruett.

McFarland, H. S. Intelligent Teaching: Professional Skills for Student Teachers. 156p. 1973. 12.00x (ISBN 0-7100-7508-1); pap. 6.95 (ISBN 0-7100-7515-4). Routledge & Kegan.

--Psychological Theory & Educational Practice: Human Development, Learning & Assessment. 1971. 21.95x (ISBN 0-7100-7009-8); pap. 8.95 (ISBN 0-7100-7010-1). Routledge & Kegan.

McFarland, Henry S. Psychology & Teaching. LC 77-7247. 1977. Repr. of 1958 ed. lib. bdg. 18.50x (ISBN 0-8371-9662-0, MCPSY). Greenwood.

McFarland, J. Postgraduate Surgery Lectures, Vol. 1. 1973. 9.95 o.p. (ISBN 0-407-36140-5). Butterworth.

--Postgraduate Surgery Lectures, Vol. 3. 1975. 11.95 o.p. (ISBN 0-407-00045-3). Butterworth.

McFarland, J., ed. Basic Clinical Surgery for Nurses & Medical Students. (Illus.). 500p. 1975. Repr. of 1973 ed. 29.95 o.p. (ISBN 0-407-80101-4). Butterworth.

McFarland, J. W. Sulfonyl Isocyanates & Sulfonyl Isothiocyanates. (Sulfur Reports Ser.). 54p. 1981. pap. 15.00 (ISBN 3-7186-0082-X). Harwood Academic.

McFarland, James W. see Ibsen, Henrik.

McFarland, Kenton & Sparks, James C., Jr. Midget Motoring & Karting. (Illus.). (gr. 7 up). 1961. 11.95 (ISBN 0-525-34880-8, 01160-350). Dutton.

McFarland, Kevin. Incredible, Vol. 1. 1977. pap. 1.75 (ISBN 0-451-07490-4, E7490, Sig). NAL.

McFarland, Philip. Sojourners: A Narrative of the Human Adventure As Lived by Some Historic Dreamers & Sufferers. LC 79-63630. (Illus.). 1979. 22.50 o.p. (ISBN 0-689-11003-0). Atheneum.

McFarland, Philip, et al. Forms in English Literature. LC 75-144318. (Literature Ser.). (Illus.). 816p. (gr. 12). 1972. text ed. 12.48 o.p. (ISBN 0-395-11202-8, 2-26560); tchr's resource bk. 5.94 o.p. (ISBN 0-395-12442-5, 2-26561). HM.
--Forms in English Literature. (Literature Ser.). (Illus.). (gr. 12). 1975. text ed. 20.88 (ISBN 0-395-20076-8); tchr's resource bk 9.96 (ISBN 0-395-20082-2). HM.
--Perceptions in Literature. (Literature Ser.). (Illus.). (gr. 10). 1972. text ed. 18.40 (ISBN 0-395-11200-1, 2-26536); tchr's resource bk. 9.04 (ISBN 0-395-12621-5, 2-26537). HM.
--Themes in American Literature. (Literature Ser.). (Illus.). 815p. (gr. 11). 1972. text ed. 11.85 o.p. (ISBN 0-395-11201-X, 2-26548); tchrs' resource bk. 5.40 o.p. (ISBN 0-395-12507-3, 2-26549). HM.
--Themes in World Literature. (Literature Ser.). 1970. text ed. 11.16 o.p. (ISBN 0-395-02875-2, 2-26380); tchrs' resource bk. 4.56 o.p. (ISBN 0-395-02876-0, 2-26382). HM.
--Themes in World Literature. (Literature Ser.). (Illus.). 1975. text ed. 15.48 (ISBN 0-395-20156-X); tchr's resource bk 5.12 (ISBN 0-395-20157-8). HM.
McFarland, Philip J., et al. Focus on Action. LC 76-53136. (Focus on Literature Ser.). (Illus.). (gr. 7). 1977. text ed. 15.48 (ISBN 0-395-24966-X); tchr's guide 5.12 (ISBN 0-395-24964-3). HM.
--Focus on People. LC 76-53136. (Focus on Literature Ser.). (Illus.). (gr. 8). 1977. text ed. 15.24 (ISBN 0-395-24965-1); tchr's guide 5.12 (ISBN 0-395-24967-8). HM.
McFarland, Richard A. Physiological Psychology: The Biology of Human Behavior. LC 80-84015. (Illus.). 437p. 1981. text ed. 20.95 (ISBN 0-87484-500-9); instructors manual avail.; study guide 7.95 (ISBN 0-87484-555-6). Mayfield Pub.
McFarland, Thomas, jt. auth. see Frank, Alan R.
McFarland, Walter B. Concepts for Management Accounting. 165p. 14.95 (ISBN 0-86641-056-2, 6640). Natl Assn Accts.
--Manpower Cost & Performance Measurement. 109p. pap. 12.95 (7790). Natl Assn Accts.
McFarland, William N., et al. Vertebrate Life. 1979. text ed. 29.95x (ISBN 0-02-378870-4). Macmillan.
MacFarlane. Automatic Control of Food Manufacturing Processes. Date not set. price not set (ISBN 0-85334-200-8). Elsevier.
MacFarlane, A. A. Architectural Supervision on Site. 1973. 30.75 (ISBN 0-85334-574-0, Pub. by Applied Sci England). Elsevier.
MacFarlane, A. G., jt. auth. see Hung, Y. S.
MacFarlane, A. G., ed. Frequency: Response Methods in Control Systems. LC 79-90572. 1979. 48.95 (ISBN 0-87942-125-8). Inst Electrical.
Macfarlane, Aidan. The Psychology of Childbirth. (Developing Child Ser.). 1977. 7.95x o.p. (ISBN 0-674-72105-5); pap. 3.95 (ISBN 0-674-72106-3). Harvard U Pr.
Macfarlane, Alan. Family Life of Ralph Josselin. LC 78-96096. (Illus.). 1970. 29.95 (ISBN 0-521-07707-9). Cambridge U Pr.
--The Justice & the Mare's Ale: Law & Disorder in Seventeenth-Century England. (Illus.). 225p. 1981. 24.95 (ISBN 0-521-23949-4). Cambridge U Pr.
--The Origins of English Individualism. LC 78-73956. 1979. 28.95 (ISBN 0-521-22587-6); pap. 8.95x (ISBN 0-521-29570-X). Cambridge U Pr.
Macfarlane, Alan, et al. Reconstructing Historical Communities. LC 77-24234. 1978. 13.95 (ISBN 0-521-21796-2). Cambridge U Pr.
Macfarlane, Alistair G. Frequency Response Methods in Control Systems. 1979. 48.95 (ISBN 0-471-06486-6, Pub. by Wiley-Interscience); pap. 31.95 (ISBN 0-471-06426-2). Wiley.
McFarlane, I. D. & Maclean, Ian. Montaigne: Essays in Memory of Richard Sayce. (Illus.). 1982. 41.00x (ISBN 0-19-815769-X). Oxford U Pr.
McFarlane, James W., ed. see Ibsen, Henrik.
McFarlane, James W., tr. see Hamsun, Knut.
McFarlane, James W. see Ibsen, Henrik.
McFarlane, John. It's Easy to Fix Your Bike. 4th ed. LC 73-185890. (Illus.). 128p. 1976. spiral bdg 3.95 o.s.i. (ISBN 0-695-80652-1). Follett.
McFarlane, Judith, jt. auth. see Whitson, Betty J.
McFarlane, Judith, et al. Contemporary Pediatric Nursing: A Conceptual Approach. LC 79-18463. 1980. 24.00 (ISBN 0-471-03908-X, Pub. by Wiley Med). Wiley.
MacFarlane, P., jt. ed. see Wolf, H. K.
Macfarlane, P. W. & Lawrie, D. Introduction to Automated Electrocardiogram Interpretation. (Computers in Medicine Ser.). 1974. 9.50x o.p. (ISBN 0-407-21899-8). Butterworth.
Macfarlane, Peter W., ed. see International Congress on Electro Cardiology, Lisbon, 7th, June 1980 & De Padua, Fernando.
McFarlane, Robert W., jt. ed. see Esch, Gerald W.
MacFarlane, W. N. Principles of Small Business Management. (Illus.). 1977. text ed. 22.50 (ISBN 0-07-044380-7, G); instr.'s manual & key 7.70 (ISBN 0-07-044381-5). McGraw.
McFarlane, William R., ed. Family Therapy in Schizophrenia. LC 82-11742. (Family Therapy Ser.). 350p. 1983. text ed. 25.00x (ISBN 0-89862-042-2, G34). Guilford Pr.
McFarling, Leslie H., jt. auth. see Heimstra, Norman.
Macfarren, Natalia, tr. see Devrient, Edward.
McFate, Patricia. The Writings of James Stephens: Variations on a Theme of Love. LC 78-13287. 1979. 20.00x (ISBN 0-312-89509-7). St Martin.
McFather, Nelle. Ecstasy's Captive. 416p. 1982. pap. 3.50 o.p. (ISBN 0-505-51861-9). Tower Bks.
McFee, Graham. Much of Jackson Pollock Is Vivid Wallpaper: An Essay in the Epistomology of Aesthetic Judgements. 1978. pap. text ed. 9.50 o.p. (ISBN 0-8191-0380-2). U Pr of Amer.
McFeely, Mary D. Women's Work in Britain & America from the Nineties to World War I: An Annotated Bibliography. 1982. lib. bdg. 24.95 (ISBN 0-8161-8504-2, Hall Reference). G K Hall.
McFeely, William s. Yankee Stepfather: General O. O. Howard & the Freedmen. 368p. 1983. pap. 6.25x (ISBN 0-393-00537-2). Norton.
McFerren, Martha. Delusions of a Popular Mind. Cassin, Maxine, ed. 80p. 1983. pap. 5.00 (ISBN 0-938498-04-5). New Orleans Poetry.
McFerron, Martha. Animals & Babies. (Science Ser.). 24p. (gr. 2-3). 1980. wkbk. 5.00 (ISBN 0-8209-0160-1, S-22). ESP.
--Basic Skills Outline & Organize Workbook. (Basic Skills Workbooks). 32p. (gr. 4-7). 1983. 0.99 (ISBN 0-8209-0581-X, OW-1). ESP.
--Learning to Outline & Organize: Grades 4-7. (Language Arts Ser.). 24p. 1979. wkbk. 5.00 (ISBN 0-8209-0327-2, LA-13). ESP.
--Mammals. (Science Ser.). 24p. (gr. 3-6). 1982. wkbk. 5.00 (ISBN 0-8209-0161-X, S-23). ESP.
--Plants. (Science Ser.). 24p. (gr. 3-6). 1982. wkbk. 5.00 (ISBN 0-8209-0162-8, S-24). ESP.
MacFie, J. M. Myths & Legends of India: An Introduction to the Study of Hinduism. 357p. Repr. of 1924 ed. pap. 5.95 o.p. (ISBN 0-567-22181-4). Attic Pr.
MacGaffey, Wyatt. Custom & Government in the Lower Congo. LC 70-85415. (Illus.). 1970. 33.00x (ISBN 0-520-01614-9). U of Cal Pr.
--Modern Kongo Prophets: Religion in a Plural Society. (African Systems of Thought Ser.). (Illus.). 304p. 1983. 22.50x (ISBN 0-253-33865-4). Ind U Pr.
--Modern Kongo Prophets: Religion in a Plural Society. (Midland Bks.). (Illus.). 304p. (Orig.). 1983. pap. 15.00x (ISBN 0-253-20307-4). Ind U Pr.
MacGahar, Aileen, jt. auth. see Krauss, Leonard I.
McGahern, John. The Dark. 1983. pap. 4.95 (ISBN 0-14-006237-8). Penguin.
--Getting Through. LC 79-3667. 1980. 12.45i (ISBN 0-06-013043-1, HarpT). Har-Row.
--The Pornographer. LC 79-1709. 1979. 11.49i (ISBN 0-06-013021-0, HarpT). Har-Row.
--The Pornographer. 1983. pap. 5.95 (ISBN 0-14-006489-3). Penguin.
McGahey, Michael J., jt. auth. see Beard, Marna L.
McGann, Anthony F., et al. Introduction to Business. LC 78-12146. 1979. text ed. 32.50 (ISBN 0-471-57240-3); study guide 11.95 (ISBN 0-471-04864-X). Wiley.
McGann, Jerome J. A Critique of Modern Textual Criticism. 144p. 1983. lib. bdg. 12.00x (ISBN 0-226-55851-7). U of Chicago Pr.
--The Romantic Ideology: A Critical Investigation. LC 82-17494. 184p. 1983. lib. bdg. 15.00x (ISBN 0-226-55849-5). U of Chicago Pr.
McGann, Michele, ed. The Business Traveller's Handbook: United States & Canada. 466p. 1982. 19.95 (ISBN 0-87196-342-6); pap. 11.95 (ISBN 0-87196-322-1). Facts on File.
McGann, Thomas F. A History of Philosophy in the West: A Synopsis from Descartes to Nietzsche. 2nd ed. LC 79-66477. 1979. pap. text ed. 9.75 (ISBN 0-8191-0833-2). U Pr of Amer.
McGarey, William A. Edgar Cayce & the Palma Christi: A Study of the Use of Castor Oil Packs As Suggested Through the Unconscious Mind of Edgar Cayce, Followed in the Practice of General Medicine. 1970. 7.95 (ISBN 0-87604-045-8). ARE Pr.
McGarry, Daniel D. Medieval History & Civilization. (Illus.). 896p. 1976. text ed. 28.95x (ISBN 0-02-379100-4). Macmillan.
McGarry, Jane & Pendleton, Sally, eds. College Admissions Data Handbook - 1982-83, 4 vols. 23rd rev. ed. 2500p. (Orig.). 1982. loose leaf 130.00x (ISBN 0-933510-24-1); Set. pap. 115.00x (ISBN 0-933510-23-3); Set Microfiche 60.00x (ISBN 0-933510-32-2); pap. 36.00x Northeast Region vol. (ISBN 0-933510-19-5); pap. 36.00x Southeast Region Vol. (ISBN 0-933510-20-9); pap. 30.00x Mid-West Region vol. (ISBN 0-933510-21-7); pap. 30.00X West Region Vol. (ISBN 0-933510-22-5). Orchard Hse MA.
McGarry, M. G. & Stainforth, J., eds. Compost, Fertilizer & Biogas Production from Human & Farm Wastes in the People's Republic of China. 94p. 1978. pap. 6.00 o.p. (ISBN 0-88936-140-1, IDRC-TS8E, IDRC). Unipub.
McGarry, Mark J. Sun Dogs. (Orig.). 1981. pap. 1.95 o.p. (ISBN 0-451-09620-7, J9620, Sig). NAL.
McGarry, Mary A., ed. see Bodle, Yvonne & Corey, Joseph.
McGarty, Terrence P. Stochastic Systems & State Estimation. LC 73-18294. 1974. 47.50 (ISBN 0-471-58400-2, Pub. by Wiley-Interscience). Wiley.
McGarvey, J. W. McGarvey's Original Commentary on Acts. 9.95 (ISBN 0-89225-119-0). Gospel Advocate.
McGauhey, P. H. Engineering Management of Water Quality. LC 67-28085. 1968. text ed. 39.50 (ISBN 0-07-044975-9, C). McGraw.
McGavin, Gary L. Earthquake Protection of Essential Building Equipment: Design, Engineering, Installation. LC 80-23067. 464p. 1981. 42.50x (ISBN 0-471-06270-7, Pub. by Wiley-Interscience). Wiley.
McGavran, Donald A., jt. auth. see Glasser, Arthur F.
McGavran, Donald A., ed. The Conciliar-Evangelical Debate: The Crucial Documents, 1964-1976. 2nd enl. ed. LC 77-1705. 1977. pap. 8.95 o.p. (ISBN 0-87808-733-8). William Carey Lib.
McGaw, Dickinson, jt. auth. see Watson, George.
McGaw, Dickinson L. & Watson, George. Political & Social Inquiry. LC 75-31913. 336p. 1976. text ed. 26.50 (ISBN 0-471-58403-7). Wiley.
McGaw, Jessie B. Chief Red Horse Tells About Custer. (Illus.). 64p. (gr. 4 up). 1981. 9.25 (ISBN 0-525-66713-X, 0898-270). Lodestar Bks.
McGaw, Martha M., Sr. Stevenson in Hawaii. LC 77-13757. (Illus.). 1978. Repr. of 1950 ed. lib. bdg. 20.25x (ISBN 0-8371-9864-X, MCSH). Greenwood.
McGeary, David, jt. auth. see Plummer, Charles C.
McGee, Dennis. The Rescue. 1981. 8.95 o.p. (ISBN 0-533-04792-7). Vantage.
McGee, Gentry R. History of Tennessee. (Illus.). 1971. Repr. of 1930 ed. 10.00 (ISBN 0-918450-02-0). C Elder.
McGee, I. J., jt. auth. see Watts, R. O.
McGee, J. D. see Marton, L.
McGee, J. D., et al see Marton, L.
McGee, J. O., jt. auth. see Patrick, R. S.
McGee, J. Vernon. Thru the Bible with J. Vernon McGee: Matthew through Romans, Vol. IV. 850p. 1983. 19.95 (ISBN 0-8407-4976-7). Nelson.
McGee, Leo & Boone, Robert, eds. The Black Rural Landowner--Endangered Species: Social, Political, & Economic Implications. LC 78-69538. (Contributions in Afro-American & African Studies: No. 44). (Illus.). 1979. lib. bdg. 25.00 (ISBN 0-313-20609-0, MCB/). Greenwood.
McGee, M. Clinton. Alabama Criminal Practice. 240p. 1969. 20.75 (ISBN 0-8173-9307-2). U of Ala Pr.
McGee, Mark G. Introductory Psychology Reader. 250p. 1980. pap. text ed. 9.95 (ISBN 0-8299-0340-2). West Pub.
McGee, Richard A. Prisons & Politics. LC 81-47003. 176p. 1981. 22.95x (ISBN 0-669-04527-6). Lexington Bks.
McGee, Robert W. Fundamentals of Accounting & Finance: A Handbook for Business & Professional People. (Illus.). 216p. 1983. 14.95 (ISBN 0-13-332437-0); pap. 6.95 (ISBN 0-13-332429-X). P-H.
McGee, Shelagh. What Witches Do: & Other Poems. (Illus.). (gr. 1-4). 1979. PLB 6.95 o.p. (ISBN 0-13-955195-6). P-H.
McGee, Thomas D. A History of the Irish Settlers in North America, from the Earliest Period to the Census of 1850. LC 78-145486. (The American Immigration Library). 240p. 1971. Repr. of 1852 ed. lib. bdg. 11.95x o.p. (ISBN 0-89198-018-0). Ozer.
McGee, Timothy J., jt. auth. see Eastman, Sheila.
McGee, Vern, tr. see Schmidt, Paul.
McGeehan, B., jt. auth. see Welk, L.
McGeer, Edith G., et al, eds. Kainic Acid As a Tool in Neurobiology. LC 78-55812. 283p. 1978. 32.00 (ISBN 0-89004-279-9). Raven.
McGeer, Patrick L., jt. ed. see Durbin, Enoch.
McGeever, Patrick J. The United States Governmental System: A Compact Introduction. 1978. pap. text ed. 7.50 (ISBN 0-8191-0392-6). U Pr of Amer.
McGeorge, H. D. General Engineering Knowledge. (Marine Engineering Ser.). 96p. 1978. pap. 9.95x (ISBN 0-540-07345-8). Sheridan.
McGeorge School of Law. Owens California Forms & Procedure, 6 vols. LC 82-80399. 1982. Set. 405.00 (ISBN 0-911110-41-0). Parker & Son.
McGeough, Charles & Jungjohan, Barbara. Directory of College Facilities & Services for the Handicapped. 336p. 1983. 80.00 (ISBN 0-89774-004-1). Oryx Pr.
McGeough, J. A. Principles of Electrochemical Machining. 1974. 35.00x o.p. (ISBN 0-412-11970-6, Pub. by Chapman & Hall). Methuen Inc.
McGerr, Celia. Rene Clair. (Filmmakers Ser.). 1980. lib. bdg. 12.95 (ISBN 0-8057-9262-7, Twayne). G K Hall.
McGerr, Pat. Pick Your Victim. LC 75-44991. (Crime Fiction Ser.). 1976. Repr. of 1946 ed. lib. bdg. 17.50 o.s.i. (ISBN 0-8240-2383-8). Garland Pub.
McGettrick, Andrew. The Definition of Programming Languages. LC 79-21635. (Cambridge Computer Science Texts: No. 11). 1980. 32.50 (ISBN 0-521-22631-7); pap. 13.95 (ISBN 0-521-29585-8). Cambridge U Pr.
McGettrick, Andrew D. ALGOL Sixty-Eight. LC 77-1104. (Computer Science Texts Ser.: No. 8). (Illus.). 1978. 49.50 (ISBN 0-521-21412-2); pap. 18.95x (ISBN 0-521-29143-7). Cambridge U Pr.
--Program Verification Using Ada. LC 81-12276. (Cambridge Computer Science Texts: No. 13). (Illus.). 350p. 1982. 39.50 (ISBN 0-521-24215-0); pap. 17.50 (ISBN 0-521-28531-3). Cambridge U Pr.
McGhee, Edward & Moore, Robin. The Chinese Ultimatum. 352p. (Orig.). 1980. pap. 2.25 o.p. (ISBN 0-523-40409-3). Pinnacle Bks.
McGhee, Jerry R. & Michalek, Suzanne M., eds. Dental Microbiology. (Illus.). 624p. 1982. text ed. 32.50 (ISBN 0-06-141590-1, Harper Medical). Lippincott.
McGhee, Paul E. & Chapman, Antony J. Children's Humour. LC 79-40648. 1980. 59.95 (ISBN 0-471-27638-3, Pub. by Wiley-Interscience). Wiley.
McGhee, Richard D. Henry Kirke White. (English Authors Ser.). 1981. 12.95 (ISBN 0-8057-6808-4, Twayne). G K Hall.
McGhee, Terence, jt. auth. see Steel, E. W.
McGibbon, Bernard M. Atlas of Breast Reconstruction: Following Radical Mastectomy. (Illus.). 1983. price not set (ISBN 0-8391-1704-3, 17647). Univ Park.
McGibony, John R. Principles of Hospital Administration. 2nd ed. (Illus.). 1969. 12.95m o.p. (ISBN 0-399-40033-8). Putnam Pub Group.
McGiffert, Michael. The Higher Learning in Colorado: A Historical Study, 1860-1940. LC 82-70597. 307p. 1964. 14.95 (ISBN 0-8040-0085-9, SB). Swallow.
MacGil, Gillis. Your Future As a Model. rev. ed. (Careers in Depth Ser). (gr. 7 up). 1971. PLB 7.97 o.p. (ISBN 0-8239-0159-9). Rosen Pr.
McGilchrist, Iain. Against Criticism. 288p. 1982. 27.95 (ISBN 0-571-11922-0). Faber & Faber.
McGill, Angus & Thomson, Kenneth. Live Wires. 256p. 1982. pap. 4.95 (ISBN 0-312-48882-3). St Martin.
McGill, Arthur C. Suffering: A Test of Theological Method. LC 82-6934. 1982. pap. 6.95 (ISBN 0-664-24448-3). Westminster.
McGill, Donald A. Punched Cards: Data Processing for Profit Improvement. (Illus.). 1962. 12.50 (ISBN 0-07-044993-7, P&RB). McGraw.
McGill, Gordon. The Final Conflict: Omen III. (Orig.). 1980. pap. 2.95 (ISBN 0-451-12258-5, AE2258, Sig). NAL.
--Omen IV: Armageddon 2000. 1982. pap. 3.50 (ISBN 0-451-11818-9, AE1818, Sig). NAL.
--War Story. 1980. 8.95 o.s.i. (ISBN 0-440-09442-9). Delacorte.
McGill, J., jt. auth. see Blaschke, W. S.
McGill, Leonard. Disco Dressing: A Complete Guide to Creating Seven Smash Disco Looks, Including Basic, Thrift Shop, Bodywear, Rock 'n' Roll Jock, Roller Disco, Futuristic Prep. (Illus.). 200p. 1980. 12.95 o.p. (ISBN 0-13-215822-1); pap. 7.95 o.p. (ISBN 0-13-215830-2). P-H.
McGill, M., jt. auth. see Salton, G.
McGill, Michael E. The Forty to Sixty-Year-Old Male. 1980. 11.95 o.s.i. (ISBN 0-671-25133-3). S&S.
McGill, Ralph. Southern Encounters: Southerners of Note in Ralph McGill's South. Logue, Calvin, ed. 240p. 1982. 23.50 (ISBN 0-86554-050-0). Mercer Univ Pr.
McGill, Raymond D. Notable Names in American Theatre. 2nd ed. 1250p. 1976. 120.00x (ISBN 0-88371-018-8, Pub. by J T White). Gale.
McGill, Shirley L. & Smith, Jean R. IV Therapy. (Illus.). 166p. 1983. pap. 11.95 (ISBN 0-89303-277-8). R J Brady.
McGill University, Blacker - Wood Library of Zoology & Ornithology. A Dictionary Catalogue of the Blacker - Wood Library of Zoology & Ornithology, 9 vols. 6300p. 1966. Set. lib. bdg. 810.00 (ISBN 0-8161-0719-X, Hall Library). G K Hall.
McGill, V. J. August Strindberg: The Bedeviled Viking. 459p. 1982. Repr. of 1930 ed. lib. bdg. 40.00 (ISBN 0-89760-568-3). Telegraph Bks.
McGill, William. The Year of the Monkey: Revolt on Campus, 1968-69. 304p. 1982. 15.95 (ISBN 0-07-044997-X). McGraw.
McGill-Franzen, Anne. The Gingerbread Boy. LC 79-62980. (Learn-a-Tale). (Illus.). (gr. k-2). 1979. PLB 11.55 (ISBN 0-8393-0184-7). Raintree Pubs.
--The Three Bears. LC 79-62977. (Learn-a-Tale). (Illus.). (gr. k-2). 1979. PLB 11.55 (ISBN 0-8393-0182-0). Raintree Pubs.
--The Three Little Pigs. LC 79-62978. (Learn-a-Tale). (Illus.). (gr. k-2). 1979. PLB 11.55 (ISBN 0-8393-0183-9). Raintree Pubs.
McGillis, K. A. & Presley, M. W. Tansill, Salado & Alibates Formations: Upper Permian Evaporite-Carbonate Strata of the Texas Panhandle. (Geological Circular Ser.: No. 81-8). 31p. 1.50 (ISBN 0-686-36596-8). Bur Econ Geology.
McGillivray, Robert G. On Road Congestion Theory. 21p. 1974. pap. 1.50 o.p. (ISBN 0-87766-118-9, 69000). Urban Inst.
McGilton, Henry & McGilton, Rachel. Introducing the UNIX System. Guty, Stephen G., ed. (Illus.). 352p. 1983. 18.95 (ISBN 0-07-045001-3, P&RB). McGraw.
McGilton, Rachel, jt. auth. see McGilton, Henry.
McGilvray, Dennis B., ed. Caste Ideology & Interaction. LC 81-18037. (Papers in Social Anthropology: No. 9). (Illus.). 258p. 1982. 34.50 (ISBN 0-521-24145-6). Cambridge U Pr.
McGilvray, James A., jt. auth. see King, J. Charles.
McGimsey, C. R. & Davis, H., eds. The Management of Archeological Resources: The Airlie House Report. 1977. pap. 4.00 (ISBN 0-686-36580-1). Am Anthro Assn.

McGinley, Patrick. Bogmail. LC 80-26135. (A Joan Kahn Bk.). 264p. 1981. 10.95 (ISBN 0-89919-031-6). Ticknor & Fields.

--Goosefoot: A Novel with Murder. 280p. 1982. 13.95 (ISBN 0-525-24142-6, 01354-410, Joan Kahn Bk). Dutton.

McGinley, Phyllis. Saint-Watching. 243p. 1982. 12.95 (ISBN 0-88347-142-6). Thomas More.

--Wonders & Surprises. LC 67-19271. 1968p. (YA) (gr. 6 up). 1960. 3.95 o.p. (ISBN 0-397-31053-6). Har-Row.

--A Wreath of Christmas Legends. (gr. 4-8). 1974. pap. 0.95 o.p. (ISBN 0-02-044450-8, Collier). Macmillan.

--Year Without a Santa Claus. (Illus.). (gr. k-3). 1957. 10.53i (ISBN 0-397-30399-8, JBL-J); PLB 10.89 (ISBN 0-397-31969-X). Har-Row.

MacGinley, T. J. Steel Structures: Practical Design Studies. 300p. 1981. 32.00x (ISBN 0-419-12560-4, E & FN Spon England); pap. 17.95x (ISBN 0-419-11710-5). Methuen Inc.

McGinn, Colin. The Character of Mind. 144p. 1982. 19.95 (ISBN 0-19-219171-3); pap. 7.50 (ISBN 0-19-289159-6). Oxford U Pr.

McGinn, Daniel F. Actuarial Fundamentals for Multiemployer Plans. 122p. (Orig.). 1982. pap. text ed. 10.00 (ISBN 0-89154-191-8). Intl Found Employ.

McGinn, Donald J. John Penry & the Marprelate Controversy. 1966. 22.50x (ISBN 0-8135-0513-5). Rutgers U Pr.

--Thomas Nashe. (English Authors Ser.). 12.95 (ISBN 0-8057-6807-6, Twayne). G K Hall.

McGinn, Noel F. & Davis, Russell G. Build a Mill, Build a City, Build a School: Industrialization, Urbanization, & Education in Ciudad Guayana. 1969. 20.00x (ISBN 0-262-13052-1). MIT Pr.

McGinness, Laurie. Surfing Fundamentals. (Illus.). 1978. 12.00 o.p. (ISBN 0-589-50055-4, Pub. by Reed Books Australia). C E Tuttle.

McGinnies, W. B., ed. see Cairo International Workshop on Applications of Science & Technology for Desert Development September 9-15, 1978.

McGinnis, Alan L. La Amistad Factor Decisivo. Orig. Title: The Friendship Factor. 204p. (Span.). 1982. pap. 5.95 (ISBN 0-311-46093-3, Edit Mundo). Casa Bautista.

--The Romance Factor. LC 81-47839. 224p. 1982. 11.49i (ISBN 0-06-065360-4, HarpR). Har-Row.

McGinnis, Dorothy J. & Smith, Dorothy E. Analyzing & Treating Reading Problems. 1982. text ed. 21.95 (ISBN 0-02-379130-6). Macmillan.

McGinnis, Harry & Ruley, M. J. Basic Woodwork Projects. (gr. 7-9). 1959. text ed. 15.28 (ISBN 0-87345-043-4). McKnight.

McGinnis, Helen J. Carnegie's Dinosaurs. Jacobs, Martina M., et al, eds. LC 82-70212. (Illus.). 120p. (Orig.). 1982. pap. 8.50 (ISBN 0-911239-00-6). Carnegie Board.

McGinnis, Lyn D., jt. auth. see Hawkins, Robert P.

McGinnis, Marilyn. Single. 1976. pap. 1.50 o.s.i. (ISBN 0-89129-164-4). Jove Pubns.

McGinnis, Michael R. & D'Amoto, Richard F. Pictorial Handbook of Medically Important Fungi & Aerobic Actinomycetes. (Illus.). 172p. 1981. pap. 17.50 (ISBN 0-03-058364-0). Praeger.

McGinnis, Terri. Dr. Terri McGinnis' Dog & Cat Good Food Book. Wood, Alan, ed. LC 77-6007. (Illus.). 1977. pap. 5.95 (ISBN 0-394-73419-X, Dist. by Random). Taylor & Ng.

McGinniss, Joe. Going to Extreme's. 1982. pap. 3.50 (ISBN 0-451-11819-7, AE1819, Sig). NAL.

McGinty, Brian. Palace Inns. LC 78-73. (Illus.). 192p. 1978. pap. 9.95 (ISBN 0-686-81982-9). Stackpole.

McGinty, Gerald P. Videocassette Recorders: Theory & Servicing. (Illus.). 1979. pap. text ed. 12.96 (ISBN 0-07-044988-0, G). McGraw.

McGinty, Patricia. Dirges to Dance By. LaRue, Jaine, ed. 23p. 1982. pap. 2.50 (ISBN 0-932884-08-3). Red Herring.

McGivney, Raymond, et al. Essential Precalculus. 464p. 1980. text ed. 21.95x o.p. (ISBN 0-534-00766-X); solutions manual 6.95 o.p. (ISBN 0-534-00842-9). Wadsworth Pub.

McGlashen, Alan. Gravity & Levity. 1976. 6.95 o.p. (ISBN 0-395-24762-4). HM.

McGlashen, M. L., ed. Manual of Symbols & Terminology for Physiochemical Quantities & Units. 44p. 1976. text ed. 7.15 o.p. (ISBN 0-08-020833-9). Pergamon.

McGlathery, James M. Desire's Sway: The Plays & Stories of Heinrich von Kleist. 272p. 1983. 17.95 (ISBN 0-8143-1734-0). Wayne St U Pr.

McGlathrey, James, ed. German Source Readings in the Arts & Sciences. 1974. 9.80x (ISBN 0-87563-083-9). Stipes.

McGlinchee, Claire. James Russell Lowell. (United States Authors Ser.). lib. bdg. 12.95 (ISBN 0-8057-0460-4, Twayne). G K Hall.

McGloin, Joseph T. Christ Lives On. (Through Him with Him & to Him Ser). (gr. 10). 1966. pap. text ed. 5.96 o.p. (ISBN 0-02-820720-3); teachers' manual 2.64 o.p. (ISBN 0-02-820740-8). Glencoe.

--Life of Man in Christ. 1967. pap. text ed. 5.96 o.p. (ISBN 0-02-820760-2). Glencoe.

--Living in God. 1965. pap. text ed. 5.96 o.p. (ISBN 0-685-07649-0, 82068); teachers' manual 2.64 o.p. (ISBN 0-685-07650-4, 82070). Glencoe.

--Living in the Kingdom. 1968. pap. text ed. 5.96 o.p. (ISBN 0-02-820800-5). Glencoe.

McGlothlin, Don C. Star to Guide Us. LC 82-61488. (Illus.). 304p. 1982. write for info. Presidential.

McGlynn, D. R. Modern Microprocessor System Design: Sixteen-BIT & BIT-Slice Architecture. 295p. 1980. 28.00 (ISBN 0-471-06492-0, Pub. by Wiley-Interscience). Wiley.

McGlynn, Daniel R. Distributed Processing & Data Communications. LC 78-1117. 1978. 31.50 (ISBN 0-471-01886-4, Pub. by Wiley-Interscience). Wiley.

--Fundamentals of Microcomputer Programming: Including Pascal. LC 82-8645. 332p. 1982. pap. 14.95 (ISBN 0-471-08769-6). Wiley.

--McGlynn's Simplified Guide to Small Computers for Business. 250p. 1983. 14.95 (ISBN 0-471-86853-1, Pub. by Wiley Interscience). Wiley.

--Microprocessors: Technology, Architecture & Applications. LC 76-137. 1976. 24.95 (ISBN 0-471-58414-2, Pub. by Wiley-Interscience). Wiley.

--Personal Computing: Home, Professional & Small Business Applications. LC 79-1005. 1979. pap. 13.50 o.p. (ISBN 0-471-05380-5, Pub. by Wiley-Interscience). Wiley.

--Personal Computing: Home, Professional, & Small Business Applications. 2nd ed. 335p. 1982. pap. 14.95 (ISBN 0-471-86164-2, Pub. by Wiley-Interscience). Wiley.

McGlynn, George H., ed. Issues in Physical Education & Sports. LC 73-91388. 228p. 1974. pap. 8.95 (ISBN 0-87484-238-7). Mayfield Pub.

McGlynn, James. Modern Ethical Theories. 1962. pap. 4.95x o.p. (ISBN 0-685-07655-5, 82106). Glencoe.

McGlynn, John & Frederick, William. Reflections on Rebellion: Indonesian Stories from the Communist Rebellions of 1949 & 1965. 160p. 1983. pap. 13.00 (ISBN 0-89680-111-X, Ohio U Ctr Intl). Ohio U Pr.

McGoldrick, Monica & Pearce, John, eds. Ethnicity & Family Therapy. LC 81-20198. (Guilford Family Therapy Ser.). 600p. 1982. text ed. 29.50x (ISBN 0-89862-040-6). Guilford Pr.

McGolrick, Charles, jt. auth. see Graham, Benjamin.

McGonagle, John J. Business Agreements: A Complete Guide to Oral & Written Contracts. LC 82-71298. (Illus.). 256p. 1982. 27.50 (ISBN 0-8019-7223-X). Chilton.

M'Gonigle, R. Michael & Zacher, Mark W. Pollution, Politics, & International Law: Tankers at Sea. 1979. 18.95x (ISBN 0-520-03690-5); pap. 10.95 (ISBN 0-520-04513-0, CAL530). U of Cal Pr.

McGonnagle, Warren J. International Advances in Nondestructive Testing, Vol. 8. 361p. 1981. 75.00 (ISBN 0-677-16240-5). Gordon.

McGonnagle, Warren J., jt. auth. see Bahr, A. J.

McGonnagle, Warren J., ed. International Advances in Nondestructive Testing, Vol. 9. 400p. 1982. write for info. (ISBN 0-677-16440-8). Gordon.

McGoon, Cliff, et al, eds. see International Association of Business Communications.

McGork, Frank C., jt. ed. see Osborne, R. Travis.

MacGorman, J. W. The Gifts of the Spirit. LC 75-55191. 1980. pap. 3.75 (ISBN 0-8054-1385-5). Broadman.

McGorray, J. J., jt. auth. see Bryant, Raymond C.

McGorray, J. J., jt. ed. see Bryant, Raymond C.

McGough, Elizabeth. Who Are You? A Teen-Ager's Guide to Self-Understanding. (Illus.). (gr. 7-9). 1976. 9.95 (ISBN 0-688-22091-6); PLB 9.55 (ISBN 0-688-32091-0). Morrow.

--Your Silent Language. LC 73-4253. (Illus.). 128p. (gr. 7 up). 1974. PLB 8.59 (ISBN 0-688-31820-7). Morrow.

McGough, James P., ed. Fei Hsiao-T'ung: The Dilemma of a Chinese Intellectual. LC 79-66094. 1979. 22.50 (ISBN 0-87332-141-3). M E Sharpe.

McGough, Robert C., jt. auth. see Finch, Curtis R.

McGovern, Ann. Nicholas Bentley Stoningpot, III. LC 81-13226. (Illus.). 32p. (gr. k-3). 1982. Reinforced bdg. 11.95 (ISBN 0-8234-0443-9). Holiday.

McGovern, Edythe M. Neil Simon: A Critical Study. LC 78-7123. 1979. 14.50 (ISBN 0-8044-2567-1). Ungar.

McGovern, J. P., jt. auth. see Knotts, G. R.

McGovern, Jill, jt. auth. see Fallen, Nancy.

McGovern, Thomas, jt. auth. see Sinema, William.

McGovern, Vincent J. Malignant Melanoma: Clinical & Histological Diagnosis. LC 76-3793. 1976. 58.95 (ISBN 0-471-58417-7, Pub. by Wiley Medical). Wiley.

--Melanoma: Histological Diagnosis & Prognosis. (Biopsy Interpretation Ser.). (Illus.). 210p. 1982. text ed. 49.00 (ISBN 0-89004-711-1). Raven.

McGovern, Vincent J. & Tiller, David J. Shock: A Clinicopathologic Correlation. LC 79-87539. (Illus.). 192p. 1980. 31.50x (ISBN 0-89352-073-X). Masson Pub.

McGovern, William M., Jr. Cases & Materials on Wills, Trusts, & Future Interests: An Introduction to Estate Planning. LC 82-20034. (American Casebook Ser.). 680p. 1982. text ed. 22.95 (ISBN 0-314-68828-5). West Pub.

McGowan, Brenda & Meezan, William. Child Welfare: Current Dilemmas--Future Directions. LC 82-61260. 510p. 1983. text ed. 21.95 (ISBN 0-87581-287-2). Peacock Pubs.

McGowan, Christopher. The Successful Dragons: A Natural History of Extinct Reptiles. (Illus.). 282p. 1983. 29.95 (ISBN 0-88866-618-7). Samuel Stevens.

McGowan, Cynthia. Robinson Crusoe Notes. (Orig.). 1976. pap. text ed. 2.75 (ISBN 0-8220-1150-6). Cliffs.

McGowan, Cynthia C. Walden Two Notes. (gr. 10-12). 1979. pap. 2.25 (ISBN 0-8220-1361-4). Cliffs.

--Who's Afraid of Virginia Woolf? Notes. (Orig.). 1979. pap. text ed. 2.50 (ISBN 0-8220-1383-5). Cliffs.

McGowan, Daniel A. Consumer Economics. 1978. 22.50 (ISBN 0-395-30668-X); Tchr's Manual 1.00 (ISBN 0-395-30669-8). HM.

--Contemporary Personal Finance. 1981. 24.95 (ISBN 0-395-30823-2); Tchrs. Manual 1.25 (ISBN 0-395-30824-0). HM.

McGowan, J. W. The Excited State in Chemical Physics, Vol. 28. 492p. 1975. 54.50 o.p. (ISBN 0-471-58425-8, Pub. by Wiley-Interscience). Wiley.

McGowan, J. William. The Excited State in Chemical Physics, Pt. Two. (Advances in Chemical Physics: Vol. 45). 609p. 1981. 76.00 (ISBN 0-471-05119-5, Pub. by Wiley-Interscience). Wiley.

McGowan, Kilian. Your Way to God. 216p. 1964. pap. 2.95 o.p. (ISBN 0-8091-1722-3). Paulist Pr.

McGowan, Pat, jt. ed. see Kegley, Charles W., Jr.

McGowan, Robert A. & Merrill, Michael J. Shared Training & Development Services for Hospitals. 96p. (Orig.). 1982. pap. 28.75 (ISBN 0-87258-342-2, AHA-088200). Am Hospital.

MacGowan, Sandra, ed. see Faiola, Theodora & Pullen, Jo A.

McGowan, Vicki, jt. ed. see Skerman, V. B.

McGowen, Drusilla. Traveling the Way. 1977. 5.95 (ISBN 0-686-20047-0). Rod & Staff.

MacGowen, Kenneth & Melnitz, W. Living Stage: A History of the World Theatre. 1955. text ed. 25.95 (ISBN 0-13-538942-9). P-H.

McGowen, Lee W. Mary Joe. 140p. 1983. 6.95 (ISBN 0-89962-319-0). Todd & Honeywell.

McGowen, Tom. Album of Astronomy. LC 79-9485. (Illus.). (gr. 4-10). 1979. 8.95 (ISBN 0-528-82048-6). Rand.

--Album of Birds. (Illus.). 72p. (gr. 5up). 1982. 8.95 (ISBN 0-528-82413-9); PLB 8.97 (ISBN 0-528-80076-0). Rand.

--Dinosaurs & Other Prehistoric Animals. LC 78-54737. (Illus.). (gr. 3-7). 1978. 7.95 o.p. (ISBN 0-528-82078-8). Rand.

McGown, Elizabeth R., jt. auth. see Hamburg, David A.

McGrade, A. S. The Political Thought of William of Ockham. LC 73-86044. (Studies in Medieval Life & Thought). 264p. 1974. 39.50 (ISBN 0-521-20284-1). Cambridge U Pr.

McGrade, A. S., ed. see Hooker, Richard.

McGrady, Donald. Jorge Isaacs. (World Authors Ser.). lib. bdg. 15.95 (ISBN 0-8057-2460-5, Twayne). G K Hall.

McGrady, Mike, jt. auth. see Aronson, Harvey.

McGrady, Patrick, Jr., jt. auth. see Pritkin, Nathan.

McGrain, John W. Pig Iron & Cotton Duck: Iron & Textile Mill Towns in Baltimore County, Maryland. (Baltimore County Heritage Publication). (Illus.). Date not set. write for info. (ISBN 0-937076-01-5). Baltimore Co Pub Lib. Postponed.

McGran, Philip. The Individual Inventor: What He Should Know about the U. S. Patent System. 48p. 1982. 5.00 (ISBN 0-682-49905-6). Exposition.

McGrath, Alice, jt. auth. see Tegner, Bruce.

McGrath, Alice, ed. see Tegner, Bruce.

McGrath, Charles, jt. auth. see Menaker, Daniel.

McGrath, Daniel F. Bookman's Price Index, Vol. 24. 780p. 1983. 115.00x (ISBN 0-8103-0624-7). Gale.

--Bookman's Price Index, Vol. 25. 800p. 1983. 115.00x (ISBN 0-8103-0638-7). Gale.

McGrath, Daniel F., ed. Bookman's Price Index: A Guide to the Values of Rare & Other Out-of-Print Books. LC 64-8723. (Bookman's Price Index Ser.: Vol. 23). 900p. 1983. 115.00 (ISBN 0-8103-0623-9). Gale.

--Bookman's Price Index: A Guide to the Values of Rare & Other Out-of-Print Books, 20 vols. Incl. 1964. Vol. 1 (ISBN 0-8103-0601-8); 1967. Vol. 2 (ISBN 0-8103-0602-6); 1968. Vol. 3 (ISBN 0-8103-0603-4); 1969. Vol. 4 (ISBN 0-8103-0604-2); 1971. Vol. 5 (ISBN 0-8103-0605-0); 1973. Vol. 6 (ISBN 0-8103-0606-9); 1973. Vol. 7 (ISBN 0-8103-0607-7); 1974. Vol. 8 (ISBN 0-8103-0608-5); 1974. Vol. 9 (ISBN 0-8103-0609-3); Vol. 10 (ISBN 0-8103-0635-2); Vol. 11. 1976. Vol. 11 (ISBN 0-8103-0611-5); 1977 (ISBN 0-8103-0612-3); 1978. Vol. 13 (ISBN 0-8103-0613-1); 1978. Vol. 14 (ISBN 0-8103-0614-X); 1979. Vol. 15 (ISBN 0-8103-0615-8); Vol. 16. 1979 (ISBN 0-8103-0616-6); Vol. 17. 1979 (ISBN 0-8103-0617-4); Vol. 18. 1979 (ISBN 0-8103-0618-2); Vol. 19. 1980 (ISBN 0-8103-0619-0); Vol. 20. 1980 (ISBN 0-8103-0620-4). LC 64-8723. (Bookman's Price Index Ser.). 115.00x ea. Gale.

--Bookman's Price Index: A Guide to the Values of Rare & Other Out-of-Print Books. LC 64-8723. (Bookman's Price Index Ser.: Vol. 21). 900p. 1981. 115.00x (ISBN 0-8103-0621-2). Gale.

McGrath, Earl J. Should Students Share the Power? A Study of Their Role in College & University Governance. LC 70-133135. 124p. 1970. 9.95 (ISBN 0-87722-020-4); pap. 9.95 o.p. (ISBN 0-87722-003-4). Temple U Pr.

McGrath, Edward & Krauss, Bob, eds. A Child's History of America. (Illus.). (gr. 3 up). 1976. 9.95 (ISBN 0-316-55934-2); pap. 5.95 (ISBN 0-316-55935-0). Little.

McGrath, J. B., jt. auth. see Weiss, Harold.

McGrath, James J. & Barnes, Charles D., eds. Air-Pollution-Physiological Effects. (Research Topics in Physiology Ser.). 1982. 44.00 (ISBN 0-12-483880-4). Acad Pr.

McGrath, John. The Cheviot, the Stag, & the Black, Black Oil. 80p. 1981. pap. 6.95 (ISBN 0-413-48880-2). Methuen Inc.

--Fish in the Sea. 96p. (Orig.). 1981. pap. 3.95 (ISBN 0-686-91739-1). Pluto Pr.

--A Good Night Out: Popular Theatre - Audience, Class & Form. 144p. 1981. pap. 8.25 (ISBN 0-413-48700-8). Methuen Inc.

McGrath, John H. & Scarpitti, Frank R. Youth & Drugs: Perspectives on a Social Problem. 1970. pap. 4.95x o.p. (ISBN 0-673-07558-3). Scott F.

McGrath, Joseph E. & Martin, Joanne. Judgement Calls in Research. (Studying Organizations: Innovations in Methodology Ser.). (Illus.). 128p. 1982. 17.95 (ISBN 0-8039-1873-9); pap. 7.95 (ISBN 0-8039-1874-7). Sage.

McGrath, Judy, intro. by. Karoo Ashevak: Spirits. (Illus.). 1973. pap. 2.50 o.p. (ISBN 0-913456-21-7). Interbk Inc.

McGrath, Kay. The Seeds of Singing. (Orig.). 1983. pap. 3.95 (ISBN 0-440-19120-3). Dell.

McGrath, Lee P., jt. auth. see Scoby, Joan.

McGrath, Patrick J. & Firestone, Philip, eds. Pediatric & Adolescent Behavioral Medicine: Issues in Treatment. (Springer Series on Behavior Therapy & Behavioral Medicine: Vol. 10). 1983. text ed. 24.95 (ISBN 0-8261-4010-6). Springer Pub.

McGrath, Philomena & Mills, P. Atlas of Sectional Anatomy. (Illus.). viii, 232p. 1983. bound 82.25 (ISBN 3-8055-3624-0). S Karger.

McGrath, Phyllis S. Communicating with Professional Investors. (Report Ser: No. 644). 1974. pap. 25.00 (ISBN 0-8237-0010-0). Conference Bd.

McGrath, Richard F. California Criminal Law Workbook. 4th ed. 1978. pap. text ed. 12.95 (ISBN 0-8403-0165-0). Kendall-Hunt.

McGrath, Robert L. Early Vermont Wall Paintings, 1790-1850. LC 73-177448. (Illus.). 124p. 1972. 12.50x (ISBN 0-87451-062-7). U Pr of New Eng.

McGrath, Robert L., intro. by. John Sloan: Paintings, Prints, Drawings. LC 82-100263. (Illus.). 98p. 1981. pap. 10.00 o.p. (ISBN 0-87451-234-4, Pub. by Dartmouth College). U Pr of New Eng.

McGrath, Ruth E. Developing Concepts of Health in Early Childhood. (Illus.). 1977. 2.95 o.p. (ISBN 0-914634-44-5, 7703). DOK Pubs.

--Developing Concepts of Safety in Early Childhood. (Illus.). 1977. 2.50 o.p. (ISBN 0-914634-42-9, 7704). DOK Pubs.

McGrath, Thomas. Letter to an Imaginary Friend, Pt. 1 & 2. LC 82-71199. 214p. 1969. 12.95 (ISBN 0-8040-0185-5); pap. 6.95x (ISBN 0-8040-0186-3). Swallow.

--The Movie at the End of the World: Collected Poems. LC 82-73286. 188p. 1980. 10.95 o.p. (ISBN 0-8040-0605-9); pap. 6.95x (ISBN 0-8040-0606-7). Swallow.

McGrath, William. The Anabaptists: Neither Catholics nor Protestants. pap. 0.60 (ISBN 0-686-32317-3). Rod & Staff.

--Watch Out for These Three Leavers. pap. 0.60 (ISBN 0-686-32336-X). Rod & Staff.

--Why Alert Christians Object to Radio, TV & Theater. pap. 0.60 (ISBN 0-686-32337-8). Rod & Staff.

McGrath, William R. Bio-Nutronics. 224p. (RL 10). 1974. pap. 1.50 o.p. (ISBN 0-451-06065-2, W6065, Sig). NAL.

McGravie, Anne V. It's Easy to Be Liked. (Illus.). 72p. (gr. 4 up). 1980. wkbk 2.25 (ISBN 0-912486-34-1). Finney Co.

McGraw, Eloise J. Mara: Daughter of the Nile. (Illus.). (gr. 5-8). 1953. 7.95 o.p. (ISBN 0-698-20087-X, Coward). Putnam Pub Group.

--The Moccasin Trail. (Illus.). (gr. 5-8). 1952. 8.95 (ISBN 0-698-20092-6, Coward). Putnam Pub Group.

--Sawdust in His Shoes. (Illus.). (gr. 7 up). 1971. PLB 4.99 o.p. (ISBN 0-698-30303-2, Coward). Putnam Pub Group.

McGraw-Hill. McGraw-Hill Encyclopedia of World Biography, 12 vols. 1973. Set. 450.00 (ISBN 0-07-079633-5, P&RB). McGraw.

--McGraw-Hill Encyclopedia of World Drama, 4 vols. LC 70-37382. (Illus.). 2000p. 1972. Set. 139.50 o.p. (ISBN 0-07-079567-3, P&RB). McGraw.

McGraw-Hill Book Co. McGraw-Hill Encyclopedia of Energy. 2nd ed. Parker, Sybil P., ed. LC 80-18078. (Illus.). 856p. 1980. 44.50 (ISBN 0-07-045268-7). McGraw.

McGraw-Hill Book Company, ed. Author's Book. 2nd ed. LC 68-6295. (Illus.). 1968. Repr. of 1922 ed. 15.95 (ISBN 0-07-045051-X, C). McGraw.

McGraw Hill-Chemical Engineering Editors. Effective Communication for Engineers. 216p. 1975. pap. text ed. 19.95 (ISBN 0-07-045032-3, C). McGraw.

--Supplementary Readings in Engineering Design. 224p. 1975. text ed. 12.50 o.p. (ISBN 0-07-045031-5). McGraw.

McGraw-Hill Editors. Basic Bibliography of Science & Technology. 1966. 25.00 (ISBN 0-07-045218-0, P&RB). McGraw.

--Dictionary of the Life Sciences. (Illus.). 1976. 29.50 (ISBN 0-07-045262-8, P&RB). McGraw.

--McGraw-Hill Dictionary of Scientific & Technical Terms. 2nd ed. (Illus.). 1978. 59.50 (ISBN 0-07-045258-X, P&RB). McGraw.

--McGraw-Hill Encyclopedia of Environmental Science. (Illus.). 750p. 1974. 26.95 o.p. (ISBN 0-07-045260-1, P&RB). McGraw.

--McGraw-Hill Encyclopedia of Food, Agriculture, & Nutrition. (Illus.). 1977. 41.50 (ISBN 0-07-045263-6, P&RB). McGraw.

--McGraw-Hill Yearbook of Science & Technology. Incl. 1972. 32.50 (ISBN 0-07-045250-4); 1975. 28.50 (ISBN 0-07-045342-X); 1976. 29.50 (ISBN 0-07-045343-8); 1977. 29.50 (ISBN 0-07-045344-6); 1978. 34.50 (ISBN 0-07-045348-9); 1979. 34.50 (ISBN 0-07-045349-7, P&RB). McGraw.

McGraw-Hill Encyclopedia of Science & Technology Staff. McGraw-Hill Encyclopedia of Ocean & Atmospheric Sciences. Parker, Sybil P., ed. (Illus.). 1979. 44.50 (ISBN 0-07-045267-9). McGraw.

--McGraw-Hill Encyclopedia of Science & Technology. 4th ed. 1977. 497.00 (ISBN 0-07-079590-8, P&RB); to institutions 447.00 (ISBN 0-686-66166-4). McGraw.

McGraw-Hill Management Awareness Program Editors. McGraw-Hill Management Awareness Program No. 8. 1976. 8.00 o.p. (ISBN 0-07-045188-5, P&RB). McGraw.

--McGraw-Hill Management Awareness Program No. 7. 1976. 8.00 o.p. (ISBN 0-07-045187-7, P&RB). McGraw.

McGraw-Hill Publishing Co. Encyclopedia of Astronomy. 464p. 1983. 44.50 (ISBN 0-07-045251-2, P&RB). McGraw.

McGraw-Hill Staff. Final Examination for Illustrated Electrical Courses. 1976. 10.00 o.p. (ISBN 0-07-045704-2). McGraw.

McGraw, James R., ed. see Gregory, Dick.

McGraw, Lora, jt. auth. see Getz, Donald J.

McGraw, Marsha, jt. ed. see Brown, Gordon.

McGraw Pub. Co. Encyclopedia of Environmental Science. 2nd ed. 1980. 44.50 (ISBN 0-07-045264-4). McGraw.

--Encyclopedia of Science & Technology, 15 Vols. 4th ed. 1977. Set. 497.00 (ISBN 0-07-079590-8); 43.00 ea.; suppl. materials avail. McGraw.

McGraw, Robert P., ed. see Breyfogle, Newell D.

McGraw, Tug & Witte, Mike. Scroogie No. 2: Hello There Ball. 1977. pap. 1.25 o.p. (ISBN 0-451-07521-8, Y7521, Sig). NAL.

McGreal, Cathleen E., jt. ed. see Fitzgerald, Hiram.

McGreevey, William P., ed. Third-World Poverty: New Strategies for Measuring Development Progress. LC 78-75318. (Human Affairs Research Center Ser.). 240p. 1980. 23.95x (ISBN 0-669-02839-8). Lexington Bks.

McGreevy, John, ed. Cities. (Illus.). 256p. 1981. 17.95 (ISBN 0-517-54469-5, C N Potter Bks). Crown.

McGreevy, Susan B. Maria: The Legend, the Legacy. Smith, James C., Jr., ed. LC 81-14512. (Illus.). 64p. (Orig.). 1982. 3.50 (ISBN 0-86534-005-6). Sunstone Pr.

MacGregor, A. & Greenwood, C. T. Polymers in Nature. LC 79-41787. 391p. 1981. 64.95 (ISBN 0-471-27762-2, Pub. by Wiley-Interscience); pap. write for info. (ISBN 0-471-27794-0). Wiley.

McGregor, Alexander C. Counting Sheep: From Open Range to Agribusiness on the Columbia Plateau. LC 82-15903. (Illus.). 500p. 1982. 25.00 (ISBN 0-295-95894-4). U of Wash Pr.

Macgregor, Annie & Macgregor, Scott. Domes. (Illus.). (gr. 3 up). 1982. PLB 9.55 (ISBN 0-688-00869-0); pap. 6.00 (ISBN 0-686-94108-X). Morrow.

MacGregor, Arthur. Anglo-Scandinavian Finds from Lloyds Bank, Pavement & Other Sites. (Archaeology of York-Small Finds 17-3). 174p. 1982. pap. text ed. 15.00x (ISBN 0-906780-02-0, 40256, Pub. by Coun Brit Archaeology England). Humanities.

MacGregor, Bruce A. & Truesdale, Richard. South Pacific Coast: A Centennial. 1982. 34.95 (ISBN 0-87108-545-3). Pruett.

MacGregor, Carol. The Fairy Tale Cookbook. LC 82-7742. (Illus.). 96p. (gr. 3 up). 1983. 8.95 (ISBN 0-02-761970-2). Macmillan.

McGregor, Craig. The Great Barrier Reef. (The World's Wild Places Ser.). (Illus.). 1977. lib. bdg. 12.68 (ISBN 0-8094-2008-2). Silver.

MacGregor, David R. Merchant Sailing Ships, Seveteen Seventy-Five to Eighteen Fifteen. (Illus.). 218p. 1981. 21.95 (ISBN 0-87021-942-1). Naval Inst Pr.

--The Tea Clippers: Their History & Development 1833-1875. LC 82-61670. (Illus.). 200p. 1982. 24.95 (ISBN 0-87021-884-0). Naval Inst Pr.

McGregor, Douglas. Human Side of Enterprise. 1960. 25.95 (ISBN 0-07-045092-7, C). McGraw.

--Professional Manager. 1967. 14.95 o.p. (ISBN 0-07-045093-5, C). McGraw.

MacGregor, Ellen. Miss Pickerell & the Geiger Counter. (Illus.). (gr. 4-6). 1963. PLB 6.95 o.p. (ISBN 0-07-044554-0, GB). McGraw.

--Miss Pickerell Goes to Mars. (Illus.). (gr. 4-6). 1951. 8.95 (ISBN 0-07-044560-5); PLB 5.72 (ISBN 0-07-044559-1). McGraw.

--Miss Pickerell Goes Undersea. (Illus.). (gr. 4-6). PLB 8.95 (ISBN 0-07-044558-3, GB). McGraw.

MacGregor, Ellen & Pantell, Dora. Miss Pickerell & the Blue Whale. (Miss Pickerell Ser.). (gr. 3-7). Date not set. 9.95 (ISBN 0-686-82191-2). McGraw.

--Miss Pickerell & the Supertanker. (Illus.). (gr. 4-6). 1978. 8.95 (ISBN 0-07-044588-5, GB). McGraw.

--Miss Pickerell Meets Mr. H. U. M. new ed. (Illus.). 160p. (gr. 2-6). 1974. 5.95 o.p. (ISBN 0-07-044577-X, GB); PLB 9.95 o.p. (ISBN 0-07-044578-8). McGraw.

--Miss Pickerell Meets Mr. H.U.M, No. 3. (Miss Pickerell Ser.). (Illus.). (gr. 4-6). 1980. pap. 1.75 o.p. (ISBN 0-671-56028-X). Archway.

--Miss Pickerell on the Moon. (Miss Pickerell Ser.: No. 1). (Illus.). (gr. 4-6). 1980. pap. 1.95 (ISBN 0-671-44230-9). Archway.

--Miss Pickerell Tackles the Energy Crisis. LC 79-24149. (Illus.). (gr. 4-6). 1980. 9.95 (ISBN 0-07-044589-3). McGraw.

--Miss Pickerell to the Earthquake Rescue. (Illus.). 160p. (gr. 4-6). 1977. 8.95 (ISBN 0-07-044586-9, GB). McGraw.

Macgregor, Frances C. After Plastic Surgery: Adaptation & Adjustment. LC 79-11808. (Praeger Special Studies Ser.). 160p. 1980. 26.95 (ISBN 0-03-052131-9). Praeger.

MacGregor, Geddes. The Bible in the Making. LC 82-17499. 318p. 1983. pap. 12.75 (ISBN 0-8191-2810-4). U Pr of Amer.

--Introduction to Religious Philosophy. LC 81-40257. 380p. 1981. lib. bdg. 23.25 (ISBN 0-8191-1669-6); pap. text ed. 12.50 (ISBN 0-8191-1670-X). U Pr of Amer.

--Philosophical Issues in Religious Thought. LC 78-65851. pap. text ed. 12.25 (ISBN 0-8191-0677-1). U Pr of Amer.

McGregor, Gordon, jt. auth. see Bright, John.

McGregor, Ian P. & Gardner, Alvin F. Contact Lens Guidelines. (Allied Health Professions Monograph Ser.). 1983. write for info. (ISBN 0-87527-321-1). Green.

McGregor, James L., jt. auth. see Berg, Paul W.

McGregor, John C. Southwestern Archaeology. 2nd ed. LC 65-10079. (Illus.). 1965. 20.00 o.p. (ISBN 0-252-72659-6). U of Ill Pr.

--Southwestern Archaeology. 2nd ed. LC 65-10079. (Illus.). 518p. 1982. pap. 14.95 (ISBN 0-252-00989-4). U of Ill Pr.

McGregor, Lynn. Developments in Drama Teaching. (Changing Classroom). 1976. text ed. 11.25 o.p. (ISBN 0-7291-0007-3); pap. text ed. 4.00x o. p. o.p. (ISBN 0-7291-0002-2). Humanities.

MacGregor, Morris J., jt. ed. see Nalty, Bernard C.

McGregor, Patricia. Odiham Castle Twelve Hundred to Fifteen Hundred. 192p. 1982. text ed. 18.75x (ISBN 0-86299-030-0, Pub. by Sutton England). Humanities.

MacGregor, Ronald N. Art Plus. (Illus.). 1978. pap. text ed. 12.00x (ISBN 0-07-082450-9, C). McGraw.

Macgregor, Scott, jt. auth. see Macgregor, Annie.

Macgregor-Morris, Pamela, ed. The Book of the Horse. LC 79-84551. (Illus.). 1979. 20.00 o.p. (ISBN 0-399-12424-1). Putnam Pub Group.

MacGregory, G. Reincarnation as a Christian Hope. 1982. 60.00x (ISBN 0-333-31986-9, Pub. by Macmillan England). State Mutual Bk.

McGrew, D. R. Traffic Accident Investigation & Physical Evidence. (Illus.). 132p. 1976. spiral 16.75x (ISBN 0-398-03503-2). C C Thomas.

McGriff, Erline P. & Cooper, Signe. Accountability to the Consumer through Continuing Education in Nursing. 32p. 1974. 3.00 (ISBN 0-686-38242-0, 14-1507). Natl League Nurse.

McGriffin, Robert F., Jr. Furniture Care & Conservation. (Illus.). 256p. 1983. text ed. write for info. (ISBN 0-910050-62-7). AASLH.

McGrigor. Wage & Salary Administration: A Handbook for School Business Officials. (Research Bulletin: No. 5). pap. 1.00 o.p. (ISBN 0-685-57184-X). Assn Sch Busn.

McGuane, Thomas. Nobody's Angel. 14.50 (ISBN 0-394-52264-8); pap. 6.95 (ISBN 0-394-70565-3). Random.

--Nobody's Angel. 224p. 1983. pap. 2.95 (ISBN 0-345-30271-0). Ballantine.

McGucken, William. The Social Relations of Science Movement: Great Britain, 1931-1947. 450p. 1983. price not set (ISBN 0-8142-0351-5). Ohio St U Pr.

McGuckian, Medbh. The Flower Master. 1982. pap. 9.95 (ISBN 0-19-211949-4). Oxford U Pr.

McGuffey. Competencies Needed by Chief School Business Administrators. 1980. 11.50 (ISBN 0-910170-17-7). Assn Sch Busn.

McGuffey, William H. Old Favorites from the McGuffey Readers. Minnich, Harvey C., ed. LC 79-76081. 1969. Repr. of 1936 ed. 37.00x (ISBN 0-8103-3854-8). Gale.

McGuigan, F. J. Experimental Psychology: Methods of Research. 4th ed. (Illus.). 416p. 1983. 23.95 (ISBN 0-13-295188-6). P-H.

McGuigan, Frank J. Experimental Psychology: A Methodological Approach. 3rd ed. LC 77-25206. (Illus.). 1978. ref. ed. 22.95 o.p. (ISBN 0-13-295162-2). P-H.

McGuigan, James R. & Moyer, R. Charles. Managerial Economics. 3rd ed. (Illus.). 668p. 1982. text ed. 23.95 (ISBN 0-314-69666-0); write for info. study guide (ISBN 0-314-71110-4). West Pub.

McGuigan, Patrick B. & Rader, Randall R., eds. Criminal Justice Reform. 1983. 14.00 (ISBN 0-89526-841-8). Regnery-Gateway.

McGuiness, Kenneth C. How to Take a Case Before the National Labor Relations Board. 4th ed. LC 74-32565. (Illus.). 558p. 1976. 20.00 (ISBN 0-87179-211-7). BNA.

McGuinn, S., jt. auth. see Watson, H. W.

McGuinness, B. F., tr. see Wittgenstein, Ludwig.

McGuinness, William J. & Stein, Benjamin. Building Technology: Mechanical & Electrical Systems. LC 76-14961. 1977. text ed. 37.95 (ISBN 0-471-58433-9). Wiley.

McGuire, jt. auth. see Rayshich, Hale.

McGuire, Brian P. The Cistercians in Denmark: Their Attitudes, Roles, & Functions in Medieval Society. (Cistercian Studies: No. 35). 1982. 35.00 (ISBN 0-87907-835-9). Cistercian Pubns.

McGuire, Carl, jt. auth. see El Mallakh, Ragaei.

McGuire, Chester C. International Housing Policies: A Comparative Analysis. LC 80-8815. 272p. 1981. 27.95x (ISBN 0-669-04385-0). Lexington Bks.

McGuire, Christine H., et al. Construction & Use of Written Simulations. LC 76-50475. 1976. pap. text ed. 21.00 o.p. (ISBN 0-15-800113-3). HarBraceJ.

McGuire, David C. Evaluation of Music Faculty in Higher Education. 24p. 1979. 2.00 (ISBN 0-686-37914-4). Music Ed.

McGuire, E. Patrick. Customer Relations in Financial Institutions. (Report No. 761). (Illus., Orig.). 1979. pap. 15.00 (ISBN 0-8237-0197-2). Conference Bd.

--Evaluating New-Product Proposals. (Report Ser: No. 604). 108p. (Orig.). 1973. pap. 22.50 (ISBN 0-8237-0017-8). Conference Bd.

McGuire, E. Patrick, ed. Managing Product Recalls. (Report Ser: No. 632). 1974. pap. 17.50 (ISBN 0-8237-0037-2). Conference Bd.

McGuire, Francis, jt. ed. see Osgood, Nancy J.

McGuire, Gertrude M., jt. ed. see Hudson, Randolph H.

McGuire, Hilary. Hopie & the Los Homes Gang. (Illus.). 1978. pap. 1.95 o.p. (ISBN 0-8189-1150-6). Alba.

MacGuire, J. W., jt. auth. see Parker, Harry.

McGuire, James E. & Lee, Jasper S. Advertising & Display: Promotion in Agribusiness. (Career Preparation for Agriculture-Agribusiness). (Illus.). 1979. pap. text ed. 6.96 (ISBN 0-07-045129-X); activity guide 4.96 (ISBN 0-07-045130-3). teacher's manual & key 3.00 (ISBN 0-07-045131-1). McGraw.

McGuire, Jerry & Warner, Emily H. Learning How to Fly an Airplane. (Modern Aviation Ser.). (Illus.). 1979. 9.95 (ISBN 0-8306-9827-2); pap. 5.95 o.p. (ISBN 0-8306-2253-5, 2253). TAB Bks.

McGuire, Joseph W. Business & Society. 1963. pap. 3.95 (ISBN 0-07-045097-8, SP). McGraw.

--Theories of Business Behavior. LC 82-15550. xix, 268p. 1982. Repr. of 1964 ed. lib. bdg. 35.00x (ISBN 0-313-23567-8, MCTH). Greenwood.

McGuire, M. J., jt. ed. see Suffet, I. H.

McGuire, Meredith B. Pentecostal Catholics: Power, Charisma, & Order in a Religious Movement. 270p. 1982. 27.95 (ISBN 0-87722-235-5). Temple U Pr.

McGuire, Paula. It Won't Happen to Me. LC 82-72754. 224p. 1983. 14.95 (ISBN 0-440-04099-X). Delacorte.

--It Won't Happen to Me: Teenagers Talk about Pregnancy. 1983. pap. 6.95 (ISBN 0-440-53845-9, Delta). Dell.

McGuire, Peter J., jt. auth. see Leonard, David C.

McGuire, Phillip. Taps for a Jim Crow Army. LC 82-22689. 250p. 1983. text ed. 22.50 (ISBN 0-87436-024-2); pap. text ed. 12.75 (ISBN 0-87436-041-2). ABC-Clio.

McGuire, S. W., jt. auth. see DeRose, Peter.

McGuire, Sarah. The Daughters of the House. 256p. 1981. 9.95 o.p. (ISBN 0-312-18344-5). St Martin.

McGuire, Thomas. Financing Psychotherapy: Costs Effects & Public Policy. 264p. 1981. prof ref 30.00x (ISBN 0-88410-711-6). Ballinger Pub.

McGuire, W. L., et al, eds. Estrogen Receptors in Human Breast Cancer. LC 74-14484. 298p. 1975. 30.00 (ISBN 0-89004-015-X). Raven.

McGuire, W. L., jt. ed. see Cavalli, F.

McGuire, William. Steel Structures. 1968. text ed. 45.00 (ISBN 0-13-846493-6). P-H.

McGuire, William & Gallagher, Richard H. Matrix Structural Analysis. LC 78-8471. 1979. text ed. 42.50 (ISBN 0-471-03059-7). Wiley.

McGuire, William, ed. Dream Analysis: C. J. Jung Seminars, Vol. 1. LC 82-42787. (Bollingen Ser.: No. XCIX-1). (Illus.). 500p. 1983. 30.00 (ISBN 0-691-09896-4). Princeton U Pr.

McGuire, William L., ed. Hormones, Receptors, & Breast Cancer. LC 77-90595. (Progress in Cancer Research & Therapy Ser.: Vol. 10). 383p. 1978. 34.50 (ISBN 0-89004-261-6). Raven.

McGuire, William L., et al, eds. Progesterone Receptors in Normal & Neoplastic Tissues. LC 77-72065. (Progress in Cancer Research & Therapy Ser.: Vol. 4). 357p. 1977. 34.50 (ISBN 0-89004-163-6). Raven.

McGuiston, Frank W., Jr. & Shoemaker, Robert S. Gold & Silver Cyanidation Plant Practice. McLaughlin, Donald H., ed. (Illus.). 263p. 1981. 39.00x (ISBN 0-89520-281-6). Soc Mining Eng.

McGurdy, David, jt. auth. see Spradley, James P.

McGurk, H., ed. Ecological Factors in Human Development. LC 76-30321. (Illus.). 1977. 38.50 (ISBN 0-7204-0488-6, North-Holland). Elsevier.

McGurk, Harry. Growing & Changing. (Essential Psychology Ser.). 1975. pap. 4.50x (ISBN 0-416-82830-2). Methuen Inc.

McGurk, Harry, ed. Issues in Childhood Social Development. (Psychology in Progress Ser.). 1979. 25.00x (ISBN 0-416-70560-X); pap. 12.95x (ISBN 0-416-71500-1). Methuen Inc.

Mach, Ernst. The Science of Mechanics. 6th ed. McCormack, T. J., tr. from Ger. (Illus.). 634p. 1960. pap. 12.00x (ISBN 0-87548-202-3). Open Court.

Mach, Kaye, et al. College Typewriting: A Mastery Approach. Incl. Beginning. pap. text ed. 11.95 (ISBN 0-574-20540-3, 13-3590); beg. working papers 3.95 (ISBN 0-574-20541-1, 13-3541); Intermediate. pap. text ed. 12.95 (ISBN 0-574-20542-X, 13-3592); instructor's guide 3.25 (ISBN 0-574-20547-0, 13-3547). Set Of 45. trans. masters 27.50 (ISBN 0-574-20548-9); intermediate working papers 6.95 (ISBN 0-574-20543-8, 13-3543); Advanced. text ed. 13.95 (ISBN 0-574-20655-8, 13-3655); advanced working papers 6.95 (ISBN 0-574-20657-4, 13-3657); model answer key 3.95 (ISBN 0-574-20658-2, 13-3658). pap. 150.00 set (ISBN 0-686-66313-6). SRA.

Machado, Antonio. Juan de Mairena: Epigrams, Maxims, Memoranda, & Memoirs of an Apocryphal Professor. Belitt, Ben, tr. (Illus.). 1963. 15.95x o.p. (ISBN 0-520-00792-1); pap. 1.50 (ISBN 0-520-00794-8, CAL89). U of Cal Pr.

--Times Alone: Twelve Poems from Soledades. Bly, Robert, tr. from Span. 44p. 1982. 50.00x (ISBN 0-915308-37-1); pap. 5.00 (ISBN 0-915308-38-X). Graywolf.

Machado, Jeanne. Early Childhood Experiences in Language Arts. LC 78-55972. 1980. pap. 11.20 (ISBN 0-8273-1573-2); instructor's guide 3.75 (ISBN 0-8273-1574-0). Delmar.

Machado, Manuel A., Jr. Aftosa: A Historical Survey of Foot & Mouth Disease & Inter-American Relations. LC 69-11317. 1969. 29.50x (ISBN 0-87395-040-2). State U NY Pr.

Machado de Assis, Joaquim M. Counselor Ayres' Memorial. Caldwell, Helen, tr. from Port. LC 72-187876. 1973. 19.95x (ISBN 0-520-02227-0); pap. 5.95 (ISBN 0-520-04775-3, CAL 587). U of Cal Pr.

Machal, Jan see MacCulloch, John A.

MacHale, John. A Ballad-History of Ireland. 1983. pap. 5.95 (ISBN 0-934906-01-7). R J Liederbach.

McHale, John. Changing Information Environment. (Westview Environmental Studies: Vol. 4). 1976. lib. bdg. 18.00 o.p. (ISBN 0-89158-623-7). Westview.

McHale, John & McHale, Magda C. The Futures Directory. LC 76-51285. 1977. lib. bdg. 52.50x o.p. (ISBN 0-89158-224-X). Westview.

McHale, Magda C., jt. auth. see McHale, John.

McHale, Mary C., jt. auth. see McHale, Thomas R.

McHale, T. J. & Witzke, P. T. Advanced Algebra. (Milwaukee Area Technical College Mathematics Ser.). 1972. pap. 17.95 (ISBN 0-201-04633-4); test bklt. 3.95 (ISBN 0-201-04634-2). A-W.

--Arithmetic Module Series: One Volume Non-Programmed Edition. 400p. 1976. pap. text ed. 16.95 (ISBN 0-201-04757-8); tests 4.95 (ISBN 0-686-77108-7). A-W.

--Arithmetic Modules. 125p. 1975. module 1 whole nos. 6.95 (ISBN 0-201-04751-9); module 2 fractions 6.95 (ISBN 0-201-04752-7); module 3 decimal nos. 6.95 (ISBN 0-201-04753-5); module 4 perfect ratio 6.95 (ISBN 0-201-04754-3); module 5 6.95 (ISBN 0-201-04756-X); test bklt 4.95 (ISBN 0-201-04758-6); ans. keys avail. (ISBN 0-685-52163-X). A-W.

--Basic Algebra. (Milwaukee Area Technical College Mathematics Ser.). 1971. pap. 17.95 (ISBN 0-201-04625-3); test bklt. 3.95 (ISBN 0-201-04591-5). A-W.

--Basic Trigonometry. (Milwaukee Area Technical College Mathematics Ser.). 1971. pap. 17.95 (ISBN 0-201-04631-8); test bklt. 3.95 (ISBN 0-201-04632-6). A-W.

McHale, Thomas J. & Witzke, Paul T. Applied Algebra I. 1979. text ed. 17.95 (ISBN 0-201-04767-5); tests 4.00 (ISBN 0-201-04768-3). A-W.

--Applied Algebra II. 1980. pap. text ed. 16.95 (ISBN 0-201-04775-6); test booklet 3.50 (ISBN 0-201-04776-4). A-W.

--Calculation & Calculators. 1977. pap. text ed. 17.95 (ISBN 0-201-04771-3); tests avail. (ISBN 0-201-04772-1). A-W.

McHale, Thomas J., et al. Introductory Algebra: Programmed. 544p. 1977. text ed. 17.95 (ISBN 0-201-04747-0). A-W.

McHale, Thomas R. & McHale, Mary C. Early American-Philippine Trade: The Journal of Nathaniel Bowditch in Manila, 1796. (Monograph Ser.: No. 2). viii, 63p. 1962. 4.75x (ISBN 0-686-30905-7). Yale U SE Asia.

McHale, Tom. Dear Friends. 384p. 1983. pap. 3.50 (ISBN 0-425-05866-2). Berkley Pub.

McHale, Vincent & Skowronski, Sharon, eds. Political Parties of Europe, 2 vols. LC 82-15408. (Greenwood Encyclopedia of the World's Political Parties). (Illus.). 1983. Set. lib. bdg. 95.00 (ISBN 0-313-21405-0, MPP/). Greenwood.

Machamer, Peter K. & Turnbull, Robert G., eds. Studies in Perception: Interrelations in the History of Philosophy & Science. LC 77-10857. (Illus.). 1978. 30.00x (ISBN 0-8142-0244-6). Ohio St U Pr.

Machan, Tibor, jt. ed. see Lucey, Kenneth.

Machan, Tibor R. & Johnson, M. Bruce. Regulation & Deregulation: Economic Policy & Justice. (Pacific Institute). 1983. price not set prof ref (ISBN 0-88410-928-3). Ballinger Pub.

Machanick, Sonia. Sound Travels Too, Bks. 1-4. pap. text ed. 3.50x ea. o.p.; Bk. 1. pap. text ed. (ISBN 0-435-01460-9); Bk. 2. pap. text ed. (ISBN 0-435-01461-7); Bk. 3. pap. text ed. (ISBN 0-435-01462-5); Bk. 4. pap. text ed. (ISBN 0-435-01463-3). Heinemann Ed.

Machant, Douglas J. & Nyirjesy, Istvan, eds. Breast Disease: Proceedings of an International Symposium. (Illus.). 336p. 1979. 29.50 (ISBN 0-8089-1177-5). Grune.

McHardy, A. K., ed. The Church in London, 1375-1392. 1977. 50.00x (ISBN 0-686-96608-2, Pub by London Rec Soc England). State Mutual Bk.

McHargue, Georgess. Funny Bananas. 1976. pap. 0.95 o.p. (ISBN 0-440-42771-1, YB). Dell.

--Meet the Vampire. Gammell, Stephen, tr. (Eerie Ser.). (Illus.). 144p. (YA) (gr. 7-12). 1983. pap. 1.95 (ISBN 0-440-96180-7, LFL). Dell.

--Meet the Werewolf. (Eerie Ser.). (Illus.). (YA) (gr. 7-12). 1983. pap. 1.95 (ISBN 0-440-96182-3, LFL). Dell.

--Mummies. LC 72-2324. (Illus.). 160p. (gr. 5-9). 1972. 9.57i o.p. (ISBN 0-397-31516-3, JBL-J). Har-Row.

--The Talking Table Mystery. (Illus.). (gr. 1-4). Date not set. pap. 1.95 (ISBN 0-440-48786-2, YB). Dell.

McHargue, Georgess, tr. see Schouten, Alet.

Machem, J. Gresham. The New Testament: An Introduction to Its History & Literature. 1976. 9.95 (ISBN 0-85151-240-2). Banner of Truth.

Machen, J. Gresham. New Testament Greek for Beginners. 1923. text ed. 21.95x (ISBN 0-02-373480-9). Macmillan.

--Virgin Birth of Christ. 427p. 1958. Repr. of 1930 ed. 13.95 (ISBN 0-227-67630-0). Attic Pr.

--Virgin Birth of Christ. (Twin Brooks Ser). 1967. pap. 9.95 (ISBN 0-8010-5885-6). Baker Bk.

McHenry, Albert L., jt. auth. see McCurdy, Lyle B.

McHenry, Dean, jt. auth. see Ferguson, John.

McHenry, Dean E., jt. auth. see Ferguson, John H.

McHenry, Dean E., Jr. Ujama Villages in Tanzania: A Bibliography. 69p. 1982. pap. 12.50 (ISBN 0-686-97518-9). Holmes & Meier.

McHenry, Donald. United States Firms in South Africa. (African Humanities Ser.). 74p. (Orig.). 1975. pap. text ed. 4.00 (ISBN 0-941934-15-2). Ind U Afro-Amer Arts.

McHenry, J. Patrick. Short History of Mexico. 6.00 (ISBN 0-8446-2261-3). Peter Smith.

McHenry, Lawrence C., Jr., ed. Garrison's History of Neurology. (Illus.). 568p. 1969. 22.75x (ISBN 0-398-01261-X). C C Thomas.

McHenry, Lawrence M., Jr. Cerebral Circulation & Stroke. LC 77-73722. 320p. 1978. 22.50 o.p. (ISBN 0-87527-163-4). Green.

McHenry, Ruth W. Self-Teaching Tests in Arithmetic for Nurses. 10th. ed. LC 80-10859. (Illus.). 184p. 1980. pap. text ed. 12.95 (ISBN 0-8016-2505-X). Mosby.

McHenry, Sherry, jt. ed. see L'Abate, Luciano.

Machi, Antonio, tr. see De Finetti, Bruno.

Machiavelli, Niccolo. The Discourses, 2 vols. Walker, Leslie J., tr. 1975. Set. 45.00 (ISBN 0-7100-8076-X); 24.50x ea. Routledge & Kegan.

--Machiavelli's Thoughts on the Management of Men. (A Human Development Library Bk.). (Illus.). 112p. 1983. 49.85 (ISBN 0-86654-053-9). Inst Econ Finan.

--Prince. 1978. Repr. of 1908 ed. 9.95x (ISBN 0-460-00280-5, Evman). Biblio Dist.

--Prince. 1952. pap. 1.50 (ISBN 0-451-62123-9, MW2123, Ment). NAL.

--Il Principe (De Principatibus) Richardson, Brian, ed. & intro. by. 153p. (Orig., Ital.). 1979. pap. 6.95x (ISBN 0-7190-0742-9, Pub. by Manchester England). S F Vanni.

Machiavelli, Noccolo. The Prince. Donno, Daniel, ed. (Bantam Classics Ser.). 146p. (gr. 9-12). 1981. pap. 1.50 (ISBN 0-553-21029-7). Bantam.

Machin, Howard. The Prefect in French Public Administration. LC 76-27185. 1977. 26.00x (ISBN 0-312-63805-1). St Martin.

Machin, Noel see Allen, W. S.

Machina, Kenton. Basic Applied Logic. 1981. text ed. 20.95x (ISBN 0-673-15359-2). Scott F.

Machlachlan, Lewis. God Face to Face. 160p. 1968. pap. 3.50 (ISBN 0-227-67728-5). Attic Pr.

Machleder, Herbert I., ed. Vascular Disorders of the Upper Extremity. LC 82-84504. 1983. price not set monograph (ISBN 0-87993-193-0). Futura Pub.

Machlin, Edda S. The Classic Cuisine of the Italian Jews: Traditional Recipes & Menus & a Memoir of a Vanished Way of Life. 256p. 1981. 19.95 (ISBN 0-686-30959-6, An Everest House Book). Dodd.

Machlin, Evangeline. Teaching Speech for the Stage: A Manual for Classroom Instruction. 1980. pap. 3.95 (ISBN 0-87830-573-4). Theatre Arts.

Machlin, Lawrence J., ed. see New York Academy of Sciences Annals, Nov. 11-13, 1981.

Machlin, Milt. Pipeline. (Orig.). 1976. pap. 2.50 o.s.i. (ISBN 0-515-05408-9). Jove Pubns.

Machlin, Milt & Beckley, Tim. UFO. (Illus.). 192p. 1981. pap. 8.95 (ISBN 0-8256-3182-3, Quick Fox). Putnam Pub Group.

Machlis, Joseph. The Enjoyment of Music. 4th ed. LC 76-62482. (Illus.). 1977. 19.95x (ISBN 0-393-09118-X); shorter 19.45x (ISBN 0-393-09125-2); workbk 5.95x (ISBN 0-393-09122-8). Norton.

--Introduction to Contemporary Music. 2nd ed. (Illus.). 1979. text ed. 19.95x (ISBN 0-393-09026-4); instructor's guide o.p. free (ISBN 0-393-95023-9). Norton.

Machlup, Fritz, ed. see Congress of the International Economic Association, 4th, Budapest, Hungary.

Macho, Linda. Crocheting Ruffled Doilies. (Knitting, Crocheting, Tatting Ser.). (Illus.). 48p. (Orig.). 1983. pap. 2.25 (ISBN 0-486-24400-8). Dover.

Macho, Linda, ed. Knitting Fashion Sweaters Forties. (Knitting, Crocheting, Tatting Ser.). (Illus.). 48p. (Orig.). 1983. pap. 2.95 (ISBN 0-486-24409-1). Dover.

--Treasury of Pineapple Designs for Crocheting. (Illus.). 48p. (Orig.). 1983. pap. 2.25 (ISBN 0-486-24494-6). Dover.

Machol, R. E., jt. ed. see Ladany, S. P.

Machol, Robert E., et al. System Engineering Handbook. 1965. 59.50 o.p. (ISBN 0-07-039371-0, P&RB). McGraw.

Macholoitz, Marilyn. Workaholics: Living with Them, Working with Them. 1981. pap. 2.95 (ISBN 0-451-61971-4, ME1971, Ment). NAL.

McHose, Allen I. Contrapuntal Harmonic Technique of the Eighteenth Century. 1947. 25.95 (ISBN 0-13-171843-6). P-H.

MacHovec, Frank J., ed. Nostradamus: His Prophecies for the Future. pap. 3.95 o.p. (ISBN 0-686-91688-3). Peter Pauper.

Machover, M., jt. auth. see Bell, J.

Machu, W. Handbook of Electropainting Technology. 1980. 150.50x (ISBN 0-901150-06-1, Pub. by Electrochemical Scotland). State Mutual Bk.

McHugh. Young People Talk About Death. (gr. 7 up). 1980. PLB 8.90 (ISBN 0-531-02884-4, C10). Watts.

McHugh, Elisabet. Raising a Mother Isn't Easy. LC 82-11714. 160p. (gr. 5-7). 1983. 9.00 (ISBN 0-688-01827-0). Greenwillow.

McHugh, Gretchen. The Hungry Hiker's Book of Good Cooking. (Illus.). 288p. 1982. 17.95 (ISBN 0-394-51261-8); pap. 8.95 (ISBN 0-394-70774-5). Knopf.

McHugh, James, jt. auth. see Carlsen, Robert.

McHugh, James F., jt. auth. see Carlsen, Robert D.

McHugh, John J. Finding a Job. LC 80-18455. (Practical Job Skills Ser.). (gr. 9-12). 1981. pap. 3.95 (ISBN 0-88436-783-5, 25252); wkbk 2.95 (ISBN 0-88436-784-3, 25652). EMC.

McHugh, John J., Jr. Filling Out Job Application Forms. LC 80-18255. (Practical Job Skills Ser.). (gr. 9-12). 1980. pap. 3.95 (ISBN 0-88436-785-1, 25253); wkbk 2.95 (ISBN 0-88436-786-X, 25653). EMC.

--Getting Ready to Work. LC 81-5447. (Practical Job Skills Ser.). (gr. 9-12). 1982. pap. text ed. 3.95 (ISBN 0-88436-781-9, 25251); wkbk. 2.95 (ISBN 0-88436-782-7, 25651). EMC.

--Interviewing for Jobs. LC 80-18230. (Practical Job Skills Ser.). (gr. 9-12). 1981. pap. 3.95 (ISBN 0-88436-787-8, 25254); wkbk 2.95 (ISBN 0-88436-788-6, 25654). EMC.

--Keeping & Changing Jobs. LC 81-5585. (Practical Job Skills Ser.). (gr. 9-12). 1982. pap. text ed. 3.95 (ISBN 0-88436-791-6, 25256); wkbk. 2.95 (ISBN 0-88436-792-4, 25656). EMC.

--Starting a New Job. LC 81-7819. (Practical Job Skills Ser.). (gr. 9-12). 1982. pap. text ed. 3.95 (ISBN 0-88436-789-4, 25255); wkbk. 2.95 (ISBN 0-88436-790-8, 25655). EMC.

McHugh, Joseph & Harris, Latif. Journey to the Moon: Plato & Dore. LC 74-9757. (Illus.). 1974. pap. 4.95 o.p. (ISBN 0-912310-73-1). Celestial Arts.

McHugh, Paul. Prostitution & Victorian Social Reform: The Campaign Against the Contagious Diseases Acts. 1980. 29.00 (ISBN 0-312-65211-9). St Martin.

McHugh, Peter, et al. On the Beginning of Social Inquiry. 1974. 18.95x (ISBN 0-7100-7765-3); pap. 7.95 (ISBN 0-7100-7766-1). Routledge & Kegan.

McHugh, Stuart D. Knock on the Nursery Door: Tales of the Dickens Children. 1973. 9.95 o.p. (ISBN 0-7181-1031-5). Transatlantic.

McHugh, Thomas P. The Complete Weight Training Manual. 168p. 1982. pap. text ed. 9.95 (ISBN 0-8403-2751-X). Kendall-Hunt.

McHugh, Vincent. Caleb Catlum's America. LC 71-156927. 1971. Repr. of 1936 ed. 34.00x (ISBN 0-8103-3717-7). Gale.

McHugh, Vincent, jt. tr. see Kwock, C. H.

Machwe, Prabhakar. Four Decades of Indian Literature. LC 76-901763. 1976. 10.00x o.p. (ISBN 0-88386-806-7). South Asia Bks.

Maciariello, Joseph A. Dynamic Benefit-Cost Analysis. LC 75-522. (Illus.). 192p. 1975. 22.95 o.p. (ISBN 0-669-98020-X). Lexington Bks.

--Program-Management Control Systems. LC 77-20030. (Systems & Controls for Financial Management Ser.). 1978. 42.95 (ISBN 0-471-01566-0, Pub. by Wiley-Interscience). Wiley.

Maciel, Gary E., et al. Chemistry. 1978. text ed. 29.95x (ISBN 0-669-84830-1); instr's manual 1.95 (ISBN 0-669-99945-8); lab manual 12.95 (ISBN 0-669-00999-7); study guide 8.95x (ISBN 0-669-01000-6); solutions manual 4.95 (ISBN 0-669-01027-8). Heath.

McIlhany, William H., 2nd. The Tax-Exempt Scandal: America's Leftist Foundations. 1980. 20.00 o.p. (ISBN 0-87000-380-1, Arlington Hse). Crown.

MacIlquham, Frances. Complete Fish & Game Cookery of North America. (Illus.). 304p. 1983. 29.95 (ISBN 0-8329-0284-5). Winchester Pr.

McIlrath, T. J., ed. see AIP Conference, 90th, Boulder, 1982.

McIlroy, Gary. Employers Manual for Health Promotion. Travis, Marlene, ed. (Illus.). 1981. 129.00 o.p. (ISBN 0-941344-01-0). Healthstyles Pubns.

McIlroy, Kenneth D. Pragma, the Simplistic Computer Application Design Methodology. LC 82-179537. (Illus.). 134p. (Orig.). 1982. pap. 12.95 (ISBN 0-9608426-0-8). Pragma Applications.

McIlvain, John. Worth Avenue. 288p. 1983. 16.95 (ISBN 0-399-31020-7). Seaview Bks.

McIlvain, Thomas. Tales of Freddy Fox. 1978. 5.95 o.p. (ISBN 0-533-03318-7). Vantage.

McIlwain, C. H. Constitutionalism & the Changing World. 1969. 44.50 (ISBN 0-521-07776-1). Cambridge U Pr.

McIlwain, Charles H. The American Revolution: A Constitutional Interpretation. LC 74-166335. (Era of the American Revolution Ser.). 198p. 1973. Repr. of 1923 ed. lib. bdg. 27.50 (ISBN 0-306-70249-5). Da Capo.

McIlwain, K., jt. auth. see Pender, H.

McIlwaine, Ia & McIlwaine, John, eds. Bibliography & Reading: A Festschrift in Honour of Ronald Staveley. LC 82-21489. 180p. 1983. 15.00 (ISBN 0-8108-1601-6). Scarecrow.

McIlwaine, John, jt. ed. see McIlwaine, Ia.

McIlwraith, C. Wayne, jt. auth. see Turner, A. Simon.

McInerney, Judith W. Judge Benjamin: The Superdog Secret. LC 82-48752. (Illus.). 144p. (gr. 3-7). 1983. 9.95 (ISBN 0-8234-0484-6). Holiday.

McInerny, Constance, tr. see Paredi, Angelo.

McInerny, Paul M., jt. auth. see Thomsen, Gregory.

McInerny, Ralph. Connolly's Life. LC 82-73021. 256p. 1983. 13.95 (ISBN 0-689-11356-0). Atheneum.

--Ethica Thomistica: The Moral Philosophy of Thomas Aquinas. 1982. pap. 8.95x (ISBN 0-8132-0561-1) Cath U Pr.

--A Loss of Patients. (A Fathers Dowling Mystery Ser.). 256p. 1982. 10.95 (ISBN 0-8149-0864-0). Vanguard.

--St. Thomas Aquinas. (World Author Ser.: Italy: No. 408). 1977. lib. bdg. 8.95 o.p. (ISBN 0-8057-6248-5, Twayne). G K Hall.

McInerny, Ralph, tr. see Paredi, Angelo.

McInery, Ralph. Rhyme & Reason: St. Thomas & Modes of Discourse. LC 81-80234. (Aquinas Lecture Ser.). 84p. 1981. 7.95 (ISBN 0-87462-148-8). Marquette.

Macinko, George, jt. ed. see Platt, Rutherford H.

McInnes, Betty. Controlling the Spread of Infection: A Programmed Presentation. 2nd ed. LC 76-48945. (Illus.). 123p. 1977. pap. text ed. 9.00 o.p. (ISBN 0-8016-3334-6). Mosby.

--The Vital Signs with Related Clinical Measurements: A Programmed Approach. 3rd ed. (Illus.). 150p. 1979. pap. 12.50 (ISBN 0-8016-3333-8). Mosby.

MacInnes, C. Malcolm. Bristol: Gateway of Empire. LC 68-23841. (Illus.). Repr. of 1939 ed. 25.00x (ISBN 0-678-05609-9). Kelley.

MacInnes, Colin. Absolute Beginners. 208p. 1980. 13.95 (ISBN 0-8052-8039-1, Pub. by Allison & Busby England); pap. 5.95 (ISBN 0-8052-8038-3). Schocken.

MacInnes, Helen. Agent in Place. 1976. Repr. lib. bdg. 17.95 o.p. (ISBN 0-8161-6401-0, Large Print Bks). G K Hall.

--Assignment in Brittany. LC 42-17993. 1971. 6.95 o.p. (ISBN 0-15-109620-1). HarBraceJ.

--Cloak of Darkness. 1982. 13.95 (ISBN 0-15-118171-3). HarBraceJ.

--Cloak of Darkness. (General Ser.). 1983. lib. bdg. 18.95 (ISBN 0-8161-3486-3, Large Print Bks). G K Hall.

--I & My True Love. LC 52-13765. 6.95 o.p. (ISBN 0-15-143403-4). HarBraceJ.

--Pray for a Brave Heart. LC 55-5241. 1955. 7.50 o.p. (ISBN 0-15-173901-3). HarBraceJ.

MacInnes, Hugh. Turbochargers. LC 81-83821. (Illus.). 1976. pap. 7.95 (ISBN 0-912656-49-2). H P Bks.

McInnes, James. Video in Education & Training. (Illus.). 192p. 1980. 19.95 (ISBN 0-240-51071-2). Focal Pr.

McInnes, John. The Chocolate Chip Mystery. LC 72-1773. (Venture Ser). (Illus.). 64p. (gr. 2). 1972. PLB 6.89 (ISBN 0-8116-6964-5). Garrard.

--Drat the Dragon. LC 72-5285. (Venture Ser). (Illus.). 40p. (gr. 1). 1973. PLB 6.69 (ISBN 0-8116-6720-0). Garrard.

--The Ghost Said Boo. LC 73-20392. (Easy Venture Ser.). (Illus.). (gr. k-1). 1974. PLB 6.69 (ISBN 0-8116-6055-9). Garrard.

--Goodnight Painted Pony. LC 76-155572. (Venture Ser). (Illus.). (gr. 1). 1971. PLB 6.69 (ISBN 0-8116-6707-3). Garrard.

--Have You Ever Seen a Monster? LC 73-20394. (Easy Venture Ser). (Illus.). 32p. (gr. k-2). 1974. PLB 6.69 (ISBN 0-8116-6054-0). Garrard.

--How Pedro Got His Name. LC 73-22082. (Easy Venture Ser). (Illus.). 32p. (gr. k-2). 1974. PLB 6.69 (ISBN 0-8116-6064-8). Garrard.

--Leo Lion Paints It Red. LC 73-21586. (Easy Venture Ser). (Illus.). 32p. (gr. k-2). 1974. PLB 6.69 (ISBN 0-8116-6060-5). Garrard.

--On with the Circus. LC 72-5283. (Venture Ser). (Illus.). 40p. (gr. 1). 1973. PLB 6.69 (ISBN 0-8116-6722-7). Garrard.

--Who Ever Heard of a Tiger in a Tree. LC 72-155571. (Venture Ser). (Illus.). (gr. 1). 1971. PLB 6.69 (ISBN 0-8116-6706-5). Garrard.

McInnes, John, jt. auth. see Ryckman, John.

MacInnes, Margo. A Guide to the Campus of the University of Michigan. LC 77-95134. (Illus.). 1978. pap. 4.95 (ISBN 0-472-61300-6). U of Mich Pr.

McInnes, Mary E., ed. Essentials of Communicable Disease. 2nd ed. LC 74-28353. 402p. 1975. 14.95 o.p. (ISBN 0-8016-2545-9). Mosby.

McInnis, Donna, ed. see Junior League of Nashville.

McInnis, Edgar, jt. auth. see Soward, Frederic H.

McInnis, Philip. Decoding Keys for Reading Success. (gr. k-9). 1981. 429.00 (ISBN 0-8027-9129-8); Primary Level. 145.00 (ISBN 0-8027-9130-1); Intermediate Level. 142.00 (ISBN 0-8027-9131-X); Advanced Level. 142.00 (ISBN 0-8027-9132-8); manual 9.90 (ISBN 0-8027-9133-6). Walker & Co.

McIntire, C. T., ed. God, History & Historians: Modern Christian Views of History. 1977. pap. 9.95 (ISBN 0-19-502204-1, GB496, GB). Oxford U Pr.

Macintire, Elizabeth J., tr. see Gad, Carl.

McIntire, Robert H., jt. auth. see Rogers, Rolf E.

McIntire, Thomas C. Software Interpreters for Microcomputers. LC 78-6608. 1978. text ed. 32.95 (ISBN 0-471-02678-6). Wiley.

McIntosh, jt. ed. see Rock.

Macintosh, A. A. Isaiah XXI: A Palimpsest. LC 79-41375. 160p. 1980. 32.50 (ISBN 0-521-22943-X). Cambridge U Pr.

McIntosh, C. Eliphas Levi & the French Occult Revival. 6.95 (ISBN 0-87728-252-8). Weiser.

McIntosh, C. Alison. Population Policy in Western Europe: Responses to Low Fertility in France, Sweden, & West Germany. LC 82-5840. (Illus.). 288p. 1983. 25.00 (ISBN 0-87332-226-6). M E Sharpe.

McIntosh, Carol P. & Cole, Carole O. What Price Zion. 200p. 1983. 6.95 (ISBN 0-87747-927-5). Deseret Bk.

McIntosh, D. H. Meteorological Glossary. (Illus.). 1972. 25.00 o.p. (ISBN 0-8206-0228-0). Chem Pub.

Macintosh, Duncan. Chinese Blue & White Porcelain. LC 77-70845. 1977. 20.50 (ISBN 0-8048-1208-X). C E Tuttle.

Macintosh, H. G. Assessment & the Secondary School Teacher. (Students Library of Education Ser.). 1976. text ed. 14.95x (ISBN 0-7100-8472-2); pap. 4.95 (ISBN 0-7100-8473-0). Routledge & Kegan.

McIntosh, Hugh. Is Christ Infallible & the Bible True? 1981. lib. bdg. 27.00 (ISBN 0-86524-076-0, 8603). Klock & Klock.

McIntosh, J. Richard & Satir, Birgit H., eds. Modern Cell Biology: Spatial Organization of Eukaryotic Cells. (Modern Cell Biology Ser.: Vol. 2). 550p. 1983. 50.00 (ISBN 0-8451-3301-2). A R Liss.

McIntosh, J. Rieman. A History of the Elkridge Fox Hunting Club, the Elkridge Hounds, the Elkridge-Harford Hunt Club, 1878 to 1978. 121p. 1978. pap. 15.00 (ISBN 0-686-36669-7). Md Hist.

McIntosh, James C., tr. from Fr. The Committed Observer, Raymond Aron: Interviews with Jean-Louis Missika & Dominque Wolton. 1983. 17.00. Regnery-Gateway.

McIntosh, Mary, jt. auth. see Barrett, Michele.

McIntosh, N. A., jt. auth. see Woodley, A.

McIntosh, Naomi E., et al. A Degree of Difference: The Open Uninversity of the United Kingdom. LC 77-23034. (Praeger Special Studies). 1977. 33.95 o.p. (ISBN 0-03-040341-3). Praeger.

MacIntosh, Olding C. Use & Abuse of Diagnostic Services: The Canadian Experience. 1982. text ed. 19.50 (ISBN 0-88831-130-3). Eden Pr.

McIntosh, Peter C. Physical Education in England Since 1800. 2nd ed. (Illus.). 320p. 1974. pap. 13.50x (ISBN 0-7135-0689-X). Intl Pubns Serv.

McIntosh, R. P., ed. Phytosociology. LC 77-20258. (Benchmark Papers in Ecology: Vol. 6). 388p. 1978. 41.50 (ISBN 0-87933-312-X). Hutchinson Ross.

MacIntyre, A. Logic Colloquium 1977. (Studies in Logic & the Foundations of Mathematics: Vol. 96). 1978. 55.50 (ISBN 0-444-85178-X, North Holland). Elsevier.

MacIntyre, Alasdair, jt. ed. see Hauerwas, Stanley.

McIntyre, Alice. Role Playing: A Real Estate Training Tool. Gerth, Dawn M., ed. LC 82-83133. (Illus.). 151p. (Orig.). 1982. pap. text ed. 14.95 (ISBN 0-913652-43-1, 152). Realtors Natl.

McIntyre, Anthony. British Buildings. (Illus.). 352p. 1983. 31.50 (ISBN 0-7153-8122-9). David & Charles.

MacIntyre, C. F., tr. see Rilke, Rainer M.

McIntyre, D. A. Indoor Climate. 1980. 63.75 (ISBN 0-85334-868-5, Pub. by Applied Sci England). Elsevier.

McIntyre, Ida M. Unicorn Magic. LC 72-1922. (Venture Ser.). (Illus.). (gr. 2). 1972. PLB 6.89 (ISBN 0-8116-6965-3). Garrard.

McIntyre, James M., jt. auth. see Kolb, David A.

McIntyre, Joan. The Delicate Art of Whale Watching. LC 82-5714. (Illus.). 160p. 1982. 12.50 (ISBN 0-87156-323-1). Sierra.

McIntyre, John R., jt. ed. see Bertsch, Gary K.

McIntyre, Marie. Unify, Unify: Reflections of a Religion Teacher. LC 69-18882. 1969. 4.95 o.p. (ISBN 0-685-07671-7, 80482). Glencoe.

McIntyre, Melody. Dinosaur ABC's. (Illus.). 1981. 6.95 (ISBN 0-89051-075-X); pap. 3.95 (ISBN 0-89051-072-5); 2.95x (ISBN 0-686-85806-9). CLP Pubs.

McIntyre, Michael P. Physical Geography. 3rd ed. LC 79-19207. 1980. text ed. 28.95 (ISBN 0-471-05629-4); study guide 10.95 (ISBN 0-471-05933-1); tchrs'. manual 5.50 (ISBN 0-471-06367-3). Wiley.

McIntyre, Mildred C., ed. see Wenger, Nanette K., et al.

McIntyre, R. L. Electric Motor Control Fundamentals. 3rd ed. (Illus.). 448p. 1974. text ed. 22.95 (ISBN 0-07-045103-6, G). McGraw.

McIntyre, Ralph L. Big Ideas for Small Sunday Schools. (Teaching Helps Ser.). 64p. 1976. pap. 1.95 o.p. (ISBN 0-8010-6005-2). Baker Bk.

McIntyre, Raymond W., jt. auth. see Tedeschi, Frank P.

MacIntyre, Stuart. A Proletarian Science: Marxism in Britain, 1917-1933. LC 79-50241. (Illus.). 1980. 32.50 (ISBN 0-521-22621-X). Cambridge U Pr.

Macintyre, Sylvia, jt. ed. see Martin, G. H.

McIntyre, Vonda. Star Trek II: The Wrath of Kahn. 1982. pap. 2.50 (ISBN 0-686-97771-8). Bantam.

McIntyre, William. Christ's Cabinet. Rev. ed. 143p. 1982. Repr. of 1937 ed. 2.95 (ISBN 0-86544-017-4). Salvation Army.

MacIsaac, David. Strategic Bombing in World War II: The Story of the United States Strategic Bombing Survey. LC 75-27037. 1976. 15.00 o.s.i. (ISBN 0-8240-2025-1). Garland Pub.

MacIsaac, Fred. The Hothouse World. (YA) 1971. 6.95 (ISBN 0-685-23398-7, Avalon). Bouregy.

MacIver, Joyce. Mercy. 1976. pap. 1.95 o.p. (ISBN 0-380-00843-2, 31096). Avon.

Maciver, R. M. The Elements of Social Science. 186p. 1982. Repr. of 1921 ed. lib. bdg. 40.00 (ISBN 0-8495-3600-6). Arden Lib.

--The Ramparts We Guard. 1952. 27.50x (ISBN 0-686-51296-0). Elliots Bks.

--Society: A Textbook of Sociology. 596p. 1982. Repr. of 1937 ed. lib. bdg. 50.00 (ISBN 0-89987-587-4). Darby BKs.

McJimsey, George. Dividing & Reuniting of America: 1848-1877. LC 80-68811. (Orig.). 1981. pap. text ed. 10.95x (ISBN 0-88273-108-4). Forum Pr IL.

McJunkin, James N., jt. auth. see Crace, Max D.

Mack, Alison. Toilet Learning: The Picture Book Technique for Children & Parents. 1978. 8.95 (ISBN 0-316-54233-4). Little.

--Toilet Learning: The Picture Book Technique for Children & Parents. (Illus.). 120p. 1983. pap. 6.70 (ISBN 0-316-54237-7). Little.

Mack, Bruce. Jesse's Dream Skirt. LC 79-89892. 36p. (ps-1). 1979. pap. 3.25 (ISBN 0-914996-20-7). Lollipop Power.

Mack, Donald W. Lenin & the Russian Revolution. Reeves, Marjorie, ed. (Then & There Ser.). (Illus.). 104p. (Orig.). (gr. 7-12). 1970. pap. text ed. 3.10 (ISBN 0-582-20457-7). Longman.

Mack, Dorothy. The Belle of Bath. (Candelight Romance Ser.). (Orig.). 1981. pap. 1.50 o.s.i. (ISBN 0-440-10617-6). Dell.

--A Companion in Joy. (Orig.). 1980. pap. 1.50 o.s.i. (ISBN 0-440-11263-X). Dell.

Mack, Elsie. Magic Is Fragile. 256p. (YA) 1973. 6.95 (ISBN 0-685-27366-0, Avalon). Bouregy.

Mack, Glenn. Adventures in Improvisation at the Keyboard. 64p. 1970. pap. text ed. 8.35 (ISBN 0-87487-076-3). Summy.

--Adventures in Modes & Keys. 32p. (gr. 3-12). 1973. pap. text ed. 5.05 (ISBN 0-87487-625-7). Summy.

Mack, Harold C. The Ovary. (Illus.). 228p. 1968. photocopy ed.spiral 22.75x (ISBN 0-398-01185-0). C C Thomas.

Mack, Heinz, jt. auth. see Piene, Otto.

Mack, John. Zulus. LC 80-50951. (Surviving Peoples Ser.). PLB 12.68 (ISBN 0-382-06360-0). Silver.

Mack, John & Hickler, Holly. Vivienne. 1982. pap. 2.95 (ISBN 0-451-62135-2, ME2135, Ment). NAL.

Mack, M., et al. Modern Poetry. 2nd ed. 1961. pap. 10.95 o.p. (ISBN 0-13-281410-2). P-H.

Mack, Maynard, ed. The Last & Greatest Art: Some Unpublished Poetical Manuscripts of Alexander Pope. LC 81-50304. 448p. 1983. 35.00 (ISBN 0-87413-183-9). U Delaware Pr.

Mack, Maynard & Lord, George D., eds. Poetic Traditions of the English Renaissance. LC 82-1941. 336p. 1982. 22.50x (ISBN 0-300-02785-0). Yale U Pr.

Mack, Maynard, ed. see Pope, Alexander.

Mack, Maynard, ed. see Shakespeare, William.

Mack, Maynard, et al, eds. The Norton Anthology of World Masterpieces, 2 vols. 4th ed. 1979. text ed. 19.95x (ISBN 0-393-95036-0); Vol II. text ed. 19.95x (ISBN 0-393-95040-9); Vol I. pap. text ed. 17.95x (ISBN 0-393-95045-X); Vol II. pap. text ed. 17.95x (ISBN 0-393-95050-6). Norton.

Mack, Maynard, et al, eds. see Pope, Alexander.

Mack, Nancy. Tracy. LC 76-12557. (Moods & Emotions Ser.). (Illus.). 32p. (gr. k-4). 1976. PLB 12.85 o.p. (ISBN 0-8172-0013-4). Raintree Pubs.

--Why Me? LC 76-13175. (Moods & Emotions Ser.). (Illus.). 32p. (gr. k-3). 1976. PLB 12.85 o.p. (ISBN 0-8172-0012-6). Raintree Pubs.

Mack, Newell B., et al. Energy Research Guide: Journals, Indexes, & Abstracts. 344p. 1983. ref 37.50x (ISBN 0-88410-097-9). Ballinger Pub.

Mack, Raymond. Transforming America: Patterns of Social Change. 1967. pap. text ed. 3.75 (ISBN 0-685-55632-8). Phila Bk Co.

Mack, Raymond W., ed. Changing South. LC 72-91467. 115p. 1970. 9.95 (ISBN 0-87855-060-7); pap. 3.95 (ISBN 0-87855-557-9). Transaction Bks.

Mack, Ruth P. Planning & Uncertainty: Decision Making in Business & Government Administration. LC 79-155905. 233p. 1971. 20.25 (ISBN 0-471-56280-7, Pub. by Wiley). Krieger.

Mack, Stan. Stan Mack's Real Life Funnies: Guarantee All Dialogue Is Reported Verbatim. LC 78-22071. (Illus.). 1979. 9.95 o.p. (ISBN 0-399-12273-7); pap. 5.95 o.p. (ISBN 0-399-12306-7). Putnam Pub Group.

Mack, Walter S. & Buckley, Peter. No Time Lost. LC 82-71061. 224p. 1982. 12.95 (ISBN 0-689-11326-9). Atheneum.

Mack, William P., jt. auth. see Konetzni, Albert H., Jr.

Mack, Zella. California Paralegal's Guide. 2nd ed. LC 77-71561. 872p. 1977. incl. 1983 suppl. 47.50 (ISBN 0-911110-23-2). Parker & Son.

McKaig, Thomas H. Applied Structural Design of Buildings. 3rd ed. 1965. 32.50 o.p. (ISBN 0-07-045109-5, P&RB). McGraw.

--Building Failures: Case Studies of Construction & Design. 1962. 23.95 o.p. (ISBN 0-07-045107-9, P&RB). McGraw.

Mackail, J. W. Lectures on Greek Poetry. LC 66-23520. 1910. 10.00x (ISBN 0-8196-0180-2). Biblo.

Mackail, John W. Latin Literature. LC 66-16865. 1966. 12.50 (ISBN 0-8044-2570-1). Ungar.

McKain, David. The Common Life. LC 82-71818. 71p. 1982. 12.95 (ISBN 0-914086-41-3); pap. 4.95 (ISBN 0-914086-38-3). Alicejamesbooks.

Mackal, P. K. Psychological Theories of Agression. 216p. 1979. 40.50 (ISBN 0-444-85350-2, North Holland). Elsevier.

Mackal, Roy P. The Monsters of Loch Ness: The First Complete Scientific Study & Its Startling Conclusions. LC 82-75778. (Illus.). 401p. 1980. pap. 8.95 (ISBN 0-8040-0704-7). Swallow.

Mackaman, Frank H., ed. Understanding Congressional Leadership. LC 81-17447. 304p. 1981. 22.50 (ISBN 0-87187-213-7). Congr Quarterly.

McKamy, K. Books for Businessmen: A Bibliography. LC 65-27747. (Business Almanac Ser: No. 1). 1967. 5.95 o.p. (ISBN 0-379-11201-9). Oceana.

Mackaness, George, ed. see Bligh, William.

Mackarness, Richard. Living Safely in a Polluted World: How to Protect Yourself & Your Children from Chemicals in Your Food & Environment. LC 80-51062. 216p. 1982. pap. 8.95 (ISBN 0-8128-6143-4). Stein & Day.

McKaughan, Howard, et al. Verb Studies in Five New Guinea Languages. (Publications in Linguistics & Related Fields Ser.: No. 10). 182p. 1964. pap. 3.00 o. p. (ISBN 0-88312-010-0); microfiche o. p. 1.50 (ISBN 0-88312-410-6); microfiche 2.25 (ISBN 0-88312-314-2). Summer Inst Ling.

McKaughan, Howard P. & Macaraya, Batua A. Maranao Dictionary. LC 67-13668. 1967. pap. 15.00x o.p. (ISBN 0-87022-505-7). UH Pr.

McKaughan, Howard P., ed. see Benton, Richard A.

McKaughan, Howard P., ed. see Bernabe, Emma, et al.

McKaughan, Howard P., ed. see Bunye, Maria V. & Yap, Elsa P.

McKaughan, Howard P., ed. see Constantino, Ernesto.

McKaughan, Howard P., ed. see Forman, Michael L.

McKaughan, Howard P., ed. see Mintz, Malcolm W.

McKaughan, Howard P., ed. see Mirikitani, Leatrice T.

McKaughan, Howard P., ed. see Motus, Cecile L.

McKaughan, Howard P., ed. see Ramos, Teresita V.

McKaughan, Howard P., ed. see Ramos, Teresita V. & De Guzman, Videa.

McKaughan, Howard P., ed. see Wolfenden, E. P.

McKaughan, Howard P., ed. see Yap, Elsa P. & Bunye, Maria V.

Mckay & Hill. A History of Western Society, 2 vols. 2d ed. 1982. text ed. 23.95 (ISBN 0-686-84597-8, HS1976); write for info. HM.

Mackay, Alan L. Scientific Quotations: The Harvest of a Quiet Eye. Ebison, Maurice, ed. LC 76-48396. 192p. 1977. 22.50xo.s.i. (ISBN 0-8448-1050-9); pap. 9.95x (ISBN 0-8448-1414-8). Crane-Russak Co.

McKay, Alexander G. Houses, Villas, & Palaces of the Roman World. Scullard, H. H., ed. LC 74-20425. (Aspects of Greek & Roman Life Ser). (Illus.). 312p. 1975. 27.50x (ISBN 0-8014-0948-9). Cornell U Pr.

McKay, Alexander G. & Shepherd, D. M., eds. Roman Satire: Horace, Juvenal, Persius, Petronius, & Seneca. LC 75-29860. 1976. 16.95x o.p. (ISBN 0-312-69090-8). St Martin.

Mackay, Alice, jt. auth. see Mackay, Edward.

Mackay, Andy. Electronic Music. (Illus.). 128p. 1981. 19.95 (ISBN 0-89893-504-0); pap. 10.95 (ISBN 0-89893-302-1). CDP.

MacKay, Angus. Spain in the Middle Ages: From Frontier to Empire, 1000-1500. LC 76-52257. (New Studies in Medieval History). 1977. 17.95x o.p. (ISBN 0-312-74978-3). St Martin.

Mackay, Charles. Dictionary of Lowland Scotch. LC 68-17998. 1968. Repr. of 1888 ed. 45.00x (ISBN 0-8103-3284-1). Gale.

--Extraordinary Popular Delusions & the Madness of Crowds. (Illus.). 752p. 1980. pap. 5.95 (ISBN 0-517-53919-5, Harmony). Crown.

McKay, Charles L. Five Simple Keys to Effective Evangelism: You Too Can Do It. 1978. pap. text ed. 11.50 (ISBN 0-8191-0397-7). U Pr of Amer.

McKay, Claude. Selected Poems of Claude McKay. LC 70-78698. 1969. pap. 3.95 (ISBN 0-15-680649-5, Harv). HarBraceJ.

--Selected Poems of Claude McKay. 1971. lib. bdg. 6.00 o.p. (ISBN 0-8057-5848-8, Twayne). G K Hall.

McKay, David. Planning & Politics in Western Europe. LC 81-21233. 256p. 1982. 27.50x (ISBN 0-312-61399-7). St Martin.

Mackay, David, ed. Flock of Words: An Anthology of Poetry for Children & Others. LC 77-91070. (gr. 10 up). 1970. 8.50 (ISBN 0-15-228599-7, HJ). HarBraceJ.

Mckay, Derek & Scott, H. M. The Rise of the Great Powers: The Great Powers & European States Systems, 1648-1815. LC 82-159. 1983. text ed. 23.00x (ISBN 0-582-48553-3); pap. text ed. 11.95x (ISBN 0-686-37799-0). Longman.

MacKay, Donald. Empire of Wood: The MacMillian Bloedel Story. (Illus.). 416p. 1983. 24.95 (ISBN 0-295-95984-3). U of Wash Pr.

MacKay, Donald & Paterson, Sally, eds. Physical Behavior of PCBs In the Great Lakes. LC 82-72347. (Illus.). 442p. 1982. 39.95 (ISBN 0-250-40584-9). Ann Arbor Science.

MacKay, Donald I. & Mackay, George A. The Political Economy of North Sea Oil. LC 75-25633. 208p. 1976. 30.00 (ISBN 0-89158-515-X). Westview.

McKay, Douglas R. Carlos Arniches. (World Authors Ser.). lib. bdg. 15.95 (ISBN 0-8057-2068-5, Twayne). G K Hall.

--Enrique Jardiel Poncela. (World Authors Ser.). 1974. lib. bdg. 15.95 (ISBN 0-8057-2462-1, Twayne). G K Hall.

--Miguel Mihura. (World Authors Ser.). 1977. lib. bdg. 15.95 (ISBN 0-8057-6191-8, Twayne). G K Hall.

Mackay, E. J. Chanhu-Daro Excavations, 1935-1936. Repr. of 1942 ed. pap. 45.00 (ISBN 0-527-02694-8). Kraus Repr.

Mackay, Edward & Mackay, Alice. Elementary Principles of Acting. 1934. 5.00 o.p. (ISBN 0-573-69008-1). French.

McKay, Eleanor, ed. The West Tennessee Historical Society: Guide to Archives & Collections. 1979. pap. 4.95x o.p. (ISBN 0-87870-050-1). Memphis St Univ.

McKay, G. W., ed. see Rilke, Rainer M.

Mackay, George A., jt. auth. see MacKay, Donald I.

McKay, George L., ed. American Book Auction Catalogues, 1713-1934. 1967. Repr. of 1937 ed. 37.00x (ISBN 0-8103-3311-2). Gale.

McKay, Hugh B., jt. auth. see Ross, Robert R.

Mckay, J. H. Football Coaching. 242p. 1966. 22.95 (ISBN 0-471-07147-1). Wiley.

MacKay, James. The Guinness Book of Stamp Facts & Feats. (Illus.). 256p. 1983. 19.95 (ISBN 0-85112-241-8, Pub. by Guinness Superlatives England); pap. 12.95 (ISBN 0-85112-285-X, Pub. by Guinness Superlatives England). Sterling.

--Numismatics. 144p. 1982. 25.00x (ISBN 0-584-11017-0, Pub. by Muller Ltd). State Mutual Bk.

MacKay, James A. Encyclopedia of World Stamps, 1945-1975. LC 76-17283. (Illus.). 1976. 24.95 o.p. (ISBN 0-07-044595-8, GB). McGraw.

--Rural Crafts in Scotland. (Illus.). 1977. 10.00 o.p. (ISBN 0-7091-5460-7). Transatlantic.

--Value in Coins & Medals. (Illus.). 1969. 8.75 o.p. (ISBN 0-85307-013-X). Transatlantic.

McKay, John P. & Hill, Benneth D. A History of Western Society, 2 Vols. 2nd ed. LC 82-81320. 592p. 1982. Vol. 1. pap. text ed. 17.95 (ISBN 0-395-32798-9); Vol. 2. pap. text ed. 17.95 (ISBN 0-395-32799-7); study guide for Vol. 1 5.95 (ISBN 0-395-32805-5); study guide for Vol. 2 5.95 (ISBN 0-395-32806-3). HM.

--A History of Western Society, 3 Vols. 2nd ed. LC 82-81321. 416p. 1982. Vol. 1. pap. text ed. 15.95 (ISBN 0-395-32800-4); Vol. 2. pap. text ed. 15.95 (ISBN 0-395-32801-2); Vol. 3. pap. text ed. 15.95 (ISBN 0-395-32802-0); write for info. instr's manual (ISBN 0-395-32803-9). HM.

McKay, John P. & Hill, Bennett D. A History of Western Society. 2nd ed. LC 82-81316. 1072p. 1982. text ed. 23.95 (ISBN 0-395-32804-7). HM.

McKay, John P., et al. A History of Western Society. LC 78-69592. (Illus.). 1979. pap. text ed. 23.50 1-vol. ed. (ISBN 0-395-27276-9); pap. text ed. 17.50 ea. 2-vol. ed.; pap. text ed. 15.50 ea. 3-vol. ed.; instr's. manual 1.00 (ISBN 0-395-27421-4); wkbk.-study guide 10.50 (ISBN 0-395-27420-6); test item suppl. 0.75 (ISBN 0-395-30362-1). HM.

MacKay, R. & Mountford, A. English for Specific Purposes. (Applied Linguistics & Language Study). 1978. pap. text ed. 10.75 (ISBN 0-582-55090-4). Longman.

MacKay, R. J. Mental Handicap in Child Health Practice. (Postgraduate Pediatric Ser.). 1976. 19.95x o.p. (ISBN 0-407-00113-1). Butterworth.

MacKay, Ray. New Guinea. (The World's Wild Places Ser.). (Illus.). 1978. lib. bdg. 15.96 (ISBN 0-8094-2058-9). Silver.

Mackay, Richard V. Guardianship & the Protection of Infants. 2nd ed. LC 57-14961. (Legal Almanac Ser.: No. 6). 1957. 4.95 o.p. (ISBN 0-379-11006-7, LA). Oceana.

McKay, Robert. The Girl Who Wanted to Run the Boston Marathon. LC 79-20928. (YA) 1980. 7.95 o.p. (ISBN 0-525-66663-X). Lodestar Bks.

McKay, Robert B., ed. American Constitutional Law Reader. LC 57-12993. (Docket Ser.: Vol. 12). 256p. (Orig.). 1958. 15.00 (ISBN 0-379-11312-0); pap. 2.50 (ISBN 0-379-11300-7). Oceana.

McKay, Ron, et al, eds. Monoclonal Antibodies to Neural Antigens. LC 81-10185. (Reports in the Neurosciences: Vol. 2). 286p. 1981. 38.00x (ISBN 0-87969-138-7). Cold Spring Harbor.

Mackay, Ronald & Palmer, Joe, eds. Languages for Specific Purposes: Program Design & Evaluation. 144p. (Orig.). 1981. pap. text ed. 10.95 (ISBN 0-88377-184-5). Newbury Hse.

Mackay, Ronald, et al. Reading in a Second Language: Hypotheses, Organization & Practice. 1979. pap. text ed. 11.95 (ISBN 0-88377-134-9). Newbury Hse.

McKay, Sandra. Verbs for a Specific Purpose. (Illus.). 256p. 1982. pap. text ed. 10.95 (ISBN 0-13-941617-X). P-H.

McKay, Sandra & Rosenthal, Linda. Writing for a Specific Purpose. (Illus.). 1980. pap. text ed. 10.95 (ISBN 0-13-970269-5). P-H.

McKay, Susan. Assertive Childbirth: The Future Parent's Guide to a Positive Pregnancy. (Illus.). 256p. 1983. 19.95 (ISBN 0-13-049635-9); pap. 9.95 (ISBN 0-13-049627-8). P-H.

MacKay, William. Salesman Surgeon. 1978. 9.95 o.p. (ISBN 0-07-044390-4, GB). McGraw.

Mackaye, Marion M. Emma: A Play. 1976. 5.95 o.s.i. (ISBN 0-87027-189-X). Cumberland Pr.

Mackaye, Percy. My Lady Dear Arise. 1976. 6.95 o.s.i. (ISBN 0-87027-190-3). Cumberland Pr.

--Mystery of Hamlet, King of Denmark. 1976. ltd. ed. 125.00 (ISBN 0-87027-177-6); pap. 9.95 (ISBN 0-87027-176-8). Cumberland Pr.

--Poog & the Caboose Man. 1976. 3.95 o.s.i. (ISBN 0-87027-175-X). Cumberland Pr.

--Poog's Pasture. 1976. 3.95 o.s.i. (ISBN 0-87027-174-1). Cumberland Pr.

McKaye-Ege, Arvia. The Secret Iron of the Heart. 192p. 1982. 10.00 (ISBN 0-932776-05-1); pap. 7.50 (ISBN 0-932776-06-X). Adonis Pr.

McKeag, R. M., jt. auth. see Welsh, J.

McKeag, R. M. & MacNaghten, A. M., eds. On the Construction of Programs. 432p. 1980. 27.95 (ISBN 0-521-23090-X). Cambridge U Pr.

McKeague, Charles P. Intermediate Algebra: A Text-Workbook. 1981. 16.00 (ISBN 0-12-484763-3); instr's Manual 3.50 (ISBN 0-12-484761-7). Acad Pr.

McKeague, Patricia M. Writing about Literature: Step by Step. 144p. 1982. pap. text ed. 8.95 (ISBN 0-8403-2712-9). Kendall-Hunt.

McKean, Gerald, jt. auth. see Brabb, George J.

McKean, Hugh F. The Treasures of Tiffany. (Illus.). 64p. 1982. pap. 9.95 (ISBN 0-914091-18-2). Chicago Review.

McKean, Margarett. This Wild Heart. (Second Chance at Love Ser.: No. 91). 1982. pap. 1.75 (ISBN 0-686-81794-X). Jove Pubns.

McKeand, Alice B. Blue Feather. pap. 2.00 (ISBN 0-685-08695-X). Creative Pr.

McKearin, Helen & Wilson, Kenneth M. American Bottles & Flasks & Their Ancestry. (Illus.). 1978. 12.95 (ISBN 0-517-53147-X). Crown.

McKeating, Henry. Studying the Old Testament. LC 82-70960. 224p. (Orig.). 1982. pap. 7.95 (ISBN 0-8066-1935-X, 10-6141). Augsburg.

McKechnie, A., jt. auth. see Roblee, C.

Mackechnie, John, compiled by. Catalogue of Gaelic Manuscripts in Selected Libraries in Great Britain & Ireland. 2 vols. 1973. Set. 230.00 (ISBN 0-8161-0832-3, Hall Library). G K Hall.

McKee. King Rollo Boxed Set. 6.95 o.s.i. (ISBN 0-316-56044-8). Little.

McKee, Bates. Cascadia: The Geologic Evolution of the Pacific Northwest. (Illus.). 416p. 1972. pap. text ed. 15.95 o.p. (ISBN 0-07-045133-8, C). McGraw.

McKee, Bill. Life After Birth. 1975. pap. 2.45 (ISBN 0-8423-2190-X). Tyndale.

McKee, Carol. Lenci Clothes. 124p. 1982. 17.95 (ISBN 0-87588-191-2). Hobby Hse.

McKee, David. Day the Tide Went Out.. & Out.. & Out.. & Out.. & Out.. & Out. LC 75-18940. (Illus.). 1976. PLB 10.89 (ISBN 0-200-00160-4, AbS-J). Har-Row.

--King Rollo & the Breakfast. (King Rollo Ser.). 32p. (gr. k-2). 1982. lib. bdg. 5.95 (ISBN 0-87191-902-8). Creative Ed.

--King Rollo & the Comic. (King Rollo Ser.). 32p. (gr. k-2). 1982. lib. bdg. 5.95 (ISBN 0-87191-900-1). Creative Ed.

--King Rollo & the Dog. (King Rollo Ser.). 32p. (gr. k-2). 1982. lib. bdg. 5.95 (ISBN 0-87191-901-X). Creative Ed.

--King Rollo & the Playroom. (King Rollo Ser.). 32p. (gr. k-2). 1982. lib. bdg. 5.95 (ISBN 0-87191-899-4). Creative Ed.

McKee, David, illus. Not Now, Bernard. (Illus.). 32p. (gr. k-4). 1981. 8.95 (ISBN 0-416-30781-7). Methuen Inc.

McKee, Donald. The Strategies of Politics. 1980. 10.00 o.p. (ISBN 0-8022-2360-5). Philos Lib.

McKee, Gerald, ed. Audio-Cassette Directory. 1983. pap. 20.00t (ISBN 0-914624-04-0). Cassette Info.

McKee, Harley J. Recording Historic Buildings. Rev. ed. (Landmark Reprint Ser.). (Illus.). 176p. 1983. 14.95 (ISBN 0-89133-105-0). Preservation Pr.

McKee, James D. Martin Luther King Jr. (Lives to Remember Ser). (gr. 6 up). 1969. PLB 4.97 o.p. (ISBN 0-399-60451-0). Putnam Pub Group.

McKee, John. William Allen White: Maverick on Main Street. LC 74-5991. (Contributions in American Studies: No. 17). (Illus.). 1975. lib. bdg. 27.50 (ISBN 0-8371-7533-X, MAW/). Greenwood.

McKee, Louis. Shuykill County. 64p. 1983. pap. 4.95 (ISBN 0-931694-18-3). Wampeter Pr.

McKee, Martha. Circles. 72p. 1976. pap. 4.95 (ISBN 0-913428-26-4). Landfall Pr.

--Single Circles. 132p. 1982. 8.95 (ISBN 0-913428-42-6); pap. 5.95 (ISBN 0-913428-43-4). Landfall Pr.

Mackee, Monique M. Handbook of Comparative Librarianship. 3rd ed. 550p. 1983. price not set (ISBN 0-85157-348-7, Pub. by Bingley England). Shoe String.

McKee, Patrick L., ed. Philosophical Foundations of Gerontology. LC 81-2922. 352p. 1982. 29.95x (ISBN 0-89885-040-1); pap. 14.95x (ISBN 0-89885-041-X). Human Sci Pr.

McKeehan, Wallace L., jt. ed. see Boynton, Alton L.

McKeeman, William M., et al. Compiler Generator. LC 76-117205. (Automatic Computation Ser). 1970. ref. ed. 34.95 (ISBN 0-13-155077-2). P-H.

McKeever, Harry P. British Columbia. LC 81-21746. (Illus.). 192p. 1982. pap. 8.95 (ISBN 0-87701-266-0). Chronicle Bks.

McKeever, J. Ross, ed. Dollars & Cents of Shopping Centers: A Study of Receipts & Expenditures, 1972. 5th ed. LC 70-81240. (Special Publications Ser.). (Illus.). 1972. pap. 24.25 o.p. (ISBN 0-87420-906-4). Urban Land.

McKeever, Jim. How You Can Know the Will of God. 24p. 1982. 1.00 (ISBN 0-86694-095-2). Omega Pubns OR.

Mackeever, Samuel A., ed. see Sutton, Charles.

MacKeith, R. C., ed. see Kolvin, I.

McKellar, J. F. & Allen, N. S. Photochemistry of Man-Made Polymers. (Illus.). 1979. 57.50 (ISBN 0-85334-799-9, Pub. by Applied Sci England). Elsevier.

MacKellar, Jean, jt. auth. see Blouin, Andree.

MacKellar, William. Terror Run. LC 82-45382. 192p. (gr. 6 up). 1982. PLB 9.95 (ISBN 0-396-08091-X). Dodd.

McKellen, J., et al. Communication for Business. 1982. 12.00 (ISBN 0-08-027256-8); pap. 5.95 (ISBN 0-686-82954-9). Pergamon.

McKellips, Art. Woodcarving for Beginners. LC 77-99159. (Illus.). 1977. pap. 8.95 (ISBN 0-917304-11-X). Timber.

McKelvey, Bill. Organizational Systematics: Taxonomy, Evolution Classification. LC 81-43691. (Illus.). 500p. 1982. 29.95x (ISBN 0-520-04225-5). U of Cal Pr.

McKelvey, Blake. American Urbanization: A Comparative History. 1973. pap. 6.95x (ISBN 0-673-07616-4). Scott F.

--The Emergence of Metropolitan America, 1915-1966. LC 68-18695. (Illus.). 1968. 25.00x (ISBN 0-8135-0571-2). Rutgers U Pr.

McKelvey, F. X., jt. auth. see Horonjeff, R.

McKelvey, Jean T., ed. The Duty of Fair Representation. 120p. 1977. 10.95 (ISBN 0-87546-260-X); pap. 6.95 (ISBN 0-87546-234-0). ILR Pr.

McKelvey, Jean T., ed. see National Academy Of Arbitrators, Meetings 1-7.

McKelvey, Jean T., ed. see National Academy of Arbitrators-11th Annual Meeting.

McKelvey, Jean T., ed. see National Academy of Arbitrators-12th Annual Meeting.

McKelvey, Jean T., ed. see National Academy of Arbitrators-13th Annual Meeting.

McKelvey, John J., Jr., jt. auth. see Shorey, H. H.

McKelvey, John P. Solid State & Semiconductor Physics. LC 81-19390. 526p. 1982. Repr. of 1966 ed. 26.50 (ISBN 0-89874-396-6). Krieger.

McKelvie, Colin, ed. see Swift, Jonathan.

McKelvy, James. Music for Conducting Class. LC 77-76862. 1977. wire bound 12.95 (ISBN 0-916656-10-1). Mark Foster Mus.

--Music for Conducting Class. LC 77-76862. 1977. pap. 11.95 (ISBN 0-916656-05-5). Mark Foster Mus.

Macken, Bob, et al. The Rock Music Source Book. LC 78-1196. 648p. (Orig.). 1980. pap. 9.95 o.p. (ISBN 0-385-14139-4, Anch). Doubleday.

McKendrick, Neil & Brewer, John. The Birth of a Consumer Society: The Commercialization of Eighteenth-Century England. LC 82-47953. 356p. 1982. 29.95x (ISBN 0-253-31205-1). Ind U Pr.

MacKendrick, Paul. The Greek Stones Speak: The Story of Archaeology in Greek Lands. 1979. pap. 7.95 o.p. (ISBN 0-393-00932-7). Norton.

--The Greek Stones Speak: The Story of Archaeology in Greek Lands. 2nd ed. (Illus.). 576p. 1983. pap. 9.95 (ISBN 0-393-30111-7). Norton.

--The Mute Stones Speak: The Story of Archaeology in Italy. 2nd ed. 1983. 25.50 (ISBN 0-393-01678-1). Norton.

McKenna, Brian, ed. Irish Literature, Eighteen Hundred-Eighteen Seventy-Five: A Guide to Information Sources. LC 74-11540. (American Literature, English Literature & World Literatures in English Information Guide Ser.: Vol. 13). 1978. 42.00x (ISBN 0-8103-1250-6). Gale.

McKenna, Chris, jt. auth. see Joll, Caroline.

McKenna, Christopher K. Quantitative Methods for Business Decisions. (Quantitative Methods for Management). (Illus.). 1980. text ed. 26.50 (ISBN 0-07-045351-9); instrs.' manual 12.95 (ISBN 0-07-045352-7). McGraw.

McKenna, David L. The Communicator's Commentary-Mark, Vol. 2. Ogilvie, Lloyd, ed. (The Communicator's Commentaries Ser.). 1982. 14.95 (ISBN 0-8499-0155-3). Word Pub.

Mackenna, David W., ed. see Seminar on Grant Proposal Development.

Mackenna, F. S. Eighteenth Century English Porcelain. 39.50x (ISBN 0-87245-535-1). Textile Bk.

McKenna, G. American Politics: Ideals & Realities. 1976. text ed. 18.95 (ISBN 0-07-045355-1, C); instructor's manual 7.95 (ISBN 0-07-045356-X). McGraw.

McKenna, George G. Introduction to Criminal Law: New York Edition. LC 76-62961. 1977. pap. text ed. 10.95 (ISBN 0-8403-1680-1). Kendall-Hunt.

McKenna, George L. Repeated Exposure: Photographic Imagery in the Print Media. LC 81-86054. (Illus.). 104p. (Orig.). 1982. pap. 12.00x (ISBN 0-942614-07-0). Nelson-Atkins.

McKenna, J. J. Sarah & Joshua. 1979. pap. 2.50 o.p. (ISBN 0-380-41053-2, 41053). Avon.

McKenna, James A. Black Range Tales: Adventures in the Southwest. LC 37-15022. (Beautiful Rio Grande Classic Ser). (Illus.). 342p. 1981. Repr. of 1936 ed. lib. bdg. 10.00 (ISBN 0-87380-009-5). Rio Grande.

McKenna, John W., jt. auth. see Guth, Delloyd J.

McKenna, M., jt. auth. see Wood, Merle W.

McKenna, Mary. A Family. LC 77-95168. 1978. 7.95 (ISBN 0-89310-029-3); pap. 3.95 o.p. (ISBN 0-89310-030-7). Carillon Bks.

McKenna, Marylou. Bodypower. 1976. 7.95 o.p. (ISBN 0-671-22217-1). S&S.

McKenna, Michael. Stein & Day Dictionary of Definitive Quotations. LC 81-48453. 192p. 1982. 18.95 (ISBN 0-8128-2864-X). Stein & Day.

McKenna, Tate. Kindle the Trees. (Candlelight Ecstasy Ser.: No. 142). (Orig.). 1983. pap. 1.95 (ISBN 0-440-14506-6). Dell.

--Legacy of Love. (Candlelight Ecstasy Ser.: No. 126). (Orig.). 1983. pap. 1.95 (ISBN 0-440-15096-5). Dell.

McKenna, Terence, jt. ed. see Rabin, David.

McKenna, Thomas, jt. auth. see Spicer, Jerry.

McKenna, Tom, jt. auth. see Parker, Faye.

McKenna, Wendy, jt. auth. see Kessler, Suzanne.

McKenna, William. Husserl's Introduction to Phenomenology. 1982. lib. bdg. 41.50 (ISBN 90-247-2665-4, Pub. by Martinus Nijhoff Netherlands). Kluwer Boston.

McKenney, James L., jt. auth. see McFarlan, F. Warren.

McKenney, Kenneth. The Plants. LC 75-34725. 1976. 7.95 o.p. (ISBN 0-399-11627-3). Putnam Pub Group.

McKenney, Ruth. Industrial Valley. Repr. of 1939 ed. lib. bdg. 18.75x (ISBN 0-8371-0585-4, MCIV). Greenwood.

--My Sister Eileen. LC 38-17844. (YA) 1968. pap. 0.60 (ISBN 0-15-663890-8, Harv). HarBraceJ.

McKenney, Ruth & Bransten, Richard. Here's England: A Highly Informal Guide. rev. 3rd ed. LC 75-123949. (Illus.). 1971. 15.34i (ISBN 0-06-012917-4, HarpT). Har-Row.

McKensie, R. B., jt. ed. see Walton, Richard E.

McKenzie, A. & McKenzie, J., eds. Stories from Three Worlds. 1978. pap. text ed. 6.95x o.p. (ISBN 0-85859-184-7, 00535). Heinemann Ed.

McKenzie, A. E. The Major Achievements of Science. 1973. pap. 7.95 o.p. (ISBN 0-671-21488-8, Touchstone Bks). S&S.

McKenzie, Alan T. Thomas Gray: A Reference Guide. 320p. 1982. lib. bdg. 35.00 (ISBN 0-8161-8451-8, Hall Reference). G K Hall.

MacKenzie, Alec & Waldo, Kay C. About Time! A Woman's Guide to Time Management. (McGraw-Hill Paperback Ser.). 224p. (Orig.). 1981. pap. 5.95 (ISBN 0-07-044651-2, GB). McGraw.

MacKenzie, Andrew. Hauntings & Apparitions. 12p. 1982. 40.00x (ISBN 0-434-44051-5, Pub. by Heinemann England). State Mutual Bk.

McKenzie, Barbara. Mary McCarthy. (U. S. Authors Ser.: No. 108). 12.95 o.p. (ISBN 0-8057-0480-9, Twayne). G K Hall.

MacKenzie, Charles A. Experimental Organic Chemistry. 4th ed. LC 70-138824. (Illus.). 1971. pap. text ed. 23.95 (ISBN 0-13-294785-4). P-H.

Mackenzie, Charles E. Coded-Character Sets: History & Development. LC 77-90165. (IBM Ser.). 1980. text ed. 26.95 (ISBN 0-201-14460-3). A-W.

MacKenzie, Clara C. Sarah Barnwell Elliot. (United States Author Ser.). 1980. lib. bdg. 12.95 (ISBN 0-8057-7300-2, Twayne). G K Hall.

Mackenzie, Colin. Many a Slip. 10.50x (ISBN 0-392-07132-0, SpS). Sportshelf.

Mackenzie, Colin F. Chest Physiotherapy in the Critical Care Unit. (Illus.). 270p. 1981. pap. 23.00 (ISBN 0-683-05328-0). Williams & Wilkins.

McKenzie, D. P., ed. see Royal Society of London.

Mackenzie, David. A Manual of Manuscript Transcription for the Dictionary of the Old Spanish Language. 2nd ed. 128p. 1981. pap. 15.00 (ISBN 0-942260-15-5). Hispanic Seminary.

McKenzie, David. Wolfhart Pannenberg & Religious Philosophy. LC 80-8171. 169p. 1980. lib. bdg. 19.75 (ISBN 0-8191-1314-X); pap. text ed. 9.75 (ISBN 0-8191-1315-8). U Pr of Amer.

McKenzie, Dennis J. & Betts, Richard M. Essentials of Real Estate Economics. 2nd ed. (California Real Estate Ser.). 304p. 1980. text ed. 24.95 (ISBN 0-471-08334-8). Wiley.

McKenzie, Dennis J., et al. California Real Estate Principles. LC 80-23243. (California Real Estate Ser.). 339p. 1981. text ed. 25.95 (ISBN 0-471-01729-9). Wiley.

MacKenzie, Donald. Raven After Dark. 192p. 1981. pap. 1.95 o.p. (ISBN 0-425-04716-4). Berkley Pub.

--Raven After Dark. 1979. 7.95 o.s.i. (ISBN 0-395-28209-8). HM.

--Raven & the Paperhangers. 1982. pap. 2.25 o.p. (ISBN 0-425-05198-6). Berkley Pub.

--Raven in Flight. 1981. pap. 1.95 o.p. (ISBN 0-425-04718-0). Berkley Pub.

--Raven Settles a Score. 1981. pap. 1.95 o.p. (ISBN 0-425-04717-2). Berkley Pub.

McKenzie, Donald A. Death Notices from The Christian Guardian, 1836-1850. 368p. 1982. lib. bdg. 21.00 (ISBN 0-912606-09-6). Hunterdon Hse.

MacKenzie, Donald A. Egyptian Myth & Legend. 404p. 1983. pap. 8.25 (ISBN 0-88072-016-6). Tanager Bks.

--Migration of Symbols & Their Relations to Beliefs & Customs. LC 68-18029. 1968. Repr. of 1926 ed. 34.00x (ISBN 0-8103-3074-1). Gale.

McKenzie, E. C. Fourteen Hundred Bible Facts: A Bible Quiz Book. (Quiz & Puzzle Bks.). Orig. Title: It's in the Bible Quiz Book. 1974. pap. 3.50 (ISBN 0-8010-5965-8). Baker Bk.

--Mixed Nuts. 1978. pap. 1.50 (ISBN 0-451-11367-5, AW1367, Sig). NAL.

McKenzie, Edna. Freedom in the Midst of a Slave Society. LC 80-7495. (Illus.). 86p. 1980. pap. text ed. 8.50 (ISBN 0-8191-1036-1). U Pr of Amer.

MacKenzie, Fred T., jt. auth. see Garrels, Robert M.

MacKenzie, G. The Aristocracy of Labor. LC 73-80484. (Studies in Sociology). (Illus.). 208p. 1973. pap. 11.95 (ISBN 0-521-09825-4). Cambridge U Pr.

Mackenzie, Gavin. Class Theory & the Division of Labour. (Studies in Sociology). Date not set. pap. price not set (ISBN 0-391-01128-6). Humanities.

Mackenzie, Gavin, jt. ed. see Giddens, Anthony.

McKenzie, George. Measuring Economic Welfare: New Methods. LC 82-4422. 208p. Date not set. 32.50 (ISBN 0-521-24862-0). Cambridge U Pr.

McKenzie, Henry. Fundamentals the Church Needs. LC 70-148557. 1971. 3.95x o.s.i. (ISBN 0-8418-4583-2). University Pr.

MacKenzie, Henry. Julia de Roubiggne. 2 vols. Paulson, Ronald, ed. LC 78-60840. (Novel 1720-1805 Ser.: Vol. 7). 1979. Set. lib. bdg. write for info. o.s.i. (ISBN 0-8240-3656-5); lib. bdg. 50.00 ea. o.s.i. Garland Pub.

--The Man of the World, 2 vols. in 1. LC 74-17142. (Novel in England, 1700-1775 Ser). 1974. Repr. of 1773 ed. lib. bdg. 50.00 o.s.i. (ISBN 0-8240-1202-X). Garland Pub.

Mackenzie, Ian. Collecting Old Toy Soldiers. 1975. 32.50 (ISBN 0-7134-3036-2, Pub by Batsford, England). David & Charles.

McKenzie, J., jt. ed. see McKenzie, A.

Mackenzie, J. S., ed. Viral Diseases in South East Asia & the Western Pacific. 672p. 1982. 36.50 (ISBN 0-12-484820-6). Acad Pr.

McKenzie, James S. A Broad Education Abroad. 1978. 7.95 o.p. (ISBN 0-533-03384-5). Vantage.

MacKenzie, Jeanne, jt. auth. see MacKenzie, Norman.

MacKenzie, Jeanne, jt. ed. see Webb, Beatrice.

McKenzie, Jimmy C. & Hughes, Robert J. Office Machines: A Practical Approach. 2nd ed. 300p. 1983. write for info. wire coil (ISBN 0-697-08088-9); instr's solutions manual avail. (ISBN 0-697-08194-X); practice set avail. (ISBN 0-697-08096-X). Wm C Brown.

McKenzie, Jimmy C. & Kelley, J. Roland. Business Mathematics. 17.95 (ISBN 0-395-30672-8); tchr's annotated ed. 18.95 (ISBN 0-395-30673-6). HM.

McKenzie, John G. Nervous Disorders & Religion: A Study of Souls in the Making. LC 79-8719. 183p. 1981. Repr. of 1951 ed. lib. bdg. 20.75x (ISBN 0-313-22192-8, MCND). Greenwood.

McKenzie, John L. Light on the Epistles: A Reader's Guide. 204p. 1975. 12.95 (ISBN 0-88347-057-8); pap. 7.95 (ISBN 0-8190-0625-4). Thomas More.

--The Old Testament Without Illusion. LC 79-8503. 1980. pap. 4.50 o.p. (ISBN 0-385-15831-9, Im). Doubleday.

--A Theology of the Old Testament. LC 72-76190. 4.95 (ISBN 0-385-12108-3, Im). Doubleday.

MacKenzie, Joy & Bledsoe, Shirley. A Big Book of Bible Games & Puzzles. 192p. 1982. pap. 6.95 (ISBN 0-310-70271-2). Zondervan.

MacKenzie, Joy, jt. auth. see Forte, Imogene.

MacKenzie, K. A. Edith Simcox & George Eliot. LC 78-1538. 1978. Repr. of 1961 ed. lib. bdg. 17.50x (ISBN 0-313-20269-9, MCES). Greenwood.

Mackenzie, Kenneth D. Organizational Structures. LC 77-86209. (Organizational Behavior Ser.). 1978. pap. text ed. 13.95x (ISBN 0-88295-452-0). Harlan Davidson.

MacKenzie, Kenneth D., ed. see Jabes, Jak.

Mackenzie, Kenneth D., ed. see Kiesler, Sara B.

Mackenzie, Kenneth D., ed. see Pfeffer, Jeffrey.

Mackenzie, Kenneth D., ed. see Simmons, Richard E.

Mackenzie, Kenneth D., ed. see Tuggle, Francis D.

McKenzie, Leon. Adult Education & the Burden of the Future. LC 78-50845. 1978. pap. text ed. 8.25 (ISBN 0-8191-0470-1). U Pr of Amer.

MacKenzie, M., ed. The Letters of Sidney & Bearice Webb. Incl. Vol. 1. (ISBN 0-521-21681-8); Vol. 2. (ISBN 0-521-21682-6); Vol. 3. 74.50 ea. (ISBN 0-521-21837-3); Set. 199.50. LC 77-1665. 1978. 69.95 ea.; Set. 185.00 (ISBN 0-521-22015-7). Cambridge U Pr.

MacKenzie, Norman & MacKenzie, Jeanne. Dickens: A Life. (Illus.). 1979. 22.50 (ISBN 0-19-211741-6). Oxford U Pr.

--The Fabians. (Illus.). 1978. pap. 6.95 o.p. (ISBN 0-671-24072-2, Touchstone Bks). S&S.

MacKenzie, Ossian & Christensen, Edward, eds. Changing World of Correspondence Study: International Readings. LC 70-127384. 1971. 22.50x (ISBN 0-271-01135-1). Pa St U Pr.

Mackenzie, R. Auditorium Acoustics. 1975. 47.25 (ISBN 0-85334-646-1). Elsevier.

Mackenzie, R. Alec. The Time Trap. LC 72-82874. (Illus.). 208p. 1975. pap. 3.95 (ISBN 0-07-044650-4, SP). McGraw.

McKenzie, Richard. Economic Issues in Public Policy. (Illus.). 1979. pap. text ed. 12.95 (ISBN 0-07-045650-X). McGraw.

McKenzie, Richard & Tullock, Gordon. Modern Political Economy: An Introduction to Economics. (Illus.). 1978. 24.95 (ISBN 0-07-045159-1, C); instr.'s manual 15.95 (ISBN 0-07-045160-5); Cases & Problems in Modern Political Economy by Keating & Martin 9.95 (ISBN 0-07-045173-7); transparency masters 15.00 (ISBN 0-07-074731-8). McGraw.

McKenzie, Richard B. The Limits of Economic Science. 1982. lib. bdg. 23.00 (ISBN 0-89838-116-9). Kluwer-Nijhoff.

Mackenzie, Robert E., jt. auth. see Auslander, Louis.

Mackenzie, Ross. Trying New Sandals: What It Means to Be a Christian Today? LC 73-5348. 1977. pap. 3.95 o.p. (ISBN 0-88489-091-0). St Mary's.

McKenzie, S. L., jt. ed. see Nixon, D. W.

McKenzie, Sheila C. Aging & Old Age. 1980. pap. 13.50x (ISBN 0-673-15250-2). Scott F.

MacKenzie, Susan T. Group Legal Services. (Key Issues Ser.: No. 18). 72p. 1975. pap. 3.00 (ISBN 0-87546-231-6). ILR Pr.

--Noise & Office Work. (Key Issues Ser.: No. 19). 52p. 1975. pap. 3.00 (ISBN 0-87546-232-4). ILR Pr.

Mackenzie, W. J. Biological Ideas in Politics: An Essay in Political Adaptivity. LC 78-20278. 1979. 10.95x o.p. (ISBN 0-312-07869-2). St Martin.

--Political Identity. LC 77-26851. 1978. 18.95 (ISBN 0-312-62308-9). St Martin.

MacKenzie, W. S., et al. Atlas of Igneous Rock & Their Textures. 1982. 27.95X (ISBN 0-470-27339-9). Halsted Pr.

McKenzie, Wesley M., ed. see Douglas, Charles H.

Mackenzie, William. Practical Treatise on the Diseases of the Eye. 1979. Repr. of 1833 ed. Leather Bdg. Sold By Set Only. write for info (ISBN 0-88275-947-7); lib. bdg. 36.50 (ISBN 0-88275-841-1). Krieger.

McKenzie, William H. Mountain to Mill. LC 82-18862. (Illus.). 1982. 32.95 (ISBN 0-936206-16-0). MAC Pub Inc.

MacKenzie, William R. The English Moralities from the Point of View of Allegory. (Harvard Studies in English). Repr. of 1914 ed. 23.00 (ISBN 0-384-34880-7). Johnson Repr.

Mackenzie-Grieve, Averil. Clara Novello, 1818-1908. (Music Reprint Ser.). 1980. Repr. of 1955 ed. lib. bdg. 32.50 (ISBN 0-306-76009-6). Da Capo.

Mackenzie-Lamb, Eric. Labyrinth. LC 78-11875. 1979. 9.95 o.p. (ISBN 0-688-03422-5). Morrow.

--Labyrinth. 1980. pap. 2.25 o.p. (ISBN 0-451-09062-4, E9062, Sig). NAL.

McKeon, Richard, ed. see Abailard, P.

McKeon, Richard, ed. see Aristotle.

McKeon, Richard, ed. see United Nations Educational Scientific & Cultural Organization.

McKeon, Zahava K. Novels & Arguments: Inventing Rhetorical Criticism. LC 82-2677. 1982. pap. 22.50x (ISBN 0-226-56034-1). U of Chicago Pr.

McKeone, Dermot. Small Computers for Business & Industry. 1979. text ed. 34.25x (ISBN 0-566-02096-3). Gower Pub Ltd.

McKeough, D. Michael. The Neuroscience Coloring Book. 1982. pap. text ed. 9.95 (ISBN 0-316-56210-6). Little.

McKeown, Beverly. Guitar Songbook with Instructions. 1975. pap. text ed. 13.50 (ISBN 0-395-18648-X). HM.

McKeown, James M. & McKeown, Joan C. Price Guide to Antique & Classic Still Cameras, 1983-1984. (Illus., Orig.). 1983. pap. 15.95 (ISBN 0-931838-05-3). Centennial Photo Serv.

McKeown, Joan A., et al, eds. see Boyd, Marcia.

McKeown, Joan C., jt. auth. see McKeown, James M.

McKeown, Pamela. Reading: A Basic Guide for Parents & Teachers. 170p. 1974. 19.95x (ISBN 0-7100-7418-2); pap. 7.95 (ISBN 0-7100-7424-7). Routledge & Kegan.

McKeown, Patrick G., jt. auth. see Davis, K. Roscoe.

McKeown, Robin J., jt. auth. see Michaelis, John U.

McKeown, Tom. Driving to New Mexico. 1974. pap. 2.25 (ISBN 0-913270-31-8). Sunstone Pr.

Mackerness, E. D., ed. Hazlitt-the Spirit of the Age. 448p. 1969. 25.00x (ISBN 0-7121-0143-8, Pub. by Macdonald & Evans). State Mutual Bk.

Mackerness, Eric D. A Social History of English Music. LC 75-40994. (Illus.). 307p. 1976. Repr. of 1964 ed. lib. bdg. 20.25x (ISBN 0-8371-8705-2, MAHEM). Greenwood.

Mackerras, Colin, ed. & tr. from Chinese. The Uighur Empire According to the T'ang Dynastic Histories: A Study in Sino-Uighur Relations, 744-840. LC 73-1708. (Asian Publications Ser.: No. 2). xiv, 228p. 1973. 19.95x o.s.i. (ISBN 0-87249-279-6). U of SC Pr.

McKerrow, Ray E., et al, eds. Explorations in Rhetoric: Studies in Honor of Douglas Ehninger. 1981. text ed. 13.50x (ISBN 0-673-15518-8). Scott F.

McKerrow, Ronald B. Introduction to Bibliography for Literary Students. (Illus.). 1927. 24.95x o.p. (ISBN 0-19-818103-5). Oxford U Pr.

McKerrow, W. Stuart, ed. The Ecology of Fossils: An Illustrated Guide. (Illus.). 1978. text ed. 27.50x (ISBN 0-262-13144-7). MIT Pr.

MacKert, M., jt. auth. see Hemelt, M.

Mackes, Shy. The Overcoming Power. LC 82-73708. 1983. pap. text ed. 5.00 (ISBN 0-932050-17-4). New Puritan.

Mackesy, Piers. The Coward of Minden: The Affair of Lord George Sackville. LC 78-26204. (Illus.). 1979. 22.50 (ISBN 0-312-17060-2). St Martin.

McKetta. Encyclopedia of Chemical Processing & Design. 1983. price not set (ISBN 0-8247-2469-0). Dekker.

--Encyclopedia of Chemical Processing & Design, Vol. 16. 1982. write for info. (ISBN 0-8247-2466-6). Dekker.

--Encyclopedia of Chemical Processing & Design, Vol. 18. 1983. price not set (ISBN 0-8247-2468-2). Dekker.

McKetta, John J., Jr., intro. by. Chemical Technology: An Encyclopedic Treatment, 7 vols. Incl. Vol. 1. Air, Water, Inorganic Chemicals & Nucleonics. 1968. o.p. (ISBN 0-06-491102-0); Vol. 2. Non-Metallic Ores, Silicate Industries & Solid Minerals Fuels. (Illus.). 1971. Pgs. 828 (ISBN 0-06-491103-9); Vol. 3. Metals & Ores. (Illus.). 1970. Pgs. 918 (ISBN 0-06-491104-7); Vol. 4. Petroleum & Organic Chemicals. (Illus.). 1972. Pgs. 792 (ISBN 0-06-491105-5); Vol. 5. Natural Organic Materials & Related Synthetic Products. (Illus.). 1972. Pgs. 898 (ISBN 0-06-491106-3); Vol. 6. Wood, Paper, Textiles, Plastics & Photographic Materials. 1973 (ISBN 0-06-491107-1); Vol. 7. Vegetable Food Products & Luxuries. (Illus.). 1975. Pgs. 905 (ISBN 0-06-491108-X); Vol. 8. Edible Oils & Fats & Animal Food Products: Material Resources. (Illus.). 1975. Pgs. 600 (ISBN 0-06-491109-8). (Illus.). 45.00x ea. B&N Imports.

Mackey, A. G. Symbolism of Freemansonry. 6.95x (ISBN 0-685-22122-9). Wehman.

Mackey, Bertha. A Saloon Keeper's Daughter Saved. 15p. 1982. pap. 0.15 (ISBN 0-686-36264-0); pap. 0.25 2 copies (ISBN 0-686-37285-9). Faith Pub HSe.

Mackey, Carol, jt. auth. see Moseley, Michael E.

Mackey, Douglas A. The Rainbow Quest of Thomas Pynchon. LC 80-11219. (The Milford Ser.: Popular Writers of Today: Vol. 28). 1980. lib. bdg. 9.95x (ISBN 0-89370-142-4); pap. 3.95x (ISBN 0-89370-242-0). Borgo Pr.

Mackey, G. F. Gregory's Modern Building Practice in Australia. pap. 8.50x (ISBN 0-392-03145-0, ABC). Sportshelf.

Mackey, Howard. Wit & Whiggery: The Rev. Sydney Smith (1771-1845) LC 79-64194. 1979. pap. text ed. 17.75 (ISBN 0-8191-0756-5). U Pr of Amer.

Mackey, J. Price Guide to Collectable Antiques. (Illus.). 1975. 29.50 (ISBN 0-902028-08-1). Apollo.

Mackey, J. P. Church: Its Credibility Today. 1970. pap. 3.50 o.p. (ISBN 0-02-804200-X). Glencoe.

Mackey, James P. The Christian Experience of God As Trinity. 320p. 1983. 17.50 (ISBN 0-8245-0561-1). Crossroad NY.

--Jesus, the Man & the Myth. LC 78-61627. 320p. 1979. pap. 9.95 (ISBN 0-8091-2169-7). Paulist Pr.

Mackey, Janet & World Without War Council, eds. Terrorism & Political Self-Determination: A Tragic Marriage We Could Help Decouple. 64p. 1980. 1.00 (ISBN 0-686-81728-1). World Without War.

Mackey, Joan, jt. auth. see Abraham, Paul.

Mackey, Mary. The Last Warrior Queen. 1983. 15.95 (ISBN 0-399-31016-9). Seaview Bks.

Mackey, Mary S. & Mackey, Maryette G., eds. The Pronunciation of Ten Thousand Proper Names. 1979. Repr. of 1922 ed. 55.00x (ISBN 0-8103-4137-9). Gale.

Mackey, Maryette G., jt. ed. see Mackey, Mary S.

Mackey, Robert, jt. ed. see Mitcham, Carl.

Mackey, Samson A. Mythological Astronomy of the Ancients Demonstrated, Pt. 1. Bd. with Pt. 2. The Key to Urania. LC 73-84043. (Secret Doctrine Reference Ser.). 380p. 1973. Repr. of 1822 ed. 16.00 (ISBN 0-913510-06-8). Wizards.

Mackey, William F. & Andersson, Theodore, eds. Bilingualism in Early Childhood. 1977. pap. 16.95 o.p. (ISBN 0-88377-075-X). Newbury Hse.

McKibben, Jorge F., tr. see Davis, Guillermo H.

McKibben-Stockwell. Nuevo Lexico Griego Espanol. 316p. 1981. pap. 10.50 (ISBN 0-311-42058-3, Edit Mundo). Casa Bautista.

Mackichan, Kenneth A., jt. auth. see Hammer, Mark J.

Mackie, Annebeth, tr. Bible Speaks Again. LC 79-75400. (Dutch). 1969. pap. 4.95 o.p. (ISBN 0-8066-0931-1, 10-0704). Augsburg.

Mackie, Beatrice C. It Can Happen to You. 75p. 1983. 12.00 (ISBN 0-682-49960-9). Exposition.

Mackie, Bob & Bremer, Gerry. Dressing for Glamour. LC 79-14907. (Illus.). 192p. 1979. 14.95 o.s.i. (ISBN 0-89479-053-6). A & W Pubs.

McKie, Christine, jt. auth. see McKie, Duncan.

McKie, David & Cook, Christopher. The Decade of Disillusion: Britain in the Sixties. LC 72-83416. 1972. 26.00 (ISBN 0-312-18900-1). St Martin.

McKie, Duncan & McKie, Christine. Crystalline Solids. LC 73-34. 628p. 1974. text ed. 27.95x o.p. (ISBN 0-470-58455-6). Halsted Pr.

McKie, Duncan, tr. see Kern, Raymond & Weisbrod, Alain.

Mackie, Dustin & Decker, Douglas. Group & Ipa Hmo's. LC 81-2096. 492p. 1981. text ed. 42.95 (ISBN 0-89443-341-5). Aspen Systems.

Mackie, Euan W. Science & Society in Prehistoric Britain. LC 76-48755. 1977. 35.00x (ISBN 0-312-70245-0). St Martin.

Mackie, J. A., ed. The Chinese in Indonesia: Five Essays. LC 76-139. 296p. 1976. text ed. 14.00x (ISBN 0-8248-0449-X). UH Pr.

Mackie, J. L. Problems from Locke. (Illus.). 1976. text ed. 19.95x (ISBN 0-19-824555-6); pap. text ed. 8.95x (ISBN 0-19-875036-6); op 13.95 (ISBN 0-686-96829-8). Oxford U Pr.

McKie, James D., ed. Social Responsibility & the Business Predicament. (Studies in the Regulation of Economic Activity). 361p. 1975. 19.95 (ISBN 0-8157-5608-9); pap. 8.95 (ISBN 0-8157-5607-0). Brookings.

Mackie, Lindsay & Patullo, Polly. Women at Work. (Tavistock Women's Studies). 1977. pap. 9.95x (ISBN 0-422-75990-2, Pub. by Tavistock England). Methuen Inc.

MacKie, Marie D., tr. see Prunieres, Henry.

McKie, R., jt. auth. see Beard, H.

MacKie, Roan M. Eczema & Dermatitis. LC 82-11390. (Positive Health Guides Ser.). (Illus.). 112p. 1983. lib. bdg. 12.95 (ISBN 0-668-05629-0); pap. 7.95 (ISBN 0-668-05634-7). Arco.

Mackie, Robert, ed. Literacy & Revolution: The Pedagogy of Paulo Freire. 172p. 1981. pap. 7.95 o.p. (ISBN 0-8264-0055-8). Continuum.

Mackie, Rona M., ed. Malignant Melanoma. (Pigment Cell Ser.: Vol. 6). (Illus.). vi, 220p. 1983. 88.25 (ISBN 3-8055-3690-9). S Karger.

McKie, Roy. The Alphabet Block Book. LC 79-63611. (Shape Bks.). (Illus.). (ps-1). 1979. 2.95 (ISBN 0-394-84269-3, BYR). Random.

--The Riddle Book. LC 77-85237. (Picturebacks Ser.). (ps-2). 1978. PLB 4.99 (ISBN 0-394-93732-5, BYR); pap. 1.50 (ISBN 0-394-83732-0). Random.

McKie, Roy & Eastman, Philip D. Snow. LC 62-15114. (Illus.). (gr. 1-2). 1962. 4.95 (ISBN 0-394-80027-3); PLB 5.99 (ISBN 0-394-90027-8). Beginner.

McKie, Roy, jt. auth. see Beard, Henry.

McKigney, John I. & Munro, Hamish N., eds. Nutrient Requirements in Adolescence. LC 75-38724. 392p. 1976. text ed. 20.00x (ISBN 0-262-13119-6). MIT Pr.

McKillip, Patricia. The Forgotten Beasts of Eld. 1975. pap. 2.75 (ISBN 0-380-00480-1, 62505-9). Avon.

--The House on Parchment Street. (Illus.). 1978. pap. 1.95 (ISBN 0-689-70451-8, A-88, Aladdin). Atheneum.

McKillip, Patricia A. The Night Gift. 1980. pap. 1.95 (ISBN 0-689-70470-4, A-99, Aladdin). Atheneum.

Mckillip, Rebecca. Art Nouveau Abstract Designs. (The International Design Library). (Illus.). 48p. (Orig.). 1983. pap. 2.95 (ISBN 0-88045-023-1). Stemmer Hse.

McKillop, A., jt. auth. see Taylor, E. C.

McKillop, Allan A., et al see Heat Transfer & Fluid Mechanics Institute.

McKillop, Menzies see Lion, Eugene & Ball, David.

McKillop, Susan R. Franciabigio. (California Studies in the History of Art). (Illus.). 1974. 90.00x (ISBN 0-520-01688-2). U of Cal Pr.

McKim, Donald K., ed. The Authoritative Word: Essays on the Nature of Scripture. 288p. 1983. pap. 10.95 (ISBN 0-8028-1948-6). Eerdmans.

McKim, Elizabeth. Burning Through. LC 78-540035. (Wampeter Firsts Ser: No. 1). (Illus.). 1978. pap. 3.95 o.p. (ISBN 0-931694-01-9). Wampeter Pr.

McKim, Elizabeth, jt. auth. see Steinbergh, Judith.

McKim, Robert H. Experiences in Visual Thinking. 2nd ed. LC 80-437. (Orig.). 1980. pap. text ed. 16.95 (ISBN 0-8185-0411-0). Brooks-Cole.

--Thinking Visually: A Strategy Manual for Problem-Solving. rev. ed. LC 80-16526. 1980. 25.95 (ISBN 0-534-97988-2); pap. 14.95 (ISBN 0-534-97978-5). Lifetime Learn.

McKim, Ruby S. One Hundred & One Patchwork Patterns. rev. ed. (Illus.). 1962. pap. 3.50 (ISBN 0-486-20773-0). Dover.

Mackin, Dorothy. Melodrama Classics: Six Plays & How to Stage Them. LC 81-8856. (Illus.). 256p. (YA) (gr. 8 up). 1981. 14.95 (ISBN 0-8069-7036-7); lib. bdg. 17.79 (ISBN 0-8069-7037-5). Sterling.

Mackin, Ronald, jt. auth. see Cowie, A. P.

MacKinder, Hanford J. Britain & the British Seas. Repr. of 1902 ed. lib. bdg. 17.50x (ISBN 0-8371-2754-8, MABR). Greenwood.

Mckinlay, John B., ed. The Milbank Readers, 9 vols. 1982. write for info. MIT Pr.

McKinley, Albert E., ed. see Jameson, J. Franklin.

McKinley, Daniel, jt. ed. see Shepard, Paul.

McKinley, J. L., jt. auth. see Bent, R. D.

McKinley, James L., jt. auth. see Bent, Ralph D.

Mackinley, Malcolm S. Garcia the Centenarian & His Times. LC 75-40206. (Music Reprint Ser.). 1975. Repr. of 1908 ed. lib. bdg. 35.00 (ISBN 0-306-70671-7). Da Capo.

McKinley, Mary B. Words in a Corner: Studies in Montaigne's Latin Quotations. LC 80-70810. (French Forum Monograraphs: No. 26). 134p. (Orig.). 1981. pap. 9.50x (ISBN 0-917058-25-9). French Forum.

McKinley, Mary B., jt. ed. see Frame, Donald M.

McKinley, Robert L. The Neurotic's Handbook. 131p. 1977. pap. 5.00 (ISBN 0-9609644-0-1). Candle Bks.

McKinley, Robin. The Blue Sword. LC 82-2895. 256p. (YA) (gr. 7 up). 1982. 11.00 (ISBN 0-688-00938-7). Greenwillow.

--The Blue Sword. (gr. 7 up). 1982. 11.50 (ISBN 0-688-00938-7). Greenwillow.

McKinley, T. D. The Electron Microprobe. LC 65-26849. (Electrochemical Soc. Ser.). 1035p. 1966. 54.00 (ISBN 0-470-58460-2). Krieger.

McKinney, B. Pathology of the Cardiomyopathies. Crawford, T., ed. (Postgraduate Pathology Ser.). 1974. 49.00 o.p. (ISBN 0-407-62000-1). Butterworth.

McKinney, Douglas. Sam Peckinpah. (Filmmakers Ser.). 1979. lib. bdg. 11.95 (ISBN 0-8057-9264-3, Twayne). G K Hall.

McKinney, Eleanor & Baechtold, Marquerite. Library Service for Families. (Orig.). 1983. 22.50 (ISBN 0-208-01856-5, Lib Prof Pubns); pap. cancelled (ISBN 0-208-01855-7). Shoe String.

McKinney, Fred, et al. Effective Behavior & Human Development. (Illus.). 512p. 1976. text ed. 22.95x (ISBN 0-02-379340-6). Macmillan.

McKinney, J. Evans. Decoys of the Susquehanna Flats & Their Makers. (Illus.). 96p. 1978. pap. 12.95 (ISBN 0-686-36762-6). Md Hist.

McKinney, James D. Environmental Health Chemistry: The Chemistry of Environmental Agents As Potential Human Hazards. LC 80-65510. (Illus.). 656p. 1981. 49.95 (ISBN 0-250-40352-8). Ann Arbor Science.

McKinney, James D. & Feagans, Lynne, eds. Current Topics in Learning Disabilities, Vol. 1. (Current Topics in Learning Disabilities Ser.). 1983. text ed. 32.50 (ISBN 0-89391-089-9). Ablex Pub.

McKinney, Jerome B. & Howard, Lawrence C. Public Administration: Balancing Power & Accountability. LC 79-12796. (Orig.). 1979. pap. 12.50x (ISBN 0-935610-06-5). Moore Pub IL.

McKinney, John. California Coastal Trails: Mexican Border to Big Sur, Vol. I. (Illus.). 240p. (Orig.). 1983. pap. 8.95 (ISBN 0-88496-198-2). Capra Pr.

--How to Start Your Own Community Newspaper. LC 77-78181. 1977. pap. 19.95 o.p. (ISBN 0-931058-01-5). Meadow Pr.

McKinney, Peter & Cunningham, Bruce L. Handbook of Plastic Surgery. (Illus.). 272p. 1981. softcover 16.95 (ISBN 0-683-05865-7). Williams & Wilkins.

McKinney, R. E. Microbiology for Sanitary Engineers. (Sanitary & Water Resources Engineering). 1962. text ed. 33.95 (ISBN 0-07-045180-X, C). McGraw.

McKinnis, Jerry. Bass Fishing. (Illus.). 96p. pap. 3.95 o.p. (ISBN 0-88317-056-6). Stoeger Pub Co.

Mackinnon, Alasdair, tr. see Krzisnik, Zoran.

Mackinnon, Alasdair, tr. see Stele, France.

McKinnon, Alastair. Falsification & Belief. 1979. lib. bdg. 23.00 (ISBN 0-917930-33-9); pap. text ed. 5.50x (ISBN 0-917930-13-4). Ridgeview.

McKinnon, Alastair, ed. see Malantschuk, Gregor.

MacKinnon, Catharine A. Sexual Harassment of Working Women: A Case of Sex Discrimination. LC 78-9645. (Fastback Ser.: No. 19). 1979. 30.00x (ISBN 0-300-02298-0); pap. 7.95x (ISBN 0-300-02299-9). Yale U Pr.

MacKinnon, Charles. Farthingale's Folly. LC 78-55656. 1978. 8.95 o.p. (ISBN 0-672-52347-7). Bobbs.

MacKinnon, D. M. The Problem of Metaphysics. LC 73-79309. 180p. 1974. 24.95 (ISBN 0-521-20275-2). Cambridge U Pr.

MacKinnon, Donald W. In Search of Human Effectiveness: Identifying & Developing Creativity. LC 78-62345. 1978. pap. 9.50 (ISBN 0-930222-03-2). Creat Educ Found.

MacKinnon, Edward M. Scientific Explanation & Atomic Physics. LC 82-2702. (Illus.). 464p. 1982. lib. bdg. 27.50X (ISBN 0-226-50053-5). U of Chicago Pr.

Mackinnon, G. E., jt. ed. see Waller, T. G.

Mackinnon, G. E., jt. ed. see Waller, T. Gary.

McKinnon, Gordon P., ed. see Brannigan, Francis L.

MacKinnon, John. Borneo. (The World's Wild Places Ser.). (Illus.). 1978. lib. bdg. 15.96 (ISBN 0-8094-2020-1). Silver.

MacKinnon, Kenneth. Language, Education & Social Processes in a Gaelic Communtiy. (Direct Editions Ser.). (Orig.). 1977. pap. 12.95 (ISBN 0-7100-8466-8). Routledge & Kegan.

Mackinnon, Lillias. Music by Heart. LC 80-26551. xi, 141p. 1981. Repr. of 1954 ed. lib. bdg. 19.25x (ISBN 0-313-22810-8, MAMB). Greenwood.

McKinnon, Lise S., tr. see Friis, Babbis.

MacKinnon, Roger A. & Michels, Robert. Psychiatric Interview in Clinical Practice. LC 70-151680. 1971. 22.00 (ISBN 0-7216-5973-X). Saunders.

McKinnon, Ronald I. Money & Capital in Economic Development. 1973. 18.95 (ISBN 0-8157-5614-3); pap. 7.95 (ISBN 0-8157-5613-5). Brookings.

--Money in International Exchange: The Convertible Currency System. 1979. text ed. 19.95x (ISBN 0-19-502408-7); pap. text ed. 11.95x (ISBN 0-19-502409-5). Oxford U Pr.

McKinnon, Ronald I. & Mathieson, Donald J. How to Manage a Repressed Economy. LC 81-20283. (Essays in International Finance Ser.: No. 145). 1981. pap. text ed. 2.50x (ISBN 0-88165-052-8). Princeton U Int Finan Econ.

McKinnon, Sharon M., jt. auth. see Edmonds, Thomas P.

McKinnon, William T. Apollo's Blended Dream: A Study of the Poetry of Louis MacNeice. 1971. 12.75x o.p. (ISBN 0-19-211299-6). Oxford U Pr.

--Aspects of Modern Business Style. 196p. 1983. pap. 21.00 (ISBN 82-00-06444-1, Universitet). Columbia U Pr.

McKinon, DeShae. Struggle for Existence. 1983. 10.95 (ISBN 0-533-05662-4). Vantage.

McKinstry, Sam W. The Brokerage Role of Rajasthani Lawyers in Three Districts of Rajasthan, India: As Evidenced Through Lawyer-Client Relations-Fact or Fiction? LC 80-5232. 90p. 1980. pap. text ed. 7.00 o.p. (ISBN 0-8191-1062-0). U Pr of Amer.

McKinstry, Steven R. The Attic Treasure. LC 82-82457. (Illus.). 32p. 1982. 6.95 (ISBN 0-910079-00-5). T Henry Pub.

MacKintosh, C. H. Short Papers on Scriptural Subjects, 2 vols. Set. 13.95 (ISBN 0-88172-115-8). Believers Bkshelf.

Mackintosh, Carlos H. La Oracion y los Cultos de Oracion. 2nd ed. Daniel, Roger P., ed. Bautista, Sara, tr. from Eng. (La Serie Diamante). 40p. (Span.). 1982. pap. 0.85 (ISBN 0-942504-08-9). Overcomer Pr.

--El Perdon de los Pecados. 2nd ed. Bennett, Gordon H., ed. Bautista, Sara, tr. from Eng. (La Serie Diamante). 36p. (Span.). 1982. pap. 0.85 (ISBN 0-942504-02-X). Overcomer Pr.

Mackintosh, Charles H., tr. Tao. 1971. pap. 2.75 (ISBN 0-8356-0426-8, Quest). Theos Pub Hse.

MacKintosh, Douglas R. Systems of Health Care. LC 78-3134. (Illus.). 1978. lib. bdg. 31.50 (ISBN 0-89158-330-0); pap. text ed. 16.50 (ISBN 0-89158-818-3). Westview.

Mackintosh, John J., ed. British Prime Ministers in the Twentieth Century, Vol. 1. LC 77-76542. 1977. 25.00 (ISBN 0-312-10517-7). St Martin.

Mackintosh, John P., ed. British Prime Ministers in the Twentieth Century, Vol. 2. LC 77-76542. 1978. 25.00 (ISBN 0-312-10518-5). St Martin.

Mackintosh, Mary, tr. see Kozintzev, Grigori.

MacKintosh, N. J., jt. auth. see Sutherland, N. S.

McKinzie, Edith. Hawaiian Genealogies, Vol. 1. (Source Bulletin Ser.: No. 1). 100p. 1983. 4.50 (ISBN 0-939154-28-5). Inst Polynesian.

McKitrick, M. Financial Security. (Contemporary Consumer Ser.). 1974. text ed. 6.68 (ISBN 0-07-045315-2, G); tchr's. manual & key 6.50 (ISBN 0-07-045316-0). McGraw.

--Money Management. (Contemporary Consumer Ser.). 1974. text ed. 6.68 (ISBN 0-07-045318-7, G); tchr's. manual & key 6.50 (ISBN 0-07-045319-5). McGraw.

McKitrick, M. O., jt. auth. see Idleman, H. K.

Macklem, Francesca. Tomorrow & Forever. 256p. (Orig.). Date not set. pap. cancelled o.p. (ISBN 0-505-51839-2). Tower Bks.

Macklem, Peter T., ed. Current Concepts in Pulmonary Function & Therapy. (Illus.). 77p. (Orig.). 1979. pap. text ed. 6.00 (ISBN 0-910133-05-0). MA Med Soc.

Macklin, Eleanor D. & Rubin, Roger H. Contemporary Families & Alternative Lifestyles: Handbook on Research & Theory. 416p. 1982. 29.95 (ISBN 0-8039-1053-3). Sage.

Macklin, Ronald R. The Logging Business Management Handbook. LC 82-83344. (Illus.). 176p. 1983. pap. 48.50 (ISBN 0-87930-146-5). Miller Freeman.

Macklin, Ruth. Man, Mind & Morality: The Ethics of Behavior Control. 160p. 1982. 8.50 (ISBN 0-13-551127-5). P-H.

McKlveen, John W. Fast Neutron Activation Analysis: Elemental Data Base. LC 80-84680. 306p. 1981. text ed. 49.95 (ISBN 0-250-40406-0). Ann Arbor Science.

Mackmin, David, jt. auth. see Baum, Andrew.

McKnew, Donald H., Jr., et al. Why Isn't Johnny Crying? Coping with Depression in Children. 1983. 15.50 (ISBN 0-393-01724-9). Norton.

Macknight, Anthony D. & Leader, John P., eds. Epithelial Ion & Water Transport. 392p. 1981. 46.00 (ISBN 0-89004-537-2). Raven.

McKnight, Brian E. The Quality of Mercy: Amnesties & Traditional Chinese Justice. LC 80-26650. 184p. 1981. 15.00x (ISBN 0-8248-0736-7). UH Pr.

--Village & Bureaucracy in Southern Sung China. LC 72-159834. xii, 220p. 1971. pap. 6.95 (ISBN 0-226-56060-0). U of Chicago Pr.

McKnight, Daniel L., Jr. The Complete Partnership Manual & Guide with Tax, Financial & Managerial Strategies. LC 82-5799. 304p. 1982. 39.50 (ISBN 0-13-162230-7, Busn). P-H.

McKnight Staff. Exploring Careers in Child Care. LC 74-82448. (gr. 8-12). 1974. text ed. 16.64 (ISBN 0-87345-573-8); teacher's guide 32.00 (ISBN 0-87345-576-2); activity manual 6.64 (ISBN 0-87345-574-6). McKnight.

--Exploring Careers in Hospitality & Food Service. LC 75-18678. (gr. 8-12). 1975. text ed. 19.68 (ISBN 0-87345-605-X); teacher's guide 34.64 (ISBN 0-87345-606-8). McKnight.

--Exploring Fabrics. LC 76-53072. (gr. 7-12). 1977. text ed. 18.36 (ISBN 0-87345-613-0); tchr's ed. 42.67 (ISBN 0-87345-615-7). McKnight.

--Exploring Living Environments. LC 77-82245. (gr. 7-12). 1977. text ed. 17.28 (ISBN 0-87345-619-X); tchr's ed. 38.60 (ISBN 0-87345-620-3). McKnight.

McKnight Staff Members & Miller, Wilbur R. Electricity. LC 78-53389. (Basic Industrial Arts Ser.). (Illus.). 1978. 7.28 (ISBN 0-87345-794-3); softbound 5.28 (ISBN 0-87345-786-2). McKnight.

--Graphic Arts. LC 78-53390. (Basic Industrial Arts Ser.). (Illus.). 1978. 7.28 (ISBN 0-87345-795-1); softbound 5.28 (ISBN 0-87345-787-0). McKnight.

--Metalworking. LC 78-53387. (Basic Industrial Arts Ser.). (Illus.). 1978. 7.28 (ISBN 0-87345-792-7); softbound 5.28 (ISBN 0-87345-784-6). McKnight.

--Photography. LC 78-53393. (Basic Industrial Arts Ser.). (Illus.). 1978. 7.28 (ISBN 0-87345-797-8); softbound 5.28 (ISBN 0-87345-789-7). McKnight.

--Plastics. LC 78-53391. (Basic Industrial Arts Ser.). (Illus.). 1978. 7.28 (ISBN 0-87345-796-X); softbound 5.28 (ISBN 0-87345-788-9). McKnight.

--Power Mechanics. LC 78-53394. (Basic Industrial Arts Ser.). (Illus.). 1978. 7.28 (ISBN 0-87345-798-6); softbound 5.28 (ISBN 0-87345-790-0). McKnight.

--Woodworking. LC 78-53386. (Basic Industrial Arts Ser.). (Illus.). 1978. 7.28 (ISBN 0-87345-791-9); softbound 5.28 (ISBN 0-87345-783-8). McKnight.

MacKnight, William J., jt. auth. see Aklonis, John J.

McKoski, Martin M. & Hahn, Lynne C. The Developing Writer: A Guide to Basic Skills. 1981. pap. text ed. 13.50x (ISBN 0-673-15691-5). Scott F.

McKown, Robin. Crisis in South Africa. (World Crisis Areas Ser.). (gr. 7 up). 1972. PLB 4.49 o.p. (ISBN 0-399-60110-4). Putnam Pub Group.

--Marie Curie. (World Pioneer Biographies Ser.). (Illus.). (gr. 4-8). 1971. PLB 4.29 o.p. (ISBN 0-399-60447-2). Putnam Pub Group.

Mackrodt, W. C., jt. ed. see Catlow, C. R.

MacKsey, Kenneth. Kesselring: The Making of the Luftwaffe. 1978. 24.00 o.p. (ISBN 0-7134-0862-6, Pub. by Batsford England). David & Charles.

--The Tanks, Nineteen Forty-Five - Nineteen Seventy-Five. (Illus.). 336p. 1981. 23.95 (ISBN 0-85368-293-3). Stackpole.

Mack Smith, Denis. Italy: A Modern History. rev. & enl. ed. LC 69-15851. (History of the Modern World Ser.). (Illus.). 1969. 19.95 (ISBN 0-472-07051-7). U of Mich Pr.

Macksy, Kenneth. The Tank Pioneers. (Illus.). 224p. 1981. 18.95 (ISBN 0-86720-563-6). Sci Bks Intl.

McKuen, Rod. Fields of Wonder. 1971. 6.95 o.p. (ISBN 0-394-40348-7); ltd. ed. 10.00 o.p. (ISBN 0-394-47250-0). Random.

--Listen to the Warm. (Pocket ed.). 1969. 7.95 (ISBN 0-394-40378-9); deluxe ed. 5.00 o.p. (ISBN 0-394-40380-0). Random.

--The Outstretched Hand: Poems, Prayers, & Meditations. LC 78-20589. 160p. 1980. 9.57i (ISBN 0-06-250568-8, HarpR). Har-Row.

--The Power Bright & Shining. 1980. 8.95 o.p. (ISBN 0-671-41392-9, 41392); deluxe ed. 20.00 o.p. (ISBN 0-671-41393-7). S&S.

--Rod McKuen's Book of Days. 1982. gift ed. 24.04i (ISBN 0-06-250570-X). Har-Row.

--Watch for the Wind. 1983. pap. 2.95 (ISBN 0-686-43183-9). PB.

--We Touch the Sky. 1979. 8.95 (ISBN 0-671-24828-6); deluxe ed. 15.00 o.p. S&S.

McKusick, Victor. Human Genetics. 2nd ed. (Foundations of Modern Genetics Ser). 1969. pap. 13.95x ref. ed. (ISBN 0-13-445106-6). P-H.

McKusick, Victor A. Heritable Disorders of Connective Tissue. 4th ed. LC 72-77492. (Illus.). 878p. 1972. 43.50 o.p. (ISBN 0-8016-3288-9). Mosby.

Mackworth, Cecily. English Interludes: Mallarme, Verlaine, Paul Valery, Valery Larbaud in London, 1860-1912. (Illus.). 232p. 1975. 21.50x (ISBN 0-7100-7878-1). Routledge & Kegan.

Mackworth-Young, Robin, jt. auth. see Johnson, Michael.

McLachlan, A. D., jt. auth. see Carrington, A.

MacLachlan, Colin M. Criminal Justice in Eighteenth Century Mexico: A Study of the Tribunal of the Acordada. LC 72-97737. 1975. 27.50x (ISBN 0-520-02416-8). U of Cal Pr.

McLachlan, Gordon, ed. see Blanpain, Jan & Delesie, Luk.

McLachlan, Gordon, jt. ed. see Douglas-Wilson, J.

MacLachlan, Lewis. Commonsense About Prayer. 141p. 1965. pap. 3.25 (ISBN 0-227-67653-X). Attic Pr.

--How to Pray for Healing. 112p. 1977. pap. 3.95 (ISBN 0-227-67486-3). Attic Pr.

--Intelligent Prayer. 104p. 1965. pap. 3.95 (ISBN 0-227-67496-0). Attic Pr.

Maclachlan, Morgan D. Why They Did Not Starve: Biocultural Adaptation in a South Indian Village. LC 81-20203. (Illus.). 350p. 1983. text ed. 27.50x (ISBN 0-89727-001-0). Inst Study Human.

MacLachlan, Patricia. Arthur, For the Very First Time. LC 79-2007. (Illus.). 128p. (gr. 4-7). 1980. 9.57i (ISBN 0-06-024045-8, HarpJ); PLB 9.89 (ISBN 0-06-024047-4). Har-Row.

--Arthur, for the Very First Time. (Illus.). (gr. 3 up). Date not set. pap. 1.95 (ISBN 0-590-32257-5). Schol Bk Serv.

--Moon. Stars, Frogs & Friends. (Illus.). (ps-3). 1980. 6.95 o.p. (ISBN 0-394-84138-7); PLB 6.99 (ISBN 0-394-94138-1). Pantheon.

--Seven Kisses in a Row. LC 82-47718. (A Charlotte Zolotow Bk.). (Illus.). 64p. (gr. 2-5). 1983. 8.61i (ISBN 0-06-024083-0, HarpJ); PLB 8.89g (ISBN 0-06-024084-9). Har-Row.

McLafferty, Fred W. & Abrahamsson, Sixten. Computer Tape of the Registry of Mass Spectral Data. 3rd ed. 1982. 4000.00x (ISBN 0-471-86932-5, Pub. by Wiley-Interscience). Wiley.

Maclagan, Michael, jt. auth. see Louda, Jiri.

MacLaine, Allan, intro. by. The Beginnings to Fifteen Fifty-Eight. 96p. 1981. pap. 4.95 o.p. (ISBN 0-312-07190-6). St Martin.

McLanathan, Richard. Art in America: A Brief History. (Illus.). 1973. pap. text ed. 10.95 (ISBN 0-15-503466-9, HC). HarBraceJ.

--East Building: A Profile. LC 78-606059. (Illus.). pap. 4.00 (ISBN 0-89468-037-4). Natl Gallery Art.

--World Art in American Museums: A Personal Guide. 384p. 1983. 15.95 (ISBN 0-385-18515-4, Anchor Pr). Doubleday.

McLane, Gretel B. Kailia & the King's Horse. (Illus.). 96p. 1982. 7.95 (ISBN 0-916630-28-5). Pr Pacifica.

MacLane, Saunders & Birkhoff, Garrett. Algebra. 2nd ed. 1979. 28.95x (ISBN 0-02-374310-7). Macmillan.

MacLane, Saunders, jt. auth. see Birkhoff, Garrett.

McLaren. Chemical Manipulation of Crop Growth. 1982. text ed. 89.95 (ISBN 0-408-10767-7). Butterworth.

Maclaren, A. Allan. Religion & Social Class: The Disruption. (The Scottish Ser.). 1974. 24.00x (ISBN 0-7100-7789-0). Routledge & Kegan.

MacLaren, Alexander D. Christ in the Heart. (A Shepherd Illustrated Classic Ser.). Date not set. pap. 0.00 (ISBN 0-87983-293-2). Keats. Postponed.

MacLaren, Alxander. The Psalms, 3 Vols. 1981. 45.00 set (ISBN 0-86524-038-8, 7902). Klock & Klock.

McLaren, Angus. Sexuality & Social Order: Birth Control in Nineteenth-Century France. 240p. 1982. text ed. 29.50x (ISBN 0-8419-0744-7). Holmes & Meier.

McLaren, Annabel. Going to the Hospital. LC 80-52526. (Starters Ser.). PLB 8.00 (ISBN 0-382-06480-1). Silver.

McLaren, Dell. The Seduction of Lucy Mattson. (Inflation Fighters Ser.). 192p. 1982. pap. cancelled o.s.i. (ISBN 0-8439-1137-9, Leisure Bks). Nordon Pubns.

McLaren, Diane J. Schistosoma Mansoni: The Parasite Surface in Relation to Host Immunity. LC 80-40955. (Tropical Medicine Research Studies Ser.). 229p. 1980. 61.95 (ISBN 0-471-27869-6, Pub. by Res Stud Pr). Wiley.

McLaren, Donald S. Nutrition in the Community: A Critical Look at Nutrition Policy Planning & Programmes. 2nd ed. 1983. write for info. (ISBN 0-471-10294-6, Pub. by Wiley-Interscience). Wiley.

Maclaren, Ian. The Days of Auld Lang Syne. 366p. 1982. Repr. of 1895 ed. lib. bdg. 20.00 (ISBN 0-89984-804-4). Century Bookbindery.

McLaren, Ian A. Education in a Small Democracy, New Zealand. (World Education Ser.). 1974. 17.95x (ISBN 0-7100-7798-X). Routledge & Kegan.

McLaren, Robert B. The World of Philosophy: An Introduction. LC 82-14214. (Illus.). 272p. 1983. text ed. 23.95x (ISBN 0-8304-1000-7); pap. text ed. 10.95x (ISBN 0-88229-815-1). Nelson-Hall.

McLaren, Robert I. Organizational Dilemmas. 120p. 1982. 24.95 (ISBN 0-471-10155-9, Pub. by Wiley-Interscience). Wiley.

McLaren, Roy C., jt. auth. see Wilson, O. W.

McLarn, Jack C. Writing Part Time for Fun & Money. LC 78-50474. 1980. pap. 4.95 o.p. (ISBN 0-913864-39-0). Enterprise Del.

McLarney, William. The Freshwater Aquaculture Book: A Handbook for Small Scale Fish Culture. (Illus.). 600p. 1983. 38.50 (ISBN 0-88930-046-1, Pub. by Cloudburst Canada). Madrona Pubs.

McLauchlan, William P. American Legal Processes. LC 76-26579. (Viewpoints on American Politics Ser.). 1977. pap. text ed. 12.95 (ISBN 0-471-58561-0). Wiley.

McLaughlin, jt. auth. see Bronthon.

McLaughlin, A. C. Report on the Diplomatic Archives of the Department of State, 1789-1840. rev. ed. 1906. Repr. of 1840 ed. pap. 10.00 (ISBN 0-527-00682-3). Kraus Repr.

McLaughlin, Andrew C. The Courts, the Constitution & Parties. LC 70-87405. (The American Scene Ser.). 312p. 1972. Repr. of 1912 ed. lib. bdg. 39.50 (ISBN 0-306-71549-X). Da Capo.

McLaughlin, B. K., jt. auth. see Guth, Hans P.

McLaughlin, Barry. Second-Language Acquisition in Childhood. LC 75-52304. 230p. 1978. lib. bdg. 19.95 (ISBN 0-89859-180-5). L Erlbaum Assocs.

McLaughlin, Charles B. The Elm Is Green. (Illus.). 1974. 4.50 o.p. (ISBN 0-686-05516-0). Dnomro Pubns.

--Ouch It Hurts. (Illus.). 158p. (gr. 5-9). 1972. 3.00 o.p. (ISBN 0-686-01899-0). Dnomro Pubns.

McLaughlin, Clara J. The Black Parents Handbook: A Guide to the Facts of Pregnancy, Birth & Child Care. (Illus.). 256p. 1975. 10.00 o.p. (ISBN 0-15-113185-6, Harv). HarBraceJ.

McLaughlin, David J. The Executive Money Map. 1975. 26.50 o.p. (ISBN 0-07-045390-X, P&RB). McGraw.

McLaughlin, Donald H., ed. see McGuiston, Frank W., Jr. & Shoemaker, Robert S.

McLaughlin, Eleanor, jt. auth. see Ruether, Rosemary.

McLaughlin, Frank S. & Pickhardt, Robert C. Quantitative Techniques for Management Decisions. LC 78-69586. (Illus.). 1979. text ed. 25.95 (ISBN 0-395-26669-6); instr's. manual 3.50 (ISBN 0-395-26668-8). HM.

McLaughlin, Glenn C. Growth of American Manufacturing Areas. Repr. of 1938 ed. lib. bdg. 16.25x (ISBN 0-8371-2895-1, MCMA). Greenwood.

McLaughlin, Iona H. Triumph Over Tragedy. 128p. 1981. pap. 1.50 (ISBN 0-687-42640-5, Festival). Abingdon.

McLaughlin, John B. Gypsy Lifestyles. LC 80-7572. 160p. 1980. 16.95x (ISBN 0-669-03754-0). Lexington Bks.

McLaughlin, Loretta. The Pill, John Rock & the Church: The Biography of a Revolution. 1983. 15.45i (ISBN 0-316-56095-2). Little.

McLaughlin, Mark, jt. auth. see Johnson, Curt.

McLaughlin, Phillip J., jt. auth. see Wehman, Paul.

McLaughlin, Robert E., jt. auth. see Carron, Harold.

McLaughlin, Roberta & Wood, Lucille. Sing a Song of People. (ps-3). 1973. songbook 9.63 (ISBN 0-8372-2375-X); 3 lp records 9.09 ea.; sets 1-3, incl. 2 filmstrips, lp record & 20 minibks 57.90 ea.; minibks. sep. sets of 10 9.90; complete kit cassette ed. 199.95 (ISBN 0-8372-0219-1); complete kit record ed. 199.95 (ISBN 0-8372-0218-3). Bowmar-Noble.

McLaughlin, Stephen D. The Wayside Mechanic: An Analysis of Skills Acquisition in Ghana. (Orig.). 1980. pap. 6.00 (ISBN 0-932288-58-8). Ctr Intl Ed U of Ma.

McLaughlin, Terence. If You Like It Don't Eat It: Dietary Fads and Fancies. LC 78-61206. 1979. 10.00x o.p. (ISBN 0-87663-332-7). Universe.

McLaughlin, Tom. The Greatest Escape, or How to Live in Paradise, in Luxury, for 250 Dollars per Month. (Illus.). 200p. 1983. pap. write for info. (ISBN 0-918464-52-8). Thompson Roberts.

McLaughlin, W. L., ed. Trends in Radiation Dosimetry. (Illus.). 320p. 1982. pap. 25.00 (ISBN 0-08-029143-0). Pergamon.

McLaurin. Middle East Foreign Policy. 336p. 1982. 34.95 (ISBN 0-03-057753-5); student ed. avail. (ISBN 0-03-057754-3). Praeger.

McLaurin, A. Virginia Woolf: The Echoes Enslaved. LC 72-83589. 300p. 1973. 34.95 (ISBN 0-521-08704-X). Cambridge U Pr.

McLaurin, Melton. Paternalism & Protest: Southern Mill Workers & Organized Labor, 1875-1905. LC 70-111261. (Contributions in Economics & Economic History, No. 3). 1971. 27.50 (ISBN 0-8371-4662-3). Greenwood.

McLaurin, Melton A. The Knights of Labor in the South. LC 77-87916. (Contributions in Labor History: No. 4). (Illus.). 1978. lib. bdg. 27.50 (ISBN 0-313-20033-5, MCK/). Greenwood.

McLaurin, R. D., et al. Foreign Policy Making in the Middle East: Domestic Influences on Policy in Egypt, Iraq, Israel, & Syria. LC 76-24360. (Special Studies). 330p. 1977. text ed. 34.95 (ISBN 0-275-23870-9); pap. 10.95 (ISBN 0-275-65010-3). Praeger.

McLaurin, Robert L., ed. Myelomeningocele. LC 77-80637. 896p. 1977. 89.50 o.p. (ISBN 0-8089-1001-9). Grune.

--Pediatric Neuropsychology: Surgery of the Developing Nervous System. Date not set. price not set (ISBN 0-8089-1490-1). Grune.

--Pediatric Neurosurgery: Surgery of the Developing Nervous System. 1982. 100.00 (792846). Grune.

MacLaverty, Bernard. A Time to Dance & Other Stories. LC 82-4342. 174p. 1982. 10.95 (ISBN 0-8076-1045-3). Braziller.

McLay, A. L. & Toner, Peter G., eds. Subcelluar Taxonomy: A Classification System with Diagnostic Applications. (An Ultrastructural Pathology Publication Ser.). Date not set. text ed. 34.50 (ISBN 0-89116-293-3). Hemisphere Pub.

Maclay, Joanna Hawkins. Readers Theatre: Toward a Grammar of Practise. 1970. pap. text ed. 3.50x (ISBN 0-394-30371-7). Phila Bk Co.

Maclay, Joanna M. & Sloan, Thomas O., eds. Interpretation: An Approach to the Study of Literature. 1972. pap. text ed. 3.95x (ISBN 0-685-69594-8). Phila Bk Co.

Maclay, K. T. K. T. Maclay's Total Beauty Catalog. LC 77-21522. (Illus.). 1978. pap. 7.95 o.p. (ISBN 0-698-10835-3, Coward). Putnam Pub Group.

Maclean. Haemoglobin. (Studies in Biology: No. 93). 1978. 5.95 o.p. (ISBN 0-7131-2698-1). Univ Park.

MacLean, A. D., ed. Winter's Tales Twenty-Eight. 224p. 1983. 11.95 (ISBN 0-312-88421-4). St Martin.

McLean, A. J., et al. Organization Development in Transition: Evidence of an Evolving Profession. 200p. 1982. 24.95x (ISBN 0-471-10142-7, Pub. by Wiley-Interscience). Wiley.

McLean, Alan see Allen, W. S.

McLean, Albert F., Jr. William Cullen Bryant. (United States Authors Ser.). 1964. lib. bdg. 11.95 (ISBN 0-8057-0108-7, Twayne). G K Hall.

MacLean, Alistair. Circus. LC 74-33988. 192p. 1975. 8.95 o.p. (ISBN 0-385-11003-0). Doubleday.

--Goodbye California. LC 77-80897. 1978. 10.95 o.p. (ISBN 0-385-12853-3). Doubleday.

--Partisans. LC 82-45836. 256p. 1983. 14.95 (ISBN 0-385-18262-7). Doubleday.

--River of Death. 224p. 1983. pap. 3.50 (ISBN 0-449-20058-2, Crest). Fawcett.

--Seawitch. LC 76-47825. 1977. 7.95 o.p. (ISBN 0-385-12852-5). Doubleday.

MacLean, Andrew, jt. auth. see MacLean, Janet.

McLean, Andrew J. How to Manage Real Estate Profitably. (Illus.). 1978. pap. 4.95 (ISBN 0-930648-02-1). JWP Dev.

--The Power of Real Estate: And How to Acquire It in Your Spare Time. 1977. pap. 4.95 (ISBN 0-930648-01-3). JWP Dev.

Maclean, Charles. The Watcher. 350p. 1983. 14.95 (ISBN 0-671-25531-2). S&S.

--The Wolf Children. 1980. pap. 3.95 o.p. (ISBN 0-14-005053-1). Penguin.

McLean, Colleen J., jt. auth. see Woollerton, Henry.

McLean, D. Mechanical Properties of Metals. LC 75-11898. 430p. 1977. Repr. of 1962 ed. 24.50 (ISBN 0-88275-298-7). Krieger.

MacLean, D. J. Broadband Feedback Amplifiers. LC 82-2066. (Electronic Circuits & Systems Ser.). 295p. 1982. 38.95 (ISBN 0-471-10214-8, Pub. by Res Stud Pr). Wiley.

MacLean, David. Engine Maintenance & Repair. (Boatowners How-to Guides). (Illus.). 1977. pap. 5.95 o.p. (ISBN 0-8306-6943-4, 943). TAB Bks.

MacLean, David A., jt. auth. see Wein, Ross W.

Maclean, Diana. Birds. LC 80-52517. (Starters Ser.). PLB 8.00 (ISBN 0-382-06477-1). Silver.

MacLean, Douglas & Brown, Peter G., eds. Energy & the Future. LC 82-18609. 224p. 1983. text ed. 35.95x (ISBN 0-8476-7149-6); pap. text ed. 18.50x (ISBN 0-8476-7225-5). Rowman.

MacLean, Douglas, jt. ed. see Brown, Peter G.

McLean, Emma W. Sawney Webb: Maker of Men. (Orig.). pap. 3.00 (ISBN 0-685-03408-9). Creative Pr.

McLean, Ephraim R. & Soden, John V. Strategic Planning for MIS. LC 77-58483. 1977. 39.95 (ISBN 0-471-58562-9, Pub. by Wiley-Interscience). Wiley.

Maclean, Fitzroy. Tito: A Pictorial Biography. LC 80-18683. (Illus.). 128p. 1980. 14.95 o.p. (ISBN 0-07-044671-7); pap. 9.95 o.p. (ISBN 0-07-044660-1). McGraw.

McLean, Gary N. & Elvin, Margo. Multi-Ethnic Timed Writings. (gr. 10-12). 1978. pap. text ed. 7.24x (ISBN 0-912036-05-2). Forkner.

Maclean, Harrison John. The Fate of the Griffon. LC 82-73724. (Illus.). 118p. 1975. 8.95 (ISBN 0-8040-0674-1). Swallow.

McLean, Hugh & Vickery, Walter N., eds. The Year of Protest, 1956. LC 74-8359. 269p. 1974. Repr. of 1961 ed. lib. bdg. 15.75x (ISBN 0-8371-7575-5, MCYP). Greenwood.

McLean, Hulda H. Genealogy of the Herbert Hoover Family: Errata & Addenda. (Special Project). 1976. 2.00x o.p. (ISBN 0-8179-4112-6). Hoover Inst Pr.

Maclean, I. The Renaissance Notion of Woman. LC 79-52837. (Monographs on the History of Medicine). 1980. 19.95 (ISBN 0-521-22906-5). Cambridge U Pr.

McLean, Iain. Dealing in Votes. LC 82-10421. 1982. 25.00 (ISBN 0-312-18535-9). St Martin.

Maclean, Ian, jt. auth. see McFarlane, I. D.

McLean, Isabel & Jarvi, Edith. Canadian Selection: Books & Periodicals for Libraries (Supplement) 1977-79. 544p. 1980. 35.00x (ISBN 0-8020-4593-6). U of Toronto Pr.

McLean, J. E. & Yoder, D. E., eds. Language Intervention with the Retarded. (Illus.). 280p. 1972. text ed. 19.95 (ISBN 0-8391-0675-0). Univ Park.

MacLean, Jack. Secrets of a Superthief. 192p. (Orig.). 1983. pap. 5.95 (ISBN 0-425-05645-7). Berkley Pub.

MacLean, Jan. All Our Tomorrows. (Harlequin Romances Ser.). 192p. 1983. pap. 1.75 (ISBN 0-373-02547-5). Harlequin Bks.

MacLean, Janet & MacLean, Andrew. The Steam Train Crew. (Illus.). 32p. (ps). 1983. bds. 9.95 (ISBN 0-19-554320-3, Pub by Oxford U Pr Childrens). Merrimack Bk Serv.

McLean, Janice, jt. ed. see Wasserman, Paul.

MaClean, Jelorma, jt. auth. see Martin, Wanda J.

Maclean, Joan. English in Basic Medical Science. (English in Focus Ser.). (Illus.). 1975. pap. text ed. 9.95x (ISBN 0-19-437515-3); tchr's ed. 12.00x (ISBN 0-19-437503-X). Oxford U Pr.

MacLean, John. In the Rapids of Revolution. Milton, Nan, ed. 256p. 1980. 14.00x (ISBN 0-8052-8029-4, Pub. by Allison & Busby England); pap. 7.95 (ISBN 0-8052-8028-6, Pub. by Allison & Busby England). Schocken.

McLean, John, jt. tr. see Hadas, Moses.

McLean, John G. & Haigh, Robert W. The Growth of Integrated Oil Companies. Repr. of 1954 ed. 54.00 o.p. (ISBN 0-08-022306-0). Pergamon.

MaClean, Katherine. The Diploids. 1981. PLB 13.95 (ISBN 0-8398-2510-2, Gregg). G K Hall.

--The Trouble with You Earth People. Freas, Polly & Freas, Kelly, eds. LC 79-15246. (Illus.). 1980. pap. 5.95 (ISBN 0-915442-95-7, Starblaze). Donning Co.

MacLean, L. History of the Celtic Language. 288p. 1982. pap. 9.95 (ISBN 0-912526-29-7). Lib Res.

MacLean, L. D. Advances in Surgery, Vol. 16. 1982. 39.95 (ISBN 0-8151-5704-5). Year Bk Med.

McLean, Malcolm. Fine Texas Horses, Their Pedigrees & Performance: 1830-1845. LC 66-29218. (History & Culture Monograph Ser. No.1). 1966. 6.00 (ISBN 0-912646-11-X). Tex Christian.

McLean, Malcolm D., ed. Papers Concerning Robertson's Colony in Texas. Incl. Vol. I, 1788-1822, The Texas Association. LC 73-78014. (Illus.). lxxi, 567p. 1980. Repr. of 1974 ed. lib. bdg. 30.00 (ISBN 0-932408-01-X); Vol. II, 1823 Through September, 1826, Leftwich's Grant. LC 75-21900. (Illus.). 687p. 1975. lib. bdg. 20.00 (ISBN 0-932408-02-8); Vol. III, October, 1826, Through April, 1830, The Nashville Colony. LC 73-78014. (Illus.). 577p. 1976. lib. bdg. 20.00 (ISBN 0-932408-03-6); Vol. IV, May Through October 10, 1830, Tenoxtitlan, Dream Capital of Texas. LC 73-78014. (Illus.). 627p. 1977. lib. bdg. 20.00 (ISBN 0-932408-04-4); Vol. V, October 11, 1830, Through March 5, 1831, The Upper Colony. LC 73-78014. (Illus.). 628p. 1978. lib. bdg. 25.00 (ISBN 0-932408-05-2); Vol. VI, March 6 Through December 5, 1831, The Campaigns Against the Tawakoni, Waco, Towash, & Comanche Indians. LC 73-78014. (Illus.). 632p. 1979. lib. bdg. 25.00 (ISBN 0-932408-06-0); Vol. VII, December 6, 1831, Through October, 1833, **Those Eleven-League Grants. LC 73-78014. (Illus.). 664p. 1980. lib. bdg. 25.00 (ISBN 0-932408-07-9); Vol. VIII, November, 1833, Through September, 1834, Robertson's Colony. LC 73-78014. (Illus.). 608p. 1981. lib. bdg. 25.00 (ISBN 0-932408-08-7). UTA Pr.**

--Papers Concerning Robertson's Colony in Texas. Vol. IX: October, 1834, Through March 20, 1835, Sarahville de Viesca. LC 73-78014. (Illus.). 610p. 1982. lib. bdg. 25.00 (ISBN 0-932408-09-5). UTA Pr.

McLean, Mervyn. Oceanic Music & Dance: An Annotated Bibliography. 1977. pap. text ed. 11.00x (ISBN 0-8248-0589-5). UH Pr.

--Supplement: An Annotated Bibliography of Oceanic Music & Dance. 74p. 1982. pap. text ed. 8.00x (ISBN 0-8248-0862-2). UH Pr.

McLean, Mick. The Japanese Electronics Challenge. LC 82-42710. 170p. 1982. 27.50x (ISBN 0-312-44066-9). St Martin.

MacLean, Norman. The Differentiation of Cells. LC 77-16202. (Genetics - Principles & Persectives). 224p. 1978. pap. text ed. 19.95 (ISBN 0-8391-1194-0). Univ Park.

--A River Runs Through It & Other Stories. LC 75-20895. 232p. 1976. 12.50 (ISBN 0-226-50055-1); pap. 5.95x (ISBN 0-226-50057-8, P821, Phoen). U of Chicago Pr.

MaClean, Richard, jt. auth. see Penner, Peter.

McLean, Robert, ed. India in Transition. 1982. 15.00x o.p. (ISBN 0-8364-0011-9). South Asia Bks.

McLean, Robert A., jt. auth. see Anderson, Virgil L.

McLean, Roderick M. The Theology of Marcus Garvey. LC 81-43759. 212p. (Orig.). 1982. lib. bdg. 22.25 o.p. (ISBN 0-8191-2335-8); pap. text ed. 10.75 o.p. (ISBN 0-8191-2336-6). U Pr of Amer.

McLean, Ruari. Victorian Book Design & Colour Printing. 2nd ed. (Illus.). 256p. 1972. 70.00x (ISBN 0-520-02078-2). U of Cal Pr.

--Victorian Publishers' Book Bindings in Cloth & Leather. (Illus.). 1974. 70.00x (ISBN 0-520-02078-2). U of Cal Pr.

McLean, Scott, ed. see Snyder, Gary.

McLean, Sheila, ed. Legal Issues in Medicine. 219p. 1981. text ed. 39.00x (ISBN 0-566-00428-3). Gower Pub Ltd.

Maclean, Una. Nursing in Contemporary Society. 184p. 1974. 14.00x o.p. (ISBN 0-7100-7751-3); pap. 6.95 o.p. (ISBN 0-7100-7752-1). Routledge & Kegan.

McLean, W. G. & Nelson, E. W. Schaum's Outline of Engineering Mechanics. 3rd ed. (Schaum's Outline Ser.). 1978. pap. 8.95 (ISBN 0-07-044816-7, SP). McGraw.

MacLean, William C., Jr. & Graham, George G. Pediatric Nutrition for the Primary Care Physician. 1982. text ed. 28.95 (ISBN 0-201-15900-7, 15900, Med-Nurse). A-W.

McLeavy, Roy, ed. Jane's Surface Skimmers, 1982. (Jane's Yearbooks). (Illus.). 400p. 1982. 99.50 (ISBN 0-86720-614-4). Sci Bks Intl.

--Jane's Surface Skimmers 1983. 16th ed. (Jane's Yearbooks). (Illus.). 1983. 99.50x (ISBN 0-86720-644-6). Sci Bks Intl.

McLeay, Alison. The World of the Onedin Line. 1977. 5.95 o.p. (ISBN 0-7153-7398-6). David & Charles.

MacLeish, Archibald. J. B. 1958. 4.95 (ISBN 0-395-07949-7). HM.

--Land of the Free. LC 77-9353. (Photography Ser.). (Illus.). 1977. lib. bdg. 21.50 (ISBN 0-306-77435-6); pap. 7.95 (ISBN 0-306-80080-2). Da Capo.

MacLeish, Archibald see Moon, Samuel.

McLeish, John. The Theory of Social Change: Four Views Considered. LC 73-77571. 1969. 4.00x o.p. (ISBN 0-8052-3261-3). Schocken.

McLeish, K., jt. auth. see Nichols, R.

McLeish, K., jt. tr. see Raphael, F.

McLeish, Kenneth. Greek Art & Architecture. McLeish, Valerie, ed. (Aspects of Greek Life Ser.). (Illus.). 64p. (gr. 7-12). 1975. pap. text ed. 3.50 (ISBN 0-582-20673-1). Longman.

--Greek Exploration & Seafaring. McLeish, Valerie, ed. (Aspects of Greek Life Ser.). (Illus.). 64p. (gr. 7-12). 1972. pap. text ed. 3.50 (ISBN 0-582-34402-6). Longman.

--The Greek Theatre. McLeish, Valerie, ed. (Aspects of Greek Life Ser.). (Illus.). 64p. (gr. 7-12). 1972. pap. text ed. 3.50 (ISBN 0-582-34400-X). Longman.

McLeish, Kenneth & McLeish, Valerie. Brahms: Composers & Their World. (Illus.). 90p. (gr. 9-12). 1983. 5.95 (ISBN 0-434-95128-5, Pub. by Heinemann England). David & Charles.

--Composers & Their Music. (Illus.). 32p. pap. 4.75 laminated (ISBN 0-19-321438-5). Oxford U Pr.

--Instruments & Orchestras. (Illus.). 32p. pap. 4.75 laminated (ISBN 0-19-321435-0). Oxford U Pr.

--Mozart. (Composers & their World Ser.). (Illus.). 90p. (gr. 9-12). 1983. 5.95 (ISBN 0-434-95125-0, Pub. by Heinemann England). David & Charles.

--Music Round the World. (Illus.). 32p. pap. 4.75 laminated (ISBN 0-19-321434-2). Oxford U Pr.

--The Oxford First Companion to Music. (Illus.). 1982. 19.95 (ISBN 0-19-314303-8). Oxford U Pr.

--Schubert. (Composers & their World Ser.). (Illus.). 90p. (gr. 9-12). 1983. 5.95 (ISBN 0-434-95127-7, Pub. by Heinemann England). David & Charles.

--Singing & Dancing. (Illus.). 32p. pap. 4.75 laminated (ISBN 0-19-321436-9). Oxford U Pr.

--The Story of Music. (Illus.). 32p. pap. 4.75 laminated (ISBN 0-19-321437-7). Oxford U Pr.

McLeish, Kenneth & McLeish, Vallerie. Stravinsky. (Composers & their World Ser.). (Illus.). 90p. (gr. 9-12). 1983. 5.95 (ISBN 0-434-95126-9, Pub. by Heinemann England). David & Charles.

McLeish, Kenneth, jt. auth. see Vautier, Ghislaine.

McLeish, Kenneth, ed. see Buchanan, David.

McLeish, Kenneth, ed. see McLellan, Elizabeth.

McLeish, Kenneth, ed. see Nichols, Roger & Nichols, Sarah.

McLeish, Kenneth, ed. see Sargent, Michael.

McLeish, Kenneth, adapted by see Vautier, Ghislaine.

McLeish, Kenneth, tr. see Catullus.

MacLeish, R. Second Annual Report of the Belize Archaic Archaeological Reconnaissance. 1981. 4.00 o.p. (ISBN 0-939312-18-2). Peabody Found.

MacLeish, Roderick. Prince Ombra. LC 82-7990. 1982. 14.95 (ISBN 0-312-92658-8). Congdon & Weed.

McLeish, Valerie, jt. auth. see McLeish, Kenneth.

McLeish, Valerie, ed. see Buchanan, David.

McLeish, Valerie, ed. see McLeish, Kenneth.

McLeish, Valerie, ed. see McLellan, Elizabeth.

McLeish, Valerie, ed. see Nichols, Roger & Nichols, Sarah.

McLeish, Valerie, ed. see Sargent, Michael.

McLeish, Vallerie, jt. auth. see McLeish, Kenneth.

McLellan, A. G. The Classical Thermodynamics of Deformable Materials. LC 76-2277. (Cambridge Monographs on Physics). (Illus.). 1980. 75.00 (ISBN 0-521-21237-5). Cambridge U Pr.

McLellan, David. Marxism After Marx: An Introduction. LC 79-1675. 1980. 19.18i (ISBN 0-06-013026-1, HarpT). Har-Row.

McLellan, David S., jt. auth. see Olson, William C.

McLellan, Elizabeth. Minoan Crete. McLeish, Kenneth & McLeish, Valerie, eds. (Aspects of Greek Life Ser.). (Illus.). 64p. (Orig.). (gr. 7-12). 1976. pap. text ed. 3.50 (ISBN 0-582-20671-5). Longman.

McLellan, H. J. Elements of Physical Oceanography. 1965. 19.25 (ISBN 0-08-011320-6). Pergamon.

McLellan, Hugh D. History of Gorham, Maine. 1000p. 1981. Repr. 45.00x (ISBN 0-89725-021-4). NH Pub Co.

McLellan, John. AC & Cobra. (Illus.). 176p. 1982. 29.95 (ISBN 0-901564-57-5, Pub. by Dalton England). Motorbooks Intl.

McLellan, Joyce. Days of the Year. (gr. 2-6). 1971. 3.15 (ISBN 0-08-006799-9). Pergamon.

McLellan, Vern. People Proverbs. LC 82-83841. (Illus.). 1983. pap. 2.95 (ISBN 0-89081-326-4). Harvest Hse.

McLellan, Vernon K. Quips, Quotes & Quests. LC 81-85544. 176p. (Orig.). 1982. pap. 3.25 (ISBN 0-89081-310-8, 3108). Harvest Hse.

McLellan, Vin, jt. auth. see Avery, Paul.

McLelland, Joseph. Trabajo y Justicia. 128p. 1978. 2.50 (ISBN 0-311-46060-7). Casa Bautista.

McLelland, Robert, jt. ed. see Feig, Stephen A.

McLemore, Clinton W. The Scandal of Psychotherapy. 191p. (Orig.). 1982. pap. 6.95 (ISBN 0-8423-5852-8). Tyndale.

McLemore, William P., ed. Foundations of Urban Education. 1977. pap. text ed. 10.25 (ISBN 0-8191-0172-9). U Pr of Amer.

McLendon, James. Eddie Macon's Run. 1980. 10.95 o.p. (ISBN 0-670-28855-1). Viking Pr.

McLendon, Jonathon C., jt. auth. see Haskew, Laurence D.

McLenigham, Valjean. Know When to Stop. (Illus.). 32p. (Orig.). 1980. PLB 4.39 (ISBN 0-695-41371-6, Dist. by Caroline Hse); pap. 1.95 (ISBN 0-695-31371-1). Follett.

McLenighan, Valjean. Diana: Alone Against the Sea. Bennett, Russell, ed. LC 79-21518. (Quest, Adventure, Survival Ser.). (Illus.). 46p. (gr. 4-9). 1982. pap. 7.93g (ISBN 0-8172-2055-0). Raintree Pubs.

--Three Strikes & You're Out. (Beginning-to-Read Ser.). 32p. 1980. PLB 4.39 (ISBN 0-695-41462-3, Dist. by Caroline Hse); pap. 1.95 (ISBN 0-695-31462-9). Follett.

--Turtle & Rabbit. (Beginning-to-Read Ser.). 32p. 1980. PLB 4.39 (ISBN 0-695-41461-5, Dist. by Caroline Hse); pap. 1.95 (ISBN 0-695-31461-0). Follett.

--What You See Is What You Get. (Illus.). 32p. 1980. PLB 4.39 (ISBN 0-695-41370-8, Dist. by Caroline Hse); pap. 1.95 (ISBN 0-695-31370-3). Follett.

--You Are What You Are. (Beginning-to-Read Ser.). (Illus.). (gr. 1-3). 1977. PLB 4.39 (ISBN 0-695-40748-1, Dist. by Caroline Hse); pap. 1.95 (ISBN 0-695-30748-7). Follett.

--You Can Go Jump. (Beginning-to-Read Ser.). (Illus.). (gr. 1-3). 1977. PLB 4.39 (ISBN 0-695-40744-9, Dist. by Caroline Hse); pap. 1.95 (ISBN 0-695-30744-4). Follett.

Maclennan, Douglas. How to Keep Fit at Your Desk. 1980. 1.75 o.s.i. (ISBN 0-8431-0693-X). Price Stern.

MacLennan, Duncan. The Economics of Housing. (Illus.). 300p. (Orig.). 1982. pap. text ed. 17.50x (ISBN 0-582-44381-4). Longman.

McLennan, Gregor. Marxism & the Methodologies of History. 304p. 1982. 24.00 (ISBN 0-8052-7115-5, Pub. by NLB England); pap. 9.50 (ISBN 0-8052-7116-3). Schocken.

McLennan, Gregor, jt. ed. see Johnson, Richard.

MacLeod & Clark. Research Nursing. 1981. 9.95x (ISBN 0-471-25642-0). Wiley.

MacLeod, jt. auth. see Muller.

MacLeod, A. J., jt. ed. see Morton, I. D.

McLeod, A. L., ed. see Wilkes, G. A. & Reid, J. C.

Macleod, Charlotte. The Bilbao Looking Glass. LC 82-45500. (Crime Club Ser.). 192p. 1983. 11.95 (ISBN 0-385-18336-4). Doubleday.

--Cirak's Daughter. LC 82-1727. 192p. (gr. 7 up). 1982. 10.95 (ISBN 0-689-30930-9). Atheneum.

--The Family Vault. LC 78-14687. 1979. 10.95 o.p. (ISBN 0-385-14871-2). Doubleday.

--King Devil. LC 78-5981. 1978. 8.95 o.p. (ISBN 0-689-30659-8). Atheneum.

--Rest You Merry. 1979. pap. 2.50 (ISBN 0-380-47530-8, 61903-2). Avon.

--Rest You Merry. (General Ser.). 1979. lib. bdg. 13.50 (ISBN 0-8161-3000-0, Large Print Bks). G K Hall.

--The Withdrawing Room. LC 80-920. (Crime Club Ser.). 192p. 1980. 8.95 o.p. (ISBN 0-385-17181-1). Doubleday.

--Wrack & Rune. 208p. 1983. pap. 2.75 (ISBN 0-380-61911-3, 61911-3). Avon.

--Wrack & Rune. large type ed. LC 82-10009. 322p. 1982. Repr. of 1982 ed. 10.95 (ISBN 0-89621-372-2). Thorndike Pr.

MacLeod, Chris. Entries: Excerpta From Lovelife. 172p. 1982. pap. 10.00 (ISBN 0-686-37640-4). Solus Impress.

McLeod, D. G. & Mittemeyer, B. T. The Urinary System: Disease, Diagnosis, Treatment. (Clinical Monographs Ser.). (Illus.). 1973. pap. 7.95 o.p. (ISBN 0-87618-059-4). R J Brady.

MacLeod, D. J. Slavery, Race & the American Revolution. LC 74-77382. 269p. 1975. 39.50 (ISBN 0-521-20502-6); pap. 11.95x (ISBN 0-521-09877-7). Cambridge U Pr.

MacLeod, Doug. In the Garden of Badthings. (Illus.). (gr. k-3). 1982. pap. 3.95 (ISBN 0-14-050412-5, Puffin). Penguin.

McLeod, Enid, tr. see Colette.

MacLeod, Fiona. Iona. 1982. pap. 7.25 (ISBN 0-86315-500-6, Pub. by Floris Books). St George Bk Serv.

Macleod, Gordon K. Health Care Capital: Competition & Control. Perlman, Mark, ed. LC 77-22166. 432p. 1977. prof ref 27.50x (ISBN 0-88410-521-0). Ballinger Pub.

McLeod, Hugh. Religion & the People of Western Europe, 1789-1970. 1981. 15.95x (ISBN 0-19-215832-5); pap. 6.95x (ISBN 0-19-289101-4). Oxford U Pr.

Macleod, Ianin. Bridge Is an Easy Game. rev. ed. 1980. pap. 8.50 (ISBN 0-575-02811-4, Pub. by Gollancz England). David & Charles.

McLeod, J. G., jt. auth. see Lance, J. G.

MacLeod, Jean S. Heir, Cet Inconnu. (Harlequin Romantique Ser.). 192p. 1983. pap. 1.95 (ISBN 0-373-41179-0). Harlequin Bks.

--La Malediction De Chrichton. (Harlequin Romantique Ser.). 192p. 1983. pap. 1.95 (ISBN 0-373-41190-1). Harlequin Bks.

Macleod, Julia H., jt. auth. see Wright, Louis B.

McLeod, Mary Alice & Dudley, Cliff. I Almost Murdered this Child (by Abortion) 128p. 1983. pap. 4.95 (ISBN 0-89221-101-6). New Leaf.

McLeod, Maxwell G., jt. ed. see Kumar, Krishna.

MacLeod, Murdo J. Spanish Central America: A Socioeconomic History, 1520-1720. LC 70-174456. 1973. pap. 9.95x o.p. (ISBN 0-520-02632-2). U of Cal Pr.

Macleod, P., ed. see International Symposium on Olfaction & Taste, 6th, Gif Sur Yvette, France, 1977.

McLeod, Raymond. Management Information Systems. LC 78-14983. 1979. text ed. 23.95 (ISBN 0-574-21245-0, 13-4245); instr's guide avail. (ISBN 0-574-21246-9, 13-4246); casebook 6.95 (ISBN 0-574-21247-7, 13-4247). SRA.

McLeod, Raymond & Forkner, Irvine. Computerized Business Information Systems: An Introduction to Data Processing. 2nd ed. LC 81-10471. 583p. 1982. text ed. 25.95 (ISBN 0-471-02575-5); tchr's ed. 37.50 (ISBN 0-471-02576-3); tests 37.50 (ISBN 0-471-86775-6); tests 25.00 (ISBN 0-471-86775-6). Wiley.

McLeod, Raymond, Jr. Management Information Systems. 2nd ed. 160p. 1983. price not set (ISBN 0-574-21410-0, 13-4410); write for info. casebook (ISBN 0-574-21412-7, 13-4412); write for info. tchr's. guide (ISBN 0-574-21411-9, 13-4411). SRA.

MacLeod, Robert. Appaloosa. 144p. 1981. Repr. 9.95 (ISBN 0-8027-4004-9). Walker & Co.

MacLeod, Robert & Scapagnini, Umberto, eds. Central & Peripheral Regulation of Prolactin Function. 418p. 1980. text ed. 43.00 (ISBN 0-89004-489-9). Raven.

MacLeod, Robert M., jt. auth. see Lamberts, Steven W.

McLeod, Robert W. & Lampert, Lyndon J. The Life & Times of the Little Book Cliff Railway. 1983. price not set (ISBN 0-87108-638-7). Pruett.

MacLeod, Roy M., et al. The Corresponding Societies of the British Association for the Advancement of Science, 1883-1929. 168p. 1975. 15.00 o.p. (ISBN 0-7201-0445-9, Pub. by Mansell England). Wilson.

MacLeod, Stuart M. & Radde, Ingeborg C. Textbook of Pediatric Clinical Pharmacology. 1984. text ed. price not set (ISBN 0-7236-7036-6). Wright-PSG.

McLinn, Dianne, jt. auth. see Kysar, Ardis.

MacLochlainn, Alf, ed. see National Library of Ireland.

McLone, R. R., jt. ed. see Andrews, J. G.

McLoughlin, James & Lewis, Rena. Assessing Special Students. (Special Education Ser.). (Illus.). 640p. 1981. text ed. 22.50 (ISBN 0-675-08151-3). Merrill.

McLoughlin, John C. The Canine Clan: A New Look at Man's Best Friend. LC 81-65280. (Illus.). 176p. 1983. 15.75 (ISBN 0-670-20264-9). Viking Pr.

McLoughlin, Wayne. Space Freighter: Future Supply Ship: A Complete Kit in a Book. (The Build-It-Yourself Ser.). 40p. 1982. pap. 8.95 (ISBN 0-316-56215-7). Little.

--The Space Shuttle: A Complete Kit in a Book. (The Build-It-Yourself Ser.). (Illus.). 40p. 1982. 8.95 (ISBN 0-316-56216-5). Little.

McLoughlin, William G., ed. see Backus, Isaac.
Mac Low, jt. auth. see Jackson.
Mac Low, Jackson. From Pearl Harbor Day to FDR's Birthday. (Contemporary Literature Ser.: No. 14). 72p. 1982. 10.95 (ISBN 0-940650-18-5); pap. 5.95 (ISBN 0-940650-19-3). Sun & Moon MD.
MacLow, Jackson. The Pronouns: A Collection of Forty Dances for the Dancers - February 3rd to March 22nd 1964. LC 79-64919. 88p. 1979. ltd., signed ed. 20.00 (ISBN 0-930794-07-9); pap. 4.45 (ISBN 0-930794-06-0); ltd., signed dancer's ed. on coated cards, boxed 50.00 (ISBN 0-930794-74-5). Station Hill Pr.
--A Vocabulary for Annie Brigitte Gilles Tardos. 1980. ltd. signed ed. 50.00 (ISBN 0-930794-73-7). Station Hill Pr.
McLucas, Glennda B., jt. auth. see Moen, Wayne S.
McLucas, Suzanne. Provencal Kitchen in America. 368p. 1982. 17.95 (ISBN 0-686-97818-8). Johnson Bks.
McLuhan, Marshall. Understanding Media: The Extensions of Man. 320p. 1973. pap. 3.95 (ISBN 0-451-62170-0, ME2170, Ment). NAL.
McLuhan, T. C. Touch the Earth: A Self Portrait of Indian Existence. 1976. pap. 7.75 (ISBN 0-671-22275-9, Touchstone Bks). S&S.
McLure, Charles E. Once Is Enough: The Taxation of Corporate Equity Income. LC 77-670132. 2.00 o.p. (ISBN 0-917616-23-5). ICS Pr.
McLure, Charles E., Jr. Must Corporate Income be Taxed Twice? LC 78-27905. (Studies of Government Finance). 1979. 18.95 (ISBN 0-8157-5620-8); pap. 7.95 (ISBN 0-8157-5619-4). Brookings.
McLure, Charles E., Jr. & Mieszkowski, Peter, eds. Fiscal Federalism & the Taxation of Natural Resources: Nineteen Eighty One Tred Conference. LC 81-48561. (A Lincoln Institute of Land Policy Bk.). 272p. 1982. 35.95 (ISBN 0-669-05436-4). Lexington Bks.
MacLure, Margaret, jt. ed. see French, Peter.
McMackin, et al. Mathematics of the Shop. 4th ed. LC 76-6726. 1978. 18.80 (ISBN 0-8273-1297-0); tchr's. ed. 3.75 (ISBN 0-8273-1298-9). Delmar.
McMackin, Lorin. Thoughts on Freedom: Two Essays. 1982. 12.50 (ISBN 0-8093-1076-7). S Ill U Pr.
McMahan, Elizabeth. A Crash Course in Composition. 3rd ed. 272p. 1980. pap. text ed. 11.94 (ISBN 0-07-045458-2, C); instructor's manual 15.00 (ISBN 0-07-045459-0). McGraw.
McMahan, Elizabeth & Day, Susan. The Writer's Handbook. (Illus.). 1980. pap. text ed. 12.95 (ISBN 0-07-045423-X); wkbk. 9.95 (ISBN 0-07-016150-X). McGraw.
--The Writer's Rhetoric & Handbook. (Illus.). 1980. text ed. 13.50x (ISBN 0-07-045421-3); instructor's manual 17.00 (ISBN 0-07-045422-1); wkbk. avail. McGraw.
McMahan, Elizabeth, jt. auth. see Day, Susan.
McMahan, Forrest R. Human Mutation. LC 82-99887. (Illus.). 72p. (Orig.). 1982. pap. 3.95 (ISBN 0-910217-00-9). Synergetics WV.
McMahan, John. The McGraw-Hill Real Estate Pocket Guide: Up-to-Date Terms & Tables for the Real Estate Professional. 1979. 13.95 (ISBN 0-07-045454-X). McGraw.
McMahan, John W. Property Development: Effective Decision Making in Uncertain Times. new ed. 1976. 29.95 (ISBN 0-07-045450-7, P&RB). McGraw.
MacMahon, A. W., et al. The Administration of Federal Work Relief. LC 73-167845. (FDR & the Era of the New Deal Ser.). 408p. 1971. Repr. of 1941 ed. lib. bdg. 49.50 (ISBN 0-306-70326-2). Da Capo.
MacMahon, Alice T. All about Childbirth. 2nd ed. LC 82-70472. (Illus.). 1982. write for info. (ISBN 0-931128-01-3). Family Pubns.
McMahon, Bob & Leopold, Jay. Who Are the Best? The Sports Survey Book. LC 82-83930. (Illus.). 128p. (Orig.). 1983. pap. 6.95 (ISBN 0-686-82531-4). Leisure Pr.
McMahon, Ed. Here's Ed: Or How to Be a Second Banana from Midway to Midnight. Carroll, ed. LC 75-37084. 1976. 8.95 o.p. (ISBN 0-399-11691-5). Putnam Pub Group.
McMahon, Edward T., jt. auth. see Arbetman, Lee P.
Mcmahon, Edward T., jt. auth. see Arbetman, Lee P.
McMahon, F. Gilbert, ed. Future Trends in Therapeutics. new ed. LC 76-27218. (Principles & Techniques of Human Research & Therapeutics: Vol. 15). (Illus.). 1978. monograph 15.00 o.p. (ISBN 0-87993-087-X). Futura Pub.
McMahon, J. J. Between You & You: The Art of Listening to Yourself. LC 79-89628. 224p. 1980. 9.95 o.p. (ISBN 0-8091-0300-1). Paulist Pr.
McMahon, J. J., jt. auth. see Jason, Kathryn.
McMahon, Judi & Odell, Zia. A Year of Beauty & Exercise for the Pregnant Woman. LC 80-7853. (Illus.). 224p. 1981. 14.37i (ISBN 0-690-01865-7). Har-Row.
McMahon, Judi, jt. auth. see Reardon, James J.
McMahon, Kathryn K., jt. auth. see Azevedo, Milton M.
McMahon, Morgan E. Vintage Radio. rev. ed. (Illus.). 263p. 1973. 12.95 o.p. (ISBN 0-914126-01-6); pap. 9.95 (ISBN 0-914126-02-4). Vintage Radio.
MacMahon, Percy A. Combinatory Analysis, 2 Vols. in 1. LC 59-10267. 24.95 (ISBN 0-8284-0137-3). Chelsea Pub.
MacMahon, Percy A; see Klein, Felix.
McMahon, Sarah Lynne, jt. ed. see Carney, Clarke G.
McMahon, T. A. & Mein, R. G. Reservoir Capacity & Yield. (Developments in Water Science: Vol. 9). 1978. 53.75 (ISBN 0-444-41670-6). Elsevier.
McMahon, Thomas. McKay's Bees. LC 78-20211. 1979. 10.53i (ISBN 0-06-012974-3, HarpT). Har-Row.
--The Mass Explained. LC 78-59320. 1978. 8.95 o.p. (ISBN 0-89310-041-2); pap. 3.95 o.p. (ISBN 0-89310-042-0). Carillon Bks.
McMahon, Thomas A. Muscles, Reflexes, & Locomotion. LC 82-61378. (Illus.). 384p. 1983. 50.00 (ISBN 0-686-43259-2); pap. 15.00. Princeton U Pr.
McMahon, William E. Dreadnought Battleships & Battle Cruisers. LC 78-50769. (Illus.). 1978. lib. bdg. 13.25 (ISBN 0-8191-0465-5). U Pr of Amer.
McMains, Harvey & Wilcox, Lyle, eds. Alternatives for Growth: The Engineering & Economics of Natural Resources Development. LC 77-11870. (Published for the National Bureau of Economic Research). 278p. 1978. prof ref 20.00x (ISBN 0-88410-480-X). Ballinger Pub.
McManama, Jerre, jt. auth. see Shondell, Donald S.
McMane, Fred. Track & Field Basics. (Illus.). 48p. (gr. 3-7). 1983. 8.95 (ISBN 0-13-925966-X). P-H.
McManis, Charles R. Unfair Trade Practices in a Nutshell. LC 82-13597. (Nutshell Ser.). 444p. 1982. text ed. 7.95 (ISBN 0-314-68094-2). West Pub.
McManners, J. French Ecclesiastical Society under the Ancien Regime. 1960. 28.50 (ISBN 0-7190-0340-7). Manchester.
McManners, John. Death & the Enlightenment: Changing Attitudes to Death Among Christians & Unbelievers in Eighteenth-Century France. 1982. 29.95x (ISBN 0-19-826440-2). Oxford U Pr.
--The French Revolution & the Church. LC 82-15532. x, 161p. 1982. Repr. of 1969 ed. lib. bdg. 22.50x (ISBN 0-313-23074-9, MCFR). Greenwood.
McManners, Kelsey. Underwater Attack: The First Submarines. LC 78-15101. (Famous Firsts Ser.). (Illus.). 1978. PLB 10.76 (ISBN 0-89547-044-6). Silver.
McManus, Edwin G., et al. Palauan-English Dictionary. LC 76-9058. (Pali Language Texts: Micronesia). 1977. pap. text ed. 14.50x (ISBN 0-8248-0450-3). UH Pr.
MacManus, Seumas. A Lad of the O'Friels. 7.95 (ISBN 0-8159-6100-6). Devin.
--The Story of the Irish Race. rev. ed. 12.50 (ISBN 0-8159-6827-2). Devin.
Macmanus, Shelia. Community Action Sourcebook Toward Empowerment of People. LC 82-60854. 1982. pap. 6.95 (ISBN 0-8091-2472-6). Paulist Pr.
McManus, T., jt. auth. see King, J. N.
McManus, Una & Cooper, John C. Ni con un Millon de Dolares. Carrodeguas, Andy & Marosi, Esteban, eds. Powell de Lobo, Virginia, tr. 224p. (Span.). 1982. pap. 2.50 (ISBN 0-8297-1256-9). Life Pubs Intl.
MacManus, Yvonne. Deadly Legacy. 256p. 1981. pap. 2.50 o.p. (ISBN 0-523-41259-2). Pinnacle Bks.
McManus, Yvonne. So You Want to Write a Romance. 1983. pap. write for info. PB.
McMartin, Barbara. Discover the Adirondacks One: From Indian Lake to the Hudson River,A Four-Season Guide to the Out-of-Doors. LC 79-52961. (Illus.). 1979. pap. 6.95 (ISBN 0-89725-010-9). Backcountry Pubns.
--Discover the Adirondacks, Two: Walks, Waterways, & Winter Treks in the Southern Adirondacks. rev. ed. LC 79-90812. Orig. Title: Walks & Waterways. (Illus.). 1980. pap. 7.95 (ISBN 0-89725-012-5). Backcountry Pubns.
McMaster, Carolyn. Malawi: Foreign Policy & Development. LC 74-80653. 288p. 1974. 25.00 (ISBN 0-312-50925-1). St Martin.
McMaster, Dale. Vocabulary Development. (Language Arts Ser.). 24p. (gr. 6-9). 1976. wkbk. 5.00 (ISBN 0-8209-0312-4, VD-4). ESP.
Macmaster, Eve. God Gives the Land. (Story Bible Ser.: Vol. 3). (Illus.). 168p. (Orig.). 1982. pap. 5.95 (ISBN 0-8361-3332-3). Herald Pr.
McMaster, James H., ed. The ABC's of Sports Medicine. LC 80-20636. 1982. lib. bdg. 16.50 (ISBN 0-88275-890-X). Krieger.
McMaster, John & Stone, Frederick B. Pennsylvania & the Federal Constitution 1787-1788, 2 vols, Vol. 1. LC 74-87406. (American Constitutional & Legal History Ser). 1970. Repr. of 1888 ed. Set. lib. bdg. 79.50 (ISBN 0-306-71550-3). Da Capo.
McMaster, John M. Skills in Social & Educational Caring. 148p. 1982. text ed. 32.00x (ISBN 0-566-00385-6). Gower Pub Ltd.
McMaster, John M., ed. Methods in Social & Educational Caring. 140p. 1982. text ed. 32.00x (ISBN 0-566-00386-4). Gower Pub Ltd.
McMaster, Mary. To Him Who Waits. (Aston Hall Romances Ser.). 192p. 1981. pap. 1.75 o.p. (ISBN 0-523-41129-4). Pinnacle Bks.
McMaster, R. D., ed. see Dickens, Charles.
McMaster, R. E. Wealth For All: Inflation, Gold, Debt, Real Estate & Society, Book 4. rev. ed. 250p. 1982. 14.95 o.p. (ISBN 0-9605316-3-7). AN Inc.
McMasters, Dale. American Holidays & Special Occasions. (Social Studies). 14p. (gr. 3-6). 1980. wkbk. 5.00 (ISBN 0-8209-0266-7, AH-1). ESP.
--Basic Skills Buying Skills Workbook. (Basic Skills Workbooks). 32p. (gr. 5-8). 1983. 0.99 (ISBN 0-8209-0570-4, MW-3). ESP.
--Basic Skills Dictionary Workbook. (Basic Skills Workbooks). 32p. (gr. 4-7). 1983. 0.99 (ISBN 0-8209-0536-4, DW-1). ESP.
--Basic Skills Holidays Workbook. (Basic Skills Workbook). 32p. (gr. 4-7). 1983. 0.99 (ISBN 0-8209-0560-7, SSW-8). ESP.
--Basic Skills How to Study Workbook. (Basic Skills Workbooks). 32p. (gr. 5-9). 1983. 0.99 (ISBN 0-8209-0534-8, HSW-1). ESP.
--Basic Skills Library Workbook. (Basic Skills Workbooks). 32p. (gr. 4-7). 1983. 0.99 (ISBN 0-686-42990-7, LW-1). ESP.
--Basic Skills Word Building Workbook. (Basic Skills Workbooks). 32p. (gr. 4-7). 1983. 0.99 (ISBN 0-8209-0568-2, WBW-1). ESP.
--Basic Skills Written Problems in Math Workbook. (Basic Skills Workbooks). 32p. (gr. 3-4). 1983. 0.99 (ISBN 0-8209-0574-7, MW-7). ESP.
--Basic Study & Research. (Language Arts Ser.). 24p. (gr. 5-9). 1979. wkbk. 5.00 (ISBN 0-8209-0304-3, BSR-1). ESP.
--Beginning Vocabulary. (Language Arts Ser.). 24p. (gr. 3-5). 1976. wkbk. 5.00 (ISBN 0-8209-0309-4, VD-1). ESP.
--The Dictionary. (Language Arts Ser.). 24p. (gr. 6 up). 1980. wkbk. 5.00 (ISBN 0-8209-0308-6, D-1). ESP.
--Everyday Vocabulary. (Language Arts Ser.). 24p. (gr. 4-6). 1976. wkbk. 5.00 (ISBN 0-8209-0310-8, VD-2). ESP.
--How to Study. (Language Arts). 24p. (gr. 5-9). 1979. wkbk. 5.00 (ISBN 0-8209-0306-X, HS-1). ESP.
--Learning Buying Skills. (Math Ser.). 24p. (gr. 5-9). 1981. wkbk. 5.00 (ISBN 0-8209-0125-3, A-35). ESP.
--Using the Library. (Language Arts Ser.). 24p. (gr. 4-8). 1979. wkbk. 5.00 (ISBN 0-8209-0307-8, LIB-1). ESP.
--Vocabulary Study. (Language Arts Ser.). 24p. (gr. 5-7). 1976. wkbk. 5.00 (ISBN 0-8209-0311-6, VD-3). ESP.
--Word Building. (Language Arts Ser.). 24p. (gr. 4-7). 1976. wkbk. 5.00 (ISBN 0-8209-0305-1, WB-1). ESP.
--Written Problems in Math: Grade 4. (Math Ser.). 24p. 1981. wkbk. 5.00 (ISBN 0-8209-0124-5, A-34). ESP.
McMenamin, James F., ed. see Shaw, William T.
McMichael, A. & Fabre, J., eds. Monoclonal Antibodies in Clinical Medicine. 1982. 63.00 (ISBN 0-12-485580-6). Acad Pr.
McMichael, George. Anthology of American Literature: Colonial Through Romantic, 2 vols. 2nd ed. 1980. pap. text ed. 16.95x ea. Vol. I (ISBN 0-02-379570-0). Vol. II (ISBN 0-02-379580-8). Macmillan.
McMichael, George, ed. Concise Anthology of American Literature. 1974. pap. 17.95x (ISBN 0-02-379560-3). Macmillan.
McMichael, John H., jt. auth. see Maxwell, Arthur D.
McMichael, Stanley L. & O'Keepe, P. Leases: Percentage, Short & Long Term. 6th ed. 1974. 29.95 (ISBN 0-13-527309-9). P-H.
Macmillan. The Cardinals. 640p. 1983. 7.95 (ISBN 0-02-029400-X). Macmillan.
MacMillan, Annabelle, tr. see Anckarsvard, Karin.
MacMillan, Annabelle, tr. see Hamori, Laszlo.
McMillan, B. G., jt. ed. see Humphreys, K. K.
McMillan, Bruce. Here a Chick, There a Chick. LC 82-20348. (Illus.). 28p. (ps-1). 1983. 10.50 (ISBN 0-688-02000-3); PLB 10.08 (ISBN 0-688-02001-1). Lothrop.
MacMillan, Bruce. Surgical & Medical Support for Burn Patients. (Illus.). 208p. 1982. pap. 22.00 (ISBN 0-7236-7004-8). Wright-PSG.
McMillan, C. J., jt. ed. see Hickson, D. J.
McMillan, Claude. Mathematical Programming. 2nd ed. LC 74-23273. (Management & Administration Ser.). 650p. 1975. text ed. 29.95 o.p. (ISBN 0-471-58572-6). Wiley.
McMillan, Constance V. Donny & Marie Osmond: Breaking All the Rules. LC 77-24069. (Super Stars - So Young, So Far Ser.). (Illus.). 40p. (gr. 3-9). 1977. PLB 6.95 (ISBN 0-88436-408-9); pap. 3.95 (ISBN 0-88436-409-7). EMC.
--Nadia Comaneci: Enchanted Sparrow. LC 77-24082. (So Young, So Far Ser.). (Illus.). 40p. (gr. 3-9). 1977. PLB 6.95 (ISBN 0-88436-402-X); pap. 3.95 (ISBN 0-88436-403-8). EMC.
--Randy & Janet Jackson: Ready & Right! LC 77-24073. (So Young, So Far Ser.). (Illus.). 40p. (gr. 3-9). 1977. PLB 6.95 (ISBN 0-88436-404-6); pap. 3.95 (ISBN 0-88436-405-4). EMC.
--Steve Cauthen: Million Dollar Baby. LC 77-24072. (So Young, So Far Ser.). (Illus.). 40p. (gr. 3-9). 1977. PLB 6.95 (ISBN 0-88436-406-2); pap. 3.95 (ISBN 0-88436-407-0). EMC.
MacMillan, Donald. Mental Retardation in School & Society. 2nd ed. 1982. text ed. 22.95 (ISBN 0-316-54272-5); tchr's manual avail. (ISBN 0-316-54273-3). Little.
McMillan, Dorothy. Instant Readers, 18 vols. Incl. Vol. 1. Farm Animals; Vol. 2. Round the House; Vol. 3. Grown Ups; Vol. 4. My Family; Vol. 5. Father; Vol. 7. Big Brother; Vol. 8. People We Know; Vol. 8. Where Are They Kept; Vol. 9. Animals at the Zoo; Vol. 10. Traffic; Vol. 11. Busy; Vo. 12. Me; Vol. 13. Mother; Vol. 14. Big Sister; Vol. 15. Baby; Vol. 16. In the Park; Vol. 17. We Like You; Vol. 18. Pets. (Illus.). (gr. k-4). 1976. Set Of 54 - 1 Copy Of 18 Titles. pap. text ed. 29.40 set large format o.p. (ISBN 0-8372-2184-6); small format-3 copies of 18 titles, 54 bks 30.60 o.p. (ISBN 0-8372-2203-6). Bowmar-Noble.
Macmillan Educational Corporation. Health Today. 640p. 1983. pap. text ed. 19.95 (ISBN 0-02-374400-6). Macmillan.
MacMillan, Gail. Inherited Deception. 192p. (YA) 1976. 6.95 (ISBN 0-685-62626-1, Avalon). Bouregy.
Macmillan, Ian. Blakely's Ark. 1981. pap. 2.25 o.p. (ISBN 0-425-04928-0). Berkley Pub.
McMillan, Ian. The Changing Problem. (Carcanet New Poetry Ser.). 64p. (Orig.). 1981. pap. write for info o.p. (ISBN 0-85635-327-2, Pub. by Carcanet New Pr England). Humanities.
MacMillan, Ian. Strategy Formulation: Political Concepts. (West Ser.in Business Policy & Planning). (Illus.). 1978. pap. text ed. 12.50 (ISBN 0-8299-0209-0). West Pub.
MacMillan, J. A. Authority of the Believer. 96p. 1981. pap. 2.50 (ISBN 0-87509-152-0). Chr Pubns.
McMillan, J. A., jt. auth. see Douthitt, C. B.
MacMillan, John A. Encounter with Darkness. LC 80-67656. 116p. 2.50 (ISBN 0-87509-287-X). Chr Pubns.
McMillan, Julia A., et al. The Whole Pediatrician Catalog. LC 76-27060. 1977. pap. text ed. 24.50 (ISBN 0-7216-5968-3). Saunders.
--The Whole Pediatrician Catalog: A Compendium of Clues to Diagnosis & Management, Vol. 2. LC 78-1254. (Illus.). 1979. text ed. 24.50 (ISBN 0-7216-5967-5). Saunders.
MacMillan, Keith, jt. auth. see Oliver, Hugh.
Macmillan, Keith & Berkwith, John, eds. Contemporary Canadian Composers. (Illus.). 1975. 16.95x (ISBN 0-19-540244-8). Oxford U Pr.
MacMillan, Keith, jt. ed. see Taylor, Bernard.
McMillan, Lawrence G. Options as a Strategic Investment. (Illus.). 484p. 1980. 22.00 (ISBN 0-13-638387-4). NY Inst Finance.
McMillan, Mary L. & Jones, Ruth D. Beautiful North Carolina & the World of Flowers. LC 79-91037. (Illus.). 1979. 9.95 (ISBN 0-87716-110-0; Pub. by Moore Pub Co). F Apple.
Mc Millan, Mary L. & Jones, Ruth D. Make Your Own Merry Christmas. (Illus.). 1971. 10.95 (ISBN 0-87716-035-X, Pub. by Moore Pub Co). F Apple.
McMillan, Mary L. & Jones, Ruth D. My Helenka. LC 72-90714. (Illus.). 190p. 1973. 10.95 (ISBN 0-87716-037-6, Pub. by Moore Pub Co). F Apple.
MacMillan, Michael, ed. Cattulus. (Bolchazy-Carducci Textbook). 121p. (Orig.). pap. text ed. 7.50x (ISBN 0-86516-002-3). Bolchazy-Carducci.
McMillan, Michael, ed. Using Commercial Resources in Family Planning Communication Programs: The International Experience. 1973. pap. 5.00x (ISBN 0-8248-0303-5, Eastwest Ctr). UH Pr.
McMillan, Michael, jt. ed. see Richstad, Jim.
McMillan, Norman H. Marketing Your Hospital: A Strategy for Survival. 128p. (Orig.). 1981. pap. 18.75 (ISBN 0-87258-298-1, AHA-136100). Am Hospital.
--Planning for Survival: A Handbook for Hospital Trustees. LC 78-2281. 128p. (Orig.). 1978. pap. 16.25 (ISBN 0-87258-221-3, AHA-127173). Am Hospital.
McMillan, Patricia H., jt. auth. see Gilbert, Rose B.
McMillan, Priscilla J., tr. see Alliluyeva, Svetlana.
Macmillan Publishers, ed. The Stock Exchange Official Year Book: 1981-1982. 1192p. 1982. 190.00 (ISBN 0-333-31020-9, Pub. by Macmillan England). State Mutual Bk.
Macmillan, R. A. The Crowning Phase of the Critical Philosophy: A Study in Kant's Critique of Judgment. Beck, Lewis W., ed. LC 75-32041. (The Philosophy of Immanuel Kant Ser.: Vol. 4). 1977. Repr. of 1912 ed. lib. bdg. 33.00 o.s.i. (ISBN 0-8240-2328-5). Garland Pub.
McMillan, R. Bruce, jt. ed. see Wood, W. Raymond.
Macmillan, R. H., jt. auth. see Lockwood, Edward H.
McMillen, Donald H. Chinese Communist Power & Policy in Xinjiang, 1949-1977. 1979. lib. bdg. 35.00 o.p. (ISBN 0-89158-452-8). Westview.
McMillen, Harlow. History of Staten Island, New York, During the American Revolution. Orig. Title: Historical Study of Staten Island, New York During the American Revolution. (Illus.). 1976. pap. 3.00 (ISBN 0-686-20332-1). Staten Island.
McMillen, Loretta, jt. auth. see Fingado, Dorothy.
McMillen, S. I. None of These Diseases. 160p. 1963. pap. 2.50 (ISBN 0-8007-8030-2, Spire Bks). Revell.
McMillen, Wheeler. Farmer. LC 66-14227. (U.S.A. Survey Ser.). (Illus.). 126p. 1966. 4.95 (ISBN 0-87107-004-9). Potomac.
McMillin, S. I. None of These Diseases. 1982. pap. 2.50 (ISBN 0-515-06722-9). Jove Pubns.

McMinn, Howard E. An Illustrated Manual of California Shrubs. 1939. 37.50x (ISBN 0-520-00847-2). U of Cal Pr.

McMinn, Winston G. A Constitutional History of Australia. 1979. text ed. 42.00x (ISBN 0-19-550562-X). Oxford U Pr.

McMordie, Tabor. By Executive Arrangement. 1979. 9.95 o.p. (ISBN 0-07-045490-6, GB). McGraw.

McMorrow, Ellen & Malarkey, Louise. Prentice-Hall R.N. Review Manual for State Board Examinations. 2nd ed. (Illus.). 512p. 1983. 15.95 (ISBN 0-13-696567-9). P-H.

McMorrow, Mary E. & Malarkey, Louise M. Prentice-Hall R. N. Review for State Board Examinations. (Illus.). 352p. 1980. pap. text ed. 15.95 (ISBN 0-13-696559-8). P-H.

McMullan, J. T. Physical Techniques in Medicine, 2 vols. Incl. Vol. 1. LC 76-30281. 1977. 79.95 (ISBN 0-471-99468-5); Vol. 2. LC 79-42909. 160p. 1980. 51.00 (ISBN 0-471-27695-2). Pub. by Wiley-Interscience). Wiley.

McMullan, J. T. & Morgan, R. Heat Pumps. 156p. 1981. 50.00x o.p. (ISBN 0-85274-419-6, Pub. by A Hilger). State Mutual Bk.

McMullan, J. T. & Murray, R. B. Energy Resources. (Resources & Environmental Sciences Ser.). 208p. 1983. pap. text ed. price not set (ISBN 0-7131-2665-5). E Arnold.

McMullan, J. T., et al. Energy Resources & Supply. LC 75-6973. 1976. 75.50 o.p. (ISBN 0-471-58975-6, Pub. by Wiley-Interscience). Wiley.

McMullan, Randall. Physical Science for Technicians I. 1978. pap. text ed. 11.95 (ISBN 0-408-00332-4). Butterworth.

McMullen, Charles. Real Estate Investments: A Step by Step Guide. LC 80-20704. (Real Estate for Professional Practitioners Ser.). 174p. 1981. 22.95 (ISBN 0-471-08365-8, Pub. by Wiley-Interscience). Wiley.

McMullen, Charles W. Estate Planning for Real Estate Investments. (Real Estate for Professional Practioners Ser.). 88p. 1983. pap. 19.95x (ISBN 0-471-09613-X). Ronald Pr.

McMullen, Christopher J. Resolution of the Yemen Crisis, 1963: A Case Study in Mediation. LC 80-25944. 56p. 1980. 3.00 (ISBN 0-934742-07-3, Inst Study Diplomacy). Geo U Sch For Serv.

McMullen, David & McMullen, Susan. First into the Air: The First Airplanes. LC 78-15141. (Famous Firsts Ser.). (Illus.). 1978. PLB 10.76 (ISBN 0-89547-052-7). Silver.

McMullen, Haynes & Barr, Larry. Library Articles in Periodicals Before 1876: Bibliography & Abstracts. 600p. 1983. lib. bdg. 65.00x (ISBN 0-89950-066-8). McFarland & Co.

McMullen, Lorraine. Sinclair Ross. (World Authors Ser.: No. 504). 1979. lib. bdg. 15.95 (ISBN 0-8057-6385-6, Twayne). G K Hall.

McMullen, Mary. Better Off Dead. (Nightingale Ser.). 1982. pap. 7.95 (ISBN 0-8161-3409-X, Large Print Bks). G K Hall.

--But Nellie Was So Nice. LC 78-22823. (Crime Club Ser.). 1979. 10.95 o.p. (ISBN 0-385-15290-6). Doubleday.

--My Cousin Death. LC 79-8048. (Crime Club Ser.). 1980. 8.95 o.p. (ISBN 0-385-15748-7). Doubleday.

--The Other Shoe. (Nightingale Ser.). 1982. pap. 8.95 (ISBN 0-8161-3457-X, Large Print Bks). G K Hall.

--Something of the Night. (General Ser.). 1981. lib. bdg. 12.95 (ISBN 0-8161-3244-5, Large Print Bks). G K Hall.

McMullen, Neil. The Newly Industrializing Countries in the World Economy. (British-North American Committee Ser.). 1982. 7.00. Natl Planning.

McMullen, R. Environmental Science. 1982. 55.00x (ISBN 0-333-32755-1, Pub. by Macmillan England). State Mutual Bk.

MacMullen, Ramsay. Paganism in the Roman Empire. LC 80-54222. 384p. 1981. 30.00x (ISBN 0-300-02655-2); pap. text ed. 7.95x (ISBN 0-300-02984-5). Yale U Pr.

--Paganism in the Roman Empire. pap. 7.95 (ISBN 0-686-42822-6, Y-454). Yale U Pr.

McMullen, Susan, jt. auth. see McMullen, David.

McMullen, W. A. Posthumous Meditations: A Dialogue in Three Acts. LC 82-916. (HPC Dialogue Ser.). 84p. 1982. lib. bdg. 12.50 o.p. (ISBN 0-915145-36-7); pap. text ed. 2.50 (ISBN 0-915145-35-9). Hackett Pub.

McMullin, Ernan, ed. Death & Decision. LC 77-18444. (AAAS Selected Symposium Ser.: No. 18). 1978. lib. bdg. 17.00 (ISBN 0-89158-152-9). Westview.

McMurrain, T. Thomas. Intervention in the Human Crisis. LC 75-7974. 102p. (Orig.). 1977. pap. 7.95 (ISBN 0-89334-071-5). Humanics Ltd.

McMurran, Marshall. Programming Microprocessors. (Illus.). 1977. 14.95 (ISBN 0-8306-7985-5); pap. 6.95 o.p. (ISBN 0-8306-6985-X, 985). TAB Bks.

McMurrary, John, et al, eds. Annual Reports in Organic Synthesis, Vol. 12. (Serial Publication). 1982. 26.00 (ISBN 0-12-040812-0). Acad Pr.

McMurray, David, ed. see Guillen, Nicolas.

McMurray, George R. Gabriel Garcia Marquez. LC 76-20409. (Literature and Life Ser.). 1977. 11.95 (ISBN 0-8044-2620-1). Ungar.

--Jorge Luis Borges. LC 78-20939. (Literature and Life Ser.). 1980. 14.50 (ISBN 0-8044-2608-2). Ungar.

--Jose Donoso. (World Authors Ser.). 1979. lib. bdg. 15.95 (ISBN 0-8057-6358-9, Twayne). G K Hall.

McMurray, Georgia L. & Kazanjian, Dolores P. Day Care & the Working Poor: The Struggle for Self-Sufficiency. LC 82-199119. 140p. 1982. pap. 7.50 (ISBN 0-88156-001-4). Comm Serv Soc NY.

MacMurray, John. Self As Agent. 1978. text ed. 6.75x o. p. (ISBN 0-571-06705-0); pap. text ed. 4.50x (ISBN 0-391-02043-9). Humanities.

McMurray, Linda O. George Washington Carver: Scientist & Symbol. (Illus.). 1981. 25.00 o.p. (ISBN 0-19-502971-2); pap. 8.95 o.p. (ISBN 0-19-503205-5). Oxford U Pr.

McMurray, W. C. Synopsis of Human Biochemistry: With Medical Applications. (Illus.). 336p. 1982. pap. text ed. 15.75 (Harper Medical). Lippincott.

McMurray, William J., et al. History of the Twentieth Tennessee Regiment Volunteer Infantry, C.S.A. LC 8-19472. (Illus.). 1976. Repr. of 1904 ed. 20.00 (ISBN 0-918450-12-8). C Elder.

McMurry, Linda O. George Washington Carver: Scientist & Symbol. (Illus.). 1982. pap. 7.95 (ISBN 0-19-503205-5, GB 705, GB). Oxford U Pr.

McMurry, Richard M. John Bell Hood & the War For Southern Independence. LC 82-40175. (Illus.). 256p. (YA) 1982. 19.50 (ISBN 0-8131-1457-8). U Pr of Ky.

McMurry, Richard M., jt. ed. see Robertson, James I., Jr.

McMurtrie, Douglas C. Wings for Words: The Story of Johann Gutenberg & His Invention of Printing. LC 78-167061. (Tower Bks). (Illus.). 175p. 1972. Repr. of 1940 ed. 37.00x (ISBN 0-8103-3936-6). Gale.

McMurtrie, P., jt. auth. see Skimin, E.

McMurtry, James G., 3rd. Neurological Surgery. 2nd ed. McMurtry, James G., ed. (Medical Examination Review Bk.: Vol. 19). 1975. spiral bdg. 23.00 (ISBN 0-87488-119-6). Med Exam.

McMurtry, Larry. Cadillac Jack. 416p. 1982. 15.95 (ISBN 0-671-45445-5); deluxe ed. 75.00 (ISBN 0-671-45983-X). S&S.

McMurtry, R. Gerald, jt. auth. see Harkness, David J.

McMurty, Larry. In a Narrow Grave. 1971. pap. 3.95 o.p. (ISBN 0-671-20475-0, Touchstone Bks). S&S.

--Terms of Endearment. 1976. pap. 1.95 (ISBN 0-451-07173-5, J7173, Sig). NAL.

McNabb, J. W., jt. auth. see Mudvi, B. B.

MacNaghten, A. M., jt. ed. see McKeag, R. M.

MacNaghten, R. D., tr. see Paoli, Ugo Enrico.

McNair, Arnold D., ed. Selected Papers & Bibliography. LC 73-85761. 395p. 1974. lib. bdg. 32.00 (ISBN 0-379-00228-0). Oceana.

McNair, Joseph. An Odyssey: Poetry & Music. LC 76-7152. (Illus.). 1976. pap. 4.25 (ISBN 0-916692-06-X). Black River.

McNair, Will. Electric Drilling Rig Handbook. 222p. 1980. 43.95x (ISBN 0-87814-120-0). Pennwell Pub.

McNall, Neil A. An Agricultural History of the Genesee Valley, 1790-1860. LC 75-25260. (Illus.). 1976. Repr. of 1952 ed. lib. bdg. 19.75x (ISBN 0-8371-8396-0, MCGV). Greenwood.

McNall, Scott. Political Economy: A Critique of American Society. 1981. pap. text ed. 9.95x o.p. (ISBN 0-673-15424-6). Scott F.

McNall, Scott G. & Howe, Gary N. Current Perspectives in Social Theory, Vol. 2. 375p. 1981. 45.00 (ISBN 0-89232-190-3). Jai Pr.

McNall, Scott G. & Howe, Gary N., eds. Current Perspectives in Social Theory, Vol. 1. 394p. 1980. 45.00 (ISBN 0-89232-154-7). Jai Pr.

McNally, Clare. Ghostlight. 1982. pap. 2.95 (ISBN 0-553-22520-0). Bantam.

McNally, D. Desolate Angel: Jack Kerouac, the Beat Generation & America. 1980. pap. 6.95 (ISBN 0-07-045670-4). McGraw.

McNally, Fiona. Women for Hire: A Study of the Female Office Worker. LC 79-12793. 1979. 22.50x (ISBN 0-312-88735-3). St Martin.

McNally, Rand. Campgrounds & Trailer Parks. 1983. 9.95x (ISBN 0-685-83174-4). Wehman.

--Mobil Travel Guide, 7 bks. Incl. California & West; Great Lakes Area; Mid-Atlantic States; North Eastern States; Northwest & Great Plains; Southeastern States; Southwest & South Central. 1983. 6.95x ea. Wehman.

--Road Atlas: U.S., Canada & Mexico. 1983. 5.95x (ISBN 0-685-83176-0). Wehman.

McNally, Raymond T. Dracula Was a Woman: In Search of the Blood Countess of Transylvania. LC 82-17264. (Illus.). 288p. 1983. 14.95 (ISBN 0-07-045671-2). Galley OR.

McNally, Robert E. Council of Trent, the Spiritual Exercises & the Catholic Reform. Anderson, Charles S., ed. LC 70-96863. (Facet Bks). 64p. 1970. pap. 1.00 o.p. (ISBN 0-8006-3056-4, 1-3056). Fortress.

McNally, Tom. Fishing. LC 74-125025. (All-Star Sports Bk). 128p. (gr. 5 up). 1972. 3.95 o.s.i. (ISBN 0-695-80198-8); lib. ed. 5.97 o.s.i. (ISBN 0-695-40198-X). Follett.

--Fly Fishing. LC 77-12448. (Outdoor Life Bk.). (Illus.). 1979. 15.34i (ISBN 0-06-012868-2, HarpT). Har-Row.

--Hunting. LC 77-125023. (All Star Sports Bk). (Illus.). 128p. (gr. 4 up). 1972. 3.95 o.s.i. (ISBN 0-695-80194-5); lib. ed. 5.97 o.s.i. (ISBN 0-695-40194-7). Follett.

MacNamara. Everyday Life of the Etruscans. 17.95 o.p. (ISBN 0-7134-1691-2, Pub. by Batsford England). David & Charles.

McNamara, Brooks. American Playhouse in the Eighteenth Century. LC 68-54021. (Illus.). 1969. 11.00x o.p. (ISBN 0-674-02725-6). Harvard U Pr.

McNamara, Brooks, ed. American Popular Entertainments: A Collection of Jokes, Monologues & Comedy Routines. 1983. 19.95 (ISBN 0-933826-36-2); pap. 6.95 (ISBN 0-933826-37-0). Performing Arts.

McNamara, Charlotte & Howell, Leonore. The Before & After Dinner Cookbook. LC 77-5374. (Illus.). 1977. 10.95 o.p. (ISBN 0-689-10824-9). Atheneum.

McNamara, Jo A. & Harris, Barbara J. Women & the Structures of Social Order: Selected Research from the Fifth Berkshire Conference on the History of Women. 300p. Date not set. text ed. 27.50 (ISBN 0-8223-0558-5). Duke.

McNamara, John E. Technical Aspects of Data Communication. 387p. 1982. 32.00 (ISBN 0-686-98097-2). Telecom Lib.

McNamara, Kathleen T., jt. auth. see Webb, James T.

McNamara, Lynne & Morrison, Jennifer. Separation, Divorce & After. LC 82-2718. 192p. 1983. pap. 9.95 (ISBN 0-7022-1931-2). U of Queensland Pr.

McNamara, Martin. Palestinian Judaism & the New Testament. Date not set. pap. 12.95 (ISBN 0-89453-274-X). M Glazier.

McNamara, Walter, jt. auth. see Kalstone, Shirlee.

McNamara, William. Earthy Mysticism: Contemplation & the Life of Passionate Presence. 128p. 1983. pap. 5.95 (ISBN 0-8245-0562-X). Crossroad NY.

--The Human Adventure-Contemplation for Modern Man. LC 73-10862. 192p. 1974. 5.95 o.p. (ISBN 0-385-08993-7). Doubleday.

--Mystical Passion: Spirituality for a Bored Society. LC 77-80801. 144p. 1977. pap. 5.95 o.p. (ISBN 0-8091-2053-4). Paulist Pr.

McNaspy, Clement J. Worship & Witness. (Faith & Life Bk). 1970. pap. 3.50 o.p. (ISBN 0-02-805110-6). Glencoe.

McNaught, Brian R. Disturbed Peace: Selected Writings of an Irish Catholic Homosexual. LC 81-67627. 125p. (Orig.). 1981. pap. 5.95 (ISBN 0-940680-00-9). Dignity Inc.

McNaught, Harry. Baby Animals. LC 75-36462. (Board Bks.). (Illus.). 14p. (ps-1). 1976. 3.95 (ISBN 0-394-83241-8, BYR). Random.

--Muppets in My Neighborhood. LC 77-74472. (Illus.). (ps-k). 1977. bds. 3.50 (ISBN 0-394-83593-X, BYR). Random.

--The Truck Book. LC 77-79851. (Picturebacks Ser.). (ps-2). 1978. pap. 1.50 (ISBN 0-394-83703-7, BYR); PLB 4.99 (ISBN 0-394-93703-1). Random.

--Trucks. LC 75-36463. (Illus.). 14p. (ps-1). 1976. 3.50 (ISBN 0-394-83240-X). Random.

McNaught, L. W. Nuclear, Biological & Chemical Warfare. (Brassey's Battlefield Weapons Systems & Technology: Vol. 4). 60p. 1983. 26.01 (ISBN 0-08-028328-4); pap. 13.01 (ISBN 0-08-028329-2). Pergamon.

McNaughton, Colin. Anton B. Stanton & the Pirates. LC 79-7905. (Benn Bk.). 32p. (ps-3). 1980. 8.95a o.p. (ISBN 0-385-15759-2); PLB 8.95a (ISBN 0-385-15760-6). Doubleday.

--Crazy Bear. (Illus.). 32p. (gr. k-2). 1983. 10.95 (ISBN 0-03-063043-6). HR&W.

MacNaughton, E. G. & McDougall, T. W. A New Approach to Latin: 1. (Illus.). 1973. pap. text ed. 6.25x (ISBN 0-05-002185-0). Longman.

--A New Approach to Latin: 2. (Illus.). 1974. pap. text ed. 6.25x (ISBN 0-05-002365-9). Longman.

MacNaughton, Edgar. Elementary Steam Power Engineering. 3rd ed. 1948. text ed. 34.95x o.p. (ISBN 0-471-56034-0). Wiley.

Macnaughton, Edwin, jt. auth. see Paterson, James.

McNaughton, Howard. New Zealand Drama. (World Authors Ser.). 1981. lib. bdg. 15.95 (ISBN 0-8057-6468-2, Twayne). G K Hall.

McNaughton, Kenneth J., et al. Controlling Corrosion in Process Industry. (Chemical Engineering Book Ser.). 288p. 1980. 30.25 (ISBN 0-07-010691-6). McGraw.

McNaughton, Lenor. Turtles, Tadpoles & Take-Me-Homes. (ps-k). 1981. 5.95 (ISBN 0-916456-98-6, GA 273). Good Apple.

MacNaughton, Mary D., jt. auth. see Alloway, Lawrence.

McNaughton, Robert. Elementary Computability, Formal Languages & Automata. (Illus.). 464p. 1982. text ed. 27.95 (ISBN 0-13-253500-9). P-H.

McNaughton, Robert & Papert, Seymour. Counter-Free Automata. 1971. 20.00x (ISBN 0-262-13076-9). MIT Pr.

MacNaughton, Robin. How to Transform Your Life Through Astrology. 224p. 1983. pap. 3.50 (ISBN 0-553-23203-7). Bantam.

McNaughton, William, jt. tr. see Mayhew, Lenore.

Macnaughton, William R. Critical Essays on John Updike. (Critical Essays on American Literature). 1982. lib. bdg. 28.50 (ISBN 0-8161-8467-4, Twayne). G K Hall.

McNaugton, Colin. At Home. 16p. 1982. 3.95 (ISBN 0-399-20878-X, Philomel). Putnam Pub Group.

--At Playschool. 16p. 1982. 3.95 (ISBN 0-399-20875-5, Philomel). Putnam Pub Group.

--At the Park. 16p. 1982. 3.95 (ISBN 0-399-20879-8, Philomel). Putnam Pub Group.

--At the Party. 16p. 1982. 3.95 (ISBN 0-399-20877-1, Philomel). Putnam Pub Group.

--At the Stores. 16p. 1982. 3.95 (ISBN 0-399-20876-3, Philomel). Putnam Pub Group.

McNay, Mike. Portrait of a Kentish Village. 1980. 22.50 o.p. (ISBN 0-575-02876-9, Pub. by Gollancz England). David & Charles.

McNeal, James U. Consumer Behavior: An Integrative Approach. 1982. 22.95 (ISBN 0-316-56309-9); tchrs.' manual avail. (ISBN 0-316-56311-0). Little.

McNeal, James U. & McDaniel, Stephen W. Consumer Behavior: Classical & Contemporary Dimensions. (Orig.). 1982. pap. text ed. 16.95 (ISBN 0-316-56310-2). Little.

McNeary, M., jt. auth. see Warner, Frank M.

McNee, Robert B. Primer on Economic Geography. 1970. pap. text ed. 5.95 (ISBN 0-394-44150-8). Random.

McNeel, R. W. Beating the Stock Market. 1963. Repr. of 1921 ed. flexible cover 4.00 (ISBN 0-87034-008-5). Fraser Pub Co.

McNeely, Edwin. La Musica En el Evangelismo. Canclini, Arnoldo, tr. 96p. 1977. pap. 2.50 (ISBN 0-311-13829-2). Casa Bautista.

McNeely, Richard A., ed. see Dunton, Sabina M. & Fanning, Melody S.

McNeely, Richard A., ed. see Dunton, Sabina & Miller, Kathy A.

McNeer, May. The Hudson: River of History. LC 62-15313. (Rivers of the World Ser.). (Illus.). (gr. 4-7). 1962. PLB 3.98 (ISBN 0-8116-6356-6). Garrard.

McNeese, Paul F. Salespower Through Successful Seminars. LC 82-61431. 72p. 1982. pap. text ed. 5.95 (ISBN 0-911041-00-1). Southland Spec.

MacNeice, Louis. Astrology. LC 64-18633. (Windfall Bks.). (Illus.). 1964. 6.95 (ISBN 0-385-05245-6). Doubleday.

--The Revenant: A Song-Cycle for Hedli Anderson. 1975. text ed. 19.50x o.p. (ISBN 0-391-01597-4). Humanities.

--Varieties of Parable. 1966. 29.95 (ISBN 0-521-05654-3). Cambridge U Pr.

McNeil. How Things Began. (Books of the World). (gr. 2-5). 1975. 6.95 (ISBN 0-86020-027-2, Usborne-Hayes); PLB 9.95 (ISBN 0-88110-114-1); pap. 3.95 (ISBN 0-686-36304-3). EDC.

McNeil, Alex. Total Television: A Comprehensive Guide to Programming from 1948 Through 1979. (Illus.). 1980. pap. 9.95 o.p. (ISBN 0-14-004911-8). Penguin.

McNeil, B., jt. ed. see Horbury, W.

McNeil, Barbara & Herbert, Miranda. Author Biographies Master Index: Supplement. 1980. pap. 90.00x (ISBN 0-8103-1088-0). Gale.

McNeil, Barbara & Herbert, Miranda, eds. Performing Arts Biography Master Index: A Consolidated Guide to Over 270,000 Biographical Sketches of Persons Living & Dead, As They Appear in Over 100 of the Principal Biographical Dictionaries Devoted to the Performing Arts. 2nd ed. (Gale Biographical Index Ser.: No. 5). 700p. 1982. 94.00x (ISBN 0-8103-1097-X). Gale.

McNeil, Barbara & Herbert, Miranda C., eds. Historical Biographical Dictionaries Master Index. LC 80-10719. (Biographical Index Ser.: No. 7). 1980. 200.00x (ISBN 0-8103-1089-9). Gale.

McNeil, Barbara, jt. ed. see Herbert, Miranda C.

McNeil, Bill & Wolfe, Morris. Signing On: The Birth of Radio in Canada. LC 82-45257. (Illus.). 320p. 1983. 29.95 (ISBN 0-385-17742-9); pap. 19.95 (ISBN 0-385-18379-8). Doubleday.

McNeil, D., ed. Interactive Statistics. 1980. 57.50 (ISBN 0-444-85412-6). Elsevier.

McNeil, Donald R. Interactive Data Analysis: A Practical Primer. LC 76-46571. 1977. text ed. 21.95 (ISBN 0-471-02631-X, Pub. by Wiley-Interscience). Wiley.

McNeil, E. L. Airborne Care of the Ill & Injured. (Illus.). 208p. 1983. pap. 14.95 (ISBN 0-387-90754-8). Springer-Verlag.

McNeil, Elton B. Neurosis & Personality Disorders. (Lives in Disorder Ser). 1970. pap. 11.95 ref. ed. (ISBN 0-13-611491-1). P-H.

--Psychoses. (Lives in Disorder Ser.). 1970. pap. 11.95 ref. ed. (ISBN 0-13-736413-X). P-H.

McNeil, Elton B., jt. auth. see Rubin, Zick.

McNeil, Genna R. Groundwork: Charles Hamilton Houston & the Struggle for Civil Rights. LC 82-40483. (Illus.). 320p. 1983. 27.50x (ISBN 0-8122-7878-X). U of Pa Pr.

McNeil, John. The Consultant: A Novel of Computer Crime. LC 77-27034. 1978. 8.95 o.p. (ISBN 0-698-10907-4, Pub. by Coward). Putnam Pub Group.

--Spy Game. 332p. 1980. 11.95 (ISBN 0-698-11046-3, Coward). Putnam Pub Group.

--Spy Game. 1982. pap. 2.95 (ISBN 0-686-97470-0). Zebra.

McNeil, John D., jt. auth. see Lucio, William H.

McNeil, John D., et al. How to Teach Reading Successfully. (Illus.). 404p. 1980. text ed. 18.95 (ISBN 0-316-56306-4); instructor's manual avail. (ISBN 0-316-56307-2). Little.

McNeil, John S. & Wright, Roosevelt, Jr. Military Retirement: Socio-Economic & Mental Health Dilemmas. 220p. 1983. text ed. 24.95x (ISBN 0-86598-078-0). Allanheld.

McNeil, Katherine, jt. auth. see Langworthy, J. Lamont.

MacNeil, Neil. The President's Medal 1789-1977. 1977. 12.95 o.p. (ISBN 0-517-52917-3, C N Potter Bks). Crown.

McNeil, Robert, jt. auth. see Allaire, Barbara.

MacNeil, Ruth. Always Another Tomorrow. 284p. text ed. 9.95 o.s.i. (ISBN 0-932970-19-2). Prinit Pr.

MacNeilage, P. F., ed. The Production of Speech. (Illus.). 302p. 1983. 29.95 (ISBN 0-387-90735-1). Springer-Verlag.

McNeill, David. Acquisition of Language: The Study of Developmental Psycholinguistics. (Holtzman Ser). (Illus.). 183p. 1972. pap. text ed. 12.50 scp o.p. (ISBN 0-06-044379-0, HarpC). Har Row.

McNeill, J. T. The History & Character of Calvinism. 1967. pap. 11.95 (ISBN 0-19-500743-3, GB). Oxford U Pr.

McNeill, Janet. The Three Crowns of King Hullabaloo. LC 75-42151. (Stepping Stones Ser.). (Illus.). 24p. (gr. k-3). 1976. 7.00 (ISBN 0-516-03593-2). Childrens.

McNeill, John T. & Calvin Institutes of the Christian Religion, eds. Calvin, 2 vols. LC 60-5379. (Library of Christian Classics). 1982. Set. 27.95 (ISBN 0-664-22028-2). Westminster.

McNeill, John T., ed. see Calvin, John.

McNeill, Malvina R. Guidelines to Problems of Education in Brazil: A Review & Selected Bibliography. LC 76-120599. 1970. text ed. 7.95x (ISBN 0-8077-1789-4). Tchrs Coll.

McNeill, Moyra. Quilting for Today. (Illus.). 64p. 1976. 9.50 o.p. (ISBN 0-263-05601-5). Transatlantic.

Macneill, Norma, jt. auth. see Noyes, Joan.

McNeill, Pat, jt. auth. see Bishop, Beata.

McNeill, William H. The Contemporary World: Nineteen Fourteen to Present. rev. ed. 1975. pap. 9.95x (ISBN 0-673-07908-2). Scott F.

--The Metamorphosis of Greece Since World War II. LC 77-26105. (Illus.). 1978. 12.95x (ISBN 0-226-56156-9). U of Chicago Pr.

--Plaques & People. LC 76-2798. (Illus.). 1977. pap. 5.50 (ISBN 0-385-12122-9, Anch). Doubleday.

--The Shape of European History. 1974. 14.95x (ISBN 0-19-501806-0). Oxford U Pr.

McNeill, William H. & Sedlar, Jean W. Classical India. (Oxford Readings in World History Ser: Vol. 4). (Orig.). 1969. pap. text ed. 6.95x (ISBN 0-19-500972-X). Oxford U Pr.

--Classical Mediterranean World. (Oxford Readings in World History Ser.: Vol. 3). (Illus., Orig.). 1969. pap. text ed. 6.95x (ISBN 0-19-500971-1). Oxford U Pr.

McNeill, William H. & Houser, Schuyler O., eds. Medieval Europe. (Oxford Readings in World History Ser: Vol. 8). 1971. pap. 6.95x (ISBN 0-19-501312-3). Oxford U Pr.

--Modern Europe & America. (Readings in World History). 1973. pap. text ed. 6.95x (ISBN 0-19-501631-9). Oxford U Pr.

McNeill, William H. & Sedlar, Jean W., eds. Ancient Near East. (Oxford Readings in World History Ser: Vol. 2). 1968. pap. 7.95x (ISBN 0-19-500970-3). Oxford U Pr.

--China, India & Japan: The Middle Period. 1971. pap. 5.95x o.p. (ISBN 0-19-501439-1). Oxford U Pr.

--Origins of Civilization. (Oxford Readings in World History Ser: Vol. 1). 1968. pap. text ed. 6.95x (ISBN 0-19-500969-X). Oxford U Pr.

McNeilly, D. T., jt. auth. see Bradshaw, A. D.

McNeilly, F. S. Anatomy of Leviathan. LC 68-12304. 1969. 16.95 o.p. (ISBN 0-312-03430-X). St Martin.

MacNeish, R. S., jt. ed. see Byers, Douglas S.

MacNeish, Richard S. & Johnson, Frederick, eds. The Prehistory of the Tehuacan Valley. Incl. Vol. 3. Ceramics. 318p. 1970. 35.00x (ISBN 0-292-70068-7); Vol. 4. Chronology & Irrigation. 302p. 1972. 35.00x (ISBN 0-292-70155-1). (Illus.). 35.00x ea. U of Tex Pr.

MacNeish, Richard S., et al. Prehistory of the Ayacucho Basin, Peru, Vol. IV: The Preceramic Way of Life. (Illus.). 312p. 1983. text ed. 45.00x (ISBN 0-472-04967-4). U of Mich Pr.

McNelly, Theodore. Politics & Government in Japan. 2nd ed. LC 74-186377. (Contemporary Government Ser.). (Illus.). 256p. (Orig.). 1972. pap. text ed. 12.95 (ISBN 0-395-12649-5). HM.

McNemar, Quinn. Psychological Statistics. 4th ed. 1969. 30.95 (ISBN 0-471-58708-7). Wiley.

McNerney. The Influence of Ausias March on Castilian Golden Age Poetry. (Biblioteca Hispanoamericana y Espanola de Amsterdam: Vol. 3). 128p. 1982. pap. text ed. 14.00x (ISBN 90-6203-654-6, Pub. by Rodopi Holland). Humanities.

McNerney, Walter J., ed. Working for a Healthier America. 304p. 1980. prof ref 29.00x (ISBN 0-88410-718-3). Ballinger Pub.

McNett, Ian, ed. Early Alert: The Impact of Federal Education on the States. 64p. (Orig.). 1983. pap. write for info. (ISBN 0-937846-99-6). Inst Educ Lead.

--Let's Not Reinvent the Wheel: Profiles of School-Business Collaboration. 72p. (Orig.). 1983. pap. write for info. (ISBN 0-937846-97-X). Inst Educ Lead.

MacNicholas, John. James Joyce's Exiles: A Textual Companion. LC 78-67061. (Reference Library Ser.). 1979. lib. bdg. 35.00 o.s.i. (ISBN 0-8240-9781-5). Garland Pub.

MacNicholas, John, ed. Twentieth-Century American Dramatists, 2 vols. (Dictionary of Literary Biography Ser.: Vol. 7). (Illus.). 300p. 1981. 148.00x set (ISBN 0-8103-0928-9, Bruccoli Clark). Gale.

McNichols, Thomas. Policymaking & Executive Action. 6th ed. (Illus.). 832p. 1983. text ed. 27.95x (ISBN 0-07-045680-1); instr's manual 10.95x (ISBN 0-07-045681-X). McGraw.

McNichols, Thomas J. Executive Policy & Strategic Planning. (Illus.). 192p. 1977. pap. 14.00 (ISBN 0-07-045683-6, C). McGraw.

McNickle, D'Aracy. Native American Tribalism: Indian Survivals & Renewals. 1973. pap. 6.95x (ISBN 0-19-501724-2). Oxford U Pr.

McNickle, D'Arcy. Native American Tribalism. new ed. (Illus.). 1973. 12.95x (ISBN 0-19-501723-4). Oxford U Pr.

McNickle, Roma K., ed. see Western Resources Conference, 3rd, Colorado State University, 1961.

Macnicol, John. Movement for Family Allowances Nineteen Eighteen to Forty-Five. (Studies in Social Policy & Welfare). 1981. text ed. 30.00x (ISBN 0-435-82555-0). Heinemann Ed.

McNicoll, Geoffrey, jt. auth. see Hicks, George L.

MacNiece, jt. auth. see Brandwein.

McNitt, Frank. The Indian Traders. LC 62-16469. 393p. 1962. 17.95 o.p. (ISBN 0-8061-0531-3). U of Okla Pr.

McNitt, Lawrence. Invitation to COBOL for the TRS-80. (Illus.). 330p. 1983. text ed. 15.00 (ISBN 0-89433-209-0). Petrocelli.

--Invitation to FORTRAN for the TRS-80. (Illus.). 240p. 1983. pap. 15.00 (ISBN 0-89433-210-4). Petrocelli.

McNitt, Lawrence L. Thirty-Six Statistical Analysis Programs in BASIC for the TRS-80. 250p. 1983. pap. write for info. (ISBN 0-88056-087-8). Dilithium Pr.

--Thirty-Two Management Programs for the TRS-80. 250p. pap. write for info (ISBN 0-88056-088-6). Dilithium Pr.

McNown, Robert F. & Lee, Dwight R. Economics in Our Time: Macro Issues. LC 76-374. 224p. 1976. pap. text ed. 7.95 (ISBN 0-574-19260-3, 13-2260); instr's guide avail. (ISBN 0-574-19261-1, 13-2261). SRA.

McNown, Robert F., jt. auth. see Lee, Dwight R.

McNulty, Charles. India. (Orig.). (gr. 9). 1982. pap. text ed. 5.66 (ISBN 0-87720-628-7). AMSCO Sch.

McNulty, Elizabeth, jt. auth. see Hilderby, Robert.

McNulty, Elizabeth G., jt. auth. see Covert, Richard P.

McNulty, Faith. How to Dig a Hole to the Other Side of the World. LC 78-22479. (Illus.). (ps-3). 1979. 8.95i o.p. (ISBN 0-06-024147-0, HarpJ); PLB 10.89 (ISBN 0-06-024148-9). Har-Row.

--Hurricane. LC 79-2672. (Illus.). 64p. (gr. 3-5). 1983. 8.61i (ISBN 0-06-024142-X, HarpJ); PLB 8.89g (ISBN 0-06-024143-8). Har-Row.

--Prairie Dog Summer. (Illus.). (gr. 4-8). 1972. PLB 4.64 o.p. (ISBN 0-698-30442-X, Coward). Putnam Pub Group.

McNulty, James G., jt. auth. see Walsh, Anthony.

McNulty, John K. Federal Estate & Gift Taxation in a Nutshell. 3rd ed. LC 82-24726. (Nutshell Ser.). 493p. 1983. pap. text ed. 7.95 (ISBN 0-314-71766-8). West Pub.

McNulty, Paul J. The Origins & Development of Labor Economics. 320p. 1980. text ed. 20.00x (ISBN 0-262-13162-5). MIT Pr.

McNulty, Thomas F., jt. auth. see Stevens, Mary O.

McNutt, David R., jt. auth. see McNutt, Kristen W.

MacNutt, Francis. Healing. LC 74-81446. (Illus.). 336p. 1974. pap. 3.95 (ISBN 0-87793-074-0). Ave Maria.

McNutt, Kristen W. & McNutt, David R. Nutrition & Food Choices. LC 77-13636. 1978. text ed. 21.95 (ISBN 0-574-20500-4, 13-3500). SRA.

McNutt, Kristen W., jt. ed. see Sipple, Horace.

McNutt, Randall E. Cal Stewart: Your Uncle Josh. LC 81-50758. (Illus.). 115p. 11.95 (ISBN 0-940152-00-2); pap. 7.95 (ISBN 0-940152-01-0). McNutt Pubns.

McNutt, Robert D. West's Book of Legal Forms. 162p. 1981. pap. text ed. 6.95 (ISBN 0-8299-0516-2). West Pub.

Macomber, William F. A Catalogue of Ethiopian Manuscripts, Vol. III: Project Numbers 701-1100. LC 76-365354. 1978. pap. 34.50 (ISBN 0-8357-0303-7, IS00048, Hill Monastic Manuscript Library). Univ Microfilms.

Macon, Jorge & Merino Manon, Jose. Financing Urban & Rural Development Through Betterment Levies: The Latin American Experience. LC 76-24359. (Special Studies). 1977. 28.95 o.p. (ISBN 0-275-23970-5). Praeger.

Macor, Alida. And Sew On... (Illus.). 56p. 1983. pap. 3.95 (ISBN 0-9610632-0-3). Alida Macor.

Macovski, Albert. Medical Imaging Systems. (Illus.). 256p. 1983. 29.95 (ISBN 0-13-572685-9). P-H.

Macoy Publishing & Masonic Supply Co. Book of the Scarlet Line; Heroines of Jericho Ritual & Ceremonies. 1981. Repr. of 1948 ed. 6.95. Macoy Pub.

Macoy, Robert. The Adoptive Rite. 1981. Repr. 5.50 (ISBN 0-88053-300-5). Macoy Pub.

McPartland, Joseph F. McGraw-Hill's National Electrical Code Handbook. 17th ed. 928p. 1981. 26.50 (ISBN 0-07-045693-3). McGraw.

--McGraw-Hill's National Electrical Code Handbook. 16th ed. (Illus.). 1979. 21.50 (ISBN 0-07-045690-9). McGraw.

McPartland, Joseph F. & Novak, W. J. Electrical Design Details. 1960. 19.50 o.p. (ISBN 0-07-045692-5, P&RB). McGraw.

--Electrical Equipment Manual. 3rd ed. (Illus.). 1965. 30.25 (ISBN 0-07-045697-6, P&RB). McGraw.

--Practical Electricity. 1964. 30.25 (ISBN 0-07-045694-1, P&RB). McGraw.

McPartland, Pamela. Take It Easy: American Indians & Two Word Verbs for Students of English As a Foreign Language. (ESL Ser.). 176p. 1981. pap. text ed. 8.95 (ISBN 0-13-882902-0). P-H.

McPartlnd, Joseph F. Handbook of Practical Electrical Design. Crawford, Harold B., ed. (Illus.). 672p. 1983. 24.50 (ISBN 0-07-045695-X, P&RB). McGraw.

McPeek, Mary, tr. & intro. by. Bobbin Lace, First Series: Les Dentelles Aux Fuseaux, 3 pts. rev. ed. LC 73-18373. (Illus.). 255p. 1974. Repr. Set. 67.00x (ISBN 0-8103-3955-2); 25 corner patterns incl. (ISBN 0-685-49538-8). Gale.

McPhail, David. The Cereal Box. (Illus.). 32p. (gr. k-3). 1974. 4.95g o.p. (ISBN 0-316-56314-5, Pub. by Atlantic Monthly Pr). Little.

--Great Cat. (Illus.). 32p. (all ages). 1982. 9.75 (ISBN 0-525-45102-1, 0947-280, Unicorn Bks). Dutton.

--Snow Lion. (Illus.). 48p. (ps-3). 1983. 5.50 (ISBN 0-8193-1097-2); PLB 5.95 (ISBN 0-8193-1098-0). Parents.

McPhail, Peter. Social & Moral Education. (Theory & Practice in Education Ser.: No. 4). 216p. 1982. text ed. 19.95x (ISBN 0-631-12792-5, Pub. by Basil Blackwell England); pap. text ed. 9.95x (ISBN 0-631-12947-2). Biblio Dist.

McPhater, Donald. Well-Site Geologists Handbook. MacTiernan, Brian, ed. 96p. 1983. 19.95x (ISBN 0-87814-217-7). Pennwell Books Division.

McPhatter, William. The Business Beat: Its Impact & Its Problems. LC 80-16599. (ITT Key Issue Lecture Ser.). 168p. 1980. pap. text ed. 6.50 (ISBN 0-672-97702-8). Bobbs.

McPhaul, John J. Deadlines & Monkeyshines. LC 72-6201. (Illus.). 308p. 1973. Repr. of 1962 ed. lib. bdg. 20.00x (ISBN 0-8371-6471-0, MCDM). Greenwood.

McPhedran, Margaret G., jt. auth. see Taylor, Norman B.

McPhee, Arthur G. Friendship Evangelism: The Caring Way to Share Your Faith. 1979. pap. 3.95 (ISBN 0-310-37311-5). Zondervan.

McPhee, Carol & FitzGerald, Ann, eds. Feminist Quotations: Voices of Rebels, Reformers & Visionaries. LC 78-3308. 1979. 14.37i (ISBN 0-690-01770-7). T Y Crowell.

McPhee, Colin. Music in Bali. LC 76-4979. (Music Reprint Ser.). 1976. Repr. of 1966 ed. lib. bdg. 49.50 (ISBN 0-306-70778-0). Da Capo.

McPhee, J. R. & Phil, D. The Mothproofing of Wool. 58p. 1971. 39.00x (ISBN 0-686-97038-1, Pub. by Meadowfield Pr England). State Mutual Bk.

McPhee, John. Basin & Range. (Illus.). 1981. 10.95 (ISBN 0-374-10914-1); pap. 5.95 (ISBN 0-374-51690-1). FS&G.

--The Crofter & the Laird. LC 77-113774. (Illus.). 160p. 1970. 8.95 (ISBN 0-374-13192-9); pap. 6.25 (ISBN 0-374-51465-8). FS&G.

--In Suspect Terrain. 1983. 12.95 (ISBN 0-374-17650-7). FS&G.

--Levels of the Game. 160p. 1969. 9.95 (ISBN 0-374-18568-9); pap. 5.95 (ISBN 0-374-51526-3). FS&G.

--Oranges. 1967. 7.50 (ISBN 0-374-22688-1); pap. 5.25 (ISBN 0-374-51297-3). FS&G.

--A Sense of Where You Are: A Profile of William Warren Bradley. (Illus.). 1969. 9.95 (ISBN 0-374-26093-1); pap. 3.95 (ISBN 0-374-51485-2). FS&G.

--The Survival of the Bark Canoe. (Illus.). 146p. 1975. 7.95 (ISBN 0-374-27207-7); pap. 5.95 (ISBN 0-374-51693-6). FS&G.

McPhee, John, jt. auth. see Rowell, Galen.

McPhee, Nancy. The Book of Insults Ancient & Modern. LC 78-19201. (Illus.). 1978. 6.95 o.p. (ISBN 0-312-08929-5). St Martin.

--The Second Book of Insults. 1983. pap. 3.95 (ISBN 0-14-006474-5). Penguin.

McPhee, Norma. More Programs & Skits for Young Teens. 1980. pap. 3.95 o.p. (ISBN 0-8024-5669-3). Moody.

McPhee, Norma H. Programs & Skits for Young Teens. 1978. pap. 3.95 o.p. (ISBN 0-8024-6892-6). Moody.

MacPhee, Tracey, ed. Management Vision. 1981. 28.00 (ISBN 0-686-36322-1). Master Teacher.

McPherson, A. & Gray, J. Reconstruction of Secondary Education: Theory, Myth & Practice Since the War. (Routledge Education Bks.). 300p. 1983. 34.95 (ISBN 0-7100-9268-7); pap. 18.50 (ISBN 0-7100-9268-7). Routledge & Kegan.

Macpherson, Alan, ed. Atlantic Provinces. (Studies in Canadian Geography). 1972. 12.50x o.p. (ISBN 0-8020-1916-1); pap. 6.00x (ISBN 0-8020-6158-3). U of Toronto Pr.

McPherson, Alexander. Preparation & Analysis of Protein Crystals. LC 81-16442. 371p. 1982. 50.00x (ISBN 0-471-08524-3, Pub. by Wiley-Interscience). Wiley.

McPherson, Bruce. Between Two Worlds: Victorian Ambivalence about Progress. LC 82-23814. 92p. (Orig.). 1983. lib. bdg. 17.25 (ISBN 0-8191-2972-0); pap. text ed. 7.25 (ISBN 0-8191-2973-9). U Pr of Amer.

Macpherson, C. B. Democratic Theory: Essays in Retrieval. 1973. 13.95 o.p. (ISBN 0-19-827187-5); pap. text ed. 9.95x (ISBN 0-19-827189-1). Oxford U Pr.

--Real World of Democracy. 1966. pap. 4.95x (ISBN 0-19-501534-7). Oxford U Pr.

Macpherson, C. B., ed. see Locke, John.

McPherson, E. & Ashton, D. L. Metric Engineering Drawing Examples. 69p. 1979. pap. 9.95x (ISBN 0-87201-539-4). Gulf Pub.

McPherson, Edward. Handbook of Politics, 12 vols. in 4. LC 72-146558. (Law, Politics & History Ser.). 1973. Repr. of 1894 ed. lib. bdg. 55.00 ea.; Set. lib. bdg. 225.00 (ISBN 0-306-70030-1). Da Capo.

--The Political History of the U. S. A. During the Period of Reconstruction. Hyman, Harold & Trefousse, Hans, eds. LC 77-127288. (Studies in American History & Government Ser.). 648p. 1973. Repr. of 1871 ed. lib. bdg. 85.00 (ISBN 0-306-71206-7). Da Capo.

--Political History of the United States of America During the Great Rebellion. LC 73-127287. (American Constitutional & Legal History Ser). 1972. Repr. of 1865 ed. lib. bdg. 75.00 (ISBN 0-306-71207-5). Da Capo.

McPherson, Elizabeth, jt. auth. see Cowan, Gregory.

McPherson, George. An Introduction to Electrical Machines & Transformers. LC 80-19632. 557p. 1981. text ed. 29.95 (ISBN 0-471-05586-7). Wiley.

McPherson, Gertrude. Small Town Teacher. LC 71-188349. (Illus.). 449p. 1972. 14.00x (ISBN 0-674-81100-3); pap. 5.95x o.p. (ISBN 0-674-81101-1). Harvard U Pr.

MacPherson, Harriet D. Censorship Under Louis XIV, Sixteen Sixty-One to Seventeen Fifteen: Some Aspects of Its Influence. (Perspectives in European History Ser.: No. 40). xvi, 176p. Repr. of 1929 ed. lib. bdg. 17.50x (ISBN 0-87991-055-0). Porcupine Pr.

MacPherson, Ian. Illustrated Sermon Outlines. (Pocket Pulpit Library). 96p. (Orig.). 1982. pap. 3.50 (ISBN 0-8010-6141-5). Baker Bk.

McPherson, James M. The Negro's Civil War: How American Negroes Felt & Acted during the War for the Union. 1982. pap. 8.95 (ISBN 0-252-00949-5). U of Ill Pr.

MacPherson, Kenneth. Canada's Fighting Ships. 1975. 15.95 o.p. (ISBN 0-88866-566-0); pap. 9.95 (ISBN 0-685-53614-9). Samuel Stevens.

MacPherson, Malcolm. The Lucifer Key. 1981. 13.50 o.p. (ISBN 0-525-14985-6, 01311-390). Dutton.

McPherson, Michael. Singing with the Owls. 64p. 1983. pap. 5.95 (ISBN 0-932136-05-2). Petronium Pr.

MacPherson, Myra. The Power Lovers: An Intimate Look at Politics & Marriage. LC 75-18581. 448p. 1975. 10.00 o.p. (ISBN 0-399-11495-5). Putnam Pub Group.

MacPherson, R. C. Collision Repair Guide. 1971. 16.95 (ISBN 0-07-044690-3); instr.'s manual 3.50 (ISBN 0-07-044691-1); student notebook 6.95 (ISBN 0-07-044693-8); instructor's kit 95.00 (ISBN 0-07-079615-7); slides avail. (ISBN 0-07-044692-X). McGraw.

MacPherson, Robert C. Automotive Collision Appraisal. (Illus.). 240p. 1974. pap. text ed. 15.95 (ISBN 0-07-044695-4); instructors' manual 4.50 (ISBN 0-07-044696-2); slides 70.00 (ISBN 0-07-044697-0); instr.'s pkg. 135.00 (ISBN 0-07-079374-3). McGraw.

Macpherson, Ruth. That's Entertaining. (Illus., Orig.). 1981. pap. 8.95 (ISBN 0-8437-3377-2). Hammond Inc.

McPherson, Sandra. Patron Happiness. new ed. (American Poetry Ser.). 88p. 1983. 9.95 (ISBN 0-88001-021-5). Ecco Pr.

McPherson, Steven P. Respiratory Therapy Equipment. 2nd ed. LC 80-21627. (Illus.). 514p. 1980. text ed. 29.95 (ISBN 0-8016-3313-3). Mosby.

MacPherson, Stewart. Social Policy in the Third World: The Social Dilemmas of Underdevelopment. LC 82-6837. 220p. 1983. pap. text ed. 14.85x (ISBN 0-86598-090-X). Allanheld.

MacPherson, Stewart, jt. ed. see Bean, Philip.

McPherson, Thomas. The Argument from Design. LC 72-77774. (New Studies in the Philosophy of Religion). 96p. 1972. 12.95 o.p. (ISBN 0-312-04865-3). St Martin.

MacPherson, Tom. Dragging, Driving, & Basic Customizing. (Putnam Sports Shelf). (Illus.). (gr. 5-11). 1972. PLB 6.29 o.p. (ISBN 0-399-60712-9). Putnam Pub Group.

--Keep Your Car Running: How to Be an Auto Genius. LC 76-818. (Illus.). 128p. (gr. 5 up). 1976. 6.95 o.p. (ISBN 0-399-20512-8). Putnam Pub Group.

McPhillips, Martin. The Solar Energy Almanac. (Illus.). 256p. 1983. pap. 8.95 (ISBN 0-89696-152-4, An Everest House Book). Dodd.

McPhillips, Martin, ed. The Solar Energy Almanac. LC 82-9362. 256p. 1982. 15.95x (ISBN 0-87196-727-8). Facts on File.

McPhum, Malcolm. Kites. LC 80-50943. (Whizz Kids Ser.). 8.00 (ISBN 0-382-06437-2). Silver.

McQuade, Donald & Atwan, Robert, eds. Popular Writing in America: The Interaction of Style & Audience. shorter, alternate ed. (Illus.). 1977. pap. text ed. 9.95x (ISBN 0-19-502195-9). Oxford U Pr.

McQuaid, Clement, ed. Gambler's Digest. (DBI Bks). 1971. pap. 7.95 o.s.i. (ISBN 0-695-80104-X). Follett.

McQuaid, Kim. Big Business & Presidential Power: From FDR to Reagan. LC 82-6382. 375p. 1982. 17.50 (ISBN 0-688-01313-9). Morrow.

McQuaig, Douglas J. College Accounting Fundamentals. 2nd ed. Incl. Westside Lanes: A Sole-Proprietorship Service Business for Chapters 1-10. Practice Set I 9.50 (ISBN 0-395-29412-6); Driscoe's Rugs: A Sole-Proprietorship Merchandising Business for Chapters 1-15. Practice Set II 9.50 (ISBN 0-395-29413-4); Claverton Outdoor Store: A Voucher System for Business for Chapters 16-29. Practice Set III 8.50 (ISBN 0-395-29414-2). 1981. 19.95 (ISBN 0-395-29408-8); chapters 1-15 14.95 (ISBN 0-395-29409-6); chapters 1-10 14.50 (ISBN 0-395-29410-X); instr's manual 3.50 (ISBN 0-395-29411-8); Chapters 1-29 21.50 (ISBN 0-395-29408-8). HM.

--College Accounting Fundamentals. 2nd ed. 1983. 29 chaps. 21.50 (ISBN 0-395-29408-8); supplementary materials avail.; computer assisted practice set, denton appliance, with workbook & solutions manual 9.95; medical practice set, CW Hale with workbook & solutions manual 9.95; legal practice set, Mt. Chandler with workbook & solutions manual 9.95. HM.

McQuaig, Jack, et al. How to Interview & Hire Productive People. LC 80-70952. 320p. 1981. 15.95 (ISBN 0-8119-0332-X). Fell.

McQuaker, R. J. Computer Choice: A Manual for the Practitioner. 1979. 49.00 (ISBN 0-444-85250-6, North Holland). Elsevier.

McQuarie, Donald. Marx: Sociology-Social Change-Capitalism. 15.95 (ISBN 0-7043-3221-3, Pub. by Quartet England); pap. 6.95 (ISBN 0-686-82876-3). Charles River Bks.

McQuarrie, Donald A. Quantum Chemistry. LC 82-51234. (Physical Chemistry Ser.). (Illus.). 1983. text ed. 22.00x (ISBN 0-935702-13-X). Univ Sci Bks.

McQuarrie, Donald A., ed. see Rock, Peter A.

MacQuarrie, Gordon. Stories of the Old Duck Hunters. 1979. pap. 7.95 (ISBN 0-932558-10-0). Willow Creek.

Macquarrie, John. In Search of Humanity: A Theological & Philosophical Approach. 288p. 1983. 16.95 (ISBN 0-8245-0564-6). Crossroad NY.

--Martin Heidegger. LC 68-11970. (Makers of Contemporary Theology Ser). 1968. pap. 3.95 (ISBN 0-8042-0659-7). John Knox.

--Mystery & Truth. (Pere Marquette Theology Lectures). 1970. 6.95 (ISBN 0-87462-518-1). Marquette.

--New Directions in Theology Today & God & Secularity. (Vol. 3). 1967. pap. 2.85 o.p. (ISBN 0-664-24787-3). Westminster.

--Paths in Spirituality. (Student Christian Movement Press Ser.). 1972. pap. 7.95x (ISBN 0-19-520329-1). Oxford U Pr.

--Studies in Christian Existentialism. 1966. 10.00x o.p. (ISBN 0-7735-0024-3). McGill-Queens U Pr.

Macquarrie, John, ed. Dictionary of Christian Ethics. LC 67-17412. 1967. 16.95 (ISBN 0-664-20646-8). Westminster.

McQuarrie, Ralph. Return of the Jedi Portfolio. (Orig.). 1983. pap. 9.95 (ISBN 0-345-30961-8). Ballantine.

McQuay, Mike. The Odds Are Murder. (Mathew Swain Ser.: No. 4). 213p. 1983. pap. 2.50 (ISBN 0-686-82105-X). Bantam.

MacQueen, Don. On the Piano. (Contemporary Poets Ser.: No. 4). 48p. (Orig.). 1983. pap. 3.95 (ISBN 0-916982-29-7, RL229). Realities.

McQueen, Iris. Sexual Harassment in the Workplace: The Management View. Levers, Joan & Moss, Lowell, eds. (Illus.). 138p. (Orig.). 1983. text ed. 24.95 (ISBN 0-9609354-1-X); pap. 14.95 (ISBN 0-9609354-0-1). McQueen & Son.

MacQueen, Jean & Hanes, Ted. The Living World: Exploring Modern Biology. LC 78-2601. (Illus.). 1978. 17.95 (ISBN 0-13-538975-5, Spec); pap. 9.95 o.p. (ISBN 0-13-538967-4). P-H.

MacQueen, John & MacQueen, Winifred, eds. A Choice of Scottish Verse. 224p. 1972. pap. 4.95 (ISBN 0-571-09686-7). Faber & Faber.

MacQueen, John & Scott, Tom, eds. Oxford Book of Scottish Verse. 1966. 29.00 (ISBN 0-19-812131-8). Oxford U Pr.

McQueen, M. Britain, the EEC & the Developing World. (Studies in the British Economy). 1977. pap. text ed. 5.50x o.p. (ISBN 0-435-84562-4). Heinemann Ed.

McQueen, William A. A Short Guide to English Composition. 3rd ed. 1979. pap. text ed. 6.95x o.p. (ISBN 0-534-00703-1). Wadsworth Pub.

McQueen, William A. & Rockwell, Kiffin A. Latin Poetry of Andrew Marvell. (University of North Carolina Studies in Comparative Literature: No. 34). Repr. of 1964 ed. 16.00 (ISBN 0-384-34916-1). Johnson Repr.

McQueen, William A., jt. auth. see Hanford, James H.

MacQueen, Winifred, jt. ed. see MacQueen, John.

McQueen-Williams, Morvyth & Appisson, Barbara. A Diet for One Hundred Healthy, Happy Years. 1978. pap. 1.95 o.s.i. (ISBN 0-515-04523-3). Jove Pubns.

McQuesten, Fern W. Oh, Tante Anna Has the Answer! 1979. 6.50 o.p. (ISBN 0-533-04280-1). Vantage.

McQuigg, James D. & Harness, Alta M. Flowcharting. (Modern Mathematics Ser). (Illus.). (gr. 7-12). 1970. pap. 5.40 (ISBN 0-395-03244-X). HM.

McQuilkin, Robert. How to Photograph Sports & Action, Vol. 15. 160p. 1982. pap. 9.95 (ISBN 0-89586-145-3). H P Bks.

--Runner's World: Outdoor Sports Photography Book. 195p. 1982. pap. 9.95 (ISBN 0-89037-243-8). Anderson World.

McQuilkin, Robertson. Understanding & Applying the Bible. (Orig.). 1983. pap. 9.95 (ISBN 0-8024-0457-X). Moody.

McQuillan, Florence. Realities of Nursing Management: How to Cope. LC 78-8298. 384p. 1978. text ed. 19.95 o.p. (ISBN 0-87618-991-5). R J Brady.

McQuillan, Mary T. Somatostatin, Vol. 1. Horrobin, D. F., ed. (Annual Research Reviews Ser.). 1979. 24.00 (ISBN 0-88831-040-4). Eden Pr.

--Somatostatin, Vol. 2. Horrobin, D. F., ed. (Annual Research Reviews). 238p. 1980. 30.00 (ISBN 0-88831-077-3). Eden Pr.

McQuillen, K., jt. ed. see Mandelstam, J.

McQuillen, Kevin. System 360-370 Assembler Language (DOS) Murach, Mike, ed. LC 74-76436. (Illus.). 407p. (Orig.). 1974. pap. text ed. 22.50 (ISBN 0-911625-01-1). M Murach & Assoc.

--System 360-370 Assembler Language (OS) Murach, Mike, ed. LC 74-29645. (Illus.). 450p. (Orig.). 1975. pap. text ed. 22.50 (ISBN 0-911625-02-X). M Murach & Assoc.

McQuiston, Faye C. & Parker, Jerald D. Heating, Ventilating, & Air Conditioning: Analysis & Design. LC 77-8033. 1977. 29.95 o.p. (ISBN 0-471-01722-1). Wiley.

McQuiston, Frank W., Jr. & Shoemaker, Robert S. Primary Crushing Plant Design. (Illus.). 1978. 33.00x (ISBN 0-89520-252-2). Soc Mining Eng.

McQuiston, L., jt. ed. see Bicknell, J.

MacQuitty, William. Tutankhamun: The Last Journey. (Illus.). 1976. 10.95 o.p. (ISBN 0-517-53170-4); pap. 4.95 o.p. (ISBN 0-517-53171-2). Crown.

McQuown, Judith H. Inc. Yourself: How to Profit by Setting up Your Own Corporation. 1981. pap. 6.95 (ISBN 0-446-37656-6). Warner Bks.

--INC. Yourself: Profit by Setting up Your Own Corporation. (Illus.). 352p. 1982. 13.95 (ISBN 0-686-32943-0). Macmillan.

McQuown, Judith H. & Laugier, Odile. The Fashion Survival Manual. (Illus.). 256p. 1981. 15.95 (ISBN 0-89696-120-6, An Everest House Book); pap. 10.95 (ISBN 0-89696-139-7). Dodd.

Macracken, Mary. A Circle of Children. (RL 9). 1975. pap. 2.50 (ISBN 0-451-12048-5, AE2048, Sig). NAL.

McRae. Fire Department Operations with Modern Elevators. 1977. pap. 12.95 o.p. (ISBN 0-87618-713-0). R J Brady.

McRae, Bradley. Time Management. 160p. 1983. pap. 3.95 (ISBN 0-8120-2486-9). Barron.

MacRae, C. Duncan, jt. auth. see Andreassi, Michael W.

MacRae, Donald L., et al. You & Others: An Introduction to Interpersonal Communication. (Illus.). 1976. pap. text ed. 18.95 (ISBN 0-07-082256-5, C). McGraw.

McRae, Gail C. How to Raise & Train a Borzoi. (Illus., Orig.). pap. 2.95 (ISBN 0-87666-250-5, DS1043). TFH Pubns.

MacRae, George W. Hebrews. Karris, Robert J., ed. (Collegeville Bible Commentary Ser.: No. 10). 64p. 1983. pap. 2.50 (ISBN 0-8146-1310-1). Liturgical Pr.

--Invitation to John: A Commentary on the Gospel of John with Complete Text from the Jerusalem Bible. LC 77-91559. 1978. pap. 3.95 (ISBN 0-385-12212-8, Im). Doubleday.

Macrae, Jack, ed. see Hospital, Janette.

Macrae, James. With Lord Byron in the Sandwich Islands. 90p. pap. 4.75 (ISBN 0-912180-14-5). Petroglyph.

MacRae, Norma M. Canning & Preserving Without Sugar. 132p. (Orig.). 1982. pap. 6.95 (ISBN 0-914718-71-1). Pacific Search.

--How to Have Your Cake & Eat It! rev. ed. (Illus.). 1982. pap. 8.95 (ISBN 0-88240-226-9). Alaska Northwest.

McRae, S. G. & Burnham, C. P. Land Evaluation. (Monographs on Soil Survey). (Illus.). 1981. 42.00x (ISBN 0-19-854518-5). Oxford U Pr.

McRae, T. W. Computer & Accounting. LC 75-6793. 1976. 27.95 (ISBN 0-471-58985-3, Pub. by Wiley-Interscience). Wiley.

--Statistical Sampling for Audit & Control. LC 73-19329. 288p. 1974. 49.95 (ISBN 0-471-58991-8, Pub. by Wiley-Interscience). Wiley.

McRae, William. The Dynamics of Spiritual Gifts. 144p. 1983. pap. 4.95 (ISBN 0-310-29091-0). Zondervan.

McRae, William J. The Dynamics of Spiritual Gifts. 160p. 1976. pap. 2.95 o.p. (ISBN 0-310-29092-9). Zondervan.

Macrakis, Michael S., ed. Energy: Demand, Conservation, & Institutional Problems. LC 74-2257. 450p. 1974. 40.00x (ISBN 0-262-13091-2). MIT Pr.

MacRauch, Earl. New York, New York. 1977. 9.95 o.p. (ISBN 0-671-22633-9). S&S.

McRaven, Charles. Building with Stone. (Illus.). 1980. 15.34i (ISBN 0-690-01879-7); pap. 9.95 (ISBN 0-690-01912-2). Har-Row.

McReynolds. Single-Subject Design Experimental Designs in Communicative Disorders. 1982. text ed. 27.95 (ISBN 0-8391-1714-0). Univ Park.

Macreynolds, George. Place Names in Bucks County Pennsylvania: Historical Narratives. 1976. Repr. of 1955 ed. 8.95 (ISBN 0-910302-11-1). Bucks Co Hist.

McReynolds, Ginny. Alone on a Desert Island. Bennett, Russell, ed. LC 79-22144. (Quest, Adventure, Survival Ser.). (Illus.). 46p. (gr. 4-9). 1982. pap. 7.93g (ISBN 0-8172-2050-X). Raintree Pubs.

McReynolds, Paul, ed. Advances in Psychological Assessment, Vol. 1. LC 68-21578. 1968. 9.50x o.p. (ISBN 0-8314-0017-X). Sci & Behavior.

--Four Early Works on Motivation, 4 vols. in 1. Incl. An Inquiry Concerning Beauty, Order, etc. Hutcheson, Francis. Repr. of 1726 ed; Concerning the Constitution of Human Nature & the Supreme Good. Hutcheson, Francis. Repr. of 1755 ed; An Inquiry into the Origins of Human Affections. Long, James. Repr. of 1747 ed; A Tale of the Springs of Action. Bentham, Jeremy. Repr. of 1815 ed. LC 72-81360. (History of Psychology Ser.). (Illus.). 1969. 60.00x (ISBN 0-8201-1057-4). Schol Facsimiles.

Macri, Angelika, tr. see Hartmann, Sven & Hartner, Thoman.

Macridis, Roy C. Contemporary Political Ideologies: Movements & Regimes. (Orig.). 1980. pap. text ed. 12.95 (ISBN 0-316-54279-2). Little.

--Modern Political Systems: Europe. 4th ed. 1978. ref. 22.95 (ISBN 0-13-597187-X). P-H.

--Modern Political Systems: Europe. 5th ed. (Illus.). 576p. 1983. prof. ref. 22.95 (ISBN 0-13-597195-0). P-H.

--Study of Comparative Government. (Orig.). 1955. pap. text ed. 2.45 (ISBN 0-685-19771-9). Phila Bk Co.

Macridis, Roy C., ed. Foreign Policy in World Politics. 5th ed. 1976. 14.95 (ISBN 0-13-326488-2). P-H.

McRobbie, K., tr. see Gombos, Karoly.

MacRoberts, Barbara R., jt. auth. see MacRoberts, Michael H.

MacRoberts, Michael H. & MacRoberts, Barbara R. Social Organization & Behavior of the Acorn Woodpecker in Central Coastal California. 115p. 1976. 7.50 (ISBN 0-943610-21-4). Am Ornithologists.

McRoberts, Robert. Lip Service. LC 76-55803. 59p. 1976. 3.50 (ISBN 0-87886-078-9). Ithaca Hse.

Macsai, John, et al. Housing. 2nd ed. LC 81-7584. 590p. 1982. 56.50 (ISBN 0-471-08126-4, Pub. by Wiley-Interscience). Wiley.

--Housing. LC 75-38736. 1976. 54.50 (ISBN 0-471-56312-9, Pub. by Wiley-Interscience). Wiley.

MacShane, Denis. Francois Mitterand: A Political Odyssey. LC 82-23793. 288p. 1983. 14.95 (ISBN 0-87663-418-8). Universe.

McShane, E. J. Order-Preserving Maps & Integration Processes. (Annals of Mathematics Studies). Repr. of 1953 ed. pap. 12.00 (ISBN 0-527-02747-2). Kraus Repr.

McShane, E. J., ed. Unified Integration. LC 82-16266. (Pure & Applied Mathematics Ser.). Date not set. price not set (ISBN 0-12-486260-8). Acad Pr.

MacShane, Frank. The Life & Work of Ford Madox Ford. 328p. (Orig.). 1983. pap. 9.95 (ISBN 0-8180-0252-2). Horizon.

--The Life of John O'Hara. (Illus.). 300p. 1981. 15.95 o.p. (ISBN 0-525-13720-3). Dutton.

MacShane, Frank, ed. see Ford, Ford M.

MacShane, Frank, tr. see Serrano, Miguel.

McShane, J. Learning to Talk. LC 79-19875. (Illus.). 1980. 27.95 (ISBN 0-521-22478-0). Cambridge U Pr.

McShane, Philip. Lonergan's Challenge to the University & the Economy. LC 79-3809. 1980. text ed. 20.00 (ISBN 0-8191-0933-9); pap. text ed. 10.25 (ISBN 0-8191-0934-7). U Pr of Amer.

--Music That is Soundless: An Introduction to God for the Graduate. 1977. pap. text ed. 8.00 (ISBN 0-8191-0236-9). U Pr of Amer.

--The Shaping of the Foundations: Being at Home in the Transcendental Method. 10.50 (ISBN 0-8191-0209-1). U Pr of Amer.

--Wealth of Self & Wealth of Nations: Self-Axis of the Great Ascent. LC 81-40712. 134p. 1982. lib. bdg. 19.75 (ISBN 0-8191-1915-6); pap. text ed. 9.50 (ISBN 0-8191-1916-4). U Pr of Amer.

McShean, Gordon. Bum Ticker: A Hearty Traveler's Tale. LC 76-13744. 1976. 9.95 (ISBN 0-917112-01-6); pap. 4.95 (ISBN 0-917112-62-8). Multinational Media.

--Mr. Chillhead. LC 76-13743. (Illus.). (gr. 2-6). 1977. pap. 4.95 (ISBN 0-917112-03-2). Multinational Media.

McSheehy, William R. Skid Row. 1979. lib. bdg. 14.50 (ISBN 0-8161-9008-9, Univ Bks). G K Hall.

McSherry, James E. Computer Typesetting: A Guide for Authors, Editors, & Publishers. 95p. 1983. pap. 9.50x (ISBN 0-912162-05-8). Open-Door.

McSorley, Joseph. Isaac Hecker & His Friends. 314p. 1972. pap. 1.45 (ISBN 0-8091-1605-7). Paulist Pr.

McSpadden, J. W. The Book of Holidays. 346p. 1983. Repr. of 1917 ed. lib. bdg. 35.00 (ISBN 0-89984-823-0). Century Bookbindery.

McSpadden, William, jt. auth. see Dearholt, Donald.

McStay, William. True Book About Royal Air Force. (Illus.). (gr. 7 up). 12.75x (ISBN 0-392-05154-0, LTB). Sportshelf.

MacStravic, Robin E. Marketing Health Care. LC 76-58967. 250p. 1977. 31.95 (ISBN 0-912862-41-6). Aspen Systems.

MacStravic, Robin S. Marketing by Objectives for Hospitals. LC 80-10903. 280p. 1980. text ed. 34.95 (ISBN 0-89443-174-9). Aspen Systems.

MacStravic, Suellen. Print Making. LC 72-13344. (Early Craft Bks.). (Illus.). 36p. (gr. 1-4). 1973. PLB 3.95g (ISBN 0-8225-0859-1). Lerner Pubns.

MacSwain, J. W., jt. auth. see Linsley, E. G.

McSwain, Norman E., Jr. Traumatic Surgery. (Medical Outline Ser.). 1976. spiral bdg. 21.00 (ISBN 0-87488-619-8). Med Exam.

McSwain, Romola. The Past & Future People: Tradition & Change on a New Guinea Island. (Illus.). 1977. 26.50x o.p. (ISBN 0-19-550521-2). Oxford U Pr.

McSweeney, Kerry. Four Contemporary Novelists: Angus Wilson, Brian Moore, John Fowles, V. S. Naipaul. 232p. 1983. 24.95 (ISBN 0-7735-0399-4). McGill-Queens U Pr.

McSweeney, William. Roman Catholicism: The Search for Relevance. 1980. 25.00 (ISBN 0-312-68969-1). St Martin.

MacSwiggan, Amelia E. Fairy Lamps. (Illus.). 180p. 1983. text ed. 17.95x (ISBN 0-686-83979-X). Irvington.

McTaggart, John. Some Dogmas of Religion. LC 68-57622. (Illus.). 1969. Repr. of 1906 ed. lib. bdg. 17.25x (ISBN 0-8371-0587-0, MCDR). Greenwood.

McTavish, Thistle & Swenson, Allan. Bush Country by George. (Illus.). 144p. (Orig.). 1982. pap. 7.95 (ISBN 0-930096-29-0). G Gannett.

McTeer, Ed. Fifty Years As a Low Country Witch Doctor. 1976. 12.95 (ISBN 0-910206-02-3). Beaufort Bk Co.

McTeigue, Susan. Dining for Two. LC 79-56406. 128p. (Orig.). 1980. pap. 5.95 (ISBN 0-935000-00-3). Bloom Bks.

MacTiernan, Brian, ed. see McPhater, Donald.

MacUlsten, Liam. Post Mortem. (Irish Play Ser.). pap. 2.50x (ISBN 0-912262-43-5). Proscenium.

Macura, P. Dictionary of Botany, 2 vols. 1982. Set. 213.00 (ISBN 0-686-94134-9); Vol. 1. write for info.; Vol. 2: General Terms. 110.75 (ISBN 0-444-41977-2). Elsevier.

--Elsevier's Dictionary of Botany, Vol. 1: Plant Names. LC 79-15558. 580p. 1979. 110.75 (ISBN 0-444-41787-7). Elsevier.

MacVane, John. On the Air in World War II. LC 79-18973. (Illus.). 1979. 12.95 o.p. (ISBN 0-688-03558-2). Morrow.

McVaugh, Rogers. Flora Novo-Galiciana: A Descriptive Account of the Vascular Plants of Western Mexico. Anderson, William R., ed. LC 82-13537. (Graminae Ser.: Vol. 14). (Illus.). 384p. 1983. text ed. 38.00 (ISBN 0-472-04814-7). U of Mich Pr.

McVay, Chester B., jt. auth. see Anson, Barry J.

McVay, Kipling L. & Stubbs, Robert S. Governmental Ethics & Conflicts of Interest in Georgia. 227p. 1980. with 1981 suppl. 20.00 (ISBN 0-87215-304-5); 1981 suppl. 7.50 (ISBN 0-87215-396-7). Michie-Bobbs.

McVean, James. Seabird Nine. 1981. 12.95 (ISBN 0-698-11063-3, Coward). Putnam Pub Group.

McVeigh, J. C. Sun Power: An Introduction to the Applications of Solar Energy. 2nd ed. (Illus.). 240p. 1983. 40.00 (ISBN 0-08-026148-5); pap. 15.00 (ISBN 0-08-026147-7). Pergamon.

McVeigh, Malcolm. God in Africa. 1982. 10.00 (ISBN 0-686-96557-4). Branden.

McVeigh, Malcolm J. God in Africa: Conceptions of God in African Traditional Religion & Christianity. LC 74-76005. (God Ser.: No. 201). (Illus.). 235p. 1974. 10.00 (ISBN 0-89007-003-2). C Stark.

Macvey, John W. Space Weapons-Space Wars. LC 78-24147. (Illus.). 264p. 1982. pap. 7.95 (ISBN 0-8128-6111-6). Stein & Day.

McVey, Mary A. Bridge Basics: An Introduction to the Game. 2d ed. 120p. 1982. pap. 5.50x (ISBN 0-910475-01-6). KET.

McVey, Richard C. Why So Many of Us? 1978. 8.95 o.p. (ISBN 0-533-03201-6). Vantage.

McVicar, Marjorie & Craig, Julia F. Minding My Own Business: Entrepreneurial Women Share Their Secrets for Success. LC 80-29423. 425p. 1981. 13.95 (ISBN 0-399-90116-7, Marek). Putnam Pub Group.

McVoy, D. Stevens, jt. auth. see Baldwin, Thomas F.

McVoy, Gary R., jt. auth. see Cohn, Louis F.

McWaters, Barry. Conscious Evolution. 1981. pap. 7.95 (ISBN 0-87613-096-1). New Age.

--Conscious Evolution: Personal & Planetary Transformation. (Illus.). 177p. (Orig.). 1981. pap. 7.95 (ISBN 0-87613-071-6). New Age.

McWeeny, R., ed. see Farina, John E.

McWeeny, Roy, rev. by see Coulson, C. A.

McWhan, D. B., ed. Crystal Structure at High Pressure. pap. 5.00 (ISBN 0-686-60376-1). Polycrystal Bk Serv.

McWhinney, Edward. Canada & the Constitution 1979-1982: Patriation & the Charter of Rights. 240p. 1982. 29.50x o.p. (ISBN 0-8020-2478-5); pap. 10.95 (ISBN 0-8020-6501-5). U of Toronto Pr.

McWhinney, Edward & Bradley, Martin A. The Freedom of the Air. LC 68-56077. 259p. 1968. lib. bdg. 19.00 (ISBN 0-379-00372-4). Oceana.

McWhinney, Ian R. An Introduction to Family Medicine. (Illus.). 1981. text ed. 16.95x (ISBN 0-19-502807-4); pap. text ed. 11.95x (ISBN 0-19-502808-2). Oxford U Pr.

McWhinnie, Mary A., ed. Polar Research: To the Present & the Future. LC 78-52068. (AAAS Selected Symposium Ser.: No. 7). (Illus.). 1978. lib. bdg. 31.50 (ISBN 0-89158-435-8). Westview.

McWhirr, Alan. Roman Gloucestershire. 224p. 1982. text ed. 18.00x (ISBN 0-904387-63-1, Pub. by Sutton England); pap. text ed. 9.00x (ISBN 0-904387-60-7). Humanities.

McWhirter, Norris. Guinness Book of Amazing Animals. LC 81-50983. (Illus.). 96p. (YA) (gr. 9 up). 1981. 6.95 (ISBN 0-8069-0222-1); lib. bdg. 8.99 (ISBN 0-8069-0223-X). Sterling.

--Guinness Book of Essential Facts. LC 78-66314. (Illus.). 1979. 12.95 o.p. (ISBN 0-8069-0160-8); lib. bdg. 11.69 o.p. (ISBN 0-8069-0161-6). Sterling.

--Guinness Book of Sports Spectaculars. LC 81-50983. (Illus.). 96p. 1981. 6.95 (ISBN 0-8069-0222-1); PLB 8.99 (ISBN 0-8069-0223-X). Sterling.

--Guinness Book of Superstunts & Staggering Statistics. LC 79-91387. (Guinness Illustrated Collection of World Records for Young Readers Ser.). (Illus.). 96p. (gr. 3-12). 1980. 6.95 (ISBN 0-8069-0180-2); PLB 6.69 (ISBN 0-8069-0181-0). Sterling.

--Guinness Book of World Records, 1983. LC 65-24391. (Illus.). 544p. 1982. 12.95 (ISBN 0-8069-0246-9); lib. bdg. 15.69_o. p. (ISBN 0-8069-0247-7). Sterling.

--Guinness Book of World Records 1984. LC 64-4984. (Illus.). 544p. 1983. 12.95 (ISBN 0-8069-0256-6); lib. bdg. 15.69 (ISBN 0-8069-0257-4). Sterling.

--Guinness: The Stories Behind the Records. LC 81-85584. 128p. 1982. 9.95 (ISBN 0-8069-0244-2); pap. 4.95 (ISBN 0-8069-7618-7); lib. bdg. 12.49 (ISBN 0-8069-0245-0). Sterling.

McWhirter, Norris & McWhirter, Ross. Guinness Book of Astounding Feats & Events. LC 75-14503. (Guinness Illustrated Collection for Young People Ser.). 96p. (YA) 1975. 6.95 (ISBN 0-8069-0036-9); lib. bdg. 8.99 (ISBN 0-8069-0037-7). Sterling.

--Guinness Book of Daring Deeds & Fascinating Facts. LC 78-66312. (Illus.). (gr. 3 up). 1979. 6.95 (ISBN 0-8069-0158-6); PLB 8.99 (ISBN 0-8069-0159-4). Sterling.

--Guinness Book of Extraordinary Exploits. LC 77-79505. (Guinness Illustrated Collection of World Records for Young Readers). (Illus.). (gr. 3 up). 1977. 6.95 (ISBN 0-8069-0118-7); PLB 8.99 (ISBN 0-8069-0119-5). Sterling.

--Guinness Book of Startling Acts & Facts. LC 78-57791. (Guinness Illustrated Collection of World Records for Young Readers). (Illus.). (gr. 2 up). 1978. 6.95 (ISBN 0-8069-0128-4); PLB 6.69 (ISBN 0-8069-0129-2). Sterling.

McWhirter, Norris & Pallas, Norvin. Guinness Game Book. LC 77-93311. (Illus.). (gr. 3 up). 1978. 5.95 o.p. (ISBN 0-8069-0122-5); PLB 5.89 o.p. (ISBN 0-8069-0123-3). Sterling.

McWhirter, Norris, jt. auth. see McWhirter, Ross.

McWhirter, Norris & McWhirter, Ross, eds. Guinness Book of Phenomenal Happenings. LC 76-1162. (Illus.). 96p. (gr. 4 up). 1976. 5.95 o.p. (ISBN 0-8069-0040-7); PLB 6.69 o.p. (ISBN 0-8069-0041-5). Sterling.

McWhirter, Norris, et al. Guinness Book of Sports Records, Winners & Champions. Rev. ed. LC 81-85045. (Illus.). 352p. 1982. 12.95 (ISBN 0-8069-0234-5); PLB 15.69 (ISBN 0-8069-0235-3). Sterling.

McWhirter, Ross & McWhirter, Norris. Guinness Book of Dazzling Endeavors. LC 80-52330. (Guinness Illustrated Collection of World Records for Young Readers). (Illus.). 96p. (gr. 3 up). 1980. 6.95 (ISBN 0-8069-0194-2); PLB 8.99 (ISBN 0-8069-0195-0). Sterling.

McWhirter, Ross, jt. auth. see McWhirter, Norris.

McWhirter, Ross, jt. ed. see McWhirter, Norris.

McWhorter, Gene. Understanding Digital Electronics. LC 78-57024. (Understanding Ser.). (Illus.). 264p. 1978. pap. text ed. 6.95 (ISBN 0-89512-017-8, LCB-3311). Tex Instr Inc.

McWhorter, Jane. Meet My Friend David. 4.60 (ISBN 0-89137-420-5). Quality Pubns.

McWhorter, Kathleen T. College Reading & Study Skills. (Illus.). 321p. 1980. pap. text ed. 10.95 (ISBN 0-316-56400-1); instructor's manual avail. (ISBN 0-316-56402-8). Little.

McWhorter, Margaret L., ed. see Andrecht, Venus C.

McWilliam, H. O. Muhammad & the World of Islam. Reeves, Marjorie, ed. (Then & There Ser.). (Illus.). 96p. (Orig.). (gr. 7-12). 1977. pap. text ed. 3.10 (ISBN 0-582-20537-9). Longman.

McWilliam, J. Book of Freezing. 1977. Repr. 12.00 (ISBN 0-85941-010-2). State Mutual Bk.

McWilliams, Bernard F, tr. see Dussel, Enrique.

McWilliams, Betty J. & Morris, Hughlett H. Cleft Palate Speech. 300p. 1983. text ed. 28.00 (ISBN 0-941158-11-X, D3339-7). Mosby.

McWilliams, Betty J., jt. auth. see Cohn, Ellen R.

McWilliams, Carey. California, the Great Exception. LC 75-138398. xiii, 377p. Repr. of 1949 ed. lib. bdg. 16.00x (ISBN 0-8371-5926-1, MCCA). Greenwood.

--A Mask for Privilege: Anti-Semitism in America. LC 78-26197. 1979. Repr. of 1948 ed. lib. bdg. 20.50x (ISBN 0-313-20880-8, MCMP). Greenwood.

--North from Mexico, the Spanish Speaking People of the United States. LC 68-28595. lib. bdg. 15.50x (ISBN 0-8371-0180-8, MCNM); pap. 5.95 (ISBN 0-8371-7352-3). Greenwood.

--Prejudice: Japanese-Americans, Symbol of Racial Intolerance. LC 77-122415. 1971. Repr. of 1944 ed. 22.50 o.p. (ISBN 0-208-01087-4, Archon). Shoe String.

--Witch Hunt. LC 74-20311. 361p. 1975. Repr. of 1950 ed. lib. bdg. 18.25x (ISBN 0-8371-7849-5, MCWH). Greenwood.

McWilliams, Dean. The Narratives of Michel Butor: The Writer As Janus. LC 77-92254. x, 150p. 1978. 13.00x (ISBN 0-8214-0389-3, 82-82824). Ohio U Pr.

McWilliams, Dean, tr. see Weisgerber, Jean.

MacWilliams, F. J. & Sloane, N. J. The Theory of Error Correcting Codes, 2 Pts. in 1 vol. (Mathematical Library: Vol. 16). 1978. 47.00 (ISBN 0-444-85193-3, North-Holland). Elsevier.

McWilliams, Jerry. The Preservation & Restoration of Sound Recordings. LC 79-17173. (Illus., Orig.). 1979. pap. text ed. 10.00 (ISBN 0-910050-41-4). AASLH.

McWilliams, John P., Jr. Political Justice in a Republic: James Fenimore Cooper's America. LC 75-182283. 1973. 30.00x (ISBN 0-520-02175-4). U of Cal Pr.

McWilliams, Margaret. Food Fundamentals. 3rd ed. LC 78-65888. 1979. 26.95 (ISBN 0-471-02691-3). Wiley.

--Illustrated Guide to Food Preparation. 4th ed. 1982. 14.95x (ISBN 0-8087-3420-2). Burgess.

--Illustrated Guide to Food Preparation. 4th ed. LC 76-13996. (Illus.). 1982. spiral bdg. 14.95x (ISBN 0-8087-3420-2). Plycon Pr.

--Nutrition for the Growing Years. 3rd ed. LC 80-453. 491p. 1980. text ed. 27.50 (ISBN 0-471-02692-1). Wiley.

MacWilliams, Margaret. Toria. (Candlelight Edwardian Special Ser.: No. 670). (Orig.). 1981. pap. 1.50 o.s.i. (ISBN 0-440-19031-2). Dell.

McWilliams, Margaret, jt. auth. see Kotschevar, L. H.

McWilliams, Margaret, jt. auth. see Stare, Frederick J.

McWilliams, Margaret, jt. auth. see Stare, Fredrick J.

McWilliams, Peter A. The Personal Computer Book. (Illus.). 289p. 1982. pap. 9.95 (ISBN 0-931580-90-0). Prelude Press.

--The Word Processing Book: A Short Course in Computer Literacy. 252p. 1982. pap. 8.95 (ISBN 0-931580-98-6). Prelude Press.

McWilliams, R. O., jt. auth. see Christenson, R. M.

McWilliams, Wilson C. The Idea of Fraternity in America. LC 73-101339. 1973. 30.00x (ISBN 0-520-01650-5); pap. 4.95 (ISBN 0-520-02772-8). U of Cal Pr.

Macy, Christopher, jt. auth. see Falkner, Frank.

Macy, Jesse. Anti-Slavery Crusade. 1919. text ed. 8.50 (ISBN 0-686-83472-0). Elliots Bks.

Macy, Joanna. Dharma & Development: Religion As Resource in the Sarvodaya Movement. LC 82-83015. (K. P. Monograph: No. 2). 104p. 1983. pap. 6.75x (ISBN 0-931816-11-4); 13.75x (ISBN 0-931816-74-2). Kumarian Pr.

Macy, John W., Jr. To Irrigate a Wasteland: The Struggle to Shape a Public Television System in the United States. 1974. 17.95x (ISBN 0-520-02498-2). U of Cal Pr.

Macy, Ralph. Wooden Sidewalks. 350p. (Orig.). 1983. pap. 10.95 (ISBN 0-913244-59-7). Hapi Pr.

Macy, Ralph W. & Berntzen, Allen K. Laboratory Guide to Parasitology: With Introduction to Experimental Methods. (Illus.). 316p. 1971. spiral 17.75x (ISBN 0-398-02154-6). C C Thomas.

Maczuley, J. V. Lands of Contrast. 14.50x (ISBN 0-392-03629-0, ABC). Sportshelf.

Mad Editors. Mad Around the Town. (Mad Ser.: No. 63). 192p. 1983. pap. 1.95 (ISBN 0-446-30588-X). Warner Bks.

Mad Magazine Editors. The Non-Violent Mad. (Mad Ser.: No. 33). (Illus.). 1972. pap. 1.75 o.p. (ISBN 0-446-94593-5). Warner Bks.

Madach, Imre. The Tragedy of Man. 8th ed. Horne, J. C., tr. 4.00x o.p. (ISBN 0-89918-336-0, H336). Vanous.

Madame De Stael. Lettres Sur les Ouvrages et la Caractere De J. J. Rousseau. (Rousseauism: 1788-1797). (Fr.). 1978. Repr. of 1788 ed. lib. bdg. 42.00x o.p. (ISBN 0-8287-0793-6). Clearwater Pub.

Madam Sadat, ed. see Schulze, Helmut.

Madan, Raj, compiled by. Colored Minorities in Great Britain: A Comprehensive Bibliography, 1970-1977. 1979. lib. bdg. 29.95 (ISBN 0-313-20705-4, MCM/). Greenwood.

Madan, T. N. Way of Life: King, Householder, Renouncer; Essays in Honour of Louis Dumont. 400p. 1982. text ed. 45.00x (ISBN 0-7069-1843-6, Pub. by Vikas India). Advent NY.

Madan, T. N., jt. ed. see Beteille, Andre.

Madaras, Lynda. What's Happening to My Body? The Growing-Up Book for Mothers & Daughters. (Illus.). 192p. (gr. 4 up). 1983. 14.95 (ISBN 0-937858-25-0); pap. 7.95 (ISBN 0-937858-21-8). Newmarket.

Madaras, Lynda, jt. auth. see Palewicz-Rousseau, Pam.

Madariaga, Salvador de. Don Quixote: An Introductory Essay in Psychology. LC 79-16911. 159p. 1980. Repr. of 1935 ed. lib. bdg. 18.50x (ISBN 0-313-22011-5, MADQ). Greenwood.

--The World's Design. 1938. 7.50x (ISBN 0-686-17395-3). R S Barnes.

Madaus, G. & Scriven, M. S. Conceptual Issues in Evaluation. (Evaluation & Education in Human Services Ser.). 1983. lib. bdg. 38.00 (ISBN 0-89838-123-1). Kluwer Nijhoff.

Madaus, George F., jt. auth. see Bloom, Benjamin S.

Madaus, George F., ed. The Courts, Validity & Minimum Competency Testing. (Evaluation in Education & Human Services Ser.). 1982. lib. bdg. 20.00 (ISBN 0-89838-113-4). Kluwer-Nijhoff.

Madaus, George F., et al. School Effectiveness: A Reassessment of the Evidence. 1980. text ed. 18.50 (ISBN 0-07-039378-8). McGraw.

Madauss, Martyria. Jesus: A Portrait of Love. 3.25 o.p. (ISBN 3-872-09603-6). Evang Sisterhood Mary.

--The Shield of Faith. 1974. gift edition 0.75 (ISBN 3-87209-659-1). Evang Sisterhood Mary.

Maddala, G. S. Econometrics. 1977. 30.95 (ISBN 0-07-039412-1). McGraw.

--Limited-Dependent & Qualitative Variables in Econometrics. LC 82-9554. (Econometric Society Monographs in Quantitative Economics 3). 416p. Date not set. 39.50 (ISBN 0-521-24143-X). Cambridge U Pr.

Madden. Guide to Alcohol & Drug Dependence. 256p. 1979. pap. 20.00 (ISBN 0-7236-0504-1). Wright-PSG.

Madden, A. F. & Morris-Jones, W. H., eds. Australia & Britain: Studies in a Changing Relationship. 191p. Date not set. 29.50x (ISBN 0-7146-3149-3, F Cass Co). Biblio Dist.

Madden, Anne, ed. The Best of Sail Cruising. (Illus.). 1978. 14.95 (ISBN 0-914814-11-7). Sail Bks.

Madden, Carl H. Clash of Culture: Management & the Age of Changing Values. LC 72-88236. 132p. 1976. 5.00 (ISBN 0-89068-006-X). Natl Planning.

Madden, Chris C. Baby Hints Handbook. Date not set. pap. 3.95 (ISBN 0-449-90078-9, Columbine). Fawcett.

Madden, D. J. & Lion, J. R., eds. Rage, Hate, Assault & Other Forms of Violence. (Aggression & Violence Ser.). 265p. 1976. 15.00x o.s.i. (ISBN 0-470-15022-X). Halsted Pr.

Madden, David. Pleasure-Dome. LC 79-10664. 1979. 10.00 o.p. (ISBN 0-672-52553-4). Bobbs.

--The Suicide's Wife. 1979. pap. 1.95 o.p. (ISBN 0-380-47522-7, 47522). Avon.

--The Suicide's Wife. LC 78-55644. 1978. 8.95 o.p. (ISBN 0-672-52492-9). Bobbs.

Madden, David, jt. ed. see Sever, John L.

Madden, Donald L. Management Accounting. LC 80-17277. (Self Teaching Guides Ser.). 326p. 1980. 8.95x (ISBN 0-471-03135-6, Pub. by Wiley-Interscience). Wiley.

Madden, Frederic, jt. ed. see Forshall, Josiah.

Madden, Frederick & Fieldhouse, David K., eds. Oxford & the Idea of Commonwealth: Essays Presented to Sir Edgar Williams. 168p. 1982. text ed. 26.00x (ISBN 0-7099-1021-5, Pub. by Croom Helm Ltd England). Biblio Dist.

Madden, James F. My First Atlas. new ed. LC 74-32520. (Illus.). 64p. (gr. 3-6). 1980. pap. 3.33x (ISBN 0-8437-7400-2). Hammond Inc.

Madden, L. How to Find Out About the Victorian Period. LC 74-116777. 1970. 24.00 o.s.i. (ISBN 0-08-015834-X); pap. text ed. 10.75 (ISBN 0-08-015833-1). Pergamon.

Madden, Mary A. Maybe He's Dead. 1981. 10.95 o.p. (ISBN 0-394-51190-5); pap. 5.95 (ISBN 0-394-74918-9). Random.

Madden, Mary J. Thinward Bound: Medical Management & Weight Loss. Hoel, Donna, ed. (Illus.). 112p. 1982. pap. 8.95 (ISBN 0-89303-228-X). R J Brady.

Madden, R. Father Madden's Life of Christ. 1960. pap. 1.75 o.p. (ISBN 0-685-01125-9, 80424). Glencoe.

Madden, Richard. Boy & His Teens. (Orig.). 1963. pap. 1.25 o.p. (ISBN 0-685-07614-8, 80422). Glencoe.

Madden, Samuel. Memoirs of the Twentieth Century: Being Original Letters of State Under George the Sixth. LC 74-170588. (Foundations of the Novel Ser.: Vol. 58). lib. bdg. 50.00 o.s.i. (ISBN 0-8240-0570-8). Garland Pub.

Madden, Thomas A., et al. Health Fact Almanac. 368p. 1982. pap. text ed. 14.95 (ISBN 0-89004-757-X). Raven.

Madden, Virginia M. Across America on the Yellow Brick Road. (Illus.). 1980. pap. 8.95 o.p. (ISBN 0-937760-00-5). Crow Canyon.

Madden, Walter. Jason's Orchid. 1982. pap. 1.95 (ISBN 0-686-97515-4, 39-1076). Concordia.

Madden, William, jt. auth. see Levine, George.

Madders, Jane. Stress & Relaxation. Hay, Kenneth, ed. LC 78-24489. (Positive Health Guides Ser.). (Illus.). 1979. 7.95 o.p. (ISBN 0-668-04674-0, 4674-0); pap. 4.95 (ISBN 0-668-04680-5, 4680-5). Arco.

Maddex, Diane, ed. Whole Preservation Catalog. (Illus.). 400p. 1983. 29.95 (ISBN 0-89133-107-7); pap. 19.95 (ISBN 0-89133-108-5). Preservation Pr.

Maddex, Diane & Marsh, Ellen, eds. The Little Brown Book: A Desk Reference for the Preservationist. 144p. 1983. pap. 9.95 (ISBN 0-89133-106-9). Preservation Pr.

Maddi, Salvatore R. & Kobasa, Suzanne. The Hardy Executive: Health Under Stress. LC 82-73631. (Dorsey Professional Ser.). 325p. 1983. 22.50 (ISBN 0-87094-381-2). Dow Jones-Irwin.

Maddin, R., jt. auth. see Kimura, H.

Maddin, Stuart. Current Dermatologic Therapy. (Illus.). 637p. 1982. 60.00 (ISBN 0-7216-5987-X). Saunders.

Maddison, Angus. Phases of Capitalist Development. (Illus.). 288p. 1982. 29.95x (ISBN 0-19-828450-0); pap. 8.95 (ISBN 0-19-828451-9). Oxford U Pr.

--Unemployment: The European Perspective. LC 81-21264. 220p. 1982. 20.00 (ISBN 0-312-83261-3). St Martin.

Maddison, R., jt. auth. see Vetter, M.

Maddison, R. E., tr. see Schmidt, Helmut & Von Stackelberg, Mark.

Maddock, R. J. Intermediate Network Theory. (Bk I). 1973. pap. 6.95 o.p. (ISBN 0-408-70513-2). Butterworth.

Maddock, Shirley & Easther, Michael. A Christmas Garland: A New Zealand Christmas Album, 1642-1900, In Twelve Parts. (Illus.). 96p. 1983. 15.95 (ISBN 0-00-216981-9, Pub. by W Collins Australia). Intl Schol Bk Serv.

Maddock, V., jt. ed. see Gillibrand, P.

Maddocks, Melvin. The Atlantic Crossing. LC 80-26891. (Seafarers Ser.). PLB 19.92 (ISBN 0-8094-2727-3). Silver.

--The Great Liners. LC 78-1366. (The Seafarers Ser.). (Illus.). 1978. lib. bdg. 19.92 (ISBN 0-8094-2663-3). Silver.

Maddox & Fuquay. State & Local Government. 4th ed. Date not set. pap. text ed. price not set o.s.i. (ISBN 0-442-24454-1). Van Nos Reinhold.

Maddox, Bill & Beeson, Harold. Rags & Patches. LC 78-3218. (Illus.). 1978. 3.96 (ISBN 0-695-80966-0, Dist. by Caroline Hse); PLB 5.31 (ISBN 0-695-40966-2). Follett.

Maddox, Brenda. The Half-Parent. 1976. pap. 1.95 o.p. (ISBN 0-451-09365-8, J9365, Sig). NAL.

Maddox, Everette. The Everette Maddox Songbook. Cassin, Maxine, ed. (New Orleans Poetry Journal Press Books). (Illus.). 80p. 1982. pap. 5.00 (ISBN 0-938498-02-9). New Orleans Poetry.

Maddox, George, jt. auth. see Fann, William E.

Maddox, I. J. Elements of Functional Analysis. LC 71-85726. 1970. text ed. 29.95 (ISBN 0-521-07617-X); pap. 13.95x (ISBN 0-521-29266-2). Cambridge U Pr.

Maddox, Irene, ed. Campfire Songs. 192p. 1983. pap. 7.95 (ISBN 0-914788-68-X). East Woods.

Maddox, John. The Doomsday Syndrome. LC 72-3844. 336p. 1972. 8.95 o.p. (ISBN 0-07-039428-8, GB). McGraw.

Maddox, John, jt. auth. see Beaton, Leonard.

Maddox, Lucy B. Nabokov's Novels in English. LC 82-4893. 208p. 1983. text ed. 15.00 (ISBN 0-8203-0626-6). U of Ga Pr.

Maddox, Robert, tr. see Hahn, Ferdinand.

Maddox, Russell W. & Fuquay, Robert F. State & Local Government. 3rd ed. 628p. 1975. text ed. 13.95x (ISBN 0-442-25078-9). Van Nos Reinhold.

Maddox, William P. Foreign Relations in British Labour Politics: A Study of the Formation of Party Attitudes on Foreign Affairs, & the Application of Political Pressure Designed to Influence Government Policy, 1900-1924. (Perspectives in European History Ser.: No. 34). Repr. of 1934 ed. lib. bdg. 19.50x (ISBN 0-87991-635-4). Porcupine Pr.

Maddrell, Simon H. & Nordmann, Jean J. Neurosecretion. LC 79-63655. (Tertiary Level Biology Ser.). 173p. 1979. 29.95x o.s.i. (ISBN 0-470-26711-9). Halsted Pr.

Maddux, Bob. Gem of the Wanderer. 1979. 4.95 (ISBN 0-89728-009-1). Omega Pubns OR.

Maddux, Cleborne D. How to Use Scripsit. Willis, Jerry, ed. 200p. 1983. pap. 9.95 (ISBN 0-88056-110-6). Dilithium Pr.

Maddux, James F. & Desmond, David P. Careers of Opioid Users. 256p. 1981. 27.95 (ISBN 0-03-059817-6). Praeger.

Maddux, Rachel, et al. Fiction into Film: A Walk in the Spring Rain. LC 72-111050. (Illus.). 1970. 16.50x (ISBN 0-87049-112-1). U of Tenn Pr.

Maddy, A. H., ed. Biochemical Analysis of Membranes. 1976. 68.00x (ISBN 0-412-12440-8, Pub. by Chapman & Hall England). Methuen Inc.

Madeira, Louis C., compiled by. Annals of Music in Philadelphia & History of the Musical Fund Society. LC 78-169650. (Music Reprint Ser.). (Illus.). 234p. 1973. Repr. of 1896 ed. lib. bdg. 25.00 (ISBN 0-306-70260-6). Da Capo.

Madeja, Stanley, jt. auth. see Hurwitz, Al.

Madell, Robert. Picturing Multiplication & Division. 1979. 8.50 (ISBN 0-88488-122-9). Creative Pubns.

Madell, Robert & Stahl, Elizabeth L. Picturing Addition. (gr. k-3). 1977. wkbk 10.50 (ISBN 0-88488-072-9). Creative Pubns.

--Picturing Numeration. (gr. k-3). 1977. wkbk 10.50 (ISBN 0-88488-071-0). Creative Pubns.

--Picturing Subtraction. (gr. k-3). 1977. wkbk 10.50 (ISBN 0-88488-073-7). Creative Pubns.

Madelung, Otfried. Physics of Three-Five Compounds. LC 64-23849. 409p. 1964. text ed. 22.00 (ISBN 0-471-56316-1, Pub. by Wiley). Krieger.

Mademoiselle Magazine Editors. Make It with Mademoiselle. 1977. pap. 5.95 o.p. (ISBN 0-517-52865-7, Harmony). Crown.

Mader, Charles L., et al, eds. Los Alamos Explosives Performance Data. LC 82-40391. (Los Alamos Series on Dynamic Material Properties: Vol. 7). 824p. 1983. 45.00x (ISBN 0-520-04014-7). U of Cal Pr.

Mader, Chris. Information Systems: Technology, Economics, Applications, Management. 2nd ed. LC 78-13048. 1979. text ed. 21.95 (ISBN 0-574-21150-0, 13-4150); instr's guide avail. (ISBN 0-574-21151-9, 13-4151). SRA.

Mader, Chris & Bortz, John. Dow Jones-Irwin Guide to Real Estate Investing. rev. ed. LC 82-73928. 1983. 19.95 (ISBN 0-87094-214-X). Dow Jones-Irwin.

Madero, Thomas P., tr. see Thies, Dagmar.

Mades, Leonard, tr. see Donoso, Jose.

Madge, Nicola, jt. auth. see Brown, Muriel.

Madge, Sidney J. Domesday of Crown Lands. LC 67-31560. (Illus.). Repr. of 1938 ed. 20.00x (ISBN 0-678-05071-6). Kelley.

Madgic, R., et al. The American Experience. 3rd ed. (gr. 11). 1979. text ed. 20.96 (ISBN 0-201-04671-7, Sch Div); tchr's ed. 12.88 (ISBN 0-201-04672-5). A-W.

Madgic, R. F., jt. auth. see Coombs, A. J.

Madglin, Nel. Where Love Is... LC 82-71489. 56p. (Orig.). 1982. pap. 7.95 (ISBN 0-931494-17-6). Brunswick Pub.

Madgwick, H. I., jt. auth. see Sattoo, T.

Madgwick, P. J. American City Politics. (Library of Political Studies). 1970. 8.95x o.p. (ISBN 0-7100-6807-7). Routledge & Kegan.

Madgwick, Peter & Rose, Richard, eds. The Territorial Dimension in United Kingdom Politics. 256p. 1982. text ed. 42.00x (ISBN 0-333-29403-3, Pub. by Macmillan England). Humanities.

Madhavananda, Swami, tr. Brhadaranyaka Upanishad. (Sanskrit & Eng.). 1965. 12.00 o.p. (ISBN 0-87481-063-9). Vedanta Pr.

Madigan, Margaret. Good Night, Aunt Lilly. LC 82-84022. (Little Golden Bk.). (Illus.). 24p. (ps-2). 1983. 0.89 (ISBN 0-307-02084-3, Golden Pr); PLB price not set (ISBN 0-307-60218-4). Western Pub.

Madigan, Mary J. Steuben Glass: An American Tradition in Crystal. LC 81-22907. (Illus.). 320p. 1982. 55.00 (ISBN 0-8109-1642-8). Abrams.

Madigan, Mary Jean & Colgan, Susan, eds. Early American Furniture: From Settlement to City - Aspects of Form, Style, & Regional Design from 1620-1830. 160p. 1983. 25.00 (ISBN 0-8230-8007-2, Art & Antiques). Watson-Guptill.

--Prints & Photographs: Understanding, Appreciating, Collecting. 160p. 1983. pap. text ed. 25.00 (ISBN 0-8230-8006-4, Art & Antiques). Watson-Guptill.

Madigan, Thomas F. Word Shadows of the Great: The Lure of Autograph Collecting. LC 70-145705. (Illus.). 1971. Repr. of 1930 ed. 37.00x (ISBN 0-8103-3378-3). Gale.

Madill, W., jt. auth. see Bartlett, R. E.

Madis, George. Winchester Dates of Manufacture. (Illus.). 1981. 4.95 (ISBN 0-910156-05-0). Art & Ref.

--The Winchester Model Twelve. (Illus.). 1982. 14.95 (ISBN 0-910156-06-9). Art & Ref.

Madison, Arnold. Arson! LC 78-6877. (Illus.). (gr. 5 up). 1978. PLB 7.90 s&l (ISBN 0-531-02243-9). Watts.

--Aviation Careers. (Career Concise Guides Ser.). (Illus.). 1977. lib. bdg. 8.90 (ISBN 0-531-01300-6). Watts.

--Great Unsolved Cases. (gr. 7-12). 1980. pap. 1.75 (ISBN 0-440-93099-5, LFL). Dell.

--Runaway Teens: An American Tragedy. LC 79-11683. 1979. 8.95 (ISBN 0-525-66636-2, 0801-240). Lodestar Bks.

--Suicide & Young People. LC 77-13240. 144p. (gr. 6 up). 1978. 8.95 (ISBN 0-395-28913-0, Clarion). HM.

Madison, Arnold & Drotar, David L. Pocket Calculators: How to Use & Enjoy Them. LC 78-707. (Illus.). (gr. 6 up). 1978. 8.95 (ISBN 0-525-66580-3). Lodestar Bks.

Madison, Bernice. The Meaning of Social Policy: The Comparative Dimension in Social Welfare. 336p. 1980. text ed. 15.00 (ISBN 0-89158-914-7). Westview.

Madison, Eddie, ed. see Chamblee, Ronald F. & Evans, Marchsll C.

Madison, G. B. The Phenomenology of Merleau-Ponty: A Search for the Limits of Consciousness, Vol. 3. LC 81-4026. (Continental Thought Ser.). xxxvi, 345p. 1981. text ed. 24.95x (ISBN 0-8214-0448-2, 82-83400); pap. text ed. 12.95 (ISBN 0-8214-0644-2, 82-83418). Ohio U Pr.

Madison, James. Notes of Debates in the Federal Convention of 1787 Reported by James Madison. LC 65-18705. 1976. 25.00x (ISBN 0-8214-0011-8, 82-80125). Ohio U Pr.

--The Virginia Report of 1799-1800, Touching the Alien & Sedition Laws. Bd. with Virginia Resolutions of December 21, 1789. LC 75-107626. (Civil Liberties in American History Ser.). 1970. Repr. of 1850 ed. lib. bdg. 35.00 (ISBN 0-306-71860-X). Da Capo.

Madison, James, jt. auth. see Mancini, Janet K.

Madison, John H. Principles of Turfgrass Culture. LC 80-39763. 440p. 1983. Repr. of 1971 ed. lib. bdg. write for info. with corr. & suppl. matl. (ISBN 0-89874-197-1). Krieger.

Madison, Virginia & Stillwell, Hallie. How Come It's Called That? rev. ed. 130p. 1979. Repr. of 1968 ed. 8.95 (ISBN 0-686-38928-X). Big Bend.

Madison, Winifred. Getting Out. LC 75-34629. (gr. 7 up). 1976. 6.95 o.s.i. (ISBN 0-695-80634-3); PLB 6.99 o.s.i. (ISBN 0-695-40634-5). Follett.

--The Party That Lasted All Summer. (Illus.). 240p. (gr. 5-7). 1976. 6.95 o.p. (ISBN 0-316-54362-4). Little.

Madlee, Dorothy, jt. auth. see Norton, Andre.

Madlener, Judith Cooper. The Sea Vegetable Book: Foraging & Cooking Seaweed. 1977. 14.95 (ISBN 0-517-52905-X, C N Potter); pap. 6.95 (ISBN 0-517-52906-8, C N Potter Bks). Crown.

Madler, Trudy. Why Did Grandma Die? LC 79-23892. (Life & Living from a Child's Point of View Ser.). (Illus.). (gr. k-5). 1980. PLB 13.30 (ISBN 0-8172-1354-6). Raintree Pubs.

Madnick, Myra E., ed. Consumer Health Education: A Guide to Hospital Based Programs. 239p. 1980. Repr. 25.00 (ISBN 0-913654-61-2). Aspen Systems.

Madnick, S., jt. auth. see Donovan, J.

Madnick, Stuart & Donovan, John. Operating Systems. (Illus.). 640p. 1974. text ed. 35.00 (ISBN 0-07-039455-5, C); solutions manual 25.00 (ISBN 0-07-039456-3). McGraw.

Madore, B. F., jt. ed. see Hanes, D. A.

Madow, Leo. Anger, How to Recognize & Cope with It. 3.95 o.p. (ISBN 0-686-92286-7, 6310). Hazelden.

--Love: How to Understand & Enjoy It. 192p. 1982. pap. 4.95 (ISBN 0-686-37895-4, ScribT). Scribner.

Madow, Leo & Snow, Laurence H. The Psychodynamic Implications of Physiological Studies on Sensory Deprivation. photocopy ed. (Illus.). 120p. 1970. photocopy ed. spiral 12.50x (ISBN 0-398-01195-8). C C Thomas.

Madow, William G., jt. ed. see Nisselson, Harold.

Madrigal, Margarita. Invitation to Italian. 1965. 7.95 o.p. (ISBN 0-671-38120-2). S&S.

--See It & Say It in Spanish. (Orig.). pap. 1.95 (ISBN 0-451-11314-4, AJ1314, Sig). NAL.

Madrigal, Margarita & Dulac, Collette. See It & Say It in French. (Orig.). pap. 2.50 (ISBN 0-451-12182-1, AE2182, Sig). NAL.

Madrigal, Margarita & Halpert, Inge. See It & Say It in German. (Orig.). pap. 2.25 (ISBN 0-451-12203-8, AE2203, Sig). NAL.

Madrigal, Margarita & Salvadori, Giuseppina. See It & Say It in Italian. (Orig.). pap. 1.95 (ISBN 0-451-11327-6, AJ1327, Sig). NAL.

Madron, Thomas. Microcomputers in Large Organizations. 182p. 1983. 19.95 (ISBN 0-13-580795-6); pap. 12.95 (ISBN 0-13-580787-5). P-H.

Madruga, Lenor. One Step at a Time. 1980. pap. 2.25 o.p. (ISBN 0-451-09407-7, E9407, Sig). NAL.

Madry, Bobbi R., jt. auth. see Gerson, Joel.

Madsen. Preventing Childhood Epilepsy. 280p. 1983. 21.50 (ISBN 0-87527-221-5). Green.

Madsen, Ann M., jt. auth. see Dailey, Charles A.

Madsen, Axel. Living for Design. (Illus.). 1979. 12.95 o.s.i. (ISBN 0-440-05358-7). Delacorte.

--Private Power: Multinational Corporations & the Survival of Our Planet. 256p. 1981. pap. 8.00 (ISBN 0-688-00800-3). Quill NY.

Madsen, Brigham D. A Forty-Niner in Utah with the Stansbury Exploration of Great Salt Lake: Letters & Journal of John Hudson, 1858-60. (Utah, the Mormans, & the West Ser.: No. 11). 244p. 1982. 22.50 (ISBN 0-686-95945-0). U of Utah Pr.

Madsen, Clifford K., jt. auth. see Yarbrough, Cornelia.

Madsen, David. Black Plume. 1980. 11.95 o.p. (ISBN 0-671-25599-1). S&S.

--Successful Dissertations & Theses: A Guide to Graduate Student Research from Proposal to Completion. LC 82-49039. 1983. text ed. 12.95x (ISBN 0-87589-555-7). Jossey-Bass.

Madsen, David A. Geometric Dimensioning & Tolerancing. LC 81-902. 128p. 1982. pap. 6.00 (ISBN 0-87006-399-5). Goodheart.

Madsen, David A. & Shumaker, Terence M. Civil Drafting Technology. (Illus.). 144p. 1983. 17.95 (ISBN 0-13-134890-6, 402-403). P-H.

Madsen, George F. Iowa Title Opinions & Standards, Annotated. 2nd ed. 1978. text ed. 45.00x incl. 1982 supplement (ISBN 0-87473-107-0). A Smith Co.

Madsen, Harold S. & Bowen, J. Donald. Adaptation in Language Teaching. 1978. pap. text ed. 9.95 o.p. (ISBN 0-88377-105-5). Newbury Hse.

Madsen, Jane M., et al. Please Don't Tease Me. 32p. 1980. pap. 3.95 (ISBN 0-8170-0876-4). Judson.

Madsen, Richard W. & Moeschberger, Melvin E. Introductory Statistics for Business & Economics. (Illus.). 752p. 1983. 26.95 (ISBN 0-13-501577-4). P-H.

Madsen, Stephan T. Sources of Art Noveau. Christopherson, Ragnar, tr. LC 74-34464. (Architecture & Decorative Arts Ser). (Illus.). 488p. 1975. Repr. of 1956 ed. lib. bdg. 49.50 (ISBN 0-306-70733-0). Da Capo.

Madsen, Truman. Eternal Man. LC 66-26092. 80p. 5.95 (ISBN 0-87747-082-0). Deseret Bk.

Madsen, William. Virgin's Children: Life in an Aztec Village Today. Repr. of 1960 ed. lib. bdg. 45.00x (ISBN 0-8371-2098-5, MAVC). Greenwood.

Madsen, William G., ed. see Milton, John.

Madubuike, Ihechukwu. The Senegalese Novel: A Sociological Study of the Impact of the Politics of Assimilation. LC 81-51650. (Illus.). 182p. 1983. 18.00 (ISBN 0-89410-000-9); pap. 7.00 (ISBN 0-89410-001-7). Three Continents.

Madubuike, Ihechukwu, jt. auth. see Chinweizu, Onwuchekwa J.

Madunagu, Edwin. Problems of Socialism: The Nigerian Challenge. 128p. 1982. pap. 8.95 (ISBN 0-86232-027-5, Pub. by Zed Pr England). Lawrence Hill.

Madurga, G. & Lozano, M. Heavy-Ion Colision, La Rabida, Spain, 1982: Proceedings. (Lecture Notes in Physics: Vol. 168). 429p. 1983. pap. 21.00 (ISBN 0-387-11945-0). Springer-Verlag.

Madvig, Donald, tr. see Schweizer, Eduard.

Maecha, Alberto, ed. see Bourgeois, Jean-Francois.

Mae-Chu-Chang. Asian-Pacific-American Perspectives in Bilingual Education. (Bilingual Education Ser.). 1983. pap. text ed. write for info. (ISBN 0-8077-2723-7). Tchrs Coll.

Maeda, Kiyoshige. Alor Janggus: A Chinese Community in Malaya. (Center for Southeast Asian Studies Monographs' Kyoto University). 152p. 1967. 10.00xboxed o.p. (ISBN 0-8248-0375-2). UH Pr.

Maeder, Edward, et al. An Elegant Art: Fashion & Fantasy in the Eighteenth Century. Freshman, Phil, ed. (Illus.). 256p. (Orig.). 1983. 45.00 (ISBN 0-8109-0864-6); pap. 16.95 (ISBN 0-87587-111-9). LA Co Art Mus.

Maeder, Herbert & Och, Armin, eds. Beautiful Switzerland-Mervelileuse Suisse. (Illus., Fr. & Eng.). 1975. 35.00 o.p. (ISBN 3-7263-6186-3). Heinman.

Maeder, Thomas. The Unspeakable Crimes of Dr. Petiot. 1980. 12.95 (ISBN 0-316-54366-7, Pub. by Atlantic Monthly Pr). Little.

Maedke, Wilmer O., et al. Consumer Education. LC 77-73301. 528p. (gr. 11-12). 1979. text ed. 12.36 (ISBN 0-02-475720-9); student act. guide 4.95 (ISBN 0-02-475730-6); tchrs. manual & key 7.50 (ISBN 0-02-475740-3). Glencoe.

--Information & Records Management. LC 73-7362. (Illus.). 480p. 1974. text ed. 19.95x (ISBN 0-02-470800-3). Glencoe.

Maehler, Herwig. Die Lieder des Bakchylides. Erster Teil. Incl. Edition des Textes mit einleitung un Ubersetzung. xviii, 137p; Kommentar. v, 307p. (Mnemosyn Ser.: Suppl. 62). 1982. pap. write for info. (ISBN 90-04-06409-5). E J Brill.

Maehlum, B., ed. see Symposium On Ionospheric Physics - Alpbach - 1964.

Maekawa, M. & Belady, L. A., eds. Operating Systems Engineering, Amagi, Japan 1980: Proceedings. (Lecture Notes in Computer Science: Vol. 143). 465p. 1983. pap. 19.00 (ISBN 0-387-11604-4). Springer-Verlag.

Maenchen-Helfen, Otto J. The World of the Huns: Studies in Their History & Culture. Knight, Max, ed. LC 79-94985. 1973. 44.00x (ISBN 0-520-01596-7). U of Cal Pr.

Maeroff, Gene I. Don't Blame the Kids: The Trouble with America's Public Schools. 224p. 1982. 16.95 (ISBN 0-07-039465-2). McGraw.

Maes-Jelinek, Hena. Wilson Harris. (World Authors Ser.). 1982. lib. bdg. 17.95 (ISBN 0-8057-6506-9, Twayne). G K Hall.

Maestas, Roberto, jt. auth. see Johansen, Bruce.

Maestas, Roberto F, jt. auth. see Johansen, Bruce E.

Maestri, William. Bioethics: A Parish Resource. LC 81-40822. 64p. (Orig.). 1982. lib. bdg. 17.50 (ISBN 0-8191-2171-1); pap. text ed. 6.50 (ISBN 0-8191-2172-X). U Pr of Amer.

--The God for Every Day. 204p. 1981. 9.95 (ISBN 0-88347-123-X). Thomas More.

Maestro, Betsy. Busy Day: A Book of Action Words. LC 77-15635. (Illus.). (ps-1). 1978. reinforced lib. bdg. 5.95 o.p. (ISBN 0-517-53288-3). Crown.

--A Wise Monkey Tale. LC 75-9749. (Illus.). (gr. k-3). 1975. reinforced lib. bdg. 6.95 o.p. (ISBN 0-517-52328-0). Crown.

Maestro, Betsy & Maestro, Guilio. Traffic: A Book of Opposites. (Illus.). 32p. 1981. 6.95 (ISBN 0-517-54427-X). Crown.

Maestro, Guilio, jt. auth. see Maestro, Betsy.

Maestro, Marcello. Cesare Beccaria & the Origins of Penal Reform. LC 72-91133. 179p. 1973. 19.95 (ISBN 0-87722-024-7). Temple U Pr.

Maeterlinck, M. Maurice Maeterlinck: A Biographical Study with Two Essays. Allinson, Alfred, tr. from French. 142p. 1982. lib. bdg. 30.00 (ISBN 0-89760-579-9). Telegraph Bks.

Maeterlinck, Maurice. The Intruder. Brown, Edmund R., ed. (International Pocket Library). pap. 3.00 (ISBN 0-686-77243-1). Branden.

Maeterlinck, Maurice see Brown, Edmund R.

Maevis, Alfred C., ed. see Rapid Excavation & Tunneling Conference, 1979.

Maffei, Paolo. Beyond the Moon. O'Connell, D. J., tr. LC 77-27091. 1978. text ed. 17.50 (ISBN 0-262-13133-1). MIT Pr.

--Monsters in the Sky. (Illus.). 1980. 17.50x (ISBN 0-262-13153-6). MIT Pr.

Maffeo, Dante. Duty Charts & Schedules Made Easy. 222p. 1982. spiral 22.75x (ISBN 0-398-04720-0). C C Thomas.

Magagna, Anna M., illus. First Prayers. LC 82-60742. (Illus.). 64p. (ps-2). 1983. 7.95 (ISBN 0-02-762120-0). Macmillan.

Magalaner, Marvin, jt. auth. see Volpe, Edmond L.

Magalit, Henry, jt. auth. see Hackenberg, Robert.

Magalnick, B. English Reader. 1979. text ed. 5.62 (ISBN 0-07-039470-9). McGraw.

Magan, Geralyn G., ed. Aging, Race & Culture: Issues in Long Term Care. LC 82-72776. 150p. 1983. pap. 6.50 (ISBN 0-943774-11-X). AAHA.

Magann, Julia H. Municipal Financial Disclosure: An Empirical Investigation. Farmer, Richard N., ed. LC 82-4905. (Research for Business Decisions: No. 58). 1983. write for info. (ISBN 0-8357-1394-6). Univ Microfilms.

Magar, Magar E. Incorporation & Business Guide for Oregon. 114p. 1978. 9.95 (ISBN 0-88908-810-1); incorporation forms 6.95 (ISBN 0-686-35987-9). Self Counsel Pr.

Magara, K. Compaction & Fluid Migration: Practical Petroleum Geology. (Developments in Petroleum Science Ser.: Vol. 9). 1978. 74.50 (ISBN 0-444-41654-4). Elsevier.

Magarello, Anthony. Good Reading-Good Writing, A. (Effective Lang. Arts Program Ser.). (Illus.). 59p. 1981. 4.75 (ISBN 0-9602800-7-3). Comp Pr.

--Good Reading-Good Writing, C. (Effective Lang. Arts Program Ser.). (Illus.). 50p. 1983. 4.75 (ISBN 0-9602800-8-1). Comp Pr.

Magarian, Judy, jt. auth. see Fioretti, Sandra.

Magarick, Pat. Casualty Investigation Checklists. 2nd ed. LC 77-24444. 1977. spiral bdg. 25.00 o.p. (ISBN 0-87632-154-6). Boardman.

--Excess- Liability - Duties & Responsibilities of the Insurer. LC 75-44308. 1976. with 1978 suppl. 35.00 (ISBN 0-87632-157-0). Boardman.

--Successful Handling of Casualty Claims. LC 73-91720. 1974. 45.00 (ISBN 0-87632-168-6). Boardman.

Magaro, Peter A., et al. The Mental Health Industry: A Cultural Phenomenon. LC 77-14434. (Series on Personality Processes). 1978. 29.95 (ISBN 0-471-02406-6, Pub. by Wiley- Interscience). Wiley.

Magarshac, David, tr. see Tolstoy, Leo.

Magarshack, David. Chekhov, a Life. Repr. of 1953 ed. lib. bdg. 29.75 (ISBN 0-8371-4095-1, MACH). Greenwood.

Magarshack, David, tr. see Dostoyevsky, Fyodor.

Magarshack, David, tr. see Leskov, Nikolai S.

Magarshack, David, tr. from Rus. see Saltykov-Shchedrin, Mikhail.

Magary, Alan & Magary, Kirsten. South of San Francisco. LC 82-48520. 192p. (Orig.). 1983. pap. 5.72i (ISBN 0-06-091035-6, CN 1035, CN). Har-Row.

Magary, Kirsten, jt. auth. see Magary, Alan.

Magat, Wesley A. Reform of Environmental Regulation. 208p. 1982. prof ref 26.50x (ISBN 0-88410-908-9). Ballinger Pub.

Magaziner, Ira & Reich, Robert. Minding America's Business. 387p. 1982. pap. text ed. 11.95 (ISBN 0-15-558835-4, HC). HarBraceJ.

Magaziner, Ira C. & Hout, Thomas M. Japanese Industrial Policy. LC 81-80791. (Policy Papers in International Affairs: No. 15). (Illus.). 120p. 1981. pap. 6.50x (ISBN 0-87725-515-6). U of Cal Intl St.

Magaziner, Ira C. & Reich, Robert B. Minding America's Business: The Decline & Rise of the American Economy. LC 81-47901. 1981. 14.95 (ISBN 0-15-159954-8). HarBraceJ.

--Minding America's Business: The Decline & Rise of the American Economy. LC 81-13663. (Illus.). 400p. 1983. pap. 5.95 (ISBN 0-394-71538-1, Vin). Random.

Magdics, Klara. Studies in the Acoustic Characteristics of Hungarian Speech Sounds. LC 68-65314. (Uralic & Altaic Ser: Vol. 97). (Illus.). 1969. pap. text ed. 7.00x o.p. (ISBN 0-87750-041-X). Res Ctr Lang Semiotic.

Magdoff, Harry. Imperialism: From the Colonial Age to the Present. LC 77-7617. 1979. pap. 5.00 (ISBN 0-85345-498-1, PB4981). Monthly Rev.

Magdol, Edward. A Right to the Land: Essays on the Freedmen's Community. LC 76-39707. (Contributions in American History: No. 61). (Illus.). 1977. lib. bdg. 29.95 (ISBN 0-8371-9409-1, MFC/). Greenwood.

Magee, Bryan. Modern British Philosophy. LC 70-175934. 1971. text ed. 17.95 o.p. (ISBN 0-312-53760-3); pap. 7.95 o.p. (ISBN 0-312-53725-5). St Martin.

Magee, Doug. What Murder Leaves Behind: The Victim's Family. (Illus.). 1983. 12.95 (ISBN 0-396-08153-3). Dodd.

Magee, Heno. Hatchet. signed 7.50 (ISBN 0-912262-47-8); pap. 2.95x (ISBN 0-912262-48-6). Proscenium.

Magee, John. Northern Ireland: Crises & Conflict. (World Studies). (Illus.). 212p. 1974. 16.00x o.p. (ISBN 0-7100-7946-X); pap. 7.95 (ISBN 0-7100-7947-8). Routledge & Kegan.

Magee, John, jt. auth. see Edwards, Robert D.

Magee, John B. Religion & Modern Man: A Study of the Religious Meaning of Being Human. 1967. text ed. 23.50 scp (ISBN 0-06-044167-4, HarpC); instructor's manual avail. (ISBN 0-06-364109-7). Har-Row.

Magee, John F. Physical Distribution Systems. (Illus.). 1967. pap. 9.50 o.p. (ISBN 0-07-039483-0, C). McGraw.

Magee, John R. & Boodman, D. M. Production Planning & Inventory Control. 2nd ed. 1982. pap. text ed. 36.95 (ISBN 0-07-039488-1, C). McGraw.

Magee, Malachy. One Thousand Years of Irish Whiskey. (Illus.). 144p. 1982. 15.95 (ISBN 0-905140-71-0, Pub. by Salem Hse Ltd.). Merrimack Bk Serv.

Magee, Michael & Bayes, Pat. Champions. (Illus.). 1980. 29.95 o.p. (ISBN 0-688-03716-X). Morrow.

Magee, Michael C. Basic Science for the Practicing Urologist. LC 82-4561. (Illus.). 250p. Date not set. price not set (ISBN 0-521-24567-2). Cambridge U Pr.

Magee, Peter N., ed. Banbury Report 12: Nitrosamines & Human Cancer. LC 82-12952. (Banbury Report Ser.: Vol. 12). 500p. 1982. 67.00X (ISBN 0-87969-211-1). Cold Spring Harbor.

Magee, Susan F. MesoAmerican Archaeology: A Guide to the Literature & Other Information Sources. (Guides & Bibliographics Ser.: No. 12). 81p. 1981. pap. text ed. 5.95x (ISBN 0-292-75053-6). U of Tex Pr.

Magel, Charles R. A Bibliography on Animal Rights & Related Matters. LC 80-5636. 622p. 1981. lib. bdg. 30.50 (ISBN 0-8191-1488-X). U Pr of Amer.

Mager, Marcia. A Woman of New York. (Woman's Destiny Ser.: No. 4). (Orig.). 1983. pap. 2.95 (ISBN 0-440-08968-9). Dell.

Mager, P. S. Power Writing, Power Speaking: Two Hundred Ways to Make Your Words Count. LC 79-3507. 1980. pap. 5.95 (ISBN 0-688-08295-5). Quill NY.

Mager, Robert F. Developing Attitude Toward Learning. LC 68-54250. 1968. pap. 6.95 (ISBN 0-8224-2000-7). Pitman Learning.

--Goal Analysis. LC 77-189630. 1972. pap. 6.95 (ISBN 0-8224-3476-8). Pitman Learning.

--Mager Library, 6 vols. Incl. Analyzing Performance Problems. Pipe, Peter; Developing Attitude Toward Learning; Developing Vocational Instruction. Beach, Kenneth M; Goal Analysis; Measuring Instructional Intent. Set. pap. 34.50 slipcase (ISBN 0-8224-4333-3). Pitman Learning.

--Measuring Instructional Intent, or Got a Match? LC 73-80970. 1973. pap. 6.95 (ISBN 0-8224-4462-3). Pitman Learning.

--Preparing Instructional Objectives. 2nd. ed. LC 75-16518. 1975. pap. 6.95 (ISBN 0-8224-5601-X). Pitman Learning.

Mager, Robert F. & Beach, Kenneth M., Jr. Developing Vocational Instruction. LC 67-26846. 1967. pap. 6.95 (ISBN 0-8224-2060-0). Pitman Learning.

Mager, Robert F. & Pipe, Peter. Analyzing Performance Problems; or, You Really Oughta Wanna. LC 73-140896. 1970. pap. text ed. 6.95 (ISBN 0-8224-0301-3); Quick Reference checklist, set of 25 4.95 (ISBN 0-8224-0302-1); Performance Analysis Poster 4.00 (ISBN 0-8224-0303-X). Pitman Learning.

Magerman, W. D. Zay Jeffries. 1973. 16.00 (ISBN 0-686-95225-1). ASM.

Maggenti, A. R. General Nematology. (Springer Series in Microbiology). (Illus.). 372p. 1982. 29.80 (ISBN 0-387-90588-X). Springer-Verlag.

Maggs, Chistopher. The Origins of General Nursing. 176p. 1983. text ed. 25.25x (ISBN 0-7099-1734-1, Pub. by Croom Helm Ltd England). Biblio Dist.

Maggs, Margaret. The Classroom Survival Book: A Practical Manual for Teachers. 1979. pap. 7.95 (ISBN 0-531-01302-2). Watts.

Maggs, Peter B., jt. auth. see Berman, Harold J.

Maghroori, Ray & Gorman, Stephen M. The Yom Kippur War: A Case Study in Crisis Decision Making in American Foreign Policy. LC 80-5811. 98p. 1981. lib. bdg. 16.75 (ISBN 0-8191-1373-5); pap. text ed. 7.00 (ISBN 0-8191-1374-3). U Pr of Amer.

Maghroori, Ray & Ramberg, Bennett. Globalism vs Realism: International Relations' Third Debate. 225p. (Orig.). 1982. lib. bdg. 25.00 (ISBN 0-86531-346-6); pap. 12.00 (ISBN 0-86531-347-4). Westview.

Magi, Aldo P., ed. see Hoagland, Clayton & Hoagland, Kathleen.

Magid, Leonard M. Electromagnetic Fields, Energy, & Waves. LC 80-16458. 808p. 1981. Repr. of 1972 ed. text ed. 41.00 (ISBN 0-89874-221-8). Krieger.

Magid, Renee, jt. auth. see Kaplan-Sanoff, Margot.

Magidoff, Robert. Yehudi Menuhin. LC 73-10753. (Illus.). 319p. 1974. Repr. of 1955 ed. lib. bdg. 17.75x (ISBN 0-8371-7020-6, MAYM). Greenwood.

Magill, Frank N. McGill's Literary Annual, 1977: Essay Review of 200 Outstanding Books Published in the United States During 1976, 2 Vols. 50.00x set (ISBN 0-686-94005-9, Pub. by Salem Pr). Gale.

--McGill's Literary Annual, 1978: Essay Review of 200 Outstanding Books Published in the United States During1977, 2 Vols. 952p. 50.00x set (ISBN 0-686-94010-5, Pub. by Salem Pr). Gale.

--McGill's Literary Annual, 1979: Essay Review of 200 Outstanding Books Published in the United States During 1978, 2 Vols. 936p. 50.00x set (ISBN 0-686-94008-3, Pub. by Salem Pr). Gale.

--McGill's Literary Annual, 1981: Essay Review of 200 Outstanding Books Published in the United States During 1980, 2 Vols. 900p. 1981. 50.00x set (ISBN 0-686-94003-2, Pub. by Salem Pr). Gale.

--McGill's Literature Annual, 1980: Essay Review of 200 Outstanding Books Published in the United States During 1979, 2Vols. 898p. 50.00x set (ISBN 0-686-93999-9, Pub. by Salem Pr). Gale.

Magill, Frank N., ed. Magill's Literary Annual, 1982, 2 vols. 900p. 1982. Set. 50.00x (ISBN 0-686-95221-9, Pub. by Salem Pr). Gale.

--Masterpieces of World Literature in Digest Form, 4 vols. Incl. Series 1. 1952. o.p. (ISBN 0-06-003870-5); Series 2. 1956. o.p. (ISBN 0-06-003690-7); lib. bdg. 19.79 (ISBN 0-06-003900-0); Series 3. 1960. 22.50i (ISBN 0-06-003750-4); lib. bdg. 22.79i (0-06-003930-2); Series 4. 1969. 24.04i (ISBN 0-06-003751-2); lib. bdg. 22.79i (ISBN 0-06-003752-0). HarpT). Har-Row.

--Masterpieces of World Philosophy in Summary Form. 1961. 24.04i (ISBN 0-06-003780-6, HarpT). Har-Row.

Magill, Jane M. & Moore, John B., Jr. Experiments in Biochemistry. 100p. (Orig.). 1978. pap. text ed. 4.95x (ISBN 0-89641-007-2). American Pr.

--Experiments in Metabolism. 118p. (Orig.). 1979. pap. text ed. 4.95x plastic comb. bdg. (ISBN 0-89641-013-7). American Pr.

Magill, Kathleen. Meagan. LC 82-22133. 1983. 10.95 (ISBN 0-686-84720-2). Dodd.

Magill, L. M. & Ault, Nelson A. Synopses of Shakespeare's Complete Plays. (Quality Paperback: No. 22). (Orig.). 1968. pap. 3.95 (ISBN 0-8226-0022-6). Littlefield.

Magill, Richard A. & Ash, Michael J., eds. Children in Sport. 2nd ed. LC 82-82668. 327p. 1982. pap. text ed. 10.95x (ISBN 0-931250-34-X). Human Kinetics.

Magill, Robert S. Social Policy in American Society. 192p. 1983. text ed. 19.95 (ISBN 0-89885-138-6). Human Sci Pr.

Magilton, J. R. The Church of St. Helen-on-the Walls, Aldwark, York. (Archaeology of York Ser.: Vol. 10). 64p. 1980. pap. text ed. 14.95x (ISBN 0-900312-98-X, Pub. by Coun Brit Archaeology). Humanities.

Maginley, C. J. Historic Models of Early America: & How to Make Them. LC 47-11432. (Illus.). (gr. 4-6). 1966. pap. 0.60 (ISBN 0-15-640371-4, VoyB). HarBraceJ.

--Toys You Can Build. 1975. pap. 6.25 (ISBN 0-8015-7860-4, 0607-180, Hawthorn). Dutton.

Maginn, John & Tuttle, Donald, eds. Managing Investment Portfolios. 47.50 (ISBN 0-686-84714-8); student ed. 23.75 (ISBN 0-88262-874-7). Warren.

Maginnis, Hayden B., ed. see Meiss, Millard.

Magliato, Joe. The Wall Street Gospel. LC 80-84629. (Orig.). 1981. pap. 4.95 o.p. (ISBN 0-89081-279-9). Harvest Hse.

Maglio, Rodolfo, jt. auth. see Jaffe, Philip M.

Magliocco, Peter. Among a Godly Few. LC 82-81129. (Illus.). 179p. (Orig.). 1982. pap. 6.95 (ISBN 0-88100-003-5). Limited Ed.

Maglis, J. V. & Ricca, A. B. Dental & Skeletal Morphology of the Earliest Elephants. Date not set. 10.25 (ISBN 0-7204-8448-0, North Holland). Elsevier.

Maglischo, Ernest W. Swimming Faster: A Comprehensive Guide to the Science of Swimming. (Illus.). 472p. 1982. 19.95 (ISBN 0-87484-548-3). Mayfield Pub.

Magloire-Holly, Helene, ed. see Lefebvre, Claire.

Magnani, Bruno, ed. Beta-Adrenergic Blocking Agents in the Management of Hypertension & Angina Pectoris. LC 74-15629. 202p. 1974. 21.50 (ISBN 0-89004-013-3). Raven.

Magnani, Bruno & Hansson, Lennart, eds. Potassium, the Heart & Hypertension: A Symposium Sponsored by the Italian Society of Cardiology. LC 82-51013. (Illus.). 200p. 1982. write for info. (ISBN 0-88137-000-2). TransMedica.

Magnani, Franco. One Room Interiors. (Illus.). 1979. 22.50 (ISBN 0-8230-7379-3, Whitney Lib). Watson-Guptill.

Magnarella, Paul J. The Peasant Venture: Tradition, Migration, & Change Among Georgian Peasants in Turkey. 1979. lib. bdg. 15.50 (ISBN 0-8161-8271-X, Univ Bks). G K Hall.

--Tradition & Change in a Turkish Town. LC 74-14927. 199p. 1974. 11.00 (ISBN 0-470-56338-9, Pub. by Wiley). Krieger.

--Tradition & Change in a Turkish Town. 2nd ed. (Illus.). 256p. 1982. 16.95x (ISBN 0-87073-153-X); pap. 8.95x (ISBN 0-87073-152-1). Schenkman.

Magner, D. Classic Encyclopedia of the Horse. (Illus.). Repr. 6.98 o.p. (ISBN 0-517-32168-8). Crown.

Magner, Thomas F. & Matejka, Ladislav. Word Accent in Modern Serbo-Croatian. LC 77-145826. 1971. 18.95x (ISBN 0-271-01138-6). Pa St U Pr.

Magner, Thomas F., ed. Slavic Linguistics & Language Teaching. x, 309p. 1976. soft cover 16.95 (ISBN 0-89357-037-0). Slavica.

Magner, Thomas F. & Schmalstieg, William R., eds. Baltic Linguistics. LC 71-79842. 1970. 17.50x (ISBN 0-271-00094-5). Pa St U Pr.

Magni, Roberto, jt. auth. see Guidoni, Enrico.

Magnifico, G. European Monetary Unification. LC 73-303. 227p. 1973. 39.95x (ISBN 0-470-56525-X). Halsted Pr.

Magnotta, Miguel. Historia y Bibliografia De la Critica Sobre el "Poemade Mio Cid" (1750-1971) (Studies in the Romance Languages & Literatures: No. 145). 300p. 1976. 16.50x (ISBN 0-685-88881-9). U of NC Pr.

Magnotti, Shirley. Library Science Research. 140p. 1983. 15.00 (ISBN 0-87875-235-8). Whitston Pub.

Magnum Publications Ltd., ed. Wire Industry Yearbook, Wire Industry Machinery Guide & Encyclopaedia of Wire. 1981. 80.00x (ISBN 0-686-96971-5, Pub. by Magnum England). State Mutual Bk.

Magnus, Albertus. Albertus Magnus: Egyptian Secrets. 3.95 (ISBN 0-685-72555-3). Wehman.

Magnus, Gunter H. Dumonts Handbook for Graphic Artists: A Practical Introduction. (Illus.). 256p. 1984. 19.95 (ISBN 0-8120-5466-0). Barron.

Magnus, K. Trends in Cancer Incidences: Causes & Practical Implications. 1982. 79.50 (ISBN 0-07-039501-2). McGraw.

Magnus, Laurie. A Dictionary of European Literature, Designed As a Companion to English Studies. rev. ed. LC 74-6269. xii, 605p. 1975. Repr. of 1927 ed. 56.00x (ISBN 0-8103-4014-3). Gale.

Magnus, Laury, jt. auth. see Epstein, Jane.

Magnus, Leonard A. Russian Folk-Tales with Introduction & Notes. LC 74-6486. 1974. Repr. of 1916 ed. 37.00x (ISBN 0-8103-3654-5). Gale.

Magnus, Margaret. Fundamentals of Nursing. (Nursing Examination Review Books: Vol. 11). 1972. pap. 7.50 o.p. (ISBN 0-87488-511-6). Med Exam.

Magnus, Ralph H., jt. auth. see Khairzada, Faiz.

Magnus, W., jt. auth. see Chandler, B.

Magnus, W., et al. Formulas & Theorems for the Special Functions of Mathematical Physics. 3rd ed. (Grundlehren der Mathematischen Wissenschaften: Vol. 52). 1966. 46.00 o.p. (ISBN 0-387-03518-4). Springer-Verlag.

Magnus, Wilhelm, et al. Combinational Group Theory: Presentations of Groups in Terms of Generators & Relations. 1976. pap. text ed. 7.95 (ISBN 0-486-63281-4). Dover.

Magnusen, Karl O. Organizational Design, Development, & Behavior. 1977. pap. 10.95x (ISBN 0-673-15042-9). Scott F.

Magnuson, James & Petrie, Dorothea G. Orphan Train. 1979. lib. bdg. 14.95 o.p. (ISBN 0-8161-6666-8, Large Print Bks). G K Hall.

Magnuson, Paul. Coleridge's Nightmare Poetry. LC 74-4422. (Illus.). 140p. 1974. 12.95x (ISBN 0-8139-0534-6). U Pr of Va.

Magnuson, Teodore. A Small Gust of Wind: A Novel of Action & Intrigue. LC 80-677. 256p. 1980. 10.00 o.p. (ISBN 0-672-52663-8). Bobbs.

Magnuson, Torgil. Rome in the Age of Bernini, Vol. 1. 388p. 1982. text ed. 45.00x (ISBN 0-391-02586-4). Humanities.

Magnussen, S. Iceland: Country & People. (Illus.). 66p. (Orig.). pap. 5.00x (ISBN 0-89918-113-9). Vanous.

Magnusson, D., et al. Adjustment: A Longitudinal Study. LC 75-11593. 266p. 1975. 21.95x o.p. (ISBN 0-470-56347-8). Halsted Pr.

Magnusson, David. Test Theory. 1966. 20.95 (ISBN 0-201-04395-5). A-W.

Magnusson, David & Endler, Norman S. Personality at the Crossroads: Current Issues in Interactional Psychology. LC 77-4190. 454p. 1977. text ed. 24.95 (ISBN 0-89859-293-3). L Erlbaum Assocs.

Magnusson, Magnus. Archaeology of the Bible. (Illus.). 1978. 12.95 o.p. (ISBN 0-671-24010-2). S&S.

Magnusson, Sigurdur A., tr. from Icelandic. The Postwar Poetry of Iceland. LC 82-8606. (Iowa Translations Ser.). 288p. (Orig.). 1982. pap. text ed. 12.50x (ISBN 0-87745-115-X). U of Iowa Pr.

Magocsi, Paul R. Galicia: A Historical Survey & Bibliographic Guide. (Illus.). 336p. 1983. 19.50x (ISBN 0-8020-2482-3). U of Toronto Pr.

--Vienna Nineteen Eighty-Two: The Rusyn-Ukrainians of Czechoslovakia, An Historical Survey. (Bausteine Zur Ethnopolitischen Forschung: Ethnos Vol. 6). (Illus.). 94p. (Orig.). 1982. pap. 7.95 (ISBN 3-7003-0312-2, Pub. by Wm Braumuller Univ Vlg Vienna). Res Ctr.

--Vienna Nineteen Eighty-Two: Wooden Churches in the Carpathians, Holzkirchen in den Karpaten, the Photographs of Florian Zapletal. (Illus.). 176p. (Ger. & Eng.). 1982. 24.95 (ISBN 0-686-38725-2, Pub. by Wm Braumuller Univ Vlg Vienna). Res Ctr.

Magono, C. Thunderstorms. (Developments in Atmospheric Science Ser.: Vol. 12). 1980. 61.75 (ISBN 0-444-15179-6). Elsevier.

Magoon, Robert A. Education & Psychology: Past, Present, & Future. LC 72-91623. 384p. 1973. pap. text ed. 10.95 o.p. (ISBN 0-675-09012-1). Merrill.

Magor, J. T. Outbreaks of the Australian Plague Locust (Hortoicetes Terminifera Walk.) During the Seasons 1937 to 1962, with Particular Reference to Rainfall. 1970. 35.00x (ISBN 0-85135-002-X, Pub. by Centre Overseas Research). State Mutual Bk.

Magor, J. T. & Ward, P. Illustrated Descriptions, Distribution Maps & Bibliography of the Species of Quelea (Weaverbirds; Ploceidae) (Illus.). 1972. 35.00x (ISBN 0-85135-058-5, Pub. by Centre Overseas Research). State Mutual Bk.

Magorian, Christopher, jt. auth. see Morell, David.

Magorian, James. Fimperings & Torples. LC 81-69872. 44p. 1981. 3.00 (ISBN 0-930674-06-5). Black Oak.

--Ketchup Bottles. 2nd ed. Wolman, Arnold, ed. (James Magorian Ser.). (Illus., Orig.). pap. 6.95 (ISBN 0-686-97650-9). Peradam Pub Hse.

--Revenge. 1979. pap. 1.00 o.p. (ISBN 0-686-25266-7). Samisdat.

--Taxidermy Lessons. LC 82-73156. 68p. 1982. 5.00 (ISBN 0-930674-08-1). Black Oak Press.

--Training at Home to be a Locksmith. LC 80-68264. 112p. 1981. 6.00 (ISBN 0-930674-05-7). Black Oak.

Magos, Eunice, jt. auth. see Hornnes, Esther.

Magoun, Francis P., Jr., tr. see Grimm Brothers.

Magrab, E. B., ed. Vibration Testing - Instrumentation & Data Analysis: AMD Vol. 12. 142p. 1975. pap. text ed. 14.00 o.p. (ISBN 0-685-62577-X, I00091). ASME.

Magrab, Edward B. Environmental Noise Control. LC 75-20233. 299p. 1975. 42.50 (ISBN 0-471-56344-7, Pub. by Wiley-Interscience). Wiley.

Magrab, Phyllis R. Early Life Conditions & Chronic Diseases. (Psychological Management of Pediatric Problems Ser.). 366p. 1978. text ed. 27.95 (ISBN 0-8391-1218-1). Univ Park.

Magrab, Phyllis R., ed. Sensorineural Conditions & Social Concerns, Vol. II. (Psychological Management of Pediatric Problems Ser.). 334p. 1978. text ed. 27.95 (ISBN 0-8391-1245-9). Univ Park.

Magrab, Phyllis R., jt. ed. see Johnston, Robert B.

Magri, Iole F. S. A Ciascuno Il Suo. LC 75-29713. 1976. pap. text ed. 9.50 (ISBN 0-395-13398-X). HM.

Magriel, Paul, ed. Chronicles of the American Dance. (Series in Dance). (Illus.). 1978. Repr. of 1948 ed. lib. bdg. 27.50 (ISBN 0-306-77566-2). Da Capo.

--Nijinsky, Pavlova, Duncan: Three Lives in Dance. LC 76-30403. (Series in Dance). 1977. lib. bdg. 25.00 (ISBN 0-306-70845-0); pap. 6.95 (ISBN 0-306-80035-7). Da Capo.

Magrill, Rose Mary & Rinehart, Constance, eds. Library Technical Services: A Selected, Annotated Bibliography. LC 76-27130. 248p. 1977. lib. bdg. 27.50 (ISBN 0-8371-9286-2, MAB/). Greenwood.

Magubane, Bernard & Nzongola-Ntalaja, eds. Proletarianization & Class Struggle in Africa. (Contemporary Marxism Ser.). (Illus., Orig.). 1983. pap. 6.50 (ISBN 0-89935-019-4). Synthesis Pubns.

Maguire, Anne. Nurse in las Palmas. (YA) 1980. 6.95 (ISBN 0-686-73916-7, Avalon). Bouregy.

--Run Before Midnight. 1981. pap. 6.95 (ISBN 0-686-84705-9, Avalon). Bouregy.

--Strings to Love. (YA) 1981. 6.95 (ISBN 0-686-73959-0, Avalon). Bouregy.

--Substitute Nurse. (YA) 1978. 6.95 (ISBN 0-685-53393-X, Avalon). Bouregy.

Maguire, Byron. Carpentry: Framing & Finishing. (Illus.). 1979. 20.95 (ISBN 0-8359-0701-5); instrs manual avail. (ISBN 0-8359-0702-3). Reston.

--The Complete Book of Woodworking & Cabinetmaking. (Illus.). 1974. 16.95 (ISBN 0-87909-153-3); pap. text ed. 9.95 (ISBN 0-87909-182-7). Reston.

Maguire, Byron W. Construction Materials. 375p. 1981. text ed. 21.95 (ISBN 0-8359-0935-2). Reston.

Maguire, Daniel C. Death by Choice. LC 74-26729. 236p. 1975. pap. 5.95 (ISBN 0-8052-0478-4). Schocken.

--A New American Justice: Ending the White Male Monopolies. LC 78-20084. (Illus.). 240p. 1980. 9.95 o.p. (ISBN 0-385-14325-7). Doubleday.

Maguire, Doris D. French Ensor Chadwick: Selected Letters & Papers. LC 81-40169. 656p. (Orig.). 1982. lib. bdg. 35.00 (ISBN 0-8191-1923-7); pap. text ed. 24.00 (ISBN 0-8191-1924-5). U Pr of Amer.

Maguire, Eliza D. Kona Legends. (Illus.). 1966. pap. 3.25 (ISBN 0-912180-05-6). Petroglyph.

Maguire, J. M. Marx's Theory of Politics. LC 77-90214. 1979. 32.50 (ISBN 0-521-21955-8). Cambridge U Pr.

Maguire, John M. Evidence of Guilt: Restrictions Upon Its Discovery or Compulsory Disclosure. 295p. 1982. Repr. of 1959 ed. lib. bdg. 32.50x (ISBN 0-8377-0843-5). Rothman.

--The Lance of Justice: A Semi-Centennial History of the Legal Aid Society 1876-1926. xi, 305p. 1982. Repr. of 1928 ed. lib. bdg. 30.00x (ISBN 0-8377-0847-8). Rothman.

Maguire, John T., jt. auth. see Yeck, John D.

Maguire, Mike & Bennett, Trevor. Burglary in a Dwelling: The Offence, the Offender & the Victim, No. XLIX. Radzinowicz, Leon, ed. (Cambridge Studies in Crimonology). 204p. 1982. text ed. 40.00x (ISBN 0-435-82567-4). Heinemann Ed.

Magyar, B. Guidelines to Planning Atomic Spectometric Analysis. Date not set. 70.25 (ISBN 0-444-99699-0). Elsevier.

Magyar, K., ed. Symposium on Pharmacological Agents & Biogenic Amines in the Central Nervous System. (Hungarian Pharmacological Society, First Congress Ser.: Vol. I). (Illus.). 274p. 1973. 20.00 (ISBN 0-686-43332-7). Intl Pubns Serv.

Magyari, E., jt. auth. see Constantinescu, F.

Mahabir, Cynthia. Nation Building Today, & the Legacy of Legal Barriers. 224p. 1983. 16.95 (ISBN 0-87073-601-9); pap. 8.95 (ISBN 0-87073-602-7). Schenkman.

Mahadevan. Biochemical Aspects of Plant Disease Resistance: Post-Infectional Defense Mechanisms, Pt. II. (International Bio Science Monograph: No. 13). 1982. write for info. (ISBN 0-88065-244-6, Pub. by Messers Today & Tomorrow Printers & Publishers). Scholarly Pubns.

Mahadevan, T. M. Invitation to Indian Philosophy. 300p. 1973. text ed. 13.50x o.p. (ISBN 0-391-00262-7). Humanities.

--Invitation to Indian Philosophy. (Orig.). 1979. pap. 7.50 (ISBN 0-89684-090-5, Pub. by Arnold Heinemann India). Orient Bk Dist.

--Ramana Maharshi: The Sage of Arunacala. (Unwin Paperbacks). 1976. 12.50 o.p. (ISBN 0-04-149040-1); pap. 6.25 (ISBN 0-04-149041-X). Allen Unwin.

--Spiritual Perspectives. 1975. 12.00 o.p. (ISBN 0-88386-589-0). South Asia Bks.

Mahadevan, T. M., tr. see Sankaracharya.

Mahadevan, T. M. P. & Saroja, G. V. Contemporary Indian Philosophy. 282p. 1981. 32.50x (ISBN 0-940500-51-5, Pub. by Sterling India). Asia Bk Corp.

Mahaffey, Denis, tr. see Frechet, Alec.

Mahaffey, Mary J. & Mennes, Mary E. Food Service Manual for Health Care Institutions. (Illus.). 392p. 1981. pap. 25.00 (ISBN 0-87258-330-9, AHA-046170). Am Hospital.

Mahaffey, Maryann & Hanks, John, eds. Practical Politics: Social Work & Political Responsibility. 1982. text ed. 17.95x (ISBN 0-686-86374-7); pap. text ed. 18.95x (ISBN 0-87101-093-3, CBL-093-C). Natl Assn Soc Workers.

Mahaffey, Michael L. & Perrodin, Alex F. Teaching Elementary School Mathematics. LC 76-138646. (Illus.). 375p. 1973. text ed. 14.95 (ISBN 0-87581-084-5). Peacock Pubs.

Mahajan, B. N. Consumer Behaviour in India: An Econometric Study. 1980. text ed. 21.50x (ISBN 0-391-01834-5). Humanities.

Mahajani, Usha. The Role of Indian Minorities in Burma & Malaya. LC 72-12144. 344p. 1973. Repr. of 1960 ed. lib. bdg. 18.75x (ISBN 0-8371-6716-7, MAIN). Greenwood.

Mahak, Francine, tr. see SATPREM.

Mahammed, N. & Piccininni, R. Some Applications of Topological K-Theory. (Mathematical Ser.: Vol. 45). 1980. 40.50 (ISBN 0-444-86113-0, North Holland). Elsevier.

Mahan, A. & Preston, A. Influence of Seapower in History. 29.95 o.p. (ISBN 0-13-464537-5). P-H.

Mahan, Alfred T. From Sail to Steam: Recollections of Naval Life. LC 68-26817. (American Scene Ser.). 1968. Repr. of 1907 ed. lib. bdg. 37.50 (ISBN 0-306-71148-6). Da Capo.

--The Panama Canal & the Sea Power in the Pacific. (The Great Issues of History Library). (Illus.). 107p. 1983. Repr. of 1913 ed. 79.85 (ISBN 0-86722-027-9). Inst Econ Pol.

Mahan, Bill. The Boy Who Looked Like Shirley Temple. 256p. 1983. pap. 2.95 (ISBN 0-449-20261-5, Crest). Fawcett.

Mahan, Bruce H. University Chemistry. 3rd ed. LC 74-19696. 1975. text ed. 26.95 (ISBN 0-201-04405-6). A-W.

Mahan, Colleen. The Lodge. 1981. pap. 2.75 o.p. (ISBN 0-686-71645-0, E9969, Sig). NAL.

Mahan, David J., jt. auth. see Moeller, Gerald.

Mahan, Don, jt. auth. see Hart, Jack.

Mahan, Harold D., jt. auth. see Wallace, George J.

Mahan, Kathleen L., jt. auth. see Krause, Marie V.

Mahan, William. What Is Your Name & Telephone Number? Young, Billie, ed. LC 74-76434. 1975. 7.95 (ISBN 0-87949-028-4). Ashley Bks.

Mahanand, Marilyn, jt. auth. see Cunningham, William.

Mahaney, William E., ed. Francis Verney's "Antipoe" & John Speed's "The Converted Robber". Old-Spelling Editions with an Introduction & Notes. (Salzburg Studies in English Literature: Elizabethan & Renaissance Studies: No. 42). 1979. pap. text ed. 25.00x o.p. (ISBN 0-391-01472-2). Humanities.

Mahanthappa, K. T., et al, eds. see Boulder Conference on High Energy Physics.

Mahany, Gene. Mahany on Sales Promotion. LC 81-67753. 120p. 1982. pap. 8.95 (ISBN 0-87251-066-2). Crain Bks.

Mahany, Patricia. The Lollipop Dragon Goes for a Walk. (Coloring Bks.). (Illus.). 16p. (Orig.). (gr. k-3). 1982. pap. 0.89 (ISBN 0-87239-602-9, 2391). Standard Pub.

--Lollipop Keeps His Promise. (Happy Day Bks.). (Illus.). 24p. (ps-2). 1983. 1.29 (ISBN 0-87239-638-X, 3558). Standard Pub.

--Party Ideas. (Ideas Ser). (Illus.). 1977. pap. text ed. 1.75 (ISBN 0-87239-121-3, 7961). Standard Pub.

--Stories Jesus Told. (Coloring Bks.). (Illus.). 16p. (Orig.). (gr. k-3). 1982. pap. 0.89 (ISBN 0-87239-601-0, 2390). Standard Pub.

Mahany, Patricia, compiled by. Bible Finger Plays for Young Children. (Standard Ideas Ser.). (Illus.). 1978. pap. 1.75 o.s.i. (ISBN 0-87239-212-0, 2813). Standard Pub.

Mahany, Patricia, ed. see Brooks, Sandra.

Mahany, Patricia, ed. see Cachiaras, Dot.

Mahany, Patricia, ed. see Claire, Anne.

Mahany, Patricia, ed. see Curie, Barbara.

Mahany, Patricia, ed. see Downs, Kathy.

Mahany, Patricia, ed. see Flournoy, Fran.

Mahany, Patricia, ed. see Gambill, Henrietta.

Mahany, Patricia, ed. see Humphrey, Rilda.

Mahany, Patricia, ed. see Hutson, Joan.

Mahany, Patricia, ed. see Irland, Nancy.

Mahany, Patricia, ed. see Kayser, Rita.

Mahany, Patricia, ed. see Knoepfel & Farber.

Mahany, Patricia, ed. see Milner, Wanda.

Mahany, Patricia, ed. see Patterson, Y.

Mahany, Patricia, ed. see Phillips, Cara L.

Mahany, Patricia, ed. see Stewart, K. K.

Mahany, Patricia, ed. see Truitt, Gloria.

Mahany, Patricia, ed. see Watson, E. Elaine.

Mahany, Patricia, ed. see Witherow, Lucy.

Mahany, Patricia, ed. see Wright, Beverly W.

Mahany, Patricia S. Charlie's "Be Kind" Day. LC 81-50673. (A Happy Day Bk.). (Illus.). 24p. (Orig.). (ps-1). 1981. pap. 1.29 (ISBN 0-87239-462-X, 3595). Standard Pub.

Mahar, Dennis J. Brazil: Intergrated Development of the Northwest Frontier. vi, 101p. 1981. pap. 10.00 (ISBN 0-686-36098-2, RC-8101). World Bank.

Mahar, J. Michael. India: A Critical Bibliography. rev. ed. Date not set. cancelled (ISBN 0-8165-0635-3). U of Ariz Pr. Postponed.

Maharaj, B., jt. auth. see Charran, R.

Maharam-Stone, D., jt. ed. see Koelzow, D.

Maharani & Mitra, S. M. The Position of Women in Indian Life. 358p. 1981. Repr. text ed. 26.00x (ISBN 0-391-02259-8, Pub. by Concept India). Humanities.

Mahaut, A. Maandelyks Musikaels Tydverdryf: Bestaende in Nieuwe Hollandsche Canzonetten of Zang-Liederen Op D'italiaensche Trant In't Musiek Gebragt. 1979. 57.50 o.s.i. (ISBN 90-6027-294-3, Pub. by Frits Knuf Netherlands); complete in 12 issues 37.50 o.s.i. (ISBN 90-6027-293-5). Pendragon NY.

--Nieuwe Manier Om Binnen Korte Tijd Op De Dwarsfluit Te Leeren Speelen: Nouvelle Methode Pour Apprendre En Peu De Temps a Jouer De la Flute Traversiere. (The Flute Library: Vol. 4). 36p. 1981. 25.00 o.s.i. (ISBN 90-6027-292-7, Pub. by Frits Knuf Netherlands). Pendragon NY.

Mahecha, Alberto, ed. see Pollock, Algernon J.

Mahendra Nath Gupta, see M, pseud.

Maher, Brendan, ed. Clinical Psychology & Personality: The Selected Papers of George Kelly. LC 78-10716. 372p. 1979. Repr. of 1969 ed. lib. bdg. 16.00 (ISBN 0-88275-772-5). Krieger.

Maher, Brendan & Maher, W., eds. Progress in Experimental Personality Research, Vol. 11. (Serial Publication Ser.). 1982. 32.00 (ISBN 0-12-541411-0). Acad Pr.

Maher, Carolyn. General Math Two. Gafney, Leo, ed. (General Math Ser.). (Illus.). 464p. (gr. 9-12). 1981. text ed. 15.52 (ISBN 0-07-039595-0, W); tchr's ed. 17.08 (ISBN 0-07-039596-9); tchr's wkbk. 6.48 (ISBN 0-07-039598-5); wkbk. 5.92 (ISBN 0-07-039597-7). McGraw.

Maher, Carolyn A., et al. Math, No. 1. Gafney, Leo, ed. (General Math Ser.). (Illus.). (gr. 7-9). 1981. text ed. 13.44 pupil's ed. (ISBN 0-07-039591-8, W); tchr's ed., 448 p. 16.44 (ISBN 0-07-039592-6); wkbk. to pupils ed. 5.92 (ISBN 0-07-039593-4); tchrs' ed. wkbk. 6.48 (ISBN 0-07-039594-2). McGraw.

Maher, Donald J., jt. auth. see Mehta, Nitin H.

Maher, J. Peter. Papers on Language Theory & History I: Creation & Tradition in Language. (Current Issues in Linguistic Theory Ser.). xx, 171p. 1977. 23.00 (ISBN 90-272-0904-9, 3). Benjamins North Am.

Maher, J. Peter & Koerner, Konrad, eds. Papers from the Third International Conference on Historical Linguistics, Hamburg, August 22-26, 1977. (Current Issues in Linguistic Theory Ser,: 13). 400p. 1982. 40.00 (ISBN 90-272-3505-8). Benjamins North Am.

Maher, James T., ed. see Wilder, Alec.

Maher, Michael. Psychology. (Stonyhurst Philosophical Ser.). 608p. 1982. pap. text ed. 5.95x (ISBN 0-87343-051-4). Magi Bks.

Maher, Ramona. Alice Yazzie's Year. LC 77-24963. (Illus.). (gr. 3-6). 1977. 7.95 o.p. (ISBN 0-698-20432-8, Coward). Putnam Pub Group.

--When Windwagon Smith Came to Westport. (Illus.). 48p. (gr. 3-6). 1977. 5.95 o.p. (ISBN 0-698-20407-7, Coward). Putnam Pub Group.

Maher, Richard P. Introduction to Construction Operations. LC 82-1884. 402p. 1982. 32.95x (ISBN 0-471-86136-7, Pub. by Wiley-Interscience). Wiley.

Maher, Vanessa. Women & Property in Morocco. LC 74-80351. (Studies in Social Anthropology: No. 10). (Illus.). 164p. 1975. 32.50 (ISBN 0-521-20548-4). Cambridge U Pr.

Maher, W., jt. ed. see Maher, Brendan.

Mahesh, Virendra B., jt. ed. see Muldoon, Thomas G.

Mahesh, Vivenda B., ed. see Symposium on the Pituitary, Medical College of Georgia, Augusta, Georgia, May 20-22, 1976.

Maheu, R., pref. by. Main Trends of Research in the Social & Human Sciences, Pt. 1: Social Sciences. LC 70-114641. 1970. 158.00 o.p. (ISBN 92-3-100828-5, U363, UNESCO). Unipub.

Maheu, Rene. UNESCO in Perspective. rev. ed. 129p. (Orig.). 1975. pap. 4.00 o.p. (ISBN 92-3-101187-1, UNESCO). Unipub.

Mahfouz, Nagrib. The Crime. (Arabic.). pap. 5.50x (ISBN 0-86685-147-X). Intl Bk Ctr.

Mahillon, Victor C. Catalogue descriptif et Analytique du Musee Instrumental de Conservatoire Royal de Musique de Bruxelles(1893-1922, 5 vols. 1978. 162.50 o.s.i. (ISBN 90-6027-295-1, Pub. by Frits Knuf Netherlands). Pendragon NY.

Mahler, Gregory S., ed. Readings on the Israeli Political System: Structures & Processes. LC 81-40031. 450p. (Orig.). 1982. lib. bdg. 27.50 (ISBN 0-8191-2117-7); pap. text ed. 15.00 (ISBN 0-8191-2118-5). U Pr of Amer.

Mahler, Henry R. & Cordes, Eugene H. Biological Chemistry. 2nd ed. (Illus.). 1971. text ed. 50.50 scp (ISBN 0-06-044172-0, HarpC). Har-Row.

Mahler, Kurt. P-Adic Numbers & Their Functions. 2nd ed. LC 79-20103. (Cambridge Tracts in Mathematics Ser.: No. 76). 1981. 49.95 (ISBN 0-521-23102-7). Cambridge U Pr.

Mahlstede, John P. & Haber, E. S. Plant Propagation. LC 57-5924. 1957. 29.95 o.s.i. (ISBN 0-471-56364-1). Wiley.

Mahlum, D. D., ed. Developmental Toxicology of Energy-Related Pollutants: Proceedings. Sikov, M. R. LC 78-606139. (DOE Symposium Ser.). 660p. 1978. pap. 24.50 (ISBN 0-87079-113-3, CONF-771017); microfiche 4.50 (ISBN 0-87079-178-8, CONF-77107). DOE.

Mahlum, D. Dennis, jt. ed. see Sikov, Melvin R.

Mahlum, Dennis D., et al, eds. Coal Conversion & the Environment: Chemical, Biomedical, & Ecological Considerations Proceedings. LC 81-607088. (DOE Symposium Ser.). 620p. 1981. pap. 24.75 (ISBN 0-87079-128-1, CONF-801039); microfiche 4.50 (ISBN 0-87079-401-9, CONF-801039). DOE.

Mahmood, Tahir. Muslim Personal Law. 1977. text ed. 14.75x (ISBN 0-7069-0532-6). Humanities.

Mahmud, A. el-Sayed. A New Temple for Hathor at Memphis. (Egyptology Today Ser.: No. 1, 1978). (Illus.). 22p. 1978. pap. text ed. 22.00x (ISBN 0-686-86104-3, Pub. by Aris & Phillips England). Humanities.

Mahnke, Susan, ed. Yankee Magazine's Great New England Recipes. (Illus.). 320p. 1983. 15.95 (ISBN 0-911658-36-X). Yankee Bks.

Mahoe, Noelani K., jt. ed. see Elbert, Samuel H.

Mahon, John K. The American Militia, Decade of Decision, 1789-1800. LC 60-63132. (Social Science Monographs: No. 6). 1960. pap. 3.25 (ISBN 0-8130-0153-6). U Presses Fla.

--History of the Militia & the National Guard. 1983. 19.95 (ISBN 0-686-83899-8). Macmillan.

Mahon, Maureen. Thomas Hardy's Novels: A Study Guide. 1976. pap. text ed. 3.95x o.p. (ISBN 0-435-18552-7). Heinemann Ed.

Mahoney, Bertha & Whitney, Elinor. Contemporary Illustrators of Children's Books. LC 79-185381. (Illus.). 1978. Repr. of 1930 ed. 55.00x (ISBN 0-8103-4308-8). Gale.

Mahoney, E. R. Human Sexuality. Nave, Patricia S., ed. (Illus.). 608p. 1983. text ed. 21.95 (ISBN 0-07-039650-7, C); write for info instr's manual (ISBN 0-07-039651-5). McGraw.

Mahoney, Elizabeth A. & Flynn, Jean P. The Handbook of Medical-Surgical Nursing. 600p. 1983. 18.50 (ISBN 0-471-86982-1, Pub. by Wiley Med). Wiley.

Mahoney, Irene. An Accidental Grace. LC 82-5648. 368p. 1982. 14.95 (ISBN 0-312-00223-8). St Martin.

Mahoney, John L. The English Romantics. 1978. text ed. 20.95x (ISBN 0-669-01030-8). Heath.

--The Enlightenment & English Literature: Prose & Poetry of the Eighteenth Century with Selected Modern Critical Essays. 1980. text ed. 24.95 (ISBN 0-669-02321-3). Heath.

Mahoney, Marnie & Lichtman, Ronnie. The Family Health History Workbook. 1982. pap. 12.45 (ISBN 0-688-01005-9). Morrow.

Mahoney, Michael. The Drawings of Salvator Rosa, 2 vols. LC 76-23637. (Outstanding Dissertations in the Fine Arts - 17th Century). (Illus.). 1977. Repr. of 1965 ed. Set. lib. bdg. 133.00 o.s.i. (ISBN 0-8240-2707-8). Garland Pub.

Mahoney, Michael J. Cognition & Behavior Modification. LC 74-13019. 384p. 1974. prof ref 19.50x (ISBN 0-88410-500-8). Ballinger Pub.

--The Scientist As Subject: The Psychological Imperative. LC 76-5878. 264p. 1976. prof ref 19.50 (ISBN 0-88410-505-9); pap. text ed. 11.00x prof ref (ISBN 0-88410-514-8). Ballinger Pub.

--Self-Change: Strategies for Solving Personal Problems. 224p. 1981. pap. 4.95 o.p. (ISBN 0-393-00067-2). Norton.

Mahoney, Ralph. Drawing Closer to God. 60p. 1982. pap. 2.95 (ISBN 0-930756-72-X). Women's Aglow.

Mahood, Kenneth. Losing Willy. LC 77-6267. (Illus.). (ps-2). 1978. PLB 6.95 o.p. (ISBN 0-13-540583-1); pap. 2.95 o.p. (ISBN 0-13-540591-2). P-H.

--The Secret Sketchbook of Bloomsbury Lady. (Illus.). 64p. 1983. pap. 10.95 (ISBN 0-312-70873-4). St Martin.

Mahowald, Mary B., ed. Philosophy of Woman: Classical to Current Concepts. LC 77-16638. 1977. 15.00 (ISBN 0-915144-49-2); pap. text ed. 6.95 (ISBN 0-915144-48-4). Hackett Pub.

Mahrer, Alvin R. Experiencing: A Humanistic Theory of Psychology & Psychiatry. LC 77-27269. 1978. 30.00 (ISBN 0-87630-160-X). Brunner-Mazel.

--Experiential Psychotherapy: Basic Practices. 400p. 1983. 27.50 (ISBN 0-87630-318-1). Brunner-Mazel.

Mahrous, Haroun, jt. auth. see Seidman, Arthur H.

Mahy, Margaret. The Boy Who Was Followed Home. (Illus.). 32p. (ps-3). 1983. pap. 3.95 (ISBN 0-8037-0903-X, 0383-120). Dial Bks Young.

--The Bus Under the Leaves. (Illus.). 64p. 1975. Repr. of 1974 ed. 6.50x o.p. (ISBN 0-460-05899-1, Pub. by J. M. Dent. England). Biblio Dist.

--Clancy's Cabin. (Illus.). 96p. 1976. Repr. of 1974 ed. 6.50x o.p. (ISBN 0-460-05900-9, J M Dent England). Biblio Dist.

--The Great Millionaire Kidnap. (Illus.). 40p. 1975. 9.00x o.p. (ISBN 0-460-06693-5, Pub. by J. M. Dent England). Biblio Dist.

--The Haunting. LC 82-3983. 144p. (gr. 5-9). 1982. 8.95 (ISBN 0-689-50243-5, McElderry Bk). Atheneum.

Maiano, William E., jt. auth. see Cohen, Ronald J.

Maibach, Howard, jt. auth. see Reeves, John.

Maibach, Howard I., jt. ed. see Marzulli, Francis N.

Maibaum, Matt. Hope is a Waking Man's Dream. LC 81-80147. 200p. 1981. 10.95 (ISBN 0-86666-019-4). GWP.

Maickel, Roger P., jt. auth. see Sokol, Gerald H.

Maiden, Cecil & Knight, Hilary. Beginning with Mrs. McBee. LC 60-15411. (Illus.). (gr. k-3). 1959. 5.95 o.s.i. (ISBN 0-8149-0356-8). Vanguard.

Maiden, Lewis S. Highlights of the Nashville Theater: Eighteen Seventy-Six to Eighteen Ninety. 1979. 8.95 o.p. (ISBN 0-533-04122-8). Vantage.

Maidens, Ena. The Techniques of Crocheted & Openwork Lace. (Illus.). 144p. 1982. 22.50 (ISBN 0-7134-2568-7, Pub. by Batsford England). David & Charles.

Maidens, Melinda, ed. American Technology: Are We Falling Behind? (Editorials on File Ser.). 192p. 1982. 19.95x (ISBN 0-87196-677-8). Facts on File.

Maidment, Patricia. How to Make & Furnish A Dollhouse for a Hundred Dollars or Less. new ed. 192p. 1983. 16.95 (ISBN 0-672-52742-1); pap. 10.95 (ISBN 0-672-52745-6). Bobbs.

Maidment, R. A., jt. auth. see Lees, J. D.

Maidment, Robert. Straight Talk: A Guide to Saying More with Less. LC 82-12211. 112p. (Orig.). 1983. pap. 5.95 (ISBN 0-88289-340-8). Pelican.

Maidment, Robert & Bronstein, Russell. Simulation Games: Design & Implementation. LC 73-75051. 1973. pap. text ed. 6.95 o.p. (ISBN 0-675-08968-9). Merrill.

Maier, Arlee, jt. auth. see Guerin, Gilbert.

Maier, D. J. Priests & Power: The Case of the Dente Shrine in Nineteenth-Century Ghana. LC 82-48582. (Illus.). 272p. 1983. 18.50x (ISBN 0-253-34602-9). Ind U Pr.

Maier, Elaine C. How to Prepare a Legal Citation. 1983. pap. 8.95 (ISBN 0-8120-2382-X). Barron.

Maier, Ernest L. & McAfee, R. Bruce. Cases in Selling. (Illus.). 1979. pap. text ed. 12.95 (ISBN 0-07-039720-1, T&D); leader's guide 4.95 (ISBN 0-07-039721-X). McGraw.

Maier, Eugene, ed. see Ashley, John P. & Harvey, E. R.

Maier, Joseph B. & Waxman, Chaim I., eds. Ethnicity, Identity & History: Essays in Memory of Werner J. Cahnman. (Illus.). 350p. 1983. 35.95 (ISBN 0-87855-461-0). Transaction Bks.

Maier, L., jt. auth. see Kosolapoff, G. M.

Maier, Mathilde. All the Gardens of My Life. 1983. 7.95 (ISBN 0-533-05486-9). Vantage.

Maier, Monika. How to Succeed at Skating. (Illus.). 128p. 1982. 12.95 (ISBN 0-686-97815-3); lib. bdg. 15.69 (ISBN 0-8069-4157-X); pap. 6.95 (ISBN 0-8069-4154-5). Sterling.
Maier, Norman R. Problem-Solving Discussions & Conferences: Leadership Methods & Skills. 1963. text ed. 25.95 (ISBN 0-07-039715-5, C). McGraw.
--Psychology in Industrial Organizations. 4th ed. LC 74-4797. 750p. 1973. text ed. 19.95 o.p. (ISBN 0-395-14046-3); instr's. manual 2.70 o.p. (ISBN 0-395-15102-3, 3-34270). HM.
Maier, Norman R. & Verser, Trudy G. Psychology in Industrial Organizations. 5th ed. LC 81-81702. (Illus.). 672p. 1982. text ed. 21.95 (ISBN 0-395-31740-1); instr's. Manual 1.00 (ISBN 0-395-31741-X). HM.
Maier, Norman R. F., et al. The Role-Play Technique: A Handbook for Management & Leadership Practice. LC 74-30943. Orig. Title: Supervisory & Executive Development. 290p. 1975. pap. 15.50 (ISBN 0-88390-104-8). Univ Assocs.
Maier, Paul. The Flames of Rome: A Documentary Novel. LC 80-2561. (Illus.). 456p. 1981. 15.95 (ISBN 0-385-17091-2, Galilee). Doubleday.
Maier, Paul L. A Man Spoke, a World Listened. 1980. pap. 8.95 (ISBN 0-570-03822-7, 12-2762). Concordia.
Maier, Paul L., jt. ed. see Cornfeld, Gaalyah.
Maier, Pauline. Boston & New York in the Eighteenth Century. 19p. 1982. pap. 3.50 (ISBN 0-912296-54-2, Dist. by U Pr of Va). Am Antiquarian.
--From Resistance to Revolution: Colonial Radicals & the Development of American Opposition to Britain, 1765-1776. 1973. pap. 4.95 (ISBN 0-394-71937-9, Vin). Random.
Maieru, A., ed. English Logic in Italy in the 14th & 15th Centuries. (History of Logic Ser.: Vol. I). 388p. 1982. 45.00x (ISBN 88-7088-054-0, Pub. by Bibliopolis Italy); pap. text ed. 24.95x (ISBN 88-7088-057-5). Humanities.
Maiken, Peter T., jt. auth. see Sullivan, Terry.
Maikowski, Stephen, jt. ed. see Hammerman, Susan.
Mailer, Norman. Advertisements for Myself. 540p. 1981. pap. 6.95 (ISBN 0-399-50538-5, Perige). Putnam Pub Group.
--Ancient Evenings. 800p. 1983. 19.45i (ISBN 0-316-54410-8). Little.
--Armies of the Night. 1971. pap. 3.95 (ISBN 0-451-12317-4, AE2317, Sig). NAL.
--Barbary Shore. LC 79-26233. 312p. 1980. Repr. of 1951 ed. 21.50x (ISBN 0-86527-218-2). Fertig.
--The Deer Park. LC 79-20163. 375p. 1980. Repr. of 1955 ed. 21.50x (ISBN 0-86527-235-2). Fertig.
--The Deer Park. 384p. 1981. pap. 5.95 (ISBN 0-399-50531-8, Perige). Putnam Pub Group.
--Existential Errands. 320p. 1973. pap. 1.75 o.p. (ISBN 0-451-05422-9, E5422, Sig). NAL.
--Marilyn. LC 73-6899. (Illus.). 272p. 1981. pap. 11.95 (ISBN 0-448-11813-0, G&D). Putnam Pub Group.
--Naked and the Dead. 1971. pap. 3.50 o.p. (ISBN 0-451-09702-5, E9702, Sig). NAL.
--Of a Fire on the Moon. 1971. pap. 1.75 o.p. (ISBN 0-451-04765-6, E4765, Sig). NAL.
--Of Women & Their Elegance. 256p. 1981. pap. 3.50 (ISBN 0-523-48015-6). Pinnacle Bks.
--Of Women & Their Elegance. (Illus.). 1980. 29.95 o.p. (ISBN 0-671-24020-X). S&S.
--Pieces & Pontifications. 1983. pap. 7.95 (ISBN 0-316-54420-5). Little.
--The Short Fiction of Norman Mailer. LC 79-20189. 285p. 1980. Repr. of 1967 ed. 21.50x (ISBN 0-86527-303-0). Fertig.
Mailer, Paul L. The Flames of Rome. 1982. pap. 3.95 (ISBN 0-451-11737-9, AE1737, Sig). NAL.
Maillard, Keith. Cutting Through. 1983. 16.95 (ISBN 0-8253-0120-3). Beaufort Bks NY.
Maillard, Robert, ed. New Dictionary of Modern Sculpture. 1971. 12.50 o.p. (ISBN 0-8148-0479-9). L Amiel Pub.
Maiman, Joan M., et al. Vietnam Heroes: A Tribute: An Anthology of Poems by Veterans & Their Friends. Topham, J., ed. LC 82-3955. 21p. 1982. pap. text ed. 3.95 (ISBN 0-933486-34-0). Am Poetry Pr.
Maimon, Elaine P., et al. Writing in the Arts & Sciences. 1981. text ed. 12.95 (ISBN 0-316-54424-8); tchr's ed. avail. (ISBN 0-316-54425-6). Little.
Maimonides, Moses. Guide for the Perplexed. 2nd ed. 10.50 (ISBN 0-8446-2512-4). Peter Smith.
--The Reason of the Laws of Moses. Townley, James, ed. LC 78-97294. 451p. 1975. Repr. of 1827 ed. lib. bdg. 18.50x (ISBN 0-8371-2618-5, MARL). Greenwood.
Main, I. G. Vibration & Waves in Physics. LC 77-5546. (Illus.). 1978. 69.95 (ISBN 0-521-21662-1); pap. 19.95x (ISBN 0-521-29220-4). Cambridge U Pr.
Main, Jackson T. The Antifederalists: Critics of the Constitution, 1781-1788. 320p. 1974. pap. 6.95 (ISBN 0-393-00760-X, Norton Lib). Norton.
Main, Jackson T; see Weaver, Glenn.
Main, Jody & Portugal, Nancy. Sprout Booklet & Stainless Steel Screen. (Illus.). 1978. pap. 1.50 (ISBN 0-9601088-6-6). Wild Horses Potted Plant.
Main, Jody, jt. auth. see Portugal, Nancy.
Main, Robert S. & Baird, Charles W. Elements of Microeconomics. (Illus.). 1977. pap. text ed. 12.95 o.s.i. (ISBN 0-8299-0136-1). West Pub.
Mainardi, F., ed. Wave Propagation with Viscoelastic Media. (Research Notes in Mathematics Ser.: No. 52). 280p. (Orig.). 1982. text ed. 25.00 (ISBN 0-273-08511-5). Pitman Pub MA.
Mainardi, Patricia. Quilts: The Great American Art. LC 77-95430. (Illus.). 1978. 7.95x o.p. (ISBN 0-917300-06-8); pap. 2.95 o.p. (ISBN 0-917300-01-7). Miles & Weir.
Mainardus, G., jt. ed. see Collatz, L.
Maine, Henry J. S. Ancient Law. 1972. Repr. of 1917 ed. 10.95x (ISBN 0-460-00734-3, Evman). Biblio Dist.
Maine Historical Society. The Maine Bicentennial Atlas: An Historical Survey. (Illus.). 1976. 10.00 (ISBN 0-915592-24-X); pap. 6.00 o.p. (ISBN 0-915592-23-1). Maine Hist.
Maine Studies Curriculum Project. Natural History of Maine: Physical Science Ser, Vol. 1. Bennett, Dean B., ed. (Illus.). 224p. 1982. Tchrs'. Guide 29.95 (ISBN 0-89272-146-4). Down East.
Maines, David R., jt. ed. see Lopata, Helena Z.
Maini, Darshan S. Studies in Punjabi Poetry. 1979. text ed. 10.50x (ISBN 0-7069-0709-4). Humanities.
Maini, R. N., jt. ed. see Dumonde, D. C.
Mainiero, Lina, ed. American Women Writers: A Critical Reference Guide. LC 78-20945. 1981. Vol. 2, F-Le. 55.00 (ISBN 0-8044-3152-3); Vol. 3, Li-R. 55.00 (ISBN 0-8044-3153-1). Ungar.
Mainous, Frank D., jt. auth. see Ottman, Robert W.
Mains, Karen B. The Fragile Curtain. 1981. 9.95 o.p. (ISBN 0-89191-474-9, 54742). Cook.
--Open Heart, Open Home. 1980. pap. 4.95 (ISBN 0-89191-111-1). Cook.
Mainstone, Madeleine & Mainstone, Rowland. The Seventeenth Century. LC 80-40039. (Cambridge History of Art Ser.: No. 4). (Illus.). 100p. 1981. 19.95 (ISBN 0-521-22162-5); pap. 7.50 (ISBN 0-521-29376-6). Cambridge U Pr.
Mainstone, Rowland, jt. auth. see Mainstone, Madeleine.
Mainstone, Rowland J. Developments in Structural Form. (Illus.). 352p. 1983. pap. 17.50 (ISBN 0-262-63088-5). MIT Pr.
Mainwaring, John. Memoirs of the Life of the Late George Frederic Handel. (Facsimilies of Early Biographies Ser.: Vol. 2). 1975. Repr. of 1760 ed. 17.50 o.s.i. (ISBN 90-6027-016-9, Pub. by Frits Knuf Netherlands). Pendragon NY.
Mainwaring, R. M., jt. auth. see Honour, T. F.
Mainzer, Lewis C. Political Bureaucracy: The American Public Service. 192p. 1973. pap. 8.95x (ISBN 0-673-05913-8). Scott F.
Maio, Gerald De see Kushner, Harvey W. & De Maio, Gerald.
Maiolo, John & Orbach, Michael K. Modernization & Marine Fisheries Policy. LC 81-69470. 300p. 1982. text ed. 29.95 (ISBN 0-250-40515-6). Ann Arbor Science.
Maiolo, Joseph & Brantley, Jill, eds. From Three Sides: Reading for Writers. 288p. 1976. pap. 12.95 (ISBN 0-13-331876-1). P-H.
Maione, M., ed. see International Society for Paediatric Ophthalmology, 2nd Meeting.
Maiorana, Victor P. How to Learn & Study in College. (Illus.). 1980. pap. text ed. 12.95 (ISBN 0-13-415059-7). P-H.
Maiorano, Robert. A Little Interlude. LC 79-21521. (Illus.). (gr. 4-8). 1980. 5.95 (ISBN 0-698-20496-4, Coward). Putnam Pub Group.
--Worlds Apart: The Autobiography of a Dancer from Brooklyn. (Illus.). 176p. (gr. 6-8). 1980. 9.95 (ISBN 0-698-20505-7, Coward). Putnam Pub Group.
Maiori, Rachel, jt. auth. see Martin, Genevieve A.
Mair, George. The Sex-Book Digest. LC 82-12413. 1982. 16.50 (ISBN 0-688-01528-X); pap. 8.50 (ISBN 0-688-01336-8). Morrow.
Mair, Graig. A Time in Turkey. (Illus.). 160p. 1974. 9.50 o.p. (ISBN 0-7195-2836-4). Transatlantic.
Mair, Lucy. African Kingdoms. (Illus.). 1977. text ed. 24.95x (ISBN 0-19-821698-X); pap. text ed. 10.95x (ISBN 0-19-874075-1). Oxford U Pr.
--African Societies. LC 73-93398. (Illus.). 236p. 1974. 32.50 (ISBN 0-521-20442-9); pap. 10.95x (ISBN 0-521-09854-8). Cambridge U Pr.
--An Introduction to Social Anthropology. 2nd ed. 1972. pap. text ed. 7.95x (ISBN 0-19-874011-5). Oxford U Pr.
Mair, S. E., jt. auth. see Ducan, J. P.
Mair, Victor H., ed. Experimental Essays on Chuang-tzu. (Asian Studies at Hawaii: No. 29). 200p. 1983. pap. 10.00x (ISBN 0-8248-0836-3). UH Pr.
Maire, Susan S. How to Raise & Train an English Setter. (Illus.). pap. 2.95 (ISBN 0-87666-292-0, DS1074). TFH Pubns.
Mairet, Philip. Autobiographical & Other Papers. Sisson, C. H., ed. 288p. (Orig.). 1981. pap. text ed. 17.00 (ISBN 0-85635-326-4, Pub. by Carcanet New Pr England). Humanities.
Maisel, Eric. Dismay. LC 82-61850. 211p. (Orig.). 1983. pap. 5.95 (ISBN 0-686-38108-4). Maya Pr.
Maisel, Herbert. Computers: Programming & Applications. LC 75-30547. (Illus.). 416p. 1976. text ed. 19.95 (ISBN 0-574-21070-9, 13-4070); instructor's guide 2.50 (ISBN 0-574-21071-7, 13-4071). SRA.
Maisel, Herbert & Gnugnoli, Guiliano. Simulation of Discrete Stochastic Systems. LC 72-80761. (Illus.). 465p. 1972. 24.95 (ISBN 0-574-16133-3, 13-1565). SRA.
Maisel, Louis. Probability, Statistics & Random Processes. (Tech Outlines Ser.). pap. 4.95 o.p. (ISBN 0-671-18915-8). Monarch Pr.
Maisel, Sherman J. Macroeconomics: Theories & Policies. 1982. text ed. 19.95x (ISBN 0-393-01490-8); instrs.' manual avail. (ISBN 0-393-95210-X); 7.95x (ISBN 0-393-95207-X). Norton.
Maisel, Sherman J. & Roulac, Stephen E. Real Estate Investment & Finance. (Illus.). 1976. text ed. 25.95x (ISBN 0-07-039730-9, C); instr's manual 7.95 (ISBN 0-07-039731-7). McGraw.
Maislen, Ruth, et al. Eat, Think & Be Thinner: The Weigh of Life Way. LC 76-19810. 1976. 8.95 o.p. (ISBN 0-8069-0150-0); lib. bdg. 8.29 o.p. (ISBN 0-8069-0151-9). Sterling.
Maison, Della. The Care Bears' Garden. LC 82-61566. (Care Bear Mini-Storybooks). (Illus.). 32p. (gr. 1-6). 1983. pap. 1.25 saddle-stitched (ISBN 0-394-85827-1). Random.
Maiss, Otto. Yemen Arab Republic: Development of a Traditional Economy. xxviii, 303p. 1979. pap. 20.00 (ISBN 0-686-36125-3, RC-7901). World Bank.
Maissel, L. & Glang, R. Handbook of Thin Film Technology. (Classic Handbook Program). 1970. 65.00 (ISBN 0-07-039742-2, P&RB). McGraw.
Maister, David H. Management of Owner-Operator Fleets. LC 79-5112. 256p. 1980. 26.95x (ISBN 0-669-03197-6). Lexington Bks.
Maister, David H., jt. auth. see Wyckoff, D. Daryl.
Maister, Philippa. The Insider's Atlanta. (Illus.). 252p. (Orig.). 1982. pap. 7.95 (ISBN 0-9608596-0-8). Good Hope GA.
Maistre, Joseph de see De Maistre, Joseph.
Maistre, Joseph M. de. Essay on the Generative Principle of Political Constitutions. LC 77-24972. 1977. Repr. of 1847 ed. 25.00x (ISBN 0-8201-1294-1). Schol Facsimiles.
Maital, Schlomo & Meltz, Noah, eds. Lagging Productivity Growth: Causes & Remedies. 328p. 1980. prof ref 27.50x (ISBN 0-88410-689-6). Ballinger Pub.
Maital, Shlomo. Minds, Markets, & Money: Psychological Foundations of Economic Behavior. LC 81-68410. 320p. 1982. 14.95 (ISBN 0-465-04623-1). Basic.
Maitland, David. Against the Grain: Coming through Mid-Life Crises. 208p. 1981. pap. 8.95 (ISBN 0-8298-0675-X). Pilgrim NY.
Maitland, Derek. Firecracker Suite: Comic Tales of Cultural Collision. 1981. 8.95 (ISBN 962-7031-01-1, Pub. by CFW Pubns Hong Kong). C E Tuttle.
Maitland, Derek, ed. Hong Kong in Focus. (The "In Focus" Ser.). (Illus.). 64p. (Orig.). 1981. pap. 5.95 (ISBN 962-7031-14-3). C E Tuttle.
Maitland, Derek, ed. see Lockhart, Saul.
Maitland, Edward. By & By. 1977. Repr. of 1873 ed. lib. bdg. 20.00 (ISBN 0-8398-2379-7, Gregg). G K Hall.
Maitland, Edward, jt. auth. see Kingsford, Anna.
Maitland, F. W., ed. Bracton's Note Book: A Collection of Cases Decided in the King's Courts During the Reign of Henry the Third, Annotated by a Lawyer of That Time, Seemingly by Henry of Bratton, 3 Vols. 1983. Repr. of 1887 ed. lib. bdg. 145.00x (ISBN 0-8377-0334-4). Rothman.
Maitland, Frederic W. Constitutional History of England. 1908. text ed. 69.50x (ISBN 0-521-05656-X); pap. text ed. 19.95x (ISBN 0-521-09137-3). Cambridge U Pr.
--Forms of Action at Common Law. 1936. text ed. 17.50x (ISBN 0-521-05657-8); pap. text ed. 8.95x (ISBN 0-521-09185-3). Cambridge U Pr.
Maitland, Frederic W., jt. auth. see Pollock, Edward.
Maitland, Frederick W. Life & Letters of Leslie Stephen. LC 67-23873. 1968. Repr. of 1906 ed. 30.00x (ISBN 0-8103-3058-X). Gale.
Maitland, Ian. The Causes of Industrial Disorder: A Comparison of a British & a German Factory. (Routledge Direct Edition Ser.). 192p. 1983. pap. 12.95 (ISBN 0-7100-9207-5). Routledge & Kegan.
Maitland, Sara. The Languages of Love. LC 80-943. 288p. 1981. 10.95 o.p. (ISBN 0-385-17203-6). Doubleday.
--A Map of the New Country: Women & Christianity. LC 82-13142. 218p. 1983. 12.95 (ISBN 0-7100-9326-8). Routledge & Kegan.
Maitland, Terrence & Weiss, Stephen. Raising the Stakes. Manning, Robert, ed. LC 82-71280. (The Vietnam Experience Ser.: Vol. 3). (Illus.). 192p. 1982. 14.95 o.s.i. (ISBN 0-939526-02-6). Boston Pub Co.
Maity, S. K. Cultural History of Ancient India. 120p. 1982. text ed. 12.00x (ISBN 0-391-02809-X). Humanities.
Maizell, Robert E. How to Find Chemical Information: A Guide for Practicing Chemists, Teachers & Students. LC 78-23222. 1979. 29.00 (ISBN 0-471-56531-8, Pub. by Wiley-Interscience). Wiley.
Maizels, Alfred. Industrial Growth & World Trade. 47.50 (ISBN 0-521-05662-4); pap. 12.95x (ISBN 0-521-09527-1). Cambridge U Pr.
Maizlish, Steven E., jt. ed. see Kushma, John J.
Majaro, Simon. International Marketing: A Strategic Approach to World Markets. 2nd ed. 320p. 1982. pap. text ed. 13.95x (ISBN 0-04-658240-1). Allen Unwin.
Majault, Joseph. James Joyce. Stewart, Jean, tr. from Fr. 1971. 6.00x (ISBN 0-685-74779-4). Pendragon Hse.
Majax, Gerard. Secrets of the Card Sharps. LC 76-51187. (Illus.). 156p. 1977. pap. 8.95 (ISBN 0-8069-4548-6). Sterling.
Majda, Andrew. The Stability of Multi-Dimensional Shock Fronts. LC 82-206000036. (Memoirs of the American Mathematics Society Ser.: No. 275). 6.00 (ISBN 0-8218-2275-6, MEMO/275). Am Math.
Majer, V., jt. auth. see Benes, P.
Majid, Kamal I. Optimum Design of Structures. LC 73-15015. 264p. 1974. text ed. 38.95x o.s.i. (ISBN 0-470-56533-0). Halsted Pr.
Majka, Linda C. & Majka, Theo J. Farm-Workers, Agribusiness, & the State. 320p. 1982. 24.95 (ISBN 0-87722-256-8). Temple U Pr.
Majka, Theo J., jt. auth. see Majka, Linda C.
Majkowski, E. Polish Textiles. 22.50x (ISBN 0-87245-333-2). Textile Bk.
Majno, Guido & Cotran, Ramzi. The Inflammatory Process & Infectious Diseases. (International Academy of Pathology Ser.: Vol. 23). (Illus.). 239p. 1982. lib. bdg. 39.00 (ISBN 0-683-05401-5). Williams & Wilkins.
Majone, Giandomenico & Quade, Edward S. Pitfalls of Analysis. LC 79-41700. (Wiley IIASA International Series on Applied Systems Analysis). 224p. 1980. 41.95 (ISBN 0-471-27746-0, Pub. by Wiley-Interscience). Wiley.
Major, A. Hyatt. Popular Prints of the Americas. (Illus.). 1973. 15.95 o.p. (ISBN 0-517-50601-7). Crown.
Major, Alan, jt. auth. see Russell, Ian.
Major, Beverly. The Magic Pizza. LC 77-26993. (Illus.). (gr. 2-5). 1978. 5.95 (ISBN 0-13-545202-3). P-H.
--Porcupine Stew. LC 82-2268. (Illus.). 40p. (gr. k-3). 1982. 9.50 (ISBN 0-688-01272-8). Morrow.
Major, Clarence. The Dark & the Feeling. LC 73-83162. 5.95 o.p. (ISBN 0-89388-119-8). Okpaku Communications.
Major, Constance J. Contemporary Patchwork Quilts: A Stitch in Our Time. LC 82-50545. (Illus.). 128p. 1982. 19.99 (ISBN 0-8069-5472-6); lib. bdg. 19.99 (ISBN 0-8069-5473-6); pap. 8.95 (ISBN 0-8069-7634-9). Sterling.
Major, David A., jt. ed. see Miller, Howard A.
Major, David C. Multiobjective Water Resources Planning. LC 77-899. (Water Resources Monograph: No. 4). 1977. pap. 10.00 (ISBN 0-87590-305-3). Am Geophysical.
Major, David C. & Lenton, Roberto L. Applied Water Resource Systems Planning. (Environmental Sciences Ser.). (Illus.). 1979. text ed. 29.95 (ISBN 0-13-043364-0). P-H.
Major, Francis J., jt. auth. see Silverberg, Steven G.
Major, J. Kenneth & Watts, Martin. Victorian & Edwardian Windmills & Watermills. 1977. 19.95 o.p. (ISBN 0-7134-0621-6, Pub. by Batsford England). David & Charles.
Major, Jack, jt. ed. see Barbour, Michael G.
Major, James R. Representative Institutions in Renaissance France, 1421-1559. LC 82-25305. ix, 182p. 1983. Repr. of 1960 ed. lib. bdg. 35.00x (ISBN 0-313-23569-4, MAJR). Greenwood.
Major, Jill C., jt. auth. see Chapman, Eugenia.
Major, John. The Oppenheimer Hearing. LC 76-156939. 344p. 1983. pap. 9.95 (ISBN 0-8128-6179-5). Stein & Day.
Major, John M., ed. Sir Thomas Elyot's: The Book Named the Governor. LC 75-108883. 1970. text ed. 10.50 (ISBN 0-8077-1796-7). Tchrs Coll.
Major, Kevin. Far from Shore. (YA) (gr. 7-12). 1983. pap. 2.50 (ISBN 0-440-92585-1, LFL). Dell.
--Hold Fast. (gr. 7 up). 1981. pap. 2.25 (ISBN 0-440-93756-6, LE). Dell.
Major-Poetzl, Pamela. Michel Foucault's Archaeology of Western Culture: Toward a New Science of History. LC 81-19689. xiii, 276p. 1982. 24.00x (ISBN 0-8078-1517-9). U of NC Pr.
Majors, Judith S. Sugar Free...Sweets & Treats. LC 82-73049. 1982. pap. 4.95 (ISBN 0-9602238-6-X). Apple Pr.
Majstorovic, Stevan. Cultural Policy in Yugoslavia. LC 75-187097. (Illus.). 81p. (Orig.). 1972. pap. 5.00 o.p. (ISBN 92-3-100920-6, U139, UNESCO). Unipub.
Majul, Cesar A. The Names of God in Relation to the Mathematical Structure of Quran. 35p. (Orig.). 1983. 1.50 (ISBN 0-934894-04-3). Islamic Prods.
Majumdar, B. Joyce Cary: An Existentialist Approach. 220p. 1982. text ed. 18.50x (ISBN 0-391-02807-3). Humanities.
Majumdar, Badiul A. Innovations, Product Developments & Technology Transfers: An Empirical Study of Dynamic Competitive Advantage, The Case of Electronic Calculators. LC 80-1451. (Illus.). 198p. (Orig.). 1982. lib. bdg. 22.00 (ISBN 0-8191-2065-0); pap. text ed. 10.25 (ISBN 0-8191-2066-9). U Pr of Amer.
Majumdar, R. C. & Chopra, P. N. Main Currents of Indian History. 1980. text ed. 9.00x (ISBN 0-391-00961-3). Humanities.
Majumdar, S. K. Irrigation Engineering. 350p. Date not set. 9.95x (ISBN 0-07-451756-2). McGraw.
Majumdar, Tapas. Investment in Education & Social Choice. LC 82-12829. (Illus.). 160p. Date not set. 29.95 (ISBN 0-521-25143-5). Cambridge U Pr.

Majupuria, Trilok C. Glimpses of Nepal. (Illus.). 327p. 1980. pap. 17.95x (ISBN 0-686-92276-X); pap. text ed. 17.95x (ISBN 0-686-98496-X). Asia Bk Corp.

Majupuria, Trilok C. & Gupta, S. P. Nepal: The Land of Festivals (Religious, Cultural, Social & Historical Festivals) (Illus.). 152p. 1981. 14.95x (ISBN 0-940500-83-3, Pub by S Chand India). Asia Bk Corp.

Makanowitzky, Barbara, tr. see Chekhov, Anton.

Makanowitzky, Barbara, tr. see Turgenev, Ivan.

Makari, Victor E. Ibn Taymiyyah's Ethics: The Social Factor. LC 81-1019. (American Academy of Religion Academy Ser.). pap. write for info. o.s.i. (ISBN 0-89130-477-0). Scholars Pr CA.

Makarim, Sami N., ed. see Al-Fawaris, Abu.

Makaroff, Dmitri, jt. auth. see Duff, Charles.

Makdisi, George. Islam & the Medieval West: Aspects of Intercultural Relations. Semaan, Khalil I., ed. LC 79-18678. 1979. 39.50x (ISBN 0-87395-409-2); pap. 14.95x (ISBN 0-87395-455-6). State U NY Pr.

Makepeace, Christopher. Ephemera. 1983. write for info. (ISBN 0-566-03439-5, 06086-0, Pub. by Gower Pub Co England). Lexington Bks.

Makepeace, John, et al. The Art of Making Furniture. LC 80-52623. (Illus.). 192p. 1981. 21.95 (ISBN 0-8069-5426-4); lib. bdg. 19.99 o.p. (ISBN 0-8069-5427-2). Sterling.

Makepeace, LeRoy M. Sherman Thatcher & His School. 1941. text ed. 49.50x (ISBN 0-686-83739-8). Elliots Bks.

Maker, C. June. Teaching Models in Education of the Gifted. LC 82-1692. 475p. 1982. 30.50 (ISBN 0-89443-682-1). Aspen Systems.

Maker, Janet & Lenier, Minnette. College Reading. 416p. 1982. pap. text ed. 12.95x (ISBN 0-534-01092-X). Wadsworth Pub.

Maker, Janet, jt. auth. see Lenier, Minette.

Maker, Janet, jt. auth. see Lenier, Minnette.

Makhijani, Arjun & Poole, Alan. Energy & Agriculture in the Third World. LC 75-4777. (Ford Foundation Energy Pology Project Ser.). 168p. cancelled prof ref (ISBN 0-88410-341-2); pap. text ed. cancelled (ISBN 0-88410-342-0). Ballinger Pub.

Makhlis, F. A. Radiation Physics & Chemistry of Polymers. LC 74-13587. 287p. 1975. 54.95 o.s.i. (ISBN 0-470-56537-3). Halsted Pr.

Maki, Alan W., jt. ed. see Dickson, Kenneth L.

Maki, Daniel & Thompson, Maynard. Finite Mathematics. 2nd ed. (Illus.). 544p. 1983. text ed. 22.95 (ISBN 0-07-039747-3); PNS instr's manual (ISBN 0-07-039748-1). McGraw.

--Mathematical Models & Applications: With Emphasis on the Social, Life, & Management Sciences. (Illus.). 464p. 1973. ref. ed. 28.95 (ISBN 0-13-561670-0). P-H.

Maki, Daniel P. & Thompson, Maynard. Finite Mathematics. (Illus.). 1978. text ed. 19.95 (ISBN 0-07-039745-7, C); instr's manual 15.00 (ISBN 0-07-039746-5). McGraw.

Makielski, S. J., Jr. Pressure Politics in America. LC 80-5529. 372p. 1980. lib. bdg. 23.50 (ISBN 0-8191-1129-5); pap. 13.00 (ISBN 0-8191-1130-9). U Pr of Amer.

Makin, Peter. Provence & Pound. LC 77-76186. 1979. 37.50x (ISBN 0-520-03488-0). U of Cal Pr.

Makinson, Randell L. Greene & Greene: Architecture As a Fine Art. LC 76-57792. (Illus.). 1977. 29.95 (ISBN 0-87905-023-3); pap. 0.19.95 (ISBN 0-87905-126-4). Peregrine Smith.

--Greene & Greene: Furniture & Related Designs. LC 76-57792. (Illus.). 1978. 29.95 o.p. (ISBN 0-87905-060-8); pap. 19.95 o.p. (ISBN 0-87905-125-6). Peregrine Smith.

Makinster, Genie. Ravensloch: Gothic Mystery. (Illus.). 141p. (Orig.). 1982. pap. 1.95 (ISBN 0-9608742-0-8). Gemak Pub.

Makita, Akira & Handa, Shizuo, eds. New Vistas in Glycolipid Research. (Advances in Experimental Medicine & Biology Ser.: Vol. 152). 504p. 1982. 62.50x (ISBN 0-306-41108-3, Plenum Pr). Plenum Pub.

Makkai, Adam, ed. see Boetner, Maxine & Gates, John E.

Makkai, Adam, ed. see Gate, John E. & Gates, John E.

Makki, M. S. Medina, Saudi Arabia: A Geographic Analysis of the City & the Region. 1981. 75.00x o.p. (ISBN 0-86127-301-X, Pub. by Avebury Pub England). State Mutual Bk.

Maklad, Nabil F. Ultrasonic Diagnosis of Ectopic Pregnancy. 260p. (Orig.). 1983. 27.50 (ISBN 0-87527-222-3). Green.

Maklin, Ruth, jt. auth. see Gorovitz, Sam.

Mako, William P. U. S. Ground Forces & the Defense of Central Europe. LC 82-45977. (Studies in Defense Policy). 200p. 1983. 22.95; pap. 8.95 (ISBN 0-8157-5443-4). Brookings.

Makogon, Yuri F. Hydrates of Natural Gas. Cieslewicz, W. J., tr. from Russian. 237p. 1981. 37.95x (ISBN 0-87814-165-0). Pennwell Books Division.

Makovsky, A., jt. auth. see Fleichits, Ye.

Makower, Joel. Office Hazards: How Your Job Can Make You Sick. 1982. pap. 6.95 o.p. (ISBN 0-686-34586-X). Caroline Hse.

Makowski, Pete, jt. auth. see Halfin, Ross.

Makowsky, Veronica A., ed. see Blackmur, R. P.

Makrakis, Apostolos, jt. auth. see Stratman, Chrysostomos H.

Makram-Ebeid, S. & Tuck, B., eds. Semi-Insulating Three-Four Materials: Evian 1982. 420p. 1982. text ed. 62.95x (ISBN 0-906812-22-4). Birkhauser.

Makridakis, Spyros & Wheelwright, Steven C. Forecasting: Methods & Applications. LC 77-18806. (Management & Administration Ser.). 1978. 39.95 (ISBN 0-471-93770-3). Wiley.

Makridakis, Spyros & Wheelwright, Steven C., eds. The Handbook of Forecasting: A Managers Guide. LC 81-16269. 602p. 1982. 49.95 (ISBN 0-471-08435-2, Pub. by Wiley-Interscience). Wiley.

Maksimovic, Desanka. Shaggy Little Dog. LC 82-24180. (Illus.). 24p. (gr. 3-6). PLB 11.95 (ISBN 0-571-12521-2). Faber & Faber.

Maksymowych, R. Analysis of Leaf Development. LC 72-83585. (Developmental & Cell Biology Monographs: No. 1). (Illus.). 112p. 1973. 37.50 (ISBN 0-521-20017-2). Cambridge U Pr.

Mal, M. K., jt. auth. see Hausner, H. H.

Malabre, Alfred, Jr. Understanding the Economy: For People Who Can't Stand Economics. 1977. pap. 3.50 (ISBN 0-451-62140-9, ME2140, Ment). NAL.

Malabre, Alfred L., Jr. America's Dilemma: Jobs vs. Prices. LC 78-18809. 1978. 9.95 o.p. (ISBN 0-396-07586-X). Dodd.

--Investing for Profit in the Eighties: The Business Cycle System. LC 80-2971. (Illus.). 192p. 1982. 15.95 (ISBN 0-385-17047-5). Doubleday.

Malacara, D. Optical Shop Testing. 523p. 1978. 47.50 (ISBN 0-471-01973-9, Pub. by Wiley-Interscience). Wiley.

Malaga, Rose C. Cesar Visits the Floating Island of the Uros. LC 81-90139. (Illus.). 32p. (gr. 4-6). 1981. 7.95 (ISBN 0-939642-00-X). Malaga.

Malagalada, J. R. & Holtermuller, K. H., eds. Advances in Ulcer Disease. (International Congress Ser.: No. 537). 1981. 119.25 (ISBN 0-444-90192-2). Elsevier.

Malagoda, Kirsiri. Buddhism in Sinhalese Society, 1750-1900: A Study of Religious Revival & Change. LC 74-22966. 1976. 40.00x (ISBN 0-520-02873-2). U of Cal Pr.

Malakoff, Anna & Powdrrell, Fances D. Minkapee. LC 81-86202. (Illus.). 88p. 1983. 11.95 (ISBN 0-86666-072-0). GWP.

Malamed, Stanley F. Handbook of Local Anesthesia. LC 80-17546. (Illus.). 249p. 1980. pap. text ed. 22.95 (ISBN 0-8016-3072-X). Mosby.

--Handbook of Medical Emergencies in the Dental Office. 2nd ed. LC 81-18687. (Illus.). 408p. 1982. pap. text ed. 25.95 (ISBN 0-8016-3075-4). Mosby.

Malamud, Bernard. The Magic Barrel. 214p. 1958. 14.95 (ISBN 0-374-19576-5); pap. 6.25 (ISBN 0-374-50412-1). FS&G.

Malamud, Nathan & Hirano, Asao. Atlas of Neuropathology. (Illus.). 1975. 90.00x (ISBN 0-520-02221-1). U of Cal Pr.

Malan, David H. Individual Psychotherapy & the Science of Psychodynamics. LC 78-40691. (Postgraduate Psychiatic Ser.). 1979. 24.95 (ISBN 0-407-00088-7). Butterworth.

Maland, Charles J. Frank Capra. (Filmmakers Ser.). 1980. lib. bdg. 11.95 (ISBN 0-8057-9273-2, Twayne). G K Hall.

Malandro, Loretta A. & Barker, Larry L. Nonverbal Communication. 400p. Date not set. pap. text ed. 13.95 (ISBN 0-201-05336-5). A-W.

Malanga, Gerald. This Will Kill That. 160p. 1983. pap. 8.50 (ISBN 0-87685-495-1); 25.00 (ISBN 0-87685-496-X). Black Sparrow.

Malantschuk, Gregor. The Controversial Kierkegaard. McKinnon, Alastair, ed. Hong, Howard V. & Hong, Edna H., trs. (The Kierkegard Monograph). 82p. 1980. pap. text ed. 9.00x (ISBN 0-88920-093-9, Pub. by Wilfrid Laurier U Pr Canada). Humanities.

Malaparte, Curzio. Kaputt. Foligno, Cesare, tr. from Italian. LC 82-61436. 407p. 1982. 16.95 (ISBN 0-910395-00-4); pap. 9.50 (ISBN 0-910395-01-2). Marlboro Pr.

Malarkey, Louise, jt. auth. see McMorrow, Ellen.

Malarkey, Louise M., jt. auth. see McMorrow, Mary E.

Malasanos, Lois. Health Assessment. 2nd ed. LC 80-27518. (Illus.). 723p. 1981. text ed. 31.95 (ISBN 0-8016-3073-8). Mosby.

Malaschak, Dolores. Run in the Morning. 1969. 4.00 o.p. (ISBN 0-8233-0127-3). Golden Quill.

Malatesha, Rattihalli N. Neuropsychology & Cognition. 1982. lib. bdg. 135.00 (ISBN 90-247-2752-9, Pub. by Martinus Nijhoff Netherlands). Kluwer Boston.

Malatesta, Edward. The Spirit of God in Christian Life. LC 77-74589. 160p. 1977. pap. 1.95 o.p. (ISBN 0-8091-2033-X). Paulist Pr.

Malatesta, Errico. Malatesta: Life & Ideas. Richards, Vernon, ed. 309p. 1965. pap. 4.00 (ISBN 0-900384-15-8). Left Bank.

Malaurie, Jean. The Last Kings of Thule: With the Polar Eskimos As They Face Their Destiny. Foulke, Adrienne, tr. (Illus.). 608p. 1982. 25.75 (ISBN 0-525-03052-2, 02501-740). Dutton.

Malcolm, A. Treatise of Musick, Speculative, Practical & Historical. LC 69-16676. (Music Ser). 1970. Repr. of 1721 ed. lib. bdg. 59.50 (ISBN 0-306-71099-4). Da Capo.

Malcolm, Andrew. The Tyranny of the Group. (Quality Paperback: No. 294). 190p. (Orig.). 1975. pap. 3.95 (ISBN 0-8226-0294-6). Littlefield.

Malcolm, Douglas R., Jr. Fundamentals of Electronics. 1982. text ed. 24.95x (ISBN 0-534-01179-9). Breton Pubs.

Malcolm, Janet. Diana & Nikon: Essays on the Aesthetic of Photography. LC 78-74547. (Illus.). 176p. 1981. pap. 7.95 (ISBN 0-87923-387-7). Godine.

Malcolm, Margaret. Not Less Than All, The Lonely Road, Cherish the Wayward Heart. (Harlequin Romance Ser.). 192p. 1983. pap. 1.75 (ISBN 0-373-20072-2). Harlequin Bks.

Malcolm, Norman & Von Wright, Georg H. Ludwig Wittgenstein: A Memoir. 1967. pap. 5.95 (ISBN 0-19-500282-2, 218, GB). Oxford U Pr.

Malcolmson, Reginald & Wachsmann, Konrad, eds. Visionary Projects for Buildings & Cities. LC 74-79132. (Illus.). 1974. pap. 2.00 (ISBN 0-88397-071-6, Pub. by Intl Exhibit Foun). C E Tuttle.

Malcolmson, Robert W. Life & Labor in England Seventeen Hundred to Seventeen Eighty. LC 81-9379. 208p. 1982. 22.50x (ISBN 0-312-48390-2). St Martin.

--Popular Recreations in English Society: Seventeen Hundred to Eighteen Fifty. LC 72-91958. (Illus.). 1980. pap. 14.95 (ISBN 0-521-29595-5). Cambridge U Pr.

--Popular Recreations in English Society, 1700-1850. LC 72-91958. (Illus.). 300p. 1973. 34.50 (ISBN 0-521-20147-0). Cambridge U Pr.

Malcomson, William L. How to Survive in the Ministry. 88p. 1982. pap. 5.95 (ISBN 0-8170-0964-7). Judson.

Maldonado, Luis & Power, David, eds. Symbol & Art in Worship. (Concilium Ser.: Vol. 132). 128p. (Orig.). 1980. pap. 5.95 (ISBN 0-8164-2274-5). Seabury.

Maldonado, Luis A. Cuando Llora un Guerrillero. 89p. 1981. pap. 1.95 (ISBN 0-311-37014-4). Casa Bautista.

Maleady, Antoinette O. Index to Record & Tape Reviews: A Classical Music Buying Guide, 1981. LC 72-3355. 57.50x (ISBN 0-917600-07-X). Chulainn Press.

Malebranche, Nicolas. Entretiens sur la Metaphysique: Dialogues on Metaphysics. Doney, Willis, tr. from Fr. (Janus Ser.). 359p. 1980. 20.00 (ISBN 0-913870-57-9). Abaris Bks.

Malecki & Donaldson. Commercial Liability Risk Management & Insurance, 2 vols. 1978. 18.00 ea. o.p. IIA.

Malecki, Donald S. & Donaldson, James H. Commercial Liability Risk Management & Insurance, 2 Vols. LC 78-67497. 978p. Date not set. text ed. 18.00 (ISBN 0-686-82665-5). Am Inst Property.

Maleev, Vladimir L. Diesel Engine Operation & Maintenance. 1954. text ed. 26.95 (ISBN 0-07-039770-8, G). McGraw.

Malehorn, Hal. K to Three Teacher's Classroom Almanac: A Treasury of Learning Activities & Games. LC 80-20422. 325p. 1981. 16.50 (ISBN 0-13-514422-1, Parker). P-H.

--Open to Change: Options for Teaching Self-Directed Learners. LC 77-28653. 1978. text ed. 10.95x (ISBN 0-673-16407-1). Scott F.

Malek, James S. & Backscheider, Paula R., eds. The Plays of John Home. LC 78-66641. (Eighteenth-Century English Drama Ser.: Vol. 22). 1980. lib. bdg. 50.00 o.s.i. (ISBN 0-8240-3596-8). Garland Pub.

Malek, Jaromir, jt. auth. see Baines, John.

Malek, P. & Bartos, V., eds. Lymphology: Proceedings of the 6th International Conference. LC 78-24681. (Illus.). 532p. 1979. text ed. 49.50 o.p. (ISBN 0-88416-280-X). Wright-PSG.

Maleka, Leo, jt. auth. see Moore, John B.

Malekin, Peter. Liberty & Love: English Literature & Society, 1640-88. 224p. 1981. 25.00x (ISBN 0-312-48358-9). St Martin.

Maler, George J., jt. auth. see Pearson, S. Ivar.

Malerstein, Abraham J. & Ahern, Mary. A Piagetian Model of Character Structure. LC 81-6305. 252p. 1982. 26.95 (ISBN 0-89885-002-9). Human Sci Pr.

Malet, Marianne D. Violet; or the Danseuse: A Portraiture of the Human Passions & Character, 2 vols. in 1. LC 79-8167. Date not set. Repr. of 1836 ed. 44.50 (ISBN 0-404-62018-3). AMS Pr.

Maletsky, Evan, jt. auth. see Sobel, Max.

Malewicki, Douglas J. How to Build the One Hundred Fifty-Five MPG at 55 MPH California Commuter. 2nd ed. 50p. 1982. pap. 15.00 (ISBN 0-941730-00-X); pap. text ed. 15.00 (ISBN 0-941730-01-8). Aero Vis.

Maley, A. & Duff, A. Drama Techniques in Language Learning. (English Language Learning Ser.). 1978. limp bdg 8.95x (ISBN 0-521-21877-2). Cambridge U Pr.

Maley, Alan & Duff, Alan. Drama Techniques in Language Learning: A Resource Book of Communication Activities for Language Teachers. (Cambridge Handbooks for Language Teachers Ser.). (Illus.). 240p. 1983. 19.95 (ISBN 0-521-24907-4); pap. 8.95 (ISBN 0-521-28868-1). Cambridge U Pr.

Malgonkar, Manohar. The Sea Hawk. (Orient Paperbacks Ser.). 293p. 1980. pap. 4.95 (ISBN 0-86578-069-2); 9.95 (ISBN 0-86578-136-2). Ind-US Inc.

Malgonkar, Monohar. A Bend in the Ganges. 382p. 1981. Repr. of 1975 ed. pap. 4.00 (ISBN 0-88253-772-5). Ind-US Inc.

Malhotra, S. L. Gandhi: An Experiment with Communal Politics. LC 75-903635. 1975. 10.00x o.p. (ISBN 0-88386-192-5). South Asia Bks.

Malhotra, V. M., ed. Developments in the Use of Superplasticizers. LC 81-65667. (SP-68). 572p. (Orig.). 1981. pap. 38.95 (ISBN 0-686-95243-X). ACI.

Mali, Millicent S. Madame Campan: Educator of Women, Confidante of Queens. LC 78-65428. 1978. pap. text ed. 10.50 (ISBN 0-8191-0662-3). U Pr of Amer.

Mali, Paul. How to Manage by Objectives: A Short Course for Managers. LC 75-27387. (Wiley Professional Development Programs, Business Administration Ser.). 288p. 1975. text ed. 55.95 (ISBN 0-471-56574-1, Pub. by Wiley-Interscience). Wiley.

--Improving Total Productivity: MBO Strategies for Business, Government & Not-for-Profit Organizations. LC 77-26191. 1978. 36.95 (ISBN 0-471-03404-5, Pub. by Wiley-Interscience). Wiley.

--Management Handbook Operating Guidelines & Techniques & Practices. LC 80-20514. 1522p. 1981. 59.50 (ISBN 0-471-05263-9). Wiley.

--Managing by Objectives: An Operating Guide to Faster & More Profitable Results. LC 72-1803. (Illus.). 314p. 1972. 36.95 (ISBN 0-471-56575-X, Pub. by Wiley-Interscience). Wiley.

Malian, Ida, jt. auth. see Charles, C. M.

Malibran, Maria. Album Lyrique & Dernieres Pensees. (Women Composers Ser.: No. 14). 62p. 1983. Repr. of 1831 ed. lib. bdg. 22.50 (ISBN 0-306-76194-7). Da Capo.

Malick, Jeffrey B., et al, eds. Anxiolytics: Neurochemical, Behavioral, & Clinical Perspectives. (Central Nervous System Pharmacology Ser.: Vol. 2). 1982. text ed. write for info. (ISBN 0-89004-731-6). Raven.

Malik, Amita. India Watching: The Media Game. 1978. 9.50x o.p. (ISBN 0-8364-0167-0). South Asia Bks.

Malik, Charles. The Two Tasks. 37p. 1980. pap. 1.95 (ISBN 0-89107-212-8). Crossway Bks.

Malik, Imam & Din, M. R. Muwata. 24.95 (ISBN 0-686-83588-3). Kazi Pubns.

Malik, Rex, jt. auth. see Fedida, Sam.

Malik, Rex, ed. Future Imperfect: Science Fact & Science Fiction. 219p. 1982. 25.00 (ISBN 0-686-42971-0). F Pinter Pubs.

Malik, S. C. Principles of Real Analysis. LC 82-20051. 1982. 19.95x (ISBN 0-470-27369-0). Halsted Pr.

Malik, S. C., ed. Dissent, Protest & Reform in Indian Civilization. 1977. 18.50x o.p. (ISBN 0-8364-0104-2). South Asia Bks.

Malik, Suneila. Social Integration of Scheduled Castes. 1979. 12.50x o.p. (ISBN 0-8364-0359-2). South Asia Bks.

Malik, Z. I. Democracy in Islam. 1.95 (ISBN 0-686-83891-2). Kazi Pubns.

Malik, Zahiruddin. A Mughal Statesman of the Eighteenth Century: Khan-I-Dauran Mir Bashshi of Mumammad Shah 1719-1739. 120p. 1973. 2.75x o.p. (ISBN 0-210-40544-9). Asia.

Malin, Edward. A World of Faces: Masks of the Northwest Coast Indians. 158p. 1978. write for info. (ISBN 0-917304-03-9); pap. 10.95 (ISBN 0-917304-05-5). Timber.

Malin, Irving. Isaac Bashevis Singer. LC 73-185350. (Literature and Life Ser.). 128p. 1972. 11.95 (ISBN 0-8044-2588-4). Ungar.

Malina, Frank J., ed. Kinetic Art: Selections from the Journal Leonardo. (Illus.). 1974. pap. 6.50 o.p. (ISBN 0-486-21284-X). Dover.

Malina, Robert M. & Roche, Alex F., eds. Manual of Physical Status & Performance in Childhood, Vol. I. 1456p. 1983. 195.00x (ISBN 0-306-41136-9, Plenum Pr). Plenum Pub.

--Manual of Physical Status & Performance in Childhood, Vol. II. 814p. 1983. 115.00x (ISBN 0-306-41137-7, Plenum Pr). Plenum Pub.

Malinchak, Alan A. Crime & Gerontology. (Ser. in Criminal Justice). (Illus.). 1980. text ed. 24.95 (ISBN 0-13-192815-5); pap. text ed. 19.95 (ISBN 0-13-192807-4). P-H.

Malinconico, S. Michael & Fasana, Paul. The Future of the Catalog: The Library's Choices. LC 79-16619. (Professional Librarian Ser.). 1979. text ed. 24.50x softcover (ISBN 0-914236-32-6). Knowledge Indus.

Maling, Arthur. Bent Man. 1975. Repr. lib. bdg. 12.50 o.p. (ISBN 0-8161-6361-8, Large Print Bks). G K Hall.

--From Thunder Bay. LC 80-8397. 1981. 12.45i (ISBN 0-06-014832-2, HarpT). Har-Row.

--Lucky Devil. LC 77-11782. 1979. pap. 1.95i o.p. (ISBN 0-06-080482-3, P 482, PL). Har-Row.

--Ripoff. LC 75-25091. 1979. pap. 1.95i o.p. (ISBN 0-06-080483-1, P 483, PL). Har-Row.

--Schroeder's Game. LC 76-5547. 1979. pap. 1.95i o.p. (ISBN 0-06-080484-X, P 484, PL). Har-Row.

--A Taste of Treason. LC 82-48580. 256p. 1983. 14.50 (ISBN 0-06-015128-5, HarpT). Har-Row.

Malinowski, B. Crime & Punishment in Primitive Societies. (A Science of Man Library Book). (Illus.). 131p. 1983. Repr. of 1926 ed. 98.75 (ISBN 0-89901-080-6). Found Class Reprints.

Malinowski, Bronislaw. Crime & Custom in Savage Society. (Quality Paperback: No. 210). 1976. pap. 3.95 (ISBN 0-8226-0210-5). Littlefield.

--The Dynamics of Culture Change. Kaberry, Phyllis M., ed. LC 75-14599. 171p. 1976. Repr. of 1961 ed. lib. bdg. 18.25x (ISBN 0-8371-8216-6, MADCC). Greenwood.

--Malinowski in Mexico: The Economics of a Mexican Market System. Drucker-Brown, Susan & De La Fuente, Julio, eds. (International Library of Anthropology). 260p. 1982. 25.00 (ISBN 0-7100-9197-4). Routledge & Kegan.

Malinowski, Edmund R. & Howery, Darryl G. Factor Analysis in Chemistry. LC 79-27081. 1980. 33.95 (ISBN 0-471-05881-5, Pub. by Wiley Interscience). Wiley.

Malinowski, Janet S. & DeLoach, Carolyn P. Nursing Care of the Labor Patient. (Illus.). 350p. 1983. pap. text ed. 12.95 (ISBN 0-8036-5802-8, 5802-8). Davis Co.

Malinowski, Ruth K. Miracle Cuisine Minceur. LC 77-73082. 144p. 1977. pap. 3.95 o.s.i. (ISBN 0-89104-080-3, A & W Visual Library). A & W Pubs.

Malinowski, Stanley B. & Melodia, Thomas V. The Easter Bunny Comes to Forgottenville. 48p. (gr. 3-12). 1983. write for info (ISBN 0-941316-02-5). TSM Prods.

Malinowsky, H. Robert & Richardson, Jeanne M. Science & Engineering Literature: A Guide to Reference Sources. 3rd ed. LC 80-21290. (Library Science Text Ser.). 342p. 1980. lib. bdg. 33.00x (ISBN 0-87287-230-0); pap. text ed. 21.00 (ISBN 0-87287-245-9). Libs Unl.

Malinski, M. & Muller, Alois, eds. Pope John Paul II: The Life of Karol Wojtyla. 278p. 1981. 12.95 (ISBN 0-686-95524-2). Crossroad NY.

Malinski, Mieczyslaw. Joyful, Sorrowful, Glorious Reflections on Life & the Rosary. (Illus.). 1979. pap. 1.95 o.p. (ISBN 0-89570-160-X, CP-313, Jubilee). Claretian Pubns.

Malinvaud, A. Statistical Methods in Econometrics. 3rd ed. (Studies in Mathematical & Managerial Economics Ser.: Vol. 6). 1980. 51.00 (ISBN 0-444-85473-8). Elsevier.

Malinvaud, E. Lectures on Microeconomic Theory. (Advanced Textbooks on Economics Ser: Vol. 2). 1972. text ed. 32.50 (ISBN 0-444-10389-9, North-Holland); pap. 18.00 (ISBN 0-7204-3092-5). Elsevier.

--Profitability & Unemployment. LC 79-21472. 1980. 16.95 (ISBN 0-521-22999-5). Cambridge U Pr.

Malinvaud, E. & Bacharach, M. O., eds. Activity Analysis. (International Economic Assn. Ser). 1967. 25.00 (ISBN 0-312-00385-4). St Martin.

Malits, Elena. The Solitary Explorer: Thomas Merton's Transforming Journey. LC 80-7744. 192p. (Orig.). 1980. pap. 6.95i o.p. (ISBN 0-06-065411-2, RD 331, HarpR). Har-Row.

Maliyamkono, T. L. & Ishumi, A. G. Higher Education & Development in Eastern Africa. (Eastern Africa Universities Research Project Ser.). 336p. 1982. text ed. 40.00x (ISBN 0-435-89580-X). Heinemann Ed.

--Training & Productivity in Eastern Africa. (Eastern African Universities Research Project Ser.). 400p. 1982. text ed. 60.00x (ISBN 0-435-89582-6). Heinemann Ed.

Malkemes, Fred & Pires, Deborah S. Looking at English, Bk. III. (Illus.). 288p. 1983. pap. text ed. 10.95 (ISBN 0-13-540435-5). P-H.

--Looking at English: An ESL Text-Workbook for Beginners, Bk. 1. (English As a Second Language Ser.). (Illus.). 256p. 1981. pap. text ed. 10.95 (ISBN 0-13-540401-0). P-H.

Malkevitch, Joseph & Meyer, Walter. Graphs, Models & Finite Mathematics. (Illus.). 480p. 1974. ref. ed. 24.95 (ISBN 0-13-363465-5). P-H.

Malkiel, Burton G. A Random Walk Down Wall Street. rev. ed. (Illus.). 1973. 13.95 (ISBN 0-393-05500-0); pap. 5.95x (ISBN 0-393-09246-1). Norton.

--A Random Walk Down Wall Street. 2nd ed. 1981. 7.95x (ISBN 0-393-95117-0). Norton.

--Winning Investment Strategies: The Inflation-Beater's Investment Guide. New ed. 192p. 1982. pap. 4.95 (ISBN 0-393-30031-5). Norton.

Malkiel, Burton G. & Quandt, Richard E. Strategies & Rational Decisions in the Securities Options Market. 1969. 15.00x o.p. (ISBN 0-262-13056-4); pap. 4.95 (ISBN 0-262-63051-6). MIT Pr.

Malkiel, Burton G., jt. auth. see Cragg, John G.

Malkiel, Yakov. From Particular to General Linguistics: Selected Essays 1965-1978. (Studies in Language Companion: No. 3). 650p. 1983. 59.00 (ISBN 90-272-3002-1). Benjamins North Am.

Malkiel, Yakov, jt. auth. see Lehmann, Winfred P.

Malkin, Carole. The Journeys of David Toback. LC 80-22962. 224p. (Orig.). 1982. 10.95 (ISBN 0-8052-3756-9); pap. 6.95 (ISBN 0-8052-0700-7). Schocken.

Mall, David. In Good Conscience: Abortion & Moral Necessity. xii, 212p. 1982. 18.50 (ISBN 0-9608410-1-6); pap. 8.50 (ISBN 0-9608410-0-8). Kairos Bks.

Mall, E. Jane. Abingdon Manual of Installation Services. 80p. (Orig.). 1983. pap. 4.95 (ISBN 0-687-00367-9). Abingdon.

--How to Become Wealthy Publishing a Newsletter. 110p. 1983. pap. 17.50 (ISBN 0-914306-83-9). Intl Wealth.

Mall, Jeanette, jt. ed. see Kelman, Barbara.

Mallakh, Ragaei E., jt. auth. see Waterbury, John.

Mallakh, Ragaei El see El Mallakh, Ragaei.

Mallakh, Ragaei El, jt. ed. see El Mallakh, Dorthea.

Mallakh, Ragaei E. & El Mallakh, Ragael E., eds. Saudi Arabia: Energy, Developmental Planning, & Industrialization. LC 81-47746. 224p. 1982. 23.95 (ISBN 0-669-04801-1). Lexington Bks.

Mallalieu, J. P. Sporting Days. 9.50 (ISBN 0-392-06949-0, SpS). Sportshelf.

Mallan, John T., jt. auth. see Welton, David A.

Mallaris, A. G. Stochastic Methods in Economics & Finance. (Advanced Textbooks in Economics: Vol. 17). 1982. 38.50 (ISBN 0-444-86201-3). Elsevier.

Mallas, J. H. & Kreimer, E. The Messier Album. LC 79-16714. (Illus.). 1979. 15.95 (ISBN 0-521-23015-2). Cambridge U Pr.

Mallea, Eduardo. History of an Argentine Passion. Miller, Yvette E., ed. Litchblau, Myron, tr. 184p. 1982. pap. 10.95 (ISBN 0-935480-10-2). Lat Am Lit Rev Pr.

Mallen, Bruce. Principles of Marketing Channel Management: Interorganizational Distribution Design & Relations. LC 76-27923. (Illus.). 384p. 1977. 25.95 (ISBN 0-669-00985-7). Lexington Bks.

Mallen, Bruce E. The Marketing Channel: A Conceptual Viewpoint. LC 67-17344. 308p. 1967. 13.50 (ISBN 0-471-56580-6, Pub. by Wiley). Krieger.

Maller, Allen S. God, Sex & Kabbalah. LC 82-12318. (Orig.). 1983. pap. write for info. (ISBN 0-86628-019-7). Ridgefield Pub.

--Jewish Time Machine. LC 82-10207. 1982. write for info. (ISBN 0-86628-030-8). Ridgefield Pub.

Mallery, Garrick. Picture-Writing of the American Indians, 2 vols. (Illus.). 1972. pap. 8.50 (ISBN 0-686-85908-1); Vol. 1. pap. (ISBN 0-486-22842-8); Vol. 2. pap. 8.50 (ISBN 0-486-22843-6). Dover.

Mallery, Mary S. & DeVore, Ralph E. Sign System for Libraries. LC 82-11612. 40p. 1982. pap. text ed. 5.00 (ISBN 0-8389-0377-0). ALA.

Mallery, Paul. The Complete Handbook of Model Railroad Operations. (Illus.). 1978. 9.95 (ISBN 0-8306-9894-9); pap. 6.95 o.p. (ISBN 0-8306-1021-9, 1021). TAB Bks.

Malleson, George B. Battlefields of Germany, from the Outbreak of the Thirty-Years' War. Repr. of 1884 ed. lib. bdg. 17.75x (ISBN 0-8371-5017-5, MABG). Greenwood.

Mallet, J. Fire Engines of the World. (Illus.). 224p. 1982. 25.95 (ISBN 0-86710-051-6). Edns Vilo.

Mallet Du Pan, Jacques. Considerations on the Nature of the French Revolution & on the Causes Which Prolong Its Duration. LC 74-13491. xxii, 114p. 1975. Repr. of 1793 ed. 17.50x (ISBN 0-86527-032-5). Fertig.

Mallett, Jerry J. Library Skills Activity Puzzles Series, 5 bks. Incl. Book Bafflers (ISBN 0-87628-188-9); Dictionary Puzzlers (ISBN 0-87628-273-7); Lively Locators (ISBN 0-87628-539-6); Reading Incentives (ISBN 0-87628-719-4); Resource Rousers (ISBN 0-87628-741-0). 64p. (gr. 2-6). 1982. pap. 6.95 ea. (ISBN 0-686-81680-3). Ctr Appl Res.

Mallett, Richard. University of Maine at Farmington. LC 74-20199. (Illus.). 304p. 1975. 10.95 (ISBN 0-87027-157-1); pap. 6.95 (ISBN 0-87027-158-X). Cumberland Pr.

Mallett, Sandy. A Year with New England's Birds: A Guide to Twenty-Five Field Trips. LC 77-26352. (Illus.). 120p. 1978. 10.00 o.p. (ISBN 0-912274-91-3); pap. 2.95 (ISBN 0-912274-87-5). Backcountry Pubns.

Mallette, M. Frank, et al. Introductory Biochemistry. LC 78-23388. 824p. 1979. Repr. of 1971 ed. lib. bdg. 27.50 (ISBN 0-88275-807-1). Krieger.

Mallick. Case Presentations: In Renal Medicine. 1982. text ed. write for info (ISBN 0-407-00234-0). Butterworth.

Mallick, K., jt. auth. see Patra, H. P.

Mallik, David & Moss, Peter, eds. New Essays in the Teaching of Literature. 1982p. (Orig.). pap. text ed. 10.25 (ISBN 0-909955-38-7). Boynton Cook Pubs.

Mallin, Jay. Fulgencia Batista, Ousted Cuban Dictator. Rahmas, D. Steve, ed. (Outstanding Personalities Ser.: No. 70). 32p. (Orig.). (gr. 7-12). 1974. lib. bdg. 2.95 incl. catalog cards (ISBN 0-87157-570-1); pap. 1.95 vinyl laminated covers (ISBN 0-87157-070-X). SamHar Pr.

--General Vo Nguyen Giap, North Vietnamese Military Leader. Rahmas, D. Steve, ed. LC 73-87629. (Outstanding Personalities Ser.: No. 66). 32p. (Orig.). (gr. 7-12). 1973. lib. bdg. 2.95 incl. catalog cards (ISBN 0-87157-566-3); pap. 1.95 vinyl laminated covers (ISBN 0-87157-066-1). SamHar Pr.

--The Great Managua Earthquake. Rahmas, D. Steve, ed. (Events of Our Times Ser.: No. 14). 32p. (Orig.). (gr. 7-12). 1974. lib. bdg. 2.95 incl. catalog cards (ISBN 0-87157-715-1); pap. 1.95 vinyl laminated covers (ISBN 0-87157-215-X). SamHar Pr.

Mallin, Jay, ed. Terror & Urban Guerillas: A Study of Tactics & Documents. LC 79-163842. 1971. 10.95x (ISBN 0-87024-223-7). U of Miami Pr.

Mallinson, G. & Brake, B. J. Language Typology. (North Holland Linguistic Ser.: Vol. 46). 1981. 53.25 (ISBN 0-444-86311-7). Elsevier.

Mallinson, G. G. A Summary of Research in Science Education, 1975. (ERIC Bibliography Ser.). 1977. 21.95 o.s.i. (ISBN 0-471-04359-1). Wiley.

Mallinson, J. H. Chemical Plant Design with Reinforced Plastics. 1969. 49.50 o.p. (ISBN 0-07-039793-7, P&RB). McGraw.

Mallis, A. George, jt. auth. see VanAllen, Leroy C.

Mallison, Ruth. Education As Therapy: Suggestions for Work with Neurologically Impaired Children. LC 68-57925. (Illus., Orig.). 1968. pap. 6.50x o.p. (ISBN 0-87562-014-0). Spec Child.

Malloch, Theodore R. Beyond Reductionism. 290p. 1983. text ed. 24.50x (ISBN 0-8290-1292-3). Irvington.

Malloch, Theodore R., jt. ed. see Harper, William A.

Mallock, W. H. A Romance of the Nineteenth Century, 1881. LC 75-1528. (Victorian Fiction Ser.). 1975. lib. bdg. 60.00 o.s.i. (ISBN 0-8240-1600-9). Garland Pub.

Mallock, W. H. see Gould, Frederick J.

Mallon, Thomas. Edmund Blunden. (English Authors Ser.). 158p. 1983. lib. bdg. 17.95 (ISBN 0-8057-6829-7, Twayne). G K Hall.

Mallon, V. M. First Gear. (Illus.). 1979. pap. text ed. 6.50x o.p. (ISBN 0-435-42240-5). Heinemann Ed.

Mallone, George, et al. Those Controversial Gifts. 168p. (Orig.). 1983. pap. 4.95 (ISBN 0-87784-823-8). Inter-Varsity.

Mallory, Bob F. & Cargo, David M. Physical Geology. (Illus.). 1979. text ed. 26.00 (ISBN 0-07-039795-3, C); instructor's manual 4.95 (ISBN 0-07-039796-1). McGraw.

Mallory, Charlotte. The Clinic. 352p. (Orig.). 1981. pap. 2.95 o.p. (ISBN 0-523-48017-2). Pinnacle Bks.

Mallory, Delores, jt. ed. see Hackel, Emanuel.

Mallory, Franklin B. Serial Numbers of U. S. Martial Arms. 96p. 1983. 10.00 (ISBN 0-9603306-1-5). Springfield Res Serv.

Mallory, George. Boswell the Biographer. LC 73-18423. 1971. Repr. of 1912 ed. 37.00x (ISBN 0-8103-3675-8). Gale.

Mallory, Michael. The Sienese Painter Paolo Di Giovanni Fei (c.1345-1411) LC 75-23802. (Outstanding Dissertations in the Fine Arts - 15th Century). (Illus.). 1976. lib. bdg. 41.00 o.s.i. (ISBN 0-8240-1997-0). Garland Pub.

Mallory, Thomas. King Arthur & His Knights of the Round Table. Lanier, Sidney & Pyle, Howard, eds. (Illus.). (gr. 4-6). 5.95 (ISBN 0-448-05816-2, G&D); deluxe ed. 8.95 (ISBN 0-448-06016-7). Putnam Pub Group.

Mallory, Walter H. Political Handbook of the World: Parliaments, Parties & Press as of January 1, 1931. 1931. text ed. 49.50x (ISBN 0-686-83706-1). Elliots Bks.

Mallowan, Agatha C. Come Tell Me How You Live. (Illus.). 226p. 1976. 8.95 o.p. (ISBN 0-396-07320-4). Dodd.

--Star Over Bethlehem. 1965. 4.95 o.p. (ISBN 0-396-05232-0). Dodd.

Malloy, Edward A. The Ethics of Law Enforcement & Criminal Punishment. LC 82-20015. 102p. (Orig.). 1983. lib. bdg. 16.75 (ISBN 0-8191-2842-2); pap. 6.75 (ISBN 0-8191-2843-0). U Pr of Amer.

--Homosexuality & the Christian Way of Life. LC 81-40385. 382p. (Orig.). 1981. lib. bdg. 25.75 (ISBN 0-8191-1794-3); pap. text ed. 14.00 (ISBN 0-8191-1795-1). U Pr of Amer.

Malloy, J. F., jt. auth. see Turner, W. C.

Malloy, Loncie L. The Wedding of Butternut Kisses & Fresco the Great. 1982. 4.95 (ISBN 0-533-05138-X). Vantage.

Malloy, Merrit. Things I Meant to Say to You When We Were Old. LC 76-26353. 144p. 1977. pap. 6.95 (ISBN 0-385-12326-4, Dolp). Doubleday.

--We Hardly See Each Other Any More. LC 82-452066. 208p. 1983. 12.95 (ISBN 0-385-15943-9); pap. 6.95 (ISBN 0-385-15944-7, Dolp). Doubleday.

Malloy, Ruth L. The Morrow Travel Guide To the Peoples' Republic of China. 2nd ed. 1982. pap. 12.50 (ISBN 0-686-94110-1). Morrow.

--Travel Guide to the People's Republic of China. LC 80-16428. (Illus.). 416p. 1980. 17.50 o.p. (ISBN 0-688-03690-2); pap. 10.95 o.p. (ISBN 0-688-08690-X). Morrow.

Malloy, Terry. Montessori & Your Child: A Primer for Parents. LC 73-90684. (Illus.). 96p. 1976. 6.00x (ISBN 0-8052-3538-8); pap. 5.95 (ISBN 0-8052-0520-9). Schocken.

Malm, William P. & Sweeney, Amin. Studies in Malaysian Oral & Musical Traditions: Music in Kelantan - Malaysia & Some of Its Cultural Implications. LC 74-83599. (Michigan Papers on South & Southeast Asia, No. 8). (Illus.). 100p. 1974. pap. 3.50x o.p. (ISBN 0-89148-008-0). Ctr S&SE Asian.

Malmfors, T. & Thoenen, T. Six-Hydroxydopamine & Catecholamine Neurons. 1971. 30.00 (ISBN 0-444-10087-3). Elsevier.

Malmstad, John, ed. see Khodasevich, Vladislav.

Malmstadt, et al. Electronics & Instrumentation for Scientists. 1982. 28.95 (ISBN 0-8053-6917-1, 800D00); pap. 4.95 solutions manual (ISBN 0-8053-6919-8, 36919). Benjamin-Cummings.

Malmstadt, H. V., et al. Electronics for Scientists. 1962. 19.95 o.p. (ISBN 0-8053-6900-7). Benjamin-Cummings.

Malmstrom, Jean. Grammar Basics: A Reading-Writing Approach. LC 77-23235. (gr. 10 up). 1977. pap. text ed. 6.00 (ISBN 0-8104-6025-4). Boynton Cook Pubs.

Malmstrom, Jean & Weaver, Constance. Transgrammar: English Structure, Style & Dialects. 1973. pap. 12.50x (ISBN 0-673-07802-7). Scott F.

Malmstrom, Ruth, jt. auth. see Malmstrom, Vincent.

Malmstrom, Vincent & Malmstrom, Ruth. British Isles. rev. ed. LC 77-83908. (World Cultures Ser). (Illus.). 164p. (gr. 6 up). 1978. text ed. 11.20 ea. 1-4 copies o.s.i. (ISBN 0-88296-173-X); text ed. 8.96 ea. 5 or more copies o.s.i.; tchrs'. guide 8.94 o.s.i. (ISBN 0-686-85953-7). Fideler.

Malmstrom, Vincent H., et al. British Isles & Germany. rev. ed. LC 77-83891. (World Cultures Ser.). (Illus.). 320p. (gr. 6 up). 1978. text ed. 12.43 ea. 1-4 copies o.s.i. (ISBN 0-88296-148-9); text ed. 9.94 ea. 5 or more copies o.s.i.; tchrs' guide 8.94 o.s.i. (ISBN 0-686-85954-5). Fideler.

Malnic, J., jt. auth. see Godden, E.

Malnig, Lawrence R. & Morrow, Sandra. What Can I Do with a Major in...? 101p. 8.95 (ISBN 0-930568-01-X). Garrett Pk.

Malo, David. Hawaiian Antiquities. (Special Publication Ser: No. 2). (Illus.). 278p. 1971. pap. 8.00 (ISBN 0-910240-15-9). Bishop Mus.

Malocsay, Zoltan. Galloping Wind. LC 77-9997. 1978. 6.95 o.p. (ISBN 0-399-20619-1). Putnam Pub Group.

Malocsay, Zoltan & Shapiro, Jed. How to Stay Healthy in Spite of Your Habits. (Illus.). 225p. Date not set. price not set o.p. (ISBN 0-87364-222-8). Paladin Ent. Postponed.

Malone, Ann. Women in Texas. (Southwestern Studies: No. 70). 72p. 1983. pap. 4.00 (ISBN 0-87404-130-9). Tex Western.

Malone, Barbara, jt. auth. see Sims, Dorothy.

Malone, Bill C. Country Music, U.S.A. A Fifty-year History. LC 68-66367. (American Folklore Society Memoir Ser.: No. 54). (Illus.). 438p. 1969. 0.00 o.p.; pap. 9.95 (ISBN 0-292-71029-1). U of Tex Pr.

Malone, Dandridge M. Small Unit Leadership. (Illus.). 160p. (Orig.). 1983. pap. 8.95 (ISBN 0-89141-173-9). Presidio Pr.

Malone, Dumas, ed. see Jefferson, Thomas.

Malone, John W., Jr., jt. auth. see Epp, Donald J.

Malone, Leo J. Basic Concepts of Chemistry. LC 80-19501. 454p. 1981. text ed. 23.95 (ISBN 0-471-06381-9). Wiley.

Malone, Maggie. Classic American Patchwork Quilt Patterns. LC 77-80195. (Illus.). 1978. 8.95 (ISBN 0-8069-8212-8). Sterling.

--One Hundred-Twenty Patterns for Traditional Patchwork Quilts. LC 82-19671. (Illus.). 240p. 1983. 19.95 (ISBN 0-8069-5488-4); pap. 9.95 (ISBN 0-8069-7716-7). Sterling.

--One Thousand & One Patchwork Designs. LC 81-85037. (Illus.). 224p. 1982. 16.95 (ISBN 0-8069-5460-4); lib. bdg. 19.99 (ISBN 0-8069-5461-2); pap. 9.95 (ISBN 0-8069-7604-7). Sterling.

Malone, Margaret G. Dolly the Dolphin. LC 78-3797. (Illus.). 96p. (gr. 4 up). 1978. PLB 7.29 o.p. (ISBN 0-671-32903-0). Messner.

Malone, Mary. Annie Sullivan. LC 71-121943. (See & Read Biographies). (Illus.). (gr. 2-4). 1971. PLB 5.99 o.p. (ISBN 0-399-60031-0). Putnam Pub Group.

--Liliuokalani: Queen of Hawaii. LC 75-6783. (Discovery Ser.). (Illus.). 84p. (gr. 2-5). 1975. PLB 6.69 (ISBN 0-8116-6320-5). Garrard.

--Milton Hershey: Chocolate King. LC 74-131020. (Americans All Ser). (Illus.). (gr. 3-6). 1971. PLB 7.12 (ISBN 0-8116-4565-7). Garrard.

Malone, Thomas F., intro. by. Weather & Climate Modification: Problems & Progress. LC 79-22479. 1980. Repr. of 1973 ed. 38.00x (ISBN 0-8103-1017-1). Gale.

Malone, Tom. Rejoicing with Creation. pap. 6.50 (ISBN 0-8042-1420-4). John Knox.

Malone, Tyrone. Little Irvy: A Tale of a Whale. LC 80-25338. (Adventures of Tyrone Malone Ser.). (Illus.). 48p. (gr. 4 up). 1981. PLB 10.60 (ISBN 0-516-01862-0); pap. 3.95 (ISBN 0-516-41862-9). Childrens.

--The Million Dollar Truck Display. LC 80-39622. (Adventures of Tyrone Malone Ser.). (Illus.). 48p. (gr. 4 up). 1981. PLB 10.60 (ISBN 0-516-01863-9); pap. 3.95 (ISBN 0-516-41863-7). Childrens.

--Super Boss: King of Diesel Truck Drag Racing. LC 80-28992. (Adventures of Tyrone Malone Ser.). (Illus.). 48p. (gr. 4 up). 1981. PLB 10.60 (ISBN 0-516-01861-2); pap. 3.95 (ISBN 0-516-41861-0). Childrens.

Malone, William E. & Suarez, J. C., eds. The Literary Dog. LC 78-14536. (Illus.). 1978. 14.95 o.p. (ISBN 0-399-12301-6, Pub. by Berkley). Putnam Pub Group.

Malone, William F., jt. auth. see Tylman, Stanley D.

Malone, William F., ed. Tissue Management in Restorative Dentistry. (Illus.). 352p. 1982. 32.50 (ISBN 0-88416-154-4). Wright-PSG.

Maloney, Clarence. People of the Maldive Islands. (Illus.). 432p. 1980. text ed. 27.95x (ISBN 0-86131-158-2, Pub. by Orient Longman Ltd India). Apt Bks.

Maloney, Elliott C. Semitic Interference in Marcan Syntax. LC 80-13016. (Society of Biblical Literature Dissertation Ser.: No. 51). pap. 15.00 (ISBN 0-89130-406-1, 06-01-51). Scholars Pr CA.

Maloney, George S. A Theology of Uncreated Energies of God. (Pere Marquette Lecture Ser.). 1978. 7.95 (ISBN 0-87462-516-5). Marquette.

Maloney, J. J. I Speak for the Dead. 241p. 1982. 12.95 (ISBN 0-8362-6118-6). Andrews & McMeel.

Maloney, L., tr. see Buhler, Walther.

Maloney, Martin & Rubenstein, Paul M. Writing for the Media. 1980. text ed. 18.95 (ISBN 0-13-970558-9). P-H.

Maloney, Mary Ann, jt. auth. see Pensis, Nancy T.

Maloney, Pat, Sr. & Pasqual, Jack. Winning the Million Dollar Lawsuit. LC 82-21175. 280p. 1982. text ed. 89.50 (ISBN 0-87624-848-2). Inst Busn Plan.

Maloney, Timothy J. Industrial Solid State Electronics: Devices & Systems. (Illus.). 1980. text ed. 28.95 (ISBN 0-13-463406-3). P-H.

Maloney, Tom. Edward Steichen. (Illus.). 320p. 1981. 24.95 o.p. (ISBN 0-517-54263-3). Crown.

Malony, H. Newton. Wholeness & Holiness: Readings in the Psychology, Theology of Mental Health. 304p. (Orig.). 1983. pap. 12.95 (ISBN 0-8010-6147-4). Baker Bk.

Malony, H. Newton, jt. auth. see Vande Kempe, Hendrika.

Malony, H. Newton, ed. A Christian Existential Psychology: The Contributions of John G. Finch. LC 80-8158. 353p. 1980. lib. bdg. 24.00 (ISBN 0-8191-1259-3); pap. text ed. 13.25 (ISBN 0-8191-1260-7). U Pr of Amer.

--Psychology & Faith: The Christian Experience of Eighteen Psychologists. LC 78-63271. 1978. pap. text ed. 11.00 (ISBN 0-8191-0621-6). U Pr of Amer.

Malory, Thomas. King Arthur & His Knights. Vinaver, Eugene, ed. (Illus.). 1975. pap. 7.95 (ISBN 0-19-501905-9, 434, GB). Oxford U Pr.

--Le Morte d'Arthur. LC 72-78185. (Illus.). 6000p. 1972. 50.00 o.p. (ISBN 0-312-47600-0). St Martin.

--Morte D'Arthur. 1962. 6.00 o.p. (ISBN 0-517-02060-2, C N Potter Bks). Crown.

--Le Morte D'Arthur, Vol. 1. 1953. 9.95x (ISBN 0-460-00045-4, Evman); pap. 3.95x (ISBN 0-460-01045-X, Evman). Biblio Dist.

--Morte D'Arthur: King Arthur & the Knights of the Round Table. Baines, Keith, tr. (Orig.). 1962. pap. 3.95 (ISBN 0-451-62220-0, ME6220, Ment). NAL.

Malotki, Ekkehart. Hopi-Raum. Eine Sprachwissenschaftliche Analyse der Raumvorstellungen in der Hopi Sprache. (Tubinger Beitrage zur Linguistik: 81). 406p. (Ger.). 1979. 62.00 (ISBN 3-87808-081-6). Benjamins North Am.

Malotki, Ekkehart, et al. Hopi Tales. Malotki, Ekkehart, tr. (Special Publications Ser.). (Illus.). 1978. pap. 8.00 o.p. (ISBN 0-89734-001-9). Mus Northern Ariz.

Malott, Richard W. & Whaley, Donald. Pyschology. 680p. text ed. 19.95 (ISBN 0-918452-43-0). Learning Pubs.

Malouet, Pierre-Victor. Memoire sur l'Esclavage des Negres dans Lequel On Discute les Motifs Proposes pour Leur Affranchissement, Ceux Qui S'y Opposent et les Moyens Practicables pour Ameliorer Leur Sort. (Slave Trade in France Ser., 1744-1848). 156p. (Fr.). 1974. Repr. of 1788 ed. lib. bdg. 47.50x o.p. (ISBN 0-8287-0566-6, TN110). Clearwater Pub.

Malouf, Pyrrha. Metamassage: How to Massage Your Way to a Beautiful Complexion - All Over. (Illus.). 1983. 6.95 (ISBN 0-87795-472-0, Pub. by Priam). Arbor Hse.

Malparte, Curzio. Kaputt (Goes Europe!) Foligno, Cesare, tr. from Italian. LC 82-60881. (Mission Rescue Ser.). 410p. 1983. pap. 8.00 (ISBN 0-916288-13-7). Micah Pubns.

Malpass, E. Deanne, pref. by. Personalities & Policies: Essays on English & European History. LC 76-43381. (Illus.). 1977. lib. bdg. 6.00x (ISBN 0-912646-39-X). Tex Christian.

Malpede, Karen, ed. Women in Theatre: Compassion & Hope. LC 81-12488. 304p. 1983. 19.95x (ISBN 0-89676-054-5); pap. 12.50 o.p. (ISBN 0-89676-055-3). Drama Bk.

Malpezzi, S., jt. auth. see Follain, James R., Jr.

Malphurs, J. G. Amusement for Your Bible Hour. 1961. pap. 0.60 (ISBN 0-88027-100-0). Firm Foun Pub.

--Let's Do Something. 1958. pap. 0.60 (ISBN 0-88027-099-3). Firm Foun Pub.

Malraux, Andre. Man's Fate. Chevalier, Haakon M., tr. 1965. pap. 3.95 (ISBN 0-686-38913-1, Mod LibC). Modern Lib.

--Man's Hope. Gilbert, Stuart & MacDonald, Alastair, trs. from Fr. LC 79-2333. 1979. pap. 12.50 (ISBN 0-394-17093-8, E740, Ever). Grove.

--Metamorphosis of the Gods. LC 60-10395. 1964. 15.00 (ISBN 0-385-00955-0). Doubleday.

Malsch, Brownson. Sunbelt Gardening Made Easy. (Illus.). 128p. (Orig.). 1982. pap. cancelled (ISBN 0-88319-064-8). Shoal Creek Pub.

Malseed, Roger T. Pharmacology: Drug Therapy & Nursing Considerations. (Illus.). 784p. 1982. text ed. 19.75 (ISBN 0-397-54248-8, Lippincott Medical). Lippincott.

--Quick Reference to Drug Therapy & Nursing Considerations. (Quick References for Nurses Ser.). 974p. 1982. pap. text ed. 14.50 (ISBN 0-397-54420-0, Lippincott Nursing). Lippincott.

Malsky, Stanley J. Hospital Administration for Middle Management: A Practical Approach. 320p. 1983. 27.50 (ISBN 0-87527-170-7). Green.

Malt, R. A. & Williamson, R., eds. Colonic Carcinogenesis. (Illus.). 406p. 1981. text ed. 65.00 (ISBN 0-85200-443-5, Pub. by MTP Pr England). Kluwer Boston.

Maltby, Arthur. The Government of Northern Ireland Nineteen Twenty-Two to Seventy-Two: A Catalogue & Breviate of Parliamentary Papers. 258p. 1974. text ed. 30.00x (ISBN 0-7165-2151-2, Pub by Irish Academic Pr). Biblio Dist.

Maltby, Arthur, ed. Sayers Manual of Classification. rev. ed. 336p. 1975. 26.50 (ISBN 0-233-96603-X, 05805-X, Pub. by Gower Pub Co England). Lexington Bks.

Maltby, Richard. Harmless Entertainmnet: Hollywood & the Ideology of Concensus. LC 82-10344. 425p. 1983. 26.50 (ISBN 0-8108-1548-6). Scarecrow.

Maltese, John A., ed. The Accompanist: Autobiography of Andre Benoist. (Illus.). 384p. 1978. 17.95 (ISBN 0-87666-614-4, Z-26). Paganiniana Pubns.

Maltha, D. J. Agricultural Science: Wageningen in Focus. (Illus.). 92p. 1981. pap. 13.75 (ISBN 0-686-93145-9, PDC243, Pudoc). Unipub.

--Technical Literature Search & the Written Report. 1976. 14.95 (ISBN 0-444-19501-7). Elsevier.

Malthus, Thomas R. An Essay on the Principle of Population. 1976. 10.95x o.p. (ISBN 0-460-10692-9, Evman). Biblio Dist.

--Essay on the Principle of Population or a View of Its Past & Present Effects on Human Happiness. 7th ed. LC 70-144322. Repr. of 1872 ed. lib. bdg. 35.00x (ISBN 0-678-00838-8). Kelley.

--Essays on Principle of Population. (Penguin English Library). 1983. pap. write for info. (ISBN 0-14-043206-X). Penguin.

Malthus, Thomas R., et al. The Malthus Library Catalogue: The Personal Collection of Thomas Robert Malthus at Jesus College, Cambridge University. 150p. 1983. 19.50 (ISBN 0-08-029386-7). Pergamon.

Maltin, Leonard. The Great Movie Comedians. (Illus.). 1978. 12.95 o.p. (ISBN 0-517-53241-7). Crown.

--Great Movie Comedians from Charlie Chaplin to Woody Allen. (Illus.). 256p. 1982. pap. 5.95 o.p. (ISBN 0-517-54606-X, Harmony). Crown.

--The Great Movie Shorts. (Illus.). 1972. 9.95 o.p. (ISBN 0-517-50455-3). Crown.

--Of Mice & Magic: A History of American Animated Cartoons. LC 79-21923. (Illus.). 488p. 1980. 24.95 (ISBN 0-07-039835-6, P&RB). McGraw.

--Of Mice & Magic: A History of American Animated Cartoons. 1980. pap. 9.95 (ISBN 0-452-25240-7, Z5240, Plume). NAL.

Maltin, Leonard, ed. T.V. Movies: 1983-84 Edition. 1982. pap. 4.95 (ISBN 0-451-11847-2, AE1847, Sig). NAL.

--The Whole Film Sourcebook. 1982. pap. 8.95 (ISBN 0-452-25361-6, Z5361, Plume). NAL.

--The Whole Film Sourcebook. LC 82-84314. 476p. 1983. 14.95 (ISBN 0-87663-416-1). Universe.

Maltoni, C., et al, eds. see International Symposium on Cancer Detection & Prevention.

Maltz, Maxwell. Psycho-Cybernetics. pap. 3.00 (ISBN 0-87980-127-1). Wilshire.

--Psycho-Cybernetics. 2.95 o.p. (ISBN 0-686-92398-7, 6600). Hazelden.

--Psycho-Cybernetics: The New Way to a Successful Life. 1960. 14.95 o.p. (ISBN 0-13-732255-0, Parker). P-H.

Maluccio, Anthony N. & Sinaoglu, Paula A. Social Work with Parents of Children in Foster Care: A Bibliography. 96p. 1981. 2.75 (ISBN 0-87868-210-4, F-60). Child Welfare.

Maluccio, Anthony N. & Sinanoglu, Paula A., eds. The Challenge of Partnership: Working with Parents of Children in Foster Care. (Orig.). 1981. 14.00 (ISBN 0-87868-198-1, F-57); pap. 8.95 (ISBN 0-87868-180-9). Child Welfare.

Maluccio, Anthony N., jt. ed. see Sinanoglu, Paula A.

Malum, Amadu. Amadu's Bundle. Moody, Ronald & Gulla, Kell, trs. (African Writers Ser.). 1972. pap. text ed. 3.00x (ISBN 0-435-90118-4). Heinemann Ed.

Malushitsky, Yuri N. Centrifugal Model Testing of Waste-Heap Embankments. Schofield, A. N., ed. LC 78-67431. (Illus.). 1981. 77.50 (ISBN 0-521-22423-3). Cambridge U Pr.

Malvern, Gladys. Six Wives of Henry Eighth. LC 71-134678. (Illus.). (gr. 7 up). 1969. 7.95 o.s.i. (ISBN 0-8149-0665-6). Vanguard.

Malvern, Lawrence E. Engineering Mechanics, 2 vols. Incl. Vol. 1. Statics. ref. ed. 27.95 (ISBN 0-13-278663-X); Vol. 2. Dynamics. ref. ed. 24.95x (ISBN 0-13-278671-0). (Illus.). 352p. 1976. P-H.

--Introduction to the Mechanics of a Continuous Medium. 1969. ref. ed. 34.95 (ISBN 0-13-487603-2). P-H.

Malvino, A. P. & Leach, Donald. Digital Principles & Applications. 2nd ed. (Illus.). 608p. 1975. text ed. 26.50 (ISBN 0-07-039837-2, G); answer 1.95 (ISBN 0-07-039838-0). McGraw.

Malvino, Albert. Experiments for Electronic Principles. (Illus.). 216p. 1973. 9.95 o.p. (ISBN 0-07-039840-2, G). McGraw.

Malvino, Albert P. Digital Computer Electronics. (Illus.). 1976. text ed. 23.95 (ISBN 0-07-039861-5, G); answer key 1.50 (ISBN 0-07-039862-3). McGraw.

--Electronic Instrumentation Fundamentals. (Illus.). 1967. text ed. 23.95 (ISBN 0-07-039847-X, G); answers to even-numbered problems 1.50 (ISBN 0-07-039848-8). McGraw.

--Electronic Principles. 2nd ed. (Illus.). 1979. text ed. 26.50 (ISBN 0-07-039867-4, G); inst's manual 3.00 (ISBN 0-07-039869-0); experiments 15.95 (ISBN 0-07-039868-2). McGraw.

--Resistive & Reactive Circuits. new ed. (Illus.). 640p. 1974. text ed. 22.95 (ISBN 0-07-039856-9, G); answer to even-numbered problems 1.50 (ISBN 0-07-039857-7). McGraw.

--Transistor Circuit Approximations. 3rd ed. LC 79-18580. (Illus.). 1980. text ed. 25.50x (ISBN 0-07-039878-X); experiments 11.95 (ISBN 0-07-039880-1); answer key 2.00 (ISBN 0-07-039879-8). McGraw.

--Transistor Circuit Approximations. 2nd ed. (Illus.). 512p. 1973. text ed. 17.25 o.p. (ISBN 0-07-039858-5, G). McGraw.

Malvino, Albert P. & Leach, Donald. Digital Principles & Applications. LC 68-31663. (Illus.). 1968. text ed. 16.50 o.p. (ISBN 0-07-039849-6, G). McGraw.

Malvino, Albert P. & Leach, Donald P. Digital Principles & Applications. 3rd ed. LC 80-19631. (Illus.). 496p. 1980. text ed. 26.50x (ISBN 0-07-039875-5); answers 2.50 (ISBN 0-07-039876-3). McGraw.

Malvino, Albert P., jt. auth. see Zbar, Paul B.

Malvins, A. P. Digital Computer Electronics: An Introduction to Microcomputers. 2nd ed. 384p. 1982. text ed. 23.95x (ISBN 0-07-039901-8); experiments 9.95 (ISBN 0-07-039902-6); instr's manual 3.00 (ISBN 0-07-039903-4). McGraw.

Malyala, Panduranga R. Bhaguadgeeta - Bible - Khuran (Krishna - Jesus Mohammad) Date not set. 3.99 (ISBN 0-938924-04-4). Sri Shirdi Sai.

--Mantras-Meaning (from Physics & Chemistry Stand Point of View) Date not set. 3.99 (ISBN 0-938924-05-2). Sri Shirdi Sai.

--Sri Ganesh Puja (Worship of God of Obstacles) (Illus.). 56p. 1982. 1.99 (ISBN 0-938924-03-6). Sri Shirdi Sai.

Malyusz, Csaszar, ed. Theater & National Awakening. 350p. 1981. pap. 19.50 o.p. (ISBN 0-686-77620-8). Carrollton Pr.

Malz, Betty. Prayers That Are Answered. 1981. pap. 2.50 (ISBN 0-451-11991-6, AE1991, Sig). NAL.

Malz, Wilfried. Studien Zum Problem des Metaphorischen Redens Am Beispiel Von Texten Aus Shakeskpeares "Richard II" und Marlowes "Edward II". 251p. (Ger.). 1982. write for info. (ISBN 3-8204-5824-7). P Lang Pubs.

Malzan, Jerry, jt. auth. see Djokovic, D. Z.

Malzberg, Barry N. Galaxies. 1980. lib. bdg. 12.50 (ISBN 0-8398-2548-X, Gregg). G K Hall.

Malzberg, Barry N., jt. auth. see Pronzini, Bill.

Mamak, Alexander, ed. see Young Nations Conference, Sydney, 1976.

Mamak, Alexander F. Colour, Culture & Conflict: A Study of Pluralism in Fiji. (Illus.). 1979. 31.00 (ISBN 0-08-023354-6); pap. 15.50 (ISBN 0-08-023353-8). Pergamon.

Maman, Andre, et al. France: Ses Grandes Heures Litteraires. (Level 4 or 5). (gr. 9-12). 1968. text ed. 32.50 (ISBN 0-07-039851-8, C); inst. manual 10.95 (ISBN 0-07-039852-6); exercises 9.95 (ISBN 0-07-039853-4); tapes 230.00 (ISBN 0-07-097885-9). McGraw.

Mamayev, O. I. Temperature-Salinity Analysis of World Ocean Waters. (Oceanography Ser.: Vol. 11). 374p. 1975. 85.00 (ISBN 0-444-41251-4). Elsevier.

Mamber, Stephen. Cinema Verite in America: Studies in Uncontrolled Documentary. (Illus.). 288p. 1974. 15.00x o.p. (ISBN 0-262-13092-0); pap. 6.95 (ISBN 0-262-63058-3). MIT Pr.

Mambert, W. A. Effective Presentation: A Short Course for Professionals. (Professional Development Ser.). 1976. text ed. 55.95 (ISBN 0-471-56630-6); 3.00 o.p. leader's guide (ISBN 0-471-02130-X). Wiley.

--Presenting Technical Ideas: A Guide to Audience Communication. LC 67-28335. (Wiley Series on Human Communication). 1968. 23.95 o.p. (ISBN 0-471-56629-2, Pub. by Wiley-Interscience). Wiley.

Mamchak, Susan & Mamchek, Steven R. School Administrator's Encyclopedia. LC 81-22492. 414p. 1982. 27.50 (ISBN 0-13-792390-2, Parker). P-H.

Mamchek, Steven R., jt. auth. see Mamchak, Susan.

Mamdani, Mahmood. The Myth of Population Control: Family, Caste & Class in an Indian Village. LC 72-81761. (Illus.). 176p. 1973. 7.95 (ISBN 0-85345-236-9, CL2369); pap. 4.50 (ISBN 0-85345-284-9, PB2849). Monthly Rev.

--Politics & Class Formation in Uganda. LC 75-15348. 1978. pap. 5.95 (ISBN 0-85345-425-6). Monthly Rev.

Mamet, David. Edmond. 112p. 1983. 15.00 (ISBN 0-394-53104-3). Grove.

--Edmond. 112p. 1983. pap. 6.95 (ISBN 0-394-62445-9, Ever). Grove.

Mamis, Justin. How to Buy: An Insider's Guide to Making Money in the Stock Market. 1983. pap. 6.95 (ISBN 0-346-12586-3). Cornerstone.

Mammen, Edward W., jt. auth. see Gondin, William R.

Mammitzsch, Ulrich & Takemoto, Toru. Mandala in Japanese Buddhism. Date not set. price not set o.p. West Wash Univ.

Mammitzsch, Ulrich, tr. see Wu Han.

Man, J. Jungle Nomads of Equador: The Waorani. (Peoples of the Wild Ser.). 1982. write for info. (ISBN 0-7054-0704-7, Pub. by Time-Life). Silver.

Man-Made Lakes Stock Assessment Working Group, Jinji, Uganda, 1970. Report. (FAO Fisheries Report: No. 87). 13p. 1970. pap. 7.50 (ISBN 0-686-93051-7, F1688, FAO). Unipub.

Manach, Jorge. Frontiers in the Americas: A Global Perspective. Phenix, Philip H., tr. from Span. LC 74-34325. 125p. 1975. 11.95x (ISBN 0-8077-2481-5); pap. 7.50x (ISBN 0-8077-2480-7). Tchrs Coll.

--Marti: Apostle of Freedom. (Illus.). 6.50 (ISBN 0-8159-6201-0). Devin.

Management Analysis Center, Inc. Implementing Strategy: Making Strategy Happen. 200p. 1982. prof ref 25.00x (ISBN 0-88410-904-6). Ballinger Pub.

Management Information Exchange, Inc. Business Services & Information: The Guide to the Federal Government. LC 78-65641. 1978. 49.50 (ISBN 0-471-05366-X, Pub by Wiley-Interscience). Wiley.

Manak, James P. Standards Relating to Prosecution. (Juvenile Justice Standards Project Ser.). 112p. 1980. 20.00x (ISBN 0-88410-238-6); pap. 10.00x (ISBN 0-88410-814-7). Ballinger Pub.

Manaka, Y. Chinese Massage: Quick & Easy. 5.95x o.s.i. (ISBN 0-685-70676-1). Wehman.

Manaka, Yoshio & Uquahart, Ian A. Chinese Massage. (Quick & Easy Ser.). (Illus.). 60p. (Orig.). 1973. pap. 3.95 (ISBN 0-8048-1399-X, Pub. by Shufanmato Co. Ltd Japan). C E Tuttle.

Manakar, George H. Interior Plantscapes: Installation Maintenance & Management. 1981. 21.95 (ISBN 0-13-469312-4). P-H.

Manalang, Priscilla S. A Philippine Rural School: Its Cultural Dimension. 1976. 13.50x (ISBN 0-8248-0473-2). UH Pr.

Manamori, H. Earthquakes: Observation, Theory & Interpretation. (Enrico Fermi Summer School Ser.: Vol. 85). Date not set. price not set. Elsevier.

Manas, Vincent T., ed. National Plumbing Code Handbook. (Illus.). 1957. 39.00 (ISBN 0-07-039850-X, P&RB). McGraw.

Manaser, J. C. & Werner, A. M. Instruments for Study of Nurse-Patient Interaction. 1964. pap. text ed. 9.95x (ISBN 0-02-375260-2). Macmillan.

Manashil, Gordon B. Clinical Sialography. (Illus.). 112p. 1978. 19.50x o.p. (ISBN 0-398-03770-1). C C Thomas.

Manassah, Jamal T., ed. Alternate Energy Sources. 1981. Pt. A. 56.00 (ISBN 0-12-467101-2); Pt. B. 51.50 (ISBN 0-12-467102-0). Acad Pr.

Manasse, Fred K. Semiconductor Electronics Design. LC 76-13638. (Illus.). 1977. text ed. 31.95 (ISBN 0-13-806273-0). P-H.

Manasse, Sylvia. Take Me with You. 1978. 5.95 o.p. (ISBN 0-533-03443-4). Vantage.

Manassewitsch, Vadim. Frequency Synthesizers: Theory & Design. 2nd ed. LC 80-13345. 544p. 1980. 42.95 (ISBN 0-471-07917-0, Pub. by Wiley Interscience). Wiley.

Manaster, Guy J. & Corsini, Raymond J. Individual Psychology: Theory & Practice. LC 81-82887. 322p. 1982. pap. text ed. 12.95 (ISBN 0-87581-274-0). Peacock Pubs.

Mancall, Jacqueline C. & Drott, M. Carl. Measuring Student Information Use: A Guide for School Library Media Specialists. 175p. 1983. lib. bdg. 19.50 (ISBN 0-87287-366-8). Libs Unl.

Manceron, Claude. The French Revolution IV: Toward the Brink. LC 82-47836. 1983. 20.00 (ISBN 0-394-51533-1). Knopf.

--Toward the Brink: The French Revolution Vol. 4. LC 82-47836. (Illus.). 480p. 1983. 20.00 (ISBN 0-394-51533-1). Knopf.

Mancha, Donald L. Nobody Wants My Resume. LC 79-14986. 1980. 9.95 o.p. (ISBN 0-07-039870-4). McGraw.

Manchel. Great Sports Movies. (gr. 5 up). 1980. PLB 8.90 (ISBN 0-531-01501-7, E46). Watts.

Manchel, Frank. The Box-Office Clowns: Bob Hope, Jerry Lewis, Mel Brooks, Woody Allen. LC 79-10276. (Illus.). (gr. 7 up). 1979. PLB 8.90 s&l (ISBN 0-531-02881-X). Watts.

--Gangsters on the Screen. LC 78-5953. (Illus.). (gr. 6 up). 1978. PLB 8.90 s&l (ISBN 0-531-01471-1). Watts.

Manchester, Alden C. The Public Role in the Dairy Economy: How & Why Governments Intervene in the Dairy Business. (Special Studies in Agriculture-Aquaculture Science & Policy). 304p. 1983. price not set (ISBN 0-86531-590-6). Westview.

Manchester, Frederick, tr. see Prabhavananda, Swami.

Manchester, Frederick, jt. tr. see Prabhavananda, Swami.

Manchester, Frederick A. & Shepard, Odell, eds. Irving Babbitt, Man & Teacher. Repr. of 1941 ed. lib. bdg. 17.50x (ISBN 0-8371-1859-X, MAIB). Greenwood.

Manchester, P. W., jt. auth. see Chujoy, Anatole.

Manchester, Richard B. Grab a Pencil Book of Crossword Puzzles. (Grab a Pencil Ser.). 256p. (Orig.). 1983. pap. 4.95 (ISBN 0-89104-326-8, A & W Visual Library). A & W Pubs.

--Grab a Pencil Book of Word Games. (Grab a Pencil Ser.). 256p. (Orig.). 1983. pap. 4.95 (ISBN 0-89104-325-X, A & W Visual Library). A & W Pubs.

Manchester, William. American Caesar: Douglas MacArthur 1880-1964. LC 78-8004. (Illus.). 1978. 15.00 (ISBN 0-316-54498-1). Little.

--H. L. Mencken: Disturber of the Peace. 1962. pap. 0.95 o.p. (ISBN 0-02-004830-0, Collier). Macmillan.

--The Last Lion: Winston Spencer Churchill Visions of Glory, 1874-1932. LC 82-24972. (Illus.). 1983. 25.00i (ISBN 0-316-54503-1). Little.

Mancinelli. Catacombs & Basilkns. pap. 9.95 (ISBN 0-935748-13-X). ScalaBooks.

Mancini, Anthony. Minnie Santangelo & the Evil Eye. LC 77-4494. 224p. 1977. 7.95 o.p. (ISBN 0-698-10818-3, Coward). Putnam Pub Group.

Mancini, Janet K. & Madison, James. Strategic Styles: Coping in the Inner City. LC 79-56773. (Illus.). 348p. 1981. 20.00x (ISBN 0-87451-179-8). U Pr of New Eng.

Mancini, Janet K. & Robbins, Franklyn A. Encountering Society: Introductory Readings in Sociology. LC 80-8253. 219p. 1980. pap. text ed. 11.00 (ISBN 0-8191-1181-3). U Pr of Amer.

Mancini, Marguerite R. & Gale, Alice T. Emergency Care & the Law. LC 81-4364. 255p. 1981. text ed. 24.50 (ISBN 0-89443-337-7). Aspen Systems.

Mancini, Pat. Friday's Child. (Orig.). 1977. pap. 1.50 o.p. (ISBN 0-451-07395-9, W7395, Sig). NAL.

Mancroft, Lord. A Chinaman in My Bath. 188p. 1974. 6.50 o.p. (ISBN 0-85974-010-2). Transatlantic.

Mancusi, Richard J. Ophthalmic Surfacing for Plastic & Glass Lenses. LC 81-84855. 1982. 28.00 (ISBN 0-87873-041-9). Prof Press.

Mancuso, Anthony. California Non-Profit Corporation Book. 3rd ed. LC 80-82465. (Illus.). 1983. pap. 17.95. Nolo Pr.

--Computed Tomography of the Head & Neck. (Illus.). 296p. 1981. lib. bdg. 55.00 (ISBN 0-683-05475-9). Williams & Wilkins.

Mancuso, Anthony & Honigsberg, Peter. California Professional Corporations Handbook. (Orig.). 1982. pap. 19.95 (ISBN 0-917316-46-0). Nolo Pr.

Mancuso, Arlene, jt. ed. see Norman, Elaine.

Mancuso, James C., jt. auth. see Sarbin, Theodore R.

Mancuso, Joseph R. How to Prepare & Present a Business Plan. (Illus.). 320p. 1983. 19.95 (ISBN 0-13-430629-5); pap. 9.95 (ISBN 0-13-430611-2). P-H.

--How to Start, Finance & Manage Your Own Small Business. LC 77-14303. (Illus.). 1978. 18.95 (ISBN 0-13-434928-8); pap. 9.95 (ISBN 0-13-434910-5). P-H.

Mancuso, Joseph R., jt. auth. see Baumback, Clifford M.

Mancy, K. H. & Weber, W. J. Analysis of Industrial Wastewaters. 1972. pap. 12.00 (ISBN 0-471-56640-3, Pub. by Wiley). Krieger.

Mancy, K. H., et al. Applied Chemistry of Wastewater Treatment, 8 vols. LC 73-80194. (Vol. 8, 0-250-40031-6). 1977. pap. 76.00 set (ISBN 0-250-40037-5); pap. 14.50 ea. Vol. 1 (ISBN 0-250-40024-3). Vol. 2 (ISBN 0-250-40025-1). Vol. 3 (ISBN 0-250-40026-X). Vol. 4 (ISBN 0-250-40027-8). Vol. 5 (ISBN 0-250-40028-6). Vol. 6 (ISBN 0-250-40029-4). Vol. 7 (ISBN 0-250-40030-8). Ann Arbor Science.

Mandal, R. B. Introduction to Rural Settlements. 1979. text ed. 19.50x (ISBN 0-391-01817-5). Humanities.

Mandal, R. B. & Sinha, V. N., eds. Recent Trends & Concepts in Geography, 3 vols. Incl. Vol. 1. 1980 (ISBN 0-391-01820-5); Vol. 2. 1980 (ISBN 0-391-01821-3); Vol. 3. 1980 (ISBN 0-391-01822-1). text ed. 29.25x ea. Humanities.

Mandalesvara dasa, ed. see Das Goswami, Satsvarupa.

Mande, C., jt. ed. see Bonnelle, C.

Mandekic, Anthony V. Your Heavenly Children--Alleluia! LC 82-90171. 160p. (Orig.). 1983. pap. text ed. 6.00 (ISBN 0-9608312-0-7). Mandekic.

Mandel, Charlotte, et al, eds. Saturday's Women. (Eileen W. Barnes Award Anthology Ser.). 102p. (Orig.). 1982. pap. 6.50 (ISBN 0-938158-02-3). Saturday Pr.

Mandel, Ernest. From Stalinism to Eurocommunism. 1978. text ed. 19.00x (ISBN 0-8052-7049-3, Pub by NLB); pap. 7.75 (ISBN 0-8052-7048-5, Pub. by Verso). Schocken.

--Late Capitalism. (Illus.). 1978. 24.00x o.p. (ISBN 0-8052-7048-5); pap. 12.50 (ISBN 0-86091-703-7, Pub by Verso). Schocken.

--Revolutionary Marxism Today. 236p. (Orig.). 1980. 23.00x (ISBN 0-8052-7072-8, Pub. by NLB); pap. 10.70 (ISBN 0-8052-7073-6, Pub. by NLB). Schocken.

--The Second Slump: A Marxist Analysis of Recession in the Seventies. 1979. 12.95 (ISBN 0-86091-012-1, Pub. by NLB); pap. 6.95 (ISBN 0-8052-7084-1). Schocken.

--Trotsky: A Study in the Dynamic of His Thought. 156p. (Orig.). 1980. 18.00x (ISBN 0-8052-7075-2, Pub. by NLB); pap. 6.75 (ISBN 0-86091-027-X, Pub. by Verso). Schocken.

Mandel, Leon. American Cars. LC 82-5609. (Illus.). 448p. 1982. 60.00 (ISBN 0-941434-19-2, 8004). Stewart Tabori & Chang.

Mandel, Morris. Thirteen: A Teenage Guide to Judaism. LC 61-8452. (Illus.). (gr. 7 up). 1961. 10.00 o.p. (ISBN 0-8246-0096-7). Jonathan David.

Mandel, N., tr. see Vdovenko, V. M. & Dubasov, Yu V.

Mandel, Oscar. A Definition of Tragedy. LC 82-8505. 184p. 1982. pap. text ed. 9.25 (ISBN 0-8191-2530-X). U Pr of Amer.

Mandel, Oscar, tr. from Fr. Five Comedies of Medieval France. LC 82-13499. 158p. 1982. pap. text ed. 8.00 (ISBN 0-8191-2668-3). U Pr of Amer.

Mandel, Paul, jt. ed. see DeFeudis, Francis V.

Mandel, Robert. Perception, Decision Making & Conflict. LC 78-65350. 1978. pap. text ed. 9.50 (ISBN 0-8191-0652-6). U Pr of Amer.

Mandel, S., tr. see Trakl, Georg.

Mandel, Sally. Change of Heart. 1980. 9.95 o.s.i. (ISBN 0-440-01475-1). Delacorte.

--Quinn. 1982. 13.95 (ISBN 0-440-07205-0). Delacorte.

--Quinn. 1983. pap. 3.50 (ISBN 0-440-17176-8). Dell.

Mandel, Siegfried. Writing for Science & Technology. 1970. pap. 3.95 o.s.i. (ISBN 0-440-59712-9, Delta). Dell.

Mandel, Siegfried, ed. see Rilke, Rainer M.

Mandel, William M. Soviet Women Update. (Illus.). 96p. 1983. pap. 2.50 (ISBN 0-87867-091-2). Ramparts.

Mandelbaum, Allan, tr. see Virgil.

Mandelbaum, Allen. Chelmaxioms: The Maxims, Axioms, Maxioms of Chelm. LC 77-78398. 1977. 30.00x o.p. ltd. ed. (ISBN 0-87923-229-3); 12.50x (ISBN 0-87923-214-5). Godine.

--Journeyman: Poems. LC 67-13155. 1967. 4.50 o.p. (ISBN 0-8052-3129-3). Schocken.

Mandelbaum, Allen, tr. see Alighieri, Dante.

Mandelbaum, Allen, tr. see Dante.

Mandelbaum, Allen, tr. see Virgil.

Mandelbaum, David G. Human Fertility in India: Social Components & Policy Perspectives. 1974. 22.50x (ISBN 0-520-02551-2). U. of Cal Pr.

Mandelbaum, David G., ed. see Sapir, Edward.

Mandelbaum, Maurice, jt. ed. see Freeman, Eugene.

Mandelbaum, Maurice, et al, eds. Philosophic Problems. 2nd ed. 1967. text ed. 22.95x (ISBN 0-02-375360-9). Macmillan.

Mandelbaum, Michael. The Nuclear Question. LC 79-388. 1979. 24.95 (ISBN 0-521-22681-3); pap. 9.95 (ISBN 0-521-29614-5). Cambridge U Pr.

--The Nuclear Revolution: International Politics Before & After Hiroshima. LC 80-24194. 256p. 1981. 29.95 (ISBN 0-521-23819-6); pap. 9.95 (ISBN 0-521-28239-X). Cambridge U Pr.

Mandelik, Peter & Schatt, Stanley, eds. Concordance to the Poetry of Langston Hughes. LC 74-11251. (Illus.). 296p. 1975. 70.00x (ISBN 0-8103-1011-2). Gale.

Mandelker & Montgomery. Housing in America: Problems & Perspectives. LC 73-7689. 1973. pap. 19.95 o.p. (ISBN 0-672-61346-8). Bobbs.

Mandelker, Daniel R. Environment & Equity: A Regulatory Challenge. (Regulation of American Business & Industry (RABI) Ser.). 240p. 1981. 27.95 (ISBN 0-07-039864-X, P&RB). McGraw.

--Land Use Law. 400p. 1982. 35.00 (ISBN 0-87215-525-0). Michie-Bobbs.

--Managing Our Urban Environment. 2nd ed. (Contemporary Legal Education Ser). 1971. 21.00 o.p. (ISBN 0-672-81707-1, Bobbs-Merrill Law). Michie-Bobbs.

--New Developments in Land Use & Environmental Controls. (Contemporary Legal Education Ser). 1974. 5.50 o.p. (ISBN 0-672-81964-3, Bobbs-Merrill Law). Michie-Bobbs.

--Zoning Dilemma. 1971. 14.50 (ISBN 0-672-81663-6, Bobbs-Merrill Law). Michie-Bobbs.

Mandelker, Daniel R. & Netsch, Dawn C. State & Local Government in a Federal System, Cases & Materials. (Contemporary Legal Education Ser.). 1977. with 1981 suppl. 25.00 (ISBN 0-672-83047-7, Bobbs-Merrill Law); 1981 suppl. only 7.00 (ISBN 0-672-84388-9). Michie-Bobbs.

Mandell, Alan. Science Projects & Science Teaching. 50p. (Orig.). 1982. pap. write for info. o.p. (ISBN 0-87355-023-4). Natl Sci Tchrs.

Mandell, Arnold J., ed. Neurobiological Mechanisms of Adaptation & Behavior. LC 74-14475. (Advances in Biochemical Psychopharmacology Ser.: Vol. 13). 314p. 1975. 30.00 (ISBN 0-89004-001-X). Raven.

Mandell, Barbara & McCreedy, James. First the Dream. (Illus.). 1982. pap. 4.95 (ISBN 0-932616-09-7). New Poets.

Mandell, Betty, jt. auth. see Schram, Barbara.

Mandell, Betty R. & Schram, Barbara. Human Services: An Introduction. 600p. 1983. text ed. 18.95 (ISBN 0-471-08574-X); tchrs.' ed avail. (ISBN 0-471-87198-2). Wiley.

Mandell, Colleen J. & Fiscus, Edward D. Understanding Exceptional People. (Illus.). 538p. 1981. text ed. 23.50 (ISBN 0-8299-0394-1). West Pub.

Mandell, Colleen J., jt. auth. see Fiscus, Edward D.

Mandell, Ernest. The Long Waves of Capitalist Development. LC 80-16244. (Studies in Modern Capitalism). 112p. 1980. 16.95 (ISBN 0-521-23000-4). Cambridge U Pr.

Mandell, Fran G., jt. auth. see Mandell, Marshall.

Mandell, Judith J. Buffalo Blinkie & the Crazy Circus Caper. (Illus.). (gr. 3-5). 1977. 5.00x (ISBN 0-89039-196-3); tchr's ed. 4.00 (ISBN 0-89039-198-X). Ann Arbor Pubs.

Mandell, Lewis. Consumer Economics. 448p. 1980. pap. text ed. 17.95 (ISBN 0-574-19290-5, 13-2290); instr's guide avail. (ISBN 0-574-19291-3, 13-2291). SRA.

--Credit Card Use in the United States. LC 72-86124. 120p. 1972. pap. 8.00x (ISBN 0-87944-129-1). Inst Soc Res.

--Economics from the Consumer's Perspective. LC 74-34343. (Illus.). 300p. 1975. text ed. 18.95 (ISBN 0-574-18205-5, 13-2205); instr's guide avail. (ISBN 0-574-18206-3, 13-2206). SRA.

Mandell, Lewis, et al. Surveys of Consumers 1971-72: Contributions to Behavioral Economics. LC 72-619718. 352p. 1973. 16.00x (ISBN 0-87944-140-2); pap. 10.00x (ISBN 0-87944-139-9). Inst Soc Res.

Mandell, M. & Rosenberg, L. Marketing. 2nd ed. 1981. 26.95 (ISBN 0-13-556225-2); pap. 9.95 study guide (ISBN 0-13-556233-3). P-H.

Mandell, Mark. Butcher Block. (Nazi Hunter Ser.: No. 4). 208p. 1983. pap. 2.25 (ISBN 0-523-41447-1). Pinnacle Bks.

Mandell, Marshall. Dr. Mandell's Lifetime Arthritis Relief System. 252p. 1983. 13.95 (ISBN 0-698-11176-1, Coward). Putnam Pub Group.

Mandell, Marshall & Mandell, Fran G. The Mandell's: It's Not Your Fault You're Fat Diet. LC 82-48124. (Illus.). 224p. 1983. 13.41i (ISBN 0-06-015114-5, HarpT). Har-Row.

Mandell, Marshall & Scanlon, Lynne W. Dr. Mandell's Five-Day Allergy Relief System. LC 78-3309. (Illus.). 1979. 10.95i o.p. (ISBN 0-690-01471-6). T Y Crowell.

Mandell, Muriel & Wood, Robert E. Make Your Own Musical Instruments. rev. ed. LC 57-11535. (Illus.). (gr. 3-8). 1959. 8.95 (ISBN 0-8069-5022-6); PLB 10.99 (ISBN 0-8069-5023-4). Sterling.

--Make Your Own Musical Instruments. (Illus.). 218p. (gr. 4 up). 1982. pap. 4.95 (ISBN 0-8069-7658-6). Sterling.

Mandell, Robert W. Financing the Capital Requirements of the U. S. Airline Industry in the 1980's. LC 79-7747. 192p. 1979. 23.95 (ISBN 0-669-03215-8). Lexington Bks.

Mandell, Stephen R., jt. auth. see Kirszner, Laurie.

Mandell, Steven L. Computers & Data Processing: Concepts & Applications. (Data Processing & Information Systems Ser.). (Illus.). 1979. text ed. 18.95 (ISBN 0-8299-0198-1). West Pub.

--Computers & Data Processing: Concepts & Applications, with BASIC. 2nd ed. (Illus.). 600p. 1982. text ed. 22.95 (ISBN 0-314-63263-8); instr's. manual avail. (ISBN 0-314-63264-6); study guide avail. (ISBN 0-314-63265-4). West Pub.

--Computers & Data Processing: Concepts & Applications with BASIC Appendix. (Data Processing & Information System Ser.). (Illus.). 1979. text ed. 19.95 (ISBN 0-8299-0247-3); instrs.' manual avail. (ISBN 0-8299-0633-9); study guide avail. (ISBN 0-8299-0254-6). West Pub.

--Computers & Data Processing Today. (Illus.). 350p. 1983. pap. text ed. 15.95 (ISBN 0-314-69663-6); instrs.' manual avail. (ISBN 0-314-71105-8); study guide avail. (ISBN 0-314-71106-6). West Pub.

--Computers & Data Processing Today with BASIC. (Illus.). 510p. pap. text ed. 8.95 (ISBN 0-314-70646-1). West Pub.

--Computers & Data Processing Today with PASCAL. (Illus.). 450p. 1983. pap. text ed. 8.95 (ISBN 0-314-70647-X). West Pub.

--Introduction to BASIC Programming. New ed. (Illus.). 160p. 1982. pap. 7.95 (ISBN 0-314-68082-9). West Pub.

--Principles of Data Processing. 2nd ed. (West Series in Data Processing & Information Systems). (Illus.). 160p. 1981. pap. text ed. 10.50 (ISBN 0-8299-0392-5). West Pub.

--Principles of Data Processing. (Mass Communication Ser.). (Illus.). 1978. pap. text ed. 7.95 o.s.i. (ISBN 0-8299-0212-0); instrs.' manual avail. o.s.i. (ISBN 0-8299-0554-5). West Pub.

Mandell, Steven L., et al. Introduction to Business: Concepts & Applications. 1981. write for info. Alternate Test Bank (ISBN 0-8299-0528-6). West Pub.

--Introduction to Business: Concepts & Applications. (Illus.). 640p. 1981. text ed. 21.50 (ISBN 0-8299-0393-3). West Pub.

Mandelstam, J. & McQuillen, K., eds. Biochemistry of Bacterial Growth. 3rd ed. LC 72-12036. 582p. 1973. pap. text ed. 34.95x (ISBN 0-470-27249-X). Halsted Pr.

Mandelstam, Joel, et al. Biochemistry of Bacterial Growth. 3rd. ed. LC 81-68495. 500p. 1982. pap. 39.95x (ISBN 0-470-27249-X). Halsted Pr.

Mandelstam, Osip. Osip Mandelstam: Fifty Poems. Meares, Bernard, tr. LC 76-52274. (Poetry in Translation Ser.). 1977. o. p. 7.95 (ISBN 0-89255-005-8); pap. 5.95 (ISBN 0-89255-006-6). Persea Bks.

Mandelstam, S. L., ed. Spectrochemical Analysis in the U. S. S. R. 112p. 1982. pap. 16.00 (ISBN 0-08-028747-6). Pergamon.

Mandelstam, Stanley, jt. auth. see Yourgrau, Wolfgang.

Mander, Anica V. & Rush, Anne K. Feminism As Therapy. LC 74-8097. (Illus.). 1975. pap. 5.95 (ISBN 0-394-70937-3). Random.

Mander, Gertrud. Moliere. Peters, Diana, tr. from Ger. LC 70-163147. (Literature and Life Ser.). (Illus.). 1973. 11.95 (ISBN 0-8044-2662-7). Ungar.

Mander, Jerry. Four Arguments for the Elimination of Television. 371p. 1978. pap. 5.95 (ISBN 0-688-08274-2). Quill NY.

Mander, John. Berlin: The Eagle & the Bear. LC 78-12860. 1979. Repr. of 1959 ed. lib. bdg. 18.25x (ISBN 0-313-21209-0, MABN). Greenwood.

--Our German Cousins: Anglo-German Relations in the 19th & 20th Centuries. 273p. 1975. 12.50 o.p. (ISBN 0-7195-2894-1). Transatlantic.

Mander, M. R. & Pargeter, F. W. Metals & Alloys. 1974. pap. text ed. 4.00x o.p. (ISBN 0-435-65966-9); tchr's guide 5.00x o.p. (ISBN 0-435-65967-7). Heinemann Ed.

Mander, Nicholas, ed. Gloucestershire: A Concise Guide. (Illus.). 192p. 1982. pap. text ed. 9.00x (ISBN 0-904387-72-0, Pub. by Sutton England). Humanities.

Mander-Jones, Phyllis, ed. Manuscripts in the British Isles Relating to Australia, New Zealand & the Pacific. LC 78-172122. 1972. text ed. 35.00x (ISBN 0-8248-0204-7). UH Pr.

Manderson, Lenore. Women, Politics, & Change: The Kaum Ibu UMNO Malaysia, 1945-1972. (East Asian Social Science Monographs). (Illus.). 1981. 34.95x (ISBN 0-19-580437-6). Oxford U Pr.

Mandeville, Bernard. Free Thoughts on Religion, the Church, & National Happiness. LC 77-17171. 1981. Repr. of 1720 ed. lib. bdg. 50.00x (ISBN 0-8201-1300-X). Schol Facsimiles.

--A Treatise of the Hypochondriack & Hysterick Diseases. LC 76-45623. 1976. Repr. of 1732 ed. 50.00x (ISBN 0-8201-1277-1). Schol Facsimiles.

--The Virgin Unmask'd. LC 75-14288. 256p. 1975. Repr. of 1709 ed. lib. bdg. 35.00x (ISBN 0-8201-1155-4). Schol Facsimiles.

Mandeville, Mildred S., ed. Used Book Price Guide: Five Year Edition, 1977 Supplement. 479p. 1977. 49.00 (ISBN 0-911182-76-4). Price Guide.

--Used Book Price Guide: Five Year, 1983 Edition. 536p. 1983. 79.00. Price Guide.

Mandeville, Sylvia. Amigos de Dios. Gutierrez, Edna L., tr. from Eng. (Serie Apunta Con Tu Dedo). 24p. 1980. pap. 9.95 (ISBN 0-311-38532-X, Edit Mundo). Casa Bautista.

Mandeville, Sylvia & Pierson, Lance. Conoce a Jesus. Gutierrez, Edna L., tr. from Eng. (Pointing Out Bk.). 24p. 1980. pap. 9.95 (ISBN 0-311-38531-1, Edit Mundo). Casa Bautista.

Mandeville, Terry M. Backpacking Menus. 1980. pap. 3.95 o.p. (ISBN 0-685-70087-9). Price Guide.

Mandi, Peter. Education & Economic Growth in the Developing Countries. 225p. 1981. text ed. 25.00x (ISBN 963-05-2781-2, 50012, Pub. by Kultura Pr Hungary). Humanities.

Mandich, Donald R., et al, eds. Foreign Exchange Trading Techniques & Controls. LC 76-21912. 1976. 15.00 (ISBN 0-89982-000-X, 230600); non-members 22.50. Am Bankers.

Mandino, Og. The Christ Commission. 240p. 1980. 11.49i (ISBN 0-690-01914-9). T Y Crowell.

--The Greatest Miracle in the World. 7.95 o.p. (ISBN 0-686-92331-6, 6065). Hazelden.

--The Greatest Success in the World. 1982. pap. 2.75 (ISBN 0-553-22771-8). Bantam.

Mandino, Og, jt. auth. see Dewey, Edward R.

Mandl, F. Statistical Physics. (Manchester Physics Ser). 1971. 19.95 (ISBN 0-471-56658-6, Pub. by Wiley-Interscience). Wiley.

Mandl, Matthew. Basics of Electricity & Electronics. (Illus.). 448p. 1975. ref. ed. 21.95 (ISBN 0-13-060228-0). P-H.

Mandle, Bill. Conflict in the Promised Land. (Studies in 20th Century History Ser.). 1976. pap. text ed. 4.50x o.p. (ISBN 0-435-31760-1). Heinemann Ed.

Mandle, J. R. Patterns of Caribbean Development: An Interpretive Essay on Economic Change. (Carribean Studies: Vol. 2). 162p. 32.50 (ISBN 0-677-06000-9). Gordon.

Mandle, Jay. The Plantation Economy: Population & Economic Change in Guyana, 1838-1960. LC 72-95883. 170p. 1973. 19.95x (ISBN 0-87722-054-9). Temple U Pr.

Mandle, Jay R. The Roots of Black Poverty: The Southern Plantation Economy After the Civil War. LC 78-52026. 1978. pap. 8.25 (ISBN 0-8223-0436-8). Duke.

Mandle, Joan D. Women & Social Change in America. LC 79-84301. 240p. 1979. pap. 9.95x (ISBN 0-916622-11-8). Princeton Bk Co.

Mandlebaum, Bernard. Live with Meaning. 1980. pap. 4.95 (ISBN 0-87677-182-7). Hartmore.

Mandler, George. Mind & Emotion. LC 81-14291. 296p. 1982. Repr. of 1975 ed. lib. bdg. 14.50 (ISBN 0-89874-350-8). Krieger.

Mandler, George & Kessen, William. The Language of Psychology. LC 74-34051. 320p. 1975. Repr. of 1959 ed. 16.50 (ISBN 0-88275-276-6). Krieger.

Mandlin, Harvey, photos by. Early Childhood Series, 18 Bks. large type ed. Incl. Apple Is Red. Curry, Nancy. LC 67-31186 (ISBN 0-8372-0252-3); Beautiful Day for a Picnic. Curry, Nancy. LC 67-31187. o.p. (ISBN 0-8372-0255-8); Benny's Four Hats. Jaynes, Ruth M. Curry, Nancy, ed. LC 67-26370 (ISBN 0-8372-0243-4); The Biggest House. Jaynes, Ruth M. Curry, Nancy, ed. LC 67-31188 (ISBN 0-8372-0254-X); Box Tied with a Red Ribbon. Jaynes, Ruth M. Curry, Nancy, ed. LC 68-17034 (ISBN 0-8372-0261-2); Colors. Radlauer, Ruth & Radlauer, Ed. Curry, Nancy, ed. LC 68-17026. o.p. (ISBN 0-8372-0259-0); Do You Know What. Jaynes, Ruth M. Curry, Nancy, ed. LC 67-31189 (ISBN 0-8372-0253-1); Do You Suppose Miss Riley Knows. Curry, Nancy. LC 67-31327. o.p. (ISBN 0-8372-0263-9); Evening. Radlauer, Ruth & Radlauer, Ed. Curry, Nancy, ed. LC 68-17033. o.p. (ISBN 0-8372-0269-8); Father Is Big. Radlauer, Ruth & Radlauer, Ed. (ISBN 0-8372-0240-X); Follow the Leader. Crume, Marion W. o.p. (ISBN 0-8372-0242-6); Friends, Friends, **Friends. Jaynes, Ruth M. Curry, Nancy, ed. LC 67-26371 (ISBN 0-8372-0245-0); Funny Mr. Clown. Crume, Marion W. Curry, Nancy, ed. LC 67-27124 (ISBN 0-8372-0248-5); Furry Boy. Crume, Marion W. Curry, Nancy, ed. LC 67-31474 (ISBN 0-8372-0264-7); I Like Cats. Crume, Marion W. Curry, Nancy, ed. LC 67-31475. o.p. (ISBN 0-8372-0260-4); Let Me See You Try. Crume, Marion W. Curry, Nancy, ed. LC 67-31185 (ISBN 0-8372-0256-6); Listen. Crume, Marion W. LC 68-54580. o.p. (ISBN 0-8372-0251-5); The Littlest House. Curry, Nancy. LC 68-17032. o.p. (ISBN 0-8372-0258-2); Melinda's Christmas Stocking. Jaynes, Ruth M. Curry, Nancy, ed. LC 68-17031. o.p. (ISBN 0-8372-0265-5); Morning. Crume, Marion W. Curry, Nancy, ed. LC 68-17030 (ISBN 0-8372-0268-X); My Friend Is Mrs. Jones. Curry, Nancy. LC 67-26369 (ISBN 0-8372-0244-2); My Tricycle & I. Jaynes, Ruth M. o.p. (ISBN 0-8372-0266-3); Tell Me, Please, What's That. Jaynes, Ruth M. Curry, Nancy, ed. LC 68-17028 (ISBN 0-8372-0267-1); That's What It Is. Jaynes, Ruth M. Curry, Nancy, ed. LC 67-31543 (ISBN 0-8372-0250-7); Three Baby Chicks (ISBN 0-8372-0257-4); What Do You Say (ISBN 0-8372-0262-0); What Is a Birthday Child (ISBN 0-8372-0247-7); Where Is Whiffen (ISBN 0-8372-0246-9). (ps-3). 1967-68. 6.39 ea. Bowmar-Noble.**

--Early Childhood Series. large-type ed. Incl. Three Baby Chicks. Jaynes, Ruth M. Curry, Nancy, ed. LC 72-165174 (ISBN 0-8372-0257-4); Watch Me Indoors. Jaynes, Ruth M. Curry, Nancy, ed. LC 67-31476. o.p. (ISBN 0-8372-0249-3); Watch Me Outdoors. Jaynes, Ruth M. LC 67-25574. o.p. (ISBN 0-8372-0241-8); What Do You Say. Crume, Marion W. Curry, Nancy, ed. LC 67-31328 (ISBN 0-8372-0262-0); What Is a Birthday Child. Jaynes, Ruth M. Curry, Nancy, ed. LC 67-27125 (ISBN 0-8372-0247-7); Where Is Whiffen. Jaynes, Ruth M. Curry, Nancy, ed. LC 67-27126 (ISBN 0-8372-0246-9). (ps-3). 1967-68. 6.39 ea. o.p. Bowmar-Noble.

M&MR Mars, Sweet Treat Cookery. LC 78-61008. (Illus.). 1978. pap. cancelled o.p. (ISBN 0-89586-013-9). H P Bks.

Mandrell, Louise & Collins, Ace. The Mandrell Family Album. (Illus.). 168p. 1983. 14.95 (ISBN 0-8407-4109-X). Nelson.

Mandt, Mikkel G. & Bell, Bruce A. Oxidation Ditches in Wastewater Treatment. LC 82-70700. (Illus.). 169p. 1982. 29.95 (ISBN 0-250-40430-3). Ann Arbor Science.

Mandyczewski, Eusebius, ed. see Brahms, Johannes.

Mandyczewski, Eusebius, ed. see Schubert, Franz.

Maneker, M., jt. auth. see Foley, J.

Manell, P. & Johansson, S. G., eds. The Impact of Computer Technology on Drug Information: Proceedings of the IFIP-IMIA Working Conference, Uppsala, Sweden, October 26-28, 1981. 262p. 1982. 34.00 (ISBN 0-444-86451-2, North Holland). Elsevier.

Manella, Douglas. Amphoto Guide to Black-&-White Processing & Printing. (Illus.). 1979. 12.95 (ISBN 0-8174-2461-X, Amphoto); pap. 7.95 (ISBN 0-8174-2135-1). Watson-Guptill.

Manella, Raymond L., jt. ed. see Amos, William E.

Manely, Robert N. Kansas: Our Pioneer Heritage. (Illus.). 88p. 1982. pap. 6.75 tchr's. guide (ISBN 0-939644-05-3). Media Prods & Mktg.

Maner, Robert E. Making the Small Church Grow. 101p. 1982. pap. 2.95 (ISBN 0-8341-0741-4). Beacon Hill.

Manera, Anthony S. Solid-State Electronic Circuits for Engineering Technology. (Illus.). 672p. 1973. text ed. 26.95 (ISBN 0-07-039871-2, G); solutions & ans. 2.95 (ISBN 0-07-039872-0). McGraw.

Manera, Elizabeth S. & Wright, Robert E. Annotated Writer's Guide to Professional Educational Journals. 188p. 1982. pap. 9.95 (ISBN 0-9609782-0-8). Bobets.

Manes, Esther & Manes, Stephen. The Bananas Move to the Ceiling. (Easy-Read Story Bks.). (Illus.). 32p. (gr. k-3). 1983. 3.95 (ISBN 0-531-03575-1); PLB 8.60 (ISBN 0-531-04517-X). Watts.

Manes, Stephen. The Boy Who Turned into a TV Set. LC 78-31436. (Illus.). (gr. 3-5). 1979. 7.95 (ISBN 0-698-20491-3, Coward). Putnam Pub Group.

--The Boy Who Turned into a TV Set. (Illus.). 32p. 1983. pap. 1.95 (ISBN 0-380-62000-6, 62000-6, Camelot). Avon.

--The Hooples' Haunted House. LC 81-2216. (Illus.). 128p. (gr. 3-7). 1981. 8.95 o.p. (ISBN 0-440-03733-6); PLB 8.89 (ISBN 0-440-03736-0). Delacorte.

--Hooples on the Highway. LC 78-1710. (gr. 3-5). 1978. 6.95 o.p. (ISBN 0-698-20459-X, Coward). Putnam Pub Group.

--I'll Live. 160p. 1982. pap. 2.25 (ISBN 0-380-81737-3, 81737, Flare). Avon.

--Mule in the Mail. LC 77-26193. (Illus.). (gr. 3-5). 1978. 6.95 o.p. (ISBN 0-698-20453-0, Coward). Putnam Pub Group.

--Pictures of Motion & Pictures that Move: Eadweard Muybridge & the Photography of Motion. (Illus.). 64p. 1982. 9.95 (ISBN 0-698-20550-2, Coward). Putnam PubGroup.

--Socko: Every Riddle Your Feet Will Ever Need. (Illus.). 32p. 1982. 5.95 (ISBN 0-698-20538-3, Coward). Putnam Pub Group.

--That Game from Outer Space. (Illus.). 64p. (gr. 3-5). 1983. 8.95 (ISBN 0-525-44056-9, 0869-260). Dutton.

--Video War. 272p. pap. 2.25 (ISBN 0-380-83303-4, Flare). Avon.

Manes, Stephen, jt. auth. see Manes, Esther.

Maness, Bill. Recreation Ministry: A Guide for all Congregations. LC 81-85324. 102p. 1983. pap. 11.95 (ISBN 0-8042-1186-8). John Knox.

Manesson-Mallet, Allain. Descriptions de l'Univers Contenant les Differents Systemes du Monde. (Bibliotheque Africaine Ser.). 276p. (Fr.). 1974. Repr. of 1683 ed. lib. bdg. 74.50x o.p. (ISBN 0-8287-0567-4, 72-2156). Clearwater Pub.

Manetti, Antonio. Life of Brunelleschi. Saalman, Howard, ed. Enggass, Catherine, tr. LC 68-8183. (Illus.). 1970. 16.95x (ISBN 0-271-00075-9). Pa St U Pr.

Maney, Margaret, jt. auth. see Grasso, Mary E.

Manfred, Frederick. The Buckskin Man Tales, 5 bks. 1980. Set. lib. bdg. 70.00 (ISBN 0-8398-2734-2, Gregg). G K Hall.

--Conquering Horse. 1980. lib. bdg. 15.95 (ISBN 0-8398-2590-0, Gregg). G K Hall.

--King of Spades. 1980. lib. bdg. 14.95 (ISBN 0-8398-2592-7, Gregg). G K Hall.

--Lord Grizzly. 1980. lib. bdg. 14.95 (ISBN 0-8398-2591-9, Gregg). G K Hall.

--Lord Grizzly. (Buckskin Man Tales Ser.). 288p. 1982. pap. 7.95 (ISBN 0-8032-8118-8, BB 837, Bison). U of Nebr Pr.

--Riders of Judgment. 1980. lib. bdg. 15.95 (ISBN 0-8398-2593-5, Gregg). G K Hall.

--Scarlet Plume. 1980. lib. bdg. 15.95 (ISBN 0-8398-2594-3, Gregg). G K Hall.

--Sons of Adam. 352p. 1980. 12.95 o.p. (ISBN 0-517-54186-6, Michelman Bks). Crown.

--This Is the Year. 1979. lib. bdg. 14.95 (ISBN 0-8398-2580-3, Gregg). G K Hall.

Manfred, Frederick F. Lord Grizzly. (RL 9). 1971. pap. 1.75 o.p. (ISBN 0-451-08311-3, E8311, Sig). NAL.

Manfreda, Marguerite L. & Krampitz, Sydney D. Psychiatric Nursing. 10th ed. LC 77-2836. (Illus.). 525p. 1977. text ed. 12.95x o.p. (ISBN 0-8036-5822-2). Davis Co.

Manfredi, John. The Social Limits of Art. LC 82-8661. (Illus.). 208p. 1982. lib. bdg. 15.00x (ISBN 0-87023-372-6). U of Mass Pr.

Mang, Karl. Viennese Architecture Eighteeen Sixty to Nineteen Thirty in Drawings. LC 79-64900. (Illus.). 1980. 32.50 (ISBN 0-8478-0257-4). Rizzoli Intl.

Mangan, Celine. One-Two Chronicles, Ezra, Nehemiah, Vol. 13. 1982. 12.95 (ISBN 0-89453-247-2); pap. 6.95 (ISBN 0-686-32766-7). M Glazier.

Mangan, Doreen & Fehr, Terry. How to Be a Super Camp Counselor. (Concise Guides Ser.). (Illus.). (gr. 7 up). 1979. PLB 8.90 s&l (ISBN 0-531-02893-3). Watts.

Mangan, Frances S. Intermediate Algebra. new ed. (Mathematics Ser). (Illus.). 480p. 1975. pap. text ed. 17.95 o.p. (ISBN 0-675-08742-2). Additional supplements may be obtained from publisher. Merrill.

Mangan, G. The Biology of Human Personality. (International Series in Experimental Psychology: Vol. 25). 470p. 1982. 72.00 (ISBN 0-08-026781-5). Pergamon.

Mangano, Antonio. Sons of Italy: A Social & Religious Study of the Italians in America. LC 75-145488. (American Immigration Library). xii, 264p. 1971. Repr. of 1917 ed. lib. bdg. 15.95x (ISBN 0-89198-020-2). Ozer.

Mangen, David J. & Peterson, Warren A., eds. Research Instruments in Social Gerontology: Social Roles & Social Participation, Vol. 2. LC 81-16449. 600p. 1982. 35.00x (ISBN 0-8166-1096-7). U of Minn Pr.

Mangenot, jt. auth. see Du Mesnil.

Manger, W. M. Catecholamines in Normal & Abnormal Cardiac Function. (Advances in Cardiology: Vol. 30). (Illus.). xxiv, 152p. 1982. 58.75 (ISBN 3-8055-3516-3). S Karger.

Mangham, Evelyn. Great Missionaries in a Great Work. Schroeder, E. H., ed. (Illus.). 85p. 1970. pap. 1.75 (ISBN 0-87509-091-5). Chr Pubns.

Mangham, Iain. The Politics of Organizational Change. LC 79-23. (Contributions in Economics & Economic History: No. 26). 1979. lib. bdg. 27.50 (ISBN 0-313-20981-2, MPC/). Greenwood.

Mangham, Iain, ed. Interactions & Interventions in Organizations. LC 78-2602. (Wiley Series on Individuals, Groups & Organizations). 1978. 34.95 (ISBN 0-471-99622-X, Pub. by Wiley-Interscience). Wiley.

Mangham, Ian, jt. auth. see Bate, Paul.

Manghnani, M. H., jt. auth. see Akimoto, S.

Mangieri, J., et al. Elementary Reading. 1982. 22.50x (ISBN 0-07-039886-0). McGraw.

Mangin, Marie F. Suzette & Nicholas & the Seasons Clock. (Illus.). 32p. 1982. 8.95 (ISBN 0-399-20832-1, Philomel). Putnam Pub Group.

Mangin, Marie-France, jt. auth. see Lochak, Michele.

Mangiola, Stelio & Ritota, Michael C. Cardiac Arrythmias: Practical ECG Interpretations. 2nd ed. (Illus.). 272p. 1982. text ed. 37.50 (ISBN 0-397-50511-6, Lippincott Medical). Lippincott.

Mangione, Jerre. The Dream & the Deal: The Federal Writers Project 1935-1943. LC 75-187787. (Illus.). 1972. 12.50 o.s.i. (ISBN 0-916224-22-8). Banyan Bks.

--An Ethnic at Large: A Memoir of America in the Thirties & Forties. LC 77-27447. (Illus.). 1978. 12.50 o.p. (ISBN 0-399-11774-1). Putnam Pub Group.

--An Ethnic at Large: A Memoir of America in the Thirties & Forties. LC 82-40494. (Illus.). 416p. 1983. pap. 10.95 (ISBN 0-8122-1140-5). U of Pa Pr.

Mangione, Jerry. The Dream & the Deal: The Federal Writers Project, 1935-1943. LC 82-40495. (Illus.). 432p. 1983. pap. 10.95 (ISBN 0-8122-1141-3). U of Pa Pr.

Mangold, Edward, et al. Coal Liquefaction & Gasification Technologies. LC 81-69550. (Illus.). 266p. 1981. text ed. 29.95 (ISBN 0-250-40494-X). Ann Arbor Science.

Mangold, H. K. & Paltavy, F., eds. Ether Lipids: Biomedical Aspects. LC 82-11619. Date not set. price not set (ISBN 0-12-468780-6). Acad Pr.

Mangold, Peter. Superpower Intervention in the Middle East. LC 77-9237. 1978. 26.00x (ISBN 0-312-77668-3). St Martin.

Mangold, Tom, jt. auth. see Summers, Anthony.

Mangone, Gerard J. Marine Policy for America: The United States at Sea. LC 77-243. 1977. 28.95 (ISBN 0-669-01432-X). Lexington Bks.

--A Short History of International Organization. LC 74-10653. 326p. 1975. Repr. of 1954 ed. lib. bdg. 18.25x (ISBN 0-8371-7652-2, MAIO). Greenwood.

Mangrum, Charles T. Learning to Study: Study Skills-Strategies Book F. (Learning to Study Ser.). 1983. pap. text ed. 3.95 (ISBN 0-89061-287-0); tchr's ed 5.25 (ISBN 0-89061-293-5). Jamestown Pubs.

--Learning to Study: Study Skills-Study Strategies Book B-C. (Learning to Study Ser.). 80p. 1983. pap. text ed. 3.95 (ISBN 0-89061-284-6); tchr's ed 5.25 (ISBN 0-89061-290-0). Jamestown Pubs.

--Learning to Study: Study Skills-Study Strategies Book D. (Learning to Study Ser.). 80p. 1983. pap. text ed. 3.95 (ISBN 0-89061-285-4); tchr's ed 5.25 (ISBN 0-89061-291-9). Jamestown Pubs.

--Learning to Study: Study Skills-Study Strategies Book E. (Learning to Study Ser.). 96p. 1983. pap. text ed. 3.95 (ISBN 0-89061-286-2); tchr's ed 5.25 (ISBN 0-89061-292-7). Jamestown Pubs.

--Learning to Study: Study Skills-Study Strategies Book G. (Learning to Study Ser.). 96p. 1983. pap. text ed. 3.95 (ISBN 0-89061-288-9); tchr's ed 5.25 (ISBN 0-89061-294-3). Jamestown Pubs.

--Learning to Study: Study Skills-Study Strategies Book H. (Learning to Study Ser.). 96p. 1983. pap. text ed. 3.95 (ISBN 0-89061-289-7); tchr's ed 5.25 (ISBN 0-89061-295-1). Jamestown Pubs.

Mangrum, Charles T. & Forgan, Harry W. Developing Competencies in Teaching Reading: A Modular Program for Preservice & Inservice Elementary & Middle School Teachers. Heilman, Arthur W., ed. (Elementary Education Ser.). 1979. pap. text ed. 18.95 (ISBN 0-675-08367-2). Additional supplements may be obtained from publisher. Merrill.

Mangrum, Charles T., jt. auth. see Forgan, Harry W.

Mangus, A. L. Changing Aspects of Rural Relief. LC 74-165685. (Research Monograph Series: Vol. 14). 1971. Repr. of 1938 ed. lib. bdg. 29.50 (ISBN 0-306-70346-7). Da Capo.

Mangus, A. R., jt. auth. see Asch, Berta.

Manhaimer. Cataloging & Classification: A Workbook. 2nd, rev. ed. (Books in Library & Information Ser.: Vol 30). 1980. 11.50 (ISBN 0-8247-1027-4). Dekker.

Manhas, Maghar S. Chemistry of Penicillins & Other Beta-Lactams. LC 78-27100. 248p. 1983. Repr. of 1971 ed. write for info. (ISBN 0-88275-830-6). Krieger.

Manhattan, Avro. The Vacation Moscow Washington Alliance. 352p. (Orig.). pap. 6.95 (ISBN 0-937958-12-3). Chick Pubns.

Manheim, Frank T., jt. auth. see Fanning, Kent A.

Manheim, Jarol B. & Rich, Richard C. Empirical Political Analysis: Research Methods in Political Science. (Illus.). 432p. 1981. text ed. 22.95 (ISBN 0-13-274605-0). P-H.

Manheim, Mary, tr. see Bertholle, Louisette.

Manheim, Ralph, tr. see Auerbach, Erich.

Manheim, Ralph, tr. see Cassirer, Ernst.

Manheim, Ralph, tr. see Celine, Louis-Ferdinand.

Manheim, Ralph, tr. see Grass, Gunter.

Manheim, Ralph, tr. see Jaspers, Karl.

Manheim, Ralph, tr. see Maass, Joachim.

Manheim, Ralph, tr. see Oberski, Jona.

Manheim, Ralph, tr. see Proust, Marcel.

Manheim, Ralph, tr. see Reich, Wilhelm.

Manheim, Ralph, tr. see Von Lang, Jochen.

Manheim, Werner. Martin Buber. (World Authors Ser.: Austria: No. 269). 1974. lib. bdg. 10.95 o.p. (ISBN 0-8057-2182-7, Twayne). G K Hall.

Manheimer, Ronald J. Kierkegaard As Educator. LC 76-24587. 1978. 22.50x (ISBN 0-520-03312-4). U of Cal Pr.

Manheimer, Wallace M. An Introduction to Trapped-Particle Instability in Tokamaks. LC 77-8530. (ERDA Critical Review Ser.: Advances in Fusion Science & Engineering). 104p. 1977. pap. 10.50 (ISBN 0-87079-105-2, TID-27157); microfiche 4.50 (ISBN 0-87079-251-2, TID-27157). DOE.

Mani, Vettam. Puranic Encyclopedia: Comprehensive Dictionary with Special Reference to the Epics & the Puranas. LC 76-900024. 1976. 65.00x o.p. (ISBN 0-88386-755-9). South Asia Bks.

Manian, Victor, jt. auth. see Gardner, Thomas J.

Manicas, Peter T. & Krugar, A. N. Logic: The Essentials. 1976. text ed. 23.95 (ISBN 0-07-039893-3, C); instructors' manual 15.00 (ISBN 0-07-039894-1). McGraw.

Manila, Gabriel J. Marcos: Wild Child of the Sierra Morena. Bonner, Deborah, tr. 167p. 1982. text ed. 17.50x (ISBN 0-285-64924-8, Pub. by Condor Bk England). Humanities.

Manion, L., jt. auth. see Cohen, L.

Manion, Paul D. Tree Disease Concepts in Relation to Forest & Urban Tree Management Practice. (Illus.). 400p. 1981. text ed. 24.95 (ISBN 0-13-930701-X). P-H.

Maniruzzaman, Talukder. Group Interests & Political Changes: Studies of Pakistan & Bangladesh. 1982. 24.00x (ISBN 0-8364-0892-6). South Asia Bks.

Manis, Laura G. Womanpower: A Manual for Workshops in Personal Effectiveness. LC 76-54156. 1977. pap. text ed. 5.75x (ISBN 0-910328-10-2). Carroll Pr.

Manis, Michael S. Real Estate Investment Analysis. (Real Estate Ser.). 272p. 1983. text ed. 25.95 (ISBN 0-471-86503-6). Wiley.

Maniscalco, Joe. Bible Hero Stories. LC 74-28725. (Illus.). 144p. (gr. 3-6). 1975. 6.95 (ISBN 0-87239-036-5, 2746). Standard Pub.

--Joseph. LC 74-28725. (Bible Hero Stories). (Illus.). 48p. (Orig.). (gr. 3-6). 1975. pap. 2.00 (ISBN 0-87239-332-1, 2737). Standard Pub.

Maniscalco, Nancy. Lesser Sins. 1979. pap. 1.95 o.p. (ISBN 0-380-46029-7, 46029). Avon.

Manka, Dan, ed. Automated Stream Analysis for Processed Control, Vol. 1. LC 82-8822. 336p. 1982. 39.50 (ISBN 0-12-469001-7). Acad Pr.

Mankabady, S. Collision at Sea: A Guide to the Legal Consequences. 1978. 59.75 (ISBN 0-444-85155-0, North-Holland). Elsevier.

Mankekar, D. R. Leaves from a War Reporter's Diary. 1977. text ed. 11.95x o.p. (ISBN 0-7069-0505-9, Pub. by Vikas India). Advent NY.

Man Keung Ho. Group Work with Probation & After-Care Youth. 102p. 1977. 8.50 (ISBN 0-686-74263-X). U Pr of Amer.

--Social Work Methods, Techniques & Skills. LC 80-5319. 559p. 1980. pap. text ed. 19.50 (ISBN 0-8191-1077-9). U Pr of Amer.

Mankiewicz, Rene H., ed. Yearbook of Air & Space Law, 1967. 536p. 1971. 27.50x o.p. (ISBN 0-7735-0064-2). McGill-Queens U Pr.

Mankin, Don. Toward a Post-Industrial Psychology: Emerging Perspectives on Technology, Work, Education & Leisure. LC 78-5302. 1978. pap. text ed. 16.95 (ISBN 0-471-02086-9). Wiley.

Mankin, Don & Ames, Russell E., Jr., eds. Classics of Industrial & Organizational Psychology. LC 80-15699. (Classics Ser.). (Orig.). 1980. pap. 12.50x (ISBN 0-935610-11-1). Moore Pub IL.

Mankin, Paul & Szogyi, Alex. Anthologie d'humour Francais. 1970. pap. 7.95x o.p. (ISBN 0-673-05111-0). Scott F.

Manko, Howard H. Effective Technical Speeches & Sessions: A Guide for Speakers & Program Chairmen. LC 69-18731. (Illus.). 1969. 24.75 (ISBN 0-07-039896-8, P&RB). McGraw.

--Solders & Soldering. 2nd ed. LC 79-9714. (Illus.). 1980. 31.25 (ISBN 0-07-039897-6). McGraw.

Mankoff, Milton, jt. auth. see Chambliss, William J.

Mankoff, Robert. Elementary: The Cartoonist Did It. 128p. 1982. pap. 4.95 (ISBN 0-380-75317-0, 75317). Avon.

Manley, Deborah. Finding Out About Bible Times. 1980. 7.95 o.p. (ISBN 0-89191-339-4). Cook.

Manley, Gregory, jt. auth. see Crotty, Robert.

Manley, Mary D. The Adventures of Rivella. Bd. with The Adventures & Surprizing Deliverances of James Dubourdieu & His Wife Who Were Taken by Pyrates. Evans, Ambrose. LC 73-170534. LC 70-170533. (Foundations of the Novel Ser.: Vol. 22). lib. bdg. 50.00 o.s.i. (ISBN 0-8240-0534-1). Garland Pub.

--Novels, 1705-1714, 7 Vols. in Two. LC 75-161934. 1971. 150.00x set (ISBN 0-8201-1094-9). Schol Facsimiles.

--Secret Memoirs & Manners of Several Persons of Quality of Both Sexes from the New Atalantis. LC 74-170520. (Foundations of the Novel Ser.: Vol. 15). lib. bdg. 50.00 o.s.i. (ISBN 0-8240-0527-9). Garland Pub.
Manley, Michael. Jamaica: Struggle in the Periphery. (Illus.). 259p. 1982. 15.95 (ISBN 0-906495-97-0); pap. 7.95 (ISBN 0-906495-98-9). Writers & Readers.
Manley, Paula J., jt. auth. see Hanft, Ethel W.
Manley, Robert G., ed. see Wells, Theodora.
Manley, Robert H. Guyana Emergent: The Post-Independence Struggle for Nondependent Development. 1979. lib. bdg. 14.50 (ISBN 0-8161-9001-1, Univ Bks). G K Hall.
--International & Comparative Public Policy, 2 vols. in 3 pts. (International Public Policy Institute Ser.). 1982. Repr. Vol. 1, No. 1, 286p. lib. bdg. 20.00 (ISBN 0-8191-2103-7); Vol. 1, No. 2, 152p. lib. bdg. 20.00 (ISBN 0-8191-2104-5); Vol. 2, 146p. lib. bdg. 20.00 (ISBN 0-8191-2105-3). U Pr of Amer.
Manley, Robert H., ed. Building Positive Peace: Actors & Factors. LC 81-43025. 242p. 1981. lib. bdg. 21.50 (ISBN 0-8191-1516-9); pap. text ed. 10.75 (ISBN 0-8191-1517-7). U Pr of Amer.
Manley, Robert N. Kansas, Our Pioneer Heritage. (Illus.). 215p. 1982. 12.50 (ISBN 0-939644-03-7). Media Prods & Mktg.
Manley, Seon. A Present for Charles Dickens. (Illus.). 120p. (gr. 5-7). 1983. price not set (ISBN 0-664-32706-0). Westminster.
Manley, Seon & Lewis, Gogo. The Haunted Dolls. LC 79-7608. (Illus.). 336p. 1980. 10.95a o.p. (ISBN 0-385-15363-5); PLB 10.95a (ISBN 0-385-15654-5). Doubleday.
Manley, Seon & Lewis, Gogo, eds. To You with Love: A Treasury of Great Romantic Literature. LC 77-87987. (Illus.). (gr. 5 up). 1969. 6.25 (ISBN 0-8255-5520-5). Macrae.
Manley, Timothy M. Outline of Sca Structure. (Oceanic Linguistics Ser.: No. 12). 250p. (Orig.). 1972. pap. text ed. 8.00x (ISBN 0-8248-0238-1). UH Pr.
Manley, Will. Snowballs in the Bookdrop: Talking It Over with Your Library's Community. 216p. (Orig.). 1982. pap. 14.50 o.p. (ISBN 0-208-01944-8, Lib Prof Pubns). Shoe String.
Manley-Casimir, Michael E., ed. Family Choice in Schooling: Issues & Dilemmas. LC 81-47024. 224p. 1981. 23.95 (ISBN 0-669-04546-2). Lexington Bks.
Manley-Tucker, Audrie. Shetland Summer. (Aston Hall Romances Ser.: No. 110). 192p. (Orig.). 1980. pap. 1.50 o.p. (ISBN 0-523-41122-7). Pinnacle Bks.
Manlove, C. N. The Impulse of Fantasy Literature. LC 82-15335. xiii, 174p. 1983. 17.50 (ISBN 0-87338-273-0). Kent St U Pr.
--Literature & Reality, Sixteen Hundred to Eighteen Hundred. LC 78-6934. 1978. 26.00x (ISBN 0-312-48747-9). St Martin.
--Modern Fantasy: Five Studies. LC 74-31798. 320p. 1975. 42.50 (ISBN 0-521-20746-0); pap. 11.95 (ISBN 0-521-29386-3). Cambridge U Pr.
Manlove, Colin N. The Gap in Shakespeare: The Motif of Division from 'Richard II to I the Tempest. (Critical Studies). 200p. 1981. 26.50x (ISBN 0-389-20111-1). B&N Imports.
Manlove, Donald C. The Best of James Whitcomb Riley. LC 82-74958. 192p. (Orig.). 15.00 (ISBN 0-253-10610-9); pap. 7.95 (ISBN 0-253-20299-X). Ind U Pr.
Manly, John M. & Rickert, Edith. Contemporary American Literature, Bibliographies & Study Outlines. LC 74-17631. 378p. 1975. Repr. of 1929 ed. lib. bdg. 20.25x (ISBN 0-8371-7254-3, MAAL). Greenwood.
Manly, R. H. Durable Press Treatment of Fabrics-Recent Developments. LC 76-2322. (Chemical Technology Review: No. 68). 372p. 1976. 39.00 (ISBN 0-8155-0617-1). Noyes.
Manly, William. Death Valley in Forty-Nine. (Classics of the Old West). 1982. lib. bdg. 17.28 (ISBN 0-686-42771-8). Silver.
Manly, William L. Death Valley in '49. 1977. 16.95 (ISBN 0-912494-22-0); pap. 13.95 (ISBN 0-912494-23-9). Chalfant Pr.
Manmohan, Mehra. Harley Granville Barker: A Critical Study of the Major Plays. 1982. 16.00x (ISBN 0-686-38375-3). South Asia Bks.
Mann. Marijuana Alert. 1983. write for info. (ISBN 0-07-039907-7); pap. write for info. (ISBN 0-07-039906-9). McGraw.
Mann, jt. auth. see Weiss.
Mann, A. T. The Round Art: Space Time & Astrology. LC 78-50947. (Illus.). cancelled (ISBN 0-89169-503-6); pap. cancelled (ISBN 0-89169-502-8). Reed Bks.
Mann, Arthur. The One & the Many: Reflections on the American Identity. LC 78-27849. 1979. 12.95x (ISBN 0-226-50337-2). U of Chicago Pr.
Mann, C. S., jt. ed. see Albright, William F.
Mann, Charles E., ed. see Hutchinson, John Wallace.
Mann, Dale. Policy Decision Making in Education: An Introduction to Calculation & Control. LC 74-13962. 1975. text ed. 15.50x (ISBN 0-8077-2548-X); pap. text ed. 8.50x o.p. (ISBN 0-8077-2468-8). Tchrs Coll.
Mann, Dale & Skinulis, Richard. The Complete Log House Book. (Illus., Orig.). 1979. pap. 12.95 (ISBN 0-07-082817-2). McGraw.
Mann, Dale, ed. Making Change Happen? LC 78-21849. (Orig.). 1978. pap. text ed. 14.95x o.p. (ISBN 0-8077-2548-X). Tchrs Coll.
Mann, Dale, et al. Chasing the American Dream: Jobs, Schools, & Employment Training Programs in New York State: Technical Report. 47p. (Orig.). 1980. 10.00 (ISBN 0-88156-006-5); pap. 2.00 (ISBN 0-88156-005-7). Comm Serv Soc NY.
Mann, David D. Sir George Etherege: A Reference Guide. 1981. lib. bdg. 24.00 (ISBN 0-8161-8171-3, Hall Reference). G K Hall.
Mann, Dean, ed. Environmental Policy. (Orig.). 1980. pap. 6.00 (ISBN 0-918592-43-7). Policy Studies.
Mann, Dean E., ed. Environmental Policy Formation: The Impacts of Values, Ideology & Standards. LC 79-3828. (A Policy Studies Organization). 256p. 1981. 26.95x (ISBN 0-669-03518-1). Lexington Bks.
--Environmental Policy Implementation: The Impacts of Values, Ideology, & Standards. LC 79-3829. (A Policy Studies Organization). 272p. 1982. 29.95x (ISBN 0-669-03516-5). Lexington Bks.
Mann, Fritz A. Legal Aspects of Money. 4th ed. (Illus.). 1982. 79.00x (ISBN 0-19-825367-2). Oxford U Pr.
Mann, George A. Recovery of Reality. 9.95 o.p. (ISBN 0-686-92065-1). Hazelden.
--Recovery of Reality: Overcoming Chemical Dependency. LC 78-19496. (Illus.). 1979. 11.95i (ISBN 0-06-250560-2, HarpR). Har-Row.
Mann, Gertrude, jt. auth. see Rabinsky, Leatrice.
Mann, Golo. Secretary of Europe: The Life of Fredrich Gentz, Enemy of Napoleon. 1946. text ed. 18.50x (ISBN 0-686-83734-7). Elliots Bks.
Mann, I. Animal By-Products: Processing & Utilization. (FAO Agricultural Development Paper No. 75, FAO Animal Pruduction & Health Ser.: No. 9). 246p. 1962. pap. 13.75 (ISBN 0-686-93109-2, F1474, FAO). Unipub.
Mann, J. Y. & Milligan, I. S., eds. Aircraft Fatigue: Design, Operational & Economic Aspects. LC 71-125094. 570p. 1975. 105.00 (ISBN 0-08-017526-0). Pergamon.
Mann, James H. Reducing Made Easy: The Elments of Microfilm. LC 76-25335. 12.00 (ISBN 0-87716-069-4, Pub. by Moore Pub Co). F Apple.
Mann, Jessica. Funeral Sites. LC 81-43617. (Crime Club Ser.). 192p. 1982. 10.95 (ISBN 0-385-18045-4). Doubleday.
--The Sting of Death. LC 82-45868. (Crime Club Ser.). 192p. 1983. 11.95 (ISBN 0-385-18701-7). Doubleday.
Mann, Jill. Chaucer & Medieval Estates Satire. LC 72-90490. 384p. 1972. 49.50 (ISBN 0-521-20058-X); pap. 15.95 (ISBN 0-521-09795-9). Cambridge U Pr.
Mann, Jim. Solving Publishing's Toughest Problems. Date not set. 49.95 (ISBN 0-918110-07-6). Folio.
Mann, Jim & Oxford Dietetic Group. The Diabetics' Diet Book. LC 81-22875. (Illus.). 123p. 1983. 12.95 (ISBN 0-668-05325-9, 5325). Arco.
Mann, K. H. Ecology of Coastal Waters: A Systems Approach. LC 81-40321. (Studies in Ecology: Vol. 8). (Illus.). 300p. 1981. 36.00x (ISBN 0-520-04526-2); pap. 18.00x (ISBN 0-520-04734-6). U of Cal Pr.
Mann, Klaus. Mephisto: Movie Tie-In Edition. Smith, Robin, tr. from Ger. 1983. pap. 4.95 (ISBN 0-14-006578-4). Penguin.
Mann, Lawrence. Maintenance Management. 320p. 1976. 26.95 (ISBN 0-669-00143-0). Lexington Bks.
Mann, Lawrence, Jr. Maintenance Management. LC 81-47628. 384p. 1983. 32.95x (ISBN 0-669-04715-5). Lexington Bks.
Mann, Lester, jt. auth. see Sabatino, David.
Mann, Lester, et al. Teaching the Learning-Disabled Adolescent. LC 77-74377. (Illus.). 1978. pap. text ed. 22.95 (ISBN 0-395-25434-5). HM.
Mann, M. Workers on the Move: The Sociology of Relocation. (Studies in Sociology: No. 6). (Illus.). 1973. 34.50 (ISBN 0-521-08701-5); pap. 10.95x (ISBN 0-521-09787-8). Cambridge U Pr.
Mann, M., jt. ed. see Sharp, J. R.
Mann, Marjorie B. The Big Feed: Twenty Three Course French Dinners for Six with Wine Selections. LC 79-11931. 1979. 13.95 (ISBN 0-89594-022-1); pap. 5.95 (ISBN 0-89594-019-1). Crossing Pr.
Mann, Marty. Marty Mann's New Primer on Alcoholism. 5.95 o.p. (ISBN 0-686-92265-4, 4288). Hazelden.
Mann, Mary. Elvis, Why Don't They Leave You Alone? 1982. pap. 2.95 (ISBN 0-451-11877-4, AE1877, Sig). NAL.
Mann, Michael, jt. auth. see Blackburn, R. M.
Mann, Nancy R., et al. Methods for the Statistical Analysis of Reliability & Life Data. LC 73-20461. (Ser. in Probability & Mathematical Statistics). 576p. 1974. 44.95 (ISBN 0-471-56737-X, Pub. by Wiley-Interscience). Wiley.
Mann, Nancy W. Tylers & Gardiners on the Village Green: Williamsburg, Va. & East Hampton, Long Island. 1983. 9.50 (ISBN 0-533-05556-3). Vantage.
Mann, Peggy. Amelia Earhart: First Lady of Flight. (Illus.). (gr. 5-8). 1970. PLB 6.99 (ISBN 0-698-30008-4, Coward). Putnam Pub Group.
--Clara Barton: Battlefield Nurse. (Illus.). (gr. 3-5). 1969. PLB 3.99 o.p. (ISBN 0-698-30047-5, Coward). Putnam Pub Group.
--Golda: The Story of Israel's Prime Minister. (Illus.). (gr. 5-8). 1971. 6.95 o.p. (ISBN 0-698-20052-7, Coward). Putnam Pub Group.
--King Laurence, the Alarm Clock. LC 74-16156. 48p. (ps). 1976. PLB 7.95 (ISBN 0-385-04972-2). Doubleday.
--Luis Munoz Marin: The Man Who Remade Puerto Rico. LC 76-6117. (Illus.). 128p. (gr. 6 up). 1976. PLB 5.86 o.p. (ISBN 0-698-30614-7, Coward). Putnam Pub Group.
--My Dad Lives in a Downtown Hotel. 1974. pap. 1.75 o.p. (ISBN 0-380-00096-2, 55038, Camelot). Avon.
--The Secret Dog of Little Luis. (Illus.). 96p. (gr. 3-5). 1973. PLB 4.97 o.p. (ISBN 0-698-30528-0, Coward). Putnam Pub Group.
--The Street of the Flower Boxes. (Illus.). (gr. 4-6). 1966. PLB 4.49 o.p. (ISBN 0-698-30341-5, Coward). Putnam Pub Group.
--There Are Two Kinds of Terrible. (gr. 5 up). 1979. pap. 1.50 o.p. (ISBN 0-380-45823-3, 45823, Camelot). Avon.
--There Are Two Kinds of Terrible. LC 76-42372. (gr. 3-7). 1977. PLB 7.95a o.p. (ISBN 0-385-08185-5). Doubleday.
--Twelve Is Too Old. LC 78-14705. (gr. 4). 1980. 8.95a (ISBN 0-385-05099-2); PLB o.p. (ISBN 0-385-05110-7). Doubleday.
--When Carlos Closed the Street. (Illus.). (gr. 3-5). 1969. PLB 4.97 o.p. (ISBN 0-698-30401-2, Coward). Putnam Pub Group.
Mann, Peggy, jt. auth. see Hersch, Giselle.
Mann, Peggy, jt. auth. see Kluger, Ruth.
Mann, Pete M. Correspondence Models for Educators. LC 82-80826. 105p. (Orig.). 1982. pap. 6.95x (ISBN 0-89950-065-X). McFarland & Co.
Mann, Peter. From Author to Reader: A Social Study of Books. 160p. 1982. 17.95 (ISBN 0-7100-9089-7). Routledge & Kegan.
Mann, Philip, ed. see Pearson, Bill.
Mann, Phillip. Eight Days a Week. (Australian Theatre Workshop Ser.). 1972. pap. text ed. 4.50x o.p. (ISBN 0-85859-027-1, 00536). Heinemann Ed.
--Eye of the Queen. 1983. 13.50 (ISBN 0-87795-462-3). Arbor Hse.
Mann, Robert. Rails 'Neath the Palms. (Illus.). 1983. write for info. (ISBN 0-933506-08-2). Darwin Pubns.
Mann, Robert W., jt. auth. see Taylor, Angus E.
Mann, Roger, ed. Exotic Species in Mariculture. (Illus.). 1979. text ed. 20.00x (ISBN 0-262-13155-2). MIT Pr.
Mann, Roger A. DuVries' Surgery of the Foot. 4th ed. LC 78-10829. (Illus.). 624p. 1978. text ed. 57.50 (ISBN 0-8016-2333-2). Mosby.
Mann, Stella T. How to Analyze & Overcome Your Fears. 2nd ed. 179p. 1972. pap. 4.95 (ISBN 0-87516-175-8). De Vorss.
--How to Live in the Circle of Prayer & Make Your Dreams Come True. (Illus.). 180p. 1975. pap. 4.95 (ISBN 0-87516-206-1). De Vorss.
Mann, Stephanie, jt. auth. see Henke, Shirley.
Mann, Stuart H., jt. auth. see Johnson, Edward R.
Mann, T. K. Administration of Justice in India. 1979. text ed. 14.25x (ISBN 0-391-01854-X). Humanities.
Mann, Thomas. Black Swan. 1954. 11.50 (ISBN 0-394-41708-9). Knopf.
--Buddenbrooks. 1961. pap. 6.95 (ISBN 0-394-70180-1, Vin). Random.
--Death in Venice. Heller, Erich, tr. (YA) 1970. pap. 3.25 (ISBN 0-394-30999-5, T99, Mod LibC). Modern Lib.
--Doctor Faustus. 1966. 3.95 o.s.i. (ISBN 0-394-60365-6, M365). Modern Lib.
--Magic Mountain. (YA) 1956. 20.50 (ISBN 0-394-43458-7). Knopf.
--Reflections of a Nonpolitical Man. Morris, Walter, tr. from Ger. LC 82-40249. 600p. 1983. 29.50x (ISBN 0-8044-2585-X). Ungar.
--Stories of Three Decades. Lowe-Porter, H. T., tr. 6.95 (ISBN 0-394-60483-0). Modern Lib.
--Tod in Venedig. Hornsey, A. W., ed. 1971. pap. text ed. 6.95 (ISBN 0-395-11925-1, 3-34397). HM.
Mann, Victor. He Remembered to Say "Thank You". (Arch Bks: No. 13). (Illus.). 32p. (ps-4). 1976. pap. 0.89 (ISBN 0-570-06103-2, 59-1221). Concordia.
Mann, Wayne M. Obliquely Wild. Hammack, Susan M. & Hammack, Edie, eds. 476p. 1982. pap. 9.95 (ISBN 0-9608904-0-8). Mann Found.
Mann, William. The Operas of Mozart. LC 76-9279. (Illus.). 1977. 39.95 o.p. (ISBN 0-19-519891-3). Oxford U Pr.
Mann, William, tr. see Rath, Wilhelm.
Mann, William E. The Language of Logic. LC 79-66151. 1979. pap. text ed. 10.50 (ISBN 0-8191-0795-6). U Pr of Amer.
Manna & the Agricultural Marketing Project. Eclipse of the Blue Moon Foods. 104p. 1979. tchr's guide 7.95 (ISBN 0-686-95681-8). Alternatives.
Manna, Z. Lectures on the Logic of Computer Programming. LC 79-93153. (CBMS-NSF Regional Conference Ser.: No. 31). iv, 49p. 1980. pap. 8.00 (ISBN 0-89871-164-9). Soc Indus-Appl Math.
Manna, Zohar. Introduction to Mathematical Theory of Computation. (Computer Science Ser). (Illus.). 360p. 1974. text ed. 43.00 (ISBN 0-07-039910-7, C). McGraw.
Manne, A. S., jt. auth. see Goreux, L. M.
Manne, Henry G. The Economics of Legal Relationships. LC 75-4884. (Illus.). 660p. 1975. text ed. 28.95 (ISBN 0-8299-0048-9). West Pub.
Mannello, George. Americans All, 2 vols. in 1. (Orig.). (gr. 10-11). 1982. pap. text ed. 13.33 (ISBN 0-87720-629-5); text ed. 24.83 (ISBN 0-87720-630-9). AMSCO Sch.
Mannello, Timothy A. Problem Drinking among Railroad Workers: Extent, Impact & Solutions. 4.95 o.p. (ISBN 0-686-92163-1, 9130). Hazelden.
Manner, Harold. Metabolic Therapy "A". 1.00x (ISBN 0-686-29836-5). Cancer Control Soc.
Mannerberg, Donald & Roth, Jane. Aerobic Nutrition: The Long-Life Plan for Ageless Health & Vigor. 1981. 13.50 (ISBN 0-8015-0070-2, 01311-390, Hawthorn). Dutton.
Mannerheim, C. G. Across Asia from West to East in 1906-1908: Record of the Journey, Vol. 1 & 2. 1969. Set. text ed. 58.25x o.p. (ISBN 9-0623-4053-9). Humanities.
Manners, Alexandra. Candles in the Wood. LC 74-79657. 256p. 1974. 6.95 o.p. (ISBN 0-399-11371-1). Putnam Pub Group.
--Cardigan Square. LC 76-57200. 1977. 8.95 o.p. (ISBN 0-399-11918-3). Putnam Pub Group.
--The Singing Swans. LC 75-18580. 256p. 1975. 7.95 o.p. (ISBN 0-399-11593-5). Putnam Pub Group.
--Wildford's Daughter. LC 78-2636. 1978. 8.95 o.p. (ISBN 0-399-12198-6). Putnam Pub Group.
Manners, David. Here's Power for You: Body Building Courses & Exercises. LC 74-29790. (Orig.). (YA) 1972. pap. 3.95 (ISBN 0-668-03242-1). Arco.
--The Soundless Voice: A Discovery in Stillness. Date not set. pap. cancelled o.p. (ISBN 0-916108-10-4). Seed Center. Postponed.
Manners, George E., Jr. & Louderback, Joseph G. Managing Return on Investment: Implications for Pricing, Volume, & Funds Flow. LC 80-8817. 192p. 1981. 23.95x (ISBN 0-669-04383-4). Lexington Bks.
Manners, Gerald. Coal in Britain. (The Resource Management Ser., No 4.). (Illus.). 1981. text ed. 25.00x (ISBN 0-04-333018-5); pap. text ed. 11.95x (ISBN 0-04-333019-3). Allen Unwin.
Manners, Gerald, et al. Regional Development in Britain. 2nd ed. LC 79-42901. 1980. 62.95 (ISBN 0-471-27636-7, Pub. by Wiley-Interscience). Wiley.
Manners, John. Irish Crafts & Craftsmen. (Illus.). 130p. 1983. pap. 7.95 (ISBN 0-904651-92-4, Pub by Salem Hse Ltd). Merrimack Bk Serv.
Manners, Robert, jt. auth. see Kaplan, David.
Manners, Robert A. Hualapai Indians, Vol. 2: An Ethnological Report on the Hualapai (Walapai) Indians of Arizona. (American Indian Ethnohistory Ser: Indians of the Southwest). (Illus.). lib. bdg. 42.00 o.s.i. (ISBN 0-8240-0723-9). Garland Pub.
Manners, Ruth A. & Mannners, William. The Quick & Easy Vegetarian Cookbook. LC 78-2259. 288p. 1978. 12.50 (ISBN 0-87131-260-3); pap. 6.95 (ISBN 0-87131-303-0). M Evans.
Mannes, David. Music Is My Faith: An Autobiography. (Music Reprint, 1978 Ser.). (Illus.). 1978. Repr. of 1938 ed. lib. bdg. 29.50 (ISBN 0-306-77595-6). Da Capo.
Mannes, Marya. Who Owns the Air. 1960. pap. 1.95 o.p. (ISBN 0-87462-413-4). Marquette.
Mannhardt, Werner G., tr. see Muller, Herbert W.
Mannheim, Hermann. Group Problems in Crime & Punishment. 2nd, enl. ed. LC 73-108234. (Criminology, Law Enforcement, & Social Problems Ser.: No. 117). 1972. 20.00x (ISBN 0-87585-117-7). Patterson Smith.
--Juvenile Delinquency in an English Middletown. LC 73-108226. (Criminology, Law Enforcement, & Social Problems Ser.: No. 109). (Illus., With intro. added). 1970. Repr. of 1948 ed. 9.00x (ISBN 0-87585-109-6). Patterson Smith.
--Pioneers of Criminology. 2nd, enl. ed. LC 78-108238. (Criminology, Law Enforcement, & Social Problems Ser.: No. 121). 1972. 20.00x (ISBN 0-87585-121-5); pap. 11.95x (ISBN 0-87585-902-X). Patterson Smith.
Mannheim, Karl. From Karl Mannheim. Wolff, Kurt H., ed. (Orig.). 1971. pap. 10.95 (ISBN 0-19-501394-8, GB). Oxford U Pr.
Mannheim, Karl & Stewart, W. A. Introduction to the Sociology of Education. (International Library of Sociology & Social Reconstruction). 1970. text ed. 8.50x (ISBN 0-7100-3416-4); pap. text ed. 3.75x (ISBN 0-7100-6897-2). Humanities.
Mannheim, L. A. The Olympus OM Way. (Camera Way Bks.). (Illus.). 1979. 29.95 (ISBN 0-240-50985-4). Focal Pr.
--Rollei Way. 10th ed. (Camera Way Bks.). 1974. 22.95 (ISBN 0-240-44911-8). Focal Pr.
--Rolleiflex SL 66 & SLX Way. (Camera Way Bks.). (Illus.). 1974. 33.95 (ISBN 0-240-50788-6). Focal Pr.
Mannheim, L. A., jt. auth. see Jacobson, C. I.
Mannheimer, Jeffrey S. & Lampe, Gerald N. Clinical Transcutaneous Electrical Nerve Stimulation. (Illus.). 350p. 1983. 34.95 (ISBN 0-8036-5832-X). Davis Co.

Manniche, Lise. The Prince Who Knew His Fate: An Ancient Egyptian Story Translated from Hieroglyphs. 40p. 1982. 30.00x (ISBN 0-7141-8043-2, Pub. by Brit Mus Pubns England). State Mutual Bk.

Manniche, Lise, tr. The Prince Who Knew His Fate. (Illus.). 40p. 1982. 10.95 (ISBN 0-399-20850-X, Philomel). Putnam Pub Group.

Manniche, Peter. Living Democracy in Denmark. Repr. of 1952 ed. lib. bdg. 17.00x (ISBN 0-8371-3985-6, MADD). Greenwood.

Mannin, Ethel. The Kennedys Abroad: Ann & Peter in Sweden. 10.50 (ISBN 0-392-15926-0, SpS). Sportshelf.

Manning & Vanmaanen. Policing: A View from the Street. LC 77-19343. 1978. pap. text ed. 15.95x o.p. (ISBN 0-673-16317-2). Scott F.

Manning, Al G. Helping Yourself with Psycho-Cosmic Power. LC 68-12433. 1983. pap. 5.95 (ISBN 0-941698-06-8). Pan Ishtar.

Manning, Al. G. Miracle of Universal Psychic Power: How to Build Your Way to Prosperity. 1976. pap. 14.95 o.p. (ISBN 0-13-585794-5, Parker). P-H.

Manning, Al G. Your Golden Key to Success: A Self Help Odyssey. LC 82-60767. 1982. 12.95 (ISBN 0-941698-04-1); pap. 5.95 (ISBN 0-941698-05-X). Pan-Ishtar.

Manning, Alan. The Argentaye Tract: A Critical Edition. (Toronto Medieval Texts & Translations). (Illus.). 132p. 1983. 30.00x (ISBN 0-8020-5590-7). U of Toronto Pr.

Manning, Barbara S. Dictionary for the World of Work. Wilson, Roberta & Robson, Sherry, eds. 1983. pap. text ed. 6.95x (ISBN 0-89262-053-6). Career Pub.

Manning, Brian, ed. Politics, Religion & the English Civil War. LC 73-87138. 288p. 1974. text ed. 19.95 o.p. (ISBN 0-312-62755-6). St Martin.

Manning, Clarence A. History of the Slavic Studies in the United States. 1957. 10.95 (ISBN 0-87462-304-9). Marquette.

Manning, Clarence A., ed. see Franko, Ivan.

Manning, D. J., ed. The Form of Iceology. 1980. text ed. 22.50x (ISBN 0-04-320138-5); pap. text ed. 9.95x (ISBN 0-04-320139-3). Allen Unwin.

Manning, Elsie & Food Editors of Farm Journal. The Farm Journal's Meal & Menu Planner Cookbook. (Illus.). 448p. 1980. 12.95 o.p. (ISBN 0-525-93116-3). Dutton.

Manning, Francis, jt. auth. see Canjar, Lawrence.

Manning, Frank. Creative Chip Carving. rev. ed. (Illus.). 48p. 1983. pap. 2.50 (ISBN 0-486-23735-4). Dover.

Manning, Frank E., ed. The World of Play. LC 82-83395. (Annual Proceedings of the American Anthropological Association Study of Play (TAASP)). 240p. (Orig.). 1983. pap. text ed. 14.95 (ISBN 0-88011-059-7). Leisure Pr.

Manning, Frank V. Managerial Dilemmas & Executive Growth. 1981. text ed. 19.95 (ISBN 0-8359-4231-7). Reston.

Manning, G., jt. auth. see Reece, B.

Manning, Gerald L. & Reece, Barry L. Selling Today: A Personal Approach. 460p. 1980. text ed. write for info. (ISBN 0-697-08032-3); instr's manual avail. (ISBN 0-697-08070-6). Wm C Brown.

Manning, Gerry. Cobol Basics: A Structured Approach. 352p. 1980. text ed. 20.00 (ISBN 0-394-32359-9). Random.

Manning, Harvey. Backpacking: One Step at a Time, New 1980's Edition. 3rd ed. LC 79-3580. (Illus.). 1980. pap. 5.95 (ISBN 0-394-74290-7, Vin). Random.

--Footsore Four: Walks & Hikes Around Puget Sound. LC 77-23727. (Footsore Ser.). (Illus.). 240p. (Orig.). 1979. pap. 7.95 (ISBN 0-916890-81-3). Mountaineers.

--Footsore One: Walks & Hikes Around Puget Sound. 2nd ed. (Illus.). 240p. 1982. pap. 7.95 (ISBN 0-89886-065-2). Mountaineers.

--Footsore One: Walks & Hikes Around Puget Sound. LC 77-23727. (Footsore Ser.). (Illus.). 216p. (Orig.). 1977. pap. 6.95 o.p. (ISBN 0-916890-53-8). Mountaineers.

--Footsore Three: Walks & Hikes Around Puget Sound. LC 77-23727. (Footsore Ser.). (Illus.). 232p. (Orig.). 1978. pap. 7.95 (ISBN 0-916890-65-1). Mountaineers.

--Footsore Two: Walks & Hikes Around Puget Sound. LC 77-23727. (Footsore Ser.). (Illus.). 224p. (Orig.). 1978. pap. 7.95 (ISBN 0-916890-54-6). Mountaineers.

--One Hundred Two Hikes in the Alpine Lakes, South Cascades & Olympics. 3rd ed. (Illus.). 224p. 1983. pap. 7.95 (ISBN 0-89886-067-9). Mountaineers.

Manning, Harvey, jt. auth. see Spring, Ira.

Manning, Hiram. Manning on Decoupage. (Illus.). 1969. 10.00 (ISBN 0-8208-0316-2). Hearthside.

Manning, Jack. Fine Thirty-Five mm Portrait. (Illus.). 1978. 25.00 o.p. (ISBN 0-8174-2438-5, Amphoto). Watson-Guptill.

--Young Brazil. LC 71-99178. (Illus.). (gr. 3 up). 1970. 4.95 o.p. (ISBN 0-396-07183-X). Dodd.

--Young Puerto Rico. LC 62-15499. (Illus.). (gr. 3 up). 1962. PLB 4.95 o.p. (ISBN 0-396-06594-5). Dodd.

Manning, Jerome A. Estate Planning. 2nd ed. 441p. 1982. text ed. 55.00 (ISBN 0-686-97892-7, D1-0153). PLI.

Manning, Joseph F. The Miracle of Agape Love. 160p. 1977. pap. 2.95 (ISBN 0-88368-079-3). Whitaker Hse.

Manning, Kenneth V., jt. auth. see White, Marsh W.

Manning, M. J. Phylogeny of Immunological Memory. (Developments in Immunology Ser.: Vol. 10). 1980. 58.00 (ISBN 0-444-80255-X). Elsevier.

Manning, Olivia. The Balkan Trilogy. 1982. pap. 8.95 (ISBN 0-14-005936-9). Penguin.

--The Levant Trilogy. 1983. pap. 7.95 (ISBN 0-14-005962-8). Penguin.

--Summer Companions. (Inflation Fighter Ser.). 192p. 1982. pap. cancelled o.s.i. (ISBN 0-8439-1120-4, Leisure Bks). Nordon Pubns.

Manning, Olivia, ed. Romanian Short Stories. (World's Classics). 1971. 7.95 (ISBN 0-19-250615-3). Oxford U Pr.

Manning, Peter J. Byron & His Fictions. LC 78-7943. 1978. 17.50x (ISBN 0-8143-1600-X). Wayne St U Pr.

Manning, Peter K. The Narc's Game: Organizational & Informational Limits on Drug Law Enforcement. 1980. 22.50x (ISBN 0-262-13154-4). MIT Pr.

--Police Work: The Social Organization of Policing. 1977. 25.00x (ISBN 0-262-13130-7); pap. 8.95 (ISBN 0-262-63070-2). MIT Pr.

Manning, Peter K., jt. ed. see Smith, Robert B.

Manning, Robert, ed. see Dougan, Clark & Weiss, Stephen.

Manning, Robert, ed. see Doyle, Edward G. & Lipsman, Samuel L.

Manning, Robert, ed. see Maitland, Terrence & Weiss, Stephen.

Manning, Robert E., ed. Mountain Passages: An Appalachia Anthology. (Illus.). 320p. (Orig.). 1983. pap. 9.95 (ISBN 0-910146-43-8). Appalach Mtn.

Manning, Robert T., jt. auth. see Delp, Mahlon H.

Manning, Robert T., jt. ed. see Delp, Mahlon H.

Manning, S. A. Nature in the West Country. 1979. 6.50 (ISBN 0-437-09502-9, Pub. by World's Work). David & Charles.

Manning, Sidney A. Child & Adolescent Development: A Basic Self-Instructional Guide. LC 76-30876. (McGraw-Hill Basic Self Instructional Guide Ser.). 1977. pap. text ed. 13.95 (ISBN 0-07-039915-8, C); instr's manual 15.00 (ISBN 0-07-039916-6). McGraw.

Manning, Steve. The Jacksons. LC 76-11634. (gr. 4 up). 1976. pap. 4.95 o.p. (ISBN 0-672-52275-6). Bobbs.

Manning, W. A. & Garnero, R. S. Fortran IV Problem Solver. 1970. 13.50 o.p. (ISBN 0-07-039918-2, C). McGraw.

Manning, W. J. & Feder, W. A. Biomonitoring Air Pollutants with Plants. 1980. 26.75 (ISBN 0-85334-916-9, Pub. by Applied Sci England). Elsevier.

Manning, William & Vinton, Jean, eds. Harmfully Involved. (Orig.). 1978. pap. 7.95 (ISBN 0-89486-056-9). Hazelden.

Manning, William R. Early Diplomatic Relations Between the United States & Mexico. LC 68-55101. 1968. Repr. of 1916 ed. lib. bdg. 21.00x (ISBN 0-8371-0558-7, MAUM). Greenwood.

Manningham, Daniel. Crossfeed. LC 82-6698. 256p. 1983. 20.00 (ISBN 0-87668-602-1). Aronson.

Manningham, John. The Diary of John Manningham of the Middle Temple, 1602-1603. Sorlien, Robert P., ed. LC 74-22553. 481p. 1976. text ed. 32.50x (ISBN 0-87451-113-5). U Pr of New Eng.

Manningham, Mary. A Mary Mixture. LC 76-46913. (Illus.). 92p. 1976. 6.00 (ISBN 0-911838-49-X). Windy Row.

--Thoughts & Verses. 1971. 5.00 (ISBN 0-911838-15-5). Windy Row.

Manning-Sanders, Ruth. A Book of Charms & Changelings. LC 71-179053. 128p. (gr. 2-6). 1972. 8.95 (ISBN 0-525-26775-1). Dutton.

--A Book of Spooks & Spectres. LC 79-17673. (Illus.). (gr. 2-6). 1980. 10.95 (ISBN 0-525-27045-0, 01063-320). Dutton.

Mannino, F. V., et al, eds. The Practice of Mental Health Consultation. 255p. 1975. 13.95x o.p. (ISBN 0-470-56774-0). Halsted Pr.

Mannino, Mary J., ed. The Nurse Anesthetist & the Law. Date not set. price not set (ISBN 0-8089-1496-0). Grune.

Mannison, D. S., et al, eds. Environmental Philosophy. (Monograph: No. 2). vi, 386p. 1980. pap. 10.00x (ISBN 0-909596-39-5). Ridgeview.

Mannix, Jeffrey. Food Combining: The Revolutionary Diet Plan for Health & Longevity. 160p. 1983. 13.95 (ISBN 0-8092-5662-2). Contemp Bks.

--The Mannix Method: A Twelve-Week Program for Weight Control Through Behavior Therapy. LC 78-31219. 1979. 9.95 o.p. (ISBN 0-399-90048-9, Marek). Putnam Pub Group.

Mannners, William, jt. auth. see Manners, Ruth A.

Mannoia, V. James, Jr. What Is Science? An Introduction to the Structure & Methodology of Science. LC 79-47988. (Illus.). 149p. 1980. pap. text ed. 7.50 (ISBN 0-8191-0989-4). U Pr of Amer.

Manns, Peter. Martin Luther. LC 82-14972. (Illus.). 224p. 1982. 50.00 (ISBN 0-8245-0510-7). Crossroad NY.

--Martin Luther: An Illustrated Biography. (Illus.). 128p. 1983. 14.95 (ISBN 0-8245-0563-8). Crossroad NY.

Mannucci, P. M. & D'Angelo, A., eds. Urokinase: Basic & Clinical Aspects. LC 81-68958. (Serono Symposium Ser.: Vol. 48). 276p. 1982. 36.00 (ISBN 0-12-469280-X). Acad Pr.

Mano, E. B., ed. see International Symposium on Macromolecules.

Mano, M. Digital Logic & Computer Design. 1979. 33.95 (ISBN 0-13-214510-3). P-H.

Mano, M. Morris. Computer Logic Design. (Automatic Computation Ser.). (Illus.). 464p. 1972. 32.95 (ISBN 0-13-165472-1). P-H.

--Computer System Architecture. (Illus.). 528p. 1976. ref. ed. 28.00 o.p. (ISBN 0-13-166363-1). P-H.

Mano, Morris. Computer System Architecture. 2nd ed. (Illus.). 544p. 1982. 31.95 (ISBN 0-13-166611-8). P-H.

Manocha, Sohan L. Malnutrition & Retarded Human Development. (Illus.). 400p. 1972. photocopy ed. spiral 39.50x (ISBN 0-398-02548-7). C C Thomas.

Manoff, Tom. The Music Kit. 1976. pap. text ed. 18.95x (ISBN 0-393-09179-1); tchrs. manual avail. (ISBN 0-393-09157-0). Norton.

Manohar, M. & Krishnamachar, P. Fluid Mechanics. 500p. Date not set. text ed. 37.50x (ISBN 0-7069-1188-1, Pub. by Vikas India). Advent NY.

--Hydraulic Machinery & Advanced Hydraulics. 600p. 1982. text ed. 50.00x (ISBN 0-7069-1194-6, Pub. by Vikas India). Advent NY.

Manohar, R., jt. auth. see Tremblay, J. P.

Manoogian, Torkom. The Gold Sheaf of My Days & Other Poems by Shen Mah. Der Hovanessian, Diana & Margossian, Marzbed, trs. 64p. 1983. pap. 5.00 (ISBN 0-934728-06-2). St Vartan.

Manor, Giora. Gospel According to Dance. (Illus.). 160p. 1980. 12.95 o.p. (ISBN 0-312-34052-4). St Martin.

Manougian, Manoug, jt. auth. see Isaak, Samuel.

Manougian, Manoug N. & Northcutt, Robert. Ordinary Differential Equations: An Introduction. LC 72-95281. 1973. text ed. 19.95 (ISBN 0-675-09004-0). Merrill.

Manoukian, Edward B. Remoralization. (Pure & Applied Mathematics Ser.). Date not set. price not set (ISBN 0-12-468450-5). Acad Pr.

Manpower Demonstration Research Corp. Summary & Findings of the National Supported Work Demonstration. 1980. prof ref 20.00x (ISBN 0-88410-687-X). Ballinger Pub.

Manpower Demonstration Research Group. Tenant Management: Findings from a Three-Year Experiment in Public Housing. 296p. 1981. prof ref 24.50x (ISBN 0-88410-696-9). Ballinger Pub.

Manpower Research Associates. Arco Handbook of Job & Career Opportunities. LC 77-12559. 1978. lib. bdg. 3.95 (ISBN 0-668-04465-9, 4328); pap. 3.95 (ISBN 0-668-04328-8). Arco.

Manring, A. B. Exporting from the U. S. A. How to Develop Export Markets & Cope with Foreing Customs. 114p. (Orig.). 1981. pap. 12.95 (ISBN 0-88908-908-6). Self Counsel Pr.

Manrique. Termodinamica. 2nd ed. 352p. (Span.). 1981. pap. text ed. write for info. (ISBN 0-06-315510-9, Pub. by HarLA Mexcio). Har-Row.

--Transferencia de Calor. 216p. (Span.). 1982. pap. text ed. write for info. (ISBN 0-06-315514-1, Pub. by HarLA Mexcio). Har-Row.

Manrique, Jaime. Colombian Gold. 1983. write for info. (ISBN 0-517-54649-3, C N Potter Bks). Crown.

Manrique, Jose. Termodinamica Para Ingenieros. 1976. pap. text ed. 12.40 o.p. (ISBN 0-06-315512-5, IntlDept). Har-Row.

--Transferencia De Calor. 1977. pap. text ed. 11.40 o.p. (ISBN 0-06-315511-7, IntlDept). Har-Row.

Mansbach, jt. auth. see Flemming.

Mansbach, R. W. & Ferguson, Y. H. The Web of World Politics: Nonstate Actors in the Global System. (Illus.). 336p. 1976. pap. text ed. 13.95x (ISBN 0-13-947952-X). P-H.

Mansbach, Richard W. & Vasquez, John A. In Search of Theory: A New Paradigm for Global Politics. 1983. pap. 12.50 (ISBN 0-231-05061-5). Columbia U Pr.

Mansbach, Richard W., ed. Northern Ireland: Half a Century of Partition. LC 72-81732. 221p. (Orig.). 1974. lib. bdg. 17.50x o.p. (ISBN 0-87196-182-2). Facts on File.

Mansbridge, Jane J. Beyond Adversary Democracy. xiv, 412p. 1980. pap. 10.95 (ISBN 0-226-50355-0). U of Chicago Pr.

Manschreck, Clyde L. Melanchthon: The Quiet Reformer. LC 73-21263. (Illus.). 350p. 1975. Repr. of 1958 ed. lib. bdg. 27.25x (ISBN 0-8371-6131-2, MAMQ). Greenwood.

Manschreck, Theo C. & Kleinman, Arthur M., eds. Renewal in Psychiatry: A Critical Rational Perspective. LC 77-1244. (The Ser. in Clinical & Community Psychology). 346p. 1977. 23.50x o.p. (ISBN 0-470-99108-9). Halsted Pr.

Manschrek, Clyde L. A History of Christianity in the World: From Persecution to Uncertainty. (Illus.). 384p. 1974. text ed. 20.95 (ISBN 0-13-389346-4). P-H.

Mansell, William C. North American Birds of Prey. LC 80-81423. (Illus.). 176p. 1980. 7.00 (ISBN 0-688-03707-0). Morrow.

Manser, Anthony. Bradley's Logic. LC 82-24407. 230p. 1983. text ed. 29.95x (ISBN 0-389-20379-3). B&N Imports.

Manser, Jose & Manser, Michael. Planning Your Kitchen. LC 77-78531. (Design Centre Books). (Illus.). 1977. pap. 4.95 o.p. (ISBN 0-85072-020-6, 030081, Quick Fox). Putnam Pub Group.

Manser, Michael, jt. auth. see Manser, Jose.

Mansergh, Nicholas. The Commonwealth Experience, 2 vols. rev. ed. Incl. Vol. 1. The Durham Report to the Anglo-Irish Treaty. 27.50x (ISBN 0-8020-2491-2); pap. 12.95 (ISBN 0-8020-6515-5); Vol. 2. From British to Multiracial Commonwealth. 27.50 (ISBN 0-8020-2492-0); pap. 12.95 (ISBN 0-8020-6516-3). 1982. 50.00x (ISBN 0-8020-2477-7); Set. pap. 25.00 (ISBN 0-8020-6497-3). U of Toronto Pr.

Mansfeld, J. Pseudo-Hippocratic Tract & Greek Philosophy. (Philosophy Texts & Studies: No. 20). 1970. text ed. 33.75x o.p. (ISBN 9-0232-0701-7). Humanities.

Mansfield, A., ed. see Kelly, F. M.

Mansfield, Carl M. Therapeutic Radiology: New Directions in Therapy. 1982. 55.00 (ISBN 0-87488-694-5). Med Exam.

Mansfield, D. Electrochemistry. 1974. pap. text ed. 4.00x o.p. (ISBN 0-435-65952-9); tchr's guide 5.00x o.p. (ISBN 0-435-65953-7). Heinemann Ed.

--Radiochemistry. 1974. pap. text ed. 4.00x o.p. (ISBN 0-435-65968-5); pap. text ed. 5.00x tchrs'. guide o.p. (ISBN 0-435-65969-3). Heinemann Ed.

Mansfield, E. A., jt. auth. see Hillhouse, Marion S.

Mansfield, Edwin. Economics: Principles, Problems, & Decisions. 4th ed. 1982. pap. 24.95x (ISBN 0-393-95265-7); study guide avail. (ISBN 0-393-95271-1); instr's manual avail. (ISBN 0-393-95273-8); test item file avail. (ISBN 0-393-95269-X). Norton.

--Economics: Principles, Problems, Decisions. 3rd ed. 1980. text ed. 20.95x (ISBN 0-393-95118-9). Norton.

--Economics: Readings, Issues & Cases. 1983. pap. write for info o.p. (ISBN 0-393-95268-1). Norton.

--Microeconomics: Selected Readings, Theory & Applications. 4th ed. (Illus.). 1982. 20.45x (ISBN 0-393-95232-0); pap. 12.95x (ISBN 0-393-95208-8). Norton.

--Microeconomics: Theory & Application. 4th ed. (Illus.). 1981. 20.95x (ISBN 0-393-95218-5); instrs'. manual avail. (ISBN 0-393-95215-0). Norton.

--Principles of Macroeconomics. 4th ed. 600p. 1982. text ed. 14.95x (ISBN 0-393-95266-5). Norton.

--Principles of Macroeconomics: Reading Issues & Cases. 4th ed. 1982. text ed. write for info (ISBN 0-393-95340-8); write for info study guide. Norton.

--Principles of Macroeconomics. 3rd ed. pap. text ed. 14.95x (ISBN 0-393-95120-0); instrs' manual free (ISBN 0-393-95124-3); study guide 5.95x (ISBN 0-393-95140-5); cases 4.95x (ISBN 0-393-95134-0); test item free (ISBN 0-393-95125-1); transparency masters free (ISBN 0-393-95131-6). Norton.

--Principles of Microeconomics. 3rd ed. 1980. pap. text ed. 14.95x (ISBN 0-393-95128-6); instrs' manual free (ISBN 0-393-95124-3); cases 4.95x (ISBN 0-393-95144-8); study guide 5.95x (ISBN 0-393-95147-2); test item free (ISBN 0-393-95125-1); transparency masters free (ISBN 0-393-95131-6). Norton.

--Principles of Microeconomics. 4th ed. 1983. 14.95x (ISBN 0-393-95267-3). Norton.

--Principles of Microeconomics: Readings, Issues & Cases. 4th ed. 1982. text ed. write for info. (ISBN 0-393-95331-9); write for info. tchr's manual (ISBN 0-393-95273-8); write for info. study guide (ISBN 0-393-95334-3); write for info. test item file. Norton.

--Statistics for Business & Economics: Methods & Applications. 2nd ed. 1983. text ed. 22.95x (ISBN 0-393-95293-2); write for info. Problems & Case Studies (ISBN 0-393-95333-5); write for info. solutions manual; write for info. test item file. Norton.

--Statistics for Business & Economics. 1980. text ed. 21.95x (ISBN 0-393-95057-3); May 1980. pap. 8.95x Readings & Cases (ISBN 0-393-95066-2); pap. 6.95x Problems, Exercises & Case Studies (ISBN 0-393-95062-X); solutions manual 1.95x (ISBN 0-393-95070-0). Norton.

Mansfield, Edwin, ed. Managerial Economics & Operations Research. 4th ed. 1980. 24.95 o.p. (ISBN 0-393-01271-9); pap. text ed. 8.95x (ISBN 0-393-95060-3). Norton.

Mansfield, Edwin, et al. Technology Transfer, Productivity, & Economic Policy. 1983. 35.00x (ISBN 0-393-95222-3). Norton.

Mansfield, Elizabeth. Her Heart's Captain. 192p. 1983. pap. 2.25 (ISBN 0-425-05501-9). Berkley Pub.

--Love Lessons. 208p. (Orig.). 1983. pap. 2.50 (ISBN 0-425-05938-3). Berkley Pub.

--The Phantom Lover. 256p. (Orig.). 1981. pap. 2.25 o.p. (ISBN 0-425-05078-5). Berkley Pub.

Mansfield, Elizabeth, ed. see Lawrence, D. H.

Mansfield, Ellen K., et al. Basic Language Skills. LC 82-3893. 192p. (Orig.). 1982. pap. 6.95 (ISBN 0-668-05127-2, 5127). Arco.

Mansfield, Harvey C., Jr., ed. Thomas Jefferson: Selected Writings. LC 77-86039. (Crofts Classics Ser.). 1979. pap. text ed. 3.75x (ISBN 0-88295-120-3). Harlan Davidson.

Mansfield, Helene. Contessa. LC 81-43536. 504p. 1982. 18.95 (ISBN 0-385-17300-8). Doubleday.

Mansfield, Irving & Block, Jean L. Life with Jackie. 320p. 1983. 16.95 (ISBN 0-553-05020-6). Bantam.

Mansfield, J. & Derijk, L. M., eds. Kephalaion: Studies in Greek Philosophy & Its Continuation Offered to Prof. C. J. DeVogel. (Philosophical Texts & Studies: No. 23). 272p. 1975. text ed. 43.25x o.p. (ISBN 9-0232-1212-6). Humanities.

Mansfield, J. B. History of the Great Lakes, Vols. 1-2. (Illus.). 2000p. 1972. Repr. 125.00 set (ISBN 0-686-01098-1). Freshwater.

Mansfield, John M., jt. auth. see Hall, G. Stanley.

Mansfield, Katherine. The Aloe. O'Sullivan, Vincent, ed. 164p. 1983. text ed. 14.75x (ISBN 0-85635-455-4, Pub. by Carcanet New Pr England). Humanities.

--Journal of Katherine Mansfield. LC 82-11541. (Illus.). 255p. 1983. pap. 6.95 (ISBN 0-88001-023-1). Ecco Pr.

--The Scrapbook of Katherine Mansfield. LC 74-16042. 288p. 1975. Repr. of 1939 ed. 29.50x (ISBN 0-86527-299-9). Fertig.

--The Short Stories of Katherine Mansfield. 688p. 1983. pap. 9.95 (ISBN 0-88001-025-8). Ecco Pr.

--Stories. Bowen, Elizabeth, ed. 1956. pap. 4.95 (ISBN 0-394-70036-8, Vin). Random.

Mansfield, P. H. Electrical Transducers for Industrial Measurement. 1973. text ed. 16.95 o.p. (ISBN 0-408-70465-9). Butterworth.

Mansfield, Peter. The Arab World. LC 76-45442. 1976. 19.18i (ISBN 0-690-01170-9). T Y Crowell.

--The Middle East: A Political & Economic Survey. (Illus.). 1980. 32.50x (ISBN 0-19-215851-1). Oxford U Pr.

--The New Arabians. LC 81-43385. 288p. 1982. 14.95 (ISBN 0-385-17911-1). Doubleday.

--The Ottoman Empire & Its Successors. LC 73-86362. (Making of the Twentieth Century Ser). 224p. 1973. 17.95 (ISBN 0-312-59010-5); pap. 8.95 (ISBN 0-312-58975-1). St Martin.

Mansfield, Roger & Poole, Micael. International Perspectives on Management & Organization. 164p. 1981. text ed. 36.75x (ISBN 0-566-00469-0). Gower Pub Ltd.

Mansfield, Roger, jt. auth. see Poole, Michael.

Mansfield, Sue, ed. see Mill, John S.

Mansfield, T. A., ed. Effects of Air Pollutants on Plants. LC 75-32449. (Society for Experimental Biology Seminar Ser.: No. 1). (Illus.). 180p. 1976. 42.50 (ISBN 0-521-21087-9); pap. 16.95x (ISBN 0-521-29039-2). Cambridge U Pr.

Manship, Darwin & Cornwell, Robert C. Business English. 256p. 1981. pap. text ed. write for info. o.p. (ISBN 0-697-08047-1). Wm C Brown.

Mansion, J. E., tr. see Daudet, A.

Mansir, A. Richard. The Art of Ship Modeling. 320p. 1982. 35.00 (ISBN 0-940620-03-0). Van Nos Reinhold.

Manske, R. & Rodrigo, R., eds. The Alkaloids: Chemistry & Pharmacology, Vol. 20. 1982. 59.50 (ISBN 0-12-469520-5). Acad Pr.

Manske, R. H., et al, eds. The Alkaloids: Chemistry & Physiology. Incl. Vol. 1. 1965. 76.00 (ISBN 0-12-469501-9); Vol. 2. 1952. 76.00 (ISBN 0-12-469502-7); Vol. 3. 1965. 68.00 (ISBN 0-12-469503-5); Vol. 4. 1965. 65.00 (ISBN 0-12-469504-3); Vol. 5. Pharmacology. 1965. 65.00 (ISBN 0-12-469505-1); Vol. 6. Supplement to Volumes 1 & 2. 1965. 65.00 (ISBN 0-12-469506-X); Vol. 7. Supplement to Volumes 2, 3, 4 & 5. 1960. 72.50 (ISBN 0-12-469507-8); Vol. 8. The Indole Alkaloids. 1965. 89.00 (ISBN 0-12-469508-6); Vol. 9. 1967. 78.50 (ISBN 0-12-469509-4); Vol. 10. 1968. 78.50 (ISBN 0-12-469510-8); Vol. 11. 1968. 78.50 (ISBN 0-12-469511-6); Vol. 12. 1970. o.s. 78.50 (ISBN 0-12-469512-4); Vol. 13. 1971. 67.00 (ISBN 0-12-469513-2); Vol. 14. 1973. 83.00 (ISBN 0-12-469514-0); Vol. 15. 1975. 67.00 (ISBN 0-12-469515-9); Vol. 16. 1977. 83.50 (ISBN 0-12-469516-7); Vol. 17. 1979. 66.50 (ISBN 0-12-469517-5). Acad Pr.

Manski, Charles F. & Wise, David A. College Choice in America. (Illus.). 272p. 1983. text ed. 22.50x (ISBN 0-674-14125-3). Harvard U Pr.

Manski, Charles F. & McFadden, Daniel, eds. Structural Analysis of Discrete Data with Econometric Applications. 588p. 1981. text ed. 32.50x (ISBN 0-262-13159-5). MIT Pr.

Manso, Peter, jt. auth. see Hawkes, Ellen.

Manso, Susan, jt. ed. see Kaplan, Patricia.

Manson, Connie J., ed. Index to Geologic & Geophysical Mapping of Washington. (Information Circular Ser.: No. 73). (Illus.). 63p. 4.00 (ISBN 0-686-38468-7). Geologic Pubns.

Manson, Edward, jt. ed. see Macdonnell, John.

Manson, G., jt. auth. see Cherryholmes, C.

Manson, S. S. Thermal Stress & Low-Cycle Fatigue. 1966. 39.50 o.p. (ISBN 0-07-039930-1, P&RB). McGraw.

Manson-Bahr, P. E. & Apted, F. I., eds. Manson's Tropical Diseases. 1000p. 1982. text ed. 75.00 (ISBN 0-02-858440-6, Bailliere-Tindall). Saunders.

Manson-Hing, Lincoln R., jt. auth. see Wuehrmann, Arthur H.

Mansour, Norman, jt. auth. see Ribbens, William B.

Manstead, S. R., jt. ed. see Semin, Gun R.

Mansuelli, Guido A. Art of Etruria & Early Rome. (Art of the World Library). (Illus.). 1965. 6.95 o.p. (ISBN 0-517-50839-7). Crown.

Mansukhani, H. L. The Jungle of Customs Law & Procedures. LC 74-900717. (Illus.). 722p. 1974. 24.00x o.p. (ISBN 0-7069-0283-1). Intl Pubns Serv.

Mansum, C. J. Van see Van Mansum, C. J.

Mansur, Ina. A New England Church: Its First Hundred Years. LC 74-76868. (Illus.). 256p. 1974. 10.95 (ISBN 0-87027-139-3); pap. 5.95 (ISBN 0-87027-140-7). Cumberland Pr.

Mansvelt-Beck, Frederick W. & Wiig, Karl M. The Economics of Offshore Oil & Gas Supplies. LC 76-54558. (Illus.). 176p. 1977. 18.95 o.p. (ISBN 0-669-01306-4). Lexington Bks.

Mant, A. K., ed. Modern Trends in Forensic Medicine, Vol. 3. (Illus.). 288p. 1973. 26.95 o.p. (ISBN 0-407-29202-0). Butterworth.

Mant, Alistair. The Dynamics of Management Education: Observations on the Mid-Career Development Process. 104p. 1981. text ed. 23.50x (ISBN 0-566-02282-6). Gower Pub Ltd.

Mant, Richard. Verses to the Memory of Joseph Warton DD, Repr. Of 1800. Reiman, Donald H., ed. Bd. with The Slave & Other Poetical Pieces: Being an Appendix to Poems. Repr. of 1807 ed; Poems. Repr. of 1806 ed; The Simpliciad: a Satirico Didactic Poem (Dedicated to Wordsworth, Southey & Coleridge) Repr. of 1808 ed. LC 75-31229. (Romantic Context Ser: Poetry 1789-1830). 1979. lib. bdg. 47.00 o.s.i. (ISBN 0-8240-2178-9). Garland Pub.

Mantegazza, Paolo. The Legends of Flowers. Kennedy, Mrs. Alexander, tr. LC 73-180973. (Illus.). 190p. 1975. Repr. of 1927 ed. 30.00x (ISBN 0-8103-4051-8). Gale.

Mantel, Linda H. & Bliss, Dorothy E., eds. The Biology of Crustacea: Vol. 5: Physiological Regulation. 400p. 1983. 57.00 (ISBN 0-12-106405-0). Acad PR.

Mantell, Charles L. Solid Wastes: Origin, Collection, Processing & Disposal. LC 74-26930. 1152p. 1975. 99.95 (ISBN 0-471-56777-9, Pub by Wiley-Interscience). Wiley.

Mantell, David M. True Americanism: Green Berets & War Resisters: A Study of Commitment. LC 74-2230. 1974. pap. 10.95 (ISBN 0-8077-2452-1). Tchrs Coll.

Mantell, Laurie. Murder & Chips. 160p. 1982. 10.95 o.s.i. (ISBN 0-8027-5463-5). Walker & Co.

--Murder in Fancy Dress. 1981. 9.95 o.s.i. (ISBN 0-8027-5446-5). Walker & Co.

Mantellini, Rafael, tr. see D'Annunzio, Gabriele.

Mantero, F. & Biglieu, E. G. Endocrinology of Hypertension - Symposium. 55.00 (ISBN 0-12-469980-4). Acad Pr.

Mantey, J. R., jt. auth. see Dana, H. E.

Mantey, R., jt. auth. see Dana, H. E.

Manthuruthil, Jose, jt. ed. see Hamilton, Joseph H.

Mantinband, Gerda. Bing, Bong, Bang & Fiddle, Dee, Dee. LC 78-18562. 1979. PLB 6.95a o.p. (ISBN 0-385-14212-9). Doubleday.

Mantinband, Gerda B. Papa & Mama Biederbeck. LC 82-15619. (Illus.). 48p. (gr. 2-5). 1983. lib. bdg. 7.95 (ISBN 0-395-33228-1). HM.

Mantinband, James H. Concise Dictionary of Greek Literature. Repr. of 1962 ed. lib. bdg. 17.25x (ISBN 0-8371-2289-9, MAGL). Greenwood.

Mantinband, James H., tr. Four Plays of Aristophanes: The Clouds, the Birds, Lysistrata, the Frogs. LC 82-21910. 320p. (Orig.). 1983. pap. text ed. 12.75 (ISBN 0-8191-2930-5). U Pr of Amer.

Mantinband, James H., jt. tr. see Passage, Charles E.

Mantle, J. Gregory. Better Things from Above. 1971. pap. 3.75 (ISBN 0-87509-051-6). Chr Pubns.

Manton, Jo. Mary Carpenter & the Children of the Streets. 1976. text ed. 32.95x o.p. (ISBN 0-435-32569-8). Heinemann Ed.

Mantoux, Paul. The Industrial Revolution in the Eighteenth Century: An Outline of the Beginnings of the Modern Factory System in England. LC 82-20219. iv, 528p. 1983. pap. 12.50 (ISBN 0-226-50384-4). U of Chicago Pr.

Mantovani, E. & Marconi, W. Aspects of Biomedicine: Perspectives & Progress in Blood Detoxification. 180p. 1982. 23.75x (ISBN 0-86187-269-X). F Pinter Pubs.

Manucy, Albert & Torres-Reyes, Ricardo. The Forts of Old San Juan. LC 73-83358. (Illus.). 96p. 1973. pap. 6.95 (ISBN 0-85699-085-X). Chatham Pr.

Manuel, David, jt. auth. see Marshall, Peter.

Manuel, Don J. El Conde Lucanor. (Span.). 9.95 (ISBN 84-241-5615-3). E Torres & Sons.

--Tales from Count Lucanor. Talbot, Toby, tr. from Span. LC 73-120294. (Illus.). 64p. (gr. 4-6). 1970. 4.95 o.s.i. (ISBN 0-8037-8497-X); PLB 4.58 o.s.i. (ISBN 0-8037-8498-8). Dial.

Manuel, Frank E. The Changing of the Gods. 180p. 1983. text ed. 14.00x (ISBN 0-87451-254-9). U Pr of New Eng.

--The Realities of American-Palestine Relations. LC 72-596. 378p. 1975. Repr. of 1949 ed. lib. bdg. 17.75x (ISBN 0-8371-5999-7, MARA). Greenwood.

Manuel, Frank E. & Manuel, Fritzie P. Utopian Thought in the Western World. LC 79-12382. 1979. text ed. 30.00x (ISBN 0-674-93185-8, Belknap Pr); pap. 12.95 (ISBN 0-674-93186-6). Harvard U Pr.

Manuel, Fritzie P., jt. auth. see Manuel, Frank E.

Manuel, Herschel T. Spanish-Speaking Children of the Southwest: Their Education & the Public Welfare. 236p. 1965. pap. text ed. 6.95x (ISBN 0-292-70097-0). U of Tex Pr.

Manuel, R. L. British Anthozoa. LC 80-41264. (Synopses of the British Fauna Ser.: No. 18). 1981. 18.00 o.s.i. (ISBN 0-12-470050-0). Acad Pr.

Manus, Willard. Mott the Hoople. 224p. 1980. pap. 2.25 o.p. (ISBN 0-523-41147-2). Pinnacle Bks.

Manushkin, Fran. Bubblebath! LC 72-14329. (Illus.). 32p. (gr. k-2). 1974. 6.95i o.p. (ISBN 0-06-024058-X, HarpJ); PLB 4.79 o.p. (ISBN 0-06-024059-8). Har-Row.

--Shirleybird. LC 73-5489. (Illus.). (ps-3). 1975. 5.95i o.p. (ISBN 0-06-024063-6, HarpJ). Har-Row.

--Swinging & Swinging. LC 74-2621. (Illus.). (gr. k-3). 1976. 2.95 o.p. (ISBN 0-06-024066-0); PLB 5.79 o.p. (ISBN 0-06-024067-9). Har-Row.

Manuso, James S. Occupational Clinical Psychology. 350p. 1983. 35.95 (ISBN 0-03-059006-X). Praeger.

Manvell, Roger. Films & the Second World War. 388p. 1976. pap. 4.95 o.s.i. (ISBN 0-440-52555-1, Delta). Dell.

Manvell, Roger & Fraenkel, Heinrich. The Hundred Days to Hitler. LC 73-89867. 240p. 1974. 8.95 o.p. (ISBN 0-312-40040-3). St Martin.

Manville, Bill. Saloon Society. 192p. 1980. pap. 2.25 o.s.i. (ISBN 0-515-05490-9). Jove Pubns.

Manwell, A. R. The Generalized Tricomi Equation: With Applications to the Theory of Plane Transonic Flow. (Research Notes in Mathematics Ser.). (Illus.). 1979. pap. cancelled o.p. (ISBN 0-8224-8428-5). Pitman Pub MA.

--The Tricomi Equation with Applications to the Theory of Plane Transonic Flow. (Research Notes in Mathematics Ser.: No. 35). 176p. (Orig.). 1979. pap. text ed. 20.95 (ISBN 0-273-08428-3). Pitman Pub MA.

Manyeto, Rex. ABC of Modern Africa. 2nd ed. 228p. 1981. 31.00 (ISBN 0-9608056-0-5); pap. 15.00 (ISBN 0-9608056-1-3). African Am Trading.

Manyon, L. A., tr. see Bloch, Marc.

Manypenny, George Washington. Our Indian Wards. LC 68-54844. (The American Scene Ser). 1972. Repr. of 1880 ed. lib. bdg. 35.00 (ISBN 0-306-71140-0). Da Capo.

Manz, A. F. The Welding Power Handbook. 1974. 13.00 (ISBN 0-685-65956-9, WPH). Am Welding.

Manz, H. P. International Film Bibliography: 1979-80. 165p. (Ger. Fr. & Eng.). 29.95 (ISBN 3-88690-045-2, Pub. by Filmland Pr). NY Zoetrope.

Manzalaoui, Mahmoud, ed. Arabic Writing Today: Drama, Vol. 2. (American Research Center in Egypt, Publications Ser.: Vol. 2). 643p. (Orig.). 1977. pap. 10.00x (ISBN 0-686-30892-1, Pub by Am Res Ctr Egypt). Undena Pubns.

Manzione, James V., Jr., jt. auth. see Bodak-Gyovai, Levente Z.

Manzler, David, jt. auth. see Buechner, Robert.

Manzler, David L., jt. auth. see Buechner, Robert W.

Manzolillo, Deborah, jt. auth. see Harding, Diana.

Manzoni, Pablo. Instant Beauty: The Complete Way to Perfect Make up. (Illus.). 1978. 9.95 o.p. (ISBN 0-671-22555-3). S&S.

Mao, J. C. Quantitative Analysis of Financial Decisions. 1969. text ed. 28.95x (ISBN 0-02-375820-1). Macmillan.

Mao, James C. Corporate Financial Decisions. LC 75-18149. (Illus.). 600p. 1976. text ed. 19.95 (ISBN 0-915944-00-6). Pavan Pubs.

Mao, Nathan K. Li Yu. (World Authors Ser.). 1977. lib. bdg. 15.95 (ISBN 0-8057-6283-3, Twayne). G K Hall.

--Pa Chin. (World Authors Ser.). 1978. 15.95 (ISBN 0-8057-6337-6, Twayne). G K Hall.

Mao, Nathan K., tr. see Ch'ien Chung-shu.

Mao, Nathan K., jt. ed. see Yang, Winston L.

Mao Dun. Spring Silkworms & Other Stories. 2nd ed. 1980. 6.95 (ISBN 0-8351-0615-2). China Bks.

Mao Tse-Tung. Selected Military Writings, 1928-1949. 1967-1968. 7.95 (ISBN 0-8351-0321-8); red plastic 7.95 (ISBN 0-8351-0323-4); pap. 5.95 (ISBN 0-8351-0322-6). China Bks.

--Selected Works, 4 vols. Incl. Vol. 1. 1924-37. 1965 (ISBN 0-8351-0328-5) (ISBN 0-8351-0329-3); Vol. 2. 1937-41. 1965 (ISBN 0-8351-0330-7) (ISBN 0-8351-0331-5); Vol. 3. 1941-45. 1965 (ISBN 0-8351-0332-3). pap. (ISBN 0-8351-0333-1); Vol. 4. 1945-49. 1965.. 7.95 ea. (ISBN 0-8351-0334-X); pap. 5.95 ea. (ISBN 0-8351-0335-8). China Bks.

--Selected Works of Mao Tse-Tung, 5 vols. LC 77-30658. 1978. Set. text ed. 65.00 (ISBN 0-08-022262-5); text ed. 15.00 (ISBN 0-686-68045-6); Vol. I. text ed. 15.00 (ISBN 0-08-022980-8); Vol. II. text ed. 15.00 (ISBN 0-08-022981-6); Vol. III. text ed. 15.00 (ISBN 0-08-022982-4); Vol. IV. text ed. 15.00 (ISBN 0-08-022983-2); Vol. V. text ed. 15.00 (ISBN 0-08-022984-0). Pergamon.

Ma'Oz, Moshe, ed. Studies on Palestine During the Ottoman Period. 582p. 1975. text ed. 34.50x (ISBN 0-686-74322-9, Pub. by Magnes Israel). Humanities.

Maoz, Zeev. Paths to Conflict: International Dispute Initiation, 1816-1976. 270p. 1982. softco ver 21.50 (ISBN 0-86531-933-2). Westview.

Map Workshop Panel, June 3, 1969 Special Libraries Association Annual Conference, Montreal. Recent Practices in Map Libraries, Geography & Map Division: Proceedings. LC 78-182056. 1971. 4.50 o.p. (ISBN 0-87111-204-3). SLA.

Mapes, Lola R. Name Games. 80p. (gr. 3-5). 1983. pap. text ed. 5.95 (ISBN 0-86530-077-1, IP 77-1). Incentive Pubs.

Maple & Humblestone. Mysterious Powers & Strange Forces. (Supernatural Guides Ser.). (gr. 5-9). 1979. 5.95 (ISBN 0-86020-244-5, Usboren-Hayes); PLB 8.95 (ISBN 0-88110-012-9); pap. 2.95 (ISBN 0-86020-245-3). EDC.

Maple, Eric. The Ancient Art of Occult Healing. (Paths to Inner Power Ser.). 1974. pap. 1.25 o.p. (ISBN 0-87728-231-5). Weiser.

--Deadly Magic. 1976. pap. 3.95 o.p. (ISBN 0-87728-354-0). Weiser.

Maple, M. B. & Fischer, O., eds. Superconductivity in Ternary Compounds II: Superconductivity & Magnetism. (Topics in Current Physics: Vol. 34). (Illus.). 335p. 1982. 32.00 (ISBN 0-387-11814-4). Springer-Verlag.

Maple, M. Brian, jt. ed. see Suhl, Harry.

Maples, Evelyn. The Many Selves of Ann-Elizabeth. (Illus.). (ps-3). 1973. 6.50 o.p. (ISBN 0-8309-0093-4, 15-0104-6). Ind Pr MO.

Mapp, Alf J., Jr. The Virginia Experiment. rev. ed. 588p. 1974. 27.50x (ISBN 0-87548-309-7); pap. 12.00x (ISBN 0-87548-308-9). Open Court.

Mapp, Alfred J., Jr. The Golden Dragon: Alfred the Great & His Times. LC 74-8983. 1974. 15.50x (ISBN 0-87548-293-7). Open Court.

Mappes, Thomas & Zembaty, Jane. Biomedical Ethics. (Illus.). 640p. 1980. text ed. 23.50 (ISBN 0-07-040123-3). McGraw.

--Social Ethics: Morality & Social Policy. (Illus.). 1976. pap. text ed. 15.75 (ISBN 0-07-040120-9, C). McGraw.

Mappes, Thomas A. & Zembaty, Jane S. Social Ethics: Morality & Social Policy. 2nd ed. (Illus.). 448p. 1982. pap. 14.95x (ISBN 0-07-040121-7). McGraw.

Mapplethorpe, Robert & Chatwin, Bruce. Lady: Lisa Lyon. (Illus.). 112p. 1983. 31.25 (ISBN 0-670-43012-9, Studio); pap. 19.95 (ISBN 0-670-43013-7). Viking Pr.

Maquet, J. & Greenberg, J., eds. On Linguistic Anthropology: Essays in Honor of Harry Hoijer, 1979. LC 80-50214. (Other Realities Ser.: Vol. 2). 139p. text ed. 12.00x (ISBN 0-686-70972-1); pap. text ed. 9.00x (ISBN 0-89003-062-6). Undena Pubns.

Maquet, J. P. The Sociology of Knowledge. Locke, John F., tr. from Fr. LC 70-168963. 318p. 1973. Repr. of 1951 ed. lib. bdg. 19.75x (ISBN 0-8371-6236-X, MASK). Greenwood.

Maquet, Jacques. Civilizations of Black Africa. Rayfield, Joan, tr. 1972. pap. 7.95x (ISBN 0-19-501464-2). Oxford U Pr.

Mar, Alexander Del see Del Mar, Alexander.

Mar, James W., ed. Structures Technology for Large Radio & Radar Telescope Systems. 1969. 40.00x (ISBN 0-262-13046-7). MIT Pr.

Mar, Timothy T. Face Reading. 1975. pap. 1.50 o.p. (ISBN 0-451-06539-5, W6539, Sig). NAL.

Mar, Virginia A. La see Shakespeare, William.

Mar, W. Del see Pender, H. & Del Mar, W.

Mara. Tracings. LC 80-67934. (Earth Song Ser.). 84p. 1980. pap. 4.95 (ISBN 0-9605170-0-6). Earth-Song.

Mara, D. Duncan, ed. see Feachem, Richard G. & Bradley, David J.

Mara, Duncan. Sewage Treatment in Hot Climates. LC 75-23421. 240p. 1976. 41.95 (ISBN 0-471-56784-1, Pub by Wiley-Interscience). Wiley.

Mara, Thalia. First Steps in Ballet. LC 75-37100. (Illus.). 64p. (YA) 1976. Repr. of 1955 ed. pap. 3.75 (ISBN 0-87127-082-X). Dance Horiz.

--Third Steps in Ballet. LC 70-181475. (Illus.). 63p. pap. 3.75 (ISBN 0-87127-040-4). Dance Horiz.

Marable, Manning. How Capitalism Underdeveloped Black America. 285p. 1982. 20.00 (ISBN 0-89608-166-4); pap. 7.50 (ISBN 0-89608-165-6). South End Pr.

Maraccini, Jim. Read & Do with Professor Riddle. 1972. 2.75x (ISBN 0-88323-091-7, 195). Richards Pub.

Maracotta, Lindsay. Caribe. (Orig.). 1980. pap. 2.25 o.s.i. (ISBN 0-515-04692-2). Jove Pubns.

Maradudin, A., jt. ed. see Horton, G.

Maradudin, A. A., jt. auth. see Horton, G. K.

Maraini, Fosco. Tokyo. (The Great Cities Ser.). (Illus.). (gr. 6 up). 1976. PLB 12.00 (ISBN 0-8094-2267-0, Pub by Time-Life). Silver.

Marais, G. V., jt. auth. see Loewenthal, R. E.

Maraldo, John C., tr. see Dumoulin, Heinrich.

Maraldo, John C., tr. see Lassalle, H. M.

Maramorosch, K., ed. see Symposium Of The Entymological Society Of America - Atlantic City - 1960.

Maramorosch, Karl & Koprowski, Hilary, eds. Methods in Virology, Vols. 1-6. Incl. Vol. 1. 1967. 71.50, by subscription 60.50 (ISBN 0-12-470201-5); Vol. 2. 1968. 71.50, by subscription 60.50 (ISBN 0-12-470202-3); Vol. 3. 1967. by subscription 60.50 71.50 (ISBN 0-12-470203-1); Vol. 4. 1968. 74.50, by subscription 64.00 (ISBN 0-12-470204-X); Vol. 5. 1971. 63.00, by subscription 51.50 (ISBN 0-12-470205-8); Vol. 6. 1977. 62.50 (ISBN 0-12-470206-6); subscription 51.50 (ISBN 0-686-66775-1). Acad Pr.

Maramorosch, Karl & Mitsuhashi, Jun, eds. Invertebrate Cell Culture Applications. 245p. 1982. 23.00 (ISBN 0-12-470290-2). Acad Pr.

Maran, Rene. Batouala. (African Writers Ser.). (Orig.). 1973. pap. text ed. 4.00x o.p. (ISBN 0-435-90135-4). Heinemann Ed.

Marana, Giovanni P. Letters Writ by a Turkish Spy. Weitzman, Arthur J., ed. 252p. 1970. 24.95 (ISBN 0-87722-000-X). Temple U Pr.

Marana, Robert W., et al. Perceptions of Life Quality in Rural America: An Analysis of Survey Data from Four Studies. 118p. 1980. pap. 12.00x (ISBN 0-87944-252-2). Inst Soc Res.

Maranell, Gary M. Responses to Religion: Studies in the Social Psychology of Religious Belief. LC 73-19860. (Illus.). xviii, 313p. 1974. 17.95x (ISBN 0-7006-0114-7). Univ Pr KS.

Marano, Joseph & Kaufman, Kenneth. Fundamentals of Mathematics. (Illus.). 480p. 1973. text ed. 19.95 (ISBN 0-13-341081-1). P-H.

Marano, Russell. Poems from a Mountain Ghetto. (Illus.). 76p. (Orig.). 1979. pap. 5.00x (ISBN 0-686-37048-1). Back Fork Bks.

Marans, Robert W. & Fly, J. Mark. Recreation & the Quality of Urban Life: Recreational Resources, Behaviors & Evaluations of People in the Detroit Region. 240p. 1981. pap. 16.00x (ISBN 0-87944-273-5). Inst Soc Res.

Marans, Robert W. & Spreckelmeyer, Kent F. Evaluting Built Enviroment Environments: A Behavioral Approach. (Illus.). 249p. 1981. text ed. 20.00x (ISBN 0-87944-272-7, 81-6709). Inst Soc Res.

Marans, Robert W. & Wellman, John D. The Quality of NonMetropolitan Living: Evaluations, Behaviors, & Expectations of Northern Michigan Residents. LC 78-69913. (Illus.). 280p. 1978. 20.00x (ISBN 0-87944-227-1); pap. 12.00x (ISBN 0-87944-226-3). Inst Soc Res.

Marans, Robert W., et al. Waterfront Living: A Report on Permanent & Seasonal Residents in Northern Michigan. LC 76-620083. 301p. 1976. pap. 12.00x (ISBN 0-87944-218-2). Inst Soc Res.

--Youth & the Environment: An Evaluation of the 1971 Youth Conservation Corps. LC 72-81090. 257p. 1972. pap. 6.00x (ISBN 0-87944-121-6). Inst Soc Res.

Marans, Robert W., jt. auth. see King, Jonathan.

Marasco, Michael C., ed. The Complete Commodity Futures Directory. 2nd ed. 250p. 1982. 3 ring binder 49.00 (ISBN 0-9610034-0-5). Christopher Res.

Marascuilo, Leonard A. & Levin, Joel R. Multivariate Statistics in the Social Sciences: A Researcher's Guide. (Statistics Ser.). 576p. 1983. text ed. 32.95 (ISBN 0-686-83031-8). Brooks-Cole.

Marasinghe, M. L., ed. Third World Legal Studies: Law in Alternative Strategies of Rural Development. 313p. 1982. pap. 15.00 (ISBN 0-686-37983-7). Intl Ctr Law.

Marat, J. P. Decouvertes Sur le Feau, L'electricite et la Lumiere Constatees Par une Suite D'experiences Nouvelles Qui Viennent D'etre Verifiees Par Mm. les Commissaires De L'academie Des Sciences. Repr. of 1779 ed. 20.00 o.p. (ISBN 0-8287-0568-2). Clearwater Pub.

Marateck, Samuel. BASIC. 2nd ed. 1975. 19.75 (ISBN 0-12-470455-7); instr's manual 3.50 (ISBN 0-12-470456-5). Acad Pr.

Marateck, Samuel L. Fortran. 1977. 19.75 (ISBN 0-12-470460-3); instr's. manual 3.50 (ISBN 0-12-470462-X). Acad Pr.

Maratsos, M. P. The Use of Definite & Indefinite Reference in Young Children. (Illus.). 160p. 1976. 29.95 (ISBN 0-521-20924-2). Cambridge U Pr.

Maravall, Jose. Dictatorship & Political Dissent: Workers & Students in Franco's Spain. 1979. 26.00 (ISBN 0-312-20012-9). St Martin.

--Transition to Democracy in Spain. LC 81-21317. 230p. 1982. 30.00x (ISBN 0-312-81459-3). St Martin.

Marazzi, Rich & Fiorito, Len. Aaron to Zuverink: A Nostalgic Look at the Baseball Players of the Fifties. LC 80-5893. 352p. 1981. 19.95 (ISBN 0-8128-2775-9). Stein & Day.

Marbach, Ethel. The Cabbage Moth & the Shamrock. 6.95 (ISBN 0-914676-15-6); pap. 4.95 (ISBN 0-686-95971-X). Green Tiger Pr.

--A Christmas Tree For All Seasons. (Illus.). 12p. (Orig.). 1982. pap. 2.50 (ISBN 0-914676-60-1, Pub. by Envelope Bks). Green Tiger Pr.

--Soup Pot. (Illus.). 12p. (Orig.). 1982. pap. 2.50 (ISBN 0-914676-49-0, Pub. by Envelope Bks). Green Tiger Pr.

Marban, Edilberto. Ancient & Medieval History. (Blue Bks.). pap. 1.25 o.p. (ISBN 0-671-18102-5). Monarch Pr.

Marbeau, J. B. Des Creches Ou Moyen De Diminuer la Misere En Augmentant la Population. (Conditions of the 19th Century French Working Class Ser.). 139p. (Fr.). 1974. Repr. of 1845 ed. lib. bdg. 44.00x o.p. (ISBN 0-8287-0570-4, 1113). Clearwater Pub.

--Du Pauperisme En France et Des Moyens D'y Remedier, Ou Principes D'economie Charitable. (Conditions of the 19th Century French Working Class Ser.). 195p. (Fr.). 1974. Repr. of 1847 ed. lib. bdg. 56.00x o.p. (ISBN 0-8287-0571-2, 1022). Clearwater Pub.

Marberger, Michael & Dreikorn, Kurt. Renal Preservation. (International Perspectives In Urology: Vol. 8). (Illus.). 352p. 1983. lib. bdg. price not set (ISBN 0-683-05585-2). Williams & Wilkins.

Marble, Annie R. Pen Names & Personalities. 256p. 1983. Repr. of 1930 ed. lib. bdg. 40.00 (ISBN 0-89984-824-9). Century Bookbindery.

Marble, Harriet C. James Monroe: Patriot & President. LC 78-113516. (Lives to Remember Ser.). (gr. 5-8). 1970. PLB 4.97 o.p. (ISBN 0-399-60309-3). Putnam Pub Group.

Marbot, Bernard. After Darauerre: Masterworks of French Photography from the Bibliotheque Nationale. Eigsti, Mary S., tr. from Fr. (Illus.). 202p. 1980. 35.00 (ISBN 0-87099-257-0). Metro Mus Art.

Marbury, Edward. Obadiah & Habakkuk. 1979. 23.95 (ISBN 0-86524-007-8, 7003). Klock & Klock.

Marcantonio, Alfredo, intro. by. Is the Bug Dead? LC 82-19202. (Illus.). 144p. 1983. pap. 9.95 (ISBN 0-941434-24-9). Stewart Tabori & Chang.

Marcel, Gabriel. Man Against Mass Society. 288p. 1962. pap. 4.95 (ISBN 0-89526-945-7). Regnery-Gateway.

--The Mystery of Being, 2 vols. Incl. Vol. 1. Reflections & Mystery. 236p. pap. 5.95 (ISBN 0-89526-929-5); Vol. 2. Faith & Reality. 200p. pap. 5.95 (ISBN 0-89526-930-9). 1960. Repr. Regnery-Gateway.

--Royce's Metaphysics. Ringer, Virginia & Ringer, Gordon, trs. from Ger. LC 74-33746. 180p. 1975. Repr. of 1956 ed. lib. bdg. 20.50 (ISBN 0-8371-7978-5, MARO). Greenwood.

Marcel, Pierre Ch. Relevance of Preaching. (Notable Books on Preaching). 1977. pap. 2.95 o.p. (ISBN 0-8010-6037-0). Baker Bk.

Marcell, David W. Progress & Pragmatism: James, Dewey, Beard & the American Idea of Progress. LC 72-818. (Contributions in American Studies: No. 9). 402p. 1974. lib. bdg. 29.95 (ISBN 0-8371-6387-0, MPR/). Greenwood.

Marcell, David W., ed. American Studies: A Guide to Information Sources. LC 73-17559. (Information Guide Library: Vol. 10). 250p. 1982. 42.00x (ISBN 0-8103-1263-8). Gale.

March, Frederick, et al. Wind Power for the Electric-Utility Industry: Policy Incentives for Fuel Conservation. LC 81-48267. (An Arthur D. Little Bk.). 176p. 1982. 19.95x (ISBN 0-669-05321-X). Lexington Bks.

March, Harold. Frederic Soulie: Novelist & Dramatist of the Romantic Period. 1931. text ed. 26.00x (ISBN 0-686-83553-0). Elliots Bks.

March, J. G., jt. auth. see Cyert, Richard M.

March, James G. & Simon, Herbert A. Organizations. LC 58-13464. 1958. 25.95 (ISBN 0-471-56793-0). Wiley.

March, Jerry. Advanced Organic Chemistry. 2nd ed. (Advanced Chemistry Ser.). (Illus.). 1977. text ed. 47.50 (ISBN 0-07-040247-7, C). McGraw.

March, Joseph M. Wild Party, a Certain Wildness, the Set-up. LC 68-27623. (Illus.). 310p. 1968. ltd. autographed ed. 25.00 (ISBN 0-87027-104-0); 10.95 (ISBN 0-87027-103-2). Cumberland Pr.

March, L., ed. The Architecture of Form. LC 74-80354. (Cambridge Urban & Architectural Studies: No. 4). (Illus.). 552p. 1976. 84.50 (ISBN 0-521-20528-X). Cambridge U Pr.

March, L., jt. ed. see Martin, Leslie.

March, Lionel & Steadman, Philip. The Geometry of Environment: An Introduction to Spatial Organization in Design. 1974. pap. 12.50x o.p. (ISBN 0-262-63055-9). MIT Pr.

March, Marion & McEvers, Joan. The Only Way to Learn Astrology: Horoscope Analysis, Vol. 3. 1982. pap. 9.95 (ISBN 0-917086-43-0, Pub. by Astro Comp Serv). Para Res.

March, N. H. & Tosi, M. P. Atomic Dynamics in Liquids. LC 76-16040. 330p. (Orig.). 53.50 (ISBN 0-470-15145-5). Krieger.

March, Norman H., et al. Many-Body Problem in Quantum Mechanics. (Cambridge Monographs on Physics). 1968. 59.50 (ISBN 0-521-05671-3). Cambridge U Pr.

March, Peyton C. Nation at War. Repr. of 1932 ed. lib. bdg. 30.00x (ISBN 0-8371-4269-5, MANW). Greenwood.

March, Robert H. Physics for Poets. 2nd ed. (Illus.). 1977. text ed. 24.50 (ISBN 0-07-040243-4, C); instructor's manual 15.00 (ISBN 0-07-040244-2). McGraw.

--Physics for Poets. (Illus.). 304p. 1983. pap. 7.95 (ISBN 0-8092-5532-4). Contemp Bks.

March, William. Bad Seed. 1983. pap. 2.95 (ISBN 0-553-20820-9). Bantam.

Marchac, Daniel & Renier, Dominique. Craniofacial Surgery for Craniosynostosis. 1982. text ed. 48.50 (ISBN 0-316-54582-1). Little.

Marchak, John P., ed. see Educational Research Council of America.

Marchall, Joanne. The Peacock Bed. (Orig.). 1980. pap. 1.25 o.s.i. (ISBN 0-440-16883-X). Dell.

Marchand, Alan P. Stereochemical Applications of NMR Studies in Rigid Bicyclic Systems. LC 82-13648. (Methods in Stereochemical Analysis: Vol. 1). (Illus.). xiii, 231p. 1982. 92.50x (ISBN 0-89573-112-6). Verlag Chemie.

Marchand, James W., jt. ed. see Fink, Karl J.

Marchand, Leslie A., ed. see Byron, George G.

Marchand, P. R. Du Pauperisme. (Conditions of the 19th Century Working Class Ser.). 536p. (Fr.). 1974. Repr. of 1845 ed. lib. bdg. 132.00x o.p. (ISBN 0-8287-0573-9, 1023). Clearwater Pub.

Marchant. Design for Fire Safety. 1983. text ed. write for info (ISBN 0-408-00487-8). Butterworth.

Marchant, Catherine. The Fen Tiger. LC 79-84694. 1979. 8.95 o.p. (ISBN 0-688-03448-9). Morrow.

Marchant, E. C., ed. see Thucydides.

Marchant, E. C., ed. see Xenophon.

Marchant, J. P. & Pegg, D. Digital Computers. 2nd ed. 214p. (Figs). 1969. 7.00x (ISBN 0-216-88873-5). Intl Pubns Serv.

Marchant, Leslie. Aboriginal Administration in Western Australia: 1889-1905. (Australian Aboriginal Studies - New Ser.: No. 31). 89p. 1981. pap. text ed. 6.75x (ISBN 0-391-02320-9, Pub. by Australian Inst Australia). Humanities.

Marchant, Maurice P. Participative Management in Academic Libraries. LC 76-8740. (Contributions in Librarianship & Information Science: No. 16). 320p. 1977. lib. bdg. 29.95 (ISBN 0-8371-8935-7, MPM/). Greenwood.

Marchant, W. T. In Praise of Ale, or Songs, Ballads, Epigrams & Anecdotes Relating to Beer Malt, & Hops. LC 68-22038. 1968. Repr. of 1888 ed. 42.00x (ISBN 0-8103-3511-5). Gale.

Marchant, William. Firebird. 288p. 1980. 10.95 o.p. (ISBN 0-517-53922-5). Crown.

Marchbank, Pearce, ed. With the Beatles: The Historic Photographs of Dezo Hoffmann. (Illus.). 96p. (Orig.). 1983. pap. 12.95 (ISBN 0-399-41009-0). Delilah Bks.

Marchbanks, John B. Great Doctrines Relating to Salvation. LC 73-123612. 1970. pap. 2.95 (ISBN 0-87213-640-X). Loizeaux.

Marchenko, Anatoly. From Tarusa to Siberia. Rubenstein, Joshua, ed. 1980. 12.50 (ISBN 0-931554-16-0); pap. 6.00 (ISBN 0-931554-17-9). Strathcona.

--My Testimony. Scammell, Michael, tr. from Rus. 480p. 1983. Repr. of 1969 ed. 22.95 (ISBN 0-931554-20-9). Strathcona.

Marchesi, Blanche. Singer's Pilgrimage. LC 77-1941. (Music Reprint Ser.: 1978). (Illus.). 1978. Repr. of 1923 ed. lib. bdg. 29.50 (ISBN 0-306-70878-7). Da Capo.

Marchesi, Mathilde. Marchesi & Music: Passages from the Life of a Famous Singing-Teacher. LC 77-27354. (Music Reprint Ser., 1978). 1978. Repr. of 1898 ed. lib. bdg. 29.50 (ISBN 0-306-77577-8). Da Capo.

Marchesi, Vincent T. & Gallo, Robert C., eds. Differentiation & Function of Hematopoietic Cell Surfaces. LC 82-6557. (UCLA Symposia on Molecular & Cellular Biology Ser.: Vol. 1). 320p. 1982. 56.00 (ISBN 0-8451-2600-8). A R Liss.

Marchet, Jean-Francois, jt. auth. see Coltrin, Peter.

Marchette, Nyven J. Ecological Relationships & Evolution of the Rickettsiae, Vol. I. 192p. 1982. 60.00 (ISBN 0-8493-6125-7). CRC Pr.

Marchetti, Victor & Marks, John D. The CIA & the Cult of Intelligence. 1983. pap. 3.95 (ISBN 0-440-31298-1, LE). Dell.

Marchington, John. Your Book of Photographing Wild Life. (gr. 7 up). 1973. 4.95 o.p. (ISBN 0-571-09601-8). Transatlantic.

Marchington, M. Managing Industrial Relations. 208p. 1982. 19.00 (ISBN 0-07-084580-8). McGraw.

--Responses to Participation at Work. 232p. 1980. text ed. 31.25x (ISBN 0-566-02148-X). Gower Pub Ltd.

Marchione, Margherita. Clemente Rebora. (World Authors Ser.). 1979. lib. bdg. 15.95 (ISBN 0-8057-6362-7, Twayne). G K Hall.

--L' Imagine Tesa: The Life & Works of Clemente Rebora. enl. ed. 410p. 1974. 10.00 (ISBN 0-686-84873-X). Am Inst Ital Stud.

Marchione, Margherita, ed. Lettere Di Clemente Rebora 1897-1930, Vol. I. 680p. 1976. 20.00 (ISBN 0-686-84877-2). Am Inst Ital Stud.

Marchione, Margherita & Scalia, S. Eugene, eds. Carteggio Di Giovanni Boine, Vol. I_IV. Incl. Vol. I. Bione-Prezzolini, 1908-1915. Prezzolini, Giuseppe, pref. by. 264p. 1971. 10.00 (ISBN 0-686-84878-0); Vol. II. Boine-Emilio Cecchi 1911-1917. Martini, Carlo, pref. by. 252p. 1972. 10.00 (ISBN 0-686-84879-9); Vol. III. Boine-Amici Del Rinnovamento, 1905-1917. Vigorelli, Giancarlo, pref. by. 1132p. 1977. 25.00 (ISBN 0-686-84880-2); Boine-Amici De La Voce Ed Altri, 1900-1917. Amoretti, Giovanni, pref. by. 15.00 (ISBN 0-686-84881-0). Date not set. Am Inst Ital Stud.

Marchione, Margherita, tr Philip Mazzei: Jefferson's "Zealous Whig". 352p. 1975. 9.95 (ISBN 0-686-84875-6); pap. 5.95 (ISBN 0-686-84876-4). Am Inst Ital Stud.

--Twentieth Century Italian Poetry: A Bilingual Anthology. 302p. 1974. 10.00 (ISBN 0-686-84882-9). Am Inst Ital Stud.

Marchiore, Giuseppe, ed. see Delacroix, Eugene.

Marchuk, G. I. & Kagan, B. A. Ocean Tides: Mathematical Models & Numerical Experiments. Cartwright, D. E., tr. LC 82-18898. (Illus.). 240p. 1983. 65.00 (ISBN 0-08-026236-8). Pergamon.

Marciano, John, jt. auth. see Griffen, William L.

Marcin, Marietta. The Complete Book of Herbal Teas. (Illus.). 224p. 1983. 8.95 (ISBN 0-312-92098-9). Congdon & Weed.

Marcinkowski, M. J. Unified Theory of Mechanical Behavior of Matter. LC 78-27799. 1979. 44.95 o.s.i. (ISBN 0-471-05434-8, Pub by Wiley-Interscience). Wiley.

Marcinowski, Bettina. Die Frau In Afrika. 246p. (Ger.). 1982. write for info. (ISBN 3-8204-7237-1). P Lang Pubs.

Marck, E. E. Van see Gigase, P. L. & Van Marck, E. E.

Marck, Jan V. D. Arman Selected Works. (Illus.). 48p. 1974. 8.00x (ISBN 0-686-99820-0). La Jolla Mus Contemp Art.

Marck, Jan Van Der see Van Der Marck, Jan.

Marck, Jan Van Der see Van der Marck, Jan.

Marck, Louis, jt. auth. see Rechtschaffen, Bernard.

Marckwardt, Albert H. American English. rev. ed. Dillard, J. L., ed. 225p. 1980. 16.95x (ISBN 0-19-502600-4); pap. 6.95x (ISBN 0-19-502609-8). Oxford U Pr.

--The Place of Literature in the Teaching of English As a Second or Foreign Language. LC 77-25360. 1978. pap. text ed. 4.50x (ISBN 0-8248-0606-9, Eastwest Ctr). UH Pr.

Marckwardt, Albert H. & Moore, Samuel. Historical Outlines of English Sounds & Inflections. 1957. pap. 7.50x (ISBN 0-685-21787-6). Wahr.

Marco, Carolyn, jt. auth. see Gach, Michael.

Marco, Guy A., tr. see Zarlino, Gioseffo.

Marco, S. M., jt. auth. see Brown, Aubrey I.

Marcolungo, G., ed. see Pretto, G., et al.

Marcon, Mike. The TNT Job Getting System. Taylor, Margot W., ed. 128p. (Orig.). 1983. 9.95 (ISBN 0-911529-00-4). Worthington Co.

Marconi, W., jt. auth. see Mantovani, E.

Marcosson, Isaac F. Marse Henry: A Biography of Henry Watterson. LC 74-156200. (Illus.). 1971. Repr. of 1951 ed. lib. bdg. 15.50x (ISBN 0-8371-6150-9, MAMH). Greenwood.

Marcotty, Michael. Structured Programming with Pl-One: An Introduction. (Illus.). 1977. pap. text ed. 17.95 (ISBN 0-13-854885-4). P-H.

Marcoux, Paul & LoCigno, Joseph P., eds. Reading, Preaching & Celebrating the Word. pap. 9.95 (ISBN 0-941850-00-5). Sunday Pubn.

Marcovicz, Digne M. Martin Heidegger. 65p. 1980. 10.00 o.p. (ISBN 0-88254-644-9, Pub. by Fey Verlag Germany). Hippocrene Bks.

Marcucci, Robert, jt. auth. see Schoen, Harold L.

Marcue-Roberts, Helen, jt. auth. see Pai, Anna C.

Marcum, James. Khrushchev & the Legacy of Stalinism. Date not set. pap. 9.95 (ISBN 0-8120-5279-X). Barron.

Marcum, John A. Angolan Revolution Vol. 1: The Anatomy of an Explosion, 1950-1962. (Studies in Communism, Revisionism & Revolution). 1969. 35.00x (ISBN 0-262-13048-3). MIT Pr.

--The Angolan Revolution Volume II: Exile Politics & Guerrilla Warfare, 1962-1976. LC 69-11310. 1978. 37.00x (ISBN 0-262-13136-6). MIT Pr.

Marcum, John A., ed. Education, Race, & Social Change in South Africa. LC 82-60256. (Perspectives on Southern Africa: Vol. 34). 180p. 1982. 25.00x (ISBN 0-520-04855-5); pap. 6.50 (ISBN 0-520-04899-7). U of Cal Pr.

Marcus, jt. auth. see Heistad.

Marcus, Aaron. Soft Where, Inc, Vol. 2. (Illus.). 92p. (Orig.). 1982. pap. text ed. 5.00 (ISBN 0-915596-27-X). West Coast.

Marcus, Abraham. Electronics for Technicians. LC 69-10789. 1969. ref. ed. 21.95 (ISBN 0-13-252387-6). P-H.

Marcus, Abraham & Thrower, James R. Introduction to Applied Physics. 450p. 1980. text ed. 23.95x (ISBN 0-534-00825-9, Breton Pubs). Wadsworth Pub.

Marcus, Adrianne. The Chocolate Bible. LC 78-25784. 1979. 12.95 o.p. (ISBN 0-399-12042-4). Putnam Pub Group.

Marcus, Alfred A. Promise & Performance: Choosing & Implementing an Environmental Policy. LC 79-8290. (Contributions in Political Science: No. 39). 1980. lib. bdg. 25.00 (ISBN 0-313-20707-0, MPT/). Greenwood.

Marcus, Bruce W. Competing for Capital: A Financial Relations Approach. LC 75-19280. 265p. 1975. 18.00 o.p. (ISBN 0-471-56863-5, Pub. by Wiley). Krieger.

Marcus, Burton, et al. Modern Marketing Management. rev. ed. 709p. 1980. text ed. 21.00 (ISBN 0-394-32254-1); wkbk 6.95 (ISBN 0-394-32489-7). Random.

Marcus, David. A Manual of Akkadian. LC 78-63068. 1978. pap. text ed. 9.50 (ISBN 0-8191-0608-9). U Pr of Amer.

--A Manual of Babylonian Jewish Aramaic. LC 80-6073. 104p. (Orig.). 1981. pap. text ed. 8.25 (ISBN 0-8191-1363-8). U Pr of Amer.

Marcus, Dora, jt. auth. see Dressel, Paul L.

Marcus, Edward & Marcus, Mildred R. Economic Progress & the Developing World. 1971. pap. 7.95x (ISBN 0-673-05140-4). Scott F.

Marcus, Elizabeth. Our Wonderful Seasons. LC 82-17372. (Question & Answer Bks.). (Illus.). 32p. (gr. 3-6). 1983. PLB 8.59 (ISBN 0-89375-896-5); pap. text ed. 1.95 (ISBN 0-89375-897-3). Troll Assocs.

--Rocks & Minerals. LC 82-17424. (Question & Answer Bks.). (Illus.). 32p. (gr. 3-6). 1983. PLB 8.59 (ISBN 0-89375-876-0); pap. text ed. 1.95 (ISBN 0-89375-877-9). Troll Assocs.

Marcus, Frank, tr. see Schnitzler, Arthur.

Marcus, Fred H. Short Story-Short Film. (Illus.). 1977. pap. text ed. 13.95 (ISBN 0-13-809558-2). P-H.

Marcus, George & Marcus, Nancy. Forbidden Fruits & Forgotten Vegetables: A Guide to Cooking with Ethnic, Exotic & Neglected Produce. (Illus.). 160p. 19.95 (ISBN 0-312-29826-9); pap. 8.95 (ISBN 0-312-29827-7). St Martin.

Marcus, George E. The Nobility & the Chiefly Tradition in the Modern Kingdom of Tonga. 1980. pap. text ed. 15.00x (ISBN 0-8248-0683-2, Pub. by Polynesian Soc). UH Pr.

Marcus, Greil. Mystery Train: Images of America in Rock 'n' Roll Music. 1976. pap. 5.50 o.p. (ISBN 0-525-47422-6). Dutton.

Marcus, Harold G. The Life & Times of Menelik II: Ethiopia 1844-1913. (Oxford Studies in African Affairs). (Illus.). 1975. 39.00x (ISBN 0-19-821674-2). Oxford U Pr.

Marcus, Henry S., et al. Federal Port Policy in the United States. LC 76-10853. 376p. 1976. 30.00x (ISBN 0-262-13125-0). MIT Pr.

Marcus, Irving. The Portable Dictionary of Real Estate Terminology. 120p. 1983. pap. 4.95 (ISBN 0-686-96560-4). Branden.

Marcus, Isabel. Dollars for Reform: The OEO Neighborhood Health Center Experience. LC 79-2198. 208p. 1981. 24.95x (ISBN 0-669-03092-9). Lexington Bks.

Marcus, Jerry. Fat Kat, No. II. 128p. (Orig.). 1983. pap. 1.75 (ISBN 0-523-49038-0). Pinnacle Bks.

--Fatkat. 128p. 1981. pap. 1.75 (ISBN 0-523-49021-6). Pinnacle Bks.

Marcus, John T. French Socialism in the Crisis Years, 1933-1936. LC 75-28666. 1976. Repr. of 1958 ed. lib. bdg. 17.25x (ISBN 0-8371-8480-0, MAFRS). Greenwood.

Marcus, Joyce, jt. ed. see Flannery, Kent V.

Marcus, Judith, jt. auth. see Marcus, Rebecca B.

Marcus, Lyn. Dialectical Economics: An Introduction to Marxist Political Economy. 544p. 1975. text ed. 18.95x o.p. (ISBN 0-669-85308-9). Heath.

Marcus, Marie. Diagnostic Teaching of the Language Arts. LC 76-52400. 1977. text ed. 31.95x (ISBN 0-471-56854-6). Wiley.

Marcus, Marvin. Discrete Mathematics: A Computational Approach Using BASIC. 1983. price not set (ISBN 0-914894-38-2). Computer Sci.

Marcus, Matityahu, jt. auth. see Baumol, William J.

Marcus, Michael & Brown, Leroy. The Computer in Your Legal Practice. (Illus.). 240p. 1983. 24.95 (ISBN 0-13-164400-9); pap. 19.95 (ISBN 0-13-164392-4). P-H.

Marcus, Mildred R., jt. auth. see Marcus, Edward.

Marcus, Mitchell P. Switching Circuits for Engineers. 3rd ed. (Illus.). 336p. 1975. ref. ed. 28.95 (ISBN 0-13-879908-3). P-H.

Marcus, Mordecai. The Assistant Notes. 1972. pap. 2.95 (ISBN 0-8220-0214-0). Cliffs.

Marcus, Nancy, jt. auth. see Marcus, George.

Marcus, Pillip L., ed. see Yeats, W. B.

Marcus, Rebecca B. & Marcus, Judith. Fiesta Time in Mexico. LC 73-12834. (Around the World Holidays Ser). (Illus.). 96p. (gr. 4-7). 1974. PLB 7.12 (ISBN 0-8116-4953-9). Garrard.

Marcus, Richard, ed. Digital Video Three. Rev. ed. (Illus.). 230p. (Orig.). 1982. pap. text ed. 25.00 (ISBN 0-940690-04-7). Soc Motion Pic & TV Engrs.

Marcus, Robert. The Principles of Specification Design Workbook. Weinberg, Gerald, ed. (Illus.). 284p. 1979. pap. text ed. 19.95 o.p. (ISBN 0-87619-459-5). R J Brady.

Marcus, Robert & Burner, David. American Voices: A Historical Reader, 2 vols. 1979. pap. 10.95x ea. Vol. 1 (ISBN 0-673-15172-7). Vol. 2 (ISBN 0-673-15173-5). Scott F.

Marcus, Samuel H. Basics of Structural Steel Design. 2nd ed. 480p. 1980. text ed. 27.95 (ISBN 0-8359-0419-9); soln. manual avail. (ISBN 0-8359-0420-2). Reston.

Marcus, Sharon, ed. see Muhaiyaddeen, Bawa.

Marcus, Shlomo, jt. ed. see Leibowitz, J. O.

Marcus, Stanley. His & Hers: The Fantasy World of the Neiman-Marcus Catalogue. LC 82-71029. (Illus.). 224p. 1982. 25.00 (ISBN 0-670-37263-3). Viking Pr.

--Minding the Store. 1975. pap. 2.95 (ISBN 0-451-11374-8, AE1374, Sig). NAL.

Marcus, Steven, ed. World of Modern Fiction, 2 Vols. 1966. Set. 17.50 o.p. (ISBN 0-671-82956-4). S&S.

Marcus, William & Levy, Alex. Elements of Radio Servicing. 3rd ed. (gr. 9-12). 1967. text ed. 21.95 (ISBN 0-07-040290-6, G). McGraw.

--Practical Radio Servicing. 2nd ed. LC 79-26498. 632p. 1980. Repr. of 1963 ed. lib. bdg. 29.50 (ISBN 0-89874-061-4). Krieger.

--Practical Radio Servicing. 2nd ed. 1963. 33.50 o.p. (ISBN 0-07-040283-3, P&RB). McGraw.

Marcus, Y. Introduction to Liquid State Chemistry. LC 76-40230. 1977. 57.95 (ISBN 0-471-99448-0, Pub. by Wiley-Interscience). Wiley.

Marcuse, Dietrich, ed. Integrated Optics. LC 72-92691. (Illus.). 304p. 1973. 22.95 (ISBN 0-87942-021-9). Inst Electrical.

Marcuse, Katherine. The Devil's Workshop. LC 78-24121. (Illus.). (gr. 3-7). 1979. 6.50g o.p. (ISBN 0-687-10506-4). Abingdon.

Marcussen, Henrik & Torp, Jens. The Internationalization of Capital. 192p. 1982. 23.50 (ISBN 0-905762-90-8, Pub. by Zed Pr England); pap. 10.50 (ISBN 0-905762-77-0). Lawrence Hill.

Marcuvitz, Nathan & Felsen, L. B. Radiation & Scattering of Waves. LC 78-167786. 1973. ref. ed. 42.00 (ISBN 0-13-750364-4). P-H.

Marcy, Barton C., Jr., jt. ed. see Schubel, Jerry R.

Marcy, Carl. Presidential Commissions. LC 72-8109. (Studies in American History & Government). 156p. 1973. Repr. of 1945 ed. lib. bdg. 25.00 (ISBN 0-306-70532-X). Da Capo.

Marcy, Janis, jt. auth. see Marcy, Steve.

Marcy, Michel, jt. auth. see Marcy, Teresa.

Marcy, Randolph B. The Prairie Traveler. LC 81-8790. (Classics of the Old West Ser.). PLB 17.28 (ISBN 0-8094-3975-1). Silver.

Marcy, Randolph B. & McClellan, G. B. Adventure on Red River: A Report on the Exploration of the Headwaters of the Red River. Foreman, Grant, ed. (American Exploration & Travel Ser.: Vol. 1). (Illus.). 1968. Repr. of 1938 ed. 8.95 o.p. (ISBN 0-8061-0067-2). U of Okla Pr.

Marcy, Sam. Anatomy of the Economic Crisis. 120p. 1982. pap. 3.25 (ISBN 0-89567-077-1). WV Pubs.

--China, Suppression of the Left. 111p. 1977. pap. 2.00 (ISBN 0-686-84043-7). WV Pubs.

--Czechoslovakia Nineteen Sixty-Eight: The Class Character of the Events. 62p. 1978. pap. 1.50 (ISBN 0-89567-002-X). WV Pubs.

--Eurocommunism, New Form of Reformism. 52p. 1978. pap. 1.00 (ISBN 0-89567-026-7). WV Pubs.

--Imperialism & the Crisis in the Socialist Camp. 57p. 1979. pap. 1.50 (ISBN 0-89567-030-5). WV PUbs.

--Poland: Behind the Crisis. 168p. 1982. pap. 3.95 (ISBN 0-89567-076-3). WV Pubs.

--Selected Articles by Sam Marcy, 1979-1980. 73p. 1981. pap. 2.00 o.s.i. (ISBN 0-89567-043-7). WV Pubs.

--Selected Articles: 1976-1977. 78p. 1977. pap. 2.00 (ISBN 0-89567-010-0). WV Pubs.

--Selected Articles: 1977-1978. 72p. 1978. pap. 2.00 (ISBN 0-89567-029-1). WV Pubs.

--Selected Articles: 1980-1981. 63p. 1981. pap. 2.00 (ISBN 0-89567-048-8). WV Pubs.

--Selected Articles: 1980-1981. 89p. 1982. pap. 2.50 (ISBN 0-89567-078-X). WV Pubs.

--Selected Articles: 1981-82. 89p. 1982. pap. 2.50 (ISBN 0-89567-078-X). WV Pubs.

Marcy, Sam & Griswold, Deirdre. China, the Struggle Within. 2nd ed. 116p. 1972. pap. 2.00 (ISBN 0-89567-079-8). WV Pubs.

Marcy, Steve & Marcy, Janis. Addition & Subtraction with a Happy Ending. (Illus.). (gr. 4-7). 1976. wkbk. 5.85 (ISBN 0-88488-051-6). Creative Pubns.

--Algebra With Pizzazz! Incl. Book A (ISBN 0-88488-244-6); Book B (ISBN 0-88488-240-3); Book C (ISBN 0-88488-246-2); Book D (ISBN 0-88488-247-0). (gr. 9-12). 1982. 7.50 (ISBN 0-686-37852-0). Creative Pubns.

--Mathimagination. Incl. Bk. A. Beginning Multiplication & Division (ISBN 0-88488-029-X); Bk. B. Operations with Whole Numbers (ISBN 0-88488-030-3); Bk. C. Number Theory, Sets, & Number Bases (ISBN 0-88488-031-1); Bk. D. Fractions (ISBN 0-88488-025-7); Bk. E. Decimals & Per Cent (ISBN 0-88488-026-5); Bk. F. Geometry, Measurement, & Cartesian Coordinates (ISBN 0-88488-032-X). (Illus.). (gr. 4-9). 1973. wkbk. 5.85 ea. Creative Pubns.

--Pre-Algebra with Pizzazz! AA. (YA) 1978. wkbk. 7.50 (ISBN 0-88488-096-6). Creative Pubns.

--Pre-Algebra with Pizzazz! BB. (YA) 1978. wkbk. 7.50 (ISBN 0-88488-097-4). Creative Pubns.

--Pre-Algebra with Pizzazz! CC. (YA) 1978. wkbk. 7.50 (ISBN 0-88488-098-2). Creative Pubns.

--Pre-Algebra with Pizzazz! DD. (YA) 1978. wkbk. 7.50 (ISBN 0-88488-099-0). Creative Pubns.

Marcy, Teresa & Marcy, Michel. Cortina-Grosset Basic French Dictionary. Berberi, Dilaver & Berberi, Edel A., eds. LC 73-18522. 384p. 1975. pap. 3.50 (ISBN 0-448-14031-4, G&D). Putnam Pub Group.

Marczewski, Jan. Crisis in Socialist Planning: Eastern Europe & the USSR. Lindsay, Noel, tr. from Fr. LC 73-15190. (Special Studies). (Illus.). 270p. 1974. 34.95 o.p. (ISBN 0-275-08140-0). Praeger.

Marden, C. C., ed. Libro De Apollonio, an Old Spanish Poem, 2 pts. Incl. Pt. 1. (Elliott Monographs: Vols. 11 - 12). Repr. of 1917 ed. pap. 15.00 (ISBN 0-527-02610-7); Pt. 2. Repr. of 1922 ed. pap. 12.00 (ISBN 0-527-02615-8). (Elliott Monographs: Vol. 6). (Span.). Kraus Repr.

Marden, Charles F. & Meyer, Gladys. Minorities in American Society. 5th ed. 1978. text ed. 13.95 (ISBN 0-442-23460-0). Van Nos Reinhold.

Marden, Margaret A. The Bargain Shopper's Guide to Northern New England. LC 81-66701. 208p. (Orig.). 1981. pap. 7.95 (ISBN 0-89272-122-7, PIC474). Down East.

Marder, Arthur J. From the Dreadnought to Scapa Flow: The Royal Navy in the Fisher Era, 1904-1919, 5 vols. Incl. Vol. 1. The Road to War, 1904-1914. 1961. 37.50x (ISBN 0-19-215122-3); Vol. 3. Jutland & After. 2nd ed. 1978. 34.50x (ISBN 0-19-215841-4); Vol. 4. 1917: Year of Crisis. 1969. 24.00x (ISBN 0-19-215170-3); Vol. 5. Victory & Aftermath. 1970. 37.50x (ISBN 0-19-215187-8). Oxford U Pr.

Marder, Estelle, jt. auth. see Marder, William.

Marder, William & Marder, Estelle. Anthony, The Man, The Company, The Cameras. Duncan, Bob, ed. LC 81-90597. 1982. 59.95 (ISBN 0-9607480-0-8); pap. 29.95 (ISBN 0-686-99447-7). Marder.

Mardesic, S. & Segal, J. Shape Theory. (Mathematical Library Ser.: Vol. 26). Date not set. 74.50 (ISBN 0-444-86286-2, North Holland). Elsevier.

Mardh, P., jt. auth. see Holmes, K. K.

Mardh, P. A. & Holmes, K. K., eds. Chlamydial Infections: Proceedings, 5th International Symposium, Lund, Sweden, June 15-19, 1982. (Fernstrom Foundation Ser.: Vol. 2). 454p. 1982. 62.75 (ISBN 0-444-80431-5, Biomedical Pr). Elsevier.

Mardh, Per-Anders, jt. auth. see Holmes, King K.

Mardia, K. V., et al. Multivariate Analysis. LC 79-40922. (Probability and Mathematical Statistics Ser.). 1980. 63.50 (ISBN 0-12-471250-9); pap. 35.50 (ISBN 0-12-471252-5). Acad Pr.

Mardiguian, Steven Y., et al, eds. Specialized Catalogue of Canadian Stamps & Covers 1982. (Illus.). 144p. (Orig.). 1981. pap. 3.50 o.p. (ISBN 0-89487-043-2). Scott Pub Co.

Mardock, Robert. Reformers & American Indians. 1977. 12.50 (ISBN 0-686-95805-5). Jefferson Natl.

Mardon, D. K. An Illustrated Catalogue of the Rothschild Collection of Fleas, Vol. VI: Pygiopsyllidae. 298p. 1981. 200.00x (ISBN 0-686-82365-6, Pub. by Brit Mus England). State Mutual Bk.

Mardon, Deidre. Canvas of Passion. (Harlequin American Romance Ser.). 256p. 1983. pap. 2.25 (ISBN 0-373-16009-7). Harlequin Bks.

Mare, Margaret. Eduard Morike: The Man & the Poet. LC 72-7860. (Illus.). 275p. 1973. Repr. of 1957 ed. lib. bdg. 15.50x (ISBN 0-8371-6538-5, MEMO). Greenwood.

Mare, P. De La see De La Mare, P. B.

Mare, Walter de la see De la Mare, Walter.

Marec, J. P. Optimal Space Trajectories. LC 79-14664. (Studies in Astronautics Ser.: Vol. 1). 1979. 70.25 (ISBN 0-444-41812-1). Elsevier.

Marechal, Ernest, jt. auth. see Kennedy, Joseph P.

Marechal, Sylvain. Apologues Modernes, a L'usage Du Dauphin. Repr. of 1788 ed. 28.00 o.p. (ISBN 0-8287-0575-5). Clearwater Pub.

--Catechisme Du Cure Meslier. Repr. of 1790 ed. 11.50 o.p. (ISBN 0-8287-0576-3). Clearwater Pub.

--Dame Nature a la Barre De L'assemblee Nationale. Repr. of 1791 ed. 9.50 o.p. (ISBN 0-8287-0578-X). Clearwater Pub.

Marek, George R. Cosima Wagner. LC 80-7591. (Illus.). 256p. 1981. 17.26i (ISBN 0-06-012704-X, HarpT). Har-Row.

--A Front Seat at the Opera. LC 71-138161. 307p. 1972. Repr. of 1948 ed. lib. bdg. 17.50x (ISBN 0-8371-5618-1, MAFS). Greenwood.

Marek, Joseph, tr. see Herling, Gustaw.

Marek, Miroslav, et al. Cultural Policy in Czechoslavakia. (Studies & Documents on Cultural Policies Ser.). 77p. 1970. pap. 5.00 (ISBN 92-3-100853-6, U115, UNESCO). Unipub.

Marek, Richard, jt. auth. see King, Harold.

Marek, Wiktor. Elements of Logic & Foundations of Mathematics in Problems. 1982. 39.50 (ISBN 90-277-1084-8, Pub. by Reidel Holland). Kluwer Boston.

Marek Marzi Kronlandu, Jan. Thaumantias, Liber De Arcu Coelesti Deque Colorum Apparentium Natura Ortu et Causis. (Lat). Repr. of 1648 ed. slip case 26.00 (ISBN 0-384-35320-7). Johnson Repr.

Marel, R. Van Der see Van der Marel, R. & Beutelspacher, H.

Marelli, Leonard R., jt. auth. see Nadler, Harvey.

Marenbon, J. From the Circle of Alcuin to the School of Auxerre. (Cambridge Studies in Medieval Life & Thought: Third Ser., Vol. 15). (Illus.). 248p. 1981. 49.50 (ISBN 0-521-23428-X). Cambridge U Pr.

Marengo, Franco. The Code of British Trade Union Behavior. 1979. text ed. 31.25x (ISBN 0-566-00300-7). Gower Pub Ltd.

Marengo, Franco D. Rules of the Italian Political Game. 134p. 1981. text ed. 35.50x (ISBN 0-566-00301-5). Gower Pub Ltd.

Marer, Paul, ed. see Pecsi, Kalman.

Mares, F. M., ed. see Jonson, Ben.

Mares, William J., jt. auth. see Simmons, John.

Maresca, Carmela C. Careers in Marketing: A Woman's Guide. 240p. 1982. 16.95 (ISBN 0-13-115139-8); pap. 8.95 (ISBN 0-13-115121-5). P-H.

Marett, Cora B. & Leggon, Cheryl B., eds. Research in Race & Ethnic Relations, Vol. 1. 199p. 1979. 40.00 (ISBN 0-89232-064-8). Jai Pr.

Marett, Robert R. Psychology & Folk-Lore. LC 74-10825. 275p. Repr. of 1920 ed. 34.00x (ISBN 0-8103-4045-3). Gale.

Maretzek, Max. Crochets & Quavers: Or Revelations of an Opera Manager in America. 2nd ed. LC 65-23397. (Music Ser). 1966. Repr. of 1855 ed. lib. bdg. 32.50 (ISBN 0-306-70915-5). Da Capo.

Marfia, Jim, tr. see Nimzovich, Aron.

Marg, Elwyn. Computer-assisted Eye Examination. LC 78-65159. (Illus.). 1980. 12.00 (ISBN 0-911302-40-9). San Francisco Pr.

Margadant, Guillermo F. An Introduction to the History of Mexican Law. Date not set. lib. bdg. 30.00 (ISBN 0-379-20744-3). Oceana.

Margand, Peter, et al. Pre-Operative Pulmonary Preparation: A Clinical Guide. (Illus.). 141p. 1981. pap. 15.95 (ISBN 0-683-05587-9). Williams & Wilkins.

Margaris, N., jt. auth. see Koedam, A.

Marge, M., jt. auth. see Irwin, J.

Margenau, Henry. The Nature of Physical Reality: A Philosophy of Modern Physics. LC 77-86356. 1977. 26.00 (ISBN 0-918024-02-1); pap. text ed. 14.00 (ISBN 0-918024-03-X). Ox Bow.

--Thomas & the Physics of Nineteen Fifty-Eight: A Confrontation. (Aquinas Lecture). 1958. 7.95 (ISBN 0-87462-123-2). Marquette.

Marger, Martin. Elites & Masses: An Introduction to Political Sociology. 1980. text ed. 15.95 (ISBN 0-442-25410-5); instr's. manual 2.00 (ISBN 0-442-24628-5). Van Nos Reinhold.

Margeret, Jacques. The Russian Empire & Grand Duchy of Muscovy: A Seventeenth-Century French Account. Dunning, Chester S., ed. & tr. from Fr. LC 82-20126. (Illus.). 235p. 1983. 19.95 (ISBN 0-8229-3805-7). U of Pittsburgh Pr.

Margerie, Bertrand de see De Margerie, Bertrand.

Margerison, C. J. Managerial Problem Solving. 1975. 25.95 (ISBN 0-07-084445-3, P&RB). McGraw.

Margerison, D. & East, G. C. An Introduction to Polymer Chemistry. 1966. 27.00 o.s.i. (ISBN 0-08-011891-7); pap. 12.75 (ISBN 0-08-011890-9). Pergamon.

Margerison, D., jt. auth. see Green, J. R.

Margherita, Marchione. Clemente Rebora: A Man's Quest for the Absolute. (Twayne's World Authors Ser.). 180p. 1979. 12.50 (ISBN 0-686-84874-8). Am Inst Ital Stud.

Margie, Joyce D., jt. auth. see Block, Abby.

Margiotta, Franklin D. & Brown, James. Changing U. S. Military Manpower Realities. (Special Studies in Military Affairs). 290p. 1983. lib. bdg. 25.00 (ISBN 0-89158-935-X). Westview.

Margiotta, Franklin D., ed. The Changing World of the American Military. (Westview Special Studies in Military Affairs). 1978. lib. bdg. 33.00 (ISBN 0-89158-331-9); pap. 14.00 (ISBN 0-89158-309-2). Westview.

Margol, M., jt. auth. see Dubin, F.

Margolies, B. L. Princes of the Earth: Subcultural Diversity in a Mexican Municipality. 1975. pap. 4.00 (ISBN 0-686-36567-4). Am Anthro Assn.

Margolies, Edward & Bakish, David, eds. Afro-American Fiction, Eighteen Fifty-Three to Nineteen Seventy-Six: A Guide to Information Sources. LC 73-16976. (American Literature, English Literature, & World Literatures in English Information Guide Ser.: Vol. 25). 1979. 42.00x (ISBN 0-8103-1207-7). Gale.

Margolies, Eva L. Sensual Pleasure: A Woman's Guide. 192p. (Orig.). 1981. pap. 5.95 (ISBN 0-380-78006-2, 83592-4). Avon.

Margolies, Marjorie. The Girls in the Newsroom. 1983. pap. 3.50 (ISBN 0-441-28929-0, Pub. by Charter Bks). Ace Bks.

Margolies, Marjorie & Gruber, Ruth. They Came to Stay. (Illus.). 1976. 8.95 o.p. (ISBN 0-698-10662-8, Coward). Putnam Pub Group.

Margolin, Edythe. Teaching Young Children at School & Home. 448p. 1982. text ed. 22.95 (ISBN 0-02-375980-1). Macmillan.

Margolin, Jean-Claude. Douze Annees De Bibliographie Erasmienne (1950-1961) 1977. pap. 25.00x o.p. (ISBN 0-8020-2277-4). U of Toronto Pr.

--Quatorze Annees De Bibliographie Erasmienne (1936-1949) 1977. pap. 45.00x o.p. (ISBN 0-8020-2278-2). U of Toronto Pr.

Margolin, Judith B. The Individual's Guide to Grants. 325p. 1983. 15.95x (ISBN 0-306-41309-4, Plenum Pr). Plenum Pub.

Margolin, Malcolm. The Ohlone Way: Indian Life in the San Francisco & Monterey Bay Areas. LC 78-56826. (Illus., Orig.). 1978. 8.95 o.p. (ISBN 0-930588-02-9); pap. 5.95 (ISBN 0-930588-01-0). Heyday Bks.

Margolin, Victor & Bricta, Ira. The Promise & the Product: Two Hundred Years of American Advertising Posters. (Illus.). 1979. 19.95 o.s.i. (ISBN 0-02-579480-9); pap. 9.95 o.p. (ISBN 0-02-011880-5). Macmillan.

Margoliouth, H. M., et al, eds. see Marvell, Andrew.

Margolis, Diane R. The Managers: Corporate Life in America. 312p. 1981. pap. 5.95 (ISBN 0-688-00351-6). Quill NY.

Margolis, Gary. The Day We Still Stand Here. 1983. 8.95x (ISBN 0-8203-0634-7); pap. 4.95x (ISBN 0-8203-0635-5). U of Ga Pr.

Margolis, J. & Guitton, H., eds. Public Economics: An Analysis of Public Production & Consumption & Their Relations to the Private Sector. LC 70-84182. (International Economics Association Ser.). 1969. 36.00 (ISBN 0-312-65415-4). St Martin.

Margolis, Joseph. Negativities: The Limits of Life. new ed. (Philosophy Ser). 176p. 1975. text ed. 10.95 (ISBN 0-675-08729-5); pap. text ed. 6.95x o.p. (ISBN 0-675-08732-5). Merrill.

Margolis, Joseph, ed. An Introduction to Philosophical Inquiry. 2nd ed. 1978. text ed. 21.95 (ISBN 0-394-31274-0). Knopf.

--Philosophy Looks at the Arts: Contemporary Readings in Aesthetics. rev. ed. LC 77-95028. 492p. 1978. 29.95 (ISBN 0-87722-123-5); pap. 12.95 (ISBN 0-87722-134-0). Temple U Pr.

Margolis, Joseph, ed. see Braude, Stephen E.
Margolis, Joseph, ed. see Muyskens, James L.
Margolis, Julius, jt. auth. see Haveman, Robert.
Margolis, Matthew, jt. auth. see Siegal, Mordecai.
Margolis, Michael. Viable Democracy. LC 79-5053. 1979. 22.50x (ISBN 0-312-83886-7). St Martin.
Margolis, Neal & Harmon, N. Paul. Accounting Essentials. LC 72-4756. (Self-Teaching Guides Ser.). 320p. 1972. pap. text ed. 8.95 (ISBN 0-471-56867-8). Wiley.
Margolis, S., jt. auth. see Mayne, R.
Margon, Lester. Construction of American Furniture Treasures. (Illus.). 168p. 1975. pap. 6.00 (ISBN 0-486-23056-2). Dover.
--Masterpieces of American Furniture. 1965. 15.00 o.s.i. (ISBN 0-8038-0150-5). Architectural.
--More American Furniture Treasures. 16.50 o.s.i. (ISBN 0-8038-0163-7). Architectural.
Margossian, Marzbed, tr. see Manoogian, Torkom.
Margoulias, Harry J. Byzantine Christianity: Emperor, Church & the West. LC 81-13089. 206p. 1982. 13.95 (ISBN 0-8143-1704-9); pap. 6.50 (ISBN 0-8143-1705-7). Wayne St U Pr.
Margrie, Janet. Pictures & Patterns. LC 77-8005. (Beginning Crafts Ser.). (Illus.). (gr. k-3). 1977. PLB 9.30 o.p. (ISBN 0-8393-0117-0). Raintree Pubs.
Marguilies, S., tr. see Pauli, Wolfgang.
Margulies, N. & Raia, A. Organizational Development: Values Process & Technology. 1971. 19.95 o.p. (ISBN 0-07-040357-0, C). McGraw.
Margulies, Newton & Raia, Anthony P. Conceptual Foundations of Organizational Development. (Management Ser.). (Illus.). 1978. text ed. 25.95 (ISBN 0-07-040360-0, C). McGraw.
Margulies, Newton & Wallace, John. Organizational Change: Techniques & Applications. 1973. pap. 10.95x (ISBN 0-673-07761-6). Scott F.
Margulis, Alexander R. & Burhenne, H. Joachim. Alimentary Tract Radiology, 2 Vols. 3rd ed. LC 82-8076. (Illus.). 2494p. 1983. text ed. 225.00 (ISBN 0-8016-3170-X). Mosby.
Margulis, Alexander R. & Burhenne, H. Joachim, eds. Alimentary Tract Roentgenology, Vols. 1 & 2. 2nd ed. LC 72-14444. 1689p. 1973. Set. 165.00 o.p. (ISBN 0-8016-3131-9); Vol.1. 118.00 o.p. (ISBN 0-8016-3149-1); Vol. 2. 118.00 o.p. (ISBN 0-8016-3150-5). Mosby.
Margulis, Alexander R. & Gooding, Charles A., eds. Diagnostic Radiology, 1979. LC 76-1666. (Illus.). 1024p. 1979. 100.00 (ISBN 0-89352-056-X). Masson Pub.
Margulis, Daniel, ed. A Century at Cornell. (Illus.). 232p. 1980. 19.95 (ISBN 0-938304-00-3). Cornell Daily.
Margulis, Lynn, ed. see Interdisciplinary Conference 2nd.
Marharishi Mahesh Yogi. Transcendental Meditation. 320p. 1973. pap. 3.95 (ISBN 0-451-12184-8, AE2184, Sig). NAL.
Maria, Richard De see De Maria, Richard.
Mariah, Paul. Personae Non Gratae. new ed. 24p. 1976. pap. 2.95 (ISBN 0-915288-07-9). Shameless Hussy.
Mariani, Paul. Crossing Cocysus & Other Poems. LC 81-48539. 1982. 12.50 o.p. (ISBN 0-394-52829-8, GP853). Grove.
--Crossing Cocytus & Other Poems. LC 81-48539. (Grove Press Poetry Ser.). 94p. 1982. 12.50 (ISBN 0-394-52829-8); pap. 5.95 (ISBN 0-394-17978-1, E801, Ever). Grove.
Marianna Junior Woman's Club. Chipola River Revisited. 384p. Date not set. pap. 10.00 (ISBN 0-939114-78-X). Marianna Jr.
Mariante, Benjamin R. Pluralistic Society, Pluralistic Church. LC 80-69058. 212p. (Orig.). 1982. lib. bdg. 21.75 (ISBN 0-8191-1933-4); pap. text ed. 10.75 (ISBN 0-8191-1934-2). U Pr of Amer.
Marichal, Juan & Einstein, Charles. Pitcher's Story. LC 67-19069. 1967. 8.95 o.p. (ISBN 0-385-08502-8). Doubleday.
Marichev, O. I. Handbook of Integral Transforms of Higher Transcendental Functions: Theory & Algorithmic Tables. (Mathematics & Its Applications). 350p. 1983. 79.95x (ISBN 0-470-27364-X). Halsted Pr.
Maricondo, Barbara & Puccio, Denise. Muppet Music Dictionary. (Illus.). 210p. (gr. 3-7). 1983. 14.95 (ISBN 0-89524-164-1, 8603); pap. 9.95 (ISBN 0-89524-153-6, 8608). Cherry Lane.
Marie, jt. auth. see Evelyn.
Marie, Geraldine. The Magic Box. LC 80-26096. (Illus.). 32p. (ps-3). 1983. 5.95 (ISBN 0-525-66721-0). Dandelion Pr.
Mariechild, Diane. Mother Wit: A Feminist Guide to Psychic Development. LC 81-4159. (Illus.). 200p. 1981. 15.95 (ISBN 0-89594-050-7); pap. 7.95 (ISBN 0-89594-051-5). Crossing Pr.
Marier, Donald & Stoiaken, Larry. Alternative Sources of Energy Housing-Greenhouses, No. 59. (Orig.). 1983. pap. 3.50 (ISBN 0-917328-49-3). ASEI.
--Alternative Sources of Energy Photovoltaics-Wind, No. 60. (Orig.). 1983. pap. 3.50 (ISBN 0-917328-50-7). ASEI.
Marier, Donald & Winkle, Carl. Alternative Sources of Energy-Wind-Photovoltaics, No. 58. (Orig.). 1982. pap. 3.50 (ISBN 0-917328-48-5). ASEI.
Marieskind, Helen I. Women in the Health System: Patients, Providers & Programs. LC 80-19961. (Illus.). 330p. 1980. pap. text ed. 15.95 (ISBN 0-8016-3106-8). Mosby.
Mariken, Gene & Scheimann, Eugene. A Doctor's Sensible Approach to Alcohol & Alcoholism. (Illus.). 1969. pap. 2.50 o.p. (ISBN 0-685-56948-9). Budlong.
Maril, Nadja. Me, Molly Midnight, the Artist's Cat. (Illus.). (gr. k up). 1977. 9.95 (ISBN 0-916144-15-1); pap. 5.95 (ISBN 0-916144-16-X). Stemmer Hse.
Maril, Robert L. Texas Shrimpers: Community, Capitalism, & the Sea. LC 82-45897. (Illus.). 256p. 1983. 18.00x (ISBN 0-89096-147-6). Tex A&M Univ Pr.
Marill, Alvin H. Movies Made for Television: The Telefeature & the Mini-Series, 1964-1979. (Illus.). 1979. 29.95 o.p. (ISBN 0-517-54816-X, Arlington Hse). Crown.
Marilla, E. L. Comprehensive Bibliography of Henry Vaughan. 44p. 1948. pap. 1.45 o.p. (ISBN 0-8173-9500-8). U of Ala Pr.
--The Secular Poems of Henry Vaughan: Essays & Studies on English Language & Literature. Liljergren, S. B., ed. 337p. 1983. Repr. of 1958 ed. lib. bdg. 50.00 (ISBN 0-89760-571-3). Telegraph Bks.
Marilla, Esmond L. & Simmonds, James D., eds. Henry Vaughan: A Bibliographical Supplement. LC 63-17400. 24p. 1963. pap. 1.25 o.p. (ISBN 0-8173-9501-6). U of Ala Pr.
Marillac, Charles de. Man, Know Thyself & the Equation of Love. 1979. 10.00 o.p. (ISBN 0-533-03693-3). Vantage.
Marilue. Bobby Bear Meets Cousin Boo. LC 80-82952. (Bobby Bear Ser.). (Illus.). (ps-1). PLB 6.75x (ISBN 0-87783-155-6). Oddo.
--Bobby Bear's Christmas. LC 77-83628. (Illus.). (ps-1). 1978. PLB 6.75x (ISBN 0-87783-142-4); pap. 2.75x deluxe ed. o.p. (ISBN 0-87783-146-7); cassette 5.95x (ISBN 0-87783-182-3). Oddo.
--Bobby Bear's New Home. LC 78-190265. (Bobby Bear Ser.). (Illus.). (ps-1). 1973. PLB 6.75x (ISBN 0-87783-054-1); pap. 2.75x deluxe ed. o.p. (ISBN 0-87783-085-1); cassette 5.95x (ISBN 0-87783-184-X). Oddo.
--Bobby Bear's Red Raft. LC 71-190266. (Bobby Bear Ser.). (Ilus.). (ps-1). 1973. PLB 6.75x (ISBN 0-87783-055-X); pap. 2.75x deluxe ed.o.p. (ISBN 0-87783-086-X); cassette 5.95x (ISBN 0-87783-185-8). Oddo.
--Bobby Bear's Thanksgiving. LC 77-83623. (Bobby Bear Ser.). (Illus.). (ps-1). 1978. PLB 6.75x (ISBN 0-87783-143-2); pap. 2.75x deluxe ed. o.p. (ISBN 0-87783-147-5); cassette 5.95x (ISBN 0-87783-187-4). Oddo.
Marin, jt. auth. see Chong.
Marin, Diego. La Intriga Secundaria en el Teatro de Lope De Vega. LC 59-48361. 200p. 1958. 15.00x o.p. (ISBN 0-8020-7010-8). U of Toronto Pr.
Marin, Genaro. Guaimi. LC 80-67818. 120p. (Orig.). 1981. pap. write for info. o.p. Ediciones.
Marin, Javier J., tr. see Barclay, William.
Marin, Peter & Cohen, Allan Y. Understanding Drug Use: An Adult's Guide to Drugs & the Young. 10.95 o.p. (ISBN 0-686-92267-0, 4200). Hazelden.
Marin, Peter & Cohen, Allen Y. Understanding Drug Use: An Adult's Guide to Drugs & the Young. LC 69-15318. 1971. 12.45i (ISBN 0-06-012768-6, HarpT). Har-Row.
Marinaccio, Anthony & Marinaccio, M. Maxine. Human Relations & Cooperative Planning in Education & Management. 1978. pap. text ed. 8.95 (ISBN 0-8403-0921-X). Kendall-Hunt.
Marinaccio, M. Maxine, jt. auth. see Marinaccio, Anthony.
Marinaro, vincent. In the Ring of the Rise. write for info. N Lyons Bks.
--A Modern Dry-Fly Code. write for info. N Lyons Bks.
Marinaro, Vincent C. In the Ring of the Rise. 1976. limited ed. 12.95 o.p. (ISBN 0-517-52550-X). Crown.
Marine Aquaculture Association & Northeast Regional Coastal Information Center. Directory of Aquaculturists in the Northeast. 56p. 1980. pap. 1.00 (ISBN 0-938412-22-1, P856). URI Mas.
Marine Biological Laboratory & Woods Hole Oceanographic Institution, Woods Hole, Massachusetts. Catalog of the Library of the Marine Biological Laboratory & the Woods Hole Oceanographic Institution, 12 vols. 1971. lib. bdg. 1140.00 set (ISBN 0-8161-0937-0, Hall Library); journal catalog o.p. 55.00 (ISBN 0-8161-0115-9). G K Hall.
Marine, William M. British Invasion of Maryland, Eighteen Twelve to Eighteen Fifteen. Dielman, Louis H., ed. LC 66-128. (Illus.). xx, 519p. Repr. of 1913 ed. 34.00x (ISBN 0-8103-5036-X). Gale.
Marinelli, Peter V. Pastoral. (Critical Idiom Ser.). 1971. pap. 4.95x (ISBN 0-416-08710-8). Methuen Inc.
Marinero, Hazel. Arzneimittelhaftung In Den USA und Deutschland. xxvii, 292p. (Ger.). 1982. write for info. (ISBN 3-8204-7121-9). P Lang Pubs.
Mariners Museum Library - Newport News - Virginia. Catalog of Maps, Ships' Papers & Logbooks. 1964. lib. bdg. 95.00 (ISBN 0-8161-0686-X, Hall Library). G K Hall.
--Catalog of Marine Photographs, 5 Vols. 1964. Set. lib. bdg. 475.00 (ISBN 0-8161-0685-1, Hall Library). G K Hall.
--Catalog of Marine Prints & Paintings, 3 Vols. 1964. Set. lib. bdg. 285.00 (ISBN 0-8161-0684-3, Hall Library). G K Hall.
--Dictionary Catalog of the Library of the Mariners Museum, 9 Vols. 1964. Set. lib. bdg. 855.00 (ISBN 0-8161-0674-6, Hall Library). G K Hall.
Marini, John J. Respiratory Medicine & Intensive Care for the House Officer. (House Officer Ser.). 275p. 1981. pap. 9.95 (ISBN 0-683-05551-8). Williams & Wilkins.
Marini, Lucio, ed. Repertorio Terapeutico. 6th ed. 1048p. (Orig., Ital. & Eng.). 1979. pap. 65.00x (ISBN 88-7076-001-4). Intl Pubns Serv.
Marini-Bettolo, G. B., ed. Natural Products & the Protection of Plants: Proceedings of a Study Week of the Pontifical Academy of Sciences, Oct., 1976. 1978. 170.25 (ISBN 0-444-41620-X). Elsevier.
Marino, John, et al. John Marino's Bicycling Book. LC 79-57652. (Illus.). 320p. 1981. 10.95 (ISBN 0-87477-131-5); pap. 6.95 (ISBN 0-87477-245-1). J P Tarcher.
Marino, M. A. & Luthin. Seepage & Groundwater. (Developments in Water Science Ser.: Vol. 13). 1982. 106.50 (ISBN 0-444-41975-6). Elsevier.
Marino, Raul, jt. ed. see Rasmussen, Theodore.
Marinoff, K. Getting Started in Handmade Rugs. 1971. pap. 2.95 o.p. (ISBN 0-685-01117-8, 80430). Glencoe.
Mario, D. Adapting Working Hours to Modern Needs: The Time Factor in the New Approach to Working Conditions. viii, 50p. 1980. 14.95 (ISBN 92-2-101659-5); pap. 8.55 (ISBN 92-2-101658-7). Intl Labour Office.
Mario, Thomas. Playboy's New Bar Guide. 400p. 1983. pap. 3.95 (ISBN 0-515-07267-2). Jove Pubns.
Mariolopoulos, E. Compendium in Astronomy. 1982. 49.50 (ISBN 90-277-1373-1, Pub. by Reidel Holland). Kluwer Boston.
Marion, Frances. How to Write & Sell Film Scripts. Kupelnick, Bruce S., ed. LC 76-52115. (Classics of Film Literature Ser.). 1978. lib. bdg. 18.00 o.s.i. (ISBN 0-8240-2884-8). Garland Pub.
Marion, J. B. Essential Physics in the World Around Us. 444p. 1977. 27.95 o.s.i. (ISBN 0-471-56905-4). Wiley.
Marion, Jerry. Classical Dynamics of Particles & Systems. 2nd ed. 1970. text ed. 29.50 (ISBN 0-12-472252-0). Acad Pr.
--Instructor's Manual for Physics in the Modern World. 2nd ed. 1980. 3.50 (ISBN 0-12-472282-2). Acad Pr.
--Physics in the Modern World. 2nd ed. 1980. 27.00 (ISBN 0-12-472280-6). Acad Pr.
Marion, Jerry & Heald, Mark A. Classical Electromagnetic Radiation. 2nd ed. 1980. 27.00 (ISBN 0-12-472257-1). Acad Pr.
Marion, Jerry B. General Physics with Bioscience Essays. LC 78-4487. 1979. text ed. 29.95x (ISBN 0-471-56911-9); tchrs. manual 4.00 (ISBN 0-471-03672-2); study guide 8.95 (ISBN 0-471-03673-0). Wiley.
--Our Physical World. 1978. pap. text ed. 8.95 (ISBN 0-675-08409-1); 8 cassettes 8 filmstrips o.p. 257.00 (ISBN 0-686-86338-0). Merrill.
Marion, Jerry E. Physics & the Physical Universe. 3rd ed. LC 79-9387. 1980. text ed. 26.95 (ISBN 0-471-03430-4). study guide 7.95 (ISBN 0-471-05815-7). Wiley.
Marios, G. H. Dutch Painters of the Nineteenth Century. Rev. ed. (Illus.). 307p. 32.50 (ISBN 0-686-91879-7). Newbury Bks.
Mariotti, F. A., tr. see Hunter, Emily.
Mariotti, Federico A., tr. see Hunter, Wayne & Hunter, Emily.
Mariotti, Mario, illus. Hanimals. (Illus.). 40p. 1982. pap. 5.95 o.p. (ISBN 0-914676-90-3, Star & Eleph Bks). Green Tiger Pr.
Mariotti, Maryanne, jt. auth. see Crowell, Lynda.
Marique, Pierre J. Philosophy of Christian Education. Repr. of 1939 ed. lib. bdg. 17.00x (ISBN 0-8371-4271-7, MAED). Greenwood.
Maris, Edward. Coins of New Jersey. 1982. Repr. of 1878 ed. pap. 15.00 (ISBN 0-915262-64-9). S J Durst.
Maritain, Jacques. Approaches to God. O'Reilly, Peter, tr. from Fr. LC 78-16555. 1978. Repr. of 1954 ed. lib. bdg. 18.25x (ISBN 0-313-20606-6, MATG). Greenwood.
--The Education of Man: Educational Philosophy. Gallagher, Donald & Gallagher, Idella, eds. LC 75-28667. 1976. Repr. of 1967 ed. lib. bdg. 17.00x (ISBN 0-8371-8479-7, MAEOM). Greenwood.
--Notebooks. Evans, Joseph, tr. from Fr. 288p. 1983. 12.95 (ISBN 0-87343-050-6). Magi Bks.
--On the Use of Philosophy: Three Essays. LC 81-13338. 71p. 1982. Repr. of 1961 ed. lib. bdg. 19.25x (ISBN 0-313-23199-0, MAUP). Greenwood.
--Saint Thomas & the Problem of Evil. (Aquinas Lecture). 1942. 7.95 (ISBN 0-87462-106-2). Marquette.
Maritano, Adela. Flight for Dreamers. (Orig.). 1980. pap. 1.50 o.s.i. (ISBN 0-440-12465-4). Dell.
Marius, Richard. Bound for the Promised Land. (RL 9). 1977. pap. 3.50 (ISBN 0-451-11772-7, AE1772, Sig). NAL.
--Coming of Rain. pap. 1.95 o.p. (ISBN 0-451-07474-2, J7474, Sig). NAL.
Marivaux, P. C. L' Isle de la Raison. (Utopias in the Enlightenment Ser.). 178p. (Fr.). 1974. Repr. of 1727 ed. lib. bdg. 52.50x o.p. (ISBN 0-8287-0580-1, 004). Clearwater Pub.
--L' Isle des Esclaves. (Utopias in the Enlightenment Ser.). 72p. (Fr.). 1974. Repr. of 1725 ed. 20.00x o.p. (ISBN 0-8287-0581-X, 002). Clearwater Pub.
Marivaux, Pierre C. De Chamblain De see De Chamblain De Marivaux, Pierre C.
Marjani, Fatollah, tr. see Shariati, Ali.
Marjoribanks, K. Environments for Learning. 320p. 1974. pap. text ed. 22.00x (ISBN 0-85633-040-X, Nfer). Humanities.
Marjorie, Palmer. God Helps David. (My Bible Story Reader Ser.: Vol. 1). (Illus.). (gr. 2 up). 1983. pap. price not set (ISBN 0-8024-0191-0). Moody.
--God Saves Noah. (My Bible Story Reader Ser.: Vol. 2). (Illus., Orig.). (gr. 2). 1983. pap. price not set (ISBN 0-8024-0192-9). Moody.
Mark. Handbook of Physical & Mechanical Testing of Paper & Paperboard, Vol. 1. 821p. 1983. price not set (ISBN 0-8247-1871-2). Dekker.
Mark, Ber. Uprising in the Warsaw Ghetto. Freidlin, Gershon, tr. from Yiddish. LC 74-26913. 222p. (Orig.). 1976. 11.00x (ISBN 0-8052-3578-7); pap. 4.95 (ISBN 0-8052-0515-2). Schocken.
Mark, Charles, ed. Research Studies in Comparative Sociology. 147p. 1973. pap. text ed. 8.95x (ISBN 0-8422-0308-7). Irvington.
Mark, Charles & Mark, Paula F., eds. Sociology of America: A Guide to Information Sources. LC 73-17560. (American Studies Information Guide Ser.: Vol. 1). 564p. 1976. 42.00x (ISBN 0-8103-1267-0). Gale.
Mark, Charles C. A Study of Cultural Policy in the United States. 1970. pap. 5.00 o.p. (ISBN 92-3-100739-4, UNESCO). Unipub.
Mark, H., jt. auth. see Overberger, C.
Mark, H. F., et al. Encyclopedia of Polymer Science & Technology, 16 vols. Incl. Vol. 1. 1964. 85.00 (ISBN 0-470-56970-0); Vol. 2. 1965. 85.00 (ISBN 0-470-56973-5); Vol. 3. 1965. 85.00 (ISBN 0-470-56975-1); Vol. 4. 1966. 85.00 (ISBN 0-470-56977-8); Vol. 5. 1966. 85.00 (ISBN 0-470-56979-4); Vol. 6. 1967. 85.00 (ISBN 0-470-56980-8); Vol. 7. 1967. 85.00 (ISBN 0-470-56981-6); Vol. 8. 1968. 85.00 (ISBN 0-470-56982-4); Vol. 9. 1968. 85.00 (ISBN 0-470-56983-2); Vol. 10. 1969. 85.00 (ISBN 0-471-56984-4); Vol. 11. 1969. 85.00 (ISBN 0-471-56969-0); Vol. 12. 1970. 85.00 (ISBN 0-471-56992-5); Vol. 13. 1970. 85.00 (ISBN 0-471-56993-3); Vol. 14. 1971. 85.00 (ISBN 0-471-56994-1); Vol. 15. 1971. 85.00 (ISBN 0-471-56995-X); Vol. 16. Index. 1972 (ISBN 0-471-56996-8). LC 64-22188. 85.00 ea.; Set. write for info. (ISBN 0-471-04184-X); supplements for vols. 1-2 85.00 (ISBN 0-686-86895-1). Supplement, Vol. 1 O.s.i (ISBN 0-471-56997-6). Supplement, Vol. 2 (ISBN 0-471-56998-4). Wiley.
Mark, H. F., et al, eds. Man-Made Fibers, 2 vols. 1967-68. Vol. 1. 29.00 o.p. (ISBN 0-87245-426-6); Vol. 2. 53.95x (ISBN 0-87245-427-4); Vol. 3. 77.95x (ISBN 0-87245-428-2). Textile Bk.
Mark, Harry B., Jr., jt. ed. see Fujiwara, Shizuo.
Mark, Harry H. Optokinetics: A Treatise on the Motions of Lights. LC 81-71626. (Illus.). 150p. 1982. 18.50 (ISBN 0-9608152-0-1). H Mark-Corbett.
Mark, Lester C., ed. Pain Control: Practical Aspects of Patient Care. LC 81-12359. (Illus.). 128p. 1981. 19.50x (ISBN 0-89352-145-0). Masson Pub.
Mark, Lester C. & Ngai, S. H., eds. Highlights of Clinical Anesthesiology. (Illus.). 1971. 12.75 (ISBN 0-06-141697-5, Harper Medical). Lippincott.
Mark, Lynn, ed. see Hart, Leon A.
Mark, Mary E. Passport. LC 74-13170. 58p. 1976. pap. 9.95 (ISBN 0-912810-14-9). Lustrum Pr.
Mark, Michael L. Source Readings in Music Education. 1982. text ed. 16.95x (ISBN 0-02-871910-7). Schirmer Bks.
Mark, Paula F., jt. ed. see Mark, Charles.
Mark, Polly. Jungle Nurse. (YA) 1981. 6.95 (ISBN 0-686-73953-1, Avalon). Bouregy.
--Nurse Molly's Search. (YA) 1978. 6.95 (ISBN 0-685-86410-3, Avalon). Bouregy.
Mark, Richard F. Memory & Nerve Cell Connections: Criticisms & Contributions from Developmental Neurophysiology. (Illus.). 1974. pap. text ed. 9.95x (ISBN 0-19-857129-1). Oxford U Pr.
Mark, Ted. A Stroke of Lightning. (Stroke Ser.). 1982. pap. cancelled (ISBN 0-8217-1078-8). Zebra.
Mark, Theonie. Greek Islands Cooking. 1979. 22.50 o.p. (ISBN 0-7134-1283-6, Pub. by Batsford England). David & Charles.
Markakis, Pericles, ed. Anthocyanins As Food Colors. LC 81-22902. (Food Science & Technology Ser.). 1982. 35.00 (ISBN 0-12-472550-3). Acad Pr.
Markandaya, Kamala. The Golden Honeycomb. 1978. pap. 2.50 o.p. (ISBN 0-451-07907-8, E7907, Sig). NAL.
--Handful of Rice. (John Day Bk.). 1966. 10.53i (ISBN 0-381-98152-5, A32460). T Y Crowell.
--Nectar in a Sieve. pap. 2.50 (ISBN 0-451-12291-7, AE2291, Sig). NAL.
--Shalimar. LC 82-48838. (Bessie Bks.). 344p. 1983. price not set (ISBN 0-06-039022-0, HarpT). Har-Row.

--Two Virgins. LC 73-4293. (John Day Bk.). 256p. 1973. 10.53i (ISBN 0-381-98244-0). T Y Crowell.

Markarian, Ohannes, jt. auth. see Daniels, George.

Marke, Julius J. A Catalogue of the Law Collection at New York University: Published by the Law Center of N.Y.U. LC 53-6439. 1372p. 1953. 85.00 (ISBN 0-379-00125-X). Oceana.

Marke, Julius J. & Bander, Edward J. Commercial Law Information Sources. LC 73-120909. (Management Information Guide Ser.: No. 17). 1970. 42.00x (ISBN 0-8103-0817-7). Gale.

Markel, Bob, ed. see Schwartz, Stephan.

Markel, Geraldine P., jt. auth. see Bizer, Linda S.

Markel, J. E. & Gray, A. H. Linear Prediction of Speech. (Communications & Cybernetics Ser.: Vol. 12). (Illus.). 305p. 1976. 34.00 (ISBN 0-387-07563-1). Springer-Verlag.

Markel, John D., jt. ed. see Schafer, Ronald W.

Markel, Michael H. & Lucier, R. J. Make Your Point: A Guide to Improving Your Business & Technical Writing. (Illus.). 156p. 1983. 12.95 (ISBN 0-13-547760-3); pap. 5.95 (ISBN 0-13-547752-2). P-H.

Markel, Michael N. Hilaire Belloc. (English Authors Ser.). 1982. lib. bdg. 15.95 (ISBN 0-8057-6833-5, Twayne). G K Hall.

Markel, Robert, ed. see Ginott, Haim G.

Markell. Somebody Love Me. 1979. pap. 2.25 (ISBN 0-8423-6065-4). Tyndale.

Markell, Edward K. & Voge, Marietta. Medical Parasitology. 4th ed. LC 76-8580. (Illus.). 1976. text ed. 16.95 o.p. (ISBN 0-7216-6083-5); filmstrips 55.00 o.p. (ISBN 0-7216-9919-7); slides 165.00 o.p. (ISBN 0-7216-9920-0). Saunders.

Markell, Jane & Winn, Jane. Overcoming Stress. 1982. pap. 4.50 (ISBN 0-686-82562-4). Victor Bks.

Marken, Jack W., et al, eds. see Godwin, William.

Marken, Richard. Methods in Experimental Psychology. LC 80-20320. 375p. (Orig.). 1981. pap. text ed. 15.95 (ISBN 0-8185-0431-5). Brooks-Cole.

Marker, Carolyn G. & Quigley, Edward J. Cardiovascular Assessment Update: Cardiovascular Nursing Mastery Module Program. (Illus.). 32p. 1982. pap. text ed. 12.00 (ISBN 0-916730-53-0). InterMed Comm.

Marker, Frederick J. Kjeld Abell. (World Authors Ser.). 1976. lib. bdg. 15.95 (ISBN 0-8057-6236-1, Twayne). G K Hall.

Marker, Frederick J., ed. see Bergman, Ingmar.

Marker, Lise-Lone, ed. see Bergman, Ingmar.

Markesinis, B. S., jt. auth. see Lawson, F. H.

Market Linkage Project for Special Education, ed. Educational Products for the Exceptional Child. 1981. 74.50x (ISBN 0-912700-84-X). Oryx Pr.

Markey, Edward J. Nuclear Peril: The Politics of Nuclear Proliferation. LC 82-13854. 204p. 1982. prof ref 14.95 (ISBN 0-88410-892-9). Ballinger Pub.

Markey, T. L. H. C. Branner. (World Authors Ser.). 1973. lib. bdg. 15.95 (ISBN 0-8057-2172-X, Twayne). G K Hall.

Markham, Beryl. West with the Night. 304p. 1983. pap. 12.50 (ISBN 0-86547-118-5). N Point Pr.

Markham, Chris. Mississippi Odyssey. 1980. 15.00 (ISBN 0-89002-166-X); pap. 7.95 (ISBN 0-89002-165-1). Northwoods Pr.

Markham, Felix M. Napoleon. (Illus.). pap. 2.95 (ISBN 0-451-62120-4, ME2120, Ment). NAL.

Markham, George. Japanese Infantry Weapons of World War II. LC 76-390. (Illus.). 100p. 1976. 10.00 o.p. (ISBN 0-88254-374-1). Hippocrene Bks.

Markham, Jesse W. & Teplitz, Paul V. Baseball Economics & Public Policy. LC 79-6032. 208p. 1981. 23.95 (ISBN 0-669-03607-2). Lexington Bks.

Markham, Jesse W., et al. Horizontal Divestiture & the Petroleum Industry. LC 77-3350. 184p. 1977. prof ref 27.50x (ISBN 0-88410-471-0). Ballinger Pub.

Markham, K. R. Techniques of Flavonoid Identification. (Biological Techniques Ser.). 1982. 17.50 (ISBN 0-12-472680-1). Acad Pr.

Markham, Margaret, jt. auth. see Schwartz, Gordon F.

Markham, Marion M. The Halloween Candy Mystery. (gr. 2-5). 1982. PLB 7.95 (ISBN 0-395-32437-8); 7.70. HM.

Markham, R., ed. Modification of Cells. LC 74-81326. 350p. 72.50 (ISBN 0-444-10699-5, North-Holland). Elsevier.

Markin, Rom. Marketing: Strategy & Management. 2nd ed. LC 81-11463. (Wiley Ser. in Marketing). 672p. 1982. 24.95 (ISBN 0-471-08522-7); tchrs'. ed. 25.95 (ISBN 0-471-09466-8); 10.95 (ISBN 0-471-09465-X). Wiley.

Markison, Francina. Tichina. 1983. 16.95 (ISBN 0-533-05604-7). Vantage.

Markland, Robert E. Topics in Management Science. LC 78-17932. (Management & Administration Ser.). 1979. text ed. 32.95 (ISBN 0-471-01745-0). Wiley.

Markle, A. The Law of Arrest & Search & Seizure. (Illus.). 320p. 1974. 19.75x o.p. (ISBN 0-398-03188-6). C C Thomas.

Markle, Allan & Rinn, Roger C., eds. Author's Guide to Journals in Psychology, Psychiatry & Social Work. LC 76-50377. (Author's Guide to Journals Ser.). 1977. 19.95 (ISBN 0-917724-00-3, B0). Haworth Pr.

Markle, George B., IV. The Teka Stone. 128p. (Orig.). 1982. pap. write for info. (ISBN 0-9606262-1-2). Yesnaby Pubs.

Markle, Geraldine, jt. auth. see Karn, Joan.

Markle, Susan M. Good Frames & Bad: A Grammer of Frame Writing. 2nd ed. LC 71-91153. 1969. pap. 20.95 o.p. (ISBN 0-471-57013-3). Wiley.

Markley, Klare S. Fatty Acids: Their Chemistry, Properties, Production & Uses, 5 pts. 2nd ed. LC 82-8934. 724p. 1983. Set. lib. bdg. 312.50 (ISBN 0-89874-521-7). Krieger.

Markley, R. W., jt. auth. see Sheeler, W. D.

Markley, Rayner W. Handwriting Workbook. Evans, A. R., ed. (Welcome to English Ser.). 1977. wkbk. 3.45 (ISBN 0-89285-043-4). English Lang.

Markman, ed. see Nadel & Sherrer, Jr.

Markman, Alan M. & Steinberg, Erwin R. Exercises in the History of English. LC 82-23769. 100p. 1983. pap. text ed. 7.25 (ISBN 0-8191-2971-2). U Pr of Amer.

Markman, Sidney D. Architecture & Urbanization in Colonial Chipas. (Memoirs Ser.: Vol. 153). 1983. 35.00 (ISBN 0-87169-153-1). Am Philos.

--Horse in Greek Art. LC 72-88057. (Illus.). 1969. Repr. of 1943 ed. 12.00x (ISBN 0-8196-0247-7). Biblo.

Markoe, Karen, jt. auth. see Phillips, Louis.

Markoosie. Harpoon of the Hunter. (Illus.). 1970. 9.95 (ISBN 0-7735-0102-9); pap. 4.95 (ISBN 0-7735-0232-7). McGill-Queens U Pr.

Markos, Carol, jt. auth. see Awtrey, Amy.

Markov, A. I. Ultrasonic Machining of Intractable Materials. 17.00x o.p. (ISBN 0-685-20645-9). Transatlantic.

Markova, A. K. The Teaching & Mastery of Language. Szekely, Beatrice B., ed. Vale, Michel, tr. from Rus. LC 78-65595. 1979. 27.50 (ISBN 0-87332-131-6). M E Sharpe.

Markova, Ivana. Paradigms, Thought & Language. LC 81-22022. 229p. 1982. 36.95 (ISBN 0-471-10196-6, Pub. by Wiley-Interscience). Wiley.

--The Social Context of Language. LC 77-3861. 1978. 49.95 (ISBN 0-471-99511-8, Pub. by Wiley-Inerscience). Wiley.

Markovic, Mihailo. From Affluence to Praxis: Philosophy & Social Criticism. 1980. 6.95 o.p. (ISBN 0-472-64000-3). U of Mich Pr.

--The Philosophy of Democratic Socialism. LC 81-21283. 224p. 1982. 25.00x (ISBN 0-312-19383-1). St Martin.

Markovits, Andrei S., ed. The Political Economy of West Germany: Modell Deutschland. 240p. 1982. 27.95 (ISBN 0-03-060617-9). Praeger.

Markow. Drawing & Selling Cartoons. 2nd ed. (The Grosset Art Instruction Ser.: No. 4). (Illus.). 48p. Date not set. pap. price not set (G&D). Putnam Pub Group.

--Drawing Funny Pictures. (Pitman Art Ser.: Vol. 65). pap. 2.95 (ISBN 0-448-00574-3, G&D). Putnam Pub Group.

Markow, Herbert L. Small Boat Law. LC 77-154289. 435p. Date not set. pap. 36.00 (ISBN 0-686-84262-6). Banyan Bks.

--Small Boat Law 1978 Supplement. 144p. Date not set. pap. 18.00 (ISBN 0-686-84270-7). Banyan Bks.

--Small Boat Law 1979-1980 Supplement. 174p. Date not set. pap. 21.00 (ISBN 0-686-84271-5). Banyan Bks.

Markowitz, Arnold L., ed. Historic Preservation: A Guide to Information Sources. LC 80-14313. (Art & Architecture Information Guide Ser.: Vol. 13). 220p. 1980. 42.00x (ISBN 0-8103-1460-6). Gale.

Markowitz, Endel. Abracadabra. (Illus.). write for info. Haymark.

--Below the Belt. 78p. Date not set. T.V. Shooting Script. price not set. Haymark.

--Kid-Ish Yiddish. (Illus.). 90p. (gr. 8-10). 1982. 8.95g (ISBN 0-686-97548-0). Haymark.

Markowitz, Grace, jt. auth. see McDonald, Anne.

Markowitz, Sidney L. What You Should Know About Jewish Religion, History, Ethics, & Culture. 226p. 1973. pap. 5.95 (ISBN 0-8065-0028-X). Citadel Pr.

Markowski, Michael A. Ultralight Flight: The Pilot's Handbook of Ultralight Knowledge. LC 81-71889. (Ultralight Aviation Ser.: No. 3). (Illus.). 204p. (Orig.). 1982. 21.95 (ISBN 0-938716-07-7); pap. 14.95 (ISBN 0-938716-06-9). Ultralight Pubns.

Marks, Alfred H. & Bort, Barry D. Guide to Japanese Prose. 155p. 1975. lib. bdg. 12.00 (ISBN 0-8161-1110-3, Hall Reference). G K Hall.

Marks, Alfred H., tr. see Ihara Saikaku.

Marks, Alfred H., tr. see Mishima, Yukio.

Marks, Bailey. An Ordinary Businessman. LC 78-71247. 1980. pap. 4.95 o.p. (ISBN 0-89840-003-1). Heres Life.

Marks, Barry A. E. E. Cummings. (United States Authors Ser.). 1963. lib. bdg. 11.95 (ISBN 0-8057-0176-1, Twayne). G K Hall.

Marks, Burton & Marks, Rita. Puppets & Puppet-Making. (Illus., Orig.). (gr. 3-8). 1982. pap. 6.95 (ISBN 0-8238-0256-6). Plays.

Marks, Charles E. Commissurotomy, Consciousness & Unity of Mind. 64p. 1980. pap. 4.00x (ISBN 0-262-63076-1). MIT Pr.

Marks, Edith, jt. auth. see Lewis, Adele.

Marks, Edward. Jensen on Mechanics' Liens: New York. 4th ed. LC 63-14740. 1963. with 1980 suppl. 50.00 (ISBN 0-87632-068-X). Boardman.

Marks, Edwin S., jt. auth. see Hyde, Margaret O.

Marks, Elaine & De Courtivron, Isabelle, eds. New French Feminisms, An Anthology. LC 81-40413. (Women's Studies Ser.). 304p. 1981. pap. 8.95 (ISBN 0-8052-0681-7). Schocken.

Marks, Elaine, ed. see Gide, Andre.

Marks, Ethel M., jt. auth. see Marks, Stanley J.

Marks, Frederick W., 3rd. Independence on Trial: Foreign Affairs & the Making of the Constitution. LC 73-77652. 272p. 1973. 17.50x o.p. (ISBN 0-8071-0052-8). La State U Pr.

Marks, G., jt. auth. see Raben, J.

Marks, Henry S. Who Was Who in Alabama. LC 74-188627. 1972. 12.95 o.p. (ISBN 0-87397-017-9). Strode.

--Who Was Who in Florida. LC 73-83503. 1973. 12.95 (ISBN 0-87397-039-X). Strode.

Marks, Isaac. Cure & Care of Neuroses: Theory & Practice of Behavioral Psychotherapy. LC 80-26600. 331p. 1981. 29.95x (ISBN 0-471-08808-0, Pub. by Wiley-Interscience). Wiley.

Marks, Isaac M. Living with Fear: You As a Therapist. 1978. 17.95 (ISBN 0-07-040395-3, P&RB). McGraw.

Marks, J., ed. The Treatment of Parkinsonism with L-Dopa. 1974. 21.95 (ISBN 0-444-19537-8). Elsevier.

Marks, J., ed. see Corneille.

Marks, J., jt. ed. see Glatt, M. M.

Marks, Jane. Help: A Guide to Counseling & Therapy Without a Hassle. LC 76-23375. 192p. (gr. 7 up). 1976. PLB 7.79 o.p. (ISBN 0-671-32811-5). Messner.

Marks, Jeannette. The Family of the Barrett: A Colonial Romance. LC 75-136937. (Illus.). 709p. 1973. Repr. of 1938 ed. lib. bdg. 37.50x o.p. (ISBN 0-8371-5409-X, MAFB). Greenwood.

Marks, Joan, jt. auth. see Hendin, David.

Marks, John D., jt. auth. see Marchetti, Victor.

Marks, John L. Teaching Elementary School Mathematics for Understanding. 4th ed. (Illus.). 512p. 1975. text ed. 27.50 (ISBN 0-07-040422-4, C). McGraw.

Marks, Leonard, jt. auth. see Walsh, Charles V.

Marks, Linda G., jt. ed. see Benton, Mildred.

Marks, M. I. Common Bacterial Infections in Infancy & Childhood. 160p. 1979. pap. text ed. 14.95 o.p. (ISBN 0-8391-1345-5). Univ Park.

Marks, Micky K. Easy-to-Do Sculpture with Wax, Sand & Slate. rev. ed. (Illus.). 48p. 1982. pap. 2.25 (ISBN 0-486-24303-6). Dover.

Marks, Morton, jt. auth. see Taylor, Martha.

Marks, Nolan. On the Spot Repair Manual for Commercial Food Equipment. (Illus.). 80p. 1982. pap. write for info. (ISBN 0-941712-01-X). INtl Pub Corp OH.

Marks, Percy. The Craft of Writing. 231p. 1982. Repr. of 1932 ed. lib. bdg. 30.00 (ISBN 0-89760-581-0). Telegraph Bks.

Marks, R. & Payne, P. A. Bioengineering & the Skin. (Illus.). 320p. 1981. text ed. 59.00 (ISBN 0-85200-314-5, Pub. by MTP Pr England). Kluwer Boston.

Marks, R. & Plewig, G., eds. Stratum Corneum. (Illus.). 300p. 1983. pap. 35.00 (ISBN 0-387-11704-0). Springer-Verlag.

Marks, Richard & Morgan, Nigel. Golden Age of English Manuscript Painting, 1200-1500. (Illus.). 1981. 27.75x (ISBN 0-686-82197-1). Intl Pubns Serv.

Marks, Rita, jt. auth. see Marks, Burton.

Marks, Robert. Non-Renewable Resources & Disequilibrium Macrodynamics. LC 78-75018. write for info. (ISBN 0-8240-4053-8). Garland Pub.

Marks, Russell. The Idea of I.Q. LC 81-40166. 320p. (Orig.). 1981. lib. bdg. 24.00 (ISBN 0-8191-2062-6); pap. text ed. 12.75 (ISBN 0-8191-2063-4). U Pr of Amer.

Marks, S. & Rathbone, R., eds. Industrialisation & Social Change in South Africa: African Class, Culture & Consciousness, 1870-1930. (Illus.). 368p. 1982. text ed. 35.00x (ISBN 0-582-64338-4); pap. text ed. 10.95x (ISBN 0-582-64337-6). Longman.

Marks, Sally. The Illusion of Peace: International Relations 1918-1933. (The Making of the Twentieth Century Ser.). (Illus.). 1976. 16.95x o.p. (ISBN 0-312-40600-2); pap. text ed. 8.95x (ISBN 0-312-40635-5). St Martin.

Marks, Stanley J. The Two Christs; Or, the Decline & Fall of Christianity. 1983. pap. 14.95 (ISBN 0-686-38796-1). Bur Intl Aff.

Marks, Stanley J. & Marks, Ethel M. The Blue Book of the U. S. Consumer Market, 1983. 1983. pap. 50.00 (ISBN 0-686-38795-3). Bur Intl Aff.

Marks, Stephen E., jt. auth. see Walter, Gordon A.

Marks, Thomas J. More Bible Study Puzzles. (Orig.). 1983. pap. 2.50 (ISBN 0-8054-9108-2). Broadman.

Marks, Tracy. How to Handle Your T-Square. LC 79-66937. (Illus., Orig.). 1979. pap. 12.00 (ISBN 0-933620-04-7). Sag Rising.

Marks, Vic. Cloudburst: A Handbook of Rural Skills & Technology. 2nd ed. (Illus.). 128p. 1977. lib. bdg. 11.95 o.p. (ISBN 0-88930-038-0, Pub. by Cloudburst Canada); pap. 5.95 o.p. (ISBN 0-88930-016-X). Madrona Pubs.

Marks, Walter & Nystrand, Raphael O. Strategies for Educational Change. (Illus.). 1980. text ed. 21.95x (ISBN 0-02-376180-6). Macmillan.

Markson, Elizabeth & Batra, Gretchen, eds. Public Policies for an Aging Population. LC 79-3249. (The Boston University Ser. in Gerontology). 1980. 16.95 (ISBN 0-669-03398-7). Lexington Bks.

Markson, Elizabeth W., jt. auth. see Hess, Beth B.

Markson, Elizabeth W., ed. Older Women: Issues & Prospects. LC 81-48025. (Boston University Gerontology Ser.). 352p. 1983. 29.95x (ISBN 0-669-05245-0). Lexington Bks.

Markstein, George. The Ultimate Issue. 336p. (Orig.). 1982. pap. 2.75 (ISBN 0-345-29031-3). Ballantine.

Markstein, Linda & Grunbaum, Dorien. What's the Story? Photographs for Language Practice, 4 bks. (English As a Second Language Bk.). 1981. pap. text ed. 3.05x ea. Bk. 1: Beginning (ISBN 0-582-79783-7). Bk. 2: Low-Intermediate (ISBN 0-582-79784-5). Bk. 3: High-Intermediate (ISBN 0-582-79785-3). Bk. 4: Advanced (ISBN 0-582-79786-1). tchr's manual 2.95x (ISBN 0-582-79787-X); wall charts 32.00x (ISBN 0-582-79788-8). Longman.

Markstein, Linda & Hirasawa, Louise. Developing Reading Skills, Intermediate. (Orig.). (gr. 11-12). 1981. pap. text ed. 8.95 (ISBN 0-88377-236-1). Newbury Hse.

--Expanding Reading Skills: Intermediate. 224p. (gr. 11-12). 1982. pap. text ed. 8.95 (ISBN 0-88377-242-6). Newbury Hse.

Markstein, Linda, jt. auth. see O'Neill, Robert.

Markstein, Linda R. & Hirasawa, Louise. Expanding Reading Skills: Advanced. 1977. pap. text ed. 8.95 (ISBN 0-88377-074-1). Newbury Hse.

Markstein, Linda R., jt. auth. see Hirasawa, Louise.

Markun, Maloney P. The Panama Canal. rev. ed. (First Bks.). (Illus.). (gr. 4 up). 1979. PLB 8.90 s&l (ISBN 0-531-04075-5). Watts.

Markun, Patricia M. Central America & Panama. rev. ed. (First Bks.). (Illus.). 96p. (gr. 4 up). 1983. PLB 8.90 (ISBN 0-531-04523-4). Watts.

--Witnesses for Oil. Canes, Michael, ed. 1976. 6.95 (ISBN 0-685-76766-3, 877-82100). Am Petroleum.

Markus, J. Electronics Dictionary. 4th ed. 1978. 32.95 (ISBN 0-07-040431-3). McGraw.

Markus, John. Communications Circuits Ready-Reference. (Illus.). 160p. 1982. pap. 12.50 (ISBN 0-07-040460-7). McGraw.

--Electronic Circuits Manual. 1971. 65.00 (ISBN 0-07-040444-5, P&RB). McGraw.

--Guidebook of Electronic Circuits. (Illus.). 992p. 1974. 65.00 (ISBN 0-07-040445-3, P&RB). McGraw.

--Modern Electronic Circuits Reference Manual. (Illus.). 1980. 61.50 (ISBN 0-07-040446-1, P&RB). McGraw.

--Sourcebook of Electronic Circuits. 1967. 65.00 (ISBN 0-07-040443-7, P&RB). McGraw.

--Television & Radio Repairing. 2nd ed. (Illus.). 1961. 29.50 o.p. (ISBN 0-07-040453-4, P&RB). McGraw.

Markus, Julia. American Rose. 1982. pap. 2.95 (ISBN 0-686-97170-1). Berkley Pub.

Markus, L., jt. auth. see Lee, E. B.

Markus, R. A. Saeculum: History & Society in the Theology of St Augustine. LC 71-87136. 1970. 47.50 (ISBN 0-521-07621-8). Cambridge U Pr.

Markushevich, A. I. Theory of Functions of a Complex Variable, 3 vols. in 1. 2nd ed. Silverman, Richard A., tr. from Russian. LC 77-8515. 1977. text ed. 35.00 (ISBN 0-8284-0296-5). Chelsea Pub.

Marlar, Robin, jt. auth. see Lillywhite, Fred.

Marler, E. E., compiled by. Pharmacological & Chemical Synonyms: A Collection of Names of Drugs, Pesticides & Other Compounds Drawn from the Medical Literature of the World. 7th ed. Date not set. 76.75 (ISBN 0-444-90227-9). Elsevier.

Marler, George C. The Admiral Issue of Canada. 566p. 1982. 35.00 (ISBN 0-933580-08-8). Am Philatelic.

Marley, D. Maryland Plan. 1973. 9.96 o.p. (ISBN 0-02-821100-6). Glencoe.

Marley, Ross. Pollution & Politics in the Phillipines. LC 76-620091. (Papers in International Studies: Southeast Asia: No. 43). (Illus.). 1977. pap. 7.00 (ISBN 0-89680-029-6, Ohio U Ctr Intl). Ohio U Pr.

Marlin, Herb & Savitt, Sam. How to Take Care of Your Horse Until the Vet Comes. LC 75-11727. (Illus.). 96p. (gr. 5 up). 1975. 5.95 o.p. (ISBN 0-396-07145-7). Dodd.

Marling, Karal A. Wall-to-Wall America: A Cultural History of Post Office Murals in the Great Depression. LC 82-2622. (Illus.). 344p. 1982. 35.00x (ISBN 0-8166-1116-5); pap. 14.95 (ISBN 0-8166-1117-3). U of Minn Pr.

Marling, Karal A., intro. by. Seven American Women: The Depression Decade. (Illus.). 40p. 1976. pap. 4.00 (ISBN 0-89062-130-6, Pub by A.I.R. Gallery). Pub Ctr Cult Res.

Marlo, J., jt. auth. see Wright, G. R.

Marlor. History of the Brooklyn Art Association with an Index of Exhibitions. 1970. 45.00 (ISBN 0-686-43147-2). Apollo.

Marlow, A. W. Classic Furniture Projects. (Illus.). 1979. pap. 9.95 (ISBN 0-8128-6034-9). Stein & Day.

--The Early American Furnituremaker's Manual. LC 72-91257. 144p. 1983. pap. 8.95 (ISBN 0-8128-6184-1). Stein & Day.

--Fine Furniture. LC 55-13928. 1977. pap. 12.95 (ISBN 0-8128-2250-1). Stein & Day.

Marlow, Andrew, jt. auth. see Hoard, F.

Marlow, David. Winning is Everything. 352p. 1983. 15.95 (ISBN 0-399-12801-8). Putnam.
Marlow, Dorothy R. Textbook of Pediatric Nursing. 5th ed. LC 77-72819. (Illus.). 1977. text ed. 27.50 (ISBN 0-7216-6099-1). Saunders.
Marlow, Eugene. Managing the Corporate Media Center. LC 81-8155. (The Video Bookshelf Ser.). (Illus.). 224p. 1981. text ed. 24.95 (ISBN 0-914236-68-7). Knowledge Indus.
--Video & the Corporation. (Video Bookshelf). 200p. 1983. 29.95 (ISBN 0-86729-026-9). Knowledge Indus.
Marlow, Joan. The Great Women. 384p. 1983. pap. 7.95 (ISBN 0-89104-327-6, A & W Visual Library). A & W Pubs.
Marlow, Joan, ed. The Great Women. LC 79-65342. (Illus.). 352p. 1979. 14.95 o.s.i. (ISBN 0-89479-056-0). A & W Pubs.
Marlow, Joyce. The Tolpuddle Martyrs. 1972. 12.50 o.p. (ISBN 0-233-95820-7). Transatlantic.
Marlow, W. H. Mathematics for Operations Research. LC 78-534. 1978. 48.50 (ISBN 0-471-57233-0, Pub. by Wiley-Interscience). Wiley.
Marlow, W. H., ed. Modern Trends in Logistics Research. LC 75-43617. 480p. 1976. text ed. 30.00x (ISBN 0-262-13122-6). MIT Pr.
Marlowe, Christopher. Doctor Faustus. Jump, John, ed. (Methuen English Classics). 1965. pap. 4.25 (ISBN 0-423-75710-5). Methuen Inc.
--Doctor Faustus. Barnet, Sylvan, ed. 1969. pap. 2.50 (ISBN 0-451-51710-5, CE1710, Sig Classics). NAL.
--Tamburlaine the Great, Parts I & II. Jump, John D., ed. LC 67-10666. (Regents Renaissance Drama Ser). xxvi, 205p. 1967. pap. 6.50x (ISBN 0-8032-5271-4, BB 222, Bison). U of Nebr Pr.
Marlowe, Francine. Male Modeling: An Inside Look. (Illus.). 192p. 1980. 12.95 o.p. (ISBN 0-517-53194-1); pap. 5.95 o.p. (ISBN 0-517-53195-X). Crown.
Marlowe, John. Spoiling the Egyptians. LC 74-21749. 288p. 1975. 18.95 o.p. (ISBN 0-312-75285-7). St Martin.
Marlowe, Olwen C. Outdoor Design: A Handbook for the Architect & Planner. 301p. 1977. text ed. 76.00x o.p. (ISBN 0-258-97017-0, Pub. by Granada England). Renouf.
Marlowe, Stephen. The Valkyrie Encounter. 1978. pap. 1.95 o.s.i. (ISBN 0-515-04705-8). Jove Pubns.
--The Valkyrie Encounter. LC 77-11177. 1978. 9.95 o.p. (ISBN 0-399-12068-8). Putnam Pub Group.
Marly, Diana De see De Marly, Diana.
Marly, Diana de see De Marly, Diana.
Marme & Marre. Plasmalemma & Tonoplast: Their Functions in the Plant Cell. (Developments in Plant Biology: Vol. 7). 1982. 76.75 (ISBN 0-444-80409-9). Elsevier.
Marmier, Pierre & Sheldon, Eric. Physics of Nuclei & Particles, Vols. 1-2. 1969-70. 21.75 ea. Vol. 1 (ISBN 0-12-473101-5). Vol. 2 (ISBN 0-12-473102-3). Acad Pr.
Marmier, Xavier. Lettres sur la Russie, la Finlande et la Pologne. (Nineteenth Century Russia Ser.). 419p. (Fr.). 1974. Repr. of 1851 ed. lib. bdg. 106.00 o.p. (ISBN 0-8287-0582-8, R76). Clearwater Pub.
Marmion, Daniel M. Handbook of U. S. Colorants for Foods, Drugs & Cosmetics. LC 78-10949. 1979. 40.00 (ISBN 0-471-04684-1, Pub. by Wiley-Interscience). Wiley.
Marmo, V. Granite Petrology & the Granite Problem. (Developments in Petrology Ser.: Vol. 2). 1971. 78.75 (ISBN 0-444-40852-5). Elsevier.
Marmor, Judd. Psychiatrists & Their Patients: A National Study of Private Office Practice. LC 75-18676. 181p. 1975. pap. 9.00 (ISBN 0-89042-518-3). Am Psychiatric.
Marmor, Judd, ed. Homosexual Behavior: A Modern Reappraisal. 1982. pap. 10.50 (ISBN 0-465-03046-7). Basic.
Marmor, Solomon. Laboratory Methods in Organic Chemistry. LC 81-65304. 1981. text ed. 23.95x (ISBN 0-8087-3997-2). Burgess.
Marmorstein, Emile, tr. see Rosenthal, Franz.
Marmur, Mildred, tr. see Flaubert, Gustave.
Marney, John. Chiang Yen. (World Authors Ser.). 1981. lib. bdg. 15.95 (ISBN 0-8057-6471-2, Twayne). G K Hall.
--Liang Chien-Wen Ti. (World Authors Ser.). 1976. lib. bdg. 15.95 (ISBN 0-8057-6221-3, Twayne). G K Hall.
Marnham, Patrick. Lourdes: A Modern Pilgrimage. (Illus.). 244p. 1981. 12.95 (ISBN 0-686-74811-5, Coward). Putnam Pub Group.
--Lourdes: A Modern Pilgrimage. LC 82-45299. 272p. 1982. pap. 4.95 (ISBN 0-385-18252-X, Im). Doubleday.
Marois, M. Development of Chemotherapeutic Agents for Parasitic Diseases. 1976. 38.50 (ISBN 0-444-10996-X, North-Holland). Elsevier.
--Towards a Plan of Actions for Mankind. 558p. 1975. 68.00 (ISBN 0-444-10722-3, North-Holland). Elsevier.
Marois, M., ed. Biological Balance & Thermal Modifications. 1975. pap. 17.00 (ISBN 0-444-10719-3). Elsevier.
--Theoretical Physics & Biology. 1969. 20.50 (ISBN 0-444-10243-4, North-Holland-). Elsevier.
Marol, Jean-Claude. Vagabul & His Shadow. (Vagabul Ser.). (Illus.). 32p. (gr. k-6). 1982. lib. bdg. 5.95 (ISBN 0-87191-889-7). Creative Ed.
--Vagabul Escapes. (Vagabul Ser.). (Illus.). 32p. (gr. k-6). 1982. lib. bdg. 5.95 (ISBN 0-87191-888-9). Creative Ed.
--Vagabul Goes Skiing. (Vagabul Ser.). (Illus.). 32p. (gr. k-6). 1982. lib. bdg. 5.95 (ISBN 0-87191-886-2). Creative Ed.
--Vagabul in the Clouds. (Vagabul Ser.). (Illus.). 32p. (gr. k-6). 1982. lib. bdg. 5.95 (ISBN 0-87191-887-0). Creative Ed.
Marom, E., et al, eds. Applications of Holography & Optical Data Processing: Proceedings of an International Conference, Jerusalem, 1976. 1977. write for info. o.p. (ISBN 0-08-021625-0). Pergamon.
Maron, Margaret B. One Coffee With. (Raven House Mysteries Ser.). 224p. 1983. pap. cancelled (ISBN 0-373-63052-2, Pub. by Worldwide). Harlequin Bks.
Maron, Melvin J. Applied Numerical Analysis. 1982. text ed. 27.95 (ISBN 0-02-475670-9). Macmillan.
Maron, Michael P., jt. auth. see Hopps, Marti.
Marone, G., jt. ed. see Ricci, M.
Marosi, Antonio, tr. see Cabral, J.
Marosi, Antonio, tr. see Henrichsen, Walter A.
Marosi, Esteban, ed. see Barber, Cyril J.
Marosi, Esteban, ed. see BOyer, Orlando.
Marosi, Esteban, ed. see Boyer, Orlando.
Marosi, Esteban, ed. see Cabral, J.
Marosi, Esteban, ed. see Caldwell, E. S.
Marosi, Esteban, ed. see Carlson, G. Raymond.
Marosi, Esteban, ed. see Charles, J. Norman & Charles, Sharon.
Marosi, Esteban, ed. see Coleman, William L.
Marosi, Esteban, ed. see Cornwall, Judson.
Marosi, Esteban, ed. see Ekvall, Robert B.
Marosi, Esteban, ed. see Henrichsen, Walter A.
Marosi, Esteban, ed. see Hook & Boren.
Marosi, Esteban, ed. see Hutchison, Becky & Farish, Kay.
Marosi, Esteban, ed. see Kerstan, Reinhold.
Marosi, Esteban, ed. see Lin, Yi.
Marosi, Esteban, ed. see McManus, Una & Cooper, John C.
Marosi, Esteban, ed. see Mayhall, Jack & Mayhall, Carole.
Marosi, Esteban, ed. see Nee, T. S.
Marosi, Esteban, ed. see Nee, Watchman.
Marosi, Esteban, ed. see Petersen, William J.
Marosi, Esteban, ed. see Strauss, Richard.
Marosi, Esteban, ed. see Tenney, Merrill C.
Marosi, Esteban, ed. see Wirt, Sherwood E.
Marosi, Esteban, et al, eds. see Gossett, Don.
Marosi, Esteban, et al, eds. see Ortlund, Raymond C.
Marosi, Estenan, ed. see Brights, Bill.
Marotta, Michael. The Code Book: All About Unbreakable Codes & How to Use Them. 1982. pap. 7.95 o.p. (ISBN 0-686-26030-9). Loompanics.
Marotta, Theodore, jt. auth. see Herubin, Charles.
Marotz-Braden, Ramon, jt. ed. see Tallman, Irving.
Marovic, D. Play the King's Indian Defense. (Pergamon Chess Ser.). (Illus.). 176p. 1983. 19.90 (ISBN 0-08-029727-7); pap. 12.90 (ISBN 0-08-029726-9). Pergamon.
Marowitz, Charles, tr. see Ionesco, Eugene.
Marowitz, Charles, et al, eds. New Theatre Voices of the Fifties & Sixties: Selections from "Encore" Magazine 1956-1963. 308p. 1981. 22.00x (ISBN 0-413-48900-0); pap. 10.95 (ISBN 0-413-48910-8). Methuen Inc.
Marple, Raymond P. Toward a Basic Accounting Philosophy. 117p. 12.95 (ISBN 0-86641-057-0, 6435). Natl Assn Accts.
Marple, V. A. & Liu, B. Y. H., eds. Aerosol In the Mining & Industrial Work Environments: Fundamentals & Status, 3 vol. set, Vol. 1. LC 82-70701. (Illus.). 360p. 1983. 37.50 (ISBN 0-250-40531-8); Set. 93.75 (ISBN 0-250-40533-4). Ann Arbor Science.
--Aerosols In the Mining & Industrial Work Environments: Characterization, 3 vol. set, Vol. 2. LC 82-70701. (Illus.). 283p. 1983. 18.75 (ISBN 0-250-40532-6); Set. 93.75 (ISBN 0-250-40533-4). Ann Arbor Science.
--Aerosols In the Mining & Industrial Work Environment: Instrumentation, 3 Vols, Vol. 3. LC 82-70701. (Illus.). 500p. 1983. 37.50 (ISBN 0-250-40597-0). Ann Arbor Science.
Marples, Morris. White Horses & Other Hill Figures. 224p. 1982. pap. text ed. 9.00x (ISBN 0-904387-59-3, 61083, Pub. by Sutton England). Humanities.
Marquadt, Mervin. Grandfather's Story. LC 59-1239. (Arch Bk Ser.: No. 15). (Illus.). (gr. k-3). 1978. 0.89 (ISBN 0-570-06121-0, 59-1239). Concordia.
Marquand, David, ed. John P. Mackintosh: On Parliament & Social Democracy. LC 81-14240. 320p. 1982. pap. 15.95x (ISBN 0-582-29587-4). Longman.
Marquand, J. P. Thank You, Mr. Moto & Mr. Moto Is So Sorry from the Saturday Evening Post. LC 77-90931. 320p. 1977. 5.95 (ISBN 0-89387-016-1, Co-Pub. by Sat Eve Post). Curtis Pub Co.
Marquard, Leo. Peoples & Policies of South Africa. 4th ed. 1969. pap. 5.95x o.p. (ISBN 0-19-285030-X, OPB). Oxford U Pr.
Marquard, Ralph L. Jokes & Anecdotes for All Occasions. (Illus.). 448p. (Orig.). 1977. pap. 5.95 o.s.i. (ISBN 0-89104-185-0, A & W Visual Library). A & W Pubs.
Marquardt, Charles E., jt. auth. see Swanson, Richard W.
Marquardt, Dorothy A. A Guide to the Supreme Court. LC 76-47338. (Illus.). 1977. 7.95 o.p. (ISBN 0-672-52167-7); pap. 7.95 o.p. (ISBN 0-672-52168-7). Bobbs.
Marquardt, J., jt. auth. see Peterson, H.
Marquardt, Merv. Song for Joseph. (Arch Bks.: No. 18). (gr. k-4). 1981. pap. 0.89 (ISBN 0-570-06146-6, 59-1263). Concordia.
Marquardt, Mervin. Good Little King Josiah. (Arch Bk Ser.: No. 15). (Illus.). (gr. k-3). 1978. 0.89 (ISBN 0-570-06118-0, 59-1236). Concordia.
Marquardt, Michael & Stump, Robert W. Training: Issues & Answers for the Eighties. 1982. pap. 6.00 (ISBN 0-87771-030-9). Grad School.
Marquardt, R. A., et al. Retail Management. 3rd ed. LC 78-56199. 1983. text ed. 26.95 (ISBN 0-03-062608-0). Dryden Pr.
Marquart, Frank. An Auto Worker's Journal: The UAW from Crusade to One-Party Union. LC 75-11993. 200p. 1975. 14.95x (ISBN 0-271-01196-3). Pa St U Pr.
Marquart, M. Jesus' Second Family. (Arch Book Series Fourteen). (gr. k-2). 1977. pap. 0.89 (ISBN 0-570-06111-3, 59-1229). Concordia.
Marques, Rene. The Docile Puerto Rican: Essays. Aponte, Barbara B., tr. from Span. LC 75-14688. 163p. 1976. 24.95 (ISBN 0-87722-048-4). Temple U Pr.
Marquess of Anglesey. A History of the British Cavalry, 1872-1898, Vol. III. (Illus.). 520p. 1983. 75.00 (ISBN 0-436-27327-6, Pub. by Secker & Warburg). David & Charles.
Marquez, Gabriel G. Chronicle of a Death Foretold. LC 82-48884. 1983. 10.95 (ISBN 0-394-53074-8). Knopf.
--One Hundred Years of Solitude. 1971. pap. 3.95 (ISBN 0-380-01503-X, 62224-6, Bard). Avon.
Marquez, Robert, ed. see Guillen, Nicolas.
Marquez, Sandra, jt. auth. see Wagner, Candy.
Marquis, Alice G. Marcel Duchamp: Eros, C'est la Vie. LC 79-57325. 429p. 1981. 22.50x (ISBN 0-87875-187-4); pap. 10.95 (ISBN 0-87875-266-8). Whitston Pub.
Marquis, Don. Archy & Mehitabel. LC 62-56573. 6.95 (ISBN 0-385-04572-7). Doubleday.
--Archy & Mehitabel. (Anchor Literary Library). 1982. pap. 4.50 (ISBN 0-686-42701-7, Anch). Doubleday.
--Lives & Times of Archy & Mehitabel. LC 50-5335. 1940. 10.95 (ISBN 0-385-04262-0). Doubleday.
Marquis, Vivienne, jt. auth. see Haskell, Patricia.
Marquit, Erwin. The Socialist Countries: General Features of Political, Economic, & Cultural Life. LC 77-92870. (Studies in Marxism: Vol. 3). 200p. 1978. 14.95x (ISBN 0-930656-05-9); pap. 6.50 (ISBN 0-686-96784-4). Marxist Educ.
Marquit, Erwin, et al, eds. Dialectical Contradictions: Contemporary Marxist Discussions. LC 81-8462. (Studies in Marxism: Vol. 10). 220p. 1982. 19.95x (ISBN 0-930656-19-9); pap. 9.95 (ISBN 0-930656-20-2). MEP Pubns.
Marr, C. D. Ramaria of Western Washington. 1973. 20.00 (ISBN 3-7682-0902-4). Lubrecht & Cramer.
Marr, David. Barwick. (Illus.). 336p. 1981. text ed. 25.00x (ISBN 0-86861-058-5). Allen Unwin.
Marr, David G. Vietnamese Anticolonialism, 1885-1925. (Center for South & Southeast Asia Studies, UC Berkeley). 1971. 20.00x (ISBN 0-520-04278-6); pap. 8.95x (ISBN 0-520-04277-8, CAMPUS59). U of Cal Pr.
Marr, David G., ed. see Phan Boi Chau & Ho Chi Minh.
Marr, G. W. & Layton, R. C. General Engineering Science in SI Units, 2 vols. 2nd ed. 1971. Vol. 1. 12.00 o.p. (ISBN 0-08-015805-6); Vol. 2. 12.00 o.p. (ISBN 0-08-015807-2); Vol. 1. pap. 4.80 o.p. (ISBN 0-08-015804-8); Vol. 2. pap. 4.80 o.p. (ISBN 0-08-015806-4). Pergamon.
Marr, John, ed. Kuroshio: A Symposium on the Japan Current. 1970. 30.00x (ISBN 0-8248-0090-7, Eastwest Ctr). UH Pr.
Marr, Phebe. The Modern History of Iraq. 275p. 1983. lib. bdg. 25.00x (ISBN 0-86531-119-6). Westview.
Marram, Gwen & Barrett, Margaret W. Primary Nursing: A Model for Individualized Care. 2nd ed. LC 79-54. (Illus.). 216p. 1979. pap. text ed. 12.95 (ISBN 0-8016-3125-4). Mosby.
Marram, Gwen & Flynn, Kathleen. Cost-Effectiveness of Primary & Team Nursing. LC 76-11326. 91p. 1976. pap. 13.95 (ISBN 0-913654-28-0). Aspen Systems.
Marranca, Bonnie, ed. see Breuer, Lee.
Marre, jt. auth. see Marme.
Marrero, J. Espada. Madre y Hogar. 50p. (Span.). 1980. pap. 1.25 (ISBN 0-311-07302-6). Casa Bautista.
Marrer-Tising, Carlee. The Reception of Herman Hesse by the Youth in the United States: A Thematic Analysis. 487p. 1982. write for info. (ISBN 3-261-05006-3). P Lang Pubs.
Marrese, Michael & Vanous, Jan. Soviet Subsidization of Trade with Eastern Europe: A Soviet Perspective. (Research Ser.: No. 52). (Illus.). xxvi, 250p. 1983. pap. 11.50x (ISBN 0-87725-152-5). U of Cal Intl St.
Marrett, Cora B. & Leggon, Cheryl, eds. Research in Race & Ethnic Relations, Vol. 2. 250p. 1980. lib. bdg. 40.00 (ISBN 0-89232-141-5). Jai Pr.
Marriage, Ellen, tr. see Balzac, Honore De.
Marrie, Alain, jt. auth. see Hollender, Louis F.
Marrin, Albert. Nicholas Murray Butler. (World Leaders Ser.). 1976. lib. bdg. 12.95 (ISBN 0-8057-7706-7, Twayne). G K Hall.
--Norman Angell. (World Leaders Ser.). 1979. lib. bdg. 14.95 (ISBN 0-8057-7725-3, Twayne). G K Hall.
--Overlord: D-Day & The Invasion of Europe. LC 82-1745. (Illus.). 224p. (gr. 5 up). 1982. 12.95 (ISBN 0-689-30931-7). Atheneum.
--Victory in the Pacific. LC 82-6707. (Illus.). 224p. (gr. 5 up). 1983. 12.95 (ISBN 0-689-30948-1). Atheneum.
Marriner, Ann. Contemporary Nursing Management: Issues & Practice. LC 81-14165. (Illus.). 403p. 1982. pap. text ed. 13.95 (ISBN 0-8016-3168-8). Mosby.
--Current Perspectives in Nursing Management, Vol. I. LC 78-31446. (Illus.). 1979. text ed. 12.50 o.p. (ISBN 0-8016-3119-X); pap. text ed. 9.50 o.p. (ISBN 0-8016-3120-3). Mosby.
--Guide to Nursing Management. LC 79-24241. (Illus.). 242p. 1980. pap. 14.50 (ISBN 0-8016-3121-1). Mosby.
--The Nursing Process: A Scientific Approach to Nursing Care. 3rd ed. LC 82-3466. (Illus.). 402p. 1983. pap. text ed. 12.95 (ISBN 0-8016-3117-3). Mosby.
--The Nursing Process: A Scientific Approach to Nursing Care. 2nd ed. LC 78-21093. (Illus.). 276p. 1979. pap. 13.50 o.p. (ISBN 0-8016-3122-X). Mosby.
Marriott, jt. auth. see Rachlin.
Marriott, Alice. The Ten Grandmothers. LC 45-1584. (The Civilization of the American Indians Ser.: Vol. 26). 306p. 1983. pap. 10.95 (ISBN 0-8061-1825-3). U of Okla Pr.
Marriott, Alice & Rachlin, Carol. Plains Indian Mythology. LC 75-26554. (Illus.). 224p. 1975. 14.37i (ISBN 0-690-00694-2). T Y Crowell.
Marriott, Alice & Rachlin, Carol K. Peyote. 1972. pap. 2.50 (ISBN 0-451-62034-8, ME2034, Ment). NAL.
Marriott, Alice L. Greener Fields: Experiences Among the American Indians. Repr. of 1953 ed. lib. bdg. 15.00 o.p. (ISBN 0-8371-0562-5, MAGF). Greenwood.
Marriott, F. H. Basic Mathematics for the Biological & Social Sciences. LC 73-99863. 1970. text ed. 18.50 o.p. (ISBN 0-08-006663-1); pap. 9.25 (ISBN 0-08-006664-X). Pergamon.
Marriott, Henry J. Practical Electrocardiography. 7th ed. (Illus.). 560p. 1983. text ed. price not set (ISBN 0-683-05574-7). Williams & Wilkins.
Marriott, Henry J. & Conover, Mary H. Advanced Concepts in Arrhythmias. LC 82-3447. (Illus.). 354p. 1983. text ed. 24.95 (ISBN 0-8016-3110-6). Mosby.
Marriott, John, jt. ed. see Royal United Services Institute for Defence Studies, London.
Marriott, John A. Crisis of English Liberty, a History of the Stuart Monarchy & the Puritan Revolution. Repr. of 1930 ed. lib. bdg. 20.75x (ISBN 0-8371-4272-5, MAEL). Greenwood.
--Dictatorship & Democracy. 231p. 1982. Repr. of 1935 ed. lib. bdg. 30.00 (ISBN 0-8495-3937-4). Arden Lib.
--The Makers of Modern Italy: Napoleon to Mussolini. LC 74-30842. (Illus.). 228p. 1975. Repr. of 1931 ed. lib. bdg. 16.25x (ISBN 0-8371-7936-X, MAMA). Greenwood.
Marriott, Sir John A. Commonwealth or Anarchy: A Survey of Projects of Peace from the Sixteenth to the Twentieth Century. LC 79-1636. 1983. Repr. of 1937 ed. 19.50 (ISBN 0-88355-939-0). Hyperion Conn.
Marriott, Peter. The Amazing Fact Book of Balloons, Vol. 5. LC 80-65592. (Illus.). 32p. (Orig.). (gr. 4 up). 1980. 5.95 (ISBN 0-86550-008-8); lib. bdg. 8.95 (ISBN 0-686-96969-3); pap. 2.95 (ISBN 0-86550-009-6). A & P Bks.
--The Amazing Fact Book of Monsters, Vol. 10. LC 80-65593. (Illus.). 32p. (gr. 4 up). 1980. 5.95 (ISBN 0-86550-018-5); PLB 8.95 (ISBN 0-686-96982-0); pap. 2.95 (ISBN 0-86550-019-3). A & P Bks.
Marris, Andrew W. & Stoneking, Charles E. Advanced Dynamics. LC 76-8007. 318p. 1976. Repr. of 1967 ed. 18.00 (ISBN 0-88275-403-3). Krieger.
Marris, Peter. Loss & Change. (Reports of the Institute of Community Studies). 184p. 1974. 15.95 (ISBN 0-7100-7890-0). Routledge & Kegan.
--Meaning & Action: Dilemmas of Inner City Planning. 208p. 1983. 19.95 (ISBN 0-7100-9349-7). Routledge & Kegan.
Marris, Peter & Somerset, Anthony. African Entrepreneur: A Study of Entrepreneurship & Development in Kenya. LC 70-180668. 288p. 1972. 22.50 (ISBN 0-8419-0098-1). Holmes & Meier.
Marris, Robin. A Survey & Critique of World Bank Supported Research in International Comparisons of Real Product. (Working Paper: No. 365). ii, 56p. 1979. 3.00 (ISBN 0-686-36093-1, WP-0365). World Bank.
Marron, Carol A. Mother Told Me So. (Illus.). 32p. (Orig.). (ps-3). 1982. 11.95 (ISBN 0-940742-00-4); pap. 4.75 (ISBN 0-940742-03-9). Carnival Pr.
Marron, Henri, jt. auth. see Leclercq, Dom H.

Marron, J. P., jt. auth. see Lewis, B. T.

Marron, John, ed. Visual Syntax. (Illus.). 150p. (Orig.). Date not set. lib. bdg. write for info. (ISBN 0-918842-01-8); pap. write for info. Asis So&So.

Marron, John, ed. see Walsh, Charlie.

Marrone, Nila Gutierrez. El Estilo de Juan Rulfo: Estudio linguistico. LC 77-93114. 1978. lib. bdg. 13.95x (ISBN 0-916950-08-5); pap. 8.95x (ISBN 0-916950-07-7). Bilingual Pr.

Marrone, Steven P. William Auvergne & Robert Grosseteste: New Ideas of Truth in the Early Thirteenth Century. LC 82-61375. 328p. 1983. 32.50 (ISBN 0-691-05383-9). Princeton U Pr.

Marrow, Alfred J. Practical Theorist: The Life & Work of Kurt Lewin. LC 77-1400. 1977. pap. text ed. 9.95x (ISBN 0-8077-2525-0). Tchrs Coll.

Marrow, Deborah. The Art Partronage of Maria de'Il Medici. Harris, Ann S., ed. LC 82-1951. (Studies in Baroque Art History: No. 4). 192p. 1982. 39.95 (ISBN 0-8357-1303-2, Pub. by UMI Res Pr). Univ Microfilms.

Marrow, Stanley B. The Words of Jesus in Our Gospel. LC 79-52105. 160p. 1979. pap. 5.95 (ISBN 0-8091-2215-4). Paulist Pr.

Marrs, Texe. You & the Armed Forces: Career & Educational Oportunities fo a Secure Future. LC 82-16386. 176p. 1983. lib. bdg. 12.95 (ISBN 0-668-05685-1); pap. 7.95 (ISBN 0-668-05693-2). Arco.

Marrucci, G., jt. auth. see Astarita, G.

Marrus, Michael R. The Politics of Assimilation: The French Jewish Community at the Time of the Dreyfus Affair. (Illus.). 1980. pap. 19.95 (ISBN 0-19-822591-1). Oxford U Pr.

Marrus, Michael R. & Paxton, Robert O. Vichy France & the Jews. LC 80-70307. 442p. 1981. 20.95 (ISBN 0-465-09005-2). Basic.

--Vichy France & the Jews. LC 82-16869. 432p. (Orig.). 1983. pap. 12.95 (ISBN 0-8052-0741-4). Schocken.

Marryat, Capt see Swan, D. K.

Marryat, Captain. Mr. Midshipman Easy. 1983. pap. 4.95 (ISBN 0-14-005295-X). Penguin.

Marryat, F. The Children of the New Forest. (Childrens Illustrated Classics Ser). (Illus.). 325p. 1977. Repr. of 1955 ed. 9.00x o.p. (ISBN 0-460-05032-X, Pub. by J. M. Dent. England). Biblio Dist.

Marryat, Frank. Mountains & Molehills. LC 74-7775. (Illus.). 233p. 1975. Repr. of 1962 ed. lib. bdg. 15.25x o.p. (ISBN 0-8371-7593-3, MAMM). Greenwood.

--Mountains & Molehills. (Classics of the Old West). 1982. lib. bdg. 17.28 (ISBN 0-8094-3999-9). Silver.

Mars, Alastair. British Submarines at War 1939-45. LC 73-82476. (Illus.). 256p. 1973. 10.00 o.p. (ISBN 0-87021-811-5). Naval Inst Pr.

Mars, Diana. Sweet Abandon. (Second Chance at Love Ser.: No. 122). 1983. pap. 1.75 (ISBN 0-515-07210-9). Jove Pubns.

--Sweet Surrender. (Second Chance at Love Ser.: No. 95). 192p. 1983. pap. 1.75 (ISBN 0-515-06859-4). Jove Pubns.

Mars, G., et al. Manpower Problems in the Hotel & Catering Industry. 180p. 1979. text ed. 28.25x (ISBN 0-566-00214-0). Gower Pub Ltd.

Mars, Gerald. Cheats at Work: An Anthropology of Workplace Crime. 256p. text ed. 16.95x (ISBN 0-04-301151-9). Allen Unwin.

Mars, Leonard. The Village & the State. 1980. text ed. 35.50x (ISBN 0-566-00337-6). Gower Pub Ltd.

Marsac, J., jt. ed. see Chretien, J.

Marsack, Robyn. The Cave of Making: The Poetry of Louis MacNeice. 140p. 1982. 17.95 (ISBN 0-19-811718-3). Oxford U Pr.

Marsack, Robyn, ed. see Blunden, Edmund.

Marsak, L. M., ed. The Nature of Historical Inquiry. LC 74-16092. 220p. 1977. pap. 7.50 (ISBN 0-88275-221-9). Krieger.

Marsan, C. Ajmone, jt. ed. see Caputto, R.

Marsboom, R. P., jt. ed. see Lewi, P. J.

Marschall, Laurence A., jt. ed. see Crowner, David L.

Marsden, Andrew K., ed. see Casualty Surgeons Association of Great Britain.

Marsden, Brian G. Catalog of Cometary Orbits. 128p. 1983. pap. text ed. 10.00 (ISBN 0-89490-095-1). Enslow Pubs.

Marsden, C. D., jt. ed. see Meldrum, B. S.

Marsden, E., jt. auth. see Inns, E. G.

Marsden, George M. Fundamentalism & American Culture: The Shaping of Twentieth Century Evangelicalism, 1870-1925. (Illus.). 1980. 19.95 (ISBN 0-19-502758-2). Oxford U Pr.

--Fundamentalism & American Culture: The Shaping of Twentieth-Century Evangelicalism, 1870-1925. 1982. pap. 7.95 (ISBN 0-19-503083-4, GB 684, GB). Oxford U Pr.

Marsden, H. B. & Steward, J. K. Tumours in Children. (Recent Results in Cancer Research: Vol. 13). (Illus.). 1968. 54.00 (ISBN 0-387-07632-8). Springer-Verlag.

Marsden, Hilda, ed. see Bronte, Emily.

Marsden, J. F., jt. auth. see Stoneman, C. F.

Marsden, Jerrold & Weinstein, Alan. Calculus. 2nd ed. 1980. 31.95 (ISBN 0-8053-6930-9); study guide 8.95 (ISBN 0-8053-6933-3). Benjamin-Cummings.

--Calculus Unlimited. 1980. pap. text ed. 11.95 (ISBN 0-8053-6932-5). Benjamin-Cummings.

Marsden, Michael T. & Nachbar, John G. Movies as Artifacts: Cultural Criticism of Popular Film. LC 82-6300. 288p. 1982. text ed. 22.95 (ISBN 0-88229-453-9); pap. text ed. 11.95 (ISBN 0-88229-803-8). Nelson-Hall.

Marsden, Norman, ed. A Jewish Life Under the Tsars: The Autobiography of Chaim Aronson, 1825-1888, Vol. 3. LC 81-10963. (Publications of the Oxford Centre for Postgraduate Hebrew Study). 368p. 1983. 19.95 (ISBN 0-86598-066-7). Allanheld.

Marsden, Peter V. & Lin, Nan. Social Structure & Network Analysis. (Sage Focus Editions). (Illus.). 300p. 1982. 25.00 (ISBN 0-8039-1888-7); pap. 12.50 (ISBN 0-8039-1889-5). Sage.

Marsden, Ralph W., ed. Politics, Minerals, & Survival. LC 74-27310. 104p. 1975. 17.50 (ISBN 0-299-06810-2); pap. 9.95 (ISBN 0-299-06814-5). U of Wis Pr.

Marsden, Walter. Lapland. (The World's Wild Places Ser.). (Illus.). 1979. lib. bdg. 15.96 (ISBN 0-8094-2055-4). Silver.

--Lincolnshire. 1977. 19.95 o.p. (ISBN 0-7134-0683-6, Pub. by Batsford England). David & Charles.

Marsella, Anthony J., jt. auth. see Corsini, Raymond J.

Marsella, Anthony J., et al, eds. Perspectives on Cross-Cultural Psychology. LC 79-6950. 1979. 38.50 (ISBN 0-12-473550-9). Acad Pr.

Marsh, jt. auth. see Olivo.

Marsh, A. I., ed. Concise Encyclopedia of Industrial Relations. 1979. text ed. 46.00x (ISBN 0-566-02095-5). Gower Pub Ltd.

Marsh, A. R. Protein Chemistry. 1970. text ed. 6.00x o.p. (ISBN 0-435-65565-5). Heinemann Ed.

Marsh, Angela. Pirate Treasure. LC 78-26275. (Raintree Great Adventures Ser.). (Illus.). (gr. 3-6). 1979. PLB 12.85 (ISBN 0-8393-0155-3). Raintree Pubs.

Marsh, Arthur. Employee Relations Policy & Decision Making. 248p. 1982. text ed. 41.50x (ISBN 0-566-00540-9). Gower Pub Ltd.

--Trade Union Handbook. 2nd ed. 396p. 1980. text ed. 61.00x (ISBN 0-566-02208-7). Gower Pub Ltd.

Marsh, Arthur & Ryan, Victoria. Historical Directory of Trade Unions: Vol. 1: Non-Manual Unions. 256p. 1981. text ed. 52.25x (ISBN 0-686-79653-5). Gower Pub Ltd.

Marsh, Carole. The Backyard Searcher's Extra Terrestrial Log Book. (Tomorrow's Books). (Illus.). 28p. 1983. 2.95 (ISBN 0-935326-27-8). Gallopade Pub Group.

--Bugs & Bytes: Computer for Kids. (Tomorrow's Books). (Illus.). 56p. 1983. 5.95 (ISBN 0-935326-15-4). Gallopade Pub Group.

--Go Queen Go! Chess for Kids. (Tomorrow's Books). (Illus.). 48p. 1983. 3.95 (ISBN 0-935326-14-6). Gallopade Pub Group.

--How to Find An Extra Terrestrial in Your Own Backyard. (Tomorrow's Books). (Illus.). 74p. 1983. 2.95 (ISBN 0-935326-09-X). Gallopade Pub Group.

--A Kid's Book of Smarts: How to Think, Make Decisions, Figure Things Out, Budget your Time, Money, Plan your Day, Week, Life & Other Things Adults Wish They'd Learned When They Were Kids! (Tomorrow's Books). (Illus.). 68p. 1983. 7.95 (ISBN 0-935326-18-9). Gallopade Pub Group.

--Life Isn't Fair: Murphy-like Lanes for Kids. (Tomorrow's Books). (Illus.). 74p. 1983. 2.95 (ISBN 0-935326-08-1). Gallopade Pub Group.

--Meet in the Middle: The Parents Test - The Kids Test. (Tomorrow's Books). (Illus.). 48p. 1983. 3.95 (ISBN 0-935326-24-3). Gallopade Pub Group.

--Mystery of the Lost Colony. (History Mystery Ser.). (Illus.). 160p. 1983. 4.95 (ISBN 0-935326-05-7). Gallopade Pub Group.

--Of All the Gaul: Latin for Kids. (Tomorrow's Books). (Illus.). 62p. 1983. 5.95 (ISBN 0-935326-17-0). Gallopade Pub Group.

--Six Puppy Feet: Bridge for Kids. (Tomorrow's Bks.). (Illus.). 48p. 1983. 3.95 (ISBN 0-935326-13-8). Gallopade Pub Group.

--The Teddy Bear Company: Easy Economics for Kids. (Tomorrow's Books). (Illus.). 62p. 1983. 5.95 (ISBN 0-935326-16-2). Gallopade Pub Group.

--The Teddy Bear's Annual Report: Tomorrow's Books. (Illus.). 48p. 1983. 7.95 (ISBN 0-935326-26-X). Gallopade Pub Group.

--Typing in Ten Minutes: On Any Keyboard - At Any Age. (Tomorrow's Books). (Illus.). 56p. 1983. 5.95 (ISBN 0-935326-12-X). Gallopade Pub Group.

Marsh, Charles R. Share Your Faith with a Muslim. LC 75-15883. 1975. pap. 2.95 (ISBN 0-8024-7900-6). Moody.

Marsh, Chelsea. If you Can't Find It in the Dark, Turn on A Light. LC 81-86205. (Illus.). 176p. 1983. pap. 6.95 (ISBN 0-86666-068-2). GWP.

Marsh, Dave & Stein, Kevin. The Book of Rock Lists. (Orig.). 1981. pap. 10.95 (ISBN 0-440-57580-X, Dell Trade Pbks). Dell.

Marsh, David. Paul Simon. LC 77-93716. 1978. pap. 7.95 (ISBN 0-8256-3916-6, Quick Fox). Putnam Pub Group.

Marsh, David C., ed. Introducing Social Policy. 1979. 21.50x (ISBN 0-7100-0132-0); pap. 9.95 (ISBN 0-7100-0133-9). Routledge & Kegan.

Marsh, Ellen, jt. ed. see Maddex, Diane.

Marsh, Ellen T. Reap the Savage Wind. 1982. pap. 4.95 (ISBN 0-686-82572-1). Ace Bks.

Marsh, Elsie A., ed. see Hollander, Jacob H.

Marsh, F. E. Marsh Bible Study Series, 6 vols. 1981. 48.00 (ISBN 0-8254-3236-7). Kregel.

Marsh, Frank B. The Founding of the Roman Empire. LC 75-18360. 329p. 1975. Repr. of 1922 ed. lib. bdg. 18.00x (ISBN 0-8371-8324-3, MAFRE). Greenwood.

Marsh, Frank H. The Emerging Rights of Children in Treatment for Mental & Catastrophic Illnesses. LC 79-66481. 1979. text ed. 16.75 (ISBN 0-8191-0829-4); pap. text ed. 8.25 (ISBN 0-8191-0830-8). U Pr of Amer.

Marsh, George E. & Price, Barrie Jo. Methods for Teaching the Mildly Handicapped Adolescent. LC 80-13396. (Illus.). 354p. 1980. pap. text ed. 16.95 (ISBN 0-8016-3115-7). Mosby.

Marsh, George E., et al. Teaching Mildly Handicapped Children: Methods & Materials (A Generic Approach to Comprehensive Teaching Ser.) LC 82-3440. (Illus.). 448p. 1983. pap. text ed. 18.95 (ISBN 0-8016-3177-7). Mosby.

Marsh, Glenda, jt. auth. see Marsh, Roger.

Marsh, Hadleigh. Newsom's Sheep Diseases. LC 65-10735. (Illus.). 470p. 1973. Repr. of 1965 ed. 29.50 (ISBN 0-88275-123-9). Krieger.

Marsh, Harold, Jr., jt. auth. see Jennings, Richard W.

Marsh, Jack. You Can Help the Alcoholic: A Christian Plan for Intervention. LC 82-74499. 88p. (Orig.). 1983. pap. 2.95 (ISBN 0-87793-270-0). Ave Maria.

Marsh, James. Selected Works of James Marsh, 3 vols. LC 76-42199. 2400p. 1976. lib. bdg. 200.00x set (ISBN 0-8201-1275-5). Schol Facsimiles.

Marsh, Janet. Janet Marsh's Nature Diary. LC 79-66030. (Illus.). 1979. 24.95 o.p. (ISBN 0-688-03559-0). Morrow.

Marsh, Jean. Loving Partnership. (Aston Hall Romances Ser.). 192p. (Orig.). 1981. pap. 1.75 o.p. (ISBN 0-523-41132-4). Pinnacle Bks.

Marsh, John. Amos & Micah. (Student Christian Movement Press, Torch Bible Ser.). (Orig.). 1959. pap. 7.95x (ISBN 0-19-520300-3). Oxford U Pr.

--Jesus in His Lifetime. 262p. 1982. 19.95 (ISBN 0-283-98638-7, Pub. by Sidgwick & Jackson). Merrimack Bk Serv.

--Saint John. LC 77-81619. (Westminster Pelican Commentaries Ser.). 1978. 19.50 (ISBN 0-664-21346-4). Westminster.

Marsh, John S. European Agriculture in an Uncertain World. (The Atlantic Papers: No. 75/1). 72p. (Orig.). 1975. pap. text ed. 4.75x (ISBN 0-686-83633-2). Allanheld.

--European Economic Issues: Agriculture, Economic Security, Industrial Democracy, the OECD. LC 76-30359. (Special Studies). 1977. 33.95 o.p. (ISBN 0-275-24410-5). Praeger.

Marsh, John S. & Swanney, Pamela J. Agriculture & the European Community. (Studies on Contemporary Europe: No. 2). (Illus.). 96p. (Orig.). 1980. text ed. 17.95x (ISBN 0-04-338092-1); pap. text ed. 6.95x (ISBN 0-04-338093-X). Allen Unwin.

Marsh, Judy & Dyer, Carole, eds. The Maine Way -- a Collection of Maine Fish & Game Recipes. (Illus.). 96p. (Orig.). 1978. pap. 4.95 (ISBN 0-686-69324-8). DeLorme Pub.

Marsh, L. G. Let's Explore Mathematics, 4 bks. Incl. Bk. 1. (Illus.). 96p. (gr. 6). 1964. pap. text ed. 2.45 (ISBN 0-668-01511-X); Bk. 2. (Illus.). 112p. (gr. 7). 1964. pap. text ed. 2.45 (ISBN 0-668-01512-8); Bk. 3. (Illus.). 112p. (gr. 8). 1964. pap. text ed. 2.45 (ISBN 0-668-01513-6); Bk. 4. (Illus.). 96p. (gr. 9). 1968. pap. 2.45 o.p. (ISBN 0-668-01825-9); Teacher's Guide: Children Explore Mathematics. 152p. 1967. 3.00 (ISBN 0-668-02077-6). LC 66-22887. (YA) Arco.

Marsh, Lillian. The Forgotten Bride. (Second Chance at Love Ser.: No. 99). 1983. pap. 1.75 (ISBN 0-686-82153-X). Jove Pubns.

Marsh, Margaret. Anarchist Women: 1870-1920. Davis, Allen F., ed. (American Civilization Ser.). (Illus.). 256p. 1980. 27.95 (ISBN 0-87722-202-9). Temple U Pr.

Marsh, Matthew E. California Mechanics' Lien Law Handbook. 3rd ed. LC 72-83952. 673p. 1979. 55.00 (ISBN 0-911110-30-5); 1983 suppl. incl. (ISBN 0-685-44105-9). Parker & Son.

Marsh, Meredith. Eating Cake. LC 78-20955. 1979. 10.95 (ISBN 0-698-10985-6, Coward). Putnam Pub Group.

--I Had Wild Jack for a Lover. LC 77-7473. 1977. 9.95 o.p. (ISBN 0-698-10848-5, Coward). Putnam Pub Group.

Marsh, Michael. Gemini. 1975. pap. 1.00 o.p. (ISBN 0-686-20746-7). Samisdat.

Marsh, Moreton. Easy Expert in American Antiques: Knowing, Finding, Buying & Restoring Early American Furniture. rev. ed. LC 78-9050. Orig. Title: The Easy Expert in Collecting & Restoring American Antiques. 1978. 14.37i (ISBN 0-397-01287-X, LP-139); pap. 7.95i (ISBN 0-397-01288-8). Har-Row.

Marsh, Neville. Fibrinolysis. LC 80-42309. 272p. 1981. 41.50x (ISBN 0-471-28029-1, Pub. by Wiley-Interscience). Wiley.

Marsh, Ngaio. Artists in Crime. pap. 1.95 (ISBN 0-515-05414-3). Jove Pubns.

--The Clutch of Constables. (Ngaio Marsh Mystery Ser.). 224p. 1983. pap. 2.50 (ISBN 0-515-07105-6). Jove Pubns.

--Death & the Dancing Footman. (Ngaio Marsh Mysteries Ser.). pap. 2.50 (ISBN 0-515-06715-6). Jove Pubns.

--Death in a White Tie. (Ngaio Marsh Mysteries Ser.). pap. 2.50 (ISBN 0-515-06224-3). Jove Pubns.

--Death in Ecstasy. 256p. 1981. pap. 2.50 (ISBN 0-515-06166-2). Jove Pubns.

--Death of a Fool. (Ngaio Marsh Mystery Ser.). 288p. 1981. pap. 2.50 (ISBN 0-515-06177-8). Jove Pubns.

--Final Curtain. 288p. 1983. pap. 2.50 (ISBN 0-515-07074-2). Jove Pubns.

--Grave Mistake. 1983. pap. 2.50 (ISBN 0-515-06178-6). Jove Pubns.

--Hand in Glove. 1978. pap. 2.25 (ISBN 0-515-06136-0). Jove Pubns.

--Killer Dolphin. (Ngaio Marsh Mystery Ser.). 256p. 1983. pap. 2.50 (ISBN 0-515-06820-9). Jove Pubns.

--Last Ditch. (Ngaio Marsh Mystery Ser.). 288p. 1983. pap. 2.50 (ISBN 0-515-06821-7). Jove Pubns.

--Light Thickens. 12.95 (ISBN 0-316-54675-5). Little.

--Light Thickens. (General Ser.). 1983. lib. bdg. 16.95 (ISBN 0-8161-3509-6, Large Print Bks). G K Hall.

--A Man Lay Dead. 1978. pap. 2.50 (ISBN 0-515-06496-3). Jove Pubns.

--Ngaio Marsh: Black Beech & Honeydew. (Illus.). 1982. 19.95 (ISBN 0-00-216367-5, Pub. by W Collins Australia). Intl Schol Bk Serv.

--Night at the Vulcan. (Ngaio Marsh Mystery Ser.). 256p. 1981. pap. 1.75 o.s.i. (ISBN 0-515-05293-0). Jove Pubns.

--Nursing Home Murder. 1978. pap. 1.50 o.s.i. (ISBN 0-515-04530-6). Jove Pubns.

--Overture to Death. (Ngaio Marsh Mysteries Ser.). 320p. 1981. pap. 2.50 (ISBN 0-515-06822-5). Jove Pubns.

--Scales of Justice. 256p. 1980. pap. 2.50 (ISBN 0-515-06497-1). Jove Pubns.

--Spinsters in Jeopardy. (Ngaio Marsh Mystery Ser.). pap. 2.50 (ISBN 0-515-06179-4). Jove Pubns.

--Tied up in Tinsel. 1978. pap. 2.50 (ISBN 0-515-06015-1). Jove Pubns.

Marsh, P. D. V. Contracting for Engineering & Construction Projects. 2nd ed. 257p. 1981. text ed. 44.00x (ISBN 0-566-02232-X). Gower Pub Ltd.

Marsh, Patrick O. Messages That Work: A Guide to Communication Design. 460p. 1983. 32.95 (ISBN 0-87778-184-2). Educ Tech Pubns.

Marsh, Peter. Aggro: The Illusion of Violence. 160p. 1978. 17.50x (ISBN 0-460-12026-3, Pub by J. M. Dent England). Biblio Dist.

Marsh, R. W. Systemic Fungicides. 351p. (Orig.). pap. 18.00 (ISBN 0-470-57250-7). Krieger.

Marsh, R. Warren & Olivo, Thomas. Basics of Refrigeration. 2nd ed. 1979. 18.95 o.p. (ISBN 0-442-26273-6). Van Nos Reinhold.

Marsh, Robert W. A Taste of Steel. 224p. 1982. pap. 2.50 o.s.i. (ISBN 0-8439-1155-7, Leisure Bks). Nordon Pubns.

Marsh, Robin R. Development Strategies in Rural Colombia: The Case of Caaueta. LC 82-620032. (Latin American Studies: Vol. 55). 1983. text ed. write for info. (ISBN 0-87903-055-0). UCLA Lat Am Ctr.

Marsh, Roger. Monoprints for the Artist. (gr. 10 up). 1969. pap. 7.50 o.s.i. (ISBN 0-85458-549-4). Transatlantic.

Marsh, Roger & Marsh, Glenda. Imaginative Collage. (Illus.). 136p. 1975. 14.95x o.p. (ISBN 0-8464-0501-6). Beekman Pubs.

Marsh, S. B. & Soulsby, J. Outlines of English Law. 304p. 1982. write for info. (ISBN 0-07-084655-3). McGraw.

Marsh, William & Dozier, Jeffrey. Landscape: An Introduction to Physical Geography. LC 80-68120. (Geography Ser.). (Illus.). 656p. 1981. text ed. 26.95 (ISBN 0-201-04101-4); slides avail. (ISBN 0-201-14099-3); wkbk. avail. (ISBN 0-201-04102-2); tchr's manual & test file 3.00 (ISBN 0-201-04103-0). A-W.

Marsh, William H., jt. auth. see Kuniansky, Harry R.

Marsh, William M. Environmental Analysis: For Land-Use & Site Planning. (Illus.). 1977. 37.50 (ISBN 0-07-040490-9, P&RB). McGraw.

--Landscape Applications. LC 82-13889. (Earth Science Ser.). (Illus.). 225p. 1981. pap. text ed. 12.95x (ISBN 0-201-04102-2). A-W.

Marsh, Zoe & Kingsnorth, G. W. A History of East Africa. 4th ed. LC 72-171677. (Illus.). 1972. 22.95 (ISBN 0-521-08346-X); pap. 7.95x o.p. (ISBN 0-521-09677-4). Cambridge U Pr.

Marshak, David, ed. see Tobin, Catherine.

Marshak, R. E. Perspectives in Modern Physics. 673p. Repr. of 1966 ed. text ed. 25.50 (ISBN 0-470-57295-7). Krieger.

Marshak, Richard H. & Lindner, Arthur E. Radiology of the Small Intestine. 2nd ed. LC 75-5053. (Illus.). 705p. 1976. text ed. 50.00 o.p. (ISBN 0-7216-6127-0). Saunders.

Marshak, Robert E. Academic Renewal in the 1970's: Memoirs of a City College President. LC 82-16111. 300p. (Orig.). 1983. lib. bdg. 23.25 (ISBN 0-8191-2779-5); pap. text ed. 11.25 (ISBN 0-8191-2780-9). U Pr of Amer.

Marshak, S. In the Van. 12p. 1982. pap. 1.25 (ISBN 0-8285-2289-8, Pub. by Progress Pubs USSR). Imported Pubns.

Marshak, Samuil & Harms, David. The Merry Starlings. Rottenberg, Dorian, tr. from Rus. LC 82-47725. (Illus.). 24p. (ps-3). 1983. 9.57i (ISBN 0-06-024089-X, HarpJ); PLB 9.89g (ISBN 0-06-024090-3). Har-Row.

Marshall. Cryptorchidism & Related Anomalies. 128p. 1982. 19.50 (ISBN 0-03-059282-8). Praeger.

Marshall & Williams. Textbook of Zoology: Invertebrates. 7th ed. 1972. text ed. 16.95 (ISBN 0-444-19579-3). Elsevier.

Marshall, A. B. Ices, Plain & Fancy: A Reprint of Book of Ices by A. B. Marshall. LC 76-18215. (Illus.). 1976. 6.95 o.s.i. (ISBN 0-87099-150-7). Metro Mus Art.

Marshall, A. J., jt. auth. see Armstrong, C. N.

Marshall, Alan see Allen, W. S.

Marshall, Alan G. Biophysical Chemistry: Principles, Techniques & Applications. LC 77-19136. 1978. text ed. 39.95 (ISBN 0-471-02718-9); students manual 8.95 (ISBN 0-471-03674-9). Wiley.

Marshall, Alejandro & Bennett, Gordon H. La Salvacion y las Dudas de Algunas Personas. 2nd ed. Bautista, Sara, tr. from Span. (La Serie Diamante). 36p. (Eng.). 1982. pap. 0.85 (ISBN 0-942504-01-1). Overcomer Pr.

Marshall, Andrew. Brazil. (Illus.). 1966. 8.50x o.s.i. (ISBN 0-8027-2102-8); pap. 3.50 o.s.i. (ISBN 0-8027-7010-X, 55). Walker & Co.

Marshall, Anthony, jt. auth. see Cournoyer, Norman G.

Marshall, Brenda. The Charles Dickens Cookbook: Or Mr. Pickwick's Plentiful Portions. (Illus.). 176p. 1981. gift ed. 12.95 (ISBN 0-920510-40-X, Pub. by Personal Lib). Dodd.

Marshall, C. Edmund. The Physical Chemistry & Mineralogy of Soils: Soils in Place, Vol. II. LC 64-20074. 1977. 42.50 (ISBN 0-471-02957-2, Pub. by Wiley-Interscience). Wiley.

--The Physical Chemistry & Mineralogy of Soils: Volume 1: Soil Materials. LC 75-22180. 398p. 1975. Repr. of 1964 ed. 22.50 (ISBN 0-88275-351-7). Krieger.

Marshall, Catherine. Adventures in Prayer. 1975. 11.95 (ISBN 0-912376-89-9). Chosen Bks Pub.

--Algo Mas. 171p. Date not set. 3.75 (ISBN 0-88113-001-X). Edit Betania.

--Aventuras en la Oracion. 192p. Date not set. 2.50 (ISBN 0-88113-005-2). Edit Betania.

--El Ayudador. 208p. Date not set. 3.25 (ISBN 0-88113-009-5). Edit Betania.

--Beyond Our Selves. large print ed. 512p. 1982. 14.95 (ISBN 0-8007-1321-4). Revell.

--Christy. 1967. 11.95 (ISBN 0-07-040605-7, GB). McGraw.

--Christy. 1968. pap. 3.50 (ISBN 0-8007-8008-6, Spire Bks). Revell.

--Man Called Peter. 1971. pap. 3.25 (ISBN 0-380-00894-7, 61838-9). Avon.

--Something More. 1975. Repr. lib. bdg. 13.95 o.p. (ISBN 0-8161-6276-X, Large Print Bks). G K Hall.

--Story Bible. (Illus.). 220p. 1982. PLB 17.50 (ISBN 0-912376-94-5). Chosen Bks Pub.

Marshall, Catherine & LeSourd, Leonard. Mi Diario Personal de Oracion. 416p. Date not set. 5.95 (ISBN 0-88113-306-X). Edit Betania.

Marshall, Catherine & Le Sourd, Leonard. My Personal Prayer Diary. (Epiphany Bks.). 1983. pap. 3.95 (ISBN 0-345-30612-0). Ballantine.

Marshall, Catherine, ed. see Marshall, Peter.

Marshall Cavendish Editorial Board. The Home Bread Baker. LC 74-14119. (Illus.). 96p. 1975. 6.95 o.p. (ISBN 0-668-03640-0). Arco.

Marshall, Christopher. Physical Basis of Computerized Tomography. 1982. 37.50 (ISBN 0-87527-314-9). Green.

Marshall, D. S. The Black & White of Love: A Collection of Love Poetry. 1982. 5.95 (ISBN 0-533-05503-2). Vantage.

Marshall, Dale & Montgomery, Roger, eds. Housing Policy for the Eighties. 1979. pap. 6.00 (ISBN 0-918592-36-4). Policy Studies.

Marshall, Dale R., jt. ed. see Leonard, David K.

Marshall, Dale R., jt. ed. see Montgomery, Roger.

Marshall, Daniel P. & Rabold, J. Gregory. Staying Healthy Without Medicine: A Manual of Home Prevention & Treatment. (Illus.). 336p. 1983. lib. bdg. 27.95x (ISBN 0-88229-635-3). Nelson-Hall.

Marshall, Don. R. Successful Techniques for Solving Employee Compensation Problems. LC 77-17964. 1978. 38.50 o.s.i. (ISBN 0-471-57297-7, Pub. by Wiley-Interscience). Wiley.

Marshall, Dorothy. The Life & Times of Victoria. Fraser, Antonia, ed. (Kings & Queens of England Ser.). (Illus.). 224p. 1972. text ed. 17.50x (ISBN 0-686-36954-8, Pub. by Weidenfeld & Nicolson England). Biblio Dist.

Marshall, Edmund. Parliament & the Public. 150p. 1982. 15.00x (ISBN 0-8448-1454-7). Crane-Russak Co.

Marshall, Edward. Fox at School. LC 82-45506. (Illus.). 48p. (ps-3). 1983. 3.95 (ISBN 0-8037-2674-0, 0383-120); lib. bdg. 8.89 (ISBN 0-8037-2675-9). Dial Bks Young.

--Fox in Love. LC 82-70190. (Easy-to-Read Ser.). 56p. (ps-3). 1982. pap. 3.75 (ISBN 0-8037-2426-8); PLB 8.89 (ISBN 0-8037-2433-0). Dial.

Marshall, Eldon K. & Kurtz, P. David. Interpersonal Helping Skills: A Guide to Training Methods, Programs, & Resources. LC 82-48070. (Social & Behavioral Science Ser.). 1982. text ed. 29.95x (ISBN 0-87589-551-4). Jossey Bass.

Marshall, Eric & Hample, Naomi C. They Keep Their Promises: Children Talk About Grandparents. LC 78-69822. (Illus.). 1978. pap. 3.95 o.p. (ISBN 0-448-16456-6, G&D). Putnam Pub Group.

Marshall, F. Ray. Illegal Immigration: The Problem, the Solutions. 1982. pap. text ed. 2.50 (ISBN 0-935776-02-8). F A I R.

Marshall, G. I., jt. auth. see Hanneman, L. J.

Marshall, Geoffrey. Constitutional Theory. (Clarendon Law Ser). 1971. 17.95x (ISBN 0-19-876022-1). Oxford U Pr.

Marshall, George C. Selected Speeches & Statements of General of the Army George C. Marshall. DeWeerd, H. A., ed. LC 72-10365. (FDR & the Era of the New Deal Ser.). 1973. Repr. of 1945 ed. lib. bdg. 37.50 (ISBN 0-306-70556-7). Da Capo.

Marshall, George N. Buddha: The Quest for Serenity. LC 78-53787. (Illus.). 1978. 12.02 o.p. (ISBN 0-8070-1346-3); pap. 4.95 o.p. (ISBN 0-8070-1347-1, BP580). Beacon Pr.

Marshall, Gordon. In Search of the Spirit of Capitalism: An Essay on Max Weber's Protestant Ethic Thesis. 233p. 1982. 22.50 (ISBN 0-231-05498-X); pap. 10.00 (ISBN 0-686-82236-6). Columbia U Pr.

Marshall, H. Creative Writers' Bibliography & Resource File. 32p. 1982. pap. 10.95 (ISBN 0-686-94768-1). Creative Bk Co.

Marshall, H., ed. Yevgeny Yevtushenko: Bilingual Edition. 1967. text ed. 13.75 o.p. (ISBN 0-08-012464-X). Pergamon.

Marshall, H. H. From Dependence to Statehood in Commonwealth Africa: Selected Documents, World War I to Independence, 2 vols. Incl. Vol. 1. Southern Africa (ISBN 0-379-20348-0); Vol. 2. Central Africa. LC 80-10407. 1982. lib. bdg. 75.00 ea. Oceana.

Marshall, Helen, tr. see Scharfetter, C.

Marshall, Helen L. Aim for a Star. 1966. 4.95 (ISBN 0-385-08258-4). Doubleday.

--Bright Horizons. 1954. 3.95 o.p. (ISBN 0-385-08266-5). Doubleday.

Marshall, Howad I. Biblical Inspiration. 128p. 1983. pap. 4.95 (ISBN 0-8028-1959-1). Eerdmans.

Marshall, Howard. How to Save Your Teeth. LC 79-51197. (Illus.). 312p. 1980. 14.95 o.p. (ISBN 0-89696-039-0, An Everest House Book). Dodd.

Marshall, Howard I. One & Two Thessalonians. (New Century Bible Commentary Ser.). 256p. 1983. pap. 6.95 (ISBN 0-8028-1946-X). Eerdmans.

Marshall, Hugh. Orestes Brownson & the American Republic. 1971. pap. 14.95x o.p. (ISBN 0-8132-0581-6). Cath U Pr.

Marshall, I. H. Composite Structures. (Applied Science Ser.). 1981. 129.50 (ISBN 0-85334-988-6). Elsevier.

Marshall, I. H., ed. Composite Structures. (Illus.). xvi, 732p. 1981. 139.50 (ISBN 0-85334-988-6, Pub. by Applied Sci England). Elsevier.

Marshall, I. Howard. The New International Commentary on the New Testament: The Epistles of John. 1978. 12.95 (ISBN 0-685-87177-0). Eerdmans.

Marshall, I. Howard, ed. see Wells, David F.

Marshall, J., jt. auth. see Cooper, C. L.

Marshall, J. D. The Old Poor Law Seventeen Ninety Five to Eighteen Thirty Four. (Studies in Economic & Social History). 49p. 1968. pap. text ed. 5.25x (ISBN 0-333-09365-8). Humanities.

Marshall, J. D. & Walton, J. K. The Lake Counties from Nineteen-Thirty to the Mid Twentieth Century. 320p. 1982. 30.00 (ISBN 0-7190-0824-7). Manchester.

Marshall, J. F. Victor Jacquemont: Letters to Achille Chaper. LC 60-10142. (Memoirs Ser: Vol. 50). (Illus.). 1960. 5.00 o.p. (ISBN 0-87169-050-0). Am Philos.

Marshall, James. Going, Going, Gone? The Waste of Our Energy Resources. LC 75-44014. (New Conservation Ser.). (Illus.). 96p. (gr. 7 up). 1976. PLB 5.99 o.p. (ISBN 0-698-30607-4, Coward). Putnam Pub Group.

--What's the Matter with Carruthers? LC 72-75607. (Illus.). 32p. (gr. k-3). 1972. reinforced bdg. 9.95 (ISBN 0-395-13895-7). HM.

--Yummers! LC 72-5400. (Illus.). 32p. (gr. k-3). 1973. reinforced bdg. 9.95 (ISBN 0-395-14757-3). HM.

Marshall, James, jt. auth. see Allard, Harry.

Marshall, James F., tr. De Stael-Du Pont Letters: Correspondence of Madame de Stael & Pierre Samuel du Pont de Nemours, & of Other Members of the Necker & Du Pont Families. (Illus.). 428p. 1968. 35.00 (ISBN 0-299-05061-0). U of Wis Pr.

Marshall, James L. Carbon-Carbon & Carbon-Proton NMR Couplings: Applications to Organic Stereochemistry & Conformational Analysis. LC 82-16117. (Methods in Sterochemical Analysis Ser.: Vol. 2). (Illus.). 1983. 49.95x o.p. (ISBN 0-89573-113-4). Verlag Chemie.

Marshall, James V. Still Waters. LC 82-2308. 175p. 1982. 10.50 (ISBN 0-688-01254-X). Morrow.

Marshall, Jan. Still Hanging in There...Confessions of a Totaled Woman. (Orig.). 1979. pap. 4.95 o.p. (ISBN 0-523-40622-3). Pinnacle Bks.

Marshall, Janet, et al. The Fiat Book of Common Birds of New Zealand: Mountain, Bush & Shore Birds, Vol. 2. LC 72-79069. (Illus.). 97p. 1972. pap. 3.95 o.p. (ISBN 0-589-00759-9, Dist. by C E Tuttle). Reed.

Marshall, Jay, ed. How to Perform Instant Magic. LC 79-55634. (Illus.). 1980 (Domus Bks). pap. 8.95 o.p. (ISBN 0-89196-043-0). Quality Bks IL.

Marshall, Joanne. The Peacock Bed. LC 77-99125. 1978. 8.95 o.p. (ISBN 0-312-59941-2). St Martin.

Marshall, Joe T. Systematics of Smaller Asian Night Birds Based on Voice. 58p. 1978. 7.00 (ISBN 0-943610-25-7). Am Ornithologists.

Marshall, John. An Autobiographical Sketch by John Marshall. Adams, John S., ed. LC 71-160849. (American Constitutional Legal History Ser.). (Illus.). 74p. 1973. Repr. of 1937 ed. lib. bdg. 19.50 (ISBN 0-306-70216-9). Da Capo.

--The Infertile Period. 1980. 16.00x o.p. (ISBN 0-686-75608-8, Pub. by Darton-Longman-Todd England). State Mutual Bk.

--Man Oh Man. (Illus.). 14.50 (ISBN 0-392-03856-0, SpS). Sportshelf.

--The Original Starch-Blocker Diet. 1982. pap. 3.50 (ISBN 0-440-04078-7). Dell.

--Rail Facts & Feats. (Illus.). 252p. 1980. 19.95 (ISBN 0-900424-56-7, Pub by Guinness Superlatives England). Sterling.

Marshall, John A. American Bastille. LC 71-121115. (Civil Liberties in American History Ser). 1970. Repr. of 1869 ed. lib. bdg. 85.00 (ISBN 0-306-71963-0). Da Capo.

Marshall, John B., jt. auth. see Cornelius, Temple H.

Marshall, John C., jt. ed. see Morton, John.

Marshall, John L. & Barbash, Heather. The Sports Doctor's Fitness Book for Women. 320p. 1981. 13.95 o.s.i. (ISBN 0-440-08201-3). Delacorte.

Marshall, Judi, jt. auth. see Cooper, Cary L.

Marshall, Judi & Cooper, Cary L., eds. Coping with Stress at Work. 236p. 1981. text ed. 38.00x (ISBN 0-566-02338-5). Gower Pub Ltd.

Marshall, K. C. Advances in Microbial Ecology, Vol. 6. 252p. 1982. 39.50x (ISBN 0-306-41064-8, Plenum Pr). Plenum Pub.

Marshall, Kenneth, ed. see Newbourne, Malcolm J.

Marshall, Kenneth G. & Attia, E. L. Disorders of the Ear: Diagnosis & Management. 320p. 1983. text ed. 27.50 (ISBN 0-7236-7056-0). Wright-PSG.

Marshall, Kevin C., jt. ed. see Bitton, Gabriel.

Marshall, Larry G. Evolution of the Borhyaenidae, Extinct South American Predaceous Marsupials. (Publications in Geological Sciences: Vol. 117). 1978. pap. 15.50x (ISBN 0-520-09571-5). U of Cal Pr.

Marshall, Lauriston C. & Sahlin, Harry L., eds. Electrostatic & Electromagnetic Confinement of Plasmas & the Phenomenology of the Relativistic Electron Beam. (Annals of the New York Academy of Sciences Ser.: Vol. 251). 711p. 1975. 83.75x (ISBN 0-89072-005-3). NY Acad Sci.

Marshall, Lydie. Cooking with Lydie Marshall. LC 82-47832. 1982. 18.95 (ISBN 0-394-52022-X). Knopf.

Marshall, Madeleine F. & Todd, Janet M. English Congregational Hymns in the Eighteenth Century. LC 82-40176. 192p. 1982. 15.50x (ISBN 0-8131-1470-5). U Pr of Ky.

Marshall, Margaret R. An Introduction to the World of Children's Books. 190p. 1982. 17.95x (ISBN 0-566-03437-9, 05806-8, Pub by Gower Pub Co England). Lexington BKs.

--Libraries & Literature for Teenagers. 304p. 1975. 20.00 (ISBN 0-233-96604-8, 05807-6, Pub. by Gower Pub Co England). Lexington Bks.

--Libraries & the Handicapped Child. 206p. 1981. 26.50 (ISBN 0-233-97299-4, 05808-4, Pub. by Gower Pub Co England). Lexington Bks.

Marshall, Marilyn. The Turquoise Talisman. (Adventures in Love Ser.: No. 38). 1982. pap. 1.95 (ISBN 0-451-11931-2, AJ1931, Sig). NAL.

Marshall, Martha. What Child Is This. LC 82-7239. (Illus.). (gr. 1-2). 1982. lib. bdg. 4.95 (ISBN 0-686-83149-7). Dandelion Hse.

Marshall, Mel. Cooking Over Coals. (Illus.). 320p. pap. 5.95 o.p. (ISBN 0-88317-022-1). Stoeger Pub Co.

--Gato. (Orig.). 1980. pap. 1.95 o.s.i. (ISBN 0-440-12933-8). Dell.

--How to Choose & Use Lumber, Plywood, Panelboards, & Laminates. LC 79-4710. 1980. pap. 4.95i o.p. (ISBN 0-06-090724-X, CN 724, CN). Har-Row.

--Lannigan's Revenge. (Orig.). 1980. pap. 1.75 o.s.i. (ISBN 0-440-15014-0). Dell.

Marshall, Michael. Top Hat & Tails: The Story of Jack Buchanan. (Illus.). 1978. 24.00 o.p. (ISBN 0-241-89602-9, Pub. by Hamish Hamilton England). David & Charles.

Marshall, Nancy, jt. auth. see Bouton, Bobbie.

Marshall, Norman. Pocket Encyclopedia of Ocean Life. (Illus.). (gr. 7 up). 1971. 8.95 o.p. (ISBN 0-02-580180-5). Macmillan.

Marshall, Norton L., jt. auth. see Mason, William H.

Marshall, P. J. East Indian Fortunes: The British in Bengal in the Eighteenth Century. (Illus.). 1976. 45.00x (ISBN 0-19-821566-5). Oxford U Pr.

Marshall, P. J., ed. British Discovery of Hinduism in the Eighteenth Century. LC 73-111132. (Illus.). 1970. 39.50 (ISBN 0-521-07737-0). Cambridge U Pr.

Marshall, P. T., jt. auth. see Hughes, David T.

Marshall, Paule. Praisesong for the Widow. 256p. 1983. 13.95 (ISBN 0-399-12754-2). Putnam Pub Group.

--Soul Clap Hands & Sing. 177p. 1971. Repr. of 1961 ed. 7.95x o.p. (ISBN 0-911860-06-1). Chatham Bkseller.

Marshall, Peter. First Easter. 137p. 1978. PLB 6.95 o.p. (ISBN 0-912376-28-7). Chosen Bks Pub.

--Heaven Can't Wait. 222p. 1978. pap. 4.95 o.p. (ISBN 0-912376-44-9). Chosen Bks Pub.

--Jean Baptiste Anteine Guillemet Eighteen Hundred Forty-One to Nineteen Hundred Eighteen. (Illus.). 63p. 1983. 20.00 (ISBN 0-8390-0303-X). Allanheld & Schram.

--Keepers of the Springs. 1962. 3.95 o.p. (ISBN 0-8007-1011-8). Revell.

--Let's Keep Christmas. 34p. 1978. PLB 5.95 o.p. (ISBN 0-912376-25-2). Chosen Bks Pub.

--Mister Jones, Meet the Master: Sermons & Prayers of Peter Marshall. Marshall, Catherine, ed. pap. 5.95 (ISBN 0-8007-5095-0, Power Bks). Revell.

Marshall, Peter & Manuel, David. The Light & the Glory. 352p. 1977. 12.95 (ISBN 0-8007-0886-5); pap. 6.95 (ISBN 0-8007-5054-3, Power Bks). Revell.

--The Light & the Glory. 1980. pap. 6.95 (ISBN 0-8007-5054-3, Power Bks). Revell.

--The Light & the Glory Study Guide. 1981. pap. 3.95 (ISBN 0-8007-1279-X); photo enrichment pack 12.50 (ISBN 0-8007-1285-4). Revell.

Marshall, R., jt. auth. see Skitok, J.

Marshall, R. G., et al. Fuente Hispana. (Level 3). (gr. 10-12). 1971. text ed. 16.95 (ISBN 0-07-040575-1, C); instructors' manual 9.95 (ISBN 0-07-040579-4); tapes 250.00 (ISBN 0-07-098975-3). McGraw.

Marshall, R. T., jt. auth. see Campbell, J. R.

Marshall, Randall G., et al. La Fuente Hispana. 2nd ed. (Illus.). 448p. (gr. 3). 1977. text ed. 21.95 (ISBN 0-07-040580-8, C); exercises 10.95 (ISBN 0-07-040582-4); instr's manual 10.95 (ISBN 0-07-040581-6); tapes 495.00 (ISBN 0-07-098976-1); tests 139.95 (ISBN 0-07-040583-2); tests replacements 49.95 (ISBN 0-07-040584-0). McGraw.

Marshall, Ray. The Negro Worker. 1967. pap. text ed. 3.60x (ISBN 0-394-30735-6). Phila Bk Co.

Marshall, Ray & Paul, Korkey. Hey Diddle Diddle. Klimo, Kate, ed. (Chubby Pop-Ups Ser.). (Illus.). 10p. 1983. 3.95 (ISBN 0-671-46239-3, Little). S&S.

Marshall, Ray & Paul, Korky. Humpty Dumpty. Klimo, Kate, ed. (Chubby Pop-Ups Ser.). (Illus.). 10p. 1983. 3.95 (ISBN 0-671-46236-9, Little). S&S.

--Jack & Jill. Klimo, Kate, ed. (Illus.). 10p. 1983. 3.95 (ISBN 0-671-46238-5, Little). S&S.

--Sing a Song of Sixpence. Klimo, Kate, ed. (Chubby Pop-Ups Ser.). (Illus.). 10p. (ps-k). 1983. 3.95 (ISBN 0-671-46237-7, Little). S&S.

Marshall, Richard, jt. auth. see Merrick, David.

Marshall, Robert G., ed. Short-Title Catalogue of Books Printed in Italy & of Books in Italian Printed Abroad, 1501-1600, Held in Selected North American Libraries, 3 Vols. 1970. Set. lib. bdg. 150.00 (ISBN 0-8161-0852-8, Hall Library). G K Hall.

Marshall, Robert H. & Swanson, Rodney B. The Monetary Process: Essentials of Money & Banking. 2nd ed. 450p. 1980. text ed. 24.95 (ISBN 0-395-26530-4); instr's. manual 1.00 (ISBN 0-395-26527-4). HM.

Marshall, Robert J. Resistant Interactions: Child, Family & Psychotherapist. LC 82-947. 240p. 1982. 29.95x (ISBN 0-89885-116-5). Human Sci Pr.

Marshall, Robert L., ed. Studies in Renaissance & Baroque Music in Honor of Arthur Mendel. 1974. 37.00 (ISBN 0-913574-26-0, OSMARS). Eur-Am Music.

Marshall, Roger. Sailing Techniques Illustrated. (Illus.). 1983. 29.45x (ISBN 0-393-03276-0). Norton.

Marshall, Rush P. Control of Cedar-Apple Rust on Red Cedar. 1941. pap. 22.50x (ISBN 0-686-51364-9). Elliots Bks.

Marshall, S. L. A. Vietnam: Three Battles. (Quality Paperbacks Ser.). (Illus.). 242p. 1982. pap. 7.95 (ISBN 0-306-80174-4). Da Capo.

Marshall, Shelly, ed. Young, Sober, & Free. 1978. 5.95 (ISBN 0-89486-055-0). Hazelden.

Marshall, Sol H. Editors Don't Always Hate Publicists. 130p. 1983. pap. 8.95 (ISBN 0-88409-103-1). Creative Bk Co.

--Fund-Raising with Your Own Cookbook. 1983. pap. 8.95 (ISBN 0-88409-084-1). Creative Bk Co.

Marshall, Sol H., ed. Recipes in Rhyme. 120p. (Orig.). 1983. pap. 8.95 (ISBN 0-88409-108-2). Creative Bk Co.

Marshall, Sol H. & Medress, Dolly, eds. Recipes My Milwaukee Mother Taught Me. 120p. (Orig.). 1983. pap. 8.95 (ISBN 0-88409-107-4). Creative Bk Co.

Marshall, Stephen E., ed. Randax Education Guide: A Guide to Colleges Seeking Students, 1983 Edition. 12th ed. (Illus.). 128p. (Orig.). 1983. pap. 8.95 (ISBN 0-914880-13-6). Educ Guide.

Marshall, Steven F. Public Relations for Theatre. 130p. 1983. pap. 8.95 (ISBN 0-88409-104-X). Creative Bk Co.

Marshall, Suzanne R. A Falling Leaf & Other Poetry Activities. LC 82-83777. 92p. 1982. pap. text ed. 10.45 (ISBN 0-918452-41-4). Learning Pubns.

Marshall, Sybil. Experiment in Education. (Illus.). 31.95 (ISBN 0-521-05680-2); pap. 11.95 (ISBN 0-521-09372-4). Cambridge U Pr.

Marshall, T. H. Social Policy in the Twentieth Century. 4th rev. ed. 1975. text ed. 12.00x (ISBN 0-09-105130-4, Hutchinson U Lib); pap. text ed. 9.25x (ISBN 0-09-122621-X, Hutchinson U Lib). Humanities.

Marshall, T. J. & Holmes, J. W. Soil Physics. LC 78-73809. (Illus.). 1980. 80.00 (ISBN 0-521-22622-8); pap. 24.95x (ISBN 0-521-29579-3). Cambridge U Pr.

Marshall, T. M. History of the Western Boundary of the Louisiana Purchase, 1819-1841. LC 73-87411. (American Scene Ser). (Illus.). 1970. Repr. of 1914 ed. lib. bdg. 35.00 (ISBN 0-306-71554-6). Da Capo.

Marshall, Tony M., jt. auth. see Rose, Gordon.

Marshall, Walter H. I've Met Them All. (Illus.). 186p. 1983. 12.95; pap. 8.95. W H Marshall.

--I've Met Them All. LC 82-91157. (Illus.). 186p. (Orig.). 1983. 12.95 (ISBN 0-934318-10-7); pap. 8.95 (ISBN 0-934318-09-3). Falcon Pr MT.

Marshall, William. Perfect End. LC 82-15502. 204p. 1983. 13.50 (ISBN 0-03-047481-7). HR&W.

Marshall, William H., ed. see Byron, George G.

Marshall, Woodville K., ed. The Colthurst Journal. LC 76-56884. (Caribbean Monographs). 1978. lib. bdg. 30.00 (ISBN 0-527-61830-6). Kraus Intl.

Marshall-Ball, Robin. The Sporting Shotgun. (Illus.). 168p. 1982. 23.95 (ISBN 0-913276-38-3). Stone Wall Pr.

Marshaw, Jerry L. Bureaucratic Justice: Administrative Law from an Internal Perspective. LC 82-17506. 240p. 1983. text ed. 25.00x (ISBN 0-300-02808-3). Yale U Pr.

Marshbum, Sandra, jt. auth. see RanDelle, B. J.

Marshner, William H. Annulment or Divorce? 96p. (Orig.). 1978. pap. 2.95 o.p. (ISBN 0-931888-00-X, Chris. Coll. Pr.). Christendom Pubns.

Marsili, Juan, tr. see Taylor, W. Carey.

Marsingill, Leroy. I Have Seen Visions of God. 1978. 6.95 o.p. (ISBN 0-533-03636-4). Vantage.

Marsischky, Trudy. Come Take My Hand. 1983. 6.95 (ISBN 0-533-05548-2). Vantage.

Marsland, Amy L., jt. auth. see Marsland, William D.

Marsland, William D. & Marsland, Amy L. Venezuela Through Its History. LC 75-40919. (Illus.). 277p. 1976. Repr. of 1954 ed. lib. bdg. 18.50x (ISBN 0-8371-8690-0, MAVE). Greenwood.

Marson, Chuck. Great Plains Gardening. (Illus.). 208p. 1983. pap. 6.95 (ISBN 0-941974-01-4). Baranski Pub Corp.

Marson, Chuck & Parker, Roy. In Your Own Backyard: A Gardener's Guide & the Great Plains. (Illus.). 208p. (Orig.). 1983. pap. 6.95 (ISBN 0-941974-01-4). Baranski Pub Corp.

Marson, Eric, et al. Kafka's Trial: The Case Against Josef K. 353p. 1975. text ed. 21.00x o.p. (ISBN 0-7022-0890-6). Humanities.

Marson, Philip. Yankee Voices. 192p. 1981. pap. 7.95x (ISBN 0-87073-190-4). Schenkman.

Marson, Ron. Electricity. (Science with Simple Things Ser.: No. 32). (Illus.). 80p. 1983. pap. text ed. 12.95 (ISBN 0-941008-32-0). Tops Learning.

--Magnetism. (Science with Simple Things Ser.: No. 33). (Illus.). 80p. 1983. pap. 12.95 (ISBN 0-941008-33-9). Tops Learning.

Marsteller, Phyllis, ed. Peterson's Annual Guides to Graduate & Undergraduate Study, 1983, 6 vols. 7200p. (Orig.). 1982. pap. 105.00 set (ISBN 0-87866-190-5); pap. 2.00 ea. Indexes 6 vols. 45 pgs. o.p. (ISBN 0-87866-191-3). Petersons Guides.

--Peterson's Guides to Graduate Study: Biological, Agricultural, & Health Sciences, 1983. 1800p. 1982. pap. 21.95 (ISBN 0-87866-187-5). Petersons Guides.

Marston, A. N. Encyclopedia of Angling. 2nd ed. 1963. 15.00 o.p. (ISBN 0-600-40092-1). Transatlantic.

Marston, Albert R. The Undiet: A Psychological Approach to Permanent Weight Control. (Illus.). 240p. 1983. 13.95 (ISBN 0-13-936815-9); pap. 6.95 (ISBN 0-13-936807-8). P-H.

Marston, Elsa. The Cliffs of Cairo. 1982. pap. 1.75 (ISBN 0-451-11530-9, Sig Vista). NAL.

Marston, Garth & Kelleher, Hugh. Creative Real Estate Financing: A Guide to Buying & Selling Homes in the 1980's. 224p. 1983. 19.95 (ISBN 0-471-86678-4). Ronald Pr.

Marston, Hope I. Machines on the Farm. LC 82-5106. (Illus.). 64p. (gr. 2-5). 1982. PLB 8.95 (ISBN 0-396-08070-7). Dodd.

Marston, John E. Modern Public Relations. (Illus.). 1979. text ed. 23.95 (ISBN 0-07-040619-7, C). McGraw.

--Nature of Public Relations. 1963. text ed. 23.95 (ISBN 0-07-040618-9, C). McGraw.

Marston, Leslie R. From Age to Age a Living Witness. 1960. 10.95 (ISBN 0-685-14209-4). Light & Life.

Marston, R. C., jt. auth. see Herring, R. J.

Marston, V. Paul. The Biblical Family. LC 80-68332. 208p. 1980. pap. 5.95 (ISBN 0-89107-192-X, Crossway Bks). Good News.

Marszal, Barbara, tr. see Lem, Stanislaw.

Martan, Susan, jt. auth. see Eheart, Brenda.

Martech Strategies, Inc. Present & Projected Business Utilization of International Telecommunications. 1981. 75.00 (ISBN 0-686-37964-0). Info Gatekeepers.

Marteena, Constance H. The Lengthening Shadow of a Woman: A Biography of Charlotte Hawkins Brown. 1977. 6.50 o.p. (ISBN 0-682-48597-7). Exposition.

Martelet, Gustave. The Risen Christ & the Eucharistic World. 1977. 3.00 (ISBN 0-8164-0316-3). Seabury.

Martell, et al. Developments in Iron Chelators for Clinical Use. 1981. 60.00 (ISBN 0-444-00650-8, Pub. by Applied Sci England). Elsevier.

Martell, Dwane K. The Enigma of God & Man's Proclivity to Evil. (Institute for Religious Research Library Books). (Illus.). 77p. 1983. 37.75 (ISBN 0-89920-049-4). Am Inst Psych.

Martelli, George. Livingstone's River. LC 71-101881. 1970. 7.50 o.p. (ISBN 0-671-20466-1). S&S.

Martelli, L. & Graham, A. Communities. (Our Nation, Our World Ser.). (gr. 3). 1983. 11.96 (ISBN 0-07-039943-3); supplementary materials avail. McGraw.

--Earth's Regions. (Our Nation, Our World Ser.). (gr. 4). Date not set. text ed. 13.72 (ISBN 0-07-039944-1); tchr's. ed. 25.00 (ISBN 0-07-039954-9); suppl. materials avail. McGraw.

--Going Places. (Our Nation, Our World Ser.). (gr. 2). 1983. pap. text ed. 10.40 (ISBN 0-07-039942-5); tchr's. ed. 22.00 (ISBN 0-07-039952-2); suppl. materials avail. McGraw.

Martelli, Len & Graham, Alma. Meeting People. (Our Nation, Our World Ser.). 48p. (gr. 1). 1983. 9.32 (ISBN 0-07-039941-7, W). Supplementary material avail. McGraw.

--United States. (Our Nation, Our World Ser.). 128p. (gr. 5). 1983. 15.68 (ISBN 0-07-039945-X, W); supp. materials avail. (ISBN 0-07-039955-7). McGraw.

--The World. (Our Nation, Our World Ser.). 480p. (gr. 6). 1983. 15.96 (ISBN 0-07-039946-8, W); supplementary materials 330 avail. (ISBN 0-686-91830-4). McGraw.

Martello, William E. & Butler, Jeffrey E. The History of Sub-Saharan Africa: A Select Bibliography of Books & Reviews, 1945-1975. 1978. lib. bdg. 26.00 (ISBN 0-8161-8002-4, Hall Reference). G K Hall.

Marten, Elizabeth & Crosby, Nina. Creative Writing in Action. (gr. 3-8). 1981. 5.95 (ISBN 0-86653-004-5, GA232). Good Apple.

Marten, Elizabeth, jt. auth. see Crosby, Nina.

Marten, J. L., ed. see Symposium on Theory of Argumentation, Groningen, October 11-13, 1978.

Marten, Michael, jt. auth. see May, John.

Martenhoff, Jim. The Powerboat Handbook. (Stoeger Bks). (Illus.). 1977. pap. 5.95 o.s.i. (ISBN 0-695-80735-8). Follett.

Martens, Anne C. Popular Plays for Teen-Agers. LC 68-13724. (YA) (gr. 7 up). 1968. 12.95 o.p. (ISBN 0-8238-0063-6). Plays.

Martens, Frederick H., tr. see Bachmann, Alberto.

Martens, Frederick K. A Thousand & One Nights of Opera. LC 77-25416. (Music Reprint Ser., 1978). 1978. Repr. of 1926 ed. lib. bdg. 35.00 (ISBN 0-306-77565-4). Da Capo.

Martens, Frederick T., jt. auth. see Dintino, Justin J.

Martens, Hinrich R., jt. auth. see Cadzow, James A.

Martens, Phyllis, ed. see Becker, Nancy & Braun, Jack.

Martens, Rachel. The How-to Book of Repairing, Rewiring & Restoring Lamps & Lighting Fixtures. LC 78-66997. (Illus.). 1979. pap. 5.95 o.p. (ISBN 0-385-14747-3, Dolp). Doubleday.

Martens, Rainer. Sport Competition Anxiety Test. LC 77-150176. (Illus.). 158p. 1977. pap. text ed. 10.00x o.p. (ISBN 0-931250-04-8); pap. 10.00x o.p. (ISBN 0-931250-04-8). Human Kinetics.

Martens, Rainer, ed. Joy & Sadness in Children's Sports. 375p. 1978. pap. text ed. 10.95x (ISBN 0-931250-15-3). Human Kinetics.

Martens, Robert W., jt. auth. see Sisson, James E.

Martens, Tom, jt. auth. see Jeneid, Michael.

Martensson, Bertil. Growing Terror. Murray, Steven T., tr. from Swedish. (Jan Erelius Police Mystery Ser.). Orig. Title: Vaexande Hot. 192p. (Orig.). 1983. pap. cancelled (ISBN 0-940242-02-8). Fjord Pr.

Martensson, Kerstin. Kwik-Sew Method for Easy Sewing. (Illus.). pap. 8.50 (ISBN 0-913212-09-1). Kwik Sew.

--Kwik Sew Method for Sewing Mens Wear. (Illus.). 1977. pap. 8.50 (ISBN 0-913212-06-7). Kwik Sew.

--Professional Pattern Alterations Made Easy. (Illus.). 1976. pap. 8.50 (ISBN 0-913212-05-9). Kwik Sew.

--Sew for Baby the Fun Way. (Illus.). 1974. pap. 8.95 (ISBN 0-913212-00-8). Kwik Sew.

Martensson, Kerstin, illus. Kwik Sew Method for Sewing Lingerie. (Illus.). 1978. pap. 8.95 (ISBN 0-913212-07-5). Kwik Sew.

--Sew for Toddlers. (Illus.). 1979. pap. 8.95 (ISBN 0-913212-08-3). Kwik Sew.

Marter, Jean M., jt. auth. see Ashton, Dore.

Marth, Del & Marth, Martha. Florida Almanac 1982. rev. ed. LC 71-618243. pap. write for info. (ISBN 0-498-02550-0). A S Barnes.

Marth, Del & Marth, Martha J., eds. The Florida Almanac, 1983-84 Edition. 5th ed. LC 71-618243. 444p. 1983. pap. 9.95 (ISBN 0-88289-322-X). Pelican.

Marth, E. H., jt. auth. see Minor, T.

Marth, Martha, jt. auth. see Marth, Del.

Marth, Martha J., jt. ed. see Marth, Del.

Marti, Fritz. Religion & Philosophy: Collected Papers. LC 78-68801. 1979. pap. text ed. 10.25 (ISBN 0-8191-0702-6). U Pr of Amer.

--Unpopular Truths. LC 81-40174. (Illus.). 163p. (Orig.). 1981. lib. bdg. 19.00 (ISBN 0-8191-1671-8); pap. text ed. 9.50 (ISBN 0-8191-1672-6). U Pr of Amer.

Marti, Fritz, tr. see Medicus, Fritz.

Marti, Jose. Inside the Monster: Writings on the United States & American Imperialism. Foner, Philip, ed. Randall, Elinor, tr. from Span. LC 74-21475. 384p. 1975. 16.50 (ISBN 0-85345-359-4, CL3594). Monthly Rev.

--Inside the Monster: Writings on the United States and American Imperialism. Foner, Philip, ed. Randall, Elinor, tr. from Span. LC 74-21475. 1977. pap. 5.95 (ISBN 0-85345-403-5, PB4035). Monthly Rev.

--Jose Marti: Major Poems. Foner, Philip S., ed. Randall, Elinor, tr. 200p. 1982. 22.50x (ISBN 0-8419-0761-7); pap. text ed. 12.50x (ISBN 0-8419-0834-6). Holmes & Meier.

--On Art & Literature: Critical Writings. Foner, Philip S., ed. Randall, Elinor, tr. LC 81-81697. 416p. 1982. 18.00 (ISBN 0-85345-589-9, CL5899); pap. 10.00 (ISBN 0-85345-590-2, PB5902). Monthly Rev.

--On Education: Articles on Educational Theory & Pedagogy, & Writings for Children from the Age of Gold. Foner, Philip, ed. Randall, Elinor, tr. LC 79-2326. 1979. 14.00 (ISBN 0-85345-483-3); pap. 7.50 (ISBN 0-85345-565-1). Monthly Rev.

Marti, Peter. Plastic Analysis of Reinforced Concrete Shear Walls. (IBA Ser.: No. 87). 19p. 1979. pap. text ed. 8.25x (ISBN 3-7643-1065-0). Birkhauser.

Martial & Pliny. Selections. Kennedy, E. C., ed. text ed. 6.50x (ISBN 0-521-05683-7). Cambridge U Pr.

Martignoni, Margaret E., ed. Illustrated Treasury of Children's Literature. (Illus.). 512p. (gr. 5-8). 1955. 13.95 (ISBN 0-448-04101-4, G&D). Putnam Pub Group.

Martigny. Voyage d'Alcimedon. (Utopias in the Enlightenment Ser.). 146p. (Fr.). 1974. Repr. of 1751 ed. lib. bdg. 45.50x o.p. (ISBN 0-8287-0583-6, 031). Clearwater Pub.

Marti-Ibanez, Felix, ed. Adventure of Art. (Illus.). 1970. 25.00 o.p. (ISBN 0-517-50630-0, C N Potter Bks). Crown.

Martimort, A. G., ed. The Church At Prayer: Part One-The Liturgy. 264p. 1969. text ed. 15.00x (ISBN 0-7165-0511-8, Pub. by Irish Academic Pr Ireland). Biblio Dist.

Martin. Future Developments in Telecommunications. 2nd ed. 624p. 1977. text ed. 39.95 (ISBN 0-13-345850-4). P-H.

Martin & Ellis. Cage & Aviary Birds. pap. 16.95 (ISBN 0-686-42725-4, Collins Pub England). Greene.

Martin & Whattam. The Early Days in Photographs: Indians. 16p. 1976. pap. 2.29 o.p. (ISBN 0-918146-04-6). Peninsula WA.

Martin, jt. ed. see Bentz.

Martin, et al. Comprehensive Rehabilitation Nursing. (Illus.). 816p. 1980. text ed. 29.95 (ISBN 0-07-040611-1, HP). McGraw.

Martin, A. E. Infrared Interferometric Spectrometers: A Series of Advances. (Vibrational Spectra & Structure Ser.: Vol. 8). 1980. 64.00 (ISBN 0-444-41907-1). Elsevier.

Martin, A. E., ed. Small-Scale Resource Recovery Systems. LC 81-18944. (Pollution Technology Review: No. 89). (Illus.). 364p. 1982. 42.00 (ISBN 0-8155-0885-9). Noyes.

Martin, Alan & Harbison, Samuel A. Introduction to Radiation Protection. 2nd ed. 1980. 25.00x (ISBN 0-412-16240-7, Pub. by Chapman & Hall England); pap. 13.95x (ISBN 0-412-16230-X). Methuen Inc.

Martin, Alexander C. & Barkely, William D. Seed Identification Manual. 1973. 30.00x (ISBN 0-520-00814-6). U of Cal Pr.

Martin, Alexander C., jt. auth. see Zim, Herbert S.

Martin, Alexander C., et al. American Wildlife & Plants: A Guide to Wildlife Food Habits. 1951. pap. 6.50 (ISBN 0-486-20793-5). Dover.

Martin, Alexander H., jt. auth. see Francis, Carl C.

Martin, Alfred. Isaiah: The Salvation of Jehovah. (Everyman's Bible Commentary Ser.). 1967. pap. 4.50 (ISBN 0-8024-2023-0). Moody.

Martin, Alfred & Martin, Dorothy. The Holy Spirit. (Personal Bible Study Guide). 64p. 1974. pap. 2.95 o.p. (ISBN 0-8024-1104-5). Moody.

Martin, Alfred & Martin, John A. Isaiah: The Glory of the Messiah. (Orig.). 1983. pap. 7.95 (ISBN 0-8024-0168-6). Moody.

Martin, Alfred G. Hand-Taming Wild Birds at the Feeder. LC 63-13599. pap. 2.25 (ISBN 0-87027-145-8). Cumberland Pr.

Martin, Allan W. Henry Parkes: A Biography. 504p. 1980. 45.00x (ISBN 0-522-84174-0, Pub. by Melbourne Univ Pr Australia). Intl Schol Bk Serv.

Martin, Alvin, ed. The Means of World Evangelization: Missiological Education at Fuller School of World Mission. LC 74-9185. 544p. (Orig.). 1974. pap. 9.95 o.p. (ISBN 0-87808-143-7). William Carey Lib.

Martin, Ann. Bummer Summer. LC 82-48755. (Illus.). 160p. (gr. 5-9). 1983. 10.95 (ISBN 0-8234-0483-8). Holiday.

Martin, Anneliese, tr. see Barthel, Thomas.

Martin, Augustine. Anglo-Irish Literature. (Aspects of Ireland Ser.: Vol. 7). (Illus.). 71p. 1981. pap. 6.95 (ISBN 0-906404-07-X, Pub. by Dept Foreign Ireland). Irish Bks Media.

Martin, B. G. Muslim Brotherhoods in 19th Century Africa. LC 75-35451. (African Studies Ser.: No. 18). 1977. 39.50 (ISBN 0-521-21062-3). Cambridge U Pr.

Martin, Barclay. Abnormal Psychology. 1973. pap. 9.95x (ISBN 0-673-05014-9). Scott F.

--Anxiety & Neurotic Disorders. LC 76-151033. (Approaches to Behavior Pathology Ser). 1971. pap. text ed. 16.50 (ISBN 0-471-57353-1). Wiley.

Martin, Bernard & Chien-Tung, Shui. Makers of China: Confucius to Mao. LC 72-3114. 238p. 1972. 9.50 (ISBN 0-470-57359-7, Pub. by Wiley). Krieger.

Martin, Bernard, jt. auth. see Silver, Daniel J.

Martin, Bernard, ed. Movements & Issues in American Judaism: An Analysis & Sourcebook of Developments Since 1945. LC 77-87971. 1978. lib. bdg. 29.95 (ISBN 0-313-20044-0, MCJ/). Greenwood.

--A Shestov Anthology. LC 74-81453. xvii, 328p. 1970. 17.00x (ISBN 0-8214-0070-3, 82-80760). Ohio U Pr.

Martin, Bernard, tr. see Bergelson, David.

Martin, Bernard, tr. see Shestov, Lev.

Martin, Betty. The Principal's Handbook on the School Library Media Center. Carson, Ben, ed. 1978. pap. 8.95 o.s.i. (ISBN 0-915794-22-5, 6553). Gaylord Prof Pubns.

--The School Library Media Specialist's Survival Handbook. 1983. price not set (ISBN 0-208-01997-9, Lib Prof Pubns); pap. price not set (ISBN 0-208-01998-7). Shoe String.

Martin, Betty B. & Quilling, Joan. Positive Approaches to Classroom Discipline. 1981. 4.00 (ISBN 0-686-38742-2). Home Econ Educ.

Martin, Bill, commentary by. Bill Martin: Paintings Nineteen Sixty-Nine to Nineteen Seventy-Nine. (Illus.). 96p. 16.95 o.p. (ISBN 0-517-53895-4, Harmony); pap. 9.95 o.p. (ISBN 0-517-53896-2, Harmony). Crown.

Martin, Bill, Jr. Bill Martin Freedom Book Series, 10 bks. Incl. Adam's Balm. Foreman, Michael, illus (ISBN 0-8372-2052-1); America, I Know You. Rand, Ted, illus (ISBN 0-8372-2048-3); Freedom's Apple Tree. Rambola, John, illus (ISBN 0-8372-2047-5); Gentle, Gentle Thursday. Maitin, Samuel, illus (ISBN 0-8372-2055-6); I Am Freedom's Child. Shimin, Symeon, illus (ISBN 0-8372-2046-7); I Reach Out to the Morning. Markowitz, Henry, illus (ISBN 0-8372-2054-8); It's America for Me. Glanzman, Lou, illus (ISBN 0-8372-2049-1); Once There Were Bluebirds. Martin, Bernard, illus. o.p. (ISBN 0-8372-0652-9); Poor Old Uncle Sam. Murdocca, Sal, illus (ISBN 0-8372-2051-3); Spoiled Tomatoes. Ells, Jay, illus (ISBN 0-8372-2050-5). (gr. 5-12). pap. 12.60 pkg. of 6 copies o.p. (ISBN 0-685-29088-3); tchrs' guide 4.68 o.p. (ISBN 0-8372-0708-8). 10 records 90.90 o.p. (ISBN 0-8372-0230-2). complete lab: 60 s-c, 50 activity cards & teacherhs guide 211.95 set o.p. (ISBN 0-8372-2449-7); bks., guide, activitycards, & **cassettes 211.95 set o.p. (ISBN 0-8372-2044-0); book pack, 6 copies of one title avail. o.p.; activity cards 22.86 o.p. (ISBN 0-8372-1949-3). Bowmar-Noble.**

Martin, Billy & Golenbock, Peter. Number One. 1980. 11.95 o.s.i. (ISBN 0-440-06416-3). Delacorte.

Martin, Bob. Hiking Trails of Central Colorado. (Illus.). 1983. pap. price not set (ISBN 0-87108-635-2). Pruett.

Martin, Brian V., jt. auth. see Wohl, Martin.

Martin, Brian W. John Henry Newman: His Life & Work. (Illus.). 250p. 1982. 19.95 (ISBN 0-19-520387-9). Oxford U Pr.

Martin, Briton, Jr. New India, 1885: British Official Policy & the Emergence of the Indian National Congress. LC 70-98140. (Center for South & Southeast Asia Studies, UC Berkeley). 1969. 35.00x (ISBN 0-520-01580-0). U of Cal Pr.

Martin, Bruce K. Philip Larkin. (English Author Ser.). 1978. 14.95 (ISBN 0-8057-6705-3, Twayne). G K Hall.

Martin, C. D., jt. auth. see Heller, Rachelle.

Martin, C. Leslie. Architectural Graphics. 2nd ed. (Illus.). 1970. text ed. 26.95x (ISBN 0-02-376570-4). Macmillan.

--Design Graphics. 2nd ed. (Illus.). 1968. text ed. 28.95x (ISBN 0-02-376640-9). Macmillan.

Martin, Calvin. Keepers of the Game. 1978. 10.95 (ISBN 0-686-95787-3). Jefferson Natl.

--Keepers of the Game: Indian-Animal Relationship & the Fur Trade. LC 77-78381. 1978. 12.95x (ISBN 0-520-03519-4). U of Cal Pr.

--Keepers of the Game: Indian-Animal Relationships & the Fur Trade. (Illus.). 238p. 1982. pap. 6.95 (ISBN 0-520-04637-4). U of Cal Pr.

Martin, Carolyn A. Games, Contest & Relays. 285p. 1981. pap. text ed. 8.95x (ISBN 0-89641-094-3). American Pr.

Martin, Carter W., ed. see O'Connor, Flannery.

Martin, Cecil P. Psychology, Evolution & Sex: A Study of the Mechanisms of Evolution Based on a Comprehensive View of Biology. 176p. 1956. photocopy ed. spiral 15.75x (ISBN 0-398-01224-5). C C Thomas.

Martin, Charles. Sierra Whitewater. LC 74-48882. (Illus.). 192p. 1982. pap. 11.95 (ISBN 0-9609984-0-3). C F Martin.

Martin, Charles E. Dunkel Takes a Walk. (Illus.). 24p. (gr. k-3). 1983. 10.00 (ISBN 0-688-01815-7); PLB 9.55 (ISBN 0-688-01816-5). Greenwillow.

Martin, Christopher. The Wonders of Prehistoric Man. (The Wonders of Science Library). (Illus.). (gr. 5-9). 1964. PLB 4.49 o.p. (ISBN 0-399-60681-5). Putnam Pub Group.

Martin, Chryssee B., jt. auth. see Martin, Esmond.

Martin, Chryssee B., jt. auth. see Martin, Esmond B.

Martin, Claude R., Jr., jt. ed. see Leigh, James H.

Martin, Cliff & Scott, Frank, eds. Rhythm & Blues Records: An Encyclopedic Discography 1943 to 1975. (Ethnic Music Ser.: Vol. 1). pap. write for info (ISBN 0-936518-05-7). Nighthawk Pr.

Martin, Clyde I., jt. auth. see Espy, Rosalie.

Martin, Clyde I., jt. auth. see Rickard, J. A.

Martin, Constance R. Textbook of Endocrine Physiology. (Illus.). 1976. 24.95x (ISBN 0-19-502295-5). Oxford U Pr.

Martin, Cort. Bolt, No. 1: First Blood. (Orig.). 1981. pap. 2.25 (ISBN 0-89083-767-8). Zebra.

--Bolt, No. 2: Dead Man's Bounty. 1981. pap. 2.25 (ISBN 0-89083-783-X). Zebra.

--Bolt, No. 3: Showdown at Black Mesa. (Orig.). 1981. pap. 2.25 (ISBN 0-89083-812-7). Zebra.

--Bolt, No. 4: The Guns of Taos. (Orig.). 1981. pap. 2.25 (ISBN 0-89083-873-9). Zebra.

--Bolt, No. 5: Shootout at Sante Fe. (Orig.). 1982. pap. 2.25 (ISBN 0-89083-943-3). Zebra.

--Bolt, No. 6: The Tombstone Honeypot. 1982. pap. 2.25 (ISBN 0-8217-1009-5). Zebra.

--Bolt, No. 8: Hard in the Saddle. 1982. pap. 2.25 (ISBN 0-8217-1095-8). Zebra.

--Bolt, No. 9: Badman's Bordello. 1983. pap. 2.25 (ISBN 0-8217-1127-X). Zebra.

Martin, Cy & Martin, Jeannie. Gold! & Where They Found It: A Guide to Ghost Towns & Mining Camp Sites in the West, Southwest, Northwest, Tennessee, British Columbia & the Yukon. 2nd, rev. ed. Crump, Spencer, ed. LC 79-67767. (Illus.). 160p. 1980. 9.95 (ISBN 0-87046-053-6, Pub. by Trans-Anglo). Interurban.

Martin, D., tr. see Oberman, H. A.

Martin, D. Roger. Classic Summer. 12p. 1982. pap. 1.00 (ISBN 0-686-37935-7). Samisdat.

Martin, D. W., tr. see Soloukhin, Vladimir.

Martin, Daniel W. Three Mile Island: Prologue or Epilogue? 272p. 1980. prof ref 20.00x (ISBN 0-88410-629-2). Ballinger Pub.

Martin, Darwin J. How to Raise & Train a Schipperke. (Orig.). pap. 2.95 (ISBN 0-87666-381-1, DS1114). TFH Pubns.

Martin, David. Breaking the Image: The Sociology of Christian Theory & Practice. 1980. 26.00 (ISBN 0-312-09522-8). St Martin.

--Teaching English. pap. 1.60 (ISBN 0-686-32333-5). Rod & Staff.

Martin, David & Jacobus, Lee. Humanities Through the Arts. 2nd ed. (Illus.). 24.50 (ISBN 0-07-040614-6, C); pap. text ed. 17.50 (ISBN 0-07-040613-8). McGraw.

Martin, David & Johnson, Phyllis. The Struggle for Zimbabwe. LC 81-84556. (Orig.). 1982. pap. 8.95 (ISBN 0-85345-599-6, PB5996). Monthly Rev.

--Struggle for Zimbabwe. 378p. 1981. 25.00 (ISBN 0-571-11066-5). Faber & Faber.

Martin, David, jt. auth. see Bernhardt, Roger.

Martin, David, et al, eds. Sociology & Theology. 170p. 1980. 26.00x (ISBN 0-312-74007-7). St Martin.

Martin, David E., et al. The High Jump Book. (Illus.). 158p. Date not set. pap. 8.95 (ISBN 0-911521-09-7). Tafnews.

Martin, David L. Running City Hall: Municipal Administration in America. LC 81-14646. (Illus.). 225p. 1982. text ed. 17.75 (ISBN 0-8173-0154-2); pap. text ed. 7.95 (ISBN 0-8173-0155-0). U of Ala Pr.

Martin, David L., jt. auth. see Morlan, Robert L.

Martin, Del. Battered Wives. rev. ed. LC 75-24031. 288p. 1981. pap. 10.00 (ISBN 0-912078-70-7). Volcano Pr.

Martin, Dennis, jt. auth. see Schultz, Don E.

Martin, Derald. Professional Industrial Photography. (Illus.). 176p. 1980. 19.95 (ISBN 0-8174-4008-9, Amphoto). Watson-Guptill.

Martin, Diane. Child Growth & Development. O'Neill, Martha, ed. 32p. 1982. tchr's manual 4.44 (ISBN 0-07-040698-7). McGraw.

Martin, Dianne, jt. auth. see Heller, Rachelle.

Martin, Dolores M., ed. Handbook of Latin American Studies, Vol. 43: Social Sciences. 969p. 1983. text ed. 65.00x (ISBN 0-292-73022-5). U of Tex Pr.

Martin, Don. The Completely Mad Don Martin. 192p. 1974. pap. 4.95 o.s.i. (ISBN 0-446-87989-4). Warner Bks.

--Don Martin Bounces Back. (Illus., Orig.). pap. 0.95 o.p. (ISBN 0-451-06294-9, Q6294, Sig). NAL.

--Don Martin Cooks up More Tales. (Illus.). 192p. 1976. pap. 1.95 (ISBN 0-446-30445-X). Warner Bks.

--Don Martin Forges Ahead. (Illus., Orig.). 1977. pap. 1.95 (ISBN 0-446-30447-6). Warner Bks.

--Mad's Don Martin Cooks up More Tales. (Orig.). 1969. pap. 0.95 o.p. (ISBN 0-451-06295-7, Q6295, Sig). NAL.

--Mad's Don Martin Cooks up More Tales, No. 5. 192p. 1982. pap. 1.95 o.p. (ISBN 0-446-30445-X). Warner Bks.

--Mad's Maddest Artist Don Martin Bounces Back. (Illus.). 192p. 1976. pap. 1.95 (ISBN 0-446-30453-0). Warner Bks.

Martin, Donald L. & Schwartz, Warren C., eds. Deregulating American Industry: Legal & Economic Problems. LC 77-5273. (Illus.). 144p. 1977. 18.95 (ISBN 0-669-01603-9). Lexington Bks.

Martin, Dorothy. Chapter Closed for Peggy. (Peggy Ser.). (gr. 8 up). 1966. pap. 2.95 (ISBN 0-8024-7608-2). Moody.

--Light at the Top of the Stairs. 256p. 1974. pap. 3.95 (ISBN 0-8024-4748-1). Moody.

--Mystery of the Jade Earring. LC 80-10195. (Vickie Ser.). (Orig.). 1980. pap. 2.95 (ISBN 0-8024-5702-9). Moody.

--Mystery of the Missing Bracelets. LC 79-25799. (Vickie Ser.). (gr. 4-7). 1980. pap. 2.95 (ISBN 0-8024-5701-0). Moody.

--Mystery of the Missing Dog. LC 82-6276. (Vickie Adventure Ser.). 144p. 1982. pap. 2.95 (ISBN 0-8024-5704-5). Moody.

--Mystery on the Fourteenth Floor. LC 79-24718. (Vickie Ser.). 128p. (Orig.). (gr. 6-9). 1980. pap. 2.95 (ISBN 0-8024-5700-2). Moody.

--No Place to Hide. 1975. pap. 3.95 (ISBN 0-8024-5939-0). Moody.

--The Other Side of Yesterday. LC 77-18069. 1978. pap. 3.95 (ISBN 0-8024-6095-X). Moody.

--Prayer Answered for Peggy. LC 75-45474. (Peggy Ser.). 128p. 1976. pap. 2.95 (ISBN 0-8024-7610-4). Moody.

--The Story of Billy Carrell. 160p. (Orig.). 1983. pap. 3.95 (ISBN 0-8024-0519-3). Moody.

Martin, Dorothy, jt. auth. see Martin, Alfred.

Martin, Dorothy, jt. auth. see Smith, G. Barnett.

Martin, Dwight. The Triad Imperative. LC 80-67860. 288p. 1980. 10.95 o.p. (ISBN 0-312-92829-7). Congdon & Weed.

Martin, Edward C., jt. auth. see Rozwenc, Edwin C.

Martin, Edwin. Southeast Asia & China: The End of Containment. LC 76-53510. 1977. lib. bdg. 18.00 (ISBN 0-89158-219-3). Westview.

Martin, Edwin M. Conference Diplomacy-A Case Study: The World Food Conference, Rome, 1974. LC 79-91018. 58p. 1979. 3.00 (ISBN 0-934742-01-4, Inst Study Diplomacy). Geo U Sch For Serv.

Martin, Edwin M, jt. auth. see Atlantic Council Working Group on the U.S. & the Developing Countries.

Martin, Eleanor J. Rene Marques. (World Authors Ser.). 1979. lib. bdg. 15.95 (ISBN 0-8057-6357-0, Twayne). G K Hall.

Martin, Elizabeth. The Over Thirty, Six Week, All Natural Health & Beauty Plan. 1982. 12.95 (ISBN 0-517-54439-3, C N Potter); pap. 8.95 (ISBN 0-517-54630-2, C N Potter Bks). Crown.

Martin, Ernest. Histoire Des Monstres Depuis L'antiquite Jusqu'a Nos Jours. Repr. of 1880 ed. 116.00 o.p. (ISBN 0-8287-0584-4). Clearwater Pub.

Martin, Ernest T. The Warlock. Kirkland, David, ed. (Illus.). 330p. (Orig.). 1982. 9.50 (ISBN 0-686-38126-2); pap. 3.95 (ISBN 0-910759-00-6). Mars Pubns.

Martin, Esmond & Martin, Chryssee B. Run Rhino Run. 1983. 19.95 (ISBN 0-686-38875-5, Pub. by Chatto & Windus). Merrimack Bk Serv.

Martin, Esmond B. & Martin, Chryssee B. Run Rhino Run. (Illus.). 136p. 1983. 19.95 (ISBN 0-7011-2632-9, Pub. by Chatto & Windus). Merrimack Bk Serv.

Martin, F., jt. auth. see Barrot, J.

Martin, F. David & Jacobus, Lee A. The Humanities Through the Arts. 3rd ed. (Illus.). 520p. 1983. pap. text ed. 19.95 (ISBN 0-07-040639-1, C). McGraw.

Martin, F. L., jt. auth. see Haltiner, G. J.

Martin, Fay Carrozza see Hauser-Cram, Penny & Carrozza-Martin, Fay.

Martin, Fenton, jt. auth. see Goehlert, Robert.

Martin, Florence. Observing National Holidays & Church Festivals: A Weekday Church School Unit in Christian Citizenship Series for Grades Three & Four. LC 76-174077. 1971. Repr. of 1940 ed. 42.00x (ISBN 0-8103-3804-1). Gale.

Martin, Francis, tr. see Bavarel, Michel.

Martin, Frederick. Clinical Audiometry & Masking. LC 74-183115. (Studies in Communicative Disorders Ser). 1972. pap. 3.25 (ISBN 0-672-61282-8). Bobbs.

Martin, Frederick N. Introduction to Audiology. 2nd ed. (Illus.). 480p. 1981. text ed. 26.95 (ISBN 0-13-478131-7). P-H.

Martin, Frederick N., ed. Medical Audiology: Disorders of Hearing. (Illus.). 512p. 1981. text ed. 39.95 (ISBN 0-13-572677-8). P-H.

Martin, G. F., ed. see Kuypers, H. G.

Martin, G. H. & Macintyre, Sylvia, eds. A Bibliography of British & Irish Municipal History, Vol. 2. 1980. text ed. 20.00x o.p. (ISBN 0-391-01198-7, Leicester). Humanities.

Martin, G. W. Revision of the North Central Tremellales. 1969. Repr. of 1952 ed. 16.00 (ISBN 3-7682-0636-X). Lubrecht & Cramer.

Martin, Gary & Pear, Joseph. Behavior Modification: What Is It & How to Do It. LC 77-10849. (Illus.). 1978. pap. text ed. 19.95 (ISBN 0-13-066787-0). P-H.

Martin, Gene & Martin, Mary. Trail Dust. (Illus.). 56p. (Orig.). 1972. pap. 1.95x (ISBN 0-87315-047-3). Golden Bell.

Martin, Genevieve A. & Maiori, Rachel. Living English for Italian-Speaking People. 1957. 15.95, with 4 lp records conversation manual & dictionary (ISBN 0-517-50200-3). Crown.

Martin, Geoffrey J., jt. auth. see James, Preston E.

Martin, George. The Ballet Guide. 1982. pap. 13.95 (ISBN 0-396-08098-7). Dodd.

--Reading Scripture As the Word of God. (Orig.). 1975. pap. 3.95 o.p. (ISBN 0-89283-023-9). Servant.

--Red Shirt & the Cross of Savoy: The Story of Italy's Risorgimento, 1748-1871. LC 68-8279. (Illus.). 1969. 15.00 o.p. (ISBN 0-396-05908-2). Dodd.

Martin, George, tr. see Calvino, Italo.

Martin, George A. The Family Horse: Its Stabling, Care, and Feeding. LC 77-3503. (Illus.). 1977. Repr. of 1895 ed. 15.00 (ISBN 0-88427-020-3). North River.

--Fences, Gates & Bridges: A Practical Manual. LC 74-19255. (Illus.). 196p. 1974. 7.95 o.p. (ISBN 0-8289-0240-2); pap. 6.95 (ISBN 0-8289-0458-8). Greene.

Martin, George H. Kinematics & Dynamics of Machines. LC 69-12261. (Mechanical Engineering Ser). (Illus.). 1969. text ed. 24.95 o.p. (ISBN 0-07-040637-5, C); solutions manual 5.95 o.p. (ISBN 0-07-040638-3). McGraw.

--Kinematics & Dynamics of Machines. 2nd ed. (Illus.). 544p. 1982. 33.50x (ISBN 0-07-040657-X); instr's manual 11.00 (ISBN 0-07-040658-8). McGraw.

Martin, George R. Dying of the Light. 1977. 10.95 o.p. (ISBN 0-671-22861-7). S&S.

--Night Flyers. Bd. with True Names. Vinge, Vernor. (Binary Star: No. 5). (Orig.). 1981. pap. 2.50 o.s.i. (ISBN 0-440-10757-1). Dell.

Martin, George R., ed. New Voices: Fourth Annual Volume: the John W. Campbell Award Nominees. (Orig.). 1981. pap. 2.25 o.p. (ISBN 0-425-05033-5). Berkley Pub.

Martin, George R., jt. ed. see Asimov, Isaac.

Martin, George V. Are There a Beginning & an End to Man's Existence? 1983. 8.95 (ISBN 0-533-05562-8). Vantage.

Martin, George W. The Opera Companion. LC 82-7438. 1979. pap. 13.95 (ISBN 0-396-08097-9). Dodd.

Martin, Gerald D. & Clay, William C., Jr. How to Win Maximum Awards for Lost Earnings: A Guide to Estimating Damages Fairly & Proving Them in Court. 1980. 89.50 (ISBN 0-13-440669-9). Exec Reports.

Martin, Gordon P., jt. auth. see Berry, Dorothea M.

Martin, Grace B. Oregon Schoolma'am: The Depression Years, Bk.2. (Illus.). 200p. pap. 7.95 (ISBN 0-934784-26-4). Calapooia Pubns.

Martin, Graham D., tr. see Labe, Louise.

Martin, Gregory. Canaletto. (Illus.). 1971. 12.00 (ISBN 0-912728-00-0). Newbury Bks.

Martin, Hansborg. Kein Schnaps Fur Tamara. (Easy Readers, B). (Illus.). 1975. pap. text ed. 3.95 (ISBN 0-88436-282-5). EMC.

Martin, Hardie St. see Donoso, Jose.

Martin, Harold C. Introduction to Matrix Methods of Structural Analysis. 1966. text ed. 35.50 o.p. (ISBN 0-07-040633-2, C). McGraw.

Martin, Harold C. & Carey, G. F. Introduction to Finite Element Analysis. text ed. 33.95 o.p. (ISBN 0-07-040641-3, C); solutions to problems 18.00 o.p. (ISBN 0-07-009830-1). McGraw.

Martin, Harold P., ed. The Abused Child: A Multidisciplinary Approach to Developmental Issues & Treatment. LC 76-11766. 336p. 1976. prof ref 19.50x (ISBN 0-88410-218-1); pap. 12.95 (ISBN 0-88410-394-3). Ballinger Pub.

Martin, Helen P., jt. auth. see Sohner, Charles P.

Martin, Helmut. Cult & Canon: The Origins & Development of State Maoism. Vale, Michael, tr. from Ger. LC 82-16811. Orig. Title: China Ohne Maoismus? 250p. 1982. 37.50 (ISBN 0-87332-150-2). M E Sharpe.

Martin, Henri. La Russie et l'Europe. (Nineteenth Century Russia Ser.). 439p. (Fr.). 1974. Repr. of 1866 ed. lib. bdg. 110.50 o.p. (ISBN 0-8287-0586-0, R77). Clearwater Pub.

Martin, Hubert & Woodcock, David. The Scientific Principles of Crop Protection. 480p. 1983. text ed. 72.50 (ISBN 0-7131-3467-4). E Arnold.

Martin, Hubert, Jr. Alcaeus. (World Authors Ser.). lib. bdg. 14.95 (ISBN 0-8057-2016-2, Twayne). G K Hall.

Martin, Hugh. Jonah. (Geneva Series Commentaries). 1978. 11.95 (ISBN 0-85151-115-5). Banner of Truth.

Martin, Hugh, ed. see Bernard de Clairvaux, St.

Martin, I. & Levey, A. B. Genesis of the Classical Conditioned Response. 164p. 1969. 27.00 (ISBN 0-08-013360-6). Pergamon.

Martin, Ian K. Rekill. LC 77-7646. 1977. 8.95 o.p. (ISBN 0-399-11986-8). Putnam Pub Group.

Martin, Inge, tr. see Groddeck, Marie.

Martin, Irene & Venables, Peter H., eds. Techniques in Psychophysiology. LC 79-42925. 1980. 69.95 (ISBN 0-471-27637-5, Pub. by Wiley-Interscience). Wiley.

Martin, J. Computer Data-Base Organization. 2nd ed. 1977. 36.00 (ISBN 0-13-165423-3). P-H.

--Design of Real Time Computer Systems. 1967. ref. ed. 32.95 (ISBN 0-13-201400-9). P-H.

--End User's Guide to Data Base. 1981. 24.95 (ISBN 0-13-277129-2). P-H.

--Telecommunications & the Computer. 2nd ed. 1976. 39.95 (ISBN 0-13-902494-8). P-H.

Martin, J. B. Plasticity: Fundamentals Concepts & General Results. 1975. 45.00x o.p. (ISBN 0-262-13114-5). MIT Pr.

Martin, J. D., et al. Personal Financial Management. 560p. 1982. 22.95 (ISBN 0-07-040615-4); instr's manual 12.50 (ISBN 0-07-040616-2); study guide 8.95 (ISBN 0-07-040620-0). McGraw.

Martin, J. I. The Migrant Presence. LC 78-57602. (Studies in Society). 1978. text ed. 22.50x (ISBN 0-86861-272-3); pap. text ed. 9.95x (ISBN 0-86861-280-4). Allen Unwin.

Martin, J. P., ed. Violence & the Family. LC 77-21846. 1978. 54.95 (ISBN 0-471-99576-2, Pub. by Wiley-Interscience). Wiley.

Martin, J. R., jt. auth. see Wallace, Hugh A.

Martin, J. R., jt. ed. see Halliday, N. A.

Martin, J. S. E. M. Forster, the Endless Journey. LC 76-4755. (British Authors Ser). 1976. 27.95 (ISBN 0-521-21272-3); pap. 8.95 (ISBN 0-521-29082-1). Cambridge U Pr.

Martin, J. T. & Juniper, B. E. Cuticles of Plants. 1970. 29.95 o.p. (ISBN 0-312-18025-X). St Martin.

Martin, J. W. Micromechanisms in Particle-Hardened Alloys. LC 78-70411. (Cambridge Solid State Science Ser.). (Illus.). 1980. 59.50 (ISBN 0-521-22623-6); pap. 17.95 (ISBN 0-521-29580-7). Cambridge U Pr.

Martin, J. W. & Doherty, R. D. Stability of Microstructure in Metallic Systems. LC 75-38179. (Cambridge Solid State Science Ser.). (Illus.). 298p. 1980. pap. 18.95x (ISBN 0-521-29883-0). Cambridge U Pr.

Martin, James. Application Development Without Programmers. 345p. 1982. 32.50 (ISBN 0-686-98081-6). Telecom Lib.

--Communications Satellite Systems. 398p. 1978. 39.50 (ISBN 0-686-98090-5). Telecom Lib.

--Computer Networks & Distributed Processing. 562p. 1981. 34.00 (ISBN 0-686-98085-9). Telecom Lib.

--Computer Networks & Distributed Processing: Software, Techniques, & Architecture. (Illus.). 544p. 1981. text ed. 37.95 (ISBN 0-13-165258-3). P-H.

--Design & Strategy for Distributed Data Processing. (Illus.). 672p. 1981. text ed. 39.95 (ISBN 0-13-201657-5). P-H.

--Design of Man-Computer Dialogues. (Illus.). 496p. 1973. ref. ed. 35.00 (ISBN 0-13-201251-0). P-H.

--Design Strategy for Distributed Processing. 624p. 1981. 37.50 (ISBN 0-686-98083-2). Telecom Lib.

--Future Developments in Telecommunications. 668p. 1977. 37.00 (ISBN 0-686-98074-3). Telecom Lib.

--Introduction to Teleprocessing. 267p. 1972. 22.95 (ISBN 0-686-98120-0). Telecom Lib.

--Managing the Data Base Environment. (Illus.). 720p. 1983. text ed. 35.00 (ISBN 0-13-550582-8). P-H.

--Systems Analysis for Data Transmission. (Automatic Computation Ser). 1972. ref. ed. 45.95 (ISBN 0-13-881300-0). P-H.

--Systems Analysis for Data Transmission. 910p. 1972. 39.95 (ISBN 0-686-98100-6). Telecom Lib.

--Telecommunications & the Computer. 670p. 1976. 37.50 (ISBN 0-686-98073-5). Telecom Lib.

--Telematic Society. 244p. 1981. 12.95 (ISBN 0-686-98077-8). Telecom Lib.

Martin, James & Norman, Adrian. The Computerized Society. 560p. 1970. 18.95 (ISBN 0-686-98121-9). Telecom Lib.

Martin, James A. Conflict of Laws: Cases & Materials. 1978. text ed. 24.50 (ISBN 0-316-54851-0); 1982 suppl. 7.95. Little.

--Conflict of Laws, 1982 Supplement. 1982. pap. text ed. cancelled (ISBN 0-316-54849-9). Little.

--Perspectives on Conflict of Laws: Choice of Law. 1980. pap. text ed. 7.95 (ISBN 0-316-54853-7). Little.

Martin, James A., jt. auth. see Epstein, David G.

Martin, James A., jt. auth. see Landers, Jonathan M.

Martin, James A., jt. auth. see Landers, Jonathon.

Martin, James C., jt. auth. see Martin, Robert S.

Martin, James D., tr. see Noth, Martin.

Martin, James G. & Franklin, Clyde W. Minority Group Relations. LC 72-97539. 1973. text ed. 16.95 (ISBN 0-675-08953-0). Merrill.

Martin, James J. American Liberalism & World Politics, 1931-1941, 2 vol. set. 1963. 22.50 (ISBN 0-8159-5005-5). Devin.

Martin, James J., ed. see Stirner, Max.

Martin, James K. In the Course of Human Events: An Interpretive Exploration of the American Revolution. LC 79-50878. (Illus.). 1979. text ed. 19.95x (ISBN 0-88295-794-5); pap. text ed. 12.95x (ISBN 0-88295-795-3). Harlan Davidson.

Martin, James K. & Lender, Mark E. A Respectable Army: The Military Origins of the Republic, 1763-1789. (American History Ser.). (Illus.). 256p. (Orig.). 1982. pap. 8.95x (ISBN 0-88295-812-7). Harlan Davidson.

Martin, James K., jt. auth. see Lender, Mark E.

Martin, James T. Programming Real-Time Computer Systems. (Illus.). 1965. ref. ed. 27.95 (ISBN 0-13-730507-9). P-H.

Martin, James T. & Norman, Adrian R. Computerized Society. (Automatic Computation Ser). 1970. ref. ed. 20.95 (ISBN 0-13-165977-4). P-H.

Martin, James W. & Martin, Thomas J. Surface Mining Equipment. LC 82-81951. (Illus.). 450p. 1982. 77.00 (ISBN 0-9609060-0-2). Martin Consult.

Martin, Jay. Always Merry & Bright: The Life of Henry Miller. 1980. pap. 10.95 o.p. (ISBN 0-14-005548-7). Penguin.

--Winter Dreams: An American in Moscow. 1979. 10.95 o.s.i. (ISBN 0-395-27589-X). HM.

Martin, Jay, ed. A Singer in the Dawn: Reinterpretations of Paul Laurence Dunbar. LC 74-104. 350p. 1974. 10.95 o.p. (ISBN 0-396-06944-4). Dodd.

Martin, Jean-Hubert. Man Ray: Photographs. (Illus.). 266p. 1982. 35.00 (ISBN 0-500-54079-9). Thames Hudson.

Martin, Jeannie, jt. auth. see Martin, Cy.

Martin, Jeff. Thou Shalt Meditate. 40p. 1980. pap. 1.50 (ISBN 0-686-83199-3). Harrison Hse.

Martin, Jerry, jt. auth. see Lutzker, John.

Martin, Joan, ed. see Golos, Natalie & Golbitz, Frances G.

Martin, Joanne, jt. auth. see McGrath, Joseph E.

Martin, Joe. My First Fifty Years in Politics. LC 74-28530. (Illus.). 261p. 1975. Repr. of 1960 ed. lib. bdg. 16.50x o.p. (ISBN 0-8371-7919-X, MAMF). Greenwood.

Martin, John. Blackmail Eighty-Seven. LC 81-80164. 226p. 1983. pap. text ed. 7.95 (ISBN 0-86666-023-2). GWP.

--Construction Materials. 1981. text ed. 20.95 (ISBN 0-8359-0933-6); instrs.' manual free (ISBN 0-8359-0934-4). Reston.

Martin, John, jt. auth. see Copeland, Peter.

Martin, John A., jt. auth. see Martin, Alfred.

Martin, John D., et al. Basic Financial Management. 2nd ed. (Illus.). 704p. 1982. text ed. 25.95 (ISBN 0-13-060525-5); study guide 9.95 (ISBN 0-13-060608-1). P-H.

--Cases in Basic Financial Management. 1979. pap. text ed. 13.95 (ISBN 0-13-117556-4). P-H.

Martin, John E. Atlas of Mammography: Histologic & Mammographic Correlations. (Illus.). 353p. 1982. lib. bdg. 69.00 (ISBN 0-683-05601-8). Williams & Wilkins.

Martin, John F. Civil Rights & the Crisis of Liberalism: The Democratic Party, 1945-1976. 1979. lib. bdg. 28.50 (ISBN 0-89158-454-4). Westview.

Martin, John H., jt. auth. see Leonard, Warren H.

Martin, John H., et al. Principles of Field Crop Production. 3rd ed. (Illus.). 1056p. 1976. text ed. 31.95x (ISBN 0-02-376720-0). Macmillan.

Martin, Joseph. A Guide to Marxism. LC 79-20376. 1980. 17.95 (ISBN 0-312-35297-2). St Martin.

Martin, Joseph B., et al, eds. Neurosecretion & Brain Peptides: Implications for Brain Function & Neurological Disease. (Advances in Biochemical Psychopharmacology Ser.: Vol. 28). 725p. 65.00 o.p. (ISBN 0-89004-535-6). Raven.

Martin, Joseph C. No Laughing Matter: Chalk Talks About Alcohol. LC 82-47750. 192p. 1982. 11.49i (ISBN 0-06-065440-6, HarpR). Har-Row.

Martin, Joseph P. Private Yankee Doodle. rev. ed. Scheer, George F., ed. (Orig.). 1979. pap. 1.95 (ISBN 0-89062-047-4). Eastern Acorn.

Martin, Judith. Everybody, Everybody: A Collection from the Paper Bag Players. (Illus.). 80p. (gr. 3-7). 1981. 10.25 (ISBN 0-525-66736-9, 0995-300). Lodestar Bks.

--Gender-Related Behaviors of Children in Abusive Situations. LC 81-86006. 125p. (Orig.). 1983. pap. 14.95 (ISBN 0-88247-685-8). R & E Res Assoc.

--Gilbert. LC 82-71060. 288p. 1982. 14.95 (ISBN 0-689-11327-7). Atheneum.

Martin, Judith A. & Lanegran, David. Where We Live: The Residential Districts of Minneapolis & St. Paul. LC 82-11064. (Illus.). 144p. 1983. 29.50x (ISBN 0-8166-1093-2); pap. 14.95 (ISBN 0-8166-1094-0). U of Minn Pr.

Martin, Julio, et al, eds. Etiology & Pathogenesis of Insulin-Dependent Diabetes Mellitus. 315p. 1981. text ed. 37.00 (ISBN 0-89004-613-1). Raven.

Martin, Kenneth R. Whalemen's Paintings & Drawings: Selections from the Kendall Whaling Museum Collection. LC 81-50343. (Illus.). 176p. 1982. 30.00 (ISBN 0-87413-191-X). U Delaware Pr.

Martin, Knute, jt. auth. see Katz, Alfred H.

Martin, L. E. Mental Health-Mental Illness: Revolution in Progress. 1970. pap. 6.95 o.p. (ISBN 0-07-040644-8, C). McGraw.

Martin, L. H., jt. auth. see Holmes, Mike.

Martin, L. John & Lambert, Richard D., eds. Role of the Mass Media in American Politics. LC 76-11898. (Annals Ser: No. 427). 200p. 1976. pap. 7.95 (ISBN 0-87761-205-6). Am Acad Pol Soc Sci.

Martin, Lance, jt. auth. see Aagre, Scott.

Martin, Laurence. The Two-Edged Sword: Armed Force in the Modern World, The Reith Lectures 1981. 1982. 13.95 (ISBN 0-393-01655-2). Norton.

Martin, Laurence, ed. The Management of Defense. LC 76-12233. 136p. 1976. 25.00x (ISBN 0-312-51275-9). St Martin.

Martin, Laurence W., jt. ed. see Wolfers, Arnold.

Martin, Lawrence. The Presidents & the Prime Ministers. LC 82-45259. 320p. 1983. 19.95 (ISBN 0-385-17981-2). Doubleday.

Martin, Lawrence M., tr. see Zahan, Dominique.

Martin, Leda B. & Barbaresi, Sara M. How to Raise & Train a Miniature Schnauzer. (Orig.). pap. 2.95 (ISBN 0-87666-338-2, DS1026). TFH Pubns.

Martin, Lee J. & Kroitor, Harry P. The Five Hundred Word Theme. 3rd ed. (Illus.). 1979. pap. text ed. 11.95 (ISBN 0-13-321588-1). P-H.

Martin, Leslie & March, L., eds. Urban Space & Structures. (Studies in Architecture: Vol. 1). 1972. 32.50 (ISBN 0-521-08414-8); pap. 14.50x (ISBN 0-521-09934-X). Cambridge U Pr.

Martin, Lester H. This Is the Poodle. (Illus.). 1960. 12.95 (ISBN 0-87666-361-7, PS616). TFH Pubns.

Martin, Loren D. Isaiah: An Ensign to the Nations. (Isaiah Ser.: Vol. 1). (Illus.). 180p. 1982. 7.95 (ISBN 0-9608244-0-5); Set of Multivolumes. write for info. (ISBN 0-9608244-2-1). Valiant Pubns.

--Utah Criminal Code. (Orig.). plastic comb bdg. 6.50 (ISBN 0-9608244-3-X). Valiant Pubns.

--Utah Probate Handbook. 352p. (Orig.). 1982. pap. 19.95 (ISBN 0-9608244-1-3). Valiant Pubns.

Martin, Lowell. Library Response to Urban Change: A Study of the Chicago Public Library. LC 76-104040. 1969. 12.00 (ISBN 0-8389-0077-1). ALA.

Martin, Lynne. Puffin, Bird of the Open Seas. LC 76-3486. (Illus.). (gr. 3-7). 1976. 8.95 (ISBN 0-688-22074-6); PLB 8.59 (ISBN 0-688-32074-0). Morrow.

Martin, M. H. & Coughtrey, P. J. Biological Monitoring of Heavy Metal Pollution: Land & Air. (Pollution Monitor Ser.: No. 5). (Illus.). x, 468p. 1982. 80.00 (ISBN 0-85334-136-2, Pub. by Applied Sci England). Elsevier.

Martin, M. J. & Denison, R. A., eds. Case Exercises in Operations Research. LC 75-146548. 1971. 29.95 (ISBN 0-471-57355-8, Pub. by Wiley-Interscience). Wiley.

Martin, M. W. Miracles in Medicine. LC 73-80419. (Illus.). 1974. 9.95 o.p. (ISBN 0-8246-0159-9). Jonathan David.

Martin, Malachi. The Decline & Fall of the Roman Church. 1981. 14.95 (ISBN 0-399-12665-1). Putnam Pub Group.

--The Encounter. 488p. 1970. 10.00 o.p. (ISBN 0-374-14816-3). FS&G.

--King of Kings. 560p. 1982. pap. 3.95 (ISBN 0-671-44217-1). PB.

Martin, Margaret, jt. auth. see Ausberger, Carolyn.

Martin, Margaret E. Merchants & Trade of the Connecticut River Valley 1750-1820. (Perspectives in American History Ser.: No. 68). vii, 284p. Repr. of 1939 ed. lib. bdg. 22.50x (ISBN 0-87991-382-7). Porcupine Pr.

Martin, Margaret J. & Ausberger, Carolyn. Frequent Error Pairs. 96p. (gr. k-8). 1982. 35.00 (ISBN 0-88450-835-8, 3127-B). Communication Skill.

Martin, Margaret J., jt. auth. see Ausberger, Carolyn.

Martin, Marie T., tr. see Coleman, William.

Martin, Marilyn. Pedro. 152p. 1980. 6.00 (ISBN 0-686-30765-8). Rod & Staff.

Martin, Marla. Caterpillar Green. 1977. 5.95 (ISBN 0-686-23330-1). Rod & Staff.

--Kitten in the Well. 1978. 6.45 (ISBN 0-686-24051-0). Rod & Staff.

--The Locust Story. 1977. pap. 2.75 (ISBN 0-686-23331-X). Rod & Staff.

--A Sweet Singer. (gr. 2-4). 1976. 2.75 (ISBN 0-686-15487-8). Rod & Staff.

Martin, Marlo, ed. see Birdahl, Paul, et al.

Martin, Marta S., jt. auth. see Bonachea, Ramon L.

Martin, Martha E. The Friendly Stars. rev. ed. Menzel, Donald H., ed. (Illus.). 1964. pap. 2.95 (ISBN 0-486-21099-5). Dover.

Martin, Marty. Gertrude Stein Gertrude Stein Gertrude Stein. LC 80-5488. 96p. 1980. pap. 3.95 (ISBN 0-394-74624-4, Vin). Random.

Martin, Marvin. Britannica Junior Encyclopaedia, 15 vols. (Illus.). 1982. Set. 263.00 (ISBN 0-85229-888-9). Ency Brit Ed.

--Compton's Precyclopedia, 16 vols. 1981. per set 199.00 (ISBN 0-85229-323-2). Ency Brit Ed.

Martin, Mary, jt. auth. see Martin, Gene.

Martin, Mary L. The Fables of Marie de France: An English Translation. 16.00 (ISBN 0-917786-34-3). French Lit.

Martin, Maurice H., jt. auth. see Allaud, Louis.

Martin, Michael. Concepts of Science Education: A Philosophical Analysis. 1972. pap. 6.95x (ISBN 0-673-07540-0). Scott F.

--Social Science & Philosophical Analysis: Essays in Philosophy of the Social Sciences. LC 78-51142. 1978. pap. text ed. 12.50 (ISBN 0-8191-0478-7). U Pr of Amer.

Martin, Michael & Gelber, Leonard. Dictionary of American History. rev. & enl. ed. (Quality Paperback: No. 124). 1978. pap. 9.95 (ISBN 0-8226-0124-9). Littlefield.

--New Dictionary of American History. Repr. of 1952 ed. lib. bdg. 26.50x o.p. (ISBN 0-8371-2099-3, MADA). Greenwood.

Martin, Michael & Schinzinger, Roland. Ethics in Engineering. 1st ed. (Illus.). 384p. 1983. pap. text ed. 21.50 (ISBN 0-07-040701-0, C); write for info. instr's manual (ISBN 0-07-040702-9). McGraw.

Martin, Michael R. & Harrier, Richard A. Concise Encyclopedic Guide to Shakespeare. 1975. pap. 2.65 o.p. (ISBN 0-380-00238-8, 16832, Discus). Avon.

Martin, Murray S. Budgetary Control in Academic Libraries, Vol. 5. LC 76-5648. (Foundations in Library & Information Science Ser.). 1978. lib. bdg. 37.50 (ISBN 0-89232-010-9). Jai Pr.

--Issues in Personnel Management, Vol. 14. Stueart, Robert D., ed. LC 81-81649. (Foundations in Library & Information Sciences). 250p. 1981. 40.00 (ISBN 0-89232-136-9). Jai Pr.

Martin, Murray S., ed. Financial Planning for Libraries. LC 82-23346. (Journal of Library Administration Ser.: Vol. 3, Nos. 3 & 4). 1983. 20.00 (ISBN 0-86656-118-8, B118). Haworth Pr.

Martin, N. F. G. & England, J. W. Encyclopedia of Mathematics & Its Applications, Vol. 12: Mathematical Theory of Entropy. 1981. 34.50 (ISBN 0-201-13511-6). A-W.

Martin, Nancy. Selected Essays. 192p. (Orig.). 1983. pap. text ed. 8.50x (ISBN 0-86709-069-3). Boynton Cook Pubs.

Martin, Nancy, ed. Writing Across the Curriculum Pamphlets. 160p. (Orig.). 1983. pap. text ed. 8.00x (ISBN 0-86709-101-0). Boynton Cook Pubs.

Martin, Nancy, et al. Understanding Children Talking. 208p. 1976. pap. 4.75x (ISBN 0-14-080348-3). Boynton Cook Pubs.

--Writing & Learning Across the Curriculum 11-16. 176p. 1979. pap. text ed. 7.75 (ISBN 0-86709-095-2, 6063-7, Pub. by Ward Lock Educational England). Boynton Cook Pubs.

Martin, Nancy J. The Basics of Quilted Clothing. (Illus.). 68p. 1982. pap. 8.00 (ISBN 0-943574-12-9). That Patchwork.

--Nostalgic Noel. (Illus.). 38p. 1982. pap. 6.00 (ISBN 0-943574-14-5). That Patchwork.

--Sew Easy Strip Quilting. (Illus.). 20p. 1980. pap. 5.00 (ISBN 0-943574-00-5). That Patchwork.

Martin, P. W. Experiment in Depth: A Study of the Work of Jung, Eliot & Toynbee. 275p. 1982. Repr. of 1955 ed. lib. bdg. 40.00 (ISBN 0-89987-649-8). Darby Bks.

Martin, Pat, compiled by. The Czech Book: Recipes & Traditions. (Illus.). 60p. pap. 4.75 (ISBN 0-9603858-6-X). Penfield.

Martin, Patricia M. Abraham Lincoln. (See & Read Biographies). (Illus.). (gr. k-3). 1964. PLB 4.49 o.p. (ISBN 0-399-60002-7). Putnam Pub Group.

--Andrew Jackson. (See & Read Biographies). (Illus.). (gr. k-3). 1966. PLB 4.49 o.p. (ISBN 0-399-60023-X). Putnam Pub Group.

--Daniel Boone. (See & Read Biographies). (Illus.). (gr. k-3). 1965. PLB 5.99 o.p. (ISBN 0-399-60119-8). Putnam Pub Group.

--The Dog & the Boat Boy. (Illus.). (gr. k-3). 1969. PLB 4.69 o.p. (ISBN 0-399-60130-9). Putnam Pub Group.

--James Madison. (See & Read Biographies). (gr. k-4). 1970. PLB 3.96 o.p. (ISBN 0-399-60307-7). Putnam Pub Group.

--John Fitzgerald Kennedy. (See & Read Biographies). (Illus.). (gr. k-4). 1964. PLB 5.99 o.p. (ISBN 0-399-60319-0). Putnam Pub Group.

--Kumi & the Pearl. (Illus.). (gr. 2-4). 1968. PLB 3.86 o.p. (ISBN 0-399-60343-3). Putnam Pub Group.

--A Long Ago Christmas. (Illus.). (gr. k-2). 1968. PLB 4.99 o.p. (ISBN 0-399-60427-8). Putnam Pub Group.

--The Lucky Little Porcupine. (See & Read Storybooks). (Illus.). (gr. k-3). 1963. PLB 3.96 o.p. (ISBN 0-399-60432-4). Putnam Pub Group.

--Pocahontas. (See & Read Biographies). (Illus.). (gr. k-4). 1964. PLB 5.99 o.p. (ISBN 0-399-60515-0). Putnam Pub Group.

--The Pumpkin Patch. (Illus.). (gr. 2-5). 1966. PLB 4.69 o.p. (ISBN 0-399-60524-X). Putnam Pub Group.

--The Raccoon & Mrs. McGinnis. (See & Read Storybookser). (Illus.). (gr. k-3). 1961. PLB 3.96 o.p. (ISBN 0-399-60530-4). Putnam Pub Group.

--Thomas Alva Edison. (See & Read Biographies). (Illus.). (gr. 2-4). 1971. PLB 5.99 o.p. (ISBN 0-399-60631-9). Putnam Pub Group.

--Two Plays About Foolish People. new ed. LC 70-181413. (Illus.). 48p. (gr. 1-5). 1972. PLB 3.69 o.p. (ISBN 0-399-60751-X). Putnam Pub Group.

--Zachary Taylor. (See & Read Biographies). (Illus.). (gr. 2-4). 1969. PLB 4.49 o.p. (ISBN 0-399-60696-3). Putnam Pub Group.

Martin, Patricia P. & Bernal, Louis C. Images & Conversations: Mexican Americans Recall a Southwestern Past. 1983. 25.00 (ISBN 0-8165-0801-1); pap. 12.50 (ISBN 0-8165-0803-8). U of Ariz Pr.

Martin, Patrick, jt. auth. see Schaefer, Halmuth.

Martin, Paul. Have a Good Day. 1972. 1.50 (ISBN 0-8341-0236-6). Beacon Hill.

Martin, Paul & Brady, Peggy. Port Angeles-Washington: A History. (Illus.). 228p. 1983. pap. 18.95x (ISBN 0-918146-23-2). Peninsula WA.

Martin, Paul J., ed. see Edge, Nellie.

Martin, Paul K., ed. The Airline Handbook: 7th Annual. (Illus.). 476p. (Orig.). 1982. pap. 14.00 (ISBN 0-686-32833-7). AeroTravel Resear.

Martin, Peter. Pursuing Innocent Pleasures: The Gardening World of Alexander Pope. 1983. price not set (ISBN 0-208-02011-X, Archon Bks). Shoe String.

Martin, Peter, jt. ed. see Toon, Peter.

Martin, Philip L. Labor Displacement & Public Policy. LC 82-48099. 144p. 1982. 18.95 (ISBN 0-669-05969-2). Lexington Bks.

Martin, Philip R. Auto Mechanics for the Complete Dummy. 2nd, Rev. ed. Ritums, John & Guido, Dennis, eds. LC 74-14655. (Illus.). 1982. pap. 4.95 (ISBN 0-930968-01-8). Motormatics.

--Auto Mechanics for the Complete Dummy. 2nd ed. LC 82-62322. (Illus.). 192p. 1983. pap. 4.95 (ISBN 0-930968-02-6). Motormatics.

Martin, Phillip A., jt. auth. see Miller, Mark J.

Martin, Prudence. Heart's Shadow. (Candlelight Ecstasy Ser.: No. 119). (Orig.). 1983. pap. 1.95 (ISBN 0-440-13694-6). Dell.

--Love on the Run. (Candlelight Ecstasy Supreme Ser.: No. 2). (Orig.). 1983. pap. 2.95 (ISBN 0-440-15013-2). Dell.

--Love Song. (Candlelight Ecstasy Ser.). (Orig.). 1983. pap. 1.95 (ISBN 0-440-14849-9). Dell.

--Moonlight Rapture. (Candlelight Ecstasy Ser.: No. 148). (Orig.). 1983. pap. 1.95 (ISBN 0-440-15825-7). Dell.

Martin, R. A., jt. auth. see Elliott, John H.

Martin, R. D. Primate Origins. 1981. 35.00x o.p. (ISBN 0-412-12710-5, Pub. by Chapman & Hall). Methuen Inc.

Martin, R. H., ed. Terence, the Adelphoe. LC 75-36173. (Cambridge Greek & Latin Classics Ser.). 250p. 1976. 42.50 (ISBN 0-521-20936-6); pap. 13.95x (ISBN 0-521-29001-5). Cambridge U Pr.

Martin, R. L., et al, eds. Towards the Dynamic Analysis of Spatial Systems. 210p. 1980. 21.50x (ISBN 0-85086-072-5, Pub. by Pion England). Methuen Inc.

Martin, R. M. Semiotics & Linguistic Structure. LC 78-6873. 1978. 44.50x (ISBN 0-87395-381-9). State U NY Pr.

Martin, Ralph. A Crisis of Truth: The Attack on Faith, Morality & Mission in the Catholic Church. 250p. 1982. 10.95 (ISBN 0-89283-328-3). Servant.

--Hungry for God. 1976. pap. write for info o.p. (ISBN 0-515-09587-7). Jove Pubns.

Martin, Ralph, ed. New Wine, New Skins. LC 76-2855. 182p. 1976. pap. 2.95 o.p. (ISBN 0-8091-1942-0, Deus). Paulist Pr.

--Sent by the Spirit. LC 76-5671. 296p. 1976. pap. 2.95 o.p. (ISBN 0-8091-1946-3). Paulist Pr.

--The Spirit & the Church. LC 76-9366. 352p. 1976. pap. 2.95 o.p. (ISBN 0-8091-1947-1). Paulist Pr.

Martin, Ralph & Toon, Peter, eds. Reconciliation: A Study of Paul's Theology. LC 80-16340. (New Foundations Theological Library). 272p. 1981. 12.95 (ISBN 0-8042-3709-3); pap. 11.95 (ISBN 0-8042-3729-8). John Knox.

Martin, Ralph, ed. see Avis, Paul D.

Martin, Ralph, ed. see Carson, D. A.

Martin, Ralph G. Jennie, Vol. 1: The Life of Lady Randolph Churchill, the Romantic Years 1854-1895. 1970. pap. 3.95 (ISBN 0-451-12109-0, AE2109, Sig). NAL.

--The Woman He Loved. (Illus.). 480p. 1974. 9.95 o.p. (ISBN 0-671-21810-7). S&S.

Martin, Ralph P. Mark: Evangelist & Theologian. (Contemporary Evangelical Perspective Ser.). 249p. 1973. kivar 7.95 (ISBN 0-310-28801-0). Zondervan.

--The Worship of God: Some Theological, Pastoral & Practical Reflections. 238p. (Orig.). 1982. pap. 7.95 (ISBN 0-8028-1934-6). Eerdmans.

Martin, Rhona. Gallows Wedding. LC 78-14974. 1978. 9.95 o.p. (ISBN 0-698-10951-1, Coward). Putnam Pub Group.

Martin, Ricardo & Selowsky, Marcelo. Energy Prices, Substitution & Optimal Borrowing in the Short Run: An Analysis of Adjustment in Oil-Importing Developing Countries. (Working Papers: No. 466). 77p. 1981. 5.00 (ISBN 0-686-36164-4, WP-0466). World Bank.

Martin, Richard. A Parent's Guide to Childhood Symptoms: Understanding the Signals of Illness from Infancy through Adolescence. 384p. 1982. 14.95 (ISBN 0-312-59658-8). St Martin.

--Primordiality, Science, & Value. LC 80-14724. 336p. 1980. 39.50x (ISBN 0-87395-418-1); pap. 14.95x (ISBN 0-87395-444-0). State U NY Pr.

Martin, Richard J., jt. auth. see Fanaroff, Avroy.

Martin, Richard M. How to Keep Softbilled Birds in Cage or Aviary. (Illus.). 96p. 1980. 3.95 (ISBN 0-7028-8010-8). Avian Pubns.

--The Mammals of the Oceans. LC 76-56957. (Illus.). 1977. 12.95 o.p. (ISBN 0-399-11590-0). Putnam Pub Group.

Martin, Robert A. & Poland, Elizabeth Y. Learning to Change: A Self-Management Approach to Adjustment. 1980. pap. text ed. 13.95 (ISBN 0-07-040635-9); instructor's manual 10.00 (ISBN 0-07-040636-7). McGraw.

Martin, Robert B. The Triumph of Wit: A Study of Victorian Comic Theory. 1974. 22.00x (ISBN 0-19-812057-5). Oxford U Pr.

Martin, Robert E., Jr. Ordinary Differential Equations. (Illus.). 448p. 1983. text ed. 25.95 (ISBN 0-07-040687-1, C); write for info. instr's manual (ISBN 0-07-040688-X). McGraw.

Martin, Robert J. Teaching Through Encouragement: Techniques to Help Students Learn. 208p. 1980. 10.95t (ISBN 0-13-896266-9, Spec); pap. 4.95 (ISBN 0-13-896258-8). P-H.

Martin, Robert L. Studies in Feedback Shift-Register Synthesis of Sequential Machines. (Press Research Monographs: No. 50). 1969. 20.00x (ISBN 0-262-13047-5). MIT Pr.

Martin, Robert L., ed. The Paradox of the Liar. 1979. lib. bdg. 23.00 (ISBN 0-917930-30-4); pap. text ed. 7.00x (ISBN 0-917930-10-X). Ridgeview.

Martin, Robert S. & Martin, James C. Contours of Discovery: Pointed Maps Delineating the Texas & Southern Chapters in the Cartographic History of North America, 1513-1930. LC 82-83547. 35.00 (ISBN 0-87611-058-8). Tex St Hist Assn.

Martin, Roderick. New Technology & Industrial Relations in Fleet Street. 1981. 39.50x (ISBN 0-19-827243-X). Oxford U Pr.

Martin, Roger D. No Dreams for Sale: New & Selected Poems. 1983. price not set signed & numbered 1-25 (ISBN 0-938566-16-4); pap. text ed. price not set (ISBN 0-938566-15-6). Adastra Pr.

Martin, Roger H. Evangelicals United: Ecumenical Stirrings in Pre-Victorian Britain, 1795-1830. LC 82-10784. (Studies in Evangelicalism: No. 4). 244p. 1983. 17.50 (ISBN 0-8108-1586-9). Scarecrow.

Martin, Rose L. Fabian Freeway: High Road to Socialism in the U.S.A. LC 66-28199. 1966. 8.95 (ISBN 0-88279-209-1). Western Islands.

Martin, Rupert. Looking at Spain. LC 73-78938. (Looking at Other Countries Ser). (Illus.). (gr. 4-6). 1970. 10.53i (ISBN 0-397-31137-0, JBL-J). Har-Row.

Martin, Ruth. Wonderful Ways with Chicken. 6.00x (ISBN 0-392-06272-0, LTB). Sportshelf.

Martin, S. J. The Biochemistry of Viruses. LC 77-8231. (Texts in Chemistry & Biochemistry Ser.). (Illus.). 1978. 39.50 (ISBN 0-521-21678-8); pap. 13.95 (ISBN 0-521-29229-8). Cambridge U Pr.

Martin, Samuel, jt. auth. see Chaplin, Hamako.

Martin, Samuel P., jt. ed. see Kovner, Anthony R.

Martin, Sara H., ed. see Tapia, Fernando.

Martin, Sarah C. Old Mother Hubbard & Her Dog. Jensen, Virginia A., tr. LC 75-21967. (Illus.). (ps-3). 1976. 6.95 o.p. (ISBN 0-698-20348-8, Coward). Putnam Pub Group.

Martin, Shan. Managing Without Managers: Alternative Work Arrangements in Public Organizations. (Sage Library of Social Research). (Illus.). 176p. 1983. 22.00 (ISBN 0-8039-1960-3); pap. 10.95 (ISBN 0-8039-1961-1). Sage.

Martin, Stephen J., jt. auth. see French, William B.

Martin, Steve. Cruel Shoes. LC 78-12473. 1979. 6.95 (ISBN 0-399-12304-0); 12 copy pre-pack 83.40 (ISBN 0-399-12340-7). Putnam Pub Group.

--Cruel Shoes. 1980. pap. 2.25 o.p. (ISBN 0-446-92070-3). Warner Bks.

--Jerk. (Illus., Orig.). 1979. pap. 2.25 o.p. (ISBN 0-446-92523-3). Warner Bks.

Martin, Sue, jt. auth. see Green, Harriet.

Martin, Susan E. Breaking & Entering: Policewoman on Patrol. LC 79-63555. 275p. 1980. 15.95x (ISBN 0-520-03908-4). U of Cal Pr.

Martin, Susan K., ed. Information Politics: Proceedings of the ASIS 39th Annual Meeting. LC 64-8303. (Annual Meeting Ser.: Vol. 13). 1976. 17.50 (ISBN 0-87715-413-9). Am Soc Info Sci.

Martin, Susan K., jt. ed. see Butler, Brett.

Martin, Sydney. Beacon Bible Expositions, Vol. 10. Greathouse, William M & Taylor, Willard H., eds. 1978. 6.95 (ISBN 0-8341-0321-4). Beacon Hill.

--The Gospel of Power. 1973. pap. 1.50 (ISBN 0-8341-0242-0). Beacon Hill.

Martin, T. E. Beacon Bible Expositions: The Revelation. Greathouse, M., ed. (Beacon Bible Exposition Ser.: Vol. 12). 230p. 1983. 6.95 (ISBN 0-8341-0809-7). Beacon Hill.

Martin, Ted. Pavlov...Dog Pounds. 104p. 1983. pap. 3.95 (ISBN 0-8362-2050-1). Andrews & McMeel.

Martin, Terence. Nathaniel Hawthorne. (United States Authors Ser.). 1964. lib. bdg. 11.95 (ISBN 0-8057-0348-9, Twayne). G K Hall.

--Nathaniel Hawthorne. rev. ed. (United States Authors Ser.). 233p. 1983. lib. bdg. 13.95 (ISBN 0-8057-7384-3, Twayne). G K Hall.

Martin, Thomas B., jt. ed. see Dixon, N. Rex.

Martin, Thomas J., jt. auth. see Martin, James W.

Martin, Thomas L., Jr. Malice in Blunderland. LC 73-4376. 156p. 1973. 9.95 (ISBN 0-07-040617-0, GB). McGraw.

Martin, Thomas L., Jr. & Latham, Donald C. Strategy for Survival. LC 63-17720. (Illus.). 389p. 1963. 1.95x o.p. (ISBN 0-8165-0088-6). U of Ariz Pr.

Martin, Tony. Race First: The Ideological & Organizational Struggles of Marcus Garvey & the Universal Negro Improvement Assoc. LC 75-16968. (Contributions in Afro-American & African Studies: No. 19). 448p. 1976. lib. bdg. 25.00 (ISBN 0-8371-8280-8, MMG/). Greenwood.

Martin, Toy. Pre-School Crafts Book. (Illus.). 64p. (Orig.). (gr. k-1). 1983. pap. 3.95 (ISBN 0-7137-1330-5, Pub. by Blandford Pr England). Sterling.

Martin, Van J. & Mitchell, Wm. R., Jr. Landmark Homes of Georgia, 1733-1983. (Illus.). 1982. 45.00 (ISBN 0-932958-01-X). Golden Coast.

Martin, Vicky. Changing Partners. 1980. 10.95 o.p. (ISBN 0-312-12965-3). St Martin.

Martin, W. C. & Hutchins, R. Flora of New Mexico, 2 vols. (Illus.). 3000p. 1980. Set. lib. bdg. 160.00 (ISBN 3-7682-1263-7). Lubrecht & Cramer.

Martin, Wallace E., compiled by. Sail & Steam on the Northern California Coast, 1850-1900. LC 82-60604. 351p. 1982. bds. write for info (ISBN 0-9605182-0-7). Natl Maritime.

Martin, Walter. Mormonismo. 48p. Date not set. 1.50 (ISBN 0-88113-208-X). Edit Betania.

--Los Testigos de Jehova. 80p. Date not set. 1.75 (ISBN 0-88113-285-3). Edit Betania.

Martin, Wanda J. & MacLean, Jelorma. Car Free Connexions: Discover the Northwest by Boat, Plane, Train, & Bus. (Illus.). 112p. (Orig.). 1983. pap. 6.95 (ISBN 0-940546-00-0). Connexions.

Martin, Warren B. A College of Character. LC 82-48392. (Higher Education Ser.). 1982. text ed. 15.95x (ISBN 0-87589-554-9). Jossey Bass.

Martin, Wayne. We Can Do Without Heart Attacks. 1983. 9.75 (ISBN 0-8062-1974-2). Carlton.

Martin, Wendy. Love's Journey. 192p. (YA) 1976. 6.95 (ISBN 0-685-66479-1, Avalon). Bouregy.

--Two Hearts Adrift. 192p. (YA) 1976. 6.95 (ISBN 0-685-62026-3, Avalon). Bouregy.

Martin, Will. Everybody's Guitar Manual: How to Buy, Maintain & Repair an Acoustic Guitar. (Illus.). 96p. (Orig.). 1983. pap. 7.50 (ISBN 0-912528-30-3). John Muir.

Martin, William, jt. auth. see Chapman, E. N.

Martin, William O. Metaphysics & Ideology. (Aquinas Lecture). 1959. 7.95 (ISBN 0-87462-124-0). Marquette.

--Order & Integration of Knowledge. LC 68-54425. (Illus.). 1968. Repr. of 1957 ed. lib. bdg. 17.50x (ISBN 0-8371-0161-1, MAKN). Greenwood.

Martin, William R. & Drossin, Julius. Music of the Twentieth Century. (Illus.). 1980. text ed. 19.95 (ISBN 0-13-608927-5). P-H.

Martin, William R., jt. auth. see Duderstadt, James J.

Martin, William T., et al. Elementary Differential Equations. 3rd ed. Date not set. text ed. price not set (ISBN 0-8162-5435-4). Holden-Day. Postponed.

Martinas-Miller, Orlando, tr. see Fisher, J. & Dryer, R.

Martindale. The Triumphs of Caesar by Andrea Mantegna. 1979. 95.00 o.p. (ISBN 0-905203-16-X, Pub. by H Miller England). Wiley.

Martindale, Andrew. The Triumphs of Caesar by Andrea Mantegna in the Collection of Her Majesty the Queen at Hampton Court. (Illus.). 342p. 1982. 74.00x (ISBN 0-19-921025-X). Oxford U Pr.

Martindale, Colin. Romantic Progression: The Psychology of Literary History. LC 74-26559. 225p. 1975. 17.50 o.p. (ISBN 0-470-57365-1, Pub. by Wiley). Krieger.

Martindale, David. Earth Shelters. (Illus.). 160p. 1981. 18.50 (ISBN 0-525-93199-6, 01796-540); pap. 10.25 (ISBN 0-525-93200-3, 0995-330). Dutton.

--How to Be a Freelance Writer. 256p. 1982. 12.95 (ISBN 0-517-54785-6). Crown.

Martindale, Don. Personality & Milieu: The Shaping of Social Science Culture. 208p. 1983. text ed. 15.95 (ISBN 0-88105-001-6). Cap & Gown.

--The Scope of Social Theory: Essays & Sketches. 500p. 1983. text ed. 19.95 (ISBN 0-88105-003-2). Cap & Gown.

Martindale, Don & Hanson, R. Galen. Small Town & the Nation: The Conflict of Local & Translocal Forces. LC 79-90793. (Contributions in Sociology: No. 3). 1970. lib. bdg. 25.00 (ISBN 0-8371-1854-9, MAT/); pap. 4.95 (ISBN 0-8371-4991-6). Greenwood.

Martindale, Don & Martindale, Edith. Social Dimensions of Mental Illness, Alcoholism, & Drug Dependence. LC 72-133499. 332p. lib. bdg. 29.95 (ISBN 0-8371-5175-9, MAM/); pap. 5.95 (ISBN 0-8371-8924-1). Greenwood.

Martindale, Don, jt. ed. see Mohan, Raj P.

Martindale, Don, et al, trs. see Weber, Max.

Martindale, Don A. The Nature & Types of Sociological Theory. 2nd ed. LC 80-68142. (Illus.). 640p. 1981. text ed. 24.95 (ISBN 0-395-29732-X). HM.

Martindale, Edith, jt. auth. see Martindale, Don.

Martindale, William, ed. Extra Pharmacopoeia. 28th ed. 2050p. 1982. 130.00 (ISBN 0-85369-160-6, Pub. by Pharmaceutical). Rittenhouse.

Martine. The Only Astrology Book You'll Ever Need. LC 80-5403. 288p. 1981. 22.95 (ISBN 0-8128-2726-0). Stein & Day.

Martine, James J. Critical Essays on Arthur Miller. (Critical Essays on American Literature Ser.). 1979. lib. bdg. 25.00 (ISBN 0-8161-8258-2, Hall Reference). G K Hall.

Martine, James J., ed. American Novelists Nineteen Ten to Nineteen Forty-Five, 3 vols. (Dictionary of Literary Biography Ser.: Vol. 9). (Illus.). 800p. 1981. Set. 222.00x (ISBN 0-8103-0931-9, Bruccoli Clark). Gale.

Martine, Roddy, jt. auth. see Cambell, Andrew.

Martineau, Richard & Girolami, Anne-Marie. Vient De Paraitre. LC 74-20593. 1975. pap. text ed. 4.95 (ISBN 0-88436-174-8). EMC.

Martine-Barnes, Adrienne. The Dragon Rises. 2.75 (ISBN 0-441-16655-5, Pub. by Ace Science Fiction). Ace Bks.

Martinell, Cesar. Gaudi: His LIfe, His Theories, His Work. Ribalta, Marta, ed. (Illus.). 127p. 1982. pap. 12.95 (ISBN 84-7031-218-9, Pub. by Editorial Blume Spain). Intl Schol Bk Serv.

Martinell, Patricia & Seaman, Patricia. National Certification Examinations: For Nurse Practitioners & Other primary Health Care Providers Study Guide & Manual. 125p. 1983. pap. text ed. 9.95x (ISBN 0-8290-1279-6). Irvington.

Martinelli, F. N. Studies on the Use of Helicopters for Oil Spill Clearance, 1980. 1981. 40.00x (ISBN 0-686-97140-X, Pub. by W Spring England). State Mutual Bk.

Martinelli, F. N. & Cormack, D. Investigation of the Effects of Oil Viscosity & Water-in-Oil Emulsion Formation on Dispersant Efficiency, 1979. 1981. 40.00x (ISBN 0-686-97091-8, Pub. by W Spring England). State Mutual Bk.

Martinelli, F. N. & Lynch, B. W. Factors Affecting the Efficiency of Dispersants, 1980. 1981. 30.00x (ISBN 0-686-97076-4, Pub. by W Spring England). State Mutual Bk.

Martinengo, Luciano, tr. see Pasolini, Pier P.

Martinet, Andre. Elements of General Linguistics. Palmer, Elisabeth, tr. LC 64-19845. 1964. 5.00 o.p. (ISBN 0-226-50873-0). U of Chicago Pr.

--Elements of General Linguistics. Palmer, Elisabeth, tr. LC 64-19845. (Midway Reprint Ser.). 206p. 1982. pap. 8.00x (ISBN 0-226-50875-7). U of Chicago Pr.

Martinet, Andre & Walter, Henriette. Dictionnaire De la Prononciation Francaise Dans Son Usage Reel. (Fr.). 1977. lib. bdg. 59.00x o.p. (ISBN 0-685-74923-1). Clearwater Pub.

Martinet, Jean. Singularities of Smooth Functions & Maps. Simon, C. P., tr. LC 81-18034. (London Mathematical Society Lecture Note Ser.: No. 58). 180p. 1982. pap. 19.95 (ISBN 0-521-23398-4). Cambridge U Pr.

Martinez & Martinez. Neuroanatomy. 1982. text ed. 42.00 (ISBN 0-7216-6147-5). Saunders.

Martinez, Adolfo & Diamond, Ray B. Fertilizer Use Statistics in Crop Production. LC 82-15856. (Technical Bulletin Ser.: No. T-24). 37p. (Orig.). 1982. pap. text ed. 4.00 (ISBN 0-88090-042-3). Intl Fertilizer.

Martinez, Bernice Bass de see Sims, William E. & Bass de Martinez, Bernice B.

Martinez, Eliud. The Art of Mariano Azuela: Modernism in la Malhora, el Desquite, la Luciernaga. Miller, Yvette E., ed. 101p. 1980. pap. 5.95 (ISBN 0-935480-02-1). Lat Am Lit Rev Pr.

Martinez, Eluid L. & Smith, James C., Jr. What Is a New Mexico Santo? LC 77-78519. (Illus.). 1978. pap. 2.95 (ISBN 0-913270-76-8). Sunstone Pr.

Martinez, J., jt. auth. see Kalman, R.

Martinez, J. D. Combat Mime: A Non-Violent Approach to Stage Violence. (Illus.). 224p. 1982. text ed. 24.95x (ISBN 0-88229-730-9); pap. text ed. 12.95x (ISBN 0-88229-809-7). Nelson-Hall.

Martinez, J. R., jt. ed. see Quinton, P. M.

Martinez, Jose L., ed. see Neighbour, Ralph.

Martinez, Jose Luis, ed. see Haney, David.

Martinez, Maria. Sterling Silver Roses. Fidillino, Tony & Branzuela, Len B., eds. LC 81-90579. 73p. 1982. 9.95x (ISBN 0-686-36306-X); text ed. 9.95x (ISBN 0-686-99438-8). La Morenita.

Martinez, Nancy C. & Kuntz, Joseph M. Poetry Explication: A Checklist of Interpretation Since 1925 of British and American Poems Past and Present. 1980. lib. bdg. 40.00 (ISBN 0-8161-8313-9, Hall Reference). G K Hall.

Martinez, Pam. Sugarless Cooking. 5.95 o.p. (ISBN 0-934230-05-6). Green Hill.

Martinez, Raul C. Organizational Behavior Management: A Manual for Supervisors. (Illus.). 148p. (Orig.). 1980. pap. 9.50 (ISBN 0-937230-00-6). NPD Corp.

Martinez, Raymond J., jt. auth. see Hardy, Helen H.

Martinez, Tomas M. The Gambling Scene: Why People Gamble. (Illus.). 294p. 1983. 24.50x (ISBN 0-398-04745-6). C C Thomas.

Martinez-Alier, Verena. Marriage, Class & Colour in Nineteenth Century Cuba. LC 73-82463. 224p. 1974. 30.95 o.p. (ISBN 0-521-20412-7); pap. 13.95 (ISBN 0-521-09846-7). Cambridge U Pr.

Martinez-Miller, Orlando, tr. see Irvin, Judith L. & Downey, Joan M.

Martinez-Palomo, Adlofo. The Biology of Entamoeba Histolytica. (Tropical Medicine Research Studies). 161p. 1982. 39.95 (ISBN 0-471-10404-3, Pub. by Res Stud Pr). Wiley.

Martinez Sierra, Gregorio. Sueno De Una Noche De Agosto. Walsh, Donald, ed. (Span). 1952. pap. 3.95x o.p. (ISBN 0-393-09477-4, NortonC). Norton.

Martini, Anna. Mondadori Regional Italian Cookbook. 1983. 18.95 (ISBN 0-517-54873-9, Harmony). Crown.

Martini, Carlo see Marchione, Margherita & Scalia, S. Eugene.

Martini, L. & Ganong, W. F., eds. Frontiers in Neuroendocrinology, Vol. 4. LC 77-82030. 304p. 1976. 32.50 (ISBN 0-89004-033-8). Raven.

Martini, L. & James, V. H., eds. Current Topics in Experimental Endocrinology, Vol. 4. (Serial Publication). Date not set. price not set (ISBN 0-12-153204-6). Acad Pr.

Martini, L., jt. ed. see Ganong, W. F.

Martini, Luciano & Ganong, William F. Frontiers in Neuroendocrinology, 1971. (Illus.). 1971. text ed. 29.50x o.p. (ISBN 0-19-501415-4). Oxford U Pr.

Martini, Luciano & Ganong, William F., eds. Frontiers in Neuroendocrinology, Vol. 6. 430p. 1979. text ed. 47.00 (ISBN 0-89004-404-X). Raven.

Martini, Luciano & James, V. H., eds. Current Topics in Experimental Endocrinology: Vol. 5: Fetal Endocrinology & Metabolism. (Serial Publication). Date not set. price not set (ISBN 0-12-153205-4). Acad Pr.

Martini, Luciano, jt. ed. see Besser, G. M.

Martini, Luciano, jt. ed. see Ganong, William F.

Martini, Luciano, jt. ed. see Serio, Mario.

Martini, N., jt. ed. see Ostino, G.

Martini, R. & Jager, E. M. Geometric Techniques in Gauge Theory: The Netherlands Proceedings, 1981. (Lecture Notes in Mathematics: Vol. 926). 219p. 1982. pap. 12.50 (ISBN 0-387-11497-1). Springer-Verlag.

Martini, Teri. Cowboys. LC 81-10049. (The New True Bks.). (Illus.). 48p. (gr. k-4). 1981. PLB 9.25 (ISBN 0-516-01611-3). Childrens.

--John Marshall. LC 73-11430. (Illus.). (gr. 4-7). 1974. 5.25 o.s.i. (ISBN 0-664-32540-8). Westminster.

Martinis, M., et al, eds. Particle Physics. 400p. 1975. 30.00 (ISBN 0-444-10648-0, North-Holland). Elsevier.

Martinko, Mark, jt. auth. see Luthans, Fred.

Martino, A. A. Deontic Logic, Computational Linguistics & Legal Information Systems. 1982. 66.00 (ISBN 0-444-86415-6). Elsevier.

Martino, J. P. Technological Forecasting for Decision-Making. 384p. 1983. pap. 29.00 (ISBN 0-444-00722-9, North Holland). Elsevier.

Martino, James. The Purest Sight. 1979. 4.95 o.p. (ISBN 0-533-03896-0). Vantage.

Martino, Mario. Emergence: A Transsexual Biography. (Illus.). 1979. pap. 2.50 o.p. (ISBN 0-451-08520-5, E8520, Sig). NAL.

Martino, R. L. Critical Path Networks. 1970. 21.95 o.p. (ISBN 0-07-040654-5, P&RB). McGraw.

--Information Management: The Dynamics of MIS. 1970. 19.95 o.p. (ISBN 0-07-040651-0, P&RB). McGraw.

--Project Management. 118p. 1968. 64.00x (ISBN 0-677-61070-X). Gordon.

--Resources Management. 1970. 22.50 (ISBN 0-07-040652-9, P&RB). McGraw.

Martins, J. B., ed. Numerical Methods in Geomechanics. 1982. 69.50 (ISBN 90-277-1461-4, Pub. by Reidel Holland). Kluwer Boston.

Martins, Peter & Cornfield, Robert. Far from Denmark. 1982. 24.95 (ISBN 0-316-54855-3). Little.

Martins, R. E. & Engie, A. Electrical Interference in Electronic Systems: Its Avoidance Within High-Voltage Substations & Elsewhere. 198p. 1979. 42.95 (ISBN 0-471-27887-4, Pub. by Research Studies Pr). Wiley.

Martinson, I., et al, eds. Beam-Foil Spectroscopy. (Journal of Nuclear Instruments & Methods Ser.: Vol. 90). (Proceedings - 2nd Conference). 1970. 64.75 (ISBN 0-7204-0198-4, North Holland). Elsevier.

Martire. Antisemitism in the U. S. A. Study of Prejudice in the 1980's. 188p. 1982. 23.95 (ISBN 0-03-061907-6). Praeger.

Martis, Kenneth C. The Historical Atlas of United States Congressional Districts, 1789-1983. 1982. lib. bdg. 150.00x (ISBN 0-02-920150-0). Macmillan.

Martland, Richard E. & Welsby, Derek A. Basic Cookery. 1980. pap. 12.50 (ISBN 0-434-92232-3, Pub. by Heinemann). David & Charles.

Martland, T. R. Religion As Art. LC 80-27104. (Ser. in Philosophy). 265p. 1981. 24.50x (ISBN 0-87395-520-X); pap. 11.95x (ISBN 0-87395-521-8). State U NY Pr.

Martlew, Margaret. The Psychology of Written Language: A Developmental Approach. 432p. 1983. 49.95 (ISBN 0-471-10291-1, Pub. by Wiley-Interscience). Wiley.

Martome, Michael. Dark Light. LC 73-88291. (Illus., Orig.). 1973. pap. 6.95 (ISBN 0-912810-11-4). Lustrum Pr.

Marton, Beryl M. The Coupon Saver's Cookbook: Nearly Three Hundred Inventive Ways to Use Your Food Coupons in Delectable Dishes with a Special Section for the Calorie-Conscious Couponer. 1980. 12.95 o.p. (ISBN 0-517-54154-8); pap. 6.95 o.p. (ISBN 0-517-54035-5). Crown.

Marton, C. & Harmuth, H. F., eds. Advances in Electronics & Electron Physics, Supplement 14: Nonsinusoidal Waves for Radar & Radio Communication. (Serial Publication Ser.). 1981. 51.50 (ISBN 0-12-014575-8). Acad Pr.

Marton, C. & Septier, A., eds. Advances in Electronics & Electron Physics Supplement, No. 13C. (Serial Publication). 544p. 1983. price not set (ISBN 0-12-014576-6). Acad Pr.

Marton, C., jt. ed. see Marton, L.

Marton, Claire, ed. Methods of Experimental Physics: Fluid Dynamics, Vol. 18A. LC 79-26343. 1981. 57.00 (ISBN 0-12-475960-2). Acad Pr.

Marton, Claire, jt. ed. see Marton, L.

Marton, Clare & Lecar, Harold, eds. Methods of Experimental Physics: Biophysics, Vol. 20. 568p. 1982. 74.50 (ISBN 0-12-475962-9). Acad Pr.

Marton, Kati. Wallenberg. 1982. 15.50 (ISBN 0-394-52360-1). Random.

Marton, L. Early History of the Electron Microscope. Gabor, intro. by. LC 68-19314. (History of Technology Monographs). (Illus.). 1968. 5.00 (ISBN 0-911302-07-7). San Francisco Pr.

Marton, L. see Marton, L.

Marton, L., ed. Advances in Electronics & Electron Physics. Incl. Vols. 1-5. 1948-53. 63.00 ea. Vol. 1 (ISBN 0-12-014501-4). Vol. 2 (ISBN 0-12-014502-2). Vol. 3 (ISBN 0-12-014503-0). Vol. 4 (ISBN 0-12-014504-9). Vol. 5 (ISBN 0-12-014505-7); Vols. 6-8. 1954-56. 63.00 ea. Vol. 6 (ISBN 0-12-014506-5). Vol. 7 (ISBN 0-12-014507-3). Vol. 8 (ISBN 0-12-014508-1); Vols. 9-10. 1957-58. 63.00 ea. Vol. 9 (ISBN 0-12-014509-X). Vol. 10 (ISBN 0-12-014510-3); Vol. 11. 1959. 56.50 (ISBN 0-12-014511-1); Vol. 12. Proceedings. Symposium on Photo-Electronic Image Devices - 1st. McGee, J. D. & Wilcock, W. L., eds. 1960. 42.00 (ISBN 0-12-014512-X); Vols. 13-15. 1960-61. 63.00 ea. Vol. 13 (ISBN 0-12-014513-8). Vol. 14 (ISBN 0-12-014514-6). Vol. 15 (ISBN 0-12-014515-4); Vol. 16. Proceedings. Symposium on Photo-Electronic Image Devices - 2nd. McGee, J. D., et al, eds. 1962. 78.00 (ISBN 0-12-014516-2); Vol. 17. 1963. 63.00 (ISBN 0-12-014517-0); Vol. 18. 1963. 63.00 (ISBN 0-12-014518-9); Vol. 19. 1964. 56.50 (ISBN **0-12-014519-7); Vols. 20-21. 1965-66. 63.00 ea. Vol. 20 (ISBN 0-12-014520-0). Vol. 21 (ISBN 0-12-014521-9); Vol. 22. Proceedings. Symposium on Photo-Electronic Image Devices - 3rd. McGee, J. D., et al, eds. 1966. Pt. A. 79.50 (ISBN 0-12-014522-7); Pt. B. 47.50 (ISBN 0-12-014542-1); Vol. 23. 1967. 63.00 (ISBN 0-12-014523-5); Vol. 24. 1968. 63.00 (ISBN 0-12-014524-3); Vol. 25. 1968. 63.00 (ISBN 0-12-014525-1); Vol. 26. 1969. 63.00 (ISBN 0-12-014526-X); Vol. 27. 1970. 63.00 (ISBN 0-12-014527-8); Vol. 28. Proceedings. Symposium on Photo-Electronic Image Devices - 4th. McGee, J. D., et al, eds. 1969. Pt. A. 87.50 (ISBN 0-12-014528-6); Pt. B, 1970. 89.00 (ISBN 0-12-014548-0); Vol. 29. 1970. 63.00 (ISBN 0-12-014529-4); Vol. 30. 1971. 63.00 (ISBN 0-12-014530-8); Vol. 31. 1972. 56.50 (ISBN 0-12-014531-6); Vol. 32. 1973. 63.00 (ISBN 0-12-014532-4); Vol. 33. Proceedings. Symposium on Photo-Electronic Image Devices - 5th. McGee, J. D., et al, eds. 1972. Pt. A, 1972. 72.50 (ISBN 0-12-014533-2); Pt. B. 96.50 (ISBN 0-12-014553-7). Pt. B, 1973. Acad Pr.**

--Advances in Electronics & Electron Physics. Incl. Vol. 36. 1974. 63.00 (ISBN 0-12-014536-7); Vol. 37. 1975. 63.00 (ISBN 0-12-014537-5); lib. ed. 80.00 (ISBN 0-12-014584-7); microfiche 47.50 (ISBN 0-12-014585-5); Vol. 38. 1975. 63.00 (ISBN 0-12-014538-3); lib. ed. 80.00 (ISBN 0-12-014586-3); microfiche 47.50 (ISBN 0-12-014587-1); Vol. 39. 1975. 63.00 (ISBN 0-12-014539-1); lib. ed. 80.00 (ISBN 0-12-014588-X); microfiche 47.50 (ISBN 0-12-014589-8); Vol. 40a. Photo-Electronics Image Devices: Proceedings. Imperial College, London, Sept. 9-13, 1974, 6th Symposium, et al. Morgan, B. L., ed. 1976. 98.50 (ISBN 0-12-014540-5); lib. ed. 128.50 (ISBN 0-12-014590-1); microfiche 68.50 (ISBN 0-12-014591-X); Vol. 40B. Photo-Electronic Image Devices. 1977. 98.50 (ISBN 0-12-014554-5); Vol. 42. 1976. 63.00 (ISBN 0-12-014642-8); lib. ed. 79.00 (ISBN 0-12-014684-3); microfiche 45.50 (ISBN 0-12-014685-1); Vol. 45. 1978. 58.50 (ISBN 0-12-014645-2); lib. ed. 75.50 (ISBN 0-12-014690-8); microfiche 42.00 (ISBN 0-12-014691-6). (Serial Publication). Acad Pr.

--Advances in Electronics & Electron Physics, Vol. 60. (Serial Publication). 424p. Date not set. 60.00 (ISBN 0-12-014660-6). Acad Pr.

--Advances in Electronics & Electron Physics: Supplements. Incl. Suppl. 1. Electroluminescence & Related Effects. Ivey, Henry F. 1963. 58.00 (ISBN 0-12-014561-8); Suppl. 2. Optical Masers. Birnbaum, George. 1964. 53.50 (ISBN 0-12-014562-6); Suppl. 3. Narrow Angle Electron Guns & Cathode Ray Tubes. Moss, Hilary. 1968. 43.50 (ISBN 0-12-014563-4); Suppl. 5. Linear Ferrite Devices for Microwave Applications. Von Aulock, W. H. & Fay, C. E. 1969. 54.00 (ISBN 0-12-014565-0); Suppl. 6. Electron Probe Microanalysis. Tousimis, A. J. & Marton, L. 1969. 63.00 (ISBN 0-12-014566-9); Suppl. 7. Quadruples in Electron Lens Design. Hawkes, P. W. 1970. 63.00 (ISBN 0-12-014567-7); Suppl. 9. Sequency Theory Foundations & Applications. Harmuth, Henning F., ed. 1977. 65.00 (ISBN 0-12-014569-3); Suppl. 11. Acoustic Imaging with Electronic Circuits. Harmuth, Henning F., ed. 1979. 36.50 (ISBN 0-12-014571-5). Acad Pr.

--Methods of Experimental Physics Vol. 15A: Quantum Electronics. (Methods of Experimental Physics Ser.). 1979. 52.50 (ISBN 0-12-475915-7). Acad Pr.

Marton, L. & Marton, C., eds. Advances in Electronics & Electron Physics, Vol. 51. LC 49-7504. (Serial Publication). 1980. 44.50 (ISBN 0-12-014651-7); lib. ed. 69.50 (ISBN 0-12-014702-5); microfiche ed. 38.00 (ISBN 0-12-014703-3). Acad Pr.

--Advances in Electronics and Electron Physics, Vol. 52. 1980. 86.50 (ISBN 0-12-014652-5); lib. bdg. 97.50 lib. ed. (ISBN 0-12-014704-1); microfiche ed. 52.50 (ISBN 0-12-014705-X). Acad Pr.

Marton, L. & Marton, Claire, eds. Advances in Electronics & Electron Physics, Vol. 50. LC 49-7504. 1980. 59.50 (ISBN 0-12-014650-9); lib. ed. 75.00 (ISBN 0-12-014700-9); 42.50 (ISBN 0-12-014701-7). Acad Pr.

Martonosi, Anthony N., ed. Membrane & Transport, Vol. 1. LC 82-3690. 675p. 1982. 75.00x (ISBN 0-306-40853-8, Plenum Pr); Set with Vol. 2. 130.00 (ISBN 0-686-97452-2). Plenum Pub.

Martorana, S. V., jt. ed. see Kuhns, Eileen.

Martorella, Rosanne, jt. ed. see Kamerman, Jack B.

Martos, B. Nonlinear Programming Theory & Methods. 280p. 1975. 47.00 (ISBN 0-444-10738-X, North-Holland). Elsevier.

Martos, B., jt. ed. see Kornai, J.

Martos, Joseph. Doors to the Sacred: A Historical Introduction to Sacraments in the Catholic Church. LC 82-45148. 552p. 1982. pap. 9.95 (ISBN 0-385-18180-9, Im). Doubleday.

Marts, J. A. Paying Your Way. 1975. 24.00 (ISBN 0-07-086495-0, G). McGraw.

Marty, Martin, ed. see James, William.

Marty, Martin E. The New Shape of American Religion. LC 78-1576. 1978. Repr. of 1959 ed. lib. bdg. 19.00x (ISBN 0-313-20353-9, MANE). Greenwood.

--Our Faiths. 1976. pap. 1.75 o.s.i. (ISBN 0-515-09588-5). Jove Pubns.

--Righteous Empire. 1977. pap. text ed. 4.95xi o.p. (ISBN 0-06-131931-7, TB 1931, Torch). Har-Row.

Marty, Martin E., ed. Where the Spirit Leads: Seventeen American Denominations Today. LC 80-82197. 208p. (Orig.). 1980. pap. 4.25 (ISBN 0-8042-0868-9). John Knox.

Marty, Myron A., jt. auth. see Kyvig, David.

Marty, Myron A., jt. auth. see Kyvig, David E.

Martyrologe Colonial, No. 1-3. Tableau de l'Esclavage aux Colonies Francaises. (Slave Trade in France Ser., 1744-1848). 24p. (Fr.). 1974. Repr. of 1848 ed. 23.50 o.p. (ISBN 0-8287-0323-X, TN 143). Clearwater Pub.

Martz, Edwine M., ed. see Walpole, Horace.

Martz, Harry F. & Waller, Ray A. Bayesian Reliability Analysis. LC 81-21878. (Wiley Series in Probability & Mathematical Statistics: Applied Probability & Statistic Section). 745p. 1982. 44.95x (ISBN 0-471-86425-0, Pub. by Wiley-Interscience). Wiley.

Martz, Jim. Hurricane Strikes: University of Miami Baseball. 200p. 1983. 10.95 (ISBN 0-87397-248-1). Strode.

Martz, Louis. The Paradise Within: Studies in Vaughan, Traherne, & Milton. 236p. 1983. pap. 7.95x (ISBN 0-300-00164-9). Yale U Pr.

Martz, Mary Reid Jeanne. The Central American Soccer War: Historical Patterns & Internal Dynamics of OAS Settlement Procedures. LC 78-11595. (Papers in International Studies: Latin American: No. 4). 1978. pap. 7.00 (ISBN 0-89680-077-6, Ohio U Ctr Intl). Ohio U Pr.

Martz, William J. Beginnings in Poetry. 2nd ed. 1973. pap. 9.95x (ISBN 0-673-07713-6). Scott F.

--Distinctive Voice: Twentieth Century American Poetry. 1966. pap. 9.95x (ISBN 0-673-05642-2). Scott F.

Maru, Olavi. Digest of Bar Association Ethics Opinion: 1975 Supplement. Sikes, Bette, ed. 1977. lib. bdg. 20.00 (ISBN 0-910058-84-9). Am Bar Foun.

Maru, Olavi, ed. Supplement to the Digest of Bar Association Ethics Opinions, 1980: Including 1970 & 1975 Supplements & Index. ix, 835p. Date not set. 50.00 (ISBN 0-910059-01-2). Am Bar Foun.

Maruki, Toshi. Hiroshima No Pika. LC 82-15365. (Illus.). 48p. (gr. 7 up). 1982. 12.00 (ISBN 0-688-01297-3). Lothrop.

Marulli, Luciana, tr. see Lunati, Rinaldo.

Marvan, Jiri. Prehistoric Slavic Contraction. Gray, Wilson, tr. LC 78-23498. (Illus.). 1979. text ed. 18.50x (ISBN 0-271-00210-7). Pa St U Pr.

Marvell, Andrew. Andrew Marvell: Selected Poems. Hutchings, Bill, ed. (Fyfield). 96p. 1979. pap. text ed. 5.25x (ISBN 0-85635-258-6, Pub. by Carcanet New Pr England). Humanities.

--The Garden. LC 79-123434. (Illus.). 1970. ltd. ed. 140.00 (ISBN 0-87923-011-8). Godine.

--Poems & Letters of Andrew Marvell, 2 vols. 3rd ed. Margoliouth, H. M., et al, eds. (Oxford English Texts Ser). (Illus.). 1971. 78.00x set (ISBN 0-19-811853-8). Oxford U Pr.

--The Poems of Andrew Marvell. MacDonald, Hugh, ed. (Muses' Library). 206p. 1969. pap. 8.95 (ISBN 0-7100-4920-X). Routledge & Kegan.

Marvell, E. N., jt. auth. see Kice, J. L.

Marvell, Thomas B. Appellate Courts & Lawyers: Information Gathering in the Adversary System. LC 77-94743. (Contributions in Legal Studies: No. 4). 1978. lib. bdg. 29.95x (ISBN 0-313-20312-1, MAA/). Greenwood.

Marvelle, James. The Sound of Our Bodies. (Contemporary Poets Ser.: No. 5). 48p. (Orig.). 1983. pap. 3.95 (ISBN 0-916982-30-0, RL230). Realities.

Marvell-Mell, Linnaea. NLP Skillbuilders: Advanced Techniques in Neuro-Linguistic Programming, Book II. (NLP Skillbuilders Ser.). (gr. 9-12). 1982. 34.95 (ISBN 0-686-38220-X); write for info. Metamorphous Pr.

--NLP Skillbuilders: Basic Techniques in Neuro-Linguistic Programming, Book I. (NLP Skillbuilders Ser.). (Illus.). (gr. 9-12). 1982. 34.95 (ISBN 0-686-38226-9); write for info. Metamorphous Pr.

Marvick, Elizabeth W., jt. auth. see Leites, N.

Marvin, Edgar. When the Movies Began: The First Film Star. LC 78-15167. (Famous First in History Ser.). PLB 10.76 (ISBN 0-89547-055-1). Silver.

Marvin, Frederic R. Last Words (Real & Traditional) of Distinguished Men & Women. LC 72-140424. 1971. Repr. of 1910 ed. 34.00x (ISBN 0-8103-3187-X). Gale.

Marvin, Mark C. Expert Protein Combining for Vegetarians. 20p. 1982. pap. 2.95 cancelled (ISBN 0-9604336-2-7). Marvanco.

--New Vitamin Cures. new ed. LC 80-81401. 284p. 1980. 10.95 (ISBN 0-9604336-1-9); pap. 6.50 (ISBN 0-9604336-0-0). Marvanco.

Marvin, Philip. Managing Your Successful Career. 1978. text ed. 12.95 (ISBN 0-8403-1876-6). Kendall Hunt.

Marvin, Stephen. Africa Below the Sahara. rev. ed. (World Studies Inquiry Ser.). (gr. 7-12). 1979. pap. text ed. 7.32 (ISBN 0-201-42665-X, Sch Div); tchr's ed. 3.32 (ISBN 0-201-42666-8). A-W.

Marwah, Onkar & Pollack, Jonathan D., eds. Military Power & Policy in Asian States: Toward the 1980's. (Special Studies in Military Affairs Ser.). 1979. lib. bdg. 25.00 (ISBN 0-89158-407-2). Westview.

Marwah, Onkar & Schulz, Ann, eds. Nuclear Proliferation & the Near-Nuclear Countries. 1975. 22.50x (ISBN 0-88410-605-5). Ballinger Pub.

Marwah, Onkar S., jt. auth. see Katz, James E.

Marwick, Arthur. British Society since Nineteen Forty-Five. 304p. 1982. 40.00x o.p. (ISBN 0-7139-1075-5, Pub. by Penguin Bks). State Mutual Bk.

--British Society Since '45. 1983. pap. cancelled (ISBN 0-14-021906-4, Pelican). Penguin.

Marx, jt. auth. see Heath.

Marx, Anne. By Way of People. 1970. 4.00 o.p. (ISBN 0-8233-0147-8). Golden Quill.

Marx, Bob. Rx: Take Two Joints & Go to Bed. LC 81-86204. 208p. 1983. pap. 5.95 (ISBN 0-86666-077-1). GWP.

Marx, Bomer Von see Von Marx, Bomer.

Marx, Emanuel. The Social Context of Violent Behaviour: A Social Anthropological Study in an Israeli Immigrant Town. (Direct Editions Ser.). (Orig.). 1976. text ed. 14.50x (ISBN 0-7100-8420-X). Routledge & Kegan.

Marx, Fredrick, jt. auth. see Sharpe, John C.

Marx, G. F. & Bassell, G. M. Obstetric Analgesia & Anesthesia. (Monographs in Anesthesia Ser.: Vol. 7). 1980. 82.75 (ISBN 0-444-80137-5); pap. 41.50 (ISBN 0-444-00437-8). Elsevier.

Marx, Gary, jt. auth. see Goodman, Norman.

Marx, Groucho & Anobile, Richard. The Marx Brothers Scrapbook. 1974. 13.95 o.p. (ISBN 0-517-51546-6, Darien Hse). Crown.

Marx, Groucho & Arce, Hector. The Secret Word Is Groucho. LC 76-458. 1976. 7.95 o.p. (ISBN 0-399-11690-7). Putnam Pub Group.

Marx, K. & Engels, F. Mega, Vol. 4, pt. 2. 911p. 60.00x (ISBN 0-8285-2205-7, Pub. by Diet Germany). Imported Pubns.

Marx, Karl. Capital. 1936. 5.95 o.s.i. (ISBN 0-394-60726-0, G26). Modern Lib.

--Capital & Other Writings. 1932. 3.95 o.s.i. (ISBN 0-394-60202-1, M202). Modern Lib.

--The Communist Manifesto. (Illus.). 1983. 3.25 (ISBN 0-7178-0600-6). Intl Pub Co.

--Early Writings. 1963. pap. 4.95 (ISBN 0-07-040671-5, SP). McGraw.

--The Portable Karl Marx. Kamenka, Eugene, ed. 704p. 1983. pap. 6.95 (ISBN 0-14-015096-X). Penguin.

--Wages, Price & Profit. 55p. 1976. pap. 0.95 (ISBN 0-8285-0060-6, Pub. by Progress Pubs USSR). Imported Pubns.

Marx, Karl & Engels, Frederick. Cologne Communist Trial. Livingstone, Rodney, tr. from Ger. 298p. 1974. 15.00x (ISBN 0-8464-0256-4). Beekman Pubs.

--Revolution in Spain. LC 74-27667. 255p. 1975. Repr. of 1939 ed. lib. bdg. 17.00x (ISBN 0-8371-7909-2, MARS). Greenwood.

Marx, Karl & Engels, Friedrich. Communist Manifesto. Huberman, Leo, ed. Bd. with Principles of Communism. Friedrich, Engels. LC 64-21175. 1964. 5.50 o.p. (ISBN 0-85345-019-6, CL0196); pap. 3.95 (ISBN 0-85345-062-5, PB0625). Monthly Rev.

--On Religion. LC 82-17032. (Classics in Religious Studies). 384p. 1982. Repr. of 1964 ed. 10.50x (ISBN 0-89130-599-8, 00 05 03). Scholars Pr CA.

Marx, Karl & Engles, Friedrich. Harold J. Laski on the Communist Manifesto. 1982. pap. 2.25 (ISBN 0-451-62125-5, ME2125, Ment). NAL.

Marx, Leo. Machine in the Garden: Technology & the Pastoral Ideal in America. (Illus.). 1967. pap. 8.95 (ISBN 0-19-500738-7, GB). Oxford U Pr.

Marx, M., jt. auth. see Larsen, R.

Marx, Maxine. Growing up with Chico. LC 80-15387. 1980. 9.95 o.p. (ISBN 0-13-367821-0). P-H.

Marx, Melvin H. & Hillix, William A. Systems & Theories in Psychology. 3rd ed. (Illus.). 1979. text ed. 27.50 (ISBN 0-07-040679-0, C). McGraw.

Marx, Melvin H., jt. auth. see Hillix, William A.

Marx Memorial Library, London. Catalog of the Marx Memorial Library. 1979. lib. bdg. 285.00 (ISBN 0-8161-0280-5, Hall Library). G K Hall.

Marx, Patricia & Stuart, Sarah. How To Regain Your Virginity: And Ninety-Nine Other Recent Discoveries About Sex. (Illus.). 144p. 1983. pap. 4.95 (ISBN 0-89480-365-4). Workman Pub.

Marx, Robert F. Spanish Treasure in Florida Waters: A Billion Dollar Graveyard. LC 78-65775. (Illus.). 1979. 15.00 (ISBN 0-913352-06-3). Mariners Boston.

Marx, Samuel & Clayton, Jan. Rodgers & Hart: Bewitched, Bothered & Bedeviled. LC 76-12494. (Illus.). 1976. 10.00 o.p. (ISBN 0-399-11786-5). Putnam Pub Group.

Marx, Werner. Heidegger Memorial Lectures. 125p. 1982. 10.00x (ISBN 0-8207-0154-8). Humanities.

Marx, Werner, ed. Heidegger: The University of Freiburg Memorial Lectures. 125p. 1981. text ed. 12.50x (ISBN 0-8207-0154-8). Duquesne.

Marx, Wesley. Acts of God, Acts of Man. (Illus.). 256p. 1977. 8.95 o.p. (ISBN 0-698-10631-8, Coward). Putnam Pub Group.

--The Protected Ocean: How to Keep the Seas Alive. (New Conservation Ser.). (Illus.). (gr. 7 up). 1972. PLB 4.99 o.p. (ISBN 0-698-30428-4, Coward). Putnam Pub Group.

Marxhausen, Ben, jt. auth. see Marxhausen, Joanne.

Marxhausen, Evelyn. The Man Who Slept Through a Sermon. (Arch Bk.: No. 16). (Illus.). 1979. 0.89 (ISBN 0-570-06128-8, 59-1246). Concordia.

--When God Laid Down the Law. LC 59-1259. (Arch Bk.). 1981. pap. 0.89 (ISBN 0-570-06142-3). Concordia.

--When God Made Baalam's Donkey Talk. 1980. pap. 0.89 (ISBN 0-570-06135-0, 59-1253, Arch Bk). Concordia.

Marxhausen, Joanne. The Mysterious Star. (Illus.). 48p. (gr. 1-3). 1974. 7.95 (ISBN 0-570-03433-7, 56-1188). Concordia.

Marxhausen, Joanne & Marxhausen, Ben. I Am a Cloud. (Illus.). 1979. 1.95 (ISBN 0-570-07951-9, 56-1320). Concordia.

--I Am a Tree. (Illus.). 1979. 1.95 (ISBN 0-570-07952-7, 56-1321). Concordia.

--I Am People. (Illus.). 1979. 1.95 (ISBN 0-570-07953-5, 56-1322). Concordia.

--I Am the Sun. (Illus.). 1979. 1.95 (ISBN 0-570-07950-0, 56-1319). Concordia.

Marxist-Leninist Party, U. S. A. El Avance del Movimiento Revolucionario Require de una Enconada Lucha Contra la Socialdemocracia y el Liquidacionismo. 93p. (Span.). pap. 1.00 (ISBN 0-86714-023-2). Marxist-Leninist.

--Songbook: Down with Ronald Reagan, Chieftain of Capitalist Reaction & Other Songs of Revolutionary Struggle & Socialism. (Illus.). 84p. 1982. pap. 1.00 (ISBN 0-86714-024-0). Marxist-Leninist.

--La Verdad sobre las Relaciones entre el Partido Marxista de los EUA y el Partido Communista del Canada. 86p. (Span.). 1982. pap. 1.00 (ISBN 0-86714-022-4). Marxist-Leninist.

Mary, Mother & Ware, Archimandrite K., trs. The Lenten Triodion. 700p. 1979. 32.00 (ISBN 0-571-11253-6). Faber & Faber.

Mary Francis, Sr. Right to Be Merry. LC 73-6850. 1973. pap. 1.95 o.p. (ISBN 0-8199-0506-2). Franciscan Herald.

Maryland Chapter Arthritis Foundation. Beyond Beer & Crabs: Cooking in Maryland. Streich, Marianne, ed. (Illus.). 192p. (Orig.). 1982. pap. 6.50. Wimmer Bks.

Maryland Historical Society in Connection with the Celebration of the 150th Anniversary of the Settlement of Baltimore. Proceedings. 123p. 1880. 9.50 (ISBN 0-686-36844-4). Md Hist.

Maryland Historical Society, 50th Anniversary. Proceedings. 6.00 (ISBN 0-686-36717-0). Md Hist.

Maryland Historical Trust. Inventory of Historic Sites in Calvert County, Charles Country, & St. Mary's County. rev. ed. (Illus.). 179p. 1980. 14.00 (ISBN 0-686-36815-0). Md Hist.

Maryland Hospital Education Institute. Controlling Hospital Liability: A Systems Approach. (Illus.). 40p. (Orig.). 1976. pap. 10.00 (ISBN 0-87258-199-3, AHA-178134). Am Hospital.

--Hospital-Sponsored Ambulatory Care: The Governing Board's Role. LC 80-18004. (Illus.). 116p. (Orig.). 1980. pap. 18.75 (ISBN 0-87258-308-2, AHA-016077). Am Hospital.

Maryland State Dept. of Education, ed. see Cyzyk, Janet L.

Mary Of Agreda. The City of God, 4 vols. Set. 35.00 o.s.i. (ISBN 0-686-74594-9). Prow Bks-Franciscan.

Marz, Roy. The Island-Maker. LC 82-17282. 100p. (Orig.). 1982. pap. 6.00 (ISBN 0-87886-120-3). Ithaca Hse.

Marzan, Betty, jt. auth. see Mattil, Edward L.

Marzano, Dale. Roller Disco. LC 78-24717. (Illus.). 1979. pap. 4.95 o.p. (ISBN 0-89196-039-2, Domus Bks). Quality Bks IL.

Marzano, Dale A. Disco Roller Skating. (Illus.). 96p. 1979. 5.98 o.p. (ISBN 0-89196-048-1, Bk Value Intl). Quality Bks IL.

Marzell, Ernst S. Great Inventions. LC 77-171532. (Real Life Bks). (Illus.). 32p. (gr. 5-9). 1973. PLB 4.95g (ISBN 0-8225-0705-6). Lerner Pubns.

Marzik, Thomas D., jt. ed. see Miller, Randall M.

Marzilli, jt. auth. see Eichorn, G. L.

Marzine, Carl. The Alpha & the Omega. Bd. with The Rebel Drug Addict. 1982. 6.95 (ISBN 0-533-04411-1). Vantage.

Marzio, Peter, ed. A Nation of Nations. LC 75-25051. (Illus.). 416p. (YA) 1976. 28.80i (ISBN 0-06-012834-8, HarpT); pap. 8.95 o.p. (ISBN 0-06-012836-4, TD-256, HarpT). Har-Row.

Marzollo, Claudio, jt. auth. see Marzollo, Jean.

Marzollo, Jean. Birthday Parties for Children: How to Give Them, How to Survive Them. LC 82-48234. (Illus.). 160p. 1983. pap. 4.76i (ISBN 0-06-091014-3, CN 1014, CN). Har-Row.

--Birthday Parties for Children: How to Give Them, How to Survive Them. LC 82-48234. (Illus.). 160p. 1983. 12.95 (ISBN 0-06-015119-6, HarpT); pap. 4.95 (ISBN 0-06-091014-3). Har-Row.

--Do You Love Me, Harvey Burns? LC 82-73218. 224p. 1983. 10.95 (ISBN 0-8037-1668-0, 01063-320). Dial Bks Young.

--Superkids. LC 80-8691. (Illus.). 1982. pap. 4.76i (ISBN 0-06-090939-0, CN939, CN). Har-Row.

--Supertot: Creative Learning Activities for Children 1-3 & Sympathetic Advice for Their Parents. LC 76-47265. (Illus.). 1978. 12.45i (ISBN 0-06-012847-X, HarpT). Har-Row.

Marzollo, Jean & Lloyd, Janice. Learning Through Play. LC 78-144182. (Illus.). 192p. 1972. 14.37i (ISBN 0-06-012819-4, HarpT). Har-Row.

Marzollo, Jean & Marzollo, Claudio. Red Sun Girl. LC 82-45507. (Illus.). 56p. (ps-3). 1983. lib. bdg. 8.89 (ISBN 0-8037-7494-X, 0383-120); pap. 3.95 (ISBN 0-8037-7494-X). Dial Bks Young.

--Robin of Bray. (Dial Easy-to-Read ser.). 56p. (ps-3). 1982. 8.89 (ISBN 0-8037-7332-3); pap. 3.75 (ISBN 0-8037-7329-3). Dial.

Marzollo, Jean & Savage, Beth. Letter Sounds. (Learning Workbooks Language Arts). (gr. k-2). pap. 1.50 (ISBN 0-8224-4175-6). Pitman.

--Number & Number Values. (gr. k-2). pap. 1.50 (ISBN 0-8224-4183-7). Pitman.

Marzuki, S. & Dilts, R. Bintang Anda: A Game Process for Community Development. (Technical Note Ser.: No. 18). 21p. (Orig.). 1982. pap. 1.00 (ISBN 0-686-84116-6). Ctr Intl Ed U of MA.

Marzulli, Francis N. & Maibach, Howard I., eds. Dermatotoxicology. 2nd ed. LC 82-9234. (Illus.). 605p. 1982. text ed. 59.95 (ISBN 0-89116-250-X). Hemisphere Pub.

Masamune, S. Organic Synthesis. (Organic Synthesis Ser.: Vol. 55). 1976. 18.95 o.s.i. (ISBN 0-471-57390-6, Pub. by Wiley-Interscience). Wiley.

Masani, P., ed. see Weiner, Norbert.

Masani, P., ed. see Wiener, Norbert.

Masaryk, Thomas G. Suicide & the Meaning of Civilization. Weist, William B. & Batson, Robert G., trs. from Ger. LC 74-108777. (Heritage of Sociology Ser). 1970. 17.50x o.s.i. (ISBN 0-226-50931-1). U of Chicago Pr.

Masaryk, Tomas G. Modern Man & Religion. Kennedy, H. E., ed. Repr. of 1938 ed. lib. bdg. 15.75x (ISBN 0-8371-4273-3, MAMR). Greenwood.

Masayesva, Victor & Younger, Erin, eds. Hopi Photographers-Hopi Images. (Sun Tracks Ser.). 1983. 25.00 (ISBN 0-8165-0809-7); pap. 14.95 (ISBN 0-8165-0804-6). U of Ariz Pr.

Mascarenhas, R. C. Technology Transfer & Development: India's Hindustan Machine Tools Company. 235p. 1982. softcover 19.50 (ISBN 0-86531-934-0). Westview.

Mascari, Claude J., et al, eds. see Reid, Charles F., III.

Mascari, Claude J., et al, eds. see Reid, Charles, 3rd.

Mascaro, Juan, tr. Bhagavad Gita. (Classics Ser.). (Orig.). 1962. pap. 2.95 (ISBN 0-14-044121-2). Penguin.

Mascelli, Joseph V. The Five C's of Cinematography. lib. bdg. 29.50 o.p. (ISBN 0-9600240-0-X). Calif Pubns.

Mascetta, Joseph A. Chemistry the Easy Way. (Easy Way Ser.). 320p. (gr. 10-12). 1983. pap. write for info. (ISBN 0-8120-2624-1). Barron.

Maschke, Joachim. Moose Als Bioindikatoren Von Schwermetall-Immissionen. (Bryophytorum Bibliotheca: No. 22). (Illus.). 492p. (Ger.). 1981. lib. bdg. 60.00x (ISBN 3-7682-1320-X). Lubrecht & Cramer.

Maschke, Ruby. Bible People Story-N-Puzzle Book. Sparks, Judith Ann, ed. 48p. (Orig.). (gr. 7 up). 1983. pap. 1.50 (ISBN 0-87239-673-8, 2773). Standard Pub.

--Blinkety Blanks. Zapel, Arthur L., ed. (Illus., Orig.). (gr. 6-12). 1981. 1.50 (ISBN 0-916260-10-0). Meriwether Pub.

--Disciples of Christ Story-N-Puzzle Book. 48p. (Orig.). (gr. 7 up). 1983. pap. 1.50 (ISBN 0-87239-675-4, 2775). Standard Pub.

--Promises of Jesus From the Gospel: Puzzle Book. (Illus.). 48p. 1983. pap. 1.50 (ISBN 0-87239-591-X, 2789). Standard Pub.

Mascia, L. Thermoplastics: Materials Engineering. (Illus.). xiii, 440p. 1983. 78.00 (ISBN 0-85334-146-X, Pub. by Applied Sci England). Elsevier.

Mas-Colell, Andrew, ed. Noncooperative Approaches to the Theory of Perfect Competition. LC 82-13936. 1982. 25.00 (ISBN 0-12-476750-8). Acad Pr.

Mascona, A., ed. Current Topics in Development Biology, Vol. 17. Hunt. 309p. 1982. 42.00 (ISBN 0-12-153117-1). Acad Pr.

Mascott, Holly A. Cherish the Dream. (Orig.). 1983. pap. 3.95 (ISBN 0-440-11614-7). Dell.

Mase, G. E. Continuum Mechanics. (Schaum's Outline Ser). 1970. pap. 7.95 (ISBN 0-07-040663-4, SP). McGraw.

Masefield, G. B. Food & Nutrition Procedures in Times Of Disaster. (FAO Nutritional Studies: No. 21). 96p. 1967. pap. 9.00 o.p. (ISBN 0-686-92767-2, F189, FAO). Unipub.

Masefield, Geoffrey B. A Short History of Agriculture in the British Colonies. LC 77-26015. 1978. Repr. of 1950 ed. lib. bdg. 18.25x (ISBN 0-313-20094-7, MAAG). Greenwood.

Masello, Robert. What Do Men Want from Women? 160p. (Orig.). 1983. pap. 4.95 (ISBN 0-345-30822-0). Ballantine.

Masereel, Frans. The City. Orig. Title: Die Stadt. (Illus.). 1970. pap. 2.00 o.p. (ISBN 0-486-22448-1). Dover.

Maserve, Robert L., jt. auth. see Camp, Thomas.

Masetto, Antonio Dal see Dal Masetto, Antonio.

Mashayekhi, Afsaneh. Shadow Prices for Project Appraisal in Turkey. (Working Paper: No. 392). 57p. 1980. 5.00 (ISBN 0-686-36091-5, WP-0392). World Bank.

Mashelkar, R. A., jt. auth. see Mujumdar, A. S.

Masi, Dale A. Human Services in Industry. 272p. 1981. 28.95 (ISBN 0-669-05104-7). Lexington Bks.

--Organizing for Women: Issues, Strategies, & Services. LC 78-19577. (Illus.). 240p. 1981. 24.95 (ISBN 0-669-02577-1). Lexington Bks.

Masi, Edoarda. China Winter: Workers, Mandarins & the Purge of the Gang of Four. Foulke, Adrienne, tr. LC 81-12502. 367p. 1982. 19.95 (ISBN 0-525-10764-9, 01937-580). Dutton.

Masi, Michael. Boethian Number Theory: A Translation of the De Institutione Arithmetica. Date not set. pap. text ed. price not set (ISBN 0-85635-155-5). Humanities.

Masia, Seth, jt. auth. see Bennet, John.

Masin, Herman L. The Funniest Moments in Sports. LC 73-86219. (Illus.). 128p. (gr. 4 up). 1974. 5.95 (ISBN 0-87131-133-X); pap. 1.95 (ISBN 0-87131-152-6). M Evans.

Maskaleris, Thanasis. Kostis Palamas. (World Authors Ser.). lib. bdg. 15.95 (ISBN 0-8057-2666-7, Twayne). G K Hall.

Maskell. Urinary Tract Infections. (Current Topics in Infections Ser.: Vol. 3). 1982. 29.50 (ISBN 0-444-00459-9). Elsevier.

Maskell, Alfred. Ivories. LC 66-20572. (Illus.). 551p. 1966. 57.50 (ISBN 0-8048-0269-6). C E Tuttle.

Maskelyne, Nevil. Maskelyne on the Performance of Magic. LC 75-22648. 160p. 1976. pap. 2.00 o.p. (ISBN 0-486-23238-7). Dover.

Maslach, Christina, jt. auth. see Zimbardo, Philip.

Maslak, Paul. Strategy in Unarmed Combat. LC 80-130558. (Illus.). 136p. 1980. pap. 6.95 (ISBN 0-86568-000-0). Unique Pubns.

--What the Masters Know. LC 80-130491. (Illus.). 108p. 1980. pap. 6.95 (ISBN 0-86568-001-9). Unique Pubns.

Masland, John W., jt. auth. see Lyons, Gene M.

Masling, J., ed. Empirical Studies of Psychoanalytical Theories. (Illus.). 320p. 1982. text ed. 29.95 (ISBN 0-88163-000-4). L Erlbaum Assocs.

Maslov, Norman, jt. auth. see Bacon, David.

Maslow, Abraham H. Psychology of Science: A Reconnaissance. LC 66-11479. 190p. 1966. pap. 3.95 (ISBN 0-89526-972-4). Regnery-Gateway.

--Religions, Values, & Peak-Experiences. 1976. pap. 3.95 (ISBN 0-14-004262-8). Penguin.

Maslow, Abraham H., ed. New Knowledge in Human Values. LC 58-11501. 1970. pap. 5.95 (ISBN 0-89526-978-3). Regnery-Gateway.

Maslow, P. Chemical Materials for Construction. 1981. 32.50 o.p. (ISBN 0-07-040664-2). McGraw.

Maslow, William C., et al. Practical Diagnosis: Hematologic Disease. 1980. kroydenflex bdg. 25.00 (ISBN 0-471-09488-9, Pub. by Wiley Med). Wiley.

Maslowski, Peter. Treason Must Be Made Odious: Military Occupation & Wartime Reconstruction in Nashville, Tennessee. 1862-65. LC 78-16799. (KTO Studies in American History). 1979. lib. bdg. 25.00 (ISBN 0-527-62185-4). Kraus Intl.

Maslowski, Stanley. What's the Good Word. LC 67-29591. 1967. 3.95 o.p. (ISBN 0-685-07676-8, 80434). Glencoe.

Masnick, George & Bane, Mary Jo. The Nation's Families: 1960-1990. LC 80-20531. (Illus.). 200p. (Orig.). 1980. 19.95 (ISBN 0-86569-050-2); pap. 10.95 (ISBN 0-86569-051-0). Auburn Hse.

Masnick, George & Pitkin, John. The Changing Population of State & Regions: Analysis & Projections, 1970-2000. (Illus.). 250p. (Orig.). 1982. pap. 12.00 (ISBN 0-943142-01-6). Joint Cen Urban.

Mason. Forensic Medicine for Lawyers. 2nd ed. 1983. text ed. write for info. (ISBN 0-407-00244-8). Butterworth.

--Plaid for Business & Economic Statistics. rev. ed. 1978. 5.95 o.p. (ISBN 0-256-00119-7, 10-0506-02). Dow Jones-Irwin.

Mason, A. These Unmusical Days. 90p. 1951. 8.95 o.p. (ISBN 0-8173-8500-2). U of Ala Pr.

Mason, A. T. & Beaney, Wiliam M. American Constitutional Law: Introductory Essays & Selected Cases. 6th ed. 1978. text ed. 27.95 (ISBN 0-13-024778-2). P-H.

Mason, Abelle. Understanding Academic Lectures. (Illus.). 208p. 1983. pap. text ed. 9.95 (ISBN 0-13-936419-6). P-H.

Mason, Alexander. The Real Estate Broker's Inside Guide to Selling Your Own Home. 288p. 1982. 12.95 (ISBN 0-698-11138-9, Coward). Putnam Pub Group.

Mason, Alpheus T. Free Government in the Making: Readings in American Political Thought. 3rd ed. 1965. 22.50x (ISBN 0-19-500963-0). Oxford U Pr.

--The States Rights Debate: Anti-Federalism & the Constitution. 2nd ed. 1972. pap. text ed. 5.95x (ISBN 0-19-501553-3). Oxford U Pr.

Mason, Alpheus T. & Beaney, William M. American Constitutional Law: Introductory Essays & Selected Cases. 7th ed. 704p. 1983. text ed. 27.95 (ISBN 0-13-024695-6). P-H.

Mason, Alpheus T. & Leach, Richard H. In Quest of Freedom: American Political Thought & Practice. LC 80-5749. 432p. 1981. pap. text ed. 13.25 (ISBN 0-8191-1473-1). U Pr of Amer.

Mason, Anne. Cook for Tomorrow. 1966. 7.50 o.p. (ISBN 0-233-95914-9). Transatlantic.

Mason, B. J. Clouds, Rain & Rainmaking. 2nd ed. LC 74-16991. (Illus.). 160p. 1976. 22.95x (ISBN 0-521-20650-2). Cambridge U Pr.

Mason, Bernard, ed. The American Colonial Crisis: The Daniel Leonard - John Adams Letters to the Press 1774-1775. 5.50 o.p. (ISBN 0-8446-4584-2). Peter Smith.

Mason, Bernard S. Boomerangs: How to Make & Throw Them. LC 73-94346. (Illus.). 1974. pap. 2.50 (ISBN 0-486-23028-7). Dover.

--How to Make Drums, Tom Toms & Rattles. (Illus.). 208p. 1974. pap. 4.00 (ISBN 0-486-21889-9). Dover.

--Primitive & Pioneer Sports for Recreation Today: Rope Spinning, Lariat Throwing, Tumblesticks, Whip Cracking, Boomerangs, Log Rolling, Boomabirds, Tomahawks, Darts, Blowguns, & Many Others. LC 76-162516. (Illus.). 342p. 1975. Repr. of 1937 ed. 37.00x (ISBN 0-8103-4029-1). Gale.

Mason, Betty. I Go to School. LC 73-157406. (Illus.). (gr. k-1). 1971. 3.50 o.p. (ISBN 0-8054-4221-9). Broadman.

Mason, Beverly & Finley, Virginia. A Cat Called Room 8. (Illus.). (gr. 2-6). 1966. PLB 4.97 o.p. (ISBN 0-399-60085-X). Putnam Pub Group.

Mason, Bill. Path of the Paddle: An Illustrated Guide to the Art of Canoeing. 192p. 1980. 24.95 o.p. (ISBN 0-442-29630-4). Van Nos Reinhold.

Mason, Bobbie A. Shiloh & Other Stories. LC 82-47541. 288p. 1982. 12.45i (ISBN 0-06-015062-9, HarpT). Har-Row.

Mason, Brian. Principles of Geochemistry. 3rd ed. LC 66-26752. 1966. 30.95 (ISBN 0-471-57521-6). Wiley.

Mason, Brian & Moore, Carleton B. Principles of Geochemistry. 4th ed. 368p. 1982. text ed. 29.95 (ISBN 0-471-57522-4). Wiley.

Mason, C. F. Decomposition. (Studies in Biology: No. 74). 64p. 1977. pap. text ed. 8.95 (ISBN 0-7131-2589-6). E Arnold.

Mason, C. M., jt. auth. see Witherick, M. E.

Mason, C. R. Art & Science of Protective Relaying. LC 56-8694. 1956. 44.95 (ISBN 0-471-57552-6, Pub. by Wiley-Interscience). Wiley.

Mason, C. W., jt. auth. see Chamot, E. M.

Mason, C. W., jt. auth. see Chamot, Emile M.

Mason, Charles, jt. auth. see Melges, Buddy.

Mason, Charles W. The Value-Philosophy of Alfred Edward Taylor: A Study in Theistic Implication. LC 79-52512. 1979. pap. text ed. 15.00 (ISBN 0-8191-0772-7). U Pr of Amer.

Mason, D., ed. see Meigs, Walter B. & Meigs, Robert F.

Mason, D. K. & Chisolm, D. M. Salivary Glands in Health & Disease. LC 75-1402. (Illus.). 320p. 1975. text ed. 15.00 (ISBN 0-7216-6135-1). Saunders.

Mason, D. T. & Neri Serneri, G. G., eds. Myocardial Infarction, 2 vols. (International Congress Ser.: Vol. 491). 1980. Set. 148.00 (ISBN 0-686-95522-6). Elsevier.

Mason, Daniel G. Dilemma of American Music, & Other Essays. Repr. of 1928 ed. lib. bdg. 16.00x (ISBN 0-8371-1155-2, MAAM). Greenwood.

--Romantic Composers. Repr. of 1906 ed. lib. bdg. 17.50 (ISBN 0-8371-4096-X, MARC). Greenwood.

Mason, David & Dyller, Fran. Pharmaceutical Dictionary & Reference for Prescriptions Drugs. Rev. ed. (Illus.). 270p. 1982. pap. 3.50 (ISBN 0-87216-998-7). Playboy.

Mason, David, jt. auth. see Hunt, Robert.

Mason, David K. Time & Providence: An Essay Based on an Analysis of the Concept of Time in Whitehead & Heidegger. LC 81-40007. 464p. (Orig.). 1982. lib. bdg. 29.50 (ISBN 0-8191-2131-2); pap. text ed. 17.25 (ISBN 0-8191-2132-0). U Pr of Amer.

Mason, David M, et al see Heat Transfer & Fluid Mechanics Institute.

Mason, Dean T., ed. Advances in Heart Disease, Vol. 3. (Clinical Cardiology Monograph). 811p. 1980. 56.50 (ISBN 0-8089-1284-4). Grune.

Mason, Donald G., ed. see Woltz, Phebe M. & Arlen, Richard T.

Mason, E. A. & Spurling, T. H. The Viral Equation of State. LC 69-17903. 1970. text ed. 47.00 o.s.i. (ISBN 0-08-013292-8); pap. text ed. 31.00 (ISBN 0-08-018988-1). Pergamon.

Mason, E. J. Caves & Caving in Britain. (Illus.). 1977. 12.00 o.p. (ISBN 0-7091-6195-6). Transatlantic.

Mason, Edite. To Be a Writer: A Course in Creative Writing. 1971. pap. 4.95 o.p. (ISBN 0-7195-2059-2). Transatlantic.

Mason Editorial Staff, ed. see Eisberg, John F.

Mason, Edward S. & Asher, Robert E. The World Bank Since Bretton Woods. LC 73-1089. 1973. 25.95 (ISBN 0-8157-5492-2). Brookings.

Mason, Edwin. Collaborative Learning. LC 72-166549. 1973. pap. 2.95 o.p. (ISBN 0-8052-0396-6). Schocken.

Mason, Elizabeth B. & Starr, Louis M., eds. The Oral History Collection of Columbia University. 4th ed. (Illus.). xxx, 306p. 1979. text ed. 23.75 (ISBN 0-9602492-0-6). Oral History.

Mason, Elliott, jt. auth. see Spence, Alexander.

Mason, Emanuel J. & Bramble, William J. Understanding & Conducting Research: Applications in Education & the Behavioral Sciences. (Illus.). 1977. text ed. 29.00 (ISBN 0-07-040697-9, C). McGraw.

Mason, Eudo C. Goethe's Faust: Its Genesis & Purport. 1967. 30.00x (ISBN 0-520-00821-9). U of Cal Pr.

--Rilke, Europe, & the English-Speaking World. 1961. 44.50 (ISBN 0-521-05687-X). Cambridge U Pr.

Mason, Eugene, ed. Aucassin & Nicolette & Other Medieval Romances & Legends. 1958. pap. 3.45 o.p. (ISBN 0-525-47019-0). Dutton.

Mason, Eugene, tr. see Wace, Robert & Layamon.

Mason, Evelyn. A Sister for Sam. (Illus.). 40p. (ps-3). 1983. 4.99 (ISBN 0-910313-03-2). Parker Bro.

Mason, F. H., jt. auth. see Jensen, C. H.

Mason, Francis K. Harrier. (Illus.). 185p. 1982. 18.95 o.p. (ISBN 0-85059-501-0). Naval Inst Pr.

Mason, Gene. Save Your License: A Driver's Survival Guide. LC 78-2218. (Illus.). 150p. 1978. 10.95 (ISBN 0-87364-103-5). Paladin Pr.

Mason, George E. A Primer on Teaching Reading: Basic Concepts & Skills of the Early Elementary Years. LC 80-52458. 220p. 1981. pap. text ed. 9.95 (ISBN 0-87581-262-7). Peacock Pubs.

Mason, George F. Animal Habits. (Illus.). (gr. 5-9). 1959. PLB 8.16 (ISBN 0-688-31034-6). Morrow.

--Animal Sounds. (Illus.). (gr. 5-9). 1948. PLB 8.16 (ISBN 0-688-31036-2). Morrow.

Mason, Herbert, tr. Gilgamesh: A Verse Narrative. 128p. 1972. pap. 1.95 (ISBN 0-451-62199-9, MJ2199, Ment). NAL.

Mason, Herbert L. A Flora of the Marshes of California. LC 57-7960. (Illus.). 1957. 34.50x (ISBN 0-520-01433-2). U of Cal Pr.

Mason, Herbert M., Jr. Duel for the Sky: Fighter Planes & Fighting Pilots of World War II. LC 76-108914. (Elephant Bks). (Illus.). (gr. 4-8). 1977. pap. 2.95 o.p. (ISBN 0-448-12982-5, G&D). Putnam Pub Group.

--Famous Firsts in Exploration. (Famous Firsts Ser.). (Illus.). (gr. 5 up). 1967. PLB 4.49 o.p. (ISBN 0-399-60159-7). Putnam Pub Group.

Mason, J. A. Archaeology of Santa Maria, Colombia: The Tairona Culture. (Chicago Field Museum of Natural History Fieldiana Anthropology Ser). Repr. of 1939 ed. pap. 72.00 (ISBN 0-527-01880-5). Kraus Repr.

Mason, J. Alden. Ancient Civilizations of Peru. rev. ed. (Illus., Orig.). 1957. pap. 4.95 o.p. (ISBN 0-14-020395-8, Pelican). Penguin.

--Language of the Papago of Arizona. (Museum Monographs). 84p. 1950. soft bound 2.00 o.p. (ISBN 0-934718-00-8). Univ Mus of U PA.

Mason, J. W. Furniture Trade Catalog of J. W. Mason & Co. (Illus.). 116p. Date not set. pap. 25.00 (ISBN 0-87556-495-X). Saifer.

Mason, Jackie. Jackie Mason's America. 192p. 1983. 12.00 (ISBN 0-8184-0338-1). Lyle Stuart.

Mason, James H. The Dudley Genealogies. LC 82-62705. 200p. 1983. 20.00 (ISBN 0-9609032-1-6). J H Mason.

Mason, James J., ed. AIREA Financial Tables. 473p. 1982. 22.50 (ISBN 0-911780-68-8). Am Inst Real Estate Appraisers.

Mason, John. Financial Management of Commercial Banks. LC 78-24809. 442p. 1979. text ed. 17.95 o.p. (ISBN 0-88262-309-5). Warren.

Mason, John F., ed. Petroleum Geology in China. 264p. 1981. 43.95x (ISBN 0-87814-163-4). Pennwell Books Division.

Mason, John H. The Irresistible Diderot. 403p. 1982. 29.50 (ISBN 0-686-95247-2). Quartet Bks.

Mason, John M. Financial Management of Commercial Banks. LC 78-24809. 442p. 1982. text ed. 25.50 (ISBN 0-471-87745-X); tchrs.' ed avail. (ISBN 0-471-89511-3). Wiley.

Mason, John P. Island of the Blest: Islam in a Libyan Oasis Community. LC 77-620016. (Papers in International Studies: Africa: No. 31). (Illus.). 1977. pap. 10.00x (ISBN 0-89680-063-6, Ohio U Ctr Intl). Ohio U Pr.

Mason, Joseph. History of Housing in the U.S. 1930-1980. (Illus.). 280p. 1982. 22.50 (ISBN 0-686-96538-8); collector's ed. 35.00 (ISBN 0-686-99786-7). Natl Assn Home.

Mason, Joseph & Cox, Andrew. Great Black Men of Masonry: Qualitative Black Achievers Who Were Freemasons. 211p. 1982. 15.00 (ISBN 0-686-82377-X); pap. 8.00 (ISBN 0-686-82378-8). Blue Diamond.

Mason, K. L. Advanced Spanish Course. 1967. text ed. 11.40 o.s.i. (ISBN 0-08-012272-8); pap. text ed. 9.80 (ISBN 0-08-012271-X). Pergamon.

Mason, K. L., jt. auth. see Lawrence, M. J.

Mason, L. C. Scale Model Traction Engine Building Featuring 'Minnie' (Illus.). 232p. 1973. 12.50x (ISBN 0-85344-077-8). Intl Pubns Serv.

Mason, L. Ryder. California Family Law Handbook. LC 79-90704. 459p. 1980. 42.00 (ISBN 0-911110-31-3); 1982 suppl. incl. Parker & Son.

Mason, Lauris & Ludman, Joan. The Lithographs of George Bellows: A Catalogue Raisonne. LC 77-4348. 1977. 60.00 (ISBN 0-527-62200-1). Kraus Intl.

Mason, Lauris & Ludman, Joan, eds. Print Reference Sources: A Selected Bibliography, 18th-20th Centuries. 2nd ed. LC 78-31889. 1979. lib. bdg. 55.00 (ISBN 0-527-62190-0). Kraus Intl.

Mason, Linda & Brown, Roger. Rice, Rivalry & Politics: Managing Cambodian Relief. 256p. 1983. text ed. 19.95 (ISBN 0-268-01615-1); pap. text ed. 9.95 (ISBN 0-268-01616-X). U of Notre Dame Pr.

Mason, Lowell. Musical Letters from Abroad. 2nd ed. LC 67-13035. (Music Ser). 1967. Repr. of 1854 ed. lib. bdg. 29.50 (ISBN 0-306-70940-6). Da Capo.

Mason, Lowell & Webb, George J. The Boston Glee Book. LC 76-52481. (Music Reprint Ser., 1977). 1977. Repr. of 1844 ed. lib. bdg. 29.50 (ISBN 0-306-70860-4). Da Capo.

Mason, Lowell, ed. The Boston Handel & Haydn Society Collection of Church Music. LC 77-171078. (Earlier American Music Ser.: Vol. 15). 324p. 1973. Repr. of 1822 ed. lib. bdg. 29.50 (ISBN 0-306-77315-5). Da Capo.

Mason, M. A., jt. auth. see Smola, B. K.

Mason, M. J. How to Write Meaningful Nursing Standards. 355p. 1978. pap. 18.95x (ISBN 0-471-04439-3, Pub. by Wiley Med). Wiley.

Mason, Marcus M. Bibliography of the Dog. facsimile ed. 1959. pap. 13.50x o.p. (ISBN 0-8138-2210-6). Iowa St U Pr.

Mason, Marilyn G. The Federal Role in Library & Information Services. 150p. 1983. 34.50 (ISBN 0-86729-010-2); pap. 27.50 (ISBN 0-86729-009-9). Knowledge Indus.

Mason, Marion, et al. The Dynamics of Clinical Dietetics. LC 77-21936. 1977. pap. text ed. 18.95 o.p. (ISBN 0-471-02172-5, Pub. by Wiley Medical). Wiley.

--The Dynamics of Clinical Dietetics. 2nd ed. LC 81-16160. 354p. 1982. 18.95 (ISBN 0-471-06088-7, Pub. by Wiley Med). Wiley.

Mason, Mary G. & Green, Carol H., eds. Journeys: Autobiographical Writings by Women. 1979. lib. bdg. 14.95 (ISBN 0-8161-8310-4, Univ Bks). G K Hall.

Mason, Miriam E. Frances Willard: Girl Crusader. (Childhood of Famous Americans Ser.). (Illus.). (gr. 3-7). 1961. 3.95 o.p. (ISBN 0-672-50055-8). Bobbs.

--Mary Mapes Dodge: Jolly Girl. (Childhood of Famous Americans Ser). (Illus.). (gr. 3-7). 1949. 3.95 o.p. (ISBN 0-672-50131-7). Bobbs.

Mason, Needra E. Feelings. 1983. 6.95 (ISBN 0-533-05327-7). Vantage.

Mason, Nicholas, jt. auth. see Lovesey, John.

Mason, Nina B. Marah: The Woman at the Well. 1982. pap. 3.50 (ISBN 0-8423-4032-7). Tyndale.

Mason, Peter. The Light Fantastic. 1983. pap. 5.95 (ISBN 0-14-022449-1). Penguin.

Mason, Philip. The English Gentleman. LC 82-47651. (Illus.). 240p. 1982. 18.00 (ISBN 0-688-01400-3). Morrow.

--Kipling: The Glass, the Shadow & the Fire. LC 74-29175. 336p. (YA) 1975. 10.00i (ISBN 0-06-012833-X, HarpT). Har-Row.

Mason, Philip, ed. India & Ceylon: Unity & Diversity: A Symposium. 1967. pap. 5.95x o.p. (ISBN 0-19-500351-9). Oxford U Pr.

Mason, Philip P., ed. see Schoolcraft, Henry R.

Mason, Polly C. Records of Colonial Gloucester County, Virginia. (Illus.). 146p. (Repr. of 1946-1948 eds.). write for info o.p. (ISBN 0-685-65079-0). Va Bk.

Mason, R. Essentials of Statistics. 1976. pap. text ed. 17.95 (ISBN 0-13-289561-7). P-H.

Mason, R., et al. Marketing Practices & Principles. 3rd ed. (Illus.). 1980. text ed. 15.00 (ISBN 0-07-040693-6, G); activity guide 6.52 (ISBN 0-07-040694-4); tchr's manual & key 6.00 (ISBN 0-07-040695-2). McGraw.

Mason, R. A., jt. auth. see Armitage, M. M.

Mason, R. E. & Rath, P. M. Marketing & Distribution. 1968. text ed. 12.96 o.p. (ISBN 0-07-040675-8, G); tchr's manual & key 5.05 o.p. (ISBN 0-07-040678-2). McGraw.

Mason, R. H., ed. Photography Yearbook, 1983. LC 36-13575. (Illus.). 256p. 1982. 35.00x (ISBN 0-85242-806-5). Intl Pubns Serv.

Mason, R. M., jt. auth. see Eisele, J. A.

Mason, R. O., jt. auth. see Rowe, A. J.

Mason, Ralph. Native Clays & Glazes for North American Potters: A Manual for the Utilization of Local Clay & Glaze Materials. 150p. 1981. cloth 24.95 (ISBN 0-686-86210-4); pap. 17.95 (ISBN 0-917304-02-0). Timber.

Mason, Ralph E., et al. Marketing & Distribution. 2nd ed. LC 73-2826. (Illus.). 576p. (gr. 11-12). 1974. text ed. 12.96 o.p. (ISBN 0-07-040690-1, G); teachers manual & key 4.95 o.p. (ISBN 0-07-040692-8); project activity guide 6.52 o.p. (ISBN 0-07-040691-X). McGraw.

Mason, Richard H. & Swanson, E. Burton. Measurement for Management Decision. (Computer Science: Decision Support Ser.). (Illus.). 448p. 1981. text ed. 23.95 (ISBN 0-201-04646-6). A-W.

Mason, Richard O. & Mitroff, Ian I. Challenging Strategic Planning Assumptions: Theory, Cases & Techniques. LC 80-29657. 324p. 1981. 35.95 (ISBN 0-471-08219-8, Pub. by Wiley-Interscience). Wiley.

Mason, Richard O., jt. auth. see Mitroff, Ian I.

Mason, Rita A. A Guide to Dental Radiography. 2nd ed. (Illus.). 176p. 1982. pap. text ed. 16.50 casebound (ISBN 0-7236-0623-4). Wright-PSG.

Mason, Robert D. Business & Economic Statistics. 4th ed. (Plaid Ser.). 166p. 1983. pap. 11.95 (ISBN 0-87094-287-5). Dow Jones-Irwin.

Mason, Roger. Conspicious Consumption. 1980. 29.00 (ISBN 0-312-16424-6). St Martin.

Mason, Roger D., jt. auth. see O'Brien, Michael.

Mason, Ronald M. Participatory & Workplace Democracy: A Theoretical Development in Critique of Liberalism. 268p. 1982. 24.00 (ISBN 0-8093-0992-0). S Ill U Pr.

Mason, Russell E. Basic, Intermediate Systematic Substitution Training, Set-IS. 1973. Tape 3, t-10, t-11. pap. 25.00x (ISBN 0-89533-017-2). F I Comm.

--Positive Substitution, Purposeful Relaxation, & Goal Achievement Training: A Beginning, Set-PS. 1975. pap. 50.00x (ISBN 0-89533-014-8); Clinical Applications, rev. ed., 1979, Brief Outlines 1, Relaxation Training, Brief Outlines 3, Substitution Training incl.; tape-1A; t-2; t-4; t-5 (ISBN 0-89533-035-0); t-6 (ISBN 0-89533-036-9); t-10. F I Comm.

Mason, S. F. Molecular Optical Activity & the Chiral Discriminations. LC 82-1125. (Illus.). 250p. 1982. 39.50 (ISBN 0-521-24702-0). Cambridge U Pr.

Mason, Sally. Take a Trip to China. (Take a Trip to Ser.). (Illus.). 32p. (gr. 1-3). 1981. lib. bdg. 8.40 (ISBN 0-531-04317-7). Watts.

Mason, Sammy. Stalls, Spins & Safety. (McGraw-Hill in Aviation Ser.). (Illus.). 192p. 1982. 21.95 (ISBN 0-07-040696-0). McGraw.

Mason, Scott A., ed. see American Hospital Association.

Mason, Sharon, ed. see Guinther, John.

Mason, Shirlene. Daniel Defoe & the Status of Women. LC 78-59369. 1978. 12.95 (ISBN 0-88831-025-0). Eden Pr.

Mason, Theodore C. Battleship Sailor. LC 81-85440. (Illus.). 352p. 1982. 16.95 (ISBN 0-87021-095-5). Naval Inst Pr.

Mason, Theodore K. The South Pole Ponies. LC 79-52052. (Illus.). (gr. 7 up). 1979. 7.95 o.p. (ISBN 0-396-07729-3). Dodd.

--Two Against the Ice: Amundsen & Ellsworth. LC 82-45383. (Illus.). 224p. (gr. 7 up). 1982. PLB 13.95 (ISBN 0-396-08092-8). Dodd.

Mason, Thomas A., jt. ed. see Rutland, Robert A.

Mason, Tony. Association Football in English Society. 1980. text ed. 36.25x o.p. (ISBN 0-391-01718-7). Humanities.

Mason, Warren & Thurston, Robert, eds. Physical Acoustics: Principles & Methods, Vol. 16. LC 63-22327. 512p. Date not set. 72.00 (ISBN 0-12-477916-6). Acad Pr.

Mason, Warren P., ed. Physical Acoustics: Principles & Methods. Incl. Vol. 1A. Methods & Devices. 1964. 67.00 (ISBN 0-12-477901-8); Vol. 1B. Methods & Devices. 1964. 63.50 (ISBN 0-12-477941-7); Vol. 2A. Properties of Gases, Liquids & Solutions. 1965. 67.00 (ISBN 0-12-477902-6); Vol. 2B. Properties of Polymers & Nonlinear Acoustics. 1965. 63.50 (ISBN 0-12-477942-5); Vol. 3A. Applications to the Study of Imperfections & Lattice Dynamics. 1966. o.s. 67.00 (ISBN 0-12-477903-4); Vol. 3B. Applications to the Study of Imperfections & Lattice Dynamics. 1966. 61.00 (ISBN 0-12-477943-3); Vol. 4A. Applications to Quantum & Solid State Physics. 1966. 63.50 (ISBN 0-12-477904-2); Vol. 4B. Applications to Quantum & Solid State Physics. 1968. 67.00 (ISBN 0-12-477944-1); Vol. 5. 1968. 63.50 (ISBN 0-12-477905-0); Vol. 6. Thurston, R., ed. 1970. 64.50 (ISBN 0-12-477906-9); Vol. 7. 1970. 64.50 (ISBN 0-12-477907-7); Vol. 8. 1971. 64.50 (ISBN 0-12-477908-5); Vol. 9. 1972. 63.50 (ISBN 0-12-477909-3); Vol. 10. 1973. **68.50 (ISBN 0-12-477910-7); Vol. 13. Thurston, R. N., ed. 1977. 58.00 (ISBN 0-12-477913-1); Vol. 14. Thurston, R. N., ed. 1979. 66.50 (ISBN 0-12-477914-X). Acad Pr.**

Mason, William. Memories of a Musical Life. LC 70-125056. (Music Ser). 1970. Repr. of 1901 ed. lib. bdg. 35.00 (ISBN 0-306-70021-2). Da Capo.

--Rubik's Revenge. 154p. 1982. 10.95 (ISBN 0-13-783571-X); pap. 3.95 (ISBN 0-13-783563-9). P-H.

Mason, William H. & Lawrence, Faye B. Laboratory Manual & Study Guide in Animal Biology. 176p. 1982. pap. text ed. 13.95 (ISBN 0-8403-2740-4). Kendall-Hunt.

Mason, William H. & Marshall, Norton L. General Biology Laboratory Manual. 2nd ed. 144p. 1980. pap. text ed. 8.95 (ISBN 0-8403-0125-1). Kendall-Hunt.

--The Human Side of Biology. 592p. 1983. text ed. 29.95 scp (ISBN 0-06-044239-5, HarpC); instr's. manual avail. (ISBN 0-06-364170-4); study guide scp 9.50 (ISBN 0-06-044242-5). Har-Row.

Masoro, E. J., ed. Pharmacology of Lipid Transport & Atherosclerotic Processes. 1975. text ed. 115.00 (ISBN 0-08-017762-X). Pergamon.

Masotti, L., jt. auth. see Collins, J. H.

Masotti, Louis, jt. ed. see Lineberry, Robert.

Masotti, Louis H. & Lineberry, Robert L., eds. The New Urban Politics. LC 76-5869. 288p. 1976. prof ref 15.00x (ISBN 0-88410-422-2); pap. 9.95x (ISBN 0-88410-472-9). Ballinger Pub.

Masotti, Louis H., jt. ed. see Linesberry, Robert L.

Masotto, Rosemarie, jt. auth. see Drotning, Jayne.

Masouredis, Serafeim P., ed. Hybridomas & Monoclonal Antibodies. (Illus.). 57p. 1981. 8.00 (ISBN 0-914404-69-5). Am Assn Blood.

Maspero, Henri. Taoism & Chinese Religion. Kierman, Frank A., Jr., tr. from Fr. LC 80-13444. Orig. Title: Le Taoisme et les religions Chinoises. 612p. 1981. lib. bdg. 37.50x (ISBN 0-87023-308-4). U of Mass Pr.

Mass, Nathaniel J. Economic Cycles: An Analysis of Underlying Causes. LC 75-10485. 1975. 37.50x (ISBN 0-262-13139-0). MIT Pr.

Mass, Nathaniel J., ed. Readings in Urban Dynamics, Vol. 1. LC 73-89545. (Illus.). 1974. 32.50x (ISBN 0-262-13140-4). MIT Pr.

Massa, Ana. American Literature in Context, Four: 1900-1930. 1982. 22.00x (ISBN 0-416-73920-2); pap. 8.95x (ISBN 0-416-73930-X). Methuen Inc.

Massa, Frank, illus. Contando Para Divertirme. Kreps, Georgian, tr. from Eng. (Shape Board Play Books). Orig. Title: Counting for Fun. (Illus.). 14p. (Span.). (ps-3). 1981. bds. 3.50 plastic com bdg (ISBN 0-89828-203-9, 15003). Tuffy Bks.

Massa, Jack. Mooncrow. 1979. pap. 1.95 o.p. (ISBN 0-425-04287-1). Berkley Pub.

Massachusettes Historical Society. Proceedings of the Massachusettes Historical Society, Vol. 93. 1982. 25.00 (ISBN 0-686-37595-5); pap. 20.00 (ISBN 0-686-37596-3). Mass Hist Soc.

Massachusetts Bar Association Staff & Massachusetts Society of Certified Public Accountants Staff. Massachusetts Corporate Tax Manual with 1982 Supplement. 300p. 1983. write for info. looseleaf binder (ISBN 0-88063-021-3). Butterworth Legal Pubs.

Massachusetts Board of Bar Overseers, compiled by. Massachusetts Attorney Discipline Reports, Vol. II. 250p. Date not set. price not set (ISBN 0-88063-026-4). Butterworth Legal Pubs.

Massachusetts General Hospital. Clinical Anesthesia Procedures of the Massachusetts General Hospital. Lebowitz, Philip W., ed. 1978. pap. text ed. 13.95 o.p. (ISBN 0-316-54957-6). Little.

--Department of Nursing Staff Education Manual. Stetler, Cheryl B., et al, eds. 1981. text ed. 34.95 (ISBN 0-8359-4251-1). Reston.

Massachusetts Historical Society. Catalog of Manuscripts of the Massachusetts Historical Society: First Supplement. 1980. lib. bdg. 220.00 (ISBN 0-8161-0850-1, Hall Library). G K Hall.

Massachusetts Historical Society, Boston. Catalog of Manuscripts of the Massachusetts Historical Society, Boston, 7 Vols. 1969. Set. 700.00 (ISBN 0-8161-0822-6, Hall Library). G K Hall.

Massachusetts Horticultural Society, Boston. Dictionary Catalog of the Library of the Massachusetts Horticultural Society, 3 Vols. 1963. Set. lib. bdg. 250.00 (ISBN 0-8161-0648-7, Hall Library). G K Hall.

--Dictionary Catalog of the Library of the Massachusetts Horticultural Society, First Supplement. 1972. lib. bdg. 105.00 (ISBN 0-8161-1038-7, Hall Library). G K Hall.

Massachusetts Society of Certified Public Accountants Staff, jt. auth. see Massachusetts Bar Association Staff.

Massam, B. H. Spatial Search: Applications to Planning Problems in the Public Sector. (The Urban & Regional Planning Ser.: Vol. 23). 1980. 35.00 (ISBN 0-08-024286-3). Pergamon.

Massar, Phyllis D. Presenting Stefano della Bella: Seventeenth-Century Printmaker. LC 70-162340. (Illus.). 1971. 7.95 (ISBN 0-87099-109-4). Metro Mus Art.

Massar, Phyllis D. & De Vesme, Alexandre. Stefano Della Bella: Catalogueraisonne, 2 Vols. LC 78-110443. (Illus., Fr. & Eng.). 1971. lib. bdg. 95.00 o.p. (ISBN 0-87681-042-3). Hacker.

Massarik, Fred. Participative Management. 1983. 35.00 (ISBN 0-08-029509-6). Pergamon.

Massaro, D. W. Letter & Word Perception: Orthographic Structure & Visual Processing in Reading. (Advances in Psychology Ser.: Vol. 4). 1980. 38.50 (ISBN 0-444-85493-2). Elsevier.

Massart, D. L. & Kaufman, Leonard. The Interpretation of Analytical Chemical Data by the Use of Cluster Analysis. (Chemical Analysis Ser.: Monographs on Analytical Chemistry & Its Applications). 191p. 1983. 45.00 (ISBN 0-471-07861-1, Pub. by Wiley Interscience). Wiley.

Massart, D. L., et al. Evaluation & Optimization of Laboratory Methods & Analytical Procedures. (Techniques & Instrumentation in Analytical Chemistry Ser.: Vol. 1). 1978. 66.00 (ISBN 0-444-41743-5). Elsevier.

Masschelein, W. J. Ozonization Manual for Water & Wastewater Treatment. LC 81-21986. 324p. 1982. 41.95 (ISBN 0-471-10198-2, Pub. by Wiley-Interscience). Wiley.

Masschelein, Willy J. Chlorine Dioxide: Chemistry & Enviromental Impact of Oxychlorine Compounds. Rice, Rip C., ed. LC 77-92595. 1979. 39.95 (ISBN 0-250-40224-6). Ann Arbor Science.

MassCOSH Legal Committee. Injured on the Job: A Handbook for Massachusetts Workers. 4th rev. ed. Schwartz, Robert M., ed. LC 82-81398. 256p. (Orig.). 1982. pap. 4.75 (ISBN 0-9608416-3-6). Mass Coalition.

Masse, H. J. Chats on Old Pewter. rev. ed. Michaelis, R. F., ed. LC 72-138803. (Illus.). 1971. pap. 3.00 o.p. (ISBN 0-486-22129-6). Dover.

Massee, Bill, jt. auth. see Ivens, Dorothy.

Massee, Robin, tr. see Evans, David & Hoxeng, James.

Massee, William E. Joyous Anarchy: The Search for Great American Wines. LC 77-26007. (Illus.). 1978. 10.95 o.p. (ISBN 0-399-12069-6). Putnam Pub Group.

--Massee's Wine Almanac. LC 80-13391. 240p. 1980. 12.95 o.p. (ISBN 0-13-559658-0); pap. 6.95 o.p. (ISBN 0-13-559641-6). P-H.

Massee, William E., jt. auth. see Ivens, Dorothy.

Masselman, George. Cradle of Colonialism. 1963. 49.50x (ISBN 0-685-69840-8). Elliots Bks.

Massenet, Jules E. My Recollections. Barnett, H. Villiers, tr. Repr. of 1919 ed. lib. bdg. 15.75x (ISBN 0-8371-4276-8, MARE). Greenwood.

Massengale, John D. The Principles & Problems of Coaching. 392p. 1975. 19.75x (ISBN 0-398-03258-0); pap. 15.50x o.p. (ISBN 0-398-03259-9). C C Thomas.

Masser, I. Theory & Practice in Regional Science. (London Papers in Regional Science). 166p. 1980. pap. 12.50x (ISBN 0-85086-051-2, Pub. by Pion England). Methuen Inc.

Masserman, J. H. & Schwab, John J., eds. Social Psychiatry, Vol. 1. LC 73-19790. 224p. 1974. text ed. 39.50 (ISBN 0-8089-0001-3). Grune.

Masserman, Jules H., ed. Current Psychiatric Therapies, Vol. 21. Date not set. price not set (ISBN 0-8089-1517-7). Grune.

Massett, Larry, 3rd & Sutherland, Earl W. Everyman's Guide to Drugs & Medicines. LC 74-7833. 224p. 1975. 9.95 o.p. (ISBN 0-88331-069-4). Luce.

Massey, Craig. Adjust or Self Destruct. LC 77-4088. pap. 2.95 (ISBN 0-8024-0136-8). Moody.

--Adjustarse O Autodestruirse. 128p. 1981. pap. 3.50 (ISBN 0-8024-0148-1). Moody.

--I Love You, I Hear You. 160p. 1980. text ed. 7.95 o.p. (ISBN 0-8024-3957-8). Moody.

Massey, Doreen & Meegan, Richard. Anatomy of Job Loss. 1982. 25.00x (ISBN 0-416-32350-2); pap. 11.95x (ISBN 0-416-32360-X). Methuen Inc.

Massey, Doreen B. & Batey, P. W., eds. Alternative Frameworks for Analysis. (London Papers in Regional Science). 168p. 1977. pap. 12.50x (ISBN 0-85086-061-X, Pub. by Pion England). Methuen Inc.

Massey, E. Wayne & Lashner, Robert T., eds. Mononeuropathies. (Illus.). 1983. price not set (ISBN 0-8391-1817-1, 18066). Univ Park.

Massey, F. J., Jr., jt. auth. see Dixon, Wilfrid J.

Massey, H. S. Electronic & Ionic Impact Phenomena, 2 vols. Incl. Vol. 1. Collision of Electrons with Atoms. Massey, H. S. & Burhop, E. H. 79.00x (ISBN 0-19-851247-3); Vol. 2. Electron Collisions with Molecules & Photoionization. Massey, H. S. 79.00x (ISBN 0-19-851249-X). 1969. Oxford U Pr.

Massey, H. S. & McDaniel, Earl, eds. Applied Atomic Collision Physics: Gas Laser, Vol. 3. (Pure & Applied Physics). 544p. 1982. 67.00. Acad Pr.

Massey, H. S., et al. Electronic & Ionic Impact Phenomena: Slow Collisions of Heavy Particles, Vol. 3. 1971. 85.00x (ISBN 0-19-851252-X). Oxford U Pr.

Massey, H. S., et al, eds. Applied Atomic Collision Physics, Vol. 5. (Pure & Applied Physics Ser.). 426p. 1982. 62.00 (ISBN 0-12-478805-X). Acad Pr.

Massey, Harrie. Negative Ions. 3rd ed. LC 74-31792. (Cambridge Monographs on Physics). (Illus.). 600p. 1976. 139.50 (ISBN 0-521-20775-4). Cambridge U Pr.

Massey, Harrie, et al. Applied Atomic Collision Physics: Atmospheric Physics & Chemistry, Vol. 1. (Pure & Applied Physics Ser.). 482p. 1982. 67.50 (ISBN 0-12-478801-7). Acad Pr.

--Electronic & Ionic Impact Phenomena: Slow Position & Muon Collisions & Notes on Recent Advances, Vol. 5. (International Series of Monographs on Physics). (Illus.). 1974. 79.00x (ISBN 0-19-851283-X). Oxford U Pr.

Massey, Irving. The Gaping Pig: Literature & Metamorphoses. LC 74-22967. 1976. 26.50x (ISBN 0-520-02887-2). U of Cal Pr.

Massey, James, jt. ed. see McCown, Wayne.

Massey, James A., ed. see Schleiermacher, Friedrich.

Massey, James A., tr. see Feuerbach, Ludwig.

Massey, L. D. Probability & Statistics. 1971. 28.50 (ISBN 0-07-040720-7, P&RB). McGraw.

Massey, Linton R. William Faulkner-Man Working, 1919-1962: A Catalogue of the William Faulkner Collections at the University of Virginia. LC 68-19477. (Illus.). 288p. 1968. 27.50x (ISBN 0-8139-0174-X, Bibliographic Society, University of Virginia). U Pr of Va.

Massey, Marilyn C. Christ Unmasked: The Meaning of "The Life of Jesus" in German Politics. LC 82-8547. (Studies in Religion Ser.). xi, 175p. 1982. 23.00x (ISBN 0-8078-1524-1). U of NC Pr.

Massey, Michael. Roman Religion. Hodge, Peter, ed. (Aspects of Roman Life Ser.). 48p. (Orig.). (gr. 7-12). 1979. pap. text ed. 3.50 (ISBN 0-582-21573-0). Longman.

Massey, Penelope P., ed. Colorado. (Travel Ser.). (Illus.). 72p. (Orig.). 1982. write for info. (ISBN 0-938440-09-8). Colourpicture.

Massey, Robert. Personality Theories: Comparisons & Syntheses. 1981. text ed. write for info. (ISBN 0-442-23892-4). Van Nos Reinhold.

Massey, William C., jt. auth. see Driver, Harold E.

Massialas, Byron G. & Zevin, Jack. Creative Encounters in the Classroom. LC 81-19375. 286p. 1983. lib. bdg. write for info. (ISBN 0-89874-437-7). Krieger.

Massialas, Byron G., jt. auth. see Kazamias, Andreas M.

Massie, Diane R. Cocoon. LC 82-45578. (Illus.). 32p. (gr. 2 up). 1983. 7.64i (ISBN 0-690-04273-6, TYC-J); PLB 7.89g (ISBN 0-690-04274-4). Har-Row.

Massie, Joseph L. Essentials of Management. 3rd ed. (Essentials of Management Ser.). (Illus.). 1979. ref. 18.95 (ISBN 0-13-286351-0); pap. 12.95 ref. (ISBN 0-13-286344-8). P-H.

Massie, Joseph L. & Douglas, John. Managing: A Contemporary Introduction. 3rd ed. (Illus.). 544p. 1981. text ed. 23.95 (ISBN 0-13-550327-2); pap. 9.95 student resource manual (ISBN 0-13-550368-X). P-H.

Massie, Joseph L., et al. Management: Analysis, Concepts, Cases. 3rd ed. (Illus.). 800p. 1975. ref. ed. 24.95 (ISBN 0-13-548412-X). P-H.

Massie, Philip E. Executive Guide to Wordstar. (Illus.). 24p. 1982. pap. text ed. 5.75 (ISBN 0-910517-00-2). Culver City.

Massie, Robert & Sweezey, Marilyn P. The Romanov Family Album. Gregory, Alexis K. & Wheeler, Daniel, eds. LC 82-7098. (Illus.). 1982. 25.00 (ISBN 0-86565-019-5). Vendome.

Massie, Suzanne. Land of the Firebird. 1982. pap. 12.95 (ISBN 0-671-46059-5, Touchstone Bks). S&S.

Massinger, Philip. A New Way to Pay Old Debts: A Comedy. Byrne, M. St. Clare, ed. LC 75-40928. 168p. 1976. Repr. of 1956 ed. lib. bdg. 16.00x (ISBN 0-8371-8691-9, MANWP). Greenwood.

--Plays & Poems of Philip Massinger, 5 vols. Edwards, Philip & Gibson, Colin, eds. (Oxford English Texts Ser). 1976. Set. 179.00x set (ISBN 0-19-811894-5). Oxford U Pr.

Massingham, Betty. A Century of Gardeners. (Illus.). 288p. 1983. 24.95 (ISBN 0-571-11811-9). Faber & Faber.

Massion, J., ed. Cerebro-Cerebellar Interactions. Sasaki, K. LC 79-18156. (Developments in Neuroscience Ser.: Vol. 6). 1979. 62.25 (ISBN 0-444-80147-2, North Holland). Elsevier.

Massis, Bruce E. & Cylke, Kurt, eds. Library Service for the Blind & Physically Handicapped: An International Approach, Vol. 2. (IFLA Publications: No. 23). 100p. 1983. 18.00 (ISBN 3-598-20385-3, Pub. by K G Saur). Shoe String.

Masson, C. F. Memoires Secrets sur la Russie. (Nineteenth Century Russia Ser.). 369p. (Fr.). 1974. Repr. of 1800 ed. lib. bdg. 95.00x o.p. (ISBN 0-8287-0588-7, R32). Clearwater Pub.

Masson, Charles. Nouveau Traite Des Regles Pour La Composition De la Musique. 2nd ed. LC 67-25446. (Music Ser). 1967. Repr. of 1699 ed. lib. bdg. 18.50 (ISBN 0-306-70941-4). Da Capo.

Masson, Francois. The End of Our Era. Horwege, Richard A., ed. Steinberg, David M., tr. from Fr. 136p. 1983. pap. 6.95 (ISBN 0-89865-202-2). Donning Co.

Masson, G. M., jt. auth. see Thurber, Kenneth J.

Masson, Georgina. Companion Guide to Rome. (Illus.). 560p. 1983. 16.95 (ISBN 0-13-154609-0); pap. 8.95 (ISBN 0-13-154591-4). P-H.

Masson, J., jt. auth. see Pender, J. A.

Masson, J. Moussaieff, jt. tr. see Merwin, W. S.

Masson, M., ed. The Compleat Cook: The Secrets of a Seventeenth-Century Housewife - Rebecca Price. 1974. 20.00 o.p. (ISBN 0-7100-7444-1). Routledge & Kegan.

Masson, Paul Marie. L' Opera de Rameau. LC 70-168675. (Music Ser). (Illus.). 596p. 1972. Repr. of 1930 ed. lib. bdg. 59.00 (ISBN 0-306-70262-2). Da Capo.

Masson, Robert. The Pedagogy of God's Image. LC 82-16812. (College Theology Society Annual Publication). 214p. 1982. 18.00 (ISBN 0-89130-598-X, 34 10 81). Scholars Pr CA.

Masson, Robert T. & Qualls, P. David, eds. Essays on Industrial Organization: In Honor of Joe S. Bain. LC 76-3610. 296p. 1976. prof ref 20.00x (ISBN 0-88410-416-8). Ballinger Pub.

Massonnet, C. C., jt. auth. see Save, M. A.

Massot, R., jt. auth. see Cornu, A.

Massot, R., ed. see Cornu, A.

Massoud, Aly, jt. ed. see Hart, Ronald.

Massry, Shaul G. & Glassock, Richard J. Textbook of Nephrology, 2 Vols. (Illus.). 1800p. 1983. 110.00 (ISBN 0-683-05619-0). Williams & Wilkins.

Massucci, Edoardo. Cars for Kids. LC 82-42764. (Illus.). 128p. (gr. 3up). 1983. 27.50 (ISBN 0-8478-0469-0). Rizzoli Intl.

Massy, William F., jt. auth. see Frank, Ronald E.

Massy, William F., et al. Stochastic Models of Buying Behavior. 1970. 25.00x (ISBN 0-262-13039-4); pap. 6.95x (ISBN 0-262-63052-4). MIT Pr.

Mast, Ben V., tr. see Baumgart, Winfried.

Mast, Gerald. Howard Hawks, Storyteller. (Illus.). 375p. 1982. 29.95 (ISBN 0-19-503091-5). Oxford U Pr.

--Howard Hawks, Storyteller. (Galaxy Ser.: No. 718). (Illus.). 375p. 1982. pap. cancelled o.p. (ISBN 0-19-503233-0). Oxford U Pr.

--Movies in Our Midst: Documents in the Cultural History of Film in America. LC 81-16223. (Illus.). xxiv, 766p. 1983. pap. 12.50 (ISBN 0-226-50981-8). U of Chicago Pr.

--A Short History of the Movies. 3rd ed. LC 79-14309. 1981. pap. 16.50 o.p. (ISBN 0-672-61521-5). Pegasus.

Mast, Gerald & Cohen, Marshall, eds. Film Theory & Criticism: Introductory Readings. 2nd ed. (Illus.). 1979. 29.95x (ISBN 0-19-502503-2); pap. text ed. 14.95x (ISBN 0-19-502498-2). Oxford U Pr.

Mastalerz, John W. The Greenhouse Environment: The Effect of Environmental Factors on Flower Crops. LC 77-6793. 1977. 30.95x (ISBN 0-471-57606-9). Wiley.

Masten, Ric. The Deserted Roster. 1982. pap. 5.00 (ISBN 0-931104-11-4). Sunflower Ink.

--Even as We Speak. 1982. pap. 5.50 (ISBN 0-931104-12-2). Sunflower Ink.

Master, Melvyn C., jt. auth. see Livingstone-Learmonth, John.

Master, Richard Le see Le Master, Richard.

Master, Roy. How to Survive Your Parents. LC 82-71162. 182p. 1982. pap. 6.50 (ISBN 0-933900-10-4). Foun Human Under.

Master Ch'ing Liang. Flower Adornment Sutra Preface. Bilingual ed. Ch'an Master Hua, commentary by. Heng Hsien, Bhikshuni, et al, trs. from Chinese. (Illus.). 244p. (Orig.). 1980. pap. 7.00 (ISBN 0-917512-28-6). Buddhist Text.

--Flower Adornment Sutra Prologue, Vol. II. Ch'an Master Hua, commentary by: Bhikshuni Heng Hsien, tr. from Chinese. (Illus.). 280p. (Orig.). 1981. pap. 10.00 (ISBN 0-917512-73-1). Buddhist Text.

Master Hua, Ch'an, commentary by. Dharma Flower Sutra, Vol IV. Heng Yin, Bhikshuni, tr. from Chinese. (Illus.). 371p. (Orig.). 1980. pap. 8.95 (ISBN 0-917512-62-6). Buddhist Text.

--Dharma Flower Sutra, Vol. VII. Heng Yin, Bhikshuni, tr. from Chinese. (Illus.). 250p. (Orig.). 1980. pap. 7.95 (ISBN 0-917512-93-6). Buddhist Text.

--Dharma Flower Sutra, Vol. VIII. Heng Yin, Bhikshuni, tr. from Chinese. (Illus.). 160p. (Orig.). 1980. pap. 6.95 (ISBN 0-917512-71-5). Buddhist Text.

--Flower Adornment (Avatamsaka) Sutra: Chapter 26, The Ten Grounds, Pt. One. Bhiksuni Heng Hsien, tr. from Chinese. (Illus.). 234p. (Orig.). 1980. pap. 7.00 (ISBN 0-917512-29-4). Buddhist Text.

--Flower Adornment Sutra: Chapter 39: Entering the Dharma Realm., Part 1. Heng Tao, Bhikshuni, et al, trs. from Chinese. (Illus.). 284p. (Orig.). 1980. pap. 8.50 (ISBN 0-917512-68-5). Buddhist Text.

--Flower Adornment Sutra: Chapter 39, Entering the Dharma Realm, Part II. Heng Tao, Bhikshuni, et al, trs. from Chinese. (Illus.). 312p. (Orig.). 1980. pap. 8.50 (ISBN 0-917512-70-7). Buddhist Text.

--Shurangama Sutra, Vol. 3. Heng Ch'ih, Bhikshuni, tr. from Chinese. (Illus.). 240p. (Orig.). 1980. pap. 8.50 (ISBN 0-917512-94-4). Buddhist Text.

--Shurangama Sutra, Vol. 4. Heng Ch'ih, Bhikshuni, et al, trs. from Chinese. (Illus.). 285p. (Orig.). 1980. pap. 8.50 (ISBN 0-917512-90-1). Buddhist Text.

--Shurangama Sutra, Vol. 5. Heng Ch'ih, Bhikshuni, et al, trs. from Chinese. (Illus.). 250p. (Orig.). 1980. pap. 8.50 (ISBN 0-917512-91-X). Buddhist Text.

Masterman, J. C. An Oxford Tragedy. ii, 187p. 1981. pap. 3.50 (ISBN 0-486-24165-3). Dover.

Master Ni, Hua-Ching. The Reflecting Book of Changes. (Illus.). 825p. (Orig.). 1983. 35.00 (ISBN 0-686-84582-X); pap. 25.00 (ISBN 0-937064-04-1). SEBT.

Masterpace, Victor I. The Approaching Historical Geopolitical Conflicts Threatening with Collapse of the World Order. (The Great Currents of History Library Bk.). (Illus.). 133p. 1983. 67.85 (ISBN 0-86722-026-0). Inst Econ Pol.

Masters, Anthony. The Devil's Dominion: The Complete Story of Hell & Satanism in the Modern World. LC 78-14863. (Illus.). 1979. 9.95 o.p. (ISBN 0-399-12232-X). Putnam Pub Group.

--The Natural History of the Vampire. 259p. 1972. 8.95 o.p. (ISBN 0-399-10931-5). Putnam Pub Group.

Masters, C. Homogeneous Transition-Metal Catalysis: A Gentle Art. 1980. 33.00x (ISBN 0-412-22110-1, Pub. by Chapman & Hall). Methuen Inc.

Masters, Charles O. The Encyclopedia of Live Foods. (Illus.). 336p. 1975. 14.95 (ISBN 0-87666-093-6, PS-730). TFH Pubns.

--Encyclopedia of the Water-Lily. (Illus.). 512p. 1974. text ed. 19.95 (ISBN 0-87666-168-1, H-944). TFH Pubns.

Masters, David. German Jet Genesis. (Illus.). 160p. 1982. 19.95 (ISBN 0-86720-622-5). Sci Bks Intl.

Masters, Edgar L. Mark Twain: A Portrait. LC 66-15216. 1938. 10.00x (ISBN 0-8196-0171-3). Biblo.

--Spoon River Anthology. new ed. 1962. pap. 3.50 (ISBN 0-02-070010-5, Collier). Macmillan.

--Spoon River Anthology with Additional Poems. 1963. text ed. 10.95 o.s.i. (ISBN 0-02-581740-X); text ed. 12.95 1916 ed. (ISBN 0-02-581730-2). Macmillan.

--Vachel Lindsay: A Poet in America. LC 68-56452. (Illus.). 1969. Repr. of 1935 ed. 10.00x (ISBN 0-8196-0239-6). Biblo.

Masters, G. Mallary. Rabelaisian Dialectic & the Platonic-Hermetic Tradition. LC 69-11316. 1969. 24.50x (ISBN 0-87395-039-9). State U NY Pr.

Masters, Geofferey N., jt. auth. see Wright, Benjamin D.

Masters, Gilbert. Introduction to Environmental Science & Technology. LC 73-23088. 352p. 1974. text ed. 30.95 (ISBN 0-471-57607-7). Wiley.

Masters, Hilary. Last Stands: Notes from Memory. 320p. 1982. 14.95 (ISBN 0-87923-443-1). Godine.

Masters, J. By the Green of the Spring. 1981. 13.95 (ISBN 0-07-040783-5). McGraw.

Masters, Janet F., tr. see Smith, Joyce M.

Masters, John. Heart of War. LC 80-12491. (Loss of Eden Ser.). 608p. 1980. 13.95 (ISBN 0-07-040782-7). McGraw.

Masters, John C., jt. auth. see Rimm, David C.

Masters, Judith R., tr. see Rousseau, Jean-Jacques.

Masters, Lowell F. & Mori, Allen A. Adapted Physical Education: A Practitioner's Guide. 350p. 1983. 29.50 (ISBN 0-89443-669-4). Aspen Systems.

Masters, M. The Case of the Chocolate Snatcher & Other Stories. Delagran, Louise & Grooms, Kathe, eds. (Can You Solve It Mystery Ser.: Vol. 2). (Illus.). 108p. (Orig.). (gr. 2-6). 1983. pap. 1.95 (ISBN 0-915658-85-2). Meadowbrook Pr.

--The Case of the Mysterious Dognapper & Other Stories. Delagran, Louise & Grooms, Kathe, eds. (Can You Solve It Mystery Ser.: Vol. 4). (Illus.). 108p. (Orig.). (gr. 2-6). 1983. pap. 1.95 (ISBN 0-915658-95-X). Meadowbrook Pr.

--The Case of the Video Game Smugglers & Other Stories. Delagran, Louise & Grooms, Kathe, eds. (Can You Solve It Mystery Ser.: Vol. 3). (Illus.). 108p. (Orig.). (gr. 2-6). 1983. pap. 1.95 (ISBN 0-915658-88-7). Meadowbrook Pr.

--The Secret of the Long-Lost Cousin & Other Stories. Delagran, Louise & Grooms, Kathe, eds. (Can You Solve It Mystery Ser.: Vol. 1). (Illus.). 108p. (Orig.). (gr. 2-6). 1983. pap. 1.95 (ISBN 0-915658-81-X). Meadowbrook Pr.

Masters, Margaret. Australian House & Garden Book of Chrysanthemums. pap. 8.50x (ISBN 0-392-06885-0, ABC). Sportshelf.

Masters, Mildred. The House on the Hill. LC 82-909. 160p. (gr. 5-9). 1982. 9.50 (ISBN 0-688-01306-6). Greenwillow.

Masters, Olga. The Home Girls. LC 82-2709. 194p. 1983. text ed. 14.50 (ISBN 0-7022-1811-1); pap. 8.50 (ISBN 0-7022-1821-9). U of Queensland Pr.

Masters, P. M. & Fleming, N. C., eds. Quarternary Coastlines & Marine Archaeology: Towards the Prehistory of Land Bridges & Continental Shelves. LC 82-45021. Date not set. price not set (ISBN 0-12-479250-2). Acad Pr.

Masters, Robert & Houston, Jean. Listening to the Body. 1979. pap. 6.95 (ISBN 0-440-54960-4, Delta). Dell.

--Mind Games. 1973. pap. 6.95 (ISBN 0-440-55634-1, Delta). Dell.

--Mind Games: The Guide to Inner Space. LC 71-186738. 320p. 1972. 10.95 o.p. (ISBN 0-670-47632-3). Viking Pr.

Masters, Robert V., compiled by. Complete Book of Karate & Self-Defense. (Illus.). 542p. (gr. 10 up). 1974. 13.95 (ISBN 0-8069-4084-0); PLB 16.79 (ISBN 0-8069-4085-9). Sterling.

Masters, Roger D., ed. see Rousseau, Jean-Jacques.

Masters, William H., et al. Human Sexuality. 1982. text ed. 20.95 (ISBN 0-316-54990-8); tchrs.' manual avail. (ISBN 0-316-54991-6); student guide 7.95 (ISBN 0-316-54992-4). Little.

Masters, William M. How You Can Earn One Hundred Thousand Dollars a Year Without Working: Legally, Honestly, Tax-Free. 128p. (Orig.). 1983. pap. text ed. 17.95 (ISBN 0-686-38785-6). Jadestone.

Masters, Zeke. Long Odds. (Faro Blake Ser.: No. 23). (Orig.). 1982. pap. 2.25 (ISBN 0-671-45182-0). PB.

Masterson, Amanda R. Bibliography & Index of Texas Geology, Nineteen Seventy-Five to Nineteen Eighty. 334p. 1981. 8.00 (ISBN 0-686-36602-6). Bur Econ Geology.

Masterson, Audrey N. The Day the Gypsies Came to Town. (Illus.). 32p. (Orig.). (gr. 2-6). 1982. 11.95 (ISBN 0-940742-01-2); pap. 4.95 (ISBN 0-940742-04-7). Carnival Pr.

Masterson, Graham. The Manitou. 1977. pap. 2.95 (ISBN 0-523-48070-9). Pinnacle Bks.

--Rich. 1979. 12.95 o.p. (ISBN 0-671-24673-9). S&S.

Masterson, James F. Treatment of the Borderline Adolescent: A Developmental Approach. LC 78-39721. (Personality Processes Ser). 1972. 35.95 (ISBN 0-471-57615-8, Pub. by Wiley-Interscience). Wiley.

Masterson, James R. Writings on American History, 1962-73: A Subject Bibliography of Books & Monographs, 10 vols. LC 82-49027. (Writings on American History Ser.). (Orig.). 1983. Set. lib. bdg. 1200.00 (ISBN 0-527-98268-7). Kraus Intl.

Masterson, John T., jt. auth. see Beebe, Steven A.

Masterson, K. & Bohn, M. Scatterplate Mapping for Solar Concentrators. (Progress in Solar Energy Supplements SERI Ser.). 1983. pap. text ed. 7.50x (ISBN 0-89553-089-9). Am Solar Energy.

Masterson, Keith & Solar Energy Research Institute. Matrix Approach for Testing Mirrors, Pt. 2. (Progress in Solar Energy Ser.: Suppl.). 125p. 1983. pap. 13.00x (ISBN 0-89553-133-X). Am Solar Energy.

Masterson, Whit. The Hunter of the Blood. 1977. 6.95 o.p. (ISBN 0-396-07417-0). Dodd.

--The Man with Two Clocks. LC 74-6808. 196p. 1974. 5.95 o.p. (ISBN 0-396-06988-6). Dodd.

Masterson, William H. William Blount. Repr. of 1954 ed. lib. bdg. 17.00x (ISBN 0-8371-2308-9, MABL). Greenwood.

Masterton, Graham. Charnel House. (Orig.). 1978. pap. 2.95 (ISBN 0-523-48072-5). Pinnacle Bks.

--The Devils of D-Day. 1978. pap. 2.95 (ISBN 0-523-48069-5). Pinnacle Bks.

--The Djinn. 192p. 1977. pap. 2.75 (ISBN 0-523-48068-7, 40-523-0). Pinnacle Bks.

--Revenge of the Manitou. 1979. pap. 2.95 (ISBN 0-523-48071-7). Pinnacle Bks.

--Solitaire. LC 82-14197. 576p. 1982. 15.95 (ISBN 0-688-01555-7). Morrow.

--The Sphinx. 1978. pap. 2.95 (ISBN 0-523-48067-9). Pinnacle Bks.

--Tengu. (Tor Bks.). 1983. pap. 3.50 (ISBN 0-686-42720-3). Pinnacle Bks.

Masterton, Thomas & Salmon, Raymond. The Principles of Objective Testing in Geography. 1974. text ed. 11.95x o.p. (ISBN 0-435-35700-X). Heinemann Ed.

Mastin, Venita. A Rose for Carlie. 1981. pap. 6.95 (ISBN 0-686-84682-6, Avalon). Bouregy.

Maston, T. B. Consejos a la Juventud. Duffer, H. F., Jr., tr. Orig. Title: Advice to Youth. 60p. (Span.). 1980. pap. 1.25 (ISBN 0-311-46005-4). Casa Bautista.

--The Ethic of the Christian Life. Hogg, Gayle, ed. (Religious Education Ser.). 152p. 1982. kivar 10.75 (ISBN 0-311-72605-4). Casa Bautista.

--Etica De la Vida Cristiana Sus Principios Basicos. Ureta, Floreal, tr. from English. 200p. (Span.). 1981. pap. 6.50 (ISBN 0-311-46076-3). Casa Bautista.

--Etica del Cristiano en el Mundo en Crisis. Adams, Bob, tr. from Eng. 224p. (Span.). Date not set. pap. price not set (ISBN 0-311-46084-4). Casa Bautista.

Maston, T. B. & Tillman, William A. The Bible & Family Relations. LC 81-67196. 1983. 7.95 (ISBN 0-8054-6124-8). Broadman.

Mastorakis, Nico, jt. auth. see Conrad, Barnaby.

Mastors, Charlotte. School Volunteers: Who Needs Them? LC 74-34501. (Fastback Ser.: No. 55). (Illus., Orig.). 1975. pap. 0.75 o.p. (ISBN 0-87367-055-8). Phi Delta Kappa.

Mastroberti, Angela, jt. auth. see Mastroberti, Raun R.

Mastroberti, Raun R. & Mastroberti, Angela. You: The Complete Guide to Beauty for Today & Tomorrow. (Illus.). 95p. 1980. 10.95 (ISBN 0-686-37959-4). Bracale & Assoc.

Mastroianni, Luigi, Jr., jt. auth. see Garcia, Celso-Ramon.

Mastroianni, Luigi, Jr., jt. auth. see Reeder, Sharon R.

Mastromarino, Anthony J., jt. ed. see Ingall, R. F.

Mastronarde, Donald. Contact & Discontinuity: Some Conventions of Speech & Action on the Greek Tragic Stage. (University of California Publications in Classical Studies: Vol. 21). 1979. pap. 19.00x (ISBN 0-520-09601-0). U of Cal Pr.

Mastronarde, Donald J. & Bremer, Jan M. The Textural Tradition of Euripides' Phoinissai. LC 82-13492. (Publications in Classical Studies: Vol. 27). 464p. 1982. pap. text ed. 30.50x (ISBN 0-520-09664-9). U of Cal Pr.

Masuda, Yoneji. The Information Society: As Post-Industrial Society. (Illus.). 178p. 1980. pap. text ed. 12.50x (ISBN 0-930242-15-7). Transaction Bks.

Masui, Shigeo, jt. ed. see Bereday, George Z.

Masunaga, Reiho, tr. see Dogen.

Masunaga, Shizuto & Ohashi, Wataru. Zen Shiatsu: How to Harmonize Yin and Yang for Better Health. (Illus.). 176p. 1977. pap. 11.50 (ISBN 0-87040-394-X). Japan Pubns.

Masur, Harold Q. The Broker. (Fingerprint Mysteries Ser.). 304p. 1983. pap. 5.95 (ISBN 0-312-10596-7). St Martin.

Masuy, L., jt. auth. see Chaballe, L. Y.

Maszkiewicz, Ruth C., jt. auth. see Lewis, Eloise R.

Mata, Leonardo J. The Children of Santa Maria Cauque: A Prospective Field Study of Health & Growth. LC 78-70. (International Nutrition Policy Ser.: No. 2). 1978. 27.50x (ISBN 0-262-13135-8). MIT Pr.

Mataix, Claudio. Mecanica De Fluidos y Maquinas Hidraulicas. (Span). 1970. pap. text ed. 16.20 o.p. (ISBN 0-06-315590-7, IntlDept). Har-Row.

Matar, Sami. Synfuels: Hydrocarbons of the Future. 293p. 1982. 39.95x (ISBN 0-87814-189-8). Pennwell Books Division.

Matarazzo, James H., jt. ed. see Kyed, James M.

Matasa, Claudius & Tonca, Eugenia. Basic Nitrogen Compounds. 1972. 56.50 o.p. (ISBN 0-8206-0009-1). Chem Pub.

Matchan, Don C. We Mind If You Smoke. 1977. pap. 1.95 o.s.i. (ISBN 0-515-03680-3). Jove Pubns.

Matchett, D., jt. ed. see Kilpatrick, F.

Matchett, Kathy, tr. see Brandenburg, Hans.

Matchett, William H. Fireweed & Other Poems. LC 80-52963. (Illus.). 64p. (Orig.). 1980. 15.00 (ISBN 0-930954-14-9); pap. 9.00 o.p. (ISBN 0-930954-15-7). Tidal Pr.

Matchett, William M., ed. see Shakespeare, William.

Matczak, S. A., ed. & intro. by see Smith, William A.

Matczak, Sebastian A. Philosophy: A Select, Classified Bibliography of Ethics, Economics, Law, Politics, Sociology. LC 72-80678. (Philosophical Questions Ser.: No. 3). 1970. 38.00x (ISBN 0-912116-02-1). Learned Pubns.

--Philosophy: Its Nature, Methods & Basic Sources. LC 70-183043. (Philosophical Questions Ser: No. 4). 300p. 1976. 38.00x (ISBN 0-912116-09-9). Learned Pubns.

Matczak, Sebastian A., ed. see Barral, R. M.

Matczak, Sebastian A., ed. see Van Tyeese, Glenn J.

Mate, Ferenc. Best Boats To Build: From Bare Hull Up. (Illus.). 1982. 29.95 (ISBN 0-920256-06-6). Norton.

Mateene, Kahombo C., jt. ed. see Biebuyck, Daniel.

Mateescu, Gh., jt. auth. see Avram, Margareta.

Matejcek, Z., jt. auth. see Langmeier, J.

Matejic, Mateja & Milivojevic, Dragan. An Anthology of Medieval Serbian Literature in English. (Illus.). 205p. 1979. pap. 9.95 (ISBN 0-89357-055-9). Slavica.

Matejka, Ladislav, jt. auth. see Magner, Thomas F.

Matejka, Ladislav & Stolz, Benjamin A., eds. Cross Currents. (Michigan Slavic Materials Ser.: No. 19). 1982. pap. 8.00 (ISBN 0-930042-43-3). Mich Slavic Pubns.

Matejka, Ladislav & Titunik, Irwin R., eds. Semiotics of Art: Prague School Contributions. LC 75-32405. 336p. 1976. 25.00x o.p. (ISBN 0-262-13117-X). MIT Pr.

Mateles, Richard I. & Wogan, Gerald N., eds. Biochemistry of Some Foodborne Microbial Toxins. 1967. 20.00x (ISBN 0-262-13034-3). MIT Pr.

Materials Advisory Board. Ceramic Processing. (Illus.). 1968. 17.00 (ISBN 0-309-01576-6). Natl Acad Pr.

Maternity Center Assn. Birth Atlas. 6th ed. (Illus.). 1978. Repr. of 1968 ed. spiral bdg. 35.00 (ISBN 0-912758-00-7). Maternity Ctr.

Maternity Center Association. A Baby Is Born. 3rd ed. (Illus.). (gr. 7 up). 1964. 6.95 o.p. (ISBN 0-448-01335-5, G&D). Putnam Pub Group.

Materson, Richard S., jt. auth. see Kaplan, Paul E.

Mates, Barbara. Psychology. (College Outlines Ser.). pap. 4.95 o.p. (ISBN 0-671-08053-9). Monarch Pr.

Mates, Benson. Elementary Logic. 2nd ed. 1972. text ed. 15.95x (ISBN 0-19-501491-X). Oxford U Pr.

Mates, Julian. The American Musical Stage Before 1800. 1962. 25.00 (ISBN 0-8135-0393-0). Rutgers U Pr.

Mates, R. E. & Smith, C. R., eds. Advances in Bioengineering, 1976. 1976. pap. text ed. 7.00 o.p. (ISBN 0-685-75519-3, G00105). ASME.

Matesky, Ralph & Rush, Ralph E. Playing & Teaching Stringed Instruments, Pt. I. (Orig.). 1963. pap. text ed. 15.95 (ISBN 0-13-683789-1). P-H.

Math, Irwin. Bits & Pieces: Understanding & Building Computing Devices. (Illus.). 96p. (gr. 7 up). 1983. 12.95 (ISBN 0-684-17879-6). Scribner.

Mathams, R. J. Sub Rosa: Memoirs of an Australian Intelligence Analyst. 200p. 1983. text ed. 19.95x (ISBN 0-86861-380-0). Allen Unwin.

Mathe, G. & Rappaport, H. Histological & Cytological Typing of Neoplastic Diseases of Haematopoietic & Lymphoid Tissues. (World Health Organization: International Histological Classification of Tumours Ser.). (Illus.). 45p. 1976. 52.00 (ISBN 92-4-176014-1, 70-0-014-20); incl. slides 139.00 (ISBN 0-89189-126-9, 70-1-014-00). Am Soc Clinical.

--Histological & Cytological Typing of Neoplastic Diseases of Haematopoietic & Lymphoid Tissues. (WHO: No. 14). (Illus.). 45p. 52.00 (ISBN 0-686-95514-5, 70-1--14-20). Am Soc Clinical.

Mathe, Georges & DeJaeger, Robert, eds. Anthracyclines Nineteen Eighty-One: Current Status & Future Developments. LC 82-12691. (Illus.). 288p. 1983. write for info. (ISBN 0-89352-188-4). Masson Pub.

Mathe, S., tr. see Tardieu, Jean.

Mathein, J. Daniel & Squire, Morris B. How to Make Decisions That Pay Off. LC 81-85832. 128p. 1982. pap. write for info. (ISBN 0-931028-28-0); pap. 14.95 (ISBN 0-931028-27-2). Pluribus Pr.

Matheny, Kenneth, jt. auth. see Steffire, Buford.

Matheny, Kenneth B., jt. auth. see Richardson, Joseph A.

Matheopoulos, Helena. Maestro: Encounters with Conductors of Today. LC 82-48125. (Illus.). 512p. 1983. 24.95 (ISBN 0-06-015103-X, HarpT). Har-Row.

Mather, Anne. An Elusive Desire. (Harlequin Presents Ser.). 192p. 1983. pap. 1.95 (ISBN 0-373-10586-X). Harlequin Bks.

--Leopard in the Snow. (Alpha Book Ser.). 96p. 1974. pap. 2.95 (ISBN 0-19-424166-1). Oxford U Pr.

Mather, Arthur. The Mind Breaker. 1980. 10.95 o.s.i. (ISBN 0-440-05294-7). Delacorte.

Mather, Berkely. The Hour of the Dog. 356p. 1982. 14.95 (ISBN 0-312-39251-6). St Martin.

Mather, Betty Bang & Lasocki, David. The Art of Preluding, 1700-1830. 1983. 10.00 (ISBN 0-941084-08-6). McGinnis & Marx.

Mather, Cotton. Christian Philosopher: A Collection of the Best Discoveries in Nature, with Religious Improvements. LC 68-29082. 1968. Repr. of 1721 ed. 38.00x (ISBN 0-8201-1033-7). Schol Facsimiles.

--Day of Humiliation: Times of Affliction & Disaster. LC 68-24211. 1970. 46.00x (ISBN 0-8201-1067-1). Schol Facsimiles.

--Paterna: The Autobiography of Cotton Mather. Bosco, Ronald A., ed. LC 76-10595. (Center for Editions of American Authors). 504p. 1976. lib. bdg. 55.00x (ISBN 0-8201-1273-9). Schol Facsimiles.

Mather, Eleanore P. & Miller, Dorothy C. Edward Hicks: Primitive Master. LC 81-71405. (Illus.). 300p. 1982. 40.00 (ISBN 0-87413-208-8). U Delaware Pr.

Mather, Frank L., ed. Who's Who of the Colored Race. LC 79-178669. 1976. Repr. of 1915 ed. 65.00x (ISBN 0-8103-4247-2). Gale.

Mather, Frank T., Jr. American Spirit in Art. 1927. text ed. 22.50x (ISBN 0-686-83466-6). Elliots Bks.

Mather, Increase. An Essay for the Recording of Illustrious Providences. LC 77-17526. 1977. Repr. of 1684 ed. lib. bdg. 47.00x (ISBN 0-8201-1299-2). Schol Facsimiles.

Mather, John R. The Climatic Water Budget in Environmental Analysis. LC 77-17726. (Illus.). 1978. 25.95 (ISBN 0-669-02087-7). Lexington Bks.

Mather, K. The Elements of Biometry. 1967. pap. 4.95 o.p. (ISBN 0-412-20940-3, Pub. by Chapman & Hall). Methuen Inc.

--Genetical Structures of Populations. 1973. 16.95x (ISBN 0-412-12140-9, Pub. by Chapman & Hall). Methuen Inc.

Mather, Lynn M. Plea Bargaining or Trial? The Process of Criminal Case Disposition. LC 75-41560. (Illus.). 176p. 1979. 21.95 (ISBN 0-669-00467-7). Lexington Bks.

Mather, P. M. Computational Methods of Multivariate Analysis in Physical Geography. 1976. 74.95 (ISBN 0-471-57626-3, Pub. by Wiley-Interscience). Wiley.

Mathers, Edward P., ed. Coloured Stars (Oriental Love Poetry) pap. 3.00 (ISBN 0-8283-1432-2, 11). Branden.

Mathers, Michael. Riding the Rails. LC 73-80844. (Illus.). 128p. 1973. 12.95 (ISBN 0-87645-078-8). Gambit.

Mathers, S. I. The Kabbalah Unveiled. LC 71-16504. 373p. 1983. Repr. of 1900 ed. 9.95 (ISBN 0-87728-557-8). Weiser.

Mathers, S. L. The Book of the Sacred Magic of Abramelin the Mage. LC 75-12248. 320p. 1975. pap. 5.00 (ISBN 0-486-23211-5). Dover.

Mathes, J. H. & Huett, Lenora. The Amnesia Factor. LC 75-9446. 1975. pap. 4.95 o.p. (ISBN 0-89087-023-3). Celestial Arts.

Mathes, J. Harvey. The Old Guard in Gray: Researches in the Annals of the Confederate Historical Association. (Illus.). 446p. 1976. Repr. of 1897 ed. 18.00 o.p. (ISBN 0-937130-02-8). Burke's Bk Store.

Mathes, Stephen J. & Nahai, Foad. Clinical Applications for Muscle & Musculocutaneous Flaps. LC 81-18913. (Illus.). 733p. 1982. text ed. 129.50 (ISBN 0-8016-3164-5). Mosby.

--Clinical Atlas of Muscle & Musculocutaneous Flaps. LC 79-10739. (Illus.). 520p. 1979. text ed. 59.95 (ISBN 0-8016-3141-6). Mosby.

Matheson, Andrew. Leica & Leicaflex Way. 11th ed. (Illus.). 500p. 1974. 29.95 (ISBN 0-240-50670-7, 659). Focal Pr.

Matheson, Douglas W. Introductory Psychology: The Modern View. 2nd ed. (Illus.). 416p. 1982. pap. text ed. 15.95x (ISBN 0-88295-213-7). Harlan Davidson.

Matheson, Helen C., tr. see Ehrenburg, Ilya G.

Matheson, John, jt. auth. see Kelsey, Hugh.

Matheson, John R. Canada's Flag: A Search for a Country. 1980. lib. bdg. 20.00 o.p. (ISBN 0-8161-8426-7, Hall Reference). G K Hall.

Matheson, Maureen, ed. The College Handbook, 1982-83. 20th ed. 1700p. (Orig.). 1982. pap. 12.95 (ISBN 0-87447-144-3, 001443). College Bd.

Matheson, Neil. The Rules of the Game of Superpower Military Intervention in the Third World: 1975-1980. LC 81-43825. 168p. (Orig.). 1982. lib. bdg. 21.25 (ISBN 0-8191-2495-8); pap. text ed. 9.75 (ISBN 0-8191-2496-6). U Pr of Amer.

Matheson, Richard. The Shrinking Man. 1979. lib. bdg. 12.50 (ISBN 0-8398-2547-1, Gregg). G K Hall.

--What Dreams May Come. LC 78-2817. 1978. 9.95 o.p. (ISBN 0-399-12148-X). Putnam Pub Group.

Matheson, Susan B. Dura-Europos: The Ancient City & the Yale Collection. (Illus.). 42p. 1983. pap. 3.00 (ISBN 0-8143-1752-9, Dist. by the Yale Univ. Art Gallery). Wayne St U Pr.

Matheson, Virginia, jt. tr. see Andaya, Barbara W.

Mathew, Brian. Crocus. (Illus.). 224p. 1982. 50.00 (ISBN 0-917304-23-3). Timber.

--Lilies & Related Flowers. (Illus.). 240p. 1982. 60.00 (ISBN 0-87951-135-4). Overlook Pr.

Mathew, Brian, jt. auth. see Grey-Wilson, Christopher.

Mathew, David. Ethiopia, the Study of a Polity, 1540-1935. LC 73-19309. (Illus.). 254p. 1974. Repr. of 1947 ed. lib. bdg. 17.25x (ISBN 0-8371-7324-8, MAET). Greenwood.

Mathew, Jan, ed. see Junior League of Sarasota FL, Inc.

Mathew, W. M. The House of Gibbs & the Peruvian Guano Monopoly. (Royal Historical Society - Studies in History: Vol. 25). 281p. 1981. text ed. 38.50x (ISBN 0-901050-61-X, Pub. by Swiftbks England). Humanities.

Mathews, jt. auth. see Elmer, Irene.

Mathews, jt. auth. see Kramer, Janice.

Mathews, jt. auth. see Latourette, Jane.

Mathews, jt. auth. see Warren, Mary P.

Mathews, Arthur G. Take It Easy: The Art of Conquering Your Nerves. (Illus.). 1945. 8.95x (ISBN 0-911378-25-1). Sheridan.

Mathews, Betty W. How to get the Nittie Gritties Out of that Move. 64p. 1983. pap. 3.50 (ISBN 0-86666-087-9). GWP.

Mathews, C. Weldon, jt. ed. see Rao, K. N.

Mathews, Donald G. Religion in the Old South. LC 77-587. 1979. pap. 6.95 (ISBN 0-226-51002-6, P819, Phoen). U of Chicago Pr.

Mathews, F. Neil. Entomology: Investigative Activities for Could-Be Bug Buffs. Smith, Linda H., ed. 1978. pap. 4.95 (ISBN 0-936386-03-7). Creative Learning.

Mathews, F. Schuyler. Field Book of American Trees & Shrubs. (Putnam's Nature Field Bks.). (Illus.). 1915. 7.95 o.p. (ISBN 0-399-10281-7). Putnam Pub Group.

Mathews, G. Vinyl & Allied Polymers, Vol. 2. 1972. text ed. 39.95 o.p. (ISBN 0-592-05443-8). Butterworth.

Mathews, George B. Theory of Numbers. 2nd ed. LC 61-17958. 13.95 (ISBN 0-8284-0156-X). Chelsea Pub.

Mathews, Gregory R. Respect is a Higher Form of Love. (Illus.). 11p. (Orig.). 1982. pap. 1.75 (ISBN 0-941830-01-2). Explorations Pr.

Mathews, Harry. Selected Declarations of Dependence. (Illus.). 1978. pap. 5.00 (ISBN 0-915990-09-1). Z Pr.

--Trial Impressions. (Burning Deck Poetry Ser). 1978. pap. 4.00 (ISBN 0-930900-44-8). Burning Deck.

Mathews, Helen. What? Why? How? (Illus., Orig.). 1979. pap. 3.95 o.p. (ISBN 0-89260-135-3). Hwong Pub.

Mathews, J. P. Was Tammy Thinking Metric? 1978. 4.95 o.p. (ISBN 0-533-03122-2). Vantage.

Mathews, Jan. A Flame Too Fierce, No. 70. 1982. pap. 1.75 o.s.i. (ISBN 0-515-06681-8). Jove Pubns.

Mathews, Janet. Wurley & Wommera. (Illus.). (gr. 5 up). 1979. 8.95 o.p. (ISBN 0-529-05501-5, Philomel). Putnam Pub Group.

Mathews, Jay, et al, trs. see Andors, Stephen.

Mathews, John J. Osages: Children of the Middle Waters. (Civilization of the American Indian Ser.: No. 60). (Illus.). 1981. pap. 16.95 (ISBN 0-8061-1770-2). U of Okla Pr.

--Sundown. 1979. lib. bdg. 11.95 (ISBN 0-8398-2588-9, Gregg). G K Hall.

Mathews, Jon & Walker, Robert L. Mathematical Methods of Physics. 2nd ed. 1970. text ed. 29.95 (ISBN 0-8053-7002-1). Benjamin-Cummings.

Mathews, Joseph J. George W. Smalley: Forty Years a Foreign Correspondent. LC 72-87496. x, 229p. 1973. 18.00x (ISBN 0-8078-1205-6). U of NC Pr.

--Reporting the Wars. LC 72-4005. 322p. 1972. Repr. of 1957 ed. lib. bdg. 17.00x (ISBN 0-8371-6431-1, MARW). Greenwood.

Mathews, Marcia M. The Freedom Star. (Illus.). (gr. 3-6). 1971. PLB 4.39 o.p. (ISBN 0-698-30094-7, Coward). Putnam Pub Group.

Mathews, Marie A. The Social Work Mystique: Toward a Sociology of Social Work. LC 81-40723. 190p. (Orig.). 1982. lib. bdg. 20.75 (ISBN 0-8191-1903-2); pap. text ed. 10.00 (ISBN 0-8191-1904-0). U Pr of Amer.

Mathews, Mitford. American Words. LC 76-20613. (Illus.). (gr. 7 up). 1976. 6.95 o.p. (ISBN 0-529-03550-2, Philomel). Putnam Pub Group.

Mathews, P. M. & Venkatesan, K. A Textbook of Quantum Mechanics. 1979. pap. text ed. 29.95x (ISBN 0-07-096510-2, C). McGraw.

Mathews, Richard. The Clockwork Universe of Anthony Burgess. LC 78-14552. (The Milford Ser.: Popular Writers of Today: Vol. 19). 1978. lib. bdg. 9.95x (ISBN 0-89370-127-0); pap. 3.95x (ISBN 0-89370-227-7). Borgo Pr.

--Lightning from a Clear Sky: Tolkien, the Trilogy & the Silmarillion. LC 78-922. (The Milford Ser: Popular Writers of Today: Vol. 15). 1978. lib. bdg. 9.95x (ISBN 0-89370-121-1); pap. 3.95x (ISBN 0-89370-221-8). Borgo Pr.

--Worlds Beyond the World: The Fantastic Vision of William Morris. LC 78-247. (The Milford Ser: Popular Writers of Today Vol. 13). 1978. lib. bdg. 9.95x (ISBN 0-89370-118-1); pap. 3.95x (ISBN 0-89370-218-8). Borgo Pr.

Mathews, Richard W. Aldiss Unbound: The Science Fiction of Brian Aldiss. LC 77-24582. (The Milford Ser.: Popular Writers of Today Vol. 9). 1977. lib. bdg. 9.95x (ISBN 0-89370-113-0); pap. 3.95x (ISBN 0-89370-213-7). Borgo Pr.

Mathews, Shailer & Smith, Gerald B., eds. Dictionary of Religion & Ethics. LC 70-145713. 1971. Repr. of 1921 ed. 45.00x (ISBN 0-8103-3196-9). Gale.

Mathews, Thomas. Puerto Rican Politics & the New Deal. LC 76-1934. 345p. 1976. Repr. of 1960 ed. lib. bdg. 39.50 (ISBN 0-306-70752-7). Da Capo.

Mathews, Thomas, jt. ed. see Garsoian, Nina.

Mathews, Tom, jt. auth. see Wilkins, Roy.

Mathews, Wiliam. The Great Conversers, & Other Essays. 304p. 1982. Repr. of 1878 ed. lib. bdg. 50.00 (ISBN 0-89987-644-7). Darby Bks.

Mathews, William B. Life's Abiding Resources. LC 78-66872. 1978. 6.95 o.p. (ISBN 0-8158-0371-0). Chris Mass.

Mathews, Willis W. Atlas of Descriptive Embryology. 3rd ed. 1982. text ed. 13.95x (ISBN 0-02-377130-5). Macmillan.

--Laboratory Studies in Animal Development. (Illus.). 1978. pap. text ed. 10.95 (ISBN 0-02-377120-8). Macmillan.

Mathews, Zena & Jonaitis, Aldona. Native North American Art History--Selected Readings. (Illus.). 500p. (Orig.). 1982. text ed. cancelled (ISBN 0-917962-78-8); pap. text ed. 14.95 (ISBN 0-917962-73-7). Peek Pubns.

Mathewson, et al. Fundamentals of Dentistry for Children. 1982. cancelled (ISBN 0-931386-40-3). Quint Pub Co.

Mathewson, Christopher C. Engineering Geology. (Illus.). 416p. 1981. text ed. 29.95 (ISBN 0-675-08032-0). Additional supplements may be obtained from publisher. Merrill.

Mathewson, Hugh S. Pharmacology for Respiratory Therapists. 2nd ed. LC 80-25212. (Illus.). 97p. 1981. pap. text ed. 12.95 (ISBN 0-8016-3161-0). Mosby.

Mathewson, Joe. Up Against Daley: The Story of Illinois Independents. LC 74-13055. 1974. 21.00x (ISBN 0-87548-284-8). Open Court.

Mathewson, Robert. Birds. (How & Why Wonder Books Ser.). (Illus., Orig.). (gr. 4-6). 1960. deluxe ed. 1.95 o.p. (ISBN 0-448-04007-7, G&D). Putnam Pub Group.

Mathewson, Stephen. Manual for Production of Alcohol Fuel. 208p. 7.95 (ISBN 0-686-35945-3). Rutan Pub.

Mathewson, Stephen W. The Manual for the Home & Farm Production of Alcohol Fuel. LC 80-51216. 224p. 1980. 12.95 (ISBN 0-89815-030-2); pap. 7.95 (ISBN 0-89815-029-9). Ten Speed Pr.

Mathewson, William. Immediate Release. 1982. 10.95 (ISBN 0-671-43036-X). S&S.

Mathias, John, ed. see Hass, Robert, et al.

Mathias, Peter, ed. Science & Society, 1600-1900. (Illus.). 176p. 1972. 27.95 (ISBN 0-521-08375-3). Cambridge U Pr.

Mathias, Peter & Postan, Michael, eds. Cambridge Economic History of Europe: The Industrial Economies: Capital, Labour & Enterprise, Part 1: Britain, France, Germany & Scandinavia. 1982. 19.95 (ISBN 0-521-28800-2). Cambridge U Pr.

--Cambridge Economic History of Europe: The Industrial Economies: Capital, Labour, & Enterprise, Part 2: The United States, Japan, & Russia. 1982. 17.95 (ISBN 0-521-28801-0). Cambridge U Pr.

Mathias, William, et al. Foundations of Criminal Justice. (Criminal Justice Ser.). (Illus.). 1980. text ed. 22.95 (ISBN 0-13-329276-2). P-H.

Mathies, F. The Ultimate Inflation Shelter. 1980. 25.00 o.s.i. (ISBN 0-686-58614-X). Windsor.

Mathies, M. Lorraine & Watson, Peter G. Computer Based Reference Services. LC 73-9967. 270p. 1973. pap. text ed. 15.00 (ISBN 0-8389-0156-5). ALA.

Mathiesen, Elva. Sourdough. LC 75-24122. 1974. pap. 2.50 (ISBN 0-917412-01-X). Mathiesen Edns.

Mathiesen, Thomas J. A Bibliography of Sources for the Study of Ancient Greek Music. (Music Indexes & Bibliographies: No. 10). 1974. pap. 5.00 (ISBN 0-913574-10-4). Eur-Am Music.

Mathieson, Donald J., jt. auth. see McKinnon, Ronald I.

Mathieson, Elizabeth L. The Complete Book of Crochet. rev. ed. LC 76-28737. (Illus.). 1977. 16.30i (ISBN 0-690-01156-3). T Y Crowell.

Mathieson, Eric. The True Story of Jumbo the Elephant. (Illus.). (gr. 4-6). 1964. PLB 3.86 o.p. (ISBN 0-698-30377-6, Coward). Putnam Pub Group.

Mathieson, Margaret. The Preachers of Culture: A Study of English & Its Teachers. 231p. 1975. 15.00x o.p. (ISBN 0-87471-752-3). Rowman.

Mathiessen, Peter. Blue Meridian. 176p. (RL 9). 1973. pap. 1.50 o.p. (ISBN 0-451-05359-1, W5359, Sig). NAL.

Mathieu, Alix & Burke, John, eds. Infection & the Perioperative Period: Pactical Considerations for Anesthesiologists & Surgeons. (Scientific Basis of Clinicla Anesthesia Ser.). 1982. 44.50 (ISBN 0-8089-1325-5). Grune.

Mathieu, Gustave B., jt. auth. see Haas, Werner.

Mathieu, J. P., ed. Advances in Raman Spectroscopy, Vol. 1. 1973. 114.00 (ISBN 0-471-25866-0, Pub. by Wiley Heyden). Wiley.

Mathieu, Joe. The Olden Days. (Pictureback Ser.). (Illus.). 32p. (ps-3). 1981. PLB 4.99 (ISBN 0-394-94085-7); pap. 1.50 (ISBN 0-394-84085-2). Random.

Mathieu-Castellani, Gisele, ed. La Metamorphose Dans la Poesis Baroque, Francaise et Anglaise: Variations et Reaurgences. (Etudes Litteraires Francaises Ser.: No. 7). 250p. (Fr.). 1980. pap. 33.80 (ISBN 0-686-35915-1). Benjamins North Am.

Mathiot, Madeleine. A Dictionary of Papago Usage: Vol. 2 Ku-U. (Language Science Monographs: No. 8/2). pap. text ed. 25.00x o.p. (ISBN 0-87750-168-8). Res Ctr Lang Semiotic.

Mathis, Cleopatra. The Bottom Land. 96p. 1983. 13.95 (ISBN 0-686-84592-7); pap. 7.95 (ISBN 0-935296-41-7). Sheep Meadow.

Mathis, F. John, ed. Offshore Lending by U. S. Commercial Banks. 2nd ed. LC 80-83082. (Illus.). 366p. 1981. 22.00 (ISBN 0-936742-01-1). Robt Morris Assocs.

Mathis, Jack. Valley of the Cliffhangers. LC 75-195. 456p. 1975. 66.00 (ISBN 0-686-11863-4). J Mathis Adv.

Mathis, James L. Psychiatric Medicine Handbook. Gradner, Alvin F., ed. (Allied Health Professions Monograph Ser.). 1983. price not set (ISBN 0-87527-320-3). Green.

Mathis, Robert L. & Jackson, John H. Personnel: Contemporary Perspectives & Applications. 3rd ed. (Illus.). 606p. 1982. text ed. 23.50 (ISBN 0-314-63270-0). West Pub.

--Personnel: Contemporary Perspectives & Applications. 2nd ed. (Illus.). 1979. text ed. 19.95 (ISBN 0-8299-0199-X); readings & exercises by Sally Coltrin 6.95 (ISBN 0-8299-0282-1); instrs.' manual avail. (ISBN 0-8299-0555-3); study guide 8.50 (ISBN 0-686-96921-9). West Pub.

Mathis, Sharon B. Listen for the Fig Tree. (gr. 7 up). 1975. pap. 1.95 o.p. (ISBN 0-380-00390-2, 51854). Avon.

--Ray Charles. LC 72-7552. (Biography Ser.). (Illus.). (gr. 1-5). 1973. 9.57i o.p. (ISBN 0-690-67065-6, TYC-J); PLB 6.89 o.p. (ISBN 0-690-67066-4). Har-Row.

--Teacup Full of Roses. (YA) (gr. 7 up). 1973. pap. 1.75 o.p. (ISBN 0-380-00780-0, 54312). Avon.

--Teacup Full of Roses. 128p. (gr. 7 up). 1972. 10.95 (ISBN 0-670-69434-7). Viking Pr.

Mathisen, Marilyn. Apparel & Accessories. Lynch, Richard, ed. (Career Competencies in Marketing). (Illus.). 1979. pap. text ed. 7.32 (ISBN 0-07-040905-6, G); teachers' manual & key 4.00 (ISBN 0-07-040906-4). McGraw.

Mathisen, Robert R., ed. The Role of Religion in American Life: An Interpretive Historical Anthology. LC 80-6246. 420p. (Orig.). 1982. pap. text ed. 14.75 (ISBN 0-8191-2514-8). U Pr of Amer.

Mathisen, Trygve. Methodology in the Study of International Relations. LC 74-3753. 265p. 1974. Repr. of 1959 ed. lib. bdg. 17.25x (ISBN 0-8371-7472-4, MASI). Greenwood.

Mathison, Sandra, jt. ed. see House, Ernest R.

Mathre, D. E., ed. Compendium of Barley Diseases, No. 8. LC 82-72159. 96p. 1982. pap. 12.00 (ISBN 0-89054-047-0). Am Phytopathol.

Mathur, D. P. Management in Small Poultry Farms. 1979. 11.50x o.p. (ISBN 0-8364-0324-X). South Asia Bks.

Mathur, Hari M., ed. Anthropology in the Development Process. 1977. text ed. 23.50x (ISBN 0-7069-0541-5). Humanities.

Mathur, Iqbal. Introduction to Financial Management. (Illus.). 1979. text ed. 23.95x (ISBN 0-02-377250-6); student study guide avail.; intrs'. manual avail. Macmillan.

Mathur, Iqbal & Scherr, Frederick C. Cases in Financial Management. 1979. pap. text ed. 9.95x (ISBN 0-02-377260-3); instrs'. manual avail. Macmillan.

Mathur, Iqbal & Snodgrass, Coral. Introductory to Financial Management: Study Guide. 1979. pap. text ed. 7.95x (ISBN 0-02-377280-8). Macmillan.

Mathur, K. Bureaucracy & the New Agricultural Strategy. (Illus.). 103p. 1982. text ed. 13.00x (ISBN 0-391-02725-5, Pub. by Concept India). Humanities.

Mathur, M. V. & Narain, I., eds. Panchayati Raj Planning & Democracy. 17.50x o.p. (ISBN 0-210-22548-3). Asia.

Mathur, S. S. & Kandpal, T. C. Solar Concentrators: A Bibliography. (Energy). 220p. 1982. pap. 45.00x (ISBN 0-910661-01-4). Innovative Inform.

Mathur, Y. B. British Administration of Punjab. 1975. 11.00x o.p. (ISBN 0-88386-624-2). South Asia Bks.

Mathurin, Owen C. Henry Sylvester Williams & the Origins of the Pan-African Movement, 1869-1911. LC 75-35348. (Contributions in Afro-American & African Studies: No. 21). 224p. 1976. lib. bdg. 25.00 (ISBN 0-8371-8594-7, MHW/). Greenwood.

Mathy, Francis. Shiga Naoya. (World Authors Ser.). lib. bdg. 15.95 (ISBN 0-8057-2648-9, Twayne). G K Hall.

Mathy, Francis, tr. see Soseki, Natsume.

Matich, Olga & Heim, Michael. The Third Wave: Russian Literature in Emigration. 300p. 1983. 27.50 (ISBN 0-88233-782-3); pap. 8.00 (ISBN 0-88233-783-1). Ardis Pubs.

Matick, Richard E. Computer Storage Systems & Technology. LC 77-5812. 1977. 49.95 (ISBN 0-471-57629-8, Pub. by Wiley-Interscience). Wiley.

Matin, Philip. Clinical Nuclear Medicine. (Medical Outline Ser.). 1981. 34.00 (ISBN 0-87488-609-0); pap. 26.00 (ISBN 0-87488-610-4). Med Exam.

Matin, Ralph P. Carmen Christi: Philippians 2: 5-11 in Recent Interpretations & in the Setting of Early Christian Worship. 378p. 1983. pap. 7.95 (ISBN 0-8028-1960-5). Eerdmans.

Matisse, Herni. Matisse Line Drawings & Prints. (Illus.). 1980. pap. 2.50 (ISBN 0-486-23877-6). Dover.

Matisse, Paul, ed. Marcel Duchamp, Notes. (Documents of Twentieth Century Art). (Illus.). 270p. 1983. lib. bdg. 65.00 (ISBN 0-8057-9955-9, Twayne). G K Hall.

Matkin, A. M., jt. auth. see Molloy, Julia S.

Matko, jt. auth. see Clark.

Matlaw, Myron. American Popular Entertainment: Paper & Proceedings of the Conference on the History of American Popular Entertainment. LC 78-74655. (Contributions in Drama & Theatre Studies: No. 1). (Illus.). lib. bdg. 29.95 (ISBN 0-313-21072-1, MEN/). Greenwood.

Matlaw, Ralph, ed. see Dostoevsky, Fyodor.

Matlaw, Ralph E., ed. see Chekhov, Anton.

Matlaw, Ralph E., tr. see Dostoevsky, Fedor.

Matley, Jay & Chemical Engineering Magazine. Practical Process Instrumentation & Control. (Chemical Engineering Ser.). 512p. 1980. 35.75 (ISBN 0-07-010712-2). McGraw.

Matlock, Bill, jt. auth. see Schell, Frank R.

Matlock, Bill J., jt. auth. see Schell, Frank R.

Matlock, W. G. Realistic Planning for Arid Lands: Natural Resource Limitations to Agricultural Development, Vol. 2. 284p. 1981. 45.00 (ISBN 3-7186-0051-X). Harwood Academic.

Matochik, Michael J., ed. The Civil War, 1861-1865: Part I, a Classified Title List for the Microfilm Collection. 127p. 1981. write for info. o.p. (ISBN 0-667-00633-8). Microfilming Corp.

Matolek, Marmie, ed. see Kvasnicker, Ted, et al.

Matos, Antonio, ed. Guide to Reviews of Books from & about Hispanic America, 1980. LC 66-96537. 1780p. 1980. 90.00 (ISBN 0-87917-084-0). Ethridge.

Matossian, Mary K., jt. auth. see Villa, Susie H.

Matoth, Yehuda, ed. see Tel Aviv University Conference on Erythropoiesis, July, 1970, Petah Tikva.

Matras, Judah. Introduction to Population Studies: A Sociological Approach. (Illus.). 1977. text ed. 22.95 (ISBN 0-13-493122-X). P-H.

--Social Inequality, Stratification, & Mobility. LC 74-18070. (Illus.). 448p. 1975. text ed. 22.95 (ISBN 0-13-815803-7). P-H.

Matreyek, W. A. Communicating in English: Examples & Models-Interpersonal Functions, Vol. 1. (Materials for Language Practice Ser.). 128p. 1983. 6.95 (ISBN 0-08-028616-X). Pergamon.

Matricardi, Paolo, jt. auth. see Angelucci, Enzo.

Matsch, Charles L. North America & the Great Ice Age. new ed. (Earth Science Paperback Ser.). (Illus.). 1976. pap. text ed. 11.95 (ISBN 0-07-040935-8, C). McGraw.

Matsch, Lee A., jt. auth. see Gross, William.

Matsen, John M., jt. ed. see Wannamaker, Lewis W.

Matson, Alexander, tr. see Sillanpaa, Frans E.

Matson, Clive. Equal in Desire. 1982. pap. 15.00 signed ed. (ISBN 0-686-37447-9). Man-Root.

Matson, Debra, ed. see Brannigan, Francis L.

Matson, Donald D., jt. auth. see Shillito, John, Jr.

Matson, Hollis N., jt. auth. see Gray, Stephen E.

Matson, Johnny L. & Andrasik, Frank, eds. Treatment Issues & Innovations in Mental Retardation. (Applied Clinical Psychology Ser.). 666p. 1983. text ed. 49.50x (ISBN 0-306-40935-6, Plenum Pr). Plenum Pub.

Matson, Johnny L. & Barrett, Rowland P., eds. Psychopathology in the Mentally Retarded. Date not set. price not set (ISBN 0-8089-1511-8). Grune.

Matson, Johnny L. & Mulick, James A., eds. Handbook of Mental Retardation. 650p. 1983. 75.00 (ISBN 0-08-028060-9); before 7/83 55.00 (ISBN 0-08-029421-9). Pergamon.

Matson, Robert W., ed. see Paulaharju, Samuli.

Matson, Tim. Earth Ponds: The Country Pond Maker's Guide. (Illus.). 104p. 1982. 14.95 o.p. (ISBN 0-914378-85-6); pap. 9.95 (ISBN 0-914378-86-4). Countryman.

Matson, Wallace I. Sentience. LC 75-3774. 160p. 1976. 17.95x (ISBN 0-520-02987-9). U of Cal Pr.

--Sentience. (Illus.). 200p. 1982. 17.95x (ISBN 0-520-02987-9); pap. 6.95 (ISBN 0-520-04776-1, CAL 588). U of Cal Pr.

Matsuda, Mitsugu. Japanese in Hawaii: An Annotated Bibliography. (Social Science & Linguistics Institute Special Publications). 1975. pap. 8.00x (ISBN 0-8248-0290-X). UH Pr.

Matsuda, Mitsugu, tr. see Yazaki, Takeo.

Matsuda, Ryuichi. Morphology & Evolution of the Insect Head. (Memoirs Ser: No. 4). (Illus.). 334p. 1965. 12.00 o.p. (ISBN 0-686-00423-X). Am Entom Inst.

Matsui, Hideji & Kobayashi, Kando, eds. Biomechanics VIII, 2 vols. (International Series on Biomechanics). 1983. text ed. price not set (ISBN 0-931250-42-0). Human Kinetics.

--Biomechanics VIII, Vol. A. (International Series on Biomechanics). 1983. text ed. price not set (ISBN 0-931250-43-9). Human Kinetics.

--Biomechanics VIII, Vol. B. (International Series on Biomechanics). 1983. text ed. price not set (ISBN 0-931250-44-7). Human Kinetics.

Matsui, Yoshiichi. Goldfish Guide. (Illus.). 256p. 1981. 14.95 (ISBN 0-87666-545-8, PL-2011). TFH Pubns.

Matsujoto, H., jt. auth. see Umezsiva, H.

Matsumoto, A. see Young, Leo.

Matsumoto, Nancy, ed. The United States & the Global Environment: A Guide to American Organizations Concerned with International Environment Issues. LC 79-53313. (Who's Doing What Ser.: No. 9). 100p. (Orig.). 1981. pap. 25.00x (ISBN 0-912102-45-4). Cal Inst Public.

Matsumoto, T. Age & Nature of the Circum-Pacific Orogenesis. 1967. 42.50 (ISBN 0-686-43415-3). Elsevier.

Matsumoto, Teruo. Current Management of Acute Gastrointestinal Hemorrhage. (Illus.). 272p. 1977. 25.00x o.p. (ISBN 0-398-03582-2). C C Thomas.

Matsumura, Gentaro. The Emperor's Island: The Story of Japan. 240p. 1977. pap. 6.95 (ISBN 0-914778-47-1, Pub. by Lotus Japan). Phoenix Bks.

Matsunaga, Alicia & Matsunaga, Daigan. Foundation of Japanese Buddhism: The Mass Movement, Vol. 2. LC 74-83654. 1976. 14.95x (ISBN 0-914910-27-2); pap. 8.50 (ISBN 0-914910-28-0). Buddhist Bks.

Matsunaga, Daigan, jt. auth. see Matsunaga, Alicia.

Matsuno, Masako. A Pair of Red Clogs. (Illus.). (gr. 1-4). 1981. 3.95 (ISBN 0-399-20796-1, Philomel). Putnam Pub Group.

Matsushima, Seizo. High-Yielding Rice Cultivation: A Method for Maximizing Rice Yield Through "Ideal Plants". (Illus.). 1976. 32.50x (ISBN 0-86008-164-8, Pub. by Japan Sci Soc). Intl Schol Bk Serv.

--Rice Cultivation for the Million. 350p. 1980. 35.00x (ISBN 0-89955-203-X, Pub. by Japan Sci Soc Japan). Intl Schol Bk Serv.

Matt, Paul, et al. Historical Aviation Album, Vol. 13. Rust, Thomas & Foxworth, Thomas, eds. LC 74-16736. (All American Ser.). (Illus.). 72p. (Orig.). 1974. pap. 7.50 o.p. (ISBN 0-911852-12-3). Hist Aviation.

Matt, Paul R. Historical Aviation Album, Vol. 14. Rust, Kenn C. & Foxworth, Thomas G., eds. (All American Collector's Ser.). (Illus.). 72p. 1975. pap. 7.50 (ISBN 0-911852-13-1, Pub. by Hist Aviation). Aviation.

Matt, Stephen R. Electricity & Basic Electronics. LC 81-20008. (Illus.). 1982. text ed. 14.00 (ISBN 0-87006-401-0). Goodheart.

Matta, Michael S. & Wilbraham, Antony C. Chemistry: Atoms, Molecules, Life. 1981. 23.95 (ISBN 0-8053-9640-3); study guide by Dennis D. Staley 7.95 (ISBN 0-8053-9642-X); lab manual 9.95 (ISBN 0-686-73684-2). Benjamin-Cummings.

Matte, Jaqueline A. The History of Washington County: First County in Alabama. LC 82-70721. (Illus.). 486p. 1982. 30.00 (ISBN 0-9608434-0-X). WA County Hist.

Mattelart, Armand. Transnationals & the Third World: The Struggle for Culture. Buxton, David, tr. from French. (Illus.). 224p. 1983. text ed. 22.95x (ISBN 0-89789-030-2). J F Bergin.

Mattera, Joanne, ed. The Quiltmaker's Art: Contemporary Quilts & Their Motifs. LC 82-82472. (Illus.). 132p. (Orig.). 1982. 24.95 (ISBN 0-937274-04-6); pap. 15.95 (ISBN 0-937274-05-4). Lark Comm.

Matters, Marion, compiled by. Minnesota State Archives Preliminary Check List. 94p. 1979. pap. 3.00 (ISBN 0-87351-136-0). Minn Hist.

Mattes, Larry. Classroom Oral Language Development: An Elementary School Oral Language Curriculum. 150p. 1982. pap. 16.75x spiral (ISBN 0-398-04584-4). C C Thomas.

Matteson, David M. Organization of the Government Under the Constitution. LC 72-118201. (American Constitutional & Legal History Ser). 1970. Repr. of 1943 ed. lib. bdg. 47.50 (ISBN 0-306-71935-5). Da Capo.

Matteson, Marilee, ed. Small Feasts: Delectable Meals with Soups, Salads, & Sandwiches. (Clarkson N. Potter Bks.). 1980. 17.95 (ISBN 0-517-54052-5, C N Potter Bks). Crown.

Matteson, Michael & Ivancevich, John. Management Classics. 2nd ed. 1981. pap. text ed. 16.50x (ISBN 0-673-16102-1). Scott F.

Matteson, Michael T., jt. auth. see Ivancevich, John M.

Matteson, Peggy, ed. Handbook in Prepared Childbirth. (Avery's Childbirth Education Ser.). (Illus.). 112p. 1982. pap. 5.50 (ISBN 0-89529-204-1). Avery Pub.

Matthaei, Julie A. An Economic History of Women in America: Women's Work, the Sexual Division of Labor & the Development of Capitalism. LC 81-84111. 384p. 1983. 29.95 (ISBN 0-8052-3804-2); pap. 11.95 (ISBN 0-8052-0744-9). Schocken.

Matthaei, Margaret B., et al. Reading about Psychology & You. 1979. pap. text ed. 9.95x (ISBN 0-673-15164-6). Scott F.

Matthaei, Renate. Luigi Pirandello. Young, Simon & Young, Erika, trs. LC 72-79937. (Literature Life Ser.). (Illus.). 1973. 11.95 (ISBN 0-8044-2592-2). Ungar.

Matthais, John, tr. see Ostergren, Jan.

Matthay, Tobias. Visible & Invisible in Pianoforte Technique: Being a Digest of the Author's Technical Techniques up to Date. 1932. 11.95x (ISBN 0-19-318412-5). Oxford U Pr.

Matthes, Georg. The Properties of Groundwater. Harvey, John C., tr. LC 81-7481. 406p. 1982. 49.95 (ISBN 0-471-08513-8, Pub. by Wiley-Interscience). Wiley.

Matthes, K., et al. Infinitely Divisible Point Processes. (Wiley Series in Probability & Mathematical Statistics-Probability & Mathematical Statistics Section). 84.95 (ISBN 0-471-99460-X, Pub. by Wiley-Interscience). Wiley.

Mattheson, Johann. Critica Musica, D.I. Grundrichtige Untersuch- und Beurtheilung: So in Alten und Neuen, Gedruckten und Ungedruckten, Musicalischen Schrifften Zu Finden. 784p. 100.00 o.s.i. (ISBN 90-6027-005-3, Pub. by Frits Knuf Netherlands). Pendragon NY.

Matthew, C. D. & Seamark, R. F., eds. Pineal Function. 1981. 73.75 (ISBN 0-444-80313-0). Elsevier.

Matthew, Christopher. The Long-Haired Boy. LC 79-55594. 1980. 9.95 o.p. (ISBN 0-689-11051-0). Atheneum.

Matthew, Donald. The Medieval European Community. LC 76-24996. 1977. 32.50 (ISBN 0-312-52710-1). St Martin.

--The Norman Monasteries & Their English Possessions. LC 78-26293. (Oxford Historical Ser.). 1979. Repr. of 1962 ed. lib. bdg. 20.75x (ISBN 0-313-20847-6, MANM). Greenwood.

Matthew, H., ed. Acute Barbiturate Poisoning. 1973. 41.00 (ISBN 0-444-15003-X). Elsevier.

Matthew, H. C., ed. see Gladstone, William E.

Matthew, James E. Literature of Music. LC 69-12688. (Music Ser). 1969. Repr. of 1896 ed. lib. bdg. 29.50 (ISBN 0-306-71227-X). Da Capo.

Matthew, James E., tr. see Borren, Charles V.

Matthew, James S. My Fifty Years in Canada. 5.75 (ISBN 0-8062-2129-1). Carlton.

Matthew, Marie-Louise & Fergersen, Lorraine. All-in-One: Basic Writing Skills. 1980. pap. text ed. 13.95 (ISBN 0-13-022509-6). P-H.

Matthew, Paris. The Holy City. LC 79-828. 1979. pap. 5.95x (ISBN 0-914140-05-1). Carpenter Pr.

Matthew, Scott. The First Woman of Medicine: The Story of Elizabeth Blackwell. LC 78-16305. (Famous Firsts Ser.). (Illus.). 1978. PLB 10.76 (ISBN 0-89547-042-X). Silver.

Matthews, A. Warren. Abraham Was Their Father. LC 81-146. vii, 290p. 1981. 18.95 (ISBN 0-86554-005-5). Mercer Univ Pr.

Matthews, Alfred W. The Development of St. Augustine from Neoplatonism to Christianity, 386-391 A.D. LC 79-5497. 1980. text ed. 19.50 (ISBN 0-8191-0895-2); pap. text ed. 12.25 (ISBN 0-8191-0896-0). U Pr of Amer.

Matthews, Allayne, jt. auth. see Rimmer, Bob.

Matthews, Allen R. The Assault. LC 80-14926. (Great Classic Stories of World War II Ser.). 1980. 8.95 o.p. (ISBN 0-396-07874-5); pap. 5.95 o.p. (ISBN 0-396-07875-3). Dodd.

Matthews, Arthur C. Radio Production Handbook: A Beginner's Guide to Broadcasting & Cablecasting. Zapel, Arthur L. & Meyer, Sheila, eds. LC 82-60762. (Illus.). 225p. (Orig.). 1982. pap. text ed. 9.95 (ISBN 0-916260-19-4). Meriwether Pub.

Matthews, B. & Hill, R. G., eds. Anatomical, Physiological, & Pharmacological Aspects of Trigeminal Pain: Proceedings of the Third World Congress on Pain; International Association for the Study of Pain, Dunblane, Perthshire, U.K., September 11-12, 1981. (International Congress Ser.: No. 588). 312p. 1982. 78.75 (ISBN 0-444-90269-4, Excerpta Medica). Elsevier.

Matthews, Brander. Historical Novel & Other Essays. LC 68-30586. 1969. Repr. of 1901 ed. 30.00x (ISBN 0-8103-3218-3). Gale.

Matthews, Brander, ed. Ballads of Books. LC 70-141032. 1971. Repr. of 1887 ed. 30.00x (ISBN 0-8103-3384-8). Gale.

Matthews, C. D., jt. auth. see Blaikie, W. G.

Matthews, C. S. The Church: Learning about God's People. (Concept Bks.: Ser. 4). 1983. pap. 3.50 (ISBN 0-570-08525-X); Set. pap. 12.95. Concordia.

Matthews, Clayton. The Birthright. (Orig.). 1980. pap. 2.50 o.p. (ISBN 0-523-40630-4). Pinnacle Bks.

--Disinherited. 1983. pap. 3.50 (ISBN 0-553-22846-3). Bantam.

--The Harvesters. 1979. pap. 2.50 o.p. (ISBN 0-523-40448-4). Pinnacle Bks.

--The Power Seekers. 1978. pap. 2.25 o.p. (ISBN 0-523-40116-7). Pinnacle Bks.

Matthews, Clayton, jt. auth. see Matthews, Patricia.

Matthews, Daryl B. Disposable Patients. LC 77-25778. 128p. 1980. 16.95 (ISBN 0-669-02164-4). Lexington Bks.

Matthews, Donald R. & Prothro, James W. Negroes & the New Southern Politics. LC 66-28289. (Illus.). 551p. 12.50 o.p. (ISBN 0-15-165011-X). HarBraceJ.

Matthews, Donald R., jt. auth. see Keech, William R.

Matthews, Donald R., ed. Perspectives on Presidential Selection. (Studies in Presidential Selection). 1973. 18.95 (ISBN 0-8157-5508-2); pap. 7.95 (ISBN 0-8157-5507-4). Brookings.

Matthews, Dorothy, ed. Producing Award Winning Student Poets: Tips from Succesful Teachers. 67p. 3.00 (ISBN 0-686-95314-2); members 2.75 (ISBN 0-686-99493-0). NCTE.

Matthews, E., tr. see Runciman, Walter G.

Matthews, Edward. Celebrating Mass with Children: A Commentary on the Directory of Masses with Children. pap. 6.95 o.p. (ISBN 0-8091-2160-3). Paulist Pr.

Matthews, Ellen. Culture Clash. LC 81-85714. 35p. (Orig.). 1982. 11.95x (ISBN 0-686-82921-2); pap. text ed. 7.50 (ISBN 0-933662-48-3). Intercult Pr.

--Putting up with Sherwood. LC 80-17574. (Illus.). (gr. 3-5). 1980. 9.95 (ISBN 0-664-32672-2). Westminster.

Matthews, Florence, jt. auth. see Kulick, Florence.

Matthews, G. A., ed. Polymer Mixing Technology. (Illus.). 280p. 1982. 51.25 (ISBN 0-85334-133-8, Pub. by Applied Sci England). Elsevier.

Matthews, G. V. Bird Navigation. 3rd ed. LC 68-23181. (Cambridge Monographs in Experimental Biology). (Illus.). 1968. 34.50 (ISBN 0-521-07271-9); pap. 11.95x (ISBN 0-521-09541-7). Cambridge U Pr.

Matthews, Geoffery. Calculus. 1969. 6.95 o.p. (ISBN 0-7195-0898-3). Transatlantic.

Matthews, H. Surface Wave Filters: Design, Construction, & Use. LC 77-3913. 1977. 48.50 o.p. (ISBN 0-471-58030-9). Wiley.

Matthews, H. R., jt. auth. see Gould, H.

Matthews, J. H. Benjamin Peret. LC 74-30229. (World Authors Ser.). 1975. lib. bdg. 15.95 (ISBN 0-8057-2691-8, Twayne). G K Hall.

--Eight Painters: The Surrealist Context. LC 82-10801. (Illus.). 288p. 1982. text ed. 24.00x (ISBN 0-8156-2274-0). Syracuse U Pr.

--Imagery of Surrealism. (Illus.). 320p. 1977. 27.95x (ISBN 0-8156-2183-3); pap. text ed. 12.95x (ISBN 0-8156-2281-3). Syracuse U Pr.

--Surrealism & American Feature Films. (Filmmakers Ser.). 1979. lib. bdg. 11.95 (ISBN 0-8057-9265-1, Twayne). G K Hall.

--Surrealist Poetry in France. LC 71-96815. 1969. 15.95x (ISBN 0-8156-2144-2). Syracuse U Pr.

Matthews, J. H., tr. The Custom-House of Desire: A Half-Century of Surrealist Stories. LC 74-16712. 375p. 1976. 26.50x (ISBN 0-520-02865-1); pap. 6.95 (ISBN 0-520-03274-8). U of Cal Pr.

Matthews, J. I. Experiments in Solid State Electronics. 1972. text ed. 15.95 (ISBN 0-07-040961-7, G). McGraw.

Matthews, J. L. Solid State Electronics Concepts. 1971. text ed. 24.95 (ISBN 0-07-040960-9, G). McGraw.

Matthews, Jack. Collecting Rare Books for Pleasure & Profit. LC 81-81193. (Illus.). 307p. 1981. 18.95 (ISBN 0-8214-0610-8, 82-83962); pap. 10.95 (ISBN 0-8214-0611-6, 82-83970). Ohio U Pr.

--Collecting Rare Books for Pleasure & Profit. LC 76-21863. (Illus.). 1977. 12.95 o.p. (ISBN 0-399-11775-X). Putnam Pub Group.

Matthews, Jack, jt. auth. see Clevenger, Theodore, Jr.

Matthews, Jack, ed. Archetypal Themes in Modern Story. 256p. 1973. text ed. 8.95 o.p. (ISBN 0-312-04795-9). St Martin.

Matthews, Jacqueline D. Association System of the European Community. LC 76-12865. 1977. 26.95 o.p. (ISBN 0-275-23270-0). Praeger.

Matthews, James. Voices: A Life of Frank O'Connor. LC 81-69161. (Illus.). 320p. 1983. 25.00 (ISBN 0-689-11272-6). Atheneum.

Matthews, James M., ed. Kime's International Law Directory for 1981. 89th ed. 810p. 1981. 52.50x o.p. (ISBN 0-900503-13-0). Intl Pubns Serv.

Matthews, James N., ed. Kime's International Law Directory for 1982. 90th ed. LC 9-19874. 810p. 1982. 60.00x (ISBN 0-900503-15-7). Intl Pubns Serv.

Matthews, Janice R., jt. auth. see Matthews, Robert W.

Matthews, Jean V. Rufus Choate: The Law & Civic Virtue. 328p. 1980. 29.95 (ISBN 0-87722-178-2). Temple U Pr.

Matthews, John. American Bi-Centennial Book of Do It Yourself Natural Wood Sculpture. (Illus.). 82p. 1975. 10.95x o.p. (ISBN 0-8464-0128-2). Beekman Pubs.

--The Restoration of Organs. (Music Ser.). (Illus.). 170p. 1981. Repr. of 1920 ed. lib. bdg. 21.50 (ISBN 0-306-76098-3). Da Capo.

Matthews, John, jt. auth. see Cornell, Tim.

Matthews, John M. Legislative & Judicial History of the Fifteenth Amendment. LC 77-129081. (American Constitutional & Legal History Ser). 1971. Repr. of 1909 ed. lib. bdg. 22.50 (ISBN 0-306-70063-8). Da Capo.

Matthews, Joseph. Sourcebook for Older Americans. (Orig.). 1983. pap. 10.95 (ISBN 0-917316-55-X). Nolo Pr.

Matthews, Joseph & Berman, Dorothy. Your Rights & Benefits over Fifty-Five. 224p. 1983. pap. 11.95 (ISBN 0-201-05539-2). A-W.

Matthews, Joseph R. Choosing an Automated Library System: A Planning Guide. LC 80-17882. 128p. 1980. 12.50 (ISBN 0-8389-0310-X). ALA.

--Public Access to Online Catalogs: A Planning Guide for Managers. 345p. 1982. pap. text ed. 28.50 (ISBN 0-910965-00-5). Online.

Matthews, Kathy. On Your Own: Ninety-Nine Alternatives to a 9-5 Job. 1977. 10.00 o.p. (ISBN 0-394-40980-9); pap. 3.45 (ISBN 0-394-72090-3). Random.

Matthews, L. Harrison. Man & Wildlife. LC 75-4336. 250p. 1975. 18.95 o.p. (ISBN 0-312-51240-6). St Martin.

Matthews, Laura. A Very Proper Widow. 1982. pap. 2.25 (ISBN 0-451-11919-3, AE1919, Sig). NAL.

Matthews, Lawrence M. Estimating Manufacturing Costs. (Illus.). 288p. 1982. 24.95 (ISBN 0-07-040951-X). McGraw.

--Practical Operating Budgeting. (Illus.). 1977. 31.00 (ISBN 0-07-040950-1, P&RB). McGraw.

Matthews, Leslie G. The Antiques of Perfume. (Illus.). 88p. 1976. 15.00 o.p. (ISBN 0-7135-1756-5). Transatlantic.

Matthews, Martine, tr. see Segalen, Martine.

Matthews, Mary. Preparing Your Child for School: A Primer for Parents of Kindergarten & First Grade Students. (Illus.). 16p. (Orig.). 1981. pap. 3.95x. Parents Pointers.

Matthews, Mervyn. Privilege in the Soviet Union. (Illus.). 1978. text ed. 19.95x (ISBN 0-04-323020-2); pap. text ed. 7.95x (ISBN 0-04-323021-0). Allen Unwin.

Matthews, P. H. Inflectional Morphology: A Theoretical Study Based on Aspects of Latin Verb Conjugation. LC 76-171678. (Studies in Linguistics Ser., No. 6). (Illus.). 500p. 1972. 49.50 (ISBN 0-521-08372-9); pap. 19.95x (ISBN 0-521-29065-1). Cambridge U Pr.

--Morphology: An Introduction to the Theory of Word-Structure. LC 73-91817. (Cambridge Textbooks in Linguistics Ser.). 256p. 1974. 44.50 (ISBN 0-521-20448-8); pap. 12.95 (ISBN 0-521-09856-4). Cambridge U Pr.

--Syntax. LC 80-41664. (Cambridge Textbooks in Linguistics Ser.). (Illus.). 325p. 1981. 39.50 (ISBN 0-521-22894-8); pap. 12.95 (ISBN 0-521-29709-5). Cambridge U Pr.

Matthews, Patricia. Flames of Glory. 1983. pap. 6.95 (ISBN 0-686-82123-8). Bantam.

--Love Forever More. 1977. pap. 3.25 (ISBN 0-523-41857-4). Pinnacle Bks.

--Love's Avenging Heart. 1977. pap. text ed. 2.95 (ISBN 0-523-41513-3). Pinnacle Bks.

--Love's Daring Dream. (Orig.). 1978. pap. 3.50 (ISBN 0-523-42012-9). Pinnacle Bks.

--Love's Magic Moment. 1979. pap. 3.25 (ISBN 0-523-41873-6). Pinnacle Bks.

--Love's Pagan Heart. 1978. pap. 2.50 (ISBN 0-523-41834-5). Pinnacle Bks.

--Love's Raging Tide. (Orig.). 1980. pap. 3.25 (ISBN 0-523-41969-4). Pinnacle Bks.

Matthews, Patricia & Matthews, Clayton. Empire. 368p. 1982. pap. 3.50 (ISBN 0-553-22577-4). Bantam.

Matthews, Peter. Track & Field Athletics: Facts & Feats. (Guinness Superlatives Ser.). (Illus.). 288p. 1982. 19.95 (ISBN 0-85112-238-8, Pub. by Guinness Superlatives England). Sterling.

Matthews, Phoebe. Honeymoon House. 1979. pap. 1.75 o.p. (ISBN 0-380-45153-0, 45153). Avon.

--The Unsuitable Lovers. (Candlelight Regency Special Ser.: No. 682). (Orig.). 1981. pap. 1.75 o.s.i. (ISBN 0-440-14953-3). Dell.

Matthews, Ralph. The Creation of Regional Dependency. 336p. 1983. 40.00x (ISBN 0-8020-5617-2); pap. 12.95 (ISBN 0-8020-6510-4). U of Toronto Pr.

Matthews, Robert W. & Matthews, Janice R. Insect Behavior. LC 78-7869. 1978. 35.95 (ISBN 0-471-57685-9, Pub. by Wiley-Interscience). Wiley.

Matthews, Robley K. Dynamic Stratigraphy: An Introduction to Sedimentation & Stratigraphy. 1974. 27.95 (ISBN 0-13-222273-6). P-H.

Matthews, Rodney, illus. Back to Earth. (Blue Planet Ser.). (Illus.). 1975. 1.65 (ISBN 0-85953-058-2, Pub. by Child's Play England). Playspaces.

Matthews, Ronald, tr. see Servan-Schreiber, Jean-Jacques.

Matthews, Sallie R; see Holden, Frances M.

Matthews, Sanford J. & Brinley, Maryann B. Through the Motherhood Maze. LC 81-43011. 216p. 1982. 13.95 (ISBN 0-385-17210-9). Doubleday.

Matthews, Velda. Basic Bible Dictionary: Simplified Descriptions of Bible People. (Illus.). 64p. (gr. 4 up). 1978. pap. 1.95 (ISBN 0-87239-250-3, 2781). Standard Pub.

--Basic Bible Dictionary: Simplified Descriptions of Bible Places. (Illus.). 64p. (gr. 4 up). 1978. pap. 1.95 (ISBN 0-87239-254-6, 2782). Standard Pub.

Matthews, Velda & Beard, Ray. Basic Bible Dictionary: Simplified Definitions of Bible Words. (Illus.). 64p. (gr. 4 up). 1977. pap. 1.95 (ISBN 0-87239-249-X, 2780). Standard Pub.

Matthews, W. H. Mazes & Labyrinths. LC 70-75946. 1969. Repr. of 1922 ed. 34.00x (ISBN 0-8103-3839-4). Gale.

Matthews, W. K. Russian Historical Grammar. (London East European: No. 1). 1960. text ed. 36.75x (ISBN 0-485-17509-6, Athlone Pr). Humanities.

Matthews, William. Cockney Past & Present. 1972. 22.50 (ISBN 0-7100-7303-8). Routledge & Kegan.

--Cockney Past & Present: A Short History of the Dialect of London. LC 68-30638. 1970. Repr. of 1938 ed. 30.00x (ISBN 0-8103-3609-X). Gale.

Matthews, William, ed. see Pepys, Samuel.

Matthews, William H. Fossils: An Introduction to Prehistoric Life. (Orig.). 1962. pap. 3.95 o.p. (ISBN 0-06-463280-6, EH 280, EH). B&N NY.

Matthews, William H., ed. Man's Impact on the Global Environment: Assessment & Recommendations for Action. (Study of Critical Environmental Problems). 1970. 20.00x (ISBN 0-262-19086-9); pap. 4.95 (ISBN 0-262-69027-6). MIT Pr.

Matthews, William H., et al. Resource Materials for Environmental Management & Education. LC 75-28368. 272p. 1976. text ed. 15.00x (ISBN 0-262-13118-8). MIT Pr.

Matthews, William H., et al, eds. Man's Impact on the Climate. (Study of Critical Environmental Problems). 1971. 37.00x o.p. (ISBN 0-262-13075-0). MIT Pr.

Matthews, William Kleesmann, ed. Anthology of Modern Estonian Poetry. LC 77-1634. 1977. Repr. of 1953 ed. lib. bdg. 16.25x (ISBN 0-8371-9557-8, MAAN). Greenwood.

Matthews, Z. K. Freedom for My People: The Autobiography of Z. K. Matthews: Southern Africa 1901-1968. Wilson, Monica, ed. 264p. 1981. text ed. 26.50x (ISBN 0-8476-4739-0). Rowman.

Matthewson. Beginner's Guide to Video. (Illus.). 1982. pap. 9.95 (ISBN 0-408-00577-7). Focal Pr.

Matthias, E. & Shirley, D. A., eds. Hyperfine Structure & Nuclear Radiations. 1968. 59.75 (ISBN 0-444-10246-9, North-Holland). Elsevier.

Matthias, John. Bucyrus. LC 82-72601. (New Poetry Ser.: No. 42). 102p. 1971. 8.95 (ISBN 0-8040-0522-2); pap. 4.95 (ISBN 0-8040-0523-0). Swallow.

--Crossing. LC 82-76008. 125p. 1980. 12.95 (ISBN 0-8040-0829-9); pap. 7.95 (ISBN 0-8040-0830-2). Swallow.

--Turns. LC 82-73807. 111p. 1975. 8.95 (ISBN 0-8040-0689-X). Swallow.

Matthias, John, ed. Twenty-Three Modern British Poets. LC 71-150757. 338p. 1971. 15.00x o.s.i. (ISBN 0-8040-0507-9); pap. 8.95x (ISBN 0-8214-0508-X). Swallow.

Matthias, John & Printz-Pahlson, Goran, trs. Contemporary Swedish Poetry. LC 82-75976. 136p. 1980. 18.95x (ISBN 0-8040-0811-6); pap. 9.95 (ISBN 0-8040-0812-4). Swallow.

Matthias, Karl E. Citizen "M" Speaks, Vol. 1. LC 82-74183. (Illus.). 120p. 1982. pap. 6.95 (ISBN 0-9609110-0-6). Creative Lit.

Matthias, Margaret & Thiessen, Diane. Children's Mathematics Books: A Critical Bibliography. LC 79-11896. 1979. pap. 6.00 (ISBN 0-8389-0285-5). ALA.

Matthies, H., jt. ed. see Ajmone-Marsan, Cosimo.

Matthies, Leslie H. Documents to Manage By. LC 82-81937. (Illus.). 1982. 14.00x (ISBN 0-911054-06-5). Office Pubns.

--The Management System: Systems Are for People. LC 76-4572. (Wiley Series on Systems & Controls for Financial Management). 240p. 1976. 38.50 (ISBN 0-471-57697-2, Pub. by Wiley-Interscience). Wiley.

Matthiesen, Thomas, photos by. ABC, an Alphabet Book. (Illus.). 64p. (gr. 3 up). 1981. 3.95 (ISBN 0-448-41054-0, G&D). Putnam Pub Group.

--A Child's Book of Everyday Things. (Illus.). 72p. (ps-1). 1981. 3.95 (ISBN 0-448-41057-5, G&D). Putnam Pub Group.

Matthiessen, F. O. American Renaissance: Art & Expression in the Age of Emerson & Whitman. 1968. pap. 12.95 (ISBN 0-19-500759-X, 230, GB). Oxford U Pr.

--From the Heart of Europe. 1948. 19.50x (ISBN 0-686-51389-4). Elliots Bks.

--Henry James: The Major Phase. 1944. 14.95 (ISBN 0-19-501225-9). Oxford U Pr.

--Theodore Dreiser. LC 72-7876. (American Men of Letters Ser.). (Illus.). 267p. 1973. Repr. of 1951 ed. lib. bdg. 20.50x (ISBN 0-8371-6550-4, MATD). Greenwood.

Matthiessen, Lars. The Impact of Rising Oil Prices on the World Economy. 211p. 1982. text ed. 37.00x (ISBN 0-333-33185-0, Pub. by Macmillan England). Humanities.

Matthiessen, Peter. In the Spirit of Crazy Horse. (Illus.). 704p. 1983. 20.95 (ISBN 0-670-39702-4). Viking Pr.

--Wildlife in America. 1978. pap. 4.95 (ISBN 0-14-004793-X). Penguin.

Matthys, Robert J. Crystal Oscillator Circuits. 240p. 1983. write for info. (ISBN 0-471-87401-9, Pub. by Wiley-Interscience). Wiley.

Matthyse, S., ed. Attention & Information Processing in Schizophrenia: Proceedings of the Scottish Rite Schizophrenia Research Program Conference, Rochester, 1976. 1979. text ed. 108.00 (ISBN 0-08-023126-8). Pergamon.

Matthysse, Steven, jt. auth. see Snyder, Solomon H.

Matti, Jonathan C., jt. auth. see Murphy, Michael.

Mattick, Paul. Anti-Bolshevik Communism. LC 78-68639. 1979. 25.00 (ISBN 0-87332-135-9). M E Sharpe.

Mattick, Paul, Sr. Economic Crisis & Crisis Theory. LC 80-5459. Orig. Title: Krisen und Krisentheorien. 228p. 1980. 22.50 (ISBN 0-87332-179-0). M E Sharpe.

Mattiessen, Peter. The Tree Where Man Was Born. 353p. 1983. pap. 7.95 (ISBN 0-525-48032-3, 0772-230, Obelisk). Dutton.

Mattil, Edward L. Meaning in Crafts. 3rd ed. LC 73-123087. 1971. ref. ed. 19.95 (ISBN 0-13-567156-6). P-H.

Mattil, Edward L. & Marzan, Betty. Meaning in Children's Art: Projects for Teachers. 324p. 1981. 23.95 (ISBN 0-13-567115-9); pap. 17.95 (ISBN 0-13-567107-8). P-H.

Mattingly, H. Roman Coins. 1977. 25.00 (ISBN 0-685-51532-X, Pub by Spink & Son England). S J Durst.

Mattingly, Harold. Roman Imperial Civilization. (Illus.). 1957. 18.95 o.p. (ISBN 0-312-69020-7). St Martin.

Mattingly, Ignatius G., jt. ed. see Kavanagh, James F.

Mattingly, P. Biology of Mosquito Borne Diseases. 1970. 15.00 (ISBN 0-444-19723-0). Elsevier.

Mattinson, Janet. Marriage & Mental Handicap: A Study of Subnormality in Marriage. LC 70-137335. (Contemporary Community Health Ser). 1971. 9.95 o.p. (ISBN 0-686-31671-1). U of Pittsburgh Pr.

Mattioli, Massimo, illus. Animalisms One. (Cartoon Bks.). (Illus.). 96p. 1976. pap. 2.50 (ISBN 0-85953-059-0, Pub. by Child's Play England). Playspaces.

Mattis, Ann, ed. The Emerging Global Village: Society for International Development World Conference, 25th. 250p. Date not set. text ed. 25.00 (ISBN 0-8223-0561-5); pap. text ed. 11.00 (ISBN 0-8223-0562-3). Duke.

Mattison, Donald R., ed. Reproductive Toxicology. LC 83-927. (Progress in Clinical & Biological Research Ser.: Vol. 117). 408p. 1983. 58.00 (ISBN 0-8451-0117-X). A R Liss.

Mattison, Judith. Mom Has a Second Job: Prayer Thoughts for Working Mothers. LC 80-65548. 96p. (Orig.). 1980. pap. 4.50 (ISBN 0-8066-1793-4, 10-4534). Augsburg.

Mattmuller, Felix. We Want a Little Sister. LC 65-25946. (Foreign Lands Bks.). (Illus.). (gr. k-5). 1965. PLB 3.95g (ISBN 0-8225-0355-7). Lerner Pubns.

Mattoon, Mary Ann. Applied Dream Analysis: A Jungian Approach. 248p. 1978. 13.95x o.p. (ISBN 0-470-26418-7). Halsted Pr.

Mattox, Douglas E., jt. auth. see Holt, G. Richard.

Mattox, Phil, jt. auth. see Giammatteo, M. C.

Mattox, Robert F. Financial Management for Architects. LC 80-69832. (Financial Management System). (Illus.). 212p. 1980. 35.00x (ISBN 0-913962-29-5, 2M724). Am Inst Arch.

--Standardized Accounting for Architects. 3rd ed. (Illus.). 188p. 1982. write for info (ISBN 0-913962-48-1). Am Inst Arch.

Mattran, Kenneth. Speak English, Wkbk. 5. (Speak English Ser.). (Illus.). 64p. (Orig.). 1983. pap. 4.95 (ISBN 0-88499-660-3). Inst Mod Lang.
--Speak English, Text 5. (Speak English Ser.). (Illus.). 80p. (Orig.). 1983. pap. 4.95 (ISBN 0-88499-659-X). Inst Mod Lang.
Mattson, Guy C., jt. auth. see Clausen, Chris A., III.
Mattson, J. S., et al, eds. Computer-Assisted Instruction in Chemistry: Pt. A, General Approach. (Computers in Chemistry & Instrumentation Ser: Vol. 4). 288p. 1974. 50.50 (ISBN 0-8247-6103-0). Dekker.
--Computer Assisted Instruction in Chemistry: Pt. B, Applications. (Computers in Chemistry & Instrumentation Ser.: Vol. 4). 280p. 1974. 50.50 (ISBN 0-8247-6104-9). Dekker.
Mattson, K., jt. auth. see Fuchs, E.
Mattson, Lloyd, jt. ed. see Graendorf, Werner.
Mattson, Mark T., jt. auth. see Cuff, David J.
Mattson, Marylu & Leshing, Sophia. Help Yourself: A Guide To Writing & Rewriting. 320p. 1983. pap. text ed. 9.95 (ISBN 0-675-20027-X). Additional supplements may be obtained from publisher. Merrill.
Mattson, Peter H. see Alexandrov, Eugene.
Mattson, Phyllis H. Holistic Health in Perspective. LC 81-83086. 200p. 1981. pap. text ed. 6.95 (ISBN 0-87484-554-8). Mayfield Pub.
Mattson, Ralph & Miller, Arthur. Finding the Job You Can Love. 1982. pap. 5.95 (ISBN 0-8407-5817-0). Nelson.
--The Truth About You. 160p. 1977. 10.95 (ISBN 0-8007-0887-3). Revell.
Mattsson, Ingrid, jt. auth. see Finn, Jeremy D.
Mattuck, Richard D. A Guide to Feynman Diagrams in the Many-Body Problem. 2nd ed. LC 75-20063. (Illus.). 1976. text ed. 39.50 (ISBN 0-07-040954-4, C). McGraw.
Mattysse, S., ed. Psychiatry & the Biology of the Human Brain: A Symposium Dedicated to Seymour S. Kety. 1981. 51.00 (ISBN 0-444-00649-4). Elsevier.
Matulich, Serge & Heitger, Lester E. Financial Accounting: An Introduction. 1980. text ed. 24.95 (ISBN 0-07-040921-8); study guide 9.95 (ISBN 0-07-040922-6); exam questions 16.50 (ISBN 0-07-040928-5); overhead transparencies 325.00 (ISBN 0-07-074794-6); solns. manual 25.00 (ISBN 0-07-040925-0); working papers 10.95 (ISBN 0-07-040924-2). McGraw.
Matulich, Serge, jt. auth. see Heitger, Lester E.
Matuschka, A. G. von see Von Matuschka, A. G.
Matusita, K., ed. Recent Developments in Statistical Inference & Data Analysis. 1980. 64.00 (ISBN 0-444-86104-1). Elsevier.
Matusow, Alice, jt. auth. see Kohn, Barry.
Matusow, Allen J. Joseph R. McCarthy. 1970. 8.95 (ISBN 0-13-566729-1, Spec); pap. 8.95 o.p. (ISBN 0-13-566711-9, S720, Spec). P-H.
Matusow, Allen J., jt. ed. see Bernstein, Barton J.
Matuszek, D. L. Quick Pascal. 179p. 1982. pap. text ed. 11.95 (ISBN 0-471-86644-X). Wiley.
Matuszeski, Bill, jt. auth. see Procter, Mary.
Matute, Ana Maria. Historias de la Artamila. (Easy Reader, C. Ser.). 112p. (Span.). 1981. pap. text ed. 3.95 (ISBN 0-88436-889-0). EMC.
Matyas, Stephen, jt. auth. see Meyer, Carl.
Matz, Mary J. Opera Stars in the Sun. LC 73-2642. (Illus.). 349p. 1973. Repr. of 1955 ed. lib. bdg. 19.00x (ISBN 0-8371-6813-9, MAOS). Greenwood.
Matza, D. Deliquency & Drift. LC 64-18135. 1964. pap. text ed. 12.95 (ISBN 0-471-57708-1). Wiley.
Matza, David. Becoming Deviant. 1969. pap. text ed. 13.95 (ISBN 0-13-073171-4). P-H.
Matzer, John F., Jr., ed. Capital Financing Strategies. (Practical Management Ser.). (Illus.). 224p. (Orig.). 1983. pap. 19.50 (ISBN 0-87326-037-6). Intl City Mgt.
Matzke, Howard A. & Foltz, Floyd M. Synopsis of Neuroanatomy. 4th ed. (Illus.). 185p. 1983. pap. 7.95 (ISBN 0-19-503244-6). Oxford U Pr.
Matzkin, Myron A. Super Eight Millimeter. (Illus.). 96p. 1975. pap. 4.95 o.p. (ISBN 0-8174-0186-5, Amphoto). Watson-Guptill.
--The Super 8 Film-Makers Handbook. LC 75-45778. (Illus.). 1976. 21.95 (ISBN 0-240-50755-X). Focal Pr.
Mau. Create Word Puzzles with Your Microcomputer. 14.95 (ISBN 0-686-82004-5, 6251). Hayden.
Mau, Ernest E. Create Word Games With Your Microcomputer. (Illus.). 304p. 1982. pap. 14.95 (ISBN 0-8104-6251-6). Hayden.
Mau, James, jt. ed. see Bell, Wendell.
Maubouche, Robert & Hadjitarkhani, Naimeh. Seychelles: Economic Memorandum. ii, 71p. 1980. pap. 10.00 (ISBN 0-686-36119-9, RC-8009). World Bank.
Mauceri, Joe. Steps: A Collection of Poems. 1978. 4.50 o.p. (ISBN 0-533-02926-0). Vantage.
Mauch & Birch. Guide to the Successful Thesis & Dissertation, Vol. 19. (Library & Informations Ser.). 352p. 1983. price not set (ISBN 0-8247-1800-3). Dekker.
Mauck, Diane & Jenkins, Janet. Teaching Primaries. write for info. (ISBN 0-89137-610-0). Quality Pubns.
Mauck, JoAnn, jt. auth. see Pelstring, Linda.
Mauck, Scott. Oldsmobile Cutlass. 331p. 1982. pap. 11.95 (ISBN 0-85696-658-4). Haynes Pubns.
Maud, Marjory V. The Self Sufficience System: Steps to Personal, Financial, & Household Organization, 12 vols. Incl. Vol. 1. Getting It All Together (Organization) 95p. 1981. 7.50 o.p. (ISBN 0-938562-02-9); Vol. 2. Beating the Budget Blues. 99p. 1982. 7.50 o.p. (ISBN 0-938562-03-7); Vol. 3. Be Sure About Insurance. 35p. 1982. 3.50 o.p. (ISBN 0-938562-04-5); Vol. 14. Automobile Awareness. 35p. 1982. 3.50 o.p. (ISBN 0-938562-05-3); Vol. 5. Making Money Multiply. 80p. 1982. 6.40 o.p. (ISBN 0-938562-06-1); Vol. 6. In Case of...Planning for Emergency. 75p. 1982. 5.00 o.p. (ISBN 0-938562-07-X); Vol. 7. The Smart Shopping System. 100p. 1982. 7.50 o.p. (ISBN 0-686-86746-7); Vol. 8. The Busy Woman's Wardrobe Wisdom. 75p. 1982. 5.00 o.p. (ISBN 0-938562-09-6); Vol. 9. Terror-Free Taxes. 75p. 1982. 5.50 o.p. (ISBN 0-938562-10-X); Vol. 10. The Working Wo(Man) 's Practical Plan for Carefree Home Maintenance. 25p. 1982. 3.50 o.p. (ISBN 0-938562-11-8); Vol. 11. Letters of Complaint & Other Correspondences. **25p. 1982. 3.00 o.p. (ISBN 0-938562-12-6); Vol. 12. Kids & Cash. 60p. 1982. 3.50 o.p. (ISBN 0-938562-13-4). Set. 30.00 o.p. (ISBN 0-938562-01-0). Single Impressions.**
--The Self Sufficiency System-Steps to Personal, Financial & Household Organization, 12 vols. (The Self Sufficiency System Ser.). 965p. 1982. Set. 45.00 o.p. (ISBN 0-938562-01-0). Single Impressions.
--Step Eight: The Busy Woman's Wardrobe Wisdom. (The Self Sufficency System Ser.). 75p. 1982. cancelled (ISBN 0-938562-09-6). Single Impressions.
--Step Eleven: Letters of Complaint & Other Correspondence. (The Self Sufficiency System Ser.). 25p. 1982. cancelled (ISBN 0-938562-12-6). Single Impressions.
--Step Five: Making Money Multiply (Investments) (The Self Sufficiency System Ser.). 80p. 1982. cancelled (ISBN 0-938562-06-1). Single Impressions.
--Step Four: Automobile Awareness. (The Self Sufficiency System Ser.). 35p. 1982. 3.50 o.p. (ISBN 0-938562-05-3). Single Impressions.
--Step One: Getting It All Together (Organization) (The Self Sufficiency System Ser.). 161p. 1982. 9.50 o.p. (ISBN 0-938562-02-9). Single Impressions.
--Step Seven: The Smart Shopping System. (The Self Sufficiency System Ser.). 100p. 1982. cancelled (ISBN 0-938562-08-8). Single Impressions.
--Step Six: In Case of... Planning for Emergency. (The Self Sufficiency System Ser.). 75p. 1982. cancelled (ISBN 0-938562-07-X). Single Impressions.
--Step Three: Be Sure About Insurance. (The Self Sufficiency System Ser.). 35p. 1982. 3.50 o.p. (ISBN 0-938562-04-5). Single Impressions.
--Step Twelve: Kids & Cash. (The Self Sufficiency System Ser.). 60p. (gr. 1-6). 1982. cancelled (ISBN 0-938562-13-4). Single Impressions.
--Step Two: Beating the Budget Blues. (The Self Sufficiency System Ser.). 165p. 1982. 9.50 o.p. (ISBN 0-938562-03-7). Single Impressions.
Maudadi, A. A. Tafhimul - Quaran: Urdu Translation & Commentary. 75.00 (ISBN 0-686-18523-4). Kazi Pubns.
Maude. Enlarging. (Photographer's Library). (Illus.). 1983. pap. 12.95x (ISBN 0-240-51118-2). Focal Pr.
Maude, A. Leo Tolstoy. LC 75-20491. (Studies in Tolstoy, No. 62). 1974. lib. bdg. 55.95x (ISBN 0-8383-2001-5). Haskell.
--Leo Tolstoy & His Works. LC 74-6377. (Studies in Tolstoi, No. 62). 1974. lib. bdg. 26.95x (ISBN 0-8383-2009-0). Haskell.
--Tolstoy on Art. LC 72-2134. (Studies in European Literature, No. 56). 1972. Repr. of 1924 ed. lib. bdg. 50.95x (ISBN 0-8383-1459-7). Haskell.
Maude, Aylmer, tr. see Tolstoy, Leo.
Maude, H. C. & Maude, H. E. String Figures from the Gilbert Islands. 1958. pap. 6.00x o.p. (ISBN 0-8248-0588-7). UH Pr.
Maude, H. E. Of Islands & Men: Studies in Pacific History. 1968. 23.50x o.p. (ISBN 0-19-550177-2). Oxford U Pr.
Maude, H. E., jt. auth. see Maude, H. C.
Maudslay, A. P. Archaeology: Biologia Centrali-America or, Contibutions to the Knowledge of the Fauna & Flora of Mexico & Central America. Godman, F. Ducane & Salvin, Osbert, eds. LC 74-30688. (Illus.). 907p. 1983. 250.00x (ISBN 0-8061-9919-9, Pub. by Milpatron Publishing Corp). U of Okla Pr.
Maudsley, Henry. The Pathology of Mind. Lewis, Aubrey, ed. (Classics of Psychology & Psychiatry Ser.). 608p. 1983. Repr. of 1867 ed. write for info. (ISBN 0-904014-42-8). F Pinter Pubs.
Maududi. What Islam Stands For. Date not set. price not set (ISBN 0-89259-024-6). Am Trust Pubns.
Maududi, A. A. The Meaning of the Quran, 8 vols. 7.95 ea. Kazi Pubns.
--The Prophet of Islam. pap. 1.00 o.p. (ISBN 0-686-18420-3). Kazi Pubns.
--Purdah & the Status of Women in Islam. pap. 6.50 (ISBN 0-686-18464-5). Kazi Pubns.
--The Road to Salvation. pap. 1.00 (ISBN 0-686-18583-8). Kazi Pubns.
--Towards Understanding Islam. pap. 4.95 (ISBN 0-686-18479-3). Kazi Pubns.
Maue, Kenneth. Water in the Lake: Real Events for the Imagination. LC 78-4737. 1979. pap. 4.95i o.p. (ISBN 0-06-090670-7, CN-670, CN). Har-Row.
Mauer, George J., ed. Crises in Campus Management: Case Studies in the Administration of Colleges & Universities. LC 75-23981. (Special Studies). 1976. text ed. 19.95 o.p. (ISBN 0-275-55710-3). Praeger.
Mauermayer, W. Transurethral Surgery. (Illus.). 477p. 1983. 148.00 (ISBN 0-387-11869-1). Springer-Verlag.
Mauet, Thomas & Wolfson, Warren. Problems in Trial Advocacy. LC 81-84116. 744p. 1982. text ed. 15.00 (ISBN 0-316-55083-3). Little.
Mauger, Gaston. Cours De Langue et De Civilization Francaises, 4 Vols. (Fr). Vol. 1. 8.25 (ISBN 0-685-20231-3); Vol. 2. 9.25 (ISBN 0-685-20232-1); Vol. 3. 10.50 (ISBN 0-685-20233-X); Vol. 4. 13.50 (ISBN 0-685-20234-8). Schoenhof.
Mauger, Ivan & Oakes, Peter, eds. Ivan Mauger's Speedway Spectacular. (Illus.). 136p. 1976. 11.50 o.p. (ISBN 0-7207-0780-3). Transatlantic.
Mauger, Peter. British People Nineteen Two to Nineteen Seventy-Five. 2nd ed. 1976. pap. text ed. 13.95x o.p. (ISBN 0-435-31570-6). Heinemann Ed.
Maugham, Robin. The Boy from Beirut & Other Stories. Burton, Peter, ed. (Illus.). 160p. (Orig.). 1982. 20.00 (ISBN 0-917342-89-5); pap. 7.95 (ISBN 0-917342-90-9); ltd., specially bd. ed. 35.00 (ISBN 0-917342-99-2). Gay Sunshine.
--Somerset & All the Maughams. LC 75-22759. (Illus.). 1977. Repr. of 1966 ed. lib. bdg. 20.75x (ISBN 0-8371-8236-0, MASOM). Greenwood.
Maugham, W. Somerset. The Merry-Go-Round. 1978. pap. 3.95 (ISBN 0-14-003373-4). Penguin.
--The Narrow Corner. 1977. pap. 3.95 (ISBN 0-14-001859-X). Penguin.
--Of Human Bondage. 1959. 3.95 o.p. (ISBN 0-394-60176-9, M176). Modern Lib.
--Of Human Bondage. 685p. Date not set. pap. 3.95 (ISBN 0-394-60176-9, Vin). Random.
--The Summing Up. 1978. pap. 3.95 (ISBN 0-14-001852-2). Penguin.
--Up at the Villa. 1978. pap. 3.95 (ISBN 0-14-002670-3). Penguin.
Maughan, Jackie. Hiker's Guide to Idaho. (Illus.). 256p. 1983. pap. 7.95 (ISBN 0-934318-18-2). Falcon Pr MT.
Maugham, Joyce B. Talks for Tots. (gr. 1-7). 3.95 o.p. (ISBN 0-87747-289-0). Deseret Bk.
Mauk, Paul, illus. El Gran Passo en Tren. Kreps, Georgian, tr. from Span. (Shape Board Play Book). Orig. Title: The Great Train Ride. (Illus.). 14p. (Eng.). (ps-3). 1981. bds. 3.50 plastic comb bdg. (ISBN 0-89828-201-2, 15005). Tuffy Bks.
--Incendios De Bomba. Kreps, Georgian, tr. from Eng. (Shape Board Play Book). Orig. Title: Fire Engines. (Illus., Span.). (ps-3). 1981. bds. 3.50 plastic comb bdg (ISBN 0-89828-202-0, 15006). Tuffy Bks.
Maul, Gail & Maul, Terry. Beyond Limit: Ways to Growth & Freedom. 1982. pap. text ed. 9.95x (ISBN 0-673-15422-X). Scott F.
Maul, Gerd G. The Nuclear Envelope & the Nuclear Matrix, Vol.2. LC 82-15259. (The Wistar Symposium Ser.). 334p. 1982. 34.00 (ISBN 0-8451-2001-8). A R Liss.
Maul, Terry, jt. auth. see Conrad, Eva.
Maul, Terry, jt. auth. see Maul, Gail.
Maulana-Muhammad-Ali. Religion of Islam. 1978. 42.50x (ISBN 0-8002-1916-3). Intl Pubns Serv.
Mauldin, Bill. Bill Mauldin's Army. 384p. 1983. pap. 12.95 (ISBN 0-89141-159-3). Presidio Pr.
Mauldon, E. & Redfern, H. B. Games Teaching. 144p. 1981. 30.00x (ISBN 0-7121-0739-8, Pub. by Macdonald & Evans). State Mutual Bk.
Mauler, Cliff. Read Me: A Course of Study to Improve Your Reading Speed, Comprehension, Memory, & Concentration. (Illus.). 191p. (gr. 9-12). 1979. spiral bdg. 14.95 (ISBN 0-9602842-0-6). Read Me Pub.
Maull, H. Europe & World Energy. LC 80-40488. (Illus.). 1980. text ed. 39.95 (ISBN 0-408-10629-8). Butterworth.
Maull, Hanns W. Natural Gas & Economic Security. (The Atlantic Papers: No. 43). 60p. (Orig.). 1981. pap. text ed. 6.50X (ISBN 0-86598-082-9). Allanheld.
Maull, Kimball I. & Griffen, Ward O., Jr. Trauma Surgery. (Medical Examination Review Book: Vol. 36). 1981. spiral bdg. 26.50 (ISBN 0-87488-179-X). Med Exam.
Maultsby, Maxie C. Help Yourself to Happiness. pap. 7.95 (ISBN 0-686-36747-2). Inst Rat liv.
Maultsby, Maxie C., Jr. A Million Dollars for Your Hangover. 10.95 (ISBN 0-686-36765-0). Inst Rat Liv.
Maumenee, Irene H., jt. ed. see Cotlier, Edward.
Maund, Constance. Hume's Theory of Knowledge: A Critical Examination. LC 74-184234. xxiii, 310p. 1972. Repr. of 1937 ed. 18.00x o.p. (ISBN 0-8462-1645-0). Russell.
Maunder, A. H. & Hirsch, G. P. Farm Amalgamation in Western Europe. 132p. 1979. text ed. 26.00x (ISBN 0-566-00253-1). Gower Pub Ltd.
Maunder, Allen, jt. ed. see Johnson, Glenn.
Maunder, C. R. Algebraic Topology. LC 79-41610. (Illus.). 1980. 59.50 (ISBN 0-521-23161-2); pap. 23.95 (ISBN 0-521-29840-7). Cambridge U Pr.
Maunder, L., frwd. by. Engineering Challenges in the 1980's, Vol. 1. (Proceedings of the Engineering Section of the British Association for the Advancement of Science Ser.). (Illus.). 192p. 1982. text ed. 69.95 (ISBN 0-89116-348-4, Pub. by Cambridge Info & Res Serv England). Hemisphere Pub.
Maunder, Peter, ed. Government Intervention in the Developed Economy. LC 78-72590. 226p. 1979. 28.95 (ISBN 0-03-049501-6). Praeger.
Maunder, Peter, ed. see Button, Kenneth & Gillingwater, David.
Maunder, Peter, ed. see Llewellyn, D., et al.
Maunder, Peter, ed. see Presley, J. R., et al.
Maunder, Robert. The Z-X Companion. LC 82-73856. 131p. 1981. pap. 9.95 (ISBN 0-916688-26-7). Creative Comp.
Maunder, W. F. & Alderson, eds. Health Surveys & Related Studies. LC 78-40963. (Reviews of United Kingdom Statistical Sources Ser.: Vol. IX). 1979. 59.00 (ISBN 0-08-022459-8). Pergamon.
Mauner, George. Manet, Peintre-Philosophe: A Study of the Painter's Themes. LC 74-31056. 230p. 1975. 24.50x o.s.i. (ISBN 0-271-01187-4). Pa St U Pr.
--The Nabis: Their History & Their Art, 1888-1896. LC 77-94708. (Outstanding Dissertations in the Fine Arts Ser.). 1979. lib. bdg. 45.00 o.s.i. (ISBN 0-8240-3240-3). Garland Pub.
Mauntz, Alfred Von see Von Mauntz, Alfred.
Maupas, P. & Guesry, P., eds. Hepatitis B Vaccine. (INSERM Symposium Ser.: No. 18). 1981. 67.00 (ISBN 0-444-80325-4). Elsevier.
Maupassant. Mon Oncle Jules. (Easy Reader, D). pap. 3.95 (ISBN 0-88436-044-X, 40251). EMC.
Maupassant, Guy De see De Maupassant, Guy.
Maupertuis, Pierre-Louis Moreau De. Discours Sur les Differentes Figures Des Astres Avec une Exposition Des Systemes De Mm.Descartes et Newton. Repr. of 1732 ed. 33.00 o.p. (ISBN 0-8287-0592-5). Clearwater Pub.
--La Figure De la Terre Determinee Par les Observations Faites Par Ordre Du Roy Au Cercle Polaire. Repr. of 1738 ed. 61.00 o.p. (ISBN 0-8287-0593-3). Clearwater Pub.
--Venus Physique. Repr. of 1745 ed. 63.00 o.p. (ISBN 0-8287-0594-1). Clearwater Pub.
Maupin, Armistead. Further Tales of the City. 256p. 1982. 16.30i (ISBN 0-06-014991-4, CN-916); pap. 8.61i (ISBN 0-06-090916-1). Har-Row.
--More Tales of the City. LC 79-1710. 240p. (Orig.). 1980. pap. 9.57i (ISBN 0-06-090726-6, CN 726, CN). Har-Row.
Maupin, B., ed. Blood Platelets, 1971. 1973. pap. 32.75 (ISBN 0-444-15052-8). Elsevier.
Maurer, A. E. see Dryden, John.
Maurer, Armand A. St. Thomas & Historicity. LC 79-84278. (Aquinas Lecture Ser.). 1979. 7.95 (ISBN 0-87462-144-5). Marquette.
Maurer, David J., ed. United States Politics & Elections: A Guide to Information Sources. LC 78-13669. (American Government & History Information Guide Ser.: Vol. 3). 1978. 42.00x (ISBN 0-8103-1367-7). Gale.
Maurer, David W. & Vogel, Victor H. Narcotics & Narcotic Addiction. 4th ed. (Illus.). 496p. 1973. photocopy ed. spiral 47.75x (ISBN 0-398-02906-7). C C Thomas.
Maurer, Doug. APPLE Assembly Language. write for info (ISBN 0-914894-85-4). Computer Sci.
Maurer, Edward L. Practical Applied Roentgenology. 212p. 1983. lib. bdg. 36.00 (ISBN 0-683-05650-6). Williams & Wilkins.
Maurer, H. A. Data Structures & Programming Techniques. Price, T. T., tr. LC 76-21733. (Illus.). 1977. 20.95 (ISBN 0-13-197038-0). P-H.
Maurer, Isobel M. Hospital Hygiene. 1978. pap. text ed. write for info (ISBN 0-7131-4319-3). E Arnold.
Maurer, Joan H., jt. auth. see Lenburg, Jeff.
Maurer, Robert & Krauskopf, K. B. Experiments & Exercises in Physical Science. 2nd ed. (Illus.). 1969. text ed. 6.95 o.p. (ISBN 0-07-040982-X, C); instructors' manual 1.50 o.p. (ISBN 0-07-040977-3). McGraw.
Maurer, Stephen G. & Bass, William G. Eternal Solitude & Sunshine: A Grand Canyon Childhood. 1983. write for info. (ISBN 0-87108-639-5). Pruett.
Maurer, Stephen G., ed. Grand Canyon by Stage. (Illus.). 24p. (Orig.). 1982. pap. 3.85 (ISBN 0-910467-00-5). Heritage Assocs.
Maurer, T. Toxicology of Skin Irritation & Skin Sensitization: Standard Methods. (Lectures in Toxicology: No. 19). (Illus.). 12p. 1982. 60.00 (ISBN 0-08-029790-0). Pergamon.
Maurer, Walter. Englische und Anglo-Deutsche Lehnubersetzungen Im Russichen. 192p. (Ger.). 1982. write for info. (ISBN 3-261-05033-0). P Lang Pubs.
Maurer, Warren. Gerhart Hauptmann. (World Authors Ser.). 1982. lib. bdg. 17.95 (ISBN 0-8057-6517-4, Twayne). G K Hall.
Maurer, William. Advanced Drilling Techniques. 698p. 1980. 63.95x (ISBN 0-87814-117-0). Pennwell Book Division.
Mauriac, Francois. Therese Desqueuyroux. Collignon, Jean, ed. (Fr). 1963. pap. text ed. 7.95x (ISBN 0-02-377480-0). Macmillan.

Mauriber, Saul, ed. Portraits: The Photography of Carl Van Vechten. LC 78-55643. (Illus.). 1978. 29.95 o.p. (ISBN 0-672-52427-9). Bobbs.

Maurice, Arthur B. & Cooper, Frederic T. History of the Nineteenth Century in Caricature. LC 79-136560. (Tower Bks). (Illus.). 1971. Repr. of 1904 ed. 47.00x (ISBN 0-8103-3909-9). Gale.

Maurice, Charles E. Revolutionary Movement of Eighteen Forty-Eight to Eighteen Forty-Nine in Italy, Austria-Hungary, & Germany: With Some Examination of the Previous Thirty-Three Years. LC 68-57624. (Illus.). 1969. Repr. of 1887 ed. lib. bdg. 16.25x (ISBN 0-8371-1004-1, MARM). Greenwood.

Maurice, Dominique. The Tale About the Owl. (Illus.). 8p. (Orig.). 1982. pap. 2.50 (ISBN 0-914676-59-8, Pub. by Envelope Bks). Green Tiger Pr.

Maurice, Frederick D. Theological Essays. 436p. (Orig.). pap. 9.95 (ISBN 0-87921-048-6). Attic Pr.

Maurice, Klaus & Mayr, Otto. The Clockwork Universe: German Clocks & Automata 1550-1650. LC 80-16780. (Illus.). 331p. 1980. 19.95 (ISBN 0-87474-628-0). Smithsonian.

Maurice, Nancy, ed. The Maurice Case: From the Papers of Major-General Sir Fredrick Maurice. 240p. (Orig.). 1972. 17.50 o.p. (ISBN 0-208-00871-3, Archon). Shoe String.

Maurier, Daphne Du see Du Maurier, Daphne.

Maurino, Ferdinand. Modern Language Dictionary: English-Spanish, Spanish-English. 448p. 1974. pap. 4.95 o.p. (ISBN 0-671-18725-2). Monarch Pr.

Mauro, Alexander, ed. Muscle Regeneration. (Illus.). 576p. 1979. text ed. 65.50 (ISBN 0-89004-284-5). Raven.

Mauro, R., jt. auth. see Buchbaum, W. H.

Mauro, R., jt. auth. see Buchsbaum, W. H.

Maurois, Andre. Captains & Kings. 155p. 1983. Repr. of 1925 ed. lib. bdg. 20.00 (ISBN 0-89760-570-5). Telegraph Bks.

--Chateaubriand, Poet, Statesman, Lover. Fraser, Vera, tr. Repr. of 1938 ed. lib. bdg. 16.25x (ISBN 0-8371-2705-X, MAC). Greenwood.

Maurois, Michelle. Contes De Michelle Maurois. Meiden, Walter, ed. (Fr). 1966. pap. text ed. 11.50 (ISBN 0-395-04878-8). HM.

Maurus, J. Creative Emotions. LC 77-88327. 1978. pap. 1.75 o.p. (ISBN 0-8189-1155-7, 155, Pub. by Alba Bks). Alba.

--Growing Old Gracefully. LC 76-21590. 1977. pap. 1.75 o.p. (ISBN 0-8189-1137-9, Pub. by Alba Bks.). Alba.

Maurus, Walt. All About Bettas. (Orig.). 1976. pap. 8.95 (ISBN 0-87666-783-3, PS-654). TFH Pubns.

Maury de, Eric, jt. ed. see Selwyn, Victor.

Maus, Heinz. Short History of Sociology. 1962. 6.00 o.p. (ISBN 0-8022-1095-3). Philos Lib.

--A Short History of Sociology. (International Library of Sociology). 226p. 1965. pap. 8.95 (ISBN 0-7100-7168-X). Routledge & Kegan.

Mauser, Ferdinand F. Selling: A Self-Management Approach. (Illus.). 1977. text ed. 16.50 o.p. (ISBN 0-15-579630-5, HC); instructor's manual with tests & transparency masters avail. o.p. (ISBN 0-685-80210-8). HarBraceJ.

Mauser, Ferdinand F. & Schwartz, David J. American Business: An Introduction. 5th ed. (Illus.). 598p. 1982. text ed. 21.95 (ISBN 0-15-502295-4, HC); instructor's guide avail. (ISBN 0-15-502283-0); student guide 6.95 (ISBN 0-15-502284-9); manual of student assignments 7.95 (ISBN 0-15-502285-7); key to manual avail. (ISBN 0-15-502286-5); test pkgs.forms A & B avail. (ISBN 0-15-502290-3); keys to tests A & B avail. (ISBN 0-15-502291-1); instructor's tests forms A & B avail. (ISBN 0-15-502294-6); transparency masters avail. (ISBN 0-15-502287-3). HarBraceJ.

Mauskopf, Seymour H., ed. Reception of Unconventional Science by the Scientific Community. 1979. lib. bdg. 17.00 (ISBN 0-89158-297-5). Westview.

Mauss, Evelyn A. & Ullmann, John E., eds. Conservation of Energy Resources. (Annals of the New York Academy of Sciences: Vol. 324). 83p. (Orig.). 1979. 17.00x o.p. (ISBN 0-89766-016-1); pap. 17.00 (ISBN 0-89766-015-3). NY Acad Sci.

Mauss, Marcel, jt. auth. see Hubert, Henri.

Mautz, R. K. & Winjum, James. Criteria for Management Control Systems. LC 81-67794. 1981. 5.50 (ISBN 0-910586-41-1). Finan Exec.

Maves, Paul B. A Place to Live in Later Years. LC 82-72650. 112p. 1982. pap. 4.95 (ISBN 0-8066-1957-0, 10-4987). Augsburg.

Mavor, J. & Jack, M. A. Introduction to MOS LSI Design. 350p. 1982. 35.00 (ISBN 0-201-11440-2, Adv Bk Prog). A-W.

Mavragis, Edward P., jt. auth. see Craz, Albert G.

Mavrogordato, Jack. A Hawk for the Bush: A Treatise on the Training of the Sparrow Hawk & Other Short-Wings Hawks. (Illus.). 224p. 1974. 12.50 o.p. (ISBN 0-517-51434-6, C N Potter Bks). Crown.

Mavrogordatos, George T. Stillborn Republic: Social Strategies in Greece, 1922-1936. LC 82-2781. 416p. 1983. text ed. 40.00x (ISBN 0-520-04358-8). U of Cal Pr.

Mavros, Donald O. Getting Started in Ceramics. (Getting Started in Ser). (Illus.). 1971. 2.95 o.p. (ISBN 0-685-03348-1, 80446). Glencoe.

Maw, G. A. Biochemistry of S-Methyl-L-Systeine & its Principal Derivatives. (Sulfur Reports Ser.). 31p. (Orig.). 1982. pap. text ed. 23.00 (ISBN 3-7186-0112-5). Harwood Academic.

Mawby, Rob. Policing the City. 1979. text ed. 33.25x (ISBN 0-566-00277-9). Gower Pub Ltd.

Maw-Cheng Yang, jt. auth. see Thigpen, M. Elton.

Mawhin, J., jt. auth. see Rouche, N.

Mawhinney, Paul C., ed. Musicmaster: The 45 R.P.M. Record Directory, 2 vols. 2500p. (Orig.). 1983. Title directory. pap. write for info. (ISBN 0-910925-01-1); Artist directory. pap. write for info. (ISBN 0-910925-00-3); Set. pap. 150.00 (ISBN 0-910925-02-X). Record-Rama.

Mawhood, Philip. Local Government for Development: The Experience of Tropical Africa. (Public Administration in Developing Countries Ser.). 250p. 1983. price not set (ISBN 0-471-10510-4, Pub. by Wiley-Interscience). Wiley.

Mawson, C. A. Management of Radioactive Wastes. 196p. 1965. 12.50 (ISBN 0-442-05172-7, Pub. by Van Nos Reinhold). Krieger.

Mawson, C. O. Dictionary of Foreign Terms. rev. 2nd ed. Berlitz, Charles, ed. LC 74-12492. 384p. 1976. 9.95i o.s.i. (ISBN 0-690-00171-1, TYC-T). T Y Crowell.

Mawson, C. O., ed. see Roget, Peter M.

Mawson, Monica. Cooking with Herbs & Spices. LC 78-56371. (Illus.). 112p. 1980. 8.95 o.p. (ISBN 0-89196-023-6, Domus Bks). Quality Bks IL.

Max, Barbara. Whispers of Love. (Candlelight Romance Ser.: No. 673). (Orig.). 1981. pap. 1.75 o.s.i. (ISBN 0-440-19523-3). Dell.

Max, Bill see Le Corbusier.

Max, Gerry. Concerto for Ten Broken Fingers. 162p. 1978. pap. 4.95 (ISBN 0-686-38100-9, 101). William of Orange.

--Ixion's Wheel. 120p. 1979. pap. 4.95 (ISBN 0-686-38099-1, 102). William of Orange.

Max, Leslie. Barney's Picnic. (Play & Learn Shape Board Bks). 14p. (gr. k-3). 1981. bds. 3.50 comb bdg. o.s.i. (ISBN 0-89828-101-6, 06002, Ottenheimer Pubs Inc). Tuffy Bks.

--Dino's Happy & Sad Book. (Play & Learn Shape Board Bks). 14p. (gr. k-3). 1981. bds. 3.50 comb bdg. o.s.i. (ISBN 0-89828-103-2, 06004, Ottenheimer Pubs Inc). Tuffy Bks.

--Fred Flintstone's Counting Book. (Play & Learn Shape Board Bks.). 14p. (gr. k-3). 1981. bds. 3.50 comb bdg. o.s.i. (ISBN 0-89828-100-8, 06001, Pub. by Ottenheimer Pubs Inc). Tuffy Bks.

--Huckleberry Hound Takes a Trip. (Play & Learn Shape Board Bks). 14p. (gr. k-3). 1981. bds. 3.50 comb bdg. o.s.i. (ISBN 0-89828-105-9, 06006, Ottenheimer Pubs Inc). Tuffy Bks.

Max, Stefan. Dialogues et Situations. 2nd ed. 1979. text ed. 18.95 (ISBN 0-669-01788-4); cahier de travaux practiques 7.95 (ISBN 0-669-01789-2); cahier de travaux practiques 5.95 (ISBN 0-669-01907-0); cassettes 40.00 (ISBN 0-669-01908-9); demonstration tape 1.95 (ISBN 0-686-86035-7); transcript 1.95 (ISBN 0-669-01906-2). Heath.

Maxcy, Spencer J. Educational Philosophy for the Future. LC 77-18479. 1978. pap. text ed. 11.25 (ISBN 0-8191-0420-5). U Pr of Amer.

--Practical Thinking for Educators. LC 82-45040. 50p. (Orig.). 1982. pap. text ed. 5.50 (ISBN 0-8191-2380-3). U Pr of Amer.

Maxey, Virginia. Sunbird. 1978. write for info. (ISBN 0-686-05262-5). Cassandra Pubns.

--Sunbird Singing. 1978. pap. 4.00 (ISBN 0-686-14355-8). Cassandra Pubns.

Maxim, George. The Very Young: Guiding Children from Infancy Through the Early Years. 576p. 1980. text ed. 22.95x (ISBN 0-534-00820-8). Wadsworth Pub.

Maxim, George M. Social Studies & the Elementary School Child. 544p. 1983. text ed. 18.95 (ISBN 0-675-20017-2). Additional supplements may be obtained from publisher. Merrill.

Maxim, George W. Learning Centers for Young Children. 208p. 1977. 12.95 o.s.i. (ISBN 0-89104-239-3, A & W Visual Library); pap. 7.95 o.s.i. (ISBN 0-89104-238-5). A & W Pubs.

--Methods of Teaching Social Studies to Elemenatry School Children. (Elementary Education Ser.). 1977. text ed. 18.95 (ISBN 0-675-08545-4). Additional supplements may be obtained from publisher. Merrill.

Maxim, John R. Platforms. 348p. 1981. 11.95 o.p. (ISBN 0-399-12535-3). Putnam Pub Group.

Maxker, Donna. The Boatcook. (Illus.). 128p. pap. 15.00 (ISBN 0-915160-31-5). Seven Seas.

Maxmen, Jerrold S. The Post-Physician Era: Medicine in the 21st Century. LC 76-2442. (Health, Medicine & Society Ser.). 1976. 26.95 o.p. (ISBN 0-471-57880-0, Pub. by Wiley-Interscience). Wiley.

Maxon, Olivia J. The Stories of Two Grunches. 1978. 4.50 o.p. (ISBN 0-533-03268-7). Vantage.

Maxon, R. M. John Ainsworth & the Making of Kenya. LC 80-8165. 472p. 1980. lib. bdg. 26.50 (ISBN 0-8191-1155-4); pap. text ed. 16.50 (ISBN 0-8191-1156-2). U Pr of Amer.

Maxson, Marilyn M., jt. ed. see Hunt, Thomas C.

Maxson, Robin, jt. auth. see Bucheli, Fausto.

Maxson, Robin, jt. auth. see Friesen, Garry.

Maxtone-Graham, John. The Only Way to Cross. (Illus.). 434p. 1972. 15.95 (ISBN 0-02-582350-7); 10.95. Macmillan.

Maxtone-Graham, Katrina. An Adopted Woman. LC 82-71563. 1983. 15.95 (ISBN 0-943362-00-8). Remi Bks.

Maxwell. Skimming & Scanning Skills. (Basic Skills System). 1969. 14.95 (ISBN 0-07-051386-4). McGraw.

Maxwell, A. E. Basic Statistics for Medical & Social Science Students. 2nd ed. 1978. pap. 5.95x (ISBN 0-412-15580-X, Pub. by Chapman & Hall). Methuen Inc.

--Multivariate Analysis in Behavioral Research: For Medical & Social Science Students. 2nd ed. 1978. 15.95x (ISBN 0-412-15580-X, Pub. by Chapman & Hall). Methuen Inc.

--Steal the Sun. 288p. 1982. 13.95 (ISBN 0-399-90129-9, Marek). Putnam Pub Group.

Maxwell, A. K., et al. Faber's Anatomical Atlas for Nurses & Students. 62p. 1962. pap. text ed. 3.95 (ISBN 0-571-06461-2). Faber & Faber.

Maxwell, Ann. Dancer's Luck. 171p. 1983. pap. 2.50 (ISBN 0-686-43168-5, Sig). NAL.

--Fire Dancer. 208p. 1982. pap. 2.50 (ISBN 0-451-11939-8, AE1939, Sig). NAL.

Maxwell, Arthur D. & McMichael, John H. Elementary Accounting. (Quality Paperback: No. 3). (Orig.). 1977. pap. 3.95 (ISBN 0-8226-0003-X). Littlefield.

Maxwell, Arthur E., et al. Sea, Vol. 4 Pts 1-3. LC 62-18366. 1971. Pt. 1. 77.50 o.p. (ISBN 0-471-57910-6, Pub. by Wiley-Interscience). Wiley.

Maxwell, C. Bede. The New German Shorthaired Pointer. 4th ed. LC 82-3059. (Illus.). 320p. 1982. 14.95 (ISBN 0-87605-157-3). Howell Bk.

Maxwell, Charlotte T. So Many Things. (Illus.). 1978. 4.95 o.p. (ISBN 0-533-03732-8). Vantage.

Maxwell, Edwin A. Analytical Calculus, 4 vols. 1954. Vol. 1. 15.95x (ISBN 0-521-05696-9); Vol. 2. 23.95x (ISBN 0-521-05697-7); Vol. 3. 18.95x (ISBN 0-521-05698-5); Vol. 4. 23.95x (ISBN 0-521-05699-3). Cambridge U Pr.

--Fallacies in Mathematics. 1959. 15.95 (ISBN 0-521-05700-0). Cambridge U Pr.

Maxwell, Emma. Take Care, Mama. 1979. 7.95 o.p. (ISBN 0-533-03673-9). Vantage.

Maxwell, Fowden G. & Jennings, Peter R. Breeding Plants Resistant to Insects. LC 79-13462. (Environmental Science & Technology: Texts & Monographs). 1980. 32.50 (ISBN 0-471-03268-9, Pub. by Wiley-Interscience). Wiley.

Maxwell, G. M. Principles of Pediatrics. (Illus.). 1978. text ed. 36.95x (ISBN 0-7022-1412-4); pap. text ed. 19.25x (ISBN 0-7022-1413-2). U of Queensland Pr.

Maxwell, G. W., jt. auth. see Giordano, Al.

Maxwell, Gordon & Hanson, William. Rome's Most Northerly Frontier: The Antonine Wall. (Illus.). 250p. 1983. 30.00x (ISBN 0-85224-416-9, Pub. by Edinburgh U Pr Scotland). Columbia U Pr.

Maxwell, Gordon S. The Authors' Thames: A Literary Ramble Through the Thames Valley. (Illus.). 324p. 1982. Repr. of 1924 ed. lib. bdg. 40.00 (ISBN 0-89984-806-0). Century Bookbindery.

Maxwell, J. B. Data Book on Hydrocarbons: Application to Process Engineering. LC 74-30163. 268p. 1975. Repr. of 1950 ed. text ed. 16.50 (ISBN 0-88275-257-X). Krieger.

Maxwell, James A. & Aronson, J. Richard. Financing State & Local Governments. 3rd ed. LC 76-54871. (Studies of Government Finance). 1977. 22.95 (ISBN 0-8157-5512-0); pap. 8.95 (ISBN 0-8157-5511-2). Brookings.

Maxwell, Jessica. The Eye-Body Connection. (Illus., Orig.). 1980. pap. 9.95 (ISBN 0-446-37599-3). Warner Bks.

Maxwell, John. Think on These Things. 128p. 1979. pap. 2.50 (ISBN 0-8341-0600-0). Beacon Hill.

Maxwell, John A., jt. auth. see Johnson, Wesley M.

Maxwell, K. R. Conflicts & Conspiracies, Brazil & Portugal, 1750-1808. LC 72-89813. (Cambridge Latin American Studies). (Illus.). 320p. 1973. 32.50 (ISBN 0-521-20053-9). Cambridge U Pr.

Maxwell, Mervyn. Tell It to the World. LC 76-6619. 1976. 7.95 o.p. (ISBN 0-8163-0217-0, 20077-4). Pacific Pr Pub Assn.

Maxwell, Morton H. & Kleeman, Charles R., eds. Clinical Disorders of Fluid & Electrolyte Metabolism. 3rd ed. (Illus.). 1979. text ed. 85.00 (ISBN 0-07-040994-3, HP). McGraw.

Maxwell Museum of Anthropology, Univ. of New Mexico. Seven Families in Pueblo Pottery. LC 75-17376. (Illus.). 116p. 1975. pap. 6.95 (ISBN 0-8263-0388-9). U of NM Pr.

Maxwell, Neal A. Even as I Am. 128p. 1982. 6.95 (ISBN 0-87747-943-7). Deseret Bk.

Maxwell, Robert. Health & Wealth: An International Study of Health-Care Spending. LC 80-8472. 192p. 1981. 24.95 (ISBN 0-669-04109-2). Lexington Bks.

Maxwell, Robert, jt. auth. see Stirling, James.

Maxwell, Robert J., jt. auth. see Watson, Wilbur H.

Maxwell, Robert S. Texas Economic Growth, 1890 to World War II: From Frontier to Industrial Giant. Rosenbaum, Robert J., ed. (Texas History Ser.). (Illus.). 42p. 1982. pap. text ed. 1.95x (ISBN 0-89641-099-4). American Pr.

Maxwell, Robert S. & Baker, Robert D. Sawdust Empire: The Texas Lumber Industry 1830-1940. LC 82-40442. (Illus.). 256p. 1983. 24.95 (ISBN 0-89096-148-4). Tex A&M Univ Pr.

Maxwell, Ruth. The Booze Battle. 7.95 o.p. (ISBN 0-686-92091-0); pap. 2.50 o.p. (ISBN 0-686-98481-1). Hazelden.

Maxwell, Stephen, jt. auth. see Archer, Clive.

Maxwell, Stephen, ed. Scotland, Multinationals & the Third World. 160p. 1982. text ed. 13.75 (ISBN 0-906391-28-8, 40980, Pub. by Mainstream Scotland). Humanities.

Maxwell, William. The Folded Leaf. LC 80-67031. 288p. 1981. pap. 7.95 (ISBN 0-87923-351-6, Nonpareil Bks). Godine.

--Time Will Darken It. 320p. 1983. pap. 8.95 (ISBN 0-87923-448-2). Godine.

Maxwell, William, ed. The Letters of Sylvia Townsend Warner. 320p. 1983. 26.00 (ISBN 0-670-42729-2). Viking Pr.

--Thinking: The Expanding Frontier. (Problem Solving Ser.). 400p. 1983. text ed. write for info. (ISBN 0-89168-047-0). Franklin Inst Pr.

Maxwell, William E. & Crain, Ernest. Texas Politics Today. 2nd ed. (Illus.). 585p. 1981. pap. text ed. 13.50 (ISBN 0-8299-0395-X). West Pub.

--Texas Politics Today. (Illus.). 1978. pap. text ed. 10.95 o.s.i. (ISBN 0-8299-0216-3); instrs.' manual avail. o.s.i. (ISBN 0-8299-0556-1). West Pub.

Maxwell, William H. The Fortunes of Hector O'Halloran & His Man, Mark Anthony O'Toole. Wolff, Robert L., ed. (Ireland Nineteenth Century Fiction - Ser. Two: Vol. 51). 416p. 1979. lib. bdg. 32.00 (ISBN 0-8240-3500-3). Garland Pub.

Maxwell-Cook, John C. Structural Notes & Details. (C & CA Viewpoint Publication Ser.). (Illus.). 1976. text ed. 20.00x (ISBN 0-7210-1006-7). Scholium Intl.

Maxwell-Hudson, Clare. A Spa of One's Own: How to Turn Your Home Into a Health Beauty Spa. (Illus.). 238p. 1982. 18.95 (ISBN 0-13-823989-4); pap. 8.95 (ISBN 0-13-823971-1). P-H.

May, Antionette. Different Drummers: They Did What They Wanted. LC 76-11373. (Illus.). 160p. 1976. pap. 4.95 o.p. (ISBN 0-89087-907-9). Les Femmes Pub.

May, Bernie. Under His Wing: Adventures in Trusting God. rev. ed. (Illus.). 1983. pap. 6.95 (ISBN 0-930014-94-4). Multnomah.

May, Bonnie C. De see Choate, Sharr & De May, Bonnie C.

May, Brian. The Indonesian Tragedy. (Illus.). 1978. 30.00 (ISBN 0-7100-8834-5). Routledge & Kegan.

May, Charles E., ed. Short Story Theories. LC 75-36982. xiv, 251p. 1976. 13.00x (ISBN 0-8214-0189-0, 82-81917); pap. 6.95x (ISBN 0-8214-0221-8, 82-81925). Ohio U Pr.

May, Donald C., Jr., jt. auth. see Burington, Richard S.

May, Dorothy. Dulcimer Classics. (Illus.). 48p. (Orig.). 1980. pap. 2.95 (ISBN 0-941126-02-1). Meadowlark.

May, Elaine T. Great Expectations: Marriage & Divorce in Post-Victorian America. LC 80-10590. (Illus.). 1980. 15.00x (ISBN 0-226-51166-9); pap. 6.95 (ISBN 0-226-51170-7). U of Chicago Pr.

May, Elizabeth. T.S.K.H. Tickle, Snug, Kiss, Hug. LC 77-70643. 1977. 10.00 o.p. (ISBN 0-8091-0226-9); pap. 6.95 (ISBN 0-8091-2022-4). Paulist Pr.

May, Elizabeth, ed. Musics of Many Cultures: An Introduction. LC 76-50251. (Illus.). 454p. 1982. 38.50x (ISBN 0-520-03393-0); pap. 19.95 (ISBN 0-520-04778-8). U of Cal Pr.

May, Elizabeth E., et al. Independent Living for the Handicapped & the Elderly. 1974. text ed. 24.95 (ISBN 0-395-18108-9). HM.

May, Ernest R. Boom & Bust, 1917-1932. LC 63-8572. (Life History of the United States). (Illus.). (gr. 5 up). 1974. PLB 12.00 (ISBN 0-8094-0559-8, Pub. by Time-Life). Silver.

--Lessons of the Past: The Use & Misuse of History in American Foreign Policy. 1973. 16.95x (ISBN 0-19-501698-X). Oxford U Pr.

--The Progressive Era, 1901-1917. LC 63-8572. (Life History of the United States). (Illus.). (gr. 5 up). 1974. PLB 10.60 (ISBN 0-8094-0558-X, Pub. by Time-Life). Silver.

May, Ernest R. & Fraser, Janet. Campaign Seventy-Two: The Managers Speak. LC 73-85182. 224p. 1973. 12.50x (ISBN 0-674-09141-8); pap. 4.95x (ISBN 0-674-09143-4). Harvard U Pr.

May, Frank B. To Help Children Communicate. (Elementary Education Ser.: No. C22). 472p. 1980. pap. text ed. 17.95 (ISBN 0-675-08197-1). Additional supplements may be obtained from publisher. Merrill.

May, Frank B. & Eliot, Susan B. To Help Children Read. 2nd ed. (Elementary Education Ser.). 1978. pap. text ed. 15.95 o.p. (ISBN 0-675-08370-2); suppl. material avail. o.p. Merrill.

May, G. H. Le see Le May, G. H.

May, Gary. China Scapegoat: The Diplomatic Ordeal of John Carter Vincent. LC 79-4129. (Illus.). 1979. 15.95 (ISBN 0-915220-49-0). New Republic.

--China Scapegoat: The Diplomatic Ordeal of John Carter Vincent. 370p. 1982. Repr. of 1979 ed. pap. 8.95x (ISBN 0-917974-98-0). Waveland Pr.

May, George W. History of Massac County, Illinois. (Illus.). 232p. 1983. Repr. of 1955 ed. 6.00x (ISBN 0-9605566-4-8). G W May.

--Massac County Nineteen Fifty-Five to Nineteen Eighty-Two: Accompanies History of Massac County. 1983. 1.00 (ISBN 0-686-42830-7). G W May.

May, Georges. D'Ovid a Racine. (Yale Romanic Studies). 1949. pap. 37.50x (ISBN 0-685-69841-6). Elliots Bks.

May, Gerald. The Open Way: A Meditation Handbook. LC 77-70641. 192p. 1977. 8.95 o.p. (ISBN 0-8091-0228-5). Paulist Pr.

May, Gerald G. Will & Spirit: A Comtemplative Psychology. LC 82-47751. 384p. 1982. 23.99i (ISBN 0-686-98141-3, HarpR). Har-Row.

May, Glenn A. Social Engineerng in the Phillipines: The Aims, Execution & Impact of American Colonial Policy, 1900-1913. LC 79-7467. (Contributions in Comparative Colonial Studies: No. 2). 1980. lib. bdg. 29.95 (ISBN 0-313-20978-2, MAE/). Greenwood.

May, Hal, ed. Contemporary Authors, Vol. 107. 600p. 1983. 74.00x (ISBN 0-8103-1907-1). Gale.

May, Harriett J. Enterostomal Therapy. LC 76-19894. 286p. 1977. pap. 14.50 (ISBN 0-89004-144-X). Raven.

May, Harry S. Francisco Franco: The Jewish Connection. 1978. pap. text ed. 10.00 (ISBN 0-8191-0363-2). U Pr of Amer.

May, Henry F. The End of American Innocence: A Study of the First Years of Our Own Time, 1912-1917. 1979. pap. 9.95 (ISBN 0-19-502528-8, GB574, GB). Oxford U Pr.

--The Enlightenment in America. LC 75-32349. 1978. pap. 7.95 (ISBN 0-19-502367-6, GB529, GB). Oxford U Pr.

--Ideas, Faiths, & Feelings: Essays on American Intellectual & Religious History, 1952-1982. 256p. 1983. 17.95 (ISBN 0-19-503235-7, GB); pap. 6.95 (ISBN 0-19-503236-5). Oxford U Pr.

--Ideas, Faiths, & Feelings: Essays on American Intellectual & Religious History, 1952-1982. 256p. 1983. pap. 4.95 (ISBN 0-19-503236-5, GB 719, GB). Oxford U Pr.

May, Herbert G. & Hunt, G. H., eds. Oxford Bible Atlas. 2nd ed. (Illus.). 1974. 14.95 (ISBN 0-19-211556-1); pap. 8.95x (ISBN 0-19-211557-X). Oxford U Pr.

May, Herbert K. The Multinational Corporations in Latin America. 1977. pap. 8.25 (ISBN 0-685-79717-1, COA 11, CoA). Unipub.

May, Irvin M., Jr., jt. auth. see Dethloff, Henry C.

May, Isopel, et al, eds. Putnam's Contemporary Italian Dictionary. (Eng. & It.). 1973. 3.50 o.p. (ISBN 0-399-11146-8). Putnam Pub Group.

May, J. Peter. Simplicial Objects in Algebraic Topology. LC 82-51078. vi, 162p. 1982. pap. text ed. 7.00x (ISBN 0-226-51180-4). U of Chicago Pr.

May, James L., jt. auth. see Sahney, Vinod K.

May, Janice, et al. Texas Government. 8th ed. Munson, Eric M., ed. (Illus.). 416p. 1980. pap. text ed. 15.50 (ISBN 0-07-041015-1); instr's manual 16.00 (ISBN 0-07-041016-X). McGraw.

May, Janis S. Where Shadows Linger. (Orig.). 1980. pap. 1.25 o.s.i. (ISBN 0-440-19777-5). Dell.

May, John & Marten, Michael. The Book of Beasts. LC 82-40374. (Illus.). 192p. 1983. pap. 12.95 (ISBN 0-670-17915-9). Viking Pr.

May, John A. De see DeMay, John A.

May, John R., jt. auth. see Ferlita, Ernest.

May, John R. & Bird, Michael, eds. Religion in Film. LC 81-23983. (Illus.). 232p. 1982. text ed. 16.50x (ISBN 0-87049-352-3); pap. text ed. 7.95x (ISBN 0-87049-368-X). U of Tenn Pr.

May, Julian. Before the Indians. (Illus.). 40p. (gr. k-3). 1969. PLB 7.95 (ISBN 0-8234-0005-0). Holiday.

--Brede's Tale: Miniature Book; Excerpt from "The Golden Tore". LC 82-5516. (Illus.). 1982. deluxe ed. 85.00 (ISBN 0-916732-31-2); special ed. 45.00 (ISBN 0-916732-32-0). Starmont Hse.

--Hillary & Tenzing: Conquerors of Mt. Everest. LC 72-85045. 40p. (gr. 2-5). 1972. PLB 7.95 (ISBN 0-87191-219-8). Creative Ed.

--The Many-Colored Land. Date not set. pap. 6.95 (ISBN 0-449-90071-1, Columbine). Fawcett.

--Millions of Years of Eggs. Publication Associates, ed. LC 73-84732. (Illus.). (gr. 1-4). 1969. PLB 7.95 (ISBN 0-87191-034-9). Creative Ed.

--New Baby Comes. Publication Associates, ed. LC 70-84731. (Illus.). (gr. 1-4). 1969. PLB 7.95 o.p. (ISBN 0-87191-033-0). Creative Ed.

--The Nonborn King. 1983. 16.95 (ISBN 0-395-32211-1). HM.

--The Saga of Pliocene Exile: The Nonborn King, Vol. 3. (Illus.). 395p. 1983. 16.95 (ISBN 0-686-82648-5). HM.

--The Warm-Blooded Dinosarus. LC 77-24642. (Illus.). 48p. (gr. 1-3). 1978. reinforced bdg 7.95 o.p. (ISBN 0-8234-0312-2). Holiday.

--Weather. (Beginning Science Ser.). (Illus.). (gr. 2-4). 1966. PLB 5.97 o.s.i. (ISBN 0-695-89210-X). Follett.

--Wildlife in the City. Publication Associates, ed. LC 70-104927. (gr. 2-4). 1970. PLB 7.95 o.p. (ISBN 0-87191-040-3). Creative Ed.

May, Keith M. Out of the Maelstrom: Psychology & the Modern Novel. LC 76-44599. 168p. 1977. 22.50x (ISBN 0-312-59115-2). St Martin.

May, Lynn, ed. Encyclopedia of Southern Baptists, Vol. IV. LC 81-66989. 1982. 19.95 (ISBN 0-8054-6556-1). Broadman.

May, Mark A. A Social Psychology of War & Peace. 1943. 37.50x (ISBN 0-686-51314-2). Elliots Bks.

May, Phillip T. Programming Business Applications in FORTRAN IV. LC 72-7634. 1973. pap. text ed. 18.50 (ISBN 0-395-14047-1); solutions manual 1.65 (ISBN 0-395-17159-8). HM.

May, R. & Weber, J., eds. Pelvic & Abdominal Veins. (International Congress Ser.: No. 550). 1981. 81.00 (ISBN 0-444-90215-5). Elsevier.

May, R. M., jt. ed. see Anderson, R. C.

May, Robert. Physicians of the Soul: The Psychologies of the World's Great Spiritual Teachers. (Great Spiritual Teachers Ser.). 320p. 1983. 17.50 (ISBN 0-8245-0511-5). Crossroad NY.

May, Robert & Koster, Jan, eds. Levels of Syntactic Representation. 350p. 1981. 39.50x (ISBN 0-686-32120-0); pap. 24.50x (ISBN 90-70176-30-0). Foris Pubns.

May, Robert, et al. A Brief Introduction to Managerial & Social Uses of Accounting. 1975. pap. text ed. 13.95 (ISBN 0-13-082008-3). P-H.

May, Robert L. Rudolph the Red-Nosed Reindeer. (Illus.). 48p. 1980. text ed. 6.95 (ISBN 0-695-81471-0, Dist. by Caroline Hse). Follett.

May, Robin. A Companion to the Opera. LC 76-52790. 1977. 12.95 o.p. (ISBN 0-88254-439-X). Hippocrene Bks.

--North American Indians. LC 80-50428. (Fact Finders Ser.). PLB 8.00 (ISBN 0-382-06367-8). Silver.

--The Wild West. LC 79-64160. (Adventures in History Ser.). PLB 12.68 (ISBN 0-382-06297-3). Silver.

--The Wild West. LC 80-50430. (Fact Finders Ser.). PLB 8.00 (ISBN 0-382-06385-6). Silver.

May, Rollo. Art of Counseling. (Series B). 1978. pap. 4.50 o.p. (ISBN 0-687-01766-1). Abingdon.

--Freedom & Destiny. 1983. pap. 7.95 (ISBN 0-440-53012-1, Delta). Dell.

--Love & Will. 1973. pap. 5.95 o.s.i. (ISBN 0-440-55027-0, Delta). Dell.

--Man's Search for Himself. 1973. pap. 6.95 (ISBN 0-440-55296-6, Delta). Dell.

--Power & Innocence. 1976. pap. 6.95 (ISBN 0-440-57023-9, Delta). Dell.

--Psychology & the Human Dilemma. 240p. 1980. pap. 5.95 (ISBN 0-393-00978-5). Norton.

May, Ruth G., jt. auth. see Sowell, Judith B.

May, Thomas. The Tragoedy of Cleopatra Queene of Aegypt. Smith, Denzell S. & Orgel, Stephen, eds. LC 78-66784. (Renaissance Drama Ser.). 1979. lib. bdg. 35.00 o.s.i. (ISBN 0-8240-9732-7). Garland Pub.

May, William & Westley, Richard. The Right to Die. (Catholic Perspectives Ser.). 112p. 1980. pap. 6.95 (ISBN 0-88347-115-9). Thomas More.

May, William E. Contraception, Humanae Vitae & Catholic Moral Thought. (Synthesis Ser.). 1983. 1.75 (ISBN 0-8199-0925-4). Franciscan Herald.

May, Wynne. Peacock in the Jungle. (Harlequin Romances Ser.). 192p. 1983. pap. 1.50 (ISBN 0-373-02532-7). Harlequin Bks.

--Wayside Flower. (Harlequin Romance Ser.). 192p. 1983. pap. 1.75 (ISBN 0-686-38749-X). Harlequin Bks.

Mayakovsky, Vladimir. Wi the Haill Voice. Morgan, Edwin, tr. from Rus. (Translation Ser.). (Scots.). 1979. 6.95 o.p. (ISBN 0-902145-41-X, Pub. by Carcanet New Pr England). Humanities.

Mayakovsky, Vladimir & Brik, Lily. Enchained in Film. Segall, Helen, tr. (Illus.). 1982. cancelled 15.00x; pap. 6.50 cancelled. Translation Pr.

Mayall, jt. ed. see Goodwin.

Mayall, Margaret W., jt. auth. see Mayall, R. Newton.

Mayall, Margaret W., jt. auth. see Mayall, Robert N.

Mayall, R. Newton & Mayall, Margaret W. Sundials: How to Know, Use, & Make Them. 2nd ed. LC 73-76242. (Illus.). 1973. 12.95 (ISBN 0-933346-11-5). Sky Pub.

Mayall, R. Newton, jt. auth. see Olcott, William.

Mayall, Robert N. & Mayall, Margaret W. Skyshooting: Photography for Amateur Astronomers. rev. ed. pap. 4.00 (ISBN 0-486-21854-6). Dover.

Maybeck, Peter S. Stochastic Models, Estimation & Control, Vol. 2. (Mathematics in Science & Engineering Ser.). 289p. 1982. 39.50 (ISBN 0-12-480702-X). Acad Pr.

--Stochastic Models, Estimation & Control, Vol. 3. (Mathematics in Science & Engineering Ser.). 270p. 1982. 39.50 (ISBN 0-12-480703-8). Acad Pr.

Mayberry, Susanah. My Amiable Uncle: Reminiscences about Booth Tarkington. LC 82-81021. (Illus.). 160p. 1983. 12.50 (ISBN 0-911198-66-0). Purdue.

Mayburg, Arnim H., jt. auth. see Stopher, Peter R.

Maybury-Lewis, David. Akwe-Shavante Society. (Illus.). 1974. pap. 5.95x o.p. (ISBN 0-686-76959-7). Oxford U Pr.

Maycock, Paul D. & Stirewalt, Edward N. Photovoltaics: Sunlight to Electricity in One Step. 224p. (Orig.). 1981. 24.95 (ISBN 0-471-88646-7, Pub. by Brick Hse Pub.). Wiley.

--Photovoltaics: Sunlight to Electricity in One Step. 1981. 19.95 (ISBN 0-931790-24-7). Brick Hse Pub.

Maycock, Susan E. An Architectural History of Carbondale, Illinois. (Illus., Orig.). 1983. price not set (ISBN 0-8093-1128-3); pap. price not set (ISBN 0-8093-1120-8). S Ill U Pr.

Mayer. American Ideas & Education. 1964. text ed. 12.95 (ISBN 0-675-09812-2). Merrill.

--Capital Expenditure Analysis: For Managers & Engineers. LC 77-84052. 1978. text ed. 19.95x (ISBN 0-917974-12-3). Waveland Pr.

Mayer, Adele. Incest: A Treatment Manual for Therapy with Victims, Spouses & Offenders. LC 82-83779. 275p. 1982. lib. bdg. 24.95x (ISBN 0-918452-36-8). Learning Pubns.

Mayer, Adrian C. Peasants in the Pacific: A Study of Fiji Indian Rural Society. 2nd, rev. ed. LC 72-91618. (Illus.). 1973. 26.50x o.s.i. (ISBN 0-520-02333-1). U of Cal Pr.

Mayer, Albert I., Jr. Olympiad. LC 61-12875. (Illus.). (gr. 7-11). 1938. 8.00x (ISBN 0-8196-0115-2). Biblo.

Mayer, Albert J. & Gordon, Leonard. Urban Life & the Struggle to Be Human. 1979. pap. text ed. 12.95 (ISBN 0-8403-2035-3). Kendall-Hunt.

Mayer, Allan J. Madam Prime Minister: Margaret Thatcher & Her Rise to Power. Kelly, Curtis, ed. LC 79-3025. (Illus.). 1979. 8.95 o.p. (ISBN 0-88225-285-2). Newsweek.

Mayer, Andre & Wheeler, Michael. The Crocodile Man: A Case of Brain Chemistry & Criminal Violence. 224p. 1982. 12.95 (ISBN 0-395-31840-8). HM.

Mayer, Ann M. & Mayer, Harry F. Who's Out There? UFO Encounters. LC 79-14802. (Illus.). 96p. (gr. 4-6). 1979. PLB 7.29 o.p. (ISBN 0-671-32986-3). Messner.

Mayer, Anna. El Mundo de Santiago. 22p. (Sp.). (gr. 3-4). 1980. pap. text ed. 5.95 (ISBN 0-933982-18-6). Bradt Ent.

Mayer, Carl, jt. auth. see Meringer, Rudolf.

Mayer, David, ed. Henry Irving & The Bells. (Illus.). 160p. 1982. 20.00 (ISBN 0-7190-0798-4). Manchester.

Mayer, David & Richards, Kenneth, eds. Western Popular Theatre. 1980. 18.95x o.p. (ISBN 0-416-82220-7); pap. 9.95x (ISBN 0-416-73150-3). Methuen Inc.

Mayer, Debby. Sisters. LC 81-19888. 272p. 1982. 13.95 (ISBN 0-399-12700-3). Putnam Pub Group.

Mayer, Dorothy M. The Forgotten Master: The Life & Times of Louis Spohr. LC 80-27659. (Music Reprint Ser.). 208p. 1981. Repr. of 1959 ed. 25.00 (ISBN 0-306-76099-1). Da Capo.

Mayer, E., jt. ed. see Bolton, R.

Mayer, Egon. From Suburb to Shtetl: The Jews of Boro Park. (Illus.). 196p. 1979. 24.95 (ISBN 0-87722-161-8). Temple U Pr.

Mayer, Elizabeth, tr. see Goethe, Johann W.

Mayer, Elizabeth, tr. see Von Goethe, Johann W.

Mayer, Elizabeth, et al, trs. see Von Goethe, Johann W.

Mayer, Eva, tr. see Korschunow, Irina.

Mayer, Eva, tr. see Lang, Othmar F.

Mayer, Eva L., tr. see Roser, Wiltrud.

Mayer, Frederick J., ed. see Johnson, George C.

Mayer, Frederick J., ed. see Munn, H. Warner.

Mayer, Garry F., pref. by. Ecological Stress & the New York Bight: Science & Management. LC 82-71795. (Illus.). x, 717p. (Orig.). 1982. pap. text ed. 10.00 (ISBN 0-9608990-0-6). Estuarine Res.

Mayer, Gloria G., jt. ed. see Ciske, Karen L.

Mayer, Harold M. & Hayes, Charles R. Land Uses in American Cities. LC 82-81036. (Illus.). 200p. (Orig.). 1983. pap. text ed. 6.95 (ISBN 0-941226-02-6). Park Pr Co.

Mayer, Harry F., jt. auth. see Mayer, Ann M.

Mayer, Hartwig. Die Althochdeutschen Griffelglossen der Handschrift Ottob. Lat. 3295 (Biblioteca Vaticana) 192p. (Ger.). 1982. write for info. (ISBN 3-261-04965-0). P Lang Pubs.

Mayer, Henry & Garde, Pauline. The Media: Questions & Answers Australian Surveys, 1940 to 1980. 224p. 1983. text ed. 37.50x (ISBN 0-86861-348-7). Allen Unwin.

Mayer, Herbert. C.O.M.E. Leader's Manual. pap. 21.50 o.p. (ISBN 0-686-25773-1). Morse Pr.

--C.O.M.E. Members Manual. pap. 15.00 o.p. (ISBN 0-933350-24-4). Morse Pr.

Mayer, Herbert A., jt. auth. see Meyer, Daniel P.

Mayer, Herbert T. Pastoral Care: Its Roots & Renewal. LC 78-52444. 1978. 7.25 (ISBN 0-8042-1130-2). John Knox.

Mayer, Jakob P. Sociology of Film: Studies & Documents. LC 75-160239. (Moving Pictures Ser). 328p. 1971. Repr. of 1946 ed. lib. bdg. 18.95x (ISBN 0-89198-040-7). Ozer.

Mayer, James W., jt. auth. see Poate, John M.

Mayer, Jean. Health. Orig. Title: Health & the Patterns of Life. 550p. 1974. text ed. 12.95 (ISBN 0-442-25183-1). Van Nos Reinhold.

--Public Acceptance Assessment Checklist. 1977. 2.95 (ISBN 0-686-98028-X). Timber.

Mayer, Jean & Goldberg, Jeanne. Dr. Jean Mayer's Family Nutrition Book. Harris, Diane F., ed. 320p. 1983. 14.95 (ISBN 0-525-93265-8, 01602-480). Dutton.

Mayer, Jean, jt. ed. see Moss, N. Henry.

Mayer, John E. & Timms, Noel. The Client Speaks: Working Class Impressions of Casework. 1970. 18.95x (ISBN 0-7100-6906-5); pap. 9.95 (ISBN 0-7100-7673-8). Routledge & Kegan.

Mayer, John E. & Filstead, William, eds. Adolescence & Alcohol. LC 79-21226. 304p. 1980. prof ref 19.50x (ISBN 0-88410-513-X). Ballinger Pub.

Mayer, John S. IBM-PC Survivor's Manual: A Primer for the IBM Personal Computer. 35p. (Orig.). 1982. pap. 11.95 (ISBN 0-9609092-0-6). Mayer Assocs.

Mayer, Joseph E. & Mayer, Maria G. Statistical Mechanics. 2nd ed. LC 76-20668. 1977. 47.95 o.s.i. (ISBN 0-471-57985-8, Pub. by Wiley-Interscience). Wiley.

Mayer, K. & Greenwood, Ernest. The Design of Social Policy Research. (Illus.). 1980. text ed. 26.95 (ISBN 0-13-201558-7). P-H.

Mayer, Karel, tr. see Stanek, Jaroslav, et al.

Mayer, Klaus, ed. Guidelines to Transfusion Practices. 175p. 1980. 21.00 (ISBN 0-914404-52-0). Am Assn Blood.

Mayer, Lawrence C. & Burnett, John H. Politics in Industrial Societies: A Comparative Perspection. LC 76-54694. 1977. text ed. 27.50 o.s.i. (ISBN 0-471-57986-6). Wiley.

Mayer, Levy, ed. see Rorer, David.

Mayer, Mancy. The Male Mid-Life Crisis: Fresh Starts After 40. 1970. pap. 3.95 (ISBN 0-451-12178-3, AE2178, Sig). NAL.

Mayer, Maria G., jt. auth. see Mayer, Joseph E.

Mayer, Mercer. All by Myself. (Little Critter Library). (Illus.). 32p. 1983. price not set (ISBN 0-307-10604-7). Western Pub.

--I Was So Bad. LC 82-84109. (Little Critter Library). (Illus.). 32p. 1983. price not set (ISBN 0-307-10603-9, Golden Pr). Western Pub.

--Just Go to Bed. LC 82-84107. (Little Critter Library). (Illus.). 32p. 1983. price not set (Golden Pr). Western Pub.

--Little Monster's Scratch & Sniff Mystery. 32p. 1980. 5.95 (ISBN 0-307-13546-2); PLB 10.69 (ISBN 0-307-64546-0). Western Pub.

--Me, Too! LC 82-84106. (Little Critter Library). (Illus.). 32p. 1983. price not set (ISBN 0-307-10606-3, Golden Pr). Western Pub.

--The New Baby. (Little Critter Library). (Illus.). 32p. 1983. price not set (ISBN 0-307-10601-2, Golden Pr). Western Pub.

--When I Get Bigger. LC 82-84110. (Little Critter Library). (Illus.). 32p. 1983. price not set (ISBN 0-307-10602-0, Golden Pr). Western Pub.

Mayer, Milton S., ed. Tradition of Freedom. LC 57-12989. (Classics Ser.). 766p. (Orig.). 1957. 10.00 (ISBN 0-379-11701-0). Oceana.

Mayer, Morris F. A Guide for Child Care Workers. LC 58-10171. 1958. pap. 5.95 (ISBN 0-87868-066-7, I-29). Child Welfare.

Mayer, Morris F. & Richman, Leon H. Group Care of Children: Crossroads & Transitions. LC 77-80155. 1977. pap. text ed. 8.95 (ISBN 0-87868-165-5, GC-11). Child Welfare.

Mayer, Paul. Blender Cookbook. LC 77-670106. (Illus.). 224p. (Orig.). 1975. pap. 4.95 o.p. (ISBN 0-911954-07-4). Nitty Gritty.

--Fresh Vegetable. rev. ed. (Illus.). 192p. 1982. pap. 5.95 (ISBN 0-911954-34-1). Nitty Gritty.

Mayer, Peter. Cohesion & Conflict in International Communism: A Study of Marxist-Leninist Concepts & Their Application. 1968. 15.00x o.p. (ISBN 90-247-0414-6). Intl Pubns Serv.

Mayer, Ralph. A Dictionary of Art Terms & Techniques. LC 80-8854. (Illus.). 464p. 1981. pap. 6.95 (ISBN 0-06-463531-7, EH 531, EH). B&N NY.

--Dictionary of Art Terms & Techniques. (Illus.). 1969. 14.37i (ISBN 0-690-23673-5). T Y Crowell.

--A Dictionary of Art Terms & Techniques. LC 69-15414. (Apollo Eds.). (Illus.). 464p. 1975. pap. 6.95i o.s.i. (ISBN 0-8152-0371-3, A-371, TYC-T). T Y Crowell.

Mayer, Raymond. Production & Operations Management. 4th ed. (Illus.). 688p. 1982. 25.95x (ISBN 0-07-041025-9); instr's manual 12.00 (ISBN 0-07-041026-7). McGraw.

Mayer, Raymond E. Production & Operations Management. 3rd ed. (Illus.). 672p. 1975. text ed. 25.95 (ISBN 0-07-041023-2, C); instr's manual 18.95 (ISBN 0-07-041024-0). McGraw.

Mayer, Richard, jt. auth. see Tarpy, Roger.

Mayer, Richard E. Thinking & Problem Solving: An Introduction to Human Cognition & Learning. 1977. pap. 10.95x (ISBN 0-673-15055-0). Scott F.

Mayer, Richard E., jt. auth. see Tarpy, Roger M.

Mayer, Robert. Los Angeles: A Chronological & Documentary History, 1542-1976. (American Cities Chronology Ser.). 153p. 1978. 8.50 (ISBN 0-379-00612-X). Oceana.

Mayer, Robert R. Social Science & Institutional Change. LC 81-2705. 202p. 1982. text ed. 19.95 (ISBN 0-87855-432-7). Transaction Bks.

Mayer, Rosemary. Pontormo's Diary. (Illus.). 200p. 1983. 26.95 (ISBN 0-915570-17-3); pap. 16.95 (ISBN 0-686-86541-3). Oolp Pr.

Mayer, S. L. The Biography of General of the Army Douglas MacArthur. (The Commanders Ser.). (Illus.). 160p. 1981. 9.98 o.p. (ISBN 0-89196-105-4, Bk Value Intl). Quality Bks IL.

Mayer, Thomas. Elements of Monetary Policy. 1968. pap. text ed. 3.95x (ISBN 0-685-77203-9). Phila Bk Co.

Mayerchak, Patrick M., ed. Scholars' Guide to Washington DC for Southeast Asian Studies. (Scholars' Guides to Washington, D.C. Series: Vol. 9). 350p. 1983. text ed. 29.95x (ISBN 0-87474-626-4); pap. text ed. 12.50x (ISBN 0-87474-625-6). Smithsonian.

Mayeroff, Milton. On Caring. 1972. pap. 2.95i (ISBN 0-06-080242-1, P242, PL). Har-Row.
Mayers, David G. Applications of Econometrics. (Illus.). 432p. 1982. pap. 24.95 (ISBN 0-13-039180-8). P-H.
Mayers, Harry R. Drafting Patent License Agreements. LC 74-167750. 282p. 1971. 25.00 o.p. (ISBN 0-87179-131-5). BNA.
Mayers, Lewis. The Machinery of Justice: An Introduction to Legal Structure & Process. (Quality Paperback: No. 261). 115p. 1976. pap. 3.95 (ISBN 0-8226-0261-X). Littlefield.
Mayers, Marvin K. A Look at Filipino Lifestyles. LC 79-91446. (Museum of Anthropology Ser.: No. 8). 166p. (Orig.). pap. 8.45x (ISBN 0-88312-158-1); microfiche 2.25x (ISBN 0-88312-245-6). Summer Inst Ling.
--A Look at Latin America Lifestyles. (Museum of Anthropology Publications Ser.: No. 2). 119p. 1976. pap. 6.45x (ISBN 0-88312-151-4); microfiche 2.25x (ISBN 0-88312-238-3). Summer Inst Ling.
Mayers, P. L., jt. auth. see Wright, B. D.
Mayers, Patrick. Lost Bear, Found Bear. LC 72-13353. (Self Starter Ser.). (Illus.). 32p. (ps-1). 1973. 7.75g o.p. (ISBN 0-8075-4760-3). A Whitman.
Mayers, Ronald B. Religious Ministry in a Transcendentless Culture. LC 79-3424. 1980. pap. text ed. 9.50 (ISBN 0-8191-0889-8). U Pr of Amer.
Mayers, William F. Chinese Reader's Manual. LC 68-30660. 1968. Repr. of 1910 ed. 37.00x (ISBN 0-8103-3335-X). Gale.
Mayersdorf, Assa & Schmidt, Richard P., eds. Secondary Epileptogenesis. 188p. 1982. text ed. 23.00 (ISBN 0-89004-578-X). Raven.
Mayerson, Evelyn W. If Birds Are Free. LC 80-7864. 288p. 1980. 12.45i (ISBN 0-690-01890-8). Har-Row.
Mayerson, Phil. Classic Mythology in Literature, Art, & Music. 1971. text ed. 29.95x (ISBN 0-673-15690-7). Scott F.
Mayerthaler, Willi, jt. auth. see Dressler, Wofgang U.
Mayes, David G., jt. ed. see Corner, Desmond C.
Mayes, Edythe B. Mrs. Patty's Place. LC 76-532. 1976. 8.95 (ISBN 0-89002-061-2); pap. 5.00 (ISBN 0-89002-060-4). Northwoods Pr.
--Never Too Old. 1978. 15.00 (ISBN 0-89002-092-2); pap. 5.00 (ISBN 0-89002-091-4). Northwoods Pr.
--The Valiant Sex. LC 78-59067. 1978. 15.00 (ISBN 0-89002-108-2); pap. 5.00 (ISBN 0-89002-107-4). Northwoods Pr.
--Washington: God's Workshop. LC 73-92388. 1973. 13.95 (ISBN 0-89002-021-3); pap. 4.95 (ISBN 0-89002-020-5). Northwoods Pr.
Mayes, Frances. January Sixth, Quarter of Four. (Flowering Quince Poetry Ser.). (Illus.). 20p. (Orig.). 1978. pap. 4.00 (ISBN 0-940592-02-9). Heyeck Pr.
--Very Rich Hours. LC 82-84509. (Lost Roads Ser.: No. 23). 55p. (Orig.). 1983. pap. 5.95 (ISBN 0-918786-26-6). Lost Roads.
Mayes, Janet. Writing & Rewriting. 2nd ed. 1981. pap. text ed. 12.95x (ISBN 0-02-378200-5). Macmillan.
Mayes, Jim. How to Make Your Own Knives. LC 78-57407. (Illus.). 1982. 10.95 (ISBN 0-89696-018-8, An Everest House Book); pap. 7.95 (ISBN 0-89696-146-X). Dodd.
Mayes, Joseph R., ed. Virginia Lawyer: A Basic Practice Handbook. 1979. with 1981 suppl. 50.00 (ISBN 0-87215-125-5); 1981 suppl. 20.00 (ISBN 0-87215-433-5). Michie-Bobbs.
Mayes, Stanley. Makarios. LC 80-13765. 300p. 1981. 26.00x (ISBN 0-312-50488-8). St Martin.
Mayesky, et al. Creative Activities for Young Children. LC 78-52620. 1980. pap. 13.80 (ISBN 0-8273-1571-6); instructor's guide 2.50 (ISBN 0-8273-1572-4). Delmar.
Mayeur, Francoise. L' Enseignement Secondaire des-Jeunes Filles sous la Troisieme Republique. 1977. lib. bdg. 50.00x o.p. (ISBN 2-7246-0384-2); pap. text ed. 42.50x o.p. (ISBN 2-7246-0383-4). Clearwater Pub.
Mayeux, Mansel M. Retailing Farm & Light Industrial Equipment. 2nd ed. (Illus.). 1983. lib. bdg. 19.00 (ISBN 0-87055-414-X). AVI.
Mayfield, A., intro. by. Odhams Knitting Encyclopaedia. (Illus.). 1971. 8.95 o.p. (ISBN 0-600-72123-X). Transatlantic.
Mayfield, Anne. The Wayward Widow, No. 81. 1982. pap. 1.75 (ISBN 0-515-06692-3). Jove Pubns.
Mayfield, J. M. & Webber, B. M. Fundamentals of Senior Physics Textbook, 2 bks. 1973. pap. text ed. 12.95x o.p. (ISBN 0-686-86036-5). Bk. 1 (ISBN 0-686-77463-9, 00501). Bk. 2. pap. text ed. 13.95x o.p. (ISBN 0-686-77464-7, 000502). Heinemann Ed.
Mayfield, Peggy, et al. Health Assessment: A Modular Approach. Browning, Martha, ed. (Illus.). 1980. pap. text ed. 17.50 (ISBN 0-07-041027-5); ans. bklt. 6.95 (ISBN 0-07-041028-3). McGraw.
Mayhall, Carole, jt. auth. see Mayhall, Jack.
Mayhall, Jack & Mayhall, Carole. Amor Y Algo Mas. Carrodeguas, Andy & Marosi, Esteban, eds. De Powell, Elsie R., tr. Orig. Title: Marriage Takes More Than Love. 201p. 1982. pap. 2.25 (ISBN 0-8297-1209-7). Life Pubs Intl.
Mayhall, Jane. Givers & Takers 2. LC 68-55445. 78p. 1973. pap. 1.95 (ISBN 0-87130-033-8). Eakins.
Mayhall, P. D. & Geary, D. P. Community Relations & the Administration of Justice. 2nd ed. LC 78-135200. 1979. text ed. 22.95x (ISBN 0-471-04135-1); study guide 9.95x (ISBN 0-471-05314-7). Wiley.
Mayhar, Ardath. Golden Dream. Date not set. pap. price not set (Pub. by Ace Science Fiction). Ace Bks.
--Khi to Freedom. 1983. pap. 1.95 (ISBN 0-441-66957-3, Pub. by Ace Science Fiction). Ace Bks.
--Lords of the Triple Moons. LC 82-16241. 156p. (gr. 6 up). 1983. 10.95 (ISBN 0-689-30978-3, Argo). Atheneum.
--The Runes of the Lyre. LC 82-1730. 228p. 1982. 10.95 (ISBN 0-689-30932-5, Argo). Atheneum.
Mayhar, Ardath, jt. auth. see Dunn, Marylois.
Mayhead, Robin. John Keats. (British Authors Ser). (Orig.). 1967. 24.95 (ISBN 0-521-05706-X); pap. 8.95 (ISBN 0-521-09419-4). Cambridge U Pr.
--Understanding Literature. (Orig.). 1965. 34.50 (ISBN 0-521-05705-1); pap. 8.95 (ISBN 0-521-09282-5). Cambridge U Pr.
--Walter Scott. LC 72-88622. (British Authors Ser.). 128p. 1973. 27.95 (ISBN 0-521-20115-2); pap. 8.95 (ISBN 0-521-09781-9). Cambridge U Pr.
Mayhem, Y. R., jt. auth. see Rogers, G. F.
Mayhem, Y. R., jt. auth. see Rogers, G. R.
Mayhew, jt. auth. see Ince.
Mayhew, Catherine M. Genealogical Periodical Annual Index, Vol. 18, 1979. Towle, Laird C., ed. xiv, 179p. 1982. 15.00 (ISBN 0-917890-24-8). Heritage Bk.
Mayhew, Henry. London Labour & the London Poor, 4 vols. (Illus.). 1968. pap. 8.95 ea.; Vol. 1. pap. (ISBN 0-486-21934-8); Vol. 2. pap. (ISBN 0-486-21935-6); Vol. 3. pap. (ISBN 0-486-21936-4). Dover.
Mayhew, John. Hair Techniques & Alternatives to Baldness. (Illus.). 250p. 1983. 29.95 (ISBN 0-932426-25-5). Trado-Medic.
Mayhew, Lenore & McNaughton, William, trs. A Gold Orchid: Love Poems of Tsu Yeh. LC 72-79019. (Illus.). 1972. 6.25 (ISBN 0-8048-0211-4). C E Tuttle.
Mayhew, Lewis B., jt. auth. see Dressel, Paul L.
Mayhew, Vic & Long, Doug. Fireball. 1979. pap. 1.95 o.p. (ISBN 0-451-08701-1, J8701, Sig). NAL.
Mayhue, Richard. Divine Healing Today. 1983. pap. 5.95 (ISBN 0-8024-0453-7). Moody.
Mayio, Albert, jt. auth. see Morris, Milton D.
Maykapar, Samuel. Pedal Preludes. 32p. (gr. 4-12). 1974. pap. text ed. 5.05 (ISBN 0-87487-650-8). Summy.
Mayland, Hans J. The Complete Home Aquarium. LC 76-20307. (Illus.). 1981. pap. 10.95 (ISBN 0-448-12722-9, G&D). Putnam Pub Group.
Mayle, Peter. Chilly Billy. 1983. pap. 4.95 (ISBN 0-517-54959-X, Harmony). Crown.
--How to Be a Pregnant Father? 1977. 12.00 (ISBN 0-8184-0245-8). Lyle Stuart.
--What's Happening to Me? LC 75-14410. (Illus.). 56p. 1975. 12.00 (ISBN 0-8184-0221-0). Lyle Stuart.
--Where Did I Come From. 48p. 1973. 12.00 (ISBN 0-8184-0161-3). Lyle Stuart.
Mayle, Peter & Robbins, Arthur. Grownups & Other Problems: Help for Small People in a Big World. (Illus.). 64p. 1983. 12.50 (ISBN 0-02-582550-X). Macmillan.
Maynard, Christopher. All About Ghosts. LC 77-17613. (The World of the Unknown). (Illus.). (gr. 4-5). 1978. PLB 7.95 (ISBN 0-88436-469-0). EMC.
--Exploring the Great Ice Age. LC 78-67833. (Explorer Bks.). (Illus.). (gr. 3-5). 1979. 2.95 (ISBN 0-531-09128-7, Warwick Press); PLB 7.90 s&l (ISBN 0-531-09113-9). Watts.
--The Young Scientist Book of Stars & Planets. LC 78-17545. (Young Scientist Ser.). (Illus.). (gr. 3-5). 1978. text ed. 7.95 (ISBN 0-88436-528-X). EMC.
Maynard, Christopher, jt. auth. see Holmes, Edward.
Maynard, D. N., jt. auth. see Lorenzo, O. A.
Maynard, Geoffrey. Economic Development & the Price Level. LC 72-85018. (Reprints of Economic Classics). (Illus.). 1972. Repr. of 1962 ed. lib. bdg. 25.00x (ISBN 0-678-07016-4). Kelley.
Maynard, Glenn, jt. auth. see Behrens, Herman D.
Maynard, Harold B. Handbook of Business Administration. 1967. 76.95 (ISBN 0-07-041090-9, P&RB). McGraw.
--Handbook of Modern Manufacturing Management. 1970. 72.50 o.p. (ISBN 0-07-041087-9, P&RB). McGraw.
--Industrial Engineering Handbook. 3rd ed. 1971. 72.95 (ISBN 0-07-041084-4, P&RB). McGraw.
--Top Management Handbook. 1960. 72.95 (ISBN 0-07-041085-2, P&RB). McGraw.
Maynard, L. A., et al. Animal Nutrition. 7th ed. (Illus.). 1979. text ed. 32.50 (ISBN 0-07-041049-6, C). McGraw.
Maynard, Leonard A. & Loosli, J. K. Animal Nutrition. 6th ed. (Agricultural Sciences Ser.). 1969. text ed. 19.50 o.p. (ISBN 0-07-041048-8, C). McGraw.
Maynard, Richard. Celluloid Curriculum: How to Use Movies in the Classroom. (Film Attitudes & Issues Ser.). 1971. 9.15x o.p. (ISBN 0-8104-5893-4); pap. 6.85x o.p. (ISBN 0-8104-5892-6). Boynton Cook Pubs.
Mayne, A. Database Management Systems: A Technical Review. 220p. 1982. pap. 35.00x (ISBN 0-85012-323-2). Intl Pubns Serv.
Mayne, A. J. Fever, Squalor & Vice: Sanitation & Social Policy in Victorian Sydney. LC 82-2054. (Scholars' Library). (Illus.). 263p. 1982. text ed. 34.50x (ISBN 0-7022-1950-9). U of Queensland Pr.
Mayne, Alan J. The Videotex Revolution. 1982. 95.00x (ISBN 0-686-94055-5, Pub. by October Pr). State Mutual Bk.
Mayne, Lynn. Fabric Games. 1978. 12.95 o.s.i. (ISBN 0-395-27084-7); pap. 6.95 o.s.i. (ISBN 0-395-27209-2). HM.
Mayne, R. & Margolis, S. Introduction to Engineering. 1982. 22.50 (ISBN 0-07-041137-9); solutions manual 10.00 (ISBN 0-07-041138-7). McGraw.
Mayne, Richard. The Europeans. LC 70-39632. 206p. 1972. 15.50x (ISBN 0-912050-22-5, Library Pr). Open Court.
Mayne, Roger, jt. auth. see Jellicoe, Ann.
Mayne, William. The Patchwork Cat. LC 81-3735. (Illus.). 32p. (ps-3). 1981. 8.95 (ISBN 0-394-85021-1); PLB 9.99 (ISBN 0-394-95021-6). Knopf.
Maynes, E. Scott. Decision Making for Consumers. 1976. 21.95x (ISBN 0-02-378300-1). Macmillan.
Maynes, J. O. Hispanic Heroes of the U.S.A. (English Version, 4 bks. Incl. Bk. 1. Raul H. Castro, Tony Nunez, & Vikki Carr. LC 75-40234. PLB 6.95 (ISBN 0-88436-240-X); pap. 3.95 (ISBN 0-88436-241-8); Bk. 2. Henry Gonzalez, Trini Lopez, & Edward Roybal. LC 75-40232. PLB 6.95 (ISBN 0-88436-242-6); pap. 3.95 (ISBN 0-88436-243-4); Bk. 3. Carmen R. Maymi, Roberto Clemente, & Jose Feliciano. LC 75-40230. PLB 6.95 (ISBN 0-88436-244-2); pap. 3.95 (ISBN 0-88436-245-0); Bk. 4. Tony Perez, Lee Trevino, Jim Plunkett. LC 75-40231. PLB 5.95 o.p. (ISBN 0-88436-246-9); pap. 3.95 (ISBN 0-88436-247-7). (Illus.). 48p. (gr. 4-10). 1975. EMC.
--Ilustres Hispanos De los Estados Unidos. Incl. Bk. 1. Raul Castro, Tony Nunez, & Vikke Carr. PLB 6.95 (ISBN 0-88436-248-5); pap. 3.95 (ISBN 0-88436-249-3); Bk. 2. Henry Gonzalez, Trini Lopez, & Edward Roybal. PLB 6.95 (ISBN 0-88436-250-7); pap. 3.95 (ISBN 0-88436-251-5); Bk. 3. Carmen Maymi, Roberto Clemente, & Jose Feliciano. PLB 6.95 (ISBN 0-88436-252-3); pap. 3.95 (ISBN 0-88436-253-1); Bk. 4. Tony Perez, Lee Trevino, Jim Plunkett. PLB 6.95 (ISBN 0-88436-254-X); pap. 3.95 (ISBN 0-88436-255-8). (Illus.). 48p. (gr. 4-10). 1975. EMC.
Mayo, jt. auth. see Shank, W. H.
Mayo, A. History of Mexico: From Pre-Columbia to Present. 1978. 17.95 (ISBN 0-13-390203-X). P-H.
Mayo, Bernard, ed. Instructions to the British Ministers to the United States, 1791-1812. LC 70-75280. (Law, Politics & History Ser). 1971. lib. bdg. 55.00 (ISBN 0-306-71303-9). Da Capo.
Mayo, Clark. Kurt Vonnegut: The Gospel from Outer Space or, Yes We Have No Nirvanas. LC 77-24460. (The Milford Ser: Popular Writers of Today Vol. 7). 1977. lib. bdg. 9.95x (ISBN 0-89370-111-4); pap. 3.95x (ISBN 0-89370-211-0). Borgo Pr.
Mayo, Henry B. Introduction to Democratic Theory. 1960. pap. 6.95x (ISBN 0-19-500965-7). Oxford U Pr.
Mayo, Margaret. L'Ete Commence A Peine. (Collection Harlequin Ser.). 192p. 1983. pap. 1.95 (ISBN 0-373-49333-9). Harlequin Bks.
Mayo, Marjorie, jt. auth. see Jones, David.
Mayo, Patricia T. The Sugarless Baking Book: The Natural Way to Prepare America's Favorite Breads, Pies, Cakes, Puddings & Desserts. LC 82-42757. (Illus.). 116p. (Orig.). 1983. pap. 4.95 (ISBN 0-394-71429-6). Shambhala Pubns.
Mayo, R. Britton & Social Systems, Inc. Corporate Planning & Modeling with Simplan. 1978. pap. text ed. 25.00 (ISBN 0-201-05227-X). A-W.
Mayo, S. M. The Relevance of the Old Testament for the Christian Faith: Biblical Theology & Interpretive Methodology. 228p. (Orig.). 1982. lib. bdg. 22.00 (ISBN 0-8191-2656-X); pap. text ed. 10.75 (ISBN 0-8191-2657-8). U Pr of Amer.
Mayo, Welington de see Palis, Jacob, Jr. & De Mayo, Welington.
Mayor, A. Hyatt. Prints & People. (Illus.). 1972. Repr. of 1972 ed. 37.50 (ISBN 0-87099-108-6); pap. 12.95 (ISBN 0-691-00326-2). Hispanic Soc.
Mayor, A. Hyatt, ed. see Faithorne, W.
Mayor, Andreas, tr. see Proust, Marcel.
Mayor, F., ed. Scientific Research & Social Goals: Toward a New Development Model. 248p. 1982. 35.00 (ISBN 0-08-028118-4). Pergamon.
Mayor, Georges & Zingg, Ernst J. Urologic Surgery: Diagnosis, Techniques Postoperative Treatment. 1976. 175.00 o.p. (ISBN 0-471-01408-7, Pub. by Wiley Medical). Wiley.
Mayor, Joseph B. The Epistle of Saint James. 1977. 20.25 (ISBN 0-86524-971-7, 5902). Klock & Klock.
--The Epistle of St. Jude & the Second Epistle of Peter. 1978. 16.50 (ISBN 0-86524-115-5, 7101). Klock & Klock.
Mayorcas, M. J. English Needlework Carpets, 16th-19th Centuries. (Illus.). 1963. 33.50x (ISBN 0-87245-210-7). Textile Bk.
Mayo-Smith, Ian. Guidelines to Writing Official Reports. (Guideline Ser.). 34p. (Orig.). 1978. pap. 2.25x (ISBN 0-931816-00-9). Kumarian Pr.
--Managing People: Three International Case Studies. 12p. (Orig.). 1981. pap. 3.95x (ISBN 0-931816-12-2). Kumarian Pr.
Maypole, Donald E., jt. auth. see Keefe, Thomas.
Mayr, D. & Sussmann, G. Space, Time, & Mechanics. 1983. lib. bdg. 34.95 (ISBN 90-277-1525-4, Pub. by Reidel Holland). Kluwer Boston.
Mayr, Ernst. Birds of the Southwest Pacific. (Illus.). 1968. pap. 13.50 (ISBN 3-7682-0533-9). Lubrecht & Cramer.
--Principles of Systematic Zoology. LC 68-54937. (Illus.). 1969. text ed. 42.50 (ISBN 0-07-041143-3, C). McGraw.
Mayr, Ernst & Short, Lester L. Species Taxa of North American Birds: A Contribution to Comparative Systematics. (Illus.). 127p. 1970. 7.00 (ISBN 0-686-35797-3). Nuttall Ornithological.
Mayr, Marlene. Modern Masters of Religious Education. 380p. (Orig.). 1983. pap. 14.95 (ISBN 0-89135-033-0). Religious Educ.
Mayr, Otto. Origins of Feedback Control. 1970. 8.95x o.p. (ISBN 0-262-13067-X); pap. 3.95x (ISBN 0-262-63056-7). MIT Pr.
Mayr, Otto, jt. auth. see Maurice, Klaus.
Mayr-Harting, Henry. The Coming of Christianity to England. LC 74-169818. (Fabric of British History Ser). (Illus.). 300p. 1972. 12.50x o.p. (ISBN 0-8052-3436-5). Schocken.
Mayrhofer, '. & Poelt, J. Die Saxicolen Arten der Flechtengattung Rinodina in Europa. (Bibliotheca Lichenologica: No. 12). (Illus., Ger.). 1979. lib. bdg. 24.00 (ISBN 3-7682-1237-8). Lubrecht & Cramer.
Mayros & Werner. Data Bases for Business: A Manager's Guide. LC 82-70653. 224p. 1982. 27.50 (ISBN 0-8019-7255-8); pap. 19.95 (ISBN 0-8019-7256-6). Chilton.
Mayros, Van & Werner, D. M. Data Basis for Business. 224p. 1982. 27.50 (ISBN 0-8019-7256-6); pap. 19.95 (ISBN 0-686-82152-1). Chilton.
Mayrose, V., jt. auth. see Battaglia, R. A.
Mays, Buddy. Ancient Cities of the Southwest. LC 81-21732. (Illus.). 120p. 1982. pap. 7.95 (ISBN 0-87701-191-5). Chronicle Bks.
Mays, Carl. Celebration: A Writer in Search of a Play. 1972. pap. 1.50 (ISBN 0-8054-9720-X). Broadman.
Mays, David, ed. see Barton, Andrew.
Mays, James L. Leviticus, Numbers. LC 59-10454. (Layman's Bible Commentary Ser: Vol. 4). 1963. pap. 3.95 (ISBN 0-8042-3064-1). John Knox.
Mays, James L., jt. ed. see Westermann, Claus.
Mays, James L., ed. see Williamson, Lamar, Jr.
Mays, Jeb & Wheaton, Philip, eds. Jamaica: Caribbean Challenge. (Illus.). 119p. 1979. pap. text ed. 3.75 o.s.i. (ISBN 0-918346-03-7). EPICA.
Mays, John, et al, eds. Penelope Hall's Social Services of England & Wales. 9th ed. (International Library of Sociology). 352p. 1975. 22.50x o.p. (ISBN 0-7100-8251-7). Routledge & Kegan.
Mays, Laura. Genetics: A Molecular Approach. 1981. text ed. 26.95x (ISBN 0-02-378320-6). Macmillan.
Mays, Lois B. Settlers of the Okefenokee. 208p. 1975. 7.95x (ISBN 0-9601606-0-4). Okefenokee Pr.
Mays, Madeleine. Dot to Dot. (gr. 2up). pap. 0.99 (ISBN 0-695-90165-6, Dist. by Caroline Hse). Follett.
--Fun with Dots. (gr. 2up). pap. 0.99 (ISBN 0-695-90255-5, Dist. by Caroline Hse). Follett.
Mays, Willie & Berger, Maxine. Willie Mays, "Play Ball!". LC 80-13352. (Illus.). 160p. (gr. 7 up). 1980. PLB 8.29 o.p. (ISBN 0-671-41314-7). Messner.
Mays, Willie & Einstein, Charles. Born to Play Ball. (Putnam Sport Shelf). (Illus.). 1955. PLB 6.29 o.p. (ISBN 0-399-10900-5). Putnam Pub Group.
Mays, Wolfe, tr. see Piaget, Jean.
Mayston, David J. The Idea of Social Choice. LC 71-24815. 96p. 1975. text ed. 20.00 (ISBN 0-312-40425-5). St Martin.
Mazar, Benjamin & Avi-Yonah, Michael. Illustrated World of the Bible Library, 5 vols. Incl. Vol. 1. The Laws. 40.00 (ISBN 0-8088-1167-3); Vol. 2. The Early Prophets. 40.00 (ISBN 0-8088-1168-1); Vol. 3. The Late Prophets. 40.00 (ISBN 0-8088-1169-X); Vol. 4. The Writings. 40.00 (ISBN 0-8088-1170-3); Vol. 5. The New Testament. Avi-Yonah, Michael. 40.00 (ISBN 0-8088-1171-1). 1961. Vols. 1-4. old testament ed. 160.00 (ISBN 0-8088-1080-4); Vols. 1-5. new testament ed. 200.00 (ISBN 0-8088-1081-2). Davey.
Mazda, F. F. Discrete Electronic Components. 200p. 1981. 39.95 (ISBN 0-521-23470-0). Cambridge U Pr.
--Integrated Circuits. LC 77-71418. (Illus.). 1978. 39.50 (ISBN 0-521-21658-3). Cambridge U Pr.
Maze, J. R. The Meaning of Behavior. 216p. 1983. text ed. 29.50x (ISBN 0-04-150081-4). Allen Unwin.
Mazel, Judy & Schultz, Susan. Beverly Hills Diet Lifetime Plan. 1983. pap. 3.95 (ISBN 0-686-43053-0). Bantam.

Mazer, Bill. Answer Book of Sports. Duroska, Lud, ed. LC 72-86698. (Illus.). (gr. 6 up). 1969. 6.95 (ISBN 0-448-04475-7, G&D). Putnam Pub Group.
--The New Answer Book of Sports. LC 82-81047. (Illus.). 160p. (gr. 8 up). 1982. pap. 5.95 (ISBN 0-448-04474-9, G&D). Putnam Pub Group.
--Sports Answer Book. (gr. 6 up). 1966. 5.95 o.s.i. (ISBN 0-448-01163-8, G&D). Putnam Pub Group.
Mazer, Bill & Fischler, Stan. The Amazin' Bill Mazer's Baseball Trivia Book. 224p. (Orig.). 1981. pap. 2.50 o.s.i. (ISBN 0-446-91784-2). Warner Bks.
Mazer, Harry. I Love You, Stupid! 192p. 1983. pap. 2.50 (ISBN 0-380-61432-4, 61432, Flare). Avon.
--The Last Mission. LC 79-50674. (gr. 7 up). 1979. 7.95 o.s.i. (ISBN 0-440-05774-4). Delacorte.
--Snow Bound. LC 72-7958. 128p. (gr. 5-9). 1973. 9.95 o.s.i. (ISBN 0-440-08087-8). Delacorte.
--Snow Bound. 144p. 1975. pap. 1.95 (ISBN 0-440-96134-3, LFL). Dell.
--The War on Villa Street: A Novel. LC 78-50454. (gr. 7 up). 1978. 7.95 o.s.i. (ISBN 0-440-09349-X). Delacorte.
Mazer, Norma. A Figure of Speech. LC 73-6239. 192p. (gr. 7 up). 1973. 8.95 o.s.i. (ISBN 0-440-02638-5). Delacorte.
--I, Trissy. LC 72-156047. (gr. 4-7). 1971. 6.95 o.s.i. (ISBN 0-440-03986-X); PLB 6.46 o.s.i. (ISBN 0-440-03997-5). Delacorte.
Mazer, Norma F. Saturday, the Twelfth of October. LC 75-8006. 240p. (gr. 7 up). 1975. 7.95 o.s.i. (ISBN 0-440-05947-X). Delacorte.
--Saturday, the Twelfth of October. 1976. pap. 2.25 (ISBN 0-440-99592-2, LFL). Dell.
--Someone to Love. LC 82-72755. 240p. (YA) (gr. 10 up). 1983. 13.95 (ISBN 0-440-08311-7). Delacorte.
--When We First Met. (YA) (gr. 7 up). Date not set. 9.95 (ISBN 0-686-42719-X, Four Winds). Schol Bk Serv.
Mazja, W. G., jt. auth. see Gelman, I. W.
Mazlack, L. J. PL-C Essentials. text ed. 18.95 (ISBN 0-07-041170-0). McGraw.
Mazliak, P. Biogenesis & Function of Plant Lipids: Proceedings of the Paris Meeting, June 1980. (Developments in Plant Biology Ser.: Vol. 6). 1980. 80.50 (ISBN 0-444-80273-8). Elsevier.
Mazlish, Bruce & Diamond, Ed. Jimmy Carter. 1980. 11.95 o.p. (ISBN 0-671-22763-7). S&S.
Mazlish, Bruce, ed. Railroad & the Space Program: An Exploration in Historical Analogy. 1965. 18.00x o.p. (ISBN 0-262-13021-1). MIT Pr.
Mazlish, Elaine, jt. auth. see Faber, Adele.
Mazmanian, Daniel & Sabatier, Paul, eds. Successful Policy Implementation. (Orig.). 1980. pap. 6.00 (ISBN 0-918592-37-2). Policy Studies.
Mazmanian, Daniel & Sabatier, Paul A., eds. Effective Policy Implementation. LC 79-3041. (Policy Study Organization Bks.). 240p. 1981. 25.95x (ISBN 0-669-03311-1). Lexington Bks.
Mazmanian, Daniel A. Third Parties in Presidential Elections. LC 74-281. (Studies in Presidential Selection). 140p. 1974. 14.95 (ISBN 0-8157-5522-8); pap. 5.95 (ISBN 0-8157-5521-X). Brookings.
Mazmanian, Daniel A. & Nienaber, Jeanne. Can Organizations Change? Environmental Protection, Citizen Participation, & the Army Corps of Engineers. 1979. 22.95 (ISBN 0-8157-5524-4); pap. 8.95 (ISBN 0-8157-5523-6). Brookings.
Mazmanian, Daniel A. & Sebatier, Paul A. Implementation & Public Policy. 1983. 11.95x (ISBN 0-673-16561-2). Scott F.
Mazo, Joseph H. Dance Is a Contact Sport. LC 76-6557. (Paperback Ser.). 1976. pap. 7.95 (ISBN 0-306-80044-6). Da Capo.
--Prime Movers: The Makers of Modern Dance in America. LC 82-62346. (Illus.). 322p. 1983. pap. text ed. 12.95x (ISBN 0-916622-27-4). Princeton Bk Co.
Mazor, L. Analytical Chemistry of Organic Halogen Compounds. LC 75-5934. 400p. 1976. text ed. 54.00 (ISBN 0-08-017903-7). Pergamon.
Mazour, Anatole G. Modern Russian Historiography. rev. ed. LC 75-16962. (Illus.). 224p. 1975. lib. bdg. 27.50 (ISBN 0-8371-8285-9, MRH/). Greenwood.
Mazow, Julia W., ed. The Woman Who Lost Her Names: Selected Writings by American Jewish Women. LC 79-2986. 240p. 1981. pap. text ed. 6.68i (ISBN 0-06-250567-X, CN 4017, HarpR). Har-Row.
Mazria, Edward. The Passive Solar Energy Book. 1979. 16.95 o.p. (ISBN 0-87857-260-0); pap. 14.95 (ISBN 0-87857-238-4); professional 29.95 (ISBN 0-87857-237-6). Rodale Pr Inc.
Mazrui, A. The African Condition. LC 79-9657. 192p. 1980. 22.95 (ISBN 0-521-23265-1); pap. 7.95 (ISBN 0-521-29884-9). Cambridge U Pr.
Mazrui, Ali A. Africa's International Relations: The Diplomacy of Dependency & Change. LC 77-595. 1978. pap. 15.00 o.p. (ISBN 0-89158-671-7). Westview.
--Political Values & the Educated Class in Africa. LC 76-19999. 1978. 34.50x (ISBN 0-520-03292-6). U of Cal Pr.
Mazumdar, Dipak. Paradigmsin the Study of Urban Labor Markets in LDCs: A Reassessment in the Light of an Empirical Survey in Bombay City. (Working Paper: No. 366). ii, 49p. 1979. 3.00 (ISBN 0-686-36090-7, WP-0366). World Bank.
Mazumdar, Maxim. Dance for Gods. (Drama Ser.). 1981. pap. 4.95 (ISBN 0-686-30997-9, Pub. by Personal Lib). Dodd.
--Invitation to the Dance. (Drama Ser.). 96p. 1981. pap. 6.95 (ISBN 0-920510-25-6, Pub. by Personal Lib). Dodd.
--Oscar Remembered. (Drama Ser.). 72p. 1981. pap. 6.95 (ISBN 0-920510-00-0, Pub. by Personal Lib). Dodd.
Mazur, B. see Zariski, Oscar.
Mazur, B. W. Colloquial Polish. (Colloquial Ser.). 224p. 1983. pap. 12.95 (ISBN 0-7100-9030-7). Routledge & Kegan.
Mazur, Ken, ed. The Creative TRS-Eighty. (Illus.). 250p. 1983. pap. 15.95 (ISBN 0-916688-36-4). Creative Comp.
Mazur, Mary Ann, jt. auth. see Katz, Sedelle.
Mazur, Michael P. Economic Growth & Development in Jordan. (Special Studies on the Middle East). 1979. lib. bdg. 33.50 (ISBN 0-89158-455-2). Westview.
Mazure, F. A. Vie De Voltaire. Repr. of 1821 ed. 100.00 o.p. (ISBN 0-8287-0595-X). Clearwater Pub.
Mazurkiewicz, B. K. Design & Construction of Dry Docks. 390p. 1981. 54.95x (ISBN 0-87201-209-3). Gulf Pub.
Mazursky, Paul & Capetanos, Leon. Tempest: A Screenplay. LC 82-81975. (Illus.). 1982. 11.95 (ISBN 0-933826-40-0); pap. 4.95 (ISBN 0-933826-41-9). Performing Arts.
Mazuzan, George T., jt. ed. see Fausold, Martin L.
Mazzaferri, Ernest L. Endocrinology Case Studies. 3rd ed. 1981. pap. 32.50 (ISBN 0-87488-008-4). Med Exam.
Mazzaferri, Ernest L., ed. Endocrinology: A Review of Clinical Endocrinology. LC 79-91978. (Medical Outline Ser). 1980. pap. 26.50 (ISBN 0-87488-614-7). Med Exam.
Mazzaoui, Maureen F. The Italian Cotton Industry in the Later Middle Ages: 1100 to 1600. LC 80-41023. (Illus.). 272p. 1981. 54.50 (ISBN 0-521-23095-0). Cambridge U Pr.
Mazzara, Laure, jt. auth. see Moreau, Jean-Francois.
Mazzara, Richard A., tr. see Rodrigues, Jose H.
Mazzarino, Santo. The End of the Ancient World. LC 76-7479. 1976. Repr. of 1966 ed. lib. bdg. 16.25x (ISBN 0-8371-8864-4, MAEW). Greenwood.
Mazze, Edward. Personal Selling: Choice Against Chance. LC 75-35859. (Illus.). 350p. 1976. pap. text ed. 16.50 (ISBN 0-8299-0067-5); pap. text ed. 9.95 (ISBN 0-8299-0114-0). West Pub.
Mazzella, Donald P. Landing That Job. (Illus.). 160p. 1983. 9.95 (ISBN 0-87396-085-8). Stravon.
Mazzeo, jt. auth. see Kisselle.
Mazzeo, Donatella & Antonini, Chiara S. Ancient Cambodia. (Monuments of Civilization Ser.). (Illus.). 1978. Repr. of 1972 ed. 25.00 (ISBN 0-448-02026-2, G&D). Putnam Pub Group.
Mazzeo, Joseph A. Medieval Cultural Tradition in Dante's Comedy. LC 68-23313. (Illus.). 1968. Repr. of 1960 ed. lib. bdg. 20.00x (ISBN 0-8371-0166-2, MADC). Greenwood.
Mazzini, Giuseppe. Mazzini's Letters. Jervis, Alice D., tr. from Ital. LC 78-27617. 1979. Repr. of 1930 ed. lib. bdg. 18.75x (ISBN 0-313-20934-0, MALR). Greenwood.
--Selected Writings. Gangulee, N., ed. LC 74-9397. (Illus.). 253p. 1974. Repr. of 1945 ed. lib. bdg. 15.50x (ISBN 0-8371-7664-6, MASW). Greenwood.
Mazzola, Reparata & Gibson, Sonny. Mafia Kingpin. LC 81-47703. (Illus.). 512p. 1981. 14.95 (ISBN 0-448-11990-0, G&D). Putnam Pub Group.
Mazzolini, R. Government Controlled Enterprises: International Strategic & Policy Decisions. LC 78-10961. 1979. 53.95 (ISBN 0-471-99727-7, Pub. by Wiley-Interscience). Wiley.
Mazzoni, Tim L., Jr., jt. auth. see Campbell, Roald F.
Mazzullo, Sal, jt. ed. see Zenger, Donald.
Mba, Nina E. Nigerian Women Mobilized: Women's Political Activity in Southern Nigeria, 1900-1965. LC 82-15477. (Illus.). xii, 348p. 1982. pap. 12.95x (ISBN 0-87725-148-7). UCB Intl Studies.
Mberi, Antar S. A Song Out of Harlem. LC 80-12500. (Vox Humana Ser.). 96p. 1980. 8.95 (ISBN 0-89603-018-0); pap. 3.50 (ISBN 0-89603-021-0). Humana.
Meacham, Beth, jt. auth. see Searles, Baird.
Meacham, J. A., jt. ed. see Kuhn, D.
Meacham, Mary, ed. Reading for Young People: The Northwest. LC 80-24192. 152p. 1981. pap. 11.00 (ISBN 0-8389-0318-5). ALA.
Meachem, William A. Easy Guide to African Violets. rev. ed. 2.95 (ISBN 0-8208-0002-3). Hearthside.
Mead. Pardon Me Dearie--Your Values Are Showing. 1979. pap. 2.95 (ISBN 0-8423-4832-8). Tyndale.
Mead, C. David, jt. auth. see Wagner, Linda W.
Mead, Carver & Conway, Lynn. Introduction to VLSI Systems. LC 78-74688. 1979. text ed. 33.95 (ISBN 0-201-04358-0). A-W.
Mead, Daniel R. Encyclopedia of Slot Machines. (Illus.). 300p. 1983. write for info (ISBN 0-934422-17-6). Mead Co.
Mead, Edna. The Bronx Triangle: A Portrait of Norwood. Hermalyn, Gary & Ultan, Lloyd, eds. (Illus.). 141p. 1982. 9.95 (ISBN 0-941980-09-X). Bronx County.
Mead, Frank S. Encyclopedia of Religious Quotations. 1976. pap. 2.50 o.s.i. (ISBN 0-89129-194-6). Jove Pubns.
--Handbook of Denominations in the United States. 7th ed. LC 79-20252. 1980. 8.95 (ISBN 0-687-16570-9). Abingdon.
Mead, Frank S. & Barker, William P., eds. Tarbell's Teacher's Guide, 1983 to 1984. 416p. 1982. pap. 6.95 (ISBN 0-8007-1347-8). Revell.
--Tarbell's Teacher's Guide 1983-1984. (Tarbell's Teacher's Guide Ser.: Vol. 79). 320p. (Orig.). 1983. pap. 6.95 (ISBN 0-8007-1347-8). Revell.
Mead, G. R. Fragments of a Faith Forgotten, 3 Vols. 1982. Vol 1, 192pp. text ed. 13.50 (ISBN 0-7224-0211-2); Vol 2, 302pp. text ed. 18.95 (ISBN 0-7224-0212-0); Vol 3, 216pp. text ed. 13.50 (ISBN 0-7224-0213-9). Robinson & Watkins.
--Pistis Sophia. 216p. 1982. pap. 22.95 (ISBN 0-7224-0214-7). Robinson & Watkins.
Mead, George C., jt. auth. see Miller, Herbert E.
Mead, George H. Philosophy of the Present. Murphy, Arthur E., ed. (Paul Carus Lecture Ser.). xl, 239p. 1959. 16.00x (ISBN 0-87548-103-5). Open Court.
Mead, Gilbert D., ed. Pioneer Ten Mission: Jupiter Encounter. (Illus.). 1974. pap. 5.00 o.p. (ISBN 0-87590-219-7). Am Geophysical.
Mead, H. T. & Mitchell, G. L. Plant Hire for Building & Construction. 1972. text ed. 29.95 (ISBN 0-408-00080-5). Butterworth.
Mead, Jean. Wyoming in Profile. (Illus.). 250p. 1982. 16.95 (ISBN 0-87108-600-X); pap. 7.95 (ISBN 0-87108-601-8). Pruett.
Mead, Leon & Newell, Gilbert F. Manual of Forensic Quotations. LC 68-26591. 1968. Repr. of 1903 ed. 30.00x (ISBN 0-8103-3188-8). Gale.
Mead, Lucia A. Swords & Ploughshares; or, the Supplanting of the System of War by the System of Law. LC 71-143431. (Peace Movement in America Ser.). xiv, 249p. 1972. Repr. of 1912 ed. lib. bdg. 16.95x (ISBN 0-89198-079-2). Ozer.
Mead, Majorie L., ed. see Lewis, Warren H.
Mead, Margaret. Coming of Age in Samoa. 1971. pap. 6.95 (ISBN 0-688-30974-7). Morrow.
--Letters from the Field: Nineteen Twenty-Five to Nineteen Seventy-Five. Anshen, Ruth N., ed. LC 73-4110. (World Perspectives Ser.). (Illus.). 1978. 14.37i (ISBN 0-06-012961-1, HarpT). Har-Row.
--New Lives for Old. LC 75-21699. 576p. 1976. pap. 9.95 (ISBN 0-688-07169-4). Morrow.
--The School in American Culture. LC 51-9913. (Inglis Lectures Ser: 1950). 1951. 5.95x o.p. (ISBN 0-674-79260-2). Harvard U Pr.
--Soviet Attitudes Toward Authority: An Interdisciplinary Approach to Problems of Soviet Character. LC 78-10846. 1979. Repr. of 1951 ed. lib. bdg. 16.00x (ISBN 0-313-21081-0, MESO). Greenwood.
Mead, Matthew. Identities & Other Poems. 1971. pap. 2.95 o.p. (ISBN 0-85391-047-2). Transatlantic.
Mead, Rita. Henry Cowell's New Music, 1925-1936: The Society, the Music Editions, & the Recordings. Buelow, George, ed. (Studies in Musicology: No. 40). 636p. 1981. 69.95 (ISBN 0-8357-1170-6, Pub. by UMI Res Pr). Univ Microfilms.
Mead, Robert D. The Canoer's Bible. LC 74-33610. 176p. 1976. pap. 4.95 (ISBN 0-385-07276-7). Doubleday.
--Hellas & Rome: The Story of Greco-Roman Civilization. 1972. pap. 1.95 o.p. (ISBN 0-451-61146-2, MJ1146, Ment); tchr's. manual 1.00 o.p. (ISBN 0-451-61185-3, MN1185). NAL.
Mead, Russel. The Moses Bottle. (Raven House Mysteries Ser.). 224p. 1981. pap. 2.25 (ISBN 0-373-63003-4). Harlequin Bks.
Mead, Russell. The Third One. (Raven House Mysteries Ser.). 224p. 1983. pap. cancelled (ISBN 0-373-63056-5, Pub. by Worldwide). Harlequin Bks.
Mead, S. M., et al. The Lapita Pottery Style of Fiji & Its Associations. 1975. text ed. 12.50x o.p. (ISBN 0-8248-0590-9). UH Pr.
Mead, Shepherd, jt. auth. see Williams, Dakin.
Mead, Sidney. The Old Religion in the Brave New World: Reflections on the Relation Between Christendom & the Republic. LC 76-24588. (Jefferson Memorial Lecture). 1977. 13.95x (ISBN 0-520-03322-1). U of Cal Pr.
Mead, Sidney M., ed. Exploring the Visual Art of Oceania. LC 79-12707. (Illus.). 1979. text ed. 25.00x (ISBN 0-8248-0598-4). UH Pr.
Mead, W. L. & Institute of Petroleum, eds. Advances in Mass Spectrometry. (Vol. 3). 1966. 90.25 (ISBN 0-444-39973-9). Elsevier.
Mead, Walter J., jt. ed. see Utton, Albert E.
Mead, William B., jt. auth. see Feinsilber, Mike.
Meade, Andre T., jt. auth. see Friedman, Carol A.
Meade, Chris. Careers with a Railroad. LC 74-11906. (Early Career Bks.). (Illus.). 36p. (gr. 2-5). 1975. PLB 5.95g (ISBN 0-8225-0325-5). Lerner Pubns.
Meade, Frank H. & Zimmerman, Arnold W., eds. Illustrated Study Bible. LC 72-9567. (Illus.). 192p. 1973. tanalin 5.95 o.p. (ISBN 0-8170-0583-8). Judson.
Meade, George P. & Chen, James C. Cane Sugar Handbook: A Manual for Cane Sugar Maufacturers & Their Chemists. 10th ed. LC 76-51046. 1977. 95.00 (ISBN 0-471-58995-0, Pub. by Wiley-Interscience). Wiley.
Meade, J. E. The Stationary Economy: Vol. 1, the Principles of Political Economy. 1966. pap. text ed. 11.50x (ISBN 0-04-330065-0). Allen Unwin.
Meade, James E. Principles of Political Economy, 4 vols. Incl. Vol. 1. The Stationary Economy. LC 65-26549. 1965. 21.50x o.p. (ISBN 0-87395-202-2); Vol. 2. The Growing Economy. LC 79-26549. 1968. 44.50x (ISBN 0-87395-203-0); Vol. 3. The Controlled Economy. LC 79-37998. 1972. 45.50x (ISBN 0-87395-204-9); Vol. 4. The Just Economy. LC 65-26549. 1976. 34.50x (ISBN 0-87395-205-7). State U NY Pr.
--The Theory of Customs Unions. LC 80-10885. (Professor Dr. F. De Vries Lectures). 121p. 1980. Repr. of 1955 ed. lib. bdg. 16.25x (ISBN 0-313-22379-3, METC). Greenwood.
Meade, L. E., intro. by. Material & Process Advances '82. (National SAMPE Technical Conference Ser.). (Illus.). 1982. 60.00 (ISBN 0-938994-21-2). Soc Adv Material.
Meade, M. Stealing Heaven: The Love Story of Heloise & Abelard. LC 79-1182. 1979. 10.95 o.p. (ISBN 0-688-03477-2). Morrow.
Meade, Marion. Eleanor of Aquitaine: A Biography. Orig. Title: Eagle in the Court of Love: the Life of Eleanor of Aquitaine. (Illus.). 1977. 13.95 (ISBN 0-8015-2231-5, Hawthorn). Dutton.
--Eleanor of Aquitaine: A Biography. (Illus.). 1980. pap. 9.95 (ISBN 0-8015-2232-3, 0966-290, Hawthorn). Dutton.
--Madame Blavatsky: The Woman Behind the Myth. (Illus.). 1980. 19.95 o.p. (ISBN 0-399-12376-8). Putnam Pub Group.
--Sybille. Golbitz, Pat, ed. 432p. 1983. 15.95 (ISBN 0-688-00808-9). Morrow.
Meade, P. J. Meteorological Aspects of Peaceful Uses of Atomic Energy, Pt. 1. (Technical Note Ser.). 1968. pap. 7.00 (ISBN 0-685-22320-5, W13, WMO). Unipub.
Meade, Richard. Big Bend. 1981. pap. 1.95 o.p. (ISBN 0-451-09981-8, J9981, Sig). NAL.
Meader, Robert E. Iranxe: Notas Gramaticais e Lista Vocabular. 193p. 1967. pap. 2.00x (ISBN 0-88312-777-6); microfiche 2.25 (ISBN 0-88312-397-5). Summer Inst Ling.
Meader, Stephen W. Lumberjack. LC 34-31292. (Illus.). (gr. 7-9). 1934. 4.95 o.p. (ISBN 0-15-249904-0, HJ). HarBraceJ.
--Sparkplug of the Hornets. LC 53-7868. (Illus.). (gr. 7 up). 1968. pap. 0.75 (ISBN 0-15-684710-8, VoyB). HarBraceJ.
--Who Rides in the Dark? LC 37-27469. (Illus.). (gr. 7 up). 1966. pap. 0.75 (ISBN 0-15-696315-9, VoyB). HarBraceJ.
Meador, Billie. Critical Care Nursing Review & Self-Test. 250p. 1983. softcover 16.95 (ISBN 0-87489-300-3). Med Economics.
Meador, C. Lawrence, jt. ed. see Davidson, Frank P.
Meador, Daniel J. Preludes to Gideon. 1967. 12.50 (ISBN 0-87215-009-7). Michie-Bobbs.
Meador, Roy. Cogeneration & District Heating. LC 81-67258. (Illus.). 203p. 1981. 19.95 (ISBN 0-250-40420-6). Ann Arbor Science.
--Future Energy Alternatives. LC 77-92590. 1978. pap. 15.95 (ISBN 0-250-40221-1). Ann Arbor Science.
Meador, Roy, jt. auth. see Watkins, Bruce O.
Meador, Roy, jt. ed. see Gordon, Howard.
Meadors, William J., jt. auth. see Gallahue, David L.
Meadow. Telecommunications for Management. 1983. write for info. (ISBN 0-07-041198-0). McGraw.
Meadow, Charles. The Analysis of Information Systems. 2nd ed. LC 72-11518. (Information Sciences Ser.). 416p. 1973. 36.95 (ISBN 0-471-59002-9, Pub. by Wiley-Interscience). Wiley.
Meadow, Charles T. Applied Data Management. LC 76-181. (Information Sciences Ser.). 1976. 39.95 (ISBN 0-471-59011-8, Pub. by Wiley-Interscience). Wiley.
Meadow, Charles T. & Cochrane. Basics of Online Searching. LC 80-23050. (Information Science Ser.). 245p. 1981. 19.95 (ISBN 0-471-05283-3, Pub. by Wiley-Interscience). Wiley.
Meadow, Kathryn P., jt. auth. see Schlesinger, Hilde S.
Meadow, Robert G. Politics As Communication. (Communication & Information Science Ser.). 288p. 1980. 27.50 (ISBN 0-89391-031-7); pap. 15.95 (ISBN 0-89391-119-4). Ablex Pub.
Meadowbrook Medical Reference Group. The Parents' Guide to Baby & Child Medical Care. Hart, Terril H., ed. LC 82-14120. (Illus., Orig.). 1982. 12.95 (ISBN 0-915658-58-5); pap. 6.95 (ISBN 0-915658-57-7). Meadowbrook Pr.
Meadowbrook Press. Our Baby's First Years. (Illus.). 32p. 1983. 9.95 (ISBN 0-915658-98-4). Meadowbrook Pr.
Meadowbrook Reference Group. Economy Motel Guide. Delagran, Louise, ed. (Orig.). 1982. 12.95 (ISBN 0-915658-87-9); pap. 5.95 (ISBN 0-915658-56-9). Meadowbrook Pr.
Meadowbrook Reference Group, ed. The Household Handbook. LC 81-17226. (Illus.). 180p. (Orig.). 1981. 8.95 o.p. (ISBN 0-915658-46-1); pap. 3.95 o.p. (ISBN 0-915658-41-0). Meadowbrook Pr.
Meadowcourt, Richard. Milton's Paradise Regained: Two Eighteenth-Century Critiques, 2 vols. in 1. Wittreich, Joseph A., Jr., ed. LC 76-161937. 1971. Repr. of 1732 ed. 40.00x (ISBN 0-8201-1087-6). Schol Facsimiles.
Meadowcroft, Enid L. Crazy Horse: Sioux Warrior. LC 65-10090. (Indian Books Ser). (Illus.). (gr. 2-5). 1965. PLB 6.69 (ISBN 0-8116-6600-X). Garrard.

Meadowcroft, James, II. Beginning Algebra for Mature Students. 1971. pap. text ed. 19.95 (ISBN 0-13-073726-7). P-H.

Meadowes, Alicia. A Woman of Boston. (Woman's Destiny Ser.: No. 3). (Orig.). 1983. pap. 2.95 (ISBN 0-440-09750-9). Dell.

Meadows, A. J. Science & Controversy: A Biography of Sir Norman Lockyer. 280p. 1972. 10.00 o.p. (ISBN 0-262-13079-3). MIT Pr.

Meadows, A. J., ed. Development of Science Publishing in Europe. 1981. 42.75 (ISBN 0-444-41915-2). Elsevier.

Meadows, A. J. & Gordon, M., eds. The Random House Dictionary of New Information Technology. LC 82-40026. 200p. Date not set. pap. 7.95 (ISBN 0-394-71202-1, Vin). Random.

Meadows, Dennis, ed. Alternatives to Growth: Vol. 1, A Search for Sustainable Futures. LC 77-24148. 1978. pap. 12.50x prof ref (ISBN 0-88410-078-2). Ballinger Pub.

Meadows, Dennis, et al. Dynamics of Growth in a Finite World. LC 74-84400. (Illus.). 1974. 45.00x (ISBN 0-262-13142-0). MIT Pr.

Meadows, Dennis L. Dynamics of Commodity Production Cycles. LC 70-125415. (Illus.). 1972. 20.00x (ISBN 0-262-13141-2). MIT Pr.

Meadows, Dennis L. & Meadows, Donella, eds. Toward Global Equilibrium: Collected Papers. LC 72-81804. (Illus.). 400p. 1973. 32.50x (ISBN 0-262-13143-9). MIT Pr.

Meadows, Don. Califonia Paisano: The Life of William McPherson. 1972. 10.00x (ISBN 0-87093-163-6). Dawsons.

--Historic Place Names of Orange County. (Illus.). 1966. 9.50 o.p. (ISBN 0-685-59751-2). Acoma Bks.

Meadows, Donella, jt. ed. see Meadows, Dennis L.

Meadows, Donella, et al. Groping in the Dark: The First Decade of Global Modelling. 308p. 1982. 26.95x (ISBN 0-471-10027-7, Pub. by Wiley-Interscience). Wiley.

Meadows, Eric G. Pictorial Guide to Hertfordshire. 160p. 1982. 25.00x (ISBN 0-900804-22-X, Pub. by White Crescent England). State Mutual Bk.

Meadows, Eric G. & Larkman, Simon. Pictorial Guide to Bedfordshire. 1982. 25.00x (ISBN 0-900804-10-6, Pub. by White Crescent England). State Mutual Bk.

Meadows, Robert. Renal Histopathology: A Light, Electron, & Immunofluorescent Microscopy Study of Renal Disease. 2nd ed. (Illus.). 1978. text ed. 95.00x (ISBN 0-19-261213-1). Oxford U Pr.

Meagher, John. The Gathering of the Ungifted. LC 72-3827. 176p. 1975. pap. 2.45 o.p. (ISBN 0-8091-1874-2). Paulist Pr.

--The Way of the Word. 250p. 1975. 3.00 (ISBN 0-8164-0270-1). Seabury.

Meagher, John C. Five Gospels: An Account of How the Good News Came to Be. 270p. 1983. 17.50 (ISBN 0-86683-731-0); pap. 9.95 (ISBN 0-86683-691-8). Winston Pr.

Meagher, Robert, ed. Toothing Stones: Rethinking the Political. LC 82-72981. 289p. 1972. 12.95x (ISBN 0-8040-0566-4). Swallow.

Meals, Robert W. Contemporary Potraits. LC 82-80003. 166p. 1983. pap. 5.95 (ISBN 0-86666-075-5). GWP.

Meanley, Brooke. Birdlife at Chincoteague & the Virginia Barrier. LC 79-27187. (Illus.). 128p. 1981. pap. 7.50 o.p. (ISBN 0-87033-257-0, 257-0, Pub. by Tidewater). Cornell Maritime.

Means, Gardiner. Administrative Inflation & Public Policy. 1959. 2.50 (ISBN 0-910136-04-1). Anderson Kramer.

Means, Gardiner C., jt. auth. see Berle, Adolf A.

Means, Gardiner C., jt. auth. see Berle, Adolf A., Jr.

Means, Gardiner C., jt. auth. see Bonbright, James C.

Means, L. Intramurals: Their Organization & Administration. 2nd ed. 1973. ref. ed. 20.95 (ISBN 0-13-477216-4). P-H.

Means, Pat. Mystical Maze. 1976. pap. 3.95 o.p. (ISBN 0-918956-35-8). Campus Crusade.

--The Mystical Maze Study Guide. (Illus.). 1978. pap. 1.95 o.p. (ISBN 0-918956-41-2). Campus Crusade.

Means, Philip A., tr. see Pizarro, P.

Means, Philip A., tr. see Sancho, Pedro.

Meares, Ainslie. A System of Medical Hypnosis. LC 61-5108. 484p. 1974. Repr. of 1960 ed. 15.00 o.p. (ISBN 0-517-52771-5). Crown.

Meares, Bernard, tr. see Mandelstam, Osip.

Mearns, Andrew, et al. Bitter Cry of Outcast London. Wohl, Anthony S., ed. (Victorian Library). 1970. Repr. of 1883 ed. text ed. 15.00x (ISBN 0-7185-5003-X, Leicester). Humanities.

Mearns, Hughes. Creative Power: The Education of Youth in Creative Arts. (Illus.). 1958. pap. 4.50 (ISBN 0-486-20490-1). Dover.

Mears, Dana C. External Skeletal Fixation. (Illus.). 584p. 1983. 89.95 (ISBN 0-683-05900-9). Williams & Wilkins.

--Materials in Orthopaedic Surgery. (Illus.). 776p. 1979. 75.00 (ISBN 0-683-05901-7). Williams & Wilkins.

Mears, Frederick G. & Gatchel, Robert J. Fundamentals of Abnormal Psychology. 1979. 24.95 (ISBN 0-395-30674-4); Tchrs Resource Manual 2.70 (ISBN 0-395-30675-2). HM.

Mears, Helen. Year of the Wild Boar. LC 73-7457. 346p. 1973. Repr. of 1942 ed. lib. bdg. 17.50x (ISBN 0-8371-6936-4, MEWB). Greenwood.

Mears, Henrietta C. Panorama du Nouveau Testament. Cosson, Annie, ed. Perru, Philippe Le, tr. from Eng. Orig. Title: What the Bible Is All About. 347p. (Fr.). 1982. pap. 4.75 (ISBN 0-8297-1244-5). Life Pubs Intl.

--What the Bible Is All About. rev. ed. 1982. pap. 8.95 (ISBN 0-8307-0862-6). Regal.

Mears, Peter & Raho, Louis. Basic Business BASIC: Using Microcomputers. LC 82-17881. (Computer Science Ser.). 300p. 1983. pap. text ed. 16.95 (ISBN 0-534-01352-X). Brooks-Cole.

Mears, Walter R., jt. auth. see Chancellor, John.

Measell. An Overview of Speaking Situations. Applbaum, Ronald & Hart, Roderick, eds. LC 77-11907. (MODCOM - Modules in Speech Communication). 1978. pap. text ed. 2.75 (ISBN 0-574-22530-7, 13-5530). SRA.

Measham, Terry. Picasso & His World. LC 80-68209. (Great Masters Ser.). 13.00 (ISBN 0-382-06376-7). Silver.

--Van Gogh & His World. LC 80-52517. (Great Masters Ser.). 13.00 (ISBN 0-382-06379-1). Silver.

Measures, Howard. Styles of Address: A Manual of Usage in Writing & in Speech. 3rd ed. LC 72-85142. (Griffin Ser). 150p. 1970. pap. 4.95 o.p. (ISBN 0-312-77385-4, S70905). St Martin.

Meatyard, Ralph E. The Family Album of Lucybelle Crater. Williams, Jonathan, ed. LC 74-76773. (Illus.). 88p. 1974. 10.00 (ISBN 0-912330-02-3); pap. 6.95 (ISBN 0-912330-03-1). Jargon Soc.

Mebane, Mary. Mary, Wayfarer. 252p. 1983. 16.75 (ISBN 0-686-84092-5). Viking Pr.

Mecca, Stephen J. & Ekin, Cemal A. Invitation to Basic Fitness. (Illus.). 283p. 1983. pap. 15.00 (ISBN 0-89433-211-2). Petrocelli.

Mecca, Stephen J. & Robertshaw, Joseph E. Home Energy Management: Principles & Practices. (Illus.). 160p. 1981. 12.95 (ISBN 0-89433-146-9). Petrocelli.

Mecca, Stephen J., jt. auth. see Robertshaw, Joseph E.

Mecham, John L. Francisco De Ibarra & Nueva Vizcaya. LC 68-23315. (Illus.). 1968. Repr. of 1927 ed. lib. bdg. 19.25x (ISBN 0-8371-0168-9, MEFI). Greenwood.

Mechanic, David. Mental Health & Social Policy. 2nd ed. (Ser. in Social Policy). 1980. pap. text ed. 13.95 (ISBN 0-13-576025-9). P-H.

--Students Under Stress: A Study in the Social Psychology of Adaptation. LC 77-91058. 268p. 1978. 20.00 (ISBN 0-299-07470-6); pap. text ed. 9.95 (ISBN 0-299-07474-9). U of Wis Pr.

Mechanic, David, ed. Handbook of Health, Health Care & the Health Services. (Illus.). 832p. 1983. text ed. 49.95 (ISBN 0-02-920690-1). Free Pr.

--Readings in Medical Sociology. LC 79-7578. (Illus.). 1980. pap. text ed. 10.95 (ISBN 0-02-920700-2). Free Pr.

Mechanic, Sylvia. Annotated List of Selected United States Government Publications Available to Depository Libraries. 424p. 1971. 19.00 (ISBN 0-8242-0405-0). Wilson.

Mechanical & Energy Systems Engineering Dept., Arizona University. Simplified Design Guide for Estimating Photovoltaic Flat Array & System Performance. 175p. 1982. pap. 22.95x (ISBN 0-89934-168-3). Solar Energy Info.

Mechem, Floyd R. Elements of the Law of Partnership. LC 12-36583. xxxviii, 277p. 1982. Repr. of 1896 ed. text ed. 35.00 (ISBN 0-89941-180-0). W S Hein.

--A Treatise on the Law of Agency, 2 Vols. 2nd ed. LC 14-14927. 1982. Repr. of 1914 ed. lib. bdg. 95.00 (ISBN 0-89941-165-7). W S Hein.

Mechlin, Stuart & Bonanno, Ellen. Without a Thorn: A Guide to Rose Gardening in the Pacific Northwest. LC 78-13890. (Illus., Orig.). 1978. pap. 7.50 (ISBN 0-917304-37-3). Timber.

Mechtly, E. H. The International System of Units. 1977. pap. 1.40x (ISBN 0-87563-139-8). Stipes.

Mecklenburgh, J. C. & Hartland, S. The Theory of Backmixing: The Design of Continuous Flow Chemiclal Plant with Backmixing. LC 74-32190. 517p. 1975. 113.95 (ISBN 0-471-59023-1, Pub. by Wiley-Interscience). Wiley.

Meckler, Milton. Energy Conservation in Buildings & Industrial Plants. (Illus.). 1980. 24.95 (ISBN 0-07-041195-6). McGraw.

Mecklin, John M. Ku Klux Klan: A Study of the American Mind. LC 63-15172. 1963. Repr. of 1924 ed. 15.00x o.p. (ISBN 0-8462-0384-7). Russell.

Meckstroth, Betty, jt. auth. see Webb, James T.

MECutcheon, Randall J. Get Off My Brain. (Illus.). 84p. 1982. pap. 4.95 (ISBN 0-934904-18-9). J & L Lee.

Medard, L. Gas Encyclopedia. 1976. 191.50 (ISBN 0-444-41492-4). Elsevier.

Medawar & Shelley, eds. Structure in Science & Art. (International Congress Ser.: Vol. 517). 1980. 42.25 (ISBN 0-444-90150-7). Elsevier.

Medawar, J. S., jt. auth. see Medawar, P. B.

Medawar, P. B. Advice to a Young Scientist. LC 79-1676. (Sloan Foundation Bk.). 1979. 12.95i (ISBN 0-06-013029-6, HarpT); pap. 3.95i (ISBN 0-06-090810-6, CN-0810). Har-Row.

Medawar, P. B. & Medawar, J. S. The Life Science: Current Ideas in Biology. LC 76-26245. 1977. 12.45i (ISBN 0-06-012954-9, HarpT). Har-Row.

Medawar, Peter. Pluto's Republic: Incorporating "The Art of the Soluble" & "Induction & Intuition in Scientific Thought". (Illus.). 1982. 25.00 (ISBN 0-19-217726-5). Oxford U Pr.

Medawar, Peter B. Induction & Intuition in Scientific Thought. LC 69-17272. (Memoirs Ser.: Vol. 75). 1969. 5.00 (ISBN 0-87169-075-6). Am Philos.

Medbery, James K. Men & Mysteries of Wall Street. rev. ed. LC 68-28641. (Illus.). Repr. lib. bdg. 20.75x (ISBN 0-8371-0566-8, MEMM). Greenwood.

Meddaugh, E. James. Guide to Professional Accounting Standards. 228p. 1982. 9.95 (ISBN 0-13-370700-8). P-H.

Medding, P. Y. Mapai in Israel: Political Organisation & Government in a New Society. LC 75-184900. 352p. 44.50 (ISBN 0-521-08492-X). Cambridge U Pr.

Meddis, R. Elementary Analysis of Variance for the Behavioural Sciences. LC 72-12493. 129p. (Orig.). pap. 7.00 o.p. (ISBN 0-470-59007-6). Krieger.

Meddis, Ray. A Handbook of Statistics for Non-Statisticians. (Illus.). 166p. 1975. pap. text ed. 11.00 o.p. (ISBN 0-07-084044-X, C). McGraw.

Medeiros, E. Albuquerque. The Vengeance of Felix. Goldberg, Isaac, ed. & tr. (International Pocket Library). pap. 3.00 (ISBN 0-686-77244-X). Branden.

Medeiros, Robert W. Chemistry: A Modern Perspective. 1973. text ed. 9.95x o.p. (ISBN 0-442-25331-1); instructor's manual pap 1.00x o.p. (ISBN 0-442-25335-4). Van Nos Reinhold.

Meder, Albert E., Jr., ed. see Buchanan, O. Lexton, Jr.

Meder, J. & Handbuck, Ein. Durer-Katalog. LC 75-87642. (Graphic Art Ser.: Vol. 12). (Illus.). 358p. 1971. Repr. of 1932 ed. lib. bdg. 65.00 (ISBN 0-306-71788-3). Da Capo.

Medgyessy, Pal. Decomposition of Superpositions of Density Functions & Discrete Distributions. LC 75-46231. 308p. 1977. 49.95x o.s.i. (ISBN 0-470-15017-3). Halsted Pr.

Medhaug, Eleanore. Joy in the Valley. 1978. 7.95 o.p. (ISBN 0-533-03418-3). Vantage.

Medhurst, Kenneth, ed. Allende's Chile. LC 73-81735. 212p. 1973. 19.95 o.p. (ISBN 0-312-02100-3). St Martin.

Media Horizons Editors, ed. The Video Handbook. rev. ed. 192p. 1974. 17.50 o.p. (ISBN 0-13-941799-0, Spec). P-H.

Media Institute see Theberge, Leonard J.

Media Institute, ed. see Lichter, Linda & Lichter, S. Robert.

Media Publications Staff. More of the World's Best Recipes. Everest, Anne, ed. 1983. pap. 12.95 (ISBN 0-943214-04-1). Media Pubns.

Media Referral Service. The Film File: 1982-83 Edition. 341p. (Orig.). 1982. pap. 30.00 (ISBN 0-911125-01-9). Media Ref.

Medical Academic Press, ed. The Enema. LC 79-91913. (Illus.). 1980. lib. bdg. 14.95 o.s.i. (ISBN 0-918944-01-5); pap. 9.95 o.s.i. (ISBN 0-918944-02-3). Wildwood.

Medical Arts Publishing Foundation Staff. Cancer Screening & Detection Manual for Nurses. (Illus.). 1979. pap. text ed. 19.95 (ISBN 0-07-041197-2, HP). McGraw.

Medical Information Systems, 1st Illinois Conferences, October 1974, Urbana, IL. First Illinois Conference on Medical Information Systems: Proceedings. 208p. 1974. pap. text ed. 25.00x o.p. (ISBN 0-87664-274-1). Instru Soc.

Medical Publishing House, Beijin, China, ed. see Chinese Experts & Staff of the Peoples.

Medical Tribune Editors. Questions Patients Most Often Ask Their Doctors. 256p. 1983. pap. 3.50 (ISBN 0-553-23030-1). Bantam.

Medicii, Geraldine A. Drug Dosage Calculations: A Guide for Current Clinical Practice. (Illus.). 1980. pap. text ed. 12.95 (ISBN 0-13-220764-8). P-H.

Medicine, Beatrice, jt. auth. see Albers, Patricia.

Medicus & Hubbard, L. Ron. All About Radiation. LRH Personal Compilations Bureau, ed. 1957. 9.95 (ISBN 0-88404-062-3). Bridge Pubns Inc.

Medicus, Fritz. Lectures on Logic. Marti, Fritz, tr. from Ger. LC 81-40825. (Illus.). 80p. (Orig.). 1982. pap. text ed. 7.00 (ISBN 0-8191-2114-2). U Pr of Amer.

Medina. Introduction to Spanish Literature. LC 81-8293. 360p. 1982. Repr. of 1974 ed. 16.50 (ISBN 0-89874-365-6). Krieger.

Medina, Arthur, jt. auth. see Garcia, Connie.

Medina, Barbara F. Structured System Analysis: A New Technique. 96p. 1981. 25.00 (ISBN 0-677-05570-6). Gordon.

Medinnus, Gene R. Child Study & Observation Guide. LC 75-15960. 183p. 1976. text ed. 13.95 (ISBN 0-471-59024-X). Wiley.

Medinnus, Gene R. & Johnson, Ronald C. Child & Adolescent Psychology. 2nd ed. LC 75-40112. 564p. 1976. 23.50 (ISBN 0-471-59022-3). Krieger.

Medinnus, Gene R., jt. auth. see Johnson, Ronald C.

Medish, V. The Soviet Union. pap. 14.95 (ISBN 0-13-823567-8). P-H.

Meditch, J. S. Stochastic Optimal Linear Estimation & Control. LC 69-17148. (Electronic Systems Ser.). 1969. text ed. 39.50 (ISBN 0-07-041230-8, C). McGraw.

Medjati, Z. M. & Trice, J. E. English & Continental Systems of Adminstrative Law. 1978. 42.00 (ISBN 0-444-85108-9); pap. 30.00 (ISBN 0-444-85198-4). Elsevier.

Medlen, Lynn & Quattrochi, Judy. Remediating Auditory Learning & Language Disabilities: Ideas & Activities. 1975. text ed. 9.95x (ISBN 0-8134-1732-5). Interstate.

Medley. Teacher Competency Testing & the Teacher Educator. 1982. 2.50 (ISBN 0-686-38078-9). Assn Tchr Ed.

Medley, Donald B., ed. see National Computer Conference, 1980.

Medley, E. Scott. Common Health Problems in Medical Practice. (Illus.). 360p. 1982. lib. bdg. 25.00 (ISBN 0-683-05903-3). Williams & Wilkins.

Medley, Frank, jt. auth. see Smith, Wm. Flint.

Medley, H. Anthony. Sweaty Palms: The Neglected Art of Being Interviewed. (Illus.). 191p. 1978. 6.95 (ISBN 0-534-97999-8). Lifetime Learn.

Medley, Margaret. The Chinese Potter. LC 80-68381. (Illus.). 288p. 1982. pap. 14.95x (ISBN 0-8014-9239-4). Cornell U Pr.

Medley, Margaret, ed. Transactions of the Oriental Ceramic Society 1980-1981. (Illus.). 104p. 1982. text ed. 37.50x (ISBN 0-85667-168-1, Pub. by Sotheby Pubns England). Biblio Dist.

Medlicott, W. N. & Coveney, D. Bismarck & Europe. 1972. 22.50 (ISBN 0-312-08225-8). St Martin.

Medlik, S. Business of Hotels. 1980. pap. 12.50 (ISBN 0-434-91249-2, Pub. by Heinemann). David & Charles.

Medlin, Faith. Centuries of Owls. LC 67-23636. 1975. 6.95 o.p. (ISBN 0-685-56440-1). Brown Bk.

Mednick, Sarnoff, et al. Psychology: Explorations in Behavior & Experience. LC 74-22239. 550p. 1975. text ed. 26.95 o.s.i. (ISBN 0-471-59017-7). Wiley.

Mednick, Sarnoff A. & Baert, Andre E., eds. Prospective Longitudinal Research in Europe: An Empirical Basis for the Primary Prevention of Psychosocial Disorders. (Illus.). 1981. text ed. 99.50x (ISBN 0-19-261184-4). Oxford U Pr.

Mednick, Sarnoff A. & Christiansen, K. O., eds. Biosocial Bases of Criminal Behavior. 1977. 24.95x o.s.i. (ISBN 0-470-15185-4). Halsted Pr.

Mednick, Sarnoff A. & Shoham, Sigiora, eds. New Paths in Criminology. LC 77-25739. 256p. 1979. 23.95 (ISBN 0-669-01510-5). Lexington Bks.

Mednick, Stuart E., jt. auth. see Donovan, John J.

Mednis, E. From the Opening into the Endgame. (Chess Ser.). (Illus.). 176p. 1983. 18.95 (ISBN 0-08-026917-6); pap. 10.95 (ISBN 0-08-026916-8). Pergamon.

Medoff, Francine. The Mouse in the Matzah Factory. LC 82-23349. (Illus.). 40p. (ps-2). 1983. 8.95 (ISBN 0-930494-18-0); pap. 4.95 (ISBN 0-930494-19-9). Kar Ben.

Medoff, James L., jt. auth. see Freeman, Richard B.

Medoff, Mark. The Wager, a Play, & Two Short Plays. Incl. Doing a Good One for the Red Man; The War on Tatem. LC 75-31963. 1976. 6.95 o.p. (ISBN 0-88371-016-1); pap. 3.95 o.p. (ISBN 0-88371-017-X). J T White.

Medress, Dolly, jt. ed. see Marshall, Sol H.

Medsger, Betty. Framed: The New Right Attack on Chief Justice Rose Bird & the Courts. 320p. 1983. 17.95 (ISBN 0-8298-0655-5). Pilgrim NY.

Medsger, Oliver P. Edible Wild Plants. (Illus.). 359p. 1972. pap. 6.95 (ISBN 0-02-080910-7, Collier). Macmillan.

Medsker, Dennis L. & Medsker, Paula A. Chiropractic & Pediatrics. 1979. 17.00 (ISBN 0-686-26174-7). Chiro Educational Serv.

Medsker, Leland L. & Edelstein, Stewart L. Policy Guidelines for Extended Degree Programs. 1977. pap. text ed. 4.50 o.p. (ISBN 0-8268-1389-5). ACE.

Medsker, Paula A., jt. auth. see Medsker, Dennis L.

Medved, Harry & Medved, Michael. The Golden Turkey Awards. 1980. pap. 7.95 (ISBN 0-399-50463-X, Perigee). Putnam Pub Group.

Medved, Michael. Hospital: The Hidden Lives of a Medical Center Staff. 384p. 1983. 14.95 (ISBN 0-671-42442-4). S&S.

Medved, Michael, jt. auth. see Medved, Harry.

Medvedev, Roy. Khruschev. LC 82-45545. (Illus.). 350p. 1983. 17.95 (ISBN 0-385-18387-9, Anchor Pr). Doubleday.

Medvedev, Roy A. Let History Judge: The Origins & Consequences of Stalinism. Joravsky, David & Haupt, Georges, eds. 1971. 15.00 (ISBN 0-394-44645-3); Rus. lang. o.p. 22.50 (ISBN 0-394-47972-6). Knopf.

--Nikolai Bukharin: The Last Years. 176p. 1983. pap. 6.50 (ISBN 0-393-30110-9). Norton.

--On Socialist Democracy. Kadt, Ellen De, tr. from Russian. 1977. pap. 6.95 (ISBN 0-393-00850-9, Norton Lib). Norton.

--On Stalin & Stalinsim. De Kadt, Ellen, tr. 1979. 17.95x (ISBN 0-19-215842-2). Oxford U Pr.

Medvei, V. C. A History of Endocrinology. (Illus.). 900p. 1982. text ed. 95.00 (ISBN 0-85200-245-9, Pub. by MTP Pr England). Kluwer Boston.

Medvedev, Roy A. Nikolai Bukharin: The Last Years. Briggs, A. D., tr. 1980. 10.95 (ISBN 0-393-01357-X). Norton.

Medwadowski, Stefan J., jt. ed. see Popov, Egor P.

Medway, Peter. Finding a Language: Autonomy & Learning in School. 148p. pap. 4.95x (ISBN 0-906495-41-5, Pub. by Writers & Readers). Boynton Cook Pubs.

Medway, Peter, jt. auth. see Torbe, Mike.

Medway, William, et al. Textbook of Veterinary Clinical Pathology. LC 69-13696. 536p. 1969. 22.00 (ISBN 0-686-74094-7). Krieger.

Medwin, Herman, jt. auth. see Clay, Clarence S.

Mee, A. J. & Jarvis, A. C. Certificate Physical Science, 2 bks. 1977. Bk. 1. pap. text ed. 9.00x o.p. (ISBN 0-435-57581-3); Bk. 2. pap. text ed. 7.50x o.p. (ISBN 0-435-57582-1). Heinemann Ed.

Mee, A. J., et al. Science for the Seventies, 2 bks. pap. text ed. 6.50x ea. o.p.; Bk. 1. pap. text ed. (ISBN 0-435-57574-0); Bk. 2. pap. text ed. (ISBN 0-435-57576-7); Bk. 1. tchrs'. ed. 7.95x o.p. (ISBN 0-435-57575-9); Bk. 2. tchrs'. ed. 9.95x o.p. (ISBN 0-435-57577-5). Heinemann Ed.

Mee, C. B. Rhodes in the Bronze Age. 160p. 1982. text ed. 60.00x (ISBN 0-85668-143-1, Pub. by Aris & Phillips England). Humanities.

Mee, Charles L., Jr. Erasmus: The Eye of the Hurricane. (Illus.). 128p. (gr. 7 up). 1974. 5.95 o.p. (ISBN 0-698-20251-1, Coward). Putnam Pub Group.

--Meeting at Potsdam. 370p. 1982. pap. 7.95 (ISBN 0-87131-412-6). M Evans.

--Moses, Moses. LC 76-41516. (Illus.). (gr. k-3). 1977. 4.95i (ISBN 0-06-024178-0, HarpJ); PLB 4.79 o.p. (ISBN 0-06-024179-9). Har-Row.

--Seizure. 1979. pap. 2.25 o.s.i. (ISBN 0-515-05424-0). Jove Pubns.

--Seizure. pap. 2.25 (ISBN 0-686-50199-3). Jove Pubns.

Meech, D. W. Learn That Language. 83p. 1976. pap. 3.00 o.p. (ISBN 0-88312-782-2); 1.50 o.p. (ISBN 0-88312-324-X). Summer Inst Ling.

Meech-Pekarik, Julia, jt. auth. see Valenstein, Suzanne.

Meed, Vladka. On Both Sides of the Wall. LC 78-71300. 1979. 9.95 (ISBN 0-8052-5013-1, Pub. by Holocaust Library); pap. 4.95 (ISBN 0-8052-5012-3). Schocken.

Meegan, Richard, jt. auth. see Massey, Doreen.

Meehan, Dennis B., illus. Is the Forecast Acid Rain? (Illus.). 12p. (Orig.). (gr. 7-12). 1982. pap. 1.25 20 minimum order (ISBN 0-9603716-2-1). Reddy Comm.

--Takeover: Promises vs. Realities. (Illus.). 25p. (Orig.). 1982. pap. 1.50 20 minimum order (ISBN 0-9603716-1-3). Reddy Comm.

Meehan, J., jt. auth. see Polisky, M. K.

Meehan, James R. How to Use the Calculator & Comptometer. 5th ed. 1964. text ed. 9.96 (ISBN 0-07-041303-7, G). McGraw.

Meehan, James R. & Kahn, G. How to Use Adding Machines: Ten-Key, Full-Key, Printing Calculator. 1962. text ed. 9.96 (ISBN 0-07-041307-X, G); instructor's guide 3.50 (ISBN 0-07-041310-X). McGraw.

Meehan, James R., et al. Solving Business Problems on the Electronic Calculator. 1975. text ed. 9.96 (ISBN 0-07-041279-0, G); tchrs' manual & key 2.75 (ISBN 0-07-041280-4). McGraw.

Meehan, John. With Darwin in Chile. (Illus.). (gr. 7 up). 12.75x (ISBN 0-392-01878-0, LTB). Sportshelf.

Meehan, Nathan D. & Vogel, Eric L. HP-Forty-One Reservior Engineering Manual. 364p. 1982. 59.95x (ISBN 0-87814-186-3). Pennwell Books Division.

Meek & Turner. Statistical Analysis for Business Decisions. 1983. text ed. 27.95 (ISBN 0-686-84537-4, BS31); instrs' manual avail. HM.

Meek, B. L. & Fairthorne, S. Using Computers. LC 76-26871. 1977. 29.95x o.p. (ISBN 0-470-98932-7). Halsted Pr.

Meek, G. A. & Elder, H. Y., eds. Analytical & Quantitative Methods in Microscopy. LC 76-22983. (Society for Experimental Biology Seminar Ser: No. 3). (Illus.). 1977. 49.50 (ISBN 0-521-21404-1); pap. 17.95 (ISBN 0-521-29141-0). Cambridge U Pr.

Meek, Gary E. & Turner, Stephen J. Statistical Analysis for Business Decisions. 768p. 1983. text ed. 27.95 (ISBN 0-395-32274-X); write for info. instr's. manual (ISBN 0-395-32825-X). HM.

Meek, Geoffrey A. Practical Electron Microscopy for Biologists. 2nd. ed. LC 75-4955. 548p. 1976. text ed. 89.95 (ISBN 0-471-59031-2, Pub. by Wiley-Interscience); pap. 34.95 (ISBN 0-471-99592-4). Wiley.

Meek, J. L. Matrix Structural Analysis. 1971. 24.50 o.p. (ISBN 0-07-041316-9, C). McGraw.

Meek, J. M. & Craggs, J. D. Electrical Breakdown of Gases. 878p. 1978. 179.00 o.s.i. (ISBN 0-471-99553-3). Wiley.

Meek, R. L. Social Science & the Ignoble Savage. LC 75-22985. (Cambridge Studies in the History & Theory of Politics). 262p. 1976. 37.50 (ISBN 0-521-20969-2). Cambridge U Pr.

Meek, R. L., ed. Turgot on Progress: Sociology & Economics. (Studies in the History & Theory of Politics). 29.95 (ISBN 0-521-08698-1). Cambridge U Pr.

Meek, Ronald L., ed. & tr. from Fr. Precursors of Adam Smith 1750-1775. (Rowman & Littlefield University Library). 201p. 1973. 10.00x o.p. (ISBN 0-87471-398-6). Rowman.

Meeker, Barbara F., jt. auth. see Leik, Robert K.

Meeker, Charles A. Acupuncture, 3 vols. 25.00 set (ISBN 0-686-80944-0); Vol. 1 (beginning) 10.95 (ISBN 0-686-86327-5); Vol. 2 (advanced) 10.95 (ISBN 0-686-91520-8); Vol. 3 (Index of Diseases) 10.95 (ISBN 0-686-96789-5). Meeker Pub.

Meeker, David. Jazz in the Movies. 1978. 13.95 o.p. (ISBN 0-87000-403-4, Arlington Hse). Crown.

--Jazz in the Movies. new & enl. ed. (Quality Paperbacks Ser.). (Illus.). 336p. 1982. pap. 13.50 (ISBN 0-306-80170-1). Da Capo.

Meeker, Joseph W. The Comedy of Survival: In Search of an Environmental Ethic. (Illus.). 174p. 1980. pap. 7.95 (ISBN 0-917270-03-7). Finn Hill.

Meeker, M. E. Literature & Violence in North Arabia. LC 76-47194. (Cambridge Studies in Cultural Systems). 1979. 37.50 (ISBN 0-521-22074-2); pap. 13.95 (ISBN 0-521-29399-5). Cambridge U Pr.

Meeker, Margaret H., jt. auth. see Gruendemann, Barbara J.

Meeker, Mary. Structure of Intellect: Its Interpretation & Uses. LC 69-17296. 1969. text ed. 20.95 (ISBN 0-675-09516-6). Merrill.

Meeker, Thrygve R., jt. ed. see Gagnepain, J. J.

Meeks, Carol B. Housing. (Illus.). 1980. text ed. 20.95 (ISBN 0-13-394981-8). P-H.

Meeks, Esther & Bagwell, Elizabeth. How New Life Begins. (gr. 4-6). 1969. lib. ed. 3.48 o.s.i. (ISBN 0-695-43855-7). Follett.

Meeks, M. L. Explorations in Space & Time: A Series of Computer-Generated Astronomy Films, Filmnotes. 1974. pap. 2.75 o.p. (ISBN 0-395-18866-0). HM.

Meeks, M. Littleton. Radar Propagation at Low Altitudes. (Artech Radar Library). (Illus.). 250p. 1982. 28.00 (ISBN 0-89006-118-1). Artech Hse.

Meeks, Wayne A. The First Urban Christians: The Social World of the Apostle Paul. LC 82-8447. (Illus.). 296p. 1982. 19.95 (ISBN 0-300-02876-8). Yale U Pr.

Meeks, Wayne A. & Wilken, Robert L. Jews & Christians in Antioch in the First Four Centuries of the Common Era. LC 78-3760. 1978. pap. 8.95 (ISBN 0-89130-229-8, 06-03-13). Scholars Pr Ca.

Meenaghan, Thomas M. & Washington, Robert O. Macro Practice in the Human Services. (Illus.). 288p. 1982. text ed. 15.95 (ISBN 0-02-920850-5). Free Pr.

--Social Policy & Social Welfare: Structure & Applications. LC 79-54669. (Illus.). 1980. text ed. 12.95 (ISBN 0-02-920750-9). Free Pr.

Meenes, Max. Studying & Learning. (Orig.). 1954. pap. text ed. 2.25 (ISBN 0-685-19774-3). Phila Bk Co.

Meer, Atie Van Der see Van Der Meer, Ron & Van Der Meer, Atie.

Meer, Dennis Van Der see Loehr, James E. & Van Der Meer, Dennis.

Meer, Fatima. Race & Suicide in South Africa. (International Library of Sociology). 304p. 1976. 22.95x (ISBN 0-7100-8228-2). Routledge & Kegan.

Meer, Haye Van Der see Van Der Meer, Haye S.

Meer, J. H. van der see Van Leeuwen Bookmkamp, C. & Van der Meer, J. H.

Meer, Ron Van Der see Van Der Meer, Ron & Van Der Meer, Atie.

Meerhaeghe, M. A. International Economic Institutions. 2nd ed. LC 75-179701. 1972. 26.00x (ISBN 0-312-42070-6). St Martin.

Meerloo, A. M. Delusion & Mass Delusion. (Nervous & Mental Disease Monographs). Repr. of 1949 ed. 14.00 (ISBN 0-384-37950-8). Johnson Repr.

Meerovich, B., tr. see Kirichenko, E.

Mees, A. I. Dynamics of Feedback Systems. LC 40501. 214p. 1981. 41.95 (ISBN 0-471-27822-X, Pub. by Wiley-Interscience). Wiley.

Mees, Inger, jt. auth. see Collins, Beverly.

Meesook, Oey Astra. Income, Consumption & Poverty in Thailand, 1962-63 to 1975-76. (Working Paper: No. 364). 97p. 1979. 5.00 (ISBN 0-686-36147-4, WP-0364). World Bank.

Meesook, Oey Astra, jt. auth. see Chernichovsky, Dov.

Meeter, Merle, et al. English Workbook for Christian Students. 1980. pap. 5.95x (ISBN 0-89051-066-0); tchr.'s guide 2.95x (ISBN 0-686-85807-7). CLP Pubs.

Meeth, Richard, jt. auth. see O'Connell, William R., Jr.

Meeting for Consultations on Underwater Noise, Rome, 1968. Report. (FAO Fisheries Reports: No. 76). 35p. 1970. pap. 7.50 (ISBN 0-686-93032-0, F1682, FAO). Unipub.

Meetings on Fertilizer Production, Distribution & Utilization in Latin America, Rio de Janeiro, 1951. Report. (FAO Agricultural Development Papers: No. 36). 52p. 1953. pap. 4.50 (ISBN 0-686-92856-3, F1919, FAO). Unipub.

Meeus, Jean. Astronomical Formulae for Calculators. LC 82-8495. 1982. pap. text ed. 14.95 (ISBN 0-943396-01-8). Willman-Bell.

Meezan, William & Katz, Sanford. Adoptions Without Agencies: A Study of Independent Adoptions. LC 77-99283. 1977. 12.50 (ISBN 0-87868-174-4, A-40); pap. 9.50 (ISBN 0-87868-190-6). Child Welfare.

Meezan, William, jt. auth. see McGowan, Brenda.

Mefford, Bill, jt. auth. see Trumpy, Bob.

Megarry, Jacquetta & Walker, David, eds. World Yearbook of Education, 1982: Computers & Education. LC 82-12414. 350p. 1983. 35.00 (ISBN 0-89397-138-3). Nichols Pub.

Megaw, T. M. Tunnels Planning Design Construction, 2 vols. (Engineering Science Ser.). 510p. 1981. 76.95 (ISBN 0-470-27209-0); 152.95 set (ISBN 0-470-27217-1). Halsted Pr.

Megaw, Vincent, jt. ed. see Greenhalgh, Michael.

Megged, Aharon. Asahel: A Novel. Whitehill, Robert & Lilly, Susan C., trs. from Hebrew. LC 81-8822. 256p. 1982. 11.95 (ISBN 0-8008-0410-4). Taplinger.

Meggers, Betty & Evans, Clifford, eds. New Interpretations of Aboriginal American Culture History. LC 72-78236. (Illus.). vii, 135p. 1972. Repr. of 1955 ed. 18.50x (ISBN 0-8154-0419-0). Cooper Sq.

Megginson, Leon C., et al. Management: Concepts & Applications. 576p. 1983. text ed. 24.50 scp (ISBN 0-06-044412-6, HarpC); instr's. manual avail. (ISBN 0-06-364246-8); test bank avail. (ISBN 0-06-364245-X); scp study guide 9.50 (ISBN 0-06-045596-9). Har-Row.

Meggitt, M. J., jt. ed. see Lawrence, P.

Meggs, Brown. Aria. LC 77-5188. 1978. 10.95 o.p. (ISBN 0-689-10832-X). Atheneum.

Megill, Esther. Joining the Journey: A Guide to the People & Pilgrimage of Central Africa. (Orig.). 1983. pap. write for info. (ISBN 0-377-00127-9). Friend Pr.

Megill, K. A. New Democratic Theory. LC 71-122277. 1971. pap. 4.50 (ISBN 0-02-920790-8). Free Pr.

Megill, R. E. How to Be a More Productive Employee. LC 72-9445. 122p. 1980. 24.95x (ISBN 0-87814-140-5). Pennwell Pub.

--An Introduction to Exploration Economics. 2nd ed. LC 75-153985. 180p. 1979. 37.95x (ISBN 0-87814-004-2). Pennwell Pub.

Megill, Robert E. An Introduction to Risk Analysis. 200p. 1977. 39.95x (ISBN 0-87814-034-4). Pennwell Pub.

--Life in the Corporate Orbit. 128p. 1981. 29.95x (ISBN 0-87814-150-2). Pennwell Pub.

Megister, J. Thesaurus Polyglottus. (Linguistics 13th-18th Centuries). 1613p. (Fr.). 1974. Repr. of 1603 ed. lib. bdg. 371.00x o.p. (ISBN 0-8287-0596-8, 71-5008). Clearwater Pub.

Meglin, Nick. Fountain Pen Drawing. (Grosset Art Instruction Ser.: Vol. 71). pap. 2.95 (ISBN 0-448-00584-0, G&D). Putnam Pub Group.

Megrelis, Christian. Keys to the Future: From Free Trade to Fair Trade. LC 80-5075. 176p. 1980. 22.95 (ISBN 0-669-03705-2). Lexington Bks.

Megroz, Phyllis, tr. see Shaliapin, Fedor I.

Meguido, Zola. Only the Best. 1982. 9.90 (ISBN 0-531-04066-6). Watts.

Mehaffy, Robert E. Writing for the Real World. 1980. pap. text ed. 12.50x (ISBN 0-673-15244-8). Scott F.

Mehan, Hugh & Wood, Houston. The Reality of Ethnomethodology. LC 75-1190. 259p. 1975. 23.95 o.p. (ISBN 0-471-59060-6, Pub. by Wiley-Interscience). Wiley.

--The Reality of Ethnomethodology. LC 82-20885. 274p. 1983. Repr. of 1975 ed. lib. bdg. write for info. (ISBN 0-89874-586-1). Krieger.

Mehata, K. M., jt. auth. see Srinivasan, S. K.

Mehden, Fred R. Von Der see Von der Mehden, Fred R.

Mehdevi, Anne S. Persian Folk & Fairy Tales. (Illus.). (gr. 5 up). 1965. PLB 5.99 o.p. (ISBN 0-394-91496-1). Knopf.

Mehdi, Beverlee T., ed. The Arabs in America 1492-1977: A Chronology & Fact Book. LC 77-27463. (Ethnic Chronology Ser.: No. 31). 150p. 1978. lib. bdg. 8.50 (ISBN 0-379-00527-1). Oceana.

Mehdi, M. T. Peace in Palestine. LC 75-43266. 1976. pap. 5.00 (ISBN 0-911026-08-8). New World Press NY.

Meher, jt. auth. see Puri.

Meheriuk, M., jt. auth. see Richardson, D. G.

Mehl, Dieter. The Middle English Romances of the Thirteenth & Fourteenth Centuries. 1969. 29.50x (ISBN 0-7100-6240-0). Routledge & Kegan.

Mehl, Duane. No More for the Road. 3.95 o.p. (ISBN 0-686-92063-5). Hazelden.

Mehl, Lewis, ed. see Peterson, Gayle.

Mehl, Lewis E. Mind & Matter: Foundations for Holistic Health, Vol. 1. LC 81-85518. (Holistic Approaches to Health & Disease Ser.). 335p. 1982. pap. 11.95 (ISBN 0-939508-02-8). Mindbody.

Mehl, Roger. Condition of the Christian Philosopher. Kushner, Eva, tr. 324p. 1963. 16.95 (ISBN 0-227-67654-8). Attic Pr.

--Imagenes Del Hombre. Benlliure, Felix, tr. from Fr. Orig. Title: Images Del'homme. 64p. 1980. pap. 1.35 (ISBN 0-311-05051-4). Casa Bautista.

Mehler, Jacques & Walker, Edward, eds. Perspectives on Mental Representation: Experimental & Theoretical Studies of Cognitive Processes & Capacities. Franck, Susana & Garrett, M. 512p. 1982. text ed. 39.95 (ISBN 0-89859-194-5). L Erlbaum Assocs.

Mehlin, Theodore G. Astronomy. LC 59-9347. (Illus.). 391p. 1959. text ed. 10.00 o.p. (ISBN 0-471-59037-1, Pub. by Wiley). Krieger.

Mehlinger, Howard, jt. auth. see Ehman, Lee.

Mehlinger, Howard D. & Tucker, Jan L., eds. Teaching Social Studies in Other Nations. LC 79-53231. (Bulletin Ser.: No. 60). 104p. (Orig.). 1979. pap. 7.25 (ISBN 0-87986-024-3, 498-15280). Coun Soc Studies.

Mehlman, Felice. Phaidon Guide to Glass. (Illus.). 256p. 1983. 12.95 (ISBN 0-13-662023-X); pap. 6.95 (ISBN 0-13-662015-9). P-H.

Mehlman, Jeffrey. Revolution & Repetition: Marx-Hugo-Balzac. LC 76-24589. (Quantum Ser.). 1977. 17.50x (ISBN 0-520-03111-3); pap. 2.45 (ISBN 0-520-03531-3). U of Cal Pr.

Mehlman, Jeffrey, tr. see De Fontenay, Elisabeth.

Mehlman, Myron A., ed. see Symposium Held at the University of Nebraska Medical School, Omaha, Nebr., May, 1972.

Mehmed, Pasha. Ottoman Statecraft: The Book of Council for Vezirs & Governors (Nasaih Ul-Vuzera Ve' Lumera) of Sari Mehmed Pasha, the Defterdar. Wright, Walter L., Jr., tr. from Turkish. LC 79-141262. 1971. Repr. of 1935 ed. lib. bdg. 18.75x (ISBN 0-8371-5825-7, WROS). Greenwood.

Mehmet, Ozay. Economic Planning & Social Justice in Developing Countries. LC 78-18797. 1978. 22.50x (ISBN 0-312-23443-0). St Martin.

Mehnert, Klaus. Moscow & the New Left. Fischer, Helmut, tr. LC 73-90660. 1975. 30.00x (ISBN 0-520-02652-7). U of Cal Pr.

--The Russians & Their Body. (Publication Ser.). (Illus.). 225p. 1983. price not set (ISBN 0-8179-7821-6). Hoover Inst Pr.

--Soviet Man & His World. Rosenbaum, Maurice, tr. LC 76-14778. 1976. Repr. of 1962 ed. lib. bdg. 20.75x (ISBN 0-8371-8567-X, MESOM). Greenwood.

Mehra, jt. auth. see Kantin.

Mehra, Jagdish & Rechenberg, H. The Historical Development of Quantum Theory: Quantum Theory of Planck, Einstein, Bohr & Sommerfeld Its Foundation & the Rise of its Difficulties 1900-1925, Vol. I, Pt. 1. (Illus.). 400p. 1982. 28.00 (ISBN 0-387-90642-8). Springer-Verlag.

--Historical Development of Quantum Theory, Vol. IV: Fundamental Equations of Quantum Mechanics - Reception of the New Quantum Mechanics. 322p. 1982. 38.00 (ISBN 0-387-90680-0). Springer-Verlag.

--The Historical Development of Quantum Theory, Vol. I, Pt. 2: Quantum Theory of Planck, Einstein, Bohr, & Sommerfeld - Foundation & Rise of Difficulties 1900-1925. (Illus.). 506p. 1982. 36.00 (ISBN 0-387-90667-3). Springer-Verlag.

--The Historical Development of Quantum Theory, Vol. II: The Discovery of Quantum Mechanics. (Illus.). 320p. 1982. 32.00 (ISBN 0-387-90674-6). Springer-Verlag.

Mehrabian, Albert. Tactics of Social Influence. 1970. pap. text ed. 14.95 (ISBN 0-13-882159-3). P-H.

Mehring, Franz. Karl Marx. 1981. pap. text ed. 11.95x (ISBN 0-391-02305-5). Humanities.

Mehring, M. High Resolution NMR in Solids. LC 76-10680. (NMR Ser.: Vol. 11). 1976. 27.90 o.p. (ISBN 0-387-07704-9). Springer-Verlag.

--Principles of High Resolution NMR in Solids. (Illus.). 342p. 1983. 38.00 (ISBN 0-387-11852-7). Springer-Verlag.

Mehrotra, Kewal K. Horace Walpole & the English Novel: A Study of the Influence of The Castle of Otranto, 1764-1820. LC 72-83862. (Illus.). 1970. Repr. of 1934 ed. 9.50x o.p. (ISBN 0-8462-1414-8). Russell.

Mehrotra, Raja R. Names of India. (International Library of Names). 250p. 1983. text ed. 24.50x (ISBN 0-8290-1293-1). Irvington.

Mehta, A. J., jt. auth. see Bruun, P.

Mehta, Asoka. Perception of Asian Personality. 264p. 1978. 15.95x (ISBN 0-940500-63-9). Asia Bk Corp.

Mehta, Ghanshyan. The Structure of the Keynesian Revolution. LC 77-91864. 1979. 25.00x (ISBN 0-312-76770-6). St Martin.

Mehta, Gita. Karma Cola. 1979. 9.95 o.p. (ISBN 0-671-25083-3). S&S.

--Karma Kola. 1981. pap. 5.95 o.p. (ISBN 0-671-25084-1, Touchstone Bks). S&S.

Mehta, J. L. Advanced Study in the History of Medieval India (1000-1526, 3 vols. Incl. Vol. 1. 1980. text ed. 21.00x (ISBN 0-391-01918-X); Vol. 2. 1980. text ed. price not set (ISBN 0-391-01919-8); Vol. 3. 1980. text ed. price not set (ISBN 0-391-01920-1). 345p. Humanities.

--Martin Heidegger: The Way & the Vision. rev ed. 512p. 1976. Repr. of 1967 ed. text ed. 17.50x (ISBN 0-8248-0254-3). UH Pr.

Mehta, J. L., tr. see Biemel, Walter.

Mehta, M. L., jt. auth. see Harkness, E. L.

Mehta, Mark. Intractable Pain. LC 72-97913. (Major Problems in Anaesthesia Ser.: Vol. 2). (Illus.). 290p. 1973. text ed. 15.00 (ISBN 0-7216-6262-5). Saunders.

Mehta, Nitin H. & Maher, Donald J. Hospital Accounting Systems & Controls. 272p. 1977. 32.95 (ISBN 0-686-68586-5, 14919). Healthcare Fin Man Assn.

Mehta, Rama. Inside the Haveli. 208p. 1977. pap. 4.25 (ISBN 0-86578-059-5). Ind-US Inc.

Mehta, Rama, jt. auth. see Galbraith, Catherine A.

Mehta, S. S. Productivity, Production Function & Technical Change. 1980. text ed. 10.00x (ISBN 0-391-01830-2). Humanities.

Mehta, Ved. Mahatma Gandhi & His Apostles. 260p. 1977. pap. 4.95 (ISBN 0-14-004571-6). Penguin.

--Mamaji. (Illus.). 1979. 15.95 (ISBN 0-19-502640-3); pap. 7.95 (ISBN 0-19-503214-4). Oxford U Pr.

--The Photographs of Chachaji: The Making of a Documentary Film. (Illus.). 1980. 19.95 (ISBN 0-19-502792-2). Oxford U Pr.

--Vedi. (Illus.). 1982. 16.95 (ISBN 0-19-503005-2). Oxford U Pr.

Mehta, Vinod. Soviet Economic Policy: Income Differentials in the USSR. LC 77-70009. 1977. text ed. 12.50x (ISBN 0-391-00750-5). Humanities.

Mei, Chiang C. The Applied Dynamics of Ocean Surface Waves. LC 82-8639. 808p. 1982. 75.00 (ISBN 0-471-06407-6, Pub. by Wiley-Interscience). Wiley.

Meichenbaum, Donald & Jaemko, Matt, eds. Stress Reduction & Prevention. 512p. 1983. 32.50x (ISBN 0-306-41066-4, Plenum Pr). Plenum Pub.

Meichenbaum, Donald, jt. auth. see Turk, Dennis.

Meid, Louise B. Van Der see Van Der Meid, Louise B.

Meiden, Walter, jt. auth. see Moore, Olin H.

Meiden, Walter, ed. see Maurois, Michelle.

Meidl, James. Hazardous Materials Handbook. (Fire Science Ser). 1972. pap. text ed. 15.95x (ISBN 0-02-476370-5, 47637). Macmillan.

Meidl, James H. Flammable Hazardous Materials. 2nd ed. 1978. text ed. 22.95x (ISBN 0-02-476570-8). Macmillan.

Meiehnhofer, Hohannes, jt. ed. see Gross, Erhard.

Meienhofer, Johannes, jt. ed. see Goodman, Murray.

Meienhofer, Johannes, jt. ed. see Gross, Erhard.

Meier. Black Experience: Transformation of Activism. LC 72-94820. 203p. 1970. pap. 3.95 (ISBN 0-87855-558-7). Transaction Bks.

--Facilitating Children's Development: A Systematic Guide to Open Learning, 2 vols. Incl. Vol. I. Infant & Toddler Learning Episodes. 352p. 1979. pap. text ed. 14.95 (ISBN 0-8391-1261-0); Vol. II. Learning Episodes for Older Preschoolers. 320p. 1979. pap. text ed. 14.95 (ISBN 0-8391-1339-0). 1979. Univ Park.

Meier, A., ed. see Mestwerdt.

Meier, Arnold R., et al. Understanding Democracy. 1948. 1.00 o.p. (ISBN 0-8143-1016-8). Wayne St U Pr.

Meier, August & Rudick, Elliott. CORE: A Study in the Civil Rights Movement, 1942-1968. 448p. 1973. 27.50x (ISBN 0-19-501627-0). Oxford U Pr.

Meier, August & Rudwick, Elliott. Black Detroit & the Rise of the UAW. (Illus.). 1981. pap. 7.95 (ISBN 0-19-502895-3, GB 632). Oxford U Pr.

Meier, August, jt. ed. see Franklin, John H.

Meier, August, ed. see Naison, Mark.

Meier, August, ed. see Weisbrot, Robert.

Meier, G. H., jt. auth. see Birks, N.

Meier, Gerald M. & Baldwin, Robert E. Economic Development: Theory, History, Policy. LC 75-11875. 608p. 1976. Repr. of 1957 ed. 18.50 (ISBN 0-88275-299-5). Krieger.

Meier, Gerald M., ed. Leading Issues in Economic Development. 3rd ed. 1976. pap. text ed. 17.95x (ISBN 0-19-502043-X). Oxford U Pr.

Meier, Hans W. Library of Specifications Sections, 4 vols. LC 82-10149. 1983. Set. looseleaf bdg. 250.00 (ISBN 0-686-84600-1, Busn). Vol. A (ISBN 0-13-535468-4). Vol. B (ISBN 0-13-535476-5). Vol. C (ISBN 0-13-535484-6). Vol. D (ISBN 0-13-535492-7). P-H.

Meier, J. H. Developmental & Learning Disabilities: Evaluation, Management & Prevention in Children. (Illus.). 456p. 1976. text ed. 24.95 (ISBN 0-8391-0762-5). Univ Park.

Meier, Joel. Backpacking. 2nd ed. (Exploring Sports Ser.). 109p. 1983. pap. write for info. (ISBN 0-697-09960-1). Wm C Brown.

Meier, John. Gospel According to Matthew: An Access Guide. 128p. (Orig.). pap. 5.00 o.p. (ISBN 0-8215-5925-7). Sadlier.

Meier, John, jt. auth. see Brown, Raymond.

Meier, John B. Access Guide for Scripture Study: Matthew. Date not set. 2.95 (ISBN 0-8215-5932-X); 3.95 (ISBN 0-8215-5935-4). Sadlier.

Meier, John P. The Vision of Matthew: Christ, Church & Morality in the First Gospel. LC 78-70820. 1979. pap. 6.95 (ISBN 0-8091-2171-9). Paulist Pr.

Meier, Judith. Hickory & a Smooth Dime. 23p. 1975. pap. 2.25 (ISBN 0-913270-51-2). Sunstone Pr.

Meier, Lilly, jt. auth. see Hellman, Peter.

Meier, Marie. The Development & Evaluation of A Pre-School Curriculum For Severely Disabled Children. 44p. 1970. 1.50 (ISBN 0-686-38802-X). Human Res Ctr.

Meier, Matt S. & Rivera, Feliciano, eds. Dictionary of Mexican American History. LC 80-24750. (Illus.). 472p. 1981. lib. bdg. 39.95 (ISBN 0-313-21203-1, NMD/). Greenwood.

Meier, P., et al. A Grammar of Izi. (SIL Linguistics & Related Fields Ser: No. 47). 283p. 1975. 9.00x o.s.i. (ISBN 0-88312-057-7); microfiche 3.00x (ISBN 0-88312-457-2). Summer Inst Ling.

Meier, Peg. Bring Warm Clothes. LC 81-11236. (Illus.). 340p. (Orig.). (gr. 7-12). 1981. pap. 14.95 (ISBN 0-932272-06-1). Minneapolis Tribune.

Meier, Richard. Richard Meier, Architect. LC 75-38096. (Illus.). 1976. 39.50 o.p. (ISBN 0-19-502075-8). Oxford U Pr.

--Shards by Frank Stella, Text by Richard Meier. (Illus., Orig.). 1982. pap. 5.95 (ISBN 0-902825-19-4). Petersburg Pr.

Meier, Richard L. Planning for an Urban World: The Design of Resource-Conserving Cities. 1975. 33.00x o.p. (ISBN 0-262-13112-9). MIT Pr.

--Science & Economic Development: New Patterns of Living. 2nd ed. 1966. 17.50x (ISBN 0-262-13024-6). MIT Pr.

Meier, Robert C., et al. Cases in Production & Operations Management. (Illus.). 304p. 1982. 17.95 (ISBN 0-13-118950-6). P-H.

Meier, W. M. & Olson, D. H. Atlas of Zeolite Structure Types. (Illus.). 1978. pap. text ed. 5.00 (ISBN 0-9601830-0-0, Pub by Structure Comm of Intl Zeolite). Polycrystal Bk Serv.

Meiers, Steve, ed. Basic Training: A Consumer's Guide to the Military. 52p. 1982. pap. 2.95 (ISBN 0-942046-00-5). Prog Found.

Meiggs, Russell. Trees & Timber in the Ancient Mediterranean World. (Illus.). 456p. 1983. 74.00 (ISBN 0-19-814840-2). Oxford U Pr.

Meighan, Clement & True, D. L., eds. Prehistoric Trails of Atacama. (Monumenta Archaeologica: No. 7). (Illus.). 271p. 1980. 33.00 (ISBN 0-917956-10-9). UCLA Arch.

Meighan, Clement W., ed. The Archaeology of Amapa, Nayarit. LC 76-18607. (Monumenta Archaeologica: No. 2). (Illus.). 306p. 1977. 37.50 (ISBN 0-917956-01-X). UCLA Arch.

Meighan, Clement W. & Russell, Glenn, eds. Obsidian Dates III: A Compendium of Obsidian Hydration Determinations Made at the Ucla Obsidian Hydration Laboratory. (Institute of Archaeology Monograph: No. XVI). 169p. 1981. pap. 7.50 (ISBN 0-917956-20-6). UCLA Arch.

Meighan, Clement W. & Vanderhoeven, P. I., eds. Obsidian Dates II: A Compendium of Obsidian Hydration Determinations Made at the UCLA Obsidian Hydration Laboratory. (Monograph Ser.: No. VI). (Illus.). 187p. 1978. pap. 7.50 (ISBN 0-917956-28-1). UCLA Arch.

Meighan, Clement W., jt. ed. see Taylor, R. E.

Meighan, Clement W., jt. ed. see Van Tilburg, JoAnne.

Meighen, J. Van see Landsberg, H. E.

Meigs, Cornelia. The Story of Louisa Alcott. 223p. 1982. Repr. of 1935 ed. lib. bdg. 40.00 (ISBN 0-89987-591-2). Darby Bks.

Meigs, John, ed. The Cowboy in American Prints. LC 82-73997. (Illus.). 184p. 1972. ltd. ed. 100.00 (ISBN 0-8040-0721-7). Swallow.

Meigs, Robert F., jt. auth. see Meigs, Walter B.

Meigs, Walter B. & Meigs, Robert F. Accounting: The Basis for Business Decisions. 5th ed. Singer, M. & Mason, D., eds. (Illus.). 1216p. 1980. text ed. 25.95 (ISBN 0-07-041551-X, C); study guide 9.95 (ISBN 0-07-041552-8); Learning Objectives 4.95 (ISBN 0-07-041565-X); practice set 1 8.50 (ISBN 0-07-041558-7); practice set 2 9.50 (ISBN 0-07-041559-5); solutions manual 30.00 (ISBN 0-07-041560-9); overhead transparencies 375.00 (ISBN 0-07-074714-8); wksheets. sets A & B 9.50 ea. McGraw.

--Financial Accounting. 3rd ed. (Illus.). 1978. text ed. 23.95x (ISBN 0-07-041220-0, C); study guide 9.95 (ISBN 0-07-041222-7); solutions manual 25.00 (ISBN 0-07-041221-9); wkshts 8.50 (ISBN 0-07-041225-1); practice set 8.95 (ISBN 0-07-041224-3); tests & exams 16.50 (ISBN 0-07-041223-5); overhead transp 325.00 (ISBN 0-07-074735-0); visual class disp 30.00 (ISBN 0-07-074736-9); additional exam questions 21.00 (ISBN 0-07-041226-X). McGraw.

--Financial Accounting. 4th ed. (Illus.). 735p. 1983. text ed. 24.95x (ISBN 0-07-041534-X, C); instr's manual 25.00 (ISBN 0-07-041535-8); study guide avail. (ISBN 0-07-041536-6). Supplementary material avail. McGraw.

Meigs, Walter B. & Mosich, A. N. Financial Accounting. 2nd ed. (Illus.). 648p. 1975. text ed. 19.95 o.p. (ISBN 0-07-041290-1, C); wkshts. 10.00 o.p. (ISBN 0-07-041296-0); practice set 9.95 o.p. (ISBN 0-07-041293-6). solutions manual 9.95 o.p. (ISBN 0-07-041291-X). McGraw.

Meigs, Walter B., et al. Advanced Accounting. 1966. text ed. 29.95 (ISBN 0-07-041432-7, C). McGraw.

--Intermediate Accounting. 3rd ed. (Illus.). 1104p. 1974. text ed. 16.50 o.p. (ISBN 0-07-041380-0, C); 2 sets worksheets 5.50 ea. o.p. (ISBN 0-07-041383-5); checklist 1.00 o.p. (ISBN 0-07-041382-7); FASB supplement 1.95 o.p. (ISBN 0-07-041256-1). McGraw.

--Intermediate Accounting. 4th ed. 1978. text ed. 27.95 (ISBN 0-07-041255-3, C); study guide 10.00 (ISBN 0-07-041257-X). Additional materials avail. McGraw.

--Modern Advanced Accounting. (Illus.). 680p. 1975. text ed. 20.00 o.p. (ISBN 0-07-041390-8, C). tests 25.00 o.p. (ISBN 0-07-041395-9). McGraw.

--Modern Advanced Accounting. 2nd ed. 1978. text ed. 29.00x (ISBN 0-07-041201-4, C); solution manual 30.00 (ISBN 0-07-041202-2); checklist 1.50 (ISBN 0-07-041203-0); wkshts 9.95 (ISBN 0-07-041204-9); study guide 9.95 (ISBN 0-07-041205-7); examination questions 15.00 (ISBN 0-07-041206-5); overhead transp 270.00 (ISBN 0-07-075009-2). McGraw.

Meigs, William M. Life of Charles Jared Ingersoll. LC 71-127194. (American Scene Ser). 1970. Repr. of 1897 ed. lib. bdg. 42.50 (ISBN 0-306-70041-7). Da Capo.

--Life of John Caldwell Calhoun, 2 vols. in 1. LC 75-127195. (American Scene Ser). 1970. Repr. of 1917 ed. lib. bdg. 89.50 (ISBN 0-306-70042-5). Da Capo.

--Life of Thomas Hart Benton. LC 71-126599. (American Scene Ser). 1970. Repr. of 1904 ed. lib. bdg. 65.00 (ISBN 0-306-70043-3). Da Capo.

--Relation of the Judiciary to the Constitution. LC 73-124896. (American Constitutional & Legal History Ser). 1971. Repr. of 1919 ed. lib. bdg. 35.00 (ISBN 0-306-71988-6). Da Capo.

Meij, J. L. Mechanization in Agriculture. 1960. 47.50x o.p. (ISBN 0-686-50048-2). Elliots Bks.

Meijden, R. Van Der see Van Der Meijden, R.

Meijer, Anton, jt. auth. see Peeters, Paul.

Meijering, E. P. Hilary of Poitiers on the Trinity: De Trinitate 1, 1-19, 2, 3. (Philosophia Patrum: Vol. 6). ix, 199p. 1982. write for info. (ISBN 90-04-06734-5). E J Brill.

Meijlink, Jane, ed. see De Waal, M.

Meikle, Jeffrey. Twentieth Century Limited: Industrial Design in America, 1925-1939. Davis, Allen F., ed. (American Civilization Ser.). (Illus.). 264p. 1979. 29.95 (ISBN 0-87722-158-8). Temple U Pr.

Meikle, Jeffrey L. Twentieth Century Limited: Industrial Design in America, 1925-1939. 249p. 1981. pap. 9.95 (ISBN 0-87722-246-0). Temple U Pr.

Meiklejohn, Alexander. Political Freedom: The Constitutional Powers of the People. LC 78-27616. 1979. Repr. of 1960 ed. lib. bdg. 17.75x (ISBN 0-313-20907-3, MEPF). Greenwood.

Meilach, Dona Z. Before You Buy a Computer. LC 82-18281. 1983. 15.95 (ISBN 0-517-54732-5); pap. 8.95 (ISBN 0-517-54733-3). Crown.

--Contemporary Batik & Tie-Dye. LC 72-84320. (Arts & Crafts Ser). (Illus.). 228p. 1973. 8.95 o.p. (ISBN 0-517-50088-4); pap. 6.95 (ISBN 0-517-50089-2). Crown.

--Contemporary Stone Sculpture: Aesthetics, Methods, Appreciation. (Illus.). 1970. 10.95 o.p. (ISBN 0-685-03423-2, 517K08989). Crown.

--Creating Art with Bread Dough. (Illus.). 1976. 8.95 o.p. (ISBN 0-517-52589-5); pap. 6.95 (ISBN 0-517-52590-9). Crown.

--Creating Small Wood Objects As Functional Sculpture. 1976. 12.95 o.p. (ISBN 0-517-51866-X); pap. 6.95 (ISBN 0-517-51867-8). Crown.

--Macrame Accessories: Patterns & Ideas for Knotting. (Illus.). 1972. 5.95 o.p. (ISBN 0-517-50194-5); pap. 3.95 o.p. (ISBN 0-517-50009-4). Crown.

--Macrame Gnomes & Puppets: Creative Patterns & Ideas. (Illus.). 96p. 1980. pap. 7.95 o.p. (ISBN 0-517-54010-X). Crown.

--Modern Approach to Basketry with Fibers & Grasses. (Arts & Crafts Ser.). (Illus.). 224p. 1974. 9.95 o.p. (ISBN 0-517-51588-1); pap. 5.95 o.p. (ISBN 0-517-51689-6). Crown.

--Papier-Mache Artistry. LC 78-147334. (Arts & Crafts Ser). (Illus.). 1971. 8.95 o.p. (ISBN 0-685-92704-0, 0-517-K08911). Crown.

--Soft Sculpture & Other Soft Art Forms. LC 73-41153. (Arts & Craft Ser.). (Illus.). 256p. 1974. 8.95 o.p. (ISBN 0-517-51463-X); pap. 5.95 o.p. (ISBN 0-517-51464-8). Crown.

--Tile Decorating with Gemma. (Illus.). 1978. 12.95 (ISBN 0-517-52950-5); pap. 6.95 o.p. (ISBN 0-517-52951-3). Crown.

Meilach, Dona Z. & Hoor, Elvie T. Collage & Assemblage. (Illus.). 264p. 1973. 4.95 o.p. (ISBN 0-517-50577-0). Crown.

Meilach, Dona Z., jt. auth. see Kowal, Dennis, Jr.

Meiland, Jack W. Scepticism & Historical Knowledge. (Orig.). 1965. pap. text ed. 3.95 (ISBN 0-685-19765-4). Phila Bk Co.

Meili, Janet & Meili, Philip. Who Is This Man Jesus? Zapel, Arthur L., ed. LC 82-82076. (Illus.). 205p. (Orig.). 1982. pap. text ed. 8.95 (ISBN 0-916260-17-8). Meriwether Pub.

Meili, Philip, jt. auth. see Meili, Janet.

Meili, Richard, jt. auth. see Nuttin, Joseph.

Meilin, Han. One Hundred Chickens. (Illus.). 100p. 1980. 35.00 (ISBN 0-8351-1046-X). China Bks.

--Still in the Land of the Living. (Illus.). 200p. 1980. 29.95 (ISBN 0-8351-1047-8). China Bks.

Meillassoux, C., ed. Maidens, Meal & Money. Edholm, Felicity, tr. from French. LC 79-52834. (Themes in the Social Sciences Ser.). 200p. 34.50 (ISBN 0-521-22902-2); pap. 12.95 (ISBN 0-521-29708-7). Cambridge U Pr.

Meillet, Antoine. Altarmenisches Elementarbuch. LC 80-24325. (Anatolian & Caucasian Studies Ser.). 228p. 1980. Repr. of 1913 ed. 35.00x (ISBN 0-88206-043-0). Caravan Bks.

Meillon, Botha De see Freeman, Paul & De Meillon, Botha.

Mein, R. G., jt. auth. see McMahon, T. A.

Meinardus, Otto F. St. John of Patmos & the Seven Churches of the Apocalypse. (In the Footsteps of the Saints Ser.). 160p. 15.00 (ISBN 0-89241-070-1); pap. 5.95 (ISBN 0-89241-043-4). Caratzas Bros.

--St. Paul in Ephesus & the Cities of Galatia & Cyprus. (In the Footsteps of the Saints). (Illus.). 160p. 15.00 (ISBN 0-89241-071-X); pap. 5.95 (ISBN 0-89241-044-2). Caratzas Bros.

--St. Paul in Greece. (In the Footsteps of the Saints). 160p. 15.00 (ISBN 0-89241-045-0); pap. 5.95 (ISBN 0-89241-072-8). Caratzas Bros.

--St. Paul's Last Journey. (In the Footsteps of the Saints Ser.). 160p. 15.00 (ISBN 0-686-81741-9); pap. 5.95 (ISBN 0-89241-046-9). Caratzas Bros.

Meinck, F. & Mohle, K. Dictionary of Water & Sewage Engineering. 2nd ed. (Ger., Eng., Fr., & Ital.). 1977. 127.75 (ISBN 0-444-99811-X). Elsevier.

Meindl, Robert J., tr. see Wickert, Maria.

Meinecke, Friedrich. The Age of German Liberation, 1795-1815. Paret, Peter & Fischer, Helmut, trs. from Ger. LC 74-79767. Orig. Title: Das Zeitalter der Deutschen Erhebung. 1977. 30.00x (ISBN 0-520-02792-2); pap. 5.95x (ISBN 0-520-03454-6). U of Cal Pr.

--Historism: The Rise of a New Historical Outlook. 524p. 1972. 32.00 (ISBN 0-7100-7045-4). Routledge & Kegan.

Meinel, Hans. A Course in Scientific German: German for Technicians & Scientists. 1981. 40.00x o.p. (ISBN 0-686-75664-9, Pub. by European Schoolbks England). State Mutual Bk.

Meiners, Fredericka. A History of Rice University: The Institute Years, 1907-1963. (Illus.). 270p. 1982. 29.50 (ISBN 0-89263-250-X). Rice Univ.

Meiners, H. F. Physics Demonstration Experiments, 2 vols. 1493p. 1970. Set. 72.95 (ISBN 0-471-06759-8). Wiley.

Meiners, H. F., et al. Laboratory Physics. 1972. 18.50 (ISBN 0-471-59159-9). Wiley.

Meiners, Karin. Der Besondere Weg, ein Weib Zu Werden. 236p. (Ger.). 1982. write for info. (ISBN 3-8204-7094-8). P Lang Pubs.

Meiners, Roger E. Victim Compensation. LC 77-80772. 144p. 1978. 17.95 (ISBN 0-669-01667-5). Lexington Bks.

Meiners, Roger E. & Lingleb, Al H. The Legal Environment of Business. (Illus.). 600p. 1982. text ed. 23.95 (ISBN 0-314-63273-5). West Pub.

Meinhard, Heinrich. German Wines. (Illus.). 1971. 7.95 o.p. (ISBN 0-85362-107-1, Oriel). Routledge & Kegan.

Meinhardt, F. Untersuchungen Zur Genetik Des Fortpflanzungsverhaltens und der Fruchtkoerper- und Antibiotikabbildung Des Basidiomyceten Agrocybe Aegerita. (Bibliotheca Mycologica: No. 75). (Illus.). 128p. (Ger.). 1981. pap. text ed. 16.00x (ISBN 3-7682-1275-0). Lubrecht & Cramer.

Meinhardt, H. Models of Biological Pattern Formation. 1982. 37.00 (ISBN 0-12-488620-5). Acad Pr.

Meinhardt, Peter. Inventions, Patents & Trade Marks in Great Britain. 1971 ed. 397p. 25.00 (ISBN 0-686-37380-4). Beekman Pubs.

Meinhoper, Johannes, jt. ed. see Gross, Erhard.

Meinig, D. W. Southwest: Three Peoples in Geographical Change, 1600-1970. (Historical Geography of North America Ser). (Orig.). 1971. text ed. 11.95x (ISBN 0-19-501288-7); pap. text ed. 8.95x (ISBN 0-19-501289-5). Oxford U Pr.

Meinig, D. W., ed. The Interpretation of Ordinary Landscapes. (Illus.). 1979. pap. text ed. 8.95 (ISBN 0-19-502536-9). Oxford U Pr.

Meinong, Alexius. On Assumptions. Heanue, James E., Jr., ed. LC 75-27929. 396p. Date not set. 24.50x (ISBN 0-520-03139-3). U of Cal Pr. Postponed.

Meins, Betty & Floyd, Wanita. How to Groom Your Cat. (Illus.). 1972. 4.95 o.p. (ISBN 0-87666-766-3, PS-683). TFH Pubns.

--How to Show Your Own Cat. (Illus.). 1972. pap. 7.95 (ISBN 0-87666-181-9, PS-682). TFH Pubns.

Meir, Golda, jt. auth. see Levine, Gemma.

Meirion-Jones, Gwyn. The Vernacular Architecture of Brittany. 420p. 1982. text ed. 57.00x (ISBN 0-85976-060-X, Pub. by Donald England). Humanities.

Meirovitch, L. Methods of Analytical Dynamics. 1970. 39.95 (ISBN 0-07-041455-6, C). McGraw.

Meirovitch, Leonard. Analytical Methods in Vibrations. 1967. 32.95x (ISBN 0-02-380140-9). Macmillan.

--Elements of Vibration Analysis. (Illus.). 480p. 1975. text ed. 36.00 (ISBN 0-07-041340-1, C); solutions manual 9.00 (ISBN 0-07-041341-X). McGraw.

Meirowitz, Marcus & Jacobs, Paul I. Brain Muscle Builders: Games to Increase Your Natural Intelligence. 288p. 1983. 13.95 (ISBN 0-13-080986-1); pap. 6.95 (ISBN 0-13-080978-0). P-H.

Meis, Leopoldo De see DeMeis, Leopoldo & De Meis.

Meisami, Esmail & Brazier, Mary A. Neural Growth & Differentiation. (International Brain Research Organization Monographs: Vol. 5). 546p. 1979. text ed. 57.00 (ISBN 0-89004-378-7). Raven.

Meisel, James H. The Genesis of Georges Sorel: An Account of His Formative Period Followed by a Study of His Influence. 320p. 1982. Repr. of 1951 ed. lib. bdg. 32.50x (ISBN 0-313-23658-5, HEGS). Greenwood.

Meisel, Jerome. Principles of Electromechanical-Energy Conversion. 1966. text ed. 23.50 o.p. (ISBN 0-07-041448-3, C). McGraw.
--Principles of Electromechanical-Energy Conversion. LC 82-6540. 658p. 1983. Repr. of 1966 ed. lib. bdg. price not set (ISBN 0-89874-495-4). Krieger.
Meisel, Juergen M. & Pam, Martin D., eds. Linear Order & Generative Theory. (Current Issues in Linguistic Theory Ser.). vii, 507p. 1979. 46.00 (ISBN 90-272-0908-1, 7). Benjamins North Am.
Meisel, Martin. Realizations: Narrative, Pictorial, & Theatrical Arts of the Nineteenth Century. LC 82-12292. (Illus.). 416p. 1983. 45.00x (ISBN 0-691-06553-5). Princeton U Pr.
Meisels, S. Special Education & Development. 336p. 1979. pap. text ed. 19.95 (ISBN 0-8391-1351-X). Univ Park.
Meisenholder, Robert, jt. auth. see Broun, Kenneth S.
Meiser, jt. auth. see Laidler.
Meislich, Herbert, et al. Schaum's Outline of Organic Chemistry. 1977. pap. 8.95 (ISBN 0-07-041457-2, SP). McGraw.
Meislin, Jack. Rehabilitation Medicine & Psychiatry. (Illus.). 564p. 1976. 32.75x (ISBN 0-398-03432-X). C C Thomas.
Meisner, Maurice. LiTa-Chao & the Origins of Chinese Marxism. LC 67-10904. 1970. pap. text ed. 6.95x (ISBN 0-689-70221-3, 154). Atheneum.
--Marxism, Maoism & Utopianism: Eight Essays. 276p. 1982. 16.95 (ISBN 0-299-08420-5). U of Wis Pr.
Meisner, Maurice & Murphy, Rhoads. The Mozartian Historian: Essays on the Works of Joseph R. Levenson. LC 74-82849. 250p. 1976. 24.50x (ISBN 0-520-02826-0). U of Cal Pr.
Meiss, Millard. Francesco Traini. Maginnis, Hayden B., ed. (Art History Ser.: No. VI). (Illus.). 124p. 1983. 40.00 (ISBN 0-916276-12-0). Decatur Hse.
Meissner, Boris. The Communist Party of the Soviet Union. Reshetar, John S., Jr., ed. Holling, Fred, tr. LC 75-27684. (Foreign Policy Research Institute Ser.: No. 4). 276p. 1976. Repr. of 1956 ed. lib. bdg. 18.00x (ISBN 0-8371-8461-4, MECP). Greenwood.
Meissner, Gunter, jt. auth. see Buttner, Horst.
Meissner, Loren P. & Organick, Elliot I. FORTRAN Seventy-Seven: Featuring Structured Programming. 3rd ed. LC 78-74689. 1980. pap. text ed. 18.95 (ISBN 0-201-05499-X). A-W.
Meissner, Loren P., jt. auth. see Organick, Elliot I.
Meissner, W. W., jt. auth. see Zetzel, Elizabeth.
Meissner, William. Learning to Breathe Underwater. LC 79-18881. 66p. 1980. 8.95x (ISBN 0-8214-0418-0, 82-83103); pap. 5.95 (ISBN 0-8214-0426-1, 82-83111). Ohio U Pr.
Meister, A. Advances in Enzymology & Related Areas of Molecular Biology, Vol. 54. (Advances in Enzymology). 375p. 1982. write for info (ISBN 0-471-09730-6, Pub. by Wiley-Interscience). Wiley.
Meister, Alton. Advances in Enzymology & Related Areas of Molecular Biology, Vol. 52. LC 42-9213. 456p. 1981. 42.95x (ISBN 0-471-08120-5, Pub. by Wiley-Interscience). Wiley.
--Advances in Enzymology & Related Areas of Molecular Biology, Vol. 53. LC 41-9213. (Advances in Enzymology). 460p. 1982. 45.00x (ISBN 0-471-08405-0, Pub. by Wiley-Interscience). Wiley.
Meister, Alton, ed. Advances in Enzymology & Related Areas of Molecular Biology. Vol. 45, 1977. 48.00 o.p. (ISBN 0-471-02726-X); Vol. 46, 1978. 48.00 o.p. (ISBN 0-471-02993-9); Vol. 47, 1978. 51.00 o.p. (ISBN 0-471-04116-5); Vol. 51, 1980, 225p. 42.95x (ISBN 0-471-05653-7). Wiley.
Meister, Barbara, jt. auth. see Bullock, Waneta B.
Meister, Charles W. The Year of the Lord: A. D. Eighteen Forty-Four. LC 82-23976. 272p. 1983. lib. bdg. 18.95x (ISBN 0-89950-037-4). McFarland & Co.
Meister, David. Behavioral Foundations of System Development. LC 76-1834. (Human Factors Ser.). 464p. 1976. 55.50 o.s.i. (ISBN 0-471-59195-5). Wiley.
--Human Factors: Theory & Practice. LC 77-148505. (Human Factors Ser). 1971. 49.95 (ISBN 0-471-59190-4, Pub. by Wiley-Interscience). Wiley.
Meister, Jacques-Henri. De l'Origine des Principes Religieux. (Holbach & His Friends Ser). 72p. (Fr.). 1974. Repr. of 1768 ed. lib. bdg. 21.00x o.p. (ISBN 0-8287-0597-6, 1526). Clearwater Pub.
Meister, Michael W., ed. Encyclopedia of Indian Temple Architecture: South India, Lower Dravidadesa, 300 B.C.-A.D. 1326, 2 pts, Vol. 1. LC 82-50173. (Illus.). 735p. 1983. Set. 75.00x (ISBN 0-8122-7840-2). U of Pa Pr.
Meister, Richard. Race & Ethnicity in Modern America. (Problems in American History Ser.). 1975. pap. 5.95 (ISBN 0-669-91124-0). Heath.
Meister, Richard J., jt. auth. see Gluck, Peter R.
Meister, Robert. Fathers: Daughters, Sons, Fathers Reveal Their Deepest Feelings. 224p. 1981. 11.95 (ISBN 0-399-90107-8, Marek). Putnam Pub Group.
Meistrell, Lois & Barbaresi, Sara M. How to Raise & Train a Dachshund. pap. 2.95 (ISBN 0-87666-276-9, DS1011). TFH Pubns.
Meites, Louis. Handbook of Analytical Chemistry. 1963. 75.00 o.p. (ISBN 0-07-041336-3, P&RB). McGraw.
--Polarographic Techniques. 2nd ed. LC 65-19735. (Electrochemical Data Ser.). (Illus.). 1965. 70.95 (ISBN 0-470-59205-2, Pub. by Wiley-Interscience). Wiley.
Meites, Louis & Thomas, H. C. Advanced Analytical Chemistry. 1958. text ed. 25.00 o.p. (ISBN 0-07-041335-5, C). McGraw.
Meites, Louis & Zuman, Petr. CRC Handbook of Organic Electrochemistry, Vol. 5. 472p. 1982. 75.00 (ISBN 0-8493-7225-9). CRC Pr.
--Electrochemical Data, Vol. A, Pt. 1. LC 74-14958. 742p. 1974. 60.00 (ISBN 0-471-59200-5). Krieger.
Meites, S. see Reiner, Miriam, et al.
Meitus, Irv J., jt. ed. see Weinberg, Bernd.
Mejia, Alfonso, et al. Foreign Medical Graduates: The Case of the United States. LC 80-7576. 240p. 1980. 21.95 (ISBN 0-669-03760-5). Lexington Bks.
Mejias, Hugo & Garza-Swan, Gloria. Espanol Para Hablantes Nativos. 1981. pap. text ed. 14.95x (ISBN 0-02-380170-0). Macmillan.
Mekeel, Arhtur J. The Relation of the Quakers to the American Revolution. LC 79-66173. 1979. pap. text ed. 14.00 (ISBN 0-8191-0792-1). U Pr of Amer.
Melady, John H. Home Owners' Complete Garden Handbook. (Illus.). 1960. 4.95 (ISBN 0-448-01578-1, G&D). Putnam Pub Group.
Melady, Thomas P. The Revolution of Color. LC 75-41507. 208p. 1976. Repr. of 1966 ed. lib. bdg. 18.50 (ISBN 0-8371-8701-X, MERC). Greenwood.
Melamed, Elissa. Mirror, Mirror: The Terror of Not Being Young. 1983. price not set (ISBN 0-671-43429-2, Linden). S&S.
Melamed, Lawrence E., jt. auth. see Forgus, Ronald H.
Melamerson, Larry. The Cellulite-Free Body. (Illus.). 192p. 1981. 11.95 (ISBN 0-399-12527-2). Putnam Pub Group.
Melanchthon, Philipp. Selected Writings. Flack, Elmer E. & Satre, Lowell J., eds. Hill, Charles L., tr. LC 78-5175. 1978. Repr. of 1962 ed. lib. bdg. 20.75x (ISBN 0-313-20384-9, MESW). Greenwood.
Meland, Sam. Electrical Project Management. (Illus.). 320p. 1983. 32.50 (ISBN 0-07-041338-X, P&RB). McGraw.
Melander, Ingrid. The Poetry of Sylvia Plath: A Study of Themes. (Gothenburg Studies in English). 119p. (Orig.). 1972. pap. text ed. 15.00x (ISBN 0-391-00425-5). Humanities.
Melander, Lars & Saunders, William H., Jr. Reaction Rates of Isotopic Molecules. LC 79-12368. 1980. 43.95 (ISBN 0-471-04396-6, Pub. by Wiley-Interscience). Wiley.
Melanson, Richard A., ed. Neither Cold War nor Detente? Soviet-American Relations in the 1980s. LC 81-16299. 243p. 1982. 14.95x (ISBN 0-8139-0924-4); pap. 4.95x (ISBN 0-8139-0953-8). U Pr of Va.
Melbourne House Publishers. Thirty Programs for the Timex PC 1000. 192p. 1983. 15.95 (ISBN 0-13-919019-8); pap. 9.95 (ISBN 0-13-919001-5). P-H.
Melcher, Arlyn J. Structure & Process of Organization: A Systems Approach. (Illus.). 480p. 1976. 23.95 (ISBN 0-13-855254-1). P-H.
Melcher, Daniel & Larrick. Printing & Promotion Handbook: How to Plan, Produce, & Use Printing, Advertising & Direct Mail. 3rd ed. 1966. 38.50 (ISBN 0-07-041451-3, P&RB). McGraw.
Melcher, James R. Continuum Electromechanics. (Illus.). 484p. 1981. text ed. 42.50x (ISBN 0-262-13165-X). MIT Pr.
--Field-Coupled Surface Waves: A Comparative Study of Surface-Coupled EHD & MHD Systems. 1963. 17.50x (ISBN 0-262-13015-7). MIT Pr.
Melcher, Robert A. & Warch, Willard F. Music for Advanced Study. (Orig.). 1964. pap. text ed. 17.95 (ISBN 0-13-607317-4). P-H.
--Music for Keyboard Harmony. 1966. pap. text ed. 17.95 (ISBN 0-13-607432-4). P-H.
--Music for Score Reading. LC 78-119859. (Music Ser). 1971. pap. text ed. 16.95 (ISBN 0-13-607507-X). P-H.
Melchers, Bernard. Traditional Chinese Cut-Paper Designs. LC 77-88654. (Pictorial Archives Ser.). (Illus.). 1978. pap. 2.50 (ISBN 0-486-23581-5). Dover.
Melchinger, Siegfried. Anton Chekhov. Tarcov, Edith, tr. LC 76-163146. (Literature and Life Ser.). 11.95 (ISBN 0-8044-2615-5). Ungar.
--Euripides. Rosenbaum, Samuel, tr. LC 72-79983. (Literature & Life Ser.). (Illus.). 1973. 11.95 (ISBN 0-8044-2612-0). Ungar.
--Sophocles. Scrase, David, tr. LC 72-79931. (Literature and Life Ser.). (Illus.). 1974. 11.95 (ISBN 0-8044-2617-1). Ungar.
Melchior, Ib. The Watchdogs of Abaddon. LC 78-69507. 1979. 12.45i (ISBN 0-06-012967-0, HarpT). Har-Row.
Melchiori, Giorgio. Shakespeare's Dramatic Meditations: An Experiment in Criticism. 1976. 34.00x (ISBN 0-19-812073-7). Oxford U Pr.
--The Tightrope Walkers. LC 73-14036. 277p. 1974. Repr. of 1956 ed. lib. bdg. 15.75x (ISBN 0-8371-7141-5, METW). Greenwood.
Melchoir, P. The Tides of the Planet Earth. 2nd ed. LC 82-16567. (Illus.). 648p. 1983. 90.00 (ISBN 0-08-026248-1). Pergamon.
Melchor, Jim & Lohr, Gordon. Eastern Shore, Virginia, Raised-Panel Furniture, 1730-1830. LC 82-72773. (Illus.). 136p. (Orig.). 1982. pap. 20.00 (ISBN 0-940744-39-2). Chrysler Museum.
Mel'cuk, Igor K. & Percov, Nikolaj V. Suface Syntax of English: A Formal Model within the Meaning-Text Framework. 600p. 1983. 68.00 (ISBN 90-272-1515-4). Benjamins North Am.
Meldal-Johnsen, Trevor. This Cruel Beauty. 368p. (Orig.). 1983. pap. 3.50 (ISBN 0-380-81851-5). Avon.
Melden, A. I. Ethical Theories: A Book of Readings with Revisions. 2nd ed. 1967. text ed. 23.95 (ISBN 0-13-290122-6). P-H.
--Rights & Persons. LC 77-80180. 1978. 28.50x (ISBN 0-520-03528-3); pap. 5.95 (ISBN 0-520-03839-8). U of Cal Pr.
Melden, A. I., ed. see Murphy, Arthur E.
Meldman, Monte J., et al. Occupational Therapy Manual. 88p. 1969. photocopy ed. spiral 9.75x (ISBN 0-398-01283-0). C C Thomas.
Meldrum, B. S. & Marsden, C. D., eds. Primate Models of Neurological Disorders. LC 74-21980. (Advances in Neurology: Vol. 10). 378p. 1975. 40.00 (ISBN 0-89004-002-8). Raven.
Meldysh, L. V., jt. auth. see Jeffries, C. D.
Mele, Jim, jt. auth. see Fiedler, Jean.
Mele, Pietro P. Tibet. (Illus.). 1969. text ed. 30.00 o.p. (ISBN 0-8188-0194-8, Oxford & IBH Pub Co). Paragon.
Meleager. The Poems of Meleager. Whigham, Peter, tr. LC 75-7196. 128p. 1976. 19.95x (ISBN 0-520-03003-6). U of Cal Pr.
Melek, Jacques. California Commercial Industrial Directories: Alamedia, No. 1. 200p. (Orig.). 1982. pap. write for info. (ISBN 0-942330-22-6); pap. 48.00 set of 16 (ISBN 0-686-35979-8). J Melek.
--California Commercial Industrial Directories: Central Sierra Counties, No. 60. 200p. (Orig.). 1982. pap. write for info.; of 60 48.00 set (ISBN 0-686-35977-1). J Melek.
--California Commercial Industrial Directories, No. 33. (Riverside Ser.). 200p. 1982. pap. write for info. (ISBN 0-942330-54-4); of 60 48.00 set (ISBN 0-686-35962-3). J Melek.
--California Commercial Industrial Directories: Marin, No. 21. 200p. (Orig.). 1982. pap. write for info. (ISBN 0-942330-42-0); pap. 48.00 set of 60 (ISBN 0-686-98669-5). J Melek.
--California Commercial Industrial Directories: Mendocino, No. 23. 200p. (Orig.). 1982. pap. write for info. (ISBN 0-942330-21-8); pap. 48.00 set of 60 (ISBN 0-686-98662-8). J Melek.
--California Commercial Industrial Directories: Northern State Counties, No. 58. 200p. (Orig.). 1982. pap. write for info. (ISBN 0-942330-79-X); of 60 48.00 set (ISBN 0-686-98787-X). J Melek.
--Lyrics of Love: Vol. 1, Songs & Poems. LC 81-85773. 120p. 1981. Vol. 1. write for info. (ISBN 0-942330-00-5); pap. 6.00 (ISBN 0-686-96966-9). Sunrise Pubns.
Meleka, Fikri M. Dimensions of the Cancer Problem. viii, 172p. 1983. pap. 29.50 (ISBN 3-8055-3622-4). S Karger.
Melen, R. & Buss, D. Charged Coupled Devices: Technology & Applications. LC 76-20887. (IEEE Press Reprint Ser.). 1977. 31.95 (ISBN 0-471-02570-4); pap. 18.95 o.p. (ISBN 0-471-02571-2). Wiley.
Melen, Roger & Buss, Dennis, eds. Charge-Coupled Devices: Technology & Applications. LC 76-20887. 1977. 31.95 (ISBN 0-87942-083-9). Inst Electrical.
Melendy, H. Brett. Asians in America: Filipinos, Koreans, & East Indians. (Immigrant Heritage of America Ser.). 1977. lib. bdg. 11.95 (ISBN 0-8057-8414-4, Twayne). G K Hall.
--The Oriental Americans. (Immigrant Heritage of America Ser.). 1972. lib. bdg. 11.95 o.p. (ISBN 0-8057-3254-3, Twayne). G K Hall.
Melentiev, L. A., ed. Energy Reviews: Nuclear Power Systems. (Section A - Soviet Technology Reviews Ser.: Vol. 1). 450p. 1982. write for info. (ISBN 3-7186-0071-4). Harwood Academic.
Melfi, Rudy C. Permar's Oral Embryology & Microscopic Anatomy. 7th ed. LC 82-240. (Illus.). 206p. 1982. text ed. 15.00 (ISBN 0-8121-0835-3). Lea & Febiger.
Melges, Buddy & Mason, Charles. Sailing Smart. LC 82-15557. (Illus.). 216p. 1983. 16.95 (ISBN 0-03-058579-1). HR&W.
Melges, Frederick T. Time & the Inner Future: A Temporal Approach to Psychiatric Disorders. 496p. 1982. 32.50 (ISBN 0-471-86075-1, Pub. by Wiley-Interscience). Wiley.
Melhem, D. H. Children of the House Afire: More Notes on Ninety-Fourth Street. LC 76-55950. 81p. 1976. pap. 2.95 o.p. (ISBN 0-935468-02-1, Coward). Putnam Pub Group.
Melichar, Herbert, jt. auth. see Kaneko, Erika.
Melikian-Chirvani, Assadullah S. Islamic Metalwork from the Iranian World, 8th-18th Century, Vol. 1. 500p. 1982. 200.00x (ISBN 0-686-98222-3, Pub. by HMSO). State Mutual Bk.
Melillo, G., et al, eds. Respiratory Allergy. 214p. 1980. pap. 30.50x (ISBN 0-89352-115-9). Masson Pub.
Melin, Grace H. Dorothea Dix: Girl Reformer. (Childhood of Famous Americans Ser). (Illus.). (gr. 3-7). 1963. 3.95 o.p. (ISBN 0-672-50043-4). Bobbs.
Melinek, Menachem, jt. ed. see Mullahy, Patrick.
Melinkoff, Ellen. The Flavor of Los Angeles: How to Find the Best of the Ethnic Experience in Los Angeles. (Illus., Orig.). 1983. pap. 7.95 (ISBN 0-87701-248-2). Chronicle Bks.
Melio, Nancy K., jt. auth. see Mendelson, Jack H.
Melish, J. S. & Hanna, J. Genetic Environmental Interaction in Diabetes Mellitus. (International Congress Ser.). 1982. 72.50 (ISBN 0-444-90202-3). Elsevier.
Melissinos, Adrian. Experiments in Modern Physics. 1966. text ed. 28.00 (ISBN 0-12-489850-5). Acad Pr.
Melius, Kenneth W. National Forest Campground Guide. LC 82-51299. (Illus.). 310p. 1983. pap. 8.95 (ISBN 0-9610130-0-1). Tensleep.
Melkman, Alan V. How to Handle Major Customers Profitably. 1979. text ed. 37.25x (ISBN 0-566-02097-1). Gower Pub Ltd.
Mell, Donald C. A Poetics of Augustan Elegy: Studies of Poems by Dryden, Pope, Prior, Swift, Gray & Johnson. 116p. (Orig.). 1974. pap. text ed. 11.50x o.p. (ISBN 90-6203-278-8). Humanities.
Mell, Donald C., Jr., ed. English Poetry, Sixteen Sixty to Eighteen Hundred: A Guide to Information Sources. LC 73-16974. (American Literature, English Literature, & World Literature in English Ser.: Vol. 40). 400p. 1982. 42.00x (ISBN 0-8103-1230-1). Gale.
Mell, Linnaea Marvell- see Marvell-Mell, Linnaea.
Mellach. Papercraft. (The Grosset Art Instruction Ser.: No. 62). (Illus.). 48p. Date not set. pap. price not set (ISBN 0-448-00571-9, G&D). Putnam Pub Group.
--Printmaking. (The Grosset Art Instruction Ser.: No. 54). (Illus.). 48p. Date not set. pap. price not set (ISBN 0-448-00563-8, G&D). Putnam Pub Group.
Mellafe, Rolando. Negro Slavery in Latin America. 1975. 30.00x (ISBN 0-520-02106-1). U of Cal Pr.
Mellanby, Helen. Animal Life in Fresh Water. 6th ed. 1975. pap. 11.95x (ISBN 0-412-21360-5, Pub. by Chapman & Hall). Methuen Inc.
Mellard, James M. Quaternion: Stories, Poems, Plays, Essays. 1978. pap. 12.50x (ISBN 0-673-15102-6). Scott F.
Melleby, Alexander. Y's Way to a Healthy Back. (Illus.). 224p. 1982. 13.95 (ISBN 0-8329-0252-7); pap. 8.95 (ISBN 0-8329-0147-4). New Century.
Mellen, Francis, jt. auth. see Warren, Sukanya.
Mellen, Joan. Privilege: The Enigma of Sasha Bruce. 1982. 17.95 (ISBN 0-385-27447-5). Dial.
Mellen, Joan, ed. The World of Luis Bunuel: Essays in Criticism. (Illus.). 1978. pap. 8.95 (ISBN 0-19-502399-4, GB 543, GB). Oxford U Pr.
Mellen, Kathleen D. Island Kingdom Passes. 1958. 8.95 o.p. (ISBN 0-8038-3357-1). Hastings.
Mellenthin, F. W. Von see Von Mellenthin, F. W.
Meller, H. London Cemetaries: An Illustrated Guide. 1981. 60.00x o.p. (ISBN 0-86127-003-7, Pub. by Avebury Pub England). State Mutual Bk.
Meller, Norman. Congress of Micronesia: Development of the Legislative Process in the Trust Territory of the Pacific Islands. 1969. 20.00x (ISBN 0-87022-515-4). UH Pr.
Meller, Norman & Anthony, James M. Fiji Goes to the Polls: The Crucial Legislative Council Elections of 1963. LC 68-20260. (Illus.). 1969. 10.00x (ISBN 0-8248-0080-X, Eastwest Ctr). UH Pr.
Meller, Walter C. Old Times. LC 68-26592. (Illus.). 1968. Repr. of 1925 ed. 30.00x (ISBN 0-8103-3453-4). Gale.
Mellerio, Andre. Odilon Redon. LC 67-27461. (Graphic Art Ser). (Fr). 1968. Repr. of 1913 ed. lib. bdg. 65.00 (ISBN 0-306-70975-9). Da Capo.
Mellers, W. Resources of Music: Introduction & Score. 6.95x (ISBN 0-521-07263-8). Cambridge U Pr.
Mellers, Wilfrid. Beethoven & the Voice of God. (Illus.). 447p. 1983. 49.95 (ISBN 0-19-520402-6). Oxford U Pr.
--The Twilight of the Gods: The Music of the Beatles. LC 73-3508. (Illus.). 1975. pap. 7.95 (ISBN 0-02-871390-7). Schirmer Bks.
Mellert, Robert B. What Is Process Theology? LC 74-28933. 1975. pap. 2.95 o.p. (ISBN 0-8091-1867-X). Paulist Pr.
Mellett, Peter, jt. auth. see Christie, Margaret J.
Mellichamp, Duncan A., ed. Real Time Computing: With Applications to Data Acquisition & Control. 464p. 1983. text ed. 39.50 (ISBN 0-442-21372-7). Van Nos Reinhold.
Mellick, J. S., ed. see Kingsley, Henry.
Melling, J. Liquid Membrane Processes in Hydrometallurgy, 1979. 1981. 95.00x (ISBN 0-686-97108-6, Pub. by W Spring England). State Mutual Bk.
Mellinger, James F. & Stickler, Gunnar B. Critical Problems in Pediatrics. (Illus.). 352p. 1983. text ed. price not set (ISBN 0-397-50545-0, Lippincott Medical). Lippincott.
Mellink, A. F., jt. ed. see Kossmann, E. H.
Mellink, M. J. A Hittite Cemetery at Gordion. (Museum Monographs). (Illus.). 60p. 1956. soft bound 5.00 o.p. (ISBN 0-934718-05-9). Univ Mus of U PA.
Mellinkoff, David. The Language of the Law. 526p. 1963. pap. 12.95 (ISBN 0-316-56627-6). Little.
Mellizo, Carlos. Carmela. 4.00 (ISBN 0-936204-05-2). Jelm Mtn.

Mello, Anthony De see De Mello, Anthony.

Mello, J. M., jt. auth. see Hastings, N. A.

Mello, Nancy K., ed. Advances in Substance Abuse, Vol. 1. (Orig.). 1980. lib. bdg. 47.50 (ISBN 0-89232-128-8). Jai Pr.

--Advances in Substance Abuse Behaviorial & Biological Research, Vol. 2. 400p. 1981. 49.50 (ISBN 0-89232-155-5). Jai Pr.

Mellon, Joseph. Sleeping Beauty. LC 78-72129. (Illus.). (gr. k-5). 1979. 6.75 (ISBN 0-89799-135-4); pap. 3.50 (ISBN 0-89799-050-1). Dandelion Pr.

Mellon, M. G. Chemical Publications. 5th ed. 352p. 1982. text ed. 27.00x (ISBN 0-07-041514-5, C). McGraw.

Mellon, Neville, tr. see Conze, Werner.

Mellor, Anne K. Blake's Human Form Divine. LC 72-161995. (Illus.). 1974. 44.50x (ISBN 0-520-02065-0). U of Cal Pr.

--English Romantic Irony. LC 80-10687. 228p. 1980. text ed. 17.50x (ISBN 0-674-25690-5). Harvard U Pr.

Mellor, David H. Matter of Chance. LC 70-152629. (Illus.). 1971. 32.50 (ISBN 0-521-08194-7). Cambridge U Pr.

Mellor, David H., ed. Prospects for Pragmatism. 270p. 1981. 29.95 (ISBN 0-521-22548-5). Cambridge U Pr.

--Science, Belief & Behavior. LC 79-41614. (Illus.). 240p. 1980. 29.95 (ISBN 0-521-22960-X). Cambridge U Pr.

Mellor, Isha. Honey. (Illus.). 80p. 1981. 6.95 o.p. (ISBN 0-312-92306-6). St Martin.

Mellor, J. R. Urban Sociology in an Urbanized Society. (International Library of Sociology). 1977. 25.00x (ISBN 0-7100-8683-0). Routledge & Kegan.

Mellor, Jean & Pearce, T. Austin Friars, Leicester. (CBA Research Reports Ser.: No. 35). (Illus.). 186p. 1981. pap. text ed. 49.95x (ISBN 0-900312-94-7, Pub. by Coun Brit Archaeology). Humanities.

Mellor, John. The Company Store. LC 77-89414. (Illus.). 384p. 1983. 18.95 (ISBN 0-385-12812-6). Doubleday.

Mellor, John W. India: A Rising Middle Power. (Special Studies on South & Southeast Asia). 1979. lib. bdg. 35.00 (ISBN 0-89158-298-3). Westview.

--The New Economics of Growth: A Strategy for India & the Developing World. (A Twentieth Century Fund Study). 1976. 25.00x (ISBN 0-8014-0999-3); pap. 7.95 (ISBN 0-686-31795-5). Cornell U Pr.

--The New Economics of Growth: A Strategy for India & the Developing World. LC 75-38430. (Illus.). 350p. 1980. pap. 8.95x (ISBN 0-8014-9188-6). Cornell U Pr.

Mellor, M., ed. Antarctic Snow & Ice Studies. LC 64-60078. (Antarctic Research Ser.: Vol. 2). 1964. 15.00 (ISBN 0-87590-102-6). Am Geophysical.

Mellor, M. Joanna, jt. ed. see Getzel, George S.

Mellor, Rickerby. Data Processing Documentation Standards. (Illus.). 1977. Ringbinder 168.50x (ISBN 0-85012-176-0). Intl Pubns Serv.

Mellor, William B. General Patton: The Last Cavalier. LC 75-108745. (Lives to Remember Ser.). (gr. 6 up). 1971. PLB 5.49 o.p. (ISBN 0-399-60191-0). Putnam Pub Group.

Mellors, Samantha. The Orphan. 224p. (Orig.). 1980. pap. 2.25 o.s.i. (ISBN 0-515-05402-X). Jove Pubns.

Mellott, Douglas W., Jr. Marketing: Application & Cases. (Illus.). 1978. 12.95 o.p. (ISBN 0-8359-4253-8). Reston.

--Marketing: Principles & Practices. (Illus.). 1978. ref. ed. 19.95 (ISBN 0-87909-455-9); instrs'. manual avail. Reston.

Mellow, James R. Charmed Circle: Gertrude Stein & Company. 1975. pap. 4.95 (ISBN 0-380-00257-4, 61218-6). Avon.

--Charmed Circle: Gertrude Stein & Company. 672p. 1982. pap. 4.95 (ISBN 0-380-61218-6, 61218-6). Avon.

Mellown, Elgin W. Edwin Muir. (English Authors Ser.). 1979. lib. bdg. 14.95 (ISBN 0-8057-6687-1, Twayne). G K Hall.

Melmon, K. L. Drug Therapeutics, 1982: Concepts for Physicians. 1981. 32.50 (ISBN 0-444-00647-8). Elsevier.

Melmon, K. L. & Morrelli, H. F. Clinical Pharmacology: Basic Principles in Therapeutics. 2nd ed. 1978. text ed. 36.00 (ISBN 0-02-380230-8); pap. text ed. 26.95x (ISBN 0-02-380270-7). Macmillan.

Melnechuk, Theodore, jt. ed. see Baxter, Claude.

Melnick, David. Eclogs. 39p. 1972. 1.95 o.p. (ISBN 0-87886-014-2). Ithaca Hse.

Melnick, J. L., ed. Progress in Medical Virology, Vol. 29. (Illus.). viii, 250p. 1983. 93.00 (ISBN 3-8055-3618-6). S Karger.

Melnick, R. Shep. Regulation & the Courts: The Case of the Clean Air Act. 1983. 33.95 (ISBN 0-8157-5662-3); pap. 16.95 (ISBN 0-8157-5661-5). Brookings.

Melnicoe, William B. & Mennig, Jan. Elements of Police Supervision. 2nd ed. 1978. text ed. 21.95x (ISBN 0-02-476000-5). Macmillan.

Melnicove, Betty F. Crossword Puzzle Dictionary. pap. 2.50 (ISBN 0-06-461007-1, D-7). B&N NY.

Melnicove, Bettye M., compiled by. New Webster's Crossword Puzzle Dictionary. (Hand-Thumb Index Bks.). 1976. coil binding 1.95 o.p. (ISBN 0-517-52795-2). Crown.

Mel'Nik, Y. P., ed. Precambrian Banded Iron Formations: Physicochemical Conditions of Formations. (Developments in Precambrian Geology Ser.: Vol. 5). 1982. 72.50 (ISBN 0-444-41934-9). Elsevier.

Melnitz, W., jt. auth. see MacGowen, Kenneth.

Melnychuk, Taras. From Behind Prison Bars. LC 82-50025. (Ukrainian Ser.). 83p. 1982. pap. 3.25 (ISBN 0-914834-48-7). Smoloskyp.

Melo, Jaime de & Robinson, Sherman. Trade Adjustment Policies & Income Distribution in Three Archetype Developing Economies. (Working Paper: No. 442). 91p. 1980. 5.00 (ISBN 0-686-36209-8, WP-0442). World Bank.

Melodia, Thomas V., jt. auth. see Malinowski, Stanley B.

Melody, Michael E. The Apaches: A Critical Bibliography. LC 77-6918. (Newberry Library Center for the History of the American Indian Bibliographical Ser.). 96p. 1977. pap. 6.95x (ISBN 0-253-30764-3). Ind U Pr.

Melody, William. Children's Television: Ecomonics of Exploitation. LC 73-80079. 130p. 1973. 15.00x o.p. (ISBN 0-300-01654-9, YF12); pap. 4.95x o.p. (ISBN 0-300-01707-3). Yale U Pr.

Melody, William H., et al. Culture, Communication, & Dependency: The Tradition of H. A. Innis. (Communication & Information Science Ser.). 288p. 1981. text ed. 25.95 (ISBN 0-89391-065-1); pap. 15.95 (ISBN 0-89391-079-1). Ablex Pub.

Melo e Castro, E. M. de see Macedo, Helder & De Melo e Castro, E. M.

Melograno, Vincent J. & Klinzing, James E. An Orientation to Total Fitness. 2nd ed. 1980. pap. text ed. 8.95 (ISBN 0-8403-2125-2). Kendall-Hunt.

Melone, Albert P. Lawyers, Public Policy & Interest Group Politics. 265p. 1977. pap. text ed. 10.75 (ISBN 0-8191-0297-0). U Pr of Amer.

Meloney, Jennifer. You Can Disco. (Illus.). 96p. 1979. 5.98 o.p. (ISBN 0-89196-075-9, Domus Bks). Quality Bks IL.

Meloon, Walter. Men Alive. Enlow, David, ed. 120p. 1982. pap. 3.95 (ISBN 0-87509-320-5). Chr Pubns.

Melosh, Barbara. The Physician's Hand: Nurses & Nursing in the Twentieth Century. LC 82-10537. 240p. 1982. 24.95 (ISBN 0-87722-278-9); pap. text ed. 9.95x (ISBN 0-87722-290-8). Temple U Pr.

Melosi, Martin V. Garbage in the Cities: Refuse, Reform, & the Environment, 1880-1980. LC 81-40399. (Environmental History Ser.: No. 4). (Illus.). 286p. 1982. 21.50x (ISBN 0-89096-119-0). Tex A&M Univ Pr.

Melotti, Umberto. Marx & the Third World. Ransford, Pat, tr. 1977. text ed. 22.50x (ISBN 0-391-00723-8); pap. text ed. 13.95x (ISBN 0-391-00722-X). Humanities.

Melpomene. Bagabone, Hem'i Die Now. LC 79-63147. 136p. 1980. 6.95 o.p. (ISBN 0-533-04249-6). Vantage.

Melrose, D. B. Plasma Astrophysics: Nonthermal Processes in Diffuse Magnetized Plasmas, Vol.1: The Emission,Absorption & Transfer of Waves in Plasmas. 290p. 1979. 56.00 (ISBN 0-677-02340-5). Gordon.

Melrose, John. Bucomco: A Business Communication Simulation. LC 76-30752. 1977. text ed. 9.95 (ISBN 0-574-20025-8, 13-3025); instr's guide avail. (ISBN 0-574-20026-6, 13-3026). SRA.

Melsa, J., jt. auth. see Schultz, Donald.

Melsa, James L. & Cohn, Davis L. Decision & Estimation Theory. (Illus.). 1978. text ed. 33.00 (ISBN 0-07-041468-8, C). McGraw.

Melsa, James L. & Sage, Andrew P. An Introduction to Probability & Stochastic Processes. (Illus.). 448p. 1973. ref. ed. 32.95 (ISBN 0-13-034850-3). P-H.

Melsa, James L. & Schultz, Donald. Computer Programs for Computational Assistance in the Study of Linear Control Theory. 2nd ed. 1973. text ed. 19.50 (ISBN 0-07-041498-X, C). McGraw.

--Linear Control Systems. LC 68-8664. (Electronic Systems Ser). (Illus.). 1969. text ed. 38.50 (ISBN 0-07-041481-5, C); solutions manual 7.95 (ISBN 0-07-041487-4). McGraw.

Melsa, James L., jt. auth. see Sage, Andrew P.

Melsom, Andrew. House Party Games & Amusements for the Upper Class & Other Folks. Orig. Title: Are You There, Moriarty? (Illus.). 114p. 1983. pap. 4.76i (ISBN 0-06-463577-5, EH 577). B&N NY.

Melson, Gail F. Family & Environment: An Ecosystem Perspective. LC 79-56585. 1980. 16.95x (ISBN 0-8087-1395-7). Burgess.

Melton, David. And God Created... (Illus.). 1976. 9.00 (ISBN 0-8309-0144-2). Ind Pr MO.

--A Boy Called Hopeless. 232p. (gr. 5-8). 1976. 8.00 (ISBN 0-8309-0148-5). Ind Pr MO.

--Harry S. Truman: The Man Who Walked with Giants. (Illus.). 128p. (gr. 5 up). 1980. 7.00 (ISBN 0-8309-0293-7). Ind Pr MO.

--Images of Greatness: A Special Tribute to the Wit & Wisdom of Senior Citizens. 9.95 o.p. (ISBN 0-8309-0213-9). Ind Pr MO.

--The One & Only Autobiography of Ralph Miller-- The Dog Who Knew He Was a Boy. (Illus.). (gr. 3-6). 1979. pap. 6.00 (ISBN 0-8309-0233-3). Ind Pr MO.

--Theodore. 1978. 9.00 (ISBN 0-8309-0196-5). Ind Pr MO.

Melton, Gary B., ed. Legal Reforms Affecting Child & Youth Services. LC 82-6204. (Child & Youth Services Ser.: Vol. 5, Nos. 1-2). 176p. 1983. text ed. 30.00 (ISBN 0-86656-105-6, B105). Haworth Pr.

Melton, Gary B., jt. ed. see Childs, Alan W.

Melton, Gay B. & Kooche, Gerald P., eds. Children's Competence to Consent. (Critical Issues in Social Justice Ser.). 286p. 1983. 29.50x (ISBN 0-306-41069-9, Plenum Pr). Plenum Pub.

Melton, J. Gordon & Moore, Robert L. The Cult Experience: Responding to the New Religious Pluralism. LC 82-16136. 160p. (Orig.). 1982. pap. 8.95 (ISBN 0-8298-0619-9). Pilgrim NY.

Melton, James E. Vital Enthusiasm. LC 82-81903. 232p. 1982. 12.95 (ISBN 0-9604752-1-4). Global Pubns CA.

--Your Right to Fly. LC 80-82961. (Illus.). 217p. 1978. pap. 6.95 (ISBN 0-9604752-0-6). Global Pubns CA.

Meltsner, Arnold J. The Politics of City Revenue. LC 70-129610. (Oakland Project). 1971. 26.50x (ISBN 0-520-01812-5); pap. 7.50x (ISBN 0-520-02773-6). U of Cal Pr.

Meltsner, Arnold J., ed. Politics & the Oval Office: Towards a Presidential Governance. LC 80-69617. 332p. (Orig.). 1981. text ed. 18.95 (ISBN 0-87855-428-9); pap. text ed. 7.95 (ISBN 0-917616-40-5). ICS Pr.

Meltsner, Michael & Schrag, Philip G. Public Interest Advocacy: Materials for Clinical Legal Education. 1974. pap. 12.00 o.p. (ISBN 0-316-56634-9). Little.

Meltz, Noah, jt. ed. see Maital, Schlomo.

Meltzer, jt. auth. see Findler, N.

Meltzer, A., jt. auth. see Brunner, K.

Meltzer, A. C., et al. Principles of Digital Computer Design, Vol. 1. (Illus.). 624p. 1976. 32.95 (ISBN 0-13-701524-0). P-H.

Meltzer, A. H., jt. ed. see Brunner, K.

Meltzer, A. H., jt. ed. see Brunner, Karl.

Meltzer, Alan S. Sexually Transmitted Disease: Guidelines for Physicians & Health Workers. 86p. (Orig.). 1981. handbook 5.95 (ISBN 0-88831-126-5). Eden Pr.

Meltzer, Allan H., jt. auth. see Ott, David J.

Meltzer, Bernard. Bernard Meltzer Solves Your Money Problems. 1982. 13.95 (ISBN 0-671-25343-3). S&S.

--Bernard Meltzer's Guidance for Living. LC 82-5158. 192p. 1982. 12.95 (ISBN 0-385-27657-5). Dial.

Meltzer, Bernard D. Labor Law: Cases, Materials & Problems. 2nd ed. 1221p. 1977. 29.95 (ISBN 0-316-56644-6); statutory appendix 1977 pap. 5.95 (ISBN 0-316-56645-4). Little.

--Labor Law: Cases, Materials, & Problems. 1982. pap. 9.95 suppl. (ISBN 0-316-56646-2). Little.

Meltzer, Bernard N., et al. Symbolic Interactionism: Genesis, Varieties & Criticisms. (Monographs in Social Theory). 1975. 14.95x o.p. (ISBN 0-7100-8055-7). Routledge & Kegan.

Meltzer, David. The Art-The Veil. (Illus.). 64p. 1982. pap. 3.00 (ISBN 0-87924-040-7). Membrane Pr.

--The Eyes, the Blood. (Orig.). 1973. pap. 3.00 o.p. (ISBN 0-914726-13-7). Mudra.

Meltzer, David, ed. Birth: An Anthology of Ancient Texts, Songs, Prayers & Stories. LC 80-82441. (Illus.). 288p. 1981. 22.50 (ISBN 0-86547-004-9); pap. 12.50 (ISBN 0-86547-005-7). N Point Pr.

Meltzer, H. & Nord, Walter R. Making Organizations Humane & Productive: A Handbook for Practitioners. LC 81-7590. 510p. 1981. 29.95x (ISBN 0-471-07813-1, Pub. by Wiley-Interscience). Wiley.

Meltzer, Lawrence. Intensive Coronary Care: A Manual for Nurses. 4th ed. Incl. Deal, Jacquelyn. pap. text ed. 11.95 wkbk (ISBN 0-89303-248-4). 416p. 1983. text ed. 21.95 (ISBN 0-89303-247-6). R J Brady.

Meltzer, Milton. Bread & Roses: The Struggle of American Labor, 1865-1911. (RL 7). 1977. pap. 2.50 (ISBN 0-451-62035-6, ME2035, Ment). NAL.

--Brother, Can You Spare a Dime. (RL 7). 1977. pap. 3.50 (ISBN 0-451-62178-6, ME2178, Ment). NAL.

--In Their Own Words: A History of the American Negro. Incl. 1619-1865. LC 64-22541. 1964. 3.95 (ISBN 0-8152-0348-9); 1865-1916. LC 65-23778. 1965. 1.65i (ISBN 0-8152-0349-7); 1916-1966. LC 66-1439. 1967. 1.65 (ISBN 0-8152-0350-0). (Illus.). (gr. 5 up). pap. (AE-J). Apollo Eds.

--In Their Own Words: A History of the American Negro, 1619-1865, Vol. 1. LC 64-22541. (Illus.). (gr. 5 up). 1964. 10.53 o.p. (ISBN 0-690-44691-8, TYC-J). Har-Row.

--The Jewish Americans: A History in Their Own Words. LC 81-43886. 192p. (YA) (gr. 5 up). 1982. 10.10i (ISBN 0-690-04227-2, TYC-J); PLB 10.89g (ISBN 0-690-04228-0). Har-Row.

--Never to Forget. 1977. pap. 2.50 (ISBN 0-440-96070-3, LFL). Dell.

--Never to Forget: The Jews of the Holocaust. 217p. 8.95 (ISBN 0-686-95075-5); pap. 2.50 (ISBN 0-689-99457-4). ADL.

--Violins & Shovels: The WPA Arts Project. LC 75-32916. (Illus.). (YA) (gr. 7 up). 1976. 6.95 o.s.i. (ISBN 0-440-09316-3). Delacorte.

--World of Our Fathers: The Jews of Eastern Europe. 1976. pap. 1.25 o.p. (ISBN 0-440-99422-5, LFL). Dell.

Meltzer, Milton, ed. see Child, Lydia M.

Meltzer, Murray A. Plastic Surgery of the Eye. Schachat, Walter S., ed. (Intercontinental Handbook Ser.). (Illus.). 1978. text ed. 20.00x o.p. (ISBN 0-917408-06-3). Williams & Wilkins.

Meltzer, R. S. & Roelandt, J. Contrast Echocardiography. 1982. 69.50 (ISBN 90-247-2531-3, Pub. by Martinus Nijhoff Netherlands). Kluwer Boston.

Meltzer, Ronald L., jt. auth. see Cohen, Stephen D.

Meltzer, Yale. Putting Money to Work: An Investment Primer for the 3-80's. LC 75-43923. (Illus.). 256p. 1982. pap. 7.95 (ISBN 0-13-744532-6, Spec, Spec). P-H.

Meluch, R. M. Wind Child. 202p. 1982. pap. 2.50 (ISBN 0-451-11528-7, AE1528, Sig). NAL.

Melun, Armand De see De Melun, Armand.

Melveger, A. J., ed. Resonance Raman Spectroscopy: An Analytical Tool. LC 78-19535. (Eastern Analytical Symposium Ser). (Illus.). 1978. pap. 2.85 (ISBN 0-89168-018-7). Franklin Inst Pr.

Melville, Annabelle M. Elizabeth Bayley Seton. LC 51-14503. 1977. pap. 2.25 o.p. (ISBN 0-89310-005-6). Carillon Bks.

--Elizabeth Bayley Seton. 1976. pap. 2.25 (ISBN 0-515-09682-2). Jove Pubns.

Melville, Anne. Blaize. 552p. 1981. 17.95 o.p. (ISBN 0-385-14832-1). Doubleday.

Melville, Annette. Special Collections in the Library of Congress: A Selective Guide. LC 79-607780. (Illus.). xvi, 464p. 1981. 17.00 (ISBN 0-8444-0297-4). Lib Congress.

Melville, C. P., jt. auth. see Ambraseys, N. N.

Melville, Charles, jt. auth. see Melville, Keith.

Melville, Cuthbert. The Rolling Files: A Study of the Bible. 1980. 7.95 (ISBN 0-682-48165-3). Exposition.

Melville, Herman. Battle-Pieces & Aspects of the War. LC 60-5042. 1979. Repr. of 1866 ed. lib. bdg. 36.00x (ISBN 0-8201-1252-6). Schol Facsimiles.

--Billy Budd. Stern, Milton, ed. LC 73-8967. (LL Ser: No. 43). 244p. 1975. pap. 7.95 (ISBN 0-672-61040-X). Bobbs.

--Billy Budd. (Now Age Illustrated V Ser.). (Illus.). 64p. (gr. 4-12). 1979. text ed. 5.00 (ISBN 0-88301-397-5); pap. text ed. 1.95 (ISBN 0-88301-385-1); student activity bk. 1.25 (ISBN 0-88301-409-2). Pendulum Pr.

--Billy Budd & Other Tales. pap. 1.95 (ISBN 0-451-51714-8, CE1714, Sig Classics). NAL.

--Billy Budd, Sailor. Hayford, Harrision & Sealts, Merton M., Jr., eds. LC 62-17135. (Orig.). 1962. pap. 4.95 (ISBN 0-226-32132-0, P99, Phoen). U of Chicago Pr.

--Billy Budd, Sailor & Other Stories. (Bantam Classics Ser.). 278p. (gr. 7-12). 1981. pap. 1.95 (ISBN 0-553-21008-4). Bantam.

--Confidence Man. pap. 3.50 (ISBN 0-451-51698-2, CE1698, Sig Classics). NAL.

--Confidence-Man: His Masquerade. Franklin, H. Bruce, ed. LC 66-30445. 1967. pap. 6.95 o.p. (ISBN 0-672-60986-X, LL13). Bobbs.

--Herman Melville: Authentic Anecdotes of Old Zack. Starosciak, Kenneth, ed. & intro. by. 1973. pap. 5.00x (ISBN 0-686-02647-0). K Starosciak.

--Israel Potter. LC 82-73424. 225p. Repr. of 1923 ed. lib. bdg. 13.50x (ISBN 0-88116-008-3). Brenner Bks.

--Moby Dick. Walcott, Charles C., ed. (Bantam Classics Ser.). 594p. (gr. 7-12). 1981. pap. 1.95 (ISBN 0-553-21007-6). Bantam.

--Moby Dick. (Illus.). 1981. 10.95 (ISBN 0-394-60804-6). Modern Lib.

--Moby Dick. pap. 1.95 (ISBN 0-451-51651-6, CJ1651, Sig Classics). NAL.

--Moby Dick. (Raintree Short Classics Ser.). (Illus.). 48p. (gr. 4 up). 1981. PLB 13.85 (ISBN 0-8172-1679-0). Raintree Pubs.

--Moby-Dick: Or, The Whale. (The Arion Press Edition Ser.). (Illus.). 600p. 1983. pap. 9.95 (ISBN 0-520-04548-3, CAL 540). U of Cal Pr.

--Pierre or the Ambiguities. pap. 3.95 (ISBN 0-451-51707-5, CE1707, Sig Classics). NAL.

--Portable Melville. Leyda, Jay, ed. (Portable Library: Vol. 58). 1976. pap. 6.95 (ISBN 0-14-015058-7). Penguin.

--Redburn, White-Jacket, Moby-Dick. Tanselle, Thomas G., ed. LC 82-18677. 1500p. 1983. 27.50 (ISBN 0-940450-09-7). Literary Classics.

--Selected Poems of Herman Melville. Cohen, Hennig, ed. LC 63-18037. 277p. 1964. 8.95x o.p. (ISBN 0-8093-0129-6). S Ill U Pr.

--Typee. pap. 2.50 (ISBN 0-451-51648-6, CE1648, Sig Classics). NAL.

--Typee, Omoo, Mardi: Herman Melville. Tanselle, G. Thomas, ed. Bd. with Typee, Omoo, Mardi. LC 81-186000. 1334p. 1982. 25.00 (ISBN 0-940450-00-3, Pub. by Library of America). Literary Classics.

--White Jacket. 1979. pap. 3.95 (ISBN 0-451-51732-6, CE1732, Sig Classics). NAL.

Melville, Herman see Eyre, A. G.

Melville, Herman see Swan, D. K.

Melville J. Herskovits Library of African Studies. Joint Acquisitions List of Africana, 1979. 1981. lib. bdg. 95.00 (ISBN 0-8161-0372-0, Hall Library). G K Hall.

Melville, James. The Ninth Netsuke. 160p. 1982. 9.95 (ISBN 0-312-57476-2). St Martin.

Melville, Joan. Step-by-Step Guide to Growing Bonsai Trees. LC 73-77018. (Illus.). 92p. 1975. pap. 3.50 o.p. (ISBN 0-88254-259-1). Hippocrene Bks.
Melville, Joy. Phobias & Obsessions. LC 76-47676. 1977. 7.95 o.p. (ISBN 0-698-10801-9, Coward). Putnam Pub Group.
Melville, Keith & Melville, Charles. Exploring Marriage & Family Today. (Illus.). 280p. 1980. pap. text ed. 7.00 (ISBN 0-394-32183-9). Random.
Melville, Leslie W. Forms & Agreements on Intellectual Property & International Licensing. 3rd ed. LC 78-17576. 1979. looseleaf with 1979 rev. pages 75.00 (ISBN 0-686-57648-9). Boardman.
Melville, Lewis & Hargreaves, Reginald. Famous Duels & Assassinations. LC 72-178619. (Illus.). 288p. 1974. Repr. of 1929 ed. 30.00x (ISBN 0-8103-3973-0). Gale.
Melville, Lewis & Hargreaves, Reginald, eds. Great French Short Stories. 1066p. 1982. Repr. of 1928 ed. lib. bdg. 25.00 (ISBN 0-89760-583-7). Telegraph Bks.
Melville, Margarita B. Twice a Minority: Mexican American Women. LC 80-11177. (Illus.). 1980. pap. text ed. 15.95 (ISBN 0-8016-3386-9). Mosby.
Melvin, B. L. & Smith, E. N. Rural Youth: Their Situation & Prospects. LC 71-165687. (Research Monograph Ser.: Vol. 15). 1971. Repr. of 1938 ed. lib. bdg. 22.50 (ISBN 0-306-70347-5). Da Capo.
Melvin, Billy A. Free Will Baptist Minister's Manual. 1974. ringbinder 5.95 (ISBN 0-89265-024-9). Randall Hse.
Melvin, Bruce L. Rural Youth on Relief. LC 78-165686. (Research Monograph Series: Vol. 11). 1971. Repr. of 1937 ed. lib. bdg. 19.50 (ISBN 0-306-70343-2). Da Capo.
Melvin, Bruce L. & Smith, Elna N. Youth in Agricultural Villages. LC 79-165603. (Research Monograph Ser.: Vol. 21). 1971. Repr. of 1940 ed. lib. bdg. 19.50 (ISBN 0-306-70353-X). Da Capo.
Melvin, James R. & Scheffman, David T. An Economic Analysis of the Impact of Rising Oil Prices on Urban Structure. (Ontario Economic Council Research Studies). 160p. (Orig.). 1983. pap. 10.50 (ISBN 0-8020-3395-4). U of Toronto Pr.
Melvin, Jeanne L. Rheumatic Disease: Occupational Therapy & Rehabilitation. 254p. 1977. pap. text ed. 13.95x o.p. (ISBN 0-8036-6135-5). Davis Co.
Melvin, Kenneth B. & Janzen, William B. Essentials of Psychology: A Student Mastery Guide. 1977. 6.95 (ISBN 0-394-32498-6). Random.
Melvin, Kenneth B., et al. Readings, Applications & Study Guide for Developmental Psychology Today. 3rd ed. 1979. pap. text ed. 9.95x o.p. (ISBN 0-394-32296-7). Random.
Melvin, Lawrence S., Jr., jt. auth. see Trost, Barry M.
Melzack, Ronald. The Puzzle of Pain: Revolution in Theory & Treatment. LC 73-81726. (Illus.). 232p. 1973. text ed. 11.50x o.s.i. (ISBN 0-465-06779-4); pap. 6.50x o.s.i. (ISBN 0-465-09521-6, TB5022). Basic.
Melzack, Ronald & Wall, Patrick D. The Challenge of Pain. LC 82-70851. 1983. 20.95 (ISBN 0-465-00906-9). Basic.
Melzak, Z. A. Bypasses: A Simple Approach to Complexity. 250p. 1983. write for info (ISBN 0-471-86854-X, Pub. by Wiley-Interscience). Wiley.
--Invitation to Geometry. (Pure & Applied Mathematics Ser.: A Wiley Interscience Series of Texts, Monographs & Tracts). 272p. 1983. 29.95 (ISBN 0-471-09209-6, Pub. by Wiley Interscience). Wiley.
Melzer, Dorothy G. Sullivan's Island. (Illus.). 62p. 1980. 8.00 o.p. (ISBN 0-686-30156-0). Armstrong Pr.
Members of Community at Taize, France, ed. Praise God: Common Prayer at Taize. LC 76-47437. 1977. 14.95 (ISBN 0-19-519915-4). Oxford U Pr.
Members of Junior League of Corpus Christi. Delicioso. 358p. 1982. write for info (ISBN 0-9609144-0-4). Jr League Corpus Christi.
Memmi, Albert. Colonizer & the Colonized. Greenfeld, Howard, tr. pap. 4.95x (ISBN 0-8070-0297-6, BP232). Beacon Pr.
--Jews & Arabs. Levieux, Eleanor, tr. from Fr. LC 75-10697. 224p. (Eng.). 1975. 8.95 (ISBN 0-87955-327-8); pap. 5.95 (ISBN 0-87955-328-6). O'Hara.
--Liberation of the Jew. Hyun, Judith, tr. LC 66-26539. 1967. 10.00 (ISBN 0-670-42764-0, Grossman). Viking Pr.
--The Pillar of Salt. LC 55-7841. 342p. (Eng.). 1975. 8.95 (ISBN 0-87955-907-1); pap. 5.95 (ISBN 0-87955-905-5). O'Hara.
--The Scorpion. 2nd ed. LC 79-114950. 242p. (Eng.). 1975. 8.95 (ISBN 0-87955-908-X); pap. 5.95 (ISBN 0-87955-906-3). O'Hara.
Memmler, Ruth L. & Wood, Dena L. The Human Body in Health & Disease. 4th ed. LC 76-45400. 1977. 14.75 o.p. (ISBN 0-397-54193-7, Lippincott Nursing); pap. text ed. 11.00 o.p. (ISBN 0-397-54202-X, Lippincott Nursing); wkbk. 7.50 o.p. (ISBN 0-397-54197-X). Lippincott.
--Structure & Function of the Human Body. 2nd ed. LC 76-47605. 1977. text ed. 12.00 o.p. (ISBN 0-397-54194-5, Lippincott Nursing); pap. text ed. 9.50 o.p. (ISBN 0-397-54203-8); wkbk. 6.50 o.p. (ISBN 0-397-54198-8). Lippincott.
Memory & Wilson. NMR of Aromatic Compounds. 320p. 1982. 39.95 (ISBN 0-471-08899-4, Pub. by Wiley-Interscience). Wiley.
Mena, Janet Gonzalez see Gonzalez-Mena, Janet & Eyer, Dianne W.
Menacker, Julius. From School to College: Articulation & Transfer. 230p. 1975. 10.00 o.p. (ISBN 0-8268-1295-3). ACE.
--Urban Poor Students & Guidance. (Guidance Monograph). 1971. pap. 2.40 o.p. (ISBN 0-395-12047-0, 9-78856). HM.
Menacker, Julius, jt. auth. see Pollack, Erwin.
Menage, Ronald. Woolman's Greenhouse Gardening: A Comprehensive Guide to Cultivation Under Glass. (Illus.). 253p. 1975. 12.50 o.p. (ISBN 0-241-89032-2). Transatlantic.
Menake, George T. Policy-Making in the American System: The Case of the Manpower, Development & Training Program. LC 77-18584. 1978. pap. text ed. 13.25 (ISBN 0-8191-0409-4). U Pr of Amer.
Menaker, Daniel & McGrath, Charles. The Worst. (Illus., Orig.). 1979. pap. 2.95 o.p. (ISBN 0-452-25199-0, Z5199, Plume). NAL.
Menaker, Donald. Family Trees. (Fanfare Ser.). 1983. pap. 2.00 multifolded broadsheet (ISBN 0-686-82299-4). New Poets.
Menander. The Girl from Samos. Turner, E. G., tr. from Gr. 64p. 1972. pap. text ed. 10.50x (ISBN 0-485-12019-4, Athlone Pr). Humanities.
Menase, Luc, intro. by. Mersad Berber. (Illus.). 156p. 1980. 35.00 (ISBN 0-89893-112-6). CDP.
Menashe, Abraham. The Face of Prayer. LC 82-48737. 1983. 25.00 (ISBN 0-394-52930-8); pap. 15.00 (ISBN 0-394-71315-X). Knopf.
Menashe Har-El. Man & Nature in the Bible. Landau, ed. 1983. text ed. write for info (ISBN 0-86628-025-1). Ridgefield Pub.
MENC National Committee on Instruction, ed. Selected Instructional Programs in Music. 92p. 1977. pap. 2.00x (ISBN 0-940796-16-3, 1040). Music Ed.
Mencher, Melvin. Basic News Writing. 350p. 1983. pap. text ed. write for info. (ISBN 0-697-04354-1); instr's. manual avail. (ISBN 0-697-04358-4); student wkbk. avail. (ISBN 0-697-04357-6). Wm C Brown.
Mencius. Works of Mencius. Legge, James, ed. Orig. Title: Chinese Classics, Vol. (2). 1970. pap. 9.95 (ISBN 0-486-22590-9). Dover.
--Works of Mencius. Legge, James, tr. 11.50 (ISBN 0-8446-0331-7). Peter Smith.
Mencke, Claire, ed. Solar Energy Update: A Select Guide to Federal & State Government Agencies, Trade & Professional Associations Information Systems, Centers & Publications. LC 74-79869. 1977. 25.00 o.p. (ISBN 0-89947-009-2). EIC Intell.
Mencke, Claire & Horton, Craig, eds. Energy Information Locator: A Select Guide to Information Centers, Systems, Data Bases; Abstracing Services, Directories, Newsletters, Binder Services, & Journals. LC 74-79869. 1977. 35.00 o.p. (ISBN 0-89947-009-2). EIC Intell.
Mencken, H. L. The American Language. 1977. pap. 10.95 (ISBN 0-394-73315-0). Knopf.
Mencken, Henry L. American Scene: A Reader. Cairns, Huntington, ed. (YA) 1965. 20.00 (ISBN 0-394-43594-X). Knopf.
--The Philosophy of Friedrich Nietzsche. 325p. 1982. pap. 7.00 (ISBN 0-939482-05-3). Noontide.
--Vintage Mencken. Cooke, Alistair, ed. 1955. pap. 3.95 (ISBN 0-394-70025-2, Vin). Random.
Mencken, Henry L., ed. New Dictionary of Quotations on Historical Principles from Ancient & Modern Sources. 1942. 30.00 (ISBN 0-394-40079-8). Knopf.
Mencl, V., jt. auth. see Zaruba, Q.
Menconi, Jan. The Battle for the Mind. 48p. 1983. study guide 3.95 (ISBN 0-8007-1341-9). Revell.
Mendel & Mesick. Fort Johnson: A Historic Structure Report. 54p. (Orig.). 1977. pap. 7.00 (ISBN 0-9608694-1-7). Montgomery Hist.
Mendel, Arthur, jt. auth. see Ellis, Alexander J.
Mendel, Douglas. The Politics of Formosan Nationalism. LC 78-94982. (Illus.). 1970. 30.00x (ISBN 0-520-01557-6). U of Cal Pr.
Mendel, Douglas H. Japanese People & Foreign Policy: A Study of Public Opinion in Post-Treaty Japan. LC 74-141277. (Illus.). 1971. Repr. of 1961 ed. lib. bdg. 18.75x (ISBN 0-8371-5882-6, MEJP). Greenwood.
Mendel, G. Versuche Ueber Pflanzenhybriden. 1966. Repr. of 1866 ed. pap. 7.50 (ISBN 3-7682-0013-2). Lubrecht & Cramer.
Mendel, Jeffrey, ed. see Goldwater, John.
Mendel, Otto. Practical Piping Handbook. 336p. 1981. 44.95x (ISBN 0-87814-169-3). Pennwell Books Division.
Mendele Mocher Seforim. The Travels & Adventures of Benjamin the Third. LC 49-9256. 1968. 1.50 o.p. (ISBN 0-8052-3263-X); pap. 5.50 (ISBN 0-8052-0176-9). Schocken.
Mendell, Clarence W. Jeanne D'Arc at Rouen. 1931. ltd. ed. 29.50x (ISBN 0-686-50047-4). Elliots Bks.
Mendell, Dale. Early Female Development: Current Psychoanalytic Views. 303p. 1982. text ed. 30.00 (ISBN 0-89335-135-0). Spectrum Pub.
Mendell, Elizabeth L. Romanesque Sculpture in Saintonge. (Illus.). 1940. 87.50x (ISBN 0-685-89780-X). Elliots Bks.
Mendeloff, John. Regulating Safety: A Economic & Political Analysis of Occupational Safety & Health Policy. (Illus.). 1979. text ed. 22.50x (ISBN 0-262-13147-1). MIT Pr.
Mendels, Joseph. Concepts of Depression. LC 72-5497. (Approaches to Behavior Pathology Ser). 1970. pap. text ed. 12.50x o.p. (ISBN 0-471-59351-6). Wiley.
Mendelsohn, E. Algebraic & Geometric Combinatorics. 1982. 81.00 (ISBN 0-444-86365-6). Elsevier.
Mendelsohn, Erich. Amerika: Bilderbuch Tines Architekten. LC 76-40319. (Architecture & Decorative Art Ser.). (Ger.). 1977. Repr. of 1926 ed. lib. bdg. 49.50 (ISBN 0-306-70830-2). Da Capo.
Mendelsohn, Ezra. Class Struggle in the Pale. LC 71-96097. 1970. 29.95 (ISBN 0-521-07730-3). Cambridge U Pr.
--The Jews of East Central Europe Between the World Wars. LC 81-48676. (Illus.). 320p. 1983. 27.50x (ISBN 0-253-33160-9). Ind U Pr.
Mendelsohn, H., jt. auth. see Bayley, D. H.
Mendelsohn, Isaac. Slavery in the Ancient Near East: A Comparative Study of Slavery in Babylonia, Assyria, Syria & Palestine, from the Middle of the Third Millennium to the End of the First Millenium. LC 78-6962. 1978. Repr. of 1949 ed. lib. bdg. 21.00 (ISBN 0-313-20499-3, MESA). Greenwood.
Mendelsohn, J. The Final Solution in the Extermination Camps & the Aftermath. LC 81-80320. (The Holocaust Ser.). 250p. 1982. lib. bdg. 50.00 (ISBN 0-8240-4886-5). Garland Pub.
--The Judicial System & the Jews in Nazi Germany. LC 81-80321. (The Holocaust Ser.). 245p. 1982. lib. bdg. 50.00 (ISBN 0-8240-4887-3). Garland Pub.
--Legalizing the Holocaust: The Later Phase, 1939-1943. LC 81-80310. 265p. 1982. lib. bdg. 50.00 (ISBN 0-8240-4876-8). Garland Pub.
--Punishing the Perpetrators of the Holocaust: The Brandt, Pohl & Ohlendorf Cases. LC 81-80325. 269p. 1982. lib. bdg. 50.00 (ISBN 0-8240-4891-1). Garland Pub.
--Punishing the Perpetrators of the Holocaust: The Ohlendorf & the Von Weizsaecker Cases. LC 81-80326. (The Holocaust Ser.). 310p. 1982. lib. bdg. 50.00 (ISBN 0-8240-4892-X). Garland Pub.
--Relief & Rescue of Jews from Nazi Oppression, 1943-1945. LC 81-80322. (The Holocaust Ser.). 264p. 1982. lib. bdg. 50.00 (ISBN 0-8240-4888-1). Garland Pub.
--Relief in Hungary & the Failure of the Joel Brand Mission. LC 81-80323. (The Holocaust Ser.). 256p. 1982. lib. bdg. 50.00 (ISBN 0-8240-4889-X). Garland Pub.
--Rescue to Switzerland: The Mussy & Saly Mayer Affair. LC 81-80324. (The Holocaust Ser.). 280p. 1982. lib. bdg. 50.00 (ISBN 0-8240-4890-3). Garland Pub.
--The Wannsee Protocol & a 1944 Report on Auschwitz by the Office of Strategic Services. LC 81-80319. (The Holocaust Ser.). 264p. 1982. lib. bdg. 50.00 (ISBN 0-8240-4885-7). Garland Pub.
Mendelsohn, John. The Crystal Night Pogrom. LC 81-80331. (The Holocaust Ser.). 325p. 1982. lib. bdg. 50.00 (ISBN 0-8240-4877-6). Garland Pub.
--Deportation of the Jews to the East: Settin, 1940 to Hungary 1944. LC 81-80316. (The Holocaust Ser.). 256p. 1982. lib. bdg. 50.00 (ISBN 0-8240-4882-2). Garland Pub.
--The Einsatzgruppen or Murder Commandos. LC 81-80318. (The Holocaust Ser.). 256p. 1982. lib. bdg. 50.00 (ISBN 0-8240-4884-9). Garland Pub.
--Jewish Emigration from 1933 to the Evian Conference of 1938. LC 81-80313. (The Holocaust Ser.). 260p. 1982. lib. bdg. 50.00 (ISBN 0-8240-4879-2). Garland Pub.
--Jewish Emigration: The SS St. Louis Affair & Other Cases. LC 81-80315. (The Holocaust Ser.). 274p. 1982. lib. bdg. 50.00 (ISBN 0-8240-4881-4). Garland Pub.
--Jewish Emigration 1938-1940, Rublee Negotations & Intergovernmental Committee. LC 81-80314. (The Holocaust Ser.). 250p. 1982. lib. bdg. 50.00 (ISBN 0-8240-4880-6). Garland Pub.
--Medical Experiments on Jewish Inmates of Concentration Camps. LC 81-80317. (The Holocaust Ser.). 282p. 1982. lib. bdg. 50.00 (ISBN 0-8240-4883-0). Garland Pub.
--Propaganda & Aryanization, 1938-1944. LC 81-80312. (The Holocaust Ser.). 255p. 1982. lib. bdg. 50.00 (ISBN 0-8240-4878-4). Garland Pub.
Mendelsohn, M. Stefan. Money on the Move: The Modern International Capital Market. (Illus.). 1979. 23.95 (ISBN 0-07-041474-2). McGraw.
Mendelsohn, Martin. One Hundred Thousand Rolls of the Dice. LC 82-84680. 100p. 1982. pap. 9.95 (ISBN 0-89650-500-6). Gamblers.
Mendelsohn, Robert S. Confessions of a Medical Heretic. 304p. 1980. pap. 3.95 (ISBN 0-446-30627-4). Warner Bks.
Mendelsohn, Rona, jt. auth. see Epstein, Ellen R.
Mendelson, Alexander. Plasticity: Theory & Application. LC 82-21231. 368p. 1983. Repr. of 1968 ed. lib. bdg. 21.00 (ISBN 0-89874-582-9). Krieger.
Mendelson, E. Boolean Algebra & Switching Circuits. (Schaum's Outline Ser). 1970. pap. 7.95 (ISBN 0-07-041460-2, SP). McGraw.
Mendelson, Edward. Early Auden. 432p. 1983. pap. text ed. 8.95x (ISBN 0-686-82625-6). Harvard U Pr.
Mendelson, Edward, ed. W. H. Auden: Collected Poems. 1976. 25.50 (ISBN 0-394-40895-0). Random.
Mendelson, Jack H. & Melio, Nancy K. The Diagnosis & Treatment of Alcoholism. 1979. text ed. 25.95 (ISBN 0-07-041476-9, P&RB). McGraw.
Mendelson, Lee & Schulz, Charles M. Charlie Brown & Charlie Schulz. 1971. pap. 1.50 o.p. (ISBN 0-451-07311-8, W7311, Sig). NAL.
Mendelson, Phyllis C., jt. ed. see Hall, Sharon K.
Mendelson, Robert E. & Quinn, Michael A., eds. The Politics of Housing in Older Urban Areas. LC 75-23984. (Special Studies). 288p. 1976. 36.95 o.p. (ISBN 0-275-56120-8). Praeger.
Mendelson, Robert S. Male Practice: How Doctors Manipulate Women. 1981. 10.95 o.p. (ISBN 0-8092-5974-5). Contemp Bks.
Mendelssohn, K. The Quest for Absolute Zero: The Meaning of Low Temperature Physics. 2nd ed. 281p. 1977. pap. 21.95 o.p. (ISBN 0-470-99148-8). Halsted Pr.
--The World of Walther Nernst: The Rise & Fall of German Science, 1864-1941. LC 73-7605. 1973. 14.95 (ISBN 0-8229-1109-4). U of Pittsburgh Pr.
Mendelssohn, Kurt. In China Now. 1971. 8.95 o.p. (ISBN 0-685-00342-6). Transatlantic.
Mendenhall, Don. The Truth About Cowboys & Indians & Other Myths About the West. (U. S. Western History Ser.). (Illus.). 121p. (Orig.). 1980. pap. 4.95 (ISBN 0-686-28433-X). Clarion Call.
Mendenhall, J. Howard. Understanding Copper Alloys. Brass & Olin, eds. LC 79-24502. 1980. 44.95 (ISBN 0-471-04811-9, Pub. by Wiley-Interscience). Wiley.
Mendenhall, Matthew, jt. tr. see Builder, Janine.
Mendenhall, William. Introduction to Probability & Statistics. 6th ed. 800p. 1983. text ed. write for info. (ISBN 0-87150-365-4, 4760). Duxbury Pr.
Mendes-Flohr, Paul R. & Reinharz, Jehuda. The Jew in the Modern World: A Documentary History. 1980. 27.50x (ISBN 0-19-502631-4). Oxford U Pr.
Mendes-Flohr, Paul R., ed. A Land of Two Peoples: Martin Buber on Jews & Arabs. 350p. 1983. 29.95 (ISBN 0-19-503165-2). Oxford U Pr.
Mendez, M., jt. auth. see Crottel, L.
Mendieta, Ana, intro. by. Dialectics of Isolation: An Exhibition of Third World Women Artists of the United States. (Illus.). 17p. 1980. pap. 3.00 (ISBN 0-89062-099-7, Pub by A.I.R. Gallery). Pub Ctr Cult Res.
Menditto, Joseph & Kirsch, Debbie. Genetic Engineering, DNA & Cloning: A Bibliography in the Future of Genetics. LC 82-50417. 790p. 1982. 50.00 (ISBN 0-87875-241-2). Whitston Pub.
Mendler, Allen, jt. auth. see Curwin, Richard.
Mendlewicz, ed. New Advances in the Diagnosis & Treatment of Depressive Illness. (International Congress Ser.: Vol. 531). 1980. 42.25 (ISBN 0-444-90163-9). Elsevier.
Mendlewicz, J. Biological Rhythms & Behavior. (Advances in Biological Psychiatry: Vol. 11). (Illus.). iv, 150p. 1983. pap. 54.00 (ISBN 3-8055-3672-0). S Karger.
Mendlewicz, J. & Van Pragg, H. M. Management of Depressions with Monomine Precursors. (Advances in Biological Psychiatry: Vol. 10). (Illus.). viii, 200p. 1983. pap. 57.00 (ISBN 3-8055-3645-3). S Karger.
Mendlowitz, Edward. Successful Tax Planning. rev. ed. 200p. 1983. Repr. of 1980 ed. 50.00 (ISBN 0-932648-22-3). Boardroom.
Mendoza, Carlos. Earth Refugees of the Aquarian Age. 130p. (Orig.). 1982. pap. text ed. 4.95 (ISBN 0-686-38949-2). C Mendoza.
Mendoza, Celia, tr. see Edge, Findley B.
Mendoza, E., jt. auth. see Flowers, B. H.
Mendoza, George. Alphabet Sheep. LC 81-81046. (Illus.). 48p. (gr. k-2). 1982. 5.95 (ISBN 0-448-12220-0, G&D). Putnam Pub Group.
--Counting Sheep. LC 81-84016. (Illus.). 48p. (ps-1). 1982. 5.95 (ISBN 0-448-12041-0, G&D). Putnam Pub Group.
--Need a House? Call Ms. Mouse! LC 81-80884. (Illus.). 48p. 1981. 5.95 (ISBN 0-448-16575-9, G&D). Putnam Pub Group.
--Norman Rockwell's Four Seasons. LC 82-82233. 192p. 1982. 24.95 (ISBN 0-448-16618-6, G&D). Putnam Pub Group.
--Norman Rockwell's Scrapbook for a Young Boy. (Illus.). 180p. 1979. 17.95 o.p. (ISBN 0-89659-026-7); pap. 12.95 o.p. (ISBN 0-89659-162-X). Abbeville Pr.
--The Sheepish Book of Opposites. LC 81-84017. (Illus.). 48p. (ps-1). 1982. 5.95 (ISBN 0-448-12039-9, G&D). Putnam Pub Group.
--Silly Sheep & Other Sheepish Rhymes. LC 82-81045. (Illus.). 48p. (gr. k-2). 1982. 5.95 (ISBN 0-448-12219-7, G&D). Putnam Pub Group.
Mendoza, George, jt. auth. see Segovia, Andres.
Mendoza, Jose A., jt. auth. see Papalia, Anthony.

Mendoza, Manuel G. & Napoli, Vince. Systems of Society. 2nd ed. 1977. pap. text ed. 17.95x o.p. (ISBN 0-669-00547-9); instr's manual 1.95 o.p. (ISBN 0-669-00151-1); study guide 6.95x o.p. (ISBN 0-669-00554-1). Heath.
--Systems of Society: An Introduction to Social Science. 3rd ed. 1982. pap. 19.95 (ISBN 0-669-06138-7). Heath.
Mendoza De Mann, Wilma, tr. see Hunter, Emily.
Mendras, Henri. Vanishing Peasant: Innovation & Change in French Agriculture. Lerner, Jean, tr. from Fr. Orig. Title: Fin Des Paysans. 1971. 22.50x (ISBN 0-262-13065-3). MIT Pr.
Mendyk, Dennis, ed. Living in the Reader's World, 4 bks. (Adult Reading Ser.: Levels 2-6). (Illus.). 160p. 1983. pap. 4.33 ea. Bk. 1 (ISBN 0-8428-9514-0). Bk. 2 (ISBN 0-8428-9515-9). Bk. 3 (ISBN 0-8428-9516-7). Bk. 4 (ISBN 0-8428-9517-5). test bk. 2.60 (ISBN 0-8428-9518-3). Cambridge Bk.
Mendyk, Dennis, ed. see Cyzyk, Janet.
Menefee, Selden C. Vocational Training & Employment of Youth. LC 70-166953. (Research Monograph Ser.: Vol. 25). 1971. Repr. of 1942 ed. lib. bdg. 22.50 (ISBN 0-306-70357-2). Da Capo.
Meneghini, G. B. My Wife Maria Callas. Wisneski, Henry, tr. from Ital. (Illus.). 1982. 16.50 (ISBN 0-374-21752-1). FS&G.
Meneker, Jerry S. Essays on Deviance & Marginality. LC 79-66577. 1979. pap. text ed. 8.50 (ISBN 0-8191-0844-8). U Pr of Amer.
Menen, Aubrey. Art & Money: An Irreverent History. LC 79-18359. 226p. 1980. 11.95 o.p. (ISBN 0-07-041483-1). McGraw.
--London. (The Great Cities Ser.). (Illus.). (gr. 6 up). 1976. PLB 14.94 o.p. (ISBN 0-8094-2255-7, Pub by Time-Life). Silver.
--Venice. (The Great Cities Ser.). (Illus.). (gr. 6 up). 1976. PLB 12.00 (ISBN 0-8094-2263-8, Pub by Time-Life). Silver.
Menendez, Albert J. Christmas in the White House. (Illus.). 160p. 1983. write for info. (ISBN 0-664-21392-8). Westminster.
--John F. Kennedy: Catholic & Humanist. LC 78-68139. 144p. 1979. 13.95 (ISBN 0-87975-109-6). Prometheus Bks.
Menendez, Josefa. The Way of Devine Love. 506p. pap. 3.50 (ISBN 0-686-81632-3). TAN Bks Pubs.
Menestrier, Claude. L' Art Des Emblemes, Ou S'enseigne la Morale Par les Figures De la Fable, De L'Histoire et De la Nature. Orgel, Stephen, ed. LC 78-68190. (Philosophy of Images Ser.: Vol. 18). (Illus.). 1980. lib. bdg. 66.00 o.s.i. (ISBN 0-8240-3692-1). Garland Pub.
Menez, Joseph F., rev. by see Bartholomew, Paul C.
Menezes, Ruth de. Woman Songs. (Illus.). 94p. 1982. 9.75 (ISBN 0-941358-01-1); text ed. 9.75 (ISBN 0-686-99428-0); pap. 4.85 (ISBN 0-941358-02-X). Claremont CA.
Meng, Heinz, jt. auth. see Kaufmann, John.
Meng, Wang, jt. auth. see Xinwu, Liu.
Mengel, Robert M. Birds of Kentucky. American Ornithologists' Union, ed. Ed. 581p. 1965. 15.00 (ISBN 0-943610-03-6). Am Ornithologists.
Menger, Karl. Kurventheorie. 2nd, rev. ed. LC 63-11314. (Ger). 1968. 25.00 (ISBN 0-8284-0172-1). Chelsea Pub.
Menger, Lucy. Theodore Sturgeon. LC 81-40468. (Recognitions). 144p. 1981. 11.95 (ISBN 0-8044-2618-X); pap. 5.95 (ISBN 0-8044-6492-8). Ungar.
Menghetti, D. & Birtles, T. G. North Austrralia Research Bulletin. new ed. (North Australia Research Bulletin: No. 8). 101p. (Orig.). 1982. pap. text ed. 12.95 (ISBN 0-86784-154-0, 1256, Pub. by ANUP Austr alia). Bks Australia.
Menguy, Rene. Surgery of Peptic Ulcer. LC 75-14784. (Mpcs Ser.: Vol. 18). (Illus.). 290p. 1976. text ed. 20.00 o.p. (ISBN 0-7216-6248-X). Saunders.
Menikoff, Barry, jt. auth. see Rees, Robert.
Menil, Lois P. De see De Menil, Lois P.
Menke, A. S., jt. auth. see Bohart, R. M.
Menke, Arnold, ed. The Semi-Aquatic & Aquatic Hemiptera of California (Herteroptera: Hemiptera) (California Insect Survey Ser.: Vol. 21). 1979. pap. 24.50x (ISBN 0-520-09592-8). U of Cal Pr.
Menkveld, H. Dutch Baking & Pastry. 1980. 16.50 (ISBN 0-85334-839-1, Pub. by Applied Sci England). Elsevier.
Menn, Lisa, jt. ed. see Obler, Loraine.
Mennell, John M. Foot Pain: Diagnosis & Treatment Using Manipulative Techniques. 251p. 1969. 17.95 o.p. (ISBN 0-316-56669-1). Little.
Mennell, Robert L. Community Property in a Nutshell. LC 82-11163. (Nutshell Ser.). 423p. 1982. pap. text ed. 6.95 (ISBN 0-314-66185-9). West Pub.
Mennes, Mary E., jt. auth. see Mahaffey, Mary J.
Mennig, Jan, jt. auth. see Melnicoe, William B.
Menninger, Edwin A. Flowering Trees of the World: From Tropics & Warm Climates. 18.95 (ISBN 0-8208-0039-2). Hearthside.
--Flowering Vines of the World: An Encyclopedia of Climbing Plants. LC 79-92491. 1970. 25.00 (ISBN 0-8208-0063-5). Hearthside.
--Seaside Plants of the World. (Illus.). 1964. 9.95 (ISBN 0-8208-0025-2). Hearthside.
Menninger Foundation, Topeka, Kansas. Catalog of the Menninger Clinic Library, 4 vols. 1972. Set. lib. bdg. 380.00 (ISBN 0-8161-0961-3, Hall Library). G K Hall.
Menninger, Karl. Number Words & Number Symbols: A Cultural History of Numbers. (Illus.). 1969. pap. 12.50 (ISBN 0-262-63061-3). MIT Pr.
--Theory of Psychoanalytic Technique. 5.95xi o.p. (ISBN 0-06-131144-8, TB 1144, Torch). Har-Row.
--Whatever Became of Sin? 1973. 8.95 o.p. (ISBN 0-8015-8556-2, Hawthorn); pap. 9.50 (ISBN 0-8015-8554-6, 0922-280, Hawthorn). Dutton.
Menninger, Karl A. Man Against Himself. LC 38-5962. 1938. 15.00 o.p. (ISBN 0-15-156513-9). HarBraceJ.
Menocal, Narcisco G. Architecture As Nature: The Transcendentalist Idea of Louis Sullivan. (Illus.). 256p. 1981. 25.00 (ISBN 0-299-08150-8). U of Wis Pr.
Menolascino, Frank J., ed. Psychiatric Aspects of the Diagnosis & Treatment of Mental Retardation. LC 69-20313. 1971. pap. 9.00x o.p. (ISBN 0-87562-029-9). Spec Child.
Menolascino, Frank J. & McCann, Brian, eds. Mental Health & Mental Retardation: Bridging the Gap. (Illus.). 272p. 1983. pap. text ed. 27.50 (ISBN 0-8391-1784-1, 19593). Univ Park.
Menolascino, Frank J. & Pearson, Paul H., eds. Beyond the Limits: Innovations in Services for the Severely & Profoundly Retarded. LC 74-84668. 1974. pap. 8.50x o.p. (ISBN 0-87562-053-1). Spec Child.
Menolascino, Frank J., et al. Curative Aspects of Mental Retardation: Biomedical & Behavioral Advances. LC 82-17787. 356p. 1983. text ed. 25.95 (ISBN 0-933716-29-X). P H Brookes.
Menon, Bhashkar P. Global Dialogue: The New International Economic Order. 1977. text ed. 23.00 o.p. (ISBN 0-08-021498-3); pap. text ed. 8.50 (ISBN 0-08-021499-1). Pergamon.
Menon, Kreshna. The Law of Property. (Orient Longman Law Library). 556p. 1980. pap. text ed. 18.95x (ISBN 0-86125-516-X, Pub. by Orient Longman Ltd India). Apt Bks.
Menon, Narayana, tr. see Sivasankara, Pillai T.
Menon, Premachandran R., jt. auth. see Friedman, Arthur.
Menotti, Gian-Carlo. Amahl & the Night Visitors. (Illus.). (gr. 5 up). 1962. PLB 6.95 o.p. (ISBN 0-07-041484-X, GB). McGraw.
Mensch, Gerhard. Stalemate in Technology: Innovations Overcome the Depression. LC 78-16278. 272p. 1983. 19.50 (ISBN 0-88410-611-X); pap. 11.95 (ISBN 0-88410-054-5). Ballinger Pub.
Mensing, Raymond C. Toleration & Parliament, 1660-1719. LC 79-63260. 1979. pap. text ed. 9.50 (ISBN 0-8191-0723-9). U Pr of Amer.
Mensink, O. Traditionele Muziekinstrumenten Van Japan: Traditional Musical Instruments of Japan. (Haags Gemeentemuseum, Kijkboekjes: Vol. 3). (Illus.). 64p. 1979. 15.00 o.s.i. (ISBN 90-6027-301-X, Pub. by Frits Knuf Netherlands). Pendragon NY.
Mensink, O., jt. auth. see Klerk, M.
Mente, Boye De see De Mente, Boye.
Menten, Ted. Fish & Sea Life Cut & Use Stencils. (Illus.). 64p. (Orig.). 1983. pap. 3.50 (ISBN 0-486-24436-9). Dover.
--The Illuminated Alphabet. (Illus.). 1978. pap. 2.25 coloring book (ISBN 0-486-22745-6). Dover.
--Ready-to Use Art Nouveau Borders. (Illus.). 64p. (Orig.). 1983. pap. 2.95 (ISBN 0-486-24431-8). Dover.
Menten, Theodore. Chinese Cut-Paper Designs. (Illus.). 8.00 (ISBN 0-8446-5223-7). Peter Smith.
--Illuninated Alphabet Coloring Book. (Illus.). pap. 1.50 o.p. (ISBN 0-486-22745-6). Dover.
--Japanese Cut & Use Stencils. (Illus.). 64p. (Orig.). 1980. pap. 3.50 (ISBN 0-486-23996-9). Dover.
--Ready-to-Use Banners. (Clip Art Ser.). (Illus.). 1979. pap. 2.75 (ISBN 0-486-23899-7). Dover.
Menten, Theodore, ed. Ancient Egyptian Cut & Use Stencils. (Illus.). 1978. pap. 3.50 (ISBN 0-486-23626-9). Dover.
--Art Deco Cut & Use Stencils. LC 77-80484. (Illus.). 1977. pap. 3.75 (ISBN 0-486-23551-3). Dover.
--Art Nouveau & Early Art Deco Type & Design. (Illus., From the Roman Scherer Catalogue). 9.00 (ISBN 0-8446-4632-6). Peter Smith.
--Ready-to-Use-Borders. (Clip Art Ser.). (Illus.). 1979. pap. 2.75 (ISBN 0-486-23782-6). Dover.
--Ready-to-Use Headlines. (Clip Art Ser.). 1979. pap. 2.75 (ISBN 0-486-23454-1). Dover.
Menten, Theodore, ed. see Lambert, Frederick.
Menter, Ian. Carnival. (Illus.). 32p. (gr. 1-3). 1982. 8.50 (ISBN 0-241-10828-4, Pub. by Hamish Hamilton England). David & Charles.
Mento, Wally. Alpha Awareness. rev. ed. 1977. 12.95 o.p. (ISBN 0-89036-094-4). Hawkes Pub Inc.
Menton, Seymour. Magic Realism Rediscovered, 1917-1981. LC 81-65878. (Illus.). 120p. 1982. 29.50 (ISBN 0-87982-038-1). Art Alliance.
--The Spanish American Short Story: A Critical Anthology. LC 76-7765. 1980. 30.00x (ISBN 0-520-03232-2). U of Cal Pr.
Menton, Seymour, ed. The Spanish American Short Story: A Critical Anthology. 506p. 1982. pap. 10.95 (ISBN 0-520-04641-2). U of Cal Pr.
Menton, Theodore. Mother Goose Cut & Use Stencils. (Crafts Ser.). (Illus.). 64p. (Orig.). 1982. pap. 3.95 (ISBN 0-486-24363-X). Dover.
Mentwig, Joachim & Kreuder, Manfred. Chemistry Made Easy, Part II: A Programmed Course for Self-Instruction. Rouvray, D. H., tr. from Ger. 700p. pap. write for info. (ISBN 0-89573-050-2). Verlag Chemie.
Mentzer, Mike & Friedberg, Ardy. The Mentzer Method: Weight Training for Fitness for Men & Women. (Illus., Orig.). 1980. pap. 6.95 (ISBN 0-688-08636-5). Quill NY.
--Mike Mentzer's Complete Book of Weight Training. LC 82-18632. (Illus.). 256p. (Orig.). 1983. pap. 6.95 (ISBN 0-688-01600-6). Quill NY.
Menual, Stewart. The Illustrated Encyclopedia of the Strategies, Tactics & Weapons of Russian Military Power. (Illus.). 256p. 1980. 25.00 o.p. (ISBN 0-312-40783-1). St Martin.
Menville, Douglas, ed. see Morris, Kenneth.
Menville, Douglas A. & Reginald, R. Things to Come: An Illustrated History of the Science Fiction Film. 224p. 1983. Repr. of 1977 ed. lib. bdg. 9.95x (ISBN 0-89370-019-3). Borgo Pr.
Menyuk, Paula. Acquisition & Development of Language. LC 79-135023. (Current Research in Developmental Psychology Ser). 1971. 25.95x (ISBN 0-13-003087-2). P-H.
--Language & Maturation. 1977. text ed. 17.50x (ISBN 0-262-13132-3); pap. 5.95x (ISBN 0-262-63075-3). MIT Pr.
--Sentences Children Use. (Press Research Monographs: No. 52). 176p. 1972. pap. 4.95x (ISBN 0-262-63043-5). MIT Pr.
Menze, Arnold E. Regulation of Cell Membrane Activities in Plants. 1977. 43.00 (ISBN 0-7204-0615-3, North-Holland). Elsevier.
Menze, Ernest A., tr. see Kinder, Hermann & Hilgemann, Werner.
Menzel, Barbara J. Would You Rather? LC 81-6810. (Illus.). 32p. 1982. 9.95 (ISBN 0-89885-076-2). Human Sci Pr.
Menzel, D. H., jt. auth. see Shore, B. W.
Menzel, Donald H., jt. auth. see Amir-Moez, Ali R.
Menzel, Donald H., ed. see Martin, Martha E.
Menzel, Dorothy. Pottery Style & Society in Ancient Peru: Art As a Mirror of History in the Ica Valley, 1350-1570. LC 74-29797. 1976. 55.00x (ISBN 0-520-02970-4). U of Cal Pr.
Menzel, Jiri. Closely Watched Trains. (Films Scripts Modern Ser). 1970. pap. 2.95 o.p. (ISBN 0-671-20792-X, Touchstone Bks). S&S.
Menzies, jt. auth. see Simons.
Menzies, Edna O. Wendy & Brian & the Hurt Puppy. LC 78-2640. (gr. 1-3). 1978. pap. 2.95 (ISBN 0-8024-1937-2). Moody.
Menzies, Robert. The Riches of His Grace. 175p. 1956. 9.95 (ISBN 0-227-67583-5). Attic Pr.
Mepham, John, tr. see Jakobson, Roman.
Mepham, T. B. Secretion of Mild. (Studies in Biology: No. 60). 64p. 1976. pap. text ed. 8.95 (ISBN 0-7131-2535-7). E Arnold.
Mepisashvili, Rusudan & Tsintsadze, Vakhtang. Arts of Ancient Georgia. Lang, David, tr. & intro. by. (Illus.). 1979. 29.95 o.p. (ISBN 0-500-23289-X). Thames Hudson.
Mera, Harry P. Indian Silverwork of the Southwest. rev. 2nd ed. (Illus., Orig.). 1960. Repr. 7.95 (ISBN 0-912762-03-9); thin card cover 3.95 (ISBN 0-912762-02-0). King.
--Reconnaissance & Excavation in Southeastern New Mexico. LC 39-14217. (AAA Memoirs: No. 51). 1938. pap. 12.00 (ISBN 0-527-00550-9). Kraus Repr.
Merak, A. J. The Frozen Planet. 192p. Date not set. pap. cancelled o.p. (ISBN 0-505-51827-9). Tower Bks.
Meras, Phyllis. Mermaids of Chenonceaux & Eight Hundred & Twenty-Eight Other Tales. LC 81-22135. 352p. 1983. 16.95 (ISBN 0-312-92525-5). Congdon & Weed.
--The Mermaids of Chenonceaux & Nine Hundred Eighty-Seven Other Tales. 352p. 1982. 16.95 (ISBN 0-312-92525-5). St Martin.
--Miniatures: How to Make Them, Use Them & Sell Them. LC 76-16493. 1976. o.s. 12.95 (ISBN 0-395-24344-0); pap. 7.95 (ISBN 0-395-24586-9). HM.
--Vacation Crafts. 1978. 11.95 o.s.i. (ISBN 0-395-26309-3); pap. 6.95 o.s.i. (ISBN 0-395-26498-7). HM.
Meras, Phyllis & Tenenbaum, Frances. Carry-Out Cuisine. 1982. 16.95 (ISBN 0-395-32212-X); pap. 8.95 (ISBN 0-395-33010-6). HM.
Mercado, A., tr. see Strogonov, B. P., et al.
Mercado, A., tr. see Zaika, V. E.
Mercado, Ben, ed. see Eareckson, Joni & Estes, Steve.
Mercado, Benjamin, tr. see Tenney, Merrill C.
Mercado, Benjamin E., tr. see Jensen, Irving L.
Mercatante, Anthony. Who's Who in Egyptian Mythology. 1978. 14.95 (ISBN 0-517-53445-2, C N Potter Bks); pap. 5.95 o.p. (ISBN 0-517-53446-0). Crown.
Mercer, A., et al. Operational Distribution Research: Innovative Case Studies. (ORASA Text Ser.: No. 2). 1978. pap. 24.95x o.p. (ISBN 0-470-26537-X). Halsted Pr.
Mercer, Ann, jt. auth. see Mercer, Cecil.
Mercer, Barbara. Oxford Girls. 192p. 1983. 11.95 (ISBN 0-312-59366-X). St Martin.
Mercer, Cecil & Mercer, Ann. Teaching Students with Learning Problems. (Orig.). 1981. pap. text ed. 19.95 (ISBN 0-675-08040-1). Merrill.
Mercer, Cecil D. Children & Adolescents with Learning Disabilities. (Special Education Ser.). 1979. text ed. 22.95 (ISBN 0-675-08272-2). Merrill.
--Students with Learning Disabilities. 544p. 1983. text ed. 23.95 (ISBN 0-675-20042-3). Additional supplements may be obtained from publishter. Merrill.
Mercer, Cecil D. & Snell, Martha E. Learning Theory Research in Mental Retardation: Implications for Teaching. (Special Education Ser.). 1976. text ed. 23.95 o.p. (ISBN 0-675-08531-4). Merrill.
Mercer, Charles. Gerald Ford. LC 74-24332. (Beginning Biographies Ser.). (Illus.). 64p. (gr. k-4). 1975. PLB 5.99 o.p. (ISBN 0-399-60944-X). Putnam Pub Group.
--Jimmy Carter. LC 77-1861. (Beginning Biographies Ser.). (Illus.). (gr. k-4). 1977. PLB 5.99 o.p. (ISBN 0-399-61094-4). Putnam Pub Group.
--Let's Go to Europe. (Let's Go Ser.). (Illus.). (gr. 2-4). 1968. PLB 4.29 o.p. (ISBN 0-399-60366-2). Putnam Pub Group.
--Miracle at Midway. LC 77-24116. (Illus.). (gr. 6-8). 1977. 7.95 o.p. (ISBN 0-399-20612-4). Putnam Pub Group.
--Monsters in the Earth: The Story of Earthquakes. LC 78-3755. (Illus.). (gr. 6-8). 1978. 9.95 (ISBN 0-399-20642-6). Putnam Pub Group.
--Murray Hill. 11.95 o.s.i. (ISBN 0-440-06223-3). Delacorte.
--Pacific. 1981. 14.95 o.p. (ISBN 0-671-25587-8). S&S.
--Roberto Clemente. LC 73-93753. (See & Read Biographies). (Illus.). 64p. (gr. k-4). 1974. PLB 4.49 o.p. (ISBN 0-399-60887-7). Putnam Pub Group.
--Statue of Liberty. LC 78-21305. (Illus.). (gr. 5 up). 1979. 9.95 (ISBN 0-399-20670-1). Putnam Pub Group.
Mercer, Charles, adapted by see Larson, Glen A. & Thurston, Robert.
Mercer, E. H. The Foundations of Biological Theory. LC 81-1643. 232p. 1981. 39.50x (ISBN 0-471-08797-1, Pub. by Wiley-Interscience). Wiley.
Mercer, Eileen. Let's Make Doll Furniture. LC 75-13753. (Illus.). 128p. 1975. 5.95 o.p. (ISBN 0-8052-3601-5). Schocken.
Mercer, G., jt. auth. see Long, A. F.
Mercer, Ginger, jt. auth. see Bach, Bob.
Mercer, H., jt. auth. see Davey, H.
Mercer, Henry C. Ancient Carpenters' Tools. 5th ed. (Illus.). 339p. 1975. 12.95 (ISBN 0-910302-00-6). Bucks Co Hist.
--The Bible in Iron. 3rd ed. (Illus.). 356p. 1961. pap. 15.00 (ISBN 0-910302-01-4). Bucks Co Hist.
--Dating of Old Houses. (Illus.). 28p. 1976. Repr. of 1926 ed. pap. 2.00 (ISBN 0-910302-03-0). Bucks Co Hist.
--Origin of Log Houses in the United States. (Illus.). 1976. Repr. of 1926 ed. 3.00 (ISBN 0-910302-08-1). Bucks Co Hist.
Mercer, Ian. The Changing Earth. LC 81-51499. (Exploration & Discovery Ser.). PLB 13.80 (ISBN 0-382-06613-8). Silver.
Mercer, Jean. Guided Observations in Child Development. LC 79-88267. 1979. pap. text ed. 10.00 (ISBN 0-8191-0768-9). U Pr of Amer.
Mercer, John. The Stories of Vanishing Peoples. (Illus.). 128p. 1982. 9.95 (ISBN 0-8052-8106-1, Pub. by Allison & Busby England). Schocken.
Mercer, Lloyd. Railroads & Land Grant Policy: A Study of Government Intervention. 258p. 1982. 34.00 (ISBN 0-12-491180-3). Acad Pr.
Mercer, Neil, ed. Language in School & Community. 256p. 1981. pap. text ed. 16.95 (ISBN 0-7131-6347-X). E Arnold.
Merchant, Carolyn. Death in Nature: Women, Ecology, & the Scientific Revolution. LC 79-1766. (Illus.). 268p. 1983. pap. 7.64i (ISBN 0-06-250572-6, HarpR). Har-Row.
--The Death of Nature: A Feminist Reappraisal of the Scientific Revolution. LC 79-1766. 1980. 16.95i o.p. (ISBN 0-06-250571-8, HarpR). Har-Row.
Merchant, H. C. & Geers, T. L., eds. Productive Applications of Mechanical Vibrations. (AMD Ser.: Vol. 52). 1982. 30.00 (H00238). ASME.
Merchant, Jane. The Greatest of These. (Orig.). pap. 1.25 o.s.i. Jove Pubns.
Merchant, M. N. Quranic Laws. pap. 5.50 (ISBN 0-686-18550-1). Kazi Pubns.
Merchant, Moelwyn. Comedy. (Critical Idiom Ser.). 1972. pap. 4.95x (ISBN 0-416-75050-8). Methuen Inc.
Merchant, W. M., ed. Essays & Studies-1977. (Essays & Studies: Vol. 30). 109p. 1977. text ed. 15.00x (ISBN 0-391-00701-7). Humanities.
Mercie, Christine. Sons of God. 1954. pap. 3.50 (ISBN 0-87516-059-X). De Vorss.
Mercier, Alfred. L' Habitation Saint Ybars. (Novels by Franco-Americans in New England 1850-1940 Ser.). 343p. (Fr.). (gr. 10 up). pap. text ed. 5.50 (ISBN 0-911409-22-X). Natl Mat Dev.
Mercier, Charles. Criminal Responsibility. (Historical Foundations of Forensic Psychiatry & Psychology Ser.). 256p. 1980. Repr. of 1931 ed. lib. bdg. 27.50 (ISBN 0-306-76064-9). Da Capo.

Mercier, J., ed. Anticonvulsant Drugs, Vols. 1-2. LC 72-8044. 1973. Vol. 1. text ed. 69.00 (ISBN 0-08-016840-X); Vol. 2. text ed. 59.00 (ISBN 0-08-017245-8). Pergamon.

Mercier, J. P. & Legras, R. Recent Advances in the Field of Crystallization & Fusion of Polymers. (Journal of Polymer Science Symposia). 1977. 21.95 (ISBN 0-471-04425-3, Pub. by Wiley-Interscience). Wiley.

Mercier, L. S. An Deux Mille Quatre Cent Quarante, 3 vols. (Utopias in the Enlightenment Ser.). (Fr.). 1974. Repr. of 1786 ed. Set. lib. bdg. 101.00 o.p. (ISBN 0-8287-0600-X). Vol. 1 (028). Vol. 2 (029). Vol. 3 (030). Clearwater Pub.

Mercier, Louis S. De J. J. Rousseau, Considere Comme L'un Des Premiers Auteurs De la Revolution. (Rousseauism: 1788-1797). (Fr.). 1978. Repr. of 1791 ed. lib. bdg. 170.00x o.p. (ISBN 0-8287-0601-8). Clearwater Pub.

--Memoirs of the Year Two Thousand Five Hundred. (Science Fiction Ser.). 1977. Repr. of 1795 ed. lib. bdg. 22.00 (ISBN 0-8398-2380-0, Gregg). G K Hall.

Mercier, Louis-Sebastien. L' Homme Sauvage. (Utopias in the Enlightenment Ser.). 306p. (Fr.). 1974. Repr. lib. bdg. 81.00x o.p. (ISBN 0-8287-0602-6, 040). Clearwater Pub.

Mercier, Sebastien. Memoirs of the Year Two Thousand Five Hundred, 1772, 2 vols. in 1. LC 74-16201. (Novel in England, 1700-1775 Ser). 1974. lib. bdg. 50.00 o.s.i. (ISBN 0-8240-1199-6). Garland Pub.

Mercier, Vivian. Beckett-Beckett. 1977. 16.95x (ISBN 0-19-502186-X). Oxford U Pr.

Mercier, Vivian & Greene, David H., eds. One Thousand Years of Irish Prose. 1961. pap. 4.95 o.p. (ISBN 0-448-00121-7, G&D). Putnam Pub Group.

Mercurio, Louis, illus. Instant Travel Art: Vol. 1: Cruises. (Instant Travel Art Ser.). (Illus.). 48p. 1982. pap. text ed. 15.00x (ISBN 0-916032-17-5). Merton Hse.

Merdinyan, M. E. & Mortimer, C. D. The Relationship Between the Development of Fishing Gear & the Study of It: Bibliography. (Marine Memo Ser.: No. 59). 43p. 1979. 1.00 o.p. (ISBN 0-686-36965-3, P828). URI Mas.

Meredith, D. L. Nuclear Power Plant Siting: A Handbook for the Layman. (Marine Bulletin Ser.: No. 6). 32p. 1972. 1.00 o.p. (ISBN 0-938412-11-6, P72). URI Mas.

Meredith, Dale D., et al. Design & Planning of Engineering Systems. (Civil Engineering & Engineering Mechanics Ser). (Illus.). 384p. 1973. ref. ed. 31.95 (ISBN 0-13-200196-9). P-H.

Meredith, G. Small Business Management in Australia. 2nd ed. 352p. 1982. 18.50 (ISBN 0-07-451006-1). McGraw.

Meredith, George. Egoist. (World's Classics Ser.). 9.95 (ISBN 0-19-250508-4). Oxford U Pr.

--The Egoist. Woodstock, George, ed. (English Library). 1979. pap. 4.95 (ISBN 0-14-043034-2). Penguin.

--The Ordeal of Richard Feverel: A Story of a Father & Son. 480p. 1983. pap. 6.95 (ISBN 0-486-24463-6). Dover.

--Short Stories: The Tale of Chloe, The House on the Beach, Farina, the Case of General Ople & Lady Camper. 315p. 1982. Repr. of 1914 ed. lib. bdg. 25.00 (ISBN 0-8495-3936-6). Arden Lib.

Meredith, George & Sutro, Alfred. The Egoist: A Play from the Novel by George Meredith. Sawin, Lewis, ed. LC 80-28494. 145p. 1981. text ed. 15.00x (ISBN 0-8214-0552-7, 82-83459). Ohio U Pr.

Meredith, Howard & Milan, Virginia E. A Cherokee Vision of Eloh' Proctor, Wesley, tr. 37p. (Eng. & Cherokee.). 1981. 10.00x (ISBN 0-940392-04-6); pap. write for info. Indian U Pr.

Meredith, Howard & Smith, Adeline. A Cherokee Prayerbook. 44p. (Eng. & Cherokee.). 1981. pap. 1.50x (ISBN 0-940392-02-X). Indian U Pr.

Meredith, J. M. Meredith's Second Book of Bible Lists. 272p. (Orig.). 1983. pap. 5.95 (ISBN 0-87123-319-3). Bethany Hse.

Meredith, Jack R. & Gibbs, T. E. Management of Operations. LC 79-24512. (Wiley Series in Management). 1980. text ed. 31.50x (ISBN 0-471-02574-7). Wiley.

Meredith, Joseph N. The Merediths & Selveys of Virginia & West Virginia. (Illus.). 210p. 1982. 26.00 (ISBN 0-686-82432-6). J N Meredith.

Meredith, Judy & Myer, Linda. Lobbying on a Shoestring: How to Win in Massachusetts...& Other Places, Too. LC 82-42676. (Illus.). 160p. (Orig.). 1982. pap. 6.95 (ISBN 0-910001-00-6). MA Poverty Law.

Meredith, Richard C. The Awakening. LC 78-21361. 1979. 10.95 o.p. (ISBN 0-312-06260-5). St Martin.

Meredith, Robert, jt. auth. see Smith, E. Brooks.

Meredith, Robert C. & Fitzgerald, John D. Structuring Your Novel. 1972. pap. 4.95 (ISBN 0-06-463325-X, EH 325, EH). B&N NY.

Meredith, Roy. Mathew Brady's Portrait of an Era. (Illus.). 1982. 25.95 (ISBN 0-393-01395-2). Norton.

--Mr. Lincoln's Camera Man: Mathew B. Brady. LC 73-92262. (Illus.). 384p. 1974. pap. 11.95 (ISBN 0-486-23021-X). Dover.

--Mr. Lincoln's Cameraman: Matthew B. Brady. pap. 12.50 cancelled (ISBN 0-486-23087-2). Dover.

Meredith, Scott. Writing to Sell. rev. ed. LC 74-1837. 256p. (YA) 1974. 12.45i (ISBN 0-06-012929-8, HarpT). Har-Row.

Meredith, T. J., jt. ed. see Vale, J. A.

Merejkowski, Dmitri. The Death of the Gods. Treuch, Herbert, tr. from Rus. & intro. by. LC 82-82473. 464p. 1982. Repr. of 1904 ed. 15.00 (ISBN 0-89345-407-9, Spirit Fiction). Garber Comm.

Merenda, Peter F., jt. auth. see Lindeman, Richard H.

Mereness, Newton D., jt. auth. see Leland, G. Waldo.

Meres, Francis. Palladis Tamia. LC 73-170413. (The English Stage Ser.: Vol. 10). lib. bdg. 50.00 o.s.i. (ISBN 0-8240-0593-7). Garland Pub.

--Palladis Tamia. LC 39-10093. 1978. Repr. of 1598 ed. 40.00x (ISBN 0-8201-1188-0). Schol Facsimiles.

Merezhkovsky, Dmitri S. Tolstoi As Man & Artist. Repr. of 1902 ed. lib. bdg. 25.00 (ISBN 0-8371-4098-6, METO). Greenwood.

Mergen, Bernard. Play & Playthings: A Reference Guide. LC 82-6139. (American Popular Culture Ser.). (Illus.). 288p. 1982. lib. bdg. 35.00 (ISBN 0-313-22136-7, MGT/). Greenwood.

Mergers, Thomas H., jt. auth. see Hopkins.

Mergerson, David. Medicine As a Career. 13.50x o.p. (ISBN 0-392-06398-0, LTB). Sportshelf.

Merha, Lester W. Gold-Mine Jail. 1982. pap. 6.95 (ISBN 0-686-84746-6, Avalon). Bouregy.

--Kent Dell's Warpath. (YA) 1980. 6.95 (ISBN 0-686-73943-4, Avalon). Bouregy.

--Return to Elkhorne. 1977. 6.95 (ISBN 0-685-73813-2, Avalon). Bouregy.

--Rider on Rattlesnake Hill. 1982. pap. 6.95 (ISBN 0-686-84723-7, Avalon). Bouregy.

--Roughshod Posse. 1981. pap. 6.95 (ISBN 0-686-84677-X, Avalon). Bouregy.

Merha, Lester Wayne. Long Trail to Devil's Pass. (YA) 1978. 6.95 (ISBN 0-685-19060-9, Avalon). Bouregy.

--Outlaw's Grave. (YA) 1979. 6.95 (ISBN 0-685-95877-9, Avalon). Bouregy.

Merhaut, Josef. Theory of Electroacoustics. (Illus.). 336p. 1981. 47.95 (ISBN 0-07-041478-5, C). McGraw.

Merhav, M. Technological Dependence, Monopoly & Growth. 1969. 19.25 (ISBN 0-08-012754-1). Pergamon.

Merialdi, A., jt. ed. see Salvadori, B. A.

Meriam, J. L. Dynamics. 2nd ed. LC 74-30017. 480p. (SI version). 1975. text ed. 28.95 (ISBN 0-471-59607-8). Wiley.

--Engineering Mechanics, 2 vols. Incl. Vol. 1. Statics: SI Version. text ed. 28.95 (ISBN 0-471-05558-1); Arabic ed. 19.50 (ISBN 0-471-06312-6); Vol. 2. Dynamics: SI Version. text ed. 29.95 (ISBN 0-471-05559-X); Arabic ed. 19.50 (ISBN 0-471-06311-8). LC 79-11173. 1980. Wiley.

--Engineering Mechanics, 2 vols. Incl. Vol. 1. Statics. text ed. 28.95x (ISBN 0-471-59460-1); Vol. 2. Dynamics. text ed. 27.95x (ISBN 0-471-59461-X). LC 77-24716. 1978. Wiley.

--Engineering Mechanics: Statics & Dynamics Combined. LC 78-518. 1978. text ed. 38.50x (ISBN 0-471-01979-8). Wiley.

--Statics. 2nd ed. SI Version, ed. LC 74-11459. 381p. 1975. text ed. 28.95 (ISBN 0-471-59604-3). Wiley.

Meriam, James L. Dynamics. 2nd ed. LC 71-142138. 1971. text ed. 21.95x o.p. (ISBN 0-471-59601-9). Wiley.

Merian, Wilhelm. Die Tabulaturen Des Organisten Hans Kotter: Ein Beitrag Zur Musikgeschicte Des Beginnenden 16. (Bibliotheca Oranologica: Vol. 69). 1973. Repr. of 1916 ed. 40.00 o.s.i. (ISBN 90-6027-302-8, Pub. by Frits Knuf Netherlands). Pendragon NY.

Meriaux, J. Etude Analytique et Comparative de la Vegetation Aquatique D'Etangs et Marais du Nord de la France. (Valle de la Sensee et Bassin Houillier du Nord-Pas-de-Calais) (Offprint from Documents Phytosociolgique Ser.). (Fr.). 1979. pap. 20.00x (ISBN 3-7682-1238-6). Lubrecht & Cramer.

Meriden Britannia Co. The Meriden Britannia Silver-Plate Treasury: The Complete Catalog of 1886-87. (Antiques Ser.). (Illus.). 464p. 1983. pap. 20.00 (ISBN 0-486-24364-8). Dover.

Merigan, Thomas C. & Friedman, Robert M., eds. Interferons: Symposium. 481p. 1982. 42.00 (ISBN 0-12-491220-6). Acad Pr.

Merigan, William & Weiss, Bernard, eds. Neurotoxicity of the Visual System. (Illus.). 288p. 1980. text ed. 38.00 (ISBN 0-89004-400-7). Raven.

Merikangas, James R. Brain-Behavior Relationships. LC 79-2075. 240p. 1981. 26.95x (ISBN 0-669-03082-1). Lexington Bks.

--Preventing Neurologic Syndromes. 250p. 1983. 22.50 (ISBN 0-87527-224-X). Green.

Merillat, Herbert C. Guadalcanal Remembered. LC 81-19431. (Illus.). 350p. 1982. 14.95 (ISBN 0-396-08048-0). Dodd.

Merillat, Herbert C., ed. Legal Advisors & International Organizations. LC 66-20029. 124p. 1966. 8.50 (ISBN 0-379-00294-9). Oceana.

Merimee, Prosper. Venus of Ille & Other Stories. Kimber, Jean, tr. (Oxford Library of French Classics Ser). 1966. 6.50x o.p. (ISBN 0-19-255211-2). Oxford U Pr.

Merin, Jennifer, et al. International Directory of Theatre, Dance, & Folklore Festivals. LC 79-9908. 1979. lib. bdg. 29.95 (ISBN 0-313-20993-6, MTF/). Greenwood.

Mering, T. A., jt. auth. see Adrianov, O. S.

Meringer, Rudolf & Mayer, Carl. Versprechen und Verlesen: Eine Psychologisch-Linguistische Studie. (Classics in Psycholinguistics Ser.). liv, 207p. 1978. 32.00 (ISBN 90-272-0973-1, 2). Benjamins North Am.

Merino, Barbara D., jt. auth. see Previts, Gary J.

Merino Manon, Jose, jt. auth. see Macon, Jorge.

Merino-Rodriguez, Manuel, ed. Lexicon of Plant Pests & Diseases. (Eng. Lat. Fr. Span. Ital. Ger., Polyglot). 1966. 70.25 (ISBN 0-444-40393-0). Elsevier.

Meritt, Herbert D., jt. auth. see Hall, John R.

Meritt, Herbert Dean. Old English Glosses: A Collection. 135p. 1982. Repr. of 1945 ed. lib. bdg. 30.00 (ISBN 0-89760-580-2). Telegraph Bks.

Meritt, Lucy S. History of the American School of Classical Studies at Athens, 1939-1980. Date not set. 15.00x (ISBN 0-87661-942-1). Am Sch Athens.

Merivale, John H. Orlando in Roncevalles: A Poem. Reiman, Donald H., ed. LC 75-29781. (Romantic Context Ser.: Poetry 1789-1830: Vol. 81). 1978. Repr. of 1814 ed. lib. bdg. 47.00 o.s.i. (ISBN 0-8240-2180-0). Garland Pub.

Meriwether, James B., ed. James Gould Cozzens: A Checklist. (Modern Authors Checklist Ser.). (Illus.). 85p. 1973. 24.00x (ISBN 0-8103-0904-1, Bruccoli Clark Bk). Gale.

Meriwether, Louise. Daddy Was a Numbers Runner. 1976. pap. 2.25 (ISBN 0-515-06342-8). Jove Pubns.

Merk, Federick & Merrk, Lois B. Manifest Destiny & Mission in American History: A Reinterpretation. LC 82-25146. ix, 265p. 1983. Repr. lib. bdg. 35.00x (ISBN 0-313-23844-8, MERM). Greenwood.

Merk, Frederick. Slavery & the Annexation of Texas. 1972. 10.00 o.p. (ISBN 0-394-48104-6). Knopf.

Merk, Gerard, ed. Acta Monetaria. 128p. 1980. 59.00x (ISBN 0-686-81993-4, Pub. by Macdonald & Evans). State Mutual Bk.

Merkel, J. Die Vegetation in Gebiet des Messtischblattes 6434 Hersbruck. (Dissertationes Botanica: No. 51). (Illus.). 176p. (Ger.). 1980. pap. text ed. 20.00 (ISBN 3-7682-1235-1). Lubrecht & Cramer.

Merkel, Robert A., jt. auth. see Boggs, Donald L.

Merker, Hans J., jt. ed. see Neubert, Diether.

Merkl, Peter, jt. ed. see Kim, Chong Lim.

Merkl, Peter H. German Foreign Policies, West & East: On the Threshold of a New European Era. LC 73-92506. (Studies in International & Comparative Politics: No. 3). (Illus.). 232p. 1974. text ed. 20.85 o.p. (ISBN 0-87436-133-8); pap. text ed. 6.45 o.p. (ISBN 0-686-31694-0). ABC-Clio.

Merkl, Peter H., ed. see Cassinelli, C. W.

Merkl, Peter H., ed. see Fry, Earl H. & Raymond, Gregory A.

Merkl, Peter H., ed. see Schulz, Ann.

Merkle, Judith A. Management & Ideology: The Legacy of the International Scientific Management Movement. LC 78-59447. 300p. 1980. 24.50x (ISBN 0-520-03737-5). U of Cal Pr.

Merkle, Ralph C. Secrecy, Authentication & Public Key Systems. Stone, Harold, ed. LC 82-17611. (Computer Science Systems Programming Ser.: No. 18). 112p. 1982. 34.95 (ISBN 0-8357-1384-9). Univ Microfilms.

Merklein, Helmut A. & Hardy, W. Carey. Energy Economics. 238p. 1977. 17.95 (ISBN 0-87201-222-0). Gulf Pub.

Merkley, Jay P. Marksmanship with Rifles: A Basic Guide. (Illus.). 55p. 1982. pap. text ed. 2.95x (ISBN 0-89641-079-X). American Pr.

Merlan, Philip. A Syllabus in the Humanities. 128p. 1973. text ed. 6.50 o.p. (ISBN 0-8158-0288-9). Chris Mass.

Merleau-Ponty, Jacques & Morando, Bruno. The Rebirth of Cosmology. LC 82-60404. (Illus.). xvi, 302p. 1982. pap. text ed. 9.95x (ISBN 0-8214-0606-X, 82-83921). Ohio U Pr.

Merleau-Ponty, M. Phenomenology of Perception. Rev. ed. Smith, Colin, tr. from Fr. 446p. pap. text ed. 15.95x o.p. (ISBN 0-391-02551-1, Pub. by Routledge England). Humanities.

Merleau-Ponty, Maurice. Humanism & Terror. LC 71-84797. 1969. pap. 5.95x (ISBN 0-8070-0277-1, BP343). Beacon Pr.

--Phenomenology of Perception. Smith, Colin, tr. 1962. text ed. 26.00x o.p. (ISBN 0-391-00070-5). Humanities.

Merlis, S., ed. Non-Scientific Constraints on Medical Research. LC 72-133882. 114p. 1972. pap. 3.30 (ISBN 0-911216-17-0). Raven.

Merlo, Lorenzo. Japanese Photography Today & Its Origin. 192p. 1982. pap. 12.95 (ISBN 0-906333-06-7, Pub. by Salem Hse Ltd). Merrimack Bk Serv.

Merlonghi, Fernando, et al. Oggi in Italia: A First Course in Italian. 2nd ed. LC 81-85378. 1982. 20.50 (ISBN 0-395-31872-6); instr's annot. ed. 6.50 (ISBN 0-395-31873-4); write for info.; write for info. wkbk. pap. (ISBN 0-395-31874-2); write for info (ISBN 0-395-31876-9); write for info (ISBN 0-395-31875-0). HM.

Mermall, Thomas. The Rhetoric of Humanism: Spanish Culture After Ortega y Gasset. LC 76-45293. 1976. lib. bdg. 10.95x (ISBN 0-916950-02-6); pap. 6.95x (ISBN 0-916950-16-6). Bilingual Pr.

Merman, Marian A & Herman, Marian A., eds. Semiconductor Optoelectronics: Proceedings. 648p. 1981. 59.95 (ISBN 0-471-27589-1, Pub. by Wiley-Interscience). Wiley.

Mermelstein, David. Economics: Mainstream Readings & Radical Critiques. 3rd ed. 1976. text ed. 8.95x o.p. (ISBN 0-394-30108-0). Random.

Mermet, J., ed. CAD in Medium Sized & Small Industries: Proceedings. 1981. 85.00 (ISBN 0-444-86145-9). Elsevier.

Mermin, N. David. Space & Time in Special Relativity. LC 67-30052. (Illus.). 1968. pap. text ed. 14.50 (ISBN 0-07-041499-8, C). McGraw.

Mermin, Samuel. Law & the Legal System. 2nd ed. LC 81-83102. 361p. 1982. text ed. 9.95 (ISBN 0-316-56731-0). Little.

--Law & the Legal System: An Introduction. 1973. pap. 8.95 o.p. (ISBN 0-316-56730-2). Little.

Mernit, Susan. Tree Climbing. 60p. (Orig.). 1981. pap. 2.00 (ISBN 0-87924-036-9). Membrane Pr.

Merrell, Floyd. Semiotic Foundations: Steps toward an Epistemology of Written Texts. LC 81-48631. (Advances in Semiotics Ser.). 192p. 1983. 22.50 (ISBN 0-253-35161-8). Ind U Pr.

Merrem, G. & Goldhahn, W. E. Neurosurgical Operations. (Illus.). 560p. 1983. 92.00 (ISBN 0-387-11374-6). Springer-Verlag.

Merrett, C. E. A Selected Bibliography of Natal Maps. 1979. lib. bdg. 46.00 (ISBN 0-8161-8276-0, Hall Reference). G K Hall.

Merrett, Christopher E. Map Classification: A Comparison of Schemes, with Special Reference to the Continent of Africa. (Occasional Papers: No. 153). 1982. 3.00 (ISBN 0-686-96418-7). U of Ill Lib Info Sci.

Merrett, John. Famous Voyagers in Small Boats. (Illus.). (gr. 6-9). 1957. write for info. S G Phillips.

--True Book About Albert Schweitzer. (Illus.). (gr. 7 up). 12.75x o.p. (ISBN 0-392-05073-0, LTB). Sportshelf.

Merriam, Alan P. The Arts & Humanities in African Studies. (African Humanities Ser.). 17p. (Orig.). 1972. pap. text ed. 2.00 (ISBN 0-941934-34-9). Ind U Afro-Amer Arts.

--Bibliography of Jazz. LC 75-127282. (The Roots of Jazz Ser.). 1970. Repr. of 1954 ed. lib. bdg. 19.50 (ISBN 0-306-70036-0). Da Capo.

--Culture History of the Basongye. (African Humanities Ser.). (Illus.). 76p. (Orig.). 1975. pap. text ed. 4.00 (ISBN 0-941934-13-6). Ind U Afro-Amer Arts.

Merriam, Alan P. & Benford, Robert J. Bibliography of Jazz. LC 55-1225. (American Folklore Society Bibliography Ser). Repr. of 1954 ed. 20.00 (ISBN 0-527-01128-2). Kraus Repr.

Merriam, C. W., 3rd. Fortran Computer Programs. LC 77-14792. 368p. 1978. 26.95 (ISBN 0-669-01995-X). Lexington Bks.

Merriam, Eve. Bam! Zam! Boom! LC 79-181847. (Illus.). 40p. (gr. k-3). 1972. 3.95 o.s.i. (ISBN 0-8027-6095-3); PLB 3.87 o.s.i. (ISBN 0-8027-6096-1). Walker & Co.

--The Birthday Cow. LC 78-3289. (Illus.). (gr. k-3). 1978. reinforced binding 6.99 (ISBN 0-394-93808-9). Knopf.

--The Inner City Mother Goose. pap. 3.95 o.p. (ISBN 0-671-20290-1, Touchstone Bks). S&S.

--A Word or Two with You. LC 81-1282. (Illus.). 40p. (gr. 4 up). 1981. PLB 9.95 (ISBN 0-689-30862-0). Atheneum.

Merriam, George S., ed. see Bowles, Samuel.

Merriam, Kendall A. Illustrated Dictionary of Lobstering. LC 78-61525. (Illus., Orig.). 1978. pap. 6.95 (ISBN 0-87027-192-X). Cumberland Pr.

Merriam, Lawrence C., Jr., jt. auth. see Brockman, C. Frank.

Merriam, Robert L. ABC of Revolution. 52p. (Orig.). 1976. pap. 1.75 (ISBN 0-686-32502-8). R L Merriam.

--John Carson. (Illus.). 23p. (Orig.). 1977. pap. 2.00 (ISBN 0-686-37766-4). R L Merriam.

--Maple Sugar. (Illus.). 32p. (Orig.). 1982. pap. 6.50 (ISBN 0-686-35762-0). R L Merriam.

--Six Vignettes. (Illus.). 38p. 1981. 9.50 (ISBN 0-686-32492-7). R L Merriam.

Merriam, Sharan B. Coping with Male Mid-Life: A Systematic Analysis Using Literature As a Data Source. LC 80-5124. 137p. 1980. pap. text ed. 8.25 (ISBN 0-8191-1051-5). U Pr of Amer.

Merriam, Sharon, ed. Linking Philosophy & Practice. LC 81-48476. 1982. 7.95x (ISBN 0-87589-889-0, CE-15). Jossey-Bass.

Merrick, Charles M., ed. Management Division History, 1886-1980: American Society of Mechanical Engineers. (Hive Management History Ser.: No. 84). 200p. 1983. lib. bdg. 23.75 (ISBN 0-87960-118-3). Hive Pub.

Merrick, David & Marshall, Richard. Energy: Present & Future Options, Vol. 1. LC 80-41416. 384p. 1981. 54.95x (ISBN 0-471-27922-6, Pub. by Wiley-Interscience). Wiley.

Merrick, Elliot. Northern Nurse. 1982. pap. 8.95 (ISBN 0-9603324-2-1). Sherry Urie.

Merrick, Gordon. Now Let's Talk About Music. 432p. 1981. pap. 3.50 (ISBN 0-380-77867-X, 82651-8). Avon.

Merrick, Kathryn W., jt. auth. see Feder, Jack.

Merrifield, Doris F. Praktische Anleitung Zur Interpretation Von Dichtung. LC 81-40127. 246p. (Orig.). 1982. pap. text ed. 10.75 (ISBN 0-8191-2054-5). U Pr of Amer.

Merrifield, Edward see Washburn, Wilcomb E.

Merrifield, Mary. The Art of Fresco Painting. 1971. 10.00 o.s.i. (ISBN 0-85458-918-X). Transatlantic.

Merrifield, William, ed. Studies in Otomanguean Phonology. (SIL Publications in Linguistics: No. 54). 180p. 1977. 8.00x (ISBN 0-88312-067-4); microfiche 2.25x (ISBN 0-88312-467-X). Summer Inst Ling.

Merrifield, William, et al. Laboratory Manual for Morphology & Syntax. rev. ed. 183p. 1974. pap. 7.00x (ISBN 0-88312-902-7); microfiche 3.00 (ISBN 0-88312-322-3). Summer Inst Ling.

Merrifield, William R. Palantla Chinantec Grammar. 127p. 1968. pap. 1.50x (ISBN 0-88312-794-6); microfiche 2.25x (ISBN 0-88312-359-2). Summer Inst Ling.

Merrifield, William R., jt. auth. see Baer, Phil.

Merrigan, John J., jt. auth. see Guy, Edward T.

Merrigan, Joseph A. Sunlight to Electricity: Prospects for Solar Energy Conversion by Photovoltaics. LC 75-6933. 192p. (Orig.). 1975. 15.00x o.p. (ISBN 0-262-13116-1); pap. 5.95 o.p. (ISBN 0-262-63072-9). MIT Pr.

Merril, Carl R., ed. see Kroc Foundation Conference, Oct. 12-16, 1981.

Merrilees, B., ed. see Benedeit.

Merrill, Arthur A. Confessions of Congress Park. (Illus.). (gr. 10-12). pap. 3.00 o.p. (ISBN 0-911894-43-8). Analysis.

Merrill, Boynton. Jefferson's Nephews: A Frontier Tragedy. 1977. pap. 2.95 o.p. (ISBN 0-380-01837-3, 36277, Discus). Avon.

Merrill, Daphne W. A Salute to Maine. 1983. 12.95 (ISBN 0-533-05534-2). Vantage.

Merrill, E. D. A Flora of Manila. 1968. Repr. of 1912 ed. 48.00 (ISBN 3-7682-0548-7). Lubrecht & Cramer.

Merrill, G. R. Cotton Carding. (Cotton Production, Texts & Reference Material Ser). 11.00x (ISBN 0-87245-220-4). Textile Bk.

Merrill, Gary F. & Weiss, Harvey R., eds. A Two Plus Entry Blockers, Adenosine, & Neurohumors. LC 82-17591. (Illus.). 380p. 1983. text ed. 38.00 (ISBN 0-8067-1271-6). Urban & S.

Merrill, George D., jt. ed. see Hillesheim, James W.

Merrill, George D., et al. A Handbook of Civilization, Vol. 1. 2nd ed. (Illus.). 1978. pap. text ed. 12.95 (ISBN 0-8403-1833-2). Kendall-Hunt.

Merrill, George P. First One Hundred Years of American Geology. (Illus.). 773p. 1969. Repr. of 1924 ed. lib. bdg. 15.75 (ISBN 0-686-37867-9). Lubrecht & Cramer.

Merrill, Gilbert R. Cotton Combing. 11.00x (ISBN 0-87245-221-2). Textile Bk.

--Cotton Drawing & Roving. 12.50x (ISBN 0-87245-222-0). Textile Bk.

--Cotton Opening & Picking. 1954. 11.00x (ISBN 0-87245-223-9). Textile Bk.

--Cotton Ring Spinning. 14.50x (ISBN 0-87245-224-7). Textile Bk.

Merrill, Irving R. & Drob, Harold A. Criteria for Planning the College & University Learning Resources Center. Wallington, Clint, ed. LC 77-2612. 1977. pap. 6.95 (ISBN 0-89240-003-X). Assn Ed Comm Tech.

Merrill, James. The Changing Light at Sandover. LC 81-70062. (Illus.). 512p. 1982. 25.00 (ISBN 0-689-11282-3); pap. 12.95 (ISBN 0-689-11283-1). Atheneum.

--Diblos Notebook. LC 65-12401. 1975. pap. 2.95 (ISBN 0-689-70519-0, 209). Atheneum.

--From the First Nine: Poems Nineteen Forty-six to Nineteen Seventy-six. LC 81-70062. 192p. 1983. 20.00 (ISBN 0-689-11280-7); pap. 10.95 (ISBN 0-689-11281-5). Atheneum.

--Marbled Paper. (Fine Press Poetry Ser.). (Illus.). 20p. 1982. ltd. signed ed. 75.00 (ISBN 0-931356-02-4). Seluzicki Poetry.

--Santorini: Stopping the Leak. (Metacom Limited Edition Ser.: No. 8). 24p. 1982. ltd. 37.50x (ISBN 0-911381-07-4). Metacom Pr.

Merrill, James I. Heroes & Other Enlisted Men. 192p. 1983. 12.95 (ISBN 0-8059-2851-0). Dorrance.

Merrill, John R. Using Computers in Physics. LC 80-5681. 271p. 1980. pap. text ed. 11.75 (ISBN 0-8191-1134-1). U Pr of Amer.

Merrill, Kathleen K., jt. auth. see Feldman, Shirley C.

Merrill, Margaret W. Skeletons That Fit. LC 77-24155. (Illus.). (gr. 3-6). 1978. PLB 5.99 (ISBN 0-698-30677-5, Coward). Putnam Pub Group.

Merrill, Martha, ed. New England Directory for Computer Professionals, 1983. 214p. (Orig.). 1982. pap. text ed. 28.50 (ISBN 0-686-37958-6). Bradford Co.

Merrill, Michael J., jt. auth. see McGowan, Robert A.

Merrill, R. Frank, ed. Mostellaria Titus Maccus Plautus. LC 75-190468. 1973. text ed. 10.95 o.p. (ISBN 0-312-54915-6). St Martin.

Merrill, Richard, ed. Radical Agriculture. (Orig.). 1976. pap. 6.95i o.p. (ISBN 0-06-090337-6, CN337, CN). Har-Row.

Merrill, Robert. Norman Mailer. (United States Authors Ser.). 1978. 12.95 (ISBN 0-8057-7254-5, Twayne). G K Hall.

Merrill, Robert & Jarvis, Fred. The Divas. 1978. 10.95 o.p. (ISBN 0-671-24239-3). S&S.

Merrill, Robert & Saffron, Robert. Between Acts: An Irreverent Look at Opera & Other Madness. LC 76-20467. 1976. 9.95 o.p. (ISBN 0-07-041501-3, GB). McGraw.

Merrill, Toni. Discussion Topics for Oldsters in Nursing Homes: 365 Things to Talk About. 256p. 1974. photocopy ed. spiral 24.75x (ISBN 0-398-03129-0). C C Thomas.

--Party Packets: For Hospitals & Homes Shortcuts for a Single Activity Worker. (Illus.). 196p. 1970. photocopy ed. spiral 17.50x (ISBN 0-398-01295-4). C C Thomas.

Merrill, Vinita. Atlas of Roentgenographic Positions & Standard Radiologic Procedures, 3 vols. 4th ed. LC 75-1144. 1975. Set. text ed. 99.50 (ISBN 0-8016-3412-1); Vol. 1. text ed. 49.75 (ISBN 0-8016-3404-0); Vol. 2. text ed. 49.75 (ISBN 0-8016-3405-9); Vol. 3. text ed. 49.75 (ISBN 0-8016-3406-7). Mosby.

Merrill, Virginia & Richardson, Susan M. Reproducing Period Furniture & Accessories in Miniature. (Illus.). 309p. 1981. 25.00 (ISBN 0-686-36481-3). Md Hist.

Merrill, Virginia, jt. auth. see Newman, Thelma R.

Merrill, W. C., et al. Panama's Economic Development: The Role of Agriculture. (Illus.). 1975. pap. 6.95x o.p. (ISBN 0-8138-1205-4). Iowa St U Pr.

Merrill, William K. Hunter's Bible. 1968. 4.95 (ISBN 0-385-01533-X). Doubleday.

Merrill-Oldham, Jan. Conservation & Preservation of Library Materials. LC 82-1875. 1982. pap. text ed. 10.00 (ISBN 0-917590-07-4). Univ Conn Lib.

Merriman, Beth. Fondue Cookbook. LC 79-86670. (Illus., Orig.). 1969. 3.95 o.p. (ISBN 0-448-01798-9, G&D). Putnam Pub Group.

Merriman, Christine, ed. see Sutton, Weldon L.

Merriman, John, ed. French Cities in the Nineteenth Century: Class, Power, & Urbanization. LC 81-2520. 256p. 1982. text ed. 29.50x (ISBN 0-8419-0464-2). Holmes & Meier.

Merriman, Margarita. A New Look at Sixteenth-Century Counterpoint. LC 81-40924. (Illus.). 230p. (Orig.). 1982. lib. bdg. 23.00 (ISBN 0-8191-2391-9); pap. text ed. 10.75 (ISBN 0-8191-2392-7). U Pr of Amer.

Merriman, Raymond. The Gold Book: Geocosmic Correlations to Gold Price Cycles. Robertson, Arlene, ed. 320p. (Orig.). 1982. pap. 50.00 (ISBN 0-930706-13-7). Seek-It Pubns.

Merrion, Margaret D. Instructional & Classroom Management for Music Educators. LC 82-45018. (Illus.). 118p. (Orig.). 1982. PLB 18.75 (ISBN 0-8191-2433-8); pap. text ed. 7.50 (ISBN 0-8191-2434-6). U Pr of Amer.

Merriss, B. L., et al. Recommended Specifications for Stainless Steel Piping, Fittings & Accessories for the Pulp & Paper Industry. 3rd rev. ed. (TAPPI PRESS Reports). (Illus.). 1979. pap. 9.95 (ISBN 0-89852-330-3, 01-01-R030). TAPPI.

Merrit, Walter. History for the League for Industrial Rights. LC 76-120852. (Civil Liberties in Americana History Ser.). 1970. Repr. of 1925 ed. lib. bdg. 22.50 (ISBN 0-306-71961-4). Da Capo.

Merritt, Don. One Easy Piece. 1981. 13.95 (ISBN 0-698-11112-5, Coward). Putnam Pub Group.

Merritt, F. S. Applied Mathematics in Engineering Practice. 1970. 28.50 o.p. (ISBN 0-07-041511-0, P&RB). McGraw.

Merritt, Fred, ed. see Dalzell, J. Ralph.

Merritt, Frederick, jt. auth. see Dalzell, Ralph J.

Merritt, Frederick S. Building Construction Handbook. 4th ed. 1408p. 1981. 75.00 (ISBN 0-07-041521-8). McGraw.

--Building Construction Handbook. 3rd ed. 1120p. 1975. 55.00 (ISBN 0-07-041520-X, P&RB). McGraw.

Merritt, Frederick S., ed. Standard Handbook for Civil Engineers. 2nd ed. (Illus.). 1976. 55.00 (ISBN 0-07-041510-2, P&RB). McGraw.

--Standard Handbook for Civil Engineers. 3rd ed. 1664p. 1983. 79.95 (ISBN 0-07-041515-3, P&RB). McGraw.

--Structural Steel Designer's Handbook. (Illus.). 1000p. 1972. 55.00 (ISBN 0-07-041507-2, P&RB). McGraw.

Merritt, Herbert E. Hydraulic Control Systems. LC 66-28759. 1967. 45.95 (ISBN 0-471-59617-5, Pub. by Wiley-Interscience). Wiley.

Merritt, Howard & Gerdts, William. Studies on Thomas Cole, an American Romanticist: Annual II. 1968. pap. 7.50 (ISBN 0-912298-26-X). Baltimore Mus.

Merritt, LeRoy C. Book Selection & Intellectual Freedom. LC 79-116998. 100p. 1970. 8.00 (ISBN 0-8242-0420-4). Wilson.

Merritt, Leroy C., et al. Reviews in Library Book Selection. LC 58-623836. 1958. 5.95x o.p. (ISBN 0-8143-1095-8). Wayne St U Pr.

Merritt, M. L., ed. The Environment of Amchitka Island, Alaska. LC 77-24611. (ERDA Technical Information Center). 696p. 1977. pap. 25.50 (ISBN 0-87079-106-0, TID-26712); microfiche 4.50 (ISBN 0-87079-195-8, TID-26712). DOE.

Merritt, Ricard W. & Cummins, Kenneth W. An Introduction to the Aquatic Insects of North America. 3rd ed. (Illus.). 1978. text ed. 24.95 (ISBN 0-8403-8007-0). Kendall-Hunt.

Merritt, Richard, ed. Foreign Policy. 1974. pap. 6.00 (ISBN 0-918592-09-7). Policy Studies.

Merritt, Richard L. Symbols of American Community, 1735-1775. LC 76-23442. (Yale Studies in Political Science Ser: No. 16). (Illus.). 279p. 1976. Repr. of 1966 ed. lib. bdg. 21.00x (ISBN 0-8371-9012-6, MESY). Greenwood.

Merritt, Richard L., ed. Communication in International Politics. LC 72-165042. 480p. 1972. 28.50 (ISBN 0-252-00210-5). U of Ill Pr.

--Foreign Policy Analysis. LC 75-27808. (Policy Studies Organization). 176p. 1975. 19.95 (ISBN 0-669-00251-8). Lexington Bks.

Merritt, Robert C. Extractive Metallurgy of Uranium. LC 71-157076. (Illus.). 570p. 1979. Repr. of 1971 ed. 20.00 (ISBN 0-918062-10-1). Colo Sch Mines.

Merrk, Lois B., jt. auth. see Merk, Federick.

Merry, Eleanor C. Easter: The Legends & the Fact. Merry, Eleanor C., tr. (Illus.). 153p. 1967. 5.25 (ISBN 0-88010-048-6, Pub. by New Knowledge Bks England). Anthroposophic.

Merry, Henry J. Constitutional Function of Presidential-Administrative Separation. LC 78-53415. 1978. pap. text ed. 7.75 o.p. (ISBN 0-8191-0497-3). U Pr of Amer.

Merry, Sally E. Urban Danger: Life in a Neighborhood of Strangers. 278p. 1981. 27.95 (ISBN 0-87722-219-3). Temple U Pr.

Merryman, John H, et al. Law & Social Change in Mediterranean Europe & Latin America: A Handbook of Legal & Social Indicators of Comparative Study. LC 79-67718. (Stanford Studies in Law & Development). 618p. 1979. lib. bdg. 47.50 (ISBN 0-379-20700-1). Oceana.

Merryman, John H., et al, trs. Italian Civil Code. LC 69-15387. 787p. 1969. text ed. 47.50 (ISBN 0-379-00239-6). Oceana.

Mersand, Joseph & Griffith, Francis. Spelling Your Way to Success. rev. ed. LC 73-16791. (gr. 9 up). 1982. text ed. 8.50 (ISBN 0-8120-5414-8); pap. text ed. 5.95 (ISBN 0-8120-2339-0). Barron.

Merschel, Sylvia E., jt. auth. see Perry, Donald R.

Mersenne, Marin. Cogitata Physico-Mathematica, in Quibus Tam Naturae Quam Artis Effectus Admirandi Certissimis Demonstrationibus Explicantur. Repr. of 1644 ed. 164.00 o.p. (ISBN 0-8287-0603-4). Clearwater Pub.

--Novaum Observationum Physico-Mathematicarum F. Marini Mersenni Minimi Tomus III, Quibus Accessit Aristarchus Samius De Mundi Systemate. Repr. of 1647 ed. 74.00 o.p. (ISBN 0-8287-0604-2). Clearwater Pub.

Merser, Cheryl. Honorable Intentions. LC 82-45180. 256p. 1983. 13.95 (ISBN 0-689-11311-0). Atheneum.

Mersereau, John, Jr. Russian Romantic Fiction. 270p. 1983. 25.00 (ISBN 0-88233-739-4). Ardis Pubs.

Merserve, Bruce E. & Sobel, Max A. Introduction to Mathematics. 4th ed. (Illus.). 1978. text ed. 22.95 (ISBN 0-13-487553-2). P-H.

Mersky, Roy, et al. A Manual on Medical Literature for Law Librarians: A Handbook & Annotated Bibliography. LC 73-7475. 216p. 1974. 20.00x (ISBN 0-87802-101-9, Dist. by Oceana). Glanville.

Mersky, Roy, et al, eds. Author's Guide to Journals in Law, Criminal Justice & Criminology. LC 78-18805. (Author's Guide to Journals Ser.). 1979. 24.95 (ISBN 0-917724-06-2, B6). Haworth Pr.

Mersky, Roy M., ed. see Jeaffreson, John C.

Mersky, Roy M., ed. see Van Santvoord, George.

Merta, Jan, jt. auth. see Regush, Nicholas.

Mertens, Joan R., jt. auth. see Von Bothmer, Dietrich.

Mertens, Phil. La Jeune Peinture Belge. (Illus.). 260p. French Text 32.50 (ISBN 0-912729-17-1). Newbury Bk.

Mertens, Thomas & Bennett, Alice S. Laboratory Investigations in the Principles of Biology. 3rd ed. 1973. spiral bdg. 9.95x (ISBN 0-8087-1360-4). Burgess.

Mertens, Thomas R. Human Genetics: Readings on the Implications of Genetic Engineering. LC 74-30471. 320p. 1975. text ed. 13.95x (ISBN 0-471-59628-0). Wiley.

Mertens, Thomas R., jt. auth. see Winchester, A. M.

Mertes, John, jt. auth. see Wright, John S.

Mertin, Dietz, jt. auth. see Jander, Klaus H.

Mertins, Herman & Hennigan, Patrick J., eds. Applying Professional Standards & Ethics in the Eighties: A Workbook Study Guide for Public Administrators. Date not set. price not set (ISBN 0-936678-04-6). Am Soc Pub Admin.

Merton, Andrew. Enemies of Choice: The Right-to-Life Movement & Its Threat to Abortion. LC 81-65762. 252p. 1982. pap. 6.68 (ISBN 0-8070-0485-5, BP639). Beacon Pr.

Merton, Henry A. The Big Silver Melt. 128p. 1983. 12.95 (ISBN 0-02-584360-5). Macmillan.

Merton, L. F. The Moroccan Locust (Dociostaurus Maroccanus Thunberg) 1961. 35.00X (ISBN 0-85135-021-6, Pub. by Centre Overseas Research). State Mutual Bk.

Merton, Robert K. On the Shoulders of Giants: A Shandean Postscript. LC 65-12859. (Illus.). 1967. pap. 4.95 (ISBN 0-15-668781-X, Harv). HarBraceJ.

--Science, Technology & Society in Seventeenth Century England. 1978. pap. text ed. 6.95x (ISBN 0-686-86109-4). Humanities.

--The Sociology of Science: Theoretical & Empirical Investigations. Storer, Norman, ed. LC 72-97623. 1979. pap. 11.00x (ISBN 0-226-52092-7, P846, Phoen). U of Chicago Pr.

Merton, Robert K. & Nisbet, Robert A., eds. Contemporary Social Problems. 4th ed. 782p. 1976. text ed. 21.95 (ISBN 0-15-513793-X, HC); instructors' manual avail. (ISBN 0-15-513794-8). HarBraceJ.

Merton, Robert K., ed. see Bassis, Michael S. & Gelles, Richard J.

Merton, Robert K., jt. ed. see Riley, Matilda W.

Merton, Stephen. Mark Rutherford (William H. White) (English Authors Ser.). lib. bdg. 14.95 (ISBN 0-8057-1468-5, Twayne). G K Hall.

Merton, Thomas. The Climate of Monastic Prayer. (Cistercian Studies: No. 1). 154p. 1973. Repr. of 1969 ed. 7.95 (ISBN 0-87907-801-4). Cistercian Pubns.

--The Collected Poems of Thomas Merton. LC 77-9902. 1088p. 1980. pap. 37.50 (ISBN 0-8112-0643-2); pap. 18.95 (ISBN 0-8112-0769-2, NDP504). New Directions.

--Disputed Questions. 297p. 1960. 12.50 (ISBN 0-374-14061-8); pap. 6.95 o.p. (ISBN 0-374-51375-9). FS&G.

--Mystics & Zen Masters. 1969. pap. 5.95 o.s.i. (ISBN 0-440-56263-5, Delta). Dell.

--New Seeds of Contemplation. rev. ed. LC 61-17869. 1972. pap. 4.95 (ISBN 0-8112-0099-X, NDP337). New Directions.

--The Nonviolent Alternative. Zahn, Gordon C., intro. by. 1980. 12.95 (ISBN 0-374-22312-2); pap. 7.95 (ISBN 0-374-51575-1). FS&G.

--Original Child Bomb. (Illus.). 24p. 1983. pap. 4.95 (ISBN 0-87775-158-7). Unicorn Pr.

--Seeds of Destruction. 328p. 1964. pap. 6.95 (ISBN 0-374-51586-7). FS&G.

--Thoughts in Solitude. 124p. 1976. pap. 3.95 (ISBN 0-374-51325-2, N524). FS&G.

--Way of Chuang Tzu. LC 65-27556. (Illus.). 1969. pap. 4.95 (ISBN 0-8112-0103-1, NDP276). New Directions.

--Woods, Shore, Desert. 14.95 (ISBN 0-89013-140-6); pap. text ed. 6.95 (ISBN 0-89013-139-2). Museum NM Pr.

Mervyn, Len. Vitamin E Updated. Passwater, Richard A. & Mindell, Earl R., eds. (Good Health Guide Ser.). 32p. (Orig.). 1983. pap. 1.45 (ISBN 0-87983-274-6). Keats.

Mervyn, P. Memoirs of a Mis-spent Youth. 1982. 38.00x (ISBN 0-686-99795-6, Pub. by Sycamore Pr England). State Mutual Bk.

Merwe, Alwyn Van Der see Van Der Merwe, Alwyn.

Merwe, H. W. Van Der see Van Der Merwe, H. W.

Merwin, Henry C. Life of Bret Harte, with Some Account of the California Pioneers. LC 67-23887. 1967. Repr. of 1911 ed. 37.00x (ISBN 0-8103-3042-3). Gale.

Merwin, John. Stillwater Trout. LC 80-492. 1980. 15.95 o.p. (ISBN 0-385-17140-4, NLB). Doubleday.

Merwin, Richard E., ed. see National Computer Conference, 1979.

Merwin, Sam, Jr. The House of Many Worlds. 1983. pap. 2.50 (ISBN 0-441-34446-1, Pub. by Ace Science Fiction). Ace Bks.

Merwin, W. S. Opening the Hand. LC 82-73495. 96p. 1983. 12.95 (ISBN 0-689-11383-8); pap. 7.95 (ISBN 0-689-11381-1). Atheneum.

Merwin, W. S., tr. Poem of the Cid. 1975. pap. 5.95 (ISBN 0-452-00586-8, F586, Mer). NAL.

Merwin, W. S. & Masson, J. Moussaieff, trs. from Sanskrit. The Peacock's Egg: Love Poems from Ancient India. LC 81-81688. 224p. 1981. pap. 10.50 (ISBN 0-86547-059-6), N Point Pr.

Merwin, W. S., jt. tr. see Mustard, Helen M.

Mery, Eleanor C., tr. see Schindler, Maria.

Mery, Fernand. Life History & Magic of the Cat. Street, Emma, ed. 1968. Repr. 10.95 (ISBN 0-448-01111-5, G&D). Putnam Pub Group.

--Life, History & Magic of the Dog. Richmond-Watson, Angela, tr. LC 78-117172. Orig. Title: Chien. (Illus.). 1970. 8.95 (ISBN 0-448-02144-7, G&D). Putnam Pub Group.

Meryman, Richard. Mank: The Wit, World, & Life of Herman Mankiewicz. LC 78-8276. (Illus.). 1978. 12.95 o.p. (ISBN 0-688-03356-3). Morrow.

Merz, C. Mike & Groebner, David E. Toward a Code of Ethics for Management Accountants. 160p. pap. 14.95 (ISBN 0-86641-009-0, 81129). Natl Assn Accts.

Merz, Charles, jt. auth. see Schick, William.

Merz, Florian. Pop Art in School. 1970. 15.50 o.p. (ISBN 0-7134-2288-2, Pub. by Batsford England). David & Charles.

Merz, M., jt. ed. see Guttman, V.

Merzbacher, Eugen. Quantum Mechanics. 2nd ed. LC 74-88316. 1970. 34.95 (ISBN 0-471-59670-1). Wiley.

Mesa-Lago, Carmelo, ed. Revolutionary Change in Cuba. LC 73-158190. (Pitt Latin American Ser). 1971. 21.95 (ISBN 0-8229-3232-6); pap. 7.25x (ISBN 0-8229-5244-0). U of Pittsburgh Pr.

Mesa-Lago, Carmelo & Beck, Carl, eds. Comparative Socialist Systems: Essays on Politics & Economics. 1974. text ed. 16.95x o.p. (ISBN 0-916002-14-4); pap. text ed. 7.95 (ISBN 0-8229-8251-X). U of Pittsburgh Pr.

Mesarovic, M. & Reisman, A. Systems Approach & the City. 504p. 1972. 41.00 (ISBN 0-444-10410-0, North-Holland). Elsevier.

Mesch, Abraham J., tr. see Hanover, Nathan.

Meschan, Isadore. An Atlas of Anatomy Basic to Radiology. LC 73-89936. (Illus.). 1120p. 1975. text ed. 37.00 ea. o.p.; text ed. 68.00 single vol. o.p. (ISBN 0-7216-6310-9). Vol. 1 (ISBN 0-7216-6308-7). Vol. 2 (ISBN 0-7216-6309-5). Saunders.

Meschan, Isadore & Farrer-Meschan, R. M. F. Radiographic Positioning & Related Anatomy. LC 68-11638. (Illus.). 1968. 15.75 o.p. (ISBN 0-7216-6275-7); color slides 150.00 o.p. (ISBN 0-7216-9796-8). Saunders.

Meschery, Tom, jt. auth. see Colton, Larry.

Mescon, Michael, jt. auth. see Rachman, David.

Mescon, Michael H., et al. Management: Individual & Organizational Effectiveness. 704p. 1981. text ed. 24.95 scp (ISBN 0-06-166401-4, HarpC); inst. manual avail. (ISBN 0-06-364416-9); test bank avail. (ISBN 0-06-364415-0); reader scp 8.95 (ISBN 0-06-166407-3); instr's manual for reader avail. (ISBN 0-06-360185-0). Har-Row.

Mescon, Michael M., jt. auth. see Rachman, David J.

Meselson, Matthew S. Chemicals & Cancer. 1980. pap. 2.50x (ISBN 0-87081-081-2). Colo Assoc.

Meserve, Bruce E. Fundamental Concepts of Geometry. (Illus.). 352p. 1983. Repr. of 1955 ed. pap. 6.50 (ISBN 0-486-63415-9). Dover.

Meserve, Bruce E. & Sobel, Max A. Contemporary Mathematics. 3rd ed. (Illus.). 688p. 1981. text ed. 23.95 (ISBN 0-13-170076-6). P-H.

Meserve, Ruth I., jt. ed. see Meserve, Walter J.

Meserve, Walter. Studies in Death of a Salesman. LC 79-171570. 1972. pap. text ed. 3.50 (ISBN 0-675-09259-0). Merrill.

Meserve, Walter J., ed. American Drama to Nineteen Hundred: A Guide to Information Sources. (American Literature, English Literature, & World Literature in English Information Guide Ser.: Vol. 28). 1980. 42.00x (ISBN 0-8103-1365-0). Gale.

Meserve, Walter J. & Meserve, Ruth I., eds. Modern Literature from China. LC 74-15425. 337p. 1974. 20.00x o.p. (ISBN 0-8147-5370-1). NYU Pr.

Mesesnel, Janez. France Slana. Mlacnik, Milan, tr. (Illus.). 132p. 1981. 25.00 (ISBN 0-89893-082-0). CDP.

--Joze Tisnikar. Dolenc, Danica, tr. (Illus.). 128p. 1982. 25.00 (ISBN 0-89893-118-5). CDP.

Meshenberg, Kathryn & Burns, Linda, eds. Hospital Ambulatory Care: Making It Work. 200p. 1983. 37.50 (ISBN 0-87258-402-X, AHA-016620). Am Hospital.

Meshenberg, Michael J., ed. Environmental Planning: A Guide to Information Sources. LC 73-17538. (Man & the Environment Information Guide Ser.: Vol. 3). 480p. 1976. 42.00x (ISBN 0-8103-1340-5). Gale.

Meshorer, Ya'akov. Coins of the Ancient World. Currier, Richard L., ed. LC 72-10795. (The Lerner Archaeology Ser.: Digging up the Past). (Illus.). 96p. (gr. 5 up). 1975. PLB 7.95g (ISBN 0-8225-0835-4). Lerner Pubns.

Meshover, Leonard, et al. The Monkey That Went to School. LC 77-88636. (Illus.). (gr. 3-7). 1978. PLB 5.97 o.s.i. (ISBN 0-695-40878-X); pap. 3.95 o.s.i. (ISBN 0-695-30878-5). Follett.

Mesibov, Gary & Schopler, Eric, eds. Autism in Adolescents & Adults. (Current Issues in Autism Ser.). 435p. 1983. 35.00x (ISBN 0-306-41057-5, Plenum Pr). Plenum Pub.

Mesick, jt. auth. see Mendel.

Mesick, Jane L. English Traveller in America, 1785-1835. Repr. of 1922 ed. lib. bdg. 17.75x (ISBN 0-8371-4280-6, MEEN). Greenwood.

Mesics, Emil A. Education & Training for Effective Manpower Utilization: An Annotated Bibliography. (ILR Bibliography Ser.: No. 9). 164p. 1969. pap. 2.50 (ISBN 0-87546-023-2). ILR Pr.

Mesinger, F. & Arakawa, A. Numerical Methods Used in Atmospheric Models, Vol. 1. (GARP Publications Ser: No. 17). (Illus.). 64p. 1977. pap. 15.00 o.p. (ISBN 0-685-76013-8, W304, WMO). Unipub.

Mesirow, Kip. The Care & Use of Japanese Woodworking Tools. LC 78-60055. (Illus.). 1982. pap. 8.95 (ISBN 0-918036-08-9). Woodcraft Supply.

Meskill, John. Ch'oe Pu's Diary: A Record of Drifting Across the Sea. LC 64-19165. (Association for Asian Studies Monographs: No. 17). 1965. 4.50x o.p. (ISBN 0-8165-0146-7). U of Ariz Pr.

Meskill, John T., intro. by. The Pattern of Chinese History: Cycles, Development or Stagnation. LC 82-18378. (Problems in Asian Civilizations Ser.). xx, 108p. 1983. Repr. of 1965 ed. lib. bdg. 27.50x (ISBN 0-313-23739-5, MEPC). Greenwood.

Meskin, Lawrence, jt. ed. see Kudrle, Robert T.

Mesko, Jim. A-Twenty Havoc in Action. (Illus.). 50p. 1983. 4.95 (ISBN 0-89747-131-8). Squad Sig Pubns.

Mesmer, Robert E., jt. auth. see Baes, Charles F., Jr.

Messance. Recherches Sur la Population Des Generalites D'auvergne, De Lyon, De Rouen... Repr. of 1766 ed. 46.00 o.p. (ISBN 0-8287-0607-7). Clearwater Pub.

Messec, Jerry & Kranich, Roger. English Spoken Here, Bk. 2: Consumer Information. Holzer, Eva, ed. (English Spoken Here (ESL) Ser.). (Illus.). 160p. 1982. pap. 5.66 (ISBN 0-8428-0851-5); visual aids 33.33 (ISBN 0-8428-0845-0); wkbk., 128 pgs. 3.93 (ISBN 0-8428-0855-8). Cambridge Bk.

--English Spoken Here, Bk. 4: Life in the United States. (English Spoken Here (ESL) Ser.). (Illus.). 160p. 1983. pap. 5.66 (ISBN 0-8428-0853-1); visual aids 33.33 (ISBN 0-8428-0847-7); wkbk., 128 pgs. 3.93 (ISBN 0-8428-0857-4). Cambridge Bk.

Messec, Jerry L., jt. auth. see Kranich, Roger E.

Messec, Jerry L., jt. auth. see Kranich, Rogert E.

Messel, Harry, ed. Energy for Survival. (Illus.). 368p. 1979. 20.00 (ISBN 0-08-024794-6); pap. 15.00 (ISBN 0-08-024791-1). Pergamon.

Messenger, Betty. Picking Up the Linen Threads. 1982. 40.00x (ISBN 0-85640-210-9, Pub. by Blackstaff Pr). State Mutual Bk.

Messenger, Christian. Sport & the Spirit of Play in American Fiction. 352p. 1983. pap. write for info. Columbia U Pr.

Messenger, Joseph. Lost Circulation. 112p. 1981. 34.95x (ISBN 0-87814-175-8). Pennwell Books Division.

Messenger, Maire. The Breastfeeding Book. (Illus.). 128p. 1982. 16.95 (ISBN 0-442-26577-8); pap. 8.95 (ISBN 0-442-26575-1). Van Nos Reinhold.

Messenger, Nigel P. & Watson, J. Richard. Victorian Poetry: "The City of Dreadful Night" & Other Poems. (Rowman & Littlefield University Library). 242p. 1974. 12.50x o.p. (ISBN 0-87471-518-0); pap. 6.00x (ISBN 0-87471-535-0). Rowman.

Messenger, P. S., jt. ed. see Huffaker, C. B.

Messenger, Robert C., jt. auth. see Andrews, Frank M.

Messenger, Robert C., jt. auth. see Morgan, James N.

Messent, Peter B., ed. Literature of the Occult: A Collection of Critical Essays. (Twentieth Century Views Ser.). 224p. 1981. text ed. 13.95 (ISBN 0-13-537712-9, Spec); pap. text ed. 4.95 (ISBN 0-13-537704-8, Spec). P-H.

Messer, Andrew C., jt. auth. see Alexander, Daniel E.

Messer, Ronald K. Style in Technical Writing: A Text Workbook. 1982. pap. text ed. 9.95x (ISBN 0-673-15529-3). Scott F.

Messer, Sandra S. Politics for Nursing: Threat or Opportunity? 31p. 1980. 3.95 (ISBN 0-686-38348-6, 41-1816). Natl League Nurse.

Messer, Thomas M. Sixty Works: The Peggy Guggenheim Collection. (Illus.). 68p. 1982. pap. write for info. (ISBN 0-89207-037-4). S R Guggenheim.

Messer-Davidow, Ellen & Hartman, Joan E., eds. Women in Print-One: Opportunities for Women's Studies Research in Language & Literature. LC 82-3596. (MLA Commission on the Status of Women in the Profession Ser.). 198p. 1982. 22.50x (ISBN 0-87352-336-9); pap. 12.50x (ISBN 0-87352-337-7). Modern Lang.

--Women in Print-Two: Opportunities for Women's Studies Publication in Language & Literature. (MLA Commission on the Status of Women in the Profession Ser.). 173p. 1982. 22.50x (ISBN 0-87352-338-5); pap. 12.50x (ISBN 0-87352-339-3). Modern Lang.

Messerli, Douglas, ed. The Contemporary American Fiction. Abish, Walter, et al. 370p. (Orig.). 1983. 14.95 (ISBN 0-940650-22-3); pap. 9.95 (ISBN 0-940650-23-1). Sun & Moon MD.

Messerli, Douglas, ed. see Barnes, Djuna.

Messerschmidt, Jim. The Trial of Leonard Peltier. 250p. 1982. 20.00 (ISBN 0-89608-164-8); pap. 7.50 (ISBN 0-89608-163-X). South End Pr.

Messiah, A. Quantum Mechanics. Vol. 1, 1961. pap. 24.95x (ISBN 0-471-59766-X); Vol. 2 1962. pap. 24.95x (ISBN 0-471-59768-6). Halsted Pr.

Messick, Hank & Goldblatt, Burt. The Only Game in Town: An Illustrated History of Gambling. LC 75-26583. (Illus.). 224p. 1976. 12.50i (ISBN 0-690-01061-3, TYC-T). T Y Crowell.

Messick, Janice, jt. auth. see Aguilera, Donna.

Messick, Janice M., jt. auth. see Aguilera, Donna C.

Messick, R., jt. auth. see Chapin, J.

Messick, Samuel, jt. ed. see Wainer, Howard.

Messick, William L., jt. auth. see Chaney, Earlyne.

Messimer, Dwight R. Pawns of War: The Loss of the U. S. S. Langley & the U. S. S. Pecos. (Illus.). 1983. 18.95 (ISBN 0-87021-515-9). Naval Inst Pr.

Messina, Kathlyn. The Sleeping Giant Reading Program. LC 82-83558. (Illus.). 160p. (Orig.). 1983. pap. 10.95 (ISBN 0-910569-00-2). Hampton Court Pub.

Messina, P. C. & Murli, A., eds. Problems & Methodolgies in Mathematical Software Production, Sorrento, Italy 1980: Proceedings. (Lecture Notes in Computer Sciences: Vol. 142). 271p. 1983. pap. 12.30 (ISBN 0-387-11603-6). Springer-Verlag.

Messing, J. J. Operative Dental Surgery. 2nd ed. 1982. 79.00x (ISBN 0-333-31040-3, Pub. by Macmillan England). State Mutual Bk.

Messinger, Lillian & Hansen, James C., eds. Family Therapy Collections: Collection II: Therapy with Remarriage Families. LC 82-6799. 206p. 1982. 18.00 (ISBN 0-89443-601-5). Aspen Systems.

Messmann, Jon. Jogger's Moon. (Orig.). 1980. pap. 1.95 o.p. (ISBN 0-451-09116-7, J9116, Sig). NAL.

--Phone Call. 1979. pap. 2.95 (ISBN 0-451-12301-8, AE2301, Sig). NAL.

Messner, F., ed. see International Conference on Marketing Systems for Developing Countries.

Messner, Julian, jt. auth. see Van Every, Dale.

Messner, Reinhold. The Challenge. (Illus.). 1977. 15.00 o.p. (ISBN 0-19-519974-X). Oxford U Pr.

--Everest: Expedition to the Ultimate. (Illus.). 1979. 22.50 o.p. (ISBN 0-19-520135-3). Oxford U Pr.

Messner, Stephen D., jt. auth. see Kinnard, William N., Jr.

Mesterton, Erik, tr. see Lagerkvist, Par.

Mestrow, L. E., jt. auth. see Schneider, Steven.

Mestwerdt. Atlas of Colposcopy. Meier, A., ed. 176p. 1981. text ed. 60.00 o.p. (ISBN 0-7216-6268-4). Saunders.

Mesulam, Marsel. Tracing Neural Connections with Horseradish Peroxidase. LC 81-14692. (IBO Handbook Ser.: Methods in the Neurosciences). 251p. 1982. 52.00 (ISBN 0-471-10028-5, Pub. by Wiley-Interscience); pap. 26.00x (ISBN 0-471-10029-3). Wiley.

Meszaros, E. Atmospheric Chemistry: Fundamental Aspects. (Studies in Environmental Science: Vol. 11). 1981. 38.50 (ISBN 0-444-99753-9). Elsevier.

Meszaros, I. The Necessity of Social Control. 1971. text ed. 6.00x (ISBN 0-85036-154-0). Humanities.

Meszaros, Istvan. Lukacs' Concept of Dialect. (Illus.). pap. 4.95 o.p. (ISBN 0-686-23497-9, Merlin Pr). Carrier Pigeon.

--Marx's Theory of Alienation. 352p. 15.00x (ISBN 0-87556-438-0). Saifer.

--The Work of Sartre: The Challenge of History, Vol. II. Date not set. text ed. price not set (ISBN 0-391-01199-5). Humanities.

Meszaros, J. William, jt. auth. see Bishop, Vaughn F.

Meszaros, William. Cardiac Roentgenology: Plain Films & Angiographic Findings. 600p. 1969. photocopy ed. spiral 72.50x (ISBN 0-398-01297-0). C C Thomas.

Metakides. Patras Logic Symposium. (Studies in Logic & Foundations of Mathematics: Vol. 109). 1982. 59.75 (ISBN 0-444-86476-8). Elsevier.

Metalious, Grace. Peyton Place. 1956. 7.95 o.p. (ISBN 0-671-56683-0). S&S.

Metaxa, George, tr. see Steiner, Rudolf.

Metaxas, B. N. The Economics of Tramp Shipping. (Illus.). 304p. 1971. text ed. 32.50x o.p. (ISBN 0-485-11127-6, Athlone Pr). Humanities.

Metaxas, Daphne. Classic Greek Cooking. LC 74-13560. (Illus.). 192p. (Orig.). 1974. pap. 4.95 o.p. (ISBN 0-911954-31-7). Nitty Gritty.

Metcalf & Eddy Inc. Wastewater Engineering: Collection, Treatment, Disposal & Reuse. 2nd ed. Tchobanoglous, George, ed. (Illus.). 1978. text ed. 38.50 (ISBN 0-07-041677-X, C); 25.00 (ISBN 0-07-041678-8). McGraw.

Metcalf & Eddy, Inc. & Tchobanoglous, George. Wastewater Engineering: Collection & Pumping of Wastewater. (Water Resources & Engineering Ser.). (Illus.). 448p. 1981. text ed. 36.50 (ISBN 0-07-041680-X, C); solutions manual 15.00 (ISBN 0-07-041681-8). McGraw.

Metcalf, Clell L., et al. Destructive & Useful Insects. 4th ed. (Agricultural Sciences Ser.). 1962. text ed. 49.95 (ISBN 0-07-041658-3, C). McGraw.

Metcalf, D. M. Coins of South Germany in the Thirteenth Century. 1961. 12.00 (ISBN 0-685-51539-7, Pub by Spink & Son England). S J Durst.

Metcalf, Darrel S. & Elkins, Donald M. Crop Production: Principles & Practices. 4th ed. (Illus.). 1980. text ed. 31.95x (ISBN 0-02-380710-5). Macmillan.

Metcalf, David. Low Pay, Occupational Mobility, & Minimum Wage Policy in Britain. 1981. pap. 4.25 (ISBN 0-8447-3450-0). Am Enterprise.

Metcalf, Deborah. Mouth to Mouth. 1980. 12.95 (ISBN 0-399-90086-1, Marek). Putnam Pub Group.

Metcalf, E. W., jt. ed. see Ellison, Curtis W.

Metcalf, E. W., Jr., jt. auth. see Ellison, Curtis W.

Metcalf, Frank J. American Psalmody. 2nd ed. LC 68-13274. (Music Reprint Ser). (Illus.). 1968. Repr. of 1917 ed. lib. bdg. 15.00 (ISBN 0-306-71132-X). Da Capo.

Metcalf, George R. From Little Rock to Boston: The History of School Desegregation. LC 82-15581. (Contributions to the Study of Education Ser.: No. 8). 368p. 1983. lib. bdg. 35.00 (ISBN 0-313-23470-1, MDS/). Greenwood.

Metcalf, H. Topics in Classical Biophysics. 1980. pap. 13.95 (ISBN 0-13-925255-X). P-H.

Metcalf, John C. Taxidermy: A Complete Manual. (Illus.). 166p. 1981. pap. 15.00x (ISBN 0-7156-1565-3, Pub by Duckworth England). Biblio Dist.

Metcalf, Kenneth N., ed. Transportation Information Sources. LC 65-24657. (Management Information Guide Ser.: No. 8). 1965. 42.00x (ISBN 0-8103-0808-8). Gale.

Metcalf, Keyes. Planning Academic & Research Library Buildings. 1965. text ed. 35.00 o.p. (ISBN 0-07-041657-5, P&RB). McGraw.

Metcalf, Michael. FORTRAM Optimization. (APIC Studies in Data Processing: Vol. 17). write for info. (ISBN 0-12-492480-8). Acad Pr.

Metcalf, P., jt. auth. see Huntington, R.

Metcalf, Paul. Genoa: A Telling of Wonders. 1965. 10.00 (ISBN 0-912330-01-5, Dist. by Inland Bk); pap. 5.00 (ISBN 0-912330-17-1). Jargon Soc.

--Louis the Torch. 56p. 1982. pap. 3.95 (ISBN 0-916696-20-0). Cross Country.

--The Middle Passage. LC 75-21931. 1976. 5.00 (ISBN 0-912330-33-3, Dist. by Inland Bk). Jargon Soc.

--Patagoni. LC 72-13711. 1971. 10.00 o.p. (ISBN 0-912330-18-X, Dist. by Gnomon Pr). Jargon Soc.

--Waters of Potomack. LC 82-81476. (Illus.). 320p. 1982. 17.75 (ISBN 0-86547-090-1). N Point Pr.

Metcalf, Pricilla. James Knowles: Victorian Editor & Architect. (Illus.). 1980. 42.50x (ISBN 0-19-812626-3). Oxford U Pr.

Metcalf, R. L., jt. auth. see Pitts, J. N.

Metcalf, Richard M., jt. auth. see Cavert, C. Edward.

Metcalf, Robert L. & Luckmann, William H. Introduction to Insect Pest Management. 2nd ed. LC 82-4794. (Environmental Science & Technology: A Wiley-Interscience Series of Texts & Monographs). 577p. 1982. 32.50x (ISBN 0-471-08547-2, Pub. by Wiley-Interscience). Wiley.

Metcalf, Robert L., jt. ed. see Pitts, James N.

Metcalf, Thomas R. Land, Landlords, & the British Raj: Northern India in the Nineteenth Century. LC 77-85754. (Center for South & Southeast Asia Studies, UC Berkeley). 1979. 34.50x (ISBN 0-520-03575-5). U of Cal Pr.

Metcalf, William J. The Environmental Crisis: A Systems Approach. LC 77-74803. (Illus.). 1977. 18.95 (ISBN 0-312-25707-4). St Martin.

Metcalf, Woodbridge. Native Trees of the San Francisco Bay Region. (California Natural History Guides Ser.: No. 4). (Orig.). 1959. 14.95x o.p. (ISBN 0-520-03095-8); pap. 2.95 (ISBN 0-520-00853-7). U of Cal Pr.

Metcalfe, C. R. & Chalk, L., eds. Anatomy of the Dicotyledons, Vol. 1. 2nd ed. (Illus.). 1980. Set. 64.00x (ISBN 0-19-854383-2). Oxford U Pr.

Metcalfe, J. C. Christian Paganism. 1964. pap. 1.50 (ISBN 0-87508-915-1). Chr Lit.

Metcalfe, J. E. British Mining Fields. 91p. 1969. pap. text ed. 14.50x (ISBN 0-900488-00-X). IMM North Am.

Metcalfe, James J. Love Portraits. 1953. 7.95 o.p. (ISBN 0-385-01446-5). Doubleday.

Metcalfe, T. B. Radiation Spectra of Radionuclides. LC 76-2326. 394p. 1976. 36.00 o.p. (ISBN 0-8155-0620-1). Noyes.

Metelka, Charles J., ed. The Dictionary of Tourism. LC 80-83526. 91p. 1981. 12.00 (ISBN 0-916032-10-8). Merton Hse.

Meter, Donald Van see Sharkansky, Ira & Van Meter, Donald.

Meter, Margaret Van see Yacone, Linda A.

Meter, Margaret Van see Van Meter, Margaret.

Metford, J. C. A Dictionary of Christian Lore & Legend. (Illus.). 1983. 24.95 (ISBN 0-500-01262-8). Thames Hudson.

--Illustrated Encyclopaedia of Christian Lore & Legend. (Illus.). 1983. 24.95 (ISBN 0-500-01262-8). Thames Hudson.

Metheny, Eleanor. Movement & Meaning. LC 68-13885. 1968. pap. text ed. 7.95 o.p. (ISBN 0-07-041706-7, C). McGraw.

--Vital Issues. 1977. 9.95 (ISBN 0-88314-200-7, 240-25976). AAHPERD.

Metheny, Norma & Snively, W. D., Jr. Nurses' Handbook of Fluid Balance. 4th ed. (Illus.). 512p. 1983. text ed. price not set (ISBN 0-397-54381-6, Lippincott Medical). Lippincott.

Metherell, A. J., jt. auth. see Landshoff, P. V.

Methold, K., et al. Understanding Technical English, 3 bks. (English As a Second Language Bk.). (Illus.). 60p. 1975. pap. text ed. 4.65x ea. Bk. 1, 1973 (ISBN 0-582-69032-3). Bk. 2, 1974 (ISBN 0-582-69035-8). Bk. 3, 1980 (ISBN 0-582-69036-6). Longman.

Methold, Keith, et al. Puzzles for English Practice: PEP 1, 2 & 3. (English As a Second Lanugage Bk.). 1978. pap. text ed. 2.95x ea. PEP 1: Beginning (ISBN 0-582-55260-5). PEP 2: Pre-Intermediate (ISBN 0-582-55258-3). PEP 3: Pre-Intermediate (ISBN 0-582-55259-1). Longman.

Methven, Barbara. Mini-Fryer Cookery. (Illus.). 1978. 8.95 o.p. (ISBN 0-517-53238-7). Crown.

Metlyer, A. H., jt. ed. see Brunner, K.

Metos, Thomas H., jt. auth. see Bitter, Gary G.

Metra Consulting Group Ltd., ed. Venezuela: Business Opportunities in the 1980's. 224p. 1980. 314.00x (ISBN 0-686-87315-7, Pub. by Metra England). State Mutual Bk.

Metral, Antoine. Les Esclaves, 2 vols. (Slave Trade in France, 1744-1848, Ser.). 600p. (Fr.). 1974. Repr. of 1836 ed. lib. bdg. 160.00x o.p. (ISBN 0-8287-0610-7, TN126-7). Clearwater Pub.

Metral, Yvette, jt. auth. see Lartigue, Jacques-Henri.

Metraux, Alfred. The History of the Incas. Ordish, George, tr. LC 68-20890. (Illus., Fr). 1970. pap. 5.95 (ISBN 0-8052-0248-X). Schocken.

Metress, Seamus P. The Irish-American Experience: A Guide to the Literature. LC 80-69050. 226p. (Orig.). 1981. lib. bdg. 21.25 (ISBN 0-8191-1694-7); pap. text ed. 10.75 (ISBN 0-8191-1695-5). U Pr of Amer.

Metropolitan Medical Center American Diabetes Association. Diabetes: Recipes for Health. (Illus.). 416p. 1982. pap. 14.95 (ISBN 0-89303-211-5). R J Brady.

Metropolitan Museum of Art. The Gardener's Diary. (Illus.). 1982. 12.95 (ISBN 0-374-16032-5). FS&G.

--Guest Book. 80p. 1983. 17.95 (ISBN 0-686-83828-9, ScribT). Scribner.

Metropolitan Museum of Art, jt. auth. see British Museum.

Metropolitan Museum of Art, jt. auth. see Schnurnberger, Lynn E.

Metropolitan Museum of Art Curatorial Staff. Great Paintings from the Metropolitan Museum of Art. (Library of Great Museums Ser). (Illus.). 1959. 40.00 o.p. (ISBN 0-8109-0296-6). Abrams.

Metropolitan Museum of Art, New York. Library Catalog of the Metropolitan Museum of Art, New York, 25 vols. 1960. Set. lib. bdg. 1970.00 (ISBN 0-8161-0496-4, Hall Library); Suppls. 1-5. 115.00 ea. First Suppl. 1962 (ISBN 0-8161-0579-0). Second Suppl. 1965 (ISBN 0-8161-0670-3). Third Suppl. 1968 (ISBN 0-8161-0748-3). Fourth Suppl. 1970 (ISBN 0-8161-0846-3). Fifth Suppl (ISBN 0-8161-0936-2). G K Hall.

Metropolitan Museum of Art (New York) Library Catalog of the Metropolitan Museum of Art. 2nd ed. 1980. lib. bdg. 4650.00 (ISBN 0-8161-0295-3, Hall Library). G K Hall.

Metropulous, Lyman. The Illustrated Book of the Great Ancient Temples. (The Masterpieces of World Architecture Library). (Illus.). 141p. 1983. 112.50 (ISBN 0-86650-042-1). Gloucester Art.

Metry, Amir, jt. auth. see Kiang, Yen-Hsiung.

Mettam, Roger S. & Johnson, Douglas. French History & Society: The Wars of Religion to the Fifth Republic. LC 75-2861. 168p. 1974. pap. 4.95x (ISBN 0-416-81620-7). Methuen Inc.

Mettler, Fred A. & Guiberteau, Milton J., eds. Essentials of Nuclear Medicine Imaging. Date not set. price not set (ISBN 0-8089-1538-X). Grune.

Mettler, L., jt. ed. see Semm, K.

Mettler, Lawrence E. & Gregg, Thomas G. Population Genetics & Evolution. LC 69-16809. (Foundations of Modern Genetics Ser). (Illus.). 1969. pap. 12.95x ref. ed. (ISBN 0-13-685289-0). P-H.

Mettling, Stephen R. Assumptions & Purchase Money Mortgages (A & PMM) (Creative Financing Skill Development Ser.). 49p. 1982. pap. 10.95 (ISBN 0-88462-137-5). Real Estate Ed Co.

--Buydown Agreements. (Creative Financing Skill Development Ser.). 26p. 1982. pap. 7.95 (ISBN 0-88462-134-0). Real Estate Ed Co.

--The Fannie Mae (FNMA) Resale-Refinance Program. (Creative Financing Skill Development Ser.). 23p. 1982. pap. 7.95 (ISBN 0-88462-133-2). Real Estate Ed Co.

--Graduated Payment Adjustable Mortage Loan (GPAML) (Creative Financing Skill Developing Ser.). 40p. 1982. pap. 9.95 (ISBN 0-88462-136-7). Real Estate Ed Co.

--The Graduated Payment Mortgage (GPM) Bd. with The Pledged Account Mortgage (PAM; The Flip Mortgage. (Creative Financing Skill Development Ser.). 47p. (Orig.). 1982. pap. 10.95 (ISBN 0-88462-135-9). Real Estate Ed Co.

--Selling Creative Financing. (Creative Financing Skill Development Ser.). 30p. 1982. pap. 7.95 (ISBN 0-88462-139-1). Real Estate Ed Co.

Mettrick, D. F. & Desser, S. S., eds. Parasites-Their World & Ours: Proceedings of the Fifth International Congress of Parasitology, Toronto, Canada, August 7-14, 1982. 465p. 1982. 64.00 (ISBN 0-444-80433-1, Biomedical Pr). Elsevier.

Mettrie, Julien O. De La see La Mettrie, Julien O.

Metwally, M. M. Price & Non-Price Competition: Dynamics of Marketing. 1976. lib. bdg. 11.95 o.p. (ISBN 0-210-40568-6). Asia.

Metz, Clyde. Physical Chemistry. (Schaum's Outline Ser). 256p. (Orig.). 1976. pap. 8.95 (ISBN 0-07-041709-1, SP). McGraw.

Metz, Don, ed. The Compact House Book: Thirty-two Award Winning Designs. (Illus.). 192p. (Orig.). 1982. pap. 10.95 (ISBN 0-88266-323-2). Garden Way Pub.

Metz, Donald. Studies in Biblical Holiness. 1971. 9.95 (ISBN 0-8341-0117-3). Beacon Hill.

Metz, Donald E. Teaching Music in Grades Six to Nine. (Secondary Education Ser.: No. C28). 192p. 1980. pap. text ed. 13.95 spiral bdg. (ISBN 0-675-08176-9). Merrill.

Metz, Elizabeth & Delafuente, Lucien. Sound of English for the Bilingual Spanish-Speaking. 116p. 1972. pap. text ed. 37.00 (ISBN 0-88450-182-5, 3118-B). Communication Skill.

Metz, Ella, jt. auth. see Conason, Emil.

Metz, Gary & Gorden, Kurt V. Answers to Mormons. (Orig.). 1983. pap. 4.95 (ISBN 0-88449-091-2). Vision Hse.

Metz, J. C. The Two Merry Milkmaids. Orgel, Stephen, ed. LC 78-66811. (Renaissance Drama Ser.). 1979. lib. bdg. 33.00 o.s.i. (ISBN 0-8240-9740-8). Garland Pub.

Metz, Johannes B. Poverty of Spirit. LC 68-31045. 56p. 1968. 2.45 (ISBN 0-8091-1924-2). Paulist Pr.

Metz, Johannes B., jt. ed. see Schillebeeckx, Edward.

Metz, Karen S. Information Sources in Power Engineering. LC 75-32096. 114p. 1976. lib. bdg. 25.00 (ISBN 0-8371-8538-6, MPE/). Greenwood.

Metz, Leon. The Shooters. LC 76-21578. (Illus.). 1976. 14.95 o.p. (ISBN 0-930208-04-8); Ltd. Silver Bullet Ed. 50.00 o.p. (ISBN 0-686-77223-7). Mangan Bks.

Metz, Leon C. Pat Garrett: The Story of a Western Lawman. LC 72-9261. (Illus.). 328p. 1983. pap. 9.95 (ISBN 0-8061-1838-5). U of Okla Pr.

--Pat Garrett: The Story of a Western Lawmen. (Illus.). 305p. 1974. 17.95 (ISBN 0-8061-1067-8). U of Okla Pr.

Metz, Mary. Reflets Du Monde Francais. (Level 3). (gr. 9-12). 1971. text ed. 22.95 (ISBN 0-07-041718-0, C); inst. manual 10.95 (ISBN 0-07-041722-9); wkbk 10.95 (ISBN 0-07-041719-9). McGraw.

Metz, Mary & Helstrom, Jo. Le Francais a Vivre, Learning French the Modern Way, Level 2. 3rd ed. (Illus.). (gr. 10-12). 1972. text ed. 19.24 (ISBN 0-07-041710-5, W); tchr's. ed. 21.12 (ISBN 0-07-041711-3). McGraw.

Metz, Mary, jt. auth. see Helstrom, Jo.

Metz, Mary H. Classrooms & Corridors: The Crisis of Authority in Desegregated Secondary Schools. LC 76-55566. 1978. 26.50x (ISBN 0-520-03396-5); pap. 4.95 (ISBN 0-520-03941-6). U of Cal Pr.

Metz, Mary S. Reflets Du Monde Francais. 2nd ed. 1978. text ed. 21.95 (ISBN 0-07-041791-1, C); instr's manual 10.95 (ISBN 0-07-041792-X); wkbk 11.95. McGraw.

Metz, Mary S. & Helstrom, Jo. Le Francais a Vivre. 4th ed. Rebisz, Jacqueline, ed. (Illus.). (gr. 9-12). 1978. text ed. 17.72 (ISBN 0-07-041755-5, W); tchr's. ed. 19.96 (ISBN 0-07-041756-3); wkbk. 5.32 (ISBN 0-07-041757-1). McGraw.

Metz, Mary S., jt. auth. see Helstrom, Jo.

Metz, Robert. The Today Show. (Illus.). (RL 9). 1978. pap. 2.25 o.p. (ISBN 0-451-08214-1, E8214, Sig). NAL.

Metzbower, E. Source Book on Applications of the Laser in Metalworking. 1981. 46.00 (ISBN 0-87170-117-0). ASM.

Metzbower, Edward A., ed. Applications of Lasers in Materials Processing. 1979. 36.00 o.p. (ISBN 0-87170-084-0). ASM.

Metzger, Barbara. Bething's Folly. 176p. 1982. pap. 2.50 (ISBN 0-380-61143-0, 61143). Avon.

Metzger, Bruce. The Early Versions of the New Testament. 1977. 22.50x (ISBN 0-19-826170-5). Oxford U Pr.

Metzger, Bruce M. Introduction to the Apocrypha. 1957. pap. 7.95 (ISBN 0-19-502340-4). Oxford U Pr.

--Manuscripts of the Greek Bible: An Introduction to Paleography. (Illus.). 1981. 19.95x (ISBN 0-19-502924-0). Oxford U Pr.

--New Testament: Its Background, Growth & Content. LC 65-21981. 1965. 10.95 (ISBN 0-687-27913-5). Abingdon.

--Text of the New Testament: Its Transmission, Corruption, & Restoration. 2nd ed. 1968. 12.95x (ISBN 0-19-500391-8). Oxford U Pr.

Metzger, D. Electronic Components, Instruments & Troubleshooting. 1981. 30.00 (ISBN 0-13-250266-6). P-H.

Metzger, Daniel L. Electronic Circuit Behavior. (Illus.). 448p. 1975. 22.95 o.p. (ISBN 0-13-250381-6). P-H.

--Electronic Circuit Behavior. 2nd ed. (Illus.). 400p. 1983. 24.95 (ISBN 0-13-250241-0); lab manual 12.95 (ISBN 0-13-250191-0). P-H.

Metzger, Jacques. Thiazole & Its Derivatives, 3 pts. LC 78-17740. (Chemistry of Heterocyclic Compounds Ser.: Vol. 34). 1979. Pt. 1. 150.95 (ISBN 0-471-03993-4, Pub. by Wiley-Interscience); Pt. 2. 150.95 (ISBN 0-471-04126-2); Pt. 3. 150.95 (ISBN 0-471-04127-0). Wiley.

Metzger, Jan, et al. This Land Is Our Land: The West Bank Under Israeli Occupation. (Illus.). 272p. 1983. 28.95 (ISBN 0-86232-086-0, Pub. by Zed Pr England); pap. 11.50 (ISBN 0-86232-073-9, Pub. by Zed Pr England). Lawrence Hill.

Metzger, Judith. Escape from Fear: Can Agoraphobia be Cured. LC 82-81597. Date not set. pap. price not set (ISBN 0-941712-02-8). Intl Pub Corp OH.

Metzger, Judith, jt. auth. see Perry, Lily M.

Metzger, Mendel, jt. auth. see Metzger, Therese.

Metzger, Norman. The Arbitration & Grievance Process: A Guide for Health Care Supervisors. LC 82-20654. 254p. 1983. 26.50 (ISBN 0-89443-671-6). Aspen Systems.

--Energy: The Continuing Crisis. LC 76-18270. (Illus.). 1976. 14.37i (ISBN 0-690-01161-X). T Y Crowell.

--The Health Care Supervisor's Handbook. 2nd ed. LC 82-6764. 191p. 1982. 24.00 (ISBN 0-89443-696-1). Aspen Systems.

Metzger, Norman, jt. auth. see Munn, Harry.

Metzger, Norman, ed. Handbook of Health Care Human Resources Management. LC 81-3473. 903p. 1981. text ed. 85.00 (ISBN 0-89443-363-6). Aspen Systems.

Metzger, Philip. Managing a Programming Project. 2nd ed. (Illus.). 288p. 1981. text ed. 29.95 (ISBN 0-13-550772-3). P-H.

Metzger, Therese & Metzger, Mendel. Jewish Life in the Middle Ages: Illuminated Hebrew Manuscripts of the Thirteenth to the Sixteenth Centuries. (Illus.). 316p. 85.00 (ISBN 0-933516-57-6). Alpine Fine Arts.

Metzkerf, Isaac, ed. A Bintel Brief. 192p. 1982. pap. text ed. 5.95x (ISBN 0-87441-345-1). Behrman.

Metzler, Bernadette V., jt. auth. see Krey, Isabelle A.

Metzler, David. Biochemistry: The Chemical Reactions of Living Cells. 1129p. 1977. 38.75 (ISBN 0-12-492550-2); instr's. manual 3.50 (ISBN 0-12-492552-9). Acad Pr.

Metzler, Howard C., jt. auth. see Fink, Norman S.

Metzler, K. Creative Interviewing: The Writer's Guide to Gathering Information by Asking Questions. 1977. 12.95 o.p. (ISBN 0-13-189720-9); pap. 10.95 (ISBN 0-13-189712-8). P-H.

Metzler, Paul. Advanced Tennis. rev ed. LC 68-18790. (Illus.). 192p. (gr. 5 up). 1972. 8.95 o.p. (ISBN 0-8069-4000-X); PLB 8.29 o.p. (ISBN 0-8069-4001-8). Sterling.

--Fine Points of Tennis. LC 77-93309. (Illus.). 1978. 8.95 o.p. (ISBN 0-8069-4118-9); lib. bdg. 8.29 o.p. (ISBN 0-8069-4119-7). Sterling.

Metzner, Joachim K. Agriculture & Population Pressure in Sikka, Isle of Flores. LC 81-71133. (Development Studies Centre Monograph: No. 28). 355p. (Orig.). 1982. pap. text ed. 24.95 (ISBN 0-909150-59-1, 1227). Bks Australia.

Metzner, Seymour. World History in Juvenile Books. 356p. 1973. 14.00 (ISBN 0-8242-0441-7). Wilson.

Meudt, R. O. & Hinselmann, M. Ultrasonoscopic Differential Diagnosis in Obstetrics & Gynecology. (Illus.). x, 138p. 1975. 55.00 o.p. (ISBN 0-387-06991-7). Springer-Verlag.

Meudt, Werner J., ed. Strategies of Plant Reproduction. (Beltsville Symposia in Agricultural Research: Vol. 6). (Illus.). 400p. 1983. text ed. 39.50x (ISBN 0-86598-054-3). Allanheld.

Meulen, Jan van Der see Van der Meulen, Jan & Price, Nancy W.

Meulen, S. V. Vander see Lindsey, C. H. & Vander Meulen, S. V.

Meulenbelt-Nieuwburg, Albarta. Embroidery Motifs from Dutch Samplers. 1975. 19.95 o.p. (ISBN 0-7134-2875-9, Pub. by Batsford England). David & Charles.

Meuller, Francis J. Elements of Algebra. 3rd ed. (Illus.). 496p. 1981. text ed. 20.95 (ISBN 0-13-262469-9). P-H.

Meun, Jean De see De Lorris, Guillaume & De Meun, Jean.

Meurig, H. & Thomas, W. O. Y Geiriadur Mawr: The Complete Welsh-English, English-Welsh Dictionary. Williams, S. J., ed. 859p. (Welsh & Eng.). 1981. 35.00 (ISBN 0-686-97426-3, M-9434). French & Eur.

Meuris, Jacques. La Machine et Le Monde Des Formes. (Illus.). 212p. French Text 18.50 (ISBN 0-912729-18-X). Newbury Bk.

Meurs, A. P. Van see Van Meurs, A. P.

Meuzelaar, H. L. & Haverkamp, J. Pyrolysis Mass Spectrometry of Recent & Fossil Biomaterials. (Techniques & Instrumentation in Analytical Chemistry Ser.: Vol. 3). 294p. 1982. 61.75 (ISBN 0-444-42099-1). Elsevier.

Mevburg, Arnim H., jt. ed. see Stopher, Peter R.

Mevlendyke, Eve, jt. auth. see Lipman, Jean.

Mew, Charlotte. Collected Poems & Prose. Warner, Val, ed. 445p. 1981. text ed. 21.00x (ISBN 0-85635-260-8, Pub. by Carcanet New Pr England). Humanities.

Mew, James. Traditional Aspects of Hell. LC 73-140321. 1971. Repr. of 1903 ed. 42.00x (ISBN 0-8103-3693-6). Gale.

Mew, James & Ashton, John. Drinks of the World. LC 70-78207. (Illus.). 1971. Repr. of 1892 ed. 37.00x (ISBN 0-8103-3772-X). Gale.

Mews, Hazel. Frail Vessels: Woman's Role in Women's Novels from Fanny Burney to George Eliot. 1969. text ed. 30.50x (ISBN 0-485-11105-5, Athlone Pr). Humanities.

Mews, Siegfried. Carl Zuckmayer. (World Authors Ser.). 15.95 (ISBN 0-8057-6452-6, Twayne). G K Hall.

Mews, Siegfried, ed. The Fisherman & His Wife. LC 81-69878. 1982. 29.50 (ISBN 0-404-61582-1). AMS Pr.

Mews, Siegfried & Knust, Herbert, eds. Essays on Brecht: Theatre & Politics. (Studies in Comparative Literature Ser.: No. 79). xiii, 238p. 1974. 15.00x o.p. (ISBN 0-8078-8079-5). U of NC Pr.

Mews, Stuart, ed. Religion & National Identity: Papers Read at the Nineteenth Summer Meeting & the Twentieth Winter Meeting of the Ecclesiastical History Society. (Studies in Church History: Vol. 18). 634p. 1982. 36.00x (ISBN 0-631-18060-5, Pub. by Basil Blackwell England). Biblio Dist.

Mewshaw, Michael. Land Without Shadow. LC 78-69661. 1979. 8.95 o.p. (ISBN 0-385-14504-7). Doubleday.

--Short Circuit. LC 82-48699. 320p. 1983. 12.95 (ISBN 0-689-11384-6). Atheneum.

Mey, J. De see De Brabander, M. & De Mey, J.

Mey, Marx De. The Cognitive Paradigm. (Harvester Studies in Cognitive Science). 1980. text ed. write for info. o.p. (ISBN 0-391-01062-X). Humanities.

Meyberg, Arnim, jt. auth. see Stopher, Peter R.

Meyburg, Arnim H., jt. auth. see Stopher, Peter R.

Meyburg, Arnum, jt. auth. see Stopher, Peter R.

Meyendorff, Alexander F., jt. auth. see Kohn, S.

Meyendorff, John. The Byzantine Legacy in the Orthodox Church. LC 82-797. 268p. (Orig.). 1982. pap. 8.95 (ISBN 0-913836-90-7). St Vladimirs.

--Byzantine Theology: Historical Trends & Doctrinal Themes. 2nd ed. LC 74-94167. 1978. pap. 9.00 (ISBN 0-8232-0967-9). Fordham.

Meyer, Adolphe E. Educational History of the Western World. 2nd ed. (Education Ser). 528p. 1972. text ed. 26.95 (ISBN 0-07-041740-7, C). McGraw.

--Grandmasters of Educational Thought. 302p. 1975. text ed. 22.50 o.p. (ISBN 0-07-041737-7, C); pap. text ed. 10.50 o.p. (ISBN 0-07-041750-4). McGraw.

Meyer, Alfred. Historical Aspects of Cerebral Anatomy. 1971. 25.00x (ISBN 0-19-263127-6). Oxford U Pr.

Meyer, Alfred G., ed. see Casals, Felipe G.

Meyer, B. The Organization of Prose & Its Effects on Memory. (N-H Studies in Theoretical Poetics Ser.: Vol. 1). 249p. 1975. pap. 42.75 (ISBN 0-444-10946-3, North-Holland). Elsevier.

Meyer, Balthasar Henry. A History of the Northern Securities Case. LC 70-124898. (American Constitutional & Legal History Ser). 136p. 1972. Repr. of 1906 ed. lib. bdg. 24.50 (ISBN 0-306-71989-4). Da Capo.

Meyer, Beat. Low Temperature Spectroscopy. 1971. 54.95 (ISBN 0-444-00083-6, North Holland). Elsevier.

--Urea-Formaldehyde Resins. (Illus.). 1979. text ed. 39.50 (ISBN 0-201-04558-3). A-W.

Meyer, Ben F. The Aims of Jesus. (Student Christian Movement Press Ser.). 1979. 26.95x (ISBN 0-19-520331-3). Oxford U Pr.

--Man for Others. (Faith & Life Bk). 1970. pap. 3.50 o.p. (ISBN 0-02-805200-5). Glencoe.

Meyer, Bernadine & Kolasa, Blair. Legal Systems. (Illus.). 1978. 23.95 (ISBN 0-13-529404-5). P-H.

Meyer, Bernard, et al. Introduction to Plant Physiology. 2nd ed. 1973. text ed. 17.95x (ISBN 0-442-25328-1). Van Nos Reinhold.

Meyer, Bruce L. Data Communications Practice, Vol. XI. 1979. 13.00 (ISBN 0-686-98067-0). Telecom Lib.

Meyer, C., et al. Analysis & Design of Integrated Circuits. LC 68-8035. (Illus.). 1968. text ed. 40.00 o.p. (ISBN 0-07-041723-7, C). McGraw.

Meyer, C. D., jt. auth. see Campbell, S. L.

Meyer, Carl & Matyas, Stephen. Cryptography: A New Dimension in Computer Security: A Guide for the Design & Implementation of Secure Systems. 755p. 1982. 39.95x (ISBN 0-471-04892-5, Pub. by Wiley-Interscience). Wiley.

Meyer, Carol. The Writer's Survival Manual: The Complete Guide to Getting Your Book Published Right. LC 82-2461. (Illus.). 256p. 1982. 13.95 (ISBN 0-517-54485-7); text ed. 11.95 o.p. (ISBN 0-686-85834-4). Crown.

Meyer, Carolyn. Being Beautiful: The Story of Cosmetics from Ancient Art to Modern Science. 1977. 8.95 (ISBN 0-688-22125-4); lib. bdg. 8.59 (ISBN 0-688-32125-9). Morrow.

--The Bread Book. LC 76-15973. (Illus.). (gr. 3-7). 1976. pap. 1.95 (ISBN 0-15-614070-5, VoyB). HarBraceJ.

--Coconut, the Tree of Life. LC 76-22673. (Illus.). 96p. (gr. 5-9). 1976. 8.95 (ISBN 0-688-22084-3); PLB 8.59 (ISBN 0-688-32084-8). Morrow.

--Eulalia's Island. LC 82-3946. 192p. 1982. 10.95 (ISBN 0-689-50244-3, McElderry Bk). Atheneum.

--Milk, Butter, & Cheese: The Story of Dairy Products. LC 73-13574. (Illus.). 96p. (gr. 5-9). 1974. PLB 8.59 (ISBN 0-688-30100-2). Morrow.

--Music Is for Everyone. (gr. k-6). 1980. 5.95 (ISBN 0-916456-89-7, GA 200). Good Apple.

--Yarn-the Things It Makes & How to Make Them. LC 72-76367. (Illus.). 128p. (gr. 5 up). 1972. 5.95 (ISBN 0-15-299713-X, HJ). HarBraceJ.

Meyer, Charles. China Observed. Joss, Jean, tr. (Observed Ser.). (Illus.). 1981. 29.95 (ISBN 0-19-520259-7). Oxford U Pr.

Meyer, Charles R. How to Be a Clown. (A Ringling Brothers - Barnum & Bailey Book). (Illus.). (gr. 4-7). 1977. 6.95 o.p. (ISBN 0-679-20406-7). McKay.

--How to Be an Acrobat. (Ringling Bros. & Barnum & Bailey Ser.). (Illus.). (gr. 4-7). 1978. 5.95 o.p. (ISBN 0-679-20409-1). McKay.

--Religious Belief in a Scientific World. 1983. 12.95 (ISBN 0-88347-152-3). Thomas More.

--Touch of God: A Theological Analysis of Religious Experience. LC 75-38978. 170p. 1972. 4.50 o.p. (ISBN 0-8189-0237-X). Alba.

Meyer, Charles W., jt. auth. see Davis, J. Ronnie.

Meyer, Clarence. American Folk Medicine. LC 73-4300. 1973. 3.95 (ISBN 0-452-25097-8, Pub. by NAL). Formur Intl.

Meyer, Conrad F. The Tribulations of a Boy. Huggard, E. M., tr. from Ger. (Harrap's Bilingual Ser.). 83p. 1955. 5.00 (ISBN 0-911268-43-X). Rogers Bk.

Meyer, Cord. Facing Reality: From World Federalism to the CIA. LC 79-1677. (Illus.). 416p. 1980. 17.26i (ISBN 0-06-013032-6, HarpT). Har-Row.

--Facing Reality: From World Federalism to the CIA. LC 82-13588. (Illus.). 1982. pap. text ed. 10.50 (ISBN 0-8191-2559-8). U Pr of Amer.

Meyer, Dan & Williams, Tom. Painless Bookkeeping: Simplified Procedures for the Personally Owned or Family Business. (Illus.). 150p. 1983. pap. write for info. (ISBN 0-932150-02-0). MCS.

Meyer, Daniel P. & Mayer, Herbert A. Radar Target Detection: Handbook of Theory & Practice. (Electrical Science Series). 1973. 63.50 o.s.i. (ISBN 0-12-492850-1). Acad Pr.

Meyer, David R. From Farm to Factory to Urban Pastoralism: Urban Change in Central Connecticut. LC 76-3740. (Contemporary Metropolitan Analysis Ser.). (Illus.). 72p. 1976. pap. 8.95x (ISBN 0-88410-441-9). Ballinger Pub.

Meyer, Donald H. The Democratic Enlightenment. 324p. 1976. 8.95 o.p. (ISBN 0-399-11686-9). Putnam Pub Group.

Meyer, Donald L., ed. Bayesian Statistics. LC 75-86199. 138p. 1970. 7.00 o.p. (ISBN 0-87581-045-4, Dist. by Peacock). Phi Delta Kappa.

Meyer, Erika. German Graded Readers: Alternate Series, 3 bks. Incl. Bk. 1. Ein Briefwechsel. pap. text ed. 4.95 o.p. (ISBN 0-395-04890-7, 3-37470); Bk. 2. Akademische Freiheit. pap. text ed. 4.25 o.p. (ISBN 0-685-23336-7, 3-37475); Bk. 3. Goslar. pap. text ed. 4.25 o.p. (ISBN 0-685-23337-5, 3-37480). 1954. pap. HM.

Meyer, Erika, et al. Elementary German. 3rd ed. 1976. text ed. 14.95 (ISBN 0-395-19866-6); tapes 120.00 (ISBN 0-395-19869-0); wkbk. 6.50 (ISBN 0-395-19868-2). HM.

Meyer, Ernest L. Hey Yellowbacks: The War Diary of a Conscientious Objector. LC 75-143432. (Peace Movement in America Ser.). x, 209p. 1972. Repr. of 1930 ed. lib. bdg. 13.95x (ISBN 0-89198-080-6). Ozer.

Meyer, Ernst. English Chamber Music. LC 71-127181. (Music Ser). (Illus.). 1971. Repr. of 1946 ed. lib. bdg. 32.50 (ISBN 0-306-70037-9). Da Capo.

Meyer, Eugene. Chemistry of Hazardous Materials. (Illus.). 1977. 21.95 (ISBN 0-13-129239-0). P-H.

--Introduction to Modern Chemistry. (Illus.). 1979. text ed. 26.95 (ISBN 0-13-488320-9); student manual 11.95 (ISBN 0-13-488338-1). P-H.

Meyer, F. B. Christ in Isaiah. 1970. pap. 3.50 (ISBN 0-87508-341-2). Chr Lit.

--Ephesians. 1968. pap. 3.00 (ISBN 0-87508-344-7). Chr Lit.

--F. B. Meyer Commentary. 1979. 13.95 (ISBN 0-8423-4250-8). Tyndale.

--Joseph. 1975. pap. 3.95 (ISBN 0-87508-356-0). Chr Lit.

--New Testament Men of Faith. 1979. pap. 4.95 (ISBN 0-89107-171-7). Good News.

--The Shepherd Psalm. 128p. 1976. pap. 1.25 o.p. (ISBN 0-8024-7918-9). Moody.

Meyer, F. V. International Trade Policy. LC 78-4624. 1978. 24.00x (ISBN 0-312-42357-8). St Martin.

Meyer, Faith, ed. see Piche, Thomas.

Meyer, Frank S., ed. Breathes There the Man: Heroic Ballads & Poems of the English-Speaking Peoples. LC 73-82784. 281p. 1973. 18.50x (ISBN 0-87548-143-4). Open Court.

Meyer, Franz S. Handbook of Ornament. (Illus.). 11.50 (ISBN 0-8446-0800-9). Peter Smith.

Meyer, Fred & Baker, Ralph, eds. Determinants of Law Enforcement Policy. LC 79-1540. (Policy Studies Organization Bk.). 240p. 1979. 22.95 (ISBN 0-669-02900-9). Lexington Bks.

--Law Enforcement & Police Policy. 1979. pap. 6.00 (ISBN 0-918592-31-3). Policy Studies.

Meyer, Fred, jt. ed. see Baker, Ralph.

Meyer, Fred P., jt. auth. see Hoffman, Glen L.

Meyer, Freeman see Weaver, Glenn.

Meyer, Gerd. Strukturinterne und Umstrukturierende Neuerungen Dargestellt Am Beispiel der Forschung. 339p. (Ger.). 1982. write for info. (ISBN 3-261-04998-7). P Lang Pubs.

Meyer, Gladys, jt. auth. see Marden, Charles F.

Meyer, Gregory P. English Honors Papers. 38p. 1975. pap. 1.75 (ISBN 0-686-97223-6). TSU Pr.

Meyer, H., ed. Real-Time Data Handling & Process Control. 1980. 95.75 (ISBN 0-444-85468-1). Elsevier.

Meyer, Harold E. Lifetime Encyclopedia of Letters. LC 82-13343. 403p. 1983. 25.00 (ISBN 0-13-536383-7, Busn). P-H.

Meyer, Hazel. The Gold in Tin Pan Alley. LC 77-7039. 1977. Repr. of 1958 ed. lib. bdg. 20.00x (ISBN 0-8371-9694-9, MEGO). Greenwood.

Meyer, Henry I. Corporate Financial Planning Models. LC 77-24881. (Ser. on Systems & Controls for Financial Management). 1977. 36.95 o.s.i. (ISBN 0-471-59996-4, Pub. by Wiley-Interscience). Wiley.

Meyer, Henry J., et al. Girls at Vocational High: An Experiment in Social Work Intervention. LC 65-16221. 212p. 1965. 7.95x (ISBN 0-87154-601-9). Russell Sage.

Meyer, J. & Farrar, D. Managerial Economics. 1970. 23.95 (ISBN 0-13-549972-0); pap. 9.95 ref. ed. op (ISBN 0-13-549980-1). P-H.

Meyer, J. A. The Cristero Rebellion. LC 75-35455. (Cambridge Latin American Studies: No. 24). (Illus.). 1976. 39.50 (ISBN 0-521-21031-3). Cambridge U Pr.

Meyer, J. S. & Schade, J, eds. Cerebral Blood Flow. (Progress in Brain Research: Vol. 35). 1972. 108.50 (ISBN 0-444-40952-1). Elsevier.

Meyer, J. S., et al, eds. Cerebral Vascular Disease. LC 75-32669. (Illus.). 242p. 1976. 29.00 o.p. (ISBN 0-88416-134-X). Wright-PSG.

Meyer, Jack A., ed. Meeting Human Needs: Toward a New Public Philosophy. 1982. 34.95 (ISBN 0-8447-1359-7); pap. 13.95 (ISBN 0-8447-1358-9). Am Enterprise.

Meyer, Jerome. The Big Book of Family Games. (Illus.). 208p. 1980. pap. 4.95 o.p. (ISBN 0-8015-0624-7, Hawthorn). Dutton.

--Puzzle, Quiz & Stunt Fun. 1957. pap. 3.95 (ISBN 0-486-20337-9). Dover.

Meyer, John C. Christian Beliefs & Teachings. LC 81-40353. 116p. (Orig.). 1981. lib. bdg. 18.50 (ISBN 0-8191-1757-9); pap. text ed. 8.25 (ISBN 0-8191-1758-7). U Pr of Amer.

Meyer, John R., ed. Techniques of Transport Planning. Vol. 1: Pricing & Project Evaluation. (Transport Research Program Ser.). 343p. 1971. 17.95 (ISBN 0-8157-5690-9). Brookings.

--Techniques of Transport Planning. Vol. 2: Systems Analysis & Simulation Models. (Transport Research Program Ser.). 1971. 17.95 (ISBN 0-8157-5040-4). Brookings.

Meyer, John R. & Quigley, John M., eds. Local Public Finance & the Fiscal Squeeze: A Case Study. LC 76-15619. 1977. prof ref 19.50x (ISBN 0-88410-287-4). Ballinger Pub.

Meyer, John S. & Shaw, Terry. Diagnosis & Management of Stroke & TIA's. 1981. 26.95 (ISBN 0-201-04184-7, 04184, Med-Nurse). A-W.

Meyer, John S., jt. auth. see Gilroy, John.

Meyer, Jon K. & Schmidt, Chester M., Jr. Clinical Management of Sexual Disorders. 2nd ed. 404p. 1983. lib. bdg. 39.95 (ISBN 0-683-05970-X). Williams & Wilkins.

Meyer, Joseph E. Herbalist. 10.95x (ISBN 0-916638-01-4, Pub. by Meyerbooks). Formur Intl.

--The Herbalist. (Illus.). 304p. 1981. 12.95 (ISBN 0-8069-3902-8); lib. bdg. 11.69 o.p. (ISBN 0-8069-3903-6). Sterling.

Meyer, Judith W., jt. auth. see Warkov, Seymour.

Meyer, Kathi. Bedeutung und Wesen der Musik: Der Bedeutungswandel der Musik. (Samml. Mw.Abh. Ser). 267p. 40.00 o.s.i. (ISBN 90-6027-379-6, Pub. by Frits Knuf Netherlands). Pendragon NY.

Meyer, Kathleen A. Ireland: Land of Mist & Magic. Schneider, Tom, ed. (Discovering Our Heritage Ser.). (Illus.). 144p. (gr. 5 up). 1982. PLB 9.95 (ISBN 0-87518-228-3). Dillon.

Meyer, Ken. The Shooters. LC 79-84407. (Illus.). 1979. pap. 9.95 (ISBN 0-87863-187-9). Farnswth Pub.

Meyer, Klaus. Bibliographie zur Osteuropaeischen Geschichte. 760p. 1972. 60.00x o.p. (ISBN 3-447-01437-7). Intl Pubns Serv.

Meyer, Kurt. Bitches, Bastards & Lovers. LC 81-83570. 1983. 9.95 (ISBN 0-87212-157-7). Libra.

Meyer, Laurence H., ed. Improving Money Stock Control: Problems, Solutions & Consequences. 1982. lib. bdg. 25.00 (ISBN 0-89838-115-0). Kluwer-Nijhoff.

Meyer, Leo, jt. auth. see Wray, Lynn.

Meyer, Leo A. Sheet Metal Layout. 1961. 13.95 o.p. (ISBN 0-07-041730-X, G). McGraw.

--Sheet Metal Layout. 2nd ed. (Illus.). 1979. pap. text ed. 17.95 (ISBN 0-07-041731-8, G). McGraw.

Meyer, Leonard B. Explaining Music: Essays & Explorations. LC 73-187749. (Illus.). 1973. 24.50x o.s.i. (ISBN 0-520-02216-5). U of Cal Pr.

Meyer, Lewis. Off the Sauce. 1.95 o.p. (ISBN 0-686-92064-3). Hazelden.

Meyer, Lillian Hoagland. Food Chemistry. rev. & 3rd ed. (Illus.). 1978. Repr. pap. text ed. 16.00 (ISBN 0-87055-171-X). AVI.

Meyer, Linda, ed. see Ciaramitaro, Barbara.

Meyer, Linda C., jt. auth. see McCahill, Thomas W.

Meyer, Lois. The Store-Bought Doll. LC 82-83070. (Little Golden Bk.). (Illus.). 24p. (ps-2). 1983. 0.89 (ISBN 0-307-02044-4, Golden Pr); PLB price not set (ISBN 0-307-60193-5). Western Pub.

Meyer, Luc. Left Bank Celebrity Cookbook. (Orig.). 1982. pap. 8.95 (ISBN 0-89716-064-9). Peanut Butter.

Meyer, M. W. Change in Public Bureaucracies. LC 76-47193. (Illus.). 1979. 27.50 (ISBN 0-521-22670-8). Cambridge U Pr.

Meyer, Martin J. Don't Bank on It! LC 79-3156. 1979. 9.95 o.p. (ISBN 0-87863-174-7). Farnswth Pub.

Meyer, Marvin W. The Mithras Liturgy. LC 76-18288. (Society of Biblical Literature. Texts & Translation - Graeco-Roman Religion Ser.). 1976. pap. 4.50 (ISBN 0-89130-113-5, 06-02-10). Scholars Pr Ca.

--Who Do People Say That I Am? The Interpretation of Jesus in the New Testament Gospels. 104p. 1983. pap. 5.95 (ISBN 0-8028-1961-3). Eerdmans.

Meyer, Mary K. Directory of Genealogical Societies in the U. S. A. & Canada. rev. ed. 109p. 1980. 12.00 (ISBN 0-686-36499-6). Md Hist.

--Genealogical Research in Maryland: A Guide. 1982. 15.00 (ISBN 0-686-36502-X). Md Hist.

Meyer, Mary K. & Filby, P. William, eds. Who's Who in Genealogy. LC 81-69203. 1982. 62.00x (ISBN 0-8103-1630-7). Gale.

Meyer, Michael. Several More Lives to Live: Thoreau's Political Reputation in America. LC 76-56622. (Contributions in American Studies: No. 29). 1977. lib. bdg. 25.00 (ISBN 0-8371-9477-6, MES/). Greenwood.

Meyer, Michael, tr. The Plays of Strindberg, 2 vols. LC 76-10220. 1976. Vol. 1. pap. 5.95 (ISBN 0-394-71698-1, Vin); Vol. 2. pap. 5.95 (ISBN 0-394-71873-9). Random.

Meyer, Michael, tr. see Ibsen, Henrik.

Meyer, Michael A., ed. Ideas of Jewish History. LC 73-19960. (Library of Jewish Studies). 384p. 1974. 15.95x o.p. (ISBN 0-87441-202-1). Behrman.

Meyer, Michael C. & Sherman, William L. The Course of Mexican History. (Illus.). 1979. 29.95x o.p. (ISBN 0-19-502413-3); pap. text ed. 12.95x o.p. (ISBN 0-19-502414-1). Oxford U Pr.

--The Course of Mexican History. 2nd ed. LC 81-22522. (Illus.). 768p. 1983. 29.95 (ISBN 0-19-503150-4); pap. 17.95 (ISBN 0-19-503151-2). Oxford U Pr.

Meyer, Michel. Meaning & Reading: A Philosophical Essay On Language & Literature. (Pragmatics & Beyond Ser.). 100p. (Orig.). 1983. 14.00 (ISBN 90-272-2515-X). Benjamins North Am.

Meyer, P. A., jt. auth. see Dellacherie, C.

Meyer, Paul L. Introductory Probability & Statistical Applications. 2nd ed. 1970. 22.95 (ISBN 0-201-04710-1). A-W.

Meyer, Paul R., ed. Papers in Mathematics. (Annals of the New York Academy of Sciences: Vol. 321). (Orig.). 1979. pap. 22.00x (ISBN 0-89766-026-9). NY Acad Sci.

Meyer, Peter. The Yale Murder: The Fatal Romance of Bonnie Garland & Richard Herrin. 1983. pap. 3.50 (ISBN 0-425-05940-5). Berkley Pub.

Meyer, Peter B., jt. auth. see Duffee, David E.

Meyer, Philip, jt. auth. see Olson, David J.

Meyer, Philippe. Hypertension: Mechanisms & Clinical & Therapeutic Aspects. (Illus.). 1980. text ed. 27.50x o.p. (ISBN 0-19-261240-9). Oxford U Pr.

Meyer, Phillip. Precision Journalism: A Reporter's Introduction to Social Science Methods. 2nd ed. LC 79-2172. (Midland Bks.: No. 232). 448p. 1979. 22.50x (ISBN 0-253-33405-5); pap. 8.95x (ISBN 0-253-20232-9). Ind U Pr.

Meyer, R. G. Integrated-Circuit Operational Amplifiers. LC 78-59635. (IEEE Reprint Ser.). 1978. 28.95 (ISBN 0-471-05068-7); pap. text ed. 18.95 (ISBN 0-471-05069-5, Pub. by Wiley-Interscience). Wiley.

Meyer, Richard D. Practical Infectious Diseases. (Family Practice Today: A Comprehensive Postgraduate Library). 264p. 1983. 14.95 (ISBN 0-471-09565-6, Pub. by Wiley Med). Wiley.

Meyer, Richard E. Introduction to Mathematical Fluid Dynamics. 192p. 1982. pap. 4.50 (ISBN 0-486-61554-5). Dover.

Meyer, Richard E., ed. Theory of Dispersed Multiphase Flow. (Symposium). Date not set. 28.00 (ISBN 0-12-493120-0). Acad Pr.

Meyer, Rick, jt. auth. see Sachs, Jonathan.

Meyer, Robert G. & Osborne, Yvonne H. Case Studies in Abnormal Behavior. 354p. 1982. text ed. 12.95 (ISBN 0-205-07744-7, 7977441). Allyn.

Meyer, Robert G., jt. auth. see Gray, Paul R.

Meyer, Robert G., ed. Integrated Circuit Operational Amplifiers. LC 78-59635. 1978. 14.95 (ISBN 0-87942-116-9). Inst Electrical.

Meyer, Ronald, ed. Hanz Kuchelgarten: Leaving the Theatre & Other Works. Date not set. 17.50 (ISBN 0-88233-822-6); pap. 4.50 (ISBN 0-88233-833-1). Ardis Pubs.

Meyer, Samuel, ed. Dewey & Russell: An Exchange. 1983. 9.95 (ISBN 0-8022-2406-7). Philos Lib.

Meyer, Sheila, jt. auth. see Ulmer, Louise.

Meyer, Sheila, ed. see Litherland, Janet.

Meyer, Sheila, ed. see Matthews, Arthur C.

Meyer, Sheila, ed. see Weekly, James.

Meyer, Stephen, III. The Five Dollar Day: Labor Management & Social Control in the Ford Motor Company, 1908-1921. LC 80-22795. (American Social History Ser.). 230p. 1981. text ed. 39.50x (ISBN 0-87395-508-0); pap. 10.95x (ISBN 0-87395-509-9). State U NY Pr.

Meyer, Stuart L. Data Analysis for Scientists & Engineers. LC 74-8873. (Illus.). 448p. 1975. text ed. 36.95 (ISBN 0-471-59995-6). Wiley.

Meyer, Susan. Forty Watercolorists & How They Work. (Illus., Orig.). 1976. 21.95 o.p. (ISBN 0-8230-1885-7). Watson-Guptill.

Meyer, Thomas. Bang Book. LC 76-137212. 71. 6.50 (ISBN 0-912330-19-8, Dist. by Inland Bk); pap. 3.95 (ISBN 0-912330-20-1). Jargon Soc.

--Staves Calends Legends. 1979. 17.50 (ISBN 0-912330-36-8, Dist. by Inland Bk); pap. 10.00 (ISBN 0-912330-37-6, Dist. by Inland Bk). Jargon Soc.

--The Umbrella of Aesculapius. LC 75-21930. 1975. 17.50x (ISBN 0-912330-31-7, Dist. by Inland Bk); pap. 7.50 (ISBN 0-912330-32-5). Jargon Soc.

Meyer, Ursula. German. (Blue Book Ser). pap. 1.25 o.p. (ISBN 0-671-18109-2). Monarch Pr.

Meyer, Walter, jt. auth. see Malkevitch, Joseph.

Meyer, Walter H., jt. auth. see Chapman, Herman H.

Meyer, Warren G., jt. auth. see Crawford, Lucy C.

Meyer, Warren G., et al. Retailing Principles & Practices. 7th ed. LC 80-24885. (Illus.). 560p. (gr. 11-12). text ed. 15.48 (ISBN 0-07-041693-1, G); Problems & Practices units 1-10 5.48 (ISBN 0-07-041694-X); Problems & Practices units 11-22 5.48 (ISBN 0-07-041695-8); tests 3.32 (ISBN 0-07-041697-4); tchrs. manual 5.00 (ISBN 0-07-041696-6). McGraw.

Meyer, William E., jt. auth. see Murphy, Richard C.

Meyer, William J. & Dusek, Jerome B. Child Psychology: A Developmental Perspective. 1979. text ed. 20.95x (ISBN 0-669-88971-7); instr's manual 1.95 (ISBN 0-669-97857-4). Heath.

Meyer, William R. The Making of the Great Westerns. (Illus.). 1979. 20.00 o.p. (ISBN 0-517-54809-7, Arlington Hse). Crown.

Meyer-Arendt, Jurgen. Introduction to Classical & Modern Optics. LC 71-157723. (Illus.). 1972. ref. ed. 31.95 (ISBN 0-13-479436-2). P-H.

Meyer-Denkmann, Gertrud. Experiments in Sound: New Directions in Musical Education for Young Children. Paynter, Elizabeth & Paynter, John, eds. LC 50-26923. 1977. pap. 16.00 (ISBN 0-900938-49-8). Eur-Am Music.

Meyerhof, Walter E. Elements of Nuclear Physics. 1967. text ed. 33.50 (ISBN 0-07-041745-8, C); instr's guide 7.95 (ISBN 0-07-041746-6). McGraw.

Meyerhoff, Hans. Time in Literature. (Library Reprint Ser: No. 6). 1974. 27.50x (ISBN 0-520-00856-1). U of Cal Pr.

Meyerhoff, R. W. Manufacture of Superconducting Materials. 30.00 o.p. (ISBN 0-87170-049-2). ASM.

Meyerhoff, William L., jt. auth. see Paparella, Michael M.

Meyerink, George. Appliance Service Handbook. (Illus.). 464p. 1973. ref. ed. 22.95x (ISBN 0-13-038844-0). P-H.

Meyerowitz, Joel. Cape Light: Color Photographs by Joel Meyerowitz. LC 78-13869. (Illus.). 112p. 1979. pap. 13.95 (ISBN 0-87846-131-0). Mus Fine Arts Boston.

Meyerowitz, Patricia. Making Jewelry & Sculpture Through Unit Construction. 8.50 (ISBN 0-8446-5794-8). Peter Smith.

Meyerowitz, Selma. Leonard Woolf. (English Authors Ser.: 352). 1982. lib. bdg. 14.95 (ISBN 0-8057-6838-6, Twayne). G K Hall.

Meyerriecks, Andrew J. Comparative Breeding Behavior of Four Species of North American Herons. (Illus.). 158p. 1960. pap. 4.00 (ISBN 0-686-35786-8). Nuttall Ornithological.

Meyerriecks, Andrew J., jt. auth. see Norstog, Knut J.

Meyers. Charcoal Drawing. (Pitman Art Ser.: Vol. 50). pap. 1.95 o.p. (ISBN 0-448-00559-X, G&D). Putnam Pub Group.

Meyers & Lakin. Who Will Take the Children? new ed. 228p. 1983. 13.95 (ISBN 0-672-52739-1). Bobbs.

Meyers, jt. auth. see Middleton, Robert.

Meyers, jt. ed. see Lougheed, Joyce.

Meyers, A. I. Heterocycles in Organic Synthesis. (General Heterocyclic Chemistry Ser.). 336p. 1974. 53.50 (ISBN 0-471-60065-2). Wiley.

Meyers, Alan. Writing with Confidence. 1979. pap. text ed. 13.50x (ISBN 0-673-15174-3). Scott F.

Meyers, Alan, jt. auth. see Carlson, Karen.

Meyers, Bert. The Wild Olive Tree. (Orig.). pap. 3.00 o.p. (ISBN 0-915596-23-7). West Coast.

--Windowsills. LC 79-12492. (Illus.). 1979. 7.95x o.p. (ISBN 0-933228-01-5); pap. text ed. 3.95 o.p. (ISBN 0-933228-00-7). Common Table.

Meyers, Beth. The Steady Flame. (YA) 1972. 6.95 (ISBN 0-685-25149-7, Avalon). Bouregy.

Meyers, Betty & Fellers, Frederick P., eds. Discographies of Commercial Recordings of the Cleveland Orchestra (1924-1977) and the Cincinnati Symphony Orchestra (1917-1977) LC 78-3122. 1978. lib. bdg. 27.50x (ISBN 0-313-20375-X, MDI/). Greenwood.

Meyers, Bettye B., jt. auth. see Hartwig, Marie D.

Meyers, Bill. Dr. Luke Examines Jesus. 1979. pap. 3.95 (ISBN 0-88207-768-6). Victor Bks.

Meyers, Carol L. & O'Connor, M., eds. The Word of the Lord Shall Go Forth: Essays in Honor of David Noel Freedman in Celebration of His Sixtieth Birthday. 1983. text ed. price not set (ISBN 0-89757-507-5, Pub. by Am Sch Orient Res). Eisenbrauns.

Meyers, Eric M., et al. Excavations at Ancient Meiron, Upper Galilee, Israel: 1971-72, 1974-75, 1977. LC 81-4965. (Meiron Excavation Project: Vol. III). 276p. 1981. text ed. 42.50x (ISBN 0-89757-204-1, Am Sch Orient Res). Eisenbrauns.

Meyers, Frederick B. Five Musts of the Christian Life. 1927. pap. 1.50 o.p. (ISBN 0-8024-2639-5). Moody.

Meyers, Gail & Myers, Michele. The Dynamics of Human Communication. 3rd ed. (Illus.). 1980. pap. text ed. 19.00 (ISBN 0-07-044218-5); instrs'. manual 15.00 (ISBN 0-07-044219-3). McGraw.

Meyers, Jeffrey. The Enemy: A Biography of Wyndham Lewis. 1982. 19.95 (ISBN 0-7100-0514-8); pap. 15.95 (ISBN 0-7100-9351-9). Routledge & Kegan.

--Katherine Mansfield: A Biography. LC 79-18885. (Illus.). 1980. 17.50 (ISBN 0-8112-0751-X); pap. 10.50 (ISBN 0-8112-0834-6, ND543). New Directions.

--A Reader's Guide to George Orwell. (Quality Paperback Ser.: No. 339). 1977. pap. 4.95x (ISBN 0-8226-0339-X). Littlefield.

Meyers, Joan, jt. auth. see Whitaker, George O.

Meyers, Joel, jt. auth. see Alpert, Judith L.

Meyers, M. A. Dynamic Radiology of the Abdomen: Normal & Pathological Anatomy. (Illus.). 1976. 45.00 o.p. (ISBN 0-387-90178-7). Springer-Verlag.

Meyers, Marvin, et al. Sources of the American Republic: A Documentary History of Politics, Society, & Thought, Vol. 1. rev. ed. 1967. pap. 12.50x (ISBN 0-673-05342-3). Scott F.

--Sources of the American Republic: A Documentary History of Politics, Society & Thought, Vol. 2. rev. ed. 1969. pap. 12.50x (ISBN 0-673-05762-3). Scott F.

Meyers, Mary A. A New World Jerusalem: The Swedenborgian Experience in Community Cinstruction. LC 82-11997. (Contributions in American Studies: No. 65). (Illus.). 256p. 1983. lib. bdg. 29.95 (ISBN 0-313-23602-X, MNJ/). Greenwood.

Meyers, Patricia, jt. auth. see Cabrera, Roberto.

Meyers, Perla. Perla Meyer's Market-to-Kitchen Cookbook. LC 78-20178. (Illus.). 1979. 16.30i (ISBN 0-06-013033-4, HarpT). Har-Row.

Meyers, Raymond, jt. auth. see Walpole, Ronald E.

Meyers, Richard. The TV Detectives. LC 81-3576. (Illus.). 1981. 25.00 (ISBN 0-498-02577-2); pap. 14.95 (ISBN 0-686-82840-2). A S Barnes.

Meyers, Robert A. Coal Structure. 318p. 1982. 49.50 (ISBN 0-12-493080-8). Acad Pr.

--Handbook of Energy Technology & Economics. 1088p. 1983. 62.95 (ISBN 0-471-08209-0, Pub. by Wiley-Interscience). Wiley.

--Handbook of Synfuels Technology. (Illus.). 896p. 1983. 50.00 (ISBN 0-07-041762-8, P&RB). McGraw.

Meyers, Ruth S. & Banfield, Beryle, eds. Embers: Stories for a Changing World. (Illus.). 168p. (gr. 3-7). 1983. 8.95 (ISBN 0-935312-16-1). Feminist Pr.

Meyers, Steven L., jt. ed. see Baldwin, Neil.

Meyers, V. J. Matrix Analysis of Structures. 528p. 1983. text ed. 33.50 scp (ISBN 0-06-044438-X, HarpC); solutions manual avail. (ISBN 0-06-364417-7). Har-Row.

Meyers, Walter E., jt. auth. see Rippon, Michelle.

Meyerson, Evelyn W. No Enemy but Time. LC 82-45260. 408p. 1983. 15.95 (ISBN 0-385-17966-9). Doubleday.

Meyerson, Martin, et al. Housing, People, & Cities. (Action Ser.). (Illus.). 1962. text ed. 17.50 o.p. (ISBN 0-07-041760-1, P&RB). McGraw.

Meylan, B., jt. auth. see Butterfield, B. G.

Meyman, Jay. The Gourmet Guide to Water Cookery. 128p. 1983. pap. 4.95 (ISBN 0-380-81935-X, 81935-X). Avon.

Meyn, Rodney E. & Withers, H. R., eds. Radiation Biology in Cancer Research. (M. D. Anderson Symposia on Fundamental Cancer Research Ser.). 681p. 1980. text ed. 67.50 (ISBN 0-89004-402-3). Raven.

Meynell, Elinor, jt. auth. see Meynell, G. G.

Meynell, Esther. Little Chronicle of Magdalena Bach. LC 78-129112. 10.00 (ISBN 0-8044-5685-2). Ungar.

Meynell, Francis & Simon, Herbert, eds. The Fleuron Anthology. LC 78-66190. (Illus.). 1979. pap. 32.50 (ISBN 0-87923-287-0). Godine.

Meynell, G. G. Drug-Resistance Factors & Other Bacterial Plasmids. 1973. 20.00x (ISBN 0-262-13085-8). MIT Pr.

Meynell, G. G. & Meynell, Elinor. Theory & Practice in Experimental Bacteriology. 2nd ed. LC 72-85729. (Illus.). 1970. 55.00 (ISBN 0-521-07682-X). Cambridge U Pr.

Meynell, Hugo. Freud, Marx & Morals. LC 81-146124. (New Studies in Practical Philosophy). 222p. 1981. 23.00x (ISBN 0-389-20045-X). B&N Imports.

Meynell, Hugo A. The Intelligible Universe: A Cosmological Argument. LC 81-19065. 164p. 1982. 26.50x (ISBN 0-389-20253-3). B&N Imports.

Meynen, Emil. Bibliography on German Settlements in Colonial North America. LC 66-25870. 1966. Repr. of 1937 ed. 61.00x (ISBN 0-8103-3336-8). Gale.

Meyrink, Gustav & Busson, Paul. The Golem & "The Man Who Was Born Again". Two German Supernatural Novels. Bleiler, E. F., ed. (Illus.). 479p. (Orig.). 1976. pap. 4.50 (ISBN 0-486-23327-8). Dover.

Meys. Compound Adjectives in English & the Ideal Speaker-Listener. (Linguistic Ser.: Vol. 18). 226p. 1975. pap. 32.00 (ISBN 0-444-10780-0, North-Holland). Elsevier.

Meznerics, Ivan. Law of Banking in East-West Trade. LC 72-86390. 427p. 1973. lib. bdg. 25.00 (ISBN 0-379-00016-4). Oceana.

Mezvinsky, Edward & McCormally, Kevin. A Term to Remember. 256p. 1977. 9.95 o.p. (ISBN 0-698-10751-9, Coward). Putnam Pub Group.

Mezzalira, L., jt. ed. see Sami, M.

Mezzatesta, Michael. The Art of Gianlorenzo Bernini: Selected Sculpture. LC 82-81080. (Illus.). 63p. (Orig.). 1982. pap. 8.50 (ISBN 0-912804-05-X). Kimbell Art.

MFOA Committee on Public Employee Retirement Administration. Public Employee Retirement Administration. 134p. 1977. 15.00 (ISBN 0-686-84367-3). Municipal.

M. Heerma, Van Voss see Van Voss, M. Heerma.

Mhina, George A. Maendeleo Ya Kiswahili Na Mazoezi: A Swahili Anthology. LC 70-80854. (Orig., Swahili). 1970. pap. 8.50x (ISBN 0-8419-0014-0, Africana). Holmes & Meier.

Miah, Malik, ed. see Breitman, George, et al.

Miall, Antony, jt. ed. see Baker, Richard.

Miall, Bernard, tr. see Otto, Bismarck Von.

Miall, David, ed. Metaphor-Problems & Perspectives. 260p. 1982. text ed. 32.50x (ISBN 0-391-02374-8). Humanities.

Mibar, Ltd. NRCSA Directory of Special Interest Programs, 1982-1983: Britain-Ireland. 452p. pap. 7.95 (ISBN 0-937816-21-3). Tech Data.

--NRCSA Program Directory Europe, 1982-83. 115p. (Orig.). 1982. pap. 6.95 (ISBN 0-937816-19-1). Tech Data.

Mic, Rose S., ed. The Contemporary Latin American Short Story. LC 78-73619. (Senda De Estudios y Ensayos Ser.). (Orig., Span.). 1979. pap. 9.95 (ISBN 0-918454-10-7). Senda Nueva.

Micali, Paul. The Lacy Techniques of Salesmanship. rev. ed. 182p. 1982. pap. 7.25 (ISBN 0-8015-9201-1, 0704-210, Hawthorn). Dutton.

Micha, Rene. Jean Helion. (Crown QLP Ser.). (Illus.). 1979. 7.95 (ISBN 0-517-53791-5). Crown.

Michael. My Friend's Dog. (Nursery Ser.). (Illus.). 1977. 2.00 (ISBN 0-85953-071-X, Pub. by Child's Play England). Playspaces.

--Sultana. LC 82-48685. 416p. 1983. 16.30i (ISBN 0-06-015166-8, HarpT). Har-Row.

Michael, Alfred F., jt. ed. see Cummings, Nancy B.

Michael, Aloysius. Radhakrishnan on Hindu Moral Life & Action. 1979. text ed. 15.25x (ISBN 0-391-01857-4). Humanities.

Michael, David J. Death Tour. LC 78-55652. 1978. 8.95 o.p. (ISBN 0-672-52513-5). Bobbs.

--Death Tour. 1979. pap. 2.25 o.p. (ISBN 0-451-08842-5, E8842, Sig). NAL.

Michael, George & Lindsay, Ray. George Michael's Complete Hair Program for Men. LC 82-45114. (Illus.). 192p. 1983. 14.95 (ISBN 0-385-17450-0). Doubleday.

Michael, Henry N. Neolithic Age in Eastern Siberia. LC 58-9092. (Transactions Ser.: Vol. 48, Pt. 2). (Illus.). 1958. pap. 1.50 o.p. (ISBN 0-87169-482-4). Am Philos.

Michael, I. The Treatment of Classical Material in the Libro de Alexandre. 1970. 22.00 (ISBN 0-7190-1247-3). Manchester.

Michael, Ian. The Poem of the Cid: A New Critical Edition of the Spanish Test. Hamilton, Rita & Perry, Janet, trs. from Span. LC 75-17168. (The Manchester Medieval Classics Ser.). 242p. 1975. text ed. 18.50x (ISBN 0-06-494799-8). B&N Imports.

Michael, Jack. Laboratory Studies in Operant Behavior. 1963. text ed. 16.95 (ISBN 0-07-041764-4, C). McGraw.

Michael, Jerome & Adler, Mortimer J. Crime Law & Social Science. LC 77-108235. (Criminology, Law Enforcement, & Social Problems Ser.: No. 118). (With intro. added). 1971. Repr. of 1933 ed. 15.00x (ISBN 0-87585-118-5). Patterson Smith.

--Crime, Law & Social Science. (Social Science Classics Ser.). 440p. 19.95 o.p. (ISBN 0-87855-362-2); text ed. 19.95 o.p. (ISBN 0-686-68056-1); pap. cancelled o.p. (ISBN 0-87855-786-5). Transaction Bks.

Michael, Judith. Deceptions. 1983. pap. 3.95 (ISBN 0-686-43230-4). PB.

Michael, Lord C. Policy for Peace. 128p. (Orig.). 1982. 9.95 (ISBN 0-571-11969-7); pap. 4.95 (ISBN 0-571-11975-1). Faber & Faber.

Michael, Louis G. More Corn for Bessarabia: The Russian Experience, 1910-1917. 228p. 1983. 17.95 (ISBN 0-87013-233-4). Mich St U Pr.

Michael, Louis Guy. More Corn for Bessarabia: The Russian Experience, 1910-1917. 228p. 1983. 17.95. Wayne St U Pr.

Michael, Mieke. Holland Cookery. (Illus.). 108p. 1982. pap. 3.95 (ISBN 0-9609304-0-X). Colonial Pr.

Michael P. Smith & Associates. Politics in America: Studies in Policy Analysis. LC 81-40768. 188p. 1981. pap. text ed. 9.00 (ISBN 0-8191-1828-1). U Pr of Amer.

Michael, Paul. The Paul Michael Weight Loss Plan. (Illus.). 96p. 1976. pap. 5.95 (ISBN 0-688-03051-3). Quill NY.

Michael, Robert. The Radicals & Nazi Germany: The Revolution in French Attitudes Toward Foreign Policy, 1933-1939. LC 81-43861. 148p. (Orig.). 1982. PLB 19.00 (ISBN 0-8191-2421-4); pap. text ed. 8.25 (ISBN 0-8191-2422-2). U Pr of Amer.

Michael, Stephen R., et al. Techniques of Organizational Change. LC 80-16243. (Illus.). 363p. 1981. 21.50 (ISBN 0-07-041775-X). McGraw.

Michael, W. E. The Age of Error. LC 77-4233. 1977. Repr. of 1957 ed. lib. bdg. 16.25x (ISBN 0-8371-9588-8, MIAE). Greenwood.

Michaelides, Stephen, jt. auth. see DeLuca, Michael.

Michaelis. ISR Essay Annual 1981. 1981. 47.00 o.p. (ISBN 0-85501-477-6). Wiley.

Michaelis, Cameron. Incubus. LC 81-86424. 192p. 1983. pap. 6.95 (ISBN 0-86666-118-2). GWP.

Michaelis, Carol T. Coping with Handicapped Infants & Children: A Handbook for Parents & Professionals. (Illus.). 1983. pap. text ed. price not set (ISBN 0-8391-1598-9, 17663). Univ Park.

Michaelis, David T. The Best of Friends: Profiles of Extraordinary Friendships. (Illus.). 288p. 1983. 13.95 (ISBN 0-688-01558-1). Morrow.

Michaelis, H., ed. Portuguese-German, German-Portuguese Dictionary, 2 Vols. Set. 42.00 o.p. (ISBN 0-8044-0375-9); 21.00 ea. o.p. Vol. 1 (ISBN 0-8044-0376-7). Vol. 2 (ISBN 0-8044-0377-5). Ungar.

Michaelis, John. Social Studies for Children: A Guide to Basic Instruction. 7th ed. (Illus.). 1980. text ed. 23.95 (ISBN 0-13-818880-7). P-H.

Michaelis, John, et al. New Designs for Curriculum & Instruction. 2nd ed. (Illus.). 448p. 1975. text ed. 27.50 (ISBN 0-07-041772-5, C). McGraw.

Michaelis, John U. & McKeown, Robin J. Twentieth Century Asia: An Anthology. (gr. 9-12). 1968. text ed. 5.32 o.p. (ISBN 0-07-041766-0, W). McGraw.

Michaelis, John U. & Nelson, J. Secondary Social Studies Introduction, Curriculum, Evaluation. (Illus.). 1980. text ed. 24.95 (ISBN 0-13-797753-0). P-H.

Michaelis, John U., jt. auth. see Gabelko, Nina H.

Michaelis, L. S., tr. see Miehlke, Adolf.

Michaelis, L. S., tr. see Reisner, K. & Gosepath, J.

Michaelis, Michael, ed. see A.D. Little, Inc.

Michaelis, R. F., ed. see Masse, H. J.

Michaelis-Jena, Ruth, tr. see Hobusch, Erich.

Michaelman, Herbert, ed. see Appleman, Phillip.

Michaelman, Herbert, ed. see Lesburg, Sandy.

Michaelman, Herbert, ed. see Murphy, Edward.

Michaelman, Herbert, ed. see Roberts, David.

Michaelman, Herbert, ed. see Sann, Paul.

Michaelman, Herbert, ed. see Shuldner, Herbert.

Michaels, Alan. Diamonds. 256p. 1980. 10.95 o.p. (ISBN 0-312-19923-6). St Martin.

Michaels, Barbara. Black Rainbow. LC 82-7408. 320p. 1982. 13.95 (ISBN 0-312-92054-7). Congdon & Weed.

--Dark Duet. 496p. 1983. 14.95 (ISBN 0-312-92119-5). Congdon & Weed.

--The Dark on the Other Side. (General Ser.). 1983. lib. bdg. 14.95 (ISBN 0-8161-3414-6, Large Print Bks). G K Hall.

--Wings of the Falcon. (General Ser.). 1982. lib. bdg. 13.95 (ISBN 0-8161-3415-4, Large Print Bks). G K Hall.

Michaels, Bill, jt. auth. see Orde, Lewis.

Michaels, Claire F. & Carello, Claudia A. Direct Perception. (Illus.). 224p. 1981. text ed. 19.95 (ISBN 0-13-214791-2). P-H.

Michaels, Elena. Death & the I Ching. 256p. 1980. 9.95 o.p. (ISBN 0-517-54029-0, C N Potter Bks). Crown.

Michaels, Fern. All She Can Be. (Love & Life Romance Ser.). 176p. (Orig.). 1983. pap. 1.75 (ISBN 0-345-30839-5). Ballantine.

--Golden Lasso. 192p. (Orig.). 1980. pap. 1.50 (ISBN 0-671-57032-3, Pub. by Silhouette Bks). S&S.

--Sea Gypsy. 192p. (Orig.). 1980. pap. 1.50 (ISBN 0-671-57015-3, Pub. by Silhouette Bks). S&S.

--Tender Warrior. 384p. (Orig.). 1983. pap. 3.50 (ISBN 0-345-30358-X). Ballantine.

--Whisper My Name. 192p. 1981. pap. 1.50 (ISBN 0-671-57061-7, Pub. by Silhouette Bks). S&S.

--Wild Honey. 1982. pap. 2.95 (ISBN 0-686-82569-1). PB.

Michaels, Howard, jt. auth. see Cudworth, Marsha.

Michaels, J. G. & Bloch, N. J. Intermediate Algebra. 480p. 1982. instr. manual 18.95x (ISBN 0-07-041820-9). 7.50x (ISBN 0-07-041821-7); student's manual 6.95 (ISBN 0-07-041822-5). McGraw.

Michaels, Joel L. Legal Issues in a Fee-for-Service-Prepaid Medical Group. (Going Prepaid Ser.). 75p. (Orig.). 1982. pap. 15.00 (ISBN 0-933948-75-1). Ctr Res Ambulatory.

Michaels, John G., jt. auth. see Bloch, Norman J.

Michaels, Jonathan, jt. auth. see Stern, Ellen.

Michaels, Joseph. Prime of Your Life: A Practical Guide to Your Mature Years. 1983. pap. 9.70 (ISBN 0-316-56945-3). Little.

Michaels, Kasey. The Rambunctious Lady Royston. 224p. 1982. pap. 2.50 (ISBN 0-380-81448-X, 81448). Avon.

Michaels, Kevin. The Gay Book of Etiquette. 72p. (Orig.). 1982. pap. 4.45 o.p. (ISBN 0-939020-75-0). MLP Ent.

Michaels, Kristin. Enchanted Journey. (Orig.). 1977. pap. 1.25 o.p. (ISBN 0-451-07628-1, Y7628, Sig). NAL.

--Enchanted Twilight. Bd. with Song of the Heart. 1980. pap. 2.25 o.p. (ISBN 0-451-09536-7, 9536, Sig). NAL.

--Enchanted Twilight. pap. 1.25 o.p. (ISBN 0-451-07733-4, Y7733, Sig). NAL.

--Heartsong. (Orig.). 1980. pap. 1.75 o.p. (ISBN 0-451-09212-0, E9212, Sig). NAL.

--Love on Course. (Adventures in Love Ser.: No. 26). 1982. pap. 1.75 (ISBN 0-451-11646-1, AE1646, Sig). NAL.

--Love's Pilgrimage. (Orig.). 1981. pap. 1.75 o.p. (ISBN 0-451-09681-9, E9681, Sig). NAL.

--Make Believe Love. (Orig.). 1978. pap. 1.75 o.p. (W8058, Sig). NAL.

--A Special Kind of Love. (Orig.). 1976. pap. 1.25 o.p. (ISBN 0-451-07039-9, Y7039, Sig). NAL.

--Voyage to Love. Bd. with Shadow of Love. 1981. pap. 2.50 (ISBN 0-451-11525-2, AE1525, Sig). NAL.

Michaels, L. & Chissick, S. S. Asbestos: Properties, Applications & Hazards, Vol. 1. LC 78-16535. 1979. 105.00 (ISBN 0-471-99698-X, Pub. by Wiley-Interscience). Wiley.

Michaels, Leonard. Going Places. 192p. 1969. 8.95 (ISBN 0-374-16496-7); pap. 5.95. FS&G.

Michaels, Majorie. Stay Healthy with Wine. 1982. pap. 2.95 (ISBN 0-451-11778-6, AE1778, Sig). NAL.

Michaels, Margie. Beloved Pirate. (Second Chance at Love Ser.: No. 15). 192p. (Orig.). 1981. pap. 1.75 o.p. (ISBN 0-515-06067-4). Jove Pubns.

--Mirage. 192p. 1982. pap. 1.75 (ISBN 0-686-81842-3). Jove Pubns.

Michaels, Marguerite. Showing the Flag: A Report from U. S. Embassy. 1982. 13.95 (ISBN 0-671-25616-5). S&S.

Michaels, Rick. Canon AE1, AT-1: Amphoto Pocket Companion. (Illus.). 128p. 1981. pap. 8.95 (ISBN 0-8174-5523-X, Amphoto). Watson-Guptill.

Michaels, Ross. George Harrison. LC 77-78536. (Illus.). 1977. pap. 3.95 (ISBN 0-8256-3913-1, Quick Fox). Putnam Pub Group.

Michaelsen, Mark G. Enterprize Zones: A Fresh Approach Which May Possibly Help Solve the Problem of Urban Blight? (Vital Issues Ser.: Vol. XXXI, No. 3). 0.80 (ISBN 0-686-84136-0). Ctr Info Am.

Michaelson, Arthur M. Income Taxation of Estates & Trusts: Nineteen Eighty Revision. 11th ed. 227p. 1980. 30.00 (ISBN 0-686-79997-6, J1-1434). PLI.

Michaelson, Cydney R., ed. Congestive Heart Failure. (Illus.). 592p. 1983. text ed. 24.95 (ISBN 0-8016-3443-1). Mosby.

Michaelson, Karen L., ed. And the Poor Get Children: Radical Perspectives on Population Dynamics. LC 81-38389. 272p. 1981. 16.00 (ISBN 0-85345-552-X); pap. 7.50 (ISBN 0-85345-553-8). Monthly Rev.

Michaelson, Mike. Weekend Getaway Guide: Chicago. LC 79-88688. (Illus., Orig.). 1980. pap. 6.95 (ISBN 0-528-84105-X). Rand.

Michaelson, S., jt. auth. see Morton, A. Q.

Michailidou, Anna. Knossos. (Athenon Illustrated Guides Ser.). (Illus.). 128p. 1983. pap. 12.00 (ISBN 0-686-43394-7, 8236, Pub. by Ekdotike Athenon Greece). Larousse.

Michailoff, Helen. Listen & Learn Russian Manual. 1982. pap. 3.50 (ISBN 0-486-20879-6). Dover.

Michalec, George W. Precision Gearing: Theory & Practice. LC 66-21045. 1966. 59.95 (ISBN 0-471-60142-X, Pub. by Wiley-Interscience). Wiley.

Michalek, Suzanne M., jt. ed. see McGhee, Jerry R.

Michalopoulos, Andre. Homer. LC 74-80026. (Griffin Authors Ser.). 217p. 1975. pap. 5.95 o.p. (ISBN 0-312-38885-3). St Martin.

--Homer. (World Authors Ser.). 1966. lib. bdg. 11.95 (ISBN 0-8057-2432-X, Twayne). G K Hall.

Michalos, James & Wilson, E. N. Structural Mechanics & Analysis. 1965. text ed. 33.95x (ISBN 0-02-381330-X). Macmillan.

Michalove, Ed & Delson, Donn. Delson's Dictionary of Cable, Video & Satellite Terms. Posner, Neil, ed. LC 82-17767. (Entertainment Communications Ser.: Vol. 3). (Orig.). 1982. pap. 10.00 (ISBN 0-9603574-3-2, A-4). Bradson.

Michalski, Ryszard S. & Carbonell, Jaime G., eds. Machine Learning: An Artificial Intelligence Approach. LC 82-10654. (Illus.). 600p. 1983. 39.50x (ISBN 0-935382-05-4). Tioga Pub Co.

Michal-Smith, Harold & Kastein, Shulamith. Special Child: Diagnosis, Treatment, Habilitation. LC 62-51818. 1962. pap. 9.00x o.p. (ISBN 0-87562-007-8). Spec Child.

Michalson, D. & Aires, C. Spanish Grammar: Un Buen Repaso. 1981. pap. 14.95 (ISBN 0-13-824334-4). P-H.

Michalson, G. E. The Historical Dimensions of Rational Faith: The Role of History in Kant's Religious Thought. 1977. 10.50 (ISBN 0-8191-0308-X). U Pr of Amer.

Michard, L., jt. auth. see Lagarde, A.

Michaud, Jacob-Black. Cohesive Force: Feud in the Middle East. LC 74-83518. 272p. 1975. 27.50 (ISBN 0-312-14700-7). St Martin.

Michaud, Stephen G. & Aynesworth, Hugh. The Only Living Witness. (Illus.). 464p. 1983. 16.95 (ISBN 0-671-44961-3, Linden). S&S.

Michaux, Henri. Au Pays De la Magie. Broome, Peter, ed. (Athlone French Poets Ser). 1977. text ed. 20.75x o.p. (ISBN 0-485-14711-4, Athlone Pr); pap. text ed. 10.75x o.p. (ISBN 0-485-12711-3). Humanities.

--Miserable Miracle. Varese, Louise, tr. (Orig.). pap. 1.95 o.s.i. (ISBN 0-87286-033-7). City Lights.

Micheels, William M. & Karnes, M. Ray. Measuring Educational Achievement. (Education Ser.). 1960. text ed. 32.50 (ISBN 0-07-041770-9, C). McGraw.

Michel, A. & Herget, C. Mathematical Foundations in Engineering & Science: Algebra & Analysis. 1981. 29.95 (ISBN 0-13-561035-4). P-H.

Michel, Aime. Flying Saucers & the Straight-Line Mystery. LC 58-8787. (Illus.). 1958. 15.95 (ISBN 0-87599-077-0). S G Phillips.

Michel, Andree, ed. Family Issues of Employed Women in Europe & America. (International Studies in Sociology & Social Anthropology: Vol. 11). (Illus.). 166p. 1971. text ed. 24.00x o.p. (ISBN 90-040-2633-9). Humanities.

Michel, Bernard. Banques & Banquiers En Autriche Au Debut Du 20e Siecle. (Cahier Ser.: No. 199). (Fr.). 1977. lib. bdg. 50.00x o.p. (ISBN 0-8287-1333-2, Pub. by Presses De la Fondation Nationale Des Sciences Politiques); pap. text ed. 41.00x o.p. (ISBN 2-7246-0340-0). Clearwater Pub.

Michel, Charles, jt. auth. see Waters, Ethel.

Michel, Francois, compiled by. Stendhal Fichier, 3 Vols. 1964. Set. 285.00 (ISBN 0-8161-0583-9, Hall Library). G K Hall.

Michel, Jean-Pierre & Fairbridge, Rhodes W. Dictionary of Earth Science: French-English & English-French. LC 80-80095. 340p. 1980. 16.50x (ISBN 0-89352-076-4). Masson Pub.

Michel, Lawrence. Tragedy of Philotas by Samuel Daniel. 1949. text ed. 14.50x (ISBN 0-686-83831-9). Elliots Bks.

Michel, Pierre. James Gould Cozzens. (United States Authors Ser.: No. 237). 1974. 10.95 o.p. (ISBN 0-8057-0163-X, Twayne). G K Hall.

Michel, Tim. Homeowner's Guide to Landscape Design. (Illus.). 176p. (Orig.). 1983. pap. 10.95 (ISBN 0-914378-94-5). Countryman.

Michel, Walter. Wyndham Lewis: Paintings & Drawings. LC 69-11616. (Illus.). 1970. 80.00x o.s.i. (ISBN 0-520-01612-2). U of Cal Pr.

Michelangelo. Complete Poems of Michelangelo. Tusiani, Joseph, tr. 1969. Repr. of 1959 ed. text ed. 15.00x o.p. (ISBN 0-7206-6616-3). Humanities.

--Drawings by Michelangelo. Brugnoli, Maria V., ed. (Great Masters of Drawing Ser). (Illus.). 1969. pap. 2.00 o.p. (ISBN 0-486-21991-7). Dover.

Michelbacher, G. F. Multiple-Line Insurers: Their Nature & Operation. 2nd ed. (Insurance Ser.). 1970. text ed. 24.95 (ISBN 0-07-041780-6, C). McGraw.

Michele, Arthur A. Iliopsoas: Development of Anomalies in Man. (Illus.). 572p. 1962. photocopy ed. spiral 54.75x (ISBN 0-398-01305-5). C C Thomas.

--Orthotherapy. LC 73-150795. (Illus.). 224p. 1971. pap. 8.95 (ISBN 0-87131-083-X). M Evans.

Michele, Vincenzo De see De Michele, Vincenzo.

Michelet, Jules. The Bird. 308p. 1982. 30.00x (ISBN 0-7045-0444-8, Pub. by Wildwood House). State Mutual Bk.

--Joan of Arc. Guerard, Albert, tr. 1957. pap. 4.50 (ISBN 0-472-06122-4, 122, AA). U of Mich Pr.

Micheletti. The Medici. pap. 12.50 (ISBN 0-935748-05-9). ScalaBooks.

Micheletti, Emma, ed. see Rubens, Peter P.

Michelin. Paris Index Plan, No. 14. 1982. pap. 5.95 (ISBN 2-06-000141-2). Michelin.

Michelin Guides & Map Dept. Michelin Green Guide Rome. 3rd ed. (Fr.). 1982. pap. 7.95 (ISBN 2-06-005582-2). Michelin.

Michelin Guides & Maps. Michelin Green Guide Belgique et Grand Duche du Luxembourg. 2nd ed. 1981. pap. 7.95 (ISBN 2-06-005101-0). Michelin.

--Michelin Green Guide to Causses-Cevennes. 4th ed. (Green Guide Ser.). (Fr.). 1982. pap. 7.95 (ISBN 2-06-003152-4). Michelin.

--Michelin Green Guide to Londres. 2nd ed. (Green Guide Ser.). (Fr.). 1980. pap. 7.95 (ISBN 2-06-005420-6). Michelin.

--Michelin Green Guide to Nord De la France. 6th ed. (Green Guide Ser.). (Fr.). 1982. pap. 7.95 (ISBN 2-06-003421-3). Michelin.

--Michelin Green Guide to Pyrenees. 3rd ed. (Green Guide Ser.). (Fr.). 1982. pap. 7.95 (ISBN 2-06-003662-3). Michelin.

--Michelin Green Guide to Spain. rev. 3rd ed. (Green Guide Ser.). (Avail. in Fr. & Span.). 1982. pap. 7.95 (ISBN 2-06-015211-9). Michelin.

--Michelin Green Guide to Switzerland. 7th ed. (Green Guide Ser.). (Avail. in Fr., Ger.). 1982. pap. 7.95 (ISBN 2-06-015630-0). Michelin.

--Michelin Green Guide to Vallee Du Rhone. 6th ed. (Green Guide Ser.). (Fr.). 1982. pap. 7.95 (ISBN 2-06-003692-5). Michelin.

--Michelin Red Guide to Great Britain & Ireland. (Red Guide Ser.). 1981. 12.95 o.p. (ISBN 2-06-006501-1). Michelin.

--Michelin Red Guide to Italy. (Red Guide Ser.). 1981. 14.95 o.p. (ISBN 2-06-006701-4). Michelin.

--Michelin Red Guide to London. (Red Guide Ser.). 1981. pap. 3.25 o.p. (ISBN 2-06-006601-8). Michelin.

--Michelin Red Guide to Paris: Paris Hotels & Restaurants. (Red Guide Ser.). 1981. Avail. In Fr. & Eng. pap. 3.25 o.p. (ISBN 2-06-006901-7). Michelin.

--Michelin Red Guide to Spain & Portugal. (Red Guide Ser.). 1981. 12.95 o.p. (ISBN 2-06-006301-9). Michelin.

--Paris Index & Map. 4th ed. 1980. pap. 7.95 o.p. (ISBN 2-06-000112-9). Michelin.

Michelin Guides & Maps Dept. Michelin Green Guide to Alpes. 2nd ed. (Green Guide Ser.). (Fr.). 1981. pap. 7.95 (ISBN 2-06-003001-3). Michelin.

--Michelin Green Guide to Austria. 6th ed. (Green Guide Ser.). (Avail. in Ger., Fr.). 1982. pap. 7.95 (ISBN 2-06-015121-X). Michelin.

--Michelin Green Guide to Auvergne. 3rd ed. (Green Guide Ser.). (Fr.). 1982. pap. 7.95 (ISBN 2-06-003031-5). Michelin.

--Michelin Green Guide to Corse. 4th ed. (Green Guide Ser.). (Fr.). 1982. pap. 7.95 (ISBN 2-06-003252-0). Michelin.

--Michelin Green Guide to Cote De L'atlantique. 10th ed. (Green Guide Ser.). (Fr.). 1981. pap. 7.95 (ISBN 2-06-003331-4). Michelin.

--Michelin Green Guide to Dordogne. 3rd ed. (Green Guide Ser.). (Avail. in fr.). 1982. pap. 7.95 (ISBN 2-06-013610-5). Michelin.

--Michelin Green Guide to Environs De Paris. 20th ed. (Green Guide Ser.). (Fr.). 1982. pap. 7.95 (ISBN 2-06-003361-6). Michelin.

--Michelin Green Guide to French Riviera. 8th ed. (Green Guide Ser.). (Avail. in Fr.). 1982. pap. 7.95 (ISBN 2-06-013301-7). Michelin.

--Michelin Green Guide to Germany. (Green Guide Ser.). (Avail. in Fr., Ger.). 1982. pap. 7.95 (ISBN 2-06-015031-0). Michelin.

--Michelin Green Guide to Hollande. 2ndt ed. 1982. pap. 7.95 (ISBN 2-06-005531-8). Michelin.

--Michelin Green Guide to Italy. 9th ed. (Green Guide Ser.). (Avail. in Fr., Ger., Ital.). 1982. pap. 7.95 (ISBN 2-06-015330-1). Michelin.

--Michelin Green Guide to Jura. 4th ed. (Green Guide Ser.). (Fr.). 1982. pap. 7.95 (ISBN 2-06-003392-6). Michelin.

--Michelin Green Guide to Maroc. 3rd ed. (Green Guide Ser.). (Fr.). 1981. pap. 7.95 (ISBN 2-06-005450-8). Michelin.

--Michelin Green Guide to New York City. 6th ed. (Green Guide Ser.). (Avail. in fr.). 1983. pap. 7.95 (ISBN 2-06-015511-8). Michelin.

--Michelin Green Guide to Normandy. 5th ed. (Green Guide Ser.). (Avail. in Fr.). 1981. pap. 7.95 (ISBN 2-06-013480-3). Michelin.

--Michelin Green Guide to Paris. 4th ed. (Green Guide Ser.). (Avail. in Fr., Ger.). 1982. pap. 7.95 (ISBN 2-06-013541-9). Michelin.

--Michelin Green Guide to Portugal. 3rd ed. (Green Guide Ser.). (Avail. in Fr.). 1982. pap. 7.95 (ISBN 2-06-015571-1). Michelin.

--Michelin Green Guide to Provence Eng. (Avail. Fr. & Ger.). 1982. pap. 7.95 (ISBN 2-06-013641-5). Michelin.

--Michelin Red Guide to Deutschland: Annual. (Red Guide Ser.). 1983. 14.95 (ISBN 3-92-107803-2). Michelin.

--Michelin Red Guide to Great Britain & Ireland: Annual. (Red Guide Ser.). 1983. 12.95 (ISBN 2-0600-6533-X). Michelin.

--Michelin Red Guide to Italia: Annual. (Red Guide Ser.). 1983. 14.95 (ISBN 2-0600-6733-2). Michelin.

--Michelin Red Guide to London: Annual. (Red Guide Ser.). 1983. pap. 3.25 (ISBN 2-0600-6633-6). Michelin.

--Michelin Red Guide to Paris: Paris Hotels & Restaurants: Annual. (Red Guide Ser.). (Fr. & Eng.). 1983. pap. 3.25 (ISBN 2-0600-6933-5). Michelin.

--Michelin Red Guide to Spain & Portugal: Annual. (Red Guide Ser.). 1983. 12.95 (ISBN 2-0600-6333-7). Michelin.

--Michelin Red Guide to "Twenty-Two Cities in Europe". Annual. (Red Guide Ser.). 1983. 12.95 (ISBN 2-06-007033-3). Michelin.

--Paris Street Map & Index: No. 012. 1980. pap. 4.95 o.s.i. (ISBN 2-0600-0120-X). Michelin.

Michelin Guides & Maps Division Staff. Camping Caravanning in France. (Annual Ser.). 1983. pap. 7.95 (ISBN 2-06-006133-4). Michelin.

Michell, George. The Hindu Temple: An Introduction to Its Meaning & Forms. LC 77-82075. (Icon Editions). (Illus.). 1978. 25.00i (ISBN 0-06-435750-3, HarpT). Har-Row.

Michell, George, ed. Brick Temples of Bengal: From the Archives of David McCutchion. LC 82-3872. (Illus.). 450p. 1983. 75.00x (ISBN 0-691-04010-9). Princeton U Pr.

Michell, Gillian, ed. Papers of the Dictionary Society of North America 1979. 179p. Date not set. members 6.50 (ISBN 0-686-95917-5); non-members 8.00 (ISBN 0-686-99669-0). Ind St Univ.

Michell, John. Secrets of the Stones: The Story of Astro-Archaeology. 1977. pap. 3.95 (ISBN 0-14-004491-4). Penguin.

Michell, John & Rickard, J. M. Living Wonders: Mysteries & Curiosities of the Animal World. (Illus., Orig.). 1983. pap. 9.95 (ISBN 0-500-27263-8). Thames Hudson.

Michell, R. H., jt. ed. see Finean, J. B.

Michell, S. J. Introduction to Fluid & Particle Mechanics. 1970. 44.00 (ISBN 0-08-013313-4); pap. 14.00 o.p. (ISBN 0-08-013312-6). Pergamon.

Michelle, Arthur A. You Don't Have to Ache: Orthotherapy. 224p. 1983. pap. 5.95 (ISBN 0-87131-411-8). M Evans.

Michelman, Irving S. The Roots of Capitalism in Western Civilization. LC 82-83776. 336p. 1983. 17.95 (ISBN 0-8119-0486-5). Fell.

Michelozzi, Betty N. Coming Alive from Nine to Five: The Career Search Handbook. LC 79-89921. (Illus.). 186p. 1980. pap. 8.95 (ISBN 0-87484-482-7); instructor's manual avail. Mayfield Pub.

Michels, et al. Physics: Principles & Applications. LC 76-14119. (Illus.). 1976. text ed. 31.95 (ISBN 0-395-24789-6); instr's. manual 1.65 (ISBN 0-395-24790-X). HM.

Michels, Joseph W. Dating Methods in Archaeology. LC 72-84274. (Studies in Archaeology Ser). 1973. text ed. 22.50 (ISBN 0-12-785520-3). Acad Pr.

--The Kaminaljuyu Chiefdom. LC 79-15181. (Monograph Ser. on Kaminaljuyu). (Illus.). 1979. text ed. 25.00x (ISBN 0-271-00224-7). Pa St U Pr.

Michels, Joseph W., ed. see Kobishchanov, Yuri M.

Michels, Robert, jt. auth. see MacKinnon, Roger A.

Michelsen, Neil F., compiled by. The American Ephemeris 1981 to 1990. 128p. 1977. pap. 6.00 (ISBN 0-917086-10-4, Pub. by Astro Computing Serv.). Para Res.

Michelson, Frida. Rumbuli. Goodman, Wolf, tr. from Rus. 224p. Date not set. 10.95 (ISBN 0-686-95085-2); pap. 5.95 (ISBN 0-686-99459-0). ADL.

Michelson, Hyman. The Jew in Early English Literature. LC 72-83940. (Illus.). 186p. 1973. Repr. of 1926 ed. 14.50 (ISBN 0-87203-035-0). Hermon.

Michelson, Michael, jt. auth. see Villadsen, John.

Michelson, Peter. The Eater. LC 82-73179. (New Poetry Ser.: No. 45). 119p. 1972. 8.95 (ISBN 0-8040-0586-9). Swallow.

Michelson, William, ed. Behavioral Research Methods in Environmental Design. LC 74-10937. (Community Development Ser: Vol. 8). 307p. 1975. pap. 24.50 (ISBN 0-87933-133-X). Hutchinson Ross.

Michener, Dorothy & Muschlitz, Beverly. First Place: Skills & Activities for Early Learning. 07/1982 ed. LC 82-82050. (Illus.). 96p. pap. text ed. 6.95 (ISBN 0-86530-057-7). Incentive Pubns.

Michener, James A. Bridge at Andau. (gr. 10 up). 1957. 15.95 (ISBN 0-394-41778-X). Random.

--Chesapeake. 865p. 1978. 12.95 (ISBN 0-686-36764-2). Md Hist.

--The Covenant. LC 80-5315. (Spanish Literary Reader Ser.). 1980. 17.50 (ISBN 0-394-50505-0); ltd. ed. 35.00 (ISBN 0-394-51400-9). Random.

--Sayonara. 1954. 15.50 (ISBN 0-394-44385-3). Random.

--Selected Writings. LC 57-6493. 1957. 6.95 (ISBN 0-394-60467-9). Modern Lib.

--Space. (Illus.). 640p. 1982. 17.95 (ISBN 0-394-50555-7); signed, ltd. ed. o.p. 50.00 (ISBN 0-394-52764-X). Random.

--Voice of Asia. 1951. 18.50 (ISBN 0-394-45077-9). Random.

--The Watermen. 193p. 1979. 12.95 (ISBN 0-686-36766-9). Md Hist.

Michie Company Staff. West Virginia Rules Annotated: 1982 Edition. 1981. text ed. 27.50 (ISBN 0-87215-394-0). Michie-Bobbs.

Michie Editorial. Delaware Code: Annotated, Revised 1974, 20 vols. write for info (ISBN 0-87215-247-2); write for info. 1982 suppl. (ISBN 0-87215-319-3). Michie-Bobbs.

Michie Editorial Staff. Code of Alabama 1975, 27 vols. 1980. write for info. (ISBN 0-87215-126-3); write for info. 1982 cum. suppl (ISBN 0-87215-569-2). Michie-Bobbs.

--Code of Virginia, 1950, 23 vols. with 1982 cum. suppl. Set. write for info. (ISBN 0-87215-137-9); write for info. 1982 suppl. (ISBN 0-87215-570-6). Michie-Bobbs.

--Federal Ethics Handbook. 450p. 1981. looseleaf 75.00 (ISBN 0-87215-356-8). Michie-Bobbs.

--General Statutes of North Carolina, Annotated with 1979 Cum. Suppl, 17 vols. Set. write for info. (ISBN 0-87215-132-8); write for info. 1979 suppl. & index (ISBN 0-87215-308-8); 1982 interim suppl. avail. (ISBN 0-87215-572-2). Michie-Bobbs.

--Harmer's Magistrates Manual for West Virginia, with 1965 Supplement. rev. 7th ed. 1961. 25.00 o.p. (ISBN 0-87215-102-6). Michie-Bobbs.

--Maryland Code of 1957, 32 vols., with 1980 cum. suppl. 1982. Set. write for info (ISBN 0-87215-129-8). Michie-Bobbs.

--Michie on Banks & Banking, 11 vols. with 1982 cum. suppl. Set. with 1982 cum. suppl. 400.00 (ISBN 0-87215-034-8); 1981 cum. suppl. 120.00 (ISBN 0-87215-390-8). Michie-Bobbs.

--Michie's Jurisprudence of Virginia & West Virginia, 40 vols., with 1981 cum. suppl. rev. ed. 1948. 995.00 set (ISBN 0-87215-128-X); 1981 cum. suppl. only 165.00 (ISBN 0-87215-432-7). Michie-Bobbs.

--Virginia Rules Annotated: 1981 Edition. 700p. 1981. softbnd. 27.50 (ISBN 0-87215-434-3). Michie-Bobbs.

Michie Staff, ed. Maryland Rules of Procedure: 1982 Edition, 2 vols. 1500p. 1982. pap. 37.50 (ISBN 0-87215-359-2). Michie-Bobbs.

Michiels, Ivo. Book Alpha & Orchis Militaris. Dixon, Adrienne, tr. (International Studies & Translation Program). 1979. lib. bdg. 13.95 (ISBN 0-8057-8165-X, Twayne). G K Hall.

Michigan State University,(East Lansing) Dictionary Catalog of the G. Robert Vincent Library. 1975. 75.00 (ISBN 0-8161-1149-9, Hall Library). G K Hall.

Michigan United Conservation Clubs. Michigan County Maps & Outdoor Guide. 1977. pap. 9.00 (ISBN 0-933112-04-1). Mich United Conserv.

--Michigan Hiking & Skiing Trails. 1979. 1.75 (ISBN 0-933112-08-4). Mich United Conserv.

--Michigan's Fifty Best Fishing Lakes: The State's Top Inland Waters. 1982. pap. 5.95 (ISBN 0-933112-06-8). Mich United Conserv.

--Trout Streams. 1978. pap. 2.95 (ISBN 0-933112-03-3). Mich United Conserv.

--The Wildlife Chef. new ed. 1977. pap. 3.95 (ISBN 0-933112-02-5). Mich United Conserv.

Michigan Yearbook of International Legal Studies, 1982, ed. Transnational Legal Problems of Refugees. LC 81-21707. 1982. 55.00 (ISBN 0-87632-371-9). Boardman.

Michman, Ronald D. Marketing to Changing Consumer Markets: Environmental Scanning. 188p. 1983. 27.95 (ISBN 0-03-059429-4). Praeger.

Michno, Dennis G. A Priest's Handbook: The Ceremonies of the Church. LC 81-84716. (Illus.). 288p. 1983. 29.95 (ISBN 0-8192-1300-4). Morehouse.

Michon, Jacques, jt. auth. see Vilain, Raymond.

Michon, John A. Traffic Education for Young Pedestrians: A Selection of Papers Adapted from the Proceedings of the 1978 OCED Workshop on Training Objectives for Child Pedestrians. (Accident Analysis & Prevention Ser.: No. 13). 138p. 1982. 28.80 (ISBN 0-08-028145-1). Pergamon.

Michor, P. W. Manifolds of Differentiable Mappings. (Shiva Mathematics Ser.). 163p. (Orig.). 1980. pap. text ed. 20.00 (ISBN 0-906812-03-8, Pub. by Shiva Pub England). Imprint Edns.

Michotte, J. La Diffusion du Coton Allen dans la Zone Dense a l'Ouest de Bouake. (Black Africa Ser.). 22p. (Fr.). 1974. Repr. cancelled o.p. (ISBN 0-8287-1360-X, 71-2052). Clearwater Pub.

--Essai d'Appreciation des Effets des Operations de Developpement a Partir de l'Etude d'un Groupe de Budgets Familiaux. (Black Africa Ser.). 121p. (Fr.). 1974. Repr. of 1967 ed. lib. bdg. 40.00x o.p. (ISBN 0-8287-0611-5, 71-2071). Clearwater Pub.

--Etude d'une Experience d'Animation Rurale en Cote d'Ivoire. (Black Africa Ser). 121p. (Fr.). 1974. Repr. of 1967 ed. lib. bdg. 40.00x o.p. (ISBN 0-8287-0612-3, 71-2059). Clearwater Pub.

--Groupe de Production et Niveau de Revenu dans la Zone Dense de l'Ouest de Bouake. (Black Africa Ser.). 80p. (Fr.). 1974. Repr. of 1969 ed. lib. bdg. 30.50x o.p. (ISBN 0-8287-0613-1, 71-2051). Clearwater Pub.

--Les Marches du Pays Baoule de la Zone Pense, 2 vols. Incl. Vol. 1. Typologie Organisation et Fonctionnement. 29p (71-2053); Vol. 2. Annexes Cartographiques. 27p (71-2054). (Black Africa Ser). (Fr.). 1974. Repr. of 1970 ed. Set. lib. bdg. 25.50 o.p. (ISBN 0-8287-1113-5). Clearwater Pub.

--Mouvements Migratoires et Developpement Economique dans la Zone Dense a l'Ouest de Bouake. (Black Africa Ser). 80p. (Fr.). 1974. Repr. of 1968 ed. lib. bdg. 30.50x o.p. (ISBN 0-8287-0614-X, 71-2050). Clearwater Pub.

Michotte, J., jt. auth. see Chevassu, J.

Michton, J., jt. auth. see Hughes, J.

Michunas, Lynn. Kalculator Kids. (gr. 3-7). 1982. 5.95 (ISBN 0-86653-076-2, GA 410). Good Apple.

Mick, John & Brick, James. Bit-Slice Microprocessor Design. (Illus.). 416p. 1980. 26.50 (ISBN 0-07-041781-4, P&RB). McGraw.

Mickadeit, Robert E., jt. auth. see Huntington, Whitney C.

Mickel, Emanuel J., Jr. Eugene Fromentin. (World Authors Ser.). 1982. 15.95 (ISBN 0-8057-6484-4, Twayne). G K Hall.

Mickelsen, A. Berkeley & Mickelsen, Alvera M. Understanding Scripture. 2nd ed. LC 81-52231. (Better Bible Study Ser.). 1982. pap. 3.50 (ISBN 0-8307-0795-6, 5017302). Regal.

Mickelsen, Alvera M., jt. auth. see Mickelsen, A. Berkeley.

Mickelson, Anne Z. Reaching Out: Sensitivity & Order in Recent American Fiction by Women. LC 78-26164. 1979. lib. bdg. 13.00 o.p. (ISBN 0-8108-1194-4). Scarecrow.

--Thomas Hardy's Women & Men: The Defeat of Nature. LC 76-28366. 1976. 12.00 o.p. (ISBN 0-8108-0985-0). Scarecrow.

Mickelwait, Donald R., et al, eds. New Directions in Development: Study of U. S. Aid. Sweet, Charles F. & Morse, Elliott R. 1979. lib. bdg. 25.50 (ISBN 0-89158-266-5). Westview.

Mickens, Ronald E. An Introduction to Nonlinear Oscillations. LC 80-13169. (Illus.). 320p. 1981. text ed. 75.00 (ISBN 0-521-22208-7). Cambridge U Pr.

Mickiewicz, Adam. Konrad Wallenrod, & Other Writings. Noyes, George R., ed. Parish, et al, trs. from Pol. LC 74-12764. 209p. 1975. Repr. of 1925 ed. lib. bdg. 18.00x (ISBN 0-8371-7743-X, MIKW). Greenwood.

--Les Slaves: Histoire et Litterature Des Nations Polonaise, Boheme, Serbe et Russe, 5 vols. (Nineteenth Century Russia Ser.). (Fr.). 1974. Repr. of 1849 ed. Set. lib. bdg. 586.00x o.p. (ISBN 0-8287-1420-7). Clearwater Pub.

Mickle, M. M. & Da Costa, Francisco. Say It in Portuguese. (Orig.). 1954. pap. 1.95 (ISBN 0-486-20809-5). Dover.

Mickle, Marlin H., ed. see Pittsburgh Conference on Modeling & Simulation, 12th Annual.

Mickle, Marlin H., jt. ed. see Vogt, William G.

Micklem, et al. Methods of Treatment in Analytical Psychology. Baker, Ian F., ed. 247p. 1980. 25.00 (ISBN 3-87089-197-1). Spring Pubns.

Mickley, Harold S., et al. Applied Mathematics in Chemical Engineering. 2nd ed. (Chemical Engineering Ser.). (Illus.). 1957. text ed. 24.95 (ISBN 0-07-041800-4, C). McGraw.

Mickolus, Edward F. International Terrorism: Attributes of Terrorist Events, 1968-1977 (ITERATE 2) LC 82-82385. write for info. (ISBN 0-89138-927-X, ICPSR 7947). ICPSR.

Micks, Marianne H. Future Present: The Phenomenon of Christian Worship. LC 75-103844. 1970. pap. 6.95 (ISBN 0-8164-2109-9). Seabury.

--Introduction to Theology. 1967. pap. 5.95 (ISBN 0-8164-2036-X, SP40). Seabury.

--Introduction to Theology. rev. ed. 160p. 1983. pap. 8.95 (ISBN 0-8164-2465-9). Seabury.

Mico, Paul R. Developing Your Community-Based Organization: With Special Emphasis on Community Economic Development Organizations & Community Action Agencies. LC 80-53828. (Illus.). 160p. 1981. pap. text ed. 7.95 (ISBN 0-89914-004-1). Third Party Pub.

Micoleau, T., jt. auth. see Moore, J.

Micro Ink, Inc. The Best of Micro: June 1980 to May 1981, Vol. 4. Tripp, Robert M., ed. (The Best of Micro Ser.). (Illus.). Date not set. pap. cancelled o.p. (ISBN 0-938222-04-X). Micro Ink.

Micro Staff, ed. MICRO on the Apple, Vol. 3. 1982. softcover 24.95 (ISBN 0-938222-08-2). Micro Ink.

Micronesian Community College Students. Never & Always: Legends of the Micronesian People. Ashby, Gene, ed. LC 81-86460. (Illus.). 152p. (Orig.). 1983. pap. 6.95 (ISBN 0-931742-11-0). Rainy Day Oreg.

--Some Things Of Value: Micronesian Customs As Seen by Micronesians. Ashby, Gene, ed. LC 82-60520. (Illus.). 200p. (Orig.). 1983. pap. 6.95 (ISBN 0-931742-12-9). Rainy Day Oreg.

Mid-American Solar Energy Complex. Passive Solar Products Catalog. 360p. 1982. pap. 34.50x (ISBN 0-89934-175-6, A-020). Solar Energy Info.

Mid-Atlantic Conference. Industrial Waste: Proceedings of the 14th Mid-Atlantic Conference. Alleman, James E. & Kavanagh, Joseph T., eds. LC 81-65971. (Illus.). 612p. 1982. 39.95 (ISBN 0-250-40510-5). Ann Arbor Science.

Mid-European Law Project. Church & State Behind the Iron Curtain. Gsovski, Vladimir, ed. LC 72-12333. 311p. 1973. Repr. of 1955 ed. lib. bdg. 17.25x (ISBN 0-8371-6726-4, MICS). Greenwood.

Middelkoop, J. H. van see Van Middelkoop, J. H.

Middione, Carlo. Pasta! Cooking It, Loving It. LC 82-47861. (Great American Cooking Schools Ser.). (Illus.). 84p. 1982. 8.61i (ISBN 0-06-015068-8, HarpT). Har-Row.

Middlebrook, Diane Wood. Gin Considered as a Demon. LC 82-84116. 70p. (Orig.). Date not set. pap. 3.95 (ISBN 0-941692-04-3). Elysian Pr.

Middlebrook, Martin. Convoy. LC 76-43148. (Illus.). 1977. 12.50 o.p. (ISBN 0-688-03138-2). Morrow.

--The Preenmunde Raid. 272p. 1983. 14.95 (ISBN 0-672-52759-6). Bobbs.

Middlebrook, Patricia N. Social Psychology & Modern Life. 2nd ed. 620p. 1980. text ed. 20.00 (ISBN 0-394-31248-1). Knopf.

Middlebrooks, E. J. Industrial Pollution Control: Vol. 1, Agro-Industries. LC 79-10573. (Environmental Science & Technology Texts & Monographs: Vol. 1). 1979. 52.50 (ISBN 0-471-04779-1, Pub. by Wiley-Interscience). Wiley.

Middlebrooks, E. Joe. Statistical Calculations: How to Solve Statistical Problems. LC 75-39545. 1976. 19.95 (ISBN 0-250-40122-3). Ann Arbor Science.

--Water Reuse. LC 80-70324. 1982. text ed. 56.95 (ISBN 0-250-40359-5). Ann Arbor Science.

Middlebrooks, E. Joe, et al. Lagoon Information Source Book. LC 77-85086. 1978. 24.00 (ISBN 0-250-40198-3). Ann Arbor Science.

Middlekauff, Woodrow W. & Lane, Robert S. Adult & Immature Tabanidae (Diptera) of California. (Bulletin of the California Insect Survey Ser.: Vol. 22). 1980. pap. 15.00x (ISBN 0-520-09604-5). U of Cal Pr.

Middleman, Ruth R. A Study Guide for ACSW Certification. rev. ed. 48p. 1982. pap. 5.95x (ISBN 0-87101-090-9, 6B6-090-C). Natl Assn Soc Wkrs.

Middleman, Stanley. Flow of High Polymers: Continuum & Molecular Rheology. LC 67-29460. 1968. 36.50 (ISBN 0-470-60235-X, Pub. by Wiley-Interscience). Wiley.

--Fundamentals of Polymer Processing. 1977. text ed. 34.00 (ISBN 0-07-041851-9, C); solutions manual 18.50 (ISBN 0-07-041852-7). McGraw.

Middlemiss, F. A. Fossils. (Introducing Geology Ser.). 1976. pap. text ed. 5.95x (ISBN 0-04-560005-8). Allen Unwin.

Middlemiss, F. A., et al. Faunal Provinces in Space & the Time: Geological Journal Special Issue, No. 4. (Liverpool Geological Society & the Manchester Geological Association). 1980. 43.95 (ISBN 0-471-27751-7, Pub. by Wiley-Interscience). Wiley.

Middlemiss, Ross R. Algebra for College Students. (Illus.). 1953. text ed. 15.95 o.p. (ISBN 0-07-041880-2, C). McGraw.

Middlemiss, Ross R., et al. Analytic Geometry. 3rd ed. LC 68-15472. 1968. text ed. 28.50 (ISBN 0-07-041896-9, C); instr's manual 25.00 (ISBN 0-07-041897-7). McGraw.

Middlemist, R. Dennis & Hitt, Michael A. Organizational Behavior. 512p. 1981. text ed. 20.95 (ISBN 0-574-19390-1, 13-2390); instr's. guide avail. (ISBN 0-574-19391-X, 13-2391). SRA.

--Personnel Management: Jobs, People, & Logic. (Illus.). 592p. 1983. 23.95 (ISBN 0-13-659003-9). P-H.

Middlemist, R. Dennis, jt. auth. see Hitt, Michael A.

Middleton, Allen H., et al. Epilepsy. 1982. 13.95 (ISBN 0-316-56952-6). Little.

Middleton, B. C. History of English Craft Bookbinding Techniques. (Illus.). 55.00x (ISBN 0-87556-624-3). Saifer.

Middleton, Bernard C. Restoration of Leather Bindings. LC 72-184464. (Illus.). 220p. 1972. pap. 15.00 (ISBN 0-8389-3133-2). ALA.

Middleton, Christopher. Anasphere. (Burning Deck Poetry Ser). 1978. pap. 3.00 (ISBN 0-930900-53-7); signed ed. 20.00 (ISBN 0-930900-54-5). Burning Deck.

--Carminalenia. 128p. pap. 9.95 o.p. (ISBN 0-85635-284-5, Pub. by Carcanet New Pr England). Humanities.

--Carminalenia. 120p. 1980. pap. text ed. 9.95x (ISBN 0-85635-284-5, Pub. by Carcanet New Pr England). Humanities.

--One Hundred Eleven Poems. 160p. 1983. pap. text ed. 12.50x (ISBN 0-85635-457-0, Pub. by Carcanet New Pr England). Humanities.

--Pataxanadu & Other Prose. 1979. 7.95 o.p. (ISBN 0-85635-172-5, Pub. by Carcanet New Pr England). Humanities.

--Woden Dog. (Burning Deck Poetry Ser.). 32p. (Orig.). 1982. signed ed 20.00 (ISBN 0-930901-06-1); pap. 3.00 (ISBN 0-930901-07-X). Burning Deck.

Middleton, Christopher, tr. see Walser, Robert.

Middleton, Christopher, tr. see Wolf, Christa.

Middleton, David B., ed. Cornell Journal of Architecture II. (Illus.). 160p. 1983. pap. 20.00 (ISBN 0-8478-5364-0). Rizzoli Intl.

Middleton, Drew. Crossroads of Modern Warfare. LC 79-7873. (Illus.). 312p. 1983. 17.95 (ISBN 0-385-14937-9). Doubleday.

Middleton, Drew, intro. by. Air War: Vietnam. LC 78-11429. (Illus.). 1979. 15.00 o.p. (ISBN 0-672-52616-6). Bobbs.

Middleton, E. W. Lifeboats of the World. LC 77-26247. (Arco Color Ser.). (Illus.). 1978. 8.95 (ISBN 0-668-04470-5); pap. 6.95 o.p. (ISBN 0-668-04481-0). Arco.

Middleton, John, jt. ed. see Rahim, Syed A.

Middleton, Katharine & Hess, Mary. The Art of Cooking for the Diabetic. LC 77-23701. 1978. 15.95 (ISBN 0-8092-8270-4); pap. 8.95 (ISBN 0-8092-7222-9). Contemp Bks.

Middleton, Katherine & Hess, Mary A. The Art of Cooking for the Diabetic. 1979. pap. 3.95 (ISBN 0-451-12205-4, AE2205, Sig). NAL.

Middleton, Robert. Negotiating on Non-Tariff Distortions of Trade: The EFTA Precedents. LC 74-19885. 208p. 1975. 26.00 (ISBN 0-312-56315-9). St Martin.

--Television Service Manual. 4th ed. LC 76-24074. 1977. 11.95 (ISBN 0-672-23247-2, 23247). Audel.

Middleton, Robert & Meyers. Practical Electricity. new ed. (Audel Ser.). 1983. 13.95 (ISBN 0-672-23375-4). Bobbs.

Middleton, Robert G. Digital Logic Circuits: Tests & Analysis. Date not set. pap. 16.95 (ISBN 0-672-21799-6). Sams.

--Understanding Digital Logic Circuits. Date not set. pap. 18.95 (ISBN 0-672-21867-4). Sams.

Middleton, Susan, ed. Blueprints: Building Educational Programs for People Who Care for Children. (Illus.). 238p. pap. 19.95 (ISBN 0-934140-16-2). Toys N Things.

Middleton, Thomas. Three Plays. Muir, Kenneth, ed. (Rowman & Littlefield University Library). 217p. 1975. 9.50x o.p. (ISBN 0-87471-555-5); pap. 4.75x (ISBN 0-87471-556-3). Rowman.

Middleton, Thomas H., ed. Double-Crostics by Fans, No. 5. 1969. pap. 4.80 (ISBN 0-671-20405-X). S&S.

--Double-Crostics, No. 67. 1971. 3.95 o.p. (ISBN 0-671-21095-5, Fireside). S&S.

--Simon & Schuster Crostics, No. 78. 1977. spiral 2.95 o.p. (ISBN 0-671-23021-2). S&S.

--Simon & Schuster Crostics, No. 80. 1978. spiral 4.95 (ISBN 0-671-24412-4). S&S.

--Simon & Schuster Crostics, No. 80. 1976. pap. 4.95 (ISBN 0-671-22392-5). S&S.

--Simon & Schuster Crostics Omnibus, No. 8. 1978. 4.80 (ISBN 0-671-24137-0). S&S.

Middleton, Tom. The Book of Maidenhead. 1977. 25.00x o.p. (ISBN 0-86023-006-6). State Mutual Bk.

Middleton, W. E. History of the Theories of Rain & Other Forms of Precipitation. LC 66-15982. (Oldburne History of Science Ser). 1968. 15.00x o.s.i. (ISBN 0-226-52497-3). U of Chicago Pr.

Middleton, W. E., ed. Lorenzo Magalotti at the Court of Charles II (His Relazione D'inghilterra 1668) 161p. 1980. text ed. 11.00x (ISBN 0-88920-095-5, Pub. by Wilfrid Laurier U Pr England). Humanities.

Middleton, William D. Interurban Era. LC 61-10728. (Illus.). 432p. 1961. 20.00 o.p. (ISBN 0-89024-003-5). Kalmbach.

--Railroad Scene. LC 69-20446. (Illus.). 1969. 15.95 o.p. (ISBN 0-87095-000-2). Golden West.

Midelfort, H. C. Erik, ed. see Moeller, Bernd.

Midgett, Elwin W. Accounting Primer. 1971. pap. 3.50 (ISBN 0-451-62153-0, ME2153, Ment). NAL.

Midgley, Derek & Torrance, Kenneth. Potentiometric Water Analysis. LC 77-7213. 1978. 87.95 (ISBN 0-471-99532-0, Pub. by Wiley-Interscience). Wiley.

Midgley, E. B. The Ideology of Max Weber: A Thomist Critique. LC 82-16445. 200p. 1983. text ed. 22.50x (ISBN 0-389-20343-2). B&N Imports.

Midgley, E. G., ed. see Bunyan, John.

Midgley, James. Professional Imperialism: Social Work in the Third World. 1981. text ed. 32.00x (ISBN 0-435-82588-7). Heinemann Ed.

Midgley, James, jt. auth. see Hardiman, Margaret.

Midgley, Mary. Beast & Man: The Roots of Human Nature. 1980. pap. 7.95 (ISBN 0-452-00587-6, F587, Mer). NAL.

Midgley, W., jt. auth. see Lilley, A. E.

Midler, Bette. A View from a Broad. (Illus.). 1980. 12.95 o.p. (ISBN 0-671-24780-8). S&S.

Midwest Plan Service. Professional Design Supplement to the MWPS Structures & Environment Handbook. 5th ed. LC 77-24229. (Illus.). 1978. pap. text ed. 11.50 o.p. (ISBN 0-89373-037-8, MWPS-17). Midwest Plan Serv.

--Solar Livestock Housing Handbook. 1st ed. (Illus., Orig.). 1983. pap. 4.00 (ISBN 0-89373-056-4, MWPS-23). Midwest Plan Serv.

Midwest Plan Service Engineers. Structures & Environment Handbook. 10th, rev. ed. Midwest Plan Service Staff, ed. LC 76-27983. (Illus.). 490p. 1980. pap. 12.00 (ISBN 0-686-68276-9, MWPS-1). Midwest Plan Serv.

--Swine Housing & Equipment Handbook. 4th ed. Midwest Plan Service Staff, ed. LC 82-2292. (Illus.). 1983. pap. 5.00 (ISBN 0-89373-054-8). Midwest Plan Serv.

Midwest Plan Service Engineers Staff. Structures & Environment Handbook. 11th ed. (Illus.). 700p. 1983. pap. text ed. price not set (ISBN 0-89373-057-2). Midwest Plan Serv.

Midwest Plan Service Personnel. Planning Grain-Feed Handling for Livestock & Cash-Grain Farms. 1st ed. (Illus.). 1974. pap. 4.00 (ISBN 0-89373-007-6, MWPS-13). Midwest Plan Serv.

Midwest Plan Service Staff, ed. see Midwest Plan Service Engineers.

Midwinter, John E. Optical Fibers for Transmission. LC 78-15797. (Pure & Applied Optics Ser.). 1979. 38.95 (ISBN 0-471-60240-X, Pub. by Wiley-Interscience). Wiley.

Mieczkowski, Bogdan. Social Services for Women in Eastern Europe. (ASN Series in Issues Studies (USSR & East Europe): No. 3). 128p. (Orig.). 1982. pap. 8.50 (ISBN 0-910895-00-7). Assn Study Nat.

Miedaner, Terrel. The Soul of Anna Klane. 1977. 8.95 (ISBN 0-698-10826-4, Coward). Putnam Pub Group.

Miege, J. & Lyonga, S. N. Yams. (Illus.). 1982. 69.00x (ISBN 0-19-854557-6). Oxford U Pr.

Miehe, Georg. Vegetationsgeographische Untersuchungen im Dhaulagiri-und Annapurna-Himalaya, 2 vols. (Dissertationes Botanica 66). (Illus.). 500p. 1982. lib. bdg. 67.50 (ISBN 3-7682-1356-0). Lubrecht & Cramer.

Miehlke, Adolf. Surgery of the Facial Nerve. 2nd ed. Michaelis, L. S., tr. LC 72-85770. (Illus.). 255p. 1973. text ed. 22.50 (ISBN 0-7216-6318-4). Saunders.

Miekal. Last Will & Hymn. 13p. 1982. 1.00 o.p. (ISBN 0-686-37507-6). Ptolemy Brown.

Miernyk, William H. Economics. 1971. text ed. 10.00 (ISBN 0-685-55628-X). Phila Bk Co.

--Elements of Input-Output Analysis. (Orig.). 1965. pap. text ed. 7.00 (ISBN 0-394-30393-8, RanC). Random.

--Illusions of Conventional Economics. 1982. 6.95 (ISBN 0-937058-14-9). West Va U Pr.

--Regional Analysis & Regional Policy. LC 82-6419. 128p. 1982. 14.95 (ISBN 0-89946-152-2); pap. 7.95 (ISBN 0-89946-153-0). Oelgeschlager.

Miernyk, William H. & Giarrantani, Frank. Regional Impacts on Rising Energy Prices. LC 77-25075. 160p. 1978. prof ref 25.00x (ISBN 0-88410-074-X). Ballinger Pub.

Miernyk, William H., jt. auth. see Saunders, Robert J.

Miers, David, jt. auth. see Twining, William.

Miers, Earl S. America & Its Presidents. (Illus.). 256p. (gr. 3-9). 1982. 10.95 (ISBN 0-448-12325-8, G&D). Putnam Pub Group.

--Crossroads of Freedom: The American Revolution & the Rise of a New Nation. LC 78-163953. (Illus.). 1971. 25.00 (ISBN 0-8135-0699-9). Rutgers U Pr.

Mierse, William E., jt. auth. see Hanfmann, George M.

Miert, A. S. van see Van Miert, A. S.

Miertschin, Susan, jt. auth. see Goodson, Carole E.

Mies, M. The Lace Makers of Narsapur: Indian Housewives Produce for the World Market. 196p. 1982. pap. 10.50 (ISBN 0-86232-032-1, Pub. by Zed Pr England). Lawrence Hill.

Mies, Maria. Indian Women & Patriarchy. 311p. 1980. text ed. 17.75x (ISBN 0-391-02126-5). Humanities.

Miescher, Peter A. & Mueller-Eberhard, Hans J., eds. Textbook of Immunopathology, 2 vols. 2nd ed. LC 76-155406. (Illus.). 544p. 1976. 79.50 ea. Vol. I (ISBN 0-8089-0931-2). Vol. II (ISBN 0-8089-0932-0). Set. 135.00 o.s.i. (ISBN 0-686-86007-1). Grune.

Miescher, Peter A., jt. ed. see Grabar, Pierre.

Miesel, Sandra. Against Time's Arrow, the High Crusade of Poul Anderson. LC 78-14913. (The Milford Ser: Popular Writers of Today, Vol. 18). 1978. lib. bdg. 9.95x (ISBN 0-89370-124-6); pap. 3.95x (ISBN 0-89370-224-2). Borgo Pr.

Miessner, B. F. On the Early History of Radio Guidance. LC 64-21125. (History of Technology Monographs). (Illus.). 1964. 5.00 (ISBN 0-911302-00-X). San Francisco Pr.

Mieszkowski, P. & Peterson, G., eds. Public Sector Labor Markets. 216p. 1981. pap. 10.00 (ISBN 0-87766-285-1, 29100). Urban Inst.

Mieszkowski, Peter, jt. ed. see McLure, Charles E., Jr.

Mieth, Dietmar & Pohier, Marie, eds. Christian Ethics & Economics. (Concilium Ser. Vol. 140). 128p. (Orig.). 1980. pap. 5.95 (ISBN 0-8164-2282-6). Seabury.

Miethe, Terry L. Augustinian Bibliography, 1970-1980: With Essays on the Fundamentals of Augustinian Scholarship. LC 82-6173. 248p. 1982. lib. bdg. 35.00 (ISBN 0-313-22629-6, MIA/). Greenwood.

Mietus, Micheal. Write English, Bk. 5. (Speak English Ser.). (Illus.). 64p. (Orig.). 1983. pap. text ed. 4.95 (ISBN 0-88499-688-3). Inst Mod Lang.

Mietus, Norbert J. & West, Bill W. Personal Law. 2nd ed. LC 74-34192. (Consumer Education Ser). (Illus.). 464p. 1981. text ed. 21.95 (ISBN 0-574-19505-X, 13-2505); instr's guide avail. (13-2506). SRA.

Mietus, Norbert J., jt. auth. see Hastings, Paul G.

Miewald, Robert D. Public Administration: A Critical Perspective. 1977. pap. text ed. 19.95 (ISBN 0-07-041908-6, C). McGraw.

Mifflin, Lawrie, jt. auth. see Rush, Cathy.

Migdail, Sherry R. & Vail, Priscilla L. Supplement to Alternatives Notebook. 1978. pap. 4.25 (ISBN 0-934338-10-8). NAIS.

Migdalski, Edward C. Fish Mounts & Other Fish Trophies: The Complete Book of Taxidermy. 2nd ed. LC 80-27829. 212p. 1981. 17.95 (ISBN 0-471-07990-1). Wiley.

Migel, J. Michael. The Stream Conservation Handbook. LC 73-82458. (Sportsmen's Classics Ser). 244p. 1974. 7.95 o.p. (ISBN 0-517-50614-9). Crown.

Migel, Michael, ed. The Masters on the Dry Fly. (Illus.). 1978. pap. 6.95 o.s.i. (ISBN 0-695-80925-3). Follett.

Migliaccio, Janice Cook. Follow Your Heart's Vegetarian Soup Cookbook. LC 82-21822. (Illus.). 128p. (Orig.). 1983. pap. 9.95 (ISBN 0-88007-130-3); pap. 5.95 (ISBN 0-88007-131-1). Woodbridge Pr.

Migliaro, Al & Jain, Chaman L. An Executive's Guide to Econometric Forecasting. 74p. 1983. pap. 24.95 (ISBN 0-932126-10-3). Graceway.

Migliore, Daniel L. The Power of God, Vol. 8. Mulder, John C., ed. LC 82-20037. (Library of Living Faith). 120p. (Orig.). 1983. pap. 5.95 (ISBN 0-664-24454-8). Westminster.

Migliore, R. Henry. MBO: Blue Collar to Top Executive. LC 77-8538. 198p. 1977. 17.50 (ISBN 0-87179-262-1). BNA.

Migliorini, Mario. Adopting a Dog from an Animal Shelter. LC 80-15929. (Illus.). 176p. 1981. lib. bdg. 11.95 o.p. (ISBN 0-668-04889-1); pap. 6.95 o.p. (ISBN 0-668-04890-5). Arco.

--Beagles. LC 75-913. (Pet Handbooks Ser.). (Illus.). 1975. pap. 1.95 o.p. (ISBN 0-668-03770-9). Arco.

--German Shepherds. (Arco Pet Handbooks Ser.). (Illus.). 1976. pap. 1.95 o.p. (ISBN 0-668-03875-6). Arco.

--Irish Setters. LC 75-915. (Pet Handbooks Ser.). 1975. 1.95 o.p. (ISBN 0-668-03769-5). Arco.

--Labrador Retrievers. LC 70-126569. (Arco Pet Handbooks Ser.). (Illus.). 110p. 1975. pap. 1.95 o.p. (ISBN 0-668-03901-9). Arco.

--Miniature Schnauzers. LC 75-4020. (Illus.). 96p. 1976. pap. 1.95 o.p. (ISBN 0-668-03772-5). Arco.

--Schnauzer Grooming Made Easy. (Illus.). 96p. 1983. spiral 9.95 (ISBN 0-668-05419-0, 5419). Arco.

Mignani, Rigo, jt. auth. see Bernardo, Aldo S.

Migne, J. P., ed. Dictionnaire d'Ethnographie. (Nouvelle Encyclopedie Theologique Ser.: Vol. 37). 964p. (Fr.). Date not set. Repr. of 1853 ed. lib. bdg. 121.50x (ISBN 0-686-82875-5). Caratzas Bros.

--Encyclopedie Theologique, 168 vols. in 171. (Illus.). 119060p. (Fr.). Date not set. Repr. of 1873 ed. Set. lib. bdg. 14,177.48 (ISBN 0-89241-230-5). Caratzas Bros.

--Encyclopedie Theologique (First Series, 50 vols. in 52. 34591p. (Fr.). Date not set. Repr. of 1859 ed. Set. lib. bdg. 4184.75x (ISBN 0-89241-201-1). Caratzas Bros.

Mignone, Nicholas A., jt. auth. see Dyer, Jon C.

Mignot, Claude. Nineteenth Century Architecture. LC 82-42844. (Illus.). 304p. 1983. cancelled (ISBN 0-8478-0477-1). Rizzoli Intl.

Migraine Symposium, 4th, London, 1971. Background to Migraine: Proceedings. Cumings, J. N., ed. (Illus.). 1971. 8.00 o.p. (ISBN 0-387-91086-7). Springer-Verlag.

Migraine Symposium, 5th, London, 1972. Background to Migraine: Proceedings. Cumings, J. N., ed. 1973. 26.00 o.p. (ISBN 0-387-91115-4). Springer Verlag.

Miguel, jt. auth. see De Guzman.

Miguel, Pierre. Age of Discovery. LC 80-52500. (Picture Histories Ser.). lib. bdg. 12.68 (ISBN 0-382-06474-7). Silver.

--Ancient Egyptians. LC 80-54636. (Picture Histories Ser.). PLB 12.68 (ISBN 0-382-06585-9). Silver.

Miguens, Jose E., jt. ed. see Turner, Frederick C.

Mihajlov, Marija, jt. auth. see Mihajlov, Mihajlo.

Mihajlov, Mihajlo & Mihajlov, Marija. Russian Themes. 373p. 1968. 6.95 o.p. (ISBN 0-374-25292-0). FS&G.

Mihalich, Joseph C. Sports & Athletics: Philosophy in Action. LC 81-20837. (Quality Paperback Ser.: No. 371). 236p. (Orig.). 1982. pap. text ed. 5.95 (ISBN 0-8226-0371-3). Littlefield.

--Sports & Athletics: Philosophy in Action. LC 82-3736. 236p. 1982. text ed. 17.50x (ISBN 0-8476-7076-7). Rowman.

Mihaly, Ida F., ed. Hungarian Gipsy Artist: A. Janos Balazs. Schiff, Laura & Carlson, Chas., trs. 1980. 9.95 (ISBN 0-89893-158-4). CDP.

Mihalyi, Marika, tr. see Gheorghiu, C. Virgil.

Mihalyka, Jean M., compiled by. Gravestone Inscriptions in Northampton County Virginia. 6.00 o.s.i. (ISBN 0-88490-092-4). Va State Lib.

Mihara, Yoshiaki, ed. Agricultural Meteorology of Japan. LC 74-78859. 216p. 1974. text ed. 22.50x (ISBN 0-8248-0337-X, Eastwest Ctr). UH Pr.

Mihich, Enrico. New Leads in Cancer Therapeutics. 1981. lib. bdg. 29.95 (ISBN 0-8161-2148-6, Hall Medical). G K Hall.

Mihich, Enrico, ed. Biological Responses in Cancer Progress Toward Potential Applications, Vol. 1. 300p. 1982. 37.50 (ISBN 0-306-41146-6, Plenum Pr). Plenum Pub.

Mijares, Sharon G. The Babysitter's Manual. (Illus.). 60p. (gr. 6-9). 1983. spiral bdg. 4.98 (ISBN 0-911925-00-7). Grace Pubns.

Mikalson, Elaine, jt. auth. see Bryngelson, Bryng.

Mikami, S., et al, eds. Avian Endocrinology: Environmental & Ecological Perspectives. 380p. 1983. 53.00 (ISBN 0-387-11871-3). Springer-Verlag.

Mikami, Y. The Development of Mathematics in China & Japan. 2nd ed. LC 74-6716. 383p. 1974. text ed. 17.95 (ISBN 0-8284-0149-7). Chelsea Pub.

Mikami, Yoshio, jt. auth. see Smith, David Eugene.

Mikan. The Sheepskin. (Orig. Ser.). 220p. 1983. lib. bdg. 11.95 (ISBN 0-911906-26-6); pap. 4.95 (ISBN 0-911906-27-4). Harian Creative.

Mikasinovich, Branko, et al, eds. Introduction to Yugoslav Literature. (International Studies & Translations Ser.). lib. bdg. 10.95 o.p. (ISBN 0-8057-3193-8, Twayne). G K Hall.

Mike, Valerie & Stanley, Kenneth E. Statistics in Medical Research: Methods & Issues With Applications in Cancer Research. (Probability & Mathematics Statistics Ser.). 576p. 1983. 34.95x (ISBN 0-471-86911-2, Pub. by Wiley-Interscience). Wiley.

Mikes. Any Souvenirs? 1971. 6.95 (ISBN 0-87645-058-3). Gambit.

Mikes, George. Boomerang. 5.75 o.s.i. (ISBN 0-233-96041-4). Transatlantic.

--Charlie: A Novel. 1977. 10.00 o.p. (ISBN 0-233-96842-3). Transatlantic.

--How to Be an Alien: England. (Illus.). 1946. 9.75 o.s.i. (ISBN 0-233-95500-3). Transatlantic.

--How to Run a Stately Home. (Illus.). 125p. 1972. 6.95 o.s.i. (ISBN 0-233-95848-7). Transatlantic.

--Shakespeare & Myself. 4.50 o.s.i. (ISBN 0-685-37611-7). Transatlantic.

--Switzerland for Beginners. (Illus.). 1975. 12.00 o.s.i. (ISBN 0-233-96621-8). Transatlantic.

Mikesell, John, jt. ed. see McCaffery, Jerry.

Mikesell, Raymond F. Foreign Investment in Mining Projects: Case Studies of Recent Experiences. LC 82-14113. 320p. 1983. text ed. 30.00 (ISBN 0-89946-170-0). Oelgeschlager.

Mikesell, Raymond F. & Kilmarx, Robert A. The Economics of Foreign Aid & Self-Sustaining Development. 106p. 1983. lib. bdg. 17.50x (ISBN 0-86531-577-9). Westview.

Mikesh, Robert C. Ballon Bomb Attacks on North America: Japan's World War II Assaults. 86p. 1983. 8.95 (ISBN 0-8168-3950-6). Aero.

Mikhail, E. H. English Drama, Nineteen Hundred-Nineteen Fifty: A Guide to Information Sources. LC 74-11523. (American Literature, English Literature & World Literatures in English Information Guide Ser.: Vol. 11). 1977. 42.00x (ISBN 0-8103-1216-6). Gale.

--Lady Gregory: An Annotated Bibliography of Criticism. LC 80-51874. 258p. 1981. 20.00 (ISBN 0-686-97510-3). Whitston Pub.

Mikhail, E. H., ed. Brendan Behan: Interviews & Recollections. LC 81-8042. (Interviews & Recollections Ser.). 1982. 27.50x ea.; Vol. 1, 172 Pgs. (ISBN 0-389-20221-5); Vol. 2, 206 Pgs. (ISBN 0-389-20222-3). B&N Imports.

Mikhail, Edward M. Observations & Least Squares. LC 81-43906. 510p. 1982. pap. text ed. 17.50 (ISBN 0-8191-2397-8). U Pr of Amer.

Mikhailov, B. M. & Bubnov, Yu N. Organoboron Compounds in Organic Synthesis. (Soviet Scientific Reviews Supplement Ser.). Date not set. price not set (ISBN 3-7186-0113-3). Harwood Academic.

Mikhailov, F. T. The Riddle of the Self. LC 80-17541. 1981. 4.50 (ISBN 0-7178-0569-7). Intl Pub Co.

Mikhailov, G. K., jt. ed. see Koiter, W. T.

Mikhlin & Smolitskii. Approximate Methods for Solution of Differential & Integral Equations. 1967. 20.00 (ISBN 0-444-00022-4). Elsevier.

Mikkelson, Shirley J. The Poet's Dilemma. 1982. pap. cancelled (ISBN 0-686-35869-4). Quill Bks.

--A Time to Be Free. (Illus.). 1982. pap. 12.95 (ISBN 0-943536-02-2). Quill Bks.

Mikkelson, Shirley J., ed. Wild Prairie Roses: A Collection of Verse by North Dakotans. 104p. 1980. pap. 6.95 (ISBN 0-943536-00-6). Quill Bks.

Miklos, Mary O. Mathematical Ideas. LC 80-5871. 344p. 1980. pap. text ed. 12.50 (ISBN 0-8191-1099-X). U Pr of Amer.

--Preparation for Criterion-Referenced Tests: A Brief Review of Mathematical Competencies for Teachers of Middle Grades. 110p. (Orig.). 1981. pap. text ed. 8.00 (ISBN 0-8191-1545-2). U Pr of Amer.

--Preparation for Criterion Referenced Tests: A Brief Review of Scientific Competencies for Teachers of Middle Grades. (Illus.). 246p. (Orig.). 1982. pap. text ed. 10.75 (ISBN 0-8191-2242-4). U Pr of Amer.

--Preparation for Criterion-Referenced Tests: A Brief Review of Mathamatical Competencies for Teachers of Early Childhood. LC 80-5430. 88p. 1980. pap. text ed. 6.75 (ISBN 0-8191-1092-2). U Pr of Amer.

--Preparation for Criterion-Referenced Tests: A Brief View of Scientific Competencies for Teachers of Early Childhood. 157p. 1980. pap. text ed. 9.25 (ISBN 0-8191-1397-2). U Pr of Amer.

Miklos, Stephen J. How to Prepare for the New LSAT. 488p. Date not set. 8.95 (ISBN 0-15-600032-6). HarBraceJ. Postponed.

Miklowitz, Gloria. Roller Skating Nineteen Seventy-Nine. 1979. pap. 1.95 (ISBN 0-448-17064-7, G&D). Putnam Pub Group.

--Steve Cauthen. (Orig.). (gr. 4 up). 1979. pap. 1.50 o.p. (ISBN 0-448-16189-3, G&D). Putnam Pub Group.

Miklowitz, Gloria D. Barefoot Boy. (Beginning-to-Read Bks). (Illus.). (gr. 1-3). 1964. 2.50 o.s.i. (ISBN 0-695-80680-7, Dist. by Caroline Hse); PLB 3.39 (ISBN 0-695-40680-9); pap. 1.95 (ISBN 0-695-30680-4). Follett.

--Close to the Edge. LC 82-72817. 160p. (YA) (gr. 7 up). 1983. 11.95 (ISBN 0-440-00990-1). Delacorte.

--Earthquake! LC 76-57786. (Illus.). 96p. (gr. 4-6). 1977. 7.29 o.p. (ISBN 0-671-32826-3). Messner.

--Harry S. Truman. LC 74-83008. (Beginning Biographies Ser.). 64p. (gr. 1-3). 1975. PLB 5.99 o.p. (ISBN 0-399-60918-0). Putnam Pub Group.

--The Love Bombers. (YA) (gr. 9 up). 1982. pap. 2.25 (ISBN 0-440-94999-8, LFL). Dell.

--The Marshmalow Caper. (See & Read Storybooks). (Illus.). (gr. 1-3). 1971. PLB 4.49 o.p. (ISBN 0-399-60449-9). Putnam Pub Group.

--Sad Song, Happy Song. new ed. (Illus.). 32p. (gr. 1-4). 1973. PLB 4.49 o.p. (ISBN 0-399-60791-9). Putnam Pub Group.

--Turning Off. new ed. 128p. (gr. 6 up). 1973. 6.95 o.p. (ISBN 0-399-20260-9). Putnam Pub Group.

Miklowitz, J. The Theory of Elastic Waves & Waveguides. (North-Holland Ser. in Applied Mathematics & Mechanics: Vol. 22). 1978. 95.75 (ISBN 0-7204-0551-3, North-Holland). Elsevier.

Miklowitz, Julius, jt. auth. see Miklowitz Symposium at Northwestern Univ. Sept.

Miklowitz Symposium at Northwestern Univ. Sept. & Miklowitz, Julius. Modern Problems in Elastic Wave Propagation. 561p. 1978. 68.95 (ISBN 0-471-04696-5, Pub. by Wiley-Interscience). Wiley.

Mikola, P., jt. ed. see Romberger, J. A.

Miksche, Ferdinand O. The Failure of Atomic Strategy & a New Proposal for the Defence of the West. LC 76-27852. 1976. Repr. of 1959 ed. lib. bdg. 18.00x (ISBN 0-8371-9023-1, MIFA). Greenwood.

Mikulsky, K. I., ed. CMEA: International Significance of Socialist Integration. 376p. 1982. pap. 6.00 (ISBN 0-8285-2272-3, Pub. by Progress Pubs USSR). Imported Pubns.

Mikusinski, Jan. Operational Calculus, Vol. 1. 2nd ed. (International Series in Pure & Applied Mathematics: Vol. 109). (Illus.). 320p. 1982. 27.00 (ISBN 0-08-025071-8). Pergamon.

Mikusinskii, J. Operational Calculus. 1960. 49.00 (ISBN 0-08-006367-5). Pergamon.

Milady Barber Textbook Committee. Standard Textbook of Professional Barber Styling. 1977. text ed. 17.85 (ISBN 0-87350-116-0). Milady.

Milady Editors. Tecnicas Modernas Del Peinado. (Span.). 1977. 15.85 (ISBN 0-87350-076-8). Milady.

--Total Look in Interior Design. 1969. 5.45 (ISBN 0-87350-252-3). Milady.

Milady Staff. Cosmetologist's State Board Exam Review in Spanish & English. Rivas, Daniel, tr. 1981. 15.10 (ISBN 0-87350-122-5). Milady.

Milady Textbook Committee, ed. Supplement to the Van Dean Manual. (Illus.). 1976. 3.95 (ISBN 0-87350-071-7). Milady.

Milam, Edward E., jt. auth. see Crumbley, D. L.

Milam, Mary. An Axiomatic Theory of Adolescence. 1977. pap. text ed. 9.50 o.p. (ISBN 0-8191-0347-0). U Pr of Amer.

Milan, Michael A., jt. auth. see Ayllon, Teodoro.

Milan, Virginia E., jt. auth. see Meredith, Howard.

Milani, Felix. The Convict. Barrows, Anita, tr. from Fr. LC 77-10288. 1978. 10.00 o.p. (ISBN 0-312-16948-5). St Martin.

Milanich, Jerald T., ed. see Sears, William H.

Milavec, Aaron. To Empower as Jesus Did: Acquiring Spiritual Power through Apprenticeship. LC 82-6466. (Toronto Studies in Theology: Vol. 9). 456p. 1982. 49.95x (ISBN 0-88946-966-0). E Mellen.

Milavsky, J. Ronald, et al. Television & Aggression: Results of a Panel Study. (Quantitative Studies in Social Relations). 493p. 1982. 37.50 (ISBN 0-12-495980-6). Acad Pr.

Milazzo, G. Topics in Bioelectrochemistry & Bioenergetics, Vol. 5. 350p. 1983. 90.00x (ISBN 0-471-10531-7, Pub. by Wiley-Interscience). Wiley.

Milazzo, G., ed. Energetics & Technology of Biological Elimination of Wastes. (Studies in Enviornmental Science: Vol. 9). 1981. 59.75 (ISBN 0-444-41900-4). Elsevier.

--Topics in Bioelectrochemistry & Bioenergetics, 3 vols. LC 76-18231. (Topics in Bioelectrochemistry & Bioenergetics Ser.). Vol. 1, 1978. 65.00 o.p. (ISBN 0-471-01356-0, Pub. by Wiley-Interscience); Vol. 2, 1978. 61.95 (ISBN 0-471-99533-9); Vol. 3, 1980. 115.00 o.s.i. (ISBN 0-471-99744-7, Pub. by Wiley-Interscience). Wiley.

Milazzo, Guilio, et al. Tables of Standard Electrode Potentials. LC 77-8111. 1977. 96.95 (ISBN 0-471-99534-7, Pub. by Wiley-Interscience). Wiley.

Milband, Ralph & Saville, John, eds. The Socialist Register 1981. 1981. pap. 6.50 (ISBN 0-85345-613-5, PB6135, Pub. by Merlin England). Monthly Rev.

Milbauer, Barbara & Obrentz, Bert. The Law Giveth: Legal Aspects of the Abortion Controversy. LC 82-45184. 320p. 1983. 12.95 (ISBN 0-689-11312-9). Atheneum.

Milberg, Aaron S. & Shain, Henry. How to Do Your Own Bankruptcy. 1978. pap. 5.95 o.p. (ISBN 0-07-041912-4, SP). McGraw.

Milbrath, Lester W. & Goel, M. I. Political Participation: How & Why Do People Get Involved in Politics? (Illus.). 236p. 1982. pap. text ed. 10.75 (ISBN 0-8191-2647-0). U Pr of Amer.

Milburn, Ellen. Wings of Darkness. (Inflation Fighter Ser.). 192p. 1982. pap. cancelled o.s.i. (ISBN 0-8439-1121-2, Leisure Bks). Nordon Pubns.

Milburn, Frank. The Interloper. LC 82-45837. 208p. 1983. 13.95 (ISBN 0-385-19008-5). Doubleday.

Milburn, George. Catalogue. 1977. pap. 1.95 o.p. (ISBN 0-380-01650-8, 33084, Bard). Avon.

Milburn, Josephine & Doyle, William, eds. New England Political Parties. 256p. 1983. 27.00 (ISBN 0-87073-626-4); pap. 10.95 (ISBN 0-87073-627-2). Schenkman.

Milburn, Mark. Secrets of South Sahara. 1979. 7.95 o.p. (ISBN 0-533-03302-0). Vantage.

Milby, Robert V. Plastics Technology. (Illus.). 576p. 1973. text ed. 26.95x (ISBN 0-07-041918-3, G); instr's manual 3.50 (ISBN 0-07-041919-1). McGraw.

MILC-the Center for Research Libraries, ed. Rarely Held Scientific Serials in the Midwest Inter-Library Center. 197p. (Orig.). 1963. pap. write for info o.p. (ISBN 0-932486-01-0). Ctr Research Lib.

Milch, Jerome, jt. auth. see Feldman, Elliot J.

Milch, Robert. Electra Notes. Bd. with Medea Notes. (Orig.). pap. 2.50 (ISBN 0-8220-0424-0). Cliffs.

--Oedipus the King, Oedipus at Colonus, Antigone: Notes. (Orig.). 1965. pap. 2.50 (ISBN 0-8220-0708-8). Cliffs.

Milch, Robert J. Faust, Pts. 1 & 2, Notes. (Orig.). 1965. pap. 2.75 (ISBN 0-8220-0479-8). Cliffs.

Mildren, K. W., ed. Use of Engineering Literature. 608p. 1976. 74.95 (ISBN 0-408-70714-3). Butterworth.

Mileaf, Harry. Servicing Record Changers. LC 56-7939. (Orig.). 1956. 8.95 o.p. (ISBN 0-8306-6059-3); pap. 5.95 o.p. (ISBN 0-8306-5059-8, 59). TAB Bks.

Mileck, Joseph. Hermann Hesse: Life & Art. LC 76-48020. 1978. 17.95 (ISBN 0-520-03351-5); pap. 5.95 (ISBN 0-520-04152-6). U of Cal Pr.

Mileham, James W. The Conspiracy Novel: Structure & Metaphor in Balzac's Comedie Humaine. LC 81-68004. (French Forum Monographs: No. 31). 142p. (Orig.). 1982. pap. 10.00x (ISBN 0-917058-32-1). French Forum.

Mileiko, S. T., jt. ed. see Kelly, A.

Milenky, Edward S. Argentina's Foreign Policies. LC 77-90536. 1978. lib. bdg. 32.50 o.p. (ISBN 0-89158-427-7). Westview.

Milepost Staff. The Milepost: All-the-North Travel Guide. 34th ed. (Illus.). 500p. 1982. pap. 9.95 o.p. (ISBN 0-88240-162-9). Alaska Northwest.

Miler, I. The Immunity of the Foetus & Newborn Infant. 1983. 41.50 (ISBN 90-247-2610-7, Pub. by Martinus Nijhoff Netherlands). Kluwer Boston.

Miles. Bulbs for the Home Gardener. 9.95 (ISBN 0-448-12721-0, G&D). Putnam Pub Group.

--David Bowie Black Book. (Illus.). 128p. 1981. pap. 12.95 (ISBN 0-8256-3958-1, Quick Fox). Putnam Pub Group.

--Mersey Beat: The Beginnings of the Beatles. (Illus.). 1978. pap. 6.95 (ISBN 0-8256-3928-X, Quick Fox). Putnam Pub Group.

--Mick Jagger in His Own Words. (Illus.). 128p. (Orig.). 1983. pap. 6.95 (ISBN 0-399-41011-2). Delilah Bks.

--Pink Floyd: A Visual Documentary. rev. ed. (Illus.). 120p. 1981. pap. 12.95 (ISBN 0-8256-3948-4, Quick Fox). Putnam Pub Group.

--Pink Floyd: An Illustrated Discography. (Illus.). 64p. 1981. pap. 4.95 (ISBN 0-8256-3242-0, Quick Fox). Putnam Pub Group.

--Rolling Stones: An Illustrated Discography. (Illus.). 136p. 1981. pap. 4.95 (ISBN 0-8256-3957-3, Quick Fox). Putnam Pub Group.

Miles & Randolph. The Organization Game--Participants Manual. new ed. LC 78-25699. (Illus.). 1979. pap. text ed. 14.50x (ISBN 0-673-16131-5). Scott F.

Miles, compiled by. The Beatles in Their Own Words. 1979. pap. 5.95 (ISBN 0-8256-3925-5, Quick Fox). Putnam Pub Group.

--Bob Dylan in His Own Words. 1979. pap. 4.95 (ISBN 0-8256-3924-7, Quick Fox). Putnam Pub Group.

--David Bowie in His Own Words. (Illus.). 128p. 1981. pap. 5.95 (ISBN 0-8256-3952-2, Quick Fox). Putnam Pub Group.

--John Lennon in His Own Words. (Illus.). 128p. 1981. pap. 5.95 (ISBN 0-8256-3953-0, Quick Fox). Putnam Pub Group.

Miles, A., jt. ed. see Chandler, M.

Miles, A. A., jt. ed. see Wilson, Graham S.

Miles, A. C., tr. see Wittgenstein, Ludwig.

Miles, A. J., ed. see Chandler.

Miles, Alfred H., ed. The Tennyson Reciter. 224p. 1982. Repr. of 1901 ed. lib. bdg. 35.00 (ISBN 0-89760-569-1). Telegraph Bks.

Miles, Barbara, jt. auth. see Foxe, Sonja.

Miles, Beryl. Spirit of Mexico. (Illus.). 1961. 8.95 o.p. (ISBN 0-7195-0921-1). Transatlantic.

Miles, Betty. Just the Beginning. LC 75-28545. 144p. (gr. 4-7). 1976. 5.95 o.p. (ISBN 0-394-83226-4); PLB 6.99 (ISBN 0-394-93226-9). Knopf.

--Maudie & Me & the Dirty Book. LC 79-19783. 160p. (gr. 4-6). 1980. 7.95 o.p. (ISBN 0-394-84343-6); PLB 7.99 (ISBN 0-394-94343-0). Knopf.

--The Real Me. (gr. 4-7). 1975. pap. 1.95 (ISBN 0-380-00347-3, 63057-5, Camelot). Avon.

Miles, C. W. & Seabrooke, W. Recreational Land Management. 1977. 22.00x (ISBN 0-419-11060-7, Pub. by E & FN Spon). Methuen Inc.

Miles, Cassian. The Masses of Advent. 48p. (Orig.). 1979. pap. 0.95 o.p. (ISBN 0-912228-59-8). St Anthony Mess Pr.

--The Masses of Lent. 48p. (Orig.). 1980. pap. 0.95 o.p. (ISBN 0-912228-67-9). St Anthony Mess Pr.

Miles, Clement A. Christmas Customs & Traditions: Their History & Significance. LC 76-9183. Orig. Title: Christmas in Ritual & Tradition. (Illus.). 1976. pap. 6.00 (ISBN 0-486-23354-5). Dover.

--Christmas in Ritual & Tradition, Christian & Pagan. LC 68-54858. 1968. Repr. of 1912 ed. 37.00x (ISBN 0-8103-3354-6). Gale.

Miles, Delos. Church Growth - A Mighty River. LC 80-67352. 1981. pap. 5.95 (ISBN 0-8054-6227-9). Broadman.

Miles, Dick. Sports Illustrated Table Tennis. LC 74-5313. 1974. 5.95i o.p. (ISBN 0-397-01024-9, LP-90); pap. 2.95i (ISBN 0-397-01036-2). Har-Row.

Miles, Donald. Broadcast News Handbook. LC 75-2550. 1975. pap. 9.95 o.p. (ISBN 0-672-21183-1); tchr's manual 2.75 o.p. (ISBN 0-672-21198-X). Bobbs.

Miles, Dorien K. Terror of Heartbreak House. (YA) 1979. 6.95 (ISBN 0-686-52555-8, Avalon). Bouregy.

Miles, Edward & Gibbs, Stephen. The Management of Marine Regions: The North Pacific. (Illus.). 700p. 1982. 38.50x (ISBN 0-520-04458-4); after 6-30-83 50.00x (ISBN 0-686-83120-9). U of Cal Pr.

Miles, Edward L., ed. see Law of the Sea Institute, 10th Annual Conference.

Miles, Edwin A. Jacksonian Democracy in Mississippi. LC 78-107415. (American Scene Ser). 1970. Repr. of 1960 ed. lib. bdg. 29.50 (ISBN 0-306-71884-7). Da Capo.

Miles, Edwin A., jt. ed. see Remini, Robert V.

Miles, Elaine. Many Hands: Making a Communal Quilt. (Illus.). 75p. (Orig.). 1982. 6.95 (ISBN 0-936810-02-5). R&E Miles.

Miles, Emily L. The Evolution of Emily. LC 81-71055. (Illus.). 1981. pap. 10.95 (ISBN 0-939116-06-5). Creative Comm.

Miles, Eustace. Life After Life: The Theory of Reincarnation. 180p. 8.50 (ISBN 0-686-38223-4). Sun Bks.

Miles, Gary B. Virgil's Georgics: A New Interpretation. LC 78-64460. 1980. 25.00x (ISBN 0-520-03789-8). U of Cal Pr.

Miles, H. Artificial Satellite Observing & Its Applications. 1974. 21.95 (ISBN 0-444-19544-0). Elsevier.

Miles, Herbert J. Sexual Understanding Before Marriage. 224p. 1972. pap. 3.95 (ISBN 0-310-29212-3). Zondervan.

Miles International Symposium, 12th. Polypeptide Hormones: Proceedings. Beers, Roland F. & Bassett, Edward, eds. 544p. 1980. text ed. 66.00 (ISBN 0-89004-462-7). Raven.

Miles, J. Vegetation Dynamics. LC 78-13070. (Outline Studies in Ecology). 80p. 1979. pap. 6.50x (ISBN 0-412-15530-3, Pub. by Chapman & Hall England). Methuen Inc.

Miles, J. Todd. N Series Ford Tractors. 1981. 55.00 (ISBN 0-686-30648-1). F F Farmer.

--A Vegetable Growers Primer. 2nd ed. 58p. 1980. 11.95x (ISBN 0-9605070-0-0); soft cover 6.95x (ISBN 0-9605070-1-9). F F Farmer.

Miles, James W., jt. ed. see Larid, Marshall.

Miles, John G., Jr., et al. The Law Officer's Pocket Manual: 1982-83 Edition. 1982. pap. 6.50 (ISBN 0-87179-395-4). BNA.

Miles, John W. Integral Transforms in Applied Mathematics. LC 70-172834. (Illus.). 1971. text ed. 15.95x (ISBN 0-521-08374-5). Cambridge U Pr.

Miles, John W., jt. auth. see Kagan, A. Robert.

Miles, Johnnie H., jt. auth. see Hohenshil, Thomas H.

Miles, Josephine. Collected Poems, Nineteen Thirty to Nineteen Eighty-Three. LC 82-11014. 288p. 1983. 17.50 (ISBN 0-252-01017-5). U of Ill Pr.

--The Primary Language of Poetry in the Sixteen Forties. LC 78-11614. (Univ. of California Publications in English: Vol. 19, No. 1). (Illus.). 160p. 1979. Repr. of 1948 ed. lib. bdg. 18.25x (ISBN 0-313-20661-9, MIPP). Greenwood.

--To All Appearances: Poems New & Selected. LC 74-9000. 160p. 1974. pap. 4.95 o.p. (ISBN 0-252-00443-4). U of Ill Pr.

Miles, Joyce C. House Names Around the World. LC 72-12695. 135p. 1973. 18.00x (ISBN 0-8103-2009-6). Gale.

Miles, Keith & Butler, David. Marco Polo. 1982. pap. 3.50 (ISBN 0-440-15754-4). Dell.

Miles, L., jt. auth. see Craft, M.

Miles, L. W. Chapter Seven - The Production & Properties of Printing Pastes. 75.00x (ISBN 0-686-98196-0, Pub. by Soc Dyers & Colour); pap. 50.00x (ISBN 0-686-98197-9). State Mutual Bk.

Miles, L. W., ed. Textile Printing. 293p. 1982. 69.00x (ISBN 0-901956-33-3, Pub. by Soc Dyers & Colour); pap. 45.00x (ISBN 0-686-92033-3). State Mutual Bk.

Miles, Laughton E. & Dement, William C. Sleep & Aging. (Reprint of Sleep Journal Ser.: Vol. 3, No. 2). 108p. 1980. text ed. 22.00 (ISBN 0-89004-651-4). Raven.

Miles, Lawrence D. Techniques of Value Analysis & Engineering. 2nd ed. LC 74-157484. (Illus.). 320p. 1972. 39.95 (ISBN 0-07-041926-4, P&RB). McGraw.

Miles, Leland. John Colet & the Platonic Tradition. LC 60-16716. xix, 258p. 1961. 17.00x (ISBN 0-87548-005-5); pap. 7.50x (ISBN 0-87548-006-3). Open Court.

Miles, Marc A., jt. auth. see Laffer, Arthur B.

Miles, Marshall. All Fifty-Two Cards: How to Reconstruct the Concealed Hands at the Bridge Table. (Illus.). 176p. 1982. pap. 6.95 (ISBN 0-682-49897-1, Banner). Exposition.

Miles, Martin J. Real Estate Investor's Complete Handbook. LC 82-351. 572p. 1982. 49.95 (ISBN 0-13-763086-7, Busn). P-H.

Miles, Mary L. Devotions for Pre-Teens, No. 1-2. (Pre-Teen Books Ser.). Orig. Title: Quiet Moments with God I, II. (gr. 1-5). 1970. pap. 2.95 ea. No. 1 (ISBN 0-8024-3221-2). No. 2 (ISBN 0-8024-3222-0). Moody.

Miles, Matthew B. Learning to Work in Groups. 2nd ed. 360p. 1981. pap. text ed. 13.95x (ISBN 0-8077-2586-2). Tchrs Coll.

Miles, Miska. Jenny's Coat. (Skylark Ser.). 48p. 1982. pap. 1.75 (ISBN 0-553-15125-8, Skylark). Bantam.

--This Little Pig. LC 79-20264. (Illus.). 32p. (ps-3). 1980. 7.25 (ISBN 0-525-41145-3, 0704-210, Unicorn Bk). Dutton.

--Tree House Town. (Illus.). 32p. (gr. 1-5). 1974. 4.50 o.p. (ISBN 0-316-56971-2, Pub. by Atlantic Monthly Pr). Little.

Miles, Nancy R., jt. auth. see Chaney, Clara M.

Miles, Nelson A. Personal Recollections & Observations of General Nelson A. Miles. rev. ed. LC 68-23812. (American Scene Ser). (Illus.). Repr. of 1896 ed. lib. bdg. 69.50 (ISBN 0-306-71020-X). Da Capo.

Miles, P. A., jt. ed. see Townes, C. H.

Miles, Patricia. The Gods in Winter. (gr. 4-7). 1978. 10.50 (ISBN 0-525-30748-6). Dutton.

Miles, Patrick, tr. see Chekhov, Anton.

Miles, Philip G., jt. ed. see Schwalb, Marvin N.

Miles, R. S. & Alt, M. B. The Design of Educational Exhibits. (Illus.). 224p. 1982. text ed. 29.95x (ISBN 0-04-069002-4). Allen Unwin.

Miles, Raymond. How to Price a Business. LC 81-13270. 133p. 1982. 99.50 (ISBN 0-87624-211-5). Inst Busn Plan.

Miles, Raymond E. Theories of Management: Implications for Organizational Behavior & Development. Davis, Keith, ed. (Management Ser.). (Illus.). 256p. 1975. text ed. 23.95 (ISBN 0-07-041927-2, C). McGraw.

Miles, Raymond E. & Snow, Charles C. Organizational Strategy: Structure & Process. (Management Ser.). (Illus.). 1978. text ed. 23.95 (ISBN 0-07-041932-9, C). McGraw.

Miles, Robert. Racism & Migrant Labour: A Critical Text. 206p. (Orig.). 1983. pap. 9.95 (ISBN 0-7100-9212-1). Routledge & Kegan.

Miles, Robert & Bertonasco, Marc F. Prose Style for the Modern Writer. 1977. pap. text ed. 11.95 (ISBN 0-13-731521-X). P-H.

Miles, Robert H. Macro Organizational Behavior. 1980. text ed. 25.50x (ISBN 0-673-15599-4). Scott F.

--Readings in Macro Organizational Behavior. 1980. pap. text ed. 17.95x (ISBN 0-673-16100-5). Scott F.

Miles, Rosalind. The Fiction of Sex: Themes & Functions of Sex Difference in the Modern Novel. (Critical Studies). 208p. 1974. 18.50x o.p. (ISBN 0-06-494822-6). B&N Imports.

Miles, Samuel A., ed. Learning About Alcohol: A Resource Book for Teachers. 5.00 o.p. (ISBN 0-686-92228-X, 4275). Hazelden.

Miles, Sylva. Shadow over Beauclaire. 192p. (YA) 1975. 6.95 (ISBN 0-685-51237-1, Avalon). Bouregy.

Miles, T. R. Dyslexia: The Pattern of Difficulties. 256p. 1982. 27.50x (ISBN 0-398-04747-2). C C Thomas.

Miles, T. R., jt. auth. see Harzem, P.

Miles, Timothy R., jt. auth. see Pavlidis, George.

Miles, Walter F., jt. auth. see Montgomery, Richard H.

Milesko-Pytel, Diana. Bicycling the Midwest. (Illus.). 1979. pap. 6.95 o.p. (ISBN 0-8092-7607-0). Contemp Bks.

Mileti, Dennis S., jt. auth. see Gillespie, David F.

Miley, Jeannie. Spread Wide the Curtain. LC 78-72526. 1979. pap. 3.25 o.p. (ISBN 0-8054-5270-2). Broadman.

Milford Conference. Social Case Work: Generic & Specific. LC 74-83097. (NASW Classics Ser). 92p. 1974. pap. text ed. 5.00 (ISBN 0-87101-069-0, CBO-069-I). Natl Assn Soc Wkrs.

Milford, Humphrey, ed. see Browning, Robert.

Milford, Nancy. Zelda. 1971. pap. 2.50 o.p. (ISBN 0-380-00784-3, 40014). Avon.

--Zelda: A Biography. LC 66-20742. (Illus.). 1970. 16.30i (ISBN 0-06-012991-3, HarpT). Har-Row.

Milford, T. R. Christian Decision in the Nuclear Age. Sherman, Franklin, ed. (Facet Bks). 64p. (Orig.). 1967. pap. 1.00 o.p. (ISBN 0-8006-3038-6, 1-3038). Fortress.

Milgate, Murray, ed. Capital & Employment. (Studies Political Economy Ser.). Date not set. price not set (ISBN 0-12-496250-5). Acad Pr.

Milgram, Abraham E., ed. Great Jewish Ideas. (Great Bks). 352p. pap. 4.97 o.p. (ISBN 0-686-95128-X). ADL.

Milgram, Gail G. Alcohol Education Materials: Annotated Bibliographies. Incl. Literature of 1950-1973. 1975. 20.00x (ISBN 0-911290-44-3); Literature of 1973-1978. 1980. 20.00x (ISBN 0-911290-06-0); Literature of 1978-1979. 1979. 10.00x (ISBN 0-911290-10-9); Literature of 1979-1980. 1981. 10.00x (ISBN 0-911290-11-7); Literature of 1980-1981. 10.00x (ISBN 0-911290-13-3). Rutgers Ctr Alcohol.

Milgram, J. I. & Sciarra, D. J. Childhood Revisited. 1974. pap. 11.95x (ISBN 0-02-381120-X). Macmillan.

Milgram, Morris. Good Neighborhood: The Challenge of Open Housing. 10.95x o.p. (ISBN 0-393-08768-9); pap. 3.95 1979 (ISBN 0-393-00904-1). Norton.

Milgram, Stanley. Obedience to Authority. 225p. 1975. pap. 4.95i (ISBN 0-06-090475-5, CN475, CN). Har-Row.

Milgrom, Felix, jt. ed. see Rose, Noel R.

Milgrom, Peter. Regulation & the Quality of Dental Care. LC 78-1922. 258p. 1978. text ed. 40.00 (ISBN 0-89443-034-3). Aspen Systems.

Milhaud, Darius. Notes Without Music. LC 72-87419. (Music Ser). (Illus.). 1970. Repr. of 1953 ed. lib. bdg. 39.50 (ISBN 0-306-71565-1). Da Capo.

Milhorat, Thomas H., jt. auth. see Hammock, M. Kathryn.

Milhous, Judith. Thomas Betterton & the Management of Lincoln's Inn Fields, 1695-1708. LC 78-21017. 304p. 1979. 22.50x (ISBN 0-8093-0906-8). S Ill U Pr.

Milhous, Judith & Polwhele, Eliz, eds. The Frolicks or the Lawyer Cheated. LC 77-3125. 1977. 14.50x (ISBN 0-8014-1030-4). Cornell U Pr.

Miliaras, E. S. Power Plants with Air-Cooled Condensing Systems. (Monographs in Modern Electrical Technology). 240p. 1974. 25.00x (ISBN 0-262-13093-9). MIT Pr.

Miliband, Ralph. Marxism & Politics. (Marxist Introductions Ser.). 1977. op 11.95 (ISBN 0-19-876059-0); pap. 5.95 (ISBN 0-19-876062-0). Oxford U Pr.

--The State in Capitalist Society: An Analysis of the Western System of Power. LC 78-93689. 1978. o.s.i 10.00x (ISBN 0-465-08197-5); pap. 7.95 (ISBN 0-465-09734-0, CN-5034). Basic.

Miliband, Ralph & Saville, John, eds. The Socialist Register 1977. 276p. 1977. pap. 5.95 (ISBN 0-686-31932-X, PB4353, Pub. by Merlin England). Monthly Rev.

--The Socialist Register 1979. 335p. 1979. pap. 5.95 (ISBN 0-85345-528-7, PB5827, Pub. by Merlin England). Monthly Rev.

Milic, Louis T., ed. see Gerlach, John & Gerlach, Lana.

Milic-Emili, jt. auth. see Sadoul.

Milidantri, Mary Ann. Hurray for Today, Level 1. 1979. pap. 8.95 (ISBN 0-8497-5601-4, WE1.). Kjos.

--Hurray for Today, Level 2. 1979. pap. 8.95 (ISBN 0-8497-5602-2, WE2). Kjos.

Milinaire, Caterine. Celebrations. (Illus.). 144p. 1981. 30.00 o.p. (ISBN 0-517-53106-2, Harmony). Crown.

Milinaire, Catherine & Troy, Carol. Cheap Chic. (Illus.). 250p. (YA) 1976. pap. 5.95 o.p. (ISBN 0-517-52368-X, Harmony). Crown.

Milinowski, Marta. Teresa Carreno "By the Grace of God". LC 76-58931. (Music Reprint Ser.). 1977. Repr. of 1940 ed. lib. bdg. 29.50 (ISBN 0-306-70870-1). Da Capo.

Milio, Nancy. The Care of Health in Communities. (Illus.). 1975. text ed. 17.95x (ISBN 0-02-381130-7). Macmillan.

--Primary Care & the Public Health: Judging Impacts, Goals, & Polices Public's. LC 81-47275. 272p. 1983. 27.95x (ISBN 0-669-04571-3). Lexington Bks.

Milisauskas, Sarunas. European Prehistory. (Studies in Archaeology Ser.). 1979. 19.50 (ISBN 0-12-497950-5). Acad Pr.

Miliutin, Nikolai A. Sotsgorod: The Problem of Building Socialist Cities. Collins, George R. & Alex, William, eds. Sprague, Arthur, tr. from Rus. LC 73-13429. (Illus.). 143p. 1974. 30.00x (ISBN 0-262-13089-0). MIT Pr.

Milivojevic, Dragan, jt. auth. see Matejic, Mateja.

Mill, Cyril R. Activities for Trainers: Fifty Useful Designs. LC 80-50465. 226p. 1980. pap. 18.00 (ISBN 0-88390-159-5). Univ Assocs.

Mill, Dorothy, ed. see Roberts, Helen H.

Mill, J. P. Respiration in Invertebrates. LC 72-90019. 1973. 26.00 (ISBN 0-312-67760-X). St Martin.

Mill, J. S. Mill on Bentham & Coleridge. Leavis, F. R., ed. LC 79-42833. 168p. 1980. 24.95 (ISBN 0-521-23330-5); pap. 7.95 (ISBN 0-521-29917-9). Cambridge U Pr.

--On Liberty. Himmelfarb, Gertrude, ed. (English Library). (Orig.). 1975. pap. 1.95 o.p. (ISBN 0-14-040028-1). Penguin.

Mill, James. History of British India, 3 vols. 2nd ed. 1972. Repr. of 1820 ed. Set. 65.00x (ISBN 0-8002-2629-1). Intl Pubns Serv.

Mill, James & Mill, John S. James & John Stuart Mill on Education. Cavenagh, F. A., ed. LC 78-27822. 1979. Repr. of 1931 ed. lib. bdg. 17.75x (ISBN 0-8371-4282-2, MIOE). Greenwood.

Mill, John S. Considerations on Representative Government. 365p. pap. 4.95 (ISBN 0-89526-942-2). Regnery-Gateway.

--Essays on England, Ireland, & the Empire. Robson, John M., ed. (Collected Works of John Stuart Mill Ser.: Vol. 6). 744p. 1982. 60.00x (ISBN 0-8020-5572-9). U of Toronto Pr.

--Essays on Philosophy & the Classics. Robson, John M., ed. LC 63-25876. (Collected Works of John Stuart Mill Ser.). 1978. 45.00x (ISBN 0-8020-2283-9). U of Toronto Pr.

--On Liberty. Rapaport, Elizabeth, ed. LC 77-26848. 1978. lib. bdg. 12.50 (ISBN 0-915144-44-1); pap. text ed. 2.95 (ISBN 0-915144-43-3). Hackett Pub.

--On Liberty. 1983. pap. 2.95 (ISBN 0-14-043207-8). Penguin.

--Principles of Political Economy, 2 Vols. Robson, J. M., ed. LC 65-68750. (Collected Works of John Stuart Mill). 1965. Set. 55.00x o.p. (ISBN 0-8020-5146-4). U of Toronto Pr.

--The Subjection of Women. Mansfield, Sue, ed. LC 76-3318. (Crofts Classics Ser.). 1980. text ed. 9.95 (ISBN 0-88295-123-8); pap. text ed. 3.75x (ISBN 0-88295-116-5). Harlan Davidson.

--Three Essays on Religion. Repr. of 1874 ed. lib. bdg. 18.00x (ISBN 0-8371-1986-3, MIER). Greenwood.

--Utilitarianism. Sher, George, ed. LC 78-74450. 1979. pap. text ed. 2.25 (ISBN 0-915144-41-7). Hackett Pub.

--Utilitarianism. Warnock, Mary, ed. Bd. with On Liberty; Essay on Bentham; Selected Writings of Jeremy Bentham & John Austin. pap. 4.95 o.p. (ISBN 0-452-00140-4, F140, Mer). NAL.

Mill, John S., jt. auth. see Bentham, Jeremy.

Mill, John S; see Bentham, Jeremy & Mill, John S.

Mill, John S., jt. auth. see Mill, James.

Mill, John S., jt. auth. see Wollstonecraft, Mary.

Mill, P. J. Comparative Neurobiology. 200p. 1982. pap. text ed. 19.95 (ISBN 0-7131-2810-0). E Arnold.

--Structure & Function of Proprioceptors in the Invertebrates. 686p. 1976. 54.50x (ISBN 0-412-12890-X, Pub. by Chapman & Hall England). Methuen Inc.

Millan, Ventura, tr. see Petzold, Paul.

Millan, Victor, jt. ed. see Morris, Michael A.

Millan, W. H., jt. auth. see Rogers, J. W.

Millar. Ciona. 128p. 1982. 39.00x (ISBN 0-85323-031-5, Pub. by Liverpool Univ England). State Mutual Bk.

Millar, jt. auth. see Dillard.

Millar, Cynthia. Bach & His World. LC 80-68211. (Great Masters Ser.). 13.00 (ISBN 0-382-06378-3). Silver.

Millar, David, jt. ed. see Abella, Irving.

Millar, James A., jt. auth. see Epley, Donald R.

Millar, Jean A. British Management German Management. text ed. 20.75x (ISBN 0-566-00289-2). Gower Pub Ltd.

Millar, Jeff & Hinds, Bill. Another Day, Another 11,647.63 Dollars. 128p. 1983. pap. 5.95 (ISBN 0-8362-2016-1). Andrews & McMeel.

Millar, John F. Rhode Island: Forgotten Leader of the Revolutioary Era. (Illus.). 64p. (Orig.). 1975. 7.95 (ISBN 0-937550-02-7); pap. 3.95 (ISBN 0-937550-03-5). Providence Journ.

Millar, Margaret. Banshee. 216p. 1983. 10.95 (ISBN 0-688-01897-1). Morrow.

--A Stranger in My Grave. LC 82-82889. 310p. 1983. pap. 5.00 (ISBN 0-930330-06-4). Intl Polygonics.

Millar, Oliver, ed. Dutch Pictures from the Royal Collection. LC 79-172996. (Illus.). 104p. 10.00x (ISBN 0-271-01109-2). Pa St U Pr.

Millar, R. H. British Ascidians. (Synopses of British Fauna: No. 1). 1970. 6.50 o.s.i. (ISBN 0-12-496650-0). Acad Pr.

Millar, Robert W. Civil Procedures of the Trial Court in Historical Perspective. LC 52-11758. 534p. 1952. 25.00 (ISBN 0-379-00150-0). Oceana.

Millar, Robert W., tr. see Garofalo, Raffaele.

Millar, Sally, et al, eds. Methods in Critical Care. LC 79-67786. (American Association of Critical Care Nurses Ser.). (Illus.). 484p. 1980. pap. 22.50 (ISBN 0-7216-1006-4). Saunders.

Millar, T. B. Australia in Peace & War. LC 78-19211. 1978. 30.00 (ISBN 0-312-06118-8). St Martin.

Millar, William R. Isaiah Twenty-Four to Twenty-Seven & the Origin of Apocalyptic. LC 76-3561. (Harvard Semetic Museum Ser.). 1976. 9.50 (ISBN 0-89130-102-X, 04-00-11). Scholars Pr Ca.

Millard, A. R., jt. ed. see Wiseman, D. J.

Millard, Anne. Egypt. (Young Archaelogist Ser.). (Illus.). (gr. 6-9). 1971. PLB 4.89 o.p. (ISBN 0-399-60148-1). Putnam Pub Group.

--The Incas. (Warwick Press Ser.). (gr. 5 up). 1980. PLB 9.90 (ISBN 0-531-09171-6, F23). Watts.

Millard, Anne & Halton, Frances. Atlas of World History. (Illustrated Atlas Ser.). (Illus.). 96p. 1982. PLB 12.90 (ISBN 0-531-09206-2). Watts.

Millard, Anne, et al. The Egyptians. LC 77-86182. (Peoples of the Past Ser.). (Illus.). 1977. PLB 12.68 (ISBN 0-382-06121-7). Silver.

Millard, B. J. Quantitative Mass Spectrometry. 1977. 38.00 (ISBN 0-471-25906-3, Wiley Heyden). Wiley.

--Stocks & Shares Simplified. 1980. 29.95 (ISBN 0-471-25907-1, Wiley Heyden). Wiley.

Millard, Clive & Crimp, Susan. Ice Sports. (Intersport Ser.). 13.00 (ISBN 0-382-06438-0). Silver.

Millard, Everett L. Freedom in a Federal World: How Future Generations Can Live in Peace & Liberty under World Law. 5th ed. LC 60-16492. 253p. 1969. 7.50 (ISBN 0-379-00450-X). Oceana.

Millard, P. Trade Associations & Professional Bodies of the United Kingdom. 5th ed. 1971. 26.40 o.p. (ISBN 0-08-016596-6). Pergamon.

Millard, W. F., jt. auth. see Barker, Eric J.

Millau, Gault. The Best of Paris. LC 82-13064. 608p. 1982. 22.95 (ISBN 0-517-54774-0); pap. 13.95 (ISBN 0-517-54775-9). Crown.

Millay, Edna St. Vincent. Collected Poems. LC 56-8756. 1956. 19.95i (ISBN 0-06-012935-2, HarpT). Har-Row.

--Collected Sonnets. LC 41-52020. 1941. 14.37i (ISBN 0-06-012940-9, HarpT). Har-Row.

Mille, Agnes De see De Mille, Agnes.

Millen, Bruce H. The Political Role of Labor in Developing Countries. LC 79-29735. x, 148p. 1980. Repr. of 1963 ed. lib. bdg. 20.75x (ISBN 0-313-22286-X, MIPO). Greenwood.

Millender, Dharathula H. Crispus Attucks: Black Leader of Colonial Patriots. (Childhood of Famous Americans Ser.). (gr. 3-8). 1983. pap. 3.95 (ISBN 0-686-95261-8). Bobbs.

Millenson, J. R. & Leslie, Julian C. Principles of Behavioral Analysis. 2nd ed. 1978. text ed. 26.95x (ISBN 0-02-381280-X). Macmillan.

Miller. Industrial Electricity. rev. ed. (gr. 9-12). 1982. text ed. 18.00 (ISBN 0-87002-368-3). Bennett IL.

--Industrial Electricity. (gr. 9-12). 1978. text ed. 17.28 o.p. (ISBN 0-87002-200-8); student guide 3.68 (ISBN 0-87002-244-X). Bennett IL.

--Irscot System: IR Structural Correlation Tables & Data Cards. 327.00 o.p. (ISBN 0-85501-080-0). Wiley.

--Legal Secretary's Complete Handbook. 3rd ed. (Illus.). 1980. 24.95 (ISBN 0-13-528562-3, Busn). P-H.

--Macroeconomics. 1983. text ed. 23.95 (ISBN 0-686-84543-9, EC56); instr's manual avail. (EC58); study guide 8.95 (ISBN 0-686-84544-7, EC58). HM.

--Servomechanisms: Devices & Fundamentals. 1977. text ed. 21.95 o.p. (ISBN 0-87909-760-4); solutions manual avail. o.p. (ISBN 0-87909-759-0). Reston.

--The Thirty-First of April. 1983. write for info. (ISBN 0-07-042190-0). McGraw.

Miller & Nicholls. The Fishes of Britain & Europe. pap. 8.95 (ISBN 0-686-42748-3, Collins Pub England). Greene.

Miller, jt. auth. see Nelson.

Miller, jt. auth. see O'Sullivan.

Miller, ed. see Barrett, Elizabeth.

Miller, et al. Exploring Careers in Industry. LC 74-14422. (gr. 7-9). 1975. text ed. 18.64 (ISBN 0-87345-108-2). McKnight.

Miller, A. Austin. Climatology. 1979. 19.95x (ISBN 0-416-31230-6). Methuen Inc.

Miller, A. G. The Biggest. (Pop-Up Bks.). (Illus.). (ps up). 1969. 4.95 o.p. (ISBN 0-394-80697-2). Random.

Miller, A. G. & Sullivan, J. V. Teaching Physical Activities to Impaired Youth: An Approach to Mainstreaming. 242p. 1982. 18.95 (ISBN 0-471-08534-0). Wiley.

Miller, A. G., adapted by. Aladdin & the Wonderful Lamp. (Pop-Up Classics: No. 7). (Illus.). (ps up). 1970. 3.95 o.p. (ISBN 0-394-81105-4). Random.

Miller, A. G., ed. Pop Corn. (Pop-up Bks.). (gr. 1 up). 1972. 3.95 o.p. (ISBN 0-394-82447-4, BYR). Random.

--Pop-up Book of Boats. (Pop-up Books Ser). (Illus.). (gr. 1 up). 1972. 5.95 o.p. (ISBN 0-394-82426-1, BYR). Random.

Miller, A. M. For Children on Wheels. 118p. 1980. 10.00x o.p. (ISBN 0-902628-49-6, Pub. by RAC). State Mutual Bk.

Miller, A. T., jt. auth. see Durand, John.

Miller, A. V., tr. see Hegel, G. W.

Miller, Aaron D. Search for Security: Saudi Arabian Oil & American Foreign Policy, 1939-1949. LC 79-18144. xviii, 320p. 1980. 19.00x o.p. (ISBN 0-8078-1415-6). U of NC Pr.

Miller, Abraham H. Terrorism & Hostage Negotiations. (Special Studies in National & International Terrrorism). 134p. 1981. lib. bdg. 19.00 (ISBN 0-89158-856-6); pap. text ed. 10.00 (ISBN 0-86531-238-9). Westview.

Miller, Abraham H., ed. Terrorism, the Media, & the Law. 234p. 1982. lib. bdg. 25.00 (ISBN 0-941320-04-9); pap. 9.50. Transnatl Pubs.

Miller, Agnes P. Sand Design for Aquariums and Terrariums. (Illus.). 1975. pap. 0.50 o.p. (ISBN 0-87666-625-X, P-901). TFH Pubns.

Miller, Alan. BASIC Programs for Scientists & Engineers. LC 81-84003. 1981. pap. 15.95 (ISBN 0-89588-073-3, B240). Sybex.

Miller, Alan C., et al. The Disposable Woman. Ashton, Sylvia, ed. LC 77-77865. 1977. 12.95 (ISBN 0-87949-077-2). Ashley Bks.

Miller, Alan R. The Best of CP-M Software. 250p. 1983. pap. 11.95 (ISBN 0-89588-100-4). Sybex.

--Eighty-Eighty, Eighty Assembly Language: Techniques for Improved Programming. LC 80-21492. 318p. 1981. pap. text ed. 10.95 (ISBN 0-471-08124-8). Wiley.

--Mastering CP-M. LC 81-51133. 1982. pap. 15.95 (ISBN 0-89588-068-7, C302). Sybex.

Miller, Alan S., jt. auth. see Stoel, Thomas B., Jr.

Miller, Albert & Anthes, Richard A. Meteorology. 4th ed. (Physics & Physical Science Ser.). 176p. 1980. pap. text ed. 9.95 (ISBN 0-675-08181-5). Merrill.

Miller, Albert & Thompson, Jack. Elements of Meteorology. 3rd ed. 1979. text ed. 23.95 (ISBN 0-675-08293-5). Merrill.

Miller, Albert & Thompson, Jack C. Elements of Meteorology. 4th ed. 448p. 1983. text ed. 23.95 (ISBN 0-675-20005-9). Additional supplements may be obtained from publisher. Merrill.

Miller, Albert J. Lymphatics of the Heart. (Illus.). 400p. 1982. text ed. 50.50 (ISBN 0-89004-604-2). Raven.

Miller, Albert J. & Acri, Michael J. Death: A Bibliographical Guide. LC 77-1205. 1977. 21.00 o.p. (ISBN 0-8108-1025-5). Scarecrow.

Miller, Alden D., et al. A Theory of Social Reform: Correctional Change Processes in Two States. LC 77-23094. (CCJ Ser. on Massachusetts Youth Correctional Reform). 312p. 1977. prof ref 20.00x (ISBN 0-88410-786-8). Ballinger Pub.

Miller, Alfred E. Options for Health & Health Caring of Post Clinical Medicine: The Coming of Post-Clinical Medicine. LC 80-27755. (Health, Medicine, & Society Ser.). 504p. 1981. 29.50 o.p. (ISBN 0-471-60409-7, Pub. by Wiley-Interscience). Wiley.

Miller, Alice. For Your Own Good: Hidden Cruelty in Childrearing & the Roots of Violence. Hannum, Hildegarde & Hannum, Hunter, trs. from German. 1983. 16.50 (ISBN 0-374-15750-2). FS&G.

--Prisoners of Childhood. LC 80-50535. 1981. 11.95 (ISBN 0-465-06347-0). Basic.

Miller, Alice P. The Mouse Family's Blueberry Pie. LC 81-2204. (Illus.). 32p. (ps-3). 1982. 6.75 (ISBN 0-686-98415-3). Dandelion Pr.

Miller, Amy B. Shaker Herbs. (Illus.). 1977. 12.95 o.p. (ISBN 0-517-52494-5, C N Potter Bks). Crown.

Miller, Amy B. & Fuller, Persis. The Best of Shaker Cooking. (Illus.). 480p. 1976. pap. 12.95 (ISBN 0-02-009810-3, Collier). Macmillan.

Miller, Anita, ed. see Equal Rights Amendment Project.

Miller, Ann F., ed. College in Dispersion: Women at Bryn Mawr, 1896-1975. LC 76-2735. (Special Studies in Higher Education Ser). 1976. 25.50 o.p. (ISBN 0-89158-040-9). Westview.

Miller, Anne. Finding Career Alternatives for Teacher's Program. 1982. cassettes & wkbk. 49.95. Impact VA.

Miller, Arnold I. Microbiological Laboratory Techniques. 352p. 1976. pap. text ed. 15.95x (ISBN 0-669-98384-5). Heath.

Miller, Arthur. Crucible. 1976. pap. 2.50 (ISBN 0-14-048138-9). Penguin.

--Death of a Salesman. 1976. pap. 2.95 (ISBN 0-14-048134-6). Penguin.

Miller, Arthur see Laurel Editions Editors.

Miller, Arthur, jt. auth. see Mattson, Ralph.

Miller, Arthur, jt. auth. see Miller, Warren.

Miller, Arthur see Moon, Samuel.

Miller, Arthur C., jt. auth. see Balshofer, Fred J.

Miller, Arthur C., jt. auth. see Burch, Buford H.

Miller, Arthur S. The Modern Corporate State: Private Governments & the American Constitution. LC 75-35350. (Contributions in American Studies: No. 23). 320p. 1976. lib. bdg. 29.95 (ISBN 0-8371-8589-0, MCS/); pap. 6.95 (ISBN 0-313-20159-5). Greenwood.

--Social Change & Fundamental Law: America's Evolving Constitution. LC 78-66716. (Contributions in American Studies: No. 41). 1979. lib. bdg. 29.95 (ISBN 0-313-20618-X, MSO/). Greenwood.

--The Supreme Court: Myth & Reality. LC 77-91106. (Contributions in American Studies: No. 38). 1978. lib. bdg. 29.95x (ISBN 0-313-20046-7, MSC/). Greenwood.

Miller, Arthur S., jt. auth. see Pullon, Peter A.

Miller, Arthur S., jt. auth. see Robinson, Hamilton B. G.

Miller, Augustus T., jt. auth. see Morehouse, Laurence E.

Miller, B. F., et al. Investigating Your Health. new ed. LC 74-111257. (Illus.). 564p. 1974. text ed. 18.84 (ISBN 0-395-17078-8, 2-37394). HM.

Miller, Barbara & Conn, Charles P. El Milagro de Kathy. 144p. Date not set. 2.25 (ISBN 0-88113-170-9). Edit Betania.

Miller, Barbara & Miller, Kathy. We're Gonna Win! (Illus.). 192p. 1983. 9.95 (ISBN 0-8007-1340-0). Revell.

Miller, Barbara, jt. auth. see Conn, Charles P.

Miller, Barbara L., jt. auth. see Potocki, Patricia A.

Miller, Benjamin F. & Keane, Claire B. Encyclopedia & Dictionary of Medicine & Nursing. LC 73-103569. (Illus.). 1972. text ed. 21.00 o.p. (ISBN 0-7216-6357-5); student ed. 18.95 o.p. (ISBN 0-7216-6358-3). Saunders.

Miller, Benjamin F., et al. Freedom from Heart Attacks. 1972. 7.95 o.p. (ISBN 0-671-21319-9); pap. 4.95 o.p. (ISBN 0-671-21759-3). S&S.

--Masculinity & Femininity. LC 75-134861. (Illus.). 120p. (gr. 7 up). 1971. pap. text ed. 4.23 o.p. (ISBN 0-395-03243-1, 2-37390); instructor's manual 1.17 o.p. (ISBN 0-395-11210-9). HM.

Miller, Bernard S. Humanities Approach to the Modern Secondary School Curriculum. 1972. 14.95x o.p. (ISBN 0-87628-108-0). Ctr Appl Res.

Miller, Besse M., ed. Private Secretary's Encyclopedic Dictionary. 2nd ed. 1978. 19.95 (ISBN 0-13-711085-5, Busn). P-H.

Miller, Beth, ed Women in Hispanic Literature: Icons & Fallen Idols. LC 81-14663. 480p. 1983. text ed. 27.00x (ISBN 0-520-04291-3); pap. text ed. 9.95 (ISBN 0-520-04367-7). U of Cal Pr.

Miller, Beulah. The Fires of Heaven. 1975. pap. 1.75 o.p. (ISBN 0-451-06746-0, E6746, Sig). NAL.

Miller, Bill. Alley Strewn Phrases. 44p. (Orig.). 1983. pap. 3.00 (ISBN 0-940584-04-2). Gull Bks.

Miller, Bob. Rumples & the Bugs. LC 82-14577. (Illus.). (gr. k-2). 1982. PLB 9.00g (ISBN 0-516-03636-X); pap. 2.95 (ISBN 0-516-43636-8). Childrens.

--Rumples' Supper-Time Problem. LC 82-9522. (Illus.). (gr. k-2). 1982. PLB 9.00g (ISBN 0-516-03637-8); pap. 2.95 (ISBN 0-516-43637-6). Childrens.

Miller, Boulton B. Computers & Data Processing. Woltering, Denise M. & Oberthaler, James V., eds. (Illus.). 335p. 1982. 12.95 (ISBN 0-915234-06-8); pap. text ed. 7.95 (ISBN 0-915234-05-X). Bainbridge.

Miller, Brent C., jt. ed. see Olson, David H.

Miller, Brimtom M. & Litsky, Warren. Industrial Microbiology. 1976. 32.50 o.p. (ISBN 0-07-042142-0, C). McGraw.

Miller, Brooke. The Sterns. (American Dynasty Ser.: Vol. III). 1982. pap. 3.75 (ISBN 0-440-07639-0, Emerald). Dell.

Miller, Brown, et al. Innovation in New Communities. 392p. 1972. 25.00x (ISBN 0-262-13082-3). MIT Pr.

Miller, C. Arden & Moos, Merry-K., eds. Local Health Departments: Fifteen Case Studies. LC 81-68703. 499p. 1981. 10.00x (ISBN 0-87553-094-X, 061). Am Pub Health.

Miller, C. Leslie. All About Angels. 1976. pap. 1.25 o.s.i. (ISBN 0-89129-233-0). Jove Pubns.

--All About Angels. LC 73-82096. 144p. (Orig.). 1973. pap. 2.75 (ISBN 0-8307-0467-1, 50-153-08). Regal.

Miller, C. R. I Saw a Ship A-Sailing. (Illus.). 1976. pap. 3.00 (ISBN 0-686-36723-5). Md Hist.

Miller, Calvin. Star Riders of Ren. LC 82-48408. (The Singreale Chronicles Ser.: Vol. 2). (Illus.). 224p. 1983. pap. 7.95 (ISBN 0-06-250576-9, HarpT). Har-Row.

Miller, Carey. All About Monsters. LC 77-17933. (World of the Unknown). (Illus.). (gr. 4-5). 1978. PLB 7.95 (ISBN 0-88436-467-4). EMC.

Miller, Carey D., et al. Fruits of Hawaii: Description, Nutritive Value, & Recipes. 4th ed. 1976. pap. 4.95 (ISBN 0-8248-0448-1). UH Pr.

Miller, Carl E., jt. auth. see Inman, Fred W.

Miller, Carman. The Canadian Career of the Fourth Earl of Minto: The Education of a Viceroy. 225p. 1980. text ed. 11.25 (ISBN 0-88920-078-5, Pub. by Wilfrid Laurier U Pr England). Humanities.

Miller, Carolyn. Lamb in His Bosom. LC 33-22931. 1970. pap. 13.95 (ISBN 0-910220-17-4). Berg.

Miller, Casey & Swift, Kate. The Handbook of Nonsexist Writing: For Writers, Editors, & Speakers. 1981. 10.53i (ISBN 0-690-01882-7, EH-542); pap. 3.95 (ISBN 0-06-463542-2). Har-Row.

Miller, Char. Fathers & Sons: The Bingham Family & the American Mission. 308p. 1982. 24.95 (ISBN 0-87722-248-7). Temple U Pr.

Miller, Charles, jt. auth. see Battles, Ford L.

Miller, Charles, jt. auth. see Crawley, Winston.

Miller, Charles B. How to Organize & Maintain an Efficient Hospital Housekeeping Department. (Illus.). 142p. (Orig.). 1980. pap. 18.75 (ISBN 0-87258-290-6, AHA-085140). Am Hospital.

Miller, Charles D. Beginning Algebra: Study Guide. 3rd ed. 1980. pap. text ed. 7.95x (ISBN 0-673-15331-2). Scott F.

Miller, Charles D. & Heeren, Vern E. Mathematical Ideas. 4th ed. 1982. text ed. 21.95x (ISBN 0-673-15524-2). Scott F.

--Mathematics: An Everyday Experience. 2nd ed. 1980. text ed. 23.50x (ISBN 0-673-15279-0). Scott F.

Miller, Charles D. & Lial, Margaret L. Intermediate Algebra: A Text-Workbook. 2nd ed. 1983. pap. text ed. 19.95x (ISBN 0-673-15795-4). Scott F.

--Introductory Algebra: A Text-Workbook. 2nd ed. 1982. pap. text ed. 19.95x (ISBN 0-673-15796-2). Scott F.

--Introductory Algebra: A Worktext. 1979. pap. text ed. 18.95x (ISBN 0-673-15217-0). Scott F.

--Mathematics & Calculus with Applications. 1980. text ed. 26.50x (ISBN 0-673-15352-5). Scott F.

Miller, Charles D. & Salzman, Stanley A. Arithmetic: A Text-Workbook. 1981. pap. text ed. 18.95x (ISBN 0-673-15274-X). Scott F.

--Business Mathematics. 2nd ed. 1979. pap. text ed. 18.95x (ISBN 0-673-15186-7). Scott F.

--Business Mathematics. 3rd ed. 1983. pap. text ed. 18.95x (ISBN 0-673-15792-X). Scott F.

--Business Mathematics: A Programmed Approach, Book 1. 1980. pap. text ed. 12.50x (ISBN 0-673-15347-9). Scott F.

--Business Mathematics: A Programmed Approach, Bk. 2. 1981. pap. text ed. 12.50x (ISBN 0-673-15426-2). Scott F.

--Mathematics for Business. 2nd ed. 1982. text ed. 19.95x (ISBN 0-673-15535-8). Scott F.

Miller, Charles D., jt. auth. see Lial, Margaret A.

Miller, Charles D., jt. auth. see Lial, Margaret L.

Miller, Charles H. Auden: An American Friendship. (Illus.). 208p. 1983. 13.95 (ISBN 0-684-17845-1, ScribT). Scribner.

Miller, Chuck, jt. ed. see Underwood, Tim.

Miller, Clara B. Katie. LC 66-19606. 288p. 1974. pap. 3.95 (ISBN 0-8024-4524-1). Moody.

Miller, Clarence H., intro. by see Erasmus, Desiderius.

Miller, Crane S. & Hyslop, Richard S. California: The Geography of Diversity. (Illus.). 334p. 1983. pap. 15.95t (ISBN 0-87484-441-X). Mayfield Pub.

Miller, Cyr N. Christians Are Not for Lions: Adult Religious Education. 1971. pap. 3.75x o.p. (ISBN 0-02-805350-8). Glencoe.

Miller, D. B. Peasants & Politics: Grass Roots Reactions to Change in Asia. (Illus.). 1979. 27.50x (ISBN 0-312-59993-5). St Martin.

Miller, D. L. & Farmer, R. D. The Epidemiology of Diseases. (Illus.). 496p. 1982. text ed. 57.50 (ISBN 0-632-00686-2, B3445-8). Mosby.

Miller, D. N., jt. ed. see Vanderveen, B. H.

Miller, Dallas. Fathers & Dreamers. LC 66-18616. 5.95 o.p. (ISBN 0-686-67646-7). Doubleday.

--Passage West. LC 79-3982. 1979. 12.45i (ISBN 0-06-013034-2, HarpT). Har-Row.

Miller, Dana, jt. auth. see Liebers, Arthur.

Miller, Daniel. Starting a Small Restaurant: A Guide to Excellence in the Purveying of Public Victuals. 2nd, Rev. ed. 224p. (Orig.). 1983. 12.95; pap. 8.95 (ISBN 0-916782-37-9). Harvard Common Pr.

Miller, Daniel J. & Lea, Robert N. Guide to the Coastal Marine Fishes of California. 1976. pap. 5.00x (ISBN 0-931876-13-3, 4065). Ag Sci Pubns.

Miller, David. Father of Football: The Story of Matt Busby. new ed. (Illus.). 190p. 1971. 15.00x (ISBN 0-392-01167-0, SpS). Sportshelf.

--Ophthalmology: The Essentials. (Illus.). 1979. 22.50x (ISBN 0-471-09489-7, Pub. by Wiley Med). Wiley.

--Philosophy & Ideology in Hume's Political Thought. 1982. 27.50x (ISBN 0-19-824658-7). Oxford U Pr.

--Unity. 32p. (Orig.). 1981. pap. 3.00x (ISBN 0-935162-03-8). Singing Horse.

Miller, David & Stegmann, Robert. Healon: A Comprehensive Guide. 192p. 1983. 25.00 (ISBN 0-471-09561-3, Pub. by Wiley Med). Wiley.

Miller, David & Siedentop, Larry, eds. The Nature of Political Theory. 262p. 1983. 39.95 (ISBN 0-19-827441-6). Oxford U Pr.

Miller, David H., ed. Water at the Surface of the Earth: Student Edition. LC 82-13769. (International Geophysics Ser.). text ed. 24.00 (ISBN 0-12-496752-3). Acad Pr.

Miller, David K. & Allen, T. Earl. Fitness: A Lifetime Commitment. 2nd ed. LC 81-66520. 1982. pap. text ed. 7.95x (ISBN 0-8087-3993-X). Burgess.

Miller, David L. Christs: Meditations on Archetypal Images in Christian Theology. 200p. 1981. 12.95x (ISBN 0-8164-0492-5). Seabury.

--Modern Science & Human Freedom. Repr. of 1959 ed. lib. bdg. 15.75x (ISBN 0-8371-2101-9, MIMS). Greenwood.

--The New Polytheism. 148p. (Orig.). 1981. pap. 8.50 (ISBN 0-88214-314-X). Spring Pubns.

Miller, David L., jt. ed. see Hopper, Stanley R.

Miller, David M. John Milton: Poetry. (English Authors Ser.). 1978. 12.95 (ISBN 0-8057-6724-X, Twayne). G K Hall.

Miller, David W. & Starr, Martin K. Executive Decisions & Operations Research. 2nd ed. 1969. ref. ed. 23.95 o.p. (ISBN 0-13-294538-X). P-H.

--Structure of Human Decisions. (Orig.). 1967. pap. text ed. 13.95 (ISBN 0-13-854687-8). P-H.

Miller, David W., jt. auth. see Gelin, Jacques B.

Miller, Deborah U. Poppy Seeds, Too. LC 82-84021. (Illus.). 48p. (Orig.). (ps-4). 1982. 8.95 (ISBN 0-930494-16-4); pap. 4.95 (ISBN 0-930494-17-2). Kar Ben.

Miller, Denis R. & Pearson, Howard A. Smith's Blood Diseases of Infancy & Childhood. 4th ed. LC 78-7023. 888p. 1978. pap. text ed. 65.00 (ISBN 0-8016-4691-X). Mosby.

Miller, Don. The Book of Jargon: An Essential Guide to the Inside Languages of Today. 347p. 1982. 16.95 (ISBN 0-02-584960-3); pap. 9.95 (ISBN 0-02-080970-0). Macmillan.

Miller, Don E. Bodymind. 1980. pap. 1.95 o.p. (ISBN 0-523-40858-7). Pinnacle Bks.

Miller, Donald G. Fire in Thy Mouth. (Notable Books on Preaching). 160p. 1976. pap. 2.95 o.p. (ISBN 0-8010-5986-0). Baker Bk.

--Luke. LC 59-10454. (Layman's Bible Commentary Ser.: Vol. 18). 1959. pap. 3.95 (ISBN 0-8042-3078-1). John Knox.

--Nature & Mission of the Church. LC 57-9443. (Orig.). 1957. pap. 4.50 (ISBN 0-8042-3208-3). John Knox.

Miller, Dorcas S. The Maine Coast: A Nature Lover's Guide. LC 79-10290. (Illus.). 192p. 1978. pap. 7.95 (ISBN 0-914788-12-4). East Woods.

--The New Healthy Trail Food Book. rev. ed. LC 79-28172. (Orig.). 1980. pap. 4.95 (ISBN 0-914788-25-6). East Woods.

Miller, Dorothy, jt. auth. see Miller, George.

Miller, Dorothy, ed. Runaways: Illegal Aliens in Their Own Land. 220p. 1980. 22.95x (ISBN 0-686-92312-X). J F Bergin.

Miller, Dorothy A. Poor Man's Guide to Pittsburgh. 3rd ed. (Illus.). 70p. 1981. pap. 4.95 (ISBN 0-9608484-0-1). New Pittsburgh.

Miller, Dorothy C., jt. auth. see Mather, Eleanore P.

Miller, Douglas R. & Belkin, Gary S. Educational Psychology. 715p. 1982. pap. text ed. write for info. o.p. (ISBN 0-697-06059-4); write for info. o.p. (ISBN 0-697-06060-8). Wm C Brown.

Miller, Douglas T. & Nowak, Marion. The Fifties: The Way We Really Were. LC 75-36602. (Illus.). 1977. 15.95 (ISBN 0-385-11248-3). Doubleday.

Miller, Dudley G. Radioactivity & Radiation Detection. LC 70-146446. (Illus.). 122p. 1972. 34.00x (ISBN 0-677-01490-2). Gordon.

Miller, Duncan & Soranna, Morag. OECD Directory of Food Policy Institutes. new ed. 98p. 1982. pap. text ed. 29.95. Butterworth.

Miller, Duncan & Soranna, Morag, eds. Directory of Food Policy Institutes. Date not set. 29.95 (ISBN 0-686-37446-0). OECD.

Miller, E. Introduction to Cultural Anthropology. 1979. pap. 17.95 (ISBN 0-13-480236-5); study guide & wkbk. 8.95 (ISBN 0-13-480244-6). P-H.

Miller, E. & Weitz, C. Introduction to Anthropology. 1979. 22.95 (ISBN 0-13-478008-6); study guide 7.95 (ISBN 0-13-478016-7). P-H.

Miller, E., jt. auth. see Spirer, Louise Z.

Miller, E., jt. auth. see Kellar, Jane C.

Miller, E. Eugene. Jail Management. LC 76-43590. 1978. 21.95 (ISBN 0-669-00959-8). Lexington Bks.

Miller, E. Eugene & Montilla, Robert. Corrections in the Community: Success Models in Correctional Reform. 1977. text ed. 21.95 (ISBN 0-87909-174-6); pap. text ed. 16.00 (ISBN 0-87909-173-8). Reston.

Miller, E. J. A Life Apart. Gwynne, G. V., ed. 1979. pap. 10.95x (ISBN 0-422-75660-1, Pub. by Tavistock England). Methuen Inc.

Miller, E. W. & Miller, Ruby M. Middle America & the Caribbean: A Bibliography on the Third World. (Public Aministration Ser.: Bibliography P-1063). 98p. 1982. pap. 15.00 (ISBN 0-88066-213-1). Vance Biblios.

--South America: A Bibliography on the Third World. (Public Administration Ser.: Bibliography P-1064). 81p. 1982. pap. 12.00 (ISBN 0-88066-214-X). Vance Biblios.

Miller, Ed & Flamm, Steven. Build Your Own Hot Tub. LC 79-2472. (Illus.). 96p. 1979. pap. 5.95 (ISBN 0-89815-005-1). Ten Speed Pr.

Miller, Ed L. God & Reason: A Historical Approach to Philosophical Theology. 224p. 1972. pap. text ed. 13.95x (ISBN 0-02-381270-2). Macmillan.

Miller, Edgar. Abnormal Aging: The Psychology of Senile & Presenile Dementia. LC 76-28175. 1977. 29.95 (ISBN 0-471-99439-1, Pub. by Wiley-Interscience). Wiley.

Miller, Edgar G., Jr. American Antique Furniture, 2 Vols. (Illus.). 1966. pap. 10.95 ea.; Vol. 1. pap. (ISBN 0-486-21599-7); Vol. 2. pap. (ISBN 0-486-21600-4). Dover.

Miller, Edna. Duck Duck. (Treehouse Bks). (ps-3). 1981. pap. 3.95 (ISBN 0-13-220962-4). P-H.

--Mousekin Finds a Friend. (ps-3). 1967. PLB 7.95x (ISBN 0-13-604413-1); pap. 3.95 (ISBN 0-13-604397-6). P-H.

--Mousekin Takes a Trip. (Illus.). (gr. k-3). 1976. 6.95x (ISBN 0-13-604363-1); pap. 3.95 (ISBN 0-13-604348-8). P-H.

--Mousekin's ABC's. (gr. 1-4). 1972. PLB 8.95x (ISBN 0-13-604389-5). P-H.

--Mousekin's ABC's. (Illus.). (ps-3). 1972. pap. 3.95 (ISBN 0-13-604371-2). P-H.

--Mousekin's Christmas Eve. (Illus.). (gr. k-3). 1965. PLB 7.95 (ISBN 0-13-604454-9); pap. 2.95 (ISBN 0-13-604447-6). P-H.

--Mousekin's Close Call. LC 77-27571. (Illus.). (ps-2). 1980. 9.95x (ISBN 0-13-604207-4); pap. 1.95 (ISBN 0-13-604199-X). P-H.

--Mousekin's Golden House. (gr. k-3). 1964. PLB 8.95x (ISBN 0-13-604421-2); pap. 3.95 (ISBN 0-13-604439-5). P-H.

--Pebbles: A Pack Rat. LC 76-8850. (Illus.). 32p. (gr. k-3). 1976. PLB 5.95 o.p. (ISBN 0-13-655399-0); pap. 2.50 o.p. (ISBN 0-13-655381-8). P-H.

Miller, Edward. Prince of Librarians: The Life & Times of Antonio Panizzi of the British Museum. LC 67-26123. (Illus.). 356p. 1967. 17.00x (ISBN 0-8214-0030-4, 82-80331). Ohio U Pr.

--Prince of Librarians: The Life & Times of Antonio Panizzi of the British Museum. 360p. 1967. 26.50 (ISBN 0-233-95907-6, 05809-2, Pub. by Gower Pub Co England). Lexington Bks.

--That Noble Cabinet: A History of the British Museum. LC 73-85452. (Illus.). 400p. 1974. 22.95x (ISBN 0-8214-0139-4, 82-81420). Ohio U Pr.

Miller, Edward, jt. ed. see Cushman, Kathleen.

Miller, Edward J., jt. auth. see Wolensky, Robert P.

Miller, Edwin, et al. Management of Human Resources: Newer Approaches. (Illus.). 1980. pap. text ed. 16.95 (ISBN 0-13-549410-9). P-H.

Miller, Edwin H. Melville. LC 75-7958. 1976. pap. 7.95 o.p. (ISBN 0-89255-008-2). Persea Bks.

Miller, Edwin H., ed. see Whitman, Walt.

Miller, Elizabeth & Cohen, Jane. Cat & Dog & the Mixed-up Week. LC 80-12259. (ps). 1980. 2.95 (ISBN 0-531-03529-8); PLB 6.90 (ISBN 0-531-04123-9). Watts.

--Cat & Dog Give a Party. LC 80-12048. (ps). 1980. 2.95 (ISBN 0-531-03527-1); PLB 6.90 (ISBN 0-531-04126-3). Watts.

--Cat & Dog Have a Contest. LC 80-12697. (ps). 1980. 2.95 (ISBN 0-531-03528-X); PLB 6.90 (ISBN 0-531-04125-5). Watts.

--Cat & Dog Have a Parade. LC 81-349. (Cat & Dog Ser.). (Illus.). 48p. (ps-3). 1981. PLB 6.90 (ISBN 0-531-04295-2). Watts.

--Cat & Dog Learn the ABC's. LC 80-28915. (Cat & Dog Ser.). (Illus.). 48p. (ps-3). 1981. PLB 6.90 (ISBN 0-531-04294-4). Watts.

--Cat & Dog Raise the Roof. LC 80-14432. (ps). 1980. 2.95 (ISBN 0-531-03530-1); PLB 6.90 (ISBN 0-531-04124-7). Watts.

--Cat & Dog Take a Trip. LC 80-14517. (ps). 2.95 (ISBN 0-531-03531-X); PLB 6.90 (ISBN 0-531-04127-1). Watts.

Miller, Ella M. I Am a Woman. (Orig.). 1967. pap. 2.95 (ISBN 0-8024-3925-X). Moody.

Miller, Ellen, jt. auth. see Kellar, Jane C.

Miller, Elwood L. Accounting Problems of Multinational Enterprises. LC 78-20273. (Illus.). 304p. 1979. 23.95 (ISBN 0-669-02712-X). Lexington Bks.

Miller, Eric J., ed. Task & Organization. LC 75-12606. (Wiley Series Individuals, Groups & Organizations). 480p. 1976. 54.95 (ISBN 0-471-60605-7, Pub. by Wiley-Interscience). Wiley.

Miller, Ernest G., jt. auth. see Lyden, Fremont J.

Miller, Ernest L. & Grasso, Joseph E. Removable Partial Prosthodontics. 2nd ed. 423p. 1981. 35.00 (ISBN 0-683-05990-4, 5990-4). Williams & Wilkins.

Miller, Ernest R., compiled by. Harvest of Gold. LC 72-92720. (Illus.). 96p. 1973. boxed 5.50 (ISBN 0-8378-1760-9). Gibson.

Miller, Erston V. & Munger, James I. Good Fruits & How to Buy Them. (Illus., Orig.). 1967. 4.95 (ISBN 0-910286-22-1); pap. 3.95 (ISBN 0-910286-04-3). Boxwood.

Miller, Ervin. The Microeconomic Effects of Monetary Policy. LC 77-17980. 1978. 22.50 (ISBN 0-312-53173-7). St Martin.

Miller, Ethel B., tr. see Institut Francais De Pertrole.

Miller, Eugene. Barron's Guide to Graduate Business Schools: Eastern Edition. rev. ed. 1982. pap. text ed. 6.95 (ISBN 0-8120-2446-X). Barron.

--Barrons Guide to Graduate Business Schools: Western Edition. 320p. 1982. pap. 6.95 (ISBN 0-8120-2538-5). Barron.

Miller, Evelyn. How to Raise & Train a Boston Terrier. (Illus.). pap. 2.95 (ISBN 0-87666-251-3, DS1005). TFH Pubns.

--How to Raise & Train a Bulldog. (Illus.). pap. 2.50 o.p. (ISBN 0-87666-259-9, DS1007). TFH Pubns.

--How to Raise & Train a Cocker Spaniel. pap. 2.95 (ISBN 0-87666-269-6, DS1009). TFH Pubns.

--How to Raise & Train a Fox Terrier. (Illus.). pap. 2.95 (ISBN 0-87666-294-7, DS1038). TFH Pubns.

--How to Raise & Train a Golden Retriever. (Illus.). pap. 2.95 (ISBN 0-87666-306-4, DS1018). TFH Pubns.

--How to Raise & Train a Miniature Pinscher. (Illus.). pap. 2.95 (ISBN 0-87666-337-4, DS1039). TFH Pubns.

--How to Raise & Train a Poodle. pap. 2.95 (ISBN 0-87666-355-2, DS1030). TFH Pubns.

--How to Raise & Train a Pug. (Illus.). pap. 2.95 (ISBN 0-87666-364-1, DS1031). TFH Pubns.

--How to Raise & Train a Shetland Sheepdog. (Illus.). pap. 2.95 (ISBN 0-87666-386-2, DS1033). TFH Pubns.

--How to Raise & Train an Airedale. (Illus.). pap. 2.95 (ISBN 0-87666-233-5, DS1002). TFH Pubns.

Miller, Forrest R. & Keshavamurthy, R. N. Structure of an Arabian Sea Summer Monsoon System. LC 67-29576. (International Indian Ocean Expedition Meteorological Monographs: No. 1). (Illus.). 1968. 12.00x (ISBN 0-8248-0070-2, Eastwest Ctr). UH Pr.

Miller, Francis A. Aren't You the One Who...? LC 82-13798. 240p. (gr. 7 up). 1983. 11.95 (ISBN 0-689-30961-9). Atheneum.

Miller, Francis T. Hero Tales from American Life. LC 71-174081. (Illus.). 1971. Repr. of 1909 ed. 37.00x (ISBN 0-8103-3800-9). Gale.

Miller, Frank, jt. auth. see Miller, Jay.

Miller, Frank B. & Coghill, Mary A. Historical Sources of Personnel Work: An Annotated Bibliography. (ILR Bibliography Ser.: No. 5). 116p. 1961. pap. 2.00 (ISBN 0-87546-020-8). ILR Pr.

Miller, Frank O. Minobe Tatsukichi: Interpreter of Constitutionalism in Japan. (Center for Japanese & Korean Studies, UC Berkeley). 1965. 36.50x (ISBN 0-520-00865-0). U of Cal Pr.

Miller, Frank W. Prosecution: The Decision to Charge a Suspect with a Crime. 366p. 1970. pap. 7.95 (ISBN 0-316-57346-9). Little.

Miller, Frank W., et al. Guidance: Principles & Services. 3rd ed. (Guidance Ser.). 1977. text ed. 20.95 (ISBN 0-675-08461-X). Merrill.

Miller, Fred. Passport to Better Health Through Eating. 1983. pap. 5.95 (ISBN 0-89404-028-6). Aztex.

Miller, Fred D. & Smith, Nicholas D., eds. Thought Probes: Philosophy Through Science Fiction. (Illus.). 368p. 1981. text ed. 14.95 (ISBN 0-13-920041-X). P-H.

Miller, Fredric M. & Vogel, Morris J. Still Philadelphia: A Photographic History. 1983. write for info. (ISBN 0-87722-306-8). Temple U Pr.

Miller, G. S., jt. auth. see Bergeson, J. B.

Miller, G. S., Jr. The Families & Genera of Bats. 1967. Repr. of 1907 ed. 40.00 (ISBN 3-7682-0534-7). Lubrecht & Cramer.

Miller, G. Tyler, Jr. Chemistry: A Basic Introduction. 2nd ed. 560p. 1980. text ed. 25.95x (ISBN 0-534-00878-X); lab manual 14.95x (ISBN 0-534-00894-1); study guide 9.95 (ISBN 0-534-00892-5). Wadsworth Pub.

--Chemistry: Principles & Applications. 1976. text ed. 27.95x (ISBN 0-534-00430-X). Wadsworth Pub.

--Living in the Environment. 3rd ed. 704p. 1981. text ed. 25.95x (ISBN 0-534-00994-8). Wadsworth Pub.

--Living in the Environment. 2rd ed. 1979. text ed. 23.95x o.p. (ISBN 0-534-00684-1). Wadsworth Pub.

Miller, G. William, ed. The Decline & Rise of the American Economy. (American Assembly Ser.). (Illus.). 192p. 1983. 11.95 (ISBN 0-13-198465-9); pap. 4.95 (ISBN 0-13-198457-8). P-H.

Miller, Gabriel. Daniel Fuchs. (United States Authors Ser.). 1979. lib. bdg. 14.95 (ISBN 0-8057-7240-5, Twayne). G K Hall.

--John Irving. (Literature & Life Ser.). 160p. 1982. 11.95 (ISBN 0-8044-2621-X); pap. 5.95 (ISBN 0-8044-6502-9). Ungar.

Miller, Gale. It's a Living: Work in Modern Society. 300p. 1981. text ed. 16.95 (ISBN 0-312-43907-5); pap. text ed. 9.95 (ISBN 0-312-43908-3). St Martin.

Miller, Gary. Handbook of Electronic Communications. LC 78-11347. (Illus.). 1979. 25.95 (ISBN 0-13-377374-4). P-H.

--Linear Circuits for Electronics Technology. (Illus.). 368p. 1974. ref. ed. 22.95 (ISBN 0-13-536698-4). P-H.

Miller, Gary A. & Borgen, C. Winston. Professional Selling: Inside & Out. LC 77-83518. 1979. pap. text ed. 13.80 (ISBN 0-8273-1638-0); instructor's guide 4.75 (ISBN 0-8273-1639-9). Delmar.

Miller, Gary B. Improvisation, Typology, Culture, & the New Orthodoxy: How 'Oral' is Homer? 132p. (Orig.). 1982. lib. bdg. 19.75 (ISBN 0-8191-2673-X); pap. text ed. 8.25 (ISBN 0-8191-2674-8). U Pr of Amer.

Miller, Gary J. Cities by Contract: The Politics of Municipal Incorporation. 256p. 1981. text ed. 22.50x (ISBN 0-262-13164-1). MIT Pr.

Miller, Gary M. Modern Electricity Electronics. (Illus.). 448p. 1981. text ed. 21.95 (ISBN 0-13-593160-6). P-H.

--Modern Electronic Communication. (Illus.). 1978. ref. ed. 24.95 (ISBN 0-13-593145-2). P-H.

--Modern Electronic Communications. 2nd ed. (Illus.). 592p. 1983. text ed. 26.95 (ISBN 0-13-593152-5). P-H.

Miller, Gary M. & Nemeth, Gyuri. A Consumer's Guide to the Public School. (Illus.). 256p. 1983. 24.75x (ISBN 0-398-04755-3). C C Thomas.

Miller, Gene. A Believer Speaks. 1979. 5.95 o.p. (ISBN 0-533-04111-2). Vantage.

Miller, Geoffrey F., jt. auth. see Baker, Christopher T.

Miller, George. Rambles Round the Edge Hills. 154p. 1980. 9.00x o.p. (ISBN 0-900093-27-7, Pub. by Roundwood). State Mutual Bk.

Miller, George & Miller, Dorothy. Picture Postcards in the United States. (Illus.). 1976. 15.95 o.p. (ISBN 0-517-52400-7, C N Potter Bks). Crown.

Miller, George, jt. auth. see Stueart, Robert D.

Miller, George, jt. ed. see Smith, Frank.

Miller, George A. Communication, Language & Meaning: Psychological Perspectives. LC 70-174815. 320p. 1973. 12.50x o.p. (ISBN 0-465-12833-5); pap. 6.95x (ISBN 0-465-09721-9, TB-5079). Basic.

--Spontaneous Apprentices: Children & Language. 224p. 1980. 10.95 (ISBN 0-8164-9330-8). Seabury.

Miller, George E. Edward Hyde, Earl of Clarendon. (English Authors Ser.: No. 337). 192p. 1983. lib. bdg. 18.95 (ISBN 0-8057-6823-8, Twayne). G K Hall.

Miller, George H. & Gidbeau, Kenneth W. Residential Real Estate Appraisal: An Introduction to Real Estate Appraising. (Illus.). 1980. text ed. 21.95 (ISBN 0-13-774521-4). P-H.

Miller, George W. Moral & Ethical Implications of Human Organ Transplants. (Illus.). 164p. 1971. 12.75x o.p. (ISBN 0-398-01311-X). C C Thomas.

Miller, Gerald R. & Steinberg, Mark. Between People: A New Analysis of Interpersonal Communication. LC 74-18926. (Illus.). 352p. 1975. text ed. 16.95 (ISBN 0-574-17501-6, 13-5500); 3.25 o.p. study activity guide (ISBN 0-574-17502-4, 13-5502). SRA.

Miller, Girard. Effective Budgetary Presentations: The Cutting Edge. LC 82-81886. (Illus.). 230p. 1982. pap. 23.50 nonmember (ISBN 0-686-84268-5); pap. 18.50 (ISBN 0-686-84269-3). Municipal.

--A Public Investor's Guide to Money Market Instruments. LC 82-80937. (Illus.). 111p. 1982. pap. 13.00 Nonmember (ISBN 0-686-84370-3); pap. 11.00 Member (ISBN 0-686-84371-1). Municipal.

Miller, Glenn. Quimica Elemental. (Span.). 1978. pap. text ed. 10.30 o.p. (ISBN 0-06-315625-3, IntlDept). Har-Row.

Miller, Glenn E. Chicago Psychoanalytic Literature Index, 1981. 1982. lib. bdg. 50.00 (ISBN 0-918568-09-9). Chicago Psych.

Miller, Glenn E., ed. Chicago Psychoanalytic Literature Index: 1975. 1975. lib. bdg. 50.00 (ISBN 0-918568-08-0). Chicago Psych.

--Chicago Psychoanalytic Literature Index, Nineteen Twenty-Nineteen Seventy, 3 vols. LC 76-182629. 1978. Set. lib. bdg. 350.00 (ISBN 0-918568-01-3). Chicago Psych.

Miller, Glennita. Keepers of the Kingdom. 1983. 18.95 (ISBN 0-671-42523-4). S&S.

Miller, Gloria B. Thousand Recipe Chinese Cookbook. (Illus.). 1970. 19.95 (ISBN 0-448-00674-X, G&D). Putnam Pub Group.

Miller, Gordon P. Life Choices: How to Make the Critical Decisions - About Your Education, Career, Marriage, Family, Life-Style. LC 78-3860. 1978. 12.45i (ISBN 0-690-01721-9). T y Crowell.

Miller, H., jt. auth. see Howell, Y.

Miller, H. A., et al. Bryoflora of the Atolls of Micronesia. (Illus.). 1963. pap. 16.00 (ISBN 3-7682-5411-9). Lubrecht & Cramer.

--Prodromus Florae Muscorum Polynesiae. with a Key to Genera. 1978. lib. bdg. 40.00x (ISBN 3-7682-1115-0). Lubrecht & Cramer.

Miller, Hal. Christian Community: Biblical or Optional? (Orig.). 1979. pap. 3.50 o.p. (ISBN 0-89283-068-9). Servant.

Miller, Harlan B. & Williams, William H., eds. Ethics & Animals. (Contemporary Issues in Biomedicine, Ethics, & Society Ser.). 416p. 1983. 39.50 (ISBN 0-89603-036-9). Humana.

Miller, Harold G. New Zealand. LC 82-24157. (British Empire History Ser.). 156p. 1983. Repr. lib. bdg. 27.50x (ISBN 0-313-22997-X, MINZ). Greenwood.

Miller, Harry, et al, eds. see National Passive Solar Conference, 3rd, San Jose, 1979.

Miller, Harry G. & Verduin, John R. The Adult Educator: A Handbook for Staff Development. (Building Blocks of Human Potential Ser.). 178p. 1979. 14.95 (ISBN 0-87201-233-6). Gulf Pub.

Miller, Harry H. Common Sense Puppy & Dog Care. (Illus.). 1960. 3.95 (ISBN 0-8208-0305-7). Hearthside.

Miller, Harry L., jt. auth. see Ornstein, Allan C.

Miller, Hazen L. Old Au Sable. 1974. 5.95x (ISBN 0-8028-7007-4). Eerdmans.

Miller, Heather S. A Needleworker's Botany. LC 78-59803. (Illus.). 1978. 6.95 (ISBN 0-912274-81-6); pap. 5.95 o.p. (ISBN 0-912274-99-9). Backcountry Pubns.

Miller, Helen, jt. auth. see Miller, Jeanne.

Miller, Helen M. Jedediah Smith on the Far Frontier. (American Hero Biographies). (Illus.). (gr. 3-5). 1971. PLB 4.49 o.p. (ISBN 0-399-60310-7). Putnam Pub Group.

--The San Francisco Earthquake & Fire. (Sagas of the West Ser.). (Illus.). (gr. 7-10). 1970. PLB 5.29 o.p. (ISBN 0-399-60556-8). Putnam Pub Group.

Miller, Henry. Cosmological Eye. LC 75-87589. 1969. 10.95 (ISBN 0-8112-0319-0); pap. 9.25 (ISBN 0-8112-0110-4, NDP109). New Directions.

--Joey: A Loving Portrait of Alfred Perles Together with Some Bizarre Episodes Relating to the Other Sex. (Book of Friends Ser.: Vol. 3). 1979. 8.95 (ISBN 0-88496-136-2); pap. 3.95 o.s.i. (ISBN 0-88496-137-0). Capra Pr.

--The Paintings of Henry Miller. (Illus.). 132p. (Orig.). 1982. text ed. 35.00 (ISBN 0-87701-280-6); pap. 16.95 (ISBN 0-87701-276-8). Chronicle Bks.

--Tropic of Cancer. 1961. pap. 3.95 (ISBN 0-394-17760-6, B10, BC). Grove.

--Tropic of Cancer. 7.95 (ISBN 0-394-60435-0). Modern Lib.

--Wisdom of the Heart. LC 41-28118. 1942. pap. 6.50 (ISBN 0-8112-0116-3, NDP94). New Directions.

Miller, Henry C. State Coinage of Connecticut. updated ed. (Illus.). 1981. Repr. of 1920 ed. lib. bdg. 25.00 (ISBN 0-915262-64-9). S J Durst.

Miller, Herbert E. & Mead, George C. CPA Review Manual. 5th ed. (Illus.). 1979. 30.60 (ISBN 0-13-188201-5); text ed. 22.95 (ISBN 0-686-96831-X). P-H.

Miller, Herbert S. Christian Worker's Manual. 4.95 (ISBN 0-87509-064-8); pap. 4.75 (ISBN 0-87509-065-6). Chr Pubns.

Miller, Herman P. Rich Man, Poor Man. (Illus.). 1971. 8.95i o.p. (ISBN 0-690-70039-3). T Y Crowell.

Miller, Howard & Lamb, Samuel. Oaks of North America. 1983. price not set. Naturegraph.

Miller, Howard A. & Major, David A., eds. ICU Medicine. (A Hahnemann Symposium). 1982. 29.50 (792928). Grune.

Miller, Howard L. & Siegel, Paul S. Loving: A Psychological Approach. LC 72-3770. 224p. 1972. pap. 14.95 (ISBN 0-471-60390-2). Wiley.

Miller, Hugh. The Dissector. LC 76-5377. 1976. 8.95 o.p. (ISBN 0-312-21315-8). St Martin.

Miller, Hugh M. History of Music. LC 72-81476. 288p. pap. 5.50 (ISBN 0-06-460147-1, CO 147, COS). B&N NY.

Miller, I. & Freund, J. Probability & Statistics for Engineers. 2nd ed. (Illus.). 1977. 29.95 (ISBN 0-13-711945-3). P-H.

Miller, Ian. The Secret Art of Ian Miller. (Illus.). 96p. 1980. pap. 9.95 (ISBN 0-8256-9551-1, Quick Fox). Putnam Pub Group.

Miller, Inabeth. Microcomputers in School Media Centers. 200p. Date not set. 14.95x o.p. (ISBN 0-918212-51-0). Neal-Schuman. Postponed.

Miller, Inabeth, intro. by. Microcomputer Directory: Applications in Educational Settings. 2nd ed. 316p. 1982. 15.00 (ISBN 0-943484-00-6). Gutman Lib.

Miller, Ira. Seesaw. 224p. 1983. 12.95 (ISBN 0-312-70935-8). St Martin.

Miller, Irving. Israel: The Eternal Idea. 1955. 19.50x (ISBN 0-686-50046-6). Elliots Bks.

Miller, Irwin. Primer on Statistics for Economics & Business. (Orig.). 1968. pap. text ed. 3.50x (ISBN 0-685-19753-0). Phila Bk Co.

Miller, J. Aromatic Nucleophilic Substitution. (Reaction Mechanisms in Organic Chemistry: Vol. 8). 1969. 42.75 (ISBN 0-444-40683-2). Elsevier.

--Popery & Politics in England, 1660-1688. LC 73-79306. (Illus.). 278p. 1973. 44.50 (ISBN 0-521-20236-1). Cambridge U Pr.

Miller, J., jt. auth. see Riegel, R.

Miller, J. A., jt. auth. see Hutchinson, D. W.

Miller, J. C. Statistics for Advanced Levels. LC 82-4550. (Illus.). 288p. Date not set. pap. price not set (ISBN 0-521-28930-0). Cambridge U Pr.

Miller, J. Dale & Bishop, Russell H. U. S. A.-Mexico Culture Capsules. 1977. pap. text ed. 8.95 (ISBN 0-88399-150-0). Newbury Hse.

Miller, J. Dale & Loiseau, Maurice. U. S. A.-France Culture Capsules. 1977. pap. text ed. 7.95 (ISBN 0-88377-151-9). Newbury Hse.

Miller, J. Dale, et al. U. S. A-Hispanic South America Culture Capsules. 1979. pap. text ed. 8.95 (ISBN 0-88377-154-3). Newbury Hse.

Miller, J. E., jt. auth. see Brown, E. K.

Miller, J. G. Comprehensive Gear Shop. Vol. 2. 1962. 7.00 o.p. (ISBN 0-02-821180-4). Vol. 3. 1965. Glencoe.

Miller, J. Jefferson. Eighteenth-Century Meissen Porcelain from the Margaret M. & Arthur J. Mourot Collection in the Virgina Museum. 1983. pap. write for info. (ISBN 0-917046-13-7). Va Mus Fine Arts.

Miller, J. L., et al. Sentencing Reform: A Review & Annotated Bibliography. 1981. pap. 10.00 (ISBN 0-89656-056-2). Natl Ctr St Courts.

Miller, J. Lane, jt. auth. see Miller, Madeleine S.

Miller, J. Martin & Kini, Sudha R. Needle Biopsy of the Thyroid. 304p. 1983. 39.00 (ISBN 0-03-062371-5). Praeger.

Miller, J. Maxwell. Introducing the Holy Land. 208p. 1983. 13.95x (ISBN 0-86554-034-9). Mercer Univ Pr.

Miller, J. Maxwell, jt. ed. see Hayes, John H.

Miller, J. N. & West, M. A., eds. Standards in Fluorescence Spectrometry. 160p. 1981. 19.95x (ISBN 0-412-22500-X, Pub by Chapman & Hall England). Methuen Inc.

Miller, J. P. Big & Little. LC 75-36464. (Illus.). 14p. (ps-1). 1975. 3.50 (ISBN 0-394-83239-6, BYR). Random.

Miller, J. Philip. Numbers in Presence & Absence: A Study of Husserl's Philosophy of Mathematics. 1982. lib. bdg. 29.50 (ISBN 0-686-37593-9, Pub. by Martinus Nijhoff). Kluwer Boston.

Miller, J. Q., jt. auth. see Hartshorne, Hugh.

Miller, J. R. Dying to Live. rev. ed. Zodhiates, Joan, ed. LC 79-51337. Orig. Title: Making the Most of Life. 147p. 1980. pap. 3.95 (ISBN 0-89957-045-3). AMG Pubs.

--Words of Comfort. (Illus.). 1976. 3.95 o.s.i. (ISBN 0-89957-518-8); pap. 2.95 o.s.i. (ISBN 0-89957-517-X). AMG Pubs.

Miller, Jake C. The Black Presence in American Foreign Affairs. LC 78-69860. 1978. pap. text ed. 12.50 (ISBN 0-8191-0584-8). U Pr of Amer.

Miller, James. History & Human Existence: From Marx to Merleau-Ponty. LC 78-51747. 1979. 30.00x (ISBN 0-520-03667-0). U of Cal Pr.

--History & Human Existence: From Marx to Merleau-Ponty. 299p. 1982. pap. 8.95 (ISBN 0-520-04779-6, CAL 590). U of Cal Pr.

--The Social Control of Mass Communication: A Critical Analysis of Content Shaping Forces. (Communication & Information Science Ser.). Date not set. price not set (ISBN 0-89391-105-4). Ablex Pub.

Miller, James A. see Heat Transfer & Fluid Mechanics Institute.

Miller, James D., ed. Media Canada: Guidelines for Educators. 2nd rev. ed. 1974. 4.85 (ISBN 0-08-016508-7). Pergamon.

Miller, James E., Jr. Walt Whitman. (United States Authors Ser.). lib. bdg. 10.95 (ISBN 0-8057-0792-1, Twayne). G K Hall.

Miller, James H. Designing Small Theatres. Zapel, Arthur L., ed. 1974. pap. 2.95 (ISBN 0-916260-03-8). Meriwether Pub.

--Stage Lighting in the Boondocks. Zapel, Arthur L., ed. (Illus.). 76p. (Orig.). 1981. pap. text ed. 5.50 (ISBN 0-916260-11-9). Meriwether Pub.

--Technical Aspects of Staging in the Church. Zapel, Arthur L., ed. (Illus.). 1979. pap. text ed. 2.95 (ISBN 0-916260-05-4). Meriwether Pub.

Miller, James M. Genesis of Western Culture: The Upper Ohio Valley, 1800-1825. LC 77-87420. (American Scene Ser.). 1969. Repr. of 1938 ed. lib. bdg. 29.50 (ISBN 0-306-71566-X). Da Capo.

--Separation Methods in Chemical Analysis. LC 74-13781. 320p. 1975. 39.00 (ISBN 0-471-60490-9, Pub. by Wiley-Interscience). Wiley.

Miller, James N. Spirochetes in Body Fluids & Tissues: Manual of Investigative Methods. (Illus.). 86p. 1971. photocopy ed. spiral 8.75x (ISBN 0-398-01312-8). C C Thomas.

Miller, Jan. Amphoto Guide to Framing & Display. (Illus.). 168p. 1980. 10.95 o.p. (ISBN 0-8174-2515-2, Amphoto); pap. 7.95 (ISBN 0-8174-2177-7). Watson-Guptill.

Miller, Jane. Birth of a Foal. LC 76-5402. 1977. 10.53i (ISBN 0-397-31702-6, JBL-J). Har-Row.

--Farm Counting Book. (Illus.). 32p. (ps-3). 1983. 6.95 (ISBN 0-13-304790-3). P-H.

--The Greater Leisures. LC 82-45601. 96p. 1983. 10.95 (ISBN 0-385-18414-X); pap. 5.95 (ISBN 0-385-18415-8). Doubleday.

Miller, Janice, jt. auth. see Ayres, Joe.

Miller, Janice B. Juan Nepomuceno De Quesada: Governor of Spanish East Florida, 1790-1795. LC 81-40589. (Illus.). 196p. (Orig.). 1981. lib. bdg. 20.75 (ISBN 0-8191-1833-8); pap. text ed. 10.00 (ISBN 0-8191-1834-6). U Pr of Amer.

Miller, Jay. Aerograph: General Dynamics F-16 Fighting Falcon, No.1. (Illus.). 116p. 1982. pap. 14.95 (ISBN 0-686-43364-5, Pub. by Aero Fax Inc.). Aviation.

--The X Planes: From the X-1 to the X-29. (Illus.). 192p. 1983. 29.95 (ISBN 0-686-84079-8). Specialty Pr.

Miller, Jay & Miller, Frank. Magic Tricks. LC 74-11891. (Early Craft Bks.). (Illus.). 32p. (gr. 1-4). 1975. PLB 3.95g (ISBN 0-8225-0865-6). Lerner Pubns.

--Making Gifts. LC 74-33532. (Early Craft Bks). (Illus.). 32p. (gr. 1-4). 1975. PLB 3.95g (ISBN 0-8225-0867-2). Lerner Pubns.

--Nature Crafts. LC 74-33535. (Early Craft Bks). (Illus.). 32p. (gr. 1-4). 1975. PLB 3.95g (ISBN 0-8225-0866-4). Lerner Pubns.

Miller, Jay & Eastman, Carol, eds. The Tsimshian & Other Peoples of the Northwest Coast. 1983. write for info. U of Wash Pr.

Miller, Jean R. & Janosik, Ellen. Family Focused Care. (Illus.). 1979. text ed. 21.50 (ISBN 0-07-042060-2, HP). McGraw.

Miller, Jeanne & Miller, Helen. Mamanwa Grammar. (Language Data, Asian-Pacific Ser.: No.8). 1976. pap. 6.00 o.p. (ISBN 0-88312-208-1); microfiche 2.25 (ISBN 0-685-65823-6). Summer Inst Ling.

Miller, Jeffrey. Stapleton International Airport: The First Fifty Years. (Illus.). 1983. price not set (ISBN 0-87108-614-X). Pruett.

Miller, Jeffrey C., jt. auth. see Lindley, Dennis V.

Miller, Jeffrey H. Experiments in Molecular Genetics. LC 72-78914. (Illus.). 466p. 1972. 35.00x (ISBN 0-87969-106-9). Cold Spring Harbor.

Miller, Jerome K. Applying the New Copyright Law: A Guide for Educators & Librarians. LC 79-4694. 1979. pap. 12.00 (ISBN 0-685-97224-0). ALA.

--U. S. Copyright Documents: An Annotated Collection for Use by Educators & Librarians. LC 80-24768. 292p. 1981. lib. bdg. 27.50 (ISBN 0-87287-239-4). Libs Unl.

Miller, Jerry L., jt. auth. see Hamblin, Robert L.

Miller, Jerry W. & Mills, Olive. Credentialing Educational Accomplishment. 1978. pap. 16.50 o.p. (ISBN 0-8268-1227-9, 227). ACE.

Miller, Joan M. & Chaya, Ruth K. Basic Programming for the Classroom Teacher. 200p. 1982. pap. text ed. 15.95x (ISBN 0-8077-2728-8). Tchrs Coll.

Miller, Joel S., ed. Extended Linear Chain Compounds. (Vol. 3). 549p. 1982. 55.00x (ISBN 0-306-40941-0, Plenum Pr). Plenum Pub.

Miller, Joel S. & Epstein, Arthur J., eds. Synthesis & Properties of Low-Dimensional Materials, Vol. 313. (Annals of the New York Academy of Sciences). 828p. 1978. 82.00x (ISBN 0-89766-003-X); pap. 82.00x (ISBN 0-89072-069-X). NY Acad Sci.

Miller, John. Contamination. LC 81-90463. (Illus.). 112p. (Orig.). 1982. pap. 4.00x (ISBN 0-9607244-0-0). Cave Canem Bks.

--The Life & Times of William & Mary. Fraser, Antonia, ed. (Kings & Queens of England Ser.). (Illus.). 224p. 1974. text ed. 17.50X (ISBN 0-297-76760-7, Pub. by weidenfeld & Nicolson England). Biblio Dist.

--Text. (Illus.). 64p. 1980. pap. 2.00 (ISBN 0-686-82501-2). Cave Canem Bks.

--The Workingman's Paradise. Wilding, Michael, ed. 272p. 1980. 18.50x (ISBN 0-424-00057-1, Pub. by Sydney U Pr Australia). Intl Schol Bk Serv.

Miller, John, et al. American Idea: Discovery & Settlement, Revolution & Independence. (Illus.). 1976. pap. 2.00 o.p. (ISBN 0-87104-304-1). NY Pub Lib.

Miller, John, jt. auth. see Donahue, Roy.

Miller, John A. & Neuzil, E. F. General Organic Chemistry. 1979. text ed. 23.95 (ISBN 0-669-01885-6); lab manual 9.95x (ISBN 0-669-01886-4); study guide 8.95 (ISBN 0-669-01887-2). Heath.

--Modern Experimental Organic Chemistry. 736p. 1982. pap. text ed. 24.95 (ISBN 0-669-03174-7). Heath.

Miller, John C. Federalist Era, Seventeen Eighty-Nine to Eighteen-One. LC 60-15321. (New American Nation Ser.). (Illus.). 1960. 19.18i (ISBN 0-06-012980-8, HarpT). Har-Row.

--First Frontier: Life in Colonial America. (Orig.). 1966. pap. 1.50 o.p. (ISBN 0-440-32546-3, LE). Dell.

--Petting the Lion. 1982. 10.95 (ISBN 0-533-05436-2). Vantage.

--This New Man, the American: The Beginnings of the American People. 800p. 1974. 21.95 o.p. (ISBN 0-07-042051-3, P&RB). McGraw.

--Toward a More Perfect Union: The American Republic 1783-1815. 1970. text ed. 10.95x (ISBN 0-673-05765-8). Scott F.

Miller, John E. Governor Philip F. LaFollette: The Wisconsin Progressives & the New Deal. 256p. 1982. 21.00. U of MO Pr.

Miller, John H., jt. auth. see Stanley, Philip.

Miller, John P. Pricing of Military Procurements. (Yale Studies in National Policy: No. 2). 1949. 47.50x (ISBN 0-685-69842-4). Elliots Bks.

Miller, John R., jt. auth. see Gorden, William I.

Miller, John S. Childbirth: A Manual for Pregnancy & Delivery. rev. ed. LC 74-77282. 1974. o. p 6.95 (ISBN 0-689-10625-4); pap. 7.95 (ISBN 0-689-70587-5, 254). Atheneum.

Miller, John W. The Definition of the Thing: With Some Notes on Language. 1980. 16.95 (ISBN 0-393-01377-4). Norton.

--The Definition of the Thing: With Some Notes on Language. 192p. 1983. pap. 6.25x (ISBN 0-393-30059-5). Norton.

--In Defense of the Psychological. 1983. 20.00 (ISBN 0-393-01701-X). Norton.

--The Paradox of Cause & Other Essays. 1978. 14.95x (ISBN 0-393-01172-0). Norton.

--The Paradox of Cause & Other Essays. 192p. 1981. pap. 5.95 (ISBN 0-393-00032-X). Norton.

--The Philosophy of History: With Reflections & Aphorisms. 192p. 1983. pap. 6.25x (ISBN 0-393-30060-9). Norton.

Miller, Jon D. The American People & Science Policy: The Role of Public Attitudes in the Policy Process. 350p. 1983. 35.00 (ISBN 0-08-028064-1). Pergamon.

Miller, Joseph. Money, Then & Now. 4th rev. ed. LC 70-173192. (Illus., Remedial reading level). (gr. 4-10). 1971. text ed. 5.00 (ISBN 0-912472-05-7); tchrs, manual 1.50 (ISBN 0-686-96793-3); student wkbk. 1.40 (ISBN 0-686-96794-1). Miller Bks.

Miller, Judi. Hush, Little Baby. (Orig.). 1983. pap. 2.95 (ISBN 0-671-43182-X). PB.

Miller, Judi, jt. auth. see Weber, Eric.

Miller, Judith, jt. ed. see Miller, Martin.

Miller, K. M. Psychological Testing in Personnel Assessment. LC 75-18451. 1976. 39.95x o.p. (ISBN 0-470-60392-5). Halsted Pr.

Miller, Karl, ed. see Cockburn, Henry.

Miller, Kathryn S. Blue Horses. 30p. (gr. 5-7). 1982. saddle-stitched 2.50x (ISBN 0-88020-107-X). Coach Hse.

Miller, Kathy, jt. auth. see Miller, Barbara.

Miller, Kathy A., jt. auth. see Dunton, Sabina.

Miller, Keith. Second Touch. 1976. pap. 1.75 o.s.i. (ISBN 0-89129-133-4). Jove Pubns.

--A Second Touch. 1982. 7.95 (ISBN 0-8499-0338-6). Word Pub.

Miller, Kenneth S. Partial Differential Equations in Engineering Problems. 1953. ref. ed. 24.95 (ISBN 0-13-650408-6). P-H.

Miller, Lani & Rodgers, Diane. We Love Your Body. LC 80-81842. 1980. pap. 9.95 (ISBN 0-933350-32-5). Writing.

Miller, Larry. Selling in Agribusiness. Lee, Jasper S., ed. (Career Preparation for Agriculture-Agribusiness Ser.). (Illus.). 1979. pap. text ed. 6.96x (ISBN 0-07-041962-0, G); activity guide 4.96x (ISBN 0-07-041963-9); tchr's manual & key 3.00x (ISBN 0-07-041964-7). McGraw.

Miller, Larry, ed. Minnesota's Greatest & Best Recipes: A University of Minnesota Cookbook. (Campus Cookbooks). (Illus.). 192p. (Orig.). 1982. pap. 7.95 (ISBN 0-88011-060-0). Leisure Pr.

Miller, Larry S. & Braswell, Michael C. Human Relations & Police Work. 178p. (Orig.). 1983. pap. text ed. 7.95x (ISBN 0-88133-019-1). Waveland Pr.

Miller, Lawrence C. Successful Management for Contractors. 1962. 24.50 o.p. (ISBN 0-07-041976-0, P&RB). McGraw.

Miller, Lawrence G. & Kazemi, Homayoun. Manual of Clinical Pulmonary Medicine. (PreTest Manuals of Clinical Medicine Ser.). 250p. (Orig.). 1982. manual 14.95 (ISBN 0-07-042167-6, HP). McGraw.

Miller, Lawrence M. Behavior Management: The New Science of Managing People at Work. LC 77-28602. 1978. 24.95 (ISBN 0-471-02947-5, Pub. by Wiley-Interscience). Wiley.

Miller, Lee G. Story of Ernie Pyle. Repr. of 1950 ed. lib. bdg. 20.25x (ISBN 0-8371-3743-8, MIEP). Greenwood.

Miller, Len. Gambling Times Guide to Casino Games. (Illus.). 170p. (Orig.). 1983. pap. text ed. 5.95 (ISBN 0-89746-017-0). Lyle Stuart.

Miller, Lenore, jt. auth. see Walter, Carol.

Miller, Leslie A., et al. Primavera, Vol. VIII. Heller, Janet R. & Peterson, Karen, eds. LC 76-647540. (Illus.). 100p. 1983. pap. 5.00 (ISBN 0-916980-07-3). Primavera.

Miller, Levi. Our People: The Amish & Mennonites of Ohio. (Illus.). 56p. (Orig.). 1982. pap. 2.50 (ISBN 0-8361-3331-5). Herald Pr.

Miller, Levi, ed. Family in Today's Society. LC 79-170198. 1972. pap. 1.75 o.p. (ISBN 0-8361-1659-3). Herald Pr.

Miller, Lewis. The Life You Save: A Guide to Getting the Best Possible Care from Doctors, Hospitals & Nursing Homes. LC 78-1728. 1979. 9.95 o.p. (ISBN 0-688-03461-6). Morrow.

Miller, Libuse. Knowing, Doing, & Surviving: Cognition in Evolution. LC 73-1198. 358p. 1973. 17.50 (ISBN 0-471-60512-3). Krieger.

Miller, Linda A., jt. ed. see Davis, Richard C.

Miller, Lisa. Levers. (Science Is What & Why Ser). (Illus.). (gr. k-4). 1967. PLB 4.49 o.p. (ISBN 0-698-30215-X, Coward). Putnam Pub Group.

--Sound. (Science Is What & Why Ser). (Illus.). (gr. k-4). 1965. PLB 4.49 o.p. (ISBN 0-698-30322-9, Coward). Putnam Pub Group.

Miller, Lise M., jt. auth. see Seranne, Ann.

Miller, Louis G. Touched by Christ. 1978. pap. 1.95 o.p. (ISBN 0-89243-072-9, 48200). Liguori Pubns.

Miller, Lowell. The Momentum Gap Method: The Super New Way to Discover What Stocks to Buy, When to Buy Them, When to Sell. LC 77-13850. 1978. 15.00 o.p. (ISBN 0-399-12070-X). Putnam Pub Group.

Miller, Lula, jt. auth. see Yoder, Elmina.

Miller, Lyle L. Developing Reading Efficiency. 4th ed. LC 79-55778. 1980. pap. text ed. 10.95x (ISBN 0-8087-3958-1). Burgess.

--Maintaining Reading Efficiency. 4th ed. 359p. (gr. 7 up). 1978. 12.95 (ISBN 0-910504-01-6). Develop Read Dist.

--Personalizing Reading Efficiency. LC 81-65474. 1976. pap. 10.95x (ISBN 0-8087-3990-5). Burgess.

Miller, Lynn, jt. auth. see Lieberman, Ann.

Miller, Lynn H. & Pruessen, Ronald W., eds. Reflections on the Cold War: A Quarter Century of American Foreign Policy. LC 73-88279. 215p. 1974. 24.95 (ISBN 0-87722-028-X). Temple U Pr.

Miller, Lynn R. Work Horse Handbook. (Illus.). 224p. 1983. pap. 12.95 (ISBN 0-686-83703-7, ScribT). Scribner.

Miller, M., tr. see Fisher, J. & Dryer, R.

Miller, M. Clinton & Knapp, Rebecca G. Evaluating Quality of Care: Analytic Procedures, Monitoring Techniques. LC 79-4482. 352p. 1979. 38.95 (ISBN 0-89443-091-2). Aspen Systems.

Miller, Madeleine S. & Lane, J. Harper's Bible Dictionary. rev. ed. 1973. 17.95i (ISBN 0-06-065673-5, HarpR). Har-Row.

Miller, Madeleine S. & Miller, J. Lane. Harper's Encyclopedia of Bible Life. rev ed. Bennett, Boyce M., Jr. & Scott, David H., eds. LC 78-4752. (Illus.). 1978. 16.95i o.p. (ISBN 0-06-065676-X, HarpR). Har-Row.

Miller, Malcolm E., et al. Anatomy of the Dog. LC 63-7038. (Illus.). 1964. 25.00 o.p. (ISBN 0-7216-6360-5). Saunders.

Miller, Marc, intro. by. Waging Peace. (Southern Exposure Ser.). (Illus.). 120p. (Orig.). 1982. pap. 4.00 (ISBN 0-943810-14-0). Inst Southern Studies.

Miller, Marcia. Deadly Pursuit. 192p. (YA) 1976. 6.95 (ISBN 0-685-66477-5, Avalon). Bouregy.

--Second Choice. (Adventures in Love Ser.: No. 36). 1982. pap. 1.95 (ISBN 0-451-11876-6, AJ1876, Sig). NAL.

--Spotlight on Romance-Broken Dream. 1982. pap. 2.50 (ISBN 0-451-11870-7, AE1778, Sig). NAL.

Miller, Marcia M. Post Card Views & Other Souvenirs. (Illus.). 64p. 1973. pap. 2.95 (ISBN 0-913270-24-5). Sunstone Pr.

Miller, Margaret. How Like an Angel. LC 82-82890. 278p. 1982. pap. 5.00 (ISBN 0-930330-04-8). Intl Polygonics.

--The Nurse-Manager in the Emergency Department. LC 82-2264. (Illus.). 340p. 1983. pap. text ed. 24.95 (ISBN 0-8016-3512-8). Mosby.

Miller, Margaret Y. Precious Memories. 1978. 4.50 o.p. (ISBN 0-533-03631-3). Vantage.

Miller, Marge, compiled by. Bible Adventures. rev. ed. (Basic Bible Readers Ser.). (Illus.). 128p. (gr. 3). 1983. text ed. 7.95 (ISBN 0-87239-663-0, 2953). Standard Pub.

Miller, Marge, ed. I Learn to Read About Jesus: Primer. rev. ed. (Basic Bible Readers). 128p. (gr. 1). 1983. text ed. 7.95 (ISBN 0-87239-660-6, 2950). Standard Pub.

Miller, Marge, compiled by. I Read About God's Care: Grades 1 & 2. rev. ed. (Basic Bible Readers). (Illus.). 128p. (gr. 1). 1983. text ed. 7.95 (ISBN 0-87239-662-2, 2952). Standard Pub.

Miller, Maria B., jt. auth. see Ferguson, Jeanne.

Miller, Marilee. Landis: Pillar of the Church, Hypocrite, & Murderer. LC 82-84678. (Illus.). 192p. 1982. pap. 9.95 (ISBN 0-911141-00-6). Kindred Joy.

Miller, Marjorie, ed. see Downs, Kathy.

Miller, Marjorie, ed. see Stortz, Diane.

Miller, Marjorie A., et al. Kimber-Gray-Stackpole's Anatomy & Physiology. 17th ed. (Illus.). 640p. 1977. text ed. 26.95x (ISBN 0-02-381220-6). Macmillan.

Miller, Mark. Soviet Strategic Power & Doctrine: The Quest for Superiorty. (Monographs in International Affairs). 1982. text ed. 14.95 (ISBN 0-686-84847-0); pap. text ed. 9.95 (ISBN 0-686-84848-9). AISI.

Miller, Mark J & Martin, Phillip A. Administering Foreign-Worker Programs: Lessons from Europe. LC 81-47994. (Illus.). 224p. 1982. 22.95 (ISBN 0-669-05227-2). Lexington Bks.

Miller, Mark J., jt. ed. see Papademetriou, Demetrios G.

Miller, Marshall L., ed. Toxic Substances Control Two. LC 78-50807. (Toxic Control Ser.). (Illus.). 1978. pap. text ed. 17.00 (ISBN 0-86587-051-9). Gov Insts.

Miller, Marshall Lee, ed. Toxic Substances Control Three: Implementing the Regulatory Program. LC 79-83915. (Toxic Control Ser.). pap. text ed. 18.00 (ISBN 0-86587-052-7). Gov Insts.

Miller, Martin & Miller, Judith, eds. Miller's Antique Price Guide. (Illus.). 669p. 1982. 22.50 (ISBN 0-905879-16-3, Pub. by MJM England). C E Tuttle.

Miller, Marvin D. Wunderlich's Salute: The Interrelationship of the German-American Bund, Camp Siegfried, Yaphank, Long Island, & the Young Siegfrieds & Their Relations with American & Nazi Institutions. LC 82-62515. (Illus.). 270p. 1983. pap. write for info. (ISBN 0-9610466-0-0). Malamud-Rose.

Miller, Mary R. Place-Names of the Northern Neck of Virginia. 1983. pap. write for info (ISBN 0-88490-099-1). VA State Lib.

--Thomas Campbell. (English Authors Ser.). 1978. 14.95 (ISBN 0-8057-6728-2, Twayne). G K hall.

Miller, Mary S. Bringing Learning Home: How Parents Can Play a More Active & Effective Role in Their Children's Education. LC 80-7856. 256p. 1981. 12.45i (ISBN 0-690-01952-1). Har-Row.

Miller, Maurice. Four Plays: A Collection of Three-Act Comedy Dramas. 1983. 12.95 (ISBN 0-533-05465-6). Vantage.

Miller, Max D., jt. auth. see Dyken, Paul R.

Miller, Max D., jt. auth. see Rao, P. Syamasundar.

Miller, Merl, jt. auth. see Willis, Jerry.

Miller, Merl, ed. see Rosa, Nicholas.

Miller, Merle. Lyndon: An Oral Biography. 1980. 17.95 (ISBN 0-399-12357-1). Putnam Pub Group.

Miller, Michael. Therapeutic Hypnosis. LC 78-10405. 368p. 1979. 34.95 (ISBN 0-87705-341-3). Human Sci Pr.

--What Are They Saying About Papal Primacy? (WATSA Ser.). 128p. 1983. pap. 3.95 (ISBN 0-8091-2501-3). Paulist Pr.

Miller, Michael F. Classical Greek & Roman Coins: The Investor's Handbook. LC 81-69260. (Illus.). 224p. 1982. 17.95 (ISBN 0-9607106-0-4). Altara Group.

Miller, Millie. Saguaroc: The Desert Flower Book. new ed. (Orig.). 1982. pap. 4.95 (ISBN 0-933472-69-2). Johnson Bks.

Miller, Milton G. & Schwartzman, Sylvan D. Our Religion & Our Neighbors. rev. ed. LC 63-14742. (Illus.). (gr. 9). 1971. text ed. 8.50 (ISBN 0-8074-0145-5, 141513); tchrs'. guide 3.50 (ISBN 0-8074-0146-3, 204280). UAHC.

Miller, Molly. Sicilian Colony Dates: Studies in Chronography One. LC 69-14646. (Illus.). 1970. 34.50x (ISBN 0-87395-049-6). State U NY Pr.

Miller, Molly B. Thalassocracies, Studies in Chronography 2. LC 77-91204. 1971. 29.50x (ISBN 0-87395-062-3). State U NY Pr.

Miller, Monte. Snowshoe. LC 82-83035. (Illus.). 32p. (Orig.). (ps). 1983. pap. write for info. (ISBN 0-914766-88-0, 0266). IWP Pub.

Miller, Morris & Janis, Arthur. Modern Bookkeeping & Accounting. 2nd ed. LC 72-109961. (gr. 10-12) 1973. text ed. 15.84 (ISBN 0-8224-2011-2); tchrs' manual 8.00 (ISBN 0-8224-2070-8); solutions 11.60 (ISBN 0-8224-2072-4); Workbook I (units 1-26) 6.60 (ISBN 0-8224-2068-6); Workbook II (units 27-45) 6.60 (ISBN 0-8224-2069-4); tests 46.00 (ISBN 0-8224-2071-6). Pitman Learning.

Miller, N., jt. auth. see Aya, R.

Miller, N. E., jt. auth. see Richter-Heinrich, E.

Miller, Nancy, ed. Guide to Third World Business. 330p. 1981. 25.00 (ISBN 0-89893-501-6). CDP.

Miller, Nancy & Cohen, Gene D., eds. Clinical Aspects of Alzheimer's Disease & Senile Dementia. (Aging Ser.: Vol. 15). 372p. 1981. text ed. 43.00 (ISBN 0-89004-326-4). Raven.

Miller, Nancy O., jt. auth. see Lucky, Luretha F.

Miller, Natalie. The Story of Mount Vernon. LC 82-12217. (Cornerstone of Freedom Ser.). (Illus.). 32p. (gr. 2-5). 1965. PLB 7.95 (ISBN 0-516-04624-1). Childrens.

Miller, Nathan. The Child in Primitive Society. LC 76-167074. 1975. Repr. of 1928 ed. 38.00x (ISBN 0-8103-3995-1). Gale.

--FDR: An Intimate History. LC 80-2977. (Illus.). 576p. 1983. 22.50 (ISBN 0-385-15108-X). Doubleday.

Miller, Ned A. The Complete Guide to Employee Benefit Plans. rev. ed. LC 79-88343. 1983. 29.95 (ISBN 0-87863-149-6). Farnswth Pub.

Miller, Neil. Walsh & Hoyt's Clinical Neuro-Ophthalmology. 4th ed. (Illus.). 393p. 1982. lib. bdg. 55.00 (ISBN 0-683-06020-1). Williams & Wilkins.

Miller, Neil R. Sights & Sounds in Ophthalmology: Vol. 3, the Ocular Fundus in Neuroophtalmology. Fine, Stuart L., ed. (A slide-tape presentation). 1977. pap. 199.00 (ISBN 0-8016-3446-6). Mosby.

Miller, Norman, ed. International Reserves. Exchange Rates, & Developing-Country Finance. LC 81-47765. 176p. 1982. 21.95 (ISBN 0-669-04856-9). Lexington Bks.

Miller, Norman C. Microeconomics. 750p. 1983. text ed. 23.95 (ISBN 0-395-32579-X); write for info. instr's manual (ISBN 0-395-32580-3); study guide 8.95 (ISBN 0-395-32581-1). HM.

Miller, Norman G., jt. auth. see Goebel, Paul R.

Miller, Nyle H., jt. auth. see Kansas State Historical Society Staff.

Miller, O. K., Jr. & Farr, D. F. An Index of the Common Fungi of North America (Synonymy & Common Names) 1975. pap. 18.75 o.s.i. (ISBN 3-7682-0974-1). Lubrecht & Cramer.

Miller, Olga K., ed. Genealogical Research for Czech & Slovak Americans. LC 78-13086. (Genealogy & Local History Ser.: Vol. 2). (Illus.). 1978. 42.00x (ISBN 0-8103-1404-5). Gale.

Miller, Orlo. A Century of Western Ontario: The Story of London, the Free Press, & Western Ontario, 1849-1949. LC 71-165443. (Illus.). 289p. 1972. Repr. of 1949 ed. lib. bdg. 17.50x (ISBN 0-8371-6226-2, MIWO). Greenwood.

Miller, Orson K., et al. Multi-Purpose Mushroom Calendar: 1983. (Illus.). 12p. (Orig.). 1982. pap. 5.95 without mailer (ISBN 0-916422-25-9); pap. text ed. 6.95 with mailer o.p. (ISBN 0-686-73526-9). Mad River.

Miller, Orson K., Jr. Mushrooms of North America. rev. ed. 1979. 16.95 (ISBN 0-525-16166-X, 01117-330); pap. 11.50 (ISBN 0-525-47482-X). Dutton.

Miller, P. The Gardener's Dictionary. 1969. Repr. of 1754 ed. 64.00 (ISBN 3-7682-0613-0). Lubrecht & Cramer.

Miller, Patricia G., jt. auth. see Miller, Tony.

Miller, Paul E. Down Beat's Yearbook of Swing. LC 78-6152. 1978. Repr. of 1939 ed. lib. bdg. 17.25x (ISBN 0-313-20476-4, MIYS). Greenwood.

--Esquire's Jazz Books, 3 vols. Incl. 1944 Jazz Book (ISBN 0-306-79525-6); 1945 Jazz Book (ISBN 0-306-79526-4); 1946 Jazz Book (ISBN 0-306-79527-2). (The Roots of Jazz Ser.). (Repr. of 1944-46 ed.). 1979. Set. 65.00 (ISBN 0-306-79528-0); 22.50 ea. Da Capo.

Miller, Paul E., ed. Esquire's Jazz Book: 1944-1946, 3 Vols. (Roots of Jazz Ser.). 1979. Repr. Set. lib. bdg. 65.00 (ISBN 0-306-79528-0); lib. bdg. 22.50 ea.; 1944 vol. (ISBN 0-306-79525-6); 1945 vol. (ISBN 0-306-79526-4); 1946 vol. (ISBN 0-306-79527-2). Da Capo.

Miller, Paul M. Servant of God's Servants: The Work of a Christian Minister. LC 63-15499. (Conrad Grebel Lecture Ser.). 1964. 4.50 o.p. (ISBN 0-8361-1492-2). Herald Pr.

Miller, Paul S. Business Math. (Illus.). 1980. pap. text ed. 19.95x (ISBN 0-07-042157-9); instructor's manual 20.95 (ISBN 0-07-042158-7). McGraw.

Miller, Paul W., ed. see Whitlock, Brand.

Miller, Peggy J. Amy, Wendy & Beth: Learning Language in South Baltimore. (Illus.). 208p. 1982. text ed. 18.95x (ISBN 0-292-70357-0). U of Tex Pr.

Miller, Perry. The New England Mind: From Colony to Province. 528p. 1983. pap. text ed. 8.95x (ISBN 0-674-61301-5, Belknap). Harvard U Pr.

--The New England Mind: The Seventeenth Century. 540p. 1983. pap. text ed. 8.95x (ISBN 0-674-61306-6, Belknap). Harvard U Pr.

--The Responsibility of Mind in a Civilization of Machines: Essays by Perry Miller. Crowell, John & Searl, Stanford J., Jr., eds. LC 79-4699. (New England Writers Ser.). 1979. lib. bdg. 14.50x o.p. (ISBN 0-87023-281-9). U of Mass Pr.

--Sources for The New England Mind: The Seventeenth Century. Hoopes, James, ed. LC 81-81411. 156p. (Orig.). 1981. pap. text ed. 5.95 (ISBN 0-910776-01-6). Inst Early Am.

Miller, Perry & Johnson, T. H. Puritans: A Sourcebook of Their Writings, 2 Vols. Vol. 1. 15.00; Vol. 2. 17.00. Peter Smith.

Miller, Perry & Johnson, Thomas H., eds. Puritans: A Sourcebook of Their Writings, 2 vols. (Orig.). Vol. 1. pap. 8.95xi (ISBN 0-06-131093-X, TB1093, Torch); Vol. 2. pap. 7.95x (ISBN 0-06-131094-8, TB1094, Torch). Har-Row.

Miller, Perry G. Nature's Nation. LC 67-17316. 1967. 16.50x (ISBN 0-674-60550-0, Belknap Pr). Harvard U Pr.

--New England Mind: The Seventeenth Century. LC 54-7507. 1954. 16.50x o.p. (ISBN 0-674-61305-8). Harvard U Pr.

Miller, Peter. Aces Wild: The Story of the British Grand Prix. (Illus.). 140p. 1972. 9.95 o.p. (ISBN 0-7207-0580-0). Transatlantic.

Miller, Peter, jt. auth. see Hodgson, Ray.

Miller, Peter G. How to Buy a New Car & Not Lose Your Shirt. (Orig.). 1981. pap. 3.25 (ISBN 0-939972-02-6). Springhill Pr MD.

Miller, Peter G., jt. ed. see Bregman, Douglas M.

Miller, Peter M. The Hilton Head Metabolism Diet. 256p. 1983. 14.50 (ISBN 0-446-51266-4). Warner Bks.

Miller, Philip B., ed. & tr. see Von Kleist, Heinrich.

Miller, R. Radiographic Contrast Agents. Miller, R., ed. 544p. 1977. text ed. 49.50 (ISBN 0-8391-1117-7). Univ Park.

--The Resistance. LC 79-14316. (World War II Ser.). (Illus.). 1979. lib. bdg. 19.92 (ISBN 0-8094-2523-8); 17.28 (ISBN 0-8094-2524-6). Silver.

Miller, R. Baxter. Langston Hughes & Gwendolyn Brooks: A Reference Guide. 1978. 22.00 (ISBN 0-8161-7810-0, Hall Reference). G K Hall.

Miller, R. C. Soviets Begin War in the Middle East-U.S. Counters. limited ed. 96p. 1983. pap. 2.50 (ISBN 0-682-49967-6). Exposition.

--This We Can Believe. 1976. 2.00 (ISBN 0-8164-0376-7). Seabury.

Miller, R. E. & Skucas, J. Radiological Examination of the Colon. 1983. 128.00 (ISBN 90-247-2666-2, Pub. by Martinus Nijhoff Netherlands). Kluwer Boston.

Miller, R. E., jt. auth. see Sellink, J. L.

Miller, R. G. & Stace, B. C., eds. Laboratory Methods in Infrared Spectroscopy. 2nd ed. 1972. 59.95 (ISBN 0-471-25908-X, Wiley Heyden). Wiley.

Miller, R. H. Power System Operation. 1970. 36.50 (ISBN 0-07-041974-4, P&RB). McGraw.

Miller, R. K. The Placenta. Thiede, H., ed. 390p. 1982. 69.50 (ISBN 0-03-063037-1). Praeger.

Miller, R. L. Intermediate Microeconomics. 2nd ed. 1982. 23.95x (ISBN 0-07-042159-5); study guide 8.95x (ISBN 0-07-042160-9); instr.'s manual 7.50 (ISBN 0-07-042161-7). McGraw.

Miller, R. W. Schedule, Cost & Profit Control with PERT: Comprehensive Guide for Program Management. 1963. 16.95 o.p. (ISBN 0-07-041994-9, P&RB). McGraw.

Miller, Randall M., ed. The Kaleidoscopic Lens: How Hollywood Views Ethnic Groups. 1980. lib. bdg. 13.95x o.p. (ISBN 0-89198-120-9); pap. text ed. 7.95x (ISBN 0-89198-121-7). Ozer.

Miller, Randall M. & Marzik, Thomas D., eds. Immigrants & Religion in Urban America. LC 76-62866. 208p. 1977. 22.00x (ISBN 0-87722-093-X); pap. 9.95 (ISBN 0-87722-146-4). Temple U Pr.

Miller, Randolph C. The Theory of Christian Education Practice: How Theology Affects Christian Education. LC 80-15886. 312p. (Orig.). 1980. pap. 12.95 (ISBN 0-89135-049-7). Religious Educ.

Miller, Ray. Falcon! The New Size Ford. LC 82-90194. (Ford Road Ser.: Vol. 7). (Illus.). 320p. 1982. 29.95 (ISBN 0-913056-11-1). Evergreen Pr.

Miller, Raymond C. The Importance of Being in Earnest. 1951. pap. 1.00x o.p. (ISBN 0-8143-1039-7). Wayne St U Pr.

Miller, Raymond C., ed. Twentieth-Century Pessimism & the American Dream. LC 79-26081. (Franklin Memorial Lectures: Vol. VIII). (Illus.). ix, 104p. 1980. Repr. of 1961 ed. lib. bdg. 15.50x (ISBN 0-313-22212-7, MITW). Greenwood.

Miller, Raymond E. Switching Theory, 2 vols. LC 78-11958. 618p. 1979. Repr. of 1965 ed. Set. lib. bdg. 35.00 (ISBN 0-88275-759-8). Vol. 1: Combinational Circuits. Vol. 2: Sequential Circuits & Machines. Krieger.

Miller, Raymond W. A Conservative Looks at Cooperatives. LC 64-15585. 245p. 1964. 11.95 (ISBN 0-8214-0000-2, 82-80018). Ohio U Pr.

--Monsignor Ligutti: The Pope's County Agent. LC 81-40044. 252p. (Orig.). 1982. lib. bdg. 21.75 (ISBN 0-8191-1925-3); pap. text ed. 10.75 (ISBN 0-8191-1926-1). U Pr of Amer.

Miller, Reese P., tr. see Descartes, Rene.

Miller, Rex. Refrigeration & Air-Conditioning Technology. 1982. text ed. 18.64 (ISBN 0-87002-379-9); student ed. 3.32 (ISBN 0-87002-384-5); tchr's. ed. 3.20 (ISBN 0-87002-390-X). Bennett IL.

--Residential Electrical Wiring. (Illus.). 300p. 1981. text ed. 12.80 (ISBN 0-87002-331-4); student guide 3.96 (ISBN 0-87002-332-2); tchr's. ed. 4.20 (ISBN 0-87002-339-X). Bennett IL.

Miller, Rex & Culpepper, Fred. Math for Electricity-Electronics. Vorndran, Richard A., ed. 160p. 1980. pap. text ed. 5.28 (ISBN 0-02-818220-0); manual & key 4.00 (ISBN 0-02-818230-8). Glencoe.

Miller, Rex, jt. auth. see Anderson, Edwin P.

Miller, Rex, jt. auth. see Baker, Glenn E.

Miller, Rex, jt. auth. see Fuller, Nelson.

Miller, Richard. Noise Control Solutions for the Stone Industry. (Illus.). 90p. pap. text ed. 45.00 (ISBN 0-89671-028-9). Southeast Acoustics.

Miller, Richard, jt. auth. see Fox, Frederick.

Miller, Richard, tr. see Barthes, Roland.

Miller, Richard, tr. see Brassai.

Miller, Richard A. The Magical & Ritual Use of Herbs. 144p. 1983. pap. 5.95 (ISBN 0-89281-047-5). Destiny Bks.

Miller, Richard J. Ancient Japanese Nobility: The Kabane Ranking System. (Publications in Occasional Papers, Vol. 7). 1974. pap. 22.50x (ISBN 0-520-09494-8). U of Cal Pr.

Miller, Richard K. Corporate Noise Impast Assessment Manual. 1981. pap. text ed. 55.00 (ISBN 0-89671-029-7). Southeast Acoustics.

--Industrial Noise Control 1978. new ed. 1978. pap. text ed. 35.00x o.p. (ISBN 0-89671-011-4). Southeast Acoustics.

--Industrial Noise Update. (Illus.). 87p. 1981. pap. text ed. 30.00 (ISBN 0-89671-025-4). Southeast Acoustics.

--Introductory Statistics for Business & Economics. 445p. 1980. text ed. 20.95x (ISBN 0-312-43451-0); study guide 7.95 (ISBN 0-312-43453-7); solution manual available. St Martin.

--Noise & Energy. (Illus.). 134p. text ed. 45.00 (ISBN 0-89671-022-X). Southeast Acoustics.

--Noise Control for Construction. (Illus.). 140p. text ed. 55.00 (ISBN 0-89671-023-8). Southeast Acoustics.

--Noise Control for Power Plants. (Illus.). 150p. 1983. text ed. 45.00 (ISBN 0-915586-70-3). Fairmont Pr.

--Noise Control in Buffing & Polishing. new ed. (Illus.). 1979. pap. text ed. 35.00x o.p. (ISBN 0-89671-009-2). Southeast Acoustics.

--Noise Control Solutions for Monument Manufacturing. 1979. pap. text ed. 45.00x o.p. (ISBN 0-89671-008-4). Southeast Acoustics.

--Noise Control Solutions for Printing & Publishing. (Illus.). 77p. 1981. pap. text ed. 45.00 (ISBN 0-89671-026-2). Southeast Acoustics.

--Noise Control Solutions for Printing & Publishing Industry. (Illus.). 110p. 1983. text ed. 45.00 (ISBN 0-915586-74-6). Fairmont Pr.

--Noise Control Solutions for the Chemical & Petroleum Industries. new ed. 1981. text ed. 45.00x (ISBN 0-89671-036-X). Southeast Acoustics.

--Noise Control Solutions for the Food Industry. (Illus.). 110p. text ed. 45.00 (ISBN 0-89671-034-3). Southeast Acoustics.

--Noise Control Solutions for the Food Industry, Vol. II. (Illus.). 120p. 1981. pap. text ed. 45.00 (ISBN 0-89671-024-6). Southeast Acoustics.

--Noise Control Solutions for the Footwear Industry. 90p. pap. text ed. 45.00 (ISBN 0-89671-027-0). Southeast Acoustics.

--Noise Control Solutions for the Glass Industry. 120p. pap. text ed. 90.00 (ISBN 0-89671-016-5). Southeast Acoustics.

--Noise Control Solutions for the Metal Products Industry. (Illus.). 120p. text ed. 45.00 (ISBN 0-89671-031-9). Southeast Acoustics.

--Noise Control Solutions for the Metal Products Industry, Vol. II. (Illus.). 120p. pap. text ed. 45.00 (ISBN 0-89671-021-1). Southeast Acoustics.

--Noise Control Solutions for the Paper Industry. (Illus.). 80p. text ed. 45.00 (ISBN 0-89671-033-5). Southeast Acoustics.

--Noise Control Solutions for the Rubber & Plastics Industry. new ed. (Illus.). 1981. text ed. 45.00x (ISBN 0-89671-037-8). Southeast Acoustics.

--Noise Control Solutions for the Textile Industry. (Illus.). 90p. text ed. 45.00 (ISBN 0-89671-035-1). Southeast Acoustics.

--Noise Control Solutions for the Wood Products Industry. 80p. text ed. 45.00 (ISBN 0-89671-032-7). Southeast Acoustics.

--Power Plant Noise Control. (Illus.). 130p. pap. text ed. 65.00 (ISBN 0-89671-019-X). Southeast Acoustics.

--Robots in Industry: General Applications. (Illus.). 203p. pap. 65.00 (ISBN 0-89671-043-2). Southeast Acoustics.

Miller, Richard W. Flow Measurement Engineering Handbook. (Illus.). 800p. 1983. 59.95 (ISBN 0-07-042045-9, P&RB). McGraw.

Miller, Rick. The Early West. (Illus.). 176p. 1983. 13.75 (ISBN 0-932702-25-2); pap. 8.50 (ISBN 0-932702-27-9); leatherbound limited to 25 copies 75.00. Creative Texas.

Miller, Robert F. & Rigby, T. H. Twenty Sixth Congress of the CPSU in Current Political Perspective. (Department of Political Science, Research School of Social Sciences Ser.: Occasional Paper No. 16). 94p. (Orig.). pap. text ed. 9.95 (ISBN 0-909779-03-1, 1184, Pub. by ANUP Australia). Bks Australia.

Miller, Robert H. Power System Operation. 2nd ed. (Illus.). 224p. 1983. 34.50 (ISBN 0-07-041975-2, P&RB). McGraw.

--Textbook of Basic Emergency Medicine. 2nd ed. LC 79-27337. (Illus.). 278p. 1980. pap. text ed. 16.95 (ISBN 0-8016-3449-0). Mosby.

Miller, Robert K. Oscar Wilde. LC 81-70734. (Literature and Life Ser.). 160p. 1982. 11.95 (ISBN 0-8044-2629-5). Ungar.

Miller, Robert P., ed. Chaucer: Sources & Backgrounds. (Illus.). 1977. text ed. 17.95x (ISBN 0-19-502166-5); pap. text ed. 14.95x (ISBN 0-19-502167-3). Oxford U Pr.

Miller, Robert T. & Flowers, Ronald B. Toward Benevolent Neutrality: Church, State, & the Supreme Court. rev. ed. 726p. 1982. 25.00 (ISBN 0-918954-28-2). Markham Pr Fund.

Miller, Robert W. Clock Guide Identification, No. 1. pap. 10.95 (ISBN 0-87069-360-3). Wallace-Homestead.

--Higher Education & the Community College. 1977. pap. text ed. 10.50 (ISBN 0-8191-0264-4). U Pr of Amer.

Miller, Roberta B. City & Hinterland: A Case Study of Urban Growth & Regional Developments. LC 78-55340. (Contributions in American History: No. 77). (Illus.). 1979. lib. bdg. 25.00 (ISBN 0-313-20524-8, MCH/). Greenwood.

Miller, Roberta D. Psychic Massage. (Illus.). 224p. (Orig.). 1975. pap. 8.61i (ISBN 0-06-090353-8, CN353, CN). Har-Row.

Miller, Roger L. Economic Issues for Consumers. 3rd ed. (Illus.). 656p. 1981. text ed. 21.95 (ISBN 0-8299-0396-8). West Pub.

--Economic Issues for Consumers. 2nd ed. (Illus.). 1978. text ed. 20.95 (ISBN 0-8299-0151-5); pap. text ed. 6.50 study guide (ISBN 0-8299-0217-1); instrs.' manual avail. (ISBN 0-8299-0560-X). West Pub.

--The Economics of Macro Issues. 4th ed. 160p. 1982. pap. text ed. 9.50 (ISBN 0-314-69667-9). West Pub.

--Economics Today. 4th ed. 830p. 1982. text ed. 24.50 scp (ISBN 0-06-044493-2, Harp C); Instr's. Manual Avail. (ISBN 0-06-364522-X); Trans. Master Avail. (ISBN 0-06-364524-6); Student Learning Guide 8.95 (ISBN 0-06-042323-4). Har-Row.

--Economics Today: The Macro View. 4th ed. 492p. 1982. pap. text ed. 16.50 scp (ISBN 0-06-044492-4, HarpC); scp study guide 6.50 (ISBN 0-06-042353-6); student audiocassettes mod. 1-15 scp 250.00 (ISBN 0-06-044248-4); scp wkbk. audiocassettes 7.50 (ISBN 0-06-044246-8). Har-Row.

--Economics Today: The Micro View. 4th ed. 487p. 1982. pap. text ed. 16.50 (ISBN 0-06-044491-6, HarpC); scp study guide 6.50 (ISBN 0-06-042352-8); scp student audiocasssettes mod 16-30 250.00 (ISBN 0-06-044249-2); wkbk. scp 7.50 (ISBN 0-06-044247-6). Har-Row.

--Intermediate Microeconomics: Theories, Issues, & Applications. (Illus.). 1977. text ed. 23.95 (ISBN 0-07-042150-1); instr's manual 22.50 (ISBN 0-07-042151-X); study guide 9.50 (ISBN 0-07-042152-8); transparency masters 15.00 (ISBN 0-07-042153-6). McGraw.

--Personal Finance Today. (Illus.). 1979. text ed. 21.95 (ISBN 0-8299-0233-3); pap. study guide & wkbk. by Grant J. Wells 8.50 (ISBN 0-8299-0256-2); instrs.' manual avail. (ISBN 0-8299-0561-8). West Pub.

Miller, Roger L. & Power, Fred B. Personal Finance Today. 2nd ed. (Illus.). 500p. 1983. text ed. 22.95 (ISBN 0-314-69668-7); instrs.' manual avail. (ISBN 0-314-71112-0); student guide avail. (ISBN 0-314-71113-9). West Pub.

Miller, Roger L. & Pulsinelli, Robert W. Understanding Economics. (Illus.). 1983. text ed. 19.95 (ISBN 0-314-69669-5); instrs.' manual avail. (ISBN 0-314-71114-7); study guide avail. (ISBN 0-314-71143-0). West Pub.

Miller, Roger L. & Williams, Raburn M. Unemployment & Inflation: The New Economics of the Wage-Price Spiral. LC 74-1062. 100p. 1974. text ed. 12.95 (ISBN 0-8299-0009-8). West Pub.

Miller, Roger L., jt. auth. see Clarkson, Kenneth W.

Miller, Roger L., jt. auth. see North, Douglas C.

Miller, Roger L., jt. auth. see West, Edwin G.

Miller, Roger R., jt. ed. see Parad, Howard J.

Miller, Ron & Durant, Frederick C. Worlds Beyond: The Art of Chesley Bonestell. Stine, Hank, ed. LC 82-5005. (Illus.). 150p. 1982. lib. bdg. 17.95 (ISBN 0-686-81435-5); pap. 14.95 (ISBN 0-89865-195-6); ltd. ed. 35.00 (ISBN 0-89865-226-X). Donning Co.

Miller, Ronald D., ed. Year Book of Anesthesia, 1982. (Illus.). 400p. 1982. 34.95 (ISBN 0-8151-5928-5). Year Bk Med.
--Year Book of Anesthesia 1983. 1983. 35.00 (ISBN 0-8151-5929-3). Year Bk Med.
Miller, Ronald E. Dynamic Optimization & Economic Applications. (Illus.). 1980. text ed. 32.95 o.p. (ISBN 0-07-042180-3); solutions manual 4.50 o.p. (ISBN 0-07-042181-1). McGraw.
Miller, Ronald E. & Sawer, David. The Technical Development of Modern Aviation. (Airlines History Project Ser.). Date not set. price not set (ISBN 0-404-19328-5). AMS Pr.
Miller, Ronald J. The Demolition of Skid Row. LC 81-47182. 160p. 1981. 18.95x (ISBN 0-669-04563-2). Lexington Bks.
Miller, Rosalind & Rehr, Helen. Social Work Issues in Health Care. (Illus.). 288p. 1983. 24.95 (ISBN 0-13-819532-3). P-H.
Miller, Roscoe R. Prospects of Good Fortune. 1979. 5.95 o.p. (ISBN 0-533-03354-3). Vantage.
Miller, Roy A. The Japanese Language. LC 67-16777. (History & Structure of Languages Ser.). 496p. 1980. pap. 19.00x (ISBN 0-226-52718-2, Midway). U of Chicago Pr.
Miller, Roy Arthur. Studies in the Grammatical Tradition in Tibet. (Studies in the History of Linguistics Ser.: No. 6). xix, 142p. 1976. 19.00 (ISBN 90-272-0897-2). Benjamins North Am.
Miller, Ruby M., jt. auth. see Miller, E. W.
Miller, Rupert G., et al. Biostatistics Casebook. (Applied Probability & Statistics Ser.). 1980. 19.95 (ISBN 0-471-06258-8, Pub. by Wiley-Interscience). Wiley.
Miller, Rupert G., Jr. Survival Analysis. LC 81-4437. (Wiley Series in Probability & Mathematical Statistics: Applied Probability & Statistics). 238p. 1981. pap. 18.95 (ISBN 0-471-09434-X, Pub. by Wiley-Interscience). Wiley.
Miller, Russell. The Commandos. LC 81-13600. (World War II Ser.). lib. bdg. 19.92 (ISBN 0-8094-3400-8). Silver.
--Continents in Collision. (Planet Earth Ser.). 1983. lib. bdg. 19.92 (ISBN 0-8094-4325-2, Pub. by Time-Life). Silver.
--The East Indianmen. LC 80-18008. (Seafarers Ser.). 19.92 (ISBN 0-686-79859-7). Silver.
Miller, Russell R. & Greenblatt, David J., eds. Drug Therapy Reviews, Vol. 1. LC 76-54569. (Illus.). 272p. 1977. text ed. 38.00x (ISBN 0-89352-001-2). Masson Pub.
Miller, Rusty. The Jedi Master's Quizbook. (Orig.). 1982. pap. 1.95 (ISBN 0-345-30697-X, Del Rey). Ballantine.
Miller, Ruth. Black American Literature: 1760 to the Present. 1971. pap. text ed. 21.95x (ISBN 0-02-476420-5, 47642). Macmillan.
Miller, Ruth & Greenberg, Robert A. Poetry: An Introduction. 550p. 1981. pap. 10.95x (ISBN 0-312-61804-2); instr's. manual avail. (ISBN 0-312-61805-0). St Martin.
Miller, Ruth & Dolan, Paul J., eds. Race Awareness: The Nightmare & the Vision. (Illus.). 1971. pap. 7.95x o.p. (ISBN 0-19-501363-8). Oxford U Pr.
Miller, Ruth W. The City Rose. 1978. pap. 1.50 o.s.i. (ISBN 0-380-40535-0, 40535). Avon.
Miller, Ryle, tr. see Institut Francais De Pertrole.
Miller, S. & Judd, W. Thinkerthings. (gr. 4-8). 1980. pap. 13.35 (ISBN 0-201-03453-0, Sch Div); bound duplicating masters & tchrs'. guide incl. A-W.
Miller, S., jt. ed. see Sorsby, A.
Miller, S. J. Eyes. 3rd ed. (Operative Surgery Ser.). 1976. 59.95 (ISBN 0-407-00609-5). Butterworth.
Miller, Sally & Winstead-Fry, Patricia. Family Systems Theory & Nursing Practice. 176p. 1982. text ed. 12.95 (ISBN 0-8359-1850-5); pap. text ed. 9.95 (ISBN 0-8359-1849-1). Reston.
Miller, Sally M. The Radical Immigrant. (Immigrant Heritage of America Ser.). 1974. lib. bdg. 11.95 (ISBN 0-8057-3266-7, Twayne). G K Hall.
--Victor Berger & the Promise of Constructive Socialism, 1910-1920. LC 72-175609. (Contributions in American History: No. 24). 390p. 1973. lib. bdg. 29.95 (ISBN 0-8371-6264-5, MVB/). Greenwood.
Miller, Sandra L. Womanwrit: The Poems & Photographs of Sandra Lake Miller. (Illus.). 64p. (Orig.). 1982. pap. 5.00 (ISBN 0-9609448-0-X). S L Miller.
Miller, Sandy. Smart Girl. 1982. pap. 2.25 (ISBN 0-451-11887-1, Sig Vista). NAL.
--Two Loves for Jenny. 1982. pap. 1.75 (ISBN 0-451-11531-7, Sig Vista). NAL.
Miller, Sarah W. Christmas Drama for Youth. LC 76-20255. 96p. (Orig.). (gr. 7 up). 1976. pap. 4.50 (ISBN 0-8054-7511-7). Broadman.
Miller, Shelby H. Children As Parents: Progress Report. 28p. 1981. 4.50 o.p. (ISBN 0-87868-207-4, X-15). Child Welfare.
Miller, Sherod, et al. Straight Talk: A New Way to Get Close to Others by Saying What You Really Mean. 1982. pap. 3.95 (ISBN 0-451-12047-7, AE2047, Sig). NAL.
Miller, Shirley. The Vertical File & Its Satellites: A Handbook of Acquisition, Processing, & Organization. 2nd ed. LC 79-13773. (Library Science Text Ser.). 251p. 1979. lib. bdg. 19.50 (ISBN 0-87287-164-9). Libs Unl.
Miller, Sidney L. Legal Aspects of Dentistry. 1970. pap. 9.50 o.p. (ISBN 0-399-40022-2). Putnam Pub Group.
Miller, Sigmund. Symptoms: The Complete Home Medical Encyclopedia. (Illus.). 1976. 23.99i (ISBN 0-690-01125-3). T Y Crowell.
Miller, Stanley, et al. New York's Chinese Restaurants: A Guide. LC 76-53403. 1977. pap. 4.95 o.p. (ISBN 0-689-70550-6). Atheneum.
Miller, Stanley L. & Orgel, Leslie E. The Origins of Life on the Earth. (Concepts of Modern Biology Ser). (Illus.). 208p. 1974. pap. 13.95 ref. ed. (ISBN 0-13-642074-5). P-H.
Miller, Stella. Two Groups of Thessalian Gold. LC 77-80473. (UC Publications in Classical Studies: Vol. 18). 1979. pap. 17.50x (ISBN 0-520-09580-4). U of Cal Pr.
Miller, Stephen G. The Prytaneion: Its Function & Architectural Form. LC 76-24590. 1978. 30.00x (ISBN 0-520-03316-7). U of Cal Pr.
Miller, Stephen W., ed. Memory & Storage Technolgy, Vol II. (The Information Technology Ser.). (Illus.). 182p. 1977. pap. 23.00 (ISBN 0-88283-015-5). AFIPS Pr.
Miller, Stephen W., jt. auth. see Kim, Seung H.
Miller, Steven M., jt. auth. see Ayres, Robert U.
Miller, Stuart. Men & Friendship. LC 82-18718. 206p. 1983. 13.95 (ISBN 0-395-33103-X). HM.
Miller, Stuart C. The Unwelcome Immigrant: The American Image of the Chinese, 1785-1882. 1969. 26.50x (ISBN 0-520-01380-8); pap. 3.25 (ISBN 0-520-02620-9). U of Cal Pr.
Miller, Stuart J. & Dinitz, Simon. Careers of the Violent. LC 77-10168. (The Dangerous Offender Project Ser.). 384p. 1982. 36.95x (ISBN 0-669-01778-7). Lexington Bks.
Miller, Stuart J., jt. auth. see Bartollas, Clemens.
Miller, Susann. Porche Year 1982. (Illus.). 96p. 1982. 29.95 (ISBN 0-910597-01-4); pap. 17.95 (ISBN 0-910597-00-6). Carrera Intl.
Miller, Susanne, jt. auth. see Wilkins, Gloria.
Miller, Susanne S. Whales & Sharks & Other Creatures of the Deep. (Illus.). 48p. (ps-2). 1982. PLB 9.97g (ISBN 0-671-46006-4). Messner.
Miller, Suzanne S. Whales & Sharks & Giant Squid & Other Creatures of the Deep. Klimo, Kate, ed. (Illus.). 48p. 1982. text ed. 6.95 (ISBN 0-671-45148-0, Little Simon). S&S.
Miller, T. J. Reactive Power Control in Electric Systems. LC 82-10838. 381p. 1982. 49.50 (ISBN 0-471-86933-3, Pub. by Wiley-Interscience). Wiley.
Miller, T. W., jt. auth. see Monzingo, F. A.
Miller, Tamar N. Index to Novyi Mir 1925-1934. 128p. 1983. 15.00 (ISBN 0-88233-758-0). Ardis Pubs.
Miller, Ted, jt. auth. see Adair, James R.
Miller, Ted, ed. On Being a Caring Father. LC 82-48421. 128p. (Orig.). 1983. pap. 5.72i (ISBN 0-06-061384-X, HarpR). Har-Row.
--On Meeting Life's Challenges. LC 82-4824. (Christian Reader Ser.). 128p. (Orig.). 1983. pap. 5.72i (ISBN 0-06-061388-2, HarpR). Har-Row.
Miller, Terry L., jt. auth. see Noll, Kenneth E.
Miller, Theodore K. & Winston, Roger B., Jr., eds. Administration & Leadership in Student Affairs: Actualizing Student Development in Higher Education. 600p. (Orig.). 1983. pap. text ed. 29.95 (ISBN 0-915202-35-2). Accel Devel.
Miller, Thomas L. Public Lands of Texas, 1519-1970. LC 75-160500. (Illus.). 1972. 21.95 (ISBN 0-8061-0972-6); pap. 10.95 (ISBN 0-8061-1302-2). U of Okla Pr.
Miller, Tim R. State Government: Politics in Wyoming. 224p. 1981. pap. text ed. 8.95 (ISBN 0-8403-2362-X). Kendall-Hunt.
Miller, Tony & Miller, Patricia G. Cut! Print! The Language & Structure of Filmmaking. LC 72-182494. (Theater, Film & the Performing Arts Ser.). (Illus.). 188p. 1975. pap. 5.95 o.p. (ISBN 0-306-80017-9). Da Capo.
Miller, V., jt. auth. see Jennings, K.
Miller, Valentine R., tr. see Descartes, Rene.
Miller, Victor. The Glory Sharers. (Orig.). 1979. write for info (ISBN 0-515-04890-9). Jove Pubns.
Miller, W., jt. auth. see Sattler, William M.
Miller, W. J. Dairy Cattle Feeding & Nutrition. LC 78-51234. (Animal Feeding & Nutrition Ser.). 1979. 35.00 (ISBN 0-12-497650-6). Acad Pr.
Miller, W., Jr. Symmetry & Separation of Variables. (Encyclopedia of Mathematics & Its Applications: Vol. 4). 1977. text ed. 29.50 (ISBN 0-201-13503-5, Adv Bk Prog). A-W.
Miller, W. L. Electoral Dynamics. LC 76-19226. 1978. 22.50 (ISBN 0-312-24115-1). St Martin.
Miller, W. Maureen. The French. (Orig.). 1983. pap. 3.95 (ISBN 0-440-02737-3, Emerald). Dell.
Miller, W. R. & Boyd, T. Gardner. Teaching Elementary Industrial Arts. LC 70-117395. (Illus.). 1970. text ed. 9.28 o.p. (ISBN 0-87006-115-1). Goodheart.
Miller, W. Wesley. Runaway. (Perspectives II Ser.). (Illus.). 48p. (Orig.). (gr. 7-12). 1982. pap. 2.50 (ISBN 0-87879-317-8). Acad Therapy.
Miller, Wallace T. Introduction to Clinical Radiology. 1982. 24.50x (ISBN 0-02-381170-6). Macmillan.
Miller, Walter. Daedalus & Thespis: Volume II: Sculpture, Pts. 1 & 2. 280p. 1970. Repr. of 1931 ed. 18.00x (ISBN 0-8262-0590-9). U of Mo Pr.
Miller, Walter J., ed. see Verne, Jules.
Miller, Walter L. The Life & Accomplishments of Herbert Hoover. LC 78-99300. 1970. 10.95 (ISBN 0-87716-024-4, Pub. by Moore Pub Co). F Apple.
Miller, Walter M., Jr. A Canticle for Leibowitz. 336p. 1975. Repr. of 1959 ed. lib. bdg. 14.50 (ISBN 0-8398-2309-6, Gregg). G K Hall.
--The Science Fiction Stories of Walter M. Miller, Jr. 15.00 (ISBN 0-8398-2496-3, Gregg). G K Hall.
Miller, Warren & Miller, Arthur. American National Election Study, 1976. LC 82-81969. Repr. of 1977 ed. write for info. (ISBN 0-89138-929-6, ICPSR 7381). ICPSR.
Miller, Warren, et al. American National Election Study, 1972. LC 82-81968. 1982. Repr. of 1975 ed. write for info. (ISBN 0-89138-928-8, ICPSR 7010). ICPSR.
Miller, Warren E. & National Election Studies Center for Political Studies. American National Election Study, 1980, 4 vols. LC 82-82378. 1982. Set. write for info. (ISBN 0-89138-925-3, ICPSR 7763); Vol. I, Pre & Post Election Surveys. write for info. (ISBN 0-89138-921-0); Vol. II, Major Panel File. write for info. (ISBN 0-89138-922-9); Appendix A, Contextual Data. write for info. (ISBN 0-89138-923-7); Appendix B, Notes & Questionnaires. write for info. (ISBN 0-89138-924-5). ICPSR.
Miller, Wilbur R. Drafting. LC 78-53388. (Basic Industrial Arts Ser.). (Illus.). 1978. 7.28 (ISBN 0-87345-793-5); softbound 5.28 (ISBN 0-87345-785-4). McKnight.
Miller, Wilbur R., jt. auth. see McKnight Staff Members.
Miller, William, jt. auth. see Cochran, Thomas C.
Miller, William, ed. Recent Advances in Addictions Research: Selected Proceedings from the Taos International Conference on Treatment of Addictive Disorders Held in the University of New Mexico 1979. 100p. 1980. 28.50 (ISBN 0-08-025771-2). Pergamon.
Miller, William, jt. ed. see Bronner, Felix.
Miller, William A. Big Kids' Mother Goose: Christian Counselor Finds New Insights in Old Stories. LC 75-22722. (Illus.). 112p. 1976. pap. 3.95 (ISBN 0-8066-1500-1, 10-0715). Augsburg.
Miller, William V., ed. see Rutman, Roanne.
Miller, William V., et al. Technical Methods & Procedures of the American Association of Blood Banks. rev. ed. 350p. 1974. 17.50 o.p. (ISBN 0-914404-09-1). Am Assn Blood.
Miller, Yvette, ed. see Alegria, Fernando.
Miller, Yvette E., ed. see Bianco, Jose.
Miller, Yvette E., ed. see De Oca, Marco A.
Miller, Yvette E., ed. see Donahue, Moraima.
Miller, Yvette E., ed. see Feliciano, Margarita.
Miller, Yvette E., ed. see Fraire, Isabel.
Miller, Yvette E., ed. see Lopes, Maria Luisa.
Miller, Yvette E., ed. see Mallea, Eduardo.
Miller, Yvette E., ed. see Martinez, Eliud.
Miller, Yvonne A. Through My Eyes. 64p. 1983. 5.50 (ISBN 0-682-49971-4). Exposition.
Millermaster, Ralph A. Harwood's Control of Electric Motors. 4th ed. 1970. 49.95 (ISBN 0-471-60620-0, Pub. by Wiley-Interscience). Wiley.
Milleron, Jean-Claude, jt. auth. see Champsaur, Paul.
Millers, R. R., tr. Fire & Night: Lativia's Most Famous Play by Her Greatest Poet Janis Rainis. LC 81-6708. 77p. 1981. birch binding 20.00 (ISBN 0-912852-28-3); pap. 10.00. Echo Pubs.
Millerson, Gerald. Basic TV Staging. 2nd ed. (Media Manual Ser.). (Illus.). 1982. pap. 10.95 (ISBN 0-240-51191-3). Focal Pr.
--TV Camera Operation. (Media Manual Ser.). 1973. pap. 10.95 (ISBN 0-240-50851-3). Focal Pr.
--TV Lighting Methods. 2nd ed. (Media Manuals Ser). (Illus.). 192p. 1982. pap. 10.95 o.s.i. (ISBN 0-240-51181-6). Focal Pr.
Millet, Bella, ed. Hali Meidhad. (Early English Text Society Ser.). (Illus.). 250p. 1982. 17.95x (ISBN 0-19-722286-2). Oxford U Pr.
Millet, Mrs. Edward. An Australian Parsonage: The Settler & the Savage in Western Australia. 415p. 1982. 25.00 (ISBN 0-85564-191-6, Pub. by U of W Austral Pr). Intl Schol Bk Serv.
Millet, Jean. La Belle Methode Ou l'Art De Bien Chanter. LC 71-126600. (Music Ser). 76p. 1973. Repr. of 1666 ed. lib. bdg. 19.50 (ISBN 0-306-70044-1). Da Capo.
Millett, Allan R. The General: Robert L. Bullard & Officership in the U.S. Army, 1881-1925. LC 75-68. (Contributions in Military History: No. 10). (Illus.). 499p. 1975. lib. bdg. 29.95 (ISBN 0-8371-7957-2, MIG/). Greenwood.
--Semper Fidelis: The History of the United States Marine Corps. LC 80-1059. (The Macmillan Wars of the United States Ser.). (Illus.). 1980. 29.95 (ISBN 0-02-921590-0); pap. 12.95 (ISBN 0-02-921570-6). Free Pr.
Millett, John David. The Process & Organization of Government Planning. LC 76-38753. (FDR & the Era of the New Deal Ser). 188p. 1972. Repr. of 1947 ed. lib. bdg. 29.50 (ISBN 0-306-70444-7). Da Capo.
Millett, Kate. The Basement: Meditations on a Human Sacrifice. 1979. 10.95 o.p. (ISBN 0-671-24763-8). S&S.
--Going to Iran. (Illus.). 1982. 15.95 (ISBN 0-698-11095-1, Coward). Putnam Pub Group.
Millett, Stephen H., ed. Soviet Perceptions of the World Order. 1982. cancelled. Westview.
Millett, Stephen M., ed. A Selected Bibliography of American Constitutional History. LC 75-8677. 116p. 1975. 17.50 o.p. (ISBN 0-87436-204-0). ABC-Clio.
Millgate, Jane. Macaulay. (Routledge Author Guides Ser.). 1973. cased o.p. 14.50 (ISBN 0-7100-7663-0); pap. 6.95 (ISBN 0-7100-7685-1). Routledge & Kegan.
Millgate, Linda. The Almanac of Dates. LC 76-27408. 1977. pap. 5.95 (ISBN 0-15-145773-5, Harv). HarBraceJ.
Millgate, Michael. Thomas Hardy. 1971. 10.00 (ISBN 0-394-46121-5). Random.
--Thomas Hardy: A Biography. 1982. 25.00 (ISBN 0-394-48802-4). Random.
Millgate, Michael, jt. ed. see Purdy, Richard Little.
Millgram, Abraham E. An Anthology of Medieval Hebrew Literature. 469p. 1982. lib. bdg. 100.00 (ISBN 0-89760-019-3). Telegraph Bks.
Millhiser, Marlys. The Mirror. LC 78-6141. 1979. 10.95 o.p. (ISBN 0-399-12199-4). Putnam Pub Group.
--Nightmare Country. 384p. 1981. 12.95 o.p. (ISBN 0-399-12595-7). Putnam Pub Group.
--Willing Hostage. LC 75-43666. 1976. 7.95 o.p. (ISBN 0-399-11720-2). Putnam Pub Group.
Millhone, J. P. & Willis, E. H., eds. New Energy Conservation Technologies & Their Commercialization: Proceedings, 3 vols. 1982. Set. 142.30 (ISBN 0-387-11124-7). Springer-Verlag.
Milliband, Ralph, ed. Socialist Register: Annual 1970-1979. annual 17.50 ea (ISBN 0-87556-440-2). Saifer.
Millichap, Joseph R. Hamilton Basso. (United States Authors Ser.). 1979. lib. bdg. 13.95 (ISBN 0-8057-7225-1, Twayne). G K Hall.
--Lewis Milestone. (Filmmakers Ser.). 1981. lib. bdg. 14.95 (ISBN 0-8057-9281-3, Twayne). G K Hall.
--Steinbeck & Film. LC 82-42502. (Ungar Film Library). (Illus.). 200p. 1983. 12.95 (ISBN 0-8044-2630-9); pap. 6.95 (ISBN 0-8044-6500-2). Ungar.
Millier, Jane. Many Voices: Bilingualism Culture, & Education. 250p. 1983. price not set; pap. price not set (ISBN 0-7100-9341-1). Routledge & Kegan.
Milligan & Chapman, eds. The Business Traveller's Handbook: Asia, Australia & the Pacific. 416p. 1982. 19.95 (ISBN 0-87196-340-X); pap. 11.95 (ISBN 0-87196-346-9). Facts on File.
Milligan, E. E., jt. auth. see Galpin, A. M.
Milligan, Edward E. Beginning Readings in French. (Orig.). 1961. pap. text ed. 11.95x (ISBN 0-02-381360-1). Macmillan.
--Introductory French Reader. 1963. pap. text ed. 10.95 (ISBN 0-02-381470-5). Macmillan.
Milligan, George. St. Paul's Epistles to the Thessalonians. 1980. 12.00 (ISBN 0-86524-022-1, 7104). Klock & Klock.
Milligan, I. S., jt. ed. see Mann, J. Y.
Milligan, Robert see Gospel Advocate.
Milligan, W. D., jt. auth. see Bowman, Arthur G.
Milligan, William. The Acension of Christ. 1980. 15.00 (ISBN 0-86524-061-2, 9505). Klock & Klock.
Millikan, Brent, ed. see Institute for Food & Develop Policy.
Millikan, Max F. & Rostow, W. W. A Proposal: Key to an Effective Foreign Policy. LC 76-39842. 1977. Repr. of 1957 ed. lib. bdg. 15.50x (ISBN 0-8371-9346-X, MIAPR). Greenwood.
Millikan, Robert A. Evolution in Science & Religion. 1935. 11.50x (ISBN 0-686-51381-9). Elliots Bks.
Millin, Laura J., ed. James Turrell: A Series of Installations. 30p. 1982. Boxed. 15.00 (ISBN 0-941104-02-8); Signed. deluxe ed. 100.00 postpaid (ISBN 0-941104-03-6). Real Comet.
Millin, Sarah G. Mary Glenn. 1982. lib. bdg. 12.95 (ISBN 0-89733-015-3); pap. 5.95 (ISBN 0-89733-014-5). Academy Chi Ltd.
Millingen, J. G. Curiosities of Medical Experience. LC 72-83373. 1969. Repr. of 1839 ed. 37.00x (ISBN 0-8103-3487-9). Gale.
Milling-Stanley, Jeanne, ed. World Insurance Yearbook 1981. 5th ed. 467p. 1980. 82.50x (ISBN 0-582-90305-X). Intl Pubns Serv.
Millington, Arsenio G. The Discovery of the Psychological Aspects of the Phenomena of the Will & How they Affect the Future of Man. (Illus.). 137p. (YA) 1982. 73.45 (ISBN 0-89920-043-5). Am Inst Psych.
Milliron, Robert R. How to Do Your Own Accounting for a Small Business. LC 79-53800. 200p. 1980. 12.95 (ISBN 0-913864-34-X); with practice man. 17.95 (ISBN 0-913864-62-5). Enterprise Del.
Millis, N. & Pittard, A. J., eds. The Applications of Microbial Physiology & Genetics to Industrial Processes. 250p. 1982. write for info. (ISBN 0-12-497520-8). Acad Pr.
Millis, Walter & Murray, J. C. Foreign Policy & the Free Society. LC 58-12355. 116p. 1958. 7.50 (ISBN 0-379-00077-6). Oceana.
Millman, Daniel. Whole Body Fitness: Training Mind, Body & Spirit. 192p. 1979. 10.00 o.p. (ISBN 0-517-53852-0, C N Potter Bks). Crown.
Millman, Howard L. Creating a Safe Space. 1977. pap. text ed. 6.75 (ISBN 0-8191-0284-9). U Pr of Amer.
Millman, Howard L., jt. auth. see Huber, Jack T.

Millman, Howard L., jt. auth. see Schaefer, Charles E.

Millman, Howard L., et al. Therapies for Adults: Depressive, Anxiety, & Personality Disorders. LC 82-48064. (Social & Behavioral Science Ser.). 1982. text ed. 22.95x (ISBN 0-87589-537-9). Jossey Bass.

--Therapies for School Behavior Problems. LC 80-8318. (Social & Behavioral Science Ser.). 1980. text ed. 22.95x (ISBN 0-87589-483-6). Jossey-Bass.

Millman, Jacob. Microelectronics: Digital & Analog Circuits & Systems. (Illus.). 1979. text ed. 35.95 (ISBN 0-07-042327-X, C); solution manual 15.95 (ISBN 0-07-042328-8); transparency masters 15.50 (ISBN 0-07-042329-6). McGraw.

Millman, Jacob & Halkias, Christos. Electronic Devices & Circuits. (Electrical & Electronic Engineering Ser.). 1967. text ed. 26.50 o.p. (ISBN 0-07-042380-6, C); answer book 7.95 o.p. (ISBN 0-07-042376-8); solutions manual 5.50 o.p. (ISBN 0-07-042390-3). McGraw.

--Electronic Fundamentals & Applications for Engineers & Scientists. 1975. text ed. 34.95 (ISBN 0-07-042310-5, C); solutions manual 7.95 (ISBN 0-07-042311-3). McGraw.

--Integrated Electronics: Analog Digital Circuits & Systems. Terman, F. E., ed. (Electrical & Electronic Engineering Ser.). (Illus.). 900p. 1972. text ed. 35.50 (ISBN 0-07-042315-6, C); ans. bk. 8.50 (ISBN 0-07-042317-2); soln. manual 18.00 (ISBN 0-07-042316-4). McGraw.

Millman, Jacob & Taub, H. Pulse, Digital & Switching Waveforms. 1965. text ed. 44.00 (ISBN 0-07-042386-5, C); answer manual 18.95 (ISBN 0-07-042377-6); solutions manual 3.95 (ISBN 0-07-042379-2). McGraw.

Millman, Jason & Gowin, D. Appraising Educational Research: A Case Study Approach. LC 73-18004. (Educational Movement, Research & Statistics Ser.). (Illus.). 224p. 1974. pap. 13.95 ref. ed. (ISBN 0-13-043638-0). P-H.

Millman, Lawrence. Hero Jesse. 182p. 1982. 10.95 (ISBN 0-312-37004-0). St Martin.

Millman, Lorrie, jt. ed. see Hacker, Andrew.

Millman, Michael L., jt. auth. see Davis, Edith M.

Millman, R. N., jt. auth. see Brandon, P. F.

Millman, R. N., jt. ed. see Brandon, P. F.

Millman, Richard. Britain & the Eastern Question 1875-1878. (Illus.). 1979. 67.00x (ISBN 0-19-822379-X). Oxford U Pr.

Millman, Richard S. & Parker, George D. Calculus: A Practical Introduction. (Illus.). 1979. text ed. 22.50 (ISBN 0-07-042305-9, C); answer manual 15.00 (ISBN 0-07-042306-7). McGraw.

--Elements of Differential Geometry. LC 76-28497. (Illus.). 1977. 23.95 (ISBN 0-13-264143-7). P-H.

Millner, Darrell. Minority Teachers As Change Agents: A Case Study. 1977. pap. text ed. 8.00 (ISBN 0-8191-0136-2). U Pr of Amer.

Millner, R., tr. see Campannella, Thomas.

Millon, Henry, ed. Studies in Italian Art & Architecture: 15th Through 18th Centuries. (American Academy in Rome Studies in Art History Ser.). (Illus.). 1980. 60.00x (ISBN 0-262-13156-0). MIT Pr.

Millon, Henry A. & Nochlin, Linda, eds. Art & Architecture in the Service of Politics. 1978. 45.00x (ISBN 0-262-13137-4). MIT Pr.

Millon, T. & Diessenhaus, H. I. Research Methods in Psychopathology. (Approaches to Behavior Pathology Ser.). 1972. pap. 17.50 (ISBN 0-471-60626-X). Wiley.

Millon, Theodore. Disorders of Personality: DSMIII; AXIS II. LC 80-28249. 458p. 1981. 31.50 (ISBN 0-471-06403-3, Pub. by Wiley-Interscience). Wiley.

Millon, Theodore & Green, Catherine J., eds. Handbook of Clinical Health Psychology. 632p. 1982. 50.00x (ISBN 0-306-40932-1, Plenum Pr). Plenum Pub.

Millon, Therodore. Modern Psychopathology: A Biosocial Approach to Maladaptive Learning & Functioning. (Illus.). 681p. 1983. Repr. of 1969 ed. text ed. 29.95x (ISBN 0-88133-020-5). Waveland Pr.

Millor, Manuel R. Mexico's Oil: Catalyst for a New Relationship with the U. S.? (Replica Edition). 250p. 1982. softcover 19.50 (ISBN 0-86531-923-5). Westview.

Millot, Claude-Francois-Xavier. Histoire Philosophique de l'Homme. (Holbach & His Friends Ser.). 290p. (Fr.). 1974. Repr. of 1766 ed. lib. bdg. 77.50x o.p. (ISBN 0-8287-0615-8, 1575). Clearwater Pub.

Mills. Acrylics. (The Grosset Art Instruction Ser.: No. 58). (Illus.). 48p. Date not set. pap. price not set (ISBN 0-448-00567-0, G&D). Putnam Pub Group.

--The Care of Antiques. (Desmond Elliott Bks.). (Illus.). 1980. 8.95 o.p. (ISBN 0-531-09551-7). Watts.

--Design for Holidays & Tourism. 1983. text ed. price not set (ISBN 0-408-00534-3). Butterworth.

--How to Detect Fake Antiques. (Desmond Elliott Bks.). 1980. 8.95 o.p. (ISBN 0-531-09553-3). Watts.

Mills & Broughton. Class J. (Bliss Education Classification Ser.). 1977. text ed. 22.95 (ISBN 0-408-70829-8). Butterworth.

--Class P: Religion, the Occult, Morals & Ethics. (Bliss Bibliographic Classification Ser.). 1977. 22.95 (ISBN 0-408-70832-8). Butterworth.

Mills & Redford. Machinability of Engineering Materials. Date not set. 41.00 (ISBN 0-85334-183-4, Pub. by Applied Sci England). Elsevier.

Mills, et al. Instrumental Data for Drug Analysis, Vol. 1. 1982. 95.00 (ISBN 0-444-00718-0). Elsevier.

Mills, A. R., ed. see Hall, Ellen & Hall, Emily.

Mills, Adelbert P., et al. Materials of Construction. 6th ed. LC 55-7368. 1955. text ed. 35.95x o.p. (ISBN 0-471-60654-5). Wiley.

Mills, Alden, ed. see American Association Of Hospital Consultants.

Mills, Belen C. Understanding the Young Child & His Curriculum: Selected Readings. (Illus.). 480p. 1972. pap. text ed. 13.95x (ISBN 0-02-381490-X). Macmillan.

Mills, Bobby E. Institutionalized Christianity: The Great White Lie. 1979. 5.95 o.p. (ISBN 0-533-03987-8). Vantage.

Mills, Brenda. My Bible Story Picture Book. (Illus.). 128p. (gr. k-5). 1982. text ed. 12.95 (ISBN 0-89081-319-1). Harvest Hse.

Mills, C. Wright. Power, Politics & People: The Collected Essays of C. Wright Mills. Horowitz, Irving L., ed. (YA) (gr. 9 up). 1967. pap. 10.95 (ISBN 0-19-500752-2, GB). Oxford U Pr.

--Sociological Imagination. 1959. 17.95x (ISBN 0-19-500022-6). Oxford U Pr.

--White Collar: American Middle Classes. 1956. pap. 9.95 (ISBN 0-19-500677-1, GB). Oxford U Pr.

--White Collar: The American Middle Classes. 1951. 22.50x (ISBN 0-19-500024-2). Oxford U Pr.

Mills, C. Wright, tr. see Weber, Max.

Mills, Charles W. The Causes of World War Three. LC 75-31436. 1976. Repr. of 1958 ed. lib. bdg. 20.25x (ISBN 0-8371-8513-0, MICW). Greenwood.

Mills, Charlotte, ed. see Barton, Lois.

Mills, Clark, tr. see Breton, Andre.

Mills, D. L., jt. ed. see Agranovich, V. M.

Mills, D. Q. Labor-Management Relations. 2nd ed. (Management Ser.). 656p. 1982. 24.95x (ISBN 0-07-042419-5). McGraw.

Mills, D. Quinn. Labor Management Relations. Davis, Keith, ed. (Management Ser.). (Illus.). 1978. text ed. 23.95 (ISBN 0-07-042367-9, C); instructor's manual 11.50 (ISBN 0-07-042368-7). McGraw.

Mills, Daniel Q. Industrial Relations & Manpower in Construction. 1972. 22.50x (ISBN 0-262-13078-5). MIT Pr.

Mills, Daniel Q., jt. ed. see Lange, Julian E.

Mills, David, jt. auth. see Lumiansky, R. M.

Mills, David G. You Can Profit from the Eighties. (Illus.). 236p. 1982. 13.95 (ISBN 0-943732-00-X); pap. 10.95 (ISBN 0-943732-01-8). M & S Ent.

Mills, Dennis R. Lord & Peasant in Nineteenth Century Britain. LC 80-514656. (Illus.). 232p. 1980. 31.50x (ISBN 0-8476-6806-1). Rowman.

Mills, Dick. The Four Loves. (Orig.). Date not set. pap. price not set (HH-287). Harrison Hse.

--He Spoke & I Was Strengthened. 1973. pap. 2.95 (ISBN 0-88368-026-2). Whitaker Hse.

--Hearts & Flowers. (Orig.). Date not set. pap. price not set (ISBN 0-89274-288-7, HH-286). Harrison Hse.

Mills, Dick, jt. auth. see Sterba, Gunther.

Mills, Dorothy. The Book of the Ancient Greeks. (Illus.). (gr. 6-9). 1925. 7.95 o.p. (ISBN 0-399-20021-5). Putnam Pub Group.

--The Book of the Ancient Romans. (Illus.). (gr. 6-9). 1937. 7.95 o.p. (ISBN 0-399-20022-3). Putnam Pub Group.

--The Book of the Ancient World. (Illus.). (gr. 6-9). 1923. 7.95 o.p. (ISBN 0-399-20023-1). Putnam Pub Group.

--The Middle Ages. (Illus.). (gr. 6-9). 1935. 7.95 o.p. (ISBN 0-399-20169-6). Putnam Pub Group.

Mills, Dorothy H., et al. Spanish Vocabulary & Structure for the Health Professional, Bk. 1. 2nd ed. LC 80-54900. (Illus.). 157p. (Eng., Span.). 1981. pap. text ed. 15.00 (ISBN 0-935356-02-9). Mills Pub Co.

Mills, Edward D. Planning Buildings for Health, Welfare & Religion. 9th ed. 190p. 1976. Repr. of 1936 ed. 26.50 (ISBN 0-88275-425-4). Krieger.

Mills, Edward D., ed. see Wylson, Anthony.

Mills, Edwin S. Urban Economics. 2nd ed. 1980. text ed. 20.95x (ISBN 0-673-15264-2). Scott F.

Mills, Elizabeth & Murphy, Sr. Therese, eds. Suzuki Method, or Suzuki Concept: An Introduction to a Successful Method for Early Music Education. (Illus.). 220p. 1973. 7.95 o.s.i. (ISBN 0-87297-002-7); pap. 6.95 (ISBN 0-87297-003-5). Diablo.

Mills, F. E., ed. see Ben Lee Memorial International Conference on Parity Nonconservation, Weak Neutral Currents & Gauge Theories, Fermi National Accelerator Laboratory, October 20-22, 1977.

Mills, Gayley C. & Young, C. C. English Poetry Its Principles & Progress: With Representative Masterpieces From 1390 to 1917 & With Notes. Kurtz, Benjamin P., ed. 749p. 1982. Repr. of 1951 ed. lib. bdg. 75.00 (ISBN 0-686-98397-1). Century Bookbindery.

Mills, Geoffrey. On the Board. 232p. 1982. text ed. 35.50x (ISBN 0-900488-61-1). Gower Pub Ltd.

Mills, George. Harvey Ingham & Gardner Cowles Sr. Bunke, Joan, ed. (Illus.). 1977. 7.50 (ISBN 0-8138-0155-9). Iowa St U Pr.

Mills, Glen D., ed. Elementary School Guidance & Counseling: A Reader. 1971. pap. text ed. 4.75x (ISBN 0-685-19723-9). Phila Bk Co.

Mills, Helen. Commanding Composition. 1980. pap. text ed. 13.50x (ISBN 0-673-15261-8). Scott F.

--Commanding Essays. 2nd ed. 1981. pap. text ed. 13.50x (ISBN 0-673-15568-4). Scott F.

--Commanding Paragraphs. 2nd ed. 1981. pap. text ed. 13.50x (ISBN 0-673-15442-4). Scott F.

--Commanding Sentences. 2nd ed. 1979. pap. 13.50x (ISBN 0-673-15177-8). Scott F.

--Commanding Sentences. 3rd ed. 1983. pap. text ed. 13.95x (ISBN 0-673-15826-8). Scott F.

--Connecting & Combining: In Sentence & Paragraph Writing. 1982. pap. text ed. 13.50x (ISBN 0-673-15317-7). Scott F.

Mills, Howard L. Laboratory Studies in Plant Biology. 1977. pap. text ed. 7.95 (ISBN 0-8403-0686-5). Kendall-Hunt.

Mills, J. & Broughton, V. Bliss Class A: Vol. II Case. Date not set. text ed. price not set (ISBN 0-408-70823-9). Butterworth.

--Class H: Anthropology, Human Biology, & Health Sciences. (Bliss Bibliographic Classification Ser.). 1979. text ed. 64.95 o.p. (ISBN 0-408-70828-X). Butterworth.

--Class I: Psychology & Psychiatry. (Bliss Bibliographic Classification Ser). 1978. text ed. 27.95 (ISBN 0-408-70841-7). Butterworth.

Mills, J. & Broughton, V., eds. Class K: Sociology, Social Anthropology. 2nd ed. (Bliss Bibliographic Classification Ser.). Date not set. text ed. write for info (ISBN 0-408-70830-1). Butterworth.

Mills, Jack, jt. auth. see Samovar, Larry.

Mills, Jack, jt. auth. see Samovar, Larry A.

Mills, James. Report to the Commissioner. 304p. 1972. 6.95 o.p. (ISBN 0-374-24940-7). FS&G.

--The Truth about Peter Harley. 272p. 1983. pap. 2.95 (ISBN 0-345-29005-4). Ballantine.

Mills, James C. Art Handbook for Elementary Teachers. 2nd ed. 1978. pap. text ed. 15.95 (ISBN 0-8403-1093-5). Kendall-Hunt.

Mills, John. Instructions to Young Artists. (Illus.). 13.50x o.p. (ISBN 0-392-06062-0, SpS). Sportshelf.

Mills, John F. Art Facts & Feats. (Illus.). 256p. 1980. 19.95 (ISBN 0-900424-68-0, Pub by Guinness Superlatives England). Sterling.

Mills, Joseph W. Geology of the Jumbo Mountain Nickel Deposit, Snohomish County, Washington. (Reprint: No. 6). Repr. of 1960 ed. 0.25 (ISBN 0-686-36912-2). Geologic Pubns.

Mills, Joshua E., jt. auth. see Fornatale, Peter.

Mills, K. & Paul, J. Successful Retail Sales. 1979. pap. 15.95 (ISBN 0-13-869602-0). P-H.

Mills, Katherine H., jt. auth. see Kilmann, Peter R.

Mills, Kenneth, et al. A Handbook for Alcohol Education: The Community Approach. 296p. 1982. prof ref 32.50x (ISBN 0-88410-726-4). Ballinger Pub.

Mills, Kenneth H. & Paul, Judith E. Applied Visual Merchandising. (Illus.). 320p. 1982. reference 21.95 (ISBN 0-13-043331-4). P-H.

Mills, L., jt. auth. see Ibach, H.

Mills, Lennox A. Malaya: A Political & Economic Appraisal. LC 72-12499. 234p. 1973. Repr. of 1958 ed. lib. bdg. 17.75x (ISBN 0-8371-6746-9, MIMA). Greenwood.

Mills, Liston M. Pastoral Theologian of the Year: Seward Hiltner; Special Issue PP 29, No. 1. LC 80-82467. 112p. 1980. pap. 9.95x (ISBN 0-89885-068-1). Human Sci Pr.

Mills, Maldwyn, ed. Six Middle English Romances. (Rowman & Littlefield University Library). 224p. 1973. 9.25x o.p. (ISBN 0-87471-403-6); pap. 4.00x o.p. (ISBN 0-87471-396-X). Rowman.

--Six Middle English Romances. 1982. pap. 6.50x (ISBN 0-460-11090-X, Pub. by Erman). Biblio Dist.

Mills, Nicolaus, ed. Busing U.S.A. LC 78-31327. 1979. text ed. 16.95x (ISBN 0-8077-2554-4). Tchrs Coll.

--The Great School Bus Controversy. LC 73-16469. 356p. 1973. 15.95x o.p. (ISBN 0-8077-2430-0); pap. 11.95x (ISBN 0-8077-2431-9). Tchrs Coll.

Mills, Olive, jt. auth. see Miller, Jerry W.

Mills, Olive, ed. Universal Higher Education: Costs, Benefits, Options. 1972. 10.50 o.p. (ISBN 0-8268-1405-0). ACE.

Mills, P. Managing for Profit. 160p. 1982. 22.00 (ISBN 0-07-084575-1). McGraw.

Mills, P., jt. auth. see McGrath, Philomena.

Mills, R. E. Critical Phenomena. (Materials Science & Engineering Ser.). 1971. 59.50 o.p. (ISBN 0-07-042365-2, P&RB). McGraw.

Mills, Ralph J., Jr. March Light: And Other Poems. (Vagrom Chap Bk.: No. 20). 56p. (Orig.). 1983. pap. 5.95 (ISBN 0-935552-15-4). Sparrow Pr.

Mills, Ralph J., Jr., ed. see Cintron, Ralph.

Mills, Richard G. Jackie's Home Repair & Maintenance Charts. Hostage, Jacqueline, ed. LC 82-25290. (Illus.). 128p. 1983. pap. 5.95 plastic comb bdg. (ISBN 0-932620-18-3). Betterway Pubns.

Mills, Richard L. Statistics for Applied Economics & Business. (Illus.). text ed. 27.95 (ISBN 0-07-042372-5, C); instructor's manual 7.95 (ISBN 0-07-042373-3). McGraw.

Mills, Robert. Brown Bag. 1979. pap. 2.00 (ISBN 0-933180-05-5). Spoon Riv Poetry.

Mills, Robert E. The Cheyenne's Woman. (Kansan Ser.: No. 9). 208p. (Orig.). 1982. pap. 2.25 o.s.i. (ISBN 0-8439-1171-9, Leisure Bks). Nordon Pubns.

--Dark World. (Star Quest: No. 4). 224p. (Orig.). 1982. pap. 2.25 o.s.i. (ISBN 0-8439-1178-6, Leisure Bks). Nordon Pubns.

Mills, Roger & Butler, Eric. Tackle Badminton. rev. ed. (Tackle Ser). (Illus.). 124p. (gr. 9 up). 1975. pap. text ed. 6.95x o.p. (ISBN 0-09-119221-8, SpS). Sportshelf.

Mills, Roger F., ed. see Wojowasito, Soewojo.

Mills, Theodore M. Sociology of Small Groups. (Foundations of Modern Sociology Ser). 1967. pap. 9.95 ref. ed. (ISBN 0-13-821439-5). P-H.

Mills, W. Down the Grid. (Illus.). 11.50 (ISBN 0-392-02710-0, SpS). Sportshelf.

--Four Feet Eight & One Half & All That. 14.50 (ISBN 0-392-03033-0, SpS). Sportshelf.

Mills, W. Jay, ed. see Paterson, William.

Mills, William. The Stillness in Moving Things: The World of Howard Nemerov. LC 75-31619. 160p. 1975. 9.95x o.p. (ISBN 0-87870-026-9). Memphis St Univ.

Millsap, Margaret, jt. auth. see Epstein, Rhoda B.

Millsaps, Daniel & Washington International Arts Letter Editors. National Directory of Arts Support by Private Foundations. 5th ed. LC 77-79730. (The Arts Patronage Ser.: No. 12). 340p. (Orig.). 1983. 79.95 (ISBN 0-912072-13-X). Wash Intl Arts.

--National Directory of Grants & Aid to Individuals in the Arts. 5th ed. LC 70-112695. (The Arts Patronage Ser.: No. 11). 254p. (Orig.). 1983. 15.95 (ISBN 0-912072-12-1). Wash Intl Arts.

Millspaugh, Arthur. Americans in Persia. LC 76-9837. (Politics & Strategy of World War II Ser.). 1976. Repr. of 1946 ed. lib. bdg. 37.50 (ISBN 0-306-70764-0). Da Capo.

Millspaugh, Arthur Chester. Crime Control by the National Government. LC 70-168678. (American Constitutional Legal History Ser). 306p. 1972. Repr. of 1937 ed. lib. bdg. 37.50 (ISBN 0-306-70418-8). Da Capo.

Millspaugh, Charles F. American Medicinal Plants. LC 73-91487. 1974. 12.95 (ISBN 0-486-23034-1, Pub. by Dover). Formur Intl.

Millstein, Beth & Bodin, Jeanne. We, the American Women. (Illus.). 331p. 1977. lib. bdg. 17.20 o.p. (ISBN 0-574-42003-7, 11-1003); pap. text ed. 10.60 (ISBN 0-574-42000-2, 11-1000); tchrs'. guide 2.14 (ISBN 0-574-42001-0, 11-1001); student activity bk. 3.75 (ISBN 0-574-42002-9, 11-1002). SRA.

Millward, Michael & Coe, Brian. Victorian Townscape: The Work of Samuel Smith. LC 76-16439. (Illus.). 120p. 1977. 35.00 (ISBN 0-87951-050-1). Overlook Pr.

Millward, R. Public Expenditure Economics. 11.50 o.p. (ISBN 0-07-094148-3, I). McGraw.

Millward, Roy, jt. auth. see Robinson, Adrian.

Milman, Henry H. The Belvidere Apollo: A Prize Poem, Repr. Of 1812 Ed. Bd. with Fazio: A Tragedy. Repr. of 1815 ed; Samor, Lord of the Bright City: An Heroic Poem. Repr. of 1818 ed. LC 75-31232. (Romantic Context: Poetry 1789-1830 Ser.: Vol. 83). 1977. lib. bdg. 47.00 o.s.i. (ISBN 0-8240-2182-7). Garland Pub.

Milman, Miriam. Tromp l'Oeil Painting: The Illusion of Reality. LC 82-42851. (Illus.). 130p. 1983. 27.50 (ISBN 0-8478-0470-4). Rizzoli Intl.

Milne. Bela Bartok. (Life & Times Ser.). (Illus.). 150p. 1983. 16.95 (ISBN 0-88254-659-7, Pub. by Midas Bks England). Hippocrene Bks.

Milne, A. A. House at Pooh Corner. rev. ed. (Illus.). (gr. k up). 1961. 7.95 (ISBN 0-525-32302-3, 0772-230). Dutton.

--Now We Are Six. rev. ed. (Illus.). (gr. k-4). 1961. 7.95 (ISBN 0-525-36126-X, 0772-230). Dutton.

--When We Were Very Young. (gr. 1-5). 1961. 7.95 (ISBN 0-525-42580-2, 0772-230). Dutton.

--Winnie-la-Pu. (Illus.). (gr. 3 up). 1972. 6.95x (ISBN 0-685-34702-8). Esperanto League North Am.

--Winnie the Pooh. (Illus.). (gr. 1-5). 7.95 (ISBN 0-525-43035-0, 0772-230). Dutton.

--Winnie-the-Pooh & the Blustery Day. (Tell-a-Tale Readers). (Illus.). (gr. k-3). 1979. PLB 5.00 (ISBN 0-307-68577-2, Whitman). Western Pub.

--World of Christopher Robin. (gr. 1-4). 1958. 11.00 (ISBN 0-525-43292-2, 01068-320); boxed with "World of Pooh" 20.50 (ISBN 0-525-43348-1, 01990-600). Dutton.

--World of Pooh. (gr. 1-4). 1957. 11.00 (ISBN 0-525-43320-1, 01068-320); boxed with "World of Christopher Robin" 20.50 (ISBN 0-525-43348-1, 01990-600). Dutton.

Milne, B. Lumsden see Swan, D. K.

Milne, Barbara, jt. auth. see Brosnahan, Jo A.

Milne, F. A. see Gomme, George L., et al.

Milne, George, ed. see Johnson, Samuel.

Milne, Gordon. Stephen Crane at Brede: An Anglo-American Literary Circle of the Eighteen Nineties. LC 80-8136. 69p. 1980. lib. bdg. 14.50 (ISBN 0-8191-1139-2); pap. text ed. 6.75 (ISBN 0-8191-1140-6). U Pr of Amer.

Milne, Gustave & Hobley, Brian, eds. Waterfront Archaeology in Britain & Northern Europe. (CBA Research Reports Ser.: No. 41). 170p. 1981. pap. text ed. 37.50x (ISBN 0-906780-08-X, Pub. by Coun Brit Archaeology). Humanities.

Milne, H. F. The Reed Organ: It's Design & Construction. (Bibliotheca Organologica: Vol. 58). 1930. wrappers 15.00 o.s.i. (ISBN 90-6027-303-6, Pub. by Frits Knuf Netherlands). Pendragon NY.

Milne, J. G. Catalog of Alexandrian Coins. (Illus.). 1983. Repr. of 1971 ed. lib. bdg. 50.00 (ISBN 0-942666-20-8). S J Durst.

Milne, John, jt. auth. see Jupp, T. C.

Milne, Lorus & Milne, Margery. The Audubon Society Field Guide to North American Insects & Spiders. LC 80-7620. (Illus.). 1008p. 1980. 12.50 (ISBN 0-394-50763-0). Knopf.

--The Nature of Plants. LC 78-151473. (Illus.). 224p. (gr. 7-9). 1971. 10.53i (ISBN 0-397-31282-2, JBL-J). Har-Row.

Milne, Margery, jt. auth. see Lorus, J.

Milne, Margery, jt. auth. see Milne, Lorus.

Milne, P. H. Underwater Engineering Surveys. (Illus.). 400p. 1980. 45.95x (ISBN 0-87201-884-9). Gulf Pub.

Milne, R. & Strachey, C. The Theory of Programming Language Semantics, 2 vols. 1976. Set. 81.00x (ISBN 0-412-14260-0, Pub. by Chapman & Hall). Methuen Inc.

Milne, R. D. Applied Functional Analysis: An Introductory Treatment. 528p. 1980. text ed. 49.50 (ISBN 0-273-08404-6). Pitman Pub MA.

Milne, Roseleen. Borrowed Plumes. 1977. 7.95 o.p. (ISBN 0-698-10828-0, Coward). Putnam Pub Group.

--Borrowed Plumes. 1978. pap. 2.25 (ISBN 0-451-09811-0, E9811, Sig). NAL.

Milne-Edwards, Henri. Rapport sur les Progres Recents Des Sciences Soologiques En France. Repr. of 1867 ed. 137.00 o.p. (ISBN 0-8287-0616-6). Clearwater Pub.

Milner, A., ed. African Law Reports: Malawi, 1920-1970, 5 vols. LC 67-26375. 1968-71. 45.00 ea. Vol. 1 (ISBN 0-379-12951-5). Vol. 2 (ISBN 0-379-12952-3). Vol. 3 (ISBN 0-379-12953-1). Vol. 4 (ISBN 0-379-12954-X). Vol. 5. Vol. 6 o.p (ISBN 0-379-12950-7). index vols. 1 & 2 12.50 (ISBN 0-379-12956-6). Oceana.

--African Law Reports, Sierra Leone Series, 1950-1969, 5 vols. LC 75-21503. 1969-72. 45.00 ea. (ISBN 0-379-16000-5). Oceana.

Milner, Brenda, ed. Hemispheric Specialization & Interaction. 100p. 1975. pap. text ed. 4.95x o.p. (ISBN 0-262-63057-5). MIT Pr.

Milner, Douglas. The Focalguide to Mountains. (Focalguide Ser.). (Illus.). 1977. pap. 7.95 (ISBN 0-240-50969-2). Focal Pr.

Milner, G. W. & Phillips, G. Coulometry in Analytical Chemistry. 1967. 25.00 o.s.i. (ISBN 0-08-012439-9); pap. text ed. 11.25 (ISBN 0-08-012438-0). Pergamon.

Milner, Max, ed. see Protein Advisory Group of the United Nations System.

Milner, R. A Calculus of Communicating Systems. (Lecture Notes in Computer Science Ser.: Vol. 92). 260p. 1981. pap. 13.00 o.p. (ISBN 0-387-10235-3). Springer-Verlag.

Milner, Toby, ed. The Business Traveller's Handbook: Africa. 1981. 19.95 (ISBN 0-87196-341-8); pap. 11.95 (ISBN 0-87196-347-7). Facts on File.

Milner, Wanda. Learning to Use the Bible. Mahany, Patricia, ed. (Illus.). 24p. (Orig.). 1983. pap. price not set (ISBN 0-87239-690-8, 3200). Standard Pub.

Milnes, A. G. Deep Impurities in Semiconductors. LC 73-5844. 526p. 1973. 46.00 o.p. (ISBN 0-471-60670-7, Pub. by Wiley-Interscience). Wiley.

Milnes, Janet, tr. see De Waal, Frans.

Milne-Thomson, L. M. Plane Elastic Systems. 2nd ed. LC 68-56947. (Ergebnisse der Angewandten Mathematik: Vol. 6). 1968. pap. 17.00 (ISBN 0-387-03407-2). Springer-Verlag.

Milnor, William R. Hemodynamics. (Illus.). 400p. 1981. lib. bdg. 55.00 (ISBN 0-683-06050-3). Williams & Wilkins.

Milofsky, David. Playing from Memory. 1981. 12.95 o.s.i. (ISBN 0-671-25252-6). S&S.

Milone, A. F., jt. ed. see Caglioti, G.

Milone, Michael N., Jr. Handwriting Skills, K-8. 64p. (gr. k-8). 1982. tchr's ed. 2.96 (ISBN 0-686-36883-5); wkbk. 1.96 (ISBN 0-686-37366-9). Skillcorp.

Milora, Stanley L. & Tester, Jefferson W. Geothermal Energy As a Source of Electric Power: Thermodynamics & Economic Design Criteria. LC 76-7008. 190p. 1976. text ed. 25.00x (ISBN 0-262-13123-4). MIT Pr.

Milosz, Czeslaw. Emperor of the Earth: Modes of Eccentric Vision. LC 76-20005. 1977. 19.95x (ISBN 0-520-03302-7); pap. 7.95 (ISBN 0-520-04503-3, CAL522). U of Cal Pr.

--The History of Polish Literature. rev. ed. LC 82-16084. 570p. 1983. text ed. 28.00x (ISBN 0-520-04465-7); pap. text ed. 8.95x (ISBN 0-520-04477-0). U of Cal Pr.

--Hymn O Perle: Hymn to the Pearl. 1982. 10.00 (ISBN 0-930042-45-X). Mich Slavic Pubns.

--Poeticheskii Traktat. Gorbanevskaya, Natalia, tr. from Polish. 64p. 1982. text ed. write for info. (ISBN 0-88233-828-5); pap. text ed. 4.50 (ISBN 0-88233-829-3). Ardis Pubs.

--Postwar Polish Poetry: An Anthology. rev. ed. LC 82-16084. 180p. 1983. text ed. 18.00x (ISBN 0-520-04475-4); pap. text ed. 5.95x (ISBN 0-520-04476-2). U of Cal Pr.

--Visions from San Francisco Bay. Lourie, Richard, tr. from Polish. 1983. pap. 8.25 (ISBN 0-374-51763-0). FS&G.

--The Witness of Poetry. (Charles Eliot Norton Lectures, 1981-1982). 160p. 1983. 8.95 (ISBN 0-674-95382-7). Harvard U Pr.

Milosz, Czleslaw. The Seizure of Power. Wieniewa, Celina, tr. 1982. 12.95 (ISBN 0-374-25788-4); pap. 7.95 (ISBN 0-374-51697-9). FS&G.

Milroy, Lesley. Language & Social Networks. Trudgill, Peter, ed. (Language in Society Ser.: No. 2). 232p. 1980. pap. text ed. 19.95 (ISBN 0-8391-4114-9). Univ Park.

Milroy, M. E., ed. Church Lace: Being Eight Ecclesiastical Patterns in Pillow Lace. (Illus.). 121p. 1981. Repr. of 1920 ed. 36.00x (ISBN 0-8103-3014-8). Gale.

Mil'Shteyn, Y. I., ed. see Scriabin, Alexander.

Milsom, S. F. The Legal Framework of English Feudalism. LC 75-23531. (Cambridge Studies in English Legal History). 1976. 42.50 (ISBN 0-521-20947-1). Cambridge U Pr.

Milson, Fred. An Introduction to Community Work. 168p. 1974. 15.95x (ISBN 0-7100-7840-4); pap. 5.25 (ISBN 0-7100-7841-2). Routledge & Kegan.

--An Introduction to Group Work Skill. 1973. 16.95x (ISBN 0-7100-7645-2); pap. 7.50 (ISBN 0-7100-7646-0). Routledge & Kegan.

--Youth in a Changing Society. 1972. 11.75x o.p. (ISBN 0-7100-7204-X). Routledge & Kegan.

--Youth Work in the Nineteen Seventies. 1971. 14.95x o.p. (ISBN 0-7100-6865-4). Routledge & Kegan.

Milstein, Jeff. Building Cardboard Dollhouses. (Orig.). 1978. pap. 3.95i o.p. (ISBN 0-06-090612-X, CN 612, CN). Har-Row.

--Building Cardboard Toys. LC 79-2027. (Illus., Orig.). 1979. pap. 4.95i o.p. (ISBN 0-06-090666-9, CN 666, CN). Har-Row.

--Designing Houses: An Illustrated Guide. LC 75-7684. (Illus.). 160p. 1976. 10.00 o.p. (ISBN 0-87951-035-8); pap. 5.95 o.p. (ISBN 0-87951-096-X). Overlook Pr.

Milstein, Mike M. Impact & Response: Federal Education Programs & State Agencies. LC 76-14887. 1976. text ed. 15.95 o.p. (ISBN 0-8077-2502-1). Tchrs Coll.

Milthorpe, F. L. & Moorby, J. Introduction to Crop Physiology. 2nd ed. LC 78-26380. (Illus.). 1980. 45.00 (ISBN 0-521-22624-4); pap. 16.95x (ISBN 0-521-29581-5). Cambridge U Pr.

Milthorpe, Frederick L., jt. auth. see Dale, John E.

Milton. Blind Flight. LC 79-23279. (gr. 5 up). 1980. PLB 8.90 (ISBN 0-531-04108-5, A27). Watts.

Milton, Arthur. How Your Life Insurance Policies Rob You. LC 81-4679. 178p. (Orig.). 1983. 8.95 (ISBN 0-8065-0768-3); pap. 4.95 (ISBN 0-8065-0847-7). Citadel Pr.

Milton, Charles & Milton, Daniel J. Nickel-Gold Ore of the Mackinaw Mine, Snohomish County, Washington. (Reprint Ser.: No. 4). (Illus.). 22p. 1959. 0.25 (ISBN 0-686-36913-0). Geologic Pubns.

Milton, Charles R. Human Behavior in Organizations: Three Levels of Behavior. (Illus.). 432p. 1981. text ed. 23.95 (ISBN 0-13-444596-1). P-H.

Milton, Daniel J., jt. auth. see Milton, Charles.

Milton, David. The Politics of U. S. Labor: From the Great Depression to the New Deal. LC 80-8934. 352p. 1982. 18.00 (ISBN 0-85345-569-4, CL5694). Monthly Rev.

Milton, David S. Skyline. 336p. 1982. 15.95 (ISBN 0-399-12599-X). Putnam Pub Group.

Milton, Hilary. Dognappers. 144p. (Orig.). (gr. 3-7). 1983. pap. 2.50 (ISBN 0-671-44475-1). Wanderer Bks.

--Mayday! Mayday! (gr. 5 up). 1979. PLB 8.90 s&l (ISBN 0-531-02890-9). Watts.

--Plot-Your-Own Horror Stories: Craven House Horrors, No. 1. Schneider, Meg, ed. (Illus.). 128p. (Orig.). (gr. 3-7). 1982. pap. 2.50 (ISBN 0-671-45631-8). Wanderer Bks.

--Plot-Your-Own Horror Stories: Nightmare Store, No. 2. Schneider, Meg, ed. (Illus.). 128p. (Orig.). (gr. 3-7). 1982. pap. 2.50 (ISBN 0-671-45630-X). Wanderer Bks.

--Tornado! (Single Title Fiction Ser.). 160p. (gr. 4 up). 1983. PLB 9.90 (ISBN 0-531-04542-0). Watts.

Milton, J. H. & Leach, R. M. Marine Steam Boilers. 4th ed. (Illus.). 700p. 1980. text ed. 49.95 (ISBN 0-408-00416-9). Butterworth.

Milton, J. H., et al. Running & Maintenance of Marine Machinery. 286p. 1981. 62.00x (ISBN 0-686-97120-5, Pub. by Marine Mgmt England). State Mutual Bk.

Milton, J. S. & Tsokos, J. O. Statistical Methods in the Biological & Health Sciences. 480p. 1983. 21.95 (ISBN 0-07-042359-8, C); instr's. manual 5.95 (ISBN 0-07-042360-1). McGraw.

Milton, J. Susan & Tsokos, Chris P. Probability Theory with the Essential Analysis. LC 76-27867. (Applied Mathematics & Computation Ser: No. 10). 1976. text ed. 29.50 (ISBN 0-201-07604-7, Adv Bk Prog); pap. text ed. 14.50 (ISBN 0-201-07605-5, Adv Bk Prog). A-W.

Milton, John. Areopagitica. Sabine, George H., ed. Bd. with Of Education. LC 51-6754. (Crofts Classics Ser.). 1951. pap. text ed. 3.75x (ISBN 0-88295-057-6). Harlan Davidson.

--Areopagitica. 80p. 1972. Repr. of 1644 ed. 10.00x (ISBN 0-87556-219-1). Saifer.

--Complete Prose Works of John Milton, 8 vols. Incl. Vol. 1. 1624-1642. Wolfe, Don M., ed. xvi, 1073p. 1953. 80.00x (ISBN 0-300-01055-9); Vol. 2. 1643-1648. Sirluck, Ernest, ed. 840p. 1959. 66.00x (ISBN 0-300-00956-9); Vol. 3. 1648-1649. Hughes, Merritt Y., ed. & intro. by. (Illus.). 652p. 1962. 50.00x (ISBN 0-300-00581-4); Vol. 4. 1650-1655, 2 pts. Wolfe, Don M., ed. (Illus.). xxx, 1166p. 1966. Set. 80.00x (ISBN 0-300-01056-7); Vol. 5. The History of Britain & the Miltonic State Papers, 2 pts. Fogle, French & Patrick, J. Max, eds. 928p. 1970. Set. 80.00x (ISBN 0-300-01288-8); Vol. 6. Christian Doctrine, 2 pts. Kelley, Maurice, ed. Carey, John, tr. LC 72-91302. 880p. 1973. Set. 80.00x (ISBN 0-300-01541-0); Vol. 7. 1659-1660. rev. ed. LC 52-5371. 1980. text ed. 55.00x (ISBN 0-300-02015-5); Vol. 8. 1666-1682. 632p. 1982. text ed. 65.00x (ISBN 0-300-02561-0). Yale U Pr.

--Odes, Pastorals, Masques. Broadbent, et al, eds. LC 73-94355. (Milton for Schools & Colleges). 300p. 1975. pap. text ed. 8.95x (ISBN 0-521-20456-9). Cambridge U Pr.

--Paradise Lost. Madsen, William G., ed. 1969. pap. 2.95 (ISBN 0-394-30997-9, 30997, Mod LibC). Modern Lib.

--Paradise Lost & Other Poems. pap. 2.75 (ISBN 0-451-62093-3, ME2093, Ment). NAL.

--Paradise Lost & Paradise Regained. Ricks, Christopher, ed. 1968. pap. 3.95 (ISBN 0-451-51735-0, CE1735, Sig Classics). NAL.

--Rose Question & Answer Book. 3.95 (ISBN 0-8208-0024-4). Hearthside.

--Samson Agonistes, Sonnets, Etc. Broadbent, John & Hodge, R. V., eds. LC 76-28003. (Cambridge Milton for Schools & Colleges Ser.). 1977. 8.95 (ISBN 0-521-21474-2). Cambridge U Pr.

Milton, John, ed. & intro. by. Conversations with Frank Waters. LC 82-73070. 90p. 1971. 5.00 o.p. (ISBN 0-8040-0575-3); pap. 4.25 (ISBN 0-8040-0576-1). Swallow.

Milton, Joyce. Controversy: Science in Conflict. LC 80-12923. 128p. (gr. 7 up). 1980. PLB 7.29 o.p. (ISBN 0-671-33003-9). Messner.

--A Friend of China. new ed. (Illus.). 128p. (gr. 7 up). 1980. 8.95 o.p. (ISBN 0-8038-2388-6). Hastings.

Milton, Joyce, jt. auth. see Radosh, Ronald.

Milton, Nan, ed. see MacLean, John.

Milton, Octavia. Assist Three: For Consonant Blends of L, R, & S. 50p. 1981. pap. text ed. 13.95 (ISBN 0-88450-729-7, 2063-B). Communication Skill.

Milton, Ohmer & Shoben, Edward J., Jr., eds. Learning & the Professors. LC 67-22230. xvii, 216p. 1968. 12.00x (ISBN 0-8214-0036-3, 82-80398); pap. 5.95x (ISBN 0-8214-0105-X, 82-80406). Ohio U Pr.

Milton, Sybil, jt. ed. see Friedlander, Henry.

Miluck, Nancy C. Come to the Candy Dance. (Nevada Coloring Books). (Illus.). 22p. (Orig.). (gr. 2-5). 1982. pap. 1.50 (ISBN 0-9606382-6-1). Dragon Ent.

--Nevada Coloring Books: The 20th Century, 1 of 2, Pt. II. (Illus.). 46p. 1983. pap. 3.50 (ISBN 0-686-37772-9). Dragon Ent.

Milunsky, Aubrey. Prevention of Genetic Disease & Mental Retardation. LC 74-21015. (Illus.). 450p. 1975. 29.00 o.p. (ISBN 0-7216-6395-8). Saunders.

Milutinovic, Barbara, jt. auth. see Broadwell, Lucile.

Milvy, Paul, ed. The Marathon: Physiological, Medical, Epidemiological, & Psycological Studies, Vol. 301. (Annals of the New York Academy of Sciences). 1090p. 1977. 77.00x (ISBN 0-89072-047-9). NY Acad Sci.

Milward, Alan S. The German Economy at War. 1965. text ed. 36.75x (ISBN 0-485-11075-X, Athlone Pr). Humanities.

Milward, Alan S. & Saul, S. B. The Economic Development of Continental Europe 1780-1870. 2nd ed. (Illus.). 1973. text ed. 39.95x o.p. (ISBN 0-04-330229-7); pap. text ed. 15.95x (ISBN 0-04-330299-8). Allen Unwin.

Milwaukee County Welfare Rights Organization. Welfare Mothers Speak Out: We Ain't Gonna Shuffle Anymore. (Illus.). 192p. 1972. pap. 2.95 o.p. (ISBN 0-393-01073-2). Norton.

Milwaukee Public Museum. Sioux Indian Drawings. 1961. pap. 5.00 (ISBN 0-686-95820-9). Jefferson Natl.

Milwidsky, B. & Gabriel, D. Detergent Analysis. 1982. 69.00x (ISBN 0-7114-5735-2, Pub. by Macdonald Bk). State Mutual Bk.

Milyukova, M. S. Analytical Chemistry of Plutonium. 440p. 1971. 34.95 o.s.i. (ISBN 0-470-60415-8). Halsted Pr.

Mims. One Hundred & Three Projects for Electronics Experimenters. 308p. 1981. 15.95 o.p. (ISBN 0-8306-9648-2); pap. 9.95 (ISBN 0-8306-1249-1, 1249). TAB Bks.

Mims, C. A. Pathogenesis of Infectious Disease. 2nd ed. 1982. 22.00 o.s.i. (ISBN 0-12-498254-9); pap. 10.50 o.s.i. (ISBN 0-12-498255-7). Acad Pr.

Mims, Cedric. The Pathogenesis of Infectious Disease. 1977. pap. 11.00 o.p. (ISBN 0-12-498252-2). Acad Pr.

Mims, Cedric, ed. The Pathogenesis of Infectious Disease. 1976. 23.00 o.p. (ISBN 0-8089-0981-9). Grune.

Mims, Forrest. The Forrest Mims Circuit Scrapbook. Helms, Harry L., ed. (Illus.). 170p. 1982. pap. 14.95 (ISBN 0-07-042389-X, P&RB). McGraw.

Minadeo, Richard. The Golden Plectrum: Sexual Symbolism in Horace's Odes. (Studies in Classical Antiquity: Band 4). 247p. 1982. pap. text ed. 23.00x (ISBN 90-6203-664-3, Pub. by Rodopi Holland). Humanities.

Minahan, Anne, jt. auth. see Pincus, Allen.

Minami, Hiroshi. Psychology of the Japanese People. LC 72-75736. 210p. 1972. 17.50x o.p. (ISBN 0-8020-1881-5). U of Toronto Pr.

Minan, John H., ed. Legal Aspects of Solar Energy. Lawrence, William H. 256p. 1981. 25.95x (ISBN 0-669-03761-3). Lexington Bks.

Minard & Wilson. Forbes Number Game. 1979. pap. 9.95 (ISBN 0-13-325100-4). P-H.

Minault, Gail, ed. The Extended Family: Women & Political Participation in India & Pakistan. 325p. 1981. text ed. 18.00x cancelled o.p. (ISBN 0-391-02503-1, Pub. by Chanakya India). Humanities.

Minc, Alain, jt. auth. see Nora, Simon.

Minc, Henryk. Permanents. (Encyclopedia of Mathematics & Its Applications: Vol. 6). 1978. text ed. 28.50 (ISBN 0-201-13505-1, Adv Bk Prog). A-W.

Minc, Rose. Lo Fantastico y Lo Real En la Narrativa De Juan Rulfo y Gadalupe Duenas. LC 77-76932. (Senda De Estudios y Ensayos). (Illus., Orig., Span.). 1977. pap. 9.95 (ISBN 0-918454-03-4). Senda Nueva.

Minc, Rose S., ed. see Desnoes & Edmundo.

Mincer, Deanne, jt. auth. see Mincer, Richard.

Mincer, Richard & Mincer, Deanne. The Talk Show Book: An Engaging Primer on Talking Your Way to Success. LC 81-12574. 256p. 1982. 14.95x (ISBN 0-87196-604-2). Facts on File.

Minces, Juliet. House of Obedience: Women in Arab Society. Pallis, M., tr. from Fr. 116p. 1982. 18.95 (ISBN 0-86232-012-7, Pub. by Zed Pr England); pap. 8.95 (ISBN 0-86232-063-1). Lawrence Hill.

Minchliffe, Arnold P. Harold Pinter. (English Authors Ser.). lib. bdg. 11.95x (ISBN 0-8057-1448-0, Twayne). G K Hall.

Min-Chuan Ku. Comprehensive Handbook of the U.N, 2 vols. 1978. lib. bdg. 42.50 ea o.p. (ISBN 0-671-18774-0); Vol. 1. lib. bdg. (ISBN 0-685-80284-1). Vol. 2 (ISBN 0-671-18787-2). Monarch Pr.

Mindel, C. & Habenstein, R. W., eds. Ethnic Families in America. 2nd ed. 1981. pap. 16.00 (ISBN 0-444-99090-9). Elsevier.

Mindel, Charles H. & Habenstein, Robert W., eds. Ethnic Families in America: Patterns & Variations. LC 75-40654. 456p. 1976. text ed. 19.95 (ISBN 0-444-99022-4); pap. text ed. 9.50 (ISBN 0-444-99025-9). Elsevier.

Mindell, Arnold. Dreambody: The Body's Role in Revealing the Self. Sternback-Scott, Sisa & Goodman, Becky, eds. (Orig.). 1982. 17.95 (ISBN 0-938434-05-5); pap. 11.95 (ISBN 0-938434-06-3). Sigo Pr.

Mindell, Earl. Earl Mindell's Vitamin Bible. 336p. 1981. pap. 3.95 (ISBN 0-446-30626-6). Warner Bks.

--Earl Mindell's Vitamin Bible for Kids. 1981. 6.95x (ISBN 0-89256-198-X). Cancer Control Soc.

--Earl Mindell's Vitamin Bible for your Kids. 256p. 1982. pap. 3.95 (ISBN 0-553-22660-6). Bantam.

--Vitamin Bible. 6.95x (ISBN 0-89256-114-9); pap. 3.75x (ISBN 0-446-93613-8). Cancer Control Soc.

Mindell, Earl, ed. see Bland, Jeffrey.

Mindell, Earl, ed. see Challem, Jack J.

Mindell, Earl, ed. see Heinerman, John.

Mindell, Earl, ed. see Light, Marilyn.

Mindell, Earl, ed. see Passwater, Richard A.

Mindell, Earl, ed. see Rose, Jeanne.

Mindell, Earl, ed. see Rosenburg, Harold S.

Mindell, Earl R. The Vitamin Robbers. (Good Health Guide Ser.). (Illus.). 1983. pap. 1.45 (ISBN 0-87983-275-4). Keats.

Mindell, Earl R., ed. see Garrison, Robert, Jr.

Mindell, Earl R., ed. see Goldbeck, Nikki.

Mindell, Earl R., ed. see Jones, Susan S.

Mindell, Earl R., ed. see Mervyn, Len.

Mindell, Earl R., ed. see Vogel, Jerome & Walsh, Richard.

Minden, Michael. Arno Schmidt: A Critical Study of his Prose. LC 81-21651. (Anglica Germanica Ser.: No. 2). 250p. 1982. 49.50 (ISBN 0-521-24515-X). Cambridge U Pr.

Minderhoud, J. M., ed. Cerebral Blood Flow. (The Jonxis Lectures: Vol. 7). 1982. 39.75 (ISBN 0-444-90207-4). Elsevier.

Mindess, Harvey & Munford, Paul. Psychology: The Study of People. 1980. text ed. 18.95x (ISBN 0-673-16198-6). Scott F.

Mindess, Sidney & Young, J. Francis. Concrete. (Civil Engineering & Engineering Mechanics Ser.). 4488p. 1981. text ed. 39.95 (ISBN 0-686-63384-9). P-H.

Mine, H. & Osaki, S. Markovian Decision Processes. (Modern Analytic & Computational Methods in Science & Mathematics: No. 25). 1970. 29.95 (ISBN 0-444-00079-8, North Holland). Elsevier.

Minear, Paul S. Images of the Church in the New Testament. 1970. pap. 7.95 (ISBN 0-664-24903-5). Westminster.

--Mark. LC 59-10454. (Layman's Bible Commentary, Vol. 17). 1962. pap. 3.95 (ISBN 0-8042-3077-3). John Knox.
Minear, Ralph E., jt. auth. see Reinisch, Edith H.
Minear, Roger A., jt. auth. see Vesilind, P. Aarne.
Mineka, John, jt. auth. see Hayden, Seymour.
Miner, E., tr. see Teika, Fujiwara.
Miner, Earl. An Introduction to Japanese Court Poetry. LC 68-17138. 1968. 10.00x (ISBN 0-8047-0635-2); pap. 5.95x (ISBN 0-8047-0636-0). Stanford U Pr.
Miner, Earl, ed. Illustrious Evidence: Approaches to Early Seventeenth-Century Literature. 1975. 24.50x (ISBN 0-520-02782-5). U of Cal Pr.
--Seventeenth Century Imagery: Essays on Uses of Figurative Language from Donne to Farquhar. LC 76-132417. (Seventeenth & Eighteenth Centuries Studies Group, UCLA: No. 1). 1971. 28.50c (ISBN 0-520-01825-7). U of Cal Pr.
--Stuart & Georgian Moments: Clark Library Seminar Papers on Seventeenth & Eighteenth Century Literature. (Seventeenth & Eighteenth Centuries Studies Group, UCLA: No. 3). 308p. 1972. 28.50x (ISBN 0-520-01641-6). U of Cal Pr.
Miner, Earl see Dryden, John.
Miner, Earl, tr. Japanese Poetic Diaries. (Center for Japanese & Korean Studies, UC Berkeley). (Illus.). 1969. 26.50x (ISBN 0-520-01466-9); pap. 3.95 (ISBN 0-520-03047-8). U of Cal Pr.
Miner, H. Craig. Corporation & the Indian. 1976. 11.00 (ISBN 0-686-95766-0). Jefferson Natl.
--Wichita: The Early Years, 1865-80. LC 81-23138. (Illus.). xiv, 201p. 1982. 17.50 (ISBN 0-8032-3077-X, Bison); pap. 7.50 (ISBN 0-8032-8111-0, BB 812,). U of Nebr Pr.
Miner, James. Black Hill Vision. pap. 1.75 (ISBN 0-686-84331-2, HAIKU12). Juniper Pr WI.
Miner, Jane C. A Day At a Time: Dealing With an Alcoholic. Schroeder, Howard, ed. LC 82-1400. (Crisis Ser.). (Illus.). 64p. (gr. 4-5). 1982. lib. bdg. 7.95 (ISBN 0-89686-167-8). Crestwood Hse.
--A Man's Pride: Losing a Father. Schroeder, Howard, ed. LC 82-1380. (Crisis Ser.). (Illus.). 64p. (gr. 4-5). 1982. lib. bdg. 7.95 (ISBN 0-89686-168-6). Crestwood Hse.
--Mountain Fear: When a Brother Dies. Schroeder, Howard, ed. LC 82-1405. (Crisis Ser.). (Illus.). 64p. (gr. 4-5). 1982. lib. bdg. 7.95 (ISBN 0-89686-166-X). Crestwood Hse.
--Split Decision: Facing Divorce. Schroeder, Howard, ed. LC 82-1406. (Crisis Ser.). (Illus.). 64p. (gr. 4-5). 1982. lib. bdg. 7.95 (ISBN 0-89686-170-8). Crestwood Hse.
--The Tough Guy: Black in a White World. Schroeder, Howard, ed. LC 82-1408. (Crisis Ser.). (Illus.). 64p. (gr. 4-5). 1982. lib. bdg. 7.95 (ISBN 0-89686-169-4). Crestwood Hse.
Miner, Jane Claypool. Miracle of Time: Adopting a Sister. Schroeder, Howard, ed. LC 82-1375. (Crisis Ser.). (Illus.). 64p. (gr. 4-5). 1982. lib. bdg. 7.95 (ISBN 0-89686-172-4). Crestwood Hse.
--Navajo Victory-Being a Native American. Schroeder, Howard, ed. LC 82-1422. (Crisis Ser.). (Illus.). 64p. (gr. 4-5). 1982. lib. bdg. 7.95 (ISBN 0-89686-175-9). Crestwood Hse.
--New Beginning: An Athlete is Paralyzed. Schroeder, Howard, ed. LC 82-1401. (Crisis Ser.). (Illus.). 64p. (gr. 4-5). 1982. lib. bdg. 7.95 (ISBN 0-89686-174-0). Crestwood Hse.
--She's My Sister: Having a Retarded Sister. Schroeder, Howard, ed. LC 82-1424. (Crisis Ser.). (Illus.). 64p. (gr. 4-5). 1982. lib. bdg. 7.95 (ISBN 0-89686-171-6). Crestwood Hse.
--This Day is Mine: Living With Leukemia. Schroeder, Howard, ed. LC 82-1423. (Crisis Ser.). (Illus.). 64p. (gr. 4-5). 1982. lib. bdg. 7.95 (ISBN 0-89686-173-2). Crestwood Hse.
Miner, John B. The Human Constraint: The Coming Shortage of Managerial Talent. 1974. text ed. 12.50x (ISBN 0-87179-215-X). Organizat Mea.
--The Management Process: Theory, Research, & Practice. 2nd ed. (Illus.). 1978. text ed. 23.95x (ISBN 0-02-381650-3). Macmillan.
Miner, John B. & Miner, Mary G. Personnel & Industrial Relations: A Managerial Approach. 3rd ed. 1977. text ed. 24.95x (ISBN 0-02-381660-0). Macmillan.
Miner, John B., jt. auth. see Miner, Mary G.
Miner, Lynn E., jt. auth. see Griffith, Jerry.
Miner, Margaret, jt. auth. see Chock, Judy.
Miner, Marilyn. You Are the Country. 12p. (Orig.). 1980. 5.00 (ISBN 0-931188-06-7). Seal Pr WA.
Miner, Mary G. & Miner, John B. Employee Selection Within the Law. rev. ed. LC 79-13581. 1979. 21.00 (ISBN 0-87179-264-8). BNA.
--A Guide to Personnel Management. LC 73-77272. 202p. 1973. pap. 10.00 (ISBN 0-87179-186-2). BNA.
Miner, Mary G., jt. auth. see Miner, John B.
Miner, Maryalice F. Water Fun: Swimming Instruction & Water Games for the Whole Family. (Illus.). 1980. 14.95 o.p. (ISBN 0-13-945824-7, Spec); pap. 5.95 o.p. (ISBN 0-13-945816-6). P-H.
Miner, O. Irene. Plants We Know. LC 81-9929. (The New True Bks.). 48p. (gr. k-4). 1981. PLB 9.25 (ISBN 0-516-01642-3). Childrens.
Miner, Robert. Mother's Day. LC 78-1831. 1978. 8.95 o.p. (ISBN 0-399-90012-8, Marek). Putnam Pub Group.
Miner, Roy W. Field Book of Seashore Life. (Putnam's Nature Field Bks.). (Illus.). 1950. 9.75 o.p. (ISBN 0-399-10293-0). Putnam Pub Group.
Miner, Valerie. Murder in the English Department. 176p. 1983. 9.95 (ISBN 0-312-55310-2). St Martin.
Miner, Ward L., jt. auth. see Smith, Thelma M.
Miners, Norman. The Government & Politics of Hong Kong. 3rd ed. 1981. pap. 21.00x (ISBN 0-19-581319-7). Oxford U Pr.
Mines, Allan. Respiratory Physiology. (Raven Press Ser. in Physiology). 176p. 1981. 16.00 (ISBN 0-89004-634-4); pap. 10.95 (ISBN 0-686-77675-5). Raven.
Mines, R., jt. auth. see McCabe, R.
Mines, Samuel. Conquest of Pain. rev. ed. LC 73-18528. 1979. pap. (ISBN 0-448-16532-5, G&D). Putnam Pub Group.
Minetti, L., et al, eds. Debates in Nephrology. (Contributions to Nephrology, Vol. 34). (Illus.). viii, 132p. 1982. pap. 53.50 (ISBN 3-8055-3535-X). S Karger.
Minford, John, tr. see Cao, Xueqin.
Minford, John, tr. see Cao Xuequin & Gao E.
Mingall, Harry. The Business Guide to Telephone Systems: How to Evaluate & Improve Your Communications Systems. 195p. (Orig.). 1983. pap. price not set (ISBN 0-88908-561-7). Self Counsel Pr.
Mingay, G. E., jt. auth. see Chambers, J. D.
Mingay, G. E., ed. The Agricultural Revolution: Changes in Agriculture Sixteen Fifty to Eighteen Eighty. (Documents in Economic History). 1977. text ed. 18.25x o.p. (ISBN 0-7136-1703-9). Humanities.
Mingay, Gordon. Mrs. Hurst Dancing & Other Scenes from Regency Life 1812-1823. (Illus.). 158p. 1982. 25.00 (ISBN 0-312-55129-0). St Martin.
Ming Dao, Wong see Dao, Wong Ming.
Minge, M. Ronald & Giuliani, George. Mating. 352p. 1982. pap. 9.95 (ISBN 0-940162-01-6). Red Lion.
Minger, Elda. Untamed Heart. (Harlequin American Romance). 256p. 1983. pap. 2.50 (ISBN 0-373-16012-7). Harlequin Bks.
Mingione, Enzo. Social Conflict & the City. 1981. 26.00x (ISBN 0-312-73163-9). St Martin.
Mingjie, Wang, tr. see Lanyun, Liu.
Ming Lai, tr. see Chou Ching-Wen.
Mingle, J. O. The Invariant Imbedding Theory of Nuclear Transport. LC 73-187686. (Modern Analytic & Computational Methods in Science & Mathematics Ser.: No. 39). 144p. 1973. 26.95 (ISBN 0-444-00123-9, North Holland). Elsevier.
Mingorance, Oscar. De Irlanda a Argentina Con Amor. 128p. 1981. pap. 4.50 (ISBN 0-311-37025-X). Casa Bautista.
Mingot, Tomas De Galiana. Pequeno Larousse de ciencias y tecnicas. new ed. 1056p. 1975. 26.95 (ISBN 0-685-55467-8, 21115). Larousse.
Mings, Lonnie C. Rusticus. 1978. 4.95 o.p. (ISBN 0-8024-7398-9). Moody.
Minich, Quaid, jt. auth. see Elonka, Stephen M.
Minich, Quaid W., jt. auth. see Elonka, Stephen M.
Minick, Michael. Kung Fu: Health Secrets of Ancient China. 1974. 7.95 o.p. (ISBN 0-671-21703-8). S&S.
--Kung Fu: Health Secrets of Ancient China. 1973. pap. 2.95 o.p. (ISBN 0-671-21704-6, Fireside). S&S.
Miniear, Judy & Kennedy, Timothy. Kosciusko Ladies Clubs at Their Best, Vol. 1. (Illus.). 224p. 1982. pap. 9.50 (ISBN 0-910219-05-2). Little People.
Minifie, Fred D. & Lloyd, Lyle L., eds. Communicative & Cognitive Abilities: Early Behavioral Assessment. (NICHD Mental Retardation Research Centers Ser). 624p. 1978. text ed. 39.95 (ISBN 0-8391-1235-1). Univ Park.
Mining & Metallurgy Instrumentation Symposium, 5th, Vancouver, 1976. Instrumentation in the Mining & Metallurgy Industries: Proceedings, Vol. 4. LC 73-82889. 109p. 1976. pap. text ed. 12.50x o.p. (ISBN 0-87664-320-9). Instru Soc.
Mining Information Services. Mining Methods & Equipment. 224p. 1980. 21.50 (ISBN 0-07-039794-5). McGraw.
Mining Informational Services. World Demand for Raw Materials in 1985-2000. LC 78-10538. 1980. 17.50 (ISBN 0-07-039789-9, P&RB). McGraw.
Mining Journal Books Ltd. Economics of Mineral Engineering. 223p. 1980. 25.00x (ISBN 0-900117-10-9, Pub. by Mining Journal England). State Mutual Bk.
--Negotiation & Drafting of Mining Development Agreements. 236p. 1980. 30.00x (ISBN 0-900117-11-7, Pub. by Mining Journal England). State Mutual Bk.
--Tungsten. 190p. 1980. 40.00x (ISBN 0-900117-21-4, Pub. by Mining Journal England). State Mutual Bk.
--Uranium & Nuclear Energy. 326p. 1980. 45.00x (ISBN 0-900117-20-6, Pub. by Mining Journal England). State Mutual Bk.
--Uranium: Balance of Supply & Demand Nineteen Seventy Eight to Nineteen Ninety. 60p. 1980. 45.00x1311 (ISBN 0-900117-19-2, Pub. by Mining Journal England). State Mutual Bk.
Minish, Gary & Fox, Danny. Beef Production & Management. 2nd ed. 1982. text ed. 20.95 (ISBN 0-8359-0447-4); instrs'. manual avail. (ISBN 0-8359-0449-0). Reston.
Ministere de la Marine et des Colonies. Compte-Rendu au Roi de l'Execution des Lois des 18 et 19 Juillet 1845 sur le Regime des Esclaves, la Creation d'Etablissements Agricoles par le Travail Libre, etc... (Slave Trade in France Ser., 1744-1848). 310p. (Fr.). 1974. Repr. of 1847 ed. lib. bdg. 82.00x o.p. (ISBN 0-8287-1350-2, TN 165). Clearwater Pub.
Ministere De La Marine & Des Colonies. Commission Instituee par Decision Royale. (Slave Trade in France, 1744-1848, Ser.). (Fr.). 1974. Repr. of 1843 ed. lib. bdg. 310.00 o.p. (ISBN 0-8287-1348-0, TN155-8). Clearwater Pub.
Ministry of Agriculture & Fisheries- Netherlands & Nijdam, J., eds. Elsevier's Dictionary of Horticulture. (Eng., Fr., Dutch, Ger., Danish, Swedish, Span., Ital., & Lat.). 1970. 89.50 (ISBN 0-444-40812-6). Elsevier.
Ministry Of Defence Naval Library, London. Author & Subject Catalogues of the Naval Library, Ministry of Defence, 5 Vols. 1967. Set. lib. bdg. 395.00 (ISBN 0-8161-0755-6, Hall Library). G K Hall.
Ministry of Education. Scientific Terms Meteorology: Japanese-English, English-Japanese. 140p. 1975. Leatherette 19.95 (ISBN 0-686-92205-0, M-9338). French & Eur.
Ministry of Education & Social Welfare. India (Republic). the Gazetteers Unit. The Gazetteer of India; Indian Union. Incl. Vol. 1. Country & People. (Illus.). 652p. 17.50x (ISBN 0-8002-1448-X); Vol. 2. History & Culture. (Illus.). 807p. 1973. 25.00x (ISBN 0-8002-1449-8); Vol. 3. 1975. 45.00x (ISBN 0-8002-1450-1); Vol. 4. 1975. 45.00x (ISBN 0-8002-2535-X). Intl Pubns Serv.
Ministry of Education Science & Culture. Scientific Terms Electrical Engineering. 675p. (Eng. & Japanese.). 1979. 39.95 (ISBN 0-686-97433-6, M-9330). French & Eur.
Ministry of Planning Central Statistical Organization. Annual Abstract of Statistics, Iraq, 1976. LC 72-622806. 1977. pap. 17.50x o.p. (ISBN 0-8002-0258-9). Intl Pubns Serv.
Minium, E. W. Statistical Reasoning in Psychology & Education. 2nd ed. 1978. text ed. 28.50x (ISBN 0-471-60828-9); wkbk (ISBN 0-471-03633-1). Wiley.
Minium, Edward W. & Clark, Robert. Elements of Statistical Reasoning. 496p. 1982. text ed. 20.95 (ISBN 0-471-08041-1); wkbk. 7.95 (ISBN 0-471-86463-3); tchrs.' manual 5.50 (ISBN 0-471-87590-2). Wiley.
Minix, Dean A. Small Groups & Foreign Policy Decision-Making. LC 80-8128. (Illus.). 262p. (Orig.). 1982. lib. bdg. 23.25 (ISBN 0-8191-2372-2); pap. text ed. 11.50 (ISBN 0-8191-2373-0). U Pr of Amer.
Mink, B. Washburn, jt. auth. see Roueche, N. E.
Minkin, Lewis. The Labour Party Conference: A Study in the Politics of Intra-Party Democracy. 464p. 1982. pap. 12.50 (ISBN 0-7190-0800-X). Manchester.
Minkoff, Eli C. Evolutionary Biology. (Biology Ser.). (Illus.). 650p. 1983. text ed. 22.95 (ISBN 0-201-15890-6); Instrs' Manual avail. (ISBN 0-201-15891-4). A-W.
Minkowich, Avram. Success & Failure in Israeli Elementary Education: An Evaluation Study with Special Emphasis on Disadvantaged Students. LC 80-19873. 539p. 1982. 39.95 (ISBN 0-87855-370-3). Transaction Bks.
Minkowski, A. & Relier, J. P., eds. Journees Nationales de Neonatologie XIIe, Paris, Mai 1982. (Progress en Neonatologie: Vol. 2). vi, 258p. 1983. pap. 46.75 (ISBN 3-8055-3567-8). S Karger.
Minkowski, Hermann. Diophantische Approximationen. LC 56-13056. (Ger). 13.95 (ISBN 0-8284-0118-7). Chelsea Pub.
--Gesammelte Abhandlungen, 2 Vols. in 1. LC 66-28570. (Ger). 45.00 (ISBN 0-8284-0208-6). Chelsea Pub.
Minn, Loretta. Teach Speech. (gr. 3-7). 1982. 5.95 (ISBN 0-86653-058-4, GA 418). Good Apple.
Minn, Lorretta B. Rhymes, Riddles & Research. (gr. 4-8). 1981. 4.95 (ISBN 0-86653-024-X, GA 253). Good Apple.
Minnault, Gail, jt. auth. see Papanek, Hanna.
Minneapolis Institute of Arts. Arakawa. LC 79-90281. (Illus.). 1979. 8.00 o.p. (ISBN 0-912964-02-2). Minneapolis Inst Arts.
--Leger's Le Grand Dejeuner. LC 80-80235. (Illus.). 1980. 8.00 (ISBN 0-912964-11-1). Minneapolis Inst Arts.
--Millet's Gleaners. LC 78-54599. (Illus.). 1978. 5.00 (ISBN 0-912964-12-X). Minneapolis Inst Arts.
Minneapolis Institute of Arts Staff. Sculpture from the David Daniels Collection. LC 79-90068. (Illus.). 1979. 7.50 (ISBN 0-912964-10-3). Minneapolis Inst Arts.
Minnesota Council on Foundations. Guide to Minnesota Foundations & Corporate Giving Programs. LC 82-21928. 136p. 1983. pap. 14.95x (ISBN 0-8166-1219-6). U of Minn Pr.
Minnesota Hospital Association, compiled by. The Changing Role of the Hospital: Options for the Future. (Illus.). 336p. (Orig.). 1980. pap. 35.00 (ISBN 0-87258-310-4, AHA-127186). Am Hospital.
Minnich, Harvey C. Williams Holmes McGuffey & His Readers. LC 74-19214. (Illus.). xii, 203p. 1975. Repr. of 1936 ed. 34.00x (ISBN 0-8103-4104-2). Gale.
Minnich, Harvey C., ed. see McGuffey, William H.
Minnich, Jerry. The Earthworm Book: How to Raise & Use Earthworms for Your Farm & Garden. LC 77-13405. 1977. 12.95 o.p. (ISBN 0-87857-193-0). Rodale Pr Inc.
Minnich, Jerry A. The Wisconsin Garden Guide. rev. & enl. ed. (Illus.). 1982. pap. 14.95 (ISBN 0-88361-086-8). Stanton & Lee.
Minnick. Public Speaking. 2nd ed. 1983. 13.95 (ISBN 0-686-84657-5); supplementary materials avail. HM.
Minnick, Ann. Patient Teaching by Registered Nurses. Kalisch, Philip & Kalisch, Beatrice, eds. LC 82-17623. (Studies in Nursing Management: No. 9). 100p. 1982. 34.95 (ISBN 0-8357-1378-4). Univ Microfilms.
Minnick, John & Strauss, Raymond. Beginning Algebra. 2nd ed. (Illus.). 288p. 1976. text ed. 19.95 (ISBN 0-13-073791-7). P-H.
Minnick, Thomas L., jt. auth. see Good, Donald W.
Minnick, Wayne C. Public Speaking. LC 78-69580. (Illus.). 1979. text ed. 12.50 (ISBN 0-395-26791-9); instr's. manual 0.50 (ISBN 0-395-26792-7). HM.
--Public Speaking. 2d ed. LC 82-83203. 320p. 1983. pap. text ed. 13.95 (ISBN 0-395-32627-3); write for info. instr's. manual (ISBN 0-395-32628-1). HM.
Minnis, A. J. Chaucer & Pagan Antiquity. (Chaucer Studies: No. VIII). 208p. 1982. text ed. 47.50x (ISBN 0-8476-7195-X). Rowman.
Mino, Yutaka, jt. auth. see Robinson, James.
Minogue, Kenneth R. The Concept of the University. 1973. 25.00x (ISBN 0-520-02390-0, CAL 287). U of Cal Pr.
Minogue, M. Documents on Contemporary British Government: British Government & Constitutional Change, Vol. 1. LC 76-26374. 1977. 47.50 (ISBN 0-521-21437-8); pap. 14.95x (ISBN 0-521-29148-8). Cambridge U Pr.
Minogue, M., ed. Documents on Contemporary British Government: Local Government in Britain, Vol. 2. LC 76-26374. 1977. 47.50 (ISBN 0-521-21429-7); pap. 14.95x (ISBN 0-521-29147-X). Cambridge U Pr.
Minogue, M. & Molloy, J., eds. African Aims & Attitudes: Selected Documents. LC 74-76567. 404p. 1974. 42.50 (ISBN 0-521-20426-7); pap. text ed. 15.95x (ISBN 0-521-09851-3). Cambridge U Pr.
Minogue, W. J. Hawaiian & New Zealand Teacher Education. 143p. 1971. 8.00x (ISBN 0-8248-0299-3). UH Pr.
Minor, Andrew C. Music in Medieval & Renaissance Life: Anthology of Vocal & Instrumental Music, 1200-1614. 137p. 1964. 10.00 (ISBN 0-8262-0026-5). U of Mo Pr.
Minor, Andrew C. & Mitchell, M. Bonner, eds. A Renaissance Entertainment: Festivities for the Marriage of Cosimo I, Duke of Florence, in 1539. LC 68-11348. (Illus.). 389p. 1968. 20.00x (ISBN 0-8262-8522-8). U of Mo Pr.
Minor, Dorothy, jt. auth. see Minor, Eugene E.
Minor, E. O. & Fyre, H. R. Techniques for Producing Visual Instructional Media. 1977. 28.95 (ISBN 0-07-042406-3). McGraw.
Minor, Edward O. Handbook for Preparing Visual Media. 2nd ed. (Illus.). 1978. pap. text ed. 15.95 (ISBN 0-07-042407-1, C). McGraw.
Minor, Eugene E. & Minor, Dorothy. Vocabulario Huitoto Muinane. (Peruvian Linguistic Ser: No. 5). 139p. 1970. pap. 3.00x (ISBN 0-88312-656-7); microfiche 2.25x (ISBN 0-88312-362-2). Summer Inst Ling.
Minor, Lewis J. L. J. Minor Foodservice Standards Series: Nutritional Standards, Vol. 1. (Illus.). 1983. text ed. 20.00 (ISBN 0-87055-425-5). AVI.
--L. J. Minor Foodservice Standards Series: Sanitation, Safety, Environmental Standards, Vol. 2. (Illus.). 1983. text ed. 20.00 (ISBN 0-87055-428-X). AVI.
Minor, Michael J., jt. auth. see Burt, Ronald S.
Minor, Paul S. The Industry - EPA Confrontation: Living with the Water Pollution Control Act Amendments of 1972 Today. LC 76-14470. 1976. pap. 9.00 o.p. (ISBN 0-07-042401-2, P&RB). McGraw.
Minor, T. & Marth, E. H. Staphylococci & Their Significance in Foods. 1976. 59.75 (ISBN 0-444-41339-1). Elsevier.
Minors, R. A., ed. see Bede The Venerable.
Minorsky, Nicholas N. Non-Linear Oscillation. LC 74-8918. 734p. 1974. Repr. of 1962 ed. 37.00 (ISBN 0-88275-186-7). Krieger.
Minoso, Minnie. Extra Innings. (Illus.). 1982. 10.95. Regnery-Gateway.
Minot, G. R. History of the Insurrections in Massachusetts in 1786. LC 76-148912. (Era of the American Revolution Ser). 1971. Repr. of 1788 ed. lib. bdg. 27.50 (ISBN 0-306-70100-6). Da Capo.
Minot, Stephen. Three Genres. 3rd ed. (Illus.). 350p. 1982. text ed. 14.95 (ISBN 0-13-920397-4). P-H.
Minot, Walter S. Rhetoric: Theory & Practice for Composition. (Orig.). 1981. pap. text ed. 9.95 (ISBN 0-316-57430-9); tchr's ed. avail. (ISBN 0-316-57431-7). Little.

Mins, Ferm & Swenson, Melinda. Sexuality: A Nursing Perspective. 1979. pap. text ed. 16.50 (ISBN 0-07-042388-1). McGraw.

Minshull, Evelyn W. Firebug! LC 74-1366. (gr. 6-9). 1974. 5.50 o.s.i. (ISBN 0-664-32548-3). Westminster.

Minshull, G. N. The New Europe: An Economic Geography of the EEC. LC 78-6581. 1978. pap. text ed. 17.00x o.p. (ISBN 0-8419-0391-3). Holmes & Meier.

Minshull, Roger. Regional Geography. 168p. 1967. text ed. 4.50x o.p. (ISBN 0-09-082772-4, Hutchinson U Pr); pap. text ed. 2.25x o.p. (ISBN 0-09-082773-2). Humanities.

Minshull, Ruth. Efficiency. 35p. 1976. pap. write for info. (ISBN 0-937922-03-X). SAA Pub.

--How to Choose Your People. 280p. 1972. write for info. (ISBN 0-937922-02-1). SAA Pub.

--How to Cure the Selfish, Destructive Child. (Orig.). 1980. pap. write for info. (ISBN 0-937922-07-2). SAA Pub.

--Miracles for Breakfast. rev. ed. 181p. 1982. pap. write for info. (ISBN 0-937922-01-3). SAA Pub.

--Ups & Downs. 103p. 1980. pap. write for info. (ISBN 0-937922-05-6). SAA Pub.

Minshull, Ruth, ed. see Hubbard, L. Ron.

Minski, L. & Shepperd, M. J. Non-Communicating Children. 2nd ed. (Illus.). 1970. 10.95 o.p. (ISBN 0-407-33200-6). Butterworth.

Minsky, Hyman P. Can "IT" Happen Again? Essays on Instability & Finance. LC 82-10789. 1982. 35.00 (ISBN 0-87332-213-4). M E Sharpe.

Minsky, Marvin. Computation: Finite & Infinite Machines. 1967. ref. ed. 26.95 (ISBN 0-13-165563-9). P-H.

Minsky, Marvin L., ed. Semantic Information Processing. LC 68-18239. 1969. 30.00x (ISBN 0-262-13044-0). MIT Pr.

Minson, Maxine. Angel in the Park. 1983. pap. 1.50 (ISBN 0-686-38379-6). Eldridge Pub.

--Angel in the Park. 1983. pap. 1.50 (ISBN 0-686-38757-0). Eldridge Pub.

Minster, Margaret, ed. Herbs: From Cultivation to Cooking. (Illus.). 228p. 1981. Repr. of 1980 ed. spiral bdg. 9.95 (ISBN 0-88289-288-6). Pelican.

Minteer, Catherine. Understanding in a World of Words. LC 76-122936. (gr. 6-12). 1970. pap. text ed. 6.50x o.p. (ISBN 0-918970-06-7). Intl Gen Semantics.

--Words & What They Do To You. 1983. 5.50 (ISBN 0-686-84067-4). Intl Gen Semantics.

Minter, Phyllis V., jt. auth. see Rogers, Ferial.

Minter-Dowd, Christine. Finders' Guide to Decorative Arts in the Smithsonian Institution. (Finders' Guides to the Collections in the Smithsonian Institution Ser.: Vol. 2). (Illus.). 212p. 1983. text ed. 19.95x (ISBN 0-87474-636-1); pap. text ed. 9.95x (ISBN 0-87474-637-X). Smithsonian.

Minti, Daniel J., ed. Investigating the Impact of Desegregation. LC 81-48586. 1982. 7.95x (ISBN 0-87589-928-5, TM-14). Jossey-Bass.

Minto, Arlo W. Alpha Awareness Results Book. 1978. 6.95 o.p. (ISBN 0-89036-112-6). Hawkes Pub Inc.

Minton, Arthur J. Philosophy: Paradox & Discovery. 512p. 1976. 16.95 (ISBN 0-07-042412-8, C). McGraw.

Minton, Arthur J. & Shipka, Thomas A. Philosophy: Paradox & Discovery. 2nd ed. 496p. 1982. pap. text ed. 17.50x (ISBN 0-07-042413-6, C). McGraw.

Minton, Charles E. Juan of Santo Nino. (Illus.). 1973. pap. 4.95 (ISBN 0-913270-22-9). Sunstone Pr.

Minton, David. Building Scale Model Airliners. (Illus., Orig.). 1984. pap. price not set (ISBN 0-89024-056-6). Kalmbach.

--The Motorcyclist's Handbook. 1982. 10.50 (ISBN 0-671-44118-3). S&S.

Minton, Janis. Basic Skills Map Workbook. (Basic Skills Workbooks). 32p. (gr. 4-7). 1983. 0.99 (ISBN 0-8209-0540-2, SSW-4). ESP.

--Basic Skills Understanding Instructions Workbook. (Basic Skills Workbooks). 32p. (gr. 4-7). 1983. 0.99 (ISBN 0-8209-0580-1, IW-1). ESP.

--Learning to Read Maps. (Social Studies Ser.). 24p. (gr. 4-7). 1978. wkbk. 5.00 (ISBN 0-8209-0256-X, SS-23). ESP.

--Understanding Instructions. (Language Arts Ser.). 24p. (gr. 3-6). 1979. wkbk. 5.00 (ISBN 0-8209-0322-1, LA-8). ESP.

--Understanding Maps. (Social Studies Ser.). 24p. (gr. 4-7). 1979. wkbk. 5.00 (ISBN 0-8209-0257-8, SS-24). ESP.

Mintz, Barbara, jt. auth. see Katan, Norma J.

Mintz, Elizabeth & Schmeidler, R. The Psychic Thread: Paranormal & Transpersonal Aspects of Psychotherapy. 240p. 1983. 24.95 (ISBN 0-89885-139-4). Human Sci Pr.

Mintz, Grafton K., ed. see Han, Woo-Keun.

Mintz, Kenneth. The Holy Ghost. 61p. (Orig.). 1980. pap. 2.00 (ISBN 0-9609162-1-0). Monbook Pr.

Mintz, Leigh W. Historical Geology: The Science of a Dynamic Earth. 3rd ed. (Illus.). 576p. 1981. text ed. 24.95 (ISBN 0-675-08028-2). Additional supplements may be obtained from publisher. Merrill.

Mintz, Lorelie M. How to Grow Fruits & Berries. LC 79-28753. (Illus.). 96p. (gr. 4-6). 1980. PLB 7.29g o.p. (ISBN 0-671-33086-1). Messner.

Mintz, Malcolm W. Bikol Text. McKaughan, Howard P., ed. (PALI Language Texts: Philippines). (Orig.). 1971. pap. text ed. 12.00x o.p. (ISBN 0-87022-530-8). UH Pr.

Mintz, Marilyn D. The Martial Arts Films. LC 82-74498. (Illus.). 243p. 1983. Repr. of 1978 ed. 12.95 (ISBN 0-8048-1408-2). C E Tuttle.

Mintz, Morton. By Prescription Only. Orig. Title: Therapeutic Nightmare. pap. 3.95x (ISBN 0-8070-2193-8, BP267). Beacon Pr.

Mintz, Morton, jt. auth. see Cohen, Jerry S.

Mintz, Ruth F. Modern Hebrew Poetry: A Bilingual Anthology. 1966. pap. 3.95 o.s.i. (ISBN 0-520-00868-5, CAL165). U of Cal Pr.

Mintz, Ruth F., ed. Modern Hebrew Poetry: A Bilingual Anthology. 425p. 1982. pap. 9.95 (ISBN 0-520-04781-8, CAL 591). U of Cal Pr.

Mintz, Sidney W. Worker in the Cane. LC 73-19567. (Caribbean Ser.). (Illus.). 288p. 1974. Repr. of 1960 ed. lib. bdg. 18.75x (ISBN 0-8371-7297-7, MIWC). Greenwood.

Mintz, Steven. A Prision of Expectations: The Family in Victorian Culture. 232p. 1983. text ed. 25.00X (ISBN 0-8147-5388-4). NYU Pr.

Mintzberg, Henry. Impediments to the Use of Management Information. 27p. 4.95 (ISBN 0-86641-041-4, 7474). Natl Assn Accts.

Mintzer, Richard A. Chest Imaging: An Integrated Approach. (Illus.). 200p. 1981. lib. bdg. 29.95 (ISBN 0-683-06051-1). Williams & Wilkins.

Mintzer, Richard I. The Auto Owner's Diary. 112p. (Orig.). 1982. pap. 4.95 (ISBN 0-911275-00-2). Recro Products.

Minuchin, Salvador, et al. Families of the Slums: An Exploration of Their Structure Treatment. LC 67-28507. (Illus.). 1967. 18.50 (ISBN 0-465-02330-4). Basic.

Minus, Johnny & Hare, William S. Your Introduction to Film-T.V. Copyright, Contracts & Other Law. 20.00 (ISBN 0-911370-09-9); pap. 10.00x handbook (ISBN 0-686-96680-5). Borden.

Minz, Karl-Heinz. Pleroma Trinitatis: Die Trinitatstheologie bei Matthias Joseph Scheeben. (Disputationes Theologicae Ser.: Vol. 10). 404p. 1980. write for info. (ISBN 3-8204-6182-5). P Lang Pubs.

Minzey, Jack & LeTarte, Clyde. Community Education: From Program to Process to Practice: the School's Role in a New Educational Society. rev. ed. LC 76-189279. 1979. text ed. 19.00 (ISBN 0-87812-167-6); pap. 15.75 (ISBN 0-686-67736-6). Pendell Pub.

Miossi, Alfred F., ed. see Kim, Seung H. & Miller, Stephen W.

Miquel, Pierre. Eighteenth Century Europe. LC 81-52603. (Picture Histories Ser.). PLB 12.68 (ISBN 0-382-06618-9). Silver.

--Life in Ancient Rome. LC 80-52501. (Picture Histories Ser.). PLB 12.68 (ISBN 0-382-06473-9). Silver.

--The Musketeers. LC 81-52602. (Picture Histories Ser.). PLB 12.68 (ISBN 0-382-06617-0). Silver.

Mira, Julio A. Mathematical Teasers. LC 74-101122. (Orig.). 1970. pap. 4.50 (ISBN 0-06-463230-X, EH 230, EH). B&N NY.

Mira Math Pub. Mira Math for Elementary Schools. 1973. pap. 6.25 wkbk. (ISBN 0-88488-023-0). Creative Pubns.

Mirabai & Nandy, Pritish. Krishna: Devotional Songs of Mirabai. 100p. (Orig.). 1982. pap. text ed. 3.95x (ISBN 0-7069-1495-3, Pub. by Vikas India). Advent NY.

Mirabaud, Jean-Baptiste De see De Mirabaud, Jean-Baptiste.

Mirabaud, Paul & De Reuterskiold, Alex. The Postage Stamps of Switzerland, 1843-1862. LC 74-81948. (Illus.). 304p. 1975. Repr. 35.00x o.s.i. (ISBN 0-88000-050-3). Quarterman.

Mirabel, Cecil. The Surprise Bear. LC 81-1105. (Illus.). 18p. (gr. 1-3). 1982. 6.95 o.p. (ISBN 0-316-13250-0). Little.

Mirabella, Lauren, jt. auth. see Konsler, Runelle.

Mirabito, Michael M. The Exploration of Outer Space with Cameras: A History of the NASA Unmanned Spacecraft Missions. (Illus.). 225p. 1983. lib. bdg. 19.95x (ISBN 0-89950-061-7). McFarland & Co.

Miracle, Andrew W., jt. ed. see Dunleavy, Aidan O.

Miranda, Francisco De. New Democracy in America: Travels of Francisco De Miranda in the United States 1783-1784. Ezell, John S., ed. Wood, Judson P., tr. (American Exploration & Travel Ser: Vol. 40). (Illus.). 1963. 14.95 (ISBN 0-8061-0584-4); pap. 7.95x (ISBN 0-8061-1162-3). U of Okla Pr.

Miranda, Gary. Grace Period. LC 82-61373. (Princeton Series of Contemporary Poets). 72p. 1983. 10.95x (ISBN 0-691-06571-3); pap. 5.95 (ISBN 0-691-01406-X). Princeton U Pr.

Miranda, Ruben, tr. see Horowitz, Irving L.

Miranda, Wenceslao. Ignacio Agusti: El Autor y la Obra; Interpretacion y Realismo de "Guerra Civil". LC 81-40864. 120p. (Orig., Sp.). 1982. pap. text ed. 8.00 (ISBN 0-8191-2363-3). U Pr of Amer.

Mirandola, Giovanni Pico Della see Pico Della Mirandola, Giovanni.

Mirchandani, Pitu, jt. auth. see Handler, Gabriel Y.

Mirel, Elizabeth P. Plum Crazy: A Book About Beach Plums. (Illus.). 160p. 1973. 5.95 o.p. (ISBN 0-517-50383-2, 503-832, C N Potter Bks). Crown.

Mireles, Sandra. Lady Nell. (Candlelight Regency Ser.: No. 687). 256p. (Orig.). 1981. pap. 1.75 o.s.i. (ISBN 0-440-14675-5). Dell.

Mirenda, Rose, et al. Nutrition & Diet Therapy. 2nd ed. (Nursing Examination Review Book: Vol. 8). 1972. 7.50 (ISBN 0-87488-508-6). Med Exam.

Miriam, Sr. Love Is Enough. 1962. 6.50 (ISBN 0-8159-6112-X). Devin.

Miriam-Therese, jt. auth. see Ciekot, Jerald.

Mirikitani, Janice, ed. Ayumi: Japanese American Anthology. (Illus.). 29p. (Orig.). 1980. pap. 12.00 (ISBN 0-9603222-0-5). Japan Amer Anthlgy Com.

Mirikitani, Leatrice T. Kapampangan Syntax. LC 72-79568. (Oceanic Linguistics Special Publications Ser.: No. 10). 276p. (Orig.). 1972. pap. text ed. 7.00x o.p. (ISBN 0-8248-0234-9). UH Pr.

--Speaking Kapampangan. McKaughan, Howard P., ed. LC 70-152468. (PALI Language Texts: Philippines). (Orig.). 1971. pap. text ed. 14.00x o.p. (ISBN 0-87022-532-4). UH Pr.

Mirin, Susan K. The Nurse's Guide to Writing for Publication. LC 80-84085. (Illus.). 209p. 1981. 25.00 (ISBN 0-913654-71-X); pap. 19.95 (ISBN 0-913654-73-6). Aspen Systems.

Mirin, Susan K., ed. Teaching Tomorrow's Nurse: A Nurse Educator Reader. LC 79-90378. 224p. 1980. pap. 18.50 (ISBN 0-913654-59-0). Aspen Systems.

Miringoff, Marc L. Management in Human Service Organizations. (Illus.). 1980. text ed. 19.95x (ISBN 0-02-381780-1). Macmillan.

Mirkarimi, Javad. One Love Is Too Many for an Agent. 1978. 5.95 o.p. (ISBN 0-533-03690-9). Vantage.

Mirkin, Gabe. Getting Thin: All about Fat-How You Get it, How You Lose It, How You Keep It Off For Good. (Illus.). 320p. 1983. 15.00i (ISBN 0-316-57437-6). Little.

Mirkin, Howard R. The Complete Fund Raising Guide. 14.50 (ISBN 0-686-24209-2). Public Serv Materials.

Mirman, L. J. & Spulber, D. F. Essays in the Economics of Renewable Resources. (Contributions to Economic Analysis Ser.: Vol. 143). 1982. 59.75 (ISBN 0-444-86340-0). Elsevier.

Miro, Carmen & Potter, Joseph. Research for Population Policy: Directions for the Future. 1980. 18.95 (ISBN 0-312-63158-8). St Martin.

Miro, Joan. Miro Lithographs. (Art Library). (Illus.). 48p. (Orig.). 1983. pap. 2.50 (ISBN 0-486-24437-7). Dover.

Miroff, Franklin I., jt. auth. see Smith, Jerome.

Miroiu, Mihai. Rumanian-English Conversation Book. LC 77-160435. 168p. 12.00 (ISBN 0-8044-0379-1). Ungar.

Mironer, Alan. Engineering Fluid Mechanics. (Illus.). 1979. text ed. 32.95 (ISBN 0-07-042417-9, C). McGraw.

Mirov, Nicholas T. The Genus Pinus. (Illus.). 1967. 43.50 o.s.i. (ISBN 0-471-06838-1, Pub. by Wiley-Interscience). Wiley.

Mirsky, A. E., jt. ed. see Brachet, Jean.

Mirsky, Dimitry S. History of Russian Literature: From Its Beginnings to 1900. Whitfield, Francis J., ed. 1958. pap. 3.95 (ISBN 0-394-70720-6, Vin). Random.

Mirsky, Stanley & Heilman, Joan R. Diabetes: Controlling It the Easy Way. LC 81-6047. 224p. 1982. 13.50 (ISBN 0-394-51148-4). Random.

Mirvis, Philip H. & Berg, David N. Failures in Organization Development & Change: Cases & Essays for Learning. LC 77-21625. 1977. 39.95x (ISBN 0-471-02405-8). Ronald Pr.

Mirza, Sarah M, jt. auth. see Hinnebusch, Thomas J.

Misaghi, I. J. Physiology & Biochemistry of Plant-Pathogen Interactions. 275p. 1982. 32.50x (ISBN 0-306-41059-1, Plenum Pr). Plenum Pub.

Miscall, Peter D. The Workings of Old Testament Narrative. LC 82-48570. (Semeia Studies). 160p. 1983. pap. text ed. 8.95 (ISBN 0-8006-1512-3). Fortress.

--The Workings of Old Testament Narrative. LC 82-5993. (SBL Semeia Studies). 158p. 1983. pap. 8.95 (ISBN 0-89130-584-X, 06-06-12). Scholars Pr CA.

Mischel, Harriet N. & Mischel, Walter. Essentials of Psychology. 2nd ed. 640p. 1980. text ed. 21.00 (ISBN 0-394-32290-8); wkbk. 6.95 (ISBN 0-394-32498-6). Random.

Mischel, W. Personality & Assessment. LC 67-31183. 1968. 27.95 (ISBN 0-471-60925-0). Wiley.

Mischel, Walter, jt. auth. see Mischel, Harriet N.

Misczynski, Dean J., jt. ed. see Hagman, Donald G.

Misell, D. L. Image Analysis, Enhancement & Interpretation. (Practical Methods in Electron Microscopy: Vol. 7). 1979. pap. 30.00 (ISBN 0-7204-0666-8, North Nolland). Elsevier.

Misenheimer, Helen E. Rousseau on the Education of Women. LC 80-5857. 109p. 1981. lib. bdg. 18.00 (ISBN 0-8191-1404-9); pap. text ed. 8.25 (ISBN 0-8191-1405-7). U Pr of Amer.

Misenheimer, Luther, III. Basic Skills Memory Development Workbook. (Basic Skills Workbooks). 32p. (gr. 5-9). 1983. 0.99 (ISBN 0-8209-0582-8, MDW-1). ESP.

--Basic Skills Speed Reading Workbook. (Basic Skills Workbooks). 32p. (gr. 5-9). 1983. 0.99 (ISBN 0-8209-0583-6, SRW-1). ESP.

--Memory Development. (Language Arts Ser.). wkbk. 5.00 (ISBN 0-8209-0325-6, LA-11). ESP.

--Speed Reading. (Language Arts Ser.). 24p. (gr. 6-10). 1979. wkbk. 5.00 (ISBN 0-8209-0324-8, LA-10). ESP.

Mises, Ludwig Von see Von Mises, Ludwig.

Mises, Richard Von. Probability, Statistics & Truth. Geiringer, Hilda, tr. from Ger. xii, 244p. 1981. pap. 4.00 (ISBN 0-486-24214-5). Dover.

Mises, Richard Von see Mises, Richard Von.

Mises, Richard Von see Von Mises, Richard & Von Karman, Theodore.

Misfeldt, Willard E. The Albums of James Tissot. (Illus.). 134p. 1982. 24.95 (ISBN 0-87972-209-6); pap. 12.95 (ISBN 0-87972-210-X). Bowling Green Univ.

Mishan, E., ed. Welfare Economics: An Assessment. (De Vries Lecture Ser.: Vol. 4). 1969. 21.00 (ISBN 0-7204-3406-8, North Holland). Elsevier.

Mishan, E. J. Cost Benefit Analysis. 3rd ed. 384p. 1982. pap. text ed. 14.95x (ISBN 0-04-338099-9). Allen Unwin.

--Elements of Cost-Benefit Analysis. 1976. pap. text ed. 7.95x (ISBN 0-04-300066-5). Allen Unwin.

--An Introduction to Normative Economics. (Illus., Orig.). 1981. pap. text ed. 16.95x (ISBN 0-19-502791-4). Oxford U Pr.

--Making the World Safe for Pornography. LC 73-83001. 262p. 1973. 17.00x (ISBN 0-912050-41-1, Library Pr). Open Court.

Mishan, Ezra. What Political Economy is all About: An Exposition & Critique. LC 82-12880. 256p. 1982. 32.50 (ISBN 0-521-25072-2); pap. 9.95 (ISBN 0-521-27195-9). Cambridge U Pr.

Mishara, Brian & Patterson, Robert. Consumer's Handbook of Mental Health: How to Find, Select & Use Help. 1979. pap. 2.25 o.p. (ISBN 0-451-08608-2, E8608, Sig). NAL.

Mishell, Daniel R., Jr., ed. Advances in Fertility Research, Vol. 1. 225p. 1982. text ed. 27.00 (ISBN 0-89004-577-1). Raven.

Mishima, S., ed. Diseases of the Retina & Uvea. (Journal: Ophthalmologica: Vol. 185, No. 3). (Illus.). 72p. 1982. pap. 28.75 (ISBN 3-8055-3563-5). S Karger.

Mishima, Yukio. After the Banquet. Keene, Donald, tr. (The Perigee Japanese Library). 288p. 1981. pap. 5.95 (ISBN 0-399-50486-9, Perige). Putnam Pub Group.

--Five Modern No Plays. Keene, Donald, tr. 198p. Date not set. pap. 1.95 o.p. (ISBN 0-394-71883-6, Vin). Random.

--Forbidden Colors. Marks, Alfred H., tr. (The Perigee Japanese Library). 416p. 1981. pap. 6.95 (ISBN 0-399-50490-7, Perige). Putnam Pub Group.

--The Sailor Who Fell from Grace with the Sea. Nathan, John, tr. (The Perigee Japanese Library). 192p. 1981. pap. 4.95 (ISBN 0-399-50489-3, Perige). Putnam Pub Group.

--The Sound of Waves. Weatherby, Meredith, tr. (The Perigee Japanese Library). 192p. 1981. pap. 4.95 (ISBN 0-399-50487-7, Perige). Putnam Pub Group.

--The Temple of the Golden Pavilion. Morris, Ivan, tr. (The Perigee Japanese Library). (Illus.). 288p. 1981. pap. 5.95 (ISBN 0-399-50488-5, Perige). Putnam Pub Group.

--Thirst for Love. Marks, Alfred H., tr. (The Perigee Japanese Library). 224p. 1981. pap. 4.95 (ISBN 0-399-50494-X, Perige). Putnam Pub Group.

Mishkin, Fred S. & Brashear, Richard E. Use & Interpretation of the Lung Scan. (Illus.). 136p. 1971. 15.75x o.p. (ISBN 0-398-01318-7). C C Thomas.

Mishkin, Frederic S. A Rational Expectations Approach to Macroeconomics: Testing Policy Ineffectiveness & Efficient-Markets Models. LC 82-20049. (National Bureau of Economic Research-Monograph). 192p. 1983. lib. bdg. 20.00x (ISBN 0-226-53186-4). U of Chicago Pr.

Mishler, Carolyn, tr. see Carrilo, Salvador.

Mishler, Clifford, jt. auth. see Wilhite, Robert.

Mishler, Elliot G. Social Contexts of Health, Illness, & Patient Care. LC 80-22604. 256p. 1981. 27.95 (ISBN 0-521-23559-6); pap. 11.95 (ISBN 0-521-28034-6). Cambridge U Pr.

Mishler, John M., IV. Pharmacology of Hydroxyehty Starch: Use in Therapy & Blood Banking. (Illus.). 220p. 1982. text ed. 39.50x (ISBN 0-19-261239-5). Oxford U Pr.

Mishlove, Jeffrey. PSI Development Systems. LC 81-23615. 240p. 1983. lib. bdg. 19.95x (ISBN 0-89950-035-8). McFarland & Co.

--The Roots of Consciousness. LC 75-10311. (Illus.). 1975. pap. 15.95 (ISBN 0-394-73115-8). Random.

Mishne, Judith. Clinical Work with Children. 1983. text ed. 24.95 (ISBN 0-02-921630-3). Free Pr.

Mishne, Judith M., jt. auth. see Buchholz, Ester S.

Mishra, Jagdish P. Shakespeare's Impact on Hindi Literature. 1970. text ed. 7.00x (ISBN 0-391-02049-8). Humanities.

Mishra, Kamala P. Banaras in Transition: Seventeen Thirty-Eight to Seventeen Ninety-Five. LC 75-903996. 1975. 12.50 o.p. (ISBN 0-88386-590-4). South Asia Bks.

Mishra, S. N. Politics & Leadership in Municipal Government. 1979. text ed. 9.50x (ISBN 0-391-01845-0). Humanities.

--Politics & Society in Rural India: A Case Study of Darauli Gram Panchayat, Siwan District, Bihar. 184p. 1980. text ed. 11.75x (ISBN 0-391-02123-0). Humanities.

Mishra, Sachida N. Political Socialization in India. (Illus.). 156p. 1980. pap. text ed. 15.75x (ISBN 0-391-02207-5). Humanities.
Mishra, V. B. From the Vedas to the Manu-Samhita: A Cultural Study. 160p. 1982. text ed. 19.50x (ISBN 0-391-02705-0). Humanities.
Misiorowski, Robert, jt. auth. see Lee, Robert.
Misiunas, Romuald J. & Taagepera, Rein. The Baltic States: Years of Dependence, 1940-1980. LC 82-4727. 350p. Date not set. 27.50x (ISBN 0-520-04625-0). U of Cal Pr. Postponed.
Misiunas, Romuald J., jt. ed. see Vardys, V. Stanley.
Miskel, Cecil G., jt. auth. see Hoy, Wayne K.
Miskimin, Harry A. Economy of Early Renaissance Europe. LC 75-16607. (Illus.). 204p. 1975. 29.95 (ISBN 0-521-21017-8); pap. 9.95x (ISBN 0-521-29021-X). Cambridge U Pr.
--The Economy of the Later Renaissance Europe: 1460-1600. LC 75-17120. (Illus.). 1977. pap. 32.50 (ISBN 0-521-21608-7); pap. 9.95x (ISBN 0-521-29208-5). Cambridge U Pr.
--Money, Prices, & Foreign Exchange in Fourteenth Century France. LC 63-7942. 1970. Repr. of 1963 ed. 15.00 o.p. (ISBN 0-08-022307-9). Pergamon.
Miskin, C. Library & Information Services for the Legal Profession. 1981. 45.00x (ISBN 0-905984-73-0, Pub. by Brit Lib England). State Mutual Bk.
Miskin, J. Robert. Among Lions: The Battle for Jerusalem, June 5-7, 1967. (War Library). 432p. 1983. pap. 4.95 (ISBN 0-345-29673-7). Ballantine.
Misko, James A. Creative Financing of Real Estate. LC 81-6329. 202p. 1981. 49.50 (ISBN 0-87624-108-9). Inst Busn Plan.
Miskovits, Christine. Echocardiography - A Manual for Technicians. 2nd ed. 1981. pap. 29.00 (ISBN 0-87488-987-1). Med Exam.
Miskovitz, Christine & Peters, Bruce E. Diagnostic Medical Ultrasound Examination Review. 1983. pap. text ed. price not set (ISBN 0-87488-410-1). Med Exam.
Mislin, H., jt. ed. see Bachofen, R.
Misner, Gordon, jt. auth. see Johnson, Thomas A.
Misra, A. & Agrawal, R. P. Lichens. 103p. 1978. 30.00 (ISBN 0-686-84458-0, Pub. by Oxford & I B H India). State Mutual Bk.
Misra, B. B. The Indian Political Parties: An Historical Analysis of Political Behavior up to 1947. 1977. 22.00x o.p. (ISBN 0-19-560598-5). Oxford U Pr.
Misra, Bhabagrahi. Verrier Elwin: A Pioneer Indian Anthropologist. 1974. lib. bdg. 12.95x (ISBN 0-210-40556-2). Asia.
Misra, K. S. Modern Tragedies & Aristotle's Theory. 252p. 1982. text ed. 18.75x (ISBN 0-7069-1425-2, Pub. by Vikas India). Humanities.
Misra, R. & Das, R. R. Proceedings of the School on Plant Ecology. 384p. 1971. 62.00x (ISBN 0-686-84467-X, Oxford & I B H India). State Mutual Bk.
Misra, R. C. Manual of Plant Ecology. 1980. 52.00x (ISBN 0-686-84459-9, Pub. by Oxford & I B H India). State Mutual Bk.
Misra, R. P., ed. Habitat Asia: Issues & Responses, 3 vols. Incl. Vol. 1. India (ISBN 0-391-01824-8); Vol. 2. Indonesia & the Philippines (ISBN 0-391-01825-6); Vol. 3. Japan & Singapore (ISBN 0-391-01827-2). 1979. text ed. 16.25x ea. Humanities.
Misra, Raghunath P. & Sanusi, I. Daniel. An Atlas of Skin Biopsy: Diagnosis by Light and Immuno Microscopy of Vesico-Bullous, Connective Tissue Disorders & Vasculitis of the Skin. (Illus.). 118p. 1983. 22.75x (ISBN 0-398-04744-8). C C Thomas.
Misra, S. P., jt. auth. see Shukla, A. C.
Misra, Shital P., jt. auth. see Shukla, Ashok C.
Misra, Shridhar, jt. auth. see Singh, Baljit.
Misrahi, Jean, tr. see Pichon, Charles.
Missen, R. W., jt. auth. see Smith, W. R.
Missick, Patricia. Walking in God's Love. (Illus.). 1980. pap. 3.95 o.p. (ISBN 0-89260-167-1). Hwong Pub.
Missildine, Fred & Karas, Nick. Score Better at Trap & Skeet. 1977. pap. 5.95 o.s.i. (ISBN 0-695-80856-7). Follett.
Missildine, W. Hugh & Galton, Lawrence. Your Inner Conflicts. LC 74-11370. 352p. 1974. 9.95 o.p. (ISBN 0-671-21836-0). S&S.
Missionary Research Library. New York Dictionary Catalog of the Missionary Research Library, 17 vols. 1968. Set. 1615.00 (ISBN 0-8161-0778-5, Hall Library). G K Hall.
Missirian, Agnes. The Corporate Connection: Why Executive Women Need Mentors to Reach the Top. 117p. 1982. 11.95 (ISBN 0-13-173195-5); pap. 5.95 (ISBN 0-13-173187-4). P-H.
Mistichelli, Judith A., jt. auth. see Gallagher, Edward.
MIT Faculty, ed. Nuclear Almanac: Confronting the Atom in War & Peace. LC 82-20596. 1983. 14.95 (ISBN 0-201-05331-4); pap. price not set (ISBN 0-201-05332-2). A-W.
MIT Students' System Project. Project Icarus. rev. ed. Li, Yao T. & Sandorf, Paul, eds. 1979. pap. 4.95 (ISBN 0-262-63068-0). MIT Pr.
Mital, K. V. Optimization Methods in Operations Research & Systems Analysis. LC 76-56846. 1977. 18.95x o.s.i. (ISBN 0-470-99056-2). Halsted Pr.
--Optimization Methods in Operations Research & Systems Analysis. 259p. 1980. pap. 8.95x o.s.i. (ISBN 0-470-27081-0). Halsted Pr.
Mitch, Miami. The Blues Brothers. (Orig.). 1980. pap. 2.50 o.s.i. (ISBN 0-515-05630-8). Jove Pubns.
Mitcham, Carl & Mackey, Robert, eds. Philosophy & Technology. LC 82-19818. 416p. 1982. pap. text ed. 12.95 (ISBN 0-02-921430-0). Free Pr.
--Philosophy & Technology: Readings in the Philosophical Problems of Technology. LC 70-160069. (Illus.). 434p. 1972. pap. 3.50. Free Pr.
Mitcham, Samuel W., Jr. Rommel's Last Battle. LC 82-42722. (Illus.). 224p. 1983. 17.95 (ISBN 0-8128-2905-0). Stein & Day.
Mitchel, Arthur. Five Hundred Years of Travel Books about Scotland, 1296-1796. 1982. pap. 25.00 (ISBN 0-686-37955-1). Saifer.
Mitchelhill, A. Bills of Lading: Law & Practice. 1982. 30.00x (ISBN 0-412-23960-4, Pub. by Chapman & Hall); pap. 13.95x (ISBN 0-412-23940-X). Methuen Inc.
Mitchell. Endoscopic Operative Urology. 520p. 1981. 87.00 (ISBN 0-7236-0532-7). Wright-PSG.
--A Field Guide to the Trees of Britain & Northern Europe. 29.95 (ISBN 0-686-42768-8, Collins Pub England). Greene.
--Urology & Nephrology for Undergraduates. Date not set. text ed. price not set (ISBN 0-407-00199-9). Butterworth.
Mitchell & Draper. Relevance & Ethics in Geography. LC 81-19386. (Illus.). 256p. 1982. text ed. 28.00 (ISBN 0-582-30035-5). Longman.
Mitchell & Wilkinson. The Trees of Britain & Northern Europe. 14.95 (ISBN 0-686-42737-8, Collins Pub England); pap. 8.95. Greene.
Mitchell, jt. auth. see LaBarre.
Mitchell, A., jt. auth. see Hawbolt, E. B.
Mitchell, A. R. & Griffiths, D. F. The Finite Difference Method in Partial Differential Equations. 272p. 1980. 38.95 (ISBN 0-471-27641-3, Pub. by Wiley-Interscience). Wiley.
Mitchell, A. R. & Wait, R. A. The Finite Element Method in Partial Differential Equations. LC 76-13533. 1977. 34.95 (ISBN 0-471-99405-7, Pub. by Wiley-Interscience). Wiley.
Mitchell, Abby, jt. auth. see Katz, Gerald.
Mitchell, Adrian. For Beauty Douglas. (Illus.). 256p. 1982. text ed. 14.95 (ISBN 0-8052-8082-0, Pub. by Allison & Busby England); pap. 8.95 (ISBN 0-8052-8081-2). Schocken.
--For Beauty Douglas: Collected Poems, 1953-1979. (Illus.). 1982. 14.95 (ISBN 0-85031-399-6, Pub. by Allison & Busby England); pap. 8.95 (ISBN 0-8052-8081-2). Schocken.
Mitchell, Alan. The International Book of the Forest. 1981. 35.00 o.p. (ISBN 0-671-41004-0). S&S.
Mitchell, Alice & Szerny, Carl. A Systematic Introduction to Improvisation on the Piano Forte: Opus 200. Anderson, Gordon T., ed. (Longman Music Ser.). 128p. 1983. text ed. 24.95x (ISBN 0-582-28329-9). Longman.
Mitchell, Alice M. Children & Movies. LC 70-160240. (Moving Pictures Ser). xxiv, 181p. 1971. Repr. of 1929 ed. lib. bdg. 13.95x (ISBN 0-89198-041-5). Ozer.
Mitchell, Allan & Deak, Istan. Everyman in Europe: Essays in Social History, the Industrial Centuries, Vol. 2. 464p. 1974. pap. text ed. 13.95 (ISBN 0-13-293589-9). P-H.
Mitchell, Allan, rev. by see Snell, John L.
Mitchell, Anita M., et al, eds. Social Learning & Career Decision Making. LC 78-8930. 1979. 17.50x (ISBN 0-910328-21-8); pap. 13.00x (ISBN 0-910328-22-6). Carroll Pr.
Mitchell, Arnold. The Nine American Lifestyles: Who We Are & Where We Are Going. (Illus.). 256p. 1983. 19.95 (ISBN 0-02-585310-4). Macmillan.
Mitchell, Arthur, tr. see Bergson, Henri L.
Mitchell, Audrey, ed. Compton's Encyclopedia, 1983, 26 vols. 1983. per set 419.00 (ISBN 0-85229-401-8). Ency Brit Ed.
Mitchell, B. Viaje a Madrid. (Illus.). 1975. pap. text ed. 3.95x (ISBN 0-582-36463-9). cassette 10.50x (ISBN 0-582-37359-X). Longman.
Mitchell, B. J. & Dragoon, M. M. How to See the U.S. on Twelve Dollars a Day: (Per Person, Double Occupancy) LC 82-50779. (Illus.). 112p. (Orig.). 1982. pap. 3.95 (ISBN 0-943962-00-5). Viewpoint Pr.
Mitchell, Barbara. Cornstalks & Cannonballs. LC 79-91304. (Carolrhoda on My Own Books). (Illus.). (gr. 1-2). 1980. PLB 6.95g (ISBN 0-87614-121-1). Carolrhoda Bks.
--Hush, Puppies. LC 82-4465. (Carolrhoda On My Own Bks). (Illus.). 48p. (gr. 1-4). 1983. PLB 6.95g (ISBN 0-87614-201-3). Carolrhoda Bks.
--Tomahawks & Trombones. LC 81-21661. (Carolrhoda On My Own Bks). (Illus.). 56p. (gr. 1-4). 1983. lib. bdg. 6.95g (ISBN 0-87614-191-2). Carolrhoda Bks.
Mitchell, Basil. The Justification of Religious Belief. (Orig.). 1981. pap. 5.95x (ISBN 0-19-520124-8). Oxford U Pr.
Mitchell, Betty Jo, et al. Cost Analysis of Library Functions: A Total System Approach, Vol. 6. Stueart, Robert D., ed. LC 77-2110. (Foundations in Library & Information Science). 1978. lib. bdg. 37.50 (ISBN 0-89232-072-9). Jai Pr.
Mitchell, Bob. Amphoto Guide to Travel Photography. (Illus.). 1979. 10.95 o.p. (ISBN 0-8174-2472-5, Amphoto); pap. 7.95 (ISBN 0-8174-2144-0). Watson-Guptill.
--Amphoto Pocket Companion: Konica TC & FS-I. (Illus.). 128p. 1980. pap. 4.95 spiral bdg. o.p. (ISBN 0-8174-5525-6, Amphoto). Watson-Guptill.
Mitchell, Breon. James Joyce & the German Novel, 1922-1933. LC 75-36980. xvi, 194p. 1976. 14.00x (ISBN 0-8214-0192-0, 82-81958). Ohio U Pr.
Mitchell, Brian R. & Deane, P. Abstract of British Historical Statistics. (Department of Applied Economics Monographs: No. 17). 1962. 74.50 (ISBN 0-521-05738-8). Cambridge U Pr.
Mitchell, Brian R. & Jones, H. G. Second Abstract of British Historical Statistics. LC 72-128502. (Department of Applied Economics Monographs: No. 18). (Illus.). 1971. 49.50 (ISBN 0-521-08001-0). Cambridge U Pr.
Mitchell, Bridger M. & Kleindorfer, Paul R., eds. Regulated Industries & Public Enterprise: European & United States Perspectives. LC 79-3750. 304p. 1980. 32.95 (ISBN 0-669-03474-6). Lexington Bks.
Mitchell, Bridger M., et al. Peak-Load Pricing: European Lessons for U.S. Energy Policy. LC 77-27897. 272p. 1978. prof ref 25.00x (ISBN 0-88410-670-5). Ballinger Pub.
Mitchell, Broadus. Alexander Hamilton: A Concise Biography. LC 75-16899. (Illus.). 1976. 22.50x (ISBN 0-19-501979-2). Oxford U Pr.
--Depression Decade: From New Era Through New Deal 1929-1941. LC 76-48795. (The Economic History of the United States Ser.). 1977. pap. 11.95 (ISBN 0-87332-097-2). M E Sharpe.
--Price of Independence: A Realistic View of the Price of Independence; the American Revolution. 1974. 22.50x (ISBN 0-19-501735-8). Oxford U Pr.
--Rise of Cotton Mills in the South. 2nd ed. LC 68-8128. (American Scene Ser). 1968. Repr. of 1921 ed. lib. bdg. 37.50 (ISBN 0-306-71141-9). Da Capo.
Mitchell, Broadus & Mitchell, George S. Industrial Revolution in the South. LC 68-54426. 1968. Repr. of 1930 ed. lib. bdg. 18.25x (ISBN 0-8371-0568-4, MIIR). Greenwood.
Mitchell, Broadus & Mitchell, Louise. A Biography of the Constitution of the United States: Its Origin Formation, Adoption, Interpretation. 2nd ed. 1975. 22.50x (ISBN 0-19-501932-6); pap. 6.95x (ISBN 0-19-501889-3). Oxford U Pr.
Mitchell, Bruce. A Guide to Old English. 2nd ed. LC 78-60049. 1978. pap. 10.50x o.p. (ISBN 0-06-494872-2). B&N Imports.
Mitchell, Bruce & Robinson, Fred C. A Guide to Old English: Revised With Texts & Glossary. 286p. 1982. 35.00x (ISBN 0-8020-2489-0); pap. 15.00 (ISBN 0-8020-6513-9). U of Toronto Pr.
Mitchell, Bruce, jt. auth. see Crossley-Holland, Kevin.
Mitchell, Carol A. Machine Transcription: A Comprehensive Approach for Today's Office Specialist. 176p. (Orig.). 1983. pap. text ed. 10.95 (ISBN 0-672-97986-1); instr's. guide 6.67 (ISBN 0-672-97987-X); working papers 3.95 (ISBN 0-672-97988-8); tapes 266.00 (ISBN 0-672-97989-6). Bobbs.
Mitchell, Charlie & Young, William. Career Exploration: A Self-Paced Approach. 96p. 1982. pap. text ed. 6.95 (ISBN 0-8403-2723-4). Kendall-Hunt.
Mitchell, Clifford L., ed. Nervous System Toxicology. (Target Organ Toxicity Ser.). 400p. 1982. 58.00 (ISBN 0-89004-473-2, 405). Raven.
Mitchell, Colin, jt. auth. see Heaps, Ian.
Mitchell, Craig. Effective Media Promotion. LC 82-71764. 1983. pap. write for info (ISBN 0-87251-074-3). Crain Bks.
--Media Promotion. LC 82-71765. 192p. 1983. pap. price not set (ISBN 0-87251-076-X). Crain Bks.
Mitchell, Curtis C. Let's Live! 160p. 1975. 8.95 (ISBN 0-8007-0716-8). Revell.
Mitchell, Cynthia. Halloweena Hecatee & Other Rhymes to Skip to. LC 78-60175. (Illus.). (gr. k-8). 1979. 6.95 o.p. (ISBN 0-690-03925-5, TYC-J); PLB 9.89 (ISBN 0-690-03926-3). Har-Row.
--Playtime. LC 78-13326. (Illus.). 32p. (ps-2). 1979. 6.95 o.p. (ISBN 0-529-05514-7, Philomel); PLB 6.99 o.p. (ISBN 0-529-05515-5). Putnam Pub Group.
--Under the Cherry Tree. LC 79-11579. (Illus.). 1979. 8.95 o.s.i. (ISBN 0-529-05543-0, Philomel); PLB 8.99 o.s.i. (ISBN 0-529-05544-9). Putnam Pub Group.
Mitchell, D. C. The Process of Reading: A Cognitive Analyses of Fluent Reading & Learning to Read. LC 81-21912. 244p. 1982. 39.95 (ISBN 0-471-10199-0, Pub. by Wiley-Interscience). Wiley.
Mitchell, D. S., ed. Aquatic Vegetation & Its Control. (Illus.). 135p. (Orig.). 1974. pap. 7.50 (ISBN 0-686-83001-6, U36, UNESCO). Unipub.
Mitchell, Daniel J. Unions, Wages & Inflation. 1980. 22.95 (ISBN 0-8157-5752-2); pap. 8.95 (ISBN 0-8157-5751-4). Brookings.
Mitchell, Daniel J. B., jt. auth. see Weber, Arnold R.
Mitchell, David. Introduction to Logic. 1967. text ed. 9.00x o. p. (ISBN 0-09-064633-9, Hutchinson U Lib); pap. text ed. 6.50x (ISBN 0-09-064634-7, Hutchinson U Lib). Humanities.
--The Spanish Civil War. (Illus.). 210p. 1983. 18.95 (ISBN 0-531-09896-6). Watts.
Mitchell, Dobbie, jt. auth. see Lumb, Mitchell.
Mitchell, Donald. The Language of Modern Music. 168p. 1982. pap. 4.95 (ISBN 0-571-06570-8). Faber & Faber.
Mitchell, Donald & Biss, Roderick. Gambit Book of Children's Songs. LC 74-118215. (Illus.). 1970. 12.95 (ISBN 0-87645-023-0). Gambit.
Mitchell, Donald & Keller, Hans, eds. Music Survey: New Series, 1949-1952. (Illus.). 817p. 1983. 59.95 (ISBN 0-571-10040-6). Faber & Faber.
Mitchell, Donald G. About Old Story-Tellers. LC 75-159859. 1971. Repr. of 1877 ed. 37.00x (ISBN 0-8103-3732-0). Gale.
Mitchell, Donald O., ed. see Schmitz, Andrew, et al.
Mitchell, Douglas E. Shaping Legislative Decisions: Education Policy & the Social Sciences. LC 80-8385. (Illus.). 240p. 1981. 24.95 (ISBN 0-669-04091-6). Lexington Bks.
Mitchell, Edward J., ed. Perspectives on U. S. Energy Policy: A Critique of Regulation. LC 76-23093. (American Enterprise Institute Perspectives: Vol. 3). (Illus.). 1976. 28.95 o.p. (ISBN 0-275-23640-4). Praeger.
Mitchell, Edward J., jt. ed. see Horwich, George.
Mitchell, Edwin V. Horse & Buggy Age in New England. LC 74-7066. 1974. Repr. of 1937 ed. 30.00x (ISBN 0-8103-3657-X). Gale.
--It's an Old State of Maine Custom. LC 78-8102. 1978. lib. bdg. 11.50 o.p. (ISBN 0-89621-007-3); pap. 4.95 o.p. (ISBN 0-89621-006-5). Thorndike Pr.
Mitchell, Edwin V., ed. Encyclopedia of American Politics. LC 69-10135. 1969. Repr. of 1946 ed. lib. bdg. 18.75x (ISBN 0-8371-0171-9, MIAP). Greenwood.
Mitchell, Elaine A. Fort Timiskaming & the Fur Trade. LC 76-51782. 1977. 25.00x (ISBN 0-8020-2234-0). U of Toronto Pr.
Mitchell, G., jt. auth. see Hepburn, H. R.
Mitchell, G. D., jt. auth. see Snowden, R.
Mitchell, G. Frank, et al. Treasures of Early Irish Art: 1500 B.C, to 1500 A.D. LC 77-8692. (Illus.). 1977. pap. 6.95 o.p. (ISBN 0-87099-164-7). Metro Mus Art.
Mitchell, G. L., jt. auth. see Mead, H. T.
Mitchell, George. Blow My Blues Away. (Roots of Jazz Ser.). (Illus.). xiii, 208p. 1983. Repr. of 1971 ed. lib. bdg. 25.00 (ISBN 0-306-76173-4). Da Capo.
Mitchell, George S., jt. auth. see Mitchell, Broadus.
Mitchell, Gladys. Here Lies Gloria Mundy. 192p. 1983. 9.95 (ISBN 0-312-36986-7). St Martin.
Mitchell, Harris. The Basement Book. (Illus.). 104p. (Orig.). 1982. pap. 8.95 (ISBN 0-920510-48-5, Pub. by Personal Lib). Dodd.
--Twelve Hundred Household Hints You Wanted to Know. (Illus.). 252p. (Orig.). 1982. pap. 9.95 (ISBN 0-920510-66-3, Pub. by Personal Lib). Dodd.
Mitchell, Henry. The Essential Earthman. 1983. pap. 6.25 (ISBN 0-374-51765-7). FS&G.
Mitchell, Henry H. Black Preaching. LC 78-19508. 1979. pap. 6.95i (ISBN 0-06-065761-8, RD297, HarpR). Har-Row.
--The Recovery of Preaching. LC 76-62959. 1977. pap. 7.64i (ISBN 0-06-065763-4, RD 229, HarpR). Har-Row.
Mitchell, Horace, jt. auth. see Curran, Susan.
Mitchell, I. V. & Barfoot, K. M. Particle-Induced X-Ray Emission Analysis: Application to Analytical Problems. (Nuclear Science Applications Ser.). 63p. 1981. 14.00 (ISBN 3-7186-0085-4). Harwood Academic.
Mitchell, J., jt. auth. see Wu, T. K.
Mitchell, J., ed. see Lacan, J.
Mitchell, J. A., ed. see Craighead, J. J. & Sumner, J. S.
Mitchell, J. Clyde. The Yao Village: A Study in the Social Structure of a Malawian Tribe. (Institute of African Studies Ser). (Illus.). 238p. 1971. pap. text ed. 17.50x o.p. (ISBN 0-7190-1034-9). Humanities.
Mitchell, J. F., ed. see Gaddum, John.
Mitchell, J. R., jt. auth. see Blanshard, J. M.
Mitchell, J. W. Energy Engineering. 420p. 1983. write for info. (ISBN 0-471-08772-6, Pub. by Wiley-Interscience). Wiley.
Mitchell, Jack. The Gun Digest Book of Pistolsmithing. 288p. 1980. pap. 8.95 o.s.i. (ISBN 0-695-81429-X). Follett.
--The Gun Digest Book of Riflesmithing. (Illus.). 256p. 1982. pap. 9.95 (ISBN 0-910676-47-X). DBI.
Mitchell, Jack D. The Back Page. Shelsby, Earl, ed. (Illus.). 144p. (Orig.). text ed. 20.00 (ISBN 0-686-82338-9); pap. text ed. 9.95 (ISBN 0-935998-44-6). Natl Rifle Assn.
Mitchell, James. The Evil Ones. 224p. 1983. 16.95 (ISBN 0-241-10837-3, Pub. by Hamish Hamilton England). David & Charles.
--Smear Job. LC 77-4917. 1977. 7.95 o.p. (ISBN 0-399-12024-6). Putnam Pub Group.
Mitchell, James E. Maine Probate Manual. 650p. 1983. 65.00 (ISBN 0-89442-036-4). Tower Pub Co.
Mitchell, James K. Fundamentals of Soil Behavior. LC 75-28096. (Soil Engineering Ser). 384p. 1976. text ed. 48.95 (ISBN 0-471-61168-9). Wiley.
Mitchell, James W., jt. auth. see Zief, Morris.
Mitchell, Jane F., tr. see Caesar, Julius.
Mitchell, Jean B. Great Britain: Geographical Essays. 1962. 48.00 o.p. (ISBN 0-521-05739-6); pap. 21.95x (ISBN 0-521-09986-2). Cambridge U Pr.

Mitchell, Jeffrey & Resnik, H. L. Emergency Response to Crisis. (Illus.). 256p. 1981. text ed. 19.95 (ISBN 0-87619-856-6); pap. 14.95 (ISBN 0-87619-828-0). R J Brady.

Mitchell, Jeremy, ed. The Population Census. pap. text ed. 4.00x o.p. (ISBN 0-435-82846-0). Heinemann Ed.

--Research in International Organization. pap. text ed. 4.00x o.p. (ISBN 0-435-82841-X). Heinemann Ed.

--Research in Political Science. pap. text ed. 4.00x o.p. (ISBN 0-435-82840-1). Heinemann Ed.

Mitchell, Jeremy, ed. see Wall, W. D. & Williams, H. L.

Mitchell, John. Better Fishing, Freshwater. rev. ed. LC 72-185859. (Better Sports Ser). 1978. 8.50x o.p. (ISBN 0-7182-1455-2). Intl Pubns Serv.

--Life of Wallenstein, Duke of Friedland. Repr. of 1837 ed. lib. bdg. 16.25x (ISBN 0-8371-0569-2, MILW). Greenwood.

Mitchell, John, jt. auth. see Smith, Donald M.

Mitchell, John D. Lost Mines & Buried Treasures along the Old Frontier. LC 77-121730. 1982. Repr. of 1954 ed. lib. bdg. 12.00 (ISBN 0-686-84606-0). Rio Grande.

--Lost Mines of the Great Southwest. (Illus.). lib. bdg. 10.00 o.s.i. (ISBN 0-87380-013-3). Rio Grande.

Mitchell, John D., ed. The Red Pear Garden: Three Great Dramas of Revolutionary China. LC 73-81068. 288p. 1974. 15.00 (ISBN 0-87923-073-8); pap. 6.95 (ISBN 0-87923-090-8). Godine.

Mitchell, John G. An Everlasting Love: A Devotional Commentary on the Gospel of John. LC 82-22285. 1982. 13.95 (ISBN 0-88070-005-X). Multnomah.

--The Hunt. LC 80-7621. 320p. 1980. 12.95 (ISBN 0-394-50684-7). Knopf.

Mitchell, John G. & Stallings, Constance, eds. Ecotactics: The Sierra Club Handbook for Environmental Activists. 1970. pap. 1.95 o.p. (ISBN 0-671-20779-2, Touchstone Bks). S&S.

Mitchell, John H. Court of the Connectable: A Study of a French Administrative Tribunal During the Reign of Henry IV. 1947. 39.50x (ISBN 0-686-51365-7). Elliots Bks.

--Writing for Technical & Professional Journals. LC 67-31374. (Wiley Ser. on Human Communications). 1968. 21.95 o.p. (ISBN 0-471-61170-0, Pub. by Wiley-Interscience). Wiley.

Mitchell, John, Jr. & Smith, Donald M. Aquametry: A Treatise on Methods for the Determination of Water, Part 1. 2nd ed. LC 77-518. (Chemical Analysis Ser: Vol. 5). 1977. 74.95 (ISBN 0-471-02264-0). Wiley.

--Aquametry: A Treatise on Methods for the Determination of Water, Pt. 3. 2nd ed. LC 77-518. (Chemical Analysis Ser.). 1980. 115.00 (ISBN 0-471-02266-7, Pub. by Wiley-Interscience). Wiley.

Mitchell, John S. An Introduction to Machinery Analysis & Monitoring. 256p. 1981. 44.95x (ISBN 0-87814-145-6). Pennwell Pub.

Mitchell, Johnny. Secret War of Captain Johnny Mitchell. LC 76-2963. 103p. 1976. 7.95 (ISBN 0-685-66076-1). Pacesetter Pr.

Mitchell, Joyce S. Choices & Changes: A Career Book for Men. LC 82-72389. (Illus.). 336p. (Orig.). 1982. pap. 9.95 (ISBN 0-87447-151-6). College Bd.

--I Can be Anything: A Career Book for Women. 3rd ed. (Illus.). 336p. (Orig.). 1982. pap. 9.95 (ISBN 0-87447-150-8). College Bd.

--Other Choices for Becoming a Woman. 272p. 1975. pap. 1.25 o.p. (ISBN 0-440-95760-5, LFL). Dell.

Mitchell, Juliet, ed. see Lacan, Jacques & Ecole Freudienne.

Mitchell, Larry D., jt. auth. see Shigley, Joseph E.

Mitchell, Lawrence J., jt. auth. see Danks, Maureen C.

Mitchell, Leonel. Liturgical Change: How Much Do We Need. 96p. 1975. pap. 1.00 (ISBN 0-8164-2113-7). Seabury.

Mitchell Library, the Library of New South Wales. (Sydney, Australia) Dictionary Catalog of Printed Books, 38 Vols. 1968. Set. lib. bdg. 3590.00 (ISBN 0-8161-0790-4, Hall Library); lib. bdg. 130.00 1st suppl. (ISBN 0-8161-0848-X). G K Hall.

Mitchell, Louise, jt. auth. see Mitchell, Broadus.

Mitchell, M. Bonner, jt. ed. see Minor, Andrew C.

Mitchell, Malcolm & Oettgen, Herbert F., eds. Hybridomas in Cancer Diagnosis & Treatment. (Progress in Cancer Research & Therapy Ser.: Vol. 21). 288p. 1982. text ed. 33.00 (ISBN 0-89004-768-5). Raven.

Mitchell, Marcia. Jenny. (A Heartsong Book). 160p. (Orig.). (gr. 8-12). 1983. pap. 2.95 (ISBN 0-87123-283-9). Bethany Hse.

Mitchell, Marianne, jt. auth. see Gibson, Robert L.

Mitchell, Mary. Glimpses of Georgetown, Past & Present. LC 82-62163. (Illus.). 96p. 1983. pap. 12.50. Road St Pr.

Mitchell, Memory F. North Carolina's Signers: Brief Sketches of the Men Who Signed the Declaration of Independence & the Constitution. (Illus.). 1980. pap. 1.00 (ISBN 0-86526-097-4). NC Archives.

Mitchell, Meredith. Heroes & Victims. Sternback-Scott, Sisa & Smith, Lindsay, eds. 1983. 16.95 (ISBN 0-938434-18-7); pap. 11.95 (ISBN 0-938434-15-2). Sigo Pr.

Mitchell, Michael J., jt. auth. see Cava, Michael P.

Mitchell, Otis, ed. Nazism & the Common Man: Essays in German History (1929-1939) 2nd ed. LC 80-6284. 163p. 1981. lib. bdg. 19.75 (ISBN 0-8191-1546-0); pap. text ed. 9.25 (ISBN 0-8191-1547-9). U Pr of Amer.

Mitchell, Otis C. A Concise History of Brandenburg-Prussia to Seventeen Eighty-Six. LC 80-486. 142p. 1980. pap. text ed. 7.00 (ISBN 0-8191-1014-0). U Pr of Amer.

--Fascism: An Introductory Perspective. LC 78-59115. 1978. pap. 5.50 (ISBN 0-87716-091-0, Pub. by Moore Pub Co). F Apple.

--Hitler Over Germany: The Establishment of the Nazi Dictatorship (1918-34) LC 82-3005. (Illus.). 300p. 1983. text ed. 17.50 (ISBN 0-89727-036-3). Inst Study Human.

Mitchell, P. Concepts Basic to Nursing. 3rd ed. (Illus.). 720p. text ed. 25.00 (ISBN 0-07-042582-5). McGraw.

Mitchell, P. M. Henrik Pontoppidan. (World Authors Ser.). 1979. lib. bdg. 15.95 (ISBN 0-8057-6366-X, Twayne). G K Hall.

--Vilhelm Gronbech. (World Authors Ser.: Denmark). 1978. lib. bdg. 15.95 (ISBN 0-8057-6306-6, Twayne). G K Hall.

Mitchell, P. M., jt. ed. see Billeskov-Jansen, F. J.

Mitchell, Peter. Great Flower Painters: Four Centuries of Floral Art. LC 72-95231. (Illus.). 276p. 1973. 50.00 (ISBN 0-87951-008-0). Overlook Pr.

Mitchell, Phyllis. How to Study the Bible. 95p. (Orig.). 1982. pap. 4.95 (ISBN 0-686-37607-2). Women's Aglow.

Mitchell, R. Darrieus Wind Turbine Airfoil Configurations. (Progress in Solar Energy Supplements SERI Ser.). 1983. pap. text ed. 6.00x (ISBN 0-89553-103-8). Am Solar Energy.

--Development of an Oscillating Vane Concept as an Innovative Wind Energy Conversion System. (Progress in Solar Energy Supplements SERI Ser.). 1983. pap. text ed. 9.00x (ISBN 0-89553-104-6). Am Solar Energy.

Mitchell, R. J. The Medieval Tournament. Reeves, Marjorie, ed. (Then & There Ser.). (Illus.). 44p. (Orig.). (gr. 7-12). 1958. pap. text ed. 3.10 (ISBN 0-582-20373-2). Longman.

Mitchell, Ralph, ed. Water Pollution Microbiology. LC 73-168641. 1972. Vol. 1. 35.00 (ISBN 0-471-61100-X, Pub. by Wiley-Interscience); Vol. 2 1978. 47.95 (ISBN 0-471-01902-X). Wiley.

Mitchell, Richard H. Censorship in Imperial Japan. LC 82-61440. 432p. 1983. 35.00x (ISBN 0-691-05384-7). Princeton U Pr.

--The Korean Minority in Japan. (Center for Japanese & Korean Studies, UC Berkeley). 1967. 27.50x (ISBN 0-520-00870-7). U of Cal Pr.

Mitchell, Robert. Number Power Three: Algebra. (Number Power Ser.). 176p. (Orig.). 1983. pap. 4.95 (ISBN 0-8092-5518-9). Contemp Bks.

Mitchell, Robert & Prickel, Donald. Number Power Five: Graphs, Tables, Schedules & Maps. (Number Power Ser.). 176p. (Orig.). 1983. pap. 4.95 (ISBN 0-8092-5516-2). Contemp Bks.

--Number Power Four: Geometry. (Number Power Ser.). 176p. (Orig.). 1983. pap. 4.95 (ISBN 0-8092-5517-0). Contemp Bks.

Mitchell, Robert & Zim, Herbert S. Butterflies & Moths. (Golden Guide Ser.). (Illus.). (gr. 5 up). 1964. PLB 11.54 (ISBN 0-307-63524-4, Golden Pr); pap. 2.95 (ISBN 0-307-24413-X). Western Pub.

Mitchell, Robert, jt. auth. see Tedesco, Eleanor.

Mitchell, Robert D. Commercialism & Frontier: Perspectives on the Early Shenandoah Valley. LC 76-26610. (Illus.). 251p. 1977. 14.95x (ISBN 0-8139-0661-X). U Pr of Va.

Mitchell, Robert L. Engineering Economics. 1980. 38.95 (ISBN 0-471-27640-5, Pub. by Wiley-Interscience); pap. text ed. 16.00 o.p. (ISBN 0-686-65932-5). Wiley.

Mitchell, Robert M. Calvin's & the Puritan's View of the Protestant Ethic. LC 79-66537. 1979. pap. text ed. 8.00 (ISBN 0-8191-0842-1). U Pr of Amer.

Mitchell, Roger S. & Petty, Thomas L. Synopsis of Clinical Pulmonary Disease. 3rd ed. LC 81-14154. (Illus.). 352p. 1982. pap. text ed. 17.95 (ISBN 0-8016-3474-1). Mosby.

Mitchell, Ronald. Opera-Dead or Alive: Production, Performance, & Enjoyment of Musical Theatre. LC 73-121772. (Illus.). 334p. 1970. 25.00 (ISBN 0-299-05811-5); pap. 9.95t (ISBN 0-299-05814-X). U of Wis Pr.

Mitchell, S., jt. ed. see Rosen, M.

Mitchell, S., tr. see Lukacs, Georg.

Mitchell, S. Augustus, illus. Eighteen Seventy-Two S. Augustus Mitchell Map of Florida. (Illus.). 1p. Date not set. Repr. of 1872 ed. map 2.95 (ISBN 0-941948-14-5). St Johns-Oklawaha.

Mitchell, Shirley. Spiritual Sparks for Busy Women. 1982. pap. 3.95 (ISBN 0-87397-206-6). Strode.

Mitchell, Stephen, ed. see Rilke, Rainer Maria.

Mitchell, Stewart. Horatio Seymour of New York. LC 69-19475. (American Scene Ser). 1970. Repr. of 1938 ed. lib. bdg. 75.00 (ISBN 0-306-71252-0). Da Capo.

Mitchell, Stewart, ed. see Adams, Abigail.

Mitchell, Susan. Thirty Minute Meals. Coolman, Anne L., ed. LC 82-82158. (Illus.). 96p. 1982. pap. 5.95 (ISBN 0-89721-006-9). Ortho.

Mitchell, T. R. People in Organizations: An Introduction to Organizational Behavior. 2nd ed. (Management Ser.). 1982. 22.95x (ISBN 0-07-042532-9). McGraw.

Mitchell, Terence R. People in Organizations. (Illus.). 1978. text ed. 22.95 (ISBN 0-07-042530-2, C); instructor's manual 16.95 (ISBN 0-07-042531-0). McGraw.

Mitchell, Thomas L. Journal of an Expedition into the Interior of Tropical Australia, in Search of Route from Sydney to the Gulf of Carpentaria. LC 68-55204. (Illus.). 1968. Repr. of 1848 ed. lib. bdg. 20.75x (ISBN 0-8371-1319-9, MITA). Greenwood.

Mitchell, Thornton W., ed. Norton on Archives: The Writings of Margaret Cross Norton. 288p. 1975. pap. 7.00 member (ISBN 0-686-95769-5, 1021); pap. 10.00 non-member (ISBN 0-686-99607-0). Soc Am Archivists.

Mitchell, W. J., ed. The Politics of Interpretation. 1983. pap. price not set (ISBN 0-226-53220-8). U of Chicago Pr.

Mitchell, Walter & Chenevert, C. Skip, Jr. Unopened Letters & a Virgin Page. limited ed. 64p. 1983. 5.50 (ISBN 0-682-49968-4). Exposition.

Mitchell, William, et al. College Typewriting, a Mastery Approach: Comprehensive. 416p. 1982. 17.95 (ISBN 0-574-20650-7, 13-3650); Instructor's Guide Avail. (ISBN 0-574-20651-5, 13-3651); Working Papers Avail. 8.95 (ISBN 0-574-20652-3, 13-3652); Model Answer Key 3.25 (ISBN 0-574-20653-1, 13-3653); Keyboard Tapes 150.00 (ISBN 0-574-20510-1, 13-3510); Transparency Masters Available 30.00 (ISBN 0-574-20556-X, 13-3556). SRA.

Mitchell, William E., jt. auth. see Leichter, Hope J.

Mitchell, William E., et al. Exercises in Macroeconomics: Development of Concepts. (Illus.). 432p. 1973. pap. text ed. 22.95 (ISBN 0-07-042511-6, C). McGraw.

--Readings in Macroeconomics. (Illus.). 512p. 1974. pap. text ed. 16.95 (ISBN 0-07-042510-8, C). McGraw.

Mitchell, William J. Elementary Harmony. 3rd ed. 1965. 20.95 o.p. (ISBN 0-13-257279-6). P-H.

Mitchell, Williams M. The Rise of the Revolutionary Party in the English House of Commons, 1603-1629. LC 75-31471. 209p. 1976. Repr. of 1957 ed. lib. bdg. 15.50x (ISBN 0-8371-8535-1, MIRR). Greenwood.

Mitchell, Wm. R., Jr., jt. auth. see Martin, Van J.

Mitchell, Yvonne. Colette: A Taste of Life. LC 77-3517. (Illus.). 1977. pap. 7.95 (ISBN 0-15-618550-4, Harv). HarBraceJ.

Mitchell-Thome, Raoul C. Geology of the Middle Atlantic Islands. (Beitraege zur regionalen Geologie der Erde: Vol. 12). (Illus.). 1976. lib. bdg. 109.95x (ISBN 3-443-11012-6). Lubrecht & Cramer.

Mitchelson, Marvin. Living Together. 1981. 10.95 o.p. (ISBN 0-671-24981-9). S&S.

Mitchie, James, tr. see La Fontaine, Jean de.

Mitchiner, John E. Studies in the Indus Valley Inscriptions. (Illus.). 1979. text ed. 13.00x (ISBN 0-391-01614-8). Humanities.

Mitchiner, Michael. Indo-Greek & Indo-Scythian Coinage, 9 Vols. 325.00. Numismatic Fine Arts.

--Non-Islamic States & Western Colonies A. D. 600-1979. 1979. 90.00. Numismatic Fine Arts.

--Oriental Coins & Their Values: The Ancient & Classical World, Vol. 2. 1978. lib. bdg. 95.00. Numismatic Fine Arts.

Mitchiner, Michawl. Oriental Coins & Their Values: The World of Islam, Vol. 1. 1979. 55.00. Numismatic Fine Arts.

Mitchinson, J. M. Biology of the Cell Cycle. LC 72-160100. (Illus.). 1972. 55.00 (ISBN 0-521-08251-X); pap. 17.95x (ISBN 0-521-09671-5). Cambridge U Pr.

Mitchinson, Wendy, jt. ed. see Cook, Ramsay.

Mitchison, Naomi. Alexander the Great. Reeves, Marjorie, ed. (Then & There Ser.). (Illus.). 96p. (gr. 7-12). 1964. pap. text ed. 3.10 (ISBN 0-582-20394-5). Longman.

Mitchison, R. A History of Scotland. 2nd ed. 1982. 29.95x (ISBN 0-416-33220-X); pap. 15.95 (ISBN 0-416-33080-0). Methuen Inc.

Mitchley, Hugh. Brief for the Plaintiff: Or, the Poetry of Action. 1983. 13.95 (ISBN 0-533-05144-4). Vantage.

Mitelman, Bonnie, jt. auth. see Bodin, Jeanne.

Mitford, Jessica. The American Way of Death. 1978. pap. 4.95 o.p. (ISBN 0-671-24415-9, Touchstone Bks). S&S.

Mitford, Nancy. The Pursuit of Love & Love in a Cold Climate. 6.95 (ISBN 0-394-60481-4). Modern Lib.

Mitford, Rupert, ed. Recent Archaeological Excavations in Europe. 1975. 42.00x (ISBN 0-7100-7963-X). Routledge & Kegan.

Mitford, T. B. Inscriptions of Kourion. LC 78-121295. (Memoirs Ser.: Vol. 83). (Illus.). 1971. 25.00 o.p. (ISBN 0-87169-083-7). Am Philos.

Mitra, Abhijit. Synthesis of Prostaglandins. LC 77-23268. 1977. 37.50 o.p. (ISBN 0-471-02308-6, Pub. by Wiley-Interscience). Wiley.

Mitra, Ashok, tr. see Tagore, Rabindranath.

Mitra, Asok. India's Population: Aspects of Quality & Control, 2 vols. 1978. 42.50x set o.p. (ISBN 0-8364-0267-7). South Asia Bks.

Mitra, Bimal. King, Queen & Knave. 208p. 1983. 7.00 (ISBN 0-682-49958-7). Exposition.

Mitra, Debendra B. Cotton Weavers of Bengal, 1757-1833. 1978. 8.00x o.p. (ISBN 0-8364-0164-6). South Asia Bks.

Mitra, S. K. & Ekstrom, M. P., eds. Two-Dimensional Digital Signal Processing. LC 77-25337. (Benchmark Papers in Electrical Engineering & Computer Science: Vol. 20). 400p. 1978. 52.50 (ISBN 0-87933-320-0). Hutchinson Ross.

Mitra, S. M., jt. auth. see Maharani.

Mitra, Sanjit K. Active Inductorless Filters. LC 70-179914. (IEEE Press Selected Reprint Ser). 1971. 15.95 o.p. (ISBN 0-471-61177-8, Pub. by Wiley-Interscience); pap. text ed. 7.95 o.p. (ISBN 0-471-61176-X). Wiley.

Mitra, Sanjit K., ed. Active Inductorless Filters. LC 70-179914. 1971. 17.95 o.p. (ISBN 0-87942-003-0). Inst Electrical.

Mitra, Sanjit K., jt. ed. see Temes, Gabor C.

Mitra, Sujit K., jt. auth. see Rao, C. R.

Mitrani, I. Simulation Techniques for Discrete Event Systems. LC 82-4549. (Cambridge Computer Science Texts Ser.: No. 14). (Illus.). 200p. 1983. 29.95 (ISBN 0-521-23885-4); pap. 11.95 (ISBN 0-521-28282-9). Cambridge U Pr.

Mitrany, David. The Functional Theory of Politics. LC 75-37253. 320p. 1976. 26.00 (ISBN 0-312-31010-2). St Martin.

--The Progress of International Government. 1933. 29.50x (ISBN 0-686-51293-6). Elliots Bks.

Mitre Corp. Military Communications System Control Symposium. 1980. 60.00 (ISBN 0-686-38472-5). Info Gatekeepers.

Mitres, Bohumil. D C Amplifiers. 1976. 27.95 o.p. (ISBN 0-592-02824-0). Butterworth.

Mitrevski, Pavle. Can the English Language Become Phonetic? 208p. 1983. 10.00 (ISBN 0-682-49915-3). Exposition.

Mitroff, Ian I. & Mason, Richard O. The Politics of the Nineteen-Eighty Census. LC 81-47992. 288p. 1983. 27.95x (ISBN 0-669-05224-8). Lexington Bks.

Mitroff, Ian I., jt. auth. see Mason, Richard O.

Mitropolsky, Y. A., jt. auth. see Bogoliubov, N. M.

Mitruka, Brij M. & Rawnsley, Howard M. Clinical Biochemical & Hematological Reference Values in Normal Experimental Animals & Normal Humans. 2nd, exp. ed. LC 81-17157. (Illus.). 432p. 1982. lib. bdg. 52.00x (ISBN 0-89352-163-9). Masson Pub.

Mitruka, Brij M., et al. Animals for Medical Research: Models for the Study of Human Disease. LC 80-11455. 608p. 1981. Repr. of 1976 ed. lib. bdg. 39.50 (ISBN 0-89874-156-4). Krieger.

Mitsch, W. J. & Bosserman, R. W., eds. Energy & Ecological Modelling: Proceedings of the International Symposium, Louisville, Ky, April 20-23, 1981. (Developments in Environmental Modelling Ser.: Vol. 1). 848p. 1982. 127.75 (ISBN 0-444-99731-8). Elsevier.

Mitsch, William J. Energetics & Systems. LC 81-70866. 132p. 1982. 27.50 (ISBN 0-250-40535-0). Ann Arbor Science.

Mitscher, Lester A., jt. auth. see Lednicer, Daniel.

Mitson, Eileen. Amazon Adventure. 1969. pap. 1.75 o.p. (ISBN 0-87508-589-X). Chr Lit.

Mitsuhashi, Jun, jt. ed. see Maramorosch, Karl.

Mitsuhashi, S. Drug Resistance in Bacteria. 380p. 35.00 (ISBN 0-86577-085-9). Thieme-Stratton.

Mitsui, Akira, jt. ed. see Zaborsky, Oskar R.

Mitsui, T. An Introduction to the Physics of Ferroelectrics. (Ferroelectricity & Related Phenomena Ser.). 458p. 1976. 76.00 (ISBN 0-677-30600-8). Gordon.

Mitsui, Y., jt. ed. see Mizuno, K.

Mitsumasa, Anno. Anno's Magical ABC: An Anamorphic Alphabet. (Illus.). 64p. 1981. 16.95 (ISBN 0-399-20788-0, Philomel). Putnam Pub Group.

Mittal, K. L., ed. Physiochemical Aspects of Polymer Surfaces, Vol. 1. 600p. 1983. 75.00x (ISBN 0-306-41189-X, Plenum Pr). Plenum Pub.

--Physiochemical Aspects of Polymer Surfaces, Vol. 2. 675p. 1983. 85.00x (ISBN 0-306-41190-3, Plenum Pr). Plenum Pub.

Mittal, K. L. & Fendler, E. J., eds. Solution Behavior of Surfactants: Theoretical & Applied Aspects, 2 vols. 1982. Vol. 1, 750. 85.00x (ISBN 0-306-41025-7, Plenum Pr); Vol. 2, 775. 150.00 (ISBN 0-306-41026-5, Plenum Pr); Set. 150.00 (ISBN 0-686-97756-4). Plenum Pub.

Mittal, Kewal K. Role of Materialism in Indian Thought. LC 74-901145. xvi, 328p. 1974. 14.00x o.p. (ISBN 0-8364-0461-0). South Asia Bks.

Mittal, N. Freedom Movement in Punjab, 1905-1920. 12.50x o.p. (ISBN 0-88386-979-9). South Asia Bks.

Mitteis, H. The State in the Middle Ages. (Medieval Translations Ser.: Vol. 1). 380p. 1975. pap. 27.75 (ISBN 0-444-10789-4, North-Holland). Elsevier.

Mittelbach, Frank G., jt. auth. see Grebler, Leo.

Mittelman, Arnold, jt. auth. see Murphy, Gerald P.

Mittemeyer, B. T., jt. auth. see McLeod, D. G.

Mitter, H., ed. Electroweak Interactions, Schladming (Graz), Austria 1982: Proceedings. (Acta Physia Austriaca Supplementum: Vol. 24). (Illus.). 474p. 1983. 38.00 (ISBN 0-387-81729-8). Springer-Verlag.

Mitter, Wolfgang. Secondary School Graduation: University Entrance Qualification in Socialist Countries. new ed. LC 77-30471. 1979. text ed. 25.00 (ISBN 0-08-022237-4); pap. text ed. 16.25 (ISBN 0-08-022238-2). Pergamon.

Mitterand, Frank. Major Racial Changes in the Leadership of the United States: Their Meaning for the Future of the Country & of the World. (Illus.). 1982. 49.85 (ISBN 0-686-97239-2). Am Classical Coll Pr.

Mitterling, Philip I., ed. United States Cultural History: A Guide to Information Sources. LC 79-24061. (American Government & History Information Guide Ser.: Vol. 5). 1980. 42.00x (ISBN 0-8103-1369-3). Gale.

Mittermeyer, Helen. Surrender. (Loveswept Ser.: No. 2). 1983. pap. 1.95 (ISBN 0-686-43203-7). Bantam.

Mitterrand, Francois. The Wheat & the Chaff. 352p. 1983. pap. 7.95 (ISBN 0-86579-026-4). Seaver Bks.

Mittlebeeler, Emmet V. African Custom & Western Law: The Development of the Rhodesian Criminal Law for Africans. LC 73-86268. 250p. 1976. text ed. 39.50x (ISBN 0-8419-0107-4, Africana). Holmes & Meier.

Mittlefehldt, Pamela. Minnesota Folklife: An Annotated Bibliography. Sherarts, I. Karon, ed. LC 79-23255. 42p. (Orig.). 1979. pap. 3.50 (ISBN 0-935288-00-7). Minn Hist.

Mittleman, Don. BASIC Computing. 430p. 1982. pap. text ed. 16.95 (ISBN 0-15-504910-0, HC). HarBraceJ.

Mittleman, Marvin H. Introduction to the Theory of Laser-Atom Interactions. (Physics of Atoms & Molecules Ser.). 195p. 1982. 35.00x (ISBN 0-306-41049-4, Plenum Pr). Plenum Pub.

Mittler, P., jt. auth. see Hogg, J.

Mittler, Peter. Frontiers of Knowledge in Mental Retardation, Vol. 2. 368p. 1981. text ed. 19.95 (ISBN 0-8391-1637-3). Univ Park.

Mittler, Peter, ed. Frontiers of Knowledge in Mental Retardation, Vol. 1. 494p. 1981. text ed. 19.95 (ISBN 0-8391-1636-5). Univ Park.

--Psychological Assessment of Mental & Physical Handicaps. 886p. 1974. pap. 33.00x (ISBN 0-422-75600-8, Pub. by Tavistock England). Methuen Inc.

Mittler, T. E. & Dadd, R. H., eds. Metabolic Aspects of Lipid Nutrition in Insects. (Special Study). 240p. 1982. lib. bdg. 27.50 (ISBN 0-86531-321-0). Westview.

Mittler, T. E., et al, eds. Annual Review of Entomology, Vol. 28. (Illus.). 1983. text ed. 27.00 (ISBN 0-8243-0128-5). Annual Reviews.

Mitton, Bruce H. Kites, Kites, Kites: The Ups & Downs of Making & Flying Them. LC 78-57062. (Illus.). (gr. 3 up). 1978. pap. 6.95 (ISBN 0-8069-8460-0). Sterling.

--Photo Display. LC 79-7874. (Illus., Orig.). 1980. pap. 5.95 o.p. (ISBN 0-385-15538-7, Dolp). Doubleday.

Mitton, G. E. Jane Austen & Her Times. LC 74-103206. 1970. Repr. of 1905 ed. 15.00 o.p. (ISBN 0-8046-0843-1). Kennikat.

Mitton, Jacqueline. Key Definitions in Astronomy. LC 82-183. (Quality Paperback: No. 375). 174p. (Orig.). 1982. pap. text ed. 4.95 (ISBN 0-8226-0375-6). Littlefield.

Mitton, Jeffry B. & Sturgeon, Kareen B., eds. Bark Beetles in North American Conifers: A System for the Study of Evolutionary Biology. (Corrie Herring Hooks Ser.: No. 6). 539p. 1982. text ed. 30.00x (ISBN 0-292-70735-5); pap. 17.50x (ISBN 0-292-70744-4). U of Tex Pr.

Mitton, S., jt. ed. see Hazard, C.

Mitton, Simon. Daytime Star. (Illus.). 208p. 1983. pap. 6.95 (ISBN 0-686-83737-1, ScribT). Scribner.

Mittra, Sid. Money & Banking: Theory, Analysis & Policy. 1970. pap. text ed. 6.95x (ISBN 0-685-84267-3). Phila Bk Co.

Mittra, Sid, ed. Dimensions of Microeconomics: A Book of Reading. 1971. pap. 6.95 (ISBN 0-685-55631-X, 31425). Phila Bk Co.

Mittre, Sid & Gassen, Chris. Investment Analysis & Portfolio Management. 857p. text ed. 25.95 (ISBN 0-15-546882-0); tchr's. manual 2.95 (ISBN 0-15-546883-9). HarBraceJ.

Mittwer, Marie, jt. auth. see Doyle, Maryyl.

Mityayev, A. Grishka & the Astronaut. 22p. 1981. pap. 1.60 (ISBN 0-8285-2218-9, Pub. by Progress Pubs USSR). Imported Pubns.

Mitz, Rick. The Great TV Sitcom Book. (Illus.). 440p. 1982. pap. 9.95 (ISBN 0-399-50635-7, Perige). Putnam Pub Group.

Mitzel, Harold, ed. Encyclopedia of Educational Research, 4 vols. 5th ed. LC 82-2332. 1982. Set. lib. bdg. 275.00x (ISBN 0-02-900450-0). Macmillan.

Miura, Akira. Japanese Words & Their Uses. LC 82-51099. 240p. 1983. 14.00 (ISBN 0-8048-1386-8). C E Tuttle.

Miura, Akira, tr. see Tsuboi, Sakae.

Miura, Isshu & Sasaki, Ruth F. The Zen Koan. LC 65-19104. (Illus.). 1966. pap. 4.95 (ISBN 0-15-699981-1, Harv). HarBraceJ.

Miura, Lydia, ed. see Graphic Arts Trade Journals Int'l. Inc.

Miura, Lydia, ed. see Graphics Arts Trade Journals International Inc.

Miura, Robert M., ed. Some Mathematical Questions in Biology. LC 82-18418. (Lectures on Mathematics in the Life Sciences Ser.: Vol. 15). 19.00 (ISBN 0-8218-1165-7, LLSCI/15). Am Math.

Mix, A. J. A Monograph of the Genus Taphrina. (Bibl. Myco.: Vol.18). 1969. Repr. of 1949 ed. 24.00 (ISBN 3-7682-0583-5). Lubrecht & Cramer.

Mix, Emily S., jt. auth. see Allen, Jean.

Mix, James B., ed. see Sutton, Charles.

Mix, Terence J. & Rosen, Victor J. A Question of Judgement. 368p. 1983. 10.95 (ISBN 0-86666-016-X). GWP.

Mixco, Mauricio J. Kiliwa Texts: "When I Have Donned My Crest of Stars". (Anthropological Papers: No. 107). (Illus.). xvi, 307p. (Orig.). 1983. pap. 20.00x (ISBN 0-87480-219-9). U of Utah Pr.

Mixter, Richard W., ed. see Heller, Lois J. & Mohrman, David E.

Miyachi & Katoh, eds. Photosynthetic Organelles: Structures & Functions. 1982. text ed. 37.00 (ISBN 0-686-98395-5, Pub. by Japan Sci Soc Japan). Intl Schol Bk Serv.

Miyakawa, T. Scott, jt. ed. see Conroy, Hilary.

Miyamoto, Kenro. Plasma Physics for Nuclear Fusion. (Illus.). 623p. 1979. text ed. 55.00x (ISBN 0-262-13145-5). MIT Pr.

Miyamoto, Michiko, intro. by. An Exhibition of Women Artists from Japan: A. I. R. Gallery Invitational. (Illus.). 24p. 1978. pap. 3.00 (ISBN 0-89062-128-4, Pub by A.I.R. Gallery). Pub Ctr Cult Res.

Miyamoto, Shoson. The Buddhist Philosophy of the Middle Way. 1983. 9.95x (ISBN 0-914910-07-8). Buddhist Bks.

Miyashiro, Akiho, et al. Orogeny. LC 82-8499. 242p. 1982. 45.00 (ISBN 0-471-10376-4, Pub. by Wiley-Interscience). Wiley.

Miyashita, Tadao. The Currency & Financial System of Mainland China. (China in the 20th Century Ser.). 1976. Repr. of 1966 ed. lib. bdg. 32.50 (ISBN 0-306-70758-6). Da Capo.

Miyazaki, Kojiro, tr. see Niwano, Nikkyo.

Miyazaki, M. E., et al, eds. Anaesthesiology. (International Congress Ser.: No. 292). (Proceedings). 1974. 78.00 (ISBN 0-444-15043-9). Elsevier.

Miyazawa, T., jt. auth. see Emsley.

Miyoshi. Gut Peptides. 1980. 84.00 (ISBN 0-444-80208-8). Elsevier.

Miyoshi, Masao. Accomplices of Silence: The Modern Japanese Novel. 1975. Repr. of 1974 ed. 22.50 (ISBN 0-520-04609-9). U of Cal Pr.

Mize, jt. auth. see Kuester.

Mize, Jack P., jt. auth. see Carr, William N.

Mize, Jean. Night of Anguish, Morning of Hope. LC 79-88497. (Illus., Orig.). 1979. pap. 1.95 o.p. (ISBN 0-89877-009-2). Jeremy Bks.

Mize, Joe H. & Cox, J. Essentials of Simulation. 1968. ref. ed. 19.95 (ISBN 0-13-288902-1). P-H.

Mize, Joe H., et al. Operations Planning & Control. (Illus.). 1971. ref. ed. 27.95 (ISBN 0-13-637892-7). P-H.

Mize, Terry. God's Opinion of You. 32p. 1983. pap. write for info. Harrison Hse.

Mizel, S., jt. ed. see Pick, E.

Mizer, Bob, photos by. Physique: A Pictorial History of the Athletic Model Guild. Leyland, Winston, ed. (Illus.). 96p. (Orig.). 1982. pap. 18.95 (ISBN 0-917342-94-1). Gay Sunshine.

Mizeres, N. J. Human Anatomy. (A Synoptic Approach). 1981. pap. 21.95 (ISBN 0-444-00608-7). Elsevier.

--Methods of Dissection. 176p. 1982. pap. 14.95 (ISBN 0-444-00721-0, Biomedical Pr). Elsevier.

Mizio, Emelicia & Delaney, Anita J., eds. Training for Service Delivery to Minority Clients. LC 80-234668. 1980. pap. 10.95 (ISBN 0-87304-180-1). Family Serv.

Mizler, Lorenz C. Neu Eroffnete Musikalische Bibliothek Oder Grundliche Nachricht Nebst Unpartheyischem Urteil Von Alten und Neuen Musikalischen Schriften und Buchern: Leipzig 1739-1754, 3 vols. 2250p. 1966. 200.00 set o.s.i. (ISBN 90-6027-029-0, Pub. by Frits Knuf Netherlands). Pendragon NY.

Mizohata, Sigeru. The Theory of Partial Differential Equations. LC 72-83593. 350p. 1973. 79.95 (ISBN 0-521-08727-9). Cambridge U Pr.

Mizrahi, A. & Sullivan, M. Mathematics for Business & the Social Sciences: An Applied Approach. 2nd ed. 797p. 1979. text ed. 26.95 (ISBN 0-471-03334-0). Wiley.

Mizrahi, Abe & Sullivan, Michael. Calculus with Applications to Business & the Life Sciences. LC 75-17964. 384p. 1976. text ed. 25.95x (ISBN 0-471-61192-1). Wiley.

--Finite Mathematics with Applications for Business & Social Sciences. 3rd ed. LC 78-12522. 1979. text ed. 25.95x (ISBN 0-471-03336-7). study guide 12.95x (ISBN 0-471-05499-2). Wiley.

--Finite Mathematics with Applications for Business & Social Sciences. 4th ed. LC 82-17590. 650p. 1983. text ed. write for info (ISBN 0-471-05398-8). Wiley.

Mizrahi, Avshalom & Van Wezel, Antonius L., eds. Advances in Biotechnological Processes, Vol. 1. 360p. 1983. 58.00 (ISBN 0-8451-3200-8). A R Liss.

Mizruchi, Ephraim H. Regulating Society. 224p. 1982. text ed. write for info. (ISBN 0-02-921660-5). Free Pr.

Mizuike, A. Enrichment Techniques for Inorganic Trace Analysis. (Chemical Laboratory Practice). (Illus.). 144p. 1983. 29.80 (ISBN 0-387-12051-3). Springer-Verlag.

Mizukami, Masahiro, et al, eds. Hypertensive Intracerebral Hemorrhage. 1982. text ed. write for info. (ISBN 0-89004-812-6). Raven.

Mizumura, Kazue. Blue Whale. LC 70-139107. (A Let's-Read-and-Find-Out Science Bk). (Illus.). (gr. k-3). 1971. PLB 10.89 (ISBN 0-690-14994-8, TYC-J). Har-Row.

--If I Were a Cricket... LC 73-3495. (Illus.). (ps-3). 1973. 7.95 o.p. (ISBN 0-690-00075-8, TYC-J); PLB 9.89 (ISBN 0-690-00076-6). Har-Row.

Mizuno, K. & Mitsui, Y., eds. Ophthalmology Update. (International Congress Ser.: Vol. 508). 1980. 45.00 (ISBN 0-444-90114-0). Elsevier.

Mizuno, Kogen. The Beginnings of Buddhism. Friedrich, Ralph, ed. Gage, Richard L., tr. from Japanese. Orig. Title: Bukyo No Genten. (Illus.). 232p. 1980. pap. 8.95 (ISBN 4-333-00383-0, Pub. by Kosei Publishing Co). C E Tuttle.

--Buddhist Sutras: Origin, Development, Transmission. (Illus.). 216p. 1982. pap. 8.95 (ISBN 4-333-01028-4, Pub. by Kosei Publishing Co). C E Tuttle.

Mizushina, Tokuro & Wen-Jei Yang, eds. Heat Transfer in Energy Problems. LC 82-910. 1983. text ed. 69.50 (ISBN 0-89116-251-8). Hemisphere Pub.

Mjelde, K. M. Methods of the Allocation of Limited Resources. 100p. 1983. price not set (ISBN 0-471-10439-6, Pub. by Wiley-Interscience). Wiley.

Mkangi, C. C. The Social Cost of Small Families & Land Reform: A Case Study of the Wataita of Kenya. (International Population Ser.: Vol. 2). (Illus.). 160p. 1983. 25.00 (ISBN 0-08-028952-5). Pergamon.

Mlacnik, Milan, tr. Dzevad HOZO. (Illus.). 156p. 1981. 40.00 (ISBN 0-89893-176-2). CDP.

Mlacnik, Milan, tr. see Mesesnel, Janez.

MLW Publications, ed. The Book of Proverbs from Twenty-One Translations. LC 82-61262. (Illus.). 200p. 1983. pap. 8.95 (ISBN 0-9609348-0-4). MLW Pubns Inc.

Mnookin, Robert. Child, Family & State, Cases & Materials on Children & the Law. 857p. 1978. text ed. 25.00 (ISBN 0-316-57650-6). Little.

Mo, Sam. Why Heart Attack? 1981. cancelled 6.95 (ISBN 0-8062-1546-1). Carlton.

Moak, Lennox L. Municipal Bonds: Planning, Sale, & Administration. (Debt Administration Ser.). (Illus.). 400p. nonmember 37.00 (ISBN 0-686-84287-1); member 32.00 (ISBN 0-686-84288-X). Municipal.

Moak, Lennox L. & Killian, Kathryn W. Operating Budget Manual. LC 64-12365. (Illus.). 347p. 1963. 12.00 (ISBN 0-686-84284-7). Municipal.

Moakley, Gertrude. Tarot Cards Painted by Bonifacio Bembo for the Visconti-Sforza Family. (Illus.). 1966. 15.00 (ISBN 0-87104-175-8). NY Pub Lib.

Moan, T. & Shinozuka, M., eds. Structural Safety & Reliability. (Developments in Civil Engineering Ser.: Vol. 4). 1982. 106.50 (ISBN 0-444-41994-2). Elsevier.

Moat, Albert G. Microbial Physiology. LC 79-11323. 1979. 41.50 (ISBN 0-471-07258-3, Pub. by Wiley-Interscience). Wiley.

Moates, Danny R. & Schumacher, Gary M. Introduction to Cognitive Psychology. 1979. text ed. 22.95x (ISBN 0-534-00724-4). Wadsworth Pub.

Moawad, Atef M., ed. see National Institutes of Health, the Chicago Heart Association & the University of Chicago, et al.

Mobbs, A. J. Hummingbirds. 176p. 1982. 80.00x (ISBN 0-86230-049-5, Pub. by Saiga Pub). State Mutual Bk.

Moberg. The Upper Limb in Tetraplegia. 1979. 18.95 (ISBN 0-913258-63-6). Thieme Stratton.

Moberg, David O., ed. Spiritual Well-Being: Sociological Perspectives. LC 79-52191. 1979. pap. text ed. 13.75 (ISBN 0-8191-0765-4). U Pr of Amer.

Moberg, Dennis G., jt. auth. see Brown, Warren B.

Moberg, Goran. Writing in Groups: Techniques for Good Writing Without Drills. (Illus.). 210p. 1983. pap. text ed. 12.95 (ISBN 0-911683-00-3). Writing Con.

Moberger, Marion. Dreams Come True. 1983. 8.95 (ISBN 0-533-05615-2). Vantage.

Moberly, Elizabeth R. Psychogenesis: The Early Development of Gender Identity. 120p. 1983. 17.95. Routledge & Kegan.

Moberly, Robert B. see Labor Law Group.

Moberly, Robert B., ed. see Labor Law Group.

Mobil Corporation. The Clock Is Running. Date not set. 14.95 (ISBN 0-671-43459-4). S&S.

Mobius, Helga. Woman in the Baroque Age. (Image of Women Ser.). (Illus.). 216p. 1983. 35.00 (ISBN 0-8390-0283-1). Allanheld & Schram.

Mobley, Tony A., jt. auth. see Brightbill, Charles K.

Moch, Leslie P. & Stark, Gary D., eds. Essays on the Family & Historical Change. LC 82-45900. (Walter Prescott Webb Memorial Lectures Ser.: No. 17). 136p. 1983. 17.50x (ISBN 0-89096-151-4). Tex A&M Univ Pr.

Moche, Dinah. Mars. LC 78-2762. (Easy-Read-Fact Bks.). (Illus.). (gr. 2-4). 1978. PLB 8.60 s&l (ISBN 0-531-01374-X). Watts.

--Radiation: Benefits-Dangers. (Impact Ser.). (Illus.). (gr. 7 up). 1979. PLB 8.90 s&l (ISBN 0-531-02860-7). Watts.

--Search for Life Beyond Earth. (Impact Bks.). (Illus.). (gr. 7 up). 1978. lib. bdg. 8.90 (ISBN 0-531-02204-8). Watts.

Moche, Dinah L. The Astronauts. LC 78-54955. (Pictureback Bk.). (Illus.). (ps-3). 1979. pap. 1.50 (ISBN 0-394-83901-3, BYR); 4.99 (ISBN 0-394-93901-8). Random.

--Astronomy. LC 77-27367. (Self-Teaching Guides Ser.). 1978. pap. text ed. 7.95 o.p. (ISBN 0-471-01764-7). Wiley.

--Life in Space. LC 79-51841. (Illus.). 160p. (Orig.). 1979. pap. 10.95 o.s.i. (ISBN 0-89104-155-9, A & W Visual Library); 25.00 o.s.i. (ISBN 0-89104-154-0). A & W Pubs.

Mochulsky, Konstantin. Aleksandr Blok. Johnson, Doris V., tr. 504p. 1983. 30.00 (ISBN 0-8143-1707-3). Wayne St U Pr.

Mock, James R. Censorship Nineteen Seventeen. LC 74-37864. (Civil Liberties in American History Ser). 250p. 1972. Repr. of 1941 ed. lib. bdg. 29.50 (ISBN 0-306-70436-6). Da Capo.

Mock, Lonnie. Excel in Chinese Cooking. Haggerty, Nancy, ed. LC 81-70318. (Illus.). 208p. (Orig.). 1982. pap. 7.95 (ISBN 0-941716-00-7). Alpha Gamma.

Mock, Michael B., jt. ed. see Braunwald, Eugene.

Mock, Theodore J. & Grove, Hugh D. Measurement, Accounting, & Organizational Information. LC 78-10536. (Accounting & Information Systems Ser.). 1979. text ed. 32.50x (ISBN 0-471-61202-2). Wiley.

Mock, Valerie E. Addition & Subtraction Riddles. (Learning Workbooks Mathematics). (gr. 3-5). pap. 1.50 (ISBN 0-8224-4189-6). Pitman.

--Addition Drill. (Learning Workbooks Mathematics). 1981. pap. 1.50 (ISBN 0-8224-4184-5). Pitman.

--Division Drill. (Learning Workbooks Mathematics). (gr. 3-5). pap. 1.50 (ISBN 0-686-38848-8). Pitman.

--Fractions Drill. (Learning Workbooks Mathematics). (gr. 3-5). pap. 1.50 (ISBN 0-8224-4188-8). Pitman.

--Mulitiplication & Division Riddles. (Learning Workbooks Mathematics). (gr. 3-5). pap. 1.50 (ISBN 0-686-38851-8). Pitman.

--Multiplication Drill. (Learning Workbooks Mathematics). (gr. 3-5). pap. 1.50 (ISBN 0-8224-4186-1). Pitman.

--Subtraction Drill. (Learning Workbooks Mathematics). (gr. 1-3). pap. 1.50 (ISBN 0-8224-4185-3). Pitman.

Mocker, Donald W. & Spear, George E., eds. Urban Education: A Guide to Information Sources. LC 78-13627. (Urban Studies Information Guide: Vol. 3). 1978. 42.00x (ISBN 0-8103-1431-2). Gale.

Mockler, Mike, compiled by. Flights of Imagination: An Illustrated Anthology of Bird Poetry. (Illus.). 128p. 1982. 15.95 (ISBN 0-7137-1164-7, Pub. by Blandford Pr England). Sterling.

Mocq, Louis, tr. see Raspail, F. V.

Mocquet, Jean. Voyages en Afrique, Asie, Indes Orientales et Occidentales Faits Par Jean Mocquet. (Bibliotheque Africaine Ser.). 460p. (Fr.). 1974. Repr. of 1617 ed. lib. bdg. 115.00 o.p. (ISBN 0-8287-0626-3, 72-2131). Clearwater Pub.

Model Aviation Editors, ed. see Winter, William J.

Model, Lisette, jt. auth. see Frank, Robert.

Model Railroader Staff, jt. ed. see Dolzall, Donnette.

Model Railroader Staff, jt. ed. see Warren, Bob.

Modell, Judith. Ruth Benedict: Patterns of a Life. (Illus.). 400p. 1983. 30.00x (ISBN 0-8122-7874-7). U of Pa Pr.

Modell, Michael & Boyd, Robert. Paediatric Problems in General Practice. (Illus.). 1982. pap. 23.95x (ISBN 0-19-261264-6). Oxford U Pr.

Modell, Michael & Reid, Robert C. Thermodynamics & Its Applications. (Physical & Chemical Engr. Sciences Intl Ser.). (Illus.). 528p. 1974. 33.95 (ISBN 0-13-914861-2). P-H.

--Thermodynamics & Its Applications. 2nd ed. (Illus.). 512p. 1983. text ed. 34.95 (ISBN 0-13-915017-X). P-H.

Modell, Walter. Drugs in Current Use & New Drugs 1983. 29th ed. 1983. pap. text ed. 10.95 (ISBN 0-8261-0162-3). Springer Pub.

Modell, Walter & Lansing, Alfred. Drugs. LC 67-25859. (Life Science Library). (Illus.). (gr. 5 up). 1967. PLB cancelled o.p. (ISBN 0-8094-0482-6, Pub. by Time-Life). Silver.

Modelski, Sylvia, tr. see Levi-Strauss, Claude.

Moder, Joseph J. & Phillips, Cecil R. Project Management with CPM & PERT. 2nd ed. (Illus.). 1970. 17.95x o.p. (ISBN 0-442-15666-9). Van Nos Reinhold.

Modern Language Association. Continuing Spanish. 2nd ed. 480p. 1974. text ed. 14.95 (ISBN 0-442-23718-9); wkbk. 3.95x (ISBN 0-442-23719-7); tapes 75.00 (ISBN 0-442-23721-9). Van Nos Reinhold.

Modessit, L. E. The Fires of Paratime. 205p. 1982. pap. 2.95 (ISBN 0-686-82233-1, Timescape). PB.

Modeste, Victor. Du Pauperisme en France: Etat Actuel Causes, Remedes Possibles. (Conditions of the 19th Century French Working Class Ser.). 589p. (Fr.). 1974. Repr. of 1858 ed. lib. bdg. 144.00x o.p. (ISBN 0-8287-0627-1, 1024). Clearwater Pub.

Modgil, Celia, jt. auth. see Modgil, Sohan.

Modgil, Celia, jt. ed. see Modgil, Sohan.

Modgil, Sohan & Modgil, Celia. Piagetian Research, Compilation & Commentary, No. 5: Personality, Socialization & Emotionality Reasoning Among Handicapped Children. 1976. pap. text ed. 28.25x (ISBN 0-85633-105-8, NFER). Humanities.

Modgil, Sohan & Modgil, Celia, eds. Jean Piaget: An Interdisciplinary Critique. (International Library of Psychology). 200p. 1983. price not set (ISBN 0-7100-9451-5). Routledge & Kegan.

Modi, Jivanji J. The Religious Ceremonies & Customs of the Parsees: Bombay, 1922. LC 78-74280. (Oriental Religions Ser.: Vol. 7). 563p. 1980. lib. bdg. 60.50 o.s.i. (ISBN 0-8240-3913-0). Garland Pub.

Modi, John. The Best Kitchen Remodeling Workbook. LC 77-91162. 1978. pap. 7.95 (ISBN 0-8092-7541-4). Contemp Bks.

Modica, Alfred J. Franchising. (Illus.). 192p. 1981. pap. 12.95 (ISBN 0-8256-3203-X, Quick Fox). Putnam Pub Group.

Modigliani & Hemming. The Determinants of National Savings & Wealth: Proceedings of a Conference Held by International Economic Association in Bergamo, Italy. LC 82-10377. 305p. 1982. 35.00x (ISBN 0-312-19590-7). St Martin.

Modigliani, Amadeo. Modigliani. Ponente, Nello, ed. (Art Library Ser: Vol. 25). pap. 2.95 o.p. (ISBN 0-448-00474-7, G&D). Putnam Pub Group.

Modigliani, Andre, jt. auth. see Gamson, William A.

Modigliani, Franco. The Collected Papers of Franco Modigliani, 3 vols. Abel, Andrew, ed. 1980. Vol. 1, Essays In Macroeconomics. 30.00x (ISBN 0-262-13150-1); Vol. 2, The Life Cycle Of Hypothesis Of Saving. 30.00x (ISBN 0-262-13151-X); Vol. 3, Theory Of Finance & Other Essays. 30.00x (ISBN 0-262-13152-8). MIT Pr.

Modisett, Noah F. & Luter, James G. Speaking Clearly: The Basics of Voice & Articulation. LC 79-50711. 1979. pap. text ed. 10.95x (ISBN 0-8087-3949-2). Burgess.

Modleski, Tania. Loving With A Vengence: Mass Produced Fantasies for Women. 141p. 1982. 15.00 (ISBN 0-208-01945-6, Archon). Shoe String.

Modras, Ronald. Jesus of Nazareth: A Life Worth Living. (Nazareth Bks). 120p. 1983. pap. 3.95 (ISBN 0-86683-713-2). Winston Pr.

Moe, Barbara. Pickles & Prunes. LC 75-41347. 160p. (gr. 9-12). 1976. 7.95 (ISBN 0-07-042643-0, GB). McGraw.

Moe, Christian & Payne, Darwin R., eds. Six New Plays for Children. LC 70-112391. (Illus.). 304p. 1971. 12.50x o.p. (ISBN 0-8093-0453-8). S Ill U Pr.

Moe, John H., jt. auth. see Blount, Walter P.

Moe, Ronald C. Hoover Commissions Revisited. (Replica Edition). 138p. 1982. lib. bdg. 16.00x (ISBN 0-86531-926-X). Westview.

Moe, Terry M. The Organization of Interests: Incentives & the Internal Dynamics of Political Interest Groups. LC 79-13238. (Illus.). x, 282p. 1982. pap. text ed. 9.00x (ISBN 0-226-53352-2). U of Chicago Pr.

Moehle, Natalia R. The Dimensions of Evil & Transcendence: A Sociological Perspective. LC 78-59124. 1978. pap. text ed. 11.50 (ISBN 0-8191-0550-3). U Pr of Amer.

Moeller & Liedloff. Kaleidoskop: Kultur, Literatur und Grammatik. text ed. 16.95 (ISBN 0-686-84589-7, GR15); instr's. annotated ed. 17.95 (ISBN 0-686-84590-0, GR12); write for info. supplementary materials. HM.

Moeller, Bernd. Imperial Cities & the Reformation. Midelfort, H. C. Erik & Edwards, Mark U., Jr., eds. 128p. (Orig.). 1982. pap. text ed. 4.95x (ISBN 0-939464-04-7). Labyrinth Pr.

Moeller, Beverley B. Phil Swing & Boulder Dam. LC 71-635550. (Illus.). 1971. 27.50x (ISBN 0-520-01932-6). U of Cal Pr.

Moeller, Gerald & Mahan, David J. The Faculty Team: School Organization for Results. LC 77-160581. (Dimensions in Education Ser.). (Illus.). 1971. pap. 6.95 o.p. (ISBN 0-574-17388-9, 13-0388). SRA.

Moeller, Jack, jt. auth. see Drath, Viola.

Moeller, Jack R. & Liedloff, Helmut. Deutsch Heute: Grundstufe. 2nd ed. LC 78-52718. (Illus.). 1979. text ed. 19.95 (ISBN 0-395-27175-4); instr's. annot. ed. 20.95 (ISBN 0-395-27174-6); wkbk. 7.50 (ISBN 0-395-27173-8); recordings 160.00 (ISBN 0-395-27171-1). HM.

Moeller, Jack R., et al. Blickpunkt Deutschland. LC 76-190308. 416p. 1973. text ed. 18.80 (ISBN 0-395-13690-3); instr's. ed. 18.84 (ISBN 0-395-14218-0); workbook 4.84 (ISBN 0-395-14212-1); Set of 6. recordings 142.44 (ISBN 0-395-14211-3). HM.

Moeller, Roger W. Practicing Environmental Archaeology: Methods & Interpretations. LC 82-73087. (Occasional Papers No. 3). (Illus.). 112p. 1982. pap. text ed. 10.00 (ISBN 0-936322-00-4). Am Indian Arch.

Moeller, Roger W., ed. Archaeological Bibliograph for Eastern North America. 198p. 1977. pap. 7.00 (ISBN 0-936322-03-9). Am Indian Arch.

Moeller, Therald. Inorganic Chemistry: A Modern Introduction. LC 81-16455. 848p. 1982. 34.95x (ISBN 0-471-61230-8, Pub. by Wiley-Interscience). Wiley.

Moeller Van Den Bruck, Arthur. Germany's Third Empire. 1972. 24.00x (ISBN 0-86527-085-6). Fertig.

Moen, Ann & Mace, Varian. Fairy Tales. (Illus.). 48p. 1979. pap. 2.95 (ISBN 0-89844-006-8). Troubador Pr.

Moen, Elizabeth, et al. Women & the Social Costs of Economic Development: Two Colorado Case Studies. (Illus.). 225p. 1981. lib. bdg. 31.00 (ISBN 0-89158-594-X). Westview.

Moen, Wayne S. Silver Occurrences of Washington. (Bulletin Ser.: No. 69). (Illus.). 188p. 1976. 4.00 (ISBN 0-686-38464-4). Geologic Pubns.

Moen, Wayne S. & McLucas, Glennda B. Mount St. Helen's Ash: Properties & Possible Uses. (Report of Investigations Ser.: No. 24). (Illus.). 60p. 1981. 5.00 (ISBN 0-686-34731-5). Geologic Pubns.

Moenkemeyer, Heinz. Francois Hemsterhuis. (World Authors Ser.). 1975. lib. bdg. 15.95 (ISBN 0-8057-2419-2, Twayne). G K Hall.

Moerk, Ernst L. The Mother of Eve--as a First Language Teacher. Lipsitt, Lewis P., ed. (Monographs on Infancy). 208p. 1983. text ed. 18.50 (ISBN 0-89391-160-7). Ablex Pub.

Moeschberger, Melvin E., jt. auth. see Madsen, Richard W.

Moeschlin, O. & Pallaschke, D., eds. Game Theory & Mathematical Economics. 1981. 68.00 (ISBN 0-444-86296-X). Elsevier.

Moeschlin, Sven. Poisoning: Diagnosis & Treatment. LC 63-11736. 728p. 1965. 97.50 o.p. (ISBN 0-8089-0326-8). Grune.

Moeser, John V., ed. A Virginia Profile Nineteen-Sixty to Two Thousand: Assessing Current Trends & Problems. (Commonwealth Books Public Policy). (Illus.). 290p. (Orig.). 1981. pap. write for info. (ISBN 0-940390-01-9). Comwealth Bks NJ.

Moews, Daniel. Keaton: The Silent Features Close up. 1977. 15.95 o.p. (ISBN 0-520-03126-1); pap. 4.50 (ISBN 0-520-03155-5, CAL 338). U of Cal Pr.

Moffat, Anne & Schiller, Marc. Landscape Design that Saves Energy. (Illus.). 224p. 1981. pap. 9.95 (ISBN 0-688-00395-8). Quill NY.

Moffat, Bobby. Intermediate Soccer Guide. (Illus.). 170p. (Orig.). 1982. pap. 12.95 (ISBN 0-89037-181-4). Anderson World.

Moffat, Bruce. Forty Feet Below: The Story of Chicago's Freight Tunnels. Walker, Jim, ed. (Special Ser.: No. 82). (Illus.). 84p. 1982. 9.95 (ISBN 0-916374-54-8). Interurban.

Moffat, D. B. The Mammalian Kidney. LC 74-82590. (Biological Structure & Function Ser.: No. 5). (Illus.). 272p. 1975. 55.00 (ISBN 0-521-20599-9). Cambridge U Pr.

Moffat, David V. Common Algorithms in Pascal with Programs for Reading. (Software Ser.). 192p. 1983. pap. 8.95 (ISBN 0-13-152637-5). P-H.

Moffat, Derry, ed. The Lady & the Tramp. (Disney Classics Ser.). (Illus.). (gr. k-4). 1980. pap. 0.95 (ISBN 0-448-16109-5, G&D). Putnam Pub Group.

Moffat, Donald W. Charts & Monographs for Technicians & Engineers. LC 65-16436. 1965. spiral bdg. 7.95 o.p. (ISBN 0-8306-5121-7, 121). TAB Bks.

--Plant Engineer's Handbook of Formulas, Charts & Tables. 384p. 1981. 49.50 o.p. (ISBN 0-13-680280-X, Busn). P-H.

--Plant Engineer's Handbook of Formulas, Charts & Tables. 2nd. ed. LC 81-15811. 397p. 1982. 49.50 (ISBN 0-13-680298-2, Busn). P-H.

Moffat, Frances. Dancing on the Brink of the World: The Rise & Fall of San Francisco Society. 1977. 9.95 o.p. (ISBN 0-399-11721-0). Putnam Pub Group.

Moffat, Gwen. Die Like a Dog. (Illus.). 165p. 1982. 14.95 (ISBN 0-575-03118-2, Pub. by Gollancz England). David & Charles.

Moffat, Mary J., ed. In the Midst of Winter: Selections from the Literature of Mourning. 1982. 14.00 (ISBN 0-394-52116-1). Random.

Moffat, Robert E. Money & Wealth in the Affluent Society: Some Pratical Realities. 1983. 11.95 (ISBN 0-533-05607-1). Vantage.

Moffatt, G. W., et al see Wulff, J.

Moffatt, Hancock. Torts in the Conflict of Laws. LC 42-36734. (Michigan Legal Studies). lviii, 288p. 1982. Repr. of 1942 ed. lib. bdg. 30.00 (ISBN 0-89941-166-5). W S Hein.

Moffet. Microbiologia Clinica. 2nd ed. 1983. pap. text ed. write for info (ISBN 0-06-315660-1, Pub. by HarLA Mexico). Har-Row.

Moffet, Charles S., intro. by. Monet's Years at Giverny: Beyond Impressionism. LC 78-328. (Illus.). 1978. 12.50 o.s.i. (ISBN 0-87099-175-2); pap. 6.95 o.s.i. (ISBN 0-87099-174-4). Metro Mus Art.

Moffett & Wagner. Student Centered Language Arts & Reading: K-13. 3rd ed. 1982. text ed. 24.50 (ISBN 0-686-84556-0, EA98). HM.

Moffett, C. W. Getting Merchandise Ready for Sale: Receiving, Checking, & Marking. 1968. text ed. 7.68 o.p. (ISBN 0-07-042646-5, G); tchr's manual 4.05 o.p. (ISBN 0-07-042648-1). McGraw.

Moffett, Carol G. & Strydesky, Rebecca. The Receiving-Checking-Marking-Stocking Clerk. 2nd ed. (Illus.). 160p. (gr. 10-12). 1980. pap. text ed. 8.60 (ISBN 0-07-042667-8, G); instr.'s manual 4.50 (ISBN 0-07-042668-6). McGraw.

Moffett, George D., Jr. So You Are Looking for a New Job... Now What? 112p. 1983. 6.00 (ISBN 0-682-49953-6). Exposition.

Moffett, James. Coming on Center: English Education in Evolution. LC 81-10041. 192p. (Orig.). 1981. pap. text ed. 8.25x (ISBN 0-86709-005-7). Boynton Cook Pub.

--Teaching the Universe of Discourse. (Orig.). 1968. pap. text ed. 14.95 (ISBN 0-395-04928-8). HM.

Moffett, James & Wagner, Betty J. Student Centered Language Arts & Reading, K-13: A Handbook for Teachers. 2nd ed. LC 76-11920. (Illus.). 640p. 1976. 23.50 (ISBN 0-395-20630-8). HM.

Moffett, James & Wagner, Betty Jane. Student-Centered Language Arts & Reading, K-13: A Handbook for Teachers. 3rd ed. LC 82-83368. 512p. 1983. text ed. 24.95 (ISBN 0-395-32828-4). HM.

Moffett, James & McElheny, Kenneth R., eds. Points of View: An Anthology of Short Stories. pap. 3.95 (ISBN 0-451-62158-1, ME2158, Ment). NAL.

Moffett, Kenworth. Morris Louis in the Museum of Fine Arts, Boston. LC 79-6360. (Illus.). 1979. pap. 7.95 (ISBN 0-87846-135-3). Mus Fine Arts Boston.

Moffett, Kenworth, jt. auth. see Ashbery, John.

Moffi, Larry. A Simple Progression. LC 82-72089. 1982. pap. 4.95 (ISBN 0-9604740-1-3). Ampersand RI.

Moffic, H. Steven & Adams, George L. A Clinician's Manual on Mental Health Care: A Multidisciplinary Approach. 1981. 26.95 (ISBN 0-201-05960-6, 05960, Med-Nurse); pap. 14.95 (ISBN 0-201-05961-4, 05961, Med-Nurse). A-W.

Moffit, Ian. The Australian Outback. (The World's Wild Places Ser.). (Illus.). 1976. lib. bdg. 15.96 (ISBN 0-8094-2061-9). Silver.

Moffitt, Francis H. & Bouchard, Harry. Surveying. 7th ed. 834p. 1982. text ed. 35.50 scp (ISBN 0-06-044559-9, HarpC); solutions manual avail. (ISBN 0-06-364573-4). Har-Row.

Moffitt, Frederick J. Tales from Ancient Greece. LC 78-56059. (The World Folktale Library). (Illus.). 1979. PLB 12.68 (ISBN 0-382-03352-3). Silver.

Moffitt, John. Adam's Choice. 1967. 4.00 o.p. (ISBN 0-8233-0069-2). Golden Quill.

Mogel, Leonard. The Magazine: Everything You Need to Know to Make It in the Magazine Business. (Illus.). 1979. text ed. 16.95 o.p. (ISBN 0-13-543710-5, Spec); pap. 9.95 o.p. (ISBN 0-13-543702-4). P-H.

Mogen, jt. auth. see Wark.

Mogen, David. Wilderness Visions: Science Fiction Westerns, Vol. 1. LC 80-8673. (I. O. Evans Studies in the Philosophy & Criticism of Literature: No. 1). 64p. 1982. lib. bdg. 9.95x (ISBN 0-89370-152-1); pap. text ed. 3.95x (ISBN 0-89370-252-8). Borgo Pr.

Moger, Allen W. Virginia: Bourbonism to Byrd, 1870-1925. LC 68-8538. (Illus.). 400p. 1968. 12.95 (ISBN 0-8139-0182-0). U Pr of Va.

Moger, Art. Hello, My Real Name Is.... (Illus.). 160p. 1983. pap. 6.95 (ISBN 0-8065-0802-7). Citadel Pr.

Mogey, John H., ed. see Howard, Ronald L.

Moggach, Deborah. A Quiet Drink. 224p. 1981. 9.95 o.p. (ISBN 0-312-66106-1). St Martin.

Moggi, Guido, et al. Simon & Schuster's Guide to Garden Flowers. Schuler, Stanley, ed. (Illus.). 1983. price not set (ISBN 0-671-46674-7); pap. price not set (ISBN 0-671-46678-X). S&S.

Moggridge, D. E. British Monetary Policy, Nineteen Twenty-Four to Nineteen Thirty-One. LC 76-169576. (Department of Applied Economics Monographs: No. 21). 1972. 47.50 (ISBN 0-521-08225-0). Cambridge U Pr.

Moggridge, D. E., ed. Keynes: Aspects of the Man & His Work. 112p. 1974. 20.00 (ISBN 0-312-45185-7). St Martin.

Moghaddam, Reza, jt. auth. see Harter, Lafayette G., Jr.

Mogilanski, Roy, ed. Energy Index, 1982: A Guide to Energy Documents, Laws & Statistics. LC 73-89098. 600p. 1982. 175.00 (ISBN 0-89947-017-3). EIC Intell.

--Environment Index 1982: A Guide to the Key Literature of the Year. LC 73-189498. 1982. 175.00 (ISBN 0-89947-016-5). EIC Intell.

Moglen, Helene. Charlotte Bronte: The Self Conceived. 1978. 11.95x o.p. (ISBN 0-393-07505-2, Norton Lib); pap. 3.95 o.p. (ISBN 0-393-00888-6). Norton.

Mogollon Conference, March 27-28,1980, Las Cruces, New Mexico. Mogollon Archaeology: Proceedings. Beckett, Patrick & Silverbird, Kira, eds. (Illus.). 386p. 1982. pap. 19.95 (ISBN 0-916552-26-8). Acoma Bks.

Mogridge, Jenni. Problems in Social Care. (Problems in Practice Ser.: Vol. 11). (Illus.). 175p. 1983. 16.50 (ISBN 0-8036-6281-5). Davis Co.

Mohaghegh, Mehdi, tr. see Sabzavari, Hadi Ibn Mahdi.

Mohammad, Ali. Situation of Agriculture, Food & Nutrition in Rural India. 1979. 14.00x o.p. (ISBN 0-8364-0518-8). South Asia Bks.

Mohammad, N., ed. Perspectives in Agricultural Geography, 5 vols. 2522p. 1981. text ed. 147.75x (ISBN 0-391-02267-9, Pub. by Concept India). Humanities.

Mohammed, A. E. Retarded Functional Differential Equations: A Global Point of View. (Research Notes in Mathematics Ser.). 147p. (Orig.). 1978. pap. text ed. 18.95 (ISBN 0-273-08401-1). Pitman Pub MA.

Mohammed, M. J., jt. auth. see Lambert, E. N.

Mohan, Raj, ed. Working Papers in Critical Realism & Sociological Theory. Wilke, Arthur. 376p. 1981. text ed. 26.00x (ISBN 0-391-02318-7, Pub. by Concept India). Humanities.

Mohan, Raj P., ed. Management & Complex Organizations in Comparative Perspective. LC 78-22133. (Contributions in Sociology: No. 36). (Illus.). 1979. lib. bdg. 29.95 (ISBN 0-313-20752-6, MMA/). Greenwood.

Mohan, Raj P. & Martindale, Don, eds. Handbook of Contemporary Developments in World Sociology. LC 75-70. (Contributions in Sociology: No. 17). 493p. 1975. lib. bdg. 35.00 (ISBN 0-8371-7961-0, MWS/). Greenwood.

Mohan, Rakesh. The Effects of Population Growth, of the Pattern of Demand, & of Technology on the Process of Urbanization: An Application to India. LC 82-8600. (World Bank Staff Working Papers: No. 520). (Orig.). 1982. pap. 3.00 (ISBN 0-8213-0008-3). World Bank.

--The People of Bogota: Who They Are, What They Earn, Where They Live. (Working Paper: No. 390). 153p. 1980. 5.00 (ISBN 0-686-36228-4, WP-0390). World Bank.

Mohan, Rakesh & Wagner, M. Wilhelm. Measuring Urban Malnutrition & Poverty: A Case Study of Bogota & Cali, Colombia. (Working Paper: No. 447). 80p. 1981. 5.00 (ISBN 0-686-36191-1, WP-0447). World Bank.

Mohan, Robert P. Philosophy of History. 1970. pap. text ed. 4.95 o.p. (ISBN 0-02-821250-9). Glencoe.

Mohan, Sarala J., ed. Gujarati Short Stories. (Vikas Library of Modern Indian Writing: No. 26). 144p. 1982. text ed. 20.00x (ISBN 0-7069-1962-9, Pub. by Vikas India). Advent NY.

Mohanty, J. N., jt. auth. see Shahan, Robert W.

Mohanty, Jagganath. Indian Education in the Emerging Society. 205p. 1982. 24.95x (ISBN 0-940500-52-3, Pub. by Sterling India). Asia Bk Corp.

Mohanty, Sashi B. Electron Microscopy for Biologists. (Illus.). 352p. 1982. 39.75x (ISBN 0-398-04738-3). C C Thomas.

Mohapatra, R. P. Udayagiri & Khandagiri Caves. (Illus.). 270p. 1981. text ed. 88.75x (ISBN 0-391-02263-6, Pub. by Concept India). Humanities.

Mohapatra, Ram N., jt. auth. see Regier, Mary H.

Mohilla, R. & Ferencz, B. Chemical Process Dynamics. (Fundamental Studies in Engineering: Vol. 4). 1982. 64.00 (ISBN 0-444-99730-X). Elsevier.

Mohl, Raymond, jt. auth. see Cohen, Ronald.

Mohle, K., jt. auth. see Meinck, F.

Mohlenbrock, Robert H. Where Have All the Wildflowers Gone? Region-by-Region Guide to Threatened & Endangered U. S. Wildflowers. (Illus.). 256p. 1983. 15.95 (ISBN 0-02-585450-X). Macmillan.

Mohler, Rudy. Practical Welding Technology. 250p. 1983. 27.50 (ISBN 0-8311-1143-7). Indus Pr.

Mohn, G., jt. ed. see Van Hof, M. W.

Mohn, Peter. Silver Eagles. LC 77-27728. (Performers in Uniform Ser.). (Illus.). 48p. (gr. 4-8). 1978. PLB 10.00 (ISBN 0-516-01953-8). Childrens.

Mohn, Peter B. Bicycle Touring. LC 75-16089. (Back to Nature Ser.). (gr. 4). 1975. PLB 7.95 (ISBN 0-913940-28-3). Crestwood Hse.

--Cross-Country Skiing. LC 75-40597. (Back to Nature Ser.). (gr. 4). 1975. PLB 7.95 (ISBN 0-913940-37-2). Crestwood Hse.

--Hiking. LC 75-16088. (Back to Nature Ser.). (gr. 4). 1975. PLB 7.95 (ISBN 0-913940-27-5). Crestwood Hse.

--Hot Air Ballooning. LC 75-16086. (Back to Nature Ser.). (gr. 4). 1975. PLB 7.95 (ISBN 0-913940-30-5). Crestwood Hse.

--Sailing. LC 75-40598. (Back to Nature Ser.). (gr. 4). 1975. PLB 7.95 (ISBN 0-913940-38-0). Crestwood Hse.

--Scuba Diving & Snorkeling. LC 75-16090. (Back to Nature Ser.). (gr. 4). 1975. PLB 7.95 (ISBN 0-913940-29-1). Crestwood Hse.

--Trailbiking. LC 75-16087. (Back to Nature Ser.). (gr. 4). 1975. PLB 7.95 (ISBN 0-913940-26-7). Crestwood Hse.

--Whitewater Challenge. LC 75-16085. (Back to Nature Ser.). (gr. 4). 1975. PLB 7.95 (ISBN 0-913940-25-9). Crestwood Hse.

Moholt, Ray, jt. auth. see Landis, Michael.

Moholy-Nagy, Sibyl. Experiment in Totality. 1969. 12.00x o.p. (ISBN 0-262-13053-X); pap. 5.95 (ISBN 0-262-63042-7). MIT Pr.

Mohr, C. Plant Life of Alabama. (Illus.). 1969. Repr. of 1901 ed. 32.00 (ISBN 3-7682-0622-X). Lubrecht & Cramer.

Mohr, Charles E. The World of the Bat. LC 76-7355. (Living World Ser.). (Illus.). 1976. 11.49i (ISBN 0-397-00800-7). Har-Row.

Mohr, Charles E. & Poulson, T. Life of the Cave. (Our Living World of Nature Ser.). 1966. 14.95 (ISBN 0-07-042651-1, P&RB); by subscription 12.95 (ISBN 0-07-046003-5); instr.'s manual o.p. 2.95 (ISBN 0-07-042657-0). McGraw.

Mohr, Lillian H. Frances Perkins: That Woman in FDR's Cabinet! LC 78-23597. (Illus.). 1979. 18.00 (ISBN 0-88427-019-X). North River.

Mohr, Nicholasa. In Nueva York. (YA) 1979. pap. 1.50 (ISBN 0-440-94092-3, LFL). Dell.

Mohr, Ulrich & Sellwood, A. V. Sea Raider Atlantis. (Illus.). 296p. 1980. pap. 2.25 o.p. (ISBN 0-523-40961-3). Pinnacle Bks.

Mohraz, Judy J. The Separate Problem: Case Studies of Black Education in the North, 1900-1930. LC 78-4026. (Contributions in Afro-American & African Studies: No. 42). xvi, 165p. 1979. lib. bdg. 25.00 (ISBN 0-313-20411-X, MSP/). Greenwood.

Mohrenschildt, Dimitri Von, ed. Russian Revolution of 1917: Contemporary Accounts. 1971. 19.95x (ISBN 0-19-501420-0). Oxford U Pr.

Mohri, Hideo, jt. ed. see Sakai, Hikoichi.

Mohrig, J. & Neckers, D. Laboratory Experiments in Organic Chemistry. 2nd ed. 1979. text ed. 17.95 (ISBN 0-442-25468-7); instructor's manual 2.00x (ISBN 0-442-25469-5). Van Nos Reinhold.

Mohrlang, Roger. Higi Phonology. (Language Data, African Ser.: No. 2). 106p. 1972. pap. 3.50x (ISBN 0-88312-602-8); microfiche 2.25x (ISBN 0-88312-702-4). Summer Inst Ling.

Mohrman, David E., jt. auth. see Heller, Lois J.

Mohsenin, N. N. Physical Properties of Plant & Animal Materials. 758p. 1970. 112.00x (ISBN 0-677-02300-6). Gordon.

Mohsenin, Nuri N. Physical Properties of Food & Agricultural Materials: A Teachin Manual. 157p. 1981. 25.00 (ISBN 0-677-05630-3). Gordon.

Moidel, Harriet C., et al. Nursing Care of the Patient with Medical-Surgical Disorders. 2nd ed. 1976. 29.95 o.p. (ISBN 0-07-042654-4, HP). McGraw.

Moilliet. Waterproofing & Water-Repellency. 1963. 30.80 (ISBN 0-444-40398-1). Elsevier.

Moine, Donald J. Hypnotic Sales: A Pragmatic Guide to a More Effective Sales Technique. (Orig.). 1983. 19.95 (ISBN 0-686-38216-1); pap. 12.95 (ISBN 0-686-38217-X). Metamorphous Pr.

Moinuddin, Sheikh. The Book of Sufi Healing. (Illus.). 256p. (Orig.). 1983. pap. 8.95 (ISBN 0-89281-043-2). Inner Tradit.

Moir, Alfred. Caravaggio. (Library of Great Painters). (Illus.). 168p. 1982. 40.00 (ISBN 0-8109-0757-7). Abrams.

Moir, Donald D. Obstetric Anaesthesia & Analgesia. (Illus.). 1976. text ed. 49.95 (ISBN 0-02-858600-X, Pub. by Bailliere-Tindall). Saunders.

Moir, John S. A History of Biblical Studies in Canada: A Sense of Proportion. LC 82-5979. (Society of Biblical Literature: Biblical Scholarship in North America Ser.). 132p. 1982. pap. 17.95 (ISBN 0-89130-581-5, 06 11 07). Scholars Pr CA.

Moir, May A. The Garden Watcher. LC 82-24728. (Illus.). 96p. 1983. pap. text ed. 12.00x (ISBN 0-8248-0789-8). UH Pr.

Moir, May A., jt. auth. see Moir, W. W.

Moir, W. W. & Moir, May A. Creating Oncidiinae Intergenerics. LC 81-16182. (Illus.). 120p. 1982. pap. text ed. 12.00x (ISBN 0-8248-0784-7). UH Pr.

--Laeliinae Intergenerics. LC 82-4887. (Illus.). 61p. 1982. pap. text ed. 12.00x (ISBN 0-8248-0814-2). UH Pr.

Moir, W. W., et al. Breeding Variegata Oncidiums. LC 80-15946. (Illus.). 136p. 1980. pap. text ed. 12.00x (ISBN 0-8248-0712-X). UH Pr.

Moirashine. Long Term Care of the Aging. LC 82-62399. 176p. 1982. pap. 14.50 (ISBN 0-943432-00-6). Slack Inc.

Moise, Edwin E. Land Reform in China & North Vietnam: Consolidating the Revolution at the Village Level. LC 82-15900. 330p. 1983. 18.95x (ISBN 0-8078-1547-0). U of NC Pr.

Moiser, Jeremy, jt. auth. see Hirschberger, Johannes.

Moiser, Jeremy, tr. see Delumeau, Jean.

Moivre, Abraham De see De Moivre, Abraham.

Mojares, Resil B. The Origins & Rise of the Filipino Novel: A Generic Study of the Filipino Novel until 1940. 474p. 1983. text ed. 16.50x (ISBN 0-8248-0733-2, Pub. by U of Phillipines Pr); pap. text ed. 13.50x (ISBN 0-8248-0737-5). UH Pr.

Mojekwu, Christopher C. African Society, Culture & Politics. 1977. pap. text ed. 11.00 (ISBN 0-8191-0186-9). U Pr of Amer.

Mojena, Richard, jt. auth. see Ageloff, Roy.

Mojumdar, Kanchanmoy. Nepal & the Indian Nationalist Movement. LC 76-902010. 1975. 6.50x o.p. (ISBN 0-88386-703-6). South Asia Bks.

Mokgatle, Naboth. The Autobiography of an Unknown South African. LC 79-138285. (Perspectives on Southern Africa: No. 1). 1971. 22.50x (ISBN 0-520-01845-1); pap. 3.95 (ISBN 0-520-02903-8). U of Cal Pr.

Mokherjee, Sal, jt. auth. see Allen, Michael.

Mokri, M. Kurdish-Arabic Dictionary: Al-Hadiyati 'l-Hamidiyah. 1975. 28.00x (ISBN 0-86685-126-7). Intl Bk Ctr.

Mokrzycki, E. Philosophy of Science & Sociology: From the Methodological Doctrine to Research Practice. (International Library of Sociology). 180p. 1983. price not set (ISBN 0-7100-9444-2). Routledge & Kegan.

Mol, Hans. The Fixed & the Fickle: Religion & Identity in New Zealand. (Religion & Identity-Social Scientific Studies in Religion: No. 1). 96p. 1982. text ed. 8.75x (ISBN 0-88920-113-7, Pub. by Wilfrid Laurier U Pr England). Humanities.

--Meaning & Place: An Introduction to the Social Scientific Study of Religion. (Orig.). 1983. pap. 6.95 (ISBN 0-8298-0638-5). Pilgrim NY.

Molander, Earl A. Responsive Capitalism: Case Studies in Corporate Social Conduct. (Management Ser.). (Illus.). 432p. 1980. pap. text ed. 13.95x (ISBN 0-07-042658-9, C); instr's manual 13.95 (ISBN 0-07-042659-7). McGraw.

Molarsky, Osmond. A Different Ball Game. LC 78-23793. (Illus.). (gr. 3-7). 1979. 5.95 o.p. (ISBN 0-698-20475-1, Coward). Putnam Pub Group.

--Scrappy. LC 82-45991. 128p. (gr. 4 up). 1983. PLB 8.95 (ISBN 0-396-08120-7). Dodd.

Moldafsky, Annie. The New Good Buy Book: Illinois, Wisconsin, Ohio, Michigan & Indiana. LC 76-3129. 224p. 1977. pap. 3.95 o.p. (ISBN 0-8040-0705-5). Swallow.

Moldavy, Albert & Fabian, Erika. Photographing Rome. (Amphoto Travel Guide Ser.). Orig. Title: Photographer's Guide to Rome. (Illus.). 1980. pap. 5.95 (ISBN 0-8174-2126-2, Amphoto). Watson-Guptill.

Moldea, Dan E. The Hunting of Cain: A True Story of Money, Greed & Fratricide. LC 82-73032. 320p. 1983. 12.95 (ISBN 0-689-11357-9). Atheneum.

Moldenhauer, Hans & Irvine, Demar, eds. Anton Von Webern: Perspectives. LC 77-9523. (Music Reprint Ser., 1978). (Illus.). 1978. Repr. of 1966 ed. lib. bdg. 25.00 (ISBN 0-306-77518-2). Da Capo.

Moldroski, Don, illus. The Saturday Evening Post I Can Cook Children's Cookbook. LC 80-67055. (Illus.). 96p. (gr. 1 up). 1980. 7.95 (ISBN 0-89387-049-8, Co-Pub by Sat Eve Post). Curtis Pub Co.

Moldrup, William, jt. auth. see Frates, Jeffrey.

Moldvay, Albert & Fabian, Erika. Photographing Amsterdam. (Amphoto Travel Guide Ser.). Orig. Title: Photographer's Guide to Amsterdam. (Illus.). 1980. pap. 5.95 (ISBN 0-8174-2127-0, Amphoto). Watson-Guptill.

--Photographing London. (Amphoto Travel Guide Ser.). (Illus.). 1980. pap. 5.95 o.p. (ISBN 0-8174-2125-4, Amphoto). Watson-Guptill.

--Photographing Mexico City & Acapulco. (Amphoto Travel Guide Ser.). Orig. Title: Photographer's Guide to Mexico City & Alcapulco. (Illus.). 1980. pap. 5.95 (ISBN 0-8174-2122-X, Amphoto). Watson-Guptill.

--Photographing New York City. (Amphoto Travel Guide Ser.). Orig. Title: Photographer's Guide to New York. (Illus.). 1980. pap. 5.95 (ISBN 0-8174-2123-8, Amphoto). Watson-Guptill.

--Photographing Paris. (Amphoto Travel Guide Ser.). Orig. Title: Photographer's Guide to Paris. (Illus.). 1980. pap. 5.95 (ISBN 0-8174-2124-6, Amphoto). Watson-Guptill.

Mole, John. Feeding the Lake. 1981. 11.50 (ISBN 0-436-28040-X, Pub by Secker & Warburg). David & Charles.

Mole, T. & Jeffery, E. A. Organoaluminum Compounds. LC 76-180005. 1973. 74.50 (ISBN 0-444-40911-4). Elsevier.

Molen, H. J. Van Der see Van Der Molen, H. J. & Klopper, A.

Molenda, M., jt. auth. see Heinich, R.

Moler, C., jt. auth. see Forsythe, George E.

Molesworth. The Cuckoo Clock. (Childrens Illustrated Classics Ser). (Illus.). 175p. 1974. Repr. of 1954 ed. 9.00x o.p. (ISBN 0-460-05027-3, Pub. by J. M. Dent England). Biblio Dist.

Molesworth, Mary L. Four Winds Farm, Repr. Of 1887 Ed. Bd. with The Children of the Castle. Repr. of 1890 ed. LC 75-32192. (Classics of Children's Literature, 1621-1932: Vol. 54). (Illus.). 1976. PLB 38.00 o.s.i. (ISBN 0-8240-2303-X). Garland Pub.

Moleta, Vincent. From St. Francis to Giotto. 1983. 10.00 (ISBN 0-8199-0853-3). Franciscan Herald.

Moley, Raymond. After Seven Years. LC 71-168390. (FDR & the Era of the New Deal Ser.). 446p. 1972. Repr. of 1939 ed. lib. bdg. 55.00 (ISBN 0-306-70327-0). Da Capo.

--The Hays Office. LC 73-160241. (Moving Pictures Ser). 266p. 1971. Repr. of 1945 ed. lib. bdg. 16.95x (ISBN 0-89198-042-3). Ozer.

--Tribunes of the People. 1932. 34.50x (ISBN 0-685-69844-0). Elliots Bks.

Molher, Edmond. Sur l'Amelioration du Sort des Travailleurs. (Conditions of the 19th Century French Working Class Ser.). 129p. 1974. Repr. of 1849 ed. lib. bdg. 42.00x o.p. (ISBN 0-8287-0630-1, 1073). Clearwater Pub.

Molian, S. Mechanism Design: An Introductory Text. LC 81-15552. 200p. 1982. 32.50 (ISBN 0-521-23193-0); pap. 11.95 (ISBN 0-521-29863-6). Cambridge U Pr.

Moliere. Eight Plays. Bishop, Morris, tr. 1950. pap. 3.25 (ISBN 0-686-38909-3, Mod LibC). Modern Lib.

Moliere, Jean. Tartuffe & Other Plays: Ridiculous Precieuses, School for Husbands, School for Wives, Critique for the School for Wives, Versailles Impromptu, Don Juan. Frame, Donald M., tr. 1967. pap. 2.95 (ISBN 0-451-51566-8, CE1566, Sig Classics). NAL.

Moliere, Jean B. Misanthrope & Other Plays. Frame, Donald M., tr. (Orig.). 1968. pap. 3.50 (ISBN 0-451-51721-0, CE1721, Sig Classics). NAL.

Moliere, Jean Baptiste. The Misanthrope & Tartuffe. Wilbur, Richard, tr. Bd. with Tartuffe. LC 65-29707. (Illus.). 326p. 1965. pap. 5.95 (ISBN 0-15-660517-1, Harv). HarBraceJ.

Molin, Sven E. & Goodefellowe, Robin. Dion Boucicault, the Shaughraun, Vol. 1. 11.00x (ISBN 0-912262-62-1); pap. 3.95x (ISBN 0-912262-63-X). Proscenium.

Molina, E. C. Poisson's Exponential Binomial Limit. 56p. 1973. Repr. of 1942 ed. pap. 6.50 (ISBN 0-88275-107-7). Krieger.

Molina, S. P., tr. see Dobbins, G. S.

Molina, Sara P., tr. see Edge, Findley B.

Molinari, A. From Nuclei to Particles. Date not set. 106.50 (ISBN 0-444-86158-0). Elsevier.

Molinaro, Ursule. Positions with White Roses. 104p. 1983. 9.95 (ISBN 0-914232-58-4); ltd. ed. 25.00x (ISBN 0-914232-59-2). Treacle.

Molinaro, Ursule, tr. see Best, Otto F.

Molinatti, G. M. Microprolactinoma. (International Congress Ser.: No. 584). Date not set. 57.50 (ISBN 0-444-90264-3). Elsevier.

Moline, Karen, jt. auth. see Teti, Frank.

Moline, Mary. Norman Rockwell Encyclopedia. (Illus.). 320p. pap. 9.95 (ISBN 0-89387-070-6). Curtis Pub Co.

--Norman Rockwell Encyclopedia: A Chronological Catalog of the Artist's Work 1910-1978. LC 79-90498. (Illus.). 320p. 1979. 15.95 (ISBN 0-89387-032-3, Co-Pub. by Sat Eve Post). Curtis Pub Co.

Molineu, Harold. Multinational Corporations & International Investment in Latin America: A Selected Bibliography. LC 77-620052. (Papers in International Studies: Latin America: No. 3). 1977. pap. 9.00x (ISBN 0-89680-068-7, Ohio U Ctr Intl). Ohio U Pr.

Molinie, M. D. The Struggle of Jacob. LC 77-78216. Orig. Title: Le Combat De Jacob. 136p. 1977. pap. 1.95 o.p. (ISBN 0-8091-2036-4, Deus). Paulist Pr.

Molinos, Michael. The Spiritual Guide. Edwards, Gene, ed. 110p. pap. 4.95 (ISBN 0-940232-08-1). Christian Bks.

Molinsky, Steven J. & Blass, Bill. Side by Side: English Grammar Through Guided Conversations Bk. II. 1980. pap. text ed. 6.95 (ISBN 0-13-809855-7). P-H.

Molinsky, Steven J. & Bliss, Bill. Line by Line: Reading English Through Grammar Stories, Bk. I. (Illus.). 208p. 1983. pap. text ed. 6.95 (ISBN 0-13-537076-0). P-H.

--Side by Side: English Grammar Through Guided Conversation 1A. 128p. 1983. pap. text ed. 3.95 (ISBN 0-13-809715-1); wkbk. 2.50 (ISBN 0-13-809525-6). P-H.

--Side by Side: English Grammar Through Guided Conversation 1B. 128p. 1983. pap. text ed. 3.95 (ISBN 0-13-809723-2); wkbk. 2.50 (ISBN 0-13-809582-5). P-H.

--Side by Side: English Grammar Through Guided Conversations 2A. 128p. 1983. pap. text ed. 3.95 (ISBN 0-13-809772-0); wkbk. 2.50 (ISBN 0-13-809640-6). P-H.

--Side by Side: English Grammar Through Guided Conversation 2B. 128p. 1983. pap. text ed. 3.95 (ISBN 0-13-809798-4); pap. 2.50 wkbk. (ISBN 0-13-809699-6). P-H.

Molk, Jules, jt. auth. see Tannery, Jules.

Moll, H., jt. auth. see Cummings, J. T.

Moll, Helmut. Atlas of Pediatric Diseases. Kleindienst, Walter, tr. LC 74-21016. (Illus.). 1976. text ed. 18.00 (ISBN 0-7216-6430-X). Saunders.

Moll, Lloyd & Yoder, Don. Am Schwarze Baer: Bd. with Langguth's Pennsylvania German Pioneers from the County of Wertheim. (Pennsylvania German Folklore Society Ser.: Vol. 12). Repr. of 1947 ed. 20.00 o.p. (ISBN 0-911122-20-6). Penn German Soc.

Mollan, Renee. Yes They Can! A Handbook for Effectively Parenting the Handicapped. (Illus.). 104p. 1981. Repr. 11.95. Reality Prods.

Molland, Einar. Church Life in Norway: 1800-1950. Harris, Kaasa, tr. LC 78-2711. 1978. Repr. of 1957 ed. lib. bdg. 16.00x (ISBN 0-313-20342-3, MOCL). Greenwood.

Mollat, Michel, jt. auth. see Devisse, Jean.

Mollenhauer, Peter. Friedrich Nicolais Satiren: Ein Beitrag Zur Kulturgeschichte Des 18. Jahrhunderts. (German Language & Literature Monographs: No. 2). viii, 267p. 1977. 28.00 (ISBN 90-272-4006-X). Benjamins North Am.

Mollenhoff, Clark R. Investigative Reporting. 1980. pap. text ed. 14.95x (ISBN 0-02-381870-0). Macmillan.

Mollenkott, Virginia R. The Divine Feminine: The Biblical Imagery of God As Female. 144p. 1983. 12.95 (ISBN 0-8245-0565-4). Crossroad NY.

Mollenkott, Virginia R., jt. auth. see Scanzoni, Letha.

Moller, Aage R. Auditory Physiology. 279p. 1982. 34.50 (ISBN 0-12-503450-4). Acad Pr.

Moller, Christine, jt. auth. see Furntratt, Ernst.

Moller, Hermann. Vergleichendes Indogermanisch-Semitisches Worterbuch. 316p. 1982. Repr. of 1911 ed. lib. bdg. 150.00 (ISBN 0-89984-810-9). Century Bookbindery.

Moller, K. D. & Rothschild, W. G. Far-Infrared Spectroscopy. LC 70-118624. (Wiley Ser. in Pure & Applied Optics). 1971. 74.95 o.p. (ISBN 0-471-61313-4, Pub. by Wiley-Interscience). Wiley.

Moller, Mary L., jt. ed. see Hefferren, John J.

Molli, Jeanne, jt. auth. see Cassini, Igor.

Mollison, James & Murray, Laura. The Australian National Gallery: An Introduction. (Illus.). 1983. 49.95 (ISBN 0-500-99300-9). Thames Hudson.

Mollman, H. Introduction to the Theory of Thin Shells. 180p. 1982. 41.00x (ISBN 0-471-28056-9, Pub. by Wiley-Interscience). Wiley.

Mollo, Andrew, jt. auth. see Buss, Philip H.

Mollo, John. Uniforms of the Seven Years War, 1756-1763. LC 77-4912. (Color Guides Ser.). 1977. 7.95 o.p. (ISBN 0-88254-444-6). Hippocrene Bks.

Mollo, Terry, ed. U. S. Book Publishing Yearbook & Directory: 1980-1981. LC 79-649219. (Communications Library). 225p. 1980. pap. text ed. 45.00 (ISBN 0-914236-63-6). Knowledge Indus.

Mollo, Victor. Bridge a la Carte. 144p. 1983. 16.95 (ISBN 0-7207-1385-4, Pub by Michael Joseph). Merrimack Bk Serv.

Mollon, J. D., jt. ed. see Barlow, H. B.

Mollot. Le Contrat d'Apprentissage Explique aux Maitres et aux Apprentis. (Conditions of the 19th Century French Working Class Ser.). 108p. (Fr.). 1974. Repr. of 1847 ed. lib. bdg. 37.50 o.p. (ISBN 0-8287-0631-X, 1145). Clearwater Pub.

Molloy, Al. Contemporary Squash. LC 77-91160. 1978. 6.95 o.p. (ISBN 0-8092-7551-1); pap. 3.50 o.p. (ISBN 0-8092-7591-0). Contemp Bks.

Molloy, J., jt. ed. see Minogue, M.

Molloy, Julia S. Trainable Children. rev. ed. LC 70-155017. (John Day Bk.). 256p. 1972. text ed. 21.10i (ISBN 0-381-97028-0, A82402); pap. 13.95 o.p. (ISBN 0-381-97027-2, A82401, JD-T). T y Crowell.

Molloy, Julia S. & Matkin, A. M. Your Developmentally Retarded Child Can Communicate: A Guide for Parents & Teachers in Speech, Languages, & Nonverbal Communication. (John Day Bk.). 1975. 12.45xi (ISBN 0-381-97102-3). T Y Crowell.

Molloy, M. J. Three Plays. 10.00x (ISBN 0-912262-30-3). Proscenium.

Molnar, Agnes, illus. Jack & the Beanstalk. LC 78-12524. (A Goodnight Bk.). (Illus.). (ps-1). 1979. 1.75 o.p. (ISBN 0-394-84101-8). Knopf.

Molnar, Ferenc A. On the History of Word-Final Vowels in the Permian Languages. (Studia Uralo-Altaica Ser.). 87p. 1974. pap. 12.00 (ISBN 0-686-31504-9, 5). Benjamins North Am.

Molnar, John. Nomographs: What They Are & How to Use Them. LC 81-67511. 100p. 1981. text ed. 24.75 (ISBN 0-250-40419-2). Ann Arbor Science.

Molnar, Joseph J. & Clonts, Howard A., eds. Transferring Food Production Technology to Developing Nations: Economic & Social Dimensions. (Replica Edition Ser.). 174p. 1983. softcover 19.50x (ISBN 0-86531-957-X). Westview.

Molnar, Paul J. Quotes & Notes to Share. Goebel, Patrice, ed. (Orig.). 1982. pap. 4.95 (ISBN 0-938736-06-X). Life Enrich.

Molnar, Stephen. Human Variation: Races, Types & Ethnic Groups. 2nd ed. (Illus.). 304p. 1983. pap. 15.95 (ISBN 0-13-447664-6, Busn). P-H.

Molnar, Thomas. Africa: A Political Travelogue. LC 65-16312. (Illus.). 1965. 7.50 (ISBN 0-8303-0030-9). Fleet.

--Authority & Its Enemies. LC 76-8506. 1976. 7.95 o.p. (ISBN 0-87000-340-2, Arlington Hse). Crown.

Molner, Stephen. Races, Types & Ethnic Groups: The Problem of Human Variation. LC 74-23935. (Illus.). 224p. 1975. pap. 12.95 (ISBN 0-13-750240-0). P-H.

Moloff, Ronald L. & Stein, Stephen D. Realities of Dental Therapy. 1982. text ed. 78.00 (ISBN 0-931386-42-X). Quint Pub Co.

Moloney, James C. Understanding the Japanese Mind. LC 68-23316. 1968. Repr. of 1954 ed. lib. bdg. 17.50x (ISBN 0-8371-0172-7, MOJM). Greenwood.

Moloney, Kathleen & McCarthy, Shawna, eds. Isaac Asimov's Wonders of the World. 288p. 1982. 12.95 (ISBN 0-385-27776-8). Davis Pubns.

Moloney, Thomas W., jt. ed. see Blendon, Robert J.

Molony, John N. The Emergence of Political Catholicism in Italy: Partito Popolare 1919-1926. 225p. 1977. 17.50x o.p. (ISBN 0-87471-943-7). Rowman.

Molotch, Harvey L. Managed Integration: Dilemmas of Doing Good in the City. LC 74-142049. 280p. 1973. 27.50x (ISBN 0-520-01889-3). U of Cal Pr.

Molow, Doree, jt. auth. see Molow, L. Paul.

Molow, L. Paul & Molow, Doree. Your Fantastic Mind. 3.95 o.p. (ISBN 0-533-01679-7). Vantage.

Moltgen. Line Commutated Thyristor Converters. 1972. 38.00 (ISBN 0-471-25909-8, Wiley Heyden). Wiley.

Moltmann, Jurgen. The Theology of Hope. LC 67-21550. 1976. pap. 8.61xi (ISBN 0-06-065900-9, RD127, HarpR). Har-Row.

Moltmann, Jurgen, jt. auth. see Kung, Hans.

Moltmann, Jurgen, jt. auth. see Moltmann-Wendel, Elisabeth.

Moltmann, Jurgen, jt. ed. see Kung, Hans.

Moltmann-Wendel, Elisabeth. The Women Around Jesus. LC 82-72478. 160p. 1982. pap. 7.95 (ISBN 0-8245-0535-2). Crossroad NY.

Moltmann-Wendel, Elisabeth & Moltmann, Jurgen. Humanity in God. (Illus.). 160p. 1983. 13.95 (ISBN 0-8298-0662-8); pap. 7.95 (ISBN 0-8298-0670-9). Pilgrim NY.

Molton, Warren L. Friends, Partners, & Lovers. 1979. pap. 6.95 (ISBN 0-8170-0815-2). Judson.

Molyneux, Maxine. State Policies & the Position of Women Workers in the People's Democratic Republic of Yemen, 1967-77. International Labour Office, ed. (Women, Work & Development Ser.: No. 3). viii, 87p. (Orig.). 1982. pap. 10.00 (ISBN 92-2-103144-6). Intl Labour Office.

Molz, R. Kathleen. Federal Policy & Library Support. LC 76-17102. 1976. 17.50x (ISBN 0-262-13120-X). MIT Pr.

Molz, R. Kathleen, jt. ed. see Conant, Ralph W.

Momaday. American Indian Authors. Adams, William, ed. (Multi-Ethnic Literature Ser.). (gr. 9-12). 1976. pap. text ed. 5.32 (ISBN 0-395-24040-9); instr's. guide 6.08 (ISBN 0-395-24042-5). HM.

Momaday, N. Scott. The Gourd Dancer. LC 75-30338. (Illus.). 96p. (YA) 1976. 9.95 (ISBN 0-06-012982-4, HarpT); pap. 2.95i (ISBN 0-06-012983-2, TD-250, HarpT). Har-Row.

--The Names. LC 75-138749. (Illus.). 1977. pap. 4.95i o.p. (ISBN 0-06-090582-4, CN 582, CN). Har-Row.

Momaday, N. Scott, intro. by. With Eagle Glance: American Indian Photographic Images, 1868-1931. (Illus.). 63p. 1982. pap. 6.95 (ISBN 0-934490-39-2). Mus Am Ind.

Momen, Moojan, ed. Studies in Babi & Baha'i History, Vol. 1. (Illus.). 1983. text ed. 25.00 (ISBN 0-933770-16-2). Kalimat.

Momeni, Jamshid A., ed. The Population of Iran: A Selection of Readings. 1977. pap. text ed. 6.00x o.p. (ISBN 0-8248-0565-8, Eastwest Ctr). UH Pr.

Moment, D., jt. auth. see Zaleznik, Abraham.

Moment, Gairdner B. & Habermann, Helen M. Biology: A Full Spectrum. (Illus.). 768p. 1973. 15.95x o.p. (ISBN 0-19-502292-0). Oxford U Pr.

Momeny, Gayle, jt. auth. see Mulhearn, John.

Momigliano, Arnaldo. Claudius, the Emperor & His Achievement. rev. ed. Hogarth, W. D., tr. from Ital. LC 80-26158. xv, 143p. 1981. Repr. of 1961 ed. lib. bdg. 19.25x (ISBN 0-313-20813-1, MOCE). Greenwood.

Momose, K. J. Functional Approach to the Interpretation of the Skull in Infancy & Childhood. LC 70-111805. (Illus.). 250p. 1983. 27.50 (ISBN 0-87527-225-8). Green.

Mon Tricot. Knitting Dictionary: Stitches & Patterns. 3rd ed. (Illus.). 210p. (YA) 1975. pap. 2.50 o.p. (ISBN 0-517-52206-3). Crown.

Mon Tricot Editors. Knit & Crochet, Vol. 1. (Mon Tricot Ser.). 1976. pap. 7.95 o.p. (ISBN 0-517-52537-2). Crown.

--Knit & Crochet, Vol. 2. (Mon Tricot Ser.). 1976. pap. 1.98 o.p. (ISBN 0-517-52800-2). Crown.

Mon Tricot Staff. Two-Hundred Fifty Patterns to Knit & Crochet. (Illus.). 1977. pap. 2.50 o.p. (ISBN 0-517-53065-1). Crown.

Monaco, Frank. They Dwell in Monasteries. (Illus.). 80p. (Orig.). 1982. pap. 7.95 (ISBN 0-8164-2409-8). Seabury.

Monaco, James. Alain Resnais. (Illus.). 1979. 19.95 (ISBN 0-19-520037-3). Oxford U Pr.

--Alain Resnais. (Illus.). 1979. pap. 8.95 (ISBN 0-19-520038-1, GB540, GB). Oxford U Pr.

--American Film Now: The People, the Power, the Money, the Movies. (Illus.). 1979. 22.50x (ISBN 0-19-502570-9). Oxford U Pr.

--Celebrity: The Media As Image Maker. 1978. pap. 4.95 o.s.i. (ISBN 0-440-50991-2, Delta). Dell.

--The French Revolutionary Calendar. (Illus.). 32p. 1982. pap. 5.95 (ISBN 0-918432-43-X). NY Zoetrope.

--How to Read a Film: The Art, Technology, Language, History, & Theory of Film & Media. rev. ed. (Illus.). 1981. 27.50x (ISBN 0-19-502802-3); pap. 12.95 (ISBN 0-19-502806-6). Oxford U Pr.

--Media Culture: TV, Radio, Records, Magazines, Newspaper, & Movies. 1978. pap. 4.95 o.s.i. (ISBN 0-440-59305-0, Delta). Dell.

--Media: The Compleat Guide. (Illus.). 300p. 1982. 24.95 (ISBN 0-918432-40-5); pap. 9.95 (ISBN 0-918432-41-3). NY Zoetrope.

--The New Wave: Truffaut, Godard, Chabrol, Rohmer, Rivette. LC 75-38099. 1977. pap. 8.95 (ISBN 0-19-502246-7, GB516, GB). Oxford U Pr.

Monaco, Paul. Modern European Culture & Consciousness, Eighteen Seventy through Nineteen Seventy: Interdisciplinary Perspectives in Social History. LC 82-10487. 182p. 1983. 30.50 (ISBN 0-87395-702-4); pap. 8.95 (ISBN 0-87395-703-2). State U NY Pr.

Monaco, Paul, jt. ed. see Graff, Harvey J.

Monaco, Richard. The Final Quest. 416p. 1981. 13.95 (ISBN 0-399-12501-9). Putnam Pub Group.

--The Final Quest. 320p. 1983. pap. 2.75 (ISBN 0-425-05143-9). Berkley Pub.

Monagan, Charles. The Neurotic's Handbook. LC 81-69162. 160p. 1982. pap. 5.95 (ISBN 0-689-70635-9). Atheneum.

Monaghan, E. Jennifer. A Common Heritage: Noah Webster & His Blue-Back Speller. 277p. 1982. 22.50 (ISBN 0-208-01908-1, Archon). Shoe String.

Monaghan, Forbes J. Reflections on the Synoptic Gospels. LC 70-110595. 1970. 4.95 o.p. (ISBN 0-8189-0171-3). Alba.

Monaghan, James. The Man Who Elected Lincoln. LC 73-7310. (Illus.). 334p. 1973. Repr. of 1956 ed. lib. bdg. 17.50x (ISBN 0-8371-6920-8, MOMW). Greenwood.

Monahan, Clifford P. Rhode Island. LC 65-15072. 1965. pap. 2.95 o.p. (ISBN 0-8077-1827-0). Tchrs Coll.

Monahan, Gene. The Baseball Player's Guide to Sports Medicine. LC 82-83936. (Illus.). 144p. (Orig.). 1983. pap. 7.95 (ISBN 0-88011-104-6). Leisure Pr.

Monahan, John, ed. Who Is the Client? The Ethics of Psychological Intervention in the Criminal Justice System. LC 80-14101. 1980. 12.00x (ISBN 0-912704-58-6). Am Psychol.

Monahan, Patricia. Desert. (New Reference Library Ser.). PLB 11.96 (ISBN 0-382-06390-2). Silver.

Monahan, Peter J., ed. Comic Vision. (Patterns in Literary Art Ser.). 1971. text ed. 9.16 (ISBN 0-07-042681-3, W). McGraw.

Monahan, William G. & Hengst, Herbert R. Contemporary Educational Administration. 1982. text ed. 24.95x (ISBN 0-02-381930-8). Macmillan.

Monajem, Shohreh, tr. see Radley, Gail.

Monalbano, William D. & Hiaasen, Carl. Powder Burn. 1983. pap. 2.95 (ISBN 0-441-67573-5, Pub. by Charter Bks). Ace Bks.

Monas, Sidney, tr. see Dostoyevsky, Fedor.

Monas, Sidney, tr. see Zoshchenko, Mikhail.

Monat, Alan, jt. auth. see Lazarus, Richard S.

Moncrief & Jones. Elements of Physical Chemistry. 1976. 26.95 (ISBN 0-201-04897-3). A-W.

Moncrief & Popovich. CAPD Update: Continuous Ambulatory Peritoneal Dialysis, Vol. 1. LC 81-8260. (Modern Problems in Kidney Disease Ser.). 296p. 1981. 34.25x (ISBN 0-89352-134-5). Masson Pub.

Moncrieff, C. Scott, tr. see Proust, Marcel.

Moncrieff, R. W. Man-Made Fibers. 7th ed. 1000p. 1984. text ed. price not set. Butterworth.

--Man-Made Fibres. 6th ed. 1975. 103.00x (ISBN 0-87245-555-6). Textile Bk.

Moncrieffe, Silain. Guide to Scottish Tartans. (Illus.). 64p. 1982. pap. 3.50 (ISBN 0-85683-034-8, Pub by Shepheard-Walwyn England). Flatiron Book.

Moncur, Robert H., jt. auth. see Swieringa, Robert J.

Moncure, Jane. Kindness. LC 80-15286. (What Does the Bible Say? Ser.). (Illus.). 32p. 1980. 4.95 (ISBN 0-89565-167-X, 4929). Standard Pub.

--Short A & Long A Play a Game. LC 79-10300. (Illus.). 32p. (gr. k-3). 1981. lib. bdg. 8.65 (ISBN 0-516-06451-7). Childrens.

--Short E & Long E Play a Game. LC 79-10305. (Illus.). 32p. (gr. k-3). 1981. lib. bdg. 8.65 (ISBN 0-516-06452-5). Childrens.

--Short O & Long O Play a Game. LC 79-10304. (Illus.). 32p. (gr. k-3). 1981. lib. bdg. 8.65 (ISBN 0-516-06454-1). Childrens.

--Short U & Long U Play a Game. LC 79-10306. (Illus.). 32p. (gr. k-3). 1981. lib. bdg. 8.65 (ISBN 0-516-06455-X). Childrens.

Moncure, Jane B. The ABC's of Christmas. LC 82-9652. (Illus.). 32p. (gr. k-1). 1982. PLB 4.95 (ISBN 0-89565-233-1, 4950, Pub. by Childs World). Standard Pub.

--Caring. LC 80-27506. (Values to Live by Ser.). (Illus.). 32p. (ps-3). 1981. PLB 8.65 (ISBN 0-516-06521-1). Childrens.

--Caring. Buerger, Jane, ed. LC 80-14200. 32p. 1980. 4.95 (ISBN 0-89565-166-1, 4928). Standard Pub.

--Courage. LC 80-39515. (Values to Live by Ser.). (Illus.). 32p. (ps-3). 1981. PLB 8.65 (ISBN 0-516-06522-X). Childrens.

--The Gift of Christmas. LC 79-10279. (Bible Story Books). (Illus.). (ps-3). 1979. PLB 6.50 (ISBN 0-89565-083-5). Childs World.

--Happy Healthkins. LC 82-14794. (Healthkins Ser.). (gr. k-3). 1982. 9.25 (ISBN 0-516-06314-6). Childrens.

--Happy Healthkins. LC 82-14794. (Healthkins Ser.). (Illus.). (ps-2). 1982. lib. bdg. 6.95 (ISBN 0-89565-243-9). Childs World.

--The Healthkin Exercise Book. LC 82-14712. (Healthkins Ser.). (gr. k-3). 1982. 9.25 (ISBN 0-516-06312-X). Childrens.

--Healthkin Food Train. LC 82-14710. (Healthkins Ser.). (gr. k-3). 1982. 9.25 (ISBN 0-516-06311-1). Childrens.

--The Healthkin Food Train. LC 82-14710. (Healthkins Ser.). (Illus.). 32p. (ps-2). 1982. lib. bdg. 6.95 (ISBN 0-89565-240-4). Childs World.

--Healthkin Helpers. LC 82-14713. (Healthkins Ser.). (gr. k-3). 1982. 9.25 (ISBN 0-516-06313-8). Childrens.

--Healthkins Exercise! LC 82-14712. (Healthkins Ser.). (Illus.). 32p. (ps-2). 1982. lib. bdg. 6.05 (ISBN 0-89565-241-2). Childs World.

--Healthkins Help. LC 82-14713. (Healthkins Ser.). (Illus.). 32p. (ps-2). 1982. lib. bdg. 6.95 (ISBN 0-89565-242-0). Childs World.

--Hi, Word Bird! Word Birds for Early Birds. LC 80-15919. (Illus.). 32p. (ps-1). 1981. PLB 8.65 (ISBN 0-516-06551-3). Childrens.

--Hide-and-Seek Word Bird. LC 81-18068. (Word Birds for Early Birds Ser.). (ps-2). 1982. 8.65 (ISBN 0-516-06555-6). Childrens.

--Honesty. LC 80-39571. (Values to Live by Ser.). (Illus.). 32p. (ps-3). 1981. PLB 8.65 (ISBN 0-516-06523-8). Childrens.

--Honesty. rev. ed. LC 80-39571. (What Is It? Ser.). (Illus.). 32p. (gr. k-3). 1981. PLB 6.50 (ISBN 0-89565-203-X). Childs World.

--Honesty. Buerger, Jane, ed. LC 80-14298. (Illus.). 32p. 1980. 4.95 (ISBN 0-89565-163-7, 4925). Standard Pub.

--How Beautiful God's Gifts. Buerger, Jane, ed. LC 80-15434. (Illus.). 32p. 1980. 4.95 (ISBN 0-89565-172-6, 4923). Standard Pub.

--John's Choice. LC 82-7461. (Illus.). 32p. (gr. 3-4). 1982. lib. bdg. 4.95 (ISBN 0-686-83155-1). Dandelion Hse.

--Joy. LC 82-1145. (What Does the Bible Say? Ser.). (Illus.). 32p. (gr. k-3). 1982. PLB 4.95 (ISBN 0-89565-222-6, 4940, Pub. by Childs World). Standard Pub.

--Joy. (Values to Live by Ser.). (ps-3). 1982. 8.65 (ISBN 0-516-06545-9). Childrens.

--Joy. (What is It? Ser.). (Illus.). 32p. (gr. k-3). 1982. PLB 6.50 (ISBN 0-89565-224-2). Communication Skill.

--Kindness. LC 80-39535. (Values to Live by Ser.). (Illus.). 32p. (ps-3). 1981. PLB 8.65 (ISBN 0-516-06524-6). Childrens.

--The Little Boy Samuel. LC 79-12174. (Bible Story Bks.). (Illus.). (ps-3). PLB 6.50 (ISBN 0-89565-084-3). Childs World.

--The Look Book. LC 82-4517. (The Five Senses Ser.). (Illus.). 32p. (ps-3). 1982. PLB 9.25 (ISBN 0-516-03251-8). Childrens.

--Love. LC 80-27479. (Values to Live by Ser.). (Illus.). 32p. (ps-3). 1981. PLB 8.65 (ISBN 0-516-06525-4). Childrens.

--Magic Monsters Act the Alphabet. LC 79-23841. (Magic Monsters Ser.). (Illus.). 32p. (ps-3). 1980. 8.65g (ISBN 0-516-06460-6). Childrens.

--Magic Monsters Learn About Health. LC 79-24240. (Magic Monsters Ser.). (Illus.). 32p. (ps-3). 1980. PLB 8.65g (ISBN 0-516-06461-4). Childrens.

--Magic Monsters Learn About Manners. LC 79-24528. (Magic Monsters Ser.). (Illus.). 32p. (ps-3). 1980. PLB 8.65g (ISBN 0-516-06462-2). Childrens.

--My "B" Sound Box. LC 77-23588. (Sound Box Books). (Illus.). (ps-2). 1977. PLB 6.50 (ISBN 0-913778-92-3); pap. 2.75 (ISBN 0-89565-182-3). Childs World.

--A New Boy in Kindergarten. LC 76-15634. (A Values Ser.). (Illus.). (ps-3). 1976. 5.95 (ISBN 0-913778-51-6). Childs World.

--No, No Word Bird (Word Birds for Early Birds) LC 80-29491. (Illus.). 32p. (ps-1). 1981. PLB 8.65 (ISBN 0-516-06552-1). Childrens.

--Please. LC 82-9559. (What Does it Mean? Ser.). (Illus.). 32p. (gr. 1-2). 1982. pap. 4.95 (ISBN 0-89565-238-2, 4898, Pub. by Childs World). Standard Pub.

--Rhyme Me a Rhyme. LC 76-16538. (Illus.). (ps-3). 1976. 5.95 (ISBN 0-913778-42-7). Childs World.

--Riddle Me a Riddle. LC 76-30822. (Illus.). (ps-3). 1977. 5.95 (ISBN 0-913778-80-X). Childs World.

--Sounds All Around. LC 82-4516. (The Five Senses Ser.). (Illus.). 32p. (ps-3). 1982. PLB 9.25 (ISBN 0-516-03252-6). Childrens.

--Spring Is Here! LC 75-14202. (Illus.). (ps-2). 1975. 6.50 (ISBN 0-913778-11-7). Childs World.

--Summer Is Here! LC 75-12945. (Illus.). (ps-2). 1975. 6.50 (ISBN 0-913778-12-5). Childs World.

--A Tasting Party. LC 82-4411. (The Five Senses Ser.). (Illus.). 32p. (ps-3). 1982. PLB 9.25 (ISBN 0-516-03253-4). Childrens.

--Terry's Turn-Around. LC 82-7467. (Illus.). 1982. lib. bdg. 4.95 (ISBN 0-686-83153-5). Dandelion Hse.

--The Touch Book. LC 82-4154. (The Five Senses Ser.). (Illus.). (ps-3). 1982. PLB 9.25 (ISBN 0-516-03254-2). Childrens.

--Watch Out! Word Bird. LC 81-21570. (Word Birds for Early Birds Ser.). (ps-2). 1982. 8.65 (ISBN 0-516-06556-4). Childrens.

--What Does Word Bird See? LC 81-21594. (Word Birds for Early Birds Ser.). (ps-2). 1982. 8.65 (ISBN 0-516-06557-2). Childrens.

--What Your Nose Knows. LC 82-9464. (The Five Senses Ser.). (Illus.). 32p. (ps-3). 1982. PLB 9.25 (ISBN 0-516-03255-0). Childrens.

--Winter Is Here! LC 75-14201. (ps-2). 1975. 6.50 (ISBN 0-913778-10-9). Childs World.

--Wise Owl's Days of the Week. LC 81-9971. (The Wise Owl Ser.). (Illus.). 32p. (ps-2). 1981. PLB 9.25 (ISBN 0-516-06563-7). Childrens.

--A Word Bird's Circus Surprise (Word Birds for Early Birds) LC 80-29528. (Illus.). 32p. (ps-1). 1981. PLB 8.65 (ISBN 0-516-06554-8). Childrens.

--Word Bird's Hats. LC 81-18065. (Word Birds for Early Birds Ser.). (ps-2). 1982. 8.65 (ISBN 0-516-06558-0). Childrens.

Mondadori, tr. see Guidoni, Enrico & Magni, Roberto.

Mondadori, tr. see Ivanoff, Pierre.

Mondadori, tr. see Laroche, Lucienne.

Mondadori, tr. see Tamburello, Adolfo.

Mondadori Editors, ed. The Simon & Schuster Book of the Ballet. (Illus.). 1980. 24.95 o.p. (ISBN 0-671-41223-X). S&S.

Mondale, Joan A. Politics in Art. LC 72-266. (Fine Arts Books for Young People). (Illus.). 72p. (gr. 5-12). 1972. PLB 4.95g (ISBN 0-8225-0170-8); pap. 3.95 (ISBN 0-8225-9950-3). Lerner Pubns.

Mondale, Susan. Mopeds: The Go-Everywhere Bikes. LC 79-165511. (Superwheels & Thrill Sports Bks). (gr. 4 up). 1979. PLB 7.95g (ISBN 0-8225-0428-6). Lerner Pubns.

Mondel, Alan. The Comeback Kid. (Contemporary Poets of Dorrance Ser.). 112p. Date not set. 9.95 (ISBN 0-8059-2859-6). Dorrance.

Mondelli, R. J. & Ponterotto, I. L. A Conversational Spanish Review Grammar. 186p. 1961. text ed. 7.95 o.p. (ISBN 0-471-07288-5). Wiley.

Mondello, Salvatore, jt. auth. see Iorizzo, Luciano J.

Mondey, David. The Hamlyn Concise Guide to Axis Aircraft of World War II. (Hamlyn Concise Guides Ser.). (Illus.). 224p. 1983. 9.95 (ISBN 0-686-84614-1, Pub. by Hamlyn Pub England). Presidio Pr.

--The Hamlyn Concise Guide to Commercial Aircraft of the World. (Hamlyn Concise Guides Ser.). (Illus.). 224p. 1983. 9.95 (ISBN 0-600-34950-0, Pub. by Hamlyn Pub England). Presidio Pr.

--The Hamyln Concise Guide to Axis Aircraft of World War II. (Hamlyn Concise Guides). (Illus.). 224p. 1983. 9.95 (ISBN 0-686-83851-3, Hamlyn Pub England). Presidio Pr.

--Planemakers: 2 Westland. (Planemakers Ser.). (Illus.). 160p. 1982. 15.95 (ISBN 0-86720-555-5). Sci Bks Intl.

--Women of the Air. LC 81-86277. (In Profile Ser.). PLB 12.68 (ISBN 0-382-06634-0). Silver.

Mondey, David & Taylor, Michael. Jane's 1982-83 Aviation Annual. (Illus.). 158p. 1982. 15.95 (ISBN 0-86720-632-2). Sci Bks Intl.

Mondey, David, jt. auth. see Taylor, Michael.

Mondey, David, ed. The Complete Illustrated Encyclopedia of the World's Aircraft. LC 78-56306. (Illus.). 1978. 24.95 o.s.i. (ISBN 0-89479-032-3). A & W Pubs.

--The Hamlyn Concise Guide to American Aircraft of World War II. (Hamlyn Concise Guides). (Illus.). 224p. 1982. 9.95 (ISBN 0-600-34952-7, Pub. by Hamlyn Pub England). Presidio Pr.

--The Hamlyn Concise Guide to British Aircraft of World War II. (Hamlyn Concise Guides). (Illus.). 224p. 1982. 9.95 (ISBN 0-600-34951-9, Pub by Hamlyn Pub England). Presidio Pr.

Mond-Fontaine, Isabelle & Carmean, E. A. Braque: Papier Colles. (Illus.). 1982. pap. 17.50 (ISBN 0-89468-056-0). Natl Gallery Art.

Mondlane, Eduardo. The Struggle for Mozambique. 256p. 1983. pap. 10.50 (ISBN 0-86232-016-X, Pub. by Zed Pr England). Lawrence Hill.

Mondol, Prof. Operation Tibet. 1979. 7.95 o.p. (ISBN 0-533-03879-0). Vantage.

Mondot-Bernard, J. & Labonne, M. Satisfaction of Food Requirements in Mali to 2000 A. D. 214p. (Orig.). 1982. pap. 15.00x (ISBN 92-64-12300-8). OECD.

Monegal, Emir R. & Levine, Suzanne J. Maestros Hispanicos del Siglo Viente. 194p. (Orig.). 1979. pap. text ed. 10.95 (ISBN 0-15-551270-6). HarBraceJ.

Monegon, Ltd. Solar Energy Makes Sense Now: A How to Guide to Saving Money with Free Energy from the Sun. (Illus.). 42p. (Orig.). (gr. 10-12). 1982. pap. 11.95 (ISBN 0-940520-26-5). Monegon Ltd.

Monette, Louis G. & Stevens, Cheryl J. Organ Tonal Finishing & Fine Tuning. (Illus.). 141p. (Orig.). 1981. pap. 14.00 (ISBN 0-88127-000-8). Oracle Pr LA.

Money. Teletext & Viewdata. (Illus.). 1979. pap. 15.95 (ISBN 0-408-00378-2). Focal Pr.

Money, J. & Musaph, H. Handbook of Sexology, 5 vols. Incl. Vol. 1: History & Ideology (ISBN 0-444-00279-0); Vol. 2: Genetics, Hormones & Behavior (ISBN 0-444-00280-4); Vol. 3: Procreation & Parenthood (ISBN 0-444-00281-2); Vol. 4: Selected Personal & Social Issues (ISBN 0-444-00282-0); Vol. 5: Selected Syndromes & Therapy (ISBN 0-444-00283-9). 1978. pap. 14.25 ea. (North Holland); Set. text ed. 60.25. Elsevier.

Money, J. & Musaph, H., eds. Handbook of Sexology. 1977. 142.75 (ISBN 90-219-2104-9, North Holland). Elsevier.

Money, John, jt. auth. see Wolman, Benjamon B.

Money, Keith. Anna Pavlova: Her Life & Art. LC 81-47502. (Illus.). 440p. 1982. 55.00 (ISBN 0-394-42786-6). Knopf.

--Horseman in Our Midst. 12.50 (ISBN 0-392-03291-0, SpS). Sportshelf.

--John Curry. LC 77-90928. (Illus.). 1978. 17.50 o.p. (ISBN 0-394-50134-9). Knopf.

--Salute the Horse. (Illus.). 12.50 (ISBN 0-392-04473-0, SpS). Sportshelf.

Money, L. C. Chiozza. Riches & Poverty. LC 79-56955. (The English Working Class Ser.). 1980. lib. bdg. 30.00 o.s.i. (ISBN 0-8240-0109-5). Garland Pub.

Money, S. A. Microprocessor Data Book. (Illus.). 272p. 1982. 38.00 (ISBN 0-07-042706-2, P&RB). McGraw.

Money, Steve. Questions & Answers: Video. 112p. 1981. pap. 4.95 (ISBN 0-408-00553-X). Focal Pr.

Monfalcon, J. B., jt. auth. see Terme, J. F.

Mongan, Agnes. Andrew Wyeth: Dry Brush & Pencil Drawings. LC 67-20205. (Illus.). 1966. 12.95 (ISBN 0-8212-0170-0, 039551). NYGS.

Mongeau, Sam. Directory of Nursing Homes. 704p. 1982. lib. bdg. 75.00x (ISBN 0-89774-025-4). Oryx Pr.

Mongeon, John E., jt. ed. see Ziebold, Thomas O.

Monges, Henry B., tr. see Steiner, Rudolf.

Mongia, J. N. Banking Around the World. 583p. 1982. 49.95x (ISBN 0-940500-69-8, Pub by Allied Pubs India). Asia Bk Corp.

--Economics for Administrators. 600p. 1982. text ed. 40.00x (ISBN 0-7069-1293-4, Pub by Vikas India). Advent NY.

Mongillo, John F., ed. see Holmes, Neal J. & Leake, John B.

Mongillo, John F., et al. Reading about Science, Skills & Concepts. Kane, Joanne E., ed. (Reading about Science, Skills & Concepts Ser.). (Illus.). 128p. (gr. 4-7). 1980. Bk. A. pap. text ed. 6.32 (ISBN 0-07-002421-9, W); Bk. B. pap. text ed. 6.56 (ISBN 0-07-002422-7); Bk. C. pap. text ed. 6.56 (ISBN 0-07-002423-5); Bk. D. pap. text ed. 6.72 (ISBN 0-07-002424-3); Bk. E. pap. text ed. 6.72 (ISBN 0-07-002425-1); Bk. F. pap. text ed. 7.08 (ISBN 0-07-002426-X); Bk. G. pap. text ed. 7.08 (ISBN 0-07-002427-8); tchr's guide 4.32 (ISBN 0-07-002428-6). McGraw.

Monie, J & Wise, A. Social Policy & Its Administration. 1977. 38.50 (ISBN 0-08-021943-8). Pergamon.

Monier-Williams, Monier. English-Sanskrit Dictionary. 1976. Repr. of 1851 ed. Set. text ed. 34.00x (ISBN 0-391-01069-7). Humanities.

--English-Sanskrit Dictionary. 1976. Repr. of 1851 ed. 27.50x (ISBN 0-8002-0205-8). Intl Pubns Serv.

--Indian Wisdom. 575p. 1978. Repr. of 1893 ed. 21.00 (ISBN 0-89684-105-7, Pub. by Cosmo Pubns India). Orient Bk Dist.

--Sanskrit-English Dictionary. rev. ed. 1976. text ed. 45.00x o.p. (ISBN 0-391-01103-0). Humanities.

Monin, A. S. & Yaglom, A. M. Statistical Fluid Mechanics: Mechanics of Turbulence, 2 vols. Lumley, John L., ed. 95.00x set (ISBN 0-262-13158-7); Vol. 1 1971. 50.00x (ISBN 0-262-13062-9); Vol. 2 1975. 50.00x (ISBN 0-262-13098-X). MIT Pr.

Monin, A. S., et al. Variability of the Oceans. LC 77-826. 1977. 44.50 o.p. (ISBN 0-471-61328-2, Pub. by Wiley-Interscience). Wiley.

Monismith, Carl L. Addressing Societal Needs of the 1980's Through Civil Engineering Research. LC 82-70765. 336p. 1982. pap. text ed. 34.75 (ISBN 0-87262-300-9). Am Soc Civil Eng.

Monjo, F. N. King George's Head Was Made of Lead. (Illus.). 48p. (gr. 1-3). 1974. 5.95 (ISBN 0-698-20298-8, Coward). Putnam Pub Group.

--A Namesake for Nathan: Being an Account of Captain Nathan Hale by His Twelve-Year-Old Sister Joanna. (Illus.). 96p. (gr. 6 up). 1977. 6.95 o.p. (ISBN 0-698-20411-5, Coward). Putnam Pub Group.

--The Sea Beggar's Son. LC 73-78320. (Illus.). 36p. (gr. 3-5). 1975. 5.95 o.p. (ISBN 0-698-20277-5, Coward). Putnam Pub Group.

--The Secret of the Sachem's Tree. (Break-of-Day Bk.). (Illus.). 64p. (gr. 1-7). 1972. PLB 6.59 o.p. (ISBN 0-698-30446-2, Coward). Putnam Pub Group.

--Zenas and the Shaving Mill. LC 75-32531. (Illus.). 48p. (gr. 3-6). 1976. 5.95 o.p. (ISBN 0-698-20326-7, Coward). Putnam Pub Group.

Monk, J. F., ed. see Moreau, R. E.

Monk, Robert, et al. Exploring Religious Meaning. 2nd ed. (Illus.). 1980. text ed. 17.95 (ISBN 0-13-297515-7). P-H.

Monk, Samuel A. see Dryden, John.

Monkerud, Donald & Heiny, Mary. Self-Defense for Women. (Exploring Sports Ser.). 1983. pap. write for info. (ISBN 0-697-09978-4). Wm C Brown.

Monkhouse, F. J. A Dictionary of the Natural Environment. rev. ed. Small, John, ed. 1977. 39.95 o.s.i. (ISBN 0-470-99333-2); pap. 14.95 o.s.i. (ISBN 0-470-99334-0). Halsted Pr.

--Landscape from the Air. 2nd ed. LC 70-134621. (Illus.). 1971. text ed. 5.95x (ISBN 0-521-08000-2). Cambridge U Pr.

Monkhouse, Francis & Wilkinson, Henry R. Maps & Diagrams: Their Compilation & Construction. 3rd, rev. & enl. ed. (University Paperbacks Ser.). (Illus.). 522p. 1971. pap. 14.95x (ISBN 0-416-07450-2). Methuen Inc.

Monk of the Marmion Abbey. Becoming Christ. 4.95 (ISBN 0-87193-127-3). Dimension Bks.

Monks, F. J., et al, eds. see Symposium of the International Society for the Study of Behavioral Development, University of Nijmegen, the Netherlands, July, 1971.

Monks, J. G. Operations Management. 2nd ed. (Management Ser.). 736p. 1982. 25.95x (ISBN 0-07-042720-8); instr.'s guide 15.00 (ISBN 0-07-042721-6); study guide 8.95x (ISBN 0-07-042722-4). McGraw.

Monks of the Ramakrishna Order. Meditation. Bhavyananda, Swami, ed. 1977. pap. 7.95 (ISBN 0-7025-0019-4). Vedanta Pr.

Monmonier, Mark S. Computer-Assisted Cartography: Principles & Prospects. (Illus.). 256p. 1982. reference 26.95 (ISBN 0-13-165308-3). P-H.

Monmonier, Mark S., jt. auth. see Schnell, George A.

Monney, N. T., ed. Ocean Energy Resources, OED-1977, Vol. 4. 1977. pap. text ed. 15.00 o.p. (ISBN 0-685-86877-3, G00120). ASME.

Monninger, Joseph. The Summer Hunt. LC 82-71062. 288p. 1983. 14.95 (ISBN 0-689-11325-0). Atheneum.

Monnot, Michel. Selling America: Puns, Language & Advertising. LC 81-40840. (Illus.). 134p. (Orig.). 1982. lib. bdg. 19.50 (ISBN 0-8191-2002-2); pap. text ed. 8.25 (ISBN 0-8191-2003-0). U Pr of Amer.

Monod, Adolphe. Adolphe Monod's Farewell. 1962. pap. 2.45 (ISBN 0-686-12506-1). Banner of Truth.

Monoghan, Frank J. Hypnosis in Criminal Investigation. (Orig.). 1980. pap. text ed. 7.95 (ISBN 0-8403-2132-5). Kendall-Hunt.

Monoson Microsystems, Inc. Main Street Retailer: Small Computer Applications for Independent Retailers. Date not set. cancelled (ISBN 0-8283-1784-4); cancelled (ISBN 0-686-73212-X). Branden.

Monreiffe, Iain. The Highland Clans. rev. ed. (Illus.). 264p. 1982. 24.95 (ISBN 0-517-54659-0, C N Potter Bks). Crown.

Monro, David H. Godwin's Moral Philosophy: An Interpretation of William Godwin. LC 78-5640. 1978. Repr. of 1953 ed. lib. bdg. 18.75x (ISBN 0-313-20451-9, MOGM). Greenwood.

Monro, Don. Start with Basic On the Commodore Vic-20. 1982. text ed. 14.95 (ISBN 0-8359-7071-X); pap. text ed. 10.95 (ISBN 0-8359-7070-1). Reston.

--Start with BASIC on the TRS-80 Color Computer. 1982. text ed. 17.95 (ISBN 0-8359-7073-6); pap. text ed. 12.95 (ISBN 0-8359-7072-8). Reston.

Monro, Donald M. Computing with FORTRAN IV. 248p. 1977. pap. text ed. 14.95 (ISBN 0-7131-2546-2). E Arnold.

--Fortran Seventy-Seven. 368p. 1982. pap. text ed. 19.95 (ISBN 0-7131-2794-5). E Arnold.

--Interactive Computing with BASIC. 160p. 1974. pap. text ed. 14.95 (ISBN 0-7131-2488-1). E Arnold.

Monro, H. A. Manual of Fumigation for Insect Control. rev. ed. 2nd ed. (Illus., Orig.). 1969. pap. 30.50 (ISBN 0-685-00276-4, F261, FAO). Unipub.

Monro, Hector. The Ambivalence of Bernard Mandeville. 1975. 42.00x (ISBN 0-19-812061-3). Oxford U Pr.

Monro, Isabel S. & Monro, Kate M. Index to Reproductions of American Paintings: First Supplement. 480p. 1964. 15.00 (ISBN 0-8242-0024-1); suppl. 1948 15.00 (ISBN 0-8242-0025-X). Wilson.

Monro, Isabel S., jt. ed. see Cook, Dorothy E.

Monro, Kate M., jt. auth. see Monro, Isabel S.

Monroe, Betty I. Chinese Ceramics from Chicago Collections. LC 82-18962. (Illus.). 104p. 1982. pap. 12.00 (ISBN 0-941680-01-0). M&L Block.

Monroe, Burt L., Jr. Distributional Survey of the Birds of Honduras. 458p. 1968. 14.00 (ISBN 0-943610-07-9). Am Ornithologists.

Monroe, Charles P., ed. see Smith, Max J.

Monroe, Elvira. Say Cheesecake & Smile. LC 80-54453. 168p. 1981. pap. 5.95 (ISBN 0-933174-11-X). Wide World-Tetra.

Monroe, Elvira, jt. auth. see Arnot, Phil.

Monroe, Howard C., jt. auth. see Williams, John C.

Monroe, James E., jt. auth. see Ford, James M.

Monroe, James I. & Jackson, Bonnie F. Physical Science: An Inquiry Approach. 1977. text ed. 22.50 scp (ISBN 0-06-384225-4, HarpC); tchrs manual avail. (ISBN 0-06-375690-0). Har-Row.

Monroe, James T. Hispano-Arabic Poetry: A Student Anthology. LC 72-103925. 1975. 42.50x (ISBN 0-520-01692-0). U of Cal Pr.

--Shu'Ubiyya in Al'Andalus: The Risala of Ibn Garcia & Five Refutations. (U. C. Publ. in Near Eastern Studies: Vol. 13). 1970. pap. 13.50x (ISBN 0-520-09307-0). U of Cal Pr.

Monroe, James T., ed. & tr. Risalat at-Tawabic Wa Z-Zawabi (the Treatise of Familiar Spirits - Demons) by Abu a Mir Ibn Shuhaid Al-Ashja I, Al-Andalusi. (U. C. Publ. in Near Eastern Studies: Vol. 15). 1971. pap. 12.50x (ISBN 0-520-09382-8). U of Cal Pr.

Monroe, Jane A., jt. auth. see Twaite, James A.

Monroe, Keith, jt. auth. see Harman, Bob.

Monroe, Kent. Pricing: Making Profitable Decisions. (Illus.). 1979. text ed. 24.95 (ISBN 0-07-042780-1, C); instructor's manual 7.95 (ISBN 0-07-042781-X). McGraw.

Monroe, Lynn L. Boneshakers & Other Bikes. LC 72-13330. (General Juvenile Bks.). 48p. (gr. 3-6). 1973. PLB 3.95g (ISBN 0-8225-0285-2). Lerner Pubns.

--The Old-Time Bicycle Book. LC 79-52422. (Carolrhoda on My Own Bks). (Illus.). (gr. k-3). 1979. PLB 6.95g (ISBN 0-87614-110-6). Carolrhoda Bks.

Monroe, Manus & Abrams, Carl. A Course in Experimental Chemistry. 1983. 12.50x (ISBN 0-87735-210-0). Freeman C.

Monroe, Paul. Source Book of the History of Education for the Greek & Rowan Period. 515p. 1982. Repr. of 1948 ed. lib. bdg. 65.00 (ISBN 0-8495-3940-4). Arden Lib.

Monroe, Paul, ed. Cyclopedia of Education, 5 vols. LC 68-56361. (Illus.). 1968. Repr. of 1911 ed. Set. 370.00x (ISBN 0-8103-3537-9). Gale.

Monroe, R. E., et al, eds. Psychiatric Epidemiology & Mental Health Planning. 400p. 1967. pap. 5.00 o.p. (ISBN 0-685-24861-5, P022-0). Am Psychiatric.

Monroe, Robert A. Journeys Out of the Body. LC 72-157612. 288p. 1977. pap. 7.95 (ISBN 0-385-00861-9, Anch). Doubleday.

Monroe, Russell R. Brain Dysfunction in Aggressive Criminals. LC 78-4402. (Illus.). 240p. 1978. 21.95 o.p. (ISBN 0-669-02349-3). Lexington Bks.

Monroe, Stanley, jt. auth. see Szilagye, Robert J.

Monroe, Stuart A. Nonqualified Salary Continuation Plans. 1979. looseleaf text 29.95 o.p. (ISBN 0-87863-208-5). FS&G.

Monroe, Tom. The Frisbee Book. LC 82-83937. (Illus.). 176p. (Orig.). 1983. pap. 7.95 (ISBN 0-88011-105-4). Leisure Pr.

--How to Rebuild Your Ford V-8. LC 80-80171. (Orig.). 1980. pap. 9.95 (ISBN 0-89586-036-8). H P Bks.

--How to Rebuild Your Small-Block Ford. LC 78-74545. (Illus.). 1979. pap. 9.95 (ISBN 0-912656-89-1). H P Bks.

Monroe, Walter S. Directing Learning in the Elementary School. 480p. 1982. Repr. of 1932 ed. lib. bdg. 45.00 (ISBN 0-89987-648-X). Darby Bks.

Monroe, Will S. Bibliography of Education. LC 68-30661. 1968. Repr. of 1897 ed. 30.00x (ISBN 0-8103-3337-6). Gale.

Monroy, Alberto, jt. ed. see Moscona, Aron A.

Monsell, Helen A. Robert E. Lee. new ed. (Childhood of Famous Americans Ser.). (Illus.). 204p. (Orig.). (gr. 2 up). 1983. pap. 3.95 (ISBN 0-672-52750-2). Bobbs.

Monsen, Harry, tr. see Pernkopf, Eduard.

Monsen, R. J. & Walters, K. D. Nationalized Companies: A Threat to American Business. 192p. 1983. 17.95 (ISBN 0-07-071569-6, GB). McGraw.

Monsky, Susan. Midnight Suppers. 233p. 1983. 13.95 (ISBN 0-686-82649-3). HM.

Monsman, Gerald. Walter Pater. (English Authors Ser.). 1977. lib. bdg. 13.95 (ISBN 0-8057-6676-6, Twayne). G K Hall.

Monson, Milton W., Sr. Physics Is Constipated. 1983. 19.95 (ISBN 0-533-05190-8). Vantage.

Monson, Richard S. & Shelton, John C. Fundamentals of Organic Chemistry. (Illus.). 488p. 1974. text ed. 16.95 o.p. (ISBN 0-07-042810-7, C); instructor's manual 2.95 o.p. (ISBN 0-07-042811-5). McGraw.

Monson, Samuel C. Word Building. 2nd ed. (Illus., Orig.). 1968. pap. text ed. 7.95x (ISBN 0-02-382210-4). Macmillan.

Monson, Thomas S. Pathway to Perfection. LC 73-886344. 328p. 1973. 6.95 (ISBN 0-87747-511-3); pap. 2.95 (ISBN 0-87747-797-3). Deseret Bk.

Monsour, Sally, jt. auth. see Batcheller, John M.

Mont, John Du see Du Mont, J.

Montagna, Paul D. Occupations & Society: Toward a Sociology of the Labor Market. LC 76-40121. 1977. text ed. 24.95x (ISBN 0-471-61383-5). Wiley.

Montagne. Atlas of Foot Radiology. (Illus.). 288p. 1981. 62.50x (ISBN 0-89352-097-7). Masson Pub.

Montagne, Prosper. Larousse Gastronomique: The Encyclopedia of Food, Wine, & Cooking. Turgeon, Charlotte & Froud, Nina, eds. 1961. 32.50 (ISBN 0-517-50333-6). Crown.

Montago, I. With Eisenstein in Hollywood. (Illus.). 356p. pap. 4.00 (ISBN 0-686-35919-4). Newbury Bk.

Montagu, Ashley. Man & Aggression. 2nd ed. 1973. pap. 7.95 (ISBN 0-19-501680-7, 250, GB). Oxford U Pr.

--The Nature of Human Aggression. LC 75-32360. (Illus.). 336p. 1976. 16.95x (ISBN 0-19-501822-2); pap. 7.95 (ISBN 0-19-502373-0, GB535, GB). Oxford U Pr.

--Race & IQ. 1975. 19.95x (ISBN 0-19-501884-2). Oxford U Pr.

--Touching: The Human Significance of Skin. 2nd ed. 1978. pap. 6.95i (ISBN 0-06-090630-8, CN 630, CN). Har-Row.

Montagu, Ashley, jt. auth. see Levitan, Max.

Montagu, Ashley, ed. Learning Non-Aggression: The Experience of Non-Literate Societies. (Illus.). 1978. 17.95x (ISBN 0-19-502342-0). Oxford U Pr.

--Learning Non-Aggression: The Experience of Non-Literate Societies. (Illus.). 1978. pap. 6.95 (ISBN 0-19-502343-9, GB525, GB). Oxford U Pr.

--Meaning of Love. LC 72-11335. 248p. 1974. Repr. of 1953 ed. lib. bdg. 16.25x (ISBN 0-8371-6656-X, MOML). Greenwood.

--Sociobiology Examined. 1980. 19.95x (ISBN 0-19-502711-6); pap. 7.95 (ISBN 0-19-502712-4). Oxford U Pr.

Montagu, Ewen. Beyond Top Secret Ultra. LC 77-13469. 1978. 7.95 o.p. (ISBN 0-698-10882-5, Coward). Putnam Pub Group.

Montagu, Mary W. The Complete Letters of Lady Mary Wortley Montagu, 2 vols. Halsband, Robert, ed. Incl. Vol. 1. 1708-1720. 1965. 26.50x (ISBN 0-19-811446-X); Vol. 2. 1721-1751. 1966. 49.50x (ISBN 0-19-811455-9); Vol. 3. 1752-1762. 1967. o.p. (ISBN 0-19-811456-7). Oxford U Pr.

Montague. Formal Philosophy. LC 73-77159. 1974. 20.00x o.p. (ISBN 0-300-01527-5); pap. 8.95x (ISBN 0-300-02412-6, Y-345). Yale U Pr.

Montague, Albert C., jt. auth. see Lewison, Edward F.

Montague, Arthur, jt. auth. see Klein, John F.

Montague, C. J. Sixty Years in Waifdom or, the Ragged School Movement in English History. LC 70-108225. (Criminology, Law Enforcement, & Social Problems Ser.: No. 108). (With an intro. essay by Katharine Lenroot). 1970. Repr. of 1904 ed. 14.00x (ISBN 0-87585-108-8). Patterson Smith.

Montague, Charles E. Disenchantment. LC 77-29030. 1978. Repr. of 1968 ed. lib. bdg. 17.50x (ISBN 0-313-20280-X, MODS). Greenwood.

--Dramatic Values. LC 69-10136. (Illus.). 1968. Repr. of 1925 ed. lib. bdg. 16.25x (ISBN 0-8371-0173-5, MODV). Greenwood.

Montague, Gene, et al. Experience of Literature. 2nd ed. 1970. pap. text ed. 16.95 (ISBN 0-13-294728-5). P-H.

Montague, George T. Biblical Theology of the Secular. 1968. 2.95 o.p. (ISBN 0-685-07613-X, 80546). Glencoe.

--The Holy Spirit: Growth of Biblical Tradition. LC 76-4691. 384p. 1976. pap. 9.95 (ISBN 0-8091-1950-1). Paulist Pr.

--Riding the Wind. 1977. pap. 1.25 o.s.i. (ISBN 0-89129-256-X). Jove Pubns.

Montague, Gilbert H., jt. ed. see Wickersham, Cornelius W.

Montague, John. Chosen Light. LC 82-70274. 69p. 1970. 7.50 (ISBN 0-8040-0040-9). Swallow.

--Tides. LC 82-72643. 63p. 1971. 7.50 (ISBN 0-8040-0526-5); pap. 4.95 (ISBN 0-8040-0825-6). Swallow.

Montague, John, ed. Book of Irish Verse. 400p. 1977. 14.95 o.p. (ISBN 0-02-585630-8, 58563). Macmillan.

Montague, Katherine & Montague, Peter. No World Without End: The New Threat to Our Biosphere. LC 74-30569. (Illus.). 1976. 10.00 o.p. (ISBN 0-399-11500-5). Putnam Pub Group.

Montague, Peter, jt. auth. see Montague, Katherine.

Montague, Rosie. Brazilian Three-Dimensional Embroidery: Instructions & 60 Transfer Patterns. (Embroidery, Needlework Designs Ser.). (Illus.). 64p. (Orig.). Date not set. pap. 2.95 (ISBN 0-486-24384-2). Dover. Postponed.

Montague, Sarah. Pas De Deux: Great Partnerships in Dance. LC 80-54502. (Illus.). 112p. 1982. 12.95x (ISBN 0-87663-346-7); pap. 8.85 (ISBN 0-87663-553-2). Universe.

Montague Weekley, ed. see Bewick, Thomas.

Montague, William P. Belief Unbound. 1930. text ed. 11.50x (ISBN 0-686-83485-2). Elliots Bks.

--Great Visions of Philosophy. (Paul Carus Lecture Ser.). xvii, 501p. 1950. 27.50x (ISBN 0-87548-098-5). Open Court.

Montague-Smith, P., ed. Debrett's Correct Form. 375p. 1971. 15.00x (ISBN 0-905649-00-1). Intl Pubns Serv.

Montague-Smith, Patrick, jt. auth. see Kidd, Charles.

Montague-Smith, Patrick, ed. Debrett's Peerage & Baronetage Nineteen Eighty: Comprises Information Concerning the Royal Family, the Peerage, Privy Counsellors, Scottish Lords of Session, Baronets, & Chiefs of Names & Clans in Scotland. (Illus.). 1979. 116.00x (ISBN 0-8103-0949-1, Debretts Peerage Ltd). Gale.

Montagu-Nathan, M. History of Russian Music. LC 76-82815. 1918. 10.00x (ISBN 0-8196-0251-5). Biblo.

Montagu-Nathan, Montagu. Contemporary Russian Composers. Repr. of 1917 ed. lib. bdg. 17.75x (ISBN 0-8371-4285-7, MORC). Greenwood.

Montalbano, Mike. Decision Tables: Program Structure, Data Structure. LC 73-92630. (Illus.). 210p. 1974. pap. text ed. 14.95 (ISBN 0-574-19040-6, 13-2040). SRA.

Montalbano, William L. & Hiaasen, Carl. Powder Burn. LC 81-65997. 1981. 12.95 (ISBN 0-689-11174-6). Atheneum.

--Trap Line. LC 82-45177. 256p. 1982. 13.95 (ISBN 0-689-11307-2). Atheneum.

Montalvo, Joseph G., Jr., ed. Cotton Dust-Controlling: An Occupational Health Hazard. (ACS Symposium Ser.: NO. 189). 1982. write for info. (ISBN 0-8412-0716-X). Am Chemical.

Montana, Patrick J. & Roukis, George S., eds. Managing Terrorism: Strategies for the Corporate Executive. LC 82-11224. 192p. 1983. lib. bdg. 27.95 (ISBN 0-89930-013-8, MTE/, Quorum). Greenwood.

Montandon, Pat. The Intruders. LC 74-16638. 320p. 1975. 8.95 o.p. (ISBN 0-698-10636-9, Coward). Putnam Pub Group.

Montaner, Carlos A. Cuba: Claves Para Una Concienca En Crisis. 154p. 1982. pap. text ed. 9.95x (ISBN 0-686-84095-X). Transaction Bks.

--Secret Report on the Cuban Revolution. Zayas-Bazan, Eduardo, tr. from Span. LC 79-66693. 292p. 1981. o. p. 14.95 (ISBN 0-87855-300-2); pap. 6.95 (ISBN 0-87855-720-2). Transaction Bks.

Montano, Linda. Art in Everyday Life. 160p. 1981. ltd., signed ed. o. p. 20.00 (ISBN 0-937122-04-1); pap. 10.00 (ISBN 0-937122-05-X). Station Hill Pr.

Montano, Severino. Selected Plays of Severino Montano, Vol. 1 & 2. (Illus., Orig.). 1982. Vol. 1, 234. pap. 10.75 (ISBN 0-686-37565-3, Pub. by New Day Philippines); Vol. 2, 319. pap. 13.25 (ISBN 0-686-37566-1). Cellar.

Montapert, Alfred A. The Way to Happiness. 1978. 5.95 (ISBN 0-13-946228-7, Busn). P-H.

Montapert, Alfred A. & Montapert, William D. Around the World on the QE II. LC 81-5921. 381p. 1981. 12.95 (ISBN 0-13-046615-8, Busn). P-H.

Montapert, William D. The Omega Strategy: How You Can Retire Rich by 1986. (Illus.). 208p. 1982. 10.00 (ISBN 0-88496-187-7). Capra Pr.

Montapert, William D., jt. auth. see Montapert, Alfred A.

Montaperto, Nicki. The Freelancer's Career Book. LC 82-11433. 176p. 1982. 12.95 (ISBN 0-668-05287-2); pap. 7.95 (ISBN 0-668-05293-7). Arco.

Montaperto, Ronald N. & Henderson, Jay, eds. China's Schools in Flux: Report by the State Education Leaders Delegation. LC 79-88893. 1979. 25.00 (ISBN 0-87332-138-3). M E Sharpe.

Montauban. Relation du Voyage du Sieur de Montauban en l'Annee 1695. (Bibliotheque Africaine Ser.). 44p. (Fr.). 1974. Repr. of 1698 ed. lib. bdg. 24.00x o.p. (ISBN 0-8287-0633-6, 72-2136). Clearwater Pub.

Monte, Evelyn, jt. ed. see Pisano, Beverly.

Monte, John, jt. auth. see Fred Astaire Dance Studios.

Montecalvo, J., Jr., jt. auth. see Jhaveri, S.

Montefiore, A., ed. Neutrality & Impartiality. 320p. 1975. 38.50 o.p. (ISBN 0-521-20664-2); pap. 10.95x (ISBN 0-521-09923-4). Cambridge U Pr.

Montefiore, Alan. A Modern Introduction to Moral Philosophy. 1967. Repr. of 1958 ed. 12.95x o.p. (ISBN 0-7100-1865-7). Routledge & Kegan.

Montefiore, Alan, ed. Philosophy & Personal Relations: An Anglo-French Study. 208p. 1973. 12.50x o.p. (ISBN 0-7735-0179-7). McGill-Queens U Pr.

--Philosophy in France Today. LC 82-9730. 200p. Date not set. price not set (ISBN 0-521-22838-7); pap. price not set (ISBN 0-521-29673-0). Cambridge U Pr.

Montefiore, Hugh, jt. auth. see Turner, Henry E.

Montegemery, Marion. Why Poe Drank Liquor: Vol. II in the Trilogy, The Prophetic Poet & the Spirit of the Age. 442p. 1982. 19.95 (ISBN 0-89385-026-8). Sugden.

Monteiro, E. S. Anecdota Medica. (Illus.). 112p. 1983. pap. 6.95 (ISBN 0-686-42982-6). Hippocrene Bks.

Monteiro, George & Eppard, Philip. A Guide to the Atlantic Monthly Contributors' Club. 1983. lib. bdg. 35.00 (ISBN 0-8161-8492-5, Hall Reference). G K Hall.

Monteiro, George & Murphy, Brenda, eds. John Hay-Howells Letters: The Correspondence of John Hay & William Dean Howells 1861 - 1905. (American Literary Manuscripts Ser.). 1981. lib. bdg. 17.50 (ISBN 0-8057-9652-5, Twayne). G K Hall.

Monteiro, George, intro. by see Longfellow, Henry W.

Monteiro, George, tr. see Jorge de Sena.

Monteith, J. L. & Mount, L. E., eds. Heat Loss from Animals & Man: Assessment & Control. 400p. 1974. 34.95 o.p. (ISBN 0-408-70652-X). Butterworth.

Monteith, John L. Principles of Environmental Physics. (Contemporary Biology Ser.). 254p. 1973. pap. text ed. 18.95 o.p. (ISBN 0-7131-2375-3). Univ Park.

Monteith, Lesley, jt. auth. see Dickinson, Francis.

Montel, Paul. Familles Normales. LC 73-14649. xiii, 301p. 1974. text ed. 14.95 (ISBN 0-8284-0271-X). Chelsea Pub.

Monteleone, Thomas F. Guardian. LC 78-20087. (Science Fiction Ser.). 192p. 1980. 10.95 o.p. (ISBN 0-385-13694-3). Doubleday.

Monteleone, Thomas F., jt. auth. see Bischoff, David F.

Monteleone, Tom. Dark Stars & Other Illuminations. LC 79-6872. (Double D Science Fiction Ser.). 192p. 1981. 10.95 o.p. (ISBN 0-385-15769-X). Doubleday.

Monteleone, Vittorio, ed. Techniques of Knee Surgery. (Illus.). 250p. 1983. write for info (ISBN 0-89352-180-9). Masson Pub.

Montelius, O. Civilization of Sweden in Heathen Times. LC 68-25251. (World History Ser., No. 48). (Illus.). 1969. Repr. of 1888 ed. lib. bdg. 49.95x (ISBN 0-8383-0216-5). Haskell.

Montell, William L. Don't Go Up Kettle Creek: Verbal Legacy of the Upper Cumberland. LC 82-8566. (Illus.). 288p. 1983. text ed. 16.50x (ISBN 0-87049-365-5). U of Tenn Pr.

Montemurro, Donald G. & Bruni, J. Edward. The Human Brain in Dissection. 1981. text ed. 14.95 (ISBN 0-7216-6438-5). Saunders.

Monter, E. William, ed. European Witchcraft. LC 76-89682. 1969. pap. text ed. 14.50 (ISBN 0-471-61402-5). Wiley.

Montero, Darell & Weber, Marsha I. Vietnamese Americans: Patterns of Resettlement & Socioeconomic Adaption in the United States. 1979. lib. bdg. 24.50 (ISBN 0-89158-264-9). Westview.

Montero, Lidia D., tr. see Goetz, Joan.

Montes De Oca, Marco A. The Heart of the Flute. Villasenor, Laura, tr. from Sp. LC 78-71984. (International Poetry Ser.: Vol. 1). 60p. 1978. 11.95x (ISBN 0-8214-0412-1, 82-83012); pap. 6.95 (ISBN 0-8214-0423-7, 82-83020). Ohio U Pr.

Montesquieu. Persian Letters. Betts, C. J., tr. (Classics Ser.). 1977. pap. 5.95 (ISBN 0-14-044281-2). Penguin.

--The Spirit of Laws: A Compendium of the First English Editon with an English Translation of "an Essay on Causes Affecting Mind & Characters", 1737-1743. Carrithers, David W., ed. (No. 192). 1978. 42.50x (ISBN 0-520-02566-0); pap. 7.95x (ISBN 0-520-03455-4, CAMPUS SER., NO. 192). U of Cal Pr.

Montessori, Maria. Child in the Family. 1970. pap. 1.95 o.p. (ISBN 0-380-01096-8, 42648, Discus). Avon.

Montfort, Guy. Saving the Tiger. LC 80-5363. 120p. 1981. 16.95 o.p. (ISBN 0-670-61999-X, Studio). Viking Pr.

Montfort, St. Louis Marie De see De Montfort, St. Louis Marie.

Montgomerie, Norah. This Little Pig Went to Market. (Illus.). 112p. 1983. 10.95 (ISBN 0-370-30938-3, Pub by The Bodley Head). Merrimack Bk Serv.

Montgomery, jt. auth. see Mandelker.

Montgomery, frwd. by. A History of Warfare. LC 82-82146. (Illus.). 584p. 1983. 25.00 (ISBN 0-688-01645-6). Morrow.

Montgomery, A., jt. auth. see Riley, W. B.

Montgomery, A. H., jt. auth. see Riley, W. B.

Montgomery, A. T. Financial Accounting Information: An Introduction to Its Preparation & Use. LC 77-83023. 1978. text ed. 25.95 (ISBN 0-201-04924-4); instr's man. avail. (ISBN 0-201-04923-6). A-W.

Montgomery, A. Thompson. Financial Accounting: An Introduction to Its Preparation & Uses. 2nd. ed. LC 81-2410. (Accounting Ser.). 800p. 1982. text ed. 25.95 (ISBN 0-201-05163-X); Integrative Practice Sets avail. A-W.

--Introduction to Accounting. 1980. write for info. o.p. (CPCU 8). IIA.

--Introduction to Accounting. LC 80-69850. Orig. Title: Financial Accounting Information. 286p. 1982. Repr. of 1978 ed. text ed. 14.00 (ISBN 0-89463-031-8). Am Inst Property.

--Managerial Accounting Information: An Introduction to Its Content & Usefulness. LC 78-67943. 1979. text ed. 25.95 (ISBN 0-201-04927-9). A-W.

Montgomery, Bernard. The Memoirs of Field Marshal Montgomery. (Quality Paperbacks Ser.). (Illus.). 508p. 1982. pap. 9.95 (ISBN 0-306-80173-6). Da Capo.

Montgomery, Carol F. Medical Desk Manual for Law Offices. LC 82-71194. (Illus.). 167p. 1967. pap. 15.00 (ISBN 0-941916-01-4). Assn Trial Ed.

Montgomery, Carolyn K., jt. auth. see Ruebner, Boris H.

Montgomery, Chandler. Art for Teachers of Children. 2nd ed. LC 72-97008. 1973. text ed. 19.95 (ISBN 0-675-08962-X). Merrill.

Montgomery, Clarence. The Book of Beautiful Homes with Building Instructions. (A Promotion of the Arts Library Bk.). (Illus.). 1979. 49.75 (ISBN 0-89266-194-1). Am Classical Coll Pr.

Montgomery, Dan. Courage to Love. LC 79-65421. 1979. pap. 3.50 o.p. (ISBN 0-8307-0720-4, 5413001). Regal.

Montgomery, David. The Triathlon Handbook. (Illus.). 192p. (Orig.). 1983. pap. 7.95 (ISBN 0-88011-110-0). Leisure Pr.

--Workers' Control in America: Studies in the History of Work, Technology, & Labor Struggles. LC 78-32001. (Illus.). 1979. 22.95 (ISBN 0-521-22580-9). Cambridge U Pr.

--Workers' Control in America: Studies in the History of Work, Technology, & Labor Struggles. 1980. 7.50 (ISBN 0-521-28006-0). Cambridge U Pr.

Montgomery, David, jt. auth. see Eskin, Gerald.

Montgomery, Deanne & Zippin, Leo. Topological Transformation Groups. LC 74-265. 302p. 1974. Repr. of 1955 ed. 18.00 (ISBN 0-88275-169-7). Krieger.

Montgomery, Douglas C. Design & Analysis of Experiments. 2nd ed. 1976. text ed. write for info (ISBN 0-471-86812-4). Wiley.

Montgomery, Douglas C. & Johnson, Lynwood A. Forecasting & Time Series Analysis. 1976. 27.50 (ISBN 0-07-042857-3, P&RB). McGraw.

Montgomery, Douglas C. & Peck, Elizabeth A. Introduction to Linear Regression Analysis. LC 81-11512. (Wiley Ser. in Probability & Mathematical Statistics - Applied Probability & Statistics Section). 504p. 1982. 34.95x (ISBN 0-471-05850-5, Pub. by Wiley-Interscience). Wiley.

Montgomery, Douglas C., jt. auth. see Hines, William W.

Montgomery, Douglas C., jt. auth. see Johnson, Lynwood A.

Montgomery, Douglas C. & Berry, William L., eds. Production Planning, Scheduling & Inventory Control: Concepts, Techniques, & Systems. 1974. pap. text ed. 14.00 o.p. (ISBN 0-89806-022-2, 199). Inst Indus Eng.

Montgomery, Elizabeth R. Chief Seattle: Great Statesman. LC 66-10081. (Indian Books Ser). (Illus.). (gr. 2-5). 1966. PLB 6.69 (ISBN 0-8116-6603-4). Garrard.

--Dag Hammarskjold: Peacemaker for the UN. LC 73-570. (Century Biographies Ser.). (Illus.). (gr. 4-8). 1973. PLB 3.98 (ISBN 0-8116-4757-9). Garrard.

--Duke Ellington: King of Jazz. LC 70-179401. (Americans All Ser). (Illus.). 96p. (gr. 3-6). 1972. PLB 7.12 (ISBN 0-8116-4573-8). Garrard.

--Gandhi: Peaceful Fighter. LC 75-116039. (Century Biographies Ser.). (Illus.). (gr. 4-8). 1970. PLB 3.98 (ISBN 0-8116-4751-X). Garrard.

--Henry Ford: Automotive Pioneer. LC 72-83487. (Americans All Ser.). (Illus.). (gr. 3-6). 1969. PLB 7.12 (ISBN 0-8116-4556-8). Garrard.

--The Mystery of the Boy Next Door. LC 77-14019. (For Real Ser.). (Illus.). (gr. k-6). 1978. PLB 6.69 (ISBN 0-8116-6400-7). Garrard.

--Seeing in the Dark. LC 79-11736. (For Real Ser.). (Illus.). (gr. 1-5). 1979. PLB 6.69 (ISBN 0-8116-4312-3). Garrard.

--Trouble Is His Name. LC 76-18136. (For Real Bks). (Illus.). 40p. (gr. k-3). 1976. PLB 6.69 (ISBN 0-8116-4303-4). Garrard.

--Walt Disney: Master of Make-Believe. LC 71-146705. (American All Ser). (Illus.). (gr. 3-6). 1971. PLB 7.12 (ISBN 0-8116-4568-1). Garrard.

Montgomery, G. Gene, ed. The Evolution & Ecology of Armadillos, Sloths, & Vermilinguas. (Illus.). 400p. (Orig.). 1983. pap. text ed. 35.00x (ISBN 0-87474-649-3). Smithsonian.

Montgomery, George R., tr. see Leibniz, Gottfried W.

Montgomery, Gerald W. The Selling of You: A Practical Guide to Job Hunting. new ed. 103p. 1980. 12.95 (ISBN 0-937096-01-6); pap. 9.95x o.p. (ISBN 0-937096-00-8). Montgomery Comm.

Montgomery, Guy, et al, eds. Concordance to the Poetical Works of John Dryden. LC 66-27126. 1967. Repr. of 1957 ed. 30.00x o.p. (ISBN 0-8462-0903-9). Russell.

Montgomery, H. Mongoose Magoo. LC 68-56822. (Illus.). (gr. 2-5). 1968. PLB 6.75x (ISBN 0-87783-026-6); pap. 2.95x deluxe ed. (ISBN 0-87783-100-9). Oddo.

Montgomery, Hugh. Dictionary of Political Phrases & Allusions with a Short Bibliography. LC 68-28333. 1968. Repr. of 1906 ed. 34.00x (ISBN 0-8103-3092-X). Gale.

Montgomery, James. The West Indies, Repr. Of 1810 Ed. Reiman, Donald H., ed. Bd. with The World Before the Flood; a Poem, in Ten Cantos. with Other Occasional Pieces. Repr. of 1813 ed. LC 75-31239. (Romantic Context Ser.: Poetry 1789-1830). 1979. lib. bdg. 47.00 o.s.i. (ISBN 0-8240-2187-8). Garland Pub.

Montgomery, John. The Kerovac We Knew: Unposed Portraits, Action Shots. LC 82-90227. 48p. 1982. 20.00 (ISBN 0-686-93287-0); pap. 7.50 (ISBN 0-686-99095-1). Fels & Firn.

Montgomery, John D. Technology & Civic Life: Making & Implementing Development Decisions. 200p. 1974. 17.50x (ISBN 0-262-13097-1). MIT Pr.

Montgomery, John D., frwd. by. The Administration of Economic Development Programs: Baselines for Discussion, No. 3. (Lincoln Institute Monograph: No. 79-4). 1979. pap. text ed. 6.00 o.p. (ISBN 0-686-28290-6). Lincoln Inst Land.

Montgomery, John M. Before the Crisis: Can Your Church Stand Up to an Audit? LC 82-217. 156p. (Orig.). 1982. pap. 4.95 (ISBN 0-88449-086-6, A424623). Vision Hse.

Montgomery, John W. Crisis in Lutheran Theology, 2 vols. in one. 1973. pap. 7.95 o.p. (ISBN 0-87123-050-X, 210050). Bethany Hse.

--Demon Possession. LC 75-19313. 1976. pap. 7.95 (ISBN 0-87123-102-6, 210102). Bethany Hse.

--History & Christianity. 128p. pap. 2.95 (ISBN 0-89840-045-7). Heres Life.

--Principalities & Powers. 256p. 1981. pap. 6.95 (ISBN 0-87123-470-X, 210470). Bethany Hse.

--Where Is History Going? LC 69-11659. 256p. 1969. 5.95 (ISBN 0-87123-640-0, 210640). Bethany Hse.

Montgomery, John W., ed. see Skinner, Tom.

Montgomery, John Warwick. The Shaping of America. LC 76-15682. 253p. 1982. pap. 7.95 (ISBN 0-87123-227-8, 230227). Bethany Hse.

Montgomery, L. M. Anne of Green Gables. 429p. 1977. Repr. of 1908 ed. lib. bdg. 17.95x (ISBN 0-89966-262-5). Buccaneer Bks.

Montgomery, Marion. Why Flannery O'Connor Stayed Home. (The Prophetic Poet & the Spirit of the Age Ser.: Vol. 1). 486p. 1981. 19.95 (ISBN 0-89385-013-6); pap. cancelled (ISBN 0-89385-012-8). Sugden.

--Why Hawthorne Was Melancholy: Vol. III, of the Trilogy, the Prophetic Poet & the Spirit of the Age. 486p. 1983. 19.95 (ISBN 0-89385-027-6). Sugden.

Montgomery, Michael & Stratton, John. The Writer's Hotline Handbook. (Orig.). 1981. pap. 4.95 (ISBN 0-451-62225-1, ME2225, Ment). NAL.

Montgomery, Nell. Sentimental Journeys. LC 81-90629. 60p. 1982. 6.95 (ISBN 0-533-05254-8). Vantage.

Montgomery, Paula. Canyon Girl. LC 81-82799. (Adventures of Hazel Weston Ser.). (Illus.). 228p. (Orig.). (gr. k-8). 1982. pap. 4.95 (ISBN 0-9606942-0-X). Monte Pub.

Montgomery, Paula K., jt. auth. see Walker, H. Thomas.

Montgomery, Paula K., jt. auth. see Walker, Thomas H.

Montgomery, Penelope S., jt. auth. see Gaarder, Kenneth R.

Montgomery, R. H. The Solar Decision Book: Your Guide to Making a Sound Investment. LC 79-762. 1978. pap. text ed. 21.95x (ISBN 0-471-05652-9). Wiley.

Montgomery, Ray. House of Danger. (Choose Your Own Adventure Ser). 128p. (gr. 1-8). 1982. pap. 1.95 (ISBN 0-553-22541-3). Bantam.

Montgomery, Richard H. The Home Energy Audit. LC 82-15992. 191p. 1983. pap. text ed. 10.95 (ISBN 0-471-86466-8). Wiley.

Montgomery, Richard H. & Miles, Walter F. Solar Decision Book of Homes: A Guide to Designing & Remodeling for Solar Heating. LC 81-16397. 332p. 1982. text ed. 27.95x (ISBN 0-471-08280-5). Wiley.

Montgomery, Robert, ed. see Brown, Douglas R.

Montgomery, Robert L. The Reader's Eye: Studies in Didactic Literary Theory from Dante to Tasso. LC 78-57313. 1979. 24.50x (ISBN 0-520-03700-6). U of Cal Pr.

Montgomery, Roger & Marshall, Dale R., eds. Housing Policy for the Nineteen Eighties. LC 79-3278. (A Policy Studies Organization Bk.). 272p. 1980. 25.95x (ISBN 0-669-03443-6). Lexington Bks.

Montgomery, Roger, jt. ed. see Marshall, Dale.

Montgomery, Royce L. Head & Neck Anatomy: With Clinical Correlations. (Illus.). 352p. 1981. text ed. 30.00 (ISBN 0-07-042853-0). McGraw.

Montgomery, Royce L. & Singleton, Mary C. Human Anatomy Review. 2nd ed. LC 77-20974. (Arco Medical Review Ser.). (Illus.). 1978. pap. 8.00x o.p. (ISBN 0-668-03368-1, 3368). Arco.

Montgomery, Ruth. Companions Along the Way. 245p. 1974. 6.95 o.p. (ISBN 0-698-10619-9, Coward). Putnam Pub Group.

--Strangers Among Us: Enlightened Beings from a World to Come. LC 79-10574. 1979. 9.95 (ISBN 0-698-10992-9, Coward). Putnam Pub Group.

--Threshold to Tomorrow. 256p. 1983. 13.95 (ISBN 0-399-12759-3). Putnam Pub Group.

--The World Before. LC 76-16789. 256p. 1976. 7.95 (ISBN 0-698-10749-7, Coward). Putnam Pub Group.

--A World Beyond: A Startling Message from the Eminent Psychic Arthur Ford from Beyond the Grave. 1971. 6.95 (ISBN 0-698-10404-8, Coward). Putnam Pub Group.

Montgomery Ward. Catalogue & Buyers Guide Summer & Spring 1895: No. 57. 1969. 15.00 o.p. (ISBN 0-486-22409-0); pap. 12.95 (ISBN 0-486-22377-9). Dover.

Montgomery Ward & Co. Catalogue & Buyer's Guide: Spring & Summer 1895, No. 57. 16.00 (ISBN 0-8446-0806-8). Peter Smith.

Montherlant, Henry De. The Bachelors. LC 77-10926. 1977. Repr. of 1960 ed. lib. bdg. 17.25x (ISBN 0-8371-9811-9, MOTB). Greenwood.

Monti, Laura V., jt. ed. see Bigelow, Gordon E.

Monti, Peter, jt. ed. see Curran, James P.

Monticone, Ronald C. Charles De Gaulle. (World Leaders Ser.: No. 42). 1975. lib. bdg. 7.50 o.p. (ISBN 0-8057-3663-8, Twayne). G K Hall.

Montilla, M. Robert & Harlow, Nora, eds. Correctional Facilities Planning. LC 78-19930. 240p. 1979. 21.95 o.p. (ISBN 0-669-02437-6). Lexington Bks.

Montilla, Robert, jt. auth. see Miller, E. Eugene.

Montogomery, Rex & Dryer, Robert L. Biochemistry: A Case-Oriented Approach. 4th ed. 750p. 1983. text ed. 24.95 (ISBN 0-8016-3473-3). Mosby.

Montreal Telephone Co. The Seventh International Symposium on Human Factors in Telecommunications. 1974. pap. 75.00 (ISBN 0-686-37979-9). Info-Gatekeepers.

Montroll, E. W. & Lebowitz, J. L., eds. The Liquid State of Matter: Fluids, Simple & Complex. (Studies in Statistical Mechanics: Vol. 8). 250p. 1982. 53.25 (ISBN 0-444-86334-6). Elsevier.

Montross, Constance M. Virtue or Vice? Sor Juana's Use of Thomistic Thought. LC 80-6303. 136p. (Orig.). 1981. lib. bdg. 18.00 (ISBN 0-8191-1767-6); pap. text ed. 8.25 (ISBN 0-8191-1730-7). U Pr of Amer.

Montville, John B. Mack, Living Legend of Hichway. LC 78-18896. (Illus.). 1979. pap. 19.95 (ISBN 0-89404-069-3). Aztex.

Monty, Shirlee. May's Boy. (Illus.). 186p. 1983. pap. 4.95 (ISBN 0-8407-5784-0). Nelson.

Montz, John M., jt. auth. see Sloane, Roscoe C.

Monward, Richard, ed. see American Automobile Association.

Monzingo, F. A. & Miller, T. W. Introduction to Adaptive Arrays. 543p. 1980. 44.95x (ISBN 0-471-05744-4, Pub. by Wiley-Interscience). Wiley.

Mood. Introduction to Policy Analysis. 1982. 29.50 (ISBN 0-444-00671-0). Elsevier.

Mood, Alexander M., et al. Introduction to the Theory of Statistics. 3rd ed. (Illus.). 480p. 1973. text ed. 32.50 (ISBN 0-07-042864-6, C). McGraw.

Mood, Dale & Musker, Frank F. Sports & Recreational Activities for Men & Women. 8th ed. (Illus.). 442p. 1983. pap. text ed. 14.95 (ISBN 0-8016-0290-4). Mosby.

Mood, Dale P. Numbers in Motion: A Balanced Approach to Measurement & Evaluation in Physical Education. LC 79-91835. (Illus.). 396p. 1980. text ed. 18.95 (ISBN 0-87484-503-3); instructor's manual avail. Mayfield Pub.

Mood, Eric W., ed. Public Swimming Pools: Recommended Regulations for Design & Construction, Operation & Maintenance. LC 81-68843. 64p. 1981. 5.00x (ISBN 0-87553-096-6, 055). Am Pub Health.
Moodie, Colin L., jt. ed. see Mabert, Vincent A.
Moodie, Michael, jt. auth. see Bray, Frank T.
Moodie, T. Dunbar. The Rise of Afrikanerdom: Power, Apartheid, & the Afrikaner Civil Religion. LC 72-85512. (Perspectives on Southern Africa Ser). 1975. 28.50x (ISBN 0-520-02310-2); pap. 5.95 (ISBN 0-520-03943-2). U of Cal Pr.
Moody, A. D., ed. The Waste Land in Different Voices. LC 74-19953. (Illus.). 256p. 1975. 26.00 (ISBN 0-312-85645-8). St Martin.
Moody, Alton B. Celestial Navigation in the Computer Age. 224p. 1982. 18.95 (ISBN 0-442-26359-7). Van Nos Reinhold.
Moody, Anne. Coming of Age in Mississippi. 1970. pap. 3.25 (ISBN 0-440-31488-7, LE). Dell.
Moody, Barry. The Acadians. (Focus on Canadian History Ser.). (Illus.). 96p. (gr. 6-10). 1982. PLB 8.40 (ISBN 0-531-04383-5). Watts.
Moody, Bert. Ocean Ships. 6th ed. (Illus.). 1978. 12.50x o.p. (ISBN 0-7110-0865-5). Intl Pubns Serv.
Moody, D. L. Day by Day with D. L. Moody. 1977. pap. 2.95 o.p. (ISBN 0-8024-1759-0). Moody.
Moody, Douglas, ed. Patterson's Schools Classified, 1983. 225p. (Orig.). 1983. pap. 6.00x (ISBN 0-910536-32-5). Ed Direct.
Moody, Douglas C., jt. ed. see Elliott, Norman F.
Moody, Dwight L. Doscientas Anecdotas Y Ilustraciones. (Span). pap. 2.95 (ISBN 0-8024-1490-7). Moody.
--Prevailing Prayer. pap. 2.95 (ISBN 0-8024-6814-4). Moody.
--Way to God. pap. 2.95 (ISBN 0-8024-9231-2). Moody.
Moody, Dwight L., ed. Thoughts for the Quiet Hour. pap. 2.95 (ISBN 0-8024-8729-7). Moody.
Moody, Eric N., ed. Western Carpetbagger: The Extraordinary Memoirs of Senator Thomas Fitch. LC 77-18257. (Bristlecone Paperback Ser.). (Illus.). x, 286p. 1978. pap. 5.25 (ISBN 0-87417-050-8). U of Nev Pr.
Moody, F., jt. ed. see Baron, J. H.
Moody, F. J., jt. ed. see Shin, Y. W.
Moody, Graham B. Petroleum Exploration Handbook: A Practical Manual Summarizing the Application of Earth Sciences to Petroleum Exploration. (Illus.). 1961. 65.00 o.p. (ISBN 0-07-042867-0, P&RB). McGraw.
Moody, H. L. The Teaching of Literature. (Longman Handbooks for Language Teachers Ser.). 1974. pap. text ed. 7.75x (ISBN 0-582-52602-7). Longman.
Moody, J. V. & Francke, O. F. The Ants (Hymenoptera, Formicidae) of Western Texas: Part I - Subfamily Myrmicinae. (Graduate Studies Ser.: No. 27). 80p. (Orig.). 1982. pap. 12.00 (ISBN 0-89672-107-8). Tex Tech Pr.
Moody, Jess. Too Good to Keep. 1982. pap. 3.95 (ISBN 0-89693-006-8). Victor Bks.
Moody, John. Masters of Capital. 1919. text ed. 8.50x (ISBN 0-686-83619-7). Elliots Bks.
--Railroad Builders. 1919. text ed. 8.50x (ISBN 0-686-83721-5). Elliots Bks.
Moody, Kate, jt. ed. see Logan, Ben.
Moody, Larry, jt. auth. see Boa, Kenneth.
Moody, Marvin D. The Interior Article in De-Compounds in French: Agent De Police Versus Agent De la Police. LC 79-5432. 1980. pap. text ed. 7.00 (ISBN 0-8191-0881-2). U Pr of Amer.
Moody, Michael E., jt. ed. see Cole, C. Robert.
Moody, Paul. Decision Making: Proven Methods for Better Decisions. LC 82-17196. (Illus.). 256p. 1983. 24.95 (ISBN 0-07-042868-9, P&RB). McGraw.
Moody, Penderel, ed. Devon Pillow Lace: Its History & How to Make It. (Illus.). 160p. 1981. Repr. of 1907 ed. 37.00x (ISBN 0-8103-3031-8). Gale.
Moody Press Editors. What Christians Believe. 1951. pap. 2.95 (ISBN 0-8024-9378-5). Moody.
Moody Press Editors, ed. Esto Creemos: What Christians Believe. Orig. Title: What Christians Believe. (Span). 1951. pap. 2.95 (ISBN 0-8024-1930-5). Moody.
Moody, Raymond A., Jr. Life After Life. 176p. 1981. 8.95 (ISBN 0-89176-037-7); pap. 4.95 (ISBN 0-89176-036-9). Mockingbird Bks.
Moody, Richard. The World of Dinosaurs. LC 77-73208. (Illus.). (gr. 4-8). 1977. 3.95 (ISBN 0-448-14342-9, G&D); PLB 8.45 (ISBN 0-448-13438-1). Putnam Pub Group.
Moody, Richard, jt. auth. see John, David.
Moody, Ronald, tr. see Malum, Amadu.
Moody, Sophy. What Is Your Name? (The International Library of Names Ser.). 1982. Repr. of 1863 ed. text ed. 24.50x (ISBN 0-8290-1228-1). Irvington.
--What Is Your Name: A Popular Account of the Meaning & Derivations of Christian Names. LC 73-5523. 1975. Repr. of 1863 ed. 45.00x (ISBN 0-8103-4250-2). Gale.
Moody, T. W., ed. Nationality & the Pursuit of National Independence. (Historical Studies: No. XI). 1978. text ed. 17.00x (ISBN 0-904651-31-2). Humanities.
Moody, T. W., et al, eds. A Companion to Irish History, Vol. 1. (Illus.). 1982. 140.00x (ISBN 0-19-821744-7). Oxford U Pr.
Moody, William V. & Lovett, Robert M. A First View of English Literature. 386p. 1982. Repr. of 1911 ed. lib. bdg. 40.00 (ISBN 0-89760-582-9). Telegraph Bks.
Moody-Stuart, K. Brownlow North: His Life & Work. 1961. 2.45 (ISBN 0-686-12509-6). Banner of Truth.
Moog, Helmut. The Musical Experience of the Pre-School Child. Clarke, Claudia, tr. from Ger. 1976. pap. 12.00 (ISBN 0-901938-06-8, 75-A11154). Eur-Am Music.
Moog, Shirleigh. Moog's Musical Eatery, a Cookbook for Relaxed Entertaining. LC 78-5906. (Cookbooks Ser.). 1978. 15.95 (ISBN 0-89594-000-0); pap. 6.95 (ISBN 0-89594-001-9). Crossing Pr.
Mooij, J. J. A. A Study of Metaphor. (North-Holland Linguistics Ser.: Vol. 27). 1976. 32.00 (ISBN 0-7204-6209-6, North-Holland). Elsevier.
Mook, Dean T., jt. auth. see Nayfeh, Ali H.
Mookerjee, Ajit. Kundalini: The Arousal of the Inner Energy. LC 81-5466. (Illus.). 112p. 1982. pap. 10.95 (ISBN 0-89281-020-3). Destiny Bks.
--Kundalini: The Arousal of the Inner Energy. (Illus.). 112p. 1982. pap. 10.95 (ISBN 0-89281-020-3, Destiny). Inner Tradit.
Mookerji, Tapati. The Golden Road to Samarkand. 5.00 o.p. (ISBN 0-89253-526-1). Ind-US Inc.
Moolenijzer, J. H. Hendrik Andriessen Tachtig Jaar. (Composer's Worklist Ser.: Vol. 5). (Illus.). wrappers 15.00 o.s.i. (ISBN 90-6027-375-3, Pub. by Frits Knuf Netherlands). Pendragon NY.
Moolman, Valerie. Women Aloft. LC 80-20475. (Epic of Flight Ser.). PLB 19.96 (ISBN 0-8094-3288-9). Silver.
Moon, Clarice & Luedke, Ralph D., eds. Soups for All Seasons. 1977. pap. 3.25 o.p. (ISBN 0-89542-604-8). Ideals.
Moon, E. L. Experiences with My Cockatiels. rev. ed. 1976. 7.95 (ISBN 0-87666-759-0, AP-1280). TFH Pubns.
Moon, Geoff. The Birds Around Us: New Zealand Birds; Their Habits & Habitats. (Illus.). 207p. 1983. 25.95 (ISBN 0-908592-03-5, Pub. by Heinemann Pub New Zealand). Intl Schol Bk Serv.
Moon, Harry R. Typing from Rough Drafts. 1978. 12.70 (ISBN 0-87350-312-0); tchr's manual 9.70 (ISBN 0-87350-307-4); work papers packet 4.90 (ISBN 0-87350-306-6). Milady.
Moon, Harry R. & Frazier, Lois E. Guide to Transcription. (Illus.). 1978. 5.64 (ISBN 0-87350-305-8); tchr's ed. 2.60 (ISBN 0-87350-309-0). Milady.
Moon, Henry L. Balance of Power: The Negro Vote. LC 77-4915. 1977. Repr. of 1948 ed. lib. bdg. 18.75x (ISBN 0-8371-9619-1, MOBA). Greenwood.
Moon, John. Quick Marches. LC 75-19259. (Music of the Fifes & Drums Ser: Vol. 1). 1976. pap. 3.95 (ISBN 0-87935-031-8). Williamsburg.
Moon, John C. An Instructor for the Drum. (Musick of the Fifes & the Drum Ser.: Vol. 4). (Illus.). 56p. (Orig.). 1981. pap. 3.95 with record (ISBN 0-87935-059-8); Set. pap. 8.95 (ISBN 0-87935-060-1). Williamsburg.
Moon, John C., ed. Slow Marches. LC 75-19259. (Music of Fifes & Drums Ser.: Vol. 2). 1977. pap. 3.95 (ISBN 0-87935-046-6). Williamsburg.
Moon, John C., et al. Medleys. LC 75-19259. (Music of the Fifes & Drums Ser.: Vol. 3). 1980. pap. 3.95 (ISBN 0-87935-050-4). Williamsburg.
Moon, Parker T. Imperialism & World Politics. LC 75-147502. (Library of War & Peace; The Political Economy of War). lib. bdg. 38.00 o.s.i. (ISBN 0-8240-0296-2). Garland Pub.
Moon, Parry & Spencer, Domina E. The Photic Field. 240p. 1981. text ed. 27.50x (ISBN 0-262-13166-8). MIT Pr.
Moon, Richard G. Understanding Elementary Algebra. (Mathematics Ser.). 1978. text ed. 19.95 (ISBN 0-675-08406-7). Additional supplements may be obtained from publisher. Merrill.
Moon, Robert. Applied Mathematics for Technical Programs: Arithmetic & Geometry. LC 72-96904. 1973. pap. text ed. 20.95 (ISBN 0-675-08983-2); media: audiocassettes 140.00 (ISBN 0-675-08918-2); write for info. group discounts. Additional supplements may be obtained from publisher. Merrill.
--Basic Arithmetic. 2nd ed. (Mathematics Ser.). 1977. pap. text ed. 18.95 (ISBN 0-675-08627-2); cassettes 160.00 (ISBN 0-675-08515-2). Additional supplements may be obtained from publisher. Merrill.
Moon, Robert A. & Davis, Robert D. Elementary Algebra. 3rd ed. (Mathematics Ser.). 528p. 1980. pap. text ed. 19.95 (ISBN 0-675-08158-0). Additional supplements may be obtained from publisher. Merrill.
Moon, Robert G. Applied Mathematics for Technical Programs: Algebra. LC 73-75638. 1973. pap. text ed. 20.95 (ISBN 0-675-08943-3); media: audiocassettes 140.00 (ISBN 0-675-08910-7). Additional supplements may be obtained from publisher. Merrill.
--Applied Mathematics for Technical Programs: Trigonometry. LC 73-77913. 1973. pap. text ed. 21.95 (ISBN 0-675-08923-9); media: audiocassettes 140.00 (ISBN 0-675-08900-X). Additional supplements may be obtained from publisher. Merrill.
Moon, Robert G. & Davis, Robert D. Elementary Algebra. 2nd ed. (Illus.). 480p. 1975. pap. text ed. 18.95x o.p. (ISBN 0-675-08768-6); media: audiocassettes 140.00 (ISBN 0-675-08720-1). Additional supplements may be obtained from publisher. Merrill.
Moon, Samuel, ed. One Act: Eleven Short Plays of the Modern Theater. Incl. Miss Julie. Strindberg, August; Purgatory. Yeats, William B; The Man with the Flower in His Mouth. Pirandello, Luigi; Pullman Car Hiawatha. Wilder, Thornton; Hello Out There. Saroyan, William; Twenty-Seven Wagons Full of Cotton. Williams, Tennessee; Bedtime Story. O'Casey, Sean; Cecile. Anouilh, Jean; This Music Crept by Me Upon the Waters. MacLeish, Archibald; A Memory of Two Mondays. Miller, Arthur; The Chairs. Ionesco, Eugene. 1961. pap. 7.95 (ISBN 0-394-17105-5, B107, BC). Grove.
--One Act: Eleven Short Plays of the Modern Theatre. 9.50 (ISBN 0-8446-2603-1). Peter Smith.
Moon, Susan E. & Tracy, Susie. Pritt: The True Story of a Deaf Cat & Her Family. 96p. 1982. pap. 7.95 (ISBN 0-399-50670-5). Putnam Pub Group.
Moon, Warren G. Greek Vase-Painting in Midwestern Collections. LC 79-56832. (Illus.). 231p. (Orig.). 1979. pap. 12.50 (ISBN 0-86559-041-9). Art Inst Chi.
Moonan, Willard. Martin Buber: An Annotated Bibliography of Scholarship in English. LC 78-68278. 1981. lib. bdg. 20.00 o.s.i. (ISBN 0-8240-9779-3). Garland Pub.
Moone, Eric, jt. auth. see Gale, D.
Mooney. An Introduction to Nineteen-F Nuclear Magnetic Resonance Spectroscopy. 1970. 35.00 o.p. (ISBN 0-85501-008-8). Wiley.
Mooney, Christopher F. Inequality & the American Conscience: Justice Through the Judicial System. (Woodstock Studies). 144p. 1983. pap. 5.95 (ISBN 0-8091-2500-5). Paulist Pr.
Mooney, David A. Introduction to Thermodynamics & Heat Transfer. 1955. text ed. 31.95 (ISBN 0-13-499681-X). P-H.
Mooney, E. F. Annual Reports on NMR Spectroscopy, 1982, Vol. 11B. 99.50 (ISBN 0-12-505349-5). Acad Pr.
Mooney, E. F. & Webb, G. A., eds. Annual Reports on NMR Spectroscopy, 2 Vols. Date not set. Vol. 13. 99.50 (ISBN 0-12-505313-4); Vol. 14. price not set (ISBN 0-12-505314-2). Acad Pr.
Mooney, Elizabeth. Alone: Surviving as a Widow. 320p. 1981. 13.95 (ISBN 0-399-12601-5). Putnam Pub Group.
Mooney, James & Petter, Rodolphe C. Cheyenne Indians: Sketch of the Cheyenne Grammar. LC 8-10850. Repr. of 1907 ed. pap. 8.00 (ISBN 0-527-00505-3). Kraus Repr.
Mooney, Michael M., ed. George Catlin: Letters & Notes on the North American Indians. (Illus.). 384p. 1975. 15.00 o.p. (ISBN 0-517-52016-8, C N Potter Bks). Crown.
Mooney, Pat R. Seeds of the Earth: A Private or Public Resource? (Illus.). 126p. 1980. pap. 7.00 (ISBN 0-9690149-3-7). Inst Food & Develop.
Mooney, Patrick. A Gift of Love: Remembering the Old Anew. 48p. (Orig.). 1983. pap. 1.50 (ISBN 0-89622-168-7). Twenty-Third.
Mooney, Peter. Structural Foams, P-006r. 1982. 1750.00 (ISBN 0-89336-196-8). BCC.
Mooney, Samantha. A Snowflake in My Hand. 100p. 1983. 10.95 (ISBN 0-440-07935-7, E Friede). Delacorte.
Mooney, Ted. Easy Travel to Other Planets. 240p. 1983. pap. 2.95 (ISBN 0-345-30547-7). Ballantine.
Mooney, Thomas. Arithmetic That We Need. 1966. pap. 2.75x (ISBN 0-88323-003-8, 104); tchr's. key 2.75x (ISBN 0-88323-004-6, 105). Richards Pub.
--The Getting Along Series of Skills, 5 vols. Incl. Vol. I. After School Is Out. 1963 (ISBN 0-88323-021-6, 121); Vol. II. Al Looks for a Job. 1964 (ISBN 0-88323-022-4, 122); Vol. III. A Job at Last. 1964 (ISBN 0-88323-023-2, 123); Vol. IV. Money in the Pocket. 1965 (ISBN 0-88323-024-0, 124); Vol. V. From Tires to Teeth. 1965 (ISBN 0-88323-025-9, 125). wkbk. 2.50x ea. o.p. Richards Pub.
Mooradian, A. & Killinger, D. K. Optical & Laser Remote Sensing. (Springer Ser. in Optical Sciences: Vol. 39). (Illus.). 400p. 1983. 30.00 (ISBN 0-387-12170-6). Springer-Verlag.
Mooradian, Karlen. Blood, Paint & Tears: The Life of Arshile Gorky. (Illus.). 270p. 1983. 25.00 (ISBN 0-686-97754-8). Gilgamesh Pr IL.
Moorat, Joseph. Thirty Old-Time Nursery Songs. LC 80-16025. (Illus.). 33p. (ps). 1980. 9.95 (ISBN 0-87099-242-2). Metro Mus Art.
Moorby, J., jt. auth. see Milthorpe, F. L.
Moorcock, Michael. Bane of the Black Sword: Elric Series, No. 5. rev. ed. (Science Fiction Ser.). 1977. pap. 2.25 (ISBN 0-87997-805-8, UE1805). DAW Bks.
--Byzantium Endures. LC 81-40210. (Illus.). 384p. 1982. 14.50 (ISBN 0-394-51972-8). Random.
--The Chronicles of Corum. 1978. pap. 1.95 o.p. (ISBN 0-425-03855-6, Medallion). Berkley Pub.
--The Chronicles of Corum. 400p. 1983. pap. 2.75 (ISBN 0-425-05849-2). Berkley Pub.
--The Condition of Muzak. 1978. lib. bdg. 13.50 (ISBN 0-8398-2434-3, Gregg). G K Hall.
--The End of All Songs. 1978. pap. 1.75 o.p. (ISBN 0-380-01964-7, 38471). Avon.
--The Final Programme. 1976. Repr. of 1968 ed. lib. bdg. 10.95 (ISBN 0-8398-2335-5, Gregg). G K Hall.
--Gloriana. 1979. pap. 4.95 o.p. (ISBN 0-380-42986-1, 42986). Avon.
--The Jewel in the Skull. (Science Fiction Ser.). 1977. pap. 1.95 (ISBN 0-87997-841-4, UE1841). DAW Bks.
--The Land Leviathan. (Science Fiction Ser.). 1976. pap. 2.25 (ISBN 0-87997-774-4, UE1774). DAW Bks.
--The Steel Tsar. 160p. 1982. pap. 2.50 (ISBN 0-686-95151-4). DAW Bks.
--The Swords Trilogy. 1980. lib. bdg. 17.95 (ISBN 0-8398-2623-0, Gregg). G K Hall.
--The War Hound & the World's Pain. 1982. pap. 2.50 (ISBN 0-686-82565-9, Timescape). PB.
Moorcraft, Colin. Must the Seas Die? LC 72-91818. (Illus.). 219p. 1973. 9.95 (ISBN 0-87645-069-9). Gambit.
Moore, jt. auth. see Carling.
Moore, jt. auth. see Kruglak.
Moore, A., jt. auth. see Dawber, J.
Moore, A., jt. auth. see Howard, Richard.
Moore, Alex. Ballroom Dancing. 8th ed. (Illus.). 324p. (gr. 9 up). 1980. Repr. of 1974 ed. text ed. 22.50x (ISBN 0-273-00381-X, LTB). Sportshelf.
Moore, Alexander. Life Cycles in Atchalan: The Diverse Careers of Certain Guatemalans. LC 72-93732. 220p. 1973. text ed. 11.95x (ISBN 0-8077-1831-9). Tchrs Coll.
Moore, Anne J., jt. auth. see Price, Pamela A.
Moore, Anthony L., jt. ed. see Hall, John I.
Moore, Arthur. Night Riders. 1978. pap. 1.75 o.p. (ISBN 0-523-40451-4). Pinnacle Bks.
--The Strong Americans: The Raging Heart. 384p. (Orig.). 1981. pap. 2.75 o.p. (ISBN 0-523-41144-8). Pinnacle Bks.
Moore, Arthur, jt. auth. see Dowson, Ernest.
Moore, Arthur H. & Elonka, Stephen M. Electrical Systems & Equipment for Industry. LC 77-5640. (Illus.). 368p. 1977. Repr. of 1971 ed. lib. bdg. 23.50 (ISBN 0-88275-561-7). Krieger.
Moore, Aubrey. A Son of the Rectory. 160p. 1982. text ed. 16.75x (ISBN 0-86299-035-1, Pub. by Sutton England); pap. text ed. 8.50x (ISBN 0-86299-036-X). Humanities.
Moore, Austin L. Knight Errant in Africa: A Journal. 143p. 1966. 4.95 o.p. (ISBN 0-8040-0177-4). Swallow.
Moore, B. C. An Introduction to the Psychology of Hearing. 2nd ed. LC 81-69595. 27.00 (ISBN 0-12-505620-6); pap. 11.00 (ISBN 0-12-505622-2). Acad Pr.
Moore, Ballard J. Beginning Tennis: For the "Love" of Tennis. (Illus.). 80p. (Orig.). 1976. wire coil 5.95 (ISBN 0-8403-1177-X). Kendall-Hunt.
Moore, Ballard J. & Henderson, Thomas E. Shuttlecock Action. (Illus.). 1977. pap. text ed. 5.95 (ISBN 0-8403-1773-5). Kendall-Hunt.
Moore, Barrington, Jr. Soviet Politics: The Dilemma of Power: the Role of Ideas in Social Change. LC 76-19137. 1977. pap. 10.95 (ISBN 0-87332-088-3). M E Sharpe.
Moore, Barry & Hefley, Marti. In Spite of Myself. 1982. 9.95 (ISBN 0-8423-1584-5); pap. 5.95 (ISBN 0-8423-1581-0). Tyndale.
Moore, Betty T., ed. see Cornwell, Richard E. & Victor, Buzz.
Moore, Betty T., ed. see Parker, Rosetta E.
Moore, Bobbie & Bowerman, Bill. Sports Illustrated Track: Field Events. LC 76-8268. (Illus.). 1977. 5.95i o.p. (ISBN 0-397-01137-7); pap. 2.95i (ISBN 0-397-01136-9, LP-106). Har-Row.
Moore, Bradley G. Philosophy Applied to Controversial Issues in a Democratic Society. LC 79-84650. 1979. pap. text ed. 8.25 (ISBN 0-8191-0741-7). U Pr of Amer.
Moore, Brian. The Lonely Passion of Judith Hearne. 1982. pap. 3.50 (ISBN 0-686-37707-9). WSP.
--The Luck of Ginger Coffey. 1978. pap. 2.95 o.p. (ISBN 0-14-002115-9). Penguin.
--The Mangan Inheritance. 1980. pap. 2.95 o.p. (ISBN 0-14-005671-8). Penguin.
Moore, Brian E. & Ross, Timothy L. The Scanlon Way to Improved Productivity: A Practical Guide. LC 77-14396. 1978. 31.50 (ISBN 0-471-03269-7, Pub. by Wiley-Interscience). Wiley.
Moore, Burton M., jt. auth. see Moore, Joan W.
Moore, Byron C., et al. A Dictionary of Special Education Terms. 128p. 1980. lexotone 12.75x (ISBN 0-398-04009-5). C C Thomas.
Moore, C. L. Black God's Shadow. 15.00 o.p. (ISBN 0-686-27900-X). D M Grant.
--Jirel of Joiry. 336p. 1982. pap. 2.75 (ISBN 0-441-38570-2, Pub. by Ace Science Fiction). Ace Bks.
--Northwest Smith: The Legendary Hero of the Spaceway. 1982. pap. 2.75 (ISBN 0-441-58613-9, Pub. by Ace Science Fiction). Ace Bks.
Moore, C. L. & Kuttner, Henry. Earth's Last Citadel. pap. 2.25 (ISBN 0-441-18112-0, Pub. by Ace Science Fiction). Ace Bks.

Moore, Cairl E. Concrete Form Construction. 1977. pap. text ed. 10.80 (ISBN 0-8273-1094-3); instructor's guide 2.75 (ISBN 0-8273-1093-5). Delmar.

Moore, Carleton B., jt. auth. see Mason, Brian.

Moore, Carol-Lynne. Executives in Action. 2nd ed. 112p. 1982. pap. 13.50x (ISBN 0-7121-0176-4). Intl Ideas.

Moore, Carol M., jt. auth. see Torres, Lillian S.

Moore, Cecil, tr. see Schwartz, Federico.

Moore, Charles. Daniel H. Burnham: Architect Planner of Cities. LC 68-27726. (Architecture & Decorative Art Ser). (Illus.). 1968. Repr. of 1921 ed. lib. bdg. 55.00 (ISBN 0-306-71151-6). Da Capo.

--Life & Times of Charles Follen McKim. LC 70-99857. (Architecture & Decorative Art Ser). (Illus.). 1970. Repr. of 1929 ed. lib. bdg. 37.50 (ISBN 0-306-71324-1). Da Capo.

Moore, Charles & Allen, Gerald. Dimensions: Space, Scale & Shape in Architecture. 2nd ed. LC 76-28406. (Illus.). 1976. 19.95 (ISBN 0-07-002336-0, Architectural Rec Bks). McGraw.

Moore, Charles, ed. see Burnham, Daniel H. & Bennett, Edward H.

Moore, Charles A., jt. auth. see Aiello, Joseph A.

Moore, Charles A., ed. Chinese Mind: Essentials of Chinese Philosophy & Culture. LC 66-24011. 1967. pap. text ed. 6.95x (ISBN 0-8248-0075-3). UH Pr.

--Indian Mind: Essentials of Indian Philosophy & Culture. LC 66-24012. 1967. pap. text ed. 6.95x (ISBN 0-8248-0076-1). UH Pr.

--Japanese Mind: Essentials of Japanese Philosophy & Culture. LC 67-16704. 1967. pap. text ed. 6.95x (ISBN 0-8248-0077-X). UH Pr.

--Philosophy & Culture, East & West: East-West Philosophy in Practical Perspective. 1962. 25.00x (ISBN 0-87022-541-3). UH Pr.

--Status of the Individual in East & West. 22.50x (ISBN 0-87022-542-1). UH Pr.

Moore, Charles B. & Blue, William F., Jr. Editing & Layout Techniques for The Company Editor. 1979. 32.50x (ISBN 0-686-28582-4). Ink Art Pubns.

Moore, Charlotte B., ed. Reconstructing Complex Societies: An Archaeological Colloquium. (American Schools of Oriental Research, Supplement Ser.: Vol. 20). 170p. 1974. pap. text ed. 8.00x (ISBN 0-89757-320-X, Am Sch Orient Res). Eisenbrauns.

Moore, Clare. The Visual Dimension: Aspects of Jewish Art. (Publications of the Oxford Centre for Postgraduate Hebrew Study: Vol. 5). 320p. 1983. text ed. 35.00x (ISBN 0-86598-081-0). Allanheld.

Moore, Claude, et al. Applied Math for Technicians. 2nd ed. 384p. 1982. 18.95 (ISBN 0-13-041178-7). P-H.

Moore, Clement. Night Before Christmas. LC 79-165390. (Illus.). 1971. pap. 1.75 (ISBN 0-486-22797-9). Dover.

--The Night Before Christmas. LC 80-11758. (Illus.). 32p. (ps up). 1980. PLB 12.95 (ISBN 0-8234-0414-5); pap. 4.95 (ISBN 0-8234-0417-X). Holiday.

--A Visit from St. Nicholas. (Illus.). 32p. (ps up). 1981. pap. 2.50 o.p. (ISBN 0-671-44439-5, Little Simon). S&S.

Moore, Clement C. The Night Before Christmas. LC 77-71994. (gr. 1 up). 1977. pap. text ed. 7.95a o.p. (ISBN 0-385-13275-1); PLB 7.95a (ISBN 0-385-13615-3). Doubleday.

--Night Before Christmas. (Fujikawa Picture Bks.). (ps). 1961. 4.95 (ISBN 0-448-02935-9, G&D). Putnam Pub Group.

--The Night Before Christmas. (Nursery Treasure Bks). (Illus.). (gr. k-3). 1.95 (ISBN 0-448-04205-3, G&D). Putnam Pub Group.

--The Night Before Christmas. LC 75-7511. (Picturebacks Ser). (Illus.). 32p. (gr. 2-6). 1975. pap. 1.50 (ISBN 0-394-83019-9, BYR). Random.

--Visit from St. Nicholas. (Illus.). (gr. k-3). 1968. 5.95 o.p. (ISBN 0-07-042900-6, GB). McGraw.

Moore, Clement H. Images of Development: Egyptian Engineers in Search of Industry. 336p. 1980. text ed. 27.50x (ISBN 0-262-13161-7). MIT Pr.

Moore, Clyde B. & Cole, William E. Sociology in Educational Practice. Repr. of 1952 ed. lib. bdg. 17.75x (ISBN 0-8371-2574-X, MOSE). Greenwood.

Moore, Cornelia N., ed. Insulinde: Selected Translations from Dutch Writers of Three Centuries on the Indonesian Archipelago. LC 78-139. (Asian Studies at Hawaii: No. 20). 1978. pap. text ed. 9.75x (ISBN 0-8248-0564-X). UH Pr.

Moore, D. F. The Friction of Pneumatic Tyres. 220p. 1975. 55.50 (ISBN 0-444-41323-5). Elsevier.

Moore, D. M. Plant Cytogenetics. 1976. pap. 6.50x (ISBN 0-412-13440-3, Pub. by Chapman & Hall England). Methuen Inc.

Moore, D. M., ed. Green Planet: The Story of Plant Life on Earth. LC 82-4287. (Illus.). 288p. 1982. 27.50 (ISBN 0-521-24610-5). Cambridge U Pr.

Moore, D. T., et al. Catalogue of Chemically Analyzed Igneous Rocks in the Collection of the British Museum-Natural History. 112p. 1979. 24.50x (ISBN 0-565-00809-9, Pub. by Brit Mus Nat Hist England). Sabbot-Natural Hist Bks.

Moore, Daniel G. Shoot Me a Biscuit: Stories of Yesteryear's Roundup Cooks. LC 74-79391. (Southwest Chronicles). (Illus.). 172p. 1974. pap. 4.95 o.p. (ISBN 0-8165-0431-8). U of Ariz Pr.

Moore, David P. & Poppino, Mary A. Successful Tutoring: A Practical Guide to Adult Learning Processes. (Illus.). 184p. 1983. 15.75x (ISBN 0-398-04763-4); 2.75 o.p. supervisors guide. C C Thomas.

--Supervisor's Guide to Successful Tutoring. 24p. 1983. pap. 2.75x spiral (ISBN 0-398-04764-2). C C Thomas.

Moore, David R. Islanders & Aborigines at Cape York: An Ethnographic Reconstruction Based on the 1848-1850 "Rattlesnake" Journals of O. W. Brierley. LC 78-64900. (AIAS New Ser.: No. 3). (Illus.). 1979. text ed. 20.50x (ISBN 0-391-00946-X); pap. text ed. 16.75x (ISBN 0-391-00948-6). Humanities.

Moore, David W. & Readence, John E. Prereading Activities for Content Area Reading & Learning. (Reading Aids Ser.). 72p. (Orig.). 1982. pap. 5.00 (ISBN 0-87207-228-2, 228). Intl Reading.

Moore, Deborah D. At Home in America: Second Generation New York Jews. (Illus.). 320p. 1983. pap. 10.00 (ISBN 0-231-05063-1). Columbia U Pr.

Moore, Dennis. The Politics of Spenser's Complaints & Sidney's Philsides Poems. (Salzburg - Elizabethean Studies: No. 101). 196p. 1982. pap. text ed. 25.00x (ISBN 0-391-02783-2, Pub. by Salzburg Austria). Humanities.

Moore, Desmond F. Thermodynamic Principles of Energy Degrading. (Illus.). 155p. 1981. text ed. 32.50x (ISBN 0-333-29506-4, Pub. by Macmillan England); pap. 19.50x (ISBN 0-333-29504-8, Pub. by Macmillan England). Scholium Intl.

Moore, Donald. Calvarymen. (Illus.). 48p. Date not set. 24.00 o.p. (ISBN 0-88014-060-7). Mosaic Pr OH. Postponed.

Moore, Donald R. Money for College: How to Get It. 2nd ed, 240p. 1983. pap. 3.95 (ISBN 0-8120-2348-X). Barron.

--Money for College! How to Get It. LC 78-2489. (gr. 10-12). 1979. pap. 3.50 (ISBN 0-8120-0740-9). Barron.

Moore, Dorothy, jt. auth. see Moore, Raymond.

Moore, Edith. A Girl Called Sam. (YA) 1980. 6.95 (ISBN 0-686-73936-1, Avalon). Bouregy.

Moore, Edward. Studies in Dante, First Series: Scriptures & Classical Authors in Dante. LC 68-57627. (Illus.). 1969. Repr. of 1896 ed. lib. bdg. 17.00x (ISBN 0-8371-0909-4, MODF). Greenwood.

--Studies in Dante, Second Series: Miscellaneous Essays. LC 68-57628. (Illus.). 1969. Repr. of 1899 ed. lib. bdg. 17.00x (ISBN 0-8371-0908-6, MOSD). Greenwood.

--Studies in Dante, Third Series: Miscellaneous Essays. LC 68-57629. (Illus.). 1969. Repr. of 1903 ed. lib. bdg. 17.00x (ISBN 0-8371-0917-5, MODT). Greenwood.

Moore, Eliakim H., et al. The New Haven Mathematical Colloquium. 1910. 85.00x (ISBN 0-686-51424-6). Elliots Bks.

Moore, Elisabeth. Bend with the Wind. LC 78-31664. 1981. 12.95 o.s.i. (ISBN 0-87949-142-6). Ashley Bks.

Moore, Elizabeth C. An Almanac for Music Lovers. LC 70-167078. (Tower Bks). xiv, 382p. 1972. Repr. of 1940 ed. 42.00x (ISBN 0-8103-3940-4). Gale.

Moore, Ellen, jt. auth. see Bane, Michael.

Moore, Emily. Fifty-Two Sundays of Worship for Children, Bk. 2. 1972. 4.95 (ISBN 0-8341-0253-6). Beacon Hill.

--Just My Luck. (A Unicorn Bk.). 112p. (gr. 4-7). 1983. 9.95 (ISBN 0-525-44009-7, 0966-290). Dutton.

--Something to Count On. LC 79-23277. 112p. (gr. 5 up). 1980. 9.95 (ISBN 0-525-39595-4, 0966-290, Unicorn Bk). Dutton.

Moore, Eric G., jt. ed. see Gale, Stephen.

Moore, Ernest, ed. Bases of Auditory Brain Stem Evoked Responses. 1982. 29.50 (ISBN 0-8089-1465-0). Grune.

Moore, Ethel, ed. Contemporary Art Nineteen Forty-Two to Nineteen Seventy-Two: Collection of the Albright-Knox Art Gallery. LC 70-189296. (Illus.). 1972. 18.00 (ISBN 0-914782-28-2, Pub. by Albright-Knox Art Gallery). C E Tuttle.

Moore, Eva. The Cookie Book. LC 76-190381. 64p. (gr. 1-4). 9.95 (ISBN 0-395-28866-5, Clarion). HM.

--The Great Banana Cookbook for Boys & Girls. (Illus.). 48p. (gr. 1-4). 1983. 10.50 (ISBN 0-89919-150-9, Clarion). HM.

Moore, Frances S. Blue Locket. (YA) 1972. 6.95 (ISBN 0-685-28625-8, Avalon). Bouregy.

--Fair Is My Love. (YA) 1971. 6.95 (ISBN 0-685-23395-2, Avalon). Bouregy.

--The Storm. 256p. (YA) 1973. 6.95 (ISBN 0-685-27998-7, Avalon). Bouregy.

Moore, Frank. The Magic Moving Alphabet. (Illus.). 1978. pap. 2.95 (ISBN 0-486-23593-9). Dover.

Moore, Franklin G. Management of Organizations. 592p. 1982. text ed. 27.95x (ISBN 0-471-87691-7); tchr's. ed. 18.00 (ISBN 0-471-87682-8). Wiley.

Moore, Franklin G. & Jablonski, Ronald. Production Control. 3rd ed. LC 68-28418. 1969. text ed. 31.95 (ISBN 0-07-042921-9, C). McGraw.

Moore, Fred W. Texas Short Stories & a Look at Puerto Rico. LC 78-64775. 57p. 1980. 4.95 o.p. (ISBN 0-533-04043-4). Vantage.

Moore, G. Practical Problems in Mathematics for Automotive Technicians. LC 77-82372. 1979. pap. 7.00 (ISBN 0-8273-1273-3); instructor's guide 4.25 (ISBN 0-8273-1274-1). Delmar.

Moore, G. Paul. Organic Voice Disorders. LC 72-135024. (Foundations of Speech Pathology Ser). 1971. ref. ed. 16.95 (ISBN 0-13-640888-5). P-H.

Moore, Gary, jt. auth. see Richardson, William B.

Moore, Gary S. & Jaciow, Douglas M. Mycology for the Clinical Laboratory. (Illus.). 1979. text ed. 23.95 (ISBN 0-8359-4771-8). Reston.

Moore, Gary T. & Cohen, U. Designing Environments for Handicapped Children: A Design Guide & Case Study. LC 79-89670. 1979. write for info. U of Wis Ctr Arch-Urban.

Moore, Gary T., ed. Emerging Methods in Environmental Design & Planning. 1970. 20.50x o.p. (ISBN 0-262-13057-2); pap. 6.95 o.p. (ISBN 0-262-63048-6). MIT Pr.

Moore, Gary T. & Golledge, R. G., eds. Environmental Knowing: Theories, Research & Methods. LC 76-4942. (Community Development Ser.: Vol. 23). 416p. 1976. 21.50 (ISBN 0-87933-297-2). Hutchinson Ross.

Moore, Gary W., jt. auth. see Berkley, Sandra.

Moore, Gay M. Seaport in Virginia: George Washington's Alexandria. rev. ed. LC 73-188711. 274p. 1972. Repr. 12.95 o.p. (ISBN 0-8139-0183-9). U Pr of Va.

Moore, Gaylen, jt. auth. see Gilbert, Lynn.

Moore, Gene, tr. see Karpinski, Jakub.

Moore, Geoffrey. Business Cycles, Inflation & Forecasting. LC 79-26026. 488p. 1980. prof ref 42.50x (ISBN 0-88410-685-3). Ballinger Pub.

--Business Cycles, Inflation, & Forecasting. 2nd ed. 488p. 42.50 (ISBN 0-88410-284-X); pap. 19.95 (ISBN 0-88410-285-8). Ballinger Pub.

Moore, Geoffrey, jt. auth. see Brandon, Peter S.

Moore, George. Letters to Lady Cunard: Eighteen Ninety-Five to Nineteen Thirty-Three. LC 78-12712. (Illus.). 1979. Repr. of 1957 ed. lib. bdg. 19.25x (ISBN 0-313-20645-7, MOLL). Greenwood.

--Literature at Nurse. Fletcher, Ian & Stokes, John, eds. Bd. with A Mere Accident. LC 76-20110. (Decadent Consciousness Ser.). 1978. lib. bdg. 38.00 o.s.i. (ISBN 0-8240-2769-8). Garland Pub.

--Literature at Nurse, or, Circulating Morals: A Polemic on Victorian Censorship. (Society & the Victorians). 96p. 1976. Repr. of 1885 ed. text ed. 5.25x o.p. (ISBN 0-391-00588-X). Humanities.

--Managing Corporate Relations. 1980. text ed. 29.50x (ISBN 0-566-02158-7). Gower Pub Ltd.

--Mike Fletcher. Fletcher, Ian & Stokes, John, eds. LC 76-20121. (Decadent Consciousness Ser.). 1977. Repr. of 1889 ed. lib. bdg. 38.00 o.s.i. (ISBN 0-8240-2770-1). Garland Pub.

--The Untilled Field. 1976. text ed. 12.95x o.p. (ISBN 0-7705-1378-6). Humanities.

Moore, George & Wood, Chris. Social Work & Criminal Law in Scotland. 220p. 1982. 19.50 (ISBN 0-08-025731-3). Pergamon.

Moore, George E. Philosophical Studies. 1922. text ed. 22.50x o.p. (ISBN 0-7100-3001-0). Humanities.

--Principia Ethica. 1959. 34.50 (ISBN 0-521-05753-1); pap. 9.95x (ISBN 0-521-09114-4, 114). Cambridge U Pr.

Moore, Gerald. Furthermoore: Interludes in an Accompanist's Life. 160p. 1983. 22.50 (ISBN 0-241-10909-4, Pub. by Hamish Hamilton England). David & Charles.

--Wole Soyinka. LC 74-176321. 114p. 1972. text ed. 17.50x (ISBN 0-8419-0095-7, Africana); pap. text ed. 10.50x (ISBN 0-8419-0113-9, Africana). Holmes & Meier.

Moore, Guy W. The N. I. H. How it Works. 178p. 1980. text ed. 25.50 (ISBN 0-89443-353-9). Aspen Systems.

Moore, H., jt. auth. see Town, H. C.

Moore, H. L. Eternal Questions. 1968. 2.95 o.p. (ISBN 0-934942-05-6). White Wing Pub.

Moore, Hal G. Pre-Calculus Mathematics. 2nd ed. LC 76-18678. 1977. text ed. 26.95x o.s.i. (ISBN 0-471-61454-8). Wiley.

Moore, Harvey D. & Moore, Patsie S. The Droopy Flower Mystery & Other Object Lessons for Children. LC 78-13172. 1979. pap. 3.95 o.p. (ISBN 0-687-11190-0). Abingdon.

Moore, Henry. Henry Moore's Sheep Sketchbook. 1980. 9.98 (ISBN 0-500-23315-2). Thames Hudson.

Moore, Henry, jt. auth. see Finn, David.

Moore, Herbert L., Jr. Rows of Corn. 224p. 1983. 13.95 (ISBN 0-87844-048-8). Sandlapper Pub Co.

--South Carolina Prisons. 250p. 1984. 14.95 (ISBN 0-87844-024-0). Sandlapper Pub Co.

Moore, Inga. Aktil's Bicycle Ride. (Illus.). 32p. (ps). 1983. bds. 9.95 (ISBN 0-19-554319-X, Pub by Oxford U Pr Childrens). Merrimack Bk Serv.

--Aktil's Big Swim. (Illus.). 32p. (ps). 1983. bds. 9.95 (ISBN 0-19-554250-9, Pub by Oxford U Pr Childrens). Merrimack Bk Serv.

Moore, J. & Micoleau, T. Football Techniques Illustrated. 96p. 1962. 14.95x o.p. (ISBN 0-471-07152-8, Pub. by Wiley-Interscience). Wiley.

Moore, J. A., ed. Macromolecular Syntheses Collective, Vol. 1. LC 63-18627. (Macromolecular Syntheses Ser.). 1977. 52.95 (ISBN 0-471-61451-3, Pub by Wiley-Interscience). Wiley.

Moore, J. E. Design for Good Acoustics & Noise Control. 1979. text ed. 17.50x o.p. (ISBN 0-333-24292-0); pap. 16.95x o.p. (ISBN 0-333-24293-9). Scholium Intl.

Moore, J. M. Manuscript Tradition of Polybius. (Cambridge Classical Studies). 1981. 17.95 (ISBN 0-521-05755-8); pap. 19.95 (ISBN 0-521-28517-8). Cambridge U Pr.

Moore, J. N. see Jauncey, J. H.

Moore, J. R. The Post Darwinian Controversies. LC 77-94372. 1979. 49.50 (ISBN 0-521-21989-2). Cambridge U Pr.

--Principal of Oral Surgery. (Pergamon Series on Dentistry: Vol. 3). inquire for price o.p. (ISBN 0-08-011395-8). Pergamon.

Moore, J. R. & Gillbe, G. V., eds. Principles of Oral Surgery. 3rd ed. 254p. pap. 12.50 (ISBN 0-7190-0801-8). Manchester.

Moore, J. T., jt. auth. see Kruglak, Haym.

Moore, J. W. & Pearson, R. G. Kinetics & Mechanism. 3rd ed. 480p. 1980. 32.00x (ISBN 0-471-03558-0, Pub. by Wiley-Interscience). Wiley.

Moore, Jack, jt. auth. see Burbank, Rex.

Moore, Jack B. W. E. B. Du Bois. (Twayne's United States Authors Ser.). 1981. lib. bdg. 11.95 (ISBN 0-8057-7329-0, Twayne). G K Hall.

Moore, James, jt. auth. see Baylor, Robert.

Moore, James, jt. auth. see Donald, Robert.

Moore, James A. & Keene, Arthur S., eds. Archaeological Hammers & Theories. LC 82-11669. write for info. (ISBN 0-12-505980-9). Acad Pr.

Moore, James E. Everybody's Virgin Islands. 1979. pap. 8.95i (ISBN 0-397-01324-8, LP-149). Har-Row.

Moore, James M. Plant Layout & Design. (Illus.). 1962. 28.95x (ISBN 0-02-383180-4). Macmillan.

Moore, James M., jt. auth. see Tompkins, James A.

Moore, Jane. Cityward Migration: Swedish Data. 1938. 37.50x (ISBN 0-686-51354-1). Elliots Bks.

Moore, Janet G. The Eastern Gate: An Invitation to the Arts of China & Japan. LC 78-59816. (Illus.). (gr. 7 up). 1979. 24.95 (ISBN 0-529-05434-5, Philomel). Putnam Pub Group.

--Many Ways of Seeing: An Introduction to the Pleasures of Art. LC 67-23348. (Illus.). (gr. 5 up). 1969. 9.95 o.s.i. (ISBN 0-529-00954-4, A3682, Philomel); PLB 9.91 o.s.i. (ISBN 0-529-04017-4, 2792W). Putnam Pub Group.

Moore, Jared S. Rifts in the Universe: A Study of the Historic Dichotomies & Modalities of Being. 1927. 29.50x (ISBN 0-686-51303-7). Elliots Bks.

Moore, Jeanne, tr. see Braun, Otto.

Moore, Jerome. Texas Christian University: Hundred Years of History. (Centennial Publications Ser). 1974. 10.00 (ISBN 0-912646-40-3). Tex Christian.

Moore, Jerry R., jt. ed. see Williams, Paul L.

Moore, Jesse T., Jr. A Search for Equality: The National Urban League, 1910-1961. LC 80-24302. (Illus.). 264p. 1981. 18.95x (ISBN 0-271-00302-2). Pa St U Pr.

Moore, Joan & Garcia, Robert. Homeboys: Gangs, Drugs & Prison in the Barrios of Los Angeles. LC 78-11808. (Illus.). 1978. 29.95 (ISBN 0-87722-121-9); pap. 9.95 (ISBN 0-87722-114-6). Temple U Pr.

Moore, Joan W. Mexican Americans. 2nd ed. (Ethnic Groups in American Life Ser.). 208p. 1976. pap. text ed. 10.95x (ISBN 0-13-579508-7). P-H.

Moore, Joan W. & Moore, Burton M. Social Problems. (Illus.). 464p. 1982. 22.95 (ISBN 0-13-817387-7). P-H.

Moore, Joanna. South-East Asia Today. 16.95x o.p. (ISBN 0-7182-0453-0, SpS). Sportshelf.

Moore, Joe. Japanese Workers & the Struggle for Power, 1945-1947. LC 82-70552. (Illus.). 304p. 1983. 22.50 (ISBN 0-299-09320-4). U of Wis Pr.

Moore, John. By Selkirk's Lake & Other Poems. 74p. 1972. 2.95 (ISBN 0-87886-016-9). Ithaca Hse.

--PASCAL: Text & Reference. Orig. Title: PASCAL Programming. 1982. text ed. 18.95 (ISBN 0-8359-5459-5); pap. text ed. 16.95 (ISBN 0-8359-5457-9). Reston.

Moore, John, jt. auth. see Corlett, William.

Moore, John see Sophocles.

Moore, John, ed. Jane's Fighting Ships, 1982-1983. (Jane's Yearbooks). (Illus.). 960p. 140.00 (ISBN 0-86720-590-3). Sci Bks Intl.

Moore, John, tr. see Stevenson, William.

Moore, John A. Fray Luis De Granada. (World Authors Ser.). 1977. lib. bdg. 12.50 (ISBN 0-8057-6276-0, Twayne). G K Hall.

--Ramon de la Cruz. (World Authors Ser.). lib. bdg. 15.95 (ISBN 0-8057-2252-1, Twayne). G K Hall.

Moore, John A., jt. ed. see Nicholson, William J.

Moore, John B. Four Phases of American Development: Federalism, Democracy, Imperialism, Expansion. LC 72-109551. (Law, Politics & History Ser). 1970. Repr. of 1912 ed. lib. bdg. 32.50 (ISBN 0-306-71905-3). Da Capo.

Moore, John B. & Maleka, Leo. Structured Fortran & WATFIV. Alternate ed. 567p. 1981. text ed. 21.95 (ISBN 0-8359-7104-X); pap. text ed. 17.95 (ISBN 0-8359-7103-1); soln. manual o.p. avail. (ISBN 0-8359-7105-8). Reston.

Moore, John B., jt. auth. see Anderson, Brian.

Moore, John B., Jr., jt. auth. see Magill, Jane M.

Moore, John E. Warships of the Royal Navy. rev. ed. (Illus.). 128p. 1981. 19.50 (ISBN 0-86720-566-0). Sci Bks Intl.

--Warships of the Soviet Navy. (Illus.). 224p. 19.50 (ISBN 0-86720-567-9). Sci Bks Intl.

Moore, John E., ed. Jane's 1982-83 Naval Annual. (Illus.). 158p. 1982. 15.95 (ISBN 0-86720-634-9). Sci Bks Intl.

Moore, John E., ed. see Jane's Pocket Books.

Moore, John H. & Coplan, Michael A. Building Scientific Apparatus. (Illus.). 900p. 1982. 54.95 (ISBN 0-201-05532-5, Adv Bk Prog). A-W.

Moore, John M. Aristotle & Xenophon on Democracy & Oligarchy. LC 74-16713. 1975. 30.00x (ISBN 0-520-02863-5); pap. 7.95x (ISBN 0-520-02909-7). U of Cal Pr.

Moore, John M., ed. & intro. by. Friends in the Delaware Valley: Philadelphia Yearly Meeting, 1681-1981. (Illus.). 278p. (Orig.). 1981. 8.95 (ISBN 0-9609122-0-7); pap. 4.95 (ISBN 0-9609122-1-5). Friends Hist Assn.

Moore, John N. Should Evolution Be Taught? 1977. pap. 1.00 (ISBN 0-89051-043-1). CLP Pubs.

Moore, John N., ed. see Bliss, Richard.

Moore, John R., ed. Economic Impact of TVA. LC 67-12217. 1967. 12.50x (ISBN 0-87049-072-9). U of Tenn Pr.

Moore, John T. Elementary Linear & Matrix Algebra: The Viewpoint of Geometry. (Illus.). 288p. 1972. text ed. 15.95 o.p. (ISBN 0-07-042910-3, C); solutions manual 4.50 o.p. (ISBN 0-07-042886-7). McGraw.

--Elements of Linear Algebra & Matrix Theory. (International Pure & Applied Mathematics Ser). 1968. text ed. 31.50 (ISBN 0-07-042885-9, C). McGraw.

Moore, John W. Moore's Historical, Biographical, & Miscellaneous Gatherings. LC 68-17977. 1968. Repr. of 1886 ed. 52.00x (ISBN 0-8103-3312-0). Gale.

Moore, John W., et al. Chemistry. (Illus.). 1978. text ed. 28.00 (ISBN 0-07-042925-1, C); lab manual 12.95 (ISBN 0-07-042928-6); study guide 10.95 (ISBN 0-07-042927-8); instructor's manual 7.95 (ISBN 0-07-042926-X); student-instructor solution suppl. 4.95 (ISBN 0-07-042930-8). McGraw.

Moore, Jonathan & Fraser, Janet, eds. Campaign for President: 1976 in Retrospect. LC 77-12033. 208p. 1977. 12.95 (ISBN 0-88410-664-0). Ballinger Pub.

Moore, Julie & Ferguson, Sara K., eds. The Updata Index to U.S. Department of Agriculture Agricultural Handbooks Numbers 1-540. LC 81-71639. 1982. 49.50x (ISBN 0-9607840-0-4); lib. bdg. 49.50x (ISBN 0-9607840-0-4). Updata Pubns.

Moore, K. E., jt. ed. see Rech, R.

Moore, Katherine D., jt. auth. see Van Vactor, David.

Moore, Kathryn M. & Trow, Jo Anne J. Professional Advancement Kit-What to do until the Mentor Arrives: Administrative Procedures-A Practice Manual. (Orig.). 1982. write for info. (ISBN 0-686-82337-0); pap. 13.50. Natl Assn Women.

Moore, Keith L. The Developing Human. 2nd ed. LC 76-20098. (Illus.). 1977. text ed. 21.95 o.p. (ISBN 0-7216-6471-7). Saunders.

Moore, Keith L., jt. auth. see Bertram, E. G.

Moore, Kenneth, ed. see Ortega Y Gasset, Jose.

Moore, Kristin. Gold Country: A Pictorial Guide Through California's Historic Mother Lode. (Illus., Orig.). 1983. pap. 12.95 (ISBN 0-87701-247-4). Chronicle Bks.

Moore, Kristin A. & Burt, Martha R. Private Crisis, Public Cost: Policy Perspectives on Teenage Childbearing. LC 82-60293. 166p. (Orig.). 1982. pap. text ed. 11.00 (ISBN 0-87766-314-9, 33900). Urban Inst.

Moore, Lawrie. Foundations of Programming with Pascal. LC 80-40146. (Series of Computers & Their Applications). 238p. 1980. 54.95 o.p. (ISBN 0-470-27022-5, Pub. by Halsted Pr). Wiley.

Moore, Lilian. Go with the Poem. (gr. 4 up). 1979. 9.95 (ISBN 0-07-042880-8, GB). McGraw.

--Little Raccoon & Poems from the Woods. new ed. LC 75-14303. (Illus.). 48p. (gr. 4-6). 1975. 5.95 o.p. (ISBN 0-07-042913-8, GB); PLB 6.95 o.p. (ISBN 0-07-042914-6). McGraw.

--Little Raccoon & the Thing in the Pool. (Illus.). (gr. k-4). 1963. PLB 7.95 (ISBN 0-07-042892-1, GB). McGraw.

--Riddle Walk. LC 76-157849. (Venture Ser). (Illus.). (gr. 1). 1971. PLB 6.69 (ISBN 0-8116-6715-4). Garrard.

--Snake That Went to School. (Illus.). (gr. 4-6). 1957. PLB 5.99 o.p. (ISBN 0-394-90101-0, BYR). Random.

--Something New Begins. LC 81-1723. (Illus.). 128p. (gr. 3 up). 1982. 9.95 (ISBN 0-689-30818-3). Atheneum.

Moore, Lillian. A Child's First Picture Dictionary. (Illus.). 48p. Date not set. price not set (ISBN 0-448-02248-6, G&D). Putnam Pub Group.

Moore, Lillian, jt. auth. see Adelson, Leone.

Moore, Lillian C. Images of the Dance: Historical Treasures of the Dance Collection, 1581-1861. LC 65-18552. (Illus.). 1965. 15.00 (ISBN 0-87104-093-X). NY Pub Lib.

Moore, Linda, jt. auth. see Lye, Keith.

Moore, Linda, ed. see Taylor, Ron.

Moore, Linda P. Does This Mean My Kid's a Genius? How to Identify, Educate, Motivate & Live with the Gifted Child. 1982. pap. 6.95 (ISBN 0-452-25375-6, Plume). NAL.

Moore, Lou & Kassack, Nancy, eds. Computers & the Performing Arts. (Illus.). 116p. (Orig.). 1980. pap. 7.95 (ISBN 0-930452-15-1). Theatre Comm.

Moore, Lynda J., jt. auth. see Moore, Michael C.

Moore, M. J. & Sieverding, C. H. Two-Phase Steam Flow in Turbines & Separators: Theory, Instrumentation, Engineering. LC 76-9125. 1976. text ed. 38.50 (ISBN 0-07-042992-8, C). McGraw.

Moore, Malcolm A., ed. Maturation Factors & Cancer. (Progress in Cancer Research & Therapy Ser.: Vol. 23). 1982. text ed. 54.00 (ISBN 0-89004-596-8). Raven.

Moore, Margaret L., et al. Form & Function of Written Agreements in the Clinical Education of Health Professionals. LC 72-84792. 81p. 1972. 9.00x o.p. (ISBN 0-913590-04-5). Slack Inc.

Moore, Marie. Portrait of Essex. LC 69-12343. (Illus.). 112p. 1979. pap. 5.95 (ISBN 0-87106-022-1). Globe Pequot.

Moore, Marie A. How to Raise & Train a Mastiff. (Orig.). pap. 2.95 (ISBN 0-87666-336-6, DS1099). TFH Pubns.

Moore, Marilyn M. Baking Your Own: Recipes & Tips for Better Breads. LC 82-61710. (Illus.). 96p. 1982. pap. 7.95 (ISBN 0-9603788-0-4). Prairie Craft.

Moore, Marti & Bostaph, Charles. Crossroads: A Back to School Career Guide for Adults. LC 79-7112. 128p. 1979. pap. 5.95x (ISBN 0-910328-29-3). Carroll Pr.

Moore, Mary. English Teachers' Attitudes on Language & Literacy. (Language & Literacy Monograph Ser.). 1983. pap. text ed. 14.95 (ISBN 0-88499-601-8). Inst Mod Lang.

Moore, Mary C. David Rizzio. (Women Composers Ser.: No. 12). 1981. Repr. of 1937 ed. lib. bdg. 27.50 (ISBN 0-306-76101-7). Da Capo.

Moore, Mary E. Education for Continuity & Change: A New Model for Christian Religious Education. 224p. (Orig.). 1983. pap. 11.50 (ISBN 0-687-11523-X). Abingdon.

Moore, Mary E., jt. auth. see Swartz, Morris A.

Moore, Mary L. Newborn & the Nurse. LC 72-180185. (Monographs in Clinical Nursing: Vol. 3). (Illus.). 1972. 12.50x o.p. (ISBN 0-7216-6490-3). Saunders.

Moore, Maurice G. Worlds in Motion. 46p. (Orig.). 1964. pap. text ed. 5.60 (ISBN 0-686-37062-7). Trippensee Pub.

Moore, Michael C. & Moore, Lynda J. A Complete Handbook of Holistic Health. 253p. 1983. 17.95 (ISBN 0-13-168914-2); pap. 8.95 (ISBN 0-13-168906-1). P-H.

Moore, Mick & Connell, John, eds. Village Studies: Data Analysis & Bibliography: Vol. 2, Africa, Middle East & North Africa, Asia (Excluding India), Pacific Islands, Latin America, West Indies & the Caribbean, 1950-1975. 346p. 1978. pap. text ed. 32.00 (ISBN 0-7201-0797-0, Pub. by Mansell England). Wilson.

Moore, Milton. How Much Price Competition? The Prerequisites of an Effective Canadian Competition Policy. 1970. 12.50 (ISBN 0-7735-0083-9). McGill-Queens U Pr.

Moore, Milton T., Jr. Steve Reeves: A Tribute. LC 82-90099. 152p. (Orig.). 1982. pap. 14.95 (ISBN 0-9608138-0-2). M T Moore.

Moore, Nick, ed. On-Line Information in Public Libraries: A Review of Recent British Research. 69p. 1981. 35.00x (ISBN 0-905984-76-5, Pub. by Brit Lib England). State Mutual Bk.

Moore, Norman R., ed. Free & Inexpensive Learning Materials. rev. 20th ed. LC 53-2471. 257p. 1981. pap. 4.95 o.p. (ISBN 0-933436-01-7). Peabody Coll.

Moore, Norman R., ed. see Geo. Peabody College for Teachers.

Moore, Olin H. & Meiden, Walter. Onze Contes. LC 57-674. (Fr). 1957. pap. text ed. 10.50 (ISBN 0-395-04941-5). HM.

Moore, Osbert. A Thinker's Note Book. 1978. pap. 4.00 o.p. (ISBN 0-9600288-5-4). Poet Papers.

Moore, P. D. & Bellamy, D. J. Peatlands. LC 73-76673. (Illus.). 224p. 1973. 17.90 o.p. (ISBN 0-387-91112-X). Springer-Verlag.

Moore, P. D. & Webb, J. A. An Illustrated Guide to Pollen Analysis. LC 77-8822. 1978. 24.95x (ISBN 0-470-99218-2); pap. 24.95 (ISBN 0-470-27026-8). Halsted Pr.

Moore, P. G. Marine Pollution. 66p. 1978. 39.00x (ISBN 0-686-97029-2, Pub. by Meadowfield England). State Mutual Bk.

--Principles of Statistical Techniques. LC 75-85731. (Illus.). 280p. 1976. 34.50 (ISBN 0-521-07631-5); pap. 14.95 (ISBN 0-521-29055-4). Cambridge U Pr.

Moore, Patrick. Astronomy Facts & Feats. (Illus.). 288p. 1980. 19.95 (ISBN 0-900424-44-3, Pub by Guinness Superlatives England). Sterling.

--Guinness Book of Astronomy Facts & Feats. 2nd ed. (Illus.). 304p. 1983. 19.95 (ISBN 0-85112-258-2, Pub. by Guinness Superlatives England); pap. 12.95 (ISBN 0-85112-291-4, Pub. by Guinness Superlatives England). Sterling.

--True Book About Man. (Illus.). (gr. 7 up). 12.75x (ISBN 0-392-05123-0, LTB). Sportshelf.

Moore, Patrick & Brinton, Henry. Exploring Weather. (gr. 4 up). 4.50 o.p. (ISBN 0-685-20579-7). Transatlantic.

Moore, Patrick & Cross, Charles A. Mars. 1973. 8.50 o.p. (ISBN 0-517-50527-4). Crown.

Moore, Patrick, jt. auth. see Hunt, Garry.

Moore, Patrick, jt. auth. see Tombaugh, Clyde W.

Moore, Patrick, ed. Yearbook of Astronomy, 1983. (Illus.). 1983. 15.95 (ISBN 0-393-01700-1). Norton.

Moore, Patsie S., jt. auth. see Moore, Harvey D.

Moore, Peter. God Made the Stars. (Illus.). 32p. (Orig.). (gr. k-2). 1982. pap. 4.50 (ISBN 0-933770-18-9). Kalimat.

Moore, Philip. Total Bar & Beverage Management. 1981. 21.95 (ISBN 0-86730-238-0). Lebhar-Friedman.

Moore, Philip S., jt. ed. see Corbett, James A.

Moore, Philip S., et al. Sententiae Petri Pictaviensis 2. (Mediaeval Studies Ser: No. 11). (Lat). 1950. pap. 15.95x (ISBN 0-268-00391-2). U of Notre Dame Pr.

Moore, Preston L. Drilling Practices Manual. LC 74-80812. 448p. 1974. 55.95x (ISBN 0-87814-057-3). Pennwell Pub.

Moore, R. Pit-Men, Preachers & Politics. LC 73-88307. 42.50x (ISBN 0-521-20356-2); pap. 14.95x (ISBN 0-521-29752-4). Cambridge U Pr.

Moore, R., ed. see Hillison, John & Crunkilton, John.

Moore, R. E. Methods & Applications of Interval Analysis. LC 79-67191. (SIAM Studies in Applied Mathematics). xi, 190p. 1979. 17.50 (ISBN 0-89871-161-4). Soc Indus-Appl Math.

Moore, R. I. The Origins of European Dissent. 1978. 26.00x (ISBN 0-312-58852-6). St Martin.

Moore, R. I., ed. The Birth of Popular Heresy. LC 75-32934. (Documents of Medieval History Ser.). 176p. 1976. text ed. 22.00 (ISBN 0-312-08190-1). St Martin.

Moore, R. J., jt. auth. see Wilkinson, J. B.

Moore, R. J., jt. ed. see Wilkinson, J. B.

Moore, R. Laurence. In Search of White Crows: Spiritualism, Parapsychology, & American Culture. LC 76-50720. 1977. 18.95x (ISBN 0-19-502259-9). Oxford U Pr.

Moore, Ralph. The Will of God Isn't. (Religion Ser.). 150p. (Orig.). 1982. pap. write for info. (ISBN 0-941018-05-9). Martin Pr.

Moore, Ralph L. Neutralization of Waste Water by pH Control. LC 77-94491. 160p. 1978. text ed. 29.95x (ISBN 0-87664-383-7). Instru Soc.

Moore, Ralph L., ed. Basic Instrumentation Lecture Notes & Study Guide, 2 vols. (Orig.). 1983. pap. text ed. 27.95 ea. Vol. 1; Measurement Fundamentals. 178p (ISBN 0-87664-633-X). Vol. 2; Process Analyzers & Recorders. 116p (ISBN 0-87664-677-1). Set. pap. text ed. 50.00x (ISBN 0-87664-678-X); Vol. 1. slides 445.00 (ISBN 0-686-83972-2); Vol. 2. slides 380.00 (ISBN 0-686-83973-0); Vol. 1. transparencies 510.00 (ISBN 0-686-83974-9); Vol. 2. transparencies 440.00 (ISBN 0-686-83975-7). Instru Soc.

Moore, Rayanne. Thin White Line. (American Romance Ser.). 192p. 1983. pap. 2.25 (ISBN 0-373-16008-9). Harlequin Bks.

Moore, Rayburn S. Constance F. Woolson. (U. S. Authors Ser.: No. 34). 12.50 o.p. (ISBN 0-8057-0840-5, Twayne). G K Hall.

--Paul Hamilton Hayne. (United States Authors Ser.). lib. bdg. 13.95 (ISBN 0-8057-0352-7, Twayne). G K Hall.

Moore, Rayburn S., ed. A Man of Letters in the Nineteenth-Century South: Selected Letters of Paul Hamilton Hayne. (Southern Literary Studies). 376p. 1982. text ed. 32.50x (ISBN 0-8071-1025-6). La State U Pr.

Moore, Raylyn. What Happened to Emily Goode After the Great Exhibition. Freas, Polly & Freas, Kelly, eds. LC 78-2195. (Illus.). 1978. pap. 4.95 o.p. (ISBN 0-915442-51-5, Starblaze). Donning Co.

Moore, Raymond & Moore, Dorothy. Homespun Schools. 1982. 8.95 (ISBN 0-8499-0326-2). Word Pub.

Moore, Raymond C., ed. Treatise on Invertebrate Paleontology, Pt. D: Protista 3 (Radiolaria, Tintinnina) LC 53-12913. (Illus.). 1954. 16.00x (ISBN 0-8137-3004-X). Geol Soc.

--Treatise on Invertebrate Paleontology, Part G: Bryozoa. LC 53-12913. 1953. 16.00x (ISBN 0-8137-3007-4). Geol Soc.

--Treatise on Invertebrate Paleontology, Pt. I: Mollusca 1. LC 53-12913. (Illus.). 1960. 26.00x (ISBN 0-8137-3009-0). Geol Soc.

--Treatise on Invertebrate Paleontology: Part L - Mollusca 4 (Cephalopoda, Ammonoidea) LC 53-12913. 1957. 22.50x o.p. (ISBN 0-8137-3012-0). Geol Soc.

Moore, Raymond C. & Teichert, Curt, eds. Treatise on Invertebrate Paleontology: Part T: Echinodermata 2 (Crinoidea, 3 vols. LC 53-12913. (Illus.). 1978. Set. 55.00x (ISBN 0-8137-3021-X); Vol. 1. 27.00x (ISBN 0-686-82905-0); Vol. 2. 26.00x (ISBN 0-686-82906-9); Vol. 3. 13.00x (ISBN 0-686-82907-7). Geol Soc.

Moore, Raymond C., et al. Invertebrate Fossils. 1952. text ed. 45.00 (ISBN 0-07-043020-9, C). McGraw.

Moore, Reginald, ed. Official Rules of Sports & Games: 1982-1983. (Illus.). 800p. 1982. 24.95 (ISBN 0-7182-3960-1, Pub. by Kaye & Ward). David & Charles.

Moore, Richard. That Cunning Alphabet: Melville's Aesthetics of Nature. (Costerus New Ser.: No. 35). 232p. 1982. pap. text ed. 18.50x (ISBN 90-6203-734-8, Pub. by Rodopi Holland). Humanities.

Moore, Richard J., jt. auth. see Dietz, Henry A.

Moore, Richard K. Traveling Wave Engineering. (Electrical & Electronic Engineering Ser.). 1960. text ed. 36.50 (ISBN 0-07-042980-4, C). McGraw.

Moore, Robert, jt. auth. see Ellis, Josephy.

Moore, Robert, jt. auth. see Rex, John.

Moore, Robert L. Economic Principles in Action. (Illus.). 1979. pap. text ed. 12.95 (ISBN 0-13-226845-0). P-H.

--They Know Not What They Do: Baseball. (Illus.). 112p. (Orig.). 1971. pap. 1.00x (ISBN 0-912178-03-5). Mor-Mac.

Moore, Robert L., jt. auth. see Melton, J. Gordon.

Moore, Roberta, jt. auth. see Herr, Edwin L.

Moore, Robin. Fiedler: The Colorful Mr. Pops. (Music Reprint Ser.). (Illus.). 1980. Repr. of 1968 ed. lib. bdg. 32.50 (ISBN 0-306-76008-8). Da Capo.

--The Green Berets. 352p. 1983. pap. 3.50 (ISBN 0-345-30747-X). Ballantine.

Moore, Robin & Dempsey, Al. The London Switch, No. 1. (Pulsar Ser.). (Orig.). 1979. pap. 1.75 o.p. (ISBN 0-523-40707-6). Pinnacle Bks.

Moore, Robin, jt. auth. see Dempsey, Al.

Moore, Robin, jt. auth. see McGhee, Edward.

Moore, Robin J., ed. Tradition & Politics in South Asia. 1979. text ed. 17.75x (ISBN 0-7069-0608-X). Humanities.

Moore, Ronald. Legal Norms & Legal Science: A Critical Study of Kelsen's Pure Theory of Law. LC 77-12392. 1978. text ed. 14.00x (ISBN 0-8248-0516-X). UH Pr.

Moore, Rosalind, ed. Dell Crossword Puzzles, No. 45. (Orig.). 1983. pap. 2.50 (ISBN 0-440-11901-4). Dell.

--Dell Pencil Puzzles & Word Games, No. 2. (Orig.). 1983. pap. 3.50 (ISBN 0-440-11718-6). Dell.

--Dell Word Search, No. 24. (Orig.). 1983. pap. 2.75 (ISBN 0-440-11936-7). Dell.

Moore, Ruth. Evolution. rev. ed. LC 80-52119. (Life Nature Library). PLB 13.40 (ISBN 0-8094-3855-0). Silver.

--Evolution. (Young Readers Library). (Illus.). 1977. lib. bdg. 6.80 (ISBN 0-8094-1372-8). Silver.

Moore, Ruth, jt. auth. see Washburn, S. L.

Moore, Ruth N. Danger in the Pines. LC 82-15770. 160p. (gr. 4-9). 1983. text ed. 7.95 (ISBN 0-8361-3313-7); pap. 4.50 (ISBN 0-8361-3314-5). Herald Pr.

--The Ghost Bird Mystery. LC 77-10438. (Illus.). (gr. 4-8). 1977. 4.95 (ISBN 0-8361-1829-4); pap. 3.25 (ISBN 0-8361-1830-8). Herald Pr.

--Wilderness Journey. LC 79-20489. (Illus.). (gr. 4-9). 1979. 5.95 o.p. (ISBN 0-8361-1906-1); pap. 4.50 (ISBN 0-8361-1907-X). Herald Pr.

Moore, Sally F. Power & Property in Inca Peru. LC 72-5456. 190p. 1973. Repr. of 1958 ed. lib. bdg. 16.00x (ISBN 0-8371-6441-9, MOPO). Greenwood.

Moore, Samuel & Knott, Thomas A. Elements of Old English. 1955. 6.95x o.p. (ISBN 0-685-21780-9); pap. 7.50x (ISBN 0-685-21781-7). Wahr.

Moore, Samuel, jt. auth. see Marckwardt, Albert H.

Moore, Sebastian. The Crucified Jesus Is No Stranger. 1977. 6.95 (ISBN 0-8164-0341-4); pap. 5.95 (ISBN 0-8164-2315-6). Seabury.

--The Inner Loneliness. 125p. 1982. 9.95 (ISBN 0-8245-0515-8). Crossroad NY.

Moore, Sheila. Samson Svenson's Baby. LC 82-48262. (Illus.). 48p. (gr. k-3). 1983. 9.57i (ISBN 0-06-022612-9, HarpJ); PLB 9.89g (ISBN 0-06-022613-7). Har-Row.

Moore, Shelia J., jt. ed. see Coveney, James.

Moore, Stanley B. Ornamental Horticulture As a Vocation. (gr. 11 up). 1969. text ed. 9.00x (ISBN 0-912178-01-9). Mor-Mac.

Moore, Steven. A Reader's Guide to William Gaddis's "The Recognitions". LC 81-7572. xii, 337p. 1982. 25.00x (ISBN 0-8032-3072-9). U of Nebr Pr.

Moore, Susan R. The Drama of Discrimination in Henry James. LC 82-11111. (Scholars' Library). 127p. 1983. text ed. 32.50 (ISBN 0-7022-1668-2). U of Queensland Pr.

Moore, Suzanne, jt. auth. see Benmaman, Virginia.

Moore, T. Inglis. Social Patterns in Australian Literature. LC 71-133027. 1971. 32.50x (ISBN 0-520-01828-1). U of Cal Pr.

Moore, T. V. Haggai-Malachi. (Geneva Commentaries Ser.). 1974. 8.95 o.p. (ISBN 0-85151-079-5). Banner of Truth.

--Haggai, Malachi, & Zechariah. (Banner of Truth Geneva Series Commentaries). 1979. 12.95 (ISBN 0-85151-288-7). Banner of Truth.

Moore, T. W. Educational Theory: An Introduction. (Students Library of Education Ser.). 1974. 12.95x (ISBN 0-7100-7918-4); pap. 6.95 (ISBN 0-7100-8463-3). Routledge & Kegan.

Moore, T. W., et al. Conditioning & Instrumental Learning. 2nd ed. (Illus.). 1977. pap. text ed. 14.00 (ISBN 0-07-042902-2, C). McGraw.

Moore, Thomas, jt. ed. see Sue, Stanley.

Moore, Thomas V. Heroic Sanctity & Insanity: An Introduction to the Spiritual Life & Mental Hygiene. LC 59-7827. 256p. 1959. 27.50 o.p. (ISBN 0-8089-0331-4). Grune.

Moore, Tony. Nightmares. LC 81-86422. 88p. pap. 4.95 (ISBN 0-86666-116-6). GWP.

Moore, Tood. The Dark & Bloody Ground. 16p. 1982. 1.00 (ISBN 0-686-37505-X). Ptolemy Brown.

Moore, Virginia. The Madisons: A Biography. 1979. 15.00 o.p. (ISBN 0-07-042903-0, P&RB). McGraw.

Moore, W. C. British Parasitic Fungi. 1959. 75.00 (ISBN 0-521-05758-2). Cambridge U Pr.

Moore, W. D. Iam, III. Drilling Technology. 65p. 1981. pap. 17.95x (ISBN 0-87814-176-6). Pennwell Books Division.

Moore, W. E. American Negro Slavery & Abolition. LC 73-148362. 1971. 8.95 o.p. (ISBN 0-89388-000-0). Brown Bk.

Moore, W. G. The Tutorial System & Its Future. 1968. text ed. inquire for price o.p. (ISBN 0-08-012659-6); pap. text ed. 6.25 o.p. (ISBN 0-08-012658-8). Pergamon.

Moore, W. J. The Mammalian Skull. (Biological Structure & Function Ser.: No. 8). (Illus.). 400p. 1981. 95.00 (ISBN 0-521-23318-6). Cambridge U Pr.

Moore, Walter J. Physical Chemistry. 4th ed. 1972. ref. ed. 32.95 (ISBN 0-13-665968-3); solutions manual 10.95 (ISBN 0-13-665976-4). P-H.

Moore, Wayland B. New Testament Follow-Up. (Orig.). 1963. pap. 3.95 (ISBN 0-8028-1136-1). Eerdmans.

Moore, Wilbert E. Creative & Critical Thinking. LC 67-7864. 1967. text ed. 21.95 (ISBN 0-395-04939-3); instr's. manual, o.s.i. 2.15 (ISBN 0-395-04940-7, 3-38342). HM.

--The Professions: Roles & Rules. LC 78-104184. 316p. 1970. 10.95x (ISBN 0-87154-604-3). Russell Sage.

Moore, Wilbert E., jt. auth. see Young, Donald R.

Moore, Wilbert E., jt. ed. see Sheldon, Eleanor B.

Moore, William. Digital Logic Circuits: A Laboratory Manual. 1979. pap. text ed. 9.25 (ISBN 0-89917-020-X). TIS Inc.

--Home Beermaking. 2nd ed. (Illus.). 72p. 1982. pap. 3.95 (ISBN 0-9605318-0-7). Ferment Pr.

--Metric Is Here. new ed. LC 74-79676. (Illus.). 96p. (gr. 6-9). 1974. 5.95 o.p. (ISBN 0-399-20407-5). Putnam Pub Group.

--Your Science Fair Project. (Illus.). (gr. 4-8). 1964. PLB 5.49 o.p. (ISBN 0-399-60695-5). Putnam Pub Group.

Moore, William & Berlitz, Charles. The Philadelphia Experiment. LC 78-68142. 1979. 10.00 o.p. (ISBN 0-448-15777-2, G&D). Putnam Pub Group.

Moore, William C., ed. The Evangelical Sunday School Teacher's Guide, 1982-1983. 464p. (Orig.). 1982. pap. 5.95 o.p. (ISBN 0-8007-1310-9). Revell.

--The Evangelical Sunday School Teacher's Guide 1983-1984. 448p. (Orig.). 1983. pap. 6.95 (ISBN 0-8007-1348-6). Revell.

Moore, William L., jt. auth. see Berlitz, Charles.

Moore, Wynn. Keeping it on the Road: How to Buy a Car You'll Live Over 100,000 Miles & Smile When You Kiss it Goodbye. 1982. pap. 5.50 (ISBN 0-688-01013-X). Morrow.

Moore-Betty. Cook It Now, Serve It Later. 1981. 14.95 o.p. (ISBN 0-672-52685-9). Bobbs.

Moore-Betty, Maurice, jt. auth. see Travers, P. L.

Moorehead, tr. see Gauss, Karl F.

Moorehead, Alan. The Blue Nile. LC 73-186776. 1980. pap. 6.95i (ISBN 0-06-090776-2, CN 776, CN). Har-Row.

--The Blue Nile. LC 82-48895. (Illus.). 304p. 1983. pap. 12.95 (ISBN 0-394-71449-0, Vin). Random.

--Cooper's Creek. (Illus.). 1977. 12.95 o.p. (ISBN 0-312-16957-4). St Martin.

--Gallipoli. (War Library). 352p. 1982. pap. 3.50 (ISBN 0-345-30772-0). Ballantine.

--The White Nile. LC 82-48896. (Illus.). 254p. 1983. pap. 12.95 (ISBN 0-394-71445-8, Vin). Random.

Moorehead, Warren K. Archaeology of the Arkansas River Valley. 1931. text ed. 100.00x (ISBN 0-686-83475-5). Elliots Bks.

Moorehouse, Catherine. Adriana. (Orig.). 1983. pap. 3.25 (ISBN 0-440-00036-X). Dell.

Moore-Landecker, Elizabeth. Fundamentals of the Fungi. (Biological Ser). (Illus.). 1972. ref. ed. 28.95 (ISBN 0-13-339267-8). P-H.

Moores, B. M., et al. Physical Aspects of Medical Imaging: Proceedings of a Meeting Held at the University of Manchester, June 25-27, 1980. 342p. 1981. 36.95x (ISBN 0-471-10039-0, Pub. by Wiley-Interscience). Wiley.

Moores, Donald F. Educating the Deaf: Psychology, Principles, & Practices. 2nd ed. 1982. 23.95 (ISBN 0-395-31707-X). HM.

Moorey, Roger. Excavation in Palestine. 1982. 35.00x (ISBN 0-7188-2432-6, Pub. by Lutterworth Pr England). State Mutual Bk.

Moorhead, Elizabeth. Pittsburgh Portraits. (Orig.). 1955. pap. 1.95 o.p. (ISBN 0-910286-25-6). Boxwood.

Moorhead, Jack, ed. Numerical Control Applications. LC 80-52613. (Manufacturing Update Ser.). (Illus.). 260p. 1980. 32.00 (ISBN 0-87263-058-7). SME.

--Numerical Control Fundamentals. LC 80-52723. (Manufacturing Update Ser.). (Illus.). 242p. 1980. 32.00 (ISBN 0-87263-057-9). SME.

Moorhead, Lucy. Entertaining in Washington. LC 78-17789. 1978. 9.95 o.p. (ISBN 0-399-12200-1). Putnam Pub Group.

Moorhead, Max L. The Apache Frontier: Jacobo Ugarte & Spanish-Indian Relations in Northern New Spain, 1769-1791. LC 67-64449. (Civilization of the American Indian Ser.: No. 90). (Illus.). 1968. 17.95 (ISBN 0-8061-0787-1); pap. 8.95 (ISBN 0-8061-1312-X). U of Okla Pr.

Moorhead, Paul S. & Kaplan, Martin M., eds. Mathematical Challenges to the Neo-Darwinian Interpretation of Evolution. rev. ed. (Illus.). 176p. 1983. pap. 19.95 (ISBN 0-915520-60-5). Ross-Erikson.

Moorhouse, A. C. The Syntax of Sophocles. (Mnemosyne: Suppl. 75). xiii, 353p. 1982. pap. write for info. (ISBN 90-04-06599-7). E J Brill.

Moorhouse, C. San Francisco. (The Great Cities Ser.). (Illus.). 1979. lib. bdg. 12.00 (ISBN 0-8094-2348-0). Silver.

Moorhouse, Geoffrey. India Britannica. LC 82-48127. (Illus.). 272p. 1983. 22.07i (ISBN 0-06-015115-3, HarpT). Har-Row.

Moorman, Charles. Pearl Poet. (English Authors Ser.). 1980. 14.95 (ISBN 0-8057-1432-4, Twayne). G K Hall.

Moorman, Gary B., jt. auth. see Searfoss, Lyndon W.

Moorman, Lawrence & Jones, Marilyn P. Becoming Whole: A Self-Help Guide. 2nd ed. 1979. pap. text ed. 15.95 (ISBN 0-8403-1007-2, 40100702). Kendall-Hunt.

Moorman, Mary. William Wordsworth: A Biography, 2 vols. (Vol. 1, Early Years, 1770-1803;). Vol. 1. 49.00x (ISBN 0-19-811565-2); Vol. 2. pap. 5.95x o.p. (ISBN 0-19-881146-2, OPB). Oxford U Pr.

Moorman, Mary see Wordsworth, William & Wordsworth, Dorothy.

Moorman, R. B., jt. auth. see Parcel, John I.

Moors, Kent F. Glaucon & Adeimantus on Justice: The Structure of Argument in Book 2 of Plato's Republic. LC 81-40065. 156p. (Orig.). 1981. lib. bdg. 21.50 (ISBN 0-8191-1704-8); pap. text ed. 10.50 (ISBN 0-8191-1705-6). U Pr of Amer.

--Platonic Myth: An Introductory Study. LC 81-43816. 148p. (Orig.). 1982. lib. bdg. 19.50 (ISBN 0-8191-2314-5); pap. text ed. 8.25 (ISBN 0-8191-2315-3). U Pr of Amer.

Moorthy, K. Krishna. After Tito What? (Illus.). 225p. 1980. text ed. 13.00x (ISBN 0-391-02063-3). Humanities.

Moos. Number Systems: One Plus One Equals Ten. 1970. 14.95 (ISBN 0-471-25910-1, Wiley Heyden). Wiley.

Moos, Felix, jt. ed. see Goodman, Grant K.

Moos, Merry-K., jt. ed. see Miller, C. Arden.

Moos, N. H. How to Acquire a Million. 1954. 2.00 (ISBN 0-910140-26-X). Anthony.

Moos, Rudolf H. Evaluating Correctional & Community Settings. LC 73-17450. 400p. 1975. 27.50 o.p. (ISBN 0-471-61502-1, Pub. by Wiley-Interscience). Wiley.

--Evaluating Treatment Environments: A Social Ecological Approach. LC 73-17450. (Wiley-Interscience Ser. Health, Medicine, & Society). 304p. 1974. 38.95 (ISBN 0-471-61503-X, Pub. by Wiley-Interscience). Wiley.

--The Human Context: Environmental Determinants of Behavior. LC 75-26870. 444p. 1976. 31.95 o.p. (ISBN 0-471-61504-8, Pub. by Wiley-Interscience). Wiley.

Moos, Stanislaus Von see Von Moos, Stanislaus.

Moosa, Matti. The Origins of Modern Arabic Fiction. LC 82-51657. 238p. 1983. 18.00x (ISBN 0-89410-166-8); pap. 8.00 (ISBN 0-89410-167-6). Three Continents.

Moosbrugger, Bernhard & Weigner, Gladys. A Voice of the Third World: Dom Helder Camara. LC 80-82008. (Illus.). 1972. pap. 1.95 o.p. (ISBN 0-8091-1738-X). Paulist Pr.

Mooser, Stephen. Funnyman's First Case. (Easy-Read Story Bks.). (Illus.). 32p. (gr. k-3). 1981. 8.60 (ISBN 0-686-76380-7); lib. bdg. 7.40 (ISBN 0-531-03538-7). Watts.

--The Ghost with the Halloween Hiccups. (Easy-Read Storybooks). (Illus.). (gr. k-3). 1977. Repr. lib. bdg. 8.60 s&l o.p. (ISBN 0-531-01316-2). Watts.

--Into the Unknown: Nine Astounding Stories. Stevenson, Dinah, ed. LC 79-3336. (Illus.). (gr. 5 up). 9.57i o.p. (ISBN 0-397-31855-3, JBL-J); PLB 9.89 (ISBN 0-397-31904-5). Har-Row.

Moossa, A. R., jt. auth. see Cushieri, A.

Moossy, John, ed. Cerebrovascular Diseases. (Princeton Research Conferences on Cerebrovascular Diseases Ser.: No. 12). 355p. 1981. text ed. 28.00 (ISBN 0-89004-597-6). Raven.

Moots, Patricia A. & Zak, Michele, eds. Women & the Politics of Culture: Studies in the Sexual Economy. (Illus.). 352p. (Orig.). 1983. pap. text ed. 14.50x (ISBN 0-582-28391-4). Longman.

Moots, Philip R., jt. auth. see Gaffney, Edward M.

Moo-Young, M., ed. see United Nations Environment Programme.

Mope, Warren, ed. see Thomas, Norman & Wilson, Edmund.

Moquin, Wayne, ed. Makers of America, 10 Vols. (Illus.). (gr. 7-12). 1971. Set. 159.00 (ISBN 0-87827-000-0). Ency Brit Ed.

Mora, Abdias A., tr. see Copeland, E. L.

Mora, George & Brand, Jeanne L. Psychiatry & Its History: Methodological Problems in Research. 304p. 1970. photocopy ed. spiral 27.75x (ISBN 0-398-01342-X). C C Thomas.

Moracco, John. Therapist Burnout: Descriptions & Strategies. 30p. Date not set. softcover 3.25 o.p. (ISBN 0-932930-27-1). Pilgrimage Inc.

Moracco, John & Higgins, Earl. Comprehensive Approach to Human Relations Development. 360p. 1983. pap. text ed. price not set (ISBN 0-915202-38-7). Accel Devel.

Moracco, John C., jt. auth. see D'Arienzo, Raymond V.

Morace, Robert A. & VanSpanckeren, Kathryn, eds. Critical Perspectives on John Gardner: Critical Perspectives. (Crosscurrents Modern Critiques, New Ser.). 184p. 1982. 18.95x (ISBN 0-8093-1031-7). S Ill U Pr.

Moraczewski, Albert S., ed. Genetic Medicine & Engineering: Ethical & Social Dimensions. (Orig.). 1983. pap. write for info. (ISBN 0-87125-077-2). Cath Health.

Moraes, Dom. Bombay. (Great Cities Ser.). PLB 12.00 (ISBN 0-8094-2340-5). Silver.

Moraff, Barbara. Telephone Company Repairman. LC 82-19275. (Illus.). 20p. (Orig.). 1983. pap. 15.00 (ISBN 0-915124-75-0). Toothpaste.

Moraghan Jablow, Martha. Cara: Growing with a Retarded Child. 250p. 1982. 22.95 (ISBN 0-87722-255-X); pap. 12.95 (ISBN 0-87722-269-X). Temple U Pr.

Morahan, Shirley. A Woman's Place: Rhetoric & Readings for Composing Yourself & Your Prose. LC 81-4802. 336p. 1981. 34.50x (ISBN 0-87395-549-8); pap. 10.95x (ISBN 0-87395-488-2); instructor's manual avail. (ISBN 0-87395-489-0). State U NY Pr.

Morain, Lloyd L. The Human Cougar. LC 75-46147. 175p. 1976. 9.95 o.p. (ISBN 0-87975-062-6). Prometheus Bks.

Morain, Mary, ed. Classroom Exercises in General Semantics. 1983. 5.50 (ISBN 0-686-84071-2). Intl Gen Semantics.

Morais, Robert J. Social Relations in a Philippine Town, No. 19. (No. Ill. Univ., Center for SEAsian Studies, Special report). (Illus.). 165p. 1982. pap. 11.00x (ISBN 0-686-35856-2); pap. text ed. 11.00x (ISBN 0-686-37186-0). North Ill U Ctr SE Asian.

Morales, C. Saharan Dust: Mobilization Transport Deposition. LC 78-8687. (Scientific Committee on Problems of the Environment Ser.: Scope Report 14). 1979. 49.95 (ISBN 0-471-99680-7, Pub. by Wiley-Interscience). Wiley.

Morales, Emerito S. Libre Como El Viento. (Poetry Ser.). 100p. 1982. pap. 6.00 (ISBN 0-686-37371-5). Edit Asol.

Morales, Gil. Wake Me When the Semester's Over. 96p. (Orig.). 1983. pap. 3.95 (ISBN 0-345-30714-3). Ballantine.

Morales, Golie L. Floating Petals. (Illus.). 46p. 1982. pap. 2.50 (ISBN 0-910083-09-6). Heritage Trails.

Moral-Lopez, P. & Jacoby, E. H. Principles of Land Consolidation Legislation. (FAO Legislative Ser.: No. 3). (Orig.). 1966. pap. 4.50 o.p. (ISBN 0-685-09400-6, F331, FAO). Unipub.

Moran, Cathleen, jt. auth. see Balkam, Jean.

Moran, Connie. Passions of a Lover: Music of the Soul. 1980. 4.95 (ISBN 0-8062-1482-1). Carlton.

Moran, Gabriel. Education Toward Adulthood. LC 78-65897. 160p. 1979. pap. 5.95 o.p. (ISBN 0-8091-2194-8). Paulist Pr.

--The Present Revelation: In Quest of Religious Foundations. 204p. 1972. 2.00 (ISBN 0-8164-1105-0). Seabury.

--Religious Education Development. (Images for the Future). 204p. 1983. pap. 9.95 (ISBN 0-86683-692-6). Winston Pr.

--Theology of Revelation. 1968. pap. 5.95 (ISBN 0-8164-2567-1). Seabury.

Moran, George, jt. auth. see Brandreth, Gyles.

Moran, George, jt. auth. see Erskine, Jim.

Moran, Gerard P. Aeroplanes Vought: Nineteen-Seventeen to Nineteen Seventy-Seven. LC 77-91434. (Company History Ser.). (Illus.). 168p. 1978. 16.50 o.p. (ISBN 0-911852-83-2, Pub by Hist Aviation). Aviation.

Moran, Goerge, jt. auth. see Erskine, Jim.

Moran, James. Printing Presses: History & Development from the Fifteenth Century to Modern Times. (Illus.). 1973. 45.00x (ISBN 0-520-02245-9); pap. 7.95 (ISBN 0-520-02904-6). U of Cal Pr.

Moran, James J. Marketing of Professional Accounting Services: A Practice Development Approach. 2nd ed. 199p. 1982. 34.95X (ISBN 0-471-86731-4). Ronald Pr.

Moran, Kelly. A Summer Camp Directory: A Parent's & Counselor's Guide to Over 1,000 Specialized Summer Camps. (Illus.). 192p. (Orig.). 1982. lib. bdg. 19.80 o.p. (ISBN 0-89471-176-8); pap. 8.95 o.p. (ISBN 0-89471-175-X). Running Pr.

Moran, Leila, jt. ed. see Fusonie, Alan.

Moran, Marguerite K., jt. auth. see Lowenheim, Frederick A.

Moran, Michael. Availability Analysis: A Guide to Efficient Energy Use. (Illus.). 304p. 1982. 34.95 (ISBN 0-13-054874-X). P-H.

--Standards Relating to Appeals & Collateral Review. LC 77-3982. (IJA-ABA Juvenile Justice Standards Project Ser.). 64p. 1980. prof ref 14.00x (ISBN 0-88410-776-0); pap. 7.00x prof ref (ISBN 0-88410-815-5). Ballinger Pub.

Moran, P. Ulysses S. Grant, Eighteen Twenty-Two to Eighteen Eighty-Five: Chronology, Documents, Bibliographical Aids. LC 68-23568. (Presidential Chronology Ser: No. 6). 114p. 1968. 8.00 (ISBN 0-379-12056-9). Oceana.

Moran, P., ed. Calvin Coolidge, Eighteen Seventy-Two to Nineteen Thirty-Three: Chronology, Documents, Bibliographical Aids. LC 74-116060. (Presidential Chronology Ser). 144p. 1970. 8.00 (ISBN 0-379-12079-8). Oceana.

--Warren G. Harding, 1865-1923: Chronology, Documents, Bibliographical Aids. LC 78-95013. (Presidential Chronology Ser). 1970. 8.00 (ISBN 0-379-12064-X). Oceana.

Moran, Patrick R., ed. Day by Day with Mary. 204p. 1983. pap. 6.95 (ISBN 0-87973-613-5, 613). Our Sunday Visitor.

Moran, Ricardo, jt. auth. see Knight, Peter T.

Moran, Ricardo J., jt. auth. see Knight, Peter T.

Moran, Robert T., jt. auth. see Harris, Philip R.

Moran, Thomas P., jt. auth. see Card, Stuart K.

Moran, Tom. Frisbee Disc Flying Is for Me. LC 82-244. (Sports for Me Bks.). (Illus.). 48p. (gr. 2-5). 1982. lib. bdg. 6.95g (ISBN 0-8225-1137-1). Lerner Pubns.

--Roller Skating Is for Me. LC 81-3722. (Sports for Me Bks.). (Illus.). (gr. 2-5). 1981. PLB 6.95g (ISBN 0-8225-1097-9, AACR2). Lerner Pubns.

Moran, Warren, jt. auth. see Stanford, Quentin H.

Moran, William, jt. ed. see Fagan, Ted.

Moranasee, Jess R. Children's Prize Books: An International Listing of 189 Children's Literature Prizes. 2nd, rev. & enl. ed. 1983. 36.00 (ISBN 3-598-03250-1, Pub. By K G Saur). Shoe String.

Morando, Bruno, jt. auth. see Merleau-Ponty, Jacques.

Morant, Mack B. The Insane Nigger. 2nd ed. White, Mosezelle, ed. (Illus.). 75p. (Orig.). 1982. pap. 6.95x (ISBN 0-936026-00-6). R&M Pub Co.

--Lines for the Mind. Nichols, Mosezelle, ed. 52p. (Orig.). 1978. pap. 3.50x o.s.i. (ISBN 0-936026-02-2). R&M Pub Co.

Morant, Mack B., ed. see Roberts, Bobby, III.

Morantte, M. P. God Is in the Heart: Poetical & Symbolical Essays. (Illus.). 78p. (Orig.). 1982. pap. 4.75 (ISBN 971-10-0040-7, Pub. by New Day Philippines). Cellar.

Morantz, Toby, jt. auth. see Francis, Daniel.

Morash, Merry, ed. Implementing Criminal Justice Policies: Common Problems & their Sources. (Sage Research Progress Series in Criminology: Vol. 26). 160p. 1982. 18.95 (ISBN 0-8039-1884-4); pap. 8.95 (ISBN 0-8039-1885-2). Sage.

Moratin, Leandro F. De see De Moratin, Leandro F.

Moraud, Marcel I., jt. auth. see Keating, L. Clark.

Moravia. Sette Racconti. (Easy Reader, C). pap. 3.95 (ISBN 0-88436-060-1, 55258). EMC.

Moravia, Alberto. The Fetish & Other Stories. Davidson, Angus, tr. from It. LC 75-28668. 1976. Repr. of 1965 ed. lib. bdg. 18.00x (ISBN 0-8371-8487-8, PIFE). Greenwood.

--Man As an End, a Defense of Humanism: Literary, Social & Political Essays. Wall, Bernard, tr. from It. LC 75-391. 254p. 1976. Repr. of 1966 ed. lib. bdg. 17.50x (ISBN 0-8371-8019-8, PIME). Greenwood.

--Nineteen Thirty-Four. Weaver, William, tr. from Ital. 1983. 14.50 (ISBN 0-374-22254-1). FS&G.

--Roman Tales. Davidson, Angus, tr. from Italian. LC 75-26219. 229p. 1975. Repr. of 1957 ed. lib. bdg. 15.50x (ISBN 0-8371-8412-6, PIRT). Greenwood.

--Two Adolescents. De Zoete, Beryl & Davidson, Angus, trs. from It. LC 75-25266. 268p. 1976. Repr. of 1950 ed. lib. bdg. 20.50x (ISBN 0-8371-8392-8, PITA). Greenwood.

Morawetz, C. S. Lectures on Nonlinear Waves & Shocks. (Tata Institute Lectures on Mathematics). 137p. 1982. pap. 6.70 (ISBN 0-387-10830-0). Springer-Verlag.

Morawetz, Cathleen S. Notes on Time Decay & Scattering for Some Hyperbolic Problems. (CBMS Regional Conference Ser.: Vol. 19). (Illus.). v, 81p. (Orig.). 1975. pap. text ed. 11.50 (ISBN 0-89871-016-2). Soc Indus-Appl Math.

Morawetz, David. The Andean Group: A Case Study in Economic Integration Among Developing Countries. LC 74-3070. 216p. 1974. 25.00x (ISBN 0-262-13109-9). MIT Pr.

Morawetz, Thomas A. The Philosophy of Law: An Introduction. 1980. pap. text ed. 12.95x (ISBN 0-02-383340-8). Macmillan.

Morawski, Stefan. Inquiries into the Fundamentals of Aesthetics. 1974. 37.50x (ISBN 0-262-13096-3); pap. 7.95x (ISBN 0-262-63066-4). MIT Pr.

Morbidoni, Barbara. Stars & Stoves: An Astrological Cookbook. LC 79-55651. (Illus., Orig.). 1979. pap. 5.00 (ISBN 0-933646-07-0). Aries Pr.

--Zodiantics: An Astrology Handbook. Rev. ed. LC 77-2070. (Illus.). 1982. pap. 5.00 (ISBN 0-933646-18-6). Aries Pr.

Morcos, Nabil, jt. ed. see Lambrecht, Richard M.

Mordan, Mary J., jt. auth. see Bermosk, Loretta S.

Mordden, Ethan. The American Theatre. 380p. 1981. 22.50 (ISBN 0-19-502959-3). Oxford U Pr.

--A Guide to Orchestral Music: The Handbook for Non-Musicians. (Illus.). 1980. 22.50 (ISBN 0-19-502686-1). Oxford U Pr.

--The Hollywood Musical. (Illus.). 264p. 1982. pap. 8.95 (ISBN 0-312-38838-1). St Martin.

--Opera in the Twentieth Century: Sacred, Profane, Godot. 1978. 17.95x (ISBN 0-19-502288-2). Oxford U Pr.

--That Jazz! An Idiosyncratic Social History of the American Twenties. LC 77-26759. 1978. 10.95 o.p. (ISBN 0-399-12159-5). Putnam Pub Group.

Mordecai, Pamela & Morris, Mervyn, eds. Jamaica Woman, No. 29. (Caribbean Writers Ser.). 128p. (Orig.). 1982. pap. text ed. 5.00x (ISBN 0-435-98600-7). Heinemann Ed.

Mordell, Klein, ed. Passover. 128p. pap. 4.50 (ISBN 0-686-95142-5). ADL.

Mordell, Louis J; see Klein, Felix.

Mordike, Janet, tr. see Haasen, Peter.

Morduch, Anna. Sovereign Adventure: The Grail of Mankind. 196p. 1970. 11.95 (ISBN 0-227-67754-4). Attic Pr.

More, Charles, ed. Skill & the English Working Class 1870-1914. LC 80-51895. 1980. 26.00 (ISBN 0-312-72772-0). St Martin.

More, Colleen. Bold Venture. (Candlelight Regency Special Ser.: No. 690). (Orig.). 1981. pap. 1.75 o.s.i. (ISBN 0-440-10517-X). Dell.

More, George. With Livingston in South Africa. (Illus.). (gr. 7 up). 12.75x (ISBN 0-392-01914-0, LTB). Sportshelf.

More, Harry W., ed. Principles & Procedures in the Administration of Justice. LC 74-7062. (Administration of Justice Ser.). 456p. 1975. text ed. 23.95 (ISBN 0-471-61508-0, Pub. by Wiley-Interscience). Wiley.

More, Harry W., Jr. Effective Police Administration: A Behavioral Approach. 2nd ed. (Criminal Justice Ser.). (Illus.). 1979. text ed. 22.95 (ISBN 0-8299-0251-1). West Pub.

More, Harry W., Jr., jt. auth. see Kenney, John P.

More, Harry W., Jr., ed. Contemporary Criminal Justice. 2nd ed. (Administration of Justice Ser.: Vol. 6). 304p. 1977. pap. text ed. 12.95 (ISBN 0-914526-05-7). Justice Sys.

More, Jasper. The Land of Egypt. (Illus.). 192p. 1980. 22.50 (ISBN 0-7134-1635-1, Pub. by Batsford England). David & Charles.

More, Paul E. Christ the Word. LC 72-88913. Repr. of 1927 ed. lib. bdg. 15.75x (ISBN 0-8371-2244-9, MOCW). Greenwood.

--Hellenistic Philosophies. LC 69-14003. Repr. of 1923 ed. lib. bdg. 18.50x (ISBN 0-8371-1881-6, MOHP). Greenwood.

More, Shankar S. Remodelling of Democracy for Afro-Asian Nations. LC 72-9810. 347p. 1973. Repr. of 1962 ed. lib. bdg. 18.25x (ISBN 0-8371-6599-7, MORD). Greenwood.

More, Thomas. Idee d'une Republique Heureuse. Gueudeville, Nicolas, tr. (Utopias in the Enlightenment Ser.). 459p. (Fr.). 1974. Repr. of 1730 ed. lib. bdg. 115.00 o.p. (ISBN 0-8287-0634-4, 054). Clearwater Pub.

More, St. Thomas. Utopia. 1978. 8.95x (ISBN 0-460-00461-1, Evman); pap. 2.95x (ISBN 0-460-01461-7, Evman). Biblio Dist.

More, Thomas St., et al, eds. A Dialogue Concerning Heresies: Complete Works of St. Thomas More, Vol. 6, Pts. 1 & 2. LC 63-7949. (Illus.). 910p. 1981. Set. text ed. 80.00x (ISBN 0-300-02211-5). Yale U Pr.

Morea, Peter. Guidance, Selection, & Training: Ideas & Applications. 1972. 26.50x (ISBN 0-7100-7236-8). Routledge & Kegan.

Moreau, Claude. Moulds, Toxins & Food. LC 78-8715. 1979. 89.95 (ISBN 0-471-99681-5, Pub. by Wiley-Interscience). Wiley.

Moreau, David. Look Behind You! An Alphabetical Guide to Executive Survival. LC 75-8506. (Illus.). 1975. 5.95 o.p. (ISBN 0-688-02927-2). Morrow.

Moreau, J. F., jt. ed. see Amiel, M.

Moreau, J. J., et al. Hashish & Mental Illness. Peters, H. & Nahas, G., eds. Barnett, G. J., tr. from Fr. LC 76-107227. Orig. Title: Du Haschish et De l'Alienation Mentale. 267p. 1973. pap. 20.00 (ISBN 0-911216-14-6). Raven.

Moreau, James F. Effective Small Business Management. 1980. 21.95 (ISBN 0-395-30676-0); Tchrs Manual 3.25 (ISBN 0-395-30677-9). HM.

Moreau, Jean-Francois & Mazzara, Laure. Intravenous Urography. Affre, Jean & Garel, Laurent, eds. 392p. 1983. 45.00 (ISBN 0-471-87422-1, Pub. by Wiley Med). Wiley.

Moreau, R. E. The Palaearctic-African Bird Migration System. Monk, J. F., ed. 1972. 63.00 o.s.i. (ISBN 0-12-506660-0). Acad Pr.

Moreau, R. E., jt. auth. see Hall, B. P.

Moreau-Christophe, L. M. Du Probleme de la Misere et de sa Solution Chez le Peuples Anciens et Modernes, Tome 3: Peuples Modernes. (Conditions of the 19th Century French Working Class Ser.). 580p. (Fr.). 1974. Repr. of 1851 ed. lib. bdg. 142.00x o.p. (ISBN 0-8287-0635-2, 1027). Clearwater Pub.

Moreau De Saint Mery. Considerations Presentees aux Vrais Amis du Repos et du Bonheur de la France, a l'Occasion des Nouveaux Mouvements de Quelques Soi-Disant Amis des Noirs. (Slave Trade in France Ser., 1744-1848). 74p. (Fr.). 1974. Repr. of 1791 ed. lib. bdg. 29.50x o.p. (ISBN 0-8287-0636-0, TN117). Clearwater Pub.

Morecki, A. & Ekiel, J. Cybernetic Systems of Limb Movements in Man, Animals & Robots. LC 82-15717. 250p. 1983. 79.95x (ISBN 0-470-27374-7). Halsted Pr.

Morecki, A. & Bianchi, G., eds. Theory & Practice of Robots & Manipulators, III. 1980. 110.75 (ISBN 0-444-99772-5). Elsevier.

Morecki, A. & Kedzior, K., eds. Theory & Practice of Robots & Manipulators: Proceedings of the Second CISM-IFTOMM International Symposium, Warsaw, September, 1976. 1978. 93.75 (ISBN 0-444-99812-8). Elsevier.

Morecki, Adam. Biomechanics VII-A. (International Series on Biomechanics: Vol. 3A). 300p. 1982. text ed. 34.50 (ISBN 0-8391-1383-8). Univ Park.

--Biomechanics VII-B. (International Series on Biomechanics: Vol. 3B). 300p. 1982. text ed. 34.50 (ISBN 0-8391-1384-6). Univ Park.

Morecock, Michael. Heroic Dreams: Wizardry & Wild Romance. LC 78-64551. (Illus.). pap. cancelled (ISBN 0-89169-526-5). Reed Bks.

Morehart, Thomas B., jt. auth. see Apilado, Vincent P.

Morehead, et al, eds. Hoyles Rules of Games. (RL 7). 1973. pap. 2.50 (ISBN 0-451-09701-7, E9701, Sig). NAL.

Morehead, Albert H. Complete Guide to Winning Poker. 1967. 7.95 o.p. (ISBN 0-671-15504-0). S&S.

Morehead, Albert H. & Mott-Smith, Geoffrey. Hoyle Up-to-Date. 5.95 (ISBN 0-448-01984-1, G&D). Putnam Pub Group.

Morehead, Albert H., et al, eds. New American Roget's College Thesaurus in Dictionary Form. (gr. 9 up). 1957. 4.95 (ISBN 0-448-01605-2, G&D); thumb-indexed ed. 4.95 (ISBN 0-448-01622-2). Putnam Pub Group.

Morehead, Anne E., jt. ed. see Morehead, Donald M.

Morehead, Donald M. & Morehead, Anne E., eds. Normal & Deficient Child Language. (Illus.). 488p. 1976. text ed. 19.95 (ISBN 0-8391-0857-5). Univ Park.

Morehead, Joe. Introduction to U. S. Public Documents. 2nd ed. LC 78-16866. (Library Science Text). (Illus.). 377p. 1978. lib. bdg. 28.00 (ISBN 0-87287-186-X); pap. text ed. 21.00 (ISBN 0-87287-190-8). Libs Unl.

--Introduction to United States Public Documents. 3rd ed. (Library Science Text Ser.). 377p. 1983. lib. bdg. 28.50 (ISBN 0-87287-359-5); pap. text ed. 19.50 (ISBN 0-87287-362-5). Libs Unl.

Morehead, John W. Finding & Licensing New Products & Technology from the U. S. A. 500p. 1982. 495.00 (ISBN 0-943420-00-8). Tech Search Intl.

Morehead, Loy, jt. auth. see Wilson, Tom.

Morehouse & Gross. Total Fitness. LC 74-16116. 224p. 1975. 8.95 o.p. (ISBN 0-671-21925-1); pap. 2.95 o.p. (ISBN 0-671-22308-9). S&S.

Morehouse, Laurence E. & Miller, Augustus T. Physiology of Exercise. 7th ed. LC 75-22186. (Illus.). 364p. 1976. text ed. 15.95 o.p. (ISBN 0-8016-3485-7). Mosby.

Morehouse, Thomas A., jt. auth. see McBeath, Gerald A.

Morehouse, Thomas A., ed. Alaskan Resources Development: Issues of the 1980's. 350p. 1983. lib. bdg. 25.00x (ISBN 0-86531-512-4). Westview.

Morehouse, Ward. Separate, Unequal, but More Autonomous. (Working Papers in the World Order Models Project Ser.). 50p. (Orig.). 1981. pap. 1.50 (ISBN 0-911646-11-6). Transaction Bks.

--Understanding Science & Technology in India & Pakistan. (Occasional Publication). 78p. 1967. pap. 2.00 o.p. (ISBN 0-89192-136-2). Interbk Inc.

Morehouse, Ward, jt. auth. see Ehrman, Edith.

Morehouse, Ward, ed. The Comparative Approach in Area Studies & the Disciplines. (Occasional Publication). 68p. 1966. pap. 2.00 o.p. (ISBN 0-89192-135-4). Interbk Inc.

--Foreign Area Studies & the College Library. (Occasional Publication Ser.). 80p. 1965. pap. 1.00 o.p. (ISBN 0-89192-134-6). Interbk Inc.

Morehouse, Ward, III. The Waldorf: The Story Behind America's Grandest Hotel. (Illus.). 320p. 13.95 o.p. (ISBN 0-399-12541-8). Putnam Pub Group.

Moreira, J. Roberto, jt. auth. see Havighurst, Robert J.

Morel. Biochemistry of Kidney Functions. (INSERM Symposia Ser.: Vol. 21). 1982. 81.00 (ISBN 0-444-80417-X). Elsevier.

Morel, jt. auth. see Serle.

Morel, Eve, ed. see Grimm Brothers.

Morel, Julian. Pullman. (Illus.). 192p. (Orig.). 1983. 19.95 (ISBN 0-7153-8382-5). David & Charles.

Moreland, Carroll C. & Surrency, Erwin C. Research in Pennsylvania Law. 2nd ed. LC 65-27629. 118p. 1965. 11.00 (ISBN 0-379-11651-0). Oceana.

Moreland, Donald E. & St. John, Judith B., eds. Biochemical Responses by Herbicides. (ACS Symposium Ser.: No. 181). 1982. write for info. (ISBN 0-8412-0699-6). Am Chemical.

Morell, David & Magorian, Christopher. Siting Hazardous Waste Facilities: Local Opposition & the Myth of Preemption. 288p. 1982. prof ref 25.00 (ISBN 0-88410-906-2). Ballinger Pub.

Morell, R. W. Administrative Accounting. LC 80-5440. 297p. 1980. pap. text ed. 11.50 (ISBN 0-8191-1098-1). U Pr of Amer.

Morell, R. W. & Henry, M. Daniel. The Practice of Management. LC 80-8136. 510p. 1981. lib. bdg. 29.00 (ISBN 0-8191-1489-8); pap. text ed. 17.50 (ISBN 0-8191-1490-1). U Pr of Amer.

Morella, Joseph, jt. auth. see Bliss, James.

Morellet, Andre. Le Manuel des Inquisiteurs a l'Usage des Inquisitions d'Espagne et du Portugal. (Holbach & His Friends Ser). 196p. (Fr.). 1974. Repr. of 1762 ed. lib. bdg. 56.50x o.p. (ISBN 0-8287-0638-7, 1525). Clearwater Pub.

Morello, Joseph. Jean Rotrou. (World Authors Ser.). 1980. 15.95 (ISBN 0-8057-6406-2, Twayne). G K Hall.

Morelly. Naufrage des Iles Flottante. (Utopias in the Enlightenment Ser.). 321p. (Fr.). 1974. Repr. of 1753 ed. lib. bdg. 84.00x o.p. (ISBN 0-8287-1390-1, 025). Clearwater Pub.

Morel-Seytoux, Hubert J., et al, eds. Surface & Subsurface Hydrology. LC 78-68496. 1979. 28.00 (ISBN 0-918334-28-4). WRP.

Morely-Fletcher, Hugo. Investing in Pottery & Porcelain. 1968. 7.95 (ISBN 0-517-00045-8, C N Potter Bks). Crown.

Morenas. Precis Historique de la Traite des Noirs et de l'Esclavage Colonial. (Slave Trade in France, 1744-1848, Ser.). 442p. (Fr.). 1974. Repr. of 1828 ed. lib. bdg. 111.00 o.p. (ISBN 0-8287-0641-7, 2207). Clearwater Pub.

Moreno, Elizabeth. Firm Your Fanny. (Illus.). 1980. pap. 1.95 (ISBN 0-686-62003-8, Perigee). Putnam Pub Group.

Moreno, Harriet N., et al. Test of English As a Foreign Language: TOEFL. 2nd ed. LC 77-13180. 1978. lib. bdg. 12.00 o.p. (ISBN 0-668-04446-2); pap. text ed. 10.95 (ISBN 0-668-04450-0). Arco.

Moretz, Judy, ed. see Glubetich, Dave.

Morewedge, Parviz, ed. Islamic Philosophical Theology. LC 79-14405. 1979. 55.50x (ISBN 0-87395-242-1). State U NY Pr.

--Islamic Philosophy & Mysticism. LC 80-14364. (Studies in Islamic Philosophy & Science). 1981. 40.00x (ISBN 0-88206-302-2). Caravan Bks.

Morewedge, Rosmarie T., ed. The Role of Woman in the Middle Ages. LC 74-23227. (Illus.). 1975. 29.50x (ISBN 0-87395-274-X). State U NY Pr.

Morewood, William H. Building the Raritan. LC 77-89451. (Illus.). 82p. 1977. 17.00 (ISBN 0-914104-04-7); pap. 14.50 o.p. (ISBN 0-914104-03-9). Wildwood Pubns MI.

Morey, Adrian & Brooke, C. N. Gilbert Foliot & His Letters. (Cambridge Studies in Medieval Life & Thought). 1966. 47.50 (ISBN 0-521-05764-7). Cambridge U Pr.

Morey, G. B. & Balaban, Nancy. Bibliography of Minnesota Geology, 1951-1980. (Bulletin: No. 46). 1981. 10.00 (ISBN 0-934938-01-6). Minn Geol Survey.

Morey, G. B. & Hanson, Gilbert N., eds. Selected Studies of Archean Gneisses & Lower Proterozoic Rocks, Southern Canadian Shield. LC 80-67113. (Special Paper Ser.: No. 182). (Illus., Orig.). 1980. pap. 26.00x (ISBN 0-8137-2182-2). Geol Soc.

Morey, G. B., jt. ed. see Sims, P. K.

Morey, George. English Channel. 13.50x (ISBN 0-392-02786-0, SpS). Sportshelf.

--Soviet Union. LC 75-44865. (Macdonald Countries). (Illus.). (gr. 6 up). 1976. PLB 12.68 (ISBN 0-382-06103-9, Pub. by Macdonald Ed). Silver.

--West Germany. LC 75-44866. (Macdonald Countries). (Illus.). (gr. 7 up). 1976. PLB 12.68 (ISBN 0-382-06105-5, Pub. by Macdonald Ed). Silver.

Morey, Loren. The Power Rockets. 28.00 (ISBN 0-89126-110-9). MA AH Pub.

Morey, Philip R. How Trees Grow. (Studies in Biology: No. 39). 64p. 1973. pap. text ed. 8.95 (ISBN 0-7131-2386-9). E Arnold.

Morey, Robert A. How to Answer a Mormon. 128p. (Orig.). 1983. pap. 3.95 (ISBN 0-87123-260-X). Bethany Hse.

Morey, Walt. Kavik, the Wolf Dog. LC 68-24727. (Illus.). (gr. 5-9). 1968. 10.95 (ISBN 0-525-33093-3, 01064-310); pap. 1.95 o.p. (ISBN 0-525-45018-1). Dutton.

--Sandy & the Rock Star. LC 78-12375. (gr. 4-7). 1979. 10.95 (ISBN 0-525-38785-4, 01063-320). Dutton.

Morf, Gustav. Polish Shades & Ghosts of Joseph Conrad. LC 75-18281. 1976. 12.95 o.p. (ISBN 0-913994-20-0); pap. 8.95 o.p. (ISBN 0-913994-26-X). Hippocrene Bks.

Morf, W. E. Principles of Ion-Selective Electrodes & of Membrane Transport. (Studies in Analytical Chemistry: Vol. 2). 1981. 76.75 (ISBN 0-444-99749-0). Elsevier.

Morford, Mark P. & Lenardon, Robert J. Classical Mythology. 2nd ed. 1977. pap. text ed. 15.95x (ISBN 0-582-28004-4). Longman.

Morgan, et al. American Politics: Directions of Change, Dynamics of Choice. 2nd ed. LC 81-14990. (Political Science Ser.). (Illus.). 672p. 1982. text ed. 19.95 (ISBN 0-201-05089-7); write for info. Instr's Manual (ISBN 0-201-05091-9); write for info. Student Study Guide (ISBN 0-201-05090-0). A-W.

Morgan, A. T. General Theory of Electrical Machines. 384p. 1979. 29.95 (ISBN 0-471-25911-X, Pub. by Wiley Heyden). Wiley.

Morgan, Al. The Last Cavalier. 320p. 1980. 12.95 (ISBN 0-399-90079-9, Marek). Putnam Pub Group.

Morgan, Alison. Paul's Kite. LC 82-3957. 120p. (gr. 5-9). 1982. 8.95 (ISBN 0-689-50245-1, McElderry Bk). Atheneum.

Morgan, Andrew J., jt. auth. see Tribe, Michael A.

Morgan, Ann. Field Book of Ponds & Streams. (Putnam's Nature Field Bks.). (Illus.). (gr. 7 up). 1930. 6.95 o.p. (ISBN 0-399-10291-4). Putnam Pub Group.

Morgan, Anne H. & Morgan, H. Wayne. Oklahoma: New Views of the Forty-Sixth State. (Illus.). 400p. 1982. 16.95 (ISBN 0-8061-1651-X). U of Okla Pr.

Morgan, Anne H. & Strickland, Rennard. Oklahoma Memories. LC 81-2777. 336p. 1981. 18.95 (ISBN 0-8061-1689-7); pap. 9.95 (ISBN 0-8061-1767-2). U of Okla Pr.

Morgan, Arlene. Starfire. (Aston Hall Romances Ser.: No. 106). 192p. (Orig.). 1980. pap. 1.50 o.p. (ISBN 0-523-41118-9). Pinnacle Bks.

Morgan, Arthur E. Nowhere Was Somewhere: How History Makes Utopias & Utopias Make History. LC 76-7481. (Illus.). 1976. Repr. of 1946 ed. lib. bdg. 17.00x (ISBN 0-8371-8881-4, MONO). Greenwood.

Morgan, Augustus De see De Morgan, Augustus.

Morgan, Augustus De see Smith, David E. & De Morgan, Augustus.

Morgan, B. Men & Discoveries in Chemistry. (Illus.). (gr. 9 up). 1962. 7.50 o.p. (ISBN 0-7195-0944-0). Transatlantic.

--Men & Discoveries in Electricity. (Illus.). (gr. 9 up). 6.95 o.p. (ISBN 0-7195-0943-2). Transatlantic.

Morgan, B. L. see Marton, L.

Morgan, B. Q., ed. see Von Goethe, Johann W.

Morgan, Betty M. The Teacher's Bag. 1979. pap. text ed. 10.50 (ISBN 0-8191-0743-3). U Pr of Amer.

Morgan, Brandt, jt. auth. see Brown, Tom, Jr.

Morgan, C. I & King, P. E. British Tardigrades: Keys & Notes for the Identification of the Species. (Synopses of the British Fauna Ser.). 1976. pap. 10.00 o.s.i. (ISBN 0-12-506950-2). Acad Pr.

Morgan, C. M. Dearly Beloved. 1981. cancelled 5.95 (ISBN 0-8062-1740-5). Carlton.

Morgan, Carlisle L. & Phil, M. Basic Principles of Computed Tomography. (Illus.). 448p. 1983. text ed. 57.50 (ISBN 0-8391-1705-1, 13331). Univ Park.

Morgan, Cary. Forests of the Night. 1982. pap. 3.50 (ISBN 0-451-11733-6, AE1733, Sig). NAL.

Morgan, Chris. Future Man: An Optimistic Look at What the Future Holds for Mankind. 208p. 1981. pap. 7.95 (ISBN 0-86616-005-1). Lewis Pub Co.

Morgan, Chris & Waite, Mitch. The Eight Thousand Eighty-Six-Eight Thousand Eighty-Eight Sixteen-Bit Microprocessor Primer. 224p. 1982. pap. 16.95 (ISBN 0-07-043109-4, P&RB). McGraw.

Morgan, Christopher, jt. auth. see Van Devanter, Lynda.

Morgan, Christopher, ed. The Byte Book of Computer Music. LC 78-27681. 1979. pap. 10.00 (ISBN 0-07-043097-7, BYTE Bks). McGraw.

Morgan, Clifford T. Brief Introduction to Psychology. 2nd ed. (Illus.). 1976. pap. text ed. 18.95 (ISBN 0-07-043136-1, C); instr.'s manual 15.00 (ISBN 0-07-043137-X). McGraw.

--Physiological Psychology. 3rd ed. (Psychology Ser.). 1965. text ed. 36.95 (ISBN 0-07-043060-8, C). McGraw.

Morgan, Clifford T. & King, Richard A. Introduction to Psychology. 5th ed. LC 74-26982. (Illus.). 736p. 1975. text ed. 15.95 o.p. (ISBN 0-07-043125-6, C); study guide 6.95 o.p. (ISBN 0-07-043127-2); 2.95 o.p. instructor's manual (ISBN 0-07-043126-4). McGraw.

Morgan, Clifford T., et al. Introduction to Psychology. 6th ed. (Illus.). 704p. 1979. text ed. 26.50 (ISBN 0-07-043205-8). McGraw.

Morgan, Conway L., tr. see Teynac, Francoise & Nolot, Pierre.

Morgan, Cyril P., jt. auth. see Jackson, John H.

Morgan, D., jt. auth. see Cox, H.

Morgan, D. J. Changes in British Aid Policy: 1951-1970, Vol. 4. 1980. text ed. cancelled o.p. (ISBN 0-391-01687-3). Humanities.

--Developing British Colonial Resources Nineteen Forty-Five to Nineteen Fifty-One, Vol. 2. 1980. text ed. cancelled o.p. (ISBN 0-391-01685-7). Humanities.

--Guidance Towards Self-Government in British Colonies: 1941-1971, Vol. 5. (Official History of Colonial Development Ser.). 1980. text ed. cancelled o.p. (ISBN 0-391-01688-1). Humanities.

--The Origins of British Aid Policy Nineteen Twenty-Four to Nineteen Forty-Five. (Official History of Colonial Development Ser.). 1980. text ed. cancelled o.p. (ISBN 0-391-01684-9). Humanities.

--A Reassessment of British Aid Policy: 1951-1970, Vol. 3. (Official History of Colonial Development Ser.). 1980. text ed. cancelled o.p. (ISBN 0-391-01686-5). Humanities.

Morgan, D. Lloyd, tr. see Nordenskiold, Gustaf N.

Morgan, D. V., jt. auth. see Howes, M. J.

Morgan, D. V., jt. ed. see Howes, M. J.

Morgan, Daniel. Merchants of Grain. 1980. pap. 5.95 (ISBN 0-14-005502-9). Penguin.

Morgan, David. The Capitol Press Corps: Newsmen & the Governing of New York State. LC 77-84771. (Contributions in Political Science: No. 2). 1978. lib. bdg. 25.00 (ISBN 0-8371-9883-6, MCP/). Greenwood.

--Suffragists & Liberals: The Politics of Woman Suffrage in England. 184p. 1975. 14.50x o.p. (ISBN 0-87471-583-0). Rowman.

Morgan, David, jt. auth. see Evans, Mary.

Morgan, David T., ed. The John Gray Blount Papers, Vol. IV: 1803-1833. (Illus.). xxxiv, 662p. 1982. 28.00 (ISBN 0-86526-189-X). NC Archives.

Morgan, Don, jt. auth. see Lacy, Madison S.

Morgan, E. S. Puritan Family. 10.00 (ISBN 0-8446-2609-0). Peter Smith.

Morgan, E. S., tr. see Schelling, Friedrich.

Morgan, E. Victor & Harrington, Richard. Capital Markets in the E.E.C. LC 76-27854. 1977. lib. bdg. 49.00 o.p. (ISBN 0-89158-700-4). Westview.

Morgan, Edith, jt. auth. see Jasper, James.

Morgan, Edmund M., ed. Some Problems of Proof Under the Anglo-American System of Litigation. LC 75-31438. (James S. Carpentier Lectures Ser.: 1955). 207p. 1976. Repr. of 1956 ed. lib. bdg. 15.50x (ISBN 0-8371-8517-3, MOSP). Greenwood.

Morgan, Edmund S. The Challenge of the American Revolution. 1976 10.95 (ISBN 0-393-05603-1); pap. 4.95x 1978 (ISBN 0-393-00876-2). Norton.

--The Gentle Puritan: A Life of Ezra Stiles, 1727-1795. LC 62-8257. (Institute of Early American History & Culture Ser.). 504p. 1962. 25.00x (ISBN 0-8078-1231-5). U of NC Pr.

--The Meaning of Independence: John Adams, George Washington, & Thomas Jefferson. 1978. pap. 2.95 (ISBN 0-393-00896-7, Norton Lib). Norton.

--The Puritan Dilemma: The Story of John Winthrop. (Library of American Biography). 224p. 1958. 5.00 (ISBN 0-316-58285-9); pap. 5.95 (ISBN 0-316-58286-7, 1962). Little.

Morgan, Edmund S. & Morgan, Helen M. The Stamp Act Crisis: Prologue to Revolution. 384p. 1983. 6.95 (ISBN 0-02-035280-8). Macmillan.

Morgan, Edmund S., jt. auth. see Blum, John M.

Morgan, EdmundS., ed. Puritan Family: Religion & Domestic Relations in 17th Century New England. rev. ed. pap. 4.95xi (ISBN 0-06-131227-4, TB1227, Torch). Har-Row.

Morgan, Edward. John Elias: Life & Letters. 1973. 12.95 (ISBN 0-85151-174-0). Banner of Truth.

Morgan, Edwin. Essays. (Essays & Prose Ser.). 1979. 15.00 o.p. (ISBN 0-85635-072-9, Pub. by Carcanet New Pr England). Humanities.

--Essays. 299p. 1974. text ed. 14.75x (ISBN 0-85635-072-9, Pub. by Carcanet New Pr England). Humanities.

--From Glasgow to Saturn. (Poetry Ser.). 1979. 6.95 o.p. (ISBN 0-85635-040-0, Pub. by Carcanet New Pr England). Humanities.*

--The New Divan. (Poetry Ser.). 1977. 8.95x (ISBN 0-85635-211-X, Pub. by Carcanet New Pr England); pap. 6.25x (ISBN 0-85635-212-8, Pub. by Carcanet Pr New England). Humanities.

--Poems of Thirty Years. 488p. 1982. text ed. 26.95x (ISBN 0-85635-365-5, 80304, Pub. by Carcanet New Pr England). Humanities.

Morgan, Edwin, ed. Scottish Satirical Verse: An Anthology. 236p. 1980. 15.95x (ISBN 0-85635-183-0, Pub. by Carcanet New Pr England); pap. text ed. 8.95x (ISBN 0-85635-220-9). Humanities.

Morgan, Edwin, tr. from Rus., Fr., Ger., Span., & Old English. Rites of Passage: Selected Translations. (Translation Ser.). 1979. 6.95 o.p. (ISBN 0-85635-164-4, Pub. by Carcanet New Pr England); pap. 4.95 o.p. (ISBN 0-85635-165-2, Pub. by Carcanet New Pr England). Humanities.

Morgan, Edwin, tr. see Mayakovsky, Vladimir.

Morgan, Elizabeth. The Making of a Woman Surgeon. 1980. 11.95 o.p. (ISBN 0-399-12361-X). Putnam Pub Group.

Morgan, Ernest. Dealing Creatively with Death: A Manual of Death Education & Simple Burial. 10th Rev. ed. 96p. Date not set. pap. price not set (ISBN 0-914064-25-8). Celo Pr.

--Manual of Death Education & Simple Burial. 9th rev. ed. 64p. (Orig.). 1980. pap. 3.50 (ISBN 0-914064-16-9). Celo Pr.

--Manual of Death Education & Simple Burial. 9th ed. 1980. pap. 3.50 (ISBN 0-686-28152-7). Continent Assn Funeral.

--A Manual of Death Education & Simple Burial. 9th ed. 2.50 (ISBN 0-686-95809-8). Alternatives.

Morgan, Ethelyn H., jt. auth. see Robey, Cora L.

Morgan, Fay. Trial by Fire. (Second Chance at Love Ser.: No. 104). Date not set. pap. 1.75 (ISBN 0-515-06868-3). Jove Pubns.

Morgan, Fidelis. The Female Wits: Women Playwrights of the Restoration. 468p. 1983. pap. 14.95 (ISBN 0-86068-231-5, Virago Pr). Merrimack Bk Serv.

Morgan, Fred. Uwharrie Magic. LC 73-86779. 1974. 8.95 (ISBN 0-87716-050-3, Pub. by Moore Pub Co). F Apple.

Morgan, G. Campbell. Analyzed Bible, Genesis. (G. Campbell Morgan Library). 280p. 1983. pap. 4.95 (ISBN 0-8010-6148-2). Baker Bk.

--Analyzed Bible, Romans. (G. Campbell Morgan Library). 220p. 1983. pap. 5.95 (ISBN 0-8010-6149-0). Baker Bk.

--God's Perfect Will. (Morgan Library). 1978. pap. 4.50 (ISBN 0-8010-6055-9). Baker Bk.

--Hosea: The Heart & Holiness of God. (Morgan Library). 1974. pap. 4.50 (ISBN 0-8010-5952-6). Baker Bk.

--Studies of the Four Gospels, 4 vols. Incl. The Gospel According to Matthew. 320p (ISBN 0-8007-0122-4); The Gospel According to Mark. 352p (ISBN 0-8007-0121-6); The Gospel According to Luke. 288p (ISBN 0-8007-0120-8); The Gospel According to John. 336p (ISBN 0-8007-0119-4). Set. 42.95 (ISBN 0-8007-0373-1); one-volume ed. 21.95 (ISBN 0-8007-0297-2). Revell.

--The Teaching of Christ. (G. Campbell Morgan Library). 340p. 1982. pap. cancelled (ISBN 0-8010-6139-3). Baker Bk.

--True Estimate of Life. (Morgan Library). 240p. 1975. pap. 2.95 o.p. (ISBN 0-8010-5976-3). Baker Bk.

--The Unfolding Message of the Bible: The Harmony & Unity of the Scriptures. (G. Campbell Morgan Library). 416p. 1982. pap. cancelled (ISBN 0-8010-6140-7). Baker Bk.

--The Westminster Pulpit, 10 vols. Set. 69.95 (ISBN 0-8007-0342-1). Revell.

Morgan, G. Campbell, ed. Gospel According to Mark. 352p. 10.95 (ISBN 0-8007-0121-6). Revell.

Morgan, Geoffrey. Small Boat Sailing. 5.50x (ISBN 0-392-04618-0, SpS). Sportshelf.

Morgan, Gillian. Jungles & People. LC 82-50391. (Nature's Landscape Ser.). PLB 15.96 (ISBN 0-382-06675-8). Silver.

Morgan, Griscom. Small Community, Population & the Economic Order. 1975. pap. 2.00 (ISBN 0-910420-22-X). Comm Serv.

Morgan, Gwen G. Managing the Day Care Dollars: A Financial Handbook. LC 82-50691. 112p. (Orig.). 1982. pap. 7.95 (ISBN 0-942820-02-9). Steam Pr MA.

Morgan, Gwyneth. Life in a Medieval Village. LC 81-13735. (Cambridge Topic Bks.). (Illus.). 52p. (gr. 6 up). 1982. PLB 6.95g (ISBN 0-8225-1207-6). Lerner Pubns.

Morgan, H. E., ed. Cellular Biology of the Heart: Supplement to Journal of Molecular & Cellular Cardiology. 1982. 18.00 (ISBN 0-12-506960-X). Acad Pr.

Morgan, H. G. Death Wishes? The Understanding & Management of Deliberate Self-Harm. LC 79-1044. 1980. 44.95 (ISBN 0-471-27591-3, Pub. by Wiley-Interscience). Wiley.

Morgan, H. Wayne. William McKinley. LC 63-19723. (Illus.). 1963. 19.95x (ISBN 0-8156-0032-1). Syracuse U Pr.

Morgan, H. Wayne, jt. auth. see Morgan, Anne H.

Morgan, H. Wayne, ed. Gilded Age. rev. ed. LC 75-113203. (Illus.). 6.95x (ISBN 0-8156-2150-7); pap. text ed. 4.95x (ISBN 0-8156-2151-5). Syracuse U Pr.

--Victorian Culture in America, 1865-1914. LC 72-89722. (Primary Sources in American History Ser.). 1973. pap. text ed. 6.95x (ISBN 0-88295-787-2). Harlan Davidson.

Morgan, Hal & Symmes, Daniel. Amazing 3-D. (Illus.). 1982. 29.95 (ISBN 0-316-58284-0); pap. 13.95 (ISBN 0-316-58283-2). Little.

Morgan, Harry M., et al. Elementary & Secondary Level Programs for the Gifted & Talented. Tannenbaum, Abraham J., ed. (Perspectives on Gifted & Talented Education Ser.). (Orig.). 1980. pap. text ed. 6.50x (ISBN 0-8077-2592-7). Tchrs Coll.

Morgan, Harry T. Chinese Symbols & Superstitions. LC 74-167079. (Illus.). 192p. 1972. Repr. of 1942 ed. 41.00x (ISBN 0-8103-3069-5). Gale.

Morgan, Helen L. Maria Mitchell, First Lady of American Astronomy. LC 77-5871. (gr. 7-10). 1977. 8.95 (ISBN 0-664-32614-5). Westminster.

Morgan, Helen M., jt. auth. see Morgan, Edmund S.

Morgan, Henry. Painting for Pleasure. 5.50x (ISBN 0-392-05946-0, LTB). Sportshelf.

--The Uncensored Letters of Loreeta Pernie: Bought for Three Dollars in a Garage Sale. 64p. 1982. 7.95 (ISBN 0-312-92856-4). Congdon & Weed.

--The Uncensored Letters of Loretta Pernie. (Illus.). 64p. 1982. pap. 8.95 (ISBN 0-312-92856-4). Congdon & Weed.

Morgan, Henry J. Bibliotheca Canadensis: A Bio-Bibliographical Manual of Canadian Literature. LC 68-27177. 1968. Repr. of 1867 ed. 54.00x (ISBN 0-8103-3151-9). Gale.

Morgan, Howard E. Endrocrine Control Systems. LC 72-85159. 193p. (Orig.). 1973. pap. 11.00 (ISBN 0-686-74175-7). Krieger.

Morgan, Howard W. America's Road to Empire: The War with Spain & Overseas Expansion. LC 64-8714. (America in Crisis Ser.). 124p. 1965. pap. text ed. 10.50 (ISBN 0-471-61520-X). Wiley.

Morgan, Hugh G., jt. auth. see Havighurst, Robert J.

Morgan, James E. Administrative & Supervisory Management. 2nd ed. (Illus.). 336p. 1982. reference 15.95 (ISBN 0-13-008508-1). P-H.

Morgan, James E., Jr. Principles of Administrative & Supervisory Management. (Illus.). 336p. 1973. ref. ed. 16.95 o.p. (ISBN 0-13-709386-1). P-H.

Morgan, James J., jt. auth. see Stumm, Werner.

Morgan, James N. & Messenger, Robert C. THAID: A Sequential Analysis Program for the Analysis of Nominal Scale Dependent Variables. LC 72-619720. 98p. 1973. pap. 12.00x (ISBN 0-87944-137-2). Inst Soc Res.

Morgan, James N., jt. auth. see Barfield, Richard E.

Morgan, James N., jt. auth. see Lansing, John B.

Morgan, James N., ed. A Panel Study of Income Dynamics: Complete Documentation for Interviewing Years 1968-1981, 2 vols. & 9 suppls. Economic Behavior Program Staff. Incl. Vol. 1. Study Design, Procedures, Available Data for 1968-1972 Interviewing Years. 400p. 1973. pap. 40.00 (ISBN 0-87944-141-0); Vol. 2. Tape Codes & Indexesfor 1968-1972 Interviewing Years. 904p. 1973. pap. 75.00x (ISBN 0-87944-142-9); 1973 Supplement. 240p. pap. 35.00x (ISBN 0-87944-155-0); 1974 Supplement. 280p. pap. 35.00x (ISBN 0-87944-167-4); 1975 Supplement. 298p. pap. 35.00x (ISBN 0-87944-200-X); 1976 Supplement. 516p. pap. 35.00x (ISBN 0-87944-215-8); pap. 35.00x 1977 suppl. 354p.. (ISBN 0-87944-225-5); pap. 35.00x 1978 suppl. 416p.. (ISBN 0-87944-243-3); 1979 Supplement. 512p. pap. 35.00x (ISBN 0-87944-258-1); 1980 Supplement. 590p. pap. 35.00x (ISBN 0-87944-271-9); 1981 Supplement. 704p. pap. 35.00x (ISBN 0-87944-279-4); 1980 Supplement. 590p. 1981. 35.00 (ISBN 0-686-86125-6); 1981 Supplement. 720p. 1982. 35.00 **(ISBN 0-87944-279-4). Set. pap. 330.00x 11 vol. set (ISBN 0-87944-280-8). Inst Soc Res.**

Morgan, James N. & Duncan, Greg J., eds. Five Thousand American Families: Patterns of Economic Progress, 9 vols. Incl. Vol. 1. An Analysis of the First Five Years of the Panel Study of Income Dynamics. 436p; Special Studies of the First Five Years of the Panel Study of Income Dynamics. 376p. 1974. Set Vols. 1 & 2. 30.00x (ISBN 0-87944-154-2); Set Vols. 1 & 2. pap. 22.00x (ISBN 0-87944-153-4); Vol. 3. Analyses of the First Six Years of the Panel Study of Income Dynamics. 490p. 1975. 12.50 o.p. (ISBN 0-87944-176-3); pap. 14.00x (ISBN 0-87944-175-5); Vol. 4. Family Composition Change & Other Analyses of the First Seven Years of the Panel Study of Income Dynamics. 536p. 1976. 12.50 o.p. (ISBN 0-87944-197-6); pap. 14.00x (ISBN 0-87944-196-8); Vol. 5. Components of Change in Family Well-Being & Other Analyses of the First Eight Years of the Panel Study of Income Dynamics. 536p. 1977. 22.00x (ISBN 0-87944-212-3); pap. 14.00x (ISBN 0-87944-211-5); Accounting for Race & Sex Differences in Earnings & Other Analyses of the **First Nine Years of the Panel Study of Income Dynamics. 512p. 1978. Vol. 6. 22.00x (ISBN 0-87944-223-9); Vol. 7, Analyses of the First Ten Years of The Panel Study Of Income Dynamics, 1979. 22.00x (ISBN 0-87944-234-4); Vol. 8. Analysis of the First Eleven Years of the Panel Study of Income Dynamics. 464p. 1980. 22.00x (ISBN 0-87944-250-6); Vol. 9. Analysis of the First Twelve Years of the Panel Study of Income Dynamics. 552p. 1981. 22.00x (ISBN 0-87944-267-0). Set. 140.00x (ISBN 0-87944-268-9). Inst Soc. Res.**

Morgan, James N., et al. Productive Americans: A Study of How Individuals Contribute to Economic Progress. LC 66-64924. 546p. 1966. pap. 7.00x (ISBN 0-87944-047-3). Inst Soc Res.

--Results of Two National Surveys of Philanthropic Activity. 204p. 1979. pap. 12.00x (ISBN 0-87944-246-8). Inst Soc Res.

Morgan, Jan. From Holland with Love: Delicious Dutch Recipes. (Illus.). 91p. 1980. 12.50x (ISBN 0-911268-48-0). Rogers Bk.

Morgan, Jean, jt. ed. see Wasserman, Paul.

Morgan, Jefferson, jt. auth. see Morgan, Jinx.

Morgan, Jennifer, ed. see MacAdams, Cynthia.

Morgan, Jinx & Morgan, Jefferson. Two Cooks In One Kitchen. LC 81-43573. 256p. 1983. 19.95 (ISBN 0-385-17462-4). Doubleday.

Morgan, John H. Gilbert Stuart & His Pupils. LC 72-96440. (Library of American Art Ser.). 1969. Repr. of 1939 ed. lib. bdg. 21.50 (ISBN 0-306-71827-8). Da Capo.

--In Search of Meaning: From Freud to Teilhard De Chardin (an Analysis of the Classic Statements) 1977. 8.25 (ISBN 0-8191-0251-2). U Pr of Amer.

--Paintings by John Trumbull at Yale University of Historic Scenes & Personages Prominent in the American Revolution. 1926. 57.50x (ISBN 0-686-51284-7). Elliots Bks.

Morgan, John H., ed. Understanding Religion & Culture: Anthropological & Theological Perspectives. LC 79-66684. 1979. pap. text ed. 10.25 o.p. (ISBN 0-8191-0848-0). U Pr of Amer.

Morgan, John P. & Kagan, Doreen V., eds. Society & Medication: Conflicting Signals for Prescribers & Patients. LC 81-48145. 1983. write for info. (ISBN 0-669-05290-6). Lexington Bks.

Morgan, Joseph. The History of the Kingdom of Bafauah & Three Unpublished Letters. Schatter, Richard, ed. 172p. Repr. of 1946 ed. lib. bdg. write for info. Telegraph Bks.

--Introduction to University Physics, 2 vols. LC 77-12757. 1978. Repr. of 1969 ed. Set. 33.50 (ISBN 0-88275-617-6); Vol. 1, 560. lib. bdg. 19.50 (ISBN 0-686-96766-6); Vol. 2, 512p. lib. bdg. 19.50 (ISBN 0-88275-874-8). Krieger.

--The Physical Basis of Musical Sound. LC 78-5508. (Illus.). 168p. (Orig.). 1980. lib. bdg. 11.50 (ISBN 0-88275-656-7). Krieger.

Morgan, Joseph R. Hawaii. (Geographics of the U. S.). 275p. 1983. lib. bdg. 35.00 (ISBN 0-89158-942-2); pap. 18.00 (ISBN 0-86531-488-8). Westview.

Morgan, K., jt. auth. see Lewis, R. W.

Morgan, K. Z. & Turner, J. E. Principles of Radiation Protection. LC 67-22415. 640p. 1973. Repr. of 1967 ed. 28.50 (ISBN 0-88275-128-X). Krieger.

Morgan, Kathryn L. Children of Strangers: The Stories of a Black Family. (Illus.). 144p. 1980. 17.95 (ISBN 0-87722-203-7). Temple U Pr.

Morgan, Keith, jt. ed. see Lewis, Arnold.

Morgan, Kenneth O. Rebirth of a Nation: Wales 1880-1980. (History of Wales Ser.: Vol. VI). 1981. 29.95x (ISBN 0-19-821736-6). Oxford U Pr.

Morgan, L. Peter's Pockets. LC 65-27622. (Illus.). (gr. k-2). PLB 6.75x (ISBN 0-87783-029-0). Oddo.

Morgan, Lael, ed. Alaska's Native People. LC 78-10528. (Alaska Geographic Ser.: Vol. 6, No. 3). (Illus., Orig.). 1979. pap. 24.95 album style (ISBN 0-88240-104-1). Alaska Northwest.

Morgan, Lane, ed. Northwest Experience One. (Northwest Experience Ser.). 192p. (gr. 12). 1980. PLB 10.95x (ISBN 0-914842-47-1); pap. 4.95 (ISBN 0-914842-46-3). Madrona Pubs.

--The Northwest Experience Three. 192p. 1983. lib. bdg. 10.95x (ISBN 0-914842-78-1); pap. 4.95 (ISBN 0-914842-79-X). Madrona Pubs.

--The Northwest Experience Two. 192p. 1981. lib. bdg. 10.95x (ISBN 0-914842-61-7); pap. 4.95 (ISBN 0-914842-60-9). Madrona Pubs.

Morgan, Len, jt. auth. see Bradford, George.

Morgan, Lenore. Dragons & Stuff. LC 70-108725. (Illus.). (gr. 2-4). 1970. PLB 6.75x (ISBN 0-87783-012-6); pap. 2.95x deluxe ed. (ISBN 0-87783-091-6). Oddo.

Morgan, Lord. Churchill Taken from the Diaries of Lord Morgan. new ed. LC 66-14761. (Illus.). 896p. 1976. Repr. of 1966 ed. 16.95 (ISBN 0-910220-77-8). Berg.

Morgan, Loren, jt. auth. see Swaton, J. Norman.

Morgan, M. G. Energy & Man: Technical & Social Aspects of Energy. (IEEE Selected Reprint Ser.). 521p. 1975. 32.95 (ISBN 0-471-61521-8, Pub. by Wiley-Interscience). Wiley.

Morgan, M. G., ed. Energy & Man: Technical & Social Aspects of Energy. LC 74-27680. 1975. 32.95 (ISBN 0-87942-043-X). Inst Electrical.

Morgan, Marabel. Total Joy. 224p. 1977. 6.95 o.p. (ISBN 0-8007-0816-4); pap. 2.25 (ISBN 0-8007-8326-3, Spire Bks). Revell.

--The Total Woman. 192p. 1973. 8.95 o.p. (ISBN 0-8007-0608-0). Revell.

Morgan, Margaret K., jt. auth. see Ford, Charles W.

Morgan, Margery M. The Shavian Playground: An Exploration of the Art of George Bernard Shaw. (Illus.). 1974. pap. 13.95x (ISBN 0-416-82500-1). Methuen Inc.

Morgan, Marie. Breaking Through: How to Overcome Housewives' Depression. 204p. 1983. pap. 9.95 (ISBN 0-86683-697-7). Winston Pr.

Morgan, Marilyn A. Managing Career Development. LC 79-66118. 285p. 1980. pap. text ed. 12.95x (ISBN 0-442-26238-8). Kent Pub Co.

Morgan, Mark D. Ecology of Mysidacea. 1982. text ed. 54.50 (ISBN 90-6193-761-2, Pub. by Junk Pubs Netherlands). Kluwer Boston.

Morgan, Max J. Dynamic Positioning of Offshore Vessels. 513p. 1978. 43.95x (ISBN 0-87814-044-1). Pennwell Pub.

Morgan, Michael & Briggs, D., eds. Historical Sources in Geography. (Sources & Methods in Geography Ser.). 1979. pap. 9.95 (ISBN 0-408-10609-3). Butterworth.

Morgan, Michael J. Molyneux's Question: Vision, Touch, & the Philosophy of Perception. LC 76-54066. 1977. 32.50 (ISBN 0-521-21558-7). Cambridge U Pr.

Morgan, Michaela. Madelaina. 1979. pap. 2.50 o.p. (ISBN 0-523-40151-5). Pinnacle Bks.

Morgan, Morris H., tr. see Vitruvius.

Morgan, Murray. The Mill on the Boot: The Story of the St. Paul & Tacoma Lumber Company. LC 82-16107. (Illus.). 296p. 1982. 19.95 (ISBN 0-295-95949-5). U of Wash Pr.

Morgan, Nicole S. No-Where to Go? 100p. 1981. pap. text ed. 8.95x (ISBN 0-920380-90-5, Pub. by Inst Res Pub Canada). Renouf.

Morgan, Nigel, jt. auth. see Marks, Richard.

Morgan, Patrick, jt. auth. see Knorr, Klaus.

Morgan, Patrick M. Theories & Approaches to International Politics. 3rd ed. LC 79-66439. 304p. 1981. o. p. 24.95 (ISBN 0-87855-350-9); text ed. 24.95 (ISBN 0-686-68062-6); pap. 9.95 (ISBN 0-87855-791-1); pap. text ed. 9.95. Transaction Bks.

Morgan, Paula. Say Yes! 144p. pap. 2.25 o.p. (ISBN 0-523-41408-0). Pinnacle Bks.

--Sol's Daughter. LC 78-73788. 1979. 8.95 o.p. (ISBN 0-448-16332-2, G&D). Putnam Pub Group.

Morgan, Peter. Making Hats. 1978. 14.95 (ISBN 0-7134-1078-7, Pub. by Batsford England). David & Charles.

Morgan, R., jt. auth. see King, R. D.

Morgan, R., jt. auth. see McMullan, J. T.

Morgan, R. E., jt. ed. see Potholm, C. P.

Morgan, R. P. Soil Conservation: Problems & Prospects. 576p. 1981. 66.95 (ISBN 0-471-27882-3, Pub. by Wiley-Interscience). Wiley.

Morgan, R. P., jt. auth. see Kirby, M. J.

Morgan, Richard E. The Politics of Religious Conflict: Church & State in America. 2nd ed. LC 79-48094. 118p. 1980. text ed. 17.75 (ISBN 0-8191-1007-8); pap. text ed. 8.25 (ISBN 0-8191-1008-6). U Pr of Amer.

Morgan, Robert & Pye, Michael, eds. Ernst Troeltsch: Writings on Theology & Religion. LC 77-79596. 1977. 9.95 (ISBN 0-8042-0554-X). John Knox.

Morgan, Robert F. & Wilson, Jane. Growing Younger: How to Add Years to Your Life By Measuring & Controlling Your Body Age. LC 82-42854. 264p. 1983. 19.95 (ISBN 0-8128-2918-2). Stein & Day.

Morgan, Robert P. Anthology of Modern Music. 1983. pap. write for info (ISBN 0-393-95284-3). Norton.

--Modern Music. (Norton Introduction to Music History Ser.). 1983. pap. write for info (ISBN 0-393-95272-X). Norton.

Morgan, Robin. Lady of the Beasts. 1976. 10.00 (ISBN 0-394-40758-X); pap. 6.95 (ISBN 0-394-73229-4). Random.

Morgan, Robin, ed. Going Too Far: The Personal Chronicle of a Feminist. 348p. Date not set. pap. 5.95 (ISBN 0-394-72612-X, Vin). Random.

Morgan, Roger. The United States & West Germany 1945-1973: A Study in Alliance Politics. (Royal Institute of International Affairs Ser). (Illus.). 288p. 1974. 19.95x o.p. (ISBN 0-19-218304-4). Oxford U Pr.

Morgan, Roland. Honolulu Then & Now. (Illus., Orig.). 1978. pap. 6.95 o.p. (ISBN 0-88875-003-X). Bodima.

Morgan, Roseann. The Writer's Work Workbook. 248p. 1981. pap. text ed. 8.95 (ISBN 0-13-969840-X). P-H.

Morgan, S. W. Zinc & its Alloys. 224p. 1977. 29.00x (ISBN 0-7121-0945-5, Pub. by Macdonald & Evans). State Mutual Bk.

Morgan, Sarah. Dining with the Cattle Barrons. 1981. 13.95 (ISBN 0-686-92305-7). Texian.

Morgan, Stephanie. The Witch Down the Street. (Illus.). 48p. (ps-3). 1983. 4.99 (ISBN 0-910313-02-4). Parker Bro.

Morgan, Sydney O. Missionary: An Indian Tale, 3 vols. in 1. LC 80-20308. 1980. Repr. of 1811 ed. 40.00x (ISBN 0-8201-1358-1). Schol Facsimiles.

Morgan, Ted. Churchill: Young Man in a Hurry. (Illus.). 1982. 21.75 (ISBN 0-671-25303-4). S&S.

--Maugham. 1980. 17.95 o.p. (ISBN 0-671-24077-3). S&S.

Morgan, Terry. Lockheed Constellation. (Famous Aircraft Ser). (Illus.). 1967. pap. 4.95 o.p. (ISBN 0-668-01659-0). Arco.

Morgan, Thomas. The Moral Philosopher in a Dialogue Between Philalethes, a Christian Deist, & Theophanes, a Christian Jew. LC 75-11239. (British Philosophers & Theologians of the 17th & 18th Centuries: Vol. 39). 1977. Repr. of 1737 ed. lib. bdg. 42.00 o.s.i. (ISBN 0-8240-1791-9). Garland Pub.

Morgan, Thomas H. Embryology & Genetics. LC 74-12886. (Illus.). 258p. 1975. Repr. of 1934 ed. lib. bdg. 18.25x (ISBN 0-8371-7772-3, MOEG). Greenwood.

Morgan, Thomas R. Foundations of Wave Theory for Seismic Exploration. LC 82-83805. (Illus.). 160p. 1982. text ed. 32.00 (ISBN 0-934634-34-3). Intl Human Res.

Morgan, Tom. Money, Money, Money: How to Get & Keep It. LC 78-1769. (Illus.). (gr. 6-8). 1978. 7.95 o.p. (ISBN 0-399-20641-8). Putnam Pub Group.

Morgan, W. B. Agriculture in the Third World: A Spatial Analysis. LC 77-24064. (Advanced Economic Geopraphies Ser.). (Illus.). 1978. lib. bdg. 36.00 o.p. (ISBN 0-89158-820-5). Westview.

Morgan, W. B. & Munton, R. J. Agricultural Geography. 165p. 1972. 16.95 (ISBN 0-312-01470-8). St Martin.

Morgan, W. K., et al. Pulmonary Diseases. 2nd ed. (Medical Examination Review Book: Vol. 24). 1977. spiral bdg. 23.00 (ISBN 0-87488-143-9). Med Exam.

Morgan, William. The Elements of Structure. 2nd ed. Buckle, I., ed. (Illus.). (gr. 9 up). 1978. pap. text ed. 22.50x (ISBN 0-273-01079-4, LTB). Sportshelf.

--Prehistoric American Architecture in the Eastern United States. (Illus.). 240p. 1980. 27.50 (ISBN 0-262-13160-9). MIT Pr.

Morgan, William & Stern, Robert J. The Almighty Wall: The Architecture of Henry Vaughn. 1982. 30.00 (ISBN 0-262-13187-0). MIT Pr.

Morgan, William J., Jr. Supervision & Management of Quantity Preparation: Principles & Procedures. 2nd, rev ed. LC 80-83876. (Illus.). 1981. 25.00 (ISBN 0-8211-1254-6); text ed. 21.00 (ISBN 0-686-77732-8). McCutchan.

Morgan, William T., jt. auth. see Brinkman, Marilyn S.

Morgan, Wm. T. English Political Parties & Leaders in the Reign of Queen Anne, 1702-1710. (Yale Historical Studies, Miscellany: No. VII). 1920. 57.50x (ISBN 0-685-69845-9). Elliots Bks.

Morganroth, et al. Noninvasive Cardiac Imaging. 1982. 65.00 (ISBN 0-8151-5946-3). Year Bk Med.

Morgans, W. M. Outlines of Paint Technology. 1982. 127.00x (ISBN 0-686-92043-0, Pub. by Griffin England). State Mutual Bk.

Morgans, W. M., jt. ed. see Hamburg, H. R.

Morganstern, Michael. How to Make Love to a Woman. 144p. 1983. pap. 2.95 (ISBN 0-345-30962-6). Ballantine.

Morganstern, Stanley. Legal Protection for the Consumer. 2nd rev. ed. LC 78-9170. (Legal Almanac Ser.: No. 52). 119p. 1978. lib. bdg. 5.95 (ISBN 0-379-11117-9). Oceana.

Morganston, Charles E. The Appointing & Removal Power of the President of the United States. LC 75-35372. (U.S. Government Documents Program Ser.). 224p. 1976. Repr. of 1929 ed. lib. bdg. 18.75 (ISBN 0-8371-8611-0, MOAR). Greenwood.

Morgenstein, Gary. The Man Who Wanted to Play Center Field for the New York Yankees. LC 82-73020. 288p. 1983. 12.95 (ISBN 0-689-11358-7). Atheneum.

Morgenstein, Melvin & Strongin, Harriet. Modern Retailing: Principles & Practices. 624p. 1983. text ed. 23.95x (ISBN 0-471-08059-4). Wiley.

Morgenstern, Carol. Playing the Raquets. (Orig.). 1980. pap. 8.95 o.s.i. (ISBN 0-440-57121-9, Delta). Dell.

Morgenstern, Dan. Jazz People. LC 76-14462. (Illus.). 1976. 28.50 o.p. (ISBN 0-8109-1152-3). Abrams.

Morgenstern, Dan & Nanry, Charles. Annual Review of Jazz Studies Two. (Illus.). 192p. 1983. pap. text ed. 15.00 (ISBN 0-87855-906-X). Transaction Bks.

Morgenstern, Dan, ed. & tr. see Berendt, Joachim.

Morgenstern, Joy. The Dandelion. LC 79-53925. (Illus.). 87p. 1981. 7.95 (ISBN 0-934256-00-4). Dean Co WA.

Morgenstern, Michael. How to Make Love to a Woman. 160p. 1982. 10.95 (ISBN 0-517-54706-6, C N Potter Bks). Crown.

Morgenstern, Oskar & Thompson, G. L. Mathematical Theory of Expanding & Contracting Economies. LC 75-18399. 304p. 1976. 24.95 (ISBN 0-669-00089-2). Lexington Bks.

Morgenstern, Sam, jt. ed. see Barlow, Harold.

Morgenstern, Steve. Metric Puzzles, Tricks & Games. (gr. 3 up). 1978. 8.99 (ISBN 0-8069-4588-5); PLB 6.69 (ISBN 0-8069-4589-3). Sterling.

Morgenthaler, George J. Oil & Gas Title Examination. 277p. 1982. text ed. 35.00 (ISBN 0-686-82491-1, N1-1342). PLI.

Morgenthau, Hans J. In Defense of the National Interest: A Critical Examination of American Foreign Policy. LC 82-18295. 306p. 1983. pap. text ed. 11.50 (ISBN 0-8191-2846-5). U Pr of Amer.

--Politics Among Nations: The Struggle for Power & Peace. 5th, rev. ed. 1978. 27.95 (ISBN 0-394-50085-7); text ed. 20.00 (ISBN 0-394-32193-6). Knopf.

--The Purpose of American Politics. LC 82-20057. 382p. 1983. pap. text ed. 13.25 (ISBN 0-8191-2847-3). U Pr of Amer.

Morgenthau, Hans J. & Thompson, Kenneth W., eds. Principles & Problems of International Politics: Selected Readings. LC 82-13686. 490p. 1982. pap. text ed. 17.25 (ISBN 0-8191-2636-5). U Pr of Amer.

Morgulas, Jerrold. The Torguemada Principle. 1983. pap. 2.95 (ISBN 0-553-14514-2). Bantam.

Morholt, Evelyn, et al. Sourcebook for the Biological Sciences. 2nd ed. (Teaching Science Ser). 795p. 1966. text ed. 20.95 (ISBN 0-15-582850-9, HC). HarBraceJ.

Mori, A., jt. ed. see Lowenthal, A.

Mori, Alan A. Families of Children with Special Needs: Early Intervention Techniques for the Practitioner. 300p. 1983. price not set (ISBN 0-89443-934-0). Aspen Systems.

Mori, Allen A., jt. auth. see Masters, Lowell F.

Mori, Joseph E., jt. auth. see Pahler, Arnold.

Mori, Masahiro. The Buddha in the Robot: A Robot Engineer's Thoughts on Science & Religion. Friedrich, Ralph, ed. Terry, Charles S., tr. Orig. Title: Mori Masahiro No Bukkyo & Shingan. 192p. 1981. pap. 5.95 (ISBN 4-333-01002-0, Pub. by Kosei Publishing Co). C E Tuttle.

Mori, Osamu, jt. auth. see Schaarschmidt-Richter, Irmtraud.

Mori, S., jt. auth. see Furtado, J. I.

Mori, Stephen, jt. auth. see Clowers, Myles L.

Moriarity, David M. Psychic Energy. 250p. 1983. 19.50 (ISBN 0-87527-254-1). Green.

Moriarty, Alice E. Constancy & IQ Change: A Clinical View of Relationships Between Tested Intelligence & Personality. (Illus.). 232p. 1966. photocopy ed. spiral 19.75x (ISBN 0-398-01347-0). C C Thomas.

Moriarty, Brian, jt. auth. see Roland, Harold E.

Moriarty, David M. The Loss of Loved Ones. LC 79-50189. 288p. 1983. 26.50 (ISBN 0-87527-198-7). Green.

Moriarty, F., ed. Ecotoxicology: The Study of Pollutants in Exosystems. Date not set. price not set (ISBN 0-12-506760-7). Acad Pr.

Moriarty, Rowland T. Industrial Buying Behavior: Concepts, Issues, & Applications. 208p. 1982. 28.95x (ISBN 0-669-06212-X). Lexington Bks.

Moriarty, Tim & Bereswell, Joe. The Dynamic Islanders: From Cellar to Stanley Cup. LC 80-2465. (Illus.). 144p. 1980. pap. 12.95 (ISBN 0-385-17489-6). Doubleday.

Moriber, George & Hudes, Isidore. Laboratory Studies in the Physical Sciences. rev ed. 1979. pap. text ed. 10.50 (ISBN 0-8403-2032-9). Kendall-Hunt.

Moric, Rudo. Tale of a Wild Duck. LC 66-16420. (Foreign Lands Bks). (Illus.). (gr. k-5). 1966. PLB 3.95g (ISBN 0-8225-0357-3). Lerner Pubns.

Morice, Anne. Sleep of Death. 176p. 1983. 10.95 (ISBN 0-312-72863-8). St Martin.

Morice, Dave. Happy Birthday Handbook. LC 82-19429. (Illus.). 49p. (Orig.). 1982. pap. 7.50 (ISBN 0-915124-67-X). Toothpaste.

Morice, G. P., ed. David Hume: Bicentenary Papers. LC 77-81915. 240p. 1977. 17.50x (ISBN 0-292-71515-3). U of Tex Pr.

Morici, Peter, et al. Canadian Industrial Policy. LC 82-81566. 116p. 1982. 10.00. Natl Planning.

Morick, Harold. Challenges to Empiricism. LC 72-806552. 329p. 18.50 (ISBN 0-915144-89-1); pap. text ed. 12.50 (ISBN 0-915144-90-5). Hackett Pub.

Moriei, Peter & Smith, Arthur J. Canadian Industrial Policy. 116p. (Orig.). 1982. pap. 10.00 (ISBN 0-89068-063-9). Natl Planning.

Morimando, Patricia. The Neptune Effect. 1982. pap. 3.95 (ISBN 0-87728-487-3). Weiser.

Morimoto, Kazuo, jt. auth. see Hirohata, Kazushi.

Morimoto, Kigo, ed. see Tobin, Catherine.

Morin, Anne. At The Seashore. (Illus.). 1983. 4.95 (ISBN 0-533-05270-X). Vantage.

Morin, J. Donald, jt. ed. see Crawford, John.

Morin, Jim. Famous Cats. LC 82-9145. (Illus.). 128p. 1982. pap. 3.95 (ISBN 0-688-01518-2). Quill NY.

Morin, Relman. East Wind Rising: A Long View of the Pacific Crisis. LC 73-13407. 359p. 1974. Repr. of 1960 ed. lib. bdg. 19.25x (ISBN 0-8371-7054-0, MOEW). Greenwood.

Morin, Robert B. & Gorman, Marvin, eds. Chemistry & Biology of B-Lactam Antibiotics. 402p. 1982. Vol. 1. 73.00 (ISBN 0-12-506301-6); Vol. 2. 64.00 (ISBN 0-12-506302-4); Vol. 3. 64.00 (ISBN 0-12-506303-2). Acad Pr.

Morin, Thomas D. Mariano Picon Salas. (World Authors Ser.). 1979. lib. bdg. 15.95 (ISBN 0-8057-6388-0, Twayne). G K Hall.

Morina, Michael, jt. auth. see Black, J. Thomas.

Morinaga, H. & Yamazaki, T. In-Beam Gamma-Ray Spectroscopy. 1977. 89.50 (ISBN 0-444-10569-7, North-Holland). Elsevier.

Morine, John. Riding the Recession: How Your Business Can Prosper Despite Shrinking Markets, High Inflation & the Ups & Downs of Today's Economy. (Illus.). 136p. 1983. 11.95 (ISBN 0-13-781062-8); pap. 5.95 (ISBN 0-13-781054-7). P-H.

Morisawa, Marie. Geomorphology Laboratory Manual with Report Forms. LC 76-13456. 1976. pap. text ed. 14.95 (ISBN 0-471-01847-3). Wiley.

Morisawa, Marie, ed. Fluvial Geomorphology: Binghamton Symposia in Geomorphology. (International Ser.: No. 4). 304p. 1981. Repr. of 1973 ed. text ed. 25.00x (ISBN 0-04-551046-6). Allen Unwin.

Morisawa, W. Streams: Their Dynamics & Morphology. LC 68-12267. 1968. pap. text ed. 15.95 (ISBN 0-07-043123-X, C). McGraw.

Morishima, James K., jt. auth. see Sue, Stanley.

Morishima, M. The Economic Theory of Modern Society. Anthony, D. W., tr. from Japanese. LC 75-39375. (Illus.). 332p. 1976. 54.50 (ISBN 0-521-21088-7); pap. 19.95x (ISBN 0-521-29168-2). Cambridge U Pr.

--Marx's Economics: A Dual Theory of Value & Growth. LC 72-83591. (Illus.). 224p. 1981. 34.50 (ISBN 0-521-08747-3); pap. 16.95x (ISBN 0-521-29303-0). Cambridge U Pr.

--Walras's Economics. LC 76-40833. 1977. 34.50 (ISBN 0-521-21487-4); pap. 14.95 (ISBN 0-521-28522-4). Cambridge U Pr.

Morishima, M., et al. The Working of Econometric Models. LC 79-184901. (Illus.). 300p. 1972. 49.50 (ISBN 0-521-08502-0). Cambridge U Pr.

Morishima, Michio. Equilibrium, Stability, & Growth: A Multi-Sectoral Analysis. 1964. 27.95x (ISBN 0-19-828145-5). Oxford U Pr.

--Theory of Economic Growth. 1969. 29.95x (ISBN 0-19-828164-1). Oxford U Pr.

Morison, B. J. Champagne & a Gardener: A Little Maine Murder. LC 82-16787. 229p. 1982. 10.95 (ISBN 0-89621-069-3). Thorndike Pr.

Morison, Elting E. Men, Machines, & Modern Times. 1966. 10.00x (ISBN 0-262-13025-4); pap. 3.45x (ISBN 0-262-63018-4). MIT Pr.

Morison, James. By Sea to San Francisco, Eighteen Forty Nine-Eighteen Fifty: The Journal of Dr. James Morison. White, Lonnie J. & Gillaspie, William R., eds. LC 76-40153. (Memphis State University Press Primary Source Ser). (Orig.). 1977. pap. 6.95x o.p. (ISBN 0-87870-036-6). Memphis St Univ.

--Mark. 1981. lib. bdg. 21.00 (ISBN 0-86524-069-8, 4102). Klock & Klock.

--Matthew. 1981. lib. bdg. 24.95 (ISBN 0-86524-068-X, 4001). Klock & Klock.

Morison, John L. The Eighth Earl of Elgin. LC 73-109798. (Illus.). 317p. Repr. of 1928 ed. lib. bdg. 16.25x (ISBN 0-8371-4289-X, MOEE). Greenwood.

Morison, Robert S., jt. ed. see Lappe, Marc.

Morison, Ruth. A Movement Approach to Educational Gymnastics. 1974. 10.00 (ISBN 0-8238-0153-5). Plays.

Morison, Samuel E. Admiral of the Ocean Sea: A Life of Christopher Columbus. (Illus.). 680p. pap. text ed. 9.95X (ISBN 0-930350-57-X). NE U Pr.

--The Great Explorers: The European Discovery of America. 1978. 22.95 (ISBN 0-19-502314-5). Oxford U Pr.

--The Maritime History of Massachusetts: Seventeen Eighty-Three to Eighteen Sixty. LC 79-5422. 421p. 1979. 24.95 (ISBN 0-930350-06-5); pap. text ed. 9.95x (ISBN 0-930350-04-9). NE U Pr.

--Oxford History of the American People, Vol. 1. pap. 3.95 ea. (Ment). Vol. 1 (ISBN 0-451-62192-1, ME2192). Vol. 2 (ME2054). Vol. 3 (ISBN 0-451-62055-0, ME2055). NAL.

--Samuel De Champlain: Father of New France. 1972. 10.00 o.p. (ISBN 0-316-58399-5, Pub. by Atlantic Monthly Pr). Little.

Morison, Samuel E. & Commager, Henry S. A Concise History of the American Republic. LC 76-40742. (Illus.). 1977. 29.95 o.p. (ISBN 0-19-502126-6); pap. 14.95x o.p. (ISBN 0-19-502125-8); 2 vol. ed. avail. o.p. (ISBN 0-685-99793-6); Pt. 1. 11.95x o.p. (ISBN 0-19-502124-X); Pt. 2. 11.95x o.p. (ISBN 0-19-502127-4). Oxford U Pr.

Morison, Samuel E., ed. see Bradford, William.

Morison, Samuel E., et al. A Concise History of the American Republic. 2nd ed. LC 82-3621. (Illus.). 1983. 35.00 (ISBN 0-19-503179-2); pap. 17.95 (ISBN 0-19-503180-6). Oxford U Pr.

Morison, W. A., jt. auth. see Entwistle, W. J.

Morison, W. L. John Austin. LC 82-80924. (Jurists: Profiles in Legal Theory Ser.). 256p. 1982. 20.00x (ISBN 0-8047-1141-0). Stanford U Pr.

Morison, Walter, ed. & tr. see Babel, Isaac.

Morissette, Bruce, tr. see Robbe-Grillet, Alain.

Morisson, A. Management of Sensorineural Deafness. 1975. 48.95 o.p. (ISBN 0-407-00024-0). Butterworth.

Morita, James R. Kaneko Mitsuharu. (World Authors Ser.). 1980. lib. bdg. 15.95 (ISBN 0-8057-6397-X, Twayne). G K Hall.

Moritani, Masanori. Japanese Technology: Getting the Best for the Least. Simul International, tr. (Illus.). 230p. 1982. pap. 19.95 (ISBN 0-686-42807-2, Pub. by Simul Pr Japan). Intl Schol Bk Serv.

Moritz, Alan R., et al. Handbook of Legal Medicine. 4th ed. LC 74-14826. 286p. 1975. 17.95 o.p. (ISBN 0-8016-3508-X). Mosby.

Moritz, Charles & Current Biography staff. Current Biography Yearbook 1982. 488p. 1982. 28.00 (ISBN 0-686-43233-9). Wilson.

Moritz, Derry A., jt. ed. see Kim, Mi J.

Moritz, Michael & Seaman, Barrett. Going for Broke: The Chrysler Story. LC 81-43044. (Illus.). 384p. 1981. 17.95 (ISBN 0-385-17180-3). Doubleday.

Mork, D. Wulstan. Biblical Meaning of Man. 1967. 4.95 o.p. (ISBN 0-685-07612-1, 80554). Glencoe.

Mork, Gordon R. Modern Western Civilization: A Concise History. LC 80-6198. 253p. 1981. lib. bdg. 21.75 (ISBN 0-8191-1434-0); pap. text ed. 10.75 (ISBN 0-8191-1435-9). U Pr of Amer.

Mork, Knut A., ed. Energy Prices, Inflation, & Economic Activity. 192p. 1980. prof ref 24.00x (ISBN 0-88410-691-8). Ballinger Pub.

Morken, Linda O. Lines Across My Sky. LC 72-93576. 64p. 1972. 4.00 (ISBN 0-911838-25-2). Windy Row.

Morlan, Robert L. American Government: Policy & Process. 3rd ed. LC 78-69574. (Illus.). 1979. pap. text ed. 16.50 (ISBN 0-395-26631-9); instr's. manual 1.00 (ISBN 0-395-26632-7). HM.

Morlan, Robert L. & Martin, David L. Capital, Courthouse & City Hall. 6th ed. LC 80-82016. (Illus.). 480p. 1981. pap. text ed. 14.50 (ISBN 0-395-29186-0); instr's. manual 1.25 (ISBN 0-395-31769-X). HM.

Morland, Nigel, ed. The Criminologist. LC 72-4369. (Illus.). 331p. 1972. 21.00x (ISBN 0-912050-27-6, Library Pr). Open Court.

Morland, Samuel. History of the Evangelical Churches of the Valleys of Piemont. 1983. 32.00 (ISBN 0-686-42929-X). Church History.

Morley, Andrew, jt. auth. see Baglee, Chris.

Morley, Christopher. The Haunted Bookshop. 256p. pap. 4.95 (ISBN 0-380-62695-0). Avon.

--Parnassus on Wheels. 160p. 4.95 (ISBN 0-380-62703-5). Avon.

Morley, D. Pediatric Priorities in the Developing World. 1976. 13.95 (ISBN 0-407-35113-2). Butterworth.

Morley, D. A. Mathematical Modelling in Water & Wastewater Treatment. (Illus.). 1979. 67.75 (ISBN 0-85334-842-1, Pub. by Applied Sci England). Elsevier.

Morley, David, et al, eds. Making Cities Work: The Dynamics of Urban Innovation. LC 79-5489. 288p. 1980. lib. bdg. 32.00 (ISBN 0-89158-656-3, Pub. by Croom Helm England); text ed. 15.00. Westview.

Morley, David C. & Woodland, Margaret. See How They Grow: Monitoring Child Growth for Appropriate Health Care in Developing Countries. (Illus.). 1980. text ed. 17.95x (ISBN 0-19-520160-4). Oxford U Pr.

Morley, Don. Motorcycling. LC 80-50932. (Intersport Ser.). 13.00 (ISBN 0-382-06423-2). Silver.

Morley, F. The Power in the People. (Humaine Studies). 293p. 1980. text ed. 10.00x (ISBN 0-8402-1296-8); pap. text ed. 4.95x. Humanities.

Morley, F. H., ed. Grazing Animals. (World Animal Science Ser.: Vol. 1B). 1981. 85.00 (ISBN 0-444-41835-0). Elsevier.

Morley, Frank, ed. see Boswell, James.

Morley, Henry. English Writers: An Attempt Towards a History of English Literature, 2 Vols. 1982. Repr. of 1887 ed. lib. bdg. 450.00 (ISBN 0-8495-3942-0, SET). Arden Lib.

--A First Sketch of English Literature. 1982. Repr. of 1887 ed. lib. bdg. 50.00 (ISBN 0-8495-3941-2). Arden Lib.

--Memoirs of Bartholomew Fair. LC 67-24348. 1968. Repr. of 1880 ed. 37.00x (ISBN 0-8103-3495-X). Gale.

Morley, Henry, ed. see Spenser, Edmund & Davies, John.

Morley, James W., ed. see Toshihiko, Shimada, et al.

Morley, Joan. Improving Aural Comprehension's Student's Workbook: Teacher's Book of Readings. LC 70-185904. 1972. tchrs.' bk. of readings 4.95x, free with adoption of students wkbk. (ISBN 0-472-08666-9); student's wkbk 7.95x (ISBN 0-472-08665-0). U of Mich Pr.

--Listening Dictation: Understanding English Sentence Structure. 1976. pap. 4.95x (ISBN 0-472-08667-7). U of Mich Pr.

Morley, John. Diderot & the Encyclopaedists, 2 vols. LC 74-145521. 1971. Repr. of 1923 ed. 42.00x (ISBN 0-8103-3987-0). Gale.

--Voltaire. 365p. 1982. Repr. of 1913 ed. lib. bdg. 40.00 (ISBN 0-89984-803-6). Century Bookbindery.

Morley, John, jt. auth. see Brandreth, Gyles.

Morley, John, ed. Bronchial Hyperactivity. 1982. 22.95 (ISBN 0-12-506450-0). Acad Pr.

Morley, John F. Vatican Diplomacy & the Jews During the Holocaust 1939-1943. 320p. 25.00. ADL.

Morley, Patricia. Margaret Laurence. (World Authors Ser.). 1981. lib. bdg. 13.95 (ISBN 0-8057-6433-X, Twayne). G K Hall.

Morley, Peter & Wallis, Roy, eds. Culture & Curing: Anthropological Perspectives on Traditional Medical Beliefs & Practices. LC 78-62194. (Contemporary Community Health Ser.). (Illus.). 1980. 14.95 o.p. (ISBN 0-8229-1136-1); pap. 5.95 (ISBN 0-8229-5325-0). U of Pittsburgh Pr.

Morley, Robert. Pardon Me, But You're Eating My Doily: & Other Embarrassing Moments of Famous People. 160p. 1983. 8.95 (ISBN 0-312-59656-1). St Martin.

--Robert Morley's Book of Bricks. LC 79-11856. 1979. 9.95 o.p. (ISBN 0-399-12275-3). Putnam Pub Group.

--Worry! How to Kick the Serenity Habit in Ninety-Eight Easy Steps. (Illus.). 176p. 1981. 10.00 (ISBN 0-399-12596-5). Putnam Pub Group.

Morley, S. Gladys Cooper. 1979. 10.95 (ISBN 0-07-043148-5). McGraw.

Morley, Samuel. Labor Markets & Inequitable Growth: The Case of Authoritarian Capitalism in Brazil. LC 82-4488. (Illus.). 272p. Date not set. price not set (ISBN 0-521-24439-0). Cambridge U Pr.

Morley, T. P., ed. Current Controversies in Neurosurgery. LC 75-21149. (Illus.). 1976. text ed. 42.00 o.p. (ISBN 0-7216-6557-8). Saunders.

Morley, W. M. & Nicholas, Anna K. This Is the Staffordshire Bull Terrier. (Illus.). 192p. 1982. 19.95 (ISBN 0-87666-745-0, H-1054). TFH Pubns.

Morlok, E. K. Introduction to Transportation System Engineering & Planning. (Illus.). 1978. text ed. 33.95 (ISBN 0-07-043132-9, C); soln. manual 17.50 (ISBN 0-07-043133-7). McGraw.

Morlok, Edward, Jr. An Analysis of Transport Technology & Network Structure. 143p. 1970. 8.00 (ISBN 0-686-94023-7, Trans). Northwestern U Pr.

Mormand, J. M. A Lie Group: Rotation in Quantum Mechanics. Date not set. 70.00 (ISBN 0-444-86125-4). Elsevier.

Mornay, Philippe de. A Woorke Concerning the Trewnesse of the Christian Religion. Sidney, Philip, tr. from Fr. LC 75-45384. 680p. 1976. Repr. of 1587 ed. lib. bdg. 70.00x (ISBN 0-8201-1166-X). Schol Facsimiles.

Mornay, Philippe De see Mornay, Philippe de.

Morneau, R. H., Jr. Sex Crimes Investigation: A Major Case Approach. (Illus.). 304p. 1983. text ed. price not set (ISBN 0-398-04832-0). C C Thomas.

Morneau, Robert F. Mantras for the Evening. LC 82-83587. (Illus.). 116p. (Orig.). 1982. pap. text ed. 4.25 (ISBN 0-8146-1269-5). Liturgical Pr.

Mornell, Pierre. Passive Men, Wild Women. 1979. 8.95 o.p. (ISBN 0-671-24579-1). S&S.

Morner, Nils-Axel. Earth Rheology, Isostasy & Eustasy. LC 79-1473. 560p. 1980. 124.95 (ISBN 0-471-27593-X). Wiley.

Morningside Associates. Basic Guide to Research Sources. new ed. O'Brian, Robert & Soderman, Joanne, eds. 256p. 1975. pap. 5.95 o.p. (ISBN 0-671-18744-9). Monarch Pr.

Morningstar, Mildred. Danger at the Sheep Ranch. (Orig.). (gr. 3 up). 1983. pap. 2.95 (ISBN 0-8024-0267-4). Moody.

Morningstar, Mona, jt. auth. see Suppes, Patrick.

Morny, Claude, compiled by. A Wine & Food Bedside Book. (International Wine & Food Society Ser.). (Illus.). 4.50 o.p. (ISBN 0-7153-5864-2). David & Charles.

Morogues, Bigot De see De Morogues, Bigot.

Morokuma, K., jt. auth. see Ohno, K.

Morones, Gregorio. Practicas de Laboratorio de Fisica. (Span.). 1979. pap. text ed. 7.00 o.p. (ISBN 0-06-315700-4, Pub. by HarLA Mexico). Har-Row.

Moroney, John R. Income Inequality: Trends & International Comparisons. LC 79-4726. 192p. 1979. 22.95 (ISBN 0-669-03058-9). Lexington Bks.

Moroney, John R., ed. Advances in the Economics of Energy & Resources, Vol. 3. 300p. 1980. 45.00 (ISBN 0-89232-175-X). Jai Pr.

Moroney, Paul. Issues in the Implementation of Digital Feedback Compensators. (Signal Processing, Optimization, & Control Ser.). (Illus.). 224p. 1983. 30.00x (ISBN 0-262-13185-4). MIT Pr.

Morowitz, H. & Quastler, Henry, eds. First National Biophysics Conference, Columbus, Ohio, March 4-6th 1957: Proceedings. 1959. text ed. 75.00x (ISBN 0-686-83712-6). Elliots Bks.

Morowitz, Harold J. Energy Flow in Biology. LC 79-89841. 1979. 16.00 (ISBN 0-918024-12-9); pap. text ed. 10.00 (ISBN 0-918024-13-7). Ox Bow.

Morpha, Margery C. He Is Risen. 1980. pap. 1.95 o.s.i. (ISBN 0-88479-024-X). Arena Lettres.

Morphet, jt. auth. see Green.

Morphet, Edgar, et al. Educational Organization & Administration: Concepts Practices & Issues. 4th ed. (Illus.). 448p. 1982. reference 25.95 (ISBN 0-13-236729-7). P-H.

Morphet, Edgar L., jt. auth. see Johns, Roe L.

Morrall, John B. Aristotle. (Political Thinkers Ser.). 1977. text ed. 19.95x o.p. (ISBN 0-04-320121-0); pap. text ed. 12.50x (ISBN 0-04-320122-9). Allen Unwin.

Morray, Joseph P. From Yalta to Disarmament: Cold War Debate. LC 73-19225. 368p. 1974. Repr. of 1961 ed. lib. bdg. 21.00x (ISBN 0-8371-7306-X, MOYD). Greenwood.

Morreall, John. Taking Laughter Seriously. 192p. 1983. 39.00x (ISBN 0-87395-642-7); pap. 12.95 (ISBN 0-87395-643-5). State U NY Pr.

Morreall, John S. Analogy & Talking about God: A Critique of the Thomistic Approach. LC 77-18494. 1978. pap. text ed. 8.25 (ISBN 0-8191-0423-X). U Pr of Amer.

Morrell. The Future of Dollar & World Reserve System. 1981. text ed. 19.95 (ISBN 0-408-10674-3); pap. text ed. 12.50 (ISBN 0-408-10675-1). Butterworth.

Morrell, David. Blood Oath. 192p. 1982. 11.95 (ISBN 0-312-08447-1, Pub. by Marek). St Martin.

--John Barth: An Introduction. LC 75-27284. (Illus.). 256p. 1976. 16.50x (ISBN 0-271-01220-X). Pa St U Pr.

Morrell, Jack & Thackray, Arnold. Gentlemen of Science: Early Years of the British Association for the Advancement of Science. (Illus.). 1981. 49.95x (ISBN 0-19-858163-7); pap. 14.95x (ISBN 0-19-520396-8). Oxford U Pr.

Morrell, James. Britain Through the Nineteen Eighties. 1980. Vol. I, Framework & Issues, 320p. text ed. 187.25x set (sold as one only) (ISBN 0-566-02217-6). Vol. II, The Forecaster, 96 p. Gower Pub Ltd.

Morrell, Janet M., ed. Four English Comedies. Incl. Volpone. Johnson, Ben; Way of the World. Congreve, William; She Stoops to Conquer. Goldsmith, Oliver; School for Scandal. Sheridan, Richard B. (Penguin Plays Ser.). (Orig.). (YA) (gr. 9 up). 1969. pap. 3.95 o.p. (ISBN 0-14-048033-1). Penguin.

Morrell, Jonathan A., jt. ed. see Hermalin, Jared.

Morrell, S. H., ed. Progress in Rubber Technology, Vol. 44. 139p. 1981. 47.25 (ISBN 0-85334-984-3, Pub. by Applied Sci England). Elsevier.

Morrelli, H. F., jt. auth. see Melmon, K. L.

Morresi, Angelo C., jt. auth. see Cheremisinoff, Paul N.

Morrey, C. B., jt. auth. see Protter, M. H.

Morrey, Charles B., Jr., jt. auth. see Protter, Murray H.

Morrill, Chester, Jr. Computers & Data Processing Information Sources. LC 70-85486. (Management Information Guide Ser.: No. 15). 1969. 42.00x (ISBN 0-8103-0815-0). Gale.

Morrill, Chester, Jr., ed. Systems & Procedures Including Office Management Information Sources. LC 67-31261. (Management Information Ser.: No. 12). 1967. 42.00x (ISBN 0-8103-0812-6). Gale.

Morrill, J. S. Seventeenth Century Britain, Sixteen Hundred & Three to Seventeen Fourteen. (Critical Bibliographies Ser.). 188p. 1980. 17.50 o.p. (ISBN 0-208-01785-2, Archon). Shoe String.

Morrill, Joan, jt. auth. see Hagstrom, Julie.

Morrill, L. G., et al. Organic Compounds in Soils: Sorption, Degradation & Persistence. 1982. text ed. 29.50 (ISBN 0-250-40514-8). Ann Arbor Science.

Morrill, Richard L. & Wohlenberg, Ernest H. The Geography of Poverty in the United States. (Illus.). 160p. 1972. text ed. 10.95 o.p. (ISBN 0-07-043131-0, C); pap. text ed. 6.95 (ISBN 0-07-043130-2). McGraw.

Morrill, Terence C., ed. see Silverstein, Robert M. & Bassler, G. Clayton.

Morrill, Weston H. & Hurst, James C., eds. Dimensions of Intervention for Student Development. Otting, E. R., tr. LC 80-16939. (Counseling & Human Development Ser.). 339p. 1980. text ed. 29.95 (ISBN 0-471-05249-3, Pub. by Wiley-Interscience). Wiley.

Morris. Soft Ionization Biological Mass Spectrometry. 1981. 42.95 (ISBN 0-471-26188-2, Wiley Heyden). Wiley.

--Xerox Dictionary Thumb. 10.95 (ISBN 0-448-02905-7, G&D). Putnam Pub Group.

Morris & Rohrer. Decade of Creation: Acts-Facts-Impacts, Vol. 4. LC 80-67426. 320p. 1980. pap. 7.95 (ISBN 0-89051-069-5). CLP Pubs.

Morris, A. J. C. P. Trevelyan, Eighteen Seventy - Nineteen Fifty Eight: Portrait of a Radical. 1979. 25.00 (ISBN 0-312-11242-4). St Martin.

--Edwardian Radicalism 1900-1914. 288p. 1974. 23.95x (ISBN 0-7100-7866-8). Routledge & Kegan.

--Foundations of Structural Optimization: A Unified Approach. LC 81-21882. (Numerical Method in Engineering Ser.). 1982. 72.00 (ISBN 0-471-10200-8, Pub. by Wiley-Interscience). Wiley.

Morris, Aldyth. Damien. LC 79-22915. 1980. 3.50 (ISBN 0-8248-0693-X). UH Pr.

Morris, Alison, et al. Justice for Children. 176p. 1980. text ed. 26.00x (ISBN 0-333-27486-5); pap. text ed. 9.95x (ISBN 0-686-64581-2). Humanities.

Morris, Allen. Florida Place Names. LC 74-13949. 160p. 1974. 7.95 o.s.i. (ISBN 0-87024-256-3). U of Miami Pr.

Morris Animal Foundation. Zoo & Wild Animal Medicine. Fowler, Murray E., ed. LC 77-72803. (Illus.). 1978. text ed. 75.00 (ISBN 0-7216-6559-4). Saunders.

Morris, Anne C., ed. see Morris, Gouverneur.

Morris, Arthur S. South America. LC 79-13729. (Illus.). 1979. text ed. 26.50x (ISBN 0-06-494981-8); pap. text ed. 17.50x o.p. (ISBN 0-06-494982-6). B&N Imports.

Morris, Audrey S. One Thousand Inspirational Things. (Library of Beautiful Things: Vol. 2). (YA) (gr. 9-12). 1956. 9.95 o.p. (ISBN 0-8015-5568-X, Hawthorn). Dutton.

Morris, B. D., jt. auth. see Palmer, D. C.

Morris, B. R., jt. auth. see Bartholomew, D. J.

Morris, Ben. Objectives & Perspectives in Education: Studies in Educational Theory, 1955-70. 284p. 1972. 23.95x (ISBN 0-7100-7247-3). Routledge & Kegan.

Morris, Brenda, jt. ed. see Wing, J. K.

Morris, Brian, ed. Ritual Murder. 128p. (Orig.). pap. 7.95 o.p. (ISBN 0-85635-295-0, Pub. by Carcanet New Pr England). Humanities.

--William Congreve. (New Mermaid Critical Commentaries Ser.). 176p. 1972. 10.00x o.p. (ISBN 0-87471-128-2). Rowman.

Morris, Brian, ed. see Shakespeare, William.

Morris, C. B. Generation of Spanish Poets, Nineteen Twenty to Nineteen Thirty-six. LC 69-11270. (Illus.). 1969. 48.00 (ISBN 0-521-07381-2); pap. 13.95x (ISBN 0-521-29481-9). Cambridge U Pr.

--This Loving Darkness: Silent Films & Spanish Writers 1920 - 1936. 1980. 39.50x (ISBN 0-19-713440-8). Oxford U Pr.

Morris, Carl & Rolph, John. Introduction to Data Analysis & Statistical Inference. (Illus.). 416p. 1981. pap. text ed. 17.95 (ISBN 0-13-480582-8). P-H.

Morris, Charles. Psychology: An Introduction. 4th ed. 1982. text ed. 23.95 (ISBN 0-13-734293-4). P-H.

--Signification & Significance: A Study of the Relations of Signs & Values. 1964. pap. 5.95x (ISBN 0-262-63014-1). MIT Pr.

Morris, Charles G. Psychology, an Introduction: PSI Unit Mastery Workbook. (Illus.). 384p. 1982. 11.95 (ISBN 0-13-734335-3). P-H.

Morris, Charles J., et al, eds. Developing Labor Law: The Board, the Courts, & the National Labor Relations Act, 2 Vols. 2nd ed. 1983. Set. 90.00 (ISBN 0-87179-360-1). BNA.

Morris, Charles R. Locke, Berkeley, Hume. LC 79-17847. 1979. Repr. of 1931 ed. lib. bdg. 18.25x (ISBN 0-313-22091-3, MOLO). Greenwood.

Morris, Charles W. Six Theories of Mind. 1932. 10.50x o.s.i. (ISBN 0-226-54004-9). U of Chicago Pr.

Morris, Charlotte, ed. From Showgirl to Skidrow. (Illus.). 160p. 1983. 12.50 (ISBN 0-89962-308-5). Todd & Honeywell.

Morris, Colin. The Discovery of the Individual, 1050-1200. LC 72-84235. 208p. 1973. 4.50xi o.p. (ISBN 0-06-131718-7, TB1718, Torch). Har-Row.

Morris, D. J. Communication for Command & Control Systems. (International Series on Systems & Control: Vol. 5). 470p. 1983. 70.00 (ISBN 0-08-027597-4); 23.50 (ISBN 0-08-027596-6). Pergamon.

Morris, D. S., jt. auth. see Haigh, R. H.

Morris, Dan & Morris, Inez. The Complete Fish Cookbook. (Illus.). 1978. pap. 5.95 o.s.i. (ISBN 0-695-80937-7). Follett.

--The Complete Fish Cookbook. (Illus.). 416p. pap. 7.95 (ISBN 0-88317-078-7). Stoeger Pub Co.

Morris, Danny. Aces & Wingmen. 488p. 35.00x o.p. (ISBN 0-686-75476-X, Pub. by Spearman England). State Mutual Bk.

Morris, David J. The New City-States. LC 82-82572. (Illus.). 76p. Date not set. pap. 4.95 (ISBN 0-917582-49-7). Inst Local Self Re.

Morris, David J., Jr. The Wizard's Bartending Guide: Beginners Through Professionals. (Illus.). 1979. pap. 5.95 (ISBN 0-933528-01-9). ANKH.

--The Wizard's Building, Cleaning & Repairing Fireplace Guide. (Illus.). Date not set. pap. 5.95 (ISBN 0-686-24590-3). ANKH.

--The Wizard's Structural & Mechanical Guide to Buying Your Own Home. Date not set. pap. 5.95 (ISBN 0-933528-03-5). ANKH.

--You're off to See the Wizard. 1978. 5.95 (ISBN 0-933528-00-0). ANKH.

Morris, Dean. Animals That Burrow. LC 77-8114. (Read About Animals Ser.). (Illus.). (gr. k-3). 1977. PLB 13.30 (ISBN 0-8393-0012-3). Raintree Pubs.

--Animals That Live in Shells. LC 77-7911. (Read About Animals Ser.). (Illus.). (gr. k-3). 1977. PLB 13.30 (ISBN 0-8393-0013-1). Raintree Pubs.

--Birds. LC 77-8302. (Read About Animals Ser.). (Illus.). (gr. k-3). 1977. PLB 13.30 (ISBN 0-8393-0006-9). Raintree Pubs.

--Butterflies & Moths. LC 77-7912. (Read About Animals Ser.). (Illus.). (gr. k-3). 1977. PLB 13.30 (ISBN 0-8393-0010-7). Raintree Pubs.

--Cats. LC 77-8118. (Read About Animals Ser.). (Illus.). (gr. k-3). 1977. PLB 13.30 (ISBN 0-8393-0002-6). Raintree Pubs.

--Dinosaurs & Other First Animals. LC 77-23398. (Read About Animals Ser.). (Illus.). (gr. k-3). 1977. PLB 13.30 (ISBN 0-8393-0000-X). Raintree Pubs.

--Endangered Animals. LC 77-8365. (Read About Animals Ser.). (Illus.). (gr. k-3). 1977. PLB 13.30 (ISBN 0-8393-0011-5). Raintree Pubs.

--Frogs & Toads. LC 77-8116. (Read About Animals Ser.). (Illus.). (gr. k-3). 1977. PLB 13.30 (ISBN 0-8393-0003-4). Raintree Pubs.

--Horses. LC 77-8243. (Read About Ser.). (Illus.). 40p. (gr. k-3). 1983. PLB 13.30 (ISBN 0-8393-0008-5). Raintree Pubs.

--Insects That Live in Families. LC 77-8254. (Read About Animals Ser.). (Illus.). (gr. k-3). 1977. PLB 13.30 (ISBN 0-8393-0001-8). Raintree Pubs.

--Monkeys & Apes. LC 77-8148. (Read About Animals Ser.). (Illus.). (gr. k-3). 1977. PLB 13.30 (ISBN 0-8393-0005-0). Raintree Pubs.

--Snakes & Lizards. LC 77-8147. (Read About Animals Ser.). (Illus.). (gr. k-3). 1977. PLB 13.30 (ISBN 0-8393-0007-7). Raintree Pubs.

--Spiders. LC 77-8115. (Read About Animals Ser.). (gr. k-3). 1977. PLB 13.30 (ISBN 0-8393-0004-2). Raintree Pubs.

--Underwater Life: The Oceans. LC 77-23051. (Read About Animals Ser.). (Illus.). (gr. k-3). 1977. PLB 13.30 (ISBN 0-8393-0009-3). Raintree Pubs.

Morris, Derek J., jt. auth. see Hay, Donald A.

Morris, Desmond. Human Zoo. 1970. pap. 2.75 o.s.i. (ISBN 0-440-53912-9, Delta). Dell.

--Manwatching: A Field Guide to Human Behavior. (Illus.). 1979. pap. 16.95 (ISBN 0-8109-2184-7). Abrams.

--Manwatching: A Field Guide to Human Behavior. (Illus.). 1977. 25.00 (ISBN 0-8109-1310-0). Abrams.

Morris, Donald. Washing of the Spears: The Rise & Fall of the Zulu Nation. LC 65-12594. 1969. pap. 7.95 o.p. (ISBN 0-671-20233-2, Touchstone Bks). S&S.

Morris, Dwight A. & Morris, Lynne D., eds. Health Care Administration: A Guide to Information Sources. LC 78-53431. (Health Affairs Information Guide Ser.: Vol. 1). 1978. 42.00x (ISBN 0-8103-1378-2). Gale.

Morris, Earl W. & Winter, Mary. Housing, Family, & Society. LC 77-24772. 1978. text ed. 24.95x (ISBN 0-471-61570-6). Wiley.

Morris, Edmund. The Rise of Theodore Roosevelt. LC 78-23789. (Illus.). 1979. 15.95 (ISBN 0-698-10783-7, Coward). Putnam Pub Group.

Morris, Edward E. Austral English. LC 68-18003. 1968. Repr. of 1898 ed. 58.00x (ISBN 0-8103-3287-6). Gale.

Morris, Ellen. Her Own Business. 1980. cancelled (ISBN 0-698-11000-5, Coward). Putnam Pub Group.

Morris, Eric. Being & Doing. (Illus.). 204p. 1981. pap. 8.95 (ISBN 0-8256-9922-3, Quick Fox). Putnam Pub Group.

--Salerno. LC 82-48511. 560p. 1983. 19.95 (ISBN 0-8128-2893-3). Stein & Day.

Morris, Eric & Hotchkis, Joan. No Acting Please. 1979. pap. 6.95 (ISBN 0-8256-3150-5, Quick Fox). Putnam Pub Group.

Morris, Floyd. One Hundred & Ninety-Eight Easy Wood Projects. (Illus.). 1970. pap. 5.40 (ISBN 0-87006-111-9). Goodheart.

--Two Hundred & Seventy Two Artistic Silhouettes. (Illus.). 1972. pap. 5.40 (ISBN 0-87006-158-5). Goodheart.

Morris, Freda. Self-Hypnonis in Two Days. 1975. pap. 5.95 (ISBN 0-525-47403-X, 0578-170). Dutton.

Morris, G. S. How to Change the Games Children Play. 2nd ed. LC 79-56429. 1980. pap. 7.95x (ISBN 0-8087-3967-0). Burgess.

Morris, George H. George H. Morris Teaches Beginners How to Ride: A Clinic for Instructors, Parents, & Students. LC 79-7224. (Illus.). 144p. 1981. 12.95 (ISBN 0-385-14226-9). Doubleday.

Morris, Gouverneur. Diary & Letters of Gouverneur Morris, 2 Vols. Morris, Anne C., ed. LC 70-98691. (American Public Figures Ser). 1970. Repr. of 1888 ed. lib. bdg. 130.00 (ISBN 0-306-71835-9). Da Capo.

Morris, Harry W., jt. auth. see Simmons, Charles W.

Morris, Helen. Where's That Poem? An Index of Poems for Children Arranged by Subject, with a Bibliography of Books of Poetry. rev & enl ed. 287p. 1979. pap. 10.50x o.p. (ISBN 0-631-11791-1, Pub. by Basil Blackwell). Biblio Dist.
Morris, Henry. Bible & Modern Science. 1956. pap. 2.95 (ISBN 0-8024-0572-X). Moody.
Morris, Henry M. The Beginning of the World. LC 77-71005. (Illus.). 1977. pap. 3.95 (ISBN 0-916406-66-0). Accent Bks.
--Genesis Record. 17.95 (ISBN 0-8010-6004-4). Baker Bk.
--The Genesis Record. LC 76-2265. 1976. 17.95 (ISBN 0-89051-026-1). CLP Pubs.
--Many Infallible Proofs. LC 74-81484. 384p. 1974. 9.95 (ISBN 0-89051-006-7); pap. 7.95 (ISBN 0-89051-005-9). CLP Pubs.
--The Remarkable Birth of Planet Earth. 124p. 1973. pap. 2.50 (ISBN 0-89051-000-8). CLP Pubs.
--The Revelation Record. 1982. 16.95 (ISBN 0-8423-5511-1). Tyndale.
--The Troubled Waters of Evolution. 2nd ed. LC 82-15254. (Illus.). 225p. 1975. pap. 5.95 (ISBN 0-89051-087-3). CLP Pubs.
Morris, Henry M. & Clark, Martin. The Bible Has the Answer. LC 76-20206. 1976. pap. 7.95 (ISBN 0-89051-021-0). CLP Pubs.
Morris, Henry M. & Gish, Duane T. The Battle for Creation: Acts, Facts, Impacts, Vol. 2. LC 74-75429. (Illus.). 1976. pap. 5.95 (ISBN 0-89051-020-2). CLP Pubs.
Morris, Henry M. & Wiggert, James M. Applied Hydraulics in Engineering. 2nd ed. 600p. 1972. 34.50 (ISBN 0-471-06669-9); instr's solution 3.00 (ISBN 0-471-07503-5). Wiley.
Morris, Henry M., et al. Scientific Creationism. LC 74-14160. 1974. pap. 7.95 (ISBN 0-89051-003-2). CLP Pubs.
--Scientific Creationism: Public School Edition. LC 74-14159. 1974. 9.95 (ISBN 0-89051-002-4); pap. 7.95 (ISBN 0-89051-001-6). CLP Pubs.
Morris, Henry M., et al, eds. Creation: Acts-Facts-Impacts, Vol. I. LC 74-75429. 197p. 1974. pap. 3.95 (ISBN 0-89051-014-8). CLP Pubs.
Morris, Henry, 3rd. Explore the Word. LC 78-55611. 1978. pap. 7.95 (ISBN 0-89051-047-4). CLP Pubs.
Morris, Herbert. Peru. LC 82-48128. (Poetry Ser.). 64p. 1983. pap. 5.72i (ISBN 0-06-091020-8, CN 1020, CN). Har-Row.
--Peru. LC 82-48128. (Poetry Ser.). 64p. 1983. 10.95 (ISBN 0-06-015116-1, HarpT). Har-Row.
Morris, Hughlett H., jt. auth. see McWilliams, Betty J.
Morris, Inez, jt. auth. see Morris, Dan.
Morris, Ivan. The Nobility of Failure. 1976. pap. 5.95 (ISBN 0-452-00522-1, F522, Mer). NAL.
--The World of the Shining Prince: Court Life in Ancient Japan. 1979. pap. 5.95 (ISBN 0-14-005479-0, Peregrine). Penguin.
Morris, Ivan, tr. see Mishima, Yukio.
Morris, J. Gareth. A Biologist's Physical Chemistry. 408p. 1974. pap. text ed. 16.50 (ISBN 0-7131-2414-8). E Arnold.
Morris, J. Gareth, jt. ed. see Rose, A. H.
Morris, J. L. Computational Methods in Elementary Numerical Analysis. LC 82-2778. 450p. 1983. 41.95 (ISBN 0-471-10419-1, Pub. by Wiley-Interscience); pap. 24.95 (ISBN 0-471-10420-5, Pub. by wiley-Interscience). Wiley.
Morris, J. N., jt. auth. see Lesser, M. X.
Morris, J. S., jt. ed. see Bouchier, I. A.
Morris, J. Scott. Forms-1981 Supplement. LC 76-54017. 150p. 1984. pap. 55.00 o.p. (ISBN 0-316-58393-6). Little.
--Real Estate Tax Planning. 1977. text ed. 47.50 (ISBN 0-316-58390-1). Little.
--Real Estate Tax Planning: 1981 Supplement. 1981. pap. text ed. 15.00 (ISBN 0-316-58393-6). Little.
--Supplement to Real Estate Tax Planning Forms 1981. LC 80-84025. 1981. pap. 15.00 o.p. (ISBN 0-316-58393-6). Little.
Morris, Jack. Crime Analysis Charting. (Illus.). 70p. 1982. 9.95 (ISBN 0-686-37558-0). Palmer Pub CA.
Morris, Jacquelyn M. & Elkins, Elizabeth A. Library Searching: Resources & Strategies with Examples from the Environmental Sciences. (Library Resources Ser.). 1978. text ed. 8.95x o.p. (ISBN 0-88432-004-9); pap. text ed. 5.95x o.p. (ISBN 0-88432-005-7). J Norton Pubs.
Morris, James. Farewell the Trumpets: The Decline of an Empire. LC 79-24253. (Illus.). 576p. 1980. pap. 8.95 (ISBN 0-15-630286-1, Harv). HarBraceJ.
--The World of Venice. rev. ed. LC 73-18461. (Helen & Kurt Wolff Bk). (Illus.). 1973. 8.95 o.p. (ISBN 0-15-199086-7). HarBraceJ.
--The World of Venice. rev. ed. LC 73-18461. (Illus.). 328p. 1974. pap. 3.95 o.p. (ISBN 0-15-698355-9, HB281, Harv). HarBraceJ.
Morris, James M. Our Maritime Heritage: Maritime Developments & Their Impact on American Life. 1979. pap. text ed. 11.50 (ISBN 0-8191-0700-X). U Pr of Amer.
Morris, James O. A Bibliography of Industrial Relations in the Railroad Industry. LC 75-8878. (ILR Bibliography Ser.: No. 12). 172p. 1975. 5.00 (ISBN 0-87546-058-5). ILR Pr.
--Conflict Within the AFL. LC 73-22506. (Cornell Studies in Industrial & Labor Relations: Vol. 10). 319p. 1974. Repr. of 1958 ed. lib. bdg. 18.25x (ISBN 0-8371-6371-4, MOCA). Greenwood.
--Elites, Intellectuals, & Consensus: A Study of the Social Question & the Industrial Relations System in Chile. LC 66-65151. (International Report Ser.: No. 7). 312p. 1966. 6.00 (ISBN 0-87546-011-9). ILR Pr.
Morris, James O. & Cordova, Efren. Bibliography of Industrial Relations in Latin America. LC 67-64729. (ILR Bibliography Ser.: No. 8). 308p. 1967. 10.00 (ISBN 0-87546-022-4). ILR Pr.
Morris, Jan. Conundrum. 1975. pap. 1.50 o.p. (ISBN 0-451-06413-5, W6413, Sig). NAL.
--Destinations: Essays from Rolling Stone. (Illus.). 1980. 15.95 (ISBN 0-19-502708-6). Oxford U Pr.
--A Venetian Bestiary. (Illus.). 1982. 14.95 (ISBN 0-500-23354-3). Thames Hudson.
Morris, Jan, compiled by. Wales. (Small Oxford Bks.). (Illus.). 100p. 1982. 9.95 (ISBN 0-19-214118-X). Oxford U Pr.
Morris, Jane. The Food Book Activity Guide. 128p. (Orig.). 1983. wkbk. 3.80 (ISBN 0-87006-425-8). Goodheart.
Morris, Janet. Cruiser Dreams. (Dream Dancer Trilogy Ser.: Bk. 2). 276p. 1981. 14.95 (ISBN 0-399-12633-3). Putnam Pub Group.
--Dream Dancer. 312p. 1981. 12.95 (ISBN 0-399-12591-4). Putnam Pub Group.
--Earth Dreams. 240p. 1982. 14.95 (ISBN 0-399-12686-4). Putnam Pub Group.
Morris, Joan, jt. auth. see Fotheringham, John.
Morris, Joe A. Deadline Every Minute: The Story of the United Press. LC 69-10137. 1969. Repr. of 1957 ed. lib. bdg. 20.75x (ISBN 0-8371-0175-1, MOUP). Greenwood.
Morris, Joe A., jt. auth. see Vandenberg, Arthur H., Jr.
Morris, John. Managing the Library Fire Risk. 2nd, rev. ed. LC 78-22603. (Illus.). 1979. 15.50 (ISBN 0-9602278-1-4). U Cal Risk Management.
Morris, John, jt. auth. see Paulsen, Gary.
Morris, John D. Creative Metal Sculpture. 1971. 8.95 o.p. (ISBN 0-685-01116-X, 80555). Glencoe.
--Tracking Those Incredible Dinosaurs & the People Who Know Them. LC 80-67760. (Illus.). 1980. pap. 5.95 (ISBN 0-89051-067-9). CLP Pubs.
Morris, John O. Make Yourself Clear: Morris on Business Communication. (Illus.). 192p. 1972. 23.95 (ISBN 0-07-043180-9, P&RB). McGraw.
Morris, John R. Davis H. Waite: The Ideology of a Western Populist. LC 82-40106. (Illus.). 240p. (Orig.). 1982. PLB 23.00 (ISBN 0-8191-2445-1); pap. text ed. 10.75 (ISBN 0-8191-2446-X). U Pr of Amer.
Morris, John W. World Geography. 3rd ed. (Illus.). 672p. 1972. text ed. 29.00 o.p. (ISBN 0-07-043138-8, C); 3.95 o.p. instr.'s manual (ISBN 0-07-043142-6); 5.95 o.p. study guide (ISBN 0-07-061120-3). McGraw.
Morris, Joseph & Adams, St. Claire, eds. Facing Forward: Poems of Courage. 257p. 1982. Repr. of 1925 ed. lib. bdg. 30.00 (ISBN 0-89987-645-5). Darby Bks.
Morris, Judy K. The Crazies & Sam. 144p. (gr. 3-8). 1983. 11.50 (ISBN 0-670-24545-3). Viking Pr.
Morris, Kelly, ed. see Zafran, Eric & Ackerman, Gerald M.
Morris, Kenneth. The Fates of the Princes of Dyfed. Reginald, R. & Menville, Douglas, eds. LC 80-19430. (Newcastle Forgotten Fantasy Library: Vol. 15). 362p. 1980. Repr. of 1978 ed. lib. bdg. 11.95x o.p. (ISBN 0-89370-514-4). Borgo Pr.
--The Fates of the Princes of Dyfed. (Forgotten Fantasy Library: Vol. 15). 1978. pap. 4.95 o.p. (ISBN 0-87877-114-X). Newcastle Pub.
--Golden Threads in the Tapestry of History. (Illus.). 246p. 1975. pap. 4.75 (ISBN 0-913004-27-8). Point Loma Pub.
Morris, Kenneth T. & Kanitz, H. Mike. Rational-Emotive Therapy. 1975. pap. 2.40 o.p. (ISBN 0-395-20036-9). HM.
Morris, L. W. Critical Path: Construction & Analysis. 1967. text ed. 27.00 o.s.i. (ISBN 0-08-012472-0); pap. text ed. 12.75 (ISBN 0-08-012471-2). Pergamon.
Morris, Leon. First & Second Epistles to the Thessalonians. (New International Commentary of the New Testament). 1959. 11.95 (ISBN 0-8028-2187-1). Eerdmans.
Morris, Linda, jt. auth. see Zender, Karl.
Morris, Lorenzo & Henry, Charles. The Chit'lin Controversy: Race & Public Policy in America. 1978. pap. text ed. 8.50 (ISBN 0-8191-0471-X). U Pr of Amer.
Morris, Louis, et al, eds. Banbury Report 6: Product Labeling. LC 80-22728. (Banbury Report Ser.: Report 6). 325p. 1980. 45.00x (ISBN 0-87969-205-7). Cold Spring Harbor.
Morris, Lynne D., jt. ed. see Morris, Dwight A.
Morris, Mary. Crossroads. 211p. 1982. 13.95 (ISBN 0-395-33104-8). HM.
--Vanishing Animals. LC 79-52637. (Illus.). 192p. 1979. 12.95 (ISBN 0-87923-286-2). Godine.
Morris, Melinda. The First Babyfood Cookbook. (Illus.). 128p. Date not set. pap. price not set (ISBN 0-448-01252-9, G&D). Putnam Pub Group.
Morris, Mervyn, jt. ed. see Mordecai, Pamela.
Morris, Michael A. International Politics & the Sea: The Case of Brazil. (Westview Replica Edition). 1979. lib. bdg. 30.00 o.p. (ISBN 0-89158-456-0). Westview.
Morris, Michael A. & Millan, Victor, eds. Controlling Latin American Conflicts: Ten Approaches. Replica ed. 300p. 1982. softcover 21.50 (ISBN 0-86531-938-3). Westview.
Morris, Michelle. If I Should Die Before I Wake. 204p. 1982. 10.95 (ISBN 0-87477-224-9). J P Tarcher.
Morris, Milton D. & Mayio, Albert. Curbing Illegal Immigration. Carroll, Alice M., abridged by. LC 82-70892. 70p. 1982. pap. 4.95 (ISBN 0-8157-5839-1). Brookings.
Morris, N. M. Control Engineering. 3rd ed. 256p. 1983. write for info. (ISBN 0-07-084666-9). McGraw.
Morris, Neil & Morris, Ting. Find the Canary. (Mystery Picture Book Ser.). 24p. (gr. k-3). 1983. 5.70i (ISBN 0-316-58375-8). Little.
--Hide & Seek. (Mystery Picture Book Ser.). 24p. (gr. k-3). 1983. 5.70i (ISBN 0-316-58376-6). Little.
--Search for Sam. (Mystery Picture Bk. Ser.). (Illus.). 24p. (gr. k-3). 1983. 5.70 (ISBN 0-316-58378-2). Little.
--Where's My Hat? (Mystery Picture Book Ser.). (Illus.). 24p. (gr. k-3). 1983. 5.70i. Little.
Morris, Noel M. Digital Electronics for Works Electricians. (Illus.). 148p. 1980. pap. 19.50 o.p. (ISBN 0-07-084523-9). McGraw.
Morris, Norman & Arthur, Humphrey. Sterilization as a Means of Birth Control in Men & Women. (Illus.). 125p. 1982. 14.95 (ISBN 0-7206-0363-3, Pub. by Peter Owen). Merrimack Bk Serv.
Morris, Norval. Madness & the Criminal Law. LC 82-13435. (Studies in Crime & Justice). 168p. 1983. 20.00 (ISBN 0-226-53907-5). U of Chicago Pr.
Morris, Norval, jt. ed. see Tonry, Michael.
Morris, O. E. Handbook of Structural Design. 822p. 1963. 38.00 (ISBN 0-442-12104-0, Pub. by Van Nos Reinhold). Krieger.
Morris, Pauline & Beverly, Farida. On License - a Study of Parole. LC 74-12067. 178p. 1975. 28.25 o.p. (ISBN 0-471-61575-7, Pub. by Wiley-Interscience). Wiley.
Morris, Pauline, jt. auth. see Byles, Anthea.
Morris, Peter, tr. see Sadoul, Georges.
Morris, R. J. Parliament & the Public Libraries: A Survey of Legislative Activity Promoting the Municipal Library Service in England & Wales 1850-1976. 492p. 1977. 36.00 o.p. (ISBN 0-7201-0554-4, Pub. by Mansell England). Wilson.
Morris, R. L. Ladies of the Sun: Three Modern Comedies Apapted from the Work of Euripedes. 1982. 8.00 (ISBN 0-682-49912-9). Exposition.
Morris, Raymond N. Sixth Form & College Entrance. (International Library of Sociology). 1969. 10.95x o.p. (ISBN 0-7100-6319-9). Routledge & Kegan.
Morris, Reginald O. Foundations of Practical Harmony & Counterpoint. 2nd ed. LC 79-10541. (Illus.). xii, 148p. 1980. Repr. of 1931 ed. lib. bdg. 17.50x (ISBN 0-313-21465-4, MOPH). Greenwood.
Morris, Richard B. The American Revolution Reconsidered. LC 78-27608. 1979. Repr. of 1967 ed. lib. bdg. 17.75x (ISBN 0-313-20909-X, MOAM). Greenwood.
--Great Presidential Decisions: State Papers That Changed the Course of History from Washington to Nixon. new & enl. ed. 7.50 (ISBN 0-8446-5858-8). Peter Smith.
--The Making of a Nation, 1775-1789. LC 63-8572. (Life History of the United States Ser.). (Illus.). (gr. 5 up). 1974. PLB 10.60 (ISBN 0-8094-0551-2, Pub. by Time-Life). Silver.
--The New World: Before 1775. LC 63-8572. (Life History of the United States). (Illus.). (gr. 5 up). 1974. PLB 10.60 (ISBN 0-8094-0550-4, Pub. by Time-Life). Silver.
--The Peacemakers: The Great Powers & American Independence. (Illus.). 572p. 1983. 24.95X (ISBN 0-930350-35-9); pap. text ed. 9.95X. NE U Pr.
Morris, Richard B. & Woodress, James, eds. Hope & Anguish in Foreign Relations, 1962-1975. 2nd ed. (Voices from America's Past Ser.). (Illus.). (gr. 7-12). 1976. pap. text ed. 2.64 o.p. (ISBN 0-07-043276-7, W). McGraw.
--Years of National Turmoil, 1962-1975. 2nd ed. (Voices from America's Past Ser.). (Illus.). (gr. 7-12). 1976. pap. text ed. 2.64 o.p. (ISBN 0-07-043275-9, W). McGraw.
Morris, Richard B., ed. see Savage, Henry, Jr.
Morris, Richard B., ed. see Smelser, Marshall.
Morris, Richard B., ed. see Thomas, Emory M.
Morris, Richard B., et al, eds. Encyclopedia of American History. 6th ed. LC 81-47668. (Illus.). 1328p. 1981. 28.80i (ISBN 0-06-181605-1, HarpT). Har-Row.
Morris, Richard E., jt. auth. see Ferris, Robert G.
Morris, Richard J. & Kratochwill, Thomas R. Treating Children's Fears & Phobias: A Behavioral Approach. LC 82-10186. (Pergamon General Psychology Ser.: No. 114). (Illus.). 375p. 1982. 35.00 (ISBN 0-08-025999-5, J115); pap. 12.95 (ISBN 0-08-025998-7). Pergamon.
Morris, Richard J., ed. Perspectives in Abnormal Behavior. 570p. 1975. text ed. 28.00 (ISBN 0-08-017738-7); pap. text ed. 10.50 (ISBN 0-08-017739-5); test items 0.50 (ISBN 0-686-67339-5). Pergamon.
Morris, Richard J. & Kratochwill, Thomas R., eds. Practice of Therapy with Children: A Textbook of Methods. (General Psychology Ser.). 500p. 1983. 45.01 (ISBN 0-08-028033-1); pap. 19.50 (ISBN 0-08-028032-3). Pergamon.
Morris, Richard S., ed. see Smelser, Marshal L.
Morris, Robert. Allocating Health Resources for the Aged & Disabled: Technology Versus Politics. LC 80-8613. 160p. 1981. 18.95x (ISBN 0-669-04329-X). Lexington Bks.
--Select Architecture. LC 72-87427. (Architecture & Decorative Art Ser.). 102p. 1973. Repr. of 1757 ed. lib. bdg. 29.50 (ISBN 0-306-71573-2). Da Capo.
--Social Policy of the American Welfare State: An Introduction to Policy Analysis. (Boehm Ser.). 1979. text ed. 17.50 scp o.p. (ISBN 0-06-044618-8, HarpC). Har-Row.
--The Truth About the Betsy Ross Story. LC 82-70798. 1982. 15.95 (ISBN 0-9601476-3-2); pap. 12.95 (ISBN 0-9601476-4-0). Wynnehaven.
Morris, Robert B. Principles of Dental Treatment Planning. LC 82-15370. (Illus.). 300p. 1983. text ed. write for info (ISBN 0-8121-0841-8). Lea & Febiger.
Morris, Robert C. International Arbitration & Procedure. 1911. 29.50x (ISBN 0-686-51404-1). Elliots Bks.
Morris, Robert C., jt. auth. see Skemer, Don C.
Morris, Robert K. Consolations of Ambiguity: An Essay on the Novels of Anthony Burgess. LC 70-167599. (Literary Frontiers Ser). 96p. 1971. pap. 7.00x (ISBN 0-8262-0112-1). U of Mo Pr.
--Paradoxes of Order: Some Perspectives on the Fiction of V. S. Naipaul. LC 74-23752. (Literary Frontiers Ser.). 112p. 1975. pap. 7.00x (ISBN 0-8262-0172-5). U of Mo Pr.
Morris, Roger. The Genie in the Bottle: Unraveling the Myths about Wine. (Illus.). 228p. 1981 (ISBN 0-89104-213-X, A & W Visual Library). pap. 5.95 (ISBN 0-89104-198-2, A & W Visual Library). A & W Pubs.
Morris, Rosemary. The Character of King Arthur in Medieval Literature. LC 82-3712. (Arthurian Studies IV). 224p. 1982. text ed. 47.50x (ISBN 0-8476-7118-6). Rowman.
Morris, Rudolph M. Where? on Huntington Avenue. (Illus.). 1977. 9.75 o.p. (ISBN 0-8158-0357-5). Chris Mass.
Morris, S. A. Pontryagin Duality & the Structure of Locally Compact Abelian Groups. LC 76-53519. (London Mathematical Society Lecture Note Ser.: No. 29). 1977. 20.95x (ISBN 0-521-21543-9). Cambridge U Pr.
Morris, Sally M. Favorite Seafood Recipes. (Illus.). 216p. (Orig.). 1983. pap. 6.95 (ISBN 0-911954-78-3). Nitty Gritty.
Morris, Scot. Omni Games. (Illus.). 192p. 1983. pap. 9.95 (ISBN 0-03-060297-1). HR&W.
Morris, Sidney. If This Isn't Love! (JH Press Gay Play Script Ser.). 80p. (Orig.). 1982. pap. 5.95 (ISBN 0-935672-08-7). JH Pr.
Morris, Sidney, jt. auth. see Stones, Edgar.
Morris, Sylvia. Edith Kermit Roosevelt. LC 79-17851. 1980. 16.95 o.p. (ISBN 0-698-10994-5, Coward). Putnam Pub Group.
Morris, Sylvia, ed. Use of Group Services in Permanency Planning for Children. LC 82-23389. (Social Work with Groups: Vol. 5, No. 4). 100p. 1983. text ed. 16.00 (ISBN 0-86656-199-4, B199). Haworth Pr.
Morris, Terry, jt. auth. see Stallings, James D.
Morris, Ting, jt. auth. see Morris, Neil.
Morris, Van C. & Pai, Young. Philosophy & the American School. 2nd ed. LC 75-26083. (Illus.). 544p. 1976. text ed. 23.50 (ISBN 0-395-18620-X). HM.
Morris, W. D. Heat Transfer & Fluid Flow in Rotating Coolant Channels, Vol. 2. (Mechanical Engineering Research Studies). 248p. 1982. 38.00 (ISBN 0-471-10121-4). Res Stud Pr.
Morris, W. David. Heat Transfer & Fluid Flow in Rotating Coolant Channels. (Mechanical Engineering Research Studies: Vol. 2). 228p. 1982. 38.00x (ISBN 0-471-10121-4, Pub. by Wiley-Interscience). Wiley.
Morris, Walter, tr. see Mann, Thomas.
Morris, William. A Book of Verse. 1982. 12.95 (ISBN 0-517-54902-6, C N Potter). Crown.
--The Ideal Book: Essays & Lectures on the Arts of the Book. Peterson, William S., ed. LC 81-51339. (Illus.). 176p. Date not set. 45.00x (ISBN 0-520-04563-7). U of Cal Pr. Postponed.
--News from Nowhere. Redmond, James, ed. (Routledge English Texts). 1970. pap. 6.95x (ISBN 0-7100-6799-2). Routledge & Kegan.
--The Wood Beyond the World. (Facsimile of the Kelmscott Press Edition). Repr. of 1894 ed. 9.50 (ISBN 0-8446-4589-3). Peter Smith.
Morris, William, ed. The Novel on Blue Paper. 79p. 1982. pap. 4.50 (ISBN 0-904526-51-8, Pub. by Journeyman England). Lawrence Hill.
--The Weekly Reader Beginning Dictionary. (Illus.). 352p. (gr. 2-3). 1974. 7.95 o.s.i. (ISBN 0-448-11569-7, G&D). Putnam Pub Group.
--Xerox Intermediate Dictionary. (Illus.). 800p. (gr. 4-6). 1973. Repr. 9.95 (ISBN 0-448-02849-2, G&D). Putnam Pub Group.

Morris, William C. & Sashkin, Marshal. Organization Behavior in Action: Skill Building Experiences. LC 76-490. (Illus.). 288p. 1976. pap. text ed. 14.50 (ISBN 0-8299-0080-2); instrs.' manual avail. (ISBN 0-8299-0562-6). West Pub.

Morris, Willie. Good Old Boy: A Delta Boyhood. LC 80-52627. 143p. 1980. 10.95 (ISBN 0-916242-09-9); pap. 6.95 (ISBN 0-686-91819-3). Yoknapatawpha.

--James Jones: A Friendship. LC 78-4709. (Illus.). 1978. 11.95 o.p. (ISBN 0-385-14432-6). Doubleday.

--North Toward Home. LC 67-25803. 488p. 15.95 (ISBN 0-916242-15-3); pap. 9.95 (ISBN 0-916242-16-1). Yoknapatawpha.

--A Southern Album. Glusker, Irwin, ed. LC 76-49690. 1977. 8.95 o.s.i. (ISBN 0-89104-058-7). A & W Pubs.

Morris, Woodrow W. & Bader, Iva M. Hoffman's Daily Needs & Interests of Older People. 2nd ed. (Illus.). 400p. 1983. text ed. 36.50x (ISBN 0-398-04782-0). C C Thomas.

Morris, Wright. Earthly Delights, Unearthly Adornments: American Writers As Image Makers. LC 78-2154. 1978. 12.45i (ISBN 0-06-013107-1, HarpT). Har-Row.

--The Home Place. LC 48-1792. (Illus.). xii, 178p. 1968. pap. 7.95 (ISBN 0-8032-5139-4, BB 386, Bison). U of Nebr Pr.

--In Orbit. LC 75-14359. 153p. 1976. 10.95x (ISBN 0-8032-0882-0); pap. 5.95 (ISBN 0-8032-5830-5, BB 612, Bison). U of Nebr Pr.

--The Inhabitants. LC 70-115681. (Photography Ser). (Illus.). 114p. 1972. Repr. of 1946 ed. lib. bdg. 19.50 (ISBN 0-306-71931-2). Da Capo.

--Photographs & Words. Alinder, James, ed. LC 82-82471. (Illus.). 120p. 1982. 32.50 (ISBN 0-933286-28-7). Friends Photography.

--Plains Song. LC 79-2655. (Illus.). 1980. 11.49i (ISBN 0-06-013047-4, HarpT). Har-Row.

--Solo. LC 82-48674. (An American Dreamer in Europe: 1933-34 Ser.). 192p. 1983. 13.41i (ISBN 0-06-015165-X, HarpT). Har-Row.

Morrisey, Francis G. The Canonical Significance of Papal & Curial Pronouncements. 23p. (Orig.). 1981. pap. 1.50x (ISBN 0-943616-00-X). Canon Law Soc.

Morrish, Allan H. The Physical Principles of Magnetism. LC 78-2480. 696p. 1980. Repr. of 1965 ed. lib. bdg. 32.50 (ISBN 0-88275-670-2). Krieger.

Morrish, Ivor. Aspects of Educational Change. (Unwin Education Books). 1976. pap. text ed. 9.95x (ISBN 0-04-370069-1). Allen Unwin.

--Obeah, Christ, & Rashaman: Jamaica & Its Religion. 1983. 14.95 o.p. (ISBN 0-227-67831-1). Attic Pr.

Morris-Jones, W. H. & Fischer, Georges, eds. Decolonisation & After: The British & French Experience. (Studies in Commonwealth Politics & History: No. 7). 369p. 1980. 32.50x (ISBN 0-7146-3095-0, F Cass Co). Biblio Dist.

Morris-Jones, W. H., jt. ed. see Madden, A. F.

Morrison. Andes. (World's Wild Places Ser.). PLB 15.96 (ISBN 0-8094-2052-X). Silver.

Morrison, Alex. Early Man in Britain & Ireland. 1980. 36.00 (ISBN 0-312-22463-X). St Martin.

Morrison, Blake. Seamus Heaney. (Contemporary Writers Ser.). 1982. pap. 4.25 (ISBN 0-416-31900-9). Methuen Inc.

Morrison, Bonnie M., jt. auth. see Nattrass, Karen.

Morrison, Cathryn & Reiss, Wilhelm. Real Estate Licensing Examinations. 224p. 1980. pap. 6.50 (ISBN 0-06-463515-5, EH 515, EH). B&N NY.

Morrison, Chaplain W. Democratic Politics & Sectionalism: The Wilmot Proviso Controversy. LC 67-15101. x, 244p. 1967. 18.00x (ISBN 0-8078-1017-7). U of NC Pr.

Morrison, Charles E. & Suhrke, Astri. Strategies of Survival: The Foreign Policy Dilemmas of Smaller Asian States. LC 78-14152. 1979. 32.50x (ISBN 0-312-76453-7). St Martin.

Morrison, Charles E., jt. ed. see Valeo, Francis R.

Morrison, Christopher S. How to Reach the Top. (The Library of Business Psychology). (Illus.). 98p. 1981. 33.45 o.p. (ISBN 0-89266-309-X). Am Classical Coll Pr.

Morrison, D. F. Multivariate Statistical Methods. 2nd ed. 1976. 32.50 (ISBN 0-07-043186-8, C). McGraw.

Morrison, David, ed. Satellites of Jupiter. 785p. 1982. text ed. 49.50x (ISBN 0-8165-0762-7). U of Ariz Pr.

Morrison, Donald F. Applied Linear Statistical Methods. 544p. 1983. 30.95 (ISBN 0-13-041020-9). P-H.

Morrison, Dorothy. The Romans in Britian. (Exploring History Workbook Ser.). (Illus.). 48p. (Orig.). (gr. 7-12). 1978. pap. text ed. 3.15 (ISBN 0-05-003056-6); wkguides 12.50 (ISBN 0-05-002422-1). Longman.

Morrison, Eleanor S. & Price, Mila U. Values in Sexuality: A New Approach to Sex Education. 224p. (Orig.). 1974. pap. 6.95 o.s.i. (ISBN 0-89104-165-6, A & W Visual Library). A & W Pubs.

Morrison, Elting. From Know-How to Nowhere. (RL 9). pap. 1.95 o.p. (ISBN 0-451-61539-5, MJ1539, Ment). NAL.

Morrison, G. C. Emergencies in Child Psychiatry: Emotional Crises of Children, Youth and Their Families. 516p. 1975. 32.75x (ISBN 0-398-03229-7). C C Thomas.

Morrison, G. H. Morrison on Galations through Hebrews. LC 82-71841. (Glasgow Pulpit Ser.). 1982. pap. 3.50 (ISBN 0-89957-557-9). AMG Pubs.

--Morrison on John, Vol. I. new ed. (The Glasgow Pulpit Ser.). 1979. pap. 3.50 (ISBN 0-89957-534-X). AMG Pubs.

--Morrison on John, Vol. II. new ed. (The Glasgow Pulpit Ser.). 1979. pap. 3.50 (ISBN 0-89957-535-8). AMG Pubs.

--Morrison on Luke, Vol. I. new ed. (The Glasgow Pulpit Ser.). 1979. pap. 3.50 (ISBN 0-89957-532-3). AMG Pubs.

--Morrison on Luke, Vol. II. new ed. (The Glasgow Pulpit Ser.). 1979. pap. 3.50 (ISBN 0-89957-533-1). AMG Pubs.

--Morrison on Mark. new ed. (The Glasgow Pulpit Ser.). 1979. pap. 3.50 (ISBN 0-89957-531-5). AMG Pubs.

--Morrison on Matthew, Vol. I. new ed. (The Glasgow Pulpit Ser.). 1979. pap. 3.50 (ISBN 0-89957-528-5). AMG Pubs.

--Morrison on Matthew, Vol. II. new ed. (The Glasgow Pulpit Ser.). 1979. pap. 3.50 (ISBN 0-89957-529-3). AMG Pubs.

--Morrison on Matthew, Vol. III. new ed. (The Glasgow Pulpit Ser.). 1979. pap. 3.50 (ISBN 0-89957-530-7). AMG Pubs.

--Morrison on Romans & Corinthians. (Glasgow Pulpit Ser.). 96p. 1982. pap. 3.50 (ISBN 0-89957-547-1). AMG Pubs.

Morrison, G. H., ed. Morrison on Genesis. (Glasgow Pulpit Ser.). 72p. 1976. pap. 3.50 (ISBN 0-89957-520-X). AMG Pubs.

Morrison, George H. Morrison on Acts. rev. ed. Zodhiates, Joan, ed. LC 80-69541. (Glasgow Pulpit Ser.). 1981. pap. 3.50 (ISBN 0-89957-050-X). AMG Pubs.

Morrison, George S. Early Childhood Education Today. 2nd ed. (Early Childhood Education Ser.: No. C24). 456p. 1980. text ed. 20.95 (ISBN 0-675-08133-5). Additional supplements may be obtained from publisher. Merrill.

--Parent Involvement in the Home, School & Community. (Early Childhood Education Ser.). 1978. pap. text ed. 12.95 (ISBN 0-675-08393-1). Merrill.

Morrison, Harry, ed. Quantum Theory of Many-Particle Systems. (International Science Review Ser.). (Illus.). 360p. 1962. 40.00 (ISBN 0-677-00550-4). Gordon.

Morrison, Helen L., ed. Children of Depressed Parents: Risk Identification & Intervention. Date not set. price not set (ISBN 0-8089-1545-2). Grune.

Morrison, Irma L., jt. auth. see Freedman, Alan.

Morrison, Irma Lee, jt. auth. see Freedman, Alan.

Morrison, Ishbel. Knot of Love. (Illus.). 1969. pap. 1.95x (ISBN 0-685-09065-5). Dothard.

Morrison, James. Cruising Yacht Maintenance. (Illus.). 144p. Date not set. write for info. o.p. (ISBN 0-668-04993-6, 4993-6). Arco.

--Engineering in Training Examination Study Guide, EIT. LC 76-12515. (Orig.). 1976. pap. 8.00 o.p. (ISBN 0-668-04009-2). Arco.

Morrison, James D. Masterpieces of Religious Verse. 1977. pap. 9.95 o.p. (ISBN 0-8010-6038-9). Baker Bk.

--Organic Chemistry. 1979. text ed. 23.95x (ISBN 0-534-00605-1); study guide 9.95x (ISBN 0-534-00720-1); lab manual 10.95 (ISBN 0-534-00690-6). Wadsworth Pub.

Morrison, James E. Twenty Four Early American Country Dances Cotillions & Reels for the Year 1976. LC 76-3969. (Illus.). 1976. spiral bdg. 4.50 (ISBN 0-917024-04-4). Country Dance & Song.

Morrison, James L., Jr. Memoirs of Henry Heth. LC 72-820. (Contributions in Military History: No. 6). 1974. lib. bdg. 29.95 (ISBN 0-8371-6389-7, MHH/). Greenwood.

Morrison, James W. Instrument Pilot Examination. LC 78-11103. 1979. pap. 12.95 o.p. (ISBN 0-668-04592-2, 4592). Arco.

--Veterianary College Admission Test. 384p. 1983. pap. 10.95 (ISBN 0-668-05545-6, 5545). Arco.

Morrison, Jennifer, jt. auth. see McNamara, Lynne.

Morrison, Jim. The Bank of America of Louisiana. 1975. pap. 7.95 (ISBN 0-915628-00-7); case bound 5.95 (ISBN 0-685-64473-1). Zeppelin.

--The Lords & the New Creatures. 1971. pap. 5.75 (ISBN 0-671-21044-0, Touchstone Bks). S&S.

Morrison, Joel see Espenshade, Edward B., Jr.

Morrison, Joel L., jt. ed. see Espenshade, Edward B.

Morrison, Joel L., jt. ed. see Espenshade, Edward B., Jr.

Morrison, John. Modern Japanese Fiction. LC 75-11954. 1975. Repr. of 1955 ed. lib. bdg. 17.25x (ISBN 0-8371-8053-8, MOMJ). Greenwood.

Morrison, John S. & Williams, R. T. Greek Oared Ships, Nine Hundred - Three Hundred Twenty-Two B.C. LC 67-19504. (Illus.). 1968. 79.50 (ISBN 0-521-05770-1). Cambridge U Pr.

Morrison, Kenneth & Havens, Robert I. Value Clarification in Counseling. Sorenson, Don L., ed. LC 75-43284. 1976. pap. 3.50x o.s.i. (ISBN 0-932796-00-1). Ed Media Corp.

Morrison, Kristin. Cantors & Chronicles: The Use of Narrative in the Plays of Samuel Beckett & Harold Pinter. LC 82-16086. 240p. 1983. lib. bdg. 20.00x (ISBN 0-226-54130-4). U of Chicago Pr.

Morrison, L. Robert, jt. auth. see Eckhouse, Richard H., Jr.

Morrison, Leger & Birt, Robert F. Illustrated Guide for Term Papers, Reports, Theses, & Dissertations: With Index & Rules for Punctuation & for Expression of Numbers. (Illus.). ix, 102p. 1971. pap. text ed. 3.85 (ISBN 0-686-38130-0). Morrison Pub Co.

Morrison, Leger R. & Birt, Robert F. End-of-Line Division Manual. xx, 342p. (Orig.). pap. text ed. 7.95 (ISBN 0-686-38128-9). Morrison Pub Co.

--Guide to Confused Words. xxvi, 272p. (Orig.). 1972. pap. 6.55 (ISBN 0-686-38127-0). Morrison Pub Co.

Morrison, Leonard A. & Sharples, Stephen P. History of the Kimball Family in America from Sixteen Thirty-Four to Eighteen Ninety-Seven. 1981. Repr. of 1897 ed. 35.00x (ISBN 0-932334-02-4). Heart of the Lakes.

Morrison, Lester & Nugent, Nancy. Dr. Morrison's Heart-Saver Program. Gottlieb, Bill, ed. (Illus.). 304p. 1982. cancelled (ISBN 0-87857-418-2, 05-781-0). Rodale Pr Inc.

Morrison, Lillian, ed. Diller, a Dollar: Rhymes & Sayings for the Ten O'Clock Scholar. LC 55-9213. (Illus.). (gr. 4 up). 1955. 9.95 o.p. (ISBN 0-690-23957-2, TYC-J). Har-Row.

Morrison, Louis. Monarch Notes on Tolkien's Fellowship of the Ring. 1976. pap. 1.95 (ISBN 0-671-00971-0). Monarch Pr.

Morrison, M. A., et al. Quantum States of Atoms, Molecules & Solids. 204p. 1976. 34.95 (ISBN 0-13-747980-8). P-H.

Morrison, Malcolm, rev. by see Turner, J. Clifford.

Morrison, Martin E., ed. Official Rules of Chess. (Tartan Paperback). (Illus.). 1978. pap. 3.95 (ISBN 0-679-14043-3). McKay.

Morrison, Marvin L. Word City: A New Language Tool. LC 82-80928. 380p. (Orig.). 1982. pap. 4.95 (ISBN 0-9608376-0-4). Pilot Light.

Morrison, Minion K. Ethnicity & Political Integration: The Case of Ashanti, Ghana. (Foreign & Comparative Studies Program, African Ser.: No. 38). (Orig.). 1982. pap. text ed. 10.00x (ISBN 0-915984-59-8). Syracuse U Foreign Comp.

Morrison, Minion K. & Gutkind, Peter C., eds. Housing the Urban Poor in Africa. (Foreign & Comparative Studies Program, African Ser.: No. 37). (Orig.). 1982. pap. text ed. 10.00x (ISBN 0-915984-61-X). Syracuse U Foreign Comp.

Morrison, Nan. Katherine Tree. (YA) 6.95 (ISBN 0-685-07440-4, Avalon). Bouregy.

Morrison, Peter. Basic Math Skills. 1972. text ed. 8.75 (ISBN 0-07-043197-3, G). McGraw.

Morrison, Peter & Twing, J. W. Getting the Right Job. (Career in the Modern Office Ser: Bk. 4). 1970. text ed. 7.32 (ISBN 0-07-043193-0, G); tchr's manual for series 8.95 (ISBN 0-07-043194-9). McGraw.

--Making the Most of Your Skills. 1969. text ed. 5.36 o.p. (ISBN 0-07-043192-2, G). McGraw.

Morrison, Peter, et al. Making the Most of Yourself. 1969. text ed. 7.32 (ISBN 0-07-043191-4, G). McGraw.

--Opportunities in Today's Office. (Career in the Modern Office Ser: Bk. 1). 1969. text ed. 7.32 (ISBN 0-07-043190-6, G). McGraw.

Morrison, Philip W. Environmental Control in Electronic Manufacturing. LC 73-9518. 488p. (Orig.). 1973. 26.50 (ISBN 0-686-92631-5). Krieger.

Morrison, Phyllis & Twing, J. W. The Business Office. (Illus.). 1977. text ed. 14.92 (ISBN 0-07-043231-7, G); office career guide 27.80 (ISBN 0-07-043232-5); tchr's. manual & key 3.70 (ISBN 0-07-043235-X); office skills 1 4.40 (ISBN 0-07-043233-3); office skills 2 4.40 (ISBN 0-07-043234-1). McGraw.

Morrison, R., jt. auth. see Cole, A. J.

Morrison, R., jt. auth. see Davie, J. T.

Morrison, Ralph. Grounding & Shielding Techniques in Instrumentation. 2nd ed. LC 77-3265. 1977. 23.95 (ISBN 0-471-02992-0, Pub. by Wiley-Interscience). Wiley.

Morrison, Robert E. Behold This Dreamer, Vol. II. LC 78-57833. 1979. 5.95 o.p. (ISBN 0-533-03796-4). Vantage.

--The Bird of Fire, Vol. 1. 1979. 5.95 o.p. (ISBN 0-533-03797-2). Vantage.

--Mary, Vol. III. 1979. 5.95 o.p. (ISBN 0-533-03798-0). Vantage.

Morrison, Robert H., ed. Why S.O.B.'s Succeed & Nice Guys Fail in a Small Business. 387p. 1976. pap. 20.00 (ISBN 0-930566-01-7). FMA Bus.

Morrison, Samuel E. Oxford History of the American People. Incl. Vol. 2. pap. 3.50 (ISBN 0-451-62054-2, ME2054); Vol. 3. pap. 3.50 (ISBN 0-451-62055-0, ME2055). Ment). NAL.

Morrison, Sean. The Amoeba: A Photomicrographic Book. (Illus.). (gr. 4-6). 1971. PLB 5.99 (ISBN 0-698-30010-6, Coward). Putnam Pub Group.

Morrison, Stanley, jt. auth. see Bott, Raymond.

Morrison, Stanley, jt. auth. see Fairman, Charles.

Morrison, T. A. Cornwall's Central Mines: The Northern District, 1810-1895. 400p. 1980. 40.00x o.p. (ISBN 0-906720-10-9, Pub. by Hodge England). State Mutual Bk.

Morrison, Theodore, ed. see Chaucer, Geoffrey.

Morrison, Toni. Song of Solomon. (RL 7). 1978. pap. 3.50 (ISBN 0-451-12315-8, AE2315, Sig). NAL.

--Sula. Date not set. pap. 5.95 (ISBN 0-452-25333-0, Z5333, Plume). NAL.

--Tar Baby. 1982. pap. 6.95 (ISBN 0-452-25326-8, Z5326, Plume). NAL.

Morrison, Tony & Hawkins, Gerald S. Pathways to the Gods: The Secret of the Nasca Lines. LC 78-2156. (Illus.). 1979. 14.37i (ISBN 0-06-013057-1, HarpT). Har-Row.

Morrison, Velma F. There's Only One You: The Story of Heredity. LC 78-12659. (Illus.). 64p. (gr. 4-6). 1978. PLB 6.97 o.p. (ISBN 0-671-32943-X). Messner.

Morrison, W. I., jt. auth. see Smith, P.

Morrison, Wilbur H. Above & Beyond: Nineteen Forty-One to Nineteen Forty-Five. (Illus.). 336p. 1983. 16.95 (ISBN 0-312-00185-1). St Martin.

Morrison, William D. Juvenile Offenders. LC 70-172589. (Criminology, Law Enforcement, & Social Problems Ser.: No. 179). 1975. 12.50x (ISBN 0-87585-179-7). Patterson Smith.

Morrison, Winifrede. Drying & Preserving Flowers. 1973. 17.95 o.p. (ISBN 0-7134-2324-2, Pub. by Batsford England). David & Charles.

Morriss, Frank & Garvey, John. Catholic Perspectives: Abortion. (Orig.). 1979. pap. 6.95 (ISBN 0-88347-100-0). Thomas More.

Morriss, John, tr. see Bro, Bernard.

Morriss, John M., tr. see Bro, Bernard.

Morrissett, Irving, ed. Social Studies in the 1980's: A Report of Project SPAN. LC 82-72766. 147p. (Orig.). 1982. pap. text ed. 8.75 (ISBN 0-87120-114-3). Assn Supervision.

Morrissey, Dianne J. I Died in Order to Live. LC 81-71488. (Illus.). 135p. (Orig.). 1982. pap. 4.95 (ISBN 0-9604664-1-X). Artemis Pr.

Morrissey, Kathleen M. Speech Bingo, Set 1. (Illus.). 1980. pap. 7.95x (ISBN 0-8134-2144-6). Interstate.

Morrissey, L. J. Henry Fielding: A Reference Guide. 1980. lib. bdg. 35.00 (ISBN 0-8161-8139-X, Hall Reference). G K Hall.

Morrissy, Lois E., jt. auth. see Burns, Margaret A.

Morris-Vann, Artie M. Once Upon a Time... A Guide to the Use of Bibliotherapy. (Illus.). 100p. (Orig.). 1979. pap. text ed. 12.00 (ISBN 0-940370-00-X). Aid-U Pub.

Morris Wu, Eleanor B. Human Efflorescence: A Study in Man's Evolutionary & Historical Development. 352p. 1983. write for info. (ISBN 0-87527-323-8). Green.

Morrow, Betty, jt. auth. see Selsam, Millicent E.

Morrow, Bradford & Lafourcade, Bernard. A Bibliography of the Writings of Wyndham Lewis. (Illus.). 350p. 1978. 40.00 (ISBN 0-87685-419-6). Black Sparrow.

Morrow, Bradford, ed. Conjunctions One: A Festschrift for James Laughlin. (Illus.). 312p. 1981. 22.50 (ISBN 0-941964-02-7); pap. 9.00 (ISBN 0-941964-01-9). Conjunctions.

--Conjunctions Two. (Illus.). 240p. 1982. 22.50 (ISBN 0-941964-04-3); pap. 7.50 (ISBN 0-941964-03-5). Conjunctions.

--Conjunctions: 3. (Conjunctions Bi-Annual Volumes of New Writing). (Illus.). 240p. 1982. 22.50; pap. 7.50. Conjunctions.

--Conjunctions: 4. (Conjunctions Bi-Annual Volumes of New Writing). (Illus.). 240p. 1983. 22.50; pap. 7.50. Conjunctions.

Morrow, C. Paul & Townsend, Duane E. Synopsis of Gynecologic Oncology. LC 80-22384. (Clinical Monographs in Obstetrics & Gynecology). 500p. 1981. 37.50 (ISBN 0-471-06504-8, Pub. by Wiley-Med). Wiley.

Morrow, C. T., et al, eds. see Symposium on Ballistic Missile & Space Technology, 6th, Los Angeles, 1961.

Morrow, Carol K. Health Care Guidance: Commercial Health Insurance & National Health Policy. LC 76-14415. 1976. 25.95 o.p. (ISBN 0-275-56950-0). Praeger.

Morrow, Carolyn C. Conservation Treatment Procedures: A Manual of Step-by-Step Procedures for the Maintenance & Repair of Library Materials. LC 82-181. 191p. 1982. pap. text ed. 18.50 (ISBN 0-87287-294-7). Libs Unl.

--The Preservation Challenge: A Guide to Conserving Library Materials. LC 82-18726. (Professional Librarian Ser.). 231p. 1982. text ed. 34.50 (ISBN 0-86729-003-X); pap. text ed. 27.50 (ISBN 0-86729-002-1). Knowledge Indus.

Morrow, David A. Current Therapy in Theriogenology: Diagnosis, Treatment & Prevention of Reproductive Diseases in Animal. LC 77-84675. (Illus.). 1287p. 1980. text ed. 75.00 (ISBN 0-7216-6564-0). Saunders.

Morrow, Gray & Lawrence, Jim. Buck Rogers in the Twenty-Fifth Century. (Illus.). 193p. 1981. pap. 12.95 (ISBN 0-8256-3221-8, Quick Fox). Putnam Pub Group.

Morrow, Gray, jt. auth. see Weaver, Lydia.

Morrow, Harold W. Statics & Strengths of Materials. (Illus.). 512p. 1981. text ed. 23.95 (ISBN 0-13-844720-9). P-H.

Morrow, Honore. On to Oregon. (Illus.). (gr. 5-9). 1946. Repr. of 1926 ed. 10.75 (ISBN 0-688-21639-0). Morrow.

Morrow, James. The Wine of Violence. 320p. 1982. pap. 2.75 (ISBN 0-441-89441-0, Pub. by Ace Science Fiction). Ace Bks.

Morrow, James & Suid, Murray. Media & Kids: Real-World Learning in the Schools. LC 76-39941. 1977. 9.50 (ISBN 0-8104-5798-9). Boynton Cook Pubs.

Morrow, John. Euraryotic Cell Genetics. (Cell Biology Ser.). write for info. (ISBN 0-12-507360-7). Acad Pr.

Morrow, John, intro. by. Materials Overview for 1982. (The Science of Advanced Materials & Process Engineering Ser.). (Illus.). 1982. 60.00 (ISBN 0-686-37996-9). Soc Adv Material.

Morrow, Joseph M. The Thousand Yard Dash. LC 81-86210. 168p. 10.95 (ISBN 0-86666-073-9). GWP.

Morrow, K. & Johnson, K. Communicate One. (Cambridge English Language Learning Ser.). 1980. students' ed. 5.95 (ISBN 0-521-21850-0); tchr's. ed. 6.50 (ISBN 0-521-21849-7); cassette 13.95 (ISBN 0-521-21848-9). Cambridge U Pr.

Morrow, L. C., jt. auth. see Higgins, L. R.

Morrow, Margot D., jt. ed. see Edwards, Mary I.

Morrow, Patrick D. Growing up in North Dakota. 1979. pap. text ed. 2.25 o.p. (ISBN 0-8191-0650-X). U Pr of Amer.

Morrow, Robert M., jt. auth. see Brewer, Allen A.

Morrow, Sandra, jt. auth. see Malnig, Lawrence R.

Morrow, Skip. The End. LC 82-83314. 96p. 1983. pap. 4.95 (ISBN 0-03-063401-6). HR&W.

Morrow, Steve, tr. see Shiv Brat Lal.

Morrow, Theodore, tr. see Boff, Leonardo.

Morrow, William L. Public Administration: Politics, Policy & the Political System. 2nd ed. 387p. 1980. pap. text ed. 17.00 (ISBN 0-394-32426-9). Random.

Morrow, William R., et al. Behavior Therapy Bibliography, 1950-1969. LC 73-633730. 166p. 1971. 13.00x (ISBN 0-8262-0596-8). U of Mo Pr.

Morsberger, Katherine M., jt. auth. see Morsberger, Robert E.

Morsberger, Robert & Lesser, Stephen, eds. American Screenwriters, 2 vols. (Dictionary of Literary Biography Ser.). (Illus.). Date not set. Set. 148.00x (ISBN 0-8103-0917-3, Bruccoli Clark Book). Gale.

Morsberger, Robert E. Commonsense Grammar & Style. rev. ed. LC 72-78273. 448p. 1972. 12.45 (ISBN 0-690-20337-3). T Y Crowell.

--James Thurber. (United States Author Ser.). 1964. lib. bdg. 11.95 (ISBN 0-8057-0728-X, Twayne). G K Hall.

Morsberger, Robert E. & Morsberger, Katherine M. Lew Wallace: Militant Romantic. (Illus.). 384p. 1980. 17.95 o.p. (ISBN 0-07-043305-4). McGraw.

Morschauser, Joseph, III, jt. auth. see Becton, F. Julian.

Morscher, Betsey & Jones, Barbara S. Risk-Taking for Women. 224p. 1982. 12.95 (ISBN 0-89696-183-4, An Everest House Book). Dodd.

Morse. The Eighty Eighty-Six to Eighty Eighty-Eight Primer: An Introduction to Their Architecture, System Design, & Programming. 2nd ed. Date not set. 10.95 (ISBN 0-686-82002-9, 6255). Hayden.

Morse & Kaskell. New York State in Story, Pts. 1 & 2. 1962. wkbk. 2.50x (ISBN 0-88323-100-X, 283). Richards Pub.

Morse, A. P., ed. A Theory of Sets: Monographs. Rev. & Enlarged ed. (Pure & Applied Mathematics Ser.). Date not set. price not set (ISBN 0-12-507952-4). Acad Pr.

Morse, A. Reynolds. Lewd Limericks & Worse Verse. Aman, Reinhold A., ed. 1983. pap. 15.00 (ISBN 0-916500-10-1). Maledicta.

Morse, Albert L. The Tattooists. Walsh, John A., ed. (Illus.). 1977. 39.95x (ISBN 0-918320-01-1). A L Morse.

Morse, Ann. Forward Roll. LC 73-14698. (Just Like You, Just Like Me Ser.). 6.95 (ISBN 0-88436-033-4); pap. 3.95 (ISBN 0-88436-034-2). EMC.

--Max-i-Fish. LC 73-14783. (Just Like You, Just Like Me Ser.). 6.95 (ISBN 0-88436-029-6); pap. 3.95 (ISBN 0-88436-030-X). EMC.

--On a Tight Rope. LC 73-14685. (Just Like You, Just Like Me Ser.). 6.95 (ISBN 0-88436-031-8); pap. 3.95 (ISBN 0-88436-032-6). EMC.

Morse, Ann, jt. auth. see Morse, Charles.

Morse, Arthur D. While Six Million Died: A Chronicle of American Apathy. LC 82-22291. 432p. 1983. Repr. of 1966 ed. 18.95 (ISBN 0-87951-174-5). Overlook Pr.

Morse, C. G. Torts in Private International Law. LC 78-5881. (Problems in Private International Law Ser.: Vol. 2). 1979. 66.00 (ISBN 0-444-85168-2, North Holland). Elsevier.

Morse, Carmel L. Audio Visual Primer. (Illus.). 60p. (Orig.). pap. 3.95 (ISBN 0-686-38776-7). Backwoods Pubns.

Morse, Chandler, ed. see Copeland, Morris A.

Morse, Charles & Morse, Ann. Jean Claude Killy. LC 74-4489. (Creative's Superstars Ser). 32p. (gr. 7-9). 1974. 6.95 o.p. (ISBN 0-87191-343-7). Creative Ed.

Morse, Dan F. & Morse, Phyllis A., eds. Archaeology of the Central Mississippi Valley. LC 82-22734. (New World Archaeological Record). Date not set. price not set (ISBN 0-12-508180-4). Acad Pr.

Morse, David. Romanticism: A Structural Analysis. 288p. 1981. 39.00x (ISBN 0-333-28297-3, Pub. by Macmillan England). State Mutual Bk.

Morse, David A. The Origin & Evolution of the I.L.O. & Its Role in the World Community. LC 68-66942. (Pierce Ser.: No. 2). 136p. 1969. 3.50 (ISBN 0-87546-025-9). ILR Pr.

Morse, Dean & Gray, Susan. Early Retirement: Boon or Bane, a Study of Three Large Corporations. LC 79-54970. (Conservation of Human Resources Ser.: No. 14). (Illus.). 145p. 1981. text ed. 23.00x (ISBN 0-916672-44-1). Allanheld.

Morse, Dean W. & Dutka, Anna B. Life after Early Retirement: The Experience of Lower Level Workers. LC 81-70970. (Conservation of Human Resources Ser.: Vol. 17). 220p. 1982. pap. text ed. 25.00x (ISBN 0-916672-62-X). Allanheld.

Morse, Dryden, et al. A Guide to Cardiac Pacemakers. LC 82-7302. (Illus.). 380p. 1983. text ed. 65.00 (ISBN 0-8036-6323-4). Davis Co.

Morse, Edward L., ed. see Morse, Samuel F.

Morse, Edwards S. Japan Day by Day: 1877-78-79, 1882-3. LC 17-28348. (Illus.). 1978. lib. bdg. 24.95 (ISBN 0-910220-93-X). Berg.

Morse, Elisabeth, jt. ed. see Hollingsworth, Dorothy.

Morse, Elliott R. see Mickelwait, Donald R., et al.

Morse, Harriet L. Gardening in the Shade. (Illus.). 1982. 12.95 (ISBN 0-917304-16-0). Timber.

Morse, Hosea B. Trade & Administration of China. 3rd ed. LC 64-24734. (Illus.). 1967. Repr. of 1921 ed. 12.50x o.p. (ISBN 0-8462-0881-4). Russell.

Morse, J. Mitchell. The Irrelevant English Teacher. LC 72-80762. 152p. 1972 19.95 (ISBN 0-87722-016-6); pap. 8.95 1974 (ISBN 0-87722-032-8). Temple U Pr.

--Prejudice & Literature. LC 76-20169. 192p. 1976. 19.95 (ISBN 0-87722-072-7). Temple U Pr.

Morse, Jerome G. Energy Resources in Colorado: Coal, Oil Shale & Uranium. (Special Studies in Natural Resources & Energy Management). 1979. lib. bdg. 39.50 (ISBN 0-89158-457-9). Westview.

--Nuclear Methods in Mineral Exploration & Production. (Developments in Economic Geology: Vol. 7). 1977. 61.75 (ISBN 0-444-41567-X). Elsevier.

Morse, Jerome G., ed. see Technology Proceedings, Seminar III.

Morse, L. A., jt. auth. see Yorio, Carlos A.

Morse, Marston. Topological Methods in the Theory of Functions of a Complex Variable. 1947. pap. 12.00 (ISBN 0-527-02731-6). Kraus Repr.

--Variational Analysis: Critical Extremals & Sturmian Extensions. LC 72-8368. (Pure & Applied Mathematics Ser.). 304p. 1973. 43.95 o.p. (ISBN 0-471-61700-8, Pub. by Wiley-Interscience). Wiley.

Morse, Milton A., Jr. & Taylor, Conway. Modern Real Estate Practice in Texas. 4th rev. ed. 550p. 1982. pap. text ed. 19.95 (ISBN 0-88462-336-X). Real Estate Ed Co.

Morse, P. & Brand, L. Home-Style Learning: Activities for Young Children & Their Parents. 1981. pap. 5.95 (ISBN 0-13-392944-2); 11.95 (ISBN 0-13-392951-5). P-H.

Morse, Peter. Jean Charlot's Prints: A Catalogue Raisonne. (Illus.). 470p. 1976. 85.00 (ISBN 0-8248-0364-7); ltd. ed.,boxed, with etching 175.00 (ISBN 0-8248-0474-0). UH Pr.

Morse, Peter & Adamson, Ian. Computerlab. 1983. pap. price not set (ISBN 0-671-47069-8, Touchstone Bks). S&S.

Morse, Philip M. In at the Beginnings: A Physicist's Life. LC 76-40010. 1977. text ed. 20.00x (ISBN 0-262-13124-2). MIT Pr.

Morse, Philip M. & Feshbach, H. Methods of Theoretical Physics, 2 Pts. (International Ser. in Pure & Applied Physics). (Illus.). 1953. Pt. 1. text ed. 65.00 (ISBN 0-07-043316-X, C); Pt. 2. text ed. 62.50 (ISBN 0-07-043317-8). McGraw.

Morse, Philip M. & Ingard, K. U. Theoretical Acoustics. (International Ser. in Pure & Applied Physics). 1968. text ed. 60.00 (ISBN 0-07-043330-5, C). McGraw.

Morse, Phyllis A., jt. ed. see Morse, Dan F.

Morse, Roger. A Year in the Beeyard. (Illus.). 192p. 1983. 14.95 (ISBN 0-686-83827-0, ScribT). Scribner.

Morse, Roger A. The Complete Guide to Beekeeping. rev. ed. 8.95 (ISBN 0-87690-126-7); pap. 5.95 (ISBN 0-525-93105-8). Dutton.

Morse, Ronald A., ed. The Politics of Japan's Energy Strategy. (Research Papers & Policy Studies: No. 3). (Orig.). 1981. pap. 7.00 (ISBN 0-912966-45-9). IEAS.

Morse, Samuel, tr. see Anno, Mitsumasa.

Morse, Samuel F. Changes. LC 82-70225. 91p. 1964. 6.95 (ISBN 0-8040-0034-4). Swallow.

--Samuel F. B. Morse: His Letters & Journals, 2 vols. Morse, Edward L., ed. LC 76-75279. (Library of American Art Ser.). (Illus.). 1080p. 1973. Repr. of 1914 ed. Set. lib. bdg. 79.50 (ISBN 0-306-71304-7). Da Capo.

Morse, Samuel F., et al. Wallace Stevens Checklist & Bibliography of Stevens Criticism. LC 82-72247. 98p. 1963. 8.95x (ISBN 0-8040-0316-5). Swallow.

Morse, Stephen, jt. auth. see Shapiro, Michael H.

Morse, Stephen P., jt. auth. see Palmer, John F.

Morse, Sterns A., jt. auth. see Stoiber, Richard E.

Morse, Thomas S. A Gift of Courage. LC 81-43733. 336p. 1982. 16.95 (ISBN 0-385-17777-1). Doubleday.

Morse, Wayne J. Cost Accounting: Processing, Evaluating, & Using Cost Data. (Illus.). 752p. 1981. text ed. 27.95 (ISBN 0-201-04677-6); 5.95 (ISBN 0-201-04674-1); instr's manual 9.95 (ISBN 0-201-04678-4); test bank avail. (ISBN 0-201-04737-3). A-W.

Morse, Willard S. & Brinckle, Gertrude. Howard Pyle. LC 68-31099. 1969. Repr. of 1921 ed. 30.00x (ISBN 0-8103-3493-3). Gale.

Morse, William C. & Wingo, G. Max. Psychology & Teaching. 3rd ed. 1969. text ed. 16.50x (ISBN 0-673-05854-9). Scott F.

Morselli, P. L., et al, eds. Basic & Therapeutic Aspects of Perinatal Pharmacology. LC 74-21981. (Monograph of the Mario Negri Institute of Pharmacological Research). 456p. 1975. 41.50 (ISBN 0-89004-016-8). Raven.

--Neurotransmitters, Seizures, & Epilepsy. 378p. 1981. text ed. 46.00 (ISBN 0-89004-753-7). Raven.

--Drug Interactions. LC 74-77802. (Monograph of the Mario Negri Institute for Pharmacological Research). 416p. 1974. 41.50 (ISBN 0-911216-59-6). Raven.

Morselli, Paolo L., ed. Drug Disposition During Development. LC 76-47570. (Monographs in Pharmacology & Physiology: Vol. 2). 1977. 40.00x o.p. (ISBN 0-470-99178-X). Halsted Pr.

Morsink, Johannes. Aristotle on the Generation of Animals: A Philosophical Study. LC 81-43685. 192p. (Orig.). 1982. lib. bdg. 20.75 (ISBN 0-8191-2606-3); pap. text ed. 10.00 (ISBN 0-8191-2607-1). U Pr of Amer.

Morsman, Edgar M., Jr. Effective Loan Management. LC 82-60387. 224p. 1982. RMA members 28.50 (ISBN 0-936742-06-2); non-members 38.50 (ISBN 0-686-35761-2). Robt Morris Assocs.

Morson, B. C. Histological Typing of Intestinal Tumours. (World Health Organization). (Illus.). 69p. 1976. text ed. 56.00 (ISBN 92-4-176015-X, 70-1-015-20); text & slides 149.50 (ISBN 0-89189-114-5, 70-1-015-00). Am Soc Clinical.

Morson, Bosil C. The Pathogenesis of Colorectal Cancer. LC 78-1792. (Major Problems in Pathology: Vol. 10). 1978. text ed. 20.00 (ISBN 0-7216-6558-6). Saunders.

Morss, Elliot R. & Morss, Victoria A. U. S. Foreign Aid: An Assessment of New & Traditional Development Strategies. (Replica Edition). 150p. 1982. softcover 15.00 (ISBN 0-86531-919-7). Westview.

Morss, Elliott R. & Gow, David D., eds. Implementing Rural Development Projects: Nine Critical Problems. 325p. 1983. softcover 23.50x (ISBN 0-86531-942-1). Westview.

Morss, Elliott R., et al. Strategies for Small Farmer Development: An Empirical Study of Rural Development Projects in the Gambia, Ghana, Kenya, Lesotho, Nigeria, Bolivia, Colombia, Mexico, Paraguay & Peru, 2 vols. LC 75-30811. (Special Studies in Social, Political & Economic Development Ser.). 1000p. 1976. lib. bdg. 50.00 o.p. (ISBN 0-89158-017-4). Westview.

Morss, Noel. Archaeological Explorations on the Middle Chinlee. LC 28-11557. 1927. pap. 10.00 (ISBN 0-527-00533-9). Kraus Repr.

Morss, Victoria A., jt. auth. see Morss, Elliot R.

Mort, J. & Pfister, G. Electronic Properties of Polymers. 336p. 1982. 44.95 (ISBN 0-471-07696-1). Wiley.

Mort, J. & Pai, C. M., eds. Photoconductivity & Related Phenomena. LC 76-16160. 1976. 81.00 (ISBN 0-444-41463-0). Elsevier.

Morte, Michael W. La see La Morte, Michael W.

Mortell, Arthur. Anatomy of a Successful Salesman. rev. ed. LC 72-97792. 1982. 10.95 (ISBN 0-87863-041-4). Farnswth Pub.

Mortensen, C. David. Communication: The Study of Human Interaction. 480p. 1972. text ed. 25.50 (ISBN 0-07-043395-X, C); 6.95 o.p. study guide (ISBN 0-07-043396-8). McGraw.

Mortensen, Donald & Schmüller, Alan. Guidance in Today's Schools. 3rd ed. LC 75-35989. 1976. text ed. 33.95 o.s.i. (ISBN 0-471-61779-2). Wiley.

Mortensen, Neils, jt. auth. see Conrad, Barnaby.

Mortensen, V. Harvey. It's Time to Backdate. 107p. 1983. pap. 2.00 (ISBN 0-89036-149-5). Hawkes Pub Inc.

Mortenson, W. P., jt. auth. see Luening, R. A.

Mortenson, William P., jt. auth. see Brickbauer, Elwood A.

Mortenson, William P., jt. auth. see Juergenson, Elwood M.

Morth, H. T., tr. see Breuer, Georg.

Mortillaro, Nicholas A., ed. The Physiology & Pharmacology of the Microcirculation, Vol. 1. LC 82-20562. (Physiologic & Pharmacologic Basis of Drug Therapy Ser.). Date not set. price not set (ISBN 0-12-508301-7). Acad Pr.

Mortimer. Mathematics for Physical Chemistry. 1981. pap. text ed. 14.95 o.p. (ISBN 0-02-384000-5). Macmillan.

Mortimer, C. D., jt. auth. see Merdinyan, M. E.

Mortimer, C. H., jt. ed. see Graf, W. H.

Mortimer, Carole. Captive Loving. (Harlequin Presents Ser.). 192p. 1982. pap. 1.95 (ISBN 0-373-10603-3). Harlequin Bks.

--De Haine et de Passion. (Collection Harlequin). 192p. 1983. pap. 1.95 (ISBN 0-373-49325-8). Harlequin Bks.

--Golden Fever. (Harlequin Presents Ser.). 192p. 1983. pap. 1.95 (ISBN 0-373-10579-7). Harlequin Bks.

--Hidden Love. (Harlequin Presents Ser.). 192p. 1983. pap. 1.95 (ISBN 0-373-10587-8). Harlequin Bks.

--Love's Only Deception. (Harlequin Presents Ser.). 192p. 1983. pap. 1.95 (ISBN 0-373-10594-0). Harlequin Bks.

--Perfect Partner. (Harlequin Presents Ser.). 192p. 1983. pap. 1.75 (ISBN 0-373-10571-1). Harlequin Bks.

Mortimer, Charles E. Chemistry: A Conceptual Approach. 4th ed. 1979. text ed. 20.95 (ISBN 0-442-25545-4); ans. bklet 1.00 (ISBN 0-442-25547-0); solution manual 2.95 (ISBN 0-442-25546-2); study guide by Shive & Shive 5.95 (ISBN 0-442-25548-9). Van Nos Reinhold.

Mortimer, E. A. Library Books: Their Care & Repair. 1981. 9.00x o.p. (ISBN 0-86025-904-8, Pub. by Ian Henry Pubns England). State Mutual Bk.

Mortimer, Edward. Faith & Power: The Politics of Islam. LC 82-40038. 448p. 1982. pap. text ed. 6.95 (ISBN 0-394-71173-4, Vin). Random.

--Faith & Power: The Politics of Islam. (Illus.). 425p. 1982. 19.95 (ISBN 0-394-51333-9). Random.

Mortimer, Ernest. Blaise Pascal: The Life & Work of a Realist. LC 76-847. (Illus.). 240p. 1976. Repr. of 1959 ed. lib. bdg. 17.75x (ISBN 0-8371-8747-8, MOBP). Greenwood.

Mortimer, G., et al, eds. Coach (Automoblie) Trimming: Part One, 2 vols. (Engineering Craftsmen: No. E3). (Illus.). 1969. Set. spiral bdg. 47.50x set (ISBN 0-85083-041-9). Intl Ideas.

--Coach (Automoblie) Trimming: Part Two. (Engineering Craftsmen: No. E23). (Illus.). 1970. spiral bdg. 33.50x (ISBN 0-85083-124-5). Intl Ideas.

Mortimer, G. W., ed. Weakness of Will. LC 70-124950. (Controversies in Philosophy Ser.). 320p. 1971. 18.95 o.p. (ISBN 0-312-85925-2); pap. 7.50 o.p. (ISBN 0-312-85890-6). St Martin.

Mortimer, J. F. History of the Boilermakers' Society 1906-1939, Vol.2. 392p. 1982. text ed. 60.00x (ISBN 0-04-331085-0). Allen Unwin.

Mortimer, James & Pirozzolo, Francis J., eds. The Aging Motor System, Vol. 3. 270p. 1982. 29.95 (ISBN 0-03-059283-6). Praeger.

Mortimer, James A. & Schuman, Leonard M., eds. The Epidemiology of Dementia. (Illus.). 1981. text ed. 23.95x (ISBN 0-19-502906-2). Oxford U Pr.

Mortimer, John. Clinging to the Wreckage: A Part of Life. LC 82-5728. (Illus.). 224p. 1982. 12.95 (ISBN 0-89919-133-9). Ticknor & Fields.

--Come As You Are. 1971. pap. 6.95 o.p. (ISBN 0-416-63280-7). Methuen Inc.

--Rumpole's Return. 1982. pap. 2.95 (ISBN 0-14-005571-1). Penguin.

--Voyage Round My Father. 1983. pap. 4.95 (ISBN 0-14-048169-9). Penguin.

Mortimer, John, ed. see Ingersoll Engineers.

Mortimer, Mildred P., ed. Contes Africains. LC 71-168855. (Illus., Orig.). 1972. pap. text ed. 9.50 (ISBN 0-395-12078-0, 3-39210). HM.

Mortimer, Ray A. Edouard Manet & the Folies-Bergere. (Great Masters Art Book). (Illus.). 1979. deluxe ed. 41.25 (ISBN 0-930582-23-3). Gloucester Art.

Mortimer, Richard L. Stained Glass Menagerie. (Illus.). 96p. (Orig.). 1982. pap. 7.95 (ISBN 0-9608356-0-1). Glass Art.

Mortimer, Ruth, ed. The Landscape Alphabet. (Illus.). 48p. 1981. pap. 3.50 (ISBN 0-87391-023-0). Smith Coll.

Mortimore, Jo & Blackstone, Tessa. Disadvantage & Education. (SSRC-DHSS Studies in Deprivation & Disadvantage: No. 4). 216p. 1982. text ed. 25.00x (ISBN 0-435-82608-5). Heinemann Ed.

Mortland, M. M. & Farmer, V. C., eds. International Clay Conference, 1978. (Developments in Sedimentology: Vol. 27). 1979. 65.25 (ISBN 0-444-41773-7). Elsevier.

Mortley, R., jt. ed. see Dockrill, D. W.

Mortley, Raoul. Womanhood: The Feminine in Ancient Hellenism, Gnosticism, Christianity & Islam. 119p. 1983. text ed. 21.75x (ISBN 0-85668-912-2, Pub. by Aris & Phillips England); pap. text ed. 11.75x (ISBN 0-85668-913-0). Humanities.

Morton. Guts. 2nd ed. (Studies in Biology: No. 7). 1979. 5.95 o.p. (ISBN 0-8391-0154-6). Univ Park.

--A Study Guide to Epidemiology & Biostatistics. 168p. 1978. pap. text ed. 12.95 (ISBN 0-8391-1310-2). Univ Park.

--Use of Medical Literature. 2nd ed. 1978. 64.95 o.p. (ISBN 0-408-70916-2). Butterworth.

Morton & Morton, Desmond. Rebellions in Canada. (gr. 6-10). 1980. PLB 8.40 (ISBN 0-531-00449-X). Watts.

Morton, A. G. History of Botanical Science: An Account of the Development of Botany from the Ancient Time to the Present. LC 81-67891. 1981. 45.50 o.s.i. (ISBN 0-12-508380-7); pap. 21.50 o.s.i. (ISBN 0-12-508382-3). Acad Pr.

Morton, A. H., jt. auth. see Shepherd, J.

Morton, A. L., tr. see Sperber, D.

Morton, A. Q. & Michaelson, S. Critical Concordance to the Pastoral Epistles, I, II Timothy, Titus, Philemon. Baird, Arthur & Freedman, David N., eds. (The Computer Bible Ser.: Vol. XXV). 1982. pap. 35.00 (ISBN 0-935106-20-0). Biblical Res Assocs.

Morton, A. Q., et al. A Critical Concordance to the Letter of Paul to the Ephesians. Baird, J. Arthur & Freedman, David, eds. (The Computer Bible Ser.: Vol. XXII). (Orig.). 1980. pap. text ed. 20.00 (ISBN 0-935106-17-0). Biblical Res Assocs.

Morton, Alexander C. The Official Career Guide to Food Service & Hospitality Management. (Illus.). 128p. 1983. pap. 7.95 (ISBN 0-686-82173-4). Arco.

--The Official 1981-82 Guide to Airline Careers. (Illus.). 192p. 1981. pap. 7.95 (ISBN 0-931794-07-2). Arco.

Morton, Arthur L. & Tate, George. The British Labour Movement, 1770-1920: A Political History. LC 74-25892. 313p. 1975. Repr. of 1973 ed. lib. bdg. 19.25x (ISBN 0-8371-7865-7, MOBL). Greenwood.

Morton, B. R. Numerical Approximation. (Library of Mathematics). 1969. pap. 5.00 o.p. (ISBN 0-7100-4354-6). Routledge & Kegan.

Morton, C., jt. auth. see Morton, Ian.

Morton, Carl P. Desiring Stone. LC 72-83298. 112p. 1972. 5.00 (ISBN 0-911838-22-8). Windy Row.

Morton, Craig & Burger, Robert. The Courage to Believe. (Epiphany Bks.). (Illus.). 1983. pap. 2.75 (ISBN 0-345-30564-7). Ballantine.

Morton, David. The Traditional Music of Thailand. LC 70-142048. 1976. 40.00x (ISBN 0-520-01876-1). U of Cal Pr.

Morton, Desmond. Labour in Canada. (Focus on Canadian History Ser.). (Illus.). 96p. (gr. 6-10). 1982. PLB 8.40 (ISBN 0-531-04572-2). Watts.

--The Last War Drum. Swettenham, John, ed. LC 72-80054. (Canadian War Museum Historical Publications Ser.: No. 5). (Illus.). xxii, 193p. 1972. 10.95 o.p. (ISBN 0-88866-512-1); pap. 5.95 o.p. (ISBN 0-88866-513-X). Samuel Stevens.

--A Peculiar Kind of Politics: Canada's Overseas Ministry in the First World War. 280p. 1982. 22.50x (ISBN 0-8020-5586-9). U of Toronto Pr.

Morton, Desmond, jt. auth. see Morton.

Morton, Donald E. Vladimir Nabokov. LC 74-76128. (Literature and Life Ser.). 176p. 1974. 11.95 (ISBN 0-8044-2638-4). Ungar.

Morton, Eugene S., jt. ed. see Keast, Allen.

Morton, George, ed. see Riegel, E. C.

Morton, H. V. The Splendour of Scotland. (Illus.). 1977. 12.50 o.p. (ISBN 0-396-07397-2). Dodd.

--A Traveller in Italy. (Illus.). pap. 13.95 o.p. (ISBN 0-396-08046-4). Dodd.

--A Traveller in Southern Italy. LC 74-86851. (Illus.). 1969. 10.00 o.p. (ISBN 0-396-05991-0). Dodd.

Morton, Harry. The Whale's Wake. (Illus.). 396p. 1982. text ed. 32.50x (ISBN 0-8248-0830-4). UH Pr.

Morton, I. D. & MacLeod, A. J., eds. Food Flavors: Pt. A: Introduction. (Developments in Food Science Ser.: Vol. 3A). 1982. 117.00 (ISBN 0-444-41857-1). Elsevier.

Morton, Ian & Morton, C. Elsevier's Dictionary of Food Science & Technology. 1977. 42.75 (ISBN 0-444-41559-9). Elsevier.

Morton, J., ed. see Raudive, Konstantin.

Morton, J., et al. Winning Tennis after Forty. 9.95 o.p. (ISBN 0-13-961169-X). P-H.

Morton, Jacqueline, ed. see Goldman, Norma & Szymanski, Ladislas.

Morton, John. Young Artists Companion. 14.50x (ISBN 0-392-06059-0, LTB). Sportshelf.

Morton, John & Marshall, John C., eds. Psycholinguistics Two: Structures & Processes. (Psycholinguistics Ser.). 1979. text ed. 17.50x (ISBN 0-262-13148-X). MIT Pr.

Morton, Joyce. Edge of Fear. (YA) 1978. 6.95 (ISBN 0-685-84747-0, Avalon). Bouregy.

--Legal Secretarial Procedures. LC 78-23892. 1979. pap. text ed. 16.95 (ISBN 0-13-528489-9). P-H.

--Speak No Evil. (YA) 1979. 6.95 (ISBN 0-685-59937-X, Avalon). Bouregy.

Morton, Judy C., et al. Dental Teamwork Strategies: Interpersonal & Organizational Approaches. LC 79-20229. 182p. 1979. pap. 13.95 (ISBN 0-8016-0979-8). Mosby.

--Building Assertive Skills: A Practical Guide to Professional Development for Allied Dental Health Providers. LC 80-19456. (Illus.). 283p. 1981. pap. text ed. 13.95 (ISBN 0-8016-3520-9). Mosby.

Morton, Julia F. Plants Poisonous to People in Florida & Other Warm Areas. 2nd Rev. ed. (Illus.). 170p. 1982. pap. 19.75 (ISBN 0-9610184-0-2). J F Morton.

Morton, K. M. & Baines, M. J., eds. Numerical Methods for Fluid Dynamics. LC 82-11627. Date not set. 55.50 (ISBN 0-12-508360-2). Acad Pr.

Morton, K. W., jt. auth. see Richtmyer, Robert D.

Morton, Margaret A., jt. auth. see Green, Helen H.

Morton, Margaret A., jt. auth. see Hopkins, Charles R.

Morton, Maurice. Rubber Technology. 2nd ed. LC 81-8317. 614p. 1981. Repr. of 1973 ed. 28.50 (ISBN 0-89874-372-9). Krieger.

Morton, Maurice, ed. Anionic Polymerization. LC 82-11627. 268p. 1983. 39.00 (ISBN 0-12-508080-8). Acad Pr.

Morton, Michael S. Management Decision Systems: Computer-Based Support for Decision Making. LC 72-132152. (Illus.). 1971. 12.50x (ISBN 0-87584-090-6). Harvard Busn.

Morton, N. Structural Engineering Design Programs: Software Project. 1982. (users manual & 4 diskettes) 495.00 (ISBN 0-07-079572-X, P&RB). McGraw.

Morton, Nancy A. Picnics with Pizzazz. (Orig.). 1981. pap. 5.95 o.p. (ISBN 0-8092-5922-2). Contemp Bks.

Morton, Nathaniel. New England's Memorial. LC 38-10717. Repr. of 1669 ed. 30.00x (ISBN 0-8201-1184-8). Schol Facsimiles.

Morton, Newton E., ed. Genetic Structure of Populations. (Population Genetics Monographs: No. 3). 1974. 20.00x (ISBN 0-8248-0326-4). UH Pr.

--A Genetics Program Library. 69p. 1969. 10.00x (ISBN 0-87022-522-7). UH Pr.

Morton, Pamela. Basics of Disco Dancing. (Illus.). 67p. 1981. pap. text ed. 2.95x (ISBN 0-89641-084-6). American Pr.

Morton, R., et al. The Home, It's Furnishings & Equipment. 1979. text ed. 20.84 (ISBN 0-07-043417-4); tchr's manual avail. McGraw.

Morton, R. S. The Vendor of Sweets. 1983. pap. 4.95 (ISBN 0-14-006258-0). Penguin.

Morton, Richard, jt. ed. see Browning, John.

Morton, Richard A. The Tooth, the Whole Tooth, & Nothing but... 1978. 6.50 o.p. (ISBN 0-533-03644-5). Vantage.

Morton, Robert. Living with the Texas Shore. (Living with the Shore). (Illus.). 180p. Date not set. 20.00 (ISBN 0-8223-0499-6); pap. 9.75 (ISBN 0-8223-0500-3). Duke.

Morton, Ruth. Interior Design: The Home-Its Furnishing & Equipment. Zinkus, Dan & Newman, Carol, eds. (Illus.). 184p. (Orig.). (gr. 9-12). 1979. pap. 10.44 (ISBN 0-07-043426-3, W). McGraw.

Morton, Ruth, et al. Home: Its Furnishing & Equipment. (Illus.). (gr. 11-12). 1970. text ed. 21.40 o.p. (ISBN 0-07-043415-8, W); tchr's manual 3.68 o.p. (ISBN 0-07-043416-6). McGraw.

Morton, Sarah W. My Mind & Its Thoughts, in Sketches, Fragments, & Essays. LC 74-28388. 336p. 1975. Repr. of 1823 ed. lib. bdg. 39.00x (ISBN 0-8201-1150-3). Schol Facsimiles.

Morton, Sean. Exhibit Boston: Gallery Approach Guide for Artists. LC 81-72013. 60p. 1982. pap. 5.00 (ISBN 0-9607908-0-2). Exhibit Pr.

Morton, Terry B., ed. I Feel I Should Warn You: Historic Preservation Cartoons. LC 75-12480. (Illus.). 1975. o.p. (ISBN 0-89133-028-3); pap. 6.95 (ISBN 0-89133-027-5). Preservation Pr.

Morton, Thomas. Texas Real Estate Finance: A Practical Approach. 1982. text ed. 24.50x (ISBN 0-673-16009-2). Scott F.

Morton, Tom. Real Estate Finance: A Practical Approach. 1983. text ed. 21.95x (ISBN 0-673-16580-9). Scott F.

Morton, Virgil L., jt. auth. see Ellfeldt, Lois.

Morton, W. L. The Progressive Party in Canada. (Scholarly Reprint Ser.). 1980. Repr. 35.00x o.p. (ISBN 0-8020-7096-5). U of Toronto Pr.

Morton, W. Scott. China: Its History & Culture. (Illus.). 1982. pap. 7.95 (ISBN 0-07-002456-1). McGraw.

Morton, William L. Manitoba: A History. 2nd ed. LC 67-4598. (Illus.). 1967. 27.50x o.p. (ISBN 0-8020-1711-8); pap. 12.50 (ISBN 0-8020-6070-6). U of Toronto Pr.

Moruzzi, Giuseppe, et al. Brain Mechanisms. (Progress in Brain Research: Vol. 1). 1964. 124.00 (ISBN 0-444-40402-3, North Holland). Elsevier.

Morwood, William. Duel for the Middle Kingdom: The Struggle Between Chiang Kai-Shek & Mao-Tse-Tung for Control of China. LC 79-51193. 1980. 15.95 o.p. (ISBN 0-89696-047-1, An Everest House Book). Dodd.

--Traveler in a Vanished Landscape. (Illus.). 352p. 1973. 7.95 o.p. (ISBN 0-517-50064-7). Crown.

Moryadas, S., jt. auth. see Lowe, John C.

Mosak, B., jt. auth. see Mosak, Harold H.

Mosak, Harold H. & Mosak, B. A Bibliography for Adlerian Psychology. LC 74-26938. 320p. 1975. 17.50x o.s.i. (ISBN 0-470-61852-3). Halsted Pr.

Mosatche, Harriet. Searching: Practices & Beliefs of the Religious Cults & Human Potential Movements. (Illus.). 256p. 1983. 12.95 (ISBN 0-87396-092-0). Stravon.

Mosbacher, Eric, tr. see Freud, Sigmund.

Mosbacher, Eric, tr. see Paleologue, Maurice.

Mosbacher, Eric, tr. see Silone, Ignazio.

Mosbacher, Eric, tr. see Verga, Giovanni.

Mosbarger, Ellen. A Is for Applique. (Illus.). 36p. 1982. pap. 4.95 (ISBN 0-943134-00-5). Calico Mse Pubns.

Mosburg, Lewis G. Leveraged Oil & Gas Programs. 1982. 50.00 (ISBN 0-89419-209-4). Inst Energy.

--Mosburg Oil Venture Capital from Tax-Oriented Investors, 2 vols. 1982. Vol. I. (ISBN 0-89419-169-1); Vol. II. (ISBN 0-89419-170-5); Set. 90.00 (ISBN 0-89419-172-1). Inst Energy.

--Private Placements in Oil under SEC Regulation D, 2 vols. Incl. Vol. 1. 1982. 80.00 (ISBN 0-89419-203-5); Vol II. 1982. 80.00 (ISBN 0-89419-204-3). Inst Energy.

Mosburg, Lewis G., ed. Problems & Pitfalls in Exploration Agreements. 1982p. 50.00 (ISBN 0-89419-225-6). Inst Energy.

--Raising Money Without Registration. 1982. 45.00 (ISBN 0-89419-230-2). Inst Energy.

--Sample Offering Documents. 1982. 50.00 (ISBN 0-89419-210-8). Inst Energy.

Mosburg, Lewis G., Jr. Basic Principles of the Oil & Gas Lease. 1982. 50.00 (ISBN 0-89419-194-2). Inst Energy.

--Contract Use in Oil & Gas Operations. 1981. cancelled 55.00 (ISBN 0-89419-130-6). Inst Energy.

--The Economics of Oil & Gas Investment. (Illus.). 23p. (Orig.). 1982. Broker-Dealer Version. pap. text ed. 5.25 (ISBN 0-910649-00-6); Investor Version. pap. text ed. 5.25 (ISBN 0-910649-01-4). Energy Textbks.

--Handbook on Petroleum Land Titles. 1976. 32.00 (ISBN 0-685-83432-8); pap. 14.00 perfect bound (ISBN 0-89419-000-8). Inst Energy.

--Land Support Personnel, 2 vols. 1982. Vol. 1. write for info. (ISBN 0-89419-231-0); Vol. II. write for info.; Set. 55.00 (ISBN 0-89419-232-9). Inst Energy.

--Profiting from the Energy Crisis, 2 Vols. 1982. Vol. I. 40.00 ea. (ISBN 0-89419-220-5). Vol. II (ISBN 0-89419-221-3). 80.00 set (ISBN 0-89419-222-1). Inst Energy.

Mosburg, Lewis G., Jr., ed. Basics of Structuring Exploration Deals. 1948. 48.00 (ISBN 0-89931-006-0). Inst Energy.

--Contracts Used in Oil & Gas Operations: Phase 1 & 2. 1978. Phase 1. 45.00 o.p. (ISBN -089419-228-0); Phase 2. 45.00 o.p. (ISBN 0-89419-246-9). Inst Energy.

--Petroleum Land Practices. 1981. 49.00 (ISBN 0-89931-024-9). Inst Energy.

Mosby, Jack & Dapkus, Dave. Alaska Paddling Guide. (Illus.). 120p. (Orig.). 1982. pap. 7.95 (ISBN 0-9608550-0-9). J & R Enter.

Mosby, W. L., ed. Heterocyclic Compounds: Bridgehead Nitrogen Atoms. 758p. 1961. Vol. 15, Pt. 1. 75.00 o.p. (ISBN 0-470-38049-7); Vol. 15, Pt. 2. 85.50 (ISBN 0-470-38082-9). Krieger.

Moscarello, L. C., et al. Retail Accounting & Financial Control. 4th ed. 520p. 1976. 49.95 (ISBN 0-471-06793-8, Pub. by Wiley-Interscience). Wiley.

Moscatelli, V. B., jt. auth. see Hogbe-Nlend, H.

Moscheles, Ignatz. Recent Music & Musicians As Described in the Diaries & Correspondence of Ignatz Moscheles. LC 73-125057. (Music Ser). 1970. Repr. of 1873 ed. lib. bdg. 35.00 (ISBN 0-306-70022-0). Da Capo.

Moschella, Samuel L., et al. Dermatology. 1st ed. LC 73-88263. (Illus.). 1975. text ed. 95.00 set (ISBN 0-7216-6562-4); Vol. 1. text ed. 47.50 (ISBN 0-7216-6565-9); Vol. 2. 47.50 (ISBN 0-7216-6566-7). Saunders.

Moschini, Francesco, ed. Massimo Scolari. LC 80-50657. (Illus.). 240p. 1981. pap. 19.95 (ISBN 0-8478-0317-1). Rizzoli Intl.

Moschner, Meinhard. Fernsehen In Lateinamerika. 308p. (Ger.). 1982. write for info. (ISBN 3-8204-5795-X). P Lang Pubs.

Moschovakis, Y. N. Descriptive Set Theory. (Studies in Logic & the Foundations of Mathematics: Vol. 100). 640p. 1979. 85.00 (ISBN 0-444-85305-7, North Holland). Elsevier.

Moschytz, G. S. Active Filter Design Handbook: For Use with Programmable Pocket Calculators & Minicomputers. LC 80-40845. 324p. 1981. 49.95 (ISBN 0-471-27850-5, Pub. by Wiley-Interscience). Wiley.

Moschytz, George S. Linear Integrated Networks: Design. LC 74-13707. 712p. 1975. 21.00 (ISBN 0-442-25582-9). Krieger.

Mosco, Vincent. Broadcasting in the United States: Innovative Challenge & Organizational Control. LC 78-16246. (Communication & Information Science Ser.). 1979. 19.50x (ISBN 0-89391-009-0). Ablex Pub.

Mosco, Vincentf. Pushbotton Fantasies. Voight, Melvin J., ed. (Communication & Information Science Ser.). 1983. text ed. 22.50 (ISBN 0-89391-125-9); pap. text ed. 10.95 (ISBN 0-89391-132-1). Ablex Pub.

Moscona, Aron, ed. The Cell Surface in Development. LC 74-7308. 1974. 48.95 o.p. (ISBN 0-471-61855-1, Pub. by Wiley Medical). Wiley.

Moscona, Aron A. & Monroy, Alberto, eds. Current Topics in Developmental Biology: Vol. 18: Genome Function, Cell Interactions, & Differentiation. (Serial Publication). Date not set. price not set (ISBN 0-12-153118-X). Acad Pr.

Moscotti, Albert D. British Policy & the Nationalist Movement in Burma, 1917-1937. (Asian Studies at Hawaii Ser.: No. 11). 288p. (Orig.). 1973. pap. text ed. 8.50x (ISBN 0-8248-0279-9). UH Pr.

Moscove, Stephen. Accounting Fundamentals: A Self-Instructional Approach. 2nd ed. 1980. pap. text ed. 13.95 (ISBN 0-8359-0061-4); wkbk. 4.95 (ISBN 0-8359-0072-X); instr's. manual avail. (ISBN 0-8359-0062-2). Reston.

Moscove, Stephen A. & Simkin, Mark G. Accounting Information Systems: Concepts & Practice for Effective Decision Making Systems. LC 80-15445. (Accounting & Information Systems Ser.). 616p. 1981. 32.95 (ISBN 0-471-03369-3); tchr's manual 65.00 (ISBN 0-471-03371-5). Wiley.

Moscovice, I. S., jt. auth. see Rosenblatt, R. A.

Moscovici, Serge. The Human History of Nature. (European Ideas Ser.). 1977. text ed. 16.25x o.p. (ISBN 0-391-01080-8). Humanities.

Moscow, Alvin. Collision Course. LC 81-47698. (Illus.). 384p. 1981. Repr. of 1959 ed. 12.95 (ISBN 0-448-12019-4, G&D). Putnam Pub Group.

Moscow, Henry. The Street Book: An Encyclopedia of Manhattan's Street Names & Their Origins. Tracy, Thomas, ed. LC 78-66990. (Illus.). 1978. 14.95 o.p. (ISBN 0-910684-08-1, 1602515); pap. 7.95 o.p. (ISBN 0-910684-07-3, 1602507). Hagstrom Map.

Moscow, Warren. Politics in the Empire State. LC 78-23664. 1979. Repr. of 1948 ed. lib. bdg. 20.50x (ISBN 0-313-20780-1, MOPE). Greenwood.

Moscowitz, Ira, ed. see Serrulaz, Maurice.

Mosedale, F. Philosophy & Science: The Wide Range of Interaction. 1979. pap. 17.95 (ISBN 0-13-662577-0). P-H.

Mosedale, John. The Men Who Invented Broadway: Damon Runyon, Walter Winchell, & Their World. 1981. 15.00 o.s.i. (ISBN 0-399-90085-3, Marek). Putnam Pub Group.

Mosel, Arlene. The Funny Little Woman. (ps-4). 8.95 (ISBN 0-525-30265-4, 0383-120); pap. 3.95 (ISBN 0-525-45036-X, Anytime Bks). Dutton.

Moseley & Saunders. Computerized Tomography in Neuro-Opthalmology. Date not set. cancelled (ISBN 0-8151-5972-2). Year Bk Med.

Moseley, Charles. Nine Hours to Fly. LC 79-99145. 1970. 10.00 (ISBN 0-87716-022-8, Pub. by Moore Pub Co). F Apple.

Moseley, David V. Special Provision for Reading: When Will They Ever Learn ? (General Ser). 240p. 1975. pap. text ed. 20.00x o.p. (ISBN 0-85633-063-9, NFER). Humanities.

Moseley, Elizabeth, jt. auth. see Wilkie, Katharine.

Moseley, Elizabeth R. Davy Crockett: Hero of the Wild Frontier. LC 67-11949. (Discovery Books Ser). (Illus.). (gr. 2-5). 1967. PLB 6.69 (ISBN 0-8116-6301-9). Garrard.

Moseley, F., jt. auth. see Wright, A. E.

Moseley, George V., 3rd. Consolidation of the South China Frontier. (Center for Chinese Studies, UC Berkeley). 1973. 30.00x (ISBN 0-520-02102-9). U of Cal Pr.

Moseley, H. Jewel & Clift, Virgil A. Cultural Dimensions in the Baccalaureate Nursing Curriculum. 108p. 1977. 5.95 (ISBN 0-686-38249-8, 15-1662). Natl League Nurse.

Moseley, Keith, designed by see Seymour, Peter.

Moseley, Lloyd W. Customer Service: The Road to Greater Profits. rev. ed. LC 72-85929. (Illus.). 1978. 21.95 (ISBN 0-86730-303-4). Lebhar Friedman.

Moseley, Malcolm. Growth Centres in Spatial Planning. LC 74-9962. 1974. text ed. write for info. (ISBN 0-08-018055-8). Pergamon.

Moseley, Michael E. & Mackey, Carol. Twenty-Four Architectural Plans of Chan Chan, Peru. LC 73-92493. 1974. maps 50.00x (ISBN 0-87365-778-0). Peabody Harvard.

Moseley, Roy, jt. auth. see Higham, Charles.

Moseley, Spencer & Reed, Gervais. Walter F. Isaacs: An Artist in America, 1886-1964. LC 74-28489. (Index of Art in the Pacific Northwest Ser.: No. 8). (Illus.). 124p. 1982. 14.95 (ISBN 0-295-95389-6). U of Wash Pr.

Moselle, Gary. Building Cost Manual Nineteen Eighty-Two. 240p. (Orig.). 1981. pap. 10.00 o.p. (ISBN 0-910460-31-0). Craftsman.

--National Construction Estimator 1982. 288p. (Orig.). 1981. pap. 10.75 o.p. (ISBN 0-910460-30-2). Craftsman.

Mosely, ed. see Cowles, Julia.

Moser, et al. Better Living & Breathing: A Manual for Patients. 2nd ed. LC 80-17943. (Illus.). 94p. 1980. pap. text ed. 5.95 (ISBN 0-8016-3565-9). Mosby.

Moser, Charles A. Denis Fonvizin. (World Authors Ser.). 1979. lib. bdg. 15.95 (ISBN 0-8057-6402-X, Twayne). G K Hall.

Moser, Don. Central American Jungles. LC 75-14284. (American Wilderness Ser.). (Illus.). (gr. 6 up). 1975. PLB 15.96 (ISBN 0-8094-1343-4, Pub. by Time-Life). Silver.

--China-Burma-India. LC 77-93742. (World War II Ser.). PLB 19.92 (ISBN 0-8094-2483-5). Silver.

--The Snake River Country. LC 74-80283. (American Wilderness Ser.). (Illus.). (gr. 6 up). 1974. PLB 15.96 (ISBN 0-8094-1242-X, Pub. by Time-Life). Silver.

Moser, Harold D., ed. see Webster, Daniel.

Moser, Kenneth M. & Spragg, Roger G. Respiratory Emergencies. 2nd ed. LC 81-14176. (Illus.). 316p. 1982. pap. text ed. 25.50 (ISBN 0-8016-4584-0). Mosby.

Moser, Kenneth M., jt. auth. see Shibel, Elaine.

Moser, Lida. Amphoto Guide to Special Effects. (Illus.). 168p. 1980. 10.95 o.p. (ISBN 0-8174-3523-9, Amphoto); pap. 7.95 (ISBN 0-8174-3524-7). Watson-Guptill.

--Fun in Photography. (Illus.). 1974. 9.95 o.p. (ISBN 0-8174-0564-X, Amphoto). Watson-Guptill.

--Grants in Photography: How to Get Them. (Illus.). 1978. 12.50 o.p. (ISBN 0-8174-2445-8, Amphoto). Watson-Guptill.

Moser, Linda. Photography Contests: How to Enter, How to Win. (Illus.). 144p. 1981. 14.95 o.p. (ISBN 0-8174-5403-9, Amphoto); pap. 8.95 (ISBN 0-8174-5404-7). Watson-Guptill.

Moser, M. Fungorum Rariorum Icones Coloratae, Part 7. (Illus.). 1979. pap. text ed. 14.00x (ISBN 3-7682-0413-8). Lubrecht & Cramer.

Moser, M. & Horak, E. Cortinarius Fr. und nahe Verwandte Gottungen in Suedamerika. 1975. 100.00 (ISBN 3-7682-5452-6). Lubrecht & Cramer.

Moser, Meinhard. Die Pilze Mitteleuropas: Vol. 4, Die Gattung Phlegmacium (Schleimkoepfe) (Illus.). 1960. 88.00 (ISBN 3-7682-0523-1). Lubrecht & Cramer.

Moser, Michael J. Law & Social Change in a Chinese Community: A Case Study from Rural Taiwan. 1982. text ed. 45.00 (ISBN 0-379-20062-7). Oceana.

Moser, Robert E. Mental & Astral Projection. 1982. 3.50 (ISBN 0-686-97348-8). Esoteric Pubns.

Moser, Thomas, ed. see Conrad, Joseph.

Moser, Thos. Thos. Moser's Windsor Chairmaking. LC 82-50543. (Illus.). 192p. 1982. 19.95 (ISBN 0-8069-5470-1); lib. bdg. 23.59 (ISBN 0-8069-5471-X); pap. 8.95 (ISBN 0-8069-7630-6). Sterling.

Moser, W. O., jt. auth. see Coxeter, H. S.

Moser, William R. & Happel, John R., eds. Catalytic Chemistry of Solid-State Inorganics, Vol. 272. (Annals of the New York Academy of Sciences). 1976. 10.00 (ISBN 0-89072-051-7). NY Acad Sci.

Moses, A. Elfin & Hawkins, Robert O., Jr. Counseling Lesbian Women & Gay Men: A Life-Issues Approach. LC 81-11233. 263p. 1982. pap. text ed. 14.95 (ISBN 0-8016-3563-2). Mosby.

Moses, A. J. Nuclear Techniques in Analytical Chemistry. LC 64-15736. (International Series on Analytical Chemistry: Vol. 20). 1965. inquire for price o.p. (ISBN 0-08-010695-1). Pergamon.

Moses, Alice E. Identity Management in Lesbian Women. (Praeger Special Studies). 1978. 24.95 o.p. (ISBN 0-03-047641-0). Praeger.

Moses, Harold, jt. auth. see Zaccaria, Joseph S.

Moses, James A., Jr. & Golden, Charles, eds. Interpretation of the Luria-Nebraska Neuropsychological Battery, Vol. 2. Date not set. text ed. price not set (ISBN 0-8089-1537-1). Grune.

Moses, James A., Jr., et al, eds. Interpretation of the Luria-Nebraska, Vol. 1. Date not set. price not set (ISBN 0-8089-1532-0). Grune.

Moses, Joel, jt. ed. see Dertouzos, Michael L.

Moses, Joel C. The Politics of Women & Work in the Soviet Union & the United States: Alternative Work Schedules & Sex Discrimination. LC 82-23307. (Research Ser.: No. 50). xii, 184p. 1983. pap. 9.50x (ISBN 0-87725-150-9). U of Cal Intl St.

Moses, John. Trade Unionism in Germany from Bismarck to Hitler: 1869-1933, 2 vols. Incl. Vol. 1. 1869-1918. 314p (ISBN 0-389-20072-7); Vol. 2. 1919-1933. 295p (ISBN 0-389-20073-5). 1982. 25.00x ea. B&N Imports.

Moses, Joseph L. & Byham, William C., eds. Applying the Assessment Center Method. 322p. 26.00 (ISBN 0-686-84783-0). Work in Amer.

Moses, L. E., jt. auth. see Chernoff, Herman.

Moses, Leon N. Transport & the Spatial Structure of Cities & Regions. 375p. 1981. 25.00 (ISBN 0-686-94041-5, Trans). Northwestern U Pr.

Moses, Leon N., jt. auth. see Northwestern University Transportation Center Forum.

Moses, Leon N., jt. auth. see Northwestern University Transportation Center June 11-12,1979.

Moses, Leon N., jt. auth. see U.S. Department of Transportation Contract DOT-OS-60163, Feb. 29 - March 1, 1976.

Moses, Montrose J. Children's Books & Reading. LC 74-23680. 1975. Repr. of 1907 ed. 37.00x (ISBN 0-8103-3767-3). Gale.

--Famous Actor-Families in America. LC 68-8938. (Illus.). 1968. Repr. of 1906 ed. lib. bdg. 21.00x (ISBN 0-8371-0177-8, MOAF). Greenwood.

Moses, Phillip J. How to Use the Inside Secrets of a Super Land Salesman to Make Big Money in Any Kind of Real Estate. 1976. 79.50 (ISBN 0-13-436188-1). Exec Reports.

Moses, Robert A. Adler's Physiology of the Eye: Clinical Application. 7th ed. LC 80-16862. (Illus.). 747p. 1981. text ed. 49.50 (ISBN 0-8016-3541-1). Mosby.

Moses, Stanley, jt. ed. see Gross, Bertram M.

Moses, V. & Springham, D. G. Bacteria & the Enhancement of Oil Recovery. 1982. 33.00 o.s.i. (ISBN 0-85334-995-9). Elsevier.

Moses, Wilson J. Black Messiahs & Uncle Toms: Social & Literary Manipulations of a Religious Myth. LC 81-9645. 304p. 1982. 19.75x (ISBN 0-271-00294-8). Pa St U Pr.

Mosesson, G. & Scher, S. Guinea Pigs & Other Laboratory Animals. 1972. text ed. 9.95 (ISBN 0-87666-200-9, PS689). TFH Pubns.

Mosey, Anne C. Occupational Therapy: The Configuration of a Profession. 186p. 1981. text ed. 20.50 (ISBN 0-89004-655-7); pap. text ed. 14.00 (ISBN 0-89004-699-9). Raven.

Moshansky, Mozelle. Mendelssohn: His Life & Times. enl. ed. (Life & Times Ser.). (Illus.). 180p. 1981. Repr. of 1981 ed. 12.95 (ISBN 0-87666-633-0, Z-63). Paganiniana Pubns.

Mosher, David B., jt. auth. see Ortonne, Jean-Paul.

Mosher, Doug. Your Color Computer. 350p. 1983. pap. text ed. 12.95 (ISBN 0-89588-097-0). Sybex.

Mosher, Edith K. & Wagoner, Jennings L., Jr., eds. The Changing Politics of Education Prospects for the 1980's. LC 77-75609. (Education Ser.). 1978. 21.95 o.p. (ISBN 0-8211-1252-X); text ed. 19.95 ten copies o.p. (ISBN 0-685-04968-X). McCutchan.

Mosher, Frederick C., ed. Basic Documents of American Public Administration, 1776-1950. LC 76-13866. 1976. text ed. 17.50x (ISBN 0-8419-0275-5); pap. text ed. 10.95x (ISBN 0-8419-0276-3). Holmes & Meier.

--Basic Literature of American Public Administration, 1787-1950. LC 79-28553. 1981. text ed. 25.00x (ISBN 0-8419-0574-6); pap. text ed. 12.00x (ISBN 0-8419-0575-4). Holmes & Meier.

Mosher, Frederick C., jt. ed. see Stillman, Richard.

Mosher, Frederick D. The GAO: The Quest for Accountability in American Government. 1979. pap. 13.50 (ISBN 0-89158-459-5); lib. bdg. 32.50 (ISBN 0-89158-458-7). Westview.

Mosher, Lynn S. & Lear, George. Motorcycle Mechanics. (Illus.). 272p. 1977. 18.95 (ISBN 0-13-604090-X). P-H.

Mosher, Ralph L., ed. Adolescents' Development & Education: A Janus Knot. LC 78-62642. 1979. 24.75 (ISBN 0-8211-1253-8); text ed. 22.25 10 copies or more (ISBN 0-686-67279-8). McCutchan.

Mosher, Ralph L., et al. Supervision: The Reluctant Profession. LC 72-158636. (Orig.). 1972. pap. text ed. 15.50 (ISBN 0-395-12509-X). HM.

Moshinsky, Julius. A Grammar of Southeastern Pomo. (Publications in Linguistics Vol. 72). 1974. pap. 16.50x (ISBN 0-520-09450-6). U of Cal Pr.

Moshinsky, M. Many Body Problems & Other Selected Topics Theoretical Physics. 452p. 1966. 200.00x (ISBN 0-677-11500-8); pap. 54.00x (ISBN 0-677-12935-1). Gordon.

Mosich, A. N. & Larsen, E. A. Intermediate Accounting. 5th ed. 1982. 31.95x (ISBN 0-07-041580-3); Chapters 1-13. worksheets 10.95x (ISBN 0-07-041582-X); Chapters 14-25. worksheets 10.95x (ISBN 0-07-041583-8); 30.00 (ISBN 0-07-041584-6); 11.00x (ISBN 0-07-041585-4); study guide 10.95x (ISBN 0-07-041581-1); cancelled accounting worksheets (ch. 1-13, 0-07-041582-x; ch. 14-25, 0-07-041583-8). McGraw.

Mosich, A. N. & Larsen, E. J. Modern Advanced Accounting. 3rd ed. 768p. 1983. 29.95x (ISBN 0-07-040127-6, C). Supplementary materials avail. McGraw.

Mosich, A. N. & Larsen, John. CPA Review Manual. (Illus.). 1978. text ed. 32.95 (ISBN 0-07-043435-2, C). McGraw.

Mosich, A. N., jt. auth. see Meigs, Walter B.

Mosier, Alice & Pace, Frank J. Medical Records Technology. LC 74-18676. (Allied Health Ser). 1975. pap. 9.95 o.p. (ISBN 0-672-61396-4). Bobbs.

Mosier, John, jt. auth. see Gaillard, Dawson.

Mosk, Carl, ed. Patriarchy & Fertility: The Evolution of Natality in Japan & Sweden 1880-1960. (Population & Social Structure: Advances in Historical Demography). Date not set. price not set (ISBN 0-12-508480-3). Acad Pr.

Moskalew, Walter. Formular Language & Poetic Design in the Aneid. (Mnemosyne: Suppl. 73). xi, 273p. 1982. pap. write for info. (ISBN 90-04-06580-6). E J Brill.

Moskin, J. R. The U. S. Marine Corps Story. Abr. ed. 800p. 1979. pap. 12.95 (ISBN 0-07-043454-9). McGraw.

Moskin, Marietta. Adam & the Wishing Charm. (Illus.). (gr. 3-5). 1977. 5.95 o.p. (ISBN 0-698-20404-2, Coward). Putnam Pub Group.

--Day of the Blizzard. LC 78-6461. (Illus.). (gr. 3-7). 1978. 7.95 (ISBN 0-698-20468-9, Coward). Putnam Pub Group.

--Lysbet & the Fire Kittens. LC 73-97315. (Break-of-Day Bk). (Illus.). 48p. (gr. 1-3). 1974. PLB 6.99 o.p. (ISBN 0-698-30522-1, Coward). Putnam Pub Group.

--A Royal Gift. (Break-of-day Ser.). (Illus.). 64p. lib. bdg. 6.99 (ISBN 0-698-30734-8, Coward). Putnam Pub Group.

--Toto. (Illus.). (gr. 1-3). 1972. PLB 4.69 o.p. (ISBN 0-698-30372-5, Coward). Putnam Pub Group.

--Waiting for Mama. LC 74-21068. (Illus.). 98p. (gr. 2-6). 1975. 7.95 (ISBN 0-698-20319-4, Coward). Putnam Pub Group.

Moskof, Martin S., jt. auth. see Hefter, Richard.

Moskos, C. C., Jr. & Papajohn, J. C. Greek Orthodox Youth Today. Vaporis, N. M., intro. by. (Saints Peter & Paul Youth Ministry Lectures Ser.). 56p. (Orig.). 1983. pap. 3.00 (ISBN 0-916586-56-1). Holy Cross Orthodox.

Moskos, Charles C., Jr. Greek Americans: Struggle & Success. 1980. text ed. 11.95 (ISBN 0-13-365106-1); pap. text ed. 10.95 (ISBN 0-13-365098-7). P-H.

Moskovits, Martin & Ozin, Geoffrey A., eds. Cryochemistry. LC 76-11841. 592p. 1976. 47.50 o.p. (ISBN 0-471-61870-5, Pub. by Wiley-Interscience). Wiley.

Moskovitz, et al. California Tenant's Handbook. 7th ed. LC 80-117696. 1982. pap. 9.95 (ISBN 0-917316-51-7). Nolo Pr.

Moskow, M., jt. auth. see Lowenberg, J.

Moskowitz. Everybody's Business Nineteen Eighty-Two Update. LC 81-47876. 96p. 1982. pap. 0.91i (ISBN 0-06-250623-4, CN 4031). Har-Row.

Moskowitz, David. Exclusionary Zoning Litigation: Issues, Cases, Strategies. LC 76-17799. 424p. 1977. prof ref 20.00x (ISBN 0-88410-454-0). Ballinger Pub.

Moskowitz, Gertrude. Caring & Sharing in the Foreign Language Class: A Sourcebook on Humanistic Techniques. 1978. pap. 14.95 (ISBN 0-88377-098-9). Newbury Hse.

Moskowitz, H. & Wright, G. Operations Research Techniques for Management. 1979. 29.95 (ISBN 0-13-637389-5). P-H.

Moskowitz, Herbert, ed. Drugs & Driving. 1976. text ed. 28.00 (ISBN 0-08-020537-2). Pergamon.

Moskowitz, Ira, ed. Great Drawings of All Time, 4 vols. LC 75-19869. (Illus.). 2250p. 1976. Repr. of 1962 ed. Set. 515.00 (ISBN 0-686-96765-8). Vol. 1 (ISBN 0-87011-263-5). Vol. 2 (ISBN 0-87011-291-0). Vol. 3 (ISBN 0-87011-292-9). Vol. 4 (ISBN 0-87011-294-5). Kodansha.

Moskowitz, Moses. International Concern with Human Rights. LC 74-79801. 239p. 1974. lib. bdg. 22.00 (ISBN 0-379-00086-5). Oceana.

Moskowitz, Robert. How to Organize Your Work & Your Life. LC 80-1815. (Illus.). 312p. 1981. pap. 8.95 (ISBN 0-385-17012-2, Dolp). Doubleday.

Moskowitz, Roland W. Clinical Rheumatology: A Problem Oriented Approach. 2nd ed. LC 82-242. (Illus.). 421p. 1982. text ed. 25.00 (ISBN 0-8121-0847-7). Lea & Febiger.

Moskowitz, Sam. Seekers of Tomorrow. LC 73-15073. (Classics of Science Fiction Ser.). 441p. 1974. 16.50 o.s.i. (ISBN 0-88355-129-2); pap. 5.95 (ISBN 0-88355-158-6). Hyperion Conn.

Moskowitz, Stewart. Fred's Pyramid. Klimo, Kate, ed. (Moskowitz Bks.). (Illus.). 32p. Date not set. 4.95 (ISBN 0-671-44563-4, Little Simon). S&S.

--The Legend of the American Rabbit. Klimo, Kate, ed. (Moskowitz Bks.). (Illus.). 32p. 1982. 4.95 (ISBN 0-671-45544-3, Little Simon). S&S.

--Patchwork Fish Tale. Klimo, Kate, ed. (Moskowitz Bks.). (Illus.). 32p. 1982. 4.95 (ISBN 0-671-45327-0, Little Simon). S&S.

--Tooloose the Chocolate Moose. Klimo, Kate, ed. (Moskowitz Bks.). (Illus.). 32p. 1982. 4.95 (ISBN 0-671-45329-7, Little Simon). S&S.

Moskvitin, Jurij. Essay on the Origin of Thought. LC 72-85540. 297p. 1974. 15.00x o.p. (ISBN 0-8214-0156-4). Ohio U Pr.

Mosler, Gerard. People Puzzles, No. 4. 128p. 1982. pap. 1.95 (ISBN 0-445-04727-5). Popular Lib.

Mosley, D. J., jt. auth. see Adock, Francis.

Mosley, Doris Y. Nursing Students' Perceptions of the Urban Poor. (League Exchange Ser.: No. 115). 56p. 1977. 5.50 (ISBN 0-686-38344-3, 23-1694). Natl League Nurse.

Mosley, L. Battle of Britain. LC 76-45540. (World War II Ser.). (Illus.). (gr. 6 up). 1977. PLB 19.92 (ISBN 0-8094-2459-2, Pub. by Time-Life). Silver.

Mosley, M. Paul, jt. ed. see Laronne, Jonathan.

Mosley, Paul M., jt. ed. see Schumm, Stanley A.

Mosley, W. H. & Bungey, J. H. Reinforced Concrete Design. (Illus., Orig.). 1976. pap. text ed. 21.50x (ISBN 0-333-19524-8). Scholium Intl.

Mosmann, Charles, jt. auth. see Rothman, Stanley.

Mosoo, Vincent & Wasks, Janet, eds. Labor, the Working Class & Media. (Critical Communication Review Ser.: Vol. 1). 1983. 29.50 (ISBN 0-89391-122-4). Ablex Pub.

Mosqueda, John. Jesus, Emotions & You. 128p. 1983. pap. 5.95 (ISBN 0-686-82090-8). Good News.

Moss. Pediatrics Update, 1982: Reviews for Physicians. 1982. 48.95 (ISBN 0-444-00682-6). Elsevier.

--Pediatrics Update, 1984. (Reviews for Physicians Ser.). Date not set. price not set (ISBN 0-444-00729-6). Elsevier.

Moss, A. J., ed. Pediatrics Update, 1981: Reviews for Physicians. 1981. 38.50 (ISBN 0-444-00588-9). Elsevier.

Moss, Albert A., ed. Computed Tomography, Ultrasound & X-Ray: An Integrated Approach, 1979. Goldberg, Henry I. (Illus.). 574p. 1979. 68.75x (ISBN 0-89352-055-1). Masson Pub.

Moss, Brian. The Ecology of Fresh Waters. 360p. 1980. pap. 32.95x (ISBN 0-470-26942-1). Halsted Pr.

Moss, C. N. The Wreck of the Pied Piper. (Pathfinder Ser.). (Illus.). (gr. 2-6). 1979. pap. 2.95 o.p. (ISBN 0-310-37831-1). Zondervan.

Moss, Donald, tr. see Straus, Erwin.

Moss, Elaine. From Morn to Midnight. LC 77-2548. (Illus.). (gr. k-3). 1977. 8.95i (ISBN 0-690-01393-0, TYC-J); PLB 8.79 o.p. (ISBN 0-685-85787-5). Har-Row.

Moss, Ezra H. Flora of Alberta. LC 60-20369. 1959. student ed. 15.00x o.p. (ISBN 0-8020-5236-3). U of Toronto Pr.

Moss, Frank, ed. The Lore of Sportfishing. 1976. 29.95 o.p. (ISBN 0-517-52109-1). Crown.

Moss, Frank E. & Halamandaris, Val J. Too Old, Too Sick, Too Bad: Nursing Homes in America. LC 77-72515. 326p. 1977. 30.00 (ISBN 0-912862-43-2). Aspen Systems.

Moss, Gordon E. Illness, Immunity & Social Interaction. LC 80-22080. 298p. 1983. Repr. of 1973 ed. text ed. 22.95 (ISBN 0-89874-266-8). Krieger.

Moss, Henry S. Birth of the Middle Ages: 395-814. (Illus.). 1935. pap. 6.95x (ISBN 0-19-500260-1). Oxford U Pr.

Moss, Hilary see Marton, L.

Moss, Howard. Buried City. LC 74-77853. 1975. 6.95 (ISBN 0-689-10626-2); pap. 5.95 (ISBN 0-689-11293-9). Atheneum.

Moss, Howard & Gorey, Edward. Instant Lives. 1976. pap. 1.95 o.p. (ISBN 0-380-00812-2, 30866). Avon.

Moss, Howard, jt. auth. see Kagan, Jerome.

Moss, Howard, ed. The Poet's Story. 1977. pap. 6.95 (ISBN 0-671-23082-4, Touchstone Bks). S&S.

Moss, Howard A., ed. Early Intervention Programs for Infants. LC 82-15608. (Prevention in Human Services Ser.: Vol. 1, No. 4). 176p. 1982. text ed. 20.00 (ISBN 0-917724-54-2, B54). Haworth Pr.

Moss, Joanna. The Lome Conventions & Their Implications for the United States. Replica ed. 225p. 1982. softcover 19.50 (ISBN 0-86531-935-9). Westview.

Moss, John. Introduction to Data Processing. 1978. 20.00 (ISBN 0-905897-25-0). State Mutual Bk.

Moss, John R., et al. Establishing a Teaching Program for Learning Disabled College Students. (Illus.). 1982. pap. 16.95 o.p. (ISBN 0-937660-07-8). PIP.

Moss, Leonard. Arthur Miller. rev. ed. (United States Author Ser.). 1980. lib. bdg. 10.95 (ISBN 0-8057-7311-8, Twayne). G K Hall.

Moss, Lowell, ed. see McQueen, Iris.

Moss, Lydia & Conway, Madeleine. Gourmet to Go: The New York Guide to Dining out at Home. 290p. (Orig.). 1982. pap. 5.95 (ISBN 0-9609862-0-0). MC Prods.

Moss, Matthew, tr. see O'Maolmorda, Sheila.

Moss, Michael, jt. auth. see Green, Edwin.

Moss, Mitchell L. Telecommunications & Productivity. 416p. 1980. text ed. 39.50 (ISBN 0-201-04649-0). A-W.

Moss, Morris H. & Cashin, James A. Schaum's Outline of Tax Accounting. (Orig.). 1979. pap. 6.95 (ISBN 0-07-043470-0, SP). McGraw.

Moss, N. Henry & Mayer, Jean, eds. Food & Nutrition in Health & Disease. (Annals of the New York Academy of Sciences: Vol. 300). 474p. 1977. 42.00x (ISBN 0-89072-046-0). NY Acad Sci.

Moss, Orlando. Complete Handbook for Teaching Small Vocal Ensembles. (Illus.). 1978. 13.95 o.p. (ISBN 0-13-161273-5, Parker). P-H.

Moss, P. D., jt. auth. see Higgins, C. S.

Moss, Peter, jt. ed. see Mallik, David.

Moss, R., jt. auth. see Porter, B.

Moss, R. L., jt. auth. see Pope, D.

Moss, Ralph W., jt. auth. see Randolph, Theron G.

Moss, Robert & De Borchgrave, Arnaud. Monimbo. 1983. 16.50 (ISBN 0-671-43541-8). S&S.

Moss, Robert A., jt. auth. see Jones, Maitland.

Moss, Robert A., jt. auth. see Tiffany, James R.

Moss, Robert A., jt. ed. see Jones, Maitland, Jr.

Moss, Robert A., Jr. & Jones, Maitland, Jr. Carbenes, Vol. 2. LC 80-11836. (Reactive Intermediates in Organic Chemistry Ser.). 390p. 1983. Repr. of 1975 ed. lib. bdg. write for info. (ISBN 0-89874-160-2). Krieger.

Moss, Robert A., Jr. & Jones, Maitland, eds. Carbenes, Vol. 1. LC 80-11836. 368p. 1983. Repr. of 1973 ed. lib. bdg. write for info. (ISBN 0-89874-216-1). Krieger.

Moss, Stirling. How to Watch Motor Racing. 1976. 7.95 o.p. (ISBN 0-396-07275-5). Dodd.

Moss, Sylvia, jt. auth. see Tubbs, Stewart L.

Moss, T. S., jt. auth. see Balkanski, M.

Moss, T. S., jt. auth. see Keller, S. P.

Moss, T. S. & Wolfe, W. L., eds. Infrared Physics. 1976. text ed. 50.00 (ISBN 0-08-020880-0). Pergamon.

Moss, T. S., jt. ed. see Hilsum, C.

Moss, T. S., jt. ed. see Paul, W.

Moss, T. S., ed. see U. S. Specialty Group on Infrared Detectors.

Moss, Thelma. The Probability of the Impossible: Scientific Discoveries & Exploration in the Psychic World. 1975. pap. 8.95 (ISBN 0-452-25419-1, Z5419, Plume). NAL.

Moss, Thomas H. & Sills, David L., eds. The Three Mile Island Nuclear Accident: Lessons & Implications, Vol. 365. 343p. 1981. 68.00 (ISBN 0-89766-115-X). NY Acad Sci.

Moss, Thylias. Hosiery Seams on a Bowlegged Woman. 52p. (Orig.). 1983. pap. 4.50 (ISBN 0-914946-33-1). Cleveland St Univ Poetry Ctr.

Moss, W. D. Radar Watchkeeping: For the Professional Seaman. 2nd ed. (Illus.). 128p. 1973. 12.00x o.p. (ISBN 0-8464-0777-9). Beekman Pubs.

Moss, Walter, jt. auth. see Goff, Richard.

Moss, William T., et al. Radiation Oncology: Rationale, Technique, Results. 5th ed. LC 79-14367. (Illus.). 660p. 1979. text ed. 64.50 (ISBN 0-8016-3556-X). Mosby.

Mossavar-Rahmani, Bijan & Mossavar-Rahmani, Sharmir B. OPEC & Natural Gas Trade: Prospects & Problems. (Special Study in International Economics & Business). 175p. 1983. lib. bdg. 22.50X (ISBN 0-86531-354-7). Westview.

Mossavar-Rahmani, Sharmir B., jt. auth. see Mossavar-Rahmani, Bijan.

Mossberg, Howard E., jt. auth. see Rosser, James M.
Mosse, Claude. Athens in Decline 404-86 B. C. Stewart, Jean, tr. (Illus.). 1973. 24.00 o.p. (ISBN 0-7100-7649-5). Routledge & Kegan.
Mosse, G. L. Calvinism: Authoritarian or Democratic? 25p. 1957. pap. 1.50 o.p. (ISBN 0-03-009215-9). Krieger.
Mosse, George L. The Crisis of German Ideology: Intellectual Origins of the Third Reich. LC 78-19126. viii, 373p. 1981. Repr. of 1964 ed. 27.50x (ISBN 0-86527-036-8). Fertig.
--Crisis of German Ideology: Intellectual Origins of the Third Reich. (Orig.). 1964. pap. 3.95 o.p. (ISBN 0-448-00173-X, G&D). Putnam Pub Group.
--Masses & Man: Nationalist & Fascist Perceptions of Reality. LC 80-15399. xi, 362p. 1980. 32.50 (ISBN 0-86527-334-0). Fertig.
--Toward the Final Solution: A History of European Racism. LC 77-24356. (Illus.). 1980. pap. 4.95i o.p. (ISBN 0-06-090756-8, CN 756, CN). Har-Row.
Mosse, George L., ed. Nazi Culture. (Illus.). 1968. pap. 4.95 o.p. (ISBN 0-448-00187-X, G&D). Putnam Pub Group.
Mosse, W. E. Liberal Europe: The Age of Bourgeois Realism, 1848-1875. (Library of European Civilization). (Illus.). 180p. 1974. 10.00 o.s.i. (ISBN 0-500-32032-2). Transatlantic.
Mossi, John P. Modern Liturgy Handbook: A Study & Planning Guide for Worship. LC 76-12648. 240p. 1976. pap. 7.95 o.p. (ISBN 0-8091-1952-8). Paulist Pr.
Mossin, Jan. The Economic Efficiency of Financial Markets. 176p. 1977. 21.95 (ISBN 0-669-01004-9). Lexington Bks.
Mossiv, Jan, jt. ed. see Borch, C.
Mossman, Frank. Logistics Systems Analysis. rev. ed. 375p. 1977. pap. text ed. 14.75 (ISBN 0-8191-0360-8). U Pr of Amer.
Mossman, Frank H., et al. Financial Dimensions of Marketing Management. LC 77-14990. (Wiley Series on Marketing Management). 1978. 32.95 o.s.i. (ISBN 0-471-03376-6). Wiley.
Mossman, Harland W. & Duke, Kenneth L. Comparative Morphology of the Mammalian Ovary. LC 72-143765. (Illus.). 492p. 1973. 35.00 (ISBN 0-299-05930-8, 593); pap. 12.50 (ISBN 0-299-05934-0). U of Wis Pr.
Mossman, Jennifer. New Pseudonyms & Nicknames--Supplements: Supplements to Pseudonyms & Nicknames Dictionary, 2 vols. 1981. 75.00x set, softbound (ISBN 0-8103-0548-8). Gale.
Mossman, Jennifer, ed. Pseudonyms & Nicknames Dictionary. rev. 2nd ed. LC 80-13274. 980p. 1982. 145.00x (ISBN 0-8103-0547-X). Gale.
--Pseudonyms & Nicknames Dictionary. LC 80-13274. 700p. 1980. 70.00 o.p. (ISBN 0-8103-0549-6). Gale.
Mossner, Ernest C. The Life of David Hume. 2nd ed. LC 78-41137. 1980. 59.00x (ISBN 0-19-824381-2). Oxford U Pr.
Mosston, Muska. Developmental Movement. 1965. pap. text ed. 13.95 spiral bdg. (ISBN 0-675-09932-3). Merrill.
--Teaching Physical Education. 2nd ed. (Illus.). 256p. 1981. pap. text ed. 12.95 (ISBN 0-675-08036-3). Merrill.
Most, Bernard. If the Dinosaurs Came Back. LC 77-23911. (Illus.). (ps-2). 1978. 7.95 (ISBN 0-15-238020-5, HJ). HarBraceJ.
--There's an Ant in Anthony. LC 79-23089. (Illus.). 32p. (gr. k-3). 1980. 8.75 (ISBN 0-688-22226-9); PLB 8.40 (ISBN 0-688-32226-3). Morrow.
--There's an Ape Behind the Drape. LC 80-24280. (Illus.). 32p. (gr. k-3). 1981. 7.95 (ISBN 0-688-00380-X); PLB 7.63 (ISBN 0-688-00381-8). Morrow.
Most, Glenn W. & Stowe, William W., eds. The Poetics of Murder: Detective Fiction & Literary Theory. 416p. cloth 22.95 (ISBN 0-15-172280-3). HarBraceJ.
--The Poetics of Murder: Detective Fiction & Literary Theory. 416p. pap. 9.95 (ISBN 0-15-672312-3, Harv). HarBraceJ.
Mostawski, A., jt. auth. see Kuratowski, K.
Mostecky, Vaclav, ed. see Harvard Law School Library.
Mosteller, F., jt. auth. see Hoaglin, David C.
Mosteller, F. R. & Rourke, Robert E. Sturdy Statistics: Nonparametrics & Order Statistics. LC 70-184162. 1973. text ed. 23.95 (ISBN 0-201-04868-X). A-W.
Mosteller, Frederick & Tukey, John W. Data Analysis & Regression: A Second Course in Statistics. LC 76-15465. (Behavioral Science: Quantitative Methods). 1977. text ed. 27.95 (ISBN 0-201-04854-X). A-W.
Moster, Mary B. When Mom Goes to Work. LC 19-906. 180p. 1980. text ed. 8.95 (ISBN 0-8024-9442-0). Moody.
Moster, Mary Beth. Living with Cancer. LC 78-23665. 1979. 3.95 (ISBN 0-8024-4947-6). Moody.
Moster, Mary Beth, jt. auth. see Collins, Nell.
Mostert, Noel. Supership. (Illus.). 364p. 1976. pap. 2.50 o.p. (ISBN 0-446-81840-2). Warner Bks.
Mostofi, F. K. Histological Typing of Testis Tumours. (World Health Organization: International Histological Classification of Tumours Ser.). (Illus.). 1976. pap. text ed. 62.50 (ISBN 92-4-176016-8, 70-1-016-20); with slides 197.50 (ISBN 0-89189-129-3, 70-1-016-00). Am Soc Clinical.
Mostofi, F. K., jt. ed. see Helwig, Elson B.
Mostowski, Andrej. Sentences Undecidable in Formalized Arithmetic: An Exposition of the Theory of Kurt Godel. LC 82-11886. (Studies in Logic & the Foundations of Mathematics). viii, 117p. 1982. Repr. of 1952 ed. lib. bdg. 25.00x (ISBN 0-313-23151-6, MOSU). Greenwood.
Mostowski, J. & Stark, M. Introduction to Higher Algebra. 1964. inquire for price (ISBN 0-08-010152-6). Pergamon.
Mostwin, Danuta. Social Dimension of Family Treatment. LC 79-92201. (Illus.). 245p. 1980. pap. 12.95x (ISBN 0-87101-081-X, CBF-083-C). Natl Assn Soc Wkrs.
--The Transplanted Family: A Study of Social Adustment of the Polish Immigrant Family to the United States After the Second World War. Cordasco, Francesco, ed. LC 80-881. (American Ethnic Groups Ser.). 1981. lib. bdg. 35.00x (ISBN 0-405-13442-8). Ayer Co.
Mostyn, David. Cars. LC 80-52534. (Starters Ser.). PLB 8.00 (ISBN 0-382-06484-4). Silver.
--Train. LC 1-52495. (Srarters Ser.). PLB 8.00 (ISBN 0-382-06487-9). Silver.
Mostyn, Trevor, ed. Bahrain: A Middle East Economic Digest Guide. (Illus.). 240p. 1983. pap. write for info. (ISBN 0-7103-0030-1, Kegan Paul). Routledge & Kegan.
--Jordan: A Middle East Economic Digest Guide. 240p. (Orig.). 1983. pap. write for info. (ISBN 0-7103-0029-8, Kegan Paul). Routledge & Kegan.
--United Arab Emirates: A Middle East Economic Digest Guide. 324p. (Orig.). 1982. pap. 15.00 (ISBN 0-7103-0014-X, Kegan Paul). Routledge & Kegan.
Mota, A. Teixeira da see Da Mota, A. Teixeira.
Motamen, Homa. Expenditure of Oil Revenue: An Optimal Control Approach with Application to the Iranian Economy. LC 29-20567. 1979. 32.50x (ISBN 0-312-27605-2). St Martin.
Motchenbacher, C. D. & Fitchen, F. C. Low-Noise Electronic Design. LC 72-8713. 1973. 44.95x (ISBN 0-471-61950-7, Pub. by Wiley-Interscience). Wiley.
Mother Goose. Mother Goose in Hieroglyphics. Bleiler, E. F., ed. pap. 1.95 (ISBN 0-486-20745-5). Dover.
Mother Immaculata. Consecration & the Spirit of Carmel. LC 82-72203. (Living Meditation & Prayerbook ser.). (Illus.). 270p. (Orig.). 1983. pap. text ed. 6.00 (ISBN 0-932406-08-4). AFC.
Mother Jones. Mother Jones Speaks: Collected Writings & Speeches. Foner, Philip S., ed. 650p. 1983. lib. bdg. 35.00 (ISBN 0-913460-88-5); pap. 14.95 (ISBN 0-913460-89-3). Monad Pr.
Mother Mary & Archimandrite Kallistos Ware, trs. The Festal Menaion. 248p. 1977. pap. 10.95 (ISBN 0-571-11137-8). Faber & Faber.
Mother Teresa. A Gift for God: Prayers & Meditations. LC 76-351371. 96p. 1980. 7.95i (ISBN 0-06-068233-7). Har-Row.
--Words to Love By. LC 82-73373. (Illus.). 80p. (Orig.). 1983. pap. 4.95 (ISBN 0-87793-261-1). Ave Maria.
Mother Teresa of Calcutta. The Love of Christ: Spiritual Counsels. LC 81-48216. 128p. 1982. 7.64i (ISBN 0-06-068229-9, HarpR). Har-Row.
Motherwell, Robert, ed. The Dada Painters & Poets: An Anthology. 2nd ed. (Documents of 20th Century Art). 1981. lib. bdg. 40.00 (ISBN 0-8057-9951-6, Twayne). G K Hall.
Motherwell, William. Minstrelsy Ancient & Modern. LC 68-24477. 1968. Repr. of 1873 ed. 37.00x (ISBN 0-8103-3415-1). Gale.
Motil, John M. Digital System Fundamentals. Truxal, J. G. & Rohrer, R., eds. (Electronic Systems Ser.). (Illus.). 416p. 1972. 37.50 (ISBN 0-07-043515-4, C); 3.95 o.p. instr's manual (ISBN 0-07-043516-2). McGraw.
Motion, Andrew. Philip Larkin. (Contemporary Writers Ser.). 1982. pap. 4.25 (ISBN 0-416-32270-0). Methuen Inc.
--The Pleasure Steamers. (Poetry Ser.). 58p. 1978. pap. text ed. 6.25x (ISBN 0-85635-247-0, Pub. by Carcanet New Pr England). Humanities.
Motion Picture Producers & Distributors of America, jt. auth. see National Conference on Motion Pictures, New York, 1929.
Motley. Orientations to Language & Communication. Applbaum, Ronald & Hart, Roderick, eds. LC 77-12329. (MODCOM - Modules in Speech Communication). 1978. pap. text ed. 2.75 (ISBN 0-574-22534-X, 13-5534). SRA.
Motley, Marion B. A. E.'s Paintings. (Collected Edition of the Writings of G. W. Russell II Ser.: No. 8). text ed. write for info (ISBN 0-391-01201-0). Humanities.
Motley, Wilma E. Ethics, Jurisprudence & History for the Dental Hygienist. 3rd ed. LC 82-23926. (Illus.). 200p. 1983. text ed. price not set (ISBN 0-8121-0870-1). Lea & Febiger.
Motorola Inc. Microprocessor Applications Manual. 1975. 53.50 (ISBN 0-07-043527-8, P&RB). McGraw.
Motsinger, Marilyn, ed. see Thompson, Bruce.
Mott, Charles H. Accounting & Financial Management for Construction. LC 81-10502. (Construction Management & Engineering Ser.). 214p. 1981. 24.95 (ISBN 0-471-07959-6, Pub. by Wiley-Interscience). Wiley.
Mott, Frank L. A History of American Magazines, 5 vols. Incl. Vol. 1. 1741-1850. 848p. 1930. o.s.i (ISBN 0-674-39550-6); Vol. 2. 1850-1865. (Illus.). 608p. 1938. 27.50x (ISBN 0-674-39551-4); Vol. 3. 1865-1885. (Illus.). 649p. 1938. 27.50x (ISBN 0-674-39552-2); Vol. 4. 1885-1905. (Illus.). 858p. 1957. o.si. (ISBN 0-674-39553-0); Vol. 5. Sketches of 21 Magazines, 1905-1930. (Illus.). 595p. 1968. o.s.i (ISBN 0-674-39554-9). LC 39-2823 (Belknap Pr). 27.50x ea. Harvard U Pr.
Mott, George F. & Lambert, Richard D., eds. Urban Change & the Planning Syndrome. new ed. LC 72-93250. (Annals of the American Academy of Political & Social Science: No. 405). 250p. 1973. 15.00 (ISBN 0-87761-158-0, 87761); pap. 7.95 (ISBN 0-87761-157-2). Am Acad Pol Soc Sci.
Mott, Kenneth F. The Supreme Court & the Living Constitution. LC 80-8140. 282p. 1981. lib. bdg. 22.25 (ISBN 0-8191-1528-2); pap. text ed. 11.50 (ISBN 0-8191-1529-0). U Pr of Amer.
Mott, Paul, et al. From Farm to Factory: The Development of Modern Society. LC 72-87429. 1973. pap. text ed. 6.95 (ISBN 0-675-09045-8). Merrill.
--Sociological Perspectives: Understanding Human Society. LC 72-87428. 1973. pap. text ed. 6.95 (ISBN 0-675-09044-X). Merrill.
Mott, Robert L. Applied Fluid Mechanics. 2nd ed. (Mechanical Technology Ser.). 1979. text ed. 23.95 (ISBN 0-675-08305-2). Additional supplements may be obtained from publisher. Merrill.
--Applied Strength of Materials. (Illus.). 1978. ref. 22.95 (ISBN 0-13-043299-7). P-H.
Mott, Rodney L. Due Process of Law. LC 72-165604. (American Constitutional & Legal History Ser.). 702p. 1973. Repr. of 1926 ed. lib. bdg. 85.00 (ISBN 0-306-70225-8). Da Capo.
Mott, Stephen C. Biblical Ethics & Social Change. 1982. 17.95 (ISBN 0-19-502947-X); pap. 6.95x (ISBN 0-19-502948-8). Oxford U Pr.
Motta, Dick, jt. auth. see Isaacs, Neil D.
Motta, M. & Zanishi, M., eds. Pitiary Hormones & Related Peptides. (Serono Symposium: No. 49). 1982. 59.50 (ISBN 0-12-509160-5). Acad Pr.
Motta, Marcella, ed. Endocrine Functions of the Brain. (Comprehensive Endocrinology Ser.). 493p. 1980. text ed. 59.50 (ISBN 0-89004-343-4). Raven.
Motta, Marcelo, jt. auth. see Crowley, Aleister.
Mottershead, Allen. Introduction to Electricity & Electronics: Conventional Current. LC 81-10472. 674p. 1982. 25.95x (ISBN 0-471-05751-7); avail. solutions manual. Wiley.
Mottley, Harry E., Jr., jt. auth. see Norbert, Enrick.
Motto, Sytha. More Than Conquerers: Makers of History. (Illus.). 228p. 1980. 15.00 (ISBN 0-913270-88-1); ltd. signed 22.50 (ISBN 0-913270-94-6). Sunstone Pr.
Mottram, Maxine & McDonald, Susan. Preparacion para el Examen de la Licencia En Cosmetologia. LC 81-7920. Date not set. pap. 6.95 cancelled (ISBN 0-668-05306-2, 5306). Arco. Postponed.
Mott-Smith, Geoffrey, jt. auth. see Morehead, Albert H.
Motulsky, A., ed. Birth Defects. (Abstracts). 1974. 22.00 (ISBN 0-444-15060-9). Elsevier.
Motulsky, A., et al, eds. Birth Defects. (Proceedings). 1974. 88.50 (ISBN 0-444-15072-2). Elsevier.
Motulsky, Arno G., jt. ed. see Goodman, Richard M.
Motus, Cecile L. Hiligaynon Lessons. McKaughan, Howard P., ed. (PALI Language Texts: Philippines). (Orig.). 1971. pap. text ed. 7.00x o.p. (ISBN 0-87022-546-4). UH Pr.
Motyl, Alexander, jt. auth. see Karatnycky, Adrian.
Motz, Lloyd, ed. Rediscovery of the Earth. 288p. 1980. text ed. 35.00 o.p. (ISBN 0-442-26779-7). Van Nos Reinhold.
Mouat, Lucia. Back to Business: A Woman's Guide to Reentering the Job Market. 1980. pap. 1.95 o.p. (ISBN 0-451-09304-6, J9304, Sig). NAL.
Moudgal, N. R. Gonadotropins & Gonadal Function. 1974. 45.50 (ISBN 0-12-508850-7). Acad Pr.
Moudud, Hasna J. Women in China. (Illus.). 120p. 1980. text ed. 15.00x (ISBN 0-7069-1084-2, Pub. by Vikas India). Advent NY.
Moudy, James M., jt. auth. see Clark, Joseph A.
Mouffe, Barbara S., ed. see Hawthorne, Nathaniel.
Mouillesseaux, Harold R. Ethan Allen, Gunmaker: His Partners, Patents & Firearms. LC 72-94038. (Illus.). 184p. 1973. 19.95 (ISBN 0-919316-68-9). Museum Restoration.
Moul, Keith R. Theodore Roethke's Career: An Annotated Bibliography. 1977. lib. bdg. 25.00 (ISBN 0-8161-7892-5, Hall Reference). G K Hall.
Moulaert, Frank & Salinas, Wilson. Regional Analysis & the New International Division of Labor. (Studies in Applied Regional Science). 1982. lib. bdg. 24.00 (ISBN 0-89838-107-X). Kluwer-Nijhoff.
Mould, Elmer K., et al. Essentials of Bible History. 3rd ed. (Illus.). 1966. 30.50 (ISBN 0-471-07017-3). Wiley.
Moulder, F. V. Japan, China & the Modern World Economy. LC 76-2230. (Illus.). 1977. 29.95 (ISBN 0-521-21174-3); pap. 8.95x (ISBN 0-521-29736-2). Cambridge U Pr.
Moule, Charles F. Essays in New Testment Interpretation. LC 81-10141. (Illus.). 260p. 1982. 34.50 (ISBN 0-521-23783-1). Cambridge U Pr.
--Idiom Book of New Testament Greek. 2nd ed. 1959. 39.50 (ISBN 0-521-05774-4); pap. text ed. 11.95 (ISBN 0-521-09237-X). Cambridge U Pr.
--The Origin of Christology. LC 76-11087. 1977. 27.95 (ISBN 0-521-21290-1); pap. 8.95 (ISBN 0-521-29363-4). Cambridge U Pr.
Moule, H. C. Romans. 1982. lib. bdg. 16.25 (ISBN 0-86524-086-8, 4502). Klock & Klock.
Moule, H. C. & Orr, J. The Resurrection of Christ. 1980. 20.00 (ISBN 0-86524-062-0, 9506). Klock & Klock.
Moule, H. C. G. Colossian & Philemon Studies. 1981. 12.00 (ISBN 0-86524-052-3, 7106). Klock & Klock.
Moullade, M. & Nairn, A. E., eds. The Phanerozoic Geology of the World: The Mesozoic, Vol. 2A. 1978. 102.25 (ISBN 0-444-41671-4). Elsevier.
Moulton, D., jt. auth. see Iskandar, A.
Moulton, Eugene R. & Held, McDonald W. Communication: A Creative Process. LC 76-1043. 1976. pap. text ed. 10.95x o.p. (ISBN 0-8087-1378-7). Burgess.
Moulton, Gary E. Atlas of the Lewis & Clark Expedition. LC 82-675167. (Journals of the Lewis & Clark Expedition Ser.). 132p. 1982. 80.00x (ISBN 0-8032-2861-9). U of Nebr Pr.
Moulton, Gene. Conducting Fire Inspections: A Guidebook for Field Use. LC 82-61920. 302p. 1982. 18.00 (ISBN 0-87765-230-9, SPP-75). Natl Fire Prot.
Moulton, H. J. Houdini's History of Magic in Boston, 1792-1915. (Illus.). 176p. 1983. 35.00 (ISBN 0-916638-27-8). Meyerbooks.
Moulton, Harland B. From Superiority to Parity: The United States and the Strategic Arms Race, 1961-1971. LC 79-140920. 1973. lib. bdg. 27.50 (ISBN 0-8371-5822-2, MNS/). Greenwood.
Moulton, Harold G. Can Inflation Be Controlled. 1958. 6.95 (ISBN 0-910136-02-5). Anderson Kramer.
--Reparation Plan. Repr. of 1924 ed. lib. bdg. 16.00x (ISBN 0-8371-4290-3, MORP). Greenwood.
Moulton, Harold G., et al. The Recovery Problem in the United States. LC 73-176337. (FDR & the Era of the New Deal Ser.). (Illus.). 1972. Repr. lib. bdg. 85.00 (ISBN 0-306-70421-8). Da Capo.
Moulton, Harold K., ed. The Analytical Greek Lexicon Revised. rev. ed. 1978. 15.95 (ISBN 0-310-20280-9). Zondervan.
Moulton, Jack, ed. Tumors in Domestic Animals. 2nd ed. 1978. 52.50x (ISBN 0-520-02386-2). U of Cal Pr.
Moulton, Janice & Robinson, George M. Organization of Language. LC 80-19052. 400p. 1981. 47.50 (ISBN 0-521-23129-9); pap. 15.95 (ISBN 0-521-29851-2). Cambridge U Pr.
Moulton, LeArta. The Gluten Book. rev. ed. (Illus.). 165p. (Orig.). 1981. pap. 6.95 (ISBN 0-935596-11-9). Gluten Co.
--Nature's Medicine Chest, Set 1. 96p. 1974. 5.00 (ISBN 0-935596-04-6). Gluten Co.
Moulton, Nancy. Defiant Destiny. 368p. 1982. pap. 2.95 (ISBN 0-380-81430-7, 81430). Avon.
Moulton, Peter. Foundation of Programming through BASIC. LC 78-21569. 1979. text ed. 19.95 (ISBN 0-471-03311-1); tchrs. manual avail. (ISBN 0-471-05414-3). Wiley.
Moulton, Ron. Kites. (Illus.). 1979. 24.95 o.p. (ISBN 0-7207-0829-X). Transatlantic.
Moulton, Ron G. Control Line Manual. (Illus.). 216p. 1970. 7.50x o.p. (ISBN 0-85242-113-3). Intl Pubns Serv.
--Flying Scale Models. 1956. 7.25x o.p. (ISBN 0-85344-070-0). Intl Pubns Serv.
Mouly, G. J. Test Items in Education. 1962. pap. 5.95 (ISBN 0-07-043540-5, SP). McGraw.
Mounce, Earl W., jt. auth. see Dawson, Townes L.
Mounce, Robert. A Living Hope: A Commentary on 1 & 2 Peter. 1982. pap. 4.95 (ISBN 0-8028-1915-X). Eerdmans.
Mound, L. A. & Halsey, S. H. Whitefly of the World: A Systematic Catalogue of the Aleyrodidoe (Homoptera) with Host Plant & Natural Enemy Data. 1978. 53.95 (ISBN 0-471-99634-3, Pub. by Wiley-Interscience). Wiley.
Mounier, Jean J. On the Influence Attributed to Philosophers, Free-Masons, & to the Illuminati, on the Revolution of France. LC 74-13148. 280p. (Eng.). 1974. Repr. of 1801 ed. 33.00x (ISBN 0-8201-1135-X). Schol Facsimiles.
Mount, Ellis. University Science & Engineering Libraries. LC 74-34562. (Contributions in Librarianship & Information Science: No. 15). (Illus.). 214p. 1975. lib. bdg. 25.00 (ISBN 0-8371-7955-6, MSE/). Greenwood.
Mount, Ellis, ed. Cataloging & Indexing in Sci-Tech Libraries. (Science & Technology Libraries: Vol. 2, No. 3). 92p. 1982. pap. text ed. 15.00 (ISBN 0-86656-204-4, B204). Haworth Pr.
--Document Delivery for Sci-Tech Libraries. (Science & Technology Libraries: Vol. 2, No. 4). 133p. 1982. pap. text ed. 15.00 (ISBN 0-86656-200-1, B200). Haworth Pr.
--Micrographs in Sci-Tech Libraries. LC 82-23435. (Science & Technology Libraries, Vol. 3, No. 3). 73p. 1983. text ed. 20.00 (ISBN 0-86656-218-4, B218). Haworth Pr.
--Networking in Sci-Tech Libraries & Information Centers. (Science & Technology Libraries: Vol 1, No. 2). 125p. 1981. pap. text ed. 15.00 (ISBN 0-917724-72-0, B72). Haworth Pr.

--Online vs. Manual Searching in Sci-Tech Libraries. (Science & Technology Libraries: Vol. 3, No. 1). 89p. 1982. pap. text ed. 15.00 (ISBN 0-86656-203-6, B203). Haworth Pr.
--Planning for Online Search Services in Sci-Tech Libraries. (Science & Technology Libraries: Vol. 1, No. 1). 149p. (Orig.). 1981. pap. text ed. 15.00 (ISBN 0-917724-73-9, B73). Haworth Pr.
--Role of Translations in Sci-Tech Libraries. LC 82-23353. (Science & Technology Libraries: Vol. 3, No. 2). 96p. 1983. 20.00 (ISBN 0-86656-213-3). Haworth Pr.
--Scientific & Technical Libraries in the Seventies: A Guide to Information Sources. (Books, Publishing & Libraries Information Guide Ser.: Vol. 4). 300p. 1980. 42.00x (ISBN 0-8103-1483-5). Gale.
--Training of Sci-Tech Librarians & Library Users. LC 81-6975. (Science & Technology Libraries: Vol. 1, No. 3). 78p. (Orig.). 1981. pap. text ed. 15.00 (ISBN 0-917724-75-5, B75). Haworth Pr.

Mount, L. E., jt. ed. see Monteith, J. L.

Mount, Laurence E. Energy Metabolism. LC 80-40265. (Studies in the Agricultural & Food Sciences). (Illus.). 416p. 1980. text ed. 86.95 (ISBN 0-408-10641-7). Butterworth.

Mount, M. S. & Lacy, George, eds. Phytopathogenic Prolaryotes, Vol. I. LC 82-13954. 488p. 1982. 59.50 (ISBN 0-12-509001-3); subscription 51.00. Acad Pr.

Mount, Marianne & Shea, Victoria. How to Arrange the Environment to Stimulate and Teach Pre-Language Skills in the Severley Handicapped. 1982. pap. 3.95 (ISBN 0-686-84109-3). H & H Ent.
--How to Recognize & Assess Pre-Language Skills in the Severely Handicapped. 1982. pap. 3.95 (ISBN 0-89079-070-1). H & H Ent.

Mount, Mark S. & Lacy, George. Phytopathogenic Prokaryotes, Vol. II. 448p. 1982. 57.00 (ISBN 0-12-509002-1). Acad Pr.

Mountain, Lee. Dragon Don & John: Dragon Donaldo y Juan. Gunning, Monica, tr. (Storybooks for Beginners Ser.: Bk. 2). (Illus.). 15p. (Eng. & Span.). 1980. pap. 12.00 set (ISBN 0-89061-213-7, 432). Jamestown Pubs.
--Dragon Don: Dragon Donaldo. Gunning, Monica, tr. (Storybooks for Beginners Ser.: Bk. 1). (Illus.). 15p. 1980. pap. 12.00 set (ISBN 0-89061-212-9, 432). Jamestown Pubs.
--Jungle Trip. (Attention Span Stories Ser). (Illus.). 48p. (Orig.). (gr. 6-10). 1978. pap. text ed. 4.00x (ISBN 0-89061-148-3, 584). Jamestown Pubs.
--Sports Trip. (Attention Span Stories Ser). (Illus.). 48p. (Orig.). (gr. 2-3). 1978. pap. text ed. 4.00x (ISBN 0-89061-147-5, 583). Jamestown Pubs.
--Star Trip. (Attention Span Stories Ser). (Illus.). 48p. (Orig.). (gr. 2-3). 1978. pap. text ed. 4.00x (ISBN 0-89061-149-1, 585). Jamestown Pubs.
--Survival Trip. (Attention Span Stories Ser). (Illus.). 48p. (Orig.). (gr. 2-3). 1978. pap. text ed. 4.00x (ISBN 0-89061-146-7, 582). Jamestown Pubs.
--Time Trip. (Attention Span Ser). (Illus.). 48p. (Orig.). (gr. 2-3). 1978. pap. text ed. 4.00x (ISBN 0-89061-145-9, 581). Jamestown Pubs.
--Uncle Sam & the Flag. LC 77-83633. (Illus.). (gr. 2-3). 1978. PLB 6.75x (ISBN 0-87783-145-9); pap. 2.95 (ISBN 0-87783-148-3); cassette 5.95x (ISBN 0-87783-232-3). Oddo.

Mountain, Lee H. Early Reading Instruction: How to Teach Reading Before First Grade. (Illus.). 155p. (Orig.). 1981. pap. text ed. 10.00x (ISBN 0-89061-218-8, 755S). Jamestown Pubs.

Mountaingrove, Jean, ed. see Mountaingrove, Ruth I.

Mountaingrove, Ruth. The Turned on Woman Songbook. (Illus.). 1975. pap. 4.50 (ISBN 0-686-23798-6). New Woman.

Mountaingrove, Ruth I. For Those Who Cannot Sleep. Mountaingrove, Jean, ed. (Illus.). 1977. pap. 5.50 (ISBN 0-686-21884-1). New Woman.

Mountcastle, Vernon B. Medical Physiology, 2 vols. 14th ed. LC 79-25943. (Illus.). 1980. Set. 64.50 (ISBN 0-8016-3560-8); Vol. 1. 49.50 (ISBN 0-8016-3562-4); Vol. 2. 44.50 (ISBN 0-8016-3566-7). Mosby.

Mountcastle, Vernon B., jt. auth. see Edelman, Gerald M.

Mountford, A., jt. auth. see MacKay, R.

Mountford, Charles P. Ayers Rock: Its People, Their Beliefs, & Their Art. (Illus.). 1966. 12.00x o.p. (ISBN 0-8248-0053-2, Eastwest Ctr). UH Pr.

Mountford, James. Keele: An Historical Critique. (Illus.). 1972. 20.00x o.p. (ISBN 0-7100-7237-6). Routledge & Kegan.

Mountfort, jt. auth. see Peterson.

Mountfort, William. Plays of William Mountfort. LC 77-21660. 1977. 33.00x (ISBN 0-8201-1292-5). Schol Facsimiles.

Mountjoy, Alan B., ed. The Third World: Problems & Perspectives. (Illus.). 1979. 25.00x (ISBN 0-312-80036-3). St Martin.

Mountjoy, Roberta J. Night Wind. 384p. 1981. 14.95 (ISBN 0-698-11102-8, Coward). Putnam Pub Group.

Mountney, Virginia R., jt. auth. see Squire, Russel.

Moura, Bernard & Smith, Eunice. Better Reading & Spelling Through Phonics. 1960. pap. 2.95 o.p. (ISBN 0-8224-0700-0). Pitman Learning.

Mourad, Leona A. Nursing Care of Adults with Orthopedic Conditions. LC 79-26251. 1980. 28.00x (ISBN 0-471-04677-9, Pub. by Wiley Med). Wiley.

Mourant, A. E., ed. Man & Cattle: Proceedings of a Symposium on Domestication. 1963. 50.00x (ISBN 0-686-98310-6, Pub. by Royal Anthro Ireland). State Mutual Bk.

Mourant, A. E., et al. The Genetics of the Jews. (Research Monographs on Human Population Biology). (Illus.). 1978. text ed. 45.00x (ISBN 0-19-857522-X). Oxford U Pr.

Mourant, John A. & Freund, E. Hans, eds. Problems of Philosophy. 1964. text ed. 21.95x (ISBN 0-02-384560-0). Macmillan.

Moure, Nancy D. William Louis Sonntag: Artist of the Ideal. (Illus.). 157p. 1980. text ed. 35.00 (ISBN 0-686-35887-2); signed ltd. edition 65.00 (ISBN 0-686-37195-X). Goldfield Pub.

Mouret, F., jt. auth. see Jean, B.

Mourey, Gabriel, et al. Art Nouveau Jewelry & Fans. (Illus.). 150p. 1973. pap. 6.00 (ISBN 0-486-22961-0). Dover.

Mourgue, Jacques-Antoine. Essai de Statistique. Repr. of 1801 ed. 14.00 o.p. (ISBN 0-8287-0648-4). Clearwater Pub.

Mourgues, Odette De see De Mourgues, Odette.

Mourier & Winding. Collins Guide to Wildlife in the House & Home. 29.95 (ISBN 0-686-42778-5, Collins Pub England). Greene.

Mourning Dove. Cogewea, the Half-Blood. LC 80-29687. xxx, 302p. 1981. 21.95x (ISBN 0-8032-3069-9); pap. 6.25 (ISBN 0-8032-8110-2, BB 754, Bison). U of Nebr Pr.

Moursund, David. Basic Programming for Computer Literacy. 1978. text ed. 18.95 (ISBN 0-07-043565-0, C); 4.95 o.p. instructor's manual (ISBN 0-07-043566-9). McGraw.
--Calculators in the Classroom. LC 80-22165. 202p. 1981. pap. text ed. 12.95x (ISBN 0-471-08113-2). Wiley.

Moursund, David, ed. see Willis, Jerry.

Moursund, Janet, jt. auth. see Geiwitz, P. James.

Mousalam, Barbara. Gut Level-Heart Level. (Illus.). 1979. pap. 3.95 (ISBN 0-933174-09-8). Wide World-Tetra.

Mouser, Bruce L., ed. Guinea Journals: Journeys into Guinea-Conakry During the Sierra Leone Phase, 1800-1821. LC 79-62896. 1979. pap. text ed. 11.25 (ISBN 0-8191-0713-1). U Pr of Amer.

Mouser, William E., Jr. Walking in Wisdom. 180p. (Orig.). 1983. pap. 5.95 (ISBN 0-87784-846-7). Inter-Varsity.

Moussavi, Fakhreddin, compiled by. Guide to the Hanna Collection & Related Archival Materials at the Hoover Institution on War, Revolution & Peace on the Role of Education in Twentieth-Century Society. (Bibliographical Ser.: No. 64). 250p. 1982. lib. bdg. 19.95 (ISBN 0-8179-2641-0). Hoover Inst Pr.

Mousseli, A. H. Offshore Pipeline Design, Analysis & Methods. 208p. 1981. 42.95x (ISBN 0-87814-156-1). Pennwell Pub.

Mousset-Jones, Pierre, ed. see International Mine Ventilation Congress, 2nd.

Mousset-Jones, Pierre F. Geostatistics. 180p. 1980. 24.75 (ISBN 0-07-043568-5). McGraw.

Moustakas, Clark E. Loneliness & Love. 1972. 8.95 (ISBN 0-13-540252-2, Spec); pap. 3.95 (ISBN 0-13-540245-X, S267, Spec). P-H.

Moustakas, Clark E., ed. The Self: Explorations in Personal Growth. 1974. pap. 5.50xi o.p. (ISBN 0-06-131950-3, TB1950, Torch). Har-Row.

Moutjoy, Roberta J. Night Wind. 512p. 1983. pap. 3.50 (ISBN 0-515-06802-0). Jove Pubns.

Mouton, Boyce. These Two Commandments. (Orig.). 1978. pap. 2.95 o.s.i. (ISBN 0-89900-138-6). College Pr Pub.

Mouton, J. B. The New Guinea Memoirs of Jean Baptiste Octave Mouton. Biskup, Peter, ed. LC 74-76379. (Pacific History Ser.: No. 7). (Illus.). 164p. 1974. 15.00x (ISBN 0-8248-0328-0). UH Pr.

Mouton, Jane S., jt. auth. see Blake, Robert R.

Mouton, R. P., ed. Aminoglycoside Assays: Methods & Clinical Relevance. (International Congress Ser.: No. 482). 1980. 22.00 (ISBN 0-444-90089-6). Elsevier.

Moutonnet De Clairfons, J. J. Les Iles Fortunees. (Utopias in the Enlightenment Ser.). 234p. (Fr.). 1974. Repr. of 1778 ed. lib. bdg. 65.00x o.p. (ISBN 0-8287-0649-2, 032). Clearwater Pub.
--Le Veritable Philanthrope. (Utopias in the Enlightenment Ser.). 167p. (Fr.). 1974. Repr. of 1790 ed. lib. bdg. 50.00x o.p. (ISBN 0-8287-0650-6, 042). Clearwater Pub.

Moutoussamy-Ashe, Jeanne. Daufuskie Island: A Photographic Essay. (Illus.). 168p. 1982. 29.95 (ISBN 0-686-95003-8); pap. 19.95 (ISBN 0-686-99449-3). U of SC Pr.

Moutsopoulos, Evanghelos. Petros Brailas-Armenis. (World Authors Ser.). 1974. lib. bdg. 15.95 (ISBN 0-8057-2170-3, Twayne). G K Hall.

Movius, Hallam L., Jr. Excavation of Abri Pataud, les Eyzies (Dordogne) Stratigraphy. LC 76-52630. (American School of Prehistoric Bulletins: No. 31). (Illus.). 1977. pap. 35.00x (ISBN 0-87365-534-6). Peabody Harvard.

Movvel, Jane. This Paradox Shadow. 112p. 1982. pap. 11.95 (ISBN 0-933180-33-0). Spoon Riv Poetry.

Mow, Anna B. The Secret of Married Love. (Trumpet Bks). 1976. pap. 1.50 o.p. (ISBN 0-87981-054-8). Holman.
--Secret of Married Love. 1976. pap. 1.50 o.s.i. (ISBN 0-89129-190-3). Jove Pubns.
--So Who's Afraid of Birthdays? (Trumpet Bks). 1976. pap. 1.25 o.p. (ISBN 0-87981-053-X). Holman.

Mowat, A. P. Liver Disorders in Childhood. Apley, J., ed. (Postgraduate Pediatric Ser.). 1979. text ed. 49.95 (ISBN 0-407-00163-8). Butterworth.

Mowat, Charles L. Britain Between the Wars: Nineteen Eighteen-Forty. LC 55-5139. 1955. 25.00x (ISBN 0-226-54370-6). U of Chicago Pr.

Mowat, Farley. Dog Who Wouldn't Be. (gr. 6-10). 1970. pap. 1.50 o.s.i. (ISBN 0-515-05617-0, N2333). Jove Pubns.
--The Great Betrayal. 1977. pap. 5.95 (ISBN 0-316-58694-3, Pub. by Atlantic Monthly Pr.). Little.
--Lost in the Barrens. (Illus.). (gr. 7 up). 1956. 11.95 (ISBN 0-316-58638-2, Pub. by Atlantic Monthly Pr). Little.
--Never Cry Wolf. 176p. 1982. pap. 2.50 (ISBN 0-553-13301-2). Bantam.
--People of the Deer. (Orig.). pap. 1.95 o.s.i. (ISBN 0-515-05131-4). Jove Pubns.
--The Serpents Coil. 224p. 1982. pap. 2.95 (ISBN 0-553-20377-0). Bantam.

Mowat, R. B. Europe in the Age of Napoleon. 80p. 1982. Repr. of 1927 ed. lib. bdg. 25.00 (ISBN 0-89987-588-2). Darby Bks.

Mowbray, Albert H., et al. Insurance: Its Theory & Practice in the United States. 6th ed. LC 78-10258. 670p. 1979. Repr. of 1969 ed. lib. bdg. 33.00 (ISBN 0-88275-768-7). Krieger.

Mowbray, Andrew, ed. see Campbell, Archibald.

Mowday, Richard & Steers, Richard. Research in Organizations: Issues & Controversy. LC 78-25809. 1979. pap. text ed. 17.95x (ISBN 0-673-16138-2). Scott F.

Mower, A. Glenn, Jr. The United States, the United Nations, & Human Rights: The Eleanor Roosevelt & Jimmy Carter Eras. LC 78-22134. (Studies in Human Rights: No. 4). 1979. lib. bdg. 27.50 (ISBN 0-313-21090-X, MUH/). Greenwood.

Mowery, Betty C. The Clock Without Hands. 1982. pap. 6.95 (ISBN 0-686-84733-4, Avalon). Bouregy.
--Fragrance of Lilacs. 1982. pap. 6.95 (ISBN 0-686-84738-5, Avalon). Bouregy.
--The Wailing Terror. 1981. pap. 6.95 (ISBN 0-686-84687-7, Avalon). Bouregy.

Mowitz, Robert J. Design of Public Decision Systems. 176p. 1980. pap. text ed. 15.95 (ISBN 0-8391-1550-4). Univ Park.

Mowll, William. S.S. Great Britian: The Model Ship. LC 82-60766. 1982. 22.95 (ISBN 0-87021-866-2). Naval Inst Pr.

Mowoe, Isaac J., ed. The Performance of Soldiers As Governors: African Politics & the African Military. LC 79-5511. 1980. text ed. 23.75 o.p. (ISBN 0-8191-0903-7); pap. text ed. 15.25 (ISBN 0-8191-0904-5). U Pr of Amer.

Mowrer, David S. Costing Data for Fire Protection in Complex Industrial Occupancies. Date not set. 4.65 (ISBN 0-686-37671-4, TR 82-7). Society Fire Protect.

Mowrer, Donald E. Methods of Modifying Speech Behaviors: Learning Theory in Speech Pathology. (Special Education Ser.). 1978. text ed. 21.95 (ISBN 0-675-08438-5). Merrill.
--Methods of Modifying Speech Behaviors. 2nd ed. 480p. 1982. text ed. 21.95 (ISBN 0-675-09888-2). Merrill.

Mowrer, Lilian T. I've Seen It Happen Twice: First Hand Reports on a World in Crisis. 1969. 6.95 (ISBN 0-8159-5822-6). Devin.

Mowrer, O. Hobart. Learning Theory & Behavior. LC 59-15671. 576p. 1973. Repr. of 1960 ed. 26.50 (ISBN 0-88275-127-1). Krieger.
--Learning Theory & Personality Dynamics: Selected Papers. LC 50-11151. 776p. 1950. 24.50 (ISBN 0-471-06920-5, Pub. by Wiley). Krieger.
--Leaves from Many Seasons: Selected Papers. 368p. 1983. 29.95 (ISBN 0-03-059147-3). Praeger.

Mowry, George E. Era of Theodore Roosevelt: 1900-1912. (New American Nation Ser). 1958. 20.00x o.p. (ISBN 0-06-013095-4, HarpT). Har-Row.

Mowry, George E., ed. Twenties: Fords, Flappers, & Fanatics. (Orig.). 1962. pap. 4.95 (ISBN 0-13-934968-5, Spec). P-H.

Mowry, Hua-yuan L. Chinese Love Stories from Ch'ing-shih. 1983. 29.50 (ISBN 0-208-01920-0, Archon). Shoe String.

Mowry, Robert G., jt. auth. see Flemming, Donald N.

Mowshowitz, A., ed. see IFIP 2nd, Conference, Baden, Austria, June 1979.

Mowvley, Harry. Reading the Old Testament Prophets Today. LC 79-87744. (Biblical Foundations Ser.). 1979. pap. 2.49 (ISBN 0-8042-0167-6). John Knox.

Moy, Jean O., tr. see Inoue, Yasushi.

Moy, Susan L. Chinese in Chicago: The First Hundred Years. 1983. pap. write for info. (ISBN 0-934584-12-5). Pacific-Asian.

Moy, Virginia. Easy Clues Make Reading Fun. 1979. 4.95 o.p. (ISBN 0-533-04264-X). Vantage.

Moye, H. Anson. Analysis of Pesticide Residues. (Chemical Analysis Ser.). 496p. 1980. 61.00 (ISBN 0-471-05461-5, Pub by Wiley-Interscience). Wiley.

Moyer, Albert E. American Physics in Transition: Conceptual Shifts in the Late Nineteenth Century. (History of Modern Physics 1800-1950 Ser.: Vol. 3). (Illus.). 1983. write for info limited edition (ISBN 0-938228-06-4). Tomash Pubs.

Moyer, Anne & Prevention Magazine Editors. The Fiber Factor. LC 76-18923. 1976. pap. 3.95 o.p. (ISBN 0-87857-127-2). Rodale Pr Inc.

Moyer, Charles R. & Kretlow, William. Contemporary Financial Management. (Illus.). 684p. 1981. text ed. 24.95 (ISBN 0-8299-0400-X). West Pub.

Moyer, Elgin. Wycliffe Biographical Dictionary of the Church. 1982. text ed. 19.95 (ISBN 0-8024-9693-8). Moody.

Moyer, Elizabeth A. Self-Assessment of Current Knowledge in Occupational Therapy. 1976. spiral bdg. 12.00 o.p. (ISBN 0-87488-249-4). Med Exam.

Moyer, Frank A. Special Forces Foreign Weapons Handbook. new ed. LC 70-93554. (Illus.). 326p. 1970. 19.95 o.p. (ISBN 0-87364-009-8). Paladin Ent.

Moyer, John H., jt. ed. see Likoff, William.

Moyer, John W. Practical Taxidermy. 2nd ed. 1979. 17.95 (ISBN 0-471-04891-7). Wiley.

Moyer, Kenneth E., ed. Physiology of Aggression & Implications for Control: An Anthology of Readings. LC 74-14476. 336p. 1976. pap. 17.00 (ISBN 0-89004-003-6). Raven.

Moyer, Miriam W. Demands of Love. 1978. 4.40 (ISBN 0-686-24048-0). Rod & Staff.

Moyer, R., et al. The Research & Report Handbook: For Business, Industry & Government. student ed. 312p. 1981. pap. text ed. 14.95x (ISBN 0-471-04258-7). Wiley.
--The Research & Report Handbook: For Managers & Executives in Business Industry & Government. 312p. 1981. 19.95x (ISBN 0-471-04257-9). Wiley.

Moyer, R. Charles, jt. auth. see McGuigan, James R.

Moyer, R. Charles, et al. Managerial Economics: Readings, Cases & Exercises. 1979. pap. text ed. 14.50 (ISBN 0-8299-0157-4); pap. text ed. solutions manual avail. (ISBN 0-8299-0632-0). West Pub.

Moyer, Reed & Hutt, Michael D. Macro Marketing: A Social Perspective. 2nd ed. LC 77-26816. (Wiley Ser. in Marketing). 1978. text ed. 17.50x (ISBN 0-471-02699-9); teacher's manual o.p. (ISBN 0-471-02768-5). Wiley.

Moyer, Ruth. Business English Basics. LC 80-64. 1980. text ed. 19.95x (ISBN 0-471-04337-0); tchr's manual 6.50 (ISBN 0-471-08249-X). Wiley.

Moyes, Elizabeth, ed. Manual of Law Librarianship: The Use & Organization of Legal Literature. LC 76-25099. 1976. lib. bdg. 55.00 o.p. (ISBN 0-89158-637-7). Westview.

Moyes, Patricia. Black Widower. (Crime Ser.). 1977. pap. 2.95 o.p. (ISBN 0-14-004334-9). Penguin.
--The Coconut Killings. (Crime Ser). 1979. pap. 1.95 o.p. (ISBN 0-14-004593-7). Penguin.
--Death & the Dutch Uncle. LC 68-24750. 256p. 1983. pap. text ed. 3.95 (ISBN 0-03-063543-8). HR&W.
--Down Among the Dead Men. (Murder Ink Ser.: No. 51). 240p. 1982. pap. 2.50 (ISBN 0-440-11627-9). Dell.
--Johnny Under Ground. (Murder Ink Ser.: No. 61). 1983. pap. 2.95 (ISBN 0-440-14211-3). Dell.
--Murder A La Mode. LC 63-12604. 224p. 1983. pap. 3.95 (ISBN 0-03-063544-6). HR&W.
--Season of Snows & Sins. LC 74-155526. 224p. 1983. pap. 3.95 (ISBN 0-03-063542-X). HR&W.
--A Six-Letter Word for Death. LC 82-18738. 252p. 1983. 13.50 (ISBN 0-03-062978-0). HR&W.

Moyes, Philip J. Modern U. S. Fighters. (Aerodata International Ser.). (Illus.). 120p. 1982. 9.95 (ISBN 0-89747-125-3, 6203). Squad Sig Pubns.

Moyle, Peter B. & Cech, Joseph J. Fishes: An Introduction to Ichthyology. (Illus.). 720p. 1982. 31.95 (ISBN 0-13-319723-9). P-H.

Moyle, Peter B. & Smith, Jerry J. Distribution & Ecology of Stream Fishes of the Sacramento-San Joaquin Drainage System, California. LC 81-13072. (University of California Publications in Zoology Ser.: Vol. 115). 264p. 1982. 15.25x (ISBN 0-520-09650-9). U of Cal Pr.

Moyle, Richard. Songs of the Pintupi. (AIAS New Ser.). (Illus.). 1980. text ed. 41.00x (ISBN 0-391-00995-8); pap. text ed. 28.00x (ISBN 0-391-00996-6). Humanities.

Moyles, R. G., ed. English-Canadian Literature to 1900: A Guide to Information Sources. LC 73-16986. (American Literature, English Literature, & World Literatures in English Information Guide Ser.: Vol. 6). 208p. 1976. 42.00x (ISBN 0-8103-1222-0). Gale.

Moynahan, Julian, ed. see Hardy, Thomas.

Moyniham, Maurice. Eamon De Valera: Speeches & Statements 1917-1973. LC 80-51761. 1980. 85.00 (ISBN 0-312-22457-5). St Martin.

Moynihan, Daniel P. & Weaver, Suzanne. A Dangerous Place. 1980. pap. 2.75 o.p. (ISBN 0-425-04459-9). Berkley Pub.

Moynihan, Daniel P., jt. auth. see Glazer, Nathan.

Moynihan, Martin. Geographic Variation in Social Behavior & in Adaptations to Competition Among Andean Birds. (Illus.). 162p. 1979. 17.50 (ISBN 0-686-35808-2). Nuttall Ornithological.

Moynihan, Martin & Rodaniche, A. F., eds. The Behaviour & Natural History of the Caribbean Reef Squid (Sepiotheuthis Sepioiodea) (Advances in Ethology Ser.: Vol. 25). (Illus.). 144p. (Orig.). 1982. pap. text ed. 21.60 (ISBN 0-686-37065-1). Parey Sci Pubs.

Moynihan, Michael, ed. Black Bread & Barbed Wire. 1979. 12.95 o.p. (ISBN 0-85052-239-0). Presidio Pr.

Moys, Elizabeth M. Manual of Law Librarianship: The Use & Organization of Legal Literature. 736p. 1976. 52.50 (ISBN 0-233-96735-4, 05811-4, Pub. by Gower Pub Co England). Lexington Bks.

Mozans, H. J. Woman in Science. 1974. pap. 5.95 o.p. (ISBN 0-262-63054-0). MIT Pr.

Mozart, Wolfgang A. Complete String Quartets. 277p. 1970. pap. 8.95 (ISBN 0-486-22372-8). Dover.

--Don Giovanni: Complete Orchestral & Vocal Score. Schunemann, Georg & Soldan, Kurt, eds. LC 73-91488. 480p. 1974. pap. 12.95 (ISBN 0-486-23026-0). Dover.

--Later Symphonies. 285p. 1974. pap. 8.95 (ISBN 0-486-23052-X). Dover.

--Piano Concertos Seventeen-Twenty Two. pap. 10.95 (ISBN 0-486-23599-8). Dover.

--Symphony Number 35 in D. K. 385: The Haffner Symphony. facsimile ed. 1968. Set. boxed 32.50 (ISBN 0-19-393180-X); pap. 8.00 (ISBN 0-19-385289-6). Oxford U Pr.

Mozes, G. Parafin Products: Properties, Technologies, Applications. (Developments in Petroleum Products Ser.: Vol. 14). Date not set. 83.00 (ISBN 0-444-99712-1). Elsevier.

Mozley, Anita V., ed. American Photography, Past into Present: Prints from the Monsen Collection of American Photography. LC 76-4145. (Illus.). 156p. 20.00 (ISBN 0-295-95508-2). U of Wash Pr.

Mozley, James F. William Tyndale. LC 70-109801. (Illus.). 1971. Repr. of 1937 ed. lib. bdg. 17.75x (ISBN 0-8371-4292-X, MOWT). Greenwood.

Mphahlele, Ezekiel. Down Second Avenue: Growing up in a South African Ghetto. 8.50 (ISBN 0-8446-4451-X). Peter Smith.

Mrachek, L. & Kromschlies, C. Technical-Vocational Mathematics. LC 76-48917. 1978. pap. 17.95 (ISBN 0-13-898569-3). P-H.

Mrak, E. M., et al, eds. Advances in Food Research, Vols. 1-24. Incl. Vol. 1. 1948 (ISBN 0-12-016401-9); Vol. 2. 1949 (ISBN 0-12-016402-7); Vols. 3-5. 1951-54. Vol. 3 (ISBN 0-12-016403-5). Vol. 4 (ISBN 0-12-016404-3). Vol. 5 (ISBN 0-12-016405-1); Vol. 6. 1955 (ISBN 0-12-016406-X); Vols. 7-8. 1957-58. Vol. 7 (ISBN 0-12-016407-8). Vol. 8 (ISBN 0-12-016408-6); Vol. 9. Chichester, C. O., et al, eds. 1960 (ISBN 0-12-016409-4); Vols. 11-13. 1963-64. Vol. 10 (ISBN 0-12-016410-8). Vol. 11 (ISBN 0-12-016411-6). Vol. 12 (ISBN 0-12-016412-4). Vol. 13 (ISBN 0-12-016413-2); Vol. 14. 1965 (ISBN 0-12-016414-0); Vol. 15. 1967 (ISBN 0-12-016415-9); Vol. 16. 1968 (ISBN 0-12-016416-7); Vol. 17. 1969 (ISBN 0-12-016417-5); Vol. 18. 1970 (ISBN 0-12-016418-3); Vol. 19. 1971 (ISBN 0-12-016419-1); Vol. 20. 1973 (ISBN 0-12-016420-5); Vol. 21. 1975 (ISBN 0-12-016421-3). lib ed. 68.00 (ISBN 0-12-016484-1); microfiche 38.50 (ISBN 0-12-016485-X); Vol. 22. 1976 (ISBN 0-12-016422-1). lib ed. 68.00 (ISBN 0-12-016486-8); microfiche **38.00 (ISBN 0-12-016487-6); Vol. 23. 1977. 50.00 (ISBN 0-12-016423-X); lib ed. 53.50 (ISBN 0-12-016488-4); microfiche 31.00 (ISBN 0-12-016489-2); Vol. 24. 1978. 46.00 (ISBN 0-12-016424-8); lib. ed. 58.50 (ISBN 0-12-016490-6); microfiche 33.50 (ISBN 0-12-016491-4). Vols. 1-22. 53.50 ea. Acad Pr.**

Mroczkowska-Brand, Katarzyna, tr. see Kapuscinski, Ryszard.

Mrowec, S. Defects & Diffusion in Solids: An Introduction. (Materials Science Monographs: Vol. 5). 468p. 1980. 72.50 (ISBN 0-444-99776-8). Elsevier.

Mroz, John E. Influence in Conflict: The Impact of Third Parties on the Arab-Israeli Dispute Since 1973. 400p. 1983. 40.00 (ISBN 0-08-028797-2); pap. 14.95 (ISBN 0-08-028796-4). Pergamon.

Mroz, Joseph H. Safety in Everyday Living. 400p. 1978. text ed. write for info. (ISBN 0-697-07371-8); tchr's manual avail. (ISBN 0-697-07230-4). Wm C Brown.

Mroz, M. Divine Vengeance. LC 77-120130. (Studies in Shakespeare, No. 24). 1970. Repr. of 1914 ed. lib. bdg. 48.95x (ISBN 0-8383-1091-5). Haskell.

Mrozek, Ronald, jt. auth. see Ramey, Ardella.

Mr. X. Double Eagle. (Espionage-Intelligence Library). 288p. 1983. pap. 2.95 (ISBN 0-345-30192-7). Ballantine.

M. S. A. The Muslim Population of the World. pap. 1.00 (ISBN 0-686-18438-6). Kazi Pubns.

--Parents Manual. pap. 4.95 (ISBN 0-686-18465-3). Kazi Pubns.

Mshigeni, K. E. Biology & Ecology of Benthic Marine Algae with Special Reference to Hypnea (Rhodophyta, Gigartinales: A Review of the Literature. (Bibliotheca Phycologica Ser.: No. 36). 1978. pap. 16.00x (ISBN 3-7682-1166-5). Lubrecht & Cramer.

Mtewa, Mekki. Consultant Connexion: Evaluation of the Federal Consulting Service. LC 80-8141. 238p. 1980. lib. bdg. 20.75 (ISBN 0-8191-1161-9); pap. text ed. 10.50 (ISBN 0-8191-1162-7). U Pr of Amer.

--Public Policy & Development Politics: The Politics of Technical Expertise in Africa. LC 79-48041. 364p. 1980. text ed. 23.25 (ISBN 0-8191-1003-5); pap. text ed. 13.50 (ISBN 0-8191-1004-3). U Pr of Amer.

Mtewa, Mekki, ed. Science, Technology & Development: Options & Policies. LC 82-42546. (Illus.). 254p. (Orig.). 1982. lib. bdg. 22.50 (ISBN 0-8191-2533-4); pap. text ed. 11.50 (ISBN 0-8191-2534-2). U Pr of Amer.

Mtshali, Oswald. Fireflames. (Illus.). 72p. (Orig.). 1983. pap. 9.95 (ISBN 0-88208-165-9). Lawrence Hill.

Mubarak, Scott J., et al. Compartment Snydromes & Volkmann's Contracture. (Saunder's Monographs in Clinical Orthopedics: Vol. 3). (Illus.). 200p. 1981. text ed. 39.50 (ISBN 0-7216-6604-3). Saunders.

Muccie, Frank J., Jr. I & the Father Are One. 180p. 1982. pap. 9.95 (ISBN 0-938520-01-6). Edenite.

Muccigrosso, Robert. American Gothic: The Mind & Art of Ralph Adams Cram. LC 79-5436. 1981. lib. bdg. 25.25 (ISBN 0-8191-1734-X); pap. text ed. 12.50 (ISBN 0-8191-0884-7). U Pr of Amer.

Muccino, Richard R. Organic Synthesis with Carbon-Fourteen. 480p. 1982. 52.50 (ISBN 0-471-05165-9, Pub. by Wiley-Interscience). Wiley.

Mucha, Jr. The Mucha Poster Coloring Book. (Illus.). 1977. pap. 2.00 (ISBN 0-486-23444-4). Dover.

Muchenberg, B. & Prosnak, J., eds. The Symphony in Poland. (The Symphony 1720-1840 Series F: Vol. 7). 1982. lib. bdg. 90.00 (ISBN 0-8240-3820-7). Garland Pub.

Muchmore, Lynn, jt. ed. see Beyle, Thad L.

Muchnick, Steven S. & Jones, Neil D. Program Flow Analysis: Theory & Application. (Software Ser.). (Illus.). 448p. 1981. 27.95 (ISBN 0-13-729681-9). P-H.

Muchow, Kenneth & Deem, Bill. Microprocessor Principles, Programming & Interfacing. 1982. text ed. 23.95 (ISBN 0-8359-4383-6); instrs.' manual avail. (ISBN 0-8359-4384-4). Reston.

Muckelroy, K. Maritime Archaeology. LC 78-5693. (New Studies in Archaeology). 1979. 54.50 (ISBN 0-521-22079-3); pap. 15.95x (ISBN 0-521-29348-0). Cambridge U Pr.

Muckerman, Norman J., selected by. The Body in the Basement. 192p. 1983. pap. 3.95 (ISBN 0-89243-177-6). Liguori Pubns.

Muckle. Injuries in Sport. 2nd ed. 162p. 1982. 21.50 (ISBN 0-7236-0620-X). Wright-PSG.

Mucsi, Andras. Catalogue of the Old Masters Gallery at the Christian Museum in Esztergom. Halapy, Lili, tr. from Hungarian. (Illus.). 136p. 1975. pap. 7.50x (ISBN 963-13-4290-5). Intl Pubns Serv.

Mud Circulation Subcommitte of the IADC. Centrifugal Pumps & Piping Systems. 1983. pap. text ed. 24.95 (ISBN 0-87201-616-1). Gulf Pub.

Mudahar, M. S. & Hignett, T. P. Energy & Fertilizer: Policy Implications & Options for Developing Countries (Executive Brief) (Technical Bulletin Ser.: No. T-19). (Illus.). 20p. (Orig.). 1981. pap. 4.00 (ISBN 0-88090-018-0). Intl Fertilizer.

--Energy & Fertilizer: Policy Implications & Options for Developing Countries. LC 82-6084. (Technical Bulletin Ser.: No. T-20). (Illus.). 241p. (Orig.). 1982. pap. 15.00 (ISBN 0-88090-019-9). Intl Fertilizer.

Mudd, Harvey. The Plain of Smokes. (Illus.). 98p. 1982. 14.00 (ISBN 0-87685-567-2); signed ed. 20.00 (ISBN 0-87685-568-0); pap. 6.50 (ISBN 0-87685-566-4). Black Sparrow.

Mudd, J. Brian, jt. auth. see Lee, S. D.

Mudditt, B. Howard, ed. Christian Worship (Hymns) 716p. 1976. text ed. 15.00 (ISBN 0-85364-194-3). Attic Pr.

Mudge, Arthur E. Value Engineering: A Systematic Approach. (Illus.). 280p. 1971. 19.50 o.p. (ISBN 0-07-043954-0, P&RB). McGraw.

Mudge, James L., jt. auth. see Leipziger, Danny M.

Mudge, Robert W. Adventures of a Yellowbird. (Airlines History Project Ser.). Date not set. price not set (ISBN 0-404-19329-3). AMS Pr.

Mudie & MacDonald. Early Years: Childhood of Famous People. 9.50 (ISBN 0-392-16624-0, SpS). Sportshelf.

Mudie, Colin. Power Boats. 1976. 6.95 o.p. (ISBN 0-600-37045-3). Transatlantic.

Mudlark, Ichabod. Gustave Dore's Primer on the Medical Profession. (Illus.). 164p. 1983. 15.00 (ISBN 0-87527-298-3). Green.

Mudrick, Marvin. Books Are Not Life but Then What Is? 1979. 18.95x (ISBN 0-19-502508-3). Oxford U Pr.

Mudroch, Vaclav. The Wyclyf Tradition. Reeves, A. Compton, ed. LC 77-92253. xvii, 91p. 1979. 15.00x (ISBN 0-8214-0403-2, 82-82949). Ohio U Pr.

Mudvi, B. B. & McNabb, J. W. Engineering Mechanics of Materials. (Illus.). 1980. text ed. 32.95x (ISBN 0-02-385750-1). Macmillan.

Muecke, Douglas C. Irony. (Critical Idiom Ser.: Vol. 13). 1970. pap. 4.95x o.p. (ISBN 0-416-65420-7). Methuen Inc.

Muehsam, Gerd. Guide to Basic Information Sources in the Visual Arts. LC 77-17430. 266p. 1978. 9.95 (ISBN 0-87436-278-4). ABC-Clio.

Mueller, jt. auth. see Slack.

Mueller, Ann, jt. auth. see Ketcham, Katherine.

Mueller, Betty. Packrat Papers, No. 2: Tips on Food (& Other Stuff) for Hikers & Campers. (Illus.). 1977. pap. 3.95 o.p. (ISBN 0-913140-20-1). Signpost Bk Pubns.

Mueller, C., jt. auth. see DePaula, H.

Mueller, Charles F. & Rund, Douglas A. Emergency Radiology: Self Assessment. (Illus.). 328p. 1982. lib. bdg. 37.00 (ISBN 0-686-94105-5). Williams & Wilkins.

Mueller, Charles W., jt. ed. see Parcel, Toby L.

Mueller, D. Sister Chromatid Exchange Test. (Illus.). 120p. 1983. 16.50 (ISBN 0-86577-069-7). Thieme-Stratton.

Mueller, D. C. Public Choice. LC 78-11197. (Surveys in Economic Literature). 1979. 42.50 (ISBN 0-521-22550-7); pap. 12.95 (ISBN 0-521-29548-3). Cambridge U Pr.

Mueller, Dennis C., ed. The Political Economy of Growth. LC 81-15955. 296p. 1983. text ed. 23.50x (ISBN 0-300-02658-7). Yale U Pr.

Mueller, Ellen C. Calamity Jane. Jones, Jean R. & Kilpatrick, Bob, eds. LC 81-8388. (Illus.). 24p. 1981. pap. 4.00 (ISBN 0-936204-28-1). Jelm Mtn.

Mueller, Ernst, ed. see Plato.

Mueller, Eva, et al. Technological Advance in an Expanding Economy: Its Impact on a Cross-Section of the Labor Force. LC 71-627965. 254p. 1969. 12.00x (ISBN 0-87944-073-2). Inst Soc Res.

Mueller, Francis J. Essential Mathematics for College Students. 3rd ed. (Illus.). 320p. 1976. pap. 19.95 (ISBN 0-13-286518-1). P-H.

--General Mathematics for College Students. LC 75-140690. 1972. pap. text ed. 16.95 (ISBN 0-13-350512-X). P-H.

--Intermediate Algebra. (Illus.). 1979. pap. 19.95 ref. (ISBN 0-13-469452-X). P-H.

Mueller, Frank P. The Burdick Family Chronology, Vol. 1. LC 82-72466. (Illus.). 200p. 1983. 24.95 (ISBN 0-9609100-0-X). Burdick Ancestry Lib.

Mueller, G. E. & Spangler, E. R. Communication Satellites. LC 64-14994. 280p. 1964. 16.50 o.p. (ISBN 0-471-62319-9, Pub. by Wiley). Krieger.

Mueller, Gene. The Forgotten Marshal: Wilhelm Keitel. LC 79-64176. 1979. 16.95 (ISBN 0-87716-105-4, Pub. by Moore Pub Co). F Apple.

Mueller, George. Answers to Prayer. pap. 2.95 (ISBN 0-8024-2958-0). Moody.

Mueller, Georgiana. How to Raise & Train a Greyhound. (Illus.). 1965. pap. 2.50 o.p. (ISBN 0-87666-312-9, DS1083). TFH Pubns.

Mueller, Gerhard G. & Choi, Frederick D. Introduction to Multinational Accounting. (Illus.). 1978. 25.95 (ISBN 0-13-489302-6). P-H.

Mueller, Gustav E. Dialectic: A Way Into & Within Philosophy. Keyes, C. D., ed. 234p. 1983. pap. text ed. 11.00 (ISBN 0-8191-2691-8). U Pr of Amer.

Mueller, H. Deutsch-Zweites Buch. rev. ed. 1972. 6.95 o.p. (ISBN 0-02-823090-6). Glencoe.

Mueller, Hugo. Deutsch, Erstes Buch. (gr. 9-12). 1958-69. student tests 2.95 o.p. (ISBN 0-685-22893-2, 82298); tchrs' key to student tests 1.50 o.p. (ISBN 0-685-22894-0, 82302); set of 12 transparancies o.p. (ISBN 0-685-22895-9, 82304); 17 tapes 150.00 o.p. (ISBN 0-685-22896-7, 82306, 82348). wall charts 126.00 o.p. (ISBN 0-686-66599-6, 82612). Glencoe.

--Deutsch-Erstes Buch, 2 pts. Incl. Pt. 1. 1960-68. tchrs' key 1.50 o.p. (ISBN 0-685-22897-5, 82318); tchrs' manual 2.95 o.p. (ISBN 0-685-22898-3, 82300); wkbk. 1.95 o.p. (ISBN 0-685-22899-1, 82328, 82320, 82322); Pt. 2. 1967-69. 5.95 o.p. (ISBN 0-685-22900-9, 82324); tchrs' key 2.95 o.p. (ISBN 0-685-22901-7, 82326); wkbk. 1.95 o.p. (ISBN 0-685-22902-5, 82360); tapes 120.00 o.p. (ISBN 0-685-22903-3, 82330). (gr. 9-12). 1968. Glencoe.

--Deutsch-Zweites Buch. rev ed. 1963-69. tchr's key 1.95 o.p. (ISBN 0-685-22890-8, 82310); wkbk. 1.95 o.p. (ISBN 0-685-22891-6, 32308); tapes 150.00 o.p. (ISBN 0-685-22892-4, 82360, 82370, 82312). Glencoe.

Mueller, Ian. Philosophy of Mathematics & Deductive Structure in Euclid's "Elements". (Illus.). 400p. 1981. 42.50x (ISBN 0-262-13163-3). MIT Pr.

Mueller, Ivan I. Spherical & Practical Astronomy As Applied to Geodesy. LC 68-31453. (Illus.). 1969. 35.00 (ISBN 0-8044-4667-9). Ungar.

Mueller, J. Gesammelte Lichenologische Schriften, 2 vols. Incl. Vol. 1. Lichenologische Beitraege 1-XXXV. o.p. (ISBN 0-686-22233-4). 1967. 176.00 set (ISBN 3-7682-0440-5). Lubrecht & Cramer.

Mueller, Jerome F. Standard Mechanical & Electrical Details. (Illus.). 1980. 28.50 (ISBN 0-07-043960-5). McGraw.

Mueller, John H., et al. Statistical Reasoning in Sociology. 3rd ed. LC 76-13097. (Illus.). 1977. text ed. 26.50 (ISBN 0-395-24417-X); solutions manual 2.50 (ISBN 0-395-24416-1). HM.

Mueller, John T. Christian Dogmatics. 1934. 17.95 (ISBN 0-570-06731-6, 15-1071). Concordia.

Mueller, K. A., ed. see International School of Physics "Enrico Fermi" Course LIX, Varenna on Lake Como, July 9-21 1973.

Mueller, Keith J. Zero-Base Budgeting in Local Government: Attempts to Implement Administrative Reform. LC 80-5860. 149p. 1981. lib. bdg. 19.00 (ISBN 0-8191-1534-7); pap. text ed. 8.25 (ISBN 0-8191-1535-5). U Pr of Amer.

Mueller, Kimberly J. The Nuclear Power Issue: A Guide to Who's Doing What in the U. S. & Abroad. LC 79-52430. (Who's Doing What Ser.: No. 8). (Illus.). 106p. (Orig.). 1981. pap. 25.00x (ISBN 0-912102-43-8). Cal Inst Public.

Mueller, Larry. Bird Dog Guide. rev. ed. (Illus.). 208p. 1976. pap. 6.95 o.s.i. (ISBN 0-695-80655-6). Follett.

--Bird Dog Guide. (Illus.). 208p. pap. 6.95 o.p. (ISBN 0-88317-068-X). Stoeger Pub Co.

Mueller, Lisel. Life of a Queen. 1979. pap. 3.00 (ISBN 0-686-65848-5). Juniper Pr WI.

Mueller, M. E., et al. Manual of Internal Fixation: Technique Recommended by the AO-Group. Schatzker, J., et al, trs. from Ger. LC 76-138812. (Illus.). 1970. 132.00 (ISBN 0-387-09227-7); slides 210.70 (ISBN 0-387-92101-X). Springer-Verlag.

Mueller, Madeleine, tr. see Diekmann, Miep.

Mueller, Marlies, jt. auth. see Slack, Anne.

Mueller, Pat & Reznik, John W. Intramural-Recreational Sports: Programming & Administration. 5th ed. LC 78-10122. 1979. text ed. 24.95x (ISBN 0-471-04911-5). Wiley.

Mueller, Peter G. & Ross, Douglas A. China & Japan: Emerging Global Powers. LC 74-33039. (Special Studies). (Illus.). 240p. 1975. 24.95 o.p. (ISBN 0-275-05400-4); pap. text ed. 13.95 o.p. (ISBN 0-275-89390-1). Praeger.

Mueller, Robert A. & Oberlander, Theodore M. Physical Geography Today: Portrait of a Planet. 2nd ed. (CRM Bks.). 1978. text ed. 27.00x (ISBN 0-394-32088-3). Random.

Mueller, Robert K. Board Compass: What It Means to Be a Director in a Changing World. (Arthur D. Little Books). (Illus.). 224p. 1979. 24.95 (ISBN 0-669-02903-3). Lexington Bks.

--Career Conflict: Management's Inelegant Dysfunction. LC 78-19240. (Arthur D. Little Bks.). 160p. 1978. 18.95 (ISBN 0-669-02471-6). Lexington Bks.

--The Incompleat Board: The Unfolding of Corporate Governance. LC 80-8639. 304p. 1981. 29.95 (ISBN 0-669-04339-7). Lexington Bks.

--Metadevelopment: Beyond the Bottom Line. LC 77-4567. 192p. 1977. 18.95 (ISBN 0-669-01372-2). Lexington Bks.

Mueller, Robert Kirk. New Directions for Directors: Behind the by-Laws. LC 77-10216. 208p. 1978. 21.95 (ISBN 0-669-01889-9). Lexington Bks.

Mueller, Rudolf. G M B H-Gesetz Betreffend Die Gesellschaften Mit Beschrankter Haftung-G M B H German Law Concerning the Companies with Limited Liability. 3rd ed. 1977. pap. 12.50x (ISBN 3-7819-2824-1). Intl Pubns Serv.

Mueller, Rudolf & Schneider, Hannes. The German Antitrust Law. 296p. 1981. 77.00x (ISBN 0-7121-5481-7, Pub. by Macdonald & Evans). State Mutual Bk.

Mueller, Siegfried. Elektrische und Dieselelektrische Triebfahrzeuge. (Illus.). 204p. (German.). 1979. 50.05x (ISBN 3-7643-1033-2). Birkhauser.

Mueller, U. & Guenther, C., eds. Post Accident Debris Cooling: Proceedings of the Fifth Post Accident Heat Removal Information Exchange Meeting, 1982, Nuclear Research Center Karlsruhe. (Illus.). 364p. (Orig.). 1983. pap. text ed. 30.00x (ISBN 3-7650-2034-6). Sheridan.

Mueller, Virginia. Clem, the Clumsy Camel. (Arch Book Ser., No. 11). (Illus.). 32p. (gr. 1-4). 1974. pap. 0.89 (ISBN 0-570-06085-0, 59-1205). Concordia.

--The King's Invitation. (Arch Bks: Set 5). (Illus.). (gr. 3-4). 1968. laminated bdg. 0.89 (ISBN 0-570-06033-8, 59-1146). Concordia.

--Secret Journey. (Arch Bks: Set 5). (Illus.). (gr. 4-6). 1968. laminated bdg. 0.89 (ISBN 0-570-06037-0, 59-1150). Concordia.

--Silly Skyscraper. (Arch Bks: Set 7). (Illus., Orig.). (ps-4). 1970. laminated bdg 0.89 (ISBN 0-570-06050-8, 59-1166, 59-1166). Concordia.

--What Is Faith? Sparks, Judith, ed. (A Happy Day Book). (Illus.). 24p. (Orig.). (gr. k-2). 1980. 1.29 (ISBN 0-87239-411-5, 3643). Standard Pub.

--Who Is Your Neighbor? Sparks, Judith, ed. (A Happy Day Book). (Illus.). 24p. (Orig.). (gr. k-2). 1980. 1.29 (ISBN 0-87239-412-3, 3644). Standard Pub.

Mueller, W. Avenues to Understanding: Dynamics of Therapeutic Interactions. 1973. text ed. 13.95 (ISBN 0-13-055012-4). P-H.

--The Knee: Form, Function, & Ligament Reconstruction. (Illus.). 314p. 1983. 110.00 (ISBN 0-387-11716-4). Springer-Verlag.

Mueller, W., jt. ed. see Schattenkirchner, M.

Mueller, William M. & Shaw, Milton C., eds. Energetics in Metallurgical Phenomena, 4 vols. Vol. 1, 1965, 438p. 97.00x (ISBN 0-677-00570-9); Vol. 2, 1965, 212p. 50.00x (ISBN 0-677-01010-9); Vol. 3, 1967, 202p. 50.00x (ISBN 0-677-11120-7); Vol. 4, 1968, 390p. 92.00x (ISBN 0-677-11680-2). Gordon.

Mueller-Dombois, Dieter & Ellenberg, Heinz. Aims & Methods of Vegetation Ecology. LC 74-5492. 432p. 1974. text ed. 33.95 (ISBN 0-471-62290-7). Wiley.

Mueller-Dombois, Dieter, ed. Island Ecosystems: Biological Organization in Selected Hawaiian Communities. Bridges, Kent W. & Carson, Hampton L. LC 80-27650. (U. S. - IBP Synthesis Ser.: Vol. 15). 608p. 1981. 34.00 (ISBN 0-87933-381-2). Hutchinson Ross.
Mueller-Eberhard, Hans J., jt. ed. see Miescher, Peter A.
Mueller-Triol, Ingrid & Hunt-Triol, Gene. How to Import-Covert-Legalize Your Investment Automobile. 47p. 1982. write for info. HIT Pubns.
Muellet, Frederick A., ed. see Spencer, William.
Muench, David & Abbey, Edward. Desert Images: An American Landscape. LC 78-4889. 1979. 100.00 o.p. (ISBN 0-15-125302-1). HarBraceJ.
Muench, David, jt. auth. see Murphy, Dan.
Muench, David, photos by. California II. LC 77-77265. (Belding Imprint Ser.). (Illus.). 192p. (Text by Donald Pike). 1977. 32.50 (ISBN 0-912856-32-7). Graphic Arts Ctr.
Muench, John. The Painter's Guide to Lithography. 125p. 1982. 22.50 (ISBN 0-89134-057-2); pap. 14.95 (ISBN 0-89134-058-0). North Light Pub.
Muensterberger, Werner & Boyer, Bryce L., eds. The Psychoanalytic Study of Society, Vol.5. 400p. 1983. text ed. price not set (ISBN 0-88163-004-7). L Erlbaum Assocs.
Muentner, Carolyn. The Wind Does Not Forget. 68p. 1983. 8.95 (ISBN 0-9606240-3-1). Pearl-Win.
Muesegaes, Mary, ed. see Educational Research Council of America.
Mueser, Anne & Liptay, Lynne. Talk & Toddle: A Commonsense Guide for the First Three Years. 160p. 1983. pap. 7.95 (ISBN 0-312-78430-9). St Martin.
Mueser, Anne M. The Picture Story of Jockey Steve Cauthen. LC 78-27884. (Illus.). 64p. (gr. 4-6). 1979. PLB 6.97 o.p. (ISBN 0-671-32990-1). Messner.
--The Picture Story of Rod Carew. LC 80-420. (Illus.). 64p. (gr. 3 up). 1980. PLB 6.97 o.p. (ISBN 0-671-33049-7). Messner.
Mueser, Anne M., ed. see Russell, David, et al.
Muessen, H. J. How the World Cooks Chicken. LC 80-51680. 395p. 1982. 19.95 o.s.i. (ISBN 0-8128-2740-6). Stein & Day.
Muessig, Raymond H., jt. auth. see Commager, Henry S.
Muessig, Raymond H., jt. auth. see Kitchens, James A.
Muessig, Raymond H., jt. auth. see Pelto, Pertti J.
Muessig, Raymond H., jt. auth. see Straayer, John A.
Muffler, L. J., jt. ed. see Rybach, L.
Muffs, Judith H. The Holocaust in Books & Films: A Selected Annotated List. 64p. 5.00 (ISBN 0-686-95068-2). ADL.
Mufich, C. J., jt. auth. see Zammuto, A. P.
Mufid, Shaykh al see Al-Mufid, Shaykh.
Muftic, Felicia. Colorado Consumer Handbook. 96p. (Orig.). 1982. pap. 5.95 (ISBN 0-933472-62-5). Johnson Bks.
Mu Fu-Sheng. The Wilting of the Hundred Flowers. LC 73-19115. 324p. 1974. Repr. of 1963 ed. lib. bdg. 19.25x (ISBN 0-8371-7303-5, MUHF). Greenwood.
Mugar, Jayson, jt. auth. see Boarman, Patrick M.
Mugford, E., jt. auth. see Legge, K.
Muggeridge, Malcolm. Chronicles of Wasted Time: The Green Stick, 1903-1933. 1982. pap. 7.50 (ISBN 0-688-00952-2). Morrow.
--The Green Stick. LC 81-17689. (Chronicles of Wasted Time: Vol. 1). 288p. 1982. pap. 7.50 (ISBN 0-688-00952-2). Quill NY.
--The Infernal Grove. LC 81-17718. 288p. 1982. pap. 7.50 (ISBN 0-688-00953-0). Quill NY.
--Like It Was: The Diaries of Malcolm Muggeridge. Bright-Holmes, John, ed. LC 81-16784. 1982. 18.50 (ISBN 0-688-00784-8). Morrow.
Muggeridge, Malcolm & Thornhill, Alan. Sentenced to Life: A Parable in Three Acts. 132p. 1983. pap. 3.95 (ISBN 0-8407-5839-1). Nelson.
Muggeridge, Malcolm, jt. auth. see Douglas-Home, William.
Muggeridge, Malcom. The Infernal Grove. (Chronicles of Wasted Time, Chronicle 2). 1974. 7.50 (ISBN 0-688-00953-0). Morrow.
Muggia, F. M. Cancer Chemotherapy I. 1983. 69.50 (ISBN 90-247-2713-8, Pub. by Martinus Nijhoff Netherlands). Kluwer Boston.
Muggia, F. M. & Young, C. W. Anthracycline Antibiotics in Cancer Therapy. 1982. text ed. 69.50 (ISBN 0-686-37594-7, Pub. by Martinus Nijhoff Netherlands). Kluwer Boston.
Muggia, Franco & Rozencweig, Marcel, eds. Lung Cancer: Progress in Therapeutic Research. LC 77-84552. (Progress in Cancer Research & Therapy Ser.: Vol. 11). 639p. 1978. 57.00 (ISBN 0-89004-223-3). Raven.
Mugler, James K. Pavilion. 480p. 1982. pap. 3.50 (ISBN 0-515-05523-9). Jove Pubns.
Mugnier, Charlotte. Paraprofessional & the Professional Job Structure. 164p. 1980. pap. text ed. 8.00 (ISBN 0-8389-0303-7). ALA.
Mugny, Gabriel. The Power of Minorities. (European Monographs in Social Psychology: No. 31). 1982. 26.50 (ISBN 0-12-509720-4). Acad Pr.
Mugomba, Agrippah T., et al, eds. Independence without Freedom. LC 80-154. (Studies in International & Comparative Politics Ser.: No. 13). 289p. 1980. 12.75 (ISBN 0-87436-293-8). ABC-Clio.
Mugridge, A. L., rev. by see Denyer, J. C.
Mugridge, Donald H. & Conover, Helen F. An Album of American Battle Art, 1755-1918. LC 72-6278. (Illus.). 340p. 1972. Repr. of 1947 ed. lib. bdg. 45.00 (ISBN 0-306-70523-0). Da Capo.
Muhaiyadeen, Bawa. Maya Veeram or the Forces of Illusion. Marcus, Sharon, ed. Ganesan, K. & Ganesan, R., trs. from Tamil. (Illus.). 232p. 1982. pap. 10.95 (ISBN 0-87728-550-0). Weiser.
Muhaiyadeen, Bawa M. Golden Words of a Sufi Sheikh. Aschenbach, Sarah, ed. 472p. 1983. 20.00 (ISBN 0-914390-24-4). Fellowship Pr PA.
--A Tasty Economical Cookbook, Vol. 2. Toomey, Lauren, ed. (Illus.). 166p. 1983. price not set spiral (ISBN 0-914390-22-8). Fellowship Pr Pa.
Muhaiyaddeen, M. R. Gems of Wisdom. 125p. 1982. 4.95 o.p. (ISBN 0-914390-21-X). Fellowship Pr PA.
Muhaiyaddeen, M. R. Bawa. My Love You, My Children: One Hundred & One Stories for Children of All Ages. LC 81-9847. (Illus.). 425p. 1981. 20.00 (ISBN 0-914390-20-1). Fellowship Pr.
Muhaiyaddeen, M. R. Bawa see Bawa Muhaiyaddeen, M. R.
Muhammad. A Shi'Ite Anthology: Passages from the Hadith. Tabataba'I, Muhammad H. & Nasr, Seyyed H., eds. Chittick, William C., tr. from Arabic. 152p. 1981. text ed. 39.50x (ISBN 0-87395-510-2); pap. 12.95x (ISBN 0-87395-511-0). State U NY Pr.
Muhammad, S. A. How to Prepare Your Own Income Tax Return. LC 82-91051. 192p. 1982. pap. 5.00 (ISBN 0-9609996-0-4). TPA Pub.
Muhammad-'Aliy-Salmani, Ustad. My Memories of Baha'u'llah: Ustad Muhammad-'Aliy-Salmani, the Barber. Gail, Marzieh, tr. from Persian. (Illus.). xii, 148p. 1982. 11.95 (ISBN 0-933770-21-9). Kalimat.
Muhlbach, O., jt. ed. see Emmelot, P.
Muhlbacher, jt. ed. see Chroust.
Muhlbauer. The Losers: Gang Delinquency in American Suburbs. 160p. 1983. 19.95 (ISBN 0-03-060313-7). Praeger.
Muhlstein, Anka. Baron James: The Rise of the French Revolution. LC 83-6898. (Illus.). 208p. 1983. 15.95 (ISBN 0-86565-028-4). Vendome.
Muia. The Four Dimensional Tooth Color System. 1982. 78.00 (ISBN 0-931386-53-5). Quint Pub Co.
Muileman, Kathryn S. & Saltzman, Marvin L. Eurail Guide: How to Travel Europe & All the World by Train 1982. 12th ed. LC 72-83072. (Illus.). 816p. (YA) 1982. pap. 9.95 o.p. (ISBN 0-912442-12-3). Eurail Guide.
Muilenburg, James. Way of Israel: Biblical Faith & Ethics. pap. 3.95xi o.p. (ISBN 0-06-130133-7, TB133, Torch). Har-Row.
Muir. Last Periods of Shakespeare, Racine, & Ibsen. 128p. 1982. 40.00x (ISBN 0-85323-012-9, Pub. by Liverpool Univ England). State Mutual Bk.
--The Singularity of Shakespeare. 243p. 1982. 49.00x (ISBN 0-85323-433-7, Pub. by Liverpool Univ England). State Mutual Bk.
Muir, Ada. Healing Herbs of the Zodiac. 72p. 1983. soft cover 2.00 (ISBN 0-87542-486-4). Llewellyn Pubns.
Muir, Bernice L. Essentials of Genetics for Nurses. LC 82-10841. 400p. 1983. 17.95x (ISBN 0-471-08238-4, Pub. by Wiley Med). Wiley.
--Pathophysiology: An Introduction to Mechanisms of Disease. LC 79-27791. 1980. 26.00x (ISBN 0-471-03202-6, Pub. by Wiley Med). Wiley.
Muir, Edwin. The Structure of the Novel. LC 29-3271. 1969. pap. 1.65 o.p. (ISBN 0-15-685688-3, Harv). HarBraceJ.
Muir, Edwin, tr. see Feuchtwanger, Lion.
Muir, Edwin, tr. see Kafka, Franz.
Muir, Edwin, tr. see Renn, Ludwig.
Muir, Frank. An Irreverent & Almost Complete Social History of the Bathroom. LC 82-42838. 160p. 1983. 14.95 (ISBN 0-8128-2912-3); pap. 6.95 (ISBN 0-8128-6186-8). Stein & Day.
Muir, Helen. Miami, USA. (Illus.). 319p. pap. 3.95 (ISBN 0-686-84217-0). Banyan Bks.
Muir, I. D. The Four-Axis Universal Stage, Vol. 49. LC 80-83455. (Illus.). 1981. 15.00 (ISBN 0-904962-08-3). Microscope Pubns.
Muir, James. A Modern Approach to English Grammar: An Introduction to Systemic English Grammar. 148p. 1972. pap. text ed. 13.00x (ISBN 0-7134-2008-1). Humanities.
Muir, James F. & Roberts, Ronald J., eds. Recent Advances in Aquaculture. 450p. 1982. lib. bdg. 49.7506679195x (ISBN 0-86531-464-0). Westview.
Muir, John. The Cruise of the Corwin: Journal of the Arctic Expedition of 1881 in Search of De Long & the Jeannette. new ed. LC 17-31765. 1974. Repr. of 1917 ed. 14.95 (ISBN 0-910220-63-8). Berg.
--Es Lebe Mein Volkswagen. Shamai, Ruth & Jeschke, Herbert, trs. (Illus.). 308p. 1978. pap. 10.00 (ISBN 3-980018-90-3). John Muir.
--Industrial Relations Procedures & Agreements. 208p. 1981. text ed. 40.00x (ISBN 0-566-02275-3). Gower Pub Ltd.
--Letters to a Friend. new ed. LC 15-5890. 194p. 1973. 8.95 (ISBN 0-910220-48-4). Berg.
--The Mountains of California. LC 11-12846. (Illus.). 403p. 1975. Repr. of 1898 ed. 15.95 (ISBN 0-910220-72-7). Berg.
--My First Summer in the Sierra. new ed. LC 11-14183. (Illus.). 361p. 1972. 15.95 (ISBN 0-910220-34-4). Berg.
--Steep Trails. Bade, William F., ed. LC 18-18667. (Illus.). 1970. 14.95 (ISBN 0-910220-19-0). Berg.
--Stickeen. LC 9-6875. pap. 4.95 o.p. (ISBN 0-910220-20-4). Berg.
--The Story of My Boyhood & Youth. new ed. LC 13-5573. (Illus.). 301p. 1975. 10.95 (ISBN 0-910220-70-0). Berg.
--A Thousand Mile Walk to the Gulf. LC 16-23580. (Illus.). 1970. 14.95 (ISBN 0-910220-18-2). Berg.
--Wilderness Essays. (Literature of the American Wilderness Ser.). 264p. 1980. pap. 3.95 (ISBN 0-87905-072-1). Peregrine Smith.
--The Yosemite. LC 62-6777. pap. 4.50 (ISBN 0-385-03032-0, Anchor). Natural Hist.
Muir, Kenneth. Aspects of Hamlet. Wells, S., ed. LC 78-18100. (Illus.). 1979. 27.95 (ISBN 0-521-22228-1); pap. 9.95x (ISBN 0-521-29400-2). Cambridge U Pr.
--Aspects of Othello. Edwards, P., ed. LC 76-57095. (Articles Reprinted from Shakespeare Survey Ser.). (Illus.). 1977. 29.95 (ISBN 0-521-21499-8); pap. 8.95 (ISBN 0-521-29175-5). Cambridge U Pr.
--An Introduction to Elizabethan Literature. 1967. pap. text ed. 3.95x (ISBN 0-685-77208-X, 0-394-30635). Phila Bk Co.
--Troilus & Cressida. Shakespeare, William, ed. (Illus.). 1982. 19.95x (ISBN 0-19-812903-3). Oxford U Pr.
Muir, Kenneth, ed. Essays & Studies-1974. (Essays & Studies: Vol. 27). 113p. 1974. text ed. 15.00x o.p. (ISBN 0-686-83197-7). Humanities.
Muir, Kenneth & Edwards, P., eds. Aspects of Macbeth: Articles Reprinted from Shakespeare Survey. LC 76-56239. (Reprint Offshoot Ser. from Shakespeare Survey). (Illus.). 1977. 29.95 (ISBN 0-521-21500-5); pap. 8.95x (ISBN 0-521-29176-3). Cambridge U Pr.
Muir, Kenneth & Wells, Stanley, eds. Aspects of King Lear. LC 82-4344. (Illus.). 112p. 1982. 29.50 (ISBN 0-521-24604-0); pap. 9.95 (ISBN 0-521-28813-4). Cambridge U Pr.
Muir, Kenneth, ed. see Middleton, Thomas.
Muir, Kenneth, ed. see Shakespeare, William.
Muir, Kenneth, et al, eds. Shakespeare, Man of the Theater. LC 82-40346. (Illus.). 272p. 1983. 28.50 (ISBN 0-87413-217-7). U Delaware Pr.
Muir, Percy H., ed. see National Book League.
Muir, Ramsey. Muir's Historical Atlas: Ancient Medieval & Modern: Including Ancient & Classical, 6th Ed. & Medieval & Modern, 11th Ed. Ancient, Medieval & Modern. 10th ed. Treharne, R. E. & Fullard, Harold, eds. (Illus.). 136p. 1964. Repr. of 1911 ed. 22.50x (ISBN 0-06-495016-6). B&N Imports.
Muir, Richard. The English Village. (Illus.). 1983. pap. 9.95 (ISBN 0-500-27213-1). Thames Hudson.
--Modern Political Geography. 262p. 1975. 24.95x o.p. (ISBN 0-470-62356-X); pap. 19.95 o.p. (ISBN 0-470-99194-1). Halsted Pr.
Muir, Richard & Paddison, Ronan, eds. Politics, Geography & Behavior. (Illus.). 196p. 1980. lib. bdg. cancelled o.p. (ISBN 0-86531-058-0). Westview.
Muir, T. A., jt. auth. see Lambert, J.
Muir, W. L. Reclamation of Surface Mined Land. (Illus.). 244p. 1979. pap. 225.00 o.p. (ISBN 0-9506461-0-5, Pub. by Muir Coal Industry Info Serv England). Miller Freeman.
Muir, Willa, tr. see Feuchtwanger, Lion.
Muir, Willa, tr. see Kafka, Franz.
Muir, Willa, tr. see Renn, Ludwig.
Muir, Willa, et al, trs. see Kafka, Franz.
Muir, William K., Jr. Legislature: California's School of Politics. LC 82-16128. 197p. 1983. 19.00x (ISBN 0-226-54627-6). U of Chicago Pr.
Muirden, James. The Amateur Astronomer's Handbook. 3rd ed. LC 81-48044. (Illus.). 480p. 1983. write for info (ISBN 0-06-181622-1, HarpT). Har-Row.
--The Amateur Astronomer's Handbook. rev. ed. LC 74-5411. (Illus.). 384p. 1974. 12.95i o.p. (ISBN 0-690-00505-9). T Y Crowell.
--Astronomy with Binoculars. LC 77-11568. (Illus.). 1979. 13.41i (ISBN 0-690-01723-5). T Y Crowell.
--Our Universe. LC 80-52127. (Warwick Pr Ser.). (YA) (gr. 7 up). 1981. PLB 10.90 (ISBN 0-531-09181-3). Watts.
--The Sun's Family. 12.75x (ISBN 0-392-16722-0, SpS). Sportshelf.
Muirden, James, jt. auth. see Robinson, J. Hedley.
Muirhead, Desmond. Palms. LC 60-16856. (Illus., Orig.). 1961. 5.95 (ISBN 0-912762-07-1); pap. 2.50 (ISBN 0-912762-06-3). King.
Muirhead, James F. America the Land of Contrasts: A Briton's View of His American Kin. LC 74-87430. (American Scene Ser). Orig. Title: Bodley Head. 1970. Repr. of 1902 ed. lib. bdg. 37.50 (ISBN 0-306-71576-7). Da Capo.
Muirhead, John H. The Use of Philosophy: Californian Addresses. LC 78-24161. 1979. Repr. of 1929 ed. lib. bdg. 18.50x (ISBN 0-313-20662-7, MUUP). Greenwood.
Muirhead, Robb J. Aspects of Multivariate Statistical Theory. (Wiley Series in Probability & Mathematic Statistics). 688p. 1982. 39.95x (ISBN 0-471-09442-0, Pub. by Wiley-Interscience). Wiley.
Muir-Wood, Helen M. A History of the Classification of the Phylum Brachipoda. (Illus.). vii, 124p. 1968. Repr. of 1955 ed. 23.25x (ISBN 0-565-00078-0, Pub. by Brit Mus Nat Hist England). Sabbot-Natural Hist Bks.
Mujal-Leon, Eusebio. Communism & Political Change in Spain. LC 81-48616. 288p. 1983. 22.50x (ISBN 0-253-31389-9). Ind U Pr.
Mujica, Barbara, jt. ed. see Zahareas, Anthony.
Mujica, Francisco. History of the Skyscraper. LC 76-57764. (Architecture & Decorative Art Ser.). 1977. Repr. of 1929 ed. lib. bdg. 95.00 (ISBN 0-306-70862-0). Da Capo.
Mujumdar, A. S. & Mashelkar, R. A. Advances in Transport Processes, Vol. 2. 432p. 1982. 37.95x (ISBN 0-470-27320-8). Halsted Pr.
Mujumdar, Arun S., ed. Advances in Drying, Vol. 2. LC 80-10432. (Advances in Drying Ser.). (Illus.). 366p. 1983. text ed. 55.00 (ISBN 0-89116-255-0). Hemisphere Pub.
Mukerjee, Gitanjali, jt. ed. see Smith, Donald A.
Mukerji, A. B. The Chamars of Uttar Pradesh: A Study in Social Geography. 155p. 1980. text ed. 11.75x (ISBN 0-391-02124-9). Humanities.
Mukerji, Chandra. From Graven Images: Patterns of Modern Materialism. (Illus.). 368p. 1983. 30.00x (ISBN 0-231-05166-2); pap. 10.00 (ISBN 0-231-05167-0). Columbia U Pr.
Mukerji, Dhan G. Gay-Neck: The Story of a Pigeon. (Illus.). (gr. 4 up). 1968. 10.95 (ISBN 0-525-30400-2, 1063-320). Dutton.
Mukerji, K. G., jt. auth. see Lakhanpal, T. N.
Mukherjee, K. C. Underdevelopment, Educational Policy & Planning. 1968. 10.75x o.p. (ISBN 0-210-26951-0). Asia.
Mukherjee, Meenakshi, tr. see Bhattacharya, Lokenath.
Mukherjee, Ramkrishna. Classification & Social Research. 192p. 1983. 42.00x (ISBN 0-87395-607-9); pap. 13.95 (ISBN 0-87395-608-7). State U NY Pr.
Mukherjee, S. Boundary Element Methods in Creep & Fracture. (Illus.). 224p. 1983. 35.00 (ISBN 0-85334-163-X, Pub. by Applied Sci England). Elsevier.
Mukherjee, S. N. Sir William Jones. (Cambridge South Asian Studies). (Illus.). 1968. 27.95 (ISBN 0-521-05777-9). Cambridge U Pr.
Mukherjee, Satyanshu K. & Scutt, Jocelynne A., eds. Women & Crime. 208p. 1982. pap. text ed. 12.50x (ISBN 0-86861-067-4). Allen Unwin.
Mukherjee, Soumyendra N., jt. auth. see Leach, Edmund R.
Mukherjee, Sudhansu B. The Age Distribution of the Indian Population: A Reconstruction for the States & Territories, 1881-1961. LC 76-28367. 1977. pap. text ed. 5.00x (ISBN 0-8248-0518-6, Eastwest Ctr.). UH Pr.
Mukherji, Narayan, tr. see Levi, Sylvain.
Muktananda, Swami. Play of Consciousness. LC 78-15841. (Illus.). 1979. pap. 7.64i (ISBN 0-06-066044-9, RD 223, HarpR). Har-Row.
Mukunda, N., jt. auth. see Sudarshan, E. C.
Mukunda, N., et al. Relativistic Models of Extended Hadrons Obeying a Mas-Spin Trajectory Constraint. (Lecture Notes in Physics: Vol. 165). 163p. 1983. pap. 8.50 (ISBN 0-387-11586-2). Springer-Verlag.
Mulac, Margaret E. Educational Games for Fun. LC 77-138752. 1971. 12.45i (ISBN 0-06-013099-7, HarpT). Har-Row.
Mulaik, Stanley A., jt. auth. see James, Lawrence R.
Mular, A. L. & Bhappu, R. B., eds. Mineral Processing Plant Design. 2nd ed. LC 79-57345. (Illus.). 958p. 1980. text ed. 30.00x (ISBN 0-89520-269-7). Soc Mining Eng.
Mular, Andrew L. & Jergensen, Gerald V., III, eds. Design & Installation of Communication Circuits. LC 82-71992. (Illus.). 1022p. 1982. 40.00x (ISBN 0-89520-401-0). Soc Mining Eng.
Mulawka, Edward J. Taming & Training Parrots. (Illus.). 1981. 19.95 (ISBN 0-87666-989-5, H-1019). TFH Pubns.
--Yellow-Fronted Amazon Parrots. (Illus.). 160p. 12.95 (ISBN 0-686-91891-6). TFH Pubns.
Mulay, L. N., jt. auth. see Boudreaux, E. A.
Mulcaby, R., jt. ed. see Das, J. P.
Mulcahy. Biology & Implications of Plant Breeding. Date not set. price not set (ISBN 0-444-00738-5). Elsevier.
Mulcahy, B. To Speak True: A Study of Poetry As a Spoken Art. 4.40 o.p. (ISBN 0-08-006444-2). Pergamon.
Mulcahy, Kevin, jt. auth. see Swaim, C. Richard.
Mulcahy, Kevin V. & Katz, Richard S. America Votes: What You Should Know About Elections Today. LC 76-15592. 1976. pap. text ed. 4.95 o.p. (ISBN 0-13-023788-4, Spec). P-H.
Mulcahy, Risteard. Beat Heart Disease! LC 78-24490. (Positive Health Guide Ser.). (Illus.). 1979. 8.95 (ISBN 0-668-04678-3, 4678-3); pap. 4.95 o.p. (ISBN 0-668-04685-6, 4685-6). Arco.
Muldary. Interpersonal Relations for Health Professionals. 1983. 13.95 (ISBN 0-02-384640-2). Macmillan.

Mulder & Caldwell, eds. Sulfate Metabolism & Sulfate Conjugation: Proceedings of an International Workshop held at Noordwijkerhout, Netherlands, Sept. 20-23, 1981. (Illus.). 323p. 1982. text ed. 37.00 (ISBN 0-85066-233-8, Pub. by Taylor & Francis England). J K Burgess.

Mulder, Donald W., ed. Diagnosis & Treatment of Amyotrophic Lateral Sclerosis. 397p. 1980. 35.00 (ISBN 0-471-09490-0, Pub. by Wiley Med). Wiley.

Mulder, John C., jt. auth. see Zikmund, Barbara B.

Mulder, John C., ed. see Migliore, Daniel L.

Mulder, John C., ed. see Oxtoby, Willard G.

Mulder, John M., jt. auth. see Wilson, John F.

Mulder, John R., ed. Religion & Literature: The Convergence of Approaches. (AAR Thematic Studies). pap. 8.95 (ISBN 0-686-95072-0, 01-24-72). Scholars Pr CA.

--Religion & Literature: The Convergence of Approaches. (Thematic Studies). 8.95 (ISBN 0-686-96200-1, 01 20 47:2). Scholars Pr CA.

Mulder, Robert L., jt. auth. see Luper, Harold L.

Mulder, Rodney J., ed. see Timmerman, John J.

Mulder, Ronald A. The Insurgent Progressives in the United States Senate & the New Deal, 1933-1939. Freidel, Frank, ed. LC 78-62389. (Modern American History Ser.: Vol. 14). 1979. lib. bdg. 30.00 o.s.i. (ISBN 0-8240-3637-9). Garland Pub.

Muldoon, Sylvan & Carrington, Hereward. Projection of the Astral Body. (Illus.). 1970. pap. 5.95 (ISBN 0-87728-069-X). Weiser.

Muldoon, Thomas G. & Mahesh, Virendra B., eds. Recent Advances in Fertility Research, Pt. A: Developments in Reproductive Endocrinology. LC 82-20327. (Progress in Clinical & Biological Research Ser.: Vol. 112A). 340p. 1982. 36.00 (ISBN 0-8451-0172-2). A R Liss.

Muldowny, John, jt. auth. see McDonald, Michael J.

Mulford, Jeremy, ed. see Spender, Humphrey.

Mulford, Prentice. Thought Forces. 172p. 7.00 (ISBN 0-686-38235-8). Sun Bks.

Mulford, Robert M., et al. Caseworker & Judge in Neglect Cases. 1956. pap. 2.00 (ISBN 0-87868-072-1, G-14). Child Welfare.

Mulgan, R. G. Aristole's Political Theory: An Introduction for Students of Political Theory. 1978. pap. text ed. 7.95x (ISBN 0-19-827416-5). Oxford U Pr.

Mulhall, B. E., jt. auth. see Rhodes, R. G.

Mulhall, Michael G. Dictionary of Statistics. LC 68-18013. 1969. Repr. of 1899 ed. 71.00x (ISBN 0-8103-3887-4). Gale.

Mulhauser, Ruth E. Maurice Sceve. (World Authors Ser.). 1977. lib. bdg. 15.95 (ISBN 0-8057-6264-7, Twayne). G K Hall.

Mulhearn, Henry J. Crime Investigation. 150p. 1976. pap. text ed. 7.50x (ISBN 0-87526-217-1). Gould.

Mulhearn, John & Momeny, Gayle. The Psychiatric Hospital Today: A Quality Profile. LC 76-2671. 160p. 1976. prof ref 16.50x (ISBN 0-88410-506-7). Ballinger Pub.

Mulhern, Chieko. Koda Rohan. (World Authors Ser.). 1977. lib. bdg. 15.95 (ISBN 0-8057-6272-8, Twayne). G K Hall.

Mulhern, Maggie, jt. auth. see Swift, Pat.

Mulholland, H., jt. auth. see Bunday, B. D.

Mulholland, Joyce, jt. auth. see Brown, Meta.

Mulick, James A., jt. ed. see Matson, Johnny L.

Mulik, J. D. & Sawicki, E. Ion Chromatographic Analysis of Environmental Pollutants, Vol. 2. LC 77-92589. 1979. 47.50 (ISBN 0-250-40322-6). Ann Arbor Science.

Mulkay, M. J. The Social Process of Innovation: A Study in the Sociology of Science. (Studies in Sociology). 1977. pap. text ed. 2.00x o.p. (ISBN 0-333-13431-1). Humanities.

Mulkay, Michael J., jt. auth. see Edge, David.

Mulkern, John R., jt. auth. see Handler, Edward.

Mulkerne, D. D. & Andrews, M. E. Civil Service, Business & Industry Tests: Clerical & Stenographic. 2nd ed. 1982. 8.96 (ISBN 0-07-043987-7); instr's guide & key 3.95 (ISBN 0-07-043988-5). McGraw.

Mulkerne, D. J. & Andrews, M. E. Civil Service Tests for Typists. 1968. text ed. 8.96 (ISBN 0-07-043985-0, G); instructor's guides & key 3.95 (ISBN 0-07-043986-9). McGraw.

Mulkerne, Donald J., jt. auth. see Kahn, Gilbert.

Mulkey, Michael, jt. ed. see Gardiner, John.

Mulkey, Michael A., jt. ed. see Gardiner, John A.

Mullahy, Patrick & Melinek, Menachem, eds. Interpersonal Psychiatry. 200p. 1983. text ed. 25.00 (ISBN 0-89335-169-5). SP Med & Sci Bks.

Mullally, Joseph, tr. Peter of Spain: Tractatus Syncategorematum. Bd. with Selected Anonymous Treatises. (Medieval Philosophical Texts in Translation: No. 13). pap. 7.95 (ISBN 0-87462-213-1). Marquette.

Mullan, Fitzhugh. Vital Signs: A Young Doctor's Struggle with Cancer. 1983. 12.50 (ISBN 0-374-29445-3). FS&G.

Mullan, Sean. Essentials of Neurosurgery for Students & Practitioners. LC 61-12028. (Illus.). 1961. text ed. 17.95 o.p. (ISBN 0-8261-0479-7). Springer Pub.

Mullen, Edward J. Carlos Pellicer. (World Authors Ser.). 1977. 15.95 (ISBN 0-8057-6288-4, Twayne). G K Hall.

Mullen, J., jt. auth. see Harrison, William.

Mullen, Kenneth, jt. auth. see Ennis, Daniel.

Mullen, Lloyd see Allen, W. S.

Mullen, R. D. & Suvin, Darko, eds. Science Fiction Studies: Selected Articles on Science Fiction 1976-1977. (Science Fiction Second, Ser.). 1978. lib. bdg. 15.00 o.p. (ISBN 0-8398-2444-0, Gregg). G K Hall.

--Science-Fiction Studies: Selected Articles on Science Fiction 1973 to 1975. (Science Fiction Ser.). 320p. 1976. lib. bdg. 15.00 o.p. (ISBN 0-8398-2338-X, Gregg). G K Hall.

Mullen, Robert W. Blacks & Vietnam. LC 80-8235. 109p. 1981. lib. bdg. 18.50 (ISBN 0-8191-1526-6); pap. text ed. 7.75 (ISBN 0-8191-1527-4). U Pr of Amer.

--Rhetorical Strategies of Black Americans. LC 80-5502. 87p. 1980. pap. text ed. 7.00 (ISBN 0-8191-1113-9). U Pr of Amer.

Mullen, Tom. Funny Things Happen on the Way to the Cemetery. 1983. 7.95 (ISBN 0-686-84763-6). Word Bks.

Mullen, William F. Presidential Power & Politics. LC 75-29941. 224p. 1976. 17.95 (ISBN 0-312-64050-1); pap. text ed. 8.95 o.p. (ISBN 0-312-64085-4). St Martin.

Muller. Foreign Aid Program of the Soviet Union. 15.00 o.p. (ISBN 0-8027-0107-8). Walker & Co.

Muller & MacLeod. Neuroendocrine Perspectives, Vol. 1. Date not set. 91.00 (ISBN 0-444-80365-3). Elsevier.

Muller, jt. auth. see Barnet.

Muller, A., jt. ed. see Rouiller, C.

Muller, A., jt. ed. see Comes, F. J.

Muller, Alois, jt. ed. see Malinski, M.

Muller, B. R., jt. auth. see Haisman, P.

Muller, Claude, jt. ed. see Attal, Pierre.

Muller, David G., Jr. China as a Maritime Power. (Special Studies on East Asia). 300p. 1983. price not set (ISBN 0-86531-098-X). Westview.

Muller, E. Reading Architectural Working Drawings. 2nd ed. 1981. 24.95 (ISBN 0-13-753939-8). P-H.

Muller, E., jt. ed. see Pecile, A.

Muller, E. E. & Agnoli, A., eds. Neuroendocrine Correlates in Neurology & Psychiatry: (Developments in Neurology Ser.: Vol. 2). 1979. 58.75 (ISBN 0-444-80121-9, North Holland). Elsevier.

Muller, Edward J. Architectural Drawing & Light Construction. 2nd ed. (Illus.). 480p. 1976. 23.95 (ISBN 0-13-044578-9). P-H.

Muller, F. Max & Fausboll, V. The Dhammapada & Suttanipata. (Sacred Bks. of the East: Vol. 10). 11.00 (ISBN 0-686-97481-6). Lancaster-Miller.

Muller, F. Max, ed. The Upanisads. (Sacred Bks. of the East: Vol 1 & 15). both vols. 22.00 (ISBN 0-686-97473-5); 11.00 ea. Lancaster-Miller.

Muller, Francis J. De Paroecia Domui Religiosae Commissa. 1956. 3.50 (ISBN 0-686-11580-5). Franciscan Inst.

Muller, Frederick, ed. The Healthy Body: The Diagram Group. 526p. 1982. 39.00x (ISBN 0-584-11031-6, Pub. by Muller Ltd). State Mutual Bk.

Muller, G., jt. auth. see Fuchtbauer, Hans.

Muller, G. H. Sets & Classes on the Work by Paul Bernays. (Studies in Logic: Vol. 84). 1976. 74.50 (ISBN 0-444-10907-2, North-Holland). Elsevier.

Muller, George H. & Kirk, Robert W. Small Animal Dermatology. 2nd ed. LC 75-14785. (Illus.). 815p. 1976. text ed. 59.00 o.p. (ISBN 0-7216-6606-X). Saunders.

Muller, Gilbert H. The McGraw-Hill Reader. 800p. (Orig.). 1982. pap. 10.95x (ISBN 0-07-043978-8); instr.'s manual 10.00 (ISBN 0-07-043979-6). McGraw.

Muller, Gilbert H. & Wiener, Harvey S. The Short Prose Reader. 2nd ed. 384p. 1982. pap. 11.50x (ISBN 0-07-043995-8); instr.'s manual 5.00 (ISBN 0-07-043996-6). McGraw.

--The Short Prose Reader. (Illus.). 1979. pap. text ed. 10.95 (ISBN 0-07-043991-5, C); instr.'s manual 7.95 (ISBN 0-07-043992-3). McGraw.

Muller, H., jt. auth. see Cremer, L.

Muller, H. Nicholas, III, ed. In a State of Nature: Readings in Vermont History. Hand, Samuel D. 423p. 1982. text ed. 16.95 o.p. (ISBN 0-934720-28-2); pap. 12.95 (ISBN 0-934720-27-4). Vt Hist Soc.

Muller, Heinrich. Guns, Pistols, & Revolvers. LC 80-52998. (Illus.). 240p. 1981. 29.95 o.p. (ISBN 0-312-35392-8). St Martin.

Muller, Herbert W. Epicyclic Drive Trains: Analysis, Sythesis, & Applications. Glover, John H., ed. Mannhardt, Werner G., tr. (Illus.). 374p. 1982. 49.00 (ISBN 0-8143-1663-8). Wayne St U Pr.

Muller, Hermann J. The Modern Concept of Nature. Carlson, Elof A., ed. LC 74-170884. (Illus.). 200p. 1973. 34.50x (ISBN 0-87395-096-8). State U NY Pr.

Muller, J., jt. ed. see Ferguson, I. K.

Muller, Jean M., jt. auth. see Podolny, Walter.

Muller, Jorg. The Changing City. LC 76-46646. (Illus.). 1977. 11.95 (ISBN 0-689-50084-X, McElderry Bk). Atheneum.

--The Changing Countryside. LC 76-46647. (Illus.). 1977. 11.95 (ISBN 0-689-50085-8, McElderry Bk). Atheneum.

Muller, Jorg & Steiner, Jorg. The Sea People. LC 82-5488. (Illus.). 40p. 1982. 14.95 (ISBN 0-8052-3813-1). Schocken.

Muller, Joseph. The Star-Spangled Banner: Words & Music Issued Between 1814-1864. LC 79-169653. (Music Ser). (Illus.). 1973. Repr. of 1935 ed. lib. bdg. 27.50 (ISBN 0-306-70263-0). Da Capo.

Muller, Joseph-Emile. Velazquez. (World of Art Ser.). (Illus.). 1976. 15.00 o.p. (ISBN 0-500-18152-7); pap. 11.50 o.p. (ISBN 0-500-20147-1). Transatlantic.

Muller, Kenneth J., et al, eds. Neurobiology of the Leech. LC 81-68893. 320p. 1981. 38.50x (ISBN 0-87969-146-8). Cold Spring Harbor.

Muller, Kurt. Konventionen und Tendenzen der Gesellschaftskritik Im Expressionistischen Amerikanischen Drama der Zwanziger Jahre. 250p. (Ger.). 1977. write for info. (ISBN 3-261-02201-9). P Lang Pubs.

Muller, Manfred J. Selected Climatic Data for a Global Set of Standard Stations for Vegetation Science. 1982. 87.00 (ISBN 90-6193-945-3, Pub. by Junk Pubs. Netherlands). Kluwer Boston.

Muller, Marcia. The Cheshire Cat's Eye: A Sharon McCone Mystery. 160p. 1983. 10.95 (ISBN 0-312-13175-5). St Martin.

Muller, Max. Ancient History of Sanskrit Literature. 1979. text ed. 21.00x (ISBN 0-391-01202-9). Humanities.

Muller, Max, ed. Sacred Bks. of the East, 50 Vols. Repr. complete series 500.00 (ISBN 0-686-97471-9); vol. 11.00 ea. Lancaster-Miller.

Muller, Max, tr. Upanishads, Pts. 1 & 2. (Sacred Books of the East Ser). 10.00 ea. (ISBN 0-8446-3101-9). Peter Smith.

Muller, Oberlander. Brief Physical Geography. 1980. text ed. 23.00 (ISBN 0-394-32543-5). Random.

Muller, Peter O. Contemporary Suburban America. (Illus.). 240p. 1981. pap. 12.95 (ISBN 0-13-170647-0). P-H.

Muller, Peter O., et al. Metropolitan Philadelphia: A Study of Conflicts & Social Cleavages. LC 76-4484. (Contemporary Metropolitan Analysis Ser.). (Illus.). 88p. 1976. pap. 8.95x prof ref (ISBN 0-88410-444-3). Ballinger Pub.

Muller, Philippe. Tasks of Childhood. (World University Library). (Illus., Orig.). 1969. 4.95 o.p. (ISBN 0-07-043999-0, SP); pap. 2.95 (ISBN 0-07-043998-2). McGraw.

Muller, R., jt. auth. see Baker, J. R.

Muller, Richard S. & Kamins, Theodore I. Device Electronics for Integrated Circuits. LC 77-1332. 1977. 32.95 (ISBN 0-471-62364-4). Wiley.

Muller, Robert. Most of All They Taught Me Happiness. LC 78-52110. 1978. 11.95 (ISBN 0-385-14310-9). Doubleday.

Muller, Robert, ed. Computer Software Protection. 113p. 1981. text ed. 48.00x (ISBN 0-566-03418-2). Gower Pub Ltd.

Muller, Robert A., jt. auth. see Oberlander, Theodore M.

Muller, Romeo. The Little Rascals. 112p. (Orig.). (gr. 3-8). 1982. pap. 2.50 (ISBN 0-553-15078-2). Bantam.

Muller, Ronald E. Revitalizing America. 1980. 13.95 o.p. (ISBN 0-671-24889-8). S&S.

--Revitalizing the U. S. & World Economy: Would a Global Marshall Plan Work? (Vital Issues, Vol. XXX 1980-81: No. 10). 0.60 (ISBN 0-686-81605-6). Ctr Info Am.

Muller, Ronald E., jt. auth. see Barnet, Richard J.

Muller, Sonia. Magnets. (Illus.). (gr. 4-9). 1970. PLB 4.29 o.p. (ISBN 0-399-60438-3). Putnam Pub Group.

Muller, Theresa G. Fundamentals of Psychiatric Nursing. (Quality Paperback: No. 308). 1974. pap. 2.95x (ISBN 0-8226-0308-X). Littlefield.

Muller, Thomas, et al. The Impact of Beltways on Central Business Districts: A Case Study of Richmond. 101p. 1978. pap. 5.50 o.p. (ISBN 0-87766-216-9, 21500). Urban Inst.

Muller, V. K., ed. English-Russian Dictionary. rev. ed. 1973. 24.75 (ISBN 0-525-09881-X, 02403-720). Dutton.

Muller, Victor H., jt. ed. see Wallas, Charles H.

Muller, W. & Lindner, R. Transplutonium 1975: Proceedings. 1976. 40.50 (ISBN 0-444-11049-6, North-Holland). Elsevier.

Muller, W., ed. Dictionary of the Graphic Arts Industry. (In Eng., Ger., Fr., Rus., Span., Pol., Slovak & Hungarian). 1981. 117.00 (ISBN 0-444-99745-8). Elsevier.

Muller, W. & Blank, H., eds. Heavy Element Properties: Proceedings of the Joint Session of the Baden Meetings, Sept. 1975. new ed. LC 75-44241. (Illus.). 1976. 15.00 (ISBN 0-444-11048-8, North Holland). Elsevier.

Muller, W. H. Early History of the Supreme Court. xii, 117p. 1982. Repr. of 1922 ed. lib. bdg. 22.50x (ISBN 0-686-81665-X). Rothman.

Muller, W. Max. Egyptian Mythology & Indochinese Mythology. Bd. with Scott, James G. LC 63-19097. (Mythology of All Races Ser.: Vol. 12). (Illus.). Repr. of 1932 ed. 27.50x (ISBN 0-8154-0160-4). Cooper Sq.

Muller, Walter H. Botany: A Functional Approach. 4th ed. 25.95x (ISBN 0-02-384700-X). Macmillan.

Muller, William G. The Twenty Fourth Infantry: Past & Present. (Illus.). 1972. 10.95 o.p. (ISBN 0-88342-012-0); pap. 4.95 (ISBN 0-88342-219-0). Old Army.

Muller, Wulf, jt. auth. see Wunderli, Peter.

Muller-Schwarz. Basic Electrical Theory & Practice. 1980. 42.95 (ISBN 0-471-25912-8, Pub. by Wiley Heyden). Wiley.

Muller-Schwarze, Dietland, ed. Evolution of Play Behavior. LC 77-2385. (Benchmark Papers in Animal Behavior: Vol. 10). 1978. 52.50x (ISBN 0-87933-272-7). Hutchinson Ross.

Muller-Vollmar, Kurt, ed. The Hermeneutics Reader. 320p. Date not set. 17.50 (ISBN 0-8264-0208-9). Crossroad NY.

Mullet, Rosa K. Fall & Winter in N.C Forests. 241p. 1982. pap. 4.15 (ISBN 0-686-35754-X). Rod & Staff.

--Spring & Summer in N.C. Forests. 238p. 1982. pap. 4.15 (ISBN 0-686-35755-8). Rod & Staff.

Mullica, Karyn, jt. auth. see Ausberger, Carolyn.

Mulligan, F. K., jt. auth. see Sanburg, Delmer E., Jr.

Mulligan, Joseph F. Practical Physics: The Production & Conservation of Energy. (Illus.). 1980. text ed. 22.50 (ISBN 0-07-044032-8); instr.'s manual 15.00 (ISBN 0-07-044033-6). McGraw.

Mulligan, Kevin. Kid Brother. (gr. 7 up). 1982. 9.50 (ISBN 0-688-00896-8). Lothrop.

Mulligan, Robert W., tr. see Thomas Aquinas, Saint.

Mulliken, Frances H. A Bite of Eve's Apple: And Other Stories. 1982. pap. 9.75 (ISBN 0-8309-0348-8). Herald Hse.

--A Restoration Heritage. LC 79-15689. 1979. pap. 8.00 (ISBN 0-8309-0244-9). Herald Hse.

Mullin, Donald C. The Development of the Playhouse: A Survey of Theatre Architecture from the Renaissance to the Present. LC 77-84532. (Illus.). 1970. 39.50x (ISBN 0-520-01391-3). U of Cal Pr.

Mullin, Gerald W. Flight & Rebellion: Slave Resistance in 18th Century Virginia. LC 73-173327. 1974. pap. 6.95 (ISBN 0-19-501788-9, GB407, GB). Oxford U Pr.

Mullin, Glen, ed. see Gyatso, Sonam & Gyatso, Tenzin.

Mullin, Glenn H., ed. see Gyatso, Kalzang.

Mullin, J. B., ed. see International Spring School on Crystal Growth, 2nd, Japan, 1974.

Mullin, Michael, compiled by. Theatre at Stratford-Upon-Avon: A Catalogue-Index to Productions of the Shakespeare Memorial-Royal Shakespeare Theatre, 1879 to 1978, 2 vols. LC 79-8578. 1980. Set. lib. bdg. 65.00 (ISBN 0-313-22126-X, MSH/). Greenwood.

Mullin, Ray C. Electrical Wiring-Residential. LC 80-75458. 1981. pap. 14.00 (ISBN 0-8273-1951-7); instr's. guide 3.75 (ISBN 0-8273-1952-5). Delmar.

Mullin, Virginia L. Chemistry Experiments for Children. LC 68-9306. (Illus.). (gr. 3-10). 1968. pap. 2.50 (ISBN 0-486-22031-1). Dover.

Mullineaux, D. R., jt. auth. see Crandall, D. R.

Mulliner, K., jt. ed. see Raymond, Wayne.

Mullineux, N., jt. auth. see Bickford, J. P.

Mullins, B. P., ed. see Shtern, V. Y.

Mullins, Barbara. Australian Wildflowers in Colour. (Reed Colourbook Ser.). (Illus.). 112p. 1969. 11.50 (ISBN 0-589-07014-2, Pub. by Reed Books Australia). C E Tuttle.

Mullins, Carolyn & West, Thomas. The Office Automation Primer: Harnessing Information Technologies for Greater Productivity. 158p. 1982. 18.95 (ISBN 0-13-631085-0); pap. 9.95 (ISBN 0-13-631077-X). P-H.

Mullins, Carolyn J. A Guide to Writing & Publishing in the Social & Behavioral Sciences. LC 77-1153. 1977. pap. 19.95 (ISBN 0-471-02708-1, Pub. by Wiley-Interscience). Wiley.

Mullins, Edgar Y. La Religion Cristiana En Su Expresion Doctrinal. Hale, Sara A., tr. Orig. Title: The Christian Religion in Its Doctrinal Expression. 522p. 1980. pap. 10.95 (ISBN 0-311-09042-7). Casa Bautista.

Mullins, June & Wolfe, Suzanne. Special People Behind the Eight-Ball. LC 74-92371. 1975. 12.95 (ISBN 0-87804-255-5); pap. 8.95 (ISBN 0-685-90519-5). Mafex.

Mullins, L. J. Ion Transport in Heart. 144p. 1981. 18.00 (ISBN 0-89004-645-X). Raven.

Mullins, L. J., compiled by. Annual Reviews Reprints: Cell Membranes, 1978-1980. LC 81-65983. (Illus.). text ed. 28.00 (ISBN 0-8243-2503-6). Annual Reviews.

Mullins, L. J., et al, eds. Annual Review of Biophysics & Bioengineering, Vol. 12. (Illus.). 535p. 1983. text ed. 47.00 (ISBN 0-8243-1812-9). Annual Reviews.

Mullish, H., jt. auth. see Chiu, Y.

Mullish, Henry. A Basic Approach to BASIC. 1982. 17.95 (ISBN 0-471-06071-2). Wiley.

--How to Use a Pocket Calculator. LC 76-28333. 1977. 8.95 o.p. (ISBN 0-668-04081-5); pap. 4.95 o.p. (ISBN 0-668-04072-6). Arco.

--Structured COBOL: A Modern Approach. 400p. 1983. pap. text ed. 20.50 scp (ISBN 0-06-044652-8, HarpC); instr's. manual avail. (ISBN 0-06-364640-4). Har-Row.

Mullner, Ross & Killingsworth, Cleve. Surveys of the American Hospital Association Hospital Data Center. 214p. (Orig.). 1982. 48.75 (ISBN 0-87258-387-2, AH-097100). Am Hospital.

Mulloy, Teresa A., ed. Guide to Graduate Departments of Geography in the United States & Canada, 1980-1981. 13th ed. LC 68-59269. 1980. pap. 6.00 o.p. (ISBN 0-89291-152-2). Assn Am Geographers.

--Guide to Graduate Departments of Geography in the United States & Canada 1982-83. 15th ed. LC 68-59269. 350p. (Orig.). 1982. pap. 9.00 (ISBN 0-89291-163-8). Assn Am Geographers.

Mulloy, William & Figueroa, Gonzalo. A Kivi-Vai Teka Complex & Its Relationship to Easter Island Architectural Prehistory. (Asian & Pacific Archaeology Ser.: No. 8). (Illus.). 1978. pap. text ed. 7.00x (ISBN 0-8248-0652-2). UH Pr.

Mulock, Dinah M. The Adventures of a Brownie, Repr. Of 1872 Ed. Bd. with The Little Lame Prince. Repr. of 1875 ed. LC 75-32175. (Classics of Children's Literature, 1621-1932: Vol. 38). (Illus.). 1977. PLB 38.00 o.s.i. (ISBN 0-8240-2287-4). Garland Pub.

--John Halifax, Gentleman. 1976. 8.95x o.p. (ISBN 0-460-00123-X, Evman). Biblio Dist.

Mulraj, R. B. Beginnings of Punjab Nationalism: Autobiography of R. B. Mulraj. 1976. 8.00x o.p. (ISBN 0-88386-775-3). South Asia Bks.

Mulroy, Thomas R. Hospital Liability Revisited: How Governing Boards Can Protect Themselves & Improve Patient Care. LC 80-18633. xi, 55p. (Orig.). 1980. pap. text ed. 6.00 (ISBN 0-914818-06-6, Inquiry Bk). Blue Cross Shield.

Mulry, Ray C. & White, Arthur H. The Portable Back School: A Home Study Program for Proper Back Care. LC 81-3960. (Illus.). 53p. 1981. pap. text ed. 27.50 (ISBN 0-8016-3597-7). Mosby.

Mulryan, John, ed. Milton & the Middle Ages. LC 81-694400. 192p. 1982. 22.50 (ISBN 0-8387-5036-2). Bucknell U Pr.

Multer, H. Gray. Field Guide to Some Carbonate Rock Environments: Florida Keys & Western Bahamas, 1977. LC 76-50173. (Illus.). 1977. pap. text ed. 17.95 (ISBN 0-8403-1646-1). Kendall-Hunt.

Mulvaney, James E., ed. Macromolecular Syntheses. LC 63-18627. (Macromolecular Syntheses Ser.: Vol. 6). 1977. 38.50 o.s.i. (ISBN 0-471-02131-8, Pub. by Wiley-Interscience). Wiley.

Mulvany, Mollie. All About Obedience Training. (All About Ser.). (Illus.). 150p. 1983. 12.95 (ISBN 0-7207-1089-8, Pub by Michael Joseph). Merrimack Bk Serv.

Mulvey, C., jt. auth. see Trevithick, J. A.

Mulvey, Charles. The Economic Analysis of Trade Unions. LC 78-9094. 1978. 22.50x (ISBN 0-312-22684-5). St Martin.

Mulvey, J. H. The Nature of Matter. (Wolfson College Lectures 1980 Ser.). (Illus.). 216p. 1981. text ed. 15.95x (ISBN 0-19-851151-5). Oxford U Pr.

Mulvihill, Edward R., ed. see Sanchez-Silva, Jose M.

Mulvihill, John, ed. Bibliography & Index of Geology: Users Guide. 160p. (Orig.). 1982. pap. text ed. write for info. (ISBN 0-913312-66-5). Am Geol.

Mulvihill, John J., jt. ed. see Riccardi, Vincent M.

Mulvihill, John J., et al, eds. Genetics of Human Cancer. LC 75-44924. (Progress in Cancer Research & Therapy: Vol. 3). 541p. 1977. 31.00 (ISBN 0-89004-110-5). Raven.

Mulvoy, Mark. Sports Illustrated Golf. LC 80-8692. (Illus.). 192p. 1983. write for info. (ISBN 0-06-014871-3, HarpT); pap. write for info. (ISBN 0-06-090868-8, CN868). Har-Row.

Mulvoy, Mark & Richardson, Ernie. Sports Illustrated Curling. LC 73-3487. 1973. 6.50i (ISBN 0-397-00832-5); pap. 2.95i (ISBN 0-397-00816-3, LP-067). Har-Row.

Muma, John R. Language Handbook: Concepts, Assessment, Intervention. (Illus.). 1978. 23.95 (ISBN 0-13-522755-0). P-H.

Mumaw, Evelyn K. Woman Alone. LC 72-109937. (Orig.). 1970. pap. 1.95 o.p. (ISBN 0-8361-1620-8). Herald Pr.

Mumey, Nolie. Professor Oscar J. Goldrick & His Denver. LC 59-11065. 1959. pap. 1.25 o.p. (ISBN 0-8040-0080-8). Swallow.

Mumford, Amy R. When Divorce Ends Your Marriage...It Hurts. (Accent Expressions Ser.). (Illus.). 24p. (Orig.). 1982. 4.95 (ISBN 0-89636-099-7). Accent Bks.

Mumford, Bob. The King & You. 256p. 1974. pap. 3.50 o.p. (ISBN 0-8007-0672-2). Revell.

--The Purpose of Temptation. 160p. 1982. pap. 3.95 (ISBN 0-8007-5110-8, Power Bks). Revell.

--Take Another Look at Guidance. LC 77-166495. 156p. 1971. pap. 4.95 (ISBN 0-912106-32-8, Pub. by Logos). Bridge Pub.

Mumford, D. see Zariski, Oscar.

Mumford, David. Tata Lecture Notes on Theta Functions, 2 Vols. (Progress in Mathematics Ser.). 1983. Vol. 1, 220pp. text ed. 15.00 (ISBN 3-7643-3109-7); Vol. 2, 200pp. text ed. 17.50 (ISBN 3-7643-3110-0). Birkhauser.

Mumford, David M., jt. auth. see Smith, Peggy B.

Mumford, E., ed. see IFIP Conference on Human Choice & Computers Apr. 1-5, 1974.

Mumford, Enid & Henshall, Don. Participative Approach to Computer Systems Design: A Case Study of the Introduction of a New Computer System. LC 78-23831. 1978. 32.95x o.s.i. (ISBN 0-470-26581-7). Halsted Pr.

Mumford, Lewis. City Development: Studies in Disintegration & Renewal. LC 73-6212. 248p. 1973. Repr. of 1945 ed. lib. bdg. 16.00x (ISBN 0-8371-6890-2, MUCD). Greenwood.

--The City in History: Its Origins, Its Transformations & Its Prospects. LC 61-7689. 1968. pap. 7.95 (ISBN 0-15-618035-9, Harv). HarBraceJ.

--The Condition of Man. new ed. LC 72-91160. (Illus.). 467p. 1973. pap. 9.95 (ISBN 0-15-621550-0, Harv). HarBraceJ.

--The Culture of Cities. LC 32-27277. 1970. pap. 9.95 (ISBN 0-15-623301-0, Harv). HarBraceJ.

--Green Memories: The Story of Geddes Mumford. LC 73-6213. (Illus.). 342p. 1973. Repr. of 1947 ed. lib. bdg. 19.25x (ISBN 0-8371-6892-9, MUGM). Greenwood.

--Sketches From Life: The Autobiography of Lewis Mumford--The Early Years. LC 82-73958. (Illus.). 1983. pap. 12.45 (ISBN 0-8070-5413-5, BP 656). Beacon Pr.

--South in Architecture. LC 67-27462. (Architecture & Decorative Art Ser). 1967. Repr. of 1941 ed. lib. bdg. 21.50 (ISBN 0-306-70972-4). Da Capo.

--Technics & Civilization. LC 63-19641. (Illus.). 1963. pap. 7.95 (ISBN 0-15-688254-X, Harv). HarBraceJ.

--The Urban Prospect. LC 68-20631. 1969. pap. 4.95 (ISBN 0-15-693201-6, Harv). HarBraceJ.

Mumford, S. Conversation Pieces: Exercises in Elementary Listening Comprehension, Teacher's Book. (Materials for Language Practice Ser.). pap. 3.95 tchr's wkbk. (ISBN 0-08-029443-X). Pergamon.

Mumford, Stephen D. Vasectomy: The Decision-making Process. LC 77-71440. (Illus.). 1978. pap. 12.00 (ISBN 0-911302-33-6). San Francisco Pr.

Mumford, Thad & Muntean, Michaela. How to Make Your Own TV Show. Duenewald, Doris, ed. LC 78-58211. (Elephant Books Ser.). 1978. pap. 2.95 o.s.i. (ISBN 0-448-16401-9, G&D). Putnam Pub Group.

Mumford, Thomas M. Horizontal Harmony of the Gospels. 169p. 1982. pap. 5.95 (ISBN 0-87747-942-9). Deseret Bk.

Mumford, Thomas M., Jr., jt. auth. see Cheney, Daniel P.

Mumley, Anne. The Hospice Experience: A New Context for Death & Dying. 256p. 1983. 17.50 (ISBN 0-465-03060-2). Basic.

Mummah, Hazel & Smith, Marsella. The Geriatric Assistant. (Illus.). 320p. 1980. pap. text ed. 15.95 (ISBN 0-07-044015-8, HP). McGraw.

Mumpton, Frederick A., jt. ed. see Pond, Wilson G.

Mumtaz Ali Khan. Scheduled Castes & Their Status in India. 276p. 1980. 22.50x (ISBN 0-940500-23-X); lib. bdg. 22.50x (ISBN 0-686-92332-4); text ed. 22.50x (ISBN 0-686-98512-5). Asia Bk Corp.

Muna. The Arab Executive. LC 80-13711. 1980. 26.00 (ISBN 0-312-04697-9). St Martin.

Munakata, Toshinori. Matrices & Linear Programming with Business Applications. LC 78-54198. 1979. text ed. 21.50x (ISBN 0-8162-6166-0); solutions manual 6.00x (ISBN 0-8162-6167-9). Holden-Day.

Munari, Bruno. Animals for Sale. LC 79-19097. Orig. Title: Il venditore di animali. (Illus.). (ps-2). 1980. 4.95 (ISBN 0-529-05567-8, Philomel). Putnam Pub Group.

--The Birthday Present. LC 79-19082. Orig. Title: L'umo del camion. (Illus.). (ps-2). 1980. pap. 4.95 o.s.i. (ISBN 0-529-05565-1, Philomel). Putnam Pub Group.

--Bruno Munari's ABC. LC 60-11461. (Illus.). (ps-2). 1960. PLB 9.99 o.p. (ISBN 0-399-61201-7, Philomel); pap. 4.95 o.p. (ISBN 0-399-20884-4). Putnam Pub Group.

--Bruno Munari's Zoo. LC 63-14773. (Illus.). (ps-3). 1963. 9.99 (ISBN 0-399-61206-8, Philomel); pap. 4.95 (ISBN 0-399-20914-X). Putnam Pub Group.

--Bruno Murari's ABC. (Illus.). 48p. 1982. pap. 5.95 (ISBN 0-399-20884-4, Philomel). Putnam Pub Group.

--The Elephant's Wish. LC 79-19030. Orig. Title: Mai contenti. (Illus.). (ps-3). 1980. Repr. of 1945 ed. 4.95 o.s.i. (ISBN 0-529-05562-7, Philomel). Putnam Pub Group.

--Jimmy Has Lost His Cap. LC 79-18841. Orig. Title: Gigi cera il suo berretto. (Illus.). (ps-2). 1980. pap. 4.95 (ISBN 0-529-05563-5, Philomel). Putnam Pub Group.

--Tic, Tac, & Toc. LC 79-18852. (Illus.). (ps-2). 1980. Repr. of 1957 ed. 4.95 (ISBN 0-529-05564-3, Philomel). Putnam Pub Group.

--Who's There? Open the Door! LC 79-19012. (Illus.). (ps-2). 1980. Repr. of 1957 ed. 4.95 (ISBN 0-529-05568-6, Philomel). Putnam Pub Group.

Munasinghe, Mohan. Electric Power Pricing Policy: Working Paper. (No. 340). 56p. 1979. 3.00 (ISBN 0-686-36156-3, WP-0340). World Bank.

Munby, A. N., compiled by. British Book Sale Catalogues 1676-1800: A Union List. Coral, Lenore. 172p. 1977. lib. bdg. 32.00x o.p. (ISBN 0-7201-0703-2, Pub. by Mansell England). Wilson.

Munby, A. N., jt. ed. see Amory, Hugh.

Munby, A. N., jt. ed. see Deane, Seamus.

Munby, John. Communicative Syllabus Design. LC 77-90216. (Illus.). 1978. 21.95x (ISBN 0-521-22071-8). Cambridge U Pr.

--Communicative Syllabus Design: A Sociolinguistic Model for Defining the Content of Purpose-Specific Language Programmes. 232p. 1981. pap. text ed. 10.95 (ISBN 0-521-28294-2). Cambridge U Pr.

Muncaster, Martin. The Yachtsman's Quiz Book. (Illus.). 128p. (Orig.). 1982. 12.50 (ISBN 0-7153-8291-8). David & Charles.

Muncaster, R. G., jt. auth. see Truesdell, C.

Munce, Howard. Drawing the Nude. (Illus.). 1980. 17.50 o.p. (ISBN 0-8230-1411-8). Watson-Guptill.

--Graphics Handbook. LC 82-8278. 160p. 1982. pap. 11.95 (ISBN 0-89134-049-1). North Light Pub.

Muncey, R. W. Heat Transfer Calculations for Buildings. (Illus.). 1979. 26.75x (ISBN 0-85334-852-9, Pub. by Applied Sci England). Elsevier.

Munch. Life Insurance in Estate Planning. LC 80-84027. 1981. text ed. 55.00 (ISBN 0-316-58930-6); 1982 supplement 20.00 (ISBN 0-316-37218-8). Little.

Munch, Charles. I Am a Conductor. Burkatt, Leonard, tr. from Fr. LC 78-3638. 1978. Repr. of 1955 ed. lib. bdg. 20.00x (ISBN 0-313-20372-5, MUIA). Greenwood.

Munch, Peter A. & Olsen, Magnus, eds. Norse Mythology: Legends of Gods & Heroes. rev. ed. Hustuedt, Sigurd B., tr. LC 68-31092. (Illus.). 1968. Repr. of 1926 ed. 34.00x (ISBN 0-8103-3454-2). Gale.

Munch, Richard W. Harry G. Travers Legends of Terror, Vol. 1. Hershey, Richard & Bush, Lee, eds. (Roller Coaster Designers Ser.). (Illus.). 175p. 1982. pap. 14.95 (ISBN 0-935408-02-9). Amusement Pk Bks.

Munch-Petersen, Thomas, tr. see Nissen, Henrik S.

Munda, I. M. Survey of the Benthis Algal Vegetation of the Dyrafjordur, Northwest Iceland. (Offprint from Nova Hedwigia Ser.: No. 29). (Illus.). 1978. pap. text ed. 16.00 (ISBN 3-7682-1201-7). Lubrecht & Cramer.

Munday, Anthony. The English Roman Life. Ayres, Phillip J., ed. (Studies in Tudor & Stewart Literature). (Illus.). 1980. 28.50x (ISBN 0-19-812635-2). Oxford U Pr.

Munday, Don. The Unknown Mountain. LC 75-36436. 268p. 1976. pap. 6.95 o.p. (ISBN 0-916890-38-4). Mountaineers.

Mundel, Marvin E., ed. Productivity: A Series from Industrial Engineering. 1978. pap. text ed. 16.00 (ISBN 0-89806-004-4, 123); pap. text ed. 8.00 members. Inst Indus Eng.

Mundhenk, N., jt. auth. see Clark, D. J.

Mundhenk, Robert T. & Siebenschuh, William R. Contact: A Guide to Writing Skills. LC 77-73468. (Illus.). 1977. pap. text ed. 13.95 (ISBN 0-395-25110-9); instr's. manual 0.50 (ISBN 0-395-25111-7). HM.

Mundis, Hester. Separate Ways. LC 77-21544. 1978. 8.95 o.p. (ISBN 0-698-10864-7, Coward). Putnam Pub Group.

--Working Girl. 1981. 12.95 (ISBN 0-698-11110-9, Coward). Putnam Pub Group.

Mundis, Jerrold, ed. The Dog Book. (Illus.). 1983. 19.95 (ISBN 0-87795-461-5). Arbor Hse.

Mundlak, Yair & Singer, Fred. Arid Zone Development: Potentialities & Problems. LC 76-44407. 320p. 1977. prof ref 22.50x (ISBN 0-88410-050-2). Ballinger Pub.

Mundo, Laura. The Mundo UFO Report. 1983. 9.95 (ISBN 0-533-04735-8). Vantage.

Mundo Lo, Sara de see De Mundo Lo, Sara.

Mundt, Barbara, jt. auth. see Halle, Antoinette.

Mundy, Bernard K., jt. auth. see Loyd, Richard B.

Mundy, Jean & Odum, Linda. Leisure Education: Theory & Practice. LC 78-12434. 1979. text ed. 23.95x (ISBN 0-471-01347-1). Wiley.

Mundy, Jon. Learning to Die. LC 76-21119. 96p. 1976. pap. cancelled o.p. (ISBN 0-89345-002-2, Freedeeds Bks). Garber Comm.

Mundy, Simon. Elgar: His Life & Times. expanded ed. (Life & Times Ser.). (Illus.). 176p. 1981. Repr. of 1980 ed. 12.95 (ISBN 0-87666-581-4, Z-50). Paganiniana Pubns.

Mundy, Talbot. I Say Sunrise. 1969. pap. 4.95 (ISBN 0-87516-068-9). De Vorss.

--Om, the Secret of Ahbor Valley. 392p. 1980. pap. 7.25 (ISBN 0-913004-39-1). Point Loma Pub.

Munem, Mustafa & Foulis, David. Calculus. LC 79-770818. (Illus.). 1978. text ed. 34.95x (ISBN 0-87901-087-8); Pt. 1, LC79-64155. 23.95x (ISBN 0-87901-105-X); Pt. 2, LC79-64155. 23.95x (ISBN 0-87901-106-8); study guide 6.95 (ISBN 0-87901-091-6); differential equations supplement 3.95x (ISBN 0-87901-102-5); study guide, pt. 1 6.95x (ISBN 0-87901-096-7); study guide, pt. 2 6.95x (ISBN 0-87901-097-5). Worth.

Munem, Mustafa & Foulis, David J. College Algebra with Applications. LC 81-52996. (Illus.). 1982. text ed. 20.95 (ISBN 0-87901-170-X); study guide 7.95 (ISBN 0-87901-173-4). Worth.

Munem, Mustafa & Tschirhart, William. Beginning Algebra. 2nd ed. LC 76-27110. (Illus.). 1977. 21.95x (ISBN 0-87901-063-0); study guide 7.95x (ISBN 0-87901-066-5). Worth.

--College Algebra. 2nd ed. LC 78-65417. 1979. text ed. 21.95x (ISBN 0-87901-098-3); study guide 7.95x (ISBN 0-87901-099-1). Worth.

--College Trigonometry. 1974. text ed. 20.95x (ISBN 0-87901-028-2); study guide 7.95x (ISBN 0-87901-029-0). Worth.

--Intermediate Algebra. 2nd ed. LC 76-27388. (Illus.). 1977. text ed. 21.95x (ISBN 0-87901-064-9); study guide 7.95x (ISBN 0-87901-067-3). Worth.

Munem, Mustafa & Yizze, James P. Precalculus. 3rd ed. LC 77-81759. (Illus.). 1978. text ed. 22.95x (ISBN 0-87901-086-X); study guide 7.95x (ISBN 0-87901-092-4). Worth.

Munem, Mustafa A. & Foulis, David J. Algebra & Trigonometry: With Applications. (Illus.). xii, 589p. 1982. text ed. 21.95x (ISBN 0-87901-133-5); study guide 7.95 (ISBN 0-87901-164-5). Worth.

--College Trigonometry with Applications. LC 81-52995. (Illus.). 1982. text ed. 20.95 (ISBN 0-87901-171-8); study guide 7.95 (ISBN 0-87901-175-0). Worth.

Munford, Kerry & Wordsworth, Morris A. Beginner's Guide to Basketball. 1974. 12.50 o.p. (ISBN 0-7207-0740-4). Transatlantic.

Munford, Paul, jt. auth. see Mindess, Harvey.

Munford, W. A. History of the Library Association, 1877 to 1977. 1976. lib. bdg. 37.95x (ISBN 0-85365-488-3, Pub. by Lib Assn England); pap. text ed. 10.00x (ISBN 0-85365-600-2). Oryx Pr.

Mungall, Constance. Probate Guide for British Columbia. 4th ed. 96p. 1982. 12.95 (ISBN 0-88908-146-8); administration forms 14.95 (ISBN 0-686-35990-9); probate forms 13.95 (ISBN 0-686-37239-5). Self Counsel Pr.

Mungall, Dennis, ed. Applied Clinical Pharmacokinetics. 1982. text ed. write for info. (ISBN 0-89004-727-8). Raven.

Mungall, William S., jt. auth. see Doyle, Michael P.

Mungazi, Dickson A. The Underdevelopment of African Education: A Black Zimbabwean Perspective. LC 82-13696. (Illus.). 274p. (Orig.). 1982. lib. bdg. 23.00 (ISBN 0-8191-2669-1); pap. text ed. 11.50 (ISBN 0-8191-2670-5). U Pr of Amer.

Mungello, David E. Leibniz & Confucianism: The Search for Accord. LC 77-4053. 1977. text ed. 12.00x (ISBN 0-8248-0545-3). UH Pr.

Munger, James I., jt. auth. see Miller, Erston V.

Mungo, Raymond. Confessions from Left Field: Baseball Pilgrimage. 192p. 1983. 12.95 (ISBN 0-525-24168-X, 01258-370). Dutton.

Munguia, E., Jr., tr. see Azuelo, Mariano.

Municipal Finance Officers Association. An Accounting Handbook for Small Cities & Other Governmental Units. LC 78-71711. 153p. 1978. 15.00 (ISBN 0-686-84267-7). Municipal.

--A Capital Improvement Programming Handbook for Small Cities & Other Governmental Units. LC 78-71712. (Illus.). 80p. 1978. 15.00 (ISBN 0-686-84280-4). Municipal.

--Community Development Block Grant Budgetary & Financial Management. 134p. 1978. 14.95 (ISBN 0-686-84366-5). Municipal.

--A Debt Management Handbook for Small Cities & Other Governmental Units. LC 78-71726. (Debt Administration Ser.). (Illus.). 69p. 1978. 15.00 (ISBN 0-686-84294-4). Municipal.

--Governmental Accounting, Auditing, & Financial Reporting. LC 80-84747. (Illus.). 314p. 1980. nonmember 35.00 (ISBN 0-686-84252-9); member 27.50 (ISBN 0-686-84253-7). Municipal.

--A Guidebook to Improved Financial Management for Small Cities & Other Governmental Units. LC 78-71709. (Illus.). 115p. 1978. 9.00 (ISBN 0-686-84362-2). Municipal.

--Guidelines for the Preparation pf a Public Employee Retirement System Comprehensive Annual Financial Report. (Illus.). 66p. 1980. pap. 10.00 Nonmember (ISBN 0-686-84368-1); pap. 10.00 Member (ISBN 0-686-84369-X). Municipal.

--Is Your City Heading For Financial Difficulty? A Guidebook for Small Cities & Other Governmental Units. (Illus.). 43p. 1978. 6.00 (ISBN 0-686-84361-4). Municipal.

--Official Statements for Offerings of Securities by Local Governments-Examples & Guidlines. 64p. 1981. Nonmember Price 12.00 (ISBN 0-686-84334-7); Member Price 10.00 (ISBN 0-686-84335-5). Municipal.

--An Operating Budget Handbook for Small Cities & Other Governmental Units. LC 78-71727. (Illus.). 148p. 1978. 15.00 (ISBN 0-686-84276-6). Municipal.

Municipal Finance Officers Association Government Finance Research Center. State & Local Government Finance & Financial Management: A Compendium of Current Research. LC 78-70328. 690p. 1978. 18.00 (ISBN 0-686-84363-0). Municipal.

Municipal Finance Officers Association. State & Local Government Fiscal Almanac 1982-MFOA Membership Directory. 400p. 1982. pap. 50.00 Nonmemmber (ISBN 0-686-84339-8); pap. 35.00 Member (ISBN 0-686-84340-1). Municipal.

--A Treasury Management Handbook for Small Cities & Other Governmental Units. LC 78-71725. (Illus.). 93p. 1978. 15.00 (ISBN 0-686-84374-6). Municipal.

Munitz, Milton K. The Ways of Philosophy. 1979. text ed. 21.95x (ISBN 0-02-384850-2). Macmillan.

Munk, W. H. The Rotation of the Earth. LC 73-130911. (Cambridge Monographs in Mechanics & Applied Mathematics). (Illus.). 323p. 1975. 32.50 (ISBN 0-521-20778-9). Cambridge U Pr.

Munkacsi, Bernat, jt. ed. see Kunos, Ignacz.

Munkres, James. Topology: A First Course. (Illus.). 448p. 1975. ref. ed. 29.95 (ISBN 0-13-925495-1). P-H.

Munn, Elijah H. The Progress of Woman. 84p. 6.95 (ISBN 0-9609828-0-9). EHM Pub.

Munn, H. Warner. The Book of Munn or "A Recipe for Roast Camel". Mayer, Frederick J., ed. (Illus.). 138p. (gr. 3-8). 1979. 25.00 (ISBN 0-686-36858-4); PLB 20.00 (ISBN 0-686-99790-5); special limited edition, signed 50.00 (ISBN 0-686-99791-3). Outre House.

Munn, Harry & Metzger, Norman. Effective Communication in Health Care: A Supervisor's Handbook. LC 81-1378. 264p. 1981. text ed. 28.95 (ISBN 0-89443-356-3). Aspen Systems.

Munn, Harry E., Jr. The Nurse's Communication Handbook. LC 80-13066. 187p. 1980. text ed. 24.95 (ISBN 0-89443-284-2). Aspen Systems.

Munn, I., jt. auth. see Borodin, A.

Munn, Michael. Great Film Epics: The Stories Behind the Scenes. (Ungar Film Library). (Illus.). 191p. 1983. pap. 11.95 (ISBN 0-8044-6532-0). Ungar.

Munn, R. E. Biometeorological Methods. LC 71-97488. (Environmental Science Ser.). 1970. 19.50 (ISBN 0-12-510250-X); pap. 9.95 (ISBN 0-12-510256-9). Acad Pr.

--Environmental Impact Assessment: Principles & Procedures, Scope Report 5. 2nd ed. LC 78-10145. (SCOPE Scientific Committee on Problems of the Environment Ser.). 1979. pap. 26.95 (ISBN 0-471-99745-5, Pub. by Wiley-Interscience). Wiley.

Munn, R. E. see Landsberg, H. E.

Munn, Sherrill. Luke, Vol. 2. (Beacon Small Group Studies). 68p. (Orig.). 1981. pap. 2.25 (ISBN 0-8341-0689-2). Beacon Hill.

Munnell, Alicia H. The Future of Social Security. LC 76-51883. (Studies in Social Economics). 1977. 16.95 (ISBN 0-8157-5896-0); pap. 7.95 (ISBN 0-8157-5895-2). Brookings.

Munnick, Harriet. Catholic Church Records of the Pacific Northwest: Vancouver & Stellamaris Mission. LC 72-83958. (Illus.). 1972. 25.00 (ISBN 0-8323-0375-5). Binford.

Munniksma, F., ed. International Business Dictionary in Nine Languages. 1974. 45.00x (ISBN 90-267-0394-5, 1526). Esperanto League North Am.

Munonye, John. Oil Man of Obange. (African Writers Ser.). 1971. pap. text ed. 4.50x (ISBN 0-435-90094-3); pap. text ed. 4.50x. Heinemann Ed.

Munoz, A. Lopez. Programas Para Dias Especiales Tomo II. 64p. 1980. Repr. of 1977 ed. pap. 1.95 (ISBN 0-311-07006-X). Casa Bautista.

Munoz, Faye U. & Endo, Russell, eds. Perspectives on Minority Group Mental Health. LC 81-40848. 192p. (Orig.). 1982. lib. bdg. 23.00 (ISBN 0-8191-2343-9); pap. text ed. 10.25 (ISBN 0-8191-2344-7). U Pr of Amer.

Munoz, Hector. Will You Hear My Confession? Bair, Robert, tr. from Span. LC 82-20597. 174p. 1983. pap. 6.95 (ISBN 0-8189-0439-9). Alba.

Munoz, Heraldo, ed. From Dependency to Development: Strategies to Overcome Underdevelopment & Inequality. (Westview Special Studies in Social, Political, & Economic Development). 300p. 1981. lib. bdg. 30.00 (ISBN 0-89158-902-3); pap. 12.50 (ISBN 0-86531-079-3). Westview.

Munoz, Lopez A. Programas Para Dias Especiales Tomo I. 107p. 1981. pap. 1.95 (ISBN 0-311-07005-1). Casa Bautista.

Munoz, Lopez A. & Lumpuy, Luis B. Tres Dramas Ocasionales. 24p. Repr. of 1976 ed. 0.80 o.p. (ISBN 0-311-07305-0). Casa Bautista.

Munoz, Olivia, jt. auth. see Lipton, Gladys.

Munro, A. & McCullough, W. Psychiatry for Social Workers. LC 75-80842. 1969. 18.50 (ISBN 0-08-006366-7); pap. 9.75 (ISBN 0-08-006365-9). Pergamon.

Munro, Alice. The Beggar Maid. 1982. pap. 2.95 (ISBN 0-686-97685-1). Bantam.

--Lives of Girls & Women. (RL 10). 1974. pap. 3.50 (ISBN 0-451-12294-1, AE2294, Sig). NAL.

--The Moons of Jupiter. LC 82-48734. 233p. 1983. 12.95 (ISBN 0-394-52952-9). Knopf.

Munro, Andrew K. Autobiography of a Thief. 155p. 1973. 8.50 o.p. (ISBN 0-7181-0944-9). Transatlantic.

Munro, C. Lynn. The Galbraithian Vision: The Cultural Criticism of John Kenneth Galbraith. 236p. 1977. pap. text ed. 10.50 (ISBN 0-8191-0255-5). U Pr of Amer.

Munro, Colin. Sailing Ships. (Illus.). 223p. 1975. 15.00 o.p. (ISBN 0-7207-0718-8). Transatlantic.

Munro, Colin R. Television Censorship & the Law. 187p. 1979. text ed. 31.50x (ISBN 0-566-00176-4). Gower Pub Ltd.

Munro, Dana C., jt. auth. see Strayer, Joseph R.

Munro, Donald, jt. ed. see Pieterse, Cosmo.

Munro, Eleanor. Originals: American Women Artists. 1982. pap. 12.95 (ISBN 0-671-42812-8, Touchstone Bks). S&S.

--Originals: Women Artists. 1979. 24.95 (ISBN 0-671-23109-X). S&S.

Munro, H. H. see Saki.

Munro, Hamish N., jt. ed. see McKigney, John I.

Munro, Hector H. The Storyteller. (Illus.). 112p. (gr. 4 up). 1982. 10.95 (ISBN 0-87923-445-8). Godine.

Munro, J. F. The Treatment of Obesity. 248p. 1979. text ed. 29.95 o.p. (ISBN 0-8391-1424-9). Univ Park.

Munro, J. M., jt. ed. see Bushrui, S. B.

Munro, John. Employment Interviewing. 224p. 1978. 30.00x (ISBN 0-7121-0570-0, Pub. by Macdonald & Evans). State Mutual Bk.

Munro, John A., jt. auth. see Munro, Robert A.

Munro, John M. Arthur Symons. (English Authors Ser.). 14.95 (ISBN 0-8057-1528-2, Twayne). G K Hall.

--James Elroy Flecker. (English Authors Ser.). 1976. lib. bdg. 14.95 (ISBN 0-8057-6656-1, Twayne). G K Hall.

--A Mutual Concern: The Story of the American University of Beirut. LC 77-22003. 1977. 25.00x (ISBN 0-88206-014-7). Caravan Bks.

--Nairn Way: Desert Bus to Baghdad. LC 80-11875. 1980. 25.00x (ISBN 0-88206-035-X). Caravan Bks.

Munro, Margaret. The Psychology & Education of the Young: A Guide to the Principles of Development, Learning & Assessment. 1969. text ed. 8.50x o.p. (ISBN 0-435-80620-3). Heinemann Ed.

Munro, Mary. This Girl Is Mine. (Aston Hall Ser.: No. 118). 192p. (Orig.). 1981. pap. 1.75 o.p. (ISBN 0-523-41134-0). Pinnacle Bks.

Munro, Pamela, ed. see Symposium on Switch Reference & Universal Grammar.

Munro, Pamela E. Topics in Mojave Syntax. LC 75-25120. (American Indian Linguistics Ser.). 1976. lib. bdg. 42.00 o.s.i. (ISBN 0-8240-1970-9). Garland Pub.

Munro, Robert A. & Munro, John A. Real Estate Periodicals Index, 1981, Vol. 1. 118p. (Orig.). 1982. pap. text ed. 60.00x (ISBN 0-911553-00-2). Munro Assocs.

Munro, Robert A & Munro, John A. Real Estate Periodicals Index, 1982, Vol. 2. 135p. (Orig.). 1983. pap. 60.00x (ISBN 0-911553-01-0). Munro Assocs.

Munro, Robert J. Grievance Arbitration Procedure: Legal & Policy Guidelines for Public Schools, Community Colleges & Higher Education. (New Studies on Law & Society Ser.). 264p. (Orig.). 1982. text ed. 26.50x (ISBN 0-86733-021-X); pap. text ed. 16.50x o.p (ISBN 0-686-98372-6). Assoc Faculty Pr.

Munro, Robert J., jt. auth. see Taylor, Betty W.

Munro, William B. Crusaders of New France. 1918. text ed. 8.50x (ISBN 0-686-83519-0). Elliots Bks.

Munro-Ashman, D., ed. see International Congress of Allergology.

Munroe, Elizabeth A. The Shade Upon My Right Hand. 1982. 7.95 (ISBN 0-533-05359-5). Vantage.

Munroe, Esther. Sprouts to Grow & Eat. LC 74-23609. (Illus.). 128p. 1974. pap. 6.95 (ISBN 0-8289-0226-7). Greene.

Munroe, John A. Colonial Delaware: A History. LC 78-18738. (History of the American Colonies Ser.). 1978. lib. bdg. 30.00 (ISBN 0-527-18711-9). Kraus Intl.

Munroe, R., tr. see Dolci, Danilo.

Munro-Smith. Applied Naval Architecture. 1967. 17.50 (ISBN 0-444-19850-4). Elsevier.

Munschauer, John L. Jobs for English Majors & Other Smart People. 180p. 1982. pap. 6.95 (ISBN 0-87866-144-1, 1441). Petersons Guides.

Munsche, P. B. Gentlemen & Poachers: The English Game Laws 1671-1831. LC 81-6168. (Illus.). 232p. 1981. 42.50 (ISBN 0-521-23284-8). Cambridge U Pr.

Munsell, Joel. Chronology of the Origin & Progress of Paper & Paper-Making. Bidwell, John, ed. LC 78-74389. (Nineteenth-Century Book Arts & Printing History Ser.: Vol. 4). 1980. lib. bdg. 27.50 o.s.i. (ISBN 0-8240-3878-9). Garland Pub.

Munsey, Brenda, ed. Moral Development, Moral Education, & Kohlberg. LC 80-50. 478p. (Orig.). 1980. pap. 14.95 (ISBN 0-89135-020-9). Religious Educ.

Munshaw, Nancy, jt. ed. see Nagel, Stuart.

Munshi, Iskander. History of Shah Abbas the Great, 2 vols. LC 78-20663. (Persian Heritage Ser.: No. 28). 1400p. 1979. 100.00x (ISBN 0-89158-296-7). Caravan Bks.

Munshi, Kiki S., jt. auth. see Kaushall, Philip.

Munshower. Diane Keaton Scrapbook. 5.95 o.p. (ISBN 0-448-16380-2, G&D). Putnam Pub Group.

Munshower, Suzanne. The Bee Gees. (Illus.). 1978. pap. 3.95 (ISBN 0-8256-3923-9, Quick Fox). Putnam Pub Group.

Munson, Albe E. Construction Design for Landscape Architects. (Illus.). 212p. 1974. 34.50 (ISBN 0-07-044046-8, P&RB). McGraw.

Munson, Carlton E. An Introduction to Clinical Social Work Supervision. LC 83-620. 300p. 1983. text ed. 24.95 (ISBN 0-86656-196-X); pap. text ed. 14.95 (ISBN 0-86656-197-8). Haworth Pr.

Munson, Carlton E., ed. Social Work Supervision: Classic Statements & Critical Issues. LC 78-72149. 1979. pap. text ed. 12.95 (ISBN 0-02-922280-X). Free Pr.

Munson, Eric, ed. see Wiederhold, Gio.

Munson, Eric M., ed. see Bone, Hugh A. & Ranney, Austin.

Munson, Eric M., ed. see Brieland, Donald, et al.

Munson, Eric M., ed. see Faunce, William.

Munson, Eric M., ed. see Ferguson, John H. & McHenry, Dean E.

Munson, Eric M., ed. see Ferguson, John & McHenry, Dean.

Munson, Eric M., ed. see May, Janice, et al.

Munson, Eric M., ed. see Palen, J. John.

Munson, Eric M., ed. see Pritchett, C. H.

Munson, Gorham B. Writers Workshop Companion. LC 69-14009. 1969. Repr. of 1969 ed. lib. bdg. 16.00x (ISBN 0-8371-0580-3, MUWW). Greenwood.

Munson, Ken. U. S. Commercial Aircraft. (Illus.). 192p. 1982. 19.95 (ISBN 0-86720-628-4). Sci Bks Intl.

Munson, Kenneth, ed. Gravity Stealers. 12.50x (ISBN 0-392-06675-0, ABC). Sportshelf.

Munson, Patrick J. & Harn, Alan D. An Archaeological Survey of the American Bottoms & Adjacent Bluffs, Illinois, 2 pts. (Reports of Investigations Ser.: No. 21). (Illus.). 123p. 1971. pap. 3.00 (ISBN 0-89792-046-5). Ill St Museum.

Munson, Paul L. see Harris, Robert S., et al.

Munson, Paul L., et al see Harris, Robert S., et al.

Munson, Robert D. Potassium, Calcium, & Magnesium in the Tropics & Subtropics. Brosheer, J. C., ed. LC 82-11944. (Technical Bulletins Ser.: T-23). (Illus.). 60p. (Orig.). pap. text ed. 8.00 (ISBN 0-88090-041-5). Intl Fertilizer.

Munson, Ronald. The Way of Words: An Informal Logic. LC 75-31028. (Illus.). 448p. 1976. 20.95 (ISBN 0-395-20625-1); ans. bk. 2.35 (ISBN 0-395-24229-0). HM.

Munson, Shirley & Nelson, Jo. Cooking with Apples. LC 75-18210. 128p. (Orig.). 1975. pap. 3.95 (ISBN 0-89795-016-X). Farm Journal.

Munson, Thomas N. Reflective Theology: Philosophical Orientations in Religion. LC 75-36099. 211p. 1976. Repr. of 1968 ed. lib. bdg. 15.75x (ISBN 0-8371-8624-2, MURT). Greenwood.

Munson, Thurman & Appel, Martin. Thurman Munson. LC 78-8924. (Illus.). 1978. 9.95 (ISBN 0-698-10917-1, Coward). Putnam Pub Group.

Munster, Andrew M. Burn Care for the House Officer. (House Officer Ser.). (Illus.). 100p. 1980. softcover 9.95 (ISBN 0-683-06157-7). Williams & Wilkins.

Munsterberg, Hugo. The Ceramic Art of Japan: A Handbook for Collectors. LC 63-20586. (Illus.). 272p. 1964. 37.50 (ISBN 0-8048-0083-9). C E Tuttle.

--The Crown of Life: Artisitc Creativity in Old Age. (Illus.). 256p. pap. 12.95 (ISBN 0-15-623202-2, Harv). HarBraceJ.

--The Crown of Life: Artistic Creativity in Old Age. (Illus.). 256p. cloth 24.95 (ISBN 0-15-123156-7); pap. 12.95 (ISBN 0-15-623202-2). HarBraceJ.

--The History of Women Artists. (Illus.). 160p. 1975. 12.95 (ISBN 0-517-52380-9, C N Potter Bks). Crown.

Munsterman. Purchasing & Supply Management Handbook for School Business Officials. 1978. 5.00 (ISBN 0-910170-08-8). Assn Sch Busn.

Muntadas, Antonio, jt. ed. see D'Agostino, Peter.

Muntean, Michaela. Family: Theodore Mouse Goes to Sea. LC 82-82290. (Little Golden Bk.). (Illus.). 24p. (ps-2). 1983. 0.89 (ISBN 0-307-02015-0, Golden Pr); PLB price not set (ISBN 0-307-60198-6). Western Pub.

--Fargo North's Do-It-Yourself Detective Book. LC 78-67488. (Electric Company Bks). (Illus.). (gr. 2-5). 1979. PLB 7.65 (ISBN 0-448-13692-9, G&D); pap. 2.95 (ISBN 0-448-16402-7). Putnam Pub Group.

--If You Could Choose a Pet. (First Little Golden Bk.). (Illus.). (ps). 1983. 0.69 (ISBN 0-686-84753-9, Golden Pr); PLB price not set (ISBN 0-307-68143-2). Western Pub.

--Panda Bear's Secret. (First Little Golden Bk.). (Illus.). 24p. (ps). 1983. 0.69 (ISBN 0-307-10136-3, Golden Pr); PLB price not set (ISBN 0-307-68136-X). Western Pub.

Muntean, Michaela, jt. auth. see Mumford, Thad.

Munter, Preston K., jt. auth. see Greiff, Barrie S.

Munting, Roger. The Economic Development of the U. S. S. R. LC 82-42545. 240p. 1982. 25.00x (ISBN 0-312-22885-6). St Martin.

Munton, Alan, ed. see Lewis, Wyndham.

Munton, R. & Stott, J. R. Refrigeration at Sea. 2nd ed. (Illus.). 1978. text ed. 53.50x (ISBN 0-85334-766-2, Pub. by Applied Sci England). Elsevier.

Munton, R. J., jt. auth. see Morgan, W. B.

Munton, Richard. London's Green Belt: Containment in Practice. (London Research Ser. in Geography: No. 3). (Illus.). 184p. 1983. text ed. 24.95x (ISBN 0-04-333020-7). Allen Unwin.

Muntz, Carrie, tr. see Graham, Billy.

Muntz, E. Phillip, jt. auth. see Logan, Wende W.

Munz, Peter. Life in the Age of Charlemagne. (European Life Ser.). (Illus.). (gr. 7-11). 1969. 6.75 o.p. (ISBN 0-399-20124-6). Putnam Pub Group.

--When the Golden Bough Breaks: Structuralism or Typology? 158p. 1973. 15.00 (ISBN 0-7100-7650-9). Routledge & Kegan.

Munz, Peter, tr. see Fichtenau, Heinrich.

Munz, Peter, tr. see Garin, Eugenio.

Munz, Philip A. A Flora of Southern California. (Illus.). 1974. 35.00x (ISBN 0-520-02146-0). U of Cal Pr.

--Supplement to a California Flora. 1968. 15.50x (ISBN 0-520-00904-5). U of Cal Pr.

Munz, Philip A. & Keck, David D. A California Flora & Supplement. 1973. Repr. 35.00x (ISBN 0-520-02405-2). U of Cal Pr.

Munzert, Alfred. Test Your Computer IQ. Levy, Valerie, ed. (Test Yourself Ser.). (Orig.). 1983. pap. 4.95 (ISBN 0-671-47171-6). Monarch Pr.

Muqiao, Xue. Current Economic Problems in China. Fung, K. K., tr. (China & East Asia Ser.). 150p. 1982. lib. bdg. 17.00 (ISBN 0-86531-404-7). Westview.

Muqiao, Xue, ed. Almanac of China's Economy 1981 with Economic Statistics 1949-1980. 1128p. 1982. Prof. Ref. 155.00x (ISBN 0-88410-894-5). Ballinger Pub.

Mura, T. Micromechanics of Defects in Solids. 1982. lib. bdg. 98.00 (ISBN 90-247-2560-7, Pub. by Martinus Nijhoff Netherlands). Kluwer Boston.

Murach, Mike. Business Data Processing. 3rd ed. 432p. 1980. 19.95 (ISBN 0-574-21275-2, 13-4275); instr's. guide avail. (ISBN 0-574-21276-0, 13-4276); study guide 6.95 (ISBN 0-574-21277-9, 13-4277); transparency masters 3.95 (ISBN 0-574-21278-7, 13-4278); FORTRAN suppl 7.95 (ISBN 0-574-21285-X, 13-4279); BASIC suppl. 7.95 (ISBN 0-574-21290-6, 13-4280); COBOL suppl. 8.95 (ISBN 0-574-21280-9, 13-4281). SRA.

--Standard COBOL. 2nd ed. LC 74-34184. (Illus.). 400p. 1975. pap. text ed. 17.95 (ISBN 0-574-18401-5, 13-4010); instr's guide avail. (ISBN 0-574-18402-3, 13-4011). SRA.

--Structured COBOL. 1980. pap. text ed. 17.95 (ISBN 0-574-21260-4, 13-4260); instr's guide avail. (ISBN 0-574-21261-2, 13-4261); os supplement 4.95 (ISBN 0-574-21263-9, 13-4263); dos supplement 4.95 (ISBN 0-574-21264-7, 13-4264). SRA.

--System-Three-Sixty RPG. LC 70-178830. (Illus.). 297p. 1972. pap. text ed. 18.95 (ISBN 0-574-16097-3, 13-1415); instr's guide avail. (ISBN 0-574-16128-7, 13-1416); transparency masters 29.95 (ISBN 0-574-16129-5, 13-1417). SRA.

Murach, Mike & Noll, Paul. Structured ANS COBOL, 2 pts. Incl. Pt. 1. A Course for Novices. 498p; Pt. 2. An Advanced Course. 458p. (Illus.). 1979. pap. text ed. 20.00 ea. (ISBN 0-911625-13-5). M Murach & Assoc.

Murach, Mike, jt. auth. see Wohl, Gerald.

Murach, Mike, ed. see Lowe, Doug.

Murach, Mike, ed. see McQuillen, Kevin.

Murach, Mike, jt. auth. see Noll, Paul.

Murai, Harold M., jt. auth. see Bradford, Ann L.

Murakami, K. & Ono, K. Chemorheology of Polymers. (Polymer Science Library: Vol. 1). 216p. 1980. 47.00 (ISBN 0-444-41831-8). Elsevier.

Murakami, Y. Logic & Social Choice. (Monographs in Modern Logic). 1968. pap. 6.95 o.p. (ISBN 0-7100-2981-0). Routledge & Kegan.

Murakami, Y., jt. auth. see Tsukui, J.

Muramatsu, R. & Dudley, N. A., eds. Production & Industrial Systems. 1340p. 1978. write for info. (ISBN 0-85066-138-2, Pub. by Taylor & Francis). Intl Pubns Serv.

Muramatsu, Takashi, et al, eds. Teratocarcinoma & Embryonic Cell Interactions. 1982. 36.00 (ISBN 0-12-511180-0). Acad Pr.

Muramoto, Naboru. Healing Ourselves. Abehsera, Michael, compiled by. (Illus.). 150p. 1974. pap. 9.95 (ISBN 0-380-00900-5, 62125-8). Avon.

--Healing Ourselves. LC 72-97039. 1973. 9.95x (ISBN 0-380-00900-5, Pub. by Avon). Formur Intl.

Murane, Elizabeth. Daga Grammar. (Publications in Linguistics & Related Fields: No. 43). 443p. 1974. pap. 14.00x (ISBN 0-88312-053-4); microfiche 4.50x (ISBN 0-88312-453-X). Summer Inst Ling.

Murants, Ivare. Play the Plectrum Guitar. (Illus.). 5.50x (ISBN 0-392-04179-0, LTB). Sportshelf.

Murao, Satoru, jt. ed. see Hayasi, Shoji.

Murari, Timeri. Goin' Home. 1980. 9.95 o.p. (ISBN 0-399-12384-9). Putnam Pub Group.

Murarka, S. P, ed. Silicides for VLSI Appreciations. Date not set. price not set (ISBN 0-12-511220-3). Acad Pr.

Muraro, Michelangelo. Paolo da Venezia. LC 77-84667. (Illus.). 1970. 60.00x (ISBN 0-271-00098-8). Pa St U Pr.

Muraro, Michelangelo & Grabar, Andre. Treasures of Venice. LC 79-92603. (Illus.). 228p. Repr. of 1963 ed. cancelled (ISBN 0-8478-0300-7). Rizzoli Intl.

Murase, Miyeko. The Arts of Japan. 1977. 22.50 o.p. (ISBN 0-07-044053-0, P&RB); cassette 3.95 o.p. (ISBN 0-07-044054-9). Cassette & Recorder Set. 26.45 o.p. (ISBN 0-07-079265-8). McGraw.

Muraskin, William A. Middle-Class Blacks in a White Society. 1975. 32.50x (ISBN 0-520-02705-1). U of Cal Pr.

Murata, Alice K. & Farquhar, Judith, eds. Issues in Pacific-Asian American Health & Mental Health. LC 82-3507. (Occasional Paper Ser.: No.8). 67p. (Orig.). 1982. pap. 4.00 (ISBN 0-934584-10-9). Pacific-Asian.

Murata, Alice K. & Salvador-Burris, Juanita, eds. Issues in Community Research: Asian American Perspectives. LC 79-89000. (Occasional Paper Ser.: No. 5). 51p. (Orig.). 1980. pap. 2.25 (ISBN 0-934584-04-4). Pacific-Asian.

Murata, Kiyoji, ed. An Industrial Geography of Japan. LC 80-13404. 1980. 35.00 (ISBN 0-312-41428-5). St Martin.

Murata, Yasuo. Optimal Control Methods for Linear Discrete-Time Economic Systems. (Illus.). 175p. 1982. 34.00 (ISBN 0-387-90709-2). Springer-Verlag.

Murawski, Kris, jt. ed. see Collins, John A.

Muray, Nickolas. Muray's Celebrity Portraits of the Twenties & Thirties. LC 77-87448. (Illus.). 1978. pap. 6.00 (ISBN 0-486-23578-5). Dover.

Murbarger, Nell. Ghosts of the Adobe Walls: Human Interest & Historical Highlights from 400 Ghost Haunts of Old Arizona. 1977. pap. Treasure Chest.
Murcer, Bill, jt. auth. see Fitzgerald, John.
Murch, A. E., tr. see Pavese, Cesare.
Murch, Alma E. Development of the Detective Novel. LC 69-10138. 1969. Repr. of 1958 ed. lib. bdg. 20.75x (ISBN 0-8371-0581-1, MUDN). Greenwood.
Murchison, Carl. Criminal Intelligence. (Historical Foundations of Forensic Psychiatry & Psychology Ser.). 291p. 1983. Repr. of 1926 ed. lib. bdg. 29.50 (ISBN 0-306-76183-1). Da Capo.
Murchison, Irene, et al. Legal Accountability in the Nursing Process. 2nd ed. LC 81-16956. (Illus.). 188p. 1982. pap. text ed. 12.50 (ISBN 0-8016-3604-3). Mosby.
Murd, Ruth E., compiled by. Exporter's Encyclopaedia. 77th ed. (Illus.). 1800p. 1983. 325.00x (ISBN 0-942526-00-7). Dun & Brad Intl.
Murd, Ruth E., compiled by see Dun & Bradstreet Intl.
Murdaugh, Elaine. Salvation in the Secular: The Moral Law in Thomas Mann's "Joseph und seine Bruder". (Stanford German Studies: Vol. 10). 117p. 1976. pap. write for info. (ISBN 3-261-01914-X). P Lang Pubs.
Murdick, Robert. Production-Operations Management for Small Business. 150p. (Orig.). 1981. pap. text ed. 9.95 (ISBN 0-942280-00-8). Pub Horizons.
Murdick, Robert C. & Ross, Joel E. Introduction to Management Information Systems. (Illus.). 1977. 24.95 (ISBN 0-13-486233-3). P-H.
Murdick, Robert G. MIS: Concepts & Design. 1980. text ed. 26.95 (ISBN 0-13-585331-1). P-H.
Murdick, Robert G. & Ross, Joel E. Information Systems for Modern Management. 2nd ed. (Illus.). 640p. 1975. ref. ed. 28.95 (ISBN 0-13-464602-9). P-H.
Murdick, Robert G., jt. auth. see Karger, Delmar W.
Murdin, Paul, et al. Catalogue of the Universe. 1979. 19.95 (ISBN 0-517-53616-1). Crown.
Murdocca, Sal. The Hero of Hamblett. LC 80-11346. (Illus.). 48p. (gr. 3 up). 1980. PLB 8.44 o.s.i. (ISBN 0-440-04458-8); pap. 4.95 o.s.i. (ISBN 0-440-04457-X). Delacorte.
Murdocca, Sol. Grover's Own Alphabet. (Illus.). (ps-1). 1978. PLB 5.00 (ISBN 0-307-68654-X, Whitman). Western Pub.
Murdoch, Beamish. Epitome of the Laws of Nova Scotia, 4 vols. LC 73-26626. 1034p. Repr. of 1833 ed. Set. lib. bdg. 95.00x (ISBN 0-912004-04-5). W W Gaunt.
Murdoch, Brian O. Old High German Literature. (World Authors Ser.). 169p. 1983. lib. bdg. 18.95 (ISBN 0-8057-6535-2, Twayne). G K Hall.
Murdoch, Derrick. Disappearances. LC 82-45302. (Illus.). 192p. 1983. 14.95 (ISBN 0-385-17711-9). Doubleday.
Murdoch, George, ed. The Advances in Orthotics. 620p. 1976. 32.00 (ISBN 0-7131-4214-6). Krieger.
Murdoch, Iris. The Black Prince. 1983. pap. 3.95 (ISBN 0-14-003934-1). Penguin.
--Henry & Cato. 1977. pap. 4.95 (ISBN 0-14-004569-4). Penguin.
--Nuns & Soldiers. 1982. pap. 5.95 (ISBN 0-14-006143-6). Penguin.
--The Philosopher's Pupil. 1983. 18.75 (ISBN 0-670-55186-4). Viking Pr.
--Under the Net. 1977. pap. 3.95 (ISBN 0-14-001445-4). Penguin.
--A Word Child. 1976. pap. 3.95 (ISBN 0-14-004286-5). Penguin.
Murdoch, J. B. Network Theory. 1970. text ed. 25.50 o.p. (ISBN 0-07-044049-2, C); 2.95 o.p. instructor's manual (ISBN 0-07-044050-6). McGraw.
Murdoch, John B., tr. see Wyatt, David K.
Murdoch, John E. Album of Science: Antiquity & the Middle Ages. (Illus.). 336p. 1982. 50.00x (ISBN 0-684-15496-X, ScribT). Scribner.
Murdoch, Joseph S. & Seagle, Janet, eds. Golf: A Guide to Information Sources. LC 79-23270. (Sports, Games & Pastimes Information Guide Ser.: Vol. 7). 1979. 42.00x (ISBN 0-8103-1457-6). Gale.
Murdoch, Mary-Helen. Why Your Salespeople Can't Sell & What You Can do About It. LC 82-81107. (Orig.). 1983. pap. 10.95 (ISBN 0-943038-00-6). Merchandising.
Murdoch, Ritchie J., jt. ed. see Waxman, Stephen G.
Murdoch, Royal. The Disrobing: Sex & Satire. 112p. (Orig.). 1982. limited lettered 30.00 (ISBN 0-917342-95-X); pap. 5.95 (ISBN 0-917342-96-8). Gay Sunshine.
Murdock, jt. auth. see Stuart.
Murdock, B. B. Human Memory: V Theory & Data. LC 74-888. 362p. (Orig.). cloth 16.50 (ISBN 0-470-62525-2). Krieger.
Murdock, Bennet B., Jr. Human Memory: Theory & Data. LC 74-888. 1974. 12.95x o.s.i. (ISBN 0-470-62525-2). Halsted Pr.
Murdock, Clark A. Defense Policy Formation: A Comparative Analysis of the McNamara Era. LC 73-18032. 204p. 1974. 29.50x (ISBN 0-87395-252-9). State U NY Pr.
Murdock, George P., et al. Outline of Cultural Materials. 5th, rev. ed. LC 81-83836. (Behavior Science Outline Ser.). 272p. 1982. pap. 15.00 (ISBN 0-87536-654-6). HRAFP.
Murdock, James. Fluid Mechanics & Its Applications. LC 75-31024. (Illus.). 384p. 1976. text ed. 30.50 (ISBN 0-395-20626-X); solutions manual 7.50 (ISBN 0-395-24216-9). HM.
Murdock, Kenneth B. Literature & Theology in Colonial New England. LC 78-104247. xi, 235p. Repr. of 1949 ed. lib. bdg. 17.50x (ISBN 0-8371-3990-2, MUCN). Greenwood.
Murdock, L. J. & Brook, K. M. Concrete Materials & Practices. 5th ed. LC 78-27476. 1979. 74.95x (ISBN 0-470-26639-2). Halsted Pr.
Murdock, Michael L. Writing Clearly & Effectively. 2nd 1883 ed. 166p. (Orig.). 1981. pap. 4.95 (ISBN 0-930124-01-4). Transemantics.
Murdock, Steve H. & Leistritz, F. Larry. Nuclear Waste: Socioeconomic Dimensions. (Special Studies in Science, Technology, & Public Policy-Society). 343p. 1983. price not set. Westview.
Murdock, Steven H., jt. auth. see Leistritz, F. Larry.
Murdock, Tony & Stuart, Nik. Gymnastics. (Illus.). 112p. (gr. 3-6). 1982. PLB 8.90 o.p. (ISBN 0-531-00849-5). Watts.
Murdoff, Ron, jt. auth. see Evans, Idella M.
Mure, G. R. Idealist Epilogue. 1978. text ed. 23.50x (ISBN 0-19-824583-1). Oxford U Pr.
Mure, Geoffrey R. An Introduction to Hegel. LC 82-15853. xviii, 180p. 1982. Repr. of 1940 ed. lib. bdg. 29.75x (ISBN 0-313-23741-7, MUIH). Greenwood.
Murfin, Fred B. & Murfin, Robin. How Did the Wise Men Know? 1983. 14.95 (ISBN 0-533-05007-3). Vantage.
Murfin, Robin, jt. auth. see Murfin, Fred B.
Murg, Gary E. & Fox, John C. Labor Relations Law: Canada, Mexico, & Western Europe, 2 vols. LC 78-58374. 1978. text ed. 30.00 (ISBN 0-685-65702-7, H6-2942). PLI.
Murgatroyd. Coping with Crisis. 220p. 1982. text ed. 21.00x (ISBN 0-06-318229-7, Pub. by Har-Row Ltd England); pap. text ed. 12.95x (ISBN 0-06-318228-9, Pub. by Har-Row Ltd England). Har-Row.
Murgatroyd, Paul. Tibullus I. A Commentary on the First Book of the Elegies of Albius Tibullus. 333p. 1980. pap. text ed. 37.50 (ISBN 0-686-72418-6). Verry.
Murgatroyd, Paul, ed. Ovid with Love: Selection from the Ars Amatoria, Books I & II. 228p. 1982. pap. text ed. 11.95x (ISBN 0-86516-015-5). Bolchazy-Carducci.
Murger, Henri. The Bohemians of the Latin Quarter. LC 76-50140. 1983. Repr. of 1895 ed. 15.00x (ISBN 0-86527-221-2). Fertig.
Muriel, Amador, jt. auth. see Chiu Hone-Yeel.
Muriel, Amador, jt. ed. see Chiu, Hong-Yee.
Murillo, Louis A. Cyclical Night: Irony in James Joyce & Jorge Luis Borges. LC 68-54022. (Illus.). 289p. 1968. 16.00x o.p. (ISBN 0-674-18040-2). Harvard U Pr.
Murin, William J., et al, eds. Public Policy: A Guide to Information Sources. LC 80-25872. (American Government & History Information Guide Ser.: Vol. 13). 400p. 1981. 42.00x (ISBN 0-8103-1490-8). Gale.
Murison, Hamish S. & Lea, John P. Housing in Third World Countries: Perspectives on Policy & Practice. LC 79-20565. 1980. 30.00x (ISBN 0-312-39350-4). St Martin.
Murison, R., jt. ed. see Ursin, H.
Murken, J. D., et al, eds. see Third European Congress.
Murli, A., jt. ed. see Messina, P. C.
Murname, William J. Guide to Ancient Egypt. 1983. pap. price not set (ISBN 0-14-046326-7). Penguin.
Murnane, William J. United with Eternity: A Concise Guide to the Monuments of Medinet Habu. (Orig.). 1981. pap. 7.98 (ISBN 0-918986-28-1). Oriental Inst.
Muro, Diane P. Police Careers for Women. LC 78-26708. (Career Bk.). (Illus.). 192p. (gr. 7 up). 1979. PLB 8.29 o.p. (ISBN 0-671-32931-6). Messner.
Muro, James J., jt. auth. see Dinkmeyer, Don C.
Muroga, Saburo. Logic Design & Switching Theory. LC 78-12407. 1979. 42.50 (ISBN 0-471-04418-0, Pub. by Wiley-Interscience). Wiley.
Murph, Roxane C. Richard III: The Making of a Legend. LC 77-4021. 1977. 11.00 o.p. (ISBN 0-8108-1034-4). Scarecrow.
Murphey, Cecil. Comforting Those Who Grieve. LC 78-71052. 64p. 1979. pap. 1.85 (ISBN 0-8042-1099-3). John Knox.
--Press On: A/Disciple's Guide to Spiritual Growth. 140p. (Orig.). 1983. pap. 4.95 (ISBN 0-89283-129-4). Servant.
Murphey, Cecil B. When in Doubt, Hug 'em: How to Develop a Caring Church. LC 77-15751. 1978. 2.99 (ISBN 0-8042-1890-0). John Knox.
Murphey, Dwight D. Socialist Thought. LC 82-24751. 436p. (Orig.). 1983. lib. bdg. 26.75 (ISBN 0-8191-3025-7); pap. text ed. 15.50 (ISBN 0-8191-3026-5). U Pr of Amer.
--Understanding the Modern Predicament. LC 81-40345. (Orig.). 1982. lib. bdg. 25.25 (ISBN 0-8191-2135-5); pap. text ed. 14.00 (ISBN 0-8191-2136-3). U Pr of Amer.
Murphey, Murrary G., jt. auth. see Flower, Elizabeth.
Murphey, Murray G., jt. auth. see Flower, Elizabeth.
Murphey, Rhoads. Fading of the Maoist Vision. 1981. 13.95 (ISBN 0-416-60201-0). Methuen Inc.
--Patterns of the Earth. 4th ed. 1978. 24.95 (ISBN 0-395-30827-5); Tchrs. Manual 1.25 (ISBN 0-395-30828-3). HM.
Murphree, Carolyn T., jt. auth. see Rutkoskie, Alice E.
Murphy. Getting the Facts. 1980. pap. text ed. 9.95x (ISBN 0-673-16263-X). Scott F.
Murphy, jt. auth. see Carlo.
Murphy, Agatha. Hush, Hush Murder. 1978. 6.50 o.p. (ISBN 0-533-03209-1). Vantage.
Murphy, Agnes. Melba: A Biography. LC 77-8029. (Music Reprint Ser.). (Illus.). 1977. Repr. of 1909 ed. lib. bdg. 35.00 (ISBN 0-306-77428-3). Da Capo.
Murphy, Albert T. Families of Hearing-Impaired Children. 1979. pap. 4.95 (ISBN 0-88200-128-0). Bell Assn Deaf.
Murphy, Alexandra see Poulet, Anne.
Murphy, Allan, jt. auth. see Campbell, Colin.
Murphy, Allan H. & Katz, Richard W., eds. Probability, Statistics, & Decision Making in Meterology. 450p. (Orig.). Nov., 1981. lib. bdg. 28.50 (ISBN 0-86531-152-8); Oct., 1981. pap. text ed. 15.00 (ISBN 0-86531-153-6). Westview.
Murphy, Arthur. Lives of Henry Fielding & Samuel Johnson, with Essays from Gray's Inn Journal, 1752-1792. LC 68-24212. 1968. 54.00x (ISBN 0-8201-1035-3). Schol Facsimiles.
Murphy, Arthur E. Theory of Practical Reason. Melden, A. I., ed. LC 64-20840. (Paul Carus Lecture Ser.). xviii, 458p. 1964. 27.00x (ISBN 0-87548-110-8). Open Court.
--The Uses of Reason. LC 75-165444. 346p. 1972. Repr. of 1943 ed. lib. bdg. 18.25x (ISBN 0-8371-6227-0, MUUR). Greenwood.
Murphy, Arthur E., ed. see Mead, George H.
Murphy, Arthur W. & Santagata, Kenneth V. The Law of Product Liability, Problems & Policies. LC 81-84335. 174p. 1982. text ed. 39.50 (ISBN 0-89834-048-9); pap. 24.50. Natl Chamber Found.
Murphy, B. Dictionary of Australian History. 340p. 1982. 19.00 (ISBN 0-07-072946-8). McGraw.
Murphy, Barbara & Baker, Norman. Thor Heyerdahl & the Reed Boat RA. LC 73-20260. (Illus.). 64p. (gr. 4-6). 1974. 10.53i (ISBN 0-397-31503-1, HarpJ). Har-Row.
Murphy, Barbara, jt. auth. see Hoover, Rosalie.
Murphy, Barbara B. No Place to Run. (gr. 7-9). 1978. pap. 1.95 (ISBN 0-671-43291-5). Archway.
--No Place to Run. LC 76-57911. (YA) (gr. 7-11). 1977. 8.95 (ISBN 0-02-767700-1). Bradbury Pr.
--One Another. LC 81-18074. 192p. (gr. 7 up). 1982. 9.95 (ISBN 0-02-767710-9). Bradbury Pr.
Murphy, Bill. Complete Book of Championship Tennis Drills. (Illus.). 228p. 1975. 12.95 o.p. (ISBN 0-686-37478-9). USTA.
Murphy, Bill, et al, eds. see National Computing Centre.
Murphy, Brenda, jt. ed. see Monteiro, George.
Murphy, Brian. C. S. Lewis. (Starmont Reader's Guide Ser.: No. 14). 96p. 1983. Repr. lib. bdg. 10.95x (ISBN 0-89370-045-2). Borgo Pr.
--Reader's Guide to C. S. Lewis. Schlobin, Roger C., ed. (Reader's Guides to Contemporary Science Fiction & Fantasy Authors Ser.: Vol. 14). (Illus., Orig.). 1983. 10.95x (ISBN 0-916732-38-X); pap. text ed. 4.95x (ISBN 0-916732-37-1). Starmont Hse.
Murphy, Bruce. Lampmaking. LC 76-16360. (Illus.). 192p. 1976. 15.95 (ISBN 0-8069-5420-5); lib. bdg. 18.79 (ISBN 0-8069-5421-3). Sterling.
Murphy, Bruce & Lopo, Ana. Lampmaking. rev. ed. LC 76-16360. (Illus.). 192p. 1980. pap. 8.95 (ISBN 0-8069-8462-7). Sterling.
Murphy, Bruce A. The Brandeis-Frankfurter Connection: The Secret Political Activities of Two Supreme Court Justices. LC 82-45546. 496p. 1983. pap. 12.95 (ISBN 0-385-18374-7, Anch). Doubleday.
Murphy, Carol, ed. see George, David L.
Murphy, Carol J. Alienation & Absence in the Novels of Marguerite Duras. LC 82-82426. (French Forum Monographs: No. 37). 172p. (Orig.). 1982. pap. 15.00x (ISBN 0-917058-36-4). French Forum.
Murphy, Charles J., III & Bryan, J. The Windsor Story. new ed. LC 79-17576. (Illus.). 1979. 17.50 o.p. (ISBN 0-688-03553-1). Morrow.
Murphy, Chet. Advanced Tennis. 3rd ed. (Physical Education & Activities Ser). 110p. 1982. pap. text ed. write for info. (ISBN 0-697-07189-8). Wm C Brown.
Murphy, Dan. Thomas Jefferson. 12p. 1978. pap. 1.25 (ISBN 0-686-95752-0). Jefferson Natl.
Murphy, Dan & Muench, David. Lewis & Clark: Voyage of Discovery. 68p. 1977. 7.95 (ISBN 0-696-95740-7); pap. 3.75 (ISBN 0-686-99595-3). Jefferson Natl.
Murphy, Daniel, jt. auth. see Ehrlich, Eugene.
Murphy, Daniel B. & Rousseau, Viateur. Foundations of College Chemistry. 3rd ed. LC 79-17521. 1980. text ed. 29.95x (ISBN 0-471-04621-3); tchrs'. manual o.p. (ISBN 0-471-05916-1); study guide avail. (ISBN 0-471-05605-7). Wiley.
Murphy, Dennis. Better Business Communications. 1957. pap. 3.95 o.p. (ISBN 0-07-044058-1, SP). McGraw.
Murphy, Dervla. A Place Apart. 1980. 15.00 (ISBN 0-8159-6516-8). Devin.
Murphy, Dwight D. Modern Social & Political Philosophies: Burkean Conservatism & Classical Liberalism. LC 81-40167. 472p. (Orig.). 1982. lib. bdg. 28.50 (ISBN 0-8191-2137-1); pap. text ed. 17.25 (ISBN 0-8191-2138-X). U Pr of Amer.
Murphy, E. F., ed. Nature, Bureaucracy & the Rules of Property. 1977. 47.00 (ISBN 0-7204-0700-1, North-Holland). Elsevier.
Murphy, E. Jefferson. The Bantu Civilization of Southern Africa. LC 73-17194. (Illus.). 256p. (gr. 7 up). 1974. 14.38i (ISBN 0-690-00399-4, TYC-J). Har-Row.
--Creative Philanthropy: Carnegie Corporation in Africa, 1953-74. LC 76-14886. 1976. text ed. 19.90 (ISBN 0-8077-2473-4); pap. text ed. 10.95 (ISBN 0-8077-2479-3). Tchrs Coll.
--History of African Civilization. 464p. 1974. pap. 9.95 (ISBN 0-440-93735-3, Delta). Dell.
--Understanding Africa. rev. ed. LC 77-11560. (Illus.). (gr. 7 up). 1978. 14.38i o.p. (ISBN 0-690-03834-8, TYC-J); PLB 14.89 (ISBN 0-690-03846-1). Har-Row.
Murphy, Eamon. Unions in Conflict: A Comparative Study Four South Indian Textile Centres, 1918-1939. 1982. 18.00x (ISBN 0-8364-0874-8, Pub. by Australia Nat Univ). South Asia Bks.
Murphy, Edward. Two Thousand Seven Hundred Fifteen One-Line Quotations for Speakers, Writers & Raconteurs. Michaelman, Herbert, ed. 1981. 10.95 o.p. (ISBN 0-517-54281-1, Michelman Books). Crown.
--Western Dancing. (Illus.). 64p. 1983. 7.95 (ISBN 0-686-82404-0). Todd & Honeywell.
Murphy, Elizabeth R. The Assistant-New Tasks, New Opportunities: A Guide to Increased Competence for the Woman Who Assists a Manager. 192p. 1982. 15.95 (ISBN 0-8144-5675-8). Am Mgmt.
Murphy, Elspeth C. I'm Listening, God: Psalm 19. (David & I Talk to God Ser.). (ps-2). 1983. misc. format 1.75 (ISBN 0-89191-583-4). Cook.
--It's My Birthday, God: Psalm 90. (David & I Talk to God Ser.). (ps-2). 1982. misc. format 1.75 (ISBN 0-89191-580-X). Cook.
--Make Way for the King: Psalm 145 & 24. (David & I Talk to God Ser.). (ps-2). 1983. 1.75 (ISBN 0-89191-581-8). Cook.
Murphy, F. H., jt. auth. see Greenberg, H. J.
Murphy, Francis, ed. Yvor Winters: The Uncollected Essays & Reviews. LC 72-91915. 320p. 1972. 15.00 o.p. (ISBN 0-8040-0604-0). Swallow.
Murphy, Francis X. Synod Nineteen Sixty-Seven: A New Sound in Rome. 1968. 4.95 o.p. (ISBN 0-685-07667-9, 80562). Glencoe.
Murphy, Frank D. Cost Management Techniques for Hospitals. (Medical Publications Ser.). 1981. lib. bdg. 37.50 o.p. (ISBN 0-8161-2240-7, Hall Medical). G K Hall.
--Model & Department Policy Statement for Hospitals. 1981. lib. bdg. 49.95 o.p. (ISBN 0-8161-2234-2, Hall Medical). G K Hall.
--Model Department Policy Statements for Hospitals: A Manual. (Medical Publications Ser.). 1981. 49.95 o.p. (ISBN 0-8161-2234-2). G K Hall.
--Model Department Safety, Environmental & Infection Control Policies for Hospitals. 1981. lib. bdg. 65.00 o.p. (ISBN 0-8161-2239-3, Hall Medical). G K Hall.
--Model Job Descriptions for Hospitals. 1981. 49.95 o.p. (ISBN 0-8161-2233-4, Pub. by Hall Medical Bks). G K Hall.
Murphy, Frederic H. & Soyster, Allen L. Economic Behavior of Electric Utilities. 1983. 29.95 (ISBN 0-13-224089-0). P-H.
Murphy, G., ed. see Cohen, I. L.
Murphy, G. J., jt. auth. see Barnes, B. A.
Murphy, Gardner. Psychological Thought from Pythagoras to Freud: An Informal Introduction. LC 68-25371. (Orig.). 1968. pap. 3.65 o.p. (ISBN 0-15-674701-4, Harv). HarBraceJ.
Murphy, Gardner & Dale, Laura A. Challenge of Psychical Research: A Primer of Parapsychology. LC 78-31335. (World Perspectives: Vol. 26). (Illus.). 1979. Repr. of 1961 ed. lib. bdg. 29.75x (ISBN 0-313-20944-8, MUCP). Greenwood.
Murphy, Gardner & Kovach, Joseph K. Historical Introduction to Modern Psychology. 3rd ed. 526p. 1972. text ed. 23.95 (ISBN 0-15-536245-3, HC). HarBraceJ.
Murphy, Genevieve. Young Pony Rider's Companion. 14.50x (ISBN 0-392-13108-0, SpS). Sportshelf.
Murphy, George E., Jr., ed. Poet's Choice: The Poem As Ideal, Vol. II. 176p. 1983. 12.95 (ISBN 0-937504-02-5); pap. 7.95 (ISBN 0-937504-04-1). Tendril.
Murphy, George E., Jr. & Shaner, Richard C., eds. Peregrine Anthology, No. 1. LC 78-64871. 1978. pap. 2.95 o.p. (ISBN 0-931694-02-7). Wampeter Pr.
Murphy, George M., ed. Separation of the Boron Isotopes. (National Nuclear Energy Ser.: Div. III, Vol. 5). 469p. 1952. pap. 34.00 (ISBN 0-87079-349-7, TID-5227); microfilm 4.50 (ISBN 0-87079-350-0, TID-5227). DOE.
Murphy, Gerald P. & Mittelman, Arnold. Chemotherapy of Urogenital Tumors. (Illus.). 288p. 1975. 32.75x o.p. (ISBN 0-398-03319-6). C C Thomas.
Murphy, Gerald P., jt. ed. see Kuss, Rene.
Murphy, Gretchen, jt. auth. see Waters, Kathleen.

Murphy, Herta A. & Peck, Mary J. Effective Business Communications. 3rd ed. (Illus.). 1980. text ed. 23.95 (ISBN 0-07-044080-8); instr.'s manual 25.00 (ISBN 0-07-044081-6). McGraw.

Murphy, Howard A. & Stringham, E. J. Creative Harmony & Musicianship: An Introduction to the Structure of Music. 1951. pap. 22.95 (ISBN 0-13-189704-7). P-H.

Murphy, Howard A., et al. Music for Study: A Sourcebook of Excerpts. 2nd ed. 192p. 1973. pap. text ed. 17.95 (ISBN 0-13-607515-0). P-H.

Murphy, Ian & Gage, Michael. Design & Detailing for Energy Conservation. 260p. 1983. 60.00 (ISBN 0-89397-117-0). Nichols Pub.

Murphy, J. A., ed. see Society Of Manufacturing Engineers.

Murphy, J. L., jt. auth. see Harnett, D. L.

Murphy, J. L., jt. auth. see Kontos, P. G.

Murphy, Jack. Abe & Me. LC 77-73233. (Illus.). 1977. 9.95 (ISBN 0-89325-005-8). Joyce Pr.

--Damn You Al Davis. LC 79-87471. 1979. 10.95 (ISBN 0-89325-014-7). Joyce Pr.

Murphy, James F. Concepts of Leisure. 2nd ed. (Illus.). 192p. 1981. text ed. 15.95 (ISBN 0-13-166512-X). P-H.

Murphy, James F., Jr. Quonsett. 1979. pap. 1.95 o.p. (ISBN 0-380-45484-X, 45484). Avon.

--They Were Dreamers. LC 81-69138. 352p. 1983. 14.95 (ISBN 0-689-11250-5). Atheneum.

Murphy, James G. Commentary on the Book of Exodus. 1979. 12.75 (ISBN 0-86524-014-0, 0201). Klock & Klock.

Murphy, James J. Medieval Eloquence: Studies in the Theory & Practice of Medieval Rhetoric. LC 76-48026. 1978. 32.50x (ISBN 0-520-03345-0). U of Cal Pr.

--Renaissance Rhetoric: A Short Title Catalogue. LC 80-8501. 400p. 1981. lib. bdg. 50.00 o.s.i. (ISBN 0-8240-9487-5). Garland Pub.

--Rhetoric in the Middle Ages, A.D. 400-1500, the Renaissance. 1974. 34.50x (ISBN 0-520-02439-7); pap. 9.95x (ISBN 0-520-04406-1). U of Cal Pr.

Murphy, James J. & Ericson, Jon M. Debater's Guide. LC 61-17897. (Orig.). 1961. pap. 4.50 (ISBN 0-685-07188-X). Bobbs.

Murphy, James J., ed. Demosthenes on the Crown. 1967. pap. text ed. 3.95 (ISBN 0-685-38351-2). Phila Bk Co.

--Renaissance Eloquence: Studies in the Theory and Practice of Renaissance Rhetoric. LC 81-13128. 528p. 1983. text ed. 27.50x (ISBN 0-520-04543-2). U of Cal Pr.

--Three Medieval Rhetorical Arts. LC 72-132416. 1971. 28.50x (ISBN 0-520-01820-6). U of Cal Pr.

Murphy, James K. Will N. Harben. (United States Authors Ser.). 1979. lib. bdg. 14.95 (ISBN 0-8057-7245-6, Twayne). G K Hall.

Murphy, James L. An Archeological History of the Hocking Valley. LC 73-92906. (Illus.). xi, 360p. 1975. 20.00 (ISBN 0-8214-0151-3, 82-81545). Ohio U Pr.

Murphy, Jane A., ed. see Foundyller, Charles M.

Murphy, Jeffrie G. Evolution, Morality & the Meaning of Life. LC 82-9782. (Philosophy & Society Ser.). 170p. 1982. 14.95 (ISBN 0-8476-7147-X). Rowman.

--The Philosophy of Law. (Philosophy & Society Ser.). 1983. 18.50x (ISBN 0-8476-6277-2); pap. 9.95x (ISBN 0-8476-6278-0). Rowman.

Murphy, Jerome. Colossians. (Scripture Discussion Outlines). 1969. pap. 0.75 o.p. (ISBN 0-685-07621-0, 80563). Glencoe.

Murphy, Jill. The Worst Witch. 72p. (gr. 3-6). 1980. 7.95 (ISBN 0-8052-8019-7, Pub. by Allison & Busby England). Schocken.

--The Worst Witch. 1982. pap. 1.95 (ISBN 0-380-60665-8, 60665, Camelot). Avon.

--The Worst Witch Strikes Again. (Illus.). 72p. (gr. 3-6). 1980. 7.95 (ISBN 0-8052-8033-2, Pub. by Allison & Busby England). Schocken.

--The Worst Witch Strikes Again. 1982. pap. 1.95 (ISBN 0-380-60673-9, 60673, Camelot). Avon.

Murphy, Jim. Two Hundred Years of Bicycles. LC 81-48608. (Illus.). 64p. (gr. 3-6). 1983. 9.57i (ISBN 0-397-32007-8, JBL-J); PLB 9.89g (ISBN 0-397-32008-6). Har-Row.

Murphy, Jimmy. Matt-United-& Me. 15.00x (ISBN 0-392-00567-0, SpS). Sportshelf.

Murphy, John. Traditional Irish Recipes. (Illus.). 74p. 1982. 14.95 (ISBN 0-904651-63-0, Pub. by Salem Hse Ltd.). Merrimack Bk Serv.

Murphy, John F. The United Nations & the Control of International Violence. LC 81-69989. 1982. text ed. 32.50x (ISBN 0-86598-079-9). Allanheld.

Murphy, John F., jt. ed. see Evans, Alona E.

Murphy, John H., jt. auth. see Patti, Charles H.

Murphy, John J., ed. see Willa Cather Pre-Centennial Conference, 1972.

Murphy, John W. The Social Philosophy of Martin Buber: The Social World as a Human Dimension. LC 82-21779. 176p. (Orig.). 1983. lib. bdg. 21.00 (ISBN 0-8191-2940-2); pap. text ed. 10.00 (ISBN 0-8191-2941-0). U Pr of Amer.

Murphy, Joseph. How to Use the Power of Prayer. pap. 1.50 (ISBN 0-87516-275-4). De Vorss.

--Infinite Power for Richer Living. 1969. pap. 4.95 (ISBN 0-13-464396-8, Reward). P-H.

--Miracle Power for Infinite Riches. 1972. 8.95 o.p. (ISBN 0-13-585638-8, Parker); pap. 3.95 o.p. (ISBN 0-13-585612-4). P-H.

Murphy, Judith. Conflict, Consensus, & Communication. 32p. 1980. 1.00 (ISBN 0-686-37911-X). Music Ed.

Murphy, Judith, jt. auth. see Gross, Ronald.

Murphy, Karen. A House Full of Kids: Running a Successful Day Care Business in Your Own Home. LC 82-73961. 320p. (Orig.). 1983. 14.37 (ISBN 0-8070-2302-7); pap. 9.57 (ISBN 0-8070-2303-5). Beacon Pr.

Murphy, Kathleen J. Macroproject Development in the Third World: An Analysis of Transnational Partnerships. (Replica Edition). 150p. 1982. softcover 17.00x (ISBN 0-86531-939-1). Westview.

Murphy, Keith. Battle of the Alamo. LC 78-26292. (Raintree Great Adventures). (Illus.). (gr. 3-6). 1979. PLB 12.85 (ISBN 0-8393-0154-5). Raintree Pubs.

Murphy, Lawrence R. Lucien Bonaparte Maxwell: The Napoleon of the Southwest. LC 82-40454. (Illus.). 280p. 1983. 19.95 (ISBN 0-8061-1807-5). U of Okla Pr.

--Philmont: A History of New Mexico's Cimarron Country. 2nd ed. LC 72-76828. (Illus.). 261p. 1976. pap. 7.95 (ISBN 0-8263-0244-0). U of NM Pr.

Murphy, Lois B. The Home Hospital: How the Family Can Cope with Catastrophic Illness. LC 82-70852. 1982. 15.50 (ISBN 0-465-03041-6). Basic.

Murphy, Margaret. How Can I Go On? Hope for Widowed Catholics. 48p. 1981. pap. 1.95 (ISBN 0-89570-201-0). Claretian Pubns.

Murphy, Margaret D. The Convection Turbo-Oven Cookbook. LC 80-68017. (Illus.). 160p. (Orig.). 1981. pap. 4.95 (ISBN 0-448-11676-6, G&D). Putnam Pub Group.

--Wonderful Ways with Food. Kostick, Marilyn G., ed. LC 82-71811. (Illus.). 144p. 1982. 10.95 (ISBN 0-916752-58-5); softcover 5.95 (ISBN 0-916752-60-7). Dorison Hse.

Murphy, Mary, tr. see Donze, Terese.

Murphy, Mary A., jt. auth. see Brown, Marie.

Murphy, Mary F., jt. auth. see Greenwood, Kathryn M.

Murphy, Michael. Golf in the Kingdom. 1973. pap. 6.95 (ISBN 0-440-53092-X, Delta). Dell.

--Names of Ireland. (International Library of Names). 250p. 1983. text ed. 24.50x (ISBN 0-8290-1286-9). Irvington.

Murphy, Michael & Matti, Jonathan C. Lower Devonian Conodonts - Hesperius-Kindlei Zones. LC 82-8638. (Publications in Geological Sciences: Vol. 123). 94p. Date not set. pap. text ed. 8.25 (ISBN 0-520-09661-4). U of Cal Pr. Postponed.

Murphy, Michael C. How to Buy a Home While You Can Still Afford to. LC 79-91390. (Illus.). 160p. 1981. 11.95 (ISBN 0-8069-7154-1); lib. bdg. 14.49 (ISBN 0-8069-7155-X); pap. 5.95 o.p. (ISBN 0-8069-8912-2). Sterling.

Murphy, Michael G. & Oberhoff, Kenneth E. Algebra for College Students. 390p. 1982. text ed. 19.95 (HC); 3.95 (ISBN 0-15-502161-3). HarBraceJ.

Murphy, Michael J. Cambridge Newspapers & Opinion: 1780-1850. 1981. 9.95x (ISBN 0-686-96935-9, Pub. by Oleander Pr). State Mutual Bk.

Murphy, Michael J., jt. auth. see Abels, Paul.

Murphy, Michael J., jt. ed. see Cresswell, Anthony M.

Murphy, Murtagh. Asia Pacific Stories. (Oxford Progressive English Readers Ser.). (Illus.). 1974. pap. text ed. 3.50x (ISBN 0-19-580718-9). Oxford U Pr.

Murphy, Oliver F., tr. see Chekhov, Anton.

Murphy, Patricia & Taylor-Gordon, Elaine. The Business-Woman's Guide to Thirty American Cities. 400p. 1982. 19.95 (ISBN 0-312-92072-5); pap. 9.95 (ISBN 0-312-92073-3). Congdon & Weed.

Murphy, Patrick T. Our Kindly Parent - the State: The Juvenile Justice System & How It Works. LC 73-19322. 192p. 1977. pap. 3.95 (ISBN 0-14-004230-X). Penguin.

Murphy, Paul I. & Arlington, R. Rene. La Popessa. 296p. 1983. 16.50 (ISBN 0-446-51258-3). Warner Bks.

Murphy, Paul L. Constitution in Crisis Times, Nineteen Eighteen to Nineteen Sixty-Nine. LC 70-156570. (New American Nation Ser.). (Illus.). 1972. 21.10i (ISBN 0-06-013118-7, HarpT). Har-Row.

Murphy, Paul R., tr. see Herbert, George.

Murphy, Raymond E. American City. 2nd ed. (Illus.). 576p. 1974. text ed. 29.00 (ISBN 0-07-044063-8, C). McGraw.

Murphy, Rhoads, jt. auth. see Meisner, Maurice.

Murphy, Richard C. & Meyer, William E. The Care & Feeding of Trees. 1983. pap. 5.95 (ISBN 0-517-54891-7). Crown.

Murphy, Richard W. World of Cezanne. LC 68-17688. (Library of Art Ser.). (Illus.). (gr. 6 up). 1968. 19.92 (ISBN 0-8094-0272-6, Pub. by Time-Life). Silver.

Murphy, Robert. An Overture to Social Anthropology. (Illus.). 1979. pap. 12.95 ref. (ISBN 0-13-647461-6). P-H.

--The Stream. LC 69-14977. 205p. 1971. 6.95 o.p. (ISBN 0-374-27092-9). FS&G.

Murphy, Robert D. Diplomat Among Warriors. LC 75-42364. (Illus.). 470p. 1976. Repr. of 1964 ed. lib. bdg. 35.00x (ISBN 0-8371-7693-X, MUDW). Greenwood.

--Mass Communication & Human Interaction. LC 76-19906. (Illus.). 1977. pap. text ed. 17.95 (ISBN 0-395-24433-1); instr's. manual 1.65 (ISBN 0-395-24434-X). HM.

Murphy, Roland E. The Psalms, Job. LC 77-78637. (Proclamation Commentaries: the Old Testament Witnesses for Preaching). (Orig.). 1977. pap. 3.95 (ISBN 0-8006-0588-8, 1-588). Fortress.

--Wisdom Literature & Psalms: Interpreting Biblical Texts. Bailey, Lloyd R. & Furnish, Victor P., eds. 160p. (Orig.). 1983. pap. 6.95 (ISBN 0-687-45759-9). Abingdon.

Murphy, Seamus. Stone Mad: A Sculptor's Life & Craft. (Illus.). 1976. pap. 7.50 o.p. (ISBN 0-7100-8542-7). Routledge & Kegan.

Murphy, Shirley R. The Flight of the Fox. LC 78-5436. (Illus.). (gr. 4-6). 1978. 8.95 (ISBN 0-689-30662-8). Atheneum.

--Tattie's River Journey. LC 82-45508. (Illus.). 32p. (ps-3). 1983. 11.95 (ISBN 0-8037-8767-7); 11.89 (ISBN 0-8037-8770-7). Dial Bks Young.

--The Wolf Bell. 176p. 1980. pap. 1.95 (ISBN 0-380-50666-1, 62216-5). Avon.

Murphy, Stanley. Martha's Vineyard Decoys. LC 78-58592. (Illus.). 1978. 50.00 (ISBN 0-87923-260-9). Godine.

Murphy, T., et al, eds. Statistical Methods for Textile Technologists. 17.00x (ISBN 0-87245-239-5). Textile Bk.

Murphy, Sr. Therese, jt. ed. see Mills, Elizabeth.

Murphy, Thomas. A Crucial Week in the Life of a Grocer's Assistant. signed 7.50x (ISBN 0-912262-51-6). Proscenium.

Murphy, Thomas, et al. Inside the Bureaucracy: The View from the Assistant Secretary's Desk. (Westview Special Studies in Public Policy & Public Systems Management). 1979. lib. bdg. 26.00 o.p. (ISBN 0-89158-154-5). Westview.

Murphy, Thomas, Jr. Sky High. 1977. 8.95 o.p. (ISBN 0-399-11648-6). Putnam Pub Group.

Murphy, Thomas P., ed. Urban Indicators: A Guide to Information Sources. LC 80-13333. (Urban Studies Information Guide Ser.: Vol. 10). 1980. 42.00x (ISBN 0-8103-1451-7). Gale.

--Urban Politics: A Guide to Information Sources. LC 78-54117. (Urban Studies Information Guide: Vol. 1). 1978. 42.00x (ISBN 0-8103-1395-2). Gale.

Murphy, Thomas P. & Kline, Robert D., eds. Urban Law: A Guide to Information Sources. (Urban Studies Information Guide: Vol. 11). 1980. 42.00x (ISBN 0-8103-1409-6). Gale.

Murphy, Thomas P., et al. Contemporary Public Administration: A Study in Emerging Realities. LC 80-83377. 572p. 1981. text ed. 19.50 (ISBN 0-87581-269-4). Peacock Pubs.

Murphy, Tom. Aspen Incident. 1979. pap. 1.95 o.p. (ISBN 0-451-08889-1, J8889, Sig). NAL.

--Aspen Incident. LC 78-4363. 1978. 8.95 o.p. (ISBN 0-312-05728-8). St Martin.

--Auction. (Orig.). 1980. pap. 2.95 o.p. (ISBN 0-451-09478-6, Sig). NAL.

--Ballet! (Orig.). (RL 7). 1978. pap. 2.25 o.p. (ISBN 0-451-08112-9, E8112, Sig). NAL.

Murphy, Tome. The Panther Throne. 1982. pap. 3.95 (ISBN 0-451-11861-8, AE1861, Sig). NAL.

Murphy, W. F., ed. Proceedings of the International Conference on Raman Spectroscopy, Ottawa, Canada, Aug. 4-9, 1980. 1980. 85.00 (ISBN 0-444-86038-X). Elsevier.

Murphy, Walter F. The Roman Enigma. 1983. pap. 3.50 (ISBN 0-440-17419-8). Dell.

Murphy, Walter F., jt. auth. see Danielson, Michael N.

Murphy, Walter F. & Pritchett, Herman C., eds. Courts, Judges & Politics: An Introduction to the Judicial Process. 2nd ed. 1974. 22.00 (ISBN 0-394-32117-0). Random.

Murphy, Walter L., jt. auth. see Lockard, Duane.

Murphy, Warren. Bay City Blast. (Destroyer Ser.: No. 38). 1979. pap. 1.95 (ISBN 0-523-41253-3). Pinnacle Bks.

--Chained Reaction. (Destroyer Ser.: No. 34). 1978. pap. 1.95 (ISBN 0-523-41249-5). Pinnacle Bks.

--Child's Play. (Destroyer No. 23). 192p. 1976. pap. 2.25 (ISBN 0-523-41884-1). Pinnacle Bks.

--Chinese Puzzle. (Destroyer Ser.: No. 3). 192p. 1980. pap. 1.75 o.p. (ISBN 0-523-40879-X). Pinnacle Bks.

--Created, the Destroyer. (Destroyer Ser.: No. 1). 1976. pap. 2.25 (ISBN 0-523-41756-X). Pinnacle Bks.

--Dangerous Games. (Destroyer Ser.: No. 40). 192p. (Orig.). 1980. pap. 1.95 (ISBN 0-523-41255-X). Pinnacle Bks.

--Death Check. (Destroyer Ser.: No. 2). 192p. 1980. pap. 2.25 (ISBN 0-523-41757-8). Pinnacle Bks.

--Destroyer, No. 10: Terror Squad. (Orig.). 1974. pap. 1.95 (ISBN 0-523-41225-8). Pinnacle Bks.

--The Destroyer, No. 14: Judgement Day. 192p. (Orig.). 1974. pap. 1.95 (ISBN 0-523-41229-0). Pinnacle Bks.

--Destroyer, No. 16: Oil Slick. 192p. (Orig.). 1974. pap. 1.95 (ISBN 0-523-41231-2). Pinnacle Bks.

--Destroyer, No. 43: Midnight Man. 192p. (Orig.). 1981. pap. 2.25 (ISBN 0-523-41909-0). Pinnacle Bks.

--The Destroyer, No. 6: Death Therapy. (Orig.). 1974. pap. 1.95 (ISBN 0-523-41221-5). Pinnacle Bks.

--The Destroyer No. 8: Summit Chase. (Orig.). 1974. pap. 2.25 (ISBN 0-523-41814-0). Pinnacle Bks.

--Firing Line. (Destroyer Ser.: No. 41). 192p. (Orig.). 1980. pap. 2.25 (ISBN 0-523-41766-7). Pinnacle Bks.

--Mafia Fix. (Destroyer Ser.: No. 4). 192p. (Orig.). 1980. pap. 2.25 (ISBN 0-523-41758-6). Pinnacle Bks.

--Murder Ward. (The Destroyer Ser., No. 15). (Orig.). 1974. pap. 2.25 (ISBN 0-523-41768-3). Pinnacle Bks.

--Power Play. (Destroyer: No. 36). 1979. pap. 1.95 (ISBN 0-523-41251-7). Pinnacle Bks.

--Shock Value. (Destroyer Ser.: No. 51). 208p. 1983. pap. text ed. 2.25 (ISBN 0-523-41561-3). Pinnacle Bks.

--Timber Lane. (Destroyer Ser.: No. 42). 192p. (Orig.). 1980. pap. 2.25 (ISBN 0-523-41767-5). Pinnacle Bks.

Murphy, Warren, jt. auth. see Sapir, Richard.

Murphy, Wendy B. Coping with the Common Cold. LC 81-1955. (Library of Health). PLB 18.60 (ISBN 0-8094-3759-7). Silver.

--Dealing with Headaches. (Library of Health). lib. bdg. 18.60 (ISBN 0-686-79853-8). Silver.

--Touch, Smell, Taste, Sight & Hearing. LC 82-5738. (Library of Health). lib. bdg. 18.60 (ISBN 0-8094-3799-6, Pub. by Time-Life). Silver.

Murphy, Wendy B., jt. auth. see Crockett, James U.

Murphy, William M. The Yeats Family & the Pollexfens of Sligo. (New Yeats Papers Ser.: Vol. 1). (Illus.). 88p. 1971. pap. text ed. 3.75x o.p. (ISBN 0-85105-196-0, Dolmen Pr). Humanities.

Murphy, William M., ed. see Yeats, J. B.

Murphy, William P., et al. Discrimination in Employment, Labor Relations & Social Problems, Unit III. 4th ed. 870p. 1979. 24.00 (ISBN 0-87179-306-7). BNA.

Murphy, William T. Robert Flaherty: A Guide to References & Resources. 1978. lib. bdg. 21.00 (ISBN 0-8161-8022-9, Hall Reference). G K Hall.

Murr, Lawrence E. Interfacial Phenomena in Metals & Alloys. 400p. 1975. text ed. 28.50 (ISBN 0-201-04884-1); pap. text ed. 14.50 (ISBN 0-201-04885-X). A-W.

Murra, John V. The Economic Organization of the Inka State. Dalton, George, ed. (Research in Economic Anthropology Supplement Ser.: No. 1). 214p. 1980. 42.50 (ISBN 0-89232-118-0). Jai Pr.

Murra, John V., ed. see American Ethnological Society, 1974.

Murray, Albert. The Omni-Americans: Black Experience & American Culture. LC 82-48899. 240p. 1983. pap. 6.95 (Vin). Random.

Murray, Alexander. Reason & Society in the Middle Ages. 1978. 49.50x (ISBN 0-19-822540-7). Oxford U Pr.

Murray, Andrew. Abide in Christ. (Large Print Christian Classic). 192p. 1983. Repr. 14.95 (ISBN 0-87983-334-3). Keats.

--Absolute Surrender. pap. 2.95 (ISBN 0-8024-0560-6). Moody.

--The Believer's Prayer Life. rev. ed. 128p. Date not set. pap. 3.95 (ISBN 0-87123-277-4). Bethany Hse.

--Entrega Absoluta. 192p. Date not set. 2.50 (ISBN 0-88113-079-6). Edit Betania.

--God's Will: Our Dwelling Place. Orig. Title: Thy Will Be Done. 144p. 1983. pap. text ed. 2.95 (ISBN 0-88368-119-6). Whitaker Hse.

--How to Raise Your Children for Christ. LC 75-29344. 288p. 1975. pap. 4.95 (ISBN 0-87123-224-3, 210224). Bethany Hse.

--Jesus Himself. 27p. 1966. pap. 0.85 (ISBN 0-87509-096-6). Chr Pubns.

--The Master's Indwelling. LC 76-23363. 192p. 1977. pap. 2.95 (ISBN 0-87123-355-X, 200355). Bethany Hse.

--The Master's Indwelling. 144p. 1983. pap. text ed. 2.95 (ISBN 0-88368-121-8). Whitaker Hse.

--La Nueva Vida. 144p. Date not set. 2.95 (ISBN 0-88113-220-9). Edit Betania.

--Prayer Life. (Andrew Murray Ser.). pap. 2.95 (ISBN 0-8024-6806-3). Moody.

--School of Obedience. (Andrew Murray Ser.). pap. 2.95 (ISBN 0-8024-7627-9). Moody.

--True Vine. (Andrew Murray Ser.). pap. 2.95 (ISBN 0-8024-8798-X). Moody.

--The True Vine. 128p. 1983. pap. text ed. 2.50 (ISBN 0-88368-118-8). Whitaker Hse.

Murray, Andrew E. The Skyline Synod: Presbyterianism in Colorado & Utah. 1971. pap. 2.95x (ISBN 0-87315-040-6). Golden Bell.

Murray, Angus W. Resurrection Shuffle. 190p. 1982. 14.95 (ISBN 0-7206-0519-9, Pub. by Peter Owen). Merrimack Bk Serv.

Murray, Annabel. Roots of Heaven. (Harlequin Romance Ser.). 192p. 1983. pap. 1.75 (ISBN 0-373-02549-1). Harlequin Bks.

Murray, Carolyn S., ed. The Los Angeles Times California Home Book. (Illus.). 216p. 1982. 35.00 (ISBN 0-8109-1276-7). Abrams.

Murray, Charles A. Travels in North America, During the Years 1834-36, Including a Summer with the Pawnees. 2nd ed. LC 68-54845. (American Scene Ser.). 878p. 1974. Repr. of 1839 ed. lib. bdg. 85.00 (ISBN 0-306-71021-8). Da Capo.

Murray, Charles S., jt. auth. see Carr, Roy.

Murray, Christopher, ed. Selected Plays of Lennox Robinson. LC 82-71455. (Irish Drama Selections Ser.: No. 1). (Illus.). 300p. 1982. 27.95 (ISBN 0-8132-0574-3); pap. 7.95 (ISBN 0-8132-0575-1). Cath U Pr.
Murray, David. Ecurie Ecosse. 14.50x (ISBN 0-392-01640-0, SpS). Sportshelf.
Murray, David J. A History of Western Psychology. (Illus.). 400p. 23.95 (ISBN 0-13-392381-9, Busn). P-H.
Murray, David R. Odious Commerce: Britain, Spain & the Abolition of the Cuban Slave Trade. LC 79-52835. (Cambridge Latin American Studies: No. 37). 435p. 1981. 49.50 (ISBN 0-521-22867-0). Cambridge U Pr.
Murray, Dennis J., jt. ed. see Keller, Peter A.
Murray, Donal. Living Catholicism. Date not set. pap. 4.95 (ISBN 0-89453-271-5). M Glazier.
Murray, Donald. Writing for Readers: Notes on the Writer's Craft from the Boston Globe. (Illus.). 160p. (Orig.). 1983. pap. 8.95 (ISBN 0-87106-975-X). Globe Pequot.
Murray, Donald M. Learning By Teaching: Selected Articles on Writing & Teaching. LC 82-20558. 192p. 1982. pap. text ed. 8.25x (ISBN 0-86709-025-1). Boynton Cook Pubs.
--Writer Teaches Writing. LC 68-6986. (Illus.). 1968. pap. text ed. 14.50 (ISBN 0-395-04989-X). HM.
Murray, Douglas P. & Lubman, Stanley B. Communicating with China: Country Orientation Ser. Kapp, Robert A., ed. LC 82-83999. 112p. (Orig.). 1983. pap. text ed. 11.95 (ISBN 0-933662-51-3). Intercult Pr.
Murray, E. C. Side-Lights on English Society: Sketches from Life, Social & Satirical. rev ed. LC 75-83371. (Illus.). xii, 436p. 1969. Repr. of 1885 ed. 37.00x (ISBN 0-8103-3285-X). Gale.
Murray, Evelyn. Showers of Blessings. 1983. 10.95 (ISBN 0-533-05693-4). Vantage.
Murray, F. The Acquisition of Reading. 192p. 1978. text ed. 22.95 (ISBN 0-8391-1281-5). Univ Park.
--Fluoride Emissions: Measurements & Effects on Plants. 246p. 1982. 29.50 (ISBN 0-12-511980-1). Acad Pr.
Murray, Francis J. Introduction to Linear Transformations in Hilbert Space. 1941. pap. 12.00 (ISBN 0-527-02720-0). Kraus Repr.
Murray, Francis X. Where We Agree: Report of the National Coal Policy Project, 2 vols. LC 78-55420. (Westview Special Studies in Natural Resources & Energy Management). 1978. Set. lib. bdg. 60.00 (ISBN 0-89158-175-8). Westview.
Murray, Frank, jt. auth. see Adams, Ruth.
Murray, Frank B. The Impact of Piagetian Theory. 256p. 1978. text ed. 24.95 (ISBN 0-8391-1293-9). Univ Park.
Murray, George. The Legacy of Al Capone. LC 74-30571. (Illus.). 384p. 1975. 10.95 o.p. (ISBN 0-399-11502-1). Putnam Pub Group.
Murray, Gilbert. Euripides & His Age. LC 79-4184. 1979. Repr. of 1965 ed. lib. bdg. 17.25x (ISBN 0-313-20989-8, MUEA). Greenwood.
Murray, Henry A. Golf Secret. (Illus.). 1954. 8.95 (ISBN 0-87523-093-8). Emerson.
--More Golf Secrets. (Illus.). 1954. 8.95 (ISBN 0-87523-099-7). Emerson.
Murray, Henry W., ed. Fever of Undetermined Origin. (Illus.). 350p. Date not set. price not set monograph (ISBN 0-87993-194-9). Futura Pub.
Murray, I. MacKay. Human Anatomy Made Simple: A Comprehensive Course for Self-Study & Review. LC 68-22473. 1969. pap. 4.50 (ISBN 0-385-01116-4, Made). Doubleday.
Murray, Iain. The Invitation System. 1973. pap. 0.80 o.p. (ISBN 0-85151-171-6). Banner of Truth.
--El Obstaculo al Evangelismo. (Span.). pap. 0.75 o.p. (ISBN 0-686-28950-1). Banner of Truth.
Murray, Iain, ed. see Houghton, S. M.
Murray, Iain H. The Puritan Hope. 1975. pap. 5.95 (ISBN 0-686-12534-7). Banner of Truth.
Murray, Isobel M., ed. see Wilde, Oscar.
Murray, J. Atlas of British Recent Foraminiferids. 1972. 24.50 (ISBN 0-444-19594-7). Elsevier.
Murray, J. & Karpovick, P. Weight Training in Athletics. 214p. 1956. 8.95 o.p. (ISBN 0-13-947986-4). P-H.
Murray, J. A., et al, eds. Oxford English Dictionary, 13 Vols. 795.00x (ISBN 0-19-861101-3). Oxford U Pr.
Murray, J. C., jt. auth. see Millis, Walter.
Murray, J. J. & Rugg-Gunn, A. J. Fluorides in Cavities Prevention: Dental Practitioner Handbook, No. 20. 1982. text ed. 22.50 (ISBN 0-7236-0644-7). Wright-PSG.
Murray, Jack. The Proustian Comedy. 17.00 (ISBN 0-917786-13-0). French Lit.
Murray, James. Continuous National Survey: A Compendium of Questionnaire Items, Articles 1 Through 12. (Report Ser: No. 125). 1974. (ISBN 0-932132-18-9). NORC.
--To Find an Image. LC 72-89707. 192p. 1973. 7.95 o.p. (ISBN 0-672-51745-0). Bobbs.
Murray, James G. Henry Adams. (World Leaders Ser.: No. 31). 1974. lib. bdg. 10.95 o.p. (ISBN 0-8057-3651-4, Twayne). G K Hall.
--Henry David Thoreau. (World Leaders Ser). lib. bdg. 11.95 (ISBN 0-8057-3723-5, Twayne). G K Hall.
Murray, James O., intro. by. Selections from the Poetical Works of William Cowper. 243p. 1982. Repr. of 1898 ed. lib. bdg. 20.00 (ISBN 0-8495-3938-2). Arden Lib.
Murray, Janet H. & Stark, Myra, eds. The Englishwoman's Review of Social & Industrial Questions, 2 Vols. 1979. lib. bdg. 44.00 ea. Vol. 13 (ISBN 0-8240-3737-5). Vol. 14 (ISBN 0-8240-3738-3). Garland Pub.
Murray, Jerome T. Introduction to Computing: IBM System 3. 1971. text ed. 15.95 o.p. (ISBN 0-07-044076-X, P&RB). McGraw.
--Programming in RPG II. 1971. text ed. 19.75 (ISBN 0-07-044078-6, G). McGraw.
Murray, Jerry. Getting into Radio-Controlled Sports. LC 78-31751. (Illus.). (gr. 7-12). 1979. 7.95 (ISBN 0-399-20686-8). Putnam Pub Group.
--The Handbook of Motocross. LC 78-919. (Illus.). (gr. 6-8). 1978. 7.95 (ISBN 0-399-20637-X). Putnam Pub Group.
--Mo-Ped: The Wonder Vehicle. LC 76-18937. (Illus.). (gr. 5 up). 1976. 6.95 o.p. (ISBN 0-399-20540-3). Putnam Pub Group.
--Your Used Car: Selecting It & Making It Like New. LC 78-11683. (Illus.). (gr. 7 up). 1979. 7.95 (ISBN 0-399-20662-0). Putnam Pub Group.
Murray, Jim, jt. auth. see Barrilleaux, Doris.
Murray, Joan. A CB Picture Dictionary. LC 80-1725. (Illus.). 64p. (gr. 5 up). 8.95a o.p. (ISBN 0-385-14782-1); PLB 8.95a (ISBN 0-385-14783-X). Doubleday.
Murray, Joan & Abramson, Paul. Bias in Psychotherapy. 412p. 1983. 38.00 (ISBN 0-03-063226-9). Praeger.
Murray, John. British Nearshore Foraminiferids: Keys & Notes for the Identification of the Species. (Synopses of the British Fauna Ser.). 1979. 9.00 o.s.i. (ISBN 0-12-511850-3). Acad Pr.
--Fifteen Plays for Today's Teen-Agers. 1982 ed. (gr. 7-12). 1979. pap. 8.95 (ISBN 0-8238-0258-2). Plays.
--The Media Law Dictionary. LC 78-63257. 1978. pap. text ed. 8.00 (ISBN 0-8191-0616-X). U Pr of Amer.
Murray, John, tr. see Guardini, Romano.
Murray, John F. The Normal Lung: The Basis for Diagnosis & Treatment of Pulmonary Disease. LC 74-25480. (Illus.). 335p. 1976. text ed. 18.50 (ISBN 0-7216-6612-4). Saunders.
Murray, John L. Infaquatics: Teaching Kids to Swim. LC 80-82072. (Illus.). 224p. 1981. Repr. of 1980 ed. pap. 6.95 (ISBN 0-688-00476-8). Quill NY.
Murray, John L., jt. auth. see Lenz, Heinz.
Murray, John P. Status Offenders: A Sourcebook. 160p. 1983. pap. text ed. 7.50 (ISBN 0-938510-03-7). Boys Town Ctr.
Murray, John W. An Atlas of British Recent Foraminiferids. 1971. text ed. 65.00x o.p. (ISBN 0-435-62430-X). Heinemann Ed.
Murray, Jon, jt. auth. see O'Hair, Madalyn Murray.
Murray, Joseph A. Police Administration & Criminal Investigation. 3rd ed. LC 66-25231. (Orig.). 1968. lib. bdg. 12.50 o.p. (ISBN 0-668-01923-9); pap. 10.00 (ISBN 0-668-00565-3). Arco.
Murray, Ken. Golden Days of San Simeon. LC 73-130962. 1971. 19.95 (ISBN 0-385-04632-4). Doubleday.
Murray, Kenneth. Down to Earth: People of Appalachia. 2nd ed. LC 74-6233. 1974. pap. 5.95 (ISBN 0-686-37451-7). Appalach Consortium.
Murray, Laura, jt. auth. see Mollison, James.
Murray, Les. The Vernacular Republic. 1982. 16.95 (ISBN 0-89255-064-3); pap. 8.95 (ISBN 0-89255-063-5). Persea Bks.
Murray, Lindley. English Grammar. LC 81-9062. (American Linguistics Ser.). 1982. Repr. of 1824 ed. 38.00x (ISBN 0-8201-1369-7). Schol Facsimiles.
Murray, M. A. & Ellis, J. C. A Street in Petra. (British School of Archaeology in Egypt Bks.). (Illus.). 38p. 1940. text ed. 16.00x (Pub. by Aris & Phillips England). Humanities.
Murray, Malinda. Fundamentals of Nursing. 2nd ed. (Illus.). 1980. text ed. 25.95 (ISBN 0-13-341313-6); pap. text ed. 9.95 study guide (ISBN 0-13-341347-0). P-H.
Murray, Margaret. God of the Witches. (Illus.). 1970. pap. 6.95 (ISBN 0-19-501270-4, GB). Oxford U Pr.
Murray, Margaret, tr. see Orff, Carl.
Murray, Margaret A. Egyptian Religious Poetry. Cranmer-Byng, J. L., ed. LC 79-8714. (The Wisdom of the East Ser.). 120p. 1980. Repr. of 1949 ed. lib. bdg. 16.25x (ISBN 0-313-21012-8, MUER). Greenwood.
--Egyptian Sculpture. Repr. of 1930 ed. lib. bdg. 17.25x (ISBN 0-8371-4293-8, MUEG). Greenwood.
Murray, Margaret F., jt. auth. see Adams, J. H.
Murray, Margaret R. & Kopech, Gertrude, eds. Bibliography of the Research in Tissue Culture, Eighteen Eighty-Four to Nineteen Fifty, 2 Vols. 1953. Set. 82.00 o.p. (ISBN 0-12-512050-8). Acad Pr.
Murray, Martin. South African Capitalism & Black Political Opposition. 600p. 1981. text ed. 28.95x (ISBN 0-87073-719-8); pap. text ed. 15.95x (ISBN 0-87073-771-6). Schenkman.
Murray, Mary E., jt. auth. see Atkinson, Leslie D.
Murray, Meg M., ed. Face to Face: Fathers, Mothers, Masters, Monsters--Essays for a Nonsexist Future. LC 82-11708. (Contributions in Women's Studies: No. 36). 360p. 1983. lib. bdg. 29.95 (ISBN 0-313-23044-7, MFF/). Greenwood.
Murray, Melba W. Engineered Report Writing. LC 68-26960. 138p. 1969. 19.95 (ISBN 0-87814-006-9). Pennwell Pub.
Murray, Michael V., tr. see Giles of Rome.
Murray, Michele, ed. A House of Good Proportion: Images of Women in Literature. LC 72-93509. 1973. pap. 4.95 o.p. (ISBN 0-671-21472-1, Touchstone Bks). S&S.
Murray, Oswyn. Early Greece. (Illus.). 320p. 1982. pap. 8.95 (ISBN 0-8047-1185-2). Stanford U Pr.
Murray, Patrick, tr. see Hobusch, Erich.
Murray, Pauli. Proud Shoes: The Story of an American Family. LC 77-11807. 1978. 12.95i (ISBN 0-06-013109-8, HarpT); pap. 4.95 (ISBN 0-06-090617-0, CN-0617). Har-Row.
Murray, Peter. Renaissance Architecture. (History of World Architecture Ser.). (Illus.). 200p. 1983. pap. 17.50 (ISBN 0-8478-0474-7). Rizzoli Intl.
Murray, Peter B. Thomas Kyd. (English Authors Ser.: No. 88). 10.95 o.p. (ISBN 0-8057-1308-5, Twayne). G K Hall.
Murray, R. Symbols of Church & Kingdom. LC 74-80363. 430p. 1975. 54.50 (ISBN 0-521-20553-0). Cambridge U Pr.
--Trade Preferences for Developing Countries. LC 76-58546. (Problems of Economic Integration Ser.). 1977. 29.95x o.s.i. (ISBN 0-470-99080-5). Halsted Pr.
Murray, R. B., jt. auth. see McMullan, J. T.
Murray, R. D. H., et al. The Natural Coumarins: Occurance, Chemistry & Biochemistry. LC 81-14776. 702p. 1982. 162.00 (ISBN 0-471-28057-7, Pub. by Wiley-Interscience). Wiley.
Murray, R., Jr., jt. auth. see Grant, H.
Murray, Rachel. Design for Enchantment. (Nightingale Series Paperbacks). 1983. pap. 8.95 (ISBN 0-8161-3501-0, Large Print Bks). G K Hall.
Murray, Randall, ed. Mutagens & Carcinogens. 147p. 1977. 18.50x (ISBN 0-8422-4119-1). Irvington.
Murray, Richard C., jt. auth. see Fisher, Charles O.
Murray, Robert, jt. auth. see Brucker, Roger.
Murray, Robert, jt. auth. see Grant, Harvey.
Murray, Robert A. The Army Moves West: Supplying the Western Indian Wars Campaigns. 1981. pap. 2.95 (ISBN 0-88342-247-6). Old Army.
--The Army or the Powder River. facs. ed. 1972. pap. 2.00 (ISBN 0-88342-203-4). Old Army.
Murray, Robert H., jt. auth. see Grant, Harvey D.
Murray, Robert K. The One Hundred & Third Ballot: The Democrats & the Disaster in Madison Square Garden. LC 75-30340. (Illus.). 352p. (YA) 1976. 12.45i (ISBN 0-06-013124-1, HarpT). Har-Row.
--The Politics of Normalcy: Governmental Theory & Practice in the Harding-Coolidge Era. (Norton Essays in American History Ser.). 160p. 1973. pap. text ed. 3.95x o.p. (ISBN 0-393-09422-7). Norton.
--Red Scare: A Study in National Hysteria, 1919-1920. 1955. pap. 4.95 (ISBN 0-07-044075-1, SP). McGraw.
Murray, Robert K. & Brucker, Roger W. Trapped! The Story of Floyd Collins. LC 82-40177. (Illus.). 336p. (YA) 1982. pap. 7.50 (ISBN 0-8131-0153-0). U Pr of Ky.
Murray, Robin, jt. ed. see White, Gordon.
Murray, Rosemary. The Essential Handbook of Weaving. LC 82-5551. (Illus.). 160p. 1982. cancelled (ISBN 0-312-26444-5); pap. 9.95 (ISBN 0-312-26445-3). St Martin.
Murray, Rosemary & Kijek, Jean C. Current Perspectives in Rehabilitation Nursing. (Illus.). 1979. text ed. 13.95 o.p. (ISBN 0-8016-3605-1); pap. text ed. 12.95 o.p. (ISBN 0-8016-3606-X). Mosby.
Murray, Sheila L. How to Organize & Manage a Seminar: What to Do & When to Do It. 204p. 1983. 13.95 (ISBN 0-13-425199-7); pap. 6.95 (ISBN 0-13-425181-4). P-H.
Murray, Sheilagh. The Peacock & the Lions. (Illus.). 240p. 1983. 25.00 (ISBN 0-686-84463-7, Oriel). Routledge & Kegan.
Murray, Steven T., tr. see Martensson, Bertil.
Murray, T., jt. auth. see Walter, I.
Murray, T. J., jt. auth. see Pryse-Phillips, William.
Murray, T. P. & Horn, R. C. Organic Nitrogen Compounds for Use as Fertilizers. (Technical Bulletin Ser.: T-14). 65p. (Orig.). 1979. pap. 4.00 (ISBN 0-88090-013-X). Intl Fertilizer.
Murray, Thomas J., jt. auth. see Bryson, Reid A.
Murray, W. Cotter, jt. auth. see Kelly, Orville.
Murray, W. H. The West Highlands of Scotland. (Illus.). 415p. 1983. pap. 17.95 (ISBN 0-00-216813-8, Collins Pub England). Greene.
Murray, William. Horse Fever. LC 76-12532. 1976. 7.95 o.p. (ISBN 0-396-07336-0). Dodd.
--Italy: The Fatal Gift. LC 81-19588. 250p. 1982. 14.95 (ISBN 0-396-08049-9). Dodd.
--Malibu. LC 79-14308. 1980. 10.95 (ISBN 0-698-10978-3, Coward). Putnam Pub Group.
Murray, William, jt. auth. see Scarborough, Chuck.
Murray-Aynsley, Harriet G. Symbolism of the East & West. LC 77-141748. (Illus.). 1971. Repr. of 1900 ed. 37.00x (ISBN 0-8103-3395-3). Gale.
Murray-Bruce, D. J. Health in Business: An Employer's Guide. 288p. 1983. pap. 25.00x (ISBN 0-7121-1527-7). Intl Ideas.
Murray-Oliver, Anthony. Augustus Earle in New Zealand. (Illus.). 1968. text ed. 22.00x o.p. (ISBN 0-391-01948-1). Humanities.
Murrell, Hywel. Motivation at Work. (Essential Psychology Ser.). 1976. pap. 4.50x (ISBN 0-416-84090-6). Methuen Inc.
Murrell, J. N. The Theory of the Electronic Spectra of Organic Molecules. 328p. 1971. 14.95x (ISBN 0-412-10260-9, Pub. by Chapman & Hall England). Methuen Inc.
Murrell, J. N. & Boucher, E. A. Properties of Liquids & Solutions. LC 81-21921. 288p. 1982. 49.95 (ISBN 0-471-10202-4, Pub. by Wiley-Interscience); pap. text ed. 21.95 (ISBN 0-471-10201-6, Pub. by Wiley-Interscience). Wiley.
Murrell, John, jt. ed. see Allen, Hazel O.
Murrell, John N., et al. Valence Theory. 2nd ed. LC 70-129161. 1970. 26.95 (ISBN 0-471-62688-0, Pub. by Wiley-Interscience). Wiley.
--The Chemical Bond. LC 77-21728. 1978. 46.95 (ISBN 0-471-99577-0, Pub. by Wiley-Interscience); pap. 19.95 (ISBN 0-471-99578-9). Wiley.
Murrell, K. F. Ergonomics: Man In His Working Environment. 1980. 21.00x (ISBN 0-412-07800-7, Pub. by Chapman & Hall); pap. 19.95x (ISBN 0-412-21990-5). Methuen Inc.
Murrell, Mary & Lester, David. Juvenile Delinquency. 1981. pap. 11.95x (ISBN 0-02-478790-6). Macmillan.
Murrill, Paul W. & Smith, Cecil L. Fortran Four Programming for Engineers & Scientists. 2nd ed. LC 73-1689. (Illus.). 322p. 1973. pap. text ed. 16.95 scp (HarpC); solution manual avail. (ISBN 0-685-28248-1). Har-Row.
--An Introduction to COBOL Programming. 2nd ed. 1974. pap. text ed. 16.50 scp o.p. (ISBN 0-7002-2457-2, HarpC); scp solution manual 4.95 o.p. (ISBN 0-685-41784-0). Har-Row.
--Introduction to Computer Science. (Illus.). 640p. 1973. text ed. 20.50 scp o.p. (ISBN 0-7002-2420-3, HarpC); scp solution manual 4.95 o.p. (ISBN 0-685-28249-X). Har-Row.
Murrill, W. A. Tropical Polypores. 1973. Repr. of 1915 ed. 20.00 (ISBN 3-7682-0914-8). Lubrecht & Cramer.
Murrow, Gene, jt. auth. see Lang, Serge.
Murry, Calvin. Prisoner on Board the S.S. Beagle. (Prison Writing Ser.). write for info. Greenfld Rev Pr.
Murry, J. Middleton. The Life of Jesus. 1982. Repr. of 1927 ed. lib. bdg. 35.00 (ISBN 0-8495-3939-0). Arden Lib.
Mursell, James L. Human Values in Music Education. 388p. 1982. Repr. of 1934 ed. lib. bdg. 35.00 (ISBN 0-89987-646-3). Darby Bks.
Murtagh, Terence, jt. auth. see Couper, Heater.
Murthy, B. Srinivasa. Mother Teresa & India. LC 82-80522. (Illus.). 144p. (Orig.). 1983. pap. 5.95 (ISBN 0-941910-00-8). Long Beach Pubns.
Murthy, H. V. & Kamath, S. U. Studies in Indian Culture. (Illus.). 184p. 1973. pap. text ed. 3.75 o.p. (ISBN 0-210-22391-X). Asia.
Murty, Katta G. Linear & Combinatorial Programming. LC 76-7047. 560p. 1976. 42.95 (ISBN 0-471-57370-1). Wiley.
Murty, T. R. Studies in Indian Thought. 1983. 24.00x (ISBN 0-8364-0866-7); text ed. 16.00x (ISBN 0-8364-0631-1). South Asia Bks.
Murtz, Harold A., ed. Gun Digest Book of Exploded Firearms Drawings. 2nd ed. (DBI Ser.). 1977. pap. 7.95 o.s.i. (ISBN 0-695-80842-7). Follett.
Murvin, H. L. The Architect's Responsibilities in the Project Delivery Process. 2nd ed. (Illus.). 200p. 1982. pap. 19.95 (ISBN 0-9608498-0-7). H L Murvin.
Murwin, Susan A. & Payne, Suzzy C. The Quick & Easy Giant Dahlia Quilt on the Sewing Machine: Step-By-Step Instructions & Full Size Templates for Three Quilt Sizes. (Illus.). 80p. (Orig.). 1983. pap. 3.95. Dover.
Murwin, Susan A., jt. auth. see Payne, Suzzy C.
Murzin, Howy. Secrets to Lower Phone Bills. 64p. (Orig.). 1983. pap. 5.00 (ISBN 0-911199-01-2). Murzin Pub.
Murzin, Howy, jt. auth. see Schiff, Irwin A.
Musaph, H., jt. auth. see Money, J.
Musaph, H., jt. ed. see Money, J.
Musashi, Miyamoto. The Overlook Book of Five Rings 1983 Business Strategy Planner. Harris, Victor, tr. (Illus.). 128p. 1982. 8.95 (ISBN 0-87951-164-8). Overlook Pr.
Muscat, E. & Lorton, P. Microcomputer Applications for the Data Processing Work Kit TRS-80 Diskette. 1982. 50.00 (ISBN 0-07-044107-3, G); wkkit 50.00 (ISBN 0-07-044108-1); user's guide 3.90 (ISBN 0-07-044109-X). McGraw.
Muscat, Eugene, jt. auth. see Robichaud, Beryl.
Muscatine, Charles. Chaucer & the French Tradition: A Study in Style & Meaning. 1957. 27.50x (ISBN 0-520-01434-0); pap. 4.95 (ISBN 0-520-00908-8, CAL104). U of Cal Pr.
Muscatine, Charles & Griffith, Marlene. The Borzoi College Reader. 675p. 1980. pap. text ed. 12.00 (ISBN 0-394-32419-6). Knopf.
Muscatine, Doris. Old San Francisco: The Biography of a City from Early Days to the Earthquake. LC 75-16409. (Illus.). 1975. 12.95 o.p. (ISBN 0-399-11594-3). Putnam Pub Group.
Muscatine, Leonard, jt. ed. see Lenhoff, Howard M.

Muschalek, Christian, jt. auth. see Kirchenmann, Jorg C.

Muschell, Helen. Wells of Inner Space. 1970. 6.95 o.p. (ISBN 0-8158-0233-1). Chris Mass.

Muschg, Adolf. Splinters of a Cross & Other Stories. Hamburger, M. & Zeller-Cambon, M., trs. from Ger. 208p. 1983. text ed. 14.75x (ISBN 0-85635-401-5, Pub. by Carcanet New Pr England). Humanities.

Muschg, Adolph. Besprechungen. (Poly Ser.: No. 10). 148p. (Ger.). 1982. 13.20 (ISBN 3-7643-1156-8). Birkhauser.

Muschler, R. A Manual Flora of Egypt, 2 vols. in one. (Illus.). 1971. Repr. of 1912 ed. 120.00 (ISBN 3-7682-0678-5). Lubrecht & Cramer.

Muschlitz, Beverly, jt. auth. see Michener, Dorothy.

Musciano, Walter A. Corsair Aces: The Bent-Wing Bird Over the Pacific. LC 78-2452. (Illus.). 1978. lib. bdg. 6.95 (ISBN 0-668-04597-3); pap. 6.95 (ISBN 0-668-04600-7). Arco.

--Messerschmitt Aces. LC 81-20614. (Illus.). 224p. 1982. 17.95 (ISBN 0-668-04887-5). Arco.

Musculus, J. Dictionary of Paper Money. 2nd ed. (Illus.). 1982. softcovered 6.00 o.p. (ISBN 0-915262-85-1). S J Durst.

Muse. Photo Two: An Advanced Text. 288p. 1977. pap. 16.95 (ISBN 0-13-665307-3). P-H.

Muse, Bill & White, Dan. We Can Teach You to Play Soccer. 160p. 1976. pap. 5.95 (ISBN 0-8015-6911-7, Hawthorn). Dutton.

Muse, Ken. Photo One: Basic Photo Text. (Illus.). 240p. 1973. pap. text ed. 14.95 (ISBN 0-13-665331-6). P-H.

--The Secrets of Professional Cartooning. (Applied Arts & Sciences Ser.). (Illus.). 336p. 1981. text ed. 17.95 (ISBN 0-13-798140-6); pap. text ed. 17.95 (ISBN 0-13-798132-5). P-H.

Museum of Fine Arts, Boston. Illustrated Handbook, Museum of Fine Arts. (Illus.). 438p. 1975. pap. 3.50 (ISBN 0-686-83419-4). Mus Fine Arts Boston.

--A Pattern Book Based on an Applique Quilt by Mrs. Harriet Powers. (Illus.). 32p. 1973. pap. 1.75 (ISBN 0-686-83418-6). Mus Fine Arts Boston.

Museum of Fine Arts, Boston & Harvard College Library see Hofer, Philip.

Museum of Modern Art, New York. Catalog of the Library of the Museum of Modern Art, New York, 14 vols. 1976. Set. lib. bdg. 1290.00 (ISBN 0-8161-0015-2, Hall Library). G K Hall.

Musgrave, A. E., jt. ed. see Lakatos, Imre.

Musgrave, Clifford. Regency Furniture, Eighteen Hundred to Eighteen Thirty. 2nd ed. 1970. 26.00 o.p. (ISBN 0-571-04694-0). Faber & Faber.

Musgrave, Frank W., ed. Health Economics & Health Care: Irreconcilable Gap? LC 78-59166. 1978. pap. text ed. 9.25 o.p. (ISBN 0-8191-0546-5). U Pr of Amer.

Musgrave, G., ed. see Symposium, Brussels, Nov. 1978.

Musgrave, P. W. The Moral Curriculum: A Sociological Analysis. 1978. 13.95x o.p. (ISBN 0-416-85600-4); pap. 6.95x (ISBN 0-416-85620-9). Methuen Inc.

--Society & Education in England Since Eighteen Hundred. 1968. pap. 5.95x (ISBN 0-416-10790-7). Methuen Inc.

Musgrave, Peggy, jt. auth. see Musgrave, Richard.

Musgrave, Peggy B. United States Taxation of Foreign Investment Income: Issues & Arguments. LC 68-58098. (Illus.). 186p. (Orig.). 1969. pap. 6.00x (ISBN 0-915506-10-6). Harvard Law Intl Tax.

Musgrave, Peter. The Economic Structure. (Aspects of Modern Sociology Ser). 1969. text ed. 7.50x (ISBN 0-582-48804-4); pap. text ed. 2.50x (ISBN 0-582-48805-2). Humanities.

Musgrave, Richard & Musgrave, Peggy. Public Finance in Theory & Practice. 3rd ed. (Illus.). 1980. text ed. 28.95 (ISBN 0-07-044122-7). McGraw.

Musgrave, Richard A. The Theory of Public Finance: A Study in Public Economy. 646p. 1981. Repr. of 1959 ed. lib. bdg. 32.50 cancelled o.p. (ISBN 0-89874-110-6). Krieger.

Musgrave, Richard A., ed. Essays in Fiscal Federalism. LC 76-49481. (Brookings Institution, Studies of Government Finance Ser.). (Illus.). 1977. Repr. of 1965 ed. lib. bdg. 28.25x (ISBN 0-8371-9366-4, MUEFF). Greenwood.

Musgrove, F. Youth & the Social Order. LC 65-12282. 192p. 1965. 10.00x o.p. (ISBN 0-253-19960-3). Ind U Pr.

Musgrove, Frank. School & the Social Order. LC 79-40738. 1980. 44.95 (ISBN 0-471-27651-0, Pub. by Wiley-Interscience); pap. 19.95 (ISBN 0-471-27653-7, Pub. by Wiley-Interscience). Wiley.

Musgrove, Gordon. Operation Gomorrah. (Illus.). 288p. 1981. 18.95 (ISBN 0-86720-562-8). Sci Bks Intl.

Musgrove, Peggy. Who's Who Among Bible Women. LC 81-81126. 128p. (Orig.). 1981. 2.50 (ISBN 0-88243-883-2, 02-0883); teacher's ed. 3.95 (ISBN 0-88243-193-5, 32-0193). Gospel Pub.

Musgrove, Philip. Consumer Behavior in Latin America: Income & Spending of Families in Ten Andean Cities. LC 77-1108. 1978. 22.95 (ISBN 0-8157-5914-2). Brookings.

Musgrove, Richard W. History of the Town of Bristol, New Hampshire. LC 76-53696. (Illus.). 1976. Repr. of 1904 ed. 55.00x (ISBN 0-912274-67-0). NH Pub Co.

Musheno. Vogue Sewing Book. rev. ed. 24.95x (ISBN 0-685-70732-6). Wehman.

Mushier, Carole L. Team Sports for Girls & Women. LC 82-60837. (Illus.). 214p. 1983. pap. text ed. 11.95x (ISBN 0-916622-25-8). Princeton Bk Co.

Mushkat, Jerome. Aaron Burr, Controversial Politician of Early America. Rahmas, D. Steve & Kurland, Gerald, eds. (Outstanding Personalities Ser.: No. 71). 32p. (Orig.). (gr. 7-12). 1974. lib. bdg. 2.95 incl. catalog cards (ISBN 0-87157-571-X); pap. 1.95 vinyl laminated covers (ISBN 0-87157-071-8). SamHar Pr.

--George Clinton, New York Governor During Revolutionary Times. Kurland, Gerald & Rahmas, D. Steve, eds. (Outstanding Personalities Ser.: No. 68). 32p. (Orig.). (gr. 7-12). 1974. lib. bdg. 2.95 incl. catalog cards (ISBN 0-87157-568-X); pap. 1.95 vinyl laminated covers (ISBN 0-87157-068-8). SamHar Pr.

Mushkat, Marion. The Third World & Peace: Some Aspects of Problems of the Inter-Relationship of Interdevelopment & International Security. LC 82-774. 356p. 1982. 27.50x (ISBN 0-312-80039-8). St Martin.

Mushkin, Selma J. Biomedical Research: Costs & Benefits. LC 79-19889. 488p. 1979. prof ref 37.50x (ISBN 0-88410-549-0). Ballinger Pub.

Mushkin, Selma J. & Sandifer, Frank H. Personnel Management & Productivity in City Government. (Illus.). 208p. 1979. 23.95 (ISBN 0-669-02805-3). Lexington Bks.

Musial, jt. auth. see Harrison.

Musial, James, jt. ed. see Heery, Joseph M.

Music Education National Conference. Study of Music in the Elementary School: A Conceptual Approach. Evenson, Flavis & Gary, Charles L., eds. LC 67-31352. 182p. (Orig.). 1967. pap. 5.50x (ISBN 0-940796-19-8, 1048). Music Ed.

Music Educators National Conference. Documentary Report of the Ann Arbor Symposium. 372p. 1981. 15.00 (ISBN 0-940796-24-4, 1010). Music Ed.

--Power of Music. LC 72-88397. (Illus.). 94p. 1972. pap. 6.00x (ISBN 0-940796-14-7, 1037). Music Ed.

Music Educators National Conference, ed. The School Music Program: Description & Standards. LC 74-18863. 46p. 1974. pap. 3.50 (ISBN 0-940796-15-5, 1039). Music Ed.

Music Educators National Conference. Selective Music Lists-1979: Vocal Solos & Ensembles. LC 74-81894. 96p. 1974. pap. 4.50x (ISBN 0-940796-18-X, 1043). Music Ed.

--Selective Music Lists-1979: Instrumental Solos & Ensembles. LC 72-75840. 176p. 1979. pap. 5.00x (ISBN 0-940796-17-1, 1042). Music Ed.

--Toward an Aesthetic Education. LC 79-148393. 1971. pap. 6.50 (ISBN 0-940796-21-X). Music Ed.

Musician Listener & Player Magazine Staff, ed. The Year in Rock 1981-82. LC 81-67649. (Illus.). 272p. (Orig.). 1981. pap. 12.95 (ISBN 0-933328-09-5). Delilah Bks.

Musielak, Julian, ed. Commentationes Mathematicae: Tomus Specialis in Honorem Ladislai Orlicz, 2 vols, Vol. I & Vol. II. LC 78-326639. 1979. 27.50x ea. Vol. 1, 384P (ISBN 0-8002-2271-7). Vol. 2, 347P (ISBN 0-8002-2272-5). Intl Pubns Serv.

Musiker, Naomi, jt. auth. see Musiker, Reuben.

Musiker, Reuben. South Africa. (World Bibliographical Ser.: No. 7). 194p. 1979. 25.25 (ISBN 0-903450-16-X). ABC-Clio.

Musiker, Reuben & Musiker, Naomi. Guide to Cape of Good Hope Official Publications: 1854-1910. 1976. lib. bdg. 37.00 (ISBN 0-8161-7867-4, Hall Reference). G K Hall.

Musil, George. Urbanization in Socialist Countries. LC 80-19066. Orig. Title: Urbanizace v socialistickych zemich. (Illus.). 192p. 1980. 22.50 (ISBN 0-87332-180-4). M E Sharpe.

Musil, Robert. The Enthusiasts. Simon, Andrea, tr. from Ger. LC 82-62098. 1983. 15.95 (ISBN 0-933826-46-X); pap. 5.95 (ISBN 0-933826-47-8). Performing Arts.

Musker, Frank F., jt. auth. see Mood, Dale.

Muskie, Stephen O. Campobello: Roosevelt's "Beloved Island". LC 81-68478. (Illus.). 152p. 1982. 19.95 (ISBN 0-89272-137-5, PIC491). Down East.

Muslin, H. L., et al. Evaluative Methods in Psychiatric Education. 220p. 1974. pap. 10.00 o.p. (ISBN 0-685-65574-1, P182-0). Am Psychiatric.

Musman, R see Allen, W. S.

Musman, Richard see Allen, W. S.

Musmanno, Michael A. Proposed Ammendments to the Constitution. LC 75-35374. (U.S. Government Documents Program Ser.). 253p. 1976. Repr. of 1929 ed. lib. bdg. 17.50x (ISBN 0-8371-8610-2, MUPAC). Greenwood.

--That's My Opinion. Brown, Wilmore, ed. 1967. 12.50 (ISBN 0-87215-035-6). Michie-Bobbs.

Musoff, Lloyd D. Uncle Sam's Private, Profitseeking Corporations: Comsat, Fannie Mae, Amtrak, & Conrail. LC 81-48687. 144p. 1982. 18.95x (ISBN 0-669-05532-8). Lexington Bks.

Musolf, Lloyd D. & Springer, J. Frederick. Malaysia's Parliamentary System: Representative Politics & Policymaking in a Divided Society. (Westview Relica Edition). 1979. lib. bdg. 22.00x o.p. (ISBN 0-89158-460-9). Westview.

Musper, H. T. Netherlandish Painting from Van Eyck to Bosch. (Illus.). 136p. 1981. 40.00 o.p. (ISBN 0-8109-0096-3). Abrams.

Mussa, M. A Study of Macroeconomics. LC 75-38905. (Studies in Monetary Economics: Vol. 3). 1976. 51.00 (ISBN 0-444-10908-0, North-Holland). Elsevier.

Musseau, Steve. Making Success A Habit. LC 81-85812. 128p. 1982. 14.95 (ISBN 0-931028-26-4); pap. 11.95 (ISBN 0-931028-24-8). Pluribus Pr.

Mussell, Harry & Staples, Richard C. Stress Physiology in Crop Plants. LC 78-27567. 1979. 48.50x (ISBN 0-471-03809-1, Pub. by Wiley-Interscience). Wiley.

Mussell, Kay. Women's Gothic & Romantic Fiction: A Reference Guide. LC 80-28683. (American Popular Culture Ser.). 176p. 1981. lib. bdg. 25.00 (ISBN 0-313-21402-6, MGF/). Greenwood.

Musselman, Vernon A. & Hughes, Eugene. Introduction to Modern Business: Issues & Environment. 8th ed. (Illus.). 640p. 1981. text ed. 23.95 (ISBN 0-13-488072-2); pap. 9.95 study guide (ISBN 0-13-488080-3). P-H.

Musselman, Vernon A., et al. Methods of Teaching Accounting, 2nd ed. (Illus.). 1978. text ed. 18.60 (ISBN 0-07-044132-4, G). McGraw.

Mussen, P. H. Carmichael's Manual of Child Psychology, 2 vols. 3rd ed. LC 69-16127. 1970. Set. 128.95 (ISBN 0-471-62697-X); Vol. 1. 86.95 (ISBN 0-471-62695-3); Vol. 2. 66.50 (ISBN 0-471-62696-1). Wiley.

Mussen, Paul. Psychological Development of the Child. 3rd ed. (Foundations of Modern Psychology). (Illus.). 1979. text ed. 17.95 (ISBN 0-13-732420-0); pap. text ed. 9.95 (ISBN 0-13-732412-X). P-H.

Mussen, Paul & Hetherington, Mavis. Handbook of Child Psychology: Vol. 3: Cognitive Development. 1250p. 1983. text ed. write for info (ISBN 0-471-09064-6). Wiley.

Mussen, Paul & Rosenzweig, Mark. Psychology: An Introduction. 2nd ed. 1977. text ed. 21.95x (ISBN 0-669-00497-9); instructor's manual 1.95 (ISBN 0-669-00521-5); study guide 7.95x (ISBN 0-669-00505-3); individualized prog. 7.95x (ISBN 0-669-00513-4); test item file avail. to adopters avail. (ISBN 0-669-00539-8); ind. ssection tests 1.95 (ISBN 0-669-01637-3). Heath.

Mussen, Paul, et al. Psychology: An Introduction. brief ed. 1979. text ed. 20.95x (ISBN 0-669-01672-1); instr's manual 1.95 (ISBN 0-669-01680-2); study guide 7.95 (ISBN 0-669-01681-0); test item file avail., to adapters (ISBN 0-669-01682-9). Heath.

Mussen, Paul H. & Hetherington, Mavis. Handbook of Child Psychology: Socialization, Personality & Social Development, Vol. 4. 1250p. 1983. text ed. write for info (ISBN 0-471-09065-4). Wiley.

--Handbook of Child Psychology: Vol. 1: History, Theories & Methods. 1250p. 1983. text ed. write for info (ISBN 0-471-09057-3). Wiley.

Mussen, Paul H., et al. Child Development & Personality. 5th ed. LC 78-9840. 1979. text ed. 24.50 scp (ISBN 0-06-044693-5, HarpC); inst. manual with test items avail. (ISBN 0-06-364703-6); scp study guide 8.50 (ISBN 0-06-045141-6). Har-Row.

Musser, Joe. The Coming World Earthquake. 1982. pap. 2.95 (ISBN 0-8423-0405-3). Tyndale.

Musser, Joe, jt. auth. see Earechson, Joni.

Musset, Anthony, jt. auth. see Stone, Janet.

Musset, Lucien. The Germanic Invasions: The Making of Europe AD 400-600. James, Edward & James, Columba, trs. from Fr. LC 75-14261. (Illus.). 388p. 1975. 22.50x (ISBN 0-271-01198-X). Pa St U Pr.

Mussett, A. E., jt. auth. see Brown, G. C.

Mussner, Franz. What Did Jesus Teach About the End of the World? (Orig.). 1975. pap. 1.75 o.p. (ISBN 0-89283-019-0). Servant.

Musso, Louis. Will Rogers, America's Cowboy Philosopher. new ed. Rahmas, D. Steve, ed. LC 74-14622. (Outstanding Personalities Ser. No.74). 32p. 1974. lib. bdg. 2.95 incl. catalog cards (ISBN 0-87157-574-4); pap. 1.95 vinyl laminated covers (ISBN 0-87157-074-2). SamHar Pr.

Musso, Louis, III. Theodore Roosevelt, Soldier, Statesman & President. Rahmas, Sigurd C., ed. (Outstanding Personalities Ser.: No. 90). 32p. (gr. 9-12). 1982. 2.95 (ISBN 0-87157-590-6); pap. text ed. 1.95 (ISBN 0-87157-090-4). SamHar Pr.

Mussolini, Benito. The Fall of Mussolini, His Own Story. Ascoli, Max, ed. Frenaye, Frances, tr. from It. LC 75-2699. 212p. 1975. Repr. of 1948 ed. lib. bdg. 20.00x (ISBN 0-8371-8035-X, MUFM). Greenwood.

--My Autobiography. LC 78-109803. (Illus.). xix, 318p. Repr. of 1928 ed. lib. bdg. 17.00x (ISBN 0-8371-4294-6, MUAU). Greenwood.

Mustafa, Nor H. Jeritan. (Karyawan Malaysia Ser.). (Malay.). 1979. pap. text ed. 3.75x o.p. (ISBN 0-686-60443-1, 00353). Heinemann Ed.

Mustard, Helen M. & Merwin, W. S., trs. Medieval Epics. LC 63-7651. 7.95 (ISBN 0-394-60455-5). Modern Lib.

Mustard, J. F., ed. New Trends In Health Sciences Education, Research, & Services: The McMaster Experience. 208p. 1982. 25.95 (ISBN 0-03-061966-1). Praeger.

Muste, A. J. Essays of A. J. Muste. Hentoff, Nat, ed. 1970. pap. 3.45 o.p. (ISBN 0-671-20529-3, Touchstone Bks). S&S.

--Non-Violence in an Aggressive World. LC 76-137551. (Peace Movement in America Ser). 220p. 1972. Repr. of 1940 ed. lib. bdg. 13.95x (ISBN 0-89198-081-4). Ozer.

Musu-Boy, R. Dizionario Italiano-Inglese, Inglese-Italiano. 463p. (Ital. & Eng.). 1979. leatherette 4.95 (ISBN 0-686-97343-7, M-9177). French & Eur.

Musulin, Stella. Vienna in the Age of Metternich: From Napoleon to Revolution, 1805-48. LC 75-19264. (Illus.). 320p. 1975. 25.00 o.p. (ISBN 0-89158-501-X). Westview.

Musurillo, Herbert A. Symbol & Myth in Ancient Poetry. LC 77-2395. 1977. Repr. of 1961 ed. lib. bdg. 18.50x (ISBN 0-8371-9554-3, MUSM). Greenwood.

Muszynska, J., jt. auth. see Fraga, S.

Mutaftschiev, B. Interfacial Aspects of Phase Transformation. 1982. 79.00 (ISBN 90-277-1440-1, Pub. by Reidel Holland). Kluwer Boston.

Mutchler, Augusta. Five Acres & Dementia. (Illus.). 96p. 1983. pap. 8.95 (ISBN 0-931722-18-7). Corona Pub.

Mutel, Cornelia. From Grassland to Glacier. LC 76-3705. 1976. pap. 4.95 o.s.i. (ISBN 0-933472-44-7). Johnson Bks.

Muth, Eginhard J. Transform Methods with Applications to Engineering & Operations Research. (Illus.). 1977. ref. ed. 29.95 (ISBN 0-13-928861-9). P-H.

Muth, Richard F. Urban Economic Problems. 402p. 1975. text ed. 24.95 scp o.p. (ISBN 0-06-044705-2, HarpC). Har-Row.

Mutharika, A. Peter. The Alien Under American Law, 2 vols. LC 80-18236. 1980. looseleaf 85.00 ea. (ISBN 0-379-20341-3); Set. 170.00. Oceana.

--The Regulation of Statelessness Under International & National Law: Text & Documents, 2 vols. LC 76-45660. 1977. looseleaf 75.00 (ISBN 0-379-10040-1); Set. 150.00; Suppl. 15.00. Oceana.

Muther, Richard. Practical Plant Layout. 1956. text ed. 33.95 (ISBN 0-07-044156-1, C). McGraw.

Muthu, S. K. Probability & Errors: For the Physical Sciences. 568p. 1982. text ed. 35.00x (ISBN 0-86131-137-X, Pub. by Orient Longman Ltd India). Apt Bks.

Mutkoski, Stephen A. & Schurer, Marcia L. Meat & Fish Management. 1981. text ed. 22.95x (ISBN 0-534-00907-7, Breton Pubs). Wadsworth Pub.

Mutlak, Suheil. In Memory of Kahil Gibran. 1982. 12.00x (ISBN 0-86685-295-6). Intl Bk Ctr.

Mutmansky, Jan M., ed. see Hartman, Howard L., et al.

Muto, Susan. Blessings That Make Us Be: Living the Beatitudes. 176p. 1982. 7.95 (ISBN 0-8245-0516-6). Crossroad NY.

Muto, Susan A., jt. auth. see Van Kamm, Adrian.

Mutoh, Nancy W., jt. auth. see Pifer, George W.

Muttalib, M. A. Democracy, Bureaucracy & Technocracy. 144p. 1980. text ed. 12.50x (ISBN 0-391-02120-6). Humanities.

Mutti, John H., jt. auth. see Gerking, Shelby D.

Muttzall, K. M., jt. auth. see Beek, W. J.

Mutuwka, Kasuka S. Politics of the Tanzania-Zambia Railproject. 1977. pap. text ed. 11.00 (ISBN 0-8191-0301-2). U Pr of Amer.

Muus & Dahlstrom. Collins Guide to the Fresh Water Fishes of Britain & Europe. 29.95 (ISBN 0-686-42788-2, Collins Pub England). Greene.

--Collins Guide to the Sea Fishes of Britain & Northwestern Europe. 29.95 (ISBN 0-686-42789-0, Collins Pub England). Greene.

Muuss, Rolf E. Theories of Adolescence. 3rd ed. 1974. pap. text ed. 5.95x o.p. (ISBN 0-394-31867-6). Random.

Muvoz, Braulio. Sons of the Wind: The Search for Identity in Spanish American Indian Literature. 344p. (Orig.). 1982. 27.50 (ISBN 0-8135-0973-4); pap. 12.95 (ISBN 0-8135-0972-6). Rutgers U Pr.

Muwanga, jt. auth. see Geranija.

Muybridge, Eadweard. Animals in Motion. Brown, Lewis S., ed. (Illus.). 1957. 15.95 (ISBN 0-486-20203-8). Dover.

--Muybridge's Complete Human & Animal Locomotion: All 781 Plates from the 1887 Animal Locomotion, 3 vols. Incl. Vol. 1 (ISBN 0-486-23792-3); Vol. 2 (ISBN 0-486-23793-1); Vol. 3 (ISBN 0-486-23794-X). (Illus.). 1979. Repr. of 1887 ed. 33.33 ea.; Set. 100.00. Dover.

Muyskens, James L. The Sufficiency of Hope: Conceptual Foundations of Religion. Margolis, Joseph, ed. (Philosophical Monographs: 3rd Annual Ser.). 186p. 1979. 24.95 (ISBN 0-87722-162-6). Temple U Pr.

Muyskens, Judith. A French Literary Reader. 1981. pap. text ed. 5.00x (ISBN 0-394-32641-5). Random.

Muyskens, Judith A. & Lundgren, Sheila. Rendez-Vous: Anthologie Litteraire. 224p. 1982. pap. text ed. 5.00 (ISBN 0-394-32641-5). Random.

Muzik, T. J. Weed Biology & Control. 1970. text ed. 19.95 o.p. (ISBN 0-07-044165-0, C). McGraw.

Muzzey, Artemas B. Reminiscences & Memorials of Men of the Revolution. LC 70-142542. 1971. Repr. of 1883 ed. 45.00x (ISBN 0-8103-3629-4). Gale.

Muzzey, David S. Thomas Jefferson. 319p. 1982. Repr. of 1918 ed. lib. bdg. 45.00 (ISBN 0-89987-590-4). Darby Bks.

Mving, E. & Werblowsky, R. J., eds. Black Africa & the Bible. 260p. 6.00 (ISBN 0-686-95028-3). ADL.

Mwaniki, Nyaga. Pastoral Societies & Resistance to Change: A Re-evaluation. (Graduate Student Paper Competition Ser.: No. 3). 40p. (Orig.). 1980. pap. text ed. 2.00 (ISBN 0-941934-32-2). Ind U Afro-Amer Arts.

Myant & Gibbons. Biochemistry of Cholesterol. 1982. 102.25 (ISBN 0-444-80348-3). Elsevier.

Myant, Martin. Poland: A Crisis for Socialism. 253p. 1982. text ed. 21.00x (ISBN 0-85315-557-7, Pub. by Lawrence & Wishart Ltd England). Humanities.

--Socialism & Democracy in Czechoslovakia, 1945-1948. LC 80-41951. (Soviet & East European Studies). 1981. 47.50 (ISBN 0-521-23668-1). Cambridge U Pr.

Mycielska, Klara, jt. auth. see Reason, James.

Mydans, Carl. More Than Meets the Eye. LC 74-19785. 310p. 1975. Repr. of 1959 ed. lib. bdg. 19.00x (ISBN 0-8371-7808-8, MYME). Greenwood.

Mydans, Shelley. The Vermilion Bridge. LC 79-7804. 1980. 14.95 o.p. (ISBN 0-385-03547-0). Doubleday.

Myddleton, D. R., jt. auth. see Reid, Walter.

Myer, John N. Accounting for Non-Accountants. rev. 2nd ed. 1980. 14.95 (ISBN 0-8015-0026-5, 01451-440, Hawthorn); manual 5.95 (ISBN 0-8015-0028-1). Dutton.

--Understanding Financial Statements: What the Executive Should Know About the Accountant's Statements. 1968. pap. 2.50 (ISBN 0-451-62051-8, ME2051, Ment). NAL.

Myer, Linda, jt. auth. see Meredith, Judy.

Myer, Richard B. Curriculum: U. S. Capacities, Developing Countries Needs. 243p. 1979. 12.95 (ISBN 0-686-95963-9). Inst Intl Educ.

Myerburg, Robert J., jt. auth. see Hurst, J. Willis.

Myerhoff, Barbara. Number Our Days. 1979. 12.95 o.p. (ISBN 0-525-16955-5). Dutton.

Myers, Alfred S. Letters for All Occasions. (Orig.). 1952. pap. 4.76i (ISBN 0-06-463237-7, EH 237, EH). B&N NY.

Myers, Alonzo F. & Williams, Clarence O. Education in a Democracy: An Introduction to the Study of Education. Repr. of 1954 ed. lib. bdg. 16.25x (ISBN 0-8371-2888-9, MYED). Greenwood.

Myers, Alpha & Temkin, Sara. Your Future in Library Careers. LC 75-29605. (Career Guidance Ser.). 160p. 1976. pap. 4.50 (ISBN 0-668-03913-2). Arco.

Myers, Arthur. The Ghost Hunters. LC 80-19668. (Illus.). 160p. (gr. 7 up). 1980. PLB 9.29 o.p. (ISBN 0-671-33076-4). Messner.

Myers, B. S. Art & Civilization. 2nd ed. 1967. text ed. 36.95 (ISBN 0-07-044251-7, C); tchr's manual 15.95 (ISBN 0-07-044257-6); study guide 15.95 (ISBN 0-07-044253-3). McGraw.

--Dictionary of Twentieth Century Art. 1974. 14.95 (ISBN 0-07-044220-7, P&RB). McGraw.

Myers, Barbara. The Chinese Restaurant Cookbook. LC 80-6229. 348p. 1982. 19.95 (ISBN 0-8128-2803-8). Stein & Day.

Myers, Bernard, ed. Encyclopedia of Painting: Painters & Paintings of the World from Prehistoric Times to the Present Day. 4th ed. (Illus.). 1979. 19.95 o.p. (ISBN 0-517-53880-6). Crown.

Myers, Bernard S. & Myers, Shirley D., eds. Dictionary of Art, 5 Vols. (Illus.). 1969. slipcased 120.00 (ISBN 0-07-079724-2, P&RB). McGraw.

Myers, Bernard S., rev. by see Dudley, Louise & Faricy, Austin.

Myers, Carol L. The Tabernacle Menorah: A Synthetic Study of a Symbol from the Biblical Cult. LC 76-17105. (Amerian Schools of Oriental Research, Dissertation Ser.: Vol. 2). 243p. 1976. text ed. 9.00x (ISBN 0-89757-102-9, Am Sch Orient Res); pap. text ed. 6.00x (ISBN 0-89757-101-0). Eisenbrauns.

Myers, Caroline C., jt. auth. see Myers, Garry C.

Myers, Caroline C. & Barbe, Walter B., eds. Challenge of a Handicap. (Highlights Handbooks). (Illus.). (gr. 2-6). 1977. pap. 1.95 o.p. Highlights.

Myers, Charles A. Computers in Knowledge-Based Fields. 1970. 9.95x o.p. (ISBN 0-262-13068-8); pap. 3.95x (ISBN 0-262-63053-2). MIT Pr.

Myers, Charles A. & Schultz, George P. The Dynamics of a Labor Market: A Study the Impact of Employment Changes on Labor Mobility, Job Satisfactions, & Company & Union Policies. LC 75-36100. 219p. 1976. Repr. of 1951 ed. lib. bdg. 18.00x (ISBN 0-8371-8620-X, MYLM). Greenwood.

Myers, Charles A., jt. auth. see Pigors, Paul.

Myers, Constance A. The Prophet's Army: Trotskyists in America 1928-1941. LC 76-15330. (Contributions in American History Ser.: No. 56). 1976. lib. bdg. 29.95 (ISBN 0-8371-9030-4, MPA/). Greenwood.

Myers, Darlene. Computer Science Resources: A Guide to Professional Literature. LC 81-559. 346p. 1981. text ed. 59.50 (ISBN 0-914236-80-6). Knowledge Indus.

Myers, David W. Medico-Legal Implications of Death & Dying. LC 79-92372. 1981. 65.00 (ISBN 0-686-35944-5). Lawyers Co-Op.

Myers, Desaix. Labor Practices of U. S. Corporations in South Africa. LC 77-3020. (Special Studies). 1977. 23.95 o.p. (ISBN 0-275-24520-9). Praeger.

--The Nuclear Power Debate: Moral, Economic, Technical, & Political Issues. LC 75-25022. (Special Studies). 1977. 25.95 o.p. (ISBN 0-275-56440-1). Praeger.

Myers, Don A. Sole Prints: A Reference Guide for Law Enforcement Personnel. (Illus.). 180p. 1982. ref. manual 24.95 (ISBN 0-9608626-0-9). S O L E Pubns.

Myers, Edward. The Chosen Few: Surviving the Nuclear Holocaust. LC 82-72604. 180p. (Orig.). 1982. pap. 7.95 (ISBN 0-89708-107-2). And Bks.

Myers, Elisabeth P. Langston Hughes. (gr. k-6). 1981. pap. 1.50 o.p. (ISBN 0-440-44723-2, YB). Dell.

Myers, Elizabeth. Thomas Paine: Common Sense Boy. (Childhood of Famous Americans Ser). (gr. 3-7). 1976. 5.95 o.p. (ISBN 0-672-71323-3). Bobbs.

Myers, Elizabeth P. William Howard Taft. LC 70-105128. (President Ser.). (Illus.). (gr. 7 up). 1970. PLB 5.95 o.p. (ISBN 0-8092-8630-0). Contemp Bks.

Myers, Ernest R. The Community Psychology Concept: Integrating Theory, Education & Practice in Psychology, Social Work & Public Administration. 1977. pap. text ed. 9.75 (ISBN 0-8191-0291-1). U Pr of Amer.

Myers, Ernest R., ed. Race & Culture in the Mental Health Service Delivery System: A Primer. LC 80-5849. 72p. (Orig.). 1982. lib. bdg. 18.50 (ISBN 0-8191-1847-8); pap. text ed. 6.25 (ISBN 0-8191-1848-6). U Pr of Amer.

Myers, F. J., jt. auth. see Harring, H. K.

Myers, G. E. Analytical Methods in Conduction Heat Transfer. 1971. text ed. 40.00 (ISBN 0-07-044215-0, C). McGraw.

Myers, G. J. Advances in Computer Architecture. 314p. 1978. 31.00x (ISBN 0-471-03475-4, Pub. by Wiley-Interscience). Wiley.

Myers, Gail & Myers, Michele. Communicating When We Speak. 2nd ed. (Illus.). 1978. pap. text ed. 18.50 (ISBN 0-07-044192-8, C); instr.'s manual 15.00 (ISBN 0-07-044193-6). McGraw.

Myers, Gail E., jt. auth. see Myers, Michele T.

Myers, Gail E., ed. see Silber, Kathleen & Speedlin, Phylis.

Myers, Garry C. Headwork. (Highlights Handbooks Ser.). (Illus., Orig.). (gr. k-5). 1968. pap. 1.95 (ISBN 0-87534-136-5). Highlights.

Myers, Garry C. & Myers, Caroline C. Getting Ready to Read. (Highlights Handbooks Ser.). (Illus.). (ps-2). 1963. pap. 1.95 o.p. (ISBN 0-87534-117-9). Highlights.

Myers, Geoffrey, tr. see Giono, Jean.

Myers, George. Piranhas. 9.95 (ISBN 0-87666-771-X, M539). TFH Pubns.

Myers, George, Jr. An Introduction to Modern Times: Collected Essays & Reviews. LC 82-8960. 160p. (Orig.). 1982. pap. 6.00 (ISBN 0-938136-05-4). Lunchroom Pr.

Myers, Gerald E. Insurance Manual for Libraries. LC 77-24524. 1977. pap. 7.00 (ISBN 0-8389-0236-7). ALA.

Myers, Glenford J. Advances in Computer Architecture. 2nd ed. LC 81-11374. 545p. 1982. 47.50x (ISBN 0-471-07878-6, Pub. by Wiley Interscience). Wiley.

--The Art of Software Testing. LC 78-12923. (Business Data Processing Ser.). 1979. 29.95 (ISBN 0-471-04328-1, Pub. by Wiley-Interscience). Wiley.

--Digital System Design with LSI Bit-Slice Logic. 1980. 37.50x (ISBN 0-471-05376-7, Pub. by Wiley-Interscience). Wiley.

--Software Reliability: Principles & Practices. LC 76-22202. (Business Data Processing Ser.). 1976. 33.95 (ISBN 0-471-62765-8, Pub. by Wiley-Interscience). Wiley.

Myers, Isabel B. & Myers, Peter B. Gifts Differing. (Orig.). 1980. 21.50x (ISBN 0-89106-015-4, 7271); pap. 14.00x (ISBN 0-89106-011-1, 7270). Consulting Psychol.

Myers, J. Arthur. Masters of Medicine: An Historical Sketch of the College of Medical Sciences of the University of Minnesota, 1888-1966. LC 68-8890. (Illus.). 942p. 1968. 22.50 (ISBN 0-87527-058-1); pap. 17.50 (ISBN 0-87527-140-5). Green.

Myers, J. Arthur & Steele, James H. Bovine Tuberculosis in Man & Animals. LC 67-30897. (Illus.). 432p. 1969. 27.50 (ISBN 0-87527-060-3). Green.

Myers, J. E., jt. auth. see Bennett, C. O.

Myers, J. E., ed. see Bennett, C. O.

Myers, J. M. Grace & Torah. LC 74-26343. 96p. 1975. pap. 3.95 o.p. (ISBN 0-8006-1099-7, 1-1099). Fortress.

Myers, Jack, et al. Science All Around Us: Things You've Wondered About, No. 1. (Highlights Handbooks Ser). (Illus.). (gr. 2-6). 1978. pap. 1.95 (ISBN 0-87534-123-3). Highlights.

Myers, Jacob M. Hosea-Jonah. LC 59-10454. (Layman's Bible Commentary: Vol. 14). 1959. pap. 3.95 (ISBN 0-8042-3074-9). John Knox.

Myers, Jacob M., tr. Anchor Bible: Esdras 1 & 2. LC 72-84935. 408p. 1974. 16.00 (ISBN 0-385-00426-5). Doubleday.

Myers, James T. The American Way: An Introduction to the U. S. Government & Politics. 1977. text ed. 21.95x (ISBN 0-669-96701-7); instr's manual 1.95 (ISBN 0-669-00351-4). Heath.

Myers, Jay A. Tuberculosis: A Half-Century of Study & Conquest. LC 75-96989. (Illus.). 378p. 1970. 17.50 (ISBN 0-87527-059-X). Green.

Myers, John. The Harp & the Blade. LC 82-5014. (Illus.). 224p. 1982. pap. 5.95 (ISBN 0-89865-193-X, AACR2, Starblaze). Donning Co.

--Once Upon a Medieval Time. Stine, Hank, ed. (Illus.). 176p. (Orig.). 1983. pap. 5.95 (ISBN 0-89865-291-X). Donning Co.

Myers, John B., jt. auth. see Ashbery, John.

Myers, John G. & Nakamura, Leonard. Saving Energy in Manufacturing: The Post-Embargo Record. LC 78-7586. 160p. 1978. prof ref 27.50x (ISBN 0-88410-082-0). Ballinger Pub.

Myers, John G., et al. Energy Consumption in Manufacturing. LC 74-8111. (Ford Foundation Energy Policy Project Ser.). 736p. 1974. prof ref 40.00 (ISBN 0-88410-307-2). Ballinger Pub.

--Marketing Research & Knowledge Development: An Assessment for Marketing Management. (Illus.). 1980. text ed. 23.95 (ISBN 0-13-557686-5). P-H.

Myers, John J., ed. Handbook of Ocean & Underwater Engineering. LC 67-27280. 1969. 66.50 (ISBN 0-07-044245-2, P&RB). McGraw.

Myers, John M. The Moon's Fire-Eating Daughter. LC 80-23268. (Illus., Orig.). 1981. pap. 5.95 (ISBN 0-89865-079-8, Starblaze). Donning Co.

Myers, John V., ed. Jehan de Lanson: Chanson de Geste of the 13th Century. (Studies in the Romance Languages & Literatures: No. 53). xiv, 231p. 1965. 12.00x o.p. (ISBN 0-8078-9053-7). U of NC Pr.

Myers, Johnnie J. Texas Electric Railway: Bulletin No. 121. King, LeRoy O., Jr., ed. LC 82-71474. (Illus.). 256p. 1982. 36.00 (ISBN 0-915348-21-7). Central Electric.

Myers, Katherine. Dark Soldier. (Avon Romance Ser.). 304p. 1983. pap. 2.95 (ISBN 0-380-82214-8, 82214-8). Avon.

Myers, Kenneth, jt. ed. see Alexander, Yonah.

Myers, Kenneth A., ed. NATO-the Next Thirty Years: The Changing Political, Economic, & Military Setting. 440p. 1980. lib. bdg. 37.00 o.p. (ISBN 0-89158-965-1); pap. 15.00 (ISBN 0-86531-331-8). Westview.

Myers, Kent E., jt. auth. see Shirts, Morris A.

Myers, Lou. Ha Ha Ha Hyenas. (Break-of-Day Bk.). (Illus.). (gr. k-3). 1971. PLB 4.49 o.p. (ISBN 0-698-30184-6, Coward). Putnam Pub Group.

--In Plenty of Time. (Break-of-Day Bk). (Illus.). 48p. (gr. 1-3). 1972. PLB 4.49 o.p. (ISBN 0-698-30429-2, Coward). Putnam Pub Group.

Myers, M. Bert, jt. ed. see Grabb, William C.

Myers, M. Scott. Every Employee a Manager. Newton, William R., ed. (Illus.). 1981. 18.95 (ISBN 0-07-044269-X, P&RB). McGraw.

Myers, Marcia J. & Jirjees, Jassim M. The Accuracy of Telephone Reference-Information Services in Academic Libraries: Two Studies. LC 82-10785. 1983. 17.50 (ISBN 0-8108-1584-2). Scarecrow.

Myers, Margaret, jt. auth. see Lynch, Mary Jo.

Myers, Mary, jt. ed. see Heron, Alastair.

Myers, Mary R. A Journey to Cuzco. 1978. 8.95 o.p. (ISBN 0-698-10840-X, Coward). Putnam Pub Group.

--A Private Matter. (Love & Life Romance Ser.). 176p. (Orig.). 1983. pap. 1.75 (ISBN 0-345-30845-X). Ballantine.

Myers, Max H., ed. see American Joint Committee on Cancer.

Myers, Michele, jt. auth. see Meyers, Gail.

Myers, Michele, jt. auth. see Myers, Gail.

Myers, Michele T. & Myers, Gail E. Managing by Communication: An Organizational Approach. (Illus.). 512p. 1981. pap. 18.50x (ISBN 0-07-044235-5); instr's manual 15.00 (ISBN 0-07-044236-3). McGraw.

Myers, Miles & Gray, James, eds. Theory & Practice in the Teaching of Composition: Processing, Distancing, & Modeling. 1983. pap. write for info. (ISBN 0-8141-5399-2). NCTE.

Myers, Norman. The Cheetah Acinonyx Jubatus in Africa. (Illus.). 1975. pap. 10.50 (ISBN 2-88032-015-1, IUCN14, IUCN). Unipub.

--A Wealth of Wild Species: Storehouse for Human Welfare. 300p. 1983. lib. bdg. 22.50 (ISBN 0-86531-132-3); pap. text ed. 10.00 (ISBN 0-86531-133-1). Westview.

Myers, Patricia L. & Hammill, Donald D. Methods for Learning Disorders. 2nd ed. LC 75-37504. 1976. text ed. 29.50 o.s.i. (ISBN 0-471-62751-8). Wiley.

Myers, Peter B., jt. auth. see Myers, Isabel B.

Myers, Philip. Patterns of Reproduction of Four Species of Vespertiliohia Bats in Paraguay. (Publ. in Zoology Ser: Vol. 107). 1977. pap. 14.50x (ISBN 0-520-09554-5). U of Cal Pr.

Myers, Phyllis. Aging in Place. LC 82-8296. 106p. (Orig.). 1982. pap. 7.50 (ISBN 0-89164-075-4). Conservation Foun.

--Neighborhood Conservation & the Elderly. LC 78-70572. 1978. pap. text ed. 4.00 o.p. (ISBN 0-89164-050-9). Conservation Foun.

Myers, R., jt. auth. see Vandenbusche, D.

Myers, R. D., ed. Methods in Psycholbiology. Incl. Vol. 1. Laboratory Techniques in Neuropsychology & Neurobiology. 1972. 56.50 o.s.i. (ISBN 0-12-512301-9); Vol. 2. Specialized Techniques in Neuropsychology & Neurobiology. 1973. 63.00 o.s.i. (ISBN 0-12-512302-7); Vol. 3. Advanced Laboratory Techniques in Neuropsychology & Neurobiology. 1977. 40.50 o.s.i. (ISBN 0-12-461003-X). Acad Pr.

Myers, Ramon H., ed. see Bush, Richard C.

Myers, Raymond E. The Zollie Tree. LC 64-15936. (Publications, Second Ser: No. 1). 200p. 1964. 6.00 (ISBN 0-9601072-0-7). Filson Club.

Myers, Robert, jt. auth. see Garcia, Anthony.

Myers, Robert E. Jack Williamson: A Primary & Secondary Bibliography. 1979. lib. bdg. 13.00 (ISBN 0-8161-8158-6, Hall Reference). G K Hall.

Myers, Robert J., jt. ed. see Thompson, Kenneth.

Myers, Robert L., tr. see Voltaire.

Myers, Robin. The British Book Trade from Caxton to the Present Day: A Bibliographical Guide. 432p. 1975. 37.00 (ISBN 0-233-96353-7, 05812-2, Pub. by Gower Pub Co England). Lexington Bks.

Myers, Rollo. Modern French Music. (Music Reprint Ser.). (Illus.). 209p. 1983. Repr. of 1971 ed. lib. bdg. 25.00 (ISBN 0-306-76158-0). Da Capo.

Myers, Rollo, tr. see Chailley, Jacques.

Myers, Rollo H. Ravel: His Life & Works. LC 73-2340. (Illus.). 239p. 1973. Repr. of 1960 ed. lib. bdg. 20.00x (ISBN 0-8371-6841-4, MYRA). Greenwood.

Myers, S. D. Gas-in-Oil Analysis vs. All Other Methods. (TMI Evaluates Ser.). 72p. 1980. 10.00 (ISBN 0-939320-02-9). Myers Inc.

--Transformer Oil Treatment vs. Transformer Desludging. (TMI Evaluates Ser.). 72p. 1980. 10.00 (ISBN 0-939320-03-7). Myers Inc.

--What to Do about Askarel (PCB) Transformers. (TMI Evaluates Ser.). 106p. 1980. 10.00 (ISBN 0-939320-05-3). Myers Inc.

Myers, Shirley D., jt. ed. see Myers, Bernard S.

Myers, Stanley. RPG II & RPG III with Business Applications. 1983. text ed. 24.95 (ISBN 0-8359-6753-0). Reston.

Myers, Stanley E. RPG II with Business Applications. (Illus.). 1979. text ed. 23.95 (ISBN 0-8359-6303-9); instrs'. manual avail. (ISBN 0-8359-6304-7). Reston.

Myers, Steven. The Enchanted Sticks. LC 78-27725. (Illus.). (gr. 3 up). 1979. 6.95 o.p. (ISBN 0-698-20483-2, Coward). Putnam Pub Group.

Myers, Stewart C., jt. auth. see Brealey, Richard.

Myers, Stewart C., jt. auth. see Robichek, Alexander A.

Myers, T. F. & Lavers, J. Cognition Representation of Speech. (Advances in Psychology Ser.: Vol. 7). 1982. 64.00 (ISBN 0-444-86162-9). Elsevier.

Myers, Virginia. Californio! 1979. pap. 2.75 o.p. (ISBN 0-523-40594-4). Pinnacle Bks.

--Come November. (Orig.). 1980. pap. 1.50 o.s.i. (ISBN 0-440-11350-4). Dell.

--This Land I Hold. 384p. 1980. pap. 2.50 o.p. (ISBN 0-523-40963-X). Pinnacle Bks.

Myers, Walter D. The Dragon Takes a Wife. LC 71-172340. (gr. 2-4). 7.95 o.p. (ISBN 0-672-51586-5). Bobbs.

--Fly, Jimmy, Fly. new ed. LC 73-88813. (Illus.). 32p. (gr. k-3). 1974. 5.95 o.p. (ISBN 0-399-20394-X). Putnam Pub Group.

--Hoops. (YA) (gr. 7-12). 1983. pap. 2.50 (ISBN 0-440-93884-8, LFL). Dell.

--Mojo & the Russians. (gr. 5 up). 1978. pap. 1.50 o.p. (ISBN 0-380-41814-2, 41814). Avon.

--The Nicholas Factor. 180p. (gr. 6 up). 1983. 11.50 (ISBN 0-670-51055-6). Viking Pr.

Myers, Wayne L. & Shelton, Ronald L. Survey Methods for Ecosystem Management. LC 79-25404. 1980. 38.95 (ISBN 0-471-62735-6, Pub. by Wiley Interscience). Wiley.

Myers, William. Dryden. 1973. text ed. 9.00x o.p. (ISBN 0-09-116540-7, Hutchinson U Lib); pap. text ed. 5.50x o.p. (ISBN 0-09-116451-6). Humanities.

Myers, William S. The Mexican War Diary of General George B. McClellan. LC 71-87641. (The American Scene Ser). 98p. 1972. Repr. of 1917 ed. lib. bdg. 22.50 (ISBN 0-306-71789-1). Da Capo.

Myerscough, P. R. Munro Kerr's Operative Obstetrics. 9th ed. (Illus.). 1977. text ed. 55.00 o.p. (ISBN 0-02-858690-5, Pub. by Bailliere-Tindall). Saunders.

Myerson, Bess & Adler, Bill. The I Love New York Diet. 272p. 1983. pap. 2.95 (ISBN 0-446-30558-8). Warner Bks.

--I Love New York Diet: How the Beautiful New Yorkers Keep Thin. LC 81-18716. 1982. 11.45 (ISBN 0-688-01102-0). Morrow.

Myerson, Joel, ed. The American Renaissance in New England. LC 77-82803. (Dictionary of Literary Biography Ser.: Vol. 1). (Illus.). 1978. 74.00x (ISBN 0-8103-0913-0, Bruccoli Clark Bk). Gale.

--Antebellum Writers in New York & the South. LC 79-15481. (Dictionary of Literary Biography Ser.: Vol 3.). (Illus.). 1979. 74.00x (ISBN 0-8103-0915-7, Bruccoli Clark Bk). Gale.

--Studies in the American Renaissance 1977. (Studies in American Renaissance). 1978. lib. bdg. 25.00 (ISBN 0-8057-9007-1, Twayne). G K Hall.

--Studies in the American Renaissance: 1978. (Studies in the American Renaissance). 1978. lib. bdg. 25.00 (ISBN 0-8057-9009-8, Twayne). G K Hall.
--Studies in the American Renaissance 1979. (Studies in American Renaissance). 1979. lib. bdg. 25.00 (ISBN 0-8057-9011-X, Twayne). G K Hall.
--Studies in the American Renaissance, 1980. (Studies in American Renaissance). 1980. lib. bdg. 30.00 (ISBN 0-8057-9013-6, Twayne). G K Hall.
--Studies in the American Renaissance 1982. (Studies in American Renaissance). 1982. lib. bdg. 45.00 (ISBN 0-8057-9015-2, Twayne). G K Hall.

Myerson, Joel, jt. ed. see Burkholder, Robert E.

Myerson, Joel, jt. ed. see Gura, Philip F.

Myfanwy, Thomas. One of These Fine Days. 164p. 1982. text ed. 14.75x (ISBN 0-85635-387-6, 80253, Pub. by Carcanet New Pr England). Humanities.

Myhill, Henry. Motor Caravanning: A Complete Guide. (Illus.). 160p. 1976. 9.75 o.p. (ISBN 0-7063-5086-3). Transatlantic.
--North of the Pyrenees. (Illus.). 190p. 1974. 12.50 o.p. (ISBN 0-571-08671-3). Transatlantic.
--Spanish Pyrenees. 1967. 9.50 o.p. (ISBN 0-571-06823-5). Transatlantic.

Mykel. Windchime Legacy. 419p. 1980. 12.95 o.p. (ISBN 0-312-88219-X). St Martin.

Myklebust, Helmer, ed. Progress in Learning Disabilities, Vol. 5. Date not set. price not set (ISBN 0-8089-1500-2). Grune.

Myklebust, Helmer R. & Johnson, Doris, eds. Learning Disabilities-Educational Principles & Practices. (Illus.). 352p. 1967. 17.00 o.p. (ISBN 0-8089-0219-9). Grune.

Mykura, H. Solid Surfaces & Interfaces. (Solid-State Physics Ser.). 1966. pap. 3.75 o.p. (ISBN 0-7100-4386-4). Routledge & Kegan.

Mykura, W., jt. ed. see Dunning, F. W.

Myles, Bruce. Jump Jet: The Revolutionary V-STOL Fighter. LC 78-856. (Illus.). 1978. 9.95 o.p. (ISBN 0-89141-021-X). Presidio Pr.

Mylonas, George E. Mycenae. (Athenon Illustrated Guides Ser.). (Illus.). 96p. 1983. pap. 10.00 (ISBN 0-88332-305-2, 8238, Pub. by Ekdotike Greece). Larousse.

Mynatt, Elaine S., ed. Koinonia Cooking. (Illus.). 149p. (Orig.). 1982. pap. 6.00 (ISBN 0-911175-00-8). Elm Pubs.

Mynors, R. A., tr. see Erasmus, Desiderius.

Myra, H. L. Escape from the Twisted Planet. 1983. pap. 5.95 (ISBN 0-8499-2949-0). Word Pub.

Myra, Harold. The New You. (gr. 9-12). 1980. pap. 3.50 (ISBN 0-88207-581-0). Victor Bks.

Myrdal, Alva. Nation & Family. 1968. pap. 5.95x o.p. (ISBN 0-262-63017-6). MIT Pr.

Myrdal, Alva, et al. Dynamics of European Nuclear Disarmament. LC 82-670083. 306p. (Orig.). 1982. 35.00 (ISBN 0-85124-320-7); pap. 10.95 (ISBN 0-85124-321-5). Dufour.

Myrdal, Gunnar. Beyond the Welfare State: Economic Planning & Its International Implications. LC 82-15819. xiii, 287p. 1982. Repr. of 1960 ed. lib. bdg. 35.00x (ISBN 0-313-23697-6, MYBW). Greenwood.

Myrdal, Jan. China Notebook, 1975 to 1978. Von Dorp, Rolf, tr. from Swedish. LC 79-88412. (Illus.). 1982. lib. bdg. 9.95x (ISBN 0-930720-59-8); pap. 4.95 (ISBN 0-930720-58-X). Lake View Pr.
--Report from a Chinese Village. (Illus.). 1972. 10.00 (ISBN 0-394-44267-9, Vin); pap. 6.95 (ISBN 0-394-74802-6). Random.

Myrer, Anton. The Big War. 1981. pap. 3.95 (ISBN 0-425-05721-6). Berkley Pub.
--A Green Desire. 528p. 1982. 14.95 (ISBN 0-399-12630-9). Putnam Pub Group.
--A Green Desire. 720p. 1983. pap. 3.95 (ISBN 0-380-61580-0, 61580-0). Avon.
--The Intruder. 1980. pap. 2.95 (ISBN 0-425-05505-1). Berkley Pub.
--The Last Convertible. 1979. pap. 3.75 (ISBN 0-425-05349-0). Berkley Pub.
--The Last Convertible. LC 77-15557. 1978. 10.95 (ISBN 0-399-12124-2). Putnam Pub Group.

Myres, John L. Political Ideas of the Greeks with Special Reference to Early Notions About Law, Authority, & Natural Order in Relation to Human Ordinance. LC 68-54428. 1968. Repr. of 1927 ed. lib. bdg. 20.00x (ISBN 0-8371-0583-8, MYIG). Greenwood.

Myres, S. D., ed. see Williams, O. W.

Myres, Sandra, ed. Force Without Fanfare: The Autobiography of K. M. Van Zandt. LC 69-19424. 1968. 7.50 (ISBN 0-912646-28-4). Tex Christian.

Myres, Sandra L. Native Americans of Texas. Rosenbaum, Robert J., ed. (Texas History Ser.). (Illus.). 45p. 1981. pap. text ed. 1.95x (ISBN 0-89641-083-8). American Pr.
--Westering Women & the Frontier Experience, 1800-1915. (Histories of the American Frontier Ser.). (Illus.). 1982. 19.95x (ISBN 0-8263-0625-X); pap. 9.95x (ISBN 0-8263-0626-8). U of NM Pr.

Myrianthopoulos, N. C., ed. Handbook of Clinical Neurology, Vol. 43: Neurogenetic Directory Pt. 2. 664p. 1982. 161.00 (ISBN 0-7204-7200-8, North Holland). Elsevier.

Myrick, Mildred. The Secret Three. LC 63-13323. (A Trophy I Can Read Bk.). 64p. (gr. k-3). 1983. pap. 2.84i (ISBN 0-06-444035-4, Trophy). Har-Row.

Myrick, Susan. White Columns in Hollywood: Reports from the GWTW Sets. Harwell, Richard, intro. by. LC 82-18881. (Illus.). 320p. 1982. 14.95 (ISBN 0-86554-044-6). Mercer Univ Pr.

Myring. Rockets & Spaceflight. (Let's Find Out about Ser.). (gr. 2-5). 1982. 5.95 (ISBN 0-86020-610-6, Usborne-Hayes); PLB 8.95 (ISBN 0-88110-017-X); pap. 2.95 (ISBN 0-86020-584-3). EDC.
--Sun, Moon & Planets. (Let's Find Out Ser.). (gr. 2-5). 1982. 5.95 (ISBN 0-86020-581-9, Usborne-Hayes); PLB 8.95 (ISBN 0-88110-018-8); pap. 2.95 (ISBN 0-86020-580-0). EDC.
--Vampires, Werewolves, & Demons. (Supernatural Guide Ser.). (gr. 5-9). 1979. 5.95 (ISBN 0-86020-248-8, Usborne-Hayes); PLB 8.95 (ISBN 0-88110-013-7); pap. 2.95 (ISBN 0-86020-249-6). EDC.

Myron. Prehistoric Art. (Pitman Art Ser.: Vol. 52). pap. 1.50 o.p. (ISBN 0-448-00561-1, G&D). Putnam Pub Group.

Myron, Robert, jt. auth. see Fanning, Ralph.

Myrsiades, Kostas. Takis Papatsonis. (World Authors Ser.). 168p. 1974. lib. bdg. 15.95 (ISBN 0-8057-2669-1, Twayne). G K Hall.

Myrvik, Quentin N., ed. Fundamentals of Immunology. Weiser, Russell S. (Illus.). 375p. 1983. price not set (ISBN 0-8121-0866-3). Lea & Febiger.

Mysak, L. A., jt. auth. see LeBond, P. H.

Myslivec, A. & Kysela, Z. Bearing Capacity of Building Foundations. (Developments in Geotechnical Engineering: Vol. 21). 1978. 53.25 (ISBN 0-444-99794-6). Elsevier.

Mystery Writers of America. Mystery Writer's Handbook. 273p. 1982. pap. 8.95 (ISBN 0-89879-080-8); pap. 12.95 o.p. (ISBN 0-89879-101-4). Writers Digest.

Mytton, Graham. The Sociology of Communications: Changing Patterns in Africa. 220p. 1982. pap. text ed. 16.95 (ISBN 0-7131-8080-3). E Arnold.

Mzimeia, Sipo E. Apartheid: South African Nazism. 1983. 8.95 (ISBN 0-533-05481-8). Vantage.

N

Naab, Maxine, jt. auth. see Green, Mimi.

Naaman, Antoine E. Prestressed Concrete: Analysis & Design. (Illus.). 736p. 1982. text ed. 32.50x (ISBN 0-07-045761-1); instr.'s manual 15.00 (ISBN 0-07-045762-X). McGraw.

Naamani, Israel T., et al, eds. Israel: Its Politics & Philosophy. rev. ed. LC 73-15645. 447p. 1973. pap. 4.95x o.p. (ISBN 0-87441-249-8). Behrman.

Naar, Maria E. Colloquial Portugese. (Trubner's Colloquial Ser.). 192p. 1972. pap. 7.95 (ISBN 0-7100-7450-6). Routledge & Kegan.

Naar, Ray. A Primer of Group Psychotherapy. LC 81-4244. 215p. 1982. 19.95 (ISBN 0-89885-027-4). Human Sci Pr.

Naas, Bernard G., ed. American Labor Unions' Officers' Reports: A Guide to the Microfiche Edition, Phase I. 2nd ed. 71p. pap. text ed. 32.50 (ISBN 0-667-00670-2). Microfilming Corp.

Naats, I. E., jt. auth. see Zuev, V. E.

Nabarro, F. R. Moving Dislocations. (Dislocations in Solids Ser.: Vol. 3). 1980. 64.00 (ISBN 0-444-85015-5). Elsevier.

Nabarro, F. R. N., ed. Dislocations in Crystals. (Dislocations in Solids Ser.: Vol. 2). 1979. 106.50 (ISBN 0-444-85004-X, North Holland). Elsevier.
--Dislocations in Metallurgy. (Dislocations in Solids Ser.: Vol. IV). 464p. 1979. 95.75 (ISBN 0-444-85025-2, North Holland). Elsevier.

Nabarro, Gerald. Severn Valley Stream. (Illus.). 1971. 14.95 o.p. (ISBN 0-7100-7064-0). Routledge & Kegan.

Nabb, Magdalen. Death of a Dutchman: A Novel of Murder in Florence. 176p. 1983. 11.95 (ISBN 0-684-17854-0, ScribT). Scribner.
--Death of an Englishman. 176p. 1982. 10.95 (ISBN 0-684-17757-9, ScribT). Scribner.

Naber, Gregory L. Methods of Topology in Euclidean Spaces. LC 79-7225. (Illus.). 1980. 26.95x (ISBN 0-521-22746-1). Cambridge U Pr.

Nabhan, Gary P. The Desert Smells Like Rain: A Naturalist in Papago Indian Country. LC 81-81505. (Illus.). 192p. 1982. 15.00 (ISBN 0-86547-049-9). N Point Pr.

Nabholz, A., jt. ed. see Folsch, D. W.

Nabi, Malik B. The Quranic Phenomenon. Kirkari, Abu B., tr. from Fr. LC 82-70460. 150p. (Orig.). 1982. pap. 8.00 (ISBN 0-89259-023-8). Am Trust Pubns.

Nabile, Jeanette. Thinking of You. 1982. pap. 1.95 (ISBN 0-553-22516-2). Bantam.

Nabokov, Dmitri, tr. see Lermontov, Mihail.

Nabokov, Nicolas. Old Friends & New Music. LC 74-7776. 294p. 1974. Repr. of 1951 ed. lib. bdg. 17.50x (ISBN 0-8371-7594-1, NAOF). Greenwood.

Nabokov, Peter, ed. Native American Testimony: An Anthology of Indian & White Relations. First Encounter to Dispossession. LC 77-11558. (Illus.). (gr. 7 up). 1978 (ISBN 0-690-01313-2, TYC-J). PLB 10.89 (ISBN 0-690-03840-2). Har-Row.

Nabokov, Vladimir. Ada or Ardor. 1969. 8.95 o.p. (ISBN 0-07-045720-4, GB). McGraw.
--Bend Sinister. LC 73-5990. 256p. 1973. pap. 5.95 (ISBN 0-07-045710-7, SP). McGraw.
--Details of a Sunset & Other Stories. LC 75-34086. 180p. 1976. 10.95 o.p. (ISBN 0-07-045709-3, GB). McGraw.
--Glory: A Novel. 1971. 6.95 (ISBN 0-07-045733-6, GB). McGraw.
--Invitation to a Beheading. 1959. 6.95 o.p. (ISBN 0-399-10452-6). Putnam Pub Group.
--Laughter in the Dark. rev. ed. LC 60-16644. 1960. 12.50 (ISBN 0-686-86501-4); pap. 4.95 (ISBN 0-8112-0708-0, NDP458). New Directions.
--Lectures on Don Quixote. Bowers, Fredson, ed. LC 82-47665. 256p. 1983. 17.95 (ISBN 0-15-149595-5). HarBraceJ.
--Lectures on Russian Literature. Bowers, Fredson, ed. LC 81-47315. (Illus.). 416p. 1982. 8.95 (ISBN 0-15-649591-0, Harv). HarBraceJ.
--Lectures on Ulysses: A Facsimile of the Manuscript. 1980. 75.00 (ISBN 0-89723-027-2). Bruccoli.
--Lolita. 1978. 10.00 (ISBN 0-399-10501-8). Putnam Pub Group.
--Lolita: A Screenplay. LC 73-15918. 228p. 1983. 6.95 (ISBN 0-07-045768-9, GB). McGraw.
--Pale Fire. pap. 3.50 (ISBN 0-425-06238-4). Berkley Pub.
--Pale Fire. 1978. 10.00 (ISBN 0-399-12161-7). Putnam Pub Group.
--Pale Fire. LC 79-26742. 320p. 1980. pap. 5.95 (ISBN 0-399-50458-3, Perigre). Putnam Pub Group.
--Pnin. 1973. pap. 2.95 (ISBN 0-380-00819-X, 62182-7, Bard). Avon.
--Pnin. LC 82-1208. 192p. 1982. Repr. of 1957 ed. 12.50 (ISBN 0-8376-0465-6). Bentley.
--Speak Memory: An Autobiography Revisted. (Illus.). 1978. 10.00 (ISBN 0-399-10763-0). Putnam Pub Group.
--Transparent Things. LC 72-3989. 128p. 1972. 9.95 (ISBN 0-07-045734-4, GB). McGraw.

Nabokov, Vladimir, tr. see Lermontov, Mihail.

Nabors, Eugene. Legislative Reference Checklist: The Key to Legislative Histories from 1789-1903. LC 82-18074. xv, 440p. 1982. text ed. 39.50x (ISBN 0-8377-0908-3). Rothman.

Nabors, James J., jt. auth. see Bracker, William.

Nabseth, L. & Ray, G. F. Diffusion of New Technology. (National Institute of Economic & Social Research Economic & Social Studies: No. 29). (Illus.). 300p. 1974. 42.50 (ISBN 0-521-20430-5). Cambridge U Pr.

Nabudere, Dan. The Political Economy of Imperialism. 2nd ed. 304p. 1980. 33.00 (ISBN 0-905762-03-7, Pub. by Zed Pr England); pap. 8.95 (ISBN 0-905762-02-9, Pub. by Zed Pr England). Lawrence Hill.

Nabudere, Dan W. Imperialism in East Africa: Vol. 1: Imperialism & Exploitation. 144p. (Orig.). 1982. 30.00 (ISBN 0-905762-99-1, Pub. by Zed Pr England). Lawrence Hill.
--Imperialism in East Africa: Vol. 2: Imperialism & Integration. 192p. (Orig.). 1982. 30.00 (ISBN 0-905762-05-3, Pub. by Zed Pr England); pap. 7.95 o.p. (ISBN 0-905762-06-1). Lawrence Hill.

Nacci, Chris N. Ignacio Manuel Altamirano. (World Authors Ser.). lib. bdg. 14.95 (ISBN 0-8057-2040-5, Twayne). G K Hall.

Nachbar, C. M., et al. American Language Today, Bks. 1-6. Incl. Bk. 1. Secret Hand. (gr. 1). 3.00 (ISBN 0-07-045771-9); tchrs' ed 4.28 (ISBN 0-07-045781-6); webstermasters 24.12 (ISBN 0-07-045787-5); Bk. 2. Tiger Tree. (gr. 2). 5.44 (ISBN 0-07-045772-7); tchr's. ed. 7.16 (ISBN 0-07-045782-4); Bk. 3. Emerald Snowflake. (gr. 3). 8.56 (ISBN 0-07-045773-5); tchr's. ed. 8.56 (ISBN 0-07-045783-2); wkbk. 2.24 (ISBN 0-07-045789-1); Bk. 4. Orange Rain. (gr. 4). text ed. 8.56 (ISBN 0-07-045774-3); tchr's. ed. 8.56 (ISBN 0-07-045784-0); wkbk. 2.24 (ISBN 0-07-045792-1); Bk. 5. Purple Sand. (gr. 5). 8.56 (ISBN 0-07-045775-1); tchr's. ed. 8.92 (ISBN 0-07-045785-9); wkbk. o.p. 1.52 (ISBN 0-07-045793-X); Bk. 6. Flying Free. (gr. 6). 8.56 (ISBN 0-07-045776-X); tchr's. ed. 9.50 (ISBN 0-07-045786-7); wkbk. 2.24 (ISBN 0-07-045794-8). (gr. 1-5). tapes, drills & tests avail. (W). McGraw.

Nachbar, John G., jt. auth. see Marsden, Michael T.

Nachbin, Leopoldo. The Haar Integral. LC 75-42042. 168p. 1976. Repr. of 1965 ed. 10.50 o.p. (ISBN 0-88275-374-6). Krieger.
--Introduction to Functional Analysis: Banach Spaces & Different Calculus. (Pure & Applied Mathematics: Monographs & Textbooks: Vol. 60). (Illus.). 184p. 1981. 19.75 (ISBN 0-8247-6984-8). Dekker.

Nachman, Gerald. Out on a Whim: Some Very Close Brushes with Life. LC 82-9412. 312p. 1983. 16.95 (ISBN 0-385-12340-X). Doubleday.

Nachman, Paul, jt. auth. see Smil, Vaclav.

Nachmias, David & Rosenbloom, David H. Bureaucratic Culture: Citizens & Administrators in Israel. LC 78-17638. 1978. 20.00 (ISBN 0-312-10808-7). St Martin.

Nachmias, Vivianne T. Microfilaments. Head, J. J., ed. LC 82-73999. (Carolina Biology Readers Ser.). (Illus.). 16p. 1983. pap. text ed. 1.60 (ISBN 0-89278-330-3, 45-9730). Carolina Biological.

Nachtigall, Lila & Heilman, Joan. The Lila Nachtigall Report: The Intelligent Woman's Guide to Menopause, Estrogen, & Her Body. LC 77-6653. 1977. 7.95 o.p. (ISBN 0-399-11992-2). Putnam Pub Group.

Nachtigall, Werner. Insects in Flight. Oldroyd, Harold & Abbott, Roger H., trs. from Ger. (Illus.). 158p. 1974. 16.95 (ISBN 0-07-045736-0, P&RB). McGraw.

Nachtmann, Francis W. Exercises in French Phonics. 79p. 1981. pap. text ed. 5.95x (ISBN 0-87563-215-7). Stipes.
--French Review for Reading Improvement. (Orig.). 1966. pap. text ed. 11.95x (ISBN 0-02-385940-7). Macmillan.

Naczi, Frances D. Without Bombast & Blunders: An Executive's Guide to Effective Writing. LC 80-17857. 1980. pap. 5.95 (ISBN 0-87863-007-4). Farnswth Pub.

Nadas, Alexander S. & Fyler, Donald C. Pediatric Cardiology. 3rd ed. LC 76-176213. (Illus.). 749p. 1972. 40.00 (ISBN 0-7216-6651-5). Saunders.

Nadas, Betsy P. Danny's Song. (I Am, I Can, I Will Ser.). 36p. (Orig.). 1975. pap. 3.95 (ISBN 0-8331-0034-3). Hubbard Sci.

Nadeau, Maurice. The Greatness of Flaubert. Bray, Barbara, tr. 307p. 1972. pap. 8.50x (ISBN 0-87548-325-9, Library Pr). Open Court.

Nadeau, Ray E. Speech-Communication: A Modern Approach. (gr. 9-12). 1973. text ed. 12.56 (ISBN 0-201-05001-3, Sch Div); text ed. 9.12 softbound (ISBN 0-201-05002-1). A-W.

Nadeau, Remi. California: The New Society. LC 73-22754. (Illus.). 303p. 1974. Repr. of 1963 ed. lib. bdg. 17.25x (ISBN 0-8371-7345-0, NACA). Greenwood.
--City-Makers: The Story of Southern California's First Boom. 4th rev. ed. LC 76-43546. 9.95 (ISBN 0-87046-039-0, Pub. by Trans-Anglo). Interurban.
--Fort Laramie & the Sioux. LC 82-2675. (Illus.). xiv, 361p. 1982. pap. 8.95 (ISBN 0-8032-8352-0, BB 809, Bison). U of Nebr Pr.

Nadel & Sherrer. Barron's How to Prepare for the CLEP Subject Exams - Analysis & Interpretations of Literature. Date not set. pap. price not set Cancelled (ISBN 0-8120-0619-4). Barron. Postponed.
--How to Prepare for the CLEP: Analysis & Interpretation of Literature. 1982. cancelled (ISBN 0-8120-0619-4). Barron.

Nadel & Sherrer, Jr. Writing Themes about Literature. Markman, ed. Date not set. pap. 2.95 (ISBN 0-8120-0595-3). Barron.

Nadel, Ira B., ed. Jewish Writers of North America: A Guide to Information Sources. LC 80-25412. (American Studies Information Guide Ser.: Vol. 8). 493p. 1981. 42.00x (ISBN 0-8103-1484-3). Gale.

Nadel, Lynn, jt. auth. see O'Keefe, John.

Nadel, Mark V. Corporations & Political Accountability. 1976. pap. 7.95x (ISBN 0-669-93013-X). Heath.

Nadel, S. N. Contempory Capitalism & the Middle Classes. LC 82-1046. 446p. 1983. 7.95 (ISBN 0-7178-0593-X). Intl Pub Co.

Nadell, Judith, jt. auth. see Langan, John.

Nader Congress Project. Ruling Congress. 1977. pap. 4.95 (ISBN 0-14-004413-2). Penguin.

Nader, George. Chrome. LC 77-17370. 1978. 9.95 o.p. (ISBN 0-399-12125-0). Putnam Pub Group.

Nader, Philip R. Options for School Health: Meeting Community Needs. LC 78-9628. 180p. 1978. text ed. 27.95 (ISBN 0-89443-038-6). Aspen Systems.

Nader, Ralph. Ralph Nader Presents a Citizens' Guide to Lobbying. 1983. 12.95 (ISBN 0-934878-26-9); pap. 6.95 (ISBN 0-934878-27-7). Dembner Bks.
--Who Runs Congress? 3rd ed. 1979. 14.95 o.p. (ISBN 0-670-76492-2). Viking Pr.

Nader, Ralph & Blackwell, Kate. You & Your Pension. 215p. 1973. pap. 1.65 (ISBN 0-686-36546-1). Ctr Responsive Law.

Nader, Ralph & Green, Mark. Verdicts on Lawyers. LC 75-23292. 1977. 10.00 o.p. (ISBN 0-690-01006-0); pap. 4.95i o.p. (ISBN 0-690-01667-0, TYC-T). T Y Crowell.

Nader, Ralph & Ross, Donald. Action for a Change. 184p. 1972. pap. 1.75 (ISBN 0-686-36535-6). Ctr Responsive Law.

Nader, Ralph & Fortun, Michael, eds. Eating Clean: Food Safety & the Chemical Harvest. 294p. 1982. 6.50 (ISBN 0-936758-05-8). Ctr Responsive Law.

Nadich, Judah. Jewish Legends of The Second Commonwealth. 480p. 1983. 25.00 (ISBN 0-8276-0212-X). Jewish Pubn.

Nadin, Mihai, ed. Energy Crisis: A Topic for Semiotics? (Kodikas Supplement Ser.: No. 3). 96p. (Orig.). 1982. pap. 8.90 (ISBN 3-87808-572-9). Benjamins North Am.
--New Elememts in the Semiotics of Communication. 190p. 1983. pap. 17.00 (ISBN 3-87808-560-5). Benjamins North Am.

Nadin, Peter. Still Life. 96p. (Orig.). 1983. 12.95 (ISBN 0-934378-35-5); pap. 5.95 (ISBN 0-934378-36-3). Tanam Pr.

Nadis, Steven J. see Kendall, Henry W.

Nadkarni, M. V. Marketable Surplus & Market Dependence: A Study of a Millet Region. 176p. 1980. 23.50x (ISBN 0-940500-80-9, Pub by Allied Pubs India). Asia Bk Corp.

Nadler, Arie, jt. ed. see Fisher, Jeffrey D.

Nadler, Bob. Advanced B & W Darkroom Book. (Illus.). 1979. pap. 6.95 (ISBN 0-8174-2947-6, Amphoto). Watson-Guptill.

--Basic Black & White Darkroom Book. (Illus.). 1978. pap. 6.95 (ISBN 0-8174-2938-7, Amphoto). Watson-Guptill.

--The Basic Illustrated Color Darkroom Book. LC 81-21047. (Illus.). 240p. 1982. Set. 24.95 (ISBN 0-13-062448-9); Vol. 1. 7.95 (ISBN 0-13-062455-1); Vol. 2. 8.95 (ISBN 0-13-062463-2). P-H.

Nadler, Burton J. Arming Yourself for a Part-Time or Summer Job. LC 81-85609. 100p. 1982. 4.95 (ISBN 0-913420-96-4). Olympus Pub Co.

Nadler, Gerald. Motion & Time Study Work Simplification. 1957. 31.00 (ISBN 0-07-045767-0, P&RB). McGraw.

--The Planning & Design Approach. LC 81-1448. 394p. 1981. 49.95x (ISBN 0-471-08102-7, Pub. by Wiley-Interscience). Wiley.

Nadler, Gerald, et al. Design Concepts for Information Systems. 1975. pap. text ed. 12.00 (ISBN 0-89806-015-X, 31); pap. text ed. 6.00 members. Inst Indus Eng.

Nadler, Harvey & Marelli, Leonard R. American English: Grammatical Structure, 4 Bks. (An Integrated Series for International Students). 1971. Bk. I. pap. 9.50 (ISBN 0-395-31009-1); Bk. II. pap. 8.50 (ISBN 0-395-31010-5); Bk. III. pap. 8.50 (ISBN 0-395-31011-3); Bk. IV. pap. 8.50 (ISBN 0-395-30992-1); Lab Wkbk. 8.50 (ISBN 0-395-30993-X). HM.

--American English: Guided Composition Paper. (An Integrated Series for International Students). 1971. pap. 10.50 (ISBN 0-395-30995-6); instructors manual 3.00 (ISBN 0-395-30996-4); Readings I 5.00, (ISBN 0-395-30997-2); Readings II 5.00, (ISBN 0-395-30998-0); Readings III 5.00, (ISBN 0-395-30999-9). HM.

Nadler, Leonard. Critical Events Training Model. LC 81-12840. (Illus.). 368p. 1982. text ed. 18.95 (ISBN 0-686-82104-1). A-W.

--Personal Skills for the Manager. LC 82-72896. 275p. 1982. ringed binder 29.95 (ISBN 0-87094-349-9). Dow Jones-Irwin.

Nadler, Leonard & Nadler, Zeace. The Conference Book. 266p. 1977. 16.95 (ISBN 0-87201-140-2). Gulf Pub.

Nadler, Leonard, jt. auth. see Bell, Chip R.

Nadler, Paul. Commercial Banking in the Economy. rev. ed. 1973. pap. text ed. 7.00 (ISBN 0-394-32271-1). Random.

Nadler, Robert. The Color Printing Manual. 1978. 27.95 (ISBN 0-8174-2435-0, Amphoto); pap. text ed. 16.95 (ISBN 0-8174-2470-9). Watson-Guptill.

Nadler, Zeace, jt. auth. see Nadler, Leonard.

Nadol, Joseph B., Jr., jt. auth. see Wilson, William B.

Nadvi. Saviors of Islamic Spirit: Vol. 1, II. 21.00 (ISBN 0-686-18312-6). Kazi Pubns.

Nadvi, A. H. Four Pillars of Islam. 12.50 (ISBN 0-686-18597-8). Kazi Pubns.

--Islam & the World. 7.50 (ISBN 0-686-18625-7). Kazi Pubns.

--Qadianism: A Critique. pap. 1.00 (ISBN 0-686-18539-0). Kazi Pubns.

--Western Civilization, Islam & Muslims. 12.50 (ISBN 0-686-18563-3). Kazi Pubns.

Nadvi, A. H. A. Glory of Iqbal. 12.50 (ISBN 0-686-18323-1). Kazi Pubns.

Nadvi, S. Arab Navigation. 8.50 (ISBN 0-686-18335-5). Kazi Pubns.

Nadwi, Abul H. Muhammad Rasulullah: The Life of the Prophet Muhammad. rev. ed. 225p. 1983. pap. 7.00 (ISBN 0-89259-034-3). Am Trust Pubns.

Nadzo, Stefan C. Being Who You Are. LC 82-84415. 140p. 1983. pap. 6.95 (ISBN 0-937226-02-5). Edens Work.

Naeem, Nadrat, ed. see Siddique, Kankab.

Naef, Hans. Die Bildniszeichnungen Von J.A.D. Ingres, 5 vols. (Illus.). 1980. Vols. 1-3 110.00x ea. (Pub. by Sotheby Pubns England). Vol. 1 (ISBN 3-7165-0087-9). Vol. 2 (ISBN 3-7165-0249-9). Vol. 3.1979 (ISBN 3-7165-0250-2). Vol. 4 (ISBN 3-7165-0122-0). Vols. 4 & 5 125.00x (ISBN 0-686-34329-8). Vol. 5 (ISBN 3-7165-0251-0). 520.00x set (ISBN 0-686-35694-2). Biblio Dist.

Naef, Weston J. Counterparts: Form & Emotion in Photographs. 106p. 1982. 35.95 (ISBN 0-525-10768-1). Dutton.

Naef, Weston J. & Wood, James N. Era of Exploration: The Rise of Landscape Photography in the America West, 1860-1885. LC 75-9694. (Illus.). 260p. 1975. 25.00 o.p. (ISBN 0-87099-128-0, Pub. by Metro Mus Art). NYGS.

Naegele, Gerhard. Die Soziale Lage Alleinstehender Alterer Frauen In Grossstadten Aus Drei Westeuropaischen Landtern. 168p. (Ger.). 1982. write for info. (ISBN 3-8204-5806-9). P Lang Pubs.

Naegeli, Bruce A., jt. auth. see Gara, Otto G.

Naess, Arne. The Pluralist & Possibilist Aspect of the Scientific Enterprise. 147p. 1973. text ed. 11.50x o.p. (ISBN 8-2000-4609-5). Humanities.

Naether, Carl & Vriends, Matthew. Building an Aviary. new ed. (Illus.). 1978. 9.95 (ISBN 0-87666-963-1, PS-763). TFH Pubns.

Naeye, Richard L., et al. Perinatal Diseases. (The International Academy of Pathology Monographs: No. 22). (Illus.). 435p. 1981. 47.00 (ISBN 0-686-77748-4, 6301-4). Williams & Wilkins.

Naffah, H., ed. Integrated Office Systems. 1980. 47.00 (ISBN 0-444-85470-3). Elsevier.

Naffah, N. Office Information Systems. 1982. 76.75 (ISBN 0-444-86398-2). Elsevier.

Naftolin, Frederick & Stubblefield, Phillip G., eds. Dilation of the Uterine Cervix: Connective Tissue Biology & Clinical Management. 406p. 1979. text ed. 42.50 (ISBN 0-89004-300-0). Raven.

Nafziger, E. Wayne. Class, Caste, & Entrepreneurship: A Study of Indian Industrialists. LC 78-16889. 1978. text ed. 12.00x (ISBN 0-8248-0575-5, Eastwest Ctr). UH Pr.

--The Economics of Political Instability: The Nigerian-Biafran War. 210p. 1982. 19.50 (ISBN 0-86531-932-4). Westview.

Nafziger, George F. Napoleon's Invasion of Russia. (Illus.). 1983. 40.00 (ISBN 0-686-87027-1). Hippocrene Bks.

Nagan, Peter. Fail Safe Investing: How to Make Money with Less Than Ten Thousand Dollars...Without Losing Sleep. 192p. 1981. 10.95 (ISBN 0-399-12616-3). Putnam Pub Group.

Nagano, Yasuiti. Virus-Inhibiting Factor: An Antiviral, Antibacterial & Antitumor Substance. 250p. 1975. 25.00x (ISBN 0-86008-126-5, Pub. by Japan Sci Soc). Intl Schol Bk Serv.

Nagao, Yoshimi see Isard, Walter.

Nagara, Susumu. Japanese Pidgin English in Hawaii: A Bilingual Description. LC 70-184352. (Oceanic Linguistics Special Publication Ser: No. 9). 400p. 1972. pap. text ed. 9.00x (ISBN 0-8248-0216-0). UH Pr.

Nagasawa, Kimiko & Condon, Camy. Eating Cheap in Japan. (Illus.). 104p. (Orig.). 1972. pap. 7.50 (ISBN 0-8048-1401-5, Pub. by Shufunotomo Co Ltd Japan). C E Tuttle.

Nagasawa, Kimiko, jt. auth. see Condon, Camy.

Nagata, J. Modern General Topology. 2nd rev. ed. (Bibliotheca Mathematica Ser: Vol. 7). 1976. 55.50 (ISBN 0-444-10690-1, North-Holland). Elsevier.

Nagata, Lynn, jt. auth. see Schmid, Rex E.

Nagata, Shinji. Mixing: Principals & Applications. LC 75-2056. 1975. 79.95 o.p. (ISBN 0-470-62863-4). Halsted Pr.

Nagel, Charles. Charles Nagel: Speeches & Writings, Nineteen Hundred to Nineteen Twenty-Eight, 2 vols. Heller, Otto, ed. 1931. 49.50x (ISBN 0-685-89740-0). Elliots Bks.

Nagel, Ernest. Principles of the Theory of Probability. LC 40-2555. (Midway Reprint Ser.). iv, 80p. 1982. pap. text ed. 7.00x (ISBN 0-226-57581-0). U of Chicago Pr.

--The Structure of Science. LC 60-15504. 1979. lib. bdg. 25.00 (ISBN 0-915144-72-7); pap. text ed. 13.75 (ISBN 0-915144-71-9). Hackett Pub.

--Teleology Revisited: And Other Essays in the Philosophy & History of Science. 360p. 1982. pap. 13.00 (ISBN 0-231-04505-0). Columbia U Pr.

Nagel, Ernest, jt. auth. see Cohen, Morris R.

Nagel, Gwen L. & Nagel, James, eds. Sarah Orne Jewett: A Reference Guide. 1977. lib. bdg. 19.00 o.p. (ISBN 0-8161-7848-8, Hall Reference). G K Hall.

Nagel, H. T., et al. An Introduction to Computer Logic. (Illus.). 544p. 1975. ref. ed. 31.95 (ISBN 0-13-480012-5). P-H.

Nagel, Harry, jt. auth. see Bosworth, Bruce.

Nagel, Harry L., jt. auth. see Bosworth, Bruce.

Nagel, Hildegard, tr. see Jung, Emma.

Nagel, Jack. The Descriptive Analysis of Power. LC 74-14087. (Illus.). 208p. 1975. 17.50x o.p. (ISBN 0-300-01729-4). Yale U Pr.

Nagel, James. American Fiction: Historical & Critical Essays. (United States Author Ser.). 1978. lib. bdg. 16.95 o.p. (ISBN 0-8057-9006-3, Twayne). G K Hall.

--Critical Essays on Hamlin Garland. (Critical Essays on American Literature). 1982. lib. bdg. 32.50 (ISBN 0-8161-8306-6, Twayne). G K Hall.

--Stephen Crane & Literary Impressionism. LC 80-16051. 200p. 1980. 17.50x (ISBN 0-271-00267-0). Pa St U Pr.

Nagel, James, ed. American Fiction: Historical & Critical Essays. LC 77-88848. 208p. 1977. 21.95x (ISBN 0-8057-9006-3). NE U Pr.

--Historical & Critical Essays. (United States Authors Ser.). 1979. lib. bdg. 15.00 (ISBN 0-8057-9006-3, Twayne). G K Hall.

Nagel, James, jt. ed. see Nagel, Gwen L.

Nagel, Paul C. Descent from Glory: Four Generations of the John Addams Family. (Illus.). 1983. 25.00 (ISBN 0-19-503172-5). Oxford U Pr.

Nagel Staff. Nagel Guide to the German Democratic Republic. (Nagel Encyclopedia Guides). 1982. 44.00 o.p. (ISBN 0-88254-246-X). Hippocrene Bks.

Nagel, Stuart & Neef, Marian. Policy Studies Directory. 1976. pap. 6.00 (ISBN 0-918592-18-6). Policy Studies.

--Political Science Utilization Directory. 1975. pap. 6.00 (ISBN 0-918592-19-4). Policy Studies.

Nagel, Stuart, ed. Basic Facilities & Institutions in Policy Studies. 1972. pap. 6.00 (ISBN 0-918592-01-1). Policy Studies.

--Basic Issues & References in Policy Studies. 1972. pap. 6.00 (ISBN 0-918592-00-3). Policy Studies.

--Environmental Policy & Political Science Fields. 1973. pap. 6.00 (ISBN 0-918592-03-8). Policy Studies.

--Interdisciplinary Approaches to Policy Studies. 1973. pap. 6.00 (ISBN 0-918592-04-6). Policy Studies.

--Policy Studies Around the World. 1973. pap. 6.00 (ISBN 0-918592-02-X). Policy Studies.

Nagel, Stuart & Munshaw, Nancy, eds. Policy Studies Personnel Directory. 1979. pap. 6.00 (ISBN 0-918592-33-X). Policy Studies.

Nagel, Stuart & Neef, Marian, eds. Policy Grants Directory. 1977. pap. 6.00 (ISBN 0-918592-25-9). Policy Studies.

--Policy Research Centers Directory. 1978. pap. 6.00 (ISBN 0-918592-30-5). Policy Studies.

Nagel, Stuart, et al. The Political Science of Criminal Justice. (Illus.). 280p. 1983. 29.75x (ISBN 0-398-04731-6). C C Thomas.

Nagel, Stuart S. The Policy-Studies Handbook. LC 80-7688. 240p. 1980. 21.95x (ISBN 0-669-03777-X). Lexington Bks.

Nagel, Stuart S. & Neef, Marion. Decision Theory & the Legal Process. LC 78-20348. 320p. 1979. 26.95x (ISBN 0-669-02742-1). Lexington Bks.

Nagel, Stuart S., ed. Environmental Politics. LC 74-3138. (Special Studies). 250p. 1974. 39.95 o.p. (ISBN 0-275-09030-2). Praeger.

Nagel, T. Mortal Questions. LC 78-58797. 1979. 29.95 (ISBN 0-521-22360-1); pap. 8.95x (ISBN 0-521-29460-6). Cambridge U Pr.

Nagell, Trygve. Introduction to Number Theory. 309p. 1981. 15.95 (ISBN 0-8284-0163-2). Chelsea Pub.

Naggar. Foraminifereda from Bottom Sediments in the Offshore Area of Kuwait. Date not set. price not set (ISBN 0-89259-017-3). Am Trust Pubns.

Nagibin, Yuri. The Peak of Success & Other Stories. Goscilo, Helena, tr. from Rus. 360p. 1983. 25.00 (ISBN 0-88233-800-5); pap. 9.50 (ISBN 0-88233-801-3). Ardis Pubs.

Nagle, Elizabeth. Other Bentley Boys. 14.50 (ISBN 0-392-04098-0, SpS). Sportshelf.

Nagle, James J. Heredity & Human Affairs. 2nd ed. LC 78-27066. (Illus.). 380p. 1979. pap. text ed. 18.95 (ISBN 0-8016-3621-3). Mosby.

--Heredity & Human Affairs. 3rd ed. (Illus.). 448p. 1983. text ed. 18.95 (ISBN 0-8016-3626-4). Mosby.

Nagle, John D. The National Democratic Party: Right-Radicalism in the Federal Republic of Germany. LC 78-101340. 1970. 30.00x (ISBN 0-520-01649-1). U of Cal Pr.

Nagle, Mary D., jt. ed. see Harpole, Patricia C.

Nagler, A. M. Theatre Festivals of the Medici, 1539-1637. LC 76-8447. 1976. Repr. of 1964 ed. lib. bdg. 27.50 (ISBN 0-306-70779-9). Da Capo.

Nagler, Alois M. Source Book in Theatrical History. Orig. Title: Sources of Theatrical History. (Illus.). 1952. pap. 7.95 (ISBN 0-486-20515-0). Dover.

Nagler, Michael. Spontaneity & Tradition: A Study in the Oral Art of Homer. 1975. 28.50x (ISBN 0-520-02244-0). U of Cal Pr.

Na Gopaleen, Myles see Gopaleen, Myles na.

Nagore, Mary. New Sounds of the English Consonants. (gr. 9-12). 1978. pap. text ed. 8.00 o.p. (ISBN 0-88450-779-3, 3088). Communication Skill.

Nagpaul, Hans, jt. auth. see Cousins, Albert N.

Nag Raj, T. R. & DiCosmo, F. A Monograph of Herknessia & Mastigospoella with Notes on Associated Teleomorphs. (Bibliotheca Mycologica: Vol. 80). (Illus.). 160p. 1981. text ed. 20.00x (ISBN 3-7682-1300-5). Lubrecht & Cramer.

Nagrath, I. J. & Gopal, M. Control Systems Engineering. 2nd ed. LC 81-17470. 525p. 1982. 15.95x (ISBN 0-470-27148-5). Halsted Pr.

Nagvi, S. M., jt. auth. see Windley, B. F.

Nagy & Verakis. Development & Control of Dust Explosions. (Occupational Safety & Health Ser.). 352p. 1983. price not set (ISBN 0-8247-7004-8). Dekker.

Nagy, Charles J., Jr. Political Parties & System Flexibility. LC 80-5846. 196p. 1981. lib. bdg. 19.25 (ISBN 0-8191-1453-7); pap. text ed. 9.50 (ISBN 0-8191-1454-5). U Pr of Amer.

Nagy, Imre. Imre Nagy on Communism. LC 73-21343. 306p. 1974. Repr. of 1957 ed. lib. bdg. 18.25x (ISBN 0-8371-6183-5). Greenwood.

Nagybakay, Peter. Summoning Tablets of Guilds in Hungary. Horn, Susan, tr. from Hungarian. LC 82-108676. (Illus.). 88p. 1981. 8.50x (ISBN 963-13-1066-3). Intl Pubns Serv.

Nagy-Talavera, Nicholas M. Green Shirts & the Others: A History of Fascism in Hungary & Rumania. LC 74-98136. (Publications Ser.: No. 85). 1970. 12.95x o.p. (ISBN 0-8179-1851-5). Hoover Inst Pr.

Naha, Ed. The Suicide Plague. 1982. pap. 2.75 (ISBN 0-553-22588-X). Bantam.

Naha, Ed, compiled by. Lillian Roxon's Rock Encyclopedia. rev. ed. (Illus.). 1978. 16.95 (ISBN 0-448-14571-5, G&D); pap. 9.95 (ISBN 0-448-14572-3). Putnam Pub Group.

Nahai, Foad, jt. auth. see Mathes, Stephen J.

Nahas, Dunia H. The Israeli Communist Party. LC 76-15052. 1976. text ed. 17.95x o.p. (ISBN 0-312-43855-9). St Martin.

Nahas, G., ed. see Moreau, J. J., et al.

Nahas, Gabriel G., ed. see International Congress of Pharmacology, 7th, Reims, 1978. Satellite Symposium.

Nahas, Rebecca. Your Acting Career. 1976. 6.95 (ISBN 0-517-52528-3); pap. 4.95 (ISBN 0-517-52529-1). Crown.

Nahem, Joseph. Psychology & Psychiatry Today: A Marxist View. LC 81-680. 250p. 1981. 15.00 (ISBN 0-7178-0581-6); pap. 5.50 (ISBN 0-7178-0579-4). Intl Pub Co.

Nahemow, Lucille & Pousada, Lidia. Geriatric Diagnostics: A Case Studies Approach. 1983. 26.95 (ISBN 0-8261-3670-2). Springer Pub.

Nahir, Moshe, ed. Hebrew Teaching & Applied Linguistics. LC 80-8142. (Illus.). 396p. (Orig.). 1981. lib. bdg. 23.25 (ISBN 0-8191-1708-0); pap. text ed. 13.50 (ISBN 0-8191-1709-9). U Pr of Amer.

Nahm, Andrew C. A Panorama of Five Thousand Years: Korean History. LC 81-84202. (Illus.). 128p. 1983. 17.95 (ISBN 0-930878-23-X). Hollym Intl.

Nahm, M. Readings in Philosophy of Art & Aesthetics. 1975. 25.95 (ISBN 0-13-760892-6). P-H.

Nahm, Milton C., ed. Selections from Early Greek Philosophy. 4th ed. (Orig.). 1964. pap. text ed. 14.95 (ISBN 0-13-800508-7). P-H.

Nahrung, Loma, jt. auth. see White, Marianne.

Nahum, Henri & Fekete, Francois. Radiology of the Postoperative Digestive Tract. Oestreich, Alan E., tr. from Fr. LC 79-83738. (Illus.). 160p. 1979. 37.50x (ISBN 0-89352-027-6). Masson Pub.

Naib, V. P. The Land Army. 1978. 15.00x o.p. (ISBN 0-7069-0695-0, Pub. by Vikas India). Advent NY.

Naib, Zuther M. & Willis, Dean, eds. Cytology Examination Review Book, Vol. 1. 2nd ed. 1978. 12.75 (ISBN 0-87488-454-3). Med Exam.

Naidech, Howard J. & Damon, Lorraine. Radiologic Technology Examination Review. LC 82-13908. (Illus.). 288p. (Orig.). 1983. pap. text ed. 12.95 (ISBN 0-668-05366-6, 5366). Arco.

Naidoo, Indres & Sachs, Albie. Robben Island: Ten Years as a Political Prisoner in South Africa's Most Notorious Penitentiary. LC 82-49085. Orig. Title: Island in Chains: Ten Years on Robben Island by Prisoner 885 63. 288p. 1983. pap. 6.95 (ISBN 0-394-71514-4, Vin). Random.

Naidoo, S., jt. auth. see Pringle, M.

Naidu, M. V. Alliances & Balance of Power. LC 74-82531. 256p. 1975. 22.50 (ISBN 0-312-02135-6). St Martin.

--Collective Security & the United Nations. LC 74-82532. 176p. 1975. 27.50 (ISBN 0-312-15015-6). St Martin.

Naidu, N. S. & Kamaraju, V. High Voltage Engineering. 384p. Date not set. 11.95 (ISBN 0-07-451786-4). McGraw.

Naidu, Ratna. The Communal Edge to Plural Societies: India & Malaysia. 1978. text ed. 14.75x (ISBN 0-7069-0922-4). Humanities.

Naifeh, Steven, jt. auth. see Smith, Gregory W.

Naigeon, Jacques-Andre & Holbach, Paul T. Le Militaire Philosophe ou Difficultes sur la Religion Proposees au R. P. Malebranche, Pretre de l'Oratoire. (Holbach & His Friends Ser). 202p. (Fr.). 1974. Repr. of 1768 ed. lib. bdg. 58.00x o.p. (ISBN 0-8287-0651-4, 1531). Clearwater Pub.

Naik, J. A. India & the Communist Countries. 224p. 1982. text ed. 31.00x (ISBN 0-391-02573-2, 90404). Humanities.

--India & the West-Documents: 1979. 231p. 1982. text ed. 31.00x (ISBN 0-391-02572-4, 90402). Humanities.

--Russia & the Communist Countries. 1980. text ed. 51.75x (ISBN 0-391-01792-6). Humanities.

--Russia & the Western World. 227p. 1980. text ed. 26.25x (ISBN 0-391-01745-4). Humanities.

Naik, J. A., ed. India in Asia & Africa: Documents, 1979. 247p. 1982. text ed. 28.50x (ISBN 0-391-02167-2). Humanities.

--Indian Politics Documents, Events & Figures 1979. 360p. 1982. text ed. 46.00x (ISBN 0-391-02831-6, Pub. by Avinash India). Humanities.

--Russia in Asia & Africa: Documents Nineteen Forty-Six to Nineteen Seventy-One. 1979. text ed. 39.25x (ISBN 0-391-01319-X). Humanities.

Naik, M. K., ed. Aspects of Indian Writing in English. 319p. (Orig.). 1980. pap. text ed. 5.75x (ISBN 0-333-90301-3). Humanities.

Nail, Simonne & Caillot, Simonne. How to Get Your Child to Read. LC 81-71138. (Illus.). 122p. 1981. pap. 9.00 (ISBN 0-942010-00-0). Famous Pr Pub.

Naill, Roger F. Managing the Energy Transition: A System Dynamics Search for Alternatives to Oil & Gas. LC 76-52752. prof ref 25.00x (ISBN 0-88410-608-X). Ballinger Pub.

Nailor, E. J., jt. ed. see Feuchtwanger, E. J.

Naim, C. M. Readings in Urdu: Prose & Poetry. 1965. pap. text ed. 10.00x (ISBN 0-8248-0029-X, Eastwest Ctr). UH Pr.

Naiman, Arnold & Rosenfeld, Robert. Understanding Statistics. 3rd ed. 368p. 1983. text ed. 22.95x (ISBN 0-07-045863-4); write for info instr's. manual (ISBN 0-07-045864-2). McGraw.

Naiman, Arnold, et al. Understanding Statistics. 2nd ed. (Illus.). 1976. text ed. 21.00 (ISBN 0-07-045860-X, C); instr.'s manual 15.00 (ISBN 0-07-045861-8). McGraw.

Naiman, Arthur. Every Goy's Guide to Common Jewish Expressions. 192p. 1983. pap. 2.75 (ISBN 0-345-30825-5). Ballantine.

Naiman, Doris. Curriculum for Multiply Handicapped Deaf Students. 196p. 1982. pap. 13.95 (ISBN 0-913072-47-8). Natl Assn Deaf.

Naiman, Doris, jt. auth. see Schein, Jerome.

Naiman, Robert J. & Solt, David L. Fishes in North American Deserts. 360p. 1981. 47.95x (ISBN 0-471-08523-5, Pub. by Wiley-Interscience). Wiley.

Naimpally, S. A. & Warrack, B. D. Proximity Spaces. LC 73-118858. (Tracts in Mathematics & Mathematical Physics: No. 59). 1971. 22.95 (ISBN 0-521-07935-7). Cambridge U Pr.

Naipaul, Shiva. The Chip-Chip Gatherers. 1983. pap. 4.95 (ISBN 0-14-003956-2). Penguin.

--Fireflies. 1983. pap. 4.95 (ISBN 0-14-003150-2). Penguin.

Naipaul, V. S. A Bend in the River. LC 79-22317. 1980. pap. 3.95 (ISBN 0-394-74314-8, Vin). Random.

--The Mystic Masseur. (Caribbean Writers Ser.). 1971. pap. text ed. 3.00x (ISBN 0-435-98646-5). Heinemann Ed.

--Three Novels. LC 82-47819. 1982. 18.95 (ISBN 0-394-52847-6). Knopf.

Nair, K. R. G. Regional Experience in a Developing Economy. 222p. 1982. 22.50 (ISBN 0-471-87341-1, Pub. by Wiley-Interscience). Wiley.

Nair, Kannan K. The Origins & Development of Efik Settlements: Southeastern Nigeria. LC 75-620111. (Papers in International Studies: Africa: No. 26). (Illus.). 1976. pap. 4.00 (ISBN 0-89680-059-8, Ohio U Ctr Intl). Ohio U Pr.

Nair, P. Krishnan. Pollen Grains of Western Himalyan Plants. 1967. 8.50x o.p. (ISBN 0-210-26961-8). Asia.

Nair, R. R., jt. auth. see Shekhar, K. C.

Nairn, A. E., jt. ed. see Moullade, M.

Nairn, Alan E. & Stehli, Francis G., eds. The Ocean Basins & Margins, Vol. 6: The Indian Ocean. 750p. 1982. 85.00x (ISBN 0-306-37776-4, Plenum Pr). PLenum Pub.

Nairobi, 1st Meeting. Meeting of the Eastern African Sub-Committee for Soil Correlation & Land Evaluation. (World Soil Resources Reports: No. 46). (Illus.). 1976. pap. 14.00 (ISBN 0-685-74257-1, F1191, FAO). Unipub.

NAIS Teacher Services Committee. Interdependence: A Handbook for Environmental Education. 1979. pap. 4.75 o.p. (ISBN 0-934338-23-X). NAIS.

Naisbitt, John. Megatrends: Ten New Directions Transforming Our Lives. 304p. 1982. pap. 15.50 (ISBN 0-446-51251-6). Warner Bks.

Naismith, A. Treasury of Notes, Quotes & Anecdotes for Sermon Building. 5.95 o.p. (ISBN 0-8010-6683-2). Baker Bk.

--Twelve Hundred Scripture Outlines. (Source Book for Ministers). 1978. pap. 5.95 (ISBN 0-8010-6692-1). Baker Bk.

Naison, Mark. Communists in Harlem During the Depression. Meier, August, ed. LC 82-10848. (Blacks in the New World Ser.). 360p. 19.95 (ISBN 0-252-00644-5). U of Ill Pr.

Naito & Ryoichi, eds. Perfluorochemical Blood Substitutes. (International Congress Ser.: Vol. 486). 1980. 100.00 (ISBN 0-444-90086-1). Elsevier.

Naito, H., ed. Nutrition & Heart Disease. (Monographs of the American College of Nutrition: Vol. 5). 365p. 1982. text ed. 35.00 (ISBN 0-89335-119-9). Spectrum Pub.

Najam, Edward W., ed. Language Learning: The Individual & the Process. LC 66-63007. (General Publications Ser: Vol. 40). (Orig.). 1965. pap. text ed. 5.50x o.p. (ISBN 0-87750-128-9). Res Ctr Lang Semiotic.

Najarian, Haig H. Patterns in Medical Parasitology. 2nd ed. LC 80-10330. 168p. 1982. 14.50 (ISBN 0-89874-031-2). Krieger.

Najean, Y., et al, eds. Safety Problems Related to Chloramphenicol & Thiamphenicol Therapy. (Monographs of the Mario Negri Institute of Pharmacological Research). 128p. 1981. text ed. 15.00 (ISBN 0-89004-547-X). Raven.

Najean, Yves, ed. Medullary Aplasia. LC 80-80966. (Illus.). 312p. 1980. 45.75x (ISBN 0-89352-064-0). Masson Pub.

Nakadate, Neil, ed. Robert Penn Warren: A Reference Guide. 1977. lib. bdg. 32.00 (ISBN 0-8161-7820-8, Hall Reference). G K Hall.

Nakae, K. Jiu Jitsu Complete. 6.95 o.p. (ISBN 0-685-21995-X); pap. 6.95x o.p. (ISBN 0-686-66565-1). Wehman.

Nakagawa, Yoiche. Nakagawa's Tenno Yugao. Ingalls, Jeremy, tr. (International Studies & Translations Program). 1975. lib. bdg. 11.95 (ISBN 0-8057-5720-1, Twayne). G K Hall.

Nakajima, Kimiko, jt. auth. see Young, John.

Nakamoto, Kazno. Spectroscopy & Structure of Metal Chelate Compounds. McCarthy, Paul J., ed. LC 67-30634. (Illus.). 382p. 1968. text ed. 23.00 (ISBN 0-471-62981-2, Pub. by Wiley). Krieger.

Nakamoto, Kazuo. Infrared & Raman Spectra of Inorganic & Coordination Compounds. 3rd ed. LC 77-15107. 1978. 39.50x (ISBN 0-471-62979-0, Pub. by Wiley-Interscience). Wiley.

Nakamura. Bonsai Miniatures. 5.95. Wehman.

Nakamura, Akira & Tsutsui, Minoru. Principles & Applications of Homogeneous Catalysis. LC 79-24754. 1980. 50.00 (ISBN 0-471-02869-X, Pub. by Wiley-Interscience). Wiley.

Nakamura, Hajime. Ansatze Modernen Denkens in den Relifionen Japans. (Zeitschrift fur Religions- und geistesgeschichte, Beihefte: 23). viii, 183p. 1982. pap. write for info. (ISBN 90-04-06725-6). E J Brill.

--Ways of Thinking of Eastern Peoples: India, China, Tibet, Japan. rev. ed. Wiener, Philip P., ed. 1964. 15.00x o.p. (ISBN 0-8248-0010-9, Eastwest Ctr); pap. text ed. 10.95x (ISBN 0-8248-0078-8). UH Pr.

Nakamura, Hiroshi. Spirulina: Food for a Hungry World; A Pioneer's Story in Aquaculture. Hills, Christopher, ed. Wargo, Robert, tr. from Japanese. (Illus.). 224p. (Orig.). 1982. pap. 10.95 (ISBN 0-916438-47-3). Univ of Trees.

Nakamura, Kichisaburo. Formation of Modern Japan: As Viewed from Legal History. 1965. 5.00x (ISBN 0-8248-0015-X, Eastwest Ctr). UH Pr.

Nakamura, Leonard, jt. auth. see Myers, John G.

Nakamura, Robert M., jt. auth. see Kirkpatrick, Anita M.

Nakamura, Robert M., et al. Immunologic Analysis: Recent Progress in Diagnostic Laboratory Immunology. (Illus.). 240p. 1982. lib. bdg. 36.25x (ISBN 0-89352-162-0). Masson Pub.

Nakamura, Shoichiro. Computational Methods in Engineering & Science: With Applications to Fluid Dynamics & Nuclear Systems. LC 77-5471. 1977. 42.50 (ISBN 0-471-01800-7, Pub. by Wiley-Interscience). Wiley.

Nakamura, T. & Nosay, G. Decorative Hand-Guards for Japanese Swords. (Illus.). 100p. Date not set. pap. 17.50 (ISBN 0-87556-578-6). Saifer.

Nakamura, Takafusa. Economic Growth in Prewar Japan. Feldman, Robert A., tr. LC 82-50444. 320p. 1983. 35.00x (ISBN 0-300-02451-7). Yale U Pr.

Nakane, Chie. Japanese Society. LC 71-100021. (Center for Japanese & Korean Studies, UC Berkeley). 1970. 26.50x (ISBN 0-520-01642-4); pap. 5.95x (ISBN 0-520-02154-1, CAMPUS74). U of Cal Pr.

Nakanishi, Don T., ed. The Education of Asian & Pacific Americans: Historical Perspectives & Prescriptions for the Future. Hirano-Nakanishi, Marsha. 250p. 1983. lib. bdg. 27.50 (ISBN 0-89774-030-0). Oryx Pr.

Nakanishi, Koji & Harada, Nobuyuki. Excition Coupled Circular Dichroism-Application in Organic & Bioorganic Stereochemistry. LC 81-51270. (Illus.). 455p. 1983. text ed. 32.00x (ISBN 0-935702-09-1). Univ Sci Bks.

Nakanishi, Motoo, jt. auth. see Cocomas Committee.

Nakano, Hidegoro. Linear Lattices. abr. ed. LC 66-24169. (Orig.). 1966. 4.95x o.p. (ISBN 0-8143-1293-4). Wayne St U Pr.

--Uniform Spaces & Transformation Groups. LC 68-13935. 260p. 1968. 15.95x o.p. (ISBN 0-8143-1341-8). Wayne St U Pr.

Nakano, Kenneth K. Neurology of Musculoskeletal & Rheumatic Disorders. (Illus.). 1979. 60.00 (ISBN 0-471-09491-9, Pub. by Wiley Med). Wiley.

Nakano, Mei T. Riko Rabbit. (gr. 2-5). 1982. PLB write for info. (ISBN 0-942610-01-6); pap. write for info. (ISBN 0-942610-00-8). Mina Pr.

Nakao, Hiroyuki. Brain Stimulation & Learning: Switch-Off Behavior. LC 79-884886. (Illus.). 151p. 1971. 20.00x o.p. (ISBN 0-8002-0689-4). Intl Pubns Serv.

Nakao, Naomi, jt. auth. see Ayal, Ora.

Nakata, Yuri, et al. Organizing a Local Government Documents Collection. 1979. pap. 6.00 (ISBN 0-8389-0284-7). ALA.

Nakayama, Ichiro. Industrialization of Japan. 1965. 4.00x (ISBN 0-8248-0016-8, Eastwest Ctr). UH Pr.

Nakayama, Masatoshi, jt. auth. see Draeger, Donn F.

Nakayama, Shigeru, et al, eds. Science & Society in Modern Japan. 1974. 35.00x (ISBN 0-262-14022-5). MIT Pr.

Nakazato, Taroemon. Karatsu. LC 82-48169. (Famous Ceramics of Japan Ser.: Vol. 9). (Illus.). 40p. 1983. 17.75 (ISBN 0-87011-551-0). Kodansha.

Nakhjavani, Bahiyyih. When We Grow up. 1979. 6.50 (ISBN 0-85398-085-3, 332-038, Pub. by G Ronald England); pap. 2.25 o.p (ISBN 0-85398-086-1, 332-039, Pub. by G Ronald England). Baha'i.

Nakhleh, Emile A. Persian Gulf & American Policy. 172p. 1982. 22.95 (ISBN 0-03-060594-6). Praeger.

Nakhleh, K. & Zureik, E. The Sociology of the Palestinians. LC 79-12706. 1979. 26.00 (ISBN 0-312-74073-5). St Martin.

Nakhnikian, George. An Introduction to Philosophy. 1981. pap. text ed. 8.50x (ISBN 0-89917-335-7). TIS Inc.

Nakhre, A. Social Psychology of Non-Violent Action: A Study of Three Satyagrahas. 207p. 1982. text ed. 15.50x (ISBN 0-391-02761-1, Pub. by Chanakya India). Humanities.

Nakhre, Amrot. Social Psychology of Nonviolent Action: A Study of Three Satyagrahas. 1982. 15.00x (ISBN 0-8364-0897-7, Pub. by Chanakya). South Asia Bks.

Nakielny, Richard, jt. auth. see Chapman, Stephen.

Nakon, Robert. Chemical Problem Solving Using Dimensional Analysis. (Illus.). 1978. pap. 15.95 (ISBN 0-13-128645-5). P-H.

Nakosteen, Mehdi. The History & Philosophy of Education. (Illus.). 1965. 26.50 o.s.i. (ISBN 0-471-07211-7). Wiley.

Nalanda Translation Committee under the Direction of Chogyam Trungpa, tr. from Tibetan. The Life of Marpa the Translator. LC 82-13183. 300p. (Orig.). 1983. pap. 10.00 (ISBN 0-87773-763-0, Prajna). Great Eastern.

Nalbandian, Louise Z. The Armenian Revolutionary Movement: The Development of Armenian Political Parties Through the Nineteenth Century. (Near Eastern Center, UCLA). 1963. 24.50x (ISBN 0-520-00914-2). U of Cal Pr.

NALCO Chemical Company. NALCO Water Handbook. (Illus.). 1979. 36.50 (ISBN 0-07-045868-5, P&RB). McGraw.

Nalder, Lanny J. Traveler's Health Guide: A Nutritional, Medical & Fitness Handbook for Travelers & People Away from Home. LC 80-82454. 120p. (Orig.). Date not set. pap. cancelled (ISBN 0-88290-094-3, 4025). Horizon Utah. Postponed.

Nale, Nell. Sand Dollar Shuffle. (Kindergarten Keys Ser). (Illus.). 1982. pap. text ed. 2.88 (ISBN 0-8332-1705-4); tchr's manual 2.88 (ISBN 0-8332-1706-2). Economy Co.

Nale, Nell, et al. Kindergarten Keys Kit. rev. ed. 1975. 531.63 (ISBN 0-8332-1701-1); Teacher's Guidebook 85.00 (ISBN 0-8332-1702-X). Economy Co.

--The Caterpillar Caper. (Kindergarten Keys Ser.). (Illus.). 1982. pap. text ed. 2.88 (ISBN 0-8332-1703-8); tchr's manual 2.88 (ISBN 0-8332-1704-6); prereading skills test 7.59 (ISBN 0-87892-664-X); math skills test 7.59 (ISBN 0-87892-663-1). Economy Co.

Nale, Sharon A. A Cry for Help: For Families of Alcohol & Other Drug-Dependent Persons. 96p. 1982. pap. 3.50 (ISBN 0-686-82063-0, 19-53). Fortress.

Nalepa, B. H., jt. auth. see Blendon, E. G.

Naley, Linda. Looking Forward to a Career: Cosmetology. 2nd ed. LC 74-4724. (Looking Forward to a Career Ser.). (Illus.). (gr. 6 up). 1976. PLB 6.95 o.p. (ISBN 0-87518-133-3). Dillon.

Nalin, Y. Detente & Anti Communism. 155p. 1980. pap. 4.45 (ISBN 0-8285-1782-7, Pub. by Progress Pubs USSR). Imported Pubns.

Nalty, Bernard C. & MacGregor, Morris J., eds. Blacks in the Military: Essential Documents. LC 80-54664. 367p. 1981. lib. bdg. 29.95 (ISBN 0-8420-2183-3). Scholarly Res Inc.

Nam, Charles B. & Gustavus, Susan O. Population: The Dynamics of Demographic Change. LC 75-31031. (Illus.). 352p. 1976. text ed. 20.95 o.p. (ISBN 0-395-20627-8). HM.

Nam, Charles B. & Powers, Mary G. The Socioeconomic Approach to Status Measurement (with a Guide to Status Scores. 1983. text ed. price not set (ISBN 0-88105-011-3); pap. text ed. price not set (ISBN 0-88105-012-1). Cap & Gown.

Nama, Prabharathie G., jt. auth. see Tetzleff, Judith.

Namba, Ayako. Chinese Cooking. Chu, Grace, ed. 1977. pap. 4.95 (ISBN 0-8120-0823-5). Barron.

Namboodir, P. K. S., et al. Intervention in the Indian Ocean. 361p. text ed. 20.75x (ISBN 0-391-02536-8, Pub. by UBS India). Humanities.

Namboodiri, P. K. & Anand, J. P. Intervention in the Indian Ocean. 361p. 1982. 34.95x (ISBN 0-940500-81-7, Pub by ABC Pub Hse India). Asia Bk Corp.

Namboodiripad, E. M. Crisis Into Chaos: Political India 1981. 172p. 1981. pap. text ed. 4.25 (ISBN 0-86131-279-1, Pub. by Orient Longman Ltd India). Apt Bks.

Nameroff, Rochelle. Body Prints. 54p. 1972. 2.95 (ISBN 0-87886-022-3). Ithaca Hse.

Names, Larry. The Legend of Eagle Claw. (gr. 6 up). 1980. 9.00 (ISBN 0-8309-0232-5). Ind Pr MO.

Names, Larry D. Bose. LC 79-6283. (DD Western Ser.). 192p. 1980. 10.95 o.p. (ISBN 0-385-15014-8). Doubleday.

Namgostar, M. Digital Equipment Troubleshooting. (Illus.). 288p. 1977. text ed. 22.95 (ISBN 0-87909-201-7). Reston.

Namier, Lewis. England in the Age of the American Revolution. 2nd ed. 1974. 26.00 (ISBN 0-312-25270-6); pap. 10.95 o.p. (ISBN 0-312-25235-8). St Martin.

Namikoshi, T. Shiatsu. (Illus.). 1974. pap. 7.95x (ISBN 0-685-52367-5, Pub. by Japan Pubns). Wehman.

Namikoshi, Ti. Shiatsu Therapy: Theory & Practice. 7.95x (ISBN 0-685-70705-9); pap. 4.50 (ISBN 0-685-70706-7). Wehman.

Namikoshi, Toru. Complete Book of Shiatsu Therapy. LC 79-1963. (Illus.). 1980. pap. 12.95 (ISBN 0-87040-461-X). Japan Pubns.

Namir, L., jt. auth. see Schlesinger, I. M.

Namuth, Hans. Hans Namuth, Artists 1950-81: A Personal View. (Illus.). 96p. (Orig.). 1981. pap. 15.95 (ISBN 0-938608-04-5). Pace Gallery Pubns.

Nanassy, Louis C. & Fries, Albert C. Business Timed Writings. LC 72-11284. 65p. 1974. pap. text ed. 3.96 o.p. (ISBN 0-02-476480-9, 47648). Glencoe.

Nanassy, Louis C. & Selden, William. Reference Manual for Office Workers. LC 74-6627. 1977. text ed. 11.20 (ISBN 0-02-476460-4); pap. text ed. 5.52 (ISBN 0-02-476470-1); worksheets 3.00 (ISBN 0-02-476560-0). Glencoe.

Nanassy, Louis C., et al. Reference Manual for Office Workers. 1977. text ed. 12.95x (ISBN 0-02-476460-4). Macmillan.

Nanavati, Manilal B. & Vakil, Chandulal N. Group Prejudices in India: A Symposium. Repr. of 1951 ed. lib. bdg. 18.00x (ISBN 0-8371-3132-4, NAGP). Greenwood.

Nancarrow, Peter. Early China & the Wall. LC 80-7446. (Cambridge Topic Bks.). (Illus.). (gr. 5-10). 1980. PLB 6.95g (ISBN 0-8225-1218-1). Lerner Pubns.

Nance, Earl C. Self Investment Theory & Academic Work. LC 81-40593. 228p. 1982. lib. bdg. 22.00 (ISBN 0-8191-1905-9); pap. text ed. 11.00 (ISBN 0-8191-1906-7). U Pr of Amer.

Nance, Guinevera, jt. auth. see Jones, Judith.

Nance, Guinevera A. & Jones, Judith. Philip Roth. (Literature and Life Ser.). 160p. 1981. 11.95 (ISBN 0-8044-2438-1); pap. 4.95 (ISBN 0-8044-6320-4). Ungar.

Nance, H., jt. auth. see Crossan, R. M.

Nance, Harold & Nolan, Robert E. Office Work Measurement. rev. ed. LC 82-8974. 192p. 1983. Repr. of 1971 ed. write for info. (ISBN 0-89874-314-1). Krieger.

Nance, Harold W., jt. auth. see Crossan, Richard M.

Nance, James V., Jr. Recreation Condominiums in Summit County, Colorado: Locational Factors & Policy Implications. 165p. 1976. 10.00 o.p. (ISBN 0-686-64163-9). U CO Busn Res Div.

Nance, John. The Mud Pie Dilemma: A Master Potter's Struggle to Make Art & Ends Meet. LC 78-13888. (Illus.). 1978. 15.95 (ISBN 0-917304-18-7). Timber.

Nance, Sherri. Premature Babies: A Handbook for Parents. 1983. 8.95 (ISBN 0-87795-502-6, Pub. by Priam). Arbor Hse.

Nance, Virginia L. & Davis, Elwood C. Golf. 5th ed. (Exploring Sports Ser.). 106p. 1983. pap. write for info. (ISBN 0-697-09961-X). Wm C Brown.

Nanda, B. R. Gokhale, Gandhi & the Nehrus: Studies in Indian Nationalism. LC 74-76991. 200p. 1974. 19.95 o.p. (ISBN 0-312-33145-2). St Martin.

Nanda, B. R., ed. Indian Foreign Policy: The Nehru Years. LC 76-15059. 1976. text ed. 14.00x (ISBN 0-8248-0486-4, Eastwest Ctr). UH Pr.

Nanda, B. R. & Joshi, V. C., eds. Studies in Modern History, No. One. 214p. 1973. pap. text ed. 8.50x (ISBN 0-391-00624-X). Humanities.

Nanda, Ned P., et al, eds. Global Human Rights. (Westview Special Study Ser.). 285p. 1981. lib. bdg. 31.00 (ISBN 0-89158-858-2). Westview.

Nanda, Ravinder & Adler, George L., eds. Learning Curves: Theory & Application. 1977. pap. text ed. 20.00 (ISBN 0-89806-002-8); pap. text ed. 10.00 members. Inst Indus Eng.

Nanda, Ved, ed. Water Needs for the Future: Political, Economic, Legal & Technological Issues in a National & International Framework. LC 77-12273. (Westview Special Studies in Natural Resources & Energy Management). 1977. lib. bdg. 31.75 (ISBN 0-89158-236-3). Westview.

Nanda, Ved P. The Law of Transnational Business Transactions, Vol. 1. LC 81-2392. 1981. 85.00 (ISBN 0-87632-342-5). Boardman.

Nandakumar, P. Dante & Sri Aurobindo. 160p. 1981. 12.00x (ISBN 0-391-02391-8). Humanities.

Nandan, Yash, compiled by. The Durkheimian School: A Systematic & Comprehensive Bibliography. LC 77-12. 1977. lib. bdg. 35.00x (ISBN 0-8371-9532-2, NAD/). Greenwood.

Nandan, Yash, ed. see Durkheim, Emile.

Nandedkar, V. G. Local Government: Its Role in Development Administration. 1979. text ed. 15.75x (ISBN 0-686-86096-9). Humanities.

Nandy, Ashis. At the Edge of Psychology: Essays on Politics & Culture. 1981. 12.95x (ISBN 0-19-561205-1). Oxford U Pr.

Nandy, Pritish, jt. auth. see Mirabai.

Nandy, Pritish, ed. The Lord is My Shepherd: Selections from the Psalms. (Orig.). 1982. pap. 7.95x (ISBN 0-7069-1492-9, Pub. by Vikas India). Advent NY.

Nanes, Allan, jt. auth. see Alexander, Yonah.

Nanji, Azim. The Nizari Ismaili Tradition in the Indo-Pakistan Subcontinent. LC 78-12990. (Monographs in Islamic Religion & Theology). 1979. 30.00x (ISBN 0-88206-020-1). Caravan Bks.

Nankani, Gobindram T. Development Problems of Mineral Exporting Countries. (Working Paper: No. 354). xii, 106p. 1979. 5.00 (ISBN 0-686-36095-8, WP-0354). World Bank.

Nankin, Howard, jt. ed. see Troen, Philip.

Nankin, Michael & Korvetz, Elliot. Fantastic Dives: A Guide to LA's Best Hole-In-the-Wall Dining. Raphalion, Robin, ed. (Illus.). 128p. 1982. pap. text ed. 6.95 (ISBN 0-87477-228-1). J P Tarcher.

Nankivell, John H. History of the Twenty Fifth Regiment: United States Infantry 1869-1926. (Illus.). 1972. pap. text ed. 10.95 o.p. (ISBN 0-88342-013-9); pap. 4.95 (ISBN 0-88342-220-4). Old Army.

Nanney, D. L. Experimental Ciliatology: An Introduction to Genetic & Developmental Analysis in Ciliates. LC 79-21918. 1980. 31.95x (ISBN 0-471-06008-9, Pub. by Wiley-Interscience). Wiley.

Nanney, J. L. & Shaffer, R. D. Arithmetic: A Review. text ed. 24.95 (ISBN 0-471-62990-1). Wiley.

Nanney, T. Ray. Computing: A Problem-Solving Approach Using FORTRAN Seventy-Seven. (Illus.). 432p. 1981. text ed. 18.95 (ISBN 0-13-165209-5). P-H.

Nannicini, Giuliana, ed. see Laroche, Lucienne.

Nannicini, Giuliana, ed. see Scerrato, Umberto.
Nannicini, Giuliana, ed. see Tamburello, Adolfo.
Nannicini, Guiuliana, ed. see Ivanoff, Pierre.
Nanry, Charles. The Jazz Text. 276p. 1982. pap. text ed. 9.95 (ISBN 0-442-25908-5). Transaction Bks.
Nanry, Charles, jt. auth. see Morgenstern, Dan.
Nansen, Fridtjof. Armenia & the Near East. LC 76-25120. (Middle East in the Twentieth Century Ser.). 1976. Repr. of 1928 ed. lib. bdg. 37.50 (ISBN 0-306-70760-8). Da Capo.
Nao, T. Van. Forest Fire Prevention & Control. 1982. text ed. 39.50 (ISBN 90-247-3050-3, Pub. by Martinus Nijhoff). Kluwer Boston.
Napalkov, N. P., ed. Cancer Control in the Countries of the Council of Mutual Economic Assistance. (Illus.). 742p. 1982. 40.00x (ISBN 963-05-3036-8). Intl Pubns Serv.
Naparstek, Arthur J., jt. auth. see Biegel, David E.
Napier & Gershenfeld. Making Groups Work: A Guide for Group Leaders. 1983. pap. text ed. 16.95 (ISBN 0-686-84567-6). HM.
Napier, jt. auth. see Whitaker.
Napier, Bill, jt. auth. see Clube, Victor.
Napier, Mary. Forbidden Places. 1981. 12.95 (ISBN 0-698-11091-9, Coward). Putnam Pub Group.
Napier, P. H. Catalogue of Primates in the British Museum (Natural History) Part 1: Families Callitrichidae & Cebidae. 1976. pap. 25.00x (ISBN 0-565-00744-0, Pub. by Brit Mus Nat Hist). Sabbot-Natural Hist Bks.
Napier, Priscilla. Imperial Winds. 300p. 1982. 16.95 (ISBN 0-698-11108-7, Coward). Putnam Pub Group.
Napier, Prue. Chimpanzees. LC 75-28009. (Illus.). 48p. (gr. 4-9). 1976. 6.95 o.p. (ISBN 0-07-045870-7, GB). McGraw.
Napier, Rodney & Gershenfeld, Matti. Groups: Theory & Experience. 2nd ed. LC 80-82844. (Illus.). 448p. 1981. text ed. 21.95 (ISBN 0-395-29703-6); instr's manual 1.00 (ISBN 0-395-29704-4). HM.
--Making Groups Work: A Guide for Group Leaders. LC 82-82242. 304p. 1983. pap. text ed. 17.95 (ISBN 0-395-29705-2). HM.
Naples, Marge. This Is the Siamese Cat. (Illus.). 1964. 12.95 (ISBN 0-87666-853-8, PS617). TFH Pubns.
Naples, Ralph V., jt. auth. see Rosenberg, R. Robert.
Napoli, Dede. The Starving Students Cookbook. (Illus.). 150p. (Orig.). 1982. pap. 4.95 (ISBN 0-686-35980-1). EZ Cookin.
Napoli, Vince, jt. auth. see Mendoza, Manuel G.
Napoli, Vince, et al. Adjustment & Growth in a Changing World. (Illus.). 534p. 1982. pap. text ed. 18.95 (ISBN 0-314-63279-4). West Pub.
Napoli, Vince, jt. auth. see Mendoza, Manuel G.
Napolitane, Catherine & Pelligrino, Victoria. Living & Loving After Divorce. 1978. pap. 2.50 (ISBN 0-451-11250-4, AE1250, Sig). NAL.
Napolitano, L. Astronautical Research, 1970. (Proceedings). 1971. 97.75 (ISBN 0-444-10101-2). Elsevier.
Napolitano, Luigi G. & International Astronautical Congress, 27th, Anaheim, Ca., Oct. 1976. Proceedings. 1978. text ed. 64.00 (ISBN 0-08-021732-X). Pergamon.
Napora, Joe. Tongue & Groove. 12p. 1982. 1.00 o.p. (ISBN 0-686-37506-8). Ptolemy Brown.
Napper, Elizabeth, ed. see Rinbochay, Lati.
Nappi, Carmine. Commodity Market Controls. LC 78-24715. (Illus.). 224p. 1979. 26.95x (ISBN 0-669-02812-6). Lexington Bks.
Napps, Mary Alice. Lady Foxchaser. 1978. 4.95 o.p. (ISBN 0-533-03166-4). Vantage.
Naps, Thomas & Singh, Bhaghat. COBOL: A Comprehensive Treatment. (Illus.). 432p. 1982. text ed. 24.95 (ISBN 0-8359-0831-3); pap. text ed. 17.95 (ISBN 0-8359-0830-5); solutions manual avail. (ISBN 0-8359-0832-1). Reston.
Nara, Harry R. Vector Mechanics for Engineers. LC 77-10175. 910p. 1977. Repr. lib. bdg. 33.50 (ISBN 0-88275-606-0). Krieger.
Narada. Narada Bhakti Sutras: The Gospel of Divine Love. Tyagisananda, Swami, tr. (Sanskrit & Eng). pap. 3.95 o.s.i. (ISBN 0-87481-427-8). Vedanta Pr.
Narain, A. K. Studies in History of Buddhism: Papers Presented at the International Conference on the History of Buddhism at the University of Wisconsin, Madison August 19-21,1976. 421p. 1980. text ed. 42.50x (ISBN 0-391-02212-1). Humanities.
Narain, Dhirendra, ed. Explorations in the Family & Other Essays: In Memory of K. M. Kapadia. 1974. text ed. 28.75x (ISBN 0-391-00403-4). Humanities.
Narain, I., jt. ed. see Mathur, M. V.
Narasimhaiah, C. D., ed. Awakened Conscience: Studies in Commonwealth Literature. 1978. 30.00x (ISBN 0-391-00920-6). Humanities.
Narasimhan, R. Analysis on Real & Complex Manifolds. 2nd ed. 1974. 27.00 (ISBN 0-444-10452-6). Elsevier.
Narasimhan, T. N. & Freeze, R. Allan, eds. Recent Trends in Hydrogeology. (Special Papers: No. 189). 1982. 32.00x (ISBN 0-8137-2189-X). Geol Soc.
Naravane, V. S. Sarojini Naidu: An Introduction to Her Life, Work & Poetry. 160p. 1980. 20.00x (ISBN 0-86131-253-8, Pub. by Orient Longman Ltd India). Apt Bks.
Naravane, Vishwanath S. Ananda K. Coomaraswamy. (World Leaders Ser.). 1978. 13.95 (ISBN 0-8057-7722-9, Twayne); lib. bdg. write for info. G K Hall.
Narayan, R. K. The Painter of Signs. 1983. pap. 4.95 (ISBN 0-14-006259-9). Penguin.
Narayanan, R., ed. Axially Compressed Structures. 300p. 1982. 61.50 (ISBN 0-85334-139-7, Pub. by Applied Sci England). Elsevier.
Naray-Szabo, G. Steric Effects in Biomolecules. (Studies in Physical Theroretical Chemistry: Vol. 18). Date not set. 98.00 (ISBN 0-444-99693-1). Elsevier.
Narcisco, John, jt. auth. see Burkett, David.
Nard, Victor Ve see Ve Nard, Victor.
Nardi, George, tr. see Valdoni, Pietro.
Nardi, Vincent, et al. How to do Your Hair Like a Pro. (Illus.). 136p. Date not set. pap. price not set spiral bound (ISBN 0-448-12968-X, G&D). Putnam Pub Group.
Nardin, Jane. Those Elegant Decorums: The Concept of Propriety in Jane Austen's Novels. LC 73-4821. 24.50x (ISBN 0-87395-236-7). State U NY Pr.
Nardizzi, Louis. Basic Circuits & Electronic Experiments. 1973. pap. text ed. 6.95x o.p. (ISBN 0-442-25906-9). Van Nos Reinhold.
Nardoff, Ellen Van see Feld, Ellen.
Nardone, Nancy K., ed. Secular Choral Music in Print: 1982 Supplement. (Music-In-Print Ser.). 179p. 1982. lib. bdg. 48.00 (ISBN 0-88478-013-9). Musicdata.
Nardone, Thomas R., ed. Choral Music in Print: Supplement 1976. LC 73-87918. (Music in Print Ser.). 419p. 1976. lib. bdg. 75.00 o.p. (ISBN 0-88478-007-4). Musicdata.
Nardulli, Peter F. The Courtroom Elite: An Organizational Perspective on Criminal Justice. LC 78-2358. 272p. prof ref 17.50x (ISBN 0-88410-757-4). Ballinger Pub.
Nardulli, Peter F., ed. The Study of Criminal Courts: Political Perspectives. LC 79-14848. 1979. prof ref 25.00x (ISBN 0-88410-797-3). Ballinger Pub.
Naremore, James. The Magic World of Orson Welles. LC 77-22470. (Illus.). 1978. 22.50x (ISBN 0-19-502303-X). Oxford U Pr.
Naremore, James, ed. Treasure of Sierra Madre. LC 78-53298. (Screenplay Ser.). (Illus.). 206p. 1979. 17.50 (ISBN 0-299-07680-6); pap. 6.95t (ISBN 0-299-07684-9). U of Wis Pr.
Nares, Robert. Glossary of Words, Phrases, Names & Allusions in the Works of English Authors. LC 66-25635. 1966. Repr. of 1905 ed. 55.00x (ISBN 0-8103-3219-1). Gale.
Nargolkar, V. The Creed of Saint Vinoba. 320p. 1963. pap. 4.50 (ISBN 0-686-96938-3). Greenlf Bks.
Nariani, T. K., jt. auth. see Rayechaudhuri, S. P.
Narita, Kikue, ed. see Condon, Camy & Nagasawa, Kimiko.
Narkiewicz, O., jt. auth. see Hayward, J.
Narkis, Bezalel & Sed-Rajna, Gabrielle, eds. Index of Jewish Art: Iconographical Index of Hebrew Illuminated Manuscripts, Vol. 2. (Illus.). 81p. Set. 200.00x (ISBN 0-686-75626-6, Pub. by K G Saur). Gale.
Narlikar, Jayant V. Introduction to Cosmology. (Illus.). 484p. 1983. text ed. 29.00 (ISBN 0-86720-015-4). Sci Bks Intl.
--Violent Phenomena in the Universe. (Illus.). 1982. 19.95x (ISBN 0-19-219160-8). Oxford U Pr.
Narramore, Bruce. Adolescence Is Not an Illness. 1980. 9.95 (ISBN 0-8007-1114-9, Power Bks); pap. 5.95 (ISBN 0-8007-5101-9). Revell.
--Adolescence Is Not an Illness. (Illus.). 192p. 1982. pap. 5.95 (ISBN 0-8007-5101-9, PowerBks). Revell.
Narramore, Clyde & Narramore, Ruth. Como Dominar la Tension Nerviosa. Ward, Rhode, tr. from Eng. 216p. (Span.). 1978. pap. 4.95 o.s.i. (ISBN 0-89922-129-7). Edit Caribe.
Narramore, Clyde M. La Disciplina en el Hogar. Zorzoli, Ruben O., tr. from Eng. 32p. Repr. of 1975 ed. 1.10 (ISBN 0-311-46051-8). Casa Bautista.
Narramore, Ruth, jt. auth. see Narramore, Clyde.
Narrol, Harvey G. & Giblon, Shirley T. Your Child's Hidden Learning Potential: An Essay on Teaching the Fourth "R"-Reasoning. 1983. pap. text ed. write for info. (ISBN 0-8391-1745-0, 18228). Univ Park.
Narrow, B. W. & Buschle, K. B. Fundamentals of Nursing Practice. 676p. 1981. 25.95x (ISBN 0-471-05950-1, Pub. by Wiley Med). Wiley.
Narrow, Barbara W. Patient Teaching in Nursing Practice: A Patient & Family Centered Approach. LC 78-10241. 1979. pap. 11.50x (ISBN 0-471-04035-5, Pub. by Wiley Medical). Wiley.
Narsavage, Robert J., Jr., jt. auth. see Kimbler, Frank S.
Narvaez, Leon. Ambientes Hispanicos One. LC 79-15478. (Illus.). 1980. 10.95 (ISBN 0-88436-544-1); pap. text ed. 7.50 (ISBN 0-88436-543-3). EMC.
--Ambientes Hispanicos Two. LC 80-12977. (Illus.). 1981. text ed. 11.70 (ISBN 0-88436-547-6); pap. text ed. 7.95 (ISBN 0-88436-546-8). EMC.
NASA-Jet Propulsion Lab. Space Images. LC 81-84668. (Illus.). 100p. 1982. 27.95 (ISBN 0-912810-37-8); pap. 15.95 (ISBN 0-912810-36-X). Lustrum Pr.
Nasar, S. A. & Boldea, I. Linear Motion Electric Machines. LC 76-6890. 192p. 1976. 26.50 o.p. (ISBN 0-471-63029-2, Pub. by Wiley-Interscience). Wiley.
Nasar, S. A. & Unnewehr, L. E. Electromechanics & Electric Machines. 2nd ed. LC 78-8967. 1979. text ed. 29.95x (ISBN 0-471-08091-8); tchrs. manual 4.00 (ISBN 0-471-03651-X). Wiley.
--Electromechanics & Electric Machines. LC 82-13371. 461p. 1983. write for info (ISBN 0-471-87154-0). Wiley.
Nasar, S. A., jt. auth. see Unnewehr, L. E.
Nasar, Syed A., jt. auth. see Paul, Clayton R.
Nasatir, Abraham P., jt. auth. see Bailey, Helen M.
Nasatir, Abraham P., jt. auth. see Loomis, Noel M.
Nasaw, David. Schooled to Order: A Social History of Public Schooling in the United States. 1979. 18.95x (ISBN 0-19-502529-6). Oxford U Pr.
--Schooled to Order: A Social History of Public Schooling in the United States. 1979. pap. 7.95 (ISBN 0-19-502892-9, GB 626). Oxford U Pr.
Nasemann, T. & Sauerbrey, W. Fundamentals of Dermatology. (Illus.). 416p. 1983. pap. 24.90 (ISBN 0-387-90738-6). Springer-Verlag.
Nasemann, Theodor. Viral Diseases of the Skin, Mucous Membranes & Genitals: Clinical Features, Differential Diagnosis & Therapy, with Basic Principles of Virology. Frosch, Peter J., tr. LC 75-25271. (Illus.). 1977. text ed. 12.00 (ISBN 0-7216-6655-8). Saunders.
Nash, Al. Ruskin College: A Challenge to Adult & Labor Education. LC 81-1231. 144p. 1981. pap. 7.95 (ISBN 0-87546-084-4). ILR Pr.
--Union Steward: Duties, Rights, & Status. (Key Issues Ser.: No. 22). 1977. pap. 3.00 (ISBN 0-87546-235-9). ILR Pr.
Nash, Alanna. Dolly. LC 78-53981. (Illus.). 1978. 9.95 (ISBN 0-89169-523-0). Reed Bks.
Nash, Alice. Collector's Handbook. (Illus.). 40p. (Orig.). 1982. 3.95 (ISBN 0-911431-00-4). Harmon-Meek Gal.
Nash, Allan. Managerial Compensation, Vol. 15. LC 80-21044. (Work in America Institute Studies in Productivity). 1980. pap. 35.00 (ISBN 0-08-029496-0). Pergamon.
Nash, Anedith, jt. auth. see Nash, Jeffrey E.
Nash, Bruce. Can I Quote You on That? (Flip-Overs Ser.). 64p. (gr. 3-7). 1982. pap. 2.25 (ISBN 0-671-44464-6). Wanderer Bks.
--Limerwrecks. (Flip-Overs Ser.). (Illus.). 64p. 1982. pap. 2.25 (ISBN 0-671-44465-4). Wanderer Bks.
--Pundles II. 96p. Date not set. pap. price not set (ISBN 0-448-15711-X, G&D). Putnam Pub Group.
--So, You Think You Know Your Best Friend? (Flip-Overs Ser.). 64p. (Orig.). (gr. 3-7). 1981. pap. 2.50 (ISBN 0-671-44428-X). Wanderer Bks.
--So You Think You Know Your Boyfriend-Girlfriend? Schneider, Meg, ed. (Flip-Overs Ser.). 64p. (Orig.). (gr. 3-7). 1982. pap. 2.95 (ISBN 0-671-45548-6). Wanderer Bks.
--So You Think You Know Your Brother-Sister? Schneider, Meg, ed. (Flip-Overs Ser.). 64p. (Orig.). (gr. 3-7). 1982. pap. 2.95 (ISBN 0-671-45549-4). Wanderer Bks.
--So, You Think You Know Your Parents? (Flip-Overs Ser.). 64p. (Orig.). (gr. 3-7). 1981. pap. 2.50 (ISBN 0-671-44430-1). Wanderer Bks.
--Whatever Happened to Blue Suede Shoes: A Nostalgia Quiz Book of the Fifties. 1978. 14.95 o.p. (ISBN 0-448-14269-4, G&D); pap. 6.95 o.p. (ISBN 0-448-14270-8, Today Press). Putnam Pub Group.
Nash, Bruce & Nash, Greg. Monty Phython's The Life of Brian. 1979. pap. 2.50 o.p. (ISBN 0-448-16867-7, G&D). Putnam Pub Group.
--Pundles. 96p. Date not set. pap. price not set (ISBN 0-448-16867-7, G&D). Putnam Pub Group.
Nash, Bruce & Weaver, Bob. Thumbs Up, Thumbs Down: Book of Puns. (Illus.). 1979. pap. 0.95 (ISBN 0-448-17016-7, G&D). Putnam Pub Group.
Nash, Carroll B. Science of Psi: ESP & PK. 308p. 1978. 16.95x (ISBN 0-398-03803-1). C C Thomas.
Nash, Constance & Artese, Robert N. Cellulite & How to Lose It. (Orig.). 1982. pap. cancelled (ISBN 0-523-41679-2). Pinnacle Bks.
Nash, Constance & Oakey, Virginia. Screenwriter's Handbook: What to Write, How to Write It, Where to Sell It. LC 77-76031. 160p. pap. 4.95 (ISBN 0-06-463454-X, EH 454, EH). B&N NY.
--Television Writer's Handbook: What to Write, How to Write It, Where to Sell It. LC 77-77788. pap. 4.95 (ISBN 0-06-463455-8, EH 455, EH). B&N NY.
Nash, D. F. & Gilling, Cynthia M. Principles & Practice of Surgery for Nurses & Allied Professions. 80p. pap. text ed. 39.50 (ISBN 0-7131-4366-5). E Arnold.
Nash, David T. Dr. Nash's Natural Diet Book. LC 77-78343. 1978. 1.95 o.p. (ISBN 0-448-14647-9, G&D). Putnam Pub Group.
Nash, E. B. Leaders in Homoeopathic Therapeutics. 1981. 5.95x (ISBN 0-685-76565-2, Pub. by Jain). Formur Intl.
Nash, E. L. Direct Marketing: Strategy, Planning, Execution. 1982. 27.50 (ISBN 0-07-046019-1). McGraw.
Nash, Elizabeth. Always First Class: The Career of Geraldine Farrar. LC 81-40107. 292p. (Orig.). 1982. lib. bdg. 22.75 (ISBN 0-8191-1882-6); pap. text ed. 11.50 (ISBN 0-8191-1883-4). U Pr of Amer.
Nash, Gary B. Red, White & Black: The Peoples of Early America. 2nd ed. (Illus.). 368p. 1982. text ed. 17.95 (ISBN 0-13-769794-5); pap. text ed. 12.95 (ISBN 0-13-769786-4). P-H.
Nash, George. Old Houses: A Rebuilder's Manual. (Illus.). 1979. 22.95 o.p. (ISBN 0-13-633875-5, Spec); pap. 12.95 (ISBN 0-686-96841-7). P-H.
Nash, George H. The Life of Herbert Hoover: The Engineer, 1874-1914. (Illus.). 1983. 24.50x (ISBN 0-393-01634-X). Norton.
Nash, Gerald D. Issues in American Economic History: Selected Readings. 3rd ed. 1980. pap. text ed. 9.95x (ISBN 0-669-02480-5). Heath.
Nash, Greg, jt. auth. see Nash, Bruce.
Nash, Harvey. How Preschool Children View Mythological Hybrid Figures: A Study of Human-Animal Body Imagery. LC 81-40106. (Illus.). 230p. 1982. lib. bdg. 21.75 (ISBN 0-8191-2324-2); pap. text ed. 10.75 (ISBN 0-8191-2325-0). U Pr of Amer.
Nash, Jay R. Crime Movie Quiz Book. LC 82-60659. (Illus.). 224p. 1982. cancelled (ISBN 0-89526-639-3); pap. cancelled (ISBN 0-89526-844-2). Regnery Gateway.
--The Dillinger Dossier. LC 82-60661. (Illus.). 320p. 1983. cancelled (ISBN 0-89526-640-7). Regnery Gateway.
--Murder America. 1980. 16.95 o.p. (ISBN 0-671-24270-9). S&S.
--Murder Among the Mighty: Celebrity Slayings That Shocked America. (Illus.). 384p. 1983. 17.95 (ISBN 0-440-05956-9). Delacorte.
--True Crime Quiz Book. 192p. (Orig.). 1981. 9.95 (ISBN 0-87131-364-2); pap. 4.95 (ISBN 0-87131-352-9). M Evans.
Nash, Jeffrey E. & Nash, Anedith. Deafness in Society. LC 81-3753. 144p. 1981. 18.95x (ISBN 0-669-04590-X). Lexington Bks.
Nash, Jerry C., jt. ed. see Lacy, Norris J.
Nash, John. Developmental Psychology: A Psychobiological Approach. 2nd ed. LC 77-27813. (Illus.). 1978. ref. ed. 24.95 (ISBN 0-13-208272-1). P-H.
Nash, Joyce. Taking Charge of Your Smoking. 250p. (Orig.). 1981. pap. 10.95 (ISBN 0-915950-50-2). Bull Pub.
Nash, June. We Eat the Mines & the Mines Eat Us: Dependence & Exploitation in Bolivian Tin Mines. 363p. 1982. pap. 13.00 (ISBN 0-231-04711-8). Columbia U Pr.
Nash, June & Safa, Helen I., eds. Sex & Class in Latin America: Women's Perspectives on Economics, Politics & the Family in the Third World. new ed. (Illus.). 356p. 1980. lib. bdg. 25.95x (ISBN 0-89789-004-3); pap. text ed. 10.95x (ISBN 0-89789-003-5). J F Bergin.
Nash, M. J. How to Save a Fortune Using Refunds & Coupons. (Orig.). 1982. pap. 5.95x (ISBN 0-934650-03-9). Sunnyside.
Nash, Manning. Peasant Citizens: Politics, Religion, & Modernization in Kelantan, Malaysia. LC 62-620027. (Papers in International Studies: Southeast Asia: No. 31). 1977. pap. 12.00x (ISBN 0-89680-018-0, Ohio U Ctr Intl). Ohio U Pr.
Nash, Michael. Managing Organizational Performance. LC 82-49040. (Management & Social & Behavioral Science Ser.). 1983. text ed. price not set (ISBN 0-87589-561-1). Jossey-Bass.
Nash, N. Richard. Aphrodite's Cave. LC 80-1069. 489p. 1980. 15.95 o.p. (ISBN 0-385-14294-3). Doubleday.
Nash, Ogden. A Penny Saved Is Impossible. (Illus.). 132p. 1983. pap. 5.70i (ISBN 0-316-59806-2). Little.
--Verses from Nineteen Twenty-Nine On. 1964. 3.95 o.s.i. (ISBN 0-394-60343-5, M343). Modern Lib.
Nash, P. Systems Modelling & Optimisation. (IEE Control Engineering Ser.: No. 16). 224p. 1981. casebound 43.00 (ISBN 0-906048-63-X). Inst Elect Eng.
Nash, Paul, ed. History & Education: The Educational Uses of the Past. 1970. text ed. 7.50x (ISBN 0-394-30422-5). Phila Bk Co.
Nash, Paul, et al. Models of Man: Explorations in the Western Educational Tradition. LC 67-29011. 1968. pap. text ed. 24.95 (ISBN 0-471-63043-8). Wiley.
--The Educated Man: Studies in the History of Educational Thought. LC 79-21952. 434p. 1980. Repr. of 1965 ed. lib. bdg. 20.50 (ISBN 0-89874-059-2). Krieger.
Nash, Paul J. Land Hermit Crabs. (Illus., Orig.). 1976. pap. 1.49 (ISBN 0-87666-907-0, A-325). TFH Pubns.
Nash, Richard. East Wind, Rain. LC 76-40433. 1977. 9.95 o.p. (ISBN 0-689-10773-0). Atheneum.
Nash, Roderick. Wilderness & the American Mind. rev. ed. LC 72-91303. 328p. 1973. 22.50x o.p. (ISBN 0-300-01648-4, Y-219); pap. 5.95x o.p. (ISBN 0-300-01649-2). Yale U Pr.
--Wilderness & the American Mind. 3rd, Rev. ed. LC 82-4874. 380p. 1982. text ed. 25.00x (ISBN 0-300-02905-5); pap. 7.95x (ISBN 0-300-02910-1, Y-440). Yale U Pr.

Nash, Ronald H. Freedom, Justice, & the State. LC 80-8145. 243p. 1980. lib. bdg. 20.00 (ISBN 0-8191-1195-3); pap. text ed. 10.00 (ISBN 0-8191-1196-1). U Pr of Amer.

--The Word of God & the Mind of Man: The Crisis of Revealed Truth in Contemporary Theology. 176p. (Orig.). 1982. pap. 6.95 (ISBN 0-310-45131-0). Zondervan.

Nash, Roy. Classrooms Observed: The Teacher's Perception & the Pupil's Performance. (Students Library of Education). 1973. pap. 8.95 (ISBN 0-7100-7694-0). Routledge & Kegan.

Nash, S. Paul Valery's Album des Vers Anciens: A Past Transfigured. 1982. 28.50 (ISBN 0-691-06526-8). Princeton U Pr.

Nash, Steven A., jt. auth. see Albright-Knox Art Gallery.

Nash, William A. Strength of Materials. 2nd ed. (Schaum Outline Ser.). 1972. 8.95 (ISBN 0-07-045894-4, SP). McGraw.

Nashat, Guity. Women & Revolution in Iran. (Replica Edition Ser.). 250p. 1982. 18.50 (ISBN 0-86531-931-6). Westview.

Nashed, M. Z., ed. Recent Applications of Generalized Inverses. (Research Notes in Mathematics Ser.: No. 23). (Illus.). 1979. pap. cancelled o.p. (ISBN 0-685-96564-3). Pitman Pub MA.

Nashelsky, L., jt. auth. see Boylestad, Robert L.

Nashelsky, Louis. Introduction to Digital Computer Technology. 2nd ed. LC 76-42245. 1977. text ed. 28.95x (ISBN 0-471-02094-X). Wiley.

--Introduction to Digital Technology. 3rd ed. LC 82-13377. 536p. 1983. text ed. 26.95 (ISBN 0-471-09646-6); solutions manual avail. (ISBN 0-471-89526-1). Wiley.

Nashelsky, Louis, jt. auth. see Boylestad, Robert.

Nasi, Andrea, et al. The Honey Handbook. LC 78-57543. (Illus.). 1979. pap. 5.95 (ISBN 0-89696-014-5, An Everest House Book). Dodd.

Nasir, Pir. Faceless Enemy. 224p. 1983. 12.50 (ISBN 0-682-49975-7). Exposition.

Naske, Claus-M. Interpretative History of Alaskan Statehood. LC 72-92091. 216p. 1973. 4.95 o.p. (ISBN 0-88240-017-7); pap. 2.95 o.p. (ISBN 0-88240-014-2). Alaska Northwest.

Nason, Donna, jt. auth. see Nason, Michael.

Nason, Michael & Nason, Donna. Robert Schuller: The Inside Story. Date not set. 8.95 (ISBN 0-8499-0300-9). Word Pub.

Nason, Thelma. Our Statue of Liberty. LC 69-10260. (Beginning-To-Read Ser). (Illus.). (gr. 2-4). 1969. 1.95 (ISBN 0-695-86700-8, Dist. by Caroline Hse); PLB 4.39 o.s.i. (ISBN 0-685-10945-3). Follett.

Nason, Thelma C. A Stranger Here, Myself. Hunting, Constance, ed. 1980. pap. 3.50 (ISBN 0-913006-11-4). Puckerbrush.

Nasr, Raja T. The Essentials of Linguistic Science. (Applied Linguistics & Language Study Ser.). 1980. pap. text ed. 8.95x (ISBN 0-582-74609-4). Longman.

Nasr, Sayyed H. Sufi Essays. 1973. 24.50x (ISBN 0-87395-233-2). State U NY Pr.

Nasr, Seyyed H. An Introduction to Islamic Cosmological Doctrines. LC 78-58184. 1978. pap. 9.50 o.p. (ISBN 0-394-73625-7). Shambhala Pubns.

--Islamic Life & Thought. LC 81-4723. 232p. 1981. 39.50x (ISBN 0-87395-490-4); pap. 12.95x (ISBN 0-87395-491-2). State U NY Pr.

--Three Muslim Sages. LC 75-14430. 192p. 1976. pap. text ed. 10.00x (ISBN 0-88206-500-9). Caravan Bks.

Nasr, Seyyed H., ed. see Muhammad.

Nasr, Seyyed H., tr. see Al-Tabataba'I, Muhammed H.

Nasrallah, G. K., ed. The Palestine Documents, 1973. (Arabic.). 1977. 30.00 (ISBN 0-686-18938-8). Inst Palestine.

--The Palestine Documents, 1974. (Arabic.). 1977. 30.00 (ISBN 0-686-18939-6). Inst Palestine.

Nass, G., ed. Modified Nucleosides & Cancer: Workshop, Freiburg, FRG, 1981. (Recent Results in Cancer Research Ser.: Vol. 84). (Illus.). 440p. 1983. 50.50 (ISBN 0-387-12024-6). Springer-Verlag.

Nass, Gilbert D. & McDonald, Gerald W. Marriage & the Family. 2nd ed. (Sociology Ser.). (Illus.). 512p. 1982. text ed. 19.95 (ISBN 0-201-06240-2); Study Guide 5.95 (ISBN 0-686-85483-7). A-W.

Nassar, Eugene P. Essays Critical & Metacritical. LC 81-70955. 192p. 1983. 22.50 (ISBN 0-8386-3128-2). Fairleigh Dickinson.

Nassau, Jason J. Practical Astronomy. 2nd ed. (Astronomical Ser.). (Illus.). 1948. text ed. 24.95 (ISBN 0-07-046089-2, C). McGraw.

Nassau, William. The Last Word: Reflections on Reality. LC 82-51052. 160p. 1982. 11.95 (ISBN 0-932966-22-5). Permanent Pr.

Nasser & Guiliani. Clinical Two-Dimensional Echcocardiography. 1983. 34.95t (ISBN 0-8151-3501-7). Year Bk Med.

Nasser, Essam. Fundamentals of Gaseous Ionization & Plasma Electronics. LC 77-125275. (Plasma Physics Ser). 1971. 42.95x o.p. (ISBN 0-471-63056-X, Pub. by Wiley-Interscience). Wiley.

Nasset, Edmund S. Nutrition Handbook. 3rd ed. (Illus.). 176p. (Orig.). pap. 6.01i. B&N NY.

Nassif, Janet Z. Health Profession Careers in Medicine's New Technology. 2nd ed. LC 78-11386. Orig. Title: Medicine's New Technology: A Career Guide. 1979. lib. bdg. 9.95 (ISBN 0-668-04443-8); pap. 5.95 (ISBN 0-668-04436-5). Arco.

Nassif, Ricardo. Methods of Teaching Librarianship. 1969. pap. 6.00 o.p. (ISBN 92-3-100758-0, U384, UNESCO). Unipub.

Nassimbene, Raymond, jt. auth. see Carmichael, Fitzhugh L.

Nassisi, Thomas & Dubanevich, Arlene. Hearts. LC 81-8161. (Illus.). 80p. 1982. 4.95 (ISBN 0-02-588340-2); prepack(12) 59.40. Macmillan.

Nast, Lenora H. & Krause, Laurence, eds. Baltimore: A Living Renaissance. (Illus.). 336p. 1982. 29.95 (ISBN 0-942460-00-6). Hist Balt Soc.

Nastasescu, C. & Van Oystaeyen, F. Graded Ring Theory. (North-Mathematical Library: Vol. 28). 340p. 1982. 42.75 (ISBN 0-444-86489-X, North Holland). Elsevier.

Nasuti, James F., jt. auth. see Nickerson, Charles A.

Natale, Peter, jt. ed. see Kaplan, Charles.

Natale, Samuel M. Ethics & Morals in Business. 190p. 1983. text ed. price not set (ISBN 0-89135-036-5). Religious Educ.

Natan, Alex, ed. German Men of Letters: Twelve Literary Essays. 1965. Vol. 1. 15.95 (ISBN 0-85496-001-5); 10.95 (ISBN 0-85496-002-3); Vol. 2. pap. 15.95 o.s.i. (ISBN 0-85496-004-X); Vol. 3. pap. 10.95 (ISBN 0-85496-073-2). Dufour.

Natapoff, jt. auth. see Wieczorek.

Natarajan. DNA Repair: Chromosome Alterations & Chromatin Structure. (Progress in Mutation Research Ser.: Vol. 4). 1982. 89.50 (ISBN 0-444-80367-X). Elsevier.

Natarajan, B. The City of the Cosmic Dance. LC 75-904414. 1975. 10.00x o.p. (ISBN 0-88386-611-0, Orient Longman). South Asia Bks.

Natarajan, T., jt. auth. see Ahmed, Nasir.

Natchez, Gladys, jt. auth. see Roswell, Florence.

Natella, Arthur A. The Spanish in America, 1513-1979: A Chronology & Fact Book. rev. ed. LC 75-9887. (Ethnic Chronology Ser.: No. 12). 141p. 1980. 8.50 (ISBN 0-379-00540-9). Oceana.

Natella, Arthur A., jt. auth. see Schoenfeld, David.

Natella, Arthur, Jr. The New Theatre of Peru. LC 81-84037. (Senda de Estudios y Ensayos Ser.). 132p. (Orig.). 1982. pap. text ed. 9.95 (ISBN 0-918454-28-X). Senda Nueva.

Natelson, Samuel, et al. Amniotic Fluid: Physiology, Biochemistry, & Clinical Chemistry. LC 74-4444. (Current Topics in Clinical Chemistry Ser.). 416p. 1974. 48.95 o.p. (ISBN 0-471-63063-2, Pub. by Wiley Medical). Wiley.

Natemeyer, Walter E., ed. Classics of Organizational Behavior. LC 78-26983. (Classics Ser.). (Orig.). 1978. pap. 10.00x (ISBN 0-935610-03-0). Moore Pub IL.

Nater, J., et al. Unwanted Effects of Cosmetics & Drugs Used in Dermatology. 494p. 1982. 116.25 (ISBN 0-444-90265-1). Elsevier.

Nath, Aman, jt. auth. see Wacziarg, Francis.

Nath, Pran, jt. ed. see Arnowitt, Richard.

Nathan, Andrew. Peking Politics, 1918-1923: Factionalism & the Failure of Constitutionalism. LC 74-79769. 1976. 34.50x (ISBN 0-520-02784-1). U of Cal Pr.

Nathan, Beverly, jt. auth. see Bizer, Linda.

Nathan, Bill, ed. The Sea Fisherman's Bedside Book. (Illus.). 166p. 1982. text ed. 12.95x (ISBN 0-7156-1537-8, Pub. by Duckworth England). Biblio Dist.

Nathan, David G. & Oski, Frank A. Hematology of Infancy & Childhood. LC 73-89190. (Illus.). 720p. 1974. text ed. 42.50 o.p. (ISBN 0-7216-6660-4). Saunders.

--Hematology of Infancy & Childhood, 2 vols. (Illus.). 1696p. 1981. Set. text ed. 125.00; Vol. 1. 62.50 (ISBN 0-7216-6676-0); Vol. 2. 62.50 (ISBN 0-7216-6677-9). Saunders.

Nathan, Dorothy. Women of Courage. (Landmark Ser: No. 107). (Illus.). (gr. 5-9). 1964. PLB 5.99 (ISBN 0-394-90407-9, BYR); pap. 0.75 o.p. (ISBN 0-394-82186-6). Random.

Nathan, Emily. I Know a Farmer. (Community Helper Bks.). (Illus.). (gr. 1-3). 1970. PLB 4.29 o.p. (ISBN 0-399-60279-8). Putnam Pub Group.

Nathan, Joan. The Jewish Holiday Kitchen. LC 79-64114. (Illus.). 1979. 14.95 (ISBN 0-8052-3712-7). Schocken.

--The Jewish Holiday Kitchen. LC 79-64114. (Illus.). 288p. 1982. pap. 8.95 spiral bdg. (ISBN 0-8052-0724-4). Schocken.

--The Larosa International Pasta Cookbook. 8.95 o.p. (ISBN 0-916752-25-9). Green Hill.

Nathan, Joe. Free to Teach: Achieving Equity & Excellence in Schools. 224p. 1983. 14.95 (ISBN 0-8298-0657-1). Pilgrim NY.

Nathan, John, tr. see Mishima, Yukio.

Nathan, Leonard. The Teachings of Grandfather Fox. LC 76-57990. 49p. 1976. 3.50 (ISBN 0-87886-079-7). Ithaca Hse.

Nathan, Leonard, tr. The Transport of Love: The Meghaduta of Kalidasa. 1976. 17.00x (ISBN 0-520-03031-1); pap. 2.95 (ISBN 0-520-03271-3, CAL348). U of Cal Pr.

Nathan, Leonard, tr. see Sen, Ramprasad.

Nathan, Mary M., jt. ed. see Nathan, Richard P.

Nathan, Norma. Boston's Most Eligible Bachelors. (Illus.). 176p. 1982. pap. 5.95 (ISBN 0-86616-022-1). Lewis Pub Co.

--Norma Nathan's Book of Boston's Most Eligible Bachelors. 1983. pap. 5.95 (ISBN 0-86616-022-1). Greene.

Nathan, Otto, ed. see Einstein, Albert.

Nathan, Peter, ed. see Behrman, Debra L.

Nathan, Peter, ed. see Kivnick, Helen Q.

Nathan, Peter, ed. see Laurence, Lance T.

Nathan, Peter E. & Harris, Sandra L. Psychopathology & Society. (Illus.). 576p. 1975. text ed. 25.50 (ISBN 0-07-046046-9); instructors' manual 3.95 (ISBN 0-07-046048-5). McGraw.

--Psychopathology & Society. 2nd ed. LC 79-15683. (Illus.). 1980. text ed. 28.50 (ISBN 0-07-046053-1); instr's. manual 15.00 (ISBN 0-07-046054-X); study guide 9.95 (ISBN 0-07-046056-6). McGraw.

Nathan, Peter E., jt. ed. see Hay, William H.

Nathan, Peter E., ed. see Heilling, Roma J.

Nathan, Peter E., ed. see Parelman, Allison.

Nathan, Peter E., ed. see Ringler, Karin E.

Nathan, Peter E., ed. see Segalla, Rosemary A.

Nathan, Richard A., ed. Fuels from Sugar Crops: Systems Study for Sugarcane, Sweet Sorghum, & Sugar Beets. LC 78-19127. (DOE Critical Review Ser.). 148p. 1978. pap. 11.75 (ISBN 0-87079-111-7, TID-22781); microfiche 4.50 (ISBN 0-87079-212-1, TID-22781). DOE.

Nathan, Richard P. The Administrative Presidency. 200p. 1983. pap. 9.95 (ISBN 0-471-86871-X). Wiley.

Nathan, Richard P. & Adams, Charles F. Revenue Sharing: The Second Round. LC 76-51884. 1977. 18.95 (ISBN 0-8157-5986-X); pap. 7.95 (ISBN 0-8157-5985-1). Brookings.

Nathan, Richard P. & Webman, Jerry A. The Urban Development Action Grant Program. 125p. 1980. pap. text ed. 7.95 (ISBN 0-938882-01-5, Dist. by Transaction Bks). PURRC.

Nathan, Richard P. & Nathan, Mary M., eds. America's Governments: A Fact Book of Census Data on the Organization, Finances & Employment of Federal, State & Local Governments. LC 79-18575. 1979. 29.95 (ISBN 0-471-05671-5, Pub. by Wiley-Interscience). Wiley.

Nathan, Richard P., et al. Monitoring Revenue Sharing. 394p. 1975. 22.95 (ISBN 0-8157-5984-3); pap. 8.95 (ISBN 0-8157-5983-5). Brookings.

--Public Service Employment: A Field Evaluation. LC 81-4596. 130p. 1981. pap. 6.95 (ISBN 0-8157-5987-8). Brookings.

Nathan, Robert L. Coal Mine, Number Seven. 320p. 1981. 12.95 o.p. (ISBN 0-312-14499-7). St Martin.

Nathan, Simon, jt. auth. see Grande, Frank.

Nathan, Stella W. Jack & the Beanstalk. (Illus.). 24p. (gr. k-3). 1976. PLB 5.00 (ISBN 0-307-60454-3, Golden Pr). Western Pub.

Nathan, THeodore R. Hotelmanship: A Guide to Hospitality Industry Marketing & Management. LC 81-7051. 264p. 1981. 54.50 (ISBN 0-87624-203-4). Inst Busn Plan.

Nathanielsz. Animal Models in Fetal Medicine I. (Monographs in Fetal Physiology: Vol. 2). 1980. 86.00 (ISBN 0-444-80153-7). Elsevier.

--Animal Models in Fetal Medicine II. Date not set. price not set (ISBN 0-444-80425-0). Elsevier.

Nathanielsz, P. W., jt. auth. see Beard, R. W.

Nathans, Sydney. The Quest for Progress: The Way We Lived in North Carolina, 1870-1920. LC 82-20133. (The Way We Lived in North Carolina Ser.). (Illus.). viii, 108p. 1983. 11.95 (ISBN 0-8078-1552-7); pap. 6.95 (ISBN 0-8078-4104-8). U of NC Pr.

Nathans, Sydney, ed. see Clayton, Thomas H.

Nathans, Sydney, ed. see Fenn, Elizabeth A. & Wood, Peter H.

Nathans, Sydney, ed. see Parramore, Thomas C.

Nathans, Sydney, ed. see Watson, Harry L.

Nathanson, Bernard N. & Ostling, Richard N. Aborting America. LC 79-7069. 1979. 10.00 o.p. (ISBN 0-385-14461-X). Doubleday.

Nathanson, Daniel A., jt. auth. see Galbraith, Jay R.

Nathanson, Fred E. Radar Design Principles: Signal Processing & the Environment. (Illus.). 1969. 60.00 (ISBN 0-07-046047-7, P&RB). McGraw.

Nathanson, Nathaniel L., jt. auth. see Jaffe, Louis L.

Nathanson, Virginia. Art of Making Bead Flowers. 8.95 (ISBN 0-8208-0302-2). Hearthside.

--Making Bead Flowers & Bouquets. (Illus.). 192p. 1983. pap. 4.95 (ISBN 0-486-24464-4). Dover.

--The Pearl & Bead Boutique Book. (Illus.). 192p. 1972. 8.95 (ISBN 0-8208-0340-5). Hearthside.

Nathanson, Virginia G. New Patterns for Bead Flowers & Decorations, Vol. 1. LC 73-92495. (Illus.). 1969. 8.95 (ISBN 0-8208-0333-2). Hearthside.

Nation, Craig R., jt. ed. see Kauppi, Mark V.

Nation, James E. & Aram, Dorothy M. Diagnosis of Speech & Language Disorders. LC 76-28212. (Illus.). 454p. 1977. text ed. 22.95 o.p. (ISBN 0-8016-3631-0). Mosby.

Nation, James E., jt. auth. see Aram, Dorothy M.

Nation, Jim G., jt. auth. see Page, J. S.

Nation, Terry. The Survivors. LC 76-30612. 288p. 1976. 8.95 o.p. (ISBN 0-698-10664-4, Coward). Putnam Pub Group.

National Academy Of Arbitrators, Meetings 1-7. Profession of Labor Arbitration: Proceedings. McKelvey, Jean T., ed. LC 55-57413. (Library of Labor Arbitration Ser). 192p. 1957. 27.50 (ISBN 0-87179-065-3). BNA.

National Academy of Arbitrators-11th Annual Meeting. Arbitrator & the Parties: Proceedings. McKelvey, Jean T., ed. LC 55-57413. (Library of Labor Arbitration Ser.). 222p. 1958. 27.50 (ISBN 0-87179-055-6). BNA.

National Academy of Arbitrators-12th Annual Meeting. Arbitration & the Law: Proceedings. McKelvey, Jean T., ed. LC 55-57413. (Library of Labor Arbitration Ser.). 1959. 27.50 (ISBN 0-87179-053-X). BNA.

National Academy of Arbitrators-13th Annual Meeting. Challenges to Arbitration: Proceedings. McKelvey, Jean T., ed. LC 55-57413. (Library of Labor Arbitration Ser). 196p. 1960. 27.50 (ISBN 0-87179-057-2). BNA.

National Academy of Arbitrators-14th Annual Meeting. Arbitration & Public Policy: Proceedings. Pollard, Spencer D., ed. LC 55-57413. (Library of Labor Arbitration Ser.). 214p. 1961. 27.50 (ISBN 0-87179-052-1). BNA.

National Academy of Arbitrators-15th Annual Meeting. Collective Bargaining & the Arbitrator's Role: Proceedings. Kahn, Mark L., ed. LC 55-57413. (Library of Labor Arbitration Ser). 302p. 1962. 27.50 (ISBN 0-87179-058-0). BNA.

National Academy of Arbitrators-16th Annual Meeting. Labor Arbitration & Industrial Change: Proceedings. Kahn, Mark L., ed. LC 55-57413. (Library of Arbitration Ser). 382p. 1963. 27.50 (ISBN 0-87179-061-0). BNA.

National Academy of Arbitrators-17th Annual Meeting. Labor Arbitration: Perspectives & Problems: Proceedings. Kahn, Mark L., ed. LC 55-57413. (Library of Labor Arbitration Ser). 344p. 1964. 27.50 (ISBN 0-87179-062-9). BNA.

National Academy Of Arbitrators - 18th Meeting. Proceedings. Jones, Dallas L., ed. LC 55-57413. (Library of Labor Arbitration Ser). 278p. 1965. 27.50 (ISBN 0-87179-066-1). BNA.

National Academy of Arbitrators-20th Annual Meeting. Arbitrator, the NLRB, & the Courts: Proceedings. Jones, Dallas L., ed. LC 55-57413. (Library of Labor Arbitration Ser.). 436p. 1967. 27.50 (ISBN 0-87179-056-4). BNA.

National Academy of Arbitrators-21st Annnual Meeting. Developments in American & Foreign Arbitration: Proceedings. Rehmus, Charles M., ed. LC 55-57413. (Library of Labor Arbitration Ser). 256p. 1968. 27.50 (ISBN 0-87179-060-2). BNA.

National Academy of Arbitrators-22nd Annual Meeting. Arbitration & Social Change: Proceedings. Somers, Gerald G., ed. LC 55-57413. (Library of Labor Arbitration Ser.). 224p. 1969. 27.50 (ISBN 0-87179-067-X). BNA.

National Academy of Arbitrators-23nd Annual Meeting. Arbitration & the Expanding Role of Neutrals: Proceedings. Somers, Gerald G., ed. LC 55-57413. (Library of Labor Arbitration Ser). 284p. 1970. 27.50 (ISBN 0-87179-068-8). BNA.

National Academy of Arbitrators-24th Annual Meeting. Arbitration & the Public Interest: Proceedings. Somers, Gerald G. & Dennis, Barbara D., eds. LC 55-57413. (Library of Labor Arbitration Ser). 356p. 1971. 27.50 (ISBN 0-87179-069-6). BNA.

National Academy of Arbitrators-25th Annual Meeting. Labor Arbitration at the Quarter-Century Mark: Proceedings. Dennis, Barbara D. & Somers, Gerald G., eds. LC 55-57413. (Library of Labor Arbitration Ser.). 474p. 1973. 27.50 (ISBN 0-87179-070-X). BNA.

National Academy of Arbitrators-26th Meeting. Arbitration of Interest Disputes: Proceedings. Dennis, Barbara D. & Somers, Gerald G., eds. LC 55-57413. (Library of Labor Arbitration Ser). 320p. 1974. 27.50 (ISBN 0-87179-071-8). BNA.

National Academy of Arbitrators-27th Annual Meeting. Arbitration, 1974: Proceedings. Dennis, Barbara D. & Somers, Gerald G., eds. LC 55-57413. (Library of Labor Arbitration Ser.). 378p. 1975. 27.50 (ISBN 0-87179-072-6). BNA.

National Academy of Arbitrators-28th Annual Meeting. Arbitration, 1975: Proceedings. Dennis, Barbara D. & Somers, Gerald G., eds. LC 76-992. (Library of Labor Arbitration Ser.). 394p. 1976. 27.50 (ISBN 0-87179-073-4). BNA.

National Academy of Arbitrators-29th Annual Meeting. Arbitration, 1976: Proceedings. Dennis, Barbara D. & Somers, Gerald G., eds. LC 76-54779. (Library of Labor Arbitraton Ser.). 412p. 1976. 27.50 (ISBN 0-87179-238-9). BNA.

National Academy of Arbitrators-30th Annual Meeting. Arbitration 1977: Proceedings. Dennis, Barbara D. & Somers, Gerald G., eds. LC 55-57413. (Library of Labor Arbitration Ser.). 402p. 1978. 27.50 (ISBN 0-87179-266-4). BNA.

National Academy of Arbitrators-32nd Annual Meeting. Arbitration of Subcontracting & Wage Incentive Disputes: Proceedings. Stern, James L. & Dennis, Barbara D., eds. LC 79-24133. (Library of Labor Arbitration Ser.). 316p. 1980. 27.50 (ISBN 0-87179-317-2). BNA.

National Academy of Arbitrators-34th Annual Meeting. Arbitration Issues for the 1980s: Proceedings. 360p. 1982. text ed. 27.50 (ISBN 0-87179-374-1). BNA.

National Academy Of Engineering. Costs of Health Care Facilities. 1968. pap. 8.75 (ISBN 0-309-01592-8). Natl Acad Pr.

National Academy of Sciences. Developing Strategies for Rangeland Management. 1000p. 1982. lib. bdg. 45.00 (ISBN 0-86531-543-4). Westview.
National Academy of Sciences, National Academy of Engineering. Man, Materials, & Environment. 252p. 1974. 17.50x (ISBN 0-262-14019-5); pap. 5.95x (ISBN 0-262-64013-9). MIT Pr.
National Agricultural Library, U.S.D.A., ed. Agricultural Journal Titles & Abbreviations. 156p. 1982. pap. 30.00x (ISBN 0-89774-071-8). Oryx Pr.
National Army Museum, London. War & Weapons. (Modern Knowledge Library). (Illus.). 48p. (gr. 5 up). 1982. PLB 9.80 (ISBN 0-531-09059-0). Watts.
National Association for Industry Education Corporation. Placement Services: A Training Manual. LC 76-62869. 1977. 8.45 o.p. (ISBN 0-911168-35-4). Prakken.
National Association of Accountants, ed. Management Accounting for Multinational Corporations, 2 vols. 24.95 ea. (7464). Vol. I, 383 p (ISBN 0-86641-063-5, 7466). Vol. II, 317 p (ISBN 0-86641-064-3). 44.95 set (ISBN 0-686-34438-3). Natl Assn Accts.
National Association of Accountants Editorial Staff, ed. Managing Price Level Accounting: The Inflation Dilemma, Part 1, Bk 1. 178p. 14.95 (ISBN 0-86641-061-9, 7579); 24.95 set. Natl Assn Accts.
--Managing the Cash Flow. 168p. 14.95 (ISBN 0-86641-062-7, 7471). Natl Assn Accts.
National Association of Accounting Editorial Staff, ed. Management Reporting Under Inflation: The Inflation Dilemma, Part 2. 169p. 14.95 (ISBN 0-86641-060-0, 7580); 24.95 set. Natl Assn Accts.
National Association of Credit Management. Digest of Commercial Laws of the World, 7 bdrs. LC 65-22163. 1968. looseleaf 595.00 set (ISBN 0-379-01025-9). Oceana.
--Patent-Trademark Law & Practice, 2 vols. LC 65-22163. 1975. binder until may 1977 110.00x (ISBN 0-379-01025-9). Oceana.
National Association of Home Builders. Accounting System for All Builders. 78p. 1977. pap. 8.00 (ISBN 0-86718-001-3). Natl Assn Home Builders.
--Construction Cost Control. Rev. ed. (Illus.). 64p. 1982. pap. text ed. 13.00 (ISBN 0-86718-153-2). Natl Assn Home.
--Cost Effective Site Planning. Rev. ed. (Illus.). 142p. 1982. pap. text ed. 20.00 (ISBN 0-86718-156-7). Natl Assn Home.
--Cost Effective Site Planning: Single-Family Development. (Illus.). 143p. 1976. pap. 16.50 o.p. (ISBN 0-86718-019-6). Natl Assn Home Builders.
--Form Builders Manual. (Illus.). 140p. 1979. Durotrans (waterproof) metal spiral 20.00 (ISBN 0-86718-098-6). Natl Assn Home Builders.
--Performance of Nominal Five-Eighths Inch Plywood Over Joists Spaced 24 Inches Spaced on Center, Research Report 1. 11p. 1981. pap. 5.50 (ISBN 0-86718-114-1). Natl Assn Home Builders.
National Association of Legal Secretaries (NALS), ed. The Career Legal Secretary. Advanced ed. LC 82-11174. 1216p. 1982. text ed. 24.95 (ISBN 0-314-68807-2); tchr's manual avail. (ISBN 0-314-70364-0); study guide avail. (ISBN 0-314-70363-2). West Pub.
National Association of Purchasing Management. Aljians Purchasing Handbook. 4th ed. Farrell, Paul V., ed. 1152p. 1982. 49.95 (ISBN 0-07-045899-5). McGraw.
National Association of Recycling Industries Inc. Recycled Metals in the Nineteen Eighties. (Illus.). 188p. 1982. 40.00 (ISBN 0-686-81901-2). Natl Recycling.
National Association of Review Appraisers. Reviewers Guide. LC 80-53456. (Illus.). 214p. 1981. 23.50 (ISBN 0-935988-20-3). Todd Pub.
--Reviewing Condominium Projects. LC 80-53455. (Illus.). 156p. 1981. 21.50 (ISBN 0-935988-21-1). Todd Pub.
National Association of School Counselors. Counselors Certification Requirements for the Fifty States, Territories & Possessions of the United States: Research Report. 102p. 1977. pap. 7.50 (ISBN 0-686-63682-1, 1396-4-06). NEA.
National Book League. Children's Books of Yesterday. Muir, Percy H., ed. LC 76-89280. 1970. Repr. of 1946 ed. 30.00x (ISBN 0-8103-3550-6). Gale.
National Bureau of Economic Research Conference on Income & Wealth. Analysis of Inflation: 1965-1974, Vol. 42. Popkin, Joel, ed. LC 77-581. 1977. prof ref 35.00x (ISBN 0-88410-477-X). Ballinger Pub.
National Bureau of Statistics, Economic Planning Board, ed. Korea Statistical Yearbook 1981. 28th ed. LC 59-23483. 615p. 1981. 35.00x (ISBN 0-8002-3004-3). Intl Pubns Serv.
National Catholic Development Conference. Bibliography of Fund Raising & Philanthropy. LC 75-12128. 1975. 22.50, incl. 1976 & 1977 supplements o.p. (ISBN 0-9603196-0-3). Natl Cath Dev.
--Bibliography of Fund Raising & Philanthropy. 2nd ed. LC 82-81523. 1982. 22.50 (ISBN 0-9603196-1-1). Natl Cath Dev.
National Center for Health Statistics. Health Interview Survey, 1975. LC 82-80685. write for info. (ISBN 0-89138-926-1, ICPSR 7672). ICPSR.
--Mortality Detail Files, 1972-1977. LC 82-80686. 1982. write for info. (ISBN 0-89138-940-7). ICPSR.
National Center for State Courts. Business Equipment & the Courts: Reference Manual. (Illus.). 1977. pap. 21.78 (ISBN 0-89656-018-X, R0030R). Natl Ctr St Courts.
--Clemency: Legal Authority, Procedure & Structure. 1978. pap. 5.00 (ISBN 0-685-05543-4, R0035). Natl Ctr St Courts.
--Computer-Aided Transcription in the Courts: Executive Summary. (Illus., Orig.). 1981. pap. write for info. o.p. (ISBN 0-89656-052-X, R0058). Natl Ctr St Courts.
--Fiscal Administration in State-Funded Courts. 150p. 1981. pap. 10.00 (ISBN 0-89656-053-8). Natl Ctr St Courts.
--Maine Traffic Court Study: Executive Summary. Steelman, David C., ed. 1975. pap. 1.50 (ISBN 0-89656-004-X). Natl Ctr St Courts.
--Maine Traffic Court Study: Full Report. Steelman, David C., ed. (Illus.). 18.50 (ISBN 0-89656-005-8). Natl Ctr St Courts.
--Managing to Reduce Delay. (Orig.). 1980. pap. 5.50 o.p. (ISBN 0-89656-041-4, R0049). Natl Ctr St Courts.
--Microfilm & the Courts: Guide for Court Managers. (Courts' Equipment Analysis Project Ser.). 1976. pap. 3.12 (ISBN 0-89656-007-4, R0026G). Natl Ctr St Courts.
--Microfilm & the Courts: Reference Manual. (Courts Equipment Analysis Project Ser.). 1976. 44.64 (ISBN 0-89656-008-2, R0026R). Natl Ctr St Courts.
--Rural Courts: The Effect of Space & Distance on the Administration of Justice. (Illus.). 1977. pap. 5.00 (ISBN 0-89656-020-1, R0032). Natl Ctr St Courts.
--A Unified Court System for Vermont: Full Report. 1974. 16.68 (ISBN 0-89656-015-5). Natl Ctr St Courts.
--Workload Measures in the Court. 1980. pap. 10.00 (ISBN 0-89656-043-0, R0051). Natl Ctr St Courts.
National College of Education. Young People's Science Encyclopedia, 20 Vols. rev. ed. LC 67-17925. (Illus.). (gr. 3-9). 1979. Set. PLB 213.25 (ISBN 0-516-00250-3). Childrens.
National Commission on the Reform of Secondary Education. The Reform of Secondary Education. 200p. 1973. pap. 3.95 (ISBN 0-07-046050-7, P&RB). McGraw.
National Committee for Citizens in Education Staff. Violence in Our Schools: What to Know About It - What to Do About It. 40p. (Orig.). 1975. pap. 3.50 (ISBN 0-934460-00-0). NCCE.
National Committee for Fluid Mechanics Films. Illustrated Experiments in Fluid Mechanics: The NCFMF Book of Film Notes. (Illus.). 1972. pap. 12.00x (ISBN 0-262-64012-0). MIT Pr.
National Computer Centre, ed. Working with Computers: A Guide to Job Careers. (Illus.). 1975. pap. 6.50x o.p. (ISBN 0-85012-126-4). Intl Pubns Serv.
National Computer Conference, 1977. AFIPS Proceedings, Vol. 46. Korfhage, Robert R., ed. LC 55-44701. (Illus.). xiv, 1026p. 1977. 69.00 (ISBN 0-88283-007-4). AFIPS Pr.
National Computer Conference, 1978. AFIPS Proceedings, Vol. 47. Ghosh, Sakti P. & Liu, Leonard Y., eds. LC 55-44701. (Illus.). xxxiv, 1300p. 1978. 69.00 (ISBN 0-88283-006-6). AFIPS Pr.
National Computer Conference, 1979. AFIPS Proceedings, Vol. 48. Merwin, Richard E., ed. LC 55-44701. (Illus.). xi, 1114p. 1979. 69.00 (ISBN 0-88283-005-8). AFIPS Pr.
National Computer Conference, 1980. AFIPS Proceedings, Vol. 49. Medley, Donald B., ed. LC 80-66206. (Illus.). 1980. 69.00 (ISBN 0-88283-003-1). AFIPS Pr.
National Computing Centre. Ensuring Program Quality. Murphy, Bill, et al, eds. 64p. (Orig.). 1980. pap. 22.50x (ISBN 0-85012-235-X). Intl Pubns Serv.
--Working with Computers: A Guide to Jobs & Careers. 3rd ed. (Illus.). 75p. (Orig.). 1982. pap. 8.50x (ISBN 0-85012-359-3). Intl Pubns Serv.
National Computing Centre, ed. Microprocessors in Industry. 280p. (Orig.). 1981. pap. 27.50x (ISBN 0-85012-322-4). Intl Pubns Serv.
--Thesaurus of Computing Terms. 8th ed. 1977. pap. 82.50x (ISBN 0-85012-169-8). Intl Pubns Serv.
National Computing Centre Ltd. Computers in the Social Sciences: A Study Guide. Penney, G., ed. LC 74-164433. (Computers & People Ser). 48p. 1973. pap. 10.00x (ISBN 0-85012-095-0). Intl Pubns Serv.
National Computing Centre Ltd., ed. ASCOP User Manual. 162p. (Orig.). 1969. 20.00x o.p. (ISBN 0-85012-016-0). Intl Pubns Serv.
National Computing Centre Ltd, ed. Computer Appreciation for the Majority. LC 72-97128. 220p. 1973. pap. 27.50x o.p. (ISBN 0-85012-153-1). Intl Pubns Serv.
National Computing Centre Ltd., ed. see Coan, D. R.
National Computing Centre (Manchester) Computing Practice: Security Aspects. 53p. (Orig.). 1979. pap. 25.00x (ISBN 0-85012-215-5). Intl Pubns Serv.
National Conference of Appellate Court Clerks. Appellate Court Administration Review, No. 2. (Orig.). 1979. pap. 5.00 o.p. (ISBN 0-934730-00-8). Natl Conf Appellate.
National Conference Of Charities And Correction. History of Child Saving in the United States. LC 70-108228. (Criminology, Law Enforcement, & Social Problems Ser.: No. 111). (With intro. & index added). 1971. Repr. of 1893 ed. 20.00x (ISBN 0-87585-111-8). Patterson Smith.
National Conference on Motion Pictures, New York, 1929 & Motion Picture Producers & Distributors of America. The Community & the Motion Picture: Report. LC 77-160242. (Moving Pictures Ser). 96p. 1971. Repr. of 1929 ed. lib. bdg. 9.75x (ISBN 0-89198-043-1). Ozer.
National Conference on Religion & Race. Race: Challenge to Religion. Ahmann, Mathew, ed. LC 78-24276. 1979. Repr. of 1963 ed. lib. bdg. 17.75x (ISBN 0-313-20796-8, NCRA). Greenwood.
National Council for the Social Studies. Racism & Sexism: Responding to the Challenge, Bulletin 61. 96p. pap. 6.95 (ISBN 0-686-95037-2). ADL.
National Council of Architectural Registration Boards. NCARB Architect Registration Examination Handbook. (Illus.). 177p. 1983. pap. text ed. 40.00 (ISBN 0-9607310-1-6). NCARB.
National Council of Jewish Women. Adolescent Girls in the Juvenile Justice System Survey Kit. 1982. pap. text ed. 3.50 (ISBN 0-686-91873-8). NCJW.
National Council of Jewish Women Greater Detroit Section. Fiddler in the Kitchen. Schonwetter, Norma, ed. (Illus.). 192p. 1982. pap. 8.50 (ISBN 0-939114-76-3). Wimmer Bks.
National Council of Teachers of English. English for Today, Book 4: Our Changing Technology. 2nd ed. (Illus.). 184p. (gr. 9-12). 1975. pap. text ed. 9.12 (ISBN 0-07-045813-8, W); tchr's. manual 4.40 (ISBN 0-07-045812-X); cassettes 45.96 (ISBN 0-07-045834-0). McGraw.
--English for Today, Book 5: Our Changing Culture. 2nd ed. (gr. 10-12). 1976. 9.12 (ISBN 0-07-045816-2, W); tchr's. manual 4.40 (ISBN 0-07-045815-4); cassettes 45.96 (ISBN 0-07-045835-9). McGraw.
--English for Today, Book 6: Literature in English. 2nd ed. (English for Today Ser.). (Illus.). 272p. (gr. 10-12). 1975. pap. text ed. 9.12 (ISBN 0-07-045819-7, W); tchr's. manual 4.40 (ISBN 0-07-045818-9); cassettes 146.52 (ISBN 0-07-045836-7). McGraw.
--English for Tomorrow: Student's Edition, 3 Bks. 3rd ed. 1983. Bk. 1. 4.38 ea. (ISBN 0-07-046581-9). Bk. 2 (ISBN 0-07-046582-7). Bk. 3 (ISBN 0-07-046583-5). McGraw.
National Council of Teachers of Mathematics. Challenge: The Mathematically Able Student. 68p. 1981. pap. 3.50 (ISBN 0-686-95379-7). NCTM.
--Measurement in School Mathematics, 1976 Yearbook. LC 75-43533. (Illus.). 256p. 1976. 14.50 (ISBN 0-87353-018-7). NCTM.
--Microcomputers. 88p. 1981. pap. 3.50 (ISBN 0-686-95385-1). NCTM.
--Organizing for Mathematics Instruction: 1977 Yearbook. (Illus.). 256p. 1977. 14.50 (ISBN 0-87353-019-5). NCTM.
--Problem Solving in School Mathematics, 1980 Yearbook. LC 79-27145. (Illus.). 241p. 1980. 14.50 (ISBN 0-87353-162-0). NCTM.
--Teaching Problem Solving. 68p. 1982. pap. 3.50 (ISBN 0-686-95389-4). NCTM.
--Teaching Statistics & Probability: 1981 Yearbook. LC 81-1679. (Illus.). 246p. 1981. 14.50 (ISBN 0-87353-170-1). NCTM.
National Council on Governmental Accounting. Governmental Accounting & Financial Reporting Principles. (NCGA Statement 1). (Illus.). 49p. 1979. pap. 10.00 (ISBN 0-686-84258-8). Municipal.
National Data Processing Institute, Inc. Computer Concepts, 2 vols. Incl. 1969. 3rd ed. Vol. 1. pap. text ed. (ISBN 0-672-96021-4). Vol. 2 (ISBN 0-672-96023-0). pap. text ed. 16.95 ea. Bobbs.
National Election Studies Center for Political Studies, jt. auth. see Miller, Warren E.
National Federation of Abstracting & Indexing Services & American Society for Information Science. Key Papers: On the Use of Computer-Based Bibliographic Services. 1973. 15.00, members 8.00 (ISBN 0-942308-02-6). NFAIS.
National Federation of Science Abstracting and Indexing Conference - 1971. Proceedings. 1971. 15.00 (ISBN 0-942308-08-5). NFAIS.
National Food Processors Association. Laboratory Manual for Food Canners & Processors, Vol. 1 Microbiology & Processing. 3rd ed. (Illus.). 1968. 32.50 (ISBN 0-87055-027-6). AVI.
National Foundation-March of Dimes Symposium, April, 1976, New York City. Diabetes & Other Endocrine Disorders During Pregnancy & in the Newborn: Proceedings. New, Maria I. & Fiser, Robert H., Jr., eds. LC 76-21204. (Progress in Clinical & Biological Research: Vol. 10). 262p. 1976. 30.00x (ISBN 0-8451-0010-6). A R Liss.
National Gallery of Canada. (Ottawa) Catalogue of the Library of the National Gallery of Canada. 1973. Eight Vols. lib. bdg. 760.00 (ISBN 0-8161-1043-3, Hall Library). G K Hall.
National Gallery of Canada, Ottawa. Catalogue of the Library of the National Gallery of Canada, First Supplement. (Library Catalogs & Supplements Ser.). 1981. lib. bdg. 695.00 (ISBN 0-8161-0291-0, Hall Library). G K Hall.
National Geographic Society. Journey into China. (Illus.). 1982. write for info. Natl Geog.
National Geographic Society Special Publications Division. America's Spectacular Northwest. LC 80-7829. (Illus.). 200p. 1982. 13.95 (ISBN 0-295-95958-4, National Geographic). U of Wash Pr.
National Heart, Lung & Blood Institute. A Handbook of Heart Terms. LC 81-12490. (Illus.). 64p. 1982. 4.95 (ISBN 0-89490-052-8). Enslow Pubs.
National Historical Society. Fighting for Time. Davis, William C. & Wiley, Bell T., eds. LC 82-45363. (The Image of War (1861-1865) Ser.: Vol. 4). (Illus.). 464p. 1983. 39.95 (ISBN 0-385-18280-5). Doubleday.
National Housing Law Project. The Subsidized Housing Handbook: How to Provide, Preserve, & Manage Housing for Lower-Income People. 500p. (Orig.). 1982. pap. 40.00 (ISBN 0-9606098-3-0). Natl Housing Law.
National Incinerator Conference, New York City, June, 1972. Proceedings. LC 70-124402. 353p. 1972. pap. 28.00 o.p. (ISBN 0-685-25546-8, I00081). ASME.
National Incinerator Conference-1970. Proceedings. pap. 25.00 o.p. (ISBN 0-685-06529-4, I00070). ASME.
National Industrial Conference Board, Inc. Trade Associations: Their Economic Significance & Legal Status. 2nd, rev. ed. LC 25-12032. xiv, 388p. 1982. Repr. of 1925 ed. lib. bdg. 26.00 (ISBN 0-89941-164-9). W S Hein.
National Information Center for Educational Media. Index to Educational Video Tapes. LC 82-60347. 1983. pap. 78.00 (ISBN 0-89320-053-0). Univ SC Natl Info.
--Index to Environmental Studies - Multimedia. 2nd ed. LC 79-66630. 1980. pap. 40.00 o.p. (ISBN 0-89320-041-7). Univ SC Natl Info.
--Index to Producers & Distributors. LC 82-60346. 1983. pap. 34.00 (ISBN 0-89320-055-7). Univ SC Natl Info.
--Index to Psychology - Multimedia. 4th ed. LC 79-66627. 1980. pap. 55.00 o.p. (ISBN 0-89320-038-7). Univ SC Natl Info.
--Index to 16mm Educational Film. LC 82-60348. 1983. pap. 164.00 (ISBN 0-89320-052-2). Univ SC Natl Info.
--Index to 35mm Educational Filmstrips. 1983. pap. 124.00 (ISBN 0-89320-054-9). Univ SC Natl Info.
--NICEM Update on Nonbook Media, 1981-82, 4 vols. (Orig.). 1981. pap. 128.00 (ISBN 0-89320-051-4). Univ SC Natl Info.
--NICSEM Special Education Thesaurus. 2nd ed. LC 80-83509. 1980. pap. 16.00 (ISBN 0-89320-048-4). Univ SC Natl Info.
--Special Education Index to Learner Materials. LC 79-84454. 462p. 1979. pap. 60.00 o.p. (ISBN 0-89320-024-7). Univ SC Natl Info.
National Information Center for Special Education Materials (NICSEM) NICSEM Mini-Index to Special Education Materials: Family Life & Sex Education. LC 80-82538. 1980. pap. 16.00 (ISBN 0-89320-043-3). Univ SC Natl Info.
--Special Education Index to Inservice Training Materials. LC 79-84458. (Orig.). 1980. pap. 12.00 o.p. (ISBN 0-89320-027-1). Univ. SC Natl Info.
National Institute for Social Work. Social Workers: Their Role & Tasks. 283p. 1982. pap. text ed. 12.25x (ISBN 0-7199-1080-3, Pub. by Bedford England). Renouf.
National Institutes of Health, the Chicago Heart Association & the University of Chicago, et al. Uterine & Placental Blood Flow: Proceedings. Moawad, Atef M. & Lindheimer, Marshall D., eds. LC 81-23625. (Illus.). 216p. 1982. text ed. 44.50 (ISBN 0-89352-146-9). Masson Pub.
National Invitational Conference on the Independent Student. Who Pays? Who Benefits? LC 74-21679. 1974. pap. 4.00 o.p. (ISBN 0-87447-100-1, 235963). College Bd.
National Lampoon Editors, ed. The Job of Sex. (Illus.). 1974. pap. 2.25 o.p. (ISBN 0-446-92837-2). Warner Bks.
National Lawyers Guild. Employee & Union Member Guide to Labor Law. LC 81-10090. 1981. looseleaf 67.50 (ISBN 0-87632-113-9). Boardman.
--Immigration Law & Defense. 2nd ed. LC 79-9735. 1979. looseleaf with 1981 revision incl. 70.00 (ISBN 0-87632-109-0). Boardman.
--Representation of Witnesses Before Federal Grand Juries. LC 76-20443. 1976. looseleaf with 1981 rev. pages 60.00 (ISBN 0-87632-107-4). Boardman.
National League for Nursing. Criteria for Departments of Nursing in Acute Care Settings: A Guide for Self-Appraisal. 2nd, rev. ed. 85p. 1980. 5.95 (ISBN 0-686-38289-7, 20-1714). Natl League Nurse.
--Criteria for Departments of Nursing in Long-Term Care Settings: A Guide for Self-Appraisal. 2nd, rev. ed. 85p. 1980. 5.95 (ISBN 0-686-38291-9, 20-1830). Natl League Nurse.
--Toward Excellence in Nursing Education: A Guide for Diploma School Improvement. 3rd ed. 58p. 1977. cancelled (ISBN 0-686-38282-X, 16-1656). Natl League Nurse.

National Library of Anthropology & History, Mexico City. Catalogo de la Biblioteca Nacional de Antropologia y Historia - Catalogs of the National Library of Anthropology & History, 10 vols. 1972. Set. lib. bdg. 950.00 (ISBN 0-8161-0918-4, Hall Library). G K Hall.

National Library of Australia. Australian National Bibliography 1981. 21st ed. LC 63-33739. 1231p. 1982. 67.50x (ISBN 0-8002-3014-0). Intl Pubns Serv.

National Library of Ireland. Manuscript Sources for the History of Irish Civilisation: First Supplement, 3 vols. MacLochlainn, Alf, ed. 1979. Set. lib. bdg. 375.00 (ISBN 0-8161-0248-1, Hall Library). G K Hall.

National Library Of Ireland - Dublin. Manuscript Sources for the History of Irish Civilisation, 11 Vols. 1965. Set. lib. bdg. 1045.00 (ISBN 0-8161-0662-2, Hall Library). G K Hall.

--Sources for the History of Irish Civilisation: Articles in Irish Periodicals, 9 vols. 1970. Set. 950.00 (ISBN 0-8161-0858-7, Hall Library). G K Hall.

National Library of New Zealand, ed. New Zealand National Bibliography 1980. 15th ed. LC 73-640530. 565p. (Orig.). 1981. pap. 35.00x (ISBN 0-8002-3003-5). Intl Pubns Serv.

National Library of Peru. Author Catalog of the Peruvian Collection of the National Library of Peru, 6 vols. De Gaviria, Maria C., ed. 1979. Set. lib. bdg. 655.00 (ISBN 0-8161-0250-3, Hall Library). G K Hall.

National Machine Tool Builders Association. Shop Math. (NMTBA Shop Practices Ser.). 160p. 1983. text ed. 10.95 (ISBN 0-471-07841-7). Wiley.

National Opinion Research Center. General Social Survey, 1976. 1977. codebk. write for info. o.p. (ISBN 0-89138-158-9). ICPSR.

National Park Foundation. The Complete Guide to America's National Parks. 1982. 7.95 (ISBN 0-9603410-2-1). Viking Pr.

National Passive Solar Conference, 2nd Conference, Philadelphia, 1978. Passive Solar State of the Art: Proceedings, 3 vols. Prowler, Don, ed. LC 78-61242. 1978. Set. pap. text ed. 60.00x (ISBN 0-89553-008-2). Am Solar Energy.

National Passive Solar Conference, 3rd, San Jose, 1979. Proceedings. Miller, Harry, et al, eds. 1979. pap. text ed. 78.00x (ISBN 0-89553-015-5). Am Solar Energy.

National Passive Solar Conference, 4th, Kansas City, 1979. Proceedings. Franta, Gregory E., ed. pap. text ed. 78.00x (ISBN 0-89553-018-X). Am Solar Energy.

National Passive Solar Conference, 5th, Amherst, 1980. Proceedings, 2 vols. Hayes, John & Snyder, Rachel, eds. (Illus.). 1980. Set. pap. text ed. 150.00x (ISBN 0-89553-025-2). Am Solar Energy.

National Press Club Of Washington. Dateline: Washington, the Story of National Affairs Journalism in the Life & Times of the National Press Club. Phillips, Cabell, et al, eds. Repr. of 1949 ed. lib. bdg. 20.00x (ISBN 0-8371-0183-2, NPCW). Greenwood.

National Press Photographers Association & University of Missouri School of Journalism. The Best of Photojournalism, No. 7: Newspaper & Magazine Pictures of the Year. Hampton, Veita J., ed. (Illus.). 256p. (Orig.). 1982. lib. bdg. 19.80 (ISBN 0-89471-180-6); pap. 12.95 (ISBN 0-89471-179-2). Running Pr.

National Radio Institute Staff. Servicing Electrical Appliances. Ruel, O. J. & Nolte, R. C., eds. Incl. Vol. 1. Electrical Fundamentals & Heat-Producing Items. text ed. 18.95 (ISBN 0-07-046128-7); Vol. 2. Motor Theory & Motor-Driven Items. text ed. 18.95 (ISBN 0-07-046129-5). 1972. McGraw.

National Referral Center in the Library of Congress. A Directory of Information Resources in the United States: Geosciences & Oceanography. LC 81-607045. xx, 375p. 1981. pap. 8.50 (ISBN 0-8444-0372-5). Lib Congress.

National Register Publishing Co. Directory of Corporate Affiliations. LC 67-22770. 1300p. 1983. 237.00 (ISBN 0-87217-002-0). Natl Register.

--The Official Museum Directory. LC 79-144805. 1983. 67.00 (ISBN 0-87217-005-5). Natl Register.

--Standard Directory of Advertisers: Classified Edition. LC 5-21147. 1982. 151.00 (ISBN 0-87217-000-4). Natl Register.

--Standard Directory of Advertisers: Geographical Edition. LC 15-21147. 1982. 151.00 (ISBN 0-87217-001-2). Natl Register.

--Standard Directory of Advertising Agencies, 3 vols. LC 66-6149. 1982. 70.00 ea.; 183.00 set (ISBN 0-87217-003-9). Natl Register.

National Research Council. Introductory Meteorology. 1918. 39.50x (ISBN 0-686-51405-X). Elliots Bks.

National Research Council Assembly of Behavioral & Social Sciences. Ability Testing: Uses, Consequences, & Controversies, 2 vols, Pt. I. 1982. Set. pap. text ed. 34.95 (ISBN 0-309-03199-0); Pt. I. pap. text ed. 13.95 (ISBN 0-309-03223-8); Pt. II. pap. text ed. 24.95 (ISBN 0-309-03229-6). Natl Acad Pr.

National Research Council of Canada, Sept. 11-15, 1967. Wind Effects on Building & Structures: Proceedings, 2 Vols. LC 76-358270. 1968. 37.50x (ISBN 0-8020-3213-3). U of Toronto Pr.

National Research Council on Diet, Nutrition & Cancer. Diet, Nutrition, & Cancer. 1982. pap. text ed. 13.50 (ISBN 0-309-03280-6). Natl Acad Pr.

National Retail Merchants Association. Telecommunications User's Handbook. 70p. 1978. 15.00 (ISBN 0-686-98125-1). Telecom Lib.

National Retired Teachers Association & American Association of Retired Persons. Learning About Aging. LC 81-1599. 72p. 1981. pap. 5.00 (ISBN 0-8389-0324-X). ALA.

National Safety Council. Making Safety Work. (gr. 8-9). 1976. text ed. 13.96 (ISBN 0-07-046085-X, G); teacher's manual & key 1.00 (ISBN 0-07-046086-8). McGraw.

National Safety Council, jt. auth. see American Hospital Association.

National School of Mines. Federal Mine Electrical Certification: Surface & Underground. LC 79-87486. 1979. text ed. 35.00 o.p. (ISBN 0-930206-02-9). M-A Pr.

National Society of Colonial Dames of America. Behind the Maryland Scene: Women of Influence 1600-1800. (Illus.). 113p. 1977. pap. 7.50 (ISBN 0-686-36714-6). Md Hist.

National Society of Patient Representatives of the American Hospital Association. Assessing the Patient Representative Program. LC 80-28949. (Illus., Orig.). 1981. pap. 8.00 (ISBN 0-87258-334-1, AHA-157148). Am Hospital.

National Society of the Colonial Dames of America. American War Songs. LC 73-156922. 1974. Repr. of 1925 ed. 34.00x (ISBN 0-8103-3722-3). Gale.

--Catalogue of the Genealogical & Historical Library of the Colonial Dames of the State of New York. LC 76-149778. 1971. Repr. of 1912 ed. 58.00x (ISBN 0-8103-3713-4). Gale.

National Symposium. The Profession in Private Practice (Surveying, Photogrammetry) Proceedings of the National Symposium, 1982. 1983. 15.00 (ISBN 0-937294-43-8). ASP.

National Task Force on Citizenship Education. Education for Responsible Citizenship: A National Task Force Report. 1977. text ed. 17.95 o.p. (ISBN 0-07-046095-7, P&RB); pap. 5.95 o.p. (ISBN 0-07-046096-5). McGraw.

National Telecommunications & Information Administration. Competition & Deregulation in International Telecommunications: An Analysis of 15 FCC Actions & Their Effects, 2 vols. 1981. 95.00 set (ISBN 0-686-37961-6). Info Gatekeepers.

National Tool, Die & Precision Machining Association. Advanced Diemaking. 1967. text ed. 24.95 (ISBN 0-07-046093-0, G). McGraw.

--Basic Diemaking: Text Edition. 1963. text ed. 24.95 (ISBN 0-07-046090-6, G). McGraw.

National Union Of Christian Schools. The Children's Hymn Book. (Illus.). 1962. 8.95x (ISBN 0-8028-9003-2, Pub. by NUCS). Eerdmans.

National Video Clearinghouse Inc. The Video Source Book. 4th ed. 1600p. 1982. 125.00 (ISBN 0-935478-18-3, Dist. by Gale). Natl Video.

National Video Clearinghouse, Inc. The Video Tape & Disc Guide to Home Entertainment. 1982. pap. 9.95 (ISBN 0-452-25381-0, Z5381, Plume). NAL.

--The Video Tape & Disc Guide to Home Entertainment. 3rd ed. 420p. 1982. 9.95 (ISBN 0-452-25381-0). Natl Video.

National Vocational Guidance Association & American Vocational Association, eds. Career Development. 1971. 1.00 (ISBN 0-686-36412-0, 72205); nonmembers 1.25 (ISBN 0-686-37310-3). Am Personnel.

National Vocational Guidance Association. Guidelines for the Preparation & Evaluation of Nonprint Career Media. 1977. 1.00 (ISBN 0-686-36417-1, 72214). Am Personnel.

National Water Well Association. Water Well Technology: Field Principles of Exploration & Drilling for Ground Water & Other Selected Minerals. 600p. 1973. 49.50 (ISBN 0-07-046097-3, P&RB). McGraw.

National Workshop Bloomington, MN 1979. Proceedings. pap. 5.00 (ISBN 0-686-36556-9). Assn Interp Naturalist.

National Workshop, Cape Cod, Mass. 1980. Program Papers: Proceedings. 18.00 (ISBN 0-686-36557-7). Assn Interp Naturalist.

National Workshop Estes Park, CO 1981. Program Papers: Proceedings. 10.00 (ISBN 0-686-36558-5). Assn Interp Naturalist.

Nations, D. The Record of Geologic Time: A Vicarious Trip. (McGraw-Hill Concepts in Introductory Geology). (Illus.). 80p. 1975. text ed. 15.95x (ISBN 0-07-012326-8, C); slides 75.00 (ISBN 0-07-074427-0). McGraw.

Natke, H. G., ed. Identification of Vibrating Structures. (CISM - International Centre for Mechanical Sciences Courses & Lectures Ser.: Vol. 272). (Illus.). 510p. 1982. pap. 36.90 (ISBN 0-387-81651-8). Springer-Verlag.

Natkiel, Richard. Atlas of the Twentieth Century. (Illus.). 256p. 1982. 29.95 (ISBN 0-87196-612-3). Facts on File.

Nato Advanced Study Institution, et al. Cytopharmacology of Secretion: Proceedings. Ceccarelli, B., et al, eds. LC 74-76090. (Advances in Cytopharmacology Ser: Vol. 2). 400p. 1974. 64.50 (ISBN 0-911216-58-8). Raven.

Natoli, Joseph. Twentieth Century Blake Criticism: Northrop Fyre to the Present. LC 80-9021. 375p. 1982. lib. bdg. 45.00 (ISBN 0-8240-9326-7). Garland Pub.

Natow, A. B. & Heslin, J. Nutrition for the Prime of Your Life. 352p. 1983. 17.95 (ISBN 0-07-028414-8, GB). McGraw.

Nattrass, Jill. The South African Economy: Its Growth & Change. (Illus.). 348p. 1981. text ed. 24.95x (ISBN 0-19-570194-1). Oxford U Pr.

Nattrass, Karen & Morrison, Bonnie M. Human Needs in Housing: An Ecological Approach. 1977. pap. text ed. 9.75 (ISBN 0-8191-0094-3). U Pr of Amer.

Natu, Bal. Glimpses of the God-Man, Meher Baba: Vol. III, February 1952 - February 1953. LC 79-913293. (Illus.). 344p. (Orig.). 1982. pap. 7.95 (ISBN 0-913078-44-1). Sheriar Pr.

Natu, Waman R. Regulation of Forward Markets. 12.95x (ISBN 0-210-34069-X). Asia.

Natural Resources & Energy Division, U. N. Dept. of Technical Co-Operation for Development. The Development Potential of Precambrian Mineral Deposits. (Illus.). 435p. 1982. 65.00 (ISBN 0-08-027193-6). Pergamon.

Naturalization, jt. auth. see President's Commission On Immigration.

Natusch, David F. & Hopke, Philip K. Analytical Aspects of Environmental Chemistry. (Chemical Analysis Monographs). 272p. 1983. 40.00x (ISBN 0-471-04324-9, Pub. by Wiley Interscience). Wiley.

Nau, Henry R. Technology Transfer & U.S. Foreign Policy. LC 76-2908. (Illus.). 1976. 34.95 o.p. (ISBN 0-275-56790-7). Praeger.

Nau, Robert H. Basic Electrical Engineering. LC 58-5633. 1958. 25.95 (ISBN 0-471-07212-5); instr's manual 5.00 (ISBN 0-471-07582-5). Wiley.

Naughton, T. Raymond, jt. auth. see Goebel, Julius.

Naugle, Helen H. Regents' Examination Preparation Guide. 1979. pap. text ed. 4.95 (ISBN 0-8403-2091-4). Kendall-Hunt.

Nault, Marianne. Saul Bellow: His Works & His Critics; an Annotated International Bibliography. LC 76-24738. (Reference Library of the Humanities Ser.: Vol. 59). 1977. lib. bdg. 22.50 o.s.i. (ISBN 0-8240-9939-7). Garland Pub.

Nauman, Eileen. American Book of Nutrition & Medical Astrology. (Illus.). 368p. (Orig.). 1982. pap. 17.95 (ISBN 0-917086-28-7, Pub. by Astro Comp Serv). Para Res.

Naumani, M. What Islam Is? 6.50 (ISBN 0-686-18477-7). Kazi Pubns.

Naumann, Jens, jt. auth. see Hufner, Klaus.

Naumburg, Margaret. An Introduction to Art Therapy: Studies of the "Free" Art Expression of Behavior Problem Children & Adolescents As a Means of Diagnosis & Therapy. rev. ed. LC 73-78074. (Illus.). 225p. 1973. text ed. 13.95x o.p. (ISBN 0-8077-2412-2); pap. text ed. 11.95x (ISBN 0-8077-2425-4). Tchrs Coll.

Naumes, William. Entrepreneurial Manager in the Small Business: Text Readings & Cases. LC 77-83029. (Illus.). 1978. text ed. 23.95 (ISBN 0-201-05201-6). A-W.

Naumov, N. P. The Ecology of Animals. Levine, Norman D., ed. Plous, Frederick K., Jr., tr. from Rus. LC 71-170965. (Illus.). 688p. 1972. 35.00 o.p. (ISBN 0-252-00219-9). U of Ill Pr.

Naunton, Robert. Fragmenta Regalia: Sixteen Thirty. Arber, Edward, ed. 272p. Date not set. pap. 17.50 (ISBN 0-87556-577-8). Saifer.

Nauroth, Holger, jt. auth. see Held, Warner.

Nauta, W. J., jt. auth. see Brady, J.

Nauta, W. T. & Rekker, R. F., eds. The Pharmacochemistry of One, Three-Indandiones. (Pharmacochemistry Library: Vol. 3). 1981. 72.50 (ISBN 0-444-41976-4). Elsevier.

Nava, Julian. Viva la Raza: Readings on Mexican Americans. 1973. pap. text ed. 4.95x (ISBN 0-442-25918-2). Van Nos Reinhold.

Navajo School Of Indian Basketry. Indian Basket Weaving. (Illus.). 1971. pap. 3.00 (ISBN 0-486-22616-6). Dover.

--Indian Basket Weaving. (Illus.). 8.00 (ISBN 0-8446-0153-5). Peter Smith.

Naval Observatory Library. Washington D.C. Catalog of the Naval Observatory Library, Washington, D.C, 6 vols. 1976. Set. lib. bdg. 490.00 (ISBN 0-8161-0031-4, Hall Library). G K Hall.

Navaretta, Cynthia. Guide to Women's Art Organizations & Directory for the Arts. rev. ed. LC 79-83876. (Illus.). 1982. pap. text ed. 8.50 (ISBN 0-9602476-3-7). Midmarch Assocs.

Navaretta, Cynthia, ed. Voices of Women: Three Critics on Three Poets on Three Heroines. LC 80-80281. (Illus.). 1980. pap. text ed. 5.50 (ISBN 0-9602476-1-0). Midmarch Assocs.

Navarette, Vincent H. The Two Most Miraculous Words in the English Language & How to Use Them Successfully. (A Human Development Library Bk.). (Illus.). 103p. 1983. 27.45 (ISBN 0-89266-395-2). Am Classical Coll Pr.

Navarra, John G. Earth, Space, & Time: An Introduction to Earth Science. LC 79-14000. 1980. text ed. 27.95x (ISBN 0-471-63061-6). Wiley.

--Earthquake. LC 79-8938. (Illus.). 96p. (gr. 6-7). 1980. 8.95a o.p. (ISBN 0-385-15080-6); PLB 8.95a (ISBN 0-385-15081-4). Doubleday.

Navarro, Antonio. Tocayo: The True Story of a Resistance Leader in Castro's Cuba. 288p. 1981. 14.95 o.p. (ISBN 0-87000-508-1, Arlington Hse). Crown.

Navarro, J. Cervos, jt. auth. see Weller, R. O.

Navarro, J. Nelson. Marine Diatoms Associated with Mangrovew Prop Roots in the Indian River, Florida, USA. (Bibliotheca Phycologica 61 Ser.). (Illus.). 151p. (Orig.). 1982. pap. text ed. 22.50 (ISBN 3-7682-1337-4). Lubrecht & Cramer.

Navarro, Jose L. Blue Day on Main Street. LC 73-88742. 1974. pap. 6.00 (ISBN 0-88412-063-5). Tonatiuh-Quinto Sol Intl.

Navarro, Vicente, ed. Policy, Politics, Health & Medicine Ser, 5 vols. (Orig.). 1983. Set. pap. text ed. 59.50 (ISBN 0-89503-026-8). Vol. 1: 160 pgs. Vol. 2: 160 pgs. Vol. 3: 288 pgs. Vol. 4: 264 pgs. Vol. 5: 312 pgs. Baywood Pub.

Navarro, Vicente & Berman, Daniel, eds. Health & Work under Capitalism: An International Perspective, Vol. 5. (Policy, Politics, Health & Medicine). 312p. 1983. pap. text ed. 16.50 (ISBN 0-89503-035-7). Baywood Pub.

Navascues, Miguel. Lecturas Modernas De Hispanoamerica: An Intermediate Spanish Reader. (Illus.). 1980. pap. text ed. 11.95 (ISBN 0-13-527804-X). P-H.

Nave, Brenda C., jt. auth. see Nave, Carl R.

Nave, Carl R. & Nave, Brenda C. Physics for the Health Sciences. 2nd ed. LC 79-64599. (Illus.). 385p. 1980. pap. text ed. 14.00 (ISBN 0-7216-6666-3). Saunders.

Nave, Patricia S., ed. see Hetherington, E. M.

Nave, Patricia S., ed. see Mahoney, E. R.

Navia, Luis E. see Capaldi, Nicholas, et al.

Navia, Luis E. & Kelly, Eugene, eds. Ethics & the Search for Values. LC 80-82123. 530p. 1980. pap. text ed. 14.95 (ISBN 0-87975-139-8). Prometheus Bks.

Navigators Staff. Growing in Discipleship. rev. ed. (Design for Discipleship Ser.: Bk. 6). 1980. pap. text ed. 1.50 (ISBN 0-934396-21-3). Churches Alive.

--Learning to Solo. LC 82-72744. 100p. 1983. pap. text ed. 3.75 (ISBN 0-934396-30-2). Churches Alive.

--Lessons on Assurance. (Growing in Christ Ser.). 32p. 1982. pap. text ed. 1.85 (ISBN 0-934396-28-0). Churches Alive.

--Walking with Christ. rev. ed. (Design for Discipleship Ser.: Bk. 3). 1980. pap. text ed. 1.50 (ISBN 0-934396-18-3). Churches Alive.

Navon, David H. Electronic Materials & Devices. 1975. text ed. 30.50 (ISBN 0-395-18917-9); solutions manual 7.50 (ISBN 0-395-19374-5). HM.

Nawab, Ali. Some Moral & Religious Teachings of Al-Ghazzali. pap. 4.50 (ISBN 0-686-18609-5). Kazi Pubns.

Nawrath, Alfred. Norway. LC 76-17134. 1976. 25.00 o.p. (ISBN 0-88331-087-2). Luce.

Nax, Beunab & Burt, Barbara J., eds. The Social Constraints on Energy-Policy Implementation. LC 81-48613. 1983. write for info. (ISBN 0-669-05466-6). Lexington Bks.

Naxon, Jan L. & Rosenthal, Beth E. Dallas Entrees: A Restaurant Guide & Celebrity Cookbook (with a Primer to California Wines) 144p. (Orig.). 1982. pap. 5.95 (ISBN 0-910163-00-6). Artichoke Pub.

Nay, Joe N. & Kay, Peg. Government Oversight & Evaluability Assessment: Its Always More Expensive When the Carpenter Types. LC 81-47750. 272p. 1982. 29.95x (ISBN 0-669-04833-X). Lexington Bks.

Nayagam, Xavier T. Tamil Culture & Civilisation: Readings, the Classical Period. 1971. 8.95x o.p. (ISBN 0-210-98163-6). Asia.

Nayanar, E. K. My Struggles: An Autobiography. 200p. 1982. text ed. 25.00x (ISBN 0-7069-1973-4, Pub. by Vikas India). Advent NY.

Nayar, Kuldip. Between the Lines. 1969. 5.00x o.p. (ISBN 0-8188-1096-3). Paragon.

Nayfeh, Ali H. Introduction to Perturbation Techniques. LC 80-15233. 475p. 1980. 40.95 (ISBN 0-471-08033-0, Pub. by Wiley-Interscience). Wiley.

Nayfeh, Ali H. & Mook, Dean T. Nonlinear Oscillations. LC 78-27102. (Pure & Applied Mathematics Texts, Monographs & Tracts). 1979. 54.95x (ISBN 0-471-03555-6, Pub. by Wiley-Interscience). Wiley.

Nayfeh, Ali-Hasan. Perturbation Methods. LC 72-8068. (Pure & Applied Mathematics Ser). 496p. 1973. 35.50x (ISBN 0-471-63059-4, Pub. by Wiley-Interscience). Wiley.

Nayler, G. H., jt. auth. see Nayler, J. L.

Nayler, J. L. & Nayler, G. H. Dictionary of Mechanical Engineering. 2nd ed. 1978. Repr. of 1975 ed. 29.95 (ISBN 0-408-00175-5). Butterworth.

Nayler, J. L., jt. auth. see Ower, E.

Naylor, A. W. & Sell, G. R. Linear Operator Theory in Engineering & Science. (Applied Mathematical Sciences Ser.: Vol. 40). (Illus.). 624p. 1982. 28.00 (ISBN 0-387-90748-3). Springer-Verlag.

Naylor, Audrey, jt. auth. see Provence, Sally.

Naylor, C. W. Heart Talks. 279p. 1982. pap. 2.50 (ISBN 0-686-36257-8). Faith Pub Hse.

Naylor, Charles, jt. auth. see Disch, Thomas M.

Naylor, Charles, jt. ed. see Disch, Thomas M.

Naylor, Colin, ed. Contemporary Artists. LC 76-54627. (Illus.). 1077p. 55.00x (ISBN 0-686-75645-2, Pub. by St James). Gale.

Naylor, Colin, jt. auth. see Held, Michael.

Naylor, D. & Shannon, P. Geology of Offshore Ireland & West Britain. 250p. 1983. 42.00x (ISBN 0-8448-1425-3). Crane-Russak Co.

Naylor, E. British Marine Isopods. (Synopses of the British Fauna Ser.). 1972. 4.50 o.s.i. (ISBN 0-12-515150-0). Acad Pr.

Naylor, E. W. An Elizabethan Virginal Book. LC 70-87638. (Music Ser). 1970. Repr. of 1905 ed. lib. bdg. 27.50 (ISBN 0-306-71792-1). Da Capo.

--An Elizabethan Virginal Book. (Keyboard Studies Ser.: Vol. 1). (Illus.). 1981. Repr. of 1905 ed. 32.50 o.s.i. (ISBN 90-6027-304-4, Pub. by Frits Knuf Netherlands). Pendragon NY.

Naylor, Edward W. Shakespeare & Music. LC 65-16244. (Music Ser). 1965. Repr. of 1931 ed. lib. bdg. 22.50 (ISBN 0-306-70908-2). Da Capo.

Naylor, Edward W., ed. Shakespeare Music. LC 75-171080. 68p. 1973. Repr. of 1927 ed. lib. bdg. 16.50 (ISBN 0-306-70275-4). Da Capo.

Naylor, Gloria. The Women of Brewster Place. (Contemporary American Fiction Ser.). 1983. pap. 5.95 (ISBN 0-14-006690-X). Penguin.

Naylor, K. Africa: The Nile Route. 160p. (Orig.). 1983. pap. 9.95 (ISBN 0-933982-26-7, Lascelles). Bradt Ent.

Naylor, Natalie A., jt. auth. see Kniker, Charles R.

Naylor, Paz B., ed. Austronesian Studies: Papers from the Second Eastern Conference on Austronesian Languages. LC 79-87814. (Michigan Papers on South & Southeast Asia: No. 15). xi, 314p. (Orig.). 1980. pap. 10.50x (ISBN 0-89148-015-3). Ctr S&SE Asian.

Naylor, Phyllis. Crazy Love. 1978. pap. 1.95 o.p. (ISBN 0-451-08077-7, J8077, Sig). NAL.

Naylor, Phyllis R. A String of Chances. LC 82-1790. 252p. (gr. 5 up). 1982. 10.95 (ISBN 0-689-30935-X). Atheneum.

Naylor, T. H., ed. Corporate Strategy: The Integration of Corporate Planning Models & Economics. (Studies in Management Science & Systems: Vol. 8). 210p. 1982. 36.25 (ISBN 0-444-86331-1). Elsevier.

Naylor, Thomas H. Corporate Planning Models. LC 77-93329. 1978. text ed. 27.95 (ISBN 0-201-05226-1). A-W.

Naylor, Thomas H., ed. Simulation in Business & Decision Making. (SCS Simulation Ser.: Vol. 9, No. 1). 30.00 (ISBN 0-686-36675-1). Soc Computer Sim.

Naylor, Thomas H., et al. Computer Simulation Techniques. LC 66-17622. 1966. 32.95 (ISBN 0-471-63060-8). Wiley.

--Managerial Economics: Corporate Economics & Strategy. (Illus.). 464p. 1983. text ed. 26.95x (ISBN 0-07-045947-9, C); instr.'s manual 10.00 (ISBN 0-07-045948-7). McGraw.

Nayman, Jacqueline. Atlas of Wildlife. LC 78-38034. (John Day Bk.). (Illus.). 128p. 1972. 14.37i (ISBN 0-381-98162-2, A06070). T y Crowell.

Nayyar, D. India's Exports & Export Policies in the 1960's. LC 75-46206. (South Asian Studies). (Illus.). 378p. 1977. 49.50 (ISBN 0-521-21135-2). Cambridge U Pr.

Nba, Nina E. Nigerian Women Mobilized: Women's Political Activity in Southern Nigeria, 1900-1965. LC 82-15477. (Research Ser.: No. 48). (Illus.). xii, 348p. 1982. pap. 12.95x (ISBN 0-87725-148-7). U of Cal Intl St.

NCHS. State Estimates of Disability & Utilization of Medical Services, 1969-1971 Derived from the United States Health Interview Survey. (Ser. 10: No. 108). 55p. 1976. pap. 1.50 (ISBN 0-8406-0076-3). Natl. Ctr Health Stats.

Ndibalema, Charles. Fimbo Ya Ulimwengu. (Swahili Literature). (Swahili.). 1978. pap. text ed. 2.50x o.p. (ISBN 0-686-74444-6, 00611). Heinemann Ed.

Nead, Benjamin M., et al. Bd. With Valley Forge & the Pennsylvania Germans: And Pennsylvania German Dialect Writings & Their Writers, Vol. 26. Repr. of 1918 ed. 30.00 (ISBN 0-911122-05-2). Penn German Soc.

Nead, Daniel W., jt. auth. see Sachse, Julius F.

Neagley, Ross L. & Evans, N. Dean. Handbook for Effective Supervision of Instruction. 3rd ed. 1980. text ed. 24.95 (ISBN 0-13-372672-X). P-H.

Neal. Custom Draperies in Interior Design. 1982. 24.95 (ISBN 0-444-00640-0). Elsevier.

Neal, A. L. Chemistry & Biochemistry: A Comprehensive Introduction. 1971. text ed. 18.95 o.p. (ISBN 0-07-046135-X, C). McGraw.

Neal, Alfred C. Business Power & Public Policy. 176p. 1981. 24.95 (ISBN 0-03-059586-X); pap. 12.95 (ISBN 0-03-060268-8). Praeger.

Neal, Arminta. Exhibits for the Small Museum: A Handbook. LC 76-21812. (Illus.). 1976. pap. 10.00 (ISBN 0-910050-23-6). AASLH.

Neal, Arthur G. Social Psychology: A Sociology Perspective. 544p. 1983. text ed. 19.95 (ISBN 0-201-05361-6). A-W.

Neal, Avon. Scarecrows. (Illus.). 1978. 12.95 o.p. (ISBN 0-517-53500-9, C N Potter Bks). Crown.

Neal, Avon & Parker, Ann. Early American Stone Sculpture Found in the Burying Grounds of New England. (Illus.). 116p. 1982. full leather 650.00 (ISBN 0-941438-03-1); half leather 395.00 (ISBN 0-941438-04-X). Sweetwater Edns.

Neal, Avon, jt. auth. see Parker, Ann.

Neal, B. G. The Plastic Methods of Structural Analysis: SI Version. 3rd ed. 1977. 15.95x (ISBN 0-412-21450-4, Pub. by Chapman & Hall). Methuen Inc.

Neal, B. G., ed. see Cheung, Y. K.

Neal, Charles L. Parabolas del Evangelio. 144p. pap. 2.50 (ISBN 0-311-04338-0). Casa Bautista.

Neal, Daniel. History of the Puritans, 3 vols. 1979. 54.95 (ISBN 0-86524-011-6, 9401). Klock & Klock.

Neal, Emily G. The Healing Power of Christ. 1972. pap. 4.50 o.p. (ISBN 0-8015-3348-1, Hawthorn). Dutton.

Neal, Ernest. Badgers. (Illus.). 1978. 19.95 o.p. (ISBN 0-7137-0816-6, Pub. by Blandford Pr England). Sterling.

Neal, Fred W., ed. Detente or Debacle: Common Sense U. S.-Soviet Relations. (Illus.). 1979. 10.95 (ISBN 0-393-05706-2); pap. text ed. 3.95x 1978 (ISBN 0-393-95008-5). Norton.

Neal, Harry E. The Secret Service in Action. (Illus.). (gr. 6 up). 1980. 8.95 (ISBN 0-525-66665-6). Lodestar Bks.

--The Story of Offshore Oil. LC 77-11175. (Illus.). 64p. (gr. 3 up). 1977. PLB 6.97 o.p. (ISBN 0-671-32888-3). Messner.

Neal, Helen. The Politics of Pain. LC 78-6168. 1978. 9.95 o.p. (ISBN 0-07-046140-6, GB). McGraw.

Neal, John. Rachel Dyer. LC 64-10667. 1979. Repr. of 1828 ed. 34.00x (ISBN 0-8201-1263-1). Schol Facsimiles.

Neal, Julia. The Kentucky Shakers. LC 76-46029. (Kentucky Bicentennial Bookshelf Ser.). (Illus.). 120p. 1977. 6.95 o.p. (ISBN 0-8131-0236-7). U Pr of Ky.

Neal, Kenneth G. & Kalbus, Barbara H. Anatomy & Physiology: A Laboratory Manual & Study Guide. 4th ed. 448p. 1983. pap. text ed. write for info. (ISBN 0-8087-1449-X). Burgess.

Neal, Kenneth G., jt. auth. see Kalbus, Barbara N.

Neal, Larry & Edginton, Chris, eds. Exetra Perspectives: Concepts in Therapeutic Recreation. 220p. 1982. 5.95 (ISBN 0-686-84021-6). U OR Ctr Leisure.

Neal, Larry L., ed. The Next Fifty Years: Health, Physical Education, Recreation, Dance. 179p. 1971. pap. 3.50 (ISBN 0-686-84034-8). U OR Ctr Leisure.

Neal, Larry L., jt. ed. see Fairchild, Effie L.

Neal, Marie C. In Gardens of Hawaii. rev. ed. (Special Publication Ser.: No. 50). (Illus.). 944p. 1965. 25.00 (ISBN 0-910240-33-7). Bishop Mus.

Neal, Patsy E. Basketball Techniques for Women. (Illus.). 1966. 19.95 o.s.i. (ISBN 0-471-07159-5). Wiley.

Neal, Peters, jt. auth. see Smith, David.

Neal, R. E., jt. auth. see Kennelly, R.

Neal-Schuman Publishers. National Directory of Mental Health. LC 80-80661. 1980. 62.50x (ISBN 0-471-03886-5, Pub. by Wiley-Interscience). Wiley.

Neal, William J., jt. auth. see Pilkey, Orrin H., Jr.

Neale, Alan D. & Goyder, D. G. Antitrust Laws of the U. S. A. 3rd ed. (Economic & Social Research Ser.: No. 19). 525p. 1981. 49.50 (ISBN 0-521-23569-3); pap. 17.95 (ISBN 0-521-28044-3). Cambridge U Pr.

Neale, Gay W. Banners Over Terre D'or. LC 82-20592. 1982. 10.95 (ISBN 0-89587-024-X). Blair.

Neale, John E. Queen Elizabeth First. 1959. 16.95 o.p. (ISBN 0-312-65940-7). St Martin.

Neale, John M. & Liebert, Robert M. Science & Behavior: An Introduction to the Methods of Research. 2nd ed. (Ser. in Social Learning Theory). (Illus.). 1980. text ed. 23.95 (ISBN 0-13-795195-7). P-H.

Neale, John M. & Oltmanns, Thomas F. Schizophrenia. LC 80-10169. 1980. text ed. 29.95 (ISBN 0-471-63086-1). Wiley.

Neale, John M., jt. auth. see Liebert, Robert M.

Neale, R. S. Class & Ideology in the Nineteenth Century. 1972. 19.95x (ISBN 0-7100-7331-3). Routledge & Kegan.

Neale, R. S., jt. auth. see Kamenka, E.

Neale, R. S., jt. ed. see Kamenka, Eugene.

Neale, Stephen see Eaton, Mick.

Neale-Silva, Eduardo. Cesar Vallejo en su fase trilcica. 664p. 1975. pap. 27.50 (ISBN 0-299-06774-2). U of Wis Pr.

Neale-Silva, Eduardo & Nicholas, Robert L. Adelante! A Cultural Approach to Intermediate Spanish. 2nd ed. 1981. text ed. 19.95x o.p. (ISBN 0-673-15412-2); pap. text ed. 7.95x wkbk. o.p. (ISBN 0-673-15440-8). Scott F.

--En Camino! A Cultural Approach to Beginning Spanish. 2nd ed. 1981. text ed. 19.95x o.p. (ISBN 0-673-15411-4); pap. text ed. 7.95x wkbk. o.p. (ISBN 0-673-15441-6). Scott F.

Neall, Beatrice S. The Concept of Character in the Apocalypse with Implications for Character Education. LC 82-23843. 236p. (Orig.). 1983. lib. bdg. 21.50 (ISBN 0-8191-2983-6); pap. text ed. 10.75 (ISBN 0-8191-2984-4). U Pr of Amer.

Nealy, William. Kayaks to Hell. (Illus.). 144p. (Orig.). 1982. pap. 4.95 (ISBN 0-89732-010-7). Thomas Pr.

Neame, Alan, jt. auth. see Stanley, Richard.

Near, D., jt. auth. see Brendel, LeRoy A.

Near, Doris, jt. auth. see Brendel, LeRoy A.

Near, Doris, jt. auth. see Brendel, Leroy A.

Near, Jean H. G. A Genealogical Study of the Descendants of Joshua & Anna Gowan. (Illus.). 559p. 1982. 75.00 (ISBN 0-9609166-0-1). J Near.

Nearing, Helen. Simple Food for the Good Life. 1980. 13.00 (ISBN 0-686-30489-6); pap. 5.00. Soc Sci Inst.

--Simple Food for the Good Life: An Alternative Cook Book. 1980. 12.95 o.s.i. (ISBN 0-440-08479-2). Delacorte.

--Wise Words on the Good Life. 1980. 10.00 (ISBN 0-686-73458-0); pap. 6.00. Soc Sci Inst.

Nearing, Helen & Nearing, Scott. Building & Using Our Sun-Heated Greenhouse: Grow Vegetables All Year-Round. LC 77-13234. (Illus.). 1977. 11.95 o.p. (ISBN 0-88266-112-4); pap. 7.95 o.p. (ISBN 0-88266-111-6). Garden Way Pub.

--Continuing the Good Life: Half a Century of Homesteading. LC 78-21151. (Illus.). 1979. 9.95 (ISBN 0-8052-3703-8); pap. 4.95 (ISBN 0-8052-0642-6). Schocken.

--The Maple Sugar Book: Together with Remarks on Pioneering As a way of Living in the Twentieth Century. LC 73-148417. (Illus.). 1971. 8.95 (ISBN 0-8052-3400-4); pap. 5.95 (ISBN 0-8052-0308-7). Schocken.

Nearing, Helen, jt. auth. see Nearing, Scott.

Nearing, Helen K. Wise Words on the Good Life: An Anthology of Quotations. LC 80-14809. 160p. 1980. 9.95 (ISBN 0-8052-3753-4); pap. 5.95 (ISBN 0-8052-0725-2). Schocken.

Nearing, Helen K., jt. auth. see Nearing, Scott.

Nearing, Scott & Nearing, Helen. Our Sun-Heated Greenhouse. (Illus.). 8.00 (ISBN 0-685-51041-7). Soc Sci Inst.

Nearing, Scott & Nearing, Helen K. Building & Using Our Sun-Heated Greenhouse. (Illus.). 1979. pap. 8.00 (ISBN 0-686-57438-9). Soc Sci Inst.

Nearing, Scott, jt. auth. see Nearing, Helen.

Neat, K. P., tr. see Averbakh, Y. & Checkover, V.

Neat, K. P., tr. see Estrin, Y. B. & Glaskov, I. B.

Neatby, L. H. Discovery in Russian & Siberian Waters. LC 72-85535. (Illus.). 226p. 1973. 15.00x (ISBN 0-8214-0124-6, 82-81263). Ohio U Pr.

Neathery, Raymond F. Applied Strength of Materials. LC 81-14732. 419p. 1982. text ed. 24.95x (ISBN 0-471-07991-X); solutions manual 10.50 (ISBN 0-471-86323-8). Wiley.

Neave, Airey. On Trial at Nuremberg. LC 78-25626. (Illus.). 1979. 12.95 (ISBN 0-316-59930-1). Little.

Neave, Edwin H. & Wiginton, John C. Financial Management: Theory & Strategies. (Illus.). 416p. 1981. text ed. 25.95 (ISBN 0-13-316109-9). P-H.

Nebeker, Helen. Jean Rhys: Woman in Passage. 250p. (Orig.). 1981. pap. 8.95 (ISBN 0-920792-04-9). Eden Pr.

Nebel, Bernard J. Environmental Science: The Way the World Works. (Illus.). 1980. text ed. 25.95 (ISBN 0-13-283002-7). P-H.

Nebel, Cecile & Fales, Frederick F. French Grammar. (College Outlines Ser.). pap. 4.95 o.p. (ISBN 0-671-08032-6). Monarch Pr.

Nebel, Frederick. Six Deadly Dames. 1980. lib. bdg. 10.95 (ISBN 0-8398-2654-0, Gregg). G K Hall.

Nebel, Henry M., Jr., tr. Selected Aesthetic Works of Sumarokov & Karamzin. LC 81-40577. 156p. 1982. lib. bdg. 21.25 (ISBN 0-8191-1909-1); pap. text ed. 10.25 (ISBN 0-8191-1910-5). U Pr of Amer.

Nebergall, William H., et al. College Chemistry with Qualitative Analysis. 6th ed. 1980. text ed. 29.95x (ISBN 0-669-02217-9); instr's. manual 1.95 (ISBN 0-669-02475-9); study guide 9.95 (ISBN 0-669-02474-0); basic laboratory studies 12.95 (ISBN 0-669-02473-2); problems & solutions manual 9.95 (ISBN 0-669-02472-4); problems & sol. supp 1.95 (ISBN 0-669-04364-8). Heath.

--General Chemistry. 6th ed. 1980. text ed. 29.95x (ISBN 0-669-02218-7); instrs'. manual 1.95 (ISBN 0-669-02475-9); study guide 8.95 (ISBN 0-669-02474-0); basic lab. studies 10.95 (ISBN 0-669-02473-2); problems & solutions manual 8.95 (ISBN 0-669-02472-4); problems & sol. supp. 1.95 (ISBN 0-669-04364-8). Heath.

Neblett, William. The Role of Feelings in Morals. LC 81-40105. 114p. (Orig.). 1981. lib. bdg. 19.50 (ISBN 0-8191-1752-8); pap. text ed. 8.75 (ISBN 0-8191-1753-6). U Pr of Amer.

Nebold, Mary A., et al. Clothing Fabrication. 2nd ed. (Illus.). 1978. pap. text ed. 9.95 (ISBN 0-8403-0977-5). Kendall-Hunt.

Nebraska Curriculum Development Center. Nebraska Curriculum for English, Grade 10: Units 99-100, Man & Moral Law. (Nebraska Curriculum for English Ser). (Orig.). 1970. pap. 3.00x tchrs' manual (ISBN 0-8032-7531-5); pap. 3.25x student manual (ISBN 0-8032-7532-3). U of Nebr Pr.

--Nebraska Curriculum for English: Grade 7, Units 71-72, the Rhetoric of Literature. (Nebraska Curriculum for English Ser). 1967. pap. 2.50x teacher manual (ISBN 0-8032-7509-9); pap. 5.25x student manual (ISBN 0-8032-7510-2). U of Nebr Pr.

--Nebraska Curriculum for English, Grade 9: Units 94-96, Language & Its Written Uses. (Nebraska Curriculum for English Ser). 1969. pap. 4.25x student's manual (ISBN 0-8032-7528-5); 3.50x, teachers manual (ISBN 0-8032-7527-7). U of Nebr Pr.

Necas, J. & Hlavacek, I. Mathematical Theory of Elastic & Elasto-Plastic Bodies: An Introduction. (Studies in Applied Mechanics: Vol. 3). 1981. 64.00 (ISBN 0-444-99754-7). Elsevier.

Necessary, James R. The Necessary Steps to Basic: A Modular Approach. 168p. 1982. pap. text ed. 5.95x (ISBN 0-917974-90-5). Waveland Pr.

Nechamkin, Howard. Chemistry of the Elements. LC 68-21849. 1968. text ed. 7.95 o.p. (ISBN 0-07-046155-4, C). McGraw.

Nechas, Jim, jt. auth. see Lowe, Carl.

Necker, Claire. The Natural History of Cats. 1977. pap. 5.95 o.s.i. (ISBN 0-440-56356-9, Delta). Dell.

Necker, Jacques. Oeuvres Completes, 1820-21, 15 vols. LC 15-20536. 1971. Repr. Set. 575.00x (ISBN 3-511-02680-6). Intl Pubns Serv.

Necker, Jacques M. The Famous Financial Statement Submitted by M. Necker to Louis XVI of France in 1781 on the Conditions of the Country Just Prior to the French Revolution. (The Most Meaningful Classics in World Culture Ser.). 105p. 1983. Repr. of 1781 ed. 117.00 (ISBN 0-89901-101-2). Found Class Reprints.

Necker, Willy. How to Train the Family Dog. 1955. pap. 2.50 (ISBN 0-448-01498-X, G&D). Putnam Pub Group.

Neckers, D., jt. auth. see Mohrig, J.

Neckers, D. C. Mechanistic Organic Photochemistry. 336p. 1967. 18.00 (ISBN 0-442-17055-6, Pub. by Van Nos Reinhold). Krieger.

Neckers, D. C. & Doyle, M. P. Organic Chemistry. 1147p. 1977. text ed. 34.95 o.s.i. (ISBN 0-471-63091-8); study guide avail. o.s.i. (ISBN 0-471-63092-6); solutions avail. o.s.i. Wiley.

Nedderman, R. M., jt. auth. see Kay, J. M.

Nederveen, Cornelis J. Acoustical Aspects of Woodwind Instruments. 1969. 45.00 o.s.i. (ISBN 90-6027-078-9, Pub. by Frits Knuf Netherlands); 30.00 o.s.i. (ISBN 90-6027-305-2). Pendragon NY.

Nedjati, Z. M. Human Rights Under the European Convention. LC 78-23469. (European Studies in Law: Vol. 8). 1979. 57.50 (ISBN 0-444-85218-2, North Holland). Elsevier.

Nedobeck, Don. Nedobeck's Twelve Days of Christmas. (Illus.). 32p. (gr. k-6). 1982. 3.25 (ISBN 0-8249-8043-3). Ideals.

Nedwell, D. B. & Brown, C. M., eds. Sediment Microbiology. (Special Publication Ser.: No. 7). 1982. 26.50 (ISBN 0-12-515380-5). Acad Pr.

Nee, T. S. El Mensajero de la Cruz. Carrodeguas, Andy & Marosi, Esteban, eds. Silva, Jose D., tr. from Eng. Orig. Title: The Messenger of the Cross. 168p. (Span.). 1982. pap. 2.00 (ISBN 0-8297-1230-5). Life Pubs Intl.

--El Testimonio de Dios. (Span.). Date not set. 1.75 o.p. (ISBN 0-686-76343-2). Life Pubs Intl.

Nee, T. S. & Arcangeli, Gianfranco. Autorita Spirituale. (Italian.). 1980. pap. 2.50 (ISBN 0-8297-0923-1). Life Pubs Intl.

Nee, T. S. Watchman. Qui Enverrai-Je? (Fr.). 1981. 1.75 (ISBN 0-8297-1102-3). Life Pubs Intl.

Nee, Watchman. A Balanced Christian Life. Koung, Stephen, tr. 1981. pap. 3.10 (ISBN 0-686-95516-1). Christian Fellow Pubs.

--The Better Covenant. Kaung, Stephen, tr. 1982. 4.50 (ISBN 0-935008-56-X); pap. 5.50 (ISBN 0-935008-55-1). Christian Fellow Pubs.

--The Church & the Work, 3 Vols. Kaung, Stephen, tr. 550p. (Chinese.). 1982. 27.00 (ISBN 0-935008-57-8); pap. text ed. 15.00 (ISBN 0-935008-58-6). Christian Fellow Pubs.

--La Liberacion del Espiritu. 112p. Date not set. 2.50 (ISBN 0-88113-255-1). Edit Betania.

--Ministerio de Oracao da Igreja. Batista, Joao, ed. De-Moraes, Moises, tr. from Eng. 127p. 1982. pap. 1.40 (ISBN 0-8297-1339-5). Life Pubs Intl.

--The Normal Christian Life. 1977. pap. 3.95 (ISBN 0-8423-4710-0). Tyndale.

--Oremos. Marosi, Esteban, ed. Lassaletta, Manuel, tr. 113p. (Span.). 1980. pap. 1.50 (ISBN 0-8297-1046-9). Life Pubs Intl.

Need, Jeffrey & Baxter, Pam. Library Use: Handbook for Psychology. 150p. (Orig.). 1983. pap. 15.00x (ISBN 0-912704-76-4). Am Psychol.

Needham, Barrie. Guidelines for a Local Employment Study. 1978. text ed. 28.00x (ISBN 0-566-00241-8). Gower Pub Ltd.

Needham, C. D. Organizing Knowledge in Libraries: An Introduction to Information Retrieval. 448p. 1971. 22.50 (ISBN 0-233-95836-3, 05813-0, Pub. by Gower Pub Co England). Lexington Bks.

Needham, Dorothy M. Machina Carnis: The Biochemistry of Muscular Contraction in Its Historical Development. (Illus.). 1972. 110.00 (ISBN 0-521-07974-8). Cambridge U Pr.

Needham, Howard, jt. auth. see Needham, Ted.

Needham, J., jt. auth. see Lu, Gwei-Djen.

Needham, James G. & Needham, Paul R. Guide to the Study of Freshwater Biology. 5th ed. LC 62-20742. (Illus.). 1962. pap. 7.50x (ISBN 0-8162-6310-8). Holden-Day.

Needham, James G. & Westfall, Minter J., Jr. A Manual of the Dragonflies of North America (Anisoptera) Including the Greater Antilles & the Provinces of the Mexican Border. (California Library Reprint Ser.). (Illus.). 632p. 1981. Repr. of 1954 ed. 60.00x (ISBN 0-520-02913-5). U of Cal Pr.

Needham, John. Development of Iron & Steel Technology in China. LC 75-22549. (Illus.). 76p. 1975. 22.95 (ISBN 0-521-21045-3). Cambridge U Pr.

Needham, Joseph. Biochemistry & Morphogenesis. 1942. 110.50 (ISBN 0-521-05797-3). Cambridge U Pr.

--Chemistry of Life: Eight Lectures on the History of Biochemistry. LC 78-85733. (Illus.). 1970. 34.50 (ISBN 0-521-07379-0). Cambridge U Pr.

--Moulds of Understanding: A Pattern of Natural Philosophy. LC 75-37252. 320p. 1976. 26.00 (ISBN 0-312-54950-4). St Martin.

--Order & Life. 1968. pap. 4.95x (ISBN 0-262-64001-5). MIT Pr.

--Science & Civilization in China, 5 vols. Incl. Vol. 1. Introductory Orientations. 1954. 55.00 (ISBN 0-521-05799-X); Vol. 2. History of Scientific Thought. 95.00 (ISBN 0-521-05800-7); Vol. 3. Mathematics & the Sciences of the Heavens & the Earth. 135.00 (ISBN 0-521-05801-5); Vol. 4. Physics & Physical Technology, 3 pts; Pt. 1. Physics. 1962. 75.00 (ISBN 0-521-05802-3); Pt. 2. Mechanical Engineering. 115.00 (ISBN 0-521-05803-1); Pt. 3. Engineering & Nautics. 1970. 135.00 (ISBN 0-521-07060-0); Vol. 5, Pt. 4. Spagyrical Discovery & Invention. 500p. 115.00 (ISBN 0-521-08573-X). Cambridge U Pr.

--Science in Traditional China. (Illus.). 256p. text ed. 12.50x (ISBN 0-674-79438-9); pap. 4.95 (ISBN 0-674-79439-7). Harvard U Pr.

Needham, Paul. Twelve Centuries of Bookbindings: Four Hundred to Sixteen Hundred. LC 79-52345. (Illus.). 368p. 1979. 75.00 (ISBN 0-19-211580-4, Co-pub by Oxford U Pr); pap. 39.95 (ISBN 0-686-68488-5). Pierpont Morgan.

Needham, Paul R., jt. auth. see Needham, James G.

Needham, R. M. & Herbert, A. J. The Cambridge Distributed Computing System. 256p. 1982. pap. 25.00 (ISBN 0-201-14092-6, Adv Bk Prog). A-W.

Needham, Rodney. Structure & Sentiment: A Test Case in Social Anthropology. LC 62-9738. 1962. 6.50x (ISBN 0-226-56991-8); pap. 1.95 o.s.i. (ISBN 0-226-56992-6). U of Chicago Pr.

--Symbolic Classification. LC 78-11508. 1979. text ed. 11.95x o.p. (ISBN 0-673-16290-7); pap. text ed. 8.95x o.p. (ISBN 0-673-16289-3). Scott F.

Needham, Ted & Needham, Howard. Alcatraz. LC 76-11350. (Illus.). 1976. pap. 4.95 o.p. (ISBN 0-89087-129-9). Celestial Arts.

Needham, William L. & Jahoda, Gerald. Improving Library Service to Physically Disabled Persons: A Self-Evaluation Checklist. 135p. 1983. lib. bdg. 18.50 (ISBN 0-686-82503-9). Libs Unl.

Needleman, Carolyn E., jt. auth. see Needleman, Martin L.

Needleman, Herbert L., ed. Low Level Lead Exposure: The Clinical Implications of Current Research. 336p. 1980. text ed. 40.00 (ISBN 0-89004-455-4). Raven.

Needleman, Jacob. The Heart of Philosophy. 1982. 14.95 (ISBN 0-394-51380-0). Knopf.

Needleman, Jacob, ed. Speaking of My Life: The Art of Living in the Cultural Revolution. LC 78-19502. (Illus., Orig.). 1979. pap. 4.95i o.p. (ISBN 0-06-250643-9, RD 216, HarpR). Har-Row.

Needleman, Jacob & Baker, George, eds. Understanding the New Religions. 1978. 17.50 (ISBN 0-8164-0403-8); pap. 8.95 (ISBN 0-8164-2188-9). Seabury.

Needleman, Jacob, et al. Religion for a New Generation. 2nd ed. Scott, Kenneth, ed. 576p. 1977. pap. text ed. 15.95x (ISBN 0-02-385990-3). Macmillan.

Needleman, Martin L. & Needleman, Carolyn E. Guerrillas in the Bureaucracy: The Community Planning Experiment in the United States. LC 73-19806. (Urban Research Ser.). 384p. 1974. 22.95 o.p. (ISBN 0-471-63099-3, Pub. by Wiley-Interscience). Wiley.

Needleman, Theodore. Microcomputers for Accountants. (Illus.). 160p. 1983. 24.95 (ISBN 0-13-580696-8); pap. 14.95 (ISBN 0-13-580688-7). P-H.

Needler, Martin C. An Introduction to Latin American Politics: The Structure of Conflict. LC 77-23222. 1977. text ed. 22.95 (ISBN 0-13-486043-8). P-H.

--An Introduction to Latin American Politics: The Structure of Conflict. 2nd ed. (Illus.). 256p. 1983. pap. 12.95 (ISBN 0-13-486035-7). P-H.

--Mexican Politics: The Containment of Conflict. Wesson, Robert, ed. (Politics in Latin America, a Hoover Institution Ser.). 172p. 1982. 23.95 (ISBN 0-03-062039-2); pap. 12.95 (ISBN 0-03-062041-4). Praeger.

--Political Development in Latin America: Instability, Violence & Evolutionary Change. 1968. pap. text ed. 3.50x (ISBN 0-685-19751-4). Phila Bk Co.

Needles. Financial Accounting. 1983. text ed. 24.95 (ISBN 0-686-84524-2); write for info. supplementary materials. HM.

Needles & Williams. The CPA Exam, 1982, 2 vols. 1982. Set. write for info. o.p. P-H.

Needles, Belverd E. & Williams, Doyle Z. The CPA Examination: A Complete Review 1981-1982, Vol. 1. (Illus.). 1056p. 1981. text ed. 23.95 o.p. (ISBN 0-13-187765-8). P-H.

Needles, Belverd E., et al. Principles of Accounting. LC 80-80503. (Illus.). 1008p. 1981. text ed. 24.95 (ISBN 0-395-29527-0); study guide 9.95 (ISBN 0-395-29529-7); test bank 1.75 (ISBN 0-395-29538-6); practice sets I-III 7.95 ea. (ISBN I: 0-395-29534-3; ISBN II: 0-395-29535-1; ISBN III: 0-395-29536-X); achievement tests 1-7A 7.00 (ISBN 0-395-29539-4); achievement tests 1-14B 7.00 (ISBN 0-395-29540-8); achievement tests 8-14A 8.00 (ISBN 0-395-29541-6); achievement tests 8-14B 8.00 (ISBN 0-395-29542-4); 745 Transparencies ISBN 295.00. HM.

Needles, Belverd E., Jr. & Williams, Doyle Z. The CPA Examination: A Complete Review, 1982-1983, Vol. I. (Illus.). 1008p. 1982. 26.95 (ISBN 0-13-187732-1). P-H.

Needles, Belverd E., Jr. & Williams, Doyle Z., eds. The CPA Examination: A Complete Review, 1982-1983, Vol. II. (Illus.). 896p. 1982. 26.95 (ISBN 0-13-187740-2). P-H.

Needles, Mark. Electronic Calculators in Business. 1981. pap. text ed. 18.95x (ISBN 0-673-16013-0). Scott F.

Needy, Charles W., ed. Classics of Economics. (Classics Ser.). (Orig.). 1980. pap. 12.50x (ISBN 0-935610-12-X). Moore Pub IL.

Neef, Marian, jt. auth. see Nagel, Stuart.

Neef, Marian, jt. ed. see Nagel, Stuart.

Neef, Marion, jt. auth. see Nagel, Stuart S.

Neel, D., ed. Tools & Notions for Program Construction: An Advanced Course. LC 82-4141. 350p. 1982. 29.95 (ISBN 0-521-24801-9). Cambridge U Pr.

Neel, L., ed. Nonlinear Behaviour of Molecules, Atoms & Ions in Electric, Magnetic or Electromagnetic Fields. 1979. 89.50 (ISBN 0-444-41790-7). Elsevier.

Neel, Peg. How To Pray According to God's Word. 72p. 1982. pap. 2.25 (ISBN 0-88144-004-3, CPS-004). Christian Pub.

Neels, Betty. All Else Confusion. (Harlequin Romances Ser.). 192p. 1983. pap. 1.75 (ISBN 0-373-02542-4). Harlequin Bks.

--Judith. (Harlequin Romances Ser.). 192p. 1982. pap. 1.50 (ISBN 0-373-02500-9). Harlequin Bks.

--Stars Through the Mist, Winter of Change & Three for a Wedding. (Harlequin Romances Ser.: 3 Vols. in 1). 576p. 1983. pap. 3.95 (ISBN 0-373-20073-0). Harlequin Bks.

Neely, Alan, tr. see Dussel, Enrique.

Neely, Alfred S. Administrative Law in West Virginia. 850p. 1982. 35.00 (ISBN 0-686-84232-4). Michie-Bobbs.

Neely, Henry M. Primer for Star-Gazers. LC 72-120090. (Illus.). 1970. 14.37i (ISBN 0-06-013167-5, HarpT); lib. bdg. 12.27i (ISBN 0-06-013168-3). Har-Row.

Neely, John. Practical Metallurgy & Materials of Industry. LC 78-19166. 1979. text ed. 24.95x (ISBN 0-471-02962-9); tchrs. manual o.p. 8.00 (ISBN 0-471-05121-7). Wiley.

Neely, John E. Practical Machine Shop. LC 81-4537. 675p. 1982. text ed. 25.95x (ISBN 0-471-08000-4); tchrs' ed. (ISBN 0-471-86377-7); student wkbk. 7.95 (ISBN 0-471-86642-3). Wiley.

Neely, John E., jt. auth. see Kibbe, Richard R.

Neely, Lois. Fire in His Bones. 1982. pap. 6.95 (ISBN 0-8423-0869-5). Tyndale.

Neely, Martina. West Virginia Italian Heritage Festival Cookbook. (Illus.). 112p. (Orig.). 1980. pap. 5.00x (ISBN 0-686-37047-3). Back Fork Bks.

Neely, Richard. How Courts Govern America. LC 81-1048. 256p. 1981. 20.00 (ISBN 0-300-02589-0). Yale U Pr.

--How Courts Govern America. LC 81-1048. 256p. 1983. pap. 7.95 (ISBN 0-300-02980-2). Yale U Pr.

--How Courts Govern America. pap. 7.95 (ISBN 0-686-42823-4, Y-455). Yale U Pr.

--The Japanese Mistress. 1979. pap. 1.75 o.s.i. (ISBN 0-515-05164-0). Jove Pubns.

--Lies. LC 77-25177. 1978. 8.95 o.p. (ISBN 0-399-11315-0). Putnam Pub Group.

--Shadows from the Past. 352p. 1983. 15.95 (ISBN 0-440-08008-8). Delacorte.

Neeman, Yaakov. Tax Consequences Upon Conversion of Property's Use: A Comparative Study. LC 79-115426. 241p. 1970. 15.00 (ISBN 0-379-00461-5). Oceana.

Ne'Emann, Yuval, ed. Jerusalem Einstein Centennial Symposium. (Illus.). 528p. 1980. text ed. 42.50 (ISBN 0-201-05289-X). A-W.

Neer, C. S. Shoulder Reconstruction. (Illus.). Date not set. text ed. price not set. Churchill.

Neeson, Jean D. & Stockdale, Connie R. The Practitioners Handbook of Ambulatory OB-GYN. LC 80-26151. 394p. 1981. 21.50x (ISBN 0-471-05670-7, Pub. by Wiley Medical). Wiley.

Neev, Elan. Wholistic Healing: How to Harmonize Your Body, Mind & Spirit with Life, for Freedom, Joy, Health, Beauty, Love, Money & Psychic Powers. LC 77-71152. (Illus.). 1977. deluxe ed. 8.95 ltd. ed. (ISBN 0-918482-01-1); pap. 4.95 (ISBN 0-686-96648-1). Ageless Bks.

Neff, Donald. Warriors at Suez: Eisenhower Takes America into the Middle East. (Illus.). 1982. 17.95 (ISBN 0-671-41010-5, Linden); pap. 7.95 (ISBN 0-671-44276-7, Linden). S&S.

Neff, Fred. Everybody's Book of Self-Defense. LC 77-88520. (Adult & Young Adult Ser). (Illus.). 1978. PLB 12.95 o.p. (ISBN 0-8225-1158-4); 7.95 o.p. (ISBN 0-8225-9952-X). Lerner Pubns.

Neff, Jerry M. Polycyclic Aromatic Hydrocarbons in the Aquatic Environment. (Illus.). 1979. 55.50 (ISBN 0-85334-832-4, Pub. by Applied Sci England). Elsevier.

Neff, Jerry M. & Anderson, Jack W. Response of Marine Animals to Petroleum & Specific Petroleum Hydrocarbons. 177p. 1981. 39.95x (ISBN 0-470-27215-5). Halsted Pr.

Neff, Larry M., ed. Selections from Arthur D. Graeff's Scholla, Vol. V. LC 79-166008. 1971. 15.00 (ISBN 0-911122-27-3). Penn German Soc.

Neff, Larry M. & Weiser, Frederick S., eds. The Account Book of Conrad Weiser: Berks County, Pennsylvania, 1746-1760. LC 81-84666. (Sources & Documents of the Pennsylvania Germans Ser.: Vol. VI). (Illus.). 1981. 12.50x (ISBN 0-911122-43-5). Penn German Soc.

Neff, Larry M., jt. ed. see Weiser, Frederick S. & Heaney, Howell J.

Neff, Lavonne. God's Gift Baby. (Arch Book Series Fourteen). 1977. pap. 0.89 (ISBN 0-570-06113-X, 59-1230). Concordia.

--Simon was Safe. (Arch Bks: No. 13). (Illus.). 32p. (ps-4). 1976. pap. 0.89 (ISBN 0-570-06104-0, 59-1222). Concordia.

Neff, Mariam. Discover Your Worth. 1979. pap. 3.95 (ISBN 0-88207-783-X). Victor Bks.

Neff, Marsha J., jt. auth. see Dietl, L. Kay.

Neff, Miriam. Women & Their Emotions. (Orig.). 1983. pap. 5.95 (ISBN 0-8024-5151-9). Moody.

Neff, Paula E., jt. auth. see Wojciechowski, William V.

Neff, Thomas L. & Jacoby, Henry D. The International Uranium Market. 1983. prof ref 20.00x (ISBN 0-88410-850-3). Ballinger Pub.

Neff, William D. Contributions to Sensory Psychology, Vol. 7. 240p. 1982. 39.50 (ISBN 0-12-151807-8). Acad Pr.

Neff, William D., ed. Contributions to Sensory Physiology, Vol. 6. 1982. 39.50 (ISBN 0-12-151806-X). Acad Pr.

Neft, David S., et al. The Sports Encyclopedia: Baseball. rev. ed. LC 73-15137. 544p. 1982. pap. 12.95 (ISBN 0-448-14047-0, G&D). Putnam Pub Group.

--The Sports Encyclopedia: Pro Basketball. LC 74-7552. 416p. 1975. 9.95 o.p. (ISBN 0-448-11801-7, G&D). Putnam Pub Group.

Neggers, Carla. Dancing Season. (Finding Mr. Right Ser.). 208p. 1983. pap. 2.75 (ISBN 0-380-82602-X). Avon.

--Matching Wits. (Loveswept Ser.: No. 5). 1983. pap. 1.95 (ISBN 0-686-43206-1). Bantam.

Negin, Elliott. Celebrities Sweepsteaks. LC 79-17133. (Illus.). 1979. pap. 4.95 o.p. (ISBN 0-416-00161-0). Methuen Inc.

Negishi, Ei-Ichi. Organometallics in Organic Synthesis: General Discussions & Organometallics of Main Group Metals in Organic Synthesis, Vol. 1. LC 79-16818. 1980. 32.50x (ISBN 0-471-03193-3, Pub. by Wiley-Interscience). Wiley.

Negishi, T. Microeconomic Foundations of Keynesian Macroeconomics. (Studies in Mathematical & Managerial Economics: Vol. 27). 264p. 1980. 47.00 (ISBN 0-444-85225-5, North Holland). Elsevier.

Neglia, Erminio & Ordaz, Luis. Repertorio Selecto del Teatro Hispanoamericano Contemporaneo. 1982. 22.50x (ISBN 0-87918-042-0). ASU Lat Am St.

Negri, Antonio. Marx Beyond Marx: Notebooks on the Grundrisse. Orig. Title: Marx Oltre Marx. 224p. 1983. 24.95x (ISBN 0-89789-018-3). J F Bergin.

Negroponte, Nicholas. Soft Architecture Machines. LC 75-95283. 140p. 1974. 20.00x (ISBN 0-262-14018-7). MIT Pr.

Negus, James. Enjoy Stamp Collecting. 1.00. StanGib Ltd.

Negus, Joan. Cosmic Combinations. 1982. pap. 7.95 (ISBN 0-917086-37-6, Pub. by Astro Comp Serv). Para Res.

Negus, Kenneth. Grimmelshausen. (World Authors Ser.: No. 291). 15.95 (ISBN 0-8057-2405-2, Twayne). G K Hall.

Negus, Robert W. Fundamentals of Finite Mathematics. LC 80-21965. 416p. 1983. Repr. of 1974 ed. text ed. write for info. (ISBN 0-89874-270-6). Krieger.

Nehari, Zeev. Conformal Mapping. LC 74-27513. (Illus.). 416p. 1975. pap. text ed. 6.50 (ISBN 0-486-61137-X). Dover.

Neher, Andre. The Exile of the Word: From the Silence of the Bible to the Silence of Auschwitz. LC 80-12612. 224p. 1980. 17.95 (ISBN 0-8276-0176-X, 465). Jewish Pubn.

Neher, William W. & Waite, David H. Nuts & Bolts: A Manual for Effective Professional Communication. 1978. pap. 10.95x (ISBN 0-89917-000-5). TIS Inc.

Nehls, Edward H., ed. D. H. Lawrence: A Composite Biography, 3 vols. 1957-59. 35.00 ea.; Vol. 1. (ISBN 0-299-81501-3); Vol. 2. (ISBN 0-299-81502-1); Vol. 3. (ISBN 0-299-81503-X). U of Wis Pr.

Nehls, Harry J. Familiar Birds of the Northwest. 2nd ed. 1983. 6.95 (ISBN 0-931686-05-9). Audobon Soc Portland.

Nehmer, Kathleen S., ed. Elementary Teachers Guide to Free Curriculum Materials. 39th rev. ed. LC 44-52255. 1982. pap. 19.00 (ISBN 0-87708-124-7). Ed Prog.

Nehmer, Kathleen S., et al, eds. Educators Grade Guide to Free Teaching Aids. 28th rev. ed. LC 56-2444. 1982. looseleaf 37.25 (ISBN 0-87708-125-5). Ed Prog.

Nehrling, Arno & Nehrling, Irene. Picture Book of Annuals. (Illus.). 1966. 7.95 (ISBN 0-8208-0022-8). Hearthside.

--Picture Book of Perennials. (Illus.). 1964. 7.95 (ISBN 0-8208-0021-X). Hearthside.

--Propagating House Plants: New - How to Grow Herbs & Vegetables Indoors. LC 70-151460. (Illus.). 1971. 7.95 (ISBN 0-8208-0020-1). Hearthside.

Nehrling, Irene, jt. auth. see Nehrling, Arno.

Nehru, Jawaharlal. Mahatma Gandhi. 1976. pap. 4.50 o.p. (ISBN 0-210-22542-4). Asia.

Nei, Masatoshi & Koehn, Richard K., eds. Evolution of Genes & Proteins. (Illus.). 380p. 1983. price not set (ISBN 0-87893-603-3); pap. price not set (ISBN 0-87893-604-1). Sinauer Assoc.

Neidecker, Elizabeth. School Programs in Speech-Language: Organization & Management. (Illus.). 1980. text ed. 23.95 (ISBN 0-13-794321-0). P-H.

Neider, Charles see Twain, Mark.

Neider, Charles, ed. see Twain, Mark.

Neiderman, Andrew, jt. auth. see Grossinger, Tania.

Neidhardt, W. S. Fenianism in North America. LC 74-31392. 216p. 1975. 16.95x (ISBN 0-271-01188-2). Pa St U Pr.

Neidle. Electrical Installation for Technology. 2nd ed. 1983. text ed. write for info. (ISBN 0-408-01146-7). Butterworth.

Neidle, Cecyle S. America's Immigrant Women. LC 75-37110. 313p. 1976. pap. 4.95 (ISBN 0-88254-369-5). Hippocrene Bks.

--America's Immigrant Women. LC 75-12738. (Immigrant Heritage of America Ser.). 1975. lib. bdg. 12.95 o.p. (ISBN 0-8057-8400-4, Twayne). G K Hall.

--Great Immigrants. (Immigrant Heritage of America Ser). 1972. lib. bdg. 9.95 o.p. (ISBN 0-8057-3222-5, Twayne). G K Hall.

--The New Americans. (Immigrant Heritage of American Ser.). lib. bdg. 11.95 (ISBN 0-8057-3247-0, Twayne). G K Hall.

Neidle, Enid A., et al. Pharmacology & Therapeutics for Dentistry. LC 80-10522. (Illus.). 758p. 1980. text ed. 31.95 (ISBN 0-8016-3635-3). Mosby.

Neier, Aryeh. Defending My Enemy: American Nazis in Skokie, Illinois, & the Risks of Freedom. 1979. 9.95 o.p. (ISBN 0-525-08972-1). Dutton.

--Only Judgment: The Limits of Litigation in Social Change. 288p. 1982. 17.95 (ISBN 0-8195-5079-5). Wesleyan U Pr.

Neifeld, Morris R. Neifeld's Manual on Consumer Credit. 1961. 11.00 (ISBN 0-912734-13-2). Mack Pub.

Neighbors, Kyle. The Lima Shays on the Greenbrier, Cheat & Elk Railroad Company. 32p. 1969. pap. 3.00 o.p. (ISBN 0-87012-070-0). McClain.

Neighbour, Ralph. Contacto con el Espiritu. Martinez, Jose L., ed. Kratzig, Guillermo, tr. Orig. Title: The Touch of the Spirit. 120p. (Span.). Date not set. pap. price not set (ISBN 0-311-09098-2). Casa Bautista.

Neighbour, Ralph W. This Gift Is Mine. LC 73-93907. 1974. 4.95 (ISBN 0-8054-5223-0). Broadman.

Neighbour, Ralph W., Jr. Sigueme. 68p. 1982. Repr. of 1981 ed. 2.75 (ISBN 0-311-13837-3); 2.65 (ISBN 0-311-13836-5). Casa Bautista.

Neigoff, Anne. Ahora Conoces las Plantas, 5 bks. (Illus.). (gr. k-3). 1973. Set. 99.00 (ISBN 0-87827-171-6). cassettes, records & tchrs' guide avail. Ency Brit Ed.

--The Energy Workers. Rubin, Caroline, ed. LC 74-23973. (Career Awareness Community Helpers Ser.). (Illus.). 32p. (gr. k-2). 1975. 5.25g o.p. (ISBN 0-8075-2049-7). A Whitman.

--Now You Know about People at Work, 5 bks. Incl. Where People Work; When People Work; Why People Work; Work You Can Do; Who Works. (Spanish edition available). 1974. 99.00 (ISBN 0-87827-181-3); tchr's guide incl. (ISBN 0-685-57300-1); inl. records & cassettes (ISBN 0-87827-180-5). Ency Brit Ed.

--Now You Know about Plants. Incl. Many Plants; Where Plants Live; How Plants Grow; Plants & Their Seeds; Plants We Need. (Illus.). 32p. (gr. k-3). 1973. 99.00 (ISBN 0-87827-104-X); avail. spanish ed. (ISBN 0-685-31654-8); cassettes avail. (ISBN 0-87827-105-8). Ency Brit Ed.

Neigott, Anne. Now You Know about: Strange Beasts, Dinosaurs, Animals of the Ice Age, Monsters & Myths, Sharks, Strange Animals of Today, 5 bks., 5 cassettes. (Illus.). 99.00 (ISBN 0-87827-257-7). Ency Brit Ed.

Neihardt, John C. Splendid Wayfaring. 1948. pap. 5.25 (ISBN 0-686-95841-1). Jefferson Natl.

Neihardt, John G. River & I. LC 68-13650. (Illus.). x, 325p. 1968. pap. 10.95 (ISBN 0-8032-5144-0, BB 378, Bison). U of Nebr Pr.

--The Song of Three Friends & the Song of Hugh Glass. 335p. 1982. Repr. of 1941 ed. lib. bdg. 25.00 (ISBN 0-89984-360-3). Century Bookbindery.

Neijs, Karel. Literacy Primers: Construction, Evaluation & Use. 1965. pap. 2.25 o.p. (ISBN 92-3-100597-9, U361, UNESCO). Unipub.

Neil, Charles, jt. ed. see Wright, Charles.

Neil, Eric, jt. auth. see Folkow, Bjoern.

Neil, Eric, ed. see Wright, Samson.

Neil, J. Meredith. Toward a National Taste: America's Quest for Aesthetic Independence. 416p. 1975. 15.00x (ISBN 0-8248-0340-X). UH Pr.

Neil, James M. Construction Cost Estimating for Project Control. (Illus.). 336p. 1982. 26.95 (ISBN 0-13-168757-3). P-H.

Neil, Randy L., jt. auth. see International Cheerleading Foundation Staff.

Neil, William. The Message of the Bible: A Concise Introduction to the Old & New Testament. LC 79-3602. 224p. (Orig.). 1980. pap. 3.95i o.p. (ISBN 0-06-066092-9, RD 322, HarpR, HarpR). Har-Row.

--Why Listen? The Difficult Sayings of Jesus. (Orig.). pap. 1.50 o.s.i. (ISBN 0-89129-227-6). Jove Pubns.

Neill, Ian. Trout from the Hills. 13.50x o.p. (ISBN 0-392-06403-0, SpS). Sportshelf.

Neill, Marilyn. Crock-Pot Cooking. (Illus.). 208p. 1975. 7.95 (ISBN 0-307-49263-X, Golden Pr). Western Pub.

Neill, Robert. The Devil's Door. 1980. 8.95 o.p. (ISBN 0-312-19807-8). St Martin.

Neill, Stephen. Anglicanism. 4th ed. 1978. pap. 9.95x (ISBN 0-19-520033-0). Oxford U Pr.

Neill, Stephen C. The Christian Society. LC 76-141280. 334p. 1972. Repr. of 1952 ed. lib. bdg. 17.00x (ISBN 0-8371-5877-X, NECS). Greenwood.

Neill, T. J., jt. auth. see Briston, J. H.

Neill, Thomas P. History of the Western Civilization. rev. ed. 1962. 12.95 o.p. (ISBN 0-02-824200-9). Glencoe.

--Renewing the Face of the Earth. 1968. 4.50 o.p. (ISBN 0-685-07663-6, 80574). Glencoe.

Neilon, J. R. & Terauchi, E. Standards & Procedures for Presentation of Processed Data in Digital Form. (World Weather Watch Planning Report Ser.: No. 29). 1969. pap. 10.00 o.p. (ISBN 0-685-22342-6, WMO). Unipub.

Neils, Jenifer. The World of Ceramics: Masterpieces from the Cleveland Museum of Art. LC 82-1308. 176p. (Orig.). 1982. pap. 19.95X (ISBN 0-910386-68-4). Ind U Pr.

Neilson, Frances, jt. auth. see Neilson, Winthrop.

Neilson, Francis. The Churchill Legend: Winston Churchill as Fraud, Fakir & War-Monger. 1983. lib. bdg. 79.95 (ISBN 0-87700-001-8). Revisionist Pr.

--In Quest of Justice. 135p. 1944. pap. 1.00 (ISBN 0-911312-31-5). Schalkenbach.

Neilson, Nancy W. Camillo Procaccini Paintings & Drawings. LC 78-68273. (Reference Library of Humanities Ser.). 1979. lib. bdg. 55.00 o.s.i. (ISBN 0-8240-9775-0). Garland Pub.

Neilson, Winthrop & Neilson, Frances. Letter to Philemon. 1973. pap. 2.50 o.p. (ISBN 0-570-03179-6, 12-2582). Concordia.

--The Ring & the River. LC 78-27372. 1979. 10.95 o.p. (ISBN 0-399-12202-8). Putnam Pub Group.

Neiman, Fraser. Matthew Arnold. (English Authors Ser.: No. 69). 1969. lib. bdg. 11.95 o.p. (ISBN 0-8057-1012-4, Twayne). G K Hall.

Neiman, LeRoy. The Prints of LeRoy Neiman. (Illus.). 364p. 1980. 100.00 (ISBN 0-686-77668-2). CDP.

Neimark, Anne. With This Gift: The Story of Edgar Cayce. (Illus.). (gr. 7 up). 1978. 9.75 (ISBN 0-688-22147-5); PLB 9.36 (ISBN 0-688-32147-X). Morrow.

Neimark, Anne E. Damien, the Leper Priest. LC 80-15141. 160p. (gr. 7-9). 1980. 9.75 (ISBN 0-688-22246-3); PLB 9.36 (ISBN 0-688-32246-8). Morrow.

Neimark, Paul. Camping & Ecology. LC 80-27736. (Wilderness World Ser.). (Illus.). 64p. (gr. 3 up). 1981. PLB 9.25 (ISBN 0-516-02451-5). Childrens.

--Cycle Cop: The True Story of Jack Muller, the Chicago Giant-Killer Who Feared No Evil. LC 76-10792. (gr. 5 up). 1976. 5.95 o.p. (ISBN 0-399-20534-9). Putnam Pub Group.

--Same Time, Next Week: Why, When & How to Leave Your Therapist. 250p. 1981. 12.95 o.p. (ISBN 0-87000-514-6, Arlington Hse). Crown.

Neimark, Paul, jt. auth. see Berkowitz, Gerald M.

Neimark, Paul, jt. auth. see Schmidt, J. H.

Neimark, Paul G., jt. auth. see Owens, Jesse.

Neimeyer, Robert A., jt. ed. see Epting, Franz R.

Neinstein, Lawrence S. Manual of Adolescent Health Care. 1983. write for info. (ISBN 0-87527-300-9). Green.

Neinstein, Murray & Kornbluh, Elaine, eds. Barron's Regents Exams & Answers Business Law. rev. ed. LC 56-39245. 300p. (gr. 10-12). 1982. pap. text ed. 4.50 (ISBN 0-8120-3189-X). Barron.

Neish, A. C., jt. auth. see Freudenberg, K.

Neish, Gordon A. & Hughes, Gilbert C. Fungal Diseases of Fishes. Axelrod, Herbert R. & Snieszko, Stanislas F., eds. (Diseases of Fishes Ser.). (Illus.). 160p. 19.95 (ISBN 0-87666-504-0, PS-213). TFH Pubns.

Neisser, Edith G. Mothers & Daughters: A Lifelong Relationship. rev. ed. LC 73-4113. 412p. 1973. 11.95i (ISBN 0-06-013171-3, HarpT). Har-Row.

Neisworth, John & Smith, Robert. Retardation: Issues, Assessment & Intervention. (Series in Special Education). (Illus.). 1978. text ed. 24.95 (ISBN 0-07-046201-1, C); instr.'s manual 16.00 (ISBN 0-07-046202-X). McGraw.

Neisworth, John, jt. auth. see Smith, Robert M.

Neisworth, John T. Assessment in Special Education. LC 82-11455. 233p. 1982. 23.95 (ISBN 0-89443-808-5). Aspen Systems.

Neisworth, John T. & Smith, Robert M. Modifying Retarded Behavior. (Illus.). 200p. 1973. text ed. 24.95 (ISBN 0-395-14049-8). HM.

Neisworth, John T., jt. auth. see Smith, Robert M.

Neitmann, Erich. Das Politische Lied Im Schulischen Musikunterricht der DDR. 246p. (Ger.). 1982. write for info. (ISBN 3-8204-7042-5). P Lang Pubs.

Neitzel, James J., ed. Canadian Conference, 10th Annual, Sept. 10-14, 1977: Proceedings. 1978. spiral bdg. 2.00 (ISBN 0-89154-071-7). Intl Found Employ.

--Public Employees Conference, Tahoe Nevada, Oct. 2-5, 1977: Proceedings. 1978. spiral bdg. 7.50 (ISBN 0-89154-074-1). Intl Found Employ.

Neizestny, Ernst. O Sinteze v Iskusste. Nichols, Alice, tr. (Illus.). 102p. (Eng. & Rus.). 1982. pap. 12.00 (ISBN 0-938920-22-7). Hermitage MI.

Nejelski, Paul, ed. Social Research in Conflict with Law & Ethics. LC 76-19082. 216p. 1976. prof ref 16.50x (ISBN 0-88410-228-9). Ballinger Pub.

Nekam, Alexander. Personality Conception of the Legal Entity. 1938. 34.50x (ISBN 0-686-51287-1). Elliots Bks.

Nekhom, Lisa M., jt. auth. see Wright, Ione S.

Nekrasov, N. Grandpa Mazai & the Hares. 15p. 1981. pap. 1.50 (ISBN 0-8285-2201-4, Pub. by Progress Pubs USSR). Imported Pubns.

Nektarios, Miltiadis. Public Pensions, Capital Formation, & Economic Growth. Replica ed. 175p. 1982. softcover 20.00 (ISBN 0-86531-936-7). Westview.

Nelken, D., ed. The Limits of the Legal Process: A Study of Landlords, Law & Crime. Date not set. price not set (ISBN 0-12-515280-9). Acad Pr.

Nelkin, Dorothy. The Creation Controversy: Science or Scripture in the Schools. 256p. 1982. 16.95 (ISBN 0-393-01635-8). Norton.

--On the Season: Aspects of the Migrant Labor System. LC 76-632774. (Paperback Ser.: No. 8). 98p. 1971. pap. 3.50 o.s.i. (ISBN 0-87546-041-0); pap. 5.25 special hard bdg. o.s.i. (ISBN 0-87546-277-4). ILR Pr.

Nelkin, Dorothy & Pollak, Michael. The Atom Besieged: Extraparliamentary Dissent. (Illus.). 256p. 1982. 20.00x (ISBN 0-262-14034-9); pap. 7.95 (ISBN 0-262-64021-X). MIT Pr.

Nelkon, M. & Humphreys, H. I. Electronics & Radio: An Introduction. 3rd ed. 1975. pap. text ed. 12.50x o.p. (ISBN 0-435-68335-7). Heinemann Ed.

Nell, Edward J., jt. auth. see Hollis, Martin I.

Nell, Edward J., ed. Growth, Profits & Property. LC 79-47192. (Illus.). 352p. 1980. 44.50 (ISBN 0-521-22396-2). Cambridge U Pr.

Nell, Varney R. & Dickenson, Richard B., eds. Entitled! Free Papers in Appalachia Concerning Antebellum Freeborn Negroes & Emancipated Blacks of Montgomery County, Virginia. LC 81-80481. 102p. lib. bdg. 18.50 (ISBN 0-915156-47-4). Natl Genealogical.

Nelli, Humbert S. The Business of Crime: Italians & Syndicate Crime in the United States. LC 75-32350. (Illus.). 1976. 22.50x (ISBN 0-19-502010-3). Oxford U Pr.

--From Immigrants to Ethnics: The Italian Americans. 228p. 1983. 24.95 (ISBN 0-19-503200-4). Oxford U Pr.

--The Italians in Chicago, 1880-1930: A Study in Ethnic Mobility. (Urban Life in America Ser.). (Illus.). 1973. 15.95 o.p. (ISBN 0-686-76957-0); pap. text ed. 6.95x (ISBN 0-19-501674-2). Oxford U Pr.

Nellis, Micki. Makin' It on the Farm: Alcohol Fuel is the Road to Independence. 88p. pap. 4.00 (ISBN 0-686-35950-X). Rutan Pub.

Nellist, Brian, ed. Milton: Poems of 1645. 272p. 1974. 19.00x (ISBN 0-7121-0149-7, Pub. by Macdonald & Evans). State Mutual Bk.

Nelms, Henning. Play Production. rev. ed. 1958. pap. 3.95 o.p. (ISBN 0-06-460073-4, CO 73, COS). B&N NY.

Nelsen, Harvey W. The Chinese Military System: An Organizational Study of the Chinese People's Liberation Army. Rev. ed. (Special Studies on China & East Asia). (Illus.). 266p. 1981. lib. bdg. 32.00 (ISBN 0-86531-069-6); pap. text ed. 15.00 (ISBN 0-86531-192-7). Westview.

Nelsen, Jane. Positive Discipline: Teaching Children Self-Discipline, Responsibility, Cooperation & Problem-Solving Skills. LC 81-83390. (Illus.). 156p. 1981. pap. 6.95 (ISBN 0-686-32832-9). Adlerian Consult.

Nelson & Miller. Modern Management Accounting. 2nd ed. 640p. 1981. 27.50x (ISBN 0-673-16115-3). Scott F.

Nelson, jt. auth. see Daphne.

Nelson, jt. auth. see Redfarn.

Nelson, jt. ed. see Daphne.

Nelson, et al. BASIC: A Simplified Structural Approach. 1980. pap. text ed. 12.95 o.p. (ISBN 0-8359-0338-9); soln. manual avail. o.p. (ISBN 0-8359-0339-7). Reston.

Nelson, Alice B. Four Ducks on a Pond. vi, 92p. 1983. 11.95 (ISBN 0-686-82663-9); pap. 6.95 (ISBN 0-686-82664-7). Vermont Bks.

Nelson, Allen H., jt. auth. see Kruegar, Janelle C.

Nelson, Alvin F. Inquiry & Reality: A Discourse in Pragmatic Synthesis. LC 75-46077. 1976. 10.00x (ISBN 0-912646-26-8). Tex Christian.

Nelson, Ann H., jt. auth. see Wertheimer, Barbara M.

Nelson, Anne H., jt. ed. see Wertheimer, Barbara M.

Nelson Associates. Public Library Systems in the United States: A Survey of Multijurisdictional Systems. LC 68-54708. (Illus.). 1969. 10.00 o.p. (ISBN 0-8389-3087-5). ALA.

Nelson, Ben A., jt. ed. see Wait, Walter K.

Nelson, Bettye, ed. see Lagal, Roy.

Nelson, Bettye, ed. see Poteet, G. Howard.

Nelson, Bill & Schmidt, Bill. Stick With It! (Illus.). 112p. (Orig.). 1983. pap. 3.95 (ISBN 0-936750-08-1). Wetherall.

Nelson, Bonnie E. Science Activities for Children Three to Nine Years Old. 102p. 1982. 20.00 (ISBN 0-931642-12-4). Lintel.

Nelson, Brian. Western Political Thought: From Theory & Ideology. 352p. 1982. 22.95 (ISBN 0-13-951640-9). P-H.

Nelson, Bryan. Azraq: Desert Oasis. LC 73-92910. (Illus.). xix, 436p. 1973. 16.00x (ISBN 0-8214-0142-4, 82-81453). Ohio U Pr.

--Seabirds: Their Biology and Ecology. (Illus.). 248p. 1980. 14.95 o.s.i. (ISBN 0-89479-042-0). A & W Pubs.

Nelson, C. Ellis. Where Faith Begins. 1968. pap. 7.25 (ISBN 0-8042-1471-9). John Knox.

Nelson, C. M. The Fortunate Years. 1983. 15.00 (ISBN 0-533-05305-6). Vantage.

Nelson, C. Michael, jt. auth. see Kerr, Mary M.

Nelson, C. V. & Geselowitz, David B. The Theoretical Basis of Electrocardiology. (Oxford Medical Engineering Series). (Illus.). text ed. 75.00x (ISBN 0-19-857374-X). Oxford U Pr.

Nelson, Carl. Just the Greatest. LC 72-184953. (Illus.). 96p. (Orig.). 1972. pap. 1.25 o.p. (ISBN 0-87784-543-3). Inter-Varsity.

Nelson, Carl & Nelson, Martha. The Ministering Couple. (Orig.). 1983. pap. 3.95 (ISBN 0-8054-3706-1); wkbk. 2.25 (ISBN 0-8054-9406-5). Broadman.

Nelson, Carl & Gruzalski, Bart, eds. Value Conflicts in Health Care Delivery. 248p. 1982. prof ref 24.50x (ISBN 0-88410-735-3). Ballinger Pub.

Nelson, Carl A. Millwrights & Mechanics Guide. new ed. (Audel Ser.). 1983. 19.95 (ISBN 0-672-23373-8). Bobbs.

Nelson, Carolyn. Basic Skills Nursery Rhymes Workbook. (Basic Skills Workbooks). 32p. (gr. k-1). 1983. 0.99 (ISBN 0-8209-0565-8, EEW-6). ESP.

Nelson, Clemens A., jt. auth. see Zumberge, James H.

Nelson, Cyril I. The Quilt Engagement Calendar, 1984. (Illus.). 116p. 1983. spiral 8.95 (ISBN 0-525-93288-7, 0869-260). Dutton.

Nelson, D. Lloyd & Stallings, John W. Nuts & Bolts in School Administration. LC 77-95156. 1978. pap. text ed. 10.50 (ISBN 0-8191-0461-2). U Pr of Amer.

Nelson, Daniel. Frederick W. Taylor & the Rise of Scientific Management. LC 79-5411. 288p. 1980. 22.50 (ISBN 0-299-08160-5). U of Wis Pr.

--Managers & Workers: Origins of the New Factory System in the United States, 1880-1920. 246p. 1975. 25.00 (ISBN 0-299-06900-1); pap. 9.95 (ISBN 0-299-06904-4). U of Wis Pr.

Nelson, Daniel & White, Stephen, eds. Communist Legislatures in Comparative Perspective. LC 81-9189. 216p. 1982. 34.50x (ISBN 0-87395-566-8); pap. 10.95x (ISBN 0-87395-567-6). State U NY Pr.

Nelson, Daniel N. Soviet Allies: The Warsaw Pact & the Issue of Reliability. 240p. 1983. lib. bdg. 20.00X (ISBN 0-86531-359-8). Westview.

Nelson, Daniel N., ed. Communism & the Politics of Inequalities. LC 81-48525. 1983. write for info. (ISBN 0-669-05415-1). Lexington Bks.

--Local Politics in Communist Countries. LC 78-58121. 240p. 1980. 17.50x (ISBN 0-8131-1398-9). U Pr of Ky.

--Romania in the Nineteen Eighties. (Westview Special Studies on the Soviet Union & Eastern Europe). 250p. 1981. lib. bdg. 24.00 (ISBN 0-86531-027-0). Westview.

Nelson, Dick & Nelson, Sharon. Hiker's Guide to the Superstition Mountains. (Illus.). 108p. (Orig.). 1978. pap. 4.95 o.p. (ISBN 0-915030-21-7). Tecolote Pr.

Nelson, Donald F. Electric, Optic, & Acoustic Interactions in Dielectrics. LC 78-25964. 1979. 51.95 (ISBN 0-471-05199-3, Pub. by Wiley-Interscience). Wiley.

Nelson, Donald M. Arsenal of Democracy: The Story of American War Production. LC 72-2378. (FDR & the Era of the New Deal Ser.). 439p. 1973. Repr. of 1946 ed. lib. bdg. 45.00. Da Capo.

Nelson, Donald T., jt. auth. see Schneiter, Paul H.

Nelson, Douglas R. The Political Structure of the New Protectionism. (Working Paper: No. 471). 57p. 1981. 5.00 (ISBN 0-686-36166-0, WP-0471). World Bank.

Nelson, E. Clifford, ed. Lutherans in North America. rev. ed. LC 74-26337. (Illus.). 576p. 1980. o. p. 22.50x o.p. (ISBN 0-8006-0409-1); pap. 14.95 o.p. (ISBN 0-8006-1409-7, 1-1409). Fortress.

--A Pioneer Churchman: J. W. C. Dietrichson in Wisconsin, 1844-1850. Rosholt, Malcolm & Kaasa, Harris, trs. from Norwegian. 1973. lib. bdg. 10.95 (ISBN 0-8057-5443-1, Twayne). G K Hall.

Nelson, E. W., jt. auth. see McLean, W. G.

Nelson, Edward, jt. auth. see Yaffe, Maurice.

Nelson, Edward W. The Eskimo About Bering Strait. (Classics of Smithsonian Anthropology Ser.). (Illus.). 520p. 1982. pap. text ed. 17.50x (ISBN 0-87474-671-X). Smithsonian.

Nelson, Edwin L., jt. auth. see Fuda, George E.

Nelson, Erland, ed. see Princeton Conference on Cerebrovascular Disease, 11th., Mar. 1978.

Nelson, Esther L. Dancing Games for Children of All Ages. LC 78-83456. (Illus.). 72p. (gr. 2 up). 1973. 10.95 (ISBN 0-8069-4522-2); PLB 13.29 (ISBN 0-8069-4523-0). Sterling.

--Holiday Singing & Dancing Games. LC 80-52331. (Illus.). 72p. (gr. k-3). 1980. 10.95 (ISBN 0-8069-4630-X); PLB 13.29 (ISBN 0-8069-4631-8). Sterling.

--Holiday Singing & Dancing Games. (Illus.). 72p. (gr. k-4). 1982. pap. 7.95 (ISBN 0-8069-7624-1). Sterling.

--Musical Games for Children of All Ages. (Illus.). 72p. (gr. k-6). 1981. pap. 7.95 spiral (ISBN 0-8069-7520-2). Sterling.

--Musical Games for Children of All Ages. LC 76-19804. (Illus.). (gr. 3 up). 1976. 10.95 (ISBN 0-8069-4540-0); PLB 13.29 (ISBN 0-8069-4541-9); pap. 6.95 (ISBN 0-686-77162-1). Sterling.

--The Silly Songbook. LC 81-50989. (Illus.). 128p. (gr. k-7). 1981. 10.95 (ISBN 0-8069-4650-4); PLB 13.29 (ISBN 0-8069-4651-2); spiral pap. 7.95 (ISBN 0-8069-7552-0). Sterling.

--Singing & Dancing Games for the Very Young. LC 77-79513. (Illus.). 1977. 10.95 (ISBN 0-8069-4568-0); lib. bdg. 13.29 (ISBN 0-8069-4569-9); pap. 6.95 spiral bd. (ISBN 0-8069-7572-5). Sterling.

Nelson, Ethel, jt. auth. see Kang, C. H.

Nelson, Florence. How to Teach a Demonstration-Type Subject. 1981. handbk. 3.50 (ISBN 0-918328-03-9); pap. 3.50.o.p. (ISBN 0-686-96688-0). Carma.

Nelson, Fred, jt. auth. see Blauvelt, Carolyn T.

Nelson, G. O. Controlled Test Atmospheres: Principles & Techniques. LC 73-141231. (Illus.). 1971. 30.00 (ISBN 0-250-97506-8). Ann Arbor Science.

Nelson, Gary J., ed. Blood Lipids & Lipoproteins: Quantitation, Composition & Metabolism. LC 78-9098. 992p. 1979. Repr. of 1972 ed. lib. bdg. 55.00 (ISBN 0-88275-695-8). Krieger.

Nelson, Gayle L. & Winters, Thomas A. ESL Operations: Techniques for Learning While Doing. (Orig.). 1980. pap. text ed. 6.95 (ISBN 0-88377-149-7). Newbury Hse.

Nelson, George. Problems of Design. (Illus.). 1979. pap. 9.95 o.p. (ISBN 0-8230-7439-0). Watson-Guptill.

Nelson, Gertrud M. Clip-Art for Feasts & Seasons. expanded ed. (Illus.). 120p. (Orig.). 1982. pap. 9.95 (ISBN 0-916134-41-5). Pueblo Pub Co.

Nelson, Gideon E. & Robinson, Gerald G. Fundamental Concepts of Biology. 4th ed. LC 81-3320. 406p. 1982. text ed. 23.95x (ISBN 0-471-03382-0); tchrs. manual 12.50x (ISBN 0-471-07819-0); student study guide 7.95x (ISBN 0-471-86271-1). Wiley.

Nelson, Gideon E., et al. Fundamental Concepts of Biology. 3rd ed. LC 73-9894. 384p. 1974. text ed. 22.95x o.p. (ISBN 0-471-63153-1); study guide 7.95 (ISBN 0-471-63146-9); experiments o.p. avail. (ISBN 0-471-63145-0). Wiley.

Nelson, Gideon E., Jr. Biological Principles with Human Perspectives. 1980. text ed. 24.95x (ISBN 0-471-02194-6). Wiley.

Nelson, Gordon. Smokehouse Bear. (Illus.). 1982. pap. 5.95 (ISBN 0-88240-227-7). Alaska Northwest.

Nelson, Gordon K., jt. auth. see Costa, Joseph H.

Nelson, H. Royce, Jr. New Technologies in Exploration Geophysics. 1983. text ed. 29.95x (ISBN 0-87201-321-9). Gulf Pub.

Nelson, Harland S. Charles Dickens. (English Author Ser.). 1981. lib. bdg. 12.95 (ISBN 0-8057-6805-X, Twayne). G K Hall.

Nelson, Harold C., et al, eds. see Keller, John J.

Nelson, Harry & Jurmain, Robert. Introduction to Physical Anthropology. 2nd ed. (Illus.). 602p. 1982. pap. text ed. 20.95 (ISBN 0-314-63283-2). West Pub.

Nelson, Harry W. Encounter at the Aquarium & Other Poems. LC 78-59594. (Illus.). 1978. pap. 3.95x (ISBN 0-915206-78-1). Blue Leaf.

Nelson, Hilda. Charles Nodier. (World Authors Ser.). lib. bdg. 15.95 (ISBN 0-8057-2654-3, Twayne). G K Hall.

Nelson, Howard J. & Clark, W. A. The Los Angeles Metropolitan Experience: Uniqueness, Generality & the Goal of the Good Life. LC 76-4795. (Contemporary Metropolitan Analysis Ser.). (Illus.). 80p. 1976. pap. 8.95x prof ref (ISBN 0-88410-438-9). Ballinger Pub.

Nelson, Hugh. Make Your Own Backpack & Other Wilderness Campgear. LC 82-75075. (Illus.). 139p. (Orig.). 1981. pap. 12.95 (ISBN 0-8040-0355-6). Swallow.

Nelson, Ilene F., jt. ed. see Barnes, Asa.

Nelson, J., jt. auth. see Michaelis, John U.

Nelson, J. C., jt. auth. see Lind, L. F.

Nelson, J. S. Fishes of the World. LC 76-14959. 1976. 41.50x (ISBN 0-471-01497-4, Pub. by Wiley-Interscience). Wiley.

Nelson, Jack. Captive Voices: The Report of the Commission of Inquiry into High School Journalism Convened by the Robert F. Kennedy Memorial. LC 74-9507. (Illus.). 288p. 1974. 10.95x o.p. (ISBN 0-8052-3573-6); pap. 1.45 o.p. (ISBN 0-8052-0471-7). Schocken.

Nelson, Jack & Roberts, Gene, Jr. The Censors & the Schools. LC 77-23390. 1977. Repr. of 1963 ed. lib. bdg. 18.50x (ISBN 0-8371-9687-6, NECE). Greenwood.

Nelson, James B. Embodiment: An Approach to Sexuality & Christian Theology. LC 78-55589. 1979. pap. 8.95 (ISBN 0-8066-1701-2, 10-2070). Augsburg.

Nelson, James E. The Practice of Marketing Research. 672p. 1982. text ed. 24.95x (ISBN 0-534-01068-7). Kent Pub Co.

Nelson, James G. Sir William Watson. (English Authors Ser.). lib. bdg. 14.95 (ISBN 0-8057-1564-9, Twayne). G K Hall.

Nelson, Jo, jt. auth. see Munson, Shirley.

Nelson, John. Drafting for Trades & Industry - Architectural. LC 77-91450. (Drafting Ser.). 138p. 1979. pap. text ed. 10.20 (ISBN 0-8273-1839-1); instructor's guide 4.75 (ISBN 0-8273-1641-0). Delmar.

--Drafting for Trades & Industry - Basic Skills. LC 77-91450. (Drafting Ser.). 464p. 1979. pap. text ed. 18.00 (ISBN 0-8273-1841-3); instructor's guide 4.75 (ISBN 0-8273-1641-0). Delmar.

--Drafting for Trades & Industry - Civil. LC 77-91450. (Drafting Ser.). 942p. 1979. pap. text ed. 6.00 (ISBN 0-8273-1844-8); instructor's guide 4.75 (ISBN 0-8273-1641-0). Delmar.

--Drafting for Trades & Industry - Mechanical & Electronic. LC 77-91450. (Drafting Ser.). 328p. 1979. pap. text ed. 14.80 (ISBN 0-8273-1846-4); instructor's guide 4.75 (ISBN 0-8273-1641-0). Delmar.

--Drafting for Trades & Industry - Technical Illustration. LC 77-91450. (Drafting Ser.). 113p. 1979. pap. text ed. 7.80 (ISBN 0-8273-1848-0); instructor's guide 4.75 (ISBN 0-8273-1641-0). Delmar.

Nelson, John see McCarthy, Charlotte.

Nelson, John D., jt. ed. see McCracken, George H.

Nelson, Jon P. Economic Analysis of Transportation Noise Abatement. LC 77-25404. 288p. 1978. prof ref 22.50x (ISBN 0-88410-456-7). Ballinger Pub.

Nelson, Judith C. Family Treatment: An Integrative Approach. 304p. 1983. 22.95 (ISBN 0-13-301895-4). P-H.

Nelson, Julius C. Five Thousand Years Among the Gods. 1977. 6.50 o.p. (ISBN 0-533-02563-X). Vantage.

--The Protest of the Gods. 1977. 4.50 o.p. (ISBN 0-533-02963-5). Vantage.

Nelson, Karin B. & Ellenberg, Jonas H., eds. Febrile Seizures. 378p. 1981. text ed. 42.00 (ISBN 0-89004-548-8). Raven.

Nelson, Kay S. The Complete International One-Dish Meal Cookbook. LC 79-65108. 296p. 1982. pap. 8.95 (ISBN 0-8128-6126-4). Stein & Day.

--The Complete International Soup Cookbook. LC 80-5409. 324p. 1980. 13.95 (ISBN 0-8128-2719-8); pap. 9.95 (ISBN 0-8128-6163-9). Stein & Day.

--Cooking with Mushrooms. LC 76-11503. (Cookbook Ser.). (Illus.). 224p. 1976. pap. 4.00 (ISBN 0-486-23414-2). Dover.

--Stews & Ragouts: Simple & Hearty One-Dish Meals. 1978. pap. 3.00 (ISBN 0-486-23662-5). Dover.

--The Yogurt Cookbook. 8.50 (ISBN 0-8446-5600-3). Peter Smith.

Nelson, Keith E., ed. Children's Language, Vol. 3. (Ongoing Ser.). 522p. 1982. text ed. 39.95 (ISBN 0-89859-264-X). L Erlbaum Assocs.

Nelson, Keith L. Victors Divided: America & the Allies in Germany, 1918-1923. (Illus.). 424p. 1975. 40.00x (ISBN 0-520-02315-3). U of Cal Pr.

Nelson, Keith L. & Olin, Spencer C. Why War? Ideology, Theory, & History. LC 78-51746. 1979. 14.95x (ISBN 0-520-03672-7); pap. 4.95 (ISBN 0-520-04279-4). U of Cal Pr.

Nelson, Kennard S. Flower & Plant Production in the Greenhouse. 3rd ed. LC 77-79741. (Illus.). (gr. 9-12). 1978. 16.50 (ISBN 0-8134-1965-4); text ed. 12.50x. Interstate.

--Greenhouse Management for Flower & Plant Production. 2nd ed. 1980. 16.50 (ISBN 0-8134-2070-9, 2070); text ed. 12.50x (ISBN 0-686-82923-9). Interstate.

Nelson, L., Jr. Cervantes: A Collection of Critical Essays. 1969. 12.95 o.p. (ISBN 0-13-123299-1, Spec). P-H.

Nelson, L. N. & Nelson, P. N., eds. The Winds of History. LC 82-90424. (Illus.). 170p. (Orig.). 1983. pap. 9.95 (ISBN 0-942652-01-0). Windriver Scribes.

Nelson, L. N., jt. ed. see Nelson, P. N.

Nelson, Lee. The Storm Testament. (Utah Frontier Ser.). 320p. 1982. 9.95 (ISBN 0-936860-09-X). Liberty Pr.

Nelson, Leonard. System of Ethics. 1956. 49.50x (ISBN 0-685-69846-7). Elliots Bks.

Nelson, Louis N. The Nature of Teaching. LC 69-16603. 324p. (Orig.). 1969. pap. 13.50 (ISBN 0-471-00393-X). Krieger.

Nelson, Lyle M., jt. ed. see Lerner, Daniel.

Nelson, M. J., et al. Denny Reading Test. 1973. text ed. write for info o.p. (ISBN 0-685-32992-5). HM.

Nelson, M. W. Los Testigos De Jehova. 130p. 1981. pap. 2.50 (ISBN 0-311-06352-7). Casa Bautista.

Nelson, Malcolm A., jt. auth. see Goerge, Diana Hume.

Nelson, Martha, jt. auth. see Nelson, Carl.

Nelson, Mary, ed. see Bignell, Steven.

Nelson, Mary C. Masters of Western Art. (Illus.). 176p. 1982. 27.50 (ISBN 0-8230-3018-0). Watson-Guptill.

Nelson, Meryl & Thoman, Frances. That to This--the Leftovers Cookbook. Sing, Shirley, ed. (Illus.). 70p. (Orig.). pap. 4.50 (ISBN 0-941900-03-7). This N That.

Nelson, Meryl, jt. auth. see Thoman, Frances.

Nelson, Nancy P., ed. Nursing Care Plans for the Pediatric Patient. 1982. pap. 25.00 (ISBN 0-295-96019-1, Pub. by Childrens Orthopedic Hosp & Med Ctr). U of Wash Pr.

Nelson, Nickola W. Planning Individual Speech & Language Intervention Programs. 240p. 1979. pap. 15.95 (ISBN 0-88450-790-4, 3099-B). Communication Skill.

Nelson, Nina. Tunisia. (Batsford Countries of Europe Ser.). (Illus.). 1974. 9.95 (ISBN 0-8038-7150-3). Hastings.

Nelson, Norbert, jt. auth. see Kowalski, Theodore J.

Nelson, O. T. The Girl Who Owned a City. LC 73-22525. (Books for Adults & Young Adults Ser.). (Illus.). 180p. (gr. 6 up). 1975. 6.95g (ISBN 0-8225-0756-0). Lerner Pubns.

Nelson, P. N. & Nelson, L. N., eds. Oregon Gold. 1983. pap. 5.95 (ISBN 0-942652-00-2). Windriver Scribes.

Nelson, P. N., jt. ed. see Nelson, L. N.

Nelson, Paul. Days Off. LC 82-20294. (Virginia Commonwealth University Series of Contemporary Poetry). 86p. 1982. 10.95x (ISBN 0-8139-0965-1). U Pr of Va.

--Greenhouse Operation & Management. 2nd ed. 520p. 1981. text ed. 20.95 (ISBN 0-8359-2576-5); instr's. manual free (ISBN 0-8359-2577-3). Reston.

Nelson, Paul & Bangs, Lester. Rod Stewart. (Illus.). 160p. (Orig.). 1981. pap. 8.95 (ISBN 0-933328-08-7). Delilah Bks.

Nelson, Paula. Where to Get Money for Everything: A Complete Guide to Today's Money Sources. 1982. 12.50 (ISBN 0-688-00536-5). Morrow.

Nelson, R., jt. ed. see Balassa, B.

Nelson, R. J. Play Within a Play. LC 72-87356. (Theater, Film & the Performing Arts Ser.). 182p. 1971. Repr. of 1958 ed. lib. bdg. 25.00 (ISBN 0-306-71580-5). Da Capo.

Nelson, Rachel W., jt. auth. see Webb, Sheyann.

Nelson, Ralph, jt. auth. see Preston, Paul.

Nelson, Ralph L. Economic Factors in the Growth of Corporation Giving. LC 70-104182. 116p. 1970. 7.95x (ISBN 0-87154-615-9). Russell Sage.

--The Investment Policies of Foundations. LC 66-30032. 204p. 1967. 10.95x (ISBN 0-87154-614-0). Russell Sage.

Nelson, Rex, jt. auth. see Hudson, Alvin.

Nelson, Richard D. The Double Redaction of the Deuteronomistic History. (Journal for the Study of the Old Testament, Supplement Ser.: No. 18). 185p. 1982. text ed. 22.50 (ISBN 0-905774-33-7); pap. text ed. 14.95 (ISBN 0-686-97732-7). Eisenbrauns.

Nelson, Richard E., jt. auth. see Garfield, Nancy J.

Nelson, Richard K. Make Prayers to the Raven: A Koyukon View of the Northern Forest. LC 82-8441. 300p. 1983. 25.00 (ISBN 0-226-57162-9). U of Chicago Pr.

--Shadow of a the Hunter: Stories of Eskimo Life. LC 80-11091. (Illus.). xiv, 282p. 1980. pap. 7.95 (ISBN 0-686-84090-9). U of Chicago Pr.

Nelson, Richard L. Soccer. 6th ed. (Exploring Sports Ser.). 82p. 1983. pap. write for info. (ISBN 0-697-09965-2). Wm C Brown.

Nelson, Richard R. & Yates, Douglas T. Innovation & Implementation in Public Organizations. LC 74-16938. 208p. 1977. 23.95 (ISBN 0-669-95596-5). Lexington Bks.

Nelson, Richard R., ed. Government & Technical Progress: Cross-Industry Analysis. (The Technical Policy & Economic Growth Ser.). (Illus.). 512p. 1982. 45.00 (ISBN 0-08-028837-5, L110). Pergamon.

Nelson, Robert H. The Making of Federal Coal Policy. (Duke Press Policy Studies). (Illus.). 250p. 1983. 25.00 (ISBN 0-8223-0497-X). Duke.

--Zoning & Property Rights. 1977. 18.50x o.p. (ISBN 0-262-14028-4); pap. 5.95x (ISBN 0-262-64019-8). MIT Pr.

Nelson, Robert L. Downhill to Uphill. LC 79-6756. 76p. 1980. pap. text ed. 6.50 (ISBN 0-8191-0946-0). U Pr of Amer.

Nelson, Robert S., ed. Technological Change & the Future of the Railways: Proceedings. Johnson, Edward M. 239p. 1961. pap. 2.50 (ISBN 0-686-94048-2, Trans). Northwestern U Pr.

Nelson, Roy P. Articles & Features. LC 77-85340. (Illus.). 1978. text ed. 18.95. HM.

--Publication Design. 3rd ed. 320p. 1983. text ed. write for info. (ISBN 0-697-04356-8). Wm C Brown.

Nelson, Roy P. & Ferris, Byron. Fell's Guide to Commercial Art. LC 66-14801. 118p. (gr. 10 up). 1966. 19.95 (ISBN 0-8119-0041-X). Fell.

Nelson, Roy P., jt. auth. see Copperud, Roy H.

Nelson, Roy P., jt. auth. see Hulteng, John L.

Nelson, S. A. The ABC of Stock Market Spectulation & the Anticipation of the Wave Theory. (Illus.). 147p. 1982. Repr. of 1918 ed. 64.75 (ISBN 0-686-83054-7). Found Class Reprints.

--The ABC of Stock Speculation. 1964. Repr. of 1903 ed. flexible cover 8.00 (ISBN 0-87034-054-9, B401). Fraser Pub Co.

--The Methods of Trading in Wall Street for the Full Utilization of Speculative Opportunities. (A New Stock Market Library Bk.). (Illus.). 129p. 1983. 49.85 (ISBN 0-86654-059-8). Inst Econ Finan.

Nelson, Sarah M. Han River Chulmuntogi: A Study of Early Neolithic Korea. LC 76-2391. (Program in E. A. Studies: No. 9). (Illus.). 176p. 1975. pap. 6.00 (ISBN 0-914584-09-X). West Wash Univ.

Nelson, Sharon, jt. auth. see Nelson, Dick.

Nelson, Sheila M. The Violin & the Viola. (Illus.). 277p. 1972. 12.50x o.p. (ISBN 0-393-02092-4). Norton.

Nelson, Stanley. The Unknowable Light of the Alien. LC 80-53431. 180p. (Orig.). 1981. pap. 5.00 (ISBN 0-912292-65-2). The Smith.

Nelson, Stanley A., compiled by. A Journey in Becoming. (Orig.). 1983. pap. 4.50 (ISBN 0-8054-6320-8). Broadman.

Nelson, Suzanne L., ed. Garden Plans. (Rodale's Grow-It Guides). (Illus.). 128p. Date not set. pap. cancelled (ISBN 0-87857-427-1, 01-124-1). Rodale Pr Inc. Postponed.

--The Gardener's Problem Solver. (Rodale's Grow-It Guides Ser.). (Illus.). 128p. Date not set. pap. 6.95 (ISBN 0-87857-426-3, 01-125-1). Rodale Pr Inc. Postponed.

Nelson, Ted & Ames, Margery E., eds. Legal & Regulatory Affairs Manual. 1982. pap. 10.00 (ISBN 0-686-37426-6). Coun NY Law.

Nelson, Truman. God in Love: The Sexual Revolution of John Humphrey Noyes. 1983. write for info (ISBN 0-393-01636-6). Norton.

Nelson, Vera J. Scent of Water. (A Western Americana Book). 104p. (Orig.). 1973. pap. 3.00x (ISBN 0-913626-19-8). S S S Pub Co.

Nelson, Vera M. Siamese Cat Book. 5th ed. (Illus.). 1958. 9.95 (ISBN 0-87666-182-7, AP4300). TFH Pubns.

Nelson, W. How to Profit from the Money Revolution. 92p. 1983. 12.95 (ISBN 0-07-046217-8, GB). McGraw.

Nelson, W. B. Applied Life Data Analysis. LC 81-14779. (Wiley Series Probability & Mathematical Statistics: Applied Probability & Statistics Section). 634p. 1982. 40.95x (ISBN 0-471-09458-7, Pub. by Wiley-Interscience). Wiley.

Nelson, W. L. Guide to Refinery Operating Costs. 3rd ed. LC 74-125557. 332p. 1976. 39.95x (ISBN 0-87814-002-6). Pennwell Pub.

Nelson, Wayne F. How to Buy Money: Investing Wisely for Maximum Return. LC 81-3751. 1982. pap. 10.95 (ISBN 0-07-046220-8); pap. 5.95 (ISBN 0-07-046221-6). McGraw.

--The Smart Investor's Guide to the Money Market. (Orig.). 1981. pap. 3.50 (ISBN 0-451-11118-4, AE1118, Sig). NAL.

Nelson, Wilbur L. Petroleum Refinery Engineering. 4th ed. (Civil Engineering Ser.). (Illus.). 1958. 74.50 (ISBN 0-07-046268-2, P&RB). McGraw.

Nelson, William. New Jersey Biographical & Genealogical Notes, Vol. 9. 222p. 1916. 6.95 (ISBN 0-686-81825-3). NJ Hist Soc.

Nelson, William, jt. ed. see Ferguson, John.

Nelson, William B. Denturists Will Not Be Denied. 83p. 1982. 10.00 (ISBN 0-89697-045-0). Intl Univ MO.

Nelson, Wilson E. The Roots of American Bureaucracy, Eighteen Thirty to Nineteen Hundred. 240p. 1982. text ed. 22.50x (ISBN 0-674-77945-2). Harvard U Pr.

Nelson, Yvette. We'll Come When It Rains. LC 82-61649. (Minnesota Voices Project Ser.: No. 11). (Illus.). 70p. 1982. pap. 3.00 (ISBN 0-89823-043-8). New Rivers Pr.

Nelson-Ericksen, Jean, et al. How to Adopt from Asia, Europe & the South Pacific: How to Adopt: No. 2. 3rd ed. (Illus.). 1983. pap. 16.95. Los Ninos.

Nelson-Heern, Laurie, jt. ed. see Harris, Diana.

Nelson-Rees, A. Paintings by Selden Connor Gile, 1877-1947. LC 82-83509. (Illus.). 72p. 1982. 20.00 (ISBN 0-938842-02-1). WIM Oakland.

Nelson-Rees, Walter A. Lillie May Nicholson: 1884-1964 an Artist Rediscovered. LC 80-53867. (Illus.). 88p. 1981. 25.00 (ISBN 0-938842-00-5). WIM Oakland.

Nelson-Richards, M. Social Change & Rural Development: Intervention or Participation - A Zambian Case Study. LC 80-5686. 162p. 1982. lib. bdg. 19.00 (ISBN 0-8191-2291-2); pap. text ed. 8.25 (ISBN 0-8191-2292-0). U Pr of Amer.

Neman, Beth S. Teaching Students to Write. (Illus.). 456p. 1980. pap. text ed. 13.95 (ISBN 0-675-08138-6). Merrill.

--Writing Effectively. 504p. 1983. text ed. 13.95 (ISBN 0-675-20047-4); tchr's ed. 13.95 (ISBN 0-675-20053-9). Additional supplements may be obtained from publisher. Merrill.

Nemat-Nasser, S. Variational Methods in the Mechanics of Solids: Proceedings of the UUTAM Symposium, Sept. 11-13, 1978. LC 80-41529. (Illus.). 426p. 1980. 110.00 (ISBN 0-08-024728-8). Pergamon.

Nemat-Nasser, S., ed. Mechanics Today, Vols. 1-3. Incl. Vol. 1. 1973. text ed. 36.00 (ISBN 0-08-017246-6); Vol. 2. 1976. text ed. 37.00 (ISBN 0-08-018113-9); Vol. 3. 1976. text ed. 37.00 (ISBN 0-08-019882-1); Vol. 4. 1978. text ed. 55.00 (ISBN 0-08-021792-3). 1978. Vols. 1-4. text ed. 121.00 (ISBN 0-08-022682-5). Pergamon.

--Three Dimensional Constitutive Relationships & Ductile Fracture. 1981. 83.00 (ISBN 0-444-86108-4). Elsevier.

Nemchin, Jack. Goalie Album. (Illus.). 50p. 1981. pap. 9.95 o.p. (ISBN 0-312-32998-9). St Martin.

Nemec, David. Bright Lights, Dark Rooms. LC 79-7876. 1980. 10.95 o.p. (ISBN 0-385-15661-8). Doubleday.

Nemeck, Francis K. & Coombs, Marie T. Contemplation. 1982. 8.95 (ISBN 0-89453-276-6); pap. 4.95 (ISBN 0-686-32774-8). M Glazier.

--Contemplation. (Ways of Prayer Ser.: Vol. 5). 151p. 1982. 8.95; pap. 4.95 (ISBN 0-686-82184-X). M Glazier.

Nemenyi, R. Controlled Atmospheres for Heat Treatment. (Illus.). 225p. 1983. text ed. 40.01 (ISBN 0-08-019883-X). Pergamon.

Nemeroff, C. B. & Dunn, A. J., eds. Peptides, Hormones & Behavior. (Illus.). 1000p. 1983. text ed. 125.00 (ISBN 0-89335-138-5). SP Med & Sci Bks.

Nemerov, Howard. Poetry & Fiction: Essays. 1963. 27.50x o.p. (ISBN 0-8135-0438-4). Rutgers U Pr.

--Sentences. LC 80-17702. 86p. 1980. pap. 4.95 (ISBN 0-226-57262-5). U of Chicago Pr.

--Stories, Fables & Other Diversions. LC 75-143388. 1971. 7.50 (ISBN 0-87923-030-4); pap. 3.95. Godine.

Nemerow, Nelson L. Industrial Solid Waste. LC 82-13866. 384p. 1983. text ed. 35.00x (ISBN 0-88410-876-7). Ballinger Pub.

--Industrial Water Pollution: Origins, Characteristics & Treatment. LC 76-46612. 1978. text ed. 30.95 (ISBN 0-201-05246-6). A-W.

Nemerowicz, Gloria M. Children's Perceptions of Gender & Work Roles. LC 79-11783. 1979. 26.95 o.p. (ISBN 0-03-049811-2). Praeger.

Nemeshegyi, Peter. The Meaning of Christianity. 128p. 1982. pap. 2.95 (ISBN 0-8091-2464-5). Paulist Pr.

Nemeskurty, Istvan. Word & Image: History of the Hungarian Cinema. (Illus.). 296p. 1982. 14.95x (ISBN 0-8044-2656-2). Ungar.

Nemeth, Doris I. & Kenzie, Peggy, eds. The Poet. (Illus.). 400p. (gr. 5 up). 1982. pap. 11.00 (ISBN 0-932192-04-1). Fine Arts Soc.

Nemeth, Gyuri, jt. auth. see Miller, Gary M.

Nemetsky, Yu., tr. see Linnik, I.

Nemhauser, George L., jt. auth. see Garfinkel, Robert.

Nemiah, John C. Foundations of Psychopathology. 1961. pap. 8.95x (ISBN 0-19-501137-6). Oxford U Pr.

Nemiro, Beverly & Von Allman, Marie. Lunchbox Cookbook. LC 82-71249. 127p. 1965. 5.95 (ISBN 0-8040-0192-8). Swallow.

Nemirovskii, A. S. Problem Complexity & Method Efficiency in Optimization. 350p. 1983. write for info. (ISBN 0-471-10345-4, Pub. by Wiley-Interscience). Wiley.

Nemmers, Erwin E. & Grunewald, Alan E. Basic Managerial Finance. 2nd ed. LC 74-17164. 750p. 1975. text ed. 24.95 (ISBN 0-8299-0025-X); avail. study guide 8.95 (ISBN 0-8299-0027-6); instrs.' manual avail. (ISBN 0-8299-0564-2). West Pub.

Nemo, John. Patrick Kavanagh. (English Authors Ser.). 1979. lib. bdg. 14.95 (ISBN 0-8057-6770-3, Twayne). G K Hall.

Nemo, John, ed. see Kavanaugh, Patrick & O'Connor, P. J.

Nemodruk, A. A. & Karalova, Z. K. Analytical Chemistry of Boron. (Analytical Chemistry of the Elements Ser.). 1971. 44.95 o.s.i. (ISBN 0-470-63168-6). Halsted Pr.

Nemser, Cindy. Eve's Delight. 320p. (Orig.). 1982. pap. 3.75 (ISBN M-523-41755-1). Pinnacle Bks.

Nenninger, Timothy K. The Leavenworth Schools & the Old Army: Education, Professionalism, & the Officer Corps of the United States Army, 1881-1918. LC 77-91105. (Contributions in Military History: No. 15). 1978. lib. bdg. 25.00 (ISBN 0-313-20047-5, NFL/). Greenwood.

Nenno, jt. auth. see Gilligan.

Nenno, Bob, jt. auth. see Gilligan, Lawrence.

Nenno, Robert, jt. auth. see Gilligan, Lawrence.

Nennsberg, Tatiana O. & Barber, Bruce. Russian Verb Wheel. 1962. 3.95x (ISBN 0-669-30684-3). Heath.

Nentl, Jerolyn. Beaver. Schroeder, Howard, ed. (Wildlife Habits & Habitat Ser.). (Illus.). 48p. (gr. 4-5). 1983. lib. bdg. 8.95 (ISBN 0-89686-219-4). Crestwood Hse.

--Bicycle Motocross. Schroeder, Howard, ed. LC 78-6840. (Funseekers Ser.). (Illus.). (gr. 3-4). 1978. PLB 6.95 o.p. (ISBN 0-913940-89-5); pap. 3.95 (ISBN 0-89686-010-8). Crestwood Hse.

--Disco Dancing. Schroeder, Howard, ed. LC 79-27801. (Funseekers Ser.). (Illus.). (gr. 3-5). 1980. lib. bdg. 7.95 (ISBN 0-89686-073-6); pap. 3.95 (ISBN 0-89686-077-9). Crestwood Hse.

--Drag Racing. LC 78-9455. (Winners Circle Ser.). (Illus.). (gr. 4). 1978. PLB 7.95 (ISBN 0-913940-80-1). Crestwood Hse.

--Freestyle Skiing. Schroeder, Howard, ed. LC 78-8032. (Funseekers Ser.). (Illus.). (gr. 3-4). 1978. PLB 7.95 (ISBN 0-913940-90-9); pap. 3.95 (ISBN 0-89686-011-6). Crestwood Hse.

--The Gram Is. LC 76-24203. (Metrics America Ser.). (gr. 4). 1976. 6.95 (ISBN 0-913940-47-X). Crestwood Hse.

--The Liter Is. LC 76-24202. (Metrics America Ser.). (gr. 4). 1976. 6.95 (ISBN 0-913940-46-1). Crestwood Hse.

--The Mallard. Schroeder, Howard, ed. (Wildlife Habits & Habitat Ser.). (Illus.). 48p. (gr. 4-5). 1983. lib. bdg. 8.95 (ISBN 0-89686-221-6). Crestwood Hse.

--Marathon Running. Schroeder, Howard, ed. LC 79-27799. (Funseekers Ser.). (Illus.). (gr. 3-5). 1980. lib. bdg. 7.95 (ISBN 0-89686-074-4); pap. 3.95 (ISBN 0-89686-078-7). Crestwood Hse.

--The Meter Is. LC 76-24200. (Metrics America Ser.). (gr. 4). 6.95 (ISBN 0-913940-45-3). Crestwood Hse.

--Metric System Is. LC 76-24199. (Metrics America Ser.). (gr. 4). 1976. 6.95 (ISBN 0-913940-44-5). Crestwood Hse.

--Mountain Climbing. Schroeder, Howard, ed. LC 80-415. (Funseekers Ser.). (Illus.). (gr. 3-5). 1979. lib. bdg. 7.95 (ISBN 0-89686-075-2); pap. 3.95 (ISBN 0-89686-079-5). Crestwood Hse.

--Roller Skating. Schroeder, Howard, ed. LC 80-10475. (Funseekers Ser.). (Illus.). (gr. 3-5). 1980. lib. bdg. 7.95 (ISBN 0-89686-072-8); pap. 3.95 (ISBN 0-89686-076-0). Crestwood Hse.

--Skydiving. Schroeder, Howard, ed. LC 78-8702. (Funseekers Ser.). (Illus.). (gr. 3-4). 1978. PLB 7.95 (ISBN 0-913940-87-9); pap. 3.95 (ISBN 0-89686-008-6). Crestwood Hse.

--Surfing. Schroeder, Howard, ed. LC 78-8723. (Funseekers Ser.). (Illus.). (gr. 3-4). 1978. PLB 7.95 (ISBN 0-913940-93-3); pap. 3.95 (ISBN 0-89686-014-0). Crestwood Hse.

Nentl, Jerolyn, jt. auth. see East, Ben.

Nentle, Jerolyn. The Celsius Thermometer. LC 76-24205. (Metrics America Ser.). (gr. 4). 1976. 6.95 (ISBN 0-913940-48-8). Crestwood Hse.

Nentwig, Joachim & Kreuder, Manfred. Chemistry Made Easy, Part I: A Programmed Course for Self-Instruction. 600p. pap. write for info. (ISBN 0-89573-049-9). Verlag Chemie.

Neogy, Prithwish, jt. auth. see Haar, Francis.

Neophitos, Angelo. The Seasons Sing of God. (Illus.). 145p. 1979. pap. 4.95 (ISBN 0-686-81994-2). St Thomas Seminary.

Nephele, Maria. Odysseus Elytis: A Poem in Two Voices. Anagnostopoulos, Athan, tr. from Greek. 64p. 1981. 10.00 (ISBN 0-395-29465-7); pap. cancelled (ISBN 0-395-31148-9). HM.

Nepos see Livy.

Neppert, Boehland M. German Textiles. (Illus.). 22.50 o.p. (ISBN 0-87245-328-6). Textile Bk.

Nerbonne, J. J. A Foreign Correspondent Looks at Taiwan. (Illus.). 1973. 10.00 (ISBN 0-685-47316-3). Heinman.

Nercessian, Y. T. Attribution & Dating of Armenian Bilingual Trams. (Illus.). 52p. (Orig.). 1983. write for info. (ISBN 0-9606842-1-2). ANS.

Nerem, R. M., jt. ed. see Skalak, R.

Nerem, Robert M., jt. ed. see Bell, Adam C.

Nering, Evar D. Linear Algebra & Matrix Theory. 2nd ed. LC 76-91646. 1970. 29.95 (ISBN 0-471-63178-7). Wiley.

Nering, Evar D., jt. auth. see Ledbetter, Carl S.

Neri Serneri, G. G., jt. ed. see Mason, D. T.

Nerlich, Uwe, ed. Soviet Power & Western Negotiating Policy, Vol. I: The Soviet Asset: Military Power in the Competition over Europe. 384p. 1983. prof ref 38.00x (ISBN 0-88410-905-4). Ballinger Pub.

--Soviet Power & Western Negotiating Policy, Vol. II: The Western Panacea: Constraining Soviet Power Through Negotiation. 400p. 1983. prof ref 38.00x (ISBN 0-88410-921-6). Ballinger Pub.

Nerlove, M., et al. Problems of Time Series Analysis. 104p. 1980. pap. text ed. 12.95x (ISBN 3-411-01587-X). Birkhauser.

Nero, pseud. By My Laugh Its Jewish. 110p. 1983. text ed. 12.50x (ISBN 0-85303-197-5, Pub. by Vallentine Mitchell England); pap. text ed. 6.50x (ISBN 0-85303-198-3). Biblio Dist.

Nero, Anthony V., Jr. A Guidebook to Nuclear Reactors. LC 77-76183. (Cal. Ser.: No. 393). 1979. 38.50x (ISBN 0-520-03482-1); pap. 11.95 (ISBN 0-520-03661-1). U of Cal Pr.

Nero, Charles. The Reverand. LC 81-86209. 304p. 1983. text ed. 10.95 (ISBN 0-86666-074-7). GWP.

Nero, Jack. If Only My Wife Could Drink Like a Lady. LC 77-86453. 1977. pap. 6.95 (ISBN 0-89638-006-8). CompCare.

Nersesian, Roy L. Ships & Shipping: A Comprehensive Guide. 256p. 1981. 3.95x (ISBN 0-87814-148-0). Pennwell Pub.

Nerubay, Jacobo, jt. ed. see Katznelson, Alexander.

Neruda, Jan. Tales of the Little Quarter. Pargeter, Edith, tr. from Czech. 1977. Repr. of 1957 ed. lib. bdg. 21.00x (ISBN 0-8371-9344-3, NELQ). Greenwood.

Neruda, Pablo. The Captain's Verses. Walsh, Donald D., tr. from Span. & intro. by. LC 72-80977. 160p. (Eng. & Span.). 1972. pap. 4.95 (ISBN 0-8112-0457-X, NDP345). New Directions.

--Extravagaria: Bilingual Edition. Reid, Alastair, tr. from Span. LC 72-84773. 304p. 1974. 8.95 (ISBN 0-374-15126-1); pap. 5.95 o.p. (ISBN 0-374-51238-8). FS&G.

--Five Decades: Poems: 1925-1970. Belitt, Ben, ed. & tr. from Span. (Bilingual ed.). 1974. pap. 8.95 (ISBN 0-394-17869-6, E636, Ever). Grove.

--Fully Empowered. Reid, Alastair, tr. from Sp. LC 75-9726. 144p. 1975. bi-lingual ed. 12.95 (ISBN 0-374-15944-0); pap. 6.95 (ISBN 0-374-51351-1). FS&G.

--Isla Negra: A Notebook. Reid, Alastair, et al, trs. from Span. 416p. 1983. 18.95 (ISBN 0-374-17759-7); pap. 10.25 (ISBN 0-374-51734-7). FS&G.

--Residence on Earth & Other Poems. Walsh, Donald D., tr. from Sp. & intro. by. LC 72-93972. Orig. Title: Residencia en la Tierra. 1973. 10.00 (ISBN 0-8112-0466-9); pap. 7.25 (ISBN 0-8112-0467-7, NDP340). New Directions.

--Selected Poems of Pablo Neruda. 1973. pap. 9.95 (ISBN 0-440-57879-5, Delta). Dell.

Neruda, Pablo & Frasconi, Antonio. Bestiary Bestiario. Neuberger, Elsa, tr. from Span. LC 74-6154. (Illus.). 48p. 1974. pap. 3.95 (ISBN 0-15-611860-2, Harv). HarBraceJ.

Nervi, Carlo, jt. ed. see Fletcher, Gilbert.

Nerys, Dee. Fortune-Telling By Playing Cards: A New Guide to the Ancient Art of Cartomancy. (Illus.). 160p. (Orig.). 1982. pap. 6.95 (ISBN 0-85030-266-8, Pub. by Aquarian Pr England). Sterling.

Nesbit, E. The Last of the Dragons. LC 79-28584. (Illus.). 32p. (gr. k-4). 1980. 8.95 (ISBN 0-07-046285-2). McGraw.

--The Magic City. 1981. 11.95 (ISBN 0-8398-2730-X, Gregg). G K Hall.

Nesbit, Edith. Railway Children. (gr. 2-5). 1961. pap. 1.95 o.p. (ISBN 0-14-030147-X, Puffin). Penguin.

--The Railway Children. (gr. 2-5). 1983. pap. 2.25 (ISBN 0-14-035005-5, Puffin). Penguin.

Nesbit, Robert C. Wisconsin: A History. LC 72-9990. (Illus.). 620p. 1973. 19.95 (ISBN 0-299-06370-4). U of Wis Pr.

Nesbit, Robert G. How to Get Super Results from Average Performers. 1979. cassette-spiral wkbk. prog. 99.50 (ISBN 0-686-98288-6). Sales & Mktg.

Nesbitt, E. A. & Wernick, J. A. Rare Earth Permanent Magnets. (Materials Science Ser). 1973. 25.00 (ISBN 0-12-515450-X). Acad Pr.

Nesbitt, Gene H. Canine & Feline Dermatology: A Systematic Approach. LC 82-12747. (Illus.). 225p. 1983. text ed. write for info (ISBN 0-8121-0859-0). Lea & Febiger.

Nesbitt, Murray B. Labor Relations in the Federal Government Service. LC 75-44255. 560p. 1976. 20.00 (ISBN 0-87179-225-7). BNA.

Nesbitt, W. H., ed. Eighteenth Boone & Crockett Big Game Awards, 1980-1982. (Illus.). 250p. 1983. 19.50 (ISBN 0-940864-05-3). Boone & Crockett.

Nesbitt, W. H. & Wright, Philip L., eds. Records at North American Big Game. 8th ed. xii, 412p. 1981. leather, limited 195.00x (ISBN 0-940864-01-0). Boone & Crockett.

Nesdale, A. & Pratt, C. Advances in Child Developement: Theory & Research. 1982. pap. 12.50 (ISBN 0-9594161-0-2, Pub. by U of W Austral Pr). Intl Schol Bk Serv.

Nesgoda, John, jt. auth. see Vernick, Judy.

Nesi, Ruth, jt. auth. see Stalberg, Roberta.

Nesmeyanov, A. & Kocheshkov, K. Vapor Pressure of the Chemical Elements. 1963. 58.75 (ISBN 0-444-40409-0). Elsevier.

Nesmith, Hayden R. Poetical Memories from the Pen of Hayden R. Nesmith. 1981. cancelled 5.75 o.p. (ISBN 0-8062-1630-1). Carlton.

Nesnow, Stephen, jt. ed. see Langenbach, Robert.

Ness, Alex W. Pioneering. LC 82-73706. 1983. pap. text ed. 5.00 (ISBN 0-932050-14-X). New Puritan.

Ness, Bethann Van see Van Ness, Bethann.

Ness, Bethann Van see Van Ness, Bethann & De Clemente, Elizabeth M.

Ness, Evaline. Fierce the Lion. LC 80-10172. (Illus.). 32p. (ps-3). 1980. PLB 8.95 (ISBN 0-8234-0412-9). Holiday.

Ness, Gayl D. Bureaucracy & Rural Development in Malaysia. 1967. 30.00x (ISBN 0-520-00922-3). U of Cal Pr.

Ness, George T., Jr. Under the Eagle's Wings: The Army on the Eve of Civil War, 2 vols. Date not set. price not set. MA AH Pub.

Ness, Gladys M. Jesus & the Twelve in 30 A. D. 64p. 1983. 6.95 (ISBN 0-8059-2863-4). Dorrance.

Ness, H. C. Van see Van Ness, H. C.

Ness, H. C. Van see Van Ness, H. C. & Abbott, M. M.

Ness, Lottye G. Van see Van Ness, Lottye G.

Ness, Pamela M. Assisi Embroidery. (Illus.). 1978. pap. 1.95 (ISBN 0-486-23743-5). Dover.

Ness, Theodore & Vogel, Eugene L. Taxation of the Closely-Held Corporation. 3rd ed. 1975. 66.00 (ISBN 0-88262-077-0, 67-15467). Warren.

Ness Blair, Ruth Van see Blair, Ruth.

Nessel, Denise D. & Jones, Margaret B. Language-Experience Approach to Reading: A Handbook for Teachers of Reading. LC 80-27822. (Orig.). 1981. 16.50x (ISBN 0-8077-2652-4); pap. 8.95x (ISBN 0-8077-2596-X). Tchrs Coll.

Nessel, Denise D., jt. auth. see Farrell, Catharine H.

Nessen, jt. auth. see Green.

Nessen, Robert L. Tax Shelters for the Nineteen Eighties. 320p. 1983. 14.45i (ISBN 0-316-60351-1). Little.

Nessmith, William C., jt. auth. see Sloshberg, Willard.

Nesteby, James R. Black Images in American Films, Eighteen Ninety-Six to Nineteen Fifty-Four: The Interplay Between Civil Rights & Film Culture. LC 80-5697. 292p. (Orig.). 1982. lib. bdg. 23.00 (ISBN 0-8191-2167-3); pap. text ed. 11.50 (ISBN 0-8191-2168-1). U Pr of Amer.

Nestel, B. & Cock, J. Cassava: The Development of an International Research Network. 70p. 1976. pap. 5.00 (ISBN 0-88936-076-6, IDRC59, IDRC). Unipub.

Nestel, Barry L., ed. African Cassava Mosaic: Report of an Interdisciplinary Workshop Held at Muguga, Kenya, 19-22 February, 1976. (Illus.). 48p. 1977. pap. 5.00 (ISBN 0-88936-096-0, IDRC71, IDRC). Unipub.

Nester, Emery, jt. auth. see Baker, Don.

Nesterenko, I. F., jt. auth. see Brekhman, I. I.

Nestle, E., ed. Novum Testamentum Latine. 11th ed. 1971. 4.40x (ISBN 3-438-05300-4, 71702). United Bible.

Nestor, William P. Into Winter: Discovering a Season. (gr. 5-8). 1982. PLB 9.95 (ISBN 0-395-32866-7); 9.70. HM.

Nestorides, E. J., ed. Handbook on Torsional Vibration. 1958. 110.00 (ISBN 0-521-04326-3). Cambridge U Pr.

Netanyahu, B. Don Isaac Abravanel. Statesman & Philosopher. LC 68-15789. 1972. pap. 6.95 (ISBN 0-8276-0213-8, 222). Jewish Pubn.

Neth, R., et al, eds. Modern Trends in Human Leukemia V: New Results in Clinical & Biological Research Including Pediatric Oncology; Proceedings, Wilsede, FRG, June 1982. (Haematology & Blood Transfusion Ser.: Vol. 28). 600p. 1983. pap. 84.00 (ISBN 0-387-11858-6). Springer-Verlag.

Netherlands. Central Bureau of Statistics. Statistical Yearbook of the Netherlands, 1980. 10th ed. LC 75-640878. (Illus.). 432p. 1981. 40.00x (ISBN 90-12-03382-9). Intl Pubns Serv.

Netherlands State Archives Service, ed. Guide to the Sources of the History of Africa South of the Sahara in the Netherlands, Vol. 9. (Guides to the Sources for the History of Nations Ser. II: Africa South of the Sahara). 241p. 1978. 36.00x (ISBN 3-7940-3819-3, Pub. by K G Saur). Gale.

Netsch, Dawn C., jt. auth. see Mandelker, Daniel R.

Netsky, Martin G. & Shuangshoti, Samruay. The Choroid Plexus in Health & Disease. LC 73-93948. 1975. 27.50x (ISBN 0-8139-0521-4). U Pr of Va.

Netsky, Martin G., jt. auth. see Sarnat, Harvey B.

Nettels, Curtis P. The Emergence of National Economy, 1775-1815. LC 76-48794. (The Economic History of the United States Ser.). 1977. pap. 10.95 (ISBN 0-87332-096-4). M E Sharpe.

Nettesheim, P., et al, eds. Morphology of Experimental Respiratory Carcinogenesis: Proceedings. LC 73-609398. (AEC Symposium Ser.). 498p. 1970. pap. 20.50 (ISBN 0-87079-277-6, CONF-700501); microfiche 4.50 (ISBN 0-87079-278-4, CONF-700501). DOE.

Nettie Lee Benson Latin American Collection, University of Texas Library, Austin, & the Library of Congress. Bibliographic Guide to Latin American Studies: 1978. 1979. lib. bdg. 195.00 o.p. (ISBN 0-8161-6857-1, Biblio Guides). G K Hall.

Netting, Robert M. Balancing on an Alp: Ecological Change & Continuity in a Swiss Mountain Community. LC 81-358. (Illus.). 436p. 1981. 42.50 (ISBN 0-521-23743-2); pap. 15.95 (ISBN 0-521-28197-0). Cambridge U Pr.

Nettis, Joseph. Creative Thirty-Five Millimeter Photography: Traveling with Your Camera. 1965. pap. 2.95 o.p. (ISBN 0-8174-0488-0, Amphoto). Watson-Guptill.

Nettl, Bruno. Folk & Traditional Music of the Western Continents. 2nd ed. (Illus.). 272p. 1973. pap. 13.95 (ISBN 0-13-322933-5). P-H.

--The Study of Ethnomusicology: Twenty-Nine Issues & Concepts. LC 82-7065. 426p. 1983. 37.50 (ISBN 0-252-00986-X); pap. 12.50 (ISBN 0-252-01039-6). U of Ill Pr.

Nettl, Bruno, et al. Contemporary Music & Music Cultures. 304p. 1974. 18.95 (ISBN 0-13-170175-4). P-H.

Nettl, Paul. Book of Musical Documents. 1948. lib. bdg. 19.00x (ISBN 0-8371-2116-7, NEMD). Greenwood.

--Forgotten Musicians. Repr. of 1951 ed. lib. bdg. 15.75x (ISBN 0-8371-2463-8, NEFM). Greenwood.

--Mozart & Masonry. LC 78-114564. (Music Ser). 1970. Repr. of 1957 ed. lib. bdg. 19.50 (ISBN 0-306-71922-3). Da Capo.

--Other Casanova: A Contribution to Eighteenth-Century Music & Manners. LC 73-107872. (Music Ser). (Illus.). 1970. Repr. of 1951 ed. lib. bdg. 32.50 (ISBN 0-306-71896-0). Da Capo.

Nettle, Gillian, jt. auth. see Leech, Julia.

Nettler, Gwynn. Explaining Crime. 2nd ed. 1977. pap. text ed. 16.00 (ISBN 0-07-046306-9); instr.'s manual 15.00 (ISBN 0-07-046307-7). McGraw.

--Social Concerns. 384p. 1975. pap. text ed. 14.50 (ISBN 0-07-046295-X, C). McGraw.

Nettles, Tom, jt. auth. see Bush, Russ.

Nettleship, Richard L. Theory of Education in the Republic of Plato. LC 68-54676. 1968. text ed. 9.50 (ISBN 0-8077-1850-5); pap. text ed. 4.50x (ISBN 0-8077-1849-1). Tchrs Coll.

Nettleton, George H. The Book of the Yale Pageant. (Illus.). 1916. 49.50x (ISBN 0-685-89735-4). Elliots Bks.

Nettleton, L. L. Gravity & Magnetics in Oil Prospecting. (International Ser. in the Earth & Planetary Sciences). 1976. 30.00 o.p. (ISBN 0-07-046303-4, C). McGraw.

Nettleton, T., jt. auth. see Harrison, H. R.

Netto, Coelho. The Pigeons. Goldberg, Isaac, ed. & tr. (International Pocket Library). pap. 3.00 (ISBN 0-686-77245-8). Branden.

Netto, Eugen. Theory of Substitutions. 2nd ed. LC 64-10289. 1964. 11.95 (ISBN 0-8284-0165-9). Chelsea Pub.

Network Editors. Design Development & Applications of ATE. 1982. 60.00x (ISBN 0-904999-73-4, Pub. by Network). State Mutual Bk.

--Design of Telecontrol & Telemetry Systems. 1982. 60.00x (ISBN 0-904999-28-9, Pub. by Network). State Mutual Bk.

--Device Technology. 1982. 80.00x (ISBN 0-904999-75-0, Pub. by Network). State Mutual Bk.

Network Editors, ed. Advanced Techniques & Future Developments. 1982. 49.00x (ISBN 0-904999-22-X, Pub. by Network). State Mutual Bk.

--Analog & Hybrid Testing Quality Assurance & Product Testing. 1982. 110.00x (ISBN 0-686-87068-9, Pub. by Network). State Mutual Bk.

--Application of Telecontrol Systems. 1982. 60.00x (ISBN 0-904999-33-5, Pub. by Network). State Mutual Bk.

--Applications & Human Factors. 1982. 50.00x (ISBN 0-904999-57-2, Pub. by Network). State Mutual Bk.

--Software & Future Developments. 1982. 95.00x (ISBN 0-904999-38-6, Pub. by Network). State Mutual Bk.

Netzer, jt. auth. see Rice.

Netzer, Aharon, jt. ed. see Rice, Rip G.

Netzer, Corinne T. Brand Name Calorie Counter. (Orig.). 1981. pap. 3.50 (ISBN 0-440-10676-1). Dell.

--Brand Name Carbohydrate Gram Counter. (Orig.). 1981. pap. 2.95 (ISBN 0-440-10658-3). Dell.

Netzer, Corrine. The Dieter's Calorie Counter. (Orig.). 1983. pap. price not set (ISBN 0-440-52086-X, Dell Trade Pbks). Dell.

Netzer, D. The Subsidized Muse. LC 77-25441. (Illus.). 289p. 1980. pap. 11.95 (ISBN 0-521-29796-6). Cambridge U Pr.

--The Subsidized Muse. LC 77-25441. (Illus.). 1978. 29.95 (ISBN 0-521-21966-3). Cambridge U Pr.

Neu, Axel D., jt. auth. see Kriegsmann, Klaus-Peter.

Neu, Charles E. An Uncertain Friendship: Theodore Roosevelt & Japan, 1906-1909. LC 67-27091. 1967. 17.50x (ISBN 0-674-92040-6). Harvard U Pr.

Neu, Clyde W., jt. auth. see Redinbaugh, Larry D.

Neu, H. C. & Sabath, L. D., eds. Ein praktischer Leitfaden fuer die therapeutische Anwendung von Cefotiam. (Pharmanual Ser.: Vol. 3). (Illus.). viii, 192p. 1983. pap. 30.00 (ISBN 3-8055-3694-1). S Karger.

Neu, Harold C., ed. New Beta-Lactam Antibiotics: A Review from Chemistry to Clinical Efficacy of the New Cephalosporins. (Symposia on Frontiers of Pharmacology). (Illus.). 341p. 1982. text ed. 40.45 (ISBN 0-943060-00-1). Wood Inst.

Neu, Irene D. Erastus Corning, Merchant & Financier: 1794-1872. LC 77-22015. (Illus.). 1977. Repr. of 1960 ed. lib. bdg. 19.25x (ISBN 0-8371-9791-0, NEEC). Greenwood.

Neu, Jerome. Emotion, Thought, & Therapy: A Study of Hume & Spinoza & the Relationship of Philosophical Theories of the Emotions to Psychological Theories of Therapy. LC 76-20010. 1977. 27.50x (ISBN 0-520-03288-8). U of Cal Pr.

Neu, John, ed. Isis Cumulative Bibliography 1966-1975, Vol. 1: Personalities & Institutions, Vol. 1. 514p. 1980. 74.00 (ISBN 0-7201-1515-9, Pub. by Mansell England). Wilson.

Neubauer, Raymond L. The Visionary Universe: A Prophecy. (Illus.). 273p. (Orig.). 1973. pap. 3.95 (ISBN 0-914220-00-4). Nova Pr.

Neubeck, Kenneth J. Social Problems: A Critical Approach. 1979. text ed. 16.95x o.p. (ISBN 0-673-15201-4). Scott F.

Neubecker, Ottfried. A Guide to Heraldry. LC 79-13611. (Illus.). 1980. 9.95 o.p. (ISBN 0-07-046312-3). McGraw.

Neubecker, William, ed. Antique Auto Body Metal Work for the Restorer. LC 82-62579. (Vintage Craft Ser.: No. 1). (Illus.). 1969. pap. 6.00 (ISBN 0-911160-01-9). Post-Era.

Neuberg, Hans. Conceptions of International Exhibitions. 1969. 37.50 (ISBN 0-8038-1138-1). Hastings.

Neuberger, A., jt. ed. see Florkin, M.

Neuberger, A., ed. see Ycas, M.

Neuberger, E., jt. auth. see Brown, A. A.

Neuberger, Egon & Tyson, Laura D., eds. The Impact of International Economic Disturbances on the Soviet Union & Eastern Europe. (Pergamon Policy Studies). 1980. 65.00 (ISBN 0-08-025102-1). Pergamon.

Neuberger, Elsa, tr. see Neruda, Pablo & Frasconi, Antonio.

Neuberger, John. Novalis. (World Authors Ser.). 1980. lib. bdg. 15.95 (ISBN 0-8057-6398-8, Twayne). G K Hall.

Neuberger, Phyllis J. Suppose You Were a Kitten. LC 82-91105. (Illus.). (gr. 1-3). 1982. pap. 2.95 (ISBN 0-9610050-0-9). P J Neuberger.

Neuberger, Richard L. & Loe, Kelley. An Army of the Aged. LC 72-2379. (FDR & the New Deal Ser). 332p. 1973. Repr. of 1936 ed. lib. bdg. 39.50 (ISBN 0-306-70518-4). Da Capo.

Neuberger, Thomas. Foundation: Building Sentence Skills. 1982. pap. 12.50 (ISBN 0-395-31805-X); instr's man. pap. 2.50 (ISBN 0-395-31806-8); instr's support pkg. 1.00 (ISBN 0-395-31891-2). HM.

Neuberstaat, Karl. The Plant World as an Inspiration for the Creation of Artistic Forms. (Illus.). 121p. 1983. 83.45 (ISBN 0-86650-063-4). Gloucester Art.

Neubert, Christopher & Withiam, Jack, Jr. The Law School Game. 1979. pap. 7.95 (ISBN 0-8069-8872-X). Sterling.

Neubert, D., et al, eds. The Role of Pharmacokinetics in Prenatal & Perinatal Toxicology. (Illus.). 654p. 1978. text ed. 38.00 o.p. (ISBN 0-88416-293-1). Wright-PSG.

--Methods in Prenatal Toxicology. LC 77-91114. (Illus.). 486p. 1977. 28.00 o.p. (ISBN 0-88416-239-7). Wright-PSG.

Neubert, Diether & Merker, Hans J., eds. New Approaches to the Evaluation of Abnormal Embryonic Development. LC 76-4619. (Illus.). 844p. 1975. 35.00 o.p. (ISBN 0-88416-140-4). Wright-PSG.

Neubert, Emil. My Ideal, Jesus Son of Mary, According to the Spirit of William Joseph Chaminade. 3rd ed. Orig. Title: Mon ideal, Jesus Fils de Marie. 160p. 1963. pap. 1.00 (ISBN 0-9608124-4-X). Marianist Com Ctr.

Neudeck, Gerold W., jt. auth. see Pierret, Robert F.

Neuder. Dictionary of Radiological Engineering. 1973. 31.90 o.p. (ISBN 0-85501-242-0). Wiley.

Neuenswander, Helen & Arnold, Dean. Cognitive Studies in Southern Mesoamerica. 1977. 10.95x (ISBN 0-88312-152-2); microfiche 3.75x (ISBN 0-88312-250-2). Summer Inst Ling.

Neufeld, E. P. The Financial System of Canada. LC 70-178200. 635p. 1972. 32.50 (ISBN 0-312-28980-4). St Martin.

Neufeld, Henry N. & Schneeweiss, Adam. Coronary Artery Disease in Infants & Children. (Illus.). 225p. 1983. price not set (ISBN 0-8121-0860-4). Lea & Febiger.

Neufeld, Herm & Chaffin, Charles. Climate in Three-D. (Orig.). (gr. 4-9). 1973. pap. 3.50 (ISBN 0-918932-04-1). Activity Resources.

Neufeld, John. Edgar Allan. 1969. pap. 1.75 (ISBN 0-451-11801-4, AE1801, Sig). NAL.

--Edgar Allan. LC 68-31175. (Illus.). (gr. 5-8). 1968. 10.95 (ISBN 0-87599-149-1). S G Phillips.

--For All the Wrong Reasons. 1980. 7.95 (ISBN 0-453-00361-3, AE2355, Sig); pap. 2.25 (ISBN 0-451-12355-7). NAL.

--Freddy's Book. (gr. 4-7). 1973. 3.95 o.p. (ISBN 0-394-82135-1). Random.

--The Fun of It: A Love Story. LC 77-18658. 1978. 8.95 o.p. (ISBN 0-399-11993-0). Putnam Pub Group.

--Lisa, Bright & Dark. (YA) (RL 7). 1970. pap. 1.95 (AE1983, Sig). NAL.

--Lisa, Bright & Dark. (gr. 7 up). 1969. 10.95 (ISBN 0-87599-153-X). S G Phillips.

--Touching. LC 76-125867. (gr. 8 up). 1970. 9.95 o.s.i. (ISBN 0-87599-174-2). S G Phillips.

--Twink. (RL 7). 1971. pap. 1.75 (ISBN 0-451-11257-1, AE1257, Sig). NAL.

Neufeld, M. Lynne & Corneg, Martha. Energy & Environment Information Resource Guide. 1982. 20.00 (ISBN 0-942308-15-8). NFAIS.

Neufeld, M. Lynne & Cornog, Martha. A Study of Data Base Access Alternatives: Final Report. 1981. 100.00 (ISBN 0-942308-14-X). NFAIS.

Neufeld, Maurice F. Poor Countries & Authoritarian Rule. LC 65-63408. (International Report Ser.: No. 6). 256p. 1965. 5.00 (ISBN 0-87546-010-0). ILR Pr.

--A Representative Bibliography of American Labor History. LC 64-63608. (ILR Bibliography Ser.: No. 6). 160p. 1964. 1.50 (ISBN 0-87546-021-6); pap. 1.00 (ISBN 0-87546-261-8). ILR Pr.

Neufeldt, Victor A. see Pratt, John C.

Neuffer, Mark, jt. auth. see Amigo, Eleanor.

Neufville, Richard De see De Neufville, Richard.

Neugarten, Bernice I. Age or Need? Public Policies for Older People. (Sage Focus Editions). (Illus.). 288p. 1982. 25.00 (ISBN 0-8039-1908-5); pap. 12.50 (ISBN 0-8039-1909-3). Sage.

Neugarten, Dail A. Improving Productivity in Public Organizations. 175p. 1983. 19.50 (ISBN 0-08-028813-8); pap. 8.95 (ISBN 0-08-028812-X). Pergamon.

Neugarten, Dail A. & Shafritz, Jay M., eds. Sexuality in Organizations: Romantic & Coercive Behaviors at Work. (Orig.). 1980. pap. 10.00x (ISBN 0-935610-14-6). Moore Pub IL.

Neugebauer, O. & Sachs, A. Mathematical Cuneiform Texts. (American Oriental Ser.: Vol. 29). 1945. 12.00 (ISBN 0-940490-29-3). Am Orient Soc.

Neugebauer, Roger, jt. ed. see Lurie, Robert.

Neugroschel, Joachim. The Shtetl. 592p. 1982. 10.95 (ISBN 0-399-50672-1, Perige). Putnam Pub Group.

Neugroschel, Joachim, ed. The Shtetl: A Creative Anthology of Jewish Life in Eastern Europe. LC 79-13624. (Illus.). 1979. box ed. 25.00 (ISBN 0-399-90033-0, Marek). Putnam Pub Group.

Neugroschel, Joachim, tr. see Canetti, Elias.

Neugroschel, Joachim, tr. see Doerner, Klaus.

Neuhaus, Richard. Time Toward Home: The American Experience As Revelation. 250p. 1975. 4.00 (ISBN 0-8164-0272-8). Seabury.

Neuhaus, Richard J., jt. auth. see Berger, Peter.

Neuhaus, Robert & Neuhaus, Ruby. Family Crises. LC 73-85104. 1974. pap. 16.95 (ISBN 0-675-08890-9). Merrill.

Neuhaus, Robert H., jt. auth. see Neuhaus, Ruby H.

Neuhaus, Ruby, jt. auth. see Neuhaus, Robert.

Neuhaus, Ruby H. & Neuhaus, Robert H. Successful Aging. LC 81-14807. 285p. 1982. text ed. 12.95x (ISBN 0-471-08448-4). Wiley.

Neuhauser, Carol, jt. auth. see Leatzow, Nancy.

Neuhauser, Duncan, jt. auth. see Wilson, Florence.

Neuhauser, Duncan, jt. auth. see Wilson, Florence A.

Neuhoff, Walther. Die Pilze Mitteleuropas: Vol. 28, Die Milchlinge (Lactarii) (Illus.). 1956. 80.00 (ISBN 3-7682-0520-7). Lubrecht & Cramer.

Neujahr, James. The Individualized Instruction Game. LC 75-22491. 1976. text ed. 9.95x (ISBN 0-8077-2485-8). Tchrs Coll.

Neuls-Bates, Carol. Women in Music. LC 81-48045. (Illus.). 288p. 1982. pap. 8.61i (ISBN 0-06-090932-3, CN 932, CN). Har-Row.

Neuls-Bates, Carol, ed. Women in Music: An Anthology of Source Readings from the Middle Ages to the Present. LC 81-48045. (Illus.). 384p. 1982. 17.79i (ISBN 0-06-014992-2, HarpT). Har-Row.

Neuls-Bates, Carol, jt. ed. see Block, Adrienne F.

Neuman, Donald B. Experiences in Science for Young Children. LC 76-53185. 1978. pap. text ed. 11.00 (ISBN 0-8273-1642-9); instructor's guide 2.75 (ISBN 0-8273-1643-7). Delmar.

Neuman, Jeffrey. Play Ball with the Los Angeles Dodgers. LC 82-20782. (Illus.). 48p. (Orig.). (gr. 4-7). 1983. pap. 2.95 (ISBN 0-689-70760-6, A-136, Aladdin). Atheneum.

Neuman, P. Anorexia Nervosa & Bulemia: A Handbook. Date not set. price not set (ISBN 0-442-26849-1). Van Nos Reinhold.

Neuman, Phyllis. Conveyancing of Freehold Property. 1980. 30.00x (ISBN 0-686-97093-4, Pub. by Fourmat England). State Mutual Bk.

Neuman, Stephanie G., ed. Small States & Segmented Societies: National Political Integration Environment. LC 75-23986. (Special Studies). 256p. 1976. 27.95 o.p. (ISBN 0-275-55730-8). Praeger.

Neuman, Susan B. & Panoff, Renee. Exploring Feelings. 225p. (Orig.). 1982. pap. 14.95 (ISBN 0-89334-037-5). Humanics Ltd.

Neumann, A. L. Beef Cattle. 7th ed. LC 76-46616. 1977. 34.95 (ISBN 0-471-63236-8). Wiley.

Neumann, Angelo. Personal Recollections of Wagner. (Music Reprint Ser.). 329p. 1976. Repr. of 1906 ed. 35.00 (ISBN 0-306-70843-4). Da Capo.

Neumann, B. H., ed. see International Conference on the Theory of Groups, 1969.

Neumann, Bill. Here Is Your Hobby: Model Car Building. (Here Is Your Hobby Ser.). (Illus.). (gr. 5-9). 1971. PLB 5.29 o.p. (ISBN 0-399-60251-8). Putnam Pub Group.

Neumann, Bill, jt. auth. see Braverman, Robert.

Neumann, Bonnie R. Robert Smith Surtees. (English Authors Ser.). 1978. 14.95 (ISBN 0-8057-6722-3, Twayne). G K Hall.

Neumann, Bruce R., jt. auth. see Suver, James D.

Neumann, E., jt. ed. see Schoffeniels, E.

Neumann, Franz L. Democratic & the Authoritarian State: Essays in Political & Legal Theory. 1964. pap. text ed. 7.95 (ISBN 0-02-922910-3). Free Pr.

Neumann, Frederick. Essays in Performance Practice. Buelow, George, ed. LC 82-6916. (Studies in Musicology: No. 58). 334p. 1982. 44.95 (ISBN 0-8357-1351-2, Pub. by UMI Res Pr). Univ Microfilms.

Neumann, Gerhard & Pierson, W. J. Principles of Physical Oceanography. (Illus.). 1966. 38.95 (ISBN 0-13-709741-7). P-H.

Neumann, I. Biotaxonomische Untersuchungen an Einigen Hefen der Gattung Saccharomyces. 1972. 16.00 (ISBN 3-7682-5440-2). Lubrecht & Cramer.

Neumann, Inge S. European War Crimes Trials: A Bibliography. Rosebaum, Robert A., ed. LC 77-18934. (Additional material furnished by the Wiener Library, London). 1978. Repr. of 1951 ed. lib. bdg. 19.25x (ISBN 0-313-20210-9, NEEW). Greenwood.

Neumann, J. J. The Polyporaceae of Wisconsin. 1971. Repr. of 1914 ed. 24.00 (ISBN 3-7682-0704-8). Lubrecht & Cramer.

Neumann, J. Von see Von Neumann, J.

Neumann, John Von. Computer & the Brain. LC 58-6542. (Silliman Lectures Ser.). 1958. 12.50x o.p. (ISBN 0-300-00793-0); pap. 3.95x (ISBN 0-300-02415-0). Yale U Pr.

Neumann, Peter H. Publishing for Schools: Textbooks & the Less Developed Countries. (Working Paper: No. 398). ii, 79p. 1980. 5.00 (ISBN 0-686-36042-7, WP-0398). World Bank.

Neumann, Seev, jt. auth. see Ahituv, Niv.

Neumayer, Lisa, ed. see Costello, Jeanne & Witty, Doreen.

Neumeyer, Fredrik & Stedman, John C. Employed Inventor in the United States. 1971. 35.00x (ISBN 0-262-14006-3). MIT Pr.

Neumeyer, Helen, tr. see Careme, Maurice.

Neumeyer, Ken. Sailing the Farm: Independence on Thirty Feet-A Survival Guide to Homesteading the Ocean. LC 81-51896. 256p. (Orig.). 1981. pap. 7.95 (ISBN 0-89815-051-5). Ten Speed Pr.

Neumeyer, Peter. Dream Cat. (Orig.). 1982. pap. 2.50 (ISBN 0-914676-84-9, Pub. by Envelope Bks). Green Tiger Pr.

--Fenstermacher's Boulder. (Illus.). 12p. (Orig.). pap. 2.50 (ISBN 0-914676-61-X, Pub. by Envelope Bks). Green Tiger Pr.

Neumeyer, Peter, jt. auth. see Gorey, Edward.

Neundorf, Norman. Computer-Aided Drawing Using the Tektronix Graphic System. (Illus.). 320p. 1983. 16.95 (ISBN 0-13-164723-7). P-H.

Neuner, Edward J. The Natural Gas Industry: Monopoly & Competition in the Field Markets. 1960. 16.95x o.p. (ISBN 0-8061-0463-5). U of Okla Pr.

Neunhoeffer, Hans & Wiley, Paul F. Chemistry of One, Two, Three-Triazines & One, Two, Four-Triazines, Tetrazines & Pentazines. LC 77-18932. (Chemistry of Heterocyclic Compounds Ser.: Vol. 33). 1978. Vol. 33. 208.50 (ISBN 0-471-03129-1, Pub. by Wiley-Interscience). Wiley.

Neunier, John, ed. Proceedings of the Sixty-Eighth A.C.S.A. Annual Meeting. 300p. 1981. pap. 17.50 o.p. (ISBN 0-8408-0506-3). Carrollton Pr.

Neurath, Hans, ed. Proteins: Composition, Structure & Function, 3 vols. 2nd ed. Incl. Vol. 4. 1966. 59.00 (ISBN 0-12-516264-2); Vol. 5. Mettaloproteins. 1970. 32.50 (ISBN 0-12-516265-0); by subscription 28.50 (ISBN 0-12-516265-0); Vol. 3 o.p. 1965. wrtie for info. (ISBN 0-12-516263-4). Acad Pr.

Neurath, Hans & Hill, Robert, eds. The Protein, Vol. 5. 736p. 1982. 78.50 (ISBN 0-12-516305-3); subscription 68.00 (ISBN 0-686-81655-2). Acad Pr.

Neurath, Maria, ed. see Neurath, Otto.

Neurath, Otto. Philosophical Papers Nineteen Thirteen to Nineteen Forty-Six. Cohen, Robert S. & Neurath, Maria, eds. 1983. lib. bdg. 65.00 (ISBN 90-277-1483-5, Pub. by Reidel Holland). Kluwer Boston.

Neuringer, Charles, ed. Psychological Assessment of Suicidal Risk. (Illus.). 256p. 1974. photocopy ed. spiral 24.75x (ISBN 0-398-03008-1). C C Thomas.

Neuringer, Charles, jt. ed. see Goldstein, Gerald.

Neuro-Opthamology Symposia of the University of Miami & the Bascom Palmer Eye Institute. Proceedings, Vol. 8. Glaser, Joel S. & Smith, J. Lawton, eds. 1975. 37.50 o.p. (ISBN 0-8016-1846-0). Mosby.

Neusch, Marcel. The Sources of Modern Atheism: One Hundred Years of Debate Over God. LC 82-60596. 1983. pap. 9.95 (ISBN 0-8091-2488-2). Paulist Pr.

Neuschel, Richard F. Management Systems for Profit & Growth. 1976. text ed. 24.95 (ISBN 0-07-046323-9, P&RB). McGraw.

Neuschel, Robert P., jt. auth. see Northwestern University Transportation Center, May 5, 1981.

Neuschloss, G., jt. auth. see Elton, W. R.

Neuschutz, Karin. The Doll Book. Schneider, Ingun, tr. from Swedish. (Illus.). 184p. (Orig.). 1983. pap. 8.95 (ISBN 0-943914-01-9). Larson Pubns Inc.

Neusner, J., et al, eds. see Vermes, Pamela.

Neusner, Jacob. The Academic Study of Judaism: Essays & Reflections. LC 75-5782. (Brown Judaic Studies). pap. 16.50 (14-00-35). Scholars Pr CA.

--Ancient Israel after Catastrophe: The Religious World View of the Mishnah. LC 82-15972. 1983. write for info. (ISBN 0-8139-0980-5). U Pr of Va.

--Formative Judaism. LC 82-16746. (Brown Judaic Studies). 182p. 1982. pap. 13.50 (ISBN 0-89130-594-7, 14 00 37). Scholars Pr CA.

--History & Torah: Essays on Jewish Learning. 128p. 1965. text ed. 8.50x (ISBN 0-686-37017-1, Pub. by Vallentine Michell England). Biblio Dist.

--Invitation to the Talmud. LC 73-6343. 288p. 1976. pap. 7.95xi (ISBN 0-06-066097-X, RD130, HarpR). Har-Row.

--Lessons of the Founders, Porle Abott: A New American Translation & Explanation. (Illus.). 128p. 1983. 25.95 (ISBN 0-940646-05-6). Rossel Bks.

--Method & Meaning in Ancient Judaism III. LC 80-19449. (Brown Judaic Studies). 1981. pap. 27.50 (ISBN 0-89130-418-5, 14-00-16). Scholars Pr CA.

--Understanding Jewish Theology: Classsical Issues & Modern Perspective. 280p. pap. 8.95 (ISBN 0-686-95185-9). ADL.

Neusner, Jacob, jt. auth. see Haas, Peter J.

Neusner, Jacob, jt. auth. see Silverman, Morris.

Neusner, Jacob, ed. The Talmud of the Land of Israel: A Preliminary Translation & Explanation Volume 34 Horayot & Niddah. LC 81-13115. (Chicago Studies in the History of Judaism). 256p. 1982. lib. bdg. 25.00x (ISBN 0-226-57694-9); Vol. 33, Abodah Zarah, x, 234p., July 1982, lib. bdg. 25.00x (ISBN 0-226-57693-0). U of Chicago Pr.

--The Talmud of the Land of Israel: A Preliminary Translation & Explanation, Volume 32, Shebuot. (Chicago Studies in the History of Judaism). 288p. 1982. lib. bdg. 22.50x (ISBN 0-226-57692-2). U of Chicago Pr.

--Understanding American Judaism: Toward the Description of Modern Religion, 2 vols. Incl. Vol.1. The Synagogue & the Rabbi; Vol.II. Reform, Orthodoxy, Conservatism, & Reconstruction. pap. 9.95 (ISBN 0-686-95149-2). ADL.

Neusner, Jacob, ed. see Bokser, Baruch M.

Neustadt, L. W., ed. see International Congress on Programming & Control, 1st.

Neustadt, Richard. The Birth of Electronic Publishing: Legal & Economic Issues in Telephone, Cable & Over-the Air Teletext & Videotext. LC 82-6614. (Communications Library). 146p. 1982. text ed. 32.95 (ISBN 0-86729-030-7). Knowledge Indus.

Neustadt, Richard & Fineberg, Harvey. The Epidemic that Never Was: Policy-Making & the Swine Flu Scare. LC 82-40023. 288p. (Orig.). 1983. pap. 7.95 (ISBN 0-394-71147-5, Vin). Random.

Neustadt, Richard E. Presidential Power: The Politics of Leadership from FDR to Carter. LC 79-19474. 1979. pap. text ed. 11.95x (ISBN 0-471-05988-9). Wiley.

Neuwirth, Robert S. Hysteroscopy. LC 75-296. (Major Problems in Obstetrics & Gynecology Ser., Vol. 8). (Illus.). 116p. 1975. 17.50 (ISBN 0-7216-6762-7). Saunders.

Neuzil, E. F., jt. auth. see Miller, John A.

Nevakivi, Jukka. Britain, France & the Arab Middle East 1914-1920. (Univ. of London Historical Studies: No. 23). 1969. text ed. 26.00x o.p. (ISBN 0-485-13123-4, Athlone Pr). Humanities.

Nevanlinna, R. Le Theoreme de Picard-Borel. LC 73-14779. 179p. 1974. Repr. of 1970 ed. text ed. 12.95 (ISBN 0-8284-0272-8). Chelsea Pub.

Nevaskar, Balwant S. Capitalists Without Capitalism: The Jains of India & the Quakers of the West. LC 72-98709. (Contributions in Sociology: No. 6). 1971. lib. bdg. 27.50 (ISBN 0-8371-3297-5, NCA/). Greenwood.

Nevdeck, Gerold W., jt. auth. see Hayt, William H.

Neverov, O., compiled by. Antique Intaglios. (Illus.). 1979. 10.95 (ISBN 0-89893-005-7). CDP.

Neveu, J. Discrete-Parameter Martingales. LC 74-79241. (Mathematical Library: Vol. 10). 236p. 1975. 47.25 (ISBN 0-444-10708-8, North-Holland). Elsevier.

Nevgroschel, Joachim, tr. see Betti, Liliana.

Nevid, Jeffrey, jt. auth. see Rathus, Spencer.

Nevill, Gale E., Jr. Programmed Principles of Statics. 184p. 1969. pap. text ed. 7.50 (ISBN 0-471-63270-8, Pub. by Wiley). Krieger.

Nevill, Tim, tr. see Fischle, Willy H.

Neville, A. M., jt. auth. see Ghali, A.

Neville, Charles. Animal Asymmetry. (Studies in Biology: No. 67). 64p. 1976. pap. text ed. 8.95 (ISBN 0-7131-2557-8). E Arnold.

Neville, Emily C. Garden of Broken Glass. LC 74-22630. 228p. (gr. 5-9). 1975. 6.95 o.s.i. (ISBN 0-440-04839-7); PLB 6.46 o.s.i. (ISBN 0-440-04842-7). Delacorte.

Neville, Eric H. Elliptic Functions: A Primer. Langford, W. J., ed. 211p. 1971. text ed. 27.00 (ISBN 0-08-016369-6). Pergamon.

Neville, Gwen K. & Westerhoff, John H., III. Learning Through Liturgy. 189p. 1983. pap. 6.95 (ISBN 0-8164-2423-3). Seabury.

Neville, John D. Bacon's Rebellion: Abstracts of Materials in the Colonial Records Project. LC 76-24548. 442p. (Orig.). 1976. pap. 5.00 (ISBN 0-917394-00-3). Jamestown Found.

Neville, K. O., jt. auth. see Lee, H. L.

Neville, Robert C. Creativity & God: A Challenge to Process Theology. 192p. 1980. 12.95 (ISBN 0-8164-0120-9). Seabury.

--Reconstruction of Thinking. LC 81-5347. 368p. 1981. 34.50x (ISBN 0-87395-494-7); pap. 10.95x (ISBN 0-87395-495-5). State U NY Pr.

--The Tao & the Daimon: Segments of a Religious Inquiry. 304p. 1982. 34.50x (ISBN 0-87395-661-3); pap. 10.95x (ISBN 0-87395-662-1). State U NY Pr.

Nevin, D. The Soldiers. LC 73-79475. (Old West Ser). (Illus.). (gr. 5 up). 1973. 17.28 (ISBN 0-8094-1463-5, Pub. by Time-Life). Silver.

Nevin, David. Architects of Air Power. LC 80-24449. (Epic of Flight Ser.). PLB 19.96 (ISBN 0-8094-3280-3). Silver.

--The Expressmen. LC 74-12941. (The Old West). (Illus.). (gr. 5 up). 1974. 17.28 (ISBN 0-8094-1486-4, Pub. by Time-Life). Silver.

--The Mexican War. LC 77-95212. (The Old West Ser.). (Illus.). 1978. 17.28 (ISBN 0-8094-2302-2). Silver.
--The Pathfinders. LC 79-10967. (Epic of Flight Ser.). 19.96 (ISBN 0-8094-3255-2). Silver.
--The Texans. LC 75-15450. (The Old West). (Illus.). (gr. 5 up). 1975. 17.28 (ISBN 0-8094-1502-X, Pub. by Time-Life). Silver.

Nevin, John A., jt. ed. see Commons, Michael.

Nevin, John A., jt. ed. see Commons, Michael L.

Nevins, Allan. New Deal & World Affairs. 1951. text ed. 8.50x (ISBN 0-686-83647-2). Elliots Bks.
--United State in a Chaotic World. 1951. text ed. 8.50x (ISBN 0-686-83837-8). Elliots Bks.

Nevins, Allan, jt. auth. see Commager, Henry S.

Nevins, Allan, ed. Letters of Grover Cleveland, 1850-1908. LC 70-123752. (American Public Figures Ser). 1970. Repr. of 1933 ed. lib. bdg. 75.00 (ISBN 0-306-71982-7). Da Capo.

Nevins, Ann. Super Stitches: A Book of Superstitions. LC 82-15875. (Illus.). 64p. (gr. 1-4). 1983. reinforced binding 8.95 (ISBN 0-8234-0476-5). Holiday.

Nevins, Francis M., Jr. Corrupt & Ensnare. LC 78-1755. 1978. 8.95 o.p. (ISBN 0-399-12203-6). Putnam Pub Group.

Nevins, Kate. Forbidden Rapture. (Second Chance at Love Ser.: No. 90). 1982. pap. 1.75 (ISBN 0-515-06852-7). Jove Pubns.

Nevinson, Henry. Thomas Hardy. LC 72-2084. (Studies in Thomas Hardy, No. 14). 1972. Repr. of 1941 ed. lib. bdg. 22.95x (ISBN 0-8383-1466-X). Haskell.

Nevison, J. M. Executive Computing. 1981. pap. text ed. 11.95 (ISBN 0-201-05248-2). A-W.

Nevison, John M. Little Book of Basic Style: How to Write a Program You Can Read. LC 77-88882. 1978. pap. text ed. 7.95 (ISBN 0-201-05247-4). A-W.

Nevitt Dupuy, Trevor see Dupuy, Trevor Nevitt.

Nevius, Blake. Cooper's Landscapes: An Essay on the Picturesque Vision. LC 74-77730. (Quantum Bks). 1976. 18.50x (ISBN 0-520-02751-5). U of Cal Pr.
--Edith Wharton: A Study of Her Fiction. (California Library Reprint Ser). 1976. 27.50x (ISBN 0-520-03180-6). U of Cal Pr.

Nevo, Ruth. Comic Transformations in Shakespeare. 1981. 25.00x (ISBN 0-416-73880-X); pap. 10.95x (ISBN 0-416-73890-7). Methuen Inc.

New. Giant Prawn Farming. (Developments in Aquaculture & Fisheries Sciences Ser.: Vol. 10). 1982. 89.50 (ISBN 0-444-42093-2). Elsevier.

New Alchemy Staff. Gardening for All Seasons: How to Feed Your Family from Your Own Garden Twelve Months a Year. (Illus.). 320p. 1983. pap. 10.95 (ISBN 0-931790-56-5). Brick Hse Pub.

New American Foundation. Unity in Diversity: An Index to the Publications of Conservative & Libertarian Institutions. Birch, Carol L., ed. LC 82-20552. 284p. 1983. 18.50 (ISBN 0-8108-1599-0). Scarecrow.

New, Christopher. Goodbye Chairman Mao. LC 78-13650. 1979. 8.95 o.p. (ISBN 0-698-10918-X, Coward). Putnam Pub Group.

New England Association for Women in Psychology, ed. Current Feminist Issues in Psychotherapy. LC 82-15721. (Women & Therapy Ser.: Vol. 1, No. 3). 133p. 1983. text ed. 20.00 (ISBN 0-86656-206-0, B206). Haworth Pr.

New England Historical Genealogical Society. The Greenlaw Index of the New England Historic Genealogical Society. 1979. lib. bdg. 195.00 (ISBN 0-8161-0312-7, Hall Library). G K Hall.

New England Marine Advisory Service. Seafood Sourcebook: A Consumer's Guide to Information on Food from Our Oceans & Lakes. 46p. 1978. 1.00 o.p. (ISBN 0-686-36979-3, P762). URI Mas.

New England Regional Commission. The New England Regional Plan: An Economic Development Strategy. LC 81-50584. (Illus.). 158p. 1981. pap. 18.00x (ISBN 0-87451-203-4). U Pr of New Eng.

New Inc.-Fourth World Movement, ed. Children of Our Time. (Symposium Ser.: Vol. 7). (Illus., Orig.). 1981. soft cover 11.95 (ISBN 0-88946-911-3). E Mellen.

New, Maria & Levine, Lenore, eds. Juvenile Hypertension. LC 76-51556. 244p. 1977. 22.00 (ISBN 0-89004-145-8). Raven.

New, Maria I., ed. see National Foundation-March of Dimes Symposium, April, 1976, New York City.

New Orleans Academy of Ophthalmology. Symposium on Glaucoma. LC 81-2326. (Illus.). 486p. 1981. text ed. 65.00 (ISBN 0-8016-3667-1). Mosby.
--Symposium on Strabismus: Transactions of the New Orleans Academy of Ophthalmology. LC 77-18281. (Illus.). 608p. 1978. 50.50 o.p. (ISBN 0-8016-3687-6). Mosby.

New Orleans Academy of Opthalmology. Symposium on Medical & Surgical Diseases of the Cornea. LC 80-13693. (Illus.). 642p. 1980. text ed. 75.50 o.p. (ISBN 0-8016-3666-3). Mosby.

New, Paul F. & Scott, William R. Computed Tomography of the Brain. LC 75-14178. 500p. 1975. 49.50 o.p. (ISBN 0-683-06455-X). Krieger.

New, Peter J. George Crabbe's Poetry. LC 75-29857. 320p. 1976. text ed. 19.95 o.p. (ISBN 0-312-32445-6). St Martin.

New, William H. Malcolm Lowry: A Reference Guide. 1978. lib. bdg. 21.00 (ISBN 0-8161-7884-4, Hall Reference). G K Hall.

New World Dictionary Editors. Misspeller's Dictionary. 1983. write for info. (ISBN 0-671-46864-2). S&S.

New York Academy Of Medicine. Author Catalog of the Library of the New York Academy of Medicine, 43 Vols. 1969. Set. lib. bdg. 3900.00 (ISBN 0-8161-0829-3, Hall Library). G K Hall.
--Author Catalog of the Library of the New York Academy of Medicine, Second Supplement. 1979. lib. bdg. 500.00 (ISBN 0-8161-1181-2, Hall Library). G K Hall.
--Author Catalog of the Library of the New York Academy of Medicine, 1st Suppl, 4 vols. 1974. Set. lib. bdg. 495.00 (ISBN 0-8161-0851-X, Hall Library). G K Hall.
--Portrait Catalog, 5 vols. 1960. Set. 215.00 (ISBN 0-8161-0233-3, Hall Library); First Suppl. 1959-65. 105.00 (ISBN 0-8161-0733-5); Second Suppl. 1965-71. 105.00 (ISBN 0-8161-0900-1). G K Hall.
--Portrait Catalog: Third Supplement, 1971-1975. 1976. lib. bdg. 98.00 (ISBN 0-8161-0034-9, Hall Library). G K Hall.
--Subject Catalog of the Library of the New York Academy of Medicine, 34 Vols. 1969. Set. lib. bdg. 3100.00 (ISBN 0-8161-0826-9, Hall Library). G K Hall.
--Subject Catalog of the Library of the New York Academy of Medicine, Second Supplement. 1979. lib. bdg. 500.00 (ISBN 0-8161-1182-0, Hall Library). G K Hall.
--Subject Catalog of the Library of the New York Academy of Medicine, 1st Supplement, 4 vols. 1974. Set. lib. bdg. 475.00 (ISBN 0-8161-0184-1, Hall Library). G K Hall.

New York Academy of Sciences Annals of, October 19-21, 1981. Immunological Tolerance to Self & Non-Self: Proceedings, Vol. 392. Battisto, Jack R. & Claman, Henry N., eds. 436p. 1982. 80.00 (ISBN 0-89766-174-5). NY Acad Sci.

New York Academy of Sciences Annals, Nov. 11-13, 1981. Vitamin E: Biochemical, Hematological, Clinical Aspects, Vol. 393. Lubin, Bertram & Machlin, Lawrence J., eds. 506p. 1982. 95.00 (ISBN 0-89766-176-1). NY Acad Sci.

New York Academy of Sciences, Dec. 17-21, 1979. Nonlinear Dynamics, Vol. 357. Helleman, Robert H., ed. LC 80-72072. (Annals of the New York Academy of Sciences Ser.). 507p. 1980. 100.00x (ISBN 0-89766-103-6); pap. 100.00x (ISBN 0-89766-104-4). NY Acad Sci.

New York Academy of Sciences, Feb 20-22, 1980. Micronutrient Interactions: Vitamins, Minerals, & Hazardous Elements, Vol. 355. Levander, O. A. & Cheng, Lorraine, eds. LC 80-25622. 372p. 1980. 74.00x (ISBN 0-89766-099-4); pap. 74.00x (ISBN 0-686-77401-9). NY Acad Sci.

New York Academy of Sciences, Feb. 4-6, 1980. Second International Conference on Carriers & Channels in Biological Systems: Transport Proteins, Vol. 358. (Annals of the New York Academy of Sciences). 387p. 1980. 77.00x (ISBN 0-89766-105-2); pap. 77.00x (ISBN 0-89766-106-0). Ny Acad Sci.

New York Academy of Sciences, March 10-12, 1980. Modulation of Cellular Interactions by Vitamin A & Derivatives: Retinoids, Vol. 359. De Luca, Luigi M. & Shapiro, Stanley S., eds. 431p. 1981. 85.00x (ISBN 0-89766-107-9). NY Acad Sci.

New York Academy of Sciences, Nov. 28-30, 1979. Genetic Variation of Viruses, Vol. 354. Palese, Peter & Roizman, Bernard, eds. LC 80-25770. (Annals of the New York Academy of Sciences). 507p. 1980. 99.00x (ISBN 0-89766-097-8); pap. 99.00x (ISBN 0-89766-098-6). NY Acad Sci.

New York Academy of Sciences, Nov. 7-9, 1979. Airborne Contagion, Vol. 353. Kundsin, Ruth B., ed. LC 80-27061. (Annals of the New York Academy of Sciences). 341p. 1980. 69.00x (ISBN 0-89766-095-1); pap. 67.00x (ISBN 0-89766-096-X). NY Acad Sci.

New York Assn. of Realtors & Harwood, Bruce. New York Real Estate. 1981. text ed. 20.95 (ISBN 0-8359-4894-3). Reston.

New York Botanical Garden. Wild Flowers of the Northeastern States. (Illus.). 1978. 24.95 (ISBN 0-07-046371-9, P&RB). McGraw.

New York Botanical Garden Library. Catalog of the Manuscript & Archival Collections & Index to the Correspondence of John Torrey. 1973. 57.50 (ISBN 0-8161-1018-2, Hall Library). G K Hall.

New York Botanical Library. Biographical Notes Upon Botanists, 3 Vols. 1965. Set. 325.00 (ISBN 0-8161-0695-9, Hall Library). G K Hall.

New York City Commission on the Status of Women. Women's Organizations: A New York City Directory. 144p. 1982. pap. 5.95 (ISBN 0-686-36270-5). NYC Comm Women.

New York City Planning Commission. Plan for New York City. Richards, Peter, ed. Incl. Vol. 1. Critical Issues. 1970. pap. 20.00x (ISBN 0-262-64004-X); Vol. 2. Bronx. 1970. pap. 17.50x (ISBN 0-262-64005-8); Vol. 3. Brooklyn. 1970. pap. 17.50x (ISBN 0-262-64006-6); Vol. 4. Manhattan. 1970. (ISBN 0-262-64007-4); Vol. 5. Queens. o.p. (ISBN 0-262-64008-2); Vol. 6. Staten Island. 20.00x (ISBN 0-262-64009-0). MIT Pr.

New York Constitutional Convention, 1821. Reports of the Proceedings & Debates. LC 72-133168. (Law, Politics & History Ser.). 1970. Repr. of 1821 ed. lib. bdg. 85.00 (ISBN 0-306-70069-7). Da Capo.

New York Historical Society. American Landscape & Genre Paintings in the New York Historical Society: A Catalog of the Collection Including Historical, Narrative & Marine Art. (Illus.). 1450p. 1981. lib. bdg. 350.00 (ISBN 0-8161-0364-X, Hall Library). G K Hall.

New York Institute of Finance. Introduction to Brokerage Operation Department Procedures. (Illus.). 175p. 1979. 8.95 (ISBN 0-13-478982-2). NY Inst Finance.

New York Institute of Technology. A Programmed Course in Basic Electricity. 2nd ed. 1970. text ed. 18.95 (ISBN 0-07-046390-5, G); instructor's manual 1.50 (ISBN 0-07-046392-1). McGraw.
--Programmed Course in Basic Electronics. 1964. text ed. 16.05 o.p. (ISBN 0-07-046351-4, G). McGraw.
--A Programmed Course in Basic Electronics. 2nd ed. 1976. text ed. 20.95 (ISBN 0-07-046391-3, G); instructor's manual 2.00 (ISBN 0-07-046393-X). McGraw.
--A Programmed Course in Basic Pulse Circuits. new ed. (Illus.). 320p. 1977. pap. text ed. 17.95 (ISBN 0-07-046375-1, G); instructor's manual 2.00 (ISBN 0-07-046376-X). McGraw.

New York-New Jersey Trail Conference Staff, jt. auth. see Houck, Walter.

New York-New Jersey Trail Conference & the American Geographical Society. The New York Walk Book. pap. 12.95 (ISBN 0-385-03256-0). Natural Hist.

New York Public Library. Dictionary Catalog of the Schomburg Collection of Negro Literature & History, Supplement 1974. 1976. lib. bdg. 105.00 (ISBN 0-8161-0062-4, Hall Library). G K Hall.
--The Eno Collection of New York City Views. Weitenkampf, Frank, ed. LC 79-162522. (Illus.). 1971. Repr. of 1925 ed. 37.00x (ISBN 0-8103-3744-4). Gale.
--Sixty-Four Treasures. (Illus.). 1964. pap. 2.00 o.p. (ISBN 0-87104-162-6). NY Pub Lib.

New York Public Library & the Library of Congress. Guide to Festschriften. (Festschriften Collection of the New York Public Library). 1977. lib. bdg. 148.00 (ISBN 0-8161-0069-1, Hall Library). G K Hall.

New York Public Library, Research Libraries. Catalog of Government Publications, Economics Division, 40 vols. 1972. Set. lib. bdg. 3800.00 (ISBN 0-8161-0781-5, Hall Library). G K Hall.
--Catalog of the Theatre & Drama Collections: First Supplement to Pt. 2, Theatre Collection, 2 vols. 1973. Set. 270.00 (ISBN 0-8161-0747-5, Hall Library). G K Hall.
--Catalog of the Theatre & Drama Collections: First Supplement to Pt. 1, Drama Collection. 1973. 105.00 (ISBN 0-8161-0745-9, Hall Library). G K Hall.
--Catalog of the Theatre & Drama Collections, 2 pts. Incl. Pt. 1, No. 1. Drama Collection: Listing by Cultural Origin, 6 vols. Set. 640.00; Pt. 1, No. 2. Drama Collection: Author Listing, 6 vols. Set. 860.00 (ISBN 0-8161-0106-X); Pt. 2. Theatre Collection: Books on the Theatre, 9 vols. Set. 690.00 (ISBN 0-8161-0107-8). 1967 (Hall Library). G K Hall.

New York Public Library Research Libraries. Catalog of the Theatre & Drama Collections, Pt. 3. 30 Vols. Non-book Collection. 1976. lib. bdg. 3485.00 (ISBN 0-8161-1195-2, Hall Library). G K Hall.

New York Public Library, Research Libraries. Dictionary Catalog & Shelf List of the Spencer Collection of Illustrated Books & Manuscripts & Fine Bindings, 2 vols. 1970. Set. lib. bdg. 190.00 (ISBN 0-8161-0862-5, Hall Library). G K Hall.
--Dictionary Catalog of Jewish Collection, 14 Vols. 1960. Set. 1190.00 (ISBN 0-8161-0409-3, Pub. by Hall Library). G K Hall.
--Dictionary Catalog of the Albert A. & Henry W. Berg Collection of English & American Literature, First Supplement. 1975. lib. bdg. 105.00 (ISBN 0-8161-0014-4, Hall Library). G K Hall.

New York Public Library Research Libraries. Dictionary Catalog of the Art & Architecture Division, The Research Libraries of The New York Public Library, 30 vols. 1975. Set. lib. bdg. 2950.00 (ISBN 0-8161-1157-X, Hall Library). G K Hall.

New York Public Library, Research Libraries. Dictionary Catalog of the Dance Collection, Performing Arts Research Center, 10 vols. 1974. Set. lib. bdg. 820.00 (ISBN 0-8161-1124-3, Hall Library). G K Hall.
--Dictionary Catalog of the Henry W. & Albert A. Berg Collection of English & American Literature, 5 Vols. 1969. Set. lib. bdg. 465.00 (ISBN 0-8161-0870-6, Hall Library). G K Hall.
--Dictionary Catalog of the History of the Americas Collection, 28 Vols. 1961. Set. lib. bdg. 2200.00 (ISBN 0-8161-0540-5, Hall Library). G K Hall.
--Dictionary Catalog of the History of the Americas Collection, First Supplement, 9 vols. 1974. Set. lib. bdg. 945.00 (ISBN 0-8161-0771-8, Hall Library). G K Hall.
--Dictionary Catalog of the Jewish Collection, First Supplement, 8 vols. 5424p. 1975. Set. lib. bdg. 840.00 (ISBN 0-8161-0773-4, Hall Library). G K Hall.
--Dictionary Catalog of the Local History & Genealogy Division, 20 vols. 1974. Set. lib. bdg. 1540.00 (ISBN 0-8161-0784-X, Hall Library). G K Hall.
--Dictionary Catalog of the Manuscript Division, 2 Vols. 1967. Set. lib. bdg. 150.00 (ISBN 0-8161-0750-5, Hall Library). G K Hall.
--Dictionary Catalog of the Map Division, 10 vols. 1971. Set. lib. bdg. 950.00 (ISBN 0-8161-0783-1, Hall Library). G K Hall.
--Dictionary Catalog of the Music Collection, 33 Vols. 1964. Set. lib. bdg. 3135.00 (ISBN 0-8161-0709-2, Hall Library). G K Hall.
--Dictionary Catalog of the Music Collection, Supplement II, 10 vols. 1973. Set. lib. bdg. 1300.00 (ISBN 0-8161-0760-2, Hall Library). G K Hall.
--Dictionary Catalog of the Oriental Collection: First Supplement, 8 vols. 1976. Set. lib. bdg. 955.00 (ISBN 0-8161-0775-0, Hall Library). G K Hall.
--Dictionary Catalog of the Oriental Collection, 16 Vols. 1960. Set. lib. bdg. 1400.00 (ISBN 0-8161-0410-7, Hall Library). G K Hall.
--The Dictionary Catalog of the Prints Division, 5 vols. 1975. Set. lib. bdg. 475.00 (ISBN 0-8161-1148-0, Hall Library). G K Hall.
--Dictionary Catalog of the Rare Book Division: First Supplement. 1973. 110.00 (ISBN 0-8161-1089-1, Hall Library). G K Hall.
--Dictionary Catalog of the Rare Book Division, 21 vols. 1971. Set. 1996.00 (ISBN 0-8161-0782-3, Hall Library). G K Hall.
--Dictionary Catalog of the Schomburg Collection of Negro Literature & History, 9 Vols. 1962. Set. 855.00 (ISBN 0-8161-0632-0, Hall Library); 1st suppl. 1967, 2 vols. 210.00 (ISBN 0-8161-0735-1); 2nd suppl., 1972, 4 vols. 420.00 (ISBN 0-8161-0820-X). G K Hall.

New York Public Library Research Libraries, Rare Book Division. The Imprint Catalog in the Rare Book Division, 21 vols. 1979. Set. lib. bdg. 1848.00 (ISBN 0-8161-0092-6, Hall Library). G K Hall.

New York Public Library, Research Libraries. Music Subject Headings, Vol. 1. 2nd enlarged ed. 1966. lib. bdg. 65.00 (ISBN 0-8161-0739-4, Hall Library). G K Hall.
--Subject Catalog of the World War One Collection, 4 Vols. 1961. Set. 280.00 (ISBN 0-8161-0559-6, Hall Library). G K Hall.
--Subject Headings, 5 Vols. 1960. Set. lib. bdg. 325.00 (ISBN 0-8161-0368-2, Hall Library). G K Hall.
--Theatre Subject Headings, Vol. 1. 2nd enlarged ed. 1966. lib. bdg. 65.00 (ISBN 0-8161-0740-8, Hall Library). G K Hall.

New York Public Library, Research Libraries, Local History & Genealogy Division. United States Local History Catalog, 2 vols. 1115p. 1974. Set. lib. bdg. 190.00 (ISBN 0-8161-1147-2, Hall Library). G K Hall.

New York Public Library, the Research Libraries. Dictionary Catalog of the Slavonic Collection, 44 vols. 2nd, rev. ed. 1974. Set. lib. bdg. 3800.00 (ISBN 0-8161-0777-7, Hall Library). G K Hall.

New York State Commission on Cultural Resources. Cultural Resource Development: A Planning Survey & Analysis. LC 75-19790. (Special Studies). (Illus.). 300p. 1976. 19.95 o.p. (ISBN 0-275-55640-9). Praeger.

New York State Legislature Joint Committee Investigating Seditious Activities. Revolutionary Radicalism, 4 vols. in 5. LC 78-12114. (Civil Liberties in American History Ser.). 1971. Repr. of 1920 ed. Set. lib. bdg. 295.00 (ISBN 0-306-71974-6). Da Capo.

New York Times. The Complete Book of Baseball. LC 79-92320. (Sports Ser.). (Illus.). 224p. 1980. 14.95 o.p. (ISBN 0-686-61137-3). Bobbs.
--The Complete Book of Football: A New York Times Scrapbook History. LC 79-92321. (Sports Ser.). (Illus.). 224p. 1980. 14.95 o.p. (ISBN 0-672-52637-9). Bobbs.
--The Complete Book of Golf. LC 79-92319. (Sports Ser.). (Illus.). 224p. 1980. 14.95 o.p. (ISBN 0-672-52636-0). Bobbs.
--The Complete Book of Tennis: A New York Times Scrapbook History. LC 79-56751. (Sports Ser.). (Illus.). 224p. 1980. 14.95 o.p. (ISBN 0-672-52638-7). Bobbs.

New York Times, jt. auth. see CBS News.

New York University. Anglo-American Legal History Series, Nos. 2-9 In 1 Vol. 1939-1944. 25.00 o.p. (ISBN 0-379-00178-0). Oceana.

New York University School of Law. Law & the Television of the 80's. 285p. 1983. text ed. 35.00 (ISBN 0-379-20046-5). Oceana.

New York University Staff. Library Catalog of the Conservation Center of the Institute of Fine Arts. 1980. lib. bdg. 95.00 (ISBN 0-8161-0303-8, Hall Library). G K Hall.

New Yorker. The New Yorker Album of Drawings. (Large Format Ser.). (Illus.). 1978. pap. 12.95 (ISBN 0-14-004968-1). Penguin.

Newall, A., jt. auth. see Bell, C. G.

Newall, A. B., jt. auth. see Wilson, James G.

Newall, Venetia, ed. The Witch Figure: Essays in Honor of Katharine M. Briggs. (Illus.). 1973. 21.00 o.p. (ISBN 0-7100-7696-7). Routledge & Kegan.

Newark, Peter. The Illustrated Encyclopedia of the Old West. (Illus.). 288p. Date not set. 29.95 (ISBN 0-89479-126-5). A & W Pubs. Postponed.

Newball. Immunopharmacology of the Lung. (Lung Biology in Health & Disease Ser.: Vol. 20). 536p. 1983. 65.00 (ISBN 0-8247-1827-5). Dekker.

Newberg, Herbert B., ed. Public Interest Practice & Fee Awards. LC 80-80441. 567p. 1980. text ed. 20.00 (ISBN 0-686-61029-6, H1-2953). PLI.

Newberg, Leslie A., jt. auth. see Lebowitz, Philip W.

Newberger, Eli H., jt. ed. see Bourne, Richard.

Newberne, J. W., jt. auth. see Fawcett, Don W.

Newberne, Paul M. & Butler, W. H., eds. Rat Hepatic Neoplasia. 1978. text ed. 30.00x (ISBN 0-262-14029-2). MIT Pr.

Newberry, Clare T. Marshmallow. LC 42-22858. (Illus.). (gr. k-3). 1942. 12.95i (ISBN 0-06-024460-7, HarpJ); PLB 12.89 (ISBN 0-06-024461-5). Har-Row.

Newberry Library. Bibliographical Inventory to the Early Music in the Newberry Library, Chicago, Illinois. Krummel, D. W., ed. 1977. lib. bdg. 75.00 (ISBN 0-8161-0042-X, Hall Library). G K Hall.

--Narratives of Captivity Among the Indians of North America, with Supplement I. LC 74-3100. 1974. Repr. of 1912 ed. 30.00x (ISBN 0-8103-3694-4). Gale.

Newberry Library - Chicago. Catalogue of the Greenlee Collection, 2 vols. 1970. Set. 190.00 (ISBN 0-8161-0903-6, Hall Library). G K Hall.

--Dictionary Catalog of the Edward E. Ayer Collection of Americana & American Indians, First Supplement, 3 vol. 1970. Set. lib. bdg. 315.00 (ISBN 0-8161-0810-2, Hall Library). G K Hall.

--Dictionary Catalog of the Edward E. Ayer Collection of Americana & American Indians, 16 Vols. 1961. Set. 1120.00 (ISBN 0-8161-0586-3, Hall Library). G K Hall.

--Dictionary Catalogue of the History of Printing from the John M. Wing Foundation, 6 Vols. 1961. Set. lib. bdg. 570.00 (ISBN 0-8161-0587-1, Hall Library). G K Hall.

--Dictionary Catalogue of the History of Printing from the John M. Wing Foundation, First Supplement, 3 vols. 1970. Set. lib. bdg. 315.00 (ISBN 0-8161-0809-9, Hall Library). G K Hall.

Newberry Library-Chicago. Genealogical Index of the Newberry Library, Chicago, 4 vols. 1960. Set. lib. bdg. 380.00 (ISBN 0-8161-0498-0, Hall Library). G K Hall.

Newberry, Lida. One-Day Adventures by Car: With Full Directions for Drivers Out of New York City. 4th. rev. ed. (Illus.). 288p. 1980. pap. 7.95 (ISBN 0-8038-5393-9). Hastings.

Newberry, P. G., jt. auth. see Wright, A.

Newberry, Wilma. The Pirandellian Mode in Spanish Literature: From Cervantes to Sastre. LC 77-171181. 232p. 1973. 29.50x (ISBN 0-87395-089-5). State U NY Pr.

Newbery, F. Cries of London. Lurie, Alison & Schiller, Justin G., eds. Incl. Cries of New York. Wood, Samuel. LC 75-32142. (Classics of Children's Literature 1621-1932 Ser.). PLB 38.00 o.s.i. (ISBN 0-8240-2258-0). Garland Pub.

Newbery, John, et al, eds. Original Mother Goose's Melody. LC 68-31093. 1969. Repr. of 1892 ed. 30.00x (ISBN 0-8103-3485-2). Gale.

Newbigging, Thomas. Fables & Fabulists, Ancient & Modern. LC 70-78212. 1971. Repr. of 1895 ed. 34.00x (ISBN 0-8103-3770-3). Gale.

Newbigin, James E. The Reunion of the Church: A Defence of the South India Scheme. LC 79-4205. 1979. Repr. of 1960 ed. lib. bdg. 19.75x (ISBN 0-313-20797-6, NERU). Greenwood.

Newbold, H. L. Dr. Newbold's Revolutionary New Discoveries About Weight Loss: How to Master the Hidden Food & Environmental Allergies That Make You Eat. 1979. pap. 2.25 (ISBN 0-451-09637-1, AE9637, Sig). NAL.

Newbolt, Henry. Rilloby-Rill. LC 73-8809. (Illus.). 32p. (ps-1). 1974. 5.95 o.p. (ISBN 0-87955-107-0); PLB 4.98 o.p. (ISBN 0-87955-707-9). O'Hara.

Newborn, Monroe, jt. auth. see Levy, David.

Newborn, Sasha. The Basement. LC 76-45983. (Illus.). 188p. 1978. pap. 4.00 (ISBN 0-930012-06-2). Bandanna Bks.

Newborn, Sasha, ed. Brasi! Contemporary Brazilian Writing. LC 77-642342. (Rockbottom Specials Ser.). (Illus., Eng. & Port.). cancelled (ISBN 0-930012-21-6); pap. 8.00 (ISBN 0-930012-20-8). Bandanna Bks.

--First Person Intense, a Prose Anthology. LC 77-642342. 192p. 1978. pap. 5.00 (ISBN 0-930012-14-3). Bandanna Bks.

Newbould, Gerald D., et al. Going International: The Experience of Smaller Companies Overseas. LC 78-15729. 1978. 39.95x o.p. (ISBN 0-470-26493-4). Halsted Pr.

Newbourne, Malcolm J. The Transportation & Distribution Manager's Guide to Time Sharing. new ed. Marshall, Kenneth, ed. LC 79-88410. 1979. 25.00 o.p. (ISBN 0-87408-016-9). Traffic Serv.

Newbrough, E. T. Effective Maintenance Management: Organization, Motivation, & Control in Industrial Maintenance. 1967. 32.95 o.p. (ISBN 0-07-046329-8, P&RB). McGraw.

Newbrough, J. R., jt. ed. see Haywood, H. Carl.

Newbrun, Ernest. Cariology. 2nd ed. 350p. 1983. 27.50 (ISBN 0-683-06461-4). Williams & Wilkins.

Newbury, Colin. Tahiti Nui: Change & Survival in French Polynesia, 1767-1945. LC 79-23609. 1980. text ed. 25.00x (ISBN 0-8248-0630-1). UH Pr.

Newbury, Josephine. Church Kindergarten Resource Book. rev. ed. 1970. pap. 4.49 (ISBN 0-8042-9505-0). John Knox.

--More Kindergarten Resources. LC 73-5349. 264p. (Orig.). 1974. pap. 3.99 (ISBN 0-8042-1360-7). John Knox.

Newby, Cliff. Canaries for Pleasure & Profit. (Orig.). 1965. pap. 2.95 (ISBN 0-87666-418-4, AP270). TFH Pubns.

Newby, H. International Perspectives in Rural Sociology. 220p. 1978. 51.95 (ISBN 0-471-99606-8). Wiley.

Newby, Hayes, jt. auth. see Anderson, Virgil A.

Newby, Howard. Deferential Worker: A Study of Farm Workers in East Anglia. LC 79-3968. 480p. 1979. Repr. of 1977 ed. 27.50 (ISBN 0-299-07890-6). U of Wis Pr.

--Social Change in Rural England. LC 79-21703. 272p. 1979. 25.00 (ISBN 0-299-08040-4). U of Wis Pr.

Newby, Howard, jt. ed. see Buttel, Frederick H.

Newby, James E. Black Authors & Education: An Annotated Bibliography of Books. LC 79-9677. 113p. 1980. text ed. 17.75 (ISBN 0-8191-0974-6); pap. text ed. 8.25 (ISBN 0-8191-0975-4). U Pr of Amer.

--Teaching Faculty in Black Colleges & Universities: A Survey of Selected Social Science Disciplines, 1977-1978. LC 82-17620. (Illus.). 112p. (Orig.). 1983. lib. bdg. 18.50 (ISBN 0-8191-2787-6); pap. text ed. 8.25 (ISBN 0-8191-2788-4). U Pr of Amer.

Newcity, Michael A. Copyright Law in the Soviet Union. LC 76-12867. (Praeger Special Studies). 1978. 29.95 o.p. (ISBN 0-275-56450-9). Praeger.

Newcom, Samuel R. & Kadin, Marshall E. Hematologic Malignancies of the Adult. 1981. 26.95 (ISBN 0-201-04356-4, 04356, Med-Nurse). A-W.

Newcomb, Dorothy & Swansburg, Russell C. The Team Plan: A Manual for Nursing Service Administrators. 2nd ed. 1971. pap. 4.95 o.p. (ISBN 0-399-40040-0). Putnam Pub Group.

Newcomb, Duane. The Apartment Farmer. 1977. pap. 1.75 o.s.i. (ISBN 0-380-00975-7, 32524). Avon.

--Fortune-Building Secrets of the Rich. LC 82-18837. 215p. 1983. pap. 4.95 (ISBN 0-13-329102-2, Reward). P-H.

--Fortune-Building Secrets of the Rich. LC 82-18837. 215p. 1983. 14.95 (ISBN 0-13-384685-7, Parker); pap. 4.95 (ISBN 0-13-329102-2). P-H.

Newcomb, Ellsworth & Kenny, Hugh. Miracle Metals. (Science Survey Ser.). (Illus.). (gr. 4-6). 1962. PLB 5.29 o.p. (ISBN 0-399-60464-2). Putnam Pub Group.

Newcomb, Franc J. Hosteen Klah: Navaho Medicine Man & Sand Painter. LC 64-20759. (Civilization of the American Indian Ser: No. 73). (Illus.). 227p. 1971. 11.95 o.p. (ISBN 0-8061-0622-0); pap. 6.95 (ISBN 0-8061-1008-2). U of Okla Pr.

Newcomb, Franc J. & Reichard, Gladys A. Sandpaintings: Navajo Shooting Chant. 1975. pap. 7.00 (ISBN 0-686-95817-9). Jefferson Natl.

Newcomb, J. A. From Darkness to Light. 1983. 7.95 (ISBN 0-533-05666-7). Vantage.

Newcomb, Loda I., jt. auth. see Knapper, Arno F.

Newcomb, R. C. Ringold Formation of Pleistocene Age in Type Locality, The White Bluffs, Washington. (Reprint Ser.: No. 1). (Illus.). 13p. 1958. 0.25 (ISBN 0-686-36909-2). Geologic Pubns.

Newcomb, Richard. Future Resources: Their Geostatistical Appraisal. 179p. 1982. 7.50 (ISBN 0-937058-13-0). West Va U Pr.

Newcomb, T. P. & Spurr, R. T. Commercial Vehicle Braking. (Illus.). 1979. text ed. 19.95 (ISBN 0-408-00362-6). Butterworth.

Newcomb, Theodore M., et al. Persistence & Change: Bennington College & Its Students After 25 Years. 292p. 1967. text ed. 15.00 (ISBN 0-471-63380-1, Pub. by Wiley). Krieger.

Newcomb, V. N. Practical Accounting for Business Studies. 200p. 1983. price not set (ISBN 0-471-90007-9, Pub. by Wiley-Interscience). Wiley.

--Practical Calculations for Business Studies: Problems & Applications for Students in Africa. LC 80-42019. 152p. 1981. 26.95 (ISBN 0-471-27966-8, Pub. by Wiley-Interscience). Wiley.

Newcomb, W. W., Jr. The Indians of Texas: From Prehistoric to Modern Times. LC 60-14312. (Texas History Paperbacks: No. 4). (Illus.). 422p. 1961. 18.95 (ISBN 0-292-73271-6); pap. 8.95 (ISBN 0-292-78425-2). U of Tex Pr.

Newcombe, Angie, jt. auth. see Newcombe, John.

Newcombe, Jack. Game of Football. LC 67-10101. (Sports Library). (Illus.). (gr. 3-6). 1967. PLB 7.12 (ISBN 0-8116-6655-7). Garrard.

Newcombe, John & Newcombe, Angie. The Family Tennis Book. 157p. 1976. pap. 4.95 o.s.i. (ISBN 0-440-52464-4, Delta). Dell.

Newcombe, Josephine M. Leonid Andreyev. LC 72-79938. (Literature and Life Ser.). 1973. 11.95 (ISBN 0-8044-2657-0). Ungar.

Newcomer, Victor D., jt. ed. see Sternberg, Thomas H.

Newell, Adnah C. Coloring, Finishing & Painting Wood. Holtrop, ed. (gr. 9-12). 1972. text ed. 19.28 o.p. (ISBN 0-87002-124-9). Bennett IL.

Newell, C. F. Application of Queuing Theory. 2nd ed. (Monographs on Statistics & Applied Probability). 1983. 29.95x (ISBN 0-412-24500-0, Pub. by Chapman & Hall). Methuen Inc.

Newell, Charldean, jt. auth. see Kraemer, Richard.

Newell, Clarence A. Human Behavior in Educational Administration: A Behavioral Science Interpretation. (Illus.). 1978. ref. ed. 23.95 (ISBN 0-13-444638-0). P-H.

Newell, D. G., ed. Campylobacter: Progress in Research. (Illus.). 400p. 1982. text ed. 69.00 (ISBN 0-85200-455-9, Pub. by MTP Pr England). Kluwer Boston.

Newell, David M. If Nothin' Don't Happen. LC 74-7745. (Illus.). 256p. 1975. 14.50 (ISBN 0-394-49312-5, 49312). Knopf.

Newell, Frank W. Ophthalmology: Principles & Concepts. 5th ed. (Illus.). 559p. 1982. text ed. 35.50 (ISBN 0-8016-3645-0). Mosby.

--Ophthalmology: Principles & Concepts. 4th ed. LC 78-6733. 628p. 1978. 34.50 o.p. (ISBN 0-8016-3640-X). Mosby.

Newell, Frank W., ed. Hereditary Disorders of the Eye & Ocular Adnexa. (Illus.). 288p. 1980. text ed. 25.00 o.p. (ISBN 0-936820-00-4). Ophthalmic.

Newell, G., ed. Traffic Flow & Transportation. 1972. 33.95 (ISBN 0-444-00128-X, North Holland). Elsevier.

Newell, G. E. & Newell, R. C. Marine Plankton: Practical Guide. 1966. pap. text ed. 11.75x (ISBN 0-09-110541-2, Hutchinson U Lib). Humanities.

Newell, G. F. Traffic Flow on Transportation Networks. (MIT Press Transportation Studies Ser.: No. 5). (Illus.). 288p. 1980. 35.00x (ISBN 0-262-14032-2). MIT Pr.

Newell, Gilbert F., jt. auth. see Mead, Leon.

Newell, Guy R. & Ellison, Neil M., eds. Nutrition & Cancer: Etiology & Treatment. (Progress in Cancer Research & Therapy Ser.: Vol. 17). 460p. 54.50 (ISBN 0-89004-631-X). Raven.

Newell, Henry H., jt. auth. see Schwerin, Horace S.

Newell, J. David, ed. Philosophy & Common Sense. LC 79-9642. 154p. 1980. pap. text ed. 8.00 (ISBN 0-8191-0968-1). U Pr of Amer.

Newell, John C. & Griswold, P. R. Narrow Gauge East From Denver: The Colorado Eastern Railroad. (Illus.). 100p. (Orig.). 1982. pap. 6.50 (ISBN 0-87108-624-7). Pruett.

Newell, Peter. The Rocket Book. LC 68-9155. 48p. (gr. 7-12). 1974. pap. 1.50 o.p. (ISBN 0-486-22044-3). Dover.

Newell, R. C., jt. auth. see Newell, G. E.

Newell, Ray. Super Profile: Morris Minor 21000. 56p. Date not set. 9.95 (ISBN 0-85429-331-0). Haynes Pubns.

Newell, Sydney B. Chemistry: An Introduction. 2nd ed. (Illus.). 563p. 1980. text ed. 20.95 (ISBN 0-316-60454-2); instructor's manual free (ISBN 0-316-60455-0); lab manual, experimental chemistry 7.95 (ISBN 0-316-05278-7); study guide 8.95 (ISBN 0-316-60456-9). Little.

Newell, Virginia K., et al, eds. Black Mathematicians & Their Works. 1980. 18.00 o.p. (ISBN 0-8059-2556-2); pap. 17.95 (ISBN 0-8059-2677-1). Dorrance.

Newell, William L. Struggle & Submission: R. C. Zaehner on Mysticisms. LC 80-6295. 402p. 1981. lib. bdg. 23.25 (ISBN 0-8191-1696-3); pap. text ed. 13.50 (ISBN 0-8191-1697-1). U Pr of Amer.

Newendorp, Paul D. Decision Analysis for Petroleum Exploration. LC 75-10936. 668p. 1976. 59.95x (ISBN 0-87814-064-6). Pennwell Books Division.

Newey, Vincent. Cowper's Poetry: A Critical Study & Reassessment. LC 82-6843. (English Texts & Studies: No. 20). 378p. 1982. text ed. 29.50x (ISBN 0-389-20079-4). B&N Imports.

Newfarmer, Richard. Transnational Conglomerates & the Economics of Dependent Development. Altman, Edward I. & Walter, Ingo, eds. LC 78-13842. (Contemporary Studies in Economic & Financial Analysis). (Orig.). 1980. lib. bdg. 45.00 (ISBN 0-89232-110-5). Jai Pr.

Newfield, Jack. Robert F. Kennedy: A Memoir. 1978. pap. 2.50 o.p. (ISBN 0-425-04047-X, Dist. by Putnam). Berkley Pub.

Newgroschel, Joachim, tr. see Heschel, Abraham J.

Newhall, Beaumont & Newhall, Nancy. Masters of Photography. (Illus.). 192p. 1983. pap. 12.50 (ISBN 0-89104-010-2, A & W Visual Library). A & W Pubs.

Newhall, Nancy, jt. auth. see Newhall, Beaumont.

Newhall, Richard A. Muster & Review: A Problem of English Military Administration, Fourteen Twenty to Fourteen Forty. 1940. 37.50x (ISBN 0-686-51420-3). Elliots Bks.

Newhall, T. The Crusades. LC 63-11881. 146p. 1963. pap. 6.50 o.p. (ISBN 0-03-082837-6, Pub. by HR&W). Krieger.

Newham, A. T., jt. auth. see Fayle, H.

Newhan, Ross. The California Angels. LC 82-700. (Illus.). 191p. 1982. 13.50 (ISBN 0-671-42059-3). S&S.

Newhouse, B. S. How to Prepare for the Graduate Management Admissions Test (GMAT) 2nd ed. (McGraw-Hill Paperback Ser.). 1982. pap. 6.95 (ISBN 0-07-046403-0). McGraw.

Newhouse, Bertha S. How to Prepare for the Graduate Management Admission Test. 1979. pap. 5.95 o.p. (ISBN 0-07-046401-4, SP). McGraw.

Newhouse, Dora. Ciudadania Immigration, Naturalization Gobierno Americano, Historia De America Primitiva: Citizenship Immigration, Naturalization: American Government, Early American History. new ed. LC 77-82188. (Illus., Spanish & english edition). 1980. text ed. 7.95o.s.i. (ISBN 0-918050-24-3); pap. text ed. 4.95 (ISBN 0-918050-07-3). Newhouse Pr.

--The Encyclopedia of Homonyms-Sound Alikes: Condensed & Abridged Edition. LC 76-50944. (Illus.). (gr. 4-12). 1978. text ed. 9.95o.s.i. (ISBN 0-918050-02-2); pap. 6.95 (ISBN 0-918050-00-6). Newhouse Pr.

--The Encyclopedia of Homonyms 'Sound-Alikes' LC 76-27486. 1977. 16.95 (ISBN 0-918050-01-4). Newhouse Pr.

--Homonyms - Homonimos: Sound-Alikes. LC 77-82190. (Illus., Eng. & Sp.). 1978. text ed. 9.95o.p. (ISBN 0-918050-09-X); pap. 6.95 (ISBN 0-918050-27-8). Newhouse Pr.

Newhouse, Flower A. Disciplines of the Holy Quest. 4th ed. LC 59-15553. (Illus.). 1959. 9.50 (ISBN 0-910378-05-3). Christward.

--Gateways into Light. 2nd ed. LC 74-75517. 160p. 1974. pap. 7.50 (ISBN 0-910378-09-6). Christward.

--Here Are Your Answers, Vol. I. 2nd ed. LC 49-16192. 1948. 8.50 (ISBN 0-910378-01-0). Christward.

--Here Are Your Answers, Vol. II. 3rd ed. LC 76-103410. 1969. 8.50 (ISBN 0-910378-06-1). Christward.

--Here Are Your Answers, Vol. III. Boult, Pamela & Boult, Pamela, eds. 150p. 1983. write for info. (ISBN 0-910378-18-5). Christward.

--The Journey Upward. Bengtson, Athene, ed. LC 78-74955. 1978. pap. 6.50 (ISBN 0-910378-15-0). Christward.

--Kingdom of the Shining Ones. 6th ed. 1955. 10.00 (ISBN 0-910378-03-7). Christward.

--The Meaning & Value of the Sacraments. LC 77-186123. 123p. 1971. 6.50 (ISBN 0-910378-07-X). Christward.

--Rediscovering the Angels & Natives of Eternity. 7th ed. (Illus.). 10.00 (ISBN 0-910378-02-9). Christward.

--The Sacred Heart of Christmas. Bengtson, Athene, ed. LC 78-74956. (Illus.). 1978. pap. 6.00 (ISBN 0-910378-14-2). Christward.

--Songs of Deliverance. LC 72-94582. 250p. 1972. 8.50 (ISBN 0-910378-08-8). Christward.

--These, Too, Shall Be Loved. LC 76-49246. 1976. pap. 5.00 (ISBN 0-910378-11-8). Christward.

Newhouse, Flower A., et al. Insights into Reality. 2nd ed. LC 75-36869. 1975. pap. 7.50 (ISBN 0-910378-10-X). Christward.

Newick, John, jt. ed. see Field, Dick.

Newitt, Jane. Future Trends in Education Policy. LC 78-19672. 192p. 1979. 18.95 (ISBN 0-669-02713-8). Lexington Bks.

Newitt, Malyn. The Comoro Islands. (Nations of Contemporary Africa Ser.). 135p. 1983. 17.50x (ISBN 0-86531-292-3). Westview.

Newkirk, Ross T. Environmental Planning for Utility Corridors: By Computer Techniques. LC 77-92593. 1979. 30.00 o.p. (ISBN 0-250-40223-8). Ann Arbor Science.

Newland, Mary R. The Saint Book: For Parents, Teachers, Homilists, Storytellers & Children. (Illus.). 208p. 1979. 10.95 (ISBN 0-8164-0210-8). Seabury.

Newland, Mary R., jt. ed. see Hill, Brennan.

Newland, T. Ernest. Gifted in Socio-Educational Perspective. (Special Education Ser.). (Illus.). 448p. 1976. 25.95 (ISBN 0-13-356287-5). P-H.

Newlander, John. Book of Love & Marriage. 1979. pap. 1.50 (ISBN 0-89485-076-8). EdMart Intl.

--How to Respond to Unfair Evaluations. 1979. 1.50 (ISBN 0-89485-063-6). EdMart Intl.

--Quotations for the Classroom Teacher: The Basic Pocket-Size Survival Kit. LC 77-70325. 1978. tchr's ed. 1.50 (ISBN 0-89485-025-3). EdMart Intl.

--The Thousand Quotations, Bk. 1. LC 77-70322. 1980. pap. 4.95 (ISBN 0-89485-009-1). EdMart Intl.

Newlander, John, ed. Teacher Author League of America Bibliography & Directory. Date not set. cancelled (ISBN 0-89485-052-0). EdMart Intl.

--Teacher Author League of New York Bibliography. 1978. tchr's ed. 1.00 (ISBN 0-89485-051-2). EdMart Intl.

Newlands, George. Theology of the Love of God. LC 80-22547. 224p. 1981. 6.25 (ISBN 0-8042-0726-7); pap. 6.95 (ISBN 0-8042-0727-5). John Knox.

Newlands, George M. Hilary of Poitiers: A Study in Theological Method, Vol.108. (European University Studies: Series 23). xiii, 216p. 1978. pap. write for info. (ISBN 3-261-03133-6). P Lang Pubs.

Newlin, D., tr. see Bauer-Lechner, Natalie.

Newlin, Dika. Schoenberg Remembered: Diaries & Recollections (Nineteen Thirty-Eight to Nineteen Seventy-Six) (Illus.). 1980. 11.35 (ISBN 0-918728-14-2). Pendragon NY.

Newlin, Dika, tr. see Leibowitz, Rene.

Newlin, Margaret. The Book of Mourning. 1981. 10.00 o.p. (ISBN 0-88233-677-0); pap. 4.00 o.p. (ISBN 0-88233-678-9). Ardis Pubs.

Newlon, Clarke. China: The Rise to World Power. LC 82-46000. 224p. (gr. 7 up). 1983. PLB 10.95 (ISBN 0-396-08136-3). Dodd.

--Police Dogs in Action. LC 73-17865. (Illus.). (gr. 5 up). 1974. 5.95 o.p. (ISBN 0-396-06912-6). Dodd.

Newlove, Donald. Eternal Life. 1976. pap. 4.95 o.s.i. (ISBN 0-380-46458-6, 46458). Avon.

Newlove, George H. Consolidated Balance Sheets. LC 82-48380. (Accountancy in Transition Ser.). 309p. 1982. lib. bdg. 30.00 (ISBN 0-8240-5325-7). Garland Pub.

Newlyn, Walter T. Theory of Money. 3rd. ed. (Illus.). 1978. pap. 34.50x (ISBN 0-19-877099-5); pap. 11.95x (ISBN 0-19-877100-2). Oxford U Pr.

Newman, jt. auth. see Buffa.

Newman, jt. auth. see Kasner.

Newman & Feldman, eds. Down's Syndrome. (Special Education Ser.). (Illus., Orig.). 1979. pap. text ed. 15.00 (ISBN 0-89568-194-3). Spec Learn Corp.

--Educable Mentally Handicapped. (Special Education Ser.). (Illus., Orig.). 1979. pap. text ed. 15.00 (ISBN 0-89568-105-6). Spec Learn Corp.

--Trainable Mentally Handicapped. (Special Education Ser.). (Illus., Orig.). 1979. pap. 15.00 (ISBN 0-89568-106-4). Spec Learn Corp.

Newman, Alyse. It's Me, Claudia! (Easy-Read Story Bks.). (Illus.). 32p. (gr. k-3). 1981. 3.95 (ISBN 0-686-76381-5); lib. bdg. 8.60 (ISBN 0-531-04301-0). Watts.

Newman, Anne & Suk, Julie, eds. Bear Crossings: An Anthology of North American Poets. 151p. 1983. pap. 6.95 (ISBN 0-917990-08-0). New South Co.

Newman, Arnold, photos by. Faces U.S.A. (Illus.). 1977. 13.95 o.p. (ISBN 0-8174-2423-7, Amphoto); pap. 5.95 o.p. (ISBN 0-8174-2105-X). Watson-Guptill.

Newman, Arthur J., ed. In Defense of the American Public School. LC 78-19570. 1979. 20.75 (ISBN 0-8211-1307-0); text ed. 18.60 ten or more copies (ISBN 0-685-59769-5). McCutchan.

Newman, B. M. & Nida, E. A. Translator's Handbook on the Gospel of John. (Helps for Translators Ser.). 1980. softcover 4.85x (ISBN 0-8267-0137-X, 08620). United Bible.

Newman, B. M., Jr. & Nida, E. A. Translator's Handbook on Paul's Letter to the Romans. (Helps for Translators Ser.). 1982. Repr. of 1973 ed. soft cover 2.95x (ISBN 0-8267-0139-6, 08517). United Bible.

--Translator's Handbook on the Acts of the Apostles. (Helps for Translators Ser.). 1979. Repr. of 1972 ed. 4.50x (ISBN 0-8267-0138-8, 08514). United Bible.

Newman, Barbara M. & Newman, Philip R. Infancy & Childhood Development & Its Contexts. LC 77-10455. 1978. text ed. 27.50x (ISBN 0-471-02212-8); tchrs. manual 6.00 (ISBN 0-471-03802-4). Wiley.

Newman, Benjamin. Forms Manual for the CPA: For Audit, Review, & Compilation of Financial Statements. LC 80-17271. 574p. 1980. 55.95x (ISBN 0-471-05762-2). Ronald Pr.

Newman, Carol, ed. see Hildebrand, Verna.

Newman, Carol, ed. see Morton, Ruth.

Newman, Carole, jt. auth. see Newman, Isadore.

Newman, Charles. A Child's History of America: Some Ribs & Riffs for the Sixties. LC 82-73500. 307p. 1973. 13.95 (ISBN 0-8040-0644-X). Swallow.

--There Must Be More to Love Than Death: Three Short Novels. LC 82-74169. 217p. 1976. 12.95 (ISBN 0-8040-0748-9). Swallow.

Newman, Charles, ed. The Art of Sylvia Plath. LC 75-85096. (Midland Bks.: No. 148). (Illus.). 324p. 1970. pap. 2.95x o.p. (ISBN 0-253-20148-9). Ind U Pr.

Newman, Charles L. & Amos, William E., eds. Parole Decision-Making. 350p. 1974. 15.00 (ISBN 0-87945-034-7); pap. 8.95 (ISBN 0-686-96715-1). Fed Legal Pubns.

Newman, Claire M., jt. auth. see Fass, Arnold L.

Newman, D. J. A Problem Seminar. (Problem Books in Mathematics). 113p. 1983. 12.95 (ISBN 0-387-90765-3). Springer-Verlag.

Newman, D. J., jt. auth. see Feinerman, R. P.

Newman, D. J., jt. auth. see Leech, J. W.

Newman, Danny. Subscribe Now: Building Arts Audiences Through Dynamic Subscription Promotion. 3rd ed. (Illus.). 288p. 1977. 12.95 (ISBN 0-930452-00-3); pap. 7.95 (ISBN 0-930452-01-1). Theatre Comm.

Newman, Donald J. Conviction: The Determination of Guilt or Innocence Without Trial. 1966. pap. 7.95 (ISBN 0-316-60483-6). Little.

Newman, Dorothy K. & Day, Dawn. The American Energy Consumer. LC 75-4865. (Energy Policy Project of the Ford Foundation). 384p. 1975. prof ref 25.00 (ISBN 0-88410-339-0); pap. 9.95 prof ref (ISBN 0-88410-340-4). Ballinger Pub.

Newman, E. Early Paper Money of America. 3rd ed. (Illus.). 1982. lib. bdg. 29.50 o.p. (ISBN 0-686-80809-6). S J Durst.

--The Life of Richard Wagner, 4 vols. 1976. pap. 16.95 ea.; Vol. 1. pap. (ISBN 0-521-29094-5); Vol. 2. pap. (ISBN 0-521-29095-3); Vol. 3. pap. (ISBN 0-521-29096-1); Vol. 4. pap. (ISBN 0-521-29097-X); pap. 55.00 set (ISBN 0-521-29149-6). Cambridge U Pr.

Newman, Edwin. A Civil Tongue. LC 76-11607. 1976. 9.95 o.p. (ISBN 0-672-52267-5). Bobbs.

--Strictly Speaking: Will America Be the Death of English? LC 74-6525. 224p. 1974. 9.95 o.p. (ISBN 0-672-51990-9). Bobbs.

--Strictly Speaking: Will America Be the Death of English? 1975. Repr. lib. bdg. 12.50 o.p. (ISBN 0-8161-6297-2, Large Print Bks). G K Hall.

Newman, Edwin S. Civil Liberty & Civil Rights. 6th ed. LC 74-127326. (Legal Almanac Ser: No. 13). 122p. 1979. 5.95 (ISBN 0-379-11110-1). Oceana.

--Freedom Reader: A Collection of Materials on Civil Rights & Civil Liberties in America. 2nd ed. LC 62-21226. (Docket Ser.: Vol. 2). 1963. 7.50 o.p.; pap. 2.50 (ISBN 0-379-11302-3). Oceana.

Newman, Edwin S. & Wypyski, Eugene M. U. S. International Trade Reports. LC 81-11181. 1981. looseleaf 100.00 ea. (ISBN 0-379-20722-2). Oceana.

Newman, Eric P. Coins of Colonial Virginia. 2nd ed. 1983. softcover 15.00 (ISBN 0-915262-67-3). S J Durst.

Newman, Eric P. & Bressett, Kenneth. Fantastic Eighteen Hundred Four Dollar. 2nd ed. 1983. lib. bdg. 15.00 (ISBN 0-915262-63-0). S J Durst.

Newman, Ernest. Essays from the World of Music. LC 77-17326. (Music Reprint Ser.). (Illus.). 1978. Repr. of 1956 ed. lib. bdg. 25.00 (ISBN 0-306-77519-0). Da Capo.

--The Man Liszt. 1969. 11.95 o.p. (ISBN 0-575-00354-5, Pub. by Gollancz England). David & Charles.

--More Essays from the World of Music. LC 77-17332. (Music Reprint Ser.: 1978). (Illus.). 1978. Repr. of 1958 ed. lib. bdg. 29.50 (ISBN 0-306-77520-4). Da Capo.

--A Musical Motley. LC 76-10332. (Music Reprint Ser.). 1976. lib. bdg. 29.50 (ISBN 0-306-70784-5). Da Capo.

--Wagner As Man & Artis. 1963. 10.00 (ISBN 0-8446-2653-8). Peter Smith.

Newman, Ernest, ed. see Chorley, Henry F.

Newman, Ernest, tr. see Schweitzer, Albert.

Newman, Francis. Phases of Faith. (Victorian Library). 1970. Repr. of 1860 ed. text ed. 15.00x (ISBN 0-391-00109-4, Leicester). Humanities.

Newman, Francis X., ed. Meaning of Courtly Love. LC 68-25571. 1968. 24.50x (ISBN 0-87395-038-0); pap. 11.95x (ISBN 0-87395-222-7); microfiche o.p. 12.00 (ISBN 0-87395-138-7). State U NY Pr.

Newman, Fred. Leaders of the Russian Revolution. LC 81-86278. (In Profile Ser.). PLB 12.68 (ISBN 0-382-06632-4). Silver.

Newman, Frederick L. & Sorenson, James E. A Guidebook for the Design & Management of Client-Oriented Systems. (Public Health Ser.). (Illus.). 500p. Date not set. cancelled (ISBN 0-534-01118-7). Lifetime Learn.

Newman, Frederick R. Zounds! The Kids' Guide to Sound Making. LC 82-16690. (Illus.). 64p. (gr. 3-8). 1983. pap. 4.95 (ISBN 0-394-85543-4). Random.

Newman, G. F. Operation Bad Apple. 1982. pap. 3.95 (ISBN 0-413-50270-8). Methuen Inc.

Newman, George. Citizenship & the Survival of Civilization. 1928. 29.50x (ISBN 0-685-89743-5). Elliots Bks.

Newman, Georgiana C. & Dawson, Mildred A. Baker's Dozen. rev. ed. (Cornerstone Ser.). (gr. 2-3). 1978. pap. text ed. 5.32 (ISBN 0-201-41024-9, Sch Div); tchr's ed. 6.76 (ISBN 0-201-41025-7). A-W.

Newman, Gerald. The Changing Eskimos. LC 78-15956. (Easy-Read Fact Bk.). (Illus.). (gr. 2-4). 1979. PLB 8.60 s&l (ISBN 0-531-02271-4). Watts.

--Lebanon. (First Bks). (Illus.). (gr. 4-6). 1978. PLB 8.90 s&l (ISBN 0-531-02237-4). Watts.

--Zaire, Gabon & the Congo. LC 80-25245. (First Bks.). (gr. 4 up). 1981. 8.90 (ISBN 0-531-04279-0). Watts.

Newman, Graeme R. Just & Painful: An Unbeatable Case for the Corporal Punishment of Criminals. (Illus.). 210p. (Orig.). 1983. text ed. 22.00 (ISBN 0-911577-00-9); pap. 9.95 (ISBN 0-911577-01-7). Harrow & Heston.

Newman, Graeme R., ed. Crime & Justice in America: Seventeen Seventy-Six to Nineteen Seventy-Six. LC 75-36472. (Annals of the American Academy of Political Science Ser.: No. 423). pap. 7.95 (ISBN 0-87761-197-1). Am Acad Pol Soc Sci.

Newman, Harold. An Illustrated Dictionary of Glass. (Illus.). 1978. 29.95 (ISBN 0-500-23262-8). Thames Hudson.

Newman, Isadore & Newman, Carole. Conceptual Statistics for Beginners. LC 79-64100. 1979. pap. text ed. 10.75 (ISBN 0-8191-0752-2). U Pr of Amer.

Newman, Isadore, jt. auth. see Fraas, John W.

Newman, J., jt. auth. see Knight, C.

Newman, James R. Science & Sensibility, 2 Vols. 1961. Set. 10.00 o.p. (ISBN 0-671-63610-3). S&S.

Newman, Jason & O'Brien, Edward. Street Law the D.C. Project: Community Legal Assistance & Street Law. (Illus.). (gr. 9-12). 1976. pap. text ed. 4.00 o.s.i. (ISBN 0-8299-1012-3). West Pub.

Newman, Jay H., jt. auth. see Newman, Lee S.

Newman, Joel & Rikko, Fritz. A Thematic Index to the Works of Salamon Rossi. (Music Indexes & Bibliographies: No. 6). 1972. pap. 12.50 (ISBN 0-913574-06-6). Eur-Am Music.

Newman, John. Electrochemical Systems. (International Series in the Physical Chemical Engineering Sciences). (Illus.). 448p. 1973. ref. ed. 33.95 (ISBN 0-13-248922-8). P-H.

Newman, John E. & Hinrichs, John R. Performance Evaluation for Professional Personnel, Vol. 14. LC 80-20739. (Studies in Productivity Highlights of the Literature). 1982. pap. 35.00 (ISBN 0-08-029495-2). Pergamon.

Newman, John H. Apologia Pro Vita Sua. 1977. pap. 5.95 o.p. (ISBN 0-385-12646-8, Im). Doubleday.

--Apologia Pro Vita Sua. DeLaura, David, ed. (Critical Editions Ser). (gr. 9-12). 1968. pap. text ed. 10.95x (ISBN 0-393-09766-8, 9766, NortonC). Norton.

--Historical Sketches. 1970. Vol. I. 10.50 o.p. (ISBN 0-686-85799-2); Vol. 3. 10.50 o.p. (ISBN 0-87061-027-9). Chr Classics.

--The Idea of a University. (Oxford English Texts). 1976. 73.00x (ISBN 0-19-811896-1). Oxford U Pr.

--The Idea of University. Svaglic, Martin J., ed. (Notre Dame Ser. in the Great Books). 428p. 1982. pap. text ed. 7.95 (ISBN 0-268-01150-8). U of Notre Dame Pr.

--Loss & Gain: The Story of a Convert, 1848. Wolff, Robert L., ed. Bd. with Callista: A Sketch of the Third Century, 1856. (Victorian Fiction Ser.). 1975. lib. bdg. 66.00 o.s.i. (ISBN 0-8240-1530-4). Garland Pub.

Newman, Kenneth. Birdlife in Southern Africa. (Illus.). 252p. 1982. 38.95 (ISBN 0-86954-083-1, Pub. by Macmillan S Africa). Intl Schol Bk Serv.

--Birds of Southern Africa, Kruger National Park. (Illus.). 241p. 1982. 22.00 (ISBN 0-686-97788-2). Intl Schol Bk Serv.

Newman, L. M. German Language & Literature: Select Bibliography of Reference Books. 2nd, enl. ed. 175p. 1979. 30.00x (ISBN 0-85457-077-2, Pub. by Inst Germanic Stud England). State Mutual Bk.

Newman, Laura. Make Your Juicer Your Drug Store. LC 66-125414. (Illus.). 192p. 1978. pap. 2.95 (ISBN 0-87904-001-7). Lust.

Newman, Lea B. A Reader's Guide to the Short Stories of Nathaniel Hawthorne. 1979. lib. bdg. 35.00 (ISBN 0-8161-8398-8, Hall Reference). G K Hall.

Newman, Lee S. & Newman, Jay H. Kite Craft. LC 73-91154. (Arts & Crafts Ser.). (Illus.). 224p. 1974. pap. 4.95 o.p. (ISBN 0-517-51471-0). Crown.

Newman, M. Standard Cantilever Retaining Walls. 1976. 32.50 o.p. (ISBN 0-07-046347-6, P&RB). McGraw.

Newman, Margaret A., jt. auth. see Downs, Florence S.

Newman, Marsha. Reflections of Eve & Her Daughters. (Illus.). 1981. 6.95 (ISBN 0-9608658-0-2). Wellspring CA.

Newman, Matt & Lemay, Nita K. The Human Reproductive System. (Illus.). (gr. 5-8). 1980. pap. text ed. 128.00 (ISBN 0-89290-101-2, A794-SATC). Soc for Visual.

Newman, Maurice S. Financial Accounting Estimates Through Statistical Sampling by Computer. LC 76-23400. (Ser. on Systems & Controls for Financial Management). 1976. 24.95 o.p. (ISBN 0-471-01567-9, Pub. by Wiley-Interscience). Wiley.

Newman, Mona. Night of a Thousand Stars. (Aston Hall Romances Ser.: No. 101). 192p. (Orig.). 1980. pap. 1.50 o.p. (ISBN 0-523-41123-5). Pinnacle Bks.

Newman, Morris. Algorithmic Matrix Theory. 1983. text ed. p.n.s. (ISBN 0-914894-47-1). Computer Sci.

Newman, Morton. Standard Structural Details for Building Construction. 1967. 41.50 (ISBN 0-07-046345-X, P&RB). McGraw.

Newman, Oscar. Community of Interest. (Illus.). 368p. 1981. pap. 10.95 o.p. (ISBN 0-385-11124-X, Anch). Doubleday.

--Unmasking of a King. 192p. 1981. 11.95 (ISBN 0-02-588890-0). Macmillan.

Newman, Pamela & Lynch, Alfred F. Behind Closed Doors: A Guide to Successful Meetings. (Illus.). 192p. 1983. pap. 9.95 (ISBN 0-13-072025-9). P-H.

Newman, Paul. Grammatical Gender in Chadic. 200p. 1983. 34.00x (ISBN 90-70176-47-5); pap. 17.50x (ISBN 90-70176-29-7). Foris Pubns.

Newman, Paul & Newman, Roxanna M., eds. Modern Hausa-English Dictionary. 168p. 1979. pap. text ed. 6.95x o.p. (ISBN 0-19-575303-8). Oxford U Pr.

Newman, Peter. King of the Castle, the Making of a Dynasty: Seagram's & the Bronfman Empire. LC 78-65198. 1979. 11.95 o.p. (ISBN 0-689-10963-6). Atheneum.

Newman, Philip R., jt. auth. see Newman, Barbara M.

Newman, Phyllis E., et al, eds. California Manufacturers Register 1983. 36th ed. LC 48-3418. 896p. 1983. text ed. 125.00 (ISBN 0-911510-87-7). Times-M Pr.

Newman, R. Fine-Line Lithography. (Materials Processing Theory & Practice Ser.: Vol. 1). 1980. 85.00 (ISBN 0-444-85351-0). Elsevier.

Newman, Richard. Bless All Thy Creatures, Lord. 160p. 1982. 9.95 (ISBN 0-02-588880-3). Macmillan.

Newman, Richard & Wright, R. Glenn. Index to Birthplaces of American Authors. 1979. lib. bdg. 19.00 (ISBN 0-8161-8230-2, Hall Reference). G K Hall.

Newman, Richard, jt. auth. see Burkett, Randall K.

Newman, Richard, jt. ed. see Wills, David W.

Newman, Roxanna M., jt. ed. see Newman, Paul.

Newman, Ruby A. Layle Jonathan, of Mountain Springs. 140p. (Orig.). 1983. pap. 5.00 (ISBN 0-932964-07-9). MN Pubs.

--Rebel Preacher. LC 78-70488. 1979. pap. 2.00 (ISBN 0-932964-02-8). MN Pubs.

--Tour for Seven. LC 77-75506. (Illus.). 1979. pap. 2.00 (ISBN 0-932964-01-X). MN Pubs.

Newman, S. J. Dickens at Play. 1981. 17.95 (ISBN 0-312-19980-5). St Martin.

Newman, Sandra C. Indian Basket Weaving. LC 73-79779. (Illus.). 108p. 1974. pap. 5.95 o.p. (ISBN 0-87358-112-1). Northland.

Newman, Sandra J. & Owen, Michael S. Residential Displacement in the U. S., 1970-1977. 104p. 1982. pap. 12.00x (ISBN 0-87944-281-6). Inst Soc Res.

Newman, Sharan. The Chessboard Queen. 320p. 1983. 13.95 (ISBN 0-312-13176-3). St Martin.

Newman, Sharon, jt. auth. see Petillon, Mary.

Newman, Simon K. March Nineteen Thirty-Nine: A Study in the Continuity of British Foreign Policy. 1976. 39.95x (ISBN 0-19-822532-6). Oxford U Pr.

Newman, Stephen A., ed. Chemical Engineering Thermodynamics. LC 82-70702. (Illus.). 540p. 1982. 49.95 (ISBN 0-250-40520-2). Ann Arbor Science.

Newman, Thelma, et al. Paper As Art & Craft. (Arts & Crafts Ser.). (Illus.). 320p. 1973. pap. 5.95 o.p. (ISBN 0-517-50378-6). Crown.

Newman, Thelma R. Contemporary African Arts & Crafts: An on-Site Working with Art Forms & Processes. LC 73-91515. (Arts & Crafts Ser.). (Illus.). 320p. 1974. pap. 5.95 o.p. (ISBN 0-517-51467-2); pap. 5.95 o.p. (ISBN 0-686-85831-X). Crown.

--Contemporary Decoupage. (Arts & Crafts Ser.). (Illus.). 224p. 1973. 9.95 o.p. (ISBN 0-517-50090-6). Crown.

--Innovative Printmaking: The Making of Two and Three Dimensional Prints & Multiples. (Illus.). 1977. 16.95 o.p. (ISBN 0-517-52959-9); pap. 9.95 o.p. (ISBN 0-517-52960-2). Crown.

--Leather As Art & Craft. (Arts & Crafts Ser.). (Illus.). 328p. 1973. 9.95 o.p. (ISBN 0-517-50574-6); pap. 7.95 o.p. (ISBN 0-517-50575-4). Crown.

Newman, Thelma R. & Merrill, Virginia. The Complete Book of Making Miniatures. (Arts & Crafts Ser.). (Illus.). 328p. (YA) 1975. 12.95 (ISBN 0-517-52318-3); pap. 8.95 (ISBN 0-517-52460-0). Crown.

Newman, Virginia H. Teaching Young Children to Swim & Dive. LC 72-76370. (Illus.). 1969. 5.95 o.p. (ISBN 0-15-188116-2). HarBraceJ.

Newman, Walter S. & Salwen, Bert S., eds. Amerinds & Their Paleoenviornments in Northeastern North America, Vol. 288. 1977. 37.00 (ISBN 0-89072-034-7). NY Acad Sci.

Newman, William. The Pianist's Problems. 3rd ed. (Illus.). 208p. 1983. Repr. of 1974 ed. lib. bdg. 22.50 (ISBN 0-306-76213-7). Da Capo.

Newman, William & Sproull, Robert. Principles of Interactive Computer Graphics. (Illus.). 640p. 1973. text ed. 24.95 o.p. (ISBN 0-07-046337-9, C). McGraw.

Newman, William A. & Ross, Arnold, eds. Antarctic Cirripedia. LC 74-129339. (Antarctic Research Ser.: Vol. 14). (Illus.). 1971. 32.00 (ISBN 0-87590-114-X). Am Geophysical.

Newman, William H. Administrative Action: The Techniques of Organization & Management. 2nd ed. 1963. ref. ed. 23.95x (ISBN 0-13-007195-1). P-H.

--Managers for the Year Two Thousand. (Illus.). 1978. ref. ed. 18.95 (ISBN 0-13-549378-1); pap. 8.95 o.p. (ISBN 0-686-77326-8). P-H.

Newman, William H. & Warren, E. Kirby. The Process of Management: Strategy, Action, Results (CPCU Edition) 5th ed. LC 81-11985. 578p. 1982. Repr. of 1982 ed. text ed. 23.00 (ISBN 0-89463-036-9). Am Inst Property.

Newman, William H., jt. auth. see Yavitz, Boris.

Newman, William M. American Pluralism: A Study of Minority Groups & Social Theory. (Illus.). 307p. 1973. pap. text ed. 12.50 scp o.p. (ISBN 0-06-044801-6, HarpC). Har-Row.

Newman, William M. & Sproull, Robert F. Principles of Interactive Computer Graphics. 2nd ed. (Illus.). 1979. text ed. 35.95 (ISBN 0-07-046338-7, C). McGraw.

Newman, William S. The Sonata in the Baroque Era. 4th ed. 1983. text ed. 18.95x (ISBN 0-393-95275-4). Norton.

--The Sonata in the Classic Era. 3rd ed. 1983. text ed. 22.50x (ISBN 0-393-95286-X). Norton.

--The Sonata Since Beethoven. 3rd ed. 1983. 22.50x (ISBN 0-393-95290-8). Norton.

Newman, Winifred B. The Spotlessly Leopard. 48p. (Orig.). (gr. 2-6). 1983. pap. 5.50 (ISBN 0-87743-700-9). Baha'i.

Newmann, Fred M. Education for Citizen Action: Challenge for the Secondary Curriculum. LC 74-30963. 250p. 1975. 19.00 (ISBN 0-8211-1305-4); text ed. 16.95 (ISBN 0-685-52139-7). McCutchan.

Newmarch, Rosa. The Music of Czechoslovakia. LC 77-26269. (Music Reprint Ser., 1978). 1978. Repr. of 1942 ed. lib. bdg. 25.00 (ISBN 0-306-77563-8). Da Capo.

--Tchaikovsky: His Life & Works, with Extracts from His Writings, & the Diary of His Tour Abroad in 1888. LC 68-25298. (Studies in Music, No. 42). 1968. Repr. of 1900 ed. lib. bdg. 49.95x (ISBN 0-8383-0310-2). Haskell.

Newmark, Eileen. Women's Roles: A Cross-Cultural Perspective. 128p. 1981. pap. 8.40 (ISBN 0-08-026073-X). Pergamon.

Newmark, Joseph & Lake, Frances. Mathematics As a Second Language. 2nd ed. LC 81-14935. (Mathematics Ser.). (Illus.). 600p. 1982. text ed. 21.95 (ISBN 0-201-05292-X). A-W.

Newmark, Leonard, jt. auth. see Bloomfield, Morton W.

Newmark, M. & Penry, J. K., eds. Photosensitivity & Epilepsy. 232p. 1979. 21.50 (ISBN 0-89004-393-0). Raven.

Newmark, M. E., ed. Genetics of Epilepsy: A Review. Penry, J. K. 132p. 1979. 17.50 (ISBN 0-89004-394-9). Raven.

Newmark, Maxim. Dictionary of Foreign Words & Phrases. Repr. of 1957 ed. lib. bdg. 18.50x (ISBN 0-8371-2103-5, NEFW). Greenwood.

Newmark, Maxim, jt. ed. see Kendris, Christopher.

Newmark, N. M. & Rosenblueth, E. Fundamentals of Earthquake Engineering. (Civil Engineering & Engineering Mechanics Ser.). (Illus.). 1972. ref. ed. 39.95 (ISBN 0-13-336206-X). P-H.

Newmark, Nathan M. Selected Papers. 904p. 1976. pap. text ed. 44.00 o.p. (ISBN 0-87262-166-9). Am Soc Civil Eng.

Newmyer, Joseph & Klentos, Gus. Intermediate Algebra. 3rd ed. 448p. 1982. pap. text ed. 19.95 (ISBN 0-675-09912-9). Additional supplements may be obtained from publisher. Merrill.

Newmyer, Joseph, Jr. & Klentos, Gus. Intermediate Algebra. 2nd ed. Kleinfeld, ed. (Mathematics Ser). (Illus.). 416p. 1975. pap. text ed. 19.95 (ISBN 0-675-08744-9); cassettes 140.00 (ISBN 0-675-08717-1). Additional supplements may be obtained from publisher. Merrill.

Newmyer, Joseph, Jr., jt. auth. see Klentos, Gus.

Newnan, Dean C., jt. auth. see Newnan, Donald D.

Newnan, Donald D. & Newnan, Dean C. Engineer-In-Training License Review. LC 80-22287. 266p. 1981. pap. 12.95 (ISBN 0-910554-33-1). Eng Pr.

Newnan, Donald G. Engineering Economic Analysis. 2nd ed. LC 82-1522. 519p. 1983. text ed. 24.95x (ISBN 0-910554-39-0). Eng Pr.

Newnan, Donald G. & Larock, Bruce E. Engineering Fundamentals: Examination Review. 2nd ed. LC 7-12592. 503p. 1978. 40.05 (ISBN 0-471-01900-3, Pub. by Wiley-Interscience). Wiley.

Newnham, Jack. Kites to Make & Fly. 1982. pap. 2.50 (ISBN 0-14-049139-2, Puffin). Penguin.

Newport, Herbert J., jt. auth. see Steinwedel, Louis W.

Newport, M. Gene. Supervisory Management: Tools & Techniques. LC 76-10379. 384p. 1976. text ed. 17.50 (ISBN 0-8299-0116-7). West Pub.

Newport, O. W. Stamps & Postal History of the Channel Islands. 1982. 9.95 (ISBN 0-434-91470-3, Pub. by Heinemann). David & Charles.

Newsholme, E. A. & Start, C. Regulation of Metabolism. LC 72-5721. 349p. 1973. text ed. 51.95 (ISBN 0-471-63530-8, Pub. by Wiley-Interscience); pap. 21.95 (ISBN 0-471-63531-6). Wiley.

Newsom, Barbara, ed. The Art Museum As Educator. LC 76-14301. 1978. 60.00x (ISBN 0-520-03248-9); pap. 14.95 o.p. (ISBN 0-520-03249-7). U of Cal Pr.

Newsom, D. E. The Newspaper: Everything You Need to Know to Make It in the Newspaper Business. (Illus.). 256p. 1981. 24.95 (ISBN 0-13-616045-X, Spec); pap. 10.95 (ISBN 0-13-616037-9). P-H.

Newsom, D. Earl. The Birth of Oklahoma. (Illus.). 278p. (gr. 5-12). 1983. 14.95 (ISBN 0-934188-08-4); PLB 14.95 (ISBN 0-686-38034-7). Evans Pubns.

Newsom, Ed. Trail to Sonora. (YA) 1979. 6.95 (ISBN 0-685-90728-7, Avalon). Bouregy.

Newsom, S., jt. auth. see Johnston, H. H.

Newsom, S. W., ed. see International Symposium, 2nd, Cambridge, Sept. 1976.

Newsome, Arden J. Egg Decorating: Plain & Fancy. (Arts & Crafts Ser.). (Illus.). 96p. 1973. pap. 3.95 o.p. (ISBN 0-517-50596-7). Crown.

Newsome, Claire, ed. Transportation & Traffic-Data Systems Source Guide (20m) LC 81-86199. 300p. 1982. 3-ring binder 65.00 (ISBN 0-934674-42-6). J J Keller.

Newsome, Claire, et al, eds, see Keller, John J.

Newsome, David. Godliness & Good Learning: Four Studies on a Victorian Ideal. (Illus.). 1961. 21.00 (ISBN 0-7195-1015-5). Transatlantic.

--Two Classes of Men: Platonism & English Romantic Thought. LC 75-10013. 180p. 1975. 16.95 o.p. (ISBN 0-312-82670-2). St Martin.

Newsome, Walter L. Government Reference Books Eighty to Eighty-One: A Biennial Guide to U. S. Government Publications-7th Biennial Volume. 350p. 1982. 37.50 (ISBN 0-87287-291-2). Libs Unl.

Newsome, Walter L., compiled by. Government Reference Books 78-79: A Biennial Guide to U. S. Government Publications, 6th Biennial Volume. LC 76-146307. 517p. 1980. lib. bdg. 30.00 (ISBN 0-87287-242-4). Libs Unl.

Newson, E. F. Management Science & the Manager: A Casebook. (Illus.). 1980. pap. text ed. 16.95 (ISBN 0-13-549444-3). P-H.

Newson, Elizabeth & Hipgrave, Tony. Getting Through to Your Handicapped Child: A Handbook for Parents, Foster-Parents, Teachers & Anyone Caring for Handicapped Children. LC 82-4310. 144p. 1983. pap. 7.95 (ISBN 0-521-27056-1). Cambridge U Pr.

Newson, Elizabeth, jt. auth. see Newson, John.

Newson, John & Newson, Elizabeth. Seven Years Old in the Home Environment. LC 75-17184. 1976. 44.95x o.p. (ISBN 0-470-63585-1). Halsted Pr.

Newspaper Enterprise Assn. World Almanac & Book of Facts, 1983. Lane, Hana U., ed. 976p. 1982. 8.95 (ISBN 0-911818-29-4); pap. 4.95 (ISBN 0-911818-28-6). World Almanac.

Newspaper Enterprise Assoc., ed. The World Almanac & Book of Facts, 1980. (Illus., Orig.). 1979. pap. 3.95 o.p. (ISBN 0-448-16550-3, G&D). Putnam Pub Group.

Newspaper Enterprise Association. TV Trivia Crossword Puzzle Book. LC 77-73141. 96p. (Orig.). 1977. pap. 2.95 o.s.i. (ISBN 0-89104-083-8). A & W Pubs.

Newspaper Enterprises Associates, Inc. World Almanac Book of Facts 1983. 976p. 1982. 10.95 (ISBN 0-385-18348-8). Doubleday.

Newstead, Martin S., jt. auth. see Coullery, Marie-Therese.

Newstead, P. E. Lectures on Introduction to Moduli Problems & Orbit Spaces. (Tata Institute Lecture Notes). 1979. pap. 12.00 o.p. (ISBN 0-387-08851-2). Springer-Verlag.

Newstrom, John, jt. auth. see Davis, Keith.

Newstrom, John, et al. Contingency Approach to Management Readings. (Illus.). 592p. 1974. pap. text ed. 24.95 (ISBN 0-07-046415-4, C). McGraw.

Newth, D. R. & Balls, M., eds. Maternal Effects in Development. LC 78-73812. (British Society for Developmental Biology Symposium Ser.: No. 4). (Illus.). 1980. 99.00 (ISBN 0-521-22685-6). Cambridge U Pr.

Newth, Philip. Roly Goes Exploring. (ps-4). 1981. spiral binding 12.95 (ISBN 0-399-20815-1, Philomel). Putnam Pub Group.

Newth, Rebecca. Finding the Lamb. 1982. pap. 4.95 (ISBN 0-940170-05-1). Open Bk Pubns.

Newton, A. P., ed. Select Documents Relating to the Unification of South Africa. 1968. Repr. of 1924 ed. 42.50x (ISBN 0-7146-1777-6, F Cass Co). Biblio Dist.

Newton, B. The Generative Interpretation of Dialect: A Study of Modern Greek Phonology. LC 72-187080. (Studies in Linguistics: No. 8). (Illus.). 240p. 1973. 39.50 (ISBN 0-521-08497-0); pap. 13.95x (ISBN 0-521-29062-7). Cambridge U Pr.

Newton, B. A., jt. ed. see Crompton, D. W.

Newton, Byron L. Statistics for Business. LC 73-75419. (Illus.). 553p. 1973. text ed. 22.95 (ISBN 0-574-18465-1, 13-1465); instructor's guide 3.25 (ISBN 0-574-18467-8, 13-1467). SRA.

Newton, Dennis W. Severe Weather Flying. (McGraw-Hill Aviation Ser.). (Illus.). 160p. 1983. 19.95 (ISBN 0-07-046402-2, P&RB). McGraw.

Newton, Francis J. The Jazz Scene. LC 75-4748. (Roots of Jazz Ser.). 303p. 1975. Repr. of 1960 ed. lib. bdg. 27.50 (ISBN 0-306-70685-7). Da Capo.

Newton, Frank & Olmedo, Esteban L. Hispanic Mental Health Research: A Reference Guide. 696p. 1982. pap. 19.95x (ISBN 0-520-04791-5). U of Cal Pr.

Newton, Gerald. The Netherlands: An Historical & Cultural Survey 1795-1977. LC 77-16100. (Nations of the Modern World Ser.). 1978. lib. bdg. 35.00 (ISBN 0-89158-802-7). Westview.

Newton, Grant & Riesen, Austin H. Advances in Psychobiology. LC 70-178148. (Advances in Psychology Ser.: Vol. 2). 330p. 1974. 35.95 o.p. (ISBN 0-471-63596-0, Pub. by Wiley-Interscience). Wiley.

Newton, Grant W. Bankruptcy & Insolvency Accounting. 2nd ed. LC 80-39886. 500p. 1981. 49.95x (ISBN 0-471-07992-8). Ronald Pr.

Newton, Harry. The Magic of Becoming Successful: How to Achieve the Success You Deserve. 154p. 1981. 10.95 (ISBN 0-686-98040-9). Telecom Lib.

--One Hundred-One-Saving Secrets Your Phone Company Won't Tell You. 96p. (Orig.). 1982. pap. text ed. 10.95 (ISBN 0-936648-15-5). Telecom Lib.

Newton, Helmut. Big Nudes. (Illus.). 80p. 1982. 27.50 (ISBN 0-937950-02-5). Xavier Moreau.

--Sleepless Nights. (Illus.). 1983. pap. 17.50 (ISBN 0-937950-07-6). Xavier-Moreau.

Newton, Isaac. Opticks. 1952. pap. text ed. 6.50 (ISBN 0-486-60205-2). Dover.

--Optique De Newton: Traduit Par Jean Paul Marat. Repr. of 1787 ed. 149.00 o.p. (ISBN 0-8287-0653-0). Clearwater Pub.

Newton, J. Extractive Metallurgy. 532p. 1959. 37.95x o.p. (ISBN 0-471-63591-X). Wiley.

Newton, James. A Forest Is Reborn. LC 81-43882. (Illus.). 32p. (gr. 2-5). 1982. 7.93i (ISBN 0-690-04231-0, TYC-J); PLB 8.89g (ISBN 0-690-04232-9). Har-Row.

Newton, James R. The March of the Lemmings. LC 75-42491. (A Lets-Read-&-Find-Out Bk). (Illus.). 40p. (gr. k-3). 1976. PLB 10.89 (ISBN 0-690-01085-0, TYC-J). Har-Row.

Newton, Jan, jt. auth. see Young, John.

Newton, John. John Newton. (Golden Oldies Ser.). 128p. (Orig.). 1983. pap. 2.95 (ISBN 0-8024-0158-9). Moody.

--Letters of John Newton. 1976. pap. 2.95 (ISBN 0-85151-120-1). Banner of Truth.

Newton, John R. Managing Patients with Intrauterine Devices. 1979. pap. 6.95 o.p. (ISBN 0-917634-07-1). Creative Infomatics.

--Managing Patients with Intrauterine Devices. 1980. pap. 7.95 (ISBN 0-686-42718-1). Creative Infomatics.

--Reading in Your School. 1960. text ed. 17.00 (ISBN 0-07-046410-3, C). McGraw.

Newton, K. & Steeds, W. Motor Vehicle. 10th ed. 1983. text ed. write for info. (ISBN 0-408-01118-1); pap. text ed. write for info. Butterworth.

Newton, Kathleen & Looney, Gerald. Doctor Discussses Making the Mid-Years the Prime of Life. (Illus.). 1978. pap. 2.50 o.p. (ISBN 0-685-46333-8). Budlong.

Newton, LaVose. Church Library Handbook. rev. ed. LC 76-189488. 1972. pap. text ed. 4.95 o.p. (ISBN 0-930014-02-2). Multnomah.

Newton, Linda. Therapy Made Fun! Set 2. 1982. text ed. 15.75x (ISBN 0-8134-2232-9). Interstate.

Newton, Marceline A. Newlife Cookbook. (Illus.). 176p. 1976. pap. 6.95 (ISBN 0-686-36736-7). Md Hist.

Newton, Margaret. Shad: A Biography of Lloyd "Shad" Heller. Jenkins, Michael, ed. LC 82-60547. (Illus.). 294p. (Orig.). 1982. pap. 7.95 (ISBN 0-910157-00-6). Pin Oak Pub Co.

Newton, Michael. Handbook of Weed & Insect Control Chemicals for Forest Resource Management. 160p. 1980. 24.95x (ISBN 0-917304-25-X); pap. 17.95x (ISBN 0-686-86209-0). Timber.

Newton, R. D., jt. auth. see Aries, R. S.

Newton, R. E. Wave Physics. 320p. 1983. pap. text ed. price not set (ISBN 0-7131-2656-6). E Arnold.

Newton, Robert P., tr. see Lasker-Schuler, Else.

Newton, Roger G., jt. auth. see Gilbert, Robert P.

Newton, S. & Settler, H. Audit Work Papers. 3rd ed. 1977. pap. 11.95 (ISBN 0-13-052712-2). P-H.

Newton, Sherwood W., jt. auth. see Stettler, Howard F.

Newton, Stanley. The Story of Saulte Ste. Marie & Chippewa County. LC 74-27236. (Illus.). 199p. 1975. 12.00 o.p. (ISBN 0-912382-17-1); pap. 6.00 o.p. (ISBN 0-912382-27-9). Black Letter.

Newton, Suzanne. M. V. Sexton Speaking. 192p. 1983. pap. 2.25 (ISBN 0-449-70049-6, Juniper). Fawcett.

--What Are You up to, William Thomas? LC 77-23460. (gr. 6-9). 1977. 7.95 o.s.i. (ISBN 0-664-32618-8). Westminster.

Newton, T. H., jt. auth. see Kitamura, K.

Newton, T. W. Kinetics of the Oxidation-Reduction Reactions of Uranium, Neptunium, Plutonium, & Americium Ions in Aqueous Solutions. LC 75-22030. (ERDA Critical Review Ser.). 140p. 1975. pap. 11.50 (TID-26506); microfiche 4.50 (ISBN 0-87079-252-0, TID-26506). DOE.

Newton, Thomas H. & Potts, D. Gordon. Radiology of the Skull & Brain: Ventricles & Cisterns, Vol. 4. LC 78-173600. 610p. 1978. text ed. 89.00 (ISBN 0-8016-3661-2). Mosby.

Newton, W. E., jt. ed. see Gibson, A. H.

Newton, William E., jt. ed. see Orme-Johnson, William.

Newton, William R., ed. see Arnold, John.

Newton, William R., ed. see Myers, M. Scott.

Newton, William R., ed. see Zand, Dale.

Newton, William T. & Donati, Robert M. Radioassay in Clinical Medicine. (Illus.). 200p. 1974. 16.50x o.p. (ISBN 0-398-03012-X). C C Thomas.

Ney, Uwe. How to Shoot Home Movies. (Illus.). 1978. 10.95 o.p. (ISBN 0-517-53390-1). Crown.

Neyland, James. How to Find a Better Job. LC 80-83384. (Practical Handbook Ser.). 108p. (Orig.). 1981. pap. 4.95 (ISBN 0-448-01571-4, G&D). Putnam Pub Group.

--The Official Battlestar Galactica Scrapbook. LC 78-71171. (Illus.). 1978. pap. 6.95 o.p. (ISBN 0-448-16295-4, G&D); blueprints 7.95 o.p. (ISBN 0-448-16296-2). Putnam Pub Group.

Neyman, J., jt. ed. see Le Cam, L.

Neyman, Jerzy & Pearson, E. S. The Selected Papers of Jerzy Neyman & E. S. Pearson, 3 vols. Incl. Vol. 1. The Selected Papers of E. S. Pearson. 1966. 17.00 o.p. (ISBN 0-520-00990-8); Vol. 2. Joint Statistical Papers. 1967. 42.00x (ISBN 0-520-00991-6); Vol. 3. A Selection of Early Statistical Papers of J. Neyman. 1967. 43.00x (ISBN 0-520-00992-4). U of Cal Pr.

Neyman, Jerzy, ed. The Heritage of Copernicus: Theories: "Pleasing to the Mind". 1974. pap. 12.50x (ISBN 0-262-64016-3). MIT Pr.

Neyrey, Jerome H. First Timothy, Second Timothy, Titus, James, First Peter, Second Peter, Jude, No. 9. Karris, Robert J., ed. (Collegeville Bible Commentary Ser.). 112p. 1983. pap. 2.50 (ISBN 0-8146-1309-8). Liturgical Pr.

Nezu, Masuo, tr. see Niwano, Nikkyo.

NFL, compiled by. The NFL Media Information Book 1983. (Illus.). 182p. 1983. pap. 7.95 (ISBN 0-89480-367-0). Workman Pub.

NFL & Walsh, Bill, eds. The Illustrated NFL Playbook. Schacter, Norm. LC 81-71436. (Illus.). 128p. 1982. pap. 6.95 (ISBN 0-89480-210-0). Workman Pub.

Ng, Ronald, jt. auth. see Deboeck, Guido.

Ngai, S. H., jt. ed. see Mark, Lester C.

Ngan, H. & James, K. W. Clinical Radiology of the Lymphomas. Trapnell, D. H., ed. (Radiology in Clinical Diagnosis Ser.: Vol. 7). Orig. Title: Radiology in Lymphomas. (Illus.). 1973. 14.95 o.p. (ISBN 0-407-13715-7). Butterworth.

Ngara, Emmanuel. Stylistic Criticism & the African Novel. 160p. 1982. 30.00x (ISBN 0-686-82316-8, Pub. by Heinemann England). State Mutual Bk.

Ngcobo, Lauretta J. Crown of Gold. (Sun-Lit Ser.). 250p. (Orig.). 1981. 10.00x o.s.i. (ISBN 0-89410-170-6); pap. 6.00x o.s.i. (ISBN 0-89410-171-4). Three Continents.

Ngcongco, L., jt. auth. see Bhebe, Ngwabi.

Ngubane, Jordan K. An African Explains Apartheid. LC 75-35338. (Illus.). 243p. 1976. Repr. of 1963 ed. lib. bdg. 19.25x (ISBN 0-8371-8565-3, NGAE). Greenwood.

Ngugi. Usilie Mpenzi Wangu. (Swahili Literature). (Orig., Swahili.). 1978. pap. text ed. 3.50x o.p. (ISBN 0-686-74462-4, 00608). Heinemann Ed.

Nguyen, O., jt. auth. see Heymann, O.

Nguyen Dinh-Hoa. Colloquial Vietnamese. rev ed. LC 74-5132. 398p. 1974. text ed. 14.95x o.p. (ISBN 0-8093-0685-9); pap. text ed. 10.95x (ISBN 0-8093-0686-7). S Ill U Pr.

Nguyen-Dinh-Hoa. Essential English-Vietnamese Dictionary. LC 82-80014. 328p. 1983. 22.50 (ISBN 0-8048-1444-9). C E Tuttle.

Ni, Hua-Ching. The Complete Works of Lao Tzu: Tao Teh Ching & Hua Hu Ching. LC 79-88745. (Illus.). 219p. (Orig.). 1979. pap. 7.50 (ISBN 0-937064-00-9). SEBT.

--Tao: The Subtle Universal Law & the Integral Way of Life. (Illus.). 166p. (Orig.). 1979. pap. text ed. 7.50 (ISBN 0-937064-01-7). SEBT.

--The Taoist Inner View of the Universe & the Immortal Realm. LC 79-91720. (Illus.). 218p. (Orig.). 1980. pap. text ed. 12.50 (ISBN 0-937064-02-5). SEBT.

Nial, Hakan. American-Swedish Private International Law. LC 64-25226. (Parker School of Bilateral Studies in Private International Law: No. 13). 111p. 1965. 15.00 (ISBN 0-379-11413-5). Oceana.

Nianpei, Li, tr. see Xianshi, Fu.

Nias, D. K., jt. auth. see Eysenck, H. J.

Nibbelink, D. & Anderson, R. Bigger & Better Enlarging. (Illus.). 288p. 1974. 10.95 o.p. (ISBN 0-8174-0579-8, Amphoto). Watson-Guptill.

Nibbelink, Don. The Handbook of Student Photography. (Illus.). 160p. 1981. pap. 12.95 (ISBN 0-8174-3950-1, Amphoto). Watson-Guptill.

Nibbelink, Don & Nibbelink, Monica. Picturing the Times of Your Life. (Illus.). 1979. 15.95 o.p. (ISBN 0-686-66116-8, Amphoto). Watson-Guptill.

--Picturing the Times of Your Life. (Illus.). 1980. 16.95 (ISBN 0-8174-2468-7, Amphoto). Watson-Guptill.

Nibbelink, Don D. Picturing People. (Illus.). 256p. 1976. 16.95 (ISBN 0-8174-0576-3, Amphoto). Watson-Guptill.

Nibbelink, Monica, jt. auth. see Nibbelink, Don.

Nibeck, Richard G., intro. by. Learning With Microcomputers Readings form Instructional Innovator-5. 80p. Date not set. pap. 10.95 (ISBN 0-89240-042-0). Assn Ed Comm Tech.

Niblett, Brian, ed. Computer Science & Law. LC 80-40071. 256p. 1980. 37.50 (ISBN 0-521-23451-4). Cambridge U Pr.

Niblock, Margaret. The Afghan Hound: A Definitive Study. LC 79-57391. (Illus.). 448p. 1980. 49.95 o.p. (ISBN 0-668-04934-0, 4934-0). Arco.

Niblock, T., ed. Social & Economic Development in the Arab Gulf. LC 80-13697. 1980. 32.50 (ISBN 0-312-73145-0). St Martin.

Niblock, Tim, ed. Iraq: The Contemporary State. LC 82-42566. 304p. 1982. 27.50 (ISBN 0-312-43585-1). St Martin.

Nica, A. A Mechanics of Aerospace Materials. (Materials Monographs: Vol. 9). 1981. 68.00 (ISBN 0-444-99729-6). Elsevier.

Nicarthy, Ginny. Getting Free: A Handbook for Women in Abusive Relationships. LC 82-80723. 304p. 1982. pap. 7.95 (ISBN 0-931188-13-X). Seal Pr WA.

Nicas, Andrew J. Induction Theorems for Groups of Homotopy Manifold Structures. LC 82-11546. (Memoirs of the American Mathematical Society Ser.: No. 267). 6.00 (ISBN 0-8218-2267-5, MEMO/267). Am Math.

Niccolini, Binora, ed. Women of Vision: Photographic Statements of 20 Women Photographers. LC 82-81435. (Illus.). 128p. (Orig.). 1982. 39.95 (ISBN 0-88101-002-2); pap. 19.95 (ISBN 0-88101-003-0). Unicorn Pub.

Niccols, Richard. Sir Thomas Overbury's Vision (1616) & Other English Sources of Nathaniel Hawthorne's "The Scarlet Letter.". LC 57-6417. 28.00x (ISBN 0-8201-1239-9). Schol Facsimiles.

Nicene & Post-Nicene Fathers. Writings of the Nicene & Post-Nicene Fathers, 28 vols. Incl. First Series, 14 Vols. 237.30 set (ISBN 0-8028-8114-9); St. Augustine only, 8 Vols. 135.60 set (ISBN 0-8028-8106-8); St. Chrysostom only, 6 Vols. 101.70 set (ISBN 0-8028-8113-0); Second Series, 14 Vols. 237.30 set (ISBN 0-8028-8129-7). 1952-56. Repr. 16.95 ea. Eerdmans.

Nichol, Jon. Battle of Agincourt. (The Middle Ages, 1066-1485 Ser.). (Illus.). 1974. pap. text ed. 12.95 10 copies & tchr's guide (ISBN 0-582-39385-X). Longman.

--The Castle. (The Middle Ages, 1066-1485 Ser.). (Illus.). 24p. 1974. pap. text ed. 12.95 10 copies & tchr's guide (ISBN 0-582-39379-5). Longman.

--The First & Third Crusades. (The Middle Ages, 1066-1485 Ser.). (Illus.). 24p. 1974. pap. text ed. 12.95 10 copies & tchr's guide (ISBN 0-582-39377-9). Longman.

--Joan of Arc. (The Middle Ages, 1066-1485 Ser.). (Illus.). 24p. 1974. pap. text ed. 12.95 10 copies & tchr's guide (ISBN 0-582-39386-8). Longman.

--King John. (The Middle Ages, 1066-1485 Ser.). (Illus.). 24p. 1974. pap. text ed. 12.95 10 copies & tchr's guide (ISBN 0-582-39378-7). Longman.

--Richard Third. (The Middle Ages, 1066-1485 Ser.). (Illus.). 24p. 1974. pap. text ed. 12.95 10 copies & tchr's guide (ISBN 0-582-39391-4). Longman.

--Ships & Voyages. (The Middle Ages, 1066-1485 Ser.). (Illus.). 24p. 1974. pap. text ed. 12.95 10 copies & tchr's guide (ISBN 0-582-39388-4). Longman.

--The Wars of the Roses. (The Middle Ages, 1066-1485 Ser.). (Illus.). 24p. 1974. pap. 12.95 10 copies & tchr's guide (ISBN 0-582-39390-6). Longman.

Nichol, Lawrence, jt. auth. see Frieden, Carl.

Nicholaides, A. International Vascular Symposium Abstracts. 320p. 1982. 39.00x (ISBN 0-686-82353-2, Pub. by Macmillan England). State Mutual Bk.

Nicholas, Anna. The Book of the Rottweiler. (Illus.). 544p. 1981. 24.95 (ISBN 0-87666-735-3, H-1035). TFH Pubns.

Nicholas, Anna K. The Book of the Poodle. (Illus.). 528p. 39.95 (ISBN 0-87666-736-1, H-1033). TFH Pubns.

--Successful Dog Show Exhibiting. (Illus.). 384p. 1981. 14.95 (ISBN 0-87666-676-4, H-993). TFH Pubns.

Nicholas, Anna K. & Brearley, Joan M. The Book of the Pekingese. (Illus.). 352p. 1975. 29.95 (ISBN 0-87666-348-X, H-953). TFH Pubns.

Nicholas, Anna K., jt. auth. see Brearley, Joan M.

Nicholas, Anna K., jt. auth. see Brearly, Joan M.

Nicholas, Anna K., jt. auth. see Morley, W. M.

Nicholas, Anna K., jt. auth. see Tottenham, Katherine.

Nicholas, Barry. Introduction to Roman Law. (Clarendon Law Ser). 1962. pap. 14.95x (ISBN 0-19-876063-9). Oxford U Pr.

Nicholas, Clara see Little Pigeon, pseud.

Nicholas, Constantine, jt. auth. see Greely, Roger.

Nicholas, Cornelius J. Auld Tayles. LC 81-81936. 64p. 1983. 6.95 (ISBN 0-86666-046-1). GWP.

Nicholas, Darrel D. Wood Deterioration & Its Prevention by Preservative Treatments. Incl. Vol. 1. Degradation & Protection of Wood. 416p. text ed. 35.00x o.p. (ISBN 0-8156-5037-X); Vol. 2. Preservatives & Preservative Systems. 448p. text ed. 37.00x (ISBN 0-8156-5038-8). LC 73-4640. (Wood Science Ser.: No. 5). (Illus.). 1973. Syracuse U Pr.

Nicholas, David, jt. auth. see Short, John.

Nicholas, Dudley, jt. auth. see Gassner, John.

Nicholas, H. G. The United Nations as a Political Institution. 5th ed. 1975. pap. 7.95x (ISBN 0-19-519826-3). Oxford U Pr.

Nicholas, J. Karl. Writing & Revising: A Workbook. 250p. 1981. pap. text ed. 11.95 (ISBN 0-13-971499-5). P-H.

Nicholas, James. New Key to Power Golf: The Secret Lever. Ruth, R. M., ed. LC 82-17749. (Illus.). 160p. (Orig.). 1983. pap. 13.95 (ISBN 0-910815-00-3). CharLee Pr.

Nicholas, James C. State Regulation: Housing Prices. 140p. 1982. pap. text ed. 10.95 (ISBN 0-88285-075-X, Dist. by Transaction Bks). Ctr Urban Pol Res.

Nicholas, Jeanne L., jt. auth. see Mc Dermott, Irene E.

Nicholas, Karl J. & Nicholl, James R. Rhetorical Models for Effective Writing. 2nd. ed. 1981. pap. 10.95 (ISBN 0-316-60622-7); avail. tchrs'. manual (ISBN 0-316-60623-5). Little.

Nicholas, P. V., jt. auth. see Dickes, G. J.

Nicholas, Robert L. El Mundo de Hoy: A First Conversational Reader in Spanish. 1971. pap. 6.95x o.p. (ISBN 0-673-07554-0). Scott F.

Nicholas, Robert L., jt. auth. see Neale-Silva, Eduardo.

Nicholas, Ted. How to Form Your Own Non-Profit Corporation Without a Lawyer for Under 75 Dollars. 1981. 14.95 o.p. (ISBN 0-913864-56-0). Enterprise Del.

Nicholes, Paul S., jt. auth. see Gebhardt, Louis P.

Nicholl, David S. Advertising. 240p. 1978. 30.00x (ISBN 0-7121-0166-7, Pub. by Macdonald & Evans). State Mutual Bk.

Nicholl, Donald, tr. see Dante Alighieri.

Nicholl, James R., jt. auth. see Nicholas, Karl J.

Nicholl, Larry & Gomez, Miguel. Quality Education for Mexican Americans-Minorities. LC 80-5650. (Si, Se Puede!- Yes, It Can Be Done!). 277p. 1980. pap. text ed. 11.50 (ISBN 0-8191-1245-3). U Pr of Amer.

Nicholls, jt. auth. see Miller.

Nicholls, A. J. Weimar & the Rise of Hitler. 2nd ed. LC 79-10134. (The Making of the Twentieth Century Ser.). 1980. 16.95 (ISBN 0-312-86066-8); pap. text ed. 8.95 (ISBN 0-312-86067-6). St Martin.

--Weimar & the Rise of Hitler. Thorne, Christopher, ed. LC 68-29506. (Making of the Twentieth Century Ser.). (Illus., Orig.). 1969. pap. 5.95 o.p. (ISBN 0-312-86065-X, W15701). St Martin.

Nicholls, Andrew. Clocks in Color. LC 75-17890. (Illus.). 176p. 1976. 6.95 o.s.i. (ISBN 0-02-589460-9, 58946). Macmillan.

Nicholls, Ann, jt. auth. see Hudson, Kenneth.

Nicholls, Bruce & Kantzer, Kenneth. In Word & Deed. 224p. 1983. pap. 10.95 (ISBN 0-8028-1965-6). Eerdmans.

Nicholls, C. S. Swahili Coast: Politics, Diplomacy & Trade on the East African Littoral, 1798-1856. LC 78-180670. 419p. 1971. text ed. 42.50x (ISBN 0-8419-0099-X, Africana). Holmes & Meier.

Nicholls, D. Inorganic Chemistry in Liquid Ammonia. (Topics in Inorganic & General Chemistry Ser.: Vol. 17). 1979. 51.00 (ISBN 0-444-41774-5). Elsevier.

Nicholls, D. F. & Quinn, B. G. Random Coefficient Autoregressive Models: An Introduction. (Lecture Notes in Statistics: Vol. 11). (Illus.). 154p. 1983. pap. 12.00 (ISBN 0-387-90766-1). Springer-Verlag.

Nicholls, David. Bioenergetics: An Introduction to the Chemiosmotic Theory. 200p. 1982. 27.50 o.s.i. (ISBN 0-12-518120-5); pap. 11.50 o.s.i. (ISBN 0-12-518122-1). Acad Pr.

--From Dessalines to Duvalier: Race, Colour & National Independence in Haiti. LC 78-56817. (Cambridge Latin American Studies: No. 34). 1979. 47.50 (ISBN 0-521-22177-3). Cambridge U Pr.

--The Pluralist State. LC 74-23710. 399p. 1975. 21.50 o.p. (ISBN 0-312-61775-5). St Martin.

--Three Varieties of Pluralism. LC 74-80654. 80p. 1974. 20.00 (ISBN 0-312-80325-7). St Martin.

Nicholls, Marion E. & Wessells, Virginia G., eds. Nursing Standards & Nursing Process. LC 76-56882. 164p. 1977. pap. 16.50 (ISBN 0-913654-31-0). Aspen Systems.

Nicholls, Mark. The Importance of Being Oscar. 240p. 1980. 10.95 o.p. (ISBN 0-312-41014-X). St Martin.

Nicholls, Peter. The Biology of Oxygen. Head, J. J., ed. LC 81-67981. (Carolina Biology Readers Ser.). (Illus.). 16p. (gr. 10 up). 1982. pap. 1.60 (ISBN 0-89278-300-1, 45-9700). Carolina Biological.

--Cytochromes & Cell Respiration. 2nd ed. Head, J. J., ed. LC 78-55322. (Carolina Biology Readers Ser.). (Illus.). 16p. (gr. 10 up). 1983. pap. 1.60 (ISBN 0-89278-266-8, 45-9666). Carolina Biological.

Nicholls, Peter & Langford, David. The Science in Science Fiction. LC 82-14834. 208p. 1983. 25.00 (ISBN 0-394-53010-1); pap. 14.95 (ISBN 0-394-71364-8). Knopf.

Nicholls, Peter, ed. Foundation: The Review of Science Fiction, Numbers 1-8, March 1972-March 1975. (Science Fiction Ser.). 1978. 35.00 o.p. (ISBN 0-8398-2442-4, Gregg). G K Hall.

Nichols. The Poetry of Sir Philip Sydney. 192p. 1982. 39.00x (ISBN 0-85323-351-9, Pub. by Liverpool Univ England). State Mutual Bk.

Nichols, Alice, tr. see Neizestny, Ernst.

Nichols, Arlene O. Pearls for Nursing Practice. LC 79-15387. 1979. pap. text ed. 10.75 (ISBN 0-397-54251-8, Lippincott Nursing); 13.75x o.p. (ISBN 0-686-65979-1). Lippincott.

Nichols, Beverley. The Gift of a Garden; or, Some Flowers Remembered. Incl. Down the Garden Path; A Thatched Roof; A Village in the Valley. (Illus.). 344p. 1972. 7.50 o.p. (ISBN 0-396-06575-9). Dodd.

Nichols, Carole. Vote & More for Women: Suffrage & After in Connecticut. (Women & History, No. 5). 88p. 1983. text ed. 20.00 (ISBN 0-86656-192-7, B192). Haworth Pr.

Nichols, Charles H., ed. Black Men in Chains: Narratives by Escaped Slaves. LC 72-78320. 320p. 1972. o. p. 8.95 (ISBN 0-88208-003-2); pap. 5.95 o.s.i. (ISBN 0-88208-004-0). Lawrence Hill.

Nichols, David & Cooke, John. Oxford Book of Invertebrates. 1971. 32.50x (ISBN 0-19-910008-X). Oxford U Pr.

Nichols, David H. Clinical Problems, Injuries & Complications of Gynecologic Surgery. (Illus.). 300p. 1983. lib. bdg. write for info. (ISBN 0-683-06495-9). Williams & Wilkins.

Nichols, David H. & Randall, Clyde L. Vaginal Surgery. 2nd ed. 395p. 1982. PLB 39.95 o.p. (ISBN 0-683-06493-2). Williams & Wilkins.

Nichols, Dudley, jt. auth. see Gassner, John.

Nichols, Egbert R. & Roskam, William E, eds. Pump-Priming Theory of Government Spending. 482p. 1982. Repr. of 1939 ed. lib. bdg. 65.00 (ISBN 0-89984-809-5). Century Bookbindery.

Nichols, Faith. Look Again. Bahr, Amy, ed. (Illus.). 32p. Date not set. 6.95 (ISBN 0-671-45310-6, Little Simon). S&S. Postponed.

--Look Again. (Illus.). 32p. (gr. 1-4). 1982. lib. bdg. cancelled (ISBN 0-671-45092-1). Messner.

Nichols, Francis H. Through Hidden Shensi. 333p. 1982. Repr. of 1902 ed. lib. bdg. 65.00 (ISBN 0-89984-808-7). Century Bookbindery.

Nichols, Frank. Theory & Practice of Body Massage. 1979. 9.95 (ISBN 0-87350-088-1). Milady.

Nichols, Fred J. Anthology of Neo-Latin Poetry. LC 78-994. 1979. text ed. 65.00x (ISBN 0-300-02017-1); pap. 24.00x (ISBN 0-300-02365-0). Yale U Pr.

Nichols, Frederic D., jt. auth. see Whitehill, Walter M.

Nichols, Frederick D. Louis Kahn & Paul Zucker-Two Bibliographers: Papers of the American Association of Architectural Bibliographers, Vol. XII. LC 77-83363. (Library of Humanities Reference Bks.: No. 116). lib. bdg. 21.00 o.s.i. (ISBN 0-8240-9851-X). Garland Pub.

Nichols, Gerald, ed. Directory of New Jersey Libraries & Media Centers. 1983. write for info. L D A Pubs.

Nichols, Geraldine C. Miguel Hernandez. (World Authors Ser.). 1978. lib. bdg. 15.95 (ISBN 0-8057-6301-5, Twayne). G K Hall.

Nichols, H. E., jt. auth. see Wood, S. R.

Nichols, J. A. Dispersant Gels for Treating Surfaces Contaminated with Residual Oils, 1975. 1981. 30.00x (ISBN 0-686-97059-4, Pub. by W Spring England). State Mutual Bk.

--Dispersant Gels for Treating Surfaces Contaminated with Residual Oils, 1979. Lynch, B., rev. by. 1981. 39.00x (ISBN 0-686-97061-6, Pub. by W Spring England). State Mutual Bk.

Nichols, J. A., jt. auth. see Cormack, D.

Nichols, J. G. The Poetry of Ben Jonson. 1969. 20.00x (ISBN 0-7100-6448-9). Routledge & Kegan.

Nichols, John. The Magic Journrey. 640p. 1983. pap. 4.95 (ISBN 0-686-84517-X). Ballantine.

--The Nirvana Blues. 608p. 1983. pap. 4.95 (ISBN 0-345-30465-9). Ballantine.

Nichols, John B. Numerical Proportions of the Sexes at Birth. LC 7-23967. 1906. pap. 12.00 (ISBN 0-527-00503-7). Kraus Repr.

Nichols, Lawrence T., jt. auth. see Alper, Benedict S.

Nichols, Lynn W., jt. auth. see Spencer, Roberta T.

Nichols, Marion. Encyclopedia of Embroidery Stitches, Including Crewel. LC 72-97816. (Illus.). 224p. (Orig.). 1974. pap. 6.50 (ISBN 0-486-22929-7). Dover.

Nichols, Mosezelle, ed. see Morant, Mack B.

Nichols, Nell B. The Farm Cook & Rule Book: The Golden Anniversary Edition. LC 76-932. 1976. pap. 6.95 o.p. (ISBN 0-15-130407-6, Harv). HarBraceJ.

Nichols, Nell B., jt. auth. see Farm Journal Editors.

Nichols, Pamela & Lester, Teri. Escape to Romance. Bd. with Everything But Love. 1982. pap. 2.50 (ISBN 0-451-11879-0, AE1879, Sig). NAL.

Nichols, Peter. Chez Nous: A Domestic Comedy in Two Acts. 84p. 1974. pap. 4.95 (ISBN 0-571-10602-1). Faber & Faber.

--Forget-Me-Not Lane. 108p. 1971. pap. 5.50 (ISBN 0-571-09857-6). Faber & Faber.

--The Pope's Divisions. 1983. pap. 6.95 (ISBN 0-14-006368-4). Penguin.

Nichols, R. & McLeish, K. Through Roman Eyes. LC 75-10043. (Illus.). 128p. 1976. 19.95 (ISBN 0-521-20345-7); pap. 6.95 (ISBN 0-521-20944-7). Cambridge U Pr.

Nichols, R. & Stevens, L. A. Are You Listening? 1957. 14.95 (ISBN 0-07-046475-8, GB). McGraw.

Nichols, R. L., jt. auth. see Stark, R. M.

Nichols, R. W. Acoustic Emission. 1976. 39.00 (ISBN 0-85334-681-X, Pub by Applied Sci England). Elsevier.

--Non-Destructive Examination in Relation to Structural Integrity. 1980. 59.50 (ISBN 0-85334-908-8, Pub. by Applied Sci England). Elsevier.

--Trends in Reactor Pressure Vessels & Circuit Development. 1980. 67.75 (ISBN 0-85334-872-3, Pub. by Applied Sci England). Elsevier.

Nichols, R. W., ed. Advances in Non-Destructive Examination for Structural Integrity: Proceedings of the International Seminar on Non-Destructive Examination in Relation to Structural Integrity, 2nd, Paris, Aug. 24-25, 1981. (Illus.). 464p. 1982. 90.25 (ISBN 0-85334-158-3, Pub. by Applied Sci England). Elsevier.

--Developments in Pressure Vessel Technology, Vols. 1-3. 1979-80. Vol. 1. 51.25 (ISBN 0-85334-802-2, Pub. by Applied Sci England); Vol. 2. 41.00 (ISBN 0-85334-806-5); Vol. 3. 71.75 (ISBN 0-85334-922-3). Elsevier.

--Developments in Pressure Vessel Technology, Vol. 4. Date not set. price not set (Pub. by Applied Sci England). Elsevier.

--Developments in Stress Analysis for Pressured Components. (Illus.). 1977. 53.50x (ISBN 0-85334-724-7, Pub. by Applied Sci England). Elsevier.

--Pressure Vessel Engineering Technology. (Illus.). 1970. 96.50 (ISBN 0-444-20061-4, Pub. by Applied Sci England). Elsevier.

Nichols, Robert. Exile. LC 79-15330. (Daily Lives in Nghsi-Altai Ser.: Bk. IV). 1979. pap. 3.95 (ISBN 0-686-86500-6, NDP485). New Directions.

Nichols, Roger & Nichols, Sarah. Greek Everyday Life. McLeish, Kenneth & McLeish, Valerie, eds. (Aspects of Greek Life Ser.). (Illus.). 48p. (gr. 7-12). 1978. pap. text ed. 3.50 (ISBN 0-582-20672-3). Longman.

Nichols, Roger, tr. Livy: Stories of Rome. LC 81-10227. (Translations from Greek & Roman Authors Ser.). (Illus.). 112p. pap. 4.95 (ISBN 0-521-22816-6). Cambridge U Pr.

Nichols, Sarah. Prospect Lane. (Marble Arch Ser.: No. 1). 224p. (Orig.). 1980. pap. 1.75 o.p. (ISBN 0-523-41061-1). Pinnacle Bks.

Nichols, Sarah, jt. auth. see Nichols, Roger.

Nichols, Stephen G., Jr. Romanesque Signs: Early Medieval Narrative & Iconography. LC 82-7028. (Illus.). 264p. 1983. text ed. 23.50x (ISBN 0-300-02833-4). Yale U Pr.

Nichols, Sue. Words on Target: For Better Christian Communication. LC 63-16410. (Illus., Orig.). 1963. pap. 4.95 (ISBN 0-8042-1476-X). John Knox.

Nichols, Talmage & Stiles, Harold. Woodworking Workbook. rev. ed. (gr. 9-12). 1971. pap. 6.44 (ISBN 0-87002-105-2); ans. sheet free. Bennett IL.

Nichols, Virginia. Show Your Own Dog. 1970. 12.95 (ISBN 0-87666-661-6, PS607). TFH Pubns.

Nichols, William I., ed. New Treasury of Words to Live By. 1959. 7.95 o.p. (ISBN 0-671-52250-7). S&S.

Nichols, Woodrow W., Jr., jt. auth. see Longbrake, David B.

Nicholsen, Margaret, ed. People in Books. LC 69-15811. 498p. 1969. 19.00 (ISBN 0-8242-0394-1). Wilson.

Nicholson. Pediatric Ocular Tumors. LC 81-2346. 320p. 1981. 68.75x (ISBN 0-89352-125-6). Masson Pub.

Nicholson, jt. auth. see Poste.

Nicholson, Alasdair. The Cold War. Yapp, Malcolm, et al, eds. (World History Ser.). (Illus.). 32p. (gr. 10). 1980. Repr. of 1977 ed. 6.95 (ISBN 0-89908-236-X); pap. text ed. 2.25 (ISBN 0-89908-211-4). Greenhaven.

Nicholson, B. E., ed. see Brightman, Frank H.

Nicholson, Christina. The Savage Sands. 1978. 9.95 o.p. (ISBN 0-698-10898-1, Coward). Putnam Pub Group.

Nicholson, Christine. The Power & the Passion. 1977. 8.95 o.p. (ISBN 0-698-10808-6, Coward). Putnam Pub Group.

Nicholson, D. Computers in Production Management Decisions. 1975. 22.95 (ISBN 0-273-31748-2). Elsevier.

Nicholson, D. & Parsonage, N. G. Computer Simulation & the Statiscal Mechanics of Adsorption. 55.00. Acad Pr.

Nicholson, Dale, jt. auth. see Friend, Diane.

Nicholson, Diana, ed. see Chapman, Marvey.

Nicholson, Diana, jt. ed. see Thwaite, Jean.

Nicholson, Diana M., ed. see Smith, Susan H.

Nicholson, Diana M., ed. see Young, Dale.

Nicholson, Dolly. Thoughts 'N' Things. 1983. 5.95 (ISBN 0-533-05547-4). Vantage.

Nicholson, Don H., ed. Ocular Pathology Update. LC 80-80967. (Illus.). 304p. 1980. 68.75x (ISBN 0-89352-051-9). Masson Pub.

Nicholson, Dwight R. Introduction to Plasma Theory. (Plasma Physics Ser.). 304p. 1983. text ed. 29.95 (ISBN 0-471-09045-X). Wiley.

Nicholson, E. W. Preaching to the Exiles: A Study of the Prose Tradition in the Book of Jeremiah. LC 74-146021. 1971. 7.50x o.p. (ISBN 0-8052-3389-X). Schocken.

Nicholson, Ernest W. Exodus & Sinai in History & Tradition. pap. 2.99 (ISBN 0-8042-0200-1). John Knox.

Nicholson, G., jt. ed. see Poste, G.

Nicholson, G. W. Canada's Nursing Sisters. 1975. 12.95 o.p. (ISBN 0-88866-567-9). Samuel Stevens.

Nicholson, Godfrey C. Death as Departure: The Johannine Descent-Ascent Schema. LC 81-18336. (SBL Dissertation Ser.). 1982. pap. 10.50 o.p. (ISBN 0-89130-555-6, 060163). Scholars Pr CA.

Nicholson, H. Structure of Interconnected Systems. (Illus.). 258p. 1978. 35.75 (ISBN 0-901223-69-7). Inst Elect Eng.

Nicholson, H., ed. Modelling of Dynamical Systems, Vol. I. (IEE Control Engineering Ser.: No. 12). (Illus.). 256p. 1980. casebound 68.00 (ISBN 0-906048-38-9). Inst Elect Eng.

Nicholson, Ian. Customizing Your Boat. 1982. pap. 9.95 (ISBN 0-442-26911-0). Van Nos Reinhold.

Nicholson, James L. & Corlew, Robert E. Grundy County. (Tennessee County History Ser.: No. 13). (Illus.). 144p. 1982. 12.50X (ISBN 0-87870-134-6). Memphis St Univ.

Nicholson, James R. Meteorological Data Catalogue. (International Indian Ocean Expedition Meteorological Monographs: No. 3). (Illus.). 1969. 15.00x (ISBN 0-8248-0082-6, Eastwest Ctr). UH Pr.

Nicholson, Joan, jt. auth. see Scala, Bea.

Nicholson, Joyce. Yap the Penguin. (Illus.). (gr. k up). 8.50x (ISBN 0-392-01976-0, ABC). Sportshelf.

Nicholson, Luree & Torbet, Laura. How to Fight Fair with Your Kids...& Win! LC 79-1837. 1980. 12.95 o.p. (ISBN 0-15-142191-9, Harv); pap. 7.95 (ISBN 0-15-642191-7, Harv). HarBraceJ.

Nicholson, Lynda, tr. see Brenan, Gerald.

Nicholson, M. Jean, jt. auth. see Hein, Eleanor C.

Nicholson, Margaret. Catalogue of Pre-Nineteen Hundred Imprints Relating to America in the Royal Library, Brussels. LC 82-48979. (Orig.). 1983. lib. bdg. write for info. (ISBN 0-527-67200-9). Kraus Intl.

--Manual of Copyright Practice for Writers, Publishers, & Agents. 2nd ed. 1956. 14.95x (ISBN 0-19-500040-4). Oxford U Pr.

--People in Books. 795p. (First suppl.). 1977. 30.00 (ISBN 0-8242-0587-1). Wilson.

Nicholson, Marjorie H. Newton Demands the Muse: Newton's "Opticks" & the Eighteenth Century Poets. LC 78-13146. 1979. Repr. of 1966 ed. lib. bdg. 18.50x (ISBN 0-313-21044-6, NIND). Greenwood.

Nicholson, Mary J. Moments in Time with Mary John. LC 81-90608. (Illus.). 40p. 1982. pap. text ed. 6.50 (ISBN 0-9607574-0-6). M J Nicholson.

Nicholson, N. Oligopoly & Conflict. 244p. 1982. 39.00x (ISBN 0-85323-220-2, Pub. by Liverpool Univ England). State Mutual Bk.

Nicholson, Nigel, ed. see Woolf, Virginia.

Nicholson, Norman. The Lakes. (Hale Topographical Ser.). (Illus.). 1979. pap. 4.50 o.p. (ISBN 0-7091-6245-6). Hippocrene Bks.

Nicholson, Normon. Selected Poems, Nineteen Forty to Nineteen Eighty-Two. 272p. 1983. 12.95 (ISBN 0-571-11949-2); pap. 5.95 (ISBN 0-571-11950-6). Faber & Faber.

Nicholson, P. W. Nuclear Electronics. LC 73-8196. 388p. 1974. 61.95 (ISBN 0-471-63697-5, Pub. by Wiley-Interscience). Wiley.

Nicholson, R. A. Idea of Personality in Sufism. 7.50 (ISBN 0-686-18606-0). Kazi Pubns.

Nicholson, Reynold A. The Mystics of Islam: An Introduction to Sufism. LC 75-10713. 192p. 1975. pap. 3.95 (ISBN 0-8052-0492-X). Schocken.

Nicholson, Reynold A., ed. Selected Poems from the Divani Shamsi Tabriz. LC 77-1340. 1977. pap. text ed. 49.50 (ISBN 0-521-21646-X); pap. 19.95x (ISBN 0-521-29217-4). Cambridge U Pr.

Nicholson, Robert. Guide to England & Wales. (Illus.). 1983. pap. 9.95 (ISBN 0-686-38863-1). Merrimack Bk Serv.

--Nicholson's Historic Britain. 1983. pap. 12.95 (ISBN 0-686-38866-6). Merrimack Bk Serv.

--Nicholson's London Guide. (Illus.). 1983. pap. 4.95 (ISBN 0-686-38865-8). Merrimack Bk Serv.

--Nicholson's New York Guide. 1983. pap. 4.95 (ISBN 0-686-38867-4). Merrimack Bk Serv.

--Streetfinder. rev. ed. 1983. pap. 4.95 (ISBN 0-686-38864-X). Merrimack Bk Serv.

Nicholson, Shirley, ed. see Besant, Annie.

Nicholson, T. R. Sprint. (Illus.). 273p. 1969. 4.95 o.p. (ISBN 0-7153-4345-9). David & Charles.

Nicholson, W. L., jt. auth. see Dixon, W. J.

Nicholson, William. The Seventh Level. 1980. pap. 2.75 o.p. (ISBN 0-451-09479-4, E9479, Sig). NAL.

Nicholson, William J. & Moore, John A., eds. Health Effects of Halogenated Aromatic Hydrocarbons. LC 79-12253. (Annals of the New York Academy of Sciences: Vol. 320). 730p. 1979. 117.00x (ISBN 0-89766-008-0). NY Acad Sci.

Nichoul, J. C., ed. Hydrodynamics of Semi-Enclosed Seas. (Oceanography Ser.: Vol. 34). 1982. 76.75 (ISBN 0-444-42077-0). Elsevier.

Nickas, Robert, jt. ed. see Battcock, Gregory.

Nickel, Gerhard, ed. Papers in Contrastive Linguistics. LC 78-149434. (Illus.). 1971. 22.95 (ISBN 0-521-08091-6). Cambridge U Pr.

Nickel, Heinrich L. Medieval Architecture in Eastern Europe. LC 82-6254. (Illus.). 210p. 1982. text ed. 35.00x (ISBN 0-8419-0811-7). Holmes & Meier.

Nickell, Molli. This Is Baker's Clay. LC 73-5550. (Illus.). 1976. pap. 6.95 o.p. (ISBN 0-8069-8716-2). Sterling.

Nickell, Paulena, et al. Management in Family Living. 5th ed. LC 75-41398. 475p. 1976. text ed. 28.95 (ISBN 0-471-63721-1). Wiley.

Nickell, S. J. The Investment Decision of Firms. LC 78-73957. (Economic Handbooks). 1975. 47.50 (ISBN 0-521-22465-9); pap. 15.95x (ISBN 0-521-29511-4). Cambridge U Pr.

Nickels, George. The Gypsy Season. LC 80-12821. 1982. 14.95 (ISBN 0-87949-187-6). Ashley Bks.

Nickels, Sylzie. Scandinavia. LC 82-61196. (Pocket Guide Ser.). (Illus.). 1983. pap. 4.95 (ISBN 0-528-84893-3). Rand.

Nickels, William G. Marketing Principles. 2nd ed. (Illus.). 640p. 1982. text ed. 26.95 (ISBN 0-13-558197-4); study guide 8.95 (ISBN 0-13-558114-1). P-H.

Nickelsburg, George W. & Stone, Michael E. Faith & Piety in Early Judaism: Texts & Documents. LC 82-71830. 272p. 1983. 19.95 (ISBN 0-8006-0679-5). Fortress.

Nickelsburg, Janet. Nature Program for Early Childhood. new ed. 1976. pap. text ed. 11.25 (ISBN 0-201-05097-8, Sch Div). A-W.

Nickens, John M., et al. Research Methods for Needs Assessment. LC 80-5126. 98p. 1980. pap. text ed. 7.25 (ISBN 0-8191-1047-7). U Pr of Amer.

Nickerson, Charles A. & Nasuti, James F. Taxes & You. 1979. text ed. 17.50 (ISBN 0-89433-079-9); pap. 14.00 (ISBN 0-89433-080-2). Petrocelli.

Nickerson, Charles A. & Nickerson, Ingeborg A. Business Mathematics: A Consumer Approach. (Illus.). 256p. 1981. pap. text ed. 14.95 (ISBN 0-675-08071-1). Additional supplements may be obtained from publisher. Merrill.

Nickerson, Clarence B. Managerial Cost Accounting & Analysis. 2nd ed. (Accounting Ser.). 1962. text ed. 20.50 o.p. (ISBN 0-07-046494-4, C). McGraw.

Nickerson, Dorothy, jt. auth. see Nickerson, Doyne.

Nickerson, Doyne & Nickerson, Dorothy. New Three Hundred Sixty-Five Ways to Cook Hamburger & Other Ground Meat. LC 82-45262. (Illus.). 240p. 1983. 12.95 (ISBN 0-385-18068-3). Doubleday.

Nickerson, Eileen T. & O'Laughlin, Kay, eds. Action Oriented Therapies. (Illus.). 346p. (Orig.). 1982. pap. text ed. 15.95x (ISBN 0-914234-62-5). Human Res Dev Pr.

Nickerson, Ingeborg A., jt. auth. see Nickerson, Charles A.

Nickerson, N. Pigmentation of Hoppers of the Desert Locust (Schistocerca Gregaria Forskal) in Relation to Phase Coloration. 1956. 35.00x (ISBN 0-85135-023-2, Pub. by Centre Overseas Research). State Mutual Bk.

Nickerson, Robert C. Fundamentals of FORTRAN Programming. 2nd ed. 1980. pap. text ed. 16.95 (ISBN 0-316-60644-8); tchr's ed. free (ISBN 0-316-60645-6). Little.

--Fundamentals of Programming in Basic. (Orig.). 1981. pap. text ed. 16.95 (ISBN 0-316-60646-4); tchr's ed. free (ISBN 0-316-60647-2). Little.

Nickerson, Roy. Robert Louis Stevenson in California. LC 82-9643. (Illus.). 128p. (Orig.). 1982. pap. 5.95 (ISBN 0-87701-246-6). Chronicle Bks.

Nickerson, Sheila B. Writer's in the Public Library. 1983. price not set (ISBN 0-208-01872-7, Lib Prof Pubns); pap. price not set (ISBN 0-208-01873-5). Shoe String.

Nickerson, William. How I Turned One Thousand Dollars into Three Million in Real Estate-in My Spare Time. rev. ed. 1980. 16.95 (ISBN 0-671-25368-9). S&S.

Nicklaus, Carol. Drawing Pets. LC 80-11847. (gr. 1-3). 1980. PLB 8.90 (ISBN 0-531-04138-7). Watts.

--Drawing Your Family & Friends. LC 80-11387. (gr. 1-3). 1980. PLB 8.90 (ISBN 0-531-04139-5). Watts.

--Flying, Gliding, & Whirling: Making Things That Fly. LC 81-3071. (Easy-Read Activity Bks.). (Illus.). 32p. (gr. 1-3). 1981. lib. bdg. 8.90 (ISBN 0-531-04313-4). Watts.

--Harry the Hider. LC 78-10250. (Easy-Read Story Bks.). (Illus.). (gr. k-3). 1979. 3.95 o.p. (ISBN 0-531-02381-8); PLB 8.60 s&l (ISBN 0-531-02298-6). Watts.

--That's Not Chester! 32p. pap. 2.25 (ISBN 0-380-63073-7, Camelot). Avon.

Nicklaus, Jack. Take a Tip from Me. 1968. 9.95 o.p. (ISBN 0-671-70207-6). S&S.

Nicklaus, Jack & Bowden, Ken. Golf My Way. (Illus.). 1974. 15.50 (ISBN 0-671-21702-X). S&S.

Nicklaus, Jack & Wind, Herbert W. Greatest Game of All: My Life in Golf. 1969. 10.95 o.p. (ISBN 0-671-20215-4). S&S.

Nickle, Keith. Collection: A Study in Paul's Strategy. LC 66-72379. (Studies in Biblical Theology: No. 48). 1966. prebound o.p. 8.45x (ISBN 0-8401-4048-7); pap. 7.95x (ISBN 0-8401-3048-1). Allenson-Breckinridge.

Nickles, Harry G. Middle Eastern Cooking. LC 70-85530. (Foods of the World Ser). (Illus.). (gr. 6 up). 1969. PLB 17.28 (ISBN 0-8094-0068-5, Pub. by Time-Life). Silver.

Nickles, Olga. The Dairy Cookbook. LC 76-11345. 264p. (Orig.). 1976. pap. 4.95 o.p. (ISBN 0-89087-172-8). Celestial Arts.

Nickless, Graham, ed. Inorganic Sulphur Chemistry. 1969. 115.00 (ISBN 0-444-40684-0). Elsevier.

Nicksic, Esther. The Plus & Minus of Fluids & Electrolytes. 1981. text ed. 19.00 (ISBN 0-8359-5561-3); pap. text ed. 13.95 (ISBN 0-8359-5560-5). Reston.

Nickson, Geoffrey. A Portrait of Salmon Fishing. 1982. 150.00x (ISBN 0-686-94030-X, Pub. by A Atha Pub). State Mutual Bk.

Nickson, Jack W. Economics & Social Choice: Microeconomics. 1975. 10.95 o.p. (ISBN 0-07-046519-3, C); instructors' manual 5.95 o.p. (ISBN 0-07-046520-7). McGraw.

Nickson, Jack W., Jr. Economics & Social Choice. 2nd ed. (Illus.). 352p. 1974. pap. text ed. 16.00 (ISBN 0-07-046523-1, C); instr.'s manual 7.95 (ISBN 0-07-046524-X). McGraw.

Nickum, James, ed. A Research Guide to Jingji Yanjiu. (Chinese Research Aid Ser.: No. 4). 1972. 6.00x (ISBN 0-912966-44-0). IEAS.

Nickum, James E., ed. Water Management Organization in China. LC 80-5458. 1981. 30.00 (ISBN 0-87332-140-5). M E Sharpe.

Nicod, Jean. Geometry & Induction: Containing Geometry in the Sensible World & the Logical Problem of Induction. Bell, J. & Wood, M., trs. LC 70-107149. 1970. 21.00x o.p. (ISBN 0-520-01689-0). U of Cal Pr.

Nicol, Abioseh. Two African Tales. 1965. text ed. 4.50x (ISBN 0-521-05826-0). Cambridge U Pr.

Nicol, C., jt. auth. see King, A.

Nicol, C. W. Moving Zen: Karate as a Way to Gentleness. LC 74-11439. (Illus.). 1982. pap. 6.50 (ISBN 0-688-01181-0). Morrow.

Nicol, D. Africa: A Subjective View 1964. pap. text ed. 4.95x (ISBN 0-686-84195-6). Humanities.

Nicol, D. M. Church & Society in the Last Centuries of Byzantium. LC 78-72092. (The Birkbeck Lectures, 1977). 1979. 29.95 (ISBN 0-521-22438-1). Cambridge U Pr.

Nicol, Davidson & Laszlo, Ervin, eds. Regionalism & the New World Order: A Strategy for Progress. 375p. 1981. 45.00 (ISBN 0-08-026318-6). Pergamon.

Nicol, Gladys. Finland. (Batsford Countries Ser.). 1975. 12.95 o.p. (ISBN 0-8038-2311-8). Hastings.

Nicol, Jean M., ed. Calendar-Keeper 1983: A Record Keeping System for Child Care Providers. 5th ed. (Illus.). 60p. (Orig.). 1982. pap. 10.95 (ISBN 0-934140-08-1); GBC Binding 6.50 (ISBN 0-934140-06-5). Toys N Things.

Nicol, M. Donald. The Last Centuries of Byzantium: Twelve Sixty-One to Fourteen Fifty-Three. LC 72-85195. 1972. 17.95 o.p. (ISBN 0-312-47040-1). St Martin.

Nicol, Malcom, et al. Experimental Studies for General Chemistry. 2nd ed. 1973. lab manual 13.50x (ISBN 0-8162-6441-4). Holden-Day.

Nicol, N. D., et al. Catalog of the Islamic Coins, Glass Weights, Dies & Medals in the Egyptian National Library, Cairo. LC 82-70788. (American Research Center in Egypt, Catalogs Ser.: Vol. 3). (Illus.). xxviii, 342p. 1982. 46.50 (ISBN 0-89003-115-0); pap. 39.50x (ISBN 0-89003-114-2). Undena Pubns.

Nicolaeff, A., tr. Selected Plays of Aleksei Arbuzov. LC 82-364. (Illus.). 336p. 1982. 19.50 (ISBN 0-08-024548-X). Pergamon.

Nicolaevsky, Boris I. Power & the Soviet Elite: "The Letter of an Old Bolshevik" & Other Essays. Zagoria, Janet D., ed. 1975. 8.95 o.p. (ISBN 0-472-09196-4). U of Mich Pr.

Nicolai, Jurgen. Bird Keeping. Bleher, Petra, tr. from Ger. (Illus.). 96p. 1980. 4.95 (ISBN 0-87666-997-6, KW034). TFH Pubns.

--Breeding Birds at Home. Friese, U. Erich, tr. from Ger. (Illus.). 160p. 1981. 19.95 (ISBN 0-87666-841-4, H-1038). TFH Pubns.

Nicolaisen, Jay. Italian Opera in Transition, 1871-1893. Buelow, George, ed. LC 80-22512. (Studies in Musicology: No. 31). 273p. 1980. 44.95 (ISBN 0-8357-1121-8, Pub. by UMI Res Pr). Univ Microfilms.

Nicolas, jt. auth. see Will.

Nicolas, A. & Poirier, J. P. Crystalline Plasticity & Solid State Flow in Metamorphic Rocks. LC 75-15981. (Selected Topics in Geological Sciences Ser.). 444p. 1976. 113.95 (ISBN 0-471-63791-2, Pub. by Wiley-Interscience). Wiley.

Nicolaus, Martin. Restoration of Capitalism in the U. S. S. R. 198p. (Orig.). 1975. pap. 6.95x (ISBN 0-686-94095-4). Lake View Pr.

Nicolay, Helen. Lincoln's Secretary: A Biography of John G. Nicolay. LC 70-138169. (Illus.). 363p. 1972. Repr. of 1949 ed. lib. bdg. 19.25x (ISBN 0-8371-5626-2, NILS). Greenwood.

Nicole, Christopher. Black Dawn. 1978. pap. 2.25 o.p. (ISBN 0-451-08342-3, E8342, Sig). NAL.

--Caribee. 1975. pap. 1.95 o.p. (ISBN 0-451-07945-0, J7945, Sig). NAL.

--The Devil's Own. 1976. pap. 1.95 o.p. (ISBN 0-451-07256-1, J7256, Sig). NAL.

--Haggard. (Orig.). 1980. pap. 2.50 o.p. (ISBN 0-451-09340-2, E9340, Sig). NAL.

--The Inheritors. (Haggard Ser.: No. 2). (Orig.). 1981. pap. 2.95 o.p. (ISBN 0-451-09763-7, E9763, Sig). NAL.

--Mistress of Darkness. 1977. pap. 1.95 o.p. (ISBN 0-451-07782-2, J7782, Sig). NAL.

--Sunset. 1979. pap. 2.25 o.p. (ISBN 0-451-08948-0, E8948, Sig). NAL.

Nicole Van, de Ven see Russell, Diana E. & Van de Ven, Nicole.

Nicolich, Lorraine, jt. auth. see Woolfolk, Anita.

Nicolini, Claudio, ed. Chemical Carcinogenesis. (NATO Advanced Study Institutes Ser. A. Life Sciences). 510p. 1982. 59.50x (ISBN 0-306-41111-3, Plenum Pr). Plenum Pub.

Nicolis, G. & Prigogine, I. Self-Organization in Non-Equilibrium Systems: From Dissipative Structures to Order Through Fluctuations. LC 76-49019. 491p. 1977. 55.00 (ISBN 0-471-02401-5, Pub. by Wiley-Interscience). Wiley.

Nicolis, G. & Lefever, R., eds. Membranes, Dissipative Structures & Evolution. LC 74-23611. (Advances in Chemical Physics Ser: Vol. 29). 390p. 1975. 60.00 o.s.i. (ISBN 0-471-63792-0, Pub. by Wiley-Interscience). Wiley.

Nicoll, A. R. Acustic Emission. (Illus.). 385p. (Eng.). 1980. 63.00 (ISBN 0-686-37418-5, Pub. by DGM Metallurgy Germany). IR Pubns.

Nicoll, A. R., tr. see Hornbogen, E. & Zum-Gahr, K. H.

Nicoll, Allardyce. English Theatre: A Short History. Repr. of 1936 ed. lib. bdg. 18.25x (ISBN 0-8371-3133-2, NIET). Greenwood.

--The Garrick Stage: Theaters & Audience in the Eighteenth Century. 192p. 1982. pap. 12.50 (ISBN 0-7190-0858-1). Manchester.

Nicoll, Bruce. House of the Seven Gables. (Orig.). 1964. pap. 2.25 (ISBN 0-8220-0595-6). Cliffs.

Nicoll, Helen & Pienkowski, Jan. Meg & Mog Birthday Book. (Meg & Mog Ser.). (Illus.). 32p. (ps-1). 1983. 8.95 (ISBN 0-434-95428-4, Pub. by Heinemann England). David & Charles.

--Meg's Car. (Meg & Mog Ser.). (Illus.). 32p. (ps-1). 1983. 8.95 (ISBN 0-434-95426-8, Pub. by Heinemann England). David & Charles.

--Meg's Veg. (Meg & Mog Ser.). (Illus.). 32p. (ps-1). 1983. 8.95 (ISBN 0-434-95639-2, Pub. by Heinemann England). David & Charles.

--Mog at the Zoo. (Meg & Mog Ser.). (Illus.). 32p. (ps-1). 1983. 8.95 (ISBN 0-434-95429-2, Pub. by Heinemann England). David & Charles.

--Mog's Mumps. (Meg & Mog Ser.). (Illus.). 32p. (ps-1). 1983. 8.95 (ISBN 0-434-95640-6, Pub. by Heinemann England). David & Charles.

--Quest for the Gloop. (Illus.). 32p. (gr. 1-3). 1983. 11.00 (ISBN 0-434-95641-4, Pub. by Heinemann England). David & Charles.

Nicoll, Helens & Pienkowski, Jan. Meg's Castle. (Meg & Mog Ser.). (Illus.). 32p. (ps-1). 1983. 8.95 (ISBN 0-434-95427-6, Pub. by Heinemann England). David & Charles.

Nicoll, Maurice. Dream Psychology. 1979. pap. 4.95 o.p. (ISBN 0-87728-475-X). Weiser.

--New Man. (Metaphysical Lib.). 1972. pap. 3.95 o.p. (ISBN 0-14-003412-9). Penguin.

Nicoll, Mildred R., tr. see Steiner, Rudolf.

Nicollian, E. H. & Brews, J. R. MOS (Metal Oxide Semiconductor) Physics & Technology. LC 81-7607. 906p. 1982. 74.50 (ISBN 0-471-08500-6, Pub. by Wiley-Interscience). Wiley.

Nicolosi, Lucille. Terminology of Communication Disorders: Speech, Language, & Hearing. 2nd ed. (Illus.). 338p. 1982. 18.50 (ISBN 0-683-06499-1). Williams & Wilkins.

Nicolosi, Lucille, et al. Terminology of Communication Disorders: Speech, Language, Hearing. (Illus.). 288p. 1978. pap. 17.50 o.p. (ISBN 0-683-06500-9). Williams & Wilkins.

Nicols, P. J. R., et al. Rehabilitation of the Severely Disabled-2: Management. 432p. 1971. 24.95x o.p. (ISBN 0-407-38512-6). Butterworth.

Nicolson, jt. ed. see Poste.

Nicolson, Adam. National Trust Book of Long Walks in England, Scotland, & Wales. LC 81-6226. (Illus.). 288p. 1981. 15.95 o.p. (ISBN 0-517-54509-8, Harmony). Crown.

Nicolson, D. H., jt. auth. see Saldanha, C. J.

Nicolson, Harold. The Congress of Vienna. LC 46-7614. 1970. pap. 4.95 (ISBN 0-15-622061-X, Harv). HarBraceJ.

--Diplomacy. 3rd ed. 1963. pap. 6.95 (ISBN 0-19-500256-3, GB). Oxford U Pr.

--Peacemaking, Nineteen-Nineteen. 1965. pap. 2.50 o.p. (ISBN 0-448-00178-0, G&D). Putnam Pub Group.

--Some People. LC 82-71254. 256p. 1982. pap. 6.95 (ISBN 0-689-70627-8, 280). Atheneum.

Nicolson, Iain. Road to the Stars. (Illus.). 1978. 14.95 o.p. (ISBN 0-688-03336-9). Morrow.

--The Road to the Stars. (Illus.). 1979. pap. 2.75 o.p. (ISBN 0-451-61780-0, ME1780, Ment). NAL.

Nicolson, Ian. Build Your Own Boat. (Illus.). 1982. 22.95 (ISBN 0-393-03273-6). Norton.

--Surveying Small Craft: Fault Finding in Boats. (Illus.). 255p. 1983. write for info (ISBN 0-229-11552-7). Sheridan.

Nicolson, M. H., ed. see Conway, Anne.

Nicolson, Marjorie H. Pepys' Diary & the New Science. LC 65-26012. (Illus.). 198p. 1965. 12.95 (ISBN 0-8139-0188-X). U Pr of Va.

Nicolson, Marjorie H., ed. see Shadwell, Thomas.

Nicolson, Nigel. The Himalayas. (The World's Wild Places Ser.). (Illus.). 1978. lib. bdg. 15.96 (ISBN 0-8094-2023-6). Silver.

Nicolson, Nigel & Trautman, Joanne, eds. The Letters of Virginia Woolf, Vol. I: 1888-1912. LC 76-40422. 1977. pap. 8.95 (ISBN 0-15-650881-8, Harv). HarBraceJ.

--The Letters of Virginia Woolf, Vol. II: 1911-1922. LC 76-40422. (Illus.). 1978. pap. 5.95 (ISBN 0-15-650882-6, Harv). HarBraceJ.

--The Letters of Virginia Woolf: 1912-1922, Vol. II. LC 75-25538. (Illus.). 1976. 14.95 o.p. (ISBN 0-15-150925-5). HarBraceJ.

Nicolson, Nigel & Trautmann, Joanne, eds. The Letters of Virginia Woolf: Nineteen Twenty-Three to Nineteen Twenty-Eight, Vol. III. LC 76-40422. (Illus.). 624p. 1980. pap. 5.95 o.p. (ISBN 0-15-650883-4, Harv). HarBraceJ.

--The Letters of Virginia Woolf: Volume I: 1888-1912. LC 75-25538. (Illus.). 531p. 1975. 14.95 o.p. (ISBN 0-15-150924-7). HarBraceJ.

--The Letters of Virginia Woolf, 1929 to 1931, Vol. IV. LC 76-40422. 1981. pap. 7.95 (ISBN 0-15-650884-2, Harv). HarBraceJ.

Nicosia, Gerald. Memory Babe: A Critical Biography of Jack Kerouac. Jordan, Fred, ed. (Illus.). 760p. 1983. 22.50 (ISBN 0-394-52270-2, GP865). Grove.

Nicoud, J. D. & Wilmink, J., eds. Microcomputer Architectures: Proceedings of the Third EUROMICRO Symposium on Microprocessing Microprogramming, October 1977, Amsterdam. 1978. 64.00 (ISBN 0-444-85097-X, North-Holland). Elsevier.

Niczow, Alexsandar. Black Book of Polish Censorship. LC 82-72611. 170p. (Orig.). 1982. pap. 7.95 (ISBN 0-89708-095-5). And Bks.

Nida, E. A. God's Word in Man's Language. 1973. pap. 3.95 o.p. (ISBN 0-686-14419-8, 08630). Am Bible.

--Translators Notes on Literacy Selections, Pt. 1. 1974. pap. 2.10 o.p. (ISBN 0-686-14407-4, 08525). Am Bible.

Nida, E. A., jt. auth. see Arichea, D. C.

Nida, E. A., jt. auth. see Arichea, D. C., Jr.

Nida, E. A., jt. auth. see Bratcher, R. G.

Nida, E. A., jt. auth. see De Waard, J.

Nida, E. A., jt. auth. see Ellingworth, P.

Nida, E. A., jt. auth. see Loh, I.

Nida, E. A., jt. auth. see Newman, B. M.

Nida, E. A., jt. auth. see Newman, B. M., Jr.

Nida, Eugene. Message & Mission: The Communication of the Christian Faith. LC 60-11785. (Applied Cultural Anthropology Ser.). 256p. 1975. pap. text ed. 3.95x o.p. (ISBN 0-87808-711-7). William Carey Lib.

Nida, Eugene A. Religion Across Cultures. 1968. 4.95 o.p. (ISBN 0-686-14420-1, 08640). Am Bible.

--Translator's Notes on Literacy Selections, Pt. 2. 1974. pap. 3.25x (ISBN 0-8267-0013-6, 08524). United Bible.

Nida, Eugene A., jt. auth. see Bratcher, Robert G.

Nida, Eugene A., jt. auth. see Price, Brynmor F.

Nida, Gail, jt. auth. see Burton, Charles.

Nidditch, P. H. The Development of Mathematical Logic. (Monographs in Modern Logic). 1971. Repr. of 1962 ed. 6.00 o.p. (ISBN 0-7100-3801-1). Routledge & Kegan.

Nidditch, P. H., ed. see Hume, David.

Nidditch, Peter H., ed. Philosophy of Science. (Orig.). 1968. pap. 8.95x (ISBN 0-19-875008-0). Oxford U Pr.

Nidditch, Peter H., ed. see Locke, John.

Nideffer, Robert M. The Ethics & Practice of Applied Sport Psychology. 1981. text ed. 14.95; pap. text ed. 8.95. Mouvment Pubns.

Nidetch, Jean. Weight Watchers Food Plan Diet Cookbook. 448p. 1982. 13.95 (ISBN 0-453-01007-5, TE7). NAL.

Nidetch, Jean, intro. by. Weight Watchers International Cookbook. (Illus.). 1980. pap. 6.95 (ISBN 0-452-25416-7, Z5416, Plume). NAL.

Nie, et al. SCSS: A User's Guide to the SCSS Conversational System. (Illus.). 592p. 1980. text ed. 33.95 (ISBN 0-07-046538-X, C); pap. text ed. 16.95 (ISBN 0-07-046533-9); SCSS slide pkg. 350.00 (ISBN 0-07-060521-1); slide pkg. manual 2.95 (ISBN 0-07-046545-2). McGraw.

Nie, N., et al. Statistical Package for the Social Sciences. 2nd ed. 1979. text ed. 28.50 (ISBN 0-07-046532-0, C); pap. text ed. 16.95 (ISBN 0-07-046531-2). McGraw.

Nie, Norman, jt. auth. see Hull, C. Hadlai.

Nie, Norman, jt. ed. see Sackman, Harold.

Nie, Norman H. & Hadlai, H. C. SPSS Pocket Guide. (Data Analysis Ser.). 56p. 1981. pap. text ed. 3.95 (ISBN 0-07-046543-6, C). McGraw.

Nie, Norman H., jt. auth. see Hull, C. Hadlai.

Niebel, B. W. & Draper, A. B. Product Design & Process Engineering. 1974. text ed. 37.50 (ISBN 0-07-046535-5, C). McGraw.

Niebel, Benjamin W. & Niebel, Douglas A. Modern Wrestling. LC 82-7478. (Illus.). 128p. (Orig.). 1982. lib. bdg. 12.95 (ISBN 0-271-00323-5); pap. text ed. 7.95 (ISBN 0-686-97721-1). Pa St U Pr.

Niebel, Douglas A., jt. auth. see Niebel, Benjamin W.

Niebrensky, Alex A. The Unholy. 1982. pap. 2.95 (ISBN 0-451-11863-4, AE1863, Sig). NAL.

Niebuhr, H. Richard. Christ & Culture. pap. 4.95xi (ISBN 0-06-130003-9, TB3, Torch). Har-Row.

--Christ & Culture. 9.00 (ISBN 0-8446-2658-9). Peter Smith.

--Meaning of Revelation. 1967. pap. 4.95 (ISBN 0-02-087750-1). Macmillan.

--Radical Monotheism in Western Culture. pap. 4.95xi (ISBN 0-06-131491-9, TB1491, Torch). Har-Row.

Niebuhr, H. Richard, jt. ed. see Beach, Waldo.

Niebuhr, Reinhold. Leaves from the Notebook of a Tamed Cynic. LC 76-27833. (Prelude to Depression Ser.). 1976. Repr. of 1929 ed. lib. bdg. 25.00 (ISBN 0-306-70852-3). Da Capo.

--Structure of Nations & Empires: A Study of the Recurring Patterns & Problems of the Political Order in Relation to the Unique Problems of the Nuclear Age. LC 72-128064. Repr. of 1959 ed. 19.50x (ISBN 0-678-02755-2). Kelley.

Nieckels, Lars. Transfer Pricing in Multinational Firms: A Heuristic Programming Approach & Case Studies. LC 76-6174. 1976. 27.95x o.p. (ISBN 0-470-15084-X). Halsted Pr.

Niedenzu, Kurt & Zimmer, Hans, eds. Annual Reports in Inorganic & General Syntheses, Vol. 1. 1973. 34.50 (ISBN 0-12-040701-9). Acad Pr.

Niederehe, Hans Josef & Haarmann, Harald, eds. In Memoriam Friedrich Diez: Proceedings of the Colloquium for the History of Romance Studies, Trier Oct. 2-4, 1975. (Studies in the History of Linguistics: No. 9). viii, 508p. 1976. 39.00 (ISBN 90-272-0900-6). Benjamins North Am.

Niederhauser, Hans R. & Frohlich, Margaret. Form Drawing: A Practical Guide to Form Drawing in Waldorf Schools. (Illus.). 1974. pap. 4.50 o.p. (ISBN 0-916786-07-2, Pub by Rudolf Steiner School). St George Bk Serv.

Niederheitmann, F., jt. auth. see Anbele, H.

Niederhoffer, Arthur & Niederhoffer, Elaine. The Police Family. LC 73-11678. 240p. 1978. 18.95 (ISBN 0-669-90498-8). Lexington Bks.

Niederhoffer, Arthur, jt. auth. see Bloch, Herbert A.

Niederhoffer, Elaine, jt. auth. see Niederhoffer, Arthur.

Niederman, Robert A., ed. Molecular Biology & Protein Synthesis. LC 76-13388. (Benchmark Papers in Microbiology Ser.: Vol. 10). 1976. 52.50 (ISBN 0-12-787130-6). Acad Pr.

Niedermayer, Franz. Jose Ortega y Gasset. Tirner, Peter, tr. from Ger. LC 71-163150. (Literature & Life Ser.). 1973. 11.95 (ISBN 0-8044-2659-7). Ungar.

Niedermeyer, Ernst. Epilepsy Guide: Diagnosis & Treatment of Epileptic Seizure Disorders. 1983. 20.00x (ISBN 0-8067-1341-0). Urban & S.

Niederreiter, H., jt. auth. see Kuipers, L.

Niedhauk, Charlotte A. Charlotte's Story. 224p. 1983. pap. 10.00 (ISBN 0-682-49938-2). Exposition.

Niedt, F. E. Musicalische Handleitung: Hamburg 1700-1721, 3 vols in 1. (Bibliotheca Organologica: Vol. 32). 1976. 75.00 o.s.i. (ISBN 90-6027-306-0, Pub. by Frits Knuf Netherlands). Pendragon NY.

Niedzielski, Henri & Runte, Hans, eds. Jean Misrahi Memorial Volume: Studies in Medieval Literature. 20.00 (ISBN 0-917786-00-9). French Lit.

Nieh, Hua-ling. Shen Ts'ung-Wen. (World Authors Ser.). lib. bdg. 15.95 (ISBN 0-8057-2818-X, Twayne). G K Hall.

Niehaus, John F., jt. auth. see Thierauf, Robert J.

Niehaus, Richard J. Computer-Assisted Human Resources Planning. LC 78-27708. 338p. 1979. 44.95 (ISBN 0-471-04081-9, Pub. by Wiley-Interscience). Wiley.

Niehaus, Theodore F. A Biosystematic Study of the Genus Brodiaea (Amaryllidaceae) (U. C. Publ. in Botany: Vol. 60). 1971. pap. 11.50x (ISBN 0-520-09390-9). U of Cal Pr.

--Sierra Wildflowers: Mt. Lassen to Kern Canyon. (California Natural History Guides). (Illus., Orig.). 1974. 14.95x (ISBN 0-520-02742-6); pap. 6.95 (ISBN 0-520-02506-7). U of Cal Pr.

Niel, Fennand. The Mysteries of Stonehenge. 1975. pap. 1.95 o.p. (ISBN 0-380-00473-9, 38620). Avon.

Niel, Robert Van see Van Niel, Robert.

Nieland, Robert G. & Doan, Rachel N. State Court Administrative Offices. 2nd ed. LC 82-82912. 1982. pap. 6.95 (ISBN 0-938870-28-9). Am Judicature.

Nield, D., jt. auth. see King, H.

Niels, Lauersen & Whitney, Stephen. It's Your Body: A Woman's Guide to Gynecology. 1977. 14.95 o.p. (ISBN 0-448-12895-0, G&D). Putnam Pub Group.

Niels-Bjorn-Anderson, et al. Information Society. 1982. 47.00 (ISBN 0-444-86422-9). Elsevier.

Nielsen, George R. Danish-Americans. (Immigrant Heritage Ser.). 1981. lib. bdg. 14.95 (ISBN 0-8057-8419-5, Twayne). G K Hall.

Nielsen, Georgia P. From Sky Girl to Flight Attendant: Women & the Making of a Union. LC 82-8210. (Illus.). 184p. 1982. 18.50 (ISBN 0-87546-093-3); pap. 9.95 (ISBN 0-87546-094-1). ILR Pr.

Nielsen, Greg & Polansky, Joseph. Pendulum Power. 190p. pap. 1.95 o.p. (ISBN 0-686-33186-9). Inner Tradit.

Nielsen, H. A. Where the Passion Is: A Reading of Kiekegaard's Philosopical Fragments. 1982. write for info. (ISBN 0-8130-0742-9). U Presses Fla.

Nielsen, J., jt. auth. see Schmid, W.

Nielsen, J. R. Niels Bohr Collected Works, Vol. 4: The System, 1920-23. 1977. 138.50 (ISBN 0-7204-1804-6, North-Holland). Elsevier.

Nielsen, J. Rud, ed. Niels Bohr Collected Works, Vol. 3: The Correspondence 1918-1923, Vol. 3. 1976. 127.75 (ISBN 0-7204-1803-8, North-Holland). Elsevier.

Nielsen, Kai. An Introduction to the Philosophy of Religion. LC 82-16843. 200p. 1982. 20.00x (ISBN 0-312-43310-7). St Martin.

Nielsen, Kai E. Scepticism. LC 72-77776. (New Studies in the Philosophy of Religion Ser.). 96p. 1973. 18.95 (ISBN 0-312-70070-9). St Martin.

Nielsen, Kaj L. Algebra: A Modern Approach. LC 68-26403. (Illus., Orig.). 1969. pap. 4.95 (ISBN 0-06-460064-5, CO 64, COS). B&N NY.

--Differential Equations. 2nd ed. (Orig.). 1969. pap. 5.50 (ISBN 0-06-460072-6, CO 72, COS). B&N NY.

--Mathematics for Practical Use. (Orig.). 1962. pap. 3.95 (ISBN 0-06-463212-1, EH 212, EH). B&N NY.

Nielsen, Kaj L. & Vanlonkhuyzen, John H. Plane & Spherical Trigonometry. rev. ed. (Orig.). 1954. pap. 5.95 (ISBN 0-06-460045-9, CO 45, COS). B&N NY.

Nielsen, Kaj L., jt. auth. see Horblit, Marcus.

Nielsen, Kay. East of the Sun & West of the Moon. (gr. 1 up). 1977. 8.95 (ISBN 0-385-13213-1). Doubleday.

Nielsen, Lauge O. Theology & Philosophy in the Twelfth Century: A Study of Gilbert Porreta's Thinking & the Theological Expositions of the Doctrin of the Incarnation during the Period 1130-1180. (Acta Theologica Danica Ser.: Vol. 15). 396p. 1982. write for info. (ISBN 90-04-06545-8). E J Brill.

Nielsen, Linda. How to Motivate Adolescents: A Guide for Parents & Teachers of Teenagers. (Illus.). 194p. 1982. 6.95 (ISBN 0-13-424002-2); pap. 12.95 (ISBN 0-13-424010-3). P-H.

Nielsen, Louis S. Standard Plumbing Engineering Design. 2nd ed. (Illus.). 384p. 1982. 30.50 (ISBN 0-07-046541-X). McGraw.

Nielsen, M. & Schmidt, E. M., eds. Automata, Languages, & Programming: Aarhus, Denmark 1982. (Lecture Notes in Computer Science: Vol. 140). 614p. 1982. pap. 27.60 (ISBN 0-387-11576-5). Springer-Verlag.

Nielsen, Niels. Die Gammafunktion, 2 vols. in 1. Incl. Integrallogarithmus. LC 64-13785. (Ger.). 1965. 19.50 (ISBN 0-8284-0188-8). Chelsea Pub.

Nielsen, Patricia H. & Sucher, Floyd. Mockingbird Flight: Music Book & Records. (Kindergarten Keys Ser.). (Illus.). 1975. pap. text ed. 10.80 (ISBN 0-87892-660-7); record set 49.50 (ISBN 0-87892-666-6). Economy Co.

Nielsen, Ralph, jt. auth. see Sandrea, Rafael.

Nielson, Bill. One & Two Thessalonians: The Distinguishing Marks of a Christian. (Beacon Small-Group Bible Studies). 56p. 1982. pap. 2.25 (ISBN 0-8341-0738-4). Beacon Hill.

Nielson, David G. Black Ethos: Northern Urban Negro Life & Thought, 1890-1930. (Contributions in Afro-American & African Studies: No. 29). 1977. lib. bdg. 27.50 (ISBN 0-8371-9402-4, NBE/). Greenwood.

Nielson, Niels C., Jr. Solzhenitsyn's Religion. 1976. pap. 1.75 o.s.i. (ISBN 0-89129-141-5). Jove Pubns.

Nieman Chair Lectures. Social Responsibility of the News Press. 1962. pap. 5.95 o.p. (ISBN 0-87462-408-8). Marquette.

Nieman, Jean. A World of Travel Tips. (Illus.). 270p. (Orig.). 1982. write for info. (ISBN 0-9609388-0-X). Travel Inter.

Nieman, Linda, jt. auth. see Smith, Wm. Flint.

Nieman, Thomas. Better Read Than Dead. (Illus.). 193p. 1982. pap. 14.95 (ISBN 0-87364-254-6). Paladin Ent.

Niemcewicz, Julian U., ed. Under Their Vine & Fig Tree: Travels Through America in 1797-1799, 1805 with Some Further Account of Life in New Jersey, Vol. 14. (Illus.). 398p. 20.00 (ISBN 0-686-81808-3). NJ Hist Soc.

Niemeijer, J. W. & De Groot, Irene. Sailing Ships in Dutch Prints. Walker, Janet, ed. LC 81-80141. (Illus.). 32p. (Orig.). 1982. pap. 7.75 (ISBN 0-88397-040-6). Intl Exhibit Foun.

Niemeyer, Carl, ed. see Carlyle, Thomas.

Niemeyer, Roy K. & Zabik, Roger. Beginning Archery. 3rd ed. 1978. pap. 5.95x o.p. (ISBN 0-534-00565-9). Wadsworth Pub.

Niemi, Adrian A. The Quest of the Sampo. 1978. 6.95 o.p. (ISBN 0-533-03577-5). Vantage.

Niemi, Albert W., Jr. State & Regional Patterns in American Manufacturing, 1860-1900. LC 73-13289. (Contributions in Economics Ser., No. 10). 209p. 1974. lib. bdg. 25.00 (ISBN 0-8371-7148-2, NAM). Greenwood.

--Understanding Economics. 1978. pap. 18.95 (ISBN 0-395-30683-3). HM.

Niemi, John A., jt. auth. see Ilsley, Paul.

Niemi, Richard & Weisberg, Herbert. Probability Models of Collective Decision Making. LC 77-172268. 416p. 1972. text ed. 13.95x (ISBN 0-675-09180-2). Merrill.

Niemi, Richard G., jt. auth. see Jennings, M. Kent.

Nienaber, Jeanne, jt. auth. see Mazmanian, Daniel A.

Nienhauser, William H., Jr. P'I Jih-Hsiu. (World Authors Ser.). 1979. lib. bdg. 15.95 (ISBN 0-8057-6372-4, Twayne). G K Hall.

Nienhauser, William H., Jr., et al. Liu Tsung-Yuan. (World Authors Ser.). 1971. lib. bdg. 15.95 (ISBN 0-8057-2538-5, Twayne). G K Hall.

Nienheuser, Helen & Simmerman, Nancy. Fifty-Five Ways to the Wilderness in Southcentral Alaska. 2nd ed. LC 72-83325. (Illus.). 168p. (Orig.). 1978. pap. 7.95 (ISBN 0-916890-84-8). Mountaineers.

Nienhuis, A., jt. ed. see Stamatoyannopoulos, G.

Niepath, E. William. Leisure Leadership: Working with People in Recreation & Park Settings. (Illus.). 416p. 1983. 21.95 (ISBN 0-13-530071-1). P-H.

Nierenberg, Gerald I., jt. auth. see Calero, Henry H.

Nierenberg, Gerard I. Fundamentals of Negotiating. 328p. 1973. 14.95 (ISBN 0-8015-2868-2, Hawthorn). Dutton.

--Fundamentals of Negotiating. new ed. 1977. 14.95 (ISBN 0-8015-2868-2, Hawthorn); pap. 6.50 (ISBN 0-8015-2869-0, Hawthorn). Dutton.

Nierenberg, Gerard I. & Calero, Henry H. Meta-Talk. 1981. pap. 4.95 (ISBN 0-686-96694-5). Cornerstone.

Nierenberg, Judith & Janovic, Florence. The Hospital Experience: A Complete Guide to Understanding & Participating in Your Own Care. LC 78-55658. (Illus.). 1978. 12.95 o.p. (ISBN 0-672-52372-8); pap. 9.95 o.p. (ISBN 0-672-52373-6). Bobbs.

Niering, W. A. Life of the Marsh. 1966. 12.95 (ISBN 0-07-046555-X, P&RB); by subscription 12.95 (ISBN 0-07-046006-X). McGraw.

Nierman, Judith, ed. Edna St. Vincent Millay: A Reference Guide. 1977. lib. bdg. 17.00 (ISBN 0-8161-7950-6, Hall Reference). G K Hall.

Nierstrasz, F. H., ed. Building for the Aged. 1960. 27.00 (ISBN 0-444-40410-4). Elsevier.

Nies, J. I. & LaBrecque, S. V. Creating Change. 1980. 3.50 (ISBN 0-686-34527-4, A261-08448). Home Econ Educ.

Nies, Judith. Seven Women: Portraits from the American Radical Tradition. 1978. pap. 4.50 (ISBN 0-14-004792-1). Penguin.

Niesen, Thomas M. The Marine Biology Coloring Book. 1982. pap. 8.61i (ISBN 0-06-460303-2, CO-303). Har-Row.

Niesewand, Peter. Fallback. 1983. pap. 3.95 (ISBN 0-686-43027-1, Sig). NAL.

Nietzel, Michael T., jt. auth. see Bernstein, Douglas A.

Nietzsche, Friedrich. Basic Writings of Nietzsche. Kaufmann, Walter, ed. & tr. 9.95 (ISBN 0-394-60406-7). Modern Lib.

--Beyond Good & Evil. Hollingdale, R. J., tr. (Classics Ser). (Orig.). 1973. pap. 3.50 (ISBN 0-14-044267-7). Penguin.

--Beyond Good & Evil. Cowan, Marianne, tr. LC 74-6868. 240p. 1955. pap. 5.95 (ISBN 0-89526-920-1). Regnery-Gateway.

--The Birth of Tragedy. Kaufmann, Walter, tr. Bd. with The Case of Wagner. (Orig.). 1967. pap. 4.95 (ISBN 0-394-70369-3, Vin). Random.

--Daybreak: Thoughts on the Prejudices of Morality. Hollingdale, R. J., tr. LC 81-18017. (Texts in German Philosophy). 220p. 1982. 19.95 (ISBN 0-521-24396-3); pap. 7.95 (ISBN 0-521-28662-X). Cambridge U Pr.

--On the Genealogy of Morals. Kaufman, Walter, tr. Bd. with Ecce Homo. 1967. pap. 4.95 (ISBN 0-394-70401-0, Vin). Random.

--Schopenhauer As Educator. LC 65-16282. 1965. pap. 3.95 (ISBN 0-89526-950-3). Regnery-Gateway.

--Thoughts Out of Season, 2 vols. Levy, Oscar, ed. Collins, Adrian, tr. LC 82-73426. 405p. Repr. of 1909 ed. Set. lib. bdg. 35.00x (ISBN 0-88116-009-1). Brenner Bks.

--Thus Spake Zarathustra. Common, Thomas, tr. 1981. 6.95 (ISBN 0-394-60808-9). Modern Lib.

--Thus Spoke Zarathustra. Kaufmann, Walter, tr. 1978. pap. 3.50 (ISBN 0-14-004748-4). Penguin.

--Twilight of the Idols & the Anti-Christ. Hollingdale, R. J., tr. (Classics Ser.). (Orig.). 1969. pap. 2.95 (ISBN 0-14-044207-3). Penguin.

--Will to Power. Kaufmann, Walter, tr. 1968. pap. 7.95 (ISBN 0-394-70437-1, Vin). Random.

Nieuwenhuijze, C. A. van. Development Begins at Home: Problems & Prospects of the Sociology of Development. LC 82-304. (Illus.). 352p. 1982. 27.50 (ISBN 0-08-027415-3). Pergamon.

Nieuwenhuis, Paul & Van den Brock, A. A., eds. In Vivo Immunology: Histophysiology of the Lymphoid System. (Advances in Experimental Medicine & Biology). 900p. 1982. 95.00x (ISBN 0-306-41039-7, Plenum Pr). Plenum Pub.

Nieuwenhuizen, P. van see Van Nieuwenhuizen, P. & Freidman, D. Z.

Nieuwenhuys, Rob. Memory & Agony: Dutch Stories from Indonesia. (International Studies & Translations Programs). 1979. lib. bdg. 13.95 (ISBN 0-8057-8166-8, Twayne). G K Hall.

--Mirror of the Indies: A History of Dutch Colonial Literature. Beekman, E. M., ed. Van Rosevelt, Frans, tr. from Dutch. LC 82-4755. (Library of the Indies). 368p. 1982. text ed. 27.50x (ISBN 0-87023-368-8). U of Mass Pr.

Nieuwenhuysen, J. P., jt. auth. see Altman, J. C.

Nieuwkoop, P. D. & Sutasurya, L. A. Primordial Germ Cells in the Chordates. LC 78-18101. (Developmental & Cell Biology Ser.: No. 7). (Illus.). 1979. 39.50 (ISBN 0-521-22303-2). Cambridge U Pr.

Nieuwolt, S. Tropical Climatology: An Introduction to the Climates of the Low Latitudes. LC 76-13454. 207p. 1977. 34.95 (ISBN 0-471-99406-5, Pub. by Wiley-Interscience). Wiley.

Nieuwstadt, F. & Van Dop, H., eds. Atmospheric Turbulence & Air Pollution. 1982. lib. bdg. 43.50 (ISBN 90-277-1365-0, Pub. by Reidel Holland). Kluwer Boston.

Nieveen, J., ed. Arrhythmias of the Heart. (The Jonxis Lectures Ser.: Vol. 6). 1981. 35.00 (ISBN 0-444-90206-6). Elsevier.

Nievergelt, J. & Coray, G., eds. Document Preparation Systems: A Collection of Survey Articles. 280p. 1982. 42.75 (ISBN 0-444-86493-8, North Holland). Elsevier.

Niewi, Albert W., Jr. U. S. Economic History. 2nd ed. 1980. 23.95 (ISBN 0-395-30682-5). HM.

Niewyk, Donald L. Socialist, Anti-Semite, & Jew: German Social Democracy Confronts the Problem of Anti-Semitism, 1918-1933. LC 79-137123. 1971. 20.00x (ISBN 0-8071-0531-7). La State U Pr.

Niezing, Johan. Strategy & Structure: Studies in Peace Research II. LC 78-319637. (Publications of the Polemological Centre of the Free University of Brussels: Vol. 8). (Illus.). 68p. 1978. pap. 11.50x (ISBN 90-265-0274-5). Intl Pubns Serv.

Nigg, Joe. Gryphons. (Illus.). 12p. (Orig.). 1982. pap. 2.50 (ISBN 0-88138-004-0, Pub. by Envelope Bks). Green Tiger Pr.

Nigg, Joe, ed. The Book of Gryphons. (Illus.). 112p. 1982. 19.95 (ISBN 0-918222-37-0). Apple Wood.

Niggli, Josefina. New Pointers on Playwriting. 1967. 6.95 o.p. (ISBN 0-87116-041-2). Writer.

Niggli, Ursula. Erkenntnis und Ernst. 167p. (Ger.). 1982. write for info. (ISBN 3-261-04961-8). P Lang Pubs.
Nighswander, Ada. The Little Martins Learn to Love. (ps-4). 6.00 (ISBN 0-686-30775-5). Rod & Staff.
Nightengale, Gay. Rabbit Keeping. (Illus.). 94p. 1979. pap. 3.95 (ISBN 0-7028-1099-1). Avian Pubns.
Nightingale, Benedict. A Reader's Guide to Fifty Modern British Plays. LC 82-11448. (Reader's Guide). 480p. 1983. text ed. 22.50x (ISBN 0-389-20239-8). B&N Imports.
Nightingale, Florence. Notes on Nursing: What It Is, & What It Is Not. LC 79-79233. 1969. pap. 3.00 (ISBN 0-486-22340-X). Dover.
Nightingale, Pamela. Trade & Empire in Western India, 1784-1806. (South Asian Studies: No. 9). (Illus.). 1970. 27.95 (ISBN 0-521-07651-X). Cambridge U Pr.
Nightingale, Pamela, jt. auth. see Viney, Elliott.
Nightingale, William G., ed. Mining International Yearbook, 1981. 94th ed. LC 50-18583. 714p. 1981. 92.50x o.p. (ISBN 0-582-90306-8). Intl Pubns Serv.
--Mining International Yearbook 1982. 95th ed. LC 50-18583. 687p. 1982. 92.50 (ISBN 0-582-90311-4). Intl Pubns Serv.
Nigro, Felix A. & Nigro, Lloyd G. The New Public Personnel Administration. 2nd ed. LC 80-83098. 465p. 1981. text ed. 19.50 (ISBN 0-87581-265-1). Peacock Pubs.
--Readings in Public Administration. 512p. 1983. pap. text ed. 11.50 scp (ISBN 0-06-044845-8, HarpC). Har-Row.
Nigro, Lloyd G., jt. auth. see Nigro, Felix A.
Nigro, Nic, jt. auth. see Scott, Robert.
Nigro, Nic, jt. auth. see Scott, Robert H.
Nigro, Robert H. Nic see Scott, Robert & Nigro, Nic.
Nihon Vogue Staff. The Best Collections of Cross Stitch Design & Handiwork. LC 82-81054. (Illus.). 84p. 1982. pap. 6.50 (ISBN 0-87040-522-5). Japan Pubns.
--Lovely Cross Stich Designs. (Illus.). 84p. (Orig.). 1983. pap. 6.95 (ISBN 0-87040-529-2). Kodansha.
Nihoul, J. C., ed. Echohydrodynamics. (Elsevier Oceanography Ser.: Vol. 32). 1981. 51.00 (ISBN 0-444-41969-1). Elsevier.
--Marine Forecasting: Predictability & Modelling in Ocean Hydrodynamics. (Elsevier Oceanography Ser.: Vol. 25). 1979. 68.00 (ISBN 0-444-41797-4). Elsevier.
--Marine Turbulence. (Oceanography Ser.: Vol. 28). 1980. 57.50 (ISBN 0-444-41881-4). Elsevier.
--Modeling of Marine Systems. LC 74-77585. (Elsevier Oceanography Ser.: Vol. 10). 272p. 1975. 61.75 (ISBN 0-444-41232-8). Elsevier.
Nijdam, J., jt. ed. see Ministry of Agriculture & Fisheries- Netherlands.
Nijkamp, P. Theory & Application of Environmental Economics. (Studies in Regional Science & Urban Economics: Vol. 1). 1977. 47.00 (ISBN 0-7204-0763-X, North-Holland). Elsevier.
Nijkamp, Peter. Environmental Policy Analysis: Operational Methods & Models. LC 79-41778. 283p. 1980. 49.95 (ISBN 0-471-27763-0, Pub. by Wiley-Interscience). Wiley.
--Multidimensional Spatial Data & Decision Analysis. LC 79-40518. 322p. 1980. 63.95 (ISBN 0-471-27603-0, Pub. by Wiley-Interscience). Wiley.
Nijssen, G. M. Modelling Data Base Management Systems: Proceedings. Nijssen, G. M., ed. 1976. 56.00 (ISBN 0-7204-0459-2, North-Holland). Elsevier.
Nijssen, G. M., ed. see IFIP Working Conference on Modelling in Data Base Management Systems.
Nikhilananda, Swami. Hinduism: Its Meaning for the Liberation of the Spirit: a Survey of Hinduism. LC 58-6155. 189p. 5.50 (ISBN 0-911206-13-2). Ramakrishna.
Nikhilananda, Swami, tr. Upanishads, 4 Vols. LC 49-9558. with notes (set) 28.00 (ISBN 0-911206-14-0); 7.50 ea.; Vol. I, 333p. (ISBN 0-911206-15-9); Vol. II, 400p. (ISBN 0-911206-16-7); Vol. III, 408p. (ISBN 0-911206-17-5); Vol. IV, 422p. (ISBN 0-911206-18-3). Ramakrishna.
Nikiforov, G. A., jt. auth. see Ershov, V. V.
Nikitin, Nikolai. Night & Other Stories. Peppard, V., tr. from Russ. 1978. 11.50x (ISBN 0-931554-10-1); pap. 6.00 (ISBN 0-931554-11-X). Strathcona.
Nikkyo, Niwano. The Wholesome Family Life. Friedrich, Ralph, ed. Alexander, Joy, tr. from Japanese. Orig. Title: Ningen o Sodateru Kokoro. 180p. 1982. pap. 3.95 (ISBN 4-333-01026-8, Pub. by Kosei Publishing Co). C E Tuttle.
Niklas, Gerald R. & Stefanics, Charlotte. Ministry to the Hospitalized. pap. 3.95 o.p. (ISBN 0-8091-1899-8). Paulist Pr.
Niklaus, R., ed. see Rousseau, Jean J.
Nikly, Michelle. The Emperor's Plum Tree. Shub, Elizabeth, tr. (ps-3). 1982. 9.50 (ISBN 0-688-01243-4); PLB 8.59 (ISBN 0-688-01244-2). Morrow.
Nikolaev, N. S., et al. Analytical Chemistry of Fluorine. LC 72-4101. (Analytical Chemistry of the Elements Ser.). 222p. 1973. 54.95 o.p. (ISBN 0-470-63860-5). Halsted Pr.
Nikolaev, Vsevolov A. & Parry, Albert. The Loves of Catherine the Great. (Illus.). 288p. 1982. 17.95 (ISBN 0-698-11201-6, Coward). Putnam PubGroup.
Nikolai, Loren A. & Bazley, John D. Financial Accounting. 864p. 1982. text ed. 25.95x (ISBN 0-534-01349-X). Kent Pub Co.
Nikolai, Loren A., et al. Principles of Accounting. 1136p. 1982. 24.95x (ISBN 0-534-01049-0); Practice Set 1. write for info. (ISBN 0-534-01052-0); Practice Set 2. pap. text ed. write for info. (ISBN 0-534-01053-9); write for info. study guide (ISBN 0-534-01050-4); write for info. working papers. Kent Pub Co.
Nikolai, Lorin A., et al. The Measurement of Corporate Environmental Activity. 105p. pap. 12.95 (ISBN 0-86641-054-6, 7684). Natl Assn Accts.
Nikolaos, Van Dam. The Struggle for Power in Syria: Sectarianism, Regionalism & Tribalism in Politics 1961-1978. LC 78-11626. (Illus.). 1979. 26.00 (ISBN 0-312-76871-0). St Martin.
Nikolaou, Takis N. The Message of the Century. 1983. 8.95 (ISBN 0-533-05379-X). Vantage.
Nikolic, M., ed. Methods in Subnuclear Physics, 2 pts, Vol. 5. 1977. pap. 180.00x set o.p. (ISBN 0-677-15960-9). Gordon.
Nikolic, M., ed. see International School of Elementary Particle Physics, Herceg-Novi.
Nikolic, S. J., tr. see Tsypkin, Ya. Z.
Nikolowa, J., et al. Bulgarish-Deutsches Phraseologishes Worterbuch. 1088p. (Bulgarian & Ger.). 1977. 45.00 (ISBN 0-686-97391-7, M-9833). French & Eur.
Nikolskii, G. V. Theory of Fish Population Dynamics As the Biological Background for Rational Exploitation & Management of Fishery Resources. Jones, R., ed. Bradley, J. E., tr. from Rus. (Illus.). 323p. 1980. Repr. of 1969 ed. lib. bdg. 32.00x (ISBN 3-87429-171-5). Lubrecht & Cramer.
Nikol'skij, L. B., jt. auth. see Svejcer, A. D.
Nikolsky, G. V. The Ecology of Fishes. rev ed. Orig. Title: The Biology of Fishes. (Illus.). 1978. pap. 19.95 (ISBN 0-87666-505-9, H-999). TFH Pubns.
Nikolsky, S. M., jt. auth. see Bugrov, Y. S.
Niland, Deborah. ABC of Monsters. (Illus.). (gr. k-2). 1978. 4.95 (ISBN 0-07-046560-6, GB). McGraw.
Niland, John R., ed. The Production of Manpower Specialists: A Volume of Selected Papers. 248p. 1971. pap. 6.50 special hard bdg. (ISBN 0-87546-279-0); pap. 3.50 (ISBN 0-87546-045-3). ILR Pr.
Niles, Cornelia D., ed. see Smithsonian Institution, Washington, D. C.
Niles, J. J. & Williams, J.intro. by. Appalachian Photographs of Doris Ulmann. LC 70-137213. 1971. pap. 8.50 (ISBN 0-912330-00-7, Dist. by Inland Bk). Jargon Soc.
Niles, Jack M., et al. The Telecommunications-Transportation Tradeoff: Options for Tomorrow. LC 76-18107. 208p. Repr. of 1976 ed. text ed. 44.50 (ISBN 0-471-01507-5). Krieger.
Niles, John J. Singing Soldiers. LC 68-26595. 1968. Repr. of 1927 ed. 30.00x (ISBN 0-8103-3416-X). Gale.
Niles, John S., jt. auth. see Gruber, William H.
Niles, Kathryn B. Food Preparation Recipes. 1955. text ed. 27.50x o.p. (ISBN 0-471-63888-9). Wiley.
Niles, N. R., jt. auth. see Bacon, R. L.
Niles, Nathan O. Modern Technical Mathematics. (Illus.). 1978. 20.95 (ISBN 0-87909-509-1); solutions manual avail. (ISBN 0-87909-508-3). Reston.
--Plane Trigonometry. 3rd ed. LC 75-28337. 394p. 1976. text ed. 25.95 (ISBN 0-471-64025-5); solutions manual. 10.00 (ISBN 0-471-01716-7). Wiley.
Nilges, Richard G. Cycles. LC 80-12889. 1983. pap. 10.95 (ISBN 0-87949-182-5). Ashley Bks.
Nilles, Jack M. Exploring the World of the Personal Computer. (Illus.). 256p. 1982. text ed. 17.95 (ISBN 0-13-297580-7); pap. text ed. 12.95 (ISBN 0-13-297572-6). P-H.
Nilles, Jack M., et al. The Telecommunications--Transportation Tradeoff: Options for Tomorrow. LC 76-18107. 196p. 1976. 44.50 o.p. (ISBN 0-471-01507-5, Pub. by Wiley-Interscience). Wiley.
Nilsen, Alleen, jt. auth. see Nilsen, Don L.
Nilsen, Alleen P., jt. auth. see Donelson, Kenneth L.
Nilsen, Don L. & Nilsen, Alleen. Language Play: An Introduction to Linguistics. 1978. pap. text ed. 13.95 (ISBN 0-88377-102-0). Newbury Hse.
Nilsen, Thomas R. Essays on Rhetorical Criticism. LC 68-13156. 1968. text ed. 8.50x (ISBN 0-685-19690-9). Phila Bk Co.
Nilson, A. H. Design of Prestressed Concrete. 526p. 1978. 39.50 (ISBN 0-471-02034-6). Wiley.
Nilson, Arthur H., jt. auth. see Winter, George H.
Nilson, Bee. Bee's Blender Book. (Illus.). 1971. 11.50 o.p. (ISBN 0-7207-0446-4). Transatlantic.
Nilsson, B. H. Competing in Cross-Country Skiing. LC 74-82340. (Illus.). 160p. (gr. 10 up). 1974. 9.95 o.p. (ISBN 0-8069-4076-X); PLB 9.29 o.p. (ISBN 0-8069-4077-8); pap. 5.95 (ISBN 0-8069-8866-5). Sterling.
Nilsson, Birgit. Birgit Nilsson: My Memoirs in Pictures. Teal, Thomas, tr. from Swedish. (Quality Paperbacks Ser.). (Illus.). 127p. 1982. pap. 14.95 (ISBN 0-306-80180-9). Da Capo.
Nilsson, James W. Electric Circuits. 1983. pap. text ed. solutions manual avail. A-W.
Nilsson, Martin P. The Mycenaean Origin of Greek Mythology. enl ed. LC 70-181440. (Sather Classical Lectures: Vol. 8). 258p. 1973. 25.00x o.s.i. (ISBN 0-520-01951-2); pap. 3.65 o.p. (ISBN 0-520-02163-0, CAMPUS76). U of Cal Pr.
Nilsson, Nils J. Learning Machines: Foundations of Trainable Pattern-Classifying Systems. (Illus.). 1965. text ed. 24.50 o.p. (ISBN 0-07-046570-3, P&RB). McGraw.
--Problem-Solving Methods in Artificial Intelligence. 1971. text ed. 41.95 (ISBN 0-07-046573-8, C). McGraw.
Nilsson, S. Autonomic Nerve Function in the Vertebrates. (Zoophysiology Ser.: Vol. 13). (Illus.). 280p. 1983. 47.50 (ISBN 0-387-12124-2). Springer-Verlag.
Nilsson, S. T., ed. Atlas of Airborne Fungal Spores in Europe. (Illus.). 145p. 1983. 50.00 (ISBN 0-387-11900-0). Springer-Verlag.
Nilsson, W. D. & Hicks, Philip. Orientation to Professional Practice. (Illus.). 400p. 1980. text ed. 22.95 (ISBN 0-07-046571-1, C). McGraw.
Niman, Helga, tr. see Fierz, Markus.
Nimley, Anthony J. The Liberian Bureaucracy: An Analysis & Evaluation of the Environment, Structures & Functions. LC 79-63561. 1979. pap. text ed. 12.75 (ISBN 0-8191-0732-8). U Pr of Amer.
Nimmo, Dan. Political Communication & Public Opinion in America. LC 77-13143. (Illus.). 1978. text ed. 18.95x (ISBN 0-673-16269-9); pap. text ed. 14.50x (ISBN 0-673-16270-2). Scott F.
Nimmo, Dan & Savage, Robert L. Candidates & Their Images: Concepts, Methods & Findings. LC 75-21173. 288p. 1976. pap. text ed. 12.50x (ISBN 0-673-16256-7). Scott F.
Nims, Bonnie. Yo Quisiera Vivir En un Parque De Juegos; I Wish I Lived at the Playground. Orellana, Ramon S., tr. LC 79-186886. (Illus.). 64p. (Span. & Eng.). (ps-3). 1972. 4.95 (ISBN 0-87955-200-X); PLB 3.48 (ISBN 0-87955-800-8). O'Hara.
Nimura, G., ed. Clinical-Genetic Genesis of Diabetes Mellitus. (International Congress Ser.: No. 597). Date not set. price not set (ISBN 0-444-90285-6). Elsevier.
Nimzovich, Aron. Carlsbad International Chess Tournament of 1929. Marfia, Jim, tr. pap. 3.50 (ISBN 0-486-24115-7). Dover.
--Chess Praxis. Orig. Title: Praxis of My System. (Illus.). 1936. pap. 5.00 (ISBN 0-486-20296-8). Dover.
--My System. rev. ed. pap. 7.95 (ISBN 0-679-14025-5, Tartan). McKay.
Nin, Anais. Children of the Albatross. LC 82-70266. 111p. 1959. pap. 4.95 (ISBN 0-8040-0039-5). Swallow.
--Cities of the Interior, 5 vols. in 1. Incl. Ladders to Fire; Children of the Albatross; The Four-Chambered Heart; A Spy in the House of Love; Seduction of the Minotaur. LC 82-73633. (Illus.). xx, 589p. 1974. 19.95 (ISBN 0-8040-0665-2); pap. 12.95 (ISBN 0-8040-0666-0). Swallow.
--Collages. LC 82-70308. 122p. 1964. 3.95 (ISBN 0-8040-0045-X). Swallow.
--D. H. Lawrence: An Unprofessional Study. LC 82-70449. 110p. (Orig.). 1964. pap. 4.95x (ISBN 0-8040-0067-0). Swallow.
--Diary of Anais Nin, 7 vols. 1978. Set. pap. 22.50 o.p. (ISBN 0-15-626034-4, Harv). HarBraceJ.
--The Diary of Anais Nin: 1966-1974, Vol. VII. Stuhlmann, Gunther, ed. LC 66-12917. (Illus.). 368p. 1981. pap. 7.95 (ISBN 0-15-626028-X, Harv). HarBraceJ.
--The Early Diary of Anais Nin Vol. 2: Nineteen Twenty to Nineteen Twenty-Three. (Illus.). 576p. 1982. 19.95 (ISBN 0-15-127183-6). HarBraceJ.
--Four-Chambered Heart. LC 82-70753. 187p. 1959. pap. 5.95 (ISBN 0-8040-0121-9). Swallow.
--House of Incest. LC 82-70910. 72p. 1958. pap. 3.95 (ISBN 0-8040-0148-0). Swallow.
--Ladders to Fire. LC 82-71165. 152p. 1959. pap. 5.95 (ISBN 0-8040-0181-2). Swallow.
--Seduction of the Minotaur. LC 82-71876. 146p. (Orig.). 1961. pap. 5.95 (ISBN 0-8040-0268-1). Swallow.
--Spy in the House of Love. LC 82-71983. 140p. 1959. pap. 5.95 (ISBN 0-8040-0280-0). Swallow.
--Under a Glass Bell. LC 82-72155. 101p. 1948. pap. 4.25 (ISBN 0-8040-0302-5). Swallow.
--Waste of Timelessness: And Other Early Stories. LC 74-28648. 105p. 1980. 7.95 (ISBN 0-8027-0569-3, 82-87716). Ohio U Pr.
--Winter of Artifice. LC 82-72288. 175p. (Orig.). 1961. pap. 5.95 (ISBN 0-8040-0322-X). Swallow.
Nind, T. E. Principles of Oil Well Production. 2nd ed. (Illus.). 384p. 1981. 32.50 (ISBN 0-07-046576-2, P&RB). McGraw.
Nineham, D. E. Saint Mark. LC 77-81621. (Westminster Pelican Commentaries Ser.). 1978. 14.95 (ISBN 0-664-21344-8). Westminster.
Nineham, D. E., ed. see Thomas, J. Heywood.
Nineham, D. E., ed. see Towers, Bernard.
Nineham, Dennis see McDonald, Durstan R., et al.
Nineham, Gillian, ed. Adventure Holidays, Nineteen Eighty-Three. 208p. (Orig.). 1983. pap. 7.95 (ISBN 0-907638-15-5, Pub. by Vacation-Work England). Writers Digest.
Ninemeier, Jack D. Planning & Control for Food & Beverage Operations. Berman, Susan, ed. 1982. text ed. 26.95 (ISBN 0-86612-014-9). Educ Inst Am Hotel.
--Purchasing, Receiving & Storage: Operational Manual for Restaurants, Hotels & Institutions. 360p. 1983. 3 ring binder 64.95 (ISBN 0-8436-2261-X). CBI Pub.
Ninnemann, John L. The Immune Consequences of Thermal Injury. (Illus.). 250p. 1980. 42.00 o.p. (ISBN 0-683-06501-7). Williams & Wilkins.
Ninnemann, John L., ed. Traumatic Injury: Infection & Other Immunologic Sequelae. (Illus.). 1983. 39.00 (ISBN 0-8391-1780-9, 19119). Univ Park.
Ninth International Summer School of Brain Research. Perspectives in Brain Research: Proceedings. Corner, M. A. & Swaab, D. F., eds. (Progress in Brain Research Ser.: Vol. 45). 1976. 121.50 (ISBN 0-444-41457-6, North Holland). Elsevier.
Ninth Open Scientific Meeting, of the Hip Society. Hip Society: Proceedings. LC 73-7515. (Illus.). 303p. 1981. text ed. 59.50 (ISBN 0-8016-0029-4). Mosby.
Nioche, Brigitte. The Sensual Dresser. (Illus.). 176p. 1981. pap. 6.95 (ISBN 0-399-50581-4, Perige). Putnam Pub Group.
Nipon, Pearl. Dining In: Philadelphia. (Dining In Ser.). 200p. (Orig.). 1982. pap. 8.95 (ISBN 0-89716-039-8). Peanut Butter.
Nipp, Susan, jt. auth. see Beall, Pamela.
Nirkind, Bob, ed. see Kownslar, Allan O. & Smart, Terry L.
Nisargadatta Maharaj. I Am That: Conversations with Sri Nisargadatta Maharaj, 2 vols. 2nd ed. Frydman, Maurice, tr. 1981. Repr. of 1976 ed. Set. 18.00 o.p. (ISBN 0-85655-406-5, Pub. by Chetana India). Acorn NC.
Nisbet, H. B., ed. see Hegel, Georg W.
Nisbet, Ian C. & Karch, Nathan J. Chemical Hazards to Human Reproduction. LC 82-14441. (Illus.). 245p. 1983. 28.00 (ISBN 0-8155-0931-6). Noyes.
Nisbet, R. M. & Gurney, W. S. Modelling Fluctuating Populations. 379p. 1981. 53.50 (ISBN 0-471-28058-5, Pub. by Wiley-Interscience). Wiley.
Nisbet, Robert. The Social Philosophers. 1983. pap. 5.95 (ISBN 0-671-44048-9). WSP.
--Sociology As an Art Form. LC 76-9278. 1976. 16.95x (ISBN 0-19-502102-9). Oxford U Pr.
--Sociology As an Art Form. 1976. pap. 6.95 (ISBN 0-19-502103-7, GB472, GB). Oxford U Pr.
--Sociology of Emile Durkheim. 1973. 17.95 o.p. (ISBN 0-19-501733-1); pap. 7.95x (ISBN 0-19-501734-X). Oxford U Pr.
--Twilight of Authority. 272p. 1975. 18.95x (ISBN 0-19-501942-3). Oxford U Pr.
--Twilight of Authority. LC 75-7357. 1977. pap. 7.95 (ISBN 0-19-502177-0, 485, GB). Oxford U Pr.
Nisbet, Robert, ed. see Bryce, James.
Nisbet, Robert A. Quest for Community. 1962. pap. 8.95 (ISBN 0-19-500703-4, GB91, GB). Oxford U Pr.
--Sociological Tradition. LC 66-28636. 1967. o. s. 10.50x (ISBN 0-465-07953-9); pap. 6.95x (ISBN 0-465-07952-0). Basic.
--Tradition & Revolt: Essays, Historical, Sociological & Critical. 1968. text ed. 6.95x (ISBN 0-685-77217-9, 0-394-30421). Phila Bk Co.
Nisbet, Robert A., jt. ed. see Merton, Robert K.
Nisbet-Snyder Drama Collection, Northern Illinois University Libraries, jt. ed. see Dubois, William R.
Nisbett, Alec. The Use of Microphones. (Media Manual Ser.). 1983. pap. 10.95 (ISBN 0-240-51199-9). Focal Pr.
Nisbett, Richard & Ross, Lee. Human Inference: Strategies & Shortcomings in Social Judgement. (Century Psychology Ser.). (Illus.). 1980. text ed. 19.95 (ISBN 0-13-445130-9). P-H.
Nischik, Reingard M. Einstraengigkeit und Mehrstraengigkeit der Handlungsfuehrung in Literarischen Texten. (Tuebinger Beitraege zur Anglistik Ser.: No. 3). 213p. (Orig., Ger.). 1981. pap. 16.00 (ISBN 3-87808-545-1). Benjamins North Am.
Nisenson, Eric. Round about Midnight: A Potrait of Miles Davis. (Illus.). 256p. 1982. pap. 9.95 (ISBN 0-385-27232-4). Dial.
Nishida, Kitaro. Art & Morality. Dilworth, D. A. & Viglielmo, V. H., trs. from Japanese. 1973. 12.00x (ISBN 0-8248-0256-X, Eastwest Ctr). UH Pr.
Nishihara, K., jt. auth. see Taniuti, T.
Nishihara, Masashi. Japanese & Sukarno's Indonesia: Tokyo-Jakarta Relations, 1951-1966. LC 75-35765. (Monographs of the Center for Southeast Asian Studies, Kyoto University). (Illus.). 272p. 1976. text ed. 12.00x o.p. (ISBN 0-8248-0458-9, Eastwest Ctr); pap. text ed. 7.50x (ISBN 0-8248-0379-5, Eastwest Ctr). UH Pr.
Nishikawa, Kyotaro & Sano, Emily J. The Great Age of Japanese Buddhist Sculpture, AD 600-1300. LC 82-82805. 152p. (Orig.). 1982. 45.00 (ISBN 0-912804-07-6, Dist by U of Wash Pr); pap. 24.95 (ISBN 0-912804-08-4). Kimbell Art.
Nishimoto, Richard, jt. auth. see Thomas, Dorothy S.
Nishimura, Eshin, jt. auth. see Sato, Giei.

Nishimura, Hideo & Okamoto, Naomasa, eds. Sequential Atlas of Human Congenital Malformations: Observations of Embryos, Fetuses & Newborns. (Illus.). 344p. 1976. text ed. 69.50 o.p. (ISBN 0-8391-0937-7). Univ Park.

Nishimura, Shizuya. Decline of Inland Bills of Exchange in the London Money Market, 1855-1913. LC 70-134613. (Illus.). 1971. 44.50 (ISBN 0-521-08055-X). Cambridge U Pr.

Nishitani, Keiji. Religion & Nothingness. Bragt, Jan Van, tr. from Japanese. LC 81-4084. 366p. 1982. 28.50x (ISBN 0-520-04329-4). U of Cal Pr.

Nishizawa, J. Semiconductor Technologies, 1982. (Jarect Ser.: Vol. 1). 1982. 124.00 (ISBN 0-444-86409-1). Elsevier.

Niskanen, William, et al. Bureaucracy: Servant or Master? (Hobart Paperbacks). pap. 4.25 o.s.i. (ISBN 0-255-36051-7). Transatlantic.

Nisle, Virginia M. Coed Volleyball: The Now Game. (Illus.). 1977. pap. text ed. 6.95 (ISBN 0-8403-1795-6). Kendall-Hunt.

Nisonoff, Alfred. Introduction to Molecular Immunology. LC 82-3343. (Illus.). 208p. (Orig.). 1982. pap. text ed. 12.95x (ISBN 0-87893-594-0). Sinauer Assoc.

Niss, Bob. Faces of Maine. (Illus., Orig.). 1982. pap. 8.95 (ISBN 0-930096-20-7). G Gannett.

Nissan, Alfred H., ed. Future Technical Needs & Trends in the Paper Industry-I. 110p. 1973. 9.95 (ISBN 0-686-98524-9, 01-02-BS10). TAPPI.

Nisselson, Harold & Madow, William G., eds. Incomplete Data in Sample Surveys: Treatise, 2 vols. Date not set. Vol. 1. price not set (ISBN 0-12-363901-8); Vol. 2. price not set (ISBN 0-12-363902-6). Acad Pr.

Nissen, Henrik S., ed. Scandinavia During the Second World War. Munch-Petersen, Thomas, tr. from Scandinavian. LC 82-2779. (Nordic Ser.: Vol. 9). (Illus.). x, 398p. 1983. 39.50 (ISBN 0-8166-1110-6). U of Minn Pr.

Nissen, M., jt. auth. see Steimann, I.

Nissenbaum, A., ed. Hypersaline Brines & Evaporitic Environments. (Developments in Sedimentology Ser.: Vol. 28). 1980. 53.25 (ISBN 0-444-41238-7). Elsevier.

Nissenbaum, Stephen. Sex, Diet & Debility in Jacksonian America: Sylvester Graham & Health Reform. LC 79-8280. (Contributions in Medical History: No. 4). xvii, 198p. 1980. lib. bdg. 25.00 (ISBN 0-313-21415-8, NSY/). Greenwood.

Nissenbaum, Stephen, jt. ed. see Boyer, Paul.

Nissenson, R. A., jt. ed. see Draper, M. W.

Nissman, David M. & Hagen, Ed. The Prosecution Function. LC 81-47442. 224p. 1981. 23.95x (ISBN 0-669-04591-8). Lexington Bks.

Nissman, David M., et al. Beating the Insanity Defense: Denying the License to Kill. LC 80-8028. 192p. 1980. 21.95 (ISBN 0-669-03943-8). Lexington Bks.

Nister, Ernest. Animal Tales. (Illus.). 7.95 (ISBN 0-399-20801-1, Philomel). Putnam Pub Group.

--Little Tales from Long Ago. LC 79-87798. (Illus.). 1979. Boxed Set. 6.95 o.s.i. (ISBN 0-440-04968-7). Delacorte.

--Magic Windows: An Antique Revolving Picture Book. (Illus.). 14p. (ps up). 1981. 7.95 (ISBN 0-399-20773-2, Philomel). Putnam Pub Group.

Nister, Ernest & Bingham, Clifton. Revolving Pictures. LC 79-12438. (Illus.). (ps-4). 1979. 6.95 (ISBN 0-399-20802-X, Philomel). Putnam Pub Group.

Niswander, G. Donald, et al. A Panorama of Suicide: A Casebook of Psychological Autopsies. 168p. 1973. 10.25x o.p. (ISBN 0-398-02875-3). C C Thomas.

Niswander, Kenneth R. Obstetrics & Gynecology. 4th ed. (Medical Examination Review Book: Vol. 4). 1971. spiral bdg. 11.95 (ISBN 0-87488-104-8). Med Exam.

Nite, Gladys, jt. auth. see Henderson, Virginia.

Nite, Norm M. Rock on: The Illustrated Encyclopedia of Rock'n Roll: the Modern Years 1964 to the Present. LC 78-3312. (Illus.). 1978. 18.22i (ISBN 0-690-01196-2). T y Crowell.

Nite, Norm N. Rock on: The Illustrated Encyclopedia of Rock 'n Roll: the Solid Gold Years, Updated. LC 74-12247. (Illus.). 448p. 1982. 18.22i (ISBN 0-06-181642-6). T Y Crowell.

Nitobe, Inazo. Bushido. 5.50x (ISBN 0-685-00901-7). Wehman.

Nitronowa, I., et al. Polish-Russian, Russian-Polish Dictionary. 575p. (Pol. & Rus.). 1980. leatherette 4.95 (ISBN 0-686-97442-5, M-9102). French & Eur.

Nitsch, Susan L. How to Become a Freelance Secretary. Pasich, William, ed. (Illus.). 53p. 1983. pap. 3.95 (ISBN 0-943544-01-7). Secretarial Pubns.

Nitsche, Richard A. & Green, Adele. Situational Exercises in Cross-Cultural Awareness. (Elementary Education Ser.). 1977. pap. text ed. 10.95 (ISBN 0-675-08472-5). Merrill.

Nitscheke. Acoustic Behavior in the Rat. 204p. 1982. 24.95 (ISBN 0-03-061973-4). Praeger.

Nitti, John & Kasten, Lloyd. Complete Concordances & Texts of the Fourteenth-Century Aragonese Manuscripts of Juan Fernandez de Heredia. (Dialect Ser.: No. 2). 1982. 125.00 (ISBN 0-942260-16-3). Hispanic Seminary.

Nitti, John, jt. auth. see Kasten, Lloyd.

Nitti, John J. Two Hundred & One Portuguese Verbs Fully Conjugated in All the Tenses. LC 68-19525. 1974. text ed. 10.50 (ISBN 0-8120-6054-7); pap. text ed. 5.95 (ISBN 0-8120-0330-6). Barron.

Nitti, John J., ed. Juan Fernandez de Heredia's Aragonese Version of the Libro de Marco Polo. xxxvi, 122p. 1980. 12.00 (ISBN 0-942260-13-9). Hispanic Seminary.

Nittrouer, C. A., ed. Sedimentary Dynamics of Continential Shelves. (Developments in Sedementology Ser.: Vol. 32). 1981. 76.75 (ISBN 0-444-41962-4). Elsevier.

Nitty Gritty Productions, ed. Family Favorites. (Illus.). 192p. (Orig.). 1981. pap. 4.95 (ISBN 0-911954-61-9). Nitty Gritty.

--My Cookbook. (Illus.). 192p. (Orig.). 1981. pap. 4.95 (ISBN 0-911954-60-0). Nitty Gritty.

Nitze, Paul H., et al. Securing the Seas: The Soviet Naval Challenge & Western Alliance Options. (Illus.). 1979. lib. bdg. 33.50 (ISBN 0-89158-359-9); pap. text ed. 15.00 (ISBN 0-89158-360-2). Westview.

Nitzig, jt. auth. see Seligmann.

Nitzke, Susan A., jt. auth. see Way, Wendy L.

Nitzsche, Jane C. Tolkien's Art: A "Mythology for England". LC 78-32102. 1979. 22.50x (ISBN 0-312-80819-4). St Martin.

Niu, M. C. Role of RNA in Reproduction & Development. 1974. 74.50 (ISBN 0-444-10539-5, North-Holland). Elsevier.

Nivedita, Sr., jt. auth. see Coomaraswamy, Ananda K.

Niven, A. D. H. Lawrence: The Novels. LC 77-8475. (British Authors Ser.). 1978. 27.95 (ISBN 0-521-21744-X); pap. 9.95 (ISBN 0-521-29272-7). Cambridge U Pr.

Niven, Alexander C. Napoleon & Alexander I: A Study in Franco-Russian Relations, 1807-1812. LC 78-60628. 1978. pap. text ed. 6.75 (ISBN 0-8191-0561-9). U Pr of Amer.

Niven, David. Bring on the Empty Horses. LC 75-17646. (Illus.). 1975. 9.95 (ISBN 0-399-11542-0). Putnam Pub Group.

Niven, David, intro. by. Heavenly Bodies: The Complete Pirelli Calender Book. (Illus.). 304p. 1975. 19.95 (ISBN 0-517-52349-3); pap. 9.95 o.p. (ISBN 0-517-52350-7). Crown.

Niven, Ivan. The Mathematics of Choice. LC 65-17470. (New Mathematical Library: No. 15). 1975. pap. 8.75 (ISBN 0-88385-615-8). Math Assn.

Niven, Ivan & Zuckerman, Herbert S. An Introduction to the Theory of Numbers. 4th ed. LC 79-24869. 355p. 1980. text ed. 29.95x (ISBN 0-471-02851-7); solutions manual 7.00 (ISBN 0-471-06394-0). Wiley.

Niven, John. Gideon Welles. (Illus.). 1973. 35.00x (ISBN 0-19-501693-9). Oxford U Pr.

--Martin Van Buren: The Romantic Age of American Politics. (Illus.). 736p. 1983. 35.00 (ISBN 0-19-503238-1). Oxford U Pr.

Niven, John see Weaver, Glenn.

Niven, Larry & Pournelle, Jerry. Inferno. 1979. lib. bdg. 12.95 (ISBN 0-8398-2450-5, Gregg). G K Hall.

--The Mote in God's Eye. 576p. 1974. 10.95 o.p. (ISBN 0-671-21833-6). S&S.

Niven, Larry, ed. The Magic Goes Away. 1983. pap. 2.50 (ISBN 0-441-51547-9, Pub. by Ace Science Fiction). Ace Bks.

--The Magic May Return. (Illus.). 1983. pap. 2.95 (ISBN 0-441-51549-5, Pub. by Ace Science Fiction). Ace Bks.

Niven, Marian. The Doctor of Souls. (The Seekers Trilogy Ser.). 348p. 1977. 10.95 (ISBN 0-8164-0098-9). Seabury.

--The Inheritors. (Seekers Trilogy Ser.). 224p. 1977. 8.95 (ISBN 0-8164-0097-0); The Seekers Trilogy 3 Vol. Set. 27.00 (ISBN 0-8164-0514-X). Seabury.

Niven, Rex. Nigerian Kaleidoscope: Memoirs of a Colonial Servant. 1982. 25.00 (ISBN 0-208-02008-X, Archon Bks). Shoe String.

Niven, William & Ohman, Anka. Basic Accounting Procedures. 3rd ed. (Illus.). 1977. text ed. 24.95 (ISBN 0-13-056606-3); wkbk. 12.95 (ISBN 0-13-056622-5); practice set 11.95 (ISBN 0-13-056630-6). P-H.

Nivens, Beatryce. Black Woman's Career Guide. LC 80-1816. (Illus.). 456p. 1982. 24.95 (ISBN 0-385-15095-4, Anchor Pr); pap. 12.95 (ISBN 0-385-15096-2, Anch). Doubleday.

Nivola, Ruth. The Messy Rabbit. LC 78-6018. (Illus.). (ps-2). 1978. 5.95 (ISBN 0-394-83764-9); 5.99g o.p. (ISBN 0-394-93764-3). Pantheon.

Niwano, Nichiko. My Father My Teacher: A Spiritual Journey. Gage, Richard L., tr. from Jap. 143p. (Orig.). 1982. pap. 3.50 (ISBN 4-333-01095-0, Pub. by Kosei Pub Co Japan). C E Tuttle.

Niwano, Nikkyo. A Buddhist Approach to Peace. Nezu, Masuo, tr. from Japanese. (Illus.). 162p. 1977. 7.95 (ISBN 4-333-00308-3, Pub. by Kosei Publishing Co). C E Tuttle.

--A Guide to the Threefold Lotus Sutra. Friedrich, Ralph, ed. Langston, Eugene, tr. from Japanese. Orig. Title: Hokke-Sambu-Kyo-Nyumon. 168p. 1981. pap. 3.95 (ISBN 4-333-01025-X, Pub. by Kosei Publishing Co). C E Tuttle.

--Lifetime Beginner: An Autobiography. Gage, Richard L., tr. from Japanese. Orig. Title: Shoshin Issho & Niwano Nikkyo Jiden. (Illus.). 344p. 1978. 14.95 (Pub. by Kosei Publishing Co). C E Tuttle.

--The Meaningful Life. Friedrich, Ralph, ed. Gage, Richard L., tr. from Japanese. Orig. Title: Nigen No Ikigai. 128p. 1982. pap. 3.50 (ISBN 4-333-01027-6, Pub. by Kosei Publishing Co). C E Tuttle.

--The Richer Life. Gage, Richard L., tr. from Japanese. Orig. Title: Ningen Rashiku Irkiru. 138p. 1975. pap. 2.95 (ISBN 4-333-00351-2, Pub. by Kosei Publishing Co). C E Tuttle.

--Shakyamuni Buddha: A Narrative Biography. rev. ed. Davis, Rebecca M., ed. Miyazaki, Kojiro, tr. from Japanese. LC 80-154779. Orig. Title: Bukkyo No Inochi Hokeyo. (Illus.). 128p. 1980. pap. 3.50 (ISBN 4-333-01001-2, Pub. by Kosei Publishing Co). C E Tuttle.

Niwayama, Gen, jt. auth. see Resnick, Donald.

Nix, J. S., jt. auth. see Barnard, C. S.

Nix, William E., jt. auth. see Geisler, Norman L.

Nix, William E., jt. auth. see Zieg, Kermit C., Jr.

Nixdorf, Bert. Hikes & Bike Rides for the Delaware Valley & Southern New Jersey: With Emphasis on the Pine Barrens, No. 1. (Illus.). 140p. (Orig.). pap. 5.50 (ISBN 0-9610474-0-2). B Nixdorf.

Nixon. Surgical Conditions in Pediatrics. Apley, M. J., ed. (Operative Surgery Ser.). 1978. 68.95 o.p. (ISBN 0-407-00090-9). Butterworth.

Nixon, Bruce, ed. New Approaches to Management Development. 112p. 1981. text ed. 35.50x (ISBN 0-566-02290-7). Gower Pub Ltd.

Nixon, D. W. & Crowley, M., eds. Marine Affairs Journal, No. 6. (Marine Bulletin Ser.: No. 36). 112p. 1979. 1.00 o.p. (ISBN 0-686-36976-9, P835). URI Mas.

Nixon, D. W. & McKenzie, S. L., eds. Marine Affairs Journal, No. 5. (Marine Bulletin Ser.: No. 29). 152p. 1978. 1.00 (ISBN 0-686-36975-0, P732). URI Mas.

Nixon, D. W., jt. ed. see Ackenhusen-Johns, A.

Nixon, D. W., jt. ed. see Ross, N. W.

Nixon, George F., jt. auth. see Sachs, Bernard J.

Nixon, Hershell H. & Lowery, Joan. Oil & Gas: From Fossils to Fuel. LC 77-1671. (Let Me Read Bk.). (Illus.). 64p. (gr. 1-4). 1977. 5.95 o.p. (ISBN 0-15-257700-9, HJ). HarBraceJ.

Nixon, Howard L. The Small Group. LC 78-13207. (P-H Ser. in Sociology). (Illus.). 1979. ref. ed. 22.95 (ISBN 0-13-814244-0). P-H.

Nixon, Howard L., II. Sport & the American Dream. LC 82-83943. (Illus.). 240p. (Orig.). 1983. pap. text ed. 14.95 (ISBN 0-88011-112-7). Leisure Pr.

Nixon, Joan L. Alligator Under the Bed. LC 72-94263. (Illus.). 32p. (gr. k-4). 1974. 6.95 o.p. (ISBN 0-399-20423-7). Putnam Pub Group.

--Bigfoot Makes a Movie. LC 78-31106. (Illus.). (gr. 1-4). 1979. 7.95 (ISBN 0-399-20684-1). Putnam Pub Group.

--The Boy Who Could Find Anything. LC 77-15061. (gr. k-3). 1978. 5.95 (ISBN 0-15-210697-9, HJ); pap. 3.95 (ISBN 0-15-613748-8, VoyB). HarBraceJ.

--Danger in Dinosaur Valley. LC 77-6397. (See & Read Storybooks). (Illus.). (gr. 1-4). 1978. PLB 6.99 (ISBN 0-399-61109-6). Putnam Pub Group.

--Days of Fear. LC 81-12655. (Illus.). 48p. (gr. 1 up). 1983. 8.95 (ISBN 0-525-45106-4, 0869-260, Skinny Bk). Dutton.

--The Gift. LC 82-17994. (Illus.). 96p. (gr. 4-7). 1983. 8.95 (ISBN 0-02-768160-2). Macmillan.

--The Mysterious Prowler. new ed. LC 75-29314. (Let Me Read Ser.). (Illus.). 64p. (gr. 1-5). 1976. 4.95 (ISBN 0-15-256355-5, HJ); pap. 1.95 (ISBN 0-15-256356-3, VoyB). HarBraceJ.

--The Mysterious Red Tape Gang. (Illus.). 160p. (gr. 3-6). 1974. 6.95 o.p. (ISBN 0-399-20391-5). Putnam Pub Group.

--The Seance. (gr. 7 up). 1981. pap. 1.95 (ISBN 0-440-97937-4, LE). Dell.

--The Secret Box Mystery. new ed. (See & Read Storybooks). (Illus.). 48p. (gr. 1-4). 1974. PLB 6.99 o.p. (ISBN 0-399-60870-2). Putnam Pub Group.

Nixon, John E., ed. see Ulrich, Celeste.

Nixon, L. A. British Rail in Colour. (Illus.). 96p. 1983. 14.95 (ISBN 0-686-84472-6). Sci Bks Intl.

Nixon, Lucille M. & Tana, Tomoe, trs. Sounds from the Unknown: A Collection of Japanese-American Tanka. LC 64-16108. 133p. (Orig.). 1963. 3.75 o.p. (ISBN 0-8040-0278-9); pap. 4.95 (ISBN 0-8040-0279-7). Swallow.

Nixon, Mary & Taft, Ronald. Psychology in Australia. 1977. text ed. 30.00 (ISBN 0-08-021043-0); pap. text ed. 16.50 (ISBN 0-08-020561-5). Pergamon.

Nixon, Nicholas. Photographs by Nicholas Nixon, No. 31. Alinder, James, ed. LC 82-84610. (Illus.). 52p. (Orig.). 1983. pap. 16.00 (ISBN 0-933286-33-3). Friends Photography.

Nixon, P. H. People & the Sea, 3 Vols. 1977. 2.00 ea. (ISBN 0-686-36988-2). URI Mas.

Nixon, Richard. Leaders. LC 82-4820. (Illus.). 416p. 1982. pap. 17.50 (ISBN 0-446-51249-4). Warner Bks.

--The Real War. 352p. (Orig.). 1980. 12.50 o.p. (ISBN 0-446-51201-X); pap. 3.95 o.p. (ISBN 0-446-30535-9). Warner Bks.

Nixon, Richard M. Memoirs. LC 77-87793. (Illus.). 1978. 19.95 (ISBN 0-448-14374-7, G&D). Putnam Pub Group.

Nixon, S. W. & Oviatt, C. A. Ecology of Small Boat Marinas. (Technical Report Ser.: No. 5). 20p. 1973. 1.00 o.p. (ISBN 0-686-36980-7, P165). URI Mas.

Nixon, Sallie. Second Grace. LC 77-82292. 1977. 7.95 (ISBN 0-87716-081-3, Pub. by Moore Pub Co). F Apple.

Nixon, Ursula, tr. see Sabatier, Ernest.

Nixon, W. C., jt. ed. see Ahmed, H.

Niyogi, P. Integral Equation Method in Transonic Flow. (Lecture Notes in Physics: Vol. 157). 189p. 1982. pap. 11.80 (ISBN 0-387-11499-8). Springer-Verlag.

Nizami. Layla & Majnun. Gelpke, R., ed. & tr. from Persian. LC 78-58219. 1978. pap. 8.95 (ISBN 0-394-73627-3). Shambhala Pubns.

Nizami, K. A., ed. Medieval India: A Miscellany, Vol. 3. 1975. lib. bdg. 15.00 o.p. (ISBN 0-210-40581-3). Asia.

Nizamuddin, Mohammed. Contribution to the Marine Algae of Libya Dictyotales. (Bibliotheca Phycologica Ser.: No. 54). (Illus.). 120p. 1982. pap. text ed. 16.00x (ISBN 3-7682-1305-6). Lubrecht & Cramer.

Nizel, Abraham E. Nutrition in Preventive Dentistry: Science & Practice. LC 74-165283. (Illus.). 1972. 18.925 o.p. (ISBN 0-7216-6809-7). Saunders.

--Nutrition in Preventive Dentistry: Science & Practice. 2nd ed. (Illus.). 704p. 1980. text ed. 27.50 (ISBN 0-7216-6806-2). Saunders.

Nizer, Louis. New Courts of Industry: Self-Regulation Under the Motion Picture Code, Including an Analysis of the Code. LC 70-160243. (Moving Pictures Ser). 344p. 1971. Repr. of 1935 ed. lib. bdg. 19.95x (ISBN 0-89198-044-X). Ozer.

--Reflections Without Mirrors. 1979. pap. 2.95 o.p. (ISBN 0-425-04637-0). Berkley Pub.

Njoku, John E. Analyzing Nigerian-Americans under a New Economic Order. LC 80-5916. 128p. (Orig.). 1981. pap. text ed. 8.25 (ISBN 0-8191-1448-0). U Pr of Amer.

--A Dictionary of Igbo Names, Culture & Proverbs. LC 78-66416. 1978. pap. text ed. 7.00 (ISBN 0-8191-0134-6). U Pr of Amer.

Nkrumah, Kwame. Challenge of the Congo: A Case Study of Foreign Pressures in an Independent State. 1967. Repr. of 1967 ed. 7.50 o.p. (ISBN 0-7178-0026-1). Intl Pub Co.

--Neo-Colonialism: The Last Stage of Imperialism. 320p. 1981. 30.00x o.p. (ISBN 0-901787-33-7, Pub. by Panaf Bks England). State Mutual Bk.

--Revolutionary Path. 536p. 1981. 20.00x o.p. (ISBN 0-901787-22-1, Pub. by Panaf Bks England). State Mutual Bk.

Nnoli, Okwudiba, ed. Path to Nigerian Development. 272p. 1981. pap. 11.50 (ISBN 0-86232-021-6, Pub. by Zed Pr England). Lawrence Hill.

Noach, Barbara. Die Zurcher Verlobung. (Easy Reader, C. Ser.). 96p. (Ger.). 1981. pap. text ed. 3.95 (ISBN 0-88436-886-6, 45270). EMC.

Noack, Horst, ed. Medical Education & Primary Health Care. 351p. 1979. text ed. 34.50 o.p. (ISBN 0-8391-1475-3). Univ Park.

Noad, Frederick. Solo Guitar Playing. (Illus., Orig.). 1968. pap. 3.95 o.p. (ISBN 0-02-870720-6, Collier). Macmillan.

Noad, Frederick M. Playing the Guitar. 2nd ed. (Quick & Easy Ser.). (Illus.). 160p. 1972. pap. 2.95 o.p. (ISBN 0-02-871710-4, Collier). Macmillan.

--Solo Guitar Playing, Book II, Bk 2. LC 77-2529. (Illus.). 1978. pap. 9.95 (ISBN 0-02-871690-6). Schirmer Bks.

Noad, Susan S. Recipes for Science Fun. (Illus.). (gr. 3-5). 1979. PLB 7.90 s&l (ISBN 0-531-02873-9). Watts.

Noakes, Ann M., jt. ed. see Hranitz, John R.

Noakes, D., jt. ed. see Bergens, A.

Noakes, David, tr. see Hodeir, Andre.

Noakes, Jeremy. The Nazi Party in Lower Saxony 1921-1933. (Oxford Historical Monographs). (Illus.). 1971. 29.50x o.p. (ISBN 0-19-821839-7). Oxford U Pr.

Noall, Cyril. Cornish Seines & Seiners. 1981. 25.00x (ISBN 0-686-97147-7, Pub. by D B Barton England). State Mutual Bk.

Noar, Gertrud. Teaching the Disadvantaged. 33p. 0.50 o.p. (ISBN 0-686-74937-5). ADL.

Noar, Gertrude. Every Child a Winner: Individualized Instruction. LC 81-4900. 150p. Date not set. Repr. of 1972 ed. lib. bdg. 7.50 (ISBN 0-89874-340-0). Krieger.

--Individualized Instruction for the Mentally Retarded. 1974. pap. 4.95 (ISBN 0-914420-50-X). Exceptional Pr Inc.

Noback, Charles & Demarest, Robert. The Human Nervous System: Basic Principles of Neurobiology. 3rd ed. (Illus.). 1980. text ed. 30.00 (ISBN 0-07-046851-6, HP). McGraw.

Noback, Charles R. The Human Nervous System: Basic Principles of Neurobiology. 2nd ed. (Illus.). 1975. text ed. 24.00 o.p. (ISBN 0-07-046848-6, HP). McGraw.

Nobauer, Wilfried, jt. auth. see Lausch, Hans.

Nobay, A. R., jt. auth. see Johnson, Harry G.

Nobay, A. R., jt. ed. see Johnson, H. G.

Nobay, A. R., jt. ed. see Parkin, J. M.

Nobay, R., jt. ed. see Currie, D.

Nobel, Barry L. Linguistics for Bilinguals. 320p. 1981. pap. text ed. 13.95 (ISBN 0-88377-200-0). Newbury Hse.

Nobel Foundation. Nobel Lectures in Literature, 1901-1967. Frenz, Horst, ed. 1969. 68.00 (ISBN 0-444-40685-9). Elsevier.

--Nobel Lectures in Peace, 1901-1970, 3 vols. 1973. Vol. 1, 1901-1925. 68.00 (ISBN 0-444-40853-3); Vol. 2, 1926-1950. 68.00 (ISBN 0-444-41009-0); Vol. 3, 1951-1970. 68.00 (ISBN 0-444-41010-4). Elsevier.

--Nobel Lectures in Physics, 1901-1970, 4 vols. Incl. Vol. 1. 1901-1921. 1967 (ISBN 0-444-40416-3); Vol. 2. 1922-1941. 1965 (ISBN 0-444-40417-1); Vol. 3. 1942-1962. 1964 (ISBN 0-444-40418-X); Vol. 4. 1963-1970. 1973 (ISBN 0-444-40993-9). 68.00 ea. Elsevier.

Nobens, C. A. The Happy Baker. LC 79-88198. (Carolrhoda on My Own Bks.). (Illus.). (gr. k-3). 1979. PLB 6.95g (ISBN 0-87614-109-2). Carolrhoda Bks.

Nobile, Sylvia & Woodhill, Joan M. Vitamin C-The Mysterious Redox-System: A Trigger of Life? (Illus.). 185p. 1981. text ed. 29.00 (ISBN 0-85200-419-2, Pub. by MTP Pr England). Kluwer Boston.

Noble, A. Generation of Biological Patterns & Form: Some Physical, Mathmatical & Logical Aspects. LC 50-11295. (Illus.). 48p. 1981. pap. 23.00 (ISBN 0-08-027133-2). Pergamon.

Noble, Andrew, ed. Robert Louis Stevenson. (Critical Studies). 240p. 1983. text ed. 27.50x (ISBN 0-389-20369-6). B&N Imports.

Noble, Ashcroft. The Sonnets in England. 1978. Repr. of 1893 ed. lib. bdg. 20.00 (ISBN 0-8492-1953-1). R West.

Noble, Ben & Daniel, James W. Applied Linear Algebra. 2nd ed. (Illus.). 1977. ref. ed. 27.95 (ISBN 0-13-041343-7). P-H.

Noble, Ben, ed. Applications of Undergraduate Mathematics in Engineering. LC 66-27577. 364p. 1967. 19.00 (ISBN 0-88385-400-7). Math Assn.

Noble, D. & Blundell, T. L., eds. Progress in Biophysics & Molecular Biology, Vol. 38. (Illus.). 210p. 1982. 77.00 (ISBN 0-08-029683-1). Pergamon.

--Progress in Biophysics & Molecular Biology, Vol. 39. (Illus.). 230p. 1983. 78.00 (ISBN 0-08-030015-4). Pergamon.

Noble, David, ed. see DeVoney, Chris & Summe, Richard.

Noble, David, ed. see Henderson, Thomas.

Noble, David F. America by Design: Science, Technology, & the Rise of Corporate Capitalism. (Galaxy Books). (Orig.). 1979. pap. 9.95 (ISBN 0-19-502618-7, GB 588, GB). Oxford U Pr.

Noble, David F., ed. see DeVoney, Chris & Summe, Richard.

Noble, David W. The Progressive Mind. 1981. pap. 9.95x (ISBN 0-8087-1441-4). Burgess.

Noble, David W., jt. auth. see Carroll, Peter.

Noble, David W., et al. Twentieth Century Limited: A History of Recent America, 2 vols. LC 79-90364. 1980. Set. pap. 18.50 (ISBN 0-395-28742-1); Vol. I: America Through World War Two. pap. 11.50; Vol. II: World War Two to the Present. pap. 11.50 (ISBN 0-395-29272-7). HM.

Noble, Donald R. Ernest Hemingway: A Revaluation. 130p. 1983. price not set (ISBN 0-87875-249-8). Whitston Pub.

Noble, Elizabeth. Essential Exercises for the Childbearing Year: A Guide to Health & Comfort Before & After Your Baby Is Born. 1976. 12.95 o.p. (ISBN 0-395-24836-1); pap. 5.95 o.p. (ISBN 0-395-24835-3). HM.

--Having Twins: A Parents Guide to Pregnancy, Birth & Early Childhood. 1980. 14.95 o.s.i. (ISBN 0-395-29140-2); pap. 7.95 o.s.i. (ISBN 0-395-29128-3). HM.

Noble, H. Bates, jt. auth. see Bachman, David C.

Noble, Iris. Contemporary Women Scientists of America. LC 78-21292. (Illus.). 160p. (gr. 7 up). 1979. PLB 7.79 o.p. (ISBN 0-671-32920-0). Messner.

--Life on the Line: Alternative Approaches to Work. (A New Conservation Book). (Illus.). 96p. (gr. 6-8). 1977. PLB 5.49 o.p. (ISBN 0-698-30662-7, Coward). Putnam Pub Group.

--Nazi Hunter: Simon Wiesenthal. LC 79-15783. 160p. (gr. 7 up). 1979. PLB 7.29 o.p. (ISBN 0-671-32964-2). Messner.

Noble, J. K. Bowmar-Noble Handwriting, 9 bks. Incl. Bk. A (ISBN 0-8372-3752-1); Bk. B (ISBN 0-8372-3753-X); Bk. C (ISBN 0-8372-3754-8); Bk. D (ISBN 0-8372-3755-6); Bk. E (ISBN 0-8372-3756-4); Bk. F (ISBN 0-8372-3757-2); Bk. G (ISBN 0-8372-3758-0); Bk. H (ISBN 0-8372-3759-9); Bk. I (ISBN 0-8372-3760-2); tchr's. ed. Bks. E-I (ISBN 0-8372-3762-9); suppl. materials avail.. (80p. ea.). (gr. k-8). pap. 2.10 ea.; tchr's eds. 2.70 ea. Bowmar-Noble.

Noble, John. The Legendary Wichita Bill: A Retrospective Exhibition of Paintings. LC 82-61985. (Illus.). 44p. 1982. pap. 5.00 (ISBN 0-939324-06-7). Wichita Art Mus.

Noble, John H., jt. ed. see Robert Long Adams & Associates.

Noble, June & Noble, William. The Private Me. 275p. 1980. 9.95 o.s.i. (ISBN 0-440-07278-6). Delacorte.

--The Psychiatric Fix: Psychiatry's Alarming Power Over Our Lives. 1981. 13.95 o.s.i. (ISBN 0-440-07281-6). Delacorte.

Noble, Peter, ed. Screen International & TV Yearbook 1982-83. 37th ed. LC 76-646393. (Illus.). 696p. 1982. 57.50x (ISBN 0-900925-14-0). Intl Pubns Serv.

--Screen International Film & TV Yearbook, 1981-82. 36th ed. LC 76-646393. (Illus.). 700p. 1981. 57.50x o.p. (ISBN 0-900925-13-2). Intl Pubns Serv.

Noble, Peter, et al. The Medieval Alexander Legend & Romance Epic. 300p. 1981. lib. bdg. 40.00 (ISBN 0-527-62600-7). Kraus Intl.

Noble, R. D., jt. auth. see Pethoe, A.

Noble, Trinka H. Hansy's Mermaid. LC 82-45509. (Illus.). 32p. (ps-2). 1983. 10.95 (ISBN 0-8037-3605-3, 01063-320); lib. bdg. 10.89 (ISBN 0-8037-3606-1). Dial Bks Young.

Noble, Valerie, ed. A Librarians Guide to Personal Development. LC 81-17485. (Bibliography Ser.: No. 7). 1980. pap. 4.75 (ISBN 0-87111-272-8). SLA.

Noble, Virginia D., ed. see DeVoney, Chris & Summe, Richard.

Noble, W. C. Microbial Skin Disease. (Current Topics in Infection Ser.). 144p. 1983. text ed. 47.50 (ISBN 0-7131-4420-3). E Arnold.

Noble, William, jt. auth. see Noble, June.

Nobles, Melvin A. Using the Computer to Solve Petroleum Engineering Problems. (Illus.). 278p. 1974. 38.95x (ISBN 0-87201-886-5). Gulf Pub.

Noblitt, James S. Nouveau Point De Vue. 1978. text ed. 20.95x (ISBN 0-669-96545-6); instr's manual 1.95 (ISBN 0-669-00335-2); wkbk. 8.95 (ISBN 0-669-96552-9); Sets. reels 75.00 (ISBN 0-669-96560-X); cassettes 55.00 (ISBN 0-669-00250-X). Heath.

Nobrega, Jose N., jt. auth. see Gaito, J.

Nocedal, Raul, ed. see Institute of Judicial Investigations.

Nochlin, L. Impressionism & Post-Impressionism, 1874-1904: Sources in Documents. 1966. pap. 13.95 (ISBN 0-13-452003-3). P-H.

Nochlin, Linda. Realism. (Style & Civilization Ser). (Orig.). 1972. pap. 6.95 (ISBN 0-14-021305-8, Pelican). Penguin.

--Realism & Tradition in Art, Eighteen Forty-Eight - Nineteen Hundred: Sources & Documents. (Orig.). 1966. pap. 13.95 ref. ed. (ISBN 0-13-766584-9). P-H.

Nochlin, Linda, jt. ed. see Millon, Henry A.

Nock, O. S. The Gresley Pacifics: Part 1 1922-1935. (Locomotive Monographs). 1973. 14.95 o.p. (ISBN 0-7153-6336-0). David & Charles.

--The Gresley Pacifics, Part 2: 1935-1974. LC 74-157265. 1975. 14.95 o.p. (ISBN 0-7153-6718-8). David & Charles.

--History of the Great Western Railway Nineteen Twenty-Three to Nineteen Forty-Eight. 22.50x (ISBN 0-392-07907-0, SpS). Sportshelf.

--Locomotive of the North Eastern Railway. 18.50x (ISBN 0-392-08071-0, SpS). Sportshelf.

--Railways of Asia & the Far East. (Illus.). 1979. 24.00 o.s.i. (ISBN 0-7136-1855-8). Transatlantic.

--Railways of Western Europe. (Illus.). 1978. 20.00 o.s.i. (ISBN 0-7136-1686-5). Transatlantic.

--Railways Then & Now. (Illus.). 1975. 15.95 o.p. (ISBN 0-517-52036-2). Crown.

Nockolds, Harold. Lucas: The First Hundred Years, Vol. 1. 1976. 17.50 o.p. (ISBN 0-7153-7306-4). David & Charles.

Nockolds, S. T., et al. Petrology for Students. 8th ed. LC 76-52186. (Illus.). 1978. 69.50 (ISBN 0-521-21553-6); pap. 21.95x (ISBN 0-521-29184-4). Cambridge U Pr.

Nodier, Charles. History of the Secret Societies of the Army, & of the Military Conspiracies Which Had As Their Object the Destruction of the Government of Bonaparte. LC 78-14740. 1978. Repr. of 1815 ed. 32.00x (ISBN 0-8201-1318-2). Schol Facsimiles.

Noe, Joel M., jt. auth. see Rudolph, Ross.

Noe, Randolph. Kentucky Probate Methods with 1979 Supplement. 1976. with 1981 supplement 35.00 (ISBN 0-672-82532-5, Bobbs-Merrill Law); 1979 suppl 7.50 (ISBN 0-672-83978-4). Michie-Bobbs.

Noel, Bernard. Magritte. (Q L P Art Ser.). 1977. 7.95 (ISBN 0-517-53009-0). Crown.

Noel, Daniel, ed. Seeing Castaneda: Reactions to the "Don Juan" Writings of Carlos Castaneda. 1976. 7.95 o.p. (ISBN 0-399-11603-6). Putnam Pub Group.

Noel, Gerard. The Anatomy of the Catholic Church: Roman Catholicism in an Age of Revolution. LC 78-22344. 1980. 10.95 o.p. (ISBN 0-385-14311-7). Doubleday.

Noel, John V., Jr. Division Officer's Guide. 7th ed. LC 75-39931. 224p. 1976. 9.95x o.p. (ISBN 0-87021-160-9). Naval Inst Pr.

Noel, Thomas J. The City and the Saloon: Denver, 1858-1916. LC 81-16067. xviii, 172p. 1982. 16.50 (ISBN 0-8032-3306-X). U of Nebr Pr.

--Denver's Larimer Street: Main Stret, Skid Row & Urban Renaissance. LC 81-83395. 1981. pap. 14.95 d (ISBN 0-914248-02-2). Hist Denver.

Noel-Baker, Philip J. Arms Race: A Programme for World Disarmament. LC 60-10966. 603p. 1960. 17.50 (ISBN 0-379-00085-7). Oceana.

Noeldeke, Theodor. Sketches from Eastern History. LC 78-15077. (Studies in Islamic History: No. 12). 288p. Repr. of 1892 ed. lib. bdg. 22.50x (ISBN 0-87991-461-0). Porcupine Pr.

Noel Hume, Audrey. Archaeology & the Colonial Gardener. LC 73-80008. (Archaeological Ser: No. 7). (Illus.). 96p. (Orig.). 1974. pap. 2.95 (ISBN 0-87935-012-1). Williamsburg.

--Food. LC 78-4683. (Archaeological Ser.: No. 9). (Illus.). 1978. pap. 2.95 (ISBN 0-87935-045-8). Williamsburg.

Noel-Hume, Audrey, jt. auth. see Noel-Hume, Ivor.

Noel Hume, Ivor. Archaeology & Wetherburn's Tavern. LC 76-84024. (Archaeological Ser: No. 3). (Illus., Orig.). 1969. pap. 2.95 (ISBN 0-910412-08-1). Williamsburg.

--Digging for Carter's Grove. LC 73-88326. (Archaeological Ser: No. 8). (Illus., Orig.). 1974. pap. 2.95 (ISBN 0-87935-016-4). Williamsburg.

--Glass in Colonial Williamsburg's Archaeological Collections. LC 79-84022. (Archaeological Ser: No. 1). (Illus., Orig.). 1969. pap. 2.95 (ISBN 0-910412-06-5). Williamsburg.

Noel-Hume, Ivor. Guide to Artifacts of Colonial America. (Illus.). 1970. 20.00 (ISBN 0-394-42754-8). Knopf.

Noel Hume, Ivor. James Geddy & Sons: Colonial Craftsmen. LC 70-115038. (Archaeological Ser: No. 5). (Illus., Orig.). 1970. pap. 2.95 (ISBN 0-910412-10-3). Williamsburg.

--Pottery & Porcelain in Colonial Williamsburg's Archaeological Collections. LC 72-84023. (Archaeological Ser: No. 2). (Illus., Orig.). 1969. pap. 2.95 (ISBN 0-910412-07-3). Williamsburg.

--Wells of Williamsburg: Colonial Time Capsules. LC 71-109382. (Archaeological Ser.: No. 4). (Illus., Orig.). 1969. pap. 2.95 (ISBN 0-910412-09-X). Williamsburg.

--Williamsburg Cabinetmakers: The Archaeological Evidence. LC 74-115039. (Archaeological Ser: No. 6). (Illus., Orig.). 1971. pap. 2.95 (ISBN 0-910412-11-1). Williamsburg.

Noel-Hume, Ivor & Noel-Hume, Audrey. Tortoises. Foyles, Christina, ed. (Foyle's Handbks). (Illus.). 1973. 3.95 (ISBN 0-685-55798-7). Palmetto Pub.

Noelle-Neumann, Elisabeth, ed. The Germans: Public Opinions Polls, 1967-1980. rev. ed. LC 81-1075. (Illus.). 552p. 1981. lib. bdg. 39.95 (ISBN 0-313-22490-0, NEG). Greenwood.

Noer, David. How to Beat the Employment Game. LC 78-70333. 1979. pap. 4.95 (ISBN 0-913668-96-6). Ten Speed Pr.

Noer, David M. Multinational People Management: A Guide for Organizations & Employees. LC 75-13802. 164p. 1975. 17.50 (ISBN 0-87179-220-6). BNA.

Noer, H. Rolf. Navigator's Pocket Calculator Handbook. LC 82-74136. (Illus.). 176p. (Orig.). 1983. pap. 16.00 (ISBN 0-87033-295-3). Cornell Maritime.

Noer, Johny, jt. auth. see Facius, Johannes.

Noerlund, Niels H. Differenzenrechung. LC 56-1592. (Ger). 25.00 (ISBN 0-8284-0100-4). Chelsea Pub.

Noether, Gottfried E. Introduction to Statistics: A Nonparametric Approach. 2nd ed. LC 75-19532. (Illus.). 336p. 1976. text ed. 24.50 (ISBN 0-395-18578-5); solutions manual 1.75 (ISBN 0-395-18789-3). HM.

Noffke, Suzanne. Prayers of Catherine of Siena. LC 82-60746. 288p. 1983. pap. 9.95 (ISBN 0-8091-2508-0). Paulist Pr.

Noffke, Suzanne, ed. Catherine of Siena: The Dialogue. LC 79-56755. (Classics of Western Spirituality Ser.). 416p. 1980. 11.95 (ISBN 0-8091-0295-1); pap. 8.95 (ISBN 0-8091-2233-2). Paulist Pr.

Noffsinger, Anne-Russell L., jt. auth. see Auvenshine, Charles D.

Noffsinger, Ella M., jt. auth. see Allen, M. W.

Nofi, Albert A., ed. Napoleon at War: Selected Writings from F. Lorraine Petre. (Illus.). 300p. (gr. 6 up). 1983. 19.95 (ISBN 0-88254-805-0). Hippocrene Bks.

Nogar, Raymond J., jt. auth. see Deely, John N.

Nogent, Guibert De see De Nogent, Guibert.

Noggle, Fritz. Introductory Plant Physiology. (Illus.). 592p. 1976. ref. ed. 26.95 (ISBN 0-13-502187-1). P-H.

Noggle, G. Ray & Fritz, George J. Introductory Plant Physiology. 2nd ed. (Illus.). 704p. 1983. text ed. 30.95 (ISBN 0-13-502096-4). P-H.

Nogotov, E. F. Applications of Numerical Methods to Heat Transfer. (Illus.). 1978. pap. text ed. 38.00 (ISBN 0-07-046852-4, C). McGraw.

Nogradi, M., tr. see Szejtli, J.

Nohel, John S., ed. see Conference on Qualitative Theory of Nonlinear Differential & Integral Equations, Wisconsin.

Nohl, Louis. Life of Liszt. LC 70-140402. 1970. Repr. of 1889 ed. 34.00x (ISBN 0-8103-3610-3). Gale.

--Life of Mozart. Lalor, John J., tr. (Music Reprint Ser.). (Illus.). 236p. (Ger.). 1982. Repr. of 1880 ed. lib. bdg. 25.00 (ISBN 0-306-76171-8). Da Capo.

Noir, T. R., jt. auth. see Whyte, R. O.

Noiseux, Ronald A., jt. auth. see Glass, Robert L.

Nojiri, Kiyohiko see Osaragi, Jiro, pseud.

Nokes, David, ed. see Fielding, Henry.

Nolan, Albert. Jesus Before Christianity. LC 78-6708. 156p. (Orig.). 1978. pap. 6.95 (ISBN 0-88344-230-2). Orbis Bks.

Nolan, Charles J., Jr. Aaron Burr & the American Literary Imagination. LC 79-8291. (Contributions in American Studies: No. 45). 1980. lib. bdg. 25.00 (ISBN 0-313-21256-2, NAB/). Greenwood.

Nolan, Christopher. Dam-Burst of Dreams. LC 81-9669. xvi, 128p. 1982. 11.95 (ISBN 0-8214-0658-2, 82-84282). Ohio U Pr.

Nolan, Daniel J. Radiological Atlas of Gastrointestinal Disease. 256p. 1982. write for info. (ISBN 0-471-25917-9, Pub. by Wiley Med). Wiley.

Nolan, Dorothy M. Metric Cooking: One Hundred & Fifteen Easy Recipes. LC 79-24696. (Illus.). 88p. 1980. pap. text ed. 5.40 (ISBN 0-87006-293-X). Goodheart.

Nolan, Frederick. Brass Target. 1979. pap. 2.25 o.s.i. (04849-6). Jove Pubns.

Nolan, Jeannette. Getting to Know the Ohio River. (Getting to Know Ser.). (Illus.). (gr. 3-4). 1974. PLB 3.97 o.p. (ISBN 0-698-30497-7, Coward). Putnam Pub Group.

Nolan, Pat. Drastic Measures. 30p. 1981. pap. 2.00 (ISBN 0-916382-25-7). Telephone Bks.

--Fast Asleep. (Orig.). pap. 5.00 (ISBN 0-915990-06-7). Z Pr.

Nolan, Paul T. Folk Tale Plays Round the World. 1982. pap. 6.95 (ISBN 0-8238-0253-1). Plays.

--John Wallace Crawford. (United States Authors Ser.). 13.95 (ISBN 0-8057-7201-4, Twayne). G K Hall.

--Marc Connelly. (U. S. Authors Ser.: No. 149). 1969. lib. bdg. 10.95 o.p. (ISBN 0-8057-0152-4, Twayne). G K Hall.

Nolan, Peter & Bigliani, Raymond. Experiments in Physics. 1982. pap. text ed. 15.95x (ISBN 0-8087-1446-5). Burgess.

Nolan, Richard see Bernard, Dan, et al.

Nolan, Richard L. Management Accounting & Control of Data Processing. 190p. pap. 14.95 (ISBN 0-86641-045-7, 7793). Natl Assn Accts.

--Managing the Data Resource Function. 2nd ed. (Illus.). 465p. 1982. text ed. 26.95 (ISBN 0-314-63285-9). West Pub.

Nolan, Robert E., jt. auth. see Nance, Harold.

Nolan, Robert L. & Schwartz, Jerome L., eds. Rural & Appalachian Health. 272p. 1973. 16.75x o.p. (ISBN 0-398-02605-X). C C Thomas.

Nolan, T. A. Retire Easy: The Bluebook to Retirement Planning. 275p. (Orig.). 1982. pap. 9.00 o.p. (ISBN 0-686-98157-X). Natural Pr.

Nolan, Val, Jr. Ecology & Behavior of the Prairie Warbler Dendroica discolor. 595p. 1978. 29.50 (ISBN 0-943610-26-5). Am Ornithologists.

Nolan, William F. Carnival of Speed: True Adventures in Motor Racing. (Putnam Sports Shelf). 160p. (gr. 5-10). 1973. PLB 5.49 o.p. (ISBN 0-399-60807-9). Putnam Pub Group.

--Dashiell Hammett: A Life on the Edge. 1983. price not set. Congdon & Weed.

--Hammett: A Life at the Edge. (Illus.). 288p. 1983. 14.95 (ISBN 0-312-92281-7). Congdon & Weed.

--McQueen! (Illus.). 240p. Date not set. 14.95 (ISBN 0-498-02582-9). A S Barnes.

--McQueen! (Illus.). 240p. Date not set. cancelled. Oak Tree Pubns.

--Steve McQueen: Star on Wheels. (Putnam Sports Shelf). (gr. 5 up). 1972. PLB 6.29 o.p. (ISBN 0-399-60778-1). Putnam Pub Group.

Nolan, William F., ed. Ray Bradbury Companion: A Life & Career History, Photolog, & Comprehensive Checklist of Writings, with Facsimiles from Ray Bradbury's Unpublished & Uncollected Works in All Media. LC 74-10397. (A Bruccoli Clark Book). (Illus.). 339p. 1974. 66.00x (ISBN 0-8103-0930-0). Gale.

Noland, George B. General Biology. 11th ed. (Illus.). 674p. 1983. text ed. 24.95 (ISBN 0-8016-3704-X). Mosby.

Nolde, Boris E. Russia in the Economic War (Economic & Social History of the World War) 1928. 49.50x (ISBN 0-686-51304-5). Elliots Bks.

Nolde, John. Blossoms from the East. 490p. 1983. 25.00 (ISBN 0-915032-05-8); pap. 12.95 (ISBN 0-686-82371-0). Natl Poet Foun.

Nolen, William A. The Baby in the Bottle: A Review of the Edelin Case. LC 78-490. 1978. 8.95 o.p. (ISBN 0-698-10899-X, Coward). Putnam Pub Group.

--Spare Parts for the Human Body. (Illus.). (gr. 5-9). 1971. PLB 4.99 o.p. (ISBN 0-394-92338-3). Random.

--Surgeon Under the Knife. LC 75-45470. (Illus.). 256p. 1976. 8.95 (ISBN 0-698-10743-8, Coward). Putnam Pub Group.

--A Surgeon's Book of Hope. 288p. 1980. 11.95 (ISBN 0-698-11044-7, Coward). Putnam Pub Group.

Nolin, Bertil. Georg Brandes. (World Authors Ser.). 1976. lib. bdg. 15.95 (ISBN 0-8057-6232-9, Twayne). G K Hall.

Noll, Edward M. Dipole & Longwire Antennas. 1969. pap. 7.50 (ISBN 0-672-24006-8). Sams.

Noll, Kenneth E. & Miller, Terry L. Air Monitoring Survey Design. LC 76-22233. 1977. 49.95 (ISBN 0-250-40133-9). Ann Arbor Science.

Noll, Kenneth E. & Davis, Wayne T., eds. Power Generation: Air Pollution Monitoring & Control. LC 75-25330. (Illus.). 1976. 39.00 o.p. (ISBN 0-250-40118-5). Ann Arbor Science.

Noll, Mark A., compiled by. The Princeton Theology: An Anthology. 432p. (Orig.). 1983. pap. 14.95 (ISBN 0-8010-6737-5). Baker Bk.

Noll, Paul. Structured Programming for the COBOL Programmer. Taylor, Judy, ed. LC 77-85445. (Illus.). 239p. (Orig.). 1977. pap. text ed. 15.00 (ISBN 0-911625-03-8). M Murach & Assoc.

--The Structured Programming Cookbook. Taylor, Judy, ed. LC 77-88256. (Illus.). 221p. 1978. pap. text ed. 15.00 (ISBN 0-911625-04-6). M Murach & Assoc.

Noll, Paul & Murach, Mike. Structured ANS COBOL Advisor's Guide. 320p. (Orig.). 1980. 3 ring bdr. 100.00 (ISBN 0-911625-09-7). M Murach & Assoc.

Noll, Paul, jt. auth. see Murach, Mike.

Noll, R. B. & Ham, N. D. Flexrotor Wind Energy: Innovative System Assessment: Supplement. (Progress in Solar Energy Ser.). 120p. 1983. pap. text ed. 12.00 (ISBN 0-89553-118-6). Am Solar Energy.

Noll, Roger G. Reforming Regulation: An Evaluation of the Ash Council Proposals. LC 75-179326. (Studies in the Regulation of Economic Activity). 1971. pap. 5.95 (ISBN 0-8157-6107-4). Brookings.

Noll, Roger G., ed. Government & the Sports Business. LC 74-279. (Studies in the Regulation of Economic Activity). 1974. 21.95 (ISBN 0-8157-6106-6); pap. 9.95 (ISBN 0-8157-6105-8). Brookings.

Noll, Roger G., et al. Economic Aspects of Television Regulation. (Studies in the Regulation of Economic Activity). 342p. 1973. 18.95 (ISBN 0-8157-6108-2); pap. 7.95 (ISBN 0-8157-6109-0). Brookings.

Noll, Victor H., et al. Introduction to Educational Measurement. 4th ed. LC 78-69587. (Illus.). 1979. text ed. 25.95 (ISBN 0-395-26871-0); 1.75 (ISBN 0-395-26872-9). HM.

Nollau, Gunther. International Communism & World Revolution: History & Methods. LC 75-14702. 357p. 1975. Repr. of 1961 ed. lib. bdg. 20.75x (ISBN 0-8371-8232-8, NOIC). Greenwood.

Noller, Ruth B. Mentoring: A Voiced Scarf. 48p. (Orig.). 1982. pap. 2.95 (ISBN 0-943456-00-2). Bearly Ltd.

Nollet, Lois. Anthea. 1983. 11.95 (ISBN 0-8027-0735-1). Walker & Co.

Nollson, John. Washington in Pieces. LC 80-713. 264p. 1981. 11.95 o.p. (ISBN 0-385-15413-5). Doubleday.

Nolot, Pierre, jt. auth. see Teynac, Francoise.

Nolte, Ernst. Three Faces of Fascism. 1969. pap. 4.95 (ISBN 0-451-62044-5, ME2044, Ment). NAL.

Nolte, R. C., ed. see National Radio Institute Staff.

Nolte, Robert C. & Ruel, Oliver J. Residential Construction Wiring: Updated for 1981 Code. LC 78-16245. 1979. 20.95 (ISBN 0-574-21520-4, 13-4545). SRA.

Nolte-Heuritsch, Ilse. Aqua-Rhythmics: Exercises for the Swimmimg Pool. LC 78-57782. (Illus.). 1978. 8.95 (ISBN 0-8069-4130-8); lib. bdg. 10.99 (ISBN 0-8069-4131-6); pap. 4.95 o.p. (ISBN 0-8069-4132-4). Sterling.

Noltingk, B. Art of Research. 1965. 8.00 (ISBN 0-444-40424-4). Elsevier.

Noma, Elliot, jt. auth. see Baird, John C.

Nomachi, Kazuyoshi. Sahara. (Illus.). 1980. Repr. of 1977 ed. 14.95 o.p. (ISBN 0-448-14729-7, G&D). Putnam Pub Group.

--Sinai. (Illus.). 1981. 24.95 (ISBN 0-686-30967-7, An Everest House Book). Dodd.

Nomani, M. M. Meaning & Message of the Traditions, 3 vols. 8.50 ea. Kazi Pubns.

Nomizu, K., jt. auth. see Kobayashi, Shoshichi.

Nomura, Yoko. Pinch & Ouch: Acting Games. 43p. 1982. pap. text ed. 4.00 (ISBN 0-940264-14-5). Lingual Hse Pub.

--Pinch & Ouch: English Through Drama. (Illus.). 136p. 1982. pap. text ed. 5.50 (ISBN 0-940264-13-7); cassette tape avail. (ISBN 0-940264-15-3). Lingual Hse Pub.

Nonet, Philippe. Administrative Justice: Advocacy & Change in a Government Agency. LC 68-58126. 248p. 1969. 9.95x (ISBN 0-87154-627-2). Russell Sage.

Nonhebel, D. C. & Tedder, J. M. Radicals. LC 78-54721. (Cambridge Texts in Chemistry & Biochemistry Ser.). (Illus.). 1979. 42.50 (ISBN 0-521-22004-1); pap. 16.95x (ISBN 0-521-29332-4). Cambridge U Pr.

Nonis, V. Mushrooms & Toadstools: A Colour Field Guide. (Illus.). 230p. (gr. 6 up). 1983. 12.95 (ISBN 0-88254-755-0). Hippocrene Bks.

Nonken, Pamela & Hirsch, Roger. Allergy Cookbook & Food Buying Guide. 320p. (Orig.). 1982. pap. 6.95 (ISBN 0-446-37173-4). Warner Bks.

Nonte, George C. Handloading for Handgunners. 1978. pap. 7.95 o.s.i. (ISBN 0-695-81199-1). Follett.

--The Pistol Guide. 256p. 1980. pap. 7.95 o.s.i. (ISBN 0-695-81122-3). Follett.

--The Revolver Guide. (Illus.). 1978. pap. 8.95 o.s.i. (ISBN 0-695-81124-X). Follett.

Nonte, George C., Jr. Black Powder Guide. (Illus.). 256p. pap. 8.95 (ISBN 0-88317-069-8). Stoeger Pub Co.

--Pistol Guide. (Illus.). 280p. pap. 9.95 (ISBN 0-88317-095-7). Stoeger Pub Co.

Noojin, Ray O. Dermatology for Students. (Illus.). 320p. 1961. photocopy ed. spiral 32.00x (ISBN 0-398-01407-8). C C Thomas.

Noojin, Ray O., et al. Dermatology: A Practitioner's Guide. 1977. spiral bdg. 18.00 (ISBN 0-87488-720-8). Med Exam.

Noonan, Daniel. The Piedmont Flyer. (Illus.). 40p. (gr. 3-8). Date not set. 5.95 (ISBN 0-686-97486-7). Oak Tree Pubns. Postponed.

Noonan, Frederick, tr. see Badura-Skoda, Eva.

Noonan, John P. General & Special Ethics. 1947. text ed. 2.90 o.p. (ISBN 0-8294-0088-5). Loyola.

Noonan, John T., Jr. The Antelope: The Ordeal of the Recaptured Africans in the Administrations of James Monroe & John Quincy Adams. LC 76-24593. 1977. 22.50x (ISBN 0-520-03319-1). U of Cal Pr.

--Persons & Masks of the Law: Cardozo, Holmes, Jefferson & Wythe As Makers of the Masks. LC 75-30991. 1976. 10.00 (ISBN 0-374-23076-5); pap. 3.95 o.p. (ISBN 0-374-51396-1). FS&G.

Noonan, Karen A. Coping with Illness. 2nd ed. LC 80-67825. (Practical Nursing Ser.). (Illus.). 288p. 1981. pap. text ed. 9.80 (ISBN 0-8273-1438-8); instr's. guide 2.50 (ISBN 0-8273-1922-3). Delmar.

Noonan, Michael. Magwitch. 224p. 1983. 11.95 (ISBN 0-312-50426-8). St Martin.

Noonberg, A., jt. auth. see Olton, D.

Noone, Richard W. Ice: The Ultimate Disaster. LC 82-73265. (Illus.). 384p. 1982. 19.95 (ISBN 0-910285-00-4). Astraea Pub.

Noor, A. K. & Housner, J. M., eds. Advances & Trends in Structural & Solid Mechanics: Proceedings of the Symposium, Washington D.C., USA, 4-7 October 1982. 590p. 1983. 165.00 (ISBN 0-08-029990-3). Pergamon.

Noor, A. K. & McComb, H. G., eds. Computational Methods in Nonlinear Structural & Solid Mechanics: Papers Presented at the Symposium on Computational Methods in Nonlinear Structural & Solid Mechanics, 6-8 October 1980. LC 80-41608. 1980. 168.00 (ISBN 0-08-027299-1). Pergamon.

Noor, Abdun. Education & Basic Human Needs. (Working Paper: No. 450). iv, 64p. 1981. 5.00 (ISBN 0-686-36051-6, WP-0450). World Bank.

Noorani, A. G. Public Law in India. 363p. 1982. 50.00x (ISBN 0-686-94080-6, Pub. by Garlandfold England). State Mutual Bk.

Noorani, A. G., ed. Public Law in India. 340p. 1982. text ed. 40.00x (ISBN 0-7069-1390-6, Pub. by Vikas India). Advent NY.

Noorbergen, Rene. Ellen G. White: Prophet of Destiny. LC 70-190456. (Illus.). 256p. 1972. 6.95 (ISBN 0-87983-014-X); pap. 2.50 (ISBN 0-87983-077-8, Pivot Paperback). Keats.

--Invitation to a Holocaust: Nostradamus Forecasts World War III. LC 81-14571. (Illus.). 200p. 1982. 9.95 o.p. (ISBN 0-312-43517-7). St Martin.

--Secrets of the Lost Races. (Illus.). 1978. pap. 3.95 (ISBN 0-06-464025-6, BN 4025, BN). B&N NY.

Noordewier, Helen C. Uncle Josh Stories. (Voyager Ser.). 64p. 1983. pap. 7.95 (ISBN 0-8010-6738-3). Baker Bk.

Noordtzij, A. Leviticus. (Bible Student's Commentary Ser.). 288p. 1982. 13.95 (ISBN 0-310-45090-X). Zondervan.

Noorjaya. Dalam Pencarian. (Karyawan Malaysia). (Malay.). 1979. pap. text ed. 4.25x o.p. (ISBN 0-686-60346-X, 00351). Heinemann Ed.

Noorlander, H. Wooden Shoes, Their Makers & Their Wearers. (Illus.). 1982. pap. 10.00 (ISBN 9-06255-023-1). Heinman.

Noot, Jan Van Der. A Theatre for Voluptuous Worldlings. LC 43-1514. 1978. Repr. of 1569 ed. 35.00x (ISBN 0-8201-1179-1). Schol Facsimiles.

Nooten, B. A. Van see Emeneau, Murray B. & Van Nooten, B. A.

Nooten, Barend A. see Van Nooten, Barend A.

Nora, Simon & Minc, Alain. The Computerization of Society. 1980. 17.50x (ISBN 0-262-14031-4); pap. 4.95 (ISBN 0-262-64020-1). MIT Pr.

Norback & Co., Inc., jt. auth. see Thomas Cook, Inc.

Norback & Company, ed. Arco's Guide to Business & Commercial Schools. (Arco Occupational Guides Ser.). 144p. 1983. lib. bdg. 11.95 (ISBN 0-668-05525-1); pap. 6.95 (ISBN 0-668-05533-2). Arco.

--Arco's Guide to Hospital Schools. (Arco's Occupational Guides Ser.). 144p. 1983. lib. bdg. 11.95 (ISBN 0-668-05527-8); pap. 6.95 (ISBN 0-668-05534-0). Arco.

--Arco's Guide to Technical, Vocational & Trade Schools. (Arco Occupational Guides Ser.). 208p. 1983. lib. bdg. 11.95 (ISBN 0-668-05524-3); pap. 6.95 (ISBN 0-668-05532-4). Arco.

Norback, C. & Norback, P. The Must Words: The 6000 Most Important Words for a Successful & Profitable Vocabulary. 312p. 1983. pap. 5.95 (ISBN 0-07-047141-X, GB). McGraw.

Norback, C. T. U. S. Publicity Directory-Business & Finance 1981 Summer. 509p. 1981. 65.00 o.p. (ISBN 0-471-10552-X, Pub. by Wiley-Interscience). Wiley.

--U. S. Publicity Directory-Communications Services 1981 Summer. 385p. 1981. 65.00 o.p. (ISBN 0-471-10553-8, Pub. by Wiley-Interscience). Wiley.

--U. S. Publicity Directory-Magazines 1981 Summer. 495p. 1981. 65.00 o.p. (ISBN 0-471-10551-1, Pub. by Wiley-Interscience). Wiley.

--U. S. Publicity Directory-Newspapers 1981 Summer. 750p. 1981. 65.00 o.p. (ISBN 0-471-10550-3, Pub. by Wiley-Interscience). Wiley.

--U. S. Publicity Directory-Radio TV 1981 Summer. 540p. 1981. 65.00 o.p. (ISBN 0-471-10549-X, Pub. by Wiley-Interscience). Wiley.

Norback, Craig. The Complete Book of American Surveys. (Orig.). 1981. pap. 3.50 o.p. (ISBN 0-451-09571-5, E9571, Sig). NAL.

--International Consumer's Yellow Pages. LC 81-12560. 288p. 1982. 19.95x (ISBN 0-87196-582-8); pap. 9.95 (ISBN 0-87196-654-9). Facts on File.

Norback, Craig & Norback, Peter. New American Guide to Athletics, Sports, & Recreation. 1979. 19.95 o.p. (ISBN 0-453-00372-9, H372). NAL.

Norback, Craig, jt. auth. see Lachenbruch, David.

Norback, Craig T. U. S. Publicity Directory, 5 vols. Incl. Vol. 1. Radio-TV (ISBN 0-471-06372-X); Vol. 2. Newspapers (ISBN 0-471-06375-4); Vol. 3. Magazines (ISBN 0-471-06373-8); Vol. 4. Business & Finance (ISBN 0-471-06371-1); Vol. 5. Communication Services (ISBN 0-471-06374-6). 1980. 65.00 ea. o.p. (Pub. by Wiley-Interscience); Set. write for info. o.p. (ISBN 0-471-06369-X). Wiley.

Norback, Craig T., jt. auth. see Norback, Peter G.

Norback, Craig T., ed. Corporate Publications in Print. 271p. 1980. 38.00 (ISBN 0-07-047140-1). McGraw.

Norback, Craig T., jt. ed. see Asthma & Allergy Foundation of America.

Norback, Judith. Signet Book of World Winners. 1980. pap. 2.95 o.p. (ISBN 0-451-09585-5, E9585, Sig). NAL.

Norback, P., jt. auth. see Norback, C.

Norback, Peter, jt. auth. see Norback, Craig.

Norback, Peter G. & Norback, Craig T. The Dow Jones-Irwin Guide to Franchises. rev. ed. LC 81-70436. 271p. 1983. 17.50 (ISBN 0-87094-270-0); pap. 8.95 (ISBN 0-87094-412-6). Dow Jones-Irwin.

--Newsweek Travel Guide of the United States. LC 78-65503. 1979. 6.95 o.p. (ISBN 0-88225-267-4). Newsweek.

Norbeck, Craig. The Dog Food Book. 296p. 1981. pap. 3.50 o.p. (ISBN 0-451-11125-7, AE1125, Sig). NAL.

Norbeck, Edward, ed. see American Ethnological Society.

Norbeck, Oscar E. Book of Authentic Indian Life Crafts. rev. ed. LC 74-81910. (Illus.). 260p. 1974. 10.95 (ISBN 0-87874-012-0). Galloway.

Norbelle, Bernard, tr. see Hedin, Sven.

Norberg, Kenneth, jt. auth. see Brown, James W.

Norberg-Schulz, Christian. Intentions in Architecture. (Illus.). 1966. pap. 9.95 (ISBN 0-262-64002-3). MIT Pr.

--Late Baroque & Rococo Architecture. (History of World Architecture Ser.). (Illus.). 220p. 1983. pap. 17.50. Rizzoli Intl.

Norbert, Enrick & Mottley, Harry E., Jr. Manufacturing Analysis for Productivity & Quality-Cost Enhancement. 2nd ed. (Illus.). 150p. Repr. of 1968 ed. 22.95 (ISBN 0-8311-1146-1). Indus Pr.

Norbie, Don. Your New Life. pap. 0.10 o.p. (ISBN 0-937396-58-3). Walterick Pubs.

Norbom, Mary Ann. Richard Dawson & Family Feud. (Illus., Orig.). 1981. pap. 1.95 o.p. (ISBN 0-451-09773-4, J9773, Sig). NAL.

Norbu, Tsampa Yeshe. Rasa Tantra: Blood Marriage-The Sacred Initiation-A Marriage of the Faiths of East & West. (Illus.). 36p. 1980. pap. 6.95 (ISBN 0-9609802-2-9). Life Science.

Norbye, Jan. The Complete Handbook of Front Wheel Drive Cars. (Illus.). 1979. 12.95 (ISBN 0-686-86785-8); pap. 9.95 (ISBN 0-8306-2052-4, 2052). TAB Bks.

Norbye, Jan P. Maserati Bora & Merak. (AutoHistory Ser.). (Illus.). 136p. 1982. 14.95 (ISBN 0-85045-471-9, Pub. by Osprey England). Motorbooks Intl.

Norcliffe, G. B. Inferential Statistics for Geographers. (Illus.). 272p. 1983. text ed. 15.00x (ISBN 0-686-84478-5). Sheridan.

Norcliffe, Glen, ed. Planning African Development: The Kenya Experience. Pinfold, Tom. 224p. 1981. lib. bdg. 28.25 (ISBN 0-86531-161-7). Westview.

Norcross, Lisabet. Masquerade of Love. (Orig.). 1978. pap. 1.50 o.s.i. (ISBN 0-515-04464-4). Jove Pubns.

--My Lady Scapegrace. (Orig.). 1979. pap. 1.75 o.s.i. (ISBN 0-515-04495-4). Jove Pubns.

Nord, F. F. Advances in Enzymology. Incl. Vol. 14. 1953. 28.50 o.p. (ISBN 0-470-64647-0); Vol. 15. 1954. 36.50 o.p. (ISBN 0-470-64680-2); Vol. 23. 1961. 39.00 o.p. (ISBN 0-470-64944-5); Vol. 25. 1963. 38.50 o.p. (ISBN 0-470-64948-8). LC 41-9213 (Pub. by Wiley-Interscience). Wiley.

Nord, F. F., ed. Advances in Enzymology, Vol. 11. 479p. (Orig.). 1951. cloth bdg. 33.50 (ISBN 0-470-64548-2). Krieger.

--Advances in Enzymology, Vol. 14. LC 41-9213. 480p. (Orig.). 1953. cloth bdg. 33.00 (ISBN 0-470-64647-0). Krieger.

Nord, F. F, ed. Advances in Enzymology, Vol. 22. 572p. 1960. 34.00 o.p. (ISBN 0-686-74191-9). Krieger.

Nord, Walter R., jt. auth. see Meltzer, H.

Nord, Walter R., ed. Concepts & Controversy in Organizational Behavior. 2nd ed. LC 75-10424. 700p. 1976. pap. text ed. 17.95x (ISBN 0-673-16079-3). Scott F.

Nordberg, Robert B. Guidance: A Systematic Approach. 1970. text ed. 7.25x (ISBN 0-685-84265-7). Phila Bk Co.

Nordby, Vernon, jt. auth. see Hall, Calvin S.

Nordby, Vernon J., jt. auth. see Hall, Calvin S.

Norden, Carroll R. Deserts. LC 77-27090. (Read About Sciences Ser.). (Illus.). (gr. k-3). 1978. PLB 13.30 (ISBN 0-8393-0082-4). Raintree Pubs.

--The Jungle. LC 77-27590. (Read About Science Ser.). (Illus.). (gr. k-3). 1978. PLB 13.30 (ISBN 0-8393-0078-6). Raintree Pubs.

Norden, Heinz, ed. see Einstein, Albert.

Norden, Hugo. Form: The Silent Language. LC 66-27691. (Illus.). 1968. 10.00 (ISBN 0-8283-1131-5). Branden.

--Modulation Re-Defined. 6.00 (ISBN 0-8283-1406-3). Branden.

--Technique of Canon. 2nd ed. (Illus.). 1979. 15.00 o.p. (ISBN 0-8283-1028-9). Branden.

--The Technique of Canon. 1982. pap. 9.00 (ISBN 0-8283-1839-5). Branden.

Norden, Rudolf F. Christian & Social Concerns. 1967. pap. text ed. 1.25 (ISBN 0-570-03529-5, 14-1332, 14-1333). Concordia.

Norden, Rudolph F. Radiant Faith. Feucht, Oscar E., ed. 1966. pap. 1.35 study guide (ISBN 0-570-03527-9, 14-1330); pap. 1.75 leader's manual (ISBN 0-570-03528-7, 14-1331). Concordia.

Nordenskiold, Gustaf N. The Cliff Dwellers of the Mesa Verde, Southwestern Colorado: Their Pottery & Implements. Morgan, D. Lloyd, tr. LC 78-32107. (A Beautiful Rio Grande Classic Ser.). 1979. lib. bdg. 25.00 (ISBN 0-87380-127-X); pap. 15.00 o.p. (ISBN 0-87380-130-X). Rio Grande.

Nordenstreng, Kaarle. Mass Media Declaration of UNESCO. (Communications & Information Science Ser.). 250p. 1983. text ed. 32.00 (ISBN 0-89391-077-5). Ablex Pub.

Nordenstreng, Kaarle & Schiller, Herbert I., eds. National Sovereignty & International Communication: A Reader. LC 78-16046. (Communication & Information Science Ser.). 1979. 34.00 (ISBN 0-89391-008-2). Ablex Pub.

Nordentoft, Kresten. Kierkegaard's Psychology. Kirmmse, Bruce, tr. from Danish. (Psychological Ser.: Vol. 7). 1978. text ed. 20.00x o.p. (ISBN 0-391-00661-4); pap. 12.50x o.p. (ISBN 0-8207-0155-6). Duquesne.

Nordham, George W. George Washington & Money. LC 81-90327. (Illus.). 166p. (Orig.). 1982. lib. bdg. 21.25 (ISBN 0-8191-2393-5); pap. text ed. 9.75 (ISBN 0-8191-2394-3). U Pr of Amer.

--George Washington & the Law. (Illus.). 156p. 12.75 (ISBN 0-686-38396-6). Adams Pr.

Nordhaus, W. D. & Goldstein, R., eds. International Studies of the Demand for Energy: Selected Papers Presented at a Conference Held by the Institute for Applied Systems Analysis, Schloss Laxenburg, Austria. (Contributions to Economic Analysis: Vol. 120). 1978. 47.00 (ISBN 0-444-85079-1, North-Holland). Elsevier.

Nordhauser, Norman. The Quest for Stability. Freidel, Frank, ed. LC 78-62510. (Modern American History Ser.: Vol. 15). 1979. lib. bdg. 24.00 o.s.i. (ISBN 0-8240-3638-7). Garland Pub.

Nordheimer, Stuart. Beginner's Photography Simplified. 2nd ed. (Illus.). 1978. pap. 4.95 o.p. (ISBN 0-8174-2142-4, Amphoto); Spanish Ed. pap. 6.95 o.p. (ISBN 0-8174-0319-1). Watson-Guptill.

--Beginner's Photography Simplified. (Illus.). 96p. 1975. pap. 4.95 o.p. (ISBN 0-8174-0182-2, Amphoto). Watson-Guptill.

Nordhoff, Charles & Hall, James N. The Bounty Trilogy. (Illus., One volume containing Mutiny On The Bounty, Men Against The Sea & Pitcairns Island). (gr. 9 up). 1982. 24.95 (ISBN 0-316-61161-1, Pub. by Atlantic Monthly Pr). Little.

Nordhoff, James. Eastwind - Westwind. LC 79-21116. 1980. 11.95 o.p. (ISBN 0-688-03590-6). Morrow.

Nordhoff, Nancy S. & Larsen, Jo. Fundamental Practices for Success with Volunteer Boards of Non-Profit Organizations, 4 vols, Vol. I. LC 82-83808. (Fundamental Practices Ser.). 140p. 1982. pap. 11.95 (ISBN 0-9609972-0-2). Fun Prax.

Nordhoff, William A. Machine Shop Estimating. 2nd ed. (Illus.). 1960. 31.00 o.p. (ISBN 0-07-047159-2, P&RB). McGraw.

Nordholt, E. H. Design of High Performance Negative-Feedback Amplifiers. (Studies in Electric & Electronic Engineering: Vol. 7). Date not set. 57.50 (ISBN 0-444-42140-8). Elsevier.

Nordin, Virginia D., jt. auth. see Edwards, Harry T.

Nordland, Rod. Names & Numbers: A Journalist's Guide to the Most Needed Information Sources & Contacts. LC 78-18903. 560p. 1978. 45.95x (ISBN 0-471-03994-2, Pub. by Wiley-Interscience). Wiley.

Nordlinger, Eric. Soldiers in Politics: Military Coups & Government. (Illus.). 1977. pap. text ed. 12.95 (ISBN 0-13-822163-4). P-H.

Nordlinger, Eric A. On the Autonomy of the Democratic State. (Center for International Affairs Ser.). 247p. 1982. pap. text ed. 7.95x (ISBN 0-674-63409-8). Harvard U Pr.

Nordlund, Donald A., et al, eds. Semiochemicals: Their Role in Pest Control. 306p. 1981. 40.50x (ISBN 0-471-05803-3, Pub. by Wiley-Interscience). Wiley.

Nordmann, Jean J., jt. auth. see Maddrell, Simon H.

Nordoff & Robbins. Music Therapy in Special Education. 1983. 13.50 (ISBN 0-918812-22-4). Magnamusic.

Nordoff, Paul & Robbins, Clive. Creative Music Therapy: Individualized Treatment for the Handicapped Child. LC 75-6898. (John Day Bk.). 1977. 30.00i (ISBN 0-381-97100-7). T Y Crowell.

--Music Therapy in Special Education. 256p. 1980. 21.00x (ISBN 0-7121-1371-1, Pub. by Macdonald & Evans). State Mutual Bk.
--Therapy in Music for Handicapped Children. 1971. text ed. 4.25x o.p. (ISBN 0-575-00755-9). Humanities.
Nordoff, Paul & Robbins, Clive E. Music Therapy in Special Education. LC 70-89312. (John Day Bk.). 1971. 10.95i (ISBN 0-381-97031-0, A52100). T Y Crowell.
Nordon, Haskell. The Education of a Polish Jew: A Physician's War Memoirs. 314p. 1983. 11.95 (ISBN 0-910563-00-4). D Grossman Pr.
Nordquist, Gunilla, jt. auth. see Turner, Barry.
Nordquist, Myron, jt. ed. see Churchill, Robin.
Nordraa, Olaf. Red Harvest. Friis, Erick J., tr. (International Studies & Translations Program). 1978. 14.95 (ISBN 0-8057-8162-5, Twayne). G K Hall.
Nordstedt, C. F. Index Desmidiacearum citationibus locupletissimus atque bibliographia & Suppl. 1978. lib. bdg. 80.00 (ISBN 3-7682-1171-1). Lubrecht & Cramer.
Nordstrom, Richard D. Introductin to Selling: An Experiential Approach to Skill Development. 350p. 1981. pap. text ed. 14.95 (ISBN 0-02-388200-X). Macmillan.
Nordtvedt, Matilda. All Things, Even Frisky. 96p. (gr. 2-4). 1973. pap. 2.95 o.p. (ISBN 0-8024-1069-3). Moody.
Nordtvedt, Matilda & Steinkuehler, Pearl. Showers of Blessing. LC 19-764. 96p. (Orig.). 1980. pap. 3.95 (ISBN 0-8024-0434-0). Moody.
--Something Borrowed, Something Blue. 96p. 1981. pap. 3.95 (ISBN 0-8024-0926-1). Moody.
--Something Old, Something New. LC 81-3770. (Orig.). 1981. pap. 3.95 (ISBN 0-8024-0927-X). Moody.
--Women's Programs for Every Season. LC 82-6391. 96p. 1982. pap. 3.95 (ISBN 0-8024-6903-5). Moody.
Nordvedt, Matilda & Steinkueler, Pearl. Ideas for Junior High Leaders. (Orig.). 1983. pap. 4.95 (ISBN 0-8024-0187-2). Moody.
Nordyke, Eleanor C. The Peopling of Hawaii. LC 77-8842. (Illus.). 1977. pap. 4.95 (ISBN 0-8248-0511-9, Eastwest Ctr). UH Pr.
Nore, Peter & Turner, Terisa, eds. Oil & Class Struggle. 324p. (Orig.). 1980. 35.00 (ISBN 0-905762-38-X, Pub. by Zed Pr England); pap. 8.95 (ISBN 0-905762-27-4, Pub. by Zed Pr England). Lawrence Hill.
Noreen, Robert G. Saul Bellow. 1978. lib. bdg. 19.50 (ISBN 0-8161-7990-5, Hall Reference). G K Hall.
Norem-Hebeisen, Ardyth A., ed. see Lynch, Mervin D., et al.
Noren, Catherine. The Way We Looked: The Meaning & Magic of Family Photographs. (Illus.). 128p. (gr. 7 up). 1983. 10.25 (ISBN 0-525-66738-5). Lodestar Bks.
Noren, Catherine H. The Camera of My Family. 1976. 20.00 o.p. (ISBN 0-394-48838-5). Knopf.
Norenberg, W. & Weidenmuller, H. A. Introduction to the Theory of Heavy-Ion Collisions. (Lecture Notes in Physics: Vol. 51). (Illus.). 1976. soft cover 21.00 (ISBN 0-387-09753-8). Springer-Verlag.
Noreng, Oystein. The Oil Industry & Government Strategy in the North Sea. 268p. 1980. 35.00x o.p. (ISBN 0-85664-850-7, Pub. by Croom Helm Ltd England). Biblio Dist.
--The Oil Industry & Government Strategy in the North Sea. LC 80-81590. 1980. 27.50x (ISBN 0-918714-02-8). Intl Res Ctr Energy.
--Oil Politics in the Nineteen-Eighties: Patterns of International Cooperation. (Illus.). 1978. text ed. 9.95x o.p. (ISBN 0-07-047185-1, P&RB); pap. 5.95x (ISBN 0-07-047186-X). McGraw.
Norfolk, Donald. The Habits of Health: The Prudent Person's Guide to Well-Being. 224p. 1977. 9.95 o.p. (ISBN 0-312-35630-7). St Martin.
Norgren, Ralph, jt. auth. see Katsuki, Yasuji.
Norgrove, Ross. Blueprint for Paradise: How to Live on a Tropical Island. LC 82-48430. (Illus.). 256p. 1983. 20.00 (ISBN 0-87742-154-4). Intl Marine.
--Cruising Rigs & Rigging. LC 81-82489. (Illus.). 272p. 1982. 27.50 (ISBN 0-87742-145-5). Intl Marine.
Norhausberber, Rudolph C. The Historical-Philosophical Significance of Comte, Darwin, Marx & Freud. (Human Development Library Book). (Illus.). 139p. 1983. 59.85 (ISBN 0-89266-392-8). Am Classical Coll Pr.
Noriaki Itoh, jt. ed. see Brown, F. C.
Noricks, Michael. Spanish for Medical Personnel: A Short Course. 64p. (Orig.). 1983. pap. price not set (ISBN 0-910669-00-7); write for info. 2 cassettes (ISBN 0-910669-01-5). Pacific Lang.
Norimatsu, Patricia. Facemetrics: Facial Exercises for a Fast Facelift. LC 81-83602. (Illus.). 42p. 1982. cancelled 16.00 (ISBN 0-9606890-0-1). Morris Pub.
--Woman-from Head to Toes. LC 82-90058. 150p. 1982. pap. 9.95 (ISBN 0-9606890-2-8). Morris Pub.
Norins, Hanley. The Compleat Copywriter: A Comprhensive Guide to All Phases of Advertising Communication. 2nd ed. LC 79-27107. 336p. 1980. Repr. lib. bdg. 19.95 (ISBN 0-89874-117-3). Krieger.
Noris, M., jt. auth. see Kibler, L.
Norkin, Cynthia & Levangie, Pamela. Joint Structure & Function: A Comprehensive Analysis. LC 82-7368. (Illus.). 462p. 1982. text ed. 24.95 (ISBN 0-8036-6576-8). Davis Co.
Norkin, Israel. Mysterious Signs in the Sky. LC 81-80165. (Illus.). 96p. 1983. text ed. 10.95 (ISBN 0-86666-022-4). GWP.
Norlen, Urban. Simulation Model Building: A Statistical Approach to Modelling in the Social Sciences with the Simulation Methods. LC 75-4935. 1976. pap. 27.95x o.p. (ISBN 0-470-65090-7). Halsted Pr.
Norman. Serbo-Croatian Phrase Book. 1979. pap. 3.50 (ISBN 0-14-003268-1). Penguin.
Norman, A. G., ed. Advances in Agronomy, 24 vols. Incl. Vol. 1. 1949 (ISBN 0-12-000701-0); Vol. 2. 1950 (ISBN 0-12-000702-9); Vol. 3. 1951 (ISBN 0-12-000703-7); Vol. 4. 1952 (ISBN 0-12-000704-5); Vol. 5. 1953 (ISBN 0-12-000705-3); Vol. 6. 1954 (ISBN 0-12-000706-1); Vol. 7. 1955 (ISBN 0-12-000707-X); Vol. 8. 1956 (ISBN 0-12-000708-8); Vol. 9. 1957 (ISBN 0-12-000709-6); Vol. 10. 1959 (ISBN 0-12-000710-X); Vol. 11. 1959 (ISBN 0-12-000711-8); Vol. 12. 1960 (ISBN 0-12-000712-6); Vol. 13. 1961 (ISBN 0-12-000713-4); Vol. 14. 1962 (ISBN 0-12-000714-2); Vol. 15. 1963 (ISBN 0-12-000715-0); Vol. 16. 1964 (ISBN 0-12-000716-9); Vol. 17. 1965 (ISBN 0-12-000717-7); Vol. 18. 1966 (ISBN 0-12-000718-5); Vol. 19. 1967 (ISBN 0-12-000719-3); Vol. 20 o.s. 1968 (ISBN 0-12-000720-7); Vol. 21. Brady, N. C., ed. 1969 (ISBN 0-12-000721-5); Vol. 22. 1970 (ISBN 0-12-000722-3); Vol. 23. 1971 (ISBN 0-12-000723-1); Vol. 24. 1972 (ISBN 0-12-000724-X). Vols. 1-24. 55.00 ea. Acad Pr.
Norman, Adrian. Electronic Document Delivery. LC 81-20774. (Communications Library). 230p. 1981. text ed. 45.00 (ISBN 0-86729-011-0). Knowledge Indus.
--Electronic Document Delivery: The Artemis Concept. 226p. 1982. 45.00 (ISBN 0-686-82554-3). Knowledge Indus.
Norman, Adrian, jt. auth. see Martin, James.
Norman, Adrian R., jt. auth. see Martin, James T.
Norman, David W. & Simmons, Emmy B. Farming Systems in the Nigerian Savanna: Research Strategies for Development. (Replica Edition). 235p. 1982. lib. bdg. 22.00 (ISBN 0-86531-925-1). Westview.
Norman, Diana. Fitzempress' Law. 294p. 1980. 11.95 o.p. (ISBN 0-312-29419-0). St Martin.
Norman, Donald A. Memory & Attention: An Introduction to Human Information Processing. 2nd ed. LC 76-236. 262p. 1976. pap. text ed. 14.50 (ISBN 0-471-65137-0). Wiley.
Norman, Donald A., jt. auth. see Lindsay, Peter H.
Norman, Donald A., ed. Perspectives on Cognitive Science. 320p. 1981. 24.95 (ISBN 0-89391-071-6). Ablex Pub.
--Perspectives on Cognitive Science. LC 80-21343. (Illus.). 320p. 1981. 19.95 (ISBN 0-89859-106-6). L Erlbaum Assocs.
Norman, E. R. Christianity & the World Order. 1979. 9.95 o.p. (ISBN 0-19-215510-5); pap. 5.95x (ISBN 0-19-283019-8). Oxford U Pr.
Norman, E. R. & St Joseph, J. K. Early Development of Irish Society: The Evidence of Aerial Photography. LC 71-85734. (Air Surveys Ser.: No. 3). (Illus.). 1969. 37.50 (ISBN 0-521-07471-1). Cambridge U Pr.
Norman, Elaine & Mancuso, Arlene, eds. Women's Issues & Social Work Practice. LC 79-91106. 276p. 1980. pap. text ed. 9.95 (ISBN 0-87581-249-X). Peacock Pubs.
Norman, Ernest L. Tempus Interludium, Vol. 2. Norman, Ruth E., ed. 251p. 1982. 8.95 (ISBN 0-932642-48-9). Unarius.
--Voice of Hermes. (Pulse of Creation Ser). (Illus.). 1959. 7.95 o.p. (ISBN 0-932642-02-0). Unarius.
Norman, F. Theses in Germanic Studies, 1903-1961. 46p. 1962. 25.00x (ISBN 0-85457-015-2, Pub. by Inst Germanic Stud England). State Mutual Bk.
Norman, F. & Hatto, A. T. Three Essays on the 'Hildebranslied' 83p. 1973. 35.00x (ISBN 0-85457-052-7, Pub. by Inst Germanic Stud England). State Mutual Bk.
Norman, F., jt. auth. see Knight, K. G.
Norman, Geoffrey. Midnight Water: A Novel. 288p. 1983. 13.95 (ISBN 0-525-15585-6, 01354-410). Dutton. Postponed.
Norman, Geraldine. Nineteenth Century Painters & Painting: A Dictionary. LC 76-24594. (Illus.). 1978. 67.50x (ISBN 0-520-03328-0). U of Cal Pr.
Norman, Gertrude. Johnny Appleseed. (Beginning Biographies Ser.). (gr. k-3). 1960. PLB 5.99 o.p. (ISBN 0-399-60323-9). Putnam Pub Group.
--A Man Named Washington. (See & Read Biographies). (Illus.). (gr. k-3). 1960. PLB 3.96 o.p. (ISBN 0-399-60445-6). Putnam Pub Group.
Norman, Hope J. & Simon, Louise A., eds. Louisiana Entertains: A Complete Menu Cookbook. LC 78-64496. 304p. (Orig.). 1978. pap. 9.95 (ISBN 0-9603758-0-5). Rapides Symphony.
Norman, Howard, tr. Where the Chill Came from: Cree Windigo Tales & Journeys. LC 81-81506. 144p. 1982. 17.50 (ISBN 0-86547-047-2); pap. 9.00 (ISBN 0-86547-048-0). N Point Pr.
Norman, James. The Obsidian Mirror. LC 77-72806. (Illus., Orig.). 1977. pap. 5.95x (ISBN 0-914140-03-5). Carpenter Pr.
--The Strange World of Reptiles. (Illus.). (gr. 5-8). 1966. PLB 6.29 o.p. (ISBN 0-399-60617-3). Putnam Pub Group.
Norman, John. Beasts of Gor. (Science Fiction Ser.). 1977. pap. 2.95 (ISBN 0-87997-677-2, UE1677). DAW Bks.
--Blood Brothers of Gor. 1982. pap. 3.50 (ISBN 0-87997-777-9, UW1777). DAW Bks.
--Imaginative Sex. (Orig.). 1975. pap. 2.25 (ISBN 0-87997-546-6, UE1546). DAW Bks.
Norman, M. J. T. Annual Cropping Systems in the Tropics: An Introduction. LC 79-10625. (Illus.). x, 276p. 1949. text ed. 20.00 (ISBN 0-8130-0632-5). U Presses Fla.
Norman, Marty, jt. auth. see Ryan, Michael.
Norman, Philip. London Signs & Inscriptions. LC 68-22039. (Camden Library Ser). (Illus.). 1968. Repr. of 1893 ed. 30.00x (ISBN 0-8103-3496-8). Gale.
Norman, R. O. Principles of Organic Synthesis. 2nd ed. 1978. pap. 29.95x (ISBN 0-412-15520-6, Pub. by Chapman & Hall). Methuen Inc.
Norman, Richard. Hegel's Phenomenology. LC 76-12235. 1976. 15.95x o.p. (ISBN 0-312-36680-9). St Martin.
Norman, Richard W. Van see Van Norman, Richard W.
Norman, Rick. Poems of Encouragement. LC 81-67750. 1982. 4.95 (ISBN 0-686-85737-2). Broadman.
Norman, Robin. ZX-81 BASIC Book. Date not set. pap. 12.95 (ISBN 0-672-21957-3). Sams.
Norman, Ruth, ed. see Dallison, Dennis.
Norman, Ruth E. History of the Universe, Vol. 2. (Illus.). 450p. 1982. 9.95x (ISBN 0-932642-72-1). Unarius.
Norman, Ruth E., ed. see Norman, Ernest L.
Norman, Ruth E., et al. Tesla Speaks, 3 vols. Incl. Vol. 1. Scientists (ISBN 0-932642-20-9); Vol. 2. Philosophers (ISBN 0-932642-21-7); Vol. 3. Presidents (ISBN 0-932642-22-5). (Illus.). 1973. 8.95 ea. Unarius.
Norman, Ursel. A Basket of Homemade Breads. LC 73-17730. (Illus.). 64p. 1979. pap. 4.95 o.p. (ISBN 0-688-05247-9). Morrow.
Norman, V. D., jt. auth. see Dixit, A.
Norman, W. H., tr. see Akutagawa, Ryunosuke.
Norman, Yvonne. Leaves on the Wind. (YA) 1978. 6.95 (ISBN 0-685-85778-6, Avalon). Bouregy.
Normand, C. E., et al. Vacuum Problems & Techniques. (National Nuclear Energy Ser.: Division I, Vol. 11). 289p. 1950. pap. 23.50 (ISBN 0-87079-356-X, TID-5210); microfilm 4.50 (ISBN 0-87079-357-8, TID-5210). DOE.
Normann, N., jt. ed. see Hwang, N. H.
Normann, Richard. Management for Growth. LC 77-2839. 210p. 1977. 44.00 o.p. (ISBN 0-471-99513-4, Pub by Wiley-Interscience). Wiley.
Normann, Sigurd J. & Sorkin, Ernst, eds. Macrophages & Natural Killer Cells. (Advances in Experimental Medicine & Biology: Vol. 155). 849p. 1982. 95.00x (ISBN 0-306-41180-6, Plenum Pr). PLenum Pub.
Normot, Tod. The Will: A Modern Day Treasure Hunt. 62p. 1982. 6.95 (ISBN 0-686-35968-2). Tricore Assoc.
Noronha, Raymond. Social & Cultural Dimensions of Tourism. (Working Paper: No.326). iv, 66p. 1979. 5.00 (ISBN 0-686-36135-0, WP-0326). World Bank.
Norquay, Karen, jt. auth. see Bernard, Carl.
Norris. Perception of Behavioral Chemicals. 1982. 87.00. Elsevier.
Norris, A. Operation of Machinery in Motorships: Main Diesels, Boilers & Auxiliary Plant. 164p. 1981. 59.00x (ISBN 0-686-97107-8, Pub. by Marine Mgmt England). State Mutual Bk.
Norris, A. C. Computational Chemistry: An Introduction to Numerical Methods. LC 80-4691. 472p. 1981. 52.95x (ISBN 0-471-27949-8, Pub. by Wiley-Interscience); pap. 24.95 (ISBN 0-471-27950-1). Wiley.
Norris, C. Winning Tournament Karate. 5.95x o.s.i. Wehman.
Norris, Carol. OJT Personnel Clerk Resource Materials. 2nd ed. (Gregg Office Job Training Program). (Illus.). 112p. 5.60 (ISBN 0-07-047225-4, G). McGraw.
--OJT Personnel Clerk Training Manual. 2nd ed. (Gregg Office Job Training Program). (Illus.). 56p. (gr. 11-12). 1980. pap. 4.16 (ISBN 0-07-047226-2, G). McGraw.
Norris, Carolyn, et al. Jean's Christmas Stocking: Storybook for Young Deaf Children. (Illus.). 24p. Date not set. pap. 4.25 (ISBN 0-686-43092-1). Modern Signs.
Norris, Carolyn B. Island of Silence. rev. ed. (Illus.). 1978. 5.95x o.p. (ISBN 0-933076-00-2); pap. 2.50x o. p. o.p. (ISBN 0-933076-01-0). Alinda Pr.
Norris, Catherine. Concept Clarification in Nursing. LC 81-83859. 428p. 1982. 31.50 (ISBN 0-89443-825-5). Aspen Systems.
Norris, Charles H., et al. Elementary Structural Analysis. 3rd ed. 1976. 34.95 (ISBN 0-07-047256-4, C). McGraw.
Norris, Christopher. Deconstruction: Theory & Practice. LC 81-22422. 157p. 1982. 13.95x (ISBN 0-416-32060-0); pap. 7.95 (ISBN 0-416-32070-8). Methuen Inc.
Norris, Clarence & Washington, Sybil D. The Last of the Scottsboro Boys: An Autobiography. LC 78-23428. 1979. 10.95 (ISBN 0-399-12018-1). Putnam Pub Group.
Norris, F. D., jt. auth. see Gunstone, F. D.
Norris, F. H., Jr., jt. ed. see Brain, R. L.
Norris, Frank. McTeague. pap. 2.50 (ISBN 0-451-51790-3, CE1790, Sig Classics). NAL.
--McTeague. Pizer, Donald, ed. LC 77-479. (Norton Critical Editions). 1977 12.95 (ISBN 0-393-04460-2); pap. text ed. 8.95x, 1978 (ISBN 0-393-09136-8). Norton.
--McTeague: A Story of San Francisco. Starr, Kevin, ed. (American Library). 1982. pap. 3.95 (ISBN 0-14-039017-0). Penguin.
--A Novelist in the Making: A Collection of Student Themes & the Novels Blix & Vandover & the Brute. Hart, James D., ed. LC 72-129124. (The John Harvard Library). (Illus.). xiv, 596p. 1970. 30.00x (ISBN 0-674-62820-9). Harvard U Pr.
--Octopus. pap. 3.50 (ISBN 0-451-51711-3, CE1711, Sig Classics). NAL.
--Vandover & the Brute. LC 78-8537. xx, 354p. 1978. 22.50x (ISBN 0-8032-3300-0); pap. 4.95x (ISBN 0-8032-8350-4, BB 675, Bison). U of Nebr Pr.
Norris, G. & Ewart, W. Choosing & Managing Information Systems for Public Administration. 1979. text ed. 28.25x (ISBN 0-566-00244-2). Gower Pub Ltd.
Norris, Graeme. The Effective University: A Management by Objectives Approach. 1978. text ed. 28.50x (ISBN 0-566-00242-6). Gower Pub Ltd.
--Justifying Research & Teaching Objectives in Universities. 1979. text ed. 31.50x (ISBN 0-566-00243-4). Gower Pub Ltd.
Norris, H. Mr. Justice Murphy & the Bill of Rights. LC 65-22168. 568p. 1965. 12.50 (ISBN 0-379-00257-4). Oceana.
Norris, H. T. The Adventures of Antar: An Early Arab Epic. (Approaches to Arabic Literature: No. 3). 264p. 1980. text ed. 35.00x (ISBN 0-85668-161-X, Pub. by Aris & Phillips England). Humanities.
--The Berbers in Arabic Literature. LC 81-18642. (Arab Background Ser.). 320p. 1982. text ed. 35.00x (ISBN 0-582-78303-8). Longman.
Norris, Hoke. It's Not Far but I Don't Know the Way. LC 70-81965. 155p. 1969. 8.95 o.p. (ISBN 0-8040-0169-3). Swallow.
Norris, J. R. Essays in Applied Microbiology. LC 80-42066. 380p. 1981. 48.95x (ISBN 0-471-27998-6, Pub. by Wiley-Interscience). Wiley.
Norris, J. R. & Richmond, M. H. Essays in Microbiology. LC 78-2828. 540p. 1978. 56.95 o.s.i. (ISBN 0-471-99556-8, Pub. by Wiley-Interscience). Wiley.
Norris, J. R. & Ribbons, D. W., eds. Methods in Microbiology. Incl. Vol. 1. 1969. 100.50 (ISBN 0-12-521501-0); Vol. 2. 1970. 68.50 (ISBN 0-12-521502-9); Vol. 3A. 1970. 79.50 (ISBN 0-12-521503-7); Vol. 3B. 1970. 59.50 (ISBN 0-12-521543-6); Vol. 4. Norris, J. R., et al, eds. 1971. 100.50 (ISBN 0-12-521504-5); Vol. 5A. 1971. o.s. 69.00 (ISBN 0-12-521505-3); Vol. 5B. 1971. 62.50 (ISBN 0-12-521545-2); Vol. 6A. 1972. 93.00 (ISBN 0-12-521506-1); Vol. 6B. 1972. 60.50 (ISBN 0-12-521546-0); Vol. 7A. 1972. 77.00 (ISBN 0-12-521507-X); Vol. 7B. 1973. 60.00 (ISBN 0-12-521547-9); Vol. 8. 1973. 48.00 (ISBN 0-12-521508-8). Acad Pr.
Norris, James A. First Afghan War: 1838-42. LC 67-21962. 1967. 69.50 (ISBN 0-521-05838-4). Cambridge U Pr.
Norris, James D. R. G. Dun & Co., Eighteen Forty-One to Nineteen Hundred: The Development of Credit-Reporting in the Nineteenth Century. LC 77-95359. (Contributions in Economics & Economic History: No. 20). (Illus.). 1978. lib. bdg. 25.00 (ISBN 0-313-20326-1, NDC/). Greenwood.
Norris, James S. Advertising. 2nd ed. (Illus.). 448p. 1980. text ed. 19.95 (ISBN 0-8359-0171-8); pap. text ed. 16.00 (ISBN 0-8359-0168-8); instrs'. manual avail. (ISBN 0-8359-0169-6). Reston.
--Selling-the How & Why: A Comprehensive Introduction to Salesmanship. (Illus.). 304p. 1982. pap. 14.95 (ISBN 0-13-805986-1). P-H.
Norris, Jeanne L., jt. auth. see McDermott, Irene E.
Norris, Jeffrey A. Contract Compliance under the Reagan Administration: A Practitioner's Guide to Current Use of the OFCCP Compliance Manual. 520p. (Orig.). 1982. pap. 24.95 (ISBN 0-937856-05-3). Equal Employ.
Norris, Jill, jt. auth. see Liddington, Jill.
Norris, John. A Collection of Miscellanies. Wellek, Rene, ed. LC 75-11242. (British Philosophers & Theologians of the 17th & 18th Centuries Ser.). 1978. Repr. of 1687 ed. lib. bdg. 42.00 o.s.i. (ISBN 0-8240-1794-3). Garland Pub.
Norris, K. A., jt. auth. see Rutgers, A.
Norris, Keith & Valzey, John. The Economics of Research & Technology. (Studies in Economics Ser.). 1973. text ed. 18.95 o.p. (ISBN 0-04-330227-0); pap. text ed. 10.95x o.p. (ISBN 0-04-330228-9). Allen Unwin.

Norris, Kenneth S., ed. Whales, Dolphins, & Porpoises. (Library Reprint Ser.). 1978. 60.00x (ISBN 0-520-03283-7). U of Cal Pr.

Norris, Louis W. Values & the Credibility of the Professor. LC 80-5501. 171p. 1980. lib. bdg. 19.00 (ISBN 0-8191-1114-7); pap. text ed. 9.50 (ISBN 0-8191-1115-5). U Pr of Amer.

Norris, M. J. Factors Affecting the Rate of Sexual Maturation of the Desert Locust (Schistocerca Gregaria Forskal) in the Laboratory. 1957. 35.00x (ISBN 0-85135-024-0, Pub. by Centre Overseas Research). State Mutual Bk.

--Laboratory Experiments on Aviposition Responses of the Desert Locust (Schistocerca Gregaria Forskal) 1968. 35.00x (ISBN 0-686-82420-2, Pub. by Centre Overseas Research). State Mutual Bk.

--Reproduction in the Red Locust (Nomadacris Septemfasciata Serville) in the Laboratory. 1959. 35.00x (ISBN 0-85135-025-5, Pub. by Centre Overseas Research). State Mutual Bk.

--Reproduction in the Sert Locust (Schistocerca Gregaria Forskal) 1952. 35.00x (ISBN 0-85135-026-7, Pub. by Centre Overseas Research). State Mutual Bk.

Norris, M. W. Local Government in Peninsular Malaysia. 121p. 1980. text ed. 27.00x (ISBN 0-566-00283-3). Gower Pub Ltd.

Norris, Margot C. The Decentered Universe of Finnegans Wake: A Structuralist Analysis. LC 76-25507. 160p. 1977. 12.00x (ISBN 0-8018-1820-6); pap. text ed. 3.95x (ISBN 0-8018-2148-7). Johns Hopkins.

Norris, Marilyn W. Caring for Kids. (Independent Living Ser.). (Illus.). 1977. pap. text ed. 7.96 (ISBN 0-07-047246-7, G); tchr's manual & key 4.00 (ISBN 0-07-047248-3); wkbk. 4.96 (ISBN 0-07-047247-5). McGraw.

Norris, Maureen. Seaswept. 192p. 1983. pap. 1.75 (ISBN 0-686-81778-8). Jove Pubns.

Norris, Nigel, jt. auth. see Schneck, Stephen.

Norris, Richard A. Understanding the Faith of the Church. (Church's Teaching Ser.: Vol. 4). 288p. 1979. 5.95 (ISBN 0-8164-0421-6); pap. 3.95 (ISBN 0-8164-2217-6, Crossroad Bks); user guide .95 (ISBN 0-8164-2224-9). Seabury.

Norris, Robert. Memoires du Regne de Bossa-Ahadee Roi du Dahome, Etat Situe dans l'Anterieur de la Guinee. (Bibliotheque Africaine Ser.). 250p. (Fr.). 1974. Repr. of 1790 ed. lib. bdg. 68.50x o.p. (ISBN 0-8287-0657-3, 72-2140). Clearwater Pub.

Norris, Robert, jt. auth. see Buergenthal, Thomas.

Norris, Robert E. & Harris, Keith. Geography: An Introductory Perspective. 448p. 1982. 25.95 (ISBN 0-675-09885-8). Additional supplement may be obtained from publisher. Merrill.

Norris, Ruth & Ahmed, A. Karim, eds. Pills, Pesticides & Profits: The International Trade in Toxic Substances. LC 81-11001. 182p. 1982. pap. 12.95 (ISBN 0-88427-050-5). North River.

Norris, Willa. The Career Information Service. 4th ed. 1979. 24.50 (ISBN 0-395-30685-X). HM.

Norrman, Ralf. The Insecure World of Henry James's Fiction: Intensity & Ambiguity. 1982. 22.50 (ISBN 0-312-41863-9). St Martin.

Norseng, Mary K. Sigbjorn Obstfelder. (World Authors Ser.). 1982. lib. bdg. 17.95 (ISBN 0-8057-6492-5, Twayne). G K Hall.

Norsk Polarinstitiutt. Bouvetoya, South Atlantic Ocean: Results from the Norwegian Antarctic Research Expeditions 1976-79 & 1978-79. (Skrifter Ser.: No. 175). 130p. (Orig.). 1982. pap. 26.00 (ISBN 82-00-29195-2). Universitet.

Norsk Polarinstitiutt, jt. auth. see Lauritzen, Ornulf.

Norster, E. R. Combustion & Heat Transfer in Gas Turbine Systems. (Cranfield International Symposium Ser: Vol. 11). (Illus.). 1971. write for info. (ISBN 0-08-016524-9). Pergamon.

Norstog, Knut J. & Meyerriecks, Andrew J. Biology. 1983. text ed. 26.95 (ISBN 0-675-20000-8); study guide 9.95 (ISBN 0-675-20036-9). Additional supplements may be obtained from publisher. Merrill.

North, A Ffrederick, et al. Raising a Healthy, Happy Child. 1980. 10.95 o.p. (ISBN 0-679-51327-2); pap. 5.95 o.p. (ISBN 0-679-51328-0). McKay.

North, A. M., jt. ed. see Ledwith, A.

North, Alan. One Hundred & One Atari Computer Programming Tips & Tricks. new ed. 128p. (Orig.). 1982. pap. 8.95 (ISBN 0-86668-022-5). ARCsoft.

--Thirty-One New Atari Computer Programs for Home, School & Office. new ed. (Illus.). 96p. (Orig.). 1982. pap. 8.95 (ISBN 0-86668-018-7). ARCsoft.

North American Prairie Conference, 6th, Ohio State Univ., Columbus, Ohio, Aug. 12-17, 1978. Prairie Peninsula, Proceedings: In the "Shadow" of Transeau. Stuckey, Ronald L. & Reese, Karen J., eds. LC 81-82059. (Illus.). 1982. text ed. 15.00 (ISBN 0-86727-090-X). Ohio Bio Survey.

North, Anthony. Introduction to European Swords. (The Victoria & Albert Museum Introductions to the Decorative Arts Ser.). (Illus.). 48p. 1982. 9.95 (ISBN 0-88045-008-8). Stemmer Hse.

North, Arielle, ed. see Franzwa, Gregory M.

North, Barbara, tr. see Duverger, Maurice.

North, Brownlow. The Rich Man & Lazarus. 1979. pap. 2.95 (ISBN 0-85151-121-X). Banner of Truth.

--Wilt Thou Go with This Man? 1966. pap. 2.25 o.p. (ISBN 0-686-12545-2). Banner of Truth.

North, Carol. The Three Bears. LC 82-82650. (First Little Golden Bk.). (Illus.). 24p. (ps). 1983. 0.69 (ISBN 0-307-10147-9, Golden Pr); PLB price not set (ISBN 0-307-68147-5). Western Pub.

North Central Regional Center for Rural Development. Rural Development: Research Priorities. 109p. 1974. pap. 3.95x o.p. (ISBN 0-8138-1450-2). Iowa St U Pr.

--Rural Health Services: Organization, Delivery, & Use. Whiting, Larry & Hassinger, E., eds. 384p. 1976. text ed. 9.50x (ISBN 0-8138-1465-0). Iowa St U Pr.

North, Christopher R. Isaiah Forty to Fifty-Five. 2nd ed. (Student Christian Movement Press, Torch Bible Ser.). (Orig.). 1964. pap. 7.95x (ISBN 0-19-520301-1). Oxford U Pr.

--Second Isaiah Introduction, Translation & Commentary to Chapters 15-55. 1964. 25.00x o.p. (ISBN 0-19-826154-3). Oxford U Pr.

North, D. C. & Thomas, R. P. The Rise of the Western World: A New Economic History. LC 73-77258. (Illus.). 192p. 1973. 29.95 (ISBN 0-521-20171-3); pap. 8.95 (ISBN 0-521-29099-6). Cambridge U Pr.

North, Douglas C. & Miller, Roger L. The Economics of Public Issues. 5th ed. 192p. 1980. pap. text ed. 6.95 scp o.p. (ISBN 0-06-044875-X, HarpC); instructor's manual avail. o.p. Har-Row.

--The Economics of Public Issues. 6th ed. 192p. 1983. pap. text ed. 7.50 scp (ISBN 0-06-044848-2, HarpC); instr's manual avail. (ISBN 0-06-364727-3). Har-Row.

North, Douglass, jt. auth. see Davis, Lance.

North, Douglass C. Economic Growth of the United States, 1790-1860. 1966. pap. 6.95 (ISBN 0-393-00346-9, Norton Lib). Norton.

--Growth & Welfare in the American Past. 2nd ed. (Illus.). 224p. 1974. pap. text ed. 13.95 (ISBN 0-13-365338-2). P-H.

--Structure & Change in Economic History. 1981. 19.95 (ISBN 0-393-01478-9); pap. 6.95x (ISBN 0-393-95241-X). Norton.

North East London Polytechnic London, England. The Psychology Readings Catalogue of the North East London Polytechnic, London, England, 2 vols. 1976. Set. lib. bdg. 145.00 (ISBN 0-8161-1179-0, Hall Library). G K Hall.

North, Eric M. The Book of a Thousand Tongues. LC 73-174087. (Tower Bks). 386p. 1972. Repr. of 1938 ed. 40.00x (ISBN 0-8103-3948-X). Gale.

North, Freddie. Bridge with Aunt Agatha. 208p. 1983. 14.95 (ISBN 0-571-13012-7); pap. 7.95 (ISBN 0-571-13014-3). Faber & Faber.

North, Gail & Anderson, Bob. Gospel Music Encyclopedia. LC 79-65072. (Illus.). 1979. 14.95 o.p. (ISBN 0-8069-0174-8); lib. bdg. 13.29 o.p. (ISBN 0-8069-0175-6). Sterling.

North, Gary. The Theology of Christian Resistance. LC 82-84286. (Christianity & Civilization Ser.: No. 2). 388p. (Orig.). 1983. pap. 9.95 (ISBN 0-939404-05-2). Geneva Divinity.

--Unconditional Surrender. LC 81-80647. 293p. 1981. 9.95 o.p. (ISBN 0-939404-00-1). Geneva Divinity.

--Unconditional Surrender: God's Program for Victory. 2nd ed. LC 82-84385. 280p. 1983. pap. text ed. 9.95 (ISBN 0-939404-06-0). Geneva Divinity.

North, Harry, jt. auth. see Debartolo, Dick.

North, J. J. English Hammered Coinage, Vol. II. 1977. 35.00 (ISBN 0-685-51542-7, Pub by Spink & Son England). S J Durst.

North, James W. History of Augusta, Maine. LC 81-80137. 1000p. 1981. Repr. of 1870 ed. 55.00x (ISBN 0-89725-020-6). NH Pub Co.

North, Jessica. Legend of the Thirteenth Pilgrim. new ed. LC 78-10281. 1979. 8.95 (ISBN 0-698-10944-9, Coward). Putnam Pub Group.

--Mask of the Jaguar. 288p. 1981. 11.95 (ISBN 0-698-11050-1, Coward). Putnam Pub Group.

--Mask of the Jaguar. 1982. pap. 2.50 (ISBN 0-451-11341-1, AE1341, Sig). NAL.

North, Oliver S. Mineral Exploration, Mining, & Processing Patents, 1980. (Illus.). 135p. 1982. 35.00x (ISBN 0-89520-294-8). Soc Mining Eng.

North, P. M., ed. Contract Conflicts: The EEC Convention on the Law Applicable to Contractual Obligations; a Comparative Study. 404p. 1982. 49.00 (ISBN 0-686-82017-7, North Holland). Elsevier.

North, R. W. Untitled. 64p. 1983. 4.00 (ISBN 0-682-49982-X). Exposition.

North, Robert, tr. see Duverger, Maurice.

North, Robert J. & Orange, Richard A., Jr. Teenage Drinking: The Number One Threat to Young People Today. 144p. 1980. 8.95 o.p. (ISBN 0-02-589990-2). Macmillan.

North, Sterling. Abe Lincoln: Log Cabin to White House. (Landmark Ser: No. 61). (Illus.). (gr. 5-11). 1956. 2.95 (ISBN 0-394-80361-2, BYR); PLB 2.95 o.p. (ISBN 0-394-90361-7). Random.

North, W. J., ed. Biology of the Giant Kelp Beds (Macrocystis) in California. 1971. 80.00 (ISBN 3-7682-5432-1). Lubrecht & Cramer.

North, Wheeler. Underwater California. LC 75-13153. (Natural History Guide Ser). (Illus.). 1976. 14.95x o.p. (ISBN 0-520-03025-7); pap. 5.95 (ISBN 0-520-03039-7). U of Cal Pr.

Northall, G. F. English Folk-Rhymes: A Collection of Traditional Verses Relating to Places & Persons, Customs, Superstitions, Etc. LC 67-23918. 1967. Repr. of 1892 ed. 32.00x (ISBN 0-8103-3455-0). Gale.

Northam, J. Ibsen: A Critical Study. LC 72-80297. (Major European Authors Ser.). 240p. 1973. 39.50 (ISBN 0-521-08682-5); pap. 12.95x (ISBN 0-521-09733-9). Cambridge U Pr.

Northam, R. M. Urban Geography. 2nd ed. 512p. 1979. 25.95 (ISBN 0-471-03292-1). Wiley.

Northcote, K. H. Factual Key for the Recognition of Australian Soils. 1982. 50.00x (ISBN 0-686-97913-3, Pub. by CSIRO Australia). State Mutual Bk.

Northcott, Douglas G. Affine Sets & Affine Groups. LC 79-41595. (London Mathematical Society Lecture Note Ser.: No. 39). 1980. pap. 27.95x (ISBN 0-521-22909-X). Cambridge U Pr.

--Finite Free Resolutions. LC 75-31397. (Tracts in Mathematics Ser.: No. 71). 250p. 1976. 54.50 (ISBN 0-521-21155-7). Cambridge U Pr.

--A First Course of Homological Algebra. LC 72-97873. 250p. 1973. 32.50 (ISBN 0-521-20196-9). Cambridge U Pr.

--A First Course of Homological Algebra. LC 72-87873. 217p. 1980. pap. 13.95x (ISBN 0-521-29976-4). Cambridge U Pr.

--Ideal Theory. (Cambridge Tracts in Mathematics & Mathematical Physics: No. 42). 1953. 22.95 (ISBN 0-521-05840-6). Cambridge U Pr.

--Introduction to Homological Algebra. 1960. 39.50 (ISBN 0-521-05841-4). Cambridge U Pr.

Northcott, Winifred H., ed. Curriculum Guide: Hearing-Impaired Children, Birth to Three Years, & Their Parents. LC 76-56634. 1977. pap. text ed. 11.95 (ISBN 0-88200-077-2, D1998). Alexander Graham.

--The Hearing Impaired Child in a Regular Classroom: Preschool, Elementary, & Secondary Years. LC 73-86074. 1973. pap. text ed. 9.95 (ISBN 0-88200-064-0, N7431). Alexander Graham.

Northcut, Allan, ed. see Knauff, Thomas.

Northcut, Debbie, ed. see Knauff, Thomas.

Northcutt, Glenn & Davis, Roger, eds. Fish Neurobiology, Vol. 1: Brain Stem & Sense Organs. (Illus.). 368p. 1983. text ed. 45.00x (ISBN 0-472-10005-X). U of Mich Pr.

Northcutt, Glenn, jt. ed. see Davis, Roger.

Northcutt, Mary Jean, ed. see Schopf, Susan.

Northcutt, Robert, jt. auth. see Manougian, Manoug N.

Northcutt, Wayne. The French Socialist & Communist Party under the Fifth Republic, 1958-1981: From Opposition to Power. 150p. 1982. text ed. 19.50x (ISBN 0-8290-1057-2). Irvington.

Northeast Midwest Institute, compiled by. Guide to Government resources for Economic Development, 1983: A Handbook for Non-Profit Agencies & Municipalities. 19.95 (ISBN 0-686-38891-7). Public Serv Materials.

Northeast Regional Coastal Information Center, jt. auth. see Marine Aquaculture Association.

Northeast Solar Energy Ctr., for U. S. Dept. of Energy, Boston, MA. Passive Solar Products Directory. 107p. 1982. pap. 16.50x (ISBN 0-89934-173-X, A019). Solar Energy Info.

Northeastern University - Dodge Library, Boston. Selective Bibliography in Science & Engineering. 1964. 75.00 (ISBN 0-8161-0701-7, Hall Library). G K Hall.

Northedge, F. S. & Donelan, M. D. International Disputes: The Political Aspects. LC 70-149885. 1971. 26.00 (ISBN 0-312-42035-8). St Martin.

Northedge, F. S. & Wells, A. Britain & Soviet Communism: The Impact of a Revolution. 280p. 1982. text ed. 31.50x (ISBN 0-333-27192-0, 41036, Pub. by Macmillan England); pap. text ed. 15.50x (ISBN 0-333-27193-9, 41104). Humanities.

Northen, E. E. & Duckworth, J. R. The Northen Family 1635-1900 & Bridging the Gap. 2nd ed. LC 82-73787. 196p. Repr. of 1906 ed. 25.00 (ISBN 0-9608266-0-2); microfische 6.00 (ISBN 0-9608266-1-0). Burnett Farm Gen.

Northen, Henry T. Introductory Plant Science. 3rd ed. (Illus.). 586p. 1968. 27.95 o.s.i. (ISBN 0-471-06816-0); instr's manual 3.00 o.s.i. (ISBN 0-471-07522-1). Wiley.

Northen, Henry T. & Northen, Rebecca T. Greenhouse Gardening. 2nd ed. (Illus.). 350p. 1973. 21.50 o.p. (ISBN 0-471-06817-9, 72583, Pub. by Wiley-Interscience). Wiley.

Northen, Rebecca T., jt. auth. see Northen, Henry T.

Northern, Jerry, jt. auth. see Wood, Raymond.

Northern, Jerry L. & Downs, M. Hearing in Children. 3rd ed. (Illus.). 350p. 1978. 24.00 o.p. (ISBN 0-683-06572-6). Williams & Wilkins.

Northern, Tamara. Royal Art of Cameroon: The Art of the Bamenda-Tikar. LC 73-78385. (Illus.). 76p. 1973. pap. 10.00 o.p. (ISBN 0-87451-103-8). U Pr of New Eng.

Northman, John E., jt. auth. see Baker, Frank.

Northouse, Cameron. Twentieth Century Operas in England & the United States. 1976. lib. bdg. 31.00 (ISBN 0-8161-7896-8, Hall Reference). G K Hall.

Northouse, Cameron & Walsh, Thomas P. John Osborne: A Reference Guide. (Series Seventy: No. 2). 1974. lib. bdg. 9.50 o.p. (ISBN 0-8161-1152-9, Hall Reference). G K Hall.

Northouse, Cameron, jt. auth. see Walsh, Thomas P.

Northover, F. Applied Diffraction Theory. 1971. 45.00 (ISBN 0-444-00085-2). Elsevier.

Northrip, John W., et al. Analysis of Sport Motion: Anatomic & Biomechanic Perspectives. 3rd ed. 365p. 1983. pap. text ed. write for info. (ISBN 0-697-07206-1). Wm C Brown.

Northrop, Fyre. The Tempest. 1981. 3.75 o.p. (ISBN 0-14-070713-1). Penguin.

Northrop Institute of Technology. Basic Science for Aerospace Vehicles. 4th ed. 1973. text ed. 16.95 o.p. (ISBN 0-07-047484-2, G). McGraw.

--Electricity & Electronics for Aerospace Vehicles. 2nd ed. 1972. text ed. 19.95 o.p. (ISBN 0-07-047485-0, G). McGraw.

Northrup, David. Trade Without Rulers: Pre-Colonial Economic Development in South-Eastern Nigeria. (Studies in African Affairs). (Illus.). 1978. 49.50x (ISBN 0-19-822712-4). Oxford U Pr.

Northrup, James P. Old Age, Handicapped, & Vietnam-Era Anti-Discrimination Legislation. LC 80-53990. (Labor Relations & Public Policy Ser.: No. 14). 248p. 1977. pap. 10.50 (ISBN 0-89546-020-3). Indus Res Unit-Wharton.

Northwest Matrix, ed. see Barton, Lois.

Northwest Regional Educational Laboratory, jt. auth. see Idaho State Department of Education.

Northwest Regional Educational Laboratory. Advertising Techniques & Consumer Fraud. (Lifeworks Ser.). (Illus.). 1979. pap. text ed. 5.28 (ISBN 0-07-047308-0). McGraw.

Northwest Regional Educational Laboratory Staff. Buying & Caring for Your Car & Insurance for Your Life, Health & Possessions. (Lifeworks Ser.). (Illus.). 1980. pap. text ed. 5.28 (ISBN 0-07-047307-2). McGraw.

Northwest Regional Educational Laboratory. Comparison Shopping & Caring for Your Personal Possessions. (Lifeworks Ser.). (Illus.). 1980. pap. text ed. 5.28 (ISBN 0-07-047309-9). McGraw.

--Counting Money & Making Change & Making a Budget. (Lifeworks Ser.). (Illus.). 1980. pap. text ed. 5.28 (ISBN 0-07-047304-8, G). McGraw.

--Housing: Buying a House, Buying a Mobile Home. (Illus.). 1980. pap. text ed. 5.28 (ISBN 0-07-047302-1, G). McGraw.

--Housing: Moving on Getting Utilities & Using Them Wisely. (Illus.). 1980. pap. text ed. 5.28 (ISBN 0-07-047303-X, G). McGraw.

--Housing: What Are Your Needs, Renting a Place to Live. 1980. pap. text ed. 5.28 (ISBN 0-07-047301-3, G). McGraw.

--Using Credit & Banking Services & Understanding Income Tax. (Lifeworks Ser.). (Illus.). 1979. pap. text ed. 5.28 (ISBN 0-07-047306-4). McGraw.

Northwestern University. Catalog of the Melville J. Herskovits Library of African Studies, Northwestern University, & Africana in Selected Libraries, Evanston, 8 vols. 1972. Set. 720.00 (ISBN 0-8161-0921-4, Hall Library). G K Hall.

--Catalog of the Transportation Center Library, Northwestern University. 1972. Subject Catalog 9 Vols. 855.00 (ISBN 0-8161-0185-X, Hall Library); Author-title Catalog. 285.00 (ISBN 0-8161-0924-9); Set Of 12 Vols. 1114.00 (ISBN 0-685-01569-6). G K Hall.

--Joint Acquisitions List of Africana: 1978. 1980. lib. bdg. 90.00 (ISBN 0-8161-0329-1, Hall Library). G K Hall.

Northwestern University Transportation Center June 11-12,1979 & Moses, Leon N. Corporate Planning under Deregulation-The Case of the Airlines: Proceedings. 104p. 1979. 15.00 (ISBN 0-686-94043-1, Trans). Northwestern U Pr.

Northwestern University Transportation Center Forum & Moses, Leon N. In Search of a Rational Liner Shipping Policy: Proceedings. 126p. 1978. 25.00 (ISBN 0-686-94044-X, Trans). Northwestern U Pr.

Northwestern University Transportation Center, May 5, 1981 & Neuschel, Robert P. Managing Effectively Under Deregulation: Proceedings. 128p. 1981. 25.00 (ISBN 0-686-94052-0, Trans). Northwestern U Pr.

Nortman, Dorothy & Fisher, Joanne. Population & Family Planning Programs: A Compendium of Data Through 1979. 11th ed. LC 82-18992. (Orig.). 1981. pap. 6.00 (ISBN 0-87834-046-7). Population Coun.

Norton, Alice, ed. Public Relations Information Sources. LC 77-137574. (Management Information Guide Ser.: No. 22). 1970. 42.00x (ISBN 0-8103-0822-3). Gale.

Norton, Aloysius A. Theodore Roosevelt. (United States Authors Ser.). 1980. lib. bdg. 11.95 (ISBN 0-8057-7309-6, Twayne). G K Hall.

Norton, Andre. The Book of Andre Norton. (Science Fiction Ser.). 1975. pap. 2.25 (ISBN 0-87997-643-8, UE1643). DAW Bks.

--Caroline. 320p. (Orig.). 1983. pap. 2.95 (ISBN 0-523-48059-8). Pinnacle Bks.

--Catseye. 1980. lib. bdg. 9.95 (ISBN 0-8398-2637-0, Gregg). G K Hall.

--The Crossroads of Time. 1978. lib. bdg. 9.95 (ISBN 0-8398-2418-1, Gregg). G K Hall.

--Crystal Gryphon. (Science Fiction Ser.). pap. 2.25 (ISBN 0-87997-701-9, UE1701). DAW Bks.

--The Defiant Agents. 1979. lib. bdg. 9.95 (ISBN 0-8398-2423-8, Gregg). G K Hall.

--The Forerunner. 288p. (Orig.). 1981. pap. 2.75 (ISBN 0-523-48558-1). Pinnacle Bks.

--Galactic Derelict. 1979. lib. bdg. 9.95 (ISBN 0-8398-2422-X, Gregg). G K Hall.
--Gryphon in Glory. 224p. 1983. pap. 2.50 (ISBN 0-345-30950-2, Del Rey). Ballantine.
--High Sorcery. 1982. pap. 2.25 (ISBN 0-441-33709-0, Pub. by Ace Science Fiction). Ace Bks.
--Key Out of Time. 1979. lib. bdg. 9.95 (ISBN 0-8398-2424-6, Gregg). G K Hall.
--Lavender Green Magic. LC 73-21941. (Illus.). (gr. 4-9). 1974. 12.95 (ISBN 0-690-00429-X, TYC-J). Har-Row.
--Lore of the Witch World. (Science Fiction Ser.). 1980. pap. 2.50 (ISBN 0-87997-750-7, UE1750). Daw Bks.
--Octagon Magic. (Illus.). (gr. 4-6). 1978. pap. 1.75 o.p. (ISBN 0-671-56074-3). Archway.
--Ordeal in Otherwhere. 1980. lib. bdg. 9.95 (ISBN 0-8398-2634-6, Gregg). G K Hall.
--Plague Ship. 208p. 1982. pap. 2.25 (ISBN 0-441-66836-4, Pub. by Ace Science Fiction). Ace Bks.
--Plague Ship. 1978. lib. bdg. 9.95 (ISBN 0-8398-2416-5, Gregg). G K Hall.
--Red Hart Magic. LC 76-3539. (Illus.). (gr. 4 up). 1976. 12.95 (ISBN 0-690-01147-4, TYC-J). Har-Row.
--Sargasso of Space. 1978. lib. bdg. 9.95 (ISBN 0-8398-2415-7, Gregg). G K Hall.
--Secret of the Lost Race. 1978. lib. bdg. 9.95 (ISBN 0-8398-2419-X, Gregg). G K Hall.
--The Sioux Spaceman. 1978. lib. bdg. 9.95 (ISBN 0-8398-2420-3, Gregg). G K Hall.
--Sorceress of the Witch World. (Witch World Ser.: No. 6). 224p. 1982. pap. 2.50 (ISBN 0-441-77556-X, Pub. by Ace Science Fiction). Ace Bks.
--Sorceress of the Witch World. 1977. lib. bdg. 9.95 (ISBN 0-8398-2360-6, Gregg). G K Hall.
--The Space Adventure Novels. 1978. 50.00 (ISBN 0-686-74233-8, Gregg). G K Hall.
--Spell of the Witch World. 1977. lib. bdg. 9.95 (ISBN 0-8398-2354-1, Gregg). G K Hall.
--Stand to Horse. LC 56-8354. (gr. 7 up). 1968. pap. 0.75 (ISBN 0-15-684890-2, VoyB). HarBraceJ.
--Star Man's Son 2250 A.D. 1980. lib. bdg. 9.95 (ISBN 0-8398-2636-2, Gregg). G K Hall.
--Storm Over Warlock. 1980. lib. bdg. 9.95 (ISBN 0-8398-2635-4, Gregg). G K Hall.
--Three Against the Witch World. 1977. lib. bdg. 9.95 (ISBN 0-8398-2358-4, Gregg). G K Hall.
--Three Against the Witch World. (Witch World Ser.: No. 4). pap. 2.50 (ISBN 0-441-80807-7, Pub. by Ace Science Fiction). Ace Bks.
--The Time Traders. 1979. lib. bdg. 9.95 (ISBN 0-8398-2421-1, Gregg). G K Hall.
--The Time Traders Series. 1979. 35.00 (ISBN 0-686-74234-6, Gregg). G K Hall.
--Voodoo Planet & Star Hunter. 1978. lib. bdg. 9.95 (ISBN 0-8398-2417-3, Gregg). G K Hall.
--Warlock of the Witch World. 1977. lib. bdg. 9.95 (ISBN 0-8398-2359-2, Gregg). G K Hall.
--Warlock of the Witch World. (Witch World Ser.: No. 5). pap. 2.50 (ISBN 0-441-87326-X, Pub. by Ace Science Fiction). Ace Bks.
--Web of the Witch World. 192p. 1976. pap. 2.25 (ISBN 0-441-87876-8, Pub. by Ace Science Fiction). Ace Bks.
--Web of the Witch World. 1977. lib. bdg. 9.95 (ISBN 0-8398-2357-6, Gregg). G K Hall.
--Witch World. 1977. lib. bdg. 9.95 (ISBN 0-8398-2355-X, Gregg). G K Hall.
--Witch World, No. 1. 288p. 1982. pap. 2.50 (ISBN 0-441-89706-1, Pub. by Ace Science Fiction). Ace Bks.
--The Witch World Novels. 1977. 62.50 (ISBN 0-686-74235-4, Gregg). G K Hall.
--Year of the Unicorn. 1977. lib. bdg. 9.95 (ISBN 0-8398-2356-8, Gregg). G K Hall.

Norton, Andre & Madlee, Dorothy. Star Ka'at World. LC 75-36018. (Illus.). 128p. 1976. 6.95 o.s.i. (ISBN 0-8027-6300-6); PLB 6.85 o.s.i. (ISBN 0-8027-6301-4). Walker & Co.

Norton, Andre, compiled by. Small Shadows Creep. 1974. 7.95 o.p. (ISBN 0-525-39505-9). Dutton.

Norton, B. Wilderness Photography. 1977. pap. 6.95 (ISBN 0-07-047464-8). McGraw.

Norton, Boyd. Alaska: Wilderness Frontier. (Illus.). 1977. pap. 10.00 o.p. (ISBN 0-88349-136-2). Readers Digest Pr.
--Wilderness Photography. (Illus.). pap. 6.95 o.p. (ISBN 0-88349-115-X). Readers Digest Pr.

Norton, Browning. Help Me, Charley Buoy. new ed. LC 74-79698. 160p. (gr. 5-11). 1974. 6.95 o.p. (ISBN 0-698-20297-X, Coward). Putnam Pub Group.
--Wreck of the Blue Plane. LC 77-18507. (gr. 5-9). 1978. 6.95 (ISBN 0-698-20448-4, Coward). Putnam Pub Group.

Norton, Caroline S. Selected Writings of Caroline Norton. LC 78-18828. 1978. 95.00x (ISBN 0-8201-1312-3). Schol Facsimiles.

Norton, Charles A. Writing Tom Sawyer: The Adventures of Mark Twain's Classic. 210p. 1983. lib. bdg. 18.95x (ISBN 0-89950-067-6). McFarland & Co.

Norton, Cynthia F. Microbiology. LC 80-23350. (Life Sciences Ser.). (Illus.). 850p. 1981. text ed. 28.95 (ISBN 0-201-05304-7); study guide 10.95 (ISBN 0-201-05307-1); tchr's manual 7.95 (ISBN 0-201-05308-X). A-W.

Norton, Don C. Ecology of Plant-Parasitic Nematodes. LC 78-1052. 268p. 1978. 39.95x (ISBN 0-471-03188-7, Pub. by Wiley-Interscience). Wiley.

Norton, Donna E. The Effective Teaching of Language Arts. (Elementary Education Ser.: No. C22). 512p. 1980. text ed. 19.95 (ISBN 0-675-08196-3). Additional supplements may be obtained from publisher. Merrill.
--Language Arts Activities for Children. (Elementary Education Ser.: No. C22). 416p. 1980. pap. text ed. 11.95 (ISBN 0-675-08134-3). Merrill.
--Through the Eyes of a Child: Introduction to Children's Literature. 600p. 1983. text ed. 18.95 (ISBN 0-675-09832-7). Additional supplements may be obtained from publishher. Merrill.

Norton, F. H. Fine Ceramics: Technology & Applications. LC 78-106. 524p. 1979. Repr. of 1970 ed. 31.50 (ISBN 0-88275-582-X). Krieger.

Norton, Frederick J. Printing in Spain, 1501-20. 1966. 85.00 (ISBN 0-521-05842-2). Cambridge U Pr.

Norton, James C. Introduction to Medical Psychology. 416p. 1982. text ed. 22.95 (ISBN 0-02-923290-2). Free Pr.

Norton, Joseph J. Regulation of Business Enterprise in the U. S. A. 1983. looseleaf, (2 binders) 95.00 (ISBN 0-379-11250-7). Oceana.

Norton, M. D., tr. see Rilke, Rainer M.

Norton, Maggie J. The Complete Book of Crochet Design: Project & Designs from Simple Motifs. LC 78-54047. (Illus.). 1978. 14.50 o.p. (ISBN 0-88332-091-6, 8040). Larousse.

Norton, Mary. Adventures of the Borrowers, 4 vols. (Illus.). 784p. (gr. 4 up). 1975. Set. pap. 11.95 (ISBN 0-15-613605-8, VoyB). HarBraceJ.
--Are All the Giants Dead? LC 78-6622. (Illus.). (gr. 4-6). 1978. pap. 2.50 (ISBN 0-15-607888-0, VoyB). HarBraceJ.
--Bed-Knob & Broomstick. LC 74-17497. (Illus.). 189p. (gr. 4-6). 1975. pap. 2.95 (ISBN 0-15-611500-X, AVB91, VoyB). HarBraceJ.
--The Borrowers. LC 53-7870. (Illus.). (gr. 3 up). 1965. pap. 2.95 (ISBN 0-15-613600-7, VoyB). HarBraceJ.
--The Borrowers Afield. LC 55-11011. (Illus.). (gr. 4 up). 1970. pap. 2.95 (ISBN 0-15-613601-5, VoyB). HarBraceJ.
--The Borrowers Afloat. LC 59-5630. (Illus.). 191p. (gr. 3 up). 1973. pap. 2.95 (ISBN 0-15-613603-1, VoyB). HarBraceJ.
--The Borrowers Aloft. LC 73-12865. (Illus.). 192p. (gr. 4-6). 1974. pap. 2.95 (ISBN 0-15-613604-X, VoyB). HarBraceJ.
--The Borrowers Avenged. (Illus.). (gr. 3 up). Date not set. 12.95 (ISBN 0-15-210530-1). HarBraceJ.
--Poor Stainless: A New Story About the Borrowers. LC 70-140781. (Illus.). (gr. 3 up). 1971. 6.95 (ISBN 0-15-263221-2, HJ). HarBraceJ.

Norton, Mary B., jt. auth. see Berkin, Carol.

Norton, Mary B., et al. A People & a Nation, Vol. I. 512p. 1982. text ed. 16.50 (ISBN 0-395-29091-0); study guide 6.50 (ISBN 0-395-29094-5). HM.
--A People & a Nation, Vol. II. 640p. 1982. text ed. 16.50 (ISBN 0-395-29092-9); study guide 6.50 (ISBN 0-395-31893-9). HM.
--A People & a Nation: A History of the United States, 1 vol. ed. LC 81-84809. (Illus.). 1040p. 1982. text ed. 24.95 (ISBN 0-395-29090-2); 1.00 (ISBN 0-395-29093-7); study guides. 2 pts. 5.95 ea.; write for info. test items (ISBN 0-395-31892-0); transparencies 35.00, set. HM.

Norton, Mary J., jt. auth. see Eckley, Mary.

Norton, Nancy R. Rainbowland. 1979. 5.95 o.p. (ISBN 0-533-03638-0). Vantage.

Norton, Paul F. Latrobe, Jefferson, & the National Capitol. LC 76-23662. (Outstanding Dissertations in the Fine Arts Ser.). 1977. lib. bdg. 56.00x o.s.i. (ISBN 0-8240-2716-7). Garland Pub.

Norton, Peter. Ships' Figureheads. (Illus.). 1976. 10.00 o.p. (ISBN 0-517-52561-5). Crown.

Norton, Philip. The Constitution in Flux. 320p. 1982. text ed. 27.50x (ISBN 0-85520-521-0, Pub. by Martin Robertson England); pap. text ed. 9.95x (ISBN 0-85520-522-9). Biblio Dist.

Norton, Philip & Aughey, Arthur. Conservatives & Conservatism. 1981. 50.00x (ISBN 0-85117-211-3, Pub. by M Temple Smith); pap. 35.00x (ISBN 0-85117-212-1). State Mutual Bk.

Norton, Reggi & Wagner, Martha. The Soy of Cooking: A Tofu & Tempeh Recipe Book. 3rd ed. 64p. 1981. pap. 3.95 (ISBN 0-9604880-2-2). White Crane Pubns.

Norton, Robert. Race & Politics in Figi. LC 77-78122. (Illus.). 1978. 25.00x (ISBN 0-312-66138-X). St Martin.

Norton, Robert F. A Treatise on Deeds. LC 81-83533. lxxxii, 772p. 1981. Repr. of 1928 ed. lib. bdg. 80.00x (ISBN 0-912004-17-7). W W Gaunt.

Norton, Theodore M. & Ollman, Bertell, eds. Studies in Socialist Pedagogy. LC 77-91734. 1979. 16.50 (ISBN 0-85345-440-X, CL440X); pap. 6.50 (ISBN 0-85345-500-7, PB5007). Monthly Rev.

Norton, Wesley. Religious Newspapers in the Old Northwest to 1861: A History, Bibliography, & Record of Opinion. LC 75-36983. xi, 196p. 1977. 12.50x (ISBN 0-8214-0193-9, 82-81966). Ohio U Pr.

Norton-Ford, Julian D., jt. auth. see Kendall, Philip C.

Norton-Kyshe, James W. Dictionary of Legal Quotations. LC 68-30648. 1968. Repr. of 1904 ed. 34.00x (ISBN 0-8103-3189-6). Gale.

Norton-Smith, Richard. Thomas E. Dewey & His & Times. 672p. 1982. 21.75 (ISBN 0-671-41741-X). S&S.

Norton-Taylor, Duncan. God's Man: A Novel of John Calvin. LC 79-52951. 1979. 9.95 o.p. (ISBN 0-8010-6729-4). Baker Bk.

Norusis, M. J. SPSS Introductory Guide: Basic Statistics & Operations. 1982. 11.95x (ISBN 0-07-047528-8). McGraw.
--SPSS-X Introducing Statistics Guide. 1983. write for info. (ISBN 0-07-046549-5). McGraw.
--SPSS-X Statistical Guide. 820p. 1983. 15.95 (ISBN 0-07-046548-7). McGraw.

Norvell. Exorcism: Overcome Black Magic with White Magic. (BN 4000 Ser.). pap. 2.50 o.p. (ISBN 0-06-464006-X, BN). B&N NY.
--The Miracle of Prosperity Magic. LC 80-29147. 214p. 1981. 14.95 o.p. (ISBN 0-13-585547-0, Parker). P-H.
--The Miracle Power of Transcendental Meditation. 208p. 1977. pap. 2.95 (ISBN 0-06-465058-8, BN 4009, BN). B&N NY.
--The One Hundred Thousand Dollar Dream & How to Make It Come True. 1976. 6.95 o.p. (ISBN 0-13-635441-6, Reward); pap. 3.45 o.p. (ISBN 0-13-635458-0). P-H.
--Think Yourself Rich: Norvell's Secrets of Money Magnetism. 224p. 1976. pap. 4.95 (ISBN 0-06-464014-0, BN 4000). B&N NY.

Norvell, Anthony. Norvell's Dynamic Mental Laws for Successful Living. 1965. 9.95 o.p. (ISBN 0-13-623785-1, Parker). P-H.

Norvell, Douglas G., jt. auth. see Branson, Robert E.

Norville, Mary F. Drug Dosage & Solutions Workbook. (Illus.). 136p. (Orig.). 1981. pap. text ed. 10.95 (ISBN 0-87619-920-1). R J Brady.

Norville, Warren. Death Tide. pap. 1.95 o.s.i. (ISBN 0-515-05146-2). Jove Pubns.

Norwak, Mary. The Complete Mixer & Blender. (Illus.). 18.95x o.p. (ISBN 0-8464-0268-8). Beekman Pubs.
--Creative Meat Cooking. LC 78-56361. (Illus.). 1979. 12.95 o.p. (ISBN 0-89696-005-6, An Everest House Book). Dodd.
--The Foolproof Cookbook. (Illus.). 192p. 1982. 24.95 (ISBN 0-7134-3907-6, Pub. by Batsford England); pap. 14.95 (ISBN 0-7134-3908-4). David & Charles.
--Mixer & Blender Cookery. (Illus.). pap. 8.95x o.p. (ISBN 0-8464-0635-7). Beekman Pubs.

Norwick, Kenneth. Lobbying for Freedom. 1975. pap. 3.95 o.p. (ISBN 0-312-49350-9). St Martin.

Norwine, Jim & Anderson, Thomas D. Geography As Human Ecology? LC 80-8148. 70p. 1980. pap. text ed. 6.50 (ISBN 0-8191-1249-6). U Pr of Amer.

Norwood, Fred W., et al. Federal Taxation: Research Planning & Procedures. 2nd ed. LC 78-27524. (Illus.). 1979. text ed. 35.95 (ISBN 0-13-308775-1). P-H.

Norwood, Frederick A. & Carr, Jo. Young Reader's Book of Church History. LC 81-20505. (Illus.). 176p. (gr. 4 up). 1982. 8.95 (ISBN 0-687-46827-2). Abingdon.

Norwood, Gilbert. Pindar. (Sather Classical Lectures: Vol. 19). 1974. 30.00x (ISBN 0-520-01952-0). U of Cal Pr.

Norwood, John. Craftsmen at Work. (Illus.). 1978. 15.00 o.p. (ISBN 0-212-97019-4). Transatlantic.

Norwood, John B. Rio Grande Narrow Gauge. Heimburger, Donald J. & Heimburger, Marilyn M., eds. (Illus.). 312p. 1983. 39.95 (ISBN 0-911581-00-6). Heimburger Hse Pub.

Norwood, Joseph, Jr. Intermediate Classical Mechanics. (Illus.). 1979. ref. 31.95 (ISBN 0-13-469635-2). P-H.

Norwood, Warren. The Windhover Tapes: Flexing the Warp. 240p. 1983. pap. 2.75 (ISBN 0-686-82109-2). Bantam.

Nosay, G., jt. auth. see Nakamura, T.

Noseda, G. F. & Fragiacomo, C. Lipoproteins & Coronary Atherosclerosis. (Giovanni Lorenzini Foundation Symposia Ser.: Vol. 13). 1982. 76.75 (ISBN 0-444-80408-0). Elsevier.

Noseda, Giorgio, et al, eds. Diet & Drug in Atherosclerosis. 347p. 1980. text ed. 42.00 (ISBN 0-89004-491-0). Raven.

Nosich, Gerald M. Reasons & Arguments. 320p. 1982. pap. text ed. 13.95x (ISBN 0-534-01076-8). Wadsworth Pub.

No Sizwe. One Azania, One Nation: The National Question in South Africa. 216p. (Orig.). 1979. 31.00 (ISBN 0-905762-40-1, Pub. by Zed Pr England); pap. 7.95 (ISBN 0-905762-41-X, Pub. by Zed Pr England). Lawrence Hill.

Noske, Frits. French Song from Berlioz to Duparc: The Origin & Development of the Melodie. 2nd & rev ed. (Illus.). 11.50 (ISBN 0-8446-0827-0). Peter Smith.

Noson, Linda, jt. auth. see Crosson, Robert S.

Noson, Linda L. & Crosson, Robert S. Compilation of Earthquake Hypo-Centers in Western Washington: 1978. (Information Circular Ser.: No. 72). (Illus.). 18p. 1980. 0.50 (ISBN 0-686-36908-4). Geologic Pubns.

Noss, John B. Man's Religion. 6th ed. (Illus.). 1980. text ed. 23.95x (ISBN 0-02-388430-4). Macmillan.

Noss, Richard R. Heavens - His Handiwork. (Illus.). 1962. 1.25 o.s.i. (ISBN 0-910840-09-1); pap. 0.75 o.s.i. (ISBN 0-910840-08-3). Kingdom.

Nossack, Hans E. Wait for November. Hein, Ruth, tr. from Ger. LC 82-1395. Orig. Title: Spatestens im November. 285p. 1982. 14.95 (ISBN 0-88064-004-9). Fromm Intl Pub.

Nossal, G. J. & Ada, G. L. Antigens, Lymphoid Cells & the Immune Response. LC 71-137602. (Monographs on Immunology: Vol. 1). 1971. 59.00 (ISBN 0-12-521950-4). Acad Pr.

Nossaman, Allen, ed. see Kaplan, Michael.

Nossel, Hymie & Vogel, Henry J., eds. Pathobiology of the Endothelial Cell. (P & S Biomedical Sciences Symposia Ser.). 1982. 63.00 (ISBN 0-12-521980-6). Acad Pr.

Nossiter, T. J. Communism In Kerala. LC 81-71762. (Illus.). 550p. Date not set. 35.00x (ISBN 0-520-04667-6). U of Cal Pr. Postponed.

Nostlinger, Christine. Konrad. (Illus.). 144p. 1983. pap. 1.95 (ISBN 0-380-62018-9, 62018-9, Camelot). Avon.

Nostrand, A. D. Van see Van Nostrand, A. D. & Knoblauch, C. H.

Nostrand, Frederic Van see Van Nostrand, Frederic.

Nostrand, Van Jeanne see Van Nostrand, Jeanne.

Notable Children's Books Re-Evaluation Committee Association for Library Service to Children. Notable Children's Books Nineteen Seventy-One to Nineteen Seventy-Five. 48p. 1981. pap. 4.00 (ISBN 0-8389-3252-5). ALA.

Notake, Y. & Suzuki, S. Biological & Clinical Aspects of the Fetus. (Illus.). 270p. 1977. text ed. 69.50 o.p. (ISBN 0-8391-0986-5). Univ Park.

Note, Gene Van see Van Note, Gene.

Notelowitz, Morris & Ware, Marsha. Stand Tall! The Informed Woman's Guide to Preventing Osteoporosis. (Illus.). 200p. 1982. 12.95 (ISBN 0-937404-12-8); pap. 6.95 (ISBN 0-937404-14-4). Triad Pub FL.

Notestein, Wallace. The Scot in History. LC 76-104225. xvii, 371p. Repr. of 1946 ed. lib. bdg. 18.00x (ISBN 0-8371-3342-4, NOSH). Greenwood.

Notestein, Wallace, et al. Commons Debates, Sixteen Twenty-One, 7 vols. 1935. 500.00x (ISBN 0-685-69847-5). Elliots Bks.

Noth, Ernst E. Contemporary German Novel. 1961. pap. 1.95 o.p. (ISBN 0-87462-422-3). Marquette.

Noth, Martin. Exodus, a Commentary. LC 62-7940. (Old Testament Library). 1962. 15.95 (ISBN 0-664-20370-1). Westminster.
--History of Israel: Biblical History. 2nd ed. LC 58-5195. 1960. 16.95xi (ISBN 0-06-066310-3, HarpR). Har-Row.
--Leviticus: A Commentary. LC 77-7656. (Old Testament Library). 1977. 15.95 (ISBN 0-664-20774-X). Westminster.
--Numbers: A Commentary. Martin, James D., tr. LC 69-12129. (Old Testament Library). 1969. 13.95 (ISBN 0-664-20841-X). Westminster.

Noth, Martin & Anderson, Berhard W. History of Pentateuchal Traditions. LC 80-24937. (Scholars Press Reproductions Ser.). 1981. pap. 17.50 (ISBN 0-89130-446-0, 00-07-05); text ed. 22.00 (ISBN 0-686-86730-0). Scholars Pr CA.

Nothaft, Anne. Breeding Cockatoos. (Illus.). 96p. 1979. 4.95 (ISBN 0-87666-877-5, KW-059). TFH Pubns.

Nothdurft, K. H. The Complete Guide to Successful Business Negotiation. LC 73-77703. 224p. 1972. 9.00x (ISBN 0-900537-16-7, Dist. by Hippocrene Books Inc.). Leviathan Hse.

Notkin, Jerome J. & Gulkin, Sydney. Beginning Science. (How & Why Wonder Books Ser.). (gr. 4-6). deluxe ed. 1.95 o.p. (ISBN 0-448-04006-9, G&D). Putnam Pub Group.

Notley, Alice. How Spring Comes. LC 81-2829. 56p. 1981. signed 30.00 (ISBN 0-915124-41-6, Bookslinger); pap. 7.50 o. p. (ISBN 0-915124-42-4). Toothpaste.
--When I Was Alive. 64p. 1979. pap. 6.00 o.p. (ISBN 0-931428-13-0). Vehicle Edns.

Notley, Alice, jt. auth. see Codrescu, Andrei.

Notman, Larry. Ad Kit Four. 5.00 (ISBN 0-686-84765-2). Newspaper Serv.
--Ad Kit Three. 5.00 (ISBN 0-686-84769-5). Newspaper Serv.
--Ad Kit Two. 5.00 (ISBN 0-686-84768-7). Newspaper Serv.
--Front Office Worker. 5.00 (ISBN 0-686-84771-7). Newspaper Serv.
--Getting Started. 5.00 (ISBN 0-686-84764-4). Newspaper Serv.
--Management: Starting Out. 10.00 (ISBN 0-686-84770-9). Newspaper Serv.
--Professional Ad Sales. 5.00 (ISBN 0-686-84766-0). Newspaper Serv.
--Promotions & Sections. (Illus.). 40p. (Orig.). 1983. pap. 5.00x (ISBN 0-918488-11-7). Newspaper Serv.
--Working Ad Kit. 5.00 (ISBN 0-686-84767-9). Newspaper Serv.

Noton, M. Modern Control Engineering. LC 72-181056. 288p. 1973. text ed. 30.00 (ISBN 0-08-016820-5). Pergamon.

Nott, Kathleen. A Soul in the Quad: The Use of Language in Philosophy & Literature. 1969. 25.00 o.p. (ISBN 0-7100-6502-7). Routledge & Kegan.

Nott, Wanda L., jt. ed. see Hitchcock, Arthur A.

Notter, Lucille. Essentials of Nursing Research. 3rd ed. 192p. 1983. pap. 9.95 (ISBN 0-8261-1595-0). Springer Pub.

Notter, Lucille E. Essentials of Nursing Research. 2nd ed. LC 78-16108. 1978. text ed. 15.95 o.p. (ISBN 0-8261-1592-6); pap. text ed. 9.50 o.p. (ISBN 0-8261-1593-4). Springer Pub.

Notterman, Joseph M. Behavior, a Systematic Approach. pap. text ed. 8.50x (ISBN 0-394-30423-3). Phila Bk Co.

--Readings in Behavior. (Orig.). 1970. pap. text ed. 5.95 (ISBN 0-685-19760-3). Phila Bk Co.

Notterman, Joseph M., ed. Laboratory Manual for Behavior. 1970. pap. 2.95x (ISBN 0-685-38352-0). Phila Bk Co.

Nottingham, Elizabeth K. Religion: A Sociological View. LC 81-40769. 348p. 1981. pap. text ed. 11.75 (ISBN 0-8191-1813-3). U Pr of Amer.

Nottingham, M. A. Principles for Principals. 1977. pap. text ed. 10.50 (ISBN 0-8191-0326-8). U Pr of Amer.

Nottingham, Pamela. Technique of Bobbin Lace. 1976. 24.95 o.p. (ISBN 0-7134-3230-6, Pub. by Batsford England). David & Charles.

--The Technique of Bobbin Lace. LC 82-81526. (Illus.). 224p. 1982. 19.95 (ISBN 0-88332-276-5, 8223). Larousse.

Nottingham, Ronald M. The Fairy Tales of Ronald M. Nottingham, Sr, Vol. II. LC 80-50531. 1982. 5.95 (ISBN 0-533-04643-2). Vantage.

Nottrot, R. Optimal Processes on Manifolds: An Application of Stokes' Theorem. (Lecture Notes on Mathematics Ser.: Vol. 963). 124p. 1983. pap. 8.00 (ISBN 0-387-11963-9). Springer-Verlag.

Nourallah, F. S. Accountant's & Lawyer's Concise Guide to Tax Saving Opportunities. 1977. 27.95 o.p. (ISBN 0-13-001172-X, Busn). P-H.

Nour-Eldin, F. Revision Haematology: With Examination Exercises. (Illus.). 1973. 7.95 o.p. (ISBN 0-407-76700-2). Butterworth.

Nourgier, Louis R. Prehistoric Times. (Picture Histories Ser.). PLB 12.68 (ISBN 0-382-06522-0). Silver.

Nourse. The Body. rev. ed. LC 80-52251. (Life Science Library). PLB 13.40 (ISBN 0-8094-4099-7). Silver.

--Weather. rev. ed. LC 80-52114. (Life Science Library). PLB 13.40 (ISBN 0-8094-4055-5). Silver.

Nourse, Alan. The Fourth Horseman. LC 81-48056. 288p. 1983. 13.95 (ISBN 0-06-038034-9, HarpT). Har-Row.

--The Giant Planets. LC 73-14515. (First Bks). (Illus.). 96p. (gr. 5 up). 1974. PLB 8.90 o.p. (ISBN 0-531-00816-9). Watts.

--Menstruation: Just Plain Talk. (gr. 4 up). PLB 8.90 (ISBN 0-686-65171-5). Watts.

--The Patient Inside the Mayo Clinic. 1979. 12.95 o.p. (ISBN 0-07-047493-1, GB). McGraw.

Nourse, Alan E. Fractures, Dislocations & Sprains. LC 78-6855. (First Bks). (Illus.). (gr. 4 up). 1978. PLB 8.90 s&l (ISBN 0-531-01494-0). Watts.

--The Giant Planets. rev. ed. (First Bks). (Illus.). 72p. (gr. 4 up). 1982. PLB 8.90 o.p. (ISBN 0-531-04383-5). Watts.

--Hormones. (Impact Ser.). (Illus.). (gr. 7 up). 1979. PLB 8.90 s&l (ISBN 0-531-02892-5). Watts.

--Viruses. LC 75-19142. (First Bks.). (Illus.). 72p. (gr. 5 up). 1976. PLB 8.90 (ISBN 0-531-00839-8). Watts.

--Viruses. rev. ed. (First Bk.). (Illus.). 72p. (gr. 4 up). 1983. PLB 8.90 (ISBN 0-531-04534-X). Watts.

--Vitamins. (Career Concise Guides Ser.). (Illus.). (gr. 6 up). 1977. PLB 8.90 (ISBN 0-531-00096-6). Watts.

--Your Immune System. (First Bks.). (Illus.). 72p. (gr. 4). 1982. lib. bdg. 8.90 (ISBN 0-531-04462-9). Watts.

Nourse, E., et al. Three Years of the Agricultural Adjustment Administration. LC 79-173654. (FDR & the Era of the New Deal Ser.). 600p. 1971. Repr. of 1937 ed. lib. bdg. 75.00 (ISBN 0-306-70365-3). Da Capo.

Nourse, Hugh, jt. auth. see Bish, Robert.

Nourse, Hugh O. Regional Economics. LC 68-11935. (Economics Handbook). 1982. text ed. 27.50 (ISBN 0-07-047547-4, C). McGraw.

Nousiainen, Jaakko. Finnish Political System. Hodgson, John H., tr. from Fin. LC 76-120320. (Illus.). 1971. 25.00x o.p. (ISBN 0-674-30211-7). Harvard U Pr.

Nouvel, Walter W., jt. auth. see Haskell, Arnold.

Nouwen, Henri J. Creative Ministry. LC 73-139050. 1978. pap. 3.50 (ISBN 0-385-12616-6, Im). Doubleday.

--A Cry for Mercy: Prayers from the Genesee. LC 80-2563. 176p. 1981. 10.95 (ISBN 0-385-17507-8). Doubleday.

--Cry for Mercy: Prayers from the Genesee. LC 80-2563. (Illus.). 175p. 1983. pap. 5.95 (ISBN 0-385-17508-6, Im). Doubleday.

--Thomas Merton: Contemplative Critic. LC 80-8898. 176p. 1981. pap. 5.72i (ISBN 0-06-066324-3, RD 357, HarpR). Har-Row.

--The Way of the Heart. (Epiphany Bks.). 1983. pap. 2.50 (ISBN 0-345-30530-2). Ballantine.

Nouwen, Henri J. & Gaffney, Walter J. Aging: The Fulfillment of Life. LC 74-1773. 160p. 1974. 3.50 (ISBN 0-385-00918-6, Im). Doubleday.

Nouwen, Henri J. M. Intimacy. LC 80-8906. 160p. 1981. pap. 6.25i (ISBN 0-06-066323-5, RD359, HarpR). Har-Row.

Nova, Craig. The Good Son. 436p. 1982. 15.95 (ISBN 0-440-02976-3, Sey Lawr). Delacorte.

Novack, George. Understanding History: Marxist Essays. Rev. ed. LC 75-186684. 1980. lib. bdg. 18.00 (ISBN 0-87348-606-4); pap. 4.95 (ISBN 0-87348-605-6). Path Pr NY.

Novack, George, ed. Existentialism Versus Marxism. (Orig.). 1966. pap. 3.95 o.s.i. (ISBN 0-440-52438-5, Delta). Dell.

Novak, Adolph. Store Planning & Design. LC 76-56649. (Illus.). 1977. 21.95 (ISBN 0-86730-514-2). Lebhar Friedman.

Novak, Barbara. Nature & Culture: American Landscape & Painting Eighteen Twenty-Five to Eighteen Seventy-Five. (Illus.). 1980. 39.95x (ISBN 0-19-502606-3). Oxford U Pr.

--Nature & Culture: American Landscape & Painting 1825-1875. (Out-of-Ser. Paperback). (Illus.). 1980. pap. 18.95 o.p. (ISBN 0-19-502935-6). Oxford U Pr.

Novak, David. Arithmetic. 514p. 1983. pap. 20.95 (ISBN 0-669-04397-4). Heath.

--Introductory Algebra. 586p. 1983. pap. 20.95 (ISBN 0-669-03804-0). Heath.

Novak, Don. Screenplay Sales Directory the Complete How, Who & Where of Selling your Film-Tv Script. rev. ed. 100p. 1983. pap. 12.95 (ISBN 0-910665-00-1); pap. text ed. 10.35. Joshua Pub Co.

--Scriptwriters Market: How & Where to Sell What You Write For Film & TV. rev ed. 100p. 1983. pap. 12.95 (ISBN 0-910665-01-X); pap. text ed. 10.35. Joshua Pub Co.

Novak, F. A. The Pictorial Encyclopedia of Plants & Flowers. 1965. 10.00 o.p. (ISBN 0-517-09540-8). Crown.

Novak, Franc. Surgical Gynecological Techniques. LC 77-92099. 421p. 1978. 100.00 o.p. (ISBN 0-471-04276-5, Pub. by Wiley Medical). Wiley.

Novak, J., ed. see Schroeder, Albert.

Novak, J., ed. see Symposium on General Topology & Its Relations to Modern Analysis & Algebra - 2nd - Prague - 1967.

Novak, Joseph D., et al. Changing World of Science. (World of Science Ser: Bk. 3). (gr. 3). 1969. text ed. 4.16 o.p. (ISBN 0-672-70699-7); tchr's ed. 4.16 o.p. (ISBN 0-685-07137-5); tchrs' manual 1.52 o.p. (ISBN 0-685-07138-3); unit tests 0.40 o.p. (ISBN 0-685-07139-1). Bobbs.

--Exciting World of Science. (World of Science Ser: Bk. 2). (gr. 2). 1969. text ed. 3.72 o.p. (ISBN 0-672-70695-4); tchrs' ed. 3.72 o.p. (ISBN 0-685-07145-6); tchrs' manual 1.52 o.p. (ISBN 0-685-07146-4). Bobbs.

--Orderly World of Science. (World of Science Ser: Bk. 5). (gr. 5). 1969. text ed. 4.68 o.p. (ISBN 0-672-70707-1); tchrs' ed. 4.68 o.p. (ISBN 0-685-07177-4); tchrs' manual 1.52 o.p. (ISBN 0-685-07178-2); unit tests 0.40 o.p. (ISBN 0-685-07179-0). Bobbs.

Novak, M. Integrated Functional Blocks. (Studies in Electrical & Electronic Engineering: Vol. 3). 1980. 68.00 (ISBN 0-444-99759-8). Elsevier.

Novak, Maximillian E. see Dryden, John.

Novak, Maximillian. English Literature in the Age of Disguise. (California Library Reprint Ser.). 316p. 1982. 24.50x (ISBN 0-520-04628-5, CLRS 114). U of Cal Pr.

Novak, Maximillian E. Realism, Myth, & History in Defoe's Fiction. LC 82-11141. xviii, 170p. 1983. 16.95x (ISBN 0-8032-3307-8). U of Nebr Pr.

Novak, Maximillian E., jt. ed. see Dudley, Edward.

Novak, Melina A., jt. auth. see Harmatz, Morton G.

Novak, Michael. Confession of a Catholic. LC 82-484236. 128p. 1983. 10.53 (ISBN 0-06-066319-7, HarpR). Har-Row.

--The Spirit of Democratic Capitalism. 1982. 19.25 (ISBN 0-671-43154-4). S&S.

Novak, Michael, ed. Liberation South, Liberation North. 1981. pap. 4.75 (ISBN 0-8447-3464-0). Am Enterprise.

Novak, Michael, jt. auth. see Petersen, William.

Novak, P. & Cabelka, J. Models in Hydraulic Engineering. LC 80-22383. (Water Resources Engineering Ser.). 480p. 1981. text ed. 85.95 (ISBN 0-273-08436-4). Pitman Pub MA.

Novak, Richie Y., jt. auth. see Stern, Henry R.

Novak, Robert. Sleeping with Sylvia Plath. 1983. 3.00 (ISBN 0-686-43216-9). Windless Orchard.

--Writing Haiku from Photographs. 1977. 2.00 o.p. (ISBN 0-685-89719-2). Windless Orchard.

Novak, Robert, jt. auth. see Evans, Rowland.

Novak, Rose, jt. auth. see Kamien, Marcia.

Novak, Vladimir, et al, eds. Atlas of Insects Harmful to Forest Trees, Vol. 1. (Illus.). 1977. 76.75 (ISBN 0-444-99874-8). Elsevier.

Novak, W. J., jt. auth. see McPartland, Joseph F.

Novakovic, L. The Pseudo-Spin Method in Magnetism & Ferroelectricity. 200p. 1975. text ed. 37.00 (ISBN 0-08-018060-4). Pergamon.

Novalis, Peter, jt. auth. see Hawes, Gene.

Novarr, David. The Disinterred Muse: Donne's Texts & Contexts. 264p. 1980. 22.50x (ISBN 0-8014-1309-5). Cornell U Pr.

Nove, Alec. An Economic History of the U.S.S.R. rev. ed. 416p. 1983. pap. 5.95 (ISBN 0-14-021403-8, Pelican). Penguin.

--The Economics of Feasible Socialism. 272p. 1983. text ed. 29.50x (ISBN 0-04-335048-8); pap. text ed. 9.95x (ISBN 0-04-335049-6). Allen Unwin.

Noveck, Simon, ed. Contemporary Jewish Thought: A Reader. (Great Bks). 326p. pap. 4.97 o.p. (ISBN 0-686-95127-1). ADL.

--Great Jewish Personalities in Ancient & Medieval Times, Vol. 1. (Great Bks). 351p. pap. 4.97 o.p. (ISBN 0-686-95124-7). ADL.

--Great Jewish Personalities in Modern Times. 366p. pap. 4.97 o.p. (ISBN 0-686-95125-5). ADL.

--Great Jewish Thinkers of the Twentieth Century. (Great Bks). 366p. pap. 4.97 o.p. (ISBN 0-686-95126-3). ADL.

Novello, Joseph R., ed. A Practical Handbook of Psychiatry. (Illus.). 648p. 1974. photocopy ed. spiral 65.00 (ISBN 0-398-02868-0). C C Thomas.

Nover. Cell Compartmentation & Metabolic Channelling: Proceedings. 1980. 90.00 (ISBN 0-444-80150-2). Elsevier.

Noverr, Douglas A., jt. ed. see Huddleston, Eugene L.

Noverraz, Ph. Pseudo-Convexite, Convexite Polynomiale et Domaines D'holomorphie En Dimension Infinie. (Mathematics Studies: Vol. 3). 1975. pap. 17.00 (ISBN 0-444-10692-8, North-Holland). Elsevier.

Novich, Max M. Training & Conditioning of Athletes. 2nd ed. LC 82-17988. (Illus.). 300p. 1983. pap. write for info (ISBN 0-8121-0833-7). Lea & Febiger.

Novick, Andrew C. & Straffon, Ralph A. Vascular Problems in Urologic Surgery. (Illus.). 361p. 1982. 47.50 (ISBN 0-7216-6875-5). Saunders.

Novick, David, et al. Wartime Production Controls. LC 76-5795. (FDR & the Era of the New Deal Ser). 1976. Repr. of 1949 ed. lib. bdg. 49.50 (ISBN 0-306-70818-3). Da Capo.

Novick, Oscar, jt. auth. see Joseph, Lou.

Novik, Jack, jt. auth. see Hayden, Trudy.

Novik, Nimrod & Starr, Joyce, eds. Challenges in the Middle East: Regional Dynamics & Western Security. 144p. 1981. 22.95 (ISBN 0-03-059247-X). Praeger.

Novikov, I. D., jt. auth. see Zel'Dovich, Ya. B.

Novikov, Igor D. Evolution of the Universe. LC 82-9475. 180p. Date not set. price not set (ISBN 0-521-24129-4). Cambridge U Pr.

Novikov, S. P., ed. Mathematical Physics Review, Vol. I, Section C. (Soviet Scietific Reviews Ser.). 222p. 1980. 54.00 (ISBN 3-7186-0019-6). Harwood Academic.

--Mathematical Physics Reviews. Hamermesh, Morton, tr. from Russian. (Soviet Scientific Reviews, Section C: Vol. 4). 240p. 1982. 72.50 (ISBN 0-686-84002-X). Harwood Academic.

--Soviet Scientific Reviews: Mathematical Physics, Vol. 2, Section C. 282p. 1981. 76.00 (ISBN 3-7186-0069-2). Harwood Academic.

--Soviet Scientific Reviews, Mathematical Physics Reviews, Vol. 1, Section C. Date not set. lib. bdg. 54.00 (ISBN 3-7186-0019-6). Harwood Academic.

Novikov, V. Artistic Truths & Dialectics of Creative Work. 342p. 1981. 10.00 (ISBN 0-8285-2296-0, Pub. by Progress Pubs USSR). Imported Pubns.

Novin, D., et al, eds. Hunger: Basic Mechanisms & Clinical Implications. LC 75-14563. 510p. 1976. 43.00 (ISBN 0-89004-059-1). Raven.

Novit, Mitchell S. Essentials of Personnel Management. (Essentials of Management Ser.). (Illus.). 1979. pap. 12.95 ref. (ISBN 0-13-286609-9). P-H.

Novitch, Miriam, ed. Sobibor: Martydom & Revolt. (Illus.). 168p. pap. 4.95 (ISBN 0-686-95087-9). ADL.

Novitski, E., jt. ed. see Ashburner, M.

Novitski, Edward. Human Genetics. 2nd ed. 1982. 25.95x (ISBN 0-02-388570-X). Macmillan.

Novosad, John P. A Management Reference & Guide. 160p. 1982. pap. text ed. 9.95 (ISBN 0-8403-2918-0). Kendall-Hunt.

Novoselov, S. P. Problems of the Communist Movement. 336p. 1981. pap. 6.00 (ISBN 0-8285-2276-6, Pub. by Progress Pubs USSR). Imported Pubns.

Novosti Press Editors. Soviet Almanac. LC 80-7938. (Illus.). 228p. 1981. 19.95 (ISBN 0-15-184601-4); pap. 10.95 o.p. (ISBN 0-15-683923-7). HarBraceJ.

Novotny, Eva. Introduction to Stellar Atmospheres & Interiors. 1973. text ed. 29.95x (ISBN 0-19-501588-6). Oxford U Pr.

Novozhilov, V. V. Problems of Cost-Benefit Analysis in Optimal Planning. LC 69-10004. 1970. 32.50 (ISBN 0-87332-010-7). M E Sharpe.

Nowacki, Wojoiech. Stress Waves in Non-Elastic Solids. 1978. text ed. 44.00 (ISBN 0-08-021294-8). Pergamon.

Nowak, H. Revision der Laubmoosgattung Mitthyridium (Mitten) Robinson Fuer Oreanien (Calymperaceae) (Bryophytorum Bibliotheca: No. 20). (Illus., Ger.). 1981. lib. bdg. 24.00x (ISBN 3-7682-1236-X). Lubrecht & Cramer.

Nowak, Jan. Courier from Warsaw. LC 82-8599. 1982. 24.95X (ISBN 0-8143-1725-1). Wayne St U Pr.

Nowak, Karl F. Collapse of Central Europe. Repr. of 1924 ed. lib. bdg. 19.00x (ISBN 0-8371-4303-9, NOCC). Greenwood.

Nowak, Marion, jt. auth. see Miller, Douglas T.

Nowak, Stefan, jt. ed. see Bottomore, Tom.

Nowak, Thomas J., jt. auth. see Emes, John H.

Nowarre, Heinz. Heinkel HE III: A Documentary History. (Illus.). 192p. 1981. 19.95 (ISBN 0-86720-585-7). Sci Bks Intl.

Nowell-Smith, Geoffrey. Visconti. 1967. pap. 8.95 (ISBN 0-436-09853-9, Pub by Secker & Warburg). David & Charles.

Nowicki, Alexander G. Ecuador: Development Problems & Prospects. xvii, 643p. 1979. pap. 20.00 (ISBN 0-686-36105-9, RC-7908). World Bank.

--Mexico: Manufacturing Sector, Prospects & Policies. 174p. 1979. pap. 15.00 (ISBN 0-686-36111-3, RC-7905). World Bank.

Nowicki, Steven, jt. auth. see Duke, Marshall.

Nowinski, Ira, photos by. Cafe Society: Photographs & Poetry from San Francisco's North Beach. LC 78-63332. 1978. pap. 8.95 o.p. (ISBN 0-916860-05-1). Bean Pub.

--No Vacancy: Urban Redevelopment & the Elderly. LC 79-88979. (Illus.). 1979. pap. 10.95 o.p. (ISBN 0-916860-06-X). Bean Pub.

Nowinski, Joseph K. Becoming Satisfied: A Man's Guide to Sexual Fulfillment. 1980. 12.95 (ISBN 0-13-073031-9, Spec); pap. 6.95 (ISBN 0-13-073007-6, Spec). P-H.

Nowitz, Jack R. Crimes of War. 1978. 7.95 o.p. (ISBN 0-533-03496-5). Vantage.

Nowlan, Kevin B. The Politics of Repeal. LC 75-35339. 248p. 1976. Repr. of 1965 ed. lib. bdg. 17.00x (ISBN 0-8371-8562-9, NOPR). Greenwood.

Nowlan, Nora. The Shannon: River of Loughs & Legends. LC 66-12285. (Rivers of the World Ser.). (Illus.). (gr. 4-7). 1965. PLB 3.98 (ISBN 0-8116-6363-9). Garrard.

--The Tiber: The Roman River. LC 67-14318. (Rivers of the World Ser.). (Illus.). (gr. 4-7). 1967. PLB 3.98 (ISBN 0-8116-6370-1). Garrard.

Nowlan, P. IPS Notebook. rev. ed. (Illus.). 128p. 1980. pap. 3.76x (ISBN 0-913688-02-9). Pawnee Pub.

Nowlan, Robert A. The College of Trivial Knowledge. 160p. 1983. 12.95 (ISBN 0-686-84638-9). Morrow.

--The College of Trivial Knowledge. 160p. pap. 6.95 (ISBN 0-688-02072-0). Quill NY.

--Lessons in College Algebra. 1978. text ed. 20.50 scp o.p. (ISBN 0-06-044862-8, HarpC); answer bklt. free o.p. (ISBN 0-06-364731-1). Har-Row.

Nowlan, Robert A. & Lowe, Cecilia. Lessons in Essential Mathematics: Book I: Arithmetic. 1976. pap. text ed. 18.50 scp o.p. (ISBN 0-06-044863-6, HarpC); supplementary tests avail. o.p. (ISBN 0-06-364728-1). Har-Row.

Nowlin, William G., Jr., ed. see Berkman, Alexander.

Nowlis, Elizabeth A., jt. auth. see Ellis, Janice R.

Nowotny, Alois, ed. Pathological Membranes. (Biomembranes Ser.: Vol. 11). 494p. 1983. 55.00x (ISBN 0-306-41065-6, Plenum Pr). Plenum Pub.

Nowzad, Bahram. The IMF & Its Critics. LC 82-958. (Essays in International Finance Ser.: No. 146). 1981. pap. text ed. 2.50x (ISBN 0-88165-053-6). Princeton U Int Finan Econ.

Noxon, Cathy, jt. auth. see Thornton, Carol A.

Noye, Irenee. Jesus: in Christian Devotion & Contemplation. Oligny, Paul, tr. LC 73-94170. (Religious Experience Ser.: Vol. 1). 1974. pap. 3.95 (ISBN 0-87029-025-8, 20094-9). Abbey.

Noye, J. Numerical Solutions of Partial Differential Questions. 1982. 85.00 (ISBN 0-444-86356-7). Elsevier.

Noyes, Alexander D. Market Place: Reminiscences of a Financial Editor. Repr. of 1938 ed. lib. bdg. 19.75x (ISBN 0-8371-0592-7, NOMP). Greenwood.

--Thirty Years of American Finance. Repr. of 1900 ed. lib. bdg. 17.75x (ISBN 0-8371-1084-X, NOTY). Greenwood.

Noyes, Ethel J. Women of the Mayflower & Women of Plymouth Colony. LC 73-12780. Repr. of 1921 ed. 31.00x (ISBN 0-8103-3668-5). Gale.

Noyes, Florence, tr. see Krasinski, Zygmunt.

Noyes, George R., ed. see Krasinski, Zygmunt.

Noyes, George R., ed. see Mickiewicz, Adam.

Noyes, Joan & Macneill, Norma. Your Child Can Win: Strategies, Activities & Games for Parents of Children with Learning Disabilities. 258p. 1983. 11.95 (ISBN 0-688-01942-0). Morrow.

Noyes, Patricia. How to Talk to Your Cat. (RL 9). 1979. pap. 1.95 (ISBN 0-451-11167-2, AJ1167, Sig). NAL.

Noyes, Robert, ed. Small & Micro Hydroelectric Power Plants: Technology & Feasibility. LC 80-19099. (Energy Tech. Rev. 60). (Illus.). 457p. 1981. 42.00 o.p. (ISBN 0-8155-0819-0). Noyes.

Noyes, Robert W. The Sun, Our Star. (Harvard Books on Astronomy). (Illus.). 304p. 1982. 20.00 (ISBN 0-674-85435-7). Harvard U Pr.

Noyes, Russell. William Wordsworth. (English Authors Ser.). lib. bdg. 11.95 (ISBN 0-8057-1580-0, Twayne). G K Hall.

Noyes, Stanley. Faces & Spirits. 1974. pap. 2.25 (ISBN 0-913270-38-5). Sunstone Pr.

Noyle, Ken. What Time's the Midnight Buffet? 2nd ed. LC 81-82179. (Illus.). 72p. (Orig.). 1982. pap. 4.00 (ISBN 0-940324-00-8). One Thousand Ways.

Nozaki, Mitsuhiro & Yamamoto, Shozo, eds. Oxygenases & Oxygen Metabolism Symposium. 654p. 1982. 48.00 (ISBN 0-12-522780-9). Acad Pr.

Nozick, M., ed. see De Unamuno, M.

Nozick, Martin. Miguel de Unamuno. (World Authors Ser.: Spain: No. 175). lib. bdg. 9.95 o.p. (ISBN 0-8057-2906-2, Twayne). G K Hall.

Nozick, Robert. Anarchy, State & Utopia. LC 73-91081. 1974. 16.95 o.s.i. (ISBN 0-465-00270-6); pap. 9.95x (ISBN 0-465-09720-0, CN5020). Basic.

--Philosophical Explanations. 792p. 1983. pap. 9.95 (ISBN 0-674-66479-5, Belknap Pr). Harvard U Pr.

Nozik, Robert M., jt. auth. see Smith, Ronald E.

Nriagu, J. O. Biogeochemistry of Mercury in the Environment. (Topics in Environmental Health Ser.: Vol. 3). 1980. 156.25 (ISBN 0-444-80110-3). Elsevier.

--Sulfur in the Environment: Ecological Impacts, Pt. 2. 482p. 1978. 68.50 (ISBN 0-471-04255-2, Pub. by Wiley-Interscience). Wiley.

Nriagu, J. O., ed. The Biogeochemistry of Lead in the Environment, 2 pts. (Topics in Environmental Health Ser.: Vol. 1). 1978. Pt. A. 105.75 (ISBN 0-444-41599-8, TEH 1:A, Biomedical Pr); Pt. B. 101.50 (ISBN 0-444-80050-6); Set. 125.75. Elsevier.

Nriagu, Jerome O. Cadmium in the Environment: Ecological Cycling, Pt. I. LC 79-25087. (Environmental Science & Technology: A Wiley-Interscience Series of Texts & Monographs). 1980. 95.00 (ISBN 0-471-06455-6, Pub. by Wiley-Interscience). Wiley.

--Cadmium in the Environment: Health Effects, Pt. II. 1980. 128.95x (ISBN 0-471-05884-X, Pub. by Wiley Interscience). Wiley.

--Copper in the Environment, 2 pts. Incl. Pt. 1. Ecological Cycling. LC 79-10875. 78.50 (ISBN 0-471-04778-3); Pt. 2. Health Effects. LC 79-15062. 75.00 (ISBN 0-471-04777-5). (Environmental Science & Technology: Texts & Monographs). 1980 (Pub. by Wiley-Interscience). Wiley.

--Lead & Lead Poisoning in Antiquity. (Environmental Science & Technology Texts & Monographs). 456p. 1983. 49.95 (ISBN 0-471-08767-X, Pub. by Wiley-Interscience). Wiley.

--Nickel in the Environment. LC 80-16600. (Environmental Science & Technology: a Wiley Interscience Ser. of Texts & Monographs). 833p. 1980. 95.50 (ISBN 0-471-05885-8, Pub. by Wiley Interscience). Wiley.

--Sulfur in the Environment: Atmospheric Cycle, Pt. 1. LC 78-6807. (Environmental Science & Technology Ser.). 464p. 1978. 80.00 (ISBN 0-471-02942-4, Pub. by Wiley-Interscience). Wiley.

--Zinc in the Environment, 2 pts. Incl. Pt. I. Ecological Cycling. 75.00 (ISBN 0-471-05888-2); Pt. II. Health Effects. 75.00 (ISBN 0-471-05889-0). LC 79-19257. (Environmental Science & Technology: a Wiley-Interscience Ser. of Texts & Monographs). 1980. 64.95x ea. (Pub. by Wiley-Interscience). Wiley.

Nsekela, Amon J., ed. Southern Africa: Toward Economic Liberation. (Illus.). 294p. 1981. text ed. 28.50x (ISBN 0-8476-4741-2). Rowman.

Ntalaja, Nzongola. Class Struggles & National Liberation in Africa. LC 82-81279. 175p. (Orig.). 1982. pap. 6.95 (ISBN 0-943324-00-9). Omenana.

Ntiri, Daphne W., ed. & intro. by. One is Not a Woman-One Becomes... The African Woman in a Transitional Society. (Orig.). 1982. pap. 8.95 (ISBN 0-937196-50-9). Sunset Prods.

Ntuk-Idem, Moses. Compensatory Education. 164p. 1978. text ed. 24.00x (ISBN 0-566-00226-4). Gower Pub Ltd.

Nuchelmans, G. Theories of the Proposition. (Linguistics Ser.: Vol. 8). 1973. 31.75 (ISBN 0-444-10513-1, North-Holland); pap. 23.25 (ISBN 0-444-10522-0). Elsevier.

Nuckolls, James L. Interior Lighting for Environmental Designers. LC 75-40413. 371p. 1976. 42.50 (ISBN 0-471-65163-X, Pub. by Wiley-Interscience). Wiley.

Nudas, Alfeo G. Telic Contemplation: A Study of Grace in Seven Filipino Writers. 1980. text ed. 12.00x (ISBN 0-8248-0659-X, Pub. by U of Philippines Pr); pap. text ed. 8.00x (ISBN 0-8248-0660-3). UH Pr.

Nudelman, Jerrold, jt. auth. see Troyka, Lynn Q.

Nuechterlein, Donald E. National Interests & Presidential Leadership: The Setting of Priorities. LC 78-2764. (Westview Special Studies in International Relations & U.S. Foreign Policy). (Illus.). 1978. lib. bdg. 24.00 o.p. (ISBN 0-89158-169-3); pap. 12.00 o.p. (ISBN 0-89158-170-7). Westview.

Nuelle, Helen. The Danger in Loving. (Orig.). 1980. pap. 1.50 o.s.i. (ISBN 0-440-11245-1). Dell.

--The Long Enchantment. (Orig.). 1980. pap. 1.25 o.s.i. (ISBN 0-440-15407-3). Dell.

--Surrender to Love. 1978. pap. 1.25 o.s.i. (ISBN 0-440-11751-8). Dell.

--The Treacherous Heart. (Orig.). 1981. pap. 1.50 o.s.i. (ISBN 0-440-18561-0). Dell.

Nuetzel, Charles, jt. auth. see Bendall, George P.

Nuffield, E. W. X-Ray Diffraction Methods. LC 66-22843. 409p. 1966. 44.50 o.p. (ISBN 0-471-65170-2, Pub. by Wiley-Interscience). Wiley.

Nuffield Foundation. Nuffield Maths Four: Math 5-11. rev. ed. Albany, Eric A., ed. 96p. 1981. tchrs.' ed 15.95 (ISBN 0-582-19174-2); pupils' book 5.50 (ISBN 0-582-19178-5); spiritmasters 39.95 (ISBN 0-582-17017-6). Longman.

--Nuffield Maths Three: Maths 5-11. rev. ed. Albany, Eric A., ed. 112p. 1980. tchrs.' manual 10.95 (ISBN 0-582-19177-7); pupils' book 3.95 (ISBN 0-582-19173-4); spiritmasters avail. (ISBN 0-582-17016-8). Longman.

--Nuffield Maths Two. rev. ed. Albany, Eric A., ed. (Maths 5-11). 50p. 1980. worksheets K-L 35.00 (ISBN 0-582-17015-X); worksheets pack J 23.95 (ISBN 0-582-17014-1); worksheets pack G 29.95 (ISBN 0-582-17011-7); worksheets pack H 29.95 (ISBN 0-582-17012-5); worksheets pack I 23.95 (ISBN 0-582-17013-3). Longman.

Nugent, Nancy, jt. auth. see Morrison, Lester.

Nugent, Neill & Lowe, David. The Left in France. 190p. 1982. 50.00x (ISBN 0-333-24135-5, Pub. by Macmillan England). State Mutual Bk.

Nugent, Robert. Paul Eluard. (World Authors Ser.). 1974. lib. bdg. 15.95 (ISBN 0-8057-2299-8, Twayne). G K Hall.

Nugent, Robert, ed. A Challenge to Love: Gay & Lesbian Catholics in the Church. 256p. 1983. pap. 9.95 (ISBN 0-8245-0518-2). Crossroad NY.

Nugent, Thomas, tr. see Condillac, Etienne Bonnot de.

Nuitter, C. & Thoinan, E. Les Origines de L'opera Francais. LC 77-4106. (Music Reprint Ser.). 1977. Repr. of 1886 ed. lib. bdg. 35.00 (ISBN 0-306-70895-7). Da Capo.

Nukols, M. L. & Smith, K. A., eds. The Characterization of Carbon Dioxide Absorbing Agents for Life Support Equipment. (OED Ser.: Vol. 10). 1982. 40.00 (H00239). ASME.

Null, Gary. Gary Null's Nutrition Sourcebook for the Eighties. 320p. 1983. 15.95 (ISBN 0-02-590900-2); pap. 7.95 (ISBN 0-02-059500-X). Macmillan.

--The New Vegetarian Cookbook. 250p. 1980. 15.95 (ISBN 0-02-590890-1); pap. 8.95 (ISBN 0-02-010040-X). Macmillan.

--Successful Pregnancy. (Orig.). 1976. pap. 1.50 o.s.i. (ISBN 0-515-03622-6). Jove Pubns.

Null, Gary & Null, Steve. The New Vegetarian. 1979. pap. 8.95 (ISBN 0-440-50743-X, Delta). Dell.

Null, Steve, jt. auth. see Null, Gary.

Numata, M., jt. auth. see Holzner, W.

Numbers, Ronald L., ed. Compulsory Health Insurance: The Continuing American Debate. LC 82-6145. (Contributions in Medical History Ser.: No. 11). 184p. 1982. 27.50 (ISBN 0-313-23436-1). Greenwood.

--The Education of American Physicians: Historical Essays. LC 77-20326. 1980. 45.00x (ISBN 0-520-03611-5). U of Cal Pr.

Numeroff, Laura J. Beatrice Doesn't Want to. LC 81-447. (Easy-Read Story Bks.). (Illus.). 32p. (gr. k-3). 1981. 3.95 o.p. (ISBN 0-686-76377-7); PLB 8.60 (ISBN 0-531-04299-5). Watts.

--Digger. LC 82-18242. (Illus.). 32p. (ps-1). 1983. 8.95 (ISBN 0-525-44043-7, 0869-260). Dutton.

Nun, Jose. Latin America: The Hegemonic Crisis & the Military Coup. (Politics of Modernization Ser.: No. 7). 1969. pap. 2.00x o.p. (ISBN 0-87725-207-6). U of Cal Intl St.

Nunally, S. W. Managing Construction Equipment. (Illus.). 1977. text ed. 21.95 (ISBN 0-13-548339-5). P-H.

Nunan, Ted. Countering Educational Design. 176p. 1983. 22.50 (ISBN 0-89397-150-2). Nichols Pub.

Nunberg, Geoffrey, ed. The American Heritage Dictionary. 1982. 13.95 (ISBN 0-686-81876-8). HM.

Nunes, Joseph. Diesel Heavy Truck Applications & Performance Factors. (Illus.). 1981. pap. text ed. 13.95 (ISBN 0-13-211102-0). P-H.

Nunes, Maria L. The Craft of an Absolute Winner: Characterization & Narratology in the Novels of Machado de Assis. LC 82-11717. (Contributions in Afro-American & African Studies: No. 71). 208p. 1983. lib. bdg. 27.95 (ISBN 0-313-23631-3, NCW/). Greenwood.

--Lima Barreto: Bibliography & Translations. 1979. lib. bdg. 22.00 (ISBN 0-8161-8212-4, Hall Reference). G K Hall.

Nunes, Susan. A Small Obligation & Other Stories of Hilo. LC 82-72555. (Orig.). 1982. pap. 5.00 (ISBN 0-910043-00-0). Bamboo Ridge Pr.

Nunes-Vais, Al. Vacation Time Sharing: Is It Right for You? (Illus.). 1983. pap. 9.95x (ISBN 0-910793-02-6). Marlborough Pr.

Nunez, jt. ed. see Dumont.

Nunez, J., jt. ed. see Dumont, J.

Nunez, J., ed. see Symposia on Hormones & Cell Regulation (INSERM), France, 1976-79.

Nunez, Paul L. Electric Fields of the Brain: The Neurophysics of EEG. (Illus.). 1981. text ed. 49.00x (ISBN 0-19-502796-5). Oxford U Pr.

Nungezer, Edwin. Dictionary of Actors & of Other Persons Associated with the Public Representation of Plays in England Before 1642. LC 68-57633. 1969. Repr. of 1929 ed. lib. bdg. 20.00x (ISBN 0-8371-0593-5, NUDI). Greenwood.

Nunis, Doyce B., Jr., ed. see Robinson, W. W.

Nunlist, Robert A. & Seibert, Joseph C. Industrial & Consumer Credit Management. 320p. 1983. text ed. 25.95 (ISBN 0-88244-258-9). Grid Pub.

Nunn, Ancel E., illus. Dreamscapes. 1982. 49.95 (ISBN 0-940672-06-5). Shearer Pub.

Nunn, C. F. Foreign Immigrants in Early Bourbon Mexico: Seventeen Hundred to Seventeen Sixty. LC 78-1159. (Cambridge Latin American Studies: No. 31). 1979. 44.50 (ISBN 0-521-22051-3). Cambridge U Pr.

Nunn, C. S., jt. ed. see Papi, G. U.

Nunn, D. M. The Dyeing of Synthetic-Polymer & Acetate Fibres. 1979p. 1979. 100.00x (ISBN 0-686-98190-1, Pub. by Soc Dyers & Colour); pap. 55.00x (ISBN 0-686-98191-X). State Mutual Bk.

Nunn, Frederick M. Yesterday's Soldiers: European Military Professionalism in South America, 1890-1940. LC 82-6961. xiv, 358p. 1983. 26.95x (ISBN 0-8032-3305-1). U of Nebr Pr.

Nunn, Henry P. Short Syntax of New Testament Greek. 5th ed. 1931. text ed. 7.95x (ISBN 0-521-09941-2). Cambridge U Pr.

Nunn, Jack H. The Soviet First Strike Threat: The U. S. Perspective. 304p. 1982. 31.95 (ISBN 0-03-060607-1). Praeger.

Nunn, R. Gregory, jt. auth. see Azrin, Nathan H.

Nunn, Richard. Easy Home Carpentry. LC 74-18643. (Family Guidebooks Ser.). (Illus.). 1975. pap. 1.95 o.p. (ISBN 0-8487-0373-1). Oxmoor Hse.

Nunn, W. C. Peace Unto You. 1.95 o.p. (ISBN 0-448-01941-8, G&D). Putnam Pub Group.

--Somervell: Story of a Texas County. LC 75-39912. 1975. 10.00 (ISBN 0-912646-27-6). Tex Christian.

Nunn, William L., et al. A Minnesota Gardener's Companion. LC 81-2480. (Illus.). 1981. pap. 7.50 o.p. (ISBN 0-932272-05-3). Minneapolis Tribune.

Nunnally, Jim C. Educational Measurement & Evaluation. 2nd ed. (Illus.). 480p. 1972. text ed. 36.95 (ISBN 0-07-047553-9, C); tchr's. manual 4.95 (ISBN 0-07-047580-6). McGraw.

--Introduction to Psychological Measurement. 1970. text ed. 36.95 (ISBN 0-07-047559-8, C); instructor's manual 3.95 (ISBN 0-07-047560-1). McGraw.

--Introduction to Statistics for Psychology & Education. LC 74-8052. (Illus.). 448p. 1975. pap. text ed. 25.95 (ISBN 0-07-047583-0, C). McGraw.

Nunnally, Jum. Psychometric Theory. (McGraw-Hill Psychology Ser.). 1978. text ed. 39.00 (ISBN 0-07-047465-6, C). McGraw.

Nunnally, S. W. Construction Methods & Management. (Illus.). 1980. text ed. 22.95 (ISBN 0-13-168807-3). P-H.

Nunnelly, Ralph B. Secret Rhythms of the Ancients. 1979. 10.00 o.p. (ISBN 0-533-04003-5). Vantage.

Nunnery. Engine Technology. 2nd ed. 1983. text ed. 19.95 (ISBN 0-408-00516-5). Butterworth.

Nunnery, Michael Y., jt. auth. see Kimbrough, Ralph B.

Nuno, Ruben B. The Art in the Great Temple. (Illus.). 189p. 1982. 65.00x (ISBN 0-86576-036-5). W Kaufmann.

Nunz, Gregory J. Electronics in Our World: A Survey. LC 70-146682. (Illus.). 1972. ref. ed. 23.95 (ISBN 0-13-252288-8). P-H.

Nurco. Ex-Addicts' Self-Help Groups: Potential & Pitfalls. 160p. 1983. 25.95 (ISBN 0-03-063346-X). Praeger.

Nurcombe, Barry. Children of the Dispossessed. (Culture Learning Institute Monographs). 350p. 1976. pap. text ed. 8.75x (ISBN 0-8248-0362-0, Eastwest Ctr). UH Pr.

Nurge, Ethel, ed. The Modern Sioux: Social Systems & Reservation Culture. LC 71-88089. (Illus.). xvi, 352p. 1970. Repr. of 1970 ed. 21.95x (ISBN 0-8032-0715-8); pap. 4.50 o.p. (ISBN 0-8032-5812-7, BB 596, Bison). U of Nebr Pr.

Nurnberg, H. George, jt. auth. see Akins, W. R.

Nurnberg, H. W. Electroanalytical Chemistry, Vol. 10. LC 73-15061. (Advances in Analytical Chemistry & Instrumentation). 609p. 1975. 129.95 (ISBN 0-471-65234-2). Wiley.

Nurnberg, Maxwell. I Always Look up the Word "Egregious". LC 81-1460. 290p. 1981. o. p. 9.95 (ISBN 0-13-448720-6); pap. 5.95 1982 (ISBN 0-13-448712-5). P-H.

Nurnberg, Maxwell & Rosenblum, Morris. All About Words: An Adult Approach to Vocabulary Building. (RL 7). 1971. pap. 3.50 (ISBN 0-451-62071-2, ME2071, Ment). NAL.

Nurnberger, John I., ed. Biological & Environmental Determinants of Early Development. (ARNMD Research Publications Ser: Vol. 51). 457p. 1973. 38.00 (ISBN 0-683-00245-7). Raven.

Nursten, H. E., jt. ed. see Land, D. G.

Nursten, J. P., jt. auth. see Kahn, J. H.

Nursten, Jean, ed. see Gore, Elizabeth.

Nurul Islam. Development Planning in Bangladesh: A Study in Political Economy. LC 77-77354. 1977. 20.00 (ISBN 0-312-19694-6). St Martin.

Nusbacher, Jacob & Berkman, Eugene, eds. Fundamentals of a Pheresis Program. 109p. 1979. 16.00 (ISBN 0-914404-45-8). Am Assn Blood.

Nusbaum, Rosemary. The City Different & the Palace. Edelman, Sandra P., ed. LC 78-17591. (Illus.). 1978. pap. 6.95 (ISBN 0-913270-79-2). Sunstone Pr.

--Tierra Dulce: The Jesse Nusbaum Papers. (Illus.). 128p. 1980. pap. 7.95 (ISBN 0-913270-83-0). Sunstone Pr.

Nusberg, Charlotte, ed. Home Help Services for the Aging Around the World. (Orig.). 1975. pap. text ed. 4.50 (ISBN 0-910473-00-5). Intl Fed Ageing.

--Mandatory Retirement: Blessing or Curse? 27p. (Orig.). 1978. pap. text ed. 3.50 (ISBN 0-910473-06-4). Intl Fed Ageing.

--Self-Determination by the Elderly. (Orig.). 1981. pap. text ed. 2.50 (ISBN 0-910473-11-0). Intl Fed Ageing.

--The Voluntary Agency as an Instrument of Social Change: Effective Advocacy on Behalf of the Aging. (Orig.). 1976. pap. text ed. 2.00 (ISBN 0-910473-01-3). Intl Fed Ageing.

Nusberg, Charlotte & Fast, Franziska, eds. The U. N. World Assembly on the Elderly: The Aging as a Resource; The Aging as a Corcern & the Situation of the Elderly in Austria. 52p. (Orig.). 1981. pap. text ed. 3.50. Intl Fed Ageing.

Nusberg, Charlotte & Osako, Masako M., eds. The Situation of the Asian-Pacific Elderly. 116p. (Orig.). 1981. pap. text ed. 5.00 (ISBN 0-910473-10-2). Intl Fed Ageing.

Nusberg, Charlotte, jt. auth. see Dunham, Arthur.

Nusom, Lynn. The New Mexico Cookbook. Browder, Robyn, ed. LC 82-17730. (Regional Cookbook Ser.). (Illus.). 250p. pap. 7.95 (ISBN 0-89865-249-9). Donning Co.

Nuss, A. Export Marketing (French) 1979. pap. text ed. 8.50x (ISBN 0-582-35157-X); casettes 30.00x (ISBN 0-582-37361-1). Longman.

Nussbaum, jt. auth. see Cassedy.

Nussbaum, A. & Phillips, R. Contemporary Optics for Scientists & Engineers. 1976. 33.95 (ISBN 0-13-170183-5). P-H.

Nussbaum, Al. Gypsy. LC 77-76671. (Pacesetters Ser.). (Illus.). 64p. (gr. 4 up). 1978. PLB 8.65 (ISBN 0-516-02170-2). Childrens.

Nussbaum, Arthur. American-Swiss Private International Law. 2nd ed. LC 58-13617. (Bilateral Studies in Private International Law: No. 1). 93p. 1958. 15.00 (ISBN 0-379-11401-1). Oceana.

Nussbaum, Bruce. The Geography of Power: The World after Oil. 1983. price not set (ISBN 0-671-44571-5). S&S.

Nussbaum, Hedda. Plants Do Amazing Things. LC 75-36471. (Step-up Bk.: No. 24). (Illus.). 72p. (gr. 2-3). 1977. 3.95 (ISBN 0-394-83232-9, BYR); PLB 4.99 (ISBN 0-394-93232-3). Random.

Nussbaum, Louis M., jt. auth. see Callahan, Parnell J.

Nussbaum, Murray. Understanding Hematology. 1973. 15.00 o.p. (ISBN 0-87488-977-4). Med Exam.

Nussbaum, Ronald A. & Brodie, Edmund D., Jr. Amphibians & Reptiles of the Pacific Northwest. LC 82-60055. (Illus.). 1983. 19.95 (ISBN 0-89301-086-3). U Pr of Idaho.

Nussbaumer, H. Fast Fourier Transform & Convolution Algorithms. 2nd ed. (Springer Series in Information Sciences). (Illus.). 280p. 1982. pap. 28.00 (ISBN 0-686-82318-4). Springer-Verlag.

Nussbaumer, Ralph, et al, eds. Teachers Tell All. LC 82-80507. (Illus.). 156p. (Orig.). 1982. pap. 5.95 (ISBN 0-942608-00-3, 419A); pap. text ed. 5.95 (ISBN 0-942608-01-1). Milwaukee Bks.

Nussdorf, Maggie & Nussdorf, Stephen. Dress for Health. 1980. 14.95x (ISBN 0-8117-0524-2). Cancer Control Soc.

Nussdorf, Stephen, jt. auth. see Nussdorf, Maggie.

Nustad, Harry L. & Wesner, Terry H. Essentials of Technical Mathematics. 600p. 1983. text ed. write for info. (ISBN 0-697-08551-1); instrs' manual avail. (ISBN 0-697-08553-8); wkbk. avail. (ISBN 0-697-08552-X). Wm C Brown.

Nustad, Harry L., jt. auth. see Wesner, Terry H.

Nutalaya, P. Geology & Mineral Resources of South East Asia. 887p. 1980. 114.00 o.s.i. (ISBN 0-471-27696-0, Pub. by Wiley-Interscience). Wiley.

Nute, Grace L. Voyageur's Highway: Minnesota's Border Lake Land. LC 65-63529. (Illus.). 113p. 1976. pap. 3.75 (ISBN 0-87351-006-2, X1941). Minn Hist.

Nutman, P. S., ed. Symbiotic Nitrogen Fixation in Plants. LC 75-2732. (International Biological Programme Ser.: No. 7). (Illus.). 652p. 1976. 115.00 (ISBN 0-521-20645-6). Cambridge U Pr.

Nutman, Peter, jt. auth. see Hayes, John.

Nutritient Search Inc. Nutrient Alamanac-Diet-Ailment Contribution. 5.95x o.p. (ISBN 0-07-034847-2). Cancer Control Soc.

Nutrition Committee for South & East Asia, 4th Session, Tokyo, 1956. Report. (FAO Nutrition Meetings Report Ser.: No. 14). 50p. 1957. pap. 4.50 (ISBN 0-686-92813-X, F361, FAO). Unipub.

Nutt, A. Fairy Mythology of Shakespeare. LC 68-24913. (Studies in Shakespeare, No. 24). 1969. Repr. of 1900 ed. lib. bdg. 22.95x (ISBN 0-8383-0929-1). Haskell.

Nuttal, Zelia & Boone, Elizabeth H. The Book of the Life of the Ancient Mexicans, 2 vol. set. LC 81-23065. (The Codex Magliabechiano). (Illus.). 1983. Set. 60.00 (ISBN 0-520-04520-3). Bk. 1, Introduction & Facsimile, 192p. Bk. 2, The Codex Magliabechiano & the Lost Prototype of the Magliabechiane Group, 256p. U of Cal Pr.

Nuttall, A. D. A Common Sky, Philosophy & the Literary Imagination. 35.00x (ISBN 0-686-96993-6, Pub. by Scottish Academic Pr Scotland). STate Mutual Bk.

--Dostoevsky's "Crime & Punishment". 30.00x (ISBN 0-686-96996-0, Pub. by Scottish Academic Pr Scotland). State Mutual Bk.

Nuttall, J., jt. auth. see Watson, K. M.

Nuttall, Jeff. King Twist: A Portrait of Frank Randle. (Illus.). 1978. 16.50 o.p. (ISBN 0-7100-8977-5). Routledge & Kegan.

Nuttall, Jeff & Carmichael, Rodick. Common Factors-Vulgar Factions. (Illus.). 1978. 14.95 o.p. (ISBN 0-7100-8592-3). Routledge & Kegan.

Nutter, Carolyn F. Resume Workbook: A Personal Career File for Job Applications. 5th ed. LC 77-17412. (gr. 9-12). 1978. softcover 5.75 (ISBN 0-910328-00-5). Carroll Pr.

Nuttin, Joseph & Meili, Richard. Experimental Psychology: Vol. 5, Motivation, Emotion & Personality. 1968. 13.50x o.p. (ISBN 0-465-04719-X). Basic.

Nuttin, Jozef. Psychoanalysis & Personality: A Dynamic Theory of Normal Personality. Lamb, George, tr. LC 75-16855. 310p. 1975. Repr. of 1953 ed. lib. bdg. 18.25x (ISBN 0-8371-8259-X, NUPP). Greenwood.

Nutting, Wallace. The Clock Book. LC 70-178648. (Illus.). 1975. Repr. of 1924 ed. 47.00x (ISBN 0-8103-4145-X). Gale.

Nutt-Powell, Thomas E. & Furlong, Michael. The States & Manufactured Housing. (Illus.). 231p. 1980. pap. 10.00 (ISBN 0-943142-02-4). Joint Cen Urban.

Nuzzi, Christina. Parisian Fashions: From the "Journal des Dames et des Modes". LC 79-88270. (Illus., Orig.). 1979. pap. 12.50 o.p. (ISBN 0-8478-0253-1). Rizzoli Intl.

--Parisian Fashions: From the "Journal des Dames et des Modes". LC 79-88270. (Illus.). 124p. 1980. Vol. 2. pap. 12.50 o.p. (ISBN 0-8478-0307-4). Rizzoli Intl.

--Umberto Brunelleschi: Fashion Stylist, Illustrator, Stage & Costume Designer. LC 79-88271. (Illus.). 1979. pap. 12.50 o.p. (ISBN 0-8478-0225-6). Rizzoli Intl.

Nuzzolo, Luccio & Vellucci, Augusto. Tissue Culture Techniques. LC 67-26015. (Illus.). 284p. 1983. 35.00 (ISBN 0-87527-117-0). Green.

Nwabueze, B. O. Judicialism in Commonwealth Africa. LC 76-27553. 1977. 27.50x (ISBN 0-312-44695-0). St Martin.

--The Presidential Constitution of Nigeria. LC 82-47637. 558p. 1982. 45.00x (ISBN 0-312-64032-3). St Martin.

--Presidentialism in Commonwealth Africa. LC 74-76990. 480p. 1975. 32.50 (ISBN 0-312-64120-6). St Martin.

Nwogugu, E. I. Family Law in Nigeria. LC 76-983596. 1977. pap. text ed. 50.00x o.p. (ISBN 0-435-89601-6). Heinemann Ed.

Ny, J. F. Le see Le Ny, J. F. & Kintsch, W.

Nyang, Sulayman. Ali A. Mazrui: The Man & His Works. (Third World Monograph Ser.). 42p. (Orig.). 1981. pap. 2.00x o.p. (ISBN 0-931494-08-7). Brunswick Pub.

Nyang, Sulayman S., ed. see Jarmon, Charles.

Nyangoni, Wellington W. The O. E. C. D. & Western Mining Multinational Corporations in the Republic of South Africa. LC 81-43671. (Illus.). 238p. (Orig.). 1982. PLB 22.25 (ISBN 0-8191-2405-2); pap. text ed. 10.75 (ISBN 0-8191-2406-0). U Pr of Amer.

Nyber, D. M. Help for Families With a Problem Child. (Trauma Bks.: Ser. 2). 1983. pap. 2.50 (ISBN 0-570-08259-5). Concordia.

Nyberg, Bartell, jt. auth. see Eells, Robert.

Nyberg, Stanley E., jt. auth. see Zechmeister, Eugene B.

Nyborg, Philip S. & McCarter, Pender M., eds. Information Processing in the United States: A Quantitative Summary. (Illus.). vii, 55p. 1977. saddle-stitch 8.00 (ISBN 0-686-68785-X). AFIPS Pr.

Nyborg, W. L. Intermediate Biophysical Mechanics. LC 75-14973. 1976. 19.95 o.p. (ISBN 0-8465-4860-7). Benjamin-Cummings.

Nycum, S., jt. auth. see Bigelow, R.

Nycum, Susan. Software Proprietary Rights. 1982. text ed. 21.95 (ISBN 0-8359-7024-8). Reston.

Nydahl, John, jt. auth. see Silver, Howard.

Nye, Alvan C. American Colonial Furniture in Scaled Drawings. (Crafts Ser.). (Illus.). 64p. 1982. pap. 3.95 (ISBN 0-486-21560-1). Dover.

Nye, B. C. & Dorr, E. L. Product Planning. (Occupational Manuals & Projects in Marketing). 1970. text ed. 5.96 o.p. (ISBN 0-07-047561-X, G); tchr's manual o.p. 3.50 o.p. (ISBN 0-07-047593-8). McGraw.

Nye, Bill. Bill Nye's Western Humor. Larson, T. A., ed. LC 67-20599. (Illus.). xxiv, 199p. 1968. 14.50x (ISBN 0-8032-0133-8); pap. 5.95 (ISBN 0-8032-5821-6, BB 605, Bison). U of Nebr Pr.

Nye, Doug. Motor Racing in Color. (Illus.). 1978. 12.95 o.p. (ISBN 0-7137-0904-9, Pub. by Blandford Pr England). Sterling.

--Motor Racing in Color. (Illus.). 214p. 1980. pap. 6.95 o.p. (ISBN 0-686-96896-4, Pub. by Blandford Pr England). Sterling.

Nye, Doug, jt. auth. see Tanner, Hans.

Nye, F. Ivan. Family Relationships & Delinquent Behavior. LC 73-8562. 168p. 1973. Repr. of 1958 ed. lib. bdg. 16.00x (ISBN 0-8371-6967-4, NYFR). Greenwood.

Nye, F. Ivan & Berardo, Felix M. The Family: Its Structure & Interaction. Scott, Kenneth J., ed. (Illus.). 658p. 1973. text ed. 22.95x (ISBN 0-02-388740-0). Macmillan.

Nye, I. W. The Generic Names of Moths of the World, Vol. I: Noctuidae, Agaristidae & Nolidae. (Illus.). 568p. 1975. 81.25x (ISBN 0-565-00770-X, Pub. by Brit Mus Nat Hist England). Sabbot-Natural Hist Bks.

Nye, I. W., jt. auth. see Fletcher, D. S.

Nye, J. Michael. Who, What & Where in Communications Security. 130p. 1981. 200.00 (ISBN 0-686-98046-8). Telecom Lib.

Nye, Joseph, jt. ed. see Deese, David.

Nye, Mary J., ed. The Question of the Atom: From the Karlsruhe Congress to the First Solvay Conference, 1860-1911. (History of Modern Physics 1800-1950 Ser.: Vol. 4). (Illus.). 1983. price not set Ltd. Ed. (ISBN 0-938228-07-2). Tomash Pubs.

Nye, Naomi S. Hugging the Jukebox: Selected by Josephine Miles. 72p. 1982. 12.50 (ISBN 0-525-24116-7, 01214-360); pap. 5.95 (ISBN 0-525-47703-9, 0577-180). Dutton.

Nye, Nelson. The Long Run. (General Ser.). 1983. lib. bdg. 11.95 (ISBN 0-8161-3454-5, Large Print Bks). G K Hall.

--Triggers for Six. 256p. 1982. pap. 2.50 o.p. (ISBN 0-505-51844-9). Tower Bks.

Nye, Nelson C. Your Western Horse. LC 63-9372. (Illus.). 1963. 7.50 o.p. (ISBN 0-668-02834-3). Arco.

Nye, Peter. The Storm. LC 82-4852. (Triumph Bks.). (Illus.). 96p. (gr. 7 up). 1982. PLB 8.90 (ISBN 0-531-04425-4). Watts.

Nye, Richard C., intro. by see Lincoln, Warren B., et al.

Nye, Robert. Beowulf. (YA) (gr. 7 up). 1982. pap. 1.95 (ISBN 0-686-85864-6, LFL). Dell.

--Falstaff. 1976. 8.95 o.p. (ISBN 0-316-61738-5). Little.

--Faust. 290p. 1981. 12.95 o.s.i. (ISBN 0-399-12606-6). Putnam Pub Group.

--Merlin. LC 78-26799. 1979. 10.00 o.p. (ISBN 0-399-12331-8). Putnam Pub Group.

--The Voyage of the Destiny. LC 82-10194. 400p. 1982. 15.95 (ISBN 0-399-12760-7). Putnam Pub Group.

Nye, Robert, jt. auth. see Nye, Vernice.

Nye, Robert, ed. The English Sermon Seventeen Hundred Fifty to Eighteen Hundred Fifty, Vol. 3. 325p. 1976. text ed. 22.25x (ISBN 0-85635-095-8, Pub. by Carcanet New Pr England). Humanities.

Nye, Robert, ed. see Barnes, William.

Nye, Robert, ed. see Ralegh, Walter.

Nye, Robert E. & Bergethon, Bjorner. Basic Music: Functional Musicianship for the Non-Music Major. 5th ed. (Illus.). 240p. 1981. pap. text ed. 14.95 (ISBN 0-13-065672-0). P-H.

Nye, Russel B. A Baker's Dozen: Thirteen Unusual Americans. LC 74-6100. 300p. 1974. Repr. of 1956 ed. lib. bdg. 17.50x (ISBN 0-8371-7495-3, NYBD). Greenwood.

--Society & Culture in America: 1830-1860. (New American Nation Ser.). 1974. pap. 6.95xi o.p. (ISBN 0-06-131826-4, TB1826, Torch). Har-Row.

--William Lloyd Garrison & the Humanitarian Reformers. (Library of American Biography). 215p. 1969. pap. 5.95 (ISBN 0-316-61736-9). Little.

Nye, Russel B., ed. American Literary History, Sixteen Seven to Eighteen Thirty. (Orig.). 1970. pap. text ed. 4.50x (ISBN 0-685-04147-6). Phila Bk Co.

Nye, Russell B. Society & Culture in America: 1830-1860. LC 73-14277. (New American Nation Ser.). (Illus.). 416p. (YA) 1974. 17.26xi (ISBN 0-06-013229-9, HarpT). Har-Row.

Nye, Valerie. Crystal Fire. (Second Chance at Love: No. 23). 192p. (Orig.). 1982. pap. 1.75 o.s.i. (ISBN 0-515-06131-X). Jove Pubns.

Nye, Vernice & Nye, Robert. Music in the Elementary School. 4th ed. (Illus.). 1977. text ed. 20.95 (ISBN 0-13-608117-7). P-H.

Nye, Vernice T. Music for Young Children. 2nd ed. 307p. 1979. pap. text ed. write for info. o.p. (ISBN 0-697-03419-4). Wm C Brown.

--Music for Young Children. 3rd ed. 240p. 1983. pap. text ed. write for info. (ISBN 0-697-03562-X). Wm C Brown.

Nye, W. P. Nectar & Pollen Plants of Utah. 81p. (Orig.). 1971. pap. 4.00 o.p. (ISBN 0-87421-040-2). Utah St U Pr.

Nye, Wilbur S. Plains Indian Raiders: The Final Phases of Warfare from the Arkansas to the Red River. LC 67-24624. (Illus.). 1974. 22.50 o.p. (ISBN 0-8061-0803-7); pap. 8.95 o.p. (ISBN 0-8061-1175-5). U of Okla Pr.

Nyerere, Julius K. Freedom & Development-Uhuru Na Maendeleo. (Illus.). 1974. pap. 6.95x (ISBN 0-19-519772-0, GB412, GB). Oxford U Pr.

--Ujamaa: Essays on Socialism. 1971. pap. 6.95 (ISBN 0-19-501474-X, GB359, GB). Oxford U Pr.

Nygaard, Joseph M. The Counselor & Student's Legal Rights. (Guidance Monograph). 1973. pap. text ed. 2.40 o.p. (ISBN 0-395-14338-1). HM.

Nygaard, Kaare & Hale, Nathan C. The Spirit of Man: The Sculpture of Kaare Nygaard. (Illus.). 160p. 1982. 25.00 (ISBN 0-292-77575-X). U of Tex Pr.

Nygard, F. & Sandstrom, A. Measuring Income Inequality. (Stockholm Studies in Statistics: Vol. 1). 436p. 1982. pap. text ed. 30.00x (ISBN 91-22-00439-4, Pub. by Almqvist & Wiksell Sweden). Humanities.

Nygards, Nils. Wood Gas Generator For Vehicles. 18p. 1979. pamphlet 3.00 (ISBN 0-686-35951-8). Rutan Pub.

Nygren, Birgitta, jt. auth. see Anell, Lars.

Nyhan, William L. & Jones, Kenneth L., eds. Dysmorphology: Pt. B of Annual Review of Birth Defects, 1981. LC 82-10006. (Birth Defects; Original Article Ser.: Vol. 18, No. 3B). 328p. 1982. 56.00 (ISBN 0-8451-1048-9). A R Liss.

--Prenatal Dianosis & Mechanisms of Teratogenesis: Pt. A of Annual Review of Birth Defects, 1981. LC 82-9992. (Birth Defects; Original Article Ser.: Vol. 18, No. 3A). 232p. 1982. 36.00 (ISBN 0-8451-1047-0). A R Liss.

Nyhart, J. D. & Carrow, Milton M., eds. Law & Science in Collaboration: Resolving Regulatory Issues of Science & Technology. LC 81-47689. 320p. 1983. 29.95x (ISBN 0-669-04907-7). Lexington Bks.

Nyhoff, Larry & Leestma, Sanford. Problem Solving with FORTRAN 77. 368p. 1983. pap. text ed. 18.95 (ISBN 0-02-388720-6). Macmillan.

Nyilas, Jozsef. The World Economy & Its Main Developmental Tendencies. 1982. lib. bdg. 49.50 (ISBN 0-686-38405-9, Pub. by Martinus Nijhoff Netherlands). Kluwer Boston.

Nyirjesy, Istvan, jt. ed. see Machant, Douglas J.

Nykiel, Ronald A. Marketing in the Hospitality Industry. (Illus.). 320p. 1983. text ed. 19.95 (ISBN 0-8436-0886-2). CBI Pub.

Nykoruk, Barbara, ed. Authors in the News, 2 vols. LC 75-13541. (Illus.). 502p. 58.00x ea.; Vol. 1 1975. (ISBN 0-8103-0043-5); Vol. 2 1976. (ISBN 0-8103-0045-1). Gale.

--Business People in the News: A Compilation of News Stories & Feature Articles from American Newspapers & Magazines Covering People in Industry, Finance & Labor. LC 76-4617. (Illus.). xl, 402p. 1976. 68.00x (ISBN 0-8103-0044-3). Gale.

Nyland, Ralph & Larson, Charles. Forestry & Its Career Opportunities. 4th ed. (Illus.). 416p. 1983. text ed. 29.95x (ISBN 0-07-056979-7). McGraw.

Nylander, Jane C. Fabrics for Historic Buildings. 3rd ed. (Illus.). 96p. 1983. pap. 9.95 (ISBN 0-89133-109-3). Preservation Pr.

Nylander, Richard. Wallpapers for Historic Buildings. (Illus.). 96p. (Orig.). 1983. pap. 9.95 (ISBN 0-89133-110-7). Preservation Pr.

Nylander, W. Prodromus Lichenographiae Galliae et Algeriae. 1968. pap. 24.00 (ISBN 3-7682-0343-3). Lubrecht & Cramer.

Nylander, William. Lichenes Scandinaviae. 1968. pap. 27.20 (ISBN 3-7682-0459-6). Lubrecht & Cramer.

Nyman, C. J., et al. Problems for General Chemistry & Qualitative Analysis. 4th ed. LC 79-24489. 342p. 1980. pap. text ed. 10.50 (ISBN 0-471-05299-X). Wiley.

Nyman, Michael. Experimental Music: Cage & Beyond. LC 74-4848. (Illus.). 1975. Repr. of 1974 ed. 15.95 (ISBN 0-02-871200-5). Schirmer Bks.

Nyman, R. Carter & Smith, E. D. Union-Management Cooperation in the "Stretch-Out". 1934. 42.50x (ISBN 0-685-69848-3). Elliots Bks.

Nyman, Tore. A Guide to the Teaching of Collective Bargaining. 91p. 1981. 2.85 (ISBN 0-686-84631-1). Intl Labour Office.

Nyquist, Robert W. Where There's a Will. 1978. 8.95 o.p. (ISBN 0-533-03570-8). Vantage.

Nyquist, Thomas E. Toward a Theory of the African Upper Stratum in South Africa. LC 72-619647. (Papers in International Studies: Africa: No. 15). (Illus.). pap. 4.50x (ISBN 0-89680-048-2, Ohio U Ctr Intl). Ohio U Pr.

Nyrop, Christopher. Kiss & Its History. Harvey, William F., tr. LC 68-22040. 1968. Repr. of 1901 ed. 30.00x (ISBN 0-8103-3512-3). Gale.

Nystrand, Raphael O., jt. auth. see Marks, Walter.

Nystrom, Carolyn. Acts 1-12: Church on the Move. (Young Fisherman Bible Studyguides). (gr. 7-12). 1979. tchrs. ed. 4.95 (ISBN 0-87788-126-X); student ed. 2.95 (ISBN 0-87788-125-1). Shaw Pubs.

--Forgive Me If I'm Frayed Around the Edges. (Illus., Orig.). 1977. pap. 3.50 o.p. (ISBN 0-8024-2823-1). Moody.

--Growing Jesus' Way. (Children's Bible Basics Ser.). 1982. text ed. 4.50 (ISBN 0-8024-5999-4). Moody.

--The Holy Spirit in Me. (Children's Bible Ser.). 32p. (ps-2). 1980. pap. 4.50 (ISBN 0-8024-5994-3). Moody.

--Jesus Is No Secret. (Children's Bible Basics Ser.). (Illus.). (gr. 2 up). 1983. 4.50 (ISBN 0-8024-0193-7). Moody.

--Mark: God on the Move. (Young Fisherman Bible Studyguides Ser.). (gr. 7-12). 1978. pap. 1.75 tchr's ed. (ISBN 0-87788-312-2); student ed. 2.95 (ISBN 0-87788-311-4). Shaw Pubs.

--Romans: Christianity on Trial. (Young Fisherman Bible Studyguides). (Illus.). 124p. 1980. pap. 4.95 tchr's ed. (ISBN 0-87788-899-X); student ed. 3.95 (ISBN 0-87788-898-1). Shaw Pubs.

--What Happens When We Die? (Children's Bible Basics Ser.). 32p. 1981. 4.50 (ISBN 0-8024-5995-1). Moody.

--What Is a Christian? (Children's Bible Basics Ser.). 32p. 1981. 4.50 (ISBN 0-8024-5997-8). Moody.

--What Is a Church? (Children's Bible Basics Ser.). 32p. 1981. 4.50 (ISBN 0-8024-5998-6). Moody.

--What Is Prayer? (Children's Bible Basics Ser.). 32p. (ps-2). 1980. pap. 4.50 (ISBN 0-8024-5991-9). Moody.

--What Is the Bible? (Children's Bible Basics Ser.). 32p. 1982. 4.50 (ISBN 0-8024-0157-0). Moody.

--Who Is God? (Children's Bible Basics Ser.). 32p. (ps-2). 1980. pap. 4.50 (ISBN 0-8024-5992-7). Moody.

--Who Is Jesus? (Children's Bible Basics Ser.). 32p. (ps-2). 1980. pap. 4.50 (ISBN 0-8024-5993-5). Moody.

--Why Do I Do Things Wrong? (Children's Bible Basics Ser.). 32p. 1981. 4.50 (ISBN 0-8024-5996-X). Moody.

Nystrom, Carolyn & Fromer, Margaret. Acts 13-28: Missions Accomplished. (Young Fisherman Bible Studyguides). (gr. 7-12). 1979. tchrs. ed. 4.95 (ISBN 0-87788-011-5); student ed. 2.95 (ISBN 0-87788-010-7). Shaw Pubs.

Nystrom, Carolyn, jt. auth. see Fromer, Margaret.

Nystrom, Dennis. Occupation & Career Education Legislation. LC 79-12548. pap. 3.40 o.p. (ISBN 0-672-97133-X); pap. 10.50 o.p. Bobbs.

Nystrom, Harry. Creativity & Innovation. LC 78-8594. 125p. 1979. 36.95 (ISBN 0-471-99682-3, Pub. by Wiley-Interscience). Wiley.

Nystuen, John D., jt. auth. see Kolars, John F.

Nyuka. Pleasure Boat. (Illus.). 24p. (Orig.). 1981. ltd. ed. signed & numbered by author 10.00 o.p. (ISBN 0-938566-09-1). Adastra Pr.

Nyvlt, J. Solid-Liquid Phase Equilibria. 1977. 53.25 (ISBN 0-444-99850-0). Elsevier.

Nyvlt, Jaroslav. Industrial Crystallisation: The Present State of the Art. 2nd ed. 1983. pap. write for info. (ISBN 0-89573-069-3). Verlag-Chemie.

Nziramasanga, Mudziviri, jt. auth. see Obidegwu, Chukwuma F.

Nzongola-Ntalaja, jt. ed. see Magubane, Bernard.

Nzula, A., et al. Forced Labour in Colonial Africa. Cohen, Robin, ed. 218p. (Orig.). 1979. 30.00 (ISBN 0-905762-30-4, Pub. by Zed Pr England); pap. 8.50 (ISBN 0-905762-31-2, Pub. by Zed Pr England). Lawrence Hill.

O

Oades, J. M. & Lewis, D. G. Red-Brown Earths of Australia. 1982. 40.00x (ISBN 0-686-97899-4, Pub. by CSIRO Australia). State Mutual Bk.

Oag, Shay. In the Presence of Death: Antonio Ordonez. (Illus.). 1969. 15.00 o.p. (ISBN 0-698-10183-9, Coward). Putnam Pub Group.

Oakes, Annalee, ed. see American Association of Critical-Care Nurses.

Oakes, Dean, jt. auth. see Hickman, John.

Oakes, George W. Turn Left at the Pub. 1977. traveltex 5.95 o.p. (ISBN 0-679-50671-3). McKay.

Oakes, Peter, jt. ed. see Mauger, Ivan.

Oakes, William. Scenery of the White Mountains. LC 77-135880. (Illus.). 1970. Repr. of 1848 ed. 45.00x (ISBN 0-912274-05-0). NH Pub Co.

Oakeshott, G. B. Volcanoes & Earthquakes. 1975. 12.50 (ISBN 0-07-047492-3, C). McGraw.

Oakeshott, Gordon B. California's Changing Landscapes. 2nd ed. (Illus.). 1978. pap. text ed. 27.50 (ISBN 0-07-047584-9, C). McGraw.

Oakeshott, Michael. On History & Other Essays. LC 82-22617. 224p. 1983. text ed. 25.75x (ISBN 0-389-20355-6). B&N Imports.

Oakeshott, Michael, ed. see Hobbes, Thomas.

Oakeshott, Walter. Sigena: Romanesque Paintings in Spain & the Winchester Bible Artists. (Illus.). 227p. 1972. 49.00x (ISBN 0-19-921006-3). Oxford U Pr.

Oakey, R. P. High Technology Industry & Industrial Location. 144p. 1981. text ed. 36.75x (ISBN 0-566-00419-4). Gower Pub Ltd.

Oakey, Virginia, jt. auth. see Nash, Constance.

Oakland, Thomas P. Divorced Fathers: Reconstructing a Viable Life. (Illus.). 176p. 1983. 16.95x (ISBN 0-89885-101-7). Human Sci Pr.

Oakley, Barry. The Great God Mogadon & Other Plays. 119p. 1980. pap. 14.95x (ISBN 0-7022-1437-X); pap. 7.95x (ISBN 0-686-37770-2). U of Queensland Pr.

Oakley, Bruce & Schafer, Rollie. Neuroanatomy: Dissection of the Sheep Brain. (Illus.). 32p. 1980. pap. text ed. 2.98x (ISBN 0-472-08691-X). U of Mich Pr.

Oakley, Carey, ed. Archaeological Investigations in the Gainesville Lake Area of the Tennessee-Tombigee Waterway, 5 vols. Incl. Vol. I. The Gainseville Lake Area Excavations. Jenkins, Ned J. & Ensor, H. Blaine. xiv, 157p. (Orig.). 1981. pap. text ed. 21.00x (ISBN 0-8173-0157-7); Vol. II. Gainesville Lake Area Ceramic Description & Chronology. Jenkins, Ned J. xx, 445p. (Orig.). 1981. pap. text ed. 46.00x (ISBN 0-8173-0158-5); Vol. III. Gainesville Lake Area Lithics: Chronology, Technology & Use. Ensor, H. Blaine. xiii, 303p. (Orig.). 1981. pap. text ed. 36.00x (ISBN 0-8173-0159-3); Vol. IV. Biocultural Studies in the Gainesville Lake Area. Caddell, Gloria M., et al. v, 334p. (Orig.). 1981. pap. text ed. 28.50x (ISBN 0-8173-0160-7); Vol. V. Archaeology of the Gainesville Lake Area. Jenkins, Ned. J. xv, 258p. (Orig.). 1982. pap. text ed. 23.50x (ISBN 0-8173-0161-5). (Illus.). 1981-82. Set. pap. text ed. 153.25x (ISBN 0-8173-0156-9). U of Ala Pr.

Oakley, Cletus O., jt. auth. see Allendoerfer, Carl B.

Oakley, Francis. Political Thought of Pierre D'Ailly. (Yale Historical Pubs. Miscellany Ser.: No. 81). 1964. 49.50x (ISBN 0-685-69849-1). Elliots Bks.

Oakley, Graham. The Church Mice in Action. LC 82-11394. (Illus.). 32p. 1983. 11.95 (ISBN 0-689-30949-X). Atheneum.

--Hetty & Harriet. LC 81-8024. (Illus.). 32p. (gr. k-4). 1982. PLB 12.95 (ISBN 0-689-30888-4). Atheneum.

Oakley, Janet & Parkin, S. F. A Textbook for Dental Surgery Assistants. (Illus.). 240p. 1983. pap. 9.95 (ISBN 0-571-18070-1). Faber & Faber.

Oakley, Mary A. Elizabeth Cady Stanton: A Biography. 2nd ed. LC 72-80249. 160p. pap. 2.95 o.s.i. (ISBN 0-912670-03-7). Feminist Pr.

Oakley, Neil, jt. auth. see Drain, Robert H.

Oakman, Barbara F. Countdown to Successful Reading. (Illus., Orig.). (gr. 5-9). 1971. pap. text ed. 14.95 (ISBN 0-13-183616-1). P-H.

Oakman, Robert L. Computer Methods for Literary Research. LC 78-31468. (Illus.). xiv, 236p. 1980. lib. bdg. 17.95x (ISBN 0-87249-381-4). U of SC Pr.

Oaks, Priscilla S. Minority Studies: An Selected Annotated Bibliography. 1976. lib. bdg. 25.00 (ISBN 0-8161-1092-1, Hall Reference). G K Hall.

Oana. Bobby Bear & the Blizzard. LC 80-82950. (Bobby Bear Ser.). (Illus.). (ps-1). PLB 6.75x (ISBN 0-87783-151-3). Oddo.

--Bobby Bear Goes to the Beach. LC 80-82951. (Bobby Bear Ser.). (Illus.). (ps-1). PLB 6.75x (ISBN 0-87783-153-X). Oddo.

--Timmy Tiger & the Butterfly Net. LC 80-82954. (Timmy Tiger Ser.). (Illus.). (ps-4). PLB 6.75x (ISBN 0-87783-160-2). Oddo.

--Timmy Tiger & the Masked Bandit. LC 80-82955. (Timmy Tiger Ser.). (Illus.). (ps-4). PLB 6.75x (ISBN 0-87783-161-0). Oddo.

Oana, Katy D. The Little Dog Who Wouldn't Be. LC 77-18351. (Illus.). (gr. 2-4). 1978. PLB 6.75x (ISBN 0-87783-150-5). Oddo.

--Robbie & the Raggedy Scarecrow. LC 77-18349. (Oddo Sound Ser.). (Illus.). (gr. 2-4). 1978. PLB 6.75 (ISBN 0-87783-154-8). Oddo.

--Shasta & the Shebang Machine. LC 77-18350. (Oddo Sound Ser.). (Illus.). (gr. 2-4). 1978. PLB 6.75x (ISBN 0-87783-152-1). Oddo.

Oandasan, William. A Branch of California Redwood. 62p. 1981. pap. 5.00 (ISBN 0-935626-03-4). U Cal AISC.

Oates. Portrait of America, 2 Vols. 3rd ed. 1983. 12.95 ea. HM.

Oates, J. A. Welding & Cutting. (Illus.). 93p. 1976. 7.50x (ISBN 0-85344-094-8). Intl Pubns Serv.

Oates, J. C. Shandyism & Sentiment, Seventy Sixty to Eighteen Hundred. 60p. 1982. Repr. of 1968 ed. lib. bdg. 10.00 (ISBN 0-89760-633-7). Telegraph Bks.

Oates, John, ed. Early Cognitive Development. LC 78-17694. 1979. 29.95x o.s.i. (ISBN 0-470-26431-4). Halsted Pr.

Oates, John A., ed. Prostaglandins & the Cardiovascular System, Vol. 9. (Advances in Prostaglandin & Thromboxane, & Leukotriene Research Ser.). 450p. 1982. 48.50 (ISBN 0-89004-580-1). Raven.

Oates, John F. & Samuel, Alan E. Yale Papryi in the Beinecte Rare Book & Manuscript Library I. (American Society of Papyrology Ser.). 30.00 (ISBN 0-686-95222-7, 31-00-02). Scholars Pr CA.

Oates, Joyce C. Bellefleur. 688p. 1981. pap. 4.50 (ISBN 0-446-30732-7). Warner Bks.

--Contraries: Essays. 1981. 17.50x (ISBN 0-19-502884-8). Oxford U Pr.

--The Profane Art: Essays & Reviews. 256p. 1983. 17.50 (ISBN 0-525-03057-3, 01699-150). Dutton.

Oates, Joyce C., ed. Night Walks. 304p. 1982. 14.95 (ISBN 0-86538-022-8). Ontario Rev NJ.

Oates, Joyce Carol. Invisible Woman. 112p. 1982. 12.95 o.p. (ISBN 0-86538-015-5); deluxe ed. 65.00 limited ed. (ISBN 0-86538-021-X); pap. 7.95 (ISBN 0-86538-016-3). Ontario Rev NJ.

--The Profane Art: Essays & Reviews. 224p. 1983. 13.95 (ISBN 0-525-24166-3, 01354-410). Dutton.

--A Sentimental Education: Stories. 192p. 1981. 11.95 (ISBN 0-525-19950-0, Obelisk). Dutton.

--A Sentimental Education: Stories. 1982. pap. 4.95 (ISBN 0-525-48021-8, 0481-140, Obelisk). Dutton.

Oates, Joyce Carol, jt. ed. see Smith, Raymond J.

Oates, Stephen. Portrait of America, Vol. 1 & 2. 3rd ed. LC 82-81984. 480p. 1982. Vol. 1. pap. text ed. 12.95 (ISBN 0-395-32778-4); Vol. 2. pap. text ed. 12.95 (ISBN 0-395-32779-2); write for info. instr's manual (ISBN 0-395-32780-6). HM.

Oates, Stephen B. The Fires of Jubilee: Nat Turner's Fierce Rebellion. 224p. 1976. pap. 3.50 (ISBN 0-451-62141-7, ME2141, Ment). NAL.

--Let the Trumpet Sound: The Life of Martin Luther King, Jr. (Illus.). 416p. 1982. 19.18i (ISBN 0-06-014993-0, HarpT). Har-Row.

--Our Fiery Trial: Abraham Lincoln, John Brown, & the Civil War Era. LC 78-16286. 1979. 11.50x (ISBN 0-87023-261-4). U of Mass Pr.

--Portrait of America: Vol. 1, from the Cliff Dwellers to the End of Reconstruction. 2nd ed. LC 77-77432. (Illus.). 1978. pap. text ed. 12.50 (ISBN 0-395-25372-1). HM.

--Portrait of America: Vol. 2, from Reconstruction to the Present. 2nd ed. LC 77-77432. (Illus.). 1978. pap. text ed. 12.50 (ISBN 0-395-25373-X). HM.

--To Purge This Land with Blood: A Biography of John Brown. 1972. pap. 7.95xi o.p. (ISBN 0-06-131655-5, TB1655, Torch). Har-Row.

--With Malice Toward None: The Life of Abraham Lincoln. (Illus.). 1978. pap. 4.50 (ISBN 0-451-62229-4, ME2229, Ment). NAL.

Oates, Wallace E., jt. auth. see Baumol, William J.

Oates, Wayne E. The Christian Pastor. rev. & enlarged ed. LC 63-18553. 1981. pap. 6.95 o.s.i. (ISBN 0-664-24334-7). Westminster.

--The Christian Pastor. Rev. 3rd ed. LC 82-4933. 1982. pap. 9.95 (ISBN 0-664-24372-X). Westminster.

--Introduction to Pastoral Counseling. 1959. 12.95 (ISBN 0-8054-2404-0). Broadman.

--Pastoral Counseling. LC 73-19719. 240p. 1982. pap. 7.95 (ISBN 0-664-24405-X). Westminster.

--The Religious Care of the Psychiatric Patient. LC 78-18454. 1978. 13.95 (ISBN 0-664-21365-0). Westminster.

--When Religion Gets Sick. LC 76-114727. 1970. pap. 4.95 (ISBN 0-664-24891-8). Westminster.

--When You Can't Find Time for Each Other. LC 81-71999. (WHEN Bks). 96p. (Orig.). 1982. pap. 2.45 (ISBN 0-87029-182-3, 20274-7). Abbey.

Oates, Wayne E. & Rowatt, Wade. Before You Marry Them: Guidebook for Pastors. LC 74-80340. 144p. 1976. bds. 6.95 o.p. (ISBN 0-8054-2408-3). Broadman.

Oates, Whitney J., ed. From Sophocles to Picasso. LC 72-6202. (Illus.). 208p. 1973. Repr. of 1962 ed. lib. bdg. 18.75 (ISBN 0-8371-6469-9, OASP). Greenwood.

Oates, Whitney J., ed. see Augustine.

Oates, William, et al. Gugu-Yalanji & Wik-Munkan Language Studies. (Occasional Papers in Aboriginal Studies: No. 2). 146p. 1964. pap. 3.75 o.p. (ISBN 0-88312-770-9); 4.70 o.p. (ISBN 0-88312-389-4); 1.50 o.p. (ISBN 0-88312-390-8). Summer Inst Ling.

Oates, William C. The War Between the U.S. & the Confederacy & Its Lost Opportunities with a History of the 15th Alabama Regiment. (Illus.). 808p. 1974. 35.00 o.p. (ISBN 0-89029-011-3). Pr of Morningside.

Oatley, C. W. The Scanning Electron Microscope. LC 70-190413. (Cambridge Physics Monographs). (Illus.). 200p. 1972. 34.50 (ISBN 0-521-08531-4). Cambridge U Pr.

O'Ballance, Edgar. Tracks of the Bear: Soviet Imprints in the Seventies. (Illus.). 320p. 1982. 15.95 (ISBN 0-89141-133-X). Presidio Pr.

O'Banion, Terry, ed. Community College Staff Development. 180p. 1980. pap. 14.00 o.p. (ISBN 0-8408-0505-5). Carrollton Pr.

O'Banyon, Constance. Savage Desire. 1983. pap. 3.50 (ISBN 0-8217-1120-2). Zebra.

O'Barr, W. M., jt. auth. see Hartwig, G. W.

O'Barr, William. Language Strategy in the Courtroom. (Studies on Law & Social Control Ser.). 1982. 23.50 (ISBN 0-12-523520-8). Acad Pr.

Obata, jt. auth. see Bergey, Alice.

Obata, M., ed. Selected Papers of Yano Kentaro. (North-Holland Mathematics Studies: No. 70). 366p. 1982. 53.25 (ISBN 0-444-86495-4, North Holland). Elsevier.

Obata, M., ed. see Japan-United States Seminar on Minimal Submanifolds, Including Geodesics, Tokyo, 1977.

Obbo, Christine. African Women: Their Struggle for Economic Independence. 176p. 1980. text ed. 18.95 o.s.i. (ISBN 0-905762-33-9, Pub. by Zed Pr England); pap. 7.95 (ISBN 0-686-77499-X, Pub. by Zed Pr England). Lawrence Hill.

Obenauer, Heidi von, ed. Dane Magazine Annual. pap. text ed. 16.00 (ISBN 0-930036-04-2). Dance Mag Inc.

Obeng-Asamoah, J. E. Poultry Education. 1983. 10.00 (ISBN 0-533-05112-6). Vantage.

Obenhaus, Victor. Ethics for an Industrial Age: A Christian Inquiry. LC 73-15317. 338p. 1975. Repr. of 1965 ed. lib. bdg. 20.75x (ISBN 0-8371-7189-X, OBIA). Greenwood.

Ober, B. Scot, jt. auth. see Grubbs, Robert L.

Ober, Kenneth H. Meir Goldschmidt. (World Author Ser.). 1976. lib. bdg. 15.95 (ISBN 0-8057-6253-1, Twayne). G K Hall.

Oberdorfer, E. Pflanzensociologische Studien in Chile. (Illus.). 1960. 24.00 (ISBN 3-7682-0011-6). Lubrecht & Cramer.

Oberer, Walter E. & Hanslowe, Kurt L. Labor Law: Collective Bargaining in a Free Society, 1982 Supplement. 2nd ed. (American Casebook Ser.). 149p. 1982. 3.95 (ISBN 0-314-68829-3). West Pub.

Oberhammer, Gerhard, ed. Epiphanie des Heils: Zur Heilsgegenwart in Indischer und Christlicher Religion. Arbeitsdokumentation Eines Symposiums. (Publications of the De Nobili Research Library: Vol. 9). 256p. 1982. pap. write for info. (ISBN 90-04-06881-3). E J Brill.

Oberhelman, Harley D. Ernesto Sabato. (World Authors Ser.). 13.95 (ISBN 0-8057-2782-5, Twayne). G K Hall.

Oberhoff, Kenneth E., jt. auth. see Murphy, Michael G.

Oberholtzer, Ellis P. Literary History of Philadelphia. LC 72-81510. 1969. Repr. of 1906 ed. 42.00x (ISBN 0-8103-3563-8). Gale.

--The Morals of the Movie. LC 74-160244. (Moving Pictures Ser). 251p. 1971. Repr. of 1922 ed. lib. bdg. 16.95x (ISBN 0-89198-045-8). Ozer.

--The Referendum in America. LC 70-153370. (American Constitutional & Legal History Ser). 1971. Repr. of 1912 ed. lib. bdg. 59.50 (ISBN 0-306-70149-9). Da Capo.

Oberlander, Theodore M. & Muller, Robert A. Essentials of Physical Geography Today. 493p. 1982. text ed. 23.00 (ISBN 0-394-32543-5). Random.

Oberlander, Theodore M., jt. auth. see Mueller, Robert A.

Oberle, Judson B., jt. ed. see English, R. William.

Oberleder, Muriel. The Aging Trap: How to Get Over Being Young. 1982. 11.95 (ISBN 0-686-94120-9). Acropolis.

--Avoid the Aging Trap. Date not set. 11.95 (ISBN 0-686-82383-4). Acropolis.

Oberley, Edith T. & Oberley, Terry D. Understanding Your New Life with Dialysis: A Patient Guide for Physical & Psychological Adjustment. 3rd ed. (Illus.). 198p. 1982. pap. 13.75x (ISBN 0-398-04734-0). C C Thomas.

--Understanding Your New Life with Dialysis: Patient Guide for Physical & Psychological Adjustment to Maintenance Dialysis. 2nd ed. (Illus.). 168p. 1979. pap. 13.75x o.p. (ISBN 0-398-03798-1). C C Thomas.

Oberley, Gertrude F. Fact & Fantasy: Poetry & Prose. 51p. 1982. 5.95 (ISBN 0-533-05263-7). Vantage.

Oberley, Terry D., jt. auth. see Oberley, Edith T.

Oberling, Charles. The Riddle of Cancer. 1944. 34.50x (ISBN 0-685-89779-6). Elliots Bks.

Oberling, Pierre. The Road to Bellapais: The Turkish Cypriot Exodus to Northern Cyprus. (Brooklyn College Studies on Society in Change). 288p. 1982. 25.00x (ISBN 0-88033-000-7). East Eur Quarterly.

Obermair, Gilbert. Matchstick Puzzles, Tricks & Games. LC 77-79510. (Illus.). (gr. 4 up). 1977. 6.95 o.p. (ISBN 0-8069-4564-8); PLB 6.69 o.p. (ISBN 0-8069-4565-6). Sterling.

Oberman, H. A. Masters of the Reformation: Rival Roads to a New Ideology. Martin, D., tr. from German. 432p. 1981. 47.50 (ISBN 0-521-23098-5). Cambridge U Pr.

Oberman, Harold A., ed. Standards for Blood Banks & Transfusion Services. 10th ed. 46p. 1981. pap. 5.00 (ISBN 0-914404-64-4). Am Assn Blood.

Oberman, Heiko A. The Harvest of Medieval Theology: Gabriel Biel & Late Medieval Nominalism. xvi, 495p. 1983. pap. 17.50x (ISBN 0-939464-05-5). Labyrinth Pr.

Oberman, Heiko A., ed. see Tierney, Brian.

Oberman, Margaret & Steckler, Doug. I Could Have Been a Contender, or The Other Book of Lists. 1979. pap. 2.95 o.s.i. (ISBN 0-380-46383-0, 46383). Avon.

Obermeyer, Thomas. Architectural Technology. 1976. 25.95 (ISBN 0-07-047496-6, G); teacher's manual & key 1.50 (ISBN 0-07-047499-0). McGraw.

Oberschall, Anthony. Social Conflict & Social Movements. 1973. text ed. 22.95 (ISBN 0-13-815761-8). P-H.

Oberschelp, Reinhard, ed. Bibliography of German-Language Publications, 1911 to 1965, 150 vols. 1981. Set. 12500.00 (Pub. by K G Saur); 90.00x ea. Gale.

Oberski, Jona. Childhood. Manheim, Ralph, tr. LC 81-43731. (Illus.). 128p. 1983. 11.95 (ISBN 0-385-17768-2). Doubleday.

Oberson, R., jt. auth. see Bradac, G. B.

Oberst, Bruce. Deuteronomy. LC 70-1070. (The Bible Study Textbook Ser.). 1968. 14.30 o.s.i. (ISBN 0-89900-009-6). College Pr Pub.

Obert & Young. Elements of Thermodynamics & Heat Transfer. 2nd ed. (Illus.). 1962. text ed. 23.50 o.p. (ISBN 0-07-047592-X, C). McGraw.

Obert, Edward F. & Young, Robert L. Elements of Thermodynamics & Heat Transfer. 2nd ed. LC 79-23780. 558p. 1980. Repr. of 1962 ed. lib. bdg. 30.00 (ISBN 0-89874-005-3). Krieger.

Obert, Jessie C. Community Nutrition. LC 77-13992. 452p. 1978. text ed. 28.50x (ISBN 0-471-65236-9). Wiley.

Obert, Leonard & Duvall, W. L. Rock Mechanics & the Design of Structures in Rock. LC 66-26753. 650p. 1967. 71.50 (ISBN 0-471-65235-0, Pub. by Wiley-Interscience). Wiley.

Oberteuffer, Del. Concepts & Convictions. 240p. 1977. text ed. 9.95 (ISBN 0-88314-049-7, 240-25940). AAHPERD.

Oberthaler, James V., ed. see Miller, Boulton B.

Oberto, Martino. Anaphilosophia. Salamone, Rosa Maria, tr. from Ital. LC 78-58984. (Illus.). 1983. pap. 17.95 (ISBN 0-915570-10-6). Oolp Pr.

Obey, Andre. Andre Obey: Three Plays: One for the Wind, Noah, & The Phoenix. Suther, Judith D. & Clowney, Earle D, trs. LC 79-10498. 1972. pap. 10.00x (ISBN 0-912646-21-7); 2 vols. together 14.00 (ISBN 0-912646-23-3). Tex Christian.

Obeyesekere, Gananath. Land Tenure in Village Ceylon. (Cambridge South Asian Studies: No. 4). 1967. 37.50 (ISBN 0-521-05854-6). Cambridge U Pr.

Obichere, Boniface I., ed. African States & the Military: Past & Present. 1983. 32.50x (ISBN 0-7146-3135-3, F Cass Co). Biblio Dist.

Obidegwu, Chukwuma F. & Nziramasanga, Mudziviri. Copper & Zambia: An Econometric Analysis. (The Wharton Econometric Studies). 240p. 1981. 27.95x (ISBN 0-669-04659-0). Lexington Bks.

Obie, Marlene. What's a Mother to Do? 176p. 1982. pap. 3.95 (ISBN 0-89081-321-3, 3213). Harvest Hse.

Obiechina, E. An African Popular Literature. 29.95 (ISBN 0-521-20015-6); pap. 11.95x (ISBN 0-521-09744-4). Cambridge U Pr.

--Culture, Tradition & Society in the West African Novel. LC 74-80358. (African Studies: No. 14). 300p. 1975. 45.00 (ISBN 0-521-20525-5); pap. 12.95x (ISBN 0-521-09876-9). Cambridge U Pr.

Obiechina, E. N. Onitsha Market Literature. LC 72-76469. 200p. 1972. text ed. 12.50x (ISBN 0-8419-0122-8, Africana). Holmes & Meier.

Obiols, J., et al, eds. Biloglical Psychiatry Today, 2 pts. (Developments in Psychiatry: Vol. 2). 1979. Set. 172.50 (ISBN 0-444-80117-0, North Holland). Elsevier.

Obitz, Harry, et al. Six Days to Better Golf. LC 76-9196. (Illus.). 1977. 13.45i (ISBN 0-06-013203-5, HarpT). Har-Row.

Oblatt, R., jt. ed. see Jones, M. J.

Obler, Loraine & Menn, Lisa, eds. Expectional Language & Linguistics. (Perspectives in Neurolinguistics, Neuropsychology & Psycholinguistics Ser.). 1982. 34.50 (ISBN 0-12-523680-8). Acad Pr.

Obler, Loraine K. & Albert, Martin L. Language & Communication in the Elderly: Clinical, Therapeutic, & Experimental Issues. LC 80-5348. 240p. 1980. 24.95x (ISBN 0-669-03868-7). Lexington Bks.

Obligado, Lilian. Faint Frogs Feeling Feverish: & Other Terrifically Tantalizing Tongue Twisters. (Illus.). 32p. (ps-3). 1983. 11.50 (ISBN 0-670-30477-8). Viking Pr.

--Little Wolf & the Upstairs Bear. LC 78-13565. (Illus.). (gr. k-3). 1979. 6.95 o.p. (ISBN 0-670-43437-X). Viking Pr.

O'Block, Robert L. Security & Crime Prevention. c ed. LC 81-1353. (Illus.). 452p. 1981. pap. text ed. 18.95 o.p. (ISBN 0-8016-3734-8). Mosby.

Obojska, Robert, jt. auth. see Reinfeld, Fred.

Obojski, Robert. A First Stamp Album for Beginners. 1983. pap. 2.95 (ISBN 0-486-23843-1). Dover.

Obojski, Robert, jt. auth. see Hobson, Burton.

Obojski, Robert, jt. auth. see Reinfeld, Fred.

Obolensky, Alexis. Backgammon, Rules & Rulings. (Illus.). 128p. 6.95 o.p. (ISBN 0-02-591360-3). Macmillan.

Obolensky, D., jt. ed. see Auty, R.

Oboler, Eli M. Defending Intellectual Freedom: The Library & the Censor. LC 79-8585. (Contributions in Librarianship & Information Science: No. 32). xix, 246p. 1980. lib. bdg. 25.00 (ISBN 0-313-21472-7, ODF/). Greenwood.

--Ideas & the University Library: Essays of an Unorthodox Academic Librarian. LC 77-11. (Contributions in Librarianship & Information Science: No. 20). 1977. lib. bdg. 25.00x (ISBN 0-8371-9531-4, OIS/). Greenwood.

--To Free the Mind: Libraries, Technology, & Intellectual Freedom. 275p. 1983. write for info. (ISBN 0-87287-325-0). Libs Unl.

Oborne, David J. Ergonomics at Work. LC 81-14642. 321p. 1982. 29.95x (ISBN 0-471-10030-7, Pub. by Wiley-Interscience). Wiley.

Oborne, David J., jt. auth. see Gruneberg, Michael M.

Obrentz, Bert, jt. auth. see Milbauer, Barbara.

O'Brian, Patrick. Picasso: A Biography. LC 75-41334. 1976. 12.95 o.p. (ISBN 0-399-11639-7). Putnam Pub Group.

O'Brian, Patrick, tr. see Erlanger, Philippe.

O'Brian, Robert, ed. see Morningside Associates.

O'Brien. The Care of the Elderly Person: A Guide for the Licensed Practical Nurse. 2nd ed. LC 74-20864. 160p. 1975. pap. text ed. 7.95 o.p. (ISBN 0-8016-3695-7). Mosby.

O'Brien, Barbara. Operators & Things: Revelations of a Schizophrenic. 1976. pap. 1.50 o.p. (ISBN 0-451-06867-X, W6867, Sig). NAL.

O'Brien, Bev. Mom, I'm Pregnant. 125p. 1982. pap. 3.95 (ISBN 0-8423-4495-0). Tyndale.

O'Brien, Bonnie B & C, Chester. The Victory of the Lamb. 182p. 1982. pap. 10.95 (ISBN 0-311-72280-6). Casa Bautista.

O'Brien, Charles H. Ideas of Religious Toleration at the Time of Joseph Second: A Study of the Enlightenment Among Catholics in Austria. LC 76-93502. (Transactions Ser.: Vol. 59, Pt. 7). 1969. pap. 2.50 o.p. (ISBN 0-87169-597-9). Am Philos.

O'Brien, Charles J. A Joyful Diabetic. (Illus.). 144p. 1983. 7.95 (ISBN 0-89962-323-9). Todd & Honeywell.

O'Brien, D. B. Saints & Politicians. LC 74-82221. (African Studies: No. 15). (Illus.). 224p. 1975. 27.95 (ISBN 0-521-20572-7). Cambridge U Pr.

O'Brien, D. P. The Classical Economists. 1979. pap. text ed. 11.50x (ISBN 0-19-877117-7). Oxford U Pr.

O'Brien, D. P. & Darnell, A. C. Authorship Puzzles in the History of Economics: A Statistical Approach. 230p. 1982. text ed. 37.00x (ISBN 0-333-30078-5, Pub. by Macmillan England). Humanities.

O'Brien, D. P., ed. Correspondence of Lord Overstone, 3 vols. 1971. Vol. 1. 54.50 (ISBN 0-521-08097-5); Vol. 2. 54.50 (ISBN 0-521-08098-3); Vol. 3. 54.50 (ISBN 0-521-08099-1). Cambridge U Pr.

O'Brien, Darcy. The Conscience of James Joyce. 274p. 1983. Repr. of 1968 ed. 13.50 (ISBN 0-87752-221-9). Gordian.

O'Brien, David M. The Public's Right To Know: The Supreme Court & the First Amendment. 218p. 1982. 24.95 (ISBN 0-03-058029-3); pap. 12.95 (ISBN 0-03-062612-9). Praeger.

O'Brien, Edward, jt. auth. see Newman, Jason.

O'Brien, Flann. Stories & Plays. 1977. pap. 3.95 (ISBN 0-14-004537-6). Penguin.

--The Third Policeman. 1976. pap. 4.95 (ISBN 0-452-25350-0, Z5350, Plume). NAL.

O'Brien, Flann, ed. see Gopaleen, Myles na.

O'Brien, George A. Economic History of Ireland from the Union to the Famine. LC 68-56554. 1972. Repr. of 1921 ed. lib. bdg. 35.00x (ISBN 0-678-00816-7). Kelley.

--Economic History of Ireland in the Seventeenth Century. LC 68-56555. 1971. Repr. of 1919 ed. lib. bdg. 22.50x (ISBN 0-678-00817-5). Kelley.

O'Brien, J. S., jt. ed. see Durand, P.

O'Brien, James. Construction Inspection Handbook. 2nd ed. 688p. 1983. 39.50 (ISBN 0-442-25741-4). Van Nos Reinhold.

O'Brien, James A. Dazai Osamu. (World Authors Ser.). 15.95 (ISBN 0-8057-2664-0, Twayne). G K Hall.

O'Brien, James F. Design by Accident. (Illus.). 11.50 (ISBN 0-8446-2673-2). Peter Smith.

O'Brien, James J. CPM in Construction Management: Project Management with CPM. 2nd ed. 1971. 39.50 (ISBN 0-07-047611-X, P&RB); scheduling handbook 55.00 (ISBN 0-07-047601-2). McGraw.

--Value Analysis in Design & Construction. (Modern Structure Ser.). 1976. 27.50 (ISBN 0-07-047566-0, P&RB). McGraw.

O'Brien, James J. & Zilly, R. G. Contractor's Management Handbook. 1971. 46.50 (ISBN 0-07-047565-2, P&RB). McGraw.

O'Brien, Joan V. Guide to Sophocles' Antigone: A Student Edition with Commentary, Grammatical Notes, & Vocabulary. LC 77-10773. 223p. 1978. pap. text ed. 6.95x (ISBN 0-8093-0780-4). S Ill U Pr.

O'Brien, John & Baumann, Edward W. The Chicago Heist. LC 81-68394. (Illus.). 280p. (Orig.). 1981. pap. 6.95 (ISBN 0-89708-053-X). And Bks.

O'Brien, Joseph V. William O'Brien & the Course of Irish Politics, 1881-1918. LC 74-22970. 350p. 1976. 33.00x (ISBN 0-520-02886-4). U of Cal Pr.

O'Brien, Justin, ed. see Gide, Andre.

O'Brien, Kate C. A Gift Horse & Other Stories. LC 80-14996. 1981. 8.95 (ISBN 0-8076-0976-5). Braziller.

O'Brien, Katherine L., et al. Advanced French. 365p. 1965. 22.95x o.p. (ISBN 0-471-00400-6). Wiley.

O'Brien, Kevin, tr. see Guro, Elena.

O'Brien, Linda. Computers. LC 78-6979. (First Bks.). (Illus.). (gr. 4-6). 1978. PLB 8.90 s&l o.p. (ISBN 0-531-01486-X). Watts.

O'Brien, Linda, ed. see Poole, Frederick K.

O'Brien, Marian M. The Collector's Guide to Dollhouses & Dollhouse Miniatures. 1974. pap. 12.95 (ISBN 0-8015-1405-3). Dutton.

O'Brien, Mark S., ed. Pediatric Neurological Surgery. LC 78-3005. (Seminars in Neurological Surgery Ser.). 216p. 1978. 28.50 (ISBN 0-89004-178-4). Raven.

O'Brien, Mary. The Politics of Reproduction. 1983. pap. 9.95 (ISBN 0-7100-9498-1). Routledge & Kegan.

O'Brien, Mary L. Netsuke: A Guide for Collectors. LC 65-11837. (Illus.). 1965. 33.50 (ISBN 0-8048-0423-0). C E Tuttle.

O'Brien, Michael. All Clever Men Who Make Their Way. LC 82-4942. 1982. 35.00 (ISBN 0-938626-09-4). U of Ark Pr.

O'Brien, Michael & Cargill, Burton F. Principles & Practices of Harvesting & Handling of Fruits & Nuts. (Illus.). lib. bdg. write for info (ISBN 0-87055-413-1). AVI.

O'Brien, Michael & Mason, Roger D. A Late Formative Irrigation Settlement below Monte Alban: Survey & Excavation on the Xoxocotlan Piedmont, Oaxaca, Mexico. (Institute of Latin American Studies Special Publications). (Illus.). 254p. 1982. text ed. 25.00x (ISBN 0-292-74628-8). U of Tex Pr.

O'Brien, Michael, et al, eds. The Cannon Reservoir Human Ecology Project: An Archaeological Study of Cultural Adaptations in the Southern Prairie Peninsula. (Studies in Archaeology). 1982. 49.50 (ISBN 0-12-523980-7). Acad Pr.

O'Brien, Muriel. Merrie's Secret Wish. (Illus.). (gr. 3-6). 1980. 5.00 o.p. (ISBN 0-682-49555-7). Exposition.

O'Brien, Patrick. The New Economic History of Railways. LC 77-81308. 1977. 18.95x (ISBN 0-312-56639-5). St Martin.

--Railways & the Economic Development of Western Europe: 1830-1914. LC 81-23261. 356p. 1982. 30.00x (ISBN 0-312-66277-7). St Martin.

O'Brien, Patrick, tr. see Berger, Yves.

O'Brien, Paul, jt. ed. see Long, Robert L.

O'Brien, R. L. Plasma Arc Metalworking Processes. 1967. 8.00 (ISBN 0-685-65957-7). Am Welding.

--Plaza Arc Metalworking Processes. 160p. 1967. 8.00 o.p. (ISBN 0-686-95634-6). Am Welding.

O'Brien, Richard. American Premium Guide to Electric Trains: Identifications & Values. 304p. (Orig.). 1982. pap. 10.95 (ISBN 0-89689-038-4). Bks Americana.

--The Ballyhoo Years. (Jazz Age Ser.: No. 3). (Orig.). 1982. pap. 3.25 (ISBN 0-440-00388-1, Emerald). Dell.

--The Bull & the Bear. (Jazz Age Ser.: No. 4). 272p. (Orig.). 1983. pap. 3.25 (ISBN 0-440-00655-4, Emerald). Dell.

--Collecting Toys: A Collector's Identification & Value Guide. rev. 3rd ed. (Illus.). 440p. 1981. pap. 9.95 o.p. (ISBN 0-517-54402-4, Americana). Crown.

--Collecting Toys: A Collector's Identification & Value Guide. (Illus., Orig.). 1979. pap. 8.95 o.p. (ISBN 0-517-53955-1, Americana). Crown.

--Collector's Toys, Identification & Value Guide. (Illus.). pap. 9.95 (ISBN 0-89689-031-7). Wallace-Homestead.

--Dust in the Wind. (Jazz Age Ser.: No. 5). (Orig.). 1983. pap. 3.25 (ISBN 0-440-02158-8). Dell.

--Publicity: How to Get It. (Everyday Handbook Ser.). pap. 2.95 o.p. (ISBN 0-06-463465-5, EH 465, EH). B&N NY.

--Publicity: How to Get It. LC 76-39686. 1977. 12.45i (ISBN 0-06-013199-3, HarpT). Har-Row.

--Storming Heaven. (Jazz Age Ser.: No. 6). (Orig.). 1983. pap. 3.25 (ISBN 0-440-08381-8, Emerald). Dell.

O'Brien, Richard & Dickinson, Alyce M., eds. Industrial Behavior Modification: A Management Handbook. 480p. 35.00 (ISBN 0-686-84781-4). Work in Amer.

O'Brien, Richard C. Dental Radiography: An Introduction for Dental Hygienists & Assistants. 3rd ed. LC 76-8581. (Illus.). 1977. text ed. 11.95 o.p. (ISBN 0-7216-6892-5). Saunders.

O'Brien, Richard J., ed. Georgetown University Round Table on Languages & Linguistics: Linguistics, Developments of the Sixties-Viewpoints for the Seventies. LC 58-31607. (Georgetown Univ. Round Table Ser.: 1971). 316p. (GURT 1971). 1971. pap. 5.50 (ISBN 0-87840-106-7). Georgetown U Pr.

O'Brien, Rita C., ed. Information, Economics, & Power: The North-South Dimension. 200p. 1983. softcover 22.50x (ISBN 0-86531-604-X). Westview.

O'Brien, Robert. Z for Zachariah. (gr. 7 up). 1977. pap. 1.95 o.p. (ISBN 0-440-99901-4, LFL). Dell.

O'Brien, Saliee. Cajun. 384p. 1982. pap. 3.50 (ISBN 0-553-20821-7). Bantam.

O'Brien, Stephen, jt. auth. see Vacca, Richard.

O'Brien, Sue M., compiled by. The Register of Americans of Prominent Descent, Vol. I. LC 81-69243. 545p. 1982. 35.00 (ISBN 0-686-36318-3). Morten Pub.

O'Brien, Thomas C., ed. see International Committee on English in the Liturgy.

O'Brien, Tim. If I Die in a Combat Zone, Box Me up & Send Me Home. 1973. 8.95 o.s.i. (ISBN 0-440-03853-7). Delacorte.

O'Brien, Timothy J, jt. auth. see Cibulka, James G.

O'Brien, Timothy R. Radiographic Diagnosis of Abdominal Disorders in the Dog & Cat: Radiographic Interpretation, Clinical Signs, Pathophysiology. LC 76-58604. (Illus.). 1978. text ed. 49.50 o.p. (ISBN 0-7216-6898-4). Saunders.

O'Brien, Tony see Bates, Martin & Dudley-Evans, Tony.

O'Brien, William & Ryge, Gunnary. An Outline of Dental Materials & Their Selection. LC 77-80751. (Illus.). 1978. pap. text ed. 21.50 (ISBN 0-7216-6896-8). Saunders.

O'Brien, William J. Stories to the Dark: Explorations in Religious Imagination. LC 77-74577. 176p. 1977. 10.00 o.p. (ISBN 0-8091-0222-6); pap. 5.95 o.p. (ISBN 0-8091-2032-1). Paulist Pr.

O'Brien, William J., jt. auth. see Craig, Robert G.

O'Brien Palinski, Christine, jt. auth. see Pizer, Hank.

Obrinsky, Mark. Profit Theory & Capitalism. LC 82-40482. (Illus.). 176p. 1983. 18.00x (ISBN 0-8122-7863-1); pap. 8.95x (ISBN 0-8122-1147-2). U of Pa Pr.

O'Brosky, James, jt. auth. see Souter, John C.

O'Bryant, D. C., jt. auth. see Hartley, T. C.

Obstfeld, Henri. Optics in Vision. 2nd ed. 1982. text ed. 49.95 (ISBN 0-407-00240-5). Butterworth.

Obudho, Constance E. Black-White Racial Attitudes: An Annotated Bibliography. LC 75-35351. 180p. 1976. lib. bdg. 25.00 (ISBN 0-8371-8582-3, OBW/). Greenwood.

Obudho, Constance E., compiled by. Human Nonverbal Behavior: An Annotated Bibliography. LC 79-7586. 1979. lib. bdg. 25.00 (ISBN 0-313-21094-2, OBH/). Greenwood.

Obudho, R. A. & Taylor, D. R. F. The Spatial Structure of Development. (Replica Edition Ser.). 315p. 1979. softcover 32.50x (ISBN 0-89158-597-4). Westview.

Obudho, R. A. & Waller, P. P. Periodic Markets, Urbanization, & Regional Planning: A Case Study from Western Kenya. LC 75-23867. (Contributions in Afro-American & African Studies: No. 22). (Illus.). 1976. lib. bdg. 29.95x (ISBN 0-8371-8375-8, OPM/). Greenwood.

Obudhowski, jt. auth. see Kassakowski.

Obukhova, Lydia. Daughter of Night: A Tale of Three Worlds. Ginsburg, Mirra, tr. 176p. 1982. pap. 2.95 (ISBN 0-380-61192-9, 61192, Bard). Avon.

O'Byrne, John C. Farm Income Tax Manual. 6th ed. 1982. text ed. 45.00x incl. 1982 supplement (ISBN 0-87473-146-1). A Smith Co.

O'Byrne, John C. & McCord, John H. Deskbook for Illinois Estate Planners. 1969. 37.50 o.p. (ISBN 0-672-81232-0, Bobbs-Merrill Law). Michie-Bobbs.

Oca, Marco A. de see De Oca, Marco A.

O'Callaghan, Dorothy. The Job Catalog: Where to Find That Creative Job in Washington D. C.-Baltimore. 4th ed. LC 81-80660. 1981. pap. 6.00 o.p. (ISBN 0-914694-06-5). Mail Order.

O'Callaghan, Edmund B. List of Editions of the Holy Scriptures & Parts Thereof Printed in American Previous to 1860. LC 66-25690. 1966. Repr. of 1861 ed. 37.00x (ISBN 0-8103-3313-9). Gale.

O'Callaghan, Maxine. Run from Nightmare. (Raven House Mysteries Ser.). 224p. 1982. pap. cancelled (ISBN 0-373-63047-6, Pub. by Worldwide). Harlequin Bks.

O'Callaghan, Michael C. Unity in Theology: Lonergan's Framework for Theology in Its New Context. LC 80-8177. 596p. 1980. lib. bdg. 25.50 (ISBN 0-8191-1151-1); pap. text ed. 18.50 (ISBN 0-8191-1152-X). U Pr of Amer.

O'Carroll, Michael. Theotokos: A Theological Encyclopedia of the Blessed Virgin Mary. 1982. 42.00 (ISBN 0-89453-268-5). M Glazier.

O'Carroll, Tom. Pedophilia: The Radical Case. 288p. (Orig.). 1982. pap. 8.95 (ISBN 0-932870-24-4). Alyson Pubns.

O'Casey, Sean. Blasts & Benedictions: Articles & Stories. Ayling, Ronald, ed. LC 75-8487. 314p. 1976. Repr. of 1967 ed. lib. bdg. 20.00x (ISBN 0-8371-8158-5, OCBB). Greenwood.

O'Casey, Sean see Laurel Editions Editors.

O'Casey, Sean see Moon, Samuel.

OCED Staff. Controls & Impediments Affecting Inward Direct Investment in OECD Member Countries. 36p. 1982. pap. 6.00 (ISBN 92-64-12344-X). OECD.

Och, Armin, jt. ed. see Maeder, Herbert.

Ochberg, Frank, ed. Victims of Terrorism. (Special Studies in National & International Terrorism). 1981. lib. bdg. 20.00 (ISBN 0-89158-463-3). Westview.

Ochi, Kaz, jt. auth. see Huges, Patricia.

Ochiai, E. Aromatic Amine Oxides. 1967. 61.00 (ISBN 0-444-40429-5). Elsevier.

Ochorowicz-Monatowa, Marja. Polish Cookery. Karsavina, Jean, ed. & tr. (International Cook Bk.). 1958. 7.95 (ISBN 0-517-50526-6). Crown.

Ochroch, Ruth, ed. The Diagnosis & Treatment of Minimal Brain Dysfunction in Children: A Clinical Approach. LC 80-15858. 303p. 1981. professional 29.95x (ISBN 0-87705-503-3). Human Sci Pr.

Ochs, Michael, jt. auth. see Bangs, Lester.

Ochsner, Alton. Smoking: Your Choice Between Life & Death. LC 74-130484. 1971. 7.95 o.p. (ISBN 0-671-20698-2). S&S.

Ockenden, Michael & Jones, Timothy. Around Town: Situational Conversation Practice. (English As a Second Language Bk.). 1981. pap. text ed. 4.70x (ISBN 0-582-79769-1); cassette 13.95x (ISBN 0-582-79772-1); book & cassette 15.95 (ISBN 0-582-79798-5). Longman.

Ockendon, J. R., jt. auth. see Elliott, C. M.

Ockenga, Earl, jt. auth. see Immerzeel, George.

Ockenga, Starr. Mirror After Mirror. (Illus.). 1976. 14.95 o.p. (ISBN 0-8174-0589-5, Amphoto). Watson-Guptill.

Ockham, Guillelmi De see De Ockham, Guillelmi.

Ockleford, C. & Whyte, A., eds. Coated Vesicles. LC 79-17280. (Illus.). 1980. 99.00 (ISBN 0-521-22785-2). Cambridge U Pr.

Ockman, Rita. Cajun Bits Cooking Ease. 1983. 5.75 (ISBN 0-8062-2134-8). Carlton.

Ocko, Jonathan K. Bureaucratic Reform in Provincial China: Ting Jih-ch'ang in Restoration Kiangsu, 1867-1870. (Harvard East Asian Monographs: No. 103). 316p. 1983. text ed. 20.00x (ISBN 0-674-08617-1). Harvard U Pr.

O'Clair, Robert, jt. ed. see Ellmann, Richard.

Ocloo, J. K., jt. auth. see Usher, M. B.

OCMA. Recommendations for the Protection of Diesel Engines Operating in Hazardous Areas. 1979. 16.95 (ISBN 0-471-25940-3, Wiley Heyden). Wiley.

O'Collins, Gerald. What Are They Saying About Jesus? LC 77-70640. 1977. pap. 2.45 o.p. (ISBN 0-8091-2017-8). Paulist Pr.

--What Are They Saying about Jesus. rev. ed. (WATSA Ser.). 96p. 1983. pap. 3.95 (ISBN 0-686-84554-4). Paulist Pr.

--What Are They Saying About the Resurrection? LC 78-51594. 1978. pap. 2.95 (ISBN 0-8091-2109-3). Paulist Pr.

O'Collins, Gerald, jt. auth. see Latourelle, Rene.

O'Con, Robert, jt. auth. see Carr, Richard.

O'Connell, April & O'Connell, Vincent. Choice & Change: Psychology of Adjustment, Growth & Creativity. rev. ed. (Illus.). 1980. pap. text ed. 19.95 (ISBN 0-13-133066-7); study guide & wkbk. 8.95 (ISBN 0-13-133082-9). P-H.

O'Connell, Brian. Effective Leadership in Voluntary Organizations. 224p. 1976. 8.95 (ISBN 0-695-81119-3). Follett.

--Greek & Celtic. 1978. 8.95 o.p. (ISBN 0-533-02474-9). Vantage.

O'Connell, Brian J. Blacks in White-Collar Jobs. LC 78-71098. (LandMark Study). (Illus.). 144p. 1979. text ed. 18.00x (ISBN 0-916672-85-9). Allanheld.

O'Connell, D. J., tr. see Maffei, Paolo.

O'Connell, D. P. The International Law of the Sea, Vol. I. Shearer, I. A., ed. (Illus.). 664p. 1982. 74.00 (ISBN 0-19-825346-X). Oxford U Pr.

O'Connell, Daniel J. Apartment Building Valuation, Finance & Investment Analysis. (Real Estate for Professional Practitioners Ser.). 256p. 1982. 29.95 (ISBN 0-471-86523-0). Ronald Pr.

O'Connell, David. Louis-Ferdinand Celine. (World Author Ser). 1976. lib. bdg. 13.95 (ISBN 0-8057-6256-6, Twayne). G K Hall.

O'Connell, David, ed. The Teachings of Saint Louis: A Critical Text. (Studies in the Romance Languages & Literatures: No. 116). 63p. 1972. pap. 7.00x (ISBN 0-8078-9216-5). U of NC Pr.

O'Connell, F. J. Batsford Fide Chess Yearbook, 1975-1976. 159p. 1976. 8.50 o.p. (ISBN 0-7134-1223-2, Pub. by Batsford England). David & Charles.

O'Connell, J. F., jt. ed. see White, J. P.

O'Connell, James & Gallagher, Tom, eds. Contemporary Irish Studies. 200p. 1982. 20.00 (ISBN 0-7190-0919-7). Manchester.

O'Connell, K. J. Batsford Fide Chess Yearbook, 1976-1977. 1977. 8.50 o.p. (ISBN 0-7134-0675-5, Pub. by Batsford England). David & Charles.

O'Connell, Kevin, jt. auth. see Levy, David.

O'Connell, M. R. Thomas Stapleton & the Counter Reformation. 1964. 34.50x (ISBN 0-685-69850-5). Elliots Bks.

O'Connell, Margaret. The Magic Cauldron: Witchcraft for Good & Evil. LC 75-26757. (Illus.). 256p. (gr. 9-12). 1975. 12.95 (ISBN 0-87599-187-4). S G Phillips.

O'Connell, Matthew J., tr. see Adam, Adolf.

O'Connell, Matthew J., tr. see Berger & Hollerweger.

O'Connell, Matthew J., tr. see Quadflieg, Josef.

O'Connell, Matthew J., tr. see Rordorf, Willy, et al.

O'Connell, Matthew J., tr. see Von Allmen, et al.

O'Connell, Merrilyn R., jt. auth. see Rath, Frederick L.

O'Connell, Nina, jt. auth. see Ewart, Neil.

O'Connell, Paul, jt. auth. see Conroy, Larry.

O'Connell, Peggy. Aim for a Job As a Waiter or Waitress. LC 79-15014. (Arco's Career Guidance Ser.). (Illus.). 1980. lib. bdg. 7.95 (ISBN 0-668-04767-4); pap. 3.95 (ISBN 0-668-04771-2). Arco.

O'Connell, Richard L., tr. see Garcia Lorca, Federico.

O'Connell, Richard L., tr. see Lorca, Federico Garcia.

O'Connell, Robert J. Teilhard's Vision of the Past: The Making of a Method. x, 205p. 1982. 22.50 (ISBN 0-8232-1090-1); pap. 9.00 (ISBN 0-8232-1091-X). Fordham.

O'Connell, Theodore. Surgical Oncology: Controversies in Cancer Treatment. 1981. lib. bdg. 55.00 (ISBN 0-8161-2157-5, Pub. by Hall Medical Bks). G K Hall.

O'Connell, Timothy E. Principles for a Catholic Morality. 256p. 1980. pap. 8.95 (ISBN 0-8164-2031-9). Seabury.

O'Connell, Vincent, jt. auth. see O'Connell, April.

O'Connell, William J. Graphic Communication in Architecture. 1972. pap. 8.60x (ISBN 0-87563-051-0). Stipes.

O'Connell, William R., Jr. & Meeth, Richard. Evaluating Teaching Improvement Programs. 2nd ed. 47p. 1978. pap. 2.00 (ISBN 0-686-95519-6). Change Mag.

O'Conner, John, ed. see Shanghai College of Traditional Medicine.

O'Conner, Karen. Women's Organizations' Use of the Courts. LC 79-2275. (Illus.). 176p. 1980. 21.95 (ISBN 0-669-03093-7). Lexington Bks.

O'Conner, Melvin C. & Chandra, Gyan. Replacement Cost Disclosure: A/Study of Compliance with the SEC Requirement. 308p. pap. 24.95 (ISBN 0-86641-021-X, 78102). Natl Assn Accts.

O'Conner, Melvin C. & Grant, Rita. Replacement Costing: Complying with Disclosure Requirements. 41p. pap. 4.95 (ISBN 0-86641-022-8, 7789). Natl Assn Accts.

O'Conner, Raymond F. Fundamentals of the Modern Chemical Laboratory. 1971. pap. 8.95x (ISBN 0-673-07599-0). Scott F.

O'Conner, William E. An Introduction to Airline Economics. LC 77-7809. (Praeger Special Studies). 1978. 21.95 o.p. (ISBN 0-03-022416-0). Praeger.

O'Connor, A. M. Urbanization in Tropical Africa: An Annotated Bibliography. 1981. lib. bdg. 40.00 (ISBN 0-8161-8262-0, Hall Reference). G K Hall.

O'Connor, Andrea. Writing for Nursing Publications. LC 76-14600. 1976. pap. text ed. 9.00 o.p. (ISBN 0-913590-36-3). Slack Inc.

O'Connor, Ann, ed. see Alexander, Herbert.

O'Connor, Ann, ed. see Baum, Lawrence.

O'Connor, Barbara H. A Color Atlas & Instruction Manual of Peripheral Blood Morphology. (Illus.). 336p. 1983. pap. text ed. price not set (ISBN 0-683-06624-2). Williams & Wilkins.

O'Connor, Carol A. A Sort of Utopia: Scarsdale, 1891-1981. (Illus.). 272p. 1982. 34.50x (ISBN 0-87395-659-1); pap. 10.95x (ISBN 0-87395-660-5). State U NY Pr.

O'Connor, Colin. Design of Bridge Superstructures. LC 76-121912. 552p. 1971. 72.50 (ISBN 0-471-65245-8, Pub. by Wiley-Interscience). Wiley.

O'Connor, Daniel J. One Hundred One Patented Solar Energy Uses. 96p. 1980. pap. 8.95 o.p. (ISBN 0-442-24432-0). Van Nos Reinhold.

O'Connor, D'Arcy. The Money Pit: The Story of Oak Island & the World's Greatest Treasure Hunt. LC 77-21882. (Illus.). 1978. 8.95 o.p. (ISBN 0-698-10877-9, Coward). Putnam Pub Group.

O'Connor, Dennis J. & Bueso, Alberto T. Personal Financial Management: A Forecasting & Control Approach. (Illus.). 560p. 1983. text ed. 21.95 (ISBN 0-13-657940-X). P-H.

O'Connor, Dick. American Olympic Stars. new ed. LC 75-44378. (Putnam Sports Shelf). 128p. (gr. 5 up). 1976. PLB 5.29 o.p. (ISBN 0-399-61005-7). Putnam Pub Group.

--Rick Barry: Basketball Ace. LC 76-41690. (Putnam Sports Shelf). (Illus.). (gr. 6-8). 1977. PLB 5.29 o.p. (ISBN 0-399-61060-X). Putnam Pub Group.

O'Connor, Edmund. Darwin. Yapp, Malcolm, et al, eds. (World History Ser.). (Illus.). 32p. (gr. 10). 1980. Repr. of 1977 ed. lib. bdg. 6.95 (ISBN 0-89908-047-2); pap. text ed. 2.25 (ISBN 0-89908-022-7). Greenhaven.

--Education. Yapp, Malcolm & O'Connor, Edmund, eds. (World History Ser.). (Illus.). 32p. (gr. 10). 1980. Repr. of 1977 ed. lib. bdg. 6.95 (ISBN 0-89908-147-9); pap. text ed. 2.25 (ISBN 0-89908-122-3). Greenhaven.

--Japan's Modernization. Yapp, Malcolm & Killingray, Marget, eds. (World History Ser.). (Illus.). (gr. 10). 1980. Repr. of 1977 ed. lib. bdg. 6.95 (ISBN 0-89908-232-7); pap. text ed. 2.25 (ISBN 0-89908-207-6). Greenhaven.

--Roosevelt. Yapp, Malcolm & Killingray, Margaret, eds. (World History Ser.). (Illus.). 32p. (gr. 10). 1980. lib. bdg. 6.95 (ISBN 0-89908-125-8); pap. text ed. 2.25 (ISBN 0-89908-100-2). Greenhaven.

--The Wealth of Japan. Yapp, Malcolm, et al, eds. (World History Ser.). (Illus.). 32p. (gr. 10). 1980. Repr. of 1977 ed. lib. bdg. 6.95 (ISBN 0-89908-237-8); pap. text ed. 2.25 (ISBN 0-89908-212-2). Greenhaven.

O'Connor, Edmund, ed. see Doncaster, Islay.

O'Connor, Edmund, ed. see Killingray, David.

O'Connor, Edmund, ed. see Killingray, Margaret.

O'Connor, Edmund, ed. see O'Connor, Edmund.

O'Connor, Edmund, ed. see Read, James & Yapp, Malcolm.

O'Connor, Edmund, ed. see Yapp, Malcolm.

O'Connor, Edward D. Pentecostal Movement in the Catholic Church. LC 70-153878. (Illus.). 304p. 1971. pap. 2.45 o.p. (ISBN 0-87793-035-X). Ave Maria.

O'Connor, Elizabeth. Call to Commitment. LC 63-10963. 224p. 1976. pap. 6.68i (ISBN 0-06-066330-8, RD131, HarpR). Har-Row.

--Our Many Selves. LC 78-124699. 1971. pap. 5.95i (ISBN 0-06-066336-7, RD-36, HarpR). Har-Row.

O'Connor, Flannery. Everything That Rises Must Converge. 269p. 1965. 10.00 (ISBN 0-374-15012-5); pap. 5.95 (ISBN 0-374-50464-4, N287). FS&G.

--Mystery & Manners: Occasional Prose. Fitzgerald, Robert & Fitzgerald, Sally, eds. LC 69-15409. 1969. 10.95 (ISBN 0-374-21792-0); pap. 5.95 (ISBN 0-374-50804-6). FS&G.

--The Presence of Grace & Other Book Reviews. Martin, Carter W., ed. LC 82-20064. 200p. 1983. 16.00 (ISBN 0-8203-0663-0). U of Ga Pr.

--The Violent Bear It Away. 243p. 1960. pap. 5.95 (ISBN 0-374-50524-1, N303). FS&G.

O'Connor, Francine. ABC's of Faith, Bk. 3. 32p. (Orig.). (gr. 1-4). 1980. pap. 1.75 (ISBN 0-89243-125-3). Liguori Pubns.

--ABC's of Faith, Bk. 4. (Illus.). (gr. 1-4). 1981. pap. 1.75 (ISBN 0-89243-138-5). Liguori Pubns.

--ABC'S of Faith, Bk. 5. 32p. (gr. 1-4). 1982. pap. 1.75 (ISBN 0-89243-165-2). Liguori Pubns.

O'Connor, Francine M. & Boswell, Kathryn. The ABC's of Faith, 2 bks. (gr. 1-4). 1979. Bk. 1. pap. 1.75 (ISBN 0-89243-113-X); Bk. 2. pap. 1.75 (ISBN 0-89243-114-8). Liguori Pubns.

O'Connor, Frank. Collected Stories. LC 82-40039. 736p. 1982. pap. 8.95 o.p. (ISBN 0-394-71048-7, Vin). Random.

O'Connor, Frank & Hunt, Hugh. The Invincibles. (Abbey Theatre Ser.). pap. 2.95x (ISBN 0-912262-67-2). Proscenium.

--Moses' Rock: A Play in Three Acts. Sherry, Ruth, ed. (Irish Dramatic Texts Ser.). Date not set. price not set (ISBN 0-8132-0584-0); pap. price not set (ISBN 0-8132-0585-9). Cath U Pr.

O'Connor, G. Richard, jt. auth. see Kraus-Machiw, Ellen.

O'Connor, G. Richard, jt. auth. see Silverstein, Arthur M.

O'Connor, Garry. Ralph Richardson: An Actor's Life. LC 82-45178. 320p. 1982. 14.95 (ISBN 0-689-11313-7). Atheneum.

O'Connor, Hyla. Cooking on Your Wood Stove. (Illus.). 78p. 1981. pap. 5.95 (ISBN 0-9608050-0-1). Turkey Hill Pr.

O'Connor, J. F. The Banking Crisis & Recovery Under the Roosevelt Administration. LC 73-171696. (FDR & the Era of the New Deal Ser.). 168p. 1971. Repr. of 1938 ed. lib. bdg. 27.50 (ISBN 0-306-70366-1). Da Capo.

O'Connor, J. J. & Boyd, J. Standard Handbook of Lubrication Engineering. (Illus.). 1968. 57.50 (ISBN 0-07-047605-5, P&RB). McGraw.

O'Connor, Jerome J. The Telephone: How It Works. (How It Works Ser.). (Illus.). (gr. 4-7). 1972. PLB 4.69 o.p. (ISBN 0-399-60624-6). Putnam Pub Group.

O'Connor, John & Brown, Lorraine. Free, Adult, Uncensored: The Living History of the Federal Theatre Project. LC 78-9292. (Illus.). 1978. 24.95 (ISBN 0-915220-37-7); pap. 11.95 (ISBN 0-915220-38-5). New Republic.

O'Connor, John, tr. see Shanghai College of Traditional Medicine.

O'Connor, John E., ed. American History - American Television: Interpreting the Video Past. (Ungar Film Library). (Illus.). 300p. 1983. 13.50 (ISBN 0-8044-2668-6); pap. 7.95 (ISBN 0-8044-6621-1). Ungar.

O'Connor, John J. Amadis De Gaule & Its Influence on Elizabethan Literature. LC 76-96031. 1970. 25.00 (ISBN 0-8135-0622-0). Rutgers U Pr.

O'Connor, Kaori. Creative Dressing: The Unique Collection of Top Designer Looks That You Can Make Yourself. LC 80-27788. (Illus.). 192p. 1981. 10.95 (ISBN 0-7100-0680-2). Routledge & Kegan.

O'Connor, Karen. Contributions of Women: Literature. (Contributions of Women Ser.). (Illus.). 112p. (gr. 6 up). 1983. PLB 8.95 (ISBN 0-87518-234-8). Dillon.

--Maybe you Belong in a Zoo! Zoo & Aquarium Careers. LC 82-45386. (Illus.). 160p. (gr. 5 up). 1982. PLB 12.95 (ISBN 0-396-08086-3). Dodd.

--Sally Ride & the New Astronauts. (Single Titles Ser.). (Illus.). 96p. (gr. 5 up). 1983. PLB 8.90 (ISBN 0-531-04602-8). Watts.

--Special Effects: A Guide for Super-8 Filmmakers. (gr. 6-8). 1981. lib. bdg. 7.90 (ISBN 0-531-02878-X). Watts.

--Try These on for Size, Melody! LC 82-45989. (Illus.). 48p. (gr. 2-5). 1983. PLB 9.95 (ISBN 0-396-08117-7). Dodd.

O'Connor, Katherine, tr. see Chukovsky, Kornei.

O'Connor, Kathleen & Elkind, David. Learning: An Introduction for Students of Education. 1971. pap. 7.95x (ISBN 0-673-07584-2). Scott F.

O'Connor, Kevin J., jt. auth. see Schaefer, Charles E.

O'Connor, Lawrence, jt. auth. see Dunne, John J.

O'Connor, Loretto, Sr. Shared Harvest: Prose of Medieval England in Modern Version. LC 81-43629. (Illus.). 184p. (Orig.). 1982. lib. bdg. 22.25 (ISBN 0-8191-2127-4); pap. text ed. 10.25 (ISBN 0-8191-2128-2). U Pr of Amer.

O'Connor, M., jt. ed. see Meyers, Carol L.

O'Connor, Maeur. Writing Scientific Papers in English. 128p. 1978. 25.00x (ISBN 0-686-98002-6, Pub. by Pitman Bks England). State Mutual Bk.

O'Connor, Maureen. First Steps in the Kitchen. (Illus.). 1971. 3.95 o.p. (ISBN 0-571-09338-8). Faber & Faber.

O'Connor, Meagan. Pippa. (Orig.). 1980. pap. 1.50 o.s.i. (ISBN 0-440-16825-2). Dell.

O'Connor, Meave. Writing Scientific Papers in English. 128p. 1979. pap. text ed. 12.95 (ISBN 0-272-79515-1). Univ Park.

O'Connor, N. Language, Cognitive Deficits, and Retardation. 376p. 1975. 33.95 o.p. (ISBN 0-407-00007-0). Butterworth.

O'Connor, P. D. Practical Reliability Engineering. 300p. 1981. text ed. 38.00x (ISBN 0-471-25919-5, Pub. by Wiley Heyden). Wiley.

O'Connor, P. J. Brendan Behan's 'The Scarperer' (Adaptations Ser.). 6.95x (ISBN 0-912262-53-2); pap. 2.95x (ISBN 0-912262-56-7). Proscenium.

O'Connor, P. J., jt. auth. see Kavanaugh, Patrick.

O'Connor, Patricia W. Gregorio & Maria Martinez Sierra. (World Authors Ser.: Spain: No. 412). 1977. lib. bdg. 15.95 (ISBN 0-8057-6252-3, Twayne). G K Hall.

O'Connor, Patrick J. Digital & Microprocessor Technology. (Illus.). 576p. 1983. 29.95 (ISBN 0-13-212514-5). P-H.

--Retailing. LC 79-54049. (Marketing Distribution Ser.). 352p. 1981. pap. 10.12 o.p. (ISBN 0-8273-1777-8); instr's. guide 1.75 o.p. (ISBN 0-8273-1778-6). Delmar.

O'Connor, Peter D., jt. auth. see Wyne, Marvin D.

O'Connor, R. F. Chemical Principles & Their Biological Implications. LC 74-3367. 413p. 1974. 25.95 (ISBN 0-471-65246-6); lab. manual 12.95 (ISBN 0-471-65247-4); tchrs.' manual 3.00 (ISBN 0-471-65250-4). Wiley.

O'Connor, Raymond G. War, Diplomacy, & History: Papers & Reviews. LC 79-88951. 1979. pap. text ed. 12.75 (ISBN 0-8191-0790-5). U Pr of Amer.

O'Connor, Richard. Gould's Millions. LC 73-5271. (Illus.). 335p. 1973. Repr. of 1962 ed. lib. bdg. 18.25x (ISBN 0-8371-6875-9, OCGM). Greenwood.

--Iron Wheels & Broken Men: The Railroad Barons & the Plunder of the West. 384p. 1973. 8.95 o.p. (ISBN 0-399-11120-4). Putnam Pub Group.

O'Connor, Richard C., ed. Immunologic Diseases of the Mucous Membranes: Pathology, Diagnosis, & Treatment. LC 81-20794. (Illus.). 176p. 1980. 34.25x (ISBN 0-89352-102-7). Masson Pub.

O'Connor, Rod. Problemas de Quimica Aplicada. 1976. pap. text ed. 8.00 o.p. (ISBN 0-06-316601-1, IntlDept). Har-Row.

--La Quimica. 1976. text ed. 15.10 o.p. (ISBN 0-06-316600-3, IntlDept). Har-Row.

O'Connor, Ronald, ed. Managing Health Systems in Developing Areas: Experiences from Afghanistan. LC 79-48060. 336p. 1980. 29.95 (ISBN 0-669-03646-3). Lexington Bks.

O'Connor, Sally, ed. The Uscia Book of Evening: The Official Handbook of the United States Combined Training Association. (Illus.). 288p. 1982. 16.95 (ISBN 0-201-05447-7). A-W.

O'Connor, Vincent F. Mathematics at the Farm. LC 77-19169. (Raintree Mathematics Ser.). (Illus.). (gr. k-3). 1978. PLB 12.50 (ISBN 0-8393-0055-7). Raintree Pubs.

--Mathematics in Buildings. LC 77-19158. (Raintree Mathematics Ser.). (Illus.). (gr. k-3). 1978. PLB 12.50 (ISBN 0-8393-0053-0). Raintree Pubs.

--Mathematics in the Circus Ring. LC 77-19168. (Raintree Mathematics Ser.). (Illus.). (gr. k-3). 1978. PLB 12.50 (ISBN 0-8393-0056-5). Raintree Pubs.

--Mathematics in the Kitchen. LC 77-19160. (Raintree Mathematics Ser.). (Illus.). (gr. k-3). 1978. PLB 12.50 (ISBN 0-8393-0054-9). Raintree Pubs.

--Mathematics in the Toy Store. LC 77-19155. (Raintree Mathematics Ser.). (Illus.). (gr. k-3). 1978. PLB 12.50 (ISBN 0-8393-0052-2). Raintree Pubs.

--Mathematics on the Playground. LC 77-19180. (Raintree Mathematics Ser.). (Illus.). (gr. k-3). 1978. PLB 12.50 (ISBN 0-8393-0051-4). Raintree Pubs.

O'Connor, W. J. Normal Renal Function: The Excretion of Water & Electrolytes Derived from Food & Drink. (Illus.). 442p. 1982. text ed. 27.50 (ISBN 0-19-520400-X). Oxford U Pr.

O'Connor, William R. Natural Desire for God: Aquinas Lectures. 1948. 7.95 (ISBN 0-87462-113-5). Marquette.

O'Corrain, Donncha, jt. ed. see Mac Curtain, Margaret.

O Crohan, Tomas. The Islandman. Flower, Robin, tr. (Illus.). 1951. pap. 4.50x o.p. (ISBN 0-19-281233-5). Oxford U Pr.

Ocsag, Imre, jt. auth. see Sarkany, Pal.

Ocvirk, Fred W., jt. auth. see Mabie, Hamilton H.

Oda, James. Heroic Struggles of Japanese Americans: Partisan Fighters from America's Concentration Camps. 3rd ed. 275p. 1982. 12.95 (ISBN 0-686-30106-4); softcover 8.00 (ISBN 0-686-31779-3). Oda.

--Heroic Struggles of Japanese Americans: Partisans Fighters from American's Concentration Camps. 3rd ed. LC 25-3182. 1982. 12.95 (ISBN 0-686-38079-7); pap. 8.00 (ISBN 0-686-38080-0). ODA.

Oda, N. & Takayanagi, K., eds. Electronic & Atomic Collisions. 1980. Abstracts. 149.00 (ISBN 0-444-85393-6); Invited Papers. 127.75 (ISBN 0-444-85434-7). Elsevier.

Oda, Stephanie, compiled by. All Things Bright & Beautiful. 1981. 3.95 (ISBN 0-8378-2027-8). Gibson.

--A True Friend is a Gift of the Lord. 1981. 3.95 (ISBN 0-8378-2028-6). Gibson.

Oda, Stephanie C., compiled by. I Will Lift Up Mine Eyes. (Illus.). 1980. 3.95 (ISBN 0-8378-2020-0). Gibson.

--A Little Treasury of Chinese Wisdom. (Illus.). 1980. 3.50 o.p. (ISBN 0-8378-2022-7). Gibson.

Oda, Takayuki. Periods of Hilbert Modular Surfaces. (Progress in Mathematics Ser.: Vol. 19). 1981. text ed. 10.00x (ISBN 3-7643-3084-8). Birkhauser.

Odabasi, H., jt. auth. see Condon, E. U.

Odabasi, Halis & Akyuz, O. Topics in Mathematical Physics. LC 77-84853. (Illus.). 1977. text ed. 18.50x (ISBN 0-87081-072-3). Colo Assoc.

Odabasi, Halis, jt. ed. see Brittin, Wesley E.

O'Daffer, P. & Clemens, S. Geometry: Laboratory Investigations. (Grades 9 up). 1976. pap. text ed. 22.00 student ed. (ISBN 0-201-05420-5, Sch Div); tchrs. ed. 8.25 (ISBN 0-201-05421-3); wkbk. 3.15 (ISBN 0-201-05422-1). A-W.

O'Daffer, P., jt. auth. see Eicholz, R.

O'Daffer, Phares, jt. auth. see Eicholz, Robert.

O'Daniel, Larry J. Missing in Action: Trail of Deceit. (Illus.). 1979. 12.95 o.p. (ISBN 0-87000-450-6, Arlington Hse). Crown.

O'Day. Sail in a Day. pap. 2.95 (ISBN 0-448-01540-4, G&D). Putnam Pub Group.

O'Day, Anita & Eells, George. High Times, Hard Times. 320p. 1981. 14.95 (ISBN 0-399-12505-1). Putnam Pub Group.

O'Day, Danton. How to Succeed at University. 1982. pap. 2.95 (ISBN 0-7723-0074-7, YE74). NAL.

O'Day, Rosemary & Heal, Felicity, eds. Continuity & Change: Personnel & Administration of the Church in England, 1500-1642. 300p. 1976. text ed. 21.00x o.p. (ISBN 0-7185-1138-7, Leicester). Humanities.

Odden, Allan & Webb, Dean, eds. School Finance & School Improvement: Linkages in the 1980's. (American Education Finance Association). 1983. price not set prof ref (ISBN 0-88410-399-4). Ballinger Pub.

Oddo, Gilbert L. Freedom & Equality: Civil Liberties & the Supreme Court. LC 78-25592. 1979. pap. text ed. 16.95x (ISBN 0-673-16262-1). Scott F.

Oddo, Sandra, jt. auth. see Powell, Peter.

Oddo, Sandra, jt. ed. see Gottlieb, Richard.

Oddy, et al. Information Retrieval Research. 1981. text ed. 49.95 (ISBN 0-408-10775-8). Butterworth.

O'Dea, D. J. Cyclical Indicators for the Post War British Economy. LC 75-2738. (National Institute of Economic & Social Research, Occasional Papers Ser.: No. 28). (Illus.). 180p. 1975. 22.95x (ISBN 0-521-09963-3). Cambridge U Pr.

O'Dea, Thomas F. Mormons. LC 57-6984. 1964. pap. 8.95 (ISBN 0-226-61744-0, P162, Phoen). U of Chicago Pr.

O'Dea, Thomas F. & Aviad, Janet O. The Sociology of Religion. 144p. 1983. 12.95 (ISBN 0-13-821066-7); pap. 8.95 (ISBN 0-13-821058-6). P-H.

Odechuck, Anne. Poems for the Fancy Free. 1978. 4.95 o.p. (ISBN 0-533-03381-0). Vantage.

Odegaard, Charles E. Minorities in Medicine - From Receptive Passivity to Positive Action 1966-76: Report of a Study. LC 77-75502. (Illus.). 1977. pap. 4.00 o.p. (ISBN 0-914362-20-8). J Macy Foun.

Odell, Catherine M. & Odell, William. The First Human Right: A Pro-Life Primer. LC 82-61466. 1983. pap. 4.95 (ISBN 0-87973-620-8, 620). Our Sunday Visitor.

O'Dell, Felicity, jt. auth. see Lane, David.

O'Dell, Felicity A. Socialisation Through Children's Literature. LC 77-91093. (Soviet & East European Studies). 1979. 42.50 (ISBN 0-521-21968-X). Cambridge U Pr.

O'Dell, Gene J., jt. auth. see Boyenga, Kirk W.

Odell, Peter R. An Economic Geography of Oil. LC 75-43868. 219p. 1976. Repr. of 1963 ed. lib. bdg. 19.75 (ISBN 0-8371-8721-4, ODGO). Greenwood.

Odell, Peter R. & Preston, David A. Economies & Societies in Latin America: A Geographical Interpretation. 2nd ed. LC 77-12400. 289p. 1978. text ed. 38.00x (ISBN 0-471-99588-6, Pub. by Wiley-Interscience); pap. text ed. 21.95 (ISBN 0-471-99636-X). Wiley.

Odell, Peter R. & Rosing, Kenneth E. The Future of Oil: World Oil Resources & Use. 2nd ed. 200p. 1983. pap. 23.95 (ISBN 0-89397-146-4). Nichols Pub.

Odell, Rice. Environmental Awakening. LC 80-10990. 344p. 1980. prof ref 17.50x (ISBN 0-88410-630-6); pap. 8.95 (ISBN 0-88410-631-4). Ballinger Pub.

O'Dell, Richard F. Reaching Out: A History of the Rotary Club of Marquette, Michigan 1916-1981. Duerfeldt, Pryse H., ed. LC 82-60037. (Illus.). 254p. 1981. 17.00x (ISBN 0-9609764-0-X). Rotary Club.

Odell, Robin, jt. auth. see Gaute, J. H.

O'Dell, Scott. The Amethyst Ring. LC 82-23388. 224p. (gr. 7 up). 1983. 12.95 (ISBN 0-395-33886-7). HM.

--The Black Pearl. 1977. pap. 1.95 (ISBN 0-440-90803-5, LFL). Dell.

--Child of Fire. 1978. pap. 1.50 o.p. (ISBN 0-440-91239-3, LFL). Dell.

--Island of the Blue Dolphins. 1978. pap. 2.25 (ISBN 0-440-94000-1, LFL). Dell.

--Island of the Blue Dolphins. (gr. 7 up). 1960. 9.95 (ISBN 0-395-06962-9). HM.

--Sarah Bishop. (gr. 7 up). 1980. 10.95 (ISBN 0-395-29185-2). HM.

--Sing Down the Moon. 1976. pap. 1.75 (ISBN 0-440-97975-7, LFL). Dell.

--The Spanish Smile. (gr. 7 up). 1982. PLB 11.95 (ISBN 0-395-32867-5); 11.45. HM.

--Zia. LC 75-44156. (Illus.). 224p. (gr. 4-8). 1976. 11.95 (ISBN 0-395-24393-9). HM.

O'Dell, Scott see Allen, W. S.

O'Dell, T. H. Magnetic Bubbles. LC 74-12048. 159p. 1974. 39.95x o.s.i. (ISBN 0-470-65259-4). Halsted Pr.

Odell, William & Frauchimont, Paul. Principles of Competitive Protein-Binding Assays. 2nd ed. LC 82-10941. 311p. 1982. 39.50x (ISBN 0-471-08924-9, Pub. by Wiley Med). Wiley.

Odell, William, jt. auth. see Odell, Catherine M.

Odell, Zia, jt. auth. see McMahon, Judi.

Oden, J. T. Applied Functional Analysis: A First Course for Students of Mechanics & Engineering Science. LC 78-541. (Illus.). 1979. ref. 37.95 (ISBN 0-13-040162-5). P-H.

--Finite Elements of Nonlinear Continua. 1972. text ed. 35.00 o.p. (ISBN 0-07-047604-7, C). McGraw.

--Mechanics of Elastic Structures. 1967. text ed. 26.95 o.p. (ISBN 0-07-047599-7, C). McGraw.

Oden, J. T. & Reddy, J. N. An Introduction to the Mathematical Theory of Finite Elements. LC 76-6953. (Pure & Applied Mathematics Ser.). 429p. 1976. 44.95x (ISBN 0-471-65261-X, Pub. by Wiley-Interscience). Wiley.

--Variational Methods in Theoretical Mechanics. (Universitext Ser.). 310p. 1976. pap. 22.00 o.p. (ISBN 0-387-07600-X). Springer-Verlag.

--Variational Methods in Theoretical Mechanics. 2nd, rev. ed. (Universitext Ser.). 308p. 1983. pap. 20.00 (ISBN 0-387-11917-5). Springer-Verlag.

Oden, J. T., ed. see International Conference on Computational Methods in Nonlinear Mechanics, 2nd, Univ. of Texas at Austin.

Oden, J. Tinsley & Carey, Graham F. Finite Elements: Mathematical Aspects, Vol. IV. (Illus.). 208p. 1983. text ed. 28.95 (ISBN 0-13-317081-0). P-H.

Oden, John T. & Ripperger, Eugene A. Mechanics of Elastic Structures. 2nd ed. LC 79-25261. (Illus.). 480p. 1980. text ed. 37.50 (ISBN 0-07-047507-5, C). McGraw.

Oden, Richard L., ed. see Dryden, John & Shadwell, Thomas.

Oden, T. J., ed. Computational Methods in Nonlinear Mechanics. 1980. 72.50 (ISBN 0-444-85382-0). Elsevier.

Oden, Thomas C. The Intensive Group Experience: The New Pietism. 1972. pap. 3.45 o.s.i. (ISBN 0-664-24951-5). Westminster.

--Pastoral Theology: Essentials of Ministry. LC 82-47753. 456p. (Orig.). 1983. pap. 14.37i (ISBN 0-06-066353-7, HarpR). Har-Row.

Odescalchi, Edmond P. Faces of Reality. LC 74-82410. (Illus.). 80p. 1983. 10.00 (ISBN 0-914226-02-9). Cyclopedia.

--The Global Arena. LC 73-87660. (Illus.). 76p. 1983. 10.00 (ISBN 0-914226-00-2). Cyclopedia.

Odescalchi, Esther K. The Little Shoe That Ran Away. LC 75-32079. (Illus.). 27p. (gr. 2-4). 1983. 10.00 (ISBN 0-914226-04-5). Cyclopedia.

Odetola, Olatunde. Military Regimes & Development: A Comparative Analysis in African Societies. 240p. 1982. pap. text ed. 12.50x (ISBN 0-04-301154-3). Allen Unwin.

Odhner, John D., ed. see Swedenborg, Emanuel.

Odian, George. Principles of Poly Merization. 2nd ed. LC 80-29226. 731p. 1981. 39.95x (ISBN 0-471-05146-2, Pub. by Wiley-Interscience). Wiley.

Odier, Daniel. Nirvana-Tao: The Secret Meditation Techniques of the Taoist & Buddhist Masters. (Illus.). 224p. (Orig.). 1983. pap. 8.95 (ISBN 0-89281-045-9). Inner Tradit.

Odievre, Michel, jt. auth. see Alagille, Daniel.

Odin, Gilles S. Numerical Dating in Stratigraphy, 2 vols, Pt. 1. LC 81-14792. 630p. 1982. 134.00 (ISBN 0-471-10085-4, Pub. by Wiley-Interscience). Wiley.

Odin, Steve. Process Metaphysics & Hua-Yen Buddhism: A Critical Study of Cumulative Penetration vs. Interpretation. LC 81-9388. 256p. 1982. 34.50x (ISBN 0-87395-568-4); pap. 10.95x (ISBN 0-87395-569-2). State U NY Pr.

Odiorne, George. Personnel & Human Resource Management. Rev. ed. 1982. pap. 8.95 (ISBN 0-87094-340-5). Dow Jones-Irwin.

Odiorne, George S. Sales Management by Objectives. 1982. 87.50 (ISBN 0-85013-139-1). Dartnell Corp.

Odishaw, H. & Ruttenberg, S., eds. Geophysics & the IGY. LC 58-60035. (Geophysical Monograph: Vol. 2). 1958. 8.00 o.p. (ISBN 0-87590-002-X). Am Geophysical.

Odishaw, Hugh, jt. ed. see Condon, E. W.

Odiyo, P. O. Seasonal Distribution & Migrations of Agrotis Ipsilon (Hufnagel) Leipidoptera, Noctuidae. 1975. 35.00x (ISBN 0-85135-070-4, Pub. by Centre Overseas Research). State Mutual Bk.

Odlozilik, Otakar. The Hussite King: Bohemia in European Affairs, 1440-1471. 1965. 32.00 (ISBN 0-8135-0497-X). Rutgers U Pr.

Odmark, John, ed. Language, Literature & Meaning II: Current Trends in Literary Research. (Linguistic & Literary Studies in Eastern Europe Ser.). 1980. 57.00 (ISBN 90-272-1503-0, 2). Benjamins North Am.

Odmark, Leif & Thornton, Pat. Cross-Country Skiing... The Natural Way. LC 77-23702. 1978. pap. 6.95 (ISBN 0-8092-7797-2). Contemp Bks.

O'Doherty, Brian. American Masters: The Voice & the Myth in Modern Art. Whitehead, Bill, ed. 384p. 1982. pap. 9.95 (ISBN 0-525-48000-5, 0966-290). Dutton.

O'Doherty, Desmond S. Handbook of Neurologic Emergencies. 1977. spiral bdg. 12.95 o.p. (ISBN 0-87488-643-0). Med Exam.

O'Doherty, Neil. The Battered Child: Recognition in Primary Care. (Illus.). 64p. 1982. text ed. 25.00 (ISBN 0-02-858720-0, Bailliere-Tindall). Saunders.

Odom, Doug. How He Got the Mule. 1979. pap. 1.00 o.p. (ISBN 0-686-25265-9). Samisdat.

Odom, Keith C. Henry Green. (English Authors Ser.: No. 235). 1978. lib. bdg. 9.95 o.p. (ISBN 0-8057-6706-1, Twayne). G K Hall.

Odom, William. German for Singers: A Textbook of Diction & Phonetics. LC 80-5493. (Illus.). 200p. (Orig.). 1981. pap. text ed. 10.95 (ISBN 0-02-871750-3). Schirmer Bks.

O'Donald, Peter. The Artic Skua: A Study of the Ecology & Evolution of a Seabird. LC 82-12782. (Illus.). 250p. Date not set. price not set (ISBN 0-521-23581-2). Cambridge U Pr.

Odoni, A., jt. auth. see Larson, R.

O'Donnell, Allen. Towards the Primitive Terror. 1979. 7.95 o.p. (ISBN 0-533-04284-4). Vantage.

O'Donnell, Asta & Lipton, June. Keeping Fit with Asta O'Donnell: An Exercise Program for Problem Backs. (Illus.). 103p. (Orig.). 1983. pap. 12.50 (ISBN 0-9610564-0-1). J L Prods.

O'Donnell, C. Patrick, Jr., ed. see Spenser, Edmund.

O'Donnell, Cyril, jt. auth. see Koontz, Harold.

O'Donnell, Cyril, jt. auth. see Koontz, Harold D.

O'Donnell, Edward. Priestly People. 64p. 1982. pap. 1.50 (ISBN 0-89243-168-7). Liguori Pubns.

O'Donnell, Harold K. & Weihrich, Heinz. Management: A Book of Readings. 5th ed. (Illus.). 736p. text ed. 28.95x (ISBN 0-07-035418-9); pap. 18.95x (ISBN 0-07-035417-0). McGraw.

O'Donnell, James H., 3rd. Southern Indians in the American Revolution. LC 76-146662. 188p. 1973. 12.50x (ISBN 0-87049-131-8). U of Tenn Pr.

O'Donnell, James J. Cassiodorus. LC 77-93470. 1979. 30.00x (ISBN 0-520-03646-8). U of Cal Pr.

--Every Vote Counts: A Teen-Age Guide to the Electoral Process. LC 76-8947. 192p. (gr. 7 up). 1976. PLB 7.29 o.p. (ISBN 0-671-32793-3). Messner.

--Fire: Its Many Faces & Moods. LC 80-10123. 192p. (gr. 7 up). 1980. PLB 7.79 o.p. (ISBN 0-671-33021-7). Messner.

--Gold: The Noble Metal. LC 78-19167. 160p. (gr. 7 up). 1978. PLB 7.29 o.p. (ISBN 0-671-32877-8). Messner.

O'Donnell, Kevin. Mayflies & Other Spaced Spirits. (Orig.). 1979. pap. text ed. 1.95 o.p. (ISBN 0-425-04290-1). Berkley Pub.

O'Donnell, Kevin, Jr. Mayflies. 304p. 1982. pap. 2.50 (ISBN 0-425-05776-3). Berkley Pub.

--Reefs: The Journeys of McGill Felighan, Book II. 224p. (Orig.). 1981. pap. 2.50 (ISBN 0-425-05059-9). Berkley Pub.

O'Donnell, Lillian. Aftershock. LC 76-52435. 1977. 7.95 o.p. (ISBN 0-399-11951-5). Putnam Pub Group.

--The Children's Zoo. 224p. 1981. 11.95 (ISBN 0-399-12632-5). Putnam Pub Group.

--Falling Star. LC 79-11060. 1979. 9.95 o.p. (ISBN 0-399-12407-1). Putnam Pub Group.

--Leisure Dying. LC 75-43795. 1976. 6.95 o.p. (ISBN 0-399-11741-5). Putnam Pub Group.

--No Business Being a Cop. LC 78-18341. 1979. 8.95 o.p. (ISBN 0-399-12276-1). Putnam Pub Group.

--Wicked Designs. 228p. 1980. 9.95 o.s.i. (ISBN 0-399-12523-X). Putnam Pub Group.

O'Donnell, M. J., jt. ed. see Wade, L. G.

O'Donnell, Martin J., jt. ed. see Wade, L. G., Jr.

O'Donnell, Michael P. Teaching the Stages of Reading Progress. 1979. three ring binder 15.95 (ISBN 0-8403-1948-7, 40194801). Kendall-Hunt.

O'Donnell, Patrick. John Hawkes. (United States Authors Ser.). 1982. lib. bdg. 13.95 (ISBN 0-8057-7351-7, Twayne). G K Hall.

O'Donnell, Terence, jt. auth. see Vaughan, Thomas.

O'Donnell, Thomas F., jt. auth. see Jackson, Harry F.

O'Donnell, Thomas J. The Confessions of T. E. Lawrence: The Romantic Hero's Presentation of Self. LC 77-92257. x, 196p. 1979. 16.95x (ISBN 0-8214-0370-2, 82-82634). Ohio U Pr.

O'Donnell, W. R. & Todd, Loreto. Variety in Contemporary English. (Illus.). 176p. (Orig.). 1980. 25.00x (ISBN 0-04-421005-1); pap. text ed. 8.50x (ISBN 0-04-421006-X). Allen Unwin.

O'Donnell, William H., ed. see Yeats, William B.

O'Donnell, William J. & Jones, David A. The Law of Marriage & Marital Alternatives. LC 80-8029. 272p. 1982. 27.95x (ISBN 0-669-03944-6). Lexington Bks.

O'Donnol, Shirley M. American Costume, 1915-1970: A Source Book for the Stage Costumer. Barton, Lucy, frwd. by. LC 81-48390. (Illus.). 288p. 1982. 27.50 (ISBN 0-253-30589-6). Ind U Pr.

O'Donoghue. Beginners Guide to Minerals. 1983. text ed. 9.95. Butterworth.

O'Donoghue, Bernard. The Courtly Love Tradition. LC 82-18180. (Literature in Context Ser.). 320p. 1983. text ed. 25.00x (ISBN 0-389-20347-5); pap. text ed. 8.95x (ISBN 0-389-20348-3). B&N Imports.

O'Donoghue, Bernard, ed. see Hoccleve, Thomas.

O'Donoghue, David J. Poets of Ireland. LC 68-30622. 1968. Repr. of 1912 ed. 47.00x (ISBN 0-8103-3152-7). Gale.

O'Donoghue, Don H. Treatment of Injuries to Athletes. 3rd ed. LC 74-17760. (Illus.). 1976. text ed. 49.50 (ISBN 0-7216-6927-1). Saunders.

O'Donoghue, Maureen. Jedder's Land. 1983. price not set (ISBN 0-671-47044-2). S&S.

O'Donoghue, Michael. Van Nostrand Reinhold Color Dictionary of Minerals & Gemstones. 160p. 1982. pap. 12.95 (ISBN 0-442-27431-9). Van Nos Reinhold.

O'Donoghue, Michael, et al. Encyclopedia of Minerals & Gemstones. LC 76-1419. (Illus.). 1976. 22.50 o.p. (ISBN 0-399-11753-9). Putnam Pub Group.

O'Donoghue, Ronan, jt. auth. see Bowman, John.

O'Donovan, Leo J., ed. Cooperation Between Theologians & the Ecclesiastical Magisterium: A Report of the Joint Committee of the Canon Law Society of America & the Catholic Theological Society of America. 200p. (Orig.). 1982. pap. 5.00x (ISBN 0-943616-12-3). Canon Law Soc.

O'Donovan, Patrick, intro. by. Irish Shop Fronts. (Illus.). 72p. 1982. pap. 7.95 (ISBN 0-312-43623-8); pap. 79.50 Prepack of 10 o.p. (ISBN 0-312-43624-6). St Martin.

O'Donovan, Thomas M. G. P. S. S. Simulation Made Simple. LC 79-40520. (Wiley Series in Computing). 127p. 1980. 33.95 (ISBN 0-471-27614-6, Pub. by Wiley-Interscience). Wiley.

O'Donovan, Thomas R., ed. Ambulatory Surgical Centers: Development & Management. LC 76-15767. 348p. 1976. 36.95 (ISBN 0-912862-21-1). Aspen Systems.

Odor, Ruth. A Child's Book of Manners. Sparks, Judith, ed. (A Happy Day Book). (Illus.). 24p. (gr. k-2). 1980. 1.29 (ISBN 0-87239-401-8, 3633). Standard Pub.

--Christmas Is a Time for Singing. Sparks, Judy, ed. LC 81-86706. (Happy Day Bks.). (Illus.). 24p. (Orig.). (ps-3). 1982. pap. 1.29 (ISBN 0-87239-535-9, 3581). Standard Pub.

--Moods & Emotions. Buerger, Jane, ed. LC 80-17567. 112p. 1980. 5.95 (ISBN 0-89565-177-7, 4934). Standard Pub.

--My Quiet Book. LC 76-44814. (Illus.). (ps-3). 1977. 5.95 (ISBN 0-913778-65-6). Childs World.

--My Wonder Book. LC 76-44309. (Illus.). (ps-3). 1977. 5.95 (ISBN 0-913778-64-8). Childs World.

--Please. LC 79-25319. (What Does It Mean Ser.). (Illus.). 32p. (ps-2). 1980. 7.95g (ISBN 0-516-06447-9). Childrens.

--Thank You God, for Quiet Things. Buerger, Jane, ed. LC 80-15099. (Illus.). 32p. 1980. 4.95 (ISBN 0-89565-169-6, 4920). Standard Pub.

--Thank You God, for Wonderful Things. Buerger, Jane, ed. LC 80-16106. (Illus.). 32p. 1980. 4.95 (ISBN 0-89565-170-X, 4921). Standard Pub.

--Thanks. LC 79-23926. (What Does It Mean Ser.). (Illus.). 32p. (ps-2). 1980. 7.95g (ISBN 0-516-06449-5). Childrens.

--The Very Special Night. Sparks, Judith, ed. (A Happy Day Book). (Illus.). 24p. (Orig.). (gr. k-2). 1980. 1.29 (ISBN 0-87239-405-0, 3637). Standard Pub.

--What's a Body to Do? Buerger, Jane, ed. LC 80-17584. (Illus.). 112p. 1980. 5.95 (ISBN 0-89565-176-9, 4933). Standard Pub.

Odor, Ruth S. Baby in a Basket. LC 79-12092. (Bible Story Books). (Illus.). (ps-3). 1979. PLB 6.50 (ISBN 0-89565-086-X). Childs World.

--Cissy, the Pup. LC 76-15633. (A Values Ser.). (Illus.). (ps-3). 1976. 6.50 (ISBN 0-913778-50-8). Childs World.

--Glad. LC 79-26076. (What Does It Mean? Ser.). (Illus.). (ps-2). 1980. PLB 5.95 (ISBN 0-89565-114-9). Childs World.

--Happiest Day. LC 79-12184. (Bible Story Bks.). (Illus.). (ps-3). 1979. PLB 6.50 (ISBN 0-89565-085-1). Childs World.

--Learning about Castles & Palaces. LC 82-9567. (The Learning About Ser.). 48p. (gr. 2-6). 1982. 9.25 (ISBN 0-516-06537-8). Childrens.

--Learning About Giants. LC 81-10101. (Learning About Ser.). (Illus.). 48p. (gr. 2-6). 1981. PLB 9.25 (ISBN 0-516-06534-3). Childrens.

--The Little Lost Lamb. LC 79-13155. (Bible Story Books). (Illus.). (ps-3). 1979. 6.50 (ISBN 0-89565-088-6). Childs World.

--Please. LC 79-25319. (What Does It Mean? Ser.). (Illus.). (ps-2). 1980. PLB 5.95 (ISBN 0-89565-115-7). Childs World.

O'Dougherty. Line Focus Receiver Heat Losses. (Progress in Solar Energy Supplements SERI Ser.). 1983. pap. text ed. 7.50x (ISBN 0-89553-095-3). Am Solar Energy.

Odoyevsky, V. Old Father Frost. 22p. 1981. pap. 2.00 (ISBN 0-8285-2216-2, Pub. by Progress Pubs USSR). Imported Pubns.

O'Driscoll, Gerald P. Inflation or Deflation? Prospects for Capital Formation, Employment, & Economic Recovery. (Pacific Institute). 1983. write for info. (ISBN 0-88410-930-5). Ballinger Pub.

O'Driscoll, Gerald P., Jr. Economics As a Coordination Problem: The Contributions of Friedrich A. Hayek. LC 77-23382. (Studies in Economic Theory). 171p. 1978. 15.00x o.p. (ISBN 0-8362-0662-2); pap. 5.00x o.p. (ISBN 0-8362-0663-0). NYU Pr.

O'Driscoll, Herbert. Crossroads: Times of Decision for People of God. 96p. 1983. pap. 5.95 (ISBN 0-8164-2432-2). Seabury.

O'Driscoll, Robert. Symbolism & Some Implications of the Symbolic Approach: W. B. Yeats During the Eighteen Nineties. (New Yeats Papers Ser.: No. 9). 84p. 1975. pap. text ed. 8.00x o.p. (ISBN 0-85105-270-3, Dolmen Pr). Humanities.

O'Driscoll, Robert & Reynolds, Lorna, eds. Yeats Studies. Incl. Vol. 1. Yeats & the 1890's. (Illus.). 1971; Vol. 2. Theatre & the Visual Arts: a Centenary Celebration of Jack Yeats & John Synge. (Illus.). 1971. 9.00x o.p.. pap. 9.00x (ISBN 0-686-34326-3, Pub. by Irish Academic Pr). Biblio Dist.

Odum, Elisabeth C., jt. auth. see Odum, Howard T.

Odum, Eugene P., et al. The Crisis of Survival. 1970. pap. 6.95x (ISBN 0-673-07665-2). Scott F.

Odum, Howard T. Environment Power & Society. LC 78-129660. (Environmental Science & Technology Ser). 331p. 1971. pap. text ed. 16.95 (ISBN 0-471-65275-X, Pub. by Wiley-Interscience). Wiley.

Odum, Howard T. & Odum, Elisabeth C. Energy Basis for Man & Nature. 2nd ed. (Illus.). 352p. 1981. text ed. 22.50 (ISBN 0-07-047511-3, C); pap. text ed. 16.95 (ISBN 0-07-047510-5, C); instr's. manual 6.00 (ISBN 0-07-047512-1). McGraw.

Odum, Howard T. & Pigeon, Robert F., eds. A Tropical Rain Forest: A Study of Irradiation & Ecology at El Verde, Puerto Rico, 3vols. LC 70-606844. (AEC Technical Information Center Ser.). 1652p. 1970. pap. 49.25 (ISBN 0-87079-230-X, TID-24270); microfiche 4.50 (ISBN 0-87079-340-3, TID-24270). DOE.

Odum, Howard T., jt. ed. see Ewel, Katherine C.

Odum, Linda, jt. auth. see Mundy, Jean.

Oduyoye, Modupe. Sons of the Gods & Daughters of Men: An Afro-Asiatic Interpretation of Genesis 1-11. 96p. (Orig.). 1983. pap. price not set (ISBN 0-88344-467-4). Orbis Bks.

O'Dwyer, Barry W., tr. from Lat. Letters from Ireland, 1228-1229. (Cistercian Fathers Ser.: No. 28). Orig. Title: Registrum epistolarum Stephani de Lexinton abbatis de Stannlegia et de Saviagnaco. 1982. 21.95 (ISBN 0-87907-428-0). Cistercian Pubns.

O'Dwyer, Frederick. Lost Dublin. (Illus.). 152p. 1982. pap. 17.95 (ISBN 0-7171-1047-8, Pub. by Salem Hse Ltd). Merrimack Bk Serv.

O'Dwyer, J. R. O'Dwyer's Directory of Public Relations Firms, 1983. 300p. (Orig.). 1983. pap. 70.00 (ISBN 0-941424-02-2). J R O'Dwyer.

O'Dwyer, Paul. Counsel for the Defense. 1979. 10.95 o.p. (ISBN 0-671-22573-1). S&S.

OECD. Annual Reports on Competion Policy in OECD Member Countries 1982-1. 85p. 1982. pap. 8.00x (ISBN 92-64-12363-6). OECD.

--Chemical Control Legislation Glossary. 170p. Date not set. pap. 13.50x (ISBN 92-64-12364-4). OECD.

--Coal Liquification: A Technology Review. 70p. (Orig.). 1982. pap. 9.25x (ISBN 92-64-12377-6). OECD.

--Combatting Oil Spills: Some Economic Aspects. 140p. (Orig.). 1982. pap. 9.50X (ISBN 92-64-12341-5). OECD.

--Confidentiality of Data & Chemical Control. 94p. 1982. pap. 10.00x (ISBN 92-64-12365-2). OECD.

--Controls on International Capital Movements: The Experience with Controls on Int.Financial Credits, Loans, & Deposits. 130p. 1982. pap. 11.00 (ISBN 92-64-12376-8). OECD.

--The Cost of Oil Spills: Expert Studies Presented to OECD Seminar. 252p. (Orig.). 1982. pap. 15.00x (ISBN 92-64-12339-3). OECD.

--Critical Flow Modeling in Nuclear Safety. 102p. 1982. pap. 13.00 (ISBN 92-64-12366-0). OECD.

--Dry Storage of Spent Fuel Elements. 272p. 1982. pap. 17.00 (ISBN 92-64-02351-8). OECD.

--European Conference of Ministers of Transport: (ECMT) 28th Annual Report-1981, Vol. 1. (Activity of the Conference Ser.). 206p. 1982. pap. 18.00x. OECD.

--Heat Pump Systems: A Technology Review. 200p. 1982. pap. 19.50 (ISBN 92-64-12378-4). OECD.

--Historical Statistics of Foreign Trade, 1956-1980. 104p. (Orig., Eng. & Fr.). 1982. pap. 11.00x (ISBN 92-64-02352-6). OECD.

--In Service Education & Training of Teachers: A Condition for Educational Change, CERI. 88p. 1982. pap. 7.00 (ISBN 92-64-12372-5). OECD.

--Int. Standardisation of Fruit & Vegetables: Sweet Peppers. 48p. 1982. pap. 13.00x (ISBN 92-64-02321-6). OECD.

--Integrated Social Policy: A Review of the Austrian Experience. 257p. (Orig.). 1981. pap. text ed. 15.00x (ISBN 92-64-12256-7). OECD.

--Marginal Employment Subsidies. 98p. pap. 8.50 (ISBN 92-64-12374-1). OECD.

--Problems of Agricultural Trade. 178p. 1982. pap. 18.00x (ISBN 92-64-12368-7). OECD.

--Prospects for Agricultural Production & Trade in Eastern Europe: Bulgaria, Czechoslavakia, Romania, Vol. 2. 216p. (Orig.). 1982. pap. 26.00x (ISBN 92-64-12369-5). OECD.

--Review of Demand Models: ECMT Round Table Fifty Eight Forecasts-Recorded Traffic Comparisons for Urban Sands Intercity Transport. (Orig.). 1982. pap. 9.00x (ISBN 92-821-1078-8). OECD.

--Reviews of National Policies for Education: Finland. 120p. 1982. pap. 13.00 (ISBN 92-64-12371-7). OECD.

--The Search of Consensus: The Role of Institutional Dialogue Between Governments, Labour & Employers. 77p. 1982. pap. 7.50x (ISBN 92-64-12373-3). OECD.

--Tourism Policy & International Tourism in OECD Member Countries 1982. 170p. (Orig.). 1982. pap. 17.50 (ISBN 0-686-37921-7). OECD.
--The University & the Community: The Problems of Changing Relationships. 162p. 1982. pap. 14.50 (ISBN 92-64-12370-9). OECD.
OECD, IEA. Energy Research, Development & Demonstration in the IEA Countries, 1981 Review of National Programmes. 157p. (Orig.). 1982. pap. 17.00x (ISBN 92-64-12383-0). OECD.
OECD Staff. Activities of OECD in 1981. 119p. 1982. pap. 8.00 (ISBN 92-64-12310-5). OECD.
--Advertising Directed At Children: Endorsements in Advertising. 64p. (Orig.). 1982. pap. 6.00x (ISBN 92-64-12276-1). OECD.
--Annual Reports on Consumer Policy in OECD Member Countries, 1981. 125p. 1982. pap. 13.00x (ISBN 92-64-12301-6). OECD.
--The Challenge of Unemployment. 165p. (Orig.). 1982. pap. 17.00x (ISBN 92-64-12332-6). OECD.
--Economic & Ecological Interdependence. 86p. (Orig.). 1982. pap. 6.50 (ISBN 92-64-12311-3). OECD.
--Employment in the Public Sector. 79p. (Orig.). 1982. pap. 7.25 (ISBN 92-64-12319-9). OECD.
--Energy Balances of OECD Member Countries, 1976-1980. 160p. 1982. pap. 15.00 (ISBN 92-64-02320-8). OECD.
--Energy Policies & Programmes of IEA Countries, 1981 Review. 300p. 1982. pap. 20.00x (ISBN 92-64-12335-0). OECD.
--The Engineering Industries in OECD Member Countries, 1976-1979. 93p. 1982. pap. 10.00 (ISBN 92-64-02283-X). OECD.
--Eutrophication of Waters: Monitoring, Assessment, & Control. 154p. 1982. pap. 11.50 (ISBN 92-64-12298-2). OECD.
--Export Credit Financing Systems in OECD Member Countries. 252p. (Orig.). 1982. pap. 12.50x (ISBN 92-64-12291-5). OECD.
--The Future of the Use of the Car. (ECMT Round Tables Ser.). 232p. (Orig.). 1982. pap. 15.50x (ISBN 92-821-1075-3). OECD.
--Improving the Management of Urban Research: City University Co-Operation. (OECD Urban Management Studies: No. 5). 158p. (Orig.). 1982. pap. 9.00x (ISBN 92-64-12294-X). OECD.
--International Aspects of Inflation. The Hidden Economy. (OECD Occasional Studies). (Orig.). 1982. pap. 14.50x (ISBN 92-64-12330-X). OECD.
--International Investment & Multinational Enterprises: Mid-Term Report on the 1976 Declaration & Decisions. 80p. (Orig.). 1982. pap. 6.00 (ISBN 92-64-12349-0). OECD.
--International Trade in Fish Products: Effects on the 200-Mile Limit. 192p. (Orig.). 1982. pap. 17.50 (ISBN 92-64-12318-0). OECD.
--Labour Force Statistics, 1969-1980. (Orig., English-French.). 1982. pap. 22.00x (ISBN 92-64-02327-5). OECD.
--Maritime Transport, 1981. 162p. (Orig.). 1982. pap. 10.00x (ISBN 92-64-12347-4). OECD.
--Meat Balances in OECD Member Countries, 1975-1980. 85p. (Orig., English-French.). 1982. pap. text ed. 8.50x (ISBN 92-64-02323-2). OECD.
--Milk, Milk Products & Egg Balances in OECD Member Countries, 1975-1980. 112p. (Orig.). 1982. pap. 12.50x (ISBN 92-64-02324-0). OECD.
--Natural Gas Prospects to 2000. 173p. 1982. pap. 24.00 (ISBN 92-64-12309-1). OECD.
--Nuclear Energy & Its Fuel Cycle: Prospects to 2025. 262p. 1982. pap. 24.00 (ISBN 92-64-12306-7). OECD.
--Nuclear Energy Prospects to 2000. 130p. (Orig.). 1982. pap. 14.00x (ISBN 92-64-12326-7). OECD.
--OECD Economic Outlook, No. 31. 150p. 1982. pap. 11.00 (ISBN 0-686-37445-2). OECD.
--OECD Economic Outlook Historical Statistics, 1960-1980. 150p. (Orig.). 1982. pap. 11.00x (ISBN 92-64-02325-9). OECD.
--Product Durability & Product Life Extension: Their Contribution to Solid Waste Management. 129p. (Orig.). 1982. pap. 10.00x (ISBN 92-64-12293-1). OECD.
--Pulp & Paper Industry 1980. 129p. (Orig.). 1982. pap. 12.50x (ISBN 92-64-02322-4). OECD.
--Review of National Policies for Education: Greece. 122p. (Orig.). 1982. pap. 9.00x (ISBN 92-64-12334-2). OECD.
--The Steel Market in 1981 & Outlook for 1982. 74p. (Orig.). 1982. pap. 9.00x (ISBN 92-64-12340-7). OECD.
--The Use of Coal in Industry. 445p. (Orig.). 1982. pap. 44.00x (ISBN 92-64-12308-3). OECD.
OECD Staff & IEA Staff. Coal Prospects & Policies in IEA Countries, 1981 Review. 170p. (Orig.). 1982. pap. 17.00x (ISBN 92-64-12336-9). OECD.
--World Energy Outlook. (Illus.). 500p. (Orig.). 1982. pap. 45.00 (ISBN 92-64-12360-1). OECD.
Oechsner, Carl. Ossining New York: An Informal Bicentennial History. LC 75-11853. (Illus.). 144p. 1975. 12.00 (ISBN 0-88427-016-5). North River.
Oeckl, Albert, ed. Taschenbuch des Oeffentlichen Lebens (Handbook of Public & Private Institutions), 1982-83. 32nd ed. 1189p. (Ger.). 1982. 57.50x (ISBN 0-8002-3074-4). Intl Pubns Serv.
Oegjo, Caleb. Mwindaji Hodari. (Swahili Literature). (Orig., Swahili.). 1978. pap. text ed. 2.95x o.p. (ISBN 0-686-74454-3, 00613). Heinemann Ed.
Oehlberg, Barbara E. Buyer's Guide to Home Furnishings: The Market of Obsolescence. 1978. 6.95 o.p. (ISBN 0-533-03117-6). Vantage.
Oehler, Gustave. Theology of the Old Testament. 1978. 22.50 (ISBN 0-86524-125-2, 8702). Klock & Klock.
Oehm, Rudolph. The Joy of Good Health. LC 80-65169. (Orig.). 1980. pap. 3.95 o.p. (ISBN 0-89081-222-5). Harvest Hse.
Oehme, Frederick W. & Prier, James E. Large Animal Surgery. (Illus.). 618p. 1974. text ed. 43.95 (ISBN 0-683-06634-X). Williams & Wilkins.
Oehmichen, Manfred. Cerebrospinal Fluid Cytology. LC 76-8049. (Illus.). 1976. text ed. 10.00 (ISBN 0-7216-6948-4). Saunders.
Oehser, Paul H. The Smithsonian Institution. (Library of Federal Departments, Agencies, & Systems). 350p. 1983. lib. bdg. 25.00 (ISBN 0-86531-300-8). Westview.
Oelhaf, Robert C. Organic Agriculture: Economic & Ecological Comparisons with Conventional Methods. LC 78-7347. 300p. 1978. text ed. 18.00x o.p. (ISBN 0-916672-16-6). Allanheld.
Oelsner, G. H. Handbook of Weaves. pap. 7.50x (ISBN 0-87245-244-1). Textile Bk.
Oelsner, Herman. The Influence of Dante on Modern Thought: Being the Le Bas Prize Essay, 1894. 120p. 1982. Repr. of 1895 ed. lib. bdg. 45.00 (ISBN 0-89984-363-8). Century Bookbindery.
Oeltien, Jody, jt. auth. see Palmer, Elsie.
Oenslager, Donald, et alcontrib. by. Artist of the Theatre: Alexandra Exter. LC 74-78230. (Illus.). 1974. pap. 7.00 (ISBN 0-87104-250-9). NY Pub Lib.
Oerke, jt. auth. see Gawne, Eleanor.
Oersted, Hans C. The Soul in Nature. 465p. 1966. Repr. of 1852 ed. 20.00x o.p. (ISBN 0-8464-0864-3). Beekman Pubs.
Oertel, Herbert, Jr., jt. ed. see Zierep, Juergen.
Oertel, William, jt. auth. see Jones, Patricia.
Oestereich, James & Pennington, Earl. Improvising & Arranging on the Keyboard. (Illus.). 208p. 1981. 16.95 (ISBN 0-13-453563-4, Spec); pap. 7.95 (ISBN 0-13-453555-3). P-H.
Oesterle, Jean T., tr. Aristotle: On Interpretation. Incl. Commentary by St. Thomas & Cajetan. (Medieval Philosophical Texts in Translation: No. 11). 288p. 1962. pap. 7.95 (ISBN 0-87462-211-5). Marquette.
Oesterle, John A. Logic: The Art of Defining & Reasoning. 2nd ed. 1963. pap. text ed. 14.95 (ISBN 0-13-539999-8). P-H.
Oestreich, Alan E., tr. see Nahum, Henri & Fekete, Francois.
Oestreich, B., ed. see Oestreich, Gerhard.
Oestreich, Gerhard. Neostoicism & the Early Modern State. Oestreich, B. & Koenigsberger, H. G., eds. LC 81-12285. (Cambridge Studies in Early Modern History Ser.). 272p. 1982. 49.50 (ISBN 0-521-24202-9). Cambridge U Pr.
Oettgen, Herbert F., jt. ed. see Mitchell, Malcolm.
Oetting. The Chieftain of Chaucer. LC 73-87806. (Oddo Sound Ser.). (Illus.). (gr. 2-5). 1974. 6.75x (ISBN 0-87783-137-8); pap. 2.95x deluxe ed. (ISBN 0-87783-138-6). Oddo.
--The Gray Ghosts of Gotham. LC 73-87804. (Oddo Sound Ser.). (Illus.). (gr. 2-5). 1974. 6.75x (ISBN 0-87783-135-1); pap. 2.95x deluxe ed. (ISBN 0-87783-136-X). Oddo.
--Keiki of the Islands. LC 71-108728. (Illus.). (gr. 3 up). PLB 6.75x (ISBN 0-87783-018-5); pap. 2.95x deluxe ed. (ISBN 0-87783-096-7). Oddo.
Oetting, Eugene R., jt. auth. see Thornton, George C., 3rd.
Oetting, R. Orderly Cricket. LC 68-16395. (Illus.). (gr. 2-3). 1967. PLB 6.75x (ISBN 0-87783-028-2). Oddo.
--Prairie Dog Town. LC 68-56829. (Illus.). (gr. 2-5). 1968. PLB 6.75x (ISBN 0-87783-030-4); pap. 2.95x deluxe ed. (ISBN 0-87783-157-2). Oddo.
--Quetico Wolf. LC 71-190274. (Illus.). (gr. 4 up). PLB 6.75x (ISBN 0-87783-059-2); pap. 2.95x deluxe ed. (ISBN 0-87783-103-3). Oddo.
--When Jesus Was a Lad. LC 68-56816. (Illus.). (gr. 2-3). PLB 6.75x (ISBN 0-87783-047-9). Oddo.
Oetting, Rae. Timmy Tiger & the Elephant. LC 73-108730. (Timmy Tiger Ser). (Illus.). (ps-2). PLB 6.75x (ISBN 0-87783-041-X); pap. 2.95x deluxe ed (ISBN 0-87783-111-4); cassette 5.95x (ISBN 0-87783-277-3). Oddo.
--Timmy Tiger to the Rescue. LC 70-108733. (Timmy Tiger Ser). (Illus.). (ps-4). PLB 6.75x (ISBN 0-87783-043-6); pap. 2.95x deluxe ed (ISBN 0-87783-112-2); cassette 5.95 (ISBN 0-87783-229-3). Oddo.
--Timmy Tiger's New Coat. LC 74-108734. (Timmy Tiger Ser). (Illus.). (ps-2). PLB 6.75x (ISBN 0-87783-044-4); pap. 2.95x deluxe ed (ISBN 0-87783-113-0); cassette 5.95x (ISBN 0-87783-230-7). Oddo.
--Timmy Tiger's New Friend. LC 77-108732. (Timmy Tiger Ser). (Illus.). (ps-2). PLB 6.75x (ISBN 0-87783-042-8); pap. 2.95x deluxe ed (ISBN 0-87783-114-9); cassette 5.95x (ISBN 0-87783-231-5). Oddo.
Oetting, Walter W. Church of the Catacombs. LC 64-24277. (Church in History Ser). (Orig.). (YA) (gr. 9-12). 1964. pap. 4.95 (ISBN 0-570-06278-0, 12-2240). Concordia.
Oettinger, Anthony G, et al. High & Low Politics: Information Resources for the 80's. LC 77-1685. (Program on Information Resources Policy, Harvard University). 280p. 1977. prof ref 19.50x (ISBN 0-88410-064-2). Ballinger Pub.
Oettinger, Marion, Jr. & Horcasitas, Fernando. The Lienzo of Petlacala: A Pictorial Document from Guerrero, Mexico, Pt. 7. LC 81-71034. (Transactions Ser.: Vol. 72). 1982. 12.00 (ISBN 0-87169-727-0). Am Philos.
Oettmeier, Timothy N., jt. auth. see Pekar, George M.
O'Fahey, R. S. & Abu, Salim M. Land in Dar Fur: Charters & Related Documents from the Dar Fur Sultanate. LC 82-4186. (Fontes Historiae Africanae Series Arabica: No. 3). (Illus.). 176p. Date not set. price not set (ISBN 0-521-24643-1). Cambridge U Pr.
O'Fahey, R. S. & Spaulding, J. L., eds. Kingdoms of the Sudan. (Studies in African History). 1974. 19.95x (ISBN 0-416-77450-4); pap. text ed. 10.95x o.p. (ISBN 0-416-77460-1). Methuen Inc.
O'Faolain, Sean. King of the Beggars. LC 75-7242. (Illus.). 338p. 1975. Repr. of 1938 ed. lib. bdg. 18.00x (ISBN 0-8371-8104-6, OFKB). Greenwood.
--The Man Who Invented Sin. (Illus.). 1974. Repr. of 1948 ed. 8.95 (ISBN 0-8159-6212-6). Devin.
O'Farrell, Patrick. Ireland's English Question: Anglo-Irish Relations, 1534-1970. LC 75-159481. (Fabric of British History Ser). 1972. 11.50x o.p. (ISBN 0-8052-3424-1); pap. 4.95 o.p. (ISBN 0-8052-0348-6). Schocken.
O'Farrell, Timothy J. & Weyand, Carolyn A. Alcohol & Sexuality: An Annotated Bibliography on Alcohol Use, Alcoholism & Human Sexual Behavior. 1983. lib. bdg. 37.50 (ISBN 0-89774-040-8). Oryx Pr.
O'Ferrall, Fergus. Daniell O'Connell. (Gill's Irish Lives Ser.). 151p. 1981. 15.95 (ISBN 0-7171-1070-2, Gill Macmillan Ireland); pap. 5.95 (ISBN 0-686-37164-X). Irish Bk Ctr.
Offe, Claus. Industry & Inequality: The Achievement Principle in Work & Social Status. LC 76-40724. 1977. 26.00x (ISBN 0-312-41580-X). St Martin.
Offenbach, Jacques. Orpheus in America: Offenbach's Diary of His Journey to the New World. MacClintock, Lander, tr. (Illus.). Repr. of 1957 ed. lib. bdg. 15.00 o.p. (ISBN 0-8371-0598-6, OFOA). Greenwood.
Offer, Avner. Property & Politics, Eighteen-Seventy to Nineteen-Fourteen: Landownership, Law, Ideology & Urban Development in England. LC 80-41010. (Illus.). 480p. 1981. 59.50 (ISBN 0-521-22414-4). Cambridge U Pr.
Office de la Recherche Scientifique et Technique Outre Mer. Direction des Etudes du Developpement, 3 vols. Incl. Vol. 1. Esquisse Regionalisee des Objectifs de Production (71-2033); Vol. 2. Resultats par Region (71-2034); Vol. 3. Superficie Necessaire a la Realisation des Objectifs Agricoles (71-2035). (Black Africa Ser.). (Fr.). 1974. Repr. Set. lib. bdg. 80.00x o.p. (ISBN 0-8287-1362-6). Clearwater Pub.
Office for History of Science & Technology. Max Planck: A Bibliography of His Non-Technical Writings. LC 77-75623. (Berkeley Papers in History of Science: No. 1). 1977. 5.00x (ISBN 0-918102-00-6). U Cal Hist Sci Tech.
--William Henry Bragg & William Lawrence Bragg: A Bibliography of Their Non-Technical Writings. LC 77-94209. (Berkeley Papers in History of Science: No. 2). 1978. pap. 5.00x (ISBN 0-918102-01-4). U Cal Hist Sci Tech.
Office of Environmental Quality Control, State of Hawaii & The Environmental Center, University of Hawaii. Hawaii Environmental Laws & Regulations, 2 vols. & supplements. rev ed. 1976. Set. 72.00 (ISBN 0-8248-0445-7). UH Pr.
Office of Information, Gov't of Papua New Guinea. Papua New Guinea. LC 75-23775. (Illus.). 68p. 1976. text ed. 9.95x (ISBN 0-8248-0400-7, Eastwest Ctr). UH Pr.
Office of International Affairs National Telecommunications & Information Administration. Profiles of International Private Lease, DATEL & Packet Switched Service Markets for the Years 1976 to 1979. 1981. 50.00 (ISBN 0-686-37966-7). Info Gatekeepers.
Office of Technical Assessment, Congress of the U. S. Technology & Handicapped People. 1983. text ed. price not set (ISBN 0-8261-4510-8). Springer Pub.
Office of Technology Assessment. Cancer Risk: Assessing & Reducing the Dangers in our Society. (Special Study). 240p. (Orig.). 1982. lib. bdg. 18.00 (ISBN 0-86531-396-2); pap. 10.95 (ISBN 0-86531-397-0). Westview.
Office of Technology Assessment, U. S. Congress. Technology & Soviet Energy Availability. 400p. 1982. lib. bdg. 25.00 (ISBN 0-86531-468-3). Westview.
Office of Technology Assessment, U.S. Congress. Energy from Biological Processes. 200p. 1981. lib. bdg. 25.00 (ISBN 0-86531-171-4). Westview.
Office Of The Foreign Secretary. Eastern European Academies of Sciences: A Directory. 1963. pap. 3.50 (ISBN 0-309-01090-X). Natl Acad Pr.
Office Strategic Services. OSS Sabotage & Demolition Manual. (Illus.). 139p. 1973. pap. 15.95 (ISBN 0-87364-005-5). Paladin Ent.
Officer, Charles B. Introduction to the Theory of Sound Transmission. (International Ser. in Earth & Planetary Sciences). 1958. 34.50 o.p. (ISBN 0-07-047612-8, 1, P&RB). McGraw.
Officer, Lawrence H. & Smith, Lawrence B. Issues in Canadian Economics. LC 73-21373. 424p. 1975. pap. text ed. 9.95 o.p. (ISBN 0-07-077447-1, SP). McGraw.
Official Satellite Symposium, International Congress of Pharmacology, Nagasaki, Japan, 8th 30-31 July 1982. New Vistas in Depression: Proceedings. Langer, S. Z., et al, eds. (Illus.). 339p. 1982. 60.00 (ISBN 0-08-027388-2). Pergamon.
Offiong, Daniel O. Imperialism & Dependency: Obstacles in African Development. 304p. 1983. 12.95 (ISBN 0-88258-126-0); pap. 6.95 (ISBN 0-88258-127-9). Howard U Pr.
Offir, Carole, jt. auth. see Tavris, Carol.
Offir, Carole W. Human Sexuality. 608p. 1982. text ed. 19.95 (ISBN 0-15-540428-8); Instructors Handbook 4.80 (ISBN 0-15-540429-6). HarBraceJ.
Offit, Avodah. Night Thoughts: Reflections of a Sex Therapist. 256p. 1982. pap. 7.95 (ISBN 0-312-92577-8). Congdon & Weed.
Offit, Avodah K. Night Thoughts: Reflections of a Sex Therapist. LC 80-68914. 284p. 1981. 12.95 o.p. (ISBN 0-312-92575-1). Congdon & Weed.
--The Sexual Self. 304p. 1983. pap. 8.95 (ISBN 0-312-92766-5). Congdon & Weed.
Offit, Sidney. Only a Girl Like You. (gr. 7 up). 1972. 5.95 o.p. (ISBN 0-698-20176-0, Coward). Putnam Pub Group.
Offler, H. S., ed. see De Ockham, Guillelmi.
Offner, Hazel. The Fruit of the Spirit: Nine Bible Studies. (Orig.). 1977. pap. 2.50 (ISBN 0-87784-628-6). Inter-Varsity.
Offord, R. E. Semisynthetic Proteins. LC 79-40521. 235p. 1980. 69.95 (ISBN 0-471-27615-4, Pub. by Wiley-Interscience). Wiley.
Offord, Robin, jt. auth. see Yudkin, Michael.
Offutt, Andrew J. The Iron Lords. 1979. pap. 1.75 o.s.i. (ISBN 0-515-04600-0). Jove Pubns.
O'Fiaich, Tomas, jt. auth. see Forristal, Desmond.
O'Flaherty, Ellen. Toxicants & Drugs: Kinetics & Dynamics. LC 80-2445. 398p. 1981. 47.95x (ISBN 0-471-06047-X, Pub. by Wiley-Interscience). Wiley.
O'Flaherty, Fred, et al, eds. The Chemistry & Technology of Leather, 4 vols. LC 76-50622. (ACS Monographs Ser.). 1978. Repr. of 1956 ed. Vol. 1 510p. 31.00 (ISBN 0-88275-474-2); Vol. 2 568p. 35.00 (ISBN 0-88275-886-1); Vol. 3 528p. 32.00 (ISBN 0-88275-887-X); Vol. 4 448. 28.00 (ISBN 0-88275-888-8); Set. 107.75 (ISBN 0-686-86250-3). Krieger.
O'Flaherty, James C. Johann Georg Hamann. (World Authors Ser.). 1979. lib. bdg. 15.95 (ISBN 0-8057-6371-6, Twayne). G K Hall.
O'Flaherty, James C., tr. see Raabe, Wilhelm.
O'Flaherty, Liam. The Wounded Cormorant & Other Stories. 256p. 1973. pap. 5.95 (ISBN 0-393-00704-9, Norton Lib). Norton.
O'Flaherty, Wendy D. Siva: The Erotic Ascetic. (Illus.). 1981. pap. 9.95 (ISBN 0-19-520250-3, GB 650). Oxford U Pr.
--Women, Androgynes, & Other Mythical Beasts. LC 79-16128. 1980. lib. bdg. 27.50x (ISBN 0-226-61849-8, Phoen); pap. 9.95 (ISBN 0-226-61850-1). U of Chicago Pr.
Ofman, William V. Affirmation & Reality: Fundamentals of Humanistic Existential Therapy & Counseling. LC 76-46878. 203p. 1976. 19.70x o.p. (ISBN 0-87424-304-1). Western Psych.
Ofori, Patrick E. Black African Traditional Religions & Philosophy: A Selected Bibliographic Survey of the Sources from the Earliest Times to 1974. 421p. 1975. lib. bdg. 45.00 (ISBN 3-262-00478-2). Kraus Intl.
--Islam in Africa South of the Sahara: A Select Bibliographic Guide. 223p. 1977. lib. bdg. 25.00 (ISBN 3-262-00003-5). Kraus Intl.
--Land in Africa: Its Administration, Law, Tenure & Use: A Select Bibliography. 199p. 1979. lib. bdg. 30.00 (ISBN 3-262-00474-X). Kraus Intl.
Ofosu-Appiah, L. H. People in Bondage: African Slavery in the Modern Era. LC 70-128799. (Real World Crisis & Conflict Ser). (Illus.). (gr. 5-11). 1971. PLB 5.95 o.p. (ISBN 0-8225-0624-6). Lerner Pubns.
Ofshe, Richard J. Sociology of the Possible. 2nd ed. 1977. pap. text ed. 15.95 (ISBN 0-13-821595-2). P-H.
Oftedal, Laura & Jacob, Nina. My First Dictionary. (Illus.). (gr. k-3). 1948. 4.50 (ISBN 0-448-02962-6, G&D). Putnam Pub Group.
Ogai, Mori. The Incident at Sakai & Other Stories. Dilworth, David & Rimer, J. Thomas, eds. Dilworth, David & Rimer, J. Thomas, trs. from Japanese. LC 76-58462. 1977. text ed. 12.95x (ISBN 0-8248-0453-8). UH Pr.
--Saiki Koi & Other Stories. Dilworth, David & Rimer, J. Thomas, eds. Dilworth, David & Rimer, J. Thomas, trs. from Japanese. LC 77-4455. 1977. text ed. 12.95x (ISBN 0-8248-0454-6). UH Pr.
Ogan, George. Murder by Proxy. (Raven House Mysteries Ser.). 224p. 1983. pap. cancelled (ISBN 0-373-63053-0, Pub. by Worldwide). Harlequin Bks.
Ogan, George, jt. auth. see Ogan, Margaret.

Ogan, Margaret & Ogan, George. Green Thirteen. LC 77-15935. (Hiway Bks. Ser). 1978. 8.95 (ISBN 0-664-32624-2). Westminster.

Ogan, Margaret N. Ruthana. (Orig.). 1980. pap. 1.25 o.s.i. (ISBN 0-440-18208-5). Dell.

O'Gara, Elaine. Travel Writer's Markets. 58p. (Orig.). 1982. pap. 6.00 (ISBN 0-9609172-0-9). R B Shapiro.

Ogarev, N. P. Essai sur la Situation Russe. (Nineteenth Century Russia Ser.). 150p. (Fr.). 1974. Repr. of 1862 ed. lib. bdg. 46.00x o.p. (ISBN 0-8287-0661-1, R40). Clearwater Pub.

Ogasapian, J. Organ Building in New York City Seventeen Hundred to Nineteen Hundred. (Bibliotheca Organologica: Vol. 61). 1977. wrappers 30.00 o.s.i. (ISBN 90-6027-309-5, Pub. by Frits Knuf Netherlands). Pendragon NY.

Ogasapian, John. Church Organs: A Guide to Selection & Purchase. 128p. (Orig.). 1983. pap. 5.95 (ISBN 0-8010-6706-5). Baker Bk.

Ogata, Katshuiko. System Dynamics. LC 77-20180. (Illus.). 1978. 35.95 (ISBN 0-13-880385-4). P-H.

Ogata, Katsuhiko. Modern Control Engineering. LC 72-84843. (Electrical Engineering Ser). 1970. ref. ed. 34.95 (ISBN 0-13-590232-0). P-H.

--State Space Analysis of Control Systems. 1966. ref. ed. 35.00 (ISBN 0-13-844530-3). P-H.

Ogawa, Dennis M. Jan Ken Po: The World of Hawaii's Japanese Americans. new ed. LC 78-9513. (Illus.). 1978. pap. 3.95 (ISBN 0-8248-0398-1). UH Pr.

--Kodomo No Tame Ni-for the Sake of the Children: The Japanese American Experience in Hawaii. LC 77-18368. 639p. 1980. pap. 8.95 (ISBN 0-8248-0730-8). UH Pr.

Ogawa, Dennis M. & Grant, Glen. Kodomo No Tame Ni-for the Sake of the Children: The Japanese American Experience in Hawaii. LC 77-18368. 1978. 17.50 (ISBN 0-8248-0528-3). UH Pr.

Ogburn, Charlton. Adventure of Birds. LC 76-13502. (Illus.). 336p. 1980. Repr. of 1976 ed. pap. 6.95 o.p. (ISBN 0-688-08080-4). Quill NY.

--The Marauders. LC 82-16149. 307p. 1982. pap. 6.50 (ISBN 0-688-01625-1, Quill). Morrow.

--The Winter Beach. LC 66-23350. (Illus.). 1979. pap. 4.95 (ISBN 0-688-07785-4). Quill NY.

Ogburn, Charlton, Jr. The Winter Beach. (Illus.). 1966. 7.95 o.p. (ISBN 0-688-02785-7). Morrow.

Ogburn, Charlton, Jr., jt. auth. see Ogburn, Dorothy.

Ogburn, Dorothy & Ogburn, Charlton, Jr. Shakespeare: The Man Behind the Name. (Illus.). 1962. 6.00 o.p. (ISBN 0-688-02457-2). Morrow.

Ogburn, Floyd, Jr. Style As Structure & Meaning: William Bradford's "Of Plymouth Plantation". LC 80-5879. 169p. 1981. lib. bdg. 19.00 (ISBN 0-8191-1590-8); pap. text ed. 9.50 (ISBN 0-8191-1591-6). U Pr of Amer.

Ogburn, Keith D. Emotional Education: How to Deal with Stress in the Classroom Before & After it Happens-Strategies & Techniques. LC 82-60528. 125p. (Orig.). 1983. pap. 14.95 (ISBN 0-88247-683-1). R & E Res Assoc.

Ogburn, William F., ed. American Society in Wartime. LC 72-2380. (FDR & the Era of the New Deal Ser.). 237p. 1972. Repr. of 1943 ed. lib. bdg. 29.50 (ISBN 0-306-70484-6). Da Capo.

--Social Changes During Depression & Recovery. LC 72-2381. (FDR & the Era of the New Deal Ser.). 117p. 1974. Repr. of 1935 ed. lib. bdg. 22.50 (ISBN 0-306-70483-8). Da Capo.

Ogden, Adele. The California Sea Otter Trade: 1784-1848. (California Library Reprint Ser.). 1975. 30.00x (ISBN 0-520-02806-6). U of Cal Pr.

Ogden, Charles K. Bentham's Theory of Fictions. (Quality Paperback: No. 202). 1959. pap. 4.95 (ISBN 0-8226-0202-4). Littlefield.

Ogden, Charles K. & Richards, Ivor A. The Meaning of Meaning. 1959. pap. 5.95 (ISBN 0-15-658446-8, Harv). HarBraceJ.

Ogden, david A. & Lee, Stanley M. Nephrology: Continuing Education Review. 1982. pap. text ed. 29.50 (ISBN 0-87488-322-9). Med Exam.

Ogden, Dunbar H. Wedding Bells. (Orig.). 1945. pap. 1.95 (ISBN 0-8042-1884-6). John Knox.

Ogden, Dunbar H., tr. The Italian Baroque Stage: Documents by Giulio Troili, Andrea Pozzo, Ferdinando Galli-Bibiena, & Baldassare Orsini. LC 75-7197. 1978. 42.50x (ISBN 0-520-03006-0). U of Cal Pr.

Ogden, Jack. Jewellery of the Ancient World. LC 82-60069. (Illus.). 250p. 1982. 45.00 (ISBN 0-8478-0444-5). Rizzoli Intl.

Ogden, Paul W. & Lipsett, Suzanne. The Silent Garden: Understanding the Hearing-Impaired Child. 240p. 1983. pap. 7.95 (ISBN 0-8092-5571-5). Contemp Bks.

Ogden, Peggy, ed. see Vrooman, Christine W.

Ogden, Robert M. Psychology & Education. 350p. 1982. Repr. of 1932 ed. lib. bdg. 40.00 (ISBN 0-89984-364-6). Century Bookbindery.

Ogden, Sheila J., jt. auth. see Radcliff, Ruth K.

Ogdin, Carol A. Microcomputer Design. (Illus.). 1978. ref. ed. 22.00 (ISBN 0-13-580977-0); pap. 16.00 (ISBN 0-13-580985-1). P-H.

Ogelsby, Mac, et al. Pet Games & Recreation. 1981. text ed. 18.95 (ISBN 0-8359-5530-3); pap. 12.95 (ISBN 0-8359-5529-X). Reston.

Ogg, C., jt. ed. see Parsons, F. M.

Ogg, Frederic A. Old Northwest. 1919. text ed. 8.50x (ISBN 0-686-83654-5). Elliots Bks.

--Opening of the Mississippi: A Struggle for Supremacy in the American Interior. LC 69-14017. 1969. Repr. of 1904 ed. lib. bdg. 19.25x o.p. (ISBN 0-8371-1103-X, OGOM). Greenwood.

--Reign of Andrew Jackson. 1919. text ed. 8.50x (ISBN 0-686-83729-0). Elliots Bks.

Ogg, Frederick A. Builders of the Republic. 1928. text ed. 22.50x (ISBN 0-686-83496-8). Elliots Bks.

Ogg, Oscar. Twenty Six Letters. 3rd rev. ed. LC 70-140646. (Illus.). 1971. 13.41i (ISBN 0-690-84115-9). T Y Crowell.

Oggel, Terry, ed. see Bibliographic Society of Northern Illinois.

Ogilvie, Bruce & Waitley, Douglas. Rand McNally Picture Atlas of the World. (Illus.). (gr. 4-7). 1979. 9.95 (ISBN 0-528-82418-X). Rand.

Ogilvie, Elizabeth. The Silent Ones. (General Ser.). 1982. lib. bdg. 16.95 (ISBN 0-8161-3343-3, Large Print Bks). G K Hall.

Ogilvie, J. C. Overcoming Multiple Sclerosis. 5.60x (ISBN 0-686-29841-1). Cancer Control Soc.

Ogilvie, Lloyd, ed. see McKenna, David L.

Ogilvie, Lloyd J. The Communicator's Commentary-Acts, Vol. 5. (The Communicator's Commentaries Ser.). 1982. 14.95 (ISBN 0-8499-0158-8). Word Pub.

--God's Will in Your Life. LC 82-82161. 192p. 1982. 8.95 (ISBN 0-89081-282-9, 2829). Harvest Hse.

--You Can Live Life as it Was Meant to Be. 1982. pap. 4.95 (ISBN 0-8307-0865-0, 5417408). Regal.

--You've Got Charisma. 176p. 1983. pap. 3.50 (ISBN 0-687-47268-7). Abingdon.

Ogilvie, Lloyd J., jt. auth. see Chafin, Kenneth L.

Ogilvie, Lloyd J., ed. see Cedar, Paul A.

Ogilvie, Lloyd J., ed. see Fredrikson, Roger L.

Ogilvie, Lloyd J., ed. see Larson, Bruce.

Ogilvie, M. A. Wildfowl of Britain & Europe. 1982. 16.95x (ISBN 0-19-217723-0). Oxford U Pr.

Ogilvie, Mardel, jt. auth. see Eisenson, Jon.

Ogilvie, R. M. Roman Literature & Society. 303p. 1980. 24.50x (ISBN 0-389-20069-7). B&N Imports.

Ogilvie, Sheilagh C., tr. see Lepage, Henri.

Ogilvie, Sheilia A., tr. see Von Vacano, Otto-Wilhelm.

Ogilvy, Charles S. Tomorrow's Math: Unsolved Problems for the Amateur. 2nd ed. 1972. 16.95x (ISBN 0-19-501508-8). Oxford U Pr.

Ogilvy, David. The Shuttleworth Collection. 1982. 45.00x (ISBN 0-906393-18-3, Pub. by Airlife England). State Mutual Bk.

Ogilvy, James A. Many Dimensional Man: Decentralizing Self, Society & the Sacred. LC 76-57273. 1977. 22.50x (ISBN 0-19-502231-9). Oxford U Pr.

--Self & World: Readings in Philosophy. 2nd ed. 507p. 1981. pap. text ed. 12.95 (ISBN 0-15-579628-3, HC). HarBraceJ.

Ogle, Jane. The Stop Smoking Diet. 168p. 1983. pap. 5.95 (ISBN 0-87131-410-X). M Evans.

Ogle, Lucille. I Spy with My Little Eye. 1970. 9.95 o.p. (ISBN 0-07-047548-2, GB). McGraw.

Ogle, Nina M., jt. auth. see Johnson, Kenneth F.

Oglesbee, Maxine. Some of Us Will Make It & Some of Us Won't. 1978. 4.50 o.p. (ISBN 0-533-03510-4). Vantage.

Oglesby, C. H., jt. auth. see Parker, Henry.

Oglesby, Carole A., et al. Psycho-Social Aspects of Physical Education. Kneer, Marian, ed. (Basic Stuff Ser.: No. 1, 4 of 6). 60p. (Orig.). 1981. pap. text ed. 6.25 (ISBN 0-88314-027-6). AAHPERD.

Oglesby, Clarkson H. Highway Engineering. 3rd ed. LC 74-16329. (Illus.). text ed. 34.95x o.p. (ISBN 0-471-65290-3); write for info arabic translation (ISBN 0-471-05141-1). Wiley.

Oglesby, Clarkson H. & Hicks, Russell G. Highway Engineering. 4th ed. LC 81-12949. 844p. 1982. text ed. 35.95x (ISBN 0-471-02936-X). Wiley.

Oglesby, Enoch H. Ethics & Theology from the Other Side: Sounds of Moral Struggle. LC 79-62897. 1979. pap. text ed. 10.00 (ISBN 0-8191-0706-9). U Pr of Amer.

Oglesby, Stuart R. The Baby Is Baptized. pap. 1.60 (ISBN 0-8042-1536-7). John Knox.

--Becoming a Member of the Presbyterian Church. pap. 1.95 (ISBN 0-8042-1560-X). John Knox.

--Prayers for All Occasions. 1940. 4.95 (ISBN 0-8042-2484-6). John Knox.

Ogletree, Earl J. Urban Education: Perspectives & Issues. 1977. pap. text ed. 13.50 o.p. (ISBN 0-8191-0273-3). U Pr of Amer.

Ogletree, Earl J., et al. The Unit Plan: A Plan for Curriculum Organizing & Teaching. LC 79-48018. 499p. 1980. pap. text ed. 15.25 (ISBN 0-8191-0996-7). U Pr of Amer.

Oglivie, E. The Road to Nowhere. 288p. 1983. 13.95 (ISBN 0-07-047700-0, GB). McGraw.

Ogorkiewicz, R. M. Thermoplastics: Properties & Design. Imperial Chemical Industries Ltd. Plastics Division, ed. LC 73-10742. 248p. 1974. 39.75 o.p. (ISBN 0-471-65306-3, Pub. by Wiley-Interscience). Wiley.

Ogorkiewicz, R. M., ed. Engineering Properties of Thermoplastics. LC 72-83219. 1970. 38.50 o.p. (ISBN 0-471-65301-2, Pub. by Wiley-Interscience). Wiley.

O'Gorman, David, tr. see Lagerkvist, Par.

O'Gorman, James F. H. H. Richardson & His Office: Selected Drawings. (Illus.). 1979. 50.00 (ISBN 0-262-15020-4). MIT Pr.

O'Gorman, Ned. The Children Are Dying. (Orig.). 1978. pap. 1.75 o.p. (ISBN 0-451-07960-4, E7960, Sig). NAL.

O'Gorman, Richard, ed. Les Braies au Cordelier: Anonymous Fabliau of the Thirteenth Century. 1983. 16.00 (ISBN 0-917786-35-1). French Lit.

O'Gorman, Richard, jt. tr. see Hellman, Robert.

Ogot, Bethwell A., ed. see Historical Association of Kenya.

Ogra, P. L. & Dayton, Delbert H., eds. The Immunology of Breast Milk. LC 79-64434. 300p. 1979. 33.00 (ISBN 0-89004-387-6). Raven.

Ogra, P. L. & Jacobs, D., eds. Regulation of the Immune Response: Eighth Annual Convocation on Immunology, Amherst, June 1982. (Illus.). x, 390p. 1983. 130.00 (ISBN 3-8055-3574-0). S Karger.

O'Grady, James P., jt. auth. see Lynn, Robert A.

O'Grady, John F. The Gospel of John: Testimony of the Beloved Disciple. Wcela, Emil A., ed. (God's Word Today: Vol. VI). (Orig.). 1982. pap. 2.95 (ISBN 0-916134-35-0). Pueblo Pub Co.

--Models of Jesus. LC 80-1726. 192p. 1981. 10.95 o.p. (ISBN 0-385-17320-2). Doubleday.

O'Grady, John M., jt. ed. see Lewis, Peter J.

O'Grady, Joseph P. How the Irish Became Americans. (The Immigrant Heritage of America Ser). lib. bdg. 11.95 o.p. (ISBN 0-8057-3229-2, Twayne). G K Hall.

O'Grady, Leslie. The Artist's Daughter. LC 78-4000. 1979. 10.95 o.p. (ISBN 0-312-05507-2). St Martin.

O'Grady, Patricia. A Recipe for Happy Days. (Illus.). 65p. (Orig.). 1982. pap. 4.25 (ISBN 0-9601846-2-7). PM Ent.

O'Grady, Ron. Tourism in the Third World: Christian Reflections. LC 82-2227. (Illus.). 96p. (Orig.). 1982. pap. 4.95 (ISBN 0-88344-507-7). Orbis Bks.

O'Grady, Terence. The Beatles: A Musical Revolution. (Music Ser.). 206p. 1983. lib. bdg. 15.95 (ISBN 0-8057-9453-0, Twayne). G K Hall.

Ogram, Ernest W., Jr., jt. auth. see Daniels, John D.

Ogston, D. & Bennett, R. Haemostasis: Biochemistry, Physiology & Pathology. LC 76-44231. 512p. 1977. 114.95 (ISBN 0-471-99459-6, Pub. by Wiley-Interscience). Wiley.

Ogston, Karen, jt. auth. see Fowler, William.

Oguibenine, Boris, tr. see Reage, Pauline.

Ogungbesan, Kolawole. The Writings of Peter Abrahams. LC 78-26133. 156p. text ed. 27.00x (ISBN 0-8419-0472-3); pap. 12.50 (ISBN 0-8419-0480-4). Holmes & Meier.

Ogunsanwo, A. China's Policy in Africa, Nineteen Fifty-Eight to Nineteen Seventy-One. (International Studies). 336p. 1974. 37.50 (ISBN 0-521-20126-8). Cambridge U Pr.

Oguntoyinbo, J. S. see Barbour, K. M., et al.

Ogus, H. D. Common Disorders of the Temporomandibular Joint. (Dental Practitioner Handbook Ser.: No. 26). (Illus.). 120p. 1981. pap. text ed. 19.50 (ISBN 0-7236-0574-2). Wright-PSG.

Oh, John. International Financial Management: Problems, Issues & Experiences, Vol. 34. Altman, Edward I. & Walter, Ingo, eds. LC 81-81655. (Contemporary Studies in Economic & Financial Analysis). 300p. 1981. 40.00 (ISBN 0-89232-228-4). Jai Pr.

Ohaegbulam, Festus U. Nationalism in Colonial & Post-Colonial Africa. 1977. pap. text ed. 8.50 o.p. (ISBN 0-8191-0150-8). U Pr of Amer.

O'Hagan, jt. auth. see Besterfield.

O'Hagan, John T. High Rise Fire & Life Safety. (Illus.). 1977. 18.50 (ISBN 0-686-12263-1). Fire Eng.

O'Hair, Madalyn M. An Atheist Looks at Gods. 1979. 3.00 o.p. (ISBN 0-685-91836-X). Am Atheist.

--Nobody Has a Prayer. 105p. (Orig.). 1982. pap. 3.00 (ISBN 0-910309-07-8). Am Atheist.

O'Hair, Madalyn Murray & Murray, Jon. All the Questions You Ever Wanted to Ask American Atheists With all the Answers, 2 Vols. 344p. (Orig.). 1982. pap. 10.00 (ISBN 0-910309-04-3). Am Atheist.

O'Hanlon, J. F. A Users Guide to Vacuum Technology. 402p. 1980. 31.95x (ISBN 0-471-01624-1, Pub. by Wiley-Interscience). Wiley.

Ohanneson, Joan. And They Felt No Shame: Christians Reclaim Their Sexuality. 200p. (Orig.). 1982. pap. 11.95 (ISBN 0-86683-676-4). Winston Pr.

--Woman: Survivor in the Church. (Orig.). 1980. pap. 5.95 (ISBN 0-03-056671-1). Winston Pr.

O'Hara, Betsy. Japan Nineteen Forty-Eight to Nineteen Fifty-Four Through One American's Eyes. Scott, Donald M., ed. Yamakawa, Reiko, tr. 72p. (Orig., Eng. - Japanese.). 16.95x o.p. (ISBN 0-9604188-0-6); pap. 12.95x (ISBN 0-9604188-1-4). B O'Hara.

O'Hara, Deborah, ed. Words on Tape: An International Guide. 450p. 1983. 69.50x (ISBN 0-930466-55-1). Meckler Pub.

O'Hara, Deborah A., ed. Publisher's Catalogs Annual 1982-1983. 75p. 1982. write for info (ISBN 0-930466-71-3). Meckler Pub.

O'Hara, Frank. In Memory of My Feelings. limited ed. LC 67-30628. (Illus.). 1967. boxed portfolio 50.00 o.p. (ISBN 0-87070-450-8). Museum Mod Art.

--Selected Plays. LC 78-9658. 1978. 17.95 (ISBN 0-916190-08-0); pap. 8.95 (ISBN 0-916190-09-9). Full Court NY.

O'Hara, Frank H. Today in American Drama. LC 40-666. (Illus.). 1969. Repr. of 1939 ed. lib. bdg. 15.50x (ISBN 0-8371-0600-1, OHAD). Greenwood.

O'Hara, Gerald J. Malsum. 320p. 1981. pap. 2.50 o.p. (ISBN 0-380-77289-2, 77289). Avon.

O'Hara, J. D. Poetry. LC 74-83893. (World of Culture Ser.). (Illus.). 192p. 1975. 12.95 o.p. (ISBN 0-88225-119-8). Newsweek.

O'Hara, John. Appointment in Samarra. LC 82-40029. 256p. 1982. pap. 3.95 o.p. (ISBN 0-394-71192-0). Random.

--Pal Joey. LC 82-40417. 224p. 1983. pap. 3.95 (ISBN 0-394-71188-2, Vin). Random.

O'Hara, M. L. Substances & Things: Aristotle's Doctrine of Physical Substance in Recent Essays. LC 81-40931. 274p. 1982. lib. bdg. 24.00 (ISBN 0-8191-2265-3); pap. text ed. 11.75 (ISBN 0-8191-2266-1). U Pr of Amer.

O'Hara, Maggie. Wild Animals & Gentle People. LC 82-71077. (Illus.). 108p. (gr. 6 up). 1982. pap. 9.95 (ISBN 0-939116-08-1). Creative Comm.

O'Hara, Mary. The Catch Colt. 126p. 1981. 9.95 (ISBN 0-7710-6843-3, HarpT). Har-Row.

--Flicka's Friend: The Autobiography of Mary O'Hara. LC 81-22665. (Illus.). 285p. 1982. 14.95 (ISBN 0-399-12727-5). Putnam Pub Group.

--Green Grass of Wyoming. (gr. 7-9). 1946. 12.45i (ISBN 0-397-00011-1). Har-Row.

--My Friend Flicka. new ed. LC 73-6611. (Illus.). 272p. (gr. 7-9). 1973. 13.41i (ISBN 0-397-00981-X); text ed. 3.40i o.p. (ISBN 0-397-00008-1). Har-Row.

--A Song for Ireland. (Illus.). 208p. 1983. 19.95 (ISBN 0-7181-2161-9, Pub by Michael Joseph). Merrimack Bk Serv.

--A Song for Ireland. 1983. 19.95 (ISBN 0-686-38871-2, Pub. by Michael Joseph). Merrimack Bk Serv.

O'Hara, William T. & Hill, John G., Jr. The Student - the College - the Law. LC 72-87116. 1972. pap. 7.95x (ISBN 0-8077-2378-9). Tchrs Coll.

O'Hare, Colette. What Do You Feed Your Donkey On? LC 77-17155. (Illus.). (ps-8). 1978. 6.95 o.p. (ISBN 0-00-183703-6, Philomel); PLB 6.99 o.p. (ISBN 0-00-183734-6). Putnam Pub Group.

O'Hare, David, ed. Psychology & the Arts. 232p. 1981. text ed. 40.00x (ISBN 0-391-02339-X, Pub. by Harvester England). Humanities.

O'Hare, G., jt. auth. see Tivy, J.

O'Hare, Joanne. Bowker Annual of Library & Book Trade Information, 1983. 55.00 (ISBN 0-686-83430-5). Bowker.

O'Hare, Padraic, ed. Education for Peace & Justice. LC 82-48412. 224p. (Orig.). 1983. pap. 9.57 (ISBN 0-06-066361-8, HarpR). Har-Row.

O'Hare, Robert. Soldiering in Rhyme. 1983. 11.95 (ISBN 0-533-05559-8). Vantage.

O'Harra, Marjorie. Ashland: The First 130 Years. (Illus.). 200p. pap. 8.95 (ISBN 0-943388-03-1). South Oregon.

Ohashi, Watari. Do-It-Yourself Shiatsu. Lindner, Vicki, ed. 1976. pap. 7.95 (ISBN 0-525-47416-1, 0772-230). Dutton.

Ohashi, Wataru, jt. auth. see Masunaga, Shizuto.

Ohashi, Yoshimasa. English Style-Grammatical & Semantic Approach. LC 78-1278. 1978. pap. text ed. 4.95 o.p. (ISBN 0-88377-103-9). Newbury Hse.

Ohasi, Wataru & Hoover, Mary. The Eastern Way of Natural Childbirth: Do-It-Yourself Shiatsu for a Healthy Pregnancy & Delivery. 224p. (Orig.). 1983. pap. 8.95 (ISBN 0-345-30089-0). Ballantine.

O Hehir, Brendan. Expans'd Hieroglyphics: A Study of Sir John Denham's Coopers Hill, with a Critical Edition of the Poem. LC 68-27163. 1968. 30.00x (ISBN 0-520-01496-0). U of Cal Pr.

--A Gaelic Lexicon for Finnegans Wake & Glossary for Joyce's Other Works. 1968. 33.00x (ISBN 0-520-00952-5). U of Cal Pr.

--Harmony from Discords: A Life of Sir John Denham. LC 68-27162. 1968. 30.00x (ISBN 0-520-00953-3). U of Cal Pr.

O'Hehir, Brendan & Dillon, John M. A Classical Lexicon for Finnegans Wake: A Glossary of the Greek & Latin in Major Works of Joyce. 1977. 42.50x (ISBN 0-520-03082-6). U of Cal Pr.

O Heithir, Breandan. Lead Us into Temptation. 1978. 14.95 o.p. (ISBN 0-7100-0030-8). Routledge & Kegan.

O'Higgins, Patrick J. Basic Instrumentation, Industrial Measurement. 1966. text ed. 25.95 (ISBN 0-07-047649-7, G); ans. to even numbered problems 1.00 (ISBN 0-07-047647-0). McGraw.

Ohio Family Historians. Eighteen Thirty Federal Population Census Index of Ohio, 2 vols. 1976. Repr. of 1964 ed. 37.00 set (ISBN 0-911060-06-5). Vol. 1 (ISBN 0-911060-04-9). Vol. 2 (ISBN 0-911060-05-7). Ohio Lib Assn.

--Eighteen Twenty Federal Population Census Index of Ohio. 1976. Repr. of 1964 ed. 26.00 (ISBN 0-911060-03-0). Ohio Lib Assn.

Ohio State University Research Foundation. Toilet Training: Help for the Delayed Learner. (Illus.). 1978. pap. text ed. 0.11.36 (ISBN 0-07-047681-0, W). McGraw.

Ohkawa, Kazushi & Key, Bernard, eds. Asian Socioeconomic Development: A National Accounts Approach. 326p. 1980. text ed. 27.50x (ISBN 0-8248-0743-X). UH Pr.

Ohlander, Solve. Phonology, Meaning, Morphology: On the Role of Semantic & Morphological Criteria in Phonological Analysis. (Gothenburg Studies in English: No. 33). 221p. 1976. pap. text ed. 13.50x (ISBN 0-686-86106-X). Humanities.

Ohles, John F. Introduction to Teaching. 1970. pap. text ed. 9.95x (ISBN 0-394-30432-2). Phila Bk Co.

--Principles & Practice of Teaching: Selected Readings. (Orig.). 1970. pap. text ed. 6.25 (ISBN 0-685-19754-9). Phila Bk Co.

Ohles, John F., ed. Biographical Dictionary of American Educators, 3 vols. LC 77-84750. 1978. lib. bdg. 150.00 (ISBN 0-8371-9893-3, OHB/). Greenwood.

Ohlin, Bertil. The Problem of Employment Stabilization. LC 76-39926. 1977. Repr. of 1949 ed. lib. bdg. 15.50x (ISBN 0-8371-9327-3, OHES). Greenwood.

Ohlin, Lloyd E., ed. Prisoners in America: Perspectives on Our Correctional System. LC 73-1221. (American Assembly Ser.). 224p. 1973. pap. 3.45 (ISBN 0-13-710814-1, Spec). P-H.

Ohlin, Lloyd E., et al. Reforming Youth Corrections: The Massachusetts Experience in the Nineteenth & Twentieth Centuries. 1980. prof ref 16.00x (ISBN 0-88410-788-4). Ballinger Pub.

Ohlrich, Walter & Ethell, Jeff. Pilot Maker: The Incredible T6. (Illus.). 144p. 1983. 17.95 (ISBN 0-933424-34-5). Specialty Pr.

Ohlsen, Merle. Introduction to Counseling. LC 82-61587. 520p. 1983. text ed. 17.95 (ISBN 0-87581-290-2). Peacock Pubs.

Ohlson, R., jt. ed. see Appelqvist, L. A.

Ohlsson, L. Engineering Trade Specialization of Sweden & Other Industrial Countries. (Studies in International Economics: Vol. 6). 1980. 42.75 (ISBN 0-444-86114-9). Elsevier.

Ohmae, Kenichi. The Mind of the Strategist. 1983. pap. 5.95 (ISBN 0-14-006722-1). Penguin.

Ohman, Anka, jt. auth. see Niven, William.

Ohmann, Richard. English in America: A Radical View of the Profession. 1976. pap. 8.95 (ISBN 0-19-501965-2, GB). Oxford U Pr.

Ohno, K. & Morokuma, K. Quantum Chemistry Literature Data Base: Bibliography of AB Initio Calculations for 1978-80. (Physical Sciences Data Ser.: Vol. 12). 1982. 95.75 (ISBN 0-444-42074-6). Elsevier.

Ohno, Y., ed. Requirements Engineering Environments: Proceedings of the International Symposium on Current Issues of Requirements Engineering Environments, Sept. 20-21, 1982, Kyoto, Japan. 174p. 1983. 42.75 (ISBN 0-444-86533-0, North Holland). Elsevier.

Ohnsorge, J. & Holm, R. Scanning Electron Microscopy. 2nd ed. LC 77-99145. (Illus.). 168p. 1978. pap. 35.00 o.p. (ISBN 0-88416-235-4). Wright-PSG.

Ohnuki-Tierney, Emiko. Illness & Healing Among the Sakhalin Ainu: A Symbolic Interpretation. LC 80-24268. (Illus.). 272p. 1981. 37.50 (ISBN 0-521-23636-3). Cambridge U Pr.

Ohringer, Fred, photos by. Portrait of the Theatre. (Illus.). 1979. 19.95 o.p. (ISBN 0-517-53928-4). Crown.

Ohrn, Steven G. Cataloguing in Context: The African Studies Program Slide Archives. (Occasional Papers on Visual Communication). 49p. (Orig.). 1975. pap. text ed. 3.00 (ISBN 0-941934-16-0). Ind U Afro-Amer Arts.

Ohrn, Steven G., jt. ed. see Riley, Rebecca R.

Ohrn, Y., jt. auth. see Lowdin, P. O.

Ohsawa, George. Cancer & the Philosophy of the Far East. 2nd ed. Aihara, Herman, ed. 162p. 1982. pap. 7.95 (ISBN 0-918860-38-5). G Ohsawa.

Ohsawa, Junko, jt. tr. see Levy, Howard S.

Ohsberg, H. Oliver. Church & Persons with Handicaps. LC 82-80342. 128p. 1982. pap. 7.95 (ISBN 0-8361-1996-7). Herald Pr.

Ohto, Masao. Cholangiography & Pancreatography. 324p. 1978. text ed. 44.95 o.p. (ISBN 0-8391-1272-6). Univ Park.

Oi, Walter Y. & Shuldiner, Paul W. An Analysis of Urban Travel Demands. 281p. 1972. pap. 3.95 (ISBN 0-686-94025-3, Trans). Northwestern U Pr.

Oikawa, Kikuo. Trace Analysis of Atmospheric Samples. LC 77-3458. 1977. 36.95x o.s.i. (ISBN 0-470-99013-9). Halsted Pr.

Oil & Gas Journal. A Guide to Petroleum Nomography. 176p. 1977. 29.95x (ISBN 0-87814-042-5). Pennwell Pub.

--Sour-Gas Processing & Sulphur Recovery. 151p. 1979. 33.95x (ISBN 0-87814-101-4). Pennwell Book Division.

--Surveillance & Maintenance of Rotating Equipment. 176p. 1978. 29.95x (ISBN 0-87814-085-9). Pennwell Book Division.

Oil Companies Materials Association. Drilling Fluid Materials: High Viscosity Carboxymethyl Cellulose. 1973. 16.95 (ISBN 0-471-25929-2, Pub by Wiley Heyden). Wiley.

Oinas, Felix J., ed. Folklore Nationalism & Politics. 1977. pap. 10.95 (ISBN 0-89357-043-5). Slavica.

Oizerman, T. I. Dialectical Materialism & the History of Philosophy. 287p. 1982. 7.90 (ISBN 0-8285-2270-7, Pub. by Progress Pubs USSR). Imported Pubns.

Oja, Carol, ed. Stravinsky in Modern Music. (Music Reprint Ser.). 1982. Repr. of 1946 ed. 32.50 (ISBN 0-306-76108-4). Da Capo.

Oja, Carol J., ed. American Music Recordings: A Discography of 20th-Century U. S. Composers. 368p. (Orig.). 1982. pap. 60.00 (ISBN 0-914678-19-1). Inst Am Music.

Ojakangas, Richard & Darby, David. The Earth: Past & Present. new ed. (Earth Science Paperback Ser.). (Illus., Orig.). 1976. pap. text ed. 15.95 (ISBN 0-07-047676-4, C). McGraw.

Ojeda, Louis. Abraham, Son of Abraham. 1979. 5.95 o.p. (ISBN 0-533-02060-3). Vantage.

Ojemann, George A., jt. auth. see Calvin, William H.

Ojemann, Robert G. & Crowell, Robert M. Surgical Management of Cerebrovascular Disease. 500p. 1983. lib. bdg. write for info (ISBN 0-683-06639-0). Williams & Wilkins.

Ojigbo, A. Okion, ed. Young & Black in Africa. (Illus.). 1971. 3.95 o.p. (ISBN 0-394-82304-4). Random.

Ojo, O. A. & Briggs, Enang. Textbook for Midwives in the Tropics. 480p. 1982. pap. text ed. 18.95 (ISBN 0-7131-4413-0). E Arnold.

Ojomo, Olatunde. Great Tortoise Stories. 1982. 4.95 (ISBN 0-533-05455-9). Vantage.

Okabe, Hideo. Photochemistry of Small Molecules. LC 78-6704. 1978. 57.50 (ISBN 0-471-65304-7, Pub. by Wiley-Interscience). Wiley.

Okada, ed. Problems in Gaba Research from Brain to Bacteria. (International Congress Ser.: Vol. 565). 1982. 110.75 (ISBN 0-444-90236-8). Elsevier.

Okada, Barbara T. Netsuke: Masterpieces from the Metropolitan Museum of Art. Howard, Kathleen, ed. Seki, Hozen & Cranston, Edwin A., trs. (Illus.). 204p. 1982. 29.50 o.s.i. (ISBN 0-87099-273-2). Metro Mus Art.

--Netsuke: Masterpieces from the Metropolitan Museum of Art. Howand, Kathleen, ed. LC 81-38344. (Illus.). 219p. 1982. 24.50 (ISBN 0-87099-273-2). Abrams.

Okada, Shigefumi see Altman, Kurt I.

Okafor, Festus C., ed. Philosophy of Education & Third World Perspective. LC 80-70581. 405p. (Orig.). 1981. 15.00x (ISBN 0-931494-06-0); pap. 10.00 (ISBN 0-931494-07-9). Brunswick Pub.

Okal, Bill. Card Magic. LC 82-14482. (Illus.). 192p. (Orig.). 1982. pap. 7.00 (ISBN 0-910199-00-0). Paragon-Reiss.

Okamoto, Naomasa, jt. ed. see Nishimura, Hideo.

O'Kane, C. P., jt. auth. see Deichman, Elizabeth S.

O'Kane, J. P. Estuarine Water-Quality Management with Moving Element Models & Optimization Techniques. LC 79-19405. (Water Resources Engineering Ser.). 155p. 1980. text ed. 58.00 (ISBN 0-273-08443-7). Pitman Pub MA.

O'Kane, James M. Pamplona: A Sociological Analysis of Migration & Urban Adaptation Patterns. LC 81-40637. (Illus.). 174p. (Orig.). 1982. lib. bdg. 20.75 (ISBN 0-8191-1959-8); pap. text ed. 10.00 (ISBN 0-8191-1960-1). U Pr of Amer.

O'Kane, Monica. Living With Adult Children. (Illus.). 208p. (Orig.). 1981. 9.95 (ISBN 0-933656-21-1); pap. 4.95 (ISBN 0-933656-20-3). Trinity Pub Hse.

O'Kane, Monica L. Living with Adult Children: A Helpful Guide for Parents & Grown Children Sharing the Same Roof. (Illus.). 190p. 1982. 9.95 (ISBN 0-9609198-1-3); pap. 4.95 (ISBN 0-9609198-0-5). Diction Bks.

Okano, I. & Sato, T. Vital Judo. 11.95 o.s.i. (ISBN 0-685-38458-6). Wehman.

Okazaki, Renji, jt. auth. see Inagaki, Yoshio.

Oke, Janette. Spunky's Diary. 99p. (gr. 5-12). 1982. pap. 3.95 (ISBN 0-934998-11-6). Bethel Pub.

--When Calls the Heart. 240p. (Orig.). 1983. pap. 4.95 (ISBN 0-87123-611-7). Bethany Hse.

Okebe, P. N. Preliminary Practical Physics. LC 80-40846. 1981. pap. write for info. o.p. (ISBN 0-471-27852-1, Pub. by Wiley-Interscience); pap. write for info. o.p. (ISBN 0-471-27851-3, Pub. by Wiley-Interscience). Wiley.

Okediji, Florence A. The Cattle Industry in Northern Nigeria, 1900-1939. (African Humanities Ser.). (Illus., Orig.). 1973. pap. text ed. 2.00 (ISBN 0-941934-07-1). Ind U Afro-Amer Arts.

O'Keefe, Daniel. The Cheese Buyer's Handbook. 1978. 12.50 o.p. (ISBN 0-07-047660-8, GB). McGraw.

O'Keefe, John & Nadel, Lynn. The Hippocampus As a Cognitive Map. (Illus.). 1978. text ed. 55.00x (ISBN 0-19-857206-9). Oxford U Pr.

O'Keeffe, Timothy J. Milton & the Pauline Tradition: A Study of Theme & Symbolism. LC 80-5842. 356p. (Orig.). 1982. PLB 25.50 (ISBN 0-8191-2453-2); pap. text ed. 14.00 (ISBN 0-8191-2454-0). U Pr of Amer.

O'Keepe, P., jt. auth. see McMichael, Stanley L.

O'Kelley, Genie R., jt. auth. see Kershner, William K.

O'Kelly, Bernard, tr. see Colet, John.

O'Kelly De Galway, A. O. Tigran Petrosian - World Champion. 1965. text ed. 9.75 (ISBN 0-08-011013-4); pap. text ed. 5.95 (ISBN 0-08-011012-6). Pergamon.

Okely, Judith. The Traveller-Gypsies. LC 82-9478. (Illus.). 228p. 1983. 34.50 (ISBN 0-521-24641-5); pap. 10.95 (ISBN 0-521-28870-3). Cambridge U Pr.

Oken, Milt. The Beatles Complete, Vols. 1 & 2. 1024p. (Orig.). 1982. pap. 39.95 (ISBN 0-553-01329-7). Bantam.

Okigbo, Christopher. Labyrinths with Path of Thunder. LC 72-90297. (Illus.). 1971. 7.50x (ISBN 0-8419-0045-0, Africana); pap. 5.50x (ISBN 0-8419-0016-7, Africana). Holmes & Meier.

Okimoto, Jean D. It's Just Too Much. 128p. (YA) (gr. 5-12). 1980. 9.95 (ISBN 0-399-20737-6). Putnam Pub Group.

--My Mother Is Not Married to My Father. LC 78-26924. (gr. 5 up). 1979. 8.95 (ISBN 0-399-20664-7). Putnam Pub Group.

--Norman Schnurman, Average Person. 128p. 1982. 9.95 (ISBN 0-399-20913-1). Putnam Pub Group.

Okin, Josee & Schmitt, Conrad J. Francais: Commencons. 1970. text ed. 17.24 (ISBN 0-07-047500-8, W); tchr's. ed. 17.72 (ISBN 0-07-047501-6). tapes 532.00 (ISBN 0-07-047503-2). filmstrips 118.52 (ISBN 0-07-047504-0). McGraw.

--Francais: Continuons. (gr. 8-10). 1970. text ed. 17.96 (ISBN 0-07-047515-6, W); ed. 18.88tchr's. (ISBN 0-07-047516-4); wkbk. 6.12 (ISBN 0-07-047517-2); tests 110.40 (ISBN 0-07-047520-2); test replacements 54.76 (ISBN 0-07-047521-0); filmstrips 118.52 (ISBN 0-07-047519-9); tapes 532.00 (ISBN 0-07-047518-0). McGraw.

--Let's Speak French, Bks. 1-3. 1966. Bk. 1. text ed. 0.00 o.p. (ISBN 0-07-047642-X, W); Bk. 2. text ed. 7.00 (ISBN 0-07-047644-6); Bk. 3. text ed. 0.00 o.p. (ISBN 0-07-047638-1); Bk. 2. tchr's guide 10.72 (ISBN 0-07-047645-4); Bk. 3. tchr's guide 12.44 (ISBN 0-07-047639-X). McGraw.

--Let's Speak French: Lectures. 1967. text ed. 15.64 (ISBN 0-07-047640-3, W); cassettes 140.32 (ISBN 0-07-097187-0). McGraw.

Okin, Josee P. & Schmitt, Conrad J. Le Francais: Commencons. 2nd ed. LC 74-18343. (Illus.). 288p. (gr. 7). 1975. text ed. 14.44 (ISBN 0-07-047731-0, W); tchr's. ed. 16.16 (ISBN 0-07-047732-9); wkbk. 4.68 (ISBN 0-07-047733-7); cassette tapes 240.00 (ISBN 0-07-097983-9); exampak 8.00 (ISBN 0-07-047746-9); reel-to-reel tapes 483.52 (ISBN 0-07-097981-2); test pkg. 98.48 (ISBN 0-07-047734-5); test replacements 49.28 (ISBN 0-07-047735-3); filmstrips 109.44 (ISBN 0-07-097982-0). McGraw.

--Le Francais: Continuons. 2nd ed. (Illus.). 288p. (Fr.). (gr. 8-10). 1975. text ed. 14.44 (ISBN 0-07-047741-8, W); tchr's. ed. 16.16 (ISBN 0-07-047742-6); wkbk. 4.68 (ISBN 0-07-047743-4); cassette tapes 316.10 (ISBN 0-07-097988-X); reel-to-reel tapes 483.52 (ISBN 0-07-097986-3); test pkg. 98.48 (ISBN 0-07-047744-2); test replacements 49.28 (ISBN 0-07-047745-0); filmstrips 19.44 (ISBN 0-07-097987-1). McGraw.

Okinshevich, Leo. United States History & Historiography in Post-War Soviet Writings, 1945-1970: A Bibliography. new ed. LC 76-3756. 431p. 1976. text ed. 26.75 o.p. (ISBN 0-87436-208-3). ABC-Clio.

Okner, Benjamin A., jt. auth. see Pechman, Joseph A.

Oko, Adolph S., compiled by see Columbia University.

Okoli, Ekwueme F. Institutional Structure & Conflict in Nigeria. LC 79-3425. 1980. pap. text ed. 8.50 (ISBN 0-8191-0888-X). U Pr of Amer.

Okolicsanyi, L. Familial Hyperbilirubinemia: Proceedings of the Workshop on Familial Disorders of Hepatic Bilirubin Metabolism Held in Venice, Italy 23rd-24th May 1980. LC 80-41457. 263p. 1981. 49.95 (ISBN 0-471-27927-7, Pub. by Wiley-Interscience). Wiley.

Okpaku, Joseph. Superfight No. II: The Story Behind the Fights Between Muhammad Ali & Joe Frazier. LC 74-74429. 1974. 6.95 o.s.i. (ISBN 0-89388-165-1). Okpaku Communications.

--Verdict: The Exclusive Picture Story of the Trial of the Chicago 8. LC 79-129568. (Illus.). 160p. 1970. 20.00 (ISBN 0-89388-008-6); pap. 8.95 (ISBN 0-89388-009-4). Okpaku Communications.

Okpaku, Joseph, ed. Nigeria, Dilemma of Nationhood: An African Analysis of the Biafran Conflict. LC 78-111266. (Contributions in Afro-American & African Studies: No. 12). 1971. lib. bdg. 29.95 (ISBN 0-8371-4668-2, OKN/). Greenwood.

--Nigeria-Dilemma of Nationhood: An African Analysis of the Biafran Conflict. LC 73-83162. 426p. 1974. pap. 5.95 o.p. (ISBN 0-89388-088-4). Okpaku Communications.

Okpaku, S. Family Planning & Preventive Psychiatry. 1981. cancelled (ISBN 0-89388-003-5). Okpaku Communications.

Okpewho, Isidore. The Victims. 200p. (Orig.). 1979. 9.00 o.s.i. (ISBN 0-89410-115-3); pap. 5.00 o.s.i. (ISBN 0-89410-114-5). Three Continents.

Okrent, Daniel. Nine Innings. 1983. 16.75 (ISBN 0-670-52679-7). Viking Pr.

Okri, Benjamin. Flowers & Shadows. (Drum Beat Ser.). 274p. 1980. pap. 6.00 o.s.i. (ISBN 0-582-64301-5). Three Continents.

Oksaar. Language Acquisition in the Early Years: An Introduction to Paedolinguistics. Turfler, Katherine, tr. LC 82-42716. 240p. 1983. 30.00x (ISBN 0-686-84414-9). St Martin.

Oksche & Pevet. Pineal Organ: Photobiology, Biochronometry & Endocrinology. (Developments in Endocrinology: Vol. 14). 1982. 64.25 (ISBN 0-444-80387-4). Elsevier.

Okubo, Mine. Citizen 13660. LC 82-20221. (Illus.). 226p. (Orig.). 1983. pap. 8.95 (ISBN 0-295-95989-4). U of Wash Pr.

Okuda, Kunio & Peters, Robert L., eds. Hepatocellular Carcinoma. LC 76-6500. (Wiley Series on Diseases of the Liver). 512p. 1976. 100.00 (ISBN 0-471-65316-0, Pub. by Wiley Medical). Wiley.

Okumo, H. see Helmcke, J. G. & Krieger, W.

Okun, Arthur M. Equality & Efficiency: The Big Tradeoff. 124p. 1975. 11.95 (ISBN 0-8157-6476-6); pap. 5.95 (ISBN 0-8157-6475-8). Brookings.

--The Political Economy of Prosperity. 1970. 11.95 (ISBN 0-8157-6478-2). Brookings.

--Prices & Quantities: A Macroeconomic Analysis. 400p. 1981. 21.95 (ISBN 0-8157-6480-4); pap. 9.95 (ISBN 0-8157-6479-0). Brookings.

Okun, Arthur M., jt. auth. see Baily, Martin.

Okun, Arthur M. & Perry, George L., eds. Curing Chronic Inflation. 1978. 18.95 (ISBN 0-8157-6474-X); pap. 7.95 (ISBN 0-8157-6473-1). Brookings.

Okun, Daniel A. Regionalization of Water Management: A Revolution in England & Wales. (Illus.). 1977. 43.00x (ISBN 0-85334-738-7, Pub. by Applied Sci England). Elsevier.

Okun, L. B. Leptons & Quarks. Date not set. 70.25 (ISBN 0-444-86002-9). Elsevier.

Okun, Morris, ed. Programs for Older Adults. LC 81-48475. 1982. 7.95x (ISBN 0-87589-888-2, CE-14). Jossey-Bass.

Okun, Sheila. A Book of Cut Flowers. (Illus.). 144p. 1983. 10.00 (ISBN 0-688-01971-4). Morrow.

Ola, C. S. Income Tax Law & Practice in Nigeria. LC 76-983597. 1977. pap. text ed. 50.00x o.p. (ISBN 0-435-89671-7). Heinemann Ed.

Olah, George A. Carbocations & Electrophilic Reactions. LC 73-86987. (Chemie Paperback). (Illus.). 1974. pap. 14.70x o.p. (ISBN 3-527-25561-3). Verlag Chemie.

Olah, George A. & Schleyer, Paul, eds. Reactive Intermediates in Organic Chemistry: Carbonium Ions, 5 vols. Set. 188.00 (ISBN 0-686-75231-7); Vol. 1 General Aspects & Methods Of Investigation. 31.50 (ISBN 0-470-65330-2); Vol. 2 Methods Of Formation & Major Types. 35.25 (ISBN 0-471-65333-0); Vol. 3 Major Types. 46.00 (ISBN 0-471-65334-9); Vol. 4 Major Types. 46.50 (ISBN 0-471-65337-3); Miscellaneous Ions, Theory & Structure. 50.50 (ISBN 0-686-75236-8). Krieger.

Olaitan, Samson O. & Agusiobo, Obiora N. Introduction to the Teaching of Home Economics. LC 80-40288. 320p. 1981. write for info. o.p. (ISBN 0-471-27807-6, Pub. by Wiley-Interscience); pap. write for info. o.p. (ISBN 0-471-27806-8). Wiley.

Olaloku, F. Akin, et al. The Structure of the Nigerian Economy. LC 78-14765. 1979. 26.00x (ISBN 0-312-76777-3). St Martin.

Olander, Donald R. Fundamental Aspects of Nuclear Reactor Fuel Elements, 2 vols. LC 76-6485. (ERDA Technical Information Center Ser.). 1976. Vol. 1, 624 pgs. pap. 23.50 (ISBN 0-87079-031-5, TID-26711-P1); Vol. 2: Solutions to Problems, 557 pgs., 1976. microfiche 4.50 (ISBN 0-87079-466-3, TID-26711-P1); pap. 22.00 (TID-26711-P2); microfiche 4.00 (ISBN 0-87079-467-1, TID-26711-P2). DOE.

Olander, Joseph D., jt. ed. see Greenberg, Martin H.

Olander, Joseph D., et al, eds. School & Society Through Science Fiction. LC 81-40587. (Illus.). 404p. 1982. lib. bdg. 25.50 (ISBN 0-8191-1996-2); pap. text ed. 13.50 (ISBN 0-8191-1997-0). U Pr of Amer.

Olaniyan, Richard, ed. African History & Culture. (Illus.). 256p. (Orig.). 1982. pap. 7.95 (ISBN 0-582-64369-4). Longman.

O'Laughlin, Kay, jt. ed. see Nickerson, Eileen T.

O'Laughlin, Michael C. The Flaherty Book. (Irish Family History Ser.). (Illus.). 50p. 1983. saddle stitch 9.95 (ISBN 0-940134-22-5). Irish Genealog.

--Handbook on Scottish Genealogy. (Celtic Heritage Ser.). (Illus.). 1983. 14.95 (ISBN 0-940134-05-5). Irish Genealog.

Olausson, Eric & Cato, Ingemar. Chemistry & Biochemistry of Estuaries. LC 79-41211. 452p. 1980. 92.95 (ISBN 0-471-27679-0, Pub. by Wiley-Interscience). Wiley.

Olberg, Robert T., jt. ed. see Funk, Hal D.

Olbricht, Thomas H. Message of the New Testament: Ephesians & Colossians. (Way of Life Ser.). 108p. 1983. pap. 3.95 (ISBN 0-89112-170-6). Biblical Research Press.

Olcheski, Bill. One Hundred Trivia Quizzes for Stamp Collectors. 130p. 1982. pap. 4.95 (ISBN 0-933580-09-6). Am Philatelic.

Olcott, Frances J. Good Stories for Anniversaries. LC 77-167093. (Tower Bks). (Illus.). 1971. Repr. of 1937 ed. 40.00x (ISBN 0-8103-3910-2). Gale.

Olcott, Henry S. Buddhist Catechism. 1971. pap. 2.75 (ISBN 0-8356-0027-0, Quest). Theos Pub Hse.

Olcott, William & Mayall, R. Newton. Field Book of the Skies. (Putnam's Nature Field Books). (Illus.). 1954. 7.95 o.p. (ISBN 0-399-10294-9). Putnam Pub Group.

Old, Bruce S., jt. auth. see Talbert, William F.

Old-House Journal Staff. The Old-House Journal 1983 Catalog: A Buyers Guide. (Illus.). 176p. (Orig.). 1983. pap. 9.95 (ISBN 0-87951-171-0). Overlook Pr.

Old, R. W. & Primrose, S. B. Principles of Gene Manipulation: An Introduction to Genetic Engineering. 2nd ed. LC 79-6740. (Studies in Microbiology: Vol. 2). 215p. 1982. 40.00x (ISBN 0-520-04143-7, CAMPUS 295); pap. 13.95x (ISBN 0-520-04626-9). U of Cal Pr.

Old Slave Mart Museum & Library. Catalog of the Old Slave Mart Museum & Library. 1978. lib. bdg. 125.00 (ISBN 0-8161-0073-X, Hall Library). G K Hall.

Olden, Marc. Black Samurai, No. 3: Killer Warrior. (Orig.). 1974. pap. 0.95 o.p. (ISBN 0-451-06015-6, Q6015, Sig). NAL.

--Dai-Sho (Big Sword vs. Little Sword) 1983. 15.95 (ISBN 0-87795-501-8). Arbor Hse.

Olden, Sam. Getting to Know Argentina. (Getting to Know Ser). (Illus.). (gr. 3-5). 1961. PLB 3.97 o.p. (ISBN 0-698-30105-6, Coward). Putnam Pub Group.

Oldenberg, Hermann. Buddha: His Life, His Doctrine, His Order. Hoey, William, tr. from Ger. LC 1-9731. 462p. 1971. Repr. of 1882 ed. 15.00x (ISBN 0-8002-0717-3). Intl Pubns Serv.

Oldenberg, Otto & Holladay, Wendell G. Introduction to Atomic & Nuclear Physics. LC 77-5544. 424p. 1977. Repr. of 1949 ed. 23.50 (ISBN 0-88275-548-X). Krieger.

Oldenberg, Otto & Rasmussen, N. Modern Physics for Engineers. 1966. text ed. 37.5003845801x (ISBN 0-07-047653-5, C). McGraw.

Oldenburg, Carl. Frog Croaks: Haiku Tongue in Cheek. (Illus.). 65p. 1975. 3.95 o.p. (ISBN 0-517-52341-8). Crown.

Oldenburg, S. S. Last Tsar! Nicholas II, His Reign & His Russia, 4 Vols. Imhalep, Leonid & Rollins, Patrick, trs. 61.50 o.p. (ISBN 0-686-83125-X). Academic Intl.

--Last Tsar! Nicholas II, His Reign & His Russia, 4 vols. Imhalep, Leonid & Rollins, Patrick, trs. Set. 61.50 (ISBN 0-686-93968-9). Vol. 1 (ISBN 0-87569-063-7). Vol. 2 (ISBN 0-87569-068-8). Vol. 3 (ISBN 0-87569-073-4). Vol. 4 (ISBN 0-87569-074-2). Academic Intl.

Oldendorf, William H. The Quest for an Image of the Brain. (Computerized Tomography in the Perspective of Past & Future Imaging Methods). 167p. 1980. text ed. 23.00 (ISBN 0-89004-429-5). Raven.

Oldenquist, Andrew. Moral Philosophy: Text & Readings. 2nd ed. LC 77-77978. (Illus.). 1978. pap. text ed. 15.50 (ISBN 0-395-25433-7). HM.

--Normative Behavior. LC 82-23699. (Illus.). 200p. (Orig.). 1983. lib. bdg. 21.75 (ISBN 0-8191-2965-8); pap. text ed. 10.00 (ISBN 0-8191-2966-6). U Pr of Amer.

Older, Jules. Touching Is Healing. LC 81-40481. 288p. 1982. 19.95 (ISBN 0-8128-2837-2). Stein & Day.

Older, Julia. Cooking Without Fuel. LC 82-50269. (The Forgotten Arts Ser.). (Illus.). 80p. 1982. pap. 4.95 (ISBN 0-911658-40-8). Yankee Bks.

--Oonts & Others. 72p. 1982. 12.50 (ISBN 0-87775-150-1); pap. 4.50 (ISBN 0-87775-151-X). Unicorn Pr.

Older, Robert A., jt. auth. see Resnick, Martin I.

Oldfield, Elizabeth. Dream Hero. (Harlequin Presents Ser.). 192p. 1983. pap. 1.95 (ISBN 0-373-10604-1). Harlequin Bks.

Oldfield, George S., Jr. Implications of Regulation on Bank Expansion: A Simulation Analysis. Altman, Edward I. & Walter, Ingo, eds. LC 76-10399. (Contemporary Studies in Economic & Financial Analysis: Vol. 10). 1980. lib. bdg. 33.00 (ISBN 0-89232-015-X). Jai Pr.

Oldfield, Harry & Durie, Bruce. New Discoveries in Kirlian Photography. 1982. 32.00x (ISBN 0-906540-21-6, Pub. by Element Bks). State Mutual Bk.

Oldfield, Margaret J. Costumes & Customs of Many Lands. (Illus.). (gr. k-3). 1982. pap. 2.95 (ISBN 0-934876-19-3). Creative Storytime.

Oldfield, P., jt. auth. see Chirgwin, F. J.

Oldfield, Pamela. The Halloween Pumpkin. LC 75-41346. (Stepping Stones Ser.). (Illus.). 24p. (gr. k-3). 1976. 7.00 (ISBN 0-516-03582-7). Childrens.

Oldfield, Phyllis, jt. auth. see Chirgwin, John F.

Oldfield, Sybil, jt. ed. see Lamont, William.

Oldham, Joe. The New Mercedes-Benz Guide. 1977. 7.95 o.p. (ISBN 0-8306-9998-8); pap. 3.95 o.p. (ISBN 0-8306-2019-2, 2019). TAB Bks.

Oldham, John. Works of Mr. John Oldham. LC 79-26304. 1980. Repr. of 1686 ed. 75.00x (ISBN 0-8201-1337-9). Schol Facsimiles.

Oldham, John, jt. auth. see Oldham, Ray.

Oldham, Michael. Accouting Systems & Practice in Europe. 2nd ed. 271p. 1981. text ed. 51.00x (ISBN 0-566-02147-1, Pub. by Gower England). Gower Pub Ltd.

Oldham, Ray & Oldham, John. Western Heritage. 13.50x (ISBN 0-392-06045-0, ABC). Sportshelf.

--Western Heritage Part 2: George Temple-Pool, Architect of the Golden Years 1885-1897. 227p. 1981. 39.95 (ISBN 0-686-98295-9, Pub. by U of W Austral Pr). Intl Schol Bk Serv.

Oldroyd, David R. & Langham, Ian G. The Wilder Domain of Evolutionary Thought. 1983. lib. bdg. 54.50 (ISBN 90-277-1477-0, Pub. by Reidel Holland). Kluwer Boston.

Oldroyd, Harold, tr. see Nachtigall, Werner.

Olds. Maternal-Infant Nursing. 1882. softcover 10.95 (ISBN 0-201-12780-6, 12780, Med-Nurse). A-W.

Olds, Helen D. Lyndon Baines Johnson. (Beginning Biographies Ser.). (Illus.). (gr. k-4). 1965. PLB 5.99 o.p. (ISBN 0-399-60433-2). Putnam Pub Group.

--Richard E. Byrd. (See & Read Biographies). (Illus.). (gr. k-4). 1969. PLB 4.29 o.p. (ISBN 0-399-60532-0). Putnam Pub Group.

--Richard Nixon. LC 74-110320. (See & Read Biographies). (Illus.). (gr. k-4). 1970. PLB 4.29 o.p. (ISBN 0-399-60533-9). Putnam Pub Group.

Olds, James. Drives & Reinforcements: Behavioral Studies of Hypothalamic Functions. LC 75-31480. 148p. 1977. pap. 11.50 (ISBN 0-89004-087-7). Raven.

Olds, Marshall. Analysis of the Interchurch World Movement Report on the Steel Strike. LC 73-139199. (Civil Liberties in American History Ser). 1971. Repr. of 1923 ed. lib. bdg. 65.00 (ISBN 0-306-70082-4). Da Capo.

--Desire Seeking Expression: Mallarme's Prose pour des Esseintes. LC 82-82431. (French Forum Monographs: No. 42). 128p. (Orig.). 1983. pap. 10.00x (ISBN 0-917058-41-0). French Forum.

Olds, Mason. Religious Humanism in America: Dietrich, Reese & Potter. 1977. 11.00 (ISBN 0-8191-0267-9). U Pr of Amer.

Olds, Nancy J., jt. auth. see Greenberg, Margaret.

Olds, Ruthanne. Big & Beautiful: Become the Big Beautiful Person You Were Meant to Be. LC 82-6724. (Illus.). 200p. 1982. 16.95 (ISBN 0-87491-088-9). Acropolis.

Olds, S. W., jt. auth. see Papalia, D.

Olds, Sally. Obstetric Nursing, 1980: Instructor's Guide. 1980. 29.95 (ISBN 0-201-02718-6, Med-Nurse); 3.95 (ISBN 0-201-02719-4, Med-Nurse); study guide avail. (ISBN 0-201-12780-6, Med-Nurse); transparencies kit 50.00 (ISBN 0-201-02710-0, Med-Nurse). A-W.

Olds, Sally W., jt. auth. see Papalia, Diane E.

Olds, Sally W., jt. auth. see Simon, Sidney B.

Olds, Sally W., jt. auth. see Stewart, Mark A.

Oldsen, A. C., jt. auth. see Kretzmann, O. P.

Oldsey, Bernard. Hemingway's Hidden Craft: The Writing of "A Farewell to Arms". LC 79-743. (Illus.). 1979. 12.00x (ISBN 0-271-00213-1). Pa St U Pr.

Oldsey, Bernard, ed. British Novelists 1930 to 1959. (Dictionary of Literary Biography Ser.: Vol. 15). (Illus.). 350p. 1982. 74.00x (ISBN 0-8103-0938-6). Gale.

O'Leary, Brian. The Fertile Stars. 160p. 1981. 14.95 (ISBN 0-89696-079-X, An Everest House Book). Dodd.

O'Leary, Brian & Beatty, J. Kelly, eds. The New Solar System. 240p. 1982. 14.95 (ISBN 0-933346-36-0); pap. 7.75 (ISBN 0-933346-37-9). Sky Pub.

O'Leary, Brian, jt. ed. see Beatty, J. Kelly.

O'Leary, Catherine S., jt. auth. see Halton, Thomas P.

O'Leary, Cornelius. Irish Elections, 1918 - 1977: Parties, Voters & Proportional Representation. 1979. 26.00x (ISBN 0-312-43597-5). St Martin.

O'Leary, Cornelius, jt. auth. see Budge, Ian.

O'Leary, De Lacy E. Islam at the Cross Roads: A Brief Survey of the Present Position & Problems of the World of Islam. LC 80-1916. 1981. Repr. of 1923 ed. 26.50 (ISBN 0-404-18983-0). AMS Pr.

O'Leary, Greg. The Shaping of Chinese Foreign Policy. LC 80-10231. 320p. 1980. 26.00 (ISBN 0-312-71620-6). St Martin.

O'Leary, James L. & Goldring, Sidney, eds. Science & Epilepsy: Neuroscience Gains in Epilepsy Research. LC 75-21860. 303p. 1976. 28.50 (ISBN 0-89004-072-9). Raven.

O'Leary, James P. Systems Theory & Regional Integration: The "Market Model" of International Politics. LC 78-66420. 1978. pap. text ed. 11.50 (ISBN 0-8191-0500-7). U Pr of Amer.

O'Leary, John. The Running Game: The Campaign Journals of John O'Leary. (Illus.). 96p. 1983. 9.95 (ISBN 0-686-43254-1). NY Zoetrope.

O'Leary, K. Daniel, jt. auth. see Wilson, G. Terence.

O'Leary, Liam. Rex Ingram: Master of the Silent Cinema. (Illus.). 224p. 1980. 28.50x (ISBN 0-686-70951-9). B&N Imports.

O'Leary, M. Organic Chemistry. 1975. text ed. 27.50 (ISBN 0-07-047694-2, C). McGraw.

O'Leary, Michael K., jt. auth. see Coplin, William D.

O'Leary, Vincent, jt. auth. see Clear, Todd R.

Oleck, Howard. Law for Living. 1967. 9.00 (ISBN 0-685-92669-9); pap. 6.00 (ISBN 0-685-92670-2). Prof Bks Serv.

Oleck, Howard L. Modern Corporation Law, 6 Vols. 1958-1960. with 1978 suppl 350.00 (ISBN 0-672-83063-9, Bobbs-Merrill Law); 1978 suppl. 115.00 (ISBN 0-672-81982-1). Michie-Bobbs.

--Non-Profit Corporations, Organizations, & Associations. 4th ed. 1251p. 1980. 59.95 o.p. (Busn). P-H.

Oleksy, Jerome E. & Rukowski, George B. Solid State Electronic Laboratory Manual. 1980. pap. 8.50 (ISBN 0-672-97316-2); instr's guide 2.50 (ISBN 0-672-20820-2). Bobbs.

Oleksy, W. Quacky & the Crazy Curve Ball. 8.95 (ISBN 0-07-047752-3). McGraw.

Oleksy, Walter. The Black Plague. LC 82-4920. (First Bks.). (Illus.). 96p. (gr. 4 up). 1982. PLB 8.90 (ISBN 0-531-04426-2). Watts.

--Careers in the Animal Kingdom. LC 79-20742. (Career Bks.). (Illus.). 256p. (gr. 7 up). 1980. PLB 8.29 o.p. (ISBN 0-671-32939-1). Messner.

--It's Women's Work, Too! LC 80-10879. (Illus.). 192p. (gr. 7 up). 1980. PLB 8.29 o.p. (ISBN 0-671-33041-1). Messner.

--The Pirates of Deadman's Cay. LC 82-8488. (Hiway Ser.). (Illus.). (gr. 7-9). 1982. 9.95 (ISBN 0-664-32693-5). Westminster.

Oleksy, Walter, jt. auth. see Babbin, Kenneth.

Oleksy, Walter G. One Thousand Tested Money-Making Markets for Writers. pap. 2.95 o.p. (ISBN 0-06-463411-6, EH 411, EH). B&N NY.

Oleron, P. Language & Mental Development. LC 76-50666. 1977. 16.50x o.p. (ISBN 0-470-99027-9). Halsted Pr.

Oles, Carole. Quarry. (Poetry Ser.). 96p. (Orig.). 1983. pap. 8.00 (ISBN 0-87480-217-2). U of Utah Pr.

Olesker, J. Bradford. Beyond Forever. (Orig.). 1981. pap. 1.95 o.p. (ISBN 0-451-09565-0, J9565, Sig). NAL.

--The Siege of Superport. LC 77-13812. 1978. 8.95 o.p. (ISBN 0-399-12127-7). Putnam Pub Group.

--The Young Dragons. 1982. pap. 3.50 (ISBN 0-451-11453-1, AE1453, Sig). NAL.

Olesky, Walter. Visitors from Outer Space: Is There Life on Other Planets? (Illus.). (gr. 7 up). 1979. 7.95 o.p. (ISBN 0-399-20668-X). Putnam Pub Group.

Olesnicki, Roman, tr. see Kononenko, Konstantyn.

Oleson, G. Harrison. Across the Big Country: An Alphabet Adventure with Donald Duck. (Disney's Wonderful World of Reading Ser: No. 5). (Illus.). (ps-3). 1973. 4.95 (ISBN 0-394-82519-5, BYR); PLB 4.99 (ISBN 0-394-92519-X). Random.

Oleson, Sandy, jt. auth. see Long, Franklin A.

Olesten, Nils O. Numerical Control. LC 78-105390. 1970. 51.00 o.p. (ISBN 0-471-65336-5, Pub. by Wiley-Interscience). Wiley.

Oleszek, Walter. Congressional Procedure & the Policy Process. LC 78-17372. (Politics & Public Policy Ser.). 272p. 1978. pap. text ed. 8.25 (ISBN 0-87187-135-1). Congr. Quarterly.

Oleszek, Walter, jt. auth. see Davidson, Roger.

Olev, Kulno. English-Estonian-Russian Maritime Dictionary. 560p. 1981. 60.00x (ISBN 0-686-82322-2, Pub. by Collets). State Mutual Bk.

O'Levenson, Jordan, ed. Irish In Memoriam Poetry: The Books of Tears. LC 82-90968. (Orig.). 1983. pap. 15.95 (ISBN 0-914442-10-4). Levenson Pr.

Olevnik, Peter P., jt. auth. see Quay, Richard H.

Olexer, Barbara. The Enslavement of the American Indian. (Illus.). 280p. 1982. 18.95 (ISBN 0-912526-06-8). Lib Res.

Olford, Stephen. Lord, Open the Heavens! A Heartcry for Revival. LC 80-52053. 144p. 1980. pap. 4.95 (ISBN 0-87788-335-1). Shaw Pubs.

Olford, Stephen O. The Secret of Soul-Winning. 1978. pap. 3.50 o.p. (ISBN 0-8024-7684-8). Moody.

Olfson, Lewy. Radio Plays from Shakespeare. (gr. 7-12). 1958. 10.95 o.p. (ISBN 0-8238-0059-8). Plays.

--Skits & Short Farces for Young Actors. (gr. 5-12). 1973. 10.95 (ISBN 0-8238-0150-0). Plays.

Olgivie-Gordon, Maria M., tr. see Von Zittel, K. A.

Olian, JoAnne. The House of Worth: The Gilded Age 1860-1918. Hayden, John P., Jr., ed. (Illus.). 52p. (Orig.). 1982. pap. 10.00x (ISBN 0-910961-00-X). Mus City NY.

Olien, Diana D. Morpeth: A Victorian Public Career. LC 82-23820. 538p. (Orig.). 1983. lib. bdg. 29.75 (ISBN 0-8191-2989-5); pap. text ed. 18.75 (ISBN 0-8191-2990-9). U Pr of Amer.

Olien, Michael D. The Human Myth: An Introduction to Anthropology. (Illus.). 1978. text ed. 21.50 scp (ISBN 0-06-044918-7, HarpC). Har-Row.

Oligny, Paul, tr. see Noye, Irenee.

Olin, ed. see Mendenhall, J. Howard.

Olin, George. Mammals of the Southwest Desert. Rev. ed. Houk, Rose, et al, eds. LC 81-86094. (Illus.). 104p. 1982. pap. 5.95 (ISBN 0-911408-60-6). SW Pks Mnmts.

Olin, John C. & Smart, James D., eds. Luther, Erasmus, & the Reformation: A Catholic-Protestant Reappraisal. LC 82-15500. x, 150p. 1982. Repr. of 1969 ed. lib. bdg. 22.50x (ISBN 0-313-23652-6, OLLE). Greenwood.

Olin, Spencer C., jt. auth. see Nelson, Keith L.

Olin, Spencer C., Jr. California Politics: 1846-1920. Hundley, Norris, Jr. & Schutz, John A., eds. LC 81-66061. (Golden State Ser.). (Illus.). 90p. 1981. pap. text ed. 5.95x (ISBN 0-87835-114-0). Boyd & Fraser.

Olinekova, Gayle. Legs! Super Legs in Six Weeks. (Illus.). 128p. 1983. pap. 7.95 (ISBN 0-671-47241-0, Fireside). S&S.

Oliner, Pearl. Teaching Elementary Social Studies: A Rational & Humanistic Approach. (Illus.). 381p. 1976. text ed. 21.95 (ISBN 0-15-588052-7, HC). HarBraceJ.

Oliphant, Dave & Zigal, Thomas, eds. Joyce at Texas. (Illus.). 172p. 1983. pap. 14.95 (ISBN 0-87959-099-8). U of Tex Hum Res.

--Perspectives on Photography. (Illus.). 180p. 1982. pap. 14.95 (ISBN 0-87959-098-X). U of Tex Hum Res.

Oliphant, Eleana. The Haunting at Lost Lake. 224p. (Orig.). Date not set. pap. price not set o.p. (ISBN 0-505-51721-3). Tower Bks.

Oliphant, Lancelot. Great Comic Scenes from English Literature. 259p. 1982. Repr. of 1930 ed. lib. bdg. 40.00 (ISBN 0-89760-632-9). Telegraph Bks.

Oliphant, Laurence. Elgin's Mission to China & Japan, 2 Vols. (Oxford in Asia Historical Reprints Ser). 1970. 22.25x o.p. (ISBN 0-19-641004-5). Oxford U Pr.

Oliphant, Laurence & Zeevy, Rechavam. Life in the Holy Land. (Illus.). 475p. 1982. text ed. 16.00 (ISBN 0-86628-042-1). Ridgefield Pub.

Oliphant, M. Rutherford-Recollections of the Cambridge Days. 1972. 16.50 o.p. (ISBN 0-444-40968-8). Elsevier.

Oliphant, Margaret. Jeanne d'Arc: Her Life & Death. 1896. 30.00 (ISBN 0-8414-6664-5). Folcroft.

Oliphant, Margaret O. Miss Marjoribanks, 1866. Wolff, Robert L., ed. (Victorian Fiction Ser.). lib. bdg. 66.00 o.s.i. (ISBN 0-8240-1615-7). Garland Pub.

--The Perpetual Curate. Wolff, Robert L., ed. LC 75-1544. (Victorian Fiction Ser). 1975. Repr. of 1864 ed. lib. bdg. 66.00 o.s.i. (ISBN 0-8240-1614-9). Garland Pub.

--Phoebe, Junior: A Last Chronicle of Carlingford, 1876. Wolff, Robert L., ed. LC 75-1548. (Victorian Fiction Ser). 1975. lib. bdg. 66.00 o.s.i. (ISBN 0-8240-1616-5). Garland Pub.

--The Rector & the Doctor's Family, 1863. Wolff, Robert L., ed. LC 75-1543. (Victorian Fiction Ser). 1975. lib. bdg. 66.00 o.s.i. (ISBN 0-8240-1613-0). Garland Pub.

Oliphant, Pat. Oliphant Four More Years: A Cartoon History of the Years 1969 Through Election Day 1972. (Illus.). 1973. 8.95 o.p. (ISBN 0-671-21522-1). S&S.

Oliphant, Robert. A Piano for Mrs. Cimino. LC 80-10776. 366p. 1980. 11.95 o.p. (ISBN 0-13-675405-8). P-H.

Oliva, L. & Veiga-Pires, J. A., eds. Intervention Radiology: Proceedings, 2nd International Symposium, Venice-Lido, Italy, September 27 October 1, 1981, No. 2. (International Congress Ser.: No. 575). 366p. 1982. 74.50 (ISBN 0-444-90252-X, Excerpta Medica). Elsevier.

Oliva, Leo E. Fort Larned on the Santa Fe Trail. LC 82-80495. (Illus.). 75p. 1982. pap. 3.00 (ISBN 0-87726-024-9). Kansas St Hist.

Oliva, Peter F. Supervision for Today's Schools. 1976. text ed. 20.95 scp o.p. (ISBN 0-690-00858-9, HarpC). Har-Row.

Oliva, Ralph A. & Dale, Charles W. Basic Electricity & DC Circuits. 2nd ed. LC 79-92192. (Basic Electricity Ser.). (Illus.). 924p. 1980. text ed. 19.95 (ISBN 0-89512-034-8, LCW8161C). Tex Instr Inc.

Oliva, Ralph A., et al. Understanding Calculator Math. LC 78-50808. (Understanding Ser.). (Illus.). 224p. (Orig.). 1978. pap. 6.95 (ISBN 0-89512-016-X, LCB3321). Tex Instr Inc.

Olivares, Angelina S., tr. see Fisher, J. & Dryer, R.

Olivares, Angelina S., tr. see Fisher, J. & Drywer, R.

Olivares, Angelina S., tr. see Yockstick, M. L.

Olive, Marsha M. & Porro, Jeffrey D., eds. Nuclear Weapons in Europe: Modernization & Limitation. 192p. 1982. 19.95x (ISBN 0-669-05655-3). Lexington Bks.

Olive, S., jt. auth. see Henrici-Olive, G.

Oliveira, Joseph De. Jacinta, Flower of Fatima. 192p. 1972. 3.95 (ISBN 0-911988-45-9). AMI Pr.

Oliveira, Paulo de see De Oliveira, Paulo.

Oliver, A. Richard. Charles Nodier, Pilot of Romanticism. LC 64-8670. (Illus.). 1964. 17.95x (ISBN 0-8156-2073-X). Syracuse U Pr.

Oliver, Albert I. Maximizing Minicourses: A Practical Guide to a Curriculum Alternative. LC 77-13942. 1978. pap. text ed. 7.50x (ISBN 0-8077-2520-X). Tchrs Coll.

Oliver, Andrew. Auguste Edouart's Silhouettes of Eminent Americans, 1839-1844. LC 76-21073. (Illus.). 553p. 1977. 24.95 (ISBN 0-8139-0632-6, National Portrait Gallery). U Pr of Va.

Oliver, Andrew & Peabody, James B. The Records of Trinity Chruch, Boston: Vol. II-1728-1830. LC 80-68230. 1094p. 1982. 25.00x (ISBN 0-8139-0982-1, Colonial Soc MA). U Pr of Va.

Oliver, Andrew & Peabody, James B., eds. The Records of Trinity Church, Boston, 1728 - 1830. LC 80-68230. 519p. 1980. 25.00x (ISBN 0-8139-0950-3, Colonial Soc Ma). U Pr of Va.

Oliver, Bernard M. & Cage, John M. Electronic Measurements & Instrumentation. (Illus.). 720p. 1971. 56.50 (ISBN 0-07-047650-0, P&RB). McGraw.

Oliver, C. Operations Manual for Machine Tool Technology. 272p. 1982. pap. 15.95 (ISBN 0-471-04744-9). Wiley.

Oliver, Caroline. Western Women in Colonial Africa. LC 81-24194. (Contributions in Comparative Colonial Studies: No. 12). 232p. 1982. lib. bdg. 29.95 (ISBN 0-313-23388-8, OWA). Greenwood.

Oliver, Chad. Mists of Dawn. 1979. lib. bdg. 9.50 (ISBN 0-8398-2520-X, Gregg). G K Hall.

Oliver, Charles. How to Take Standardized Tests. 215p. (Orig.). (gr. 10-12). 1981. pap. text ed. 5.50 (ISBN 0-89285-155-4); listening comprehension 2 cassettes 16.95 (ISBN 0-89285-157-0). English Lang.

Oliver, Chip. High for the Game. Rapoport, Ron, ed. 1971. 5.95 o.p. (ISBN 0-688-01788-6). Morrow.

Oliver, Donald W. Education & Community: A Radical Critique of Innovative Schooling. LC 76-2114. 1977. 21.75 (ISBN 0-8211-1406-9); text ed. 19.50x in copies of ten (ISBN 0-685-80407-0). McCutchan.

Oliver, Douglas. Bougainville: A Personal History. LC 73-81594. (Illus.). 232p. 1973. pap. text ed. 4.50x o.p. (ISBN 0-8248-0289-6). UH Pr.

--The Pacific Islands. rev. ed. LC 73-77010. (Illus.). 480p. 1975. pap. text ed. 5.95x (ISBN 0-8248-0397-3). UH Pr.

Oliver, Douglas L. Ancient Tahitian Society, 3 vols. LC 73-77010. (Illus.). 1500p. 1975. text ed. 65.00x boxed (ISBN 0-8248-0267-5). UH Pr.

--Two Tahitian Villages: A Study in Comparison. 1983. text ed. 24.95x (ISBN 0-939154-22-6). Inst Polynesian.

Oliver, Elizabeth M. Black Mother Goose Book. 2nd ed. LC 81-83427. (Illus.). 48p. 1981. 6.00 (ISBN 0-912444-12-6). Gaus.

Oliver, Eloise M., jt. auth. see Bryant, Rosalie.

Oliver, Eric & Wilson, John. Security Manual. 1979. text ed. 10.50x (ISBN 0-566-02116-1). Gower Pub Ltd.

Oliver, Frederick S. A Dweller on Two Planets: The Dividing of the Way. LC 73-94420. 432p. 1982. Repr. of 1974 ed. 15.00 (ISBN 0-89345-402-8). Garber Comm.

Oliver, H. J., jt. auth. see Law, J.

Oliver, H. J. & Shakespeare, William, eds. The Taming of the Shrew. 1982. 19.95x (ISBN 0-19-812907-6). Oxford U Pr.

Oliver, H. J., ed. see Shakespeare, William.

Oliver, Hugh & MacMillan, Keith. The American Limerick Book. (Illus.). 144p. 1982. pap. 3.95 (ISBN 0-89104-287-3, A & W Visual Library). A & W Pubs.

Oliver, J. L. The Development & Structure of the Furniture Industry. 1966. inquire for price o.p. (ISBN 0-08-011460-1). Pergamon.

Oliver, J. M. Law & Economics. (Economy & Society Ser.). (Orig.). 1979. text ed. 22.50x (ISBN 0-04-330297-1); pap. text ed. 8.95x (ISBN 0-04-330298-X). Allen Unwin.

--The Principles of Teaching Economics. 1973. pap. text ed. 10.00x o.p. (ISBN 0-435-84525-X). Heinemann Ed.

Oliver, John E. Climate & Man's Environment: An Introduction to Applied Climatology. LC 73-5707. 517p. 1973. text ed. 34.95 (ISBN 0-471-65338-1). Wiley.

Oliver, John S., ed. Forensic Toxicology. 320p. 1980. text ed. 32.50 o.p. (ISBN 0-8391-4117-3). Univ Park.

Oliver, June. Polysymetrics: The Art of Making Geometric Patterns. 40p. 1982. pap. 3.95 (ISBN 0-13-684381-6). P-H.

Oliver, Kenneth. Words Every College Student Should Know. 2nd, Rev. ed. LC 81-81919. 500p. (Orig.). 1982. pap. 13.95 (ISBN 0-913244-57-0). Hapi Pr.

Oliver, Louis. Muskogee Memories. (American Indian Poetry Ser.). write for info. Greenfld Rev Pr.

Oliver, M. F. Modern Trends in Cardiology, Vol. 3. 1975. 24.95 o.p. (ISBN 0-407-00018-6). Butterworth.

Oliver, M. F., jt. ed. see Riemersma, R. A.

Oliver, Margaret. Pledge of Allegiance in Signing Exact English. (Written in sign writing). 3.00 (ISBN 0-686-95275-8). Move Short Soc.

Oliver, Mary. American Primitive. 96p. 1983. 12.00i (ISBN 0-316-65002-1); pap. 6.70i (ISBN 0-316-65004-8). Little.

Oliver, Paul. Blues Fell This Morning: The Meaning of the Blues. (Illus.). 376p. 1983. pap. 9.95 (ISBN 0-8180-1222-6). Horizon.

--Conversations with the Blues. (Illus.). 238p. 1983. pap. 8.95 (ISBN 0-8180-1223-4). Horizon.

Oliver, R., jt. auth. see Sherrington, P. J.

Oliver, R. W. A. & Oliver, S. A., eds. Analysis of Children's Urine, 5 pts. loose leaf with binder 108.00 o.p. (ISBN 0-85501-051-7). Wiley.

Oliver, Raymond. Entries. LC 80-83948. (Poetry Chapbook: No. 4). 40p. 1981. 8.95 (ISBN 0-87923-366-4). Godine.

--Poems Without Names: The English Lyric, 1200-1500. LC 77-82617. 1970. 24.50x (ISBN 0-520-01403-0). U of Cal Pr.

Oliver, Revilo, tr. see Sudraka, Kind.

Oliver, Rice D. Student Atlas of California. (Illus.). 72p. (gr. 4-12). 1982. teachers ed. 7.95 (ISBN 0-936778-83-0). Calif Weekly.

Oliver, Richard & Architectural History Foundation. Bertram Grosvenor Goodhue. (American Monograph Ser.). (Illus.). 192p. 1982. 30.00x (ISBN 0-262-15024-7). MIT Pr.

Oliver, Robert A., jt. auth. see Johnson, Dewayne J.

Oliver, Robert T. Communication & Culture in Ancient India & China. LC 73-151717. 1971. 17.95x (ISBN 0-8156-0082-8). Syracuse U Pr.

--Syngman Rhee. LC 72-13864. (Illus.). 380p. 1973. Repr. of 1954 ed. lib. bdg. 20.50x (ISBN 0-8371-6759-0, OLSR). Greenwood.

Oliver, Roland & Atmore, A. Africa Since Eighteen Hundred. 3rd ed. (Illus.). 396p. 1981. 34.50 (ISBN 0-521-23485-9); pap. 10.95 (ISBN 0-521-29975-6). Cambridge U Pr.

--African Middle Ages, 1400-1800. (Illus.). 245p. 1981. 32.50 (ISBN 0-521-23301-1); pap. 10.95 (ISBN 0-521-29894-6). Cambridge U Pr.

Oliver, Roland & Fagan, B. M. Africa in the Iron Age. LC 74-25639. (Illus.). 300p. 1975. 34.50 (ISBN 0-521-20598-0); pap. 9.95x (ISBN 0-521-09900-5). Cambridge U Pr.

Oliver, Roland & Face, J. D., eds. A Short History of Africa. (African Library). 1962. pap. 4.95 (ISBN 0-14-041002-3). Penguin.

Oliver, Roland A., jt. auth. see Fage, J. D.

Oliver, S. A., jt. ed. see Oliver, R. W. A.

Oliver, Susan. Odyssey: A Daring Transatlantic Journey. 256p. 1983. 14.75 (ISBN 0-02-592920-8). Macmillan.

Oliver Brachfeld, F. Inferiority Feelings in the Individual & the Group. Gabain, Marjorie, tr. from Fr. LC 70-169849. 301p. Repr. of 1951 ed. lib. bdg. 17.25x (ISBN 0-8371-6245-9, OLIF). Greenwood.

Oliveri, Mario. The Representatives: The Real Nature & Function of Papal Legates. LC 81-108272. 192p. (Orig.). 1981. pap. 4.95 (ISBN 0-905715-20-9). Wanderer Pr.

Oliveroff, Andre. Flight of the Swan: A Memory of Anna Pavlova. (Series in Dance). 1979. Repr. of 1932 ed. 22.50 (ISBN 0-306-79580-9). Da Capo.

Oliveros, Chuck. The Pterodactyl in the Wilderness. 56p. (Orig.). 1983. pap. 3.00 (ISBN 0-911757-00-7). Dead Angel.

Olivier, D. Luther's Faith: The Cause of the Gospel in the Church. LC 12-2961. 1982. pap. 12.95 (ISBN 0-570-03868-5). Concordia.

Olivier, Daniel D., jt. auth. see Grew, James H.

Olivier, Julien. Pas De Gene: Omer Marcoux Violoneux et Sculpteur. (Oral History Ser.). (Illus.). 94p. (Fr.). (gr. 9-10). 1981. pap. 2.50x (ISBN 0-911409-06-8). Natl Mat Dev.

--Prende Le Large: Big Jim Cote Pecheur. (Oral History Ser.). (Illus.). 107p. (Fr.). (gr. 9-10). 1981. pap. 2.50x (ISBN 0-911409-08-4). Natl Mat Dev.

--Souches et Racines. (Illus.). 175p. (Fr.). 1981. pap. text ed. 4.50 (ISBN 0-911409-09-2). Natl Mat Dev.

Olivier, Julien, jt. auth. see Landry, Monica.

Olivier, Juste. Paris en 1830: Journal de Juste Olivier. Delattre, Andre & Denkinger, Marc, eds. (Studies in the Romance Languages & Literatures: No. 19). 1951. pap. 17.00x (ISBN 0-8078-9019-7). U of NC Pr.

Olivier, Laurence. Confessions of an Actor: An Autobiography. (Illus.). 330p. 1982. 16.95 (ISBN 0-671-41701-0). S&S.

Olivier, M. C. The Private Company in Germany. 128p. 1976. 35.00x (ISBN 0-7121-1665-6, Pub. by Macdonald & Evans). State Mutual Bk.

Olivier, Tanya. How to Survive When Your Husband or Wife Walks Out, Vol. I. Thuvenet, Renee, ed. LC 82-84063. 154p. (Orig.). 1983. pap. 10.95 (ISBN 0-686-38459-8). Ferrucci.

Oliviera, Celso D., et al, trs. see Ramos, Graciliano.

Olivieri, jt. auth. see Sweeney.

Olivieri, Peter & Rubin, Michael. Computers & Programming: A Neoclassical Approach. (Illus.). 448p. 1975. text ed. 17.95 o.p. (ISBN 0-07-047692-6, C); instructors' manual 2.95 o.p. (ISBN 0-07-047693-4). McGraw.

Olivo & Marsh. Principles of Refrigeration. LC 76-14089. 1979. 17.60 (ISBN 0-8273-1014-5); pap. text ed. 13.60 (ISBN 0-686-85870-0); instructor's guide 1.65 (ISBN 0-8273-1004-8). Delmar.

Olivo, C. Thomas & Olivo, Thomas P. Fundamentals of Applied Physics. LC 77-79381. 1978. text ed. 18.20 (ISBN 0-8273-1300-4); tchr's. guide 4.75 (ISBN 0-8273-1301-2). Delmar.

Olivo, C. Thomas & Payne, Albert V. Basic Blueprint Reading & Sketching. 4th ed. LC 82-71044. (Illus.). 176p. 1983. text ed. 13.60 o.p. (ISBN 0-8273-2124-4); pap. text ed. 9.80 (ISBN 0-8273-2139-2); instr's guide 2.75 (ISBN 0-8273-2140-6). Delmar.

Olivo, C. Thomas, et al. Basic Mathematics Simplified. 4th ed. LC 76-3941. (Illus.). 221p. 1977. 19.00 (ISBN 0-8273-1270-9); pap. 15.00 (ISBN 0-8273-1269-5); fundamental ed. 10.40 (ISBN 0-8273-1268-7); instr's. guide 3.75 (ISBN 0-8273-1271-7). Delmar.

Olivo, Thomas, jt. auth. see Marsh, R. Warren.

Olivo, Thomas C. Basic Machine Technology. 1980. 21.95 (ISBN 0-672-97171-2). Bobbs.

Olivo, Thomas P., jt. auth. see Olivo, C. Thomas.

Olk-Apire, P. A. Idi Amin's Rise to Power: The Inside Story. 192p. (Orig.). cancelled (ISBN 0-905762-68-1, Pub. by Zed Pr England); pap. cancelled (ISBN 0-905762-67-3, Pub. by Zed Pr England). Lawrence Hill.

Olken, Charles, et al. The Connoisseurs' Handbook of California Wines. 2nd, rev. ed. LC 81-48103. 1982. pap. 5.95 (ISBN 0-394-71005-3). Knopf.

Olken, Ilene T., ed. Racconti Del Novecento: Forti E. Deboli. 1966. pap. text ed. 11.95 (ISBN 0-13-750083-1). P-H.

Olkin, Ingram, et al. Probability Models & Applications. (Illus.). 1980. text ed. 30.95x (ISBN 0-02-389230-7). Macmillan.

Olkowski, William, jt. auth. see Carr, Anna.

Ollard, Eric A. Introductory Electroplating. 1969. 32.50x (ISBN 0-85218-027-6). Intl Pubns Serv.

Olle. Information Systems Design Methodologies: A Comparative Review. 1982. 72.50 (ISBN 0-444-86407-5). Elsevier.

Olle, T. W. The CODASYL Approach to Data Base Management. 287p. 1978. 42.95 (ISBN 0-471-99579-7, 1-320). Wiley.

Ollen, Gunnar. August Strindberg. LC 76-153125. (Literature and Life Ser.). 11.95 (ISBN 0-8044-2664-3). Ungar.

Ollendick, Thomas H., jt. ed. see Hersen, Michel.

Oller, John W., Jr. Language Tests at School: A Pragmatic Approach. (Applied Linguistics & Language Study Ser.). (Illus.). 1979. text ed. 20.95x (ISBN 0-582-55365-2); pap. text ed. 13.95x (ISBN 0-582-55294-X). Longman.

Oller, John W., Jr., ed. Issues in Language Testing Research. 512p. 1983. pap. text ed. 21.95 (ISBN 0-88377-217-5). Newbury Hse.

Oller, John W., Jr. & Richards, Jack R., eds. Focus on the Learner: Pragmatic Perspectives for the Language Teacher. 1973. pap. text ed. 11.95 (ISBN 0-912066-67-9). Newbury Hse.

Ollerenshaw, R. J. Calibration of Cascadeimpactors Using Existing Theory, 1978. 1981. 69.00x (ISBN 0-686-97041-1, Pub. by W Spring England). State Mutual Bk.

--Fundamental Processes Involved in the Formation of Metallurgical Fume, 1978. 1981. 80.00x (ISBN 0-686-97081-0, Pub. by W Spring England). State Mutual Bk.

Olley, John W. Righteousness in the Septuagint of Isaiah: A Contextual Study. LC 78-3425. (Society of Biblical Literature, Septuagint & Cognate Studies: No. 8). 1979. 12.00 (ISBN 0-89130-226-3, 06-04-08); pap. 9.95 (ISBN 0-686-86732-7). Scholars Pr Ca.

Olley, Peter M., jt. ed. see Coceani, Flavio.

Ollier, Cliff. Volcanoes. 1970. pap. 5.95 o.p. (ISBN 0-262-65008-8). MIT Pr.

Ollis, David F., jt. auth. see Bailey, James.

Ollivant, Alfred. Bob, Son of Battle. (Classics Ser.). (Illus.). (gr. 5 up). pap. 1.95 (ISBN 0-8049-0141-4, CL-141). Airmont.

Ollivier, Jacqueline. Grammaire Francaise. 454p. (Fr.). 1978. pap. text ed. 14.95 (ISBN 0-15-529675-2, HC). HarBraceJ.

Ollman, B. Alienation. 2nd ed. LC 76-4234. (Studies in the History & Theory of Politics). 1977. 37.50 (ISBN 0-521-21281-2); pap. 10.95x (ISBN 0-521-29083-X). Cambridge U Pr.

Ollman, Bertell, jt. ed. see Norton, Theodore M.

Olmedo, Alfonso, tr. see Benko, Stephen.

Olmedo, Esteban L., jt. auth. see Newton, Frank.

Olmo, Harold P., jt. auth. see Brooks, Reid M.

Olmstead, Alan L. New York City Mutual Savings Banks, 1819-1861. LC 75-28114. xiv, 236p. 1976. 19.50x (ISBN 0-8078-1265-X). U of NC Pr.

Olmstead, Barney & Smith, Suzanne. Job Sharing Handbook. 1983. pap. 6.95 (ISBN 0-14-046544-8). Penguin.

Olmstead, Frederick L. Civilizing American Cities: A Selection of Frederick Law Olmsted's Writings on City Landscapes. Sutton, S. B., ed. (Illus.). 1971. pap. 7.95 (ISBN 0-262-65012-6). MIT Pr.

Olmstead, Frederick L., Jr. & Kimball, Theodora, eds. Forty Years of Landscape Architecture: Professional Papers of Frederick Law Olmsted, Vol. 2 Central Park. 1973. pap. 5.95x (ISBN 0-262-65006-1). MIT Pr.

Olmstead, John. The Design of the Narrative. new ed. Buell, Lawrence, ed. LC 73-75456. 74p. (gr. 7-12). 1973. pap. text ed. 1.45 o.p. (ISBN 0-88301-079-8). Pendulum Pr.

Olmstead, Mary, ed. see Carroll, Margaret D. & Abraham, Sidney.

Olmstead, Mary, tr. see Dundon, Mary L. & Gay, George A.

Olmsted, Frederich L. The Cotton Kingdom. 1981. pap. 6.95 (ISBN 0-686-38905-0, Mod LibC). Modern Lib.

Olmsted, John C. A Victorian Art of Fiction Essays on the Novel in British Periodicals, 1830-1900, 3 vols. LC 77-83397. (Reference Library of Humanities). 1979. Vol. 1, 1830-1850. lib. bdg. 65.00 o.s.i. (ISBN 0-8240-9845-5); Vol. 2, 1851-1870. lib. bdg. 57.00 o.s.i. (ISBN 0-8240-9771-8); Vol. 3, 1871-1900. lib. bdg. 57.00 o.s.i. (ISBN 0-8240-9772-6). Garland Pub.

Olmsted, John C. & Welch, Jeffrey. Victorian Novel Illustration: A Selected Checklist 1900-1976. LC 78-68248. (Reference Library of Humanities Ser.). 1979. lib. bdg. 18.00 o.s.i. (ISBN 0-8240-9773-4). Garland Pub.

Olmsted, John M. Advanced Calculus. (Illus.). 1961. text ed. 29.95 (ISBN 0-13-010983-5). P-H.

Olmsted, John M., jt. auth. see Gelbaum, Bernard R.

Olmsted, Lorena A. Journey to Adventure. (YA) 1977. 6.95 (ISBN 0-685-74274-1, Avalon). Bouregy.

--Strange Inheritance. (YA) 1978. 6.95 (ISBN 0-685-86415-4, Avalon). Bouregy.

--The Tender Season. 1982. pap. 6.95 (ISBN 0-686-84726-1, Avalon). Bouregy.

Olmsted, Lorena Ann. Dangerous Memory. 192p. (YA) 1974. 6.95 (ISBN 0-685-39471-9, Avalon). Bouregy.

--Warning of Danger. (YA) 1979. 6.95 (ISBN 0-685-93882-4, Avalon). Bouregy.

Olmsted, Robert P. An Acquaintance with Alco. LC 68-58442. (Illus.). 80p. 1980. Repr. of 1968 ed. 13.50 o.p. (ISBN 0-934228-03-5). McMillan Pubns.

Olmsted, Robert W. Shadows on Cassiopeia. LC 76-528. (Illus.). 1976. 14.95 (ISBN 0-89002-073-6); pap. 5.00 (ISBN 0-89002-072-8). Northwoods Pr.

Olney, James. The Rhizome & the Flower: The Perennial Philosophy--Yeats & Jung. 1980. 33.00x (ISBN 0-520-03748-0). U of Cal Pr.

Olney, Judith. Joy of Chocolate. 1982. 12.95 (ISBN 0-8120-5435-0). Barron.

--Summer Food. LC 77-15870. 272p. 1983. pap. 7.95 (ISBN 0-689-70643-X, 292). Atheneum.

Olney, Ross. Great Auto Racing Champions. LC 73-5696. (Sports Ser). (Illus.). 96p. (gr. 3-6). 1973. PLB 7.12 (ISBN 0-8116-6666-2). Garrard.

--Windsurfing: A Complete Guide. (Illus.). 96p. (gr. 7 up). 1982. 9.95 (ISBN 0-8027-6449-5); PLB 10.85 (ISBN 0-8027-6465-7). Walker & Co.

Olney, Ross R. Auto Racing's Young Lions. LC 76-53824. (Illus.). (gr. 6-8). 1977. 6.50 o.p. (ISBN 0-399-20579-9). Putnam Pub Group.

--Great Dragging Wagons. LC 70-111528. (Putnam Sports Shelf Ser.). (Illus.). (gr. 5-8). 1970. PLB 6.29 o.p. (ISBN 0-399-60210-0). Putnam Pub Group.

--Gymnastics. (First Bks.). (Illus.). 96p. (gr. 4-6). 1976. PLB 8.90 (ISBN 0-531-00849-5). Watts.

--Hang Gliding. LC 76-16193. (Illus.). (gr. 6-8). 1976. 7.50 o.p. (ISBN 0-399-20537-3). Putnam Pub Group.

--Keeping Our Cities Clean. LC 78-26253. (Illus.). 64p. (gr. 4 up). 1979. PLB 6.97 o.p. (ISBN 0-671-32942-1). Messner.

--Kings of Motor Speed. (Putnam Sports Shelf). (Illus.). (gr. 5-8). 1970. PLB 6.29 o.p. (ISBN 0-399-60338-7). Putnam Pub Group.

--Kings of the Drag Strip. (Putnam Sports Shelf). (Illus.). (gr. 5 up). 1969. PLB 6.29 o.p. (ISBN 0-399-60336-0). Putnam Pub Group.

--Modern Speed Record Superstars: High Interest, Low Vocabulary Ser. LC 82-7400. (Illus.). 128p. (gr. 4). 1982. PLB 7.95 (ISBN 0-396-08072-3). Dodd.

--Simple Bicycle Repair & Maintenance. LC 72-76234. 112p. 1973. pap. 3.95 o.p. (ISBN 0-385-06199-4). Doubleday.

--Superstars of Auto-Racing. LC 75-10438. (Illus.). (gr. 5 up). 1976. PLB 6.29 o.p. (ISBN 0-399-60959-8). Putnam Pub Group.

--This Game Called Hockey. LC 77-16872. (Illus.). (gr. 5 up). 1978. 5.95 o.p. (ISBN 0-396-07524-X). Dodd.

--Winners! Super-Champions of Ice Hockey. (Illus.). 128p. (gr. 6 up). 1982. 11.50 (ISBN 0-89919-109-6, Clarion); pap. 4.95 (ISBN 0-89919-134-7). HM.

Olney, Ross R. & Bush, Chan. Better Kite Flying for Boys & Girls. LC 80-14817. (Better Sports Ser.). (Illus.). 64p. (gr. 4 up). 1980. PLB 6.95 o.p. (ISBN 0-396-07853-2). Dodd.

--Better Skateboarding for Boys & Girls. (Better Sports Ser.). (Illus.). (gr. 4 up). 1977. 6.95 o.p. (ISBN 0-396-07433-2). Dodd.

Olney, Ross R. & Grable, Ron. The Racing Bugs: Formula Vee & Super Vee. LC 74-78402. (Illus.). 128p. (gr. 6 up). 1974. PLB 5.69 o.p. (ISBN 0-399-60900-8). Putnam Pub Group.

Olorunsola, Vicotr A. Societal Reconstruction in Two African States. 296p. 1977. pap. text ed. 11.50 (ISBN 0-8191-0207-5). U Pr of Amer.

Olorunsola, Victor A., jt. ed. see Rothchild, Donald.

Oloyede, E. O., jt. auth. see Adesanya, M. O.

Olphen, H. Van see Van Olphen, H.

Olschki, Leonardo. Marco Polo's Asia: An Introduction to His "Description of the World" Called "Il Milione". Scott, John A., tr. 1960. 42.50x (ISBN 0-520-00975-4). U of Cal Pr.

Olsen. Electronics a Course Book for Students: 2nd. Limp. 1982. text ed. 42.50 (ISBN 0-408-01193-9); pap. text ed. 24.95 (ISBN 0-408-00491-6). Butterworth.

Olsen, jt. auth. see Brun.

Olsen, Alexandra H. Guthlac of Croyland: A Study of Heroic Hagiography. LC 81-40062. 172p. (Orig.). 1982. lib. bdg. 20.75 (ISBN 0-8191-1980-6); pap. text ed. 10.00 (ISBN 0-8191-1981-4). U Pr of Amer.

Olsen, Alfa B., jt. auth. see Efron, Marshall.

Olsen, E. A. Adrift on a Raft. LC 68-16397. (Oceanography Ser.). (Illus.). (gr. 3 up). 1970. PLB 6.75x (ISBN 0-87783-000-2); pap. 2.99x deluxe ed. (ISBN 0-87783-078-9); cassette 7.95x (ISBN 0-87783-176-9). Oddo.

--Killer in the Trap. LC 68-16399. (Oceanography Ser.). (Illus.). (gr. 3 up). 1970. PLB 6.75x (ISBN 0-87783-019-3); pap. 2.95x deluxe ed. (ISBN 0-87783-097-5); cassette 7.95x (ISBN 0-87783-190-4). Oddo.

--Lobster King. LC 68-16400. (Oceanography Ser.). (Illus.). (gr. 3 up). 1970. PLB 6.75x (ISBN 0-87783-024-X); pap. 2.95x deluxe ed. (ISBN 0-87783-099-1); cassette 7.95x (ISBN 0-87783-192-0). Oddo.

--Mystery at Salvage Rock. LC 68-16401. (Oceanography Ser.). (Illus.). (gr. 3 up). 1970. PLB 6.75x (ISBN 0-87783-027-4); pap. 2.95x deluxe ed. (ISBN 0-87783-101-7); cassette 7.95x (ISBN 0-87783-195-5). Oddo.

Olsen, E. D. Modern Optical Methods of Analysis. 1975. 39.95 (ISBN 0-07-047697-7). McGraw.

Olsen, Einar, jt. auth. see Bucher, Charles.

Olsen, Frederick L. Kiln Book. 2nd ed. 1982. 19.95 (ISBN 0-686-94135-7). Chilton.

Olsen, G. Elements of Mechanics of Materials. 4th ed. 1982. 28.95 (ISBN 0-13-267013-5). P-H.

Olsen, Helen C. To Catch the Wind. (YA) 1978. 6.95 (ISBN 0-685-86416-2, Avalon). Bouregy.

Olsen, Ib S. The Little Locomotive. LC 75-13191. (Illus.). 32p. (gr. 1-4). 1976. 6.95 o.p. (ISBN 0-698-20364-X, Coward). Putnam Pub Group.

Olsen, Jack. Have You Seen My Son? LC 82-3895. 320p. 1982. 12.95 (ISBN 0-689-11314-5). Atheneum.

--Night of the Grizzlies. 1971. pap. 2.95 (ISBN 0-451-12304-2, AE2304, Sig). NAL.

--Night of the Grizzlies. (Illus.). 1969. 7.95 o.p. (ISBN 0-399-10582-4). Putnam Pub Group.

Olsen, James. Step up Your Reading Power, 4 bks. 1966. text ed. 4.80 ea. o.p. (W). Bk. B. Bk. C (ISBN 0-07-047813-9). Bk. D (ISBN 0-07-047814-7). Bk. E (ISBN 0-07-047815-5). McGraw.

--What Job for Me Series, 18 bks. 1969. 48.00 o.p. (ISBN 0-07-079986-5, G). McGraw.

Olsen, James T. Arnold Palmer. LC 73-13861. (Superstars Ser.). 1974. PLB 6.95 (ISBN 0-87191-310-0). Creative Ed.

--Roberto Clemente. LC 76-5813. (Creative Superstars Ser.). 1974. PLB 6.95 o.p. (ISBN 0-87191-279-1). Creative Ed.

Olsen, Jody K., jt. auth. see Gelfand, Donald E.

Olsen, Johan P., ed. Organized Democracy: Political Institutions in a Welfare State-the Case of Norway. 272p. 1983. pap. 26.00x (ISBN 82-00-06442-5, Universitet). Columbia U Pr.

Olsen, L. & Ruchin, T. Principles of Communications for Science & Technology. 432p. 1983. 16.95x (ISBN 0-07-047821-X). McGraw.

Olsen, Leslie, jt. auth. see Huckin, Thomas.

Olsen, M. H., jt. auth. see Davis, G. B.

Olsen, Magnus, jt. ed. see Munch, Peter A.

Olsen, Marvin E. Participatory Pluralism: Political Participation & Influence in the United States & Sweden. LC 82-2263. 324p. 1982. text ed. 24.95x (ISBN 0-88229-711-2). Nelson-Hall.

Olsen, Michael & Solomon, Bruce. Dick Clark's the First Twenty Five Years of Rock & Roll. 512p. (Orig.). 1981. pap. 12.95 (ISBN 0-440-51763-X, Dell Trade Pbks). Dell.

Olsen, Mimi V. The Cat Lover's Book of Days. LC 82-47529. (Illus.). 96p. 1982. 19.18i (ISBN 0-06-015040-8, HarpT). Har-Row.

Olsen, Paul. Comprehensive Psychotherapy. (Advances in Integrative Psychotherapy Ser.: Vol. 1). 184p. 1980. 26.00 (ISBN 0-686-65260-6). Gordon.

Olsen, Paul, ed. Comprehensive Psychotherapy, Vol. 2. 132p. 1981. 30.00 (ISBN 0-677-16230-8). Gordon.

Olsen, Richard. Karl Marx. (World Leaders Ser.). 1978. lib. bdg. 11.95 (ISBN 0-8057-7678-8, Twayne). G K Hall.

Olsen, Richard P. The Textile Industry. LC 77-9167. (Lexington Casebook Ser. in Industry Analysis). (Illus.). 240p. 1978. 24.95 (ISBN 0-669-01807-4). Lexington Bks.

Olsen, Roger E., ed. see Riverol, Armando.

Olsen, Rolf, jt. ed. see Wing, J. K.

Olsen, Shirley A. Group Planning & Problem-Solving Methods in Engineering Management. LC 81-19675. (Construction Management & Engineering Ser.). 455p. 1982. 49.95x (ISBN 0-471-08311-9, Pub. by Wiley-Interscience). Wiley.

Olsen, Stanley J. Osteology for the Archaeologist. rev. ed. LC 79-65654. (Peabody Museum Papers: Vol. 56, Nos. 3, 4, & 5). 1979. 15.00x (ISBN 0-87365-164-2). Peabody Harvard.

Olsen, Steve, et al. An Interpretive Atlas of Narragansett Bay. (Marine Bulletin Ser.: No. 40). 1980. 2.00 o.p. (ISBN 0-938412-16-7). URI MAS.

Olsen, T. V. Blood of the Breed. LC 81-43298. (Western Ser.). 192p. 1982. 11.95 (ISBN 0-385-17555-8). Doubleday.

--Red Is the River. 416p. (Orig.). 1983. pap. 3.50 (ISBN 0-449-12407-X, GM). Fawcett.

Olsen, Tillie. Silences. 1983. pap. 4.50 (ISBN 0-440-38337-4, LE). Dell.

--Tell Me a Riddle. 1978. 8.95 o.s.i. (ISBN 0-440-08654-X, Sey Lawr). Delacorte.

--Yonnondio from the Thirties. 208p. 1974. 6.95 o.s.i. (ISBN 0-440-09196-9, Sey Lawr). Delacorte.

Olsen, V. Norskov. John Foxe & the Elizabethan Church. 1973. 33.00x (ISBN 0-520-02075-8). U of Cal Pr.

Olsen, Viggo. Daktar. 1976. pap. write for info (ISBN 0-515-09472-2). Jove Pubns.

Olsen, Violet. The Growing Season. LC 82-1763. 228p. (gr. 4-7). 1982. 10.95 (ISBN 0-689-30938-4). Atheneum.

Olshan, Neil & Dreyer, Julie. Fears & Phobias. LC 79-24044. (gr. 7 up). 1980. PLB 7.90 (ISBN 0-531-02865-8, B08). Watts.

Olsheim, Linda, ed. Creative Handicrafts Course. (Illus.). 1976. pap. 5.95 o.p. (ISBN 0-517-52631-X). Crown.

Olshen, Barry N. John Fowles. LC 78-3149. (Literature & Life Ser.). 1978. 11.95 (ISBN 0-8044-2665-1). Ungar.

Olshen, Barry N. & Olshen, Toni A. John Fowles: A Reference Guide. 1980. lib. bdg. 16.00 (ISBN 0-8161-8187-X, Hall Reference). G K Hall.

Olshen, Toni A., jt. auth. see Olshen, Barry N.

Olshevsky, George. The Amazing Spider-Man & Other Titles. rev. ed. (The Marvel Comics Index Ser.: Pt. 1). (Illus.). 300p. 1983. 12.95 (ISBN 0-943348-21-8); pap. 8.95 (ISBN 0-943348-01-3). G Olshevsky.

--The Marvel Comics Index Series. rev. ed. (Illus.). 1982. Set. write for info. (ISBN 0-943348-20-X); Set. pap. write for info. (ISBN 0-943348-00-5). G Olshevsky.

Olshtain, E., jt. auth. see Dubin, F.

Olson see Stafford, William.

Olson, Alison G. & Brown, Richard M., eds. Anglo-American Political Relations, 1675-1775. LC 73-108758. 1970. 25.00 (ISBN 0-8135-0624-7). Rutgers U Pr.

Olson, Carl, ed. The Book of the Goddess, Past & Present: An Introduction to Her Religion. 275p. 1983. 14.95 (ISBN 0-8245-0566-2). Crossroad NY.

Olson, Charles. The Maximus Poems. Butterick, George F., ed. LC 79-65759. 650p. 1983. 32.50 (ISBN 0-520-04015-5). U of Cal Pr.

Olson, Charles & Creeley, Robert. Charles Olson & Robert Creeley: The Complete Correspondence, Vol. 5. Butterick, George F., ed. (Orig.). 1983. 20.00 (ISBN 0-87685-561-3); deluxe ed. 30.00 signed ed. (ISBN 0-87685-562-1); pap. 7.50 (ISBN 0-87685-560-5). Black Sparrow.

Olson, Charles & Picconi, Mario J. Statistics for Business Decision Making. 1983. text ed. 26.95x (ISBN 0-673-16000-9). Scott F.

Olson, Chet, ed. Jesus One: The Life & Wisdom of Jesus in Scripture. 2nd ed. (Life & Wisdom of Jesus Ser.). 216p. 9.95 (ISBN 0-940298-07-4); pap. 6.95 (ISBN 0-940298-06-6). Spiritwarrior Pub.

Olson, Clarinda E. Basic Science for Dental Auxiliaries. (Illus.). 1980. pap. 15.95 ref. ed. (ISBN 0-13-069245-X). P-H.

Olson, Craig. Craig Olson's Decorating with Plants. Grooms, Kathe, ed. LC 80-29579. (Illus.). 110p. 1981. pap. 2.95 o.p. (ISBN 0-915658-31-3). Meadowbrook Pr.

Olson, D. H., jt. auth. see Meier, W. M.

Olson, David F. Stone Grinding & Polishing. LC 73-83453. (Little Craft Book Ser.). (Illus.). 48p. (gr. 7 up). 1973. 6.95 (ISBN 0-8069-5286-5); PLB 8.99 (ISBN 0-8069-5287-3). Sterling.

Olson, David G., jt. auth. see Wright, Gordon P.

Olson, David H. & Miller, Brent C., eds. Family Study Review Yearbook. (Family Study Review Yearbooks). (Illus.). 768p. 1983. 37.50 (ISBN 0-8039-1924-7). Sage.

Olson, David J. & Meyer, Philip. Governing the United States: To Keep the Republic in Its Third Century. 2nd ed. (Illus.). 1978. text ed. 24.95 (ISBN 0-07-047712-4, C); pap. text ed. 23.50 (ISBN 0-07-047713-2); instructor's manual 15.00 (ISBN 0-07-047714-0); study guide 12.95 (ISBN 0-07-047715-9). McGraw.

Olson, David M. The Legislative Process: A Comparative Approach. (Illus.). 1980. text ed. 20.95 scp (ISBN 0-06-044919-5, HarpC). Har-Row.

Olson, David R. & Bialystok, Ellen. Spatial Cognition: The Structure & Development of Mental Representations of Spatial Relations. 256p. 1983. text ed. price not set (ISBN 0-89859-252-6). L Erlbaum Assocs.

Olson, David V. Badges & Distinctive Insignia of the Kingdom of Saudi Arabia, Vol. I. (Illus.). 192p. (Orig.). Date not set. pap. 10.00 (ISBN 0-9609690-0-4). Olson QMD.

--Badges & Distinctive Insignia of the Kingdom of Saudi Arabia. 186p. 1981. pap. 10.00 (ISBN 0-686-84348-7). Olson QMD.

Olson, Donald. If I Don't Tell. LC 75-43768. 1976. 6.95 o.p. (ISBN 0-399-11722-9). Putnam Pub Group.

Olson, Donald E. How You Can Quit Work & Have the Money to Do It. LC 80-10201. 232p. (Orig.). 1980. pap. 14.95 (ISBN 0-936220-00-7). Rockport Pubns.

Olson, Donald S. The Secrets of Mabel Eastlake. 252p. Date not set. 13.95 (ISBN 0-89479-119-2). A & W Pubs. Postponed.

Olson, Eric, jt. ed. see Lifton, Robert J.

Olson, Esther L. & Petersen, Kenneth. No Place to Hide. 160p. (Orig.). 1982. pap. 4.95 (ISBN 0-8423-4721-6). Tyndale.

Olson, Gene. Sweet Agony: A Writing Manual of Sorts. (gr. 10 up). 1972. pap. 5.47x o.p. (ISBN 0-913366-03-X). Windyridge.

Olson, Gene, jt. auth. see Olson, Joan.

Olson, Gerald W. Soils & the Environment: A Guide to Their Applications. 191p. 1982. 33.00x (ISBN 0-412-23750-4, Pub by Chapman & Hall England); pap. 16.95x (ISBN 0-412-23760-1). Methuen Inc.

Olson, Glending. Literature as Recreation in the Later Middle Ages. 248p. 1982. 19.50x (ISBN 0-8014-1494-6). Cornell U Pr.

Olson, Harry E., Jr. Monday Morning Christianity. LC 75-2833. 128p. (Orig.). 1975. pap. 3.95 (ISBN 0-8066-1478-1, 10-4535). Augsburg.

--Physician Recruitment & the Hospital. (Illus.). 160p. (Orig.). 1980. 17.50 (ISBN 0-87258-301-5, AHA-145135). Am Hospital.

Olson, Helen Kronberg. The Strange Thing That Happened to Oliver Wendell Iscovitch. LC 82-45990. (Illus.). 96p. (gr. 1 up). 1983. PLB 8.95 (ISBN 0-396-08147-9). Dodd.

Olson, James C. J. Sterling Morton. LC 79-187430. 1972. Repr. 7.95 (ISBN 0-686-18152-2). Nebraska Hist.

--Red Cloud & the Sioux Problem. LC 65-10048. (Illus.). xii, 375p. 1965. 23.50x (ISBN 0-8032-0136-2); pap. 8.50 (ISBN 0-8032-5817-8, BB 602, Bison). U of Nebr Pr.

Olson, James S. The Ethnic Dimension in American History, 2 vols. new ed. LC 78-65207. (Illus.). 1979. Combined Ed. text ed. 18.95 o.p. (ISBN 0-312-26611-1); Combined Ed. pap. text ed. 12.95x (ISBN 0-312-26612-X); Vol. 1. pap. text ed. 8.95x (ISBN 0-312-26613-8); Vol. 2. pap. text ed. 8.95x (ISBN 0-312-26614-6). St Martin.

Olson, Jim. Michigan Environmental Law: A Citizens Guide in the 1980's. 344p. 1981. pap. 19.95 (ISBN 0-943806-01-1). Greenprint Pr.

--The Reindeer & the Easter Bunny. Van Vleck, Jane & Olson, Sally, eds. (Illus.). 18p. (Orig.). (gr. 1-4). 1981. pap. 3.95 (ISBN 0-943806-00-3). Greenprint Pr.

Olson, Joan & Olson, Gene. California Times & Trails. LC 70-160291. (Illus.). (gr. 7-12). 1971. pap. 7.47x (ISBN 0-913366-02-1). Windyridge.

--Oregon Times & Trails. LC 65-23503. (Illus.). (gr. 7-12). 1965. pap. 7.47x (ISBN 0-913366-00-5). Windyridge.

--Silver Dust & Spanish Wine: A Bilingual History of Mexico. De Gutierrez, Frances A., tr. LC 78-55885. (Illus.). (gr. 9 up). 1979. pap. text ed. 9.47x (ISBN 0-913366-05-6). Windyridge.

--Silver Dust & Spanish Wine: A History of Mexico. LC 80-51869. (Illus.). 336p. (Orig.). (gr. 9 up). 1980. pap. text ed. 7.97x (ISBN 0-913366-06-4). Windyridge.

--Washington Times & Trails. LC 75-83521. (Illus.). (gr. 7-12). 1970. pap. 7.47x (ISBN 0-913366-01-3). Windyridge.

Olson, Joanne P. & Dillner, Martha H. Learning to Teach Reading in the Elementary School: Utilizing a Competency Based Instructional System. 2nd ed. 608p. 1982. pap. text ed. 17.95 (ISBN 0-02-389300-1). Macmillan.

Olson, Joanne P., jt. auth. see Dillner, Martha H.

Olson, John. Building an HO Railroad with Personality: The Jerome & Southwestern. Hayden, Bob, ed. (Illus.). 96p. (Orig.). 1983. pap. price not set (ISBN 0-89024-042-6). Kalmbach.

Olson, John R. Secrets of Buying & Selling Collector Cars. LC 82-61130. (Illus.). 93p. 1982. pap. 6.95 (ISBN 0-933424-40-X, 1849A). Motorbooks Intl.

Olson, Keith W. Biography of a Progressive: Franklin K. Lane, 1864-1920. LC 78-57766. (Contributions in American History: No. 78). 1979. lib. bdg. 27.50 (ISBN 0-313-20613-9, OBP/). Greenwood.

Olson, Ken. The Art of Hanging Loose in an Uptight World. 2.50 o.p. (ISBN 0-686-92295-6, 6329). Hazelden.

Olson, Kenneth E. Music & Musket: Bands & Bandsmen of the American Civil War. LC 79-6195. (Contributions to the Study of Music & Dance: No. 1). (Illus.). xx, 299p. 1981. lib. bdg. 29.95 (ISBN 0-313-22112-X, OMM/). Greenwood.

Olson, Kenneth R., jt. ed. see Franta, Gregory E.

Olson, Kent W., jt. auth. see Sharp, Ansel M.

Olson, Laura K., jt. ed. see Browne, William P.

Olson, Lawrence. Costs of Children. LC 82-48173. 176p. 1982. 17.95 (ISBN 0-669-06040-2). Lexington Bks.

Olson, Lawrence, et al. The Elderly & the Future Economy. LC 81-47542. 224p. 1981. 20.95x (ISBN 0-669-04651-5). Lexington Bks.

Olson, Linus. You Can Grow Roses in Florida. (Illus.). 1978. pap. 4.95 o.p. (ISBN 0-8200-0407-3). Great Outdoors.

Olson, M. H., jt. auth. see Davis, G. B.

Olson, McKinley C., ed. J. W. Gitt's Sweet Land of Liberty. LC 73-88834. (Illus.). 226p. 1975. 9.95x (ISBN 0-89198-113-6). Ozer.

Olson, Mancur, ed. New Approach to the Economics of Health Care. 1982. 18.25 (ISBN 0-8447-2212-X); pap. 10.25 (ISBN 0-8447-2213-8). Am Enterprise.

Olson, Mancur, Jr. Logic of Collective Action: Public Goods & the Theory of Groups. rev. ed. LC 65-19826. (Economic Studies: No. 24). 1971. 9.95x o.p. (ISBN 0-674-53750-5); pap. 4.95x (ISBN 0-674-03751-0). Harvard U Pr.

Olson, Margot, jt. auth. see Forrest, Mary.

Olson, Marjorie E. Art Activities: To Encourage Perceptual Development. (gr. 1-4). 1977. 3.00x (ISBN 0-89039-130-0). Ann Arbor Pubs.

--Benji the Bug: Directionality Concepts for Children. (Illus.). 21p. (gr. k-1). 1973. pap. text ed. 3.00 (ISBN 0-89039-099-1). Ann Arbor Pubs.

--Finton the Fish: Visual Discriminations for Children. (Illus.). 29p. (gr. k-1). 1974. pap. text ed. 3.00x (ISBN 0-89039-100-9). Ann Arbor FL.

--Roxy the Robin: Sequence Relationships for Children. (Illus.). 48p. (gr. k-1). 1974. pap. text ed. 4.50 (ISBN 0-89039-126-2). Ann Arbor Pubs.

Olson, May, jt. auth. see Arndt, Karl J.

Olson, Michael L. Barai Sentence Structure & Embedding. (Language Data, Asian-Pacific Ser.: No. 3). 144p. 1973. pap. 3.00x (ISBN 0-88312-303-7); microfiche 3.00 (ISBN 0-685-48708-3). Summer Inst Ling.

Olson, Nancy B. A Manual of AACR2 Examples for Microcomputer Software & Video Games. Swanson, Edward, ed. 75p. 1983. pap. text ed. 7.00 (ISBN 0-936996-14-5). Soldier Creek.

Olson, Nancy B., ed. Cumulative Subject Index to the MARC Data Base, 1968-1978, 14 vols. 1978. Set. lib. bdg. 1444.00 (ISBN 0-8408-0250-1). Res Pubns Conn.

--Library of Congress Classification Number Index to the MARC Data Base, 1968-1978, 8 vols. 1978. lib. bdg. 720.00 (ISBN 0-8408-0275-7). Res Pubns Conn.

Olson, Natanael. Como Ganar a Tu Familia Para Cristo. Villarello, Ildefonso, tr. from Eng. 1981. pap. 1.50 (ISBN 0-311-13801-2). Casa Bautista.

Olson, Nathanael. How to Win Your Family to Christ. LC 77-81561. pap. 3.95 (ISBN 0-89107-149-0). Good News.

Olson, Philip. The Study of Modern Society: Perspectives from Classical Sociology. 1970. pap. text ed. 3.95x (ISBN 0-394-30792-5). Phila Bk Co.

Olson, Richard. Science Deified & Science Defied: The Historical Significance of Science in Western Culture from the Bronze Age to the Beginnings of the Modern Era ca. 3500 B.C. to ca. A.D. 1640. LC 82-40093. (Illus.). 375p. 1983. 32.50x (ISBN 0-520-04621-8); pap. 9.95 (ISBN 0-520-04716-8). U of Cal Pr.

Olson, Richard P., jt. auth. see Johnson, Wayne.

Olson, Robert L., ed. see Weigand, Dennis A.

Olson, Robert W. The Ba'ath & Syria: The Evolution of Ideology, Party & State. (Leaders, Politics, & Social Change in the Islamic World: No. 3). 330p. 1982. 19.00 (ISBN 0-940670-18-6). Kingston Pr.

Olson, Roberta J., et al. Studies in the History of Art 1978, Vol. 8. (Illus.). pap. 9.95 (ISBN 0-89468-050-1). Natl Gallery Art.

Olson, Ruth L., ed. Hymns & Songs for Church Schools. LC 62-13898. (Illus.). 1962. 4.25 ea. (12-1500). 25 or more 4.75 ea. Augsburg.

Olson, Sally, ed. see Olson, Jim.

Olson, Selma. Ana Mistral. LC 75-263. 242p. 1975. 6.00 o.s.i. (ISBN 0-915392-00-3); pap. 2.25 o.s.i. (ISBN 0-915392-01-1). Double M Pr.

Olson, Sherry. Baltimore. LC 76-4794. (Contemporary Metropolitan Analysis Ser.). (Illus.). 1976. pap. 8.95x (ISBN 0-88410-440-0). Ballinger Pub.

Olson, Sherry H. Baltimore: The Building of an American City. (Illus.). 432p. 1980. 22.95 (ISBN 0-686-36639-5). Md Hist.

Olson, Sigurd F. Listening Point. (Illus.). 1958. 13.95 (ISBN 0-394-43358-0). Knopf.

--Reflections from the North Country. 1976. 13.95 (ISBN 0-394-40265-0). Knopf.

Olson, Tillie. Silences. 1979. pap. 8.95 (ISBN 0-440-57798-5, Delta). Dell.

Olson, Toby. Changing Appearance. 1975. pap. 5.00 (ISBN 0-87924-021-0). Membrane Pr.

Olson, W. P., ed. Quantitative Modeling of Magnetospheric Processes. (Geophysical Monograph Ser.). 1979. 30.00 (ISBN 0-87590-021-6, GM2100). Am Geophysical.

Olson, William C. & McLellan, David S. The Theory & Practice of International Relations. 6th ed. (Illus.). 416p. 1983. pap. text ed. 14.95 (ISBN 0-13-914481-1). P-H.

Olsson, Axel A. & Harbison, Anne. Pliocene Mollusca of Southern Florida. LC 79-14175. (Academy of Naturl Sciences Monograph: No. 8). 602p. 1979. Repr. of 1953 ed. lib. bdg. 36.00 (ISBN 0-88275-980-9). Krieger.

Olsson, G. Birds in Egg - Eggs in Bird. 523p. 1980. 19.50x (ISBN 0-85086-077-6, Pub. by Pion England). Methuen Inc.

Olsson, G., jt. ed. see Gould, P.

Olsson, Kari. Sweden: A Good Life for All. Hopkins, Terry, ed. (Discovering Our Heritage Ser.). (Illus.). 112p. (gr. 5 up). 1982. PLB 9.95 (ISBN 0-87518-231-3). Dillon.

Olsson, Karl. The Santa Claus Who Really Was: The Story of Saint Nicholas. Hopkins, Terri, ed. (Holiday Bks). (Illus.). 64p. (gr. 3 up). 1983. PLB 9.95 (ISBN 0-87518-243-7). Dillon Pr.

Olsson, Karl A. Meet Me on the Patio: New Relational Bible Studies for Individuals & Groups. LC 77-72453. 1977. 7.95 (ISBN 0-8066-1550-8, 10-4301); pap. 4.50 (ISBN 0-8066-1590-7, 10-4300). Augsburg.

Olsson, Marie. Parking Discounts & Car Pool Formation in Seattle. 115p. (Orig.). 1980. pap. text ed. 3.50 (ISBN 0-87766-226-6). Urban Inst.

Olsson, Martin G., jt. auth. see Barger, Vernon D.

Olsthorn, T. N., jt. auth. see Huisman, L.

Olsvanger, Immanuel, ed. Royte Pomerantsen or How to Laugh in Yiddish. 1979. pap. 4.95 (ISBN 0-8052-0099-1). Schocken.

Olthuis, James. I Pledge You My Troth: Marriage, Family, Friendship. LC 74-25695. 160p. 1975. 5.95i (ISBN 0-06-066394-4, RD-155, HarpR). Har-Row.

Oltmanns, Thomas F., jt. auth. see Neale, John M.

Olton, D. & Noonberg, A. Biofeedback: Clinical Applications in Behavioral Medicine. 1980. 27.95 (ISBN 0-13-076315-2). P-H.

Olton, Roy, jt. auth. see Plano, Jack C.

Oltrogge, David & Rensch, Calvin. Two Studies in Middle American Comparative Linguistics. (SIL Publications in Linguistics: No. 55). 1977. 5.00x (ISBN 0-88312-068-2); microfiche 2.25x (ISBN 0-88312-474-2). Summer Inst Ling.

Olvera, Carol F. The Search. LC 79-84347. (Illus.). 191p. 1979. pap. 2.25 o.p. (ISBN 0-89877-006-8). Jeremy Bks.

--The Search. 1979. pap. 2.95 (ISBN 0-89877-006-8). Omega Pubns Or.

Olvin, Joann. High Fashion in the Gilded Age. 64p. 1982. 12.95 (ISBN 0-686-81964-0). Stemmer Hse.

Olvington, Ray. Tactics on Bass: How to Fish the 23 Most Common Bass "Hotspots". (Illus.). 320p. 1983. 19.95 (ISBN 0-686-83864-5, ScribT). Scribner.

Olwell, Carol & Waldhorn, Judith. A Gift to the Street. (Illus.). 220p. 1982. pap. 17.95 (ISBN 0-312-32713-7). St Martin.

Olyanova, Nadya. Psychology of Handwriting. (Illus.). pap. 5.00 (ISBN 0-87980-128-X). Wilshire.

O'Malia, Thomas J. Banker's Guide to Financial Statements. LC 75-37589. (Illus.). 1976. text ed. 24.50 o.p. (ISBN 0-87267-024-4). Bankers.

--Banker's Guide to Financial Statements. 2nd ed. LC 82-8786. 348p. 1982. 42.00 (ISBN 0-87267-038-4). Bankers.

O'Malley, Bert W., ed. Gene Regulation: UCLA Symposium Molecular Cellular Biology. LC 82-20709. (Vol. 26). 1982. 36.50 (ISBN 0-12-525960-3). Acad Pr.

O'Malley, C. Connor. With a Fishing Rod in Ireland. 3.50 o.p. (ISBN 0-533-01634-7). Vantage.

O'Malley, C. D., ed. The History of Medical Education. LC 72-85449. (UCLA Forum in Medical Sciences Ser.: No. 12). (Illus.). 1970. 67.50x (ISBN 0-520-01578-9). U of Cal Pr.

--Leonardo's Legacy: An International Symposium. LC 68-14976. (UCLA Center for Medieval & Renaissance Studies). (Illus.). 1968. 50.00x (ISBN 0-520-00956-8). U of Cal Pr.

O'Malley, C. D., et al, trs. see Harvey, William.

O'Malley, Charles D., tr. see Da Vinci, Leonardo.

O'Malley, J. Michael. Children's English & Services Study (Cess II) Educational Needs Assessment for Minority Language Children with Limited English Proficiency. LC 82-225233. 104p. (Orig.). 1982. pap. 13.50 (ISBN 0-89763-063-7). Natl Clearinghse Bilingual Ed.

--Children's English & Services Study (Cess I) Language Minority Children with Limited Proficiency in the United States. 96p. (Orig.). 1981. pap. 4.50 (ISBN 0-89763-057-2). Natl Clearinghse Bilingual Ed.

O'Malley, Jeanne, jt. auth. see Thompson, Terry.

O'Malley, John E., jt. auth. see Koocher, Gerald P.

O'Malley, John R. Circuit Analysis. 1980. text ed. 24.95 (ISBN 0-13-133827-7). P-H.

Oman, Carola. Lord Nelson. (Makers of History Ser). 1968. 14.50 o.p. (ISBN 0-208-00205-7, Archon). Shoe String.

Oman, Charles. The Sixteenth Century. LC 75-25517. 247p. 1976. Repr. of 1936 ed. lib. bdg. 16.25x (ISBN 0-8371-8118-6, OMSIC). Greenwood.

Oman, Charles W. Great Revolt of Thirteen Eighty One. Repr. of 1906 ed. lib. bdg. 15.50x (ISBN 0-8371-1860-3, OMGR). Greenwood.

Oman, Julia T., jt. auth. see Strong, Roy.

Omans, Glen A., jt. auth. see Kulik, William R.

O'Maolmorda, Sheila. Matthew Moss-the Man & the Artist. Moss, Matthew, tr. LC 82-72263. (Illus.). 100p. 1983. 50.00 (ISBN 0-943884-00-4). Conserv Pr.

O'Mara, W. Paul & Casazza, John A. Office Development Handbook. LC 82-50078. (Community Builders Handbook Ser.). (Illus.). 288p. 1982. text ed. 42.00 (ISBN 0-87420-607-3, OD1). Urban Land.

Omar Khayyam. The Ruba'iyat of Omar Khayyam. Kasra, Parichehr, tr. from Persian. LC 73-14964. (Unesco Collection of Representative Works, Asian Ser.). 264p. 1975. 30.00x (ISBN 0-8201-1139-2). Schol Facsimiles.

Omarr, Sydney. Sydney Omarr's Astrological Guide for You in 1982. (Orig.). 1981. pap. 2.50 o.p. (ISBN 0-451-09990-7, E9990, Sig). NAL.

--Sydney Omarr's Astrological Guide for You in 1983. 1982. pap. 2.95 (ISBN 0-451-11754-9, AE1754, Sig). NAL.

--Sydney Omarr's Astrological Revelation About You. 1973. pap. 1.25 o.p. (ISBN 0-451-05674-4, Y5674, Sig). NAL.

O May. Flow Instability During Direct Steam Generation in a Line Focus Solar Collector System. (Progress in Solar Energy Supplements SERI Ser.). 1983. pap. text ed. 7.50x (ISBN 0-89553-096-1). Am Solar Energy.

O'Meara, Carra F. The Iconography of the Facade of Saint-Gilles-Du-Gard. LC 76-23668. (Outstanding Dissertations in the Fine Arts - Medieval). (Illus.). 1977. Repr. of 1975 ed. lib. bdg. 52.00 o.s.i. (ISBN 0-8240-2717-5). Garland Pub.

O'Meara, Dominic J. Neoplatonism & Christian Thought. LC 81-5272. (Neoplatonism: Ancient & Modern Ser.). 270p. 1981. 44.50x (ISBN 0-87395-492-0); pap. 14.95x (ISBN 0-87395-493-9). State U NY Pr.

O'Meara, John, tr. see Gerald of Wales.

O'Meara, John J. The Voyage of Saint Brendan: Journey to the Promised Land. (Dolmen Texts: No. 1). (Illus.). 1978. text ed. 11.75x (ISBN 0-391-00710-6, Dolmen Pr); pap. text ed. 6.50x (ISBN 0-85105-384-X). Humanities.

O'Meara, John J., tr. see Cambrensis, Giraldus.

O'Meara, Patrick, jt. ed. see Carter, Gwendolen M.

O'Meara, Thomas F. Theology of Ministry: Charism within Culture. LC 82-60588. 1983. pap. 8.95 (ISBN 0-8091-2487-4). Paulist Pr.

O'Meara, Walter. Guns at the Forks. LC 79-4000. (Illus.). 1979. pap. 5.95 (ISBN 0-8229-5309-9). U of Pittsburgh Pr.

Omel, Myles. The Diet Chef's Gourmet Cookbook. LC 80-70958. 336p. 1983. 14.95 (ISBN 0-8119-0328-1); pap. 9.95 (ISBN 0-8119-0493-8). Fell.

Omenetto, N. Analytical Laser Spectroscopy, Vol. 50. (Chemical Analysis Ser.). 550p. 1979. 74.00 (ISBN 0-471-65371-3, 1-075). Wiley.

Omenn, Gilbert S., jt. auth. see Lave, Lester B.

Omenn, Gilbert S., jt. ed. see Ehrmann, Lee.

Omer, Salima M. Institution Building & Comprehensive Social Development. LC 82-20229. 290p. (Orig.). 1983. 22.75 (ISBN 0-8191-2870-8); pap. 11.75 (ISBN 0-8191-2871-6). U Pr of Amer.

Ominde, S. H., ed. Studies in East African Geography & Development. (Illus.). 1971. 40.00x (ISBN 0-520-02073-1). U of Cal Pr.

Ommanney, F. The Fishes. (Young Readers Library). (Illus.). 1977. PLB 6.80 (ISBN 0-8094-1377-9). Silver.

Ommanney, F. D. The Fishes. rev. ed. LC 80-52256. (Life Nature Library). PLB 13.40 (ISBN 0-8094-3871-2). Silver.

--Frogs, Toads & Newts. LC 74-9513. (Illus.). 48p. (gr. 2-7). 1974. 7.95 (ISBN 0-07-047705-1, GB). McGraw.

Ommanney, K. A. & Schanker, H. H. The Stage & the School. 5th ed. 1982. 19.52 (ISBN 0-07-047671-3). McGraw.

Ommanney, K. A. & Schanker, Harry H. Stage & the School. 4th ed. 1971. text ed. 20.24 (ISBN 0-07-047657-8, W). McGraw.

Omnes, Roland. Introduction to Particle Physics. LC 75-172471. 414p. 1972. 61.95 (ISBN 0-471-65372-1, Pub. by Wiley-Interscience). Wiley.

Omnibus Society. History of the Devon General. (Illus.). pap. 8.00x (ISBN 0-392-03243-0, SpS). Sportshelf.

Omohundro, John T. Chinese Merchant Families of Iloilo: Commerce & Kin in a Central Philippine City. (Illus.). viii, 206p. 1981. text ed. 16.95x (ISBN 0-8214-0441-5, 82-83285); pap. text ed. 8.95x (ISBN 0-8214-0619-1, 83293). Ohio U Pr.

O'Mongain, Eon & O'Toole, C. P., eds. Physics in Industry: Proceedings of an International Conference, Dublin, 1976. LC 76-17504. 1976. text ed. 88.00 (ISBN 0-08-020922-X). Pergamon.

O'More, Peggy, jt. auth. see Covert, Alice L.

Omoto, jt. ed. see Wagai.

O'Muircheartaigh, Colm A. & Payne, Clive. The Analysis of Survey Data, 2 vols. LC 76-951. 1977. Vol. 1 Exploring Data Structures. 54.95 (ISBN 0-471-01706-X); Vol. 2 Model Fitting. 54.95x (ISBN 0-471-99426-X); 109.95 set (ISBN 0-471-99466-9, Pub. by Wiley-Interscience). Wiley.

Omura, James K., jt. auth. see Viterbi, Andrew J.

Omura, Yoshiaki. Acupuncture Medicine. LC 79-1944. 1982. 27.50 (ISBN 0-87040-491-1). Japan Pubns.

Omura, Yoshiaki, et al. The Japanese Doctor's High Efficiency Diet. LC 77-94854. (Illus.). 1978. 10.00 o.p. (ISBN 0-448-16177-X, G&D). Putnam Pub Group.

Omvedt, Gail. We Will Smash This Prison! Indian Women in Struggle. 192p. 1980. 31.00 (ISBN 0-905762-44-4, Pub. by Zed Pr England); pap. 8.50 (ISBN 0-905762-45-2, Pub. by Zed Pr England). Lawrence Hill.

On, Danny & Sumner, David, photos by. Along the Trail: A Photographic Essay of Glacier National Park & the Northern Rockies. LC 79-53223. (Illus.). 1980. 20.00 (ISBN 0-913504-53-X); pap. 12.95 (ISBN 0-913504-54-8). Lowell Pr.

O'Nan, Michael. Linear Algebra. 2nd ed. LC 76-27597. (Illus.). 335p. 1977. text ed. 22.95 (ISBN 0-15-518560-8, HC); answer key avail. (ISBN 0-15-518561-6). HarBraceJ.

Once Upon A Planet, Inc. Auto Diary. (Illus.). 32p. pap. 1.25_cancelled (ISBN 0-88009-023-5). OUP.

Onclin, Willy, ed. see Vatican Council Two.

Oncoscl, M., jt. auth. see Gaspar, E.

Ondaatje, Michael. Running in the Family. 212p. 1982. 12.95 (ISBN 0-393-01637-4). Norton.

Ondarza, jt. auth. see Singer.

Ondori Publishing Co. Staff. Lovely Paper Flowers. (Ondori Handicrafts Ser). (Illus., Orig.). 1977. pap. 6.50 o.p. (ISBN 0-87040-413-X). Japan Pubns.

--Smocking. (Ondori Handicraft Ser). (Illus.). 64p. 1976. pap. 5.50 o.p. (ISBN 0-87040-367-2). Japan Pubns.

Ondori Staff. Elegant Cross-Stich Embroidery. (Illus.). 100p. (Orig.). 1983. pap. 9.50 (ISBN 0-87040-538-1). Japan Pubns.

--Embroidery & Cross-Stich for Framing. (Illus.). 100p. (Orig.). 1983. pap. 9.50 (ISBN 0-87040-537-3). Japan Pubns.

--Embroidery for Beginners. (Ondori Needlework Ser.). (Orig.). (gr. 6 up). 1978. pap. 5.50 o.p. (ISBN 0-87040-429-6). Japan Pubns.

--Huck Embroidery. LC 82-81056. (Illus.). 120p. 1982. pap. 7.50 (ISBN 0-87040-519-5). Japan Pubns.

Ondorisha. The Patchwork Pattern Book. (Illus.). 106p. 1981. 21.75 (ISBN 0-525-93211-9, 02112-630); pap. 11.50 (ISBN 0-525-47681-4, 01117-330). Dutton.

Ondov, Geraldine, jt. auth. see Grubb, Reba D.

One-Design. Encyclopedia of Sailing. rev. ed. LC 76-26223. (Illus.). 1978. 28.80i (ISBN 0-06-013292-2, HarpT). Har-Row.

One Hundred & One Productions. The Whole World Cookbook. (Illus.). 512p. 1983. pap. 14.95 (ISBN 0-686-83735-5, ScribT). Scribner.

O'Neal, Hank. Berenice Abbott: American Photographer. LC 82-9887. 256p. 1982. 59.95 (ISBN 0-07-047551-2, GB). McGraw.

O'Neal, James & Werner, G. A. American Communism: A Critical Analysis of Its Origins, Development & Programs. new & rev. ed. LC 75-138170. 416p. 1972. Repr. of 1947 ed. lib. bdg. 19.75x (ISBN 0-8371-5627-0, ONAC). Greenwood.

O'Neal, Lawrence W., jt. auth. see Levin, Marvin E.

O'Neal, Reagan. The Fallon Pride. (The Fallon Chronicles Ser.: Vol. 2). 1981. pap. 2.95 (ISBN 0-523-48002-4). Pinnacle Bks.

Oneal, Zibby. A Formal Feeling. LC 82-2018. (Illus.). 168p. (gr. 7 up). 1982. 10.95 (ISBN 0-670-32488-4). Viking Pr.

O'Neil, Barbara & Phillips, Richard. Biorhythms: How to Live with Your Life Cycles. 1975. pap. 4.95 o.p. (ISBN 0-517-53757-5, Pub. by Ward Ritchie). Crown.

O'Neil, Carol L. & Ruder, Avima. Complete Guide to Editorial Freelancing. 2nd ed. (Everyday Handbook Ser.). pap. 5.95 (ISBN 0-06-463473-6, EH 473, EH). B&N NY.

O'Neil, Charles J. Imprudence in Saint Thomas Aquinas. (Aquinas Lecture Ser.). 1955. 7.95 (ISBN 0-87462-120-8). Marquette.

O'Neil, Dennis, ed. The Secret Origins of the DC Superheroes. 1976. 10.95 o.p. (ISBN 0-517-52489-9, Harmony). Crown.

O'Neil, Edward N., ed. Teles: The Cynic Teacher. LC 76-41800. (Society of Biblical Literature. Texts & Translantion - Graeco-Roman Religion Ser.). 1977. pap. 6.00 (ISBN 0-89130-092-9, 060211). Scholars Pr Ca.

O'Neil, Gerard K. Two Thousand Eighty-One: A Hopeful View of the Human Future. 1981. 13.95 o.s.i. (ISBN 0-671-24257-1). S&S.

O'Neil, Gladys, jt. ed. see Helfrich, G. W.

O'Neil, Harold F., Jr. & Spielberger, Charles, eds. Cognitive & Affective Learning Strategies. LC 79-18162. (The Educational Technology Ser.). 1979. 27.50 (ISBN 0-12-526680-4). Acad Pr.

O'Neil, Isabel. The Art of the Painted Finish for Furniture & Decoration. LC 70-151928. (Illus.). 1980. pap. 10.95 (ISBN 0-688-06070-6). Quill NY.

O'Neil, Patrick & Trickett, Edison J. Community Consultation: Strategies for Facilitating Change in Schools, Hospitals, Prisons, Social Service Programs, & Other Community Settings. LC 82-48062. (Social & Behavioral Science Ser.). 1982. text ed. 17.95x (ISBN 0-87589-541-7). Jossey Bass.

O'Neil, Paul. The Frontiersmen. LC 76-47101. (Old West Ser.). (Illus.). (gr. 5 up). 1977. 17.28 (ISBN 0-8094-1547-X, Pub. by Time-Life). Silver.

--The Rivermen. LC 75-7193. (The Old West). (Illus.). (gr. 5 up). 1975. 17.28 (ISBN 0-8094-1498-8, Pub. by Time-Life). Silver.

O'Neil, Peter V. Introduction to Linear Algebra. 1979. text ed. 19.95x o.p. (ISBN 0-534-00606-X). Wadsworth Pub.

O'Neil, Sunny. The Gift of Christmas Past: A Return to Victorian Traditions. LC 81-14961. (Illus.). 1981. 14.95 (ISBN 0-910050-55-4). AASLH.

O'Neil, Thomas J., ed. Application of Computers & Operations Research in the Mineral Industry: 16th International Symposium. LC 79-52273. (Illus.). 651p. 1979. text ed. 33.00x (ISBN 0-89520-261-1). Soc Mining Eng.

O'Neill, Barbara T. & Foreman, George C. The Prairie Print Makers. LC 81-86587. (Illus.). 64p. (Orig.). 1982. pap. 6.00 (ISBN 0-9607978-0-7). Kansas Arts Com.

O'Neill, Bard. Armed Struggle in Palestine: A Political - Military Analysis. LC 78-2285. (Westview Special Studies on the Middle East Ser.). 1978. lib. bdg. 31.50 (ISBN 0-89158-333-5). Westview.

O'Neill, Barrett. Semi-Riemannian Geometry: With Applications to Relativity. (Pure & Applied Mathematics Ser.). 1982. 45.00 (ISBN 0-12-526740-1). Acad Pr.

O'Neill, Dan. The Collective Unconscience of Odd Bodkins. 108p. 1973. pap. 4.95 o.p. (ISBN 0-912078-33-2). Volcano Pr.

--Hear the Sound of My Feet Walking, Drown the Sound of My Voice Talking. rev. ed. LC 73-106020. (Illus.). 1971. pap. 4.95 o.p. (ISBN 0-912078-13-8). Volcano Pr.

O'Neill, Daniel. Troubadour for the Lord: The Story of John Michael Talbot. 192p. 1983. 9.95 (ISBN 0-8245-0567-0). Crossroad NY.

O'Neill, Daniel J. Menopause & Its Effects on the Family. LC 81-43827. 66p. (Orig.). 1982. lib. bdg. 16.75 (ISBN 0-8191-2499-0); pap. text ed. 5.75 (ISBN 0-8191-2500-8). U Pr of Amer.

O'Neill, Daniel J., jt. auth. see Damron, O. Rex.

O'Neill, Edward. The Rotterdam Delivery. 288p. 1975. 7.95 o.p. (ISBN 0-698-10678-4, Coward). Putnam Pub Group.

O'Neill, Eugene. Anna Christie. Bd. with The Emperor Jones; The Hairy Ape. LC 72-4211. 1973. pap. 3.95 (ISBN 0-394-71855-0, Vin). Random.

--Children of the Sea. Atkinson, Jennifer, ed. 15.00 (ISBN 0-910972-14-1); collector's ed 25.00 (ISBN 0-910972-15-X). Bruccoli.

--Chris Christophersen: A Play in Three Acts. LC 82-40135. 150p. 1982. 15.00 (ISBN 0-394-52531-0). Random.

--The Dreamy Kid. Brown, Edmund R., ed. (International Pocket Library). pap. 3.00 (ISBN 0-686-77246-6). Branden.

--Hughie. 1959. 7.50x o.p. (ISBN 0-300-00806-6); pap. 3.95 (ISBN 0-300-02881-4, Y-431). Yale U Pr.

--The Later Plays. Bogard, Travis, ed. 1967. pap. 3.25 (ISBN 0-686-38910-7, Mod LibC). Modern Lib.

--A Moon for the Misbegotten. 1962. 5.00 o.p. (ISBN 0-394-40636-2); pap. 2.95 (ISBN 0-394-71236-6). Random.

--Nine Plays of Eugene O'Neill. 9.95 (ISBN 0-394-60416-4). Modern Lib.

--The Plays of Eugene O'Neill, 3 vols. Date not set. 10.95 ea. Vol. I (ISBN 0-394-60805-4). Vol. II (ISBN 0-394-60806-2). Vol. III (ISBN 0-394-60807-0). Modern Lib.

--Seven Plays of the Sea. 199p. 1972. pap. 3.95 (ISBN 0-394-71856-9, Vin). Random.

--Touch of the Poet. 1957. 15.00x o.p. (ISBN 0-300-00809-0); pap. 4.95 (ISBN 0-300-00178-9, Y2). Yale U Pr.

--A Touch of the Poet. LC 82-48894. 180p. 1983. pap. 3.95 (Vin). Random.

O'Neill, Eugene see Brown, Edmund R.

O'Neill, Francis. The French Radical Party & European Integration. 150p. 1981. 22.50x (ISBN 0-312-30516-8). St Martin.

O'Neill, George, jt. auth. see O'Neill, Nena.

O'Neill, Gerard K. The High Frontier: Human Colonies in Space. LC 76-27860. (Illus.). 1977. 8.95 o.p. (ISBN 0-688-03133-1). Morrow.

O'Neill, Hugh E. Staff Analyst-Associate Staff Analyst. LC 82-11411. (Orig.). 1983. pap. text ed. 10.00 (ISBN 0-668-05522-7, 5522). Arco.

O'Neill, James A., Jr., jt. auth. see Dean, Richard H.

O'Neill, James M. Early American Furniture. (gr. 7 up). 1963. text ed. 16.64 (ISBN 0-87345-045-0). McKnight.

O'Neill, James Milton. Religion & Education Under the Constitution. LC 72-171389. (Civil Liberties in American History Ser). 338p. 1972. Repr. of 1949 ed. lib. bdg. 39.50 (ISBN 0-306-70228-2). Da Capo.

O'Neill, Jeanne L. The Make-It-Merry Christmas Book. LC 77-3013. (Illus.). 1979. pap. 6.95 (ISBN 0-688-08207-6). Quill NY.

O'Neill, John. For Marx Against Althusser: And Other Essays. LC 82-17353. (Current Continental Research Ser.). (Illus.). 192p. (Orig.). 1983. lib. bdg. 20.50 (ISBN 0-8191-2815-5); pap. text ed. 9.50 (ISBN 0-8191-2816-3). U Pr of Amer.

O'Neill, John, ed. Modes of Individualism & Collectivism. LC 73-86363. 1973. 24.00 (ISBN 0-312-54320-4). St Martin.

O'Neill, John J. & Oyer, Herbert J. Visual Communication for the Hard of Hearing: History, Research & Methods. 2nd ed. (Illus.). 224p. 1981. text ed. 19.95 (ISBN 0-13-942466-0). P-H.

O'Neill, John P. Metropolitan Cats. Feely, Margot & Wasserman, Rosanne, eds. LC 81-9590. (Illus.). 112p. 1981. 16.95 (ISBN 0-87099-276-7). Metro Mus Art.

O'Neill, John P., jt. auth. see Jullian, Philippe.

O'Neill, John P., ed. Clyfford Still. (Illus.). 222p. 1979. text ed. 22.50 o.s.i. (ISBN 0-87099-213-9, MPL D1965); pap. write for info. o.s.i. (ISBN 0-87099-214-7). Metro Mus Art.

O'Neill, John P., et al, eds. see Porter, Eliot.

O'Neill, Judith. Martin Luther. LC 78-56804. (Cambridge Topic Bks). (Illus.). (gr. 5-10). 1978. PLB 6.95g (ISBN 0-8225-1215-7). Lerner Pubns.

O'Neill, Lois D., ed. Women's Book of World Records & Achievements. LC 77-8296. 1979. 19.95 (ISBN 0-385-12732-4); pap. 9.95 o.p. (ISBN 0-385-12733-2). Doubleday.

O'Neill, Martha, jt. auth. see Snyder, Thomas F.

O'Neill, Martha, ed. see Chamberlain, Valerie & Kelly, Joan.

O'Neill, Martha, ed. see Martin, Diane.

O'Neill, Martha, ed. see Shank, et al.

O'Neill, Martha, ed. see Snyder, Thomas F.

O'Neill, Martha, ed. see Snyder, Thomas F. F.

O'Neill, Mary. Hailstones & Halibut Bones. LC 60-7138. (gr. k-12). 8.95a o.p. (ISBN 0-385-07911-7); PLB 8.95a (ISBN 0-385-07912-5). Doubleday.

O'Neill, Michael E., et al. Criminal Justice Planning: A Practical Approach. LC 75-40692. (Administration of Justice Ser: Vol. 4). 260p. 1976. 13.95 (ISBN 0-914526-02-2). Justice Sys.

O'Neill, Nena & O'Neill, George. Shifting Gears. 1975. pap. 2.50 o.p. (ISBN 0-380-00281-7, 50518). Avon.

O'Neill, Olivia. Dragon Star. 336p. 1983. pap. 2.95 (ISBN 0-441-16663-6, Pub. by Charter Bks). Ace Bks.

O'Neill, Onora & Ruddick, William, eds. Having Children: Philosophical & Legal Reflections on Parenthood. 1979. pap. text ed. 8.95x (ISBN 0-19-502412-5). Oxford U Pr.

O'Neill, Paul. Barnstormers & Speed Kings. (Epic of Flight Ser.). 19.96 (ISBN 0-8094-3276-5). Silver.
--The End & the Myth. LC 78-26389. (The Old West Ser.). (Illus.). 1979. 17.28 (ISBN 0-8094-2314-6). Silver.
O'Neill, Paul D. Lutyens: Country Houses. (Illus.). 168p. 1981. 19.95 (ISBN 0-8230-7361-0, Whitney Lib). Watson-Guptill.
O'Neill, R. V., jt. ed. see Shugart, H. H.
O'Neill, Richard. Suicide Squads: Axis & Allied Special Attack Weapons of World War II. LC 82-10829. (Illus.). 296p. 1982. 15.95 (ISBN 0-312-77529-6). St Martin.
O'Neill, Richard W. The Homebuyer's Guide for the 80's: A Complete Guide to Every Step You Need to Take for the Biggest & Best Investment You'll Ever Make. LC 79-56187. 1980. pap. 7.95 (ISBN 0-448-16182-6, G&D). Putnam Pub Group.
O'Neill, Robert & Markstein, Linda. American Kernel Lessons: Advanced Student's Tests. (American Kernel Lessons Ser.: Adv.). (Orig.). 1982. pap. text ed. 2.25 (ISBN 0-582-79807-8). Longman.
O'Neill, Robert see Allen, W. S.
O'Neill, Robert & Horner, D. M., eds. New Directions in Strategic Thinking. 318p. 1982. text ed. 28.50x (ISBN 0-04-355013-4). Allen Unwin.
O'Neill, Robert, et al. American Kernel Lessons: Beginning Level. (English As a Second Language Bk.). 1981. pap. text ed. 4.95x student's bk. (ISBN 0-582-79734-9); tchr's manual 4.95x (ISBN 0-582-79779-9); cassette set 1 22.95x (ISBN 0-582-79778-0); cassette set 2 43.95 (ISBN 0-582-79800-0); tapescript for lab drills 3.65x (ISBN 0-686-34403-0); student's tests 2.25x (ISBN 0-686-35696-9). Longman.
--American Kernel Lessons: Intermediate Level. (English As a Second Language Bk.). (Illus.). 1978. pap. text ed. 4.95x (ISBN 0-582-79706-3); tchr's manual 4.95 (ISBN 0-582-79707-1); students tests 2.25x (ISBN 0-582-79708-X); Set 1. cassettes 13.95 (ISBN 0-582-79715-2); Set 2. cassette 22.95x (ISBN 0-582-79716-0); Set 3. cassettes 43.95x (ISBN 0-582-79710-1); tapescript 2.75x (ISBN 0-582-79709-8). Longman.
O'Neill, Tom. Of Virgin Muses & of Love: Ugo Foscolo's "Dei Sepolcri". 240p. 1981. text ed. 32.00x (ISBN 0-7165-0099-X, Pub. by Irish Academic Pr Ireland). Biblio Dist.
O'Neill, William. A Better World-The Great Schism: Stalinism & the American Intellectuals. 1982. 17.95 (ISBN 0-671-43610-4). S&S.
O'Neill, William F. Selected Educational Heresies: A Book of Readings. 1969. pap. 9.95x (ISBN 0-673-05857-3). Scott F.
O'Neill, William L. The Great Schism: Stalinism & the American Intellectuals. (Illus.). 447p. 17.95 (ISBN 0-686-43340-8). S&S.
--The Last Romantic: A Life of Max Eastman. LC 78-249. (Illus.). 1978. 19.95x (ISBN 0-19-502405-2). Oxford U Pr.
O'Neill, William L., jt. auth. see Gardner, Lloyd C.
O'Neill, Ynez V. Speech & Speech Disorders in Western Thought Before 1600. LC 79-7361. (Contributions in Medical History: No. 3). 1980. lib. bdg. 27.50 (ISBN 0-313-21058-6, OSD/). Greenwood.
Ong, Walter J. American Catholic Crossroads: Religious-Secular Encounters in the Modern World. LC 80-29660. xi, 160p. 1981. Repr. of 1959 ed. lib. bdg. 20.50x (ISBN 0-313-22467-6, ONAM). Greenwood.
--Interfaces of the Word: Studies in the Evolution of Consciousness & Culture. LC 77-3124. 352p. 1982. pap. 8.95x (ISBN 0-8014-9240-8). Cornell U Pr.
--Orality & Literacy. 1982. 17.95x (ISBN 0-416-71370-X); pap. 7.95 (ISBN 0-416-71380-7). Methuen Inc.
Onicescu, O. Invariantive Mechanics. (International Centre for Mechanical Science Courses & Lectures Ser.: No. 218). 1975. soft cover 17.20 (ISBN 0-387-81349-7). Springer-Verlag.
Onigman, Marc. Day-by-Day in Athletics History. (Illus.). 300p. (Orig.). 1983. pap. 9.95 (ISBN 0-88011-033-3). Leisure Pr.
Onimode, B. & Osayimwese, Iz. Basic Mathematics for Economists. (Illus.). 192p. (Orig.). 1980. pap. text ed. 12.50x (ISBN 0-04-330304-8). Allen Unwin.
Onimode, Bade. Imperialism & Underdevelopment in Nigeria. 256p. 1983. 26.95 (ISBN 0-86232-108-5, Pub. by Zed Pr England); pap. 10.50 (ISBN 0-86232-109-3, Pub. by Zed Pr England). Lawrence Hill.
Onis, Harriet De see De Moratin, Leandro F.
Onishi, Hiroshi, jt. auth. see Sandell, E. B.
Onken, U., jt. auth. see Gmehling, J.
Onn, Gerald, tr. see Boudon, Philippe.
Ono, Dane R. & Williams, James D. Vanishing Fishes of North America. (Illus.). 272p. 1983. 27.50 (ISBN 0-913276-43-X). Stone Wall Pr.
Ono, K., jt. auth. see Murakami, K.
Ono, Koichi. Little Panda Bear. (Shaggies Ser.). (Illus.). 12p. (ps-2). 3.95 (ISBN 0-671-42549-8, Little Simon). S&S.
Onoda, George Y., Jr. & Hench, Larry L., eds. Ceramic Processing Before Firing. LC 77-10553. 1978. 49.95x (ISBN 0-471-65410-8, Pub by Wiley-Interscience). Wiley.
Onoh, J. K. Money & Banking in Africa. LC 82-15266. (Illus.). 256p. 1983. text ed. 35.00 (ISBN 0-582-64439-9). Longman.
Onokerhoraye, A. G. Social Services in Nigeria: An Introduction. 300p. 1983. 21.00 (ISBN 0-7103-0038-7, Kegan Paul); pap. 10.95 (ISBN 0-7103-0042-5). Routledge & Kegan.
O'Nolan, Brian see Gopaleen, Myles na, pseud.
Onorato, Michael P., ed. Origins of the Philippine Republic: Extracts from the Diaries Records of Francis Burton Harrison, No. 95. 258p. 1974. 6.50 (ISBN 0-87727-096-1). Cornell SE Asia.
Ontjes, David A. & D'Ercloe, A. Joseph. Medical Examination Review: Endocrinology, Vol. 33. 2nd ed. 1982. pap. text ed. 25.00 (ISBN 0-87488-131-5). Med Exam.
Ontjes, David A. & D'Ercole, Joseph A. Endocrinology. 2nd ed. (Medical Examination Review Books: Vol. 33). 1982. 25.00 (ISBN 0-87488-131-5). Med Exam.
Onuf, Nicholas G, ed. Law Making in the Global Community. LC 80-68078. 214p. 1982. lib. bdg. 29.95 (ISBN 0-89089-169-9). Carolina Acad Pr.
Onushkin, Victor G., tr. see International Institute for Educational Planning.
Onwuanibe, Richard C. A Critique of Revolutionary Humanism: Frantz Fanon. 400p. 1983. write for info. (ISBN 0-87527-296-7). Green.
Onwueme, I. C. The Tropical Tuber Crops: Yam, Cassava, Sweet Potato, Cocoyams. LC 77-20932. 1978. pap. 21.00x o.p. (ISBN 0-471-99607-6, Pub. by Wiley-Interscience). Wiley.
Onyejekwe, Okey. The Role of the Military in Economic & Social Development: A Comparative Regime Performance in Nigeria, 1960-1979. LC 80-8181. 300p. 1981. lib. bdg. 22.25 (ISBN 0-8191-1608-4); pap. text ed. 11.25 (ISBN 0-8191-1609-2). U Pr of Amer.
Onyenelukwe, J. C. see Barbour, K. M., et al.
Ooi, Wan H. Microbiology: A Laboratory Manual. 2nd ed. 169p. 1980. pap. text ed. 9.95x (ISBN 0-89641-014-5). American Pr.
Ooi, Wan H., jt. auth. see Fritchie, G. Edward.
Ooi Jin Bee. The Petroleum Resources of Indonesia. (Natural Resources of South-East Asia Ser.). (Illus.). 256p. 1982. 29.95 (ISBN 0-19-582527-6). Oxford U Pr.
Ooka, Diane, tr. see Takama, Shinji.
Ooka, Diane, tr. see Watanabe, Yuichi.
Ooms, Theodora, ed. Teenage Pregnancy in a Family Context: Implications for Policy. (Family Impact Seminar Ser.). 456p. 1981. 29.95 (ISBN 0-87722-204-5). Temple U Pr.
Oonk, H. A. Phase Theory: The Thermodynamics of Heterogeneous Equilibria. (Studies in Modern Thermodynamics Ser.: Vol. 3). 1982. 59.75 (ISBN 0-444-42019-3). Elsevier.
Oosterbaan, John. Population Dispersal: A National Imperative. LC 79-9672. 160p. 1980. 21.95 (ISBN 0-669-03615-3). Lexington Bks.
Oosterwal, Gottfried & Staples, Russell L. Servants for Christ: The Adventist Church Facing the 80's. vi, 162p. 1980. pap. 3.95 (ISBN 0-943872-78-2). Andrews Univ Pr.
Oosting, James Van see Van Oosting, James.
Opachak, Mark, ed. Industrial Fluids: Controls, Concerns & Costs. LC 82-60442. (Manufacturing Update Ser.). 262p. 1982. 32.00 (ISBN 0-87263-086-2). SME.
Oparil, S., et al. Renin, Vol. 4. Horrobin, D. F., ed. (Annual Research Reviews). 279p. 1980. 32.00 (ISBN 0-88831-070-6). Eden Pr.
Oparil, Suzanne. Renin, Vol. 1. 1977. 26.40 (ISBN 0-88831-000-5). Eden Pr.
Oparil, Suzanne & Katholi, Richard. Renin, Vol. 2. Horrobin, D., ed. 1978. 28.80 (ISBN 0-88831-014-5). Eden Pr.
--Renin, Vol. 3. Horrobin, D. F., ed. (Annual Research Reviews Ser.). 1979. 32.00 (ISBN 0-88831-052-8). Eden Pr.
Oparil, Suzanne, et al. Renin, Vol. 5. Horrobin, D. F., ed. (Annual Research Reviews Ser.). 368p. 1981. 38.00 (ISBN 0-88831-092-7). Eden Pr.
Opdahl, Keith. Novels of Saul Bellow: An Introduction. LC 67-16197. 1967. 14.50x (ISBN 0-271-73118-4). Pa St U Pr.
Op Den Orth, J. Odo. The Standard Biphasic-Contrast Examination of the Stomach & Duodenum. 1979. lib. bdg. 56.50 o.p. (ISBN 90-247-2159-8, Pub. by Martinus Nijhoff Netherlands). Kluwer Boston.
OPEC. Annual Statistical Bulletin, 1981. 16th ed. LC 74-640556. (Illus.). 236p. (Orig.). 1982. pap. 30.00 (ISBN 0-8002-3107-4). Intl Pubns Serv.
Opeke, Lawrence K. Tropical Tree Crops. 1982. 38.95x (ISBN 0-471-10060-9, Pub. by Wiley-Interscience); pap. 16.95x (ISBN 0-471-10066-8). Wiley.
Openshaw, Harry T. Laboratory Manual of Qualitative Organic Analysis. 3rd ed. 1955. 14.95x o.p. (ISBN 0-521-05865-1); pap. 10.95x (ISBN 0-521-29112-7). Cambridge U Pr.
Openshaw, K. Cost & Financial Accounting in Forestry. 1980. text ed. 35.00 (ISBN 0-08-021456-8); pap. text ed. 15.00 (ISBN 0-08-021455-X). Pergamon.
Opferkuch, W. & Rother, K., eds. Clinical Aspects of the Complement System. LC 78-54589. (Illus.). 266p. 1978. 32.50 o.p. (ISBN 0-88416-247-8). Wright-PSG.
Opgenoorth, Winfried & Lobe, Mira. Valerie & the Good-Night Swing. (Illus.). 32p. (ps). 1983. bds. 9.95 (ISBN 0-19-279769-7, Pub by Oxford U Pr Childrens). Merrimack Bk Serv.
Ophee, Matanya. Luigi Boccherini's Guitar Quintets - New Evidence. LC 82-181560. (Studies in Guitar History Ser.). (Illus.). 88p. (Orig.). pap. 15.00 (ISBN 0-936186-06-2). Edit Orphee.
Opie, Amelia. Elegy to the Memory of the Late Duke of Bedford; Written on the Evening of His Interment, Repr. Of 1820. Bd. with Mary Tighe (Nee Blackford) (1772-1810) Psyche: with Other Poems. 3rd ed. Repr. of 1811 ed. LC 75-31245. (Romantic Context Ser.: Poetry 1789-1830: Vol. 94). 1978. lib. bdg. 47.00 o.s.i. (ISBN 0-8240-2193-2). Garland Pub.
--Poems. Reiman, Donald H., ed. LC 75-31242. (Romantic Context Ser.: Poetry 1789-1830 Ser.). 1978. Repr. of 1802 ed. lib. bdg. 47.00 o.s.i. (ISBN 0-8240-2191-6). Garland Pub.
Opie, Iona & Opie, Peter. The Classic Fairy Tales. (Illus.). 1974. 25.00x o.p. (ISBN 0-19-211559-6). Oxford U Pr.
--Lore & Language of School Children. (Illus.). (gr. 9 up). 1959. 39.95 (ISBN 0-19-827206-5, OPB). Oxford U Pr.
Opie, Iona & Opie, Peter, eds. Oxford Nursery Rhyme Book. (Illus.). (ps-3). 1955. 25.00x (ISBN 0-19-869112-2). Oxford U Pr.
Opie, Peter, jt. auth. see Opie, Iona.
Opie, Peter, jt. ed. see Opie, Iona.
Opie, Redvers, tr. see Schumpeter, Joseph A.
Opienski, Henryk, ed. Chopin: Collected Letters. Voynich, E. L., tr. LC 79-163798. 424p. Date not set. Repr. of 1931 ed. price not set. Vienna Hse.
Opies, Redvers, tr. see Schumpeter, Joseph A.
Opik, Helgi. Respiration of Higher Plants. (Studies in Biology: No. 120). 64p. 1980. pap. text ed. 8.95 (ISBN 0-7131-2801-1). E Arnold.
Opinion Research Corporation. Implementation & Enforcement Codes of Ethics in Corporations & Associations. (Opinion Research Corporation Study Ser.: No. 65334). 256p. 1980. 17.50 (ISBN 0-686-81711-7). Ethics Res Ctr.
Oplatka, Avraham, ed. Biological Structures & Coupled Flows. (Illus.). 500p. 1982. 60.00 (ISBN 0-86689-016-5); until July 48.00 (ISBN 0-686-97312-7). Balaban Intl Sci Serv.
Opler, Morris E. Dirty Boy: A Jicarilla Tale of Raid & War. LC 39-14218. 1938. 8.00 (ISBN 0-527-00551-7). Kraus Repr.
Opolot, James S. Introduction to Modern Criminal Justice Systems. 163p. 1977. pap. text ed. 9.00 o.p. (ISBN 0-8191-0285-7). U Pr of Amer.
Oppeneer, Joan, jt. auth. see Vervoren, Thora.
Oppeneer, Joan E. & Vervoren, Thora M. Gerontological Pharmacology: A Resource for Health Practitioners. (Illus.). 208p. 1983. pap. 13.95 (ISBN 0-8016-3739-2). Mosby.
Oppenheim. Consumer Skills. rev. ed. (gr. 9-12). 1982. text ed. 15.44 (ISBN 0-87002-344-6). Bennett IL.
Oppenheim, A. K., ed. Gasdynamics of Explosions & Reactive Systems: Proceedings of the Sixth International Colloquium Held in Stockholm, Sweden, 22-26 August 1977. (Illus.). 782p. 1980. 240.00 (ISBN 0-08-025442-X). Pergamon.
Oppenheim, A. Leo, jt. auth. see Hartman, Louis F.
Oppenheim, Alan V. & Schafer, Ronald W. Digital Signal Processing. LC 74-17280. (Illus.). 608p. 1975. text ed. 31.95 (ISBN 0-13-214635-5). P-H.
Oppenheim, E. Phillips. The Great Impersonation. LC 77-20546. (Illus.). 1978. pap. 4.00 (ISBN 0-486-23607-2). Dover.
Oppenheim, Felix. Moral Principles in Political Philosophy. rev. ed. (Orig.). 1976. pap. text ed. 3.45 (ISBN 0-916074-00-5). Phila Bk Co.
Oppenheim, Irene. Consumer Skills. 1977. 13.28 o.p. (ISBN 0-87002-184-2); tchr's. guide 5.28 (ISBN 0-87002-358-6); student guide 4.84 (ISBN 0-87002-372-1). Bennett IL.
--Management of the Modern Home. 2nd ed. (Illus.). 368p. 1976. text ed. 21.95x (ISBN 0-02-389440-7). Macmillan.
Oppenheim, Irwin, et al. Stochastic Processes in Chemical Physics: The Master Equation. LC 76-27843. 1977. text ed. 30.00x (ISBN 0-262-15017-4). MIT Pr.
Oppenheim, J., jt. auth. see Beattie, J. A.
Oppenheim, Joanne. James Will Never Die. LC 82-45374. (Illus.). (gr. 1-4). 1982. PLB 9.95 (ISBN 0-396-08067-7). Dodd.
--Right on Time. Lawrence, Leslie, ed. (Skills to Grow Ser.). (Illus.). 20p. (Orig.). (gr. 2-4). 1983. 6.00 (ISBN 0-88049-012-8). Milton Bradley.
Oppenheim, Micha F. The Study & Practice of Judaism: A Selected, Annotated List. LC 79-20390. (Orig.). 1979. pap. 4.95 o.p. (ISBN 0-9603100-0-2). Torah Res.
Oppenheim, Micha F., jt. auth. see Cutter, Charles.
Oppenheim, N. Models in Urban & Regional Analysis. 1980. 28.95 (ISBN 0-13-041467-0). P-H.
Oppenheim, S. Chesterfield & Shields, Carrington. Newspapers & the Antitrust Laws. 531p. 1982. 35.00 (ISBN 0-87215-476-9). Michie-Bobbs.
Oppenheim, S. Chesterfield & Weston, Glen E., eds. The Lawyer's Robinson-Patman Act Sourcebook: Opinions of the FTC & the Courts, & Related Materials, 4 vols. 2723p. 1971. 175.00 set (ISBN 0-316-65089-7). Little.
Oppenheim, Shulamith. The Selchie's Seed. (Illus.). (gr. 8-12). 1977. pap. 1.25 o.p. (ISBN 0-380-01727-X, 34165, Camelot). Avon.
Oppenheimer, Andrea. Bruno Zevi on Modernism. (Illus.). 240p. 1983. pap. 15.95 (ISBN 0-8478-0487-9). Rizzoli Intl.
Oppenheimer, Bruce I., jt. auth. see Dodd, Lawrence D.
Oppenheimer, Carl H., ed. see Kuznetsov, S. I.
Oppenheimer, Edna, jt. auth. see Stimson, Gerry V.
Oppenheimer, Heinrich. Rationale of Punishment. LC 72-172579. (Criminology, Law Enforcement, & Social Problems Ser.: No. 167). 1975. 18.00x (ISBN 0-87585-167-3). Patterson Smith.
Oppenheimer, J., jt. auth. see Frolick, N. J.
Oppenheimer, Jack & Samuels, Herbert, eds. Molecular Basis of Thyroid Hormone Action. 1982. 58.00 (ISBN 0-12-527560-9). Acad Pr.
Oppenheimer, Joan. Gardine vs. Hanover. LC 81-43390. 160p. (gr. 5-7). 1982. 8.61i (ISBN 0-690-04190-X, TYC-J); PLB 8.89g (ISBN 0-690-04191-8). Har-Row.
--Working on It. (YA) (gr. 7-12). 1983. pap. 2.25 (ISBN 0-440-99514-0, LFL). Dell.
Oppenheimer, Joel. At Fifty. Bayes, Ronald H., ed. LC 82-61230. 80p. (Orig.). 1982. pap. 9.95 (ISBN 0-932662-39-0). St Andrews NC.
--Marilyn Lives. (Illus.). 128p. (Orig.). 1981. pap. 8.95 (ISBN 0-933328-02-8). Delilah Bks.
Oppenheimer, Lillian & Epstein, Natalie. Decorative Napkin Folding for Beginners. (Illus.). 1980. pap. 1.95 (ISBN 0-486-23797-4). Dover.
Oppenheimer, Lillian, jt. auth. see Lewis, Shari.
Oppenheimer, Oscar. God & Man. LC 79-64099. 1979. pap. text ed. 9.75 (ISBN 0-8191-0753-0). U Pr of Amer.
Oppenheimer, Richard, ed. see Schuyler, Arlene A.
Oppenheimer, S. L. & Borchers. Direct & Alternating Currents. 2nd ed. 1973. text ed. 24.95 (ISBN 0-07-047665-9, G); solutions manual 2.95 (ISBN 0-07-047666-7). McGraw.
Oppenheimer, Samuel. Semiconductor Logic & Switching Circuits. 2nd ed. LC 72-92573. 1973. text ed. 24.95x (ISBN 0-675-09016-4). Additional supplements may be obtained from publisher. Merrill.
Oppenheimer, Samuel L., ed. see Tocci, Ronald J.
Oppenheimer, Samuel P. Directing Construction for Profit: Business Aspects of Contracting. 34.95 (ISBN 0-07-047646-2, P&RB). McGraw.
Oppenheimer, Valerie. Work & the Family: A Study in Social Demography. (Stuides in Population Ser.). 1982. 34.00 (ISBN 0-12-527580-3). Acad Pr.
Oppenheimer, Valerie K. The Female Labor Force in the United States: Demographic & Economic Factors Governing its Growth & Changing Composition. (Population Monograph Ser.: No. 5). xii, 197p. 1976. pap. text ed. 6.95 (ISBN 0-8371-9408-3, OPL/). Greenwood.
Oppenheimer-Bluhm, Hilde. Standard of Living of German Labor Under Nazi Rule. (Social Research Suppl.: No. 5). 1943. pap. 6.00 (ISBN 0-527-00865-6). Kraus Repr.
Oppenhiem, J. J. & Rosenstreich, D. L., eds. Cellular Functions in Immunity & Inflammation. 1981. 42.50 (ISBN 0-444-00554-4). Elsevier.
Opperman, Alfred. Dictionary of Electronics. 692p. (Eng. & Ger.). 1980. 120.00x (ISBN 0-686-98305-X, K G Saur). Gale.
Opperman, Hal. Jean-Baptiste Oudry Sixteen Eighty-Six to Seventeen Fifty-Five. 250p. (Orig.). 1983. 50.00 (ISBN 0-912804-11-4); pap. 24.95 (ISBN 0-912804-12-2). Kimbell Art.
Opperman, Hal N. Jean-Baptiste Oudry (Sixteen Eighty-Six to Seventeen Fifty-Five) LC 76-23674. (Outstanding Dissertations in the Fine Arts Ser.). 1977. lib. bdg. 133.00 o.s.i. (ISBN 0-8240-2718-3). Garland Pub.
Oppermann, Alfred, ed. Dictionary of Modern Engineering, 2 vols. 3rd ed. Incl. Vol. 1. English-German. 912p. 1972. 80.00 (ISBN 3-7940-6001-6); Vol. 2. German-English. 952p. 1974. 80.00 (ISBN 3-7940-6002-4). 160.00x set (ISBN 3-7940-6003-2, Pub. by K G Saur). Gale.
Oppliger, Jeannie, ed. see Eckols, Steve.
Oppong, C., ed. Female & Male in West Africa. 280p. 1983. text ed. 35.00x (ISBN 0-04-301158-6); pap. text ed. 12.50x (ISBN 0-04-301159-4). Allen Unwin.
Opsahl, Paul D. The Holy Spirit in the Life of the Church: From Biblical Times to the Present. LC 77-84099. 1978. pap. 10.95 (ISBN 0-8066-1625-3, 10-3160). Augsburg.
Opschoor, A. Conformations of Polyethylene & Polypropylene. 78p. 1970. 20.00x (ISBN 0-677-61220-6). Gordon.
Optner, Ruth L. Writing from the Inside Out. 1977. pap. text ed. 12.50 scp (ISBN 0-06-044928-4, HarpC); instructor's manual avail. (ISBN 0-06-364930-6). Har-Row.
Optner, Stanford L. Systems Analysis for Business Management. 3rd ed. (Illus.). 400p. 1974. ref. ed. 21.95 (ISBN 0-13-881276-4). P-H.
Oputa, C. A. Conduct at the Bar & the Unwritten Law of the Legal Profession. LC 81-85780. xiv, 69p. 1982. Repr. of 1976 ed. lib. bdg. 17.50x (ISBN 0-912004-20-7). W W Gaunt.
--Modern Bar Advocacy. LC 81-85779. xix, 224p. 1982. Repr. of 1973 ed. lib. bdg. 30.00x (ISBN 0-912004-19-3). W W Gaunt.

O'Quinn, Aglaia N., jt. auth. see Thompson, Robert J., Jr.

O'Quinn, J. Frank, ed. Jesus' Lost Gospels: The Discovery at Nag Hammadi. (Illus.). 48p. 1981. pap. text ed. 6.95 (ISBN 0-9609802-0-2). Life Science.

O'Quinn, John, ed. see Lindsay, Jack.

O'Quinn, John, ed. see Ostrander, Sheila & Schroeder, Lynn.

O'Quinn, John F. Urine Therapy: Self-Healing Through Intrinsic Medicine. 40p. 1980. pap. text ed. 6.95 (ISBN 0-9609802-1-0). Life Science.

Oquist, Paul. Violence, Conflict, & Politics in Colombia. LC 79-6778. (Studies in Social Discontinuity Ser.). 1980. 27.50 (ISBN 0-12-527750-4). Acad Pr.

Orage, Alfred R. Psychological Exercises & Essays. LC 72-181083. pap. 2.25 (ISBN 0-87728-265-X). Weiser.

Orage, Alfred R., tr. see Gurdjieff, G. I.

Oram, R. B. Cargo Handling in a Modern Port. 1964. 29.00 o.p. (ISBN 0-08-011306-0); pap. 14.00 o.p. (ISBN 0-08-011305-2). Pergamon.

Oran, Daniel. Oran's Dictionary of the Law. New ed. (Illus.). 512p. 1982. pap. 9.95 (ISBN 0-314-68800-5). West Pub.

Orange, Anne. The Flower Book. LC 74-12743. (The Early Nature Picture Bks). (Illus.). 32p. (gr. k-3). 1975. PLB 4.95g (ISBN 0-8225-0294-1). Lerner Pubns.

--The Leaf Book. LC 74-12745. (The Early Nature Picture Bks). (Illus.). 32p. (gr. k-3). 1975. PLB 4.95g (ISBN 0-8225-0296-8). Lerner Pubns.

Orange County Assoc. Frases Fundamentales para Comunicarse. (gr. k-12). 1975. 3.75 (ISBN 0-89075-200-1). Crane Pub Co.

Orange, Richard A., Jr., jt. auth. see North, Robert J.

Orasanu, Judith, et al, eds. Language, Sex & Gender. (Annals of the New York Academy of Sciences: Vol. 327). (Orig.). 1979. pap. 22.00x (ISBN 0-89766-022-6). NY Acad Sci.

Oratio, A. Supervision in Speech Pathology. 168p. 1977. pap. 16.95 (ISBN 0-8391-1113-4). Univ Park.

Orazem, Frank, jt. auth. see Doll, John P.

Orbaan, Albert. Rare & Rugged Sports. new ed. (Illus.). 128p. (gr. 6-12). 1973. PLB 4.97 o.p. (ISBN 0-399-60808-7). Putnam Pub Group.

Orbach, Michael K. Hunters, Seamen & Entrepreneurs: The Tuna Seinermen of San Diego. LC 76-48361. (Illus.). 1978. 23.50x (ISBN 0-520-03348-5). U of Cal Pr.

Orbach, Michael K., jt. auth. see Maiolo, John.

Orbach, Ruth. Acorns & Stew. LC 76-1001. (Illus.). (ps-3). 1976. 5.95 o.p. (ISBN 0-529-05286-5, A4654, Philomel). Putnam Pub Group.

--Apple Pigs. (Peppercorn Book Ser.). (Illus.). (gr. 1-4). 1981. pap. 3.95 (ISBN 0-399-20797-X, Philomel). Putnam Pub Group.

--Apple Pigs. LC 76-40472. (Illus.). (ps-3). 1977. 6.95 (ISBN 0-529-05332-2, Philomel). Putnam Pub Group.

--Please Send a Panda. LC 77-20140. (Illus.). (ps-3). 1978. 6.95 o.s.i. (ISBN 0-00-183748-6, Philomel). Putnam Pub Group.

Orbach, Susie, jt. auth. see Eichenbaum, Luise.

Orbeliani, Sulkhan-Saba. The Book of Wisdom & Lies. Vivian, Katherine, tr. 1982. 14.95 (ISBN 0-686-37151-8, Pub. by Octagon Pr England). Ins Study Human.

Orben, Bob. Two Thousand New Laughs for Speakers. pap. 4.00 (ISBN 0-87980-382-7). Wilshire.

Orben, Robert. Twenty-One Hundred Laughs for All Occasions. LC 82-45448. 240p. 1983. 13.95 (ISBN 0-385-18248-1). Doubleday.

--Two Thousand Five Hundred Jokes to Start 'em Laughing. LC 78-22538. 1979. 11.95 (ISBN 0-385-14412-1). Doubleday.

Orchard, D. B. & Longstaff, R. W., eds. J. J. Griesbach. LC 77-27405. (Society for New Testament Studies Monographs: No. 34). 1979. 29.95 (ISBN 0-521-21706-7). Cambridge U Pr.

Orchard, D. F. Concrete Technology, 2 vols. 1979. Vol. 1: Properties of Materials. 45.00 (ISBN 0-85334-794-8, Pub. by Applied Sci England); Vol. 2: Practice. 47.25 (ISBN 0-85334-837-5). Elsevier.

--Concrete Technology, Vol. 2. rev. 3rd ed. LC 72-13145. 1973. 49.95x o.p. (ISBN 0-470-65539-9). Halsted Pr.

Orchin, Milton & Jaffe, H. H. Symmetry, Orbitals, & Spectra. LC 76-136720. 1971. 42.50x (ISBN 0-471-65550-3, Pub. by Wiley-Interscience). Wiley.

Orchin, Milton M., jt. auth. see Jaffe, H. H.

Orcutt, Georgia, ed. The Gardener's Advisor. LC 82-50960. (Illus.). 144p. (Orig.). 1983. pap. 8.95 (ISBN 0-911658-41-6). Yankee Bks.

Orcutt, William D. The Stradivari Memorial. LC 76-58561. (Music Reprint Series). 1977. Repr. of 1978 ed. lib. bdg. 16.50 (ISBN 0-306-70865-5). Da Capo.

Orczy, Baroness. Leatherface: A Tale of Old Flanders. 391p. 1982. Repr. of 1916 ed. lib. bdg. 20.00 (ISBN 0-89987-630-7). Darby Bks.

Orczy, Emmuska. The League of the Scarlet Pimpernel. 238p. 1981. Repr. lib. bdg. 16.95 (ISBN 0-89966-286-2). Buccaneer Bks.

--The Scarlet Pimpernel. 256p. (RL 7). 1974. pap. 2.50 (ISBN 0-451-51762-8, CE1762, Sig Classics). NAL.

Ord, J. K., jt. auth. see Cliff, A. D.

Ordang, Laurence. The Bantam Medical Dictionary. 464p. 1982. pap. 4.95 (ISBN 0-553-22673-8). Bantam.

Ordaz, Luis, jt. auth. see Neglia, Erminio.

Orde, Lewis. Heritage. 1982. pap. 3.75 (ISBN 0-8217-1100-8). Zebra.

Orde, Lewis & Michaels, Bill. The Night They Stole Manhattan. LC 79-25392. 1980. 11.95 (ISBN 0-399-12489-6). Putnam Pub Group.

Orden, Naola Van see Van Orden, Naola & Steed, S. Paul.

Ordeshook, Peter C., ed. Game Theory & Political Science. LC 78-53028. (Studies in Game Theory & Mathematical Economics). 1978. 32.50x o.p. (ISBN 0-8147-6156-9). NYU Pr.

Ord-Hume, Arthur W. Perpetual Motion: The History of an Obsession. LC 76-10560. 1977. 15.00 o.p. (ISBN 0-312-60131-X). St Martin.

Ordish, George, tr. see Metraux, Alfred.

Ordish, Olive. Dancing & Ballet. (Local Search Ser.). (Illus.). (gr. 3-8). 1978. 9.50 o.p. (ISBN 0-7100-8880-9). Routledge & Kegan.

--Dress & Fashion. (Local Search Ser.). (Illus.). 1974. 7.95 o.p. (ISBN 0-7100-7790-4). Routledge & Kegan.

--The Theatre. (Local Search Ser.). (Illus.). 1972. 8.95 (ISBN 0-7100-7223-6). Routledge & Kegan.

Ordish, Olive, tr. see Abel, Wilhelm.

Ordman, Kathryn A. & Ralli, Mary P. What People Say. 5th ed. LC 76-6143. 1976. pap. text ed. 7.75 (ISBN 0-88200-073-X, B0990). Alexander Graham.

Ordon, Edmund, ed. Ten Contemporary Polish Stories. LC 74-2842. 252p. 1974. Repr. of 1958 ed. lib. bdg. 16.25x (ISBN 0-8371-7436-8, ORPS). Greenwood.

Ordonez, Francisco. Del Odio Al Amor. 1980. pap. 1.50 (ISBN 0-311-08223-8). Casa Bautista.

--Repertorio de Navidad. 80p. 1982. pap. 1.75 (ISBN 0-311-08211-4). Casa Bautista.

Ord-Smith, R. J. & Stephenson, J. Computer Simulation of Continous Systems. LC 74-12957. (Computer Science Texts Ser.: No. 3). (Illus.). 300p. 1975. pap. text ed. 18.95x (ISBN 0-521-09872-6). Cambridge U Pr.

Ordway, jt. auth. see Tosh.

Ordway, Frederick I. & Sharpe, Mitchell R. The Rocket Team. LC 78-3313. (Illus.). 1979. 15.34i (ISBN 0-690-01656-5). T Y Crowell.

Ordway, Frederick I., III, jt. auth. see Von Braun, Wernher.

Ordway, Frederick I., 3rd. Pictorial Guide to the Planet Earth. LC 74-34291. (Illus.). 256p. 1975. 12.95i (ISBN 0-690-62193-0); pap. o.p. (ISBN 0-690-01675-1). T Y Crowell.

Ordway, Frederick I., 3rd, jt. auth. see Von Braun, Wernher.

Ordway, Frederick I., 3rd, ed. Advances in Space Science & Technology, Vols. 1-11. Incl. Vols. 1-7. 1959-65. 64.00 ea. Vol. 1 (ISBN 0-12-037301-7). Vol. 2. o.p. (ISBN 0-12-037302-5). Vol. 3 (ISBN 0-12-037303-3). Vol. 4 (ISBN 0-12-037304-1). Vol. 5. o.p. (ISBN 0-12-037305-X). Vol. 6 (ISBN 0-12-037306-8). Vol. 7 (ISBN 0-12-037307-6); Vol. 8. 1966. 64.00 (ISBN 0-12-037308-4); Vol. 9. 1967. 64.00 (ISBN 0-12-037309-2); Vol. 10. 1970. 64.00 (ISBN 0-12-037310-6); Vol. 11. 1972. 74.50 (ISBN 0-12-037311-4); Suppl. 1. Space Carrier Vehicles: Design, Development & Testing of Launching Rockets. Lange, O. H. & Stein, R. J. 1963. 57.00 (ISBN 0-12-037361-0); Suppl. 2. Lunar & Planetary Surface Conditions. Weil, N. A. 1965. 57.00 (ISBN 0-12-037362-9). Acad Pr.

Ordway, Gerald L., jt. auth. see Druley, Ray M.

Ordway, Nicholas, jt. auth. see Friedman, Jack.

Ordway, Nicholas, jt. auth. see Hinds, Dudley.

Ordway, Richard. Earth Science & the Environment. Orig. Title: Introduction to Earth Science. 448p. 1974. pap. text ed. 14.95x (ISBN 0-442-26295-7). Van Nos Reinhold.

Ordy, J. Mark & Brizzee, Ken, eds. Sensory Systems & Communication in the Elderly. LC 79-65426. (Aging Ser.: Vol. 10). 334p. 1979. text ed. 35.00 (ISBN 0-89004-235-7). Raven.

Ore, Oystein. Invitation to Number Theory. LC 67-20607. (New Mathematical Library: No. 20). 1975. pap. 7.50 (ISBN 0-88385-620-4). Math Assn.

--Niels Hendrik Abel, Mathematician Extraordinary. LC 73-14693. (Illus.). viii, 277p. 1974. Repr. of 1957 ed. text ed. 13.95 (ISBN 0-8284-0274-4). Chelsea Pub.

--Number Theory & Its History. (Illus.). 1948. text ed. 15.95 o.p. (ISBN 0-07-047675-6, C). McGraw.

Orear, Jay. Physics. (Illus.). 1979. text ed. 31.95 (ISBN 0-02-389460-1); instrs'. manual avail. Macmillan.

O'Reilly, Edward. Brown Pelican at the Pond. LC 78-58689. (gr. k-4). 1979. 6.95 (ISBN 0-931644-01-1). Manzanita Pr.

O'Reilly, Jane. The Girl I Left Behind. 240p. 1982. pap. 3.50 (ISBN 0-553-20202-2). Bantam.

O'Reilly, John, ed. Observers for Linear Systems: Mathematics Science & Engineering. Date not set. price not set (ISBN 0-12-527780-6). Acad Pr.

O'Reilly, Kenneth. Hoover & the Un-Americans: The FBI, HUAC & the Red Menace. write for info. (ISBN 0-87722-301-7). Temple U Pr.

O'Reilly, P H & Shields. Nuclear Medicine in Urology & Nephrology. (Illus.). 1979. text ed. 49.95 (ISBN 0-407-00151-4). Butterworth.

O'Reilly, Peter, tr. see Maritain, Jacques.

O'Reilly, Robert C. & Green, Edward T. School Law for the Practitioner. LC 82-11982. (Contributions to the Study of Education Ser.: No. 6). (Illus.). 320p. 1983. lib. bdg. 35.00 (ISBN 0-313-23639-9, ORS/). Greenwood.

O'Reilly, Sean. In the Image of God. 92p. 1982. 2.95 (ISBN 0-8198-3607-9, MS0308); pap. 1.95 (ISBN 0-8198-3608-7). Dghtrs St Paul.

O'Reilly, Timothy. Frank Herbert. LC 80-5345. (Recognitions Ser.). 200p. 1981. 11.95 (ISBN 0-8044-2666-X); pap. 5.95 (ISBN 0-8044-6617-3). Ungar.

Orel, Harold, ed. Kipling: Interviews & Recollections, Vol. 1 & 2. LC 82-1724. (Interviews & Recollections Ser.). 1983. Vol. 1, 421p. text ed. 26.50x (ISBN 0-389-20275-4); Vol. 2, 437p. text ed. 26.50x (ISBN 0-389-20276-2). B&N Imports.

Orellana, Ramon, tr. see Ferguson, Charles W., et al.

Orellana, Ramon S., tr. see Nims, Bonnie.

O'Relley, Z. Edward. Soviet-Type Economic Systems: A Guide to Information Sources. LC 73-17583. (Economics Information Guide Ser.: Vol. 12). 1978. 42.00x (ISBN 0-8103-1306-5). Gale.

Orelli, Hans C. von. The Prophecies of Jeremiah. 1977. 15.25 (ISBN 0-86524-102-3, 2401). Klock & Klock.

--The Twelve Minor Prophets. 1977. 15.50 (ISBN 0-86524-114-7, 7001). Klock & Klock.

O'Relly, Edward. Sexercises: Isometric & Isotonic. 1967. 4.95 o.p. (ISBN 0-517-08320-5). Crown.

Orem, Dorothea E. Nursing Concepts of Practice. 2nd ed. (Illus.). 1980. pap. text ed. 14.95 (ISBN 0-07-047718-3). McGraw.

Orem, J. & Barnes, C. D., eds. Physiology in Sleep. (Research Topics in Physiology Ser.). 1981. 39.50 (ISBN 0-12-527650-8). Acad Pr.

Orem, R. C. & Coburn, Marjorie F. Montessori: Prescriptions for Children with Learning Disabilities. LC 77-17687. 1978. 8.95 (ISBN 0-399-11802-0). Putnam Pub Group.

Oremland, Evelyn K. & Oremland, Jerome D. Sexual & Gender Development of Young Children: The Role of the Educator. LC 77-5005. 352p. 1977. prof ref 22.50x (ISBN 0-88410-169-X). Ballinger Pub.

Oremland, Jerome D., jt. auth. see Oremland, Evelyn K.

Oren, John W., jt. auth. see Brown, Ronald.

Oren, O. H., ed. Aquaculture of Grey Mullets. LC 79-53405. (International Biological Programme: No. 26). (Illus.). 450p. 1981. 130.00 (ISBN 0-521-22926-X). Cambridge U Pr.

Oren, Tuncer J., ed. Annotated Bibliographies of Simulation. (SCS Simulation Ser.: Vol. 4, No. 1). 30.00 (ISBN 0-686-36666-2). Soc Computer Sim.

Orenstein, Alex. Existence & the Particular Quantifier. LC 78-14515. (Philosophical Monographs: Second Annual Ser.). 203p. 1978. 24.95 (ISBN 0-87722-130-8); pap. 14.95 (ISBN 0-87722-126-X). Temple U Pr.

--Willard Van Orman Quine. (World Leaders Ser.: No. 15). 1977. lib. bdg. 14.95 o.p. (ISBN 0-8057-7716-4, Twayne). G K Hall.

Orenstein, Jeffrey R., jt. auth. see Fowler, Robert B.

Oresko, Robert, ed. The Works in Architecture of Robert & James Adam. (Academy Architecture Ser.). (Illus.). 184p. 1982. pap. 19.95 o.p. (ISBN 0-312-88954-2). St Martin.

Oresme, Nicole, ed. De proportionibus proportionum. Grant, Edward, tr. Bd. with Ad pauca respicientes. (Medieval Science Publications Ser.). (Illus.). 488p. 1966. 50.00x (ISBN 0-299-04000-3). U of Wis Pr.

Orfalea, Greg. Pictures at an Exhibition. 3.00 o.p. (ISBN 0-686-74490-X). Confluence Pr.

Orff, Carl. The Schulwerk, Vol. 3. Murray, Margaret, tr. from Ger. (Carl Orff Documentation Ser.). 1978. pap. 16.45 (ISBN 0-930448-06-5, 70-00065). Eur-Am Music.

Orfield, Gary. Must We Bus? Segregated Schools & National Policy. 1978. 26.95 (ISBN 0-8157-6638-6); pap. 11.95 (ISBN 0-8157-6637-8). Brookings.

Orfield, Gary, jt. auth. see Ford Foundation.

Orfield, Lester B. Amending of the Federal Constitution. LC 74-146151. (American Constitutional & Legal History Ser). (Illus.). 1971. Repr. of 1942 ed. lib. bdg. 29.50 (ISBN 0-306-70094-8). Da Capo.

Orfila, Alejandro. The Americas in the Nineteen Eighties: An Agenda for the Decade Ahead. LC 80-5935. 166p. 1980. lib. bdg. 19.00 (ISBN 0-8191-1333-6); pap. text ed. 9.25 (ISBN 0-8191-1334-4). U Pr of Amer.

Orford, Jim & Edwards, Griffith. Alcoholism: A Comparison of Treatment & Advice, with a Study of the Influence of Marriage. (Maudsley Monographs: No. 26). (Illus.). 1978. text ed. 24.95x (ISBN 0-19-712148-9). Oxford U Pr.

Orford, Jim, jt. auth. see Otto, Shirley.

Orford, Jim & Harwin, Judith, eds. Alcohol & the Family. LC 82-50090. 304p. 1982. 29.95 (ISBN 0-312-01706-5). St Martin.

Orga, Ates. Beethoven: His Life & Times. expanded ed. (Life & Times Ser.). (Illus.). 208p. 1980. Repr. of 1978 ed. 12.95 (ISBN 0-87666-646-2, Z-45). Paganiniana Pubns.

--Chopin: His Life & Times. expanded ed. (Life & Times Ser.). (Illus.). 176p. 1980. Repr. of 1976 ed. 12.95 (ISBN 0-87666-644-6, Z-43). Paganiniana Pubns.

Orga, Ates, ed. Records & Recording Classical Guide 1978. 1978. pap. 5.95 o.p. (ISBN 0-8467-0450-1, Pub. by Two Continents). Hippocrene Bks.

Organ, Troy W. Hindu Quest for the Perfection of Man. LC 73-81450. x, 439p. 1981. pap. 12.00x (ISBN 0-8214-0575-6, 82-80729). Ohio U Pr.

--Western Approaches to Eastern Philosophy. LC 75-14554. 282p. 1975. 15.00x (ISBN 0-8214-0194-7, 82-81974). Ohio U Pr.

Organic Gardening & Farming Editors. Organic Plant Protection. Yepsen, Roger, ed. LC 75-43829. 1976. 18.95 (ISBN 0-87857-110-8). Rodale Pr Inc.

Organic Gardening & Farming Magazine, ed. Encyclopedia of Organic Gardening. LC 77-25915. 1978. 24.95 (ISBN 0-87857-225-2). Rodale Pr Inc.

Organic Gardening & Farming Staff & Editors. Nuts & Seeds, the Natural Snacks. LC 72-93742. 1973. pap. 3.95 o.p. (ISBN 0-87857-064-0). Rodale Pr Inc.

Organick, E. I. A Programmer's View of the Intel 432 System. 432p. 1983. 29.95 (ISBN 0-07-047719-1, P&RB). McGraw.

Organick, Elliot I. The Multics System: An Examination of Its Structure. 1972. 30.00x (ISBN 0-262-15012-3). MIT Pr.

Organick, Elliot I. & Meissner, Loren P. Fortran Four: Standard Fortran Watfor-Watfiv. 1975. text ed. 18.95 (ISBN 0-201-05503-1). A-W.

Organick, Elliot I., jt. auth. see Meissner, Loren P.

Organisation for Economic Co-Operation & Development. Biotechnology-International Trends & Perspectives. 84p. (Orig.). 1982. pap. 11.00x (ISBN 92-64-12362-8). OECD.

Organization for Economic Cooperation & Development. The Automobile & the Environment: An International Perspective. Gakenheimer, Ralph, compiled by. (Transportation Studies Ser.). 1978. 47.50x (ISBN 0-262-07070-7). MIT Pr.

Organization of American States. Copyright Protection in the Americas, 2 vols. 1979. looseleaf 150.00 (ISBN 0-379-20675-7); 75.00 ea. Oceana.

--Index to Latin American Periodical Literature, 1929-1960, 8 Vols. 1962. Set. 520.00 (ISBN 0-8161-0501-4, Hall Library). G K Hall.

--Index to Latin American Periodical Literature 1966-1970. 1980. lib. bdg. 190.00 (ISBN 0-8161-0314-3, Hall Library). G K Hall.

--Index to Latin American Periodical Literature, 1961-1965, 2 Vols. 1967. Set. 125.00 (ISBN 0-8161-0768-8, Hall Library). G K Hall.

--Index to Latin American Periodicals Literature, 2 vols. Set. 85.00 (Hall Library). Vol. 1, 1961 (ISBN 0-8161-0502-2). Vol. 2, 1962. 78.00 (ISBN 0-8161-0236-8). G K Hall.

--Mining & Petroleum Legislation. LC 78-16150. (Binder 1 & supplement). 1978. perfect binder 100.00 (ISBN 0-379-20381-2); Vol. 1. 75.00; Release 1 & 2. 35.00 ea. Oceana.

Organos, Minnie, ed. Catalog of the Dental School Library, 8 vols. 1978. Set. lib. bdg. 720.00 (ISBN 0-8161-0239-2, Hall Library). G K Hall.

Orgel, Doris. Lohengrin. (Opera Stories for Young People). (Illus.). (gr. 2-6). 1966. PLB 4.89 o.p. (ISBN 0-399-60426-X). Putnam Pub Group.

Orgel, L. E. The Origins of Life: Molecules & Natural Selection. LC 72-10534. 144p. 1973. 13.95 (ISBN 0-471-65693-3). Wiley.

Orgel, Leslie E., jt. auth. see Miller, Stanley L.

Orgel, Michael, jt. auth. see Adams, Sallie.

Orgel, Stephen. The Illusion of Power. LC 73-80827. (Quantum Bks). (Illus.). 1975. 19.50x (ISBN 0-520-02505-9); pap. 6.25x (ISBN 0-520-02741-8). U of Cal Pr.

Orgel, Stephen, jt. ed. see Clark, James D.

Orgel, Stephen, ed. see Conti, Natale & Tritonio, Antonio M.

Orgel, Stephen, ed. see Gordon, P. J.

Orgel, Stephen, ed. see May, Thomas.

Orgel, Stephen, ed. see Menestrier, Claude.

Orgel, Stephen, ed. see Metz, J. C.

Orgel, Stephen, ed. see Richardson, George.

Orgel, Stephen, ed. see Vaenius, Otho V.

Orgel, Stephen, ed. see Waleys, Thomas.

Orgill, Douglas & Gribbin, John. Brother Esau. (Bessie Bks.). 224p. 1983. 14.37i (ISBN 0-06-039016-6, HarpT). Har-Row.

--The Sixth Winter. 1980. 10.95 o.p. (ISBN 0-671-25016-7). S&S.

Orgill, Michael. Anchored in Love. 1976. pap. write for info (ISBN 0-515-09624-5). Jove Pubns.

Orgill, Michael, et al. Mind Angel & Other Stories. Elwood, Roger, ed. LC 73-21480. (Science Fiction Bks). 48p. (gr. 4-8). 1974. PLB 3.95g (ISBN 0-8225-0958-X). Lerner Pubns.

Orians, Gordon & Angell, Tony. Four & Twenty Blackbirds. 1983. write for info. U of Wash Pr.

Orians, Gordon, jt. auth. see Purves, William.

Oriel. Infection by Chlamydia Trachomatis. 1982. 22.00 (ISBN 0-444-00700-8). Elsevier.

Orieux, Jean. Voltaire. Bray, Barbara & Lane, Helen, trs. LC 74-25095. (Illus.). 1979. 15.95 o.p. (ISBN 0-385-08567-2). Doubleday.

Origen. Homilies on Genesis & Exodus. Heine, Ronald E., tr. from Lat. LC 82-4124. (Fathers of the Church Ser.: Vol. 71). 1982. 24.95t (ISBN 0-8132-0071-7). Cath U Pr.

Original Publications, tr. from Span. Helping Yourself With Selected Prayers. pap. 3.95 (ISBN 0-942272-01-3). Original Pubns.

Origo, Iris. Images & Shadows: Part of a Life. LC 79-134574. (Helen & Kurt Wolff Bk). 1971. 8.50 o.p. (ISBN 0-15-144101-4). HarBraceJ.

Orilia, Lawrence. Introduction to Business Data Processing. 1979. text ed. 21.95 (ISBN 0-07-047830-9, C); study guide 10.95 (ISBN 0-07-047833-3); instr's. manual 11.00 (ISBN 0-07-047831-7); test files 7.95 (ISBN 0-07-047832-5). McGraw.

Orilia, Lawrence, et al. Business Data Processing Systems, 2 pts. 2nd ed. 1971. Set. text ed. 33.95x (ISBN 0-471-65700-X); tchrs.' manual 6.00 (ISBN 0-471-02612-3). Wiley.

Orilla, L. S. Introduction to Business Data Processing. 2nd ed. 1982. 21.95 (ISBN 0-07-047835-X); instr's. manual 15.00 (ISBN 0-07-047836-8); study guide 10.95 (ISBN 0-07-047838-4); tests 9.50 (ISBN 0-07-047837-6). McGraw.

Orimo, Hajime, et al, eds. Gerontology. (International Congress Ser.: Vol. 469). 1980. 133.75 (ISBN 0-444-90070-5). Elsevier.

Oring, Elliott. Israeli Humor: The Content & Structure of the Chizbat of the Palmah. LC 80-25483. (Modern Jewish Literature & Culture Ser.). 210p. 1981. 39.50x (ISBN 0-87395-512-9); pap. 11.95x (ISBN 0-87395-513-7). State U NY Pr.

Oriol, William E. Aging in All Nations: A Special Report on the United Nations World Assembly on Aging. Bd. with Aging in North America. 200p. (Orig.). 25.00 (ISBN 0-686-82411-3); pap. 14.00 (ISBN 0-910883-00-9). Natl Coun Aging.

Orion Nebula to Honor Henry Draper Symposium, Dec 4-5, 1981. Proceedings. Glassgold, A. E. & Huggins, P. J., eds. 338p. 1982. 65.00 (ISBN 0-89766-180-X). NY Acad Sci.

O'Riordain, Sean P. Antiquities of the Irish Countryside. 5th ed. (Illus.). 1979. 33.00x (ISBN 0-416-85630-6); pap. 10.95x (ISBN 0-416-85610-1). Methuen Inc.

O'Riordan, T. Perspectives on Resource Management. (Illus.). 184p. 1971. 15.00x (ISBN 0-85086-024-5, Pub by Pion England); pap. 8.80x (ISBN 0-85086-025-3). Methuen Inc.

O'Riordan, T., jt. auth. see Watson, J. W.

O'Riordan, Timothy & Sewell, W. R. Project Appraisal & Policy Review. (Studies in Environmental Management & Resource Development). 320p. 1981. 39.95 (ISBN 0-471-27853-X, Pub. by Wiley-interscience). Wiley.

O'Riordan, Timothy & Turner, R. Kerry, eds. Progress in Resource Management & Environmental Planning, Vol. 3. LC 80-42020. (Progress in Resource Management & Environmental Planning Ser.). 320p. 1981. 64.95x (ISBN 0-471-27968-4, Pub. by Wiley-Interscience). Wiley.

O'Riordan, Timothy, et al. Progress in Resource Management & Environmental Planning. LC 79-41729. Vol. 1, 1979. 59.95 (ISBN 0-471-99746-3, Pub. by Wiley-Interscience); Vol. 2, 1980, 272p. 57.95 (ISBN 0-471-27747-9). Wiley.

Oriti, Ronald, jt. auth. see Starbird, William.

Orjuela, Hector H., jt. auth. see Hesse, Everett.

Orkin, Frederick K. & Cooperman, Lee H., eds. Complications in Anesthesiology. (Illus.). 800p. 1982. text ed. 95.00 (ISBN 0-397-50409-8, Lippincott Medical). Lippincott.

Orkin, Michael & Drogin, Richard. Vital Statistics. (Illus.). 352p. 1974. text ed. 15.95 o.p. (ISBN 0-07-047720-5, C). McGraw.

Orkin, Michael, jt. auth. see Hoffman, Laurence D.

Orkin, Micheal, jt. auth. see Hoffman, Laurence D.

Orkin, Ruth. More Pictures from My Window. LC 82-42846. (Illus.). 144p. 1983. pap. 17.50 (ISBN 0-8478-0476-3). Rizzoli Intl.

Orkin, Ruth & Karlen, Arno, eds. A World Through My Window. LC 78-2156. (Illus.). 128p. 1980. pap. 8.95i o.p. (ISBN 0-06-090808-4, CN 808, CN). Har-Row.

Orland, Leonard, jt. auth. see Goldstein, Abraham S.

Orlandi, C., et al. Recent Advances in Prenatal Diagnosis. 344p. 1981. 52.95 (ISBN 0-471-09987-2, Pub. by Res Stud Pr). Wiley.

Orlandi, Enzo, ed. see Pretto, G., et al.

Orlando, tr. see Fisher, J. & Dryer, R.

Orlando, Ida. The Dynamic Nurse-Patient Relationship. 1961. pap. 3.25 o.p. (ISBN 0-399-40009-5). Putnam Pub Group.

Orlando, Ida J. Discipline & Teaching of Nursing Process. 1972. 4.95 o.p. (ISBN 0-399-40048-6). Putnam Pub Group.

Orlans, F. Barbara, jt. ed. see Dodds, W. Jean.

Orlans, Harold. Human Services Coordination. LC 82-8357. 160p. 1982. text ed. 22.50x (ISBN 0-87663-734-9). Universe.

--Stevenage: A Sociological Study of a New Town. LC 71-139142. 1971. Repr. of 1952 ed. lib. bdg. 25.00x (ISBN 0-8371-5758-7, ORST). Greenwood.

Orlansky, Michael D. & Heward, William L. Voices: Interviews with Handicapped People. (Special Education Ser.). (Illus.). 352p. (Orig.). 1981. pap. text ed. 10.95 (ISBN 0-675-08024-X). Merrill.

Orlansky, Michael D., jt. auth. see Heward, William L.

Orleans. Great Big Book of Pencil Puzzles. pap. 3.95 (ISBN 0-448-14581-2, G&D). Putnam Pub Group.

Orleans, Jacob S. & Jacobson, Edmund. Scrabble Word Guide. 96p. (Orig.). 1958. pap. 2.95 (ISBN 0-448-01574-9, G&D). Putnam Pub Group.

Orleans, Jacob S., jt. auth. see Orleans, Selma.

Orleans, Leo A. Chinese Approaches to Family Planning. LC 79-64372. 1979. 25.00 (ISBN 0-87332-139-1). M E Sharpe.

Orleans, Selma. Pencil Puzzles, Nos. 5 & 6. No. 5. pap. 1.95 (ISBN 0-448-12651-6, G&D); No. 6. pap. 1.95 (ISBN 0-448-12652-4). Putnam Pub Group.

Orleans, Selma & Orleans, Jacob S. Pencil Puzzles. Incl. No. 1. 96p. o.p. (ISBN 0-448-11646-4); No. 2. 96p. o.p. (ISBN 0-448-11647-2); No. 3 (ISBN 0-448-11929-3); No. 4 (ISBN 0-448-11930-7). (Illus.). 1975. pap. 1.95 ea. (G&D). Putnam Pub Group.

Orledge, Robert. Debussy & the Theatre. LC 82-1348. (Illus.). 350p. 1983. 49.50 (ISBN 0-521-22807-7). Cambridge U Pr.

Orlemann, J. A., et al. Fugitive Dust Control Technology. LC 82-22246. (Pollution Technology Review: No. 96). (Illus.). 534p. 1983. 48.00 (ISBN 0-8155-0933-2). Noyes.

Orlich, Donald C. Designing Sensible Surveys. (Orig.). 1979. pap. 11.90 o.p. (ISBN 0-913178-50-0, Pub. by Two Continents). Hippocrene Bks.

Orlich, Donald C. & Orlich, Patricia R. The Art of Writing Successful R & D Proposals. 1979. pap. 9.40 o.p. (ISBN 0-913178-51-9, Pub. by Two Continents). Hippocrene Bks.

Orlich, Donald C., et al. Teaching Strategies: A Guide to Better Instruction. (Orig.). 1979. pap. text ed. 15.95 (ISBN 0-669-02700-6). Heath.

Orlich, Patricia R., jt. auth. see Orlich, Donald C.

Orlicky, Joseph A. Material Requirements Planning: The New Way of Life in Production & Inventory Management. (Illus.). 288p. 1975. 25.95 (ISBN 0-07-047708-6, P&RB). McGraw.

Orlikoff, James E., et al. Malpractice Prevention & Liability Control for Hospitals. 160p. (Orig.). 1981. 24.75 (ISBN 0-87258-359-7, AHA-178155). Am Hospital.

Orlinsky, David O. & Howard, Kenneth I. Varieties of Psychotherapeutic Experience. LC 74-22011. 1975. text ed. 17.95x (ISBN 0-8077-2458-0); pap. text ed. 12.95x (ISBN 0-8077-2478-5). Tchrs Coll.

Orlob, Gerald T. Mathematical Modeling of Water Quality: Streams, Lakes & Reservoirs. (IIASA International Series on Applied Systems Analysis). 544p. 1983. 69.50 (ISBN 0-471-10031-5, Pub. by Wiley-Interscience). Wiley.

Orloff, Lynne. Can-to-Pan Cookery. (Illus.). 120p. (Orig.). Date not set. pap. text ed. price not set (ISBN 0-9605536-0-6). Can-To-Pan.

Orloff, Neil & Brooks, George. The National Environmental Policy Act in Cases & Materials. LC 80-8395. 532p. 1980. 27.50 (ISBN 0-87179-338-5). BNA.

Orlofsky, Myron & Orlofsky, Patsy. Quilting. Date not set. pap. cancelled (ISBN 0-8289-0487-1). Greene.

Orlofsky, Patsy, jt. auth. see Orlofsky, Myron.

Orlosky, Donald E. An Introduction to Education: The Dog Ate My Homework. 560p. 1982. pap. text ed. 21.95 (ISBN 0-675-09844-0). Additional supplements may be obtained from publisher. Merrill.

Orlosky, Donald E. & Smith, B. Othanel. Curriculm Development. 1978. 16.50 (ISBN 0-395-30687-6). HM.

Orlov, Yu L. Minerology of the Diamond. LC 77-12633. 1977. 49.95 (ISBN 0-471-01869-4, Pub. by Wiley-Interscience). Wiley.

Orlova, Alexandra. Trudy i Dni Musorgskogo. Brown, Malcolm, ed. LC 82-4826. (Studies in Russian Music: No. 4). (Rus.). 1983. write for info (ISBN 0-8357-1324-5, Pub. by UMI Res Pr). Univ Microfilms.

Orlova, Raisa. Vospominaniia O Neproshedshem Vremeni. 250p. (Rus.). 1983. 20.00 (ISBN 0-88233-725-4); pap. 13.50 (ISBN 0-88233-726-2). Ardis Pubs.

Orlow, Dietrich. The History of the Nazi Party, 1919-1933. LC 69-20026. 1969. 19.95 (ISBN 0-8229-3183-4). U of Pittsburgh Pr.

--The History of the Nazi Party, 1933-1945. LC 72-81795. 1973. 19.95 (ISBN 0-8229-3253-9). U of Pittsburgh Pr.

Orlowsky, Wallace & Perera, Thomas B. Who Will Wash the River? LC 78-121382. (Science Is What & Why Ser). (Illus.). (gr. k-3). 1970. PLB 4.49 o.p. (ISBN 0-698-30408-X, Coward). Putnam Pub Group.

Orlowsky, Wallace, jt. auth. see Perera, Thomas B.

Orman, H. A. Van see Van Orman, H. A.

Orman, John M. Presidential Secrecy & Deception: Beyond the Power to Persuade. LC 79-8410. (Contributions in Political Science: No. 43). (Illus.). xv, 239p. 1980. lib. bdg. 27.50 (ISBN 0-313-22036-0, OPS/). Greenwood.

Orman Quine, Willard van see Quine, Willard van Orman.

Orme, J. E. An Introduction to Abnormal Psychology. (Manuals of Modern Psychology Ser.). 1971. 7.50x o.p. (ISBN 0-416-66010-X); pap. 3.25x (ISBN 0-416-66770-8). Methuen Inc.

Orme, Nicholas. English Schools in the Middle Ages. (Illus.). 367p. 1973. 44.00x (ISBN 0-416-16080-8). Methuen Inc.

Orme-Johnson, William & Newton, William E., eds. Nitrogen Fixation, Vol. 2. 352p. 1980. text ed. 49.95 (ISBN 0-8391-1561-X). Univ Park.

Orme-Johnson, William H., ed. Nitrogen Fixation, Vol. 1. (Steenboek Symposia Ser.: No. 7). 414p. 1980. text ed. 49.95 (ISBN 0-8391-1560-1). Univ Park.

Ormerod. Piracy in the Ancient World. 286p. 1982. pap. 40.00x (ISBN 0-85323-044-7, Pub. by Liverpool Univ England). State Mutual Bk.

Ormerod, A. Management of Textile Production. (Illus.). 1979. text ed. 44.95 o.p. (ISBN 0-408-00381-2). Butterworth.

Ormerod, Allan. Modern Preparation & Weaving Machinery. new ed. 296p. text ed. 49.95 (ISBN 0-408-01212-9). Butterworth.

Ormerod, Dana E. White Rocks: A Woodland Rockshelter in Monroe County, Ohio. LC 82-21378. (Research Papers in Archaeology). 100p. 1983. pap. 6.00 (ISBN 0-87338-285-4). Kent State U Pr.

Ormerod, Jan. Moonlight. (ps). 1982. 9.50 (ISBN 0-688-00846-1); PLB 8.59 (ISBN 0-688-00847-X). Morrow.

Ormes, Robert. Tracking Ghost Railroads in Colorado. new ed. (Illus.). 156p. 1980. pap. 14.95 (ISBN 0-937080-01-2). Century One.

Ormond, Alexander T. The Philosophy of Religion: Lectures Written for the Elliott Lectureship at the Western Theological Seminary. 195p. 1982. Repr. of 1922 ed. lib. bdg. 50.00 (ISBN 0-8495-4219-7). Arden Lib.

Ormond, Clyde. How to Track & Find Game. (Funk & W Bk.). (Illus.). 160p. 1975. 8.95i o.p. (ISBN 0-308-10210-X); pap. 4.50i (ISBN 0-308-10211-8, TYC-T). T Y Crowell.

Ormond, Richard & Rogers, Malcolm, eds. Dictionary of British Portraiture. 1981. Vol. 3: The Victorians: Historical Figures Born Between 1800-1860. 59.00 (ISBN 0-19-520182-5); Vol. 4: The Twentieth Century: Historical Figures Born Before 1900, 168p. 59.00x (ISBN 0-19-520183-3). Oxford U Pr.

Ormrod. Pollution & Horticulture. (Fundamental Aspects of Pollution Control & Environmental Science Ser.: Vol. 4). 1978. 53.25 (ISBN 0-444-41726-5). Elsevier.

Ormrod, J. A., tr. see Evola, Julius.

Ormsbee, Thomas Hamilton. Early American Furniture Makers. LC 70-174089. 183p. 1975. Repr. of 1930 ed. 37.00x (ISBN 0-8103-4086-0). Gale.

Ormsby, Frank. A Store of Candles. 1977. pap. 4.50x (ISBN 0-19-211870-6). Oxford U Pr.

Ormsby, George. Hydrocyclones. (Mud Equipment Manual Ser.: No. 6). 1982. pap. text ed. 10.75 (ISBN 0-87201-618-8). Gulf Pub.

Ormsby, George S. Mud Systems Arrangements. (Mud Equipment Manual Ser.: No. 2). 1982. pap. text ed. 10.75 (ISBN 0-87201-614-5). Gulf Pub.

Ormsby, William. Emergence of the Federal Concept in Canada, 1839-1845. LC 73-459162. 1969. 15.00x o.p. (ISBN 0-8020-3212-5). U of Toronto Pr.

Orndorff, J. R., jt. auth. see Drake, Julia A.

Orne, Jerrold. Language of the Foreign Book Trade: Abbreviations, Terms, Phrases. 3rd ed. 20.00 (ISBN 0-8389-0219-7). ALA.

Orne, Peter, jt. auth. see Zbar, Paul.

Orne, R., jt. auth. see Zbar, Paul B.

Ornstein, Allan C. & Levine, Daniel U. An Introduction to the Foundations of Education. 2nd ed. 1981. 19.95 (ISBN 0-395-30690-6); instr's man. pap. 1.25 (ISBN 0-395-30691-4). HM.

Ornstein, Allan C. & Miller, Harry L. Looking into Teaching. 1980. 21.95 (ISBN 0-395-30692-2); Tchrs Manual 1.10 (ISBN 0-395-30693-0). HM.

Ornstein, Norman J. & Elder, Shirley. Interest Groups, Lobbying & Policymaking. LC 77-17492. (Politics & Public Policy Ser.). 264p. 1978. pap. 7.95 (ISBN 0-87187-134-3). Congr Quarterly.

Ornstein, Norman J. & Lambert, Richard D., eds. Changing Congress: The Committee System. LC 73-89780. (Annals Ser.: No. 411). 1974. 15.00 (ISBN 0-87761-173-4); pap. 7.95 (ISBN 0-87761-172-6). Am Acad Pol Soc Sci.

Ornstein, Norman J., et al, eds. Vital Statistics on Congress, 1982. 1982. 16.95 (ISBN 0-8447-3496-9); pap. 8.95 (ISBN 0-8447-3493-4). Am Enterprise.

Ornstein, Paul H., ed. The Search for the Self: Selected Writings of Heinz Kohut, Vol. 3. 1983. write for info (ISBN 0-8236-6017-6). Intl Univs Pr.

Ornstein, Robert E. The Psychology of Consciousness. 1975. pap. 4.95 (ISBN 0-14-021679-0, Pelican). Penguin.

Ornston, L. Nicholas & Sligar, Steve, eds. Experiences in Biochemical Perception. LC 82-1614. 1982. 47.00 (ISBN 0-12-528420-9). Acad Pr.

Orobio, Isaac. Israel Venge. (Holbach & His Friends Ser). 247p. (Fr.). 1974. Repr. of 1770 ed. lib. bdg. 68.00x o.p. (ISBN 0-8287-0662-X, 1515). Clearwater Pub.

O'Rooney, Sean. The Flip Side of Webster or How to be a Wise Guy. LC 81-66616. 220p. 1982. pap. 7.95 (ISBN 0-933298-01-3). Caspers Wine.

O'Rourke, A. Desmond. Changing Dimensions of U. S. Agricultural Policy. (Illus.). 1978. ref. ed. 19.95 (ISBN 0-13-127936-X). P-H.

O'Rourke, Edward W. Self Help Works. pap. 1.95 o.p. (ISBN 0-8091-2147-6). Paulist Pr.

O'Rourke, Frank. Ambuscade. Bd. with Thunder on the Buckhorn. 1980. pap. 1.75 (ISBN 0-451-09490-5, Sig). NAL.

--The Bravados. 1982. pap. 1.95 (ISBN 0-451-11466-3, AJ1466, Sig). NAL.

--Gold under Skull Peak. Date not set. pap. 1.75 (ISBN 0-451-11142-7, AE 1142, Sig). NAL.

--The Last Chance. 1982. pap. 1.95 (ISBN 0-451-11564-3, AJ1564, Sig). NAL.

--The Professionals. 1982. pap. 1.95 (ISBN 0-451-11352-7, AE1352, Sig). NAL.

O'Rourke, J. Nuclear Opthalmology: Dynamic Function Studies in Intraocular Disease. LC 76-1257. (Illus.). 1976. text ed. 10.00 (ISBN 0-7216-7009-1). Saunders.

O'Rourke, Joseph, jt. auth. see Dale, Edgar.

O'Rourke, Joseph J., jt. auth. see Fabrick, Martin N.

O'Rourke, Karen & Barton, S. R. Nurse Power: Unions & the Law. (Illus.). 420p. 1980. pap. text ed. 12.95 o.p. (ISBN 0-87619-669-5). R J Brady.

O'Rourke, Kevin D., jt. auth. see Ashley, Benedict M.

O'Rourke, P. S. & Kaminsky, Peter. Another Dirty Book. (Orig.). 1979. pap. 2.25 (ISBN 0-451-09844-7, E9844, Sig). NAL.

O'Rourke, R. A., jt. auth. see Ross, J.

O'Rourke, Robert. What God Did for ZEKE the Fuzzy Caterpillar. Sparks, Judith, ed. (A Happy Day Bks.). (Illus.). 24p. (Orig.). (gr. 1-3). 1980. 1.29 (ISBN 0-87239-406-9, 3638). Standard Pub.

O'Rourke, William. Idle Hands. 1981. 12.95 o.s.i. (ISBN 0-440-04064-7). Delacorte.

Orozco, C. R. Spanish-English, English-Spanish Commercial Dictionary. 1969. 23.00 o.p. (ISBN 0-08-006381-0); pap. 12.00 (ISBN 0-08-006380-2). Pergamon.

Orozco, Julio, tr. see Lewis, C. S.

Orque, Modesta S. & Bloch, Bobbie. Ethnic Nursing Care: A Multi-Cultural Approach. (Illus.). 414p. 1983. pap. text ed. 14.95 (ISBN 0-8016-3742-2). Mosby.

Orr. Managing Complaints of Sleep & Wakefulness. 1982. 15.95 (ISBN 0-8151-6558-7). Year Bk Med.

Orr, jt. auth. see Bartholomew.

Orr, Anne. Favorite Charted Designs by Anne Orr. 40p. (Orig.). 1983. pap. 2.75 (ISBN 0-486-24484-9). Dover.

Orr, Bill, jt. auth. see Lutzer, Erwin.

Orr, Carolyn & Kelley, Patricia. Sarayacu Quichau Pottery. (Museum of Anthropology Publications: No. 1). 37p. 1976. 3.00x (ISBN 0-88312-150-6); microfiche 1.50x (ISBN 0-88312-240-5). Summer Inst Ling.

Orr, Carolyn & Wrisley, Betsy. Vocabulario Quichua del Oriente. (Vocabularios Indigenas Ser.: No. 11). 129p. 1964. pap. 3.00x o.p. (ISBN 0-88312-665-6); mi crofiche 2.25 (ISBN 0-88312-577-3). Summer Inst Ling.

Orr, D., ed. see European Geophysical Symposium, August 1980, Budapest.

Orr, David. Italian Renaissance Drama in England Before 1625. (Studies in Comparative Literature: No. 49). ix, 141p. 1970. 11.00x o.p. (ISBN 0-8078-7049-8). U of NC Pr.

Orr, Francis S., jt. auth. see Bartholomew, Roy A.

Orr, Frank. Hockey Stars of the '70's. new ed. (Putnam Sports Shelf). (Illus.). 160p. (gr. 6 up). 1973. PLB 4.97 o.p. (ISBN 0-399-60831-1). Putnam Pub Group.

--Hockey's Greatest Stars. (Putnam Sports Shelf). (Illus.). (gr. 7 up). 1970. PLB 4.97 o.p. (ISBN 0-399-60262-3). Putnam Pub Group.

--The Stanley Cup: Hockey's World Series. new ed. LC 75-35869. (Putnam Sports Shelf). 100p. (gr. 5 up). 1976. 5.95 o.p. (ISBN 0-399-20489-X). Putnam Pub Group.

Orr, Gregory. The Red House. LC 80-7592. 64p. 1980. 11.49i (ISBN 0-06-013297-3, HarpT); pap. 4.95 (ISBN 0-06-090820-3, CN820, HarpT). Har-Row.

Orr, J., jt. auth. see Lidden, H. P.

Orr, J., jt. auth. see Moule, H. C.

Orr, J. M. Libraries As Communication Systems. LC 76-8739. (Contributions in Librarianship & Information Science: No. 17). 240p. 1977. lib. bdg. 25.00 (ISBN 0-8371-8936-5, ORL). Greenwood.

Orr, Jimmy. Emotions in Abstract. 1983. 7.95 (ISBN 0-533-05297-1). Vantage.

Orr, John, ed. see Iordan, Iorgu.

Orr, Leonard H., ed. see Inform Inc.

Orr, Marsha E. Acute Pancreatic & Hepatic Dysfunction. LC 81-65856. (Series in Critical Care Nursing). (Illus.). 244p. (Orig.). 1981. pap. text ed. 12.95. Wiley.

Orr, Marsha J., jt. auth. see Donovan, Ronald.

Orr, Robert P. The Meaning of Transcendence. Dietrich, Wendell, ed. LC 80-12872. (American Academy of Religion Dissertation Ser.). 1981. pap. 9.95 (ISBN 0-89130-408-8, 01-01-35). Scholars Pr CA.

Orr, Robert T. Marine Mammals of California. LC 78-165233. (California Natural History Guides Ser.: No. 29). 88p. 1972. pap. 4.95 (ISBN 0-520-02077-4). U of Cal Pr.

Orr, Sidney D., jt. auth. see Bates, Steven L.

Orr, William F. Corinthians I. (Anchor Bible Ser.: Vol. 32). 1976. 16.00 (ISBN 0-385-02853-9). Doubleday.

Orr, William I. Radio Handbook. 22nd ed. LC 40-33904. (Illus.). 1982. 39.95 (ISBN 0-672-21874-7). Editors.

--Radio Handbook. Date not set. 39.95 (ISBN 0-672-21874-7). Sams.

Orr, Willie. Deer Forests, Landlords & Crofters. 226p. 1982. text ed. 31.50x (ISBN 0-85976-081-2, Pub. by Donald England). Humanities.

Orr, Zelma. Miracles Take Longer. (American Romance Ser.). 192p. 1983. pap. 2.25 (ISBN 0-373-16007-0). Harlequin Bks.

Orrall, Frank, ed. Solar Active Regions. LC 79-565371. (Skylab Solar Workshop Ser.). 1981. 18.50x (ISBN 0-87081-085-5). Colo Assoc.

Orre, Hume. Autobiography of a Telephohe Answering Machine. 25p. 1983. pap. 7.95 (ISBN 0-939476-57-6). Biblio Pr GA.

Orrell, John. The Quest for Shakespeare's Globe. LC 82-9445. (Illus.). 220p. Date not set. price not set (ISBN 0-521-24751-9). Cambridge U Pr.

Orsagh, Thomas, et al. The Economic History of the United States Prior to 1860: An Annotated Bibliography. new ed. LC 75-1162. 100p. 1975. text ed. 17.50 o.p. (ISBN 0-87436-205-9). ABC-Clio.

Orsborn, Peggy A. Meeting: A One-Act Play. LC 67-31721. (Illus.). (gr. 6-12). 1968. tchr's ed & 20 readers 12.95 o.p. (ISBN 0-910030-06-5). Afro Am.

Orshalick, David W., jt. auth. see Dale, Nell B.

Orsini, Joseph. Papa Bear's Favorite Italian Dishes. LC 75-7479. 1975. pap. 4.95 (ISBN 0-88270-316-1, Pub. by Logos). Bridge Pub.

--El Precio de Pentecostes. (Span.). Date not set. 2.25 o.p. (ISBN 0-686-76336-X). Life Pubs Intl.

Orsini, Nicholas. The Language of Drawing: Learning the Basic Elements. LC 80-2326. (Illus.). 144p. 1982. pap. 14.95 (ISBN 0-385-15712-6). Doubleday.

Orsinsi, Leslie, jt. auth. see McDonald, Bruce.

Orskov, E. R., ed. Protein Nutrition in Ruminants. 1982. 22.00 (ISBN 0-12-528480-2). Acad Pr.

Orsy, Ladislas. Probing the Spirit. 2.45 o.p. (ISBN 0-87193-025-0). Dimension Bks.

Orszag, Steven A., jt. auth. see Bender, Carl M.

Orszag, Steven A., jt. auth. see Gottlieb, David.

Orszagh. Hungarian Deluxe Dictionary: English-Hungarian, Vol. 1. 6th ed. 1980. 95.00x (ISBN 0-686-86851-X, H-331). Vanous.

Orszagh, Laszlo. Hungarian Concise Dictionary: Hungarian-English, Vol. 2. 7th ed. 1976. 25.00x (ISBN 9-6305-0612-2, H268). Vanous.

--Hungarian-English: English Hungarian Dictionary, 2 vols. 12th rev. ed. 1982. Set. 20.00x (ISBN 963-05-2019-2). Heinman.

--Hungarian Pocket Dictionary: Hungarian-English, Vol. 2. 12th ed. 462p. 1979. 7.50x (ISBN 9-6305-0546-0, H273). Vanous.

Orszagh, Laszlo, ed. English-Hungarian Dictionary. 13th ed. 608p. 1982. 6.25x (ISBN 963-05-2975-0). Intl Pubns Serv.

Ort, Walter & Hammann, Hermann. Konsistenzprobleme der Investitionsforderung In der Regionalpolitik und Agrarstrukturpolitik. 118p. (Ger.). 1982. write for info. (ISBN 3-8204-5741-0). P Lang Pubs.

Ortega. Ortografia Programada. 3rd ed. 165p. 1982. 7.85 (ISBN 0-07-047711-6, G). McGraw.

Ortega & Gasset. On Love. Talbot, Toby, tr. pap. 2.95 o.p. (ISBN 0-452-00084-X, F84, Mer). NAL.

Ortega, Isabel. Street of the Madwoman. LC 78-592. 1978. 9.95 o.p. (ISBN 0-698-10911-2, Coward). Putnam Pub Group.

Ortega, James M. & Rheinboldt, Werner C., eds. Numerical Solutions of Nonlinear Problems: Studies om Numerical Analysis, Two. (Illus.). 143p. 1970. text ed. 12.50 (ISBN 0-89871-043-X). Soc Indus-Appl Math.

Ortega, Pedro R., tr. see Chapman, Al.

Ortega Y Gasset, Jose. The Revolt of the Masses. Moore, Kenneth, ed. Kerrigan, Anthony, tr. LC 81-40457. 240p. 1983. 14.95 (ISBN 0-686-86808-0). U of Notre Dame Pr.

--Some Lessons in Metaphysics. LC 76-80025. 5.50x o.p. (ISBN 0-393-08591-0); pap. 4.95 (ISBN 0-393-00514-3, Norton Lib.). Norton.

Ortego, Pedro R., tr. see LaFarge, Oliver.

Orth, Ghita. The Music of What Happens. (Eileen W. Barnes Poetry Award Ser.). 70p. (Orig.). 1982. pap. 5.50 (ISBN 0-938158-01-5). Saturday Pr.

Orth, Ralph H. see Emerson, Ralph W.

Orth, Ralph W. see Emerson, Ralph W.

Orth, Rene. New York: The Largest City in the United States. (Q Book: Famous Cities). (Illus.). (gr. 2-6). 1978. 3.95 o.p. (ISBN 0-8467-0447-1, Pub. by Two Continents). Hippocrene Bks.

--Paris: Capital City of France. (Q Book: Famous Cities). (Illus.). (gr. 2-6). 1978. 3.95 o.p. (ISBN 0-8467-0445-5, Pub. by Two Continents). Hippocrene Bks.

Orth, Robert, jt. auth. see Fisher, T. W.

Orth, Samuel P. Armies of Labor. 1919. text ed. 8.50x (ISBN 0-686-83479-8). Elliots Bks.

--Boss & the Machine. 1919. text ed. 8.50x (ISBN 0-686-83493-3). Elliots Bks.

--Our Foreigners. 1920. text ed. 8.50x (ISBN 0-686-83670-7). Elliots Bks.

Orth J. Odo Op, Den see Op Den Orth, J. Odo.

Orthmer, D. K. Intimate Relationships: An Introduction to Marriage & the Family. 1981. 19.95 (ISBN 0-201-05519-8); instr.'s man. 2.50 (ISBN 0-201-05520-1); student resource guide 5.95 (ISBN 0-201-05521-X). A-W.

Ortho Books Staff. All About Ground Covers. Burke, Ken, ed. LC 82-82157. (Illus.). 112p. 1982. pap. 5.95 (ISBN 0-89721-010-7). Ortho.

--All About Growing Fruits & Berries. rev. ed. Ferguson, Barbara J., ed. LC 82-82156. (Illus.). 112p. 1982. pap. 5.95 o.p. (ISBN 0-89721-009-3, Dist. by Chevron Chemical Company). McGraw.

--All About Trees. Ferguson, Barbara J., ed. LC 82-82155. (Illus.). 112p. 1982. pap. 5.95 (ISBN 0-89721-007-7). Ortho.

Ortiz. The Psychology of Human Behavior: A Study Guide for Psychology One-Hundred. 178p. 1982. write for info. West Pub.

Ortiz, Altagracia. Eighteenth-Century Reforms in the Carribean: Miguel De Muesas, Governor of Puerto Rico, 1769-76. LC 79-56408. (Illus.). 256p. 1983. 27.50 (ISBN 0-8386-3008-1). Fairleigh Dickinson.

Ortiz, Bobbye, tr. see Debray, Regis.

Ortiz, Elisabeth L. The Complete Book of Caribbean Cooking. 448p. 1983. pap. 7.95 (ISBN 0-87131-409-6). M Evans.

Ortiz, Flora I. Career Patterns in Education: Men, Women, & Minorities in Public School Administration. 192p. 1981. 24.95 (ISBN 0-03-059223-2). Praeger.

--Career Patterns in Education: Women, Men & Minorities in Public School Administration. (Illus.). 224p. 1981. 22.95x (ISBN 0-686-84384-3). J F Bergin.

Ortiz, Juan C. Discipulo. 192p. Date not set. 2.50 (ISBN 0-88113-065-6). Edit Betania.

--Living with Jesus Today. 1982. 4.95 (ISBN 0-88419-187-7). Creation Hse.

Ortiz, Victoria. Sojourner Truth. LC 73-22290. (Illus.). 160p. (gr. 7 up). 1974. 12.95i (ISBN 0-397-31504-X, JBL-J). Har-Row.

Ortiz, Victoria, ed. see Slote, Alfred.

Ortiz-Buonafina, Marta. The Impact of Import Substitution Policies on Marketing Activities: A Case Study of the Guatemalan Commercial Sector. LC 81-40523. 158p. 1982. lib. bdg. 20.75 (ISBN 0-8191-1884-2); pap. text ed. 10.00 (ISBN 0-8191-1885-0). U Pr of Amer.

Ortiz Y Pino, Jose. The Last Patron. Engestrom, Melissa, ed. LC 81-8817. 160p. 1981. 12.95 (ISBN 0-86534-006-4); pap. 8.95 (ISBN 0-86534-007-2). Sunstone Pr.

Ortiz y Pino, Jose, III. Curandero. Hausman, Gerald, ed. LC 82-19507. (Illus.). 128p. 1982. pap. 7.95 (ISBN 0-86534-020-X). Sunstone Pr.

Ortland, Gerald J. Telemarketing: High-Profit Telephone Selling Techniques. (Professional Development Programs Ser.). 256p. 1982. text ed. 55.95 (ISBN 0-471-86786-1). Wiley.

Ortlund, Anne. Children Are Wet Cement. 192p. 1981. 9.95 (ISBN 0-8007-1260-9). Revell.

--Up with Worship. rev. ed. 1982. pap. 4.95 (ISBN 0-8307-0867-7). Regal.

Ortlund, Raymond C. Be a New Christian All Your Life. 192p. 1983. 6.95 (ISBN 0-8007-5119-1, Power Bks). Revell.

--Circulo De Fortaleza El. Marosi, Esteban, et al, eds. Lacy, Susana, tr. from Eng. Orig. Title: Circle of Strength. 112p. (Span.). 1981. pap. 1.50 (ISBN 0-8297-0502-3). Life Pubs Intl.

Ortmann, Otto. The Physiological Mechanics of Piano Technique. (Music Ser.). (Illus.). xvi, 396p. 1981. Repr. of 1929 ed. lib. bdg. 42.50 (ISBN 0-306-76058-4). Da Capo.

Ortner, Donald J., ed. How Humans Adapt: A Biocultural Odyssey. (Illus.). 500p. 1983. text ed. 17.50x (ISBN 0-87474-726-0); pap. text ed. 9.95x (ISBN 0-87474-725-2). Smithsonian.

Ortner, Sherry & Whitehead, Harriet, eds. Sexual Meanings: The Cultural Construction of Gender & Sexuality. LC 80-26655. 448p. 1981. 37.50 (ISBN 0-521-23965-6); pap. 11.95 (ISBN 0-521-28375-2). Cambridge U Pr.

Ortner, Sherry B. Sherpas Through their Rituals. LC 76-62582. (Cambridge Studies in Cultural Systems). (Illus.). 196p. 1978. 27.95 (ISBN 0-521-21536-6); pap. 9.95 (ISBN 0-521-29216-6). Cambridge U Pr.

Orton, C., jt. auth. see Hodder, Ian.

Orton, Clive. Mathematics in Archaeology. LC 81-21608. (Illus.). 248p. 1982. pap. 9.95 (ISBN 0-521-28922-X). Cambridge U Pr.

Orton, Eric. Reise Nach Hamburg. (Illus.). 1972. pap. text ed. 3.95x (ISBN 0-582-36142-7); cassette, 1977 10.50x (ISBN 0-582-37529-0). Longman.

Orton, Gavin. Eyvind Johnson. (World Authors Ser.). lib. bdg. 15.95 (ISBN 0-8057-2468-0, Twayne). G K Hall.

Orton, Graham see Ibsen, Henrik.

Orton, Harold & Dieth, Eugen, eds. Survey of English Dialects, 4 vols. Incl. Vol. 1. The Six Northern Countries & the Isle of Man, 3 pts. 1962-63. o.p. (ISBN 0-8002-2038-2); Vol. 2. West Midland Counties, 3 pts. 1969-70 (ISBN 0-8002-2039-0); Vol. 3. East Midland Counties & East Anglia, 3 pts. 1969-70 (ISBN 0-8002-2040-4); Vol. 4. The Southern Counties, 3 pts. 1968 (ISBN 0-8002-2041-2). LC 67-6774. 87.50x ea. Intl Pubns Serv.

Orton, Helen F. Mystery Up the Chimney. LC 47-4012. (Illus.). (gr. 4-6). 1947. 8.95i o.p. (ISBN 0-397-30128-6, JBL-J). Har-Row.

Orton, Joe. The Complete Plays. Incl. Entertaining Mr. Sloane; The Erpingham Camp; Funeral Games; The Good & Faithful Servant; Loot; The Ruffian on the Stair; What the Butler Saw. 1977. pap. 6.95 (ISBN 0-394-17001-6, B400, BC). Grove.

Orton, Lawrence D. Polish Detroit & the Kolasinski Affair. (Illus.). 268p. 1981. 19.95 (ISBN 0-8143-1671-9). Wayne St U Pr.

Orton, Richard, ed. Electronic Music for Schools. LC 81-3838. (Cambridge Resources of Music Ser.). (Illus.). 200p. 1982. 21.95 (ISBN 0-521-22994-4); pap. 9.95 (ISBN 0-521-28026-5); cassettes 14.95 (ISBN 0-521-23661-4). Cambridge U Pr.

Orton, Richard, compiled by. Records of California Men in the War of the Rebellion: 1861-1867. LC 78-23517. 1979. Repr. of 1890 ed. 94.00x (ISBN 0-8103-3347-3). Gale.

Orton, Samuel T. Reading Writing & Speech Problems in Children. 1973. 5.00x (ISBN 0-393-01107-0). Norton.

Orton, Vrest. The American Cider Book. 136p. 1973. 6.95 o.p. (ISBN 0-374-10397-6); pap. 3.25 (ISBN 0-374-51076-8, N450). FS&G.

Orton, William A. Liberal Tradition. 1945. text ed. 12.50x (ISBN 0-686-83606-5). Elliots Bks.

Ortonne, Jean-Paul & Mosher, David B. Vitiligo & Other Hypomelanoses of Hair & Skin. (Topics in Dermatology Ser.). 680p. 1983. 79.50x (ISBN 0-306-40974-7, Plenum Med Bk). Plenum Pub.

Ortony, Andrew, ed. Metaphor & Thought. LC 78-32011. (Illus.). 1979. 49.50 (ISBN 0-521-22727-5); pap. 15.95x (ISBN 0-521-29626-9). Cambridge U Pr.

Orts, J. C., et al. Breve Diccionario Espanol-Ruso: Ruso-Espanol de Terminos Cientificos y Tecnicos. 438p. (Span. & Rus.). 1960. leatherette 6.95 (ISBN 0-686-97394-1, S-31835). French & Eur.

Ortzen, Len. Famous Stories of the Resistance. LC 79-5036. 1979. 8.95 o.p. (ISBN 0-312-28160-9). St Martin.

Orum, Anthony M. Introduction to Political Sociology. 2nd ed. (Illus.). 384p. 1983. text ed. 22.95 (ISBN 0-13-491399-X). P-H.

--Introduction to Political Sociology: The Social Anatomy of Body Politics. (P-H Series in Sociology). (Illus.). 1978. ref. ed. 22.95 (ISBN 0-13-491381-7). P-H.

Orvell, Miles. Invisible Parade: The Fiction of Flannery O'Connor. LC 72-91132. 246p. 1972. 24.95 (ISBN 0-87722-023-9). Temple U Pr.

Orvig, S. Climates of the Polar Region. Lansberg, H. E., ed. (World Survey of Climatology Ser.: Vol. 14). 1971. 121.50 (ISBN 0-444-40828-2). Elsevier.

Orville-Thomas, W. F., jt. auth. see Hargittai, I.

Orville-Thomas, W. J., jt. auth. see Ratajczak, H.

Orville-Thomas, W. J., ed. Internal Rotation in Molecules. LC 73-2791. (Wiley Monographs in Chemical Physics). 608p. 1974. 129.95 (ISBN 0-471-65707-7, Pub. by Wiley-Interscience). Wiley.

Orville-Thomas, W. J., jt. ed. see Barnes, A. J.

Orwell, George. Animal Farm. (RL 10). 1974. pap. 1.95 (ISBN 0-451-51679-6, CJ1679, Sig Classics). NAL.

--Burmese Days. LC 73-12947. 287p. 1974. pap. 3.95 (ISBN 0-15-614850-1, Harv). HarBraceJ.

--Clergyman's Daughter. LC 60-10943. 1969. pap. 3.95 (ISBN 0-15-618065-0, Harv). HarBraceJ.

--Collection of Essays. LC 54-7594. 1970. pap. 4.95 (ISBN 0-15-618600-4, Harv). HarBraceJ.

--Dickens, Dali & Others. LC 63-22950. 1970. pap. 4.95 (ISBN 0-15-626053-0, Harv). HarBraceJ.

--Keep the Aspidistra Flying. LC 56-5326. 1969. pap. 4.95 (ISBN 0-15-646899-9, Harv). HarBraceJ.

--Nineteen Eighty-Four. (RL 10). 1971. pap. 2.50 (ISBN 0-451-51675-3, CE1675, Sig Classics). NAL.

--Orwell's Nineteen Eighty-Four: Text, Sources, Criticism. 2nd ed. Howe, Irving, ed. 450p. 1982. pap. text ed. 9.95 o.p. (ISBN 0-15-565810-7, HC). HarBraceJ.

Orwen, Gifford P. Jean-Francois Regnard. (World Authors Ser.). 1982. lib. bdg. 13.95 (ISBN 0-8057-6427-5, Twayne). G K Hall.

Orwig, Gary W. & Hodges, William S. The Computer Tutor. 1977. pap. text ed. 11.95 (ISBN 0-316-66500-2). Little.

Orwig, Sara. Magic Obsession. (Super Romances Ser.). 384p. 1983. pap. 2.95 (ISBN 0-373-70057-1, Pub. by Worldwide). Harlequin Bks.

Osa, Tetsuo, jt. ed. see Kuwana, Ted.

Osaki, S., jt. auth. see Mine, H.

Osako, Masako M., jt. ed. see Nusberg, Charlotte.

Osancova, K., tr. see Parizkova, Jana.

Osaragi, Jiro, pseud. Homecoming. Horwitz, Brewster, tr. from Jap. LC 76-54833. 1977. Repr. of 1968 ed. lib. bdg. 20.00x (ISBN 0-8371-9369-9, OSHO). Greenwood.

Osawa, S., et al, eds. Genetics & Evolution of RNA Polymerase & RNA Ribosomes. 1982. 108.50 (ISBN 0-444-80288-6). Elsevier.

Osayimwese, Iz, jt. auth. see Onimode, B.

Osbakken, Mary D., et al. Techniques, Diagnostics & Advances in Nuclear Cardiology. (Illus.). 344p. 1983. text ed. 53.50x (ISBN 0-398-04772-3). C C Thomas.

Osbaldeston, Michael, jt. auth. see Hepworth, Andrew.

Osbeck, Kenneth W. My Music Workbook. 128p. 1982. pap. 4.95x (ISBN 0-8254-3415-7). Kregel.

Osberg, Lars. Economic Inequality in the United States. 268p. 1983. text ed. 17.95 (ISBN 0-87332-234-7). M E Sharpe.

Osborn. Orientations to Rhetorical Style. Applbaum, Ronald & Hart, Roderick, eds. (MODCOM Modules in Speech Communication Ser.). 1976. pap. text ed. 2.75 (ISBN 0-574-22515-3, 13-5515). SRA.

Osborn, Albert S. Questioned Documents. rev. 2nd ed. LC 73-9875. (Criminology, Law Emforcement & Social Problems Ser.: No. 207). (Illus.). 760p. 1973. lib. bdg. 27.50x (ISBN 0-87585-207-6). Patterson Smith.

Osborn, d. Keith, jt. auth. see Osborn, Janie D.

Osborn, David. Love & Treason. 272p. 1982. 13.95 (ISBN 0-453-00421-0, H421). NAL.

Osborn, E. Ethical Patterns in Early Christian Thought. LC 75-10040. 288p. 1976. 37.50 (ISBN 0-521-20835-1). Cambridge U Pr.

Osborn, E. F. The Beginning of Christian Philosophy. LC 79-8911. 256p. 1981. 54.50 (ISBN 0-521-23179-5). Cambridge U Pr.

Osborn, Fairfield, ed. Our Crowded Planet: Essays on the Pressures of Population. LC 82-21145. 240p. 1983. Repr. of 1962 ed. lib. bdg. 29.75x (ISBN 0-313-22639-3). Greenwood.

Osborn, Howard. Vector Bundles & Their Characteristic Classes: Vol. I, Vector Bundles & Stiefel-Whitney Classes. (Pure & Applied Mathematics Ser.). 1982. 49.50 (ISBN 0-12-529301-1). Acad Pr.

Osborn, J., jt. ed. see Anderson, R. C.

Osborn, Jack R. & Kornbluth, Jesse. Winning Croquet: From Backyard to Greensward. 1983. price not set (ISBN 0-671-47276-3). S&S.

Osborn, Janie D. & Osborn, d. Keith. Cognition in Early Childhood. (Illus.). 220p. 1983. lib. bdg. write for info (ISBN 0-918772-11-7); pap. text ed. write for info (ISBN 0-918772-12-5). Ed Assocs.

Osborn, Jeanne. Dewey Decimal Classification: A Study Manual. 19th ed. LC 82-21. 366p. 1982. PLB 27.50 (ISBN 0-87287-293-9). Libs Unl.

Osborn, Jeanne, jt. auth. see Herdman, Margaret.

Osborn, Lois. My Dad is Really Something. Tucker, Kathleen, ed. (Concept Bks.). (Illus.). 32p. (gr. 1-3). 1983. PLB 7.50 (ISBN 0-8075-5329-8). A Whitman.

Osborn, Mary E. Who Tempers the Wind. LC 82-72270. 115p. 1963. pap. 4.95 (ISBN 0-8040-0320-3). Swallow.

Osborn, Michael. Speaking in Public. LC 81-82563. 1982. pap. 13.50 (ISBN 0-395-29692-7); instr's manual 1.00 (ISBN 0-395-29693-5). HM.

Osborn, Norris G. Issac H. Bromley. 1920. text ed. 19.50x (ISBN 0-686-83594-8). Elliots Bks.

Osborn, Richard N., et al. Organization Theory: An Integrated Contingency Approach. (Wiley Ser. in Management). 1980. text ed. 31.95x (ISBN 0-471-02173-3); tchrs.' manual 5.00 (ISBN 0-471-02174-1). Wiley.

Osborn, Richard W. & Flach, George W. Tapping in to the NECR. Osborn, Richard W., ed. LC 82-82124. (Illus.). 178p. 1982. pap. text ed. 8.50 (ISBN 0-87765-226-0, NEC-QUE). Natl Fire Prot.

Osborn, Richard W., ed. see Osborn, Richard W. & Flach, George W.

Osborn, Robert. Osborn on Osborn. LC 81-18492. (Illus.). 192p. 1982. 35.00 (ISBN 0-89919-051-0). Ticknor & Fields.

Osborn, Royce R. A Professional Approach to Radiology Administration. (Illus.). 228p. 1980. photocopy ed. spital 29.75x (ISBN 0-398-04097-4). C C Thomas.

Osborn, Ruth H. Developing New Horizons for Women. (Illus.). 1977. pap. text ed. 21.95 (ISBN 0-07-047780-9, C); facilitators guide 1.95 (ISBN 0-07-047781-7). McGraw.

Osborn, S. The American Guide to Diet & Health. 352p. 1982. 24.95 (ISBN 0-07-069074-X, GB); pap. 12.95 (ISBN 0-07-069072-3). McGraw.

Osborn, Scott C. & Phillips, Robert, Jr. Richard Harding Davis. 2nd ed. (United States Authors Ser.). 1978. lib. bdg. 13.95 (ISBN 0-8057-7192-1, Twayne). G K Hall.

Osborn, Susan. Free Things for Teachers. LC 81-17844. (Free Things! A Bargain Hunter's Bonanza Ser.). 128p. 1982. pap. 4.95 (ISBN 0-399-50606-3, Perige). Putnam Pub Group.

Osborn, Susan, ed. see Druse, Kenneth.

Osborn, Susan, ed. see Weiss, Jeffrey.

Osborn, T. L. Faith Speaks. 1982. pap. 2.95 (ISBN 0-89274-226-7, HH-226). Harrison Hse.

--The Good Life. 299p. Date not set. pap. 2.95 (ISBN 0-89274-179-1, HH-179). Harrison Hse.

--How to Be Born Again. 160p. Date not set. pap. 2.95 (ISBN 0-89274-224-0, HH-224). Harrison Hse.

--How to Enjoy Plenty. Date not set. pap. 2.95 (ISBN 0-89274-222-4, HH-222). Harrison Hse.

--Join This Chariot: Reaching the Lost. Date not set. pap. 2.95 (ISBN 0-89274-223-2, HH-223). Harrison Hse.

--When Jesus Visited Our House. Date not set. pap. 2.95 (ISBN 0-89274-225-9, HH-225). Harrison Hse.

Osborne, ed. Consolidated List of Approved Common Names of Insecticides & Certain Other Pesticides. LC 52-44516. 1979. 3.35 o.p. (ISBN 0-686-18865-9). Entomol Soc.

Osborne, A. R. & Rizzoli, P. M., eds. Topics in Ocean Physics: Proceedings of the International School of Physics, Enrico Fermi Course LXXX, Varenna, Italy, July 7-19, 1980. (Enrico Fermi International Summer School of Physics Ser.: Vol. 80). 554p. 1982. 105.50 (ISBN 0-444-86160-2, North Holland). Elsevier.

Osborne, Adam. The Eighty Eighty-Nine I-O Processor Handbook. 128p. (Orig.). 1980. pap. 9.95 (ISBN 0-931988-39-X). Osborne-McGraw.

--Eighty-Eighty Programming for Logic Design. (Programming for Logic Design Ser.: No. 1). (Orig.). 1976. pap. text ed. 9.50 o.p. (ISBN 0-931988-04-7). Osborne-McGraw.

--Running Wild the Next Industrial Revolution. (Orig.). 1979. pap. 4.95 (ISBN 0-931988-28-4). Osborne-McGraw.

Osborne, Adam & Bunnell, David. Introduction to Microcomputers, Vol. 0: The Beginner's Book, Vol. O. rev., 3rd ed. 240p. (Orig.). 1982. pap. 12.50 (ISBN 0-931988-64-0). Osborne-McGraw.

Osborne, Adam & Kane, Jerry. An Introduction to Microcomputers: Some Real Support Devices. 1978. pap. text ed. 15.00 o.p. (ISBN 0-931988-18-7). Osborne-McGraw.

Osborne, Adam, et al. CBASIC User's Guide. 216p. 1981. pap. 16.95 (ISBN 0-931988-61-6). Osborne-McGraw.

Osborne, Anne. The Analyst. LC 79-1065. 1979. 9.95 o.p. (ISBN 0-688-03478-0). Morrow.

--Wind from the Main. LC 72-86902. 1972. 2.50 o.s.i. (ISBN 0-87844-012-7). Sandlapper Store.

Osborne, Anne R. A History of South Carolina. (gr. 4-8). 1983. 11.95 (ISBN 0-87844-023-2). Sandlapper Pub Co.

Osborne, Arthur. Ramana Maharshi & the Path of Self-Knowledge. LC 76-18194. (Illus.). 1982. pap. write for info o.p. (ISBN 0-87728-071-1). Weiser.

Osborne, C. W., ed. International Yearbook of Educational & Instructional Technology 1982-1983. 4th ed. 450p. 1982. 36.00 o.p. (ISBN 0-686-97960-5). Nichols Pub.

Osborne, Cecil G. The Art of Getting Along with People. 192p. 1980. 8.95 o.p. (ISBN 0-310-30610-8). Zondervan.

--The Art of Getting Along With People. 192p. 1982. pap. 3.95 (ISBN 0-310-30612-4). Zondervan.

--You're in Charge. 1976. pap. 1.75 o.s.i. (ISBN 0-89129-221-7). Jove Pubns.

Osborne, Charles. The Complete Operas of Mozart. LC 78-55623. 1978. 14.95 o.p. (ISBN 0-689-10886-9). Atheneum.

--The Complete Operas of Mozart. (Quality Paperbacks Ser.). (Illus.). 349p. 1983. pap. 9.95 (ISBN 0-306-80190-6). Da Capo.

--The Life & Crimes of Agatha Cristie. (Rainbow Bks.). (Illus.). 256p. 1983. 17.95 (ISBN 0-03-062784-2). HR&W.

--Rigoletto. LC 79-65707. (Masterworks of Opera Ser.). 15.96 (ISBN 0-382-06310-4). Silver.

--The World Theater of Wagner: A Celebration of 150 Years of Wagner Productions. LC 82-130. (Illus.). 224p. 1982. 36.50 (ISBN 0-02-594050-3). Macmillan.

Osborne, Charles, ed. Richard Wagner: Stories & Essays. 187p. 16.00x (ISBN 0-912050-43-8, Library Press). Open Court.

Osborne, Charles, tr. see Leider, Frida.

Osborne, Charles, tr. see Schnitzler, Arthur.

Osborne, Colin P., III. Day Dreaming-Night Thinking: Roaming in Two Worlds. LC 81-84497. (Illus.). 80p. 1982. photographic monograph 9.95 (ISBN 0-9607332-2-1). Ololon Pubns.

Osborne, Gail B., jt. auth. see Brody, Jean.

Osborne, Grant R. & Woodward, Stephen. Handbook for Bible Study. LC 78-73429. 1979. 5.95 (ISBN 0-8010-6665-4). Baker Bk.

Osborne, Grant R. & Woodward, Stephen B. Handbook for Bible Study. 188p. 1983. pap. 5.95 (ISBN 0-8010-6701-4). Baker Bk.

Osborne, Harold, ed. Aesthetics. (Oxford Readings in Philosophy Ser.). 1972. pap. text ed. 8.95x (ISBN 0-19-875020-X). Oxford U Pr.

Osborne, Harrison. In Defense of Fascism: A New Critical Evaluation of the Fascist Experience in Modern History. (Illus.). 108p. 1983. Repr. of 1957 ed. 74.85 (ISBN 0-89901-109-8). Found Class Reprints.

Osborne, Helena. The Joker. LC 78-26800. 1979. 8.95 o.p. (ISBN 0-698-10975-9, Coward). Putnam Pub Group.

--The White Poppy. 1977. 8.95 o.p. (ISBN 0-698-10763-2, Coward). Putnam Pub Group.

Osborne, Howard. Vector Bundles & Their Characteristic Classes, Vol. 2. (Pure & Applied Mathematics Ser.). Date not set. 49.50 (ISBN 0-12-529302-X). Acad Pr.

Osborne, J. W. John Cartwright. LC 74-190422. (Conference on British Studies, Biographical Ser). 168p. 1972. 37.50 (ISBN 0-521-08537-3). Cambridge U Pr.

Osborne, James G., jt. auth. see Powers, Richard.

Osborne, John. A Better Class of Person: An Autobiography. 320p. 1981. 13.75 (ISBN 0-525-06634-9, 01335-400). Dutton.

--Entertainer. LC 58-6810. 1958. 8.95 (ISBN 0-87599-082-7). S G Phillips.

--The Entertainer. 1983. pap. 4.95 (ISBN 0-14-048178-8). Penguin.

--Four Plays. Incl. West of Suez; A Patriot for Me; Time Present; The Hotel in Amsterdam. LC 72-3920. 300p. 1973. 7.50 o.p. (ISBN 0-396-06659-3). Dodd.

--Naturalist Drama in Germany. 185p. 1971. 12.50x o.p. (ISBN 0-87471-027-8). Rowman.

--A Patriot for Me & a Sense of Detachment. 192p. 1983. pap. 7.95 (ISBN 0-571-13041-0). Faber & Faber.

Osborne, John C., tr. see Christoffel von Grimmelshausen, Hans J.

Osborne, John J. The Paper Chase. 224p. 1983. pap. 2.95 (ISBN 0-446-31141-3). Warner Bks.

Osborne, John J., Jr. The Only Thing I've Done Wrong. 1977. pap. 1.75 o.p. (ISBN 0-380-01870-5, 36970). Avon.

Osborne, Juanita T. The Ashes of Windrow. 192p. (YA) 1976. 6.95 (ISBN 0-685-59251-0, Avalon). Bouregy.

--Cry of the Whippoorwill. 1981. pap. 6.95 (ISBN 0-686-84701-6, Avalon). Bouregy.

--The Dark Bayou. (YA) 1980. 6.95 (ISBN 0-686-73923-X, Avalon). Bouregy.

--Dark Season at Aerie. (YA) 1977. 6.95 (ISBN 0-685-81423-8, Avalon). Bouregy.

--Dwellers of Riven Oak. (YA) 1978. 6.95 (ISBN 0-685-05585-X, Avalon). Bouregy.

--Fury of Fenlon. (YA) 1979. 6.95 (ISBN 0-685-95872-8, Avalon). Bouregy.

--Menace at the Gate. 1982. 6.95 (ISBN 0-686-84170-0, Avalon). Bouregy.

--Peril at Dorrough. 1979. 6.95 (ISBN 0-686-52554-X, Avalon). Bouregy.

--Rendezvous at the Hallows. 192p. (YA) 1975. 6.95 (ISBN 0-685-50529-4, Avalon). Bouregy.

--Shadow over Wyndham Hall. 192p. (YA) 1976. 6.95 (ISBN 0-685-66478-3, Avalon). Bouregy.

--The Shrinking Pond. 192p. (YA) 1974. 6.95 (ISBN 0-685-39179-5, Avalon). Bouregy.

--Terror at Tolliver Hall. (YA) 1981. 6.95 (ISBN 0-686-73960-4, Avalon). Bouregy.

--Walk with a Shadow. 1982. 6.95 (ISBN 0-686-84187-5, Avalon). Bouregy.

--Web of Haefen. 1982. pap. 6.95 (ISBN 0-686-84727-X, Avalon). Bouregy.

Osborne, June. Stained Glass in England. (Illus.). 224p. 1983. 17.95 (ISBN 0-584-97293-8, Pub. by Salem Hse Ltd). Merrimack Bk Serv.

Osborne, Lucy E., tr. see Haebler, K.

Osborne, M. Region of Revolt: Focus on Southeast Asia. LC 75-133332. 1971. 16.50 (ISBN 0-08-017533-3). Pergamon.

Osborne, Maggie. Alexa. 1980. pap. 2.25 o.p. (ISBN 0-451-09244-9, E9244, Sig). NAL.

--Yankee Princess. 1982. pap. 3.50 (ISBN 0-451-11820-0, AE1820, Sig). NAL.

Osborne, Margaret. Collies. (Foyle's Handbks). 1973. 3.95 (ISBN 0-685-55800-2). Palmetto Pub.

Osborne, Martha L. Woman in Western Thought. 1978. pap. 12.00 (ISBN 0-394-32112-X). Random.

Osborne, Milton. South East Asia. rev. ed. 208p. (Orig.). 1983. pap. text ed. 8.95 (ISBN 0-86861-269-3). Allen Unwin.

Osborne, N. O. & Chader, G. J., eds. Progress in Retinal Research, Vol. 1. (Illus.). 245p. 1982. 72.00 (ISBN 0-08-028901-0). Pergamon.

Osborne, Neville N. Biology of Serotonergic Transmission. LC 81-14671. 522p. 1982. 69.95x (ISBN 0-471-10032-3, Pub. by Wiley-Interscience). Wiley.

Osborne, Noel H. The Lytton Manuscripts. 79p. 1967. 30.00x (ISBN 0-900801-10-7). State Mutual Bk.

Osborne, R. Travis & McGork, Frank C., eds. The Testing of Negro Intelligence. 402p. 1982. 18.50 (ISBN 0-936396-02-4). Foun Human GA.

Osborne, Richard H. & Bennett, Kenneth A. Centers for Training in Physical Anthropology. 1979. pap. 3.00 (ISBN 0-686-36571-2). Am Anthro Assn.

Osborne, Thomas. California Real Estate License Manual. 1983. pap. text ed. 17.95x (ISBN 0-673-16579-5). Scott F.

Osborne, Thomas M. Society & Prisons. LC 72-172587. (Criminology, Law Enforcement, & Social Problems Ser.: No. 177). 1975. 14.00x (ISBN 0-87585-177-0). Patterson Smith.

--Within Prison Walls, Being a Narrative of Personal Experience During a Week of Voluntary Confinement in the State Prison at Auburn, New York. LC 69-14940. (Criminology, Law Enforcement, & Social Problems Ser.: No. 72). 1969. Repr. of 1914 ed. 15.00x (ISBN 0-87585-072-3). Patterson Smith.

Osborne, Valerie. One Big Yo to Go. (Illus.). (gr. 1 up). 1981. 10.95 (ISBN 0-19-554265-7). Oxford U Pr.

Osborne, William, jt. ed. see Castille, Philip.

Osborne, William S. Caroline M. Kirkland. (United States Authors Ser.). lib. bdg. 13.95 (ISBN 0-8057-0424-8, Twayne). G K Hall.

--Lydia Maria Child. (United States Authors Ser.). 1980. lib. bdg. 13.95 (ISBN 0-8057-7315-0, Twayne). G K Hall.

Osborne, Yvonne H., jt. auth. see Meyer, Robert G.

Osbourne, Lloyd, jt. auth. see Stevenson, Robert L.

Osburn, Charles B. Academic Research & Library Resources: Changing Patterns in America. LC 78-20017. (New Directions in Librarianship: No. 3). (Illus.). 1979. lib. bdg. 25.00 (ISBN 0-313-20722-4, OAR/). Greenwood.

Osburn, Donald & Schneeberger, Kenneth. Modern Agricultural Management. 2nd ed. 370p. 1982. text ed. 20.95 (ISBN 0-8359-4550-2); instr's. manual free (ISBN 0-8359-4551-0). Reston.

Osburn, William, Jr. A Hebrew & English Lexicon to the Old Testament. 287p. 1981. pap. 5.95 (ISBN 0-310-20361-9). Zondervan.

Osei-Hwedie, Kwaku, jt. auth. see Agyeman-Badu, Yaw.

Osei-Kwame, Peter. A New Conceptual Model for the Study of Political Integration in Africa. LC 80-5708. 307p. 1980. lib. bdg. 23.25 (ISBN 0-8191-1316-6); pap. 12.50 (ISBN 0-8191-1317-4). U Pr of Amer.

Osen, Lynn M. Women in Mathematics. 224p. 1974. 16.50x (ISBN 0-262-15014-X); pap. 4.95 (ISBN 0-262-65009-6). MIT Pr.

Osenton, J., jt. auth. see Dorian, A. F.

Oser, Hans J., tr. see Walz, Alfred.

Oser, Jacob. Henry George. (World Leaders Ser.). 1974. lib. bdg. 12.95 (ISBN 0-8057-3682-4, Twayne). G K Hall.

Oser, Jacob & Blanchfield, William C. Evolution of Economic Thought. 3rd ed. 512p. 1975. text ed. 22.95 (ISBN 0-15-525002-7, HC). HarBraceJ.

Osers, Edward, tr. see Heiniger, E. A.

Osers, Ewald, tr. see Haffner, Sebastian.

Osers, Ewald, tr. see Strauss, Richard & Von Hofmannsthal, Hugo.

Osgood. Senior Settlers. 304p. 1982. 27.95 (ISBN 0-03-059792-7). Praeger.

Osgood, C. The Koreans & Their Culture. 387p. 1951. 25.95 o.p. (ISBN 0-471-06943-4, Pub. by Wiley-Interscience). Wiley.

Osgood, Carl C. Fatigue Design. 2nd ed. (International Ser. on the Strength & Fracture of Materials & Structures). 500p. 1982. 55.00 (ISBN 0-08-026167-1); pap. 22.50 (ISBN 0-08-026166-3). Pergamon.

Osgood, Henry O. So This Is Jazz. LC 77-17859. (Roots of Jazz Ser.). (Illus.). 1978. Repr. of 1926 ed. lib. bdg. 25.00 (ISBN 0-306-77540-9). Da Capo.

Osgood, Nancy J. & McGuire, Francis, eds. Life after Work: Retirement, Leisure, Recreation, & the Elderly. 384p. 1982. 29.95 (ISBN 0-03-060437-0). Praeger.

Osgood, Robert E. Limited War Revisited. (Westview Special Study). 1979. soft 16.50 (ISBN 0-89158-465-X). Westview.

--The Successor Generation: Its Challenges & Responsibilities. 45p. pap. 6.00 (ISBN 0-87855-874-8). Transaction Bks.

Osgood, William. Wintering in Snow Country. LC 78-58680. (Illus.). 1977. 9.95 o.p. (ISBN 0-8289-0319-0); pap. 5.95 o.p. (ISBN 0-8289-0320-4). Greene.

Osgood, William & Hurley, Leslie. The Snowshoe Book. LC 75-4769. (Illus.). 160p. 1975 (ISBN 0-8289-0222-4). pap. 7.95 (ISBN 0-8289-0221-6). Greene.

Osgood, William F. Funktionentheorie, 2 Vols. LC 63-11319. (Ger). Vol. 1. 14.50 (ISBN 0-8284-0193-4); Vol. 2. 19.50 (ISBN 0-8284-0182-9). Chelsea Pub.

Osgood, William R. Planning & Financing Your Business: A Complete Working Guide. 216p. 1983. 24.95 (ISBN 0-8436-0883-8). CBI Pub.

Osguthorpe, Russel T. Tutor-Notetaker. 98p. (Orig.). 1980. pap. text ed. 7.00 (ISBN 0-88200-131-0, N6680). Alexander Graham.

O'Sharkey, Eithne M. The Role of the Priest in the Novels of Georges Bernanos. 1983. 10.00 (ISBN 0-533-05404-4). Vantage.

O'Shaughnessy, Arthur. An Epic of Women. Fletcher, Ian & Stokes, John, eds. LC 76-20148. (Decadent Consciousness Ser.). 1978. lib. bdg. 38.00 o.s.i. (ISBN 0-8240-2780-9). Garland Pub.

O'Shaughnessy, Brian. The Will: A Dual Aspect Theory. LC 79-13524. (Cambridge Paperback Library Ser.). Date not set. Vol. 1, 251 pgs. pap. 14.95 (ISBN 0-521-27253-X); Vol. 2, 380 pgs. pap. 14.95 (ISBN 0-521-27254-8). Cambridge U Pr.

O'Shaughnessy, J. Patterns of Business Organization. LC 76-26116. 1976. 27.95x o.p. (ISBN 0-470-98927-0). Halsted Pr.

O'Shea, Donald C., et al. Introduction to Lasers & Their Applications. (Physics Ser.). 1977. text ed. 27.95 (ISBN 0-201-05509-0). A-W.

O'Shea, J. A., intro. by. Survey of Research & Investigations in Agricultural Engineering, 1978. 129p. (Orig.). 1978. pap. text ed. 20.25x (ISBN 0-85825-098-5, Pub. by Inst Engineering Australia). Renouf.

--Survey of Research & Investigations in Agricultural Engineering, 1980. 134p. (Orig.). 1980. pap. text ed. 22.50x (ISBN 0-686-42704-1, Pub. by Inst Engineering Australia). Renouf.

--Survey of Research & Investigations in Agricultural Engineering, 1982. 110p. (Orig.). 1982. pap. text ed. 18.00x (ISBN 0-85825-180-9, Pub. by Inst Engineering Australia). Renouf.

O'Shea, John A., intro. by. Agricultural Engineering: 1978. 325p. (Orig.). 1978. pap. text ed. 54.00x (ISBN 0-85825-097-7, Pub. by Inst Engineering Australia). Renouf.

O'Shea, Lester. Tampering with the Machinery: Roots of Economic & Political Malaise. 256p. 1980. 11.95 o.p. (ISBN 0-07-047749-3, GB). McGraw.

O'Shea, Patrick, jt. auth. see Kingsbury, Roy.

Osheim, Duane J. An Italian Lordship: The Bishopric of Lucca in the Late Middle Ages. (UCLA Center for Medieval & Renaissance Studies: Vol. 11). 1977. 24.50x (ISBN 0-520-03005-2). U of Cal Pr.

O'Shell, Maggie. Prisoner-Cell Block H: The Karen Travers Story, No. 3. 224p. (Orig.). 1981. pap. 2.25 (ISBN 0-523-41176-6). Pinnacle Bks.

Osherson, Daniel N. Logical Abilities in Children, 4 vols. Incl. Vol. 1. Organization of Length & Class: Empirical Consequences of a Piagetion Formulism. 11.95 o.s.i. (ISBN 0-470-65723-5); Vol. 2. Logical Inference. 11.95 o.s.i. (ISBN 0-470-65724-3); Vol. 3. Reasoning in Adolescence-Deductive Inference. LC 75-25623. 1975. 14.95 o.s.i. (ISBN 0-470-65730-8); Vol. 4. Reasoning & Concepts. 14.95 o.s.i. (ISBN 0-470-99009-0). LC 74-2298. 1974-77. Halsted Pr.

Oshinsky, David M. Conspiracy So Immense: The World of Joe McCarthy. (Illus.). 288p. 1983. 19.95 (ISBN 0-02-923490-5). Free Pr.

--Senator Joe McCarthy. LC 77-18474. 1982. 19.95 (ISBN 0-02-923490-5). Free Pr.

Oshry, Barry. Controlling the Contexts of Consciousness: The I, the We, the All of Us. LC 75-9952. (Notes on Power Ser.). (Orig.). 1976. pap. 2.75 (ISBN 0-910411-02-6). Power & Sys.

--Middle Power. (Notes on Power Ser.). (Orig.). 1980. pap. 4.95 (ISBN 0-910411-08-5). Power & Sys.

--Middles of the World, Integrate! (Orig.). 1982. pap. 5.95 (ISBN 0-910411-09-3). Power & Sys.

--Notes on the Power & Systems Perspective. LC 75-933. (Notes on Power Ser.). (Orig.). 1976. pap. text ed. 6.75 (ISBN 0-910411-01-8). Power & Sys.

--Organic Power. LC 80-4780. (Notes on Power Ser.). (Orig.). 1976. pap. text ed. 3.25 (ISBN 0-910411-03-4). Power & Sys.

--Organization Spasms. (Notes on Power Ser.). (Orig.). 1978. pap. 3.75 (ISBN 0-910411-06-9). Power & Sys.

--Power & Position. LC 88-8848. (Notes on Power Ser.). (Orig.). 1977. pap. text ed. 7.50 (ISBN 0-910411-04-2). Power & Sys.

--Success of a Business-Failure of Its Partners. (Notes on Power Ser.). (Orig.). 1980. pap. 3.50 (ISBN 0-910411-07-7). Power & Sys.

--Take a Look at Yourself: Self-in-System Sensitizers. (Notes on Power Ser.). (Orig.). 1978. pap. text ed. 5.00 (ISBN 0-910411-05-0). Power & Sys.

Osia, Kunirum. Israel, South Africa & Black Africa: A Study of the Primacy of the Politics of Expediency. LC 81-40716. 128p. (Orig.). 1982. lib. bdg. 19.00 (ISBN 0-8191-1937-7); pap. text ed. 8.25 (ISBN 0-8191-1938-5). U Pr of Amer.

Osicka, A., jt. auth. see Poldauf, J.

Osiek, Betty T. Jose Asuncion Silva. (World Authors Ser.). 1978. 15.95 (ISBN 0-8057-6346-5, Twayne). G K Hall.

Osier, Donald V. & Wozniak, Robert H. A Century of Serial Publications in Psychology, 1850-1950; An International Bibliography. (Bibliographies in the History of Psychology & Psychiatry Ser.). (Orig.). 1983. lib. bdg. 90.00 (ISBN 0-527-98196-6). Kraus Intl.

Osipow, Samuel H., jt. ed. see Walsh, W. Bruce.

Osipow, Samuel H., et al. Theories of Career Development. 2nd & rev. ed. LC 68-15785. (Illus.). 1973. pap. 23.95 (ISBN 0-13-913442-5). P-H.

Oskamp, S. Attitudes & Opinions. LC 76-52999. 1977. 23.95 (ISBN 0-13-050393-2). P-H.

Oski, Frank A. Year Book of Pediatrics 1983. 1983. 35.00 (ISBN 0-8151-6566-8). Year Bk Med.

Oski, Frank A., jt. auth. see Nathan, David G.

Oski, Frank A., jt. ed. see Kaye, Robert.

Osler, Jack. Fifty Great Mini-Trips for Michigan. (Illus.). 1977. pap. 2.50 o.p. (ISBN 0-89645-002-3). Media Ventures.

Osler, William. Aequanimitas. 3rd ed. 1932. 30.00 (ISBN 0-07-047915-1, HP). McGraw.

Oslin, Ronald, jt. auth. see Sigafoos, Robert A.

Osman, Alice H. & McConochie, Jean. If You Feel Like Singing: American Folksongs & Activities for Students of English. (English As a Second Language Bk.). (Illus.). 1979. pap. text ed. 4.95x (ISBN 0-582-79724-1); cassettes 12.95x (ISBN 0-582-79725-X); cassette & book 15.50x (ISBN 0-582-78310-0). Longman.

Osman, Betty & Blinder, Henriette. No One To Play With: The Social Side of Learning Disabilities. LC 81-40241. 1982. 12.50 (ISBN 0-394-51134-4). Random.

Osman, Colin & Turner, Peter, eds. Creative Camera Collection: No. 5. (Illus.). 1978. 27.50 o.p. (ISBN 0-685-67248-4, Pub. by Two Continents). Hippocrene Bks.

Osman, Colin, ed. see Whitney, Leon F.

Osmani, Siddiqur R. Economic Inequality & Group Welfare: A Theory of Comparison with Application to Bangladesh. 176p. 1982. 34.95x (ISBN 0-19-828425-X). Oxford U Pr.

Osmer, Harold H. U. S. Religions Journalism & the Korean War. LC 80-5441. 153p. 1980. pap. text ed. 8.25 (ISBN 0-8191-1097-3). U Pr of Amer.

Osmond, C. B., jt. ed. see Tolbert, N. E.

Osmond, D. S. see Steiner, Rudolf.

Osmond, D. S., tr. see Steiner, Rudlof.

Osmond, D. S., tr. see Steiner, Rudolf.

Osmond, Humphrey, jt. auth. see Siegler, Miriam.

Osmond, Humphry. Predicting the Past. 222p. 1981. 11.95 o.s.i. (ISBN 0-02-594020-1). Macmillan.

Osmond, J. K. & Cowart, J. B. Natural Uranium & Thorium Series Disequilibrium: New Approaches to Geochemical Problems. (Nuclear Science Applications Ser.: Section B). 50p. 1982. 19.95 (ISBN 3-7186-0131-1). Harwood Academic.

Osmond, John. Creative Conflict: The Politics of Welsh Devolution. 1978. 16.95x (ISBN 0-7100-8741-1). Routledge & Kegan.

Osmond, Marie & Davis. Marie Osmond's Guide to Beauty, Health & Style, No. 21. 1980. 12.95 o.p. (ISBN 0-671-24686-0, 24686); pap. 5.95 o.p. (ISBN 0-671-25350-6, 25350). S&S.

Osofsky, Howard. Advances in Clinical Obstetrics & Gynecology, Vol. I. (Illus.). 320p. 1982. lib. bdg. 43.00 (ISBN 0-683-06656-0). Williams & Wilkins.

Osofsky, Howard J., ed. Advances in Clinical Obstetrics & Gynecology, 2 vols. (Illus.). 306p. 1982. Vol. I. 43.00 (ISBN 0-686-94083-0); Vol. II. write for info. Williams & Wilkins.

Osofsky, Joy D., ed. The Handbook of Infant Development. LC 78-17605. (Personality Processes Ser.). 1979. 57.50 (ISBN 0-471-65703-4, Pub. by Wiley-Interscience). Wiley.

Osofsky, Stephen. Peter Kropotkin. (World Leaders Ser.). 1979. lib. bdg. 13.95 (ISBN 0-8057-7724-5, Twayne). G K Hall.

Ospovat, Dov. The Development of Darwin's Theory: Natural History, Natural Theology, & Natural Selection, 1838-1859. LC 81-4077. (Illus.). 228p. 1981. 42.50 (ISBN 0-521-23818-8). Cambridge U Pr.

Ossa, Helen. They Saved Our Birds. (Illus.). 288p. (gr. 6 up). 1983. pap. 5.95 (ISBN 0-88254-714-3). Hippocrene Bks.

Ossar, Michael. Anarchism in the Dramas of Ernst Toller. LC 79-20304. 1980. lib. bdg. 44.50x (ISBN 0-87395-393-2). State U NY Pr.

Osserman, Robert. Two-Dimensional Calculus. LC 76-50613. 476p. 1977. Repr. of 1968 ed. lib. bdg. 24.00 (ISBN 0-88275-473-4). Krieger.

Ossman, David. The Day Book of the City. 20p. 1982. 12.50x (ISBN 0-918824-36-2). Turkey Pr.

--The Rainbow Cafe. (Illus.). 20p. 1982. limited ed. 10.00x (ISBN 0-918824-37-0). Turkey Pr.

Ossowska, M. Moral Norms: A Tentative Systemization. 1980. 47.00 (ISBN 0-444-85454-1). Elsevier.

Ostberg, Donald E., jt. auth. see Finney, Ross L.

Ostberg, Donald R., jt. auth. see Lynch, Ransom V.

Ostendarp, Carol, jt. auth. see Hekelman, Francine.

Ostenfeld, E. Forms Matter & Mind. 1982. 43.50 (ISBN 90-247-3051-1, Pub. by Martinus Nijhoff Netherlands). Kluwer Boston.

Oster, Harry. Living Country Blues. LC 69-20397. (Illus.). 1969. 30.00x (ISBN 0-8103-5026-2). Gale.

Oster, Jerry. Port Wine Stain. (Orig.). 1980. pap. 1.95 o.p. (ISBN 0-451-09345-3, J9345, Sig). NAL.

Oster, Joan. Blender Recipes. LC 77-98169. 1981. 14.95 (ISBN 0-88351-003-0). Test Recipe.

Oster, Ludwig. Modern Astronomy. LC 72-83247. 500p. 1973. text ed. 22.50x (ISBN 0-8162-6523-2). Holden-Day.

Osterbind, Carter C., jt. ed. see Kraft, John.

Ostergard, Susan, et al. The Metric World: A Survival Guide. LC 75-6919. (Illus.). 176p. 1975. pap. text ed. 11.95 (ISBN 0-8299-0059-4); instrs.' manual avail. (ISBN 0-8299-0605-3). West Pub.

Ostergren, Jan. Rainmaker. Matthais, John & Printz-Pahlson, Goran, trs. from Swedish. 56p. 1983. 13.95x (ISBN 0-8214-0745-7, 82-85140); pap. 7.95 (ISBN 0-8214-0746-5, 82-85157). Ohio U Pr.

Osterhaven, Jan. Interregional Input-Output Analysis & Dutch Regional Policy Problems. 217p. 1982. text ed. 47.50x (ISBN 0-566-00521-2). Gower Pub Ltd.

Osterhaven, M. Eugene. The Faith of the Church: A Reformed Perspective on its Historical Development. 1982. pap. 11.95 (ISBN 0-8028-1916-8). Eerdmans.

Osterheld, William, jt. auth. see Slurzberg, Morris.

Osterland, C. Kirk, jt. ed. see Espinoza, Luis R.

Osterman, Paul. Getting Started: The Youth Labor Market. 352p. 1980. text ed. 22.50x (ISBN 0-262-15021-2). MIT Pr.

Osterman, Paul, jt. auth. see Gross, Ronald.

Ostermoeller, Wolfgang. Fish Breeding Recipes. (Illus.). 1973. pap. 7.95 (ISBN 0-87666-071-5, PS-693). TFH Pubns.

Osterweis, Rollin G. Romanticism & Nationalism in the Old South. LC 49-7620. x, 296p. 1967. pap. text ed. 7.95x o.p. (ISBN 0-8071-0121-4). La State U Pr.

Ostiguy, Jean-Rene. Modernism in Quebec Art, Nineteen Sixteen to Nineteen Forty-Six. (Illus.). 256p. 1982. 19.95 (ISBN 0-686-97832-3, 56435-5, Pub. by Natl Mus Canada). U of Chicago Pr.

Ostino, G. & Martini, N., eds. Progress in Clinical Pharmacy IV: Proceedings of the European Symposium, Tenth, Stresa, Italy, October 14-17, 1981. (Progress in Clinical Pharmacy: No. IV). 274p. 1982. 59.75 (ISBN 0-444-80437-4, Biomedical Pr). Elsevier.

Ostle, R. C., ed. Studies in Modern Arabic Literature. 202p. 1975. text ed. 23.00x (ISBN 0-85668-030-3, Pub. by Aris & Phillips England); pap. text ed. 14.00x (ISBN 0-686-96744-5, Pub. by Aris & Phillips England). Humanities.

Ostle, R. C., tr. see Wellhausen, Julius.

Ostler, Carolyn H. Collecting People: Your Ancestors & Mine. (gr. 6 up). 1983. 10.00x (ISBN 0-940764-16-4). Genealog Inst.

Ostling, Acton, Jr., jt. ed. see Whitwell, David.

Ostling, Richard N., jt. auth. see Nathanson, Bernard N.

Ostlund, Neil S., jt. auth. see Szabo, Attila.

Ostor, Akos & Fruzetti, Lina. Concepts of Person: Kinship, Caste, & Marriage in India. (Harvard Studies in Cultural Anthropology Ser.: Vol. 5). (Illus.). 304p. 1982. text ed. 35.00x (ISBN 0-674-15765-6). Harvard U Pr.

Ostow, Miriam & Brecher, Charles. Dollars & Service Delivery in Health Care. (Conservation of Human Resources: Vol. 19). Date not set. text ed. 27.50x (ISBN 0-916672-59-X). Allanheld.

Ostow, Miriam, jt. ed. see Hiestand, Dale L.

Ostrander, Gilman. Ideas of the Progressive Era. 1970. pap. text ed. 1.95x (ISBN 0-88273-226-9). Forum Pr IL.

Ostrander, Gilman H. Early Colonial Thought. 1970. pap. text ed. 1.95x (ISBN 0-88273-221-8). Forum Pr IL.

Ostrander, Gilman M. American Enlightenment. 1970. pap. text ed. 1.95x (ISBN 0-88273-222-6). Forum Pr IL.

--Romantic Democracy. 1970. pap. text ed. 1.95x (ISBN 0-88273-223-4). Forum Pr IL.

--Slavery in the Union. 1970. pap. text ed. 1.95x (ISBN 0-88273-224-2). Forum Pr IL.

Ostrander, Linda, jt. auth. see Owyang, Lily.

Ostrander, Norma. Ivanhoe Notes. (Orig.). 1967. pap. 2.75 (ISBN 0-8220-0663-4). Cliffs.

--Passage to India Notes. (Orig.). 1967. pap. 2.75 (ISBN 0-8220-0985-4). Cliffs.

Ostrander, Raymond H. & Dethy, Ray C. A Values Approach to Educational Administration. LC 68-4958. 426p. 1973. Repr. of 1968 ed. 21.00 (ISBN 0-88275-086-0). Krieger.

Ostrander, Sheila. Etiquette for Today. (Illus., Orig.). (gr. 9-12). 1967. pap. 3.50 o.p. (ISBN 0-06-463272-5, EH 272, EH). B&N NY.

Ostrander, Sheila & Schroeder, Lynn. Seventy-Six Psychic Techniques: A Primer in Parapsychology. O'Quinn, John, ed. 8p. 1980. pap. text ed. 2.00 (ISBN 0-9609802-5-3). Life Science.

--Superlearning. 1980. pap. 7.95 (ISBN 0-440-58099-4, Delta). Dell.

Ostrander, Sheila, et al. Superlearning. 1982. pap. 3.95 (ISBN 0-440-38424-9, LE). Dell.

Ostransky, Leroy. The Anatomy of Jazz. LC 73-11857. (Illus.). xiii, 362p. 1973. Repr. of 1960 ed. lib. bdg. 20.75x (ISBN 0-8371-7092-3, OSAJ). Greenwood.

Ostriker, Alicia. Writing Like a Woman. (Poets on Poetry Ser.). 200p. 1983. pap. 8.95 (ISBN 0-472-06347-2). U of Mich Pr.

Ostro. Liposomes. (Immunology Ser.). 408p. 1983. price not set (ISBN 0-8247-1717-1). Dekker.

Ostrogorski, Moisei. Democracy & the Organization of Political Parties, 2 Vols. LC 72-122620. (World History Ser.: No. 48). 1970. Repr. lib. bdg. 89.95x (ISBN 0-8383-1003-6). Haskell.

--Democracy & the Organization of Political Parties, 2 vols. abr. ed. LC 81-2862. (Social Science Classics Ser.). 1982. Set. pap. 29.95 (ISBN 0-686-86794-7). Vol. 1: England, 350p (ISBN 0-87855-877-2). Vol. 2: United States, 418p (ISBN 0-87855-878-0). Transaction Bks.

Ostrom, Elinor & Parks, Roger B. Patterns of Metropolitan Policing. LC 77-25466. 240p. 1978. prof ref 20.00x (ISBN 0-88410-783-3). Ballinger Pub.

Ostrom, John. Better Paragraphs. 4th ed. 1978. pap. text ed. 6.50 scp o.p. (ISBN 0-690-01526-7, HarpC). Har-Row.

--Better Paragraphs & Short Themes. 5th ed. 128p. 1983. pap. text ed. 4.95 scp (ISBN 0-06-044969-1, HarpC). Har-Row.

--The Strange World of Dinosaurs. (Illus.). (gr. 5 up). 1964. PLB 6.69 o.p. (ISBN 0-399-60615-7). Putnam Pub Group.

Ostrosky, Anthony L., Jr. & Koch, James V. Introduction to Mathematical Economics. LC 78-69569. (Illus.). 1979. text ed. 29.95 (ISBN 0-395-27052-9); solutions manual 1.20 (ISBN 0-395-27053-7). HM.

Ostrow, Eileen J., ed. Center Stage: An Anthology of 21 Contemporary Black American Plays. 2nd ed. (Illus.). 328p. (Orig.). 1983. pap. 14.00 (ISBN 0-9605208-2-1). Sea Urchin.

Ostrow, Marshal E. Breeding Killifishes. (Illus.). 1981. 4.95 (ISBN 0-87666-540-7, KW-129). TFH Pubns.

Ostrow, Marshall. Bettas. (Illus.). 96p. 1980. 4.95 (ISBN 0-87666-522-9, KW052). TFH Pubns.

--Breeding Hamsters. (Illus.). 96p. 1982. 4.95 (ISBN 0-87666-935-6, KW-134). TFH Pubns.

Ostrow, Patricia C. & Williamson, John. Quality Assurance Primer: Improving Health Care Outcomes & Productivity. 114p. 1983. 6.00, 8.00 non-members (ISBN 0-910317-10-0). Am Occup Therapy.

Ostrow, Patricia C., jt. auth. see Williams, John W.

Ostrowski, R. & Kemper, J. World History. 1976. 18.40 (ISBN 0-07-047930-5, W); tchr's ed. 20.96 (ISBN 0-07-047931-3). McGraw.

Ostroy, Sanford E., jt. ed. see Abramson, Edwin.

Osuagwu, Harold G. Investment Demand in a Developing Country: The Nigerian Case. LC 80-8183. (Illus.). 430p. (Orig.). 1982. lib. bdg. 26.75 (ISBN 0-8191-2048-0); pap. text ed. 15.50 (ISBN 0-8191-2049-9). U Pr of Amer.

O'Suilleabhain, Sean. Handbook of Irish Folklore. LC 73-129100. 1970. Repr. of 1942 ed. 50.00x (ISBN 0-8103-3561-1). Gale.

O'Sullivan & Miller. The Geography of Warfare. LC 82-42771. 176p. 1983. 19.95x (ISBN 0-312-32184-8). St Martin.

O'Sullivan, D. G. Multiple Choice Questions in Biochemistry. 78p. 1980. pap. text ed. 6.95 (ISBN 0-7131-4363-0). E Arnold.

O'Sullivan, Patrick. Geographical Economics. LC 80-39881. 199p. 1981. 29.95x o.s.i. (ISBN 0-470-27122-1). Halsted Pr.

O'Sullivan, Patrick, jt. auth. see Ahmed, Yusef.

O'Sullivan, Sally. Looking Good. 1979. pap. text ed. 6.50x o.p. (ISBN 0-435-42243-X). Heinemann Ed.

O'Sullivan, Tim. Glitter Street. 1981. pap. 2.75 o.s.i. (ISBN 0-440-12902-8). Dell.

O'Sullivan, Vincent. The Houses of Sin, Repr. Of 1897 Ed. Fletcher, Ian & Stokes, John, eds. Bd. with Poems. Sullivan, Vincent. LC 76-25930. (Decadent Consciousness Ser.: Vol. 33). 1977. lib. bdg. 38.00 o.s.i. (ISBN 0-8240-2783-3). Garland Pub.

O'Sullivan, Vincent, ed. see Mansfield, Katherine.

O'Sullivan, Ward D. An Atlas of Gastrointestnal Surgery. LC 74-12094. (Illus.). 60p. 1974. incl. slides 165.00x (ISBN 0-8036-6690-X); 8.50x (ISBN 0-8036-6691-8). Davis Co.

Osuntokun, A. Chief S. Ladoke Akintola: His Life & Times. 200p. 1983. text ed. 30.00x (F Cass Co). Biblio Dist.

Oswald, Adrian & Hildyard, R. J. English Brown Stoneware, 1670-1900. (Illus.). 296p. 1983. 60.00 (ISBN 0-571-11905-0). Faber & Faber.

Oswald, Ian. Sleeping & Waking. 1962. 42.75 (ISBN 0-444-40431-7, North Holland). Elsevier.

Oswald, Ian & Adam, Kirstine. Get a Better Night's Sleep. LC 82-4060. (Positive Health Guides Ser.). (Illus.). 128p. 1983. 12.95 (ISBN 0-668-05335-6); pap. 7.95 (ISBN 0-668-05341-0). Arco.

Oswald, J. W., jt. auth. see Krar, S. F.

Oswald, John C. Benjamin Franklin, Printer. LC 74-3020. 1974. Repr. of 1917 ed. 42.00x (ISBN 0-8103-3642-1). Gale.

Oswalt, Wendell H. An Anthropological Analysis of Food-Getting Technology. 328p. 1983. Repr. of 1976 ed. text ed. price not set (ISBN 0-89874-606-X). Krieger.

--Kolmakovskiy Redoubt: The Ethnoarchaeology of a Russian Fort in Alaska. LC 80-53304. (Monumenta Archaeologica Ser.: No. 8). (Illus.). 212p. 1980. 13.50 (ISBN 0-917956-17-6). UCLA Arch.

--This Land Was Theirs: A Study of North American Indians. 3rd ed. LC 77-14986. 1978. text ed. 25.95x (ISBN 0-471-02342-6). Wiley.

Oswalt, Wendell H., et al. An Anthropological Analysis of Food-Getting Technology. LC 76-17640. 1976. 27.50 o.p. (ISBN 0-471-65729-8, Pub. by Wiley-Interscience). Wiley.

Oswin, jt. auth. see Cairns.

Oswin, C. R. Plastic Films & Packaging. (Illus.). xi, 214p. 1975. 28.75 (ISBN 0-85334-641-0, Pub. by Applied Sci England). Elsevier.

Otaala, Barnabas. The Development of Operational Thinking in Primary School Children: An Examination of Some Aspects of Piaget's Theory Among the Iteso Children of Uganda. LC 72-90520. 1972. pap. text ed. 5.00x (ISBN 0-8077-1870-X). Tchrs Coll.

Otaka, Terumi. Lovable Mini Dolls. (Illus.). 96p. 1982. pap. 6.50 (ISBN 0-87040-518-7). Japan Pubns.

Otaki, Tadao, jt. auth. see Draeger, Donn F.

Otanes, Fe T., jt. auth. see Schachter, Paul.

Otfinoski, Steven. The Zombie Maker. Uhlich, Richard, ed. (Bluejeans Paperback Ser.). (Illus., Orig.). (gr. 7-12). 1978. pap. text ed. 1.25 o.p. (ISBN 0-8374-0043-0). Xerox Ed Pubns.

Otis, Brooks. Cosmos & Tragedy: An Essay on the Meaning of Aeschylus. Kopff, E. Christian, ed. LC 80-25320. xiii, 119p. 1981. 16.00x (ISBN 0-8078-1465-2). U of NC Pr.

Otis, D. S. The Dawes Act & the Allotment of Indian Land. (Civilization of the American Indian Ser.: Vol. 123). 215p. 1973. 9.95x o.p. (ISBN 0-8061-1039-2). U of Okla Pr.

Otis, George. Eldridge Cleaver: Ice & Fire. pap. 2.95 o.p. (ISBN 0-89728-026-1, 664956). Omega Pubns OR.

--God, Money & You. 1975. pap. 1.50 o.s.i. (ISBN 0-89129-004-4). Jove Pubns.

--High Adventure. 1977. pap. 1.50 o.s.i. (ISBN 0-89129-014-1). Jove Pubns.

--High Adventure. 1971. 8.95 (ISBN 0-8007-0483-5); pap. 1.95 o.p. (ISBN 0-686-86539-1). Omega Pubns OR.

Otis, James. Toby Tyler. (Companion Library Ser.). (gr. 4-8). 2.95 (ISBN 0-448-05483-3, G&D). Putnam Pub Group.

--Toby Tyler: Or, Ten Weeks with a Circus. LC 75-32185. (Classics of Children's Literature, 1621-1932: Vol. 48). 1977. Repr. of 1881 ed. PLB 38.00 o.s.i. (ISBN 0-8240-2297-1). Garland Pub.

Otis, Jay L. & Leukart, R. H. Job Evaluation. 2nd ed. 1954. ref. ed. 24.95 (ISBN 0-13-509562-X). P-H.

Otnes, R. K. & Enochson, L. Applied Time Series Analysis: Vol. 1, Basic Techniques. 449p. 1978. 42.95x (ISBN 0-471-24235-7, Pub. by Wiley-Interscience). Wiley.

Otnes, Robert K. & Enochson, Loren. Digital Time Series Analysis. LC 72-637. (Wiley Series in Probability & Mathematical Statistics: Applied Probability & Statistics Section). 552p. 1972. 41.95x (ISBN 0-471-65719-0, Pub. by Wiley-Interscience). Wiley.

Oton, E. U., ed. Nigeria's Educator-Statesman: Selected Writings of Eyo Ita. 1983. 30.00x (ISBN 0-7146-2731-3, F Cass Co). Biblio Dist.

O'Toole, C. P., jt. ed. see O'Mongain, Eon.

O'Toole, James, et al, eds. Working: A Courses By Newspaper Reader, Changes & Choices. Scheiber, Jane L. & Wood, Linda. LC 81-6773. 525p. 1981. pap. 12.95 reader (ISBN 0-89885-111-4); pap. 4.95 study guide (ISBN 0-89885-112-2); Article Booklet For the Fifteenth Course 4.95 (ISBN 0-89885-113-0). Human Sci Pr.

O'Toole, L. M. & Culhane, P. T. Passport to Moscow: First Year Russian Course. (Illus.). 1972. pap. text ed. 9.95x (ISBN 0-19-872072-6); tchrs. bk free (ISBN 0-19-872074-2); wkbk. o.p. 2.95x (ISBN 0-19-872073-4); tapes 15.00x ea.; tape set 195.00x (ISBN 0-19-519740-2). Oxford U Pr.

O'Toole, Thomas L. Church Learns-the People Learn. LC 73-9276. 174p. 1974. pap. 1.25 o.p. (ISBN 0-8189-1112-3, Pub. by Alba Bks). Alba.

Otsuka, Masanori & Hall, Z. W., eds. Neurobiology of Chemical Transmission. LC 78-24602. 1979. 36.50 o.p. (ISBN 0-471-03974-8, Pub. by Wiley-Medical). Wiley.

Otsuka, Sei, jt. ed. see Eliel, Ernest L.

Ott, Attiat F., jt. auth. see Ott, David J.

Ott, D. G. Syntheses with Stable Isotopes of Carbon, Nitrogen, & Oxygen. 224p. 1981. 29.95x (ISBN 0-471-04922-0, Pub. by Wiley-Interscience). Wiley.

Ott, David, et al. Macroeconomic Theory. (Illus.). 416p. 1975. text ed. 17.95 o.p. (ISBN 0-07-047918-6, C). McGraw.

Ott, David J. & Meltzer, Allan H. Federal Tax Treatment of State & Local Securities. LC 79-27915. (Brookings Institution, National Committee on Government Finance, Studies of Government Finance). (Illus.). xiv, 146p. 1980. Repr. of 1963 ed. lib. bdg. 20.75x (ISBN 0-313-22306-8, OTFT). Greenwood.

Ott, David J. & Ott, Attiat F. Federal Budget Policy. 3rd ed. (Studies of Government Finance). 1977. 16.95 (ISBN 0-8157-6710-2); pap. 7.95 (ISBN 0-8157-6709-9). Brookings.

Ott, E. Revision der Sektion Chronopus Bge. der Gattung Astragalus. L. (Phanerogamarum Monographiae Ser.: No. 9). (Illus.). 1979. lib. bdg. 20.00 (ISBN 3-7682-1187-8). Lubrecht & Cramer.

Ott, Ellis R. Process Quality Control. (Illus.). 416p. 1975. 27.95 (ISBN 0-07-047923-2, P&RB). McGraw.

Ott, Henry W. Noise Reduction Techniques in Electronic Systems. LC 75-33165. 352p. 1976. 34.95x (ISBN 0-471-65726-3, Pub. by Wiley-Interscience). Wiley.

Ott, John & Stroer, Rosemary. Work As You Like It: A Look at Unusual Jobs. LC 78-26694. (Career Bk.). (Illus.). 192p. (gr. 7 up). 1979. PLB 7.79 o.p. (ISBN 0-671-32904-9). Messner.

Ott, Jonathan & Bigwood, Jeremy, eds. Teonanacatl: Hallucinogenic Mushrooms of North America. LC 78-14794. 1978. 14.50x (ISBN 0-914842-32-3); pap. 9.95 (ISBN 0-914842-29-3). Madrona Pubs.

Ott, L., jt. auth. see Lewis, C. L.

Ott, Lyman & Hildebrand, David. Statistical Thinking for Managers. 840p. 1982. text ed. write for info. (ISBN 0-87150-401-4, 6090). Duxbury Pr.

Ott, Lyman & Larson, Richard F. Statistics: A Tool for the Social Sciences. 512p. 1982. text ed. write for info. (ISBN 0-87150-400-6, 6084). Duxbury Pr.

Ott, Richard F., ed. see Vistnes, Lars M., et al.

Ott, Sandra. The Circle of Mountains: A Basque Shepherding Community. (Illus.). 1981. 49.95x (ISBN 0-19-823199-7). Oxford U Pr.

Ott, T., jt. ed. see Disney, R.

Ott, Virginia & Swanson, Gloria. Man with a Million Ideas: Fred Jones, Genius Inventor. LC 76-22444. (Adult & Young Adult Bks). (Illus.). (gr. 6 up). 1976. PLB 6.95g (ISBN 0-8225-0761-7). Lerner Pubns.

Ott, Wayne R. Environmental Indices: Theory & Practice. LC 77-85082. 1978. 39.95 o.p. (ISBN 0-250-40191-6). Ann Arbor Science.

Ott, William G., jt. auth. see Rosenberg, R. Robert.

Ottati, Douglas F. Meaning & Method in H. Richard Niebuhr's Theology. LC 81-43707. 226p. (Orig.). 1982. lib. bdg. 22.25 (ISBN 0-8191-2341-2); pap. text ed. 10.75 (ISBN 0-8191-2342-0). U Pr of Amer.

Ottaviano, P. J. Quality Control in the Clinical Laboratory. (Illus.). 1977. 19.95 (ISBN 0-8391-1156-8). Univ Park.

Ottaviano, Victor. Energy Management. 2nd ed. (Illus.). 700p. 1983. pap. text ed. 70.00 (ISBN 0-915586-77-0). Fairmont Pr.

Ottaway, David & Ottaway, Marina. Algeria: The Politics of a Socialist Revolution. LC 70-83210. (Illus.). 1970. 31.00x (ISBN 0-520-01655-6). U of Cal Pr.

Ottaway, David, jt. auth. see Ottaway, Marina.

Ottaway, Hal N. & Edwards, Jim L. The Vanished Splendor: Postcard Views of Early Oklahoma City. LC 82-72945. (Illus.). 64p. Date not set. 15.95 (ISBN 0-910453-00-4). Abalache Bkshop.

Ottaway, J. H., jt. auth. see Datta, S. P.

Ottaway, J. M. Biochemistry of Pollution. (Studies in Biology: No. 123). 64p. 1980. pap. text ed. 8.95 (ISBN 0-686-43101-4). E Arnold.

Ottaway, J. M. & Ure, A. M. Practical Atomic Absorption Spectrometry. 1983. 30.01 (ISBN 0-08-023800-9). Pergamon.

Ottaway, John R., jt. auth. see Baer, Charles J.

Ottaway, Marina & Ottaway, David. Ethiopia: Empire in Revolution. LC 77-28370. (Illus.). 1978. text ed. 24.50x (ISBN 0-8419-0362-X, Africana); pap. text ed. 12.50x o.p. (ISBN 0-686-76866-3). Holmes & Meier.

Ottaway, Marina, jt. auth. see Ottaway, David.

Otte, Carel, jt. ed. see Kruger, Paul.

Otte, E., jt. auth. see Lockhart, J.

Otte, Elmer & Bergmann, Mark. Engaging the Aging in Ministry. 1981. pap. 6.95 (ISBN 0-570-03833-2). Concordia.

Otten, Anna, ed. Meistererzahlungen. (Orig., Ger.). 1969. pap. text ed. 11.95 (ISBN 0-13-574251-X). P-H.

Otten, C. Michael. Power, Values, & Society: An Introduction to Sociology. 1981. pap. text ed. 12.95x o.p. (ISBN 0-673-15260-X). Scott F.

--University Authority & the Student: The Berkeley Experience. LC 72-99485. (Illus.). 1970. 30.00x (ISBN 0-520-01607-6). U of Cal Pr.

Otten, Robert M. Joseph Addison. (English Authors Ser.). 1982. lib. bdg. 13.95 (ISBN 0-8057-6824-6, Twayne). G K Hall.

Ottenheimer. Holly Hobbie's Scrambled Word Find Puzzles. (Illus.). (gr. 3-6). 1979. pap. 0.95 o.s.i. (ISBN 0-448-15936-8, G&D). Putnam Pub Group.

--Holly Hobbie's Springtime Activity Book. (Illus.). 1979. pap. 0.95 (ISBN 0-448-15937-6, G&D). Putnam Pub Group.

--New Rhyming Dictionary of One & Two Syllable Rhymes. pap. 2.50 (ISBN 0-06-461009-8, BN). B&N NY.

--Pebbles & Bamm Bamm's Secret Mazes. (Illus.). (gr. 3-6). 1979. pap. 0.95 o.s.i. (ISBN 0-448-17020-5, G&D). Putnam Pub Group.

Ottenheimer, ed. German-English, English-German Dictionary. pap. 2.25 (ISBN 0-06-465028-6, BN). B&N NY.

Ottenheimerk Publishers. Charlie Brown Funny Book. LC 79-51209. (Illus.). 64p. (gr. 1-6). 1979. PLB 4.51 o.s.i. (ISBN 0-448-13124-2, G&D); pap. 2.50 o.s.i. (ISBN 0-448-16826-X). Putnam Pub Group.

--Peanuts Book of Joke & Riddles. LC 79-50328. (Illus.). 64p. (gr. 1-6). 1979. PLB 4.51 o.s.i. (ISBN 0-448-13123-4, G&D); pap. 2.50 o.s.i. (ISBN 0-448-16829-4). Putnam Pub Group.

Ottens, Allen J. Coping with Academic Anxiety. (Personal Adjustment Ser.). 140p. 1983. lib. bdg. 7.97 (ISBN 0-8239-0607-8). Rosen Pr.

Ottensoser, Milton D., jt. auth. see Sigall, Michael W.

Otterman, Lillian. Clinker Islands. LC 81-86431. (Illus.). 1983. pap. 8.95 (ISBN 0-86666-109-3). GWP.

Ottersen, Signe R., ed. see International Institute for Environment & Development (I.I.E.D.).

Otterstrom, Thorvald. A Theory of Modulation. LC 74-34379. (Music Reprint Ser). (Illus.). viii, 162p. (Ger. & Eng.). 1975. Repr. of 1935 ed. lib. bdg. 22.50 (ISBN 0-306-70721-7). Da Capo.

Otteswill, R. H., ed. Adsorption from Solution. write for info. (ISBN 0-12-530980-5). Acad Pr.

Otting, E. R., tr. see Morrill, Weston H. & Hurst, James C.

Ottinger, M. A., jt. auth. see Scanes, C. G.

Ottley, R. & Weatherby, W., eds. The Negro in New York: An Informal Social History. LC 67-21389. 328p. 1967. 12.50 (ISBN 0-379-00251-5). Oceana.

Ottley, Reginald. No More Tommorrow. LC 78-137758. (Illus.). 107p. (gr. 7 up). 1971. 5.25 (ISBN 0-15-257495-6, HJ). HarBraceJ.

Ottlik, Geza & Hugh, Kelsey. Adventures in Card Play. 1979. 18.95 (ISBN 0-575-02608-1, Pub. by Gollancz England). David & Charles.

Ottman, R. More Music for Sight Singing. 1981. pap. 14.95 (ISBN 0-13-601211-6). P-H.

Ottman, Robert W. Advanced Harmony: Theory & Practice. 2nd ed. LC 72-173655. (Illus.). 304p. 1972. text ed. 20.95 (ISBN 0-13-012955-0). P-H.

--Elementary Harmony: Theory & Practice. 2nd ed. LC 70-105451. 1970. text ed. 18.95 (ISBN 0-13-257451-9); wkbk 12.95 (ISBN 0-13-257469-1). P-H.

--Music for Sight Singing. 2nd ed. 1967. pap. text ed. 14.95 (ISBN 0-13-607440-5). P-H.

Ottman, Robert W. & Mainous, Frank D. Rudiments of Music. 1970. pap. text ed. 18.95 (ISBN 0-13-783662-7). P-H.

Otto, Bismarck Von. Kaiser vs. Bismarck. Miall, Bernard, tr. LC 75-136405. Repr. of 1921 ed. 14.50 (ISBN 0-404-00869-0). AMS Pr.

Otto, Christian F. Space into Light: The Churches of Balthasar Neumann. (Illus.). 1979. 40.00 (ISBN 0-262-15019-0). MIT Pr.

Otto, Frei. Tensile Structures. 490p. 1973. pap. 19.95x (ISBN 0-262-65005-3). MIT Pr.

Otto, Herbert & Otto, Roberta. Total Sex. pap. 2.25 (ISBN 0-451-09287-2, E9287, Sig). NAL.

Otto, Herbert A., jt. auth. see Loring, Rosalind K.

Otto, Herbert A., ed. Love Today. 1973. pap. 2.75 o.s.i. (ISBN 0-440-55062-9, Delta). Dell.

Otto, Herbert R. The Linguistic Basis of Logic Translation. LC 78-63261. 1978. pap. text ed. 10.25 (ISBN 0-8191-0617-8). U Pr of Amer.

Otto, Luther B., jt. auth. see Call, Vaughn R.

Otto, Luther B., et al. Design for a Study: Entry into Careers, Vol. 1. LC 79-48034. (Entry into Careers Ser.). (Illus.). 256p. 1981. 20.95x (ISBN 0-669-03643-9). Lexington Bks.

Otto, Luther B., jt. auth. see Spenner, Kenneth I.

Otto, Roberta, jt. auth. see Otto, Herbert.

Otto, Shirley & Orford, Jim. Not Quite Like Home: Small Hostels for Alcoholics & Others. LC 77-12664. 1978. 38.95 o.s.i. (ISBN 0-471-99589-4, Pub. by Wiley-Interscience). Wiley.

Otto, Svend S. A Christmas Book. Tate, Joan, tr. from Danish. LC 82-81485. (Illus.). 24p. 1982. 8.95 (ISBN 0-88332-286-2, 8224). Larousse.

Otto, W., jt. auth. see Pawelek, S.

Otto, Wayne & Smith, Richard J. Corrective & Remedial Teaching. 3rd ed. LC 79-89740. (Illus.). 1980. text ed. 23.50 (ISBN 0-395-28355-8). HM.

Otto, Wayne & White, Sandra, eds. Reading Expository Material. LC 82-4054. 1982. 29.50 (ISBN 0-12-531050-1). Acad Pr.

Ottoson, D. Physiology of the Nervous System. 1982. 125.00x (ISBN 0-333-30819-0, Pub. by Macmillan England). State Mutual Bk.

Ottoson, David. Physiology of the Nervous System. (Illus.). 584p. 1983. 45.00 (ISBN 0-19-520410-7); pap. 27.95 (ISBN 0-19-520409-3). Oxford U Pr.

Ottum, Bob. Busy Days with Raggedy Ann & Andy. (Golden Touch & Feel Bk.). (Illus.). (ps-k). 1976. 4.95 (ISBN 0-307-12143-7, Golden Pr). Western Pub.

Otway-Ruthven, A. J. A History of Medieval Ireland. 2nd ed. LC 79-18849. (Illus.). 1979. 30.00x (ISBN 0-312-38139-5). St Martin.

Otyce, B., jt. auth. see Froe, Otis D.

Otzen, Benedikt, et al. Myths in the Old Testament. (Student Christian Movement Press Ser.). (Orig.). 1980. pap. 11.95x o.p. (ISBN 0-19-520332-1). Oxford U Pr.

Ou, Tsuin-chen, tr. see Dewey, John.

Ouden, Bernard D. The Fusion of Naturalism & Humanism. LC 79-5348. 1979. pap. text ed. 9.75 (ISBN 0-8191-0869-3). U Pr of Amer.

--A Symposium on Ethics: The Role of Moral Values in Contemporary Thought. 104p. (Orig.). 1983. lib. bdg. 18.75 (ISBN 0-8191-2763-9); pap. text ed. 8.00 (ISBN 0-8191-2764-7). U Pr of Amer.

Ouden, P. den & Boom, B. K. Manual of Cultivated Conifers: Hardy in the Cold & Warm Temperature Zone. 1982. text ed. 59.00 (ISBN 90-247-2148-2, Pub. by Martinus Nijhoff); pap. text ed. 37.00 (ISBN 90-247-2644-1). Kluwer Boston.

Oudenaren, John Van see Van Oudenaren, John.

Ouellette, Frances, jt. auth. see Redmond, Gertrude T.

Ouellette, Robert B., jt. auth. see Roberts, Ralph.

Ouellette, Robert P. & King, John A. Chemical Week Pesticides Register. LC 76-29646. 1977. pap. 110.00 (ISBN 0-07-047948-8, P&RB). McGraw.

Ouellette, Robert P. & Thomas, L. W. Automation Impacts on Industry. LC 82-48646. (Illus.). 200p. 1983. 27.50 (ISBN 0-250-40609-8). Ann Arbor Science.

Ouellette, Robert P., et al. Low-Temperature Plasma Technology Applications. LC 80-65514. (Electrotechnology Ser.: Vol. 5). (Illus.). 148p. 1980. 39.95 (ISBN 0-250-40375-7). Ann Arbor Science.

Ouellette, Robert P., jt. auth. see Brown, Richard D.

Ouellette, Robert P., jt. auth. see Golden, Jack.

Ouellette, Robert P., jt. auth. see Walcoff, Carol.

Ouellette, Robert P., et al, eds. Applications in Manufacturing, Vol.2. LC 77-85093. (Electrotechnology Ser.). 1978. 39.95 o.p. (ISBN 0-250-40207-6). Ann Arbor Science.

--Wastewater Treatment & Separation Methods, Vol.1. LC 77-85093. (Electrotechnology Ser.). 1978. 49.95 (ISBN 0-250-40206-8). Ann Arbor Science.

Ough, Anne R. New Directions in Crochet. LC 80-52646. (Illus.). 248p. 1981. 19.95 o.p. (ISBN 0-670-40008-4, Studio). Viking Pr.

Ough, C. S., jt. auth. see Amerine, M. A.

Oughton, Frederick. The Complete Manual of Wood Finishing. LC 82-19195. (Illus.). 288p. 1983. 18.95 (ISBN 0-8128-2890-9). Stein & Day.

Ouida, pseud. Five Tales from Tuscany. 192p. 1982. 30.00x (ISBN 0-284-98633-X, Pub. by C Skilton Scotland). State Mutual Bk.

Ouida, Sebestyen. I. O. U. 192p. (gr. 7 up). 1982. 8.95 o.p. (ISBN 0-686-79042-1, Pub. by Atlantic Monthly Pr). Little.

Ouimet, Ronald P. Contemporary Furniture Plans: One Hundred Fourteen Projects You Can Build Yourself. LC 81-8811. (Illus.). 160p. (Orig.). 1981. pap. text ed. 8.95 (ISBN 0-8069-7546-6). Sterling.

Ouimette, Victor. Jose Ortega y Gasset. (World Author Ser.). 1982. lib. bdg. 15.95 (ISBN 0-8057-6466-6, Twayne). G K Hall.

Oulanoff, Hongor. The Prose Fiction of Veniamin A. Kaverin. v, 203p. 1976. soft cover 10.95 (ISBN 0-89357-032-X). Slavica.

Oulton, A. J. & Bishop, E. The Teaching of Computer Appreciation & Library Automation. 136p. 1981. pap. 40.00x (ISBN 0-905984-75-7, Pub. by Brit Lib Engalnd). State Mutual Bk.

Oursler, Fulton. The Greatest Story Ever Told. (General Ser.). 1979. lib. bdg. 15.95 (ISBN 0-8161-6778-8, Large Print Bks). G K Hall.

Ousmane, Sembene. Xala. Wake, Clive, tr. from Fr. LC 75-41811. (Illus.). 112p. 1976. 10.00 o.s.i. (ISBN 0-88208-067-9). Lawrence Hill.

Ouspensky, P. D. Fourth Way. 1971. pap. 6.95 (ISBN 0-394-71672-8, Vin). Random.

--New Model of the Universe: Principles of the Psychological Method in Its Application to Problems of Science, Religion & Art. LC 35-8632. 1971. pap. 6.95 (ISBN 0-394-71524-1, Vin). Random.

Outcalt, David, jt. auth. see Wood, June.

Outerbridge, David E., ed. Without Makeup: Liv Ullmann a Photo-Biography. (Illus.). 1979. 15.00 (ISBN 0-688-03441-1). Morrow.

Outhwaite, William. Concept Formation in Social Science. (International Library of Sociology). 240p. 1983. 30.00 (ISBN 0-7100-9195-8). Routledge & Kegan.

Outka, Darryl E., jt. auth. see Elliot, Alfred.

Outka, Gene. Agape: An Ethical Analysis. LC 78-88070. (Publications in Religion Ser.: No. 17). 336p. 1972. 27.50x (ISBN 0-300-01384-1); pap. 7.95x (ISBN 0-300-02122-4). Yale U Pr.

Outland, Barbara. Reading! The Success Formula. 432p. 1982. pap. text ed. 21.95 (ISBN 0-8403-2864-8). Kendall-Hunt.

Outlar, Jesse. Between the Hedges: A Story of Georgia Football. Rev. & enl. ed. LC 73-87002. (College Sports Ser.). 182p. 1974. 10.95 (ISBN 0-87397-218-X). Strode.

--Georgia Football. 1982. 10.95 o.p. (ISBN 0-87397-218-X). Strode.

Ouverson, Marlin. Computer Anatomy for Beginners. 1982. text ed. 15.95 (ISBN 0-8359-0920-4); pap. text ed. 10.95 (ISBN 0-8359-0919-0). Reston.

Ouvry, Phil & Langley-Price, Pat. Seamanship & Navigation. 208p. 1982. 40.00x o.p. (ISBN 0-229-11662-0, Pub. by Granada England). State Mutual Bk.

Ouweneel, W. J. What Is the Christian's Hope? 53p. pap. 2.45 (ISBN 0-88172-116-6). Believers Bkshelf.

Ovchinnikov, V. V. Britain Observed: A Russian's View. LC 80-40657. 224p. 1981. 20.50 (ISBN 0-08-023603-0); pap. 8.50 o.p. (ISBN 0-08-023608-1). Pergamon.

Ovchinnikov, Yu. A., jt. ed. see Tosteson, D. C.

Ovenden & Corbet. The Wild Animals of Britain & Europe. pap. 8.95 (ISBN 0-686-42743-2, Collins Pub England). Greene.

Ovenden, jt. auth. see Barrett.

Ovenden, jt. auth. see Corbett.

Ovenden, Graham. Aspects of Lolita. 1977. 30.00 o.p. (ISBN 0-312-05722-9). St Martin.

Ovenden, Graham, ed. A Victorian Album: Julia Margaret Cameron and Her Circle. LC 75-18728. (Photography Ser.). (Illus.). 119p. 1975. lib. bdg. 39.50 (ISBN 0-306-70749-7) (ISBN 0-685-57063-0). Da Capo.

Over, Ira Earl, jt. auth. see Chang, Huan-Yang.

Over, Raymond Van see Van Over, Raymond.

Overbeck, Carla. Systems of the Human Body. (Science Ser.). 24p. (gr. 5 up). 1979. wkbk. 5.00 (ISBN 0-8209-0150-4, S-12). ESP.

Overbeck, Cynthia. The Butterfly Book. LC 78-7235. (Early Nature Picture Bks). (Illus.). (gr. k-3). 1978. PLB 4.95g (ISBN 0-8225-1111-8). Lerner Pubns.

--Cactus. LC 82-211. (Natural Science Bks.). (Illus.). 48p. (gr. 4-10). 1982. lib. bdg. 8.95g (ISBN 0-8225-1469-9). Lerner Pubns.

--Carnivorous Plants. LC 81-17234. (Lerner Natural Science Bks.). (Illus.). 48p. (gr. 4-10). 1982. PLB 8.95g (ISBN 0-8225-1470-2). Lerner Pubns.

--Dragonflies. LC 82-7221. (Lerner Natural Science Bks.). (Illus.). 48p. (gr. 4-10). 1982. lib. bdg. 8.95g (ISBN 0-8225-1477-X). Lerner Pubns.

--Elephants. LC 80-27550. (Lerner Natural Science Bks.). (Illus.). (gr. 4-10). 1981. PLB 8.95g (ISBN 0-8225-1452-4). Lerner Pubns.

--The Fish Book. LC 78-7205. (Early Nature Picture Bks). (Illus.). (gr. k-3). 1978. PLB 4.95g (ISBN 0-8225-1110-X). Lerner Pubns.

--The Fruit Book. LC 74-12744. (The Early Nature Picture Bks). (Illus.). 32p. (gr. k-3). 1975. PLB 4.95g (ISBN 0-8225-0295-X). Lerner Pubns.

--How Seeds Travel. LC 81-17217. (Lerner Natural Science Bks). (Illus.). 48p. (gr. 4-8). 1982. PLB 8.95g (ISBN 0-8225-1474-5). Lerner Pubns.

--Lions. LC 81-1962. (Lerner Natural Science Bks.). (Illus.). (gr. 4-10). 1981. PLB 8.95g (ISBN 0-8225-1463-X, AACR2). Lerner Pubns.

--Monkeys. LC 81-1961. (Lerner Natural Science Bks.). (Illus.). (gr. 4-10). 1981. PLB 8.95g (ISBN 0-8225-1464-8, AACRZ). Lerner Pubns.

--Sunflowers. LC 80-27797. (Lerner Natural Science Bks.). (Illus.). (gr. 4-10). 1981. PLB 8.95g (ISBN 0-8225-1457-5). Lerner Pubns.

--The Vegetable Book. LC 74-12746. (The Early Nature Picture Bks). (Illus.). 32p. (gr. k-3). 1975. PLB 4.95g (ISBN 0-8225-0297-6). Lerner Pubns.

Overbeck, Cynthia, jt. auth. see Dallinger, Jane.

Overbeck, Cynthia, jt. auth. see Thompson, Brenda.

Overbeck, Daniel B. Begin at the Beginning: Teaching Basic Response Patterns. 64p. 1981. pap. text ed. 10.00 (ISBN 0-88450-742-4, 2086-B). Communication Skill.

Overbeck, Johannes. Population: An Introduction. LC 82-81687. 278p. 1982. text ed. 14.95 (ISBN 0-15-543488-8). HarBraceJ.

Overbeek, Johannes. The Population Challenge: A Handbook for Non-Specialists. LC 76-5328. (Contributions in Sociology: No. 19). (Illus.). 224p. 1976. lib. bdg. 25.00 (ISBN 0-8371-8896-2, OPC/). Greenwood.

Overbeek, Johannes, ed. The Evolution of Population Theory: A Documentary Sourcebook. LC 76-43138. (Contributions in Sociology: No. 23). 1977. lib. bdg. 27.50 (ISBN 0-8371-9313-3, OVP/). Greenwood.

Overbeek, Ross A. & Singletary, Wilson E. Assembler Language with ASSIST. LC 75-31713. (Illus.). 416p. 1976. text ed. 22.95 (ISBN 0-574-21085-7, 13-4085); tchr's ed. avail. (ISBN 0-574-21436-4). SRA.

Overbeek, Ross A., jt. auth. see Singletary, W. E.

Overberg, Kenneth R. An Inconsistent Ethic? Teachings of the American Catholic Bishops. LC 80-512. 220p. 1980. lib. bdg. 20.00 (ISBN 0-8191-1318-2); pap. text ed. 10.75 (ISBN 0-8191-1319-0). U Pr of Amer.

Overberger, C. & Mark, H. International Symposium on Macromolecules. (JPS Symposium: No. 62). 1978. 49.95 o.p. (ISBN 0-471-05602-2, Pub by Wiley-Interscience). Wiley.

Overberger, C. G., jt. auth. see Sediacek, B.

Overbey, Daniel L. Railroads: The Free Enterprise Alternative. LC 82-7503. (Illus.). 296p. 1982. lib. bdg. 29.95 (ISBN 0-89930-031-6, OVR/, Quorum). Greenwood.

Overbury, Thomas. Conceited News of Sir Thomas Overbury & His Friends: With Sir Thomas Overbury His Wife. Savage, James E., ed. LC 68-29084. 1968. 46.00x (ISBN 0-8201-1039-6). Schol Facsimiles.

Overcash, Michael R. Decomposition of Toxic & Nontoxic Organic Compounds in Soil. LC 80-65505. 1981. text ed. 79.95 (ISBN 0-250-40333-1). Ann Arbor Science.

Overcash, Michael R. & Pal, Dhiraj. Design of Land Treatment Systems for Industrial Wastes: Theory & Practice. LC 79-88908. 1979. 49.95 (ISBN 0-250-40291-2). Ann Arbor Science.

Overcash, Michael R. & Davidson, James M., eds. Environmental Impact of Nonpoint Source Pollution. LC 79-56118. (Illus.). 1980. 39.95 (ISBN 0-250-40339-0). Ann Arbor Science.

Overcast, Thomas D., jt. ed. see Edelhertz, Herbert.

Overduin, Daniel. Reflections on the Creed. 1980. pap. 1.95 (ISBN 0-570-03814-6, 12-2782). Concordia.

--Reflections on the Lord's Prayer. 1980. pap. 1.95 (ISBN 0-570-03815-4, 12-2783). Concordia.

--Reflections on the Sacraments. 1980. pap. 1.95 (ISBN 0-570-03816-2, 12-2784). Concordia.

--Reflections on the Ten Commandments. 1980. pap. 1.95 (ISBN 0-570-03813-8, 12-2781). Concordia.

Overgaard, Herman O. & Crener, Maxime A. International Business: The Canadian Way. 560p. 1982. pap. text ed. 26.95 (ISBN 0-8403-2900-8). Kendall-Hunt.

Overgard, William. The Divide. pap. 2.50 o.s.i. (ISBN 0-515-05492-5). Jove Pubns.

Overhage, Carl. Six One-Day Walks in the Pecos Wilderness. Hausman, Gerald, ed. LC 80-20061. (Illus.). 48p. (Orig.). 1980. pap. text ed. 4.25 (ISBN 0-913270-92-X). Sunstone Pr.

Overhage, Carl F. Age of Electronics. 1962. 29.50 (ISBN 0-07-047945-3, P&RB). McGraw.

Overhage, Carl F. & Harman, R. Joyce, eds. INTREX: The Report of a Planning Conference on Information Transfer Experiments. 1965. 14.50x o.p. (ISBN 0-262-15004-2). MIT Pr.

Overholser, Wayne D. Buckaroo's Code. (Orig.). 1980. pap. 1.95 o.s.i. (ISBN 0-440-11422-5). Dell.

--Cast a Long Shadow. 1981. pap. 1.95 o.s.i. (ISBN 0-440-11423-3). Dell.

Overholt, Thomas W., jt. ed. see Culley, Robert C.

Overholt, W. H. Asia's Nuclear Future. LC 77-778. 1977. lib. bdg. 30.00 o.p. (ISBN 0-89158-217-7). Westview.

Overholt, William. The Future of Brazil. (Westview Special Studies on Latin America). 1978. lib. bdg. 30.00 o.p. (ISBN 0-89158-268-1). Westview.

Overholt, William H., jt. auth. see Rotberg, Robert I.

Overholtzer, Arthur E. Classic Guitar Making. LC 74-1079. (Illus.). 360p. (Orig.). 1974. 24.95 (ISBN 0-930534-01-8); pap. 14.95 (ISBN 0-930534-00-X). Brock Pub.

Overholtzer, Merle C. Nurse Loreen's Nightmare. 1981. pap. 6.95 (ISBN 0-686-84678-8, Avalon). Bouregy.

Overlie, George. Tallest Tree. LC 65-20158. (General Juvenile Bks). (Illus.). (gr. k-5). 1965. PLB 3.95g (ISBN 0-8225-0255-0). Lerner Pubns.

Overly, Charles H. Tricorn Hat Tour Coloring Book. 1959. pap. 0.95 (ISBN 0-910412-72-3). Williamsburg.

Overman, Michael. Understanding Telecommunications. LC 75-319049. (Understanding Science Ser.). (Illus.). 192p. 1975. 9.00x o.p. (ISBN 0-7188-2003-7). Intl Pubns Serv.

Overs, Robert P. Tame Your Paper Work Tiger. (Illus.). 137p. (Orig.). 1983. pap. 12.95 (ISBN 0-9609592-0-3). Signpost Pr.

Overstad, Beth, ed. Bibliotherapy: Books to Help Young Children. 2nd ed. 80p. 1981. pap. 10.95 (ISBN 0-934140-09-X). Toys N Things.

Overstad, Elizabeth, ed. Potpourri of Child Care & Development Pamphlets. 2nd rev. ed. 25p. lib. bdg. 14.50 (ISBN 0-934140-15-4). Toys N Things.

Overstad, Elizabeth, jt. ed. see Kysar, Ardis.

Overstreet, Robert M. Comic Book Price Guide. 13th ed. (Illus.). 600p. 1983. pap. 9.95 (ISBN 0-517-54915-8). Overstreet.

--The Comic Book Price Guide, No. 13. 1983. pap. 9.95 (ISBN 0-517-54915-8, Harmony). Crown.

Overton, Barbara, jt. auth. see Carroll, James.

Overton, David. Planning the Administrative Library. (IFLA Publications: No. 26). 1983. price not set (ISBN 3-598-20388-8, Pub. by K G Saur). Shoe String.

Overton, Don. Doctoritis. 1979. 7.50 o.p. (ISBN 0-533-02766-7). Vantage.

Overton, H. P., compiled by. The Alternative Energy Index. 60p. Date not set. pap. text ed. cancelled (ISBN 0-686-82427-X). Center Self.

--The Solar Energy Index. 100p. Date not set. pap. text ed. 17.95 (ISBN 0-910811-11-3). Center Self.

--Soybeans & Its Uses: A Bibliography. 50p. Date not set. pap. text ed. 10.95 (ISBN 0-910811-03-2). Center Self.

Overton, Jenny. The Nightwatch Winter. 190p. 1973. 6.50 o.p. (ISBN 0-571-09969-6). Faber & Faber.

Overton, Richard C. Gulf to Rockies. LC 76-100234. Repr. of 1953 ed. lib. bdg. 19.75x (ISBN 0-8371-3035-2, OVGR). Greenwood.

Overy, R. The Nazi Economic Recovery Nineteen Thirty-two to Nineteen Thirty-eight. (Studies in Economic & Social History). 80p. 1982. pap. text ed. 4.75x (ISBN 0-333-31119-1, Pub. by Macmillan England). Humanities.

Overy, R. J. The Air War, Nineteen Thirty-Nine to Nineteen Forty-Five. LC 80-6200. (Illus.). 288p. pap. 9.95 (ISBN 0-8128-6156-6). Stein & Day.

Ovesey, Lionel, jt. auth. see Kardiner, Abram.

Ovey, C. D. Swanscombe: A Survey of a Pleistocene Site. 1964. 65.00x (ISBN 0-686-98309-2, Pub. by Royal Anthro Ireland). State Mutual Bk.

Oviatt, C. A., jt. auth. see Nixon, S. W.

Oviatt, Joan. The One Game. 185p. 1982. 6.95 (ISBN 0-87747-949-6). Deseret Bk.

Ovid. The Erotic Poems. Green, Peter, tr. 1983. pap. 4.95 (ISBN 0-14-044360-6). Penguin.

--Metamorphoses. Gregory, Horace, tr. (Orig.). pap. 3.95 (ISBN 0-451-62217-0, ME2217, Ment). NAL.

--Metamorphoses, Bk. 1. Lee, A. G., ed. 1953. pap. text ed. 7.95 (ISBN 0-521-05870-8). Cambridge U Pr.

Ovington, Mary W. Half a Man: The Status of the Negro in New York. LC 75-91548. (Sourcebooks in Negro History Ser.). 1969. pap. 1.95 o.p. (ISBN 0-8052-0227-7). Schocken.

Ovington, Ray. Birds of Prey in Florida. LC 75-23054. 1976. pap. 2.95 (ISBN 0-8200-0904-0). Great Outdoors.

--Tactics on Trout. (Illus.). 135p. 1983. pap. 8.95 (ISBN 0-686-83701-0, ScribT). Scribner.

Ovsiannikov, L. V. Group Analysis by Differential Equations. Ames, William, tr. 1982. 54.00 (ISBN 0-12-531680-1). Acad Pr.

Owen. Typing for Beginners. Date not set. pap. price not set (ISBN 0-448-12241-3, G&D). Putnam Pub Group.

Owen, A. L. Selig Perlman's Lectures on Capitalism & Socialism. LC 74-27312. 202p. 1976. 27.50 (ISBN 0-299-06780-7). U of Wis Pr.

Owen, Albert K. Integral Cooperation: Its Practical Application. LC 74-32103. (The American Utopian Adventure Ser.). (Illus.). 208p. Repr. of 1885 ed. lib. bdg. 19.50x (ISBN 0-87991-019-4). Porcupine Pr.

Owen, Anita Y., jt. auth. see Frankle, Reva T.

Owen, Ann. The Sands of Time. 192p. (Orig.). 1980. pap. 1.50 o.s.i. (ISBN 0-671-57041-2). S&S.

Owen, Barbara, intro. by. The American Musical Directory. (Music Reprint Ser.). (Illus.). 260p. 1980. Repr. of 1861 ed. lib. bdg. 27.50 (ISBN 0-306-76037-1). Da Capo.

Owen, Bruce, et al. Television Economics. LC 74-926. (Illus.). 240p. 1974. 21.95 o.p. (ISBN 0-669-92999-9). Lexington Bks.

Owen, Bruce M. Economics & Freedom of Expression: Media Structure & the First Amendment. LC 75-26645. 232p. 1975. prof ref 17.50x (ISBN 0-88410-044-8). Ballinger Pub.

Owen, Bruce M. & Braeutigam, Ronald. The Regulation Game: Strategic Use of the Administration Process. LC 78-558. 1978. prof ref 25.00x (ISBN 0-88410-066-9). Ballinger Pub.

Owen, Charles A., ed. Discussions of the Canterbury Tales. LC 77-20278. (Illus.). 1978. Repr. of 1961 ed. lib. bdg. 17.00x (ISBN 0-313-20012-2, OWDC). Greenwood.

Owen, Charles A., Jr. Biological Aspects of Copper: Occurrence, Assay & Interrelationships. LC 82-7931. (Copper in Biology & Medicine Ser.). 156p. 1983. 28.00 (ISBN 0-8155-0918-9). Noyes.

Owen, D. R., jt. auth. see Hinton, E.

Owen, D. W. D. W. Owen's Rock Mysteries: Death Group. LC 78-71377. (Rock Mysteries Ser.). (Illus.). pap. cancelled (ISBN 0-89169-545-1). Reed Bks.

Owen, David. Alfa Romeo Spiders. (AutoHistory Ser.). (Illus.). 136p. 1982. 14.95 (ISBN 0-85045-462-X, Pub. by Osprey England). Motorbooks Intl.

--The Manchester Ship Canal. 160p. 1983. 20.00 (ISBN 0-7190-0864-6). Manchester.

Owen, David, jt. auth. see Duton, Mark.

Owen, David, jt. auth. see Siegel, Richard.

Owen, Dawn, ed. Animal Models in Parasitology. 250p. 1982. 70.00x (ISBN 0-333-32182-0, Pub. by Macmillan England). State Mutual Bk.

Owen, Denis. Camouflage & Mimicry. LC 82-2566. (Phoenix Ser.). (Illus.). 160p. 1982. pap. 10.95 (ISBN 0-226-64188-0). U of Chicago Pr.

Owen, Ed. Playing & Coaching Wheelchair Basketball. LC 81-10456. (Illus.). 320p. 1982. pap. 16.95 (ISBN 0-252-00867-7). U of Ill Pr.

Owen, G. E., jt. ed. see Lloyd, Geoffrey E.

Owen, G. Frederick. Abraham Lincoln: His Life & Faith. 232p. 1981. pap. 6.95 (ISBN 0-8423-0000-7). Tyndale.

--Jerusalem. (Illus.). 1972. 5.95 (ISBN 0-8341-0215-3). Beacon Hill.

Owen, Guillermo. Game Theory. 2nd ed. 1982. 29.50 (ISBN 0-12-531150-8). Acad Pr.

Owen, Guy. The Flim-Flam Man & Other Stories. LC 79-90651. 1979. 10.95 (ISBN 0-87716-109-7, Pub. by Moore Pub Co). F Apple.

Owen, Guy & Willams, Mary C., eds. Contemporary Poetry of North Carolina. LC 77-20809. 1977. 12.95 (ISBN 0-910244-98-7). Blair.

Owen, Gwyneth, jt. auth. see Heater, Derek.

Owen, Henry, ed. The Next Phase in Foreign Policy. 1973. 22.95 (ISBN 0-8157-6766-8); pap. 8.95 (ISBN 0-8157-6765-X). Brookings.

Owen, J. G. The Management of Curriculum Development. LC 72-97876. 250p. 1973. 24.95 (ISBN 0-521-20195-0); pap. o.p. (ISBN 0-521-09806-8). Cambridge U Pr.

Owen, J. I., ed. Infantry Weapons of the NATO Armies. 2nd ed. 192p. 1979. pap. 24.00 (ISBN 0-08-027015-8). Pergamon.

--Infantry Weapons of the Warsaw Pact Armies. 2nd ed. 160p. 1979. pap. 24.00 (ISBN 0-08-027016-6). Pergamon.

Owen, Jackie & Laemmlen, Ann. Articles of Faith Learning Book. (Illus.). 64p. (gr. 2-7). 1982. Bk. I. pap. 3.95 (ISBN 0-87747-878-3); Bk. II, 80pgs. pap. 3.95 (ISBN 0-87747-915-1); Bk. III, 80pgs. pap. 3.95 (ISBN 0-87747-922-4). Deseret Bk.

Owen, Jean, jt. auth. see Berkowitz, Mildred N.

Owen, John. The Correspondence: With an Account of His Life & Work. Toon, Peter, ed. 214p. 1970. 14.00 (ISBN 0-227-67746-3). Attic Pr.

--Grace & Duty of Being Spiritually Minded. (Summit Bks). 1977. pap. 3.45 o.p. (ISBN 0-8010-6663-8). Baker Bk.

--Sin & Temptation: Insight into the Workings & Motives of the Human Heart. Houston, James M., ed. (Classics of Faith & Devotion). 1983. 9.95 (ISBN 0-88070-013-0). Multnomah.

--Working Hours: An Economic Analysis. LC 78-22287. (Illus.). 224p. 1979. 23.95 (ISBN 0-669-02740-5). Lexington Bks.

Owen, John B. Eighteenth Century, Seventeen Fourteen to Eighteen Fifteen. (Norton Library History of England Ser.). (Illus.). 384p. 1976. pap. 6.95x (ISBN 0-393-00366-3, Norton Lib). Norton.

--Sheep Production. (Illus.). 436p. 1976. text ed. 18.50 o.p. (ISBN 0-8121-0748-9). Lea & Febiger.

Owen, John D. Price of Leisure: An Economic Analysis of the Demand for Leisure Time. LC 78-123194. (Illus.). 1969. 12.50x o.p. (ISBN 90-237-2216-7). Intl Pubns Serv.

Owen, John E. Sociology: Readings on Human Society. 1981. pap. text ed. 8.95x o.p. (ISBN 0-673-15265-0). Scott F.

Owen, Ken. Concorde. (Illus.). 240p. 1982. 24.95 (ISBN 0-86720-630-6). Sci Bks Intl.

Owen, Maureen, ed. see Cataldo, Susan.

Owen, Maureen, ed. see Howe, Fanny.

Owen, Maureen, ed. see Weigel, Tom.

Owen, Michael S., jt. auth. see Newman, Sandra J.

Owen, Norman G. The Philippine Economy & the United States: Studies in Past & Present Interactions. (Michigan Papers on South & Southeast Asia: No. 22). 200p. (Orig.). 1983. text ed. price not set (ISBN 0-89148-024-2); pap. price not set (ISBN 0-89148-025-0). CSSEAS.

Owen, Oliver S. Natural Resource Conservation. 3rd ed. (Illus.). 1980. text ed. 24.95 (ISBN 0-02-390020-2). Macmillan.

Owen, P. John, jt. auth. see Reigel, Stanley.

Owen, Richard. The Eye of the Gods. 1979. pap. 2.25 o.p. (ISBN 0-451-08849-2, E8849, Sig). NAL.

Owen, Robert. Selected Writings of Robert Owen: A Collection of Pamphlets 1819-1850. 1979. 37.50x (ISBN 0-678-00917-1). Kelley.

--With James Bruce in Egypt. (Illus.). (gr. 7 up). 12.75x (ISBN 0-392-05607-0, SpS). Sportshelf.

Owen, Robert, et al. Scientific Foundations of Orthopaedics & Traumatology. (Illus.). 531p. text ed. 55.00 (ISBN 0-7216-7029-6). Saunders.

Owen, Robert D. Hints on Public Architecture. (Architecture & Decorative Art Ser.). (Illus.). 1978. Repr. of 1849 ed. lib. bdg. 65.00 (ISBN 0-306-77545-X). Da Capo.

Owen, Roger. Studies in the Economic & Social History of Palestine in the 19th & 20th Centuries. Date not set. 27.50x (ISBN 0-8093-1089-9). S Ill U Pr.

Owen, T. R., jt. auth. see Anderson, J. G. C.

Owen, Thomas C. Capitalism & Politics in Russia: A Social History of the Moscow Merchants, 1855 to 1905. LC 80-11279. (Illus.). 352p. 1981. 39.50 (ISBN 0-521-23173-6). Cambridge U Pr.

Owen, Tobias & Goldsmith, Donald. The Search for Life in the Universe. 1979. 17.95 (ISBN 0-8053-3325-8). Benjamin-Cummings.

Owen, Trevor A. Lancelot Andrewes. (English Authors Ser.). 1981. lib. bdg. 14.95 (ISBN 0-8057-6769-X, Twayne). G K Hall.

Owen, W. J., ed. see Wordsworth, William.

Owen, Wilfred. The Accessible City. 150p. 1972. 12.95 (ISBN 0-8157-6770-6); pap. 5.95 (ISBN 0-8157-6769-2). Brookings.

--Transportation for Cities: The Role of Federal Policy. 1976. pap. 5.95 (ISBN 0-8157-6773-0). Brookings.

Owen, William, jt. auth. see Brown, Tom, Jr.

Owen, William F. & Culp, Wesner, Culp, Inc. Energy in Wastewater Treatment. (Illus.). 368p. 1982. 38.95 (ISBN 0-13-277665-0). P-H.

Owen, William O., ed. The Medical Department of the United States Army During the Period of the Revolution 1776-1786. (Illus.). Repr. of 1920 ed. lib. bdg. 12.50x o.p. (ISBN 0-678-03771-X). Kelley.

Owens, Albert H., ed. Tumor Cell Heterogeneity: Origins & Implications. (Bristol-Myers Cancer Symposium Ser.). 1982. 39.50 (ISBN 0-12-531520-1). Acad Pr.

Owens, Bill. Documentary Photography: A Personal View. LC 78-57681. 1978. pap. 5.95 o.p. (ISBN 0-89169-037-9). Addison Hse.

--How to Build a Small Brewery. (Illus.). 72p. pap. 7.95 (ISBN 0-686-97997-4). Working Pr CA.

--Working: I Do It for the Money. 1977. 19.95 o.p. (ISBN 0-671-22820-X); pap. 9.95 o.p. (ISBN 0-671-22782-3). S&S.

Owens, Carolyn P. A Promise of Sanity. 1982. pap. 4.95 (ISBN 0-8423-4901-4). Tyndale.

Owens, Charles E. & Bell, Jimmy, eds. Blacks & Criminal Justice. LC 76-43639. 176p. 1977. 17.95 o.p. (ISBN 0-669-01101-0). Lexington Bks.

Owens, Claire M. Zen & the Lady. LC 79-50288. 311p. (Orig.). 1981. pap. 6.95 (ISBN 0-87773-780-0). Great Eastern.

Owens, D. H. Feedback & Multivariable Systems. (IEE Control Engineering Ser.). (Illus.). 320p. 1978. casebound 47.75 (ISBN 0-906048-03-6). Inst Elect Eng.

Owens, D. H., jt. auth. see Edwards, J. B.

Owens, Don B., Jr. Dark Valor. 4.98 (ISBN 0-911734-02-3). Black Hope Found.

--The Most Controversial American. 4.98 (ISBN 0-685-72448-4). Black Hope Found.

Owens, Elisabeth A., jt. auth. see Gifford, William C.

Owens, Gwinn, jt. auth. see Blumberg, Stanley.

Owens, Gwinn, jt. auth. see Blumberg, Stanley A.

Owens, Iris see Daimler, Harriet, pseud.

Owens, J. J., jt. auth. see Yates, Kyle M.

Owens, James. Management Training. LC 82-51057. 104p. 1982. Instrs' Handbook 29.95 (ISBN 0-943170-03-6). Management Ed.

--The Theory & Practice of Managing. LC 82-90070. 570p. (Orig.). 1982. pap. 17.00 (ISBN 0-943170-00-1); pap. text ed. 17.00 (ISBN 0-686-36906-8). Management Ed.

Owens, Janice B., jt. auth. see Kinard, Jesse.

Owens, Jesse & Neimark, Paul G. The Jesse Owens Story. (Putnam Sports Shelf Ser.). (gr. 5-8). 1970. PLB 5.29 o.p. (ISBN 0-399-60315-8). Putnam Pub Group.

Owens, Joan L. The Graduate's Guide to the Business World. LC 73-77700. (Illus.). 96p. 4.95x (ISBN 0-686-09301-1, Dist. by Hippocrene Books Inc.); pap. 2.50x (ISBN 0-686-09302-X). Leviathan Hse.

Owens, John R., et al. Politics & Parties in California. (Illus.). 1970. 11.95 (ISBN 0-02-390050-4); pap. text ed. 7.95 (ISBN 0-02-390060-1). Macmillan.

Owens, Joseph. Aristotle: The Collected Papers of Joseph Owens. Catan, John R., ed. LC 81-7602. 232p. 1981. 44.50x (ISBN 0-87395-534-X); pap. 13.95x (ISBN 0-87395-535-8). State U NY Pr.

--History of Ancient Western Philosophy. 1959. text ed. 19.95 (ISBN 0-13-389098-8). P-H.

--Interpretation of Existence. (Horizons in Philosophy Ser). 1968. pap. 2.95x o.p. (ISBN 0-02-824320-X). Glencoe.

--St. Thomas Aquinas on the Existence of God: Collected Papers of Joseph Owens. Catan, John R., ed. LC 79-13885. 1980. 44.50x (ISBN 0-87395-401-7); pap. 13.95x (ISBN 0-87395-446-7). State U NY Pr.

Owens, Joseph C. Saint Thomas & the Future of Metaphysics. (Aquinas Lecture). 1957. 7.95 (ISBN 0-87462-122-4). Marquette.

Owens, Milton E., Jr., ed. Outstanding Black Sermons, Vol. 3. 80p. 1982. pap. 4.95 (ISBN 0-8170-0973-6). Judson.

Owens, Paul. Stereo Troubleshooting & Repair Manual. (Illus.). 1979. ref. 19.95 (ISBN 0-8359-7082-5). Reston.

Owens, Robert G. Organizational Behavior in Education. 2nd ed. (Illus.). 368p. 1981. text ed. 24.95 (ISBN 0-13-641050-2). P-H.

Owens, Robert G. & Steinhoff, Carl R. Administering Change in Schools. (Illus.). 192p. 1976. Ref. Ed. 20.95 (ISBN 0-13-004929-8). P-H.

Owens, Rochelle. The Karl Marx Play & Others. 240p. 1974. pap. 5.95 (ISBN 0-525-47366-1). Drama Bk.

Owens, Virginia S. And the Trees Clap Their Hands: Faith, Perception & the New Physics. 160p. 1983. pap. 6.95 (ISBN 0-8028-1949-4). Eerdmans.

--A Feast of Families. 160p. 1983. 9.95 (ISBN 0-310-45850-1). Zondervan.

Owens, W. Look to the River. Trautman, R., ed. (Reading Shelf 1). 1970. 2.12 o.p. (ISBN 0-07-065133-7, W). McGraw.

Owens, William A. Sing Me a Song. 1983. 8.95xtape (ISBN 0-292-77574-1). U of Tex Pr.

--Tell Me a Story, Sing Me a Song: A Texas Chronicle. 338p. 1983. 25.00 (ISBN 0-292-75523-6); pap. 12.50 (ISBN 0-292-78056-7). U of Tex Pr.

Owens, William A., jt. auth. see Frary, Michael.

Owensby, Lou R. & Covington, Faison. Wonderful Letters to a Therapist. 151p. 1982. pap. 5.95 (ISBN 0-9609462-0-9). Meridian Pr.

Owen-Smith, M. S. High Velocity Missile Wounds. 192p. 1981. text ed. 29.50 (ISBN 0-7131-4371-1). E Arnold.

Owen-Smith, Norman. The White Rhinoceros: The Ecology & Behavior of a Megaherbivore. Date not set. lib. bdg. 27.50 o.p. (ISBN 0-8240-7119-0). Garland Pub.

Ower, E. & Nayler, J. L. High Speed Flight. 10.00 o.p. (ISBN 0-685-28366-6). Philos Lib.

Owings, Chloe. Women Police, a Study of the Development & Status of the Women Police Movement. LC 69-14941. (Criminology, Law Enforcement, & Social Problems Ser.: No. 28). 1969. Repr. of 1925 ed. 12.00x (ISBN 0-87585-028-6). Patterson Smith.

Owings, Donnell M. His Lordship's Patronage: Offices of Profit in Colonial Maryland. 214p. 1953. 10.00 (ISBN 0-686-36830-4). Md Hist.

Owings, Loren C., ed. Environmental Values, 1860-1972: A Guide to Information Sources. LC 73-17539. (Man & the Environment Information Guide Ser.: Vol. 4). 593p. 1976. 42.00x (ISBN 0-8103-1343-X). Gale.

Owings, Timothy. A Cumulative Index of New Testament Greek Grammars. 160p. 1983. pap. 7.95 (ISBN 0-8010-6702-2). Baker Bk.

Owner - Builder Center, jt. auth. see Roskind, Robert.

Owomoyela, Oyekan, jt. auth. see Lindfors, Bernth.

Owre, J. Riis, ed. see Casona, Alejandro.

Owre, Oscar T. & American Ornithologists' Union. Adaptations for Locomotion & Feeding in the Anhinga & the Double-Crested Cormorant. 138p. 1967. 6.00 (ISBN 0-943610-06-0). Am Ornithologists.

Owsley, Frank L. Plain Folk of the Old South. (Walter Lynwood Fleming Lectures in Southern History Ser.). 264p. 1982. text ed. 22.50x (ISBN 0-8071-1062-0); pap. 6.95 (ISBN 0-8071-1063-9). La State U Pr.

Owsley, Frank L., Jr., ed. see Halbert, H. S. & Ball, T. H.

Owsley, Harriet C., jt. ed. see Smith, Sam B.

Owsley, John Q., Jr. & Peterson, Rex A. Symposium on Aesthetic Surgery of the Breast, Vol. XVIII. LC 78-17489. (Symposia of the Educational Foundation of the American Society of Plastic & Reconstructive Surgeons, Inc. Ser.). 1978. 68.50 o.p. (ISBN 0-8016-3793-7). Mosby.

Owyang. Foundations of Optical Waveguides. 1981. 49.00 (ISBN 0-444-00560-9). Elsevier.

Owyang, G. H. Foundations of Dielectric Optical Waveguides. 1982. 45.00 (ISBN 0-686-80802-9). Elsevier.

Owyang, Lily & Ostrander, Linda. Creative Piano: A Modular Approach for Adult Beginners. LC 77-78909. (Illus.). 1978. pap. text ed. 17.50 spiral binding (ISBN 0-395-25569-4). HM.

Oxaal, Ivar. Black Intellectuals & Revolutionary Consciousness in the West Indies. LC 72-170653. 224p. 1982. pap. text ed. 9.95 (ISBN 0-87073-417-2); 16.95. Schenkman.

Oxenbury, Helen. The Dancing Class. (Illus.). 24p. (ps-5). 1983. 5.95 (ISBN 0-8037-1651-6). Dial Bks Young.

--Eating Out. (Illus.). 24p. (ps-1). 1983. 5.95 (ISBN 0-8037-2203-6). Dial Bks Young.

--Pig Tale. LC 73-6357. (Illus.). 32p. (gr. k-3). 1973. PLB 9.55 (ISBN 0-688-30092-8). Morrow.

--The Queen & Rosie Randall. LC 78-10375. (Illus.). (gr. k-3). 1979. 9.75 (ISBN 0-688-22171-8); PLB 9.36 (ISBN 0-688-32171-2). Morrow.

Oxender, Jean J. Kinder-Fun More Insects Series, 6 bks. (Kinder-Fun Ser.). (Illus.). 96p. (Orig.). (gr. k-3). Set. pap. text ed. 18.00 (ISBN 0-89039-224-2); 64 flash cards incl. Ann Arbor Pubs.

Oxendine, J. Psychology of Motor Learning. 1968. text ed. 22.95 (ISBN 0-13-736595-0). P-H.

Oxford Dietetic Group, jt. auth. see Mann, Jim.

Oxford Scientific Films. Bees & Honey. LC 76-45849. (Illus.). (gr. k-4). 1977. 8.95 (ISBN 0-399-20589-6). Putnam Pub Group.

--The Butterfly Cycle. LC 76-45850. (Illus.). (gr. k-4). 1977. 8.95 (ISBN 0-399-20590-X). Putnam Pub Group.

--The Chicken & the Egg. LC 78-23663. (Illus.). (gr. 1 up). 1979. 8.95 (ISBN 0-399-20676-0). Putnam Pub Group.

--Common Frog. new ed. LC 78-24038. (Illus.). (gr. 1 up). 1979. 8.95 (ISBN 0-399-20675-2). Putnam Pub Group.

--Dragonflies. (Illus.). 32p. 1980. 8.95 (ISBN 0-399-20731-7). Putnam Pub Group.

--Harvest Mouse. (Illus.). 32p. 1982. 8.95 (ISBN 0-399-20851-8). Putnam Pub Group.

--House Mouse. LC 77-6736. (Illus.). (gr. 2 up). 1978. 8.95 (ISBN 0-399-20620-5). Putnam Pub Group.

--Jellyfish & Other Sea Creatures. (Illus.). 32p. 1982. 8.95 (ISBN 0-399-20852-6). Putnam Pub Group.

--The Spider's Web. LC 77-8322. (Illus.). 28p. (gr. 3-6). 1978. 8.95 (ISBN 0-399-20621-3). Putnam Pub Group.

--The Stickleback Cycle. LC 77-28754. (Illus.). (gr. k-4). 1979. 8.95 (ISBN 0-399-20638-8). Putnam Pub Group.

--The Wild Rabbit. (Illus.). 32p. 1980. 8.95 (ISBN 0-399-20730-9). Putnam Pub Group.

Oxford Scientific Films, jt. auth. see Foy, Sally.

Oxford Scientific Films Members, jt. auth. see Thompson, Gerald.

Oxford University. Statutes, Decrees & Regulations of the University of Oxford, 1980. (Orig.). 1980. pap. 36.00x o.p. (ISBN 0-686-80305-1). Oxford U Pr.

--Statutes, Decrees & Regulations of the University of Oxford: 1981 Vol. 726p. (Orig.). 1981. pap. text ed. 29.95x (ISBN 0-19-920128-5). Oxford U Pr.

Oxley, Andrew, et al. Czechoslovakia: The Party & the People. LC 72-93032. 300p. 1973. 19.95 o.p. (ISBN 0-312-18060-8). St Martin.

Oxley, T. A. & Barry, Sheila M., eds. Biodeterioration Five: Papers Presented at the 5th International Biodeterioration Symposium Aberdeen, September, 1981. 600p. 1982. 81.00 (ISBN 0-471-10296-2, Pub. by Wiley-Interscience). Wiley.

Oxley, William. Areopagus etc. (Salzburg - Poetic Drama Ser.: No. 80). 101p. 1982. pap. text ed. 25.00x (ISBN 0-391-02782-4, Pub. by Salzburg Austria). Humanities.

--On Human Consciousness: A Philosophical Discourse. (Salzburg - Poetic Drama Ser.: Vol. 74, No. 2). 114p. 1982. pap. text ed. 25.00x (ISBN 0-391-02802-2, Pub. by Salzburg Austria). Humanities.

Oxman, Bernard, ed. The Law of the Sea: A U. S. Policy Dilemma. 250p. 1983. text ed. 22.95 (ISBN 0-917616-59-6); pap. text ed. 7.95 (ISBN 0-917616-53-7). ICS Pr.

Oxnam, Garfield B. I Protest. LC 78-21506. 186p. 1979. Repr. of 1954 ed. lib. bdg. 17.75x (ISBN 0-313-21154-X, OXIP). Greenwood.

Oxnam, Robert B. The Ch'ing Game: History & Simulation. (Occasional Publication). 80p. 1972. pap. 2.00 o.p. (ISBN 0-89192-138-9). Interbk Inc.

Oxnam, Robert B. & Bush, Richardc., eds. China Briefing, 1980. 120p. (Published in cooperation with the China Council of the Asia Society, Inc.). 1980. lib. bdg. 14.50 (ISBN 0-86531-028-9); pap. 6.50 (ISBN 0-86531-070-X). Westview.

Oxner, Ed. Power FETs & Their Applications. (Illus.). 336p. 1982. 26.95 (ISBN 0-13-686923-8). P-H.

Oxtoby, J. C. Measure & Category: A Survey of the Analogies Between Topological & Measure Spaces. LC 73-149248. (Graduate Texts in Mathematics: Vol. 2). 1971. 21.00 (ISBN 0-387-90508-1); pap. text ed. 7.50 (ISBN 0-387-05349-2). Springer-Verlag.

Oxtoby, Willard G. The Meaning of Other Faiths, Vol. 10. Mulder, John C., ed. LC 83-1090. (Library of Living Faith). 120p. (Orig.). 1983. pap. price not set (ISBN 0-664-24443-2). Westminster.

Oyama, M. Mastering Karate. 8.95x o.s.i. (ISBN 0-685-47571-9). Wehman.

Oyama, Mas. Mas Oyama's Essential Karate. LC 77-79509. (Illus.). 1979. pap. 9.95 (ISBN 0-8069-8844-4). Sterling.

Oyama, Masutatsu. Mastering Karate. 1969. pap. 7.95 (ISBN 0-448-01747-4, G&D). Putnam Pub Group.

--This Is Karate. rev. ed. LC 65-17218. (Illus.). 368p. 1973. boxed 33.50 (ISBN 0-87040-254-4). Japan Pubns.

Oyediran, Oyeleye, ed. Nigerian Government & Politics Under Military Rule 1966-1979. LC 79-15018. 1979. 27.50 (ISBN 0-312-57272-7). St Martin.

Oyen, Hendrik van see Van Oyen, Hendrik.

Oyeneye, Ibiyemi. The Government of West Africa. (Illus.). 208p. (Orig.). 1982. pap. text ed. 5.56 (ISBN 0-686-36960-2). Longman.

Oyer, E. Jane, jt. ed. see Oyer, Herbert J.

Oyer, Herbert J., jt. auth. see O'Neill, John J.

Oyer, Herbert J. & Oyer, E. Jane, eds. Aging & Communication. (Illus.). 320p. 1976. text ed. 19.95 (ISBN 0-8391-0894-X). Univ Park.

Oyola, Eliezar, tr. see Cornwall, Judson.

Oyono, Ferdinand. The Old Man & the Medal, No. 39. Reed, John, tr. from Fr. (African Writers Ser.). 176p. (Orig.). pap. text ed. 4.00x (ISBN 0-435-90039-0). Heinemann Ed.

Oz, Amos. Hill of Evil Counsel. 1982. pap. 2.95 (ISBN 0-553-22921-4). Bantam.

Ozaeta, Pablo. Canciones Dramatizadas. Frank, Marjorie & Lono, Luz P., eds. LC 75-16545. 20p. (gr. 4-8). 1975. pap. text ed. 2.95 songbook (ISBN 0-88499-240-3); cassette 7.95 (ISBN 0-88499-200-4); program package 35.00 (ISBN 0-88499-239-X). Inst Mod Lang.

Ozaki, R. Economics, Economists & the Economy. 1978. pap. 14.95 (ISBN 0-8359-1595-6). Reston.

Ozanne, Larry & Struyk, Raymond J. Housing from the Existing Stock: Comparative, Economic Analyses of Owner-Occupants & Landlords. (An Institute Paper). 196p. 1976. pap. 5.50 o.p. (ISBN 0-87766-168-5, 14900). Urban Inst.

Ozawa, Martha N. Income Maintenance & Work Incentives: Toward a Synthesis. 300p. 1982. 29.95 (ISBN 0-03-058647-X). Praeger.

Ozawa, Terutomo. People & Productivity in Japan. (Work in America Institute Studies in Productivity). 1982. 35.00 (ISBN 0-08-029506-1). Pergamon.

Ozenfant, Amadee & Le Corbusier, eds. L' Esprit Nouveau, 8 Vols. LC 68-26816. (Illus., Fr.,). 1968. Repr. of 1925 ed. Set. lib. bdg. 395.00 (ISBN 0-306-71149-4). Da Capo.

Ozer, Jerome S., ed. Film Review Annual, 1981. xiii, 1153p. 1982. lib. bdg. 75.00x (ISBN 0-89198-125-X). Ozer.

Ozer, Mark N. Solving Learning & Behavior Problems of Children: A Planning System to Integrate Assessment & Treatment. LC 79-28316. (Social & Behavioral Science Ser.). 1980. text ed. 21.95x (ISBN 0-87589-445-3). Jossey-Bass.

Ozer, Mark N. & Collins, Jean E. The Ozer Method: A Breakthrough Problem-Solving Technique for Parents & Children. LC 82-7865. 288p. 1982. 12.50 (ISBN 0-688-01317-1). Morrow.

Ozernoy, Natalia. Russko-Anglijsky Razgovornik. (Eng. & Rus.). 1982. pap. 9.50 (ISBN 0-938920-21-9). Hermitage MI.

Ozick, Cynthia. Art & Ardor. 1983. 16.95 (ISBN 0-394-53082-9). Knopf.

--Levitation: Five Fictions. 176p. 1983. pap. 4.95 (ISBN 0-525-48027-7, 0481-140, Obelisk). Dutton.

--The Pagan Rabbi, & Other Stories. LC 75-36498. 288p. 1976. pap. 4.95 (ISBN 0-8052-0509-8). Schocken.

--The Pagan Rabbi: And Other Stories. 288p. 1983. pap. 6.95 (ISBN 0-525-48026-9, 0675-200, Obelisk). Dutton.

Ozima, Minoru. The Earth: Its Birth & Growth. Wakabayashi, J. F., tr. (Illus.). 180p. 1981. 24.95 (ISBN 0-521-23500-6); pap. 9.95 (ISBN 0-521-28005-2). Cambridge U Pr.

Ozin, Geoffrey A., jt. ed. see Moskovits, Martin.

Ozisik, M. N., jt. auth. see Fraas, Arthur P.

Ozisik, M. Necati. Basic Heat Transfer. (Illus.). 1976. text ed. 33.95 (ISBN 0-07-047980-1, C); student manual 9.50 (ISBN 0-07-047981-X). McGraw.

--Heat Conduction. LC 79-990. 1980. 44.95x (ISBN 0-471-05481-X, Pub. by Wiley-Interscience). Wiley.

--Radiative Transfer & Interactions with Conduction & Convection. LC 72-12824. 608p. 1973. 54.95x (ISBN 0-471-65722-0, Pub. by Wiley-Interscience). Wiley.

Ozman. Jennifer's Birthday Present. LC 73-87798. (Illus.). (gr. k-3). 1974. PLB 6.75x (ISBN 0-87783-125-4); pap. 2.95x deluxe ed. (ISBN 0-87783-126-2). Oddo.

Ozment, Stephen. The Age of Reform Twelve Fifty to Fifteen Fifty: An Intellectual & Religious History of Late Medieval & Reformation Europe. LC 79-24162. (Illus.). 1980. 40.00x (ISBN 0-300-02477-0); pap. 10.95x (ISBN 0-300-02760-5). Yale U Pr.

Ozment, Steven E. The Reformation in the Cities: The Appeal of Protestantism to Sixteenth-Century Germany & Switzerland. LC 75-8444. 228p. 1975. 22.50x (ISBN 0-300-01898-3); pap. 6.95x (ISBN 0-300-02496-7). Yale U Pr.

Ozment, Steven E., ed. Reformation Europe: A Guide to Research. 390p. 1982. 18.50x (ISBN 0-910345-01-5); pap. 13.50x (ISBN 0-686-82436-9). Center Reform.

Ozmon, H. Twelve Great Western Philosophers. LC 68-16403. (Illus.). (gr. 4 up). 1967. PLB 6.75x (ISBN 0-87783-046-0); pap. 2.95x deluxe ed (ISBN 0-87783-115-7). Oddo.

Ozmon, Howard & Craver, Samuel. Philosophical Foundations of Education. (Coordinated Teacher Preparation Ser.). 240p. 1976. text ed. 15.95 (ISBN 0-675-08669-8). Merrill.

--Philosophical Foundations of Education. 2nd ed. (General Education Ser.). 320p. 1981. text ed. 16.95 (ISBN 0-675-08049-5). Merrill.

P

P. S. Associates see Summerlin, Lee R.

Paananen, Victor. William Blake. (English Authors Ser.). 1977. lib. bdg. 11.95 (ISBN 0-8057-6672-3, Twayne). G K Hall.

Paap, Wouter. Marius Monnikendam, Componist, Tachtig Jaar. (Composers' Worklists Ser.: Vol. 6). (Illus.). 64p. 1976. 15.00 o.s.i. (ISBN 90-6027-376-1, Pub. by Frits Knuf Netherlands). Pendragon NY.

Paar, Jack. P. S. Jack Paar. LC 82-45938. (Illus.). 360p. 1983. 14.95 (ISBN 0-385-18743-2). Doubleday.

Paas, John R. German Broadsheet Political Sheet Sixteen Hundred to Seventeen Hundred, 6 vols. LC 78-53629. (Illus.). Set. cancelled o.p. (ISBN 0-913870-70-6). Abaris Bks.

Paatz, Walter. The Arts of the Italian Renaissance: The Painting, Sculpture, Architecture. (Illus.). 264p. 1974. text ed. 17.95 (ISBN 0-13-047316-2). P-H.

Pabst, G. W. Pandora's Box. (Film Scripts-Classic Ser). 1970. pap. 2.95 o.p. (ISBN 0-671-20615-X). S&S.

--Three-Penny Opera. (Film Scripts-Modern Ser.). 1971. 1.95 o.p. (ISBN 0-671-21083-1, Touchstone Bks). S&S.

Pacala, Lynn. Self Defense. 1980. 7.95x (ISBN 0-673-16202-8). Scott F.

Pacault, A., jt. ed. see Vidal, C.

Pace, Antonio, ed. Luigi Castiglioni's Viaggio: Travels in the Unites States of America, 1785-1787. (Illus.). 560p. 1983. text ed. 39.00 (ISBN 0-8156-2264-3). Syracuse U Pr.

Pace, Dale K. A Christian's Guide to Effective Jail & Prison Ministries. 320p. 1977. 13.95 o.p. (ISBN 0-8007-0844-X). Revell.

Pace, David. Claude Levi-Strauss: The Bearer of Ashes. 330p. (Orig.). 1983. 19.95 (ISBN 0-7100-9297-0). Routledge & Kegan.

Pace, David & Hunter, John. Direct Participation in Action: The New Bureaucracy. 1978. 19.95x o.p. (ISBN 0-566-00205-1, 02012-5, Pub. by Saxon Hse England). Lexington Bks.

Pace, Dean F. Negotiation & Management of Defense Contracts. LC 69-13681. 1970. 76.95 o.p. (ISBN 0-471-65741-7, Pub. by Wiley-Interscience). Wiley.

Pace, Denny F. & Styles, Jimmie C. Organized Crime: Concepts & Control. (Law Enforcement Ser.). (Illus.). 352p. 1974. ref. ed. 17.95 o.p. (ISBN 0-13-640961-X). P-H.

--Organized Crime: Concepts & Control. 2nd ed. (Illus.). 304p. 1983. 20.95 (ISBN 0-13-640946-6). P-H.

Pace, Frank J., jt. auth. see Mosier, Alice.

Pace Gallery Publications, ed. Chuck Close, Recent Work. (Illus.). 40p. 1983. pap. write for info. (ISBN 0-938608-11-8). Pace Gallery Pubns.

Pace, Graham, jt. auth. see Brandejs, Jan F.

Pace, Kaye, ed. see Beauchamp, Tom L.

Pace, Mildred M. Pyramids: Tombs for Eternity. (Illus.). 192p. (gr. 7-10). 1981. 9.95 (ISBN 0-07-048054-0). McGraw.

--Wrapped for Eternity: The Story of the Egyptian Mummies. (Illus.). 192p. (gr. 5 up). 1974. 9.95 (ISBN 0-07-048053-2, GB). McGraw.

Pace, R. Wayne. Organizational Communication: Foundations for Human Resource Development. (Illus.). 352p. 1983. text ed. 18.95 (ISBN 0-13-641324-2). P-H.

Pace, R. Wayne & Boren, Robert. R. The Human Transaction: Facets, Functions, & Forms of Interpersonal Communication. 300p. 1973. text ed. 14.50x (ISBN 0-673-05840-9). Scott F.

Pace, Robert. Piano for Classroom Music. 2nd ed. LC 71-98966. (Music Ser). (Illus.). 1970. pap. text ed. 15.95 (ISBN 0-13-674994-1). P-H.

Pacela, Allan F. & Sloan, Anne B. Directory of Audiovisual Aids. 4th ed. LC 79-66886. 1980. pap. 8.00x o.p. (ISBN 0-930844-07-6). Quest Pub.

--Guide to Biomedical Standards. 9th ed. LC 7-640292. 1982. pap. 9.00x (ISBN 0-930844-09-2). Quest Pub.

Pacela, Allan F., jt. auth. see Forbes, Eric G.

Pacela, Allan F., ed. The Quest Guide to Essential Test Instrumentation for Medical Equipment. LC 78-66409. 1978. looseleaf 32.50x o.p. (ISBN 0-930844-05-X). Quest Pub.

Pacey, Arnold. The Maze of Ingenuity: Ideas & Idealism in the Development of Technology. LC 74-18380. 337p. 1975. text ed. 30.00x (ISBN 0-8419-0181-3). Holmes & Meier.

--The Maze of Ingenuity: Ideas & Idealism in the Development of Technology. 1976. pap. 7.95x (ISBN 0-262-66030-X). MIT Pr.

Pacey, Arnold, compiled by. Gardening for Better Nutrition. (Illus.). 64p. (Orig.). 1978. pap. 3.50x (ISBN 0-903031-50-7, Pub. by Intermediate Tech England). Intermediate Tech.

Pacey, Arnold, ed. Sanitation in Developing Countries. LC 78-4215. 1978. 42.95 (ISBN 0-471-99655-6, Pub. by Wiley-Interscience). Wiley.

Pacey, Desmond. Ethel Wilson. (World Authors Ser.). 15.95 (ISBN 0-8057-2984-4, Twayne). G K Hall.

Pacey, May. West Highland White Terriers. (Arco-Foyles Pet Handbooks Ser.). (Illus.). 1978. 2.25 o.p. (ISBN 0-668-03992-2, 3992). Arco.

--West Highland White Terriers. (Foyle's Handbks). 1973. 3.95 (ISBN 0-685-55803-7). Palmetto Pub.

Pachauri. International Energy Policy. LC 80-25976. 600p. 1981. 57.50 (ISBN 0-471-08984-2, Wiley-Interscience). Wiley.

Pachauri, R. K. The Dynamics of Electrical Energy Supply & Demand: An Economic Analysis. LC 75-19806. (Special Studies). (Illus.). 202p. 1975. 28.95 o.p. (ISBN 0-275-01530-0). Praeger.

--Energy & Economic Development in India. LC 77-12718. (Praeger Special Studies). 208p. 1977. 27.95 o.p. (ISBN 0-03-022371-7). Praeger.

Pache, Rene. Inspiration & Authority. 1970. pap. 9.95 (ISBN 0-8024-4091-6). Moody.

--Person & Work of the Holy Spirit. 1960. 5.95 (ISBN 0-8024-6471-8). Moody.

Pachman, Ludek. Complete Chess Strategy, Vol. 3. (Illus.). 192p. 1981. Repr. of 1978 ed. 17.95 o.p. (ISBN 0-7134-1532-0, Pub. by Batsford England); pap. 11.50 (ISBN 0-7134-1533-9). David & Charles.

Pachner, J. Handbook of Numerical Analysis Applications: Programs for Engineers & Scientists. 672p. 1983. 65.00 (ISBN 0-07-048057-5, P&RB). McGraw.

Pacholski, Richard A. & Copp, Charles A., eds. Priorities in Death Education & Counseling. viii, 282p. (Orig.). 1982. pap. text ed. 8.95 (ISBN 0-686-83105-5). Forum for Death Educ.

Pacholski, Richard A. & Corr, Charles A., eds. New Directions in Death Education & Counseling: Enhancing the Quality of Life in the Nuclear Age. xvi, 346p. 1981. pap. 12.95 (ISBN 0-9607394-0-8). Forum for Death Educ.

Pachow, W. Chinese Buddhism: Aspects of Interaction & Reinterpretation. LC 80-5432. 275p. 1980. lib. bdg. 21.50 (ISBN 0-8191-1090-6); pap. text ed. 11.50 (ISBN 0-8191-1091-4). U Pr of Amer.

Pacht, Otto & Alexander, J. J. Illuminated Manuscripts in the Bodleian Library Vol. 2: Italian Schools. 1970. 25.75x o.p. (ISBN 0-19-817169-2). Oxford U Pr.

Pachter, Henry M. Modern Germany: A Social, Cultural, & Political History. (Illus.). 1979. lib. bdg. 25.00 (ISBN 0-89158-166-9). Westview.

Pachter, Marc, ed. see Edel, Leon, et al.

Pachucki, Chester. Mathematics for Industrial Technicians. (Illus.). 448p. 1974. text ed. 17.95 o.p. (ISBN 0-13-563221-8). P-H.

Pacific Northwest Laboratory. Siting Guide for Large Wind Turbines. 508p. 1982. 57.50 o.p. (ISBN 0-89934-160-8); pap. 49.50 (ISBN 0-89934-161-6). Solar Energy Info.

--Wind Energy Resource Atlas: Vol. 4, The Northeast Region (Connecticut, Maine, Massachusetts, New Hampshire, New Jersey, New York, Pennsylvania, Rhode Island, Vermont) 1981. pap. 24.95x (ISBN 0-89934-132-2, W046). Solar Energy Info.

--Wind Energy Resource Atlas: Vol. 7, The South Central Region (Arkansas, Kansas, Louisiana, Missouri, Oklahoma, & Texas) 222p. 1981. pap. 24.50x (ISBN 0-89934-135-7, W049). Solar Energy Info.

Pacific Northwest Laboratory for U. S. Department of Energy. Siting Guide & Directory of Manufacturers for Small Wind Turbines. 100p. 1982. pap. 19.95 (ISBN 0-89934-165-9, W060). Solar Energy Info.

Pacifici, Sergio. Italia: Vita E Cultura. 1970. text ed. 15.00x (ISBN 0-394-30463-2, RanC). Random.

Pacifici, Sergio, jt. auth. see Ginzburg, Natalia.

Pacifico, Carl R. & Witwer, Daniel B. Practical Industrial Management: Insights for Managers. LC 80-23190. 375p. 1981. 29.95 (ISBN 0-471-08190-6, Pub. by Wiley-Interscience). Wiley.

Pacilio, Nicola. Reactor-Noise Analysis in the Time Domain. LC 79-600321. (AEC Critical Reveiw Ser.). 102p. 1969. pap. 10.50 (ISBN 0-87079-335-7, TID-24512); microfiche 4.50 (ISBN 0-87079-336-5, TID-24512). DOE.

Pacini, Kathy, ed. see Delton, Judy.

Pacione, Michael. Urban Problems & Planning in the Developed World. 1981. 35.00x (ISBN 0-312-83465-9). St Martin.

Pacione, Michael, ed. Progress in Rural Geography. LC 82-22756. (Illus.). 268p. 1983. text ed. 26.95x (ISBN 0-389-20358-0). B&N Imports.

--Progress in Urban Geography. LC 82-22757. 296p. 1983. text ed. 26.95x (ISBN 0-389-20357-2). B&N Imports.

Pack, A. J. Nelson's Blood. LC 82-61669. 1982. 14.95 (ISBN 0-87021-944-8). Naval Inst Pr.

Pack, Alice C. Prepositions. (Dyad Learning Program Ser.). 1977. pap. text ed. 8.95 bound with teacher's ed. (ISBN 0-88377-076-8); tchrs edition (ISBN 0-88377-078-4). Newbury Hse.

--Pronouns & Determiners. (Dyad Learning Program Ser.). 1977. pap. text ed. 8.95 bound with teacher's ed. (ISBN 0-88377-081-4); tchr's ed. avail. (ISBN 0-88377-082-2). Newbury Hse.

--Verb Choices & Verb Forms. (Dyad Learning Program Ser.). 1977. pap. text ed. 8.95 bound with tchrs ed (ISBN 0-88377-079-2); (ISBN 0-88377-080-6). Newbury Hse.

Pack, Alice C. & Henrichsen, Lynn. Sentence Combination: Writing & Combining Standard English Sentences, Bk. II. 128p. (Orig.). 1981. pap. text ed. 8.95 (ISBN 0-88377-174-8). Newbury Hse.

Pack, Alice C. & Henrichsen, Lynn E. Sentence Construction: Writing & Combining Standard English Sentence, Bk I. 196p. 1980. pap. text ed. 8.95 (ISBN 0-88377-173-X). Newbury Hse.
Pack, Alice C. & Joy, Robert O. Learning to Type in English as a Second Language. 1976. pap. text ed. 10.25 (ISBN 0-8191-0025-0). U Pr of Amer.
Pack, Charles P. Thomas Hatch of Barnstable & Some of His Descendants. 356p. boxed 15.00 (ISBN 0-686-81805-9). NJ Hist Soc.
Pack, Howard. Fostering the Capital-Goods Sector in LDCs: A Survey of Evidence & Requirements. (Wkorking Paper: No. 376). v, 59p. 1980. 5.00 (ISBN 0-686-36183-0, WP-0376). World Bank.
--Macroeconomic Implications of Factor Substitution in Industrial Processes. (Working Paper: No. 377). vii, 60p. 1980. 5.00 (ISBN 0-686-36185-7, WP-0377). World Bank.
Pack, Raymond, jt. auth. see Aan-Ta-T'Loot.
Pack, Robert, ed. see Jackson, Richard.
Pack, Roger A. The Greek & Latin Literary Texts from Greco-Roman Egypt. LC 65-10786. 1967. 8.50 o.p. (ISBN 0-910294-22-4). Brown Bk.
Packard, Cindy. Hell's Bells. LC 82-73024. 320p. 1983. 14.95 (ISBN 0-689-11360-9). Atheneum.
Packard, David W. Minoan Linear A. (Illus.). 1974. 30.00x (ISBN 0-520-02580-6). U of Cal Pr.
Packard, Edward. Choose Your Own Adventure. pap. 1.95 (ISBN 0-686-82861-5). Bantam.
--Deadwood City. LC 77-17501. (Illus.). 96p. (gr. 4-6). 1978. 8.95i o.p. (ISBN 0-397-31783-2, JBL-J); pap. 3.95 (ISBN 0-397-31798-0). Har-Row.
--The Forbidden Castle. 128p. 1982. 1.75 (ISBN 0-553-22515-4). Bantam.
--Gorga, the Space Monster. (Choose Your Own Adventure Ser.: No. 5). 64p. (gr. 1-8). 1982. pap. 7.95 (ISBN 0-553-05031-1). Bantam.
Packard, George R., jt. auth. see Johnson, U. Alexis.
Packard, H. Jeremy. Minority-Majority Confrontation in America. (gr. 11-12). 1977. pap. 5.50x o.p. (ISBN 0-88334-088-7). Ind Sch Pr.
Packard, Pamela M. & Clement, Paul A. Corpus Vasorum Antiquorum. (The Los Angeles County Museum of Art. Ser: Fascicule 1, U.S.A., Fascicole 18). 1977. 70.00x o.p. (ISBN 0-520-02850-3). U of Cal Pr.
Packard, Robert G. Psychology of Learning & Instruction: A Performance Based Course. new ed. (Educational Psychology Ser.). 496p. 1975. pap. text ed. 17.95x (ISBN 0-675-08761-9). Additional supplements may be obtained from publisher. Merrill.
Packard, Sidney & Carron, Alan J. Start Your Own Store: Managing, Merchandising & Evaluating. (Illus.). 272p. 1982. text ed. 21.95 (ISBN 0-13-842948-0). P-H.
Packard, Sidney & Winters, Arthur. Fashion Buying & Merchandising. 2nd ed. (Illus.). 390p. 1983. text ed. 16.50 (ISBN 0-87005-445-7). Fairchild.
Packard, Sidney R. Europe & the Church Under Innocent Third. enl. ed. LC 67-18294. 1968. Repr. of 1927 ed. 7.00x o.p. (ISBN 0-8462-1082-7). Russell.
Packard, Vance. Our Endangered Children: Growing Up in a Changing World. 352p. 1983. 17.45i (ISBN 0-316-68751-0). Little.
Packard, William, ed. Desire. 176p. 1980. 12.95 o.p. (ISBN 0-312-19469-2). St Martin.
Packe, Michael. King Edward the Third. Seaman, L. C. B, ed. 400p. 1982. 24.95x (ISBN 0-7100-9024-2). Routledge & Kegan.
Packer, J. I. The Apostle's Creed. 1983. pap. 3.95 (ISBN 0-8423-0051-1); Leader's Guide 2.95 (ISBN 0-8423-0052-X). Tyndale.
--I Want to Be a Christian. 1977. pap. 6.95 (ISBN 0-8423-1842-9). Tyndale.
Packer, J. I. & Tenney, Merrill C. All the People & Places of the Bible. 1982. pap. 5.95 (ISBN 0-8407-5819-7). Nelson.
--Daily Life in Bible Times. 1982. pap. 5.95 (ISBN 0-8407-5822-7). Nelson.
--The World of the New Testament. 1982. pap. 5.95 (ISBN 0-8407-5821-9). Nelson.
--The World of the Old Testament. 1982. pap. 5.95 (ISBN 0-8407-5820-0). Nelson.
Packer, J. I., tr. see Luther, Martin.
Packer, James I., pref. by. Knowing God: Study Guide. 1975. pap. 2.25 (ISBN 0-87784-413-5). Inter-Varsity.
Packer, Lester, jt. ed. see Colowick, Sidney.
Packer, Murland, ed. Professional Engineer (Civil) State Board Examination Review. LC 74-27435. 1975. pap. 15.00 o.p. (ISBN 0-668-03637-0). Arco.
Packer, N. H., jt. auth. see Stone, W.
Packer, Rod E. The Investor's Computer Handbook. 1982. 10.95 (ISBN 0-686-92664-1, 5203). Hayden.
Packham, John R. & Harding, David J. Ecology of Woodland Processes. 256p. 1982. pap. text ed. 19.95 (ISBN 0-7131-2834-8). E Arnold.
Packie, Robert M. Storm Treasure. LC 81-66266. (Illus.). 160p. (Orig.). (gr. 6). 1981. 8.95t (ISBN 0-89272-082-4). Down East.
Packman, David. Vladimir Nabokov: The Structure of Literary Desire. LC 82-70671. 136p. 1982. 16.00 (ISBN 0-8262-0372-8). U of Mo Pr.
Packman, Zola. The Taxes in Grain in Ptolemaic Egypt: Granary Receipts from Diospolis Magna 164-88 B. C. (American Society of Papyrology Ser.). 9.00 (ISBN 0-686-95224-3, 31-00-04). Scholars Pr CA.
--The Taxes in Grain in Ptolemaic Egypt: Granary Receipts from Diospolis Magna 164-88 B. C. (American Studies in Papyrology). 6.00 o.p. (ISBN 0-686-96303-2, 31 00 02). Scholars Pr CA.
Packo, John E. Find & Use Your Spiritual Gifts. LC 80-69967. 117p. (Orig.). 1980. pap. 3.50 (ISBN 0-87509-293-4); Leader's Guide. 3.50 (ISBN 0-87509-294-2). Chr Pubns.
Pactor, P. & Kargilis, G. Card-Punch Machine Operation, Bk. 1. 1967. text ed. 11.85 (ISBN 0-07-048031-1, G). McGraw.
--Card-Punch Machine Operation, Bk. 2. 1973. text ed. 11.85 (ISBN 0-07-048032-X, G); instructor's manual & key 3.25 (ISBN 0-07-048036-2). McGraw.
Pactor, Paul. Printing Calculator Course. (gr. 9-12). 1969. spiral bdg 3.60 o.p. (ISBN 0-8224-0254-8); key 3.60 o.p. (ISBN 0-8224-1705-7). Pitman Learning.
Padberg, M. W. Combinatorial Optimization. (Mathematical Programming Studies: Vol. 12). 1980. 30.00 (ISBN 0-444-85489-4). Elsevier.
Paddington Press. Business Traveller's Handbook: Latin America. 448p. 1981. 19.95 (ISBN 0-87196-339-6); pap. 11.95 (ISBN 0-87196-345-0). Facts on File.
--Business Traveller's Handbook: The Middle East. 288p. 1981. 19.95 (ISBN 0-87196-343-4); pap. 11.95 (ISBN 0-87196-323-X). Facts on File.
Paddison, Ronan, jt. ed. see Muir, Richard.
Paddock, Elizabeth, jt. auth. see Paddock, William.
Paddock, William & Paddock, Elizabeth. We Don't Know How. 1973. pap. 5.95x (ISBN 0-8138-1755-2). Iowa St U Pr.
Paddon, M., jt. auth. see Busfield, Joan.
Pade, Victoria. When Love Remains. (Avon Romance Ser.). 384p. (Orig.). 1983. pap. 2.95 (ISBN 0-380-82610-0, 82610). Avon.
Paden, Elaine. Exercises in Phonetic Transcription. 30p. 1971. pap. text ed. 3.25x (ISBN 0-8134-1438-5, 1438). Interstate.
Paden, I. & Schlichmann, M. Big Oak Flat Road (to Yosemite) 1975. 14.95 (ISBN 0-910740-26-7); pap. 5.95 o.p. (ISBN 0-685-89211-5). Holmes.
Paden, Irene D. Wake of the Prairie Schooner. LC 43-15419. (Arcturus Books Paperbacks). (Illus.). 535p. 1970. pap. 2.95 o.p. (ISBN 0-8093-0462-7). S Ill U Pr.
--The Wake of the Prairie Schooner. (Illus.). pap. 5.95 (ISBN 0-8093-0462-7). Patrice Pr.
Paden, John N. Religion & Political Culture in Kano. LC 74-153548. 1973. 44.00x (ISBN 0-520-02020-0). U of Cal Pr.
Paderewski, Jan I. & Lawton, Mary. The Paderewski Memoirs. (Music Ser.). 1980. Repr. of 1939 ed. 37.50 (ISBN 0-306-76046-0). Da Capo.
Padfield, Peter. Tide of Empires: Decisive Naval Campaigns in the Rise of the West 1654-1763, Vol. 2. 232p. 1982. 27.50 (ISBN 0-7100-9215-6). Routledge & Kegan.
Padgett, James E. True Gospel Revealed Anew By Jesus of Nazareth & Master of the Celestial Heavens: 1914-1923. Vol. I. pap. 7.00 (ISBN 0-686-37147-X); Vols. II, III, & IV. 9.00 ea. Foun Church New Birth.
Padgett, Ron. Toujours L'Amour: Poems. LC 76-7710. 1976. 10.00 (ISBN 0-915342-11-1); pap. 5.00 (ISBN 0-915342-10-3). SUN.
--Tulsa Kid. Elmslie, Kenward, ed. (Illus., Orig.). 1980. 10.00 (ISBN 0-915990-16-4); pap. 5.00 (ISBN 0-915990-17-2). Z Pr.
Padgett, W. J., jt. auth. see Tsokos, Chris P.
Padilla, Amado M., jt. auth. see Levine, Elaine S.
Padilla, George & McCarty, Kenneth, eds. Genetic Expression in the Cell Cycle. (Cell Biology Ser.). 1982. 54.00 (ISBN 0-12-543720-X). Acad Pr.
Padilla, Geraldine, ed. The Clinical Nurse Specialist & Improvement of Nursing Practice. LC 78-78148. 83p. 1979. pap. 12.95 (ISBN 0-913654-51-5). Aspen Systems.
Padilla, Herberto. Heroes Are Grazing in My Garden. Hurley, Andrew, tr. from Spanish. 1983. 14.50 (ISBN 0-374-16982-9). FS&G.
--Legacies: Selected Poems. bi-lingual ed. Reid, Alastair, et al, trs. 192p. (Span. & Eng.). 1982. 15.00 (ISBN 0-374-25877-5); pap. 9.25 (ISBN 0-374-51736-3). FS&G.
Padilla, Michael J., ed. Science & the Early Adolescent. 144p. 1982. 6.00 (ISBN 0-686-84080-1). Natl Sci Tchrs.
Padley, G. A. Grammatical Theory in Western Europe 1500-1700. LC 75-44573. 320p. 1976. 49.50 (ISBN 0-521-21079-8). Cambridge U Pr.
Padley, J. S., jt. auth. see Porter, D.
Padmore, George. Life & Struggles of Negro Toilers. 126p. 1971. Repr. of 1931 ed. 20.00x (ISBN 0-913330-01-9). Sun Dance Bks.
Padon, Beth, compiled by. Archaeological Reports & Manuscripts on File at UCLA: Los Angeles, Ventura, & Orange Counties. (Occasional Papers: No. 10). 162p. 1982. pap. 8.00 (ISBN 0-917956-37-0). UCLA Arch.
Padovano, Anthony J. The Process of Sculpture. LC 78-22345. (Illus.). 352p. 1981. 19.95 (ISBN 0-385-14142-4). Doubleday.
Padovano, Anthony T. The Human Journey: Thomas Merton Symbol of the Century. LC 81-43306. 216p. 1982. 13.95 (ISBN 0-385-17879-4). Doubleday.
Padover, S. Letters of Karl Marx. 1979. 15.95 o.p. (ISBN 0-13-531533-6). P-H.
Padover, Saul. Karl Marx: An Intimate Biography. 1978. 18.95 o.p. (ISBN 0-07-048072-9, GB). McGraw.
Padover, Saul K. French Institutions: Values & Politics. LC 78-5634. (Hoover Studies: No. 2). 1978. Repr. of 1954 ed. lib. bdg. 18.50x (ISBN 0-313-20459-4, PAFI). Greenwood.
--Jefferson. 459p. 1982. Repr. of 1942 ed. lib. bdg. 50.00 (ISBN 0-8495-4415-7). Arden Lib.
--Karl Marx on History & People. (Karl Marx Library: Vol. 7). 360p. 1977. 15.00 (ISBN 0-07-048100-8); pap. 7.95 o.p. (ISBN 0-07-048101-6). McGraw.
--Living U. S. Constitution. rev. ed. 1968. pap. 4.95 (ISBN 0-451-62174-3, ME2174, Ment). NAL.
Padover, Saul K., ed. Karl Marx on Education, Women, & Children. LC 78-172260. (Karl Marx Library: Vol. 6). 204p. 1975. 10.00 o.p. (ISBN 0-07-048098-2, GB); pap. 5.95 o.p. (ISBN 0-07-048099-0). McGraw.
Padua, Fernando De see International Congress on Electro Cardiology, Lisbon, 7th, June 1980 & De Padua, Fernando.
Pae, Jae S., jt. auth. see Park, Choon-Ho.
Paelinck, J. H. Qualitative & Quantitative Mathematical Economics. 1982. lib. bdg. 34.50 (ISBN 90-247-2623-9, Pub. by Martinus Nijhoff Netherlands). Kluwer Boston.
Paelinck, Jean. Urban Structure in Western Europe. 1979. Repr. pap. text ed. 31.50 (ISBN 0-566-00198-5). Gower Pub Ltd.
Paetkau, Walter. Start Where You Are: A Guide to Local Christian Service. 1965. pap. 1.00 o.p. (ISBN 0-87303-725-1). Faith & Life.
Paff, George H. Anatomy of the Head & Neck. LC 72-93117. (Illus.). 235p. 1973. text ed. 22.00 o.p. (ISBN 0-7216-7041-5). Saunders.
Pafford, F. W. Handbook of Survey Notekeeping. LC 62-17467. 1962. pap. 19.95x (ISBN 0-471-65751-4, Pub. by Wiley-Interscience). Wiley.
Pagan, F. G. A Practical Guide to Algol 68. LC 75-6925. (Computing Ser.). 31.75 o.p. (ISBN 0-471-65746-8, Pub. by Wiley-Interscience); pap. 24.95 (ISBN 0-471-65747-6, Pub. by Wiley-Interscience). Wiley.
Pagana, Kathleen D. & Pagana, Timothy J. Understanding Medical Testing. (Medical Library). (Illus.). 272p. 1983. pap. price not set (ISBN 0-452-25404-3, 3778-3). Mosby.
Pagana, Timothy J. & Deskapagana, Kathleen. Diagnostic Testing & Nursing Implications: A Case Study Approach. LC 81-14146. (Illus.). 347p. 1982. pap. text ed. 14.50 (ISBN 0-8016-3746-5). Mosby.
Pagana, Timothy J., jt. auth. see Pagana, Kathleen D.
Paganetti, J. & Seklemian, M. The Best in Retail Ads. (Illus.). 424p. 1982. 19.95 (ISBN 0-934590-09-5). Retail Report.
Pagano, Alicia L., ed. Social Studies in Early Childhood: An Interactionist Point of View. LC 78-57997. (Bulletin Ser.: No. 58). 1978. pap. 6.95 (ISBN 0-87986-022-7). Coun Soc Studies.
Pagano, Anne L., ed. Cable Advertising Directory, 1982. 508p. 1982. pap. 30.00 (ISBN 0-940272-06-7). Natl Cable.
Pagano, Robert R. Understanding Statistics in the Behavioral Sciences. (Illus.). 592p. 1981. text ed. 23.95 (ISBN 0-8299-0316-X); student guide avail. (ISBN 0-8299-0341-0). West Pub.
Pagden, A. R., ed. & tr. see De Landa, Diego.
Pagden, Anthony. The Fall of Natural Man: The American Indian & the Origins of Comparative Ethnology. LC 82-1137. (Cambridge Iberian & Latin American Studies). 272p. 1982. 39.50 (ISBN 0-521-22202-8). Cambridge U Pr.
Page & Hooper. Accounting & Information Systems. 2nd ed. 1982. text ed. 24.95 (ISBN 0-8359-0090-8); practice case 7.95 (ISBN 0-8359-0092-4); instr's. manual free (ISBN 0-8359-0091-6). Reston.
Page, A. A Dictionary of Photographic Terms. (Illus.). 1966. 17.50 (ISBN 0-685-58545-X). Heinman.
--Mathematical Analysis & Techniques, Vol. 2. (Oxford Mathematical Handbooks Ser.). (Illus.). 568p. 1974. pap. text ed. 8.00x (ISBN 0-686-86547-2); pap. text ed. (ISBN 0-19-859612-X); Vol. 2. pap. text ed. o.p. (ISBN 0-19-859613-8). Oxford U Pr.
Page, A. N. Utility Theory: Book of Readings. LC 68-30917. 454p. 1968. text ed. 17.00 (ISBN 0-471-65754-9, Pub. by Wiley); pap. 9.50 (ISBN 0-471-65755-7). Krieger.
Page, Anthea. Ancient Egypt Figured Ostraca in the Petrie Collection. (Illus.). 120p. 1983. pap. text ed. 31.50x (ISBN 0-85668-216-0, Pub. by Aris & Phillips). Humanities.
Page, B. G. & Thomson, W. T. Insecticide, Herbicide Fungicide Quick Guide, 1983. 140p. Date not set. pap. 12.00 (ISBN 0-913702-20-X). Thomson Pub CA.
Page, B. I. & Petracca, M. P. The American Presidency. 496p. 1983. 13.95x (ISBN 0-07-048109-1). McGraw.
Page, Benjamin I. Who Gets What From Government. LC 82-13454. 288p. 1983. 15.95 (ISBN 0-520-04702-8). U of Cal Pr.
Page, Beverly. Cartoon Art: An Adventure in Creativity. Smith, Linda H., ed. 1980. pap. 4.95 (ISBN 0-936386-10-X). Creative Learning.
Page, C. N. The Ferns of Britain & Ireland. LC 82-1126. (Illus.). 450p. Date not set. price not set (ISBN 0-521-23213-9); pap. price not set (ISBN 0-521-29872-5). Cambridge U Pr.
Page, Carol G. Rachel's Hope. LC 79-84168. 202p. 1979. pap. 2.25 o.p. (ISBN 0-89877-004-1). Jeremy Bks.
Page, Carole G. Heather's Choice. LC 82-3417. 128p. pap. 2.95 (ISBN 0-8024-3490-8). Moody.
--The Two Worlds of Tracy Corbett. LC 79-54117. 128p. 1980. pap. 3.50 (ISBN 0-8066-1767-5, 10-6727). Augsburg.
Page, Carole G., jt. auth. see Hernandez, David.
Page, Carole Gift. Rachel's Hope. 1979. pap. 2.95 (ISBN 0-89877-004-1). Omega Pubns Or.
Page, Charles H. Fifty Years in the Sociological Enterprise: A Lucky Journey. LC 82-7046. 288p. 1982. lib. bdg. 25.00x (ISBN 0-87023-373-4). U of Mass Pr.
Page, Charles H., ed. Sociology & Contemporary Education. (Orig.). 1964. pap. text ed. 3.50 (ISBN 0-685-19770-0). Phila Bk Co.
Page, D. L., jt. auth. see Gow, Andrew S.
Page, Daniel J. The Michigan Supplement for Modern Real Estate Practice. 130p. 1980. pap. 6.95 o.s.i. (ISBN 0-695-81402-8). Follett.
Page, David. Prelude to Partition: The Indian Muslims & the Imperia; System of Control, 1920-32. 300p. 1982. 18.95x (ISBN 0-19-561303-1). Oxford U Pr.
Page, Denys L. History & the Homeric Iliad. (Sather Classical Lectures: Vol. 31). (Illus.). 1959. 21.50x (ISBN 0-520-03246-2). U of Cal Pr.
Page, E. S. & Wilson, L. B. Information, Representation & Manipulation in a Computer. 2nd ed. (Cambridge Computer Science Texts Ser.: No. 2). (Illus.). 1978. 44.50 (ISBN 0-521-22088-2); pap. 14.95x (ISBN 0-521-29357-X). Cambridge U Pr.
--Information Representation & Manipulation Using PASCAL. LC 82-4505. (Cambridge Computer Science Texts: No. 15). (Illus.). 275p. Date not set. price not set (ISBN 0-521-24954-6); pap. price not set (ISBN 0-521-27096-0). Cambridge U Pr.
--An Introduction to Computational Combinatorics. LC 78-54722. (Cambridge Computer Science Texts Ser.: No. 9). (Illus.). 1979. 37.50 (ISBN 0-521-22427-6); pap. 13.95x (ISBN 0-521-29492-4). Cambridge U Pr.
Page, Earle C. Looking at Type. (Illus.). 1983. Comb Bdg. 5.00 (ISBN 0-935652-09-4). Ctr Applications Psych.
Page, Edward. One Hundred Timex 1000-Sinclair ZX-81 Programming Tips & Tricks. new ed. 128p. (Orig.). (gr. 7-12). 1982. pap. 7.95 (ISBN 0-86668-020-9). ARCsoft.
--Thirty Seven Timex 1000-Sinclair ZX-81 Computer Programs for Home, School & Office. (Illus.). 96p. (Orig.). 1982. pap. 8.95 (ISBN 0-86668-021-7). ARCsoft.
Page, Edward C., jt. ed. see Rose, Richard.
Page, Edward W. The Architecture of the 8048: A Self-Study Course. 130p. 1983. pap. write for info (ISBN 0-88056-071-1). Dilithium Pr.
Page, Emma. Last Walk Home. 192p. 1983. 12.95 (ISBN 0-8027-5491-0). Walker & Co.
Page, Ernest W., et al. Human Reproduction: The Core Content of Obstetrics Gynecology & Perinatal Medicine. 2nd ed. LC 75-19851. (Illus.). 510p. 1976. text ed. 18.95 o.p. (ISBN 0-7216-7042-3). Saunders.
Page, Frederick, ed. see Byron.
Page, Frederick, ed. see Tennyson, Alfred L.
Page, Gordon T. How to Buy, Love & Sell a Car Happily: A Complete Buyer's Guide & Expose of the Automotive Jungle. (Illus.). 350p. (Orig.). 1983. 9.95 (ISBN 0-9607804-0-8). Page Pub WI.
Page, Harry R. Public Purchasing & Materials Management. LC 79-2039. 528p. 1980. 34.95x (ISBN 0-669-03059-7). Lexington Bks.
Page, Helen C. & Scroeder, John S. The Whole Family Low Cholesterol Cookbook. (Illus.). 334p. Date not set. pap. price not set (ISBN 0-448-12150-6, G&D). Putnam Pub Group.
Page, Irvine. Chemistry of the Brain. (Illus.). 440p. 1937. photocopy ed. spiral 44.00x (ISBN 0-398-04382-5). C C Thomas.
Page, J. S. & Nation, Jim G. Estimator's Piping Manhour Manual. 3rd ed. (Estimators Man Hour Library). 220p. 1976. 35.00x (ISBN 0-87201-700-1). Gulf Pub.
Page, Jack. Shoot the Moon. LC 79-2031. 1979. 8.95 o.p. (ISBN 0-672-52608-5). Bobbs.
Page, Jake, jt. auth. see Page, Susanne.
Page, James A. Selected Black American Authors: An Illustrated Bio-Bibliography. 1977. lib. bdg. 35.00 (ISBN 0-8161-8065-2, Hall Reference). G K Hall.
Page, John. Cost Estimating Man-Hour Manual for Pipelines & Marine Structures. 1977. 35.00x (ISBN 0-87201-157-7). Gulf Pub.
Page, John, Jr. Shadow Prices for Trade Strategy & Investment Planning in Egypt. LC 82-8594. (World Bank Staff Working Papers: No. 521). (Orig.). 1982. pap. 5.00 (ISBN 0-8213-0009-1). World Bank.
Page, John M., Jr. Small Enterprises in African Development: A Survey. (Working Paper: No. 363). ii, 53p. 1979. 3.00 (ISBN 0-686-36186-5, WP-0363). World Bank.

Page, John S. Estimator's Man-Hour Manual on Heating, Air Conditioning, Ventilating & Plumbing. 2nd ed. (Estimators Man-Hour Library). 240p. 1978. 35.00x (ISBN 0-87201-364-2). Gulf Pub.

Page, Joseph A. The Law of Premises Liability with 1981-1982 Supplement. LC 76-11993. 1976. text ed. 47.50 (ISBN 0-87084-683-3). Anderson Pub Co.

Page, Linda & Wigginton, Eliot, eds. Aunt Arie: A Foxfire Portrait. (Illus.). 192p. 1983. 15.95 (ISBN 0-525-93292-5, 01549-460, Foxfire Pr Bk); pap. 9.95 (ISBN 0-525-93291-7, 00966-290, Foxfire Pr Bk). Dutton.

--The Foxfire Calendar, 1984: Things You Can Make with Little or No Money. (Illus.). 24p. 1983. 5.95 (ISBN 0-525-93293-3, 0577-180). Dutton.

Page, Lou W. Astronomy. (gr. 7-12). 1973. pap. text ed. 7.84 (ISBN 0-201-05651-8, Sch Div); tchr's manual 3.48 (ISBN 0-201-05652-6). A-W.

--Geology. 1973. pap. text ed. 7.04 o.p. (ISBN 0-201-05653-4, Sch Div); tchr's manual 3.48 (ISBN 0-201-05654-2). A-W.

--Rocks & Minerals. (Illus.). (gr. 2-3). 1962. PLB 2.94 (ISBN 0-695-47774-9). Follett.

Page, Marian. Furniture Designed by Architects. (Illus.). 224p. 1983. pap. 14.95 (ISBN 0-8230-7181-2, Whitney Lib). Watson-Guptill.

Page, Martin. The Pilate Plot. LC 78-7711. 1978. 8.95 o.p. (ISBN 0-698-10790-X, Coward). Putnam Pub Group.

Page, Monte M., ed. Nebraska Symposium on Motivation, 1979: Beliefs, Attitudes & Values. LC 53-11655. (Nebraska Symposium on Motivation Ser.: Vol. 27). xii, 365p. 1980. 22.50x (ISBN 0-8032-2313-7); pap. 9.95x (ISBN 0-8032-7207-3). U of Nebr Pr.

--Nebraska Symposium on Motivation, 1982: Personality--Current Theory & Research. LC 53-11655. (Nebraska Symposium on Motivation Ser.: Vol. 30). xv, 270p. 1983. 22.95x (ISBN 0-8032-3667-0); pap. 12.95x (ISBN 0-8032-8708-9). U of Nebr Pr.

Page, Myra. Daughter of the Hills: A Woman's Story of Coalmining Life. LC 77-79619. 1977. pap. 4.95 o.p. (ISBN 0-89255-026-0). Persea Bks.

Page, Norman. Thomas Hardy. 1977. 18.00 (ISBN 0-7100-8614-8). Routledge & Kegan.

Page, Norman, ed. Tennyson: Interviews & Recollections. (Interviews & Recollections Ser.). 1983. 26.50x (ISBN 0-389-20066-2). B&N Imports.

Page, P. K. Poems Selected & New. LC 74-75921. (House of Anansi Poetry Ser.: No. 31). 150p. 1974. 12.95 (ISBN 0-88784-132-5, Pub. by Hse Anansi Pr Canada); pap. 5.95 o.p. (ISBN 0-88784-031-0). U of Toronto Pr.

Page, Paul F. Picture the Dawning. 1976. pap. 4.96 (ISBN 0-89390-002-8). Resource Pubns.

Page, Peter L. Magic, Psychology & Spiritism. (Illus.). 1979. 57.50 (ISBN 0-930582-50-0). Gloucester Art.

Page, R. Good News for Landlords & Tenants. (Illus.). 184p. 1982. pap. 12.95. Jeanies Classics.

Page, Rex & Didday, Richard. FORTRAN Seventy-Seven for Humans. (Illus.). 1980. pap. 17.95 (ISBN 0-8299-0271-6); instrs.' manual avail. (ISBN 0-8299-0615-0). West Pub.

--FORTRAN Seventy-Seven for Humans. 2nd ed. (Illus.). 500p. 1983. pap. text ed. 14.95 (ISBN 0-314-69672-5). West Pub.

Page, Rex, jt. auth. see Didday, Richard.

Page, Rex L. & Didday, Richard L. WATFIV for Humans. LC 76-3433. (Illus.). 630p. 1976. pap. text ed. 17.95 (ISBN 0-8299-0100-0). West Pub.

Page, Robert M. The Origin of Radar. LC 78-25844. (Illus.). 1979. Repr. of 1962 ed. lib. bdg. 19.75x (ISBN 0-313-20781-X, PAOR). Greenwood.

Page, Ruth. Page by Page. LC 78-65648. (Illus.). 224p. 1979. 14.95 o.p. (ISBN 0-87127-102-8). Dance Horiz.

Page, S. F. Cassell Book of Austin Farina. 10.00x (ISBN 0-392-05820-0, SpS). Sportshelf.

Page, Susanne & Page, Jake. Hopi. LC 81-19037. (Illus.). 240p. 1982. 50.00 (ISBN 0-8109-1082-9). Abrams.

Page, T. E., ed. see Virgil.

Page, Thomas. The Hephaestus Plague. 256p. 1973. 5.95 o.p. (ISBN 0-399-11184-0). Putnam Pub Group.

--The Man Who Would Not Die. 1982. pap. 3.50 (ISBN 0-451-11763-8, AE1763, Sig). NAL.

Page, Thomas N. Gordon Keith. 548p. 1982. Repr. of 1903 ed. lib. bdg. 20.00 (ISBN 0-8495-4414-9). Arden Lib.

--Red Rock: A Chronicle of Reconstruction. 584p. 1982. Repr. of 1899 ed. lib. bdg. 25.00 (ISBN 0-89987-668-4). Darby Bks.

Page, Tim. Tim Page's Nam. LC 82-48704. (Illus.). 1983. 25.00 (ISBN 0-394-53005-5); pap. 14.95 (ISBN 0-394-71345-1). Knopf.

Page, Tim, ed. The Hip Pocket Guide to New York. LC 81-48167. 192p. (Orig.). 1982. pap. 5.72i (ISBN 0-06-090945-5, CN-945, CN). Har-Row.

Page, Victor W. Early V-Eight Ford Service Manual: 1932-1950. Clymer Publications, ed. (Illus.). pap. 12.00 o.p. (ISBN 0-89287-266-7, H527). Clymer Pubns.

Page, Warren. The Accurate Rifle. (Stoeger Bks). 1975. pap. 5.95 o.s.i. (ISBN 0-695-80564-9). Follett.

--Topological Uniform Structures. LC 78-930. (Pure & Applied Mathematics. Wiley-Interscience Ser. of Texts, Monographs & Tracts: A Wiley Interscience Series of Texts, Monographs & Tracts). 1978. 53.50 o.p. (ISBN 0-471-02231-4, Pub. by Wiley-Interscience). Wiley.

Page, William. The Gatekeeper. (Raccoon Book). 48p. (Orig.). 1983. pap. 3.95 (ISBN 0-918518-07-5). St Luke TN.

Pagel, W. Paracelsus. 2nd ed. (Illus.). xii, 404p. 1982. 83.25 (ISBN 3-8055-3518-X). S Karger.

Pagel, Walter. Joan Baptista Van Helmont: Reformer of Science & Medicine. LC 81-24193. (Cambridge Monographs on the History of Medicine). (Illus.). 192p. 1982. 29.95 (ISBN 0-521-24807-8). Cambridge U Pr.

Pagelow, Mildred D. Women-Battering: Victims & Their Experiences. (Sage Library of Social Research: Vol. 129). 256p. 1981. 25.00 (ISBN 0-8039-1681-7); pap. 12.50 (ISBN 0-686-82965-4). Sage.

Pagels, Heinz. The Cosmic Code: Quantum Physics As the Law of Nature. 1982. 16.95 (ISBN 0-671-24802-2). S&S.

Pagen, Dennis. Powered Ultralight Training Course. (Illus.). 48p. 1981. pap. 12.95 (ISBN 0-686-32602-4). D Pagen.

Pagen, Frank G. Formal Specifications of Programming Language: A Panoramic Primer. (Illus.). 256p. 1981. text ed. 24.95 (ISBN 0-13-329052-2). P-H.

Pagenkopf, Andrea L., jt. auth. see Peavy, Linda S.

Paget, Kathleen & Brackett, Bruce, eds. The Psychoeducational Assessment of Pre-School Children. Date not set. price not set (ISBN 0-8089-1475-8). Grune.

Paget, Kathleen D. & Bracken, Bruce A., eds. The Psychoeducational Assessment of Preschool Children. 1982. 32.50 (793230). Grune.

Paget, M. Spirituals Reborn: Melody. LC 74-76574. 96p. (gr. 9-12). 1976. Pt. 1. pap. text ed. 4.95 (ISBN 0-521-08714-7); Pt. 2. pap. text ed. 4.95 (ISBN 0-521-21332-0); choral 12.95 (ISBN 0-521-08713-9). Cambridge U Pr.

Paget, Violet, jt. auth. see Lee, Vernon.

Paget, Wilkes M. Poverty, Revolution & the Church. 142p. (Orig.). Date not set. pap. text ed. 7.95 (ISBN 0-85364-285-0). Attic Pr.

Pagliaro, Ann M., jt. ed. see Pagliaro, Louis A.

Pagliaro, Louis A. & Pagliaro, Ann M., eds. Pharmacologic Aspects of Aging. (Illus.). 480p. 1983. text ed. 24.95 (ISBN 0-8016-3748-1). Mosby.

Pagnol, Marcel. The Time of Love. 208p. 1980. 19.95 o.p. (ISBN 0-241-10009-7, Pub. by Hamish Hamilton England). David & Charles.

Paher, Stanley W. Death Valley Teamsters. (Illus.). 1973. pap. 2.00 (ISBN 0-913814-07-5). Nevada Pubns.

--Las Vegas, As It Began, As It Grew. LC 70-175144. (Illus.). 1971. 20.00 (ISBN 0-913814-01-6). Nevada Pubns.

Paher, Stanley W., jt. auth. see Spude, Robert L.

Paher, Stanley W., ed. Nevada Towns & Tales, Vol. 2. (Illus.). 1982. 9.95 (ISBN 0-913814-45-8). Nevada Pubns.

Pahl, Aleta, jt. auth. see Harris, John.

Pahl, Walther. Die Luftwege der Erde: Politische Geographie des Weltluftverkehrs. (Airlines History Project Ser.). (Illus.). Date not set. price not set (ISBN 0-404-19330-7). AMS Pr.

Pahlavi, Ashraf. Faces in a Mirror: Memoirs from Exile. LC 80-13509. 1980. 12.95 o.p. (ISBN 0-13-299131-4). P-H.

Pahlavi, Mohammad R. Answer to History. LC 80-52039. 204p. 1982. 12.95 (ISBN 0-8128-2755-4); pap. 7.95 (ISBN 0-8128-6138-8). Stein & Day.

Pahler, Arnold & Mori, Joseph E. Advanced Accounting: Concepts & Practice. 1026p. 1981. text ed. 26.95 (ISBN 0-15-501815-9, HC); solutions manual 15.95 (ISBN 0-15-501816-7); test bklt. avail. 3.95; 300.00 (ISBN 0-15-501818-3). HarBraceJ.

Pahlow, Manfried. Living Medicine: The Healing Properties of Plants. (Illus.). 96p. (Orig.). 1983. pap. 6.95 (ISBN 0-7225-0592-2, Pub. by Thorsons Pubs England). Sterling.

Pahre, P. & Stewart, J. Going to the Doctor. (The Health Ser.). (Illus.). 65p. (gr. 7-12). 1981. pap. text ed. 3.00 (ISBN 0-910839-23-9). Hopewell.

Pahre, P., jt. auth. see Husak, G.

Pai. Viscous Flow Theory: Vol. 1, Laminar Flow. LC 56-11758. 400p. 1965. 18.50 (ISBN 0-442-06417-9, Pub. by Van Nos Reinhold). Krieger.

Pai, Anna C. Foundations of Genetics: A Science for Society. (Illus.). 320p. 1974. text ed. 18.95 o.p. (ISBN 0-07-048093-1, C); pap. text ed. 23.50 (ISBN 0-07-048092-3). McGraw.

Pai, Anna C. & Marcue-Roberts, Helen. Genetics: Its Concepts & Implications. (Illus.). 736p. 1981. text ed. 27.95 (ISBN 0-13-351007-7). P-H.

Pai, C. M., jt. ed. see Mort, J.

Pai, M. A. Power System Stability: Analysis by the Direct Method of Lyapunov. (North-Holland Systems & Control Ser.: Vol. 3). 1982. 42.75 (ISBN 0-444-86310-9). Elsevier.

Pai, S. I., ed. see Symposium On The Dynamics Of Fluids And Plasmas.

Pai, Shi I., jt. auth. see Cramer, Kenneth R.

Pai, Young, jt. auth. see Morris, Van C.

Paic, Guy & Slaus, Ivo, eds. Few Body Problems, Light Nuclei & Nuclear Interactions, 2 vols. 1969. Set. 193.00x (ISBN 0-677-13440-1); Vol. 1, 442p. 103.00x (ISBN 0-677-12760-X); Vol. 2, 480p. 115.00x (ISBN 0-677-13020-1). Gordon.

Paice, Eric. The Way to Write for Television. 96p. 1982. 16.50 o.p. (ISBN 0-241-10650-8, Pub. by Hamish Hamilton England); pap. 10.50 (ISBN 0-241-10647-8). David & Charles.

Paidoussis, M. P., jt. ed. see Chen, S. S.

Paige, Connie. The Right-to-Lifers: Who They Are, What They Are, & Where They Get Their Money. 256p. 1983. 13.95. Summit Bks.

Paige, Donald D., et al. Elementary Mathematical Methods. LC 77-2683. 22.95x (ISBN 0-471-09063-8). Wiley.

Paige, Glenn D., jt. ed. see Chaplin, George.

Paige, Grace. Catering Costs & Control. 1982. limp bdg. 50.00x (ISBN 0-304-29758-5, Pub. by Cassell England). State Mutual Bk.

Paige, Grace & Paige, Jane. The Hotel Receptionist. 1982. pap. 30.00x (ISBN 0-304-29757-7, Pub. by Cassell England). State Mutual Bk.

Paige, Jane, jt. auth. see Paige, Grace.

Paige, Jeffrey M., jt. auth. see Paige, Karen E.

Paige, Karen E. & Paige, Jeffrey M. The Politics of Reproductive Ritual. 392p. 1982. 25.00 (ISBN 0-520-03071-0); pap. 8.95 (ISBN 0-520-04782-6). U of Cal Pr.

Paige, Lowell J., et al. Elements of Linear Algebra. 2nd ed. LC 73-82137. 1974. text ed. 25.50 (ISBN 0-471-00820-6); arabic translation avail. (ISBN 0-471-00820-6). Wiley.

Paige, Rae. The Sesame Street Question & Answer Book about Animals. LC 81-84709. (Illus.). 48p. (ps-3). 1983. 6.95 (ISBN 0-307-15816-0, Golden Pr); PLB price not set (ISBN 0-307-65816-3). Western Pub.

Paige, Richard E. Complete Guide to Making Money with Your Ideas & Inventions. (Everyday Handbook Ser.). pap. 3.95 o.p. (ISBN 0-06-463446-9, EH 446, EH). B&N NY.

Paige, Robert, jt. auth. see Gibbs, John W.

Paige, Vernon. CAD Revealed: Computer Aided Design. LC 81-16047. (Illus.). 64p. (Orig.). 1982. pap. 7.00 (ISBN 0-937148-07-5). Wild Horses Potted Plant.

Paijmans, K. Explanatory Notes to the Vegetation of Papua New Guinea. 1982. 40.00x (ISBN 0-686-97914-1, Pub. by CSIRO Australia). State Mutual Bk.

--New Guinea Vegetation. 1982. 49.00x (ISBN 0-686-97904-4, Pub. by CSIRO Australia). State Mutual Bk.

Paik, Woon Ki & Sangduk Kim. Protein Methylation. LC 79-19557. (Biochemistry: a Series of Monographs). 1980. 54.95 (ISBN 0-471-04867-4, Pub. by Wiley-Interscience). Wiley.

Paikeday, Thomas, ed. The New York Times Everyday Dictionary. 1982. 12.95 (ISBN 0-8129-0910-0). Times Bks.

Paillet, Jean-Pierre & Dugas, Andre. Approaches to Syntax. (Lingvisticae Investigationes Supplementa: 5). 282p. 1983. 32.00 (ISBN 90-272-3115-X). Benjamins North Am.

--Approaches to Syntax. 282p. 1982. 32.00 o.p. (ISBN 90-272-3115-X). Benjamins North Am.

Paillet De Warcy, L. Histoire De la Vie et Des Ouvrages De Voltaire. Repr. of 1824 ed. 260.00 o.p. (ISBN 0-8287-0663-8). Clearwater Pub.

Pain, F. Practical Wood Turner. rev. ed. LC 74-6436. (Illus.). 1979. pap. 6.95 (ISBN 0-8069-8580-1). Sterling.

Pain, H. J. The Physics of Vibrations & Waves. 2nd ed. 357p. 1976. 49.95 (ISBN 0-471-99407-3); pap. 19.95 (ISBN 0-471-99408-1). Wiley.

Pain, R. H. & Smith, B. J. New Techniques in Biophysics & Cell Biology, Vols. 2-3. LC 72-8611. 1976. Vol. 2. 85.95 (ISBN 0-471-65758-1, Pub. by Wiley-Interscience); Vol. 3. 40.25 o.p. (ISBN 0-471-01814-7). Wiley.

Paine. Organizational Strategy & Policy. 3rd ed. 618p. 1982. pap. 23.95 (ISBN 0-03-060067-7). Dryden Pr.

Paine, Albert B. A Short Life View of Mark Twain. 344p. 1982. Repr. of 1920 ed. lib. bdg. 25.00 (ISBN 0-89984-829-X). Century Bookbindery.

Paine, David, jt. auth. see Buzby, Walter J.

Paine, David P. Aerial Photography & Image Interpretation for Resource Management. LC 81-4287. 571p. 1981. text ed. 34.95 (ISBN 0-471-01857-0). Wiley.

Paine, Donald F. Tennessee Law of Evidence. 1974. with 1981 cum. suppl. 45.00 (ISBN 0-672-82543-0, Bobb-Merrill Law); 1981 cum. suppl. only 15.00 (ISBN 0-87215-437-8). Michie-Bobbs.

Paine, F. A. Packaging Evaluation: The Testing of Filled Transport Packages. 1974. text ed. 12.50 o.p. (ISBN 0-408-00122-4). Butterworth.

--The Packaging Media. 444p. 1978. 59.95x o.s.i. (ISBN 0-470-99369-3). Wiley.

Paine, F. A., ed. Packaging & the Law. 1973. text ed. 19.95 (ISBN 0-408-00107-0). Butterworth.

Paine, Frank T. & Anderson, Carl R. Strategic Management. 368p. 1983. text ed. 26.95 (ISBN 0-03-061828-2). Dryden Pr.

Paine, Frank T., jt. auth. see Carroll, Stephen J., Jr.

Paine, Gustavus. Men Behind the King James Version. 1977. pap. 5.95 (ISBN 0-8010-7008-2). Baker Bk.

Paine, John K. History of Music to the Death of Schubert. LC 78-127280. (Music Ser.). (Illus.). 1971. Repr. of 1907 ed. lib. bdg. 29.50 (ISBN 0-306-70038-7). Da Capo.

--Symphony No. One: Opus 23. LC 73-171077. (Earlier American Music Ser.: No. 1). 180p. 1972. Repr. of 1908 ed. lib. bdg. 27.50 (ISBN 0-306-77301-5). Da Capo.

Paine, Josiah. A History of Harwich, Barnstable County, Massachusetts Sixteen Twenty to Eighteen Hundred. 503p. 1971. Repr. of 1937 ed. 15.00 o.s.i. (ISBN 0-940160-03-X). Parnassus Imprints.

Paine, Leslie H., ed. Health Care in Big Cities. LC 78-7783. 1978. 30.00x (ISBN 0-312-36523-3). St Martin.

Paine, Ralph D. Fight For a Free Sea. 1920. text ed. 8.50x (ISBN 0-686-83550-6). Elliots Bks.

--Old Merchant Marine. 1919. text ed. 8.50x (ISBN 0-686-83653-7). Elliots Bks.

Paine, Shep & Stewart, Lane. How to Photograph Scale Models. Hayden, Bob, ed. (Illus., Orig.). 1983. pap. price not set (ISBN 0-89024-053-1). Kalmbach.

Paine, Sheperd. Modeling Tanks & Military Vehicles. Angle, Burr, ed. (Illus.). 76p. (Orig.). 1982. pap. 8.95 (ISBN 0-89024-045-0). Kalmbach.

Paine, Stephen W. Beginning Greek: A Functional Approach. (YA) (gr. 9 up). 1961. 12.50x (ISBN 0-19-501013-2). Oxford U Pr.

Paine, Suzanne. Exporting Workers. LC 74-19528. (Department of Applied Economics, Occasional Papers Ser.: No. 41). 224p. 1974. 37.50 (ISBN 0-521-20631-6); pap. 19.95x (ISBN 0-521-09879-3). Cambridge U Pr.

Paine, Thomas. Common Sense. (Penguin American Library). 1982. pap. 2.95 (ISBN 0-14-039016-2). Penguin.

--Common Sense & the Crisis. 1970. pap. 4.50 o.p. (ISBN 0-385-09527-9, Anch). Doubleday.

Paine, Thomas, jt. auth. see Burke, Edmond.

Paine, Whiton S., ed. Job Stress & Burnout: Research, Theory & Intervention Series. (Sage Focus Editions: Vol. 54). (Illus.). 320p. 1982. 25.00 (ISBN 0-8039-1847-X); pap. 12.50 (ISBN 0-8039-1848-8). Sage.

Painter, Desmond. Columbus. Yapp, Malcolm, et al, eds. (World History Ser.). (Illus.). 32p. (gr. 10). 1980. Repr. of 1977 ed. lib. bdg. 6.95 (ISBN 0-89908-042-1); pap. text ed. 2.25 (ISBN 0-89908-017-0). Greenhaven.

--Mao Tse-Tung. Yapp, Malcolm & Killingray, Margaret, eds. (World History Ser.). (Illus.). (gr. 10). 1980. lib. bdg. 6.95 (ISBN 0-89908-127-4); pap. 2.25 (ISBN 0-89908-102-9). Greenhaven.

Painter, Desmond & Shepard, John. Religion. Yapp, Malcolm & Killinger, Margaret, eds. (World History Ser.). (Illus.). 32p. (gr. 10). 1980. lib. bdg. 6.95 (ISBN 0-89908-145-2); pap. text ed. 2.25 (ISBN 0-89908-120-7). Greenhaven.

Painter, Genevieve, jt. auth. see Corsini, Raymond J.

Painter, George D. William Caxton: A Biography. (Illus.). 1977. 14.95 o.p. (ISBN 0-399-11888-8). Putnam Pub Group.

Painter, Hal. Cross-Country Ski, Cook, Look & Pleasure Book & Welcome to the Alice in Snowpeople Land. LC 73-91637. (Illus., Orig.). 1973. pap. 4.95 (ISBN 0-911824-29-4). Wilderness.

Painter, Paul C., et al. The Theory of Vibrational Spectroscopy & Its Applications to Polymeric Materials. LC 81-12969. 530p. 1982. 60.00x (ISBN 0-471-09346-7, Pub. by Wiley-Interscience). Wiley.

Painter, Sidney, jt. auth. see Tierney, Brian.

Painter, William. Corporate & Tax Aspects of Closely Held Corporations, 1982 Supplement. LC 80-83227. (Illus.). 1982. pap. 15.00. Little.

--The Palace of Pleasure, 3 Vols. Jacobs, Joseph, ed. 1966. pap. text ed. 4.00 ea.; Vol. 1. pap. text ed. o.p. (ISBN 0-486-21691-8); Vol. 2. pap. text ed. (ISBN 0-486-21692-6); Vol. 3. pap. text ed. (ISBN 0-486-21693-4). Dover.

Painter, William H. The Federal Securities Code & Corporate Disclosure. 1979. text ed. 45.000 with 1982 suppl. (ISBN 0-87215-233-2); 1982 Supplement 12.50 (ISBN 0-87215-485-8). Michie-Bobbs.

Painter, William H. & Ratner, David L., eds. Selected Securities & Business Planning Statutes Rules & Forms. 485p. 1982. pap. text ed. (ISBN 0-314-69939-2). West Pub.

Painting, Donald H. Helping Children with Specific Learning Disabilities: A Practical Guide for Parents & Teachers. 196p. 1983. 12.92 (ISBN 0-13-387258-0); pap. 6.95 (ISBN 0-13-387241-6). P-H.

Pairault, Claude. Village-Savane En Pays Adioukrou. (Black Africa Ser.). 136p. (Fr.). 1974. Repr. of 1969 ed. lib. bdg. 43.00 o.p. (ISBN 0-8287-0666-2, 71-2012). Clearwater Pub.

Pais, Abraham. Subtle Is the Lord: The Science & Life of Albert Einstein. LC 82-2273. (Illus.). 1982. 25.00 (ISBN 0-19-853907-X). Oxford U Pr.

Paish, F. W. & Briston, R. J. Business Finance. 6th ed. 176p. 1982. 40.00x (ISBN 0-273-01768-3, Pub by Pitman Bks England). State Mutual Bk.

Paish, F. W. & Henessy, Josselyn. Rise & Fall of Incomes Policy. (Institute of Economic Affairs, Hobart Papers Ser.: No. 47). (Orig.). pap. 2.75 o.p. (ISBN 0-255-36016-9); 2.75 o.p. Transatlantic.
Paisley, William, jt. ed. see Butler, Matilda.
Paisley, William J., jt. auth. see Butler, Matilda.
Paivio, Allan & Begg, Ian. The Psychology of Language. (Illus.). 448p. 1981. text ed. 23.95 (ISBN 0-13-735951-9). P-H.
Pajestka, Josef & Feinstein, C. H. The Relevance of Economic Theories. 1980. 36.00 (ISBN 0-312-67054-0). St Martin.
Pajgrt, O., et al, eds. Processing of Polyester Fibres. (Textile Science & Technology Ser.: Vol. 2). 1980. 85.00 (ISBN 0-444-99860-8). Elsevier.
PAK-FAO Seminar on Agricultural Perspective Planning, 1977. Report. (FAO Development Documents Ser.: No. 40). 488p. 1977. pap. 37.00 o.p. (ISBN 0-686-92885-7, F1239, FAO). Unipub.
Pak, Ty. The Grateful Korean & Other Stories. (Orig.). 1983. pap. write for info. (ISBN 0-910043-01-9). Bamboo Ridge Pr.
Pakakostopoulos, D., jt. ed. see Chiarenza, G. A.
Pakenham-Walsh, W. S. A Tudor Story: The Return of Anne Boleyn. 200p. 1963. 12.00 (ISBN 0-227-67678-5). Attic Pr.
Paker, Yacup, ed. Multi-Microprocessor Systems. Date not set. price not set (ISBN 0-12-543980-6). Acad Pr.
Pakin, Sandra & Computer Innovations Staff. APL: A Short Course. (Illus.). 176p. 1973. pap. 14.95x ref. ed. (ISBN 0-13-038877-7). P-H.
Pakin, Sandra, jt. auth. see Polivka, Raymond P.
Pakkala, Lorraine. Yea God! The True Story of a Spiritual Leader, Freedom, Who Led His Followers from Eastern Mysticism to Christianity. LC 80-11503. 250p. 1980. 15.95 (ISBN 0-89594-030-2); pap. 6.95 (ISBN 0-89594-029-9). Crossing Pr.
Pakula, Marion B. Needlepoint Plaids. (Illus.). 64p. 1975. 7.95 o.p. (ISBN 0-517-52041-9); pap. 5.95 o.p. (ISBN 0-517-52042-7). Crown.
Pakula, Marion B. & Goldberg, Rhoda. Needlepoint Patterns for Signs & Sayings. (Illus.). 1977. pap. 5.95 o.p. (ISBN 0-517-52859-2). Crown.
Pakula, Marion B. & Goldberg, Rhoda O. Needlecraft Sports Designs. (Illus.). 1983. 19.95 (ISBN 0-517-54968-9); pap. 10.95 (ISBN 0-517-54969-7). Crown.
Pakvasa, S., jt. ed. see Peterson, V. S.
Pal, Anjali. Jataka Tales from the Ajanta Murals. (Illus.). 103p. (gr. 4-6). 1968. 2.00 (ISBN 0-88253-330-4). Ind-US Inc.
Pal, Dhiraj, jt. auth. see Overcash, Michael R.
Pal, Pratapaditya. The Sensuous Immortals. (Illus.). 1977. 50.00 (ISBN 0-262-16068-4). MIT Pr.
Pal, Pratapaditya, jt. auth. see Fontein, Jan.
Palacio, Alfredo. Atlas of Two-D Echocardiography. Jurade, Rafael L., tr. (Illus.). 216p. 1983. text ed. 65.00 (ISBN 0-914316-35-4). Yorke Med.
Paladin Press. Mini-Fourteen Exotic Weapons Systems. (Exotic Weapons Systems Ser.). 80p. 1982. pap. 12.00 (ISBN 0-87364-250-3). Paladin Pr.
Paladin Press, jt. ed. see Henderson, Martha.
Paladino, Lyn. The Horological Tree. LC 78-64980. 1979. 5.50 (ISBN 0-911838-53-8). Windy Row.
Palamas, Kostes. The Twelve Words of the Gypsy. new ed. Stephanides, Theodore & Katsimbalis, George, trs. from Gr. LC 75-12894. 336p. 1975. text ed. 15.00x o.p. (ISBN 0-87870-025-0); pap. text ed. 6.95x o.p. (ISBN 0-87870-029-3). Memphis St Univ.
Palamas, Kostis. The Twelve Lays of the Gypsy. 146p. 1971. deluxe ed. 19.00x (ISBN 0-8464-0939-9). Beekman Pubs.
Palamountain, Joseph C. Politics of Distribution. LC 68-8070. (Illus.). 1968. Repr. of 1955 ed. lib. bdg. 17.50x (ISBN 0-8371-0186-7, PAPD). Greenwood.
Palandri, A. Jung. Yuan Chen. (World Authors Ser.). 1977. lib. bdg. 15.95 (ISBN 0-8057-6279-5, Twayne). G K Hall.
Palandri, Angela J., tr. Modern Verse from Taiwan. LC 79-161994. 1972. 26.50x (ISBN 0-520-02061-8). U of Cal Pr.
Palangyo, Peter. Kuvuli Cha Mauti. LC 78-303243. (Swahili Literature). (Orig., Swahili). 1978. pap. text ed. 3.50x o.p. (ISBN 0-686-74449-7, 00609). Heinemann Ed.
Palardy, J. Michael. Teaching Today: Tasks & Challenges. (Illus.). 480p. 1975. pap. text ed. 14.95x (ISBN 0-02-390410-0). Macmillan.
Palassis, Neketas S., ed. A Lenten Cookbook for Orthodox Christians. 260p. 1982. pap. 7.50x (ISBN 0-913026-13-1). St Nectarios.
Palazzi, F. Novissimo Dizionario della Lingua Italiana. Folena, G., ed. 1624p. (Ital.). 1981. 75.00 (ISBN 0-686-97427-1, M-9363). French & Eur.
Palazzolo, Charles. Small Groups: An Introduction. 1980. text ed. 15.95 (ISBN 0-442-25868-2). Van Nos Reinhold.
Palazzolo, Charles S., jt. auth. see Gallagher, Bernard J.
Palder, Edward L. Magic with Chemistry. (Elephant Bks). (Illus.). 96p. (gr. 5-8). 1976. pap. 2.95 o.s.i. (ISBN 0-448-12054-2, G&D). Putnam Pub Group.
Palen. City Scenes: Problems & Prospects. 2nd ed. 1981. pap. text ed. 10.95 (ISBN 0-316-68871-1). Little.
Palen, J. John. The Urban World. (Illus.). 480p. 1974. text ed. 15.95 o.p. (ISBN 0-07-048088-5, C). McGraw.
--The Urban World. 2nd ed. Munson, Eric M., ed. 480p. 1981. text ed. 22.95 (ISBN 0-07-048107-5, C); instr's. manual 4.95 (ISBN 0-07-048108-3). McGraw.
Palen, John. Social Problems. (Illus.). 1979. text ed. 25.00 (ISBN 0-07-048103-2, GB); instructor's manual 2.95 (ISBN 0-07-048104-0); study guide 11.95 (ISBN 0-07-048105-9); test file 3.95 (ISBN 0-07-048106-7). McGraw.
Paleo, Lyn, jt. auth. see Garber, Eric.
Paleologue, Maurice. An Intimate Journal of the Dreyfus Case. Mosbacher, Eric, tr. from Fr. LC 75-19326. 319p. 1975. Repr. of 1957 ed. lib. bdg. 18.00x (ISBN 0-8371-8250-6, PADC). Greenwood.
Palermo, David S. Psychology of Language. 1978. text ed. 13.50x (ISBN 0-673-07715-2). Scott F.
Palermo, Patrick F. Lincoln Steffens. (United States Authors Ser.). 1978. 11.95 (ISBN 0-8057-7253-7, Twayne). G K Hall.
Palese, Peter, ed. see New York Academy of Sciences, Nov. 28-30, 1979.
Palev, T. D., jt. ed. see Doebner, H. D.
Palewicz-Rousseau, Pam & Madaras, Lynda. The Alphabet Connection: A Parent's & Teacher's Guide to Beginning Reading & Writing. LC 79-12493. (Illus.). 1979. 10.95x (ISBN 0-8052-3726-7). Schocken.
Paley, Alan. The Spanish Civil War. Rahmas, Sigurd C., ed. (Events of Our Times Ser.: No. 23). 32p. (Orig.). 1982. 2.95x (ISBN 0-87157-724-0); pap. text ed. 1.95 (ISBN 0-87157-224-9). SamHar Pr.
Paley, Alan L. Benito Mussolini, Fascist Dictator of Italy. new ed. Rahmus, D. Steve, ed. (Outstanding Personalities Ser.). 32p. 1975. lib. bdg. 2.95 incl. catalog cards (ISBN 0-87157-581-7); pap. 1.95 vinyl laminated covers (ISBN 0-87157-081-5). SamHar Pr.
--Edgar Allan Poe, American Poet & Mystery Writer. new ed. Rahmas, D. Steve, ed. (Outstanding Personalities Ser.). 32p. 1975. lib. bdg. 2.95 incl. catalog cards (ISBN 0-87157-584-1); pap. 1.95 vinyl laminated covers (ISBN 0-87157-084-X). SamHar Pr.
--The Establishment of Communism in China. (Events of Our Times Ser.: No. 16). 32p. (Orig.). (gr. 7-12). lib. bdg. 2.95 incl. catalog cards (ISBN 0-87157-717-8); pap. 1.95 vinyl laminated covers (ISBN 0-87157-217-6). SamHar Pr.
--George Orwell, Writer & Critic of Modern Society. Rahmas, D. Steve, ed. (Outstanding Personalities Ser.: No. 72). 32p. (Orig.). (gr. 7-12). 1974. lib. bdg. 2.95 incl. catalog cards (ISBN 0-87157-548-5); pap. 1.95 vinyl laminated covers (ISBN 0-87157-072-6). SamHar Pr.
--Sigmund Freud, Father of Psychoanalysis. new ed. Rahmas, D. Steve, ed. LC 74-14694. (Outstanding Personalities Ser.). 32p. 1974. lib. bdg. 2.95 incl. catalog cards (ISBN 0-87157-573-6); pap. 1.95 vinyl laminated covers (ISBN 0-87157-073-4). SamHar Pr.
--Sinclair Lewis, Twentieth Century American Author & Nobel Prize Winner. Rahmas, D. Steve, ed. LC 73-87626. (Outstanding Personalities Ser.: No. 67). 32p. (Orig.). (gr. 7-12). 1974. lib. bdg. 2.95 incl. catalog cards (ISBN 0-87157-567-1); pap. 1.95 vinyl laminated covers (ISBN 0-87157-067-X). SamHar Pr.
Paley, Grace. The Little Disturbances of Man. 192p. 1973. pap. 5.95 (ISBN 0-452-25391-8, Z5391, Plume). NAL.
Paley, Stephen H., et al. Professional Corporations: An Advanced Tax Planning Program, 1982. LC 82-61269. (Tax Law & Estate Planning Course Handbook Ser.). 863p. 1982. pap. 30.00 (J4-3512). PLI.
Paley, William. A Treatise on the Law of Principal & Agent, Chiefly with Reference to Mercantile Transactions. xvi, 202p. 1982. Repr. of 1840 ed. lib. bdg. 25.00x (ISBN 0-8377-1010-3). Rothman.
Palfreman, David, jt. auth. see Beardshaw, John.
Palgi, Michal & Rosner, Menachem. Sexual Equality: The Israeli Kibbutz Tests the Theories. 337p. 1982. lib. bdg. 27.50 (ISBN 0-8482-5676-X). Norwood Edns.
Palgrave. Golden Treasury. pap. 1.50 o.p. (ISBN 0-451-61423-2, MW1423, Ment). NAL.
Palgrave, Robert H. Bank Rate & the Money Market in England, France, Germany, Holland, & Belgium 1844-1900. Repr. of 1903 ed. lib. bdg. 17.75x (ISBN 0-8371-0604-4, PABR). Greenwood.
--Dictionary of Political Economy, 3 vols. LC 74-31358. 1976. Repr. of 1910 ed. Set. 191.00x (ISBN 0-8103-4210-3). Gale.
Palia, Kyamas A. & Hitt, Michael A. Grand Corporate Strategy & Critical Functions: Interactive Effects of Organizational Dimensions. 236p. 1982. 26.95 (ISBN 0-03-061734-0). Praeger.
Paliakoff, Stephen. Favourite Nights & Caught on a Train. 1982. pap. 6.95 (ISBN 0-413-50100-0). Methuen Inc.
Palic, Vladimir M. Government Publications, Vol. 1. 1977. text ed. 40.00 (ISBN 0-08-021457-6). Pergamon.
Palin, G. R. Chemistry for Technologists. LC 70-142175. 355p. 1972. text ed. 27.00 o.s.i. (ISBN 0-08-016385-8); pap. text ed. 12.75 (ISBN 0-08-016386-6). Pergamon.
Paling, John, jt. auth. see Bernard, George.
Palingenius, Marcellus. The Zodiake of Life. Googe, Barnabe, tr. LC 48-275. 1977. Repr. of 1576 ed. 45.00x (ISBN 0-8201-1214-3). Schol Facsimiles.
Palinski, Christine O., jt. auth. see Pizer, Hank.
Paliouras, John D. Complex Variables for Scientists & Engineers. (Illus.). 416p. 1975. text ed. 31.95x (ISBN 0-02-390550-6). Macmillan.
Palis, Jacob, Jr. & De Mayo, Welington. Geometric Theory of Dynamical Systems: An Introduction. (Illus.). 198p. 1982. 28.00 (ISBN 0-387-90668-1). Springer-Verlag.
Palisca, Claude. Baroque Music. 2nd ed. (P-H History of Music Ser.). (Illus.). 1980. text ed. 18.95 (ISBN 0-13-055954-7); pap. text ed. 13.95 (ISBN 0-13-055947-4). P-H.
Palisca, Claude V., jt. ed. see Holoman, D. Kern.
Palisca, Claude V., tr. see Zarlino, Gioseffo.
Palissier, Vernon G. The China Collector's Classical Guide of Marks & Monograms. (A Promotion of the Arts Library Bk.). (Illus.). 198p. 1983. Repr. of 1887 ed. 98.75 (ISBN 0-89901-099-7). Found Class Reprints.
Palissot De Montenoy, C. La Moretde Voltaire. Repr. of 1780 ed. 77.00 o.p. (ISBN 0-8287-0668-9). Clearwater Pub.
Palissot De Montenoy, Ch. Le Genie De Voltaire. Repr. of 1806 ed. 119.00 o.p. (ISBN 0-8287-0669-7). Clearwater Pub.
Palissot De Montenoy, Charles. Eloge De M. De Voltaire. Repr. of 1788 ed. 36.00 o.p. (ISBN 0-8287-0670-0). Clearwater Pub.
Palit, Chittabrata. Tensions in Bengal Rural Society: Landlords, Planters & Colonial Rule, 1830-1860. 1976. 9.00x o.p. (ISBN 0-88386-777-X). South Asia Bks.
Paliwoda, Stanley. Joint East-West Marketing & Production Ventures. 215p. 1981. text ed. 43.25x (ISBN 0-566-00473-9). Gower Pub Ltd.
Palkovich, Ann M. Pueblo Population & Society: The Arroyo Hondo Skeletal & Mortuary Remains. LC 80-51310. (Arroyo Hondo Archaeological Ser.: Vol. 3). (Illus.). 1981. pap. 8.00 (ISBN 0-933452-03-9). Schol Am Res.
Palkovitz, Harry, jt. auth. see Lubic, Lowell G.
Palkovitz, Harry P., jt. auth. see Lubic, Lowell G.
Pall, Michael L. & Streit, Lois B. Let's Talk About It: The Book for Children about Child Abuse. LC 82-60527. 125p. (Orig.). (gr. 6-12). 1983. pap. 4.95 (ISBN 0-88247-682-3). R & E Res Assoc.
Palladian, Arthur. Careers in Soccer. LC 77-72423. (Early Career Bks.). (Illus.). (gr. 2-5). 1977. PLB 5.95g (ISBN 0-8225-0331-X). Lerner Pubns.
--Careers in the Air Force. LC 77-90321. (Early Career Bks.). (Illus.). (gr. 2-5). 1978. PLB 5.95g (ISBN 0-8225-0333-6). Lerner Pubns.
--Careers in the Army. LC 77-72420. (Early Career Bks.). (Illus.). (gr. 2-5). 1978. PLB 5.95g (ISBN 0-8225-0327-1). Lerner Pubns.
--Careers in the Navy. LC 77-72421. (Early Career Bks.). (Illus.). (gr. 2-5). 1977. PLB 5.95g (ISBN 0-8225-0329-8). Lerner Pubns.
Palladino, Leo & Perry, John. Hairdressing Management. 352p. 1982. 40.00x (ISBN 0-85950-338-0, Pub. by Thornes England). State Mutual Bk.
Pallain, G., ed. Ambassade De Talleyrand a Londres: 1830-1831. LC 72-12238. (Europe 1815-1945 Ser.). 464p. 1973. Repr. of 1891 ed. lib. bdg. 59.50 (ISBN 0-306-70575-3). Da Capo.
Pallain, Georges M. The Correspondence of Prince Tallyrand & King Louis XVIII During the Congress of Vienna. LC 70-126616. (Europe, 1815-1945 Ser.). 654p. 1973. Repr. of 1881 ed. lib. bdg. 69.50 (ISBN 0-306-70047-6). Da Capo.
Pallas, Nervin. Calculator Puzzles, Tricks & Games. (Illus.). 96p. (gr. 7 up). 1983. pap. 4.95 (ISBN 0-8069-7688-8). Sterling.
Pallas, Norvin. Calculator Puzzles, Tricks & Games. LC 76-1166. (Illus.). 96p. (YA) 1976. 7.95 (ISBN 0-8069-4534-6); PLB 7.49 o.p. (ISBN 0-8069-4535-4). Sterling.
--Short Short Stories. (Newbury Hse Readers Ser.: Stage 4 - Intermediate Level). (Illus.). (gr. 7-12). 1981. pap. cancelled o.p. (ISBN 0-88377-198-5). Newbury Hse.
Pallas, Norvin, jt. auth. see McWhirter, Norris.
Pallaschke, D., jt. ed. see Moeschlin, O.
Pallaschke, D., jt. auth. see Frehse, J.
Pallett, E. H. Aircraft Electrical Systems. 2nd ed. (Aerospace Engineering Ser.). 169p. 1979. text ed. 28.50 (ISBN 0-273-08445-3). Pitman Pub MA.
--Aircraft Instruments. 2nd ed. (Aerospace Engineering Ser.). 432p. 1981. text ed. 44.00 (ISBN 0-273-01539-7). Pitman Pub MA.
Palley, Howard A., jt. auth. see Palley, Marian L.
Palley, Marian & Preston, Michael, eds. Minorities & Policy Studies. 1978. pap. 6.00 (ISBN 0-918592-29-1). Policy Studies.
Palley, Marian L. & Palley, Howard A. Urban America & Public Policies. 2nd ed. 336p. 1981. pap. text ed. 10.95 (ISBN 0-669-04004-5). Heath.
Palley, Marian L. & Preston, Michael B., eds. Race, Sex, & Policy Problems. (Policy Studies Organization Ser.). (Illus.). 288p. 1979. 24.95 (ISBN 0-669-01985-2). Lexington Bks.
Palley, Marion & Hale, George. Politics of Federal Grants. Woy, Jean, ed. LC 81-960. (Congressional Quarterly Politics & Public Policy Ser.). 191p. (Orig.). 1981. pap. 8.75 (ISBN 0-87187-161-0). Congr Quarterly.
Palling, S. J., ed. Developments in Food Packaging, Vol. 1. 1980. 45.00 (ISBN 0-85334-917-7, Pub. by Applied Sci England). Elsevier.
Pallis, Christopher A. & Lewis, Paul D. Neurology of Gastrointestinal Disease. LC 73-89191. (Major Problem in Neurology Ser.: No. 3). (Illus.). 280p. 1974. text ed. 10.00 (ISBN 0-7216-7046-6). Saunders.
Pallis, M., tr. see Amin, Samir.
Pallis, M., tr. see Minces, Juliet.
Palliser. Palliser's New Cottage Homes & Details. LC 75-4887. (Architecture & Decorative Arts Ser). (Illus.). 180p. 1975. Repr. of 1887 ed. lib. bdg. 49.50 (ISBN 0-306-70744-6). Da Capo.
Palliser, Fanny M. Historic Devices, Badges, & War-Cries. LC 68-18030. (Illus.). 1971. Repr. of 1870 ed. 45.00x (ISBN 0-8103-3381-3). Gale.
--History of Lace. LC 75-78219. (Illus.). x, 454p. 1972. Repr. of 1875 ed. 54.00x (ISBN 0-8103-3941-2). Gale.
Palliser, John. Exploration - British North America: Papers, 2 Vols. LC 68-55211. (Illus.). 1968. Repr. of 1860 ed. lib. bdg. 20.75 (ISBN 0-8371-1430-6, PABN). Greenwood.
--Solitary Rambles & Adventures of a Hunter in the Prairies. LC 69-13511. (Illus.). 1969. Repr. of 1853 ed. 5.00 o.p. (ISBN 0-8048-0534-2). C E Tuttle.
Pallone, Nathaniel J., jt. auth. see Liu, William T.
Palm, Charles & Danielson, Elena. Herbert Hoover: A Register of His Papers in the Hoover Institution Archives, No. 63. LC 82-80158. (Bibliographic Ser.). 199p. 1982. 19.95 (ISBN 0-8179-2631-3). Hoover Inst Pr.
Palm, Goran. The Flight from Work. Smith, P., tr. LC 77-76077. 1977. 18.95 (ISBN 0-521-21668-0). Cambridge U Pr.
Palm, Richard S. Physical Geography: A Multimedia Approach. (Geography Ser.). 1978. pap. text ed. 16.95 (ISBN 0-675-08403-2). Additional supplements may be obtained from publisher. Merrill.
Palm, Risa, jt. auth. see Lanegrán, David.
Palm, William J. Modeling, Analysis & Control of Dynamic Systems. 800p. 1983. text ed. 36.95 (ISBN 0-471-05800-9); solutions manual avail. (ISBN 0-471-89887-2). Wiley.
Palma, Robert J. Karl Barth's Free Theology of Culture. (Pittsburgh Theological Monographs New Ser.: No. 2). 1983. pap. write for info. (ISBN 0-915138-54-9). Pickwick.
Palma, Vera Di see Di Palma, Vera.
Palmberg, Walter. Copper Paladin: The Modoc Tragedy. 208p. 1982. 12.00 (ISBN 0-8059-2823-5). Dorrance.
Palmer. A Field Guide to the Trees of Southern Africa. 29.95 (ISBN 0-686-42772-6, Collins Pub England). Greene.
Palmer, A. Planning the Office Landscape. (Architectural Ser.). 1977. 21.50 o.p. (ISBN 0-07-048415-5, P&RB). McGraw.
Palmer, A. Dean. Heinrich August Marschner, 1795-1861: His Life & Stage Works. Buelow, George, ed. LC 80-22518. (Studies in Musicology: No. 24). 612p. 1980. 69.95 (ISBN 0-8357-1114-5, Pub. by UMI Res Pr). Univ Microfilms.
Palmer, A. R., ed. Perspectives in Regional Geological Synthesis: Planning for the Geology of North America. LC 82-9331. (DNAG Special Pub. Ser.: No. 1). (Illus.). 1982. 7.50x (ISBN 0-8137-5201-9). Geol Soc.
Palmer, Abram S. Some Curios from a Word-Collector's Cabinet. LC 79-145517. Repr. of 1907 ed. 30.00x (ISBN 0-8103-3670-7). Gale.
Palmer, Adrian S. & Kimball, Margot C. Getting Along in English. (English As a Second Language Bk.). pap. text ed. 4.30x (ISBN 0-582-79723-3); cassette 9.95x (ISBN 0-582-79768-3); bk. & cassette in plastic tote 11.95x (ISBN 0-582-79781-0). Longman.
Palmer, Alan W. Dictionary of Modern History. (Reference Ser.). (Orig.). (YA) (gr. 11 up). 1964. pap. 5.95 (ISBN 0-14-051026-5). Penguin.
Palmer, Ann, jt. auth. see Cooper, Rosaleen.
Palmer, Arlene M. A Winterthur Guide to Chinese Export Porcelain. (Winterthur Ser.). (Illus.). 1976. 6.95 o.p. (ISBN 0-517-52784-7). Crown.
Palmer, Arnold & Puckett, Earl. Four Hundred & Ninety-Five Golf Lessons by Arnold Palmer. 1973. pap. 4.95 o.s.i. (ISBN 0-695-80402-2). Follett.
Palmer, B. M. Life & Letters of J. H. Thornwell. 1974. 15.95 (ISBN 0-85151-195-3). Banner of Truth.
Palmer, Barbara & Palmer, Kenneth. The Successful Meeting Master Guide for Business & Professional People. (Illus.). 288p. 1983. 18.95 (ISBN 0-13-863373-8); pap. 9.95 (ISBN 0-13-863365-7). P-H.
Palmer, Bernard. Hitched to a Star. LC 81-9636. 1981. pap. 2.95 (ISBN 0-8024-3584-X). Moody.
--McTaggart's Promise. LC 77-78499. 1977. pap. 2.95 o.p. (ISBN 0-89191-088-3, 11460). Cook.
Palmer, Birch. The Unworthy Ones. 363p. 1982. 10.00 (ISBN 0-9610168-0-9). B Palmer.
Palmer, Brooks. Treasury of American Clocks. 2nd ed. 1967. 21.95 (ISBN 0-02-594580-7). Macmillan.
Palmer, Bryan D., jt. auth. see Kealey, Gregory S.

Palmer, Carleton H. Report of the Ellis Island Committee. LC 78-145478. (The American Immigration Library). 149p. 1971. Repr. of 1934 ed. lib. bdg. 10.95x (ISBN 0-89198-021-0). Ozer.

Palmer, Charles E., jt. auth. see Brock, Horace R.

Palmer, Claude I., et al. Practical Mathematics. 6th ed. (Illus.). (gr. 10 up). 1977. text ed. 21.50 (ISBN 0-07-048253-5, G); ans. to even numbered problems 5.95 (ISBN 0-07-048252-7). McGraw.

Palmer, Colin. Quantitative Aids for Management Decision Making. 1979. text ed. 25.25x (ISBN 0-566-00284-1). Gower Pub Ltd.

Palmer, Cynthia & Horowitz, Michael, eds. Shaman Woman, Mainline Lady. 1982. 20.50 (ISBN 0-688-01387-2); pap. 12.50 (ISBN 0-688-01385-6). Morrow.

Palmer, Cynthia, ed. see Huxley, Aldous.

Palmer, D., et al. Atomic Collision Phenomena in Solids. 1970. 68.00 (ISBN 0-444-10021-0). Elsevier.

Palmer, D. C. & Morris, B. D. Computing Science. 400p. 1980. pap. text ed. 19.95 (ISBN 0-7131-2538-1). E Arnold.

Palmer, Dave R. River & the Rock: The History of Fortress West Point, 1775-1783. LC 77-79061. (Illus.). 1969. lib. bdg. 45.00x (ISBN 0-8371-1497-7, PRR/). Greenwood.

--The Way of the Fox: American Strategy in the War for America, 1775-1783. (Contributions to Military History: No. 8). 1974. lib. bdg. 27.50 (ISBN 0-8371-7531-3, PAF/). Greenwood.

Palmer, David J., ed. Writers & Their Background: Alfred Tennyson. LC 72-95818. (Writers & Their Background Ser.). xvi, 279p. 1973. 15.00x (ISBN 0-8214-0116-5, 82-81198); pap. 6.00x (ISBN 0-8214-0117-3, 821206). Ohio U Pr.

Palmer, Donald F., jt. auth. see Allison, Ira S.

Palmer, E. H., ed. The Quran. (Sacred Bks. of the East: Vols. 6, 9). both vols. 22.00 (ISBN 0-686-97479-4); 11.00 ea. Lancaster-Miller.

Palmer, E. Lawrence & Fowler, H. Seymour. Fieldbook of Natural History. 2nd. ed. 1975. 32.50 (ISBN 0-07-048196-2, GB); PLB 24.95 trade ed. (ISBN 0-07-048425-2). McGraw.

Palmer, Earl. Thessalonians I & II: A Good News Commentary. LC 82-48409. (Good News Commentary Ser.). 128p. (Orig.). 1983. pap. 6.68 (ISBN 0-06-066455-X, HarpR). Har-Row.

Palmer, Elisabeth, tr. see Martinet, Andre.

Palmer, Elsie & Oeltien, Jody. Eating the Oregon Way. LC 82-73683. (Illus.). 180p. (Orig.). pap. 7.95 (ISBN 0-686-38722-8). Berry Patch.

Palmer, Eustace, jt. ed. see Jones, Eldred D.

Palmer, F. R. Semantics. 2nd ed. LC 80-42318. (Illus.). 170p. 1981. 32.50 (ISBN 0-521-23966-4); pap. 9.95 (ISBN 0-521-28376-0). Cambridge U Pr.

Palmer, Frederick. John J. Pershing, General of the Armies, a Biography. Repr. of 1948 ed. lib. bdg. 17.00x (ISBN 0-8371-2986-9, PAJP). Greenwood.

--Practical Upholstering: And the Cutting of Slip Covers. LC 80-51766. (Illus.). 288p. 1982. 19.95 (ISBN 0-8128-2753-8); pap. 9.95 (ISBN 0-8128-6170-1). Stein & Day.

Palmer, Friend. Early Days in Detroit: Papers Written by General Friend Palmer, of Detroit, Being His Personal Reminiscences of Important Events & Descriptions of the City for Over Eighty Years. LC 74-13871. (Illus.). 1032p. 1979. Repr. of 1906 ed. 49.00x (ISBN 0-8103-4068-2). Gale.

Palmer, G. E. & Sherrard, Philip, trs. The Philokalia, Vol. 1: The Complete Text Compiled By St. Nikodimos of the Holy Mountain & St. Markarios of Corinth, Vol. 1. 384p. 1983. pap. 10.95 (ISBN 0-571-13013-5). Faber & Faber.

Palmer, G. E., tr. see Kadloubowsky, E.

Palmer, G. E., et al, eds. The Philokalia, Vol. 2: The Complete Text. 408p. 1981. 30.00 (ISBN 0-571-11725-2). Faber & Faber.

Palmer, George, jt. auth. see Dawson, John.

Palmer, George E. The Law of Restitution, 4 vols. LC 77-71510. 1978. Set. 220.00 (ISBN 0-686-82932-8); 1982 suppl. 36.00 (ISBN 0-316-69007-4). Little.

Palmer, Gladys L. & Wood, Katherine D. Urban Workers on Relief, 2 Vols. in 1. LC 75-165688. (Research Monograph Ser.: Vol. 4). 1971. Repr. of 1936 ed. Set. lib. bdg. 59.50 (ISBN 0-306-70336-X). Da Capo.

Palmer, Gregory. The McNamara Strategy & the Vietnam War: Program Budgeting in the Pentagon, 1960-1968. LC 77-94744. (Contributions in Political Science: No. 13). 1978. lib. bdg. 25.00 (ISBN 0-313-20313-X, PMS/). Greenwood.

Palmer, H. D. & Gross, M. G., eds. Ocean Dumping & Marine Pollution: Geological Aspects of Waste Disposal at Sea. LC 78-10436. 268p. 1979. 31.50 (ISBN 0-87933-343-X). Hutchinson Ross.

Palmer, H. E. A Grammar of Spoken English. 3rd ed. Kingdon, R., ed. LC 75-26276. 341p. 1975. 39.50 (ISBN 0-521-21097-6); pap. o.p. (ISBN 0-521-29040-6). Cambridge U Pr.

Palmer, H. R., tr. see Ahmed ibn Fartua.

Palmer, Harold D., jt. ed. see Swift, D. J.

Palmer, Helen. I Was Kissed by a Seal at the Zoo. LC 62-15113. (Illus.). (gr. 1-2). 1962. PLB 5.99 (ISBN 0-394-90026-X). Beginner.

--Why I Built the Boogie House. (gr. 1-2). 1964. PLB 5.99 (ISBN 0-394-90035-9). Beginner.

Palmer, Humphrey. Analogy. LC 73-75112. (New Studies in the Philosophy of Religion). 128p. 1974. text ed. 12.95 o.p. (ISBN 0-312-03255-2). St Martin.

Palmer, J. O. The Battered Parent & How Not to Be One. 1980. 8.95 o.p. (ISBN 0-13-072371-1). P-H.

Palmer, Jack H. Cave Wall Shadows. new ed. 1978. pap. 3.00 (ISBN 0-932044-17-4). M O Pub Co.

Palmer, James D. & Saeks, R. World of Large Scale Systems. 352p. 1982. 32.95 (ISBN 0-471-87298-9, Pub. by Wiley-Interscience); pap. 21.50x (ISBN 0-471-87299-7). Wiley.

Palmer, James O. Psychological Assessment of Children. LC 70-101976. 1970. 35.50 (ISBN 0-471-65772-7). Wiley.

--The Psychological Assessment of Children. 2nd ed. 750p. 1983. 40.00 (ISBN 0-471-09765-9, Pub. by Wiley-Interscience). Wiley.

Palmer, Jean. Reptiles & Amphibians. (Blandford Pet Handbooks Ser.). 96p. 1983. 7.50 (ISBN 0-686-43144-8, Pub. by Blandford Pr England). Sterling.

--Small Pets. (Blandford Pet Handbooks Ser.). (Illus.). 96p. 1983. 7.50 (ISBN 0-7137-1202-3, Pub. by Blandford Pr England). Sterling.

Palmer, Jerry. Thrillers: Genesis & Structure of a Popular Genre. 1979. 26.00x (ISBN 0-312-80347-8). St Martin.

Palmer, Joe. Names in Pedgrees. 11.00 o.p. (ISBN 0-936032-05-7). Blood-Horse.

Palmer, Joe, jt. ed. see Mackay, Ronald.

Palmer, John. Political & Comic Characters of Shakespeare. 1967. 25.00 o.p. (ISBN 0-312-62230-9). St Martin.

Palmer, John F. & Morse, Stephen P. The Eight-Zero-Eight-Seven Primer. 224p. 1983. pap. price not set (ISBN 0-471-87569-4). Wiley.

Palmer, John L., ed. Creating Jobs: Public Employment Programs & Wage Subsidies. (Studies in Social Economics). 1978. 24.95 (ISBN 0-8157-6892-3); pap. 9.95 (ISBN 0-8157-6891-5). Brookings.

Palmer, John L. & Pechman, Joseph A., eds. Welfare in Rural Areas: The North Carolina-Iowa Income Maintenance Experiment. (Studies in Social Experimentation). 1978. 22.95 (ISBN 0-8157-6896-6); pap. 8.95 (ISBN 0-8157-6895-8). Brookings.

Palmer, John L. & Sawhill, Isabel V., eds. The Reagan Experiment: An Examination of Economic & Social Policies under the Reagan Administration. 530p. 1982. 29.95 (ISBN 0-87766-315-7, 34100); pap. 12.95 (ISBN 0-87766-316-5, 34200). Urban Inst.

Palmer, John R. The Use of Accounting Information in Labor Negotiations. 69p. pap. 7.95 (ISBN 0-86641-051-1, 7791). Natl Assn Accts.

Palmer, John R., jt. auth. see Gambino, Anthony J.

Palmer, John T. Career Education For Physically Disabled Students: Development As A Lifetime Activity. LC 80-82642. 64p. 1980. 6.50 (ISBN 0-686-38799-6). Human Res Ctr.

Palmer, Julian A. Mutiny Outbreak at Meerut in 1857. (Cambridge South Asian Studies: No. 2). 1966. 24.95 (ISBN 0-521-05901-1). Cambridge U Pr.

Palmer, K. N. Dust Explosions & Fires. 1973. 43.00x (ISBN 0-412-09430-4, Pub. by Chapman & Hall). Methuen Inc.

Palmer, Kenneth, jt. auth. see Guild, Nelson.

Palmer, Kenneth, jt. auth. see Palmer, Barbara.

Palmer, Kenneth, ed. see Shakespeare, William.

Palmer, Kingsley. The Folklore of Somerset. (Folklore of the British Isles Ser.). 186p. 1976. 15.75x o.p. (ISBN 0-87471-807-4). Rowman.

Palmer, Les. Bowling. (Illus.). 54p. 1982. pap. text ed. 2.95x (ISBN 0-89641-063-3). American Pr.

Palmer, Lilli. Night Music. LC 82-48148. 320p. 1983. 14.95 (ISBN 0-06-015105-6, HarpT). Har-Row.

Palmer, Linda. Starstruck. 400p. 1981. 13.95 (ISBN 0-399-12512-4). Putnam Pub Group.

Palmer, Lloyd. Steam Towards the Sunset: The Railroads of Lincoln County. (Lincoln County Historical Society Ser.: No. 23). (Illus.). 192p. (Orig.). 1982. pap. 19.95 (ISBN 0-911443-00-2). Lincoln Coun His.

Palmer, M. D. Henry VIII. (Illus.). 1971. pap. text ed. 5.95x (ISBN 0-582-31428-3). Longman.

Palmer, Marilyn, jt. auth. see Evans, A. J.

Palmer, Marjorie. Bride's Book of Ideas. 8.95 (ISBN 0-8423-0180-1). Tyndale.

Palmer, Marjorie & Bowman, Ethel. Young Mother's Book of Ideas. 1975. gift boxed 7.95 (ISBN 0-8423-8600-9). Tyndale.

Palmer, Martha S. A Sower Went Forth. 1978. 6.30 (ISBN 0-686-24055-3). Rod & Staff.

Palmer, Mervyn L. The Science of Teaching Swimming. (Illus.). 528p. 1980. 28.00 o.s.i. (ISBN 0-7207-1117-7). Transatlantic.

Palmer, Michael. Notes for Echo Lake. LC 80-28436. 112p. 1981. 13.50 (ISBN 0-86547-023-5); pap. 8.50 (ISBN 0-86547-024-3). N Point Pr.

--The Sisterhood. 1982. pap. 3.50 (ISBN 0-553-22704-1). Bantam.

Palmer, Michael, tr. see Berger, John & Tanner, Alain.

Palmer, Michael, jt. auth. see Kimbrough, Victoria.

Palmer, Mickey, jt. auth. see Sahadi, Lou.

Palmer, Mickey A. Architect's Guide to Facility Programming. 293p. 1981. 35.95x (ISBN 0-07-001490-6). Am Inst Arch.

Palmer, Monte. Dilemmas of Political Development. 2nd ed. LC 79-91100. 291p. 1980. pap. text ed. 10.95 (ISBN 0-87581-255-4). Peacock Pubs.

Palmer, Monte & Thompson, William. Comparative Analysis of Politics. LC 77-83373. 1978. pap. text ed. 14.50 (ISBN 0-87581-211-2). Peacock Pubs.

Palmer, Monte, jt. auth. see El Fathaly, Omar I.

Palmer, Norman D. Irish Land League Crisis: Misc. 37. (Yale Hist. Pubs. Ser.). 1940. 17.50x (ISBN 0-686-51406-8). Elliots Bks.

Palmer, Norman D., jt. auth. see Leng Shao-Chuan.

Palmer, P. E., ed. Radiology in the Developing World. (Journal: Diagnostic Imaging: Vol. 51, No. 3-4). (Illus.). 102p. 1982. pap. 43.25 (ISBN 3-8055-3523-6). S Karger.

Palmer, Pati & Pletsch, Susan. Pants for Any Body. rev. & expanded ed. 128p. (Orig.). 1982. pap. 5.95 (ISBN 0-935278-08-7). Palmer-Pletsch.

Palmer, Pete, ed. see Treat, Roger.

Palmer, Peter S. History of Lake Champlain, 1609-1814. LC 82-15422. (Illus.). 1982. Repr. of 1886 ed. write for info. (ISBN 0-916346-45-5). Harbor Hill Bks.

Palmer, Philip E., jt. auth. see Reeder, Maurice M.

Palmer, Philip E., jt. auth. see Bolt, Robert J.

Palmer, R., jt. ed. see Leach, R.

Palmer, R. R., ed. Historical Atlas of the World. 1965. pap. text ed. 5.95 (ISBN 0-528-83081-3). Rand.

Palmer, Rachel. No Sweeter Song. (Superromances Ser.). 384p. 1983. pap. 2.95 (ISBN 0-373-70058-X, Pub. by Worldwide). Harlequin Bks.

Palmer, Ralph A. Real Estate Principles: The Princeton Real Estate Examination Guide. rev. ed. (Illus.). 348p. 1982. pap. text ed. 16.95 (ISBN 0-89787-905-8). Gorsuch Scarisbrick.

Palmer, Robert. Deep Blues. 1982. pap. 5.95 (ISBN 0-14-006223-8). Penguin.

Palmer, Robert L., ed. Electroconvulsive Therapy: An Appraisal. (Illus.). 1981. text ed. 49.50x (ISBN 0-19-261266-2). Oxford U Pr.

Palmer, Robert R. & Colton, Joel. A History of the Modern World, 2 vols. 5th ed. 1977. one vol. ed. 24.00 (ISBN 0-394-32039-5); 15.00 ea. Vol. 1 (ISBN 0-394-32040-9). Vol. 2 (ISBN 0-394-32041-7). Knopf.

Palmer, Robin. Land & Racial Domination in Rhodesia. LC 76-14300. (Illus.). 1977. 30.00x (ISBN 0-520-03255-1). U of Cal Pr.

Palmer, Robin & Parsons, Neil, eds. Roots of Rural Poverty in Central & Southern Africa. LC 76-24600. (Campus Ser.: No. 199). 1978. 34.50x (ISBN 0-520-03318-3); pap. 9.50x (ISBN 0-520-03505-4, CAMPUS 199). U of Cal Pr.

Palmer, Rose W., jt. auth. see Weiner, Harvey S.

Palmer, Roy. Love Is Pleasing. LC 73-94359. 88p. (YA) (gr. 8-11). 1974. pap. text ed. 3.95 (ISBN 0-521-20445-3). Cambridge U Pr.

--The Painful Plough. LC 76-187081. (Resources of Music Ser.: No. 5). 80p. 1973. 5.95 (ISBN 0-521-08512-8). Cambridge U Pr.

--Poverty Knock. LC 73-93391. (Resources of Music Ser.: No. 9). (Illus.). 64p. (gr. 9-11). 1974. pap. text ed. 5.95 (ISBN 0-521-20443-7). Cambridge U Pr.

--The Valiant Sailor. (Resources of Music Ser.: No. 6). (Illus.). 64p. (gr. 2-7). 1973. pap. text ed. 5.95 (ISBN 0-521-20101-2). Cambridge U Pr.

Palmer, Roy & Raven, J. The Rigs of the Fair. (Resources of Music Ser.: No. 12). (Illus.). 64p. 1976. 5.95 (ISBN 0-521-20908-0). Cambridge U Pr.

Palmer, Roy, ed. Everyman's Book of British Ballads. (Illus.). 256p. 1980. 22.50 (ISBN 0-460-04452-4, Evman). Biblio Dist.

--Everyman's Book of English Country Songs. (Illus.). 256p. 1979. 16.95x o.p. (ISBN 0-460-12048-4, Pub. by J. M. Dent England). Biblio Dist.

--Folk Songs Collected by Ralph Vaughan Williams. 256p. 1983. text ed. 21.95x (ISBN 0-460-04558-X, Pub by J M Dent England). Biblio Dist.

--Room for Company: Folk Songs & Ballads. 1971. piano ed 7.95 (ISBN 0-521-08173-4); pap. 3.95 melody ed (ISBN 0-521-08174-2). Cambridge U Pr.

Palmer, Russell. John Paul II: A Pictorial Celebration. LC 79-92691. (Illus.). 128p. 1980. 12.95 o.p. (ISBN 0-87973-835-9). Our Sunday Visitor.

Palmer, Stephen E. Quisling & Others. LC 81-90533. 105p. 1982. 8.95 (ISBN 0-533-05239-4). Vantage.

Palmer, Susan R., ed. Petroleum Industry Glossary. 1982. 32.00 (ISBN 0-89931-032-X). Inst Energy.

Palmer, T. S. Index Generum Mammalium: A List of the Genera & Families of Mammals. 1968. Repr. of 1904 ed. 80.00 (ISBN 3-7682-0535-5). Lubrecht & Cramer.

Palmer, Thomas. The Transfer. LC 82-5518. 416p. 1983. 14.95 (ISBN 0-89919-130-4). Ticknor & Fields.

Palmer, Vernon V. & Poulter, Sebastian M. Legal System of Lesotho. (Legal Systems of Africa Ser). 1972. 25.00 o.p. (ISBN 0-87215-147-6). Michie-Bobbs.

Palmer, Virginia A., jt. auth. see Bogue, Margaret B.

Palmer, W. J., jt. auth. see Coombs, W. E.

Palmer, W. J., ed. Rapid & Automated Methods in Microbiology & Immunology: A Bibliography, 1976-1980. 265p. 1981. pap. 36.00 (ISBN 0-904147-19-3). IRL Pr.

Palmer, William J., jt. auth. see Cushman, Robert F.

Palmer, William S. Selected Techniques for Teaching Writing. LC 77-82293. 1977. pap. text ed. 5.50 (ISBN 0-87716-082-1, Pub. by Moore Pub Co). F Apple.

Palmeri, Joseph. Conversational & Cultural French. (Fr.). 1966. text ed. 18.95 (ISBN 0-13-171900-9). P-H.

Palmieri, F., et al, eds. Vectoral Reactions in Electron & Ion Transport in Michondria & Bacteria. (Developments in Bioenergetics & Biomembranes Ser.: Vol. 5). 1982. 73.75 (ISBN 0-444-80372-6). Elsevier.

Palmore, Erdman, ed. International Handbook on Aging: Contemporary Developments & Research. LC 78-73802. (Illus.). xviii, 529p. 1980. lib. bdg. 39.95 (ISBN 0-313-20890-5, PIH/). Greenwood.

Palmore, Paul. An Actor's Handbook: A Guide for the Beginning & Intermediate Actor. (Silliman University Humanities Ser.: No. 4). (Illus.). 114p. 1982. pap. 5.75x (ISBN 0-686-37574-2, Pub. by New Day Philippines). Cellar.

Palmore, Phyllis & Andre, Nevin. Small Appliance Repair. Schuler, Charles A., ed. LC 79-19186. (Basic Skills in Electricity & Electronics Ser.). (Illus.). 192p. (gr. 9-12). 1980. 14.96 (ISBN 0-07-048361-2, G); tchrs. manual 2.00 (ISBN 0-07-048363-9); activities manual 9.96 (ISBN 0-07-048362-0). McGraw.

Palmour, Vernon E., et al. A Planning Process for Public Libraries. LC 80-13107. 320p. 1980. pap. 15.00 (ISBN 0-8389-3246-0). ALA.

Palmour, Vernon E., et alcompiled by. A Study of the Characteristics, Costs, & Magnitude of Interlibrary Loans in Academic Libraries. LC 70-39344. 1972. lib. bdg. 25.00 (ISBN 0-8371-6340-4, PIL/). Greenwood.

Palms, Roger C. The Pleasure of His Company. 1982. pap. 5.95 (ISBN 0-8423-4847-6). Tyndale.

Palnik, Paul. Couples: How Two Worlds Become One. (Orig.). 1983. pap. 3.95 (ISBN 0-440-51303-0, Dell Trade Pbks). Dell.

Palone, Joe & Di Grazia, Bob, eds. Championship Soccer by the Experts. LC 81-84786. 160p. (Orig.). Date not set. pap. cancelled (ISBN 0-918438-24-1). Leisure Pr.

Paloutzian, Raymond F. Invitation to the Psychology of Religion. 1983. pap. text ed. 11.95x (ISBN 0-673-15343-6). Scott F.

Paloyan, Daniel. Pancreatitis. 1983. text ed. price not set (ISBN 0-87488-570-1). Med Exam.

Pals, Daniel L. The Victorian "Lives" of Jesus. LC 82-81018. (Monographs in Religion). 225p. 1982. 20.00 (ISBN 0-911536-95-7). Trinity U Pr.

Paltavy, F., jt. ed. see Mangold, H. K.

Paltridge, G. & Platt, C. Radiative Processes in Meteorology & Climatology. (Developments in Atmospheric Science: Vol. 5). 1976. 70.25 (ISBN 0-444-41444-4). Elsevier.

Paltsits, Victor H., ed. Washington's Farewell Address in Facsimile with Transliterations of All the Drafts of Washington, Madison, & Hamilton. LC 74-137706. 1971. Repr. of 1935 ed. 35.00 o.p. (ISBN 0-87104-509-5). NY Pub Lib.

Paltsits, Victor H., ed. see Albany County Sessions.

Paltsits, Victor H., ed. see Stevens, Henry.

Paludan, et al, eds. Issues Past & Present: An American History Sourcebook, 2 vols. 1978. Vol. 1. pap. text ed. 9.95x (ISBN 0-669-00784-6); Vol. 2. pap. text ed. 9.95x (ISBN 0-669-00954-7). Heath.

Paludan, Ann. The Imperial Ming Tombs. LC 80-23829. (Illus.). 272p. 1981. 35.00x (ISBN 0-300-02511-4). Yale U Pr.

Palumbo, Dennis, ed. Evaluating & Optimizing Public Policy. 1980. pap. 6.00 (ISBN 0-918592-38-0). Policy Studies.

Palumbo, Dennis & Taylor, George A., eds. Urban Policy: A Guide to Information Sources. LC 78-25957. (Urban Studies Information Guide Ser.: Vol. 6). 1979. 42.00x (ISBN 0-8103-1428-2). Gale.

Palumbo, Dennis J. & Harder, Marvin A. Implementing Public Policy. LC 80-8597. (Policy Studies Organization Bks.). 1981. 22.95x (ISBN 0-669-04305-2). Lexington Bks.

Palumbo, Dennis J., et al, eds. Evaluating & Optimizing Public Policy. LC 80-8598. (Studies Organization Book). 240p. 1981. 25.95x (ISBN 0-669-04306-0). Lexington Bks.

Palumbo, Giorgio G. Catalogue of Radial Velocities of Galaxies. 550p. 1982. write for info. (ISBN 0-677-06090-4). Gordon.

Palusamy, S. S. & Sampath, S. G, eds. Aspects of Fracture Mechanics In Pressure Vessels & Piping, Vol. 58. (PVP Ser.: Vol. 58). 324p. 1982. 50.00 (H00215). ASME.

Paluszek, John L. Will the Corporation Survive? LC 77-5730. (Illus.). 1977. 11.95 o.p. (ISBN 0-87909-894-5); pap. 12.95 (ISBN 0-87909-893-7). Reston.

Palz, W. Energy from Biomass in Europe. 1980. 39.00 (ISBN 0-85334-934-7, Pub. by Applied Sci England). Elsevier.

--Photovoltaic Power Generation. 1982. 49.50 (ISBN 90-277-1386-3, Pub. by Reidel Holland). Kluwer Boston.

Palz, W., ed. Solar Radiation Data. 1982. 24.50 (ISBN 90-277-1387-1, Pub. by Reidel Holland). Kluwer Boston.

Palz, W., jt. ed. see Grassi, G.

Palz, W., et al, eds. see International Conference on Biomass 1st, Brighton, England, November, 1980.

Pam, Leslie, jt. auth. see Rossi, Sheila I.

Pam, Martin D., jt. ed. see Meisel, Juergen M.

Pama, R. P., jt. auth. see Cusens, A. R.

Pamfilov, Yu., tr. see Linnik, I.

Pamleny, E., ed. Social-Economic Researches on the History of East-Central Europe. 1970. 13.50x (ISBN 0-8002-1985-6). Intl Pubns Serv.

Pampa, Leon & Dray, Williams, eds. Substance & Form in History. 198p. 1981. 20.00 (ISBN 0-85224-413-4, Pub. by Edinburgh U Pr Scotland). Columbia U Pr.

Pampana, Emilio. Textbook of Malaria Eradication. 2nd ed. 1969. 24.00x o.p. (ISBN 0-19-264212-X). Oxford U Pr.

Pampel, Fred C. Social Change & the Aged: Recent Trends in the United States. LC 79-4752. (Illus.). 240p. 1981. 24.95 (ISBN 0-669-02928-9). Lexington Bks.

Pampillo, C. & Biloni, H. Aluminum Transformation Technology & Applications. 1980. 53.00 (ISBN 0-87170-095-6). ASM.

Pamplin, B., ed. Progress in Crystal Growth & Characterization, Vol. 3 Complete. (Illus.). 390p. 1982. 120.00 (ISBN 0-08-028405-1). Pergamon.

--Progress in Crystal Growth & Characterization, Vol. 4. (Illus.). 345p. 1982. 130.00 (ISBN 0-08-029681-5). Pergamon.

Pamplin, Brian R. Crystal Growth. LC 73-21909. 1975. text ed. 82.00 o.p. (ISBN 0-08-017003-X); pap. 37.00 o.p. (ISBN 0-08-021310-3). Pergamon.

Pamplin, Brian R., ed. Progress in Crystal Growth & Characterization, Vol. 1. Pt. 1 1977. pap. text ed. write for info (ISBN 0-08-021663-3); Pt. 2 1978. pap. text ed. write for info (ISBN 0-08-023050-4); Pt. 3 1978. pap. text ed. write for info. (ISBN 0-08-023051-2); Pt. 4. pap. text ed. write for info. (ISBN 0-08-023083-0). Pergamon.

Pamplin, Robert B., Jr., jt. auth. see Worcester, Thomas K.

Pampuch, R. Ceramic Materials: An Introduction to Their Properties. 1976. 53.25x (ISBN 0-444-99837-3). Elsevier.

Pan Am World Airways, Inc. Pan Am's World Guide. new ed. LC 76-13509. (Illus.). 1976. 6.95 o.p. (ISBN 0-07-048424-4, GB). McGraw.

Pan Am World Airways, Inc., ed. Pan Am World Guide. 26th ed. 1982. 10.95 (ISBN 0-07-048433-3). McGraw.

Pan, Charlene. Herpes Simplex: A Complete Cure. 110p. 1982. pap. 5.00 (ISBN 0-940178-12-5). Sitare Inc.

--Herpes Simplex, A Self-Cure? 110p. 1982. pap. cancelled (ISBN 0-686-97649-5). Sitare Inc.

Pan, Elizabeth, et al, eds. Annual Review of Rehabilitation, Vol. 3. 352p. 1983. text ed. 42.00 (ISBN 0-8261-3092-5). Springer Pub.

Panaccio, Tim. Beast of the East: A Game by Game History of the Penn State-Pitt Football Rivalry 1893 to 1981. LC 82-81808. (Great Rivalry Ser.). (Illus.). 400p. 1982. 9.95 (ISBN 0-88011-068-6). Leisure Pr.

Panagoulias, Panagiotis, jt. auth. see Gonis, Antonios.

Panama, Norman & Lewin, Albert E. The Glass Bed. LC 80-12804. 192p. 1980. 9.95 o.p. (ISBN 0-688-03676-7). Morrow.

Pananides, Nicholas A. & Arny, Thomas. Introductory Astronomy. 2nd ed. LC 78-55825. (Physics Ser.). (Illus.). 1979. text ed. 23.95 (ISBN 0-201-05674-7). A-W.

Panassie, Hugues. The Real Jazz. LC 73-13328. 284p. 1973. Repr. of 1960 ed. lib. bdg. 20.25 (ISBN 0-8371-7123-7, PARJ). Greenwood.

Panati, Charles & Hudson, Michael. The Silent Intruder: Surviving the Radiation Age. 256p. 1983. pap. 3.25 (ISBN 0-425-05828-X). Berkley Pub.

Panayi, G. S. Rheumatoid Arthritis & Related Conditions, Vol. 1. (Annual Research Reviews Ser.). 1977. 14.40 (ISBN 0-88831-003-X). Eden Pr.

--Rheumatoid Arthritis & Related Conditions, Vol. 2. LC 78-317911. (Annual Research Reviews Ser.). 1978. 19.20 (ISBN 0-88831-022-6). Eden Pr.

Panayi, G. S., ed. Rheumatoid Arthritis & Related Conditions, Vol. 3. (Annual Research Reviews Ser.). 1979. 22.00 (ISBN 0-88831-054-4). Eden Pr.

--Rheumatoid Arthritis & Related Conditions, Vol. 4. (Annual Research Reviews). 155p. 1980. 24.00 (ISBN 0-88831-081-1). Eden Pr.

Panayi, Gabriel S., ed. Rheumatoid Arthritis & Related Conditions Annual Research Reviews. 119p. Date not set. 18.00 (ISBN 0-88831-104-4). Eden Pr.

Pancake, Breece D'J. The Stories of Breece D'J Pancake. 1983. 13.00i (ISBN 0-316-69012-0, Pub. by Atlantic Monthly Pr). Little.

Panchen, A. L., jt. auth. see Clark, R. B.

Pancheri, Michael, jt. auth. see Flynn, David H.

Pancheri, P., jt. ed. see Zichella, L.

Pancoast, Patricia, jt. auth. see Detmer, Josephine.

Pancoast, Patricia, et al. Portland. 2nd ed. LC 72-172820. (Illus.). 236p. 1973. 18.00 (ISBN 0-9600612-2-3); pap. 6.95 (ISBN 0-9600612-1-5). Greater Portland.

Panconcelli-Calzia, Giulio. Geschichtszahlen der Phonetik (1941) Together with Quellenatlas der Phonetik (1940) (Studies in the History of Linguistics: 16). 250p. (Ger.). 1983. 32.00 (ISBN 90-272-0957-X). Benjamins North Am.

Panconcelli-Calzia, Gulio. Geschichtszahlen der Phonetik mit Quentenatlas der Phonetik. 250p. 1982. 32.00 o.p. (ISBN 90-272-0957-X). Benjamins North Am.

Pande, B. N. The Spirit of India, 2 vols. (Indira Gandhi Festschrift Ser.). (Illus.). 1976. lib. bdg. 100.00x set (ISBN 0-685-68908-5). Vol. 1 (ISBN 0-210-40560-0). Vol. 2 (ISBN 0-210-40561-9). Asia.

Pande, G. C., jt. ed. see Goudas, C. L.

Pande, G. N. & Zienkiewicz, O. C. Soil Mechanics-Transient & Cyclic Loads: Constitutive Relations & Numerical Treatment. LC 81-16485. (Numerical Methods in Engineering Ser.). 640p. 1982. 78.95x (ISBN 0-471-10046-3, Pub. by Wiley-Interscience). Wiley.

Pandey, B. N. South & South East Asia. LC 79-26753. 1980. 25.00 (ISBN 0-312-74710-1). St Martin.

Pandey, B. N., ed. Indian Nationalist Movement, Eighteen Eighty-Five to Nineteen Forty-Seven: Select Documents. LC 78-8691. 1979. 26.00x (ISBN 0-312-41385-8). St Martin.

Pandey, M. P. The Impact of Irrigation on Rural Development. 1980. text ed. 9.50x (ISBN 0-391-01846-9). Humanities.

Pandey, Raj B. Hindu Sanskaras. 1976. Repr. 13.95 (ISBN 0-8426-0853-2). Orient Bk Dist.

Pandey, S. N. & Trivedi, P. S. A Textbook of Botany, Vol. I: Algae, Fungi, Bacteria, Virus, Lichens, Mycoplasma & Elementary Plant Pathology. 1976. 18.95 o.p. (ISBN 0-7069-0516-4, Pub. by Vikas India). Advent NY.

--Textbook of Botany: Vol. I: Algae, Fungi, Bacteria, Virus, Lichens, Mycoplasma & Elementary Plant Pathology. 5th ed. viii, 628p. 1982. text ed. 25.00x (ISBN 0-7069-1975-0, Pub. by Vikas India). Advent NY.

Pandey, S. N., et al. Textbook of Botany: Vol. II: Bryophyta, Pteridophyta, Gymnosperms & Paleobotany. 2nd ed. viii, 531p. 1981. text ed. 25.00x (ISBN 0-7069-1355-8, Pub. by Vikas India). Advent NY.

--A Textbook of Botany, Vol. II: Bryophyta, Pteridophyta, Gymnosperms & Paleobotany. 1974. 17.50x o.p. (ISBN 0-7069-0213-0, Pub. by Vikas India). Advent NY.

Pandeya, Ramchandra. Indian Studies in Philosophy. 1977. 11.50x o.p. (ISBN 0-8364-0057-7). South Asia Bks.

Pandit, G. S. & Gupta, S. P. Structural Analysis: A Matrix Approach. 592p. Date not set. 14.95x (ISBN 0-07-096554-4). McGraw.

Pandit, H. N. Fragments of History: India's Freedom Movement & after. 299p. 1982. 34.99x (ISBN 0-940500-55-8, Pub. by Sterling India). Asia Bk Corp.

Pandit, M. P. Dynamics of Yoga, Vol. II. 1979. 8.00 (ISBN 0-941524-06-X). Lotus Light.

--Dynamics of Yoga, Vol. III. 1980. write for info. (ISBN 0-941524-07-8). Lotus Light.

Pandit, S. G. & Deo, S. G. Differential Systems Involving Impulses. (Lecture Notes in Mathematics Ser.: Vol. 954). 102p. 1983. pap. 8.00 (ISBN 0-387-11606-0). Springer-Verlag.

Pandit, Sri M. P., compiled by see Aurobindo, Sri.

Pandolfini, Bruce. Let's Play Chess! A Step by Step Guide for Beginners. (Illus.). 1980. pap. 4.95 (ISBN 0-671-33061-6). Wanderer Bks.

Panek, Dennis. Catastrophe Cat. LC 77-90951. (Illus.). 32p. (ps-1). 1978. 10.95 (ISBN 0-02-769770-3). Bradbury Pr.

--Catastrophe Cat at the Zoo. LC 78-26369. (Illus.). 32p. (ps-1). 1979. 10.95 (ISBN 0-02-769780-0). Bradbury Pr.

--Detective Whoo. LC 81-7703. (Illus.). 32p. (ps-1). 1981. 10.95 (ISBN 0-02-769790-8). Bradbury Pr.

--Matilda Hippo Has a Big Mouth. LC 80-13260. (Illus.). 32p. (ps-2). 1980. 10.95 (ISBN 0-02-769810-6). Bradbury Pr.

Panel on Geography in the Two-Year Colleges. Geography in the Two-Year Colleges: No. 10. LC 73-133905. 1970. pap. 1.00 o.p. (ISBN 0-89291-038-0). Assn Am Geographers.

Panella, Luis J., tr. see Petzold, Paul.

Paner, Stanley W., jt. auth. see Gamett, James.

Panero, Julius. Anatomy for Interior Designers. 3rd ed. (Illus.). 160p. 1962. 16.95 (ISBN 0-8230-7026-3, Whitney Lib). Watson-Guptill.

Panero, Julius & Zelnik, Martin. Human Dimensions & Interior Space. (Illus.). 1979. 32.50 (ISBN 0-8230-7271-1, Whitney Lib). Watson-Guptill.

Pangborn, Cyrus R. Zoroastrianism: A Beleaguered Faith. 165p. 1982. text ed. 18.95x (ISBN 0-89891-006-4). Advent NY.

Pangborn, Edgar. West of the Sun. 1980. pap. 1.95 o.s.i. (ISBN 0-440-19366-4). Dell.

Panger, Daniel. Black Ulysses. LC 82-3517. (Illus.). vi, 402p. 1982. 16.95 (ISBN 0-8214-0660-4, 82-84309); pap. 8.95 (ISBN 0-8214-0680-9, 82-84481). Ohio U Pr.

Panhuis, Dirk G. The Communicative Perspective in the Sentence: A Study of Latin Word Order. (Studies in Language Companion: No. 11). 150p. 1982. 20.00 (ISBN 9-0272-3010-2). Benjamins North Am.

Panhuys, H. F. Van. International Law in the Netherlands, 3 vols, Vol. III. 1981. lib. bdg. 50.00 ea. (ISBN 0-379-20392-8); vol. I, 1978; vol. II, 1979. Oceana.

Panichas, George A. Epicurus. (World Authors Ser.: No. 17). 10.95 o.p. (ISBN 0-8057-2300-5, Twayne). G K Hall.

Panichas, George A., ed. see Babbitt, Irving.

Panigrahi, D. N., jt. ed. see Kumar, Ravinder.

Paniker, Jayaram, jt. auth. see Ananthanarayan, R.

Panikkar, K. Ayyappa. Malayalam Short Stories: An Anthology. 157p. 1982. 37.00x (ISBN 0-686-94072-5, Pub. by Garlandfold England). State Mutual Bk.

Panikkar, K. M. An Autobiography. Krishnamurthy, K., tr. 1977. 12.50x o.p. (ISBN 0-19-560380-X). Oxford U Pr.

Panikkar, Kavalam M. Studies in Indian History. 1968. 5.00x o.p. (ISBN 0-210-22537-8). Asia.

Panikkar, Raimundo. Mantramanjari: The Vedic Experience. 1977. 50.00x (ISBN 0-520-02854-6). U of Cal Pr.

--Trinity & the Religious Experience of Man. LC 73-77329. 80p. 1974. pap. 3.95x o.p. (ISBN 0-88344-495-X). Orbis Bks.

Panikkar, Raimundo, et al. Blessed Simplicity: The Monk as Universal Archetype. 224p. (Orig.). 1982. 17.95 (ISBN 0-8164-0531-X). Seabury.

Panish, Paul. Exit Visa: The Emigration of the Soviet Jews. 1981. 14.95 (ISBN 0-698-11056-0, Coward). Putnam Pub Group.

Panitch, L. Social Democracy & Industrial Militancy. LC 75-16869. (Illus.). 306p. 1976. 39.50 (ISBN 0-521-20779-7). Cambridge U Pr.

Panizon, Hope A. The Pleasures of Being a Catholic. new enl. ed. (Illus.). 1977. 31.15 o.p. (ISBN 0-89266-075-9). Am Classical Coll Pr.

Pankhurst, Richard J. Biological Identification. 112p. 1979. pap. text ed. 14.95 o.p. (ISBN 0-8391-1344-7). Univ Park.

--Biological Identification. (Illus.). 112p. 1978. pap. text ed. 14.95 (ISBN 0-7131-2724-4). E Arnold.

Pankhurst, Sylvia. The Suffragette Movement. 632p. 1983. pap. 10.95 (ISBN 0-86068-026-6, Virago Pr). Merrimack Bk Serv.

Pankrath, J., jt. auth. see Georgii, H.

Pankratz, jt. ed. see Houston.

Pannekoek, A. A History of Astronomy. (Illus.). 521p. 1961. 19.50x o.p. (ISBN 0-87471-365-X). Rowman.

Pannell, Clifton W. & Ma, Laurence J. C. China: The Geography of Development & Modernization. (Scripts Series in Geography). 390p. 49.95 (ISBN 0-470-27376-3); pap. 19.95 (ISBN 0-470-27377-1). Halsted Pr.

Pannell, Lucille, jt. auth. see Cavanah, Frances.

Pannenberg, Wolfhart. The Apostles' Creed: In the Light of Today's Questions. Kohl, M, tr. LC 82-15984. 1972. 8.95 (ISBN 0-664-20947-5). Westminster.

--Basic Questions in Theology, Vol. I. LC 82-15984. 257p. 1983. pap. write for info. (ISBN 0-664-24466-1). Westminster.

--Basic Questions in Theology, Vol. II. LC 82-15984. 257p. 1983. pap. write for info. (ISBN 0-664-24467-X). Westminster.

--The Church. LC 82-23768. 189p. 1983. pap. write for info. (ISBN 0-664-24460-2). Westminster.

--Faith & Reality. LC 77-682. 1977. softcover 6.50 (ISBN 0-664-24755-5). Westminster.

--Jesus-God & Man. 2d ed. Wilkins, Lewis L. & Priebe, Duane A., trs. LC 76-26478. 1977. 12.50 o.s.i. (ISBN 0-664-21289-1). Westminster.

--Jesus: God & Man. 2nd ed. Wilkens, Lewis L. & Priebe, Duane A., trs. LC 76-26478. 432p. 1982. pap. 12.95 (ISBN 0-664-24468-8). Westminster.

--Theology & the Kingdom of God. LC 69-12668. 1969. pap. 5.95 (ISBN 0-664-24842-X). Westminster.

Pannes, Ernestine D. Waters of the Lonely Way: A Chronicle of Weston, Vermont from 1761-1978. LC 82-13314. (Illus.). 352p. 1982. 22.00 (ISBN 0-914016-89-X). Phoenix Pub.

Pannick, Gerald. Richard Palmer Blackmur. (United States Authors Ser.). 1981. lib. bdg. 13.95 (ISBN 0-8057-7338-X, Twayne). G K Hall.

Panoff, Renee, jt. auth. see Neuman, Susan B.

Panofsky, Erwin. Codex Huygens & Leonardo Da Vinci's Art Theory. LC 79-109814. (Illus.). 1971. Repr. of 1940 ed. lib. bdg. 18.50x (ISBN 0-8371-4306-3, PACH). Greenwood.

--Gothic Architecture & Scholasticism. (Illus.). pap. 4.95 (ISBN 0-452-00581-7, F581, Mer). NAL.

--Meaning in the Visual Arts. LC 82-13600. (Illus.). xx, 364p. 1983. pap. 9.95 (ISBN 0-226-64551-7). U of Chicago Pr.

--Renaissance & Renascences in Western Art. (Icon Edition). (Illus.). 380p. 1972. pap. 8.95i (ISBN 0-06-430026-9, IN-26, HarpT). Har-Row.

Panofsky, Hans E. A Bibliography of Africana. LC 72-823. (Contributions in Librarianship & Information Science Ser.: No. 11). 1975. lib. bdg. 29.95 (ISBN 0-8371-6391-9, PAA/). Greenwood.

Panoletti, Rodolfo, jt. ed. see Gotto, Antonio.

Panopoulos, Nickolas J. Genetic Engineering in the Plant Sciences. 288p. 1981. 32.50 (ISBN 0-03-057026-3). Praeger.

Panouf, Irina. New Pocket Romanian Dictionary. 500p. 1982. 14.95 (ISBN 0-88254-682-1). Hippocrene Bks.

Panov, Valery & Feifer, George. To Dance: The Autobiography of Valery Panov. LC 77-20362. (Illus.). 1978. 15.00 o.p. (ISBN 0-394-49882-8). Knopf.

Panovf, Irina. The New Pocket Romanian Dictionary. 828p. 1983. 14.95 (ISBN 0-88254-683-X). Hippocrene Bks.

Panshin, Alex J., et al. Forest Products. 2nd ed. 1962. text ed. 38.50 (ISBN 0-07-048444-9, C). McGraw.

Panshin, Alexei. Rite of Passage. (Science Fiction Ser.). 272p. 1976. Repr. of 1968 ed. lib. bdg. 12.00 o.p. (ISBN 0-8398-2336-3, Gregg). G K Hall.

Panshin, Alexis J., et al. Textbook of Wood Technology, Vol. 1. 3rd ed. (Illus.). 1970. text ed. 29.95 (ISBN 0-07-048440-6). McGraw.

Pansini, Anthony J. Undergrounding Telephone Lines. 112p. 1978. 7.95 (ISBN 0-686-98123-5). Telecom Lib.

Pansini, Anthony J. & Seale, Arthur C., Jr. Electrical Distribution Engineering. (Illus.). 464p. 1983. 45.95 (ISBN 0-07-048454-6, P&RB). McGraw.

Pansky, Ben. Review of Gross Anatomy. 4th ed. 1979. pap. text ed. 21.95x (ISBN 0-02-390630-8). Macmillan.

--Review of Medical Embryology. 1982. pap. text ed. 20.95x (ISBN 0-02-390620-0). Macmillan.

Pansky, Ben & Allen, Delmas J. Review of Neuroscience. (Illus.). 1980. pap. text ed. 23.95x (ISBN 0-02-390610-3). Macmillan.

Pant, Devidatt. The Commercial Policy of the Moguls. (Studies in Islamic History: No. 20). 281p. Repr. of 1930 ed. lib. bdg. 22.50x (ISBN 0-87991-078-X). Porcupine Pr.

Pant, Sushila. The Origin & Development of Stupa Architecture in India. (Illus.). 1977. 30.00x (ISBN 0-88386-943-8). South Asia Bks.

Pantaleoni, Hewitt, ed. see Serwadda, W. Moses.

Pantelidis, Veronica S. Arab Education, Nineteen Fifty-Six to Nineteen Seventy-Eight. 670p. 1982. 72.00 (ISBN 0-7201-1588-4, Mansell Pub.). Wilson.

Pantell, Dora, jt. auth. see MacGregor, Ellen.

Pantell, Dora, jt. auth. see Macgregor, Ellen.

Pantell, Dora, jt. auth. see MacGregor, Ellen.

Pantell, Robert & Bergman, David. The Parent's Pharmacy. LC 82-13837. (Illus.). 288p. 1982. 16.95 (ISBN 0-201-08153-9); pap. 8.95 (ISBN 0-686-82138-6). A-W.

Panter, P. F. Communication Systems Design: Line-of-Sight & Tropo-Scatter Systems. 1972. 37.50 o.p. (ISBN 0-07-048436-8, P&RB). McGraw.

Pantin, W. A. The English Church in the Fourteenth Century. (Medieval Academy Reprints for Teaching Ser.). 1980. pap. 6.50 (ISBN 0-8020-6411-6). U of Toronto Pr.

Pantin, William E., jt. auth. see Flewett, H. W.

Pantoga, Fritzie & Bausch, William J. Catholic Burial: A Down-to-Earth Guide & One Pastor's Perspective. 1977. 0.25 o.p. (ISBN 0-89570-142-1). Claretian Pubns.

Pantry Press & Kitchen Ladies of America. How to Turn Your Kitchen into a Gold Mine! 288p. 1981. pap. 5.95 cancelled o.p. (ISBN 0-312-39597-3). St Martin.

Pantumsinchai, Pricha & Hassan, M. Zia. Basic Programs for Production & Operations Management. (Illus.). 448p. 1983. pap. 14.95 (ISBN 0-686-38834-8). P H.

Pantzer, Eugene E. Antun Gustav Matos. (Twayne's World Authors Ser.). 1981. lib. bdg. 15.95 (ISBN 0-8057-6478-X, Twayne). G K Hall.

Panum, Hortense. Stringed Instruments of the Middle Ages. LC 73-127279. (Music Ser). (Illus.). 1971. Repr. of 1939 ed. lib. bdg. 42.50 (ISBN 0-306-70039-5). Da Capo.

Panunzio, Constantine. Immigration Crossroads. LC 79-145489. (The American Immigration Library). xii, 308p. 1971. Repr. of 1927 ed. lib. bdg. 17.95x (ISBN 0-89198-022-9). Ozer.

Panunzio, Constantine M. Deportation Cases of Nineteen-Nineteen to Nineteen-Twenty. LC 77-109547. (Civil Liberties in American History Ser). 1970. Repr. of 1921 ed. lib. bdg. 18.50 (ISBN 0-306-71901-0). Da Capo.

Panush, Richard S. Principles of Rheumatic Diseases. LC 81-1951. 492p. 1982. 42.00 (ISBN 0-471-05198-5, Pub. by Wiley Med). Wiley.

Panvini, R. S. & Alam, M. S., eds. Novel Results in Particle Physics. LC 82-73954. (AID Conf. Proc.: No. 93). 384p. 1982. lib. bdg. 35.00 (ISBN 0-88318-192-4). Am Inst Physics.

Panzar, John C. Regulation, Service Quality, & Market Performance: A Model of Airline Rivalry. LC 78-75053. (Outstanding Dissertations in Economics Ser.). 1979. lib. bdg. 16.00 o.s.i. (ISBN 0-8240-4131-3). Garland Pub.

Panzar, John C., jt. auth. see Baumol, William J.

Panzer, Marvin, jt. auth. see Levi, Enrico.

Paola, Thomas A. De see De Paola, Thomas A.

Paola, Tomie de. Four Stories for Four Seasons. LC 76-8837. (Illus.). (ps-3). 1977. PLB 9.95 o. p. (ISBN 0-13-330175-3); pap. 3.95 (ISBN 0-13-330100-1). P-H.

Paola, Tomie de see De Paola, Tomie.

Paola, Tomie De see De Paola, Tomie.

Paola, Tomie De see De Paola, Tomie.

Paola, Tomie De see De Paola, Tomie.

Paola, Tomie De see De Paola, Tomie.

Paola, Tomie De see De Paola, Tomie.

Paola, Tommy De see De Paola, Tomie.

Paoletti, A., ed. Physics of Magnetic Garnets. (Enrico Fermi International Summer School of Physics Ser.: Course 70, 1977). 1978. 95.75 (ISBN 0-444-85200-X, North Holland). Elsevier.

Paoletti, P., et al, eds. Multidisciplinary Aspects of Brain Tumor Therapy. (Neurooncology Ser.: Vol. 1). 404p. 1979. 77.00 (ISBN 0-444-80170-7, North Holland). Elsevier.

Paoletti, R. Drugs Affecting Lipid Metabolism. Date not set. 55.50 (ISBN 0-686-94149-7). Elsevier.

Paoletti, R., jt. ed. see Samuelsson, B.

Paoletti, R., jt. auth. see Galli, C. L.

Paoletti, R., et al, eds. Lipids: Proceedings, 2 vols. Incl. Vol. 1. Biochemistry. LC 75-21982. 298p. 41.50 (ISBN 0-89004-028-1); Vol. 2. Technology. LC 75-26387. 286p. 41.50 (ISBN 0-89004-029-X). 1975. Set. 75.50 (ISBN 0-685-61106-X). Raven.

Paoletti, Rodolfo & Gotto, Antonio M., eds. Atherosclerosis Reviews, Vol. 4. LC 75-14582. 279p. 1978. 31.00 (ISBN 0-89004-218-7). Raven.

--Atherosclerosis Reviews, Vol. 5. LC 75-14582. 274p. 1979. text ed. 31.00 (ISBN 0-89004-275-6). Raven.

Paoletti, Rodolfo & Gotto, Antonio M., Jr., eds. Atherosclerosis Reviews, Vol. 3. LC 75-14582. 279p. 1978. 30.00 (ISBN 0-89004-217-9). Raven.

Paoletti, Rodolfo & Kritchevsky, David, eds. Advances in Lipid Research, Vol. 19. 226p. 1982. 36.50 (ISBN 0-12-024919-7); lib. ed. 47.50 (ISBN 0-12-024984-7); microfiche 26.00 (ISBN 0-12-024985-5). Acad Pr.

Paoletti, Rodolfo, jt. ed. see Samuelsson, Bengt.

Paoli, Ugo Enrico. Rome: Its People, Life, & Customs. MacNaghten, R. D., tr. from It. LC 75-2630. (Illus.). 336p. 1975. Repr. of 1963 ed. lib. bdg. 28.25 o.p. (ISBN 0-8371-8039-2, PARO). Greenwood.

Paolini, Gilbert, ed. La Chispa Eighty-One. Selected Proceedings. LC 81-52692. 360p. (Span. & Portuguese.). 1981. pap. 20.00 (ISBN 0-9607798-0-9). Pantheon Pr.

Paolo, Tomie de see De Paola, Tomie.

Paolozzi & Sedwick. Conversation in Italian: Points of Departure. 2nd ed. (Illus., Orig.). 1981. pap. text ed. write for info. (ISBN 0-442-24474-6). Van Nos Reinhold.

Paolozzi, Gabriel J. & Sedwick, Frank. Conversation in Italian: Points of Departure. 1975. 5.95x (ISBN 0-442-26458-5). Van Nos Reinhold.

Paolucci, Anne & Warwick, Ronald, eds. Review of National Literatures: India, Vol. 10. LC 77-126039. 240p. 1979. 14.00x (ISBN 0-686-97201-5). Griffon Hse.

Paolucci, Beatrice, jt. auth. see Hall, Olive A.

Paolucci, Beatrice, et al. Family Decision Making: An Ecosystem Approach. LC 76-39953. 1977. text ed. 15.50 (ISBN 0-471-65838-3). Wiley.

--Personal Perspectives: A Guide to Decision Making. LC 72-8842. (Illus.). 480p. (gr. 11-12). 1973. text ed. 20.64 (ISBN 0-07-048437-6, W); tchrs' manual 5.44 (ISBN 0-07-034859-6). McGraw.

--Personal Perspectives. 2nd ed. (Illus.). (gr. 9-12). 1978. text ed. 20.08 (ISBN 0-07-048438-4, W); tchr's manual 5.28 (ISBN 0-07-034862-6). McGraw.

Paolucci, Henry. A Brief History of Political Thought & Stagecraft. 6.95 (ISBN 0-918680-08-5). Griffon Hse.

--War, Peace & the Presidency. LC 68-8774. 16.95. Griffon Hse.

--Zionism, the Superpowers, & the P.L.O. LC 82-15728. 80p. 1982. 6.95 (ISBN 0-918680-18-2, GHGP 708). Griffon Hse.

Paolucci, Henry, ed. see Augustine, Saint.

Pao-min, Chang. Continuity & Change: A Profile of Chinese Americans. 1983. 11.95 (ISBN 0-533-05308-0). Vantage.

Paone, Anthony J. My Life with Christ. LC 62-17359. 1962. pap. 4.95 (ISBN 0-385-03361-3, D185, Im). Doubleday.

Paor, Maire De see De Paor, Maire.

Pap, Leo. The Portuguese-Americans. (Immigrant Heritage of America Ser.). 1981. lib. bdg. 14.95 (ISBN 0-8057-8417-9, Twayne). G K Hall.

Papa, John. Fragments of Hawaiian History. rev. ed. Barrere, Dorothy B., ed. Pukui, Mary K., tr. (Special Publication Ser.: No. 70). (Illus.). 212p. 1982. pap. 8.00 (ISBN 0-910240-31-0). Bishop Mus.

Papadakis, Aristeides. Crisis in Byzantium: The Filioque Controversy of the Patriarchate of Gregory II of Cyprus (1283-1289) 320p. 1983. 50.00 (ISBN 0-8232-1088-X). Fordham.

Papadakis, C. N., jt. ed. see Webb, D. R.

Papadatos, Costas J. & Bartsocas, Christos S., eds. Skeletal Dysplasias. LC 82-17277. (Progress in Clinical & Biological Research Ser.: Vol. 104). 572p. 1982. 60.00 (ISBN 0-8451-0104-8). A R Liss.

Papademetriou, Demetrios G. & Miller, Mark J., eds. The Unavoidable Issue: U. S. Immigration Policy in the 1980's. LC 82-15650. 328p. 1983. text ed. 20.00x (ISBN 0-89727-047-9). Inst Study Human.

Papadiamantis, Alexandros. The Murderess. Levi, Peter, tr. from Gr. 127p. 1983. 13.95 (ISBN 0-904613-94-1). Writers & Readers.

Papadimitriou, Christos, jt. auth. see Steiglitz, Kenneth.

Papadimitriou, Christos H., jt. auth. see Lewis, Harry R.

Papadopoulos, A. Multilateral Diplomacy Within the Commonwealth. 1982. lib. bdg. 39.50 (ISBN 90-247-2568-2, Pub. by Martinus Nijhoff Netherlands). Kluwer Boston.

Papadopoulos, C. Photographic Star Atlas, 3 vols. Incl. Vol. 1. Southern Stars. text ed. 200.00 (ISBN 0-08-023435-6); Vol. 2. Equatorial Stars. text ed. 325.00 (ISBN 0-08-021623-4); Vol. 3. Northern Stars. text ed. 200.00 (ISBN 0-08-021626-9). 1979. Vols. 1 & 2. text ed. 590.00 set (ISBN 0-08-021622-6). Pergamon.

Papagiannis, Michael D., ed. Eighth Texas Symposium on Relativistic Astrophysics, Vol. 302. (Annals of the New York Academy of Sciences). 689p. 1977. 47.00x (ISBN 0-89072-048-7). NY Acad Sci.

Papagno, Noella C. Desairology: The Dressing of Decedents Hair. rev., 2nd. ed. LC 81-90585. (The Family, the Funeral, & the Hairdresser Ser.). (Illus.). 124p. (Orig.). (gr. 12). 1982. text ed. 19.95x (ISBN 0-9604610-2-7); pap. text ed. 15.95x (ISBN 0-9604610-3-5). JJ Pub FL.

Papahadjopoulos, Demetrios, ed. Liposomes & Their Uses in Biology & Medicine. (Annals of the New York Academy of Sciences: Vol. 308). 462p. 1978. pap. 59.00x (ISBN 0-89072-064-9). NY Acad Sci.

Papahatzis, Nicos. Ancient Corinth. (Athenon Illustrated Guides Ser.). (Illus.). 112p. 1983. pap. 10.00 (ISBN 0-88332-303-6, Pub. by Ekdotike Athenon Greece). Larousse.

Papaioannou, A. N. The Prevention of Breast Cancer. 1983. write for info. (ISBN 0-87527-227-4). Green.

Papajohn, J. C., jt. auth. see Moskos, C. C., Jr.

Papajohn, John C. Intensive Behavior Therapy: The Behavioral Treatment of Complex Emotional Disorders. (General Psychology Ser.: No. 112). 176p. 1982. 15.00 (ISBN 0-08-025544-2, J115). Pergamon.

Papalia, Anthony & Mendoza, Jose A. La Lengua y Cultura: Primera etapa. 1978. pap. text ed. 5.95 (ISBN 0-88377-109-8). Newbury Hse.

--Lengua y Cultura: Segunda Etapa. LC 78-1002. 1978. pap. text ed. 5.95 (ISBN 0-88377-110-1). Newbury Hse.

Papalia, D. & Olds, S. W. A Child's World. 3rd ed. 1982. 23.50 (ISBN 0-07-048464-3); instrs'. manual 8.00 (ISBN 0-07-048465-1); study guide 8.95 (ISBN 0-07-048466-X); test bank 10.00 (ISBN 0-07-048467-8). McGraw.

--Human Development. 2nd ed. 1981. 23.50 (ISBN 0-07-048391-4); instr's. manual 13.00 (ISBN 0-07-048392-2); study guide 10.95 (ISBN 0-07-048394-9); test file 13.00 (ISBN 0-07-048393-0). McGraw.

Papalia, Diane E. & Olds, Sally W. A Child's World: Infancy Through Adolescence. 2nd ed. LC 74-31496. (Illus.). 672p. 1975. text ed. 20.50 (ISBN 0-07-048458-9, C); instructor's manual & test file 15.00 (ISBN 0-07-048459-7). McGraw.

Papanek, Ernest. The Austrian School Reform: Its Bases, Principles & Development--The Twenty Years Between the Two World Wars. LC 78-866. 1978. Repr. of 1962 ed. lib. bdg. 17.00x (ISBN 0-313-20292-3, PAAS). Greenwood.

Papanek, Ernst & Linn, Ed. Out of the Fire. LC 74-26674. 1975. 8.95 o.p. (ISBN 0-688-00337-0). Morrow.

Papanek, Hanna & Minnault, Gail. Separate Worlds: Studies of Purdah in South Asia. 1982. 24.00 (ISBN 0-8364-0895-0). South Asia Bks.

Papanek, Hanna, jt. ed. see Jahan, Rounaq.

Papanikolas, Helen Z., ed. The Peoples of Utah. LC 76-12311. (Illus.). 499p. 1981. Repr. of 1976 ed. 12.95 o.p. (ISBN 0-913738-26-3). Utah St Hist Soc.

Papanikolas, Zeese. Buried Unsung: Louis Tikas & the Ludlow Massacre. LC 82-13475. (University of Utah Publications in the American West: Vol. 14). (Illus.). 331p. 1982. 20.00 (ISBN 0-87480-211-3). U of Utah Pr.

Papanikolas, Zeese, jt. auth. see Bergen, Frank.

Papanoutsos, Evangelos P. Foundations of Knowledge. Anton, John P., ed. Coukis, Basil P. & Anton, John P., trs. LC 68-19533. Orig. Title: Gnosiology. 1968. 39.50x (ISBN 0-87395-034-8). State U NY Pr.

Paparella, Michael & Shumrick, Donald A., eds. Otolaryngology: Basic Sciences & Related Disciplines, Vol. 1. LC 70-145563. (Illus.). 1189p. 1973. text ed. 50.00 o.p. (ISBN 0-7216-7058-X). Saunders.

Paparella, Michael M. & Meyerhoff, William L. Clinical Otology. (Ear Clinics International Ser.: Vol. 3). (Illus.). 261p. 1982. lib. bdg. 29.95 o.p. (ISBN 0-683-06748-6). Williams & Wilkins.

Paparella, Michael M. & Shumrick, Donald A., eds. Otolaryngology: Ear, Vol. 2. LC 70-145563. (Illus.). 499p. 1973. text ed. 34.00 o.p. (ISBN 0-7216-7059-8). Saunders.

--Otolaryngology: Head & Neck, Vol. 3. LC 70-145563. (Illus.). 906p. 1973. text ed. 50.00 o.p. (ISBN 0-7216-7060-1). Saunders.

Paparella, Michael M., et al. Clinical Problems in Otitis Media & Innovations in Surgical Otology, Vol. II. (Illus.). 218p. 1982. lib. bdg. 35.00 (ISBN 0-683-06749-4). Williams & Wilkins.

--Sensorineural Hearing Loss, Vertigo & Tinnitus, Vol. I. (Ear Clinics International Ser.). 196p. 1981. 26.00 (ISBN 0-683-06750-8, 6750-8). Williams & Wilkins.

Paparian, Michael, ed. California Energy Directory: A Guide to Organizations & Information Resources. LC 78-78313. (California Information Guides Ser.). (Illus.). 88p. (Orig.). 1980. pap. 16.50x (ISBN 0-912102-51-9). Cal Inst Public.

Papas, T. S., jt. ed. see Chirikjian, J. C.

Papashvily, George, jt. auth. see Papashvily, Helen.

Papashvily, Helen & Papashvily, George. Russian Cooking. LC 78-103302. (Foods of the World Ser). (Illus.). (gr. 6 up). 1969. PLB 17.28 (ISBN 0-8094-0070-7, Pub. by Time-Life). Silver.

Pape, et al. Oddo Sound Series: 1968, 1974, 1978, 10 vols. (Illus.). (gr. 2-5). 1978. Set. PLB 67.50x (ISBN 0-87783-165-3). Oddo.

Pape, D. L. King Robert, the Resting Ruler. LC 68-56823. (Oddo Sound Ser.). (Illus.). (gr. 2-5). PLB 6.75x (ISBN 0-87783-021-5). Oddo.

--Liz Dearly's Silly Glasses. LC 68-56824. (Oddo Sound Ser.). (Illus.). (gr. 2-5). PLB 6.75x (ISBN 0-87783-023-1). Oddo.

--Professor Fred & the Fid Fuddlephone. LC 68-56825. (Oddo Sound Ser.). (Illus.). (gr. 2-5). PLB 6.75x (ISBN 0-87783-032-0). Oddo.

--Scientist Sam. LC 68-56826. (Oddo Sound Ser.). (Illus.). (gr. 2-5). 1969. PLB 6.75x (ISBN 0-87783-034-7). Oddo.

--Shoemaker Fooze. LC 68-56827. (Oddo Sound Ser.). (Illus.). (gr. 2-5). 1969. PLB 6.75x (ISBN 0-87783-036-3). Oddo.

--Three Thinkers of Thay-Lee. LC 68-56828. (Oddo Sound Ser.). (Illus.). (gr. 2-5). 1969. PLB 6.75x (ISBN 0-87783-040-1). Oddo.

Pape, Donna. Count on Leo Lion. LC 72-9093. (Venture Ser). (Illus.). 40p. (gr. 1). 1973. PLB 6.69 (ISBN 0-8116-6724-3). Garrard.

--Mrs. Twitter the Animal Sitter. LC 72-1470. (Venture Ser). (Illus.). 64p. (gr. 2). 1972. PLB 7.12 (ISBN 0-8116-6960-2). Garrard.

--The Sleep-Leaping Kangaroo. LC 72-7810. (Venture Ser). (Illus.). 40p. (gr. 1). 1973. PLB 6.69 (ISBN 0-8116-6723-5). Garrard.

Pape, Donna, et al. Bible Activities For Kids. (Orig.). (gr. 2-7). 1982. Saddle Bdg. 1.95 ea.; Bk. 5, 60pp. (ISBN 0-87123-275-8, 210275); Bk. 6, 62pp. (ISBN 0-87123-276-6, 210276). Bethany Hse.

Pape, Donna L. The Big White Thing. LC 75-6747. (Easy Venture Ser.). (Illus.). 32p. (gr. k-2). 1975. PLB 6.69 (ISBN 0-8116-6066-4). Garrard.

--A Bone for Breakfast. LC 73-22079. (Easy Venture Ser). (Illus.). 32p. (gr. k-2). 1974. PLB 6.69 (ISBN 0-8116-6059-1). Garrard.

--Doghouse for Sale. LC 78-11685. (Imagination Books). (Illus.). (gr. k-6). 1979. PLB 6.69 (ISBN 0-8116-4415-4). Garrard.

--Leo Lion Looks for Books. LC 72-1078. (Venture Ser). (Illus.). 64p. (gr. 2). 1972. PLB 6.89 (ISBN 0-8116-6956-4). Garrard.

--Mr. Mogg in the Log. LC 72-1472. (Venture Ser). (Illus.). 64p. (gr. 2). 1972. PLB 6.89 (ISBN 0-8116-6961-0). Garrard.

--The Mouse at the Show. LC 80-26690. (Illus.). 32p. (ps-3). 1982. 5.95 (ISBN 0-525-66722-9). Dandelion Pr.

--The Snoino Mystery. LC 79-17908. (Mystery Ser.). (Illus.). 40p. (gr. 2). 1980. PLB 6.79 (ISBN 0-8116-6410-4). Garrard.

--Snowman for Sale. LC 76-23308. (For Real). (Illus.). (gr. k-4). 1977. lib. bdg. 6.69 (ISBN 0-8116-4304-2). Garrard.

--Taffy Finds a Halloween Witch. LC 75-11590. (Easy Venture Ser.). (Illus.). 32p. (gr. k-2). 1975. PLB 6.69 (ISBN 0-8116-6067-2). Garrard.

--A Very Special Birthday. (Illus.). 32p. (gr. 1-3). 1975. pap. 1.95 o.p. (ISBN 0-8024-9156-1). Moody.

--Where Is My Little Joey? LC 78-1022. (Imagination Ser.). (Illus.). (gr. 1-4). 1978. PLB 6.69 (ISBN 0-8116-4411-1). Garrard.

Pape, Donna L. & Kessler, Leonard. Play Ball, Joey Kangaroo! LC 79-19343. (Imagination Ser.). (Illus.). 48p. (gr. k-4). 1980. PLB 6.69 (ISBN 0-8116-4420-0). Garrard.

Pape, Gordon & Aspler, Tony. The Scorpion Sanction. LC 79-56262. 372p. 1980. 13.95 o.p. (ISBN 0-670-19965-6). Viking Pr.

Pape, Jane. Pimplified Psychiatry. 1973. pap. 9.00 o.p. (ISBN 0-913590-24-X). Slack Inc.

Papell, Catherine P. & Rothman, Beulah, eds. Co-Leadership in Social Work with Groups. LC 80-28698. (Social Work with Groups Ser.: Vol. 3, No. 4). 82p. (Orig.). 1981. pap. text ed. 15.00 (ISBN 0-917724-90-9, B90). Haworth Pr.

Papenfuse, Edward C. & Stiverson, Georgy A. Maryland, A New Guide to the Old Line State. (Illus.). 463p. pap. 5.95 (ISBN 0-686-36832-0). Md Hist.

Papenfuse, Edward C., et al. A Biographical Dictionary of the Maryland Legislature, 1635-1789, Vol. 1, A-H. 477p. 1979. 19.50 (ISBN 0-686-36831-2). Md Hist.

Papenfuss, Richard L., jt. auth. see Curtis, John D.

Paper, Jordan D. Guide to Chinese Prose, 1 vol. 1973. lib. bdg. 15.00 o.p. (ISBN 0-8161-1103-0, Hall Reference). G K Hall.

Paperno, Dmitry. Zapiski Moskovskogo Pianista. (Illus.). 190p. (Rus.). 1983. pap. 8.00 (ISBN 0-938920-26-X). Hermitage MI.

Papers of presentation at the Microcomputers in Education Seminar. Micro Computers in Education Ii. 59p. 1981. pap. 28.60x (ISBN 0-686-97776-9). Renouf.

Papert, Jean. Photomacrography: Art & Techniques. 1971. 8.95 o.p. (ISBN 0-8174-0536-4, Amphoto). Watson-Guptill.

Papert, Seymour. Mindstorms: Children, Computers, & Powerful Ideas. 1982. pap. 6.95 (ISBN 0-465-04629-0). Basic.

Papert, Seymour, jt. auth. see McNaughton, Robert.

Papi, G. U. & Nunn, C. S., eds. Economic Problems of Agriculture in Developed Societies. LC 69-11372. (International Economic Assn. Ser). 1969. 35.00 (ISBN 0-312-23485-6). St Martin.

Papillon, Alfred L. Foundations of Educational Research. 2nd ed. LC 78-69861. 1978. pap. text ed. 13.50 (ISBN 0-8191-0583-X). U Pr of Amer.

Papineau, David. For Science in the Social Sciences. LC 78-14193. 1979. 26.00 (ISBN 0-312-29812-9). St Martin.

--Theory & Meaning. 1979. text ed. 27.50x (ISBN 0-19-824585-8). Oxford U Pr.

Papini, Giovanni. The Failure. Pope, Virginia, tr. from It. LC 76-137070. 326p. 1972. Repr. of 1924 ed. lib. bdg. 17.00x (ISBN 0-8371-5533-9, PAFA). Greenwood.

Papinot, E. Historical & Geographical Dictionary of Japan. LC 71-152116. (Illus.). 1972. pap. 10.50 (ISBN 0-8048-0996-8). C E Tuttle.

Papoulis, Athanasios. Fourier Integral & Its Applications. (Electronic Science Ser.). 1962. text ed. 36.95 (ISBN 0-07-048447-3, C). McGraw.

--Probability, Random Variables & Stochastic Processes. (Sanitary & Water Resources Engineering Ser.). 1965. text ed. 35.50 (ISBN 0-07-048448-1, C); solutions manual o.p. 6.50 (ISBN 0-07-048445-7). McGraw.

--Signal Analysis. 1977. text ed. 38.50 (ISBN 0-07-048460-0, C). McGraw.

--Systems & Transforms with Applications in Optics. LC 68-25659. (Sanitary & Water Resources Engineering Ser.). (Illus.). 1968. text ed. 29.50 o.p. (ISBN 0-07-048457-0, C). McGraw.

Papousek, D. Peasant-Potters of Los Pueblos. (Studies in Developing Countries: No. 27). 182p. 1981. 15.75 (ISBN 0-686-82313-3, 41327, Pub. by Van Gorcum Holland). Humanities.

Papousek, D. & Aliev, M. R. Molecular Vibrational-Rotational Spectra. (Studies in Physical & Theoretical Chemistry: Vol. 17). 1982. 83.00 (ISBN 0-444-99737-7). Elsevier.

Papp, Charles S., jt. auth. see Swan, Lester A.

Papp, J. Gy., jt. ed. see Szekeres, L.

Pappas. Managerial Economics. 4th ed. 1983. 26.95 (ISBN 0-03-062663-3). Dryden Pr.

Pappas, Charles N. The Life & Times of G. V. Black. (Illus.). 128p. (Orig.). 1983. pap. text ed. 24.00 (ISBN 0-931386-55-1). Quint Pub Co.

Pappas, Duane R. The Romance of Money. (The Library of Business Psychology). (Illus.). 119p. 1983. 57.15 (ISBN 0-86722-024-4). Inst Econ Pol.

Pappas, James L. & Brigham, Eugene. Managerial Economics: Study Guide. 193p. 1981. pap. text ed. 9.95 (ISBN 0-03-062443-6). Dryden Pr.

Pappas, Joan & Kendall, A. Harold. Hampshire Pottery Manufactured by J. S. Tuft & Company, Keene, New Hampshire. (Illus.). 48p. 1972. spiral bdg. 4.95 o.p. (ISBN 0-517-51087-1). Crown.

Pappas, Lou. Extra-Special Crockery Pot Recipes. rev. ed. LC 75-9644. (Illus.). 192p. 1982. pap. 5.95 (ISBN 0-911954-69-4). Nitty Gritty.

Pappas, Lou S. Bread Baking. LC 75-8615. (Illus.). 192p. (Orig.). 1975. pap. 5.95 (ISBN 0-911954-12-0). Nitty Gritty.

--Casseroles & Salads - Salads & Casseroles. Walsh, Jackie, ed. LC 77-82342. (Illus., Orig.). 1977. pap. 4.95 o.p. (ISBN 0-911954-42-2). Nitty Gritty.

--Cookies. Reynolds, Maureen, ed. LC 80-81247. (Illus.). 192p. 1980. pap. 5.95 (ISBN 0-911954-57-0). Nitty Gritty.

--Crockery Pot Cookbook. LC 75-9644. (Illus.). 192p. (Orig.). 1975. pap. 4.95 o.p. (ISBN 0-911954-11-2). Nitty Gritty.

--Egg Cookery. LC 76-13015. (Illus.). 168p. (Orig.). 1976. pap. 5.95 (ISBN 0-912238-80-1). One Hund One Prods.

--Entertaining in the Light Style. LC 82-14193. (Illus.). 144p. (Orig.). 1982. pap. 6.95 (ISBN 0-89286-207-6). One Hund One Prods.

--Greek Cooking. LC 73-4115. (Illus.). 218p. 1973. 13.41i (ISBN 0-06-013273-6, HarpT). Har-Row.

--Vegetable Cookery. (Illus.). 192p. 1982. pap. 7.95 (ISBN 0-89586-193-3). H P Bks.

Pappas, Theoni. What Do You See? An Optical Illusion Study. (Illus.). 36p. 1982. pap. 14.95 (ISBN 0-933174-18-7). Wide World-Tetra.

Pappi, F. U., jt. auth. see Laumann, E. O.

Pappi, Franz Urban, jt. auth. see Klingemann, Hans D.

Pappworth. A Primer of Medicine. 4th ed. LC 77-30428. (Primer Ser.). 1978. 34.95 (ISBN 0-407-62603-4). Butterworth.

Pappworth, M. H. Passing Medical Exams. 1975. 12.95 (ISBN 0-407-00013-5). Butterworth.

Papus. The Tarot of the Bohemians. LC 70-147105. (Illus.). 335p. 1973. 8.50 (ISBN 0-913866-07-5). US Games Syst.

Paquet, Judith B., ed. see Baloff, Marsha.

Paquet, K. J., et al. Portale Hypertension. Denck, H. & Berchtold, R., eds. x, 282p. 1982. pap. 39.00 (ISBN 3-8055-3480-9). S Karger.

Paquet, Sandra P. The Novels of George Lamming. (Studies in Caribbean Literature). 144p. (Orig.). 1983. pap. text ed. 10.00x (ISBN 0-435-91831-1). Heinemann Ed.

Paquette, Gerald N. Fish Quality Improvement: A Manual for Plant Operators. Practical Everyday Procedures to Benefit Performance & Quality. LC 82-24677. (Orig.). 1983. pap. text ed. 17.50x (ISBN 0-943738-05-9). Osprey Bks.

Paquette, Mary G. Basques to Bakersfield. (Illus.). 138p. 1982. 15.00 (ISBN 0-943500-00-1). Kern Historical.

Paquette, Radnor J., et al. Transportation Engineering: Planning & Design. 760p. 32.95x o.p. (ISBN 0-471-06670-2); tchrs.' manual 5.00 (ISBN 0-471-08440-9). Wiley.

Paquin, Claude. Paquin's Master Guide to a Successful Will Practice. LC 79-15962. 1979. 59.50 (ISBN 0-87624-423-1). Inst Busn Plan.

Paquot, C., ed. Standard Methods for the Analysis of Oils, Fats & Derivatives. 6th ed. LC 78-40305. 1979. text ed. 27.00 (ISBN 0-08-022379-6). Pergamon.

Parad, Howard J., ed. Crisis Intervention: Selected Readings. LC 65-20273. 1965. 12.00 (ISBN 0-87304-010-4). Family Serv.

Parad, Howard J. & Miller, Roger R., eds. Ego-Oriented Casework: Problems & Perspectives. LC 63-14026. 1963. 9.00 o.p. (ISBN 0-87304-011-2). Family Serv.

Parad, Howard J., et al, eds. Emergency & Disaster Management: A Mental Health Sourcebook. LC 76-14816. (Illus.). 1976. text ed. 17.95 o.p. (ISBN 0-913486-77-9). Charles.

Parade Magazine Editors, ed. Parade Cookbook. 1978. 9.95 o.p. (ISBN 0-671-22579-0). S&S.

Paradis, Adrian A. Henry Ford. (See & Read Biographies). (Illus.). (gr. 2-4). 1968. PLB 4.49 o.p. (ISBN 0-399-60235-6). Putnam Pub Group.

--The Labor Almanac. 230p. 1983. lib. bdg. 22.50 (ISBN 0-87287-374-9). Libs Unl.

Paradis, James & Postlewait, Thomas, eds. Victorian Science & Victorian Values: Literary Perspectives. 362p. 1981. 72.00x o.s.i. (ISBN 0-89766-109-5). NY Acad Sci.

Paradis, Michel, ed. see Linguistic Association of Canada & the U.S.

Paradise, ed. see Ginsburg, Lev.

Paradise, Nathaniel B., jt. auth. see Brooke, Charles F.

Paradise, Paul. Gerbils. (Illus.). 96p. 1980. 4.95 (ISBN 0-87666-927-5, KW-037). TFH Pubns.

Paradise, Paul, jt. auth. see Evans, Irene.

Paradise, Paul R. African Grey Parrots. (Illus.). 1979. 4.95 (ISBN 0-87666-977-1, KW-018). TFH Pubns.

--All About Raccoons. (Illus.). 128p. (Orig.). 1976. pap. 9.95 (ISBN 0-87666-900-3, PS739). TFH Pubns.

--Amazon Parrots. (Illus.). 1979. 4.95 (ISBN 0-87666-985-2, KW-012). TFH Pubns.

--Canaries. (Illus.). 1979. 4.95 (ISBN 0-87666-983-6, KW-004). TFH Pubns.

--Rabbits. (Illus.). 1979. 4.95 (ISBN 0-87666-924-0, KW-021). TFH Pubns.

Paradise, Paul R., ed. Goldfish. (Illus.). 1979. 4.95 (ISBN 0-87666-511-3, KW-014). TFH Pubns.

Paradiso, E. Jerry. Instant Bridge. 64p. 1978. 2.95 (ISBN 0-9602114-1-1). Paradiso E J.

Paramananda, Swami. Vedanta in Practice. 3rd ed. 1917. pap. 3.00 (ISBN 0-911564-04-7). Vedanta Ctr.

Paramount. The Mork & Mindy Act Book. (Illus.). (gr. 2-6). 1979. pap. 1.25 o.s.i. (ISBN 0-448-16143-5, G&D). Putnam Pub Group.

Paramount Pictures Corporation. The Mork & Mindy Super Activity Book. 128p. (gr. 2-6). 1980. pap. cancelled o.s.i. (ISBN 0-448-15497-8, G&D). Putnam Pub Group.

Paransky, Leah. The Gentle Echo. 64p. (Orig.). 1983. pap. text ed. 3.95 (ISBN 0-931642-14-0). Lintel.

Paraquin, Charles H. Eye Teasers: Optical Illusion Puzzles. Kuttner, Paul, tr. LC 76-21844. (Illus.). (gr. 3 up). 1976. 7.95 (ISBN 0-8069-4538-9); PLB 9.99 (ISBN 0-8069-4539-7). Sterling.

Parasnis, D. S. Mining Geophysics. 2nd ed. (Methods in Geochemistry & Geophysics Ser.: Vol. 3). 395p. 1973. 19.95 (ISBN 0-444-41077-5); pap. 14.25 (ISBN 0-444-41324-3). Elsevier.

--Principles of Applied Geophysics. 3rd ed. 1979. 27.00x (ISBN 0-412-15140-5, Pub. by Chapman & Hall); pap. 15.95x (ISBN 0-412-15810-8). Methuen Inc.

Parboni, Richard. The Dollar & Its Rivals: Recession, Inflation, & International Finance. 207p. 1982. 19.50 (ISBN 0-8052-7113-9, Pub. by NLB England); pap. 7.95 (ISBN 0-8052-7114-7). Schocken.

Parcel, Guy S. Basic Emergency Care of the Sick & Injured. 2nd ed. LC 81-14210. (Illus.). 293p. 1982. pap. text ed. 12.95 (ISBN 0-8016-3754-6). Mosby.

--First Aid in Emergency Care. LC 77-322. (Illus.). 312p. 1977. 14.95 o.p. (ISBN 0-8016-3400-8); pap. 11.95 o.p. (ISBN 0-8016-3757-0). Mosby.

Parcel, Guy S., et al. Teaching Myself About Asthma. 1st ed. LC 79-13166. (Illus.). 160p. 1979. pap. 10.00 o.p. (ISBN 0-8016-3755-4). Mosby.

Parcel, John I. & Moorman, R. B. Analysis of Statically Indeterminate Structures. 1955. 49.50 (ISBN 0-471-65868-5, Pub. by Wiley-Interscience). Wiley.

Parcel, Toby L. & Mueller, Charles W., eds. Ascription & Labor Markets: Race & Sex Difference in Earnings. LC 82-22741. (Quantitative Studies Social Relations (Monograph)). Date not set. price not set (ISBN 0-12-545020-6). Acad Pr.

Parcher. Soil Mechanics & Foundations. 1968. text ed. 29.95 (ISBN 0-675-09746-0). Merrill.

Pardeck, John T. The Forgotten Children: A Study of the Stability & Continuity of Foster Care. LC 82-20007. (Illus.). 116p. (Orig.). 1983. lib. bdg. 18.50 (ISBN 0-8191-2844-9); pap. text ed. 8.25 (ISBN 0-8191-2845-7). U Pr of Amer.

Pardeck, John T., compiled by. Child Welfare Training & Practice: Annotated Bibliography. Hegar, Rebecca L., et al. LC 82-11686. 143p. 1982. 27.50 (ISBN 0-313-23383-7, PCH/). Greenwood.

Pardee, Alice D. Blithewold, Bristol, Rhode Island. LC 78-60477. (Illus.). 1978. write for info o.p. (ISBN 0-917218-10-8). Mowbray Co.

Pardee, Arthur B. & Veer Reddy, G. P. Cancer: Fundamental Ideas. Head, J. J., ed. LC 81-67986. (Biology Readers Ser.). (Illus.). 32p. 1982. pap. 2.00 (ISBN 0-89278-328-1, 45-9728). Carolina Biological.

Pardes, Herbert, jt. auth. see Simons, Richard C.

Pardey, Larry, jt. auth. see Pardey, Lin.

Pardey, Lin & Pardey, Larry. Cruising in Seraffyn. (Illus.). 192p. 1976. 12.50 (ISBN 0-915160-19-6). Seven Seas.

--Seraffyn's Oriental Adventure. (Illus.). 1983. 19.95 (ISBN 0-393-03281-7). Norton.

Pardington, G. P. Studies in Christian Doctrine, 4 Vols. Freligh, H. M. & Schrorder, E. H., eds. 312p. 1964. pap. 1.95 ea. Vol. 1. Vol. 2. Vol. 3. Vol. 4. Chr Pubns.

Pardington, George P. Outline Studies in Christian Doctrine. pap. 5.95 (ISBN 0-87509-116-4). Chr Pubns.

Pardoen, Alan, ed. see Boyle, Patrick G.

Pardoen, Alan, ed. see Seaman, Donald.

Pardon, P. H., jt. auth. see Work, T. S.

Pare, E. G., et al. Descriptive Geometry-Metric. 6th ed. 1982. text ed. 24.95x (ISBN 0-02-390930-7). Macmillan.

Pare, J. A., jt. auth. see Fraser, Robert G.

Pare, Madeline F. Arizona. LC 82-751. 1969. pap. 2.95 o.p. (ISBN 0-8077-1868-8). Tchrs Coll.

Paredes, Americo & Bauman, Richard, eds. Toward New Perspectives in Folklore. LC 74-165922. (American Folklore Society Bibliographical & Special Ser.: No. 23). 197p. 1972. 13.50x o.p. (ISBN 0-292-70142-X). U of Tex Pr.

Paredi, Angelo. A History of the Ambrosiana. McInerny, Constance & McInerny, Ralph, trs. 112p. (Orig.). 1983. pap. text ed. 9.95x (ISBN 0-268-01078-1). U of Notre Dame Pr.

Parekh, B. C., jt. ed. see King, P.

Parekh, Bhikhu, ed. The Concept of Socialism. LC 74-28393. 240p. 1975. text ed. 32.50x (ISBN 0-8419-0190-2). Holmes & Meier.

Parelius, Ann P. & Parelius, Robert J. The Sociology of Education. LC 77-10948. (P-H Series in Sociology). (Illus.). 1978. 22.95 (ISBN 0-13-821173-6). P-H.

Parelius, Robert J., jt. auth. see Parelius, Ann P.

Parella, Michael M., ed. Year Book of Otolaryngology 1983. 1983. 40.00 (ISBN 0-8151-6640-0). Year Bk Med.

Parelman, Allison. Emotional Intimacy in Marriage: A Sex-Roles Perspective. Nathan, Peter E., ed. LC 82-20218. (Research in Clinical Psychology Ser.: No. 4). 150p. 1983. 34.95 (ISBN 0-8357-1387-3, Pub. by UMI Res Pr). Univ Microfilms.

Parent, David J., ed. see DiFranco, Ralph.

Parent, Gail. The Best Laid Plans. 300p. 1980. 10.95 (ISBN 0-399-12510-8). Putnam Pub Group.

Parent-Duchatelet, A. J. B. De la Prostitution dans la Ville de Paris, 2 vols. (Conditions of the 19th Century French Working Class Ser). 1711p. (Fr.). 1974. Repr. of 1857 ed. lib. bdg. 432.00x o.p. (ISBN 0-8287-0671-9, 1088-9). Clearwater Pub.

--Hygiene Publique, 2 Vols. (Conditions of the 19th Century French Working Class Ser.). 1510p. (Fr.). 1974. Repr. of 1836 ed. lib. bdg. 330.00x o.p. (ISBN 0-8287-0047-8, 1131-2). Clearwater Pub.

Parenteau, Shirley. Crunch It, Munch It, & Other Ways to Eat Vegetables. LC 78-8582. (Illus.). (gr. k-3). 1978. 6.95 o.p. (ISBN 0-698-20466-2, Coward). Putnam Pub Group.

--Hot Springs. (Love & Life Romance Ser.). 176p. 1983. pap. 1.75 (ISBN 0-345-30963-4). Ballantine.

--Jelly & the Spaceboat. (Illus.). (gr. 4-7). 1981. 6.95 (ISBN 0-698-20514-6, Coward). Putnam Pub Group.

Parenti, Umberto. The World of Butterflies & Moths. LC 77-14627. (Illus.). 1978. 14.95 o.p. (ISBN 0-399-12071-8). Putnam Pub Group.

Pares, Richard. The Historian's Business & Other Stories. LC 74-9228. (Illus.). 240p. 1974. Repr. of 1961 ed. lib. bdg. 15.50x (ISBN 0-8371-7622-0, PAHB). Greenwood.

Paret, Peter, tr. see Meinecke, Friedrich.

Paret, Peter, tr. & intro. by see Ritter, Gerhard.

Paretsky, Sara. Indemnity Only. 224p. 1983. pap. 2.50 (ISBN 0-345-30684-8). Ballantine.

Paretti, Sandra. The Drums of Winter. 1975. pap. 1.95 o.p. (ISBN 0-451-06454-2, J6454, Sig). NAL.

--The Magic Ship. Hein, Ruth, tr. LC 78-19400. 1979. 10.95 o.p. (ISBN 0-312-50419-5). St Martin.

Parfit, Michael. The Boys Behind the Bombs. 324p. 1983. 15.45i (ISBN 0-316-69057-0). Little.

Parfitt & Patsis. Organic Coating-Science & Technology. 384p. 1983. write for info. Dekker.

Parfitt, G., ed. The Plays of Cyril Tourneur. LC 77-77014. (Plays by Renaissance & Restoration Dramatists Ser.). 1978. 32.50 (ISBN 0-521-21697-4); pap. 9.95x (ISBN 0-521-29235-2). Cambridge U Pr.

Parfitt, G. D., ed. Dispersion of Powders in Liquids: With Special Reference to Pigments. 3rd ed. (Illus.). 533p. 1981. 82.00 (ISBN 0-85334-990-8, Pub. by Applied Sci England). Elsevier.

Pargeter, Edith, tr. see Neruda, Jan.

Pargeter, F. W., jt. auth. see Mander, M. R.

Pargeter, Margaret. Clouded Rapture. (Harlequin Presents Ser.). 192p. 1983. pap. 1.95 (ISBN 0-373-10588-6). Harlequin Bks.

--Man from the Kimberleys. (Harlequin Presents Ser.). 192p. 1983. pap. 1.95 (ISBN 0-373-10595-9). Harlequin Bks.

--Prelude to a Song. (Harlequin Presents Ser.). 192p. 1983. pap. 1.75 (ISBN 0-373-10572-X). Harlequin Bks.

--Substitute Bride. (Harlequin Presents Ser.). 192p. 1983. pap. 1.95 (ISBN 0-373-10580-0). Harlequin Bks.

Pargiter, F. E. The Purana Text of the Dynasties of the Kali Age. 1976. Repr. 11.00x o.p. (ISBN 0-88386-898-9). South Asia Bks.

Parham, Joe. What Is in My Heart. LC 81-83888. 162p. 1981. 9.95 (ISBN 0-931948-31-2). Peachtree Pubs.

Parham, Russell A. & Gray, Richard L. The Practical Identification of Wood Pulp Fibers. 212p. 1982. 34.95 (ISBN 0-89852-400-8, 01 01R0100). TAPPI.

Parham, Sidney F., Jr. Title Examination in Virginia. 1965. pap. 12.50 (ISBN 0-87215-107-7). Michie-Bobbs.

Parham, William E. Syntheses & Reactions in Organic Chemistry. LC 74-1410. 558p. 1974. pap. text ed. 19.50 (ISBN 0-88275-171-9). Krieger.

Parham, William L. A Habitation of Devils. Pierce, L. R., ed. LC 81-51729. 275p. 1981. 13.95 o.s.i. (ISBN 0-938264-02-8); pap. 7.95 o.s.i. (ISBN 0-938264-03-6). Veritas Pubns.

Parikh, Bharat, ed. see Shah, Kirit N.

Parinaud, Andre, as told to see Dali, Salvador.

Parini, Jay. Anthracite Country. LC 81-10588. 68p. 1982. 10.50 (ISBN 0-394-52263-X); pap. 5.95 (ISBN 0-394-70454-1). Random.

Paris, Alain. Teeth of the Wolf. Sokolinsky, Martin, tr. 252p. Date not set. 0.15.95 (ISBN 0-03-059899-0). HR&W.

Paris, Alexander. The Coming Credit Collapse. 1980. 12.95 o.p. (ISBN 0-87000-474-3, Arlington Hse). Crown.

Paris, C., ed. Critical Readings in Planning Theory. (Urban & Regional Planning Ser.: Vol. 27). (Illus.). 260p. 1982. 27.00 (ISBN 0-08-024681-8); 15.00 (ISBN 0-08-024680-X). Pergamon.

Paris, D. T. & Hurd, F. K. Basic Electromagnetic Theory. LC 68-8775. (Physical & Quantum Electronic Ser). (Illus.). 1969. text ed. 35.50 (ISBN 0-07-048470-8, C). McGraw.

Paris-Dauphine Conference on Money & International Monetary Problems, 5th, 1981. Recent Issues in the Theory of Flexible Exchange Rates: Proceedings. Claassen, E. M. & Salin, P., eds. (Studies in Monetary Economics: Vol. 8). 274p. 1982. 42.75 (ISBN 0-444-86389-3, North Holland). Elsevier.

Paris, David C. & Reynolds, James F. The Logic of Policy Inquiry. Rockwood, Irving, ed. 256p. 1983. text ed. 20.00x (ISBN 0-582-28356-6); pap. text ed. 12.95x (ISBN 0-582-28357-4). Longman.

Paris, Don Q. Craniographic Positioning with Comparison Studies. (Illus.). 176p. 1982. 35.00 (ISBN 0-8036-6768-X). Davis Co.

Paris, I. Mark, tr. see Weelan, Guy.

Paris, James R. The Great French Films. (Illus.). 288p. 1983. 18.95 (ISBN 0-8065-0806-X). Citadel Pr.

Paris, Pierre. Manual of Ancient Sculpture. Harrison, Jane E., tr. from Fr. (Illus.). 1983. lib. bdg. 47.50x (ISBN 0-89241-373-5). Caratzas Bros.

Paris, Ruth & Baldwin, Robert. The Book of Similes. (Illus.). 132p. 1982. 13.50 (ISBN 0-7100-9285-7). Routledge & Kegan.

Paris, Scott G., et al, eds. Learning & Motivation in the Classroom. 352p. 1983. text ed. price not set (ISBN 0-89859-273-9). L Erlbaum Assocs.

Paris, Win. Super Fitness. (Illus., Orig.). 1978. pap. 3.95 o.s.i. (ISBN 0-8431-0451-1). Price Stern.

Pariser, E. R., et al. Fish Protein Concentrate: Panacea for Protein Malnutrition? LC 77-28112. (International Nutrition Policy Ser.: NO. 3). 1978. text ed. 25.00x (ISBN 0-262-16069-2). MIT Pr.

Parish. Cutaneous Infestations in Man. 304p. 1983. 36.50 (ISBN 0-03-059662-9). Praeger.

Parish & Goddard. London's Pride. 7.50x (ISBN 0-392-08605-0, SpS). Sportshelf.

Parish, et al, trs. see Mickiewicz, Adam.

Parish, D. H. Possibilities of the Improvement for Nitrogen Fertilizer Efficiency in Rice Production. (IFD Paper Sers. P-1). 1980. 4.00 (ISBN 0-686-95954-X). Intl Fertilizer.

--Research on Modified Fertilizer Materials for Use in Developing-Country Agriculture. (IFDC Paper Sers. P-2). 1980. 4.00 (ISBN 0-686-95955-8). Intl Fertilizer.

Parish, David W. State Government Reference Publications: An Annotated Bibliography. 2nd ed. LC 81-788. 360p. 1981. lib. bdg. 25.00 (ISBN 0-87287-253-X). Libs Unl.

Parish, Desmond & Parish, Marjorie. Wild Flowers: A Photographic Guide. (Illus.). 1979. 12.95 o.p. (ISBN 0-7137-0947-2, Pub by Blandford Pr England). Sterling.

Parish, Howard I., jt. auth. see Weisberg, Joseph S.

Parish, James R. Hollywood Character Actors. (Illus.). 1978. 30.00 o.p. (ISBN 0-87000-384-4, Arlington Hse). Crown.

--The Tough Guys. LC 76-16867. (Illus.). 1976. 19.95 o.p. (ISBN 0-87000-338-0, Arlington Hse). Crown.

Parish, James R. & Stanke, Don E. The All-Americans. 1977. 20.00 o.p. (ISBN 0-87000-363-1, Arlington Hse). Crown.

--The Leading Ladies. (Illus.). 1977. 25.00 o.p. (ISBN 0-517-54814-3, Arlington Hse). Crown.

--The Swashbucklers. (Illus.). 1976. 19.95 o.p. (ISBN 0-87000-326-7, Arlington Hse). Crown.

Parish, James R. & Terrace, Vincent. Actors' Television Credits, Supplement II: 1977-1981. LC 82-5961. 337p. 1982. 22.50 (ISBN 0-8108-1559-1). Scarecrow.

Parish, James R., et al. The Hollywood Beauties. (Illus.). 1978. 25.00 o.p. (ISBN 0-87000-412-3, Arlington Hse). Crown.

Parish, Lawrence C. The Decubitus Ulcer: A Twentieth Century View. (Illus.). 96p. 1983. write for info softcover (ISBN 0-89352-174-4). Masson Pub.

Parish, Marjorie, jt. auth. see Parish, Desmond.

Parish, Peggy. Amelia Bedelia. LC 63-14367. (A Trophy Picture Bk.). (Illus.). 32p. (gr. k-3). 1983. pap. 2.84i (ISBN 0-06-443036-7, Trophy). Har-Row.

--The Cats' Burglar. LC 82-11751. (Read-Alone Bks.). (Illus.). 56p. (gr. 1-3). 1983. 7.00 (ISBN 0-688-01825-4); PLB 6.67 (ISBN 0-688-01826-2). Greenwillow.

--Clues in the Woods. (gr. k-6). 1980. pap. 1.95 (ISBN 0-440-41461-X, YB). Dell.

--Haunted House. (gr. k-6). 1981. pap. 1.95 (ISBN 0-440-43459-9, YB). Dell.

--I Can--Can You, 4 bks. LC 79-26041. (Illus.). (ps). 1980. Set. 4.95 (ISBN 0-688-80279-6); write for info. pre-pack set. Greenwillow.

--Key to the Treasure. (gr. k-6). 1980. pap. 1.95 (ISBN 0-440-44438-1, YB). Dell.

--Thank You, Amelia Bedelia. LC 64-11835. (A Trophy Picture Bk.). (Illus.). 32p. (gr. k-3). 1983. pap. 2.84 (ISBN 0-06-443037-5, Trophy). Har-Row.

--Zed & the Monsters. LC 77-15876. 1979. 6.95a o.p. (ISBN 0-385-12948-3); PLB 6.95a (ISBN 0-385-12949-1). Doubleday.

Parish, Peter. The American Civil War. LC 74-84660. 750p. 1975. text ed. 39.50x (ISBN 0-8419-0176-7); pap. text ed. 19.75 (ISBN 0-8419-0197-X). Holmes & Meier.

Parish, W., jt. auth. see Kingstather, W.

Parish, William L. & Whyte, Martin K. Village & Family in Contemporary China. LC 78-3411. (Illus.). 1978. lib. bdg. 28.00x (ISBN 0-226-64590-8); pap. 10.95 (ISBN 0-226-64591-6, P899, Phoen). U of Chicago Pr.

Parisious, Roger N., et al, eds. see Ussher, Arland.

Paritsis, N. C. & Stewart, D. J. A Color Approach to Color Perception. (Studies in Cybernetics: Vol. 2). 220p. Date not set. write for info. (ISBN 0-677-05620-6). Gordon.

Parizeau, Alice. Parenting & Delinquent Youth. LC 79-47982. 208p. 1980. 24.95x (ISBN 0-669-03620-X). Lexington Bks.

Parizeau, Alice & Szabo, Denis. The Canadian Criminal Justice System. LC 77-211. (Illus.). 240p. 1977. 22.95 (ISBN 0-669-01448-6). Lexington Bks.

Parizkova, J. Nutrition, Physical Fitness & Health. 296p. 1978. text ed. 34.50 (ISBN 0-8391-1263-7). Univ Park.

Parizkova, Jana. Body Fat & Physical Fitness. Osancova, K., tr. from Czech. (Illus.). 280p. 1977. 32.50 o.p. (ISBN 90-247-1925-9, Pub. by Nijhoff). Wright-PSG.

Park, Barbara. Don't Make me Smile. 1983. pap. 1.95 (ISBN 0-380-61994-6, Camelot). Avon.

Park, C., jt. ed. see Lanzerotti, L. J.

Park, C. C. Ecology & Environmental Management: A Geographical Perspective. LC 79-5208. (Westview Studies in Physical Geography). 224p. 1980. lib. bdg. 27.50 (ISBN 0-89158-698-9). Westview.

Park, Chong Kee. Social Security in Korea: An Approach to Socio-Economic Development. 1975. text ed. 10.00x (ISBN 0-8248-0537-2). UH Pr.

Park, Chong Kee, ed. Essays on the Korean Economy: Vol. III--Macroeconomic & Industrial Development in Korea. 402p. 1981. text ed. 15.00x (ISBN 0-8248-0754-5). UH Pr.

--Essays on the Korean Economy: Vol. IV--Human Resources & Social Development in Korea. 372p. 1981. text ed. 15.00x (ISBN 0-8248-0755-3). UH Pr.

Park, Choon-Ho & Pae, Jae S. Korean International Law. (Korean Research Monographs: No. 4). 80p. 1982. pap. 8.00x (ISBN 0-912966-40-8). IEAS.

Park, Chung I. Best Sellers & Best Choices, 1981. LC 81-640911. x, 112p. (Orig.). 1982. pap. 4.00x (ISBN 0-939670-01-1). Ad Digest.
--Best Sellers & Best Choices, 1982. LC 81-640911. (Orig.). pap. 4.75x (ISBN 0-939670-02-X). Ad Digest.
Park, David. Contemporary Physics. LC 64-23458. (Illus., Orig.). 1964. pap. 2.45 (ISBN 0-15-622566-2, Harv). HarBraceJ.
Park, David A. Introduction to the Quantum Theory. 2nd ed. (International Series in Pure & Applied Physics). text ed. 45.00 (ISBN 0-07-048481-3, C). McGraw.
Park, James. Absurdity, Insecurity & Despair. (Existential Freedom Ser.: No. 8). 1975. pap. 5.00x (ISBN 0-89231-008-1). Existential Bks.
--Authentic Love: An Existential Vision. 2nd ed. LC 76-5602. 232p. 1978. pap. 20.00x (ISBN 0-89231-510-5). Existential Bks.
--Becoming More Authentic: The Positive Side of Existentialism. 96p. 1983. pap. 8.00x ltd. edition (ISBN 0-89231-100-2). Existential Bks.
--Depression, Fragmentation, & the Void. (Existential Freedom Ser.: No. 9). 1976. pap. 5.00x (ISBN 0-89231-009-X). Existential Bks.
--Existential Anxiety: Angst. (Existential Freedom Ser.: No. 5). 1974. pap. 3.00x (ISBN 0-89231-005-7). Existential Bks.
--The Existential Christian, No. 2. (Existential Freedom Ser.: No.2). 1971. pap. 5.00x o.p. (ISBN 0-89231-002-2). Existential Bks.
--Existential Freedom, No. 3. 1973. pap. 5.00x (ISBN 0-89231-003-0). Existential Bks.
--An Existential Understanding of Death: A Phenomenology of Ontological Anxiety. (Existential Freedom Ser.: No. 6). 72p. 1975. pap. 6.00x (ISBN 0-89231-006-5). Existential Bks.
--Fundamental Fulfillment. (Existential Freedom Ser.: No. 7). 1975. pap. 5.00x o.p. (ISBN 0-89231-007-3). Existential Bks.
--Loneliness & Existential Freedom. (Existential Freedom Ser.: No. 4). 1974. pap. 5.00x (ISBN 0-89231-004-9). Existential Bks.
--Obstacles to Existential Freedom. (Existential Freedom Ser.: No. 10). 1976. pap. 5.00x o.p. (ISBN 0-89231-010-3). Existential Bks.
Park, Jane M. Meaning Well is Not Enough: Perspectives on Volunteering. 232p. 1983. 19.95 (ISBN 0-916068-17-X); pap. 12.95 (ISBN 0-916068-18-8). Groupwork Today.
Park, Joe. Selected Readings in the Philosophy of Education. 4th ed. (Illus.). 367p. 1974. pap. text ed. 12.95x (ISBN 0-02-391650-8). Macmillan.
Park, Julian, ed. Culture of France in Our Time. Repr. of 1954 ed. lib. bdg. 18.50x (ISBN 0-8371-3236-3, PACF). Greenwood.
Park, Kilho P. & Duedall, Iver W. Wastes in the Ocean: Radioactive Wastes in the Ocean, Vol. 3. (Environmental Science & Technology Texts & Monographs). 870p. 1983. 33.45 (ISBN 0-471-09770-5, Pub. by Wiley Interscience). Wiley.
Park Lane Press, Inc. Biology. (Regents Review Ser). pap. 1.95 o.p. (ISBN 0-671-18141-6). Monarch Pr.
--Business Mathematics. (Regents Review Ser.). (gr. 7-12). pap. 2.50 o.p. (ISBN 0-671-18145-9). Monarch Pr.
--Chemistry. (Regents Review Ser.). pap. 2.50 o.p. (ISBN 0-671-18150-5). Monarch Pr.
--Comprehensive Social Studies. (Regents Review Ser.). pap. 2.50 o.p. (ISBN 0-671-18142-4). Monarch Pr.
Park Lane Press. Inc. Eleventh Year Math. (Regents Review Ser.). pap. 2.50 o.p. (ISBN 0-671-18147-5). Monarch Pr.
Park Lane Press, Inc. English Comprehensive. (Regents Review Ser.). pap. 2.50 o.p. (ISBN 0-671-18143-2). Monarch Pr.
--Ninth Year Math. (Regents Review Ser.). pap. 2.50 o.p. (ISBN 0-671-18146-7). Monarch Pr.
--Tenth Year Math. (Regents Review Ser.). pap. 2.50 o.p. (ISBN 0-671-18144-0). Monarch Pr.
Park, Michael A., jt. auth. see Lucas, Jack A.
Park, Myung Soo. Public Policy: Emerging Dimensions in Public Administration. LC 79-89252. 1979. pap. text ed. 8.25 (ISBN 0-8191-0813-8). U Pr of Amer.
Park, P. K., jt. auth. see Champ, Michael A.
Park, R. & Gamble, W. L. Reinforced Concrete Slabs. LC 80-10229. 618p. 1981. 41.95 (ISBN 0-471-65915-0, Pub. by Wiley-Interscience). Wiley.
Park, R. E; see Bernard, William S.
Park, R. E., jt. auth. see Caroll, S. J.
Park, Reg. Big Chest for You. (Illus., Orig.). pap. 5.00x (ISBN 0-392-02271-0, SpS). Sportshelf.
Park, Richard L., jt. auth. see Bueno De Mesquita, Bruce.
Park, Richard L. & Lambert, Richard D., eds. The American Revolution Abroad. LC 76-19935. (Annals Ser: No. 428). 200p. 1976. 15.00 (ISBN 0-87761-206-4); pap. 7.95 (ISBN 0-87761-207-2). Am Acad Pol Soc Sci.
Park, Robert & Paulay, Thomas. Reinforced Concrete Structures. LC 74-28156. 769p. 1975. 44.95 (ISBN 0-471-65917-7, Pub. by Wiley-Interscience). Wiley.
Park, Robert E. Immigrant Press & Its Control. (Illus.). Repr. of 1922 ed. lib. bdg. 17.75x (ISBN 0-8371-2887-0, PAIP). Greenwood.
Park, Robert E., jt. auth. see Washington, Booker T.
Park, Roberta J., jt. ed. see Harris, Janet C.
Park, Roy. Sale Catalogues of Libraries of Eminent Persons: Poets & Men of Letters, Vol. 9. 564p. 1975. 27.00 o.p. (ISBN 0-686-10590-7, Pub. by Mansell England). Wilson.
Park, Ruth. When the Wind Changed. (Illus.). 32p. (Orig.). (ps-3). 1981. 8.95 (ISBN 0-698-20525-1, Coward); pap. 4.95 (ISBN 0-698-20526-X). Putnam Pub Group.
Park, S. S. Growth & Development: A Physical Output & Employment Strategy. LC 77-74817. 1977. 22.50 (ISBN 0-312-35128-3). St Martin.
Park, Taisoo. Biology of the Antarctic Seas Nine Paper 2: Calanoid Copepods of the Genus Scolecithricella from Antarctic & Subantarctic Waters. Kornicker, Louis S., ed. (Antarctic Research Ser.: Vol. 31). 79p. 1980. 22.85 (ISBN 0-87590-151-4). Am Geophysical.
Park, W. B. The Costume Party. (Illus.). 32p. (gr. 1-3). 1983. 7.70i (ISBN 0-316-69077-5). Little.
--Jonathan's Friends. LC 77-5041. (Illus.). (gr. k-4). 1977. 7.95 o.p. (ISBN 0-399-20604-3). Putnam Pub Group.
--The Pig in the Floppy Black Hat. new ed. (Illus.). 48p. (ps-3). 1974. PLB 5.29 o.p. (ISBN 0-399-60843-5). Putnam Pub Group.
Park, William R. Construction Bidding for Profit. LC 79-11451. (Practical Construction Guides Ser.). 1979. 31.95 (ISBN 0-471-04104-1, Pub. by Wiley-Interscience). Wiley.
--Cost Engineering Analysis: A Guide to the Economic Evaluation of Engineering Projects. LC 72-10237. (Illus.). 373p. 1973. 44.95 (ISBN 0-471-65914-2, Pub. by Wiley-Interscience). Wiley.
Park, William R. & Chapin-Park, Sue. How to Succeed in Your Own Business. LC 77-28955. 1978. 21.95x (ISBN 0-471-03189-5, Pub. by Wiley-Interscience). Wiley.
Park, Yoon S. Oil Money & the World Economy. LC 75-40467. (Special Studies in International Economics Ser.). 1976. 36.25 o.p. (ISBN 0-89158-018-2). Westview.
Park, Yung C., jt. auth. see Cole, David C.
Parke, Caroline M., ed. see Lodo, Venerable L.
Parke, Catherine N. & Backsheider, P. R., eds. The Plays of Edward Thompson. LC 81-66631. (Eighteenth Century English Drama Ser.). lib. bdg. 50.00 (ISBN 0-8240-3608-5). Garland Pub.
Parke, D. V. The Biochemistry of Foreign Compounds. 1968. 29.00 o.p. (ISBN 0-08-012202-7). Pergamon.
Parke, Margaret B. Getting to Know Australia. (Getting to Know Ser.). (Illus.). (gr. 3-5). 1962. PLB 3.97 o.p. (ISBN 0-698-30106-4, Coward). Putnam Pub Group.
Parke, R. D., jt. auth. see Hetherington, E. M.
Parke, R. D., ed. see Hetherington, E. M.
Parke, Ross, jt. auth. see Hetherington, Mavis.
Parke, William T. Musical Memoirs, Comprising an Account of the General State of Music in England. 2 Vols. in 1. LC 77-125058. (Music Ser). 1970. Repr. of 1830 ed. lib. bdg. 65.00 (ISBN 0-306-70023-9). Da Capo.
Parker. Computing is Easy. 1982. text ed. 9.95. Butterworth.
Parker & Leimburg. Federal Income Tax Law. 7th ed. 1982. 46.00 (ISBN 0-88262-767-8); student ed. 19.25 (ISBN 0-686-96917-0). Warren.
Parker, A. H., tr. see Steiner, Rudolf.
Parker, A. Morgan. Psalms from the Sea. 1982. pap. 1.95 (ISBN 0-8341-0745-7). Beacon Hill.
Parker, A. P. Mechanics of Fracture & Fatigue: An Introduction. 1981. 29.95x (ISBN 0-419-11460-2, Pub. by E & FN Spon); pap. 14.95x (ISBN 0-419-11470-X). Methuen Inc.
Parker, Alan. BASIC for Business: For the TRS-80 Model II & III. 1982. pap. text ed. 14.95 (ISBN 0-8359-0352-4); instr's manual free (ISBN 0-8359-0354-0). Reston.
Parker, Alan & Stewart, John. Apple BASIC Business: For the Apple II. 1981. text ed. 19.95 (ISBN 0-8359-0228-5); pap. text ed. 15.95 (ISBN 0-8359-0226-9); instrs'. manual avail. (ISBN 0-8359-0229-3). Reston.
Parker, Albert D. & Barrie, Donald S. Planning & Estimating Heavy Construction. 240p. 1983. 39.95 (ISBN 0-07-048489-9, P&RB). McGraw.
Parker & Son Staff. Parker Directory of Attorneys. LC 75-41995. 1982. 16.00 (ISBN 0-911110-18-6). Parker & Son.
Parker, Ann & Neal, Avon. The Itinerant Photographers of Guatemala. 1982. 35.00 (ISBN 0-262-16086-2). MIT Pr.
Parker, Ann, jt. auth. see Neal, Avon.
Parker, Anthony. International Exchange & Trade Regulations. 1981. 125.00x (ISBN 0-686-92036-8, Pub.by Jordan & Sons England); 1st supplement 25.00 (ISBN 0-686-98454-4). State Mutual Bk.
Parker, Arthur C. The Indian How Book. LC 74-18592. (Illus.). 335p. 1975. pap. 4.50 (ISBN 0-486-21767-1). Dover.
--The Indian How Book. (Illus.). 8.50 (ISBN 0-8446-5234-2). Peter Smith.
--Parker on the Iroquois. Fenton, William N., ed. Bd. with The Code of Handsome Lake, the Seneca Prophet. 119p; The Consitution of the Five Nations. 148p. 21.95x; Iroquois Uses of Maize & Other Food Plants. 158p. LC 68-31036. (Illus.). 1968. 19.95x (ISBN 0-8156-2124-8); pap. 12.95x (ISBN 0-686-86784-X). Syracuse U Pr.
Parker, B. V. Dynamics of Supervision. (Management Ser.). 1971. 11.20 (ISBN 0-07-048490-2, G); instructor's manual 4.50 (ISBN 0-07-048491-0). McGraw.
Parker, Betty J., jt. ed. see Parker, Franklin.
Parker, Bruce & Farrell, Nigel. TV & Radio: Everybody's Soapbox. (Illus.). 176p. 1983. 13.95 (ISBN 0-7137-1306-2, Pub. by Blandford Pr England); pap. 8.95 (ISBN 0-7137-1337-2, Pub. by Blandford Pr England). Sterling.
Parker, C. E. Gunfire at Timberline. 208p. 1982. pap. 2.25 o.s.i. (ISBN 0-8439-1078-X, Leisure Bks). Nordon Pubns.
Parker, Carolyn & Leven, Deborah. The Next Move: A Workbook in Career Planning. 2nd ed. 1979. pap. text ed. 8.95 (ISBN 0-8403-2054-X). Kendall-Hunt.
Parker, Charles W., ed. Clinical Immunology, 2 vols. LC 79-63406. (Illus.). 1438p. 1980. Set. text ed. 95.00 (ISBN 0-7216-7075-X); Vol. 1. 50.00 (ISBN 0-7216-7073-3); Vol. 2. o. p. 50.00 (ISBN 0-7216-7074-1). Saunders.
Parker, Chauncey G., 3rd. The Visitor. 1981. pap. 2.75 o.p. (ISBN 0-451-09562-6, E9562, Sig). NAL.
Parker, Cherry & Bradsher, Frances. The Hand-Me-Down Cookbook. LC 70-99140. 1969. 9.50 (ISBN 0-87716-012-0, Pub. by Moore Pub Co). F Apple.
Parker, D. B. V. Polymer Chemistry. (Illus.). 1974. 24.75 (ISBN 0-85334-571-6, Pub. by Applied Sci England). Elsevier.
Parker, D. W. Calendar of Papers in Washington Archives Relating to the Territories of the United States, to 1873. 1911. pap. 36.00 (ISBN 0-527-00684-X). Kraus Repr.
--Guide to the Materials for United States History in Canadian Archives. 1913. pap. 32.00 (ISBN 0-527-00689-0). Kraus Repr.
Parker, David L. & Siegel, Esther. Guide to Dance in Films: A Guide to Information Sources. LC 76-20339. (Performing Arts Information Guide Series: Vol. 3). 1978. 42.00x (ISBN 0-8103-1377-4). Gale.
Parker, Derek & Parker, Julia. Compleat Astrologer: Regular Edition. 1971. 24.95 o.p. (ISBN 0-07-048498-8, GB). McGraw.
--The Compleat Astrologer's Love Signs. (Illus.). 192p. Date not set. pap. price not set (ISBN 0-448-16244-X, G&D). Putnam Pub Group.
--Love Signs. Incl. Aries (ISBN 0-448-11580-8); Taurus (ISBN 0-448-11581-6); Gemini (ISBN 0-448-11582-4); Cancer (ISBN 0-448-11583-2); Leo (ISBN 0-448-11584-0); Virgo (ISBN 0-448-11585-9); Libra (ISBN 0-448-11586-7); Scorpio (ISBN 0-448-11587-5); Sagittarius (ISBN 0-448-11588-3); Capricorn (ISBN 0-448-11589-1); Aquarius (ISBN 0-448-11590-5); Pisces (ISBN 0-448-11591-3). (Illus.). 48p. (Orig.). 1973. pap. 2.95 ea. o.p. (G&D). Putnam Pub Group.
Parker, DeWitt H. Experience & Substance: An Essay in Metaphysics. LC 68-19292. 1968. Repr. of 1941 ed. lib. bdg. 19.00x (ISBN 0-8371-0606-0, PAES). Greenwood.
--Philosophy of Value. LC 68-54431. (Illus.). 1968. Repr. of 1957 ed. lib. bdg. 16.00x (ISBN 0-8371-0607-9, PAPV). Greenwood.
Parker, Donald D. Local History: How to Gather It, Write It, & Publish It. LC 78-11873. 1979. Repr. of 1944 ed. lib. bdg. 17.75x (ISBN 0-313-21100-0, PLAH). Greenwood.
Parker, Donn B. Ethical Conflicts in Computer Science & Technology. vi, 201p. 1979. 23.00 (ISBN 0-88283-009-0); 30.00 set; wkbk. 9.75 (ISBN 0-88283-010-4). AFIPS Pr.
Parker, Dorothy D. Liam's Catch. (Illus.). (gr. k-3). 1972. PLB 8.95 o.p. (ISBN 0-670-42744-6). Viking Pr.
Parker, Dorothy R. Collected Poetry. 1944. 3.95 o.s.i. (ISBN 0-394-60237-4, M237). Modern Lib.
Parker, Douglas H., jt. auth. see Bowe, William J.
Parker, Douglass, tr. see Aristophanes.
Parker, Douglass, tr. see Bovie, Palmer.
Parker, E. H., jt. auth. see Croydon, W. F.
Parker, Edmund K. Secrets of Chinese Karate. 1981. pap. 5.95 (ISBN 0-13-797845-6). P-H.
Parker, Edward A., tr. see Declareuil, Joseph.
Parker, Elinor. Cooking for One. 5th, rev. ed. LC 76-15365. 1976. 11.49i (ISBN 0-690-01176-8). T Y Crowell.
Parker, F. M. Nighthawk. LC 82-45603. 192p. 1983. 11.95 (ISBN 0-385-18412-3). Doubleday.
Parker, Faye & McKenna, Tom. Maggie's Magic Teapot. (Children's Theatre Musical Playscript Ser.). 1963. pap. 2.00 o.p. (ISBN 0-88020-038-3); piano score 5.00x o.p. (ISBN 0-88020-031-6). Coach Hse.
Parker, Frances J. Home Economics: An Introduction to a Dynamic Profession. (Illus.). 1980. text ed. 17.95x (ISBN 0-02-391700-8). Macmillan.
--Home Economics: An Introduction to a Dynamic Profession. 2nd ed. 224p. 1983. text ed. 19.95 (ISBN 0-02-391710-5). Macmillan.
Parker, Francis H. Reason & Faith Revisited. (Aquinas Lecture 1971). 7.95 (ISBN 0-87462-136-4). Marquette.
Parker, Frank J. & Schoenfeld, Norman. Modern Real Estate. 1979. text ed. 24.95 (ISBN 0-669-01326-9). Heath.
Parker, Franklin & Parker, Betty J., eds. U. S. Higher Education: A Guide to Information Sources. (Education Information Guide Ser.: Vol. 9). 400p. 1980. 42.00x (ISBN 0-8103-1476-2). Gale.
Parker, Franklin D. New Era Challenges Old Patterns: A World History, 1945-1960. LC 80-6296. 880p. (Orig.). 1981. lib. bdg. 40.50 (ISBN 0-8191-1839-7); pap. text ed. 29.25 (ISBN 0-8191-1840-0). U Pr of Amer.
--Troubled Earth Acquires Lunar Perspective: A World History, 1961-1970. LC 82-45052. 922p. (Orig.). 1982. PLB 42.50 (ISBN 0-8191-2477-X); pap. text ed. 30.25 (ISBN 0-8191-2478-8). U Pr of Amer.
Parker, Gail R. Holidays for One: Vacations for the Solo Traveler. (Illus.). 64p. (Orig.). 1981. pap. 5.50 (ISBN 0-910115-00-1). Posey Pubns.
Parker, Gail T. The Writing on the Wall. 1980. 9.95 o.p. (ISBN 0-671-22922-2). S&S.
Parker, Gary. Dry Bones & Other Fossils. LC 79-51174. (Illus.). 1979. pap. 5.50 (ISBN 0-89051-056-3). CLP Pubs.
Parker, Gary E. From Evolution to Creation: A Personal Testimony. LC 77-78020. 1978. pap. 1.00 (ISBN 0-89051-035-0). CLP Pubs.
Parker, Gary E., jt. auth. see Bliss, Richard B.
Parker, Geoffrey. Army of Flanders & the Spanish Road: 1567-1659. LC 76-180021. (Cambridge Studies in Early Modern History). (Illus.). 288p. 1972. 43.95 o.p. (ISBN 0-521-08462-8); pap. 13.95x (ISBN 0-521-09907-2). Cambridge U Pr.
--The Countries of Community Europe: A Geographical Survey of Contemporary Issues. LC 78-23239. 1979. 20.00 (ISBN 0-312-17037-8). St Martin.
Parker, George. Lexico-Concordancia del Nuevo Testamento en Griego y Espanol. 1000p. (Span.). 1982. pap. 17.95 (ISBN 0-311-42066-4). Casa Bautista.
Parker, George D., jt. auth. see Millman, Richard S.
Parker, Gillian, jt. ed. see Klein, Michael.
Parker, Glen L. The Economic Consequences of Keynesian Policy: Aspects of a Crisis. 1982. 7.50 (ISBN 0-533-05411-7). Vantage.
Parker, Gordon. Maternal Overprotection: A Defined Risk Factor to Psychiatric Disorders. write for info. Grune.
Parker, Grant. Mayday: The History of a Village Holocaust. LC 80-83408. 260p. 1980. pap. 5.95 (ISBN 0-9604958-0-0). Libty Pr MI.
Parker, H. D. Observations on the Aerial Application of Dispersant Using a DC-6B Air Craft, Gulf of Campeche, Mexico, 1980. 1981. 30.00x (ISBN 0-686-97127-2, Pub. by W Spring England). State Mutual Bk.
Parker, H. D. & Cormack, D. Requirement for Remote Sensing of Oil on the Sea, 1979. 1981. 40.00x (ISBN 0-686-97150-7, Pub. by W Spring England). State Mutual Bk.
Parker, H. D. & Pitt, G. D. Oil Pollution Control Instrumentation. 272p. 1983. 37.00x (ISBN 0-8448-1436-9). Crane-Russak Co.
Parker, Harold T. Three Napoleonic Battles. (Illus.). 280p. 1983. pap. 9.95 (ISBN 0-8223-0547-X). Duke.
Parker, Harold T. & Brown, Marvin L. Major Themes in Modern European History, 3 vols. LC 74-78546. 1974. 5.95 ea. (Pub. by Moore Pub Co); bklts 1-9 2.50 (ISBN 0-685-52529-5); write for info. set (ISBN 0-87716-053-8). F Apple.
Parker, Harold T., ed. Problems in European History. LC 78-78076. 1979. pap. 10.95 (ISBN 0-87716-097-X, Pub. by Moore Pub Co). F Apple.
Parker, Harold T., jt. ed. see Iggers, Georg G.
Parker, Harry & Ambrose, James. Simplified Design of Roof Trusses. 3rd ed. LC 81-19800. 320p. 1982. 27.95 (ISBN 0-471-07722-4, Pub. by Wiley-Interscience). Wiley.
Parker, Harry & Hauf, H. D. Simplified Design of Structural Wood. 3rd ed. LC 78-9888. 1979. 26.50 (ISBN 0-471-66630-0, Pub. by Wiley-Interscience). Wiley.
Parker, Harry & Hauf, Harold D. Simplified Design of Reinforced Concrete. 4th ed. LC 75-38840. 1976. 29.95x (ISBN 0-471-66069-8, Pub. by Wiley-Interscience). Wiley.
--Simplified Design of Structural Steel. 4th ed. LC 73-13562. 326p. 1974. 26.95x (ISBN 0-471-66432-4, Pub. by Wiley-Interscience). Wiley.
--Simplified Design of Structural Steel. 5th ed. 27.95 (ISBN 0-471-89766-3, Pub. by Wiley-Interscience). Wiley.
--Simplified Engineering for Architects & Builders. 5th ed. LC 74-18068. 362p. 1975. 29.95 (ISBN 0-471-66201-1, Pub. by Wiley-Interscience). Wiley.
--Simplified Mechanics & Strength of Materials. 3rd ed. LC 76-56465. 304p. 1977. 28.95 (ISBN 0-471-66562-2, Pub. by Wiley-Interscience). Wiley.
Parker, Harry & MacGuire, J. W. Simplified Site Engineering for Architects & Builders. 1954. 27.95 (ISBN 0-471-66363-8, Pub. by Wiley-Interscience). Wiley.
Parker, Harry, jt. auth. see Kidder, Frank E.
Parker, Harry, et al. Materials & Methods of Architectural Construction. 3rd ed. LC 58-8213. 1958. 40.95 (ISBN 0-471-66297-6, Pub. by Wiley-Interscience). Wiley.

--Simplified Design of Roof Trusses for Architects & Builders. 2nd ed. LC 52-14037. 1953. 29.50x o.p. (ISBN 0-471-66330-1, Pub. by Wiley-Interscience). Wiley.

Parker, Harry L. Clinical Studies in Neurology. 384p. 1969. 12.75x (ISBN 0-398-01449-3). C C Thomas.

Parker, Helen. Light on a Dark Trail. LC 82-71560. 1982. pap. 4.95 (ISBN 0-8054-5430-6). Broadman.

Parker, Henry & Oglesby, C. H. Methods Improvement for Construction Managers. (Illus.). 320p. 1972. text ed. 35.95 (ISBN 0-07-048503-8, C). McGraw.

Parker, Hershel, ed. Gansevoort Melville's 1846 London Journal & Letters from England, 1845. LC 66-17838. (Orig.). 1966. pap. 5.00 o.p. (ISBN 0-87104-083-2). NY Pub Lib.

Parker, Homer. Wastewater Systems Engineering. (Illus.). 464p. 1975. 32.95 (ISBN 0-13-945758-5). P-H.

Parker, Homer W. Air Pollution. (Illus.). 1977. 31.95x (ISBN 0-13-021006-4). P-H.

Parker, Horatio. Hora Novissima (Opus 30) LC 75-169652. (Earlier American Music Ser.: No. 2). 167p. 1972. Repr. of 1900 ed. lib. bdg. 27.50 (ISBN 0-306-77302-3). Da Capo.

Parker, J. Carlyle, ed. City-County Index to Eighteen-Fifty Census Schedules. LC 79-11644. (Genealogy & Local History Ser.: Vol. 6). 1979. 42.00x (ISBN 0-8103-1385-5). Gale.

--An Index to the Biographees in Nineteenth Century California County Histories. LC 79-11900. (Genealogy & Local History Ser.: Vol. 7). 1979. 42.00x (ISBN 0-8103-1406-1). Gale.

--Library Service for Genealogists. LC 80-26032. (The Gale Genealogy & Local History Ser.: Vol. 15). 285p. 1981. 42.00x (ISBN 0-8103-1489-4). Gale.

Parker, J. Carlyle, compiled by. A Personal Name Index to Orton's Records of California Men in the War of the Rebellion, 1861 to 1867. LC 78-15674. (Gale's Genealogy & Local History Ser.: Vol. 5). 1978. 42.00x (ISBN 0-8103-1402-9). Gale.

Parker, J. H. Juan Perez De Montalvan. LC 74-23740. (World Authors Ser.: Spain: No. 352). 1975. lib. bdg. 12.50 o.p. (ISBN 0-8057-2625-X, Twayne). G K Hall.

Parker, J. S., ed. Aspects of Library Development Planning. 200p. 1982. 26.00 (ISBN 0-7201-1661-9, Pub. by Mansell England). Wilson.

--Library Science & Education. 200p. 1982. 26.00 (ISBN 0-7201-1661-9, Pub. by Mansell England). Wilson.

Parker, James E. Programmed Guide to Tax Research. 272p. 1979. pap. text ed. 10.95x (ISBN 0-534-00796-1). Kent Pub Co.

Parker, James F. & Voyles, J. Bruce. The Official Nineteen Eighty-Two Price Guide to Collector Knives. (Illus.). 540p. pap. 9.95 o.p. (ISBN 0-88317-109-0). Stoeger Pub Co.

Parker, James H. Ethnic Identity: The Case of the French Americans. LC 82-23718. (Illus.). 80p. (Orig.). 1983. lib. bdg. 16.50 (ISBN 0-8191-2981-X); pap. text ed. 6.75 (ISBN 0-8191-2982-8). U Pr of Amer.

--Principles of Urban Sociology. LC 81-43477. (Illus.). 228p. (Orig.). 1982. lib. bdg. 23.00 (ISBN 0-8191-2359-5); pap. text ed. 10.75 (ISBN 0-8191-2360-9). U Pr of Amer.

Parker, James L. & Bohl, Marilyn. FORTRAN Programming & WATFIV. LC 73-77126. (Illus.). 284p. 1973. pap. text ed. 14.95 (ISBN 0-574-17070-7, 13-0070). SRA.

Parker, Jay, jt. auth. see Wooden, Wayne S.

Parker, Jerald D., jt. auth. see McQuiston, Faye C.

Parker, Joan H. & Parker, Robert B. Three Weeks in Spring. LC 77-12396. 1978. 7.95 o.p. (ISBN 0-395-26282-8). HM.

Parker, John. Father of the House. 180p. 1982. 30.00 (ISBN 0-7100-9220-2). Routledge & Kegan.

Parker, John A., jt. ed. see Golub, Morton A.

Parker, John L. Living off the Country: For Fun & Profit. Lever, B., ed. (Fun & Profit Ser). (Illus.). 1978. 7.95 (ISBN 0-916302-23-7); pap. 4.95 (ISBN 0-916302-24-5). Bookworm NY.

Parker, John L., Jr. Once a Runner. 1978. pap. 4.95 (ISBN 0-686-14458-9). Cedarwinds.

--Runners & Other Ghosts on the Trail. 1979. pap. 3.95 (ISBN 0-686-23910-5). Cedarwinds.

Parker, John R., ed. The Euterpeiad or Musical Intelligencer, 3 Vols. LC 65-23389. (Music Ser). 1977. Repr. of 1820 ed. Set. lib. bdg. 85.00 (ISBN 0-306-70920-1). Da Capo.

Parker, Joseph. The Joseph Parker Treasury of Pastoral Prayers. (Pocket Pulpit Library). 128p. 1982. pap. 3.50 (ISBN 0-8010-7077-5). Baker Bk.

Parker, Joseph B., jt. auth. see Landry, David M.

Parker, Julia. Aquarius. (Pocket Guides to Astrology 1982 Ser.). (Orig.). 1981. pap. 4.95 o.p. (ISBN 0-671-43444-6). S&S.

--Aries. (Pocket Guides to Astrology 1982 Ser.). (Orig.). 1981. pap. 4.95 o.p. (ISBN 0-671-43442-X). S&S.

--Cancer. (Pocket Guide to Astrology Ser.). (Orig.). 1981. pap. 4.95 o.p. (ISBN 0-671-43439-X). S&S.

--Capricorn. (Orig.). 1981. pap. 4.95 o.p. (ISBN 0-671-43433-0). S&S.

--Gemini. (Orig.). 1981. pap. 4.95 o.p. (ISBN 0-671-43440-3). S&S.

--Leo. (Orig.). 1981. pap. 4.95 o.p. (ISBN 0-671-43438-1). S&S.

--Libra. (Orig.). 1980. pap. 4.95 o.p. (ISBN 0-671-25554-1). S&S.

--Pisces. (Orig.). 1981. pap. 4.95 o.p. (ISBN 0-671-43443-8). S&S.

--The Pocket Guides to Astrology 1982: Libra. 1981. pap. 4.95 o.p. (ISBN 0-671-43436-5). S&S.

--Sagittarius. (Orig.). 1981. pap. 4.95 o.p. (ISBN 0-671-43434-9). S&S.

--Scorpio. (Orig.). 1981. pap. 4.95 o.p. (ISBN 0-671-43435-7). S&S.

--Taurus. (Pocket Guides to Astrology 1982 Ser.). (Orig.). 1981. pap. 4.95 o.p. (ISBN 0-671-43441-1). S&S.

--Virgo. (Pocket Guides to Astrology 1982 Ser.). (Orig.). 1981. pap. 4.95 o.p. (ISBN 0-671-43437-3). S&S.

Parker, Julia, jt. auth. see Parker, Derek.

Parker, K. J., jt. ed. see Birch, G. G.

Parker, Kay. Contemporary Quilts: Designs from M. C. Escher. LC 81-4159. (Illus.). 140p. 1981. 18.95 (ISBN 0-89594-045-0); pap. 10.95 (ISBN 0-89594-044-2). Crossing Pr.

Parker, Kellis E. Modern Judicial Remedies: Cases & Materials. 870p. 1975. 25.00 (ISBN 0-316-69082-1). Little.

Parker, Kelvin M. Cronica Troyana. LC 78-8280. (ALP Medieval Studies Ser.: Vol. 3). 1978. 35.25 o.p. (ISBN 0-8357-0319-3, IS-00051, Applied Literature Pr.). Univ Microfilms.

Parker, Larry, et al. We Let Our Son Die. (Orig.). 1980. pap. 4.95 o.p. (ISBN 0-89081-219-5). Harvest Hse.

Parker, Leo N. Trinkets of Spun Gold. 1979. 4.95 o.p. (ISBN 0-533-03927-4). Vantage.

Parker, Lois & McConnell, David. A Little Peoples' Beginning on Michigan. (Illus.). 32p. (Orig.). (gr. 1-2). 1981. pap. 2.95 (ISBN 0-910726-06-X). Hillsdale Educ.

Parker, Lynn, et al. Frac's Guide to Quality School Lunch & Breakfast Programs. rev. ed. Perry, Cecilia, ed. 60p. 1983. pap. text ed. 4.00 (ISBN 0-934220-04-2). Food Res Action.

Parker, M. D. The Slave of Life: A Study of Shakespeare & the Idea of Justice. 264p. 1983. Repr. of 1955 ed. lib. bdg. 35.00 (ISBN 0-89984-830-3). Century Bookbindery.

Parker, Marjorie F. Return to Reality. 144p. 1983. 10.50 (ISBN 0-89962-304-2). Todd & Honeywell.

Parker, Mark. Horses, Airplanes, & Frogs. LC 76-54805. (Illus.). (ps-3). 1977. 6.50 o.p. (ISBN 0-913778-71-0). Childs World.

Parker, Marshall. Pipe Line Corrosion & Cathodic Protection. 2nd ed. 1982. text ed. 18.95x (ISBN 0-87201-148-8). Gulf Pub.

Parker, Meg, ed. Socrates: The Wisest & Most Just. LC 79-11761. (Translations from Greek & Roman Authors Ser.). (Illus.). 1980. pap. 5.95x (ISBN 0-521-22813-1). Cambridge U Pr.

Parker, Merren. For Goodness Sake. 169p. 1982. pap. 4.95 (ISBN 0-00-216929-0, Pub. by W Collins Australia). Intl Schol Bk Serv.

Parker, Nancy W. Love From Aunt Betty. LC 82-45988. (Illus.). 32p. (gr. k-3). 1983. PLB 10.95 (ISBN 0-396-08135-5). Dodd.

Parker, Nathan C., ed. Personal Name Index to the 1856 City Directories of California. LC 79-24246. (Gale Genealogy & Local History Ser.: Vol. 10). 250p. 42.00x (ISBN 0-8103-1414-2). Gale.

Parker, Netta. Best Dishes from Europe & the Orient: A New Collection of Recipes. 1970. 10.00 o.p. (ISBN 0-571-08442-7). Transatlantic.

Parker, Olivia. Signs of Life: Photographs by Olivia Parker. LC 78-57684. (Illus.). 72p. 1978. limited ed. 300.00 o.s.i. (ISBN 0-87923-421-0); 22.50 o.s.i. (ISBN 0-87923-251-X). Godine.

Parker, Patricia L. Charles Brockden Browne: A Reference Guide. 1980. lib. bdg. 24.00 (ISBN 0-8161-8450-X, Hall Reference). G K Hall.

Parker, Percy L., ed. see Wesley, John.

Parker, R. The Study of Benthic Communities. LC 73-20941. (Oceanography Ser.: Vol. 9). 279p. 1975. 64.00 (ISBN 0-444-41203-4). Elsevier.

Parker, R. B. Twentieth Century Interpretations of The Glass Menagerie. 1983. 13.95 (ISBN 0-686-43175-8); pap. 5.95 (ISBN 0-686-43176-6). P-H.

Parker, R. C. Management of Innovation. LC 82-2737. 221p. 1982. 29.95 (ISBN 0-471-10421-3, Pub. by Wiley Interscience). Wiley.

Parker, R. H. An Introduction to Chemical Metallurgy: In SI-Metric Units. 2nd ed. 1978. text ed. 56.00 (ISBN 0-08-022125-4); pap. text ed. 17.50 (ISBN 0-08-022126-2). Pergamon.

Parker, R. H. & Harcourt, G. C., eds. Readings in the Concept & Measurement of Income. LC 75-87137. (Illus.). 1969. 49.50 (ISBN 0-521-07463-0); pap. 15.95x o.p. (ISBN 0-521-09591-3). Cambridge U Pr.

Parker, Richard. Quarter Boy. LC 76-22665. (gr. 6-12). 1976. 6.95 o.p. (ISBN 0-525-66522-6). Lodestar Bks.

--Three by Mistake. LC 74-13214. 128p. (gr. 4-6). 1974. 7.95 o.p. (ISBN 0-525-66417-3). Lodestar Bks.

--Wildflowers. LC 81-51068. (Illus.). 128p. (Orig.). 1983. pap. 5.95 (ISBN 0-89317-034-8). Windward Pub.

Parker, Robert. Carlos Chavez: Mexico's Modern-Day Orpheus. (Music Ser.). 192p. 1983. lib. bdg. 21.95 (ISBN 0-8057-9455-7, Twayne). G K Hall.

--God Save the Child. 1983. pap. 2.95 (ISBN 0-440-12899-4). Dell.

--The Godwulf Manuscript. 1983. pap. 2.95 (ISBN 0-440-12961-3). Dell.

--Mortal Stakes. 1983. pap. 2.95 (ISBN 0-440-15758-7). Dell.

Parker, Robert, jt. auth. see Sinclair, James E.

Parker, Robert A. A Yankee Saint: John Humphrey Noyes & the Oneida Community. LC 75-187456. (The American Utopian Adventure Ser.). 322p. Repr. of 1935 ed. lib. bdg. 19.50x (ISBN 0-87991-009-7). Porcupine Pr.

Parker, Robert B. Ceremony. 1983. pap. 2.95 (ISBN 0-440-10993-0). Dell.

--Early Autumn. 1981. 10.95 o.s.i. (ISBN 0-440-02248-7, Sey Lawr). Delacorte.

--Looking for Rachel Wallace. 1981. pap. 2.95 (ISBN 0-440-15316-6). Dell.

--The Widening Gyre. 192p. 1983. 13.95 (ISBN 0-440-08740-6, Sey Lawr). Delacorte.

--Wilderness. 1979. 8.95 o.s.i. (ISBN 0-440-09328-7, Sey Lawr). Delacorte.

Parker, Robert B., jt. auth. see Parker, Joan H.

Parker, Robert P. & Collins, Gerarda M. Shih Tzu. (Illus.). 1981. 4.95 (ISBN 0-87666-703-5, KW-084). TFH Pubns.

Parker, Robert P., Jr., jt. ed. see Davis, Frances R.

Parker, Robert S. Looking for Rachel Wallace. 1980. 10.95 o.s.i. (ISBN 0-440-04764-1). Delacorte.

Parker, Roger, tr. see Baldini, Gabriele.

Parker, Roland S. Effective Decision & Emotional Fulfillment. 308p. 1980. pap. 3.95 (ISBN 0-06-464038-8, BN 4038). B&N NY.

Parker, Rolland S. Emotional Common Sense: How to Avoid Self-Destructiveness. pap. 4.95 (ISBN 0-06-464012-4, BN). B&N NY.

Parker, Rollin J. & Studders, R. J. Permanent Magnets & Their Applications. LC 62-10930. 1962. 55.95x (ISBN 0-471-66264-X, Pub. by Wiley-Interscience). Wiley.

Parker, Ron. The Sheep Book: A Handbook for the Modern Shepherd. (Illus.). 352p. 1983. 19.95 (ISBN 0-686-83867-X, ScribT). Scribner.

Parker, Rosetta E. Housing for the Elderly: The Handbook for Managers. Moore, Betty T., ed. (Institute of Real Estate Management Monographs: Series on Specific Property Types). (Illus.). 150p. (Orig.). 1983. pap. 19.95 (ISBN 0-912104-68-6). Inst Real Estate.

Parker, Roy, jt. auth. see Marson, Chuck.

Parker, Samanthe. Star Vision. (Illus.). 64p. (Orig.). 1982. pap. 4.95 (ISBN 0-910241-00-7). Shaunter Ent.

Parker, Sheila. Coloured Things: Stages 1 & 2. LC 77-83009. (Science 5-13 Ser.). (Illus.). 1977. pap. text ed. 12.85 (ISBN 0-356-04348-7). Raintree Pubs.

--Minibeasts: Stages 1 & 2. LC 77-82989. (Science 5-13 Ser.). (Illus.). 1977. pap. text ed. 12.85 (ISBN 0-356-04106-9). Raintree Pubs.

--Trees: Stages 1 & 2. LC 77-83008. (Science 5-13 Ser.). (Illus.). 1977. pap. text ed. 12.85 (ISBN 0-356-04347-9). Raintree Pubs.

--Working with Wood: Background Information. LC 77-82995. (Science 5-13 Ser.). (Illus.). 1977. pap. text ed. 11.55 (ISBN 0-356-04010-0). Raintree Pubs.

--Working with Wood: Stages 1 & 2. LC 77-82995. (Science 5-13 Ser.). (Illus.). 1977. pap. text ed. 11.55 (ISBN 0-356-04011-9). Raintree Pubs.

Parker, Sybil P., ed. Encyclopedia of Physics. 1352p. 1983. 54.50 (ISBN 0-07-045253-9, P&RB). McGraw.

--McGraw-Hill Encyclopedia of Engineering. (Illus.). 1272p. Date not set. 57.50 (ISBN 0-07-045486-8, P&RB). McGraw.

--McGraw-Hill Yearbook of Science & Technology, 1981: Annual Supplement. LC 62-12028. (Illus.). 448p. 1981. 35.50 (ISBN 0-07-045488-4). McGraw.

Parker, Sybil P., ed. see McGraw-Hill Book Co.

Parker, Sybil P., ed. see McGraw-Hill Encyclopedia of Science & Technology Staff.

Parker, T. H., tr. see Calvin, John.

Parker, T. M. English Reformation to Fifteen Fifty-Eight. 2nd ed. 1966. pap. 4.95x (ISBN 0-19-500361-6). Oxford U Pr.

Parker, Thomas. America's Foreign Policy, Nineteen Forty-Five to Nineteen Seventy-Six: Its Creators & Critics. 276p. 1982. 22.50x (ISBN 0-87196-456-2). Facts on File.

--Day by Day: The Sixties, 2 vols. 1000p. 1983. Set. 90.00x (ISBN 0-87196-648-4). Facts on File.

Parker, W. H. Mackinder: Geography as an Aid to Statecraft. (Illus.). 1982. 34.95x (ISBN 0-19-823235-7). Oxford U Pr.

Parker, W. H., ed. see Los Angeles Police Department.

Parker, Watson. Gold in the Black Hills. LC 82-6942. (Illus.). xii, 275p. 1982. 19.95x (ISBN 0-8032-3666-2, BB 803, Bison); pap. 6.95 (ISBN 0-8032-8707-0). U of Nebr Pr.

Parker, Watson & Lambert, Hugh K. Black Hills Ghost Towns. LC 82-73468. (Illus.). 215p. 1974. 21.95 (ISBN 0-8040-0637-7, SB); pap. 11.95 (ISBN 0-8040-0638-5). Swallow.

Parker, William. Milton's Contemporary Reputation. LC 70-122996. (Studies in Milton, No. 22). 1970. Repr. of 1940 ed. lib. bdg. 36.95x (ISBN 0-8383-1129-6). Haskell.

Parker, William & Dietz, Lois. Nursing at Home. 1979. 14.95 o.p. (ISBN 0-517-52836-3). Crown.

Parker, William & St. Johns, Elaine. Prayer Can Change Your Life. 288p. 1983. pap. 4.95 (ISBN 0-13-694786-7, Reward). P-H.

Parker, William B. Life & Public Services of Justin Smith Morrill. LC 79-87371. (American Scene Ser). (Illus.). 1971. Repr. of 1924 ed. lib. bdg. 49.50 (ISBN 0-306-71595-3). Da Capo.

Parker, Willie J. Game Warden: Chesapeake Assignment. LC 82-74134. (Illus.). 288p. 1983. 14.95 (ISBN 0-87033-302-X). Cornell Maritime.

Parker, Wyman W; see Weaver, Glenn.

Parker, Xenia L., ed. Wooden Toys. LC 77-92312. (Illus.). pap. cancelled o.s.i. (ISBN 0-8015-8817-0, Hawthorn). Dutton.

Parkes, Colin M. & Weiss, Robert S. Recovery from Bereavement. 1983. 17.95 (ISBN 0-465-06868-5). Basic.

Parkes, Colin M., jt. ed. see Stevenson-Hinde, Joan.

Parkes, Don & Thrift, Nigel. Times, Spaces & Places: A Chronogeographic Perspective. 1980. 82.95 (ISBN 0-471-27616-2, Pub. by Wiley-Interscience). Wiley.

Parkes, G. Richard. Railway Snowfighting Equipment Methods. 17.50x (ISBN 0-392-08846-0, SpS). Sportshelf.

Parkes, Graham, tr. see Lauf, Detlef I.

Parkes, Henry B. The American Experience: An Interpretation of the History & Civilization of the American People. LC 82-15518. xii, 355p. 1982. lib. bdg. 35.00x (ISBN 0-313-22574-5, PAAE). Greenwood.

Parkes, James. End of an Exile: Israel, the Jews & the Gentile World. LC 82-60880. 300p. 1982. PLB 18.00 (ISBN 0-916288-12-9). Micah Pubns.

Parkes, Joan. Travel in England in the Seventeenth Century. Repr. of 1925 ed. lib. bdg. 20.50x (ISBN 0-8371-4308-X, PATE). Greenwood.

Parkes, Oscar. British Battleships, Eighteen Sixty to Nineteen Fifty: A History of Design, Construction and Armament. rev. ed. (Illus.). 1970. 50.00 o.p. (ISBN 0-208-01253-2, Archon). Shoe String.

Parkes, Patricia. Queen's Lady. 504p. 1981. 14.95 o.p. (ISBN 0-312-66008-1). St Martin.

Parkes, Roger. Alice Ray Moreton's Cookham. 1981. 39.50x o.p. (ISBN 0-86023-145-3, Pub. by Barracuda England). State Mutual Bk.

Parkes, W. B. Clay Bonded Foundry Sand. (Illus.). vii, 367p. 1971. 45.00x (ISBN 0-85334-779-4, Pub. by Applied Sci England). Elsevier.

Parket, I. Robert. Statistics for Business Decision Making. 1974. text ed. 22.00x (ISBN 0-394-31095-0). Random.

Parkhill, Douglas, jt. auth. see Godfrey, Dave.

Parkhill, Joe. Health, Beauty & Happiness. spiral 5.95 o.p. (ISBN 0-936744-00-6). Green Hill.

--Wonderful World of Honey. 6.95 o.p. (ISBN 0-936744-01-4). Green Hill.

Parkhouse, Bonnie L. & Lapin, Jackie. Women Who Win: Exercising Your Rights in Sports. (Illus.). 272p. 1980. 12.95 o.p. (ISBN 0-13-962365-5, Spec); pap. 6.95 o.p. (ISBN 0-13-962357-4). P-H.

Parkhurst, Charles H. Pulpit & the Pew. 1913. text ed. 29.50x (ISBN 0-686-83717-7). Elliots Bks.

Parkhurst, L. B., jt. auth. see Finney, Charles.

Parkin, A., jt. auth. see Coats, R. B.

Parkin, Andrew. COBOL for Students. 224p. 1982. pap. text ed. 14.95 (ISBN 0-7131-3477-1). E Arnold.

--COBOL Workbook. 80p. 1981. pap. text ed. 8.95 (ISBN 0-7131-3438-0). E Arnold.

Parkin, David, ed. Semantic Anthropology. Date not set. 30.00 (ISBN 0-12-545180-6). Acad Pr.

Parkin, Frank, ed. The Social Analysis of Class Structure. (Explorations in Sociology Ser.). 1974. text ed. 25.00x o.p. (ISBN 0-422-74460-3, Pub. by Tavistock England); pap. text ed. 10.50x o.p. (ISBN 0-422-74470-0). Methuen Inc.

Parkin, J. M. & Nobay, A. R., eds. Current Economic Problems. 1975. 54.50 (ISBN 0-521-20818-1). Cambridge U Pr.

Parkin, N. & Flood, C. R. Welding Craft Practice, Pt. 1, Vols. 1-2. 1969. Pt. 1. pap. 4.40, Vol. 1 o.p. (ISBN 0-08-012980-3); Pt. 2. pap. 5.25, Vol. 1 & 2 o.p. (ISBN 0-08-013000-3). Pergamon.

Parkin, P. H., et al. Acoustics, Noise & Buildings. 4th ed. LC 79-670251. 320p. 1979. pap. 17.50 (ISBN 0-571-04953-2). Faber & Faber.

Parkin, S. F., jt. auth. see Oakley, Janet.

Parkins, R. N., ed. Corrosion Processes. 320p. 1982. 61.50 (ISBN 0-85334-147-8, Pub. by Applied Sci England). Elsevier.

Parkinson, C. Northcote. Parkinson: The Law, Complete. 224p. 1983. pap. 2.95 (ISBN 0-345-30064-5). Ballantine.

Parkinson, Cyril N. In-Laws & Outlaws. LC 77-11606. (Illus.). 1977. Repr. of 1962 ed. lib. bdg. 20.50x (ISBN 0-8371-9817-8, PAIL). Greenwood.

Parkinson, E. M. Catalogue of Medical Books in the Manchester University Library, 1480-1700. 1972. 56.50 (ISBN 0-7190-1246-5). Manchester.

Parkinson, G. H., ed. Marx & Marxisms: Royal Institute of Philosophy Lectures, 1979-1980. LC 82-4424. 240p. 1982. pap. 12.95 (ISBN 0-521-28904-1). Cambridge U Pr.

Parkinson, J. R., jt. ed. see Bates, James.

Parkinson, John. A Garden of Pleasant Flowers: Paradisi in Sole Paradisus Terrestris. LC 76-15697. (Illus.). 1976. Repr. of 1629 ed. 25.00 o.p. (ISBN 0-486-23392-8). Dover.

Parkinson, John R., jt. auth. see Faaland, Just.

Parkinson, Michael, jt. auth. see Litt, Edgar.

Parkinson, Nancy, ed. Educational Aid & National Development: An International Comparison of the Past & Recommendations for the Future. 1976. text ed. 25.00x o.s.i. (ISBN 0-8419-5015-6). Holmes & Meier.

Parkinson, R. N. Edward Gibbon. (English Authors Ser.). 1973. lib. bdg. 13.95 (ISBN 0-8057-1218-6, Twayne). G K Hall.

Parkinson, Roger. Origins of World War I. (Putnam Documentary History Ser.). (Illus.). 1970. 6.95 o.p. (ISBN 0-399-10611-1). Putnam Pub Group.

--Origins of World War II. (Putnam Documentary History Ser.). (Illus.). 1970. 6.95 o.p. (ISBN 0-399-10612-X). Putnam Pub Group.

Parkinson, Thomas. Hart Crane & Yvor Winters: Their Literary Correspondence. LC 77-80475. 1978. 17.95x (ISBN 0-520-03538-0). U of Cal Pr.

Parkinson, Thomas, ed. Hart Crane & Yvor Winters: Their Literary Correspondence. (Illus.). 198p. 1982. pap. 6.95 (ISBN 0-520-04642-0, CAL 555). U of Cal Pr.

Parkinson, Tom, jt. auth. see Fox, Charles P.

Parkman, Frances. The Oregon Trail. Feltskog, E. N., ed. (Illus.). 854p. 1969. 27.50 (ISBN 0-299-05070-X). U of Wis Pr.

Parkman, Francis. France & England in North America, 2 Vols. Levin, David, ed. LC 82-18658. 1500p. 1983. Vol. 1. each 25.00 (ISBN 0-940450-10-0). Vol. 2 (ISBN 0-940450-11-9). Literary Classics.

--Half Century of Conflict. 10.00 (ISBN 0-8446-2700-3). Peter Smith.

--Oregon Trail. (RL 8). pap. 2.25 (ISBN 0-451-51587-0, CE1587, Sig Classics). NAL.

Parkman, Francis, Jr. The Oregon Trail. Levin, David, ed. (American Library). 1982. pap. 3.95 (ISBN 0-14-039042-1). Penguin.

Parkman, R. The Cybernetic Society. 400p. 1974. text ed. 29.00 (ISBN 0-08-016949-X); pap. text ed. 12.75 (ISBN 0-08-017185-0). Pergamon.

Parks, A. Franklin, et al. Structuring Paragraphs: A Guide to Effective Writing. 200p. 1981. pap. text ed. 8.95x (ISBN 0-312-76865-6); instr's. manual avail. (ISBN 0-312-76866-4). St Martin.

Parks, Aileen W. James Oglethorpe: Young Defender. LC 60-7711. (Childhood of Famous Americans Ser.). (Illus.). (gr. 3-7). 1957. 3.95 o.p. (ISBN 0-672-50085-X). Bobbs.

Parks, Barbara A., jt. auth. see Johnson, Dewayne.

Parks, David. GI Diary. (Howard University Press Library of Contemporary Literature). 133p. 1983. pap. 6.95 (ISBN 0-88258-113-9). Howard U Pr.

Parks, E. Taylor. Colombia & the United States, Seventeen Sixty-Five- Nineteen Thirty-Four. LC 68-9545. (Illus.). 1968. Repr. of 1935 ed. lib. bdg. 24.50x o.p. (ISBN 0-8371-0187-5, PACU). Greenwood.

Parks, Gordon. Born Black. LC 78-146692. (Illus.). 1971. 12.45i (ISBN 0-397-00690-X). Har-Row.

--To Smile in Autumn. (Illus.). 1979. 14.95 o.p. (ISBN 0-393-01272-7). Norton.

Parks, Helen J. Holding the Ropes. 156p. 1983. 5.95 (ISBN 0-8054-5194-3). Broadman.

Parks, Janet B. Physical Education: The Profession. LC 79-24507. (Illus.). 146p. 1980. pap. text ed. 10.95 (ISBN 0-8016-3759-7). Mosby.

Parks, Lloyd C., tr. see Stendhal.

Parks, Lucille M. Review Mathematics for Nurses & Health Professionals: A Textbook on Solutions & Dosage Calculations. LC 76-46122. 1977. pap. text ed. 14.95 (ISBN 0-8465-4890-9); test bklt. 8.95 (ISBN 0-8465-4891-7). Benjamin-Cummings.

Parks, M. G., ed. see Howe, Joseph.

Parks, Marge, jt. ed. see Harvey, John.

Parks, Marshall M. Atlas of Strabismus Surgery. (Illus.). 240p. 1982. text ed. 45.00 (ISBN 0-06-142111-1, Harper Medical). Lippincott.

Parks, Roger B., jt. auth. see Ostrom, Elinor.

Parks, Roland D. Examination & Valuation of Mineral Property. 4th ed. (Illus.). 1957. 32.50 (ISBN 0-201-05730-1, Adv Bk Prog). A-W.

Parks, Wallace J. United States Administration of Its International Economic Affairs. LC 68-54432. (Illus.). 1968. Repr. of 1951 ed. lib. bdg. 18.00x (ISBN 0-8371-0188-3, PAEA). Greenwood.

Parlagreco, C. Dizionario Portoghese-Italiano, Italiano-Portoghese. 1138p. (Port. & Ital.). 1979. 35.00 (ISBN 0-686-97354-2, M-9183). French & Eur.

Parlett, Beresford N. The Symmetric Eigenvalue Problem. (Illus.). 1980. text ed. 28.95 (ISBN 0-13-880047-2). P-H.

Parlett, Malcolm & Dearden, Garry, eds. Introduction to Illuminative Evaluation. 155p. 1981. 50.00x (ISBN 0-686-97123-X, Pub. by Soc Res Higher Ed England). State Mutual Bk.

Parlin, Bradley W. Immigrant Professionals in the United States: Discrimination in the Scientific Labor Market. LC 75-8409. (Special Studies). 96p. 1976. 25.95 o.p. (ISBN 0-275-01050-3). Praeger.

Parlocha, Pamela Kees, jt. auth. see Hiraki, Akemi.

Parma, Clemens. Wandering Shoe. LC 66-14897. (Foreign Lands Bks). (Illus.). (gr. k-5). 1966. PLB 3.95g (ISBN 0-8225-0358-1). Lerner Pubns.

Parma, S., jt. auth. see Gulati, R. D.

Parmenter, B. R., jt. auth. see Dixon, P. B.

Parmenter, Ross. Four Lienzos of the Coixtlahuaca Valley. (Studies in Pre-Columbian Art & Archaeology: No. 26). (Illus.). 88p. 1982. pap. 12.00x (ISBN 0-88402-109-2). Dumbarton Oaks.

Parmentor, Ross. Stages in a Journey. 271p. 1983. 14.00 (ISBN 0-686-38809-7). Profile Pr.

Parmet, Herbert S. J.F.K. The Presidency of John F. Kennedy. (Illus.). 608p. 1983. 24.95 (ISBN 0-385-27419-X). Dial.

Parmet, Robert D. Labor & Immigration in Industrial America. (Immigrant Heritage Ser.). 1981. lib. bdg. 15.95 (ISBN 0-8057-8418-7, Twayne). G K Hall.

Parmley, Robert O. Field Engineer's Manual. 608p. 1981. 26.50 (ISBN 0-07-048513-5, P&RB). McGraw.

Parnell, A. C., jt. auth. see Butcher, D. G.

Parnell, Dennis, jt. auth. see Holm, Richard.

Parnell, Frances B. Homemaking: Skills for Everyday Living. LC 81-4156. (Illus.). 464p. 1981. text ed. 16.56 (ISBN 0-87006-324-3); wkbk. 3.51 (ISBN 0-87006-409-6). Goodheart.

Parnell, Richard B. Cases, Exercises & Problems for Trial Advocacy. Shellhaas, Glen W., ed. LC 82-2668. 1982. pap. text ed. 6.95 (ISBN 0-314-66859-4). West Pub.

Parnell, Richard W. Behavior & Physique: An Introduction to Practical & Applied Somatometry. LC 73-20503. (Illus.). 1978. Repr. of 1958 ed. lib. bdg. 19.00x (ISBN 0-8371-7327-2, PABE). Greenwood.

Parnes, Herbert S. Research on Labor Mobility. LC 54-9681. 1954. pap. 5.00 (ISBN 0-527-03292-1). Kraus Repr.

--Work & Retirement: A Longitudinal Study of Men. (Illus.). 320p. 1981. text ed. 32.50x (ISBN 0-262-16079-X). MIT Pr.

Parnes, Sidney J. The Magic of Your Mind. LC 81-67950. (The Classic Ser.). 235p. (Orig.). 1981. pap. 9.50 (ISBN 0-930222-05-9, Co-Pub. by Creat Educ Found). Bearly Ltd.

Parodi, Nellie. New Moon - Poems. 99p. (Orig., Span. & Eng.). 1982. pap. text ed. 4.00 (ISBN 0-686-95006-2). N P Cartwright.

Parodiz, J. J. Darwin in the New World. (Illus.). 143p. 1982. pap. text ed. 12.00x (ISBN 90-04-06546-6, Pub. by Brill Holland). Humanities.

Parr. Beginners Guide to Microprocessors. 1982. text ed. 9.95 (ISBN 0-408-00579-3). Butterworth.

Parr, Carmen S., jt. auth. see De La Vega, Sara L.

Parr, J. B., jt. ed. see Funck, R.

Parr, James F., et al, eds. Land Treatment of Hazardous Wastes. LC 82-14402. (Illus.). 422p. 1983. 45.00 (ISBN 0-8155-0926-X). Noyes.

Parr, Jeanne. The Superwives. LC 75-41348. (Illus.). 256p. 1976. 8.95 o.p. (ISBN 0-698-10716-0, Coward). Putnam Pub Group.

Parr, John. Introduction to Ophthalmology. 2nd ed. (Illus.). 1982. pap. text ed. 18.95x (ISBN 0-19-261363-4). Oxford U Pr.

Parr, Robert E. Principles of Mechanical Design. (Illus.). 1969. text ed. 23.95 (ISBN 0-07-048512-7, G). McGraw.

Parr, Roger P., tr. Geoffery of Vinsauf: Instruction in the Method & Art of Speaking & Versifying. (Medieval Philosophical Texts in Translation: No. 17). 1968. pap. 7.95 (ISBN 0-87462-217-4). Marquette.

Parra, Nicanor. Emergency Poems. Williams, Miller, ed. & tr. from Span. LC 71-181896. 160p. (Bilingual.). 1972. 4.95 (ISBN 0-8112-0340-9); pap. 2.75 o.s. (ISBN 0-8112-0134-1, NDP333). New Directions.

Parramon, J. M. Fountain Art Series, 12 pts. Incl. No. 1. Drawing. 7.50x (ISBN 0-85242-086-2); No. 2. Painting. 12.50x (ISBN 0-85242-085-4); No. 3. Oils. 10.50x (ISBN 0-85242-091-9); No. 4. Watercolours. 10.50x (ISBN 0-85242-092-7); No. 5. Drawing the Human Head & Portraits. 7.50x (ISBN 0-85242-099-4); No. 6. Drawing the Human Body. 7.50x (ISBN 0-85242-101-X); No. 7. Drawing in Perspective. 7.50x (ISBN 0-85242-332-2); No. 8. How to Compose a Picture. 11.00x (ISBN 0-85242-345-4); No. 9. Anatomy for the Artist. 7.50x (ISBN 0-85242-305-5); No. 10. Self Portraiture. 11.25x (ISBN 0-85242-315-2); No. 11. Drawing with Colour Pencil. 10.00x (ISBN 0-85242-314-4); No. 12. Light & Shade for the Artist. 12.50x (ISBN 0-85242-338-1). (Illus.). 1971-74. Intl Pubns Serv.

Parramore, Thomas C. Express Lanes & Country Roads: The Way We Lived in North Carolina, 1920-1970. Nathans, Sydney, ed. LC 82-21747. (The Way We Lived in North Carolina Ser.). (Illus.). 120p. 11.95 (ISBN 0-8078-1553-5); pap. 6.95 (ISBN 0-8078-4105-6). U of NC Pr.

Parratt, David, et al. Radioimmunoassay of Antibody & Its Clinical Applicatons. LC 81-12939. 156p. 1982. 35.95x (ISBN 0-471-10061-7, Pub. by Wiley-Interscience). Wiley.

Parratt, J. R., ed. Early Post-Infarction Arrthythmias. 366p. 1982. 79.00x (ISBN 0-333-32672-5, Pub. by Macmillan England). State Mutual Bk.

Parratt, James R. Early Arrhythmias Resulting from Myocardial Ischaemia: Mechanisms & Prevention by Drugs. 1982. 55.00 (ISBN 0-19-520401-8). Oxford U Pr.

Parravicini, Pastori, jt. auth. see Bassani, F.

Parret, Herman, et al. Le Langage En Contexte: Etudes Philosophiques et Linguistiques de Pragmatique. (Linguisticae Investigationes Supplementa Ser.). iv, 790p. 1980. 68.00 (ISBN 90-272-3112-5, 3). Benjamins North Am.

Parries, William H. Second Coming Now--With Soul: Babylon the Great Is Fallen. 1983. 8.95 (ISBN 0-533-05570-9). Vantage.

Parrillo, Vincent M. Strangers to These Shores: Race & Ethnic Relations in the United States. LC 79-87856. 1980. text ed. 20.95 (ISBN 0-395-28562-3); instr's. manual 1.00 (ISBN 0-395-28563-1). HM.

Parrinder, Geoffrey. African Traditional Religion. 3rd ed. LC 76-22490. (Illus.). 156p. 1976. Repr. of 1976 ed. lib. bdg. 15.00 (ISBN 0-8371-3401-3, PAF&, Pub. by Negro U Pr). Greenwood.

--Introduction to Asian Religions. 1976. pap. 5.95 (ISBN 0-19-519858-1, 469, GB). Oxford U Pr.

--Jesus in the Qur'an. 1977. pap. 8.95x (ISBN 0-19-519963-4). Oxford U Pr.

--Mysticism in the World's Religions. 1976. pap. text ed. 6.95 (ISBN 0-19-502185-1, 497, GB). Oxford U Pr.

--Sex in the World's Religions. 1980. 19.95x (ISBN 0-19-520193-0); pap. 8.95x (ISBN 0-19-520202-3). Oxford U Pr.

--The Wisdom of the Early Buddhists. LC 77-7945. (New Directions Wisdon Ser.). 1977. 7.50 o.p. (ISBN 0-8112-0666-1); pap. 2.95 (ISBN 0-8112-0667-X, NDP444). New Directions.

Parrinder, Patrick. Science Fiction: Its Criticism & Teaching. 1980. 13.95 (ISBN 0-416-71390-4); pap. 6.95x (ISBN 0-416-71400-5). Methuen Inc.

Parrington, Vernon L. Main Currents in American Thought, Vol. 3: Beginnings of Critical Realism in America, 1860-1920. LC 56-58467. 1963. pap. 6.95 (ISBN 0-15-611677-4, Harv). HarBraceJ.

Parrino, John J. From Panic to Power: The Positive Use of Stress. LC 79-12027. 1979. 19.95 (ISBN 0-471-05303-1, Pub. by Wiley-Interscience). Wiley.

Parris, John. Retention of Title on the Sale of Goods. 184p. 1982. text ed. 36.75x (ISBN 0-246-11612-9, Pub. by Granada England). Renouf.

Parris, Judith H. The Convention Problem: Issues in Reform of Presidential Nominating Procedures. (Studies in Presidential Selection). 176p. 1972. 12.95 (ISBN 0-8157-6928-8); pap. 5.95 (ISBN 0-8157-6927-X). Brookings.

Parris, Judith H., jt. auth. see Bain, Richard C.

Parris, Judith H., jt. auth. see Sayre, Wallace S.

Parris, N. A. Instrumental Liquid Chromatography. (Journal of Chromatography Library: Vol. 5). 1976. 53.25 (ISBN 0-444-41427-4). Elsevier.

Parris, Nina G., compiled by. Checklist of the Paintings, Prints, & Drawings in the Collection of the Robert Hull Fleming Museum. (Illus.). 166p. (Orig.). 1977. pap. 10.00x (ISBN 0-87451-989-6). U Pr of New Eng.

Parris, Ralph L. Academic Advisement for Rural & Urban Freshmen. LC 81-40942. (Illus.). 86p. (Orig.). 1982. lib. bdg. 18.00 (ISBN 0-8191-2183-5); pap. text ed. 7.00 (ISBN 0-8191-2184-3). U Pr of Amer.

Parris, Wayne, jt. auth. see Holmes, Lowell E.

Parrish, Alvin E. Handbook of Nephrologic Emergencies. 1982. pap. text ed. 14.95 (ISBN 0-87488-680-5). Med Exam.

--Kidney Disease Case Studies. 2nd. ed. 1979. pap. 17.00 (ISBN 0-87488-022-X). Med Exam.

Parrish, Darrell & DiZazzo, Ray. The Car Buyer's Art: How to Beat the Salesman at His Own Game. (Illus.). 100p. 1982. 5.95 (ISBN 0-940060-01-9). Consumer Comm Ltd.

Parrish, Frank. Bait on the Hook. 1983. 10.95 (ISBN 0-396-08150-9). Dodd.

--Fire in the Barley. LC 82-48815. 160p. 1983. pap. 2.84i (ISBN 0-686-82651-5, P651, PL). Har-Row.

--Snare in the Dark. LC 82-48814. 224p. 1983. pap. 2.84i (ISBN 0-06-080650-8, P 650, PL). Har-Row.

--Sting of the Honeybee. LC 82-48816. 192p. 1983. pap. 2.84i (ISBN 0-06-080652-4, P 652, PL). Har-Row.

Parrish, G. The Influence of Microstructure on the Properties of Case: Carburized Components. 1980. 48.00 (ISBN 0-87170-090-5). ASM.

Parrish, James R. Between Loaded Guns. (Illus.). 140p. 1982. 12.95x (ISBN 0-910779-01-5). Book Texas.

Parrish, John A. Dermatology & Skin Care. (Illus.). 320p. 1975. text ed. 20.95 (ISBN 0-07-048508-9, HP). McGraw.

Parrish, Paul A. Richard Crashaw. (English Authors Ser.). 1980. lib. bdg. 14.95 (ISBN 0-8057-6791-6, Twayne). G K Hall.

Parrish, R. G., jt. auth. see Bell, K. W.

Parrish, Roy J., Jr., jt. auth. see Beck, Henry J.

Parrish, Stephen, ed. see Austen, Jane.

Parrish, William, et al. Missouri Heart of the Nation. LC 80-66209. 1980. text ed. 24.95x (ISBN 0-88273-237-4); pap. text ed. 18.95x (ISBN 0-88273-235-8); write for info study guide (ISBN 0-88273-236-6). Forum Pr IL.

Parronchi, Allessandro. Michelangelo: The Sculptor. (Art Library Ser: Vol. 30). pap. 2.95 (ISBN 0-448-00479-8, G&D). Putnam Pub Group.

Parrott, Bob W. God's Sense of Humor. 1983. 17.50 (ISBN 0-8022-2421-0). Philos Lib.

Parrott, Ian. Method in Orchestration. (Student's Music Library Ser). 1956. 7.95 o.s.i. (ISBN 0-234-77310-3). Dufour.

Parrott, James R. TransAmerica Drink Directory. (Illus.). 1977. pap. text ed. 3.95 (ISBN 0-931164-01-X). J R Parrott.

Parrott, Leslie. Building Today's Church. (Minister's Paperback Library Ser). 1973. pap. 5.95 (ISBN 0-8010-6941-6). Baker Bk.

Parrott, Leslie, jt. auth. see Schmelzenbach, Elmer.

Parry, Adam. Studies in Fifth-Century Thought & Literature. LC 71-166948. (Yale Classical Studies: No. 22). 260p. 1972. 37.50 (ISBN 0-521-08305-2). Cambridge U Pr.

Parry, Albert, jt. auth. see Nikolaev, Vsevolov A.

Parry, Anthony & Dinnage, James. Parry & Hardy's EEC Law. 2nd ed. 531p. 1981. lib. bdg. 55.00 (ISBN 0-379-20713-3). Oceana.

Parry, Benita. Delusions & Discoveries: Studies on India in the British Imagination 1880-1930. 1972. 30.00x (ISBN 0-520-02215-7). U of Cal Pr.

Parry, C. English Through Drama. LC 72-184902. (Illus.). 250p. 1972. 26.95 (ISBN 0-521-08483-0); pap. 10.95x (ISBN 0-521-09741-X). Cambridge U Pr.

Parry, C., ed. British International Law Cases, 9 vols. Incl. Vol. 1. 1964. 42.50 (ISBN 0-379-14021-7); Vol. 2. 1965. 42.50 (ISBN 0-379-14022-5); Vol. 3. 1966. 42.50 (ISBN 0-379-14023-3); Vol. 4. 1966. 42.50 (ISBN 0-379-14024-1); Vol. 5. 1966. 42.50 (ISBN 0-379-14025-X); Vol. 6. 1967. 42.50 (ISBN 0-379-14026-8); Vol. 7. 1969. 42.50 (ISBN 0-379-14027-6); Vol. 8. 1971. 42.50 (ISBN 0-379-14028-4); Vol. 9. 1973. 60.00 (ISBN 0-379-14029-2). LC 63-22348. Oceana.

Parry, Charles H. Evolution of the Art of Music. Colles, Henry C., ed. Repr. of 1930 ed. lib. bdg. 19.00x (ISBN 0-8371-0609-5, PAEM). Greenwood.

Parry, Clive. Index-Guide to Treaties: General Chronological List Sixteen Forty-Eight - Eighteen Nine, Vol. 1. Erwin, Paul, ed. LC 79-91238. 555p. 1979. lib. bdg. 75.00 (ISBN 0-379-13002-5). Oceana.

Parry, Clive, ed. Commonwealth International Law Cases, 10 vols. LC 73-20151. 1974-78. lib. bdg. 45.00 ea (ISBN 0-379-00950-1); Set. lib. bdg. 450.00. Oceana.

--Consolidated Treaty Series, Sixteen Forty-Eight to Nineteen Eighteen: Annotated, 231 vols. LC 70-76750. 1970-1977. 45.00 ea. (ISBN 0-379-13000-9) (ISBN 0-379-13001-7). Oceana.

--Law Officers' Opinions to the Foreign Office 1793-1860, 97 vols. 1975. Set. 2000.00 (ISBN 0-379-13400-4). Oceana.

Parry, David, ed. Fibrous Proteins: Scientific, Industrial & Medical Aspects, Vol. 1. LC 79-41004. 1980. 52.50 (ISBN 0-12-545701-4). Acad Pr.

Parry, E. H. Principles of Medicine in Africa. (Illus.). 1976. text ed. 29.95x o.p. (ISBN 0-19-264223-5). Oxford U Pr.

Parry, H. B., ed. Population & Its Problems: A Plain Man's Guide. 1974. text ed. 49.00x o.p. (ISBN 0-19-857380-4). Oxford U Pr.

Parry, Idris. Hand to Mouth: & Other Essays. (Illus.). 173p. 1981. text ed. 15.00x (ISBN 0-686-91777-4, 90122, Pub. by Carcanet New Pr England). Humanities.

Parry, J. H. The Discovery of the Sea. (Illus.). 350p. 1981. pap. 8.95 (ISBN 0-520-04237-9, CAL 478). U of Cal Pr.

--Europe & a Wider World, Fourteen Seventeen to Seventeen Fifteen. 1964. Repr. of 1949 ed. text ed. 10.00x (ISBN 0-09-026812-1, Hutchinson U Lib); pap. text ed. 7.00x o. p. (ISBN 0-09-026812-1). Humanities.

Parry, John J., ed. & tr. Brut Y Brenhinedd, Cotton Cleopatra Version. 1937. 12.00x (ISBN 0-910956-10-3). Medieval Acad.

Parry, John J., ed. see Randolph, Thomas.

Parry, Jonathan, jt. ed. see Bloch, Maurice.

Parry, Keith. The Resorts of the Lancashire Coast. (Illus.). 200p. (Orig.). 1983. 19.95 (ISBN 0-7153-8304-3). David & Charles.

Parry, Leonard A. History of Torture in England. LC 74-172590. (Criminology, Law Enforcement, & Social Problems Ser.: No. 180). 1975. 12.50x (ISBN 0-87585-180-0). Patterson Smith.

Parry, Linda. William Morris Textiles. LC 82-70184. (Illus.). 192p. 1983. 46.95 (ISBN 0-670-77075-2, Studio); pap. 24.95 (ISBN 0-670-77074-4). Viking Pr.

Parry, Megan. Stenciling. 136p. 1982. pap. 9.95 (ISBN 0-442-27444-0). Van Nos Reinhold.

Parry, Pamela J., compiled by. Photography Index: A Guide to Reproductions. LC 78-20013. 1979. lib. bdg. 35.00 (ISBN 0-313-20700-3, PPI/). Greenwood.

Parry, Thomas, ed. Oxford Book of Welsh Verse. 1962. 15.50 (ISBN 0-19-812129-6). Oxford U Pr.

Parry, Thomas G. The Multinational Enterprise. Altman, Edward I. & Walter, Ingo, eds. LC 77-24394. (Contemporary Studies in Economic & Financial Analysis Ser.). 1980. lib. bdg. 36.50 (ISBN 0-89232-092-3). Jai Pr.

Parry, William. Topics in Ergodic Theory. LC 79-7815. (Cambridge Tracts in Mathematics Ser.: No. 75). 1981. 25.95 (ISBN 0-521-22986-3). Cambridge U Pr.

Parry, William & Tuncel, Selim. Classification Problems in Ergodic Theory. (London Mathematical Society Lecture Note Ser.: No. 67). 150p. 1982. pap. 14.95 (ISBN 0-521-28794-4). Cambridge U Pr.

Pars, L. A. A Treatise on Analytical Dynamics. LC 79-87498. 1979. Repr. of 1965 ed. 55.00 (ISBN 0-918024-07-2). Ox Bow.

Parse. Man-Living-Health: A Theory of Nursing. 202p. 1981. pap. 13.50x (ISBN 0-471-04443-1, Pub. by Wiley Med). Wiley.

Parse, Rosemarie R., ed. Nursing Fundamentals. (Nursing Outline Ser.). 1974. 11.50 (ISBN 0-87488-378-4). Med Exam.

Parsegian, V. L. Introduction to Natural Science, Pt. 1, The Physical Sciences. LC 68-14657. 1968. text ed. 30.50 (ISBN 0-12-545201-2); tchrs' guide 3.50 (ISBN 0-12-545241-1). Acad Pr.

--Introduction to Natural Science, Pt. 2, The Life Sciences. 1970. text ed. 27.00 o.s.i. (ISBN 0-12-545202-0); lab. suppl. 7.75 o.s.i. (ISBN 0-12-545256-X); tchrs' guide 7.75 o.s.i. (ISBN 0-12-545257-8). Acad Pr.

Parshall, G. W. Homogeneous Catalysis: The Applications & Chemistry of Catalysis by Soluble Transition Metal Complexes. 240p. 1980. 36.50x (ISBN 0-471-04552-7, Pub. by Wiley-Interscience). Wiley.

Parshall, George W. Inorganic Syntheses, Vol. 15. 1983. Repr. of 1974 ed. lib. bdg. price not set (ISBN 0-89874-386-9). Krieger.

Parsler, Ron & Shapiro, Dan. The Social Impact of Oil in Scotland. 192p. 1980. text ed. 27.75x (ISBN 0-566-00375-9). Gower Pub Ltd.

Parsler, Ron, ed. Capitalism, Class & Politics in Scotland. 176p. 1980. text ed. 33.75x (ISBN 0-566-00390-2). Gower Pub Ltd.

Parsley, Mary, ed. I Can Choose My Bedtime Story. LC 77-152557. (Illus.). 128p. (gr. k-2). 1976. 5.95 (ISBN 0-448-02820-4, G&D); PLB 10.15 (ISBN 0-448-13362-8). Putnam Pub Group.

Parslow, Percy. Hamsters. (Illus.). 1979. 4.95 (ISBN 0-685-96898-7, KW-015). TFH Pubns.

Parson. Short Wave Length Microscopy, Vol. 306. 1978. 45.00 (ISBN 0-89072-062-2). NY Acad Sci.

Parson, Diane L. Lady of Light & Darkness. 256p. (Orig.). 1982. pap. 2.75 (ISBN 0-671-45597-4, Timescape). PB.

Parson, Ruben. Ever the Land. 1980. pap. 6.95 (ISBN 0-934860-16-5). Adventure Pubns.

Parson, Ruben A., et al. Conserving American Resources. 3rd ed. 640p. 1972. 28.95 (ISBN 0-13-167767-5). P-H.

Parson, Thomas, jt. ed. see Gans, Carl.

Parson, Thomas E. How to Dance. 2nd ed. (Illus.). 1969. pap. 3.37i (ISBN 0-06-463202-4, -EH 202, EH). B&N NY.

Parsonage, N. G., jt. auth. see Nicholson, D.

Parsonage, P. Commercial Application of Solids Separation Using Paramagnetic Liquids: Economic & Technical Considerations, 1978. 1981. 69.00x (ISBN 0-686-97046-2, Pub. by W Spring England). State Mutual Bk.

--Design & Testing of Paramagnetic Liquid Separation Systems, 1978. 1981. 69.00x (ISBN 0-686-97054-3, Pub. by W Spring England). State Mutual Bk.

Parsons, Bruce V., jt. auth. see Alexander, James.

Parsons, Charles. Russian-English Dictionary of Irovat' Verbs. 34p. (Orig.). 1982. 10.00x (ISBN 0-917564-14-6). Translation Research.

--Russian-English Dictionary of...(A,E,I,Ya) tel' Words. 32p. (Orig.). 1980. pap. 6.00x (ISBN 0-917564-08-1). Translation Research.

Parsons, Charles, jt. ed. see Levi, Isaac.

Parsons, Chuck. Clay Allison, Portrait of a Shootist. 144p. 1983. 8.75 (ISBN 0-933512-36-8). Pioneer Bk Tx.

Parsons, D. S., ed. Biological Membranes. (Illus.). 1975. text ed. 24.95x (ISBN 0-19-855469-9). Oxford U Pr.

Parsons, Donald F., ed. Ultrasoft X-Ray Microscopy: Its Application to Biological & Physical Sciences. (Annals of the New York Academy of Sciences: Vol. 342). 402p. 1980. 72.00x (ISBN 0-89766-066-8); pap. 72.00x (ISBN 0-89766-067-6). NY Acad Sci.

Parsons, E. Susan, jt. ed. see Tippet, Katherine S.

Parsons, Edward B. Wilsonian Diplomacy. LC 77-80967. 1978. lib. bdg. 10.95x (ISBN 0-88273-006-1). Forum Pr IL.

Parsons, Elsie C. Hopi & Zuni Ceremonialism. LC 34-5260. 1933. pap. 12.00 (ISBN 0-527-00538-X). Kraus Repr.

--Notes on Zuni, 2 pts. 1917. pap. 12.00 ea. Pt. I (ISBN 0-527-00518-5). Pt. II (ISBN 0-527-00519-3). Kraus Repr.

--Pueblo Indian Journal. LC 65-104022. 1925. pap. 12.00 (ISBN 0-527-00531-2). Kraus Repr.

--Scalp Ceremonial of Zuni. LC 25-1663. 1924. pap. 8.00 (ISBN 0-527-00530-4). Kraus Repr.

--Social Organization of the Tewa of New Mexico. LC 30-5855. 1929. pap. 34.00 (ISBN 0-527-00535-5). Kraus Repr.

Parsons, Elsie W. Notes on the Caddo. LC 41-19360. 1941. pap. 10.00 (ISBN 0-527-00556-8). Kraus Repr.

Parsons, F. M. & Ogg, C., eds. Renal Failure: Who Cares? 200p. 1982. text ed. write for info. (ISBN 0-85200-476-1, Pub. by MTP Pr England). Kluwer Boston.

Parsons, Francis. Early Seventeenth Century Missions of the Southwest. LC 74-32368. (Illus., Orig.). 1975. 7.50 (ISBN 0-912762-21-7); pap. 3.50 (ISBN 0-912762-20-9). King.

Parsons, Frank. Legal Doctrine & Social Progress. 1982. Repr. of 1911 ed. lib. bdg. 22.50x (ISBN 0-8377-1014-6). Rothman.

Parsons, Frank A. The Psychology of Dress. LC 74-19187. (Illus.). 1975. Repr. of 1920 ed. 42.00x (ISBN 0-8103-4087-9). Gale.

Parsons, Fred. Vision from God. 1978. 4.00 o.p. (ISBN 0-682-49022-9). Exposition.

Parsons, Howard L., jt. auth. see Somerville, John.

Parsons, Howard L., ed. Marx & Engels on Ecology. LC 77-71866. (Contributions in Philosophy: No.8). 1977. lib. bdg. 29.95 (ISBN 0-8371-9538-1, PME/). Greenwood.

Parsons, J. E. see Emerson, Ralph W.

Parsons, James. The Art Fever: Passages Through the Western Art Trade. Fox, Steve & Schlede, Nancy, eds. (Illus.). 111p. 1981. 29.95 (ISBN 0-686-37628-5). Gallery West.

--Oceans. LC 80-50956. (New Reference Library Ser.). PLB 11.96 (ISBN 0-382-06391-0). Silver.

Parsons, James J. Antioqueno Colonization in Western Colombia. rev. ed. LC 68-58002. (Illus.). 1968. 30.00x (ISBN 0-520-01464-2). U of Cal Pr.

Parsons, John A. & Schapiro, Harriette. Experiments in Cell Biology. (Illus.). 144p. 1975. pap. text ed. 22.50 (ISBN 0-07-048518-6, C). McGraw.

Parsons, John A., ed. Endocrinology of Calcium Metabolism. (Comprehensive Endocrinology Ser.). 530p. 1982. 75.00 (ISBN 0-89004-344-2). Raven.

Parsons, Kitty. Ancestral Timber. (Illus.). 1957. 3.50 o.p. (ISBN 0-8233-0078-1). Golden Quill.

--Up & Down & Roundabout. (Illus.). (gr. 2-4). 1967. 4.00 o.p. (ISBN 0-8233-0080-3). Golden Quill.

Parsons, Langdon & Sommers, Sheldon C. Gynecology, 2 vols. 2nd ed. LC 75-8184. (Illus.). 1660p. 1978. text ed. 80.00 set (ISBN 0-7216-7084-9); text ed. 70.00 single vol. (ISBN 0-7216-7081-4); Vol. 1. text ed. 50.00 (ISBN 0-7216-7082-2); Vol. 2. text ed. 40.00 (ISBN 0-7216-7083-0). Saunders.

Parsons, Leonard J., jt. auth. see Dalrymple, Douglas J.

Parsons, Malcolm. Tuberculosis Meningitis: A Handbook for Clinicians. LC 78-40807. (Illus.). 1979. text ed. 13.95x o.p. (ISBN 0-19-261166-6). Oxford U Pr.

Parsons, Nancy S., ed. Stockton Springs Vital Records 1859-1891. LC 79-55454. (Orig.). 1979. pap. 14.95x (ISBN 0-918768-02-0). Cay-Bel.

Parsons, Neil, jt. ed. see Palmer, Robin.

Parsons, P. Allen. Complete Book of Fresh Water Fishing. LC 63-8071. (Outdoor Life Ser.). (Illus.). 1963. 13.95i (ISBN 0-06-071500-6, HarpT). Har-Row.

Parsons, Peter & Anastas, Peter. When Gloucester Was Gloucester, Toward an Oral History of the City. LC 73-76939. (Illus.). 1973. 3.95 (ISBN 0-930352-02-5). Nelson B Robinson.

Parsons, Peter, jt. auth. see Ehrman, Lee.

Parsons, Stanley B. The Populist Context: Rural Versus Urban Power on a Great Plains Frontier. LC 72-824. (Contributions in American History Ser.: No. 22). (Illus.). xviii, 205p. 1973. lib. bdg. 25.00 (ISBN 0-8371-6392-7, PAC/). Greenwood.

Parsons, Talcott. The Evolution of Societies. Toby, Jackson, ed. (Illus.). 304p. 1977. pap. text ed. 12.95 (ISBN 0-13-293639-9). P-H.

Parsons, Talcott, tr. see Weber, Max.

Parsons, Theophilus. Memoir of Theophilus Parsons. LC 71-118032. (American Constitutional & Legal History Ser). 1970. Repr. of 1859 ed. lib. bdg. 55.00 (ISBN 0-306-71939-8). Da Capo.

Parsons, Thornton H. John Crowe Ransom. (United States Authors Ser.). 1969. lib. bdg. 12.95 (ISBN 0-8057-0604-6, Twayne). G K Hall.

Parsons, Timothy R. & Takahashi, M. Biological Oceanographic Processes. LC 73-7758. 196p. 1973. text ed. 19.80 o.p. (ISBN 0-08-017603-8); pap. text ed. 12.10 o.p. (ISBN 0-08-017604-6). Pergamon.

Parsons, Timothy R., et al. Biological Oceanographic Processes. 2nd ed. 1978. text ed. 38.00 o.p. (ISBN 0-08-021502-5); pap. text ed. 19.75 o.p. (ISBN 0-08-021501-7). Pergamon.

Parsons, Tony. Platinum Logic. 384p. 1982. pap. 8.95 (ISBN 0-933328-13-3). Delilah Bks.

Parsons, Virginia. Pinocchio Series. Incl. Pinocchio & Geppetto. LC 78-11844. o.p. (ISBN 0-07-048531-3); Pinocchio Goes on Stage. LC 78-12323 (ISBN 0-07-048532-1); Pinocchio Plays Truant. LC 78-11843 (ISBN 0-07-048530-5); Pinocchio & the Money Tree. LC 78-12183 (ISBN 0-07-048533-X). (gr. k-3). 1979. 4.95 ea. McGraw.

Parsons, W. J. Improving Purchasing Performance. 128p. 1982. text ed. 37.00x (ISBN 0-566-02271-0). Gower Pub Ltd.

Parsons, William B. Engineers & Engineering of the Renaissance. 1968. 18.50x o.p. (ISBN 0-262-16024-2); pap. 12.00x (ISBN 0-262-66026-1). MIT Pr.

Parsons, William S., jt. auth. see Strom, Margot S.

Parsons, William T. The Pennsylvania Dutch. (Immigrant Heritage of America Ser.). 1976. lib. bdg. 12.95 (ISBN 0-8057-8408-X, Twayne). G K Hall.

Parsonson, S. L. Pure Mathematics, 2 vols. LC 70-100026. (Illus.). 1971. Vol. 1. text ed. 15.95x (ISBN 0-521-07683-8); Vol. 2. text ed. 18.95x (ISBN 0-521-08032-0). Cambridge U Pr.

Parssinen, Terry M. Secret Passions, Secret Remedies: Narcotic Drugs in British Society, 1820 to 1930. LC 82-15571. (Illus.). 250p. 1983. text ed. 17.50 (ISBN 0-89727-043-6). Inst Study Human.

Partain, Floydene. Crying in the Wilderness. (The Caribbean Chronicles: Bk. 1). 432p. (Orig.). 1982. pap. 3.50 (ISBN 0-380-82271-7, 82271-7). Avon.

Partch, Harry. The Genesis of a Music. 2nd ed. LC 73-4333. (Music Reprint Ser.). 1974. lib. bdg. 35.00 (ISBN 0-306-71597-X); pap. 9.50 (ISBN 0-306-80106-X). Da Capo.

Partee, Barbara H. Subject & Object in Modern English. Hankamer, Jorge, ed. LC 78-66576. (Outstanding Dissertations in Linguistics Ser.). 1979. lib. bdg. 15.50 o.s.i. (ISBN 0-8240-9679-7). Garland Pub.

Partee, Linda. Attribute Pattern Boards. (Illus.). 80p. 1982. 12.95 (ISBN 0-9607366-4-6, KP114). Kino Pubns.

Partee, Phillip E. The Layman's Guide to Buying & Eating a Natural Balanced Diet. 130p. (Orig.). 1983. pap. 3.95x (ISBN 0-686-84761-X). Sprout Pubns.

Parthasarathy, R., ed. Ten Twentieth Century Indian Poets. (Three Crowns New Poetry from India Ser.). 1977. pap. 5.95x o.p. (ISBN 0-19-560665-5). Oxford U Pr.

Parthasarathy, T. & Raghavan, T. E. Some Topics in Two-Person Games. (Modern Analytic & Computational Methods in Science & Mathematics: No. 22). 1971. 33.95 (ISBN 0-444-00059-3, North Holland). Elsevier.

Parthe, E. Cristallochamie De Structures Tetraedriques. 366p. 1972. 81.00x (ISBN 0-677-50280-X). Gordon.

Parthe, Erwin. Crystal Chemistry of Tetrahedral Structures. 188p. 1964. 50.00x (ISBN 0-677-00700-0). Gordon.

Parthier, B. & Boulter, D., eds. Nucleic Acids & Proteins in Plants II: Structure, Biochemistry, & Physiology of Nucleic Acids. (Encyclopedia of Plant Physiology: Vol. 14 B). (Illus.). 774p. 1983. 125.00 (ISBN 0-387-11140-9). Springer-Verlag.

Partington, David H., ed. The Middle East Annual: Issues & Events, Vol. 1. 1982. lib. bdg. 45.00 (ISBN 0-8161-8571-9, Hall Reference). G K Hall.

Partington, Geoffrey. The Idea of an Historical Education. 257p. 1981. pap. text ed. 20.75x o.p. (ISBN 0-85633-202-X, NFER). Humanities.

Partington, I., jt. auth. see Carter, H.

Partington, James R. History of Chemistry, 4 Vols. Vol. 1. 35.00 o.p. (ISBN 0-312-37625-1); Vol. 2. 45.00 o.p. (ISBN 0-312-37660-X); Vol. 3. 45.00 o.p. (ISBN 0-312-37695-2); Vol. 4. 45.00 o.p. (ISBN 0-312-37730-4). St Martin.

Partington, M., jt. auth. see Bhagwati, J. N.

Partner, Peter. The Lands of St. Peter: The Papal State in the Middle Ages & the Early Renaissance. LC 73-182793. (Illus.). 494p. 1972. 48.50x (ISBN 0-520-02181-9). U of Cal Pr.

--The Murdered Magicians: The Templars & Their Myth. (Illus.). 232p. 1982. 29.50x (ISBN 0-19-215847-3). Oxford U Pr.

--Renaissance Rome: A Portrait of a Society, 1500-1559. 1977. 36.50x (ISBN 0-520-03026-5); pap. 6.95 (ISBN 0-520-03945-9). U of Cal Pr.

Partnow, Elaine. The Quotable Woman: An Encyclopedia of Useful Quotations, Indexed by Subject & Author, 1800-on. LC 78-7765. 1978. 9.95 o.p. (ISBN 0-385-14520-9, Anch). Doubleday.

--The Quotable Woman: 1800-1981. 608p. 1983. 29.95x (ISBN 0-87196-580-1). Facts on File.

Partnow, Elaine, jt. auth. see Browne, Turner.

Parton, James. Life & Times of Benjamin Franklin, 2 vols. LC 72-126603. (American Scene Ser). (Illus.). 1971. Repr. of 1864 ed. Set. lib. bdg. 125.00 (ISBN 0-306-70048-4). Da Capo.

--Life of Thomas Jefferson. LC 76-126604. (American Scene Ser). (Illus.). 1971. Repr. of 1874 ed. lib. bdg. 79.50 (ISBN 0-306-70049-2). Da Capo.

Partridge, A. C. English Biblical Translation. (Andre Deutsch Language Library). 1973. lib. bdg. 20.00 o.p. (ISBN 0-233-96129-1). Westview.

Partridge, Bellamy. Country Lawyer. (Illus.). 330p. pap. cancelled o.p. (ISBN 0-89062-070-9, Pub. by Hughes Press). Pub Ctr Cult Res.

Partridge, Bonnie & Stock, Susan. Someone Cares. 1.50 (ISBN 0-686-84354-1). Olympus Pub Co.

Partridge, Bruce, jt. auth. see Child, John.

Partridge, Colin. The Making of New Cultures: A Literary Perspective. (Costerus New Series: Vol. 34). 131p. 1982. pap. text ed. 14.00x (ISBN 90-6203-644-9, Pub. by Rodopi Holland). Humanities.

Partridge, Elinore H., ed. American Prose & Criticism, 1820 to 1900: A Guide to Information Sources. LC 74-11519. (American Literature, English Literature, & World Literature in English Information Guide Ser.: Vol. 39). 380p. 1983. 42.00x (ISBN 0-8103-1213-1). Gale.

Partridge, Eric. A Dictionary of Catch Phrases. LC 77-8750. 1979. pap. 10.95 (ISBN 0-8128-6037-3). Stein & Day.

--Origins: A Short Etymological Dictionary of Modern English. 972p. 1977. 45.00 o.p. (ISBN 0-02-594840-7). Macmillan.

--Shakespeare's Bawdy: A Literary & Psychological Essay & a Comprehensive Glossary. rev. ed. 1960. pap. 4.95 o.p. (ISBN 0-525-47055-7). Dutton.

--Usage & Abusage: A Guide to Good English. 384p. 1963. pap. 4.95 (ISBN 0-14-051024-9). Penguin.

Partridge, Eric & Clark, John W. British & American English Since Nineteen Hundred. LC 68-9711. (Illus.). 1968. Repr. of 1951 ed. lib. bdg. 25.00x (ISBN 0-8371-0189-1, PABA). Greenwood.

Partridge, F., tr. see Wolff, Philippe.

Partridge, Jeannette. Losing a Loved One. 2.00 (ISBN 0-686-84350-9). Olympus Pub Co.

Partridge, Jenny. Dominic Sly. (Oakapple Wood Stories Ser.). (Illus.). 24p. (gr. k-3). 1983. 4.95 (ISBN 0-03-062972-1). HR&W.

--Grandma Snuffles. LC 82-21257. (Oakapple Wood Stories Ser.). (Illus.). 24p. (gr. k-3). 1983. 4.95 (ISBN 0-03-062974-8). HR&W.

--Harriet Plume. (Oakapple Wood Stories Ser.). (Illus.). 24p. (gr. k-3). 1983. 4.95 (ISBN 0-03-062971-3). HR&W.

--Lop-Ear. (Oakapple Wood Stories Ser.). (Illus.). 24p. (gr. k-3). 1983. 4.95 (ISBN 0-03-062973-X). HR&W.

Partridge, Loren & Starn, Randolph. A Renaissance Likeness: Art & Culture in Raphael's Julius II. LC 79-63549. (Quantum Ser.). (Illus.). 1980. 18.95x (ISBN 0-520-03901-7); pap. 4.95 (ISBN 0-520-04172-0). U of Cal Pr.

Partridge, Scott H. Cases in Business & Society. (Illus.). 416p. 1982. pap. text ed. 15.95 (ISBN 0-13-117606-4). P-H.

Partridge, T. C., jt. auth. see Brink, A. B.

Partsch, K. J., jt. auth. see Bothe, M.

Paruit, Bernard. Illustrated Glossary of Process Equipment. (Illus.). 1983. text ed. 40.00x (ISBN 0-87201-692-7). Gulf Pub.

Parvey, Constance F., ed. The Community of Women & Men in the Church. LC 82-71831. 288p. (Orig.). 1982. pap. 15.95 (ISBN 0-8006-1644-8, 1-1644). Fortress.

Parvez, H., jt. auth. see Parvez, S.

Parvez, H. & Ruth, V., eds. Advances in Experimental Medicine: A Centenary Tribute to Claude Bernard. 1980. 96.75 (ISBN 0-444-80259-2). Elsevier.

Parvez, S. & Parvez, H. Biogenic Amines in Development. 1980. 101.50 (ISBN 0-444-80215-0). Elsevier.

Parvin, Jack, jt. auth. see Cisin, Fred.

Parzen, Benjamin. Design of Crystal & Other Harmonic Oscillators. 1983. 44.95 (ISBN 0-471-08819-6, Pub. by Wiley-Interscience). Wiley.

Parzen, Emanuel. Modern Probability Theory & Its Applications. LC 60-6456. (Wiley Series in Probability & Statistics: Probability & Mathematical Statistics). 1960. 33.95 (ISBN 0-471-66825-7). Wiley.

--Stochastic Processes. LC 62-9243. (Illus.). 1962. pap. 15.95x (ISBN 0-8162-6664-6). Holden-Day.

Parzynski, William & Zipse, Philip. Introduction to Mathematical Analysis. (Illus.). 384p. 1982. text ed. 25.00x (ISBN 0-07-048845-2). McGraw.

Pasachoff, Jay M. & Kutner, Marc L. Invitation to Physics. 1981. text ed. 19.95x (ISBN 0-393-95152-9); tchr's manual free (ISBN 0-393-95164-2) (ISBN 0-393-95167-7). Norton.

Pasahow, E. J. Microcomputer Interfacing for Electronics Technicians. 1981. text ed. 13.95 (ISBN 0-07-048718-9); instr's manual avail. McGraw.

Pasakow, E. J. Microprocessors & Microcomputers for Electronics Technicians. 1981. text ed. 13.95 (ISBN 0-07-048713-8); instr's manual avail. McGraw.

Pasanella, Anne L. & Volkmor, Cara B. Coming Back...or Never Leaving: Instructional Programming for Handicapped Students in the Mainstream. 1977. pap. text ed. 15.50 (ISBN 0-675-08460-1). Additional supplements may be obtained from publisher. Merrill.

--Teaching Handicapped Students in the Mainstream: Coming Back...or Never Leaving. 2nd ed. (Special Education Ser.). (Illus.). 384p. 1981. pap. text ed. 14.95 (ISBN 0-675-08026-6). Merrill.

Pasano, Beverly, ed. Irish Wolfhounds. (Illus.). 128p. 1981. 4.95 (ISBN 0-87666-718-3, KW108). TFH Pubns.

Pasca, Sue-Rhee. The T. F. H. Book of Canaries. (Illus.). 108p. 6.95 (ISBN 0-87666-819-8, HP-010). TFH Pubns.

Pascal, Blaise. Blaise Pascal: The Provincial Letters. 1982. pap. 4.95 (ISBN 0-14-044196-4). Penguin.

--Thoughts: Selections. Beattie, Arthur H., ed. & tr. LC 65-12901. (Crofts Classics Ser.). 1965. pap. text ed. 3.75x (ISBN 0-88295-065-7). Harlan Davidson.

Pascal, Francine. The Hand Me Down Kid. (gr. k-6). pap. 2.25 (ISBN 0-440-43449-1, YB). Dell.

--My First Love & Other Disasters. (gr. 7-12). 1980. pap. 1.95 (ISBN 0-440-95447-9, LFL). Dell.

Pascal, Gerald R. The Practical Art of Diagnostic Interviewing. (Dorsey Professional Ser.). 275p. 1983. 17.95 (ISBN 0-87094-367-7). Dow Jones-Irwin.

Pascal, Gerald R. & Suttell, Barbara J. The Bender Gestalt Test: Its Qualification & Validity for Adults. LC 51-3749. (Illus.). 288p. 1953. 26.50 (ISBN 0-8089-0358-6); scoring forms 50 sheets per pad 11.00 (ISBN 0-8089-0359-4). Grune.

Pascal, Harold. The Marijuana Maze. 1.75 o.p. (ISBN 0-686-92231-X, 4286). Hazelden.

Pascal, Harold J. The Secret Scandal: Families in Crisis. LC 77-71027. (Orig.). 1977. pap. 1.75 o.p. (ISBN 0-8189-1146-8, 146, Pub. by Alba Bks). Alba.

Pascale, Richard T. & Athos, Anthony G. The Art of Japanese Management: Applications for American Executives. 368p. 1982. pap. 3.95 (ISBN 0-446-30784-X). Warner Bks.

Pascall, Jeremy. Privates & Privateers. LC 81-86276. (In Profile Ser.). PLB 12.68 (ISBN 0-382-06635-9). Silver.

Pascarella, Ernest T., ed. Studying Student Attrition. LC 81-48576. 1982. 7.95x (ISBN 0-87589-906-4, IR-36). Jossey-Bass.

Pasch, Marvin, jt. auth. see Rowe, John R.

Paschall, jt. ed. see Hobbs.

Paschall, Eugene F., jt. ed. see Whistler, Roy L.

Paschke, Donald V., tr. see Garcia, Manuel, II.

Paschke, V., tr. from Span. see Garcia, Manuel, II.

Pascoe, David. Toxicology. (Studies in Biology: No. 149). 64p. 1983. pap. text ed. 8.95 (ISBN 0-7131-2862-3). E Arnold.

Pascoe, K. J. Properties of Materials for Electrical Engineers. LC 72-8612. 324p. 1973. 44.00 o.p. (ISBN 0-471-66910-5, Pub. by Wiley-Interscience); pap. 24.95 (ISBN 0-471-66911-3, Pub. by Wiley-Interscience). Wiley.

Pascoe, Robert D. Fundamentals of Solid-State Electronics. LC 75-25818. 512p. 1976. text ed. 29.95 (ISBN 0-471-66905-9); 3.00 (ISBN 0-471-01554-7). Wiley.

Pascoe, Victoria. The Golden Journey. 1983. 7.95 (ISBN 0-533-05551-2). Vantage.

Pascu, Stefan. A History of Transylvania. Ladd, D. Robert, tr. 318p. 1982. 26.00X (ISBN 0-8143-1722-7). Wayne St U Pr.

Pasek, J., jt. auth. see Horak, J.

Pashigian, B. P. The Changing Role of the Corporate Attorney: Principal Paper. Carney, William J., ed. LC 81-47902. (Illus.). 160p. 1982. 0.19.95x (ISBN 0-669-05143-8). Lexington Bks.

Pashko, Stanley. Ferguson Jenkins: The Quiet Winner. LC 74-21081. (Putnam Sports Shelf). 128p. (Orig.). (gr. 5 up). 1975. PLB 6.29 o.p. (ISBN 0-399-60936-9). Putnam Pub Group.

--How to Make Your Team. (Putnam Sport Shelf). (Illus.). (gr. 5 up). 1969. PLB 4.97 o.p. (ISBN 0-399-60270-4). Putnam Pub Group.

Pasic, N. & Grozdanic, S., eds. Workers' Management in Yugoslavia: Recent Developments & Trends. viii, 198p. 1982. 19.95 (ISBN 92-2-103034-2); pap. 14.25 (ISBN 92-2-103035-0). Intl Labour Office.

Pasich, William, ed. see Nitsch, Susan L.

Pasinetti, L. L. Growth & Income Distribution. LC 74-76579. (Illus.). 180p. 1974. 34.50 (ISBN 0-521-20474-7); pap. 14.95x (ISBN 0-521-29543-2). Cambridge U Pr.

Pasinetti, Luigi. Structural Change & Economic Growth. LC 80-41496. 296p. Date not set. pap. 14.95 (ISBN 0-521-27410-9). Cambridge U Pr.

Pask, Edward H. The Ballet in Australia: The Second Act 1940-1980. (Illus.). 318p. 1981. 69.00x (ISBN 0-19-554294-0). Oxford U Pr.

--Enter the Colonies Dancing: A History of Dance in Australia Nineteen Thirty-Five to Nineteen Forty. 1980. 34.95x (ISBN 0-19-550589-1). Oxford U Pr.

Pask, G. Conversation, Cognition & Learning. 1975. 36.95 (ISBN 0-444-41193-3). Elsevier.

Pask, Gordon & Curran, Susan. Micro Man: Computers & the Evolution of Consciousness. (Illus.). 224p. 1982. 14.75 (ISBN 0-02-595110-6). Macmillan.

Pask, Joseph A. see Fulrath, Richard M.

Pask, Joseph A., jt. ed. see Fulrath, R. M.

Pask, Raymond. China's Changing Landscapes. (Orig.). 1979. pap. text ed. 47.00x o.p. (ISBN 0-435-34687-3). Heinemann Ed.

Pask, Raymond & Bryant, Lee. Australia & New Zealand: A New Geography. 1976. pap. text ed. 9.00x o.p. (ISBN 0-435-34682-2); resources pack 47.00x o.p. (ISBN 0-435-34683-0). Heinemann Ed.

Paskoff, Paul F. & Wilson, Daniel J., eds. The Cause of the South: Selections from De Bow's Review, 1846 to 1867. (Library of Southern Civilization). 304p. 1982. text ed. 27.50x (ISBN 0-8071-1009-4); pap. text ed. 8.95x (ISBN 0-8071-1039-6). La State U Pr.

Paskowicz, Patricia. Absentee Mothers. LC 82-11492. 288p. 1982. 12.50 (ISBN 0-87663-411-0). Universe.

Paskus, John M. Not Less but More Heroic: Milton's Classical & Christian Worlds. 1978. 12.00 o.p. (ISBN 0-533-03372-1). Vantage.

Pasley, Malcolm. Germany: A Companion to German Studies. 2nd ed. 1982. 32.00x (ISBN 0-416-33650-7); pap. 21.00x (ISBN 0-416-33660-4). Methuen Inc.

Pasley, Malcolm, ed. Nietzsche: Imagery & Thought. LC 77-85748. 1978. 34.50x (ISBN 0-520-03577-1). U of Cal Pr.

Pasley, Sally. The Tao of Cooking. LC 82-80235. 240p. (Orig.). 1982. 13.95 (ISBN 0-89815-072-8); pap. 7.95 (ISBN 0-89815-069-8). Ten Speed Pr.

Pasmantier, jt. auth. see Frommer.

Pasold, E. W. Ladybird, Ladybird. 720p. 1977. 31.50 (ISBN 0-7190-0682-1). Manchester.

Pasolini, Pier P. Lutheran Letters. Hood, Stuart, tr. from Ital. 192p. 1983. text ed. 14.75x (ISBN 0-85635-410-4, Pub. by Carcanet New Pr England). Humanities.

--Poems. Macafee, Norman & Martinengo, Luciano, trs. LC 81-48293. 230p. 1982. 10.50 (ISBN 0-394-52298-2); pap. 5.95 (ISBN 0-394-70824-5). Random.

--A Violent Life. Kupelnick, Bruce S., ed. LC 76-52119. (Classics of Film Literature Ser.). 1978. lib. bdg. 18.00 o.s.i. (ISBN 0-8240-2887-2). Garland Pub.

Pasqual, Jack, jt. auth. see Maloney, Pat, Sr.

Pasquale, Bruno, Jr. The Great Chicago-Style Pizza Cookbook. (Illus.). 128p. 1983. pap. 6.95 (ISBN 0-686-42922-2). Contemp Bks.

Pasquale, Michael de see De Pasquale, Michael.

Pasquali, Elaine A., et al. Mental Health Nursing: A Bio-Psycho-Cultural Approach. LC 80-25234. (Illus.). 723p. 1981. text ed. 26.95 (ISBN 0-8016-3758-9). Mosby.

Pasquariello, Anthony M., ed. see Sastre, Alfonso.

Pasquariello, Ronald D. Faith, Justice, & Our Nation's Budget. 112p. 1982. pap. 6.95 (ISBN 0-8170-0976-0). Judson.

Pasquariello, Ronald D. & Shriver, Donald W., Jr. Redeeming the City: Theology, Politics & Urban Policy. 224p. (Orig.). 1982. pap. 10.95 (ISBN 0-8298-0626-1). Pilgrim NY.

Pass, C. L., jt. auth. see Sparkes, J. R.

Pass, G. & Sutcliffe, H. Practical Inorganic Chemistry: Preparations, Reactions & Instrumental Methods. 2nd ed. 256p. 1979. pap. 12.50x (ISBN 0-412-16150-8, Pub. by Chapman & Hall England). Methuen Inc.

Passage, Charles. Character Names in Dostoevsky's Fiction. 1981. 25.00 (ISBN 0-88233-616-9). Ardis Pubs.

Passage, Charles E. Dostoevski the Adapter. (Studies in Comp. Lit.: No. 10). x, 203p. 1975. 14.50x o.s.i. (ISBN 0-8078-7010-2); pap. text ed. 7.00x o.s.i. (ISBN 0-686-82995-6). U of NC Pr.

--Friedrich Schiller. LC 74-76129. (Literature and Life Ser.). (Illus.). 180p. 1975. 13.00 (ISBN 0-8044-2734-8). Ungar.

Passage, Charles E. & Mantinband, James H., trs. Amphitryon: Three Plays in New Verse Translation. (Studies in Comparative Literature: No. 57). viii, 307p. 1974. 19.00x (ISBN 0-8078-7057-9); pap. 8.50x (ISBN 0-686-82994-8). U of NC Pr.

Passage, Charles E., tr. see Horace.

Passage, Charles E., tr. & intro. by see Schiller, Friedrich.

Passahow, Edward. Digital Integrated Circuits for Electronics Technicians. (Illus.). 1978. text ed. 17.95 (ISBN 0-07-048710-3, G); instructor's manual 2.50 (ISBN 0-07-048711-1). McGraw.

Passant, Ernest J. Short History of Germany: Eighteen Fifteen - Nineteen Forty-Five. 1962. 37.50 (ISBN 0-521-05915-1); pap. 13.95 (ISBN 0-521-09173-X). Cambridge U Pr.

Passel, Anne. Your Words: Public & Private. 2nd ed. LC 81-40773. (Illus.). 248p. 1982. pap. text ed. 10.75 (ISBN 0-8191-1867-2). U Pr of Amer.

Passen, Barry J. Introduction to IBM System 360-Assembler Language Programming: A Problem Analysis Approach for Business Data Processing. 334p. 1973. pap. text ed. write for info. (ISBN 0-697-08108-7); student manual avail. (ISBN 0-697-08109-5); instr's manual avail. (ISBN 0-697-08223-7). Wm C Brown.

--Programming Flowcharting for the Business Data Processing. LC 77-25509. 1978. pap. text ed. 23.50x (ISBN 0-471-01410-9). Wiley.

Passey, Neil, jt. auth. see Knudsen, Mark.

Passfield, Sidney J., et al. Decay of Capitalist Civilization. Repr. of 1923 ed. lib. bdg. 17.50x (ISBN 0-8371-2037-3, PACI). Greenwood.

Passim, Herbert, ed. Season of Voting: Japanese Elections of 1976 & 1977. 1979. pap. 6.25 (ISBN 0-8447-3343-1). Am Enterprise.

Passin, Herbert. Encounter with Japan: The American Army Language School. LC 82-48166. Orig. Title: Beirkugun Nihongo-Nihon to No Deai. 220p. 1983. 15.00 (ISBN 0-87011-544-8). Kodansha.

--Society & Education in Japan. LC 65-19168. (Orig.). 1965. pap. text ed. 7.00x o.p. (ISBN 0-8077-1875-0). Tchrs Coll.

--Society & Education in Japan. LC 82-48167. 347p. 1982. pap. 6.25 (ISBN 0-87011-554-5). Kodansha.

Passin, Herbert, jt. auth. see Kahn, Herman.

Passino, Roberto, ed. see Pontifical Academy of Sciences, 1975.

Passman, Donald S. The Algebraic Structure of Group Rings. LC 77-4898. (Pure & Applied Mathematics Ser.). 1977. 54.95 (ISBN 0-471-02272-1, Pub. by Wiley-Interscience). Wiley.

Passman, Jerome. The EKG: Basic Techniques for Interpretation. 1975. 17.95 (ISBN 0-07-048715-4, HP). McGraw.

Passos, John Dos see Dos Passos, John.

Passos, Joyce, jt. auth. see Beland, Irene.

Passow, A. H., et al. The National Case Study: An Empirical Comparative Study of 21 Educational Systems. LC 76-6078. (International Studies in Evaluation: Vol. 7). 379p. 1976. pap. 36.95x o.p. (ISBN 0-470-15119-6). Halsted Pr.

Passow, A. Harry, ed. Developing Programs for the Educationally Disadvantaged. LC 67-19026. 1968. text ed. 14.95 (ISBN 0-8077-1885-8); pap. text ed. 8.95x (ISBN 0-8077-1884-X). Tchrs Coll.

--Reaching the Disadvantaged Learner. LC 69-11364. 1970. text ed. 15.95x (ISBN 0-8077-1889-0); pap. text ed. 11.95x (ISBN 0-8077-1888-2). Tchrs Coll.

--Urban Education in the 1970's: Reflections & a Look Ahead. LC 73-154693. 1971. text ed. 12.95x (ISBN 0-8077-1883-1); pap. 8.95x (ISBN 0-8077-1882-3). Tchrs Coll.

Passwater, Richard. The Easy No-Flab Diet. LC 79-4684. 1979. 10.95 (ISBN 0-399-90034-9, Marek). Putnam Pub Group.

--Hair Analysis. 1982. 10.95x (ISBN 0-686-37942-X). Cancer Control Soc.

--Super-Nutrition-Healthy Hearts. 3.50x (ISBN 0-686-29823-3). Cancer Control Soc.

--Supernutrition for Healthy Hearts. 1978. pap. 3.50 (ISBN 0-515-06343-6). Jove Pubns.

Passwater, Richard, ed. see Bland, Jeffrey.

Passwater, Richard, ed. see Rose, Jeanne.

Passwater, Richard A. EPA-Marine Lipids: Good Health Guide Ser. Mindell, Earl, ed. 36p. (Orig.). 1982. pap. 1.45 (ISBN 0-87983-321-1). Keats.

Passwater, Richard A. & Cranton, Elmer M. Trace Elements, Hair Analysis & Nutrition: Fact & Myth. LC 81-83892. 1983. pap. 11.95 (ISBN 0-87983-265-7). Keats.

Passwater, Richard A., ed. see Bland, Jeffrey.

Passwater, Richard A., ed. see Challem, Jack J.

Passwater, Richard A., ed. see Garrison, Robert, Jr.

Passwater, Richard A., ed. see Goldbeck, Nikki.

Passwater, Richard A., ed. see Heinerman, John.

Passwater, Richard A., ed. see Jones, Susan S.

Passwater, Richard A., ed. see Light, Marilyn.

Passwater, Richard A., ed. see Mervyn, Len.

Passwater, Richard A., ed. see Rosenburg, Harold S.

Passwater, Richard A., ed. see Vogel, Jerome & Walsh, Richard.

Pasta, Elmer. Complete Book of Roasts, Boasts, & Toasts. LC 82-6296. 375p. 1982. 14.95 (ISBN 0-13-158311-5, Parker); pap. 4.95 (ISBN 0-13-158329-8). P-H.

Pastan, Linda. Setting the Table. LC 79-15833. 1980. letterpress limited edition 15.00 (ISBN 0-931848-25-3); offset edition 3.75 (ISBN 0-686-96707-0). Dryad Pr.

Pasternack, Marian & Silvey, Linda. Pattern Blocks Activities, Bks. A & B. (Illus., Orig., Bk A grades 2-6; bk. B grades 4-8). (gr. 2-8). 1975. Bk. A. pap. 7.95 (ISBN 0-88488-041-9); Bk. B. pap. 7.95 (ISBN 0-88488-042-7). Creative Pubns.

Pasternak, Boris. Dr. Zhivago. 1974. pap. 2.50 o.p. (ISBN 0-451-08430-6, E8430, Sig). NAL.

--My Sister-Life. Rudman, Mark, tr. 150p. 1983. 16.00 (ISBN 0-88233-784-X); pap. 7.50 (ISBN 0-88233-785-8). Ardis Pubs.

--Poems. Kayden, Eugene, tr. LC 63-14379. (Illus.). 1963. 9.00x o.p. (ISBN 0-87338-082-7). Kent St U Pr.

--The Poems of Doctor Zhivago. Davie, Donald, ed. & tr. LC 76-1980. 1977. Repr. of 1965 ed. lib. bdg. 21.00 (ISBN 0-8371-8294-8, PAPDZ). Greenwood.

--Zhenia's Childhood. 128p. 1982. 13.95 (ISBN 0-8052-8128-2, Pub. by Allison & Busby England); pap. 5.95 (ISBN 0-8052-8129-0, Pub. by Allison & Busby England). Schocken.

Pasternak, Burton. Introduction to Kinship & Social Organization. (Illus.). 208p. 1976. Ref. Ed. pap. 11.95 (ISBN 0-13-485466-7). P-H.

Pasternak, C. A. An Introduction to Human Biochemistry. (Illus.). 1979. pap. text ed. 18.95x (ISBN 0-19-261127-5). Oxford U Pr.

--Radioimmunoassay in Clinical Biochemistry. 1975. 72.00 (ISBN 0-471-25948-9, Wiley Heyden). Wiley.

Pasteur, D. The Management of Squatter Upgrading. 1979. text ed. 37.25x (ISBN 0-566-00266-3). Gower Pub Ltd.

Pastier, John. Cesar Pelli. (Illus.). 120p. 1980. 19.95 (ISBN 0-8230-7414-5, Whitney Lib). Watson-Guptill.

Pastmantier, jt. auth. see Frommer.

Pasto, Daniel & Johnson, Carl. Organic Structure Determination. 1969. ref. ed. 29.95 (ISBN 0-13-640854-0). P-H.

Pasto, Daniel G., jt. auth. see Gutsche, C. David.

Pasto, Daniel J. & Johnson, Carol R. Laboratory Text for Organic Chemistry: A Source Book of Chemical & Physical Techniques. 1979. pap. 23.95 (ISBN 0-13-521302-9). P-H.

Pastor, Lucille E. Versatile Poetry. 1978. 4.95 o.p. (ISBN 0-533-03260-1). Vantage.

Pastor, Robert A. Congress & the Politics of U. S. Foreign Economic Policy, 1929-1976. (Illus.). 350p. 1982. pap. 8.95 (ISBN 0-520-04645-5, CAL 560). U of Cal Pr.

Pastor, Terry. Space Mission. (Illus.). 12p. (gr. 1 up). 1983. 5.95 (ISBN 0-316-69333-2). Little.

--Underwater Mission. (Illus.). 12p. (gr. 1 up). 1983. 5.95 (ISBN 0-316-69334-0). Little.

Pastoral Care Office of RLDS Church, et al. Human Sexuality. 1982. pap. 4.00 (ISBN 0-8309-0350-X). Herald Hse.

Pastore, Nicholas. Selective History of Theories of Visual Perception, 1650-1950. 1971. text ed. 19.95x (ISBN 0-19-501257-7). Oxford U Pr.

Pastorelli, Pietro, ed. Carteggio (Political Correspondence, 3 vols. Incl. Vol. Primo, 1891-1913. xiv, 592p. 1982 (ISBN 0-7006-0225-9); Vol. Secondo, 1914-1916. xvi, 776p. 1975 (ISBN 0-7006-0139-2); Vol. Terzo, 1916-1922. xvi, 788p. 1976 (ISBN 0-7006-0150-3). (Opera Omnia Di--the Complete Works of--Sidney Sonnino). xvi, 592p. (Ital.). 1982. Set. 50.00x. Univ Pr KS.

Pastre, Oliver. Multinationals: Bank & Corporate Relationships, Vol. 28. Altman, Edward I. & Walter, Ingo, eds. LC 81-80869. (Contemporary Studies in Economic & Financial Analysis). 275p. 1981. 45.00 (ISBN 0-89232-219-5). Jai Pr.

Paszkiewicz, Henryk. Origin of Russia. 1955. 10.00 o.p. (ISBN 0-8022-1283-2). Philos Lib.

Pasztor, Magda. Bibliography of Pharmaceutical Reference Literature. LC 68-140058. 167p. (Orig.). 1968. pap. 5.00x (ISBN 0-85369-055-3). Intl Pubns Serv.

Pasztory, Esther. The Murals of Tepantitla, Teotihaucan. LC 75-23806. (Outstanding Dissertations in the Fine Arts - Native American Arts). (Illus.). 1976. lib. bdg. 45.00 o.s.i. (ISBN 0-8240-2000-6). Garland Pub.

Pata, Jan L. Afghan Hound Champions, 1952-1981. (Illus.). 230p. 1983. pap. 19.95 (ISBN 0-940808-21-8). Pata Pubns.

--Basenji Champions, 1945-1981. (Illus.). 125p. 1983. pap. 19.95 (ISBN 0-940808-17-X). Pata Pubns.

--Borzoi Champions, 1952-1981. (Illus.). 150p. 1983. pap. 19.95 (ISBN 0-940808-18-8). Pata Pubns.

--Brittany Champions, 1952-1981. (Illus.). 240p. 1983. 24.95 (ISBN 0-940808-20-X). Pata Pubns.

--Bull Terrier Champions, 1952-1981. (Illus.). 75p. 1983. pap. 19.95 (ISBN 0-940808-16-1). Pata Pubns.

--English Springer Spaniel Champions, 1952-1981. (Illus.). 190p. 1983. pap. 19.95 (ISBN 0-940808-19-6). Pata Pubns.

--English Toy Spaniel Champions, 1952-1982. (Illus.). 95p. 1982. pap. 19.95 (ISBN 0-940808-22-6). Pata Pubns.

--German Shepherd Champions, Nineteen Fifty-Two to Nineteen Eighty. (Illus.). 182p. 1981. pap. 19.95 o.s.i. (ISBN 0-940808-02-1). Pata Pubns.

--Golden Retriever Champions, 1952-1981. (Illus.). 190p. 1983. 19.95 (ISBN 0-940808-25-0). Pata Pubns.

--Irish Setter Champions, 1876-1981. (Illus.). 280p. 1983. pap. 24.95 (ISBN 0-940808-23-4). Pata Pubns.

--Pomeranian Champions, 1952-1981. (Illus.). 155p. 1983. pap. 19.95 (ISBN 0-940808-13-7). Pata Pubns.

--Rottweiler Champions, 1948-1981. (Illus.). 220p. 1983. 19.95 (ISBN 0-940808-24-2). Pata Pubns.

--Yorkshire Terrier Champions, Nineteen Fifty-Two to Nineteen Eighty. (Illus.). 201p. 1981. 19.95 o.s.i. (ISBN 0-940808-08-0). Pata Pubns.

Patai, jt. auth. see Stirling, C. J.

Patai, R. On Culture Contact & Its Working in Modern Palestine. LC 48-4054. (American Anthropological Association Memoirs). Repr. of 1947 ed. pap. 8.00 (ISBN 0-527-00566-5). Kraus Repr.

Patai, Raphael. The Arab Mind. rev. ed. 448p. 1983. 19.95 (ISBN 0-686-83811-4, ScribT); pap. 10.95 (ISBN 0-686-83812-2). Scribner.

--Gates to the Old City: A Book of Jewish Legends. LC 80-66154. 858p. 1981. 27.50 (ISBN 0-8143-1679-4). Wayne St U Pr.

--The Hebrew Goddess. 1978. pap. 2.95 o.p. (ISBN 0-380-39289-5, 39289, Discus). Avon.

--Israel Between East & West: A Study in Human Relations. rev. ed. LC 70-98711. 1970. lib. bdg. 29.95 (ISBN 0-8371-3719-5, PAI/). Greenwood.

--Jordan, Lebanon, & Syria: An Annotated Bibliography. LC 73-6215. 289p. 1973. Repr. of 1957 ed. lib. bdg. 15.75x (ISBN 0-8371-6894-5, PAJL). Greenwood.

--On Jewish Folklore. 524p. 27.50 (ISBN 0-8143-1707-3). Wayne St U Pr.

Patai, Raphael, jt. auth. see Graves, Robert.

Patai, S. The Chemistry of Double-Bonded Functional Groups: Supplement A, 2 pt. set. 1343p. 1977. 233.00x o.p. (ISBN 0-471-66940-7, Pub. by Wiley-Interscience). Wiley.

--The Chemistry of Quinonoid Compounds, 2 pt. set. 1274p. 1974. 248.95x (ISBN 0-471-66928-8, Pub. by Wiley-Interscience). Wiley.

--Chemistry of the Azido Group. LC 73-149579. (Chemistry of Functional Groups Ser.). 122.95x (ISBN 0-471-66925-3, Pub. by Wiley-Interscience). Wiley.

--The Chemistry of the Carbon Carbon Triple Bond. 1065p. 1978. Set. 273.95 (ISBN 0-471-99496-0, Pub. by Wiley-Interscience); Pt. 1. 136.95 (ISBN 0-471-99497-9); Pt. 2. 136.95 (ISBN 0-471-99498-7). Wiley.

--The Chemistry of the Diazonium & Diazo Groups, 2 pts. LC 75-6913. (Chemistry of Functional Groups Ser.). 1978. Set. 222.95x (ISBN 0-471-99415-4); Pt. 1. 113.95x (ISBN 0-471-99492-8); Pt. 2. 111.00x o.p. (ISBN 0-471-99493-6, Pub. by Wiley-Interscience). Wiley.

--Supplement E Chemistry of Ethers Crown Ethers Hydroxyl Group & Their Sulphur Analogs. (Chemistry of Functional Group Ser.). 1142p. 1981. Set. 323.95 (ISBN 0-471-27618-9, Pub. by Wiley-Interscience); Pt. 1 - 608 Pgs. 161.95 (ISBN 0-471-27771-1); Pt. 2 - 534 Pgs. pap. 161.95 (ISBN 0-471-27772-X). Wiley.
--Supplement F. Set. 337.95x (ISBN 0-471-27873-4, Pub. by Wiley-Interscience); Pt. 1. 169.95x (ISBN 0-471-27871-8); Pt. 2. 169.95x (ISBN 0-471-27872-6). Wiley.
Patai, S., ed. Chemistry of Acyl Halides. LC 70-37114. (Chemistry of Functional Groups Ser.). 576p. 1972. 107.95x (ISBN 0-471-66936-9, Pub. by Wiley-Interscience). Wiley.
Patai, Saul. The Chemistry of Acid Derivatives, Supplement B. (Chemistry of Functional Groups Ser.). 1979. Set. 405.00 (ISBN 0-471-99609-2); Pt. 1. 191.25 o.p. (ISBN 0-471-99610-6); Pt. 2. 191.25 o.p. (ISBN 0-471-99611-4, Pub. by Wiley-Interscience). Wiley.
--The Chemistry of Amidines & Imidates. LC 75-6913. (Chemistry of Functional Groups Ser.). 677p. 1976. 132.95x (ISBN 0-471-66923-7, Pub by Wiley-Interscience). Wiley.
--Chemistry of Carbonyl Group, Vol. 1. LC 66-18177. (Chemistry of Functional Groups Ser.). 1966. 200.00x (ISBN 0-470-66920-9, Pub. by Wiley-Interscience). Wiley.
--Chemistry of Carboxylic Acids & Esters. LC 70-82547. (Chemistry of Functional Groups Ser.). 1970. 225.95x (ISBN 0-471-66919-9, Pub. by Wiley-Interscience). Wiley.
--Chemistry of Ketenes, Allenes & Related Compounds, 2 pts. (Chemistry of Functional Groups Ser.). 1980. 105.95 ea. (Pub. by Wiley-Interscience). Pt. 1 (ISBN 0-471-99713-7). Pt. 2 (ISBN 0-471-27670-7). Wiley.
Patai, Saul, ed. Chemistry of Hydrazo, Azo & Azoxy Groups, 2 pts. LC 75-2194. 1975. Set. 231.95 (ISBN 0-471-66924-5); Pt. 1. 116.95x (ISBN 0-471-66926-1); Pt. 2. 103.00x o.p. (ISBN 0-471-66927-X, Pub. by Wiley-Interscience). Wiley.
--The Chemistry of the Cyanates & Their Thio Derivatives, 2 pts. LC 75-6913. (Chemistry of Functional Groups Ser.). 1977. Set. 280.95 (ISBN 0-471-99425-1); Pt. 1. 111.25 o.p. (ISBN 0-471-99477-4). Pt. 2. Wiley.
Pataky-Brestyanszky, Ilona, compiled by. Margit Kovacs. Horn, Susanna & West, Elisabeth, trs. (Illus.). 193p. 1980. 30.00 (ISBN 0-89893-156-8). CDP.
Patanjali. Yoga-Sutra of Patanjali. 2nd ed. Ballantyne, J. R. & Deva, Govind S., eds. LC 70-928599. 1971. 8.50x (ISBN 0-8002-0981-8). Intl Pubns Ser.
Patanjali, Swami S. The Ten Principal Upanishads. Yeats, W. B., tr. (Orig.). 1970. pap. 5.95 (ISBN 0-571-09363-9). Faber & Faber.
Patankar, Suhas V. Numerical Heat Transfer & Fluid Flow. LC 79-28286. (Hemisphere Series on Computational Methods in Mechanics & Thermal Sciences). (Illus.). 208p. 1980. text ed. 37.50 (ISBN 0-07-048740-5). McGraw.
Patchen, Kenneth. Collected Poems. LC 67-23487. 1969. pap. 11.50 (ISBN 0-8112-0140-6, NDP284). New Directions.
Patchen, Martin, et al. Some Questionnaire Measures of Employee Motivation & Morale. LC 65-65052. 82p. 1966. pap. 6.00x (ISBN 0-87944-045-7). Inst Soc Res.
Patchett. Construction Site: Personnel 4 Checkbook. 1983. text ed. write for info. (ISBN 0-408-00688-9); pap. write for info. (ISBN 0-408-00685-4). Butterworth.
Patchin, Robert I. & Cunningham, Robert. The Management & Maintenance of Quality Circles. LC 82-73407. 200p. 1983. 17.95 (ISBN 0-87094-368-5). Dow Jones-Irwin.
Pate, Robert H., Jr., jt. auth. see Brown, Jeannette A.
Patel, Aneel N., jt. auth. see Toole, James F.
Patel, Dinker I. Exurbs: Urban Residential Developments in the Countryside. LC 79-48040. 151p. 1980. text ed. 18.00 (ISBN 0-8191-1001-9); pap. text ed. 8.50 (ISBN 0-8191-1002-7). U Pr of Amer.
Patel, Kant. Dimensions of States' Education & Public Health Policies. LC 78-64563. 1978. pap. text ed. 7.75 o.p. (ISBN 0-8191-0636-4). U Pr of Amer.
Patel, S. R. Business Law: A General Introduction. 65p. 1983. text ed. 20.00x (ISBN 0-210-40641-0, Pub. by Jaisingh & Mehta India). Apt Bks.
Patel, Satyavrata. Hinduism: Religion & Way of Life. 165p. (gr. 9-12). 1980. 15.95x (ISBN 0-940500-25-6); lib. bdg. 15.95x (ISBN 0-686-96415-2); text ed. 15.95x (ISBN 0-686-99778-6). Asia Bk Corp.
Pateman, Carole. Participation & Democratic Theory. LC 71-120193. 1970. 22.95 (ISBN 0-521-07856-3); pap. 7.95 (ISBN 0-521-29004-X). Cambridge U Pr.
--The Problem of Political Obligation: A Critical Analysis of Liberal Theory. LC 78-18460. 1979. 34.95 (ISBN 0-471-99699-8, Pub. by Wiley-Interscience). Wiley.
Patent, Dorothy H. Arabian Horses. LC 81-85090. (Illus.). 80p. (gr. 3-6). 1982. PLB 11.95 (ISBN 0-8234-0451-X). Holiday.
--Evolution Goes on Every Day. LC 76-50525. (Illus.). 160p. (gr. 5 up). 1977. 10.95 (ISBN 0-8234-0297-5). Holiday.
--Fish & How They Reproduce. LC 76-10349. (Illus.). 128p. (gr. 3-7). 1976. 9.95 (ISBN 0-8234-0285-1). Holiday.
--Frogs, Toads, Salamanders & How They Reproduce. LC 74-26567. (Illus.). 144p. (gr. 4-7). 1975. 9.95 (ISBN 0-8234-0255-X). Holiday.
--Germs! (Illus.). 40p. (gr. 3-7). 1983. reinforced binding 9.95 (ISBN 0-8234-0481-1). Holiday.
--The Lives of Spiders. LC 80-14801. (Illus.). 128p. (gr. 5 up). 1980. 9.95 (ISBN 0-8234-0418-8). Holiday.
--A Picture Book of Cows. LC 82-80819. (Illus.). 40p. (ps-3). 1982. Reinforced bdg. 9.95 (ISBN 0-8234-0461-7). Holiday.
--The World of Worms. LC 77-17117. (Illus.). 160p. (gr. 5-9). 1978. 9.95 (ISBN 0-8234-0319-X). Holiday.
Patent, Trademark & Copyright Institute of the George Washington University, jt. ed. see Harris, L. James.
Pater, Alan F. & Pater, Jason R., eds. The Great Libraries of America: A Pictorial History. 1983. 35.00 (ISBN 0-917734-03-3). Monitor.
--What They Said in 1977. LC 74-111080. (Ninth Annual Vol.). 1978. lib. bdg. 19.50 (ISBN 0-917734-01-7). Monitor.
--What They Said in 1982: The Yearbook of Spoken Opinion, Vol. 14. LC 74-111080. 1983. 27.50 (ISBN 0-917734-08-4). Monitor.
Pater, Calvin A. Karlstadt as the Father of the Baptist Movements. 324p. 1983. 35.00x (ISBN 0-8020-5555-9). U of Toronto Pr.
Pater, Jason R., jt. ed. see Pater, Alan F.
Pater, Walter. The Renaissance. LC 77-12308. 1977. lib. bdg. 10.95 o.p. (ISBN 0-915864-34-7); pap. 5.00 (ISBN 0-915864-35-5). Academy Chi Ltd.
--The Renaissance: Studies in Art & Poetry. Hill, Donald L., ed. 1980. 36.00x (ISBN 0-520-03325-6); pap. 6.95 (ISBN 0-520-03664-6). U of Cal Pr.
--Selected Prose of Walter Pater. Bloom, Harold, ed. (Orig.). 1974. pap. 1.95 o.p. (ISBN 0-451-50743-6, CJ743, Sig Classics). NAL.
Pater, Walter H. Plato & Platonism. Repr. of 1910 ed. lib. bdg. 15.50x (ISBN 0-8371-1151-X, PAPP). Greenwood.
Patera, Charlotte. Cutwork Applique: Making Ornamental Fabric Designs. (Illus.). 168p. 1983. pap. 12.95 (ISBN 0-8329-0271-3). New Century.
Paternite, David, jt. ed. see Paternite, Stephen.
Paternite, Stephen & Paternite, David, eds. American Infrared Survey. LC 82-6160. (Illus.). 88p. 1982. 21.95 (ISBN 0-9609812-0-9). Photo Survey.
Paterno, Cynthia, jt. auth. see Lackner, Marie.
Paterno, Gianfranco, jt. auth. see Barone, Antonio.
Paterson, A. K., ed. see Tirso De Molina.
Paterson, Alistair, ed. Fifteen Contemporary New Zealand Poets. LC 82-47994. 224p. 1982. 19.50 (ISBN 0-394-52881-6, GP858, GP); pap. 7.95 (ISBN 0-394-17999-4, E816, Ever). Grove.
Paterson, Diane. Hey, Cowboy! LC 81-20851. (Illus.). 48p. (gr. 4-7). 1983. 9.95 (ISBN 0-394-85341-5); lib. bdg. 9.99 (ISBN 0-394-95341-X). Knopf.
Paterson, Donald G. Physique & Intellect. Repr. of 1930 ed. lib. bdg. 15.75x (ISBN 0-8371-2886-2, PAPI). Greenwood.
Paterson, E. Palmer. Indian Peoples of Canada. (Focus on Canadian History Ser.). (Illus.). (gr. 6-10). 1982. PLB 8.40 (ISBN 0-531-04570-6). Watts.
Paterson, J. Architecture & the Microprocessor. 229p. 1980. 51.95 (ISBN 0-471-27680-4, Pub. by Wiley-Interscience). Wiley.
Paterson, J. H. North America. 6th ed. (Illus.). 1979. text ed. 19.95x (ISBN 0-19-502484-2). Oxford U Pr.
Paterson, J. R. A Faith for the 1980s. 3.95x (ISBN 0-7152-0433-5). Outlook.
Paterson, James & Macnaughton, Edwin. The Approach to Latin. (Illus.). Pt. 1, 1938. text ed. 6.95x (ISBN 0-05-000292-9); Pt. 2, 1969. text ed. 6.95x (ISBN 0-05-000293-7). Longman.
Paterson, John. Information Methods: For Design & Construction. LC 76-29649. 1977. 39.95 (ISBN 0-471-99449-9, Pub. by Wiley-Interscience). Wiley.
--The Making of the Return of the Native. LC 77-18909. (University of California Publications English Ser.: No. 19). 1978. Repr. of 1963 ed. lib. bdg. 17.00x (ISBN 0-313-20064-5, PAMR). Greenwood.
Paterson, Josephine G. & Zderad, Loretta T. Humanistic Nursing. LC 75-40431. 1976. 19.95 o.p. (ISBN 0-471-66946-6, Pub. by Wiley Medical). Wiley.
Paterson, Katherine. Bridge to Terabithia. (Illus.). (gr. 10 up). 1979. pap. 2.25 (ISBN 0-380-43281-1, 62083-9, Camelot). Avon.
--Gates of Excellence: On Reading & Writing Books for Children. 128p. 1981. 10.00 (ISBN 0-525-66750-4, 0971-290). Lodestar Bks.
Paterson, Katherine, tr. see Yagawa, Sumiko.
Paterson, R. An Introduction to Ion Exchange. 1970. 29.95 (ISBN 0-85501-011-8). Wiley.
Paterson, Sally, jt. ed. see MacKay, Donald.
Paterson, Thomas. The Origins of the Cold War. 2nd ed. (Problems in European Civilization Ser.). 1975. pap. text ed. 5.95 (ISBN 0-669-91447-9). Heath.
Paterson, Thomas G. Major Problems in American Foreign Policy. 1978. Vol. 1. pap. text ed. 11.95x (ISBN 0-669-00475-8); Vol. 2. pap. text ed. 12.95x (ISBN 0-669-00476-6). Heath.
--On Every Front: The Making of the Cold War. 1979. 14.95x o.p. (ISBN 0-393-01238-7); pap. 5.95x (ISBN 0-393-95014-X). Norton.
Paterson, Thomas G. & Clifford, J. G. American Foreign Policy: A History. 2nd ed. 1983. Vol. I, 304. pap. text ed. 13.95 (ISBN 0-669-04567-5); Vol. II, 496. pap. text ed. 13.95 (ISBN 0-669-04566-7). Heath.
Paterson, Thomas G., et al. American Foreign Policy: A History. 1977. text ed. 20.95 (ISBN 0-669-94698-2). Heath.
Paterson, W. E. & Campbell, T. R. Social Democracy in Post War Europe. LC 73-88177. 64p. 1974. 20.00 (ISBN 0-312-73185-X). St Martin.
Paterson, William. Glimpses of Colonial Society & Life at Princeton College, 1766-1773, by One of the Class of 1763. Mills, W. Jay, ed. LC 72-179711. (Illus.). 182p. (Six songs). 1972. Repr. of 1903 ed. 34.00x (ISBN 0-8103-3810-6). Gale.
Paterson, William, jt. ed. see Kolinsky, Martin.
Patey, Carole. Early Stringed Instruments at the Victoria & Albert Museum. 1982. 49.00x (ISBN 0-686-98229-0, Pub. by HMSO). State Mutual Bk.
Pathak, N. N., jt. auth. see Ranjhan, S. K.
Pathak, Shankar. Social Welfare Manpower in North India. 180p. Date not set. text ed. price not set (ISBN 0-7069-1075-3, Pub. by Vikas India). Advent NY.
Pathy, T. V. Elura: Art & Culture. (Illus.). 190p. 1980. text ed. 25.00x (ISBN 0-391-01758-6). Humanities.
Patience, Allan & Head, Brian. From Whitlam to Fraser: Reform & Reaction in Australian Politics. (Illus.). 1979. text ed. 34.95x (ISBN 0-19-550580-8). Oxford U Pr.
Patient Care Magazine Editors. Medical Abbreviations Handbook. 200p. 1982. softcover 7.95 (ISBN 0-87489-309-7). Med Economics.
Patient Care Publications. Your Dog: An Owner's Manual. (Illus.). 128p. 1983. pap. 6.95 (ISBN 0-686-82185-8, 5704). Arco.
Patil, B. S. Civil Engineering Contracts & Estimates. (Illus.). 586p. 1981. pap. text ed. 20.00 (ISBN 0-86125-036-2, Pub. by Orient Longman Ltd India). Apt Bks.
Patil, P. G. Financial Issues for International Renewable Energy Opportunites: Supplement. (Progress in Solar Energy Ser.). 164p. 1983. pap. text ed. 15.50 (ISBN 0-89553-119-4). Am Solar Energy.
Patnaik, S. K. Student Politics & Voting Behaviour. 250p. 1982. text ed. 15.75x (ISBN 0-391-02757-3, Pub. by Concept India). Humanities.
Patnode, Darwin. A History of Parliamentary Procedure. 3rd ed. LC 81-86047. 85p. (Orig.). 1982. pap. 6.95x (ISBN 0-942302-00-1). Parliamentary Pub.
Patnode, Robert, jt. auth. see Hyde, R. M.
Patolichev, N. S. Measures of Maturity - My Early Life. (World Leaders Speeches & Writings). (Illus.). 320p. 1983. 50.00 (ISBN 0-08-024545-5). Pergamon.
Paton, Alan. Ah, But Your Land is Beautiful. 280p. 1983. pap. 4.95 (ISBN 0-684-17830-3, ScribT). Scribner.
--Instrument of Thy Peace. rev. ed. 128p. 1982. pap. 6.95 (ISBN 0-8164-2421-7). Seabury.
Paton, B. E., ed. Electroslag Welding. 2nd ed. (Eng.). 1962. 12.00 o.p. (ISBN 0-685-65942-9). Am Welding.
Paton, David & Goldberg, Morton F. Management of Ocular Injuries. LC 75-12492. (Illus.). 350p. 1976. 22.00 o.p. (ISBN 0-7216-7106-3). Saunders.
Paton, David M., ed. The Mechanism of Neuronal & Extraneuronal Transport of Catecholamines. LC 74-14477. 384p. 1976. 41.50 (ISBN 0-89004-014-1). Raven.
Paton, G. W., ed. see Paton, George Whitecross.
Paton, George Whitecross. A Textbook of Jurisprudence. 4th ed. Paton, G. W. & Dorham, David P., eds. 1972. text ed. 32.50 (ISBN 0-19-825314-1). Oxford U Pr.
Paton, Herbert J. Kant's Metaphysics of Experience, 2 Vols. (Muirhead Library of Philosophy). 1976. Repr. of 1961 ed. Set. text ed. 50.00x (ISBN 0-391-00673-8). Humanities.
Paton, John & Dell, Catherine. Rainbow Encyclopedia of Nature. (Illus.). 144p. (gr. 4-6). 1982. 9.95 (ISBN 0-528-82387-6). Rand.
Paton, John, ed. Children's Encyclopedia. LC 77-70935. (Illus.). (gr. 5-9). 1977. 7.95 o.p. (ISBN 0-528-82101-6); PLB 4.97 o.p. (ISBN 0-528-80206-2). Rand.
--Children's Encyclopedia of Science. LC 82-80678. (Illus.). (gr. 4-7). 1982. 9.95 (ISBN 0-528-82386-8). Rand.
Paton, T. R., tr. see Duchaufour, R.
Paton, W. D. & Crown, June, eds. Cannabis & Its Derivatives: Pharmacology & Experimental Psychology. (Illus.). 1972. text ed. 18.00x o.p. (ISBN 0-19-261115-1). Oxford U Pr.
Paton, William A. Accounting Theory. LC 73-84526. 1973. Repr. of 1962 ed. text ed. 20.00 (ISBN 0-914348-06-X). Scholars Bk.
Paton, William D., ed. see International Congress of Pharmacology, 7th, Reims, 1978. Satellite Symposium.
Paton Walsh, Jill. The Green Book. (Illus.). 96p. (gr. 5 up). 1982. 9.95 (ISBN 0-374-32778-5). FS&G.
Paton Walsh, Jill & Crossley-Holland, Kevin. Wordboard. LC 70-85364. 160p. (gr. 7 up). 1969. 3.95 o.p. (ISBN 0-374-38042-2). FS&G.
Patoski, Margaret, tr. see Von Bock, Maria P.
Patourel, John Le see Le Patourel, John.
Patra, H. P. & Mallick, K. Geosounding Principles II: Time Varying Geoelectric Soundings. (Methods in Geochemistry & Geophysics Ser.: Vol. 14B). 1980. 76.75 (ISBN 0-444-41811-3). Elsevier.
Patrick, Dale & Dugger, William E., Jr. Electricity & Electronics Laboratory Manual. rev. ed. (Illus.). 372p. (gr. 7 up). 1980. 5.28 o.p. (ISBN 0-87006-310-3). Goodheart.
Patrick, Dale R. & Fardo, Stephen W. Energy Management & Conservation. (Illus.). 304p. 1982. 25.95 (ISBN 0-13-277657-X). P-H.
Patrick, DeAnn. Kindred Spirits. (Tapestry Romance Ser.). 320p. (Orig.). 1982. pap. 2.50 (ISBN 0-671-46186-9). PB.
Patrick, Douglas. The Stamp Bug. 1979. 8.95 o.p. (ISBN 0-07-082779-6, GB). McGraw.
Patrick, Hugh & Rosovsky, Henry, eds. Asia's New Giant: How the Japanese Economy Works. 1976. 26.95 o.p. (ISBN 0-8157-6934-2); pap. 16.95 (ISBN 0-8157-6933-4). Brookings.
Patrick, J. Max & Sundell, Roger H. Milton & the Art of Sacred Song. LC 78-65014. 248p. 1979. 25.00 (ISBN 0-299-07830-2). U of Wis Pr.
Patrick, J. Max see Milton, John.
Patrick, Johnstone G. Under the Mistletoe. LC 73-102770. 1969. lib. bdg. 4.00 (ISBN 0-911838-03-1). Windy Row.
Patrick, Lynn, ed. see Savannah Junior Auxiliary.
Patrick, Maxine. The Abducted Heart. Bd. with Bayou Bride. 1981. pap. write for info. o.p. (ISBN 0-451-11220-2, 1220, Sig). NAL.
--The Abducted Heart. (Orig.). 1978. pap. 1.50 o.p. (ISBN 0-451-08094-7, W8094, Sig). NAL.
--April of Enchantment. (Orig.). 1981. pap. 1.75 o.p. (ISBN 0-451-09579-0, E9570, Sig). NAL.
--Captive Kisses. (Orig.). 1980. pap. 1.75 o.p. (ISBN 0-451-09425-5, E9425, Sig). NAL.
--Showbound Heart. LC 82-16753. 274p. 1982. Repr. of 1981 ed. 9.95 (ISBN 0-89621-392-7). Thorndike Pr.
--Snowbound Heart. 1979. pap. 1.75 o.p. (ISBN 0-451-08935-9, E8935, Sig). NAL.
--Snowbound Heart. Bd. with Captive Kisses. 1982. pap. 2.50 (ISBN 0-451-11748-4, AE1748, Sig). NAL.
Patrick, Pamela K. Health Care Worker Burnout: What It Is, What to Do About It. LC 81-38437. (Illus.). 140p. 1981. pap. 8.95 (ISBN 0-914818-07-4, Inquiry Bk). Blue Cross Shield.
Patrick, R. S. Color Atlas of Liver Pathology. (Color Atlases of Pathology Ser.). (Illus.). 192p. 1982. 75.00 (ISBN 0-19-921033-0). Oxford U Pr.
Patrick, R. S. & McGee, J. O. Biopsy Pathology of the Liver. (Illus.). 292p. 1980. text ed. 42.50 (ISBN 0-397-58267-6, Lippincott Medical). Lippincott.
Patrick, Ronald. Beyond the Threshold. 320p. (Orig.). 1980. pap. 2.50 o.p. (ISBN 0-523-41030-1). Pinnacle Bks.
Patrick, Ruth, ed. Diversity. (Benchmark Papers in Ecology Ser.: Vol. 11). 1982. cancelled. Acad Pr.
Patrick, W. B. Letter to the Ghosts. LC 77-17153. 53p. 1977. 3.50 (ISBN 0-87886-091-6). Ithaca Hse.
Patrick, Walton R. Ring Lardner. (U. S. Authors Ser.: No. 32). lib. bdg. 10.95 o.p. (ISBN 0-8057-0440-X, Twayne). G K Hall.
Patrick, Walton R., jt. auth. see Current-Garcia, Eugene.
Patrides, C. A., ed. The Cambridge Platonists. LC 79-28412. 376p. 1980. 49.50 (ISBN 0-521-23417-4); pap. 13.95 (ISBN 0-521-29942-X). Cambridge U Pr.
Patrides, C. A., ed. see Smith, John.
Patridge, David. Crimes of Passion. Repr. of 1947 ed. 25.00 o.p. (ISBN 0-89987-145-3). Darby Bks.
Patrie, James. The Genetic Relationship of the Ainu Language. (Oceanic Linguistics Special Publications Ser.: No. 17). 380p. (Orig.). 1981. pap. text ed. 7.50x (ISBN 0-8248-0724-3). UH Pr.
Patrignani, R., intro. by. Color Treasury of Motorcycle Competition. (Bounty Bk. Ser.). (Illus.). 64p. 1974. pap. 1.98 o.p. (ISBN 0-517-51433-8). Crown.
Patrikas, Elaine O., et al. Medical Records Administration Continuing Education Review. 1975. spiral bdg. 16.50 (ISBN 0-87488-369-5). Med Exam.
Patrono, Carlo, jt. ed. see Dunn, Michael J.
Patruno, Nicholas. Language in Giovanni Verga's Early Novels. (Studies in the Romance Languages & Literatures: No. 188). 128p. (Orig.). 1978. pap. 9.00x (ISBN 0-8078-9188-6). U of NC Pr.
Patsavos, L. J. & Charles, G. J. The Role of the Priest & the Apostolate of the Laity. Vaporis, N. M., ed. (Clergy Seminar Lectures Ser.). 63p. (Orig.). 1983. pap. 3.00 (ISBN 0-916586-57-X). Holy Cross Orthodox.
Patsis, jt. auth. see Parfitt.
Patt, Jerry, jt. auth. see Ladley, Betty A.
Patt, Richard. Psallite. (Psallite Ser.: Series A). 1977. pap. 2.95 o.p. (ISBN 0-570-03764-6, 12-2698). Concordia.
--Psallite-Series B. 1978. pap. 2.75 o.p. (ISBN 0-570-03784-0, 12-2738). Concordia.

Pattabhi Raman, M. Political Involvement of India's Trade Unions. 1967. 7.50x o.p. (ISBN 0-210-31197-5). Asia.

Pattanaik, Prasanta K. Voting & Collective Choice. (Illus.). 1971. 34.50 (ISBN 0-521-07961-6). Cambridge U Pr.

Pattaniak, P. Strategy & Group Choice. (Contributions to Economic Analysis: Vol. 113). 1978. 42.75 (ISBN 0-444-85126-7, North-Holland). Elsevier.

Patte, Daniel, ed. Semeia Eighteen: Genesis Two & Three: Kaleidoscopic Structural Readings. (Semeia Ser.). 9.95 (ISBN 0-686-96255-9, 06 20 18). Scholars Pr CA.

Patte, Daniel, tr. see Calloud, Jean.

Pattee, F. L., ed. see Brown, Charles B.

Patten, Bradley M. Early Embryology of the Chick. 5th ed. 1971. text ed. 13.50 o.p. (ISBN 0-07-048796-0, C). McGraw.

Patten, J. P. Neurological Differential Diagnosis: An Illustrated Approach. (Illus.). 1977. 44.90 (ISBN 0-387-90264-3). Springer-Verlag.

Patten, Lewis B. The Angry Horseman. large type ed. LC 82-10534. 233p. 1982. Repr. of 1960 ed. 9.95 (ISBN 0-89621-383-8). Thorndike Pr.

--Apache Hostage. Bd. with Law of the Gun. 1980. pap. 1.95 o.p. (ISBN 0-451-09420-4, J9420, Sig). NAL.

--Cheyenne Captives. 1979. pap. 1.50 o.p. (ISBN 0-451-08562-0, W8562, Sig). NAL.

--Death Rides a Black Horse. (General Ser.). 1979. lib. bdg. 11.95 (ISBN 0-8161-3001-9, Large Print Bks). G K Hall.

--Death Rides a Black Horse. 1979. pap. 1.50 o.p. (ISBN 0-451-08708-9, W8708, Sig). NAL.

--Killing in Kiowa: Feud at Chimney Rock. 1982. pap. 2.75 (ISBN 0-451-11425-6, AE1425, Sig). NAL.

--The Law in Cottonwood. LC 78-7764. 1978. 10.95 o.p. (ISBN 0-385-14448-2). Doubleday.

--Pursuit. 1980. pap. 1.75 o.p. (ISBN 0-451-09209-0, E9209, Sig). NAL.

--Red Runs the River. (General Ser.). 1983. lib. bdg. 12.50 (ISBN 0-686-42953-2, Large Print Bks). G K Hall.

--Redskin. Bd. with Two For Vengeance. 1982. pap. 2.75 (ISBN 0-451-11929-0, AE1929, Sig). NAL.

--Showdown at Mesilla-The Trial of Judas Wiley. 1982. pap. 2.50 (ISBN 0-451-11631-3, AE1631, Sig). NAL.

--The Trail of the Apache Kid. (General Ser.). 1980. lib. bdg. 10.95 (ISBN 0-8161-3130-9, Large Print Bks). G K Hall.

Patten, Marguerite. The Epicure's Book of Steak & Beef Dishes. (Illus.). 1979. 16.50 o.p. (ISBN 0-671-96139-X). Sovereign Bks.

--Marguerite Patten's Sunday Lunch Cookbook. (Illus.). 120p. 14.95 (ISBN 0-7153-8381-7). David & Charles.

--Patios & Pools. (Better Living Books Ser). (Illus.). 1970. pap. 2.50 o.p. (ISBN 0-600-02002-9). Transatlantic.

Patten, Thomas H., Jr. Manpower Planning & the Development of Human Resources. LC 76-137109. 1971. 59.59 (ISBN 0-471-66944-X, Pub. by Wiley-Interscience). Wiley.

--Organizational Development Through Teambuilding. LC 80-20726. 295p. 1981. 29.95 (ISBN 0-471-66945-8, Pub. by Wiley-Interscience). Wiley.

Patten, Thomas H., Jr., ed. Classics of Personnel Management. LC 79-4233. (Classics Ser.). (Orig.). 1979. pap. 12.50x (ISBN 0-935610-05-7). Moore Pub IL.

Pattenden, G. General & Synthetic Methods, Vol. 4. 388p. 1982. 125.00x (ISBN 0-85186-854-1, Pub. by Royal Soc Chem England). State Mutual Bk.

Pattern Jury Charges Committee, ed. Texas Pattern Jury Charges 1976 Cumulative Supplement, Vol. 2. LC 78-13954. 238p. includes supplement 50.00 (ISBN 0-938160-03-6, 6308). State Bar TX.

Patterson & Eisenberg. The Counseling Process. 3rd ed. 1982. pap. text ed. 12.95 (ISBN 0-686-84568-4). HM.

Patterson, A. M. German-English Dictionary for Chemists. 3rd ed. 1950. 28.50 (ISBN 0-471-66990-3, Pub. by Wiley-Interscience). Wiley.

Patterson, Angelo T., jt. auth. see Do Carmo, Pamela B.

Patterson, Archibald L. Public Pension Administration: Georgia & the Nation. 116p. (Orig.). 1982. pap. 9.50 o.p. (ISBN 0-89854-073-9). U of GA Inst Govt.

Patterson, Barbara & Dreger, Carol. The Successful Woman: Sharpening Your Skills for Personal & Professional Development. LC 82-7704. (Illus.). 252p. 1982. 15.95 (ISBN 0-13-875492-6); pap. 7.95 (ISBN 0-13-875484-5). P-H.

Patterson, Bennett B. Forgotten Ninth Amendment. 1955. 8.50 o.p. (ISBN 0-672-80034-9, Bobbs-Merrill Law). Michie-Bobbs.

Patterson, Bessie. The Wise Woman Knows. write for info. (ISBN 0-89137-422-1). Quality Pubns.

Patterson, Bob. Carl F. Henry, Makers of the Modern Theologcial Mind. 1983. pap. 6.95 (ISBN 0-8499-2951-2). Word Bks.

Patterson, Bob E., ed. see Williamson, William B.

Patterson, C. H. Theories of Counseling & Psychotherapy. 3rd ed. 1980. text ed. 25.95 scp (ISBN 0-06-045054-1, HarpC). Har-Row.

--The Wechsler-Bellevue Scales: A Guide for Counselors. 154p. 1953. photocopy ed. spiral 14.75x (ISBN 0-398-04383-3). C C Thomas.

Patterson, Charles H. Plato's Republic Notes. (Orig.). 1963. pap. 2.50 (ISBN 0-8220-1129-8). Cliffs.

Patterson, Clara E. How to Get Rid of Wrinkles. rev ed. LC 79-27184. (Illus.). 1980. 7.95 o.p. (ISBN 0-688-06546-5, Quill); pap. 2.95 o.p. (ISBN 0-688-03673-2, Quill). Morrow.

Patterson, Colin. Evolution. LC 77-78656. (Illus.). 1978. pap. 6.95x (ISBN 0-8014-9173-8). Cornell U Pr.

Patterson, David. Faith & Philosophy. LC 81-43469. 162p. (Orig.). 1982. pap. text ed. 9.25 (ISBN 0-8191-2651-9). U Pr of Amer.

Patterson, David, ed. Pigments: An Introduction to Their Physical Chemistry. (Illus.). 1967. 28.75 (ISBN 0-444-20009-6, Pub. by Applied Sci England). Elsevier.

Patterson, David, ed. see Goodman, Lenn E.

Patterson, Deryck S., jt. auth. see Barlow, Richard M.

Patterson, Donald F., jt. ed. see Desnick, Robert J.

Patterson, Dorothy, jt. auth. see Maca-Roueche, Suanne.

Patterson, E. M. Belfast & County Down Railway. (Illus.). 1982. 12.50 (ISBN 0-7153-8306-X). David & Charles.

Patterson, E. Palmer. Inuit Peoples of Canada. (Focus on Candian History Ser.). (Illus.). 96p. (gr. 6-10). 1982. PLB 8.40 (ISBN 0-531-04571-4). Watts.

Patterson, Ernest. Black City Politics. 308p. (Orig.). 1974. pap. text ed. 12.50 scp o.p. (ISBN 0-06-045058-4, HarpC). Har-Row.

Patterson, F. W. Manual De Finanzas Para Iglesias. (Illus.). 118p. 1980. pap. 2.50 (ISBN 0-311-17005-6). Casa Bautista.

Patterson, Frances. Motion Picture Continuities. Kupelnick, Bruce S., ed. LC 76-52120. (Classics of Film Literature Ser.). 1978. lib. bdg. 18.00 o.s.i. (ISBN 0-8240-2888-0). Garland Pub.

Patterson, Francine & Linden, Eugene. The Education of Kolco. LC 82-1325. (Illus.). 240p. 1983. pap. 7.95 (ISBN 0-03-063551-9). HR&W.

Patterson, Freeman. Photography of Natural Things. 164p. 1982. 26.95 (ISBN 0-7706-0020-4); pap. 15.95 (ISBN 0-7706-0022-0). Van Nos Reinhold.

Patterson, H. Robert, et al. Falconer's Current Drug Handbook: Nineteen Eighty to Nineteen Eighty-Two. LC 58-6390. 374p. 1980. pap. text ed. 11.95 o.p. (ISBN 0-7216-3572-5). Saunders.

Patterson, H. W. Small Boat Building. (Shorey Lost Arts Ser.). (Illus.). 164p. pap. 9.95 (ISBN 0-8466-6052-0). Shorey.

Patterson, Harry. Dillinger. 240p. 1983. 14.95 (ISBN 0-8128-2898-4). Stein & Day.

--To Catch a King. (General Ser.Bks.). 1979. lib. bdg. 12.95 (ISBN 0-8161-3011-6, Large Print Bks). G K Hall.

Patterson, Henry, jt. auth. see Bew, Paul.

Patterson, I. J. The Shelduck: A Study in Behavioural Ecology. LC 81-21231. 250p. 1982. 49.50 (ISBN 0-521-24646-6). Cambridge U Pr.

Patterson, J. G. Zola Dictionary. LC 68-27179. 1969. Repr. of 1912 ed. 34.00x (ISBN 0-8103-3173-X). Gale.

Patterson, J. W. & Zarefsky, David. Contemporary Debate. LC 82-82020. 356p. 1982. pap. text ed. 19.95 (ISBN 0-395-32641-9). HM.

Patterson, Jack, jt. auth. see Johnson, Don.

Patterson, James. The Jericho Commandment. 1979. 10.00 o.p. (ISBN 0-517-53626-9). Crown.

Patterson, James W. Wastewater Treatment Technology. LC 74-28653. (Illus.). 1975. 39.95 (ISBN 0-250-40086-3). Ann Arbor Science.

Patterson, Jane R., jt. auth. see Dorman, Daniel L.

Patterson, Jerry L. Blackjack: A Winners Handbook. 208p. 1982. pap. 6.95 (ISBN 0-399-50616-0, Perigee). Putnam Pub Group.

--Blackjack's Winning Formula. 91p. 1980. write for info. (ISBN 0-9605112-0-2). Casino Gaming.

--Blackjack's Winning Formula. (Illus.). 160p. 1982. 13.95 (ISBN 0-698-11151-6, Coward). Putnam Pub Group.

--Blackjack's Winning Formula. (Illus.). 160p. 1982. pap. 6.95 (ISBN 0-399-50617-9, Perigee); 13.95 (ISBN 0-698-11151-6). Putnam Pub Group.

--A Winner's Handbook. 1982. 12.95 (ISBN 0-686-98406-4, Coward). Putnam Pub Group.

Patterson, Jerry L. & Jaye, Walter. Casino Gambling: Winning Techniques for Craps, Roulette, Baccarat & Blackjack. 224p. 1983. pap. 6.95 (ISBN 0-399-50656-X, Perige). Putnam Pub Group.

Patterson, Katherine. Jacob Have I Loved. (YA) 1981. pap. 2.25 (ISBN 0-380-56499-8, 62521-0, Flare). Avon.

Patterson, Lewis P., jt. auth. see Eisenberg, Sheldon.

Patterson, Lillie. Birthdays. LC 65-21876. (Holiday Books Ser). (gr. 2-5). 1965. PLB 7.56 (ISBN 0-8116-6557-7). Garrard.

--Christmas Feasts & Festivals. LC 68-14778. (Holiday Books Ser). (Illus.). (gr. 2-5). 1968. PLB 7.56 (ISBN 0-8116-6562-3). Garrard.

--Christmas in America. LC 69-11077. (Holiday Books Ser). (Illus.). (gr. 2-5). 1969. PLB 7.56 (ISBN 0-8116-6563-1). Garrard.

--Christmas Trick or Treat. LC 78-11308. (First Holiday Ser.). (gr. 1-4). 1979. PLB 6.69 (ISBN 0-8116-7252-2). Garrard.

--Coretta Scott King. LC 76-19077. (American All Ser.). (Illus.). (gr. 3-6). 1977. lib. bdg. 7.12 (ISBN 0-8116-4585-1). Garrard.

--Easter. LC 66-10150. (Holiday Books Ser). (Illus.). (gr. 2-5). 1966. PLB 7.56 (ISBN 0-8116-6559-3). Garrard.

--Frederick Douglass: Freedom Fighter. LC 65-10154. (Discovery Books Ser.). (Illus.). (gr. 2-5). 1965. PLB 6.69 (ISBN 0-8116-6285-3). Garrard.

--The Grouchy Santa. LC 78-21936. (First Holiday Ser.). (Illus.). (gr. 1-4). 1979. PLB 6.69 (ISBN 0-8116-7254-9). Garrard.

--Halloween. LC 63-13626. (Holiday Books Ser). (Illus.). (gr. 2-5). 1963. PLB 7.56 (ISBN 0-8116-6552-6). Garrard.

--Haunted Houses on Halloween. LC 78-11382. (First Holiday Bks). (Illus.). (gr. 1-4). 1979. PLB 6.69 (ISBN 0-8116-7253-0). Garrard.

--The Jack-O'-Lantern Trick. LC 78-11307. (First Holiday Books). (Illus.). (gr. k-4). 1979. PLB 6.69 (ISBN 0-8116-7250-6). Garrard.

--Jenny, the Halloween Spy. LC 78-11538. (First Holidays Ser.). (Illus.). (gr. 1-4). 1979. PLB 6.69 (ISBN 0-8116-7251-4). Garrard.

--Martin Luther King, Jr: Man of Peace. LC 69-19152. (Americans All Ser). (Illus.). (gr. 3-6). 1969. PLB 7.12 (ISBN 0-8116-4555-X). Garrard.

--Sequoyah: The Cherokee Who Captured Words. LC 74-20966. (Indian Ser). (Illus.). 80p. (gr. 2-5). 1975. PLB 6.69 (ISBN 0-8116-6612-3). Garrard.

Patterson, Margaret C. Literary Research Guide. 2nd, Rev. ed. LC 82-20386. xxxiv, 559p. 1983. 25.00x (ISBN 0-87352-128-5); pap. 9.50x (ISBN 0-87352-129-3). Modern Lang.

Patterson, Margaret C., ed. Author Newsletters & Journals. LC 79-63742. (American Literature, English Literature, & World Literature in English Information Guide Ser.: Vol. 19). 1979. 42.00x (ISBN 0-8103-1432-0). Gale.

--Literary Research Guide. LC 75-13925. 1976. 38.00x (ISBN 0-8103-1102-X). Gale.

Patterson, Mary Ann, jt. auth. see Jackson, Sarah.

Patterson, Mavis, ed. Ladie's Choice. LC 82-5533. (Illus.). 96p. (Orig.). 1982. pap. 3.95 (ISBN 0-89621-066-9). Thorndike Pr.

Patterson, Miles, jt. auth. see Heslin, Richard.

Patterson, Morgan W. Baptist History Sourcebook. Date not set. 15.95 (ISBN 0-8054-6568-5). Broadman.

Patterson, N. S. Yearbook Planning, Editing, & Production. (Illus.). 1976. text ed. 9.95x o.p. (ISBN 0-8138-1805-2). Iowa St U Pr.

Patterson, Orlando. Slavery & Social Death: A Comparative Study. LC 82-1072. (Illus.). 544p. 1982. text ed. 30.00x (ISBN 0-674-81082-1). Harvard U Pr.

Patterson, P. G. & Pettit, D. G. Ciento Cincuenta Cosas Que Hacer Con Papel. Orig. Title: One Hundred & Fifty Things to Make with Paper. 64p. 1981. pap. 2.25 (ISBN 0-311-26604-5). Casa Bautista.

Patterson, Pat. After You've Said "I Believe". 1979. pap. 2.50 (ISBN 0-8423-0056-2). Tyndale.

Patterson, Paulina G. Animalitos Amigables. (Illus.). 32p. 1980. pap. 0.95 (ISBN 0-311-03602-3). Casa Bautista.

Patterson, Paulina G. De see De Patterson, Paulina G.

Patterson, Phillip D., ed. Recent Developments in Urban Gaming. (SCS Simulation Ser.: Vol. 2, No. 2). 30.00 (ISBN 0-686-36659-X). Soc Computer Sim.

Patterson, Robert. Pastoral Health Care: Understanding the Church's Healing Ministers. 15p. 1983. pap. 0.90 (ISBN 0-87125-080-2). Cath Health.

Patterson, Robert, jt. auth. see Mishara, Brian.

Patterson, Roger L. Overcoming Deficits of Aging: A Behavioral Approach. (Applied Clinical Psychology Ser.). 306p. 1982. 35.00x (ISBN 0-306-40947-X, Plenum Pr). Plenum Pub.

Patterson, Samuel, jt. auth. see Jewell, Malcolm E.

Patterson, Samuel C., jt. auth. see Loewenberg, Gerhard.

Patterson, Sarah. The Distant Summer. (gr. 7-9). 1977. pap. 1.95 (ISBN 0-671-44232-5). Archway.

Patterson, Sheila, tr. see Bauman, Zygmunt.

Patterson, Stella W. Dear Mad'm. (Illus.). 264p. 1982. lib. bdg. 11.95 (ISBN 0-87961-130-8); pap. 6.95 (ISBN 0-87961-131-6). Naturegraph.

Patterson, T. Archaeology: The Evolution of Ancient Societies. 1981. pap. 16.95 (ISBN 0-13-044040-X). P-H.

Patterson, Thomas. Wasatch Hiking Map. 1983. pap. 5.00 (ISBN 0-87480-220-2). U of Utah Pr.

Patterson, Thomas C. America's Past: A New World Archaeology. 168p. 1973. pap. 6.95x o.p. (ISBN 0-673-05273-7). Scott F.

Patterson, Thomas E. & McClure, Robert D. The Unseeing Eye: The Myth of Television Power in National Elections. LC 75-43834. 1976. 7.95 o.p. (ISBN 0-399-11693-1). Putnam Pub Group.

Patterson, W. F., tr. see Robertson, A. T.

Patterson, W. R. Colloquial Spanish. 4th ed. (Trubners Colloquial Manuals Ser.). 8.75 (ISBN 0-7100-4325-2); pap. 7.95 (ISBN 0-7100-6385-7). Routledge & Kegan.

Patterson, Ward. Wonders in the Midst. LC 78-62709. 96p. (Orig.). 1979. pap. 1.95 (ISBN 0-87239-237-6, 40076). Standard Pub.

Patterson, William F. Social Democratic Parties in Western Europe. Thomas, Alstair H., ed. LC 77-77314. 1977. 26.00x (ISBN 0-312-73175-2). St Martin.

Patterson, William T. The Genealogical Structure of Spanish: A Correlation of Basic Word Properties. LC 82-17597. 244p. (Orig.). 1983. lib. bdg. 22.50 (ISBN 0-8191-2791-4); pap. text ed. 11.00 (ISBN 0-8191-2792-2). U Pr of Amer.

Patterson, Y. God Made Birds. Mahany, Patricia, ed. (Happy Day Bks.). (Illus.). 24p. (ps-2). 1983. 1.29 (ISBN 0-87239-634-7, 3554). Standard Pub.

Patterson, Yvonne. Doubting Thomas. (Arch Bk.: No. 18). 1981. pap. 0.89 (59-1261). Concordia.

--My Happy Week. Sparks, Judith, ed. LC 81-86705. (Happy Day Bks.). (Illus.). 24p. (Orig.). (ps-3). 1982. pap. 1.29 (3588). Standard Pub.

--Nicodemus Learns the Way. (Arch Bks.). 1982. pap. 0.89 (ISBN 0-570-06152-0, 59-1266). Concordia.

--The Wise King & the Baby. LC 59-1258. (Arch Bk.: No. 18). (Illus.). (gr. k-4). 1981. pap. 0.89 (ISBN 0-570-06142-3). Concordia.

Patti, Archimedes L. Why Viet Nam? Prelude to America's Albatross. (Illus.). 632p. 1982. 19.50 (ISBN 0-520-04156-9); pap. 10.95 (ISBN 0-520-04783-4). U of Cal Pr.

Patti, Charles H. & Murphy, John H. Advertising Management: Cases & Concepts. Sutton, L., ed. LC 77-81538. (Advertising & Journalism Ser.). 325p. 1978. text ed. 22.95x (ISBN 0-471-86999-6); tchr's manual 12.25x (ISBN 0-471-87000-5). Wiley.

Patti, Rino, jt. ed. see Resnick, Herman.

Pattie, Alice, jt. auth. see Kreis, Bernadine.

Pattillo, J., jt. auth. see Joplin, B.

Pattillo, James W. Zero-Base Budgeting: A Planning, Resource Allocation & Control Tool. 83p. pap. 7.95 (ISBN 0-86641-042-2, 7796). Natl Assn Accts.

Pattis, Richard E. Karel the Robot: A Gentle Introduction to the Art of Programming. LC 80-26748. 106p. 1981. pap. text ed. 8.95 (ISBN 0-471-08928-1). Wiley.

Pattison, Barrie. The Seal of Dracula. (Illus.). 128p. 1975. pap. 2.95 o.p. (ISBN 0-517-52153-9). Crown.

Pattison, Bruce. Music & Poetry of the English Renaissance. LC 70-127278. (Music Ser). (Illus.). 1971. Repr. of 1948 ed. lib. bdg. 25.00 (ISBN 0-306-71298-9). Da Capo.

Pattison, Harry C. & D'Appolonia, Elio, eds. RETC Proceedings, Nineteen Seventy-Four, 2 vols. LC 74-84644. (Illus.). 1843p. 1974. Repr. of 1981 ed. 60.00x (ISBN 0-89520-024-4). Soc Mining Eng.

Pattison, J. B. A Programmed Introduction to Gas-Liquid Chromatography. 1973. 31.00 (ISBN 0-471-25950-0, Wiley Heyden). Wiley.

Pattison, J. Behrens, jt. auth. see UCLA Applied Health Professions Project.

Pattison, James. The Petronov Plan. 192p. 1980. pap. 1.95 o.p. (ISBN 0-523-40863-3). Pinnacle Bks.

Pattison, Mark. Essays & Reviews: Tendencies of Religious Thought in England. Jowett, Benjamin, ed. 434p. 1982. Repr. of 1861 ed. lib. bdg. 75.00 (ISBN 0-686-83993-5). Darby Bks.

Pattison, Polly. How to Design a Nameplate: A Guide for Art Directors & Editors. LC 81-86058. (Communications Library). 64p. 1982. pap. 18.00 (ISBN 0-931368-07-3). Ragan Comm.

Pattison, Robert. On Literacy: The Politics of the Word from Homer to the Age of Rock. LC 82-3547. 175p. 1982. 17.95 (ISBN 0-19-503137-7). Oxford U Pr.

Pattison, T. Harwood. Making of the Sermon. 1941. 16.95 (ISBN 0-8170-0096-8). Judson.

Pattison, Walter T. Benito Perez Galdos. (World Authors Ser.: Spain: No. 341). 1975. lib. bdg. 15.95 o.p. (ISBN 0-8057-2689-6, Twayne). G K Hall.

Pattison, Walter T. & Bleznick, Donald W., eds. Representative Spanish Authors, Vol. 1: From the Middle Ages Through the Eighteenth Century. 3rd ed. 1971. text ed. 20.95x (ISBN 0-19-501326-3). Oxford U Pr.

--Representative Spanish Authors, Vol. 2: The Nineteenth Century to the Present. 3rd ed. 1971. text ed. 22.00x (ISBN 0-19-501433-2). Oxford U Pr.

Patton, Bobby R. & Patton, Bonnie R. Female-Male: Living Together. (Interpersonal Communication Ser.). (Illus.). 1976. pap. text ed. 6.95 (ISBN 0-675-08643-4). Additional supplements may be obtained from publisher. Merrill.

Patton, Bobby R., et al. Responsible Public Speaking. 1982. pap. text ed. 13.95x (ISBN 0-673-15363-0). Scott F.

Patton, Bonnie R., jt. auth. see Patton, Bobby R.

Patton, Clifford W. The Battle for Municipal Reform: Mobilization & Attack, 1875 to 1900. LC 81-6541. (Illus.). 91p. 1981. Repr. of 1940 ed. lib. bdg. 18.75x (ISBN 0-313-22883-3, PABM). Greenwood.

Patton, Edward W. The Way into the Holiest: A Devotional Study of the Tabernacle in the Wilderness. 176p. 1983. pap. 4.95 (ISBN 0-8407-5833-2). Nelson.

Patton, George S. Speech of General George S. Patton to His Third Army. 1982. pap. 1.25 (ISBN 0-685-25503-4). Hope Farm.

Patton, George S., Jr. The Next War, Vol. 6. Province, Charles M., ed. (The Patton Ser.). 53p. (Orig.). 1980. pap. 2.00 o.p. (ISBN 0-932348-10-6). C M Province.

--Patton on Armor. Province, Charles M., ed. (The Patton Ser.: Vol. 8). 60p. 1980. pap. 2.00 o.p. (ISBN 0-932348-12-2). C M Province.

--Patton Principles. Province, Charles M., ed. (Patton Ser.: Vol. 1). (Illus.). 1978. pap. 3.00 (ISBN 0-932348-00-9). C M Province.

--Vintage Works by Patton. new ed. Province, Charles M., ed. 395p. (Orig.). 1982. pap. 50.00 (ISBN 0-932348-17-3). C M Province.

Patton, Grant W., jt. auth. see Kistner, Robert W.

Patton, Harry D., jt. ed. see Ruch, Theodore C.

Patton, James R., jt. auth. see Payne, James S.

Patton, John A. Indirect Labor Measurement & Control. 73p. 1980. wkbk. 60.00 (ISBN 0-89806-010-9); members 40.00. Inst Indus Eng.

Patton, Joseph D., Jr. Instructor's Resource Manual for Maintainability & Maintenance Management. LC 80-82118. 80p. 1980. pap. text ed. 6.00x (ISBN 0-87664-501-5). Instru Soc.

--Preventative Maintenance. LC 82-48557. 1982. text ed. 29.95x (ISBN 0-87664-718-2); pap. text ed. 19.95x (ISBN 0-87664-639-9). Instru Soc.

Patton, Marion & Sherwin, Mary. Know Your America, 2 vols. LC 80-2461. 1981. Set. 16.95 (ISBN 0-385-18503-0). Doubleday.

Patton, Mary A. Designing with Leather & Fur (Real & Fake) 1972. 8.95 (ISBN 0-8208-0346-4). Hearthside.

Patton, Michael J., jt. auth. see Pepinsky, Harold B.

Patton, Michael Q. Practical Evaluation. (Illus.). 320p. 1982. 25.00 (ISBN 0-8039-1904-2); pap. 12.50. Sage.

--Profile of Hazelden Patients Discharged in 1978. 1.95 (ISBN 0-89486-070-4, 1949B). Hazelden.

Patton, Peter C., jt. auth. see Thurber, Kenneth J.

Patton, Peter C. & Holoien, Renee A., eds. Computing in the Humanities. LC 79-3185. 416p. 1981. 30.95x (ISBN 0-669-03397-9). Lexington Bks.

Patton, Rob. Dare. LC 77-382. 51p. 1977. 3.50 (ISBN 0-87886-082-7). Ithaca Hse.

--Thirty-Seven Poems: One Night Stanzas. 51p. 1971. 2.95 (ISBN 0-87886-006-1). Ithaca Hse.

Patton, Sadie. The Story of Henderson County. LC 76-4904. (Illus.). 310p. 1976. Repr. of 1947 ed. 25.00 (ISBN 0-87152-233-0). Reprint.

Patton, Temple C. Paint Flow & Pigment Dispersion: A Rheological Approach to Coating & Ink Technology. 2nd ed. LC 78-10774. 1979. 72.00 (ISBN 0-471-03272-7, Pub. by Wiley-Interscience). Wiley.

Patton, Temple C., ed. Pigment Handbook, 3 vols. LC 73-529. 1973p. 1973. Set. 360.00 (ISBN 0-471-67127-4, Pub. by Wiley-Interscience). Wiley.

Patton, W. Construction Materials. 1976. 22.95 (ISBN 0-13-168724-7). P-H.

--Materials in Industry. 2nd ed. 1976. text ed. 23.95 (ISBN 0-13-560722-1). P-H.

--Mechanical Power Transmission. 1979. 19.95 (ISBN 0-13-569905-3). P-H.

Patton, Warren L. An Author's Guide to the Copywrite Law. LC 76-16329. 208p. 1980. 23.95 (ISBN 0-669-00740-4). Lexington Bks.

Patton, William J. Kinematics. (Illus.). 1979. text ed. 22.95 (ISBN 0-8359-3693-7); students manual avail. (ISBN 0-8359-3694-5). Reston.

Patty, Catherine. Basic Skills Career Exploration Workbook. (Basic Skills Workbooks). 32p. (gr. 9-12). 1983. 0.99 (ISBN 0-8209-0585-2, CEW-1). ESP.

--Basic Skills Encyclopedia Workbook. (Basic Skills Workbooks). 32p. (gr. 5-9). 1983. 0.99 (ISBN 0-8209-0537-2, UEW-1). ESP.

--Basic Skills Social Studies Workbook: Grade 3. (Basic Skills Workbooks). 32p. (gr. 3). 1982. wkbk. 0.99 (ISBN 0-8209-0398-1, SSW-D). ESP.

--Basic Skills Social Studies Workbook: Grade 4. (Basic Skills Workbooks). 32p. (gr. 4). 1982. wkbk. 0.99 (ISBN 0-8209-0399-X, SSW-E). ESP.

--Basic Skills Social Studies Workbook: Grade 6. (Basic Skills Workbooks). 32p. (gr. 6). 1982. wkbk. 0.99 (ISBN 0-8209-0401-5, SSW-G). ESP.

--Basic Skills Thinking Development Workbook. (Basic Skills Workbooks). 32p. (gr. 4-7). 1983. 0.99 (ISBN 0-8209-0584-4, TDW-1). ESP.

--Career Exploration. (Sound Filmstrip Kits Ser.). (gr. 5-8). 1981. tchrs ed. 24.00 (ISBN 0-8209-0440-6, FCW-17). ESP.

--Career Exploration. (Social Studies). 24p. (gr. 9-12). 1979. wkbk. 5.00 (ISBN 0-8209-0260-8, SS-27). ESP.

--Communications. (Social Studies). 24p. (gr. 5-8). 1979. wkbk. 5.00 (ISBN 0-8209-0250-0, SS-17). ESP.

--Community Spirit. (Social Studies). 24p. (gr. 3-5). 1976. wkbk. 5.00 (ISBN 0-8209-0251-9, SS-18). ESP.

--Comprehension Development. (Language Arts). 24p. (gr. 3-5). 1980. wkbk. 5.00 (ISBN 0-8209-0318-3, LA-4). ESP.

--Developing Citizenship. (Sound Filmstrip Kits Ser.). (gr. 3-6). 1981. tchrs ed. 24.00 (ISBN 0-8209-0439-2, FCW-16). ESP.

--Electricity. (Sound Filmstrip Kits Ser.). (gr. 3-6). 1981. tchrs ed. 24.00 (ISBN 0-8209-0437-6, FCW-14). ESP.

--The Healthy Body. (Sound Filmstrip Kits Ser.). (gr. 3-6). 1980. tchrs ed. 24.00 (ISBN 0-8209-0431-7, FCW-8). ESP.

--The Human Body. (Sound Filmstrip Kits Ser.). (gr. 3-6). 1980. tchrs ed. 24.00 (ISBN 0-8209-0428-7, FCW-5). ESP.

--Jumbo Science Yearbook: Grade 4. (Jumbo Science Ser.). 96p. (gr. 4). 1978. 14.00 (ISBN 0-8209-0025-7, JSY 4). ESP.

--Jumbo Social Studies Yearbook: Grade 3. (Jumbo Social Studies). 96p. (gr. 3). 1980. 14.00 (ISBN 0-8209-0075-3, JSSY 3). ESP.

--Jumbo Social Studies Yearbook: Grade 4. (Jumbo Social Studies). 96p. (gr. 4). 1981. 14.00 (ISBN 0-8209-0076-1, JSSY 4). ESP.

--Jumbo Social Studies Yearbook: Grade 6. (Jumbo Social Studies). 96p. (gr. 6). 1981. 14.00 (ISBN 0-8209-0078-8, JSSY 6). ESP.

--Learning to Listen. (Language Arts Ser.). 24p. (gr. 4-7). 1980. wkbk. 5.00 (ISBN 0-8209-0317-5, LA-3). ESP.

--Life's Senses. (Science Ser.). 24p. (gr. 4-8). 1979. wkbk. 5.00 (ISBN 0-8209-0152-0, S-14). ESP.

--The Orchestra. (Music Ser.). 24p. (gr. 5-9). 1977. wkbk. 5.00 (ISBN 0-8209-0273-X, MU-2). ESP.

--Using the Encyclopedia. (Language Arts Ser.). 24p. (gr. 5-9). 1979. wkbk. 5.00 (ISBN 0-8209-0313-2, UE-1). ESP.

Patty, Catherrine. Basic Skills Science Workbook: Grade 4. (Basic Skills Workbooks). 32p. (gr. 4). 1982. wkbk. 0.99 (ISBN 0-8209-0403-1, SW-E). ESP.

Patullo, Polly, jt. auth. see Mackie, Lindsay.

Paturau, J. M. By Products of the Cane Sugar Industry: An Introduction to Their Industrial Utilization. 2nd ed. (Sugar Technology Ser.: Vol. 3). 1982. 74.50 (ISBN 0-444-42034-7). Elsevier.

Patz. Nobody Knows I Have Delicate Toes. (gr. k-3). 1980. PLB 8.90 (ISBN 0-531-04096-8, C25). Watts.

Patz, et al. Sights & Sounds in Ophthalmology: Diseases of the Macula, Vol. 1. (Illus.). 1976. pap. 199.00 incl. 2 one-hr. cassettes & 100 35mm slides (ISBN 0-8016-3761-9). Mosby.

Patz, Alan. Strategic Decision Analysis: A Managerial Approach to Policy. 1981. text ed. 21.95 (ISBN 0-316-69400-2); tchrs'. manual avail. (ISBN 0-316-69401-0). Little.

Patz, Alan L. & Rowe, A. J. Management Control & Decision Systems: Text, Cases, & Readings. (Ser. on Management, Accounting & Information Systems). 1977. 30.95x o.p. (ISBN 0-471-67195-9). Wiley.

Patz, Arnall, jt. auth. see Fine, Stuart L.

Patz, Nancy. Moses Supposes His Toeses Are Roses: And Seven Other Silly Old Rhymes. LC 82-3099. (Illus.). 32p. (gr. 4-8). 12.95 (ISBN 0-15-255690-7, HJ). HarBraceJ.

Patzan, Flora, tr. see Bauman, Elizabeth.

Pau, Hans. Differential Diagnosis of Eye Diseases. Cibis, Gerhard W., tr. LC 76-1240. (Illus.). 1978. text ed. 50.00 (ISBN 0-7216-7117-9). Saunders.

Pauchet, Victor & Dupret, S. Pocket Atlas of Anatomy. 3rd ed. (Illus.). 1937. pap. 12.95x (ISBN 0-19-263131-4). Oxford U Pr.

Pauerstein, C. J., jt. auth. see Huff, R. W.

Pauk, Walter. Essential Skills Series, 20 bks. Incl. Bk. 1 (ISBN 0-89061-100-9, ESS1); Bk. 2 (ISBN 0-89061-101-7, ESS2); Bk. 3 (ISBN 0-89061-102-5, ESS3); Bk. 4 (ISBN 0-89061-103-3, ESS4); Bk. 5 (ISBN 0-89061-104-1, ESS5); Bk. 6 (ISBN 0-89061-105-X, ESS6); Bk. 7 (ISBN 0-89061-106-8, ESS7); Bk. 8 (ISBN 0-89061-107-6, ESS8); Bk. 9 (ISBN 0-89061-108-4, ESS9); Bk. 10 (ISBN 0-89061-109-2, ESS10); Bk. 11 (ISBN 0-89061-110-6, ESS11); Bk. 12 (ISBN 0-89061-111-4, ESS12); Bk. 13 (ISBN 0-89061-112-2, ESS13); Bk. 14 (ISBN 0-89061-113-0, ESS14); Bk. 15 (ISBN 0-89061-114-9, ESS15); Bk. 16 (ISBN 0-89061-115-7, ESS16); Bk. 17 (ISBN 0-89061-116-5, ESS17); Bk. 18 (ISBN 0-89061-117-3, ESS18); Bk. 19 (ISBN 0-89061-118-1, ESS19); Bk. 20 (ISBN 0-89061-119-X, ESS20). (gr. 3-12). 1976. pap. text ed. 3.20x ea; 20 bk. set (ISBN 0-89061-098-3). Jamestown Pubs.

--Getting the Author's Tone: Is He Humorous, Serious, Satirical? (A Skill at a Time Ser). 64p. (gr. 9-12). 1975. pap. text ed. 3.20x (ISBN 0-89061-024-X, ST-4). Jamestown Pubs.

--Getting the Main Point: Separating the Wheat from the Chaff. (A Skill at a Time Ser). 64p. (gr. 9-12). 1975. pap. text ed. 3.20x (ISBN 0-89061-026-6, ST-6). Jamestown Pubs.

--How to Read Factual Literature. LC 70-113589. 1970. Bk. 1, Levels 7-8. pap. text ed. 7.95 (ISBN 0-574-17061-8, 13-0061); Bk. 2, Levels 9-10. 7.95 (ISBN 0-574-17062-6, 13-0062); Bk. 3, Levels 11-12. pap. text ed. 7.95 (ISBN 0-574-17063-4, 13-0063); instr's guide 1.50 (ISBN 0-574-17065-0, 13-0065). SRA.

--How to Study in College. 2nd ed. LC 72-7923. 1974. pap. text ed. 9.95 (ISBN 0-395-17815-0). HM.

--Perceiving Structure: How Are the Ideas Organized? (A Skill at a Time Ser). 64p. (gr. 9-12). 1975. pap. text ed. 3.20x (ISBN 0-89061-030-4, ST-10). Jamestown Pubs.

--Perceiving the Author's Intent: What is the Author's Real Message? (A Skill at a Time Ser). 64p. (gr. 9-12). 1975. pap. text ed. 3.20x (ISBN 0-89061-029-0, ST-9). Jamestown Pubs.

--Reading Between the Lines: Drawing Correct Inferences. (A Skill at a Time Ser). 64p. (gr. 9-12). 1975. pap. text ed. 3.20x (ISBN 0-89061-025-8, ST-5). Jamestown Pubs.

--Recognizing Points of View: Whose Mind; Where's He Standing? (A Skill at a Time Ser). 64p. (gr. 9-12). 1975. pap. text ed. 3.20x (ISBN 0-89061-028-2, ST-8). Jamestown Pubs.

--Recognizing Traits of Characters: How Does the Author Build His Characters? (A Skill at a Time Ser). 64p. (gr. 9-12). 1975. pap. text ed. 3.00x (ISBN 0-89061-027-4, ST-7). Jamestown Pubs.

--Six-Way Paragraphs. (Illus.). 224p. (gr. 9 up). 1974. pap. text ed. 6.00x (ISBN 0-89061-009-6, 744). Jamestown Pubs.

--Six-Way Paragraphs, Advanced Level. (gr. 8-12). 1983. pap. text ed. price not set (ISBN 0-89061-303-6); price not set. Jamestown Pubs.

--Six-Way Paragraphs, Middle Level. (gr. 4-8). 1983. pap. price not set (ISBN 0-89061-302-8). Jamestown Pubs.

--Understanding Figurative Language: What Effect Did the Author Intend? (A Skill at a Time Ser.). 64p. (gr. 9 up). 1975. pap. text ed. 3.20x (ISBN 0-89061-023-1, ST-3). Jamestown Pubs.

--Using the Signal Words: Making Transitional Words Work for You. (A Skill at a Time Ser). 64p. (gr. 9 up). 1975. pap. text ed. 3.20x (ISBN 0-89061-022-3, ST-2). Jamestown Pubs.

--Vocabulary in Context: Getting the Precise Meaning. (A Skill at a Time Ser). 64p. (gr. 9 up). 1975. pap. text ed. 3.20x (ISBN 0-89061-021-5, ST-1). Jamestown Pubs.

Pauk, Walter & Wilson, Josephine M. How to Read Creative Literature. LC 76-109962. 1970. pap. text ed. 7.95 (ISBN 0-574-17050-2, 13-0050); instr's guide avail. (ISBN 0-574-17051-0, 13-0051); transparency masters avail. (13-0052). SRA.

Pauk, Walter, ed. see Conan Doyle, Arthur.

Pauk, Walter, ed. see Harte, Bret.

Pauk, Walter, ed. see Henry, O.

Pauk, Walter, ed. see London, Jack.

Pauker, Guy J., et al. Diversity & Development in Southeast Asia. LC 77-23441. (Nineteen Eighties Project, Council on Foreign Relations Ser.). 1977. text ed. 14.95 o.p. (ISBN 0-07-048917-3, P&RB); pap. 5.95 o.p. (ISBN 0-07-048918-1). McGraw.

Paukert, Felix, et al. Income Distribution, Structure of Economy & Employment: The Philippines, Iran, the Republic of Korea, & Malaysia. (Illus.). 170p. 1981. 32.00x o.p. (ISBN 0-7099-2006-7, Pub. by Croom Helm LTD England). Biblio Dist.

Paul, A. Chemistry of Glasses. 1982. 40.00x (ISBN 0-412-23020-8, Pub. by Chapman & Hall). Methuen Inc.

Paul, A., jt. auth. see Barron, J.

Paul, A. A. & Southgate, D. A. McCance & Widdowson's Composition of Food. 4th ed. 1978. 71.00 (ISBN 0-444-80027-1). Elsevier.

Paul, A. A., et al, eds. McCane & Widdowson's Composition of Food: First Supplement. 1981. 35.75 (ISBN 0-444-80220-7). Elsevier.

Paul, Aileen. Kids Cooking Without a Stove: A Cookbook for Young Children. LC 74-3553. 64p. (gr. 1-3). 1975. 7.95a (ISBN 0-385-03140-8); PLB o.p. (ISBN 0-385-03172-6). Doubleday.

--Kids' Fifty-State Cookbook. LC 76-2812. (gr. 3-7). 1976. PLB 7.95 o.p. (ISBN 0-385-11228-9). Doubleday.

--Kids Gardening. LC 73-177239. 96p. (gr. 3-7). 1972. 7.95 o.p. (ISBN 0-385-02492-4). Doubleday.

Paul, Aileen, Jr. Coloring Calendar Cookbook for Kids. Smith, James C., ed. (Illus.). 48p. (Orig.). (gr. 5 up). 1982. pap. 3.95 (ISBN 0-913270-90-3). Sunstone Pr.

Paul, Anthony. The Tiger Who Lost His Stripes. LC 81-83987. (Illus.). 32p. (gr. 2-5). 1982. 11.95 (ISBN 0-15-287681-2, HJ). HarBraceJ.

Paul, Anthony, jt. auth. see Barron, John.

Paul, Barbara. The Frenchwoman. 1977. 8.95 o.p. (ISBN 0-312-30537-0). St Martin.

--Liars & Tyrants & People Who Turn Blue. 192p. 1982. pap. 2.25 o.p. (ISBN 0-523-41607-5). Pinnacle Bks.

--Under the Canopy. 1980. pap. 1.95 o.p. (ISBN 0-451-09215-5, E9215, Sig). NAL.

Paul, Benjamin D., ed. Health, Culture & Community: Case Studies of Public Reactions to Health Programs. LC 55-10583. 494p. 1955. pap. 6.95x (ISBN 0-87154-653-1). Russell Sage.

Paul, Burton. Kinematics & Dynamics of Planar Machinery. (Illus.). 1979. text ed. 39.95 (ISBN 0-13-516062-6). P-H.

Paul, C. Kegan, tr. see Huysmans, Joris K.

Paul, Cecil & Lanham, Jan. Choices: In Pursuit of Holiness. 1982. pap. 3.95 (ISBN 0-8341-0807-0). Beacon Hill.

Paul, Charlotte. A Child Is Missing. LC 77-24469. 1978. 8.95 o.p. (ISBN 0-399-12072-6). Putnam Pub Group.

--Phoenix Island. 1976. pap. 2.50 o.p. (ISBN 0-451-09413-1, E9413, Sig). NAL.

Paul, Clayton R. & Nasar, Syed A. Introduction to Electromagnetic Fields. (Electrical Engineering "Electromagnetics" Ser.). (Illus.). 544p. 1982. 34.50x (ISBN 0-07-045884-7); instr.'s manual 8.00 (ISBN 0-07-045885-5). McGraw.

Paul, David M., tr. see Anger, Per.

Paul, David W. Czechoslovakia: Profile of a Binational Socialist Country. (Nations of Contemporary Eastern Europe Ser.). 128p. 1981. lib. bdg. 18.50 o.p. (ISBN 0-89158-861-2); pap. 9.50 o.p. (ISBN 0-86531-506-X). Westview.

Paul, Diana. The Buddhist Feminine Ideal: Queen Srimala & the Tathagatagarbha American Academy of Religion. LC 79-12031. (Dissertation Ser.: No. 30). 14.00x (ISBN 0-89130-284-0, 01-01-30); pap. 9.95 (ISBN 0-89130-303-0). Scholars Pr CA.

Paul, E. see Peterson, A.

Paul, E., et al. Elementary Particle Physics. (Tracts in Modern Physics Ser.: Vol. 79). (Illus.). 1976. 34.00 (ISBN 0-387-07778-2). Springer-Verlag.

Paul, E. V. Essays of Yesterday: A Collection of Literary Essays. 160p. 1983. text ed. 16.95x (ISBN 0-7069-1753-7, Pub. by Vikas India). Advent NY.

Paul, Edith De see De Paul, Edith.

Paul, Ellen F. Moral Revolution & Economic Science: The Demise of Laissez-Faire in Nineteenth Century British Political Economy. LC 78-73797. (Contributions in Economics & Economic History: No. 23). 1979. lib. bdg. 29.95 (ISBN 0-313-21055-1, PMR/). Greenwood.

Paul, Ellen F., jt. ed. see Jacobs, Dan N.

Paul, Elliot H. Life & Death of a Spanish Town. LC 79-138171. 1971. Repr. of 1937 ed. lib. bdg. 20.25x (ISBN 0-8371-5628-9, PAST). Greenwood.

Paul, Frances L. Kahtahah. LC 76-17804. (Illus., Orig.). (ps-8). 1976. pap. 7.95 (ISBN 0-88240-058-4). Alaska Northwest.

Paul, G. W., jt. auth. see Guiltinan, J. P.

Paul, Grace. Paramedical Careers: Your Future in the Allied Health Professions. LC 74-7669. 192p. (gr. 5 up). Date not set. 5.75 (ISBN 0-8255-7185-5). Macrae. Postponed.

Paul, Gunter. The Satellite Spin-Off. Lacy, Alan & Lacy, Barbara, trs. from Ger. LC 75-11369. Orig. Title: Die Dritte Entdeckung der Erde. 256p. 1975. 10.00 o.p. (ISBN 0-88331-076-7). Luce.

Paul, Hazel. Undersea. 1982. 14.95 (ISBN 0-316-35261-6, Pub by Atlantic Monthly Press Book). Little.

Paul, Henry. Binoculars & All Purpose Telescopes. (Illus.). 96p. 1980. 10.95 o.p. (ISBN 0-8174-3558-1, Amphoto); pap. 5.95 o.p. (ISBN 0-8174-3559-X). Watson-Guptill.

Paul, Henry E. Outer Space Photography. 4th ed. LC 67-21698. (Illus.). 160p. 1976. 10.95 o.p. (ISBN 0-8174-2407-5, Amphoto). Watson-Guptill.

--Telescopes for Stargazing. 3rd ed. LC 65-26425. (Illus.). 160p. 1976. 10.95 o.p. (ISBN 0-8174-2408-3, Amphoto). Watson-Guptill.

Paul, Hugo. Condominium Trap. LC 79-65558. 1983. 7.50 (ISBN 0-916620-36-0). Portals Pr.

Paul, Iain. Science, Theology & Einstein. (Theology & Scientific Culture Ser.). 1982. 13.95 (ISBN 0-19-520378-X). Oxford U Pr.

Paul, J., jt. auth. see Mills, K.

Paul, J. P. Computing in Medicine. 1982. 120.00x (ISBN 0-333-31886-2, Pub. by Macmillan England). State Mutual Bk.

Paul, James L. & Epachin, Betty C. Emotional Disturbance in Children: Theories & Methods for Teachers. 448p. 1982. pap. text ed. 18.95 (ISBN 0-675-09909-9). Merrill.

Paul, James L., jt. auth. see Epanchin, Betty C.

Paul, James L., jt. auth. see Rhodes, William.

Paul, James L., ed. The Exceptional Child: A Guidebook for Churches & Community Agencies. LC 82-16914. 176p. text ed. 22.00x (ISBN 0-8156-2287-2); pap. text ed. 12.95x (ISBN 0-8156-2288-0). Syracuse U Pr.

Paul, John. Modern Harpsichord Makers: Portraits of Nineteen British Craftsmen & Their Work. (Illus.). 280p. 1981. 50.00 (ISBN 0-575-02985-4, Pub. by Gollancz England). David & Charles.

Paul, Jordan & Paul, Margaret. Do I Have To Give Up Me To Be Loved By You. 204p. 1983. 12.95 (ISBN 0-89638-063-7); pap. 8.95 (ISBN 0-89638-064-5). CompCare.

Paul, Judith E., jt. auth. see Mills, Kenneth H.

Paul, Kathleen. Aries. (Sun Signs). (Illus.). (gr. 4-12). 1978. PLB 6.95 (ISBN 0-87191-641-X); pap. 3.25 (ISBN 0-89812-071-3). Creative Ed.

--Taurus. (Sun Signs Ser.). (Illus.). (gr. 4-12). 1978. PLB 6.95 (ISBN 0-87191-642-8); pap. 3.25 (ISBN 0-89812-072-1). Creative Ed.

Paul, Korkey, jt. auth. see Marshall, Ray.

Paul, Korky, jt. auth. see Marshall, Ray.

Paul, Louis. The Chosen Race. (Illus.). 111p. 1982. 6.95 (ISBN 0-9608890-1-9); pap. 4.96 (ISBN 0-9608890-0-0). L Paul Pub.

Paul, Margaret, jt. auth. see Paul, Jordan.

Paul, Margareta, tr. see Anger, Per.

Paul, Mimi F., jt. auth. see Liebing, Ralph W.

Paul, Oglesby, ed. Angina Pectoris. 135p. 1974. pap. 9.95 o.p. (ISBN 0-683-06789-3, Pub. by W & W). Krieger.

Paul, Paula G. Inn of the Clowns. 192p. (YA) 1976. 6.95 (ISBN 0-685-67081-3, Avalon). Bouregy.

Paul, Pauline C., et al, eds. Food Theory & Applications. LC 79-172953. 1972. text ed. 32.95 (ISBN 0-471-67250-5). Wiley.
Paul, R. Field Theoretical Methods in Chemical Physics. (Studies in Physical & Theoretical Chemistry: Vol. 19). 1982. 98.00 (ISBN 0-444-42073-8). Elsevier.
Paul, Richard P. Robot Manipulators: Mathematics, Programming, & Control. (MIT Press Artificial Intelligence Ser.). (Illus.). 300p. 1981. text ed. 27.50x (ISBN 0-262-16082-X). MIT Pr.
Paul, Richard S. & Haeusler, Ernest F., Jr. Algebra & Trigonometry: For College Students. (Illus.). 1978. 22.95 (ISBN 0-87909-031-6); instructor's manual free (ISBN 0-87909-032-4). Reston.
Paul, Richard S. & Shaevel, M. Leonard. Essentials of Technical Mathematics with Calculus. LC 77-17582. (P-H Ser. in Technical Mathematics). (Illus.). 1978. ref. ed. 27.95 (ISBN 0-13-289199-9). P-H.
Paul, Richard S., jt. auth. see Haelussler, Ernest F.
Paul, Roland A. American Military Commitments Abroad. 1973. 20.00 (ISBN 0-8135-0739-1). Rutgers U Pr.
Paul, Samuel. Strategic Management of Development Programmes: Guidelines for Action. International Labour Office, ed. (Management Development Ser.: No. 19). vii, 137p. (Orig.). 1982. pap. 10.00 (ISBN 92-2-103252-3). Intl Labour Office.
Paul, Sherry. Ancient Skyscrapers: The Native American Pueblos. LC 78-23992. (Famous Firsts Ser.). (Illus.). 1978. PLB 10.76 (ISBN 0-89547-064-0). Silver.
Paul, Virginia. The Homestead Cookbook: Pioneer Receipts, Remedies & Reminders. LC 76-16158. (Illus.). 1976. pap. 6.95 o.s.i. (ISBN 0-87564-340-X). Superior Pub.
Paul, W. & Moss, T. S., eds. Handbook on Semiconductors, Vol. 1: Band Theory & Transport Properties. 842p. 1982. 147.00 (ISBN 0-444-85346-4). Elsevier.
Paul, W. E., et al, eds. Annual Review of Immunology, Vol. 1. 1983. text ed. 27.00 (ISBN 0-8243-3001-3). Annual Reviews.
Paulaharju, Samuli. Arctic Twilight: Old Finnish Tales. Matson, Robert W., ed. Pitkanen, Allan M., tr. from Finnish. 1982. 10.00 (ISBN 0-686-36300-0). FALHF.
--Arctic Twilight: Old Finnish Tales. Matson, Robert W., ed. Pitkanen, Allan M., tr. from Finnish. 1982. 10.00 (ISBN 0-686-43312-2). Finnish Am Lit.
Paulaitis, Michael E. & Penninger, Johan M. L. Chemical Engineering at Supercritical Fluid Conditions. LC 82-71529. (Illus.). 600p. 1983. 39.95 (ISBN 0-250-40564-4). Ann Arbor Science.
Paulay, Thomas, jt. auth. see Park, Robert.
Paulden, S. How to Deliver on Time. 128p. 1977. text ed. 24.25x (ISBN 0-566-02075-0). Gower Pub Ltd.
Paulding, Hiram. Journal of a Cruise of the U. S. Schooner Dolphin in Pursuit of the Mutineers of the Whale Ship Globe. LC 77-119793. (Illus.). 1970. Repr. of 1831 ed. 7.50x (ISBN 0-87022-616-9). UH Pr.
Pauley, Steven. Technical Report Writing Today. 2nd ed. LC 78-69557. (Illus.). 1979. text ed. 16.95 (ISBN 0-395-27111-8); instr's. manual 0.50 (ISBN 0-395-27110-X). HM.
Pauli, L., jt. auth. see Brimer, M. A.
Pauli, W. Collected Scientific Papers, Vols. 1-2. 2451p. 1964. 102.00 (ISBN 0-470-67254-4, Pub. by Wiley). Krieger.
Pauli, Wolfgang. Pauli Lectures on Physics. Enz, C. P., ed. Marguilies, S. & Lewis, H. R., trs. Incl. Vol. 1. Electrodynamics. LC 76-155320 (ISBN 0-262-66033-4); Vol. 2. Optics & the Theory of Electrons. LC 72-7802 (ISBN 0-262-66034-2); Vol. 3. Thermodynamics & the Kinetic Theory of Gases. LC 72-7803 (ISBN 0-262-66035-0); Vol. 4. Statistical Mechanics. LC 72-7804 (ISBN 0-262-66036-9); Vol. 5. Wave Mechanics. LC 72-7805 (ISBN 0-262-66037-7); Vol. 6. Selected Topics in Field Quantization. LC 72-7807 (ISBN 0-262-66038-5). 1973. pap. text ed. 30.00x set (ISBN 0-262-66032-6); pap. text ed. 5.95x ea. MIT Pr.
Paulin, Keith, jt. auth. see Bruning, Ted.
Paulin, Tom. Liberty Tree. 80p. (Orig.). 1983. pap. 8.95 (ISBN 0-571-13025-9). Faber & Faber.
Pauling, Linus. No More War! (Illus.). 1983. pap. 7.95 (ISBN 0-396-08157-6). Dodd.
Pauling, Linus & Wilson, E. B., Jr. Introduction to Quantum Mechanics. (Illus.). 1935. text ed. 43.50 (ISBN 0-07-048960-2, C). McGraw.
Paulinus & Bartholomaeo, S. Dissertation on the Sanskrit Language. Rocher, Ludo, intro. by. (Studies in History of Linguistics Ser.: No. 12). xxviii, 224p. 1977. 30.00 (ISBN 90-272-0953-7). Benjamins North Am.
Paulist Editorial Committee, ed. Liturgy Constitution. 192p. 1964. pap. 1.95 (ISBN 0-8091-1620-0, 192, Deus). Paulist Pr.
Paullin, C. O. & Paxson, F. L. Guide to the Materials in London Archives for the History of the United States Since 1783. 1914. pap. 56.00 (ISBN 0-527-00687-4). Kraus Repr.
Paulos, John A. Mathematics & Humor. LC 80-12742. 1980. 12.95 (ISBN 0-226-65024-3, Phoen); pap. 4.95 (ISBN 0-226-65025-1). U of Chicago Pr.
Paulra, B. E., ed. System Dynamics & the Analysis of Change. 1982. 57.50 (ISBN 0-444-86251-X). Elsevier.
Pauls, Michael, jt. auth. see Facaros, Dana.
Paulsell, William O., ed. Sermons in a Monastery: Chapter Talks by Matthew Kelty Ocso, No. 59. (Cistercian Studies Ser.). 1983. p.n.s. (ISBN 0-87907-858-8); pap. p.n.s. (ISBN 0-87907-958-4). Cistercian Pubns.
Paulsen, jt. auth. see Kadish.
Paulsen, David, jt. auth. see Cederblom, Jerry.
Paulsen, Gary. Beat the System: A Survival Guide. 256p. (Orig.). 1982. pap. 3.50 (ISBN 0-523-41317-3). Pinnacle Bks.
--Compkill. 224p. (Orig.). 1981. pap. 2.25 o.p. (ISBN 0-523-48016-4). Pinnacle Bks.
--The Curse of the Cobra. LC 76-54275. (Illus.). (gr. 3-6). 1977. 10.65 o.p. (ISBN 0-8172-0928-X). Raintree Pubs.
--Dancing Carl. 144p. (gr. 5-7). 1983. 9.95 (ISBN 0-02-708480-9). Bradbury Pr.
Paulsen, Gary & Morris, John. Canoeing, Kayaking & Rafting. LC 79-15075. (Illus.). 160p. (gr. 7 up). 1979. PLB 7.29 o.p. (ISBN 0-671-32949-9). Messner.
--Hiking & Backpacking. LC 78-14535. (Illus.). 160p. (gr. 7 up). 1978. PLB 7.29 o.p. (ISBN 0-671-32899-9). Messner.
Paulsen, Gary & Peekner, Ray. The Green Recruit. LC 78-637. 1978. 6.00 (ISBN 0-8309-0202-3). Ind Pr MO.
Paulsen, Kathryn. The Complete Book of Magic & Witchcraft. rev. ed. 1980. pap. 2.25 (ISBN 0-451-09877-3, E9877, Sig). NAL.
Paulsen, Monrad G., jt. auth. see Kadish, Sanford H.
Paulsen, Timothy. Collection Techniques for the Small Business: A Practical Guide to Collection Overdue Accounts. 2nd ed. (Illus.). 112p. 1983. pap. write for info. (ISBN 0-88908-559-5). Self Counsel Pr.
Paulson, Arvid, tr. see Strindberg, August.
Paulson, Boyd C. & Barrie, Donald S. Professional Construction Management Control. (Construction Engineering Ser.). (Illus.). 1979. text ed. 39.00 (ISBN 0-07-003845-7, C); instr's manual 7.95 (ISBN 0-07-003846-5). McGraw.
Paulson, Elmer C. Facets of Frustration. 1983. 10.95 (ISBN 0-533-05561-X). Vantage.
Paulson, Gary D., jt. auth. see Dyer, Lee.
Paulson, Michael G. The Fallen Crown: Three French Mary Stuart Plays of the Seventeenth Century. LC 79-6812. 207p. 1980. text ed. 19.25 (ISBN 0-8191-0959-2); pap. text ed. 10.25 (ISBN 0-8191-0960-6). U Pr of Amer.
Paulson, Michael G., jt. ed. see Alvarez-Detrell, Tamara.
Paulson, Ronald. Book & Painting: Shakespeare, Milton, & the Bible. LC 82-2769. (Hodges Lectures Ser.). (Illus.). 280p. 1982. text ed. 19.95x (ISBN 0-87049-358-2). U of Tenn Pr.
--Representations of Revolution, 1789-1820. LC 82-13458. (Illus.). 416p. 1983. text ed. 29.95x (ISBN 0-300-02864-4). Yale U Pr.
--Rowlandson: A New Interpretation. (Illus.). 1972. 15.00 o.p. (ISBN 0-19-519711-9). Oxford U Pr.
Paulson, Ronald, jt. auth. see Bage, Robert.
Paulson, Ronald, ed. see Godwin, William.
Paulson, Ronald, ed. see Haywood, Eliza.
Paulson, Ronald, ed. see MacKenzie, Henry.
Paulson, Ross E. Women's Suffrage & Prohibition: A Comparative Study of Equality & Social Control. 160p. 1973. pap. 7.95x (ISBN 0-673-05982-0). Scott F.
Paulson, Terry & Delson, Joyce. Parents are People Too. Posner, Neil & Delson, Donn, eds. (Orig.). 1982. pap. write for info. (ISBN 0-9603574-4-0, A-5). Bradson.
Paulson, Walter G., et al. Planning a Corrugated Container Plant. 2nd ed. (TAPPI PRESS Reports Ser.). (Illus.). 117p. 1980. pap. 69.95 (ISBN 0-89852-387-7, 01-01-R087). TAPPI.
Paulston, Christina B. & Henderson, Robert T. Writing: Communicative Activities in English. (Illus.). 288p. 1983. pap. text ed. 9.95 (ISBN 0-13-970277-6). P-H.
Paulston, Roland G. Society, Schools & Progress in Peru. 336p. 1971. text ed. 25.00 (ISBN 0-08-016428-5). Pergamon.
Paulston, Rolland G. Conflicting Theories of Social & Educational Change: A Typological Review. LC 76-9951. 1976. pap. text ed. 3.95 (ISBN 0-8229-8252-8). U of Pittsburgh Pr.
--Educational Change in Sweden. LC 68-29907. (Illus.). 1968. text ed. 11.50x (ISBN 0-8077-1892-0). Tchrs Coll.
--Other Dreams, Other Schools: Folk Colleges in Social & Ethnic Movements. LC 78-21478. (Orig.). 1980. pap. text ed. 6.95 (ISBN 0-8229-8262-5, Pub. by U Ctr Intl St). U of Pittsburgh Pr.
Paulucci, Elizabeth. Cookbook from a Melting Pot. (Illus.). 288p. 1981. 11.95 (ISBN 0-448-16860-X, G&D). Putnam Pub Group.
Paulus, Andre. Civil Engineering in French. 192p. 1982. 90.00x (ISBN 0-7277-0138-X, Pub. by Telford England). State Mutual Bk.
Paulus, David A., jt. auth. see Gravenstein, J. S.
Paulus, Trina. A Diary of Hope & Love. (Illus.). 108p. 1983. 5.95 (ISBN 0-8245-0480-1). Crossroad NY.
Paul W. Van Der, Veur see The, Lian & Van Der Veur, Paul W.
Pauly, Reinhard G. Music in the Classic Period. 2nd ed. (History of Music Ser). 224p. 1973. pap. text ed. 13.95 (ISBN 0-13-607630-0). P-H.
Pauly, Thomas H. An American Odyssey: Elia Kazan & American Culture. 1983. write for info. (ISBN 0-87722-296-7). Temple U Pr.
Paunio, J. J. The New Theory of Cycles & of Economic Growth. (Illus.). 117p. 1980. deluxe ed. 67.85 (ISBN 0-918968-68-2). Inst Econ Finan.
--Theoretical Analysis of Growth & Cycles. (Illus.). 122p. 1974. 67.50 (ISBN 0-913314-38-2). Am Classical Coll Pr.
Paunio, W. W. The Static & the Dynamic Theory of Cycles. (A Managerical & Inventiveness Science Series Book). (Illus.). 109p. 1982. Repr. of 1924 ed. 87.85 (ISBN 0-89901-088-1). Found Class Reprints.
Pau On Lau, Estelle. Ellen C. Sabin: Proponent of Higher Education for Women. 1978. pap. text ed. 8.25 (ISBN 0-8191-0469-8). U Pr of Amer.
Pauson, P. L. Organometallic Chemistry. (Illus.). 1967. 19.95 o.p. (ISBN 0-312-58800-3). St Martin.
Paust, Jordan L. & Upp, Robert D. Business Law Text. 3rd ed. LC 78-23813. 928p. 1979. text ed. 23.95 (ISBN 0-8299-2019-6). West Pub.
Pautler, Albert J., Jr. Job Seeking Guide. LC 78-57903. 1979. pap. text ed. 7.20 (ISBN 0-8273-1771-9). Delmar.
Pauw, Linda G. De see De Pauw, Linda G.
Pavalko, Ronald M., ed. Sociology of Education: A Book of Readings. 2nd ed. LC 75-17322. 1976. pap. text ed. 11.50 (ISBN 0-87581-187-6, 187). Peacock Pubs.
Pavan-Langston, D., et al, eds. Adenine Arabinoside: An Antiviral Agent. LC 75-4087. 425p. 1975. 38.00 (ISBN 0-89004-024-9). Raven.
Pavelec, Barry J. & Kirschner, Stephen M. Take This Test. LC 80-972. 288p. 1980. pap. 6.95 o.p. (ISBN 0-8019-6924-7). Chilton.
Pavese, Cesare. American Literature: Essays & Opinions. Fussell, Edwin, tr. & intro. by. LC 70-101338. 1970. 23.50x (ISBN 0-520-01633-5). U of Cal Pr.
--A Mania for Solitude: Selected Poems. Crosland, Margaret, tr. 150p. 1982. 13.95 (ISBN 0-7206-5203-0, Pub. by Peter Owen). Merrimack Bk Serv.
--The Moon & the Bonfires. Ceconi, Marianne, tr. LC 75-25262. 206p. 1975. Repr. of 1953 ed. lib. bdg. 18.00x (ISBN 0-8371-8384-7, PAMB). Greenwood.
--Summer Storm. Murch, A. E., tr. 204p. 1982. 13.95 (ISBN 0-7206-8650-4, Pub. by Peter Owen). Merrimack Bk Serv.
Pavey, Peter. I'm Taggarty Toad. LC 80-16696. (Illus.). 32p. (ps-2). 1980. 9.95 (ISBN 0-02-770240-5). Bradbury Pr.
Pavey, Peter, illus. One Dragon's Dream. LC 79-12008. (Illus.). 32p. (ps-2). 1979. 9.95 (ISBN 0-02-770250-2). Bradbury Pr.
Pavitrananda, Swami, tr. see Pushpadanta.
Pavitt, Kate, jt. auth. see Pavitt, William T.
Pavitt, William. Book of Talismans, Amulets & Zodiacal Gems. pap. 5.00 (ISBN 0-87980-217-0). Wilshire.
Pavitt, William T. & Pavitt, Kate. Book of Talismans, Amulets & Zodiacal Gems. LC 72-157497. (Tower Bks). (Illus.). 1971. Repr. of 1914 ed. 45.00x (ISBN 0-8103-3901-3). Gale.
Pavka, John, jt. auth. see Corcoran, Eileen L.
Pavlic, Breda & Uranga, Raul R. The Challenges of South-South Cooperation. 450p. 1983. lib. bdg. 25.00x (ISBN 0-686-42948-6). Westview.
Pavlidis, George & Miles, Timothy R. Dyslexia Research & Its Applications to Education. LC 80-49975. 264p. 1981. 33.50 (ISBN 0-471-27841-6, Pub. by Wiley Interscience). Wiley.
Pavlidis, T. Algorithms for Graphics & Image Processing. (Illus.). 416p. 1982. 35.00 o.p. (ISBN 0-387-11338-X). Springer-Verlag.
Pavlik, Cheryl, ed. see Yorkey, Richard, et al.
Pavlik, Cheryl, jt. auth. see Cullup, Michael.
Pavlik, Milan & Uher, Vladimir. Dialogue of Forms: The Baroque Architecture of Prague. LC 74-21651. (Illus.). 1977. 17.50 o.p. (ISBN 0-312-19880-9). St Martin.
Pavlos, Andrew J. Social Psychology & the Study of Deviant Behavior. LC 78-65426. 1978. pap. text ed. 13.50 (ISBN 0-8191-0664-X). U Pr of Amer.
Pavlov, I. P. Lectures on Conditioned Reflexes. Gray, Jeffrey, ed. (Classics of Psychology & Psychiatry Ser.). 640p. 1983. Repr. of 1928 ed. write for info. (ISBN 0-904014-43-6). F Pinter Pubs.
Pavlovich, Natalie. Nursing Research: A Learning Guide. LC 77-22518. 266p. 1978. pap. text ed. 9.50 o.p. (ISBN 0-8016-3763-5). Mosby.
Pavon, jt. auth. see Francisco, Garcia.
Pavon, Francisco G. El Carnaval. (Easy Reader, B. Ser.). 96p. (Span.). 1981. pap. text ed. 3.95 (ISBN 0-88436-895-5, 70266). EMC.
--Los Carros Vacios. (Easy Readers, Ser. A). 48p. (Span.). 1976. pap. 2.95 (ISBN 0-88436-281-7, 70264). EMC.
Pavon, J., jt. auth. see Ruiz, H.
Pavoni, Joseph, et al. Handbook of Solid Waste Disposal: Materials & Energy Recovery. LC 74-26777. 566p. 1975. 31.00 (ISBN 0-686-78300-X). Krieger.
Pavoni, N. & Green, R., eds. Recent Crustal Movements. (Developments in Geotectonics: Vol. 29). 1976. Repr. 72.50 (ISBN 0-444-41420-7). Elsevier.
Pawelczynska, Anna. Values & Violence in Auschwitz: A Sociological Analysis. LC 76-3886. 1979. 17.95x (ISBN 0-520-03210-1); pap. 4.95 (ISBN 0-520-04242-5, CAL-479). U of Cal Pr.
Pawelek, S. & Otto, W. Introduction to Industrial Drafting. 1973. 7.96 o.p. (ISBN 0-02-824340-4). Glencoe.
Pawlak, Elizabeth A. & Hoag, Philip M. Essentials of Periodontics. 2nd ed. LC 80-13361. (Illus.). 174p. 1980. pap. text ed. 17.95 (ISBN 0-8016-3764-3). Mosby.
Pawley, Thomas D., jt. auth. see Reardon, William R.
Pawlicki, T. How to Build a Flying Saucer: And Other Proposals in Specultive Engineering. 1980. pap. 5.95 (ISBN 0-13-402461-3). P-H.
Pawlik, Peter S., jt. auth. see Reismann, Herbert.
Pawlikowski, John T. Catechetics & Prejudice. LC 72-94109. 160p. 1973. pap. 4.95 o.p. (ISBN 0-8091-1758-4). Paulist Pr.
--The Challenge of the Holocaust for Christian Theology. 39p. 1.95 (ISBN 0-686-74929-4). ADL.
Pawlowski, Robert. The Seven Sacraments & Other Poems. 52p. (Orig.). 1982. pap. 5.00 (ISBN 0-910655-00-6). Flower Mound Writ.
Pawsey, Margaret M. The Demon of Discord: Tensions in the Catholic Church of Victoria, 1853-1864. (Illus.). 200p. 1983. 25.00 (ISBN 0-522-84249-6, Pub. by Melbourne U Pr Australia). Intl Schol Bk Serv.
Pawson, David L. Molpadiid Sea Cucumbers (Echinodermata: Holothuroidea) of the Antarctic Seas: Paper 3 in Biology of the Antarctic Seas VI. LC 77-2320. (Antarctic Research Ser.: Vol. 26). 1977. pap. 10.70 (ISBN 0-87590-131-X). Am Geophysical.
Pawson, David L., ed. see Heron, Gayle A.
Pawson, David L., ed. see Lamb, I. Mackenzie & Zimmerman, Martin H.
Pawson, David L., ed. see Lowry, James K.
Pawson, David L., ed. see Schultz, George A.
Pawson, David L., ed. see Tibbs, John F.
Paxson, F. L., jt. auth. see Paullin, C. O.
Paxson, Frederic L. History of the American Frontier: 1763-1893. LC 24-23381. (Illus.). 1964. 14.95 (ISBN 0-910220-21-2). Berg.
Paxson, Ruth. Life on the Highest Plane, 3 Vols. 512p. 1983. Repr. of 1928 ed. 15.95 (ISBN 0-8010-7074-0). Baker Bk.
--Rios De Agua Viva. 96p. 1979. pap. 1.95 (ISBN 0-311-46065-8). Casa Bautista.
--Rivers of Living Water. pap. 2.95 (ISBN 0-8024-7367-9). Moody.
Paxton, Albert. National Repair & Remodeling Estimator 1982. 208p. 1981. pap. 10.25 o.p. (ISBN 0-910460-32-9). Craftsman.
Paxton, Albert S. National Repair & Remodeling Estimator 1983. 240p. (Orig.). 1982. pap. 15.25 (ISBN 0-910460-97-3). Craftsman.
Paxton, Geoffrey J. El Zarandeo Del Adventismo. Orig. Title: The Shaking of Adventism. 172p. (Span.). 1982. pap. 5.75 (ISBN 0-311-05604-0, Edit Mundo). Casa Bautista.
Paxton, H. W., jt. auth. see Bain, E. C.
Paxton, J. M., ed. Manual of Civil Engineering Plant & Equipment. 2nd ed. (Illus.). 1971. 123.00 (ISBN 0-85334-500-7, Pub. by Applied Sci England). Elsevier.
Paxton, Jeremy & Harris, Robert. A Higher Form of Killing: The Secret Story of Gas & Germ Warfare. (Illus.). 1983. pap. 7.25 (ISBN 0-8090-1425-4). Hill & Wang.
Paxton, John. A Dictionary of the European Communities. 2nd ed. LC 82-10375. 290p. 1982. 27.50x (ISBN 0-312-20099-4). St Martin.
--World Legislatures. LC 74-24740. 192p. 1975. 25.00 (ISBN 0-312-89145-8). St Martin.
Paxton, John, jt. auth. see Walsh, A. E.
Paxton, John, ed. Statesman's Year-Book World Gazetteer. 2nd ed. (Illus.). 800p. 1980. 25.00x (ISBN 0-312-76126-0). St Martin.
--The Statesman's Year-Book, 1982-1983. LC 4-3776. 1700p. 1982. 35.00x (ISBN 0-312-76097-3). St Martin.
--Statesman's Yearbook World Gazetteer. LC 74-16097. 1975. 15.00 o.p. (ISBN 0-312-76125-2). St Martin.
Paxton, Robert O., jt. auth. see Marrus, Michael R.
Payack, Peter. Rainbow Bridges. 1978. pap. 1.00x o.p. (ISBN 0-686-07205-7). Samisdat.
Payer, Cheryl. The World Bank: A Critical Analysis. LC 81-84738. 1982. 22.00 (ISBN 0-85345-601-1, CL6011). Monthly Rev.
Payer, I. B. Traite D'organogenie Comparee de la Fleur. Repr. of 1857 ed. 80.00 (ISBN 3-7682-0346-8). Lubrecht & Cramer.
Payer, Pierre J., tr. see Damian, Peter.
Paykel, E. S., ed. Handbook of Affective Disorders. LC 82-1049. 457p. 1982. 50.00 (ISBN 0-89862-622-6). Guilford Pr.
Paykel, E. S. & Coppen, A., eds. Psychopharmacology of Affective Disorders. (Illus.). 1979. pap. text ed. 17.95x (ISBN 0-19-261278-6). Oxford U Pr.
Paykel, E. S., ed. see Youdim, M. B. H.
Paylor, Neil & Head, Barry. Sciences From A Divorce: A Book for Friends & Relatives of a Divorcing Family. 120p. 1983. pap. 6.95 (ISBN 0-86683-635-7). Winston Pr.

Payne, A. J. The Politics of the Caribbean Community, 1961-79: Regional Integration Among New States. LC 80-10500. 1980. 26.00 (ISBN 0-312-62874-9). St Martin.

Payne, A. R., jt. auth. see Freakley, P. K.

Payne, Albert V., jt. auth. see Olivo, C. Thomas.

Payne, Anthony. Social Behaviour in Vertebrates. (Scholarship Series in Biology). 1976. text ed. 12.95x o.p. (ISBN 0-435-61670-6). Heinemann Ed.

Payne, C. J. & White, K. J., eds. Caring for Deprived Children: International Case Studies of Residential Setting. 1979. 25.00 (ISBN 0-312-12166-0). St Martin.

Payne, Charles A. & Falls, William R. Modern Physical Science: A Student Study Guide. 1976. pap. text ed. 5.95 (ISBN 0-8403-1364-0). Kendall-Hunt.

Payne, Charlotte. The Glitterati. LC 79-28638. 352p. 1980. 10.95 o.p. (ISBN 0-688-03632-5). Morrow.

Payne, Clive, jt. auth. see O'Muircheartaigh, Colm A.

Payne, Cril. Deep Cover. Gilbert, Herbert, ed. LC 79-51632. 1979. 11.95 o.p. (ISBN 0-88225-274-7). Newsweek.

Payne, Daniel H. A Guide to Resort Time Sharing. Friedman, Robert S., ed. LC 82-19798. 300p. (Orig.). 1983. pap. 7.95 (ISBN 0-89865-274-X). Donning Co.

Payne, Darwin R. Design for the Stage: First Steps. LC 74-3090. (Illus.). 285p. 1974. pap. 7.95x o.p. (ISBN 0-8093-0669-7). S Ill U Pr.

--Materials & Craft of the Scenic Model. LC 76-15230. (Illus.). 128p. 1976. pap. text ed. 7.95 (ISBN 0-8093-0783-9). S Ill U Pr.

Payne, Darwin R., jt. ed. see Moe, Christian.

Payne, David A. The Assessment of Learning: Cognitive & Affective. 1974. text ed. 16.95 o.p. (ISBN 0-669-85209-0). Heath.

Payne, David A., ed. Specification & Measurement of Learning Outcomes. (Education & Psychology Ser). (Orig.). 1960. pap. 16.95 (ISBN 0-471-00413-8). Wiley.

Payne, David F. First & Second Samuel. LC 82-16009. (The Daily Study Bible Ser.). 320p. 1983. 12.95 (ISBN 0-664-21806-7); pap. 6.95 (ISBN 0-664-24573-0). Westminster.

Payne, David L. Nasalidad En Aguaruna. (Serie Linguistica Peruana: No. 15). 1976. pap. 2.75x (ISBN 0-88312-790-3); microfiche 1.50 (ISBN 0-88312-333-9). Summer Inst Ling.

--The Phonology & Morphology of Axininca Campa. Poulter, Virgil L., ed. LC 81-52739. (Publications in Linguistics: No. 66). (Illus.). 285p. 1981. pap. text ed. 11.95x (ISBN 0-88312-084-4); microfiche 3.00. Summer Inst Ling.

Payne, Donald. IBM BASIC. 200p. 1983. 22.95 (ISBN 0-13-448696-X); pap. 15.95 (ISBN 0-13-448688-9). P-H.

Payne, Dorothy. Life after Divorce. 24p. (Orig.). 1982. pap. 1.25 booklet (ISBN 0-8298-0610-5). Pilgrim NY.

Payne, E. A. & Payne, W. F. Easily Applied Principles of Keypunching. LC 72-118315. 1970. text ed. 15.95 (ISBN 0-13-222703-7). P-H.

Payne, E. F., ed. see Schopenhauer, Arthur.

Payne, E. F., tr. see Schopenhauer, Arthur.

Payne, E. M. F., jt. auth. see Godman, A.

Payne, Elizabeth. Meet the North American Indians. (Step-up Books Ser). (Illus.). (gr. 2-6). 1965. 4.95 (ISBN 0-394-80060-5, BYR); PLB 4.99 o.p. (ISBN 0-394-90060-X). Random.

--Meet the Pilgrim Fathers. (Step-up Books Ser). (Illus.). (gr. 4 up). 1966. PLB 5.99 (ISBN 0-394-90063-4, BYR). Random.

Payne, Eugene E., et al. The Scope of Management Information Systems. 1975. pap. text ed. 12.00 (ISBN 0-89806-014-1, 45); pap. text ed. 6.00 members. Inst Indus Eng.

Payne, F. Anne. Chaucer & Menippean Satire. LC 79-5412. 304p. 1981. 27.50 (ISBN 0-299-08170-2). U of Wis Pr.

Payne, F. William, ed. see Association of Energy Engineers.

Payne, George H. History of Journalism in the United States. Repr. of 1920 ed. lib. bdg. 19.00x (ISBN 0-8371-2817-X, PAJU). Greenwood.

Payne, H. F. Organic Coating Technology, 2 Vols. LC 54-5971. 1954-61. Vol. 1. 65.00 (ISBN 0-471-67286-6); Vol. 2. 72.00 (ISBN 0-471-67353-6, Pub by Wiley-Interscience). Wiley.

Payne, Harry, ed. Studies in Eighteenth-Century Culture, Vol. 12. (SECC Ser.). (Illus.). 256p. 1983. text ed. 25.00 (ISBN 0-299-09270-4). U of Wis Pr.

Payne, Howard E. & Callahan, Raymond. As the Storm Clouds Gathered: European Perceptions of American Foreign Policy in the 1930's. LC 78-7074. 173p. 1980. 15.95x (ISBN 0-941690-06-7); pap. 9.95x (ISBN 0-87716-101-1); pap. text ed. 5.95x (ISBN 0-686-84004-6). Regina Bks.

Payne, J. A. Introduction to Simulation. 1982. 31.95 (ISBN 0-07-048945-9). McGraw.

Payne, J. H. Unit Operations in Cane Sugar Production. (Sugar Ser.: No. 4). 204p. 1982. 51.00 (ISBN 0-444-42104-1). Elsevier.

Payne, J. P. & Hill, D. W. Oxygen Measurement in Biology & Medicine. 1975. 64.95 o.p. (ISBN 0-407-00020-8). Butterworth.

Payne, J. W. Microorganisms & Nitrogen Sources Transport & Utilization of Amino Acids Peptides, Proteins & Related Subjects. LC 79-42900. 870p. 1980. 149.95 (ISBN 0-471-27697-9). Wiley.

Payne, James L. The American Threat. LC 81-805401. 1981. pap. text ed. 10.95x (ISBN 0-915728-07-9). Lytton Pub.

Payne, James R., jt. auth. see Jordan, Randolph E.

Payne, James S. & Kauffman, James M. Exceptional Children in Focus. 160p. 1983. pap. text ed. 10.95 (ISBN 0-675-20041-5). Merrill.

Payne, James S. & Patton, James R. Mental Retardation. (Special Education Ser.). (Illus.). 480p. 1981. text ed. 23.95 (ISBN 0-675-08027-4). Additional supplements may be obtained from publisher. Merrill.

Payne, James S., et al. Strategies for Teaching the Mentally Retarded. 2nd ed. (Special Education Ser.). 368p. 1981. text ed. 19.95 (ISBN 0-675-08067-3). Merrill.

Payne, K. W., jt. auth. see Albone, D. J.

Payne, Keith B. Nuclear Deterrence in U.S. Soviet Relations. replica ed. (Illus.). 265p. 1982. soft cover 20.00 (ISBN 0-86531-903-0). Westview.

Payne, Keith B., ed. Laser Weapons in Space: Policy Issues. (Replica). 150p. 1982. softcover 17.00 (ISBN 0-86531-937-5). Westview.

Payne, L. E. Improperly Posed Problems in Partial Differential Equations. (CBMS Regional Conference Ser.: Vol. 22). v, 76p. (Orig.). 1975. pap. text ed. 9.50 (ISBN 0-89871-019-7). Soc Indus-Appl Math.

Payne, Leanne. Real Presence: The Holy Spirt in the Works of C. S. Lewis. LC 78-71945. 183p. 1979. pap. 5.95 (ISBN 0-89107-164-4). Crossway Bks.

Payne, Lucille V. Lively Art of Writing. pap. 2.95 (ISBN 0-451-62161-1, ME2161, Ment). NAL.

Payne, Oliver. Defiance. (Northwest Territory Ser.: Bk. 3). 448p. (Orig.). 1983. pap. 3.50 (ISBN 0-425-05846-8). Berkley Pub.

--Warpath. (Northwest Territory Ser.: No. 1). 432p. (Orig.). 1982. pap. 3.50 (ISBN 0-425-05738-0). Berkley Pub.

Payne, P. A., jt. auth. see Marks, R.

Payne, R., jt. auth. see Cooper, C. L.

Payne, Richard. How to Get a Better Job Quicker. 1975. pap. 2.95 (ISBN 0-451-62094-1, ME2094, Men). NAL.

--Unfinished Democracy: Study Guide. 1981. pap. 7.95x (ISBN 0-673-15487-4). Scott F.

Payne, Richard A. How to Get a Better Job Quicker. rev. ed. 1980. pap. 2.95 (ISBN 0-451-62094-1, ME2094, Ment). NAL.

Payne, Robert. By Me, William Shakespeare. LC 79-512031. (Illus.). 1980. 15.95 (ISBN 0-89696-064-1, An Everest House Book). Dodd.

--Cairo Countdown. (Able Team Ser.). 192p. 1983. pap. 1.95 (ISBN 0-373-61205-2, Pub. by Worldwide). Harlequin Bks.

--Cairo Countdown. (Able Team Ser.). 192p. 1983. pap. 1.95 (ISBN 0-686-38764-3, Pub. by Worldwide). Harlequin Bks.

--The Life & Death of Trotsky. LC 77-7523. (Illus.). 1977. 14.95 o.p. (ISBN 0-07-048940-8, GB). McGraw.

--Warlord of Azatlan. (Able Team Ser.). 192p. 1983. pap. 2.25 (ISBN 0-373-61206-0, Pub. by Worldwide). Harlequin Bks.

Payne, Robert B. Behavior, Mimetic Songs & Song Dialects, & Relationships of the Parasitic Indigobirds (Vidua) of Africa. 333p. 1973. 12.50 (ISBN 0-943610-11-7). Am Ornithologists.

Payne, Robert O. The Key of Remembrance, a Study of Chaucer's Poetics. LC 72-12316. 246p. 1973. Repr. of 1963 ed. lib. bdg. 20.50 (ISBN 0-8371-6694-2, PAKR). Greenwood.

Payne, Rolce R. New England Gardens Open to the Public. LC 78-66191. (Godine Guides: No. II). (Illus.). 1979. 20.00 (ISBN 0-87923-271-4); pap. 10.00 (ISBN 0-87923-272-2). Godine.

Payne, Ronald, jt. auth. see Dobson, Christopher.

Payne, Roy, jt. auth. see Cooper, Cary L.

Payne, Roy & Cooper, Cary L., eds. Groups at Work: Wiley Series on Individuals, Groups & Organizations. LC 80-41586. (Wiley Ser. on Individuals, Groups & Organizations). 280p. 1981. 34.95 (ISBN 0-471-27934-X, Pub by Wiley-Interscience). Wiley.

Payne, Samuel B., Jr. The Soviet Union & SALT. 224p. 1980. text ed. 22.50x (ISBN 0-262-16077-3). MIT Pr.

Payne, Sherry. Wind & Water Energy. (A Look Inside Ser.). (Illus.). 48p. (gr. 4 up). 1983. PLB 14.25 (ISBN 0-8172-1418-6). Raintree Pubs.

Payne, Stanley G. Fascism: A Comparative Approach Toward a Definition. LC 79-5413. 248p. 1980. 18.75 (ISBN 0-299-08060-9). U of Wis Pr.

--Fascism: A Comparative Approach Toward a Definition. LC 79-5415. 248p. 1983. pap. 6.95 (ISBN 0-299-08064-1). U of Wis Pr.

Payne, Stephen J., jt. ed. see Green, Thomas.

Payne, Suzzy C. & Murwin, Susan A. Creative American Quilting Inspired by the Bible. (Illus.). 192p. 1982. 24.95 (ISBN 0-8007-1322-2). Revell.

Payne, Suzzy C., jt. auth. see Murwin, Susan A.

Payne, Thomas. Quantitative Techniques for Management: A Practical Approach. (Illus.). 464p. 1982. pap. text ed. 19.95 (ISBN 0-8359-6116-8); pap. text ed. 8.95 calculator manual (ISBN 0-8359-6118-4); instrs'. manual avail. (ISBN 0-8359-6117-6); sample package avail. (ISBN 0-8359-6119-2). Reston.

Payne, W. F., jt. auth. see Payne, E. A.

Payne, W. J. Denitrification. LC 81-3363. 214p. 1981. 35.00 (ISBN 0-471-04764-3, Pub. by Wiley-Interscience). Wiley.

Payne, William F. Creative Financing for Energy Conservation. (Illus.). 250p. 1983. text ed. 36.00 (ISBN 0-915586-69-X). Fairmont Pr.

Payne-Gaposchkin, Cecilia, ed. see Baade, Walter.

Paynell, T., tr. see Erasmus, Desiderius.

Paynell, Thomas, tr. see Erasmus, Desiderius.

Paynter, Elizabeth, ed. see Meyer-Denkmann, Gertrud.

Paynter, J. & Aston, P. Sound & Silence. (Illus.). 1970. 32.50 (ISBN 0-521-07511-4); pap. 13.95 (ISBN 0-521-09597-2); record 11.95 (ISBN 0-521-07759-1). Cambridge U Pr.

Paynter, John, ed. see Meyer-Denkmann, Gertrud.

Paynter, Raymond A., Jr. Avian Energetics. (Illus.). 334p. 1974. 17.00 (ISBN 0-686-35804-X). Nuttall Ornithological.

--Ornithological Gazetteer of Venezuela. (Illus.). iii, 245p. 1982. 12.50 (ISBN 0-686-38914-X). Nutall Ornithological.

Paynter, Raymond A., Jr. & Traylor, Melvin A., Jr. Ornithological Gazetteer of Colombia. (Illus.). v, 311p. 1981. 12.50 (ISBN 0-686-35831-7). Nuttall Ornithological.

Paynter, Raymond A., Jr., jt. auth. see Rand, David M.

Paynter, Raymond A., Jr., et al. Ornithological Gazetteer of Paraguay. (Illus.). iv, 43p. 1977. 1.75 (ISBN 0-686-35829-5). Nuttall Ornithological.

--Ornithological Gazetteer of Bolivia. (Illus.). vi, 80p. 1975. 1.75 (ISBN 0-686-35827-9). Nuttaal Ornithological.

--Ornithological Gazetteer of Ecuador. viii, 152p. 1977. 5.00 (ISBN 0-686-35828-7). Nuttall Ornithological.

Paynter, Robert. Models of Spatial Inequality: Settlement Patterns in the Historical Connecticut River Valley. (Studies in Historical Archaeology Ser.). 1982. 28.00 (ISBN 0-12-547580-2). Acad Pr.

Paynton, Clifford & Blackey, Robert, eds. Why Revolution: Theories & Analyses. 294p. 1971. pap. text ed. 7.95 p.b. (ISBN 0-87073-133-5). Schenkman.

Payton, George T. Patrol Procedure. 6th ed. LC 76-53527. 1982. 19.00x (ISBN 0-910874-54-9). Legal Bk Co.

Payton, George T., jt. auth. see Fricke, Charles W.

Payton, George T., jt. auth. see Gocke, B. W.

Payton, George T., ed. see Fricke, Charles W.

Payton, Joseph. Air Taxi Charter & Rental Directory of North America and Connection Points of Commuter Airlines with Other Scheduled Air Carriers. LC 75-648387. 100p. 1980. pap. 15.00 perfect bdg o.s.i. (ISBN 0-9603908-0-4). Aircraft Chart & Rent.

Paz, Carlos F. Preparacion para el Examen de Ciudadania. (Illus.). 144p. (Orig.). 1983. pap. 3.95 (ISBN 0-668-05677-0, 5677). Arco.

Paz, Jaime, jt. auth. see Blockey, Harry.

Paz, Octavio. Alternating Current. 256p. 1983. 14.95 (ISBN 0-394-53212-0); pap. 7.95 (ISBN 0-394-62470-X). Seaver Bks.

--Claude Levi-Strauss. 176p. 1974. pap. 2.95 o.s.i. (ISBN 0-440-52091-6, Delta). Dell.

--The Labyrinth of Solitude, the Other Mexico, & Other Essays. Kemp, Lysander & Talbot, Toby, trs. from Span. LC 82-47999. 448p. 1983. 22.50 (ISBN 0-394-52830-1, GP854); pap. 9.95 (ISBN 0-394-17992-7, E811, Ever). Grove.

--On Poets. Schmidt, Michael, tr. from Span. 272p. 1983. text ed. 21.00x (ISBN 0-85635-303-5, Pub. by Carcanet New Pr England). Humanities.

--Selected Poems. Tomlinson, Charles, tr. (Orig.). pap. cancelled o.s.i. (ISBN 0-14-042246-3). Penguin.

Pazdirek, Franz. Universal-Handbuch der Musikliteratur Aller Zeiten und Volker, 34 vols. in 12. ccxxxiv, 11973p. 1967. Set. 1237.50 o.s.i. (ISBN 90-6027-034-7, Pub. by Frits Knuf Netherlands). Pendragon NY.

Pazzagli, M., jt. ed. see Serio, M.

Peaboby, A. L., tr. see Smoldyrev, A. Ye.

Peabody, Berkley. The Winged Word. LC 72-91200. 1975. 54.50x (ISBN 0-87395-059-3). State U NY Pr.

Peabody, James B., jt. auth. see Oliver, Andrew.

Peabody, James B., jt. ed. see Oliver, Andrew.

Peabody Museum of Archaeology & Ethnology. Author & Subject Catalogues of the Library of the Peabody Museum of Archaeology & Ethnology: Fourth Supplement, 7 vols. 1979. lib. bdg. 980.00 set (ISBN 0-8161-0253-8, Hall Library). G K Hall.

Peabody, Richard. I'm in Love with the Morton Salt Girl. rev. ed. LC 81-85611. 50p. 1983. pap. Paycock Pr.

Peabody, Richard, ed. Mavericks: Nine Small Publishers. 90p. (Orig.). 1983. pap. 3.00 (ISBN 0-9602424-9-X). Paycock Pr.

Peace, Judy B. The Boy Child Is Dying: South African Sketches. LC 78-4445. 1978. pap. 2.25 o.p. (ISBN 0-87784-635-9). Inter-Varsity.

Peace, Philip C. More Than Candlelighting: A Guide for Training Acolytes. LC 82-18973. (Illus.). 64p. (Orig.). 1983. pap. 4.95 (ISBN 0-8298-0642-3). Pilgrim NY.

Peace, R. Learning to Love Ourselves. LC 68-12955. pap. 1.95 o.p. (ISBN 0-87784-453-4). Inter-Varsity.

--Learning to Love Packet. pap. 5.50 o.p. (ISBN 0-87784-730-4). Inter Varsity.

Peace, Richard. The Enigma of Gogol. LC 81-3867. (Cambridge Studies in Russian Literature). 320p. 1982. 45.00 (ISBN 0-521-23824-2). Cambridge U Pr.

Peace, Sheila. An International Perspective on the Status of Older Women. 100p. (Orig.). 1981. pap. text ed. 5.00 (ISBN 0-910473-08-0). Intl Fed Ageing.

Peaceman, Donald W. Fundamentals of Numerical Reservoir Simulation. (Developments in Petroleum Science: Vol. 6). 1977. 47.00 (ISBN 0-444-41578-5). Elsevier.

Peach, Bernard, ed. The Correspondence of Richard Price, Vol. 1. Thomas, D. O. (Illus.). 310p. 1983. 35.00x (ISBN 0-8223-0452-X). Duke.

Peach, Cindy. Diary of a Virgin. LC 78-1325. 1978. 7.95 o.p. (ISBN 0-698-10900-7, Coward). Putnam Pub Group.

Peacham, Henry. The Garden of Eloquence. LC 54-11900. 1977. Repr. of 1593 ed. 33.00x (ISBN 0-8201-1225-9). Schol Facsimiles.

Peachey, L. D. Muscle & Motility. (Biocore Ser: Unit 18). 1974. 24.95 (ISBN 0-07-005349-9, C). McGraw.

Peachey, L. D., ed. see Conference on Cellular Dynamics, Fifth Interdisciplinary.

Peachey, L. D., ed. see Interdisciplinary Conference-5th.

Peachment, Brian. An Aeroplane or a Grave. 1974. pap. 1.55 (ISBN 0-08-017841-3). Pergamon.

--Devil's Island. 1974. pap. 1.55 (ISBN 0-08-017613-5). Pergamon.

--Down Among the Dead Men. 1974. pap. 1.55 (ISBN 0-08-017615-1). Pergamon.

--Educated Drama. 232p. 1976. 29.00x (ISBN 0-7121-0552-2, Pub. by Macdonald & Evans). State Mutual Bk.

--The Red Cross Story. 1977. pap. 1.55 (ISBN 0-08-021036-8). Pergamon.

Peacock, A. T., jt. auth. see Rowley, C. K.

Peacock, Alan. The Credibility of Liberal Economics. (Institute of Economic Affairs Occasional Paper Ser.: 50). 1977. pap. 2.50 o.p. (ISBN 0-255-36092-4). Transatlantic.

--Economic Analysis of Government & Related Theories. LC 79-15836. 1979. 26.00x (ISBN 0-312-22678-0). St Martin.

Peacock, Alan & Shaw, G. K. The Economic Theory of Fiscal Policy. 2nd ed. LC 76-15870. 200p. 1976. 22.50x (ISBN 0-312-23660-3). St Martin.

Peacock, Arthur. The Romantic Vision in Music (Lucifer Redeemed) 256p. 1982. text ed. 21.00x (ISBN 0-85635-366-3, Pub. by Carcanet Pr England). Humanities.

Peacock, D. G., jt. ed. see Coulson, J. R.

Peacock, D. P. Pottery in the Roman World: An Ethnoarchaeological Approach. LC 81-12356. (Archaeology Ser.). (Illus.). 192p. 1982. 35.00 (ISBN 0-582-49127-4). Longman.

Peacock, Erle E. & Van Winkle, Walton. Wound Repair. 2nd ed. LC 16-8584. (Illus.). 1976. text ed. 39.50 o.p. (ISBN 0-7216-7124-1). Saunders.

Peacock, Frederick & Gaston, Thomas. Automotive Engine Repair & Overhaul. (Illus.). 480p. 1980. text ed. 19.95 (ISBN 0-8359-0276-5); instrs' manual avail. Reston.

Peacock, J. & Kirsch, A. Human Direction: An Evolutionary Approach to Social & Cultural Anthropology. 3rd ed. 1980. pap. 15.95 (ISBN 0-13-444851-0). P-H.

Peacock, James L. Muslim Puritans: Reformist Psychology in Southeast Asian Islam. LC 76-55571. 1978. 30.00x (ISBN 0-520-03403-1). U of Cal Pr.

Peacock, Nancy W. & Freisem, Deborah. Atlanta's Best Buys. (Illus.). 260p. 1982. pap. 5.95 (ISBN 0-9608196-1-4). Atlantas Best.

Peacock, Nancy W. & Freisem, Deborah K. Atlanta's Best Buys. (Illus.). 206p. (Orig.). 1981. 4.50 o.p. (ISBN 0-9608196-0-6). Atlantas Best.

Peacock, W. J., jt. ed. see Evans, L. T.

Peacock, William. English Verse, 5 vols. Incl. Vol. 1. Early Lyrics to Shakespeare. 8.95 (ISBN 0-19-250308-1); Vol. 2. Campion to the Ballads. o.p. (ISBN 0-19-250309-X); Vol. 3. Dryden to Wordsworth. o.p. (ISBN 0-19-250310-3); Vol. 4. Scott to E. B. Browning. 12.95 (ISBN 0-19-250311-1); Vol. 5. Longfellow to Rupert Brooke. 9.95 (ISBN 0-19-250312-X). (World's Classics Ser). Oxford U Pr.

Peacock, William, ed. Selected English Essays. (World's Classic Ser). 9.95 (ISBN 0-19-250032-5). Oxford U Pr.

Peacocke, A. R. Creation & the World of Science: The Bampton Lecturers. 1979. 22.50 (ISBN 0-19-826650-2). Oxford U Pr.

Peacocke, Christopher A. Holistic Explanation: Action, Space, Interpretation. 1979. 28.50x (ISBN 0-19-824605-6). Oxford U Pr.

Peake, Charles, ed. see Johnson, Samuel.

Peake, Harold & Fleure, H. J. Apes & Men. 1927. text ed. 24.50x (ISBN 0-686-83473-9). Elliots Bks.

Peake, Harold, jt. auth. see Fleure, H. F.

Peake, Harold, jt. auth. see Fleure, H. J.

Peake, Jim. Basic Mathematics, Vol. II. 560p. 1982. pap. text ed. 19.95 (ISBN 0-8403-2787-0). Kendall-Hunt.

--Basic Mathematics, Vol. I. 288p. 1982. pap. text ed. 12.95 (ISBN 0-8403-2786-2). Kendall-Hunt.

Peake, Lilian. Promise at Midnight. (Harlequin Romances Ser.). 192p. 1981. pap. 1.25 (ISBN 0-373-02404-5). Harlequin Bks.

Peaker, G. F. The Plowden Children Four Years Later. (General Ser.). 50p. 1971. pap. text ed. 7.75x o.p. (ISBN 0-901225-80-0, NFER). Humanities.

Peaker, M. & Linzell, J. L. Salt Glands in Birds & Reptiles. LC 74-12966. (Physiological Society Monographs: No. 32). (Illus.). 296p. 1975. 65.00 (ISBN 0-521-20629-4). Cambridge U Pr.

Peale, George C., et al. Antiguedad Y Actualidad de Luis Velez de Guevara: Estudios Criticos. 300p. 1982. 34.00 (ISBN 90-272-1720-3). Benjamins North Am.

Peale, Norman V. Norman Vincent Peale's Treasury of Joy & Enthusiasm. 192p. 1981. 9.95 (ISBN 0-8007-1180-7); pap. 2.50 (ISBN 0-8007-8450-2, Spire Bks). Revell.

--You Can If You Think You Can. LC 73-17323. 336p. 1974. 8.95 o.p. (ISBN 0-13-972547-4). P-H.

Peale, Norman Vincent. Bible Stories. pap. 2.25 o.s.i. (ISBN 0-89129-049-4). Jove Pubns.

Pear, Joseph, jt. auth. see Martin, Gary.

Pear, Lillian M. Pewabic Pottery. 1976. 22.50 (ISBN 0-87069-158-9, 99050). Wallace-Homestead.

Pearce. Medicine & Poisons Guide. 3rd ed. 216p. 1982. 12.00 (ISBN 0-85369-162-2, Pub. by Pharmaceutical). Rittenhouse.

Pearce, Brian, tr. see Claudin, Fernando.

Pearce, Brian, tr. see Emmanuel, Arghiri.

Pearce, Charles. Essentials of Auto Mechanics. (Auto Mechanics Motivational Program). 1973. pap. text ed. 7.95 (ISBN 0-89036-816-3); tchrs' guide 1.50 (ISBN 0-89036-821-X); vocabulary 2.95 (ISBN 0-89036-818-X); unit tests 3.50 (ISBN 0-89036-817-1); study guide pap. 7.50 (ISBN 0-89036-820-1); guide bk. 2.95 (ISBN 0-89036-815-5). Hawkes Pub Inc.

--Essentials of Drivers Education. (Drivers Education Motivational Program). 1973. pap. 5.95 (ISBN 0-89036-811-2); study guide 5.95 (ISBN 0-89036-812-0); vocabulary 2.95 (ISBN 0-89036-813-9); sample tests 2.95 (ISBN 0-89036-814-7); guide bk. 2.95 (ISBN 0-89036-815-5). Hawkes Pub Inc.

--Study Guide for California Drivers Handbook. Incl. Adapted N.Y. State Drivers Handbook. pap. 3.95 (ISBN 0-89036-823-6). 1973. pap. 1.50 (ISBN 0-89036-823-6); study guide pap. o.p. 2.95 (ISBN 0-89036-824-4); vocabulary o.p. 1.95 (ISBN 0-89036-825-2); sample tests o.p. 1.95 (ISBN 0-89036-828-7); study guide for official N.Y. state driver's manual pap. 2.50, sample tests 1.00 o.p. (ISBN 0-89036-827-9). Hawkes Pub Inc.

Pearce, Charles E. Sims Reeves, Fifty Years of Music in England. (Music Reprint Ser.). 1980. Repr. of 1924 ed. lib. bdg. 27.50 (ISBN 0-306-76007-X). Da Capo.

Pearce, Colin. Prediction Techniques for Marketing Planners: The Practical Application of Forecasting Methods to Business Problems. 254p. 1971. 17.50x o.p. (ISBN 0-304-93885-8). Intl Pubns Serv.

Pearce, D. W. Aviary Design & Construction. (Blandford Pet Handbooks Ser.). (Illus.). 96p. 1983. 7.50 (ISBN 0-7137-1218-X, Pub. by Blandford Pr England). Sterling.

Pearce, D. W., jt. auth. see Ryan, W. J.

Pearce, David W., ed. The Dictionary of Modern Economics. 512p. 1981. text ed. 35.00x (ISBN 0-262-16084-6). MIT Pr.

Pearce, G. L. The Pioneer Craftsmen of New Zealand. (Illus.). 256p. 1982. 29.95 (ISBN 0-00-216986-X, Pub. by W Collins Australia). Intl Schol Bk Serv.

Pearce, I. F., et al, eds. A Model of Output, Employment, Wages & Prices in the UK. LC 75-46134. (Illus.). 1976. 32.50 (ISBN 0-521-21210-3). Cambridge U Pr.

Pearce, J. Kenneth & Stenzel, George. Logging & Pulpwood Production. 400p. 1972. 31.50 (ISBN 0-471-06839-X, Pub. by Wiley-Interscience). Wiley.

Pearce, J. R., jt. ed. see Bacharach, A. L.

Pearce, J. Winston. Planning Your Preaching. LC 78-73135. 1979. pap. 5.95 (ISBN 0-8054-2108-4). Broadman.

--Ten Good Things I Know About Retirement. LC 82-71668. 1982. 6.95 (ISBN 0-8054-5429-2). Broadman.

Pearce, Janice, jt. auth. see Pearce, Wayne.

Pearce, Joan. The Common Agricultural Policy: Prospects for Change. (Chatham House Papers: No. 13). 122p. 1982. pap. 10.00 (ISBN 0-7100-9069-2). Routledge & Kegan.

Pearce, Joan T., jt. auth. see Williams, Patrick.

Pearce, John, jt. ed. see McGoldrick, Monica.

Pearce, M. R., et al. Introduction to Business Decision-Making. 1977. 27.95x (ISBN 0-458-92750-3). Methuen Inc.

Pearce, Mary E. Cast a Long Shadow. 256p. 1983. 11.95 (ISBN 0-312-12353-1). St Martin.

Pearce, P. L. The Social Psychology of Tourist Behaviour. (International Series in Experimental Social Psychology: Vol. 3). 142p. 1982. 19.50 (ISBN 0-08-025794-1). Pergamon.

Pearce, Peter. Structure in Nature Is a Strategy for Design. LC 77-26866. 1978. 49.50x (ISBN 0-262-16064-1); pap. 12.50 (ISBN 0-262-66045-8). MIT Pr.

Pearce, Philippa. The Minnow Leads to Treasure. 1980. PLB 9.95 (ISBN 0-8398-2609-5, Gregg). G K Hall.

Pearce, Richard. Critical Essays on Thomas Pynchon. (Critical Essays on American Literature). 1981. 25.00 (ISBN 0-8161-8320-1, Twayne). G K Hall.

--The Novel in Motion: An Approach to Modern Fiction. 200p. 1983. 17.50 (ISBN 0-8142-0345-0). Ohio St U Pr.

Pearce, Robert, jt. ed. see Hoskins, Brian.

Pearce, Robert D., jt. auth. see Dunning, John H.

Pearce, Roy H., ed. Tales & Sketches: Nathaniel Hawthorne. LC 81-20760. 1504p. 1982. 27.50 (ISBN 0-940450-03-8). Literary Classics.

Pearce, S. C. The Agricultural Field Experiment: A Statistical Examination of Theory & Practice. 400p. 1983. write for info. (ISBN 0-471-10511-2, Pub. by Wiley-Interscience). Wiley.

Pearce, T., jt. auth. see Mellor, Jean.

Pearce, T. M. Mary Hunter Austin. (United States Authors Ser.). 13.95 (ISBN 0-8057-0032-3, Twayne). G K Hall.

--Oliver La Farge. (U. S. Authors Ser.: No. 191). lib. bdg. 7.95 o.p. (ISBN 0-8057-0432-9, Twayne). G K Hall.

Pearce, T. M., ed. Literary America, Nineteen Hundred & Three to Nineteen Thirty-Four: The Mary Austin Letters. LC 78-67914. (Contributions in Women's Studies: No. 5). (Illus.). 1979. lib. bdg. 25.00 (ISBN 0-313-20636-8, PEL/). Greenwood.

Pearce, Wayne & Pearce, Janice. Tennis. (Sport Ser). (Illus.). 1971. pap. 6.95 ref. ed. (ISBN 0-13-903435-8). P-H.

Pearcey, T. Table of the Fresnal Integral to Six Decimal Places. 1982. 30.00x (ISBN 0-686-97895-1, Pub. by CSIRO Australia). State Mutual Bk.

Pearcy, G. Etzel & Stoneman, Elvyn A. Handbook of New Nations. (Illus.). (gr. 9 up). 1968. 11.49 (ISBN 0-690-36455-5). T Y Crowell.

Peare, Catherine O. FDR Story. LC 65-21418. (Illus.). (gr. 5-9). 1962. 9.95i o.p. (ISBN 0-690-29355-0, TYC-J). Har-Row.

Pearkes, Gillian. Vinegrowing in Britain. 224p. 1982. 40.00x (ISBN 0-460-04393-5, Pub. by J M Dent England). State Mutual Bk.

Pearl, jt. ed. see Benton.

Pearl, Cora. Grand Horizontal: The Erotic Memoirs of a Passionate Lady. Blatchford, William, ed. LC 82-42870. 192p. 1983. 16.95 (ISBN 0-8128-2917-4). Stein & Day.

Pearl, David & Gray, Kevin. Social Welfare Law. 320p. 1981. 36.95x (ISBN 0-85664-644-X, Pub. by Croom Helm LTD England). Biblio Dist.

Pearl, Esther E. Deeper Than Shame. 384p. (Orig.). 1980. pap. 2.50 o.s.i. (ISBN 0-515-05533-6). Jove Pubns.

Pearl, Leon. Descartes. (World Leaders Ser.). 1977. lib. bdg. 11.95 (ISBN 0-8057-7714-8, Twayne). G K Hall.

Pearl, Morris L. William Cobbett: A Bibliographical Account of His Life & Times. LC 78-136079. 1971. Repr. of 1953 ed. lib. bdg. 18.25x (ISBN 0-8371-5229-1, PEWC). Greenwood.

Pearl, Richard M. America's Mountain: Pikes Peak & the Pikes Peak Region. 4th ed. LC 64-25340. 1976. pap. 2.50 (ISBN 0-940566-00-1). Earth Science.

--Cleaning & Preserving Minerals. 5th ed. 1980. pap. 4.00 (ISBN 0-940566-02-8). Earth Science.

--Colorado Gem Trails & Mineral Guide. rev., 3rd ed. LC 82-70340. (Illus.). 223p. 1972. 12.95 (ISBN 0-8040-0052-2, SB). Swallow.

--Exploring Rocks, Minerals, Fossils in Colorado. rev. ed. LC 82-70647. (Illus.). 215p. 1969. 12.95 (ISBN 0-8040-0105-7). Swallow.

--Handbook for Prospectors. 5th ed. LC 72-11749. 544p. 1973. 29.95 (ISBN 0-07-049025-2, P&RB). McGraw.

--How to Know the Minerals & Rocks. (RL 7). pap. 1.50 o.p. (ISBN 0-451-07240-5, W7240, Sig). NAL.

--Seven Keys to the Rocky Mountains. LC 68-55439. 1968. 5.00 (ISBN 0-940566-09-5). Earth Science.

Pearl, Shirley, jt. auth. see Dozoretz, Eileen.

Pearl, Valerie, jt. ed. see Lloyd-Jones, Hugh.

Pearlman, Barbara. Barbara Pearlman's Four Week Stomach & Waist Shape-up. LC 82-45520. (Illus.). 96p. 1983. pap. 4.95 (ISBN 0-385-18353-4, Dolp). Doubleday.

Pearlman, Daniel & Pearlman, Paula R. Guide to Rapid Revision. 3rd ed. LC 81-12244. 1981. pap. text ed. 3.95 o.p. Odyssey Pr.

Pearlman, Della. No Choice: Library Services for the Mentally Handicapped. 64p. 1982. lib. bdg. 17.25x (ISBN 0-89774-013-0, Pub. by Lib Assn England). Oryx Pr.

Pearlman, Kenneth & Schmidt, Frank L. Contemporary Problems in Personnel. 3rd ed. 400p. 1983. text ed. 18.95 (ISBN 0-471-87376-4). Wiley.

Pearlman, Moshe, jt. auth. see Ben Gurion, David.

Pearlman, Paula R., jt. auth. see Pearlman, Daniel.

Pearlstein, Stanley. Psychiatry, the Law & Mental Health. 2nd ed. LC 67-16050. (Legal Almanac Ser.: No. 30). 124p. 1967. 5.95 (ISBN 0-379-11030-X). Oceana.

Pearlstien, Edward W. Three Intellectual Plays: Jack Ruby, Mariana Alcoforado, Pocahontas. 146p. 1979. pap. 1.95 (ISBN 0-917636-02-3). Edit Consult.

Pearman, Richard. Power Electronics: Solid Stare Motor Control. (Illus.). 1980. text ed. 24.95 (ISBN 0-8359-5585-0). Reston.

--Solid State Industrial Electronics. 1982. text ed. 23.95 (ISBN 0-8359-7041-8); instrs'. manual avail. (ISBN 0-8359-7042-6). Reston.

Pearn, Tony. The Secret of Successful Steeplechasing. (Illus.). 121p. 1973. 10.00 o.p. (ISBN 0-7207-0584-3). Transatlantic.

Pears, A. Dimension Theory of General Spaces. LC 74-12955. (Illus.). 440p. 1975. 92.50 (ISBN 0-521-20515-8). Cambridge U Pr.

Pears, D. F., tr. see Wittgenstein, Ludwig.

Pears, David. Ludwig Wittgenstein. (Modern Masters Ser.). 1977. pap. 2.95 o.p. (ISBN 0-14-004497-3). Penguin.

Pears, Edwin. Destruction of the Greek Empire & the Story of the Capture of Constantinople by the Turks. LC 69-14032. 1969. Repr. of 1903 ed. lib. bdg. 20.00x (ISBN 0-8371-0612-5, PEGE). Greenwood.

Pearsall, Derek, ed. see Langland, William.

Pearsall, Mile D. & Verbruggen, Hugo. Scent: Theory & Practice. (Illus.). 224p. 1982. 14.95 (ISBN 0-931866-11-1). Alpine Pubns.

Pearsall, R. Is That My Hook in Your Ear. 12.50x (ISBN 0-392-06563-0, SpS). Sportshelf.

Pearsall, R. B. Rupert Brooke: The Man & Poet. 174p. (Orig.). 1975. pap. text ed. 14.25x o.p. (ISBN 90-6203-437-3). Humanities.

Pearsall, Robert B. Robert Browning. (English Authors Ser.). 1974. lib. bdg. 12.95 (ISBN 0-8057-1065-5, Twayne). G K Hall.

Pearsall, Ronald. Victorian Popular Music. (Illus.). 250p. 1973. 21.00x (ISBN 0-8103-2002-9). Gale.

--Victorian Sheet Music Covers. LC 72-6422. (Illus.). 116p. 1972. 18.00x (ISBN 0-8103-2001-0). Gale.

--Worm in the Bud. 1983. pap. 7.95 (ISBN 0-14-006343-9). Penguin.

Pearsall, Thomas E., jt. auth. see Brown, James I.

Pearse, John S., jt. ed. see Giese, Arthur C.

Pearse, M. J. Gravity Thickening Theories: A Review, 1977. 1981. 60.00x (ISBN 0-686-97084-5, Pub. by W Spring England). State Mutual Bk.

--An Investigation of the Oxidation & Self-Heating of Metal Sulphide Concentrates, 1979. 1982. 59.00x (ISBN 0-686-97098-5, Pub. by W Spring England). State Mutual Bk.

--Laboratory Procedures for the Choice & Sizing of Dewatering Equipment in the Mineral Processing Industry, 1978. 1981. 75.00x (ISBN 0-686-97104-3, Pub. by W Green England). State Mutual Bk.

Pearse, R. O. Mountain Splendour. (Illus.). 239p. 1981. 37.50x (ISBN 0-86978-156-1, Pub. by Timmins Africa). Intl Schol Bk Serv.

Pearse, R. W., jt. auth. see Gaydon, A. G.

Pearson, jt. ed. see Polanyi, Arensberg.

Pearson, et al. On Your Own. (The Gregg McGraw-Hill Ser. for Independent Living). (Illus.). 1977. pap. text ed. 7.96 (ISBN 0-07-049051-1, G); student wkbk. 4.96 (ISBN 0-07-049052-X); tchr's. manual & key 4.00 (ISBN 0-07-049053-8). McGraw.

Pearson, A. J. The Railways & the Nation. 11.50 (ISBN 0-392-15604-0, SpS). Sportshelf.

Pearson, Alice. Heartspun & Homespun Poems. 1982. 4.95 (ISBN 0-934860-23-8). Adventure Pubns.

Pearson, Bill. Olive & Swee' Pea Wash up! Mann, Philip, ed. (Shape Board Play Book). (Illus.). 14p. (gr. k-3). 1980. bds. 3.50 comb bdg. o.p. (ISBN 0-89828-126-1, 06008). Tuffy Bks.

--Popeye & His Pals Stay in Shape. Mann, Philip, ed. (Shape Board Play Book). (Illus.). 14p. (gr. k-3). 1980. bds. 3.50 comb bdg. o.p. (ISBN 0-89828-125-3, 06007). Tuffy Bks.

--Wimpy in What's Good to Eat? Mann, Philip, ed. (Shape Board Play Book). (Illus.). 14p. (gr. k-3). 1980. bds. 3.50 comb bdg. o.s.i. (ISBN 0-89828-127-X, 06009). Tuffy Bks.

Pearson, Carl M., et al. Drugs for Rheumatic Disease. (Monographs in Clinical Pharmacology). (Illus.). Date not set. text ed. price not set (ISBN 0-443-08011-9). Churchill.

Pearson, Carol & Pope, Katherine. Who Am I This Time? Female Portraits in British & American Literature. 1976. text ed. 16.95 (ISBN 0-07-049032-5, C). McGraw.

Pearson, Charles & Eyres, Alfred. A Happier Life. LC 72-79092. 270p. 1969. 10.95 (ISBN 0-87716-005-8, Pub. by Moore Pub Co). F Apple.

Pearson, Charles & Pryor, Anthony. Environment: North & South an Economic Interpretation. LC 77-11143. 52.95 o.s.i. (ISBN 0-471-02741-3, Pub. by Wiley-Interscience). Wiley.

Pearson, Charles H. Russia: By a Recent Traveler. (Russia Through European Eyes Ser). 1971. Repr. of 1859 ed. lib. bdg. 39.50 (ISBN 0-686-85849-2). Da Capo.

Pearson, Craig M. Food & You. (Independent Living Ser.). (gr. 11-12). 1978. pap. 7.96 (ISBN 0-07-049057-0, G); tchr's manual & key 4.00 (ISBN 0-07-049059-7); wkbk. 3.96 (ISBN 0-07-049058-9). McGraw.

Pearson, Craig M., et al. Independent Living: Being on Your Own. LC 79-16892. (Independent Living Ser.). (Illus.). 464p. (gr. 11-12). 1979. text ed. 15.86 (ISBN 0-07-049061-9); tchrs. manual & key 3.50 (ISBN 0-07-049063-5); student wkbk. 7.96 (ISBN 0-07-049062-7). McGraw.

Pearson, D. Chemical Analysis of Foods. 1977. text ed. 41.00 o.p. (ISBN 0-8206-0207-8). Chem Pub.

Pearson, D. G. Race Class & Political Activism. 216p. 1980. text ed. 34.25x (ISBN 0-566-00353-8). Gower Pub Ltd.

Pearson, Drew & Allen, Robert S. The Nine Old Men. LC 73-21727. (American Constitutional & Legal History Ser). 325p. 1974. Repr. of 1966 ed. lib. bdg. 45.00 (ISBN 0-306-70609-1). Da Capo.

Pearson, Durk & Shaw, Sandy. Life Extension. 896p. 1983. pap. 12.95 (ISBN 0-446-87990-8). Warner Bks.

--Life Extension: A Practical Scientific Approach Adding Years to Your Life & Life to Your Years. LC 80-27589. (Illus.). 600p. 1982. pap. 22.50 (ISBN 0-446-51272-9). Warner Bks.

Pearson, E. S., jt. auth. see Neyman, Jerzy.

Pearson, Eileen. Hitler's Reich. Yapp, Malcolm & Killingray, Margaret, eds. (World History Ser.). (Illus.). (gr. 10). 1980. Repr. of 1977 ed. lib. bdg. 6.95 (ISBN 0-89908-208-4); pap. text ed. 2.25 (ISBN 0-89908-233-5). Greenhaven.

Pearson, Frederic S. The Weak State in International Crisis: The Case of the Netherlands in the German Invasion Crisis of 1939-1940. LC 80-69042. 182p. 1981. lib. bdg. 19.75 (ISBN 0-8191-1558-4); pap. text ed. 9.50 (ISBN 0-8191-1559-2). U Pr of Amer.

Pearson, H. F., et al. Preliminary Report on the Synagogue at Dura-Europos. (Illus.). 1936. pap. 49.50x (ISBN 0-686-51290-1). Elliots Bks.

Pearson, Hesketh. Beerbohm Tree: His Life & Laughter. LC 70-138123. (Illus.). 1971. Repr. of 1956 ed. lib. bdg. 15.50x (ISBN 0-8371-5699-8, PEBT). Greenwood.

--Dizzy: The Life & Nature of Benjamin Disraeli, Earl of Beaconsfield. LC 74-12579. (Illus.). 284p. 1975. Repr. of 1951 ed. lib. bdg. 19.75x (ISBN 0-8371-7729-4, PEDIZ). Greenwood.

--Henry of Navarre: The King Who Dared. LC 76-23244. 1976. Repr. of 1963 ed. lib. bdg. 20.75x (ISBN 0-8371-9015-0, PEHN). Greenwood.

Pearson, Howard A., jt. auth. see Miller, Denis R.

Pearson, Ian. English in Biological Science. (English in Focus Ser.). 1979. pap. text ed. 9.95x student's ed. (ISBN 0-19-437513-7); tchr's ed. 12.00x (ISBN 0-19-437505-6). Oxford U Pr.

Pearson, J. D., ed. International African Bibliography Cumulation: 1973-1978. 376p. 1982. lib. bdg. 80.00 (ISBN 0-7201-1565-5). Mansell.

Pearson, J. D. & Walsh, Ann, eds. Index Islamicus, Fourth Supplement: Part 2, 1972-73. new ed. 108p. 1974. pap. 8.00 o.p. (ISBN 0-7201-0286-3, Pub. by Mansell England). Wilson.

--Index Islamicus: Fourth Supplement, Part 4, 1974-1975. 128p. 1975. pap. 10.00x o.p. (ISBN 0-7201-0288-X, Pub. by Mansell England). Wilson.

Pearson, Jacqueline. Tragedy & Tragi-Comedy in the Plays of John Webster. 151p. 1980. 20.50x (ISBN 0-389-20030-1). B&N Imports.

Pearson, James, et al. Hawaii Home Energy Book. LC 77-79935. 1978. pap. 8.95 (ISBN 0-8248-0596-8). UH Pr.

Pearson, James D., ed. A Bibliography of Pre-Islamic Persia. LC 75-306315. 318p. 1975. 44.00 o.p. (ISBN 0-7201-0365-7, Pub. by Mansell England). Wilson.

Pearson, Jeanne. Pony in the Yard. (Third Grade Bk.). (Illus.). (gr. 3-4). PLB 5.95 o.p. (ISBN 0-513-00392-4). Denison.

Pearson, Jeffrey & Pearson, Jessica. No Time but Place. (Illus.). 256p. 1980. 16.95 o.p. (ISBN 0-07-049030-9). McGraw.

Pearson, Jessica, jt. auth. see Pearson, Jeffrey.

Pearson, John R., ed. Hiker's Guide to Trails of Big Bend National Park. 2nd ed. (Illus.). 32p. (Orig.). 1978. pap. 1.00 (ISBN 0-686-38926-3). Big Bend.

--River Guide to the Rio Grande, 4 vols. (Illus.). 72p. (Orig.). 1982. pap. 10.00 (ISBN 0-686-38924-7). Big Bend.

--Road Guide to Backcountry Dirt Roads of Big Bend National Park. (Illus.). 40p. (Orig.). 1980. pap. 1.00 (ISBN 0-686-38927-1). Big Bend.

--Road Guide to Paved & Improved Dirt Roads of Big Bend National Park. (Illus.). 48p. (Orig.). 1980. pap. 1.00 (ISBN 0-686-38925-5). Big Bend.

Pearson, John R., ed. see Deckert, Frank.

Pearson, John S. Student Guide for Principles of Life Insurance, Pt. 1. (FLMI Insurance Education Program Ser.). 140p. 1972. pap. 4.00 workbook (ISBN 0-915322-01-3). LOMA.

Pearson, Judy C. Interpersonal Communication: Clarity, Confidence, Concern. 1982. pap. text ed. 10.95x (ISBN 0-673-15379-7). Scott F.

Pearson, Katherine. American Crafts for the Home. (Illus.). 240p. 1983. 35.00 (ISBN 0-941434-30-3). Stewart Tabori & Chang.

Pearson, Kazue, tr. see Kim, Jeong-Hak.

Pearson, Lionel. The Art of Demosthenes. LC 81-16752. (American Philological Association Special Publications Ser.). 1981. pap. 18.00 (ISBN 0-89130-551-3, 40-05-04). Scholars Pr CA.

--Early Ionian Historians. LC 75-136874. 240p. 1975. Repr. of 1939 ed. lib. bdg. 18.25x (ISBN 0-8371-5314-X, PEIH). Greenwood.

Pearson, Lu E. Elizabethans at Home. LC 57-9305. (Illus.). 1957. text ed. 32.50x (ISBN 0-8047-0494-5); pap. 6.95 o.p. (ISBN 0-8047-0495-3). Stanford U Pr.

Pearson, Lucien D., tr. see Collins, Rowland L.

Pearson, M. N. Merchants & Rulers in Gujarat: The Response to the Portuguese in the Sixteenth Century. 1976. 30.00x (ISBN 0-520-02809-0). U of Cal Pr.

Pearson, M. N., jt. ed. see Kling, Blair B.

Pearson, Mark L. & Epstein, Henry F., eds. Muscle Development: Molecular & Cellular Control. LC 82-72381. 500p. 1982. 57.00X (ISBN 0-87969-154-9). Cold Spring Harbor.

Pearson, Michael. The Store. 1982. pap. 3.95 (ISBN 0-553-22657-6). Bantam.

--Those Yankee Rebels. 192p. (gr. 6 up). 1974. 6.95 o.p. (ISBN 0-399-20404-0). Putnam Pub Group.

Pearson, N. M. Coastal Western India: Studies from the Portuguese Records. Date not set. cancelled o.p. (ISBN 0-8364-0856-X, Pub by Concept India). South Asia Bks.

Pearson, Nancy & Spiegelberg, Stanley, trs. To Live Within: The Story of Five Years with a Himalayan Guru. 284p. 1974. 12.50 o.p. (ISBN 0-04-291008-0). Allen Unwin.

Pearson, Nancy, tr. see Corbin, Henry.

Pearson, Norman H., jt. ed. see Auden, W. H.

Pearson, Norman H., ed. & intro. by see Hawthorne, Nathaniel.

Pearson, Patricia C., ed. see Graber, Alan L., et al.

Pearson, Paul D. Alvar Aalto & the International Style. (Illus.). 1977. 27.50 (ISBN 0-8230-7023-9, Whitney Lib). Watson-Guptill.

Pearson, Paul H., jt. ed. see Menolascino, Frank J.

Pearson, R. G., jt. auth. see Basolo, Fred.

Pearson, R. G., jt. auth. see Moore, J. W.

Pearson, Ralph G. Symmetry Rules for Chemical Reactions: Orbital Topology & Elementary Processes. LC 76-10314. 600p. 1976. 45.95 o.s.i. (ISBN 0-471-01495-8, Pub. by Wiley-Interscience). Wiley.

Pearson, Richard J. Archaeology of the Ryukyu Islands: A Regional Chronology from 3000 B. C. to the Historic Period. LC 75-76762. (Illus.). 1969. text ed. 12.00x (ISBN 0-87022-620-7). UH Pr.

Pearson, Richard J., tr. see Kim, Jeong-Hak.

Pearson, Robert, ed. The Wisley Book of Gardening. (Illus.). 1983. 25.95 (ISBN 0-393-01676-5). Norton.

Pearson, Roger. Dictionary of Anthropology. (Orig.). 1983. write for info. (ISBN 0-89874-510-1). Krieger.

--Introduction to Anthropology. 634p. 1981. Repr. of 1974 ed. write for info. o.p. (ISBN 0-89874-378-8). Krieger.

Pearson, Roger W. & Lynch, Donald F. Alaska: A Geography. 300p. 1983. lib. bdg. 36.25 (ISBN 0-89158-903-1); text ed. 20.00 (ISBN 0-686-96922-7). Westview.

Pearson, S. Ivar & Maler, George J. Introductory Circuit Analysis. LC 74-10895. 566p. 1974. Repr. of 1965 ed. 25.50 (ISBN 0-88275-175-1). Krieger.

Pearson, Sidney A., Jr. Arthur Koestler. (English Authors Ser.). 1978. lib. bdg. 12.95 (ISBN 0-8057-6699-5, Twayne). G K Hall.

Pearson, Sindey A., Jr. The Constitutional Polity: Essays on the Founding Principles of American Politics. LC 82-15953. 364p. (Orig.). 1983. lib. bdg. 24.25 (ISBN 0-8191-2744-2); pap. text ed. 12.75 (ISBN 0-8191-2745-0). U Pr of Amer.

Pearson, T. Gilbert. Birds of America. 1936. 29.95 (ISBN 0-385-00024-3). Doubleday.

Pearson, Ted. The Blue Table. LC 76-64870. 72p. 1979. pap. 4.00 (ISBN 0-917588-03-7). Trike.

Pearson, W. N. see Sebrell, W. H., Jr. & Harris, Robert S.

Peart, Jane. Portrait in Shadows. (Orig.). 1981. pap. 1.50 o.s.i. (ISBN 0-440-16693-4). Dell.

--Spanish Masquerade. (Orig.). 1980. pap. 1.25 o.s.i. (ISBN 0-440-17745-6). Dell.

Peary, Dannis, jt. auth. see Peary, Gerald.

Peary, Gerald & Peary, Dannis. American Animated Cartoon. (Illus.). 1980. pap. 10.95 (ISBN 0-525-47639-3, 01063-320). Dutton.

Peary, Gerald, ed. Little Caesar. (Illus.). 200p. 1981. 15.00 o.p. (ISBN 0-299-08450-7); pap. 5.95 o.p. (ISBN 0-686-78006-X). U of Wis Pr.

Peary, Gerald & Kay, Karyn, eds. Women & the Cinema: A Critical Anthology. 1977. pap. 8.95 o.p. (ISBN 0-525-47459-5). Dutton.

Pease, Cynthia M., ed. Complete Index to High Fidelity's Test Reports, 1952-1979. 1980. 4.95 (ISBN 0-911656-10-3). Wyeth Pr.

Pease, Daniel C., ed. Cellular Aspects of Neural Growth & Differentiation. LC 73-126760. (UCLA Forum in Medical Sciences: No. 14). (Illus.). 1971. 77.00x (ISBN 0-520-01793-5). U of Cal Pr.

Pease, Dudley A. Basic Fluid Power. 1967. ref. ed. 21.95 (ISBN 0-13-061432-7). P-H.

Pease, Jack G. & Russell, Robert. Arithmetic Fundamentals. new ed. 240p. 1975. pap. text ed. 14.95x o.p. (ISBN 0-675-08767-8). Merrill.

Pease, Jane H. & Pease, William H. Bound with Them in Chains: A Biographical History of the Antislavery Movement. LC 74-175612. (Contributions in American History: No. 18). 284p. 1972. lib. bdg. 29.95 (ISBN 0-8371-6265-3, PEB/). Greenwood.

Pease, Ralph W., jt. auth. see Johnson, Robert A.

Pease, T. C. The Leveller Movement. 9.00 (ISBN 0-8446-1345-2). Peter Smith.

Pease, William H., jt. auth. see Pease, Jane H.

Peatman, J. B. Design of Digital Systems. (Electronic Systems Ser.). 1972. text ed. 36.00 (ISBN 0-07-049136-4, C). McGraw.

--Digital Hardware Design. 1980. 33.50 (ISBN 0-07-049132-1). McGraw.

--Microcomputer-Based Design. 1977. 35.95 (ISBN 0-07-049138-0). McGraw.

Peattie, Donald C. An Almanac for Moderns. LC 79-90410. 416p. 1981. 17.95 (ISBN 0-87923-356-7, Nonpareil Bks); pap. 8.95 (ISBN 0-87923-314-1, Nonpareil Bks). Godine.

Peattie, Lisa R. View from the Barrio. LC 68-16441. (Illus.). 1968. 9.95 (ISBN 0-472-72280-8). U of Mich Pr.

--View from the Barrio. (Illus.). 1970. pap. 4.95 (ISBN 0-472-06169-0, 169, AA). U of Mich Pr.

Peattie, Roderick. Mountain Geography: A Critique & Field Study. Repr. of 1936 ed. lib. bdg. 15.75x (ISBN 0-8371-2243-0, PEMG). Greenwood.

Peau, Andrew T. Le see Le Peau, Andrew T.

Peavy, Charles D. Larry McMurtry. (United States Authors Ser.). 1977. lib. bdg. 12.95 (ISBN 0-8057-7194-8, Twayne). G K Hall.

Peavy, Charles D., ed. Afro-American Literature & Culture, Nineteen Forty-Five to Nineteen Seventy-Three: A Guide to Information Sources. LC 73-17561. (American Studies Information Guide Ser.: Vol. 6). 1979. 42.00x (ISBN 0-8103-1254-9). Gale.

Peavy, Linda. Have a Healthy Baby: Section on What to Eat After Your Baby Is Born. LC 76-46807. 1977. 9.95 o.p. (ISBN 0-8069-8376-0); PLB 8.29 o.p. (ISBN 0-8069-8377-9). Sterling.

Peavy, Linda & Smith, Ursula. Women Who Changed Things. LC 82-21612. (Illus.). 208p. (gr. 7 up). 1983. 12.95 (ISBN 0-684-17849-4). Scribner.

Peavy, Linda S. & Pagenkopf, Andrea L. Grow Healthy Kids! LC 78-67967. 336p. 1981. pap. 7.95 (ISBN 0-448-16530-9, G&D). Putnam Pub Group.

Peay, Marilyn, jt. auth. see Winefield, Helen R.

Pebay-Peyroula, J. C., jt. auth. see Cagnoa, B.

Peberdy, John F. Developmental Microbiology. LC 80-14825. (Tertiary Level Biology Ser.). 230p. 1980. pap. 39.95x (ISBN 0-470-26989-8). Halsted Pr.

Pebworth, Ted-Larry. Owen Felltham. (English Authors Ser.). 1976. lib. bdg. 14.95 (ISBN 0-8057-6655-3, Twayne). G K Hall.

Pebworth, Ted-Larry, jt. auth. see Summers, Claude J.

Pebworth, Ted-Larry, jt. ed. see Summers, Claude J.

Pecan, Erene, jt. ed. see Woodwell, George M.

Peccei, Aurelio. One Hundred Pages for the Future. 1982. pap. 3.95 (ISBN 0-451-62139-5, ME2139, Ment). NAL.

Pecci, Ernest F., jt. auth. see Pecci, Mary F.

Pecci, Mary F. Content Areas. (Super Seatwork). (Illus.). 168p. 1977. 7.95 (ISBN 0-943220-01-7). Pecci Educ Pub.

--Letter Recognition. (Super Seatwork). (Illus.). 104p. 1978. 7.95 (ISBN 0-943220-02-5). Pecci Educ Pubs.

--Linguistic Exercises. (Super Seatwork Ser.). (Illus.). 106p. 1978. 7.95 (ISBN 0-943220-03-3). Pecci Educ Pubs.

Pecci, Mary F. & Pecci, Ernest F. At Last A Reading Method for Every Child! 3rd, rev. ed. LC 72-193681. (Illus.). 306p. 1975. pap. 19.95 Comb bdg. (ISBN 0-943220-00-9). Pecci Educ Pub.

Peccorini, Francisco L. On to the World of "Freedom". A Kantian Meditation on Finite Selfhood. LC 82-40233. 370p. (Orig.). 1982. lib. bdg. 25.25 (ISBN 0-8191-2643-8); pap. text ed. 14.00 (ISBN 0-8191-2644-6). U Pr of Amer.

Pecherer, Angela, jt. auth. see Sauve, Mary J.

Pecheux, M. Christopher. Milton: A Topographical Guide. LC 81-40626. (Illus.). 148p. (Orig.). 1982. lib. bdg. 20.00 (ISBN 0-8191-1953-9); pap. text ed. 8.25 (ISBN 0-8191-1954-7). U Pr of Amer.

Pechey, Susan. Impressions of the University of Queensland. (Illus.). 57p. 1983. text ed. 12.50x (ISBN 0-7022-1853-7). U of Queensland Pr.

Pechman, Joseph A. Federal Tax Policy. 3rd ed. LC 76-54901. (Studies of Government Finance). 1977. 16.95 (ISBN 0-8157-6978-4); pap. 8.95 (ISBN 0-8157-6977-6). Brookings.

Pechman, Joseph A. & Okner, Benjamin A. Who Bears the Tax Burden? LC 74-280. (Studies of Government Finance). 120p. 1974. 12.95 (ISBN 0-8157-6968-7); pap. 5.95 (ISBN 0-8157-6967-9). Brookings.

Pechman, Joseph A., ed. Comprehensive Income Taxation. LC 77-24246. (Studies of Government Finance). 1977. 17.95 (ISBN 0-8157-6982-2); pap. 8.95 (ISBN 0-8157-6981-4). Brookings.

--Setting National Priorities: The 1979 Budget. 1978. 14.95 (ISBN 0-8157-6984-9); pap. 5.95 (ISBN 0-8157-6983-0). Brookings.

--Setting National Priorities: The 1980 Budget. LC 76-27205. 1979. 14.95 (ISBN 0-8157-6986-5); pap. 5.95 (ISBN 0-8157-6985-7). Brookings.

--Setting National Priorities: The 1982 Budget. LC 76-27205. 250p. 1981. 22.95 (ISBN 0-8157-6990-3); pap. 8.95 (ISBN 0-8157-6989-X). Brookings.

--What Should Be Taxed: Income or Expenditure? (Studies of Government Finance). 1980. 22.95 (ISBN 0-8157-6966-0); pap. 9.95 (ISBN 0-8157-6965-2). Brookings.

Pechman, Joseph A. & Timpane, P. Michael, eds. Work Incentives & Income Guarantees: The New Jersey Negative Income Tax Experiment. (Studies in Social Experimentation). 232p. 1975. 18.95 (ISBN 0-8157-6976-8); pap. 7.95 (ISBN 0-8157-6975-X). Brookings.

Pechman, Joseph A., jt. ed. see Aaron, Henry J.

Pechman, Joseph A., jt. ed. see Palmer, John L.

Pechmeja, Jean De. Telephe en Douze Livres. (Utopias in the Enlightenment Ser.). 267p. (Fr.). 1974. Repr. of 1784 ed. lib. bdg. 72.00x o.p. (ISBN 0-8287-0672-7, 038). Clearwater Pub.

Pecile, A., ed. Calcitonin: Proceedings, Milan 1980. (International Congress Ser.: No. 540). 1982. 80.00 (ISBN 0-686-80806-1). Elsevier.

Pecile, A. & Muller, E., eds. Growth Hormones & Other Biologically Active Peptides. (International Congress Ser.: Vol. 495). 1980. 58.50 (ISBN 0-444-90122-1). Elsevier.

Peck, Abraham J. Radicals & Reactionaries: The Crisis of Conservatism in Wilhelmine Germany. LC 78-62921. (Illus.). 1978. pap. text ed. 13.50 (ISBN 0-8191-0601-1). U Pr of Amer.

Peck, Cornelius J., ed. see Labor Law Group.

Peck, Cynthia V., jt. auth. see Cox, Diane.

Peck, David & Whitlow, David. Approaches to Personality Theory. (Essential Psychology Ser.). 1975. pap. 4.50x (ISBN 0-416-82810-8). Methuen Inc.

Peck, David W. Decision at Law. LC 76-56082. 1977. Repr. of 1961 ed. lib. bdg. 20.00x (ISBN 0-8371-9419-9, PEDL). Greenwood.

Peck, Elisabeth S. & Smith, Emily A. Berea's First One Hundred Twenty-Five Years: 1855-1980. LC 82-6955. (Illus.). 312p. 1982. 17.50x (ISBN 0-8131-1466-7). U Pr of Ky.

Peck, Elizabeth A., jt. auth. see Montgomery, Douglas C.

Peck, Ellen & Granzig, William. The Parent Test: How to Measure & Develop Your Talent for Parenthood. LC 77-17668. 1978. 9.95 o.p. (ISBN 0-399-12030-0). Putnam Pub Group.

Peck, Ellen, jt. auth. see Lieberman, E. J.

Peck, Ellen, jt. auth. see Lieberman, E. James.

Peck, J. E., ed. Algol Sixty-Eight Implementation. (Proceedings). 1971. 29.50 (ISBN 0-7204-2045-8, North Holland). Elsevier.

Peck, Johanne. Young Children's Behavior: Implementing Your Goals. new ed. LC 78-56624. (Illus.). 1978. pap. text ed. 8.95 (ISBN 0-89334-015-4). Humanics Ltd.

Peck, Johanne, ed. see Goldman, Richard, et al.

Peck, Judith. Leap to the Sun: Learning Through Dynamic Play. (Illus.). 1979. 12.95 o.p. (ISBN 0-13-527275-0, Spec). P-H.

Peck, Larry, jt. auth. see Irgolic, Kurt.

Peck, Leilani B., et al. Focus on Food. (Illus.). 432p. (gr. 7-9). 1974. text ed. 17.88 (ISBN 0-07-049145-3, W). McGraw.

Peck, Lyman C. Basic Mathematics for Management & Economics. 1970. text ed. 18.95x (ISBN 0-673-05954-5). Scott F.

Peck, M. Scott. The Road Less Traveled: A New Psychology of Love, Traditional Values & Spiritual Growth. 1978. 15.95 o.s.i. (ISBN 0-671-24086-2). S&S.

Peck, Mary J., jt. auth. see Murphy, Herta A.

Peck, Michaeleen P. An Investigation of Tenth-Grade Students' Writing. LC 82-40074. (Illus.). 166p. (Orig.). 1982. lib. bdg. 22.00 (ISBN 0-8191-2562-8); pap. text ed. 10.00 (ISBN 0-8191-2563-6). U Pr of Amer.

Peck, Paul L. Footsteps along the Path. rev. ed. (Spiritual Metaphysics: Freeways to Divine Awareness Ser.). 164p. (Orig.). 1982. pap. 7.95 (ISBN 0-941600-01-7). Harmony Pr.

--Freeway to Health. (Spiritual Metaphysics: Freeways to Divine Awareness Ser.). 264p. (Orig.). 1982. pap. 7.95 (ISBN 0-941600-04-1). Harmony Pr.

--Freeway to Human Love. (Spiritual Metaphysics: Freeways to Divine Awareness Ser.). 264p. (Orig.). 1982. pap. 7.95 (ISBN 0-941600-06-8). Harmony Pr.

--Freeway to Personal Growth. (Spiritual Awareness: Freeways to Divine Awareness Ser.). 264p. (Orig.). 1982. pap. 7.95 (ISBN 0-941600-07-6). Harmony Pr.

--Freeway to Work & Health. (Spiritual Metaphysics: Freeways to Divine Awareness Ser.). 264p. (Orig.). 1982. pap. 7.95 (ISBN 0-941600-05-X). Harmony Pr.

--Inherit the Kingdom. rev. ed. (Spiritual Metaphysics: Freeways to Divine Awareness Ser.). (Orig.). 1982. pap. 7.95 (ISBN 0-941600-02-5). Harmony Pr.

--Milestones of the Way. rev. ed. (Spiritual Metaphysics: Freeways to Divine Awareness Ser.). 250p. (Orig.). 1982. pap. 7.95 (ISBN 0-941600-03-3). Harmony Pr.

Peck, Paula. Art of Fine Baking. 1961. 9.95 o.p. (ISBN 0-671-04345-5). S&S.

Peck, R. B., jt. auth. see Terzaghi, Karl.

Peck, Ralph B., et al. Foundation Engineering. 2nd ed. LC 73-9877. 544p. 1974. 36.95 (ISBN 0-471-67585-7). Wiley.

Peck, Richard. Are You in the House Alone? 1977. pap. 2.25 (ISBN 0-440-90227-4, LFL). Dell.

--Close Enough to Touch. (Young Love Romance Ser.). (gr. 7-12). 1982. pap. 2.25 (ISBN 0-440-91282-2, LFL). Dell.

--Father Figure. (Orig.). (RL 5). 1979. pap. 2.25 (ISBN 0-451-11787-5, AE1787, Sig). NAL.

--The Ghost Belonged to Me. (gr. 7 up). 1976. pap. 1.95 o.p. (ISBN 0-380-00725-8, 51847). Avon.

--Amanda Miranda. 1980. 12.95 o.p. (ISBN 0-670-11530-4). Viking Pr.

--New York Time. 224p. 1981. 11.95 o.s.i. (ISBN 0-440-06346-9). Delacorte.

--This Family of Women. 440p. 1983. 15.95 (ISBN 0-440-08588-8). Delacorte.

Peck, Robert L. American Meditation & Beginning Yoga. 1976. 6.00 (ISBN 0-685-71846-8). Personal Dev Ctr.

Peck, Robert N. A Day No Pigs Would Die. (gr. 7 up). 1972. 11.95 (ISBN 0-394-48235-2). Knopf.

--Eagle Fur. 1979. pap. 1.95 o.p. (ISBN 0-380-45039-9, 45039). Avon.

--Eagle Fur. 1978. 10.95 (ISBN 0-394-42785-8). Knopf.

--Fawn. (gr. 4-8). 1977. pap. 1.25 o.p. (ISBN 0-440-92488-X, LFL). Dell.

--Kirk's Law. LC 80-2058. 216p. 1981. 11.95a (ISBN 0-385-17242-7); PLB (ISBN 0-385-17243-5). Doubleday.

--Last Sunday. LC 76-42381. 1977. 6.95 o.p. (ISBN 0-385-12532-1). Doubleday.

--Millie's Boy. 176p. 1975. pap. 1.50 o.p. (ISBN 0-440-95657-9, LFL). Dell.

--Path of Hunters: Animal Struggle in a Meadow. (Illus.). (gr. 4-6). 1973. 4.95 o.p. (ISBN 0-394-82424-5); PLB 5.99 (ISBN 0-394-92424-X). Knopf.

--Soup. LC 73-15117. (Illus.). 104p. (gr. 3 up). 1974. o. p. 4.95 (ISBN 0-394-82700-7); PLB 6.99 (ISBN 0-394-92700-1). Knopf.

--Trig. (Illus.). (gr. 4-6). 1977. 6.95 (ISBN 0-316-69654-4). Little.

Peck, Robert Newton. Basket Case. LC 78-60298. (gr. 10 up). 1979. PLB 7.95 (ISBN 0-385-14362-1). Doubleday.

--Soup in the Saddle. LC 82-14010. (Illus.). 96p. (gr. 3-6). 1983. 9.95 (ISBN 0-394-85294-X); lib. bdg. 9.99 (ISBN 0-394-95294-4). Knopf.

Peck, Russell A. Chaucer's Lyrics & Anelida & Arcite: An Annoted Bibliography 1900 to 1980. (Chaucer Bibliographies Ser.). 256p. 1983. 36.00x (ISBN 0-8020-2481-5). U of Toronto Pr.

Peck, Stephen R. Atlas of Human Anatomy for the Artist. (Illus.). 1951. 19.95 o.p. (ISBN 0-19-500052-8); pap. text ed. 11.95x o.p. (ISBN 0-19-501020-5). Oxford U Pr.

--Atlas of Human Anatomy for the Artist. 1982. pap. 11.95 (ISBN 0-19-503095-8, GB 689, GB). Oxford U Pr.

Peck, Theodore P., ed. Chemical Industries Information Sources. LC 76-6891. (Management Information Guide Ser.: No. 29). 1979. 42.00x (ISBN 0-8103-0829-0). Gale.

--Employee Counseling in Industry & Government: A Guide to Information Sources. LC 79-16028. (Management Information Guide Ser.: No. 37). 1979. 42.00x (ISBN 0-8103-0837-1). Gale.

--Occupational Safety & Health: A Guide to Information Sources. LC 74-7199. (Management Information Guide Ser.: No. 28). 262p. 1974. 42.00x (ISBN 0-8103-0828-2). Gale.

Peck, Theresa, jt. auth. see St. Vincent Hospital Staff.

Peck, W. A. Bone & Mineral Research: Annual 1. Date not set. 81.00 (ISBN 0-444-90239-2). Elsevier.

Peckham, Gladys C. & Freeland, Jeanne H. Foundations of Food Preparation. 4th ed. (Illus.). 1979. text ed. 22.95x (ISBN 0-02-393260-0). Macmillan.

Peckham, H. Hands On BASIC: For the Apple II Plus Computer. 1982. pap. 19.95 (ISBN 0-07-049179-8). McGraw.

--Hands-On BASIC for the IBM Personal Computer. Adhesive bd. ed. 352p. 1982. 7.98 (ISBN 0-07-049184-4). McGraw.

Peckham, H., jt. auth. see Luehrmann, A.

Peckham, Herbert, jt. auth. see Luehrmann, Arthur.

Peckham, Herbert C. BASIC: A Hands-on Method. 2nd ed. (Illus.). 320p. 1981. pap. text ed. 17.95 (ISBN 0-07-049160-7); instructor's manual 4.00 (ISBN 0-07-049161-5). McGraw.

Peckham, Herbert D. Hands-On BASIC: For the IBM Computer. LC 82-81497. 352p. 1982. pap. text ed. 19.95x (ISBN 0-07-049178-X, C). Mcgraw.

--Hands-On BASIC with a PET. (Illus.). 1979. pap. 17.95 (ISBN 0-07-049157-7, C). McGraw.

--Programming Basic with the TI Small Business Computer. 1979. pap. text ed. 19.95 (ISBN 0-07-049156-9). McGraw.

Peckham, Howard H. War for Independence: A Military History. LC 58-5685. (Chicago History of American Civilization Ser). 1958. pap. 6.95 (ISBN 0-226-65316-1, CHAC15). U of Chicago Pr.

Peckham, Howard H., jt. ed. see Brown, Lloyd A.

Peckham, John M., 3rd. Master Guide to Income Property Brokerage. 1969. 59.50 (ISBN 0-13-559864-8). Exec Reports.

Peckham, Morse. Man's Rage for Chaos: Biology, Behavior, & the Arts. LC 65-22544. (Illus.). 1967. pap. 5.95 (ISBN 0-8052-0142-4). Schocken.

Peckham, Morse, ed. Robert Browning: Sordello. a Marginally Emended Edition. LC 76-58619. 468p. 1977. 18.50 (ISBN 0-87875-240-4). Whitston Pub.

Peckham, Morse, ed. see Swinburne, Algernon C.

Peckinpaugh, Angela & Hayna, Lois B. A Book of Charms. 64p. (Orig.). 1983. pap. 6.95 (ISBN 0-935306-19-6). Barnwood Pr.

Peckner, Donald & Bernstein, I. M. Handbook of Stainless Steels. (Handbook Ser.). (Illus.). 928p. 1977. 69.50 (ISBN 0-07-049147-X, P&RB). McGraw.

Peckner, Donald, ed. Strengthening of Metals. 256p. 1964. 13.95 o.p. (ISBN 0-442-15534-4, Pub. by Van Nos Reinhold). Krieger.

Pecora, Ferdinand. Wall Street Under Oath. LC 68-20529. Repr. of 1939 ed. 15.00x o.p. (ISBN 0-678-00372-6). Kelley.

Pecora, Robert, jt. auth. see Berne, Bruce J.

Pecsi, Kalman. The Future of Socialist Economic Integration. rev. ed. Marer, Paul, ed. Hajdu, George & Crane, Keith, trs. from Hungarian. LC 81-2524. Orig. Title: A KGST Termelesi Integracio Kozgazdasagi Kerdesei. 224p. 1981. 25.00 (ISBN 0-87332-186-3). M E Sharpe.

Pecsok, Robert L., jt. auth. see Laub, Richard J.

Pecsok, Robert L., et al. Modern Methods of Chemical Analysis. 2nd ed. LC 76-13894. 1976. 29.95x (ISBN 0-471-67662-4). Wiley.

Pecufflic, M. & Abdel-Malek, A. Science & Technology in the Transformation of the World. 1982. 55.00x (ISBN 0-686-42943-5, Pub. by Macmillan England). State Mutual Bk.

Pedde, Lawrence D. & Foote, Warren E. Metric Manual. 278p. 1980. Repr. of 1978 ed. 38.00x (ISBN 0-8103-1020-1). Gale.

Pedder, Jonathan R., jt. auth. see Brown, Dennis G.

Pedder, M., jt. auth. see Ryan, W.

Peddie, Robert A. Place-Names in Imprints: An Index to the Latin & Other Forms Used on Title-Pages. LC 68-30594. 1968. Repr. of 1932 ed. 30.00x (ISBN 0-8103-3239-6). Gale.

Peddle, Frank. Thought & Being: Hegel's Criticism of Kant's System of Cosmological Ideas. LC 79-9695. 204p. 1980. text ed. 20.00 (ISBN 0-8191-0987-8); pap. text ed. 10.25 (ISBN 0-8191-0988-6). U Pr of Amer.

Pedemonti, Richard D., jt. auth. see Coleman, Les.

Peden, Creighton & Chipman, Donald, eds. Critical Issues in Philosophy of Education. LC 79-66233. 1979. pap. text ed. 9.50 (ISBN 0-8191-0805-7). U Pr of Amer.

Peden, Margaret S. Emilio Carballido. (World Authors Ser.). 1980. lib. bdg. 15.95 (ISBN 0-8057-6403-8, Twayne). G K Hall.

--The Latin American Short Story: A Critical History. (Critical History of the Modern Short Story Ser.). 208p. 1983. lib. bdg. 17.95 (ISBN 0-8057-9351-8, Twayne). G K Hall.

Peden, Margaret S., tr. see Carballido, Emilio.

Peden, Margaret S., tr. see Quiroga, Horacio.

Pedersen, B. E. see Bernard, Edward, pseud.

Pedersen, Christian F. The International Flag Book in Color. (Illus.). 1971. 6.95 o.p. (ISBN 0-688-01883-1). Morrow.

Pedersen, Holgar, et al, eds. A Glance at the History of Lingustics with Particular Regard to the Historical Study of Phonology. (Studies in History of Linguistics Ser.: No. 7). 14.00 (ISBN 90-272-1720-3). Benjamins North Am.

Pedersen, Jean J. & Armbruster, Franz O. A New Twist: Developing Arithemetic Skills Through Problem Solving. 1979. text ed. 10.75 (ISBN 0-201-05712-3, Sch Div). A-W.

Pedersen, Paul B., et al, eds. Counseling Across Cultures. rev. & expanded ed. LC 80-2961. 368p. (Orig.). 1981. pap. 10.00x (ISBN 0-8248-0725-1). UH Pr.

Pederson, E. O. Transportation in Cities. 1981. 12.50 (ISBN 0-08-024666-4). Pergamon.

Pederson, Erik S. Nuclear Power: Nuclear Power Plant Design, Vol. 1. LC 77-92594. (Illus.). 1978. 49.95 (ISBN 0-250-40230-0). Ann Arbor Science.

--Nuclear Power: Nuclear Power Project Management, 2 vols. LC 77-92594. (Illus.). 1978. Vol. 1. 37.50 o.p. (ISBN 0-250-40230-0); Set. 99.90 (ISBN 0-250-40235-1); Vol. 2. 49.95 (ISBN 0-250-40231-9). Ann Arbor Science.

Pederson, Johannes. Israel: Its Life & Culture, 4 bks. Incl. Bks. 1 & 2. 1973. Repr. of 1926 ed. 59.00x o.p. (ISBN 0-19-647899-5). Oxford U Pr.

Pederson, L. G., jt. auth. see Isenhour, T. L.

Pederson, Les. Missionary Go Home? LC 80-14445. 1980. pap. 3.95 (ISBN 0-8024-4881-X). Moody.

PeDerson, Paul, jt. auth. see Douglas, Stephan A.

Pederson, Paul B., ed. Counseling Across Culture. 1978. 2.00 (ISBN 0-686-36380-9); nonmembers 2.50 (ISBN 0-686-37297-2). Am Personnel.

Pederson, Rolf A. Rolf's Collection of Wild Game Recipes: Vol. I: Upland Game Birds. Carlson, Nancy, ed. 174p. (Orig.). 1982. pap. 9.95 (ISBN 0-910579-00-8). Rolfs Gall.

Pederson, Sam, jt. auth. see Bruce, Phillip.

Pederson, Trudy Rodine. A Pioneer Experience. (Illus.). 116p. (Orig.). 1982. 10.00 (ISBN 0-686-95352-5). Directed Media.

Pedgley, David E. Windbourne Pests & Diseases: Meteorology of Airborne Organisms. 240p. 1981. 59.95 (ISBN 0-470-27516-2). Halsted Pr.

Pedicord, Harry W. & Bergmann, Frederick L., eds. The Plays of David Garrick, Vol. 4. Date not set. price not set. S Ill U Pr.

--The Plays of David Garrick, Vol. 5: Garrick's Alterations of Others, 1742-1750. 1982. 50.00x (ISBN 0-8093-0993-9). S Ill U Pr.

--The Plays of David Garrick, Vol. 6: Garrick's Alterations of Others, 1751-1756. 1982. 50.00x (ISBN 0-8093-0994-7). S Ill U Pr.

--The Plays of David Garrick, Vol. 7: Garrick's Alterations of Others, 1757-1773. 1982. 50.00x (ISBN 0-8093-1051-1). S Ill U Pr.

Pedicord, Harry W. & Bergmann, Fredrick L., eds. The Plays of David Garrick, Vol. 3: A Complete Collection of the Social Satires, French Adaptations, Pantomimes, Christmas & Musical Plays, Preludes, Interludes, & Burlesques, to Which Are Added the Alterations & Adaptations of the Plays of Shakespeare & Other Dramatists from the Sixteenth & Seventeenth Centuries. LC 79-28443. (Illus.). 496p. 1981. 50.00x (ISBN 0-8093-0968-8). S Ill U Pr.

Pedler, K. see Allen, W. S.

Pedler, Mike, jt. ed. see Boydell, Tom.

Pedley, T. J. The Fluid Mechanics of Large Blood Vessels. LC 78-73814. (Cambridge Monographs on Mechanics & Applied Mathematics). (Illus.). 1980. 97.50 (ISBN 0-521-22626-0). Cambridge U Pr.

Pedlosky, J. Geophysical Fluid Dynamics: Springer Study Edition. (Illus.). 624p. 1983. pap. 26.00 (ISBN 0-387-90745-9). Springer-Verlag.

Pedlow, J. C. Windows on the Holy Land. 150p. 1980. pap. 8.95 (ISBN 0-227-67839-7). Attic Pr.

Pedoe, D. Course of Geometry for Colleges & Universities. (Illus.). 1970. 29.95x (ISBN 0-521-07638-2). Cambridge U Pr.

Pedoe, Dan. Geometry & the Liberal Arts. LC 77-24023. (Illus.). 1978. 10.95 o.p. (ISBN 0-312-32370-0). St Martin.

--Geometry & the Visual Arts. (Illus.). 353p. 1983. pap. 6.00 (ISBN 0-486-24458-X). Dover.

Pedoe, Daniel. A Geometric Introduction to Linear Algebra. 2nd ed. LC 72-78369. xi, 224p. 1976. text ed. 12.95 (ISBN 0-8284-0286-8). Chelsea Pub.

Pedolsky, Andrea, ed. In-House Traning & Development Programs: A Guide to Schools & Colleges Offering Training Programs for Businesses, Seminar Packagers, Consultants, Audiovisual Producers & Distributors. 328p. 1981. 115.00x (ISBN 0-8103-0963-7). Gale.

Pedraz, Juan L. I Wish I Could Believe. Attanasio, Salvatore, tr. from Span. LC 82-20606. 216p. (Orig.). 1983. pap. 7.95 (ISBN 0-8189-0445-3). Alba.

Pedrell, Felipe, ed. Hispaniae Schola Musica Sacra, 8 vols. in 4. Repr. of 1894 ed. per double vol. 30.00 (ISBN 0-384-45635-9); 110.00 set (ISBN 0-686-96761-5); pap. 25.00 per double vol. (ISBN 0-686-57641-1); pap. 90.00 set (ISBN 0-685-31549-5). Johnson Repr.

Pedretti, Carlo. Catalogue of the Newly Restored Sheets of the Leonardo Da Vinci Codex Atlanticus. 1978. leather bdg. 100.00 (ISBN 0-384-32305-7); cloth bdg. 60.00 (ISBN 0-384-32304-9). Johnson Repr.

Pedretti, Lorraine W. Occupational Therapy: Practice Skills for Physical Dysfunction. LC 81-11076. (Illus.). 339p. 1981. pap. text ed. 29.95 (ISBN 0-8016-3772-4). Mosby.

Pedrick, George, jt. auth. see Goffman, Casper.

Pedrick, Jean. Greenfellow. LC 81-846411. 63p. 1981. pap. 3.00 (ISBN 0-89823-033-0). New Rivers Pr.

Peebles, Andy. The Elton John Tapes. (Illus.). 72p. 1981. pap. 3.95 (ISBN 0-312-24380-4); prepack o.p. 39.50 (ISBN 0-686-86763-7). St Martin.

Peebles, Marvin L. Directory of Consultants & Management Training Programs Intended for Local Nonprofits 1983. 100p. 1983. spiral bdg. 20.00 (ISBN 0-939020-26-2). MLP Ent.

--Directory of Consultants & Management Training Programs: 1981. 100p. 1981. 12.00x o.p. (ISBN 0-939020-25-4). MLP Ent.

--Directory of Management Resources for Community Based Organizations: Third Annual. 100p. 1981. spiral bdg. 12.00x o.p. (ISBN 0-939020-03-3). MLP Ent.

Peebles, Patrick. Sri Lanka: A Handbook of Historical Statistics. (International Historical Statistics Ser.). 387p. 1982. lib. bdg. 65.00 (ISBN 0-8161-8160-8, Hall Reference). G K Hall.

Peebles, Peyton Z. Communication System Principles. (Illus.). 1976. 29.50 (ISBN 0-201-05758-1, Adv Bk Prog); solutions manual 4.50 (ISBN 0-201-05759-X). A-W.

--Probability, Random Variables, & Random Signal Principles. (Illus.). 1980. text ed. 29.50 (ISBN 0-07-049180-1); solns. manual 25.00 (ISBN 0-07-049181-X). McGraw.

Peebles Press International & Zabronski, Ann. Cheaper & Cheaper Restaurant Guide to Manhattan. 192p. 1980. 8.95 (ISBN 0-13-128421-5, Spec); pap. 3.95 o.p. (ISBN 0-13-128413-4). P-H.

Peek, Hedley & Aflalo, F. G., eds. Encyclopaedia of Sport, 2 vols. LC 75-23210. (Illus.). 1976. Repr. of 1897 ed. Set. 175.00x (ISBN 0-8103-4207-3). Gale.

Peek, Peter & Standing, Guy, eds. State Policies & Migration: Studies in Latin America & the Caribbean. (Illus.). 422p. 1982. text ed. 32.50x (Pub. by Croom Helm Ltd England). Biblio Dist.

Peek, Walter W., jt. auth. see Sanders, Thomas E.

Peeke, Catherine. Preliminary Grammar of Auca. (Publications in Linguistics & Related Fields Ser.: No. 39). 1973. pap. 6.00x o.s.i. (ISBN 0-88312-041-0); microfiche 2.25x (ISBN 0-88312-441-6). Summer Inst Ling.

Peeke, Harmon V. & Herz, Michael J., eds. Habituation, 2 vols. Incl. Vol. 1. Behavioral Studies. 1973. 46.50 (ISBN 0-12-549801-2); Vol. 2. Electrophysiological Substrates. 1973. 40.50 (ISBN 0-12-549802-0). Set. 70.00. Acad Pr.

Peekner, Ray, jt. auth. see Paulsen, Gary.

Peel, D. A., jt. auth. see Holden, K.

Peel, J. & Potts, D. M. Textbook of Contraceptive Practice. (Illus.). 1969. 49.50 (ISBN 0-521-07515-7); pap. 15.95x (ISBN 0-521-09598-0). Cambridge U Pr.

Peel, J. D. Y. & Ranger, T. O., eds. Past & Present in Zimbabwe. 128p. 1983. pap. 9.95 (ISBN 0-7190-0896-4). Manchester.

Peel, J. H. Along the Green Roads of Britain. (Illus.). 240p. 1982. 22.50 (ISBN 0-7153-8327-2). David & Charles.

--Peel's England. LC 77-73586. 1977. 14.95 o.p. (ISBN 0-7153-7380-3). David & Charles.

Peel, John D. Story of Private Security. 168p. 1971. photocopy ed. spiral 16.75x (ISBN 0-398-01465-5). C C Thomas.

Peel, Ronald, et al. Processes in Physical & Human Geography. 1975. text ed. 33.95x o.p. (ISBN 0-435-35625-9). Heinemann Ed.

Peel, Roy V. & Donnelly, Thomas C. The Nineteen Thirty-Two Campaign: An Analysis. LC 73-454. (FDR & the Era of the New Deal Ser.). 252p. 1973. Repr. of 1935 ed. lib. bdg. 29.50 (ISBN 0-306-70567-2). Da Capo.

Peel, Roy V. & Sellin, Thorsten, eds. Ombudsman or Citizen's Defender: A Modern Institution. LC 68-21996. (Annals of the American Academy of Political & Social Science: No. 377). (Orig.). 1968. 15.00 (ISBN 0-87761-107-6); pap. 7.95 (ISBN 0-87761-106-8). Am Acad Pol Soc Sci.

Peelaert, Guy & Cohn, Nik. Rock Dreams. (Illus.). 176p. 1982. 19.95 (ISBN 0-394-52870-0); pap. 10.95 (ISBN 0-394-71000-2). Knopf.

Peele, David A., ed. Racket & Paddle Games: A Guide to Information Sources. LC 80-23977. (Sports, Games & Pastimes Information Guide Ser.: Vol. 9). 300p. 1980. 42.00x (ISBN 0-8103-1480-0). Gale.

Peele, George. The Chronicle of King Edward the First, Surnamed Longshanks: With the Life of Lluellen, Rebel in Wales. Dreher, G. K., ed. LC 74-79524. (Illus.). xliii, 96p. 1974. pap. 5.95 (ISBN 0-9601000-1-6). Longshanks Bk.

--Samples from the Love of King David & Fair Bethsabe: With Reference Portions of the Bible. Dreher, G. K., ed. LC 79-56834. 70p. (Orig.). 1980. pap. 4.95 (ISBN 0-9601000-2-4). Longshanks Bk.

Peele, Gillian & Cook, Chris, eds. The Politics of Reappraisal: Nineteen-Eighteen to Nineteen Thirty-Nine. LC 75-13591. 250p. 1975. 26.00 (ISBN 0-312-62720-3). St Martin.

Peele, R. Mining Engineers' Handbook, 2 vols. 3rd ed. (Engineering Handbook Ser.). 1941. Set. 95.95 (ISBN 0-471-67716-7, Pub. by Wiley-Interscience). Wiley.

Peele, Stanton. The Addiction Experience. 1980. pap. 1.95 (ISBN 0-89486-089-5). Hazelden.

--How Much Is Too Much? Healthy Habits of Destructive Addictions. (Illus.). 160p. 1981. 11.95 (ISBN 0-13-424192-4, Spec); pap. 5.95 (ISBN 0-13-424184-3). P-H.

--The Science of Experience: A Direction for Psychology. LC 81-48555. 1983. price not set (ISBN 0-669-05420-8). Lexington Bks.

Peele, Stanton & Brodsky, Archie. Addiction is a Social Disease. 1.95 (ISBN 0-89486-015-1, 1127B). Hazelden.

--Love & Addiction. 1976. pap. 3.50 (ISBN 0-451-12049-3, AE2049, Sig). NAL.

--Love & Addiction. 2.95 o.p. (ISBN 0-686-92376-6, 6489). Hazelden.

Peele, Talmage L. The Neuroanatomic Basis for Clinical Neurology. 3rd ed. 1976. 41.00 (ISBN 0-07-049175-5, HP). McGraw.

Peeples, Bill, ed. see Vauclair, Marguerite.

Peeples, Samuel. The Man Who Died Twice: A Novel About Hollywood's Most Baffling Murder. LC 76-7085. 1976. 7.95 o.p. (ISBN 0-399-11777-6). Putnam Pub Group.

Peeples, W. D., Jr., jt. auth. see Wheeler, Ruric E.

Peer Review Committee of the American Psychiatric Assn., et al, eds. Manual of Psychiatric Peer Review. 2nd ed. LC 80-69213. 160p. 1981. spiral bdg. 11.00 (ISBN 0-89042-116-1, P168-0). Am Psychiatric.

Peercy, P. S., jt. ed. see White, C. W.

Peerman, Frank. See You in the Morning. LC 76-5296. 96p. 1976. 4.50 o.p. (ISBN 0-8054-5237-0). Broadman.

Peers, E. Alison. The Life of Teresa of Jesus. 1960. pap. 5.50 (ISBN 0-385-01109-1, Im). Doubleday.

Peers, Edgar A. Catolonia Infelix. Repr. of 1938 ed. lib. bdg. 17.75x (ISBN 0-8371-4310-1, PECI). Greenwood.

--The Spanish Tragedy, Nineteen Thirty to Nineteen Thirty-Six. LC 75-8724. 247p. 1975. Repr. of 1936 ed. lib. bdg. 16.00x (ISBN 0-8371-8048-1, PEST). Greenwood.

Peers, W. R. The My Lai Inquiry. LC 78-14242. (Illus.). 318p. 1979. 12.95 o.p. (ISBN 0-393-01184-4). Norton.

Peery, D. J. & Azar, J. J. Aircraft Structures. 2nd ed. 1982. 36.00 (ISBN 0-07-049196-8). McGraw.

Peery, Rex & Umbach, Arnold. Wrestling. rev. ed. LC 61-12052. (Athletic Institute Ser). (Illus.). (gr. 6 up). 1967. 9.95 (ISBN 0-8069-4334-3); PLB 12.49 (ISBN 0-8069-4335-1). Sterling.

Peet, Bill. Buford the Little Bighorn. (Illus.). 48p. (gr. k-3). 1983. pap. 3.95 (ISBN 0-395-34067-5). HM.

--Caboose Who Got Loose. LC 79-155554. (Illus.). (gr. k-3). 1971. reinforced bdg. 9.95 (ISBN 0-395-14805-7); pap. 3.95 (ISBN 0-395-28715-4). HM.

--Countdown to Christmas. LC 72-78394. (Illus.). 48p. (gr. 1-4). 1972. 4.95 o.p. (ISBN 0-516-18716-3, Golden Gate); PLB 9.25 (ISBN 0-516-08716-9). Childrens.

--Encore for Eleanor. (gr. k-3). 1981. 11.95 (ISBN 0-395-29860-1). HM.

--How Droofus the Dragon Lost His Head. (Illus.). 48p. (gr. k-3). 1983. pap. 3.95 (ISBN 0-395-34066-7). HM.

--Hubert's Hair-Raising Adventure. (Illus.). (gr. k-3). 1959. reinforced bdg. 11.95 (ISBN 0-395-15083-3). HM.

--Huge Harold. (Illus.). (gr. k-3). 1961. reinforced bdg. 11.95 (ISBN 0-395-18449-5). HM.

--No Such Things. LC 82-23234. (Illus.). 32p. (gr. k-3). 1983. pap. text ed. 10.95 (ISBN 0-395-33888-3). HM.

--Randy's Dandy Lions. (Illus.). (gr. k-3). 1964. reinforced bdg. 11.95 (ISBN 0-395-18507-6). HM.

Peet, Creighton. Eye on the Sky: How Aircraft Controllers Work. (Illus.). (gr. 4 up). 1970. 6.25 (ISBN 0-8255-7200-2); PLB 5.97 (ISBN 0-8255-7201-0). Macrae.

--Man in Flight: How the Airlines Operate. (Illus.). 192p. (gr. 5 up). 1972. 6.25 (ISBN 0-8255-7220-7); PLB 5.79 (ISBN 0-8255-7221-5). Macrae.

Peet, Louis H. Handy Book of American Authors. LC 75-156928. 1971. Repr. of 1907 ed. 42.00x (ISBN 0-8103-3360-0). Gale.

Peet, Louise J., et al. Household Equipment. 8th ed. LC 78-11749. 1979. text ed. 29.95x (ISBN 0-471-02694-8); tchrs. manual o.p. avail. (ISBN 0-471-04876-3). Wiley.

Peet, Mary M., jt. auth. see Teare, Iwan D.

Peet, Richard. Radical Geography. 387p. 1978. text ed. 8.95x (ISBN 0-416-71240-1). Methuen Inc.

Peet, Richard, ed. Radical Geography: Alternative Viewpoints on Contemporary Social Issues. LC 76-55222. (Maaroufa Press Geography Ser.). (Illus.). 1977. pap. 7.95x (ISBN 0-88425-006-7). Maaroufa Pr.

Peeters, H., ed. Protides of the Biological Fluids: Proceedings of the 30th Colloquium on Protides of the Biological Fluids, May 1982, Brussels, Belguim. LC 58-5908. (Illus.). 760p. 1982. 180.00 (ISBN 0-08-029815-X, H220). Pergamon.

Peeters, Henk, jt. auth. see Ketting, Kees.

Peeters, Paul & Meijer, Anton. Computer Network Architectures. 1983. text ed. 27.95 (ISBN 0-914894-41-2). Computer Sci.

Peets, Elbert. On the Art of Designing Cities: Selected Essays of Elbert Peets. Spreiregen, Paul D., ed. 1968. 12.50 o.p. (ISBN 0-262-16022-6). MIT Pr.

Peffer, Nathaniel. Far East: A Modern History. rev. & enl. ed. LC 68-29270. (History of the Modern World Ser). (Illus.). 1968. 15.00x o.p. (ISBN 0-472-07031-2). U of Mich Pr.

Pegal, Alfred A. VW Vanagon: 1980-1981 Shop Manual. Wauson, Sydnie A., ed. (Illus.). 288p. (Orig.). 1982. pap. 11.95 (ISBN 0-89287-351-5). Clymer Pubns.

Pegels, C. Carl. Health Care & the Elderly. LC 80-24360. 225p. 1981. text ed. 29.00 (ISBN 0-89443-333-4). Aspen Systems.

Pegels, C. Carl & Verkler, R. C. BASIC: A Computer Programming Language with Business & Management Applications. 3rd ed. LC 78-61168. 1978. pap. text ed. 14.95x (ISBN 0-8162-6684-0); instr's manual 1.95x (ISBN 0-8162-6683-2). Holden-Day.

Pegels, C. Carl, ed. Systems Analysis for Production Operations: Instructors Manual. (Studies in Operations Research). Date not set. write for info. (ISBN 0-677-05380-0). Gordon.

Pegg, D., jt. auth. see Marchant, J. P.

Pegg, Mark. Broadcasting & Society Nineteen-Eighteen - Nineteen Thirty-Nine. 240p. 1983. text ed. 29.25x (ISBN 0-7099-2039-3, Pub. by Croom Helm Ltd England). Biblio Dist.

Pegis, Anton C. Saint Thomas & Philosophy. (Aquinas Lecture). 1964. 7.95 (ISBN 0-87462-129-1). Marquette.

--Saint Thomas & the Greeks. (Aquinas Lecture). 1939. 7.95 (ISBN 0-87462-103-8). Marquette.

Pegler, D. N. & Young, T. W. Basidiospore Morphology in the Agaricales. (Illus.). 1971. 64.00 (ISBN 3-7682-5435-6). Lubrecht & Cramer.

Pegler, Martin. Stores of the Year. (A Pictorial Report on Store Interiors 1979-80). 1979. 34.95 o.p. (ISBN 0-934590-02-8). Retail Report.

--Visual Merchandising & Display. (Illus.). 250p. 1983. text ed. 20.00 (ISBN 0-87005-434-1). Fairchild.

Pegler, Martin, ed. Store Windows That Sell, 1980-81. (Illus.). 178p. 1980. 34.95 o.p. (ISBN 0-934590-04-4). Retail Report.

Pegler, Martin M. Dictionary of Interior Design. (Illus.). 250p. 1983. 25.00 (ISBN 0-87005-447-3). Fairchild.

Pegler, Martin M., ed. Store Windows That Sell, Vol. II. (Illus.). 176p. 1982. 34.95 (ISBN 0-934590-08-7). Retail Report.

--Stores of the Year, Vol. II. (Illus.). 176p. 1981. 39.95 (ISBN 0-934590-07-9). Retail Report.

Pegnetter, Richard. Public Employment Bibliography, Vol. 1. 60p. 1971. pap. 2.00 (ISBN 0-87546-036-4). ILR Pr.

Pegram. Game of Patience. 1970. 4.95 (ISBN 0-87645-024-9). Gambit.

--The Pleasure Garden. 1977. 7.95 (ISBN 0-87645-096-6). Gambit.

Pegram, Don R. America: Christian or Pagan. 1982. pap. 1.00 (ISBN 0-89265-082-6). Randall Hse.

--Great Churches-Today's Essentials. 1982. pap. 1.00 (ISBN 0-89265-083-4). Randall Hse.

--Sheep Among Wolves. 1982. pap. 1.00 (ISBN 0-89265-084-2). Randall Hse.

--Sinning Against the Holy Spirit. 1982. pap. 1.00 (ISBN 0-89265-085-0). Randall Hse.

--Why We Do Not Speak in Tongues. 1982. pap. 1.00 (ISBN 0-89265-086-9). Randall Hse.

Pegrum, Dudley F. Residential Population & Urban Transport Facilities in the Los Angeles Metropolitan Area. (BBER Occasional Paper: No. 3). (Illus.). 1964. pap. 1.00 o.p. (ISBN 0-911798-13-7). UCLA Mgmt.

Pei, Mario. New Italian Self-Taught. 336p. (Ital.). 1982. pap. text ed. 4.76i (ISBN 0-06-463616-X, EH 616, EH). B&N NY.

--New Italian Self-Taught. 1982. pap. 4.76i (ISBN 0-06-463616-X, EH-616). Har-Row.

--The Story of Latin & the Romance Languages. LC 75-6352. (Illus.). 384p. (YA) 1976. 18.22i (ISBN 0-06-013312-0, HarpT). Har-Row.

--Story of the English Language. rev. ed. 1968. pap. 5.95 o.p. (ISBN 0-671-20064-X, Touchstone Bks). S&S.

--Weasel Words: The Art of Saying What You Don't Mean. LC 76-5524. 1978. 13.41i (ISBN 0-06-013342-2, HarpT). Har-Row.

--The World's Chief Languages. 1960. 18.50x (ISBN 0-913298-07-7). S F Vanni.

Pei, Mario & Ramondio, Salvatore. Dictionary of Foreign Terms. 368p. (Orig.). 1974. pap. 2.25 o.p. (ISBN 0-440-31779-7, LE). Dell.

Peich, Michael, ed. see Coover, Robert.

Peierls, Sir Rudolf. A Perspective of Physics, 2 vols. Incl. Vol. 1. Selections from 1976 Comments on Modern Physics. 280p. 1977. 43.00 (ISBN 0-677-13190-9); Vol. 2. Selections from 1977 Comments on Modern Physics. 294p. 1978. 43.00x (ISBN 0-677-12400-7). Gordon.

Peiffer, Robert L., Jr. Comparative Ophthalmic Pathology. (Illus.). 448p. 1983. 60.00x (ISBN 0-398-04780-4). C C Thomas.

Peikari, Behrouz. Fundamentals of Network Analysis & Synthesis. LC 82-13031. 512p. 1982. Repr. PLB 29.95 (ISBN 0-89874-538-1). Krieger.

Peil, Margaret. The Ghanian Factory Worker: Industrial Man in Africa. LC 73-160091. (African Studies: No. 5). (Illus.). 320p. 1972. 32.50 (ISBN 0-521-08296-X). Cambridge U Pr.

Peillon, Michael. Contemporary Irish Society: An Introduction. 231p. 1982. pap. text ed. 10.00x (ISBN 0-7171-1141-5, 90243, Pub. by Gill & Mac Ireland). Humanities.

--Irish Society: An Introduction. 1982. 39.00x (ISBN 0-7171-1141-5, Pub. by Gill & Macmillan Ireland). State Mutual Bk.

Peinkofer, Karl & Tannigel, Fritz. Handbook of Percussion Instruments. Stone, Kurt & Stone, Else, trs. from Ger. LC 76-330. 1976. pap. 22.00 (ISBN 0-930448-09-X, 70-00406). Eur-Am Music.

Peinovich, M. P. Old English Noun Morphology: A Diachronic Study. (Linguistic Ser.: Vol. 41). 1979. 34.00 (ISBN 0-444-85287-5, North Holland). Elsevier.

Peirce, Bradford K. Half Century with Juvenile Delinquents, or the New York House of Refuge & Its Times. LC 69-16242. (Criminology, Law Enforcement, & Social Problems Ser.: No. 91). (Illus., With intro. added). 1969. Repr. of 1869 ed. 18.00x (ISBN 0-87585-091-X). Patterson Smith.

Peirce, Charles S. Collected Papers of Charles Sanders Peirce, 6 vols. Hartshorne, Charles & Weiss, Paul, eds. Incl. Vol. 1 (bk. 1) Principles of Philosophy; Vol. 2 (bk. 1) Elements of Logic; Vol. 3 (bk. 2) Exact Logic (ISBN 0-674-13803-1); Vol. 4 (bk. 2) Simplest Mathematics; Vol. 5 (bk. 3) Pragmatism & Pragmaticism; Vol. 6 (bk. 3) Scientific Metaphysics; Vol. 7 (bk. 4) Science & Philosophy. Burks, A. W., ed. o.p. (ISBN 0-685-23375-8); Vol. 8 (bk. 4) Reviews, Correspondence & Bibliography. Burks, A. W., ed. o.p. (ISBN 0-685-23376-6). LC 60-9172. 3 bks. 2 vols. in ea. 50.00x ea. (Belknap Pr). Bk. 1 (ISBN 0-674-13800-7). Bk. 2 (ISBN 0-674-13801-5). Bk. 3 (ISBN 0-674-13802-3). Harvard U Pr.

Peirce, Charles S., ed. Studies in Logic: By Members of the Johns Hopkins University (1883) (Foundations of Semiotics Ser.: 1). xl, 203p. 1982. Repr. 24.00 (ISBN 90-272-3271-7). Benjamins North Am.

Peirce, Donald & Alswang, Hope. American Interiors: New England & the South. LC 82-74299. (Illus.). 64p. 1983. pap. 7.95 (ISBN 0-87663-583-4). Universe.

Peirce, F. T. & Womersley, J. R. Cloth Geometry. 80p. 1978. 29.50x (ISBN 0-900739-28-2, Pub. by Textile Inst England). State Mutual Bk.

Peirce, Henry B., jt. auth. see Durrant, Samuel W.

Peirce, J. Jeffery, et al. Hazardous Waste Management. LC 81-67509. 200p. 1981. text ed. 29.95 (ISBN 0-250-40459-1). Ann Arbor Science.

Peirce, Jeffrey J., jt. auth. see Vesilind, P. Aarne.

Peirce, Neal R. People's President: The Electoral College in American History & the Direct Vote Alternative. 1968. pap. 2.95 o.p. (ISBN 0-671-20065-8, Touchstone Bks). S&S.

Peirce, Neal R. & Hagstrom, Jerry. The Book of America. 1983. 24.50x (ISBN 0-393-01639-0). Norton.

Peires, J. B. The House of Phalo: A History of the Xhosa People in the Days of Their Independence. LC 82-2624. (Illus.). 304p. 1982. 27.50x (ISBN 0-520-04663-3); pap. 10.95x (ISBN 0-520-04793-1). U of Cal Pr.

Peiris, Kamala. Tiny Sapling-Sturdy Tree: Primary Education Reforms of the 1970's in Sri Lanka. 1983. write for info. (Universitet). Columbia U Pr.

Peithmann, Irvin M. Red Men of Fire: A History of the Cherokee Indians. (Illus.). 184p. 1964. photocopy ed. spiral 12.95x (ISBN 0-398-01470-1). C C Thomas.

Pejovic, Brian. Man & Meteorites. Stewart, T. H. & Stewart, S. M., eds. (Illus.). 120p. 1982. 14.95 (ISBN 0-907733-01-8). Sheridan.

Pejovich, Svetozar. The Codetermination Movement in the West. LC 77-18480. (Labor Participation in the Management of Business Firms). 224p. 1978. 22.95 (ISBN 0-669-02112-1). Lexington Bks.

Pejovich, Svetozar, ed. Philosophical & Economic Foundations of Capitalism. LC 82-48047. 160p. 1982. 19.95x (ISBN 0-669-05906-4). Lexington Bks.

Pekalski, A., jt. ed. see Turko, L.

Pekar, George M. & Oettmeier, Timothy N. Techniques with a Thirty-Six Inch Baton. (Illus.). 74p. 1983. spiral 6.95x (ISBN 0-398-04751-0). C C Thomas.

Pekarik, Andrew J. Japanese Lacquer, 1600-1900: Selections from the Charles A. Greenfield Collection. Wasserman, Rosanne, ed. (Illus.). 146p. 1980. 19.75 (ISBN 0-87099-247-3). Metro Mus Art.

Pekelis, Alexander H. Law & Social Action: Selected Essays of Alexander H. Pekelis. Konvitz, Milton, ed. LC 77-87376. (American Constitutional & Legal History Ser). (Illus.). 1970. Repr. of 1950 ed. lib. bdg. 37.50 (ISBN 0-306-71600-3). Da Capo.

Peking University Faculty. Modern Chinese: A Basic Course. LC 78-169835. Orig. Title: Modern Chinese Reader. 1971. Repr. of 1963 ed. pap. text ed. 4.00 (ISBN 0-486-22755-3); record & manual o.p. 14.95 (ISBN 0-486-98832-5); cassette 14.95 (ISBN 0-486-99910-6). Dover.

Pekkanen, John. American Connection. 1973. 7.95 o.s.i. (ISBN 0-695-80419-7). Follett.

--Travel Ontario. 1971. trade ed. 3.95 (ISBN 0-695-80233-X). Follett.

Peladeau, Marius B., ed. see Tyler, Royall.

Pelauzy, M. A. & Roca, F. Catala. Spanish Folk Crafts. (Illus.). 240p. 1982. 35.00 (ISBN 84-7031-060-7, Pub. by Editorial Blume Spain). Intl Schol Bk Serv.

Pelczar, Michael J., Jr., et al. Microbiology. 4th ed. 1977. text ed. 33.95 (ISBN 0-07-049229-8, C); instructor's manual 9.95 (ISBN 0-07-049231-X); lab exercises 15.95 (ISBN 0-07-049230-1); illustrated chart avail. (ISBN 0-07-049233-6); study guide 15.95 (ISBN 0-07-049232-8). McGraw.

Pelczar, Michael, Jr. & Chan, E. C. S. Elements of Microbiology. 1st ed. (Illus.). 704p. (Orig.). 1981. text ed. 27.50 (ISBN 0-07-049240-9, C); 10.95 (ISBN 0-07-049241-7); instr's. manual 15.95 (ISBN 0-07-049230-1). McGraw.

Pelczynski, Z. A., ed. Hegel's Political Philosophy: Problems & Perspectives. LC 71-160096. 1971. pap. 16.95x (ISBN 0-521-09987-0). Cambridge U Pr.

Peled, Abraham & Liu, Bede. Digital Signal Processing: Theory, Design & Implemetation. LC 76-17326. 1976. text ed. 32.95 (ISBN 0-471-01941-0). Wiley.

Pelegrin, M. J., et al, eds. Comparison of Automatic & Operations Research Techniques Applied to Large Systems Analysis. LC 80-40979. (Illus.). 240p. 1980. 49.00 (ISBN 0-08-024454-8). Pergamon.

Pelgrom, Els. The Winter When Time Was Frozen. Rudnik, Maryka & Rudnik, Raphael, trs. from Dutch. LC 80-21224. 256p. (gr. 4-6). 1980. 10.75 (ISBN 0-688-22247-1); PLB 10.32 (ISBN 0-688-32247-6). Morrow.

Pelham, David. The Penguin Book of Kites. (Illus.). 224p. 1976. pap. 8.95 (ISBN 0-14-004117-6). Penguin.

Pelham, Thomas G. State Land-Use Planning & Regulation: Florida, the Model Code, & Beyond. LC 79-2390. (Lincoln Institute of Land Policy Books). 224p. 1979. 25.95 (ISBN 0-669-03062-7). Lexington Bks.

Peli, Walden, II, compiled by. A History of St. Andrew's School: 1928-1958. (Illus.). 1973. 10.00 o.p. (ISBN 0-517-50555-X, C N Potter Bks). Crown.

Pelikan, Jaroslav. The Christian Tradition: A History of the Development of Doctrine, Vol. 3, The Growth of Medieval Theology, 600-1300. LC 78-1501. xxviii, 336p. 1980. pap. 8.95 (ISBN 0-226-65375-7, P896). U of Chicago Pr.

Pelikan, Jaroslav J. The Shape of Death: Life, Death, & Immortality in the Early Fathers. LC 78-6030. 1978. Repr. of 1961 ed. lib. bdg. 18.50x (ISBN 0-313-20458-6, PESD). Greenwood.

Pelikan, Jiri. Socialist Opposition in Eastern Europe: The Czechoslovak Example. LC 76-19161. (Motive Ser.). 1976. 20.00x (ISBN 0-312-73780-7). St Martin.

Pelin, Elin. Short Stories. (International Studies & Translations Program Ser.). 6.50 o.p. (ISBN 0-8057-5033-9, Twayne). G K Hall.

Pelkmans, Jacques, jt. auth. see Gordon, Robert.

Pell, Arthur & Sodek, Goerge. Resumes for Engineers. (Monarch's Job Finders Ser.). 128p. 1982. pap. 6.95 (ISBN 0-671-44304-6). Monarch Pr.

Pell, Erik M., ed. Proceedings: International Conference on Photoconductivity, 3rd, Stanford University, Aug. 12, 1969. 1971. 88.00 (ISBN 0-08-016137-5). Pergamon.

Pell, Jerry, jt. auth. see Hanna, Steven R.

Pell, P. S., ed. Developments in Highway-Pavement Engineering, Vol. 1. (Illus.). 1978. 57.50x (ISBN 0-85334-781-6, Pub. by Applied Sci England). Elsevier.

--Developments in Highway Pavement Engineering, Vol. 2. (Illus.). 1978. 41.00x (ISBN 0-85334-804-9, Pub. by Applied Sci England). Elsevier.

Pell, Sylvia. The Shadow of the Sun. 384p. 1981. pap. 2.50 o.p. (ISBN 0-380-50658-0, 50658). Avon.

--The Shadow of the Sun. LC 77-17877. 1978. 9.95 o.p. (ISBN 0-698-10849-3, Coward). Putnam Pub Group.

--Sun Princess. 1981. pap. 2.75 o.p. (ISBN 0-380-77628-6, 77628). Avon.

Pellat, Charles. The Life & Works of Jahiz. Hawke, D. M, tr. (Islamic World Ser.). 1969. 28.50x (ISBN 0-520-01498-7). U of Cal Pr.

Pelle, Rolland R. La see La Pelle, Rolland R.

Pellegrini, Angelo. Lean Years, Happy Years: The Kitchen, the Garden, & the Cellar. 200p. 1983. 12.95 (ISBN 0-914842-98-6). Madrona Pubs.

Pellegrini, Anthony L., jt. ed. see Bernardo, Aldo S.

Pellegrini, Anthony L., ed. see Dante Society of America, Inc.

Pellegrini, C. Developments in High Power Lasers & Their Applications. (No. 74). 1982. 88.50 (ISBN 0-444-85459-2, Pub. by Applied Sci England). Elsevier.

--Developments in High Power Lasers & Their Applications. 1982. 89.50 (ISBN 0-444-85459-2, Pub. by Applied Sci England). Elsevier.

Pellegrini, Nina, jt. auth. see Garcia, Edward.

Pellegrino, Charles R. & Stoff, Jesse A. Darwin's Universe: Origins & Crises in the History of Life. (Illus.). 256p. 1983. 18.95 (ISBN 0-442-27526-9). Van Nos Reinhold.

Pellegrino, Edmund D. & Thomasma, David C. A Philosophical Basis of Medical Practice: Toward a Philosophy & Ethic of the Healing Professions. (Illus.). 1981. 25.00x (ISBN 0-19-502790-6). Oxford U Pr.

Pellegrino, Ronald. The Electronic Arts of Sound & Light. 256p. 1982. text ed. 28.50 (ISBN 0-442-26499-2). Van Nos Reinhold.

Pellegrino, Victor C. You Can Write! Practical Writing Skills for Hawaii. LC 81-71307. (Illus.). 296p. 1982. text ed. 11.95 (ISBN 0-935848-05-3); pap. text ed. 9.95 (ISBN 0-935848-04-5). Bess Pr.

Pellens, Mildred, jt. auth. see Terry, Charles E.

Pellerin, D. & Bertin, P. Techniques of Pediatric Surgery. (Illus.). 600p. 1983. write for info. Masson Pub.

Pellerite, James J. A Modern Guide to Fingerings for the Flute. LC 72-76260. 1972. pap. text ed. 15.00 (ISBN 0-931200-68-7). Zalo.

Pelletan, Jean-Gabriel. Memoire sur la Colonie Francaise du Senegal. (Slave Trade in France, 1744-1848, Ser.). 138p. 1974. Repr. of 1800 ed. lib. bdg. 44.00x o.p. (ISBN 0-8287-0674-3, TN120). Clearwater Pub.

Pelletier, Jean, jt. auth. see Bethemont, Jacques.

Pelletier, Kenneth R. Longevity: Fulfilling Our Biological Potential. 1981. 15.95 o.s.i. (ISBN 0-440-05016-2, Sey Lawr). Delacorte.

--Mind As Healer Mind As Slayer. 1977. 10.00 o.s.i. (ISBN 0-440-05591-1, Sey Lawr). Delacorte.

--Toward a Science of Consciousness. 1978. 11.95 o.s.i. (ISBN 0-440-08972-7). Delacorte.

--Toward a Science of Consciousness. 1978. pap. 4.95 o.s.i. (ISBN 0-440-58640-2, Delta). Dell.

Pelletier, Kenneth R., ed. Holistic Medicine: From Pathology to Optimum Health. (A Merloyd Lawrence Bk.). 1979. 10.00 o.s.i. (ISBN 0-440-05288-2, Sey Lawr). Delacorte.

Pelletier, Louis, jt. auth. see Snyder, Anne.

Pelletier, Paula, jt. auth. see Rattenbury, Judith.

Pelletier, S. W. Alkaloids: Chemical & Biological Perspectives, Vol. 1. 432p. 1982. 60.00 (ISBN 0-471-08811-0, Pub. by Wiley-Interscience). Wiley.

Pelletreau, William S. Early History of Putnam County, New York. LC 75-15223. (Illus.). 880p. 1975. Repr. of 1886 ed. 16.00 (ISBN 0-89062-006-7, Pub by Landmarks Preservation Commitee of Southeast Museum). Pub Ctr Cult Res.

Pelleu, John C. Oil Painting Outdoors. (Illus.). 160p. 1976. pap. 9.95 o.p. (ISBN 0-8230-3283-3). Watson-Guptill.

Pellicer, Olga, jt. ed. see Fagen, Richard R.

Pelligrini, Anthony D. & Yawkey, Thomas D. The Development of Oral & Written Language in Social Contexts. Freedle, Roy O., ed. (Advances in Discourse Processes Ser.: Vol. 13). 320p. (Orig.). 1983. text ed. 32.50 (ISBN 0-89391-171-2); pap. text ed. 16.50 (ISBN 0-89391-172-0). Ablex Pub.

Pelligrino, Victoria, jt. auth. see Napolitane, Catherine.

Pelling, Henry. The British Communist Party: A Historical Profile. (Illus.). 204p. 1975. pap. text ed. 6.75x o.p. (ISBN 0-7136-1543-5). Humanities.

--A History of British Trade Unionism. 3rd ed. LC 76-44598. (Illus.). 1977. 22.50 (ISBN 0-312-37590-5). St Martin.

--Popular Politics & Society in Late Victorian Britain. LC 68-29377. 1968. 22.50 (ISBN 0-312-63070-0). St Martin.

--A Short History of the Labour Party. 5th ed. LC 76-40726. 1977. 20.00x (ISBN 0-312-72030-0); pap. text ed. 8.95x (ISBN 0-312-71995-7). St Martin.

--Social Geography of British Elections: 1885-1910. (Maps). 1967. 26.00 (ISBN 0-312-73290-2). St Martin.

Pelling, Henry, jt. auth. see Bealey, Frank.

Pelliprat, Henri-Paul. Everyday French Cooking. pap. 3.95 (ISBN 0-451-11680-1, AE1680, Sig). NAL.

Pellman, Donald R., jt. auth. see Glick, Ferne P.

Pellman, Rachel T., jt. ed. see Good, Phyllis P.

Pellow, Harry C. Murphy Is My Co-Pilot. 1983. 29.95 (ISBN 0-941210-07-3). HCP Res.

Pellowski, Anne. First Farm in the Valley: Anna's Story. (Illus.). 192p. 1982. 9.95 (ISBN 0-399-20887-9, Philomel). Putnam Pub Group.

--The Nine Crying Dolls: A Story from Poland. LC 79-25975. (Illus.). 32p. (gr. k-3). 1980. 6.95 (ISBN 0-399-20752-X, Philomel); PLB 6.99 (ISBN 0-399-61162-2). Putnam Pub Group.

--Stairstep Farm: Anna Rose's Story. (Illus.). 176p. (gr. 3-8). 1981. 9.95 (ISBN 0-399-20814-3, Philomel). Putnam Pub Group.

--Willow Wind Farm: Betsy's Story. (Illus.). 176p. (gr. 9-12). 1981. 8.95 (ISBN 0-399-20781-3, Philomel). Putnam Pub Group.

--Winding Valley Farm: Annie's Story. (Illus.). 192p. 1982. 9.95 (ISBN 0-399-20863-1, Philomel). Putnam Pub Group.

Pells, Richard H. Radical Visions & American Dreams. 1977. pap. 6.95xi o.p. (ISBN 0-06-131813-2, TB1813, Torch). Har-Row.

Pelly, Brian R. Thyristor Phase-Controlled Converters & Cycloconverters: Operation, Control, & Performance. LC 70-125276. 1971. 57.50x (ISBN 0-471-67790-6, Pub. by Wiley-Interscience). Wiley.

Peloubet, F. N., ed. The Every Day Bible Dictionary. Orig. Title: Peloubet's Bible Dictionary. 816p. 1983. 14.95 (ISBN 0-310-30850-X); pap. 9.95 (ISBN 0-310-30851-8). Zondervan.

Peloubet, F. N., ed. see Smith, William.

Peloubet, M. A., ed. see Smith, William.

Pelphrey, Brant. Love Was His Meaning: The Theology & Mysticism of Julain of Norwich. (Salzburg-Elizabethan Studies: Vol. 92, No. 4). 360p. 1982. pap. text ed. 25.00x (ISBN 0-391-02758-1, Pub. by Salzburg Austria). Humanities.

Pels, Gertrude. Care of Water Pets. LC 54-9768. (Illus.). (gr. 2-5). 1955. 9.57i o.p. (ISBN 0-690-17070-X, TYC-J); PLB 8.79 (ISBN 0-690-17071-8). Har-Row.

Pelson, R. L. Anyone Can Win Sweepstakes. 1980. pap. 4.95 (ISBN 0-89511-000-8). R & D Serv.

Pelson, Wickes, jt. auth. see Liebert, Robert M.

Pelstring, Linda & Mauck, JoAnn. Foods to Improve Your Health: A Complete Guide to over Three Hundred Foods for One Hundred One Common Ailments. LC 73-83298. 224p. 1974. 5.95 o.s.i. (ISBN 0-8027-7147-5). Walker & Co.

Pelt, Ethel Van see Van Pelt, Ethel.

Pelt, G. Van see Van Pelt, G.

Pelt, G. W. van see Van Pelt, G. W.

Pelt, Gertrude W. Van see Van Pelt, Gertrude W.

Pelta, Kathy. What Does a Paramedic Do? (What Do They Do? Ser.). (gr. 5 up). 1978. 6.95 (ISBN 0-396-07541-X). Dodd.

Peltason, J. W., ed. Students & Their Institutions: A Changing Relationship. 13.50 o.p. (ISBN 0-8268-1393-3, 393). ACE.

Peltchinski, V. S. La Russie En 1844 Systeme De Legislatiion, D'administration et Politique, Par un Homme D'etat Russe. (Nineteenth Century Russia Ser.). 142p. (Fr.). 1974. Repr. of 1845 ed. lib. bdg. 44.50x o.p. (ISBN 0-8287-0676-X, R31). Clearwater Pub.

Peltier, Hubert C. see Hagens, James A.

Peltier, Leslie C. Starlight Nights. LC 65-20992. (Illus.). 236p. 1980. pap. 8.95 (ISBN 0-933346-02-6, 6026). Sky Pub.

Pelto, Gretel H. & Pelto, Pertii J. Human Adventure: An Introduction to Anthropology. (Illus.). 640p. 1976. 22.95x (ISBN 0-02-393550-2). Macmillan.

Pelto, Gretel H. & Pelto, Pertti J. The Cultural Dimension: In Human Adventure. (Illus.). 1979. pap. text ed. 19.95x (ISBN 0-02-393530-8). Macmillan.

Pelto, Gretel H., jt. auth. see Pelto, Pertti J.

Pelto, Pertii J., jt. auth. see Pelto, Gretel H.

Pelto, Pertti J. & Muessig, Raymond H. The Study & Teaching of Anthropology. 2nd ed. (Social Science Seminar, Secondary Education Ser.: No. C28). 136p. 1980. pap. text ed. 7.95 (ISBN 0-675-08192-0). Merrill.

Pelto, Pertti J & Pelto, Gretel H. Anthropological Research: The Structure of Inquiry. 2d ed. LC 76-62583. 1978. 37.50 (ISBN 0-521-21673-7); pap. 12.95 (ISBN 0-521-29228-X). Cambridge U Pr.

Pelto, Pertti J., jt. auth. see Bernard, H. Russell.

Pelto, Pertti J., jt. auth. see Cone, Cynthia A.

Pelto, Pertti J., jt. auth. see Pelto, Gretel H.

Pelton, Barry. Tennis. 3rd ed. 1980. pap. text ed. 7.95x (ISBN 0-673-16205-2). Scott F.

Pelton, Dan & Pelton, Jeanette. The Microheart. 75p. Date not set. pap. price not set (ISBN 0-88056-073-8). Dilithium Pr.

Pelton, Jeanette, jt. auth. see Pelton, Dan.

Pelton, Joseph N. Global Talk. LC 80-83261. 320p. Date not set. price not set (ISBN 90-286-0240-2). Sijthoff & Noordhoff. Postponed.

Pelton, Robert D. The Trickster in West Africa: A Study of Mythic Irony & Sacred Delight. LC 77-75396. (Hermeneutics: Studies in the History of Religions). 1980. 36.50x (ISBN 0-520-03477-5). U of Cal Pr.

Pelton, Robert W. Infernal Revenue or Where Your Taxes Go. (Illus.). 1983. 6.95 (ISBN 0-916620-67-0). Portals Pr.

--Your Guide to Numerology. (Illus.). 160p. 1983. pap. 4.95 (ISBN 0-8329-0276-4). New Century.

Pelton, Sonya T. Wild Island Sands. 1983. pap. 3.75 (ISBN 0-8217-1135-0). Zebra.

Peltz, Leslie R. Merchandising Mathematics. LC 79-494. 1979. pap. 11.50 (ISBN 0-672-97273-5). Bobbs.

Peltzer, Remi, illus. Redcomb & the Fox. LC 79-635. (Goodnight Bks.). (Illus.). (ps-2). 1979. 1.75 o.p. (ISBN 0-394-84239-1). Knopf.

Peluso, Ada. Background for Calculus. 1978. pap. text ed. 15.95 (ISBN 0-8403-2295-X, 40260701). Kendall-Hunt.

Pelz, Donald C. & Andrews, Frank M. Scientists in Organizations: Productive Climates for Research & Development. rev. ed. LC 76-620038. 401p. 1976. 18.00x (ISBN 0-87944-208-5). Inst Soc Res.

Pelz, Werner. The Scope of Understanding in Sociology. 1974. 24.00x (ISBN 0-7100-7854-4); pap. 10.00 (ISBN 0-7100-8009-3). Routledge & Kegan.

Pelzer, Louis, ed. see Carleton, J. Henry.

Pember, Don. Mass Media in America. 3rd ed. 416p. 1981. pap. text ed. 14.95 (ISBN 0-574-22715-6, 13-5715); instr's. guide avail. (ISBN 0-574-22716-4, 13-5716). SRA.

Pember, Don R. Mass Media In America. 4th ed. 448p. 1983. pap. text ed. write for info. (ISBN 0-574-22725-3); write for info. instr's. guide (ISBN 0-574-22726-1). SRA.

Pember, Phoebe Y. A Southern Woman's Story. Wiley, Bell I., ed. 1982. pap. 2.25 (ISBN 0-89176-024-5, 6024). Mockingbird Bks.

Pemberton, Doris H. Juneteenth at Comanche Crossing. (Illus.). 340p. 1983. 19.95 (ISBN 0-89015-373-6). Eakin Pubns.

Pemberton, J. E. How to Find Out in Mathematics. 2nd ed. 1969. 24.00 (ISBN 0-08-006824-3); pap. 10.75 (ISBN 0-08-006823-5). Pergamon.

Pemberton, P. H. & Swindell, K. Case Studies in West African Geography. (Illus.). 96p. 1974. pap. 6.50 o.p. (ISBN 0-7179-1576-X). Transatlantic.

Pemberton, S. Macpherson. Disestablishment in Ireland: Implications for Catholic Objectives in Higher Education, 1869-1879. LC 79-64245. 1979. pap. text ed. 8.75 (ISBN 0-8191-0759-X). U Pr of Amer.

Pembrook, Linda. How to Beat Fatigue. 1975. pap. 1.75 o.p. (ISBN 0-380-00671-5, 29371). Avon.

Pemer Reeves, M. S. Round about a Pound a Week. LC 79-56968. (The English Working Class Ser.). 1980. lib. bdg. 25.00 o.s.i. (ISBN 0-8240-0119-2). Garland Pub.

Pempel, T. J. Patterns of Japanese Policy-Making: Experiences from Higher Education. 1978. lib. bdg. 24.50 o.p. (ISBN 0-89158-270-3). Westview.

--Policy & Politics in Japan: Creative Conservatism. (Policy & Politics in Industrial States Ser.). 330p. 1982. 29.95 (ISBN 0-87722-249-5); pap. 10.95 (ISBN 0-87722-250-9). Temple U Pr.

Pena, Gus, tr. see Berger, Bill & Anderson, Ken.

Pena, Lilian M., ed. see Wood, Lorraine.

Pena, Manuel S. Practical Criminal Investigation. LC 82-70470. (Illus.). 425p. 1982. text ed. 15.95 (ISBN 0-942728-08-4); pap. 12.95 (ISBN 0-942728-00-9). Custom Pub Co.

Penalosa, Fernando. Chicano Sociolinguistics: A Brief Introduction. (Sociolinguistics Ser.). 1980. pap. text ed. 13.95 (ISBN 0-88377-127-6). Newbury Hse.

Penberth, Martyann. Help with Legal Aspects of Nursing Practice. (Help Series of Management Guides). 116p. 1979. pap. 10.50 (ISBN 0-933036-18-3). Ganong W L Co.

Pencak, William. America's Burke: The Mind of Thomas Hutchinson. 258p. (Orig.). 1982. lib. bdg. 23.50 (ISBN 0-8191-2626-8); pap. text ed. 11.50 (ISBN 0-8191-2627-6). U Pr of Amer.

Pence, Christine C. How Venture Capitalists Make Investment Decisions. Dufey, Gunter, ed. LC 82-8473. (Research for Business Decisions Ser.: No. 53). 152p. 1982. 39.95 (ISBN 0-8357-1362-8, Pub. by UMI Res Pr). Univ Microfilms.

Pence, R. W. & Emery, D. W. Grammar of Present-Day English. 2nd ed. 1963. text ed. 17.95x (ISBN 0-02-393720-3). Macmillan.

Penchoen, Thomas G. Tamazight of the Ayt Ndhir. LC 73-91702. (Afro-Asiatic Dialects Ser.: Vol. 1). (Illus.). 122p. 1973. pap. 16.00x (ISBN 0-89003-000-6). Undena Pubns.

Pendagast, Edward, Jr., jt. auth. see Arnold, Peter.

Pendagast, Edward L., jt. auth. see Arnold, Peter.

Pendar, Kenneth. Adventure in Diplomacy. LC 76-5479. (World War II Ser.). 1976. Repr. of 1945 ed. lib. bdg. 29.50 (ISBN 0-306-70774-8). Da Capo.

Pendell, Elmer. Why Civilizations Self-Destruct. LC 76-40801. 196p. 1977. 10.00 (ISBN 0-914576-07-0); pap. 0.00 o.p. Howard Allen.

Pender, H. & Del Mar, W. Electrical Engineers Handbook: Electrical Power. 4th ed. (Wiley Engineers Handbook Ser.). 1949. 55.00x (ISBN 0-471-67881-3, Pub. by Wiley-Interscience). Wiley.

Pender, H. & McIlwain, K. Electrical Engineers Handbook: Electric Communication & Electronics. 4th ed. (Wiley Engineers Handbook Ser.). 1950. 49.95x (ISBN 0-471-67848-1, Pub. by Wiley-Interscience). Wiley.

Pender, J. A. Soldadura. 1973. text ed. 14.95 (ISBN 0-07-091756-6, G). McGraw.

Pender, J. A. & Masson, J. Welding Projects: A Design Approach. 1976. text ed. 17.95 (ISBN 0-07-077330-0, G). McGraw.

Pendergast, David M., ed. Palenque: The Walker-Caddy Expedition to the Ancient Maya City, 1839-1840. (American Exploration & Travel Ser: No. 52). (Illus.). 1967. 12.50 (ISBN 0-8061-0729-4); pap. 5.95 o.p. (ISBN 0-8061-1090-2). U of Okla Pr.

Pendergast, Kathleen. Say Another One about My Family. LC 82-61139. (Say Another One ser.). (Illus.). 54p. (gr. k-6). 1982. pap. 6.95 (ISBN 0-942178-01-7). Madison Park Pr.

Pendergast, Kathleen, et al. Photo Articulation Test. text ed. 17.50x (ISBN 0-8134-1064-9, 1064). Interstate.

Pendergrass, A. Edna. Missionary Journey with Steve & Ed. 1958. pap. 1.50 (ISBN 0-88027-008-X). Firm Foun Pub.

Pendery, Rosemary. A Home for Hopper. LC 70-120612. (Illus.). (gr. k-3). 1971. pap. 6.75 o.p. (ISBN 0-688-21649-8); PLB 6.00 o.p. (ISBN 0-688-31649-2). Morrow.

Pendleton, tr. see Hahnemann, Samuel.

Pendleton, Bruce. Creative Still-Life Photography. (Illus.). 175p. 1983. 14.95 (ISBN 0-13-191247-X). P-H.

Pendleton, Conrad. West: Manhattan to Oregon. LC 82-72254. 72p. 1966. 5.95 (ISBN 0-8040-0318-1). Swallow.

Pendleton, David & Hasler, John, eds. Doctor-Patient Communciation. Date not set. price not set (ISBN 0-12-549880-2). Acad Pr.

Pendleton, Don. Battle Mask. (Executioner Ser, No. 3). 1970. pap. 2.25 (ISBN 0-523-41699-7). Pinnacle Bks.

--Command Strike. (The Executioner Ser.: No. 29). 1977. pap. 1.95 (ISBN 0-523-41093-X). Pinnacle Bks.

--Dixie Convoy. (Executioner Ser: No. 27). 1976. pap. 1.95 (ISBN 0-523-41091-3). Pinnacle Bks.

--Executioner: Assault on Soho. (Executioner Ser, No. 6). (Orig.). 1971. pap. 2.25 (ISBN 0-523-41831-0). Pinnacle Bks.

--The Executioner: Boston Blitz. (The Executioner Ser., No. 12). 192p. (Orig.). 1972. pap. 2.25 (ISBN 0-523-41833-7). Pinnacle Bks.

--Executioner: California Hit. (Executioner Ser.: No. 11). 192p. (Orig.). 1972. pap. 2.25 (ISBN 0-523-41832-9). Pinnacle Bks.

--Executioner: Chicago Wipeout. (Executioner Ser., No. 8). (Orig.). 1971. pap. 2.25 (ISBN 0-523-41763-2). Pinnacle Bks.

--Executioner: Continental Contract. (Executioner Ser.: No. 5). (Orig.). 1971. pap. 2.25 (ISBN 0-523-41918-X). Pinnacle Bks.

--Executioner: Detroit Deathwatch. (Executioner der.: No. 19). (Orig.). 1974. pap. 2.25 (ISBN 0-523-41830-2). Pinnacle Bks.

--Executioner: Jersey Guns. (Executioner Ser., No. 17). 1974. pap. 2.25 (ISBN 0-523-41882-5). Pinnacle Bks.

--Executioner: Miami Massacre. (Executioner Ser.: No. 4). 1970. pap. 2.25 (ISBN 0-523-41823-X). Pinnacle Bks.

--Executioner: New Orleans Knockout. (Executioner Ser.: No. 20). (Orig.). 1974. pap. 2.25 (ISBN 0-523-41853-1). Pinnacle Bks.

--Executioner: Nightmare in New York. (Executioner Ser, No. 7). (Orig.). 1971. pap. 2.25 (ISBN 0-523-42014-5). Pinnacle Bks.

--The Executioner: Panic in Philly. (The Executioner Ser., No. 15). 192p. (Orig.). 1973. pap. 1.95 (ISBN 0-523-41079-4). Pinnacle Bks.

--Executioner: Savage Fire. (The Executioneer Ser: No. 28). 1977. pap. 1.95 (ISBN 0-523-41092-1). Pinnacle Bks.

--Executioner: Texas Storm. (Executioner Ser.: No. 18). 192p. (Orig.). 1974. pap. 2.25 (ISBN 0-523-41764-0). Pinnacle Bks.

--Executioner: Vegas Vendetta. (Executioner Ser. No. 9). (Orig.). 1971. pap. 2.25 (ISBN 0-523-42015-3). Pinnacle Bks.

--The Executioner: Washington I.O.U. (Executioner Ser., No. 13). 194p. (Orig.). 1972. pap. 2.25 (ISBN 0-523-41855-8). Pinnacle Bks.

--The Executioner's War Book. (The Executioner Ser.). 224p. 1977. pap. 1.50 o.p. (ISBN 0-523-40027-6). Pinnacle Bks.

--Friday's Feast. (Executioner Ser.: No. 37). (Orig.). 1979. pap. 2.25 (ISBN 0-523-41883-3). Pinnacle Bks.

--Hawaiian Hellground: Executioner Ser., No. 22. 192p. (Orig.). 1975. pap. 1.95 (ISBN 0-523-41086-7). Pinnacle Bks.

--The Libya Connection: The Executioner. 192p. 1982. pap. 1.95 (ISBN 0-373-61048-3). Harlequin Bks.

--Monday's Mob. (Executioner Ser.: No. 33). pap. 2.25 (ISBN 0-523-41815-9). Pinnacle Bks.

--St. Louis Showdown. (Executioner Ser.: No. 23). 192p. (Orig.). 1975. pap. 2.25 (ISBN 0-523-42036-6). Pinnacle Bks.

--Satan's Sabbath. (Executioner Ser.: No. 38). (Orig.). 1980. pap. 2.25 (ISBN 0-523-41796-9). Pinnacle Bks.

--Terrible Tuesday. (Executioner: No. 34). 1979. pap. 2.95 (ISBN 0-523-41765-9). Pinnacle Bks.

--Thermal Thursday. (Executioner Ser.: No. 36). (Orig.). 1979. pap. 2.25 (ISBN 0-523-41854-X). Pinnacle Bks.

--Wednesday's Wrath. (The Executioner Ser.: No. 35). 1979. pap. 2.25 (ISBN 0-523-41801-9). Pinnacle Bks.

Pendleton, Don & Wilson, Gar. Atlantic Scramble. (Phoenix Force Ser.). 192p. 1982. pap. 1.95 (ISBN 0-373-61303-2, Pub. by Worldwide). Harlequin Bks.

Pendleton, J. M. Compendio de Teologia Cristiana. Trevino, Alejandro, tr. Orig. Title: Christian Doctrines: Compendium of Theology. 413p. (Span.). 1981. pap. 5.50 (ISBN 0-311-09008-7). Casa Bautista.

Pendleton, James H. Christian Doctrines: A Compendium of Theology. 15.95 (ISBN 0-8170-0037-2). Judson.

Pendleton, James M. Baptist Church Manual. rev. ed. 1966. Repr. of 1867 ed. 7.50 (ISBN 0-8054-2510-1). Broadman.

Pendleton, Sally, jt. ed. see McGarry, Jane.

Pendrill, D., jt. auth. see Lewis, R.

Pene Du Bois, William. Alligator Case. LC 65-11446. (Illus.). (gr. 1-5). 1965. PLB 12.89 (ISBN 0-06-021746-4, HarpJ). Har-Row.

--Lazy Tommy Pumpkinhead. LC 66-8207. (Illus.). (gr. 1-5). 1966. PLB 12.89 (ISBN 0-06-021750-2, HarpJ). Har-Row.

--Lion. (Viking Seafarer Ser). (Illus.). (gr. 1-3). 1974. pap. 1.50 o.p. (ISBN 0-670-05093-8, Puffin). Penguin.

--Lion. (Illus.). 32p. (ps-3). 1982. pap. 3.95 (ISBN 0-14-050417-6, Puffin). Penguin.

Penelhum, Terence. Hume. LC 75-2951. (Philosophers in Perspective Ser.). 200p. 1975. text ed. 15.95 o.p. (ISBN 0-312-40005-5). St Martin.

Penelhum, Terence, jt. ed. see Coward, Harold.

Pener, M. P., jt. auth. see Shulov, A.

Penfield. The Excitable Cortex in Conscious Man. 54p. 1982. 50.00x (ISBN 0-85323-241-5, Pub. by Liverpool Univ England). State Mutual Bk.

Penfield, Elizabeth. Purpose & Pattern: A Rhetoric Reader. 1982. pap. text ed. 10.95x (ISBN 0-673-15459-9). Scott F.

Penfield, Joyce. Communicating with Quotes: The Igbo Case. LC 82-15626. (Contributions in Intercultural & Comparative Studies Ser.: No. 8). (Illus.). 152p. 1983. lib. bdg. 29.95 (ISBN 0-313-23767-0, PEN/). Greenwood.

Penfield, Paul, Jr. Frequency-Power Formulas. (Press Research Monographs: No. 8). 1960. 15.00x o.s.i. (ISBN 0-262-16005-6). MIT Pr.

Penfield, Thomas. Directory of Buried Or Sunken Treasures & Lost Mines of the United States. (True Treasure Ser.). (Illus.). 134p. (Orig.). 1979. pap. text ed. 6.95 (ISBN 0-941620-06-9). H G Carson Ent.

--A Guide to Treasure in Arizona. (True Treasure Ser.). 134p. 1982. pap. 6.95 (ISBN 0-941620-01-8). H G Carson Ent.

--A Guide to Treasure in Arkansas, Louisiana, Mississippi. (Treasure Guide Ser.). 127p. 1982. pap. 6.95 (ISBN 0-686-96970-7). H G Carson Ent.

--A Guide to Treasure in California. (Treasure Guide Ser.). 160p. (Orig.). 1983. pap. 6.95 (ISBN 0-941620-23-9). H G Carson Ent.

Peng, Fred C., ed. Sign Language & Language Acquisition in Man & Ape. (AAAS Selected Symposium Ser.: No. 15). (Illus.). 1978. lib. bdg. 23.50 (ISBN 0-89158-445-5). Westview.

Peng, Syd S. Coal Mine Ground Control. LC 78-8965. 1978. 44.95 (ISBN 0-471-04121-1, Pub. by Wiley-Interscience). Wiley.

Pengelly, Raymond D. Microwave Field-Effect Transistors: Theory, Design & Applications. (Electronic Devices & Systems Research Studies). 480p. 1982. 34.95 (ISBN 0-471-10208-3, Pub. by Res Stud Pr). Wiley.

P'eng Hsin-wei. A Monetary History of China. Kaplan, Edward H., tr. Date not set. price not set o.p. West Wash Univ.

Penick, Elizabeth. In the Room Across the Hall. 1978. 4.50 o.p. (ISBN 0-533-03601-1). Vantage.

Penick, James L., Jr. The New Madrid Earthquakes of 1811-1812. rev. ed. LC 81-50531. 192p. 1981. pap. 7.95 (ISBN 0-8262-0344-2). U of Mo Pr.

Peninou, Georges, et al. Multinational Corporations & European Public Opinion. LC 78-58894. (Praeger Special Studies). 1978. 27.95 o.p. (ISBN 0-03-046191-X). Praeger.

Penkala, Maria. European Pottery: A Guide for the Collector & Dealer. 2nd ed. (Illus.). 472p. 1968. 15.00 o.p. (ISBN 0-8048-0173-8). C E Tuttle.

Penketh. Electronic Power Control for Technical Paper. 1982. pap. text ed. 14.95 (ISBN 0-408-01154-8). Butterworth.

Penlington, Norman. Canada & Imperialism, Eighteen Ninety-Six to Ninety-Nine. 1965. 25.00x o.p. (ISBN 0-8020-5148-0). U of Toronto Pr.

Penman, Kenneth A. Planning Physical Education & Athletic Facilities in Schools. LC 76-18134. 1977. text ed. 33.95 o.s.i. (ISBN 0-471-67915-1). Wiley.

--Using Statistics in Teaching Physical Education: A Linear Programmed Presentation. LC 76-3703. 1976. text ed. 18.95x (ISBN 0-471-67916-X). Wiley.

Penn, Cordelia. Landscaping with Native Plants. LC 82-17801. 1982. pap. 14.95 (ISBN 0-89587-028-2). Blair.

Penn, Gerald M. Resolution of Monoclonal Gammopathy Problems by Electrophoresis & Associated Immunonchemical Techniques. LC 82-720308. (Illus.). 53p. 1982. includes slides & tape 50.00 (ISBN 0-89189-166-8, 21-2-002-00). Am Soc Clinical.

Penn, Irving. Flowers. (Illus.). 96p. 1980. 40.00 (ISBN 0-517-54074-6, Harmony). Crown.

Penn, J. B., jt. auth. see Knutson, Ronald.

Penn, John. An Ad for Murder. 192p. 1982. 11.95 (ISBN 0-684-17761-7, ScribT). Scribner.

Penn, Linda. Young Scientists Explore Air, Land & Water Life, Bk. 3. (gr. 1-3). 1982. 3.95 (ISBN 0-86653-071-1, GA 404). Good Apple.

--Young Scientists Explore Insects, Bk. 1. (gr. 1-3). 1982. 3.95 (ISBN 0-86653-070-3, GA 403). Good Apple.

--Young Scientists Explore the World of Nature, Bk. 1. (gr. 1-3). 1982. 3.95 (ISBN 0-86653-069-X, GA 402). Good Apple.

Penn, Margaret. The Foolish Virgin. 256p. 1981. pap. 9.95 (ISBN 0-521-28297-7). Cambridge U Pr.

--Manchester Fourteen Miles. 244p. 1981. pap. 9.95 (ISBN 0-521-28065-6). Cambridge U Pr.

--The Young Mrs. Burton. 256p. 1981. pap. 9.95 (ISBN 0-521-28298-5). Cambridge U Pr.

Penn, Ruth B. Mommies Are for Loving. (Illus.). (gr. k-3). 1962. PLB 4.99 o.p. (ISBN 0-399-60468-5). Putnam Pub Group.

Penna, et al. National Library & Information Services: A Handbook for Planners. 1977. 33.95 (ISBN 0-408-70818-2). Butterworth.

Penna, Anthony N., jt. ed. see Beyer, Barry K.

Pennacchi, Laurie. Hung up on Vegetables. 1978. 5.95 o.p. (ISBN 0-533-03677-1). Vantage.

Pennak, Robert W. Collegiate Dictionary of Zoology. 1964. 28.95x (ISBN 0-471-06790-3, Pub. by Wiley-Interscience). Wiley.

--Fresh-Water Invertebrates of the United States. 2nd ed. LC 78-8130. 1978. 42.50 (ISBN 0-471-04249-8, Pub. by Wiley-Interscience). Wiley.

Pennant, Edmund. Dream's Navel. 80p. (Orig.). 1982. pap. 4.95 (ISBN 0-931642-08-6). Lintel.

Pennar, Jaan, jt. ed. see Bereday, George Z.

Pennar, Jaan, et al. The Estonians in America, 1627-1975: A Chrononology & Fact Book. LC 75-9799. (Ethnic Chronology Ser.: No. 17). 150p. 1975. text ed. 8.50 (ISBN 0-379-00519-0). Oceana.

Pennebaker, James W. The Psychology of Physical Symptoms. (Illus.). 192p. 1982. 19.95 (ISBN 0-387-90730-0). Springer-Verlag.

Pennell, Joseph. Illustration of Books: A Manual for the Use of Students. LC 78-146921. 1971. Repr. of 1896 ed. 35.00x (ISBN 0-8103-3641-3). Gale.

Pennell, Joseph S. The History of Rome Hanks & Kindred Matters. LC 81-85726. 363p. 1982. Repr. of 1949 ed. 16.95 (ISBN 0-933256-32-9). Second Chance.

Penner, Allen R. Alan Sillitoe. LC 72-161822. (English Authors Ser.: No. 141). lib. bdg. 10.95 o.p. (ISBN 0-8057-1496-0, Twayne). G K Hall.

Penner, Donald, jt. auth. see Hatzios, Kriton K.

Penner, Louis. Social Psychology: A Contemporary Approach. 1978. text ed. 16.95x (ISBN 0-19-502394-3). Oxford U Pr.

Penner, Lucille R. The Thanksgiving Book. (Illus.). (gr. 5 up). 1983. PLB 10.95 (ISBN 0-8038-7228-3). Hastings.

Penner, N. Canadian Left: A Critical Analysis. 1977. pap. 11.25 (ISBN 0-13-113126-5). P-H.

Penner, Peter & MaClean, Richard. The Rebel Bureaucrat: Frederick John Shore 1799-1837 as Critic of William Bentinick's India. 1982. 24.00x (ISBN 0-8364-0920-5, Pub. by Chanakya). South Asia Bks.

Penner, S. S. New Sources of Oil & Gas: Gases from Coal, Liquid Fuels from Coal, Shale, Tar Sands, & Heavy Oil Sources. (Illus.). 120p. 1982. 25.00 (ISBN 0-08-029335-2). Pergamon.

Penney, Alexandra. How to Make Love to a Man. Southern, Carol, ed. 160p. 1981. 10.95 (ISBN 0-517-54145-9, C N Potter Bks). Crown.

--How to Make Love to Each Other. 144p. 1983. 11.95 (ISBN 0-399-12743-7). Putnam Pub Group.

Penney, David E., jt. auth. see Edwards, C. H.

Penney, G., ed. see National Computing Centre Ltd.

Penney, Grace J. Moki. (Illus.). (gr. 3). 1973. pap. 1.25 o.p. (ISBN 0-380-00850-5, 24091, Camelot). Avon.

Penney, Norman & Baker, Donald I. The Law of Electronic Fund Transfer Systems. LC 80-52858. 1981. 66.00 (ISBN 0-88262-489-X). Warren.

Penney, Peggy L. Surgery: From Stone Scalpel to Laser Beam. LC 77-2588. (gr. 7 up). 1977. Repr. 6.95 o.p. (ISBN 0-525-66534-X). Lodestar Bks.

Penney, Robert V. Aftermath of a Stroke. 1978. 6.95 o.p. (ISBN 0-533-03313-6). Vantage.

Pennick, Frank. Frank Pennick's Choice of Golf Courses. 1977. pap. 9.75 o.p. (ISBN 0-7136-1659-8). Transatlantic.

Pennick, Nigel. The Ancient Science of Geomancy: Man in Harmony with the Earth. (Illus.). 1979. 16.95 o.p. (ISBN 0-500-05032-5). Thames Hudson.

Penniket, J. R. Common Sea Shells. (Mobil New Zealand Nature Ser.). (Illus.). 80p. (Orig.). 1982. pap. 9.30 (ISBN 0-589-01400-5, Pub. by Reed Books Australia). C E Tuttle.

Penniman, Howar d R. Venezuela at the Polls. 1981. 15.25 (ISBN 0-8447-3418-7); pap. 7.25 (ISBN 0-8447-3391-1). Am Enterprise.

Penniman, Howard R., ed. Canada at the Polls, 1979 & 1980. 1982. 17.25 (ISBN 0-8447-3474-8); pap. 9.25 (ISBN 0-8447-3472-1). Am Enterprise.

Penning, L. & Front, D. Brain Scintigraphy. 1975. 160.00 (ISBN 0-444-15156-7). Elsevier.

Penninger, F. Elaine, ed. English Drama to Sixteen Sixty (Excluding Shakespeare): A Guide to Information Sources. LC 73-16988. (American Literature, English Literature, & World Literatures in English Information Guide Ser.: Vol. 5). vi, 520p. 1976. 42.00x (ISBN 0-8103-1223-9). Gale.

Penninger, Frieda E. William Caxton. (English Authors Ser.). 1979. lib. bdg. 12.95 (ISBN 0-8057-6759-2, Twayne). G K Hall.

Penninger, Johan M. L., jt. auth. see Paulaitis, Michael E.

Pennings, Johannes M. Interlocking Directorates: Origins & Consequences of Connections Among Organizations' Boards of Directors. LC 80-8001. (Social & Behavioral Science Ser.). 1980. text ed. 21.95x (ISBN 0-87589-469-0). Jossey-Bass.

Pennington, Anne, tr. see Popa, Vasko.

Pennington, Basil. Challenges in Prayer. 1982. 8.95 (ISBN 0-89453-275-8); pap. 4.95 (ISBN 0-686-32773-X). M Glazier.

Pennington, Donald & Thomas, Keith, eds. Puritans & Revolutionaries: Essays in Seventeenth-Century History Presented to Christopher Hill. 1978. 45.00x o.p. (ISBN 0-19-822439-7). Oxford U Pr.

Pennington, Earl, jt. auth. see Oestereich, James.

Pennington, Elisabeth A. Interdisciplinary Education in Nursing. (League Exchange Ser.: No. 130). 40p. 1981. 4.95 (ISBN 0-686-38273-0, 15-1877). Natl League Nursing.

Pennington, G. W., et al. Dental Pharmacology. 4th ed. (Illus.). 240p. 1981. pap. text ed. 21.95 (ISBN 0-632-00539-4, B-3817-8). Mosby.

Pennington, Harvard C. TRS-80 Disk & Other Mysteries. (TRS-80 Information Ser.: Vol. 1). (Illus.). 133p. (Orig.). 1979. pap. 22.50 (ISBN 0-936200-00-6). IJG Inc.

Pennington, Jean & Church, Helen N. Food Values of Portions Commonly Used. 13th ed. LC 80-7594. 200p. 1980. pap. 6.25i (ISBN 0-06-090943-9, CN943, CN). Har-Row.

--Food Values of Portions Commonly Used. 13th ed. LC 80-7594. 200p. 1980. 12.95i o.p. (HarpT); pap. 5.95i (ISBN 0-06-090819-X, CN 819). Har-Row.

Pennington, Lillian B. Snafu: The Littlest Clown. LC 73-90113. (Illus.). (gr. 1-6). 1972. PLB 6.75x (ISBN 0-685-59387-8); cassette 5.95x (ISBN 0-87783-225-0). Oddo.

Pennington, Lucinda. The Hundred Forty-Nine Ways to Profit from Your Divorce. new ed. 228p. 1983. 12.95 (ISBN 0-672-52744-8). Bobbs.

Pennington, M. Basil. A Place Apart: Monastic Prayer & Practice for Everyone. LC 81-43566. 168p. 1983. 13.95 (ISBN 0-385-17850-6). Doubleday.

Pennington, M. Basil, ed. Prayer & Liberation. LC 76-21594. (Illus.). 1977. pap. 1.75 o.p. (ISBN 0-8189-1139-5, Pub. by Alba Bks). Alba.

Pennington, Michael. Rossya: A Journey by Trans-Siberian Express. (Oleander Travel Books Ser.: Vol. 9). (Illus.). 96p. 1978. pap. 12.50 (ISBN 0-686-92599-8). Oleander Pr.

Pennington, Neil D. The Spanish Baroque Guitar with a Transcription of De Murcia's Passacalles y obras, 2 vols. Buelow, George, ed. LC 81-13016. (Studies in Musicology: No. 46). 588p. 1981. Set. 79.95 (ISBN 0-8357-1188-9, Pub. by UMI Res Pr). Vol. 1 (ISBN 0-8357-1261-3). Vol. 2 (ISBN 0-8357-1262-1). Univ Microfilms.

Pennington, Richard. A Descriptive Catalogue of the Etched Works of Wenceslaus Hollar, 1607-1677. LC 81-51828. 452p. 1982. 150.00 (ISBN 0-521-22408-X). Cambridge U Pr.

Pennington, T. H. & Ritchie, D. A. Molecular Virology. (Outline Studies in Biology). 1976. pap. 6.50x (ISBN 0-412-12590-0, Pub. by Chapman & Hall). Methuen Inc.

Pennink, Betsy. This is San Francisco, No. B18. (Heinemann Guided Readers). (Illus.). 32p. (Orig.). 1983. pap. text ed. 2.00x (ISBN 0-435-27089-3). Heinemann Ed.

Pennisi, Vincent R. Women in Jeopardy from Breast Cancer. LC 81-86160. 94p. 1983. 9.95 (ISBN 0-86666-065-8). GWP.

Penn-Lewis, Jessie. Story of Job. 1965. pap. 5.95 (ISBN 0-87508-954-2). Chr Lit.

Pennock, Michael. Moral Problems: Student Text. LC 79-51015. (Illus.). 240p. 1979. pap. text ed. 4.50 (ISBN 0-87793-177-1); tchr's manual 2.25 (ISBN 0-87793-178-X). Ave Maria.

Pennsylvania Association of Notaries. Practical Guide for Notaries Public in Pennsylvania. 18th ed. LC 63-11110. 1982. pap. write for info. Penn Assoc Not.

Penny. The Birds of the Seychelles & Outlying Islands. 23.95 (ISBN 0-686-42764-5, Collins Pub England). Greene.

Penny, Edward B., tr. see Saint-Martin, Louis Claude de.

Penny, Larry. Walking the Hamptons: A Guide to the Natural Heritage of the South Fork. 1983. 18.95 (ISBN 0-916366-20-0). Pushcart Pr.

Penny, Nicholas, jt. ed. see Clarke, Michael.

Penny, Terry, ed. Low Grade Heat Power Cycles. (Progress in Solar Energy Supplements Ser.). 1982. text ed. 25.00x (ISBN 0-89553-054-6). Am Solar Energy.

Penny, William J., jt. auth. see Peterson, James A.

Penny, William M., ed. see American Micro Systems.

Pennycook, Andrew. Codes & Ciphers: Amazing Ways to Scramble & Unscramble Secret Messages. 1978. 12.50 o.s.i. (ISBN 0-679-50856-2); pap. 7.95 o.s.i. (ISBN 0-679-50966-6). McKay.

Pennycuick, Colin J. Animal Flight. (Studies in Biology: No. 33). 72p. 1972. pap. text ed. 8.95 (ISBN 0-7131-2356-7). E Arnold.

Pennycuick, John. In Contact with the Physical World. (Muirhead Library of Philosophy). 1971. text ed. 11.50x o.p. (ISBN 0-391-00175-2). Humanities.

Pennypacker, Arabelle, ed. Reading for Young People: The Middle Atlantic. LC 80-16021. 162p. 1980. pap. 11.00 (ISBN 0-8389-0295-2). ALA.

Penoyre, Jane, jt. auth. see Penoyre, John.

Penoyre, John & Penoyre, Jane. Houses in the Landscape: A Regional Study of Vernacular Building Styles in England & Wales. (Illus.). 240p. 1978. 19.95 (ISBN 0-571-11055-X). Faber & Faber.

Penrice, John. Dictionary & Glossary of the Koran, with Copious Grammatical References & Explanations. LC 70-90039. 1969. Repr. of 1873 ed. 17.00x (ISBN 0-8196-0252-3). Biblo.

Penrod, Steven. Social Psychology. 704p. 1983. text ed. 23.95 (ISBN 0-13-817924-7). P-H.

Penrose, Barrie. Stalin's Gold: The Story of HMS Edinburgh & Its Treasures. (Illus.). 256p. 1983. 15.00i (ISBN 0-316-69877-6). Little.

Penrose, Edith T. The Theory of the Growth of the Firm. LC 79-91109. 304p. 1980. 27.50 (ISBN 0-87332-166-9). M E Sharpe.

Penrose, Ernest F. Population Theories & Their Application: With Special Reference to Japan. LC 72-136545. 347p. 1973. Repr. of 1934 ed. lib. bdg. 19.25x (ISBN 0-8371-5466-9, PEPO). Greenwood.

Penrose, L. C. A Clinical & Genetic Study of 1280 Cases of Mental Defect: The Colchester Study. 162p. Date not set. Repr. of 1981 ed. write for info. o.p. (ISBN 0-89874-191-2). Krieger.

Penrose, L. S. On the Objective Study of Crowd Behavior. 78p. 1981. Repr. of 1952 ed. text ed. write for info. o.p. (ISBN 0-89874-287-0). Krieger.

Penrose, Maryly B. Baumann-Bowman Family of the Mohawk, Susquehanna & Niagara Rivers. LC 77-6452. 1978. 35.00 (ISBN 0-918940-05-2). Libty Bell Assoc.

--Indian Affairs Papers: American Revolution. LC 80-24018. (Illus.). xviii, 395p. 1981. lib. bdg. 25.00 (ISBN 0-918940-07-9). Libty Bell Assoc.

Penrose, O. Foundations of Statistical Mechanics: A Deductive Treatment. LC 70-89513. (International Series in Natural Philosophy: Vol. 22). (Illus.). 1970. inquire for price (ISBN 0-08-013314-2). Pergamon.

Penrose, Roger. Techniques of Differential Topology in Relativity. (CBMS Regional Conference Ser.: Vol. 7). (Illus.). viii, 72p. (Orig.). 1972. pap. text ed. 7.00 (ISBN 0-89871-005-7). Soc Indus-Appl Math.

Penrose, Roland. McWilliam Sculptor. 13.50 o.p. (ISBN 0-85458-728-4). Transatlantic.

--Tapies. LC 77-88715. (Illus.). 1980. pap. 15.00 (ISBN 0-8478-0258-2). Rizzoli Intl.

Penrose, Valentine. Poems & Narrations. Edwards, Roy, tr. from Fr. (Translation Ser.). 1979. pap. 12.95 o.p. (ISBN 0-85635-207-1, Pub. by Carcanet New Pr England). Humanities.

Penry, J. K. see Newmark, M. E.

Penry, J. K., jt. ed. see Newmark, M.

Penry, J. Kiffin see Glaser, G. H., et al.

Penry, J. Kiffin, ed. Epilepsy: The Eighth International Symposium. LC 76-58059. 432p. 1977. 21.00 (ISBN 0-89004-190-3). Raven.

Penry, J. Kiffin, ed. see Epilepsy International Symposium, 10th.

Penry, J. Kiffin, ed. see Epilepsy International Symposium, 11th., et al.

Pensinger, Brenda. Diccionario Mixteco del Este De Jamiltepec. (Vocabularios Indigenas Ser.: No. 18). 156p. 1974. 7.00 (ISBN 0-88312-751-2); microfiche 2.25x (ISBN 0-88312-586-2). Summer Inst Ling.

Pensis, Nancy T. & Maloney, Mary Ann. Mealtimes for People with Handicaps: A Guide for Parents, Paraprofessionals, & Allied Health Professionals. 142p. 1983. pap. text ed. write for info. (ISBN 0-398-04819-3). C C Thomas.

Penson, John B., Jr. & Lins, David A. Agricultural Finance: An Introduction to Micro & Macro Concepts. (Illus.). 1980. text ed. 24.95 (ISBN 0-13-018903-0). P-H.

Penson, John B., Jr., et al. Personal Finance. (Illus.). 480p. 1982. 21.95 (ISBN 0-13-657320-7). P-H.

Pentecost, Dwight. Designed to Be Like Him. LC 66-16226. 1981. pap. 6.95 (ISBN 0-8024-2132-6). Moody.

--Man's Problems - God's Answers. LC 72-155685. 192p. 1972. pap. 5.95 (ISBN 0-8024-5178-0). Moody.

Pentecost, High. Death Mask. (Nightingale Series Paperbacks). 1983. pap. 9.95 (ISBN 0-8161-3500-2, Large Print Bks). G K Hall.

Pentecost, Hugh. Murder in High Places. (A Pierre Chambrun Mystery Novel & Red Badge Novel of Suspense Ser.). 1983. 10.95 (ISBN 0-396-08146-0). Dodd.

--Past, Present, & Murder: A Julian Quist Mystery Novel. LC 82-9638. 1982. 9.95 (ISBN 0-396-08103-7). Dodd.

--Sow Death, Reap Death: A Julian Quist Mystery Novel. (A Red Badge Novel of Suspense Ser.). 202p. 1981. 8.95 o.p. (ISBN 0-396-08006-5). Dodd.

--Time of Terror. (Red Badge Novel of Suspense). 194p. 1975. 5.95 o.p. (ISBN 0-396-07123-6). Dodd.

Pentecost, J. Dwight. Design for Discipleship. 1977. pap. 3.95 (ISBN 0-310-30861-5). Zondervan.

Pentecoste, Joseph. Systems of Poverty. 121p. 1977. pap. text ed. 7.50 o.p. (ISBN 0-8191-0176-1). U Pr of Amer.

Pentz, Croft M. Outlines on Revelation. (Sermon Outline Ser.). 1978. pap. 2.50 (ISBN 0-8010-7030-9). Baker Bk.

--Sermon Outlines for Special Days. (Sermon Outline Ser.). 1979. pap. 2.50 (ISBN 0-8010-7046-5). Baker Bk.

Pentzer, W. T., jt. auth. see Ryall, A. Lloyd.

Penulas, M. C. Jacintho Benavente. (World Authors Ser.: No. 57). 12.50 o.p. (ISBN 0-8057-2136-3, Twayne). G K Hall.

Penycate, J., jt. auth. see Clark, T.

Penzias, Walter & Goodman, M. W. Man Beneath the Sea: A Review of Underwater Ocean Engineering. LC 70-148506. 1973. 86.95 (ISBN 0-471-68018-4). Wiley.

Penzien, J., jt. auth. see Clough, R.

Penzler, Otto, jt. auth. see Steinbrunner, Chris.

Penzler, Otto, ed. Whodunit? Houdini? LC 76-3388. 288p. (YA) 1976. 13.41i (ISBN 0-06-013336-8, HarpT). Har-Row.

Penzoldt, Ernst. The Powenz Pack. Woods, John E., tr. from Ger. LC 81-22169. (Illus.). 255p. 1982. 13.95 (ISBN 0-88064-002-2). Fromm Intl Pub.

Peoples, Edward E. Readings in Criminal Justice: An Introduction to the System. LC 77-16552. (Illus.). 1978. pap. text ed. 11.95x o.p. (ISBN 0-673-16320-2). Scott F.

Pepe, Phil & Hollander, Zander. The Book of Sports Lists. 1979. pap. 2.95 (ISBN 0-523-41650-4). Pinnacle Bks.

Pepe, Philip S. Personal Typing Thirty. 5th ed. 64p. 1974. 9.95 (ISBN 0-07-049300-6, G); text ed. 9.32 (ISBN 0-07-049299-9). McGraw.

Pepin, Jacques. Everyday Cooking with Jacques Pepin. (Illus.). 1982. 19.18i (ISBN 0-06-014994-9, HarpT); pap. 10.53i (ISBN 0-06-090943-9, CN-943). Har-Row.

--Jacques Pepin: A French Chef Cooks at Home. LC 75-4686. 352p. 1975. 12.50 o.s.i. (ISBN 0-671-21946-4). S&S.

Pepin, Ronald E. The Entheticus of John of Salisbury: A Critical Text. 1975. pap. 4.00 o.p. (ISBN 0-8232-0075-2). Fordham.

Pepinsky, Harold B. & Patton, Michael J. The Psychological Experiment: A Practical Accomplishment. LC 75-134829. 208p. 1972. 17.25 (ISBN 0-08-016515-X). Pergamon.

Pepinsky, Harold E. Crime Control Strategies: An Introduction to the Study of Crime. 1979. pap. text ed. 11.95x (ISBN 0-19-502607-1). Oxford U Pr.

Pepinsky, Harold E., ed. Rethinking Criminology: New Premises, New Directions. (Research Progress Series in Criminology: Vol. 27). 152p. 1982. 18.95 (ISBN 0-8039-1891-7); pap. 8.95 (ISBN 0-686-82380-X). Sage.

Pepitone, Lena & Stadiem, William. Marilyn Monroe Confidential. 1979. 9.95 o.p. (ISBN 0-671-24289-X). S&S.

Peplau, Hildegarde E. Interpersonal Relations in Nursing. (Illus.). 1952. 7.50 o.p. (ISBN 0-399-40020-6). Putnam Pub Group.

Peplau, Letitia A. & Perlman, Daniel. Loneliness: A Sourcebook of Current Theory, Research & Therapy. LC 81-16272. (Wiley Series on Personality Processes). 429p. 1982. 37.95x (ISBN 0-471-08028-4, Pub. by Wiley-Interscience). Wiley.

Pepler, D. J. & Rubin, K. H., eds. The Play of Children: Current Theory & Research. (Contributions to Human Development: Vol. 6). (Illus.). x, 158p. 1982. pap. 36.75 (ISBN 3-8055-3540-6). S Karger.

Peplow, Elizabeth. Stay Slim with Herbs & Spices. 120p. 1981. 10.00 o.p. (ISBN 0-232-51464-X, Pub. by Darton-Longman-Todd England). State Mutual Bk.

Peplow, Michael W. George S. Schuyler. (United States Authors Ser.). 1980. lib. bdg. 13.95 (ISBN 0-8057-7289-8, Twayne). G K Hall.

Peplow, Michael W. & Bravard, Robert S. Samuel R. Delany: A Primary & Secondary Bibliography, 1962-1979. 1980. lib. bdg. 26.00 (ISBN 0-8161-8054-7, Hall Reference). G K Hall.

Peppard, Murray B. Friedrich Durrenmatt. (World Authors Ser.: Germany: No. 87). lib. bdg. 10.95 o.p. (ISBN 0-8057-2284-X, Twayne). G K Hall.

Peppard, V., tr. see Nikitin, Nikolai.

Peppe, Rodney. The Mice Who Lived in a Shoe. (ps-1). 1982. 9.50 (ISBN 0-688-00844-5). Morrow.

--Odd One Out. (Illus.). (gr. k-3). 1974. PLB 9.95 (ISBN 0-670-52029-2). Viking Pr.

--Rodney Peppe's Moving Toys. LC 81-50023. (Illus.). 128p. 1981. 17.79 (ISBN 0-8069-5422-1); lib. bdg. 13.29 (ISBN 0-8069-5423-X); pap. 7.95 (ISBN 0-8069-5424-8). Sterling.

Pepper, Art & Pepper, Laurie. Straight Life. 1983. pap. 9.95 (ISBN 0-02-872010-5). Schirmer Bks.

Pepper, Bert, ed. The Young Adult Chronic Patient. LC 81-48483. 1982. 7.95x (ISBN 0-87589-908-0, MHS-14). Jossey-Bass.

Pepper, Elizabeth. Witches' Almanac: Aries 1979 to Pisces 1980. new ed. LC 73-29853. (Orig.). 1979. pap. 1.95 o.p. (ISBN 0-448-16559-7, G&D). Putnam Pub Group.

Pepper, Elizabeth & Wilcock, John. A Guide to Magical & Mystical Sites: Europe & the British Isles. LC 76-5533. (Illus.). 1979. pap. 4.95 o.p. (ISBN 0-06-090656-1, CN 656, CN). Har-Row.

--Witches All. (Illus.). 1977. pap. 4.95 o.p. (ISBN 0-448-12856-X, G&D). Putnam Pub Group.

--The Witches Almanac: Aries 1978 to Pisces 1979. (Illus.). 1978. pap. 0.99 o.p. (ISBN 0-448-14639-8, G&D). Putnam Pub Group.

Pepper, George H. & Wilson, Gilbert L. Hidatsa Shrine & the Beliefs Respecting It. LC 9-5503. 1908. pap. 8.00 (ISBN 0-527-00509-6). Kraus Repr.

Pepper, Laurie, jt. auth. see Pepper, Art.

Pepper, Max, jt. auth. see Coe, Rodney M.

Pepper, Robert D., ed. Four Tudor Books on Education. LC 66-10027. 270p. 1976. lib. bdg. 33.00x (ISBN 0-8201-1271-2). Schol Facsimiles.

Pepper, Stephen C. Concept & Quality. LC 66-19679. (Paul Carus Lecture Ser). xiv, 666p. 1966. 30.00x (ISBN 0-87548-095-0). Open Court.

--The Sources of Value. 1958. 39.50x (ISBN 0-520-01798-6). U of Cal Pr.

Pepper, Thomas, jt. auth. see Kahn, Herman.

Pepper, William F. & Kennedy, Florynce R. Sex Discrimination in Employment. 337p. 1982. 25.00 (ISBN 0-87215-331-2). Michie-Bobbs.

Peppercorn, David. Bordeaux. (Wine Bks.). 448p. 1982. 24.95 (ISBN 0-571-11751-1); pap. 10.95 (ISBN 0-571-11758-9). Faber & Faber.

Peppers, Larry C., jt. auth. see Bails, Dale G.

Peppiatt, Michael & Bellony-Rewald, Alice. Imagination's Chamber. 232p. 1982. 45.00 (ISBN 0-686-42857-9). NYGS.

Peppin, Brigid. Dictionary of Book Illustrators, 1800-1980. (Illus.). 544p. 1982. 30.00 (ISBN 0-668-04366-0). Arco.

Peppler, Henry J., ed. Microbial Technology. LC 77-796. (Illus.). 464p. 1977. Repr. of 1967 ed. lib. bdg. 25.00 (ISBN 0-88275-538-2). Krieger.

Peppler, Henry J. & Perlman, David, eds. Microbial Technology, Vol. 1: Microbial Processes. 2nd ed. LC 78-67883. 1979. 55.00 o.s.i. (ISBN 0-12-551501-4). Acad Pr.

Pepys, J. The Mast Cell. 896p. 1979. pap. text ed. 34.50 o.p. (ISBN 0-272-79582-8). Univ Park.

Pepys, Samuel. The Diary of Samuel Pepys, 9 vols. Latham, Robert & Matthews, William, eds. Incl. Vol. 1. 1660. 1970. 29.50x (ISBN 0-520-01575-4); Vol. 2. 1661. 29.50 (ISBN 0-520-01576-2); Vol. 3. 1662. 29.50 (ISBN 0-520-01577-0); Vol. 4. 1663. 29.50 (ISBN 0-520-01857-5); Vol. 5. 1664. 29.50 (ISBN 0-520-01858-3); Vol. 6. 1665. 29.50 (ISBN 0-520-01859-1); Vol. 7. 1666. 29.50 (ISBN 0-520-02094-4); Vol. 8. 1667. 29.50 (ISBN 0-520-02095-2); Vol. 9. 1668-1669. 29.50 (ISBN 0-520-02096-0). U of Cal Pr.

--The Diary of Samuel Pepys, Vol. XI. Latham, Robert & Matthews, William, eds. LC 70-96950. (The Complete Diary of Samuel Pepys). 368p. 1983. 35.00 (ISBN 0-520-02098-7). U of Cal Pr.

--The Diary of Samuel Pepys, Vol. 1. 1968. Repr. of 1953 ed. 9.95x (ISBN 0-460-00053-5, Evman). Biblio Dist.

--The Diary of Samuel Pepys, Vol. 2. 1981. Repr. of 1953 ed. 9.95x (ISBN 0-460-00054-3, Evman). Biblio Dist.

--The Diary of Samuel Pepys, Vol. 3. 1981. Repr. of 1953 ed. 9.95x (ISBN 0-460-00055-1, Evman). Biblio Dist.

--The Diary of Samuel Pepys: The Companion, Vol. X. Latham, Robert, et al, eds. LC 70-96950. (The Complete Diaries of Samuel Pepys). 656p. 1983. 35.00 (ISBN 0-520-02097-9). U of Cal Pr.

--The Diary of Samuel Pepys: Vol. 10, Companion. Latham, Robert, compiled by. LC 70-96950. (Illus.). 626p. 1983. 35.00 (ISBN 0-520-02097-9). U of Cal Pr.

--A Pepysian Garland: Black-Letter Broadside Ballads of the Years 1595-1639, Chiefly from the Collection of Samuel Pepys. Rollins, Hyder E., ed. LC 74-176041. (Illus.). 491p. 1971. 25.00x (ISBN 0-674-66185-0). Harvard U Pr.

Pequegnat, Willis E. & Chace, Fenner A., Jr., eds. Contributions on the Biology of the Gulf of Mexico. LC 71-135998. (Texas A&M University Oceanographic Studies: Vol. 1). 270p. 1970. 29.95x (ISBN 0-87201-346-4). Gulf Pub.

Perachio, Joseph J., jt. auth. see Young, Edna C.

Peradotto, John. Classical Mythology: An Annotated Bibliographical Survey. (American Philological Association Pamphlets). 1981. Repr. of 1973 ed. pap. 5.95 (ISBN 0-686-32613-X, 40-06-02). Scholars Pr CA.

Perales, A. P. Fanfou dans les Bayous. LC 82-15148. 40p. 1982. pap. 4.95 (ISBN 0-88289-378-5). Pelican.

Perard. Drawing Faces & Expressions. (The Grosset Art Instruction Ser.: No. 11). (Illus.). 48p. Date not set. pap. price not set (ISBN 0-448-00520-4, G&D). Putnam Pub Group.

--Drawing Flowers. (The Grosset Art Instruction Ser.: No. 12). (Illus.). 48p. Date not set. pap. price not set (ISBN 0-448-00521-2, G&D). Putnam Pub Group.

--Drawing Trees. (The Grosset Art Instruction Ser.: No. 18). (Illus.). 48p. Date not set. pap. price not set (ISBN 0-448-00527-1, G&D). Putnam Pub Group.

Perard & Cook. Drawing Horses. (The Grosset Art Instruction Ser.: No. 16). (Illus.). 48p. Date not set. pap. 2.95 (ISBN 0-448-00525-5, G&D). Putnam Pub Group.

Perard, Victor. Drawing Animals. (Grosset Art Instruction Ser.: Vol. 5). (Illus.). 48p. Date not set. pap. 2.95 (ISBN 0-448-00514-X, G&D). Putnam Pub Group.

--Drawing Sea & Sky. (Pitman Art Ser.: Vol. 17). pap. 1.95 o.p. (ISBN 0-448-00526-3, G&D). Putnam Pub Group.

--Figure Drawing. (Grosset Art Instruction Ser.: Vol. 20). pap. 2.95 (ISBN 0-448-00529-8, G&D). Putnam Pub Group.

--Sketching Landscape. (Grosset Art Instruction Ser.: Vol. 25). pap. 2.95 (ISBN 0-448-00534-4, G&D). Putnam Pub Group.

Perard, Victor, et al. How to Sketch. (Grosset Art Instruction Ser.: Vol. 31). 1966. pap. 2.95 (ISBN 0-448-00540-9, G&D). Putnam Pub Group.

Peratta, Phyllis W. Jose Santos Chocano. (World Authors Ser.). 15.95 (ISBN 0-8057-2220-3, Twayne). G K Hall.

Percefull, Aaron. The Cambridge Program for the GED Writing Skills Test. (GED Preparation Ser.). 304p. (Orig.). 1981. pap. text ed. 5.87 (ISBN 0-8428-9387-3); Cambridge Exercise Book for the Writing Skills Test 96p. wkbk. 3.33 (ISBN 0-8428-9391-1). Cambridge Bk.

--Gymnastics. (Easy-Read Sports Bks.). 48p. (gr. 1-3). 1982. PLB 8.60 (ISBN 0-531-04377-0). Watts.

Percefull, Aaron W. Balloons, Zeppelins & Dirigibles. (First Bks.). (Illus.). 72p. (gr. 4 up). 1983. PLB 8.90 (ISBN 0-531-04535-8). Watts.

Perceval, Don & Lockett, Clay. A Navajo Sketch Book. 2nd ed. LC 62-21125. (Illus.). 1968. Repr. 14.50 o.p. (ISBN 0-87358-036-2). Northland.

Percheron, Maurice. Buddha & Buddhism. Stapleton, Edmund, tr. from Fr. LC 82-3471. (The Overlook Spiritual Masters Ser.). (Illus.). 192p. 1983. 16.95 (ISBN 0-87951-157-5). Overlook Pr.

Percival, D. & Harper, J. Solar Electric Technologies: Methods of Electric Utility Value Analysis. (Progress in Solar Energy Supplements Ser.). 65p. 1983. pap. text ed. 9.00x (ISBN 0-89553-079-1). Am Solar Energy.

Percival, Fred & Ellington, Henry. Educational Technology: A Practical Guide for Teachers. 150p. 1983. 22.95. Nichols Pub.

Percival, Harold W. Thinking & Destiny. 9th ed. LC 47-1811. (Illus.). 1000p. 1982. deluxe ed. 22.95 (ISBN 0-911650-09-1, 091); pap. 12.95 (ISBN 0-911650-06-7). Word Foun.

Percival, Ian C. & Richards, Derek. Introduction to Dynamics. LC 82-15514. (Illus.). 240p. 1983. 34.50 (ISBN 0-521-23680-0); pap. 14.95 (ISBN 0-521-28149-0). Cambridge U Pr.

Percival, John. Nureyev: Aspects of a Dancer. LC 75-21519. (Illus.). 1975. 8.95 o.p. (ISBN 0-399-11544-7). Putnam Pub Group.

--Roman Villa: A Historical Introduction. LC 76-7766. 1976. 40.00x (ISBN 0-520-03233-0). U of Cal Pr.

--The World of Diaghilev. (Illus.). 1979. 10.00 o.p. (ISBN 0-517-53902-0, Harmony); pap. 5.95 o.p. (ISBN 0-517-53903-9). Crown.

Percival, Robert V., jt. auth. see Friedman, Lawrence M.

Percov, Nikolaj V., jt. auth. see Mel'cuk, Igor K.

Percy, Bishop. Bishop Percy's Folio Manuscript Ballards & Romances, 3 vols. Hales, John W., et al, eds. LC 67-23962. 1866p. 1968. Repr. of 1868 ed. 191.00x (ISBN 0-8103-3409-7). Gale.

Percy, Eustace. John Knox. 344p. 1964. 12.00 (ISBN 0-227-67510-X). Attic Pr.

--John Knox. LC 65-11937. 1965. 7.95 (ISBN 0-8042-0924-3). John Knox.

--Maritime Trade in War. 1930. text ed. 29.50x (ISBN 0-686-83617-0). Elliots Bks.

Percy, Graham, illus. Sleeping Beauty. LC 79-18233. (Goodnight Bks). (Illus.). 24p. (gr. 1). 1980. 1.75 o.p. (ISBN 0-394-84384-3). Knopf.

Percy, Walker. The Message in the Bottle. 352p. 1975. 16.50 (ISBN 0-374-20856-5); pap. 8.25 (ISBN 0-374-51338-4). FS&G.

--The Second Coming. 416p. 1981. pap. 3.95. WSP.

Percy, William A. Sewanee. LC 82-60214. (Illus.). 56p. 1982. 12.00 (ISBN 0-913720-37-2). Beil F C.

Perdue, Theda. Nations Remembered: An Oral History of the Five Civilized Tribes, 1865-1907. LC 79-6828. (Contributions in Ethnic Studies: No. 1). xxiv, 221p. 1980. lib. bdg. 27.50 (ISBN 0-313-22097-2, PFN/). Greenwood.

Perdue, Theda, ed. Cherokee Editor: The Writings of Elias Boudinot. LC 82-11110. 248p. 1983. text ed. 18.95x (ISBN 0-87049-366-3). U of Tenn Pr.

Perea, Jose A., jt. auth. see Cabrera, Y. Arturo.

Pereda, Jose M. Jose Maria Pereda: Selections from Sotileza & Penas Arriba. Talamantes, Florence W., ed. 1978. pap. text ed. 9.50 (ISBN 0-8191-0379-9). U Pr of Amer.

Pereira, Antonio O. Marcore. Hower, Alfred & Saunders, John, trs. from Portuguese. (Texas Pan American Ser). 248p. 1970. 12.50x o.p. (ISBN 0-292-70013-X). U of Tex Pr.

Pereira, Frederick A., jt. auth. see Selmanowitz, Victor J.

Pereira, H. C. Land Use & Water Resources. LC 72-85437. (Illus.). 180p. (Orig.). 1973. 44.50 (ISBN 0-521-08677-9); pap. 14.95x (ISBN 0-521-09750-9). Cambridge U Pr.

Pereira, Jose. Elements of Indian Architecture. 1983. 34.00x (ISBN 0-8364-0868-3). South Asia Bks.

Pereira, Luis C. Bresser see Bresser Pereira, Luis C.

Perella, Frederick J. & Procopio, Mariellen. Poverty Profile U. S. A. 1976. pap. 1.95 o.p. (ISBN 0-8091-1945-5). Paulist Pr.

Perella, Nicolas J. The Kiss Sacred & Profane: An Interpretative History of Kiss Symbolism & Related Religio-Erotic Themes. LC 75-83292. (Illus.). 1969. 40.00x (ISBN 0-520-01392-1). U of Cal Pr.

Perelman, Bob. Braille. 61p. 1975. 3.50 (ISBN 0-87886-057-6). Ithaca Hse.

Perelman, Chaim. The Realm of Rhetoric. Kluback, William, tr. LC 79-66378. (Fr.). 1982. text ed. 15.95x (ISBN 0-268-01604-6); pap. text ed. 5.95x (ISBN 0-268-01605-4). U of Notre Dame Pr.

Perelman, Charles. Historical Introduction to Philosophical Thinking. Brown, Kenneth A., tr. (Orig.). 1965. pap. text ed. 6.50 o.p. (ISBN 0-394-30653-8, RanC). Random.

Perelman, Leslie, jt. auth. see Dimarco, Vincent.

Perelman, Lewis J., et al, eds. Energy Transitions: Long-Term Perspectives. (AAAS Selected Symposium: No. 48). 250p. 1981. lib. bdg. 20.00 o.p. (ISBN 0-89158-862-0). Westview.

Perelman, Michael. Classical Political Economy: Primitive Accumulation & the Social Division of Labor. 224p. 1983. text ed. 25.95x (ISBN 0-86598-095-0). Allanheld.

--Farming for Profit in a Hungry World: Capital & the Crisis in Agriculture. LC 76-43229. 250p. 1978. text ed. 16.00x (ISBN 0-916672-88-3); pap. text ed. 7.50x (ISBN 0-916672-55-7). Allanheld.

Perelman, S. J. The Last Laugh. 1981. 13.95 o.s.i. (ISBN 0-671-42515-3). S&S.

--The Last Laugh. 1982. pap. 4.80 (ISBN 0-671-42516-1, Touchstone Bks). S&S.

--Vinegar Puss. 224p. 1976. pap. 3.45 o.s.i. (ISBN 0-440-59356-5, Delta). Dell.

Perenyi, Eleanor. Green Thoughts: A Writer in the Garden. LC 81-40224. 304p. 1981. 15.50 (ISBN 0-394-50375-9). Random.

Perenyi, Imre. Town & Environs: Recreation in Town Planning. 152p. 1978. 17.50 (ISBN 0-88275-758-X). Krieger.

Perera, Frederica P. & Ahmed, A. Karim. Respirable Particles: Impact of Airborne Fine Particulates on Health & Environment. LC 79-13163. 208p. 1979. prof ref 22.50x (ISBN 0-88410-090-1). Ballinger Pub.

Perera, Gretchen & Perere, Thomas. Your Brain Power. LC 75-7862. (Science Is What & Why Ser.). (Illus.). 48p. (gr. k-4). 1975. PLB 4.64 o.p. (ISBN 0-698-30587-6, Coward). Putnam Pub Group.

Perera, Ronald C., jt. ed. see Appleton, Jon H.

Perera, Thomas B. & Orlowsky, Wallace. Who Will Clean the Air? (Science Is What & Why Ser). (Illus.). (gr. k-3). 1971. PLB 4.49 o.p. (ISBN 0-698-30407-1, Coward). Putnam Pub Group.

Perera, Thomas B., jt. auth. see Orlowsky, Wallace.

Perere, Thomas, jt. auth. see Perera, Gretchen.

Peres, Richard. Dealing with Employment Discrimination. 1977. 29.95 (ISBN 0-07-049317-0, P&RB). McGraw.

--Preventing Discrimination Complaints: A Guide for Supervisors. 1979. pap. 7.50 (ISBN 0-07-049318-9, T&D). McGraw.

Peret, Benjamin. A Marvelous World: Poem by Benjamin Peret. Jackson, Elizabeth R., ed. xxii, 112p. Date not set. text ed. 0.00 cancelled (ISBN 0-8071-0664-X). La State U Pr.

Peretz, David, et al, eds. Death & Grief: Selected Readings for the Medical Student. 270p. 1977. pap. 6.95 (ISBN 0-930194-82-9). Ctr Thanatology.

Peretz, Don. The Government & Politics of Israel. 1979. lib. bdg. 26.00 (ISBN 0-89158-086-7); pap. 10.95 (ISBN 0-89158-087-5). Westview.

Peretz, Don, et al. Islam: Legacy of the Past, Challenge of the Future. LC 80-27443. 160p. 1983. 12.95 (ISBN 0-88427-048-3, Dist. by Everest Hse). North River.

Peretz, I. L. Selected Stories. Howe, Irving & Greenberg, Eliezer, eds. LC 73-91342. 159p. 1975. pap. 4.95 (ISBN 0-8052-0496-2). Schocken.

Peretz, Paul. The Political Economy of Inflation in the United States. 264p. 1983. 28.00 (ISBN 0-226-65671-3); pap. 14.00 (ISBN 0-226-65672-1). U of Chicago Pr.

Perez, Belia. Tres Dramas De Navidad. 24p. 1981. pap. 0.80 (ISBN 0-311-08221-1). Casa Bautista.

Perez, Karen. Food Moods. 1982. text ed. 12.95 (ISBN 0-8359-2082-8); pap. text ed. 8.95 (ISBN 0-8359-2081-X). Reston.

Perez, L. M. Guide to the Materials for American History in Cuban Archives. (Carnegie Inst. Wash.: Vol. 16). 1907. pap. 21.00 (ISBN 0-527-00696-3). Kraus Repr.

Perez, Louis A., Jr. Army Politics in Cuba, 1898-1958. LC 75-35440. (Pitt Latin American Ser.). 1976. 14.95x (ISBN 0-8229-3303-9). U of Pittsburgh Pr.

--Cuba Between Empires, Eighteen Seventy-Eight to Nineteen Two. LC 82-11059. (Pitt Latin American Ser.). 465p. 1983. 34.95 (ISBN 0-8229-3472-8). U of Pittsburgh Pr.

--Historiography in the Revolution: A Bibliography of Cuban Scholarship, 1959-1979. (Reference Library of Social Science: Vol. 90). 1982. lib. bdg. 40.00 (ISBN 0-8240-9329-1). Garland Pub.

--Intervention, Revolution, & Politics in Cuba 1913-1921. LC 78-53601. (Pitt Latin American Ser.). 1978. 13.95x (ISBN 0-8229-3386-1). U of Pittsburgh Pr.

Perez, Louis C., ed. see Sabato, Ernesto.

Perez, Robert H. Southwest Borderlands: Veins of Silver & Gold. (Illus.). 160p. (YA) (gr. 10-12). 1982. pap. text ed. 7.50 (ISBN 0-940870-13-4); tchr's man. 2.50 (ISBN 0-940870-14-2). U of AZ Ed Mat.

Perez, Rosanne H. Protocols for Perinatal Nursing Practice. LC 80-27539. (Illus.). 536p. 1981. text ed. 24.95 (ISBN 0-8016-3805-4). Mosby.

Perez Castellon, Ninoska see Castellon, Ninoska Perez.

Perez Firmat, Gustavo. Idle Fictions: The Hispanic Vanguard Novel, 1926-1934. LC 82-12773. (Illus.). 220p. 1982. text ed. 25.75x (ISBN 0-8223-0528-3). Duke.

Pereznieto. Derecho Internacional Privado. 2nd ed. 332p. (Span.). 1981. pap. text ed. write for info. (ISBN 0-06-316703-4, Pub. by HarLA Mexico). Har-Row.

Pereznieto, Leonel. Derecho Internacional Privado. (Span.). 1980. pap. text ed. 11.20 o.p. (ISBN 0-06-316701-8, Pub. by HarLA Mexico). Har-Row.

Perez-Polo, J. Regino & De Vellis, Jean, eds. Growth & Trophic Factors. LC 83-954. (Progress in Clinical & Biological Research Ser.: Vol. 118). 472p. 1983. 45.00 (ISBN 0-8451-0118-8). A R Liss.

Perham, Margery. African Apprenticeship: An Autobiographical Journey in Southern Africa, 1929. LC 74-78312. 264p. 1974. 25.00x (ISBN 0-8419-0169-4, Africana). Holmes & Meier.

Perham, Margery, ed. see Wight, Martin.

Perham, Margery F. The Colonial Reckoning: End of Imperial Rule in Africa in the Light of British Experience. LC 76-25998. 1976. Repr. of 1962 ed. lib. bdg. 20.75x (ISBN 0-8371-9016-9, PECR). Greenwood.

Peri, Yoram. Between Battles & Ballots: Israeli Military in Politics. 368p. p.n.s. (ISBN 0-521-24414-5). Cambridge U Pr.

Periers, Bonaventure Des see Des Periers, Bonaventure.

Perin, Constance. With Man in Mind: An Interdisciplinary Prospectus for Environmental Design. (Illus.). 168p. 1972. pap. 4.95 o.p. (ISBN 0-262-66016-4). MIT Pr.

Perina, Jan. Coherence of Light. LC 77-141981. 318p. (Orig.). 1972. 24.50 (ISBN 0-686-92635-8). Krieger.

Perinbam, B. Marie. Holy Violence: The Revolutionary Thought of Franz Fanon; an Intellectual Biography. LC 81-51664. 224p. (Orig.). 1983. 22.00x (ISBN 0-89410-175-7); pap. 10.00x (ISBN 0-89410-176-5). Three Continents.

Perinbanayagam, R. S. The Karmic Theater: Self, Society & Astrology in Jaffna. LC 82-6997. 224p. 1982. lib. bdg. 22.50x (ISBN 0-87023-374-2). U of Mass Pr.

Perisic, Zoran. The Animation Stand. (Media Manuals Ser.). 1976. pap. 7.95 o.p. (ISBN 0-240-50863-7). Focal Pr.

--The Focalguide to Shooting Animation. (Focalguide Ser.). (Illus.). 1976. pap. 7.95 (ISBN 0-240-50973-0). Focal Pr.

--Special Optical Effects. LC 80-41005. (Illus.). 1980. 29.95 (ISBN 0-240-51007-0). Focal Pr.

Peristiany, J. G., ed. Mediterranean Family Structure. LC 75-20833. (Cambridge Studies in Social Anthropology: No. 13). (Illus.). 434p. 1976. 42.50 (ISBN 0-521-20964-1). Cambridge U Pr.

Peritz, E., jt. auth. see Abramson, J. H.

Per Jahn Lavik. Doors, Windows, & Shingles of Bergen. (Illus.). 129p. 1982. 26.00 (ISBN 82-00-05597-3). Universitet.

Perkell, Joseph S. Physiology of Speech Production: Results & Implications of a Quantitative Cineradiographic Study. (Press Research Monographs: No. 53). 1969. 14.00x o.p. (ISBN 0-262-16026-9). MIT Pr.

Perkes, Alden. The Santa Claus Book. 144p. 1982. 19.95 (ISBN 0-8184-0327-6). Lyle Stuart.

Perkes, Dan. The New Giant Crossword Puzzle Book. 13th ed. 1979. pap. 1.95 o.p. (ISBN 0-517-53687-0). Crown.

Perkes, Dan, ed. New Giant Crossword Puzzle Book: Fourteenth Ser. 64p. 1980. pap. 2.50 o.p. (ISBN 0-517-54020-7). Crown.

Perkey, Elton. Perkey's Nebraska Place-Names, Vol. XXVIII. LC 82-80300. 1982. write for info. Nebraska Hist.

Perkin, G. D. & Rose, F. Clifford. Optic Neuritis & Its Differential Diagnosis' (Illus.). 1979. text ed. 69.00x (ISBN 0-19-261156-9). Oxford U Pr.

Perkin, Harold, ed. History: An Outline for the Intending Student. (Outline Ser.). 1970. cased 14.95 o.p. (ISBN 0-7100-6814-X); pap. 7.95 o.p. (ISBN 0-7100-6815-8). Routledge & Kegan.

Perkins. Language Handicaps in Adults. (Current Therapy of Communication Disorders Ser.: Vol. 3). 1983. price not set (ISBN 0-86577-090-5). Thieme-Stratton.

Perkins, A see Hill, H.

Perkins, Al. Diggingest Dog. LC 67-21920. (Illus.). (gr. k-3). 1967. 4.95 (ISBN 0-394-80047-8); PLB 5.99 (ISBN 0-394-90047-2). Beginner.

Perkins, Al, adapted by. Hugh Lofting's Travels of Doctor Dolittle. (ps-3). 1967. 3.50 o.p. (ISBN 0-394-80048-6). Beginner.

Perkins, Al, ed. see Lofting, Hugh.

Perkins, Ann L. The Comparative Archeology of Early Mesopotamia. LC 49-10748. (Studies in Ancient Oriental Civilization: No. 25). (Illus.). xx, 201p. (Orig.). 1977. pap. text ed. 14.00x (ISBN 0-686-96827-1). Oriental Inst.

Perkins, Bob F. Deltaic Sedimentation on the Louisiana Coast. 1982. 10.00. SEPM.

Perkins, Bradford. The First Rapprochement: England & the United States, 1795-1805. 1967. Repr. 30.00x (ISBN 0-520-00998-3). U of Cal Pr.

Perkins, C. Molly. 136p. Date not set. pap. 5.95 (ISBN 0-88826-092-X). Superior Pub.

Perkins, Charles & Dwight, John. History of the Handel & Haydn Society, Vol. 1. LC 77-8152. (Music Reprint Ser.). 1977. Repr. of 1893 ed. lib. bdg. 49.50 (ISBN 0-306-77429-1); Vols. 1 & 2. 79.50 (ISBN 0-306-79658-9). Da Capo.

Perkins, Courtland D. & Hage, R. E. Airplane Performance, Stability & Control. 1949. 40.95 (ISBN 0-471-68046-X). Wiley.

Perkins, D. N. The Mind's Best Work: A New Psychology of Creative Thinking. 328p. 1983. pap. 7.95 (ISBN 0-674-57624-1). Harvard U Pr.

Perkins, Dan G., et al. Student's Resource Book & Study Guide to Accompany Psychology & You. 1978. pap. 7.95x (ISBN 0-673-15087-9). Scott F.

Perkins, David L., jt. auth. see Tanis, Norman E.

Perkins, Deborah A., jt. ed. see Steves, Ann.

Perkins, Dennis N., et al. Managing Creation: The Challenge of Building a New Organization. (Organizational Assessment & Change Ser.). 225p. 1983. 24.95 (ISBN 0-471-05204-3, Pub. by Wiley-Interscience). Wiley.

Perkins, Dexter. Charles Evans Hughes & American Democratic Statesmanship. Handlin, Oscar, ed. LC 78-5919. (The Library of American Biography Ser.). 1978. Repr. of 1956 ed. lib. bdg. 20.00x (ISBN 0-313-20463-2, PECH). Greenwood.

--History of the Monroe Doctrine. rev. ed. (Illus.). 1963. 10.00 o.p. (ISBN 0-316-69933-0). Little.

Perkins, Dexter & Snell, John L. The Education of Historians in the United States. LC 74-25597. 1975. Repr. of 1962 ed. lib. bdg. 17.00x (ISBN 0-8371-7881-9, PEEH). Greenwood.

Perkins, Donald. Charles Dickens: A New Perspective. 1982. 15.95 (ISBN 0-903540-53-3, Pub. by Floris Books). St George Bk Serv.

Perkins, Dorothy. Separation & Suffering: Hindu & Christian Views of Love. (Orig.). 1980. pap. 4.00 o.p. (ISBN 0-9604742-0-X). D J Perkins.

Perkins, Dwight, ed. Rural Small-Scale Industry in the People's Republic of China. LC 76-20015. 1977. 30.00x (ISBN 0-520-03284-5); pap. 7.95 (ISBN 0-520-04401-0, CAL449). U of Cal Pr.

Perkins, E. A., jt. auth. see Reigel, C. E.

Perkins, E. A., et al. Practice for Professional Typing. 1968. text ed. 9.00 (ISBN 0-07-049301-4, G). McGraw.

Perkins, E. J. The Biology of Estuaries & Coastal Waters. 1974. 102.00 o.s.i. (ISBN 0-12-550750-X). Acad Pr.

Perkins, Edward A., jt. auth. see Reigel, Charles E.

Perkins, Edwin J., ed. Men & Organizations: The American Economy in the Twentieth Century. LC 76-48150. 1977. 7.95 o.p. (ISBN 0-399-11890-X). Putnam Pub Group.

Perkins, Elizabeth, jt. auth. see Sprague, Stuart.

Perkins, Esther R. Backroading Through Cecil County, Maryland. LC 77-75889. (Illus.). 78p. 1977. 22.00 (ISBN 0-935968-08-3); pap. 11.75 (ISBN 0-935968-01-6). EPM Pubns.

Perkins, Esther R., jt. auth. see Sawin, Nancy C.

Perkins, G. The Ruminations of an Orthopaedic Surgeon. (Illus.). 1970. 5.95 o.p. (ISBN 0-407-38700-5). Butterworth.

Perkins, G., jt. auth. see Drummond, David A.

Perkins, H. C. Air Pollution. (Illus.). 448p. 1974. text ed. 34.95 (ISBN 0-07-049302-2, C); solutions manual 12.50 (ISBN 0-07-049303-0). McGraw.

Perkins, Henry C., jt. auth. see Reynolds, William C.

Perkins, J. M., jt. ed. see Butler, A. R.

Perkins, J. O. The Australian Financial System after the Campbell Report. 152p. 1982. pap. 14.00 (ISBN 0-522-84253-4, Pub. by Melbourne U Pr Australia). Intl Schol Bk Serv.

Perkins, James & Stevens, Jane. One Man's World: Popham Beach, Maine. LC 74-76867. (Illus.). 144p. 1974. 16.95 o.s.i. (ISBN 0-87027-141-5); pap. 9.95 o.s.i. (ISBN 0-87027-142-3). Cumberland Pr.

Perkins, James S. Experiencing Reincarnation. LC 77-5249. (Illus.). 1977. pap. 4.95 (ISBN 0-8356-0500-0, Quest). Theos Pub Hse.

--Through Death to Rebirth. new ed. LC 61-13301. (Illus.). 124p. 1974. pap. 4.25 (ISBN 0-8356-0451-9, Quest). Theos Pub Hse.

Perkins, John H., jt. ed. see Pimentel, David.

Perkins, Lynn. Let's Go to a Paper Mill. (Let's Go Ser). (Illus.). (gr. 3-6). 1969. PLB 4.29 o.p. (ISBN 0-399-60388-3). Putnam Pub Group.

Perkins, Margaret. Teaching Needlecrafts. 1972. pap. text ed. 8.50x o.p. (ISBN 0-435-42245-6). Heinemann Ed.

--Using the Sewing Machine. (Illus.). 1977. pap. text ed. 7.50x o.p. (ISBN 0-435-42840-3). Heinemann Ed.

Perkins, Marlin. My Wild Kingdom: An Autobiography. (Illus.). 320p. 1983. 15.95 (ISBN 0-525-24146-9, 01549-460). Dutton.

Perkins, Maxwell, ed. see DeJong, Dola.

Perkins, Michael. The Secret Record: Modern Erotic Literature. LC 76-18832. 1976. 7.95 o.p. (ISBN 0-688-03121-8); pap. 4.50 o.p. (ISBN 0-688-08121-5). Morrow.

Perkins, Patt & Hootman, Marcia. How to Forgive Your Ex-Husband. (Illus.). 150p. (Orig.). 1982. pap. 6.95 (ISBN 0-943172-01-2). New Wave.

--Making the Break. LC 82-6324. (Illus.). 130p. 1982. pap. 5.95 (ISBN 0-686-36311-6). New Wave.

Perkins, Pheme. The Book of Revelation. Karris, Robert J., ed. (Collegeville Bible Commentary Ser.: No. 11). 96p. 1983. Vol. 11. pap. 2.50 (ISBN 0-8146-1311-X). Liturgical Pr.

--Ministry In The Pauline Churches: Partners for Christ. LC 82-60849. 1982. pap. 4.95 (ISBN 0-8091-2473-4). Paulist Pr.

Perkins, Pheme, jt. auth. see Fuller, Reginald.

Perkins, Philip H., jt. auth. see Green, J. Keith.

Perkins, Robert. Against Straight Lines: Self-Portrait in a Landscape. 1983. 16.00i (ISBN 0-316-69930-6). Little.

Perkins, Robert F., et al, eds. The Boston Athenaeum Art Exhibition Index: 1827-1874. (Illus.). 1980. 55.00x (ISBN 0-262-16075-7). MIT Pr.

Perkins, Roger & Douglas-Morris, K. J. Gunfire in Barbary: Admiral Lord Exmouth's Battle with the Corsairs of Algiers in 1816. (Illus.). 200p. 1982. text ed. 24.50x (ISBN 0-85937-271-5). Sheridan.

Perkins, Rollin M. & Boyce, Ronald N. Criminal Law. 3rd ed. LC 82-15976. (University Textbook Ser.). 1269p. 1982. text ed. write for info. (ISBN 0-88277-067-5). Foundation Pr.

Perkins, Steve, jt. auth. see Herskowitz, Mickey.

Perkins, William. Dysarthria & Apraxia: Current Therapy of Communication Disorders, Vol. 2. (Illus.). 128p. 1983. write for info. (ISBN 0-86577-086-7). Thieme-Stratton.

--General Principles of Therapy: Current Therapy of Communication Disorders, Vol. 1. (Illus.). 80p. 1982. 10.95 (ISBN 0-86577-077-8). Thieme-Stratton.

Perkins, William H., ed. Human Perspectives in Speech & Language Disorders. LC 77-13282. (Illus.). 1978. pap. 19.95 (ISBN 0-8016-3786-4). Mosby.

Perkins, Wilma L. The Fanny Farmer Junior Cookbook. rev. ed. (Illus.). (gr. 5 up). 1957. 6.95 o.p. (ISBN 0-316-69932-2). Little.

Perkins, Y. O. The Macroeconomic Mix to Stop Stagflation. 1979. 34.95x (ISBN 0-470-26525-6). Halsted Pr.

Perkinson, Henry J. Imperfect Panacea: American Faith in Education, 1865-1968. 2nd ed. (Orig.). 1977. pap. text ed. 8.00 (ISBN 0-394-31216-3, RanC). Random.

Perkinson, Roy L., jt. auth. see Dolloff, Francis W.

Perko, Joanne E., jt. auth. see Kreigh, Helen Z.

Perkoff, Gerald T. Changing Health Care: Perspectives from a New Medical Care Setting. LC 79-20504. 160p. 1980. 18.50x (ISBN 0-914904-38-8). Health Admin Pr.

Perkowski, Jan L. Kashubian Idiolect in the United States. LC 68-64529. (Language Science Monographs Ser: Vol. 2). 1969. pap. text ed. 11.50x o.p. (ISBN 0-87750-135-1). Res Ctr Lang Semiotic.

Perks, William T. & Robinson, Ira M., eds. Urban & Regional Planning in a Federal State: The Canadian Experience. LC 78-3648. (Community Development Ser.: Vol. 41). (Illus.). 1979. 57.00 o.p. (ISBN 0-87933-315-4). Hutchinson Ross.

Perl, Lila. America Goes to the Fair: All About State & County Fairs in the U. S. A. LC 74-5938. 128p. (gr. 5-9). 1974. 7.95 o.p. (ISBN 0-688-21830-X); PLB 6.96 o.p. (ISBN 0-688-31830-4). Morrow.

--East Africa: Kenya, Tanzania, Uganda. 160p. (gr. 5-9). 1973. PLB 9.12 (ISBN 0-688-30088-X). Morrow.

--Eating the Vegetarian Way: Good Food from the Earth. LC 80-18416. (Illus.). 96p. (gr. 4-6). 1980. 9.75 (ISBN 0-688-22248-X); PLB 9.36 (ISBN 0-688-32248-4). Morrow.

--Egypt: Rebirth on the Nile. (gr. 5-9). 1977. 9.55 o.p. (ISBN 0-688-22106-8); lib. bdg. 10.51 (ISBN 0-688-32106-2). Morrow.

--Ethiopia, Land of the Lion. 160p. (gr. 5-9). 1972. PLB 7.44 o.p. (ISBN 0-688-30033-2). Morrow.

--Ghana & Ivory Coast, Spotlight on West Africa. LC 74-23106. (Illus.). 160p. (gr. 5-9). 1975. 9.55 (ISBN 0-688-31833-9). Morrow.

--Junk Food, Fast Food, Health Food What America Eats & Why. 192p. (gr. 5 up). 1980. 10.95 (ISBN 0-395-29108-9, Clarion); pap. 4.95 (ISBN 0-395-30060-6). HM.

--Mexico, Crucible of the Americas. LC 77-20203. (Illus.). (gr. 5-9). 1978. 10.75 (ISBN 0-688-22148-3); PLB 10.32 (ISBN 0-688-32148-8). Morrow.

--Puerto Rico, Island Between Two Worlds. LC 79-1130. (Illus.). (gr. 7-9). 1979. 11.25 (ISBN 0-688-22181-5); PLB 10.80 (ISBN 0-688-32181-X). Morrow.

Perl, Lila & Ada, Alma F. Pinatas & Paper Flowers-Pinatas y Flores de Papel: Holidays of the Americas in English & Spanish. (Illus.). 96p. (gr. 3-6). 1983. 11.50 (ISBN 0-89919-112-6, Clarion); pap. 3.95 (ISBN 0-89919-155-X). HM.

Perl, Martin L. High Energy Hadron Physics. LC 74-6348. 584p. 1974. 48.95x (ISBN 0-471-68049-4, Pub. by Wiley-Interscience). Wiley.

Perl, P. Ferns. (Encyclopedia of Gardening Ser.). (gr. 6 up). 1977. PLB 17.28 (ISBN 0-8094-2559-9). Silver.

Perl, Philip, jt. auth. see Crockett, James U.

Perl, Raphael. The Falkalan Island Dispute in International Law & Politics: A Documentary Sourcebook. 600p. 1983. lib. bdg. 45.00 (ISBN 0-379-11251-5). Oceana.

Perl, Susan, jt. auth. see Bayley, Monica.

Perl, Susan, jt. auth. see Dutton, June.

Perl, T., jt. auth. see Freedman, M.

Perl, William, jt. auth. see Lassen, Niels A.

Perl, William R. The Four Front War: From the Holocaust to the Promised Land. (Illus.). 1979. 12.95 o.p. (ISBN 0-517-53837-7). Crown.

--Operation Action: Rescue from the Holocaust. 1983. 16.95 (ISBN 0-8044-1725-3); pap. 9.95 (ISBN 0-8044-6645-9). Ungar.

Perlberg, Mark. The Feel of the Sun. LC 82-75679. x, 70p. 1982. 15.95x (ISBN 0-8040-0422-6); pap. 6.95 (ISBN 0-8040-0423-4). Swallow.

Perlberg, Mark, ed. see Bailey, David H. & Gottlieb, Louise.

Perle, George. Twelve-Tone Tonality. LC 76-50258. 1978. 26.50x (ISBN 0-520-03387-6). U of Cal Pr.

Perles, B. & Sullivan, C. Freund & Williams' Modern Business Statistics. rev. ed. 1969. text ed. 23.95 (ISBN 0-13-589580-4); lab. manual & wkbk. 7.95 (ISBN 0-13-589598-7). P-H.

Perles, Benjamin M., jt. auth. see Freund, John E.

Perlet, Harry F., Jr., jt. auth. see Lorimer, James J.

Perley, Michael, jt. auth. see Howard, Ross.

Perlin, George. The Tory Syndrome: Leadership Politics in the Progressive Conservative Party. 262p. 20.00x (ISBN 0-7735-0350-1); pap. text ed. 9.95 (ISBN 0-7735-0352-8). McGill-Queens U Pr.

Perlin, Seymour, jt. auth. see Beauchamp, Thom.

Perlis, jt. auth. see Galler.

Perlis, Alan, et al, eds. Software Metrics. (Computer Science Ser.). (Illus.). 350p. 1981. 27.50x (ISBN 0-262-16083-8). MIT Pr.

Perlis, Alan J., ed. see Gross, Jonathan L. & Brainerd, Walter S.

Perlis, Harlan J., jt. ed. see Cheremisinoff, Paul N.

Perlman. Fermentation: 1977: Annual Reports. 1977. 37.50 (ISBN 0-12-040301-3). Acad Pr.

Perlman, Anne S. Sorting it Out. LC 82-70744. 1982. 12.95 (ISBN 0-915604-72-8); pap. 4.95 (ISBN 0-915604-73-6). Carnegie-Mellon.

Perlman, Bennard. Robert Henri: His Life & Art. (Illus.). 375p. 1983. 39.50 (ISBN 0-8180-0136-4). Horizon.

Perlman, D. & Tsao, G. T., eds. Annual Reports on Fermentation Processes, Vol. 2. 1978. 34.50 (ISBN 0-12-040302-1). Acad Pr.

Perlman, Daniel, jt. auth. see Peplau, Letitia A.

Perlman, David, jt. ed. see Peppler, Henry J.

Perlman, Helen H. Perspectives on Social Casework. LC 70-157736. 223p. 1971 19.95 (ISBN 0-87722-009-3); pap. 7.95 (ISBN 0-87722-034-4). Temple U Pr.

--Relationship: The Heart of Helping People. LC 78-19064. x, 236p. 1979. pap. 7.95 (ISBN 0-226-66036-2). U of Chicago Pr.

Perlman, Janice E. The Myth of Marginality: Urban Poverty & Politics in Rio De Janeiro. LC 73-87246. 250p. 1976. 33.00x (ISBN 0-520-02596-2); pap. 7.95x (ISBN 0-520-03952-1). U of Cal Pr.

Perlman, Ken. Clawhammer Style Banjo: A Complete Guide for Beginning & Advanced Banjo Players. (Illus.). 192p. 1983. 19.95 (ISBN 0-13-136374-3); pap. 10.95 (ISBN 0-13-136366-2). P-H.

Perlman, M., jt. ed. see Van Door, G.

Perlman, Mark, ed. The Organization & Retrieval of Economic Knowledge. LC 76-30513. (International Economic Association Ser). 1977. lib. bdg. 40.00 o.p. (ISBN 0-89158-721-7). Westview.

Perlman, Mark, ed. see International Economic Association Conference, Tokyo.

Perlman, Mark, ed. see Macleod, Gordon K.

Perlman, Philip. Essentials of Modern Chemistry. rev. ed. 472p. (gr. 9-12). 1984. pap. text ed. 6.95 (ISBN 0-8120-2278-5). Barron.

--Essentials of Modern Chemistry. LC 78-2344. (gr. 9-12). 1979. 10.50o.p. (ISBN 0-8120-6079-2); pap. 7.95 (ISBN 0-8120-0646-1). Barron.

Perlman, Richard. The Economics of Poverty. new ed. (Illus.). 1976. pap. text ed. 9.50 o.p. (ISBN 0-07-049307-3, C). McGraw.

--Labor Theory. LC 80-12286. 250p. 1981. Repr. of 1969 ed. lib. bdg. write for info. o.p. (ISBN 0-89874-163-7). Krieger.

Perlman, Robert & Gurin, Arnold. Community Organization & Social Planning. LC 71-177887. 1972. 23.95 (ISBN 0-471-68050-8). Wiley.

Perlman, Robert & Warren, Roland L. Families in the Energy Crisis: Impacts & Implications for Theory & Policy. LC 77-24314. 256p. 1977. prof ref 20.00x (ISBN 0-88410-068-5). Ballinger Pub.

Perlman, Robert, ed. Family Home Care: Critical Issues for Services & Policies. (Home Health Care Services Quarterly, Vol. 3, No. 3-4). 328p. 1983. text ed. 29.95 (ISBN 0-86656-220-6); pap. text ed. 14.95 (ISBN 0-86656-221-4). Haworth Pr.

Perlman, William J., ed. The Movies on Trial: The Views & Opinions of Outstanding Personalities Anent Screen Entertainment Past & Present. LC 78-160245. (Moving Pictures Ser). 1971. Repr. of 1936 ed. lib. bdg. 16.95x (ISBN 0-89198-046-6). Ozer.

Perlmann, Moshe, ed. & tr. from Arabic. Ibn Kammuna's Examination of the Three Faiths: A Thirteenth-Century Essay in the Comparative Study of Religion. LC 73-102659. 1971. 30.00x (ISBN 0-520-01658-0). U of Cal Pr.

Perlmutter, Amos. Military & Politics in Israel 1948-1967. rev ed. 176p. 1983. 28.50x (ISBN 0-7146-2392-X, F Cass Co). Biblio Dist.

--The Military & Politics in Modern Times: Professionals, Praetorians & Revolutionary Soldiers. LC 76-45769. 1977. 25.50x (ISBN 0-300-02045-7); pap. 9.95x (ISBN 0-300-02353-7). Yale U Pr.

Perlmutter, Amos, jt. ed. see Gooch, John.

Perlmutter, Arnold, jt. ed. see Kursunoglu, Behram.

Perlmutter, Arnold, jt. ed. see Kursunglu, Behram N.

Perlmutter, David M., ed. Studies in Relational Grammar 1. LC 82-6945. 416p. 1983. lib. bdg. 30.00x (ISBN 0-226-66050-8). U of Chicago Pr.

Perlmutter, Felice, ed. Mental Health Promotion & Primary Prevention. LC 81-48482. 1982. 7.95x (ISBN 0-87589-907-2, MHS-13). Jossey-Bass.

Perlmutter, Felice D. & Slavin, Simon, eds. Leadership in Social Administration: Perspectives for the 1980's. 268p. 1980. 29.95 (ISBN 0-87722-172-3); pap. 12.95 (ISBN 0-87722-201-0). Temple U Pr.

Perlmutter, Marion, ed. Development & Policy Concerning Children with Special Needs. (Minnesota Symposium on Child Psychology Ser.: Vol. 16). 272p. 1983. text ed. write for info. (ISBN 0-89859-261-5). L Erlbaum Assocs.

Perlmutter, Nate. How to Win Money at the Races. updated ed. (Illus.). 1979. pap. 2.95 o.p. (ISBN 0-02-081090-3, Collier). Macmillan.

Perloff, Harvey S. Education for Planning: City, State, & Regional. LC 77-23156. (Resources for the Future, Inc.). (Illus.). 1977. Repr. of 1957 ed. lib. bdg. 15.50x (ISBN 0-8371-9474-1, PEEP). Greenwood.

--Planning the Post-Industrial City. LC 80-67753. (Illus.). 328p. (Orig.). 1980. 25.95 (ISBN 0-918286-21-2). Planners Pr.

Perloff, William H. & Baron, William. Soil Mechanics: Principles & Applications. LC 74-22543. 1976. 45.50x (ISBN 0-471-06671-0); tchrs. manual 3.00 (ISBN 0-471-07566-3). Wiley.

Perlroth, Karen A., jt. auth. see Lagerwerff, Ellen B.

Perls, Frederick, et al. Gestalt Therapy: Excitement & Growth in the Human Personality. 1954. 10.00 o.p. (ISBN 0-517-52764-2). Crown.

Perls, Fritz. The Gestalt Approach & Eyewitness to Therapy. 1973. 7.95 (ISBN 0-8314-0034-X). Sci & Behavior.

Perls, Fritz & Baumgardner. Legacy from Fritz: Gifts from Lake Cowichan. Bd. with Gifts from Lake Cowichan. Baumgardner, Patricia. LC 75-23594. 1975. 8.95 (ISBN 0-8314-0046-3). Sci & Behavior.

Perlson, Michael R. How to Understand & Influence People & Organizations: Practical Psychology for Goal Achievement. 256p. 1982. 16.95 (ISBN 0-8144-5684-7). Am Mgmt.

Perlstein, Israel. How to Relieve or Eliminate Chronic Pains - Discomforts Acquired During Sleep: A Doctor's Solution to Your Sleeping Problems. (Illus.). 64p. (Orig.). 1981. pap. 1.95 o.p. (ISBN 0-8326-2252-4, 7445). Delair.

Perman, David. Change & the Churches: An Anatomy of Religion in Britain. 1978. 18.00 o.p. (ISBN 0-370-10329-7). Transatlantic.

Perman, M. Reunion Without Compromise: The South & Reconstruction, 1865-1868. LC 72-86418. (Illus.). 384p. 1973. 44.50 (ISBN 0-521-20044-X); pap. 12.95x (ISBN 0-521-09779-7). Cambridge U Pr.

Permanent Commission of the Conference on the Use & Conservation of the Marine Resources of the South Pacific. Establishment, Structure, Functions & Activities of International Fisheries Bodies IV. 44p. 1968. pap. 7.50 (ISBN 0-686-92803-2, F1736, FAO). Unipub.

Permar, B., ed. see Schroeder, Albert.

Permutt, Cyril. Collecting Old Cameras. LC 76-14888. (Photography Ser.). 1977. lib. bdg. 22.50 (ISBN 0-306-70855-8). Da Capo.

Pern, S. Masked Dancers of West Africa: The Dogon. (Peoples of the Wild Ser.). 1982. 15.96 (ISBN 0-7054-0706-3, Pub. by Time-Life). Silver.

Perna, Albert F. Glider Gladiators of World War Two. LC 70-91840. (Illus.). 398p. 1970. 16.00 (ISBN 0-9600302-0-4). Podiatric Educ.

Pernia, Ernesto D. Urbanization, Population Growth & Economic Deveopment in the Philippines. (Studies in Population & Urban Demography: No. 3). 1977. lib. bdg. 29.95 (ISBN 0-8371-9721-X, PEU/). Greenwood.

Pernkopf, Eduard. Atlas of Topographical & Applied Human Anatomy: Head & Neck, Vol. 1. rev. 2nd ed. Ferner, Helmut, ed. Monsen, Harry, tr. from Ger. LC 79-25264. Orig. Title: Atlas der Topographischen und Angewamdten Anatomie Des Menschen. (Illus.). 308p. 1980. Repr. of 1963 ed. text ed. 98.00 (ISBN 0-7216-7198-5). Saunders.

--Atlas of Topographical & Applied Human Anatomy, 2 vols. Ferner, Helmut, ed. Incl. Vol. 1. Head & Neck. LC 63-16443. (Illus.). 356p. 1963. 75.00 o.p. (ISBN 0-7216-7200-0); Vol. 2. Thorax, Abdomen & Extremeties. LC 63-16443. (Illus.). 421p. 1964. 85.00 o.p. (ISBN 0-7216-7201-9). Saunders.

Pernoud, Regine. Joan of Arc: By Herself & Her Witnesses. LC 66-24807. 1969. pap. 10.95 (ISBN 0-8128-1260-3). Stein & Day.

Pernow, Bengt, jt. ed. see Carlson, Lars A.

Pernow, Bengt, jt. ed. see Von Euler, Ulf S.

Pero & Rovin. Always, Lana. 288p. 1982. pap. 3.50 (ISBN 0-553-20805-5). Bantam.

Peroival, J., jt. ed. see Loyn, H. R.

Peron, Michel, et al. Dictionnaire francais-anglais, anglais-francais des affaires: A French-English English-French Dictionary of Business Terms. rev. ed. 512p. 1974. 30.95 (ISBN 2-03-020609-1, 3764). Larousse.

Perone, Sam P. & Jones, David O. Digital Computers in Scientific Instrumentation: Application to Chemistry. (Illus.). 420p. 1973. pap. text ed. 19.95 (ISBN 0-07-049319-7, C). McGraw.

Peroni, Carlo, jt. auth. see Gallagher, Elizabeth.

Peroni, Peter A. The Burg: An Italian-American Community at Bay in Trenton. LC 79-63258. 1979. pap. text ed. 9.00 (ISBN 0-8191-0724-7). U Pr of Amer.

Perotti, James L. Heidegger on the Divine: The Thinker, the Poet & God. LC 73-92904. x, 134p. 1974. 10.00x (ISBN 0-8214-0144-0, 82-81479). Ohio U Pr.

Perotto, Aldo, jt. auth. see Delagi, Edward F.

Perouse, Comte De La see La Perouse, Comte De.

Perr, Harvey see Lion, Eugene & Ball, David.

Perraton, J. & Baxter, R., eds. Models, Evaluations & Information Systems for Planners. 1975. 35.95 (ISBN 0-85200-102-9). Elsevier.

Perrault, Charles. Perrault's Complete Fairy Tales. Johnson, A. E., tr. from Fr. LC 82-19873. (Illus.). 184p. 1982. pap. 7.95 (ISBN 0-396-08108-8). Dodd.

--Perrault's Fairy Tales. LC 72-79522. (Illus.). (gr. 4-6). 1969. pap. 4.00 (ISBN 0-486-22311-6). Dover.

Perreault, Robert B. La Presse Franco-Americaine et la Politique: L'Oeuvre de Charles-Roger Daoust. (Illus., Fr.). pap. text ed. 3.50 (ISBN 0-911409-39-4). Natl Mat Dev.

Perrell, O. C., jt. auth. see Pride, William M.

Perren, Richard. The Meat Trade in Britain, 1840-1914. (Studies in Economic History). 1978. 22.95x (ISBN 0-7100-8841-8). Routledge & Kegan.

Perren, S. M., jt. auth. see Allgower, M.

Perrens, S. J., intro. by. Agricultural Engineering, 1982. (Agricultural Conferences Ser.). 225p. (Orig.). 1982. pap. text ed. 42.00x (ISBN 0-85825-176-0, Pub. Inst Engineering Australia). Renouf.

Perrett, Bryan. Weapons of the Falklands Conflict. (Illus.). 1983. 9.95 (ISBN 0-7137-1315-1, Pub. by Blandford Pr England). Sterling.

Perrett, Geoffrey. A Dream of Greatness: The American People, 1945-1963. LC 78-10343. 1979. 24.95 (ISBN 0-698-10949-X, Coward). Putnam Pub Group.

Perrett, Heli & Lethem, Francis J. Human Actors in Project Work. (Working Paper: No. 397). 85p. 1980. 5.00 (ISBN 0-686-36086-9, WP-0397). World Bank.

Perreymond. Le Bilan de la France, ou la Misere et le Travail. (Conditions of the 19th Century French Working Class Ser.). 117p. (Fr.). 1974. Repr. of 1849 ed. lib. bdg. 39.00 o.p. (ISBN 0-8287-0681-6, 1032). Clearwater Pub.

Perriam, Wendy. After Purple. 384p. 1982. 14.95 (ISBN 0-312-01164-4). St Martin.

Perriche, Marlene. Caribbean Love Song. (YA) 1980. 6.95 (ISBN 0-686-73922-1, Avalon). Bouregy.

--A Heart Triumphant. (YA) 1981. 6.95 (ISBN 0-686-74799-2, Avalon). Bouregy.

--Mansion of Peril. (YA) 1981. 6.95 (ISBN 0-686-74795-X, Avalon). Bouregy.

Perrie, Maureen. The Agrarian Policy of the Russian Socialist-Revolutionary Party. LC 76-644. (Soviet & East European Studies Ser.). 1977. 29.95 (ISBN 0-521-21213-8). Cambridge U Pr.

Perrier, Donald, jt. auth. see Gibaldi, Milo.

Perriere, Guillaume De La see La Perriere, Guillaume de.

Perrigo, Lynn I. Gateway to Glorieta: A History of Las Vegas, New Mexico. (Illus.). 250p. 1982. 14.95 (ISBN 0-87108-597-6); pap. 8.95 (ISBN 0-87108-598-4). Pruett.

Perrin, Arnold, ed. see Anson, Joan.

Perrin, Bernadotte, ed. see Plutarch.

Perrin, Charles. Mathematics for Chemists. LC 79-112850. 1970. 33.95x (ISBN 0-471-68069-9, Pub. by Wiley-Interscience). Wiley.

Perrin, D. D. & Dempsey, B. Buffers for PH & Metal Ion Control. 1979. 15.95x o.p. (ISBN 0-412-11700-2, Pub. by Chapman & Hall England); pap. 13.95x (ISBN 0-412-21890-9). Methuen Inc.

Perrin, D. D., ed. Ionisation Constants of Inorganic Acids & Bases in Aqueous Solution, No.29. 2nd ed. (Chemical Data Ser.). 194p. 1982. 50.00 (ISBN 0-08-029214-3). Pergamon.

Perrin, D. D., et al. PKA Predictions for Organic Acids & Bases. 150p. 1981. 29.95x (ISBN 0-412-22190-X, Pub. by Chapman & Hall). Methuen Inc.

Perrin, Elula. So Long As There Are Women. Salemson, Harold J., tr. from Fr. LC 79-26502. 1980. 10.95 o.p. (ISBN 0-688-03596-5). Morrow.

--Women Prefer Women. Salemson, Harold J., tr. from Fr. LC 78-13330. 1979. 8.95 o.p. (ISBN 0-688-03407-1). Morrow.

Perrin, Linda. Your Career in Health Care. (Arco's Career Guidance Ser.). (Illus.). 128p. 1983. lib. bdg. 7.95 (ISBN 0-668-05503-0); pap. 4.50 (ISBN 0-668-05514-6). Arco.

Perrin, Noel. Dr. Bowdler's Legacy: A History of Expurgated Books in England & America. LC 70-86546. 216p. 1969. text ed. 15.00x (ISBN 0-87451-064-3). U Pr of New Eng.

--Giving up the Gun: Japan's Reversion to the Sword, 1543-1879. (General Ser.). 1979. lib. bdg. 9.95 (ISBN 0-8161-3010-8, Large Print Bks). G K Hall.

Perrin, Norman. Rediscovering the Teachings of Jesus. LC 67-11510. 1976. pap. 6.95xi (ISBN 0-06-066493-2, RD 151, HarpR). Har-Row.

Perrin, Norman, jt. auth. see Abernathy, David.

Perrin, Porter G. Reference Handbook of Grammar & Usage. (Derived from Writer's guide & Index to English). 1972. 9.45 (ISBN 0-688-00061-4). Morrow.

Perrine, Garrith D. Administration of Justice: Principles & Procedures. (Criminal Justice Ser.). (Illus.). 300p. 1980. text ed. 18.50 (ISBN 0-8299-0345-3). West Pub.

Perrine, Laurence. The Art of Total Relevance: Papers on Poetry. LC 76-1978. 1976. pap. text ed. 6.95 o.p. (ISBN 0-88377-055-5). Newbury Hse.

Perring, F. H. & Walters, S. M. Atlas of British Flora. (Illus.). 432p. 1976. 55.00x o.p. (ISBN 0-87471-900-3). Rowman.

Perrins, Leslie. Showing Your Dog. (Foyle's Handbks). (Illus.). 1973. 3.95 (ISBN 0-685-55790-1). Palmetto Pub.

Perris, C. & Struwe, G. Biological Psychiatry, 1981. (Developments in Psychiatry Ser.: Vol. 5). 1982. 181.00 (ISBN 0-444-80404-8). Elsevier.

Perrodin, Alex F., jt. auth. see Mahaffey, Michael L.

Perrone, N., jt. ed. see Herrmann, G.

Perrone, Nicholas & Pilkey, Walter D., eds. Structural Mechanics Software Series, Vol. IV. (Illus.). 400p. 1982. 25.00x (ISBN 0-8139-0918-X). U Pr of Va.

Perrone, Nicholas, jt. ed. see Pilkey, Walter D.

Perrot, Jean. The Organ from Its Invention in the Hellenistic Period to the End of the Thirteenth Century. Deane, Norma, tr. 1971. 37.50x (ISBN 0-19-318418-4). Oxford U Pr.

Perrot, Michelle. Enquetes sur la Condition Ouvriere au Dix-Neuvieme Siecle. (Conditions of the 19th Century French Working Class Ser.). 110p. (Fr.). 1974. pap. text ed. 11.50x o.p. (ISBN 0-8287-0682-4, 1000). Clearwater Pub.

Perrott, Ronald & Allison, Donald. PASCAL for FORTRAN Programmers. 1983. text ed. p.n.s. (ISBN 0-914894-09-9). Computer Sci.

Perrow, Charles. Complex Organizations: A Critical Essay. 2nd ed. 1979. pap. text ed. 10.95x o.p. (ISBN 0-673-15205-7). Scott F.

Perru, Philippe Le, tr. see Mears, Henrietta C.

Perrucci, Robert & Gerstl, Joel E. Profession Without Community: Engineers in American Society. (Orig.). 1969. pap. text ed. 3.50 (ISBN 0-685-19756-5). Phila Bk Co.

Perrucci, Robert, et al. Sociology: Basic Structures & Processes. 625p. 1977. text ed. write for info. (ISBN 0-697-07550-8); instr's manual avail. (ISBN 0-697-07595-8). Wm C Brown.

Perry & Smith. Mild Hypertension: To Lease of Not to Treat, Vol. 304. 1978. 57.00 (ISBN 0-89072-059-2). NY Acad Sci.

Perry, A. E. Hot-Wire Anemometry. (Illus.). 204p. 1982. 47.00x (ISBN 0-19-856327-2). Oxford U Pr.

Perry, A. H., jt. auth. see Barry, R. G.

Perry, Allen H. Environmental Hazards in the British Isles. (Illus.). 192p. (Orig.). 1981. text ed. 27.50x (ISBN 0-04-910069-6); pap. text ed. 17.95x (ISBN 0-04-910070-X). Allen Unwin.

Perry, Andrew. The Practical Carpenter. LC 78-65661. 1979. 11.95i o.p. (ISBN 0-690-01811-8); pap. 5.95i (ISBN 0-690-01819-3; TYC-T). T Y Crowell.

Perry, Anne. Resurrection Row. 192p. 1982. pap. 2.50 (ISBN 0-449-24566-7, Crest). Fawcett.

Perry, Anne G. & Potter, Patricia A. Shock: Comprehensive Nursing Management. (Illus.). 303p. 1983. pap. text ed. 19.95 (ISBN 0-8016-3827-5). Mosby.

Perry, Bliss. American Spirit in Literature. 1918. text ed. 8.50x (ISBN 0-686-83469-0). Elliots Bks.

Perry, C. Seat Weaving. 1940. pap. 4.60 (ISBN 0-87002-015-3). Bennett IL.

Perry, C. C. & Lissner, H. R. Strain Gage Primer. 2nd ed. 1962. 43.50 (ISBN 0-07-049461-4, P&RB). McGraw.

Perry, C. L., jt. auth. see Evans, George W.

Perry, C. W., jt. auth. see Sheehan, P. W.

Perry, Cecilia, ed. see Parker, Lynn, et al.

Perry, Dave. Little Fox's Airbrush Stencil Techniques. (Illus.). 125p. 1982. pap. 14.95 (ISBN 0-9603530-8-9). Southwest Screen Print.

--Little Fox's Airbrush Stencil Techniques. (Illus.). 125p. (Orig.). 1982. pap. text ed. 14.95 (ISBN 0-9603530-8-9). Southwest Screen Print.

Perry, Donald R. & Merschel, Sylvia E. Journey into a Hollow Tree. LC 80-14284. (Illus.). 64p. (gr. 5-12). 1980. PLB 8.95 (ISBN 0-89490-038-2). Enslow Pubs.

Perry, E. S., jt. auth. see Weissberger, A.

Perry, Earl. Puppets Go to Church. 1975. pap. 1.95 (ISBN 0-8341-0385-0). Beacon Hill.

Perry, Edith W. Altar Guild Manual. (Orig.). 1945. pap. 2.95 (ISBN 0-8192-1067-6). Morehouse.

Perry, Edward L. Luyties Homeopathic Practice. 165p. 1974. pap. 1.65 (ISBN 0-89378-052-9). Formur Intl.

Perry, Edward L., jt. auth. see Chapman, J. B.

Perry, Elizabeth J. Chinese Perspectives on the Nien Rebellion. LC 81-9300. 150p. 1981. 25.00 (ISBN 0-87332-191-X). M E Sharpe.

--Rebels & Revolutionaries in North China, 1845-1945. LC 79-65179. xvi, 324p. 1980. 25.00x (ISBN 0-8047-1055-4); pap. 8.95 (ISBN 0-8047-1175-5, SP 62). Stanford U Pr.

--Rebels & Revolutionaries in North China, 1845-1945. LC 79-65179. xvi, 324p. 1983. pap. 8.95 (ISBN 0-8047-1175-5, SP-62). Stanford U Pr.

Perry, Elliot. Pat Paragraphs. Turner, George T. & Stanton, Thomas E., eds. LC 81-68198. (Illus.). 1982. 55.00 (ISBN 0-930412-05-2). Bureau Issues.

Perry, Enos J. Artificial Insemination of Farm Animals. 473p. 1968. 22.50 o.p. (ISBN 0-8135-0577-1). Rutgers U Pr.

Perry, Erna, jt. auth. see Perry, John A.

Perry, Erna K., jt. auth. see Perry, John.

Perry, Erna K., jt. auth. see Perry, John A.

Perry, Estelle. Story of Maine for Young Readers. rev. ed. LC 62-20544. (Illus.). 104p. (gr. 4). 1976. pap. 4.95 o.s.i. (ISBN 0-87027-160-1). Cumberland Pr.

Perry, F. E. A Dictionary of Banking. 304p. 1979. 35.00x (ISBN 0-7121-0428-3, Pub. by Macdonald & Evans). State Mutual Bk.

Perry, Frances, ed. Simon & Schuster's Complete Guide to Plants & Flowers. (Illus.). 1976. 17.95 o.s.i. (ISBN 0-671-22246-5); pap. 9.95 (ISBN 0-671-22247-3). S&S.

Perry, Frank A. Lighthouse Point: Reflections on Monterey Bay History. LC 82-90116. (Illus.). 93p. 1982. 9.95 (ISBN 0-943896-00-2); pap. 5.95 (ISBN 0-943896-01-0). G B H Pub.

Perry, Frank L., Jr. Sex & the Bible. LC 82-72143. (Orig.). 1982. pap. 7.95 (ISBN 0-943708-00-1). Chr Educ Res Inst.

Perry, George. Movies From the Mansion: A History of Pinewood Studios. (Illus.). 192p. 1982. 19.95 (ISBN 0-241-10799-7). NY Zoetrope.

Perry, George L., jt. ed. see Okun, Arthur M.

Perry, Glenn E. The Middle East: Fourteen Islamic Centuries. (Illus.). 336p. 1983. pap. 14.95 (ISBN 0-13-581603-3). P-H.

Perry, Helen S., ed. see Sullivan, Harry S.

Perry, Henry B. & Breitner, Bina. Physician Assistants: Their Contribution to Health Care. LC 81-6260. 331p. 1982. 29.95 (ISBN 0-89885-066-5). Human Sci Pr.

Perry, James L. & Kraemer, Kenneth L. Public Management: Public & Private Perspectives. 344p. (Orig.). 1983. pap. 16.95 (ISBN 0-87484-564-5). Mayfield Pub.

Perry, James L. & Kraemer, Kenneth L., eds. Technological Innovation in American Local Governments: The Case of Computing. LC 78-26458. (Pergamon Policy Studies). (Illus.). 1980. 24.00 (ISBN 0-08-023707-X). Pergamon.

Perry, Jane G., jt. auth. see Perry, John.

Perry, Janet, tr. see Michael, Ian.

Perry, John. The Small Computer & Architectural Practice. (Illus.). 128p. 1983. pap. 19.50 (ISBN 0-89397-121-9). Nichols Pub.

--State of Russia Under the Present Czar. (Russian Through European Eyes Ser). 1968. Repr. of 1716 ed. lib. bdg. 45.00 (ISBN 0-686-85852-2). Da Capo.

Perry, John & Perry, Erna K. The Social Web: An Introduction to Sociology. 4th ed. 640p. 1983. pap. text ed. 19.50 scp (ISBN 0-06-045129-7, HarpC); study guide scp 6.50 (ISBN 0-06-045145-9); test bank & instr's. manual avail. (ISBN 0-06-365124-6). Har-Row.

Perry, John & Perry, Jane G. The Sierra Club Guide to the Natural Areas of California. LC 82-16936. (Sierra Club Books Guides to the Natural Areas of the United States). (Illus.). 380p. (Orig.). 1983. pap. 9.95 (ISBN 0-87156-333-9). Sierra.

--The Sierra Club Guide to the Natural Areas of Oregon & Washington. LC 82-16937. (The Sierra Club Books Guides to the Natural Areas of the United States). (Illus.). 380p. (Orig.). 1983. pap. 9.95 (ISBN 0-87156-334-7). Sierra.

Perry, John, jt. auth. see Barwise, Jon.

Perry, John, jt. auth. see Palladino, Leo.

Perry, John A. & Perry, Erna. Contemporary Society: An Introduction to Social Science. 3rd ed. (Illus.). 591p. 1980. pap. text ed. 17.50 scp (ISBN 0-06-045135-1, HarpC); instrs'. manual avail. (ISBN 0-06-365122-X); scp study guide 8.95 (ISBN 0-06-045136-X). Har-Row.

Perry, John A. & Perry, Erna K. The Social Web: An Introduction to Sociology. 3rd ed. LC 78-24446. 1979. pap. text ed. 17.50 scp o.p. (ISBN 0-06-045131-9, HarpC); inst. manual avail. o.p. (ISBN 0-06-365120-3); scp study guide 8.95 o.p. (ISBN 0-06-045132-7); test bank avail. o.p. (ISBN 0-06-365121-1). Har-Row.

Perry, John O. The Experience of Poems: A Text & Anthology. 544p. 1972. pap. text ed. 10.95 (ISBN 0-02-394590-7). Macmillan.

Perry, John R. A Dialogue on Personal Identity & Immortality. LC 78-52943. 1978. lib. bdg. 12.50 (ISBN 0-915144-91-3); pap. text ed. 2.50 (ISBN 0-915144-53-0). Hackett Pub.

Perry, Joseph B., Jr. & Pugh, Meredith. Collective Behavior: Response to Social Stress. (Illus.). 1978. text ed. 14.95 (ISBN 0-8299-0158-2). West Pub.

Perry, Josephine. Cookies from Many Lands. (Dover Cook Book Ser). 160p. (gr. 6-12). 1972. pap. 3.00 (ISBN 0-486-22832-0). Dover.

Perry, K. W. Accounting: An Introduction. 1971. text ed. 25.95 (ISBN 0-07-049425-8, C); study guide o.p. 6.50 (ISBN 0-07-049427-4); 8.00. Form 1 (ISBN 0-07-049428-2). Form 2. 8.95 (ISBN 0-07-049429-0); practice set 1 12.95; practice set 2 10.95; solutions manual 24.50 (ISBN 0-07-049426-6). McGraw.

Perry, Leslie A., jt. auth. see Woodington, Cynthia C.

Perry, Lilla C., illus. Lilla Cabot Perry: Impressionists. (Illus., Orig.). 1982. pap. 6.00 (ISBN 0-941430-06-5). Santa Fe E Gallery.

Perry, Lily M. & Metzger, Judith. Medicinal Plants of East & Southeast Asia: Attributed Properties & Uses. 632p. 1980. 49.50x (ISBN 0-262-16076-5). MIT Pr.

Perry, Lloyd. Getting the Church on Target. 1977. 9.95 o.p. (ISBN 0-8024-2924-6); pap. 7.95 o.p. (ISBN 0-8024-2922-X). Moody.

Perry, Lloyd & Hanson, Calvin. Romans: A Model for Bible Study Methods. LC 82-6281. 288p. 1982. pap. 8.95 (ISBN 0-8024-7374-1). Moody.

Perry, Lloyd & Sell, Charles. Speaking to Life's Problems. 1983. pap. price not set (ISBN 0-8024-0170-8). Moody.

Perry, Lloyd M. Biblical Preaching for Today's World. LC 73-7471. 256p. 1973. 12.95 (ISBN 0-8024-0707-2). Moody.

Perry, Lloyd M. & Peterson, Gilbert A. Churches in Crisis. LC 81-38427. 144p. 1981. pap. 7.95 (ISBN 0-8024-1551-2). Moody.

Perry, Lloyd M. & Shawchuck, Norman. Revitalizing the Twentieth Century Church. LC 81-16974. 1982. text ed. 9.95 (ISBN 0-8024-7317-2). Moody.

Perry, Malcolm. The Management of Acute Vascular Injuries. (Illus.). 148p. 1980. 26.00 (ISBN 0-683-06858-X). Williams & Wilkins.

Perry, Margaret. Bio-Bibliography of Countee P. Cullen, 1903-1946. 1971. 25.00 (ISBN 0-8371-3325-4, Pub. by Negro U Pr). Greenwood.

--Silence to the Drums. LC 74-19806. (Contributions in Afro-American & African Studies: No. 18). 1976. lib. bdg. 25.00 (ISBN 0-8371-7847-9, PSD/). Greenwood.

Perry, Marvin. Man's Unfinished Journey: A World History. 2nd ed. LC 79-84595. (Illus.). (gr. 10-12). 1980. text ed. 20.72 (ISBN 0-395-27563-6); instr's. guide & key. pap. 13.06 (ISBN 0-395-27557-1); activities bk. 4.88 (ISBN 0-395-27562-8); instr's. annot. ed. activities bk. 7.25 (ISBN 0-395-27558-X). HM.

Perry, Marvin, et al. Western Civilization: A Concise History, 1 vol. ed. LC 80-82843. (Illus.). 704p. 1981. pap. text ed. 22.95 (ISBN 0-395-29313-8). HM.

Perry, Marvin, et al, eds. Western Civilization: A Concise History. Incl. Vol. 1. To 1789. pap. text ed. 14.95 (ISBN 0-395-29314-6); Vol. 2. From the 1600s. pap. text ed. 14.95 (ISBN 0-395-29315-4). (Illus.). 400p. 1981. instr's manual 1.50 (ISBN 0-395-29316-2). HM.

Perry, Murvin H. Newswriting Exercises. 1975. perfect bdg. 6.95 (ISBN 0-8403-1105-2). Kendall-Hunt.

Perry, P. Scattering Theory by the Enss Method. (Mathematical Reports: Vol. 1, No. 1). 150p. 1982. write for info. (ISBN 3-7186-0093-5). Harwood Academic.

Perry, P. J. The Evolution of British Manpower Policy from the Statute of Artificers 1563 to the Industrial Training Act 1964. 1981. 55.00 (ISBN 0-686-96954-5, Pub. by BACIE England). State Mutual Bk.

Perry, Paul. Chinese Fitness: Ancient Exercise Traditions in the Modern World. (Illus.). 176p. (Orig.). Date not set. pap. cancelled o.p. (ISBN 0-88496-190-7). Capra Pr.

Perry, Philip M. Successful Secrets to Smart Retailing. 300p. 1982. 34.50 o.p. (ISBN 0-87624-528-9). Inst Busn Plan.

Perry, Phillip M. Retailer's Complete Guide to Bigger Sales-Lower Costs-Higher Profits. LC 82-878. (Illus.). 265p. (Orig.). 1982. pap. 34.50 (ISBN 0-87624-509-2). Inst Busn Plan.

Perry, R., ed. see Institute of Criminology, University of Cambridge, England.

Perry, R. A., jt. ed. see Goodall, D. W.

Perry, Ralph B. Humanity of Man. 1956. 4.50 o.s.i. (ISBN 0-8076-0028-8). Braziller.

--In the Spirit of William James. LC 78-31937. 1979. Repr. of 1938 ed. lib. bdg. 19.75x (ISBN 0-313-20715-1, PEIN). Greenwood.

--Present Philosophical Tendencies. LC 68-21318. 1968. Repr. of 1955 ed. lib. bdg. 19.00x (ISBN 0-8371-0191-3, PEPT). Greenwood.

Perry, Richard. Changes. LC 73-13224. 1974. 6.95 o.p. (ISBN 0-672-51850-3). Bobbs.

Perry, Ritchie. Brazil. LC 78-56598. (Countries Ser.). (Illus.). 1978. PLB 12.68 (ISBN 0-382-06183-7). Silver.

Perry, Robert. Owning Your Home Computer. (The Complete Illustrated Guide Ser.). (Illus.). 256p. (Orig.). 1980. pap. 10.95 (ISBN 0-89696-156-7, An Everest House Book). Dodd.

Perry, Robert, jt. auth. see Webster, Bryce.

Perry, Robert H. Engineering Manual: A Practical Reference of Design. (Handbook Ser.). (Illus.). 800p. 1976. 34.50 (ISBN 0-07-049476-2, P&RB). McGraw.

Perry, Robert H. & Chilton, C. H. Chemical Engineers' Handbook. 5th ed. 1973. 65.50 (ISBN 0-07-049478-9, P&RB). McGraw.

Perry, Robert L. Games Computers Play. 320p. 1981. cancelled o.s.i. (ISBN 0-399-90122-1, Marek). Putnam Pub Group.

Perry, Robin. Creative Color Photography of Robin Perry. (Illus.). 1974. 15.95 o.p. (ISBN 0-8174-0575-5, Amphoto). Watson-Guptill.

--The Road Rider: A Guide to on-the-Road Motorcycling. LC 73-91519. (Illus.). 128p. 1974. 5.95 o.p. (ISBN 0-517-51501-6); pap. 2.95 o.p. (ISBN 0-517-51502-4). Crown.

Perry, Roland. Program for a Puppet. 288p. 1980. 9.95 o.p. (ISBN 0-517-54101-7). Crown.

Perry, Ronald H. Canoeing for Beginners. 1967. pap. 2.50 o.s.i. (ISBN 0-8096-1775-7, Assn Pr). Follett.

Perry, Ronald W. Racial Discrimination & Military Justice. LC 76-53541. (Special Studies). 1976. 24.95 o.p. (ISBN 0-275-24180-7). Praeger.

--The Social Psychology of Civil Defense. (The Batelle Human Affairs Research Centers ser.). 144p. 1982. 18.95x (ISBN 0-669-05963-3). Lexington Bks.

Perry, Ronald W., et al. Evacuation Planning in Emergency Management. LC 81-47542. (Batelle Human Affairs Research Centers Ser.). (Illus.). 224p. 1981. 24.95x (ISBN 0-669-04650-7). Lexington Bks.

Perry, Sherryl R., jt. auth. see Cushman, Robert F.

Perry, Stewart E. San Francisco Scavengers: Dirty Work & the Pride of Ownership. LC 77-78382. 1978. 16.95x (ISBN 0-520-03518-6). U of Cal Pr.

Perry, Stuart. The New Zealand Whiskey Book. (Illus.). 144p. 1982. 13.95 (ISBN 0-00-216973-8, Pub. by W Collins Australia). Intl Schol Bk Serv.

Perry, T. M. The Discovery of Australia: The Charts & Maps of the Navigators & Explorers. (Illus.). 160p. 1983. 100.00 (ISBN 0-241-10863-2, Pub. by Hamish Hamilton England). David & Charles.

Perry, T. W., ed. Feed Formulations. 3rd ed. 1981. 16.50 (ISBN 0-8134-2174-8); text ed. 12.50x. Interstate.

Perry, Ted, ed. see Bowser, et al.

Perry, Thomas. The Butcher's Boy. 1983. pap. 2.95 (ISBN 0-441-08950-X, Pub. by Charter Bks). Ace Bks.

Perry, Thomas A. A Bibliography of American Literature Translated into Romanian. 1983. 35.00 (ISBN 0-8022-2414-8). Philos Lib.

Perry, Vincent G. Skitch: The Message of the Roses. 6.95 o.p. (ISBN 0-87714-032-4). Green Hill.

Perry, William. Our Threatened Wildlife: An Ecological Study. LC 68-23878. (New Conservation Ser). (Illus.). (gr. 6-9). 1970. PLB 4.99 o.p. (ISBN 0-698-30276-1, Coward). Putnam Pub Group.

Perry, William E. Computer Control & Security Guide for Management Systems Analysis. LC 80-39936. (Business Data Processing: a Wiley Ser.). 207p. 1981. 29.95 (ISBN 0-471-05235-3, Pub. by Wiley-Interscience). Wiley.

--Ensuring Data Base Integrity. 300p. 1983. write for info (ISBN 0-471-86526-5). Ronald Pr.

--So You Think You Need Your Own Business Computer: The Manager's Guide to Selecting, Installing & Using the Right Small Computer System. LC 82-8348. 201p. 1982. pap. 14.95 (ISBN 0-471-86196-0). Ronald Pr.

--What to Ask Your Accountant: A Reference for Those in Business & Those about to Begin. LC 81-17094. 224p. 1982. 14.95 (ISBN 0-8253-0078-9). Beaufort Bks NY.

Perry, William E. & Kuong, Javier F. Effective Computer Audit Practices Manual ECAP- Map-11: A Manual in Installments. 1980. 350.00 (ISBN 0-686-27136-X). Management Advisory Pubns.

--Generalized Computer Audit Software-Selection & Application. 1980. 50.00 (ISBN 0-686-26150-X). Management Advisory Pubns.

Perryman, M. R., jt. auth. see Anderson, O. D.

Perryman, M. R., jt. ed. see Anderson, O. D.

Perryman, Penelope & West, Kirsten. The No Cellulite Cookbook: The First Cookbook-Menu Planner to Help You Fight Those Lumps, Bumps & Bulges. 256p. 1983. 13.50 (ISBN 0-02-595900-X). Macmillan.

Persaud, T. V. Neural & Behavioural Teratol. (Vol. 4). 248p. 1980. text ed. 39.50 o.p. (ISBN 0-8391-1488-5). Univ Park.

--Teratogenic Mechanisms, Vol. 1. 252p. 1979. text ed. 39.50 o.p. (ISBN 0-8391-1428-1). Univ Park.

Perschia, Doris. The Fluger. (Science Fiction Ser.). 1980. pap. 1.95 o.p. (ISBN 0-87997-577-6, UJ1577). DAW Bks.

Perse, St. John. Anabasis. Eliot, T. S., tr. from Fr. LC 49-48962. 1970. pap. 2.95 (ISBN 0-15-607406-0, Harv). HarBraceJ.

Perse, Saint-John. Selected Poems. Caws, Mary A., ed. Eliot, T. S., et al, trs. from Fr. LC 82-8305. 160p. (Orig.). 1982. pap. 9.95 (ISBN 0-8112-0855-9, NDP547). New Directions.

--Selected Poems of Saint-John Perse. Caws, Mary Ann, ed. 160p. 1982. 9.95 (ISBN 0-686-82025-8). New Directions.

Persen, L. N. Rock Dynamics & Geophysical Exploration. LC 74-21865. (Developments in Geotechnical Engineering: Vol. 8). 276p. 1975. 61.75 (ISBN 0-444-41284-0). Elsevier.

Pershing, Marie. Maybe Tomorrow. (Orig.). 1980. pap. 1.25 o.s.i. (ISBN 0-440-14909-6). Dell.

Persico, Joseph. Imperial Rockefeller. 1983. price not set. WSP.

--The Spiderweb. 1979. 10.00 o.p. (ISBN 0-517-53925-X). Crown.

Persico, Joseph E. The Imperial Rockefeller. large type ed. LC 82-5994. 523p. 1982. Repr. of 1982 ed. 13.95 (ISBN 0-89621-371-4). Thorndike Pr.

Persing, Bobbye S. Business Communication Dynamics. (General Business Ser.). 475p. 1981. 22.95x (ISBN 0-675-08153-X). Additional supplements may be obtained from publisher. Merrill.

Perske, J., jt. auth. see Witt, U.

Persky, Lester, jt. auth. see McDougal, W. Scott.

Person. Vibrational Intensities in Infrared & Raman Spectroscopy. (Studies in Physical & Theoretical Chemistry). 1982. 95.75 (ISBN 0-444-42115-7). Elsevier.

Person, Ethel S., jt. ed. see Stimpson, Catherine.

Person, Laura, jt. auth. see Griffith, Nancy S.

Person, Peter P. Introduction to Christian Education. pap. 4.95 o.p. (ISBN 0-8010-6928-9). Baker Bk.

Person, Russell V. Essentials of Mathematics. 4th ed. LC 79-10708. 1980. text ed. 25.95x (ISBN 0-471-05184-5); study guide 9.95x (ISBN 0-471-06288-X); tchrs.' manual 7.00 (ISBN 0-686-86896-X). Wiley.

Person, Russell V. & Person, Vernon J. Practical Mathematics. LC 76-21732. 400p. 1977. 23.95x (ISBN 0-471-68216-0). Wiley.

Person, Vernon J., jt. auth. see Person, Russell V.

Persons, Stow. American Minds: A History of Ideas. rev. ed. LC 74-12326. 540p. 1975. Repr. of 1958 ed. 24.50 (ISBN 0-88275-203-0). Krieger.

Persson, Richard J. The Stock Photographer's Marketing Guide. (Illus., Orig.). 1982. pap. 9.95 (ISBN 0-9608486-0-6). R J Persson Ent.

Pertschuk, Michael. Revolt Against Regulation: The Rise & Pause of the Consumer Movement. LC 82-40108. 225p. 1982. 12.95 (ISBN 0-520-04824-5). U of Cal Pr.

Pervier, Evelyn. The Beginning Rider: A Common Sense Approach. LC 80-17821. (Illus.). 192p. (gr. 7 up). 1980. PLB 8.79 o.s.i. (ISBN 0-671-34068-9). Messner.

Pervin, L. A. Personality: Theory, Assessment, & Research. 3rd ed. 598p. 1980. 24.95 (ISBN 0-471-07908-1); tchrs.' manual 7.00 (ISBN 0-686-86902-8). Wiley.

Pervin, Lawrence A. Current Controversies & Issues in Personality. LC 78-15361. 1978. pap. text ed. 15.95x (ISBN 0-471-02035-4). Wiley.

Pervin, Lawrence A., jt. ed. see Leiblum, Sandra R.

Peryt, T., ed. Coated Grains. (Illus.). 600p. 1983. 58.00 (ISBN 0-387-12071-8). Springer-Verlag.

Peryt, T., jt. ed. see Fuchtbauer, H.

Pesaran, M. H. & Slater, L. J. Dynamic Regression: Theory & Algorithms. LC 79-41652. (Computers & Their Applications Ser.). 363p. 1980. 99.95 (ISBN 0-470-26939-1). Halsted Pr.

Pescar, S., jt. auth. see Freeman, R.

Pescar, Susan C., jt. auth. see Jackson, Douglas W.

Pescatello, Ann M. Power & Pawn: The Female in Iberian Families, Societies & Cultures. LC 75-35352. (Council on Intercultural & Comparative Studies: No. 1). 320p. 1976. lib. bdg. 29.95 (ISBN 0-8371-8583-1, PPP/); pap. text ed. 6.95x (ISBN 0-8371-8584-X, PPP/). Greenwood.

Pesce, Vince. A Complete Manual of Professional Selling: The Modular Approach to Sales Success. (Illus.). 240p. 1983. 15.95 (ISBN 0-13-162099-1); pap. 8.95 (ISBN 0-13-162081-9). P-H.

Pesch, Imelda M. Macrame. LC 76-126848. (Little Craft Book Ser.). (gr. 6 up). 1970. 5.95 o.p. (ISBN 0-8069-5158-3); PLB 6.69 o.p. (ISBN 0-8069-5159-1). Sterling.

Peschel, Enid R., tr. from Fr. Four French Symbolists Poets: Baudelaire, Rimbaud, Verlaine, Mallarme. LC 80-29625. (Illus.). xx, 359p. 1981. text ed. 28.95x (ISBN 0-8214-0557-8, 82-83517); pap. text ed. 15.95 (ISBN 0-8214-0643-4, 82-83525). Ohio U Pr.

Peschel, Enid R., tr. see Rimbaud, Arthur.

Peschl, Otto, ed. Catalog of Holdings in Slavonic Philology Including Belles-Lettres, University of Library Vienna: Katalog der Bestande auf dem Gebiet der Slawischen Philologie Einschliesslich der Belle Tristik. 1972. lib. bdg. 65.00 (ISBN 0-8161-0996-6, Hall Library). G K Hall.

Pesci, M., ed. Studies on Loess. 555p. 1980. pap. text ed. 46.50x (ISBN 963-05-2871-1, 41212, Pub. by Kultura Pr Hungary). Humanities.

Pesek, Ludek. Trap for Perseus. Bell, Anthea, tr. LC 79-24862. 192p. (YA) (gr. 8 up). 1980. 9.95 o.p. (ISBN 0-87888-160-3). Bradbury Pr.

Pesek, R., jt. ed. see Billingham, J.

Pesetsky, Bette. Author from a Savage People. LC 82-48731. 1983. 12.95 (ISBN 0-394-53033-0). Knopf.

Peshkin, Alan. The Imperfect Union: School Consolidation & Community Conflict. LC 82-16104. (Illus.). 224p. 1983. lib. bdg. 17.00x (ISBN 0-226-66166-0). U of Chicago Pr.

Peshkoff, Viacheslav C. Miracle, or, How Would You Like to Live Forever? 1978. 10.00 o.p. (ISBN 0-533-03726-3). Vantage.

Pesin, Alan. Beating the Pro Football Pointspread. 128p. (Orig.). 1981. pap. 2.50 o.p. (ISBN 0-523-41718-7). Pinnacle Bks.

--Beating the Pro Football Pointspread: 1982-83 Edition. 144p. (Orig.). 1982. pap. 2.75 (ISBN 0-523-41895-7). Pinnacle Bks.

Pesman. Meet Flora Mexicana. rev. 2nd ed. LC 62-16863. (Illus.). Date not set. cancelled (ISBN 0-912762-11-X); pap. cancelled (ISBN 0-912762-12-8). King.

Pesmen, Sandy. Writing for the Media. 160p. 1983. pap. write for info. (ISBN 0-87251-077-8). Crain Bks.

Pessagno, E. A., Jr. Radiolarian Zonation & Stratigraphy of the Upper Cretaceous Portion of the Great Valley Sequence, California Coast Ranges. (Micropaleontology Special Publications Ser.: No. 2). 95p. 1976. 20.00 (ISBN 0-686-84250-2). Am Mus Natl Hist.

Pessemier, Edgar A. New Product Decisions. 1966. pap. text ed. 12.50 (ISBN 0-07-049517-3, C). McGraw.

--Product Management: Strategy & Organization. 2nd ed. LC 81-4699. 668p. 1982. text ed. 33.95x (ISBN 0-471-05718-5). Wiley.

Pessen, Edward. The Many-Faceted Jacksonian Era: New Interpretations. (Contributions in American History: No. 67). (Illus.). 1977. lib. bdg. 29.95 (ISBN 0-8371-9720-1, PJE/). Greenwood.

--Most Uncommon Jacksonians: The Radical Leaders of the Early Labor Movement. LC 67-63761. 1967. pap. 9.95x (ISBN 0-87395-066-6). State U NY Pr.

--Riches, Class, & Power Before the Civil War. 1973. text ed. 10.95 o.p. (ISBN 0-669-84459-4). Heath.

Pessin, Allan H. & Ross, Joseph A. Words of Wall Street: 2,000 Investment Terms Defined. 225p. 1983. 15.95 (ISBN 0-87094-382-0); pap. 9.95 (ISBN 0-87094-417-7). Dow Jones-Irwin.

Pessin, Deborah. Aleph-Bet Story Book. (Illus.). (gr. 1-3). 1946. 5.95 (ISBN 0-8276-0125-5, 260). Jewish Pubn.

Pessoa, Fernando. Fernando Pessoa: Selected Poems. Rickard, Peter, ed. & tr. from Portuguese. (Edinburgh Bilingual Library: No. 4). 201p. 1971. 15.00x (ISBN 0-292-72402-0); pap. 0.00 o.p. (ISBN 0-292-72401-2). U of Tex Pr.

Pestalozzi, Johann H. Pestalozzi. Anderson, Lewis F., ed. LC 73-10877. 283p. 1974. Repr. of 1931 ed. lib. bdg. 17.50x (ISBN 0-8371-7046-X, PEP). Greenwood.

Pestana, Carlos. Fluids & Electrolytes in the Surgical Patient. 2nd ed. (Illus.). 184p. 1980. softcover 15.95 (ISBN 0-683-06860-1). Williams & Wilkins.

Pestka, Sidney, jt. ed. see Weissbach, Herbert.

Pestolesi, Robert A. & Sinclair, William A. Creative Administration in Physical Education & Athletics. LC 77-7075. (Illus.). 1978. 20.95 (ISBN 0-13-188987-7). P-H.

Peston, M. H. Theory of Macroeconomic Policy. LC 74-31043. 213p. 1974. 12.50 o.p. (ISBN 0-470-68236-1). Krieger.

Peston, Maurice. Whatever Happened to Macro-Economics? 96p. 1982. pap. 4.95 (ISBN 0-7190-0796-8). Manchester.

Peston, Maurice & Corry, Bernard, eds. Essays in Honour of Lord Robbins. LC 73-79597. (Illus.). 405p. 1973. 22.50 (ISBN 0-87332-043-3). M E Sharpe.

Peteghem, C. Van see Roncucci, R. & Van Peteghem, C.

Peter Adonis Travelling Fantasy Show. Ladies Night Out. 96p. 1982. 5.95 (ISBN 0-399-50662-4, Perige). Putnam Pub Group.

Peter, Gilbert M. & Peterson, Daniel R. An Understandable Approach to Basic Mathematics. 1981. text ed. 19.95x (ISBN 0-673-16045-9). Scott F.

Peter, Gilbert M., jt. auth. see Peterson, Daniel R.

Peter, Joseph S. Become Wealthy: Using Tax Savings & Real Estate Investments. LC 82-4299. (Orig.). 1982. lib. bdg. 14.00 (ISBN 0-943020-01-8); pap. 10.00 (ISBN 0-943020-02-6). Bottom Line Pr.

Peter, K. & Jesch, F. Inhalation Anaesthesia: Today & Tomorrow. (Anaesthesiology & Intensive Care Medicine Ser.: Vol. 150). (Illus.). 259p. 1983. 31.70 (ISBN 0-387-11757-1). Springer-Verlag.

Peter, Laurence J. Prescriptive Teaching. (Illus.). 1965. text ed. 23.95 (ISBN 0-07-049575-0, C); instructor's manual o.p. 3.95 (ISBN 0-07-049576-9). McGraw.

Peter, Laurence J. & Dana, Bill. The Laughter Prescription. (Orig.). 1982. pap. 5.95 (ISBN 0-345-29900-0). Ballantine.

Peter, Lawrence J. Peter's Almanac. LC 82-8031. (Illus.). 400p. 1982. 14.95 (ISBN 0-688-01612-X). Morrow.

Peter, Lily. The Great Riding: The Story of De Soto in America. LC 82-20269. 1983. 21.00 (ISBN 0-938626-14-0); pap. 9.95 (ISBN 0-938626-17-5). U of Ark Pr.

--In the Beginning: Great Myths of the Western World. (Illus.). 1983. 19.00 (ISBN 0-938626-15-9); pap. 9.95 (ISBN 0-938626-18-3). U of Ark Pr.

Peter, Nancy & Schiffer, Herbert F. The Brass Book. (American, English & European 15th Century thru 1850). 1978. 35.00 (ISBN 0-916838-17-X). Schiffer.

Peter, Piper. Peter Piper's Practical Principles of Plain & Perfect Pronunciation. (Illus.). 1970. 3.00 (ISBN 0-486-22660-3); pap. 1.75 (ISBN 0-486-22560-7). Dover.

Peter, Roche De Coppens see Roche De Coppens, Peter.

Peterdi, Gabor. Printmaking. rev. & expanded ed. LC 80-12888. (Illus.). 336p. 1980. 27.95 o.p. (ISBN 0-02-596060-1). Macmillan.

Peterfi, William O., ed. Issues & Trends in Contemporary Politics. LC 79-67053. 1979. pap. text ed. 7.75 o.p. (ISBN 0-8191-0864-2). U Pr of Amer.

--Issues & Trends in Contemporary Politics. rev. ed. LC 81-43762. (Illus.). 1983. pap. text ed. 8.25 (ISBN 0-8191-2667-5). U Pr of Amer.

Peterfreund, Emanuel. The Process of Psychoanalytic Therapy: Models & Strategies. 288p. 1982. text ed. 24.95 (ISBN 0-89859-274-7). L Erlbaum Assocs.

Peterfreund, Stuart. The Hanged Knife & Other Poems. 52p. 1970. 2.95 (ISBN 0-87886-000-2). Ithaca Hse.

--Harder Than Rain. LC 77-23857. 82p. 1977. 3.50 (ISBN 0-87886-084-3). Ithaca Hse.

Peteri, Zoltan & Lamm, Vanda, eds. General Reports to the Tenth International Congress of Comparative Law, 8 Vols. 1050p. 1981. 395.00x (ISBN 0-569-08701-5, Pub. by Collets). State Mutual Bk.

Peter Joyce St. Iprimavera, Elise see St. Peter, Joyce.

Peterken, George. Woodland Conservation & Management. 350p. 1981. 55.00x (ISBN 0-412-12820-9, Pub. by Chapman & Hall England). Methuen Inc.

Peterkin, Julia. Black April. new ed. LC 27-5080. 316p. 1973. Repr. of 1932 ed. 12.95 (ISBN 0-910220-42-5). Berg.

--Bright Skin. LC 32-26364. 352p. 1973. Repr. of 1932 ed. 12.95 (ISBN 0-910220-37-9). Berg.

--A Plantation Christmas. LC 34-41450. 1972. 6.95 (ISBN 0-910220-41-7). Berg.

Peterkin, Julie. Scarlet Sister Mary. LC 28-24477. 1970. 12.95 (ISBN 0-910220-22-0). Berg.

Peterle, Tony J., ed. see International Congress of Game Biologists, Thirteenth, Atlanta, Ga., March 11-15, 1977.

Peterlik, Meindrad, jt. ed. see Bronner, Felix.

Peterlin, A. Macromolecular Reviews, Vol. 15 & 16. 486p. 1980. Vol. 15. pap. 44.95 (ISBN 0-471-08889-7, Pub. by Wiley-Interscience); Vol. 16. pap. 69.95 (ISBN 0-471-09898-1). Wiley.

Petermann, Herbert & Petermann, Joan. The Many Worlds of Catalina. (Illus.). 1983. write for info. Amber Crest.

Petermann, Joan, jt. auth. see Petermann, Herbert.

Peters, A. F., ed. Impact of Offshore Oil Operations: Proceedings of the Institute of Petroleum, Aviemore, Scotland 1974. (Illus.). 1974. 35.00 (ISBN 0-85334-453-1, Pub. by Applied Sci England). Elsevier.

Peters, A. T. Ferrous Production Metallurgy. LC 81-11710. 299p. 1982. 54.95x (ISBN 0-471-08597-9, Pub. by Wiley-Interscience). Wiley.

Peters, Amalia B. de see Lombardi, Ronald P. & De Peters, Amalia B.

Peters, Anne. Rings of Green. 76p. 1982. text ed. 15.00x (ISBN 0-86140-124-7, Pub. by Colin Smythe England). Humanities.

Peters, Bruce E., jt. auth. see Miskovitz, Christine.

Peters, Cortez W., Jr. Cortez Peters Championship Typing Drills. 1979. pap. text ed. 8.20 (ISBN 0-07-049590-4, G). McGraw.

Peters, D. A. The Principles & Practice of Supervision. 1968. 16.25 o.s.i. (ISBN 0-08-012684-7); pap. 5.75 (ISBN 0-08-012683-9). Pergamon.

Peters, Diana, tr. see Gerstinger, Heinz.

Peters, Diana, tr. see Mander, Gertrud.

Peters, Don. Mondeb: An Advanced M6800 Monitor Debugger. LC 78-11814. 1978. pap. 5.00 (ISBN 0-07-049556-4, BYTE Bks). McGraw.

Peters, Donald L., jt. ed. see Walcher, Dwain N.

Peters, Edward, jt. auth. see Prasow, Paul.

Peters, Edward I. Chemical Skills. (Illus.). 416p. 1983. pap. text ed. 15.95x (ISBN 0-07-049557-2). McGraw.

Peters, Elizabeth. The Copenhagen Connection. (General Ser.). 1982. lib. bdg. 13.95 (ISBN 0-8161-3467-7, Large Print Bks). G K Hall.

--Legend in Green Velvet. LC 76-3617. 1976. 7.95 o.p. (ISBN 0-396-07283-6). Dodd.

--The Love Talker. (General Ser.). 1980. lib. bdg. 13.95 (ISBN 0-8161-3135-X, Large Prrint Bks). G K Hall.

--The Seventh Sinner. LC 78-38523. 260p. 1972. 5.95 o.p. (ISBN 0-396-06520-1). Dodd.

--Silhouette in Scarlet. 256p. 1983. 12.95 (ISBN 0-312-92773-8). Congdon & Weed.

Peters, Ellen A. Commercial Transactions: Text & Problems on Personalty, Realty & Services. 1971. text ed. 22.00 o.p. (ISBN 0-672-81703-9, Bobbs-Merrill Law). Michie-Bobbs.

Peters, Ellis. The Grass Widow's Tale. 1979. 15.00x o.p. (ISBN 0-86025-085-7, Pub. by Ian Henry Pubns England). State Mutual Bk.

--The Virgin in the Ice. Williams, Jennifer, ed. 228p. 1983. Repr. of 1981 ed. 11.95 (ISBN 0-688-01672-3). Morrow.

Peters, Erskine. William Faulkner: The Yoknapatawpha World & Black Being. 265p. 1982. lib. bdg. 25.00 (ISBN 0-8482-5675-1). Norwood Edns.

Peters, F. E. Harvest of Hellenism. LC 74-116509. 1971. pap. 8.95 o.p. (ISBN 0-671-20659-1, Touchstone Bks). S&S.

--Ours: The Making & Unmaking of a Jesuit. 192p. 1981. 11.95 (ISBN 0-399-90113-2, Marek). Putnam Pub Group.

--Ours: The Making & Unmaking of a Jesuit. 1982. pap. 4.95 o.p. (ISBN 0-14-006317-X). Penguin.

Peters, Faye L., jt. auth. see Puetz, Belinda E.

Peters, G. David & Eddins, John M. A Planning Guide to Successful Computer Instruction. 1981. 19.95 (ISBN 0-942132-00-9). Electron Course.

Peters, Gary L. & Larkin, Robert P. Population Geography: Problems, Concepts, & Prospects. 1979. pap. text ed. 10.95 (ISBN 0-8403-1976-2). Kendall-Hunt.

Peters, George N. The Theocratic Kingdom, 3 vols. LC 72-88588. (Kregel Limited Edition Library). 1984. Set. 49.95 o.p. (ISBN 0-8254-3502-1). Kregel.

Peters, Guy, jt. auth. see Hogwood, Brian.

Peters, H., jt. ed. see Byskov, A. G.

Peters, H., ed. see Moreau, J. J., et al.

Peters, H. F. My Sister, My Spouse: A Biography of Lou Andreas - Salome. (Illus.). 328p. 1974. pap. 6.95 (ISBN 0-393-00748-0, Norton Lib.). Norton.

--Rainer Maria Rilke: Masks & the Man. LC 77-24731. 240p. 1977. Repr. of 1960 ed. 10.00x (ISBN 0-87752-198-0). Gordian.

Peters, Herman. Interpreting Guidance Programs to the Public. (Guidance Monograph). 1968. pap. 2.40 o.p. (ISBN 0-395-09910-2). HM.

Peters, Herman J & Hansen, James C. Vocational Guidance & Career Development: Selected Readings. 3rd ed. 1977. pap. text ed. 14.95x (ISBN 0-02-394670-9). Macmillan.

Peters, Herman J. & Shertzer, Bruce. Guidance: Program Development & Management. 3rd ed. (Education-Guidance & Counseling Ser.). 640p. 1974. text ed. 22.95 (ISBN 0-675-08825-9). Merrill.

Peters, Herman J., jt. auth. see Cunningham, Louis.

Peters, J. Seven-Place Values of Trigonometric Functions for Every Thousandth of a Degree. 370p. 1942. 16.50 (ISBN 0-685-39872-2, Pub. by Van Nos Reinhold). Krieger.

Peters, Jean. Eight-Place Tables of Trigonometric Functions for Every Second of Arc. 1963. 59.50 (ISBN 0-8284-0174-8); thumb index ed. 69.50 (ISBN 0-8284-0185-3). Chelsea Pub.

Peters, Jean, ed. The Bookman's Glossary. rev. ed. 200p. 1983. 21.95 (ISBN 0-8352-1686-1). Bowker.

Peters, Jens. Philippines. (Travel Paperbacks Ser.). (Illus.). 192p. 1982. pap. 6.95 (ISBN 0-908086-27-X, Pub. by Lonely Planet Australia). Hippocrene Bks.

Peters, Joseph P. A Guide to Strategic Planning for Hospitals. LC 79-10063. 148p. (Orig.). 1979. 20.00 (ISBN 0-87258-259-0, AHA-127180). Am Hospital.

Peters, Joseph P., jt. auth. see James B.

Peters, Lenrie. Katchikali. (African Writers Ser.). 1971. pap. text ed. 2.50x o.p. (ISBN 0-435-90103-6). Heinemann Ed.

Peters, M., jt. auth. see Clark, N.

Peters, M. H., jt. auth. see Shirley, R. C.

Peters, M. S. Elementary Chemical Engineering. (Chemical Engineering Ser.). 1954. text ed. 33.95 (ISBN 0-07-049585-8, C). McGraw.

Peters, Margot, ed. see Shaw, George B.

Peters, Maureen. Princess of Desire. 1978. pap. 1.50 o.p. (ISBN 0-523-40275-9). Pinnacle Bks.

Peters, Max. College Algebra. rev. ed. LC 61-18891. (Orig.). 1962. 10.50 (ISBN 0-8120-5024-X); pap. 6.95 (ISBN 0-8120-0048-X). Barron.

Peters, Max, jt. ed. see Kaplan, Stanley.

Peters, Max S. & Timmerhaus, Klaus. Plant Design & Economics for Chemical Engineers. 3rd ed. (Chemical Engineering Ser.). (Illus.). 1980. text ed. 36.95 (ISBN 0-07-049582-3); solutions manual 23.50 (ISBN 0-07-049583-1). McGraw.

Peters, Michael P. & Hisrich, Robert D. Marketing a New Product: Its Planning, Development & Control. LC 77-84070. 1978. 22.95 (ISBN 0-8053-4102-1). Benjamin-Cummings.

Peters, Mike. Win One for the Geezer. LC 82-90325. (Illus.). 128p. 1982. pap. 4.50 (ISBN 0-553-01429-3). Bantam.

Peters, Mollie C., tr. see Staden, Wendelgard von.

Peters, Nancy J., et al, eds. Free Spirits: Annals of the Insurgent Imagination. (Illus.). 240p. 1982. pap. text ed. 7.95 (ISBN 0-87286-128-7). City Lights.

Peters, Natasha. The Immortals. 1983. pap. 6.95 (ISBN 0-449-90088-6, Columbine). Fawcett.

Peters, Neal & Smith, David. Ann Margaret: A Dream Come True: A Photo Extravaganza & Memoir. (Illus.). 256p. 1981. 24.95 (ISBN 0-933328-16-8); pap. 12.95 (ISBN 0-933328-10-9). Delilah Bks.

Peters, Nick. One Hundred Years of Blue & Gold: A Pictorial History of California Football. LC 82-80432. (Illus.). 203p. 1982. 25.00 (ISBN 0-938694-10-3). JCP Corp VA.

Peters, Oneita B., jt. auth. see West, Luther S.

Peters, Plym, tr. see Hammacher, A. M.

Peters, R. Textile Chemistry, Vol. 1. 1963. 37.50 (ISBN 0-444-40451-1). Elsevier.

Peters, R. H. Textile Chemistry, Vol. 3. 155.00x (ISBN 0-87245-598-X). Textile Bk.

Peters, R. S. Psychology & Ethical Development. 1974. text ed. 25.00x o.p. (ISBN 0-04-150049-0); pap. text ed. 15.95x (ISBN 0-04-150050-4). Allen Unwin.

Peters, R. s., ed. The Concept of Education. 226p. 1970. pap. 8.95 (ISBN 0-7100-7658-4). Routledge & Kegan.

--The Philosophy of Education. (Oxford Readings in Philosophy). 1973. pap. text ed. 8.95x (ISBN 0-19-875023-4). Oxford U Pr.

--The Role of the Head. (Students Library of Education). 1976. 14.95x (ISBN 0-7100-8319-X). Routledge & Kegan.

Peters, Ralph. Bravo Romeo. LC 80-20872. 226p. 1981. 11.95 o.s.i. (ISBN 0-399-90097-7, Marek). Putnam Pub Group.

Peters, Raymond H. Textile Chemistry, Vols. 2 & 3. Incl. Vol. 2: Impurities in Fibres. 1967. 66.00 (ISBN 0-444-40452-X); Vol. 3: The Physical Chemistry of Dyeing. 1975. 138.50 (ISBN 0-444-41120-8). Elsevier.

Peters, Richard. Barry Manilow: An Illustrative Biography. (Illus.). 104p. (Orig.). 1983. pap. 8.95 (ISBN 0-933328-65-6). Delilah Bks.

Peters, Richard S. Reason & Compassion: The Lindsay Memorial Lectures & the Swarthmore Lecture Delivered to the Society of Friends. 128p. 1973. 10.00x (ISBN 0-7100-7651-7); pap. 6.95 (ISBN 0-7100-7652-5). Routledge & Kegan.

Peters, Robert. Gauguin's Chair: Selected Poems 1967-1974. LC 76-47636. (Illus.). 128p. 1977. 12.95 (ISBN 0-912278-73-0); pap. 5.95 (ISBN 0-912278-74-9). Crossing Pr.

--The Picnic in the Snow: Ludwig of Bavaria. LC 82-81364. (Illus.). 103p. 1982. pap. 5.00 (ISBN 0-89823-037-3). New Rivers Pr.

--What Dillinger Meant to Me. LC 82-62111. 95p. (Orig.). 1983. pap. 5.95 (ISBN 0-933322-09-7). Sea Horse.

Peters, Robert L., jt. ed. see Okuda, Kunio.

Peters, Sharon. Animals at Night. LC 82-19226. (Now I Know Ser.). (Illus.). 32p. (gr. k-2). 1982. lib. bdg. 8.89 (ISBN 0-89375-903-1). Troll Assocs.

Peters, Stella. Bedouins. LC 80-53610. (Surviving Peoples Ser.). PLB 12.68 (ISBN 0-382-06421-6). Silver.

Peters, Susan D., ed. see McCausland, Elizabeth.

Peters, Terry, jt. ed. see Callcott, M. V.

Peters, Thelma. Biscayne Country, 1870-1926. LC 81-13020. (Illus.). viii, 323p. 1981. 14.95. Banyan Bks.

--Biscayne Country, 1870-1926. (Illus.). 300p. Date not set. pap. 14.95 (ISBN 0-686-84304-5). Banyan Bks.

Peters, Thomas J. & Waterman, Robert H., Jr. In Search of Excellence: Lessons from America's Best Run Companies. LC 82-47530. (Illus.). 384p. 1982. 19.18i (ISBN 0-06-015042-4, HarpT). Har-Row.

Peterscu, Paul & Rodna, Nicolae. Roumanian Textiles. (Illus.). 22.50x (ISBN 0-87245-334-0). Textile Bk.

Petersdorf, Robert G. & Adams, Raymond D. Harrison's Principles of Internal Medicine. 10th ed. (Illus.). 2240p. 1983. 70.00x (ISBN 0-07-049603-X); Set of 2 vols. 90.00x (ISBN 0-07-079309-3). McGraw.

Petersen, A. M. Dark Savior. 75p. 1968. 6.00 o.p. (ISBN 0-912950-02-1); pap. 4.00 o.p. (ISBN 0-912950-01-3). Blue Oak.

--Stars in Twilight. 1978. 10.00 o.s.i. (ISBN 0-912950-41-2); pap. 4.50 o.s.i. (ISBN 0-912950-42-0). Blue Oak.

Petersen, Anne C., jt. ed. see Wittig, Michele A.

Petersen, Barbara. Building Blocks: For Developing Basic Language. 560p. 1977. 24.95 (ISBN 0-86575-036-X). Dormac.

Petersen, Bill. Those Curious New Cults in the Eighties. rev. ed. LC 72-93700. 1982. pap. text ed. 3.95 (ISBN 0-87983-317-3). Keats.

Petersen, Carol. Albert Camus. Gode, Alexander, tr. LC 68-31455. (Literature and Life Ser.). 1969. 11.95 (ISBN 0-8044-2691-0); pap. 4.95 o.p. (ISBN 0-8044-6646-7). Ungar.

--Max Frisch. LaRue, Charlotte, tr. LC 72-153124. (Literature and Life Ser.). 11.95 (ISBN 0-8044-2692-9). Ungar.

Petersen, Dan. Analyzing Safety Performance. LC 79-19304. 344p. 1980. lib. bdg. 32.50 o.s.i. (ISBN 0-8240-7123-9). Garland Pub.

--The O S H A Compliance Manual. rev. ed. (Illus.). 1979. 41.50 (ISBN 0-07-049598-X, P&RB). McGraw.

--Techniques of Safety Management. 2nd ed. (Illus.). 1978. 29.00 (ISBN 0-07-049596-3, P&RB). McGraw.

Petersen, Dan & Goodale, Jerry. Readings in Industrial Ancient Prevention. (Illus.). 1980. pap. text ed. 14.95 (ISBN 0-07-049591-2). McGraw.

Petersen, Donald J., et al. Arbitration in Health Care. LC 81-10811. 300p. 1982. text ed. 31.50 (ISBN 0-89443-372-5). Aspen Systems.

Petersen, Eggert. A Reassessment of the Concept of Criminality: An Analysis of Criminal Behavior in Terms of Individual & Current Environment: the Application of a Stochastic Model. LC 76-51327. 1977. 49.95 o.s.i. (ISBN 0-470-99034-1). Halsted Pr.

Petersen, Elizabeth. Maze: How Not to Go into Business. LC 82-62505. 160p. (Orig.). 1983. 14.95 (ISBN 0-9610200-0-8); pap. 9.95 (ISBN 0-9610200-1-6). MEDA Pubns.

Petersen, Emma M., jt. auth. see Petersen, Mark E.

Petersen, Eugene T. Hunters' Heritage: A History of Hunting in Michigan. Lowe, Kenneth S., ed. (Illus.). 1979. lib. bdg. 4.00 (ISBN 0-933112-01-7). Mich United Conserv.

Petersen, Evelyn & Petersen, J. Allan. For Women Only. 1975. 6.95 (ISBN 0-8423-0895-4); pap. 6.95 (ISBN 0-8423-0896-2). Tyndale.

Petersen, Grant. Roads of Alameda, Contra Costa & Marin Counties: A Topographic Guide for Bicylists. 200p. Date not set. pap. 5.95 (ISBN 0-930588-07-X). Heyday Bks.

Petersen, Grete. Leathercrafting. LC 80-95205. (Illus.). 96p. 1980. pap. 5.95 (ISBN 0-8069-8942-4). Sterling.

Petersen, Grete & Svennas, Elsie. Handbook of Stitches. 1970. pap. 4.95 o.p. (ISBN 0-442-26533-6). Van Nos Reinhold.

Petersen, Grete, jt. auth. see Bruun-Rasmussen, Ole.

Petersen, Gwenn B. The Moon in the Water: Understanding Tanizaki, Kawabata, & Mishima. LC 79-14994. 1979. text ed. 15.95x (ISBN 0-8248-0520-8). UH Pr.

Petersen, I., jt. ed. see Kellaway, P.

Petersen, Ingemar S., jt. ed. see Kellaway, Peter.

Petersen, J. Allan. Before You Marry. 1974. pap. 2.95 (ISBN 0-8423-0104-6). Tyndale.

--For Men Only. 1973. pap. 5.95 (ISBN 0-8423-0891-1). Tyndale.

Petersen, J. Allan, jt. auth. see Petersen, Evelyn.

Petersen, J. Allan, compiled by. The Marriage Affair. pap. 8.95 (ISBN 0-8423-4171-4). Tyndale.

Petersen, J. Allan, et al. Two Become One. x ed. 1975. pap. 3.95 (ISBN 0-8423-7620-8). Tyndale.

Petersen, J. Allen. The Myth of the Greener Grass. 1983. 8.95 (ISBN 0-8423-4656-2). Tyndale.

Petersen, Johanna. Careers with a Fire Department. LC 74-11904. (Early Career Bks.). (Illus.). 36p. (gr. 2-5). 1975. PLB 5.95g (ISBN 0-8225-0309-3). Lerner Pubns.

--Careers with the Postal Service. LC 74-11905. (Early Career Bks.). (Illus.). 36p. (gr. 2-5). 1975. PLB 5.95g (ISBN 0-8225-0322-0). Lerner Pubns.

Petersen, Julius see Ball, W. Rouse, et al.

Petersen, K. E. Brownian Motion, Hardy Spaces & Bounded Mean Oscillation. LC 76-46860. (London Mathematical Society Lecture Notes: No. 28). (Illus.). 1977. limp bdg. 15.95x (ISBN 0-521-21512-9). Cambridge U Pr.

Petersen, Karl. Ergodic Theory. LC 82-4473. (Cambridge Studies in Advanced Mathematics: No. 2). (Illus.). 320p. Date not set. price not set (ISBN 0-521-23632-0). Cambridge U Pr.

Petersen, Kenneth, jt. auth. see Olson, Esther L.

Petersen, Mark E. Hear Ye Him. (Illus.). 8p. 1975. pap. 0.95 o.p. (ISBN 0-87747-582-2). Deseret Bk.

--Noah & the Flood. 97p. 1982. 6.95 (ISBN 0-87747-935-6). Deseret Bk.

Petersen, Mark E. & Petersen, Emma M. Virtue Makes Sense. new ed. LC 73-81621. 112p. 1973. 5.95 o.p. (ISBN 0-87747-500-8). Deseret Bk.

Petersen, Morris S. & Rigby, J. Keith. Interpreting Earth History: A Manual in Historical Geology. 2nd ed. 185p. 1978. wire coil write for info. o.p. (ISBN 0-697-05080-7); instrs'. manual avail. o.p. (ISBN 0-697-05081-5). Wm C Brown.

--Interpreting Earth History: A Manual in Historical Geology. 3rd ed. 210p. 1982. write for info. wire coil bdg. (ISBN 0-697-05063-7); instr's. manual avail. (ISBN 0-697-05064-5). Wm C Brown.

Petersen, Niels E., jt. auth. see Jensen, Finn.

Petersen, Nis. Whistlers in the Night: And Other Verse by Nis Petersen. Sorensen, Otto M., tr. from Danish. LC 82-62386. Orig. Title: Nis Petersen, Samlede Digte. (Illus.). 94p. 1983. 9.95 (ISBN 0-933748-04-3). Nordic Bks.

Petersen, Norman R., ed. Semeia Sixteen: Perspectives on Mark's Gospel. (Semeia Ser.). 9.95 (ISBN 0-686-96248-6, 06 20 16). Scholars Pr CA.

Petersen, P. J. Would You Settle for Improbable? (YA) (gr. 5-9). 1983. pap. 2.25 (ISBN 0-440-99733-X, LFL). Dell.

Petersen Publishing Co. How to Tune Your Car. 7th ed. (Petersen's Basic Auto Repair Ser.). (Illus.). 1000p. 1983. pap. 7.95 (ISBN 0-8227-5049-X). Petersen Pub.

Petersen, R. H. A Monograph of Ramaria Subgenus Echinoramaria. (Bibliotheca Mycologica). (Illus.). 150p. 1981. lib. bdg. 24.00x (ISBN 3-7682-1290-4). Lubrecht & Cramer.

--Ramaria, Subgenus Lentoramaria, with Emphasis on North American Taxa. (Bibliotheca Mycologica Ser.: No. 43). 1975. text ed. 20.00 (ISBN 3-7682-0961-X). Lubrecht & Cramer.

Petersen, Robert P., jt. ed. see Licata, Salvatore J.

Petersen, Ronald H. B & C: Mycological Association of M. J. Berkeley & M. A. Curtis. (Bibliotheca Mycologica: 72). (Illus.). 120p. 1980. pap. text ed. 12.00 (ISBN 3-7682-1258-0). Lubrecht & Cramer.

Petersen, W. P. & Fehr, Terry. Meditation Made Easy. (Concise Guides Ser.). (Illus.). (gr. 6 up). 1979. s&l 8.90 (ISBN 0-531-02894-1). Watts.

Petersen, William. Population. 3rd ed. (Illus.). 704p. 1974. text ed. 24.95x (ISBN 0-02-394880-9). Macmillan.

Petersen, William & Novak, Michael. Concepts of Ethnicity. (Dimensions of Ethnicity Ser.). 160p. 1982. pap. text ed. 5.95x (ISBN 0-674-15726-5). Harvard U Pr.

Petersen, William A. Interrogating the Oracle: A History of the London Browning Society. 290p. 1979. 4.40x (ISBN 0-89062-103-9, Pub. by Browning Inst). Pub Ctr Cult Res.

Petersen, William J. Another Hand on Mine. LC 67-13515. (Illus.). pap. 1.95 o.p. (ISBN 0-87983-128-6). Keats.

--Harriet Beecher Stowe had a Husband. 1983. pap. 2.95 r (ISBN 0-686-82689-2, 07-1329-X). Tyndale.

--Martin Luther Had a Wife. 1983. pap. 2.95 (ISBN 0-8423-4104-8). Tyndale.

--Meet Me on the Mountain. 1979. pap. 4.50 (ISBN 0-88207-784-8). Victor Bks.

--Those Curious New Cults. rev. ed. LC 72-93700. 240p. 1975. pap. 2.25 o.p. (ISBN 0-87983-120-0). Keats.

--Timoteo, el Hombre Fiel. Carrodeguas, Andy & Marosi, Esteban, eds. Calderon, Wilfredo, tr. 218p. (Span.). 1982. pap. 2.50 (ISBN 0-8297-1250-X). Life Pubs Intl.

Petersen, Wretha. Educational Developmental Program, Kit 1: The Educational Evaluation. 1970. 110.00 o.p. (ISBN 0-87562-015-9). Spec Child.

--An Educational Developmental Program, Kit 2: The Preacademic Instructional Program. 1975. 725.00 o.p. (ISBN 0-87562-034-5). Spec Child.

Peterseon, Evelyn H. Who Cares? A Handbook of Christian Counselling. 181p. pap. text ed. 6.95 (ISBN 0-85364-272-9). Attic Pr.

Petersohn, Henry H. Developing Computer Solutions for Your Business Problems. (Illus.). 157p. 1982. 21.95 (ISBN 0-13-204313-0); pap. 14.95 (ISBN 0-13-204305-X). P-H.

Peterson & Elman. The Great Guns. 1977. 10.95 (ISBN 0-448-02069-6, G&D). Putnam Pub Group.

Peterson & Mountfort. A Field Guide to the Birds of Britain & Europe. 27.95 (ISBN 0-686-42752-1, Collins Pub England). Greene.

Peterson, jt. auth. see Gross.

Peterson, jt. auth. see Richardson.

Peterson, A., ed. Collector's Handbook of Marks on Pottery & Porcelain. Paul, E. (Illus.). 12.50 (ISBN 0-913274-02-X). Wallace-Homestead.

Peterson, A. D. International Baccalaureate. 189p. (Harrap). 1973. 15.50x (ISBN 0-245-50521-0). Open Court.

Peterson, Anne C., jt. auth. see Conger, John J.

Peterson, Arthur G. Four Hundred Trademarks on Glass: With Separate Index. LC 68-12557. (Illus.). 52p. (Orig.). 1968. lib. bdg. 13.95x (ISBN 0-9605664-0-6); pap. 8.95x (ISBN 0-9605664-1-4). A G Peterson.

--Glass Patents & Patterns. LC 72-91628. (Illus.). 226p. 1973. lib. bdg. 18.95x (ISBN 0-9605664-2-2); pap. 14.95x (ISBN 0-9605664-3-0). A G Peterson.

--Glass Salt Shakers: One Thousand Patterns. LC 70-93972. (Illus.). 196p. 1970. lib. bdg. 15.95x (ISBN 0-9605664-4-9). A. G. Peterson.

--Viking & Cherokee. LC 79-89769. (Illus.). 170p. 1980. pap. 8.95 (ISBN 0-9605664-5-7). A G Peterson.

Peterson, Bernard. The Peripheral Spy. LC 79-1476. 1980. 8.95 (ISBN 0-698-10979-1, Coward). Putnam Pub Group.

Peterson, Brenda. River of Light. LC 77-11868. 1978. 8.95 o.p. (ISBN 0-394-41894-8). Knopf.

Peterson, Brenda, jt. auth. see Hafen, Brent Q.

Peterson, Brent D., jt. auth. see Timm, Paul R.

Peterson, Brent D., et al. Speak Easy: Introduction to Public Speaking. 320p. 1980. pap. text ed. 13.50 (ISBN 0-8299-0313-5); instrs.' manual avail. (ISBN 0-8299-0347-X). West Pub.

Peterson, C. R., jt. auth. see Hill, Philip G.

Peterson, Carl. For Anna Akhmatova & other Poems. LC 77-3193. 50p. 1977. 3.50 (ISBN 0-87886-081-9). Ithaca Hse.

Peterson, Carol A., jt. auth. see Gunn, Scout.

Peterson, Carol J. & Broderick, Mary E. Competency-Based Curriculum & Instruction. (League Exchange Ser.: No. 22). 59p. 1979. 4.50 (ISBN 0-686-38246-3). Natl League Nurse.

Peterson, Carol J. & Waters, Verle. Partners in Educational Preparation for Nursing Practice. 32p. 1982. 6.50 (ISBN 0-686-38274-9, 14-1884). Natl League Nurse.

Peterson, Carol J. & Williams, Pat E. Curriculum Development & Its Implementation Through a Conceptual Framework. 64p. 1978. 5.95 (ISBN 0-686-38250-1, 23-1723). Natl League Nurse.

Peterson, Carol W. & Connelly, Shirley. Teaching & Evaluating Synthesis in an Associate Degree Nursing Program: A Developmental Experience. (League Exchange Ser.: No.107). 79p. 1975. 5.50 (ISBN 0-686-38279-X, 23-1573). Natl League Nurse.

Peterson, Carole W. Conversation Starters for Speech-Language Pathology. 1981. pap. 2.95x (ISBN 0-8134-2186-1, 2186). Interstate.

Peterson, Carolyn S. Christmas Story Programs. (Illus.). 1981. 7.00 (ISBN 0-686-38109-2). Moonlight FL.

Peterson, Carolyn S. & Fenton, Ann D. Index to Children's Songs. 318p. 1979. 18.00 (ISBN 0-8242-0638-X). Wilson.

--Story Programs for Older Children. (Illus.). Date not set. price not set. Moonlight FL.

Peterson, Carrol P. Sugarloaf Hill. LC 81-90806. 162p. 1982. 8.95 (ISBN 0-533-05336-6). Vantage.

Peterson, Carroll V. John Davidson. (English Authors Ser.). lib. bdg. 14.95 (ISBN 0-8057-1140-6, Twayne). G K Hall.

Peterson, Craig A. & McCarthy, Claire. Handling Zoning & Land Use Litigation: A Practical Guide. 769p. 1982. 40.00 (ISBN 0-87215-451-3). Michie-Bobbs.

Peterson, D. Mathematics for Business Decisions. 320p. 1983. 11.50 (ISBN 0-07-049620-X); write for info. instr's manual & key (ISBN 0-07-049621-8). McGraw.

Peterson, Dale, ed. A Mad People's History of Madness. LC 81-50430. (Contemporary Community Health Ser.). 385p. 1981. 19.95 (ISBN 0-8229-3444-2); pap. 11.95 (ISBN 0-8229-5331-5). U of Pittsburgh Pr.

Peterson, Daniel. Functional Mathematics for the Mentally Retarded. LC 70-188780. text ed. 23.95 (ISBN 0-675-09097-0). Merrill.

Peterson, Daniel R. & Peter, Gilbert M. Introduction to Technical Mathematics. 416p. 1974. text ed. 16.50x (ISBN 0-673-07784-5). Scott F.

Peterson, Daniel R., jt. auth. see Peter, Gilbert M.

Peterson, David. Hebrews & Perfection: An Examination of the Concept of Perfection in the Epistle to the Hebrews. LC 82-4188. (Society for New Testament Monograph 47). 260p. 1982. 39.50 (ISBN 0-521-24408-0). Cambridge U Pr.

Peterson, David A. Facilitating Education for Older Learners. LC 82-49041. (Higher Education Ser.). 1983. text ed. price not set (ISBN 0-87589-565-4). Jossey-Bass.

Peterson, David M. & Thomas, Charles W. Corrections: Problems & Prospects. 2nd ed. (Criminal Justice Ser.). 1980. pap. text ed. 17.95 (ISBN 0-13-178350-5). P-H.

Peterson, Donald R. & Thomas, David B. Fundamentals of Epidemology. LC 77-11244. (Illus.). 128p. 1978. 10.95 (ISBN 0-669-01901-1). Lexington Bks.

Peterson, Donovan & Ward, Annie, eds. Due Process in Teacher Evaluation. LC 80-5233. 223p. 1980. lib. bdg. 19.25 (ISBN 0-8191-1063-9); pap. text ed. 10.50 (ISBN 0-8191-1064-7). U Pr of Amer.

Peterson, E. A. Cellulosic Ion Exchangers. (Laboratory Techniques in Biochemistry & Molecular Biology Ser.: Vol. 2, Pt. 2). 1970. pap. 15.00 (ISBN 0-444-10057-1, North-Holland). Elsevier.

Peterson, Elmer T. Big Dam Foolishness. 1954. 7.50 (ISBN 0-8159-5107-8). Devin.

Peterson, Eric. Nonprofit Arts Organizations: Formations & Maintenance. 1977. pap. 14.00 incl. suppl. o.p. (ISBN 0-912078-66-9). Volcano Pr.

Peterson, Esther A. Frederick's Alligator. LC 78-15597. (Illus.). (gr. k-3). 1979. reinforced lib. bdg. 8.95 (ISBN 0-517-53597-1). Crown.

Peterson, Eugene H. Growing up in Christ: A Guide for Families with Adolescents. LC 76-12396. 1976. pap. 4.95 (ISBN 0-8042-2026-3). John Knox.

Peterson, F. & Carmi, S., eds. Three Dimensional Turbulent Shear Flows. 160p. 1982. 30.00 (G00211). ASME.

Peterson, Franklynn. Children's Toys You Can Build Yourself. 1978. 9.95 o.p. (ISBN 0-13-132613-9); pap. 5.95 o.p. (ISBN 0-13-132506-X). P-H.

Peterson, Franklynn & Kesselman-Turkel, Judi. The Magazine Writer's Handbook. 288p. 1983. 17.95 (ISBN 0-13-543751-2); pap. 8.95 (ISBN 0-13-543744-X). P-H.

Peterson, G., jt. ed. see Mieszkowski, P.

Peterson, Gayle. Holistic Prenatal Care, Vol. I. Mehl, Lewis, ed. (Holistic Approaches to Health & Disease Ser.). 1982. pap. write for info. Mindbody.

Peterson, George. The Economic & Fiscal Accompaniments of Population Change. 44p. pap. text ed. 2.75 (ISBN 0-686-84408-4). Urban Inst.

Peterson, George, jt. auth. see Dickson, Elizabeth.

Peterson, George, et al. The Future of Boston's Capital Plant. LC 80-54775. (Illus.). 69p. (Orig.). 1981. pap. text ed. 6.00 (ISBN 0-87766-291-6). Urban Inst.

--The Future of Oakland's Capital Plant. LC 80-54776. 80p. (Orig.). 1981. pap. text ed. 6.00 (ISBN 0-87766-290-8). Urban Inst.

Peterson, George E. Tax Exempt Financing of Housing Investment. 45p. 1980. pap. text ed. 11.00 (ISBN 0-87766-251-7). Urban Inst.

Peterson, Gerald R., jt. auth. see Hill, Frederick J.

Peterson, Gilbert A., jt. auth. see Perry, Lloyd M.

Peterson, H. & Marquardt, J. Appraisal & Diagnosis of Speech & Language Disorders. 1981. 23.95 (ISBN 0-13-043505-8). P-H.

Peterson, H. E. & Isaksson, A. J., eds. Communication Networks in Health Care: Proceedings of the IFIP-IMIA Working Conference on Communication Networks in Health Care, Ulvsunda Palace, Sweden, 14-18 June, 1982. 366p. 1982. 49.00 (ISBN 0-444-86513-6, North Holland). Elsevier.

Peterson, Hans. When Peter Was Lost in the Forest. LC 74-120096. (Illus.). (gr. k-2). 1970. PLB 4.49 o.p. (ISBN 0-698-30402-0, Coward). Putnam Pub Group.

Peterson, Helen S. Abigail Adams: Dear Partner. LC 67-10099. (Discovery Books Ser.). (Illus.). (gr. 2-5). 1967. PLB 6.69 (ISBN 0-8116-6299-3). Garrard.

--Electing Our Presidents. LC 74-113495. (American Democracy Ser.). (Illus.). (gr. 3-6). 1970. PLB 7.12 (ISBN 0-8116-6503-8). Garrard.

--Give Us Liberty: The Story of the Declaration of Independence. LC 72-6426. (American Democracy Ser.). (Illus.). 96p. (gr. 3-6). 1973. PLB 7.12 (ISBN 0-8116-6507-0). Garrard.

--Making of the U. S. Constitution. LC 73-10055. (American Democracy Ser.). (Illus.). 96p. (gr. 3-6). 1974. PLB 7.12 (ISBN 0-8116-6509-7). Garrard.

--Sojourner Truth: Fearless Crusader. LC 70-182271. (Americans All Ser). (Illus.). 96p. (gr. 3-6). 1972. PLB 7.12 (ISBN 0-8116-4574-6). Garrard.

--Susan B. Anthony: Pioneer in Woman's Rights. LC 76-151991. (Americans All Ser). (Illus.). (gr. 3-6). 1971. PLB 7.12 (ISBN 0-8116-4570-3). Garrard.

Peterson, J. A. & Hashisaki, J. Theory of Arithmetic. 3rd ed. LC 70-132855. 1971. text ed. 26.95 (ISBN 0-471-68320-5); tchrs.' manual 8.00 (ISBN 0-471-68322-1). Wiley.

Peterson, James, ed. Computer Organization & Assembly Language Programming. (Computer Science & Applied Mathematics Ser.). 1978. 25.00 (ISBN 0-12-552250-9). Acad Pr.

Peterson, James, jt. auth. see Lawson, Gary.

Peterson, James A. Fitness for Women: The Nautilus Way. LC 81-86520. (Illus.). 224p. (Orig.). Date not set. pap. 7.95 (ISBN 0-88011-049-X). Leisure Pr. Postponed.

Peterson, James A. & Bertucci, Bob. Official's Manual: Volleyball. 2nd ed. LC 82-81450. (Official's Manuals Ser.). (Illus.). 80p. (Orig.). 1982. pap. 2.95 (ISBN 0-88011-078-3). Leisure Pr.

Peterson, James A. & Brown, Dale. Conditioning for Basketball: The LSU Way. LC 81-85626. (Illus.). 144p. (Orig.). Date not set. pap. text ed. 5.95 (ISBN 0-918438-87-X). Leisure Pr.

Peterson, James A. & Cromartie, Bill. Bear Bryant: Countdown to Glory. LC 81-86518. (Illus.). 352p. (Orig.). 1982. 14.95 (ISBN 0-88011-046-5). Leisure Pr.

Peterson, James A. & Harris, Dorothy. The Women's Sports Foundation's Women's Fitness Book. LC 81-85971. (Illus.). 354p. (Orig.). Date not set. pap. 9.95 (ISBN 0-88011-025-2). Leisure Pr.

Peterson, James A. & Penny, William J. A Pictorial History of the Chicago Cubs. LC 82-83951. (Illus.). 350p. 1983. 29.95 (ISBN 0-88011-116-X). Leisure Pr.

Peterson, James A., jt. auth. see Switzer, Kathrine.

Peterson, James A., jt. auth. see Wolfe, Michael.

Peterson, James A., ed. Conditioning for a Purpose. LC 76-62811. (Illus., Orig.). 1977. pap. text ed. 6.95 o.p. (ISBN 0-918438-01-2). Leisure Pr.

Peterson, James A., et al. Official's Manual: Volleyball. (Illus.). 1979. pap. text ed. 2.25 o.p. (ISBN 0-918438-48-9). Leisure Pr.

Peterson, James L. Petri Net Theory & the Modeling of Systems. (Prentice-Hall Foundations of Philosophy Ser.). (Illus.). 288p. 1980. 27.95 (ISBN 0-13-661983-5). P-H.

Peterson, James R. The Playboy Advisor on Love & Sex. (Illus.). 350p. 1983. 16.95 (ISBN 0-399-50742-6, Perigee); pap. 7.95 (ISBN 0-399-50741-8). Putnam.

Peterson, Jeanne W. That Is That. LC 77-25676. (Illus.). (gr. k-3). 1979. 7.95i o.p. (ISBN 0-06-024708-8, HarpJ); PLB 7.89 (ISBN 0-06-024709-6). Har-Row.

Peterson, John. The Littles to the Rescue. (Illus.). 48p. (ps-3). 1981. 6.95 (ISBN 0-448-47491-3, G&D). Putnam Pub Group.

Peterson, John E. Oman in the Twentieth Century: Political Foundations of an Emerging State. LC 78-761. (Illus.). 1978. text ed. 25.00x (ISBN 0-06-495522-2). B&N Imports.

Peterson, Karen. The Last Word. 137p. 1982. 12.95 (ISBN 0-9609520-0-4). Tolemac.

Peterson, Karen, ed. see Miller, Leslie A., et al.

Peterson, Kathy K., ed. Oil Shale: The Environmental Challenges II. 2nd ed. (Illus.). 402p. 1982. 20.00 (ISBN 0-918062-51-9). Colo Sch Mines.

Peterson, Kay. Directory of Informational Sources for RVers. 34p. 1983. pap. 1.95 bklet (ISBN 0-910449-03-1). Roving Pr Pub.

--Home Is Where You Park It. (Illus.). 1977. pap. 5.95 o.s.i. (ISBN 0-695-80773-0). Follett.

--Home is Where You Park It. Rev. ed. (Illus.). 200p. 1982. pap. 7.95 (ISBN 0-910449-00-7). Roving Pr Pub.

--Is Full-Time RVing for You? (Illus.). 24p. 1983. pap. 1.95 bklet (ISBN 0-910449-04-X). Roving Pr Pub.

--The Rainbow Chasers. (Illus.). 216p. 1982. pap. 6.75 (ISBN 0-910449-01-5). Roving Pr Pub.

--Survival of the Snowbirds. (Illus.). 222p. 1982. pap. 7.95 (ISBN 0-910449-02-3). Roving Pr Pub.

Peterson, Keith & Sadfie, Robert. Grasp-It: A General Review & Study Program--Interactive Testing. user's manual scp 4.00 (ISBN 0-06-045148-3, HarpC); complete package scp 250.00 (ISBN 0-06-045147-5). Har-Row.

Peterson, Levi S. The Canyons of Grace. LC 82-4720. (Illinois Short Fiction Ser.). 160p. 1982. 11.95 (ISBN 0-252-00997-5); pap. 4.95 (ISBN 0-252-00998-3). U of Ill Pr.

Peterson, Linda K. & Solt, Marilyn L. Newbery & Caldecott Medal & Honor Books: An Annotated Bibliography. 1982. lib. bdg. 39.95 (ISBN 0-8161-8448-8, Hall Reference). G K Hall.

Peterson, Lloyd R. Learning. 134p. 1975. pap. 8.95x (ISBN 0-673-05050-5). Scott F.

Peterson, Lorraine. Why Isn't God Giving Cash Prizes? (Devotionals for Teens Ser.: No. 3). 160p. (gr. 8-12). 1982. pap. 4.95 (ISBN 0-87123-626-5, 210626). Bethany Hse.

Peterson, Louis J., jt. auth. see Schifferes, Justus J.

Peterson, M., jt. auth. see Winn, Charles S.

Peterson, M. Jeanne. The Medical Profession in Mid-Victorian London. LC 76-48362. 1978. 34.50x (ISBN 0-520-03343-4). U of Cal Pr.

Peterson, Maria P., jt. auth. see Leyden, Michael B.

Peterson, Martin L. The Complete Montana Travel Guide. LC 79-88126. (Illus.). 224p. 1980. pap. 5.95 (ISBN 0-686-28763-0). Lake County.

Peterson, Marvin W., et al. Black Students on White Campuses: The Impacts of Increased Black Enrollments. LC 78-60965. 384p. 1978. 18.00x (ISBN 0-87944-221-2). Inst Soc Res.

Peterson, Maude G. How to Know Wild Fruits. LC 72-95943. (Illus.). 1973. pap. text ed. 4.00 o.p. (ISBN 0-486-22943-2). Dover.

Peterson, Merrill D. Adams & Jefferson: A Revolutionary Dialogue. LC 76-1145. (Illus.). 1978. pap. 5.95 (ISBN 0-19-502355-2). Oxford U Pr.

--Jefferson Image in the American Mind. 1960. 25.00x (ISBN 0-19-501539-8). Oxford U Pr.

--Thomas Jefferson & the New Nation: A Biography. LC 70-110394. 1970. 39.95x (ISBN 0-19-500054-4). Oxford U Pr.

--Thomas Jefferson & the New Nation: A Biography. LC 70-110394. (Illus.). 1975. pap. 12.95 (ISBN 0-19-501909-1, GB436, GB). Oxford U Pr.

Peterson, Merrill D., ed. The Portable Thomas Jefferson. 1975. pap. 14.95 (ISBN 0-670-70359-1). Viking Pr.

Peterson, N. L. & Harkness, S. D., eds. Radiation Damage in Metals. (TA 460.r23). 1976. 38.00 o.p. (ISBN 0-87170-055-7). ASM.

Peterson, Nancy L. The Ever-Single Woman: Life Without Marriage. LC 82-583. Orig. Title: Our Lives for Ourselves. 264p. 1982. pap. text ed. 7.50 (ISBN 0-688-00982-4). Quill NY.

--The Ever-Single Woman: Life Without Marriage. 1982. pap. 7.50 (ISBN 0-688-00982-4). Morrow.

--Our Lives for Ourselves: Women Who Have Never Married. 320p. 1981. 13.95 (ISBN 0-399-12476-4). Putnam Pub Group.

Peterson, Nicolas, ed. Tribes & Boundaries in Australia. LC 76-15262. (AIAS Social Anthropology Ser: No. 10). (Illus.). 1976. pap. text ed. 14.00x (ISBN 0-391-00614-2). Humanities.

Peterson, Owen, jt. auth. see Jeffrey, Robert C.

Peterson, Owen, jt. ed. see Braden, Waldo W.

Peterson, Owen see Braden, Waldo W. & Peterson, Owen.

Peterson, P. J. The Boll Weevil Express. LC 82-72816. 192p. (YA) (gr. 7 up). 1983. 12.95 (ISBN 0-440-00856-5). Delacorte.

Peterson, Paul. Readings in American Democracy. 1979. pap. text ed. 12.95 (ISBN 0-8403-2001-9). Kendall-Hunt.

Peterson, Paul, et al. Working in Animal Science. Amberson, Max, ed. (Illus.). (gr. 9-10). 1978. pap. text ed. 9.96 (ISBN 0-07-000839-6, G); tchr's manual, activity guide & tester avail. McGraw.

Peterson, Paul E., jt. auth. see Greenstone, J. David.

Peterson, Penelope L. & Walberg, Herbert J., eds. Research on Teaching: Concepts, Findings & Implications. LC 78-62102. (Education Ser.). 1979. 21.25 (ISBN 0-8211-1518-9); text ed. 19.25 in ten or more copies (ISBN 0-685-63681-X). McCutchan.

Peterson, R. Industrial Order & Social Policy. 1973. pap. 10.95 ref. ed. o.p. (ISBN 0-13-464297-X). P-H.

Peterson, R. F. Silently, by Night. 1964. 8.95 o.p. (ISBN 0-07-049600-5, GB). McGraw.

Peterson, R. V., jt. ed. see Richardson, J. H.

Peterson, Ralph. A Place for Caring & Celebration. (School Media Centers: Focus on Issues & Trends Ser.: No. 4). 1979. pap. 6.00 (ISBN 0-8389-3229-0). ALA.

Peterson, Rein & Silver, Edward A. Decision Systems for Inventory Management & Production Planning. LC 78-4980. (Ser. in Management Administration). 1979. text ed. 38.50x (ISBN 0-471-68327-2); solutions manual 6.00 (ISBN 0-471-03727-3). Wiley.

Peterson, Renno L., jt. auth. see Esperti, Robert A.

Peterson, Rex A., jt. auth. see Owsley, John Q., Jr.

Peterson, Richard. The Character Catalogue. 1983. pap. 5.95 (ISBN 0-89676-069-3). Drama Bk.

Peterson, Richard B. & Tracy, Lane. Systematic Management of Human Resources. LC 78-55826. 1979. text ed. 23.95 (ISBN 0-201-05814-6); readings book avail. 13.95 (ISBN 0-201-05815-4). A-W.

Peterson, Richard B., jt. auth. see Woodworth, Robert T.

Peterson, Richard F. Mary Lavin. (English Author Ser.). 1978. 14.95 (ISBN 0-8057-6707-X, Twayne). G K Hall.

--William Butler Yeats. (English Author Ser.). 1982. lib. bdg. 11.95 (ISBN 0-8057-6815-7, Twayne). G K Hall.

Peterson, Richard F., et al, eds. Work in Progress: Joyce Centenary Essays. 192p. 1983. 15.95x (ISBN 0-8093-1094-5). S Ill U Pr.

Peterson, Rita W. & Butts, David. Science & Society. 1983. text ed. 21.95 (ISBN 0-675-20022-9). Additional supplements may be obtained from publisher. Merrill.

Peterson, Robert C. Understand Accounting-Fast. new ed. (Illus.). 1976. 23.95 (ISBN 0-07-049615-3, P&RB). McGraw.

Peterson, Robert L. Trail of the Serpent. LC 76-21438. 1977. pap. 1.95 o.p. (ISBN 0-87983-130-8). Keats.

Peterson, Robin, jt. auth. see Gross, Charles.

Peterson, Robin, et al. Marketing in Action: An Experiential Approach. (Illus.). 1978. pap. text ed. 12.95 (ISBN 0-8299-0204-X); instrs.' manual avail. (ISBN 0-8299-0565-0). West Pub.

Peterson, Robin T. Personal Selling: An Introduction. LC 77-10979. (Marketing Ser.). 1978. text ed. 28.95x (ISBN 0-471-01743-4); tchrs.' manual 8.00 (ISBN 0-471-01744-2). Wiley.

Peterson, Robin T., jt. auth. see Gross, Charles W.

Peterson, Roger T. Audubon Birds. LC 79-57407. (Abbeville Library of Art: No. 4). (Illus.). 112p. 1980. pap. 4.95 o.p. (ISBN 0-89659-091-7). Abbeville Pr.

--The Birds. rev. ed. LC 80-52118. (Life Nature Library). (gr. 7 up). PLB 13.40 (ISBN 0-8094-3879-8). Silver.

--The Birds. (Young Readers Library). (Illus.). 1977. lib. bdg. 6.80 (ISBN 0-8094-1356-6). Silver.

--A Field Guide to the Birds: A Completely New Guide to All the Birds of Eastern and Central North America. 4th ed. 1980. 15.00 (ISBN 0-395-26621-1); ltd. ed. 50.00 (ISBN 0-686-65213-4); pap. 10.95 (ISBN 0-395-26619-X). HM.

--A Field Guide to the Birds of Texas & Adjacent States. 1963. 17.95 (ISBN 0-395-08087-8). HM.

--A Field Guide to the Birds of Texas & Adjacent States. (Peterson Field Guide Ser.). 1979. pap. 11.95 (ISBN 0-395-26252-6). HM.

--Field Guide to Western Birds. (Peterson Field Guide Ser.). 1972. 16.95 (ISBN 0-395-08085-1); pap. 10.95 (ISBN 0-395-13692-X); Set. 3 records 21.95 (ISBN 0-395-08089-4); Set. 3 cassettes 24.95 (ISBN 0-395-19430-X). HM.

--How to Know the Birds. (Illus.). (RL 7). 1971. pap. 2.50 (ISBN 0-451-09790-4, E9790, Sig). NAL.

--How to Know the Birds. 1982. pap. 2.50 (ISBN 0-451-09790-4, E9790, Sig). NAL.

--One Hundred Two Favorite Audubon Birds of America. (Illus.). 154p. 1980. Repr. 7.98 (ISBN 0-686-36483-X). Md Hist.

Peterson, Roger T. & Peterson, Virginia M. The Audubon Society Baby Elephant Folio: Audubon's Birds of America. LC 79-57407. (Illus.). 712p. 1981. text ed. 185.00 (ISBN 0-89659-231-6); collector's edition 350.00 (ISBN 0-89659-253-7); slipcased ed. 185.00 (ISBN 0-89659-261-8). Abbeville Pr.

Peterson, Roger T., et al. Gardening with Wildlife. Bourne, Russell & MacConomy, Alma D., eds. LC 74-82797. (Illus.). 192p. 1974. 12.95g o.p. (ISBN 0-912186-15-1). Natl Wildlife.

Peterson, Ronald, tr. from Rus. The Russian Symbolists: An Anthology of Critical & Theoretical Writings. 214p. 1983. 25.00 (ISBN 0-686-82223-4). Ardis Pubs.

Peterson, Rudolph E. Stress Concentration Factors. LC 53-11283. 336p. 1974. 42.95x (ISBN 0-471-68329-9, Pub. by Wiley-Interscience). Wiley.

Peterson, Russell. Technology: Its Promise & Its Problems. (Illus.). 1979. pap. 2.50 (ISBN 0-87081-123-1). Colo Assoc.

Peterson, Ruth S. Stretch Out My Golden Wing. LC 75-7014. 70p. 1975. 5.00 (ISBN 0-911838-45-7). Windy Row.

Peterson, Samiha S., et al. The Two-Career Family: Issues & Alternatives. LC 78-66418. 1978. pap. text ed. 11.50 (ISBN 0-8191-0020-X). U Pr of Amer.

Peterson, Shailer, ed. The Dentist & the Assistant. 4th ed. LC 77-8359. (Illus.). 494p. 1977. text ed. 20.95 o.p. (ISBN 0-8016-3820-8). Mosby.

Peterson, Shailer A. Preparing to Enter Dental School. 1979. text ed. 13.95 (ISBN 0-13-697326-4, Spec); pap. text ed. 6.95 (ISBN 0-13-697318-3, Spec). P-H.

--Preparing to Enter Medical School. 1980. text ed. 14.95 (ISBN 0-13-697342-6, Spec); pap. text ed. 6.95 (ISBN 0-13-697334-5). P-H.

Peterson, Susan L. Self-Defense for Women. (Illus.). 192p. (Orig.). 1983. pap. 7.95 (ISBN 0-88011-114-3). Leisure Pr.

--The Women's Stretching Book. LC 82-83927. (Illus.). 144p. (Orig.). 1983. pap. 6.95 (ISBN 0-88011-095-3). Leisure Pr.

Peterson, Thomas D. Wittgenstein for Preaching: A Model for Communication. LC 80-5802. 192p. 1980. lib. bdg. 19.75 (ISBN 0-8191-1342-5); pap. text ed. 9.75 (ISBN 0-8191-1343-3). U Pr of Amer.

Peterson, Thurman S. & Hobby, Charles R. College Algebra. 3rd ed. 1978. text ed. 23.50 scp o.p. (ISBN 0-06-045161-0, HarpC); ans. booklet avail. o.p. (ISBN 0-06-365183-1). Har-Row.

Peterson, Trudy H. Basic Archival Workshop Exercises. 86p. 1982. pap. text ed. 11.00 (ISBN 0-931828-54-6). Soc Am Archivists.

Peterson, V. S. & Pakvasa, S., eds. Proceedings of the Eighth Hawaii Topical Conference in Particle Physics, 1979. (Particle Physics Conference Proceedings). 1980. pap. text ed. 20.00x o.p. (ISBN 0-8248-0716-2). UH Pr.

Peterson, V. Z., jt. ed. see Dobson, P. N.

Peterson, Victor P. & Peterson, Victor P., Jr. Native Trees of the Sierra Nevada. (Natural History Guides Ser.: No. 36). 1974. 14.95x o.p. (ISBN 0-520-02736-1); pap. 3.95 (ISBN 0-520-02666-7). U of Cal Pr.

Peterson, Virginia M., jt. auth. see Peterson, Roger T.

Peterson, W. Introduction to Economics. 1977. pap. text ed. 16.95 (ISBN 0-13-481242-5); study guide 12.95 (ISBN 0-13-481267-0). P-H.

Peterson, W., ed. Quintilian, Institutionis Oratoriae Liber X. 130p. Repr. of 1903 ed. 8.50 (ISBN 0-86516-009-0). Bolchazy-Carducci.

Peterson, Wallace C. Income, Employment, & Economic Growth: An Intermediate Text in Aggregate Economic Analysis. 5th ed. 1983. write for info (ISBN 0-393-95274-6). Norton.

Peterson, Walter F. An Industrial Heritage: Allis-Chalmers Corporation. LC 76-57456. (Illus.). 448p. 1978. 17.50 (ISBN 0-938076-02-7). Milwaukee County.

Peterson, Warren A., jt. ed. see Mangen, David J.

Peterson, Wilfred A. Art of Living Day by Day. 1972. 10.00 o.p. (ISBN 0-671-21343-1). S&S.

--More About the Art of Living. 1966. 4.95 o.p. (ISBN 0-671-49090-7). S&S.

Peterson, Willard. Bitter Gourd: Fang-I-Chin & Intellectual Change in the 1630s. LC 78-18491. (Illus.). 1979. text ed. 27.50x (ISBN 0-300-02208-5). Yale U Pr.

Peterson, William. Japanese Americans. LC 81-40780. 282p. 1981. pap. text ed. 9.25 (ISBN 0-8191-1807-9). U Pr of Amer.

Peterson, William, jt. ed. see Stone, Richard.

Peterson, William, jt. auth. see Taylor, Joshua C.

Peterson, William J. The Discipling of Timothy. 144p. 1980. pap. 4.50 (ISBN 0-88207-217-X). Victor Bks.

Peterson, William S. Interrogating the Oracle: A History of the London Browning Society. LC 69-15916. (Illus.). xii, 276p. 1970. 16.00x (ISBN 0-8214-0056-8, 82-80620). Ohio U Pr.

--Robert & Elizabeth Barrett Browning: An Annotated Bibliography, 1951-1970. LC 74-24915. (Illus.). 1974. 26.50x (ISBN 0-930252-02-0, Pub. by Browning Inst). Pub Ctr Cult Res.

Peterson, William S., ed. see Browning, Elizabeth B.

Peterson, William S., ed. see Morris, William.

Peterson-Hunt, William S. & Woodruff, Evelyn L. Union List of Sanborn Fire Insurance Maps Held by Institutions in the United States & Canada: Volume 2 (Montana to Wyoming, Canada & Mexico, with a Supplement & Corrigenda to Volume 1. rev. ed. LC 76-6129. (Western Association of Map Libraries: Occasional Paper; No. 3). (Illus.). 216p. (Orig.). 1977. pap. 6.00x (ISBN 0-939112-03-5); pap. 10.00 Vols. 1 & 2 (ISBN 0-939112-04-3). Western Assn Map.

Peterson-Nedry, Judy. Showcase Oregon Wineries. 68p. (Orig.). 1981. 4.95 (ISBN 0-942098-00-5). Class Media Prod.

Petesch, Natalie L. Seasons Such As These: Two Novels, New Letters. LC 82-75935. 163p. 1978. 15.95 (ISBN 0-8040-0803-5). Swallow.

Petesch, Natalie L. M. Duncan's Colony: A Novel. LC 82-75463. 220p. 1982. 21.95 (ISBN 0-8040-0401-3); pap. 9.95 (ISBN 0-8040-0402-1). Swallow.

Petherbridge, Elizabeth. Paper Sculpture Step by Step. (Illus.). 112p. 1974. 12.95 o.s.i. (ISBN 0-7135-1718-2). Transatlantic.

Petherick, Karin. Per Gunnar Evander. (World Authors Ser.). 1982. lib. bdg. 16.95 (ISBN 0-8057-6493-3, Twayne). G K Hall.

Pethig, Ronald. Dielectric & Electronic Properties of Biological Materials. LC 78-13694. 1979. 61.95 (ISBN 0-471-99728-5, Pub. by Wiley-Interscience). Wiley.

Pethoe, A. & Noble, R. D. Residence Time Distribution Theory in Chemical Engineering: Proceedings of a Summer School at Bad Honnef-August 15-25, 1982. (Illus.). 1982p. pap. 57.50x (ISBN 0-89573-061-8). Verlag Chemie.

Pethrick, R. A. & Richards, R. W. Static & Dynamic Properties of the Polymeric Solid State. 1982. 56.50 (ISBN 90-277-1481-9, Pub. by Reidel Holland). Kluwer Boston.

Pethybridge, Roger. The Social Prelude to Stalinism. LC 74-75011. 1974. 21.50 o.p. (ISBN 0-312-73395-X). St Martin.

--Witnesses to the Russian Revolution. (Illus.). 1982. pap. 6.95 (ISBN 0-8065-0018-2, C274). Citadel Pr.

Petie, Haris. Billions of Bugs. (Illus.). (ps-3). 1975. 5.95 o.p. (ISBN 0-13-076240-7); pap. 2.95 o.p. (ISBN 0-13-076174-5). P-H.

--A Book of Big Bugs. (Illus.). 32p. (gr. 1-4). 1982. pap. 2.95 o.p. (ISBN 0-13-079889-4, Pub. by Treehouse). P-H.

Petievich, Gerald. Money Men. 224p. 1983. pap. 2.50 (ISBN 0-523-41154-5). Pinnacle Bks.

--One-Shot Deal. 224p. 1983. pap. 2.50 (ISBN 0-523-41155-3). Pinnacle Bks.

--To Die in Beverly Hills. 1983. 14.50 (ISBN 0-87795-487-9). Arbor Hse.

Petillon, Mary & Newman, Sharon. Olympics Made Easy. (Illus.). 202p. (gr. 5-9). 1982. pap. text ed. 8.95 (ISBN 0-910935-00-9); wkbk. 8.95. Vista Graphics.

Petit. Traite Sur le Governement des Esclaves, 2 vols. (Slave Trade in France Ser., 1744-1848). 796p. (Fr.). 1974. Repr. of 1777 ed. lib. bdg. 203.00x o.p. (ISBN 0-8287-0684-0); Vol. 1. (ISBN 0-685-49510-8, TN106); Vol. 2. (ISBN 0-685-49511-6, TN107). Clearwater Pub.

Petit, Paul. Pax Romana. Willis, James, tr. 1976. 40.00x (ISBN 0-520-02171-1). U of Cal Pr.

Petit, Ron E. The Career Connection. 161p. 1982. 8.95 (ISBN 0-941944-01-8). Impact VA.

Petit, Ronald E. The Career Connection: Keys to Employment. Atwell, Susan, ed. (Illus.). 155p. 1981. pap. 5.95 (ISBN 0-686-42916-8). Maron Pubns.

--From the Military to a Civilian Career. Atwell, Susan, ed. (Illus.). 146p. 1980. pap. 5.95 (ISBN 0-941944-02-6). Maron Pubns.

--Women & the Career Game: Play to Win! (Illus.). 147p. (Orig.). 1982. pap. 7.95 (ISBN 0-941944-03-4). Prof Dev Serv.

--Women & The Career Game: Play to Win!!! 147p. 1982. pap. 7.95 (ISBN 0-941944-03-4). Maron Pubns.

Petit, Thomas A. Fundamentals of Management Coordination: Supervisors, Middle Managers & Executives. LC 81-19364. 528p. 1983. Repr. of 1975 ed. price not set (ISBN 0-89874-433-4). Krieger.

Petit Bois, G. Tables of Indefinite Integrals. 1906. pap. text ed. 6.00 (ISBN 0-486-60225-7). Dover.

Petite, Irving. Tiger Mountain Sketchbook. 144p. (Orig.). 1983. pap. 7.95 (ISBN 0-914842-93-5). Madrona Pubs.

Petitti, Richard E. The Sensitive Man & Its OK to Be Feminine. (Illus.). 125p. 1982. pap. 10.00 (ISBN 0-686-36325-6). Rich Concepts.

Petonnet, Colette. Those People: The Subculture of a Housing Project. Smidt, Rita, tr. from Fr. LC 72-825. (Contributions in Sociology: No. 10). 1973. lib. bdg. 29.95 (ISBN 0-8371-6393-5, PTP/). Greenwood.

Petr, J. Personalized System of Instruction: P S I-Keller Plan. 1975. 12.50 (ISBN 0-07-049650-1, C). McGraw.

Petracca, M. P., jt. auth. see Page, B. I.

Petrak, F. & Sydow, H. Die Gattungen der Pyrenomyceten, Sphaeropsideen und Melanconieen, Pt. 1. (Feddes Repertorium: Beiheft 27). 551p. (Ger.). 1979. Repr. of 1926 ed. lib. bdg. 72.00x (ISBN 3-87429-071-9). Lubrecht & Cramer.

Petralia, Joseph F. Gold! Gold!-A Beginners Handbook & Recreational Guide: How to Prospect for Gold, Vol. 4. 2nd ed. LC 81-126200. (Illus.). 112p. (Orig.). 1982. 10.95 (ISBN 0-9605890-2-3); pap. 6.95 (ISBN 0-9605890-3-1). Sierra Trading.

Petrarca, Francesco. Physicke Against Fortune. Twyne, Thomas, tr. LC 80-22768. 1980. Repr. of 1579 ed. 80.00x (ISBN 0-8201-1359-X). Schol Facsimiles.

Petrarch. Petrarch: Selected Sonnets, Odes, Letters. Bergin, Thomas G., ed. LC 66-19204. (Crofts Classics Ser.). 1966. pap. text ed. 3.75x (ISBN 0-88295-066-5). Harlan Davidson.

Petras, Herman, jt. auth. see Logan, William.

Petras, James. Critical Perspectives on Imperialism & Social Class in the Third World. LC 78-13915. 1980. pap. 7.50 o.p. (ISBN 0-85345-529-5, PB5295). Monthly Rev.

--Politics & Social Forces in Chilean Development. 1969. 30.00x (ISBN 0-520-01463-4). U of Cal Pr.

Petras, James, jt. ed. see Lopez, Adalberto.

Petras, James, et al. Class, State & Power in the Third World: With Case Studies in Class Conflict in Latin America. LC 80-25938. 285p. 1981. text ed. 19.95x (ISBN 0-86598-018-7); pap. text ed. 8.95x (ISBN 0-86598-056-X). Allanheld.

Petras, James F., et al. The Nationalization of Venezuelan Oil. LC 77-7822. (Praeger Special Studies). 1977. 28.95 o.p. (ISBN 0-03-022656-2). Praeger.

Petras, John W., ed. George Herbert Mead: Essays on His Social Philosophy. LC 59-11329. 1968. 10.95x (ISBN 0-8077-1902-1). Tchrs Coll.

Petre, F. Loraine. Napoleon at Bay, 1814. LC 77-77986. 1978. 14.95 o.p. (ISBN 0-88254-447-0). Hippocrene Bks.

Petrello, George J., jt. auth. see Brown, Richard D.

Petrello, George J., jt. auth. see Burton, Robert H.

Petrescu, P. & Rodna, N. Romanian Textiles. (A Survey of World Textiles: No. 20). (Illus.). 1966. text ed. 15.00x (ISBN 0-686-86108-6, Pub. by A & C Black England). Humanities.

Petreshene, Susan S. A Complete Guide to Learning Centers. LC 76-49794. (Educational Ser.). (Illus.). 1977. pap. 11.95 (ISBN 0-916988-08-2). Pendragon Hse.

--Research Pleasers. Sussman, Ellen, ed. (Illus., Orig.). (gr. 3-6). 1982. pap. text ed. 5.95 (ISBN 0-933606-19-2, MS-618). Monkey Sisters.

--Research Teasers. Sussman, Ellen, ed. (Illus., Orig.). (gr. 3-6). 1982. pap. text ed. 5.95 (ISBN 0-933606-18-4, MS-617). Monkey Sisters.

--Supplement to the Complete Guide to Learning Centers. LC 77-71176. (Educational Ser.). (Illus.). 1977. pap. 6.00 (ISBN 0-916988-13-9). Pendragon Hse.

Petrey, Sandy. History in the Text "Quatrevingt-Treize" & the French Revolution. (Purdue University Monographs in Romance Languages). viii, 129p. 1980. 19.00 (ISBN 90-272-1713-0). Benjamins North Am.

Petri, Herbert. Motivation: Theory & Research. 400p. 1981. text ed. 25.95x (ISBN 0-534-00936-0). Wadsworth Pub.

Petri, R. Construction Estimating. 1978. ref. ed. 21.95 (ISBN 0-87909-152-5); text ed. 18.95 (ISBN 0-686-96862-X). Reston.

Petrich, Mario. Introduction to Semigroups. LC 72-78086. 1973. text ed. 21.95 (ISBN 0-675-09062-8). Merrill.

Petrick, M., jt. auth. see Chaffee, S.

Petrides, Heidrun. Hans & Peter. LC 63-1031. (Illus.). (gr. k-3). 1963. 5.95 o.p. (ISBN 0-15-233275-8, HJ). HarBraceJ.

Petrie. Cardiovascular & Respiratory Disease Therapy. (Clinically Important Adverse Drug Interactions Ser.: Vol. 1). 1981. 50.75 (ISBN 0-444-80233-9). Elsevier.

Petrie, Alexander. An Introduction to Roman History, Literature & Antiquities. 3rd ed. LC 78-25840. (Illus.). 1979. Repr. of 1963 ed. lib. bdg. 19.25x (ISBN 0-313-20848-4, PEIR). Greenwood.

Petrie, Chris J. Elongational Flows. (Research Notes in Mathematics Ser.: No. 29). 254p. (Orig.). 1979. pap. text ed. 25.00 (ISBN 0-273-08406-2). Pitman Pub MA.

Petrie, Dorothea G., jt. auth. see Magnuson, James.

Petrie, Glen. Mariamne. 1977. 9.95 o.p. (ISBN 0-698-10769-1, Pub. by Coward). Putnam Pub Group.

Petrie, Joyce. Mainstreaming in the Media Center. 232p. (Orig.). 1982. pap. text ed. 22.50x (ISBN 0-89774-006-8); lib. bdg. 22.50. Oryx Pr.

Petrie, Sidney & Stone, Robert B. Fat Destroyer Foods: The Magic Metabolizer Diet. 1974. 10.95 (ISBN 0-13-308098-6, Reward); pap. 4.95 (ISBN 0-13-308080-3). P-H.

--Helping Yourself with Autogenics. LC 82-14488. 205p. 1983. 14.95 (ISBN 0-13-387407-9, Parker); pap. 4.95 (ISBN 0-13-387399-4). P-H.

--The Wonder Protein Diet: Miracle Way to Better Health & Longer Life. 1978. 14.95 o.p. (ISBN 0-13-962498-8, Parker). P-H.

Petrie, William M. Seventy Years in Archaeology. Repr. of 1932 ed. lib. bdg. 17.75x (ISBN 0-8371-2241-4, PESA). Greenwood.

Petrik-Ott, A. J. The Pteridophytes of Kansas, Nebraska, South Dakota & North Dakota, USA Nova Hedwigia Beiheft, No. 61. 1979. lib. bdg. 30.00 (ISBN 3-7682-5461-5). Lubrecht & Cramer.

Petrikovic, John J., ed. see Tucker, Bettie C.

Petrillo. Processing Securities Transactions: Administrative Procedures of Brokerage Firms. 260p. 1969. 43.95 (ISBN 0-471-06573-0). Wiley.

Petrillo & Sanger. Emotional Care of Hospitalized Children. 2nd ed. pap. text ed. 12.00 (ISBN 0-686-97971-0, Lippincott Nursing). Lippincott.

Petrofsky, Jerrold S., jt. auth. see Phillips, Chandler A.

Petrone, Louis & Crary. Foundations of Modern Education. 1971. 11.95 o.p. (ISBN 0-394-31034-9). Knopf.

Petronko, Diane, jt. auth. see Angel, Gerry.

Petroski, Catherine. Beautiful My Mane in the Wind. LC 82-12120. (Illus.). 32p. (gr. 1 up). 1983. pap. 9.95 (ISBN 0-395-33074-2). HM.

Petrosky, Anthony. Jurgis Petraskas: Poems. LC 82-18003. 1983. text ed. 12.95 (ISBN 0-8071-1092-2); pap. 5.95 (ISBN 0-8071-1091-4). La State U Pr.

Petrov, A. A. Einstein Spaces. 1969. inquire for price o.p. (ISBN 0-08-012315-5). Pergamon.

Petrov, Vladimir. Escape from the Future: The Incredible Adventures of a Young Russian. LC 73-80380. 488p. 1973. Repr. of 1951 ed. 12.50 o.p. (ISBN 0-253-12360-7). Ind U Pr.

Petrovich, Michael B., tr. see Djilas, Milovan.

Petrow, Richard. The Bitter Years: The Invasion & Occupation of Denmark & Norway April 1940 - May 1945. LC 74-9576. (Illus.). 1979. pap. 5.95 (ISBN 0-688-05275-4). Quill NY.

Petrucci, Ralph H. General Chemistry: Principles & Modern Applications. 3rd ed. 1982. text ed. 29.95x (ISBN 0-02-395010-2). Macmillan.

Petruck, Marvin, jt. ed. see Levey, Martin.

Petruck, Peninah R. Y. American Art Criticism: 1910-1939, No. 5. LC 79-575499. (Outstanding Dissertations in the Fine Arts Ser.). 310p. 1982. lib. bdg. 33.00 o.s.i. (ISBN 0-8240-3939-4). Garland Pub.

Petrunkevich, Alexander. A Study of Amber Spiders. 1942. pap. 75.00x (ISBN 0-686-51318-5). Elliots Bks.

Petrusewicz, S. A., ed. Industrial Noise & Vibration Control. 1974. 33.95 (ISBN 0-444-19543-2). Elsevier.

Petrusz, P., jt. ed. see Bullock, G. R.

Petry, Ann. Street. (gr. 9-12). 1969. pap. 1.25 o.s.i. (ISBN 0-515-01997-6). Jove Pubns.

--Tituba of Salem Village. LC 64-20691. (gr. 7-11). 1964. 12.45i (ISBN 0-690-82677-X, TYC-J). Har-Row.

Petry, Loren C. A Beachcomber's Botany. LC 68-26716. (Illus.). 160p. 1975. 12.95 (ISBN 0-85699-119-8). Chatham Pr.

Petry, Michael J., tr. see Hegel, G. W.

Petsche, Hellmuth, jt. ed. see Brazier, Mary A.

Petschek, Joyce S. The Silver Bird: A Tale for Those Who Dream. LC 80-70049. (Illus.). 192p. 1981. pap. 14.95 (ISBN 0-89087-359-3). Celestial Arts.

Petschek, Rodolfo, jt. auth. see Bohn, Dave.

Pettengill, J. S. Labour Unions & Inequality of Earned Income. (Contributions to Economic Analysis Ser.: Vol. 129). 1980. 51.00 (ISBN 0-444-85409-6). Elsevier.

Pettengill, Robert B. & Uppal, J. S. Can Cities Survive? The Fiscal Plight of American Cities. 128p. 1974. pap. text ed. 8.95 (ISBN 0-312-11480-X). St Martin.

Petter, Martin, jt. auth. see Lee, J. M.

Petter, Rodolphe C., jt. auth. see Mooney, James.

Petterson, Alan R. Frankenstein's Aunt. 1982. pap. 1.95 (ISBN 0-380-60020-X, 60020, Camelot). Avon.

Petterson, Lindsey, ed. Black Theater. 1972. pap. 8.95 (ISBN 0-452-25313-6, Z5313, Plume). NAL.

Petterssen, Sverre. Introduction to Meteorology. 3rd ed. LC 68-15476. 1968. text ed. 39.95 (ISBN 0-07-049720-6, C). McGraw.

--Weather Analysis & Forecasting, 2 vols. 2nd ed. Incl. Vol. 1. Motion & Systems. text ed. 22.00 (ISBN 0-07-049685-4); Vol. 2. Weather & Systems. text ed. 17.00 (ISBN 0-07-049686-2). 1956 (C). McGraw.

Petteruto, Ray. How to Open & Operate a Restaurant. LC 80-67823. (Food Service Ser.). 269p. 1979. pap. 11.80 (ISBN 0-8273-1966-5); instr's. guide 3.25 (ISBN 0-8273-1967-3). Delmar.

Pettes, Dorothy E. Staff & Student Supervision: A Task Centered Approach. (National Institute Social Services Library). 1979. text ed. 19.95x (ISBN 0-04-361033-1); pap. text ed. 7.95x (ISBN 0-04-361034-X). Allen Unwin.

Pettet, E. C. Of Paradise & Light: A Study of Vaughn's Silex Scintillans. 217p. 1983. Repr. of 1960 ed. lib. bdg. 40.00 (ISBN 0-89760-050-9). Telegraph Bks.

Pettey, Richard J. In His Footsteps: The Priest in the Catholic Charismatic Renewal. LC 76-45274. 112p. 1977. pap. 2.45 o.p. (ISBN 0-8091-2007-0, Deus). Paulist Pr.

Petti, Theodore, ed. Childhood Depression. LC 83-580. (Journal of Children in Contemporary Society Ser.: Vol. 15, No. 2). 104p. 1983. text ed. 20.00 (ISBN 0-917724-95-X, B95). Haworth Pr.

Pettigrew, Grady L., Jr. Federal Bankruptcy Code: Theory Into Practice. 295p. 1982. wkbk 60.00 (ISBN 0-87179-376-8). BNA.

Pettigrew, Helen. Bible Word Quest. new ed. 96p. 1975. pap. 2.95 (ISBN 0-8010-6965-3). Baker Bk.

Pettigrew, Shirley. There Was an Old Lady. (Break-of-Day Bk). (Illus.). 48p. (gr. 1-3). 1974. PLB 6.99 o.p. (ISBN 0-698-30541-8, Coward). Putnam Pub Group.

Pettigrew, T. & Frederickson, G. Prejudice. (Dimensions in Ethnicity Ser.). 128p. 1982. pap. text ed. 4.95x (ISBN 0-674-70063-5). Harvard U Pr.

Pettigrew, T. F. Racially Separate or Together. 1971. pap. text ed. 13.95 (ISBN 0-07-049718-4, C). McGraw.

Pettigrew, Thomas F., et al. School Desegregation: The Continuing Challenge. new ed. Harvard Educational Review Editorial Board, ed. (HER Reprint Ser.). 1976. pap. text ed. 4.95 (ISBN 0-916690-13-X). Harvard Educ Rev.

Pettijohn, F. J., et al. Sand & Sandstone. LC 79-168605. 1972. 31.10 o.p. (ISBN 0-387-05528-2); pap. 24.80 (ISBN 0-387-90071-3). Springer-Verlag.

Pettil, G. R., ed. Synthetic Peptides, Vol. 5. 1980. 95.75 (ISBN 0-444-41895-4). Elsevier.

Pettingill, Olin S., ed. Bird Watcher's America. (Apollo Eds.). pap. 4.50i (ISBN 0-8152-0356-X, A-356). T Y Crowell.

Pettis, A. M. Basic Car Care. (Illustrated Guides Ser.). (Orig.). 1977. pap. 2.95 o.p. (ISBN 0-671-18778-3). Monarch Pr.

Pettis, Ashley B. Journey to the Unexpected. 320p. 1983. Repr. of 1974 ed. 24.50x (ISBN 0-8290-1305-9). Irvington.

Pettis, Ruth. The Goudy Presence at Konglomerati Press. (Illus.). 1977. pap. 4.50 (ISBN 0-686-98152-9). Konglomerati.

Pettit, D. G., jt. auth. see Patterson, P. G.

Pettit, Ernest L. Collectible Tin Containers Bk. 2. 1971. spiral bdg. 4.95 o.p. (ISBN 0-517-51084-7). Crown.

Pettit, Florence H. The Stamp-Pad Printing Book. LC 78-22504. (Illus.). (gr. 5-9). 1979. 8.61i (ISBN 0-690-03967-0, TYC-J); PLB 9.89 o.p. (ISBN 0-690-03968-9). Har-Row.

Pettit, G. R. Synthetic Peptides, Vol 4. 1977. 95.75 (ISBN 0-444-41521-1). Elsevier.

Pettit, G. R., ed. Synthetic Peptides, Vol. 6. 1982. 153.25 (ISBN 0-444-42080-0). Elsevier.

Pettit, Joseph M. Electronic Switching, Timing, & Pulse Circuits. 2nd ed. (Electronic & Electrical Engineering Ser.). 1970. text ed. 36.00 (ISBN 0-07-049726-5, C). McGraw.

Pettit, Philip. The Concept of Structuralism: A Critical Analysis. LC 74-22971. 198p. 1975. 17.95x (ISBN 0-520-02882-1); pap. 2.95 (ISBN 0-520-03416-3). U of Cal Pr.

Pettit, Ray H. ECM & ECCM Techniques for Digital Communications. (Systems Engineering Ser.). (Illus.). 180p. 1982. 30.50 (ISBN 0-534-97932-7). Lifetime Learn.

Pettit, Rhonda, ed. see Brant, Russell A.

Pettit, Rhonda, ed. see Robl, Tom & Koppenaal, Dave.

Pettit, Ted S. Bird Feeders & Shelters You Can Make. (Cub Scout Project Bks.). (Illus.). (gr. 3-6). 1970. 5.95 o.p. (ISBN 0-399-20018-5). Putnam Pub Group.

--The Long, Long Pollution Crisis. LC 74-24750. 96p. (gr. 6 up). 1975. 5.95 o.p. (ISBN 0-399-20436-9). Putnam Pub Group.

--Wildlife at Night. LC 76-13596. (Illus.). (gr. 6-8). 1976. PLB 5.89 o.p. (ISBN 0-399-61026-X). Putnam Pub Group.

Pettit, Terry, et al. Watermarks. Hollis, James, ed. (Illus., Orig.). 1971. pap. 1.45 o.p. (ISBN 0-87178-924-8). Brethren.

Pettman, Barrie O. Equal Pay for Women. LC 77-7335. (Illus.). 1977. text ed. 24.95x (ISBN 0-07-049735-4, C). McGraw.

Pettman, Barrie O., ed. Labour Turnover & Retention. LC 75-18452. 204p. 1976. 27.95 o.s.i. (ISBN 0-470-68448-8). Halsted Pr.

Pettman, Charles. Africanderisms. LC 68-18007. 1968. Repr. of 1913 ed. 47.00x (ISBN 0-8103-3289-2). Gale.

Pettman, Jan. Zambia: Security & Conflict, 1964-1973. LC 74-79129. 381p. 1974. 25.00 (ISBN 0-312-89845-2). St Martin.

Pettman, Ralph. Human Behavior & World Politics: An Introduction to International Relations. LC 75-10759. 352p. 1976. 18.95 (ISBN 0-312-39760-7); pap. text ed. 11.95 (ISBN 0-312-39795-X). St Martin.

--State & Class: A Sociology of International Affairs. 1979. 26.00 (ISBN 0-312-75602-X). St Martin.

Pettman, Ralph, ed. Moral Claims in World Affairs. LC 78-11431. 1979. 22.50 (ISBN 0-312-54755-2). St Martin.

Pettman, William R. Resources of the United Kingdom. LC 68-56563. Repr. of 1830 ed. 25.00 (ISBN 0-678-00661-X). Kelley.

Pettofrezzo, Anthony J. & Armstrong, Lee H. Arithmetic: A Programmed Approach. 1981. pap. text ed. 19.95x (ISBN 0-673-15314-2). Scott F.

--Elementary Algebra: A Programmed Approach. 1980. pap. text ed. 18.95x (ISBN 0-673-15293-6). Scott F.

--Intermediate Algebra: A Programmed Approach. 1981. pap. text ed. 18.95x (ISBN 0-673-15315-0). Scott F.

Pettofrezzo, Anthony J. & Hight, Donald W. Elementary Mathematics: Number Systems & Algebra. 1970. text ed. 17.95x (ISBN 0-673-05997-9). Scott F.

Pettus, John. Fodinae Regales (The Mines Royal) 115p. 1981. Repr. of 1670 ed. text ed. 42.75x (ISBN 0-686-32510-9). IMM North Am.

Petty, Fred C. Italian Opera in London, 1760-1800. Buelow, George, ed. LC 79-25564. (Studies in Musicology: No. 16). 1980. 44.95 (ISBN 0-8357-1073-4, Pub. by UMI Res Pr). Univ Microfilms.

Petty, J. William, II, jt. auth. see Walker, Ernest W.

Petty, Jo. An Apple a Day: Treasured Selections from Apples of Gold. 1979. pap. 5.50 (ISBN 0-8378-5025-8). Gibson.

--Life Is for Living. 160p. 1979. gift-boxed 7.95 (ISBN 0-8007-0978-0). Revell.

--Words of Silver & Gold. (General Ser.). 1979. lib. bdg. 8.95 (ISBN 0-8161-6698-6, Large Print Bks); pap. 6.95 o.p. (ISBN 0-8161-6741-9). G K Hall.

Petty, Jo, compiled by. Pathways of Gold. 1983. 5.50 (ISBN 0-8378-1709-9). Gibson.

--Wings of Silver. LC 67-21924. (Illus.). 1968. boxed 5.50 (ISBN 0-8378-1773-0). Gibson.

Petty, L. Jalik. Reducing Racial Tension in the Schools Through Values Clarification. LC 81-52146. 56p. (Orig.). 1982. pap. 5.95 (ISBN 0-942428-00-5). Universal Ministries.

Petty, Richard E., jt. ed. see Cacioppo, John T.

Petty, Robert O., jt. auth. see Korling, Torkel.

Petty, Roy. Contemporary Tennis. LC 77-91165. 1978. 6.95 o.p. (ISBN 0-8092-7548-1); pap. 5.95 (ISBN 0-8092-7574-0). Contemp Bks.

--Home Birth. LC 78-24718. (Illus.). 1979. 12.50 o.p. (ISBN 0-89196-059-7, Domus Bks); pap. 6.95 o.p. (ISBN 0-89196-026-0). Quality Bks IL.

Petty, Thomas L. Prescribing Home Oxygen for COPD. 128p. 9.95 (ISBN 0-86577-078-6). Thieme-Stratton.

Petty, Thomas L., jt. auth. see Mitchell, Roger S.

Petty, Walter T. Curriculum for the Modern Elementary School. 1976. 22.95 (ISBN 0-395-30695-7). HM.

Petuchowski, jt. auth. see Heinemann.

Petyt, K. M. The Study of Dialect: An Introduction to Dialectology. (Andre Deutsch Language Library). 240p. 1980. lib. bdg. 29.00 (ISBN 0-86531-060-2). Westview.

Petzal, David E., ed. Experts' Book of the Shooting Sports. 9.95 o.p. (ISBN 0-671-21328-8). S&S.

Petzold, jt. auth. see Geissler.

Petzold, A. & Rohrs, M. Concrete for High Temperatures. 2nd ed. Phillips, A. R. & Turner, F. H., trs. from Ger. (Illus.). 1970. text ed. 41.00x (ISBN 0-85334-033-1, Pub. by Applied Sci England). Elsevier.

Petzold, Paul. The All-in-One Cine Book. 4th ed. (Illus.). 1979. pap. 9.95 (ISBN 0-240-51024-0). Focal Pr.

--The Konica Autoreflex Book. (Camera Books). (Illus.). 1978. pap. 7.95 o.p. (ISBN 0-240-50977-3); pap. 7.95 (ISBN 0-240-51104-2). Focal Pr.

--Light on People in Photography. 2nd ed. (Illus.). 1979. 27.95 (ISBN 0-240-51033-X). Focal Pr.

--Toda la Cinematografia En un Solo Libro. Millan, Ventura & Panella, Luis J., trs. from Eng. 282p. (Span.). 1975. pap. 8.95 o.p. (ISBN 0-240-51097-6, Pub. by Ediciones Spain). Focal Pr.

Petzold, Paul, jt. auth. see Gaunt, Leonard.

Petzow, Gunter. Metallographic Etching. 1978. 31.00 (ISBN 0-87170-002-6). ASM.

Peurifoy, Robert L. Construction Planning, Equipment & Methods. 3rd ed. (Illus.). 1979. text ed. 35.50 (ISBN 0-07-049760-5, C); solutions manual 12.00 (ISBN 0-07-049761-3). McGraw.

--Estimating Construction Costs. 3rd ed. 1975. 34.50 (ISBN 0-07-049738-9, C); ans. 7.95 (ISBN 0-07-049739-7). McGraw.

--Formwork for Concrete Structures. 2nd ed. 1976. 32.50 (ISBN 0-07-049754-0, P&RB). McGraw.

Peusner, Leonardo. Concepts in Bioenergetics. (Concepts of Modern Biology Ser). (Illus.). 272p. 1974. pap. 14.95 reference ed. (ISBN 0-13-166264-3). P-H.

Pevet, jt. auth. see Oksche.

Pevet, P., jt. ed. see Ariens-Kappers, J.

Pevet, P., jt. ed. see Swaab, D. F.

Pevsner, Nikolaus. Academies of Art, Past & Present. LC 78-87379. (Illus.). 332p. 1973. Repr. of 1940 ed. lib. bdg. 35.00 (ISBN 0-306-71603-8). Da Capo.

--Outline of European Architecture. (Illus., Orig.). 1950. pap. 11.95 o.p. (ISBN 0-14-020109-2, Pelican). Penguin.

Pevsner, Stella. Call Me Heller, That's My Name. (gr. 4-6). 1981. pap. 1.95 (ISBN 0-671-43868-9). Archway.

--Cute Is a Four Letter Word. (gr. 7 up). 1981. pap. 1.95 (ISBN 0-671-42208-1). Archway.

--A Smart Kid Like You. LC 74-19320. 192p. (gr. 4-8). 1975. 10.95 (ISBN 0-395-28876-2, Clarion). HM.

Pevsner, Y. State-Monopoly Capitalism & the Labour Theory of Value. 390p. 1982. 7.95 (Pub. by Progress Pubs USSR). Imported Pubns.

Pexieder, Tomas, ed. Mechanisms of Cardiac Morphogenesis & Teratogenesis. (Perspectives in Cardiovascular Research Ser.: Vol. 5). (Illus.). 528p. 1981. text ed. 64.00 (ISBN 0-89004-460-0). Raven.

Pexton, Myron R., jt. auth. see Weiss, Robert R.

Peyman, Gholam A., et al, eds. Principles & Practice of Ophthalmology, 3 vols. (Illus.). 2000p. 1981. Set. text ed. 275.00 (ISBN 0-7216-7228-0); Vol. 1. text ed. 95.00 (ISBN 0-7216-7211-6); Vol. 2. text ed. 95.00 o. p. (ISBN 0-7216-7212-4); Vol. 3. text ed. 95.00 (ISBN 0-7216-7213-2). Saunders.

Peyo, pseud. Coloring Magic with Painter Smurf. (Illus.). 16p. (ps-3). 1983. 1.25 (ISBN 0-394-85621-X). Random.

--Romeo & Smurfette & Twelve Other Smurfy Stories. LC 82-60258. (Smurf Adventures Ser.). (Illus.). 48p. (gr. 4-7). 1983. 2.95 (ISBN 0-394-85618-X). Random.

--The Smurf Activity Book. Schwarz, Rae P. (Illus.). 64p. (gr. 1-5). 1983. 3.95 (ISBN 0-394-85383-0). Random.

Peyo. The Smurf Year-Round Coloring Book. (Illus.). 80p. (ps-3). 1983. 1.95 (ISBN 0-394-85644-9). Random.

Peyo, pseud. The Smurfs & Their Woodland Friends. LC 81-85940. (Chunky Bks.). (Illus.). 28p. (ps). 1983. pap. 2.95 (ISBN 0-394-85370-9). Random.

--Through the Seasons with Smurfette. LC 82-60093. (Smurf Hummingbird Bks.). (Illus.). 16p. (ps-3). 1983. 1.25 (ISBN 0-394-85620-1). Random.

Peyraud, J., jt. ed. see DeWitt, C.

Peyre, Henri & Seronde, Joseph, eds. Nine Classic French Plays. rev. ed. 1974. pap. text ed. 15.95x o.p. (ISBN 0-669-90241-1). Heath.

Peyrefitte, Roger. Knights of Malta. LC 59-12194. 1959. 15.95 (ISBN 0-87599-087-8). S G Phillips.

Peyser, Herbert F., jt. auth. see Biancolli, Louis L.

Peyton, K. M. Dear Fred. 1981. 9.95 (ISBN 0-399-20813-5, Philomel). Putnam Pub Group.

--Flambards. LC 68-26977. (Illus.). (gr. 6 up). 1968. PLB 4.99 o.s.i. (ISBN 0-529-00507-7, Philomel). Putnam Pub Group.

--Flambards Divided. 272p. 1982. 10.95 (ISBN 0-399-20864-X, Philomel). Putnam Pub Group.

--Going Home. (Illus.). 112p. 1982. 9.95 (ISBN 0-399-20889-5, Philomel). Putnam Pub Group.

--The Maplin Bird. 1980. 9.95 (ISBN 0-8398-2611-7, Gregg). G K Hall.

--A Midsummer Night's Death. (gr. 6 up). 1981. 8.95 o.p. (ISBN 0-399-20768-6, Philomel). Putnam Pub Group.

--A Pattern of Roses. LC 73-3387. (Illus.). 132p. (gr. 6 up). 1973. 10.53i (ISBN 0-690-61199-4, TYC-J). Har-Row.

--Prove Yourself a Hero. LC 78-18802. (gr. 6 up). 1978. 8.95 o.p. (ISBN 0-399-20836-4, Philomel). Putnam Pub Group.

Pezdek, Robert V. Public Employment Bibliography, Vol. 2. LC 73-620038. (ILR Bibliography Ser.: No. 11). 196p. 1973. pap. 3.00 (ISBN 0-87546-051-8); pap. 6.00 special hard bdg. (ISBN 0-87546-282-0). ILR Pr.

Pezzano, Chuck, jt. auth. see Sperber, Paula.

Pezzini, Wilma. The Tuscan Cookbook. LC 77-15809. 288p. 1982. 10.95 (ISBN 0-689-10866-4); pap. 6.95 (ISBN 0-689-70598-0, 279). Atheneum.

Pezzullo, Thomas R. & Brittingham, Barbara E. Salary Equity: Detecting Sex Bias in Salaries Among College & University Professors. LC 78-24634. 176p. 1979. 21.95 (ISBN 0-669-02770-7). Lexington Bks.

Pezzuti, Ella, ed. see Stewart, Jeffrey R., et al.

Pfadt, Robert. Animals Without Backbones. (Beginning-to-Read Bks.). (Illus.). (gr. 2-4). 1967. pap. 1.50 o.s.i. (ISBN 0-695-30428-3); PLB 3.39 o.s.i. (ISBN 0-695-80428-6). Follett.

Pfadt, Robert E. Fundamentals of Applied Entomology. 3rd ed. (Illus.). 1976. text ed. 28.95x (ISBN 0-02-395110-9). Macmillan.

Pfaffenberger, Bryan. Caste in Tamil Culture: The Religious Foundations of Sudra Domination in Tamil Sri Lanka. (Foreign Comparative Studies Program, South Asian Ser.: No. 7). (Orig.). 1982. pap. 12.00x (ISBN 0-915984-84-9). Syracuse U Foreign Comp.

Pfaffenberger, C., et al. Guide Dogs for the Blind: Their Selection, Development & Training. (Developments in Animal & Veterinary Sciences Ser.: Vol. 1). 1976. 38.50 (ISBN 0-444-41520-3). Elsevier.

Pfafflin, James & Ziegler, Edward, eds. Advances in Environmental Science & Engineering, Vol. 4. 174p. 1981. 68.00 (ISBN 0-677-16250-2). Gordon.

Pfafflin, Sheila M., jt. ed. see Briscoe, Anne.

Pfahl, P. Blair, Jr., jt. auth. see Pfahl, Peter B.

Pfahl, Peter B. & Pfahl, P. Blair, Jr. The Retail Florist Business. 4th ed. 500p. 1983. 19.35 (ISBN 0-8134-2250-7); text ed. 14.50x (ISBN 0-686-83989-7). Interstate.

Pfaltz, C. R., ed. Follows. (Advances in Oto-Rhino-Laryngology Ser.: Vol. 32). (Illus.). viii, 192p. 1983. 78.00 (ISBN 3-8055-3701-8). S Karger.

--Neurophysiological & Clinical Aspects of Vestibular Disorders. (Advances in Oto-Rhino-Laryngology: Vol. 30). (Illus.). viii, 250p. 1983. 90.00 (ISBN 3-8055-3607-0). S Karger.

Pfaltz, John. Computer Data Structures. (Illus.). 1977. text ed. 33.95 (ISBN 0-07-049743-5, C); instr's. manual 11.00 (ISBN 0-07-049744-3). McGraw.

Pfaltzgraff, Robert & Ra'anan, Uri. The U. S. Defense Mobilization Infrastructure: Problems & Priorities. 292p. 1982. lib. bdg. 29.50 (ISBN 0-208-01984-7, Archon). Shoe String.

Pfaltzgraff, Robert, Jr., ed. Study of International Relations: A Guide to Information Sources. LC 73-17511. (International Relations Information Guide Ser.: Vol. 5). 220p. 1977. 42.00x (ISBN 0-8103-1331-6). Gale.

Pfaltzgraff, Robert L., Jr. & Ra'anan, Uri, eds. The Projection of Power: Perspectives, Perceptions, & Problems. 341p. 1982. 32.50 (ISBN 0-208-01954-5, Archon). Shoe String.

Pfanner, Helmut F. Exile in New York: German & Austrian Writers After 1933. (Illus.). 272p. 1983. 18.95 (ISBN 0-8143-1727-8). Wayne St U Pr.

Pfannkuch, Hans-Olaf. Elsevier's Dictionary of Hydrogeology. (Eng., Fr., & Ger.). 1969. 42.75 (ISBN 0-444-40717-0). Elsevier.

Pfanzagl, J. Contributions to a General Asymptotic Statistical Theory. (Lecture Notes in Statistics Ser.: Vol. 13). (Illus.). 315p. 1983. pap. 16.80 (ISBN 0-387-90776-9). Springer-Verlag.

Pfatteicher, Philip H. Commentary on the Occasional Services. LC 82-48542. 336p. 1983. 16.95 (ISBN 0-8006-0697-3, 1-1697). Fortress.

Pfeffer, Irving & Klock, David R. Perspectives on Insurance. (Illus.). 448p. 1974. ref. ed. 22.95 o.p. (ISBN 0-13-661066-8). P-H.

Pfeffer, J., et al. Basic Spoken German Grammar. LC 73-8875. (Illus.). 384p. 1974. text ed. 18.95 (ISBN 0-13-061994-9); tapes o.p. 150.00 (ISBN 0-13-062182-X); wkbk. & guide to tapes 9.50 (ISBN 0-13-062000-9). P-H.

Pfeffer, J. Alan. Grunddeutsch: Basic (Spoken) German Dictionary for Everyday Usage. LC 73-116147. (German Ser). (Ger). 1970. ref. ed. 9.95 o.p. (ISBN 0-13-367755-9). P-H.

Pfeffer, Jeffrey. Organizational Design. Mackenzie, Kenneth D., ed. LC 77-86024. (Organizational Behavior Ser.). (Illus.). 1978. pap. text ed. 13.95x (ISBN 0-88295-453-9). Harlan Davidson.

Pfeffer, Leo. Creeds in Competition: A Creative Force in American Culture. LC 78-2308. 1978. Repr. of 1958 ed. lib. bdg. 19.00x (ISBN 0-313-20349-0, PFCC). Greenwood.

Pfeffer, Susan B. Courage, Dana. LC 82-72821. (Illus.). 160p. (gr. 4-8). 1983. 10.95 (ISBN 0-440-00922-7). Delacorte.

--Just Between Us. LC 79-53606. (gr. 4-7). 1980. 9.95 o.p. (ISBN 0-440-05045-6); PLB 9.89 (ISBN 0-440-05046-4). Delacorte.

--Kid Power. LC 77-1975. (gr. 4-6). 1977. PLB 8.90 s&l (ISBN 0-531-00123-7). Watts.

--What Do You Do When Your Mouth Won't Open? (gr. 4-8). 1982. pap. 2.25 (ISBN 0-440-49320-X, YB). Dell.

Pfeffermann, Guy P. & Webb, Richard C. The Distribution of Income in Brazil. (World Bank Staff Working Paper: No. 356). 116p. 1979. 5.00 (ISBN 0-686-36048-6, WP-0356). World Bank.

Pfeifeer, Ernst F., jt. auth. see Federlin, Konrad.

Pfeiffer & Banks. Dr. Pfeiffer's Total Nutrition. 1980. 9.95 o.p. (ISBN 0-671-24059-5, 24059). S&S.

Pfeiffer, C. Boyd. Tackle Craft. LC 73-82959. (Sportsmen's Classics Ser.). (Illus.). 288p. 1974. 10.00 o.p. (ISBN 0-517-50615-7); pap. 7.95 o.p. (ISBN 0-517-52136-9). Crown.

--Tackle Craft. write for info. N Lyons Bks.

Pfeiffer, Carl. Mental & Elemental Nutrients. 1975. 11.95x (ISBN 0-87983-114-6). Cancer Control Soc.

Pfeiffer, Carl C. & Smythies, John R., eds. International Review of Neurobiology, Vol. 24. (Serial Publication). Date not set. price not set (ISBN 0-12-366824-7). Acad Pr.

Pfeiffer, Carl J. Cancer of the Esophagus. 176p. 1982. 51.50 (ISBN 0-8493-6213-X). CRC Pr.

Pfeiffer, Charles F. Atlas Biblico: Rustica. (Span.). 1977. pap. 2.75 (ISBN 0-8297-0498-1). Life Pubs Intl.

--The Bible Atlas. LC 60-15536. 1975. 16.95 (ISBN 0-8054-1129-1). Broadman.

--Epistle to the Hebrews. (Everyman's Bible Commentary Ser.). (Orig.). 1968. pap. 4.50 (ISBN 0-8024-2058-3). Moody.

--Outline of Old Testament History. (Orig.). 1960. pap. 4.95 (ISBN 0-8024-6265-0). Moody.

Pfeiffer, Charles F. & Vos, Howard F. Wycliffe Historical Geography of Bible Lands. 1967. 19.95 (ISBN 0-8024-9699-7). Moody.

Pfeiffer, Charles F., ed. see Gama, Roberto.

Pfeiffer, Charles F., et al, eds. Wycliffe Bible Encyclopedia, 2 vols. (Illus.). 1875p. 1975. 49.95 (ISBN 0-8024-9697-0). Moody.

Pfeiffer, Eric, jt. auth. see Busse, Ewald W.

Pfeiffer, Isobel L. & Dunlap, Jane B. Supervision of Teachers: A Guide to Improving Instruction. LC 82-8150. 248p. 1982. lib. bdg. 22.50 (ISBN 0-89774-045-9). Oryx Pr.

Pfeiffer, J. William & Jones, John E. Reference Guide to Handbooks & Annuals. rev. ed. LC 75-14661. 166p. 1981. pap. 10.50 (ISBN 0-88390-069-6). Univ Assocs.

Pfeiffer, J. William & Jones, John E., eds. Annual Handbook for Group Facilitators, 1974. LC 73-92841. (Series in Human Relations Training). 289p. 1974. pap. 21.50 (ISBN 0-88390-074-2); looseleaf ntbk. 49.50 (ISBN 0-88390-082-3). Univ Assocs.

--Annual Handbook for Group Facilitators, 1972. LC 73-92841. (Series in Human Relations Training). 271p. 1972. pap. 21.50 (ISBN 0-88390-072-6); looseleaf ntbk. 49.50 (ISBN 0-88390-085-8). Univ Assocs.

--Annual Handbook for Group Facilitators, 1976. LC 73-92841. (Series in Human Relations Training). 292p. 1976. pap. 21.50 (ISBN 0-88390-088-2); looseleaf notebk. 49.50 (ISBN 0-88390-087-4). Univ Assocs.

--The Annual Handbook for Group Facilitators, 1980. LC 73-92841. (Series in Human Relations Training). 296p. 1980. pap. 21.50 (ISBN 0-88390-097-1); looseleaf notebook 49.50 (ISBN 0-88390-096-3). Univ Assocs.

--Annual Handbook for Group Facilitators, 1978. LC 73-92841. (Series in Human Relations Training). 295p. 1978. pap. 21.50 (ISBN 0-88390-099-8); looseleaf notebook 49.50 (ISBN 0-88390-098-X). Univ Assocs.

--A Handbook of Structured Experiences for Human Relations Training, 8 vols. LC 73-92840. (Series in Human Relations Training). 1973-81. pap. 10.50 ea.; Vol. 1. Rev. Ed. (ISBN 0-88390-041-6); Vol. 2. Rev. Ed. (ISBN 0-88390-042-4); Vol. 3. Rev. Ed. (ISBN 0-88390-043-2); Vol. 4. (ISBN 0-88390-044-0). Vol. 5 (ISBN 0-88390-045-9). Vol. 6 (ISBN 0-88390-046-7). Vol. 7 (ISBN 0-88390-047-5). Vol.8 (ISBN 0-88390-048-3). Univ Assocs.

--A Handbook of Structured Experiences for Human Relations Training, Vol. VIII. LC 73-92840. (Ser. in Human Relations Training). 142p. (Orig.). 1981. pap. 10.50 (ISBN 0-88390-048-3). Univ Assocs.

Pfeiffer, J. William, jt. ed. see Jones, John E.

Pfeiffer, John. The Emergence of Society: A Prehistory of the Establishment. new ed. LC 76-27308. (Illus.). 528p. 1977. text ed. 22.50 (ISBN 0-07-049758-3, C); pap. text ed. 15.00 (ISBN 0-07-049759-1). McGraw.

Pfeiffer, John E. The Creative Explosion: An Inquiry into the Origins of Art & Religion. LC 82-47531. (Illus.). 320p. 1982. 28.80i (ISBN 0-06-013345-7, HarpT). Har-Row.

--The Search for Early Man. LC 63-16371. (Horizon Caravel Bks.). 154p. (YA) (gr. 7 up). 1963. PLB 14.89 o.p. (ISBN 0-06-024696-0, HarpJ). Har-Row.

Pfeiffer, Robert H. State Letters of Assyria. 1935. pap. 23.00 (ISBN 0-527-02680-8). Kraus Repr.

Pfeiffer, Steven. Neuroscience Approached Through Cell Culture. 248p. 1982. 75.00 (ISBN 0-8493-6340-3). CRC Pr.

Pfeilschifter, B. & Schmalz, N. Shen-Fu's Story. 3.50 o.p. (ISBN 0-8199-0130-X, L38787). Franciscan Herald.

Pfeuty, Pierre & Toulouse, Gerard. Introduction to the Renormalization Group & to Critical Phenomena. Barton, G., tr. LC 76-26111. 1977. 42.95 (ISBN 0-471-99440-5, Pub. by Wiley-Interscience). Wiley.

Pfiffner, James P. The President, the Budget, & Congress: Impoundment & the 1974 Budget Act. (Special Studies in Public Policy & Public Systems Management). 1979. lib. bdg. 20.00 (ISBN 0-89158-468-4); pap. text ed. 9.00 (ISBN 0-89158-495-1). Westview.

Pfister, Adrienne, jt. auth. see Schick, Allen.

Pfister, G., jt. auth. see Mort, J.

Pflaum-Connor, Susanna. The Development of Language & Reading in the Young Child. 2nd ed. Heilman, Arthur W., ed. (Early Childhood Education Ser.). 1978. text ed. 14.95 (ISBN 0-675-08392-3). Merrill.

Pflaum-Connor, Susanna, ed. Aspects of Reading Education. LC 77-95250. (National Society for the Study of Educ., Series on Contemp Educ. Issues). 1978. 19.95 (ISBN 0-8211-1517-0); text ed. 17.95 (ISBN 0-685-04964-7). McCutchan.

Pfleeger, Charles P. Machine Organization: An Introduction to the Structure & Programming of Computer Systems. LC 81-11380. 227p. 1982. text ed. 25.95 (ISBN 0-471-07970-7). Wiley.

Pfleger, Reinhardt. Studien Zur Konstituierung Einer Rezeptionsanalytisch Fundierten Literaturdidaktik. 347p. (Ger.). 1982. write for info. (ISBN 3-8204-6296-1). P Lang Pubs.

Pfloog, Jan. Kittens. LC 77-74471. (Illus.). (ps-k). 1977. 3.50 (ISBN 0-394-83590-5, BYR). Random.

--Puppies. LC 78-64608. (Board Bks). (Illus.). (ps). 1979. 3.50 (ISBN 0-394-84132-8, BYR). Random.

--Puppies Are Like That. LC 74-2542. (Picturebacks Ser.). (Illus.). 32p. (Orig.). (ps-1). 1975. pap. 1.50 (ISBN 0-394-82923-9, BYR). Random.

Pflug, G., jt. ed. see Grossman, W.

Pfnister, Allan O. Planning for Higher Education: Background & Application. LC 76-5906. (Special Studies in Higher Education Ser). 1976. 29.50 (ISBN 0-89158-035-2). Westview.

Pfohl, Stephen J. Predicting Dangerousness. LC 77-25742. (Illus.). 272p. 1978. 23.95 (ISBN 0-669-01509-1). Lexington Bks.

Pforr, Manfred & Limbrunner, Alfred. Breeding Birds of Europe: Vol. 2-Sandgrouse to Crows. Robertson, Iian, ed. Stoneman, Richard, tr. from Ger. (Illus.). 394p. 1983. 24.00 (ISBN 0-88072-027-1). Tanager Bks.

Pfuhl, John J. Oil & Its' Impact: A Case Study of Community Change. LC 80-5090. 164p. 1980. text ed. 19.50 (ISBN 0-8191-1043-4); pap. text ed. 9.75 (ISBN 0-8191-1044-2). U Pr of Amer.

Pfund, P. A. & Yao, S. C., eds. Tube Bundle Thermal-Hydraulics. 73p. 1982. 20.00 (G00212). ASME.

Pfund, P. A., jt. ed. see Coleman, H. W.

Pfurtscheller, G. & Buser, P., eds. Rhythmic EEG Activities & Cortical Function. (Developments in Neuroscience Ser.: Vol. 10). 1980. 57.00 (ISBN 0-444-80028-X). Elsevier.

Phadnis, Urmila. Religion & Politics in Sri Lanka. LC 76-6252. 1976. 17.50x o.p. (ISBN 0-88386-754-0). South Asia Bks.

Phaigh, Bethal. Gestalt & the Wisdom of the Kahunas. LC 82-50928. 144p. 1983. pap. 5.95 (ISBN 0-87516-498-6). De Vorss.

Phair, Anthony. Amazon II: Amazing Secret Discoveries by an Expedition to the Far Amazon. (Illus.). 267p. 17.95 (ISBN 0-9608114-0-0). USA Intl Pub.

Phalon, Richard. The Takeover Barons of Wall Street: Inside the Billion-Dollar Merger Game. 264p. 1981. 13.95 (ISBN 0-399-12661-9). Putnam Pub Group.

Phan Boi Chau & Ho Chi Minh. Reflections from Captivity: Phan Boi Chau's "Prison Notes" & Ho Chi Minh's "Prison Diary". Marr, David G., ed. Jenkins, Christopher, et al, trs. LC 78-1369. (Southeast Asia Translations Ser.: Vol. 1). 113p. 1978. 12.00x (ISBN 0-8214-0375-3, 82-82707); pap. 5.00x (ISBN 0-8214-0386-9, 82-82725). Ohio U Pr.

Phan-Thuy, N., et al. Industrial Capacity & Employment Promotion: Case Studies of Sri Lanka, Nigeria, Morocco & an Overall Survey of Other Developing Countries. 404p. 1981. text ed. 44.00x (ISBN 0-566-00433-X). Gower Pub Ltd.

Phantom, D. S. & Da Gama, Bosco, eds. The Best of Kitty Torture Quarterly Magazine. 64p. 1982. pap. 2.95 (ISBN 0-934646-07-4). S & S Pr TX.

Phanuel, I. see Coscia, Louis W., pseud.

Phares, Donald, ed. A Decent Home & Suitable Environment for Every American. LC 77-2780. 224p. 1977. prof ref 18.50x (ISBN 0-88410-357-9). Ballinger Pub.

Pharmaceutical Society of Great Britain, ed. British Pharmacopoeia, 2 vols. 2nd ed. 1980. 165.00 (ISBN 0-11-320688-7, Pub. by Pharmaceutical). Vol. 1, 540 Pg. Vol. 2, 680 Pg. Rittenhouse.

Pharmaceutical Technology Conference, New York, 1982. Proceedings. 700p. 1982. pap. text ed. 75.00 (ISBN 0-943330-01-7). Pharm Tech.

Pharr, Susan J. Political Women in Japan: The Search for a Place in Political Life. LC 80-12984. 275p. 1981. 27.50x (ISBN 0-520-04071-6). U of Cal Pr.

Phatak, Arvind. International Dimensions of Management. Ricks, Davis A., ed. (International Dimensions of Business). 160p. 1982. text ed. 8.95x (ISBN 0-534-01317-1). Kent Pub Co.

Phelan, Gerald B. Saint Thomas & Analogy. (Aquinas Lecture). 1941. 7.95 (ISBN 0-87462-105-4). Marquette.

Phelan, James. Scandals, Scamps, & Scoundrels: The Casebook of An Investigative Reporter. 1982. 13.95 (ISBN 0-394-48196-8). Random.

Phelan, James & Pozen, Robert. The Company State: The Report on Dupont in Delaware. LC 70-184474. (Ralph Nader Study Group Reports). 1973. pap. 3.95 o.p. (ISBN 0-670-23358-7, Grossman). Penguin.

Phelan, John L. The Millennial Kingdom of the Franciscans in the New World. 2nd rev ed. 1970. 28.50x (ISBN 0-520-01404-9). U of Cal Pr.

Phelan, Marilyn. Museums & the Law. LC 81-22912. (Illus.). 1982. 21.00x (ISBN 0-910050-60-0). AASLH.

Phelan, Richard M. Fundamentals of Mechanical Design. 3rd ed. LC 79-98487. 1970. text ed. 35.95 (ISBN 0-07-049776-1, C); solutions manual 25.00 (ISBN 0-07-049790-7). McGraw.

Phelan, Thomas P. Catholics in Colonial Days. LC 74-145706. Repr. of 1935 ed. 34.00x (ISBN 0-8103-3685-5). Gale.

Phelger, Marjorie, jt. auth. see Phleger, Frederick.

Phelon, Sheldon & Marsar, Inc. Phelon's Women's Specialty Stores 1983-1984. 8th ed. 1982. 80.00 (ISBN 0-686-23021-3). P S & M Inc.

Phelps, Austin. The Still Hour. 1979. pap. 2.95 (ISBN 0-85151-202-X). Banner of Truth.

Phelps, E. R., jt. auth. see Wolfe, John H.

Phelps, Edmund S., ed. Altruism, Morality, & Economic Theory. LC 74-79448. 242p. 1975. 10.50x (ISBN 0-87154-659-0). Russell Sage.

--The Microeconomic Foundations of Employment & Inflation Theory. 1973. 17.95x (ISBN 0-393-09326-3). Norton.

Phelps, Elizabeth S. The Silent Partner: A Novel. Bd. with The Tenth of January. 352p. 1983. pap. 6.95 (ISBN 0-935312-08-0). Feminist Pr.

Phelps, Gilbert. The Tragedy of Paraguay. LC 74-21750. 300p. 1975. 25.00 (ISBN 0-312-81340-6). St Martin.

Phelps, Gilbert, ed. see Herriot, James, et al.

Phelps, Gilbert, intro. by see Waterton, Charles.

Phelps, Humphrey. The Forest of Dean. 192p. 1982. pap. text ed. 8.25x (ISBN 0-904387-86-0, Pub. by Sutton England). Humanities.

Phelps, J. Alfred. On Being Black in America. LC 77-94105. 1978. pap. 2.95 o.p. (ISBN 0-89260-119-1). Hwong Pub.

Phelps, John & Philbin. Complete Building Construction. new ed. (Audel Ser.). 1983. 19.95 (ISBN 0-672-23377-0). Bobbs.

Phelps, John, ed. see Herriot, James, et al.

Phelps, L. Applied Consumption Analysis. 1974. 37.50 (ISBN 0-444-10663-4); pap. 18.00 (ISBN 0-444-10714-2). Elsevier.

Phelps, Leland, jt. ed. see Loram, Ian.

Phelps, Lynn & Dewine, Sue. Interpersonal Communication Journal. LC 76-3576. (Illus.). 200p. 1976. pap. text ed. 12.50 (ISBN 0-8299-0102-7); instrs.' manual avail. (ISBN 0-8299-0566-9). West Pub.

Phelps, M. F., jt. ed. see Heiss, W. D.

Phelps, Robert, jt. auth. see Agee, James.

Phelps, Stanlee & Austin, Nancy. The Assertive Woman. 5.95 o.p. (ISBN 0-686-92303-0, 6350). Hazelden.

Phelps, Steven. Art & Artefacts of the Pacific, Africa & the Americas: The James Hooper Collection. (Illus.). 487p. 1976. 52.50x o.p. (ISBN 0-8476-1368-2). Rowman.

--Oceanic Art. LC 81-19078. (Illus.). 172p. Date not set. text ed. cancelled (ISBN 0-89659-238-3). Abbeville Pr.

Phelps, Thomas R. Juvenile Delinquency: A Contemporary View. LC 74-31511. 300p. 1976. text ed. 21.95x o.p. (ISBN 0-673-16313-X). Scott F.

Phelps, Thomas R., et al. Introduction to Criminal Justice. LC 78-31325. 1979. 20.95x o.p. (ISBN 0-673-16312-1). Scott F.

Phelps, William D. Alta California, 1840-1842: The Journal & Observations of William Dane Phelps. Busch, Briton C, ed. LC 82-71376. (Western Lands & Water Ser.: XIII). (Illus.). 364p. 1983. 29.50 (ISBN 0-87062-143-2). A H Clark.

Phelps, Winston. Cars, Kids, Cape Codders, & Other Yarns. 1983. 8.95 (ISBN 0-533-05389-7). Vantage.

Phelps Brown, E. H. The Inequality of Pay. LC 76-7768. 36.00x (ISBN 0-520-03380-9). U of Cal Pr.

Phenice, Lillian A., jt. ed. see Kostelnik, Marjorie J.

Phenix, Philip H. Realms of Meaning: A Philosophy of the Curriculum for General Education. (Curriculum & Methods in Education Ser.). 1964. text ed. 32.50 (ISBN 0-07-049781-8, C). McGraw.

Phenix, Philip H., tr. see Manach, Jorge.

Pherson, Dave Mac. The Incredible Cover-Up. 1975. 8.95 (ISBN 0-88270-143-6); pap. 3.95 (ISBN 0-88270-144-4). Omega Pubns Or.

Phialas, Peter G. Shakespeare's Romantic Comedies: The Development of Their Form & Meaning. xvi, 314p. 1969. pap. 6.00x (ISBN 0-8078-4043-2). U of NC Pr.

Phibbs, Brendan. The Human Heart: A Consumer's Guide to Cardiac Care. LC 82-2119. (Medical Library). (Illus.). 240p. 1982. pap. 8.95 (ISBN 0-452-25337-3, 3942-7). Mosby.

Phifer, Kate G. Track Talk: An Introduction to Thoroughbred Horse Racing. LC 77-94198. (Illus.). 1978. 12.00 o.p. (ISBN 0-88331-098-8). Luce.

Phifer, Keith R. The Blind Date. LC 78-61213. (Illus.). 1978. pap. 1.95 (ISBN 0-930678-02-8). Key Ray Pub.

--The Singles Directory. 3rd ed. 1978. 1.00 (ISBN 0-930678-01-X). Key Ray Pub.

--Whole in One. King, Bob, ed. (Illus.). 1977. pap. 3.95 (ISBN 0-930678-00-1). Key Ray Pub.

Phifer, Keith R., ed. see Way, Zilla S., et al.

Phifer, Kenneth G. Tales of Human Frailty & the Gentleness of God. LC 73-16914. (Orig.). 1974. pap. 1.00 (ISBN 0-8042-2197-9). John Knox.

Phiillifent, John T. King of Argent. (Science Fiction Ser). 1981. pap. 2.25 o.p. (ISBN 0-87997-649-7, UE1649). DAW Bks.

Phil, D., jt. auth. see McPhee, J. R.

Phil, M., jt. auth. see Morgan, Carlisle L.

Philbert, Francois J., jt. auth. see Vitry, Aubert De.

Philbin, jt. auth. see Phelps, John.

Philbin, Tobias R. Admiral Von Hipper: The Inconvenient Hero. (The World of History Ser.: Vol. 1). 235p. 1982. pap. text ed. 27.75x (ISBN 90-6032-200-2, Pub. by B R Gruner Netherlands). Humanities.

Philbin, Tom. Basic Plumbing. (Illus.). 1977. 18.95 (ISBN 0-87909-065-0). Reston.

Philbin, Tom & Koelbel, Fritz. The Nothing Left Out Home Improvement Book. LC 76-16515. (Illus.). 336p. 1976. 8.95 o.p. (ISBN 0-13-624353-3). P-H.

Philbrick, Helen, jt. auth. see Philbrick, John.

Philbrick, John & Philbrick, Helen. Gardening for Health & Nutrition: An Introduction to the Method of Bio-Dynamic Gardening Inaugurated by Rudolf Steiner. (Illus.). 93p. 1971. pap. 4.40 (ISBN 0-8334-1715-0, Pub. by Steinerbooks NY). Anthroposophic.

Philbrick, Marianne, ed. see Cooper, James F.

Philbrick, Thomas. St. John de Crevecoeur. (U. S. Authors Ser.: No. 154). 10.95 o.p. (ISBN 0-8057-0191-5, Twayne). G K Hall.

Philbrick, Thomas, ed. see Cooper, James F.

Philby, H. St. John. The Heart of Arabia, 2 vols. 1983. Repr. Set. 65.00x (ISBN 0-7146-3072-1, F Cass Co). Biblio Dist.

Philby, J. B. Arabian Highlands. LC 76-10643. (Middle East in the 20th Century). 1976. Repr. of 1952 ed. lib. bdg. 75.00 (ISBN 0-306-70765-9). Da Capo.

Philby, Kim. My Silent War. (Espionage-Intelligence Library). 224p. 1983. pap. 2.75 (ISBN 0-345-30843-3). Ballantine.

Philcox, Phil & Boe, Beverly. The Great Castle Hotels of Europe. (Illus.). 1983. 17.95 (ISBN 0-89651-268-1). Icarus.

Philip, A. Butt, jt. auth. see Bayliss, B. T.

Philip, A. E., jt. auth. see McCulloch, J. W.

Philip, A. G. & Hayes, D. S., eds. Astronomical Oaraneters fir Globular Clusters: IAU Colloquium, No. 88. 614p. (Orig.). 1981. 38.00 (ISBN 0-9607902-2-5); pap. 27.00 (ISBN 0-9607902-1-7). Davis Pr.

Philip, A. T. & Sivaji Rao, K. H. Indian Government & Politics. 299p. 1981. 19.95x (ISBN 0-940500-45-0, Pub. by Sterling India). Asia Bk Corp.

Philip, Alex. Dicken's Honeymoon & Where He Spent It. LC 72-6507. (Studies in Dickens, No. 52). 1972. Repr. of 1912 ed. lib. bdg. 22.95x (ISBN 0-8383-1619-0). Haskell.

Philip, Allan A. American-Danish Private International Law. LC 57-6015. (Bilateral Studies in Private International Law: No. 7). 80p. 1957. 15.00 (ISBN 0-379-11407-0). Oceana.

Philip, Andre. Counsel from an Ally: Reflections on Changes Within the Atlantic Community. LC 66-14033. 1966. 2.50 o.p. (ISBN 0-8262-0045-1). U of Mo Pr.

Philip, Davis. X-Ray Symposium 1981. 76p. 1981. pap. 8.00 (ISBN 0-9607902-0-9). Davis Pr.

Philip, Franklin, tr. see De Condillac, Etienne Bonnot.

Philip, Neil. A Fine Anger: A Critical Introduction to the Work of Alan Garner. 192p. (gr. 8 up). 1981. 14.95 (ISBN 0-399-20828-3, Philomel). Putnam Pub Group.

Philip, Thangam E. Modern Cookery for Teaching & the Trade, Vol. 1. 3rd ed. (Illus.). 1062p. 1981. pap. text ed. 30.00x (ISBN 0-86131-284-8, Pub. by Orient Longman Ltd India). Apt Bks.

--Modern Cookery for Teaching & the Trade, Vol. 2. (Illus.). 824p. 1982. pap. text ed. 30.00x (ISBN 0-86125-158-X, Pub. by Orient Longman Ltd India). Apt Bks.

Philipp, P. F., jt. ed. see Shaner, W. W.

Philippakis, A. S. & Kazmier, L. J. Advanced COBOL for Information Systems. (Illus.). 608p. 1982. 27.95x (ISBN 0-07-049806-7); instr's. manual 7.00 (ISBN 0-07-049807-5). McGraw.

Philippakis, A. S., jt. auth. see Kazmier, Leonard J.

Philippakis, Andreas & Kazmier, Leonard. Program Design Concepts with Application in COBOL. (Illus.). 240p. 1983. text ed. 22.95 (ISBN 0-07-049808-3, C). McGraw.

Philippakis, Andreas S. & Kazmier, Leonard J. Cobol for Business Applications. (Illus.). 320p. 1973. text ed. 21.95 (ISBN 0-07-049768-0, C); instr's. manual 7.95 (ISBN 0-07-049769-9). McGraw.

--Information Systems Through COBOL. 2nd ed. (Illus.). 1978. text ed. 22.95 (ISBN 0-07-049791-5, C); instructor's manual 7.95 (ISBN 0-07-049792-3). McGraw.

--Structured COBOL. 2nd ed. Stewart, Charles E., ed. (Illus.). 448p. 1981. pap. text ed. 2.95 (ISBN 0-07-049801-6); instr's. manual 12.95 (ISBN 0-07-049802-4). McGraw.

Philippe, jt. ed. see Ficat.

Philippe, Joseph. Coffee. (Q Books: Where Do Things Come from?). (Illus.). 1978. 3.95 o.p. (ISBN 0-8467-0443-9, Pub. by Two Continents). Hippocrene Bks.

--Cotton. (Q Books: Where Do Things Come from?). (Illus.). 1978. 3.95 o.p. (ISBN 0-8467-0444-7, Pub. by Two Continents). Hippocrene Bks.

Philippe, Richard, jt. auth. see Urban, Ivan.

Philippe, Robert. Political Graphics: Art As A Weapon. Ramsay, James, tr. LC 81-20540. Orig. Title: Il Linguaggio della Grafica Politica. (Illus.). 334p. 1982. 60.00 (ISBN 0-89659-272-3). Abbeville Pr.

Philippon, Catherine, tr. see Vossler, Otto.

Philips, Barbara. Don't Call Me Fatso. LC 79-23888. (Life & Living from a Child's Point of View Ser.). (Illus.). (gr. k-5). 1980. PLB 13.30 (ISBN 0-8172-1350-3). Raintree Pubs.

Philips, Clare, jt. auth. see Rachman, S. J.

Philips, David. Crime & Authority in Victorian England: The Black Country 1835-1860. 321p. 1977. 20.00x o.p. (ISBN 0-87471-866-X). Rowman.

Philips, J. P. & Dacons, J. C. Organic Electronic Spectral Data. 1152p. Repr. of 1976 ed. text ed. 54.50 (ISBN 0-471-02305-1). Krieger.

--Organic Electronic Spectral Data, Vol. 11. 1072p. Repr. of 1975 ed. text ed. 49.50 (ISBN 0-471-68802-9). Krieger.

Philips, Judson. Five Roads to Death. (Peter Styles Mystery & a Red Badge Novel of Suspense Ser.). 1977. 6.95 o.p. (ISBN 0-396-07472-3). Dodd.

--Target for Tragedy: A Peter Styles Mystery Novel. LC 82-5088. 1982. 10.95 (ISBN 0-396-08079-0). Dodd.

Philips, L. Applied Consumption Analysis. Date not set. price not set (ISBN 0-444-86531-4). Elsevier.

Philips, Susan U. The Invisible Culture: Communication in Classroom & Community on the Warm Springs Indian Reservation. LC 81-20842. (Research on Teaching Ser.). 128p. 1982. 19.50tx (ISBN 0-582-28361-2); pap. 9.95 (ISBN 0-582-28360-4). Longman.

Philipson, Julia, jt. auth. see Edes, Shirley.

Philipson, Morris. Secret Understandings. abr. ed. 384p. 1983. 16.95 (ISBN 0-671-46619-4). S&S.

--The Wallpaper Fox. 1978. pap. 1.95 o.p. (ISBN 0-515-04436-9). Jove Pubns.

Philipson, Morris & Gudel, Paul J., eds. Aesthetics Today. rev. ed. 1980. pap. 9.95 (ISBN 0-452-00574-4, F574, Mer). NAL.

Philipson, Morris, ed. see Huxley, Aldous L.

Philliber, Susan G., et al. Social Research. LC 79-91097. 189p. 1980. pap. text ed. 8.50 (ISBN 0-87581-252-X). Peacock Pubs.

Philliber, William w. Appalachian Migrants in Urban America: Cultural Conflict or Ethnic Group Formation. 156p. 1981. 22.95 (ISBN 0-03-059687-4). Praeger.

Phillimore, J. S., ed. see Statius.

Phillimore, W. P. How to Write the History of a Family: A Guide for the Genealogist. LC 70-179653. (Illus.). viii, 206p. 1972. Repr. of 1876 ed. 37.00x (ISBN 0-8103-3117-9). Gale.

Phillimore, William P. & Fry, E. A. Index to Changes of Name. LC 68-27180. 1969. Repr. of 1905 ed. 34.00x (ISBN 0-8103-3132-2). Gale.

Phillion, Numa. Numa: A Life Reading. 224p. 1983. 12.50 (ISBN 0-89962-303-4). Todd & Honeywell.

Phillip, Alban M. Prison-Breakers: A Book of Escapes from Captivity. LC 76-174093. (Illus.). 1971. Repr. of 1927 ed. 34.00x (ISBN 0-8103-3803-3). Gale.

Phillip, Perry P., jt. auth. see Shaner, W. W.

Phillipov, Vladimir, tr. see Levchev, Lyubomir.

Phillips. Baroque Art. (Pitman Art Ser.: Vol. 61). pap. 1.50 o.p. (ISBN 0-448-00570-0, G&D). Putnam Pub Group.

--Evaluation in Education. 1968. pap. text ed. 4.95 o.p. (ISBN 0-675-09688-X). Merrill.

--Viruses Associated with Human Cancer. 896p. 1983. 95.00 (ISBN 0-8247-1738-4). Dekker.

Phillips & Judd. How to Fall Out of Love. 192p. 1982. pap. 2.95 (ISBN 0-446-31038-7). Warner Bks.

Phillips, jt. auth. see Denning.

Phillips, A. R., tr. see Petzold, A. & Rohrs, M.

Phillips, Allan, et al. The Birds of Arizona. LC 64-17265. (Illus.). 1964. 30.00 (ISBN 0-8165-0012-6). U of Ariz Pr.

Phillips, Almarin, ed. Promoting Competition in Regulated Markets. (Studies in the Regulation of Economic Activity). 397p. 1975. 21.95 (ISBN 0-8157-7052-9); pap. 9.95 (ISBN 0-8157-7051-0). Brookings.

Phillips, Amelia, ed. see Houston, Ralph.

Phillips, Ann V. & Phillips, David A. The Soil to Psyche Recipe Book: New Age Menus from Australia. LC 77-79908. (Illus., Orig.). 1977. pap. 3.95 o.p. (ISBN 0-912800-44-5). Woodbridge Pr.

Phillips, Anthony C., jt. ed. see Coggins, Richard J.

Phillips, Arnold. One Man's Opinion. 1980. 5.95 o.p. (ISBN 0-533-04478-2). Vantage.

Phillips, Audrey E., ed. see University of California, Berkeley, Library.

Phillips, Barty, jt. auth. see Hills, Nicolas.

Phillips, Bernard. Sociology: From Concepts to Practice. (Illus.). 1979. text ed. 27.50 (ISBN 0-07-049787-7, C); instr's. manual 15.00 (ISBN 0-07-049788-5); study guide 11.95 (ISBN 0-07-049793-1); tests 6.50 (ISBN 0-07-049796-6). McGraw.

Phillips, Bernard, ed. & intro. by see Suzuki, Daisetz T.

Phillips, Betty L. Chris Evert: First Lady of Tennis. LC 77-14398. (Sports Book Ser.). (Illus.). 192p. (gr. 7 up). 1977. PLB 7.79 o.p. (ISBN 0-671-32890-5). Messner.

--The Picture Story of Dorothy Hamill. LC 78-18543. (Illus.). 64p. (gr. 3 up). 1978. PLB 6.97 o.p. (ISBN 0-671-32936-7). Messner.

--The Picture Story of Nancy Lopez. LC 79-25344. (Illus.). 64p. (gr. 4-6). 1980. PLB 6.97 o.p. (ISBN 0-671-33050-0). Messner.

Phillips, Billie R., jt. auth. see Baker, Rance G.

Phillips, Bob. The All American Joke Book. LC 75-34744. 1975. pap. 2.25 (ISBN 0-89081-016-8, 0168). Harvest Hse.

--The Last of the Good Clean Jokes. LC 74-24851. 1974. pap. 2.25 (ISBN 0-89081-005-2, 0052). Harvest Hse.

--More Good Clean Jokes. LC 74-24850. 1974. pap. 2.25 (ISBN 0-89081-006-0, 0060). Harvest Hse.

--Redi-Reference. 1975. pap. 1.50 (ISBN 0-89081-043-5, 0435). Harvest Hse.

--The World's Greatest Collection of Heavenly Humor. LC 81-82676. 190p. (Orig.). 1982. pap. text ed. 2.50 (ISBN 0-89081-297-7, 2977). Harvest Hse.

Phillips, Bob, jt. auth. see LaHaye, Tim.

Phillips, Bonnie D. Business Communication. 2nd ed. LC 82-73090. (Illus.). 272p. 1983. text ed. 16.00 (ISBN 0-8273-2188-0); wkbk. 5.20 (ISBN 0-8273-2190-2); cassette 12.00 (ISBN 0-8273-2192-9); instr's guide 4.20 (ISBN 0-8273-2191-0). Delmar.

Phillips, Bonnie D. & Storey, Dale A. Business Mathematics & Calculating Machines. (Illus.). 224p. 1976. pap. text ed. 13.95x (ISBN 0-02-395280-6). Macmillan.

Phillips, Burt. The Ideal Horse: How to Train Him & Yourself. (Illus.). 272p. 1982. 20.00 (ISBN 0-682-49896-3, Banner). Exposition.

Phillips, C. W. Archaeology in the Ordnance Survey Seventeen Ninety-One to Nineteen Sixty-Five. 72p. 1980. pap. text ed. 11.50x (ISBN 0-900312-90-4, Pub. by Coun Brit Archaeology). Humanities.

Phillips, Cabell, et al, eds. see National Press Club Of Washington.

Phillips, Calvin & McFadden, David. Investigating the Fireground. (Illus.). 288p. 1982. pap. 16.95 (ISBN 0-89303-074-0). R J Brady.

Phillips, Cara L. Doing Right Makes Me Happy. Mahany, Patricia, ed. LC 82-80028. (Happy Day Bks.). (Illus.). 24p. (Orig.). (ps-3). 1982. pap. 1.29 (ISBN 0-87239-536-7, 3582). Standard Pub.

Phillips, Carolyn. Michelle. Date not set. 3.25 (ISBN 0-88113-205-5). Edit Betania.

Phillips, Catherine A., tr. see Du Moulin-Eckart, Richard.

Phillips, Catherine A., tr. see Specht, Richard.

Phillips, Catherine A., tr. see Stendhal, Henry B.

Phillips, Cecil R., jt. auth. see Moder, Joseph J.

Phillips, Celeste R. Family-Centered Maternity-Newborn Care: A Basic Text. LC 80-11522. (Illus.). 374p. 1980. pap. text ed. 15.95 (ISBN 0-8016-3920-4). Mosby.

Phillips, Celeste R. & Anzalone, Joseph T. Fathering: Participation in Labor & Birth. 2nd ed. LC 82-22329. (Illus.). 168p. 1982. pap. text ed. 11.95 (ISBN 0-8016-3922-0). Mosby.

Phillips, Celeste R., jt. auth. see Sumner, Philip E.

Phillips, Chandler A. & Petrofsky, Jerrold S. Mechanics of Skeletal & Cardiac Muscle. (Illus.). 336p. 1982. 24.75x (ISBN 0-398-04721-9). C C Thomas.

Phillips, Charles. Paderewski: The Story of a Modern Immortal. LC 77-17399. (Music Reprint Ser.). (Illus.). 1978. Repr. of 1934 ed. lib. bdg. 39.50 (ISBN 0-306-77534-4). Da Capo.

Phillips, Charles D. Sentencing Councils in the Federal Courts: An Evaluation. LC 79-3784. 176p. 1980. 23.95x (ISBN 0-669-03514-9). Lexington Bks.

Phillips, Cheryl M., ed. see Stirrup Associates Inc.

Phillips, Cheryl M., ed. see Stirrup Associates, Inc.

Phillips, Christine E., jt. auth. see Sanderson, J. H.

Phillips, Christopher. Steichen at War: Naval Aviation in the Pacific. (Illus.). 256p. 40.00 o.p. (ISBN 0-8109-1639-8). Abrams.

Phillips, Claire. Manila Espionage. (Illus.). 1947. 7.95 (ISBN 0-8323-0071-3). Binford.

Phillips, Connie, ed. see Food & Nutrition Group.

Phillips, D. Catalogue of the Type & Figured Specimens of Mesozoic Ammonoidea in the British Museum (Natural History) 1977. pap. 28.75x (ISBN 0-565-00790-4, Pub. by Brit Mus Nat Hist). Sabbot-Natural Hist Bks.

Phillips, D. A. & Hornak, J. E. Measurement & Evaluation in Physical Education. 376p. 1979. text ed. 23.95x (ISBN 0-471-04962-X). Wiley.

Phillips, D. H. & Burdekin, D. A. Diseases of Forest & Ornamental Trees. 1982. 190.00x (ISBN 0-333-32357-2, Pub. by Macmillan England). State Mutual Bk.

Phillips, D. J. Quantitative Aquatic Biological Indicators. (Pollution Monitoring Ser.: No. 1). 1980. 63.75 (ISBN 0-85334-884-7). Elsevier.

Phillips, D. Z. Religion Without Explanation. 200p. 1978. pap. 9.95x (ISBN 0-631-19850-4, Pub. by Basil Blackwell England). Biblio Dist.

Phillips, D. Z., jt. auth. see Dilman, Ilham.

Phillips, D. Z., et al, eds. see Fries, Jakob F.

Phillips, David, jt. auth. see Sainsbury, Eric.

Phillips, David A., jt. auth. see Phillips, Ann V.

Phillips, David R. & Williams, Allan M. Rural Housing & the Public Sector. 174p. 1982. text ed. 26.50x (ISBN 0-566-00456-9). Gower Pub Ltd.

Phillips, Debra H., jt. auth. see Ryan, Kevin.

Phillips, Dee. The Coconut Kiss: A Novel. 1983. 14.50 (ISBN 0-393-01679-X). Norton.

Phillips, Delbert D. Spook or Spoof: The Structure of the Supernatural in Russian Romantic Tales. LC 81-40838. 168p. 1982. lib. bdg. 22.25 (ISBN 0-8191-2223-8); pap. text ed. 10.25 (ISBN 0-8191-2224-6). U Pr of Amer.

Phillips, Dennis. Cold War 2 & Australia. 144p. 1983. text ed. 18.50x (ISBN 0-86861-125-5). Allen Unwin.

Phillips, Don T. Applied Goodness of Fit Testing. 1972. pap. text ed. 12.00 (ISBN 0-89806-021-4, 71). Inst Indus Eng.

Phillips, Don T. & Garcia-Diaz, Alberto. Fundamentals of Network Analysis. (Illus.). 496p. 1981. text ed. 31.95 (ISBN 0-13-341552-X). P-H.

Phillips, Don T., et al. Operations Research: Principles & Practices. LC 75-44395. 585p. 1976. text ed. 35.95x (ISBN 0-471-68707-3). Wiley.

Phillips, Donald, jt. auth. see Beightler, Charles.

Phillips, Donald A. & Purvis, Arthur J. Turning Supervisors On: To Employee Counseling Programs. 2.50 (ISBN 0-89486-086-0). Hazelden.

Phillips, Donald E. Student Protest Nineteen Sixty-Nineteen Sixty-Nine: An Analysis of the Issues & Speeches. LC 79-3716. 1980. text ed. 13.75 o.p. (ISBN 0-8191-0911-8); pap. text ed. 9.50 (ISBN 0-8191-0912-6). U Pr of Amer.

Phillips, Donna-Lee, ed. Eros & Photography. LC 77-81897. (Illus.). pap. 100.00x (ISBN 0-917986-02-4). NFS Pr.

Phillips, Dorothy B., et al, eds. The Choice Is Always Ours. rev. ed. 480p. (Orig.). 1975. pap. 3.95 (ISBN 0-8356-0302-4, Quest). Theos Pub Hse.

Phillips, E. B. & Lane, S. Personal Finance: Text & Case Problems. 4th ed. 620p. 1980. 33.95x (ISBN 0-471-02580-1); tchrs.' manual avail. (ISBN 0-471-02581-X). Wiley.

Phillips, E. Bryant & Lane, Sylvia, eds. How to Manage Your Personal Finances: A Short Course for Professionals. (Professional Development Programs Ser.). 1978. text ed. 39.95 (ISBN 0-471-02316-7). Wiley.

Phillips, E. L., jt. auth. see Haring, Norris G.

Phillips, E. Lakin. Counseling & Psychotherapy: A Behavioral Approach. LC 77-1771. (Personality Processes Ser.). 1977. 36.50 o.s.i. (ISBN 0-471-01881-3, Pub. by Wiley-Interscience). Wiley.

--Stress, Health & Psychological Problems in the Major Professions. LC 82-17556. 478p. (Orig.). 1983. lib. bdg. 30.50 (ISBN 0-8191-2773-6); pap. text ed. 17.50 (ISBN 0-8191-2774-4). U Pr of Amer.

Phillips, Edgar. The Ultimate in Sports. 32p. 1982. pap. write for info. (ISBN 0-9608576-1-3). Busn Pro Bks.

Phillips, Elizabeth. Marianne Moore. LC 81-71399. (Literature and Life Ser.). 256p. 1982. 14.50 (ISBN 0-8044-2698-8). Ungar.

Phillips, Elizabeth D., et al. Intermediate Algebra: Applications & Problem Solving. 560p. 1983. text ed. 22.95 scp (ISBN 0-06-045219-6, HarpC); instr's. manual avail. (ISBN 0-06-365184-X). Har-Row.

Phillips, Elliott. Get a Good Night's Sleep. 228p. 1983. 13.95 (ISBN 0-13-354290-4); pap. 6.95 (ISBN 0-13-354282-3). P-H.

Phillips, Esther R., jt. auth. see Rose, Israel H.

Phillips, Florence H., tr. see Botticelli, Sandro.

Phillips, Fred M. Desert People & Mountain Men: Exploration of the Great Basin 1824-1865. LC 77-23351. (Illus.). 1977. 6.50 (ISBN 0-912494-24-7); pap. 3.95 (ISBN 0-912494-25-5). Chalfant Pr.

Phillips, G., jt. auth. see Milner, G. W.

Phillips, G. O. & Wedlock, D. J., eds. Gums & Stabilizers for the Food Industry: Interactions of Hydrocolloids. (Illus.). 420p. 1982. 110.00 (ISBN 0-08-026843-9). Pergamon.

Phillips, Gail. The Imagery of the Libro de Bucn Amor. (Spanish Ser.: No. 9). 1983. 20.00 (ISBN 0-942260-23-6). Hispanic Seminary.

Phillips, Gene D. George Cukor. (Filmmakers Ser.). 1982. lib. bdg. 16.95 (ISBN 0-8057-9286-4, Twayne). G K Hall.

--Graham Greene: The Films of His Fiction. LC 73-85252. 1974. pap. 9.50x (ISBN 0-8077-2376-2). Tchrs Coll.

--John Schlesinger. (Filmmakers Ser.). 1981. lib. bdg. 14.95 (ISBN 0-8057-9280-5, Twayne). G K Hall.

--Ken Russell. (Filmmakers Ser.). 1979. lib. bdg. 12.95 (ISBN 0-8057-9266-X, Twayne). G K Hall.

Phillips, George H., Jr. The Enduring Struggle. Hundley, Norris & Schutz, John A., eds. LC 81-66060. (Golden State Ser.). (Illus.). 110p. 1981. pap. text ed. 5.95x (ISBN 0-87835-118-3). Boyd & Fraser.

Phillips, Gerald M. & Goodall, H. Lloyd, Jr. Loving & Living: Improve Your Friendships & Marriage. 218p. 1983. 13.95 (ISBN 0-13-541136-X); pap. 6.95 (ISBN 0-13-541128-9). P-H.

Phillips, Gerald M., et al. Group Discussion: A Practical Guide to Participation & Leadership. LC 78-56441. (Illus.). 1979. text ed. 17.50 (ISBN 0-395-25415-9); instr's. manual 1.00 (ISBN 0-395-25416-7). HM.

Phillips, H. M. Basic Education: A World Challenge: Measures & Innovations for Children & Youth in Developing Countries. LC 74-6995. 259p. 1975. 54.95 o.s.i. (ISBN 0-471-68670-0, Pub. by Wiley-Interscience). Wiley.

--Educational Cooperation Between Developed & Developing Countries. LC 75-19807. (Praeger Special Studies). (Illus.). 352p. 1976. 36.95 o.p. (ISBN 0-275-55900-9). Praeger.

Phillips, Harold R. & Firth, Robert E., eds. Cases in Denominational Administration: A Management Casebook for Decision-Making. vi, 314p. 1978. pap. text ed. 4.95 (ISBN 0-943872-75-8). Andrews Univ Pr.

Phillips, Henry, Jr., jt. ed. see Chase, Alston H.

Phillips, Herbert E. Innovative Idea Bank. LC 80-65052. 192p. 1980. pap. 15.00 o.p. (ISBN 0-8408-0501-2). Carrollton Pr.

Phillips, Herbert P. Thai Peasant Personality: The Patterning of Interpersonal Behavior in the Village of Bang Chan. 1965. 28.50x (ISBN 0-520-01008-6). U of Cal Pr.

Phillips, Hosea, tr. see De Villiers du Terrage, Marc.

Phillips, I., et al, eds. Microbiological Hazards of Infusion Therapy. LC 76-47865. (Illus.). 194p. 1976. 22.00 o.p. (ISBN 0-88416-187-0). Wright-PSG.

Phillips, J. B. New Testament in Modern English. rev ed. student ed. 11.95 (ISBN 0-02-596970-6). student ed 3.95 (ISBN 0-686-67531-2, 59697). Macmillan.

--Your God Is Too Small. 1.95 o.p. (ISBN 0-686-92424-X, 6700). Hazelden.

Phillips, J. P., jt. auth. see Beckman, J. E.

Phillips, J. P., et al. Organic Electronic Spectral Data. LC 60-16428. Vol. 13, 1971. 66.00 o.p. (ISBN 0-471-03563-7, Pub. by Wiley-Interscience); Vol. 14, 1978. 96.50 o.p. (ISBN 0-471-05076-8); Vol. 15, 1979. 85.00 o.p. (ISBN 0-471-05572-7). Wiley.

Phillips, J. P., et al, eds. Organic Electronic Spectral Data, Vol. 7. LC 60-16428. 1318p. 1971. 62.50 (ISBN 0-471-68798-7). Krieger.

Phillips, Jack J. Handbook of Training Evaluation & Measurement Methods. 1982. 19.95 (ISBN 0-87201-877-6). Gulf Pub.

Phillips, James. Ancient Egyptian Architecture. (Architecture Ser.: Bibliography A-784). 73p. 1982. pap. 11.25 (ISBN 0-88066-203-4). Vance Biblios.

--Early Christian & Early Byzantine Architecture in Palestine (Including Jordan) Vol. II, the Sites. (Architecture Ser.: Bibliography A 854). 54p. 1982. pap. 8.25 (ISBN 0-88066-264-6). Vance Biblios.

Phillips, James E., ed. Twentieth Century Interpretations of Coriolanus. (Twentieth Century Interpretations Ser). 1970. 9.95 o.p. (ISBN 0-13-172676-5, Spec); pap. 1.25 o.p. (ISBN 0-13-172668-4, Spec). P-H.

Phillips, James M., jt. auth. see Holter, Wayne V.

Phillips, Janine. My Secret Diary. 160p. 1982. 25.00x (ISBN 0-85683-062-3, Pub. by Shepheard-Walwyn England). State Mutual Bk.

--My Secret Diary. 160p. 1982. 8.50 (ISBN 0-85683-062-3, Pub. by Shepheard-Walwyn). Flatiron Book Dist.

Phillips, Jayne A. Black Tickets. 1979. 8.95 o.s.i. (ISBN 0-440-00708-9, Sey Lawr). Delacorte.

--Black Tickets. (gr. 7-12). 1983. pap. 3.95 (ISBN 0-440-30924-7, LE). Dell.

--Counting. 56p. 1978. 15.00 (ISBN 0-931428-19-X); pap. 6.00 (ISBN 0-931428-18-1). Vehicle Edns.

Phillips, Jean A. For Better Reading: Lots You Need to Know about Short Vowels. (Illus.). 56p. 1981. pap. write for info. (ISBN 0-911305-00-9). J Phillips Pub Co.

--For Better Reading: Lots You Need to Know about Vowels. (Illus.). 58p. 1982. pap. 3.88 (ISBN 0-911305-01-7). J Phillips Pub Co.

Phillips, Jeremy & Hoolahan, Michael. Employee Inventions in the United Kingdom. 160p. 1982. 39.00x (ISBN 0-686-97891-9, Pub. by ESC Pub England). State Mutual Bk.

Phillips, Jill M. The Second World War in History, Biography, Diary, Poetry, Literature, & Film: A Bibliography. 1983. lib. bdg. 79.95 (ISBN 0-8490-3231-8). Gordon Pr.

Phillips, Jo. Exploring Triangles: Paper-Folding Geometry. LC 74-14862. (Young Math Ser.). (Illus.). 40p. (gr. k-3). 1975. PLB 10.89 (ISBN 0-690-00645-4, TYC-J). Har-Row.

--Right Angles: Paper-Folding Geometry. LC 72-171007. (Young Math Ser.). (Illus.). (gr. 1-4). 1972. PLB 10.89 (ISBN 0-690-60917-5, TYC-J). Har-Row.

Phillips, Joan. Gretchen & the Lost Carousel. LC 82-80871. (Illus.). 48p. (gr. k-3). 1982. 5.95 (ISBN 0-448-16576-7, G&D). Putnam Pub Group.

Phillips, Johanna. Passion's Song. (Second Chance at Love Ser.: No. 88). 1982. pap. 1.75 (ISBN 0-515-06850-0). Jove Pubns.

Phillips, John. Dear Parrot. (Illus.). 1979. 5.95 (ISBN 0-517-53868-7, C N Potter Bks). Crown.

--Exploring Genesis. LC 80-23685. 582p. 1980. 12.95 (ISBN 0-8024-2408-2); pap. 8.95 (ISBN 0-8024-2430-9). Moody.

--Exploring Hebrews. LC 76-39908. 1977. 10.95 (ISBN 0-8024-2406-6); pap. 8.95 (ISBN 0-8024-2431-7). Moody.

--Exploring Revelation. LC 74-15330. 288p. 1974. 10.95 (ISBN 0-8024-2407-4); pap. 8.95 (ISBN 0-8024-2432-5). Moody.

--Exploring Romans. 250p. 1971. 10.95 (ISBN 0-8024-2405-8); pap. 8.95 (ISBN 0-8024-2433-3). Moody.

--Exploring the Future. 400p. 1983. 14.95 (ISBN 0-8407-5275-X). Nelson.

--Exploring the Scriptures. 1965. pap. 8.95 (ISBN 0-8024-2434-1). Moody.

--Exploring the World of the Jew. LC 81-16844. 288p. 1982. pap. 11.95 (ISBN 0-8024-2411-2). Moody.

--One Hundred Sermon Outlines from the New Testament. 1979. pap. 4.95 (ISBN 0-8024-7817-4). Moody.

Phillips, John, ed. Prince Albert & the Victorian Age. LC 81-6141. (Illus.). 200p. 1981. 32.50 (ISBN 0-521-24242-8). Cambridge U Pr.

Phillips, John B. Your God Is Too Small. 8.95 (ISBN 0-02-597410-6); pap. 2.95. Macmillan.

Phillips, John P., et al. Organic Electronic Spectral Data, Vol. 16. LC 60-16428. (Data Vol. xvi, 1974). 1126p. 1980. 128.00x (ISBN 0-471-06058-5, Pub. by Wiley-Interscience). Wiley.

--Organic Electronic Spectral Data: 1975, Vol. 17. LC 60-16428. 1060p. 1981. 113.00x (ISBN 0-471-08614-2, Pub. by Wiley-Interscience). Wiley.

Phillips, John R. The Reformation of Images: Destruction of Art in England, 1530-1665. 1974. 32.50x (ISBN 0-520-02424-9). U of Cal Pr.

Phillips, Joseph W. Jedidiah Morse & New England Congregationalism. 305p. 1983. 30.00 (ISBN 0-8135-0982-3). Rutgers U Pr.

Phillips, Julien. Stars of the Ziegfeld Follies. LC 72-165324. (Pull Ahead Bks). (Illus.). (gr. 6-11). 1972. PLB 4.95g (ISBN 0-8225-0464-2). Lerner Pubns.

Phillips, Kevin P. Post-Conservative America: People, Politics & Ideology in a Time of Crisis. 1982. 14.50 (ISBN 0-394-52212-5). Random.

--Post-Conservative America: People, Politics, & Ideology in a Time of Crisis. LC 82-48898. 288p. 1983. pap. 6.95 (ISBN 0-394-71438-5, Vin). Random.

Phillips, Lawrence C. & Hoffman, William H. West's Federal Taxation: Individual Incomes Taxes, 1979. new rev. ed. 1978. text ed. 17.95 o.s.i. (ISBN 0-8299-0178-7); solutions manual avail. o.s.i. (ISBN 0-8299-0567-7). West Pub.

Phillips, Leona R. Twixt Wind & Water. LC 80-12218. 1983. 14.95 (ISBN 0-87949-179-5). Ashley Bks.

Phillips, Linda R., jt. auth. see Wolanin, Mary O.

Phillips, Louis. Celebrity Quiz. Schneider, Meg, ed. (Magic Answer Bks.). 64p. (gr. 3-7). 1983. pap. 2.75 (ISBN 0-671-49921-1). Wanderer Bks.

--How Do You Get a Horse Out of the Bathtub? Profound Answers to Preposterous Questions. (Illus.). 80p. 1983. 9.50 (ISBN 0-670-38119-5). Viking Pr.

--The Man Who Stole the Atlantic Ocean. (Illus.). 1979. pap. 1.25 (ISBN 0-380-00766-5, 48173-1, Camelot). Avon.

--The Upside Down Riddle Book. (ps). 1982. 8.50 (ISBN 0-688-00931-X); PLB 7.63 (ISBN 0-688-00932-8). Lothrop.

Phillips, Louis & Markoe, Karen. Fun Fact Fill-Ins. (Magic Answer Bks.). (Illus.). 64p. (gr. 3-7). 1983. pap. 2.75 (ISBN 0-671-44919-2). Wanderer Bks.

--Riddle Whiz Quiz. (Magic Answer Bks.). (Illus.). 64p. (gr. 3-7). 1983. pap. 2.75 (ISBN 0-671-44920-6). Wanderer Bks.

--Travel Games. (Magic Answer Bks.). 64p. (gr. 3-7). 1983. pap. 2.75 (ISBN 0-671-44922-2). Wanderer Bks.

Phillips, Marcia, jt. auth. see Kaplan, David.

Phillips, Margaret. Erasmus on His Times. 1964. pap. 7.50 (ISBN 0-521-09413-5). Cambridge U Pr.

Phillips, Marjorie. Duncan Phillips & His Collection. (Illus.). 1982. 35.00 (ISBN 0-393-01608-0); pap. 18.95 (ISBN 0-393-30041-2). Norton.

--Duncan Phillips & His Collection. Lancaster, Jan, et al, eds. LC 82-81039. 1982. text ed. 18.00; pap. text ed. 19.00 (ISBN 0-393-01608-0). Phillips Collec.

Phillips, Michael, ed. Interpreting Blake. LC 78-8322. (Illus.). 1979. 42.50 (ISBN 0-521-22176-5). Cambridge U Pr.

Phillips, Michael, ed. see MacDonald, George.

Phillips, Michael J. The Dilemma of Individualism: Status, Liberty, & American Constitutional Law. LC 82-15580. (Contributions in American Studies: No. 67). 240p. 1983. lib. bdg. 29.95 (ISBN 0-313-23690-9, KF4749). Greenwood.

--Edwin Muir: A Master of Modern Poetry. LC 78-67103. 1978. 25.00 (ISBN 0-915144-54-9). Hackett Pub.

Phillips, Michael J., jt. auth. see Fisher, Bruce D.

Phillips, Mike. Growth of a Vision. pap. 3.50 o.s.i. (ISBN 0-940652-00-5). Sunrise Chr Bks.

Phillips, Mike, ed. see MacDonald, George.

Phillips, N., jt. auth. see Phillips, W. J.

Phillips, N. V., jt. auth. see Hazewindus, Nico.

Phillips, Nigel. Sijobang: Sung Narrative Poetry of West Sumatra. LC 80-42227. (Cambridge Studies in Oral & Literate Culture: No. 1). (Illus.). 248p. 1981. 44.50 (ISBN 0-521-23737-8). Cambridge U Pr.

Phillips, Nina. Conversational English for the Non-English-Speaking Child. LC 68-23006. 1968. pap. text ed. 6.95x (ISBN 0-8077-1907-2). Tchrs Coll.

Phillips, O. M. The Dynamics of the Upper Ocean. 2nd ed. LC 76-26371. (Cambridge Monographs on Mechanics & Applied Mathematics Ser.). (Illus.). 1977. 72.50 (ISBN 0-521-21421-1). Cambridge U Pr.

--The Dynamics of the Upper Ocean. 2nd ed. LC 76-26371. (Cambridge Monographs on Mechanics & Applied Mathematics). 344p. 1980. pap. 23.95x (ISBN 0-521-29801-6). Cambridge U Pr.

Phillips, Osborne, jt. auth. see Denning, Melita.

Phillips, P. C. B. & Wickens, M. R. Exercise in Econometrics, Vols. I & II. 1979. Two Vol. Set. prof ref 35.00x (ISBN 0-88410-190-8); Vol. I, 304pgs. 20.00x (ISBN 0-88410-186-X); Vol. II, 264pgs. 20.00x (ISBN 0-88410-187-8). Ballinger Pub.

Phillips, P. T. The Sectarian Spirit: Sectarianism, Society & Politics in Victorian Cotton Towns. 224p. 1983. 30.00x (ISBN 0-8020-2406-8). U of Toronto Pr.

Phillips, Pat. Love Waits at Penrhyn. 192p. (YA) 1975. 6.95 (ISBN 0-685-53495-2, Avalon). Bouregy.

Phillips, Patricia. Contemporary Square Dance. (Physical Education Activities Ser.). 80p. 1968. pap. text ed. write for info. (ISBN 0-697-07008-5); tchr's manual avail. (ISBN 0-697-07216-9). Wm C Brown.

--Jenny. (Histoical Romance). 432p. (Orig.). 1981. pap. 2.75 o.s.i. (ISBN 0-515-05538-7). Jove Pubns.

--Touch Me with Fire. 416p. 1982. pap. 3.50 (ISBN 0-515-05908-0). Jove Pubns.

Phillips, Patty, jt. auth. see Suval, Judy.

Phillips, Paul, jt. auth. see Lazenby, David.

Phillips, Paul C. Hawaii's Democrats: Chasing the American Dream. LC 81-40876. 222p. (Orig.). 1982. lib. bdg. 22.00 (ISBN 0-8191-2143-6); pap. text ed. 10.75 (ISBN 0-8191-2144-4). U Pr of Amer.

Phillips, Philip & Brown, James A. Pre-Columbian Shell Engravings from the Craig Mound at Spiro, Oklahoma, 6 vols. LC 74-77557. (Illus.). 1978. Limited Ed. lib. bdg. 180.00t (ISBN 0-87365-777-2). Peabody Harvard.

--Pre-Columbian Shell Engravings From the Craig Mound at Spiro, Oklahoma: Vol. VI of the Limited Edition. (Peabody Museum Press Ser.). (Illus.). 220p. 1982. text ed. 60.00x (ISBN 0-87365-785-3). Peabody Harvard.

--Pre-Columbian Shell Engravings from the Craig Mound at Spiro, Oklahoma: Paperback Edition, Pt. 2. (Illus.). 600p. 1983. pap. text ed. 35.00x (ISBN 0-87365-802-7). Peabody Harvard.

Phillips, Philip G. A Very Strange Case. 1978. 5.95 o.p. (ISBN 0-533-03085-4). Vantage.

Phillips, Phoebe. The Collector's Encyclopedia of Antiques. 1973. 25.00 o.p. (ISBN 0-517-50451-0). Crown.

Phillips, Phoebe & Hatch, Pamela. The Complete Book of Good Health: The Illustrated Family Guide to Diet, Fitness & Beauty. LC 78-4768. 1978. 12.95i o.p. (ISBN 0-690-01781-2). T Y Crowell.

Phillips, R., jt. auth. see Nussbaum, A.

Phillips, R. D. & Gillis, M. F., eds. Biological Effects of Extremely Low Frequency Electromagnetic Fields: Proceedings. LC 79-607778. (DOE Symposium Ser.). 577p. 1979. pap. 22.50 (ISBN 0-87079-118-4, CONF-781016); microfiche 4.50 (ISBN 0-87079-148-6, CONF-781016). DOE.

Phillips, R. S. Malaria. (Studies in Biology: No. 152). 64p. 1983. pap. text ed. 8.95 (ISBN 0-7131-2858-5). E Arnold.

Phillips, Ralph & Webster, Susan. Group Travel Operating Procedures. 176p. 1983. text ed. 17.95 (ISBN 0-8436-0882-X). CBI Pub.

Phillips, Ralph W. Elements of Dental Materials. 3rd ed. LC 76-50152. (Illus.). 1977. text ed. 17.50 (ISBN 0-7216-7232-9). Saunders.

--Skinner's Science of Dental Materials. 7th ed. LC 72-78959. (Illus.). 682p. 1973. 25.00 o.p. (ISBN 0-7216-7234-5). Saunders.

--Skinner's Science of Dental Materials. 8th ed. (Illus.). 646p. 1982. 32.00 (ISBN 0-7216-7235-3). Saunders.

Phillips, Raphael T. Roots of Strategy: A Collection of Classics. LC 82-11890. 448p. 1982. Repr. of 1940 ed. lib. bdg. 39.75x (ISBN 0-313-23657-7, PHRS). Greenwood.

Phillips, Richard, jt. auth. see O'Neil, Barbara.

Phillips, Robert. Denton Welch. (English Authors Ser.). 1974. lib. bdg. 14.95 (ISBN 0-8057-1567-3, Twayne). G K Hall.

--Land of Lost Content. LC 70-134667. 1970. 7.95 o.s.i. (ISBN 0-8149-0674-5). Vanguard.

--The Pregnant Man. LC 77-27727. 1978. pap. 4.95 o.p. (ISBN 0-385-14013-4). Doubleday.

--Technocraton. (Australian Theatre Workshop Ser.). 1976. pap. text ed. 4.50x o.p. (ISBN 0-85859-049-2, 00528). Heinemann Ed.

--William Goyen. (United States Authors Ser.). 1979. lib. bdg. 13.95 (ISBN 0-8057-7269-3, Twayne). G K Hall.

Phillips, Robert F. To Save Bastogne. LC 82-42721. 272p. 1983. 18.95 (ISBN 0-8128-2907-7). Stein & Day.

Phillips, Robert I., jt. auth. see Stevens, Matthew.

Phillips, Robert, Jr., jt. auth. see Osborn, Scott C.

Phillips, Roger. Concise Russian Review Grammar with Exercises. 1974. pap. 6.95x (ISBN 0-299-06544-8). U of Wis Pr.

--Wild Flowers of Britain. 1978. 19.95 o.p. (ISBN 0-8256-3113-0, Quick Fox); pap. 9.95 o.p. (ISBN 0-8256-3111-4). Putnam Pub Group.

Phillips, Stella. Death in Sheep's Clothing. 192p. 1983. 12.95 (ISBN 0-8027-5489-9). Walker & Co.

Phillips, Steven. Civil Actions. LC 82-45365. 288p. 1983. 14.95 (ISBN 0-385-15988-9). Doubleday.

--No Heroes, No Villains. 1977. 8.95 o.p. (ISBN 0-394-40907-8). Random.

Phillips, Susan M. & Zecher, J. Richard. The SEC & the Public Interest. (Illus.). 184p. 1981. text ed. 25.00x (ISBN 0-262-16080-3). MIT Pr.

Phillips, Susan M., jt. auth. see Stevenson, Richard A.

Phillips, Tom. A Humument: A Treated Victorian Novel. (Illus.). 1983. pap. 12.95 (ISBN 0-500-27284-0). Thames Hudson.

Phillips, U. B. Correspondence of Robert Toombs, Alexander H. Stephens, & Howell Cobb. LC 68-54846. (American Scene Ser). 1970. Repr. of 1911 ed. lib. bdg. 95.00 (ISBN 0-306-71191-5). Da Capo.

Phillips, Uad & Yotey, H. L. Economic Analysis of Pressing Social Problems. 2nd ed. 1977. pap. 13.95 o.p. (ISBN 0-395-30696-5). HM.

Phillips, W., ed. see Franklin, Benjamin.

Phillips, W. A., jt. auth. see Sproull, R. L.

Phillips, W. J. & Phillips, N. Introduction to Mineralogy for Geologists. LC 79-42898. 344p. 1980. 59.95 (ISBN 0-471-27642-1); pap. 23.95 (ISBN 0-471-27795-9). Wiley.

Phillips, W. Louis, compiled by. Index to Plant Distribution Maps in North American Periodicals Through 1972. 1976. lib. bdg. 110.00 (ISBN 0-8161-0009-8, Hall Library). G K Hall.

Phillips, W. R., jt. auth. see Grant, I. S.

Phillips, W. Revell & Griffen, Dana T. Optical Mineralogy: The Nonopaque Minerals. LC 80-12435. (Illus.). 677p. 1981. text ed. 42.50x (ISBN 0-7167-1129-X). W H Freeman.

Phillips, Wally. The Wally Phillips People Book. (Illus.). 1979. 7.95 o.p. (ISBN 0-89803-012-9). Caroline Hse.

Phillips, Warren R. & Rimkunas, Richard. Crisis Warning: The Perception Behavior Interface. 300p. 1982. 48.50 (ISBN 0-677-05940-X). Gordon.

Phillips, Wendell. Wendell Phillips on Civil Rights & Freedom. 2nd ed. Filler, Louis, ed. LC 82-17343. 252p. 1983. pap. text ed. 10.25 (ISBN 0-8191-2793-0). U Pr of Amer.

Phillips, William, jt. ed. see Kurzweil, Edith.

Phillips, William M., Jr. The School Sociologist: A Need & an Emergent Profession. LC 81-40051. (Illus.). 272p. (Orig.). 1982. lib. bdg. 22.25 (ISBN 0-8191-1945-8); pap. text ed. 11.50 (ISBN 0-8191-1946-6). U Pr of Amer.

Phillips-McClenahan, Sallie. Touchstones. LC 82-11454. (Illus.). 300p. (Orig.). 1982. pap. 8.95 (ISBN 0-87233-066-4). Bauhan.

Phillipson, Chris. Capitalism & the Construction of Old Age. (Critical Texts in Social Work & the Welfare State). 192p. 1982. text ed. 26.25x (ISBN 0-333-28642-1, Pub. by Macmillan England); pap. text ed. 10.50x (ISBN 0-333-28644-8). Humanities.

Phillipson, Coleman. Three Criminal Law Reformers: Beccaria, Bentham, Romilly. LC 77-17157. (Criminology, Law Enforcement, & Social Problems Ser.: No. 113). 1970. 20.00x (ISBN 0-87585-113-4); pap. 7.50x (ISBN 0-87585-904-6). Patterson Smith.

Phillipson, J. Ecological Energetics. (Studies in Biology: No. 1). 64p. 1966. pap. text ed. 8.95 (ISBN 0-7131-2079-7). E Arnold.

Phillipson, John S. Thomas Wolfe: A Reference Guide. (Reference Publications Ser.). 1977. lib. bdg. 19.00 (ISBN 0-8161-7878-X, Hall Reference). G K Hall.

Phillipson, R. V. Modern Trends in Drug Dependence & Alcoholism. 1970. 21.50 o.p. (ISBN 0-407-29040-0). Butterworth.

Phillis, J. W. Veterinary Physiology. LC 75-29773. (Illus.). 882p. 1976. text ed. 10.00 (ISBN 0-7216-7238-8). Saunders.

Phillis, Susan, jt. ed. see Jenkins, Betty L.

Phillus, J. W., jt. ed. see Kernut, G. A.

Philmus, Robert M. Into the Unknown: The Evolution of Science Fiction from Frances Godwin to H.G. Wells. 186p. 1983. pap. 6.95 (ISBN 0-520-04959-4, CAL 627). U of Cal Pr.

Philmus, Robert M., ed. see Wells, H. G.

Philodemus. On Methods of Inference. De Lacy, Ph. H. & De Lacy, E. A., eds. (The School of Epicurus Ser.). 232p. 1982. text ed. 23.00x (ISBN 88-7088-009-5, 40627, Pub. by Bibliopolis Italy). Humanities.

Philosophy of Science Association, Biennial Meeting, 1976. PSA 1976: Proceedings, Contributed Papers & Special Sessions, 2 vols. Suppe, F. & Asquith, P. D., eds. LC 76-27152. 1976. Vol. 1. 8.50 (ISBN 0-917586-02-6); Vol. 2. 9.75 (ISBN 0-917586-04-2); Vol. 2. pap. 6.25 (ISBN 0-917586-03-4). Philos Sci Assn.

Philosophy of Science Biennial Meeting, 1976. PSA 1976: Symposia, Vol. 2. Asquith, Peter D. & Suppe, Frederick, eds. LC 76-27152. 1977. 9.75 o.p. (ISBN 0-917586-04-2); pap. 6.25 o.p. (ISBN 0-917586-03-4). Philos Sci Assn.

Philp, M. & Duckworth, D. Children with Disabilities & Their Families: A Review of Research. (NFER Research Publications Ser.). 131p. 1982. pap. text ed. 14.75x (ISBN 0-7005-0491-5, NFER). Humanities.

Philp, R. & Whitney, Mary. Danseur: The Male in Ballet. LC 77-5844. 1977. 19.95 o.p. (ISBN 0-07-049811-3, GB). McGraw.

Philp, Richard, jt. auth. see Witkin, Kate.

Philpot, Gordon A. The National Economy: An Introduction to Macroeconomics. LC 80-20615. 188p. 1980. pap. text ed. 13.95x (ISBN 0-471-05591-3); tchrs.' manual 6.00 (ISBN 0-471-09111-1). Wiley.

Philpott, Thomas L. The Slum & the Ghetto: Neighborhood Deterioration & Middle-Class Reform, Chicago 1880-1930. LC 76-57275. (Urban Life in America Ser.). (Illus.). 1978. 25.00x (ISBN 0-19-502276-9). Oxford U Pr.

Philpott, William. Brain Allergies. 1980. 16.95x (ISBN 0-87983-224-X). Cancer Control Soc.

Philpott, William, jt. auth. see Kalita, Dwight.

Phinney, Eleanor, ed. Librarian & the Patient. LC 76-45178. 1977. text ed. 25.00 (ISBN 0-8389-0227-8). ALA.

Phippen, George. The Life of a Cowboy. LC 70-101102. (Illus.). 108p. 1969. 15.00 o.p. (ISBN 0-8165-0205-6). U of Ariz Pr.

Phippen, Sanford. The Police Know Everything: And Other Maine Stories. Hunting, Constance, ed. 149p. (Orig.). 1982. pap. 6.95 (ISBN 0-913006-27-0). Puckerbrush.

Phipps, C. J. A Voyage Towards the Norht Pole: 1773. 1981. 45.00x (ISBN 0-686-98243-6, Pub. by Caedmon of Whitby). State Mutual Bk.

Phipps, David. Famous Modern Racing Cars of the World. 11.75x o.p. (ISBN 0-392-08149-0, SpS). Sportshelf.

Phipps, Diana. Diana Phipps' Affordable Splendor: An Ingenious Guide to Decorating Elegantly, Inexpensively & Doing Most of It Yourself. LC 81-6028. (Illus.). 320p. 1982. 20.00 (ISBN 0-394-50441-0). Random.

Phipps, Lloyd J. Mechanics in Agriculture. 2nd ed. LC 76-24049. 1977. 22.50 (ISBN 0-8134-1841-0); text ed. 16.95x (ISBN 0-686-82926-3). Interstate.

Phipps, Lloyd J., jt. auth. see Cook, G. C.

Phipps, Rita. The Successful Student's Handbook: A Step-by-Step Guide to Study, Reading & Thinking Skills. LC 80-54427. (Illus.). 160p. 1983. pap. 8.95 (ISBN 0-295-95802-2). U of Wash Pr.

Phipps, William E. Encounter Through Questioning Paul: A Fresh Approach to the Apostle's Life & Letters. LC 82-17580. (Illus.). 114p. (Orig.). 1983. lib. bdg. 19.00 (ISBN 0-8191-2785-X); pap. text ed. 8.25 (ISBN 0-8191-2786-8). U Pr of Amer.

--Influential Theologians on Wo-Man. LC 79-5431. 1980. lib. bdg. 18.00 (ISBN 0-8191-1383-2); pap. text ed. 8.25 (ISBN 0-8191-0880-4). U Pr of Amer.

Phipps, Wilma J. & Long, Barbara C. Medical-Surgical Nursing: Concepts & Clinical Practice. 2nd ed. (Illus.). 2000p. 1983. text ed. 39.95 (ISBN 0-8016-3931-X). Mosby.

Phipps, Wilma J., et al. Shafer's Medical-Surgical Nursing. 7th ed. LC 79-27334. (Illus.). 1000p. 1980. text ed. 36.95 (ISBN 0-8016-3934-4). Mosby.

Phipson, Joan. The Watcher in the Garden. LC 82-3960. 288p. 1982. 10.95 (ISBN 0-689-50246-X, Argo). Atheneum.

Phister, Montgomery, Jr. Logical Design of Digital Computers. LC 58-6082. (Illus.). 1958. 29.95 o.p. (ISBN 0-471-68805-3, Pub. by Wiley-Interscience). Wiley.

Phleger, Frederick. Whales Go By. LC 59-9740. (Illus.). (gr. 1-2). 1959. PLB 5.99 (ISBN 0-394-90009-X). Beginner.

Phleger, Frederick & Phelger, Marjorie. You Will Live Under the Sea. (Illus.). (gr. k-3). 1966. PLB 5.99 (ISBN 0-394-90043-X). Beginner.

Phongpaichit, Pasuk. From Peasant Girls to Bangkok Masseuses. International Labour Office, ed. (Women, Work & Development Ser.: No. 2). ix, 80p. (Orig.). 1982. pap. 8.55 (ISBN 92-2-103013-X). Intl Labour Office.

Photo. Maine Four Seasons. 1974. 14.95 (ISBN 0-89272-009-3). Down East.

Phyfe, William H. Five Thousand Facts & Fancies. rev. ed. LC 66-24369. 1966. Repr. of 1901 ed. 61.00x (ISBN 0-8103-0159-8). Gale.

Phyllis, Hoffman. Happy Halloween. LC 82-6803. 1982. pap. 2.95 (ISBN 0-686-84871-3, A-133, Pub. by Aladdin). Atheneum.

Phypers, David, jt. auth. see Bridge, Donald.

Physician & Sports Medicine Magazine Editors, ed. Cross-Country Skiing. (The Physician & Sportsmedicine Ser.). (Illus.). 1980. 7.95 o.p. (ISBN 0-07-049872-5). McGraw.

Physick, John. The Victoria & Albert Museum: The History of its Building. (Illus.). 304p. 1983. 45.00 (ISBN 0-7148-8001-9, Pub by Salem Hse Ltd). Merrimack Bk Serv.

Phythian, B. A., ed. A Concise Dictionary of Foreign Expressions. LC 82-13895. 158p. 1982. text ed. 15.50x (ISBN 0-389-20327-0). B&N Imports.

Pi, Ying-Hsien, jt. auth. see Jo, Yung-Hwan.

Piachaud, David. The Distribution & Redistribution of Incomes. 140p. 1982. pap. text ed. 11.00x (ISBN 0-7199-1086-2, Pub. by Bedford England). Renouf.

Piaget, J., jt. auth. see Beth, E. W.

Piaget, Jean. Child's Conception of Movement & Speed. LC 70-84025. 1969. 15.00x o.s.i. (ISBN 0-465-01082-2). Basic.

--Child's Conception of Number. 1965. pap. 5.95 (ISBN 0-393-00324-8, Norton Lib). Norton.

--Insights & Illusions of Philosophy. Mays, Wolfe, tr. pap. 3.95 o.p. (ISBN 0-452-00235-4, F235, Mer). NAL.

--Intelligence & Affectivity: Their Relationship During Child Development. Brown, T. A. & Kaegi, C. E., eds. (Illus.). 1981. text ed. 8.00 (ISBN 0-8243-2901-5). Annual Reviews.

--John Amos Comenius on Education. LC 67-21499. 1968. text ed. 11.00 (ISBN 0-8077-1911-0); pap. text ed. 6.00x (ISBN 0-8077-1908-0). Tchrs Coll.

--Mechanisms of Perception. Seagrin, G. N., tr. LC 72-78462. 1969. 14.50x o.s.i. (ISBN 0-465-04432-8). Basic.

--Psychology of Intelligence. (Quality Paperback: No. 222). 1976. Repr. of 1966 ed. pap. 4.95 (ISBN 0-8226-0222-9). Littlefield.

--To Understand Is to Invent. 1976. pap. 3.95 (ISBN 0-14-004378-0). Penguin.

Piaget, Jean & Inhelder, Barbel. Mental Imagery in the Child: A Study of the Development of Imaginal Representation. LC 79-150811. 1971. 13.50x o.s.i. (ISBN 0-465-04498-0). Basic.

--Psychology of the Child. Weaver, Helen, tr. LC 73-78449. 1969. 12.50x o.s.i. (ISBN 0-465-06735-2); pap. 5.95x o.s.i. (ISBN 0-465-09500-3, TB5001). Basic.

Piaget, Jean, jt. auth. see Inhelder, Barbel.

Pialorsi, Frank & Dunkel, Patricia. Avanced Listening Comprehension. 192p. 1982. pap. text ed. 12.95 (ISBN 0-88377-227-2). Newbury Hse.

Piana, Angelina La see La Piana, Angelina.

Pianka, Eric R. Evolutionary Ecology. 3rd ed. 416p. 1982. text ed. 26.95 scp (ISBN 0-06-045232-3, HarpC). Har-Row.

Pianka, Eric R., jt. ed. see Huey, Raymond B.

Pianka, Phyllis T. Nurse of the Island. 192p. (YA) 1976. 6.95 (ISBN 0-685-66476-7, Avalon). Bouregy.

Piano, Celeste, tr. from Fr. Oh Wicked Country! LC 82-84059. (Grove Press Victorian Library). 144p. (Orig.). 1983. pap. 3.25 (ISBN 0-394-62447-5, B485, BC). Grove.

Piasecki, Bruce. Stray Prayers. 64p. 1976. 3.50 (ISBN 0-87886-075-4). Ithaca Hse.

Piatagorsky, Gregor. Cellist. (Music Report Ser.). 1976. Repr. of 1965 ed. lib. bdg. 29.50 (ISBN 0-306-70822-1). Da Capo.

Piatigorsky, A., jt. ed. see Denwood, P.

Piatigorsky, Alexander. The Buddhist Philosophy of Thought. LC 82-3987. 320p. 1983. text ed. 23.50x (ISBN 0-389-20266-5). B&N Imports.

Piatigorsky, Alexander, jt. ed. see Denwood, Philip.

Piatti, G. Advances in Composite Materials. 1978. 98.50 (ISBN 0-85334-770-0, Pub. by Applied Sci England). Elsevier.

Piazza, Gail. World of Wok Cookery. LC 82-71462. (Illus.). 144p. 1982. pap. 5.95 (ISBN 0-916752-59-3). Dorison Hse.

Piazza, Peter B., jt. auth. see Cunliffe, Frederick.

Piazza, Robert, ed. Reading Disorders. (Special Education Ser.). (Illus., Orig.). 1978. pap. text ed. 15.00 (ISBN 0-89568-085-8). Spec Learn Corp.

--Readings in Hyperactivity. (Special Education Ser.). (Illus.). 1979. pap. text ed. 15.00 (ISBN 0-89568-107-2). Spec Learn Corp.

--Readings in Language & Writing Disorders. (Special Education Ser.). (Illus., Orig.). 1978. pap. text ed. 15.00 (ISBN 0-89568-087-4). Spec Learn Corp.

--Readings in Perception & Memory. (Special Education Ser.). (Illus., Orig.). 1978. pap. text ed. 15.00 (ISBN 0-89568-086-6). Spec Learn Corp.

--Three Models of Learning Disabilities. (Special Education Ser.). (Illus., Orig.). 1978. pap. text ed. 15.00 (ISBN 0-89568-089-0). Spec Learn Corp.

Picano, Felice. An Asian Minor: The True Story of Ganymede. LC 81-917. (Illus.). 126p. 1981. o.s.i. (ISBN 0-933322-07-0); pap. 6.95 (ISBN 0-933322-06-2). Sea Horse.

--Late in the Season. 1981. 12.95 o.s.i. (ISBN 0-440-04729-3). Delacorte.

--Late in the Season. 1982. pap. 3.50 (ISBN 0-440-14757-3). Dell.

--The Lure. 1979. 9.95 o.s.i. (ISBN 0-440-05081-2). Delacorte.

--Slashed to Ribbons in Defense of Love & Other Stories. 200p. (Orig.). 1983. pap. 6.95 (ISBN 0-9604724-2-8). Gay Pr NY.

Picano, Felice, ed. A True Likeness: An Anthology of Lesbian and Gay Writing Today. LC 80-24894. 320p. 1980. pap. 9.95 (ISBN 0-686-77525-2) (ISBN 0-933322-04-6). Sea Horse.

Picard, Barbara L., ed. see Robinson, H. S. & Wilson, K.

Picard, C. F. Graphs & Questionnaires. (Mathematical Studies Ser.: Vol. 32). 1978. 59.75 (ISBN 0-444-85239-5, North-Holland). Elsevier.

Picard, Emile & Simart, G. Theorie Des Fonctions Algebriques De Deux Variables Independantes 2 Vols. in 1. LC 67-31156. (Fr). 1971. 32.50 (ISBN 0-8284-0248-5). Chelsea Pub.

Picard, Jacques L. Marketing Decisions for European Operations in the U.S. LC 78-24322. (Research for Business Decisions Ser.: No. 4). 130p. 1978. 34.95 (ISBN 0-8357-0956-6, Pub. by UMI Res Pr). Univ Microfilms.

Picard, Max. The World of Silence. LC 53-5808. 232p. Repr. pap. 4.95 (ISBN 0-89526-939-2). Regnery-Gateway.

Picard, Raymond C., jt. ed. see Bryan, John L.

Picasso, Juan R. Senderos de Navidad. 24p. 1980. pap. 0.80 (ISBN 0-311-08218-1). Casa Bautista.

Picasso, Pablo. A Collection of the Ten Best Paintings by Picasso in Colors. (Illus.). 97p. 1980. deluxe ed. 21.45 (ISBN 0-930582-64-0). Gloucester Art.

Picayune. Picayune Creole Cookbook. (Dover Cookbook Ser.). 1971. pap. 6.95 (ISBN 0-486-22678-6). Dover.

Picchi, F. A Practical Guide for Mariners English-Italian. 319p. (Eng. & Ital.). 1980. pap. 29.95 (ISBN 0-686-97444-1, M-9193). French & Eur.

Piccininni, R., jt. auth. see Mahammed, N.

Piccione, Anthony. In a Gorge with a Friend. (Orig.). 1979. signed ed. 6.50 (ISBN 0-918092-11-6); pap. 3.50 (ISBN 0-686-51190-5). Tamarack Edns.

Piccone, Paul. Italian Marxism. LC 82-1474. 225p. 1983. text ed. 19.95x (ISBN 0-520-04798-2). U of Cal Pr.

Picconi, Mario J., jt. auth. see Olson, Charles.

Pichaske, David R. Jubilee College Diary. 224p. 1982. 14.95 o.p. (ISBN 0-933180-35-7). Ellis Pr.

--The Jubilee Diary: April 10, 1980-April 19, 1981. (Illus.). 240p. (Orig.). 1982. pap. 5.95 (ISBN 0-686-81707-9). Ellis Pr.

--The Poetry of Rock: The Golden Years. 192p. (Orig.). 1981. pap. 5.95 (ISBN 0-933180-17-9). Ellis Pr.

--Salem-Peoria, Eighteen Eighty-Three to Nineteen Eighty-Two. (Illus.). 256p. (Orig.). 1982. pap. 6.95 (ISBN 0-933180-40-3). Ellis Pr.

Piche, Thomas. Art Nouveau Glass & Pottery. Meyer, Faith, ed. (Illus.). 16p. (Orig.). 1982. pap. text ed. 4.00 (ISBN 0-932660-06-1). U of NI Dept Art.

Pichler, Joseph A., jt. ed. see DeGeorge, Richard T.

Pichon, Charles. Vatican & Its Role in World Affairs. Misrahi, Jean, tr. Repr. of 1950 ed. lib. bdg. 16.25x (ISBN 0-8371-2828-5, PIVW). Greenwood.

Pichon, Yann le see Le Pichon, Yann.

Pick. Mind & Body. (Warwick Press Ser.). (gr. 5 up). 1980. PLB 9.40 (ISBN 0-531-09174-0, F54). Watts.

Pick, A., ed. see Kozhevnikov, A. V.

Pick, A. I. Plasma Cell Dyscrasias. (Journal: Acta Haematologica: Vol. 68, No. 3). (Illus.). vi, 96p. 1982. pap. 35.50 (ISBN 3-8055-3549-X). S Karger.

Pick, Aaron. Dictionary of Old Testament Words for English Readers. LC 76-16230. 1977. kivar 12.95 (ISBN 0-8254-3511-0). Kregel.

Pick, Albert. Standard Catalog of World Paper Money, Vol. 2. 4th ed. Bruce, Colin & Shafer, Neil, eds. (Illus.). 960p. 1982. 35.00. Krause Pubns.

Pick, Bernard. The Cabala. LC 13-26188. 115p. 1974. pap. 4.00x (ISBN 0-87548-199-X). Open Court.

Pick, Christopher. Railways & Trains. LC 80-54123. (New Reference Library). PLB 11.96 (ISBN 0-382-06388-0). Silver.

--The Young Scientist Book of the Undersea. LC 78-17796. (Young Scientist Ser.). (Illus.). (gr. 4-5). 1978. text ed. 7.95 (ISBN 0-88436-529-8). EMC.

Pick, Christopher, ed. What's What in the Nineteen Eighty's: A Dictionary of Contemporary History, Literature, Arts, Technology, Medicine, Cinema, Theatre, Controversies, Fads, Movements & Events, Vol. 1. 399p. 1982. 42.00x (ISBN 0-8103-2035-5). Gale.

Pick, E. & Mizel, S., eds. Lymphokines, Vol. 7. 277p. 1982. 34.00 (ISBN 0-12-432007-4). Acad Pr.

Pick, Franz. Pick's Currency Yearbook 1980-1982. 23rd ed. LC 55-11013. 1983. 196.00x (ISBN 0-87551-278-X). Pick Pub.

Pick, Herbert L., Jr. & Saltzman, Elliot, eds. Modes of Perceiving & Processing Information. LC 77-21025. 1977. 14.95x o.s.i. (ISBN 0-470-99342-1). Halsted Pr.

Pick, John. Arts Administration. 256p. 1980. pap. 13.95x (ISBN 0-419-11540-4, Pub. by E & FN Spon). Methuen Inc.

Pick, M., et al. Theory of the Earth's Gravity Field. 1973. 98.00 (ISBN 0-444-40939-4). Elsevier.

Pick, Michael R. Childhood-Namhood-Manhood: The Writings of Michael Robert Pick, A Vietnam Veteran. Bradford, Elizabeth A., ed. LC 82-60704. 160p. (Orig.). 1982. pap. 4.95 (ISBN 0-910441-00-6). Pizzuto Ltd Pub.

Pickar, Gloria D. Dosage Calculations. LC 82-71146. (Illus.). 128p. 1982. pap. text ed. 9.00 (ISBN 0-8273-2090-6). Delmar.

Pickard, C. Glenn, jt. auth. see Denham, John W.

Pickard, G. L. Descriptive Physical Oceanography. 2nd ed. 220p. 1975. text ed. 12.10 o.p. (ISBN 0-08-018159-7); pap. text ed. 7.70 o.p. (ISBN 0-08-018158-9). Pergamon.

Pickard, H. M. Manual of Operative Dentistry. 5th ed. (Illus.). 1983. 19.50x (ISBN 0-19-261327-8). Oxford U Pr.

Pickard, Phyllis M. If You Think Your Child Is Gifted. (Illus.). 168p. (Orig.). 1976. 15.00 o.p. (ISBN 0-208-01583-3). Shoe String.

Pickard, Roy. Movies on Video. 1982. 20.00x (ISBN 0-584-11029-4, Pub. by Muller Ltd). State Mutual Bk.

Pickard, Tom. Hero Dust. 9.95 (ISBN 0-8052-8033-2, Pub. by Allison & Busby England); pap. 4.95 (ISBN 0-8052-8032-4). Schocken.

--The Jarrow March. (Illus.). 96p. 1983. 11.95 (ISBN 0-8052-8079-0, Pub. by Allison & Busby England); pap. 5.95 (ISBN 0-8052-8078-2). Schocken.

Pickell, M. R., jt. ed. see Hendricks, N. S.

Picken, Laurence, ed. Musica Asiatica, Vol. 3. (Illus.). 1981. pap. 22.50x (ISBN 0-19-323236-7). Oxford U Pr.

Pickens, Judy E. The Freelancers Handbook. 144p. 1981. 10.95 (ISBN 0-13-330696-8); pap. 4.95 (ISBN 0-13-330688-7). P-H.

Pickens, L. Self-Awareness & Drug Abuse & Drug Control. Zak, Therese A., ed. (Lifeworks Ser.). (Illus.). 128p. 1981. 6.12 (ISBN 0-07-049910-1). McGraw.

Pickens, Roy, jt. auth. see Hatsukami, Dorothy.

Pickens, Rupert T., ed. The Sower & His Seed: Essays on Chretien de Troyes. LC 82-84402. (French Forum Monographs: No. 44). 168p. (Orig.). 1983. pap. 12.50 (ISBN 0-917058-43-7). French Forum.

Picker, Fred. The Fine Print. (Illus.). 144p. 1975. 19.95 o.p. (ISBN 0-8174-0584-4, Amphoto). Watson-Guptill.

--Fred Picker Photographs. (Illus.). 1979. 19.95 o.p. (ISBN 0-8174-2524-1, Amphoto); pap. 12.50 o.p. (ISBN 0-8174-2187-4). Watson-Guptill.

--The Iceland Portfolio. (Illus.). 1976. signed 75.00 o.p. (ISBN 0-8174-9000-0, Amphoto). Watson-Guptill.

--The Zone VI Workshop. (Illus.). 128p. 1978. 9.95 (ISBN 0-8174-0574-7, Amphoto). Watson-Guptill.

Picker, Martin, jt. auth. see Bernstein, Martin.

Pickering, C. A., et al. Interstitial Lung Disease. (Topics in Respiratory Disease Ser.). 112p. 1982. 17.95 (ISBN 0-85200-427-3, Pub. by MTP Pr England). Kluwer Boston.

Pickering, F. B. Physical Metallurgy & Design of Steels. (Illus.). 1978. text ed. 67.75 (ISBN 0-85334-752-2, Pub. by Applied Sci England). Elsevier.

Pickering, F. B., ed. Source Book: Metallurgical Evolution of Stainless Steels. 1979. 42.00 o.p. (ISBN 0-87170-077-8). ASM.

Pickering, F. P. Essays on Medieval German Literature & Iconography. LC 78-73815. (Anglica Germanica Ser.). (Illus.). 1980. 39.95 (ISBN 0-521-22627-9). Cambridge U Pr.

Pickering, George. Creative Malady. 336p. 1976. pap. 3.95 o.s.i. (ISBN 0-440-54995-7, Delta). Dell.

Pickering, Hoeper. Concise Companion to Literature. 1981. pap. 9.95 (ISBN 0-02-395400-0). Macmillan.

Pickering, James H. Fiction One Hundred. 3rd ed. 1086p. 1982. pap. text ed. 12.95 (ISBN 0-02-395450-7). Macmillan.

Pickering, Jerry. Theatre: A Contemporary Introduction. 3rd ed. (Illus.). 402p. 1981. pap. text ed. 15.50 (ISBN 0-8299-0403-4). West Pub.

Pickering, Jerry V. A Treasury of Drama: Classical Through Modern. LC 75-1415. (Illus.). 515p. 1975. pap. text ed. 10.50 (ISBN 0-8299-0042-X). West Pub.

Pickering, John M., jt. ed. see Secor, Robert A.

Pickering, Miles. Investigations in General Chemistry. 208p. 1982. pap. text ed. write for info. (ISBN 0-87150-766-8, 4501). Grant Pr.

Pickering, R. J. Strength Training for Athletics. pap. 3.95x o.p. (ISBN 0-392-08944-0, SpS). Sportshelf.

Pickering, Samuel, Jr., jt. auth. see Butler, Francelia.

Pickering, Wilbur. A Framework for Discourse Analysis. (SIL Publications in Linguistics No. 64). 189p. 1980. pap. 10.95x (ISBN 0-88312-076-3); microfiche 2.25x (ISBN 0-88312-484-X). Summer Inst Ling.

Pickersgill, J. W., ed. The Mackenzie King Record, 4 vols. Incl. Vol. 1. 1939-1944. 1960. o.p. (ISBN 0-8020-1129-2); Vol. 2. 1944-1945. Forster, D. F., ed. 1968. 30.00x o.p. (ISBN 0-8020-1525-5); Vol. 3. 1945-1946. Forster, D. F., ed. 1970. 30.00x (ISBN 0-8020-1655-3); Vol. 4. 1947-1948. Forster, D. F., ed. 1970. 30.00x (ISBN 0-8020-1686-3). U of Toronto Pr.

Pickett, jt. auth. see Levitt.

Pickett, Albert J. History of Alabama. 669p. 1962. Repr. of 1878 ed. 12.95 (ISBN 0-87397-242-2). Strode.

Pickett, B. & Kovacs, D. The Baby Strawberry Book of Baby Farm Animals. 1980. 2.95 o.p. (ISBN 0-07-049909-8). McGraw.

--The Baby Strawberry Book of Pets. 1980. 2.95 o.p. (ISBN 0-07-049908-X). McGraw.

Pickett, D. J. Electrochemical Reactor Design. 2nd. rev. ed. LC 79-14364. (Chemical Engineering Monographs: Vol. 9). 1979. 70.25 (ISBN 0-444-41814-8). Elsevier.

Pickett, George E., jt. auth. see Hanlon, John J.

Pickett, Hazel. God's Perfect Way for You. 1949. pap. 1.95 (ISBN 0-910924-32-5). Macalester.

Pickett, J. M. Sounds of Speech Communications. (Perspectives in Audiology). 264p. 1980. text ed. 18.95 (ISBN 0-8391-1533-4). Univ Park.

Pickett, L. M. Centre Game & Danish Gambit. (Chess Player Ser.). 1977. pap. 4.95 o.s.i. (ISBN 0-900928-49-2, H-1157). Hippocrene Bks.

--Sicilian Defence Series 8: Lines with B-QN5. (Chess Player Ser.). 1977. pap. 5.95 o.p. (ISBN 0-900928-85-9, H-1193). Hippocrene Bks.

--Sicilian Defence Series 9: Rossolimo Variation. (Chess Player Ser.). 1977. pap. 5.95 o.p. (ISBN 0-900928-91-3, H-1185). Hippocrene Bks.

Pickett, Nell Ann, jt. ed. see Sparrow, W. Keats.

Pickett, Ronald, jt. auth. see Swets, John.

Pickett-Heaps, Jeremy D. Green Algae: Structure Reproduction & Evolution in Selected Genera. LC 74-24363. (Illus.). 640p. 1975. text ed. 30.00x o.p. (ISBN 0-87893-652-1). Sinauer Assoc.

Pickford, Kaylan. Always a Woman. (Illus.). 1982. pap. 9.95 (ISBN 0-686-82122-X). Bantam.

Pickford, M. University Expansion & Finance. 32.00x (ISBN 0-686-97028-4, Pub. by Scottish Academic Pr Scotland). State Mutual Bk.

Pickhardt, Robert C., jt. auth. see McLaughlin, Frank S.

Pickle, H. B. & Abrahson, R. L. Small Business Management. 2nd ed. LC 80-25071. (Wiley Series in Management). 560p. 1981. text ed. 25.95x (ISBN 0-471-06218-9); tchrs.' manual 9.00 (ISBN 0-471-08939-7); study guide 9.00x (ISBN 0-471-08938-9). Wiley.

Pickle, Hal, et al. Introduction to Business. 4th ed. (Illus.). 1980. text ed. 17.95 (ISBN 0-673-16094-7); instructor's manual free (ISBN 0-87620-486-8); study guide 7.95 (ISBN 0-87620-482-5); write for info. Career Sourcebook (ISBN 0-685-75092-2); instructional objectives manual 3.50 (ISBN 0-685-75093-0). transparency masters free; career cassette free. Scott F.

Pickle, Hal B. & Abrahamson, Royce L. Introduction to Business. 5th ed. 1982. text ed. 23.95x (ISBN 0-673-16571-X). Scott F.

Pickles, Dorothy. The Government & Politics of France, Vol. 1: Institutions & Parties. 1972. text ed. 18.50x o.p. (ISBN 0-416-30000-6); pap. 12.50x (ISBN 0-416-29990-3). Methuen Inc.

--Problems of Contemporary French Politics. 1982. 22.00x (ISBN 0-416-73230-5); pap. 9.95x (ISBN 0-416-73240-2). Methuen Inc.

Pickles, Dorothy M. Algeria & France. LC 75-35340. 1976. Repr. lib. bdg. 18.00x (ISBN 0-8371-8564-5, PIAF). Greenwood.

--The Fifth French Republic. LC 75-32461. 222p. 1976. Repr. of 1960 ed. lib. bdg. 16.25x (ISBN 0-8371-8544-0, PIFF). Greenwood.

--France: The Fourth Republic. LC 75-3870. 1976. Repr. of 1958 ed. lib. bdg. 18.25x (ISBN 0-8371-8089-9, PIFR). Greenwood.

Pickles, J. D. see Watson, George.

Pickowicz, Paul. Marxist Literary Thought & China: A Conceptual Framework. LC 79-620064. (Current Chinese Language Project; Studies in Chinese Terminology Ser.). 69p. 1980. pap. 3.50x (ISBN 0-912966-22-X). IEAS.

Pickthall. The Holy Quran: Text & Explanatory Translation. 22.50 (ISBN 0-686-18527-7). Kazi Pubns.

--The Meaning of the Glorious Quran. pap. 3.95 (ISBN 0-686-18531-5). Kazi Pubns.

Pickthall, M. Cultural Side of Islam. 6.50 (ISBN 0-686-18385-1). Kazi Pubns.

Pickthall, Marmaduke, tr. The Meaning of the Glorious Koran. 693p. 1982. Leather-bound Deluxe ed. 110.00x (ISBN 0-686-94070-9, Pub. by Garlandfold England). State Mutual Bk.

Pickthall, Mohammed M., tr. Meaning of the Glorious Koran. pap. 3.95 (ISBN 0-451-62144-1, ME1924, Ment). NAL.

Pickvance, C. G., ed. Urban Sociology: Critical Essays. LC 75-42546. 225p. 1976. 18.95 (ISBN 0-312-83475-6). St Martin.

Pico, Pancho. Matrimonio Sorprendente. 96p. 1981. pap. 1.75 (ISBN 0-311-37022-5). Casa Bautista.

Pico Della Mirandola, Giovanni. On the Dignity of Man. Wallis, Charles G., et al, trs. Bd. with On Being & Unity; Heptaplus. LC 65-26540. 1965. pap. 6.50 (ISBN 0-672-60483-3, LLA227). Bobbs.

Picon, Gaeton. Modern Painting: From 1800 to the Present. LC 74-83889. (World of Culture Ser.). (Illus.). 192p. 1975. 7.95 (ISBN 0-88225-113-9). Newsweek.

--Surrealists & Surrealism. (Illus.). 220p. 1983. pap. 14.95 (ISBN 0-8478-0486-0). Rizzoli Intl.

Picon, Molly & Grillo, Jean. Molly. 1980. 12.95 o.p. (ISBN 0-671-24016-1). S&S.

Picot, P. & Johan, Z. Atlas of Ore Minerals. (Illus.). 406p. Date not set. 170.25 (ISBN 0-444-99684-2). Elsevier.

Pictorius, Georg see Albricus.

Pidgeon, Mary E. Women in the Economy of the United States of America. Bd. with Employed Women Under NRA Codes. LC 75-8784. (FDR & the Era of the New Deal Ser.). 1975. Repr. of 1937 ed. lib. bdg. 29.50 (ISBN 0-306-70731-4). Da Capo.

PIE Seminar,Papers, Oxford, April 1979. Foreign Language Learning: Meeting Individual Needs. Altman, Howard B., ed. 128p. 1980. pap. 8.95 (ISBN 0-08-024604-4). Pergamon.

Piechowiak, Ann & Cook, Myra. Complete Guide to the Elementary Learning Center. 252p. 1980. pap. 8.95 o.p. (ISBN 0-13-160309-4, Reward). P-H.

Piediscalzi, N., et al. Distinguishing Moral Education, Values Clarification & Religion-Studies: Proceedings. Swyhart, B., ed. LC 76-26670. (American Academy of Religion. Section Papers). 1976. pap. 12.00 (ISBN 0-89130-082-1, 01-03-07). Scholars Pr Ca.

Piehl, Mel. Breaking Bread: The Catholic Worker & the Origin of Catholic Radicalism in America. LC 82-10327. 233p. 1982. 19.95 (ISBN 0-87722-257-6). Temple U Pr.

Piekalkiewicz, Janusz. The Battle for Cassino. LC 80-51757. 224p. 1980. 16.95 o.p. (ISBN 0-672-52667-0). Bobbs.

Piekalkiewicz, Jaroslaw. Communist Local Government: A Study of Poland. LC 72-85539. xiv, 282p. 1975. 18.00x (ISBN 0-8214-0140-8, 82-81438). Ohio U Pr.

Piekarski, Vicki, jt. auth. see Tuska, Jon.

Piel, E. Joseph & Truxal, John G. Technology: Handle with Care. 304p. 1975. pap. text ed. 13.00 (ISBN 0-07-049923-3, C). McGraw.

Pielou, E. C. Biogeography. LC 79-13306. 351p. 1979. 27.50x (ISBN 0-471-05845-9, Pub. by Wiley-Interscience). Wiley.

--Mathematical Ecology. LC 76-49441. 1977. 33.95x (ISBN 0-471-01993-3, Pub. by Wiley-Interscience). Wiley.

Pielou, Evelyn C. Ecological Diversity. LC 75-9663. 165p. 1975. 27.95 (ISBN 0-471-68925-4, Pub. by Wiley-Interscience). Wiley.

Piene, Otto & Mack, Heinz. Zero. 320p. 1973. 25.00 (ISBN 0-262-16041-2). MIT Pr.

Piening, Ekkehard, tr. see Streit, Jacob.

Piening, Jacob, tr. see Streit, Jocob.

Pienkowski, Jan. Dinnertime. 12p. 1981. pap. 5.95 (ISBN 0-8431-0961-0). Price Stern.

--The Haunted House. (Illus.). (ps-3). 1979. 9.95 (ISBN 0-525-31520-9, 0966-290). Dutton.

--Home. Klimo, Kate, ed. (Pienkowski Concept Bks.). (Illus.). 32p. (ps-k). 1983. 3.95 (ISBN 0-671-46246-6, Little). S&S.

--Size. Klimo, Kate, ed. (Pienkowski Concept Bks.). (Illus.). 32p. (ps-k). 1983. 3.95 (ISBN 0-671-46244-X, Little). S&S.

--Sizes. LC 74-83408. (Concept Bks). (Illus.). 32p. (ps-2). 1975. PLB 5.59 o.p. (ISBN 0-8178-5262-X). Harvey.

--Time. Klimo, Kate, ed. (Pienkowski Concept Bks.). (Illus.). 32p. (ps-k). 1983. 3.95 (ISBN 0-671-46247-4, Little). S&S.

--Weather. Klimo, Kate, ed. (Peinkowski Concept Bks.). (Illus.). 32p. (ps-k). 1983. 3.95 (ISBN 0-671-46245-8, Little). S&S.

Pienkowski, Jan, jt. auth. see Nicoll, Helen.

Pienkowski, Jan, jt. auth. see Nicoll, Helens.

Piepe, Anthony. Knowledge & Social Order. 1971. text ed. 5.00x o.p. (ISBN 0-435-82685-9). Heinemann Ed.

Piepe, Anthony, et al. Mass Media & Cultural Relationships. 184p. 1977. text ed. 28.00x o.p. (ISBN 0-566-00161-6). Renouf.

Pieper, Elizabeth. A School for Tommy: (Handling Difficult Times) LC 79-12309. (Illus.). 32p. (gr. 2-4). 1979. lib. bdg. 8.35 (ISBN 0-516-06432-0). Childrens.

Pieper, F. C., ed. Subject Index to Sources of Comparative International Statistics. 6th ed. 745p. 1978. 225.00x (ISBN 0-900246-23-5). Gale.

Pieper, Francis. Christian Dogmatics, 4 Vols. Engelder, Theodore, et al, trs. 1950-1957. Vol. 1. 16.95 (ISBN 0-570-06712-X, 15-1001); Vol. 2. 17.95 (ISBN 0-570-06713-8, 15-1002); Vol. 3. 17.95 (ISBN 0-570-06714-6, 15-1003); Vol. 4. 24.95 (ISBN 0-570-06711-1, 15-1000); Set. 69.95 (ISBN 0-570-06715-4, 15-1852). Concordia.

Pieper, Josef. Four Cardinal Virtues. 1966. pap. 4.95 (ISBN 0-268-00103-0). U of Notre Dame Pr.

--Leisure: The Basis of Culture. 1964. pap. 2.50 (ISBN 0-451-62042-9, ME2042, Ment). NAL.

--Problems of Modern Faith: Essays & Addresses. Van Heurck, Jan, tr. 1983. 12.00 (ISBN 0-8199-0856-8). Franciscan Herald.

--Scholasticism. 1964. pap. 4.95 (ISBN 0-07-049930-6, SP). McGraw.

Pieper, Kathleen. Hidden Heritage. (YA) 1979. 6.95 (ISBN 0-685-65271-8, Avalon). Bouregy.

--To Know Love. 1979. 6.95 (ISBN 0-686-52556-6, Avalon). Bouregy.

Pierard, Louis. Belgian Problems Since the War. 1929. text ed. 29.50x (ISBN 0-686-83484-4). Elliots Bks.

Pierard, Richard V., jt. auth. see Clouse, Robert G.

Pieratt, Asa B., Jr. & Klinkowitz, Jerome. Kurt Vonnegut, Jr. A Descriptive Bibliography & Annotated Secondary Checklist. (Illus.). xix, 138p. 1974. 15.00 o.p. (ISBN 0-208-01449-7, Archon). Shoe String.

Pierce. Edmund C. Tarbell & The Boston School of Printing, 1889-1980. (Illus.). 1980. 50.00 (ISBN 0-686-43148-0). Apollo.

Pierce, Allan D. Acoustics: An Introducton to Its Physical Principles & Applications. (Illus.). 656p. 1981. text ed. 33.50x (ISBN 0-07-049961-6, C); solutions manual 20.00 (ISBN 0-07-049962-4). McGraw.

Pierce, Anne E. & Glenn, N. E. Musicianship for the Elementary Teacher: Theory & Skills Through Songs. 1967. text ed. 11.95 o.p. (ISBN 0-07-049970-5, C). McGraw.

Pierce, Anthony. Canal People. (Junior Reference Ser.). (Illus.). 64p. (gr. 7 up). 8.95 (ISBN 0-7136-1811-6). Dufour.

Pierce, Barbara B., et al. The Design of Poetry. new ed. Buell, Lawrence, ed. LC 73-75454. 80p. (Orig.). (gr. 7-12). 1973. pap. text ed. 1.45 o.p. (ISBN 0-88301-080-1). Pendulum Pr.

Pierce, Bessie L. Public Opinion & the Teaching of History in the United States. LC 71-107416. (Civil Liberties in American History Ser.). 1970. Repr. of 1926 ed. lib. bdg. 45.00 (ISBN 0-306-71883-9). Da Capo.

Pierce, Carl W. & Cullen, Susan E., eds. Ir Genes: Past, Present, & Future. (Experimental Biology & Medicine Ser.). (Illus.). 640p. 1983. 64.50 (ISBN 0-89603-050-4). Humana.

Pierce, Charles. The Religious Life of Samuel Johnson. 1982. lib. bdg. 21.50 (ISBN 0-208-01992-8, Archon). Shoe String.

Pierce, Deirdre, jt. auth. see Altobello, Pat.

Pierce, Edith G. Horace Mann: Our Nation's First Educator. LC 78-128805. (Real Life Bks). (Illus.). (gr. 5-11). 1972. PLB 3.95g (ISBN 0-8225-0703-X). Lerner Pubns.

Pierce, Eleanor B. Tampa for Children of All Ages. McCaskey, Mary J., ed. LC 80-82486. (Illus.). 124p. Date not set. pap. 5.95 (ISBN 0-686-84249-9). Banyan Bks.

Pierce, Enneking, jt. auth. see Joseph, John.

Pierce, F. E., jt. auth. see MacCracken, H. N.

Pierce, Flora M. Sonnets of Eve. LC 72-90713. 1973. 8.95 (ISBN 0-87716-040-6, Pub. by Moore Pub Co). F Apple.

Pierce, Frank. Amadis de Gaula. (World Authors Ser.). 1976. lib. bdg. 15.95 (ISBN 0-8057-6220-5, Twayne). G K Hall.

Pierce, Frederick E. World That God Destroyed & Other Poems. 1911. text ed. 24.50x (ISBN 0-686-83865-3). Elliots Bks.

Pierce, G. Barry, et al. Cancer: A Problem of Developmental Biology. (Foundations of Developmental Biology Ser.). 1978. 22.95 (ISBN 0-13-113373-X). P-H.

Pierce, Gail. The New Age Brown Rice Cookbook. LC 81-84830. (Illus.). 172p. (Orig.). 1982. pap. 9.95 (ISBN 0-9607436-0-X). Sea-Wind Pr.

Pierce, Harold E., ed. Cosmetic Plastic Surgery in Non-white Patients. 260p. 1982. 32.50 (ISBN 0-8089-1495-2, 793303). Grune.

Pierce, Hazel. Philip K. Dick. (Starmont Reader's Guide Ser.: No. 12). 64p. 1982. Repr. lib. bdg. 10.95x (ISBN 0-89370-043-6). Borgo Pr.

--Reader's Guide to Philip K. Dick. Schlobin, Roger C., ed. (Reader's Guides to Contemporary Science Fiction & Fantasy Authors Ser.: Vol. 12). (Illus., Orig.). 1982. 10.95x (ISBN 0-916732-34-7); pap. text ed. 4.95x (ISBN 0-916732-33-9). Starmont Hse.

Pierce, J. From Abacus to Zeus: A Handbook of Art History. 1977. pap. text ed. 9.95 (ISBN 0-13-331686-6). P-H.

Pierce, J. R. The Beginnings of Satellite Communications. LC 68-19315. (History of Technology Monographs). (Illus.). 1968. 5.00 (ISBN 0-911302-05-0). San Francisco Pr.

Pierce, Jack. The Freight Train Book. LC 79-91307. (Illus.). (ps-3). 1980. PLB 7.95g (ISBN 0-87614-123-8). Carolrhoda Bks.

--The State Fair Book. LC 79-91308. (Illus.). (ps-3). 1980. PLB 7.95g (ISBN 0-87614-124-6). Carolrhoda Bks.

Pierce, James A., jt. auth. see Anzaldua, Mike M., Jr.

Pierce, Joe E. Development of Linguistic System in English Speaking American Children, Vol. 2. 130p. (Orig.). 1981. pap. 10.95 o.p. (ISBN 0-913244-51-1). Hapi Pr.

--Fairy Princess. LC 82-83473. 125p. (Orig.). 1982. pap. 5.95 (ISBN 0-913244-58-9). Hapi Pr.

Pierce, John & Doerksen, Harvey R. Water Politics & Public Involvement. LC 76-1723. (Man, Community & Natural Resources Ser.). (Illus.). 1976. 30.00 o.p. (ISBN 0-250-40128-2). Ann Arbor Science.

Pierce, John C., et al. The Dynamics of American Public Opinion: Patterns & Processes. 1981. pap. text ed. 17.95x (ISBN 0-673-16055-6). Scott F.

Pierce, John G., ed. Proteins & Peptides Hormones. LC 82-6159. (Benchmark Papers in Biochemistry: Vol. 4). 480p. 1982. 58.00 (ISBN 0-87933-417-7). Hutchinson Ross.

Pierce, John R. Almost All About Waves. 1974. pap. 5.95x (ISBN 0-262-66027-X). MIT Pr.

Pierce, John T., jt. auth. see Furuseth, Owen J.

Pierce, Josiah. Letters to Laura: Letters from Josiah Pierce, Jr. to Laura Dunham, 1884-1889. 120p. 1974. 7.50 (ISBN 0-87923-156-4). Godine.

Pierce, L. R., ed. see Parham, William L.

Pierce, Leona, jt. auth. see De Regniers, Beatrice S.

Pierce, Margaret, jt. auth. see Pierce, Robert.

Pierce, Marjorie. East of the Gabilans. LC 76-56566. (Illus.). 1977. 15.00 o.p. (ISBN 0-913548-39-1, Valley Calif). Western Tanager.

Pierce, Meredith. The Darkangel. 192p. (YA) (gr. 7 up). 1982. 11.95 (ISBN 0-316-70741-4, Pub. by Atlantic Monthly Pr). Little.

Pierce, Milton. How to Collect Your Overdue Bills: A Guide to Collection Techniques & Customer Relations. LC 80-66023. 1980. 19.95 o.p. (ISBN 0-87094-198-4). Dow Jones-Irwin.

--Money Matters: Hundreds of Ways to Save Thousands of Dollars. (Illus.). 256p. 1981. pap. 8.95 (ISBN 0-8256-3224-2, Quick Fox). Putnam Pub Group.

Pierce, Noel. Praetorius Point. LC 77-10064. 1978. 8.95 o.p. (ISBN 0-698-10858-2, Coward). Putnam Pub Group.

Pierce, Patty. Along Came Love. 192p. (Orig.). Date not set. pap. cancelled o.p. (ISBN 0-505-51842-2). Tower Bks.

Pierce, Phyllis. The Dow Jones Investor's Handbook, 1983. LC 66-17630. 136p. 1983. 11.95 (ISBN 0-87094-397-9). Dow Jones-Irwin.

Pierce, Phyllis, ed. The Dow Jones Averages, 1885-1980. LC 82-72368. 300p. 1982. 47.50 (ISBN 0-87094-353-7). Dow Jones-Irwin.

--Dow Jones Investor's Handbook, 1982. LC 82-71541. 150p. 1982. pap. 10.95 o.p. (ISBN 0-87094-323-5). Dow Jones-Irwin.

Pierce, R. C. & Tebeaux, W. Gene. Operational Mathematics for Business. 512p. 1980. text ed. 20.95x (ISBN 0-534-00789-9). Wadsworth Pub.

Pierce, R. C., Jr., jt. auth. see Anderson, Chaney.

Pierce, Richard S. Associative Algebras. (Graduate Texts in Mathematics: Vol. 88). 416p. 1982. 39.00 (ISBN 0-387-90693-2). Springer-Verlag.

Pierce, Robert. A Picture Puzzle Activity Book. LC 76-19666. (Elephant Bks). (Illus.). 1977. pap. 1.25 (ISBN 0-448-12725-3, G&D). Putnam Pub Group.

Pierce, Robert & Pierce, Margaret. High Sierra Hiking Guide to Yosemite. 3rd ed. Winnett, Thomas, ed. LC 74-75768. (High Sierra Hiking Guide Ser.: Vol. 1). (Illus.). 96p. (Orig.). 1974. pap. 4.95 (ISBN 0-911824-34-0). Wilderness.

Pierce, Robert, et al. Feeling-Expressive Psychotherapy. 1983. 24.95 (ISBN 0-89876-015-1). Gardner Pr.

Pierce, W. C., et al. Quantitative Analysis. 4th ed. LC 58-7905. 1958. 28.95 o.s.i. (ISBN 0-471-68904-1). Wiley.

Pierce, Walter D. & Gray, Charles E. Deciphering the Learning Domains: A Second Generation Classification Model for Educational Objectives. LC 79-66225. 1979. lib. bdg. 21.25 (ISBN 0-8191-1470-7); pap. text ed. 11.50 (ISBN 0-8191-0816-2). U Pr of Amer.

Pierce, Walter D., jt. auth. see Lorber, Michael A.

Piercy, Caroline B. The Shaker Cookbook. 1969. 3.00 o.p. (ISBN 0-517-01424-6). Crown.

Piercy, Frederick. Route from Liverpool to the Great Salt Lake Valley. facsimile ed. Brodie, Fawn M., ed. LC 62-19223. (The John Harvard Library). 1962. 17.50x o.p. (ISBN 0-674-77956-8). Harvard U Pr.

Piercy, Marge. Braided Lives. 576p. 1983. pap. 3.95 (ISBN 0-449-20018-3, Crest). Fawcett.

--Hard Loving. LC 70-82544. (Wesleyan Poetry Program: Vol. 46). 77p. 1969. 10.00x (ISBN 0-8195-2046-2, Pub. by Wesleyan U Pr); pap. 6.95 (ISBN 0-8195-1046-7). Columbia U Pr.

--Living in the Open. 1976. pap. 5.95 (ISBN 0-394-73171-9). Knopf.

--Parti-Colored Blocks for a Quilt: Poets on Poetry. 320p. 1982. pap. 7.95 (ISBN 0-472-06338-3). U of Mich Pr.

--Stone, Paper, Knife. LC 82-48050. 125p. 1983. 12.95 (ISBN 0-394-52802-6); pap. 5.95 (ISBN 0-394-71219-6). Knopf.

--Vida. 480p. 1981. 15.00 (ISBN 0-671-40110-6). Ultramarine Pub.

Piercy, Marge & Wood, Ira. The Last White Class: A Play About Neighborhood Terror. LC 79-18884. 160p. 1979. 12.95 (ISBN 0-89594-028-0); pap. 5.95 (ISBN 0-89594-027-2). Crossing Pr.

Piercy, Nigel. Export Strategy: Markets & Competition. 272p. 1982. text ed. 30.00x (ISBN 0-04-382037-9); pap. text ed. 13.95x (ISBN 0-04-382038-7). Allen Unwin.

Pierini, Francis P. Children's Theater in Elementary School. 88p. 1977. pap. 1.00 (ISBN 0-8164-0342-2). Seabury.

Pierman, Carol J. The Naturalized Citizen. LC 81-82537. (Illus.). 68p. 1981. pap. 3.00 (ISBN 0-89823-031-4). New Rivers Pr.

Piero & Chiara. I Giovedi Della Signora Giulia. (Easy Readers, B). 1977. pap. 3.95 (ISBN 0-88436-292-2). EMC.

Pieroni, Robert E. Family Practice Review, Vol. 2. LC 79-91973. 1980. pap. 20.00 (ISBN 0-87488-181-1). Med Exam.

--Internal Medicine Review. 2nd ed. LC 82-6777. (Illus.). 320p. 1982. text ed. 12.00x (ISBN 0-668-05488-3, 5488). Arco.

--Medical Examination Review: Behavioral Sciences. 1982. pap. text ed. 12.50 (ISBN 0-87488-221-4). Med Exam.

--National Boards Exam Review: Clinical Sciences, Pt. II. 4th ed. 1982. pap. 26.50; pap. 26.50 (ISBN 0-87488-101-3). Med Exam.

--Rheumatology. 2nd ed. (Medical Examination Review: Vol. 31). 1983. pap. text ed. 23.00 (ISBN 0-87488-144-7). Med Exam.

--Self-Assessment of Current Knowledge in Rheumatology. 3rd ed. 1982. pap. text ed. 22.00 (ISBN 0-87488-258-3). Med Exam.

Pieroni, Robert E. & Beetham, William P., Jr. Rheumatology. (Medical Examination Review Book: Vol. 31). 1974. spiral bdg. 22.00 o.p. (ISBN 0-87488-144-7). Med Exam.

Pieroni, Robert E. & Scutchfield, F. Family Practice Review. 1978. 20.00 (ISBN 0-87488-134-X). Med Exam.

Pieroth, Kuno F. The Great German Wine Book. LC 82-61708. (Illus.). 208p. 1983. 22.50 (ISBN 0-8069-0254-X). Sterling.

Pierpoint, Robert C. At the White House: Assignments to Six Presidents. (Illus.). 192p. 1981. 11.95 (ISBN 0-399-12281-8). Putnam Pub Group.

Pierpoint, S., jt. auth. see Robb, D. A.

Pierre, Dominique La see Collins, Larry & La Pierre, Dominique.

Pierre, Donald A. & Lowe, Michael J. An Introduction with Computer Programs. (Applied Mathematics & Computation Ser.: No. 9). 464p. 1975. text ed. 29.50 (ISBN 0-201-05796-4); pap. text ed. 14.50 (ISBN 0-201-05797-2). A-W.

Pierret, Robert F. & Neudeck, Gerold W. Modular Series on Solid State Devices: Semiconductor Fundamentals, Vol. I. LC 81-14978. (Electrical Engineering Ser.). (Illus.). Date not set. pap. text ed. 35.80 (ISBN 0-201-05320-9); solutions manual avail. (ISBN 0-201-05324-1). A-W.

Pierrot, Jean. The Decadent Imagination, 1880-1900. Coltman, Derek, tr. LC 81-4828. 304p. 1982. 22.50x (ISBN 0-226-66822-3). U of Chicago Pr.

Pierrot, Roland. Chemical & Determinative Tables of Mineralogy Without the Silicates. LC 79-90000. 608p. 1980. 98.75x (ISBN 0-89352-077-2). Masson Pub.

Pierrot-Bults, A. C., jt. ed. see Van der Spoel, S.

Piers, Anthony. Rings of Ice. 1974. pap. 1.50 o.p. (ISBN 0-380-00039-3, 38166). Avon.

Piers, Maria W., ed. Play & Development: A Symposium. 1977. 12.95x o.p. (ISBN 0-393-01003-1, N871, Norton Lib); pap. 2.95 (ISBN 0-393-00871-1). Norton.

Piersel. Photophonics II. (Illus.). (gr. 1-5). 1968. pap. 2.39x (ISBN 0-87783-074-6); tchr's guide 0.29x (ISBN 0-87783-202-1). Oddo.

Piersol, Allan G., jt. auth. see Bendat, Julius S.

Pierson, A. T. Acts of the Holy Spirit. 127p. 1980. pap. 2.50 (ISBN 0-87509-274-8). Chr Pubns.

--The Holy Care of the Body. 1966. pap. 0.45 (ISBN 0-87509-093-1). Chr Pubns.

Pierson, Carlos C., tr. see Le Roy.

Pierson, Carlos C., tr. see Tidwell, J. B.

Pierson, Daniel J. Man & Woman Teacher Manual. rev. ed. (To Live in Christ Ser.). 264p. 1980. pap. 4.75 (ISBN 0-697-01751-6). Wm C Brown.

Pierson, Don. Lee Roy Selmon: The Giant from Oklahoma. LC 82-4485. (Sports Stars Ser.). (gr. 2-8). 1982. 7.95 (ISBN 0-516-04324-2); pap. 2.50 (ISBN 0-516-44324-0). Childrens.

--Terry Bradshaw: Super Bowl Quarterback. LC 81-6113. (Sports Stars Ser.). (Illus.). 48p. (gr. 2-8). 1981. PLB 7.95 (ISBN 0-516-04317-X); pap. 2.50 (ISBN 0-516-44317-8). Childrens.

Pierson, Elizabeth C. & Pierson, Jan Erik. A Birder's Guide to the Coast of Maine. LC 81-67953. (Illus.). 224p. 1981. pap. 8.95 (ISBN 0-89272-118-9, PIC471). Down East.

Pierson, Jan. The Mystery of Skull Rocks Mansion. (gr. 5-10). 1983. pap. 2.95 (ISBN 0-8423-4665-1, 75-4665-1). Tyndale.

Pierson, Jan Erik, jt. auth. see Pierson, Elizabeth C.

Pierson, John H. Full Employment. 1941. text ed. 39.50x (ISBN 0-686-83556-5). Elliots Bks.

--Full Employment Without Inflation. LC 79-5446. 252p. 1980. text ed. 18.50x (ISBN 0-916672-39-5). Allanheld.

Pierson, K. K. Principles of Prosection: A Guide for the Anatomic Pathologist. 236p. 1974. 30.00x (ISBN 0-471-05811-4, Pub. by Wiley Med). Wiley.

Pierson, Lance, jt. auth. see Mandeville, Sylvia.

Pierson, Paul E. Themes from Acts. LC 82-80153. (Bible Commentary for Laymen Ser.). (Orig.). 1982. pap. 2.50 (ISBN 0-8307-0819-7, S361107). Regal.

Pierson, Raymond H. Guide to Spanish Idioms. 180p. 1981. 30.00x (ISBN 0-85950-334-8, Pub. by Thornes England). State Mutual Bk.

Pierson, Tobie W. The Yellow Fetish. 1979. 6.95 o.p. (ISBN 0-533-04069-8). Vantage.

Pierson, W. J., jt. auth. see Neumann, Gerhard.

Pierson, William H. & Jordy, William H. American Buildings & Their Architects. Incl. Vol. 1. The Colonial & Neo-Classical Styles. Pierson, William H., Jr. (Illus.). 544p. pap. (ISBN 0-385-01623-9); Vol. 3. Progressive & Academic Ideals at the Turn of the Century. Jordy, William H. (Illus.). 448p. pap. (ISBN 0-385-05702-4); Vol. 4. The Impact of European Modernism in the Mid-Twentieth Century. Jordy, William H. (Illus.). 512p. pap. (ISBN 0-385-05704-0). 1976. pap. 10.95 ea. (Anch). Doubleday.

Pierson, William H., Jr. American Buildings & Their Architects, Volume 2A: Technology & the Picturesque, the Corporate & the Early Gothic Styles. LC 76-369389. (Illus.). 1978. pap. 10.95 (ISBN 0-385-08179-0, Anch). Doubleday.

Piesarskas, B. & Baravykas, V. Lithuanian-English, English-Lithuanian Dictionary, 2 vols. 30.00 set (ISBN 0-685-39857-9). Heinman.

Pieterse, Cosmo. Echo & Choruses. LC 74-620029. (Papers in International Studies: Africa: No. 22). 1974. pap. 5.00 (ISBN 0-89680-055-5, Ohio U Ctr Intl). Ohio U Pr.

Pieterse, Cosmo & Duerden, Dennis, eds. African Writers Talking. LC 72-75255. 195p. 1972. 25.00x (ISBN 0-8419-0118-X, Africana); pap. 15.00x (ISBN 0-8419-0119-8, Africana). Holmes & Meier.

Pieterse, Cosmo & Munro, Donald, eds. Protest & Conflict in African Literature. LC 77-80856. 127p. 1969. 14.50x (ISBN 0-8419-0004-3, Africana); pap. 9.50x (ISBN 0-8419-0005-1, Africana). Holmes & Meier.

Pietersma, Albert, et al. The Apocalypse of Elijah. LC 79-24788. 1981. pap. 14.25 (ISBN 0-89130-372-3, 06-02-19). Scholars Pr CA.

Pietralunga, Mario, tr. see Lajolo, Davide.

Pietralunga, Mark see Lajolo, Davide.

Pietro, Anthony San see San Pietro, Anthony, et al.

Pietro, Phil Di see Di Pietro, Phil.

Pietro, Robert Di see Di Pietro, Robert.

Pietrocola-Rossetti, T., tr. see Carroll, Lewis.

Pietrofesa, John J., et al. Counseling. 1978. 23.50 (ISBN 0-395-30698-1). HM.

--The Authentic Counselor. 2nd ed. 1978. pap. 12.50 (ISBN 0-395-30697-3). HM.

Pietrusewsky, Michael. Prehistoric Human Skeletal Remains from Papua New Guinea & the Marquesas. LC 76-521. (Asian & Pacific Archeology Ser.: No. 7). 1976. pap. 7.00x (ISBN 0-8248-0525-9). UH Pr.

Pietrzyk, Donald J. & Frank, Clyde. Analytical Chemistry. 2nd ed. 700p. 1979. 26.00 (ISBN 0-12-555160-6); pap. text ed. 3.50 instr's manual (ISBN 0-12-555162-2). Acad Pr.

Pietsch, A. Operator Ideals. (North Holland Mathematical Library: Vol. 20). 432p. 1979. 85.00 (ISBN 0-444-85293-X, North Holland). Elsevier.

Pietsch, W. Roll Pressing. 1976. 42.95 (ISBN 0-471-25952-7, Wiley Heyden). Wiley.

Piety, Patricia & Kettering, Charles F. The Kettering Digest. (Illus.). 94p. 1982. pap. 3.95 (ISBN 0-913428-45-0). Landfall Pr.

Pietzschke, F., ed. Portuguese-English, English-Portuguese Illustrated Dictionary: The New Michaelis, 2 vols. 28th ed. 1982. Set. 125.00 (ISBN 0-685-58551-4). Portuguese-english, 24th Ed (ISBN 3-7653-0050-0). English-portuguese, 26th Ed (ISBN 3-7653-0051-9). Heinman.

Pieyre de Mandiargues, Andre. The Motorcycle. Howard, Richard, tr. from French. LC 76-40432. 1976. Repr. of 1965 ed. lib. bdg. 16.00x (ISBN 0-8371-9061-4, MAMC). Greenwood.

Pifer, Drury. Smack. (Contemporary Drama Ser.). 6.95x (ISBN 0-912262-58-3); pap. 2.95 (ISBN 0-912262-59-1). Proscenium.

Pifer, George W. & Mutoh, Nancy W. Points of View. LC 77-972. 1977. pap. text ed. 7.95 (ISBN 0-88377-072-5). Newbury Hse.

Pigeon, Robert F., jt. ed. see Odum, Howard T.

Pigg, R. Morgan, jt. auth. see Rash, J. Keogh.

Pigg, Robert M., Jr. Professional Preparation in Patient Education. 1982. pap. 3.00x (ISBN 0-941636-50-X). IN U Dept Health.

Piggins, Carol Ann, jt. auth. see Thurman, Anne.

Piggott, Derek. Beginning Gliding: The Fundamentals of Soaring Flight. (Illus.). 208p. 1982. 22.50x (ISBN 0-06-495569-9). B&N Imports.

Piggott, F. T. The Music & Musical Instruments of Japan. LC 70-155234. (Music Ser). 1971. Repr. of 1909 ed. lib. bdg. 25.00 (ISBN 0-306-70160-X). Da Capo.

Piggott, Patrick. The Life & Music of John Field, 1782-1837: Creator of the Nocturne. (Illus.). 1974. 58.50x (ISBN 0-520-02412-5). U of Cal Pr.

Piggott, Stuart. Scotland Before History. (Illus.). 200p. 1982. text ed. 15.00 (ISBN 0-85224-348-0, Pub. by Edinburgh U Pr Scotland). Columbia U Pr.

Piggott, Stuart, jt. auth. see Clark, John G.

Piggott, Stuart, ed. The Agrarian History of England & Wales, Vol. 1, Pt. 1: Prehistory. LC 66-19763. (Agrarian History of England & Wales Ser.). 1981. 64.50 (ISBN 0-521-08741-4). Cambridge U Pr.

--Approach to Archaeology. (Illus.). 1959. pap. 2.45 o.p. (ISBN 0-07-050013-4, SP). McGraw.

--Sale Catalogues of Libraries of Eminent Persons: Antiquaries, Vol. 10. 520p. 1975. 27.00 o.p. (ISBN 0-7201-0378-9, Pub. by Mansell England). Wilson.

Pigman, W. & Horton, D. The Carbohydrates. 2nd ed. Incl. Vol. 1A. 1972. 78.50 (ISBN 0-12-556301-9); subscription 67.00; Vol. 2A. 1970. 64.00, subscription 55.00 (ISBN 0-12-556302-7); Vol. 2B. 1970. 83.00, subscription 71.00 (ISBN 0-12-556352-3). Acad Pr.

Pigman, Ward & Horton, Derek, eds. Advances in Carbohydrate Chemistry & Biochemistry, Vol. 34. 1977. 71.00 (ISBN 0-12-007234-3); lib. ed. 91.00 (ISBN 0-12-007280-7); microfiche 51.00 (ISBN 0-12-007281-5). Acad Pr.

Pignataro, Louis J. Traffic Engineering: Theory & Practice. (Illus.). 512p. 1973. 34.95 (ISBN 0-13-926220-2). P-H.

Pignataro, Robert J. Say It in English for Italian-Speaking People. 1956. pap. 1.50 (ISBN 0-486-20816-8). Dover.

Pignatti, Terisio. The Golden Century of Venetian Painting. Donahue, Kenneth, ed. Baca, Murtha, tr. from It. (Illus.). 1979. 14.95 (ISBN 0-87587-088-0); 0.00 o.p. (ISBN 0-686-86270-8). LA Co Art Mus.

--Master Drawings: From Cave Art to Picasso. (Illus.). 400p. 1982. 65.00 (ISBN 0-8109-1663-0). Abrams.

--Painting One. LC 73-89393. (World of Culture Ser.). (Illus.). 192p. 1974. 12.95 o.p. (ISBN 0-88225-105-8). Newsweek.

--Veronese: L'Opera Completa, 2 vols. (Illus., It.). 1977. Set. 180.00 o.p. (ISBN 0-685-91093-8). Vol. 1 (ISBN 0-8478-5001-3). Vol. 2 (ISBN 0-8478-5297-0). Rizzoli Intl.

Pignatti, Terisio, et al. Los Angeles County Museum of Art Bulletin, 1975, Vol. 21. LC 58-35949. (Illus.). 1976. pap. text ed. 2.50 o.p. (ISBN 0-87587-069-4). LA Co Art Mus.

Pigors, Paul & Myers, Charles A. Personnel Administration: A Point of View & a Method. 9th ed. (Illus.). 560p. 1981. text ed. 24.95x (ISBN 0-07-049971-3, C); instr's. manual 15.95 (ISBN 0-07-049972-1). McGraw.

Pigou, Arthur C. Essays in Applied Economics. 199p. 1965. 29.50x (ISBN 0-7146-1240-5, F Cass Co). Biblio Dist.

--Income: An Introduction to Economics. LC 78-21487. 1979. Repr. of 1966 ed. lib. bdg. 16.25x (ISBN 0-313-20665-1, PIIN). Greenwood.

--The Veil of Money. LC 78-10214. 1979. Repr. of 1949 ed. lib. bdg. 19.25x (ISBN 0-313-20742-9, PIVM). Greenwood.

Pigrem, Sheila. Help, I Can't Draw, 3 bks. LC 77-84096. 1978. Set. pap. 9.50 (ISBN 0-8066-1628-8, 10-3004); pap. 3.95 ea. Bk. 1 (ISBN 0-8066-1629-6, 10-3001). Bk. 2 (ISBN 0-8066-1630-X, 10-3003). Bk. 3 (ISBN 0-8066-1631-8). Augsburg.

Pijl, L. Van Der see Van der Pijl, L.

Pijpers, F. W., jt. auth. see Kateman, G.

Pikarsky, Milton & Christensen, Daphne. Urban Transportation Policy & Management. (Illus.). 272p. 1976. 23.95 o.p. (ISBN 0-669-00955-5). Lexington Bks.

Pike, Arnold. Viewpoint on Nutrition. LC 80-24024. 221p. 1980. Repr. of 1973 ed. lib. bdg. 12.95x (ISBN 0-89370-621-3). Borgo Pr.

--Viewpoint on Nutrition. 224p. (Orig.). 1973. pap. 4.95 o.p. (ISBN 0-87877-021-6, H-21). Newcastle Pub.

Pike, Arthur M., jt. auth. see Popkin, Gary S.

Pike, Charles R. The Killing Trail. large print ed. LC 81-4739. 228p. 1981. Repr. of 1980 ed. 7.95x o.p. (ISBN 0-89621-279-3). Thorndike Pr.

Pike, Christopher, ed. The Futurists, the Formalists & the Marxist Critique. Andrew, Joe & Pike, Christopher, trs. from Rus. 265p. 1979. text ed. 20.00x o.p. (ISBN 0-906133-14-9). Humanities.

Pike, Christopher, tr. see Pike, Christopher.

Pike, D. Australia: The Quiet Continent. 2nd ed. (Illus.). 1970. 32.50 (ISBN 0-521-07745-1); pap. 10.95x (ISBN 0-521-09604-9). Cambridge U Pr.

Pike, Diane K. & Lorrance, Arleen. Channeling Love Energy. rev ed. LC 75-42074. 88p. 1976. pap. 3.00 o.p. (ISBN 0-916192-02-4). L P Pubns.

Pike, Douglas. Viet Cong: The Organization & Techniques of the National Liberation Front of South Vietnam. (Studies in Communism, Revisionism & Revolution). (Illus.). 1966. 20.00x (ISBN 0-262-16014-5); pap. 4.95 o.p. (ISBN 0-262-66006-7). MIT Pr.

--War, Peace, & the Viet Cong. 1969. 15.00x (ISBN 0-262-16028-5). MIT Pr.

Pike, E. G., jt. auth. see Pike, K. L.

Pike, E. Royston. Human Documents of the Lloyd George Era. (Illus.). 378p. 1972. 9.95 o.p. (ISBN 0-312-39900-6). St Martin.

Pike, E. Royston, ed. Golden Times: Human Documents of the Victorian Age. LC 67-28725. (Illus.). 386p. 1972. pap. 3.95 o.p. (ISBN 0-8052-0335-4). Schocken.

Pike, Eunice V. Dictation Exercises in Phonetics. 188p. 1963. pap. 5.00x (ISBN 0-88312-900-0); 2.25 (ISBN 0-88312-382-7). Summer Inst Ling.

Pike, Evelyn, jt. auth. see Pike, Kenneth L.

Pike, Frank. Ah! Mischief: The Writer & Televison. 160p. (Orig.). 1982. pap. 6.95 (ISBN 0-571-11881-X). Faber & Faber.

Pike, Frederick B. Spanish America: Tradition & Social Innovation. (Library of World Civilization Ser.). 1973. 7.95x (ISBN 0-393-05488-8); pap. 4.95x (ISBN 0-393-09340-9). Norton.

Pike, James. Scout & Ranger. LC 74-39282. (The American Scene Ser). (Illus.). 164p. 1972. Repr. of 1932 ed. lib. bdg. 25.00 (ISBN 0-306-70458-7). Da Capo.

Pike, James A. & Pittenger, W. Norman. Faith of the Church. (Orig.). 1951. pap. 1.00 (ISBN 0-8164-2019-X, SP3). Seabury.

Pike, Jody P. & Singer, Pamela M. On the Move: What to Do after the Moving Van Leaves. LC 82-80653. 136p. 1982. pap. 6.95 (ISBN 0-942892-00-3). Three Meadows Pr.

Pike, K. L. & Pike, E. G. Grammatical Analysis. rev. ed. (Publications in Linguistics & Related Fields Ser. No.53: No. 51). 1981. pap. 16.00x (ISBN 0-88312-066-6); microfiche 5.25x (ISBN 0-686-67824-9). Summer Inst Ling.

Pike, Kenneth L. Linguistic Concepts: An Introduction to Tagmemics. LC 81-19814. (Illus.). xvi, 146p. 1982. 19.95 (ISBN 0-8032-3664-6, BB 790, Bison); pap. 6.95x (ISBN 0-8032-8703-8). U of Nebr Pr.

--Tagmemic & Matrix Linguistics Applied to Selected African Languages. (Publications in Linguistics & Related Fields Ser.: No. 23). 122p. 1970. pap. 3.00x (ISBN 0-88312-025-9); microfiche 2.25x (ISBN 0-88312-425-4). Summer Inst Ling.

Pike, Kenneth L. & Pike, Evelyn. Instructors Guide to Grammatical Analysis. 1977. instructor's guide o. p. 16.00x (ISBN 0-88312-910-8); microfiche 2.25 (ISBN 0-88312-393-2). Summer Inst Ling.

Pike, Kenneth L., jt. ed. see Suharno, Ignatius.

Pike, Luke O. History of Crime in England, Illustrating the Changes of the Laws in the Progress of Civilization, 2 Vols. LC 68-55779. (Criminology, Law Enforcement, & Social Problems Ser.: No. 19). (Repr. 1873-76). 1968. Set. 40.00x (ISBN 0-87585-019-7). Patterson Smith.

Pike, Mary A. Town & Country Fare & Fable: A Collection of Regional Recipes & Customs. LC 78-60989. (Illus.). 1978. 11.95 o.p. (ISBN 0-7153-7720-5). David & Charles.

Pike, Nelson. God & Timelessness. LC 74-100988. (Studies in Ethics & the Philosophy of Religion). 1970. 7.00x o.p. (ISBN 0-8052-3332-6). Schocken.

Pike, Norman. The Peach Tree. (Illus.). 32p. 1983. 8.95 (ISBN 0-88045-014-2). Stemmer Hse.

Pike, Royston E. Britain's Prime Ministers from Walpole to Wilson. (Illus.). 1970. 8.95 o.p. (ISBN 0-600-72032-2). Transatlantic.

Pike, Royston E., ed. Human Documents of the Victorian Golden Age. 1967. text ed. 12.50x (ISBN 0-04-942136-0); pap. text ed. 9.50x o.p. (ISBN 0-04-942136-0). Allen Unwin.

Pike, Ruth. Penal Servitude in Early Modern Spain. LC 82-70551. (Illus.). 224p. 1983. text ed. 26.00 (ISBN 0-299-09260-7). U of Wis Pr.

Pike, Ruth L. & Brown, Myrtle L. Nutrition: An Integrated Approach. 2nd ed. LC 75-1488. 1082p. 1975. text ed. 38.50 (ISBN 0-471-68977-7). Wiley.

Pike, Trisha, jt. auth. see Gibson, Michael.

Pike, William H. Why Stocks Go Up (& Down) A Guide to Sound Investing. LC 82-71875. 298p. 1983. 19.95 (ISBN 0-87094-314-6). Dow Jones-Irwin.

Pike, Zebulon M. Account of Expeditions to the Source of the Mississippi, the Southwest, Etc, 2 vols. facsimile ed. 1965. Set. boxed 22.50 o.p. (ISBN 0-87018-049-5). Ross.

--Zebulon Pike's Arkansaw Journal. Hart, Stephen H. & Hulbert, Archer B., eds. LC 72-138172. (Illus.). 200p. 1972. Repr. of 1932 ed. lib. bdg. 16.25x (ISBN 0-8371-5629-7, PIAJ). Greenwood.

Pikunas, Justin. Fundamental Child Psychology. rev. ed. 1965. 7.95 o.p. (ISBN 0-02-824600-4). Glencoe.

--Human Development: An Emergent Science. 3rd ed. (Illus.). 1976. text ed. 26.00 (ISBN 0-07-050015-0, C); instructor's manual 7.95 (ISBN 0-07-050026-6). McGraw.

--Manual for the Pikunas Graphoscopic Scale. 3rd ed. LC 81-43841. (Illus.). 70p. (Orig.). 1982. 7.00 (ISBN 0-8191-2351-X). U Pr of Amer.

Piland, William E., jt. auth. see Weinrauch, J. Donald.

Pilapil, F. & Studva, K., eds. Programmed Instruction: Radiation Therapy. 55p. 1979. pap. 7.00x (ISBN 0-89352-099-3). Masson Pub.

--Programmed Instruction: Understanding Cancer & Chemotherapy. 80p. 1979. pap. 7.00x (ISBN 0-89352-081-0). Masson Pub.

Pilapil, Frediswinda & Studva, Kathleen V. Programmed Instruction: Immunology, No. 3. 72p. 1981. pap. 7.00x (ISBN 0-89352-150-7). Masson Pub.

Pilar, Frank L. Elementary Quantum Chemistry. 1968. text ed. 39.00 o.p. (ISBN 0-07-050025-8, C). McGraw.

Pilarski, Jan, jt. auth. see Bossong, Ken.

Pilat, Oliver. Pegler, Angry Man of the Press. LC 73-3236. (Illus.). 288p. 1973. Repr. of 1963 ed. lib. bdg. 18.50x (ISBN 0-8371-6838-4, PIPE). Greenwood.

Pilbeam, David. The Ascent of Man: An Introduction to Human Evolution. (Illus.). 224p. 1972. pap. text ed. 13.95 (ISBN 0-02-395270-9). Macmillan.

Pilbeam, John. Mammillaria: A Collector's Guide. LC 81-2956. (Illus.). 200p. 1981. text ed. 40.00x (ISBN 0-87663-360-2). Universe.

Pilborough, L. Inspection of Chemical Plants. 392p. 1977. 29.95x (ISBN 0-87201-388-X). Gulf Pub.

Pilcer, Sonia. Teen Angel. LC 78-5376. 1978. 8.95 o.p. (ISBN 0-698-10941-4, Coward). Putnam Pub Group.

Pilch, John J. What Are They Saying About the Book of Revelation? LC 78-51594. 1978. pap. 2.45 o.p. (ISBN 0-8091-2126-3). Paulist Pr.

Pilch, John J. & Karris, Robert J. Galatians & Romans, No. 6. (Collegeville Bible Commentary Ser.). 80p. 1983. pap. 2.50 (ISBN 0-8146-1306-3). Liturgical Pr.

Pilch, Michael & Wood, V. Pension Schemes. 1979. text ed. 37.25x (ISBN 0-566-02117-X). Gower Pub Ltd.

Pilcher, R. Appraisal & Control of Project Costs. 1973. 37.50 (ISBN 0-07-084412-7, P&RB). McGraw.

Pilcher, Rosamunde. The Carousel. (Nightingale Series Paperbacks). 1983. pap. 7.95 (ISBN 0-8161-3488-X, Large Print Bks). G K Hall.

Pilcher, Roy. Appraisal & Control of Project Costs. (Illus.). 324p. 1982. text ed. 27.50x (ISBN 0-88133-005-1). Waveland Pr.

Pilder, Richard J. & Pilder, William F. How to Find Your Life's Work: Staying Out of Traps & Taking Control of Your Career. 147p. 1981. 15.95 (ISBN 0-13-406710-X); pap. 4.95 (ISBN 0-13-406702-9). P-H.

Pilder, William F., jt. auth. see Pilder, Richard J.

Pile, jt. auth. see Friedmann.

Pile, jt. auth. see Leamy.

Pile, John, jt. auth. see Diekman, Norman.

Pile, John, ed. Drawings of Architectural Interiors. (Illus.). 1979. pap. 9.95 (ISBN 0-8230-7158-8, Whitney Lib). Watson-Guptill.

Pile, John, ed. see Klein, Judy G.

Pile, John F. Design: Purpose, Form, & Meaning. 1979. pap. 9.95 (ISBN 0-393-95106-5). Norton.

--Modern Furniture. LC 78-5440. 1979. 31.95x (ISBN 0-471-02667-0, Pub. by Wiley-Interscience). Wiley.

Pile, Stephen. The Incomplete Book of Failures: The Official Handbook of the Not-Terribly-Good Club of Great Britain. 1979. pap. 6.75 (ISBN 0-525-47589-3, 0655-200). Dutton.

Pilgrim. I'll Smile Again. 1978. 4.50 o.p. (ISBN 0-533-03611-9). Vantage.

Pilgrim Society Collection. Arthur Lord Collection. 1.00 (ISBN 0-686-30037-8). Pilgrim Hall.

--History of the Pilgrim Society. Date not set. 0.75 (ISBN 0-686-30039-4). Pilgrim Hall.

Pilinszky, Janos. Selected Poems. Hughes, Ted & Csokits, Janos, trs. LC 76-52273. (Poetry in Translation Ser.). 1977. o. p. 8.95 (ISBN 0-89255-017-1); pap. 4.95 o.s.i. (ISBN 0-89255-018-X). Persea Bks.

Pilkey, Orrin H., Jr. & Neal, William J. From Currituck to Calabash: Living with North Carolina's Barrier Islands. LC 80-52835. (Living with the Shore Ser.). (Illus.). 224p. 1982. pap. 9.75 (ISBN 0-8223-0548-8). Duke.

Pilkey, Walter D. & Pin Yu Chang. Modern Formulas for Statics & Dynamics: A Stress & Strain Approach. LC 77-15093. (Illus.). 1978. 34.75 (ISBN 0-07-049998-5, P&RB). McGraw.

Pilkey, Walter D. & Perrone, Nicholas, eds. The Structural Mechanics Software Series, 2 vols. (Software Ser.). 1977. 25.00x ea.; Vol. 1. (ISBN 0-8139-0735-7); Vol. 2. (ISBN 0-8139-0781-0). U Pr of Va.

Pilkey, Walter D., jt. ed. see Perrone, Nicholas.

Pilkington, John. The Heart of Yoknapatawpha. LC 80-29686. 344p. 1981. 25.00x o.p. (ISBN 0-87805-135-X). U Pr of Miss.

Pilkington, John, jt. auth. see Bradt, Hilary.

Pilkington, Roger. Small Boat Through Holland. 1979. 15.00x o.p. (ISBN 0-86025-807-6, Pub. by Ian Henry Pubns England). State Mutual Bk.

Pilkington, T. & Plonsey, R. Engineering Contributions - Biophysical Electrocardiography. 256p. 1982. text ed. 26.00 (ISBN 0-471-87027-7, Pub. by Wiley Interscience). Wiley.

Pilkington, William T. Critical Essays on the Western American Novel. (Reference Bks). 1980. lib. bdg. 25.00 (ISBN 0-8161-8351-1). G K Hall.

--Harvey Fergusson. (United States Authors Ser.). 1975. lib. bdg. 13.95 (ISBN 0-8057-7157-3, Twayne). G K Hall.

--Imagining Texas: The Literature of the Lone Star State. Rosenbaum, Robert J., ed. (Texas History Ser.). (Illus.). 37p. 1981. pap. text ed. 1.95x (ISBN 0-89641-095-1). American Pr.

Pill, Juri. Planning & Politics: The Metro Toronto Transportation Plan Review. (MIT Center for Transportation Studies: No. 5). (Illus.). 1979. 25.00x (ISBN 0-262-16073-0). MIT Pr.

Pillai, K. C. Orientalisms of the Bible, Vol. 1. 1969. 4.95x (ISBN 0-912178-02-7). Mor-Mac.

--Orientalisms of the Bible, Vol. 2. 1974. 4.95x (ISBN 0-912178-04-3). Mor-Mac.

Pillai, K. M. Crop Nutrition. 1968. pap. 4.00x o.p. (ISBN 0-210-22717-6). Asia.

Pillai, S. K. First Course on Electrical Drives. 208p. 1982. 14.95X (ISBN 0-470-27531-6). Halsted Pr.

Pillay, T. V., ed. Coastal Aquaculture in the Indo-Pacific Region. (Illus.). 497p. (Orig.). 1974. 27.50 o.p. (ISBN 0-85238-023-2, FN6, FNB). Unipub.

Pillement, Georges. Unknown France, 4 vols. Incl. Vol. 1. From Paris to the Riviera. 236p. 1963; Vol. 2. The French Alps, the Riviera. 176p. 1963. o.p.; Vol. 3. The Roads to Spain. 256p. 1964; Vol. 4. The Valley of the Loire, Brittany. 250p. 1965. o.p.. LC 66-41729. (Unknown Guides Ser). (Illus.). 12.50x ea. Intl Pubns Serv.

--Unknown Turkey, 2 vols. LC 73-159531. (Illus.). 227p. 1974. Vol. 1. 12.50x (ISBN 0-85307-120-9); Vol. 2- Anatolia, Cappadocia, The Eastern Frontiers. 12.50x ea. (ISBN 0-85307-129-2). Intl Pubns Serv.

Piller. Bulked Yarns. 31.95 o.p. (ISBN 0-87245-539-4). Textile Bk.

Pilleri, G., jt. ed. see Purves, P. E.

Pillich, William F. Social Dance. (Physical Education Activities Ser.). 76p. 1967. pap. text ed. write for info. (ISBN 0-697-07025-5); tchr's manual avail. (ISBN 0-697-07223-1). Wm C Brown.

Pillin, William. Pavanne for a Fading Memory. LC 63-16650. 82p. 1963. 5.00 o.p. (ISBN 0-8040-0240-1). Swallow.

Pilling, Doria. The Child with a Chronic Medical Problem: Cardiac Disorders, Diabetes, Haemophilia, Social, Emotional, & Educational Adjustment. (General Ser.). 60p. 1973. pap. text ed. 7.00x (ISBN 0-85633-027-2, NFER). Humanities.

Pilling, John. A Reader's Guide to Fifty Modern European Poets. LC 82-11363. (Reader's Guide). 480p. 1983. text ed. 22.50x (ISBN 0-389-20241-X). B&N Imports.

Pillon, Nancy B. Reaching Young People Through Media. 300p. 1982. lib. bdg. 23.50 (ISBN 0-87287-369-2). Libs Unl.

Pillsbury. Breads Cook Book. 1969. 3.95 o.p. (ISBN 0-671-20457-2). S&S.

--Pillsbury Bake-Offs: Main Dish Cookbook. 1969. 3.95 o.p. (ISBN 0-671-20454-8). S&S.

Pillsbury, Barbara L., jt. ed. see Joseph, Suad.

Pillsbury, Dorothy L. Star Over Adobe. LC 63-21376. (Illus.). 1977. pap. 4.95 o.p. (ISBN 0-8263-0179-7). U of NM Pr.

Pilon, A. Barbara. Teaching Language Arts Creatively in the Elementary Grades. LC 77-23508. 1978. 18.95x (ISBN 0-471-68980-7). Wiley.

Pilotta, Joseph J. Women in Organizations: Barriers & Breakthroughs. 101p. (Orig.). 1983. pap. text ed. 4.95x (ISBN 0-88133-008-6). Waveland Pr.

Pilotta, Joseph J., ed. Interpersonal Communication: Essays in Phenomenology & Hermeneutics. LC 82-40211. (Current Continental Research Ser.: No. 2). 196p. (Orig.). 1982. PLB 20.00 (ISBN 0-8191-2475-3); pap. text ed. 9.50 (ISBN 0-8191-2476-1). U Pr of Amer.

Piltch, Benjamin. Application Forms. 1972. 2.75x (ISBN 0-88323-092-5, 196). Richards Pub.

--Find the Right Letter: Letter Discrimination Practice. 1972. 2.50x (ISBN 0-88323-089-5, 193). Richards Pub.

--Find the Right Number: Number Discrimination Practice. 1972. 2.50x (ISBN 0-88323-088-7, 192). Richards Pub.

--Find the Right Word: Word Discrimination Practice. 1972. 2.50x (ISBN 0-88323-090-9, 194). Richards Pub.

--Stories About Workers. (Illus.). 1975. pap. 2.75x (ISBN 0-88323-120-4, 208). Richards Pub.

Piltch, Benjamin, ed. see Kaufman, Tanya & Wishny, Judith.

Pim, Alan. Financial & Economic History of the African Tropical Territories. 1970. Repr. of 1940 ed. 15.00 (ISBN 0-87266-046-X). Argosy.

Pim, Linda. The Invisible Additives: Environmental Contamination of Food. LC 80-2430. 288p. 1981. 17.95 (ISBN 0-385-17001-7); pap. 9.95 (ISBN 0-385-17002-5). Doubleday.

Pimentel, David. Food, Energy & Future of Society. 1980. pap. 3.50x (ISBN 0-87081-089-8). Colo Assoc.

Pimentel, David, ed. World Food, Pest Losses & the Environment. LC 77-90418. (AAAS Selected Symposium Ser.: No. 13). (Illus.). 1978. softcover 22.50 (ISBN 0-89158-441-2). Westview.

Pimentel, David & Perkins, John H., eds. Pest Control: Cultural & Environmental Aspects. LC 79-18516. (AAAS Selected Symposium: No. 43). (Illus.). 243p. 1980. lib. bdg. 22.50 (ISBN 0-89158-753-5). Westview.

Pimentel, David, jt. ed. see Smith, Edward H.

Pimentel, David, ed. see Symposium, Cornell University, Ithaca, New York, Oct. 1974.

Pimentel, George C. & Spratley, Richard D. Understanding Chemistry. LC 70-142944. 1971. 32.50x (ISBN 0-8162-6761-8); solution manual o.p. 6.95 (ISBN 0-8162-6741-3). Holden-Day.

Pimentel, Richard A. Morphometrics: The Multivariate Analysis of Biological Data. 1978. pap. text ed. 21.95 (ISBN 0-8403-1928-2). Kendall-Hunt.

Pimlott, B. Labour & the Left in the 1930's. LC 76-27906. 1977. 24.95 (ISBN 0-521-21448-3). Cambridge U Pr.

Pimlott, Ben & Cook, Chris, eds. Trade Unions in British Politics. 320p. (Orig.). 1982. pap. text ed. 13.95 (ISBN 0-582-49184-3). Longman.

Pimlott, Douglas H., jt. auth. see Rutter, Russell J.

Pimm, S. L. Food Web. (Population & Community Biology Ser.). 1981. 35.00x (ISBN 0-412-23100-X, Pub. by Chapman & Hall); pap. 16.95x (ISBN 0-412-23110-7). Methuen Inc.

Pimmel, R. L., jt. auth. see Gualt, J. W.

Pimpton, George, jt. ed. see Stein, Jean.

Pimsleur, Meira, jt. auth. see Jacobstein, J. Myron.

Pimsleur, Paul. C'est la Vie: Lectures d'aujourd'hui. 3rd ed. (Illus.). 207p. (Fr.). 1982. pap. text ed. 10.95 (ISBN 0-15-505892-4, HC). HarBraceJ.

Pimsleur, Paul & Quinn, Terence, eds. Psychology of Second Language Learning. (Illus.). 1971. 32.50 (ISBN 0-521-08236-6). Cambridge U Pr.

Pinar, William. Heightened Consciousness, Cultural Revolution, & Curriculum Theory. LC 73-17615. 1974. 19.00 (ISBN 0-8211-1511-1); text ed. 16.95 (ISBN 0-685-42641-6). McCutchan.

Pinar, William F., ed. see Fisher, Barbara.

Pinchbeck, Ivy. Women Workers & the Industrial Revolution 1750-1850. 342p. 1983. pap. 7.95 (ISBN 0-86068-170-X, Virago Pr). Merrimack Bk Serv.

Pinchera, A. & Vanhaelst, L., eds. Autoimmunity & Endocrine Diseases. (Jounal: Hormone Research: Vol. 16, No. 5). (Illus.). 84p. 1982. pap. 24.75 (ISBN 3-8055-3658-5). S Karger.

Pincherle, L. Worked Problems in Heat, Thermodynamics & Kinetic Theory. 1966. 24.00 o.s.i. (ISBN 0-08-012016-4); pap. 10.75 (ISBN 0-08-012015-6). Pergamon.

Pincherle, Marc. Corelli: His Life & His Music. (Music Reprint Ser.). 1979. Repr. of 1956 ed. lib. bdg. 25.00 (ISBN 0-306-79576-0). Da Capo.

Pinchot, Gifford. To the South Seas: The Cruise of the Schooner Mary Pinchot to the Galapogos, the Marquesas, the Tuamotu Islands & Tahiti. LC 70-174094. (Illus.). xiv, 500p. 1972. Repr. of 1930 ed. 42.00x (ISBN 0-8103-3933-1). Gale.

Pinciss, Gerald M. Christopher Marlowe. LC 72-79934. (Literature and Life Ser.). (Illus.). 144p. 1975. 11.95 (ISBN 0-8044-2694-5). Ungar.

Pinckney, Cathey & Pinckney, Edward. The Patient's Guide to Medical Tests. 336p. 1983. pap. 7.95 (ISBN 0-87196-615-8). Facts on File.

Pinckney, Edward, jt. auth. see Pinckney, Cathey.

Pinclroll, F. & Anderson, J., eds. Changes in Health Care Instrumentation Due to Microprocessor Technology: Proceedings. 1981. 42.75 (ISBN 0-444-86138-6). Elsevier.

Pincus, Allen & Minahan, Anne. Social Work Practice: Model & Method. LC 73-82647. 355p. 1973. text ed. 12.95 (ISBN 0-87581-132-9). Peacock Pubs.

Pincus, Gregory, ed. Control of Fertility. 1965. 43.50 (ISBN 0-12-557056-2). Acad Pr.

Pincus, Gregory, ed. see Laurentian Hormone Conferences.

Pincus, Harriet, jt. auth. see Grimm Brothers.

Pincus, Harriet, ed. & illus. Little Red Riding Hood. LC 68-11505. (Illus.). (gr. k-3). 1968. 6.95 o.p. (ISBN 0-15-247132-4, HJ). HarBraceJ.

Pincus, Jonathan H. & Tucker, Gary J. Behavioral Neurology. 2nd ed. (Illus.). 1978. text ed. 18.95x (ISBN 0-19-502306-4); pap. text ed. 9.95x (ISBN 0-19-502305-6). Oxford U Pr.

Pincus, Leo I. Practical Boiler Water Treatment: Including Air Conditioning Systems. 1962. 26.00 o.p. (ISBN 0-07-050027-4, P&RB). McGraw.

Pincus, Lily & Dare, Christopher. Secrets in the Family. LC 77-88763. 1980. pap. 3.95i o.p. (ISBN 0-06-090669-3, CN 669, CN). Har-Row.

Pincus, Lily, jt. auth. see Bannister, Kathleen.

Pincus-Witten, Robert. Entries (Maximalism) (Illus.). 250p. 1983. pap. 14.95 (ISBN 0-915570-20-3). Oolp Pr.

--Occult Symbolism in France: Josephin Peladan & the Salons De la Rose-Croix. LC 75-23809. (Outstanding Dissertations in the Fine Arts-20th Century). (Illus.). 1976. lib. bdg. 41.00 o.s.i. (ISBN 0-8240-2003-0). Garland Pub.

--Postminimalism: American Art of the Decade. LC 77-77010. (Illus.). 1981. pap. text ed. 11.95 o.p. (ISBN 0-915570-07-6). Oolp Pr.

Pindar. The Odes of Pindar. Bowra, C. M., tr. 1982. pap. 4.95 (ISBN 0-14-044209-X). Penguin.

Pinder, David. Regional Economic Development & Policy: Theory & Practice in the European Community. 144p. 1983. text ed. 24.95x (ISBN 0-04-320153-9); pap. text ed. 10.95x (ISBN 0-04-320152-0). Allen Unwin.

Pinder, David, jt. ed. see Hoyle, Brian.

Pinder, George F., jt. auth. see Lapidus, Leon.

Pinder-Wilson, R., ed. Paintings from Islamic Lands. LC 69-17154. (Oriental Studies: No. 4). (Illus.). 206p. 1969. 24.95x o.s.i. (ISBN 0-87249-138-2). U of SC Pr.

Pindyck, R. S. Optimal Planning for Economic Stabilization. (Contributions to Economic Analysis: Vol. 81). 1973. 30.00 (ISBN 0-444-10517-4, North-Holland). Elsevier.

Pindyck, Robert S. The Structure of World Energy Demand. (Illus.). 1979. 25.00x (ISBN 0-262-16074-9). MIT Pr.

Pindyck, Robert S. & Rubinfeld, Daniel. Econometric Models & Economic Forecasts. 1980. 28.95 o.p. (ISBN 0-07-050096-7, C); instr's. manual 20.00 o.p. (ISBN 0-07-050097-5). McGraw.

Pindyke, Robert S., ed. Advances in the Economics of Energy & Resources, Vol. 1. 310p. 1979. 42.50 (ISBN 0-89232-078-8). Jai Pr.

--Advances in the Economics of Energy & Resources, Vol. 2. 250p. 1979. 42.50 (ISBN 0-89232-079-6). Jai Pr.

Pine, Eli S. How to Enjoy Calculus. LC 80-10974. 128p. 1980. lib. bdg. 7.95 o.p. (ISBN 0-668-04949-9); pap. 4.95 o.p. (ISBN 0-668-04951-0). Arco.

Pine, L. G. A Dictionary of Mottoes. 150p. 1983. price not set (ISBN 0-7100-9339-X). Routledge & Kegan.

Pine, Stanley H., et al. Organic Chemistry. 4th ed. (Illus.). 1056p. 1980. text ed. 35.00 (ISBN 0-07-050115-7); student solution supplement 17.00 (ISBN 0-07-050116-5). McGraw.

Pine, Tillie S. & Levine, Joseph. The Arabs Knew. (Illus.). (gr. 3-5). 1976. PLB 8.95 (ISBN 0-07-050091-6, GB). McGraw.

--Energy All Around. new ed. LC 75-14323. (Illus.). 48p. (ps-3). 1975. PLB 7.95 o.p. (ISBN 0-07-050087-8, GB). McGraw.

--Eskimos Knew. (Illus.). (gr. 1-4). 1962. PLB 8.95 o.p. (ISBN 0-07-050053-3, GB). McGraw.

--Incas Knew. (Illus.). (gr. k-3). 1967. PLB 8.95 o.p. (ISBN 0-07-050078-9, GB). McGraw.

--Indians Knew. (Illus.). (gr. 1-4). 1957. PLB 8.95 (ISBN 0-07-050031-2, GB). McGraw.

--Simple Machines & How We Use Them. (Illus.). (gr. 3-5). 1965. PLB 8.95 (ISBN 0-07-050067-3, GB). McGraw.

Pine, Vanderlyn R. Introduction to Social Statistics. (Methods of Social Science Ser.). (Illus.). 1977. text ed. 21.95 o.p. (ISBN 0-13-496844-1). P-H.

Pinedo, H. M., ed. Cancer Chemotherapy 1982. (Cancer Chemotherapy Annual Ser.: No. 4). 450p. 1982. 50.00 (ISBN 0-444-90255-4, Excerpta Medica). Elsevier.

Pinell-Siles, Armando. Determinants of Private Industrial Investment in India. (Working Paper: No. 333). 51p. 1979. 3.00 (ISBN 0-686-36179-2, WP-0333). World Bank.

Pines, H., jt. ed. see Eley, D. D.

Pines, Malcolm, ed. The Evolution of Group Analysis. (International Library of Group Psychotherapy & Group Process). 280p. 1983. price not set (ISBN 0-7100-9290-3). Routledge & Kegan.

Pines, Malcolm & Rafaelsen, Lise, eds. The Individual & the Group: Boundaries & Interrelations, 2 vols. 1982. Set. text ed. 75.00 (ISBN 0-686-96854-9, Plenum Pr); Vol. 1: Theory. text ed. 55.00 (ISBN 0-306-40837-6); Vol. 2: Practice. text ed. 32.50 (ISBN 0-306-40838-4). Plenum Pub.

Pines, Maya. The Brain Changers. 1975. pap. 1.95 o.p. (ISBN 0-451-07855-1, J7855, Sig). NAL.

Pinfield, Edward R., jt. auth. see Aikawa, Jerry K.

Pinfold, Tom see Norcliffe, Glen.

Pingree, D., jt. auth. see Reiner, Erica.

Pingree, David, jt. auth. see Reiner, Erica.

Pingree, David, ed. see Hashimi, Ali Ibn Sulayman al.

Pini, Richard & Pini, Wendy. Elfquest, The Novel: Raid at Sorrow's End. (Elfquest Ser.). (Illus.). 320p. 1982. 4.95 o.p. (ISBN 0-934438-63-3). Underwood-Miller.

Pini, Richard, jt. auth. see Pini, Wendy.

Pini, Wendy & Pini, Richard. Elfquest. LC 81-5401. (Illus.). 1981. ltd. ed. o.p. 35.00 (ISBN 0-89865-166-2); pap. 9.95 (ISBN 0-89865-140-9). Donning Co.

--ElfQuest, Vol. 2. Reynolds, Kay, ed. LC 81-5401. (Illus.). 172p. (Orig.). 1982. pap. 10.95 (ISBN 0-89865-245-6). Donning Co.

Pini, Wendy, jt. auth. see Pini, Richard.

Pinion, F. B. A Jane Austin Companion. LC 72-88426. (Illus.). 1973. 16.50 o.p. (ISBN 0-312-43995-4). St Martin.

Pinion, F. B., ed. Browning: Dramatis Personae. 256p. 1969. 20.00x (ISBN 0-7121-0139-X, Pub. by Macdonald & Evans). State Mutual Bk.

Pink, A. W. Profiting from the Word. 1977. pap. 2.95 (ISBN 0-85151-032-9). Banner of Truth.

Pink, Arthur W. The Antichrist. 1980. pap. 12.00 o.p. (ISBN 0-86524-000-0). Klock & Klock.

--Divine Inspiration of the Bible. pap. 4.50 (ISBN 0-8010-7005-8). Baker Bk.

--Doctrine of Salvation. LC 75-18228. 1975. pap. 4.95 (ISBN 0-8010-7026-0). Baker Bk.

--Gleanings from Elisha. LC 79-181591. 288p. 1972. 10.95 (ISBN 0-8024-2962-9); pap. 9.95 (ISBN 0-8024-3000-7). Moody.

--Gleanings from Paul. LC 67-14379. 1967. write for info. (ISBN 0-8024-2965-3); pap. 9.95 (ISBN 0-8024-3005-8). Moody.

--Gleanings from the Scriptures: Man's Total Depravity. LC 73-80942. 1970. 10.95 (ISBN 0-8024-2966-1); pap. 9.95 (ISBN 0-8024-3006-6). Moody.

--Gleanings in Exodus. 1964. 10.95 (ISBN 0-8024-2975-0); pap. 9.95 (ISBN 0-8024-3001-5). Moody.

--Gleanings in Genesis. 1922. 10.95 (ISBN 0-8024-2968-8); pap. 9.95 (ISBN 0-8024-3002-3). Moody.

--Gleanings in Joshua. LC 64-20991. 1964. 10.95 o.p. (ISBN 0-8024-2982-3); pap. 9.95 o.p. (ISBN 0-8024-3004-X). Moody.

--Gleanings in the Godhead. LC 75-15760. 256p. 10.95 (ISBN 0-8024-2977-7); pap. 9.95 (ISBN 0-8024-3003-1). Moody.

--Holy Spirit. 1970. pap. 6.95 (ISBN 0-8010-7041-4). Baker Bk.

--Practical Christianity. pap. 5.95 (ISBN 0-8010-6990-4). Baker Bk.

Pinka, Patricia G. This Dialogue of One: The Songs & Sonnets of John Donne. LC 81-16116. 1982. 18.75 (ISBN 0-8173-0104-6). U of Ala Pr.

Pinkard, Terry P., jt. ed. see Beauchamp, Tom L.

Pinkas, Danny, jt. auth. see Golan, Aviezer.

Pinkele, Carl F. & Pollis, Adamantis. The Contemporary Mediterranean World. 394p. 1983. 32.95 (ISBN 0-03-060091-X). Praeger.

Pinker, R. A., ed. see Wilson, Dorothy.

Pinker, Robert. The Idea of Welfare. LC 79-670318. (Studies in Social Policy & Welfare). 1979. text ed. 33.95x (ISBN 0-435-82683-2); pap. text ed. 10.00x (ISBN 0-435-82684-0). Heinemann Ed.

Pinkerton, Alan. Thirty Years a Detective: A Thorough & Comprehensive Expose of Criminal Practices of All Grades & Classes. (Criminology, Law Enforcement, & Social Problems Ser.: No. 154). (Illus.). 1975. Repr. of 1884 ed. 18.00x (ISBN 0-87585-154-1). Patterson Smith.

Pinkerton, Amy, jt. auth. see Rose, Harvey.

Pinkerton, Edward C. Word for Word: A Dictionary of Etymological Cognates. 454p. 1982. 42.00x (ISBN 0-686-97794-7). Gale.

Pinkerton, Kathrene. Hidden Harbor. LC 76-18900. (Illus.). (gr. 9 up). 1966. pap. 0.75 (ISBN 0-15-640185-1, VoyB). HarBraceJ.

Pinkerton, Kathrene S. Steer North. LC 62-8346. (gr. 7 up). 1962. 4.95 o.p. (ISBN 0-15-280210-X, HJ). HarBraceJ.

Pinkerton, Percy, tr. see Artzibashev, Michael.

Pinkerton, Susan S., et al. Behavioral Medicine: Clinical Applications. LC 81-11417. (Wiley Series on Personality Processes). 376p. 1982. 32.50 (ISBN 0-471-05619-7, Pub. by Wiley-Interscience). Wiley.

Pinkham, Joan, tr. see Cesaire, Aime.

Pinkham, Mary Ellen. Mary Ellen's Help Yourself Diet Plan: The One That Worked for Me! 192p. 1983. 10.95 (ISBN 0-312-51863-3). St Martin.

Pinkham, Walter. The Second Oldest Profession. 1979. 7.95 o.p. (ISBN 0-533-03614-3). Vantage.

Pinkney, David H. Nineteenth Century, Eighteen Fifteen to Nineteen Fourteen. 1979p. 1979. pap. text ed. 2.95x (ISBN 0-88273-325-7). Forum Pr IL.

--World of Europe Since Eighteen Fifteen, Vol. 3. 1979. pap. text ed. 10.95x (ISBN 0-88273-332-X). Forum Pr IL.

Pinkney, David H., jt. auth. see De Bertier de Sauvigny, G.

Pinkney, William, Jr. Life of William Pinkney. LC 75-75276. (Law, Politics & History Ser.). 1969. Repr. of 1853 ed. lib. bdg. 49.50 (ISBN 0-306-71307-1). Da Capo.

Pinkster, Harm, ed. Theoretical & Descriptive Studies in Latin Linguistics: Proceedings of the 1st. International Colloquium on Latin Linguistics. (Studies in Language Companion: 12). 250p. 1983. 30.00 (ISBN 90-272-3011-0). Benjamins North Am.

Pinkston, Elsie M., et al. Effective Social Work Practice: Advanced Techniques for Behavioral Intervention with Individuals, Families, & Institutional Staff. LC 82-48057. (Social & Behavioral Science Ser.). 1982. text ed. 22.95x (ISBN 0-87589-534-4). Jossey Bass.

Pinkus, O. & Wilcock, D. F., eds. Strategy for Energy Conservation Through Tribology. 2nd ed. (Bk. No. H00109). 1982. 20.00 (ISBN 0-685-37585-4). ASME.

Pinkus, Theo, jt. auth. see Lukacs, Georg.

Pinkwater, Daniel. I Was a Second Grade Werewolf. LC 82-17715. (Illus.). 32p. (ps-2). 1983. 9.95 (ISBN 0-525-44038-0, 0966-290). Dutton.

--The Snarkout Boys & the Avacado of Death. (gr. 5 up). 1982. 10.50 (ISBN 0-688-00871-2). Lothrop.

Pinkwater, Daniel M., jt. auth. see Pinkwater, Jill.

Pinkwater, Jill & Pinkwater, Daniel M. Superpuppy: How to Choose, Raise & Train the Best Possible Dog for You. LC 76-8825. (Illus.). 208p. (gr. 6 up). 1976. 10.95 (ISBN 0-395-28878-9, Clarion). HM.

Pinloche, A. Dictionnaire Francais-Allemand, Deutsch-Franzosisch. 805p. (Fr. & Ger.). Date not set. pap. 6.50 (ISBN 0-686-97409-3, M-9043). French & Eur.

Pinneau, S. R. Changes in Intelligence Quotient: Infancy to Maturity. 1961. text ed. 7.88 o.p. (ISBN 0-395-09455-0). HM.

Pinner, R. & Frances, Michael, eds. Turkoman Studies, 2 vols. LC 77-90413. Vol. 1. text ed. 108.00x (ISBN 0-391-00821-8); Vol. 2. text ed. write for info (ISBN 0-391-00554-5). Humanities.

Pinner, S. H. & Simpson, W. G. Plastics Surface & Finish. 1971. text ed. 15.95 o.p. (ISBN 0-408-70062-9). Butterworth.

Pinney, John J. Your Future in the Nursery Industry. O ed. LC 67-10084. (Careers in Depth Ser). (Illus.). (gr. 7 up). 1982. PLB 7.97 o.p. (ISBN 0-8239-0331-1). Rosen Pr.

Pinney, T., ed. The Letters of Thomas Babington Macaulay, Vol. 5. LC 73-75860. (Illus.). 425p. 1981. Vol. 5. 95.00 (ISBN 0-521-22749-6). Vol. 6 (ISBN 0-521-22750-X). Cambridge U Pr.

Pinney, T., ed. see Macauley, Thomas B.

Pinney, Thomas, ed. see Macaulay, Thomas B.

Pino, DAvid. The Clarinet & Clairnet Playing. 03/1983 ed. (Illus.). 320p. pap. 9.95 (ISBN 0-686-83740-1, ScribT). Scribner.

Pino, Piero, jt. ed. see Wender, Irving.

Pinon, Fernando. Of Myths & Realities: Dynamics of Ethnic Policies. 1978. 7.50 o.p. (ISBN 0-533-03323-3). Vantage.

Pinot, Pierre, jt. auth. see Auge-Laribe, Michel.

Pinowski, J. & Kendeigh, S. C., eds. Granivorous Birds in Ecosystems. LC 76-47189. (International Biological Programme Ser.: No. 12). (Illus.). 1978. 85.00 (ISBN 0-521-21504-8). Cambridge U Pr.

Pinsker, Harold & Willis, William D., Jr., eds. Information Processing in the Nervous System. 378p. 1980. text ed. 42.00 (ISBN 0-89004-422-8). Raven.

Pinsker, Sanford. Critical Essays on Philip Roth. (Critical Essays on American Literature). 1982. lib. bdg. 28.50 (ISBN 0-8161-8423-2, Twayne). G K Hall.

Pinson, Koppel S. Modern Germany. 2nd ed. 1966. text ed. 25.95 (ISBN 0-02-395420-5). Macmillan.

Pinson, William M. The Word Topical Bible of Issues & Answers. 1983. pap. 7.95 (ISBN 0-8499-2934-2). Word Pub.

Pinstrup-Andersen, Per. Nutritional Consequences of Agricultural Projects: Conceptual Relationships & Assessment Approaches. (Working Paper: No. 456). 93p. 1981. 5.00 (ISBN 0-686-36057-5, WP-0456). World Bank.

Pinstrup-Anderson, Per. Agricultural Research & Technology in Economic Development. LC 81-14297. (Illus.). 304p. 1982. text ed. 39.95x (ISBN 0-582-46048-4). Longman.

Pint, J., ed. Pint's Passages for Aural Comprehension II: Telephone Talk. (Materials for Language Practice Ser.). (Illus.). 96p. 1983. pap. 5.95 (ISBN 0-08-028621-6); cassette 12.00 (ISBN 0-08-029456-1). Pergamon.

--Pint's Passages: Materials for Aural Comprehension. (Materials for Language Practice Ser.). (Illus.). 96p. 1983. pap. 4.95 (ISBN 0-08-028620-8); kit 15.95 (ISBN 0-08-029430-8). Pergamon.

Pinta, M., jt. auth. see Aubert, H.

Pinta, Maurice. Modern Methods for Trace Element Analysis. LC 76-50988. 1978. 49.95 (ISBN 0-250-40152-5). Ann Arbor Science.

Pintauro, Joseph. Cold Hands. 1980. pap. 2.50 o.p. (ISBN 0-451-09482-4, E9482, Sig). NAL.

--Cold Hands. 1979. 10.95 o.p. (ISBN 0-671-24726-3). S&S.

Pintel, G., jt. auth. see Diamond, J.

Pintel, Gerald & Diamond, Jay. Basic Business Mathematics. 3rd ed. (Illus.). 240p. 1982. pap. text ed. 14.95 (ISBN 0-13-057380-9). P-H.

--Retailing. 2nd ed. (Illus.). 1977. 20.95 (ISBN 0-13-777532-6); wkbk. 9.95 (ISBN 0-13-777540-7). P-H.

Pintel, Gerald, jt. auth. see Diamond, Jay.

Pinter, Harold. Other Places: A Kind of Alaska; Victoria Station: Family Voices. 96p. 1983. 15.00 (ISBN 0-394-53131-0, GP849). Grove.

--Other Places: Three Plays. 96p. 1983. pap. 6.95 (ISBN 0-394-62449-1, Ever). Grove.

Pinthus, G. Das Konzertleben in Deutdschland. (Sammlung Mw.Abh. Ser.). 160p. 35.00 o.s.i. (ISBN 90-6027-322-2, Pub. by Frits Knuf Netherlands). Pendragon NY.

Pinto, Diana, ed. Contemporary Italian Sociology: A Reader. (Illus.). 224p. 1981. 44.50 (ISBN 0-521-23738-6); pap. 16.95 (ISBN 0-521-28191-1). Cambridge U Pr.

Pinto, F. M. The Voyages & Adventures of Fernand Mendez Pinto. 318p. 1981. 49.00x (ISBN 0-686-97627-4, Pub. by Dawson). State Mutual Bk.

Pinto, J. D. Behavior & Taxonomy of the Epicauta Maculata Group (Coleoptera: Meloidae) (U. C. Publications in Entomology Ser.: Vol. 89). 1980. pap. 16.50x (ISBN 0-520-09616-9). U of Cal Pr.

Pinto, Vivian De Sola see De Sola Pinto, Vivian.

Pinto-Lopez, J. Polyporaceae, Contribuicao Rara a Sua Bio-Taxonomia (Broteriana 8) (Illus.). 1968. pap. 24.00 (ISBN 3-7682-0555-X). Lubrecht & Cramer.

Pinxten, Rik & Van Dooren, Ingrid. The Anthropology of Space. LC 82-40490. (Illus.). 336p. 1983. 32.50x (ISBN 0-8122-7879-8). U of Pa Pr.

Pin Yu Chang, jt. auth. see Pilkey, Walter D.

Pinzon, Scott. Splendini. 176p. (Orig.). (gr. 3-7). 1982. pap. 5.95 (ISBN 0-310-45601-0). Zondervan.

Pio, Padre. The Agony of Jesus. 40p. 1954. pap. 0.75 (ISBN 0-686-81635-8). TAN Bks Pubs.

--Meditation Prayer on Mary Immaculate. (Illus.). 28p. pap. 0.50 (ISBN 0-686-81640-4). Tan Bks Pubs.

Piore, Michael, jt. auth. see Berger, Suzanne.

Piore, Michael J., jt. auth. see Doeringer, Peter B.

Piore, Michael J., ed. Unemployment & Inflation: Institutional & Structuralist Views, a Reader in Labor Econonmics. LC 79-55274. 1980. 20.00 o.p. (ISBN 0-87332-143-X); pap. 9.95 (ISBN 0-87332-165-0). M E Sharpe.

Piore, Nancy K. Lightning: The Poetry of Rene Char. LC 80-22001. (Illus.). 150p. 1981. 18.95x (ISBN 0-930350-08-1). NE U Pr.

Piotrovsky, Boris, intro. by. The Hermitage Picture Gallery. 1980. 24.95 (ISBN 0-89893-079-0). CDP.

Piotrow, Phyllis, jt. auth. see Tapinos, Georges.

Piotrowska, Maria, tr. see Bigon, Mario & Regazzoni, Guido.

Piotrowski, Rufin. Souvenirs d'un Siberien. (Nineteenth Century Russia Ser.). 255p. (Fr.). 1974. Repr. of 1870 ed. lib. bdg. 69.50x o.p. (ISBN 0-8287-0694-8, R44). Clearwater Pub.

Piotrowski, Zygmunt A. Perceptanalysis: The Rorschach Method Fundamentally Reworked Expanded & Systematized. 3rd ed. LC 57-5067. (Illus.). 1977. 16.95 o.s.i. (ISBN 0-685-87743-4); scoring man 6.50 o.s.i. (ISBN 0-918924-01-4). Postgrad Intl.

Piou, Nanie, ed. see Lefebvre, Claire.

Pious, Richard M. The American Presidency. LC 78-19808. 1979. 9.95 (ISBN 0-465-00183-1); pap. text ed. 6.95x (ISBN 0-465-00184-X). Basic.

Piowaty, Kim K. Don't Look in Her Eyes. LC 82-13903. 192p. (gr. 5-9). 1983. 10.95 (ISBN 0-689-50273-7, McElderry Bk). Atheneum.

Pipe, G. R. & Veenhius, A. A. National Planning for Informatics in Developing Countries: Proceedings. 1976. 65.25 (ISBN 0-7204-0392-8, North-Holland). Elsevier.

Pipe, Peter. Practical Programming. LC 76-27984. 80p. 1977. pap. 4.50 (ISBN 0-88275-468-8). Krieger.

Pipe, Peter, jt. auth. see Mager, Robert F.

Pipe, Peter see Mager, Robert F.

Pipe, Virginia. Explore Together, Vol. 4. 128p. 1982. pap. 11.95 (ISBN 0-8170-0975-2). Judson.

Piper, David. The Artist's London. (Illus.). 1982. 19.95 (ISBN 0-19-520392-5). Oxford U Pr.

--Companion Guide to London. (Illus.). 544p. 1983. 16.95 (ISBN 0-13-154542-6); pap. 8.95 (ISBN 0-13-154534-5). P-H.

--The Image of the Poet: British Poets & Their Portraits. (Illus.). 1983. 25.00 (ISBN 0-19-817365-2). Oxford U Pr.

--The Random House Library of Painting & Sculpture, 4 vols. LC 80-28604. (Illus.). 960p. 1981. Boxed Set. boxed set 100.00 (ISBN 0-394-50092-X). Random.

Piper, David, jt. auth. see Wise, Susan.

Piper, David, ed. see Baccheschi, Edi.

Piper, F. C., jt. auth. see Hughes, D. R.

Piper, Fred, jt. auth. see Beker, Henry.

Piper, H. Beam. Uller Uprising. 1983. pap. 2.75 (ISBN 0-441-84292-5, Pub. by Ace Science Fiction). Ace Bks.

Piper, John. All About Angling. 1971. 7.50 o.p. (ISBN 0-7207-0429-4). Transatlantic.

--The Justification of God: An Exegetical & Theological Study of Romans 9: 1-23. 312p. (Orig.). 1983. pap. 8.95 (ISBN 0-8010-7079-1). Baker Bk.

--Love Your Enemies. LC 77-95449. (Society for New Testament Studies: No. 38). 1980. 27.95 (ISBN 0-521-22056-4). Cambridge U Pr.

Piper, Julia, ed. Managing Sales Promotion. 304p. 1980. text ed. 44.50x (ISBN 0-566-02206-0). Gower Pub Ltd.

Piper, Priscilla J., jt. auth. see Annual Symposium of Basic Medical Sciences, 10th.

Piper, Watty. The Little Engine That Could. (Illus.). 48p. 3.95 (ISBN 0-448-40520-2, G&D). Putnam Pub Group.

Piper, Watty, ed. The Bumper Book. (Illus.). (ps-3). 1946. 5.95 (ISBN 0-696-96853-0). Platt.

Piper, Watty, retold by. The Little Engine That Could. (Illus.). 16p. (ps). Date not set. price not set deluxe ed. (ISBN 0-448-40035-9, G&D); price not set, 8p., junior ed. Putnam Pub Group.

Piper, William, ed. see Swift, Jonathan.

Pipes, A. CAD Nineteen Eighty-Two: Proceedings. 1982. pap. text ed. 64.95 (ISBN 0-686-37585-8). Butterworth.

Pipes, L., jt. auth. see Hovanessian, S. A.

Pipes, L. A. & Harvill, L. R. Applied Mathematics for Engineers & Physicists. 3rd ed. 1970. text ed. 55.00 (ISBN 0-07-050060-6, C). McGraw.

Pipes, Peggy L., jt. ed. see Holm, Vanja A.

Pipes, Richard. U. S. Soviet Relations in the Era of Detente: A Tragedy of Errors. 230p. (Orig.). 1981. lib. bdg. 25.00 (ISBN 0-86531-154-4); pap. text ed. 10.50 (ISBN 0-86531-155-2). Westview.

Pipes, Richard, ed. Bibliography of the Published Writings of Peter Berngardovich Struve. LC 80-10274. 232p. (Orig.). 1980. pap. 20.25 o.p. (ISBN 0-8357-0503-X, SS 00127). Univ Microfilms.

Pipkin, Bernard & Cummings, David. Environmental Geology: An Exercise Textbook. (Illus.). 240p. 1983. pap. 14.95 (ISBN 0-89863-058-4). Star Pub CA.

Pipkin, H. Wayne & Potter, G. R., eds. A Zwingli Bibliography. LC 73-153549. 1972. 7.00 (ISBN 0-931222-06-0). Pitts Theolog.

Pipkin, John M. Half-a-Love. 1970. 4.00 (ISBN 0-911838-10-4). Windy Row.

--Half After Love. LC 76-46775. 1977. 8.95 (ISBN 0-87716-075-9, Pub. by Moore Pub Co). F Apple.

Pipkin, Lewis S., et al. Relation of Highway Noise to Residential Property Values in Urban Areas of Tennessee. (Illus.). 1978. pap. text ed. 35.00x o.p. (ISBN 0-89671-014-9). Southeast Acoustics.

Pippard, A. B. Elements of Classical Thermodynamics. 1966. pap. text ed. 10.95x (ISBN 0-521-09101-2). Cambridge U Pr.

Pippard, Brian. The Physics of Vibration, Vol. 1. LC 77-85685. (Illus.). 1978. 82.50 (ISBN 0-521-21899-3). Cambridge U Pr.

--The Physics of Vibration: The Simple Vibrator in Quantum Mechanics, Vol. 2. LC 77-85685. (Illus.). 200p. Date not set. price not set (ISBN 0-521-24623-7). Cambridge U Pr.

Pippenger, Dale E., jt. auth. see Spencer, John D.

Pippenger, John & Hicks, Tyler. Industrial Hydraulics. 3rd ed. (Illus.). 1979. text ed. 27.95 (ISBN 0-07-050140-8, G). McGraw.

Pippenger, John H. & Hicks, Tyler G. Industrial Hydraulics. 2nd ed. 1970. text ed. 19.95 o.p. (ISBN 0-07-050064-9, G). McGraw.

Piquet, H. S. The Economic Axioms. 1978. 8.95 o.p. (ISBN 0-533-03229-6). Vantage.

Pirandello, Luigi. Four Short Stories: Quattro Novelle. Jeffery, V. M., tr. from Italian. (Harrap's Bilingual Ser.). 58p. 1955. 5.00 (ISBN 0-911268-44-8). Rogers Bk.

--Naked Masks: Five Plays. Bentley, Eric, ed. Incl. It Is So If You Think So; Henry Fourth; Six Characters in Search of an Author; Each in His Own Way; Liola. 1957. pap. 4.50 (ISBN 0-525-47006-9, 0437-130). Dutton.

--One, None & a Hundred-Thousand. Putnam, S., tr. from Ital. LC 76-50039. 268p. 1983. Repr. of 1933 ed. 15.00x (ISBN 0-686-69134-2). Fertig.

--Shoot! (Si Gura) The Notebook of Serafino Gubbio Cinematograph Operator. Kupelnick, Bruce S., ed. LC 76-52123. (Classics of Film Literature Ser.). 1978. lib. bdg. 18.00 o.s.i. (ISBN 0-8240-2889-9). Garland Pub.

--Sicilian Comedies. LC 82-62097. 1983. 18.95 (ISBN 0-933826-50-8); pap. 6.95 (ISBN 0-933826-51-6). Performing Arts.

Pirandello, Luigi see Moon, Samuel.

Pirani, Emma. Herbarium: Natural Remedies from a Medieval Manuscript. (Illus.). 112p. pap. 12.50 o.p. (ISBN 0-8478-0305-8). Rizzoli Intl.

Pirani, F. A. & Crampin, M. Applicable Differential Geometry. LC 81-18188. (London Mathematical Society Lecture Note Ser.: No. 59). (Illus.). 200p. Date not set. pap. price not set (ISBN 0-521-23190-6). Cambridge U Pr.

Pirazzoli-t'Serstevens, Michele. The Han Dynasty. LC 82-50109. (Illus.). 224p. 1982. 50.00 (ISBN 0-8478-0438-0). Rizzoli Intl.

Pirenne, Henri. Early Democracies in the Low Countries: Urban Society & Political Conflict in the Middle Ages & the Renaissance. Saunders, J. V., tr. Orig. Title: Belgian Democracy. 1971. pap. 1.95x (ISBN 0-393-00565-8, Norton Lib). Norton.

Pirenne, M. H. Optics, Painting & Photography. LC 71-108109. (Illus.). 1970. 64.50x (ISBN 0-521-07686-2). Cambridge U Pr.

Pires, Deborah S., jt. auth. see Malkemes, Fred.

Pirie, David. William Wordsworth. 1982. 32.00x (ISBN 0-416-31300-0). Methuen Inc.

Pirie, Madsen. Trial & Error & the Idea of Progress. LC 77-8577. 1978. 16.00x (ISBN 0-87548-344-5). Open Court.

Pirie, N. W., ed. Food Protein Sources. LC 74-12962. (International Biological Programme Ser.: No. 4). (Illus.). 288p. 1975. 49.50 (ISBN 0-521-20588-3). Cambridge U Pr.

Pirie, Peter J. The English Musical Renaissance. 1980. 16.95 o.p. (ISBN 0-312-25435-0). St Martin.

Pirie, R. Gordon, ed. Oceanography: Contemporary Readings in Ocean Sciences. 2nd ed. (Illus.). 1977. pap. text ed. 12.95x (ISBN 0-19-502119-3). Oxford U Pr.

Pirie, Robert, ed. John Donne, Fifteen Seventy-Two to Sixteen Thirty-One: A Catalogue of the Anniversary Exhibition Held at the Grolier Club, 1972. LC 72-92128. (Illus.). 41p. 1973. pap. 5.00x (ISBN 0-8139-0545-1, Dist. by U Pr of Va). Grolier Club.

Pirie, Susan. Drug Calculations. 48p. 1982. 25.00x (ISBN 0-85950-367-4, Pub. by Thornes England). State Mutual Bk.

Piriou, A., jt. auth. see Chazarain, J.

Piriou, Jean-Pierre J., ed. see Green, Julien.

Pirkle, E. C. Our Physical Environment. 1980. pap. text ed. 15.95x (ISBN 0-8087-1687-5). Burgess.

Pirmantgen, Pat, jt. auth. see Butwin, Miriam.

Pirofsky, Bernard, et al. Blood Banking Principles Review Book: Essay Questions & Answers. 1973. spiral bdg. 12.50 o.p. (ISBN 0-87488-339-3). Med Exam.

Pirone, Pascal P. Diseases & Pests of Ornamental Plants. 5th ed. LC 77-26893. 1978. 29.95x (ISBN 0-471-07249-4, Pub. by Wiley-Interscience). Wiley.

Pirozzolo, Francis J., jt. ed. see Mortimer, James.

Pirruccello, Frank W. Plastic & Reconstruction Surgery of the Face: Flaps of the Head & Neck. (Illus.). 112p. 1982. 26.00 (ISBN 0-683-06889-X). Williams & Williams.

--Plastic & Reconstructive Surgery of the Face: Cosmetic Surgery. (Illus.). 88p. 1981. 26.00 (ISBN 0-686-77751-4, 6891-1). Williams & Wilkins.

Pirserchia, Doris. Doomtime. (Science Fiction Ser.). 1981. pap. 2.25 o.p. (ISBN 0-87997-619-5, UE1619). DAW Bks.

Pirson, S. J. Geologic Well Log Analysis. 2nd ed. 385p. 1978. 19.95x o.p. (ISBN 0-87201-901-2). Gulf Pub.

Pir Vilayat Inayat Khan. The Call of the Dervish. LC 81-52421. 224p. (Orig.). 1981. pap. 7.95 (ISBN 0-930872-26-6, 1013P). Omega Pr NM.

Pirz, Therese. Speak French to Your Baby. (Illus.). (gr. 5-8). 1983. spiral bdg. 14.95 (ISBN 0-9606140-0-1); pap. 11.95 (ISBN 0-9606140-1-X). Chou-Chou.

Pisa, Guido Da see Da Pisa, Guido.

Pisano, Beverly. Afghan Hounds. (Illus.). 125p. 1980. 4.95 (ISBN 0-87666-682-9, KW-077). TFH Pubns.

--Boxers. (Illus.). 1979. 4.95 (ISBN 0-87666-688-8, KW-041). TFH Pubns.

--Chow Chows. (Illus.). 125p. 4.95 (ISBN 0-87666-702-7, KW-089). TFH Pubns.

--Old English Sheepdogs. (Illus.). 128p. 1980. 4.95 (ISBN 0-87666-723-X, KW-093). TFH Pubns.

--Pekingese. (Illus.). 128p. 1981. 4.95 (ISBN 0-87666-724-8, KW-095). TFH Pubns.

--Siberian Huskies. (Illus.). 128p. 1979. 4.95 (ISBN 0-87666-677-2, KW-068). TFH Pubns.

Pisano, Beverly & Holcombe, A. D. Beagles. (Illus.). 125p. 1979. 4.95 (ISBN 0-87666-686-1, KW-080). TFH Pubns.

Pisano, Beverly & Lewis, Gloria. Miniature Schnauzers. (Illus.). 1979. 4.95 (ISBN 0-87666-690-X, KW-042). TFH Pubns.

Pisano, Beverly & Ricketts, Viva L. Pomeranians. (Illus.). 128p. 1980. 4.95 (ISBN 0-87666-707-8, KW-091). TFH Pubns.

Pisano, Beverly & Taynton, Mark. Shetland Sheepdogs. 125p. 1979. 4.95 (ISBN 0-87666-685-3, KW-079). TFH Pubns.

Pisano, Beverly & Thurmer, Tressa E. Chihuahuas. (Illus.). 128p. 1980. 4.95 (ISBN 0-87666-701-9, KW-087). TFH Pubns.

Pisano, Beverly, ed. Dalmatians. (Illus.). 128p. 1980. 4.95 (ISBN 0-87666-705-1, KW-090). TFH Pubns.

--English Setters. (Illus.). 128p. 1980. 4.95 (ISBN 0-87666-716-7, KW102). TFH Pubns.

Pisano, Beverly & Monte, Evelyn, eds. Brittany Spaniels. (Illus.). 128p. 1980. lib. bdg. 4.95 (ISBN 0-87666-708-6, KW092). TFH Pubns.

Pisano, Ronald. William Merritt Chase in the Company of Friends. (Illus.). 70p. 1979. catalogue 1.00 (ISBN 0-943526-06-X). Parrish Art.

Pisano, Ronald G. American Paintings from The Parrish Art Museum. LC 82-61450. (Illus.). 52p. pap. write for info (ISBN 0-943526-07-8). Pachyderm Pr.

--An American Place. (Illus.). 44p. (Orig.). 1981. write for info. catalogue. Parrish Art.

--American Realist & Impressionist: Paintings From the Collection of Mr. & Mrs. Haig Tashjian. (Illus., Orig.). 1982. write for info. catalogue. Parrish Art.

--The Long Island Landscape, Eighteen Sixty-Five through Nineteen Fourteen: The Halcyon Years. (Illus.). 44p. (Orig.). 1981. write for info. catalogue (ISBN 0-943526-03-5). Parrish Art.

--William Merrit Chase. (Illus.). 88p. 1979. 22.50 o.p. (ISBN 0-8230-5739-9). Watson-Guptill.

Pisar, Samual. Of Blood & Hope. (Illus.). 320p. 1982. 7.95 (ISBN 0-02-006310-5). Macmillan.

Piscatori, James P. Islam in the Political Process. LC 82-9745. 272p. Date not set. 37.50 (ISBN 0-521-24941-4); pap. 14.95 (ISBN 0-521-27434-6). Cambridge U Pr.

Pischel, Gina. Sculpture. LC 75-2273. (World of Culture Ser). (Illus.). 12.95 o.p. (ISBN 0-88225-121-X). Newsweek.

Pischel, Gina, et al. World History of Art. 2nd rev ed. La Farge, Henry A. & Bernard, Catherine, eds. LC 78-55593. (Illus.). 1978. 19.98 (ISBN 0-88225-258-5). Newsweek.

Pischke, Sibyl J. Sibyl's Legend of Mammy Jane. 1981. 14.95 (ISBN 0-9608532-0-0). Sibyl.

Piscopo, John. Kinesiology: The Science of Movement. LC 80-21545. 619p. 1981. text ed. 24.95x (ISBN 0-471-03483-5); tchr.'s manual 9.00 (ISBN 0-471-08978-8). Wiley.

Pisello, Daniel M. Gravitation, Electromagnetism & Quantized Charge: The Einstein Insight. LC 78-67493. 1979. 15.00 o.p. (ISBN 0-250-40286-6). Ann Arbor Science.

Piserchia, Doris. The Deadly Sky. 176p. 1983. pap. 2.25. NAL.

Pisk, Paul A., jt. auth. see Ulrich, Homer.

Piskac, A., jt. ed. see Bartik, M.

Pissarides, C. A. Labour Market Adjustment. LC 75-21035. 1976. 49.50 (ISBN 0-521-21064-X). Cambridge U Pr.

Pister, K., ed. Structural Engineering & Structural Mechanics: A Volume Honoring Egor P. Popov. 1980. 40.00 (ISBN 0-13-853671-6). P-H.

Pistole, Elizabeth. Serving with Love - Seasonal. 1981. gift, padded cover 6.95 (ISBN 0-87162-244-0, J1013). Warner Pr.

--Servings with Love - Special Days. 1981. gift, padded cover 6.95 (ISBN 0-87162-245-9, J1014). Warner Pr.

Pistole, Elizabeth S. Food & Fellowship. 1973. pap. 1.50 o.p. (ISBN 0-87162-148-7, D3755). Warner Pr.

Piston, Walter. Harmony. 4th ed. De Voto, Mark, ed. 500p. 1978. text ed. 18.95 (ISBN 0-393-09034-5); wkbk. 7.95x (ISBN 0-393-95071-9). Norton.

Pi-Sunyer, Oriol & Salzmann, Zdenek. Humanity & Culture: An Intro to Anthropology. LC 77-76336. (Illus.). 1978. text ed. 26.50 (ISBN 0-395-25051-X); instr's. manual 1.00 (ISBN 0-395-26239-9). HM.

Piszkiewicz, Dennis. Kinetics of Chemical & Enzyme-Catalyzed Reactions. (Illus.). 1977. text ed. 22.00x (ISBN 0-19-502096-0); pap. text ed. 12.95x (ISBN 0-19-502095-2). Oxford U Pr.

Pita, Edward G. Air Conditioning Principles & Systems: An Energy Approach. LC 80-18958. 467p. 1981. text ed. 28.95x (ISBN 0-471-04214-5); tchrs.' manual 10.00 (ISBN 0-471-09636-9). Wiley.

Pitard, J. & Proust, L. Les Iles Canaries, Flore de L'archipel. 1973. Repr. of 1908 ed. lib. bdg. 60.00x (ISBN 3-87429-050-6). Lubrecht & Cramer.

Pitavy, Francois. William Faulkner's Light in August: A Critical Casebook. LC 81-48416. 300p. 1982. lib. bdg. 40.00 (ISBN 0-8240-9385-2). Garland Pub.

Pitcairn, Leonora. Young Students' Book of Child Care. 4th ed. LC 76-58076. 1978. 7.95x (ISBN 0-521-21671-0). Cambridge U Pr.

Pitch, Irvin. The Pitch Formula for Success. 192p. 1981. 12.95 (ISBN 0-920510-37-X, Pub. by Personal Lib). Dodd.

Pitcher, Evelyn G. & Schultz, Lynn H. Boys & Girls at Play: The Development of Sex Roles. (Illus.). 192p. 1983. text ed. 22.95x (ISBN 0-89789-010-8). J F Bergin.

Pitcher, Evelyn G., et al. Helping Young Children Learn. 3rd ed. 1979. pap. text ed. 13.95 (ISBN 0-675-08256-0). Merrill.

Pitcher, Frederick W. Identification Guide to Marine Tropical Aquarium Fish. LC 77-5528. (Illus.). 1977. 5.95 o.p. (ISBN 0-668-04299-0, 4299). Arco.

Pitcher, Harvey, tr. see Chekhov, Anton.

Pitcher, Tony, jt. auth. see Hart, Paul.

Pitchford, J. D. & Turnovsky, Stephen J. Applications of Control Theory to Economic Analysis. LC 76-41254. (Contributions to Economic Analysis: Vol. 101). 1977. 59.75 (ISBN 0-7204-0455-X, North-Holland). Elsevier.

Pitchford, Kenneth, tr. see Rilke, Rainer M.

Pitcoff, Ramsey K. & Powell, Herb. Neuroradiology with Computed Tomography. 575p. 1981. text ed. write for info. o.p. (ISBN 0-7216-7444-5). Saunders.

Pither, Raymond F. Manual of Foreign Exchange. 7th ed. 1971. 15.00x o.p. (ISBN 0-273-31459-9). Intl Pubns Serv.

Pitkanen, Allan M., tr. see Paulaharju, Samuli.

Pitkin, Anne. Notes for Continuing the Performance. 1977. 3.00 (ISBN 0-918116-04-X). Jawbone Pr.

Pitkin, John, jt. auth. see Masnick, George.

Pitkin, Roy M., ed. Year Book of Obstetrics & Gynecology 1983. 1983. 35.00 (ISBN 0-8151-6692-3). Year Bk Med.

Pitkin, Timothy. Political & Civil History of the United States of America from the Year 1763 to the Close of the Administration of President Washington in March, 1797, 2 Vols. LC 79-109613. (Ear of the American Revolution Ser). 1970. Repr. of 1823 ed. Set. lib. bdg. 135.00 (ISBN 0-306-71908-8). Da Capo.

Pitkin, Walter, ed. see Lash, Joseph P.

Pitman, E. J. Some Basic Theory for Statistical Inference. LC 78-11921. (Monographs on Applied Probability & Statistics). 105p. 1979. 17.50x (ISBN 0-412-21720-1, Pub. by Chapman & Hall England). Methuen Inc.

Pitman Publishing Ltd. Editors. Peterborough Postgraduate Symposia: Cardiology. (Pitman Medical Conference Reports Ser.). (Illus.). 128p. 1975. pap. text ed. 16.95x (ISBN 0-8464-0713-2). Beekman Pubs.

Pitman, Walter C., III, jt. ed. see Talwani, Manik.

Pitot, Henry C. Fundamentals of Oncology. 2nd., rev. ed. 304p. 1981. write for info. (ISBN 0-8247-1419-9). Dekker.

Pitseolak, Peter. Peter Pitseolak's Escape from Death. Eber, Dorothy, ed. LC 77-83236. 1978. 7.95 o.s.i. (ISBN 0-440-06894-0, Sey Lawr); PLB 7.45 o.s.i. (ISBN 0-440-06896-7). Delacorte.

Pitskhelauri, G. Z. The Longliving of Soviet Georgia. Lesnoff-Caravaglia, Gari, ed. LC 81-4176. (Illus.). 158p. 1982. 16.95x (ISBN 0-89885-073-8). Human Sci Pr.

Pitsvada, Bernard T., jt. auth. see Draper, Frank D.

Pitt, Barrie. Battle of the Atlantic. LC 79-74822. (World War II Ser.). (Illus.). (gr. 6 up). 1977. PLB 19.92 (ISBN 0-8094-2467-3; Pub. by Time-Life). Silver.

Pitt, Bertram, jt. auth. see Strauss, H. William.

Pitt, Clifford S. Church, Ministry & Sacraments: A Critical Evaluation of the Thought of Peter Taylor Forsyth. LC 82-24817. 360p. (Orig.). 1983. lib. bdg. 25.00 (ISBN 0-8191-3027-3); pap. text ed. 14.00 (ISBN 0-8191-3028-1). U Pr of Amer.

Pitt, Douglas C. Telecommunications Function of the British Post Office. 1979. text ed. 27.00x (ISBN 0-566-00273-6). Gower Pub Ltd.

Pitt, G. D., jt. auth. see Parker, H. D.

Pitt, Leonard. The Decline of the Californios: A Social History of the Spanish-Speaking Californians, 1846-1890. 1966. 14.95 o.s.i. (ISBN 0-520-01019-1); pap. 5.95 (ISBN 0-520-01637-8, CAL186). U of Cal Pr.

--We Americans: A Topical History of the United States, 2 vols. Incl. Vol. 1. Colonial Times to 1877 (ISBN 0-673-15001-1); Vol. 2. 1865 to the Present (ISBN 0-673-15002-X). 1976. pap. 12.50x ea. Scott F.

Pitt, Peter. Surgeon in Nepal. (Illus.). 1971. 15.00 o.p. (ISBN 0-7195-2191-2). Transatlantic.

Pitt, Valerie & Cook, David. A Closer Look at Dogs. LC 75-4390. (Closer Look at Ser.). (Illus.). (gr. 8 up). 1979. pap. 1.95 (ISBN 0-531-03447-X). Watts.

Pitt, Valerie, jt. auth. see Hoke, Helen.

Pittard, A. J., jt. ed. see Millis, N.

Pittaway, Margaret. The Rainforest Children. (Illus.). (ps-3). 1980. 9.95 (ISBN 0-19-554238-X). Oxford U Pr.

Pittenger, Norman. The Ministry of All Christians. 96p. 1983. pap. write for info. (ISBN 0-8192-1323-3). Morehouse.

Pittenger, W. Norman, jt. auth. see Pike, James A.

Pitti, Buonaccorso & Dati, Gregorio. Two Memoirs of Renaissance Florence: The Diaries of Buonaccorso Pitti & Gregorio Dati. pap. 3.95xi (ISBN 0-06-131333-5, TB1333, Torch). Har-Row.

Pittie, H. V. Characteristic Classes of Foliations. (Research Notes in Mathematics: No. 10). 107p. (Orig.). 1976. pap. text ed. 17.50 (ISBN 0-273-00311-9). Pitman Pub MA.

Pittier De Fabrega, Henri. Ethnographic & Linguistic Notes on the Paez Indians of Tierra Adentro, Cauca, Colombia. LC 8-3129. 1907. pap. 13.00 (ISBN 0-527-00504-5). Kraus Repr.

Pittiglio, D. Harmening. Modern Blood Banking & Transfusion Practices. LC 82-17989. 600p. 1983. 30.00 (ISBN 0-8036-6948-8). Davis Co.

Pittinger, Virginia. Wait until Midnight. LC 78-58393. (Moonstone Gothic Ser.). 208p. 1978. pap. 1.75 (ISBN 0-87216-668-6). Playboy Pbks.

Pittinger, William. Daring & Suffering. (Collector's Library of the Civil War). 1982. 26.60 (ISBN 0-8094-4220-5). Silver.

Pittman, Brenda S. The Feelings Are There. 1981. cancelled 4.50 (ISBN 0-8062-1553-4). Carlton.

Pittman, David J. & Snyder, Charles R., eds. Society, Culture & Drinking Patterns. LC 65-15188. (Arcturus Books Paperbacks). 633p. 1968. pap. 12.95 o.p. (ISBN 0-8093-0326-4). S Ill U Pr.

Pittman, Margaret B. The Mystery of Who Discovered the Americas. LC 79-17203. (Unsolved Mysteries of the World Ser.). PLB 11.96 (ISBN 0-89547-076-4). Silver.

Pittman, Richard & Kerr, Harland, eds. Papers on the Languages of the Australian Aborigines. 166p. 1964. pap. 2.00x o.s.i. (ISBN 0-88312-795-4); microfiche 2.25 o.s.i. (ISBN 0-88312-338-X). Summer Inst Ling.

Pittock, A. B., et al, eds. Climatic Change & Variability: A Southern Perspective. LC 76-53521. (Illus.). 1978. 72.50 (ISBN 0-521-21562-5). Cambridge U Pr.

Pittock, Malcolm. Ernst Toller. (World Authors Ser.). 1979. lib. bdg. 15.95 (ISBN 0-8057-6350-3, Twayne). G K Hall.

Pittore, Carlo. Bern Porter Commemorative Stamp Series Book. (Illus.). 1981. 1.50x (ISBN 0-934376-15-8). Pittore Euforico.

--Post Me Stamp Series Book. (Illus.). 1981. 1.50x (ISBN 0-934376-14-X). Pittore Euforico.

Pitt-Rivers, J. The Fate of Shechem or the Politics of Sex. LC 76-27913. (Studies in Social Anthropology Ser.: No. 19). (Illus.). 1977. 27.95 (ISBN 0-521-21427-0). Cambridge U Pr.

Pitts, Audre. Each Year Is a Book. 1982p. 1982. pap. 2.95 (ISBN 0-8341-0792-9). Beacon Hill.

Pitts, Dennis. Rogue Hercules. LC 77-88904. 1978. 6.95 o.p. (ISBN 0-689-10849-4). Atheneum.

Pitts, Donald R. & Sissam, Leighton E. Heat Transfer. (Schaum's Outline Ser.). 1977. pap. 8.95 o.p. (ISBN 0-07-050203-X, SP). McGraw.

Pitts, Donald R., jt. auth. see Sissom, Leighton E.

Pitts, Forrest R. Japan. rev. ed. LC 80-69169. (World Cultures Ser.). (Illus.). 192p. (gr. 6 up). 1981. text ed. 11.20 5 or more copies 7.96 ea. (ISBN 0-88296-120-9); tchrs'. guide 8.96 (ISBN 0-88296-381-3). Fideler.

Pitts, Gerald N., jt. auth. see Bateman, Barry L.

Pitts, J. N. & Metcalf, R. L. Advances in Environmental Science & Technology. 371p. 1975. 37.50 o.p. (ISBN 0-471-69088-0, Pub. by Wiley-Interscience). Wiley.

Pitts, James N. & Metcalf, Robert L., eds. Advances in Environmental Science & Technology, Vol. 10. LC 74-644364. 1980. 61.95x (ISBN 0-471-06480-7, Pub. by Wiley-Interscience). Wiley.

Pitts, James N., et al. Advances in Photochemistry. LC 66-13592. Vol. 11, 1979. 63.95 (ISBN 0-471-04797-X); Vol. 12, 1980. 68.00x (ISBN 0-471-06286-3). Wiley.

Pitts, John D. & Finbow, Malcolm E., eds. The Functional Integration of Cells in Animal Tissues. LC 81-10213. (British Society for Cell Biology Symposium Ser.: No. 5). (Illus.). 400p. 1982. 69.50 (ISBN 0-521-24199-5). Cambridge U Pr.

Pittsburgh Conference on Modeling & Simulation, 12th Annual. Modeling & Simulation: Proceedings, 4 pts, Vol. 12. Vogt, William G. & Mickle, Marlin H., eds. LC 73-85004. 1776p. 1981. Set. pap. text ed. 149.00x (ISBN 0-87664-563-5); pap. text ed. 40.00x ea. Pt. 1 Energy & Environment (ISBN 0-87664-559-7). Pt. 2-Systems, Control & Computers (ISBN 0-87664-560-0). Pt. 3-Socio-economics & Biomedical (ISBN 0-87664-561-9). Pt. 4-General Modeling & Simulation (ISBN 0-87664-562-7). Instru Soc.

Pitty, A. F. Geography & Soil Properties. 1979. 25.95x (ISBN 0-416-75380-9); pap. 15.95x (ISBN 0-416-71540-0). Methuen Inc.

Pitz, jt. auth. see Wallace.

Pitz, Henry C. Howard Pyle: Writer, Illustrator, Founder of the Brandywine School. (Illus.). 1975. 25.00 o.p. (ISBN 0-517-51665-9, C N Potter Bks). Crown.

Pitz, Henry C., ed. & intro. by see Remington, Frederic.

Pitzer & Brewer. Thermodynamics. 2nd ed. (Advanced Chemistry Ser.). 1961. text ed. 42.50 (ISBN 0-07-037622-0, C). McGraw.

Pival, Jean G., jt. auth. see Adelstein, Michael E.

Pivar, David J. Purity Crusade: Sexual Morality & Social Control, 1868-1900. LC 70-179650. (Contributions in American History Ser.: No. 23). 308p. 1973. lib. bdg. 29.95 (ISBN 0-8371-6319-6, PPC/); pap. 4.95 (ISBN 0-8371-7890-8). Greenwood.

Pivar, William. Real Estate Ethics. 1979. pap. 13.95 o.s.i. (ISBN 0-695-81253-X). Follett.

Pivar, William H. California Real Estate License Preparation Text. 5th ed. (Illus.). 1980. text ed. 19.25 (ISBN 0-686-86551-0); pap. text ed. 19.95 (ISBN 0-13-112540-0). P-H.

--California Real Estate License Preparation Text. 6th ed. (Illus.). 320p. 1983. pap. 22.60 (ISBN 0-13-111914-1); students ed. 16.95 (ISBN 0-686-92006-6). P-H.

--Power Real Estate Listing. 170p. 1983. text ed. 12.95 (ISBN 0-88462-480-3). Real Estate Ed Co.

--Power Real Estate Sales. 170p. 1983. text ed. 12.95 (ISBN 0-88462-479-X). Real Estate Ed Co.

--The Real Estate Career Guide. LC 80-11544. 240p. 1980. lib. bdg. 11.95 (ISBN 0-668-04789-5); pap. 7.95 o.p. (ISBN 0-668-04970-7). Arco.

--Real Estate License Preperation Test. (Illus.). 272p. 1980. pap. text ed. 17.95 (ISBN 0-13-764209-1). P-H.

Pivcevic, E., ed. Phenomenology & Philisophical Understanding. LC 74-19533. 304p. 1975. 39.50 (ISBN 0-521-20637-5); pap. 12.95x (ISBN 0-521-09914-5). Cambridge U Pr.

Piven, Frances F. & Cloward, Richard A. Regulating the Poor: The Functions of Public Relief. 416p. 1972. pap. 5.95 (ISBN 0-394-71743-0, V743, Vin). Random.

Piven, Peter. Compensation Management: A Guidelenes for Small Firms. (Illus.). 32p. 1982. 15.00x (ISBN 0-913962-47-3). Am Inst Arch.

Pivka, Otto Von see Von Pivka, Otto.

Pixley, Alden F. Applied Linear Algebra. LC 80-8241. 264p. 1980. lib. bdg. 20.75 (ISBN 0-8191-1169-4); pap. text ed. 11.25 (ISBN 0-8191-1170-8). U Pr of Amer.

Pixton, William H. Some Conventions of Standard Written English. 3rd ed. 1979. pap. text ed. 6.95 (ISBN 0-8403-2643-2). Kendall-Hunt.

Pizan, Christine De see De Pizan, Christine.

Pizarro, P. Relation of the Discovery & Conquest of the Kingdoms of Peru, 2 Vols. in 1. Means, Philip A., tr. Repr. of 1921 ed. 45.00 (ISBN 0-527-19724-6). Kraus Repr.

Pizer, Donald. Critical Essays on Theodore Dreiser. (Critical Essays on American Literature). 1981. lib. bdg. 25.00 (ISBN 0-8161-8257-4, Twayne). G K Hall.

Pizer, Donald & Dowell, Richard W. Theodore Dreiser: A Primary & Secondary Bibliography. 1975. lib. bdg. 31.00 (ISBN 0-8161-1082-4, Hall Reference). G K Hall.

Pizer, Donald, ed. see London, Jack.

Pizer, Donald, ed. see Norris, Frank.

Pizer, Hank. Guide to the New Medicine: What Works, What Doesn't. 1982. 10.95 (ISBN 0-688-01314-7). Morrow.

Pizer, Hank & Garfink, Christine. The Post Partum Book: How to Cope with & Enjoy the First Year of Parenting. LC 78-19710. 1979. 9.95 o.s.i. (ISBN 0-394-50524-7, GP821). Grove.

Pizer, Hank & O'Brien Palinski, Christine. Coping with Miscarriage. (Medical Library). 192p. 1982. pap. 6.95 (ISBN 0-686-84852-7, 3945-X). Mosby.

Pizer, Hank & Palinski, Christine O. Coping with a Miscarriage. 1981. pap. 4.95 (ISBN 0-452-25371-3, Z5371, Plume). NAL.

Pizer, Stephen M. Numerical Computing & Mathematical Analysis. (Computer Science Ser). (Illus.). 544p. 1975. text ed. 25.95 (ISBN 0-574-19155-0, 13-4025). SRA.

Pizer, Stuart A. & Travers, Jeffrey. Psychology & Social Changes. (Psychology Ser.). 204p. 1974. pap. text ed. 7.95 o.p. (ISBN 0-07-050224-2, C). McGraw.

Pizer, Vernon. Ink, Ark., & All That: How American Places Got Their Names. LC 76-13176. (Illus.). (gr. 6-8). 1976. 8.95 o.p. (ISBN 0-399-20532-2). Putnam Pub Group.

--Shortchanged by History: America's Neglected Innovators. LC 78-24141. (Illus.). (gr. 6-8). 1979. 8.95 (ISBN 0-399-20665-5). Putnam Pub Group.

--You Don't Say: How People Communicate Without Speech. LC 77-12576. (Illus.). (gr. 6 up). 1978. 7.95 (ISBN 0-399-20625-6). Putnam Pub Group.

Pizetti, I. & Cocker, H. Flowers: A Guide for Your Garden, 2 vols. (Illus.). 24.95 set o.p. (ISBN 0-517-22044-X). Crown.

Pizzarelli, Alan. Zenryu & Other Works: Nineteen Seventy-Four. (Xtras Ser.: No. 2). 36p. (Orig.). 1975. pap. 2.00 o.p. (ISBN 0-89120-001-0). From Here.

Pizzarello, Donald J. & Witcofski, Richard L. Medical Radiation Biology. 2nd ed. LC 81-19311. (Illus.). 164p. 1982. text ed. 32.50 (ISBN 0-8121-0834-5). Lea & Febiger.

Pizzey, Erin. Scream Quietly or the Neighbors Will Hear. LC 77-23406. 1977. 11.95x (ISBN 0-89490-005-6). Enslow Pubs.

Pizzillo, Joseph J. Intercultural Studies: School in Diversity. 272p. 1982. pap. text ed. 10.95 (ISBN 0-8403-2860-5). Kendall-Hunt.

Pizzo, Peggy. Parent to Parent: Working Together for Ourselves & Our Children. LC 85-73875. 320p. 1983. 13.41 (ISBN 0-8070-2300-0). Beacon Pr.

Pizzo, Peggy D. Parent to Parent: A Look at Self Help & Child Advocacy by Parents. 256p. 1982. cancelled o.p. (ISBN 0-8052-3777-1). Schocken.

Pizzuti, Mary. Phoneme Baseline Recording Forms. (Illus., Orig.). 1979. pap. text ed. 15.00 (ISBN 0-88450-796-3, 3055-B). Communication Skill.

Pizzuto, J. J., et al. Fabric Science. 432p. 1975. Set. 20.00 o.s.i. (ISBN 0-87005-136-9); ring bdg 13.50 o.s.i. (ISBN 0-685-55491-0); fabric swatch kit & binder 12.50 o.s.i. (ISBN 0-87005-376-0). Fairchild.

PLA Audiovisual Committee. Guidelines for Audiovisual Materials & Services for Large Public Libraries. 40p. 1975. pap. text ed. 4.00 (ISBN 0-8389-3172-3). ALA.

--Recommendations for Audiovisual Materials & Services for Small & Medium- Sized Public Libraries. 40p. 1975. pap. text ed. 4.00 (ISBN 0-8389-3173-1). ALA.

Plaa, G. L. & Hewitt, W. R., eds. Toxicology of the Liver. (Target Organ Toxicology Ser.). 352p. 1982. text ed. 45.00 (ISBN 0-89004-584-4). Raven.

Plaat, Otto. Ordinary Differential Equations. LC 70-156869. 350p. 1971. 22.50x (ISBN 0-8162-6844-4). Holden-Day.

Placa, Alan. Contemplative Prayer: Problems & an Approach for Ordinary Christians. 1976. pap. 1.75 o.p. (ISBN 0-914544-13-6). Living Flame Pr.

Placa, Alan & Riordan, Brendan P. Desert Silence: A Way of Prayer for an Unquiet Age. (Orig.). 1977. pap. 2.50 (ISBN 0-914544-15-2). Living Flame Pr.

Place. The Vikings. (gr. 5 up). 1980. pap. 9.90 (ISBN 0-531-09170-8, G32, Warwick Press). Watts.

Place, C. M., jt. auth. see Arrowsmith, D. K.

Place, Charles A. Charles Bulfinch: Architect & Citizen. LC 68-27717. (Architecture & Decorative Art Ser). (Illus.). 1968. Repr. of 1925 ed. lib. bdg. 37.50 (ISBN 0-306-71150-8). Da Capo.

Place, Edwin B. & Behm, Herbert C., trs. Amadis of Gaul: A Novel of Chivalry of the 14th Century Presumably First Written in Spanish, Vol. 2, Bks. 3 & 4. LC 73-77256. (Studies in Romance Languages: No. 11). 752p. 1975. 28.00x (ISBN 0-8131-1313-X). U Pr of Ky.

Place, Irene & Byers, Edward E. Executive Secretarial Procedures. 5th ed. LC 79-9097. (Illus.). 1980. text ed. 21.35 (ISBN 0-07-050255-2); instrs'. manual & key 7.35 (ISBN 0-07-050257-9). McGraw.

Place, Irene M. & Popham, E. L. Filing & Records Management. 1966. text ed. 16.95 (ISBN 0-13-314625-1). P-H.

Place, J. A. The Western Films of John Ford. 1977. pap. 7.95 (ISBN 0-8065-0594-X). Citadel Pr.

Place, Jonathan. How to Save a Million. LC 82-82315. 156p. (Orig.). 1982. pap. 4.95 (ISBN 0-448-16807-3, G&D). Putnam Pub Group.

Place, Marian T. Lotta Crabtree: Gold Rush Girl. (Childhood of Famous Americans Ser.). (Illus.). (gr. 3-7). 1958. 3.95 o.p. (ISBN 0-672-50122-8). Bobbs.

--The Witch Who Saved Halloween. (Illus.). (gr. 2-5). 1974. pap. 1.75 o.p. (ISBN 0-380-00097-0, 51417, Camelot). Avon.

Place, Marian T. & Preston, Charles G. Juan's Eighteen-Wheeler Summer. LC 82-7251. 160p. (gr. 4 up). 1982. PLB 8.95 o.p. (ISBN 0-396-08078-2). Dodd.

Place, Patricia A., jt. auth. see Lillie, David L.

Place, Robin & Ross, Anne. The Celts. LC 77-86183. (Peoples of the Past Ser.). (Illus.). 1977. PLB 12.68 (ISBN 0-382-06124-1). Silver.

Place, Stan & Budd, Elaine. Stan Place's Guide to Make-Up: How to Look Like Yourself Only Better. (Illus.). 192p. 1981. 17.95 o.p. (ISBN 0-385-15537-9). Doubleday.

Placek, Paul J., ed. see Hendershot, Gerry E.

Places, Edouard des. Etudes Plantoniciennes, 1929-1979. (Etudes Preliminaires aux Religions Orientales dans l'Empire Romain Ser.: Vol. 90). (Illus.). xx, 416p. 1981. write for info. (ISBN 90-04-06473-7). E J Brill.

Placido, Bucolo, ed. The Other Pareto. LC 79-24588. 1980. 36.00 (ISBN 0-312-58955-7). St Martin.

Placket, R. L., jt. auth. see Hewlitt, P. S.

Placzek, Adolf K., ed. Macmillan Encyclopedia of Architects, 4 Vols. 1982. lib. bdg. 275.00x (ISBN 0-02-925000-5). Macmillan.

Placzek, Beverley, ed. see Reich, Wilhelm.

Placzek, Beverly, ed. Record of a Friendship: The Correspondence of Wilhelm Reich & A. S. Neill. 1983. pap. 11.95 (ISBN 0-374-51770-3). FS&G.

Plagens, Peter. DeWain Valentine. 24p. 1975. 6.50x (ISBN 0-686-99813-8). La Jolla Mus Contemp Art.

Plagens, Peter, jt. auth. see Hickey, Dave.

Plagman, Bernard K., jt. auth. see Leong-Hong, Belkis W.

Plaid, Ian. Brace Yourself, Bridget! The Official Irish Sex Manual. 96p. 1982. 5.95 (ISBN 0-312-09430-2); prepack 29.75 (ISBN 0-312-09431-0). St Martin.

Plaidy, Jean. The Bastard King. LC 78-20970. 1979. 10.00 (ISBN 0-399-12322-9). Putnam Pub Group.

--The Battle of the Queens. 320p. 1981. 10.95 (ISBN 0-399-12604-X). Putnam Pub Group.

--The Battle of the Queens. 384p. 1982. pap. 2.95 (ISBN 0-449-24565-9, Crest). Fawcett.

--Beyond the Blue Mountains. LC 75-7951. 464p. 1975. 8.95 (ISBN 0-399-11599-4). Putnam Pub Group.

--The Captive of Kensington Palace. LC 76-27122. 1976. 8.95 o.p. (ISBN 0-399-11851-9). Putnam Pub Group.

--The Follies of the King. 336p. 1982. 12.95 (ISBN 0-399-12690-2). Putnam Pub Group.

--Gaylord Robert. 1971. 6.95 (ISBN 0-399-10336-8). Putnam Pub Group.

--The Goldsmith's Wife. LC 73-91717. 320p. 1974. 6.95 o.p. (ISBN 0-399-11351-7). Putnam Pub Group.

--Hammer of the Scots. 320p. 1981. 11.95 (ISBN 0-399-12641-4). Putnam Pub Group.

--The Haunted Sisters. LC 77-23757. 1977. 8.95 o.s.i. (ISBN 0-399-12073-4). Putnam Pub Group.

--A Health Unto His Majesty. 288p. 1972. 6.95 o.p. (ISBN 0-399-10982-X). Putnam Pub Group.

--The Heart of the Lion. 344p. 1980. 10.95 o.s.i. (ISBN 0-399-12538-8). Putnam Pub Group.

--Here Lies Our Sovereign Lord. 320p. 1973. 6.95 o.p. (ISBN 0-399-11137-9). Putnam Pub Group.

--The Italian Woman. 304p. 1975. 7.95 o.p. (ISBN 0-399-11685-0). Putnam Pub Group.

--Light on Lucrezia. LC 75-45064. 1976. 8.95 (ISBN 0-399-11723-7). Putnam Pub Group.

--The Lion of Justice. LC 79-12572. 1979. 10.00 o.p. (ISBN 0-399-12355-5). Putnam Pub Group.

--Madame Serpent. LC 74-28549. 1975. 7.95 o.p. (ISBN 0-399-11506-4). Putnam Pub Group.

--Mary Queen of Scots: The Fair Devil of Scotland. LC 75-7904. (Illus.). 272p. 1975. 15.95 (ISBN 0-399-11581-1). Putnam Pub Group.

--The Murder in the Tower. LC 74-78900. 288p. 1974. 6.95 o.p. (ISBN 0-399-11396-7). Putnam Pub Group.

--Murder Most Royal. 230p. 1972. 7.95 (ISBN 0-399-10934-X). Putnam Pub Group.

--Passage to Pontefract. (Plantagenet Saga Ser.: Vol. 10). 368p. 1982. 12.95 (ISBN 0-399-12750-X). Putnam Pub Group.

--The Passionate Enemies. LC 79-12586. 1979. 10.00 (ISBN 0-399-12413-6). Putnam Pub Group.

--The Plantagenet Prelude. LC 79-24299. 1980. 10.95 (ISBN 0-399-12448-9). Putnam Pub Group.

--The Prince of Darkness. 320p. 1981. 10.95 (ISBN 0-399-12517-5). Putnam Pub Group.

--The Queen & Lord M. LC 77-3644. 1977. 7.95 (ISBN 0-399-11994-9). Putnam Pub Group.

--The Queen from Provence. 288p. 1981. 11.95 (ISBN 0-399-12656-2). Putnam Pub Group.

--Queen Jezebel. LC 76-10751. 1976. 8.95 o.p. (ISBN 0-399-11787-3). Putnam Pub Group.

--The Queen's Favourites. LC 78-1752. 1978. 10.00 (ISBN 0-399-12236-2). Putnam Pub Group.

--The Queen's Husband. LC 77-21161. 1978. 8.95 (ISBN 0-399-12128-5). Putnam Pub Group.

--The Revolt of the Eaglets. 1980. 10.95 (ISBN 0-399-12495-0). Putnam Pub Group.

--Royal Road to Fotheringay: A Novel of Mary Queen of Scots. 1968. 6.95 o.p. (ISBN 0-399-10711-8). Putnam Pub Group.

--St. Thomas's Eve. 1970. 6.95 (ISBN 0-399-10717-7). Putnam Pub Group.

--The Spanish Bridegroom. 1971. 6.95 o.p. (ISBN 0-399-10761-4). Putnam Pub Group.

--The Star of Lancaster. (Plantagenet Saga Ser.). 320p. 1982. 12.95 (ISBN 0-399-12758-5). Putnam Pub Group.

--The Three Crowns. LC 76-55937. 1977. 8.95 (ISBN 0-399-11892-6). Putnam Pub Group.

--The Vow on the Heron. 352p. 1982. 12.95 (ISBN 0-399-12708-9). Putnam Pub Group.

--The Wandering Prince. 1971. 6.95 o.p. (ISBN 0-399-10850-5). Putnam Pub Group.

--The Widow of Windsor. LC 78-20391. 1978. 10.00 o.s.i. (ISBN 0-399-12282-6). Putnam Pub Group.

Plain, Belva. Eden Burning. (General Ser.). 1982. lib. bdg. 16.95 (ISBN 0-8161-3424-3, Large Print Bks). G K Hall.

--Eden Burning. 1983. pap. 3.95 (ISBN 0-440-12135-3). Dell.

--Evergreen. 1978. 15.95 o.s.i. (ISBN 0-440-02661-X). Delacorte.

--Evergreen, 2 vols. (General Ser.). 1980. Set. lib. bdg. 23.95 o.p. (ISBN 0-8161-3114-7, Large Print Bks). G K Hall.

--Random Winds. 1980. 15.95 o.s.i. (ISBN 0-440-07124-0). Delacorte.

--Random Winds. 1981. pap. 3.95 (ISBN 0-440-17158-X). Dell.

Plaisance, D. De, jt. auth. see Gattine, M. A.

Plaister, Jean M. Computing in Laser: Regional Library Cooperation. 64p. 1982. pap. 15.00 (ISBN 0-85365-954-0). Oryx Pr.

Plaister, T. Developing Listening Comprehension for ESL Students: The Kingdom of Kochen. 1976. pap. 11.95 (ISBN 0-13-204479-X); tapes 170.00 (ISBN 0-13-204495-1). P-H.

Plaister, Ted. English Monosyllables: A Minimal Pair Locator List for English As a Second Language. 1965. pap. 2.00x o.p. (ISBN 0-8248-0022-2, Eastwest Ctr). UH Pr.

Plakogiannis, Fotios M. & Cutie, Anthony J. Self-Assessment of Current Knowledge in Pharmacy. 1976. spiral bdg. 13.00 (ISBN 0-87488-272-9). Med Exam.

Plambeck, James A. Electroanalytical Chemistry: Basic Principles & Applications. LC 82-2803. 404p. 1982. 35.00 (ISBN 0-471-04608-6, Pub. by Wiley-Interscience). Wiley.

Plamenatz, John. Karl Marx's Philosophy of Man. 1975. pap. 14.95x (ISBN 0-19-824649-8). Oxford U Pr.
Plamenatz, John P. German Marxism & Russian Communism. LC 75-1135. 356p. 1975. Repr. of 1954 ed. lib. bdg. 39.75x (ISBN 0-8371-7986-6, PLGM). Greenwood.
Plamondon, Ann L. Whitehead's Organic Philosophy of Science. LC 78-16682. 1979. 34.50x (ISBN 0-87395-387-8). State U NY Pr.
Planche, James R. The Pursuivant of Arms; or, Heraldry Founded Upon Facts. LC 72-10610. (Illus.). 299p. 1973. Repr. of 1874 ed. 30.00x (ISBN 0-8103-3171-3). Gale.
--Recollections & Reflections. (Music Reprint Ser.). (Illus.). 1978. Repr. of 1901 ed. lib. bdg. 49.50 (ISBN 0-306-79501-9). Da Capo.
Planck, Dennistown W. Ver see Ver Planck, Dennistown W. & Teare, B. R.
Plane, R. A., jt. auth. see Sienko, M. J.
Plane, Robert A., jt. auth. see Sienko, Michell J.
Planer, F. E. Superstitution. cancelled o.s.i. (ISBN 0-8180-2001-6). Horizon.
Plank, J. E. Van Der see Van Der Plank, J. E.
Plank, Tom M., jt. auth. see Blensly, Douglas L.
Plank, William G. Sartre & Surrealism. Kuspit, Donald, ed. LC 81-431. (Studies in Fine Arts: Art Theory: No. 2). 110p. 1981. 34.95 (ISBN 0-8357-1175-7, Pub. by UMI Res Pr). Univ Microfilms.
Plann, Susan. Relative Clauses in Spanish Without Overt Antecedents & Related Constructions. (U C. Publications in Linguistics Ser.: Vol. 93). 1980. pap. 15.50x (ISBN 0-520-09608-8). U of Cal Pr.
Plano, Jack C. & Olton, Roy. The International Relations Dictionary. 3rd ed. LC 82-3996. (Clio Dictionaries in Political Science Ser.: No. 2). 488p. 1982. text ed. 19.75 (ISBN 0-87436-332-2); pap. 9.75 (ISBN 0-87436-336-5). ABC-Clio.
Plano, Jack C., jt. auth. see Chandler, Ralph.
Plano, Jack C., jt. auth. see Rossi, Ernest E.
Plant, Sir Arnold. Selected Economic Essays & Addresses. Seldon, Arthur, ed. 260p. 1974. 27.95x (ISBN 0-7100-7935-4). Routledge & Kegan.
Plant, Martin A. Drinking Careers: Occupations, Drinking Habits, & Drinking Problems. (Illus.). 1979. 27.00x (ISBN 0-422-76590-2, Pub. by Tavistock England). Methuen Inc.
Plant, Michael. In & Out: Australian Usage & Abusage. pap. 6.50x (ISBN 0-392-03369-0, ABC). Sportshelf.
Plant, R. Population & Labour: A Popular Account of the Implications of Rapid Population Growth for the Training, Employment & Welfare of Workers. 1973. 10.00 (ISBN 92-2-101024-4). Intl Labour Office.
Plant, Raymond. Community & Ideology: An Essay in Applied Social Philosophy. (The International Library of Welfare & Philosophy). 96p. 1974. 9.95x o.p. (ISBN 0-7100-7856-0); pap. 3.95 o.p. (ISBN 0-7100-7857-9). Routledge & Kegan.
--Social & Moral Theory in Casework. (Library of Social Work). 1970. 10.00x o.p. (ISBN 0-7100-6808-5); pap. 3.50 o.p. (ISBN 0-7100-6809-3). Routledge & Kegan.
Plante, David. Difficult Women. LC 82-71059. 192p. 1983. 9.95 (ISBN 0-689-11329-3). Atheneum.
--Ghost of Henry James. LC 71-118217. 1970. 5.95 (ISBN 0-87645-025-7). Gambit.
Plante, Russell. Solar Domestic Hot Water: A Practical Guide to Installation & Understanding. 350p. 1983. text ed. 18.95x (ISBN 0-471-09592-3). Wiley.
Plantinga, Alvin. Does God Have a Nature? LC 80-6585. (Aquinas Lecture Ser.). 1980. 7.95 (ISBN 0-87462-145-3). Marquette.
--The Nature of Necessity. 1979. pap. 12.95x (ISBN 0-19-824414-2). Oxford U Pr.
Plantinga, John H. A Creative Alternative to Swingsets: Guidelines for Planning & Designing Creative Playgrounds. 67p. 1977. pap. 4.00 (ISBN 0-686-84035-6). U OR Ctr Leisure.
Plantinga, Leon B. Schumann As Critic. LC 76-7599. (Music Reprint Ser.). 1976. Repr. of 1967 ed. pap. 32.50 (ISBN 0-306-70785-3). Da Capo.
Plantinga, Theodore. Learning to Live with Evil. (Illus.). 1982. pap. 5.95 (ISBN 0-8028-1917-6). Eerdmans.
Plantinga, Theodore, tr. see De Boer, Theo.
Plantley. The International Civil Service: Law & Management. LC 80-82069. 472p. 1981. 68.75x (ISBN 0-89352-103-5). Masson Pub.
Plants, H. & Haynes, R. H. Programmed Topics in Statics & Strength of Materials. 1966. pap. text ed. 14.00 (ISBN 0-07-050320-6, C). McGraw.
Plants, Helen & Venable, Wallace. Introduction to Statics. LC 74-32425. (Illus.). 1045p. 1975. text ed. 24.50 (ISBN 0-8299-0023-3); tchrs' ed. avail. (ISBN 0-8299-0568-5); notebook 7.95 (ISBN 0-8299-0047-0). West Pub.
Plantz, Shereen la see La Plantz, Shereen.
Planz, Allen. Chunderhara. 2nd, rev. ed. 80p. Date not set. pap. cancelled (ISBN 0-686-87053-0). Street Pr.
--Night for Rioting. LC 82-71553. (New Poetry Ser: No.37). 53p. 1969. 8.95 (ISBN 0-8040-0227-4). Swallow.
Plas, Leendert Van Der see Van Der Plas, Leendert.
Plascov, Avi. The Palestinian Refugees in Jordan Ninteen Forty-Eight to Fifty-Seven. (Illus.). 286p. 1981. 45.00x (ISBN 0-7146-3120-5, F Cass Co). Biblio Dist.
Plascov, Avi, ed. Modernization, Political Development & Stability. LC 80-28387. (Security in the Persian Gulf Ser.: Vol. 3). 192p. 1982. pap. text ed. 10.00x (ISBN 0-86598-046-2). Allanheld.
Plaskett, L. G., jt. auth. see White, L. P.
Plaskin, Glenn. Horowitz: A Biography of Vladimir Horowitz. (Illus.). 640p. 1983. 17.95 (ISBN 0-688-01616-2). Morrow.
Plaskon, Stephen P., jt. auth. see Cohen, Sandra B.
Plaskow, Judith. Sex, Sin & Grace: Women's Experience & the Theologies of Reinhold Niebuhr & Paul Tillich. LC 79-5434. 1980. pap. text ed. 10.25 (ISBN 0-8191-0882-0). U Pr of Amer.
Plaskow, Judith, jt. auth. see Christ, Carol P.
Plasse, J. C., jt. ed. see Aulanger, G.
Plastaras, James. Creation & Convenant. 1968. pap. text ed. 3.95 o.p. (ISBN 0-685-07626-1, 82470). Glencoe.
--Witness of John: A Study of Johannine Theory. 1972. pap. 4.95 o.p. (ISBN 0-02-824360-9). Glencoe.
Plaster, Herbert J. Blast Cleaning & Allied Processes, 2 Vols. LC 73-155194. (Illus.). 1972. Vol. 1, 374p. 125.00x set (ISBN 0-901994-03-0). Vol. 2, 452p. Intl Pubns Serv.
Plastics Education Foundation. Curriculum Guide for Plastics Education. LC 77-4080. 1977. pap. 16.50 (ISBN 0-672-97113-5). Bobbs.
Plat, Hugh. Floures of Philosophie. LC 81-21324. 1982. Repr. of 1572 ed. 40.00x (ISBN 0-8201-1374-3). Schol Facsimiles.
Plate, E., ed. Engineering Methodology. (Studies in Wind Engineering & Industrial Aerodynamics: No. 1). 740p. 1982. 149.00 (ISBN 0-444-41972-1). Elsevier.
Plate, Erich J. Aerodynamic Characteristics of Atmospheric Boundary Layers. LC 70-611329. (AEC Critical Review Ser.). 191p. 1971. pap. 12.75 (ISBN 0-87079-132-X, TID-25465); microfiche 4.50 (ISBN 0-87079-133-8, TID-25465). DOE.
Plate, Kenneth, jt. auth. see Altman, Ellen.
Plath, Carl & Davis, Malcolm. This Is the Parrot. 9.95 (ISBN 0-87666-431-1, PS653). TFH Pubns.
Plath, David W. Long Engagements: Maturity in Modern Japan. LC 79-65181. 248p. 1980. 17.50x (ISBN 0-8047-1054-6); pap. 6.95 (ISBN 0-8047-1176-3, SP 75). Stanford U Pr.
--Long Engagements: Maturity in Modern Japan. xii, 235p. 1983. pap. 6.95 (ISBN 0-8047-1176-3). Stanford U Pr.
Plath, Sylvia. Ariel. LC 66-15738. 1968. 13.42i (ISBN 0-06-013358-9, HarpT); pap. 3.95i (ISBN 0-06-090890-4, CN-890, HarpT). Har-Row.
--The Bed Book. LC 76-3825. (Illus.). (ps-3). 1976. 9.57i (ISBN 0-06-024746-0, HarpJ); PLB 10.89 (ISBN 0-06-024747-9). Har-Row.
--Crossing the Water. LC 71-138756. 1971. 8.95i (ISBN 0-06-013366-X, HarpT); pap. 3.95i (ISBN 0-06-090789-4, CN-789, HarpT). Har-Row.
--Johnny Panic & the Bible of Dreams: Short Stories, Prose & Diary Excerpts. LC 77-181659. 1979. 13.41i (ISBN 0-06-013377-5, HarpT). Har-Row.
Platner, Warren. Ten by Warren Platner. (Illus.). 1975. 29.95 (ISBN 0-07-050285-4, P&RB). McGraw.
Plato. Apology. Adam, A. M., ed. (Gr). text ed. 6.50x (ISBN 0-521-05958-5). Cambridge U Pr.
--Crito. Adam, James, ed. (Gr). text ed. 16.95x with vocab. (ISBN 0-521-05959-3). Cambridge U Pr.
--Euthyphro, Apology Crito: With the Death Scene from Phaedo. Church, F. J. & Cummings, R. D., trs. Bd. with Apology; Crito. (gr. 9up). 1956. pap. 2.95 (ISBN 0-672-60166-4, LLA4). Bobbs.
--Five Dialogues. Grube, G. M., tr. from Gr. LC 81-82275. (HPC Philosophical Classics Ser.). 162p. 1981. text ed. 12.50 (ISBN 0-915145-23-5); pap. 4.25 (ISBN 0-915145-22-7). Hackett Pub.
--Phaedo. Hackforth, R., ed. 200p. 1972. 24.50 (ISBN 0-521-08458-X); pap. 7.95x (ISBN 0-521-09702-9). Cambridge U Pr.
--Phaedo. Grube, G. M., tr. LC 76-40412. 1977. pap. 2.25 (ISBN 0-915144-18-2). Hackett Pub.
--Phaedrus. Hackforth, R., ed. 200p. 1972. 24.50 (ISBN 0-521-08459-8); pap. 7.95x (ISBN 0-521-09703-7). Cambridge U Pr.
--Philebus. Hackforth, R., ed. 200p. 1972. 24.95 (ISBN 0-521-08460-1); pap. 7.95x (ISBN 0-521-09704-5). Cambridge U Pr.
--Philebus. Waterfield, Robin A., tr. from Gr. 1983. pap. 3.95 (ISBN 0-14-044395-9). Penguin.
--Portrait of Socrates Being the Apology, Crito, & Phaedo. Livingstone, Richard W., tr. 1938. pap. 9.95x (ISBN 0-19-814145-9). Oxford U Pr.
--Protagoras & Meno. Guthrie, W. K., tr. Bd. with Meno. (Classics Ser.). 1957. pap. 3.95 (ISBN 0-14-044068-2). Penguin.
--Republic. LC 68-54141. 1968. text ed. 16.95 o.s.i. (ISBN 0-465-06935-5); pap. text ed. 5.95x o.s.i. (ISBN 0-465-06936-3). Basic.
--Republic, 2 Vols. rev. ed. Adam, James, ed. (Gr.). Vol. 1, Bks. 1-5. text ed. 59.50x (ISBN 0-521-05963-1); Vol. 2, Bks. 6-10. text ed. 69.50x (ISBN 0-521-05964-X). Cambridge U Pr.
--Republic. Lindsay, A. D., tr. 1957. pap. 6.75 (ISBN 0-525-47004-2). Dutton.
--The Republic. new ed. Grube, G. M., tr. & intro. by. LC 73-91951. 288p. 1973. 12.50 (ISBN 0-915144-04-2); pap. text ed. 4.95 (ISBN 0-915144-03-4). Hackett Pub.
--The Republic. Larson, Raymond, ed. & tr. LC 77-86034. (Crofts Classics). 1979. text ed. 12.95x (ISBN 0-88295-121-1); pap. text ed. 5.95x (ISBN 0-88295-118-1). Harlan Davidson.
--Republic. Jowett, Benjamin, tr. 1982. 7.95 (ISBN 0-394-60153-X). Modern Lib.
--The Republic. Jowett, Benjamin, tr. 1982. 7.95 (ISBN 0-394-60813-5). Modern Lib.
--Symposium. Dover, K. J., ed. LC 78-67430. (Cambridge Greek & Latin Classics Ser.). 1980. 34.50 (ISBN 0-521-20081-4); pap. 12.95x (ISBN 0-521-29523-8). Cambridge U Pr.
--Symposium: A Dramatized Version. Kobler, Franz & Mueller, Ernst, eds. LC 66-25102. (Milestones of Thought Ser.). pap. 3.95 (ISBN 0-8044-6654-8). Ungar.
--Symposium of Plato. Jowett, Benjamin, tr. pap. 2.50 (ISBN 0-8283-1456-X, 17, IPL). Branden.
--Timaeus & Critias. Lee, H. D., tr. (Classics Ser.). 1972. pap. 3.50 (ISBN 0-14-044261-8). Penguin.
--The Works of Plato. Jowett, Benjamin, tr. Date not set. 7.95 (ISBN 0-394-60420-2). Modern Lib.
Platt, Alan & Weiler, Lawrence D., eds. Congress & Arms Control. LC 77-28307. (Westview Special Studies in International Relations & Foreign Policy). 1978. lib. bdg. 27.50 o.p. (ISBN 0-89158-157-X). Westview.
Platt, Alan A. The U.S. Senate & Strategic Arms Policy: 1969-1977. LC 78-7151. (A Westview Replica Edition). 1978. lib. bdg. 17.50 o.p. (ISBN 0-89158-199-5). Westview.
Platt, C., jt. auth. see Paltridge, G.
Platt, C. J. Tax Systems of Africa, Asia & the Middle East. 1982p. 1982. text ed. 37.50x (ISBN 0-566-02335-0). Gower Pub Ltd.
--Tax Systems of Western Europe: A Guide for Business & the Professions. 166p. 1980. pap. 36.00 (ISBN 0-566-02183-8). Gower Pub Ltd.
Platt, Charles. Popular Superstitions. LC 70-167114. 244p. 1973. Repr. of 1925 ed. 40.00x (ISBN 0-8103-3170-5). Gale.
Platt, Colin. The Castle in Medieval England & Wales. (Illus.). 224p. 1983. 25.00 (ISBN 0-684-17799-4, ScribT). Scribner.
Platt, D., ed. Geriatrics II: Digestive, Endocrine, Kidney Urogenital, Hematologic, Respiratory Systems, Rehabilitation, Nutrition & Drug Treatment. (Illus.). 490p. 1983. 70.00 (ISBN 0-387-10982-X). Springer-Verlag.
Platt, Gerald M., jt. auth. see Weinstein, Fred.
Platt, H. M., jt. ed. see Stone, A. R.
Platt, Harold L. City Building in the New South: The Growth of Public Services in Houston, Texas 1830-1915. LC 82-10411. (Technology & Urban Growth Ser.). 233p. 1982. text ed. 24.95 (ISBN 0-87722-281-9). Temple U Pr.
Platt, Helen, tr. see Bazin, Herve.
Platt, J. A. Realities of Social Research: An Empirical Study of British Sociologists. 35.00x (ISBN 0-686-97020-9, Pub. by Scottish Academic Pr Scotland). State Mutual Bk.
Platt, Jennifer. Realities of Social Research. LC 75-30275. 224p. 1976. 35.95x o.s.i. (ISBN 0-470-69119-0). Halsted Pr.
Platt, Jerome & Labate, Christina. Heroin Addiction: Theory, Research, & Treatment. LC 76-5794. (Personality Processes Ser.). 417p. 1976. 32.95 o.p. (ISBN 0-471-69114-3, Pub. by Wiley-Interscience). Wiley.
Platt, John. Reformed Thought & Scholasticism: The Arguments for the Existence of God in Dutch Theology, 1575-1650. (Studies in the History of Christian Thought Ser.: Vol. 29). viii, 249p. 1982. write for info. (ISBN 90-04-06593-8). E J Brill.
Platt, John & Weber, Heidi. English in Singapore & Malaysia: Status, Features, Functions. (Illus.). 1981. 37.50 (ISBN 0-19-580438-4); pap. 24.00x (ISBN 0-19-580444-9). Oxford U Pr.
Platt, Kin. The Ape Inside Me. LC 79-2402. (gr. 7 up). 1979. 7.95 o.p. (ISBN 0-397-31826-X, JBL-J); PLB 9.89 o.p. (ISBN 0-397-31863-4). Har-Row.
--Brogg's Brain. LC 79-9622. 128p. (gr. 6 up). 1981. 9.13i (ISBN 0-397-31945-2, JBL-J); PLB 9.89g (ISBN 0-397-31946-0). Har-Row.
--Chloris & the Freaks. LC 75-11113. 224p. (gr. 5-7). 1975. 9.95 (ISBN 0-02-774470-1). Bradbury Pr.
--Chloris & the Weirdos. LC 78-55214. 192p. (gr. 5-7). 1978. 9.95 (ISBN 0-02-774480-9). Bradbury Pr.
--Dracula, Go Home. LC 78-11335. (Triumph Ser.). (Illus.). (gr. 7 up). 1979. PLB 8.90 s&l (ISBN 0-531-01464-9). Watts.
--Frank & Stein & Me. (Triumph Bks). 128p. (gr. 7 up). 1982. PLB 8.90 (ISBN 0-531-04169-7). Watts.
--Headman. (gr. 8 up). 1977. pap. 1.50 o.p. (ISBN 0-440-93568-7, LFL). Dell.
Platt, Richard, jt. auth. see Kass, Edward H.
Platt, Robert T., jt. auth. see Brodsky, Carroll M.
Platt, Rutherford. River of Life. 1962. pap. 1.75 o.p. (ISBN 0-671-62451-2, Touchstone Bks). S&S.
--Wilderness, the Discovery of a Continent of Wonder. LC 72-9919. (Illus.). 310p. 1973. Repr. of 1961 ed. lib. bdg. 17.75x (ISBN 0-8371-6608-X, PLWI). Greenwood.
Platt, Rutherford H. & Macinko, George, eds. Beyond the Urban Fringe: Land-Use Issues of Nonmetropolitan America. (Illus.). 384p. 1983. 39.50x (ISBN 0-8166-1099-1). U of Minn Pr.
Platt, Tony, et al. The Iron Fist & the Velvet Glove: An Analysis of the U. S. Police. 2nd ed. (Illus.). 1977. pap. text ed. 3.50 o.p. (ISBN 0-917404-02-5). Ctr Res Criminal.
Platte, Mary K. The Beginning of Satellite Communication Airborne ITV, MPATI, & the Ohio Story. 104p. 1982. pap. text ed. 6.95 (ISBN 0-8403-2794-3). Kendall-Hunt.
Plattes, Gabriel. A Discovery of Subterraneall Treasure. 37.50 (ISBN 0-686-38306-0). IMM North Am.
--Discovery of Subterraneall Tresure. 60p. 1980. Repr. of 1639 ed. text ed. 34.50x (ISBN 0-686-97563-4). IMM North Am.
Plattner, Mark F. Human Rights in Our Time: History, Theory, Policy. 175p. 1983. 18.50x (ISBN 0-86531-606-6). Westview.
Plattner, S., ed. Formal Methods In Economic Anthropology. 1975. pap. 4.00 (ISBN 0-686-36565-8). Am Anthro Assn.
Plattner, Steven W. Witness to the Forties: Roy Stryker & the Standard Oil (New Jersey) Photography Project. (Illus.). 144p. 1983. 19.95 (ISBN 0-292-77028-6). U. of Tex Pr.
Platts, John T. A Dictionary of Urdu Classical Hindi & English. LC 78-670100. 1977. Repr. of 1884 ed. 50.00x (ISBN 0-8002-0243-0). Intl Pubns Serv.
Platvoet, J. G. Comparing Religions: A Limitative Approach. (Religion & Reason Ser.: No. 24). xiv, 350p. 1982. 49.00x (ISBN 90-279-3170-4). Mouton.
Platz, Bert L. American Flyer Plus. (Illus.). 1700p. 1978. pap. 75.00 (ISBN 0-933360-00-2). AL-DEL.
Platzer, Norbert. Commodity & Engineering Plastics: Proceedings of the National Meeting of the American Society Atlanta Symposium, 181st, Georgia, March 29 to April 8, 1981. 239p. 1982. 28.00x (ISBN 0-471-86670-9, Pub. by Wiley-Interscience). Wiley.
Platzer, Werner, jt. auth. see Reiffenstuhl, Gunther.
Platzman, P. M. & Wolff, P. A. Waves & Interactions in Solid State Plasmas. (Solid State Physics: Suppl. 13). 1973. 32.00 (ISBN 0-12-607773-8). Acad Pr.
Platzoeder, Renate, ed. Documents of the Third United Nations Conference on the Law of the Sea, 2 vols. 1982. 100.00 ea. Vol. 1 (ISBN 0-379-20724-9). Vol. 2 (ISBN 0-379-20804-0). Oceana.
Plauger, P. J., jt. auth. see Kernighan, B. W.
Plauger, P. J., jt. auth. see Kernighan, Brian W.
Plaut, W. Gunther. Deuteronomy: A Modern Commentary. (The Torah: A Modern Commentary Ser.). 528p. 1983. 20.00 (ISBN 0-8074-0045-9). UAHC.
--Exodus: A Modern Commentary. (The Torah Commentary Ser.). 571p. 1983. 20.00 (ISBN 0-8074-0040-8, 381606). UAHC.
Plautus. The Amphitruo of Plautus. Sedgwick, W. B., ed. 1960. pap. 11.00 (ISBN 0-7190-0107-2). Manchester.
--Casina. Maccary, W. T. & Willcock, M. M., eds. (Greek & Latin Classics Ser.). 220p. 1976. 42.00 (ISBN 0-521-21041-0); pap. 13.95x (ISBN 0-521-29022-8). Cambridge U Pr.
--Plautus: Rudens, Curculio, Casina. Stace, Christopher, tr. LC 81-6086. (Translations from Greek & Roman Authors Ser.). (Illus.). 160p. 1982. pap. 5.95 (ISBN 0-521-28046-X). Cambridge U Pr.
Plautus see Aristophanes.
Play, Frederic Le see Le Play, Frederic.
Playboy Editors. Playboy's Party Jokes, No. 8. 160p. 1982. pap. 2.25 (ISBN 0-86721-180-6). Playboy Pbks.
Player, Gary & Harris, Norman. Gary Player on Fitness & Success. (Illus.). 1979. pap. 4.95 (ISBN 0-437-12751-6, Pub. by World's Work). David & Charles.
Player, Mack A. Employment Discrimination Law, Cases & Materials: 1982 Supplement. (American Casebook Ser.). 174p. 1981. pap. text ed. 10.50 (ISBN 0-314-63826-1). West Pub.
Playfair, Giles. Kean. LC 73-10878. (Illus.). 346p. 1973. Repr. of 1939 ed. lib. bdg. 20.50x (ISBN 0-8371-7047-8, PLKE). Greenwood.
Playfair, Guy & Hill, Scott. The Cycles of Heaven. LC 77-15823. 1978. 10.00 o.p. (ISBN 0-312-18053-5). St Martin.
Playfair, Guy L. The Indefinite Boundary. LC 76-28051. 1977. 8.95 o.p. (ISBN 0-312-41195-2). St Martin.
Playfair, John. Illustrations of the Huttonian Theory of the Earth. 1956. pap. 5.00 o.p. (ISBN 0-486-61168-X). Dover.
Playford, John. The English Dancing Master: Or, Plaine & Easie Rules for the Dancing of Country Dances, with the Tune to Each Dance. LC 75-9161. 104p. 1977. pap. 4.95x o.p. (ISBN 0-87127-080-3). Dance Horiz.
--The English Dancing Master (Sixteen Fifty-One) Dean-Smith, Margaret, ed. 1957. 29.00 (ISBN 0-901938-44-0, 75-A11316). Eur-Am Music.
Playford, John & Purcell, Henry. An Introduction to the Skill of Musick. LC 67-27551. (Music Reprint Ser.). 282p. 1972. Repr. of 1694 ed. lib. bdg. 32.50 (ISBN 0-306-70937-6). Da Capo.

Playle, Ron. How You Can Trace Your Family Roots. (Illus., Orig.). 1982. pap. 4.95 (ISBN 0-89511-005-9). R & D Serv.
Playne, A. T. Minchinhampton & Avening. 188p. 1978. text ed. 20.50x (ISBN 0-904387-25-9, Pub. by Sutton England). Humanities.
Plaza, Lasso G. Problems of Democracy in Latin America. LC 81-36. (The Weil Lectures on American Citizenship Ser.). vi, 88p. 1981. Repr. of 1955 ed. lib. bdg. 19.25x (ISBN 0-313-22877-9, PLPD). Greenwood.
Ple, Albert. Christian Morality: Duty or Pleasure? 272p. Date not set. 14.95 (ISBN 0-8245-0522-0). Crossroad NY.
Pleasance, Simon, tr. see Bologna, Gianfranco.
Pleasance, Simon, tr. see Pretto, G., et al.
Pleasance, Simon, tr. see Tanara, Milli U.
Pleasants, Henry. Agony of Modern Music. 1962. pap. 2.95 o.p. (ISBN 0-671-01401-3, Touchstone Bks). S&S.
Pleck, Elizabeth H. Black Migration & Poverty in Boston, Eighteen Sixty-Five to Nineteen Hundred. LC 79-51684. (Studies in Social Discontinuity). 1979. 23.00 (ISBN 0-12-558650-7). Acad Pr.
Pleck, Joseph H. The Myth of Masculinity. 240p. 1983. pap. 6.95 (ISBN 0-262-66050-4). MIT Pr.
Pleck, Joseph H. & Sawyer, Jack, eds. Men & Masculinity. 192p. 1974. 8.95 (ISBN 0-13-574319-2, Spec); pap. 4.95 (ISBN 0-13-574301-X, Spec). P-H.
Pledge, H. T. Science Since Fifteen-Hundred: A Short History of Mathematics, Physics, Chemistry, Biology. 10.00 (ISBN 0-8446-0850-5). Peter Smith.
Plee, H. D. Karate: Beginner to Black Belt. (Illus.). 1967. 10.95x o.p. Wehman.
--Karate by Pictures. 5.95x o.p. (ISBN 0-685-22004-4). Wehman.
Plekhanov, George V. Development of the Monist View of History. 335p. 1974. 3.60 (ISBN 0-8285-0191-2, Pub. by Progress Pubs USSR). Imported Pubns.
--Fundamental Problems of Marxism. rev. ed. LC 69-20358. 1969. 5.95 o.p. (ISBN 0-7178-0074-1); pap. 2.25 (ISBN 0-7178-0073-3). Intl Pub Co.
Plemelj, J. Problems in the Sense of Riemann & Klein. LC 64-16626. 175p. 1964. 11.50 o.p. (ISBN 0-470-69125-5, Pub. by Wiley). Krieger.
Plenckers, L. J. The Hague Municipal Catalogue of Musical Instruments Collection, Vol. 1: Brass Instruments. LC 74-126617. (Music Reprint Ser.). (Dutch.). 1970. 13.50 o.p. (ISBN 0-306-77231-0). Da Capo.
--Hoorn-En Trompetachtige Blaasinstrumenten. (Haags Gemeente-Museum Ser.). (Illus.). 20.00 o.s.i. (ISBN 90-6027-322-2, Pub. by Frits Knuf Netherlands). Pendragon NY.
Plenzdorf, Ulrich. Die Neuen Liedew Des Jungen W. 1978. pap. text ed. 13.50x (ISBN 0-471-02855-X). Wiley.
Pleslova-Stikova, Emilie, jt. auth. see Ehrich, Robert W.
Pless, Vera. Introduction to the Theory of Error-Correcting Codes. LC 1-10417. (Wiley-Interscience Series in Discrete Mathematics). 169p. 1982. 22.95x (ISBN 0-471-08684-3, Pub. by Wiley-Interscience). Wiley.
Plesset, Milton, et al, eds. see Committee on the Safety of Nuclear Installations Specialist Meeting.
Plessis, David du see Du Plessis, David.
Plessner, Gerald. The New Testimonial Dinner & Industry Luncheon Management Manual. 39.00 (ISBN 0-686-37134-8). Public Serv Materials.
Plessner, Gerlad. The Golf Tournament Management Manual. 39.00 (ISBN 0-686-37135-6). Public Serv Materials.
Plesums, Guntis. Townframe: Environments for Adaptive Housing. LC 77-20679. (Community Development Ser.: Vol. 38). (Illus.). 1978. 35.00 (ISBN 0-87933-303-0). Hutchinson Ross.
Pletcher, R. H., et al. Computational Fluid Mechanics & Heat Transfer. 1983. price not set (ISBN 0-07-050328-1). McGraw.
Pletsch, Susan, jt. auth. see Palmer, Pati.
Pletta, Dan H. & Frederick, Daniel. Engineering Mechanics: Statics & Dynamics. LC 81-17230. xx, 674p. 1983. Repr. of 1964 ed. text ed. write for info. (ISBN 0-89874-405-9). Krieger.
Plewig, G., jt. ed. see Marks, R.
Plews, R. W. Analytical Methods Used in Sugar Refining. 1969. 43.00 (ISBN 0-444-20046-0, Pub. by Applied Sci England). Elsevier.
Plezia, Valerie. Polka Party Dances. (Ethnic Dance Bk. Ser.: No.280). 130p. (Orig.). 1982. 7.95x (ISBN 0-9609368-0-7). V Plezia.
Plimmer, Jack R., ed. Pesticides Residues & Exposure. (ACS Symposium Ser.: No. 182). 1982. write for info. (ISBN 0-8412-0701-1). Am Chemical.
Plimpton, George. The Bogey Man. (Penguin Sports Library). 306p. 1983. pap. 5.95 (ISBN 0-14-006430-3). Penguin.
--Out of My League. (Penguin Sports Library). 1983. pap. 4.95 (ISBN 0-14-006429-X). Penguin.
--Paper Lion. (RL 7). 1974. pap. 2.95 (ISBN 0-451-11296-2, AE1296, Sig). NAL.
--A Sports Bestiary. LC 82-10002. (Illus.). 112p. 1982. 14.95 (ISBN 0-07-050290-0). McGraw.
Plimpton, George, jt. ed. see Stein, Jean.
Pliner, Patricia, et al. Communication & Affect: Language & Thought. 1973. 29.50 (ISBN 0-12-558250-1). Acad Pr.
Pliny. Fifty Letters of Pliny, Vol. 3. Sherwin-White, A. N., et al, eds. 350p. 1982. 27.00x (ISBN 0-19-814591-8). Oxford U Pr.
--Selection from Pliny's Letters Handbook. Fisher, M. B. & Griffen, M. R., eds. LC 76-28002. (Cambridge Latin Texts Ser.). (Illus.). 9.95 (ISBN 0-521-20487-9). Cambridge U Pr.
--Selections from Pliny's Letters. Fisher, M. B. & Griffen, M. R., eds. LC 73-80489. (Latin Texts Ser.). (Illus.). 64p. 1973. 3.95 (ISBN 0-521-20298-1). Cambridge U Pr.
Pliny, jt. auth. see Martial.
Plischke, Elmer, ed. U. S. Foreign Relations: A Guide to Information Sources. LC 74-11516. (American Government & History Information Guide Ser.: Vol. 6). 715p. 1980. 42.00x (ISBN 0-8103-1204-2). Gale.
Pliskin, Jeffrey, jt. auth. see Gelb, Bernard.
Plog, Fred, jt. auth. see Jolly, Clifford.
Plog, Fred T. A Study of Prehistoric Change. 1974. 27.50 (ISBN 0-12-785645-5). Acad Pr.
Plog, Stephen. Stylistic Variation in Prehistoric Ceramics. (New Studies in Archaeology). (Illus.). 130p. 1980. 27.95 (ISBN 0-521-22581-7). Cambridge U Pr.
Ploghoft, Milton E. & Shuster, Albert H. Social Science Education in the Elementary School. 2nd ed. (Elementary Education Ser.). 400p. 1976. text ed. 19.95 (ISBN 0-675-08692-2). Merrill.
Ploman, Edward W., ed. International Law Governing Communications & Information: A Collection of Documents. LC 81-7036. 600p. 1982. lib. bdg. 45.00 (ISBN 0-313-23277-6, PLC/). Greenwood.
Plomer, William. Diamond of Jannina: Ali Pasha 1741-1822. LC 79-107008. 1970. 7.50 o.p. (ISBN 0-8008-2190-4). Taplinger.
Plomin, Robert, jt. auth. see Buss, Arnold H.
Plomin, Robert, jt. auth. see Buss, Arnold M.
Plonsey, R., jt. auth. see Pilkington, T.
Plonsey, Robert. Bioelectric Phenomena. 1969. text ed. 39.50 (ISBN 0-07-050342-7, C). McGraw.
Plonsey-Collin, Robert E. Principles & Applications of Electromagnetic Fields. 1961. text ed. 40.00 (ISBN 0-07-050340-0, C). McGraw.
Plonus, Martin. Applied Electromagnetics. (Illus.). 1978. text ed. 36.50 (ISBN 0-07-050345-1, C); solutions manual 15.50 (ISBN 0-07-050346-X). McGraw.
Plooij, Frans X. The Behavioral Development of Free-Living Chimpanzee Babies & Infants. (Monographs on Infancy: Vol. 3). 1983. 18.50x (ISBN 0-89391-115-1). Ablex Pub.
--The Behavioral Development of Free-Living Chimpanzee Babies & Infants. Lipsitt, Lewis P., ed. (Monographs on Infancy). (Illus.). 208p. (Orig.). 1983. text ed. 18.50 (ISBN 0-89391-114-3). Ablex Pub.
Ploski, Harry. The Negro Almanac: A Reference Work on the Afro-American. 4th ed. 1250p. 1983. 67.95 (ISBN 0-471-87710-7, Pub. by Wiley-Interscience). Wiley.
Plosser, George G., ed. see White, Marjorie L.
Plossi, George. Manufacturing Control: The Last Frontier for Profits. LC 73-8965. 1973. 22.95 (ISBN 0-87909-483-4). Reston.
Plossl, G. & Wright, O. Production & Inventory Control: Principles & Techniques. 1967. ref. ed. 29.95 (ISBN 0-13-725127-0). P-H.
Plotch, Walter, jt. ed. see Tumin, Melvin M.
Plotkin, H. C. Learning Development & Culture: Essays in Evolutionary Epistemology. LC 82-1947. 489p. 1982. 64.95 (ISBN 0-471-10219-9, Pub. by Wiley-Interscience). Wiley.
Plotnick, Charles & Leimberg, Stephen. Die Rich. LC 82-18185. (Illus.). 352p. 1983. 17.95 (ISBN 0-698-11223-7, Coward). Putnam PubGroup.
Plotnik, Arthur. The Elements of Editing: A Modern Guide for Editors & Journalists. 132p. 1982. 9.50 (ISBN 0-02-597700-8). Macmillan.
Plou, Dafne C. De see Drakeford, John W.
Plous, Frederick K., Jr., tr. see Naumov, N. P.
Plovnick, Mark S. & Fry, Ronald E. Managing Health Care Delivery: A Training Program for Primary Care Physicians. LC 77-21501. 136p. 1978. prof ref 17.50x (ISBN 0-88410-518-0). Ballinger Pub.
Plow, Sabanes De see Simmons, Paul D. & Crawford, Kenneth.
Plowden, David. An American Chronology: The Photographs of David Plowden. LC 82-70181. (Illus.). 160p. 1982. 45.00 (ISBN 0-670-11719-6, Studio). Viking Pr.
Plowden, G. F. C. Pope on Classic Ground. LC 82-14413. 184p. 1983. text ed. 20.95x (ISBN 0-8214-0664-7, 82-84333). Ohio U Pr.
Plowhead, Ruth G. Holidays with Betty Sue & Sally Lou. LC 39-2442. (Illus.). 234p. (gr. 2-4). 1939. 2.50 o.p. (ISBN 0-87004-118-5). Caxton.
Plowman, Paul D. Behavioral Objectives: Teacher Success through Student Performance. LC 76-130585. (Dimensions in Education Ser). (Illus.). 1970. pap. text ed. 6.95 o.s.i. (ISBN 0-574-17390-0, 13-0390). SRA.
Plowman, Peter. Passenger Ships of Australia & New Zealand: 1913-1981, Vol. II. 224p. 1982. 40.00x (ISBN 0-85177-247-1, Pub. by Conway Maritime England). State Mutual Bk.
--Passenger Ships of Australia & New Zealand: 1876-1912, Vol. I. 224p. 1982. 40.00x (ISBN 0-85177-246-3, Pub. by Conway Maritime England). State Mutual Bk.
Plowright, Piers. Read English. 1973. pap. text ed. 3.50x (ISBN 0-435-28705-2); tape 28.00x (ISBN 0-435-28706-0); cassette 22.00x (ISBN 0-435-28707-9). Heinemann Ed.
Pluckhan, Margaret. Human Communication: The Matrix of Nursing. (Illus.). 1977. pap. text ed. 14.95 (ISBN 0-07-050352-4, HP). McGraw.
Plucknett, Donald L. Small-Scale Processing & Storage of Tropical Root Crops. (Tropical Agriculture Ser.). 1979. lib. bdg. 35.00 (ISBN 0-89158-471-4). Westview.
Plucknett, Donald L., jt. auth. see Lumpkin, Thomas A.
Plucknett, Donald L. & Beemer, Halsey, eds. Vegetable Farming Systems in the People's Republica of China. (Westview Special Studies in Agricultural Science). 350p. 1981. lib. bdg. 33.50 (ISBN 0-89158-999-6). Westview.
Plucknett, Theodore F. A Concise History of the Common Law. 5th ed. 802p. 1956. 24.00 (ISBN 0-316-71083-0). Little.
--Statutes & Their Interpretation in the First Half of the Fourteenth Century. Helmholz, R. H. & Reams, Bernard D., Jr., eds. LC 79-91757. (Historical Writings in Law & Jurisprudence Ser.: No. 4, Bk. 4). xlii, 200p. 1980. Repr. of 1922 ed. lib. bdg. 30.00 (ISBN 0-89941-043-X). W S Hein.
Pluckrose, ed. Small World of Eskimos. (Warwick Press Ser.). (gr. k-3). 1980. PLB 7.90 (ISBN 0-531-03418-6, E38). Watts.
--Small World of Plains Indians. (Warwick Press Ser.). (gr. k-3). 1980. PLB 7.90 (ISBN 0-531-03419-4, F28). Watts.
Pluckrose, H. Let's Work Large. (Illus.). 121p. 1973. text ed. 6.50x o.p. (ISBN 0-263-70847-0). Transatlantic.
Pluckrose, Henry. Victorian Britain: History Around Us. 80p. 1982. 30.00x (ISBN 0-7135-1290-3, Pub. by Bell & Hyman England). State Mutual Bk.
Pluckrose, Henry, ed. Small World of Apes. (Small World Ser.). (Illus.). 1979. (gr. 5-8) 2.95 (ISBN 0-531-03443-7); PLB 7.90 s&l (ISBN 0-531-03407-0). Watts.
--Small World of Birds. (Small World Ser.). (Illus.). 1979. 9 (gr. 5-8) 2.95 (ISBN 0-531-03444-5); PLB 7.90 (ISBN 0-531-03408-9). Watts.
--Small World of Elephants. (Small World Ser.). (Illus.). (gr. k-3). 1979. 2.95 (ISBN 0-531-03426-7); PLB 6.90 o.p. (ISBN 0-686-83007-5). Watts.
--Small World of Horses. (Small Worlds Ser.). (Illus.). (gr. k-3). 1979. PLB 7.90 s&l (ISBN 0-531-03405-4). Watts.
--Vikings. (Small World Ser.). (Illus.). 32p. 1982. lib. bdg. 9.40 (ISBN 0-531-03457-7). Watts.
Pluckrose, Henry, compiled by. The Art & Craft Book. (Illus.). 190p. (gr. 4 up). 1975. 15.00 o.p. (ISBN 0-237-35141-2). Transatlantic.
--Art & Craft Today. (Illus.). 192p. (gr. 4 up). 1975. 15.00 o.p. (ISBN 0-237-35226-5). Transatlantic.
Plueddemann, Edwin P., ed. Silane Coupling Agents. 250p. 1982. 37.50x (ISBN 0-306-40957-7, Plenum Pr). Plenum Pub.
Plum, Fred, ed. see Association for Research in Nervous & Mental Disease.
Plum, Thomas. Learning to Program in C. (Illus.). 350p. (Orig.). 1983. pap. text ed. 25.00x (ISBN 0-911537-00-7). Plum Hall.
Plumb, Charlie. I'm No Hero: A POW Story. (Illus.). 250p. (YA) 1973. 9.00 o.p. (ISBN 0-8309-0111-6). Ind Pr MO.
Plumb, E. C. Ship Stewards Manual. 118p. 1971. pap. 6.50x o.p. (ISBN 0-540-00255-0). Sheridan.
Plumb, Gregory A. Waterfalls of the Pacific Northwest. (Illus.). 224p. 1983. pap. 9.95 (ISBN 0-916076-60-1). Writing.
Plumb, J. H. Growth of Political Stability in England, Sixteen Seventy-Five to Seventeen Twenty-Five. (Repr. of 1967 ed.). 1977. text ed. 20.00x o. p. (ISBN 0-333-02331-5); pap. text ed. 10.50x (ISBN 0-391-01908-2). Humanities.
Plumb, John H., jt. auth. see Lancaster, Bruce.
Plumbley, Philip, jt. auth. see Golzen, Godfrey.
Plume, Ilse. The Bremen Town Musicians. LC 79-6622. (Illus.). 32p. (ps-3). 1980. 9.95a (ISBN 0-385-15161-6); PLB (ISBN 0-385-15162-4). Doubleday.
--The Story of Befana: An Italian Christmas Tale. (gr. k-3). 1981. 11.95 (ISBN 0-87923-420-2). Godine.
Plumer, W. S. Psalms. (Geneva Commentaries Ser.). 1978. 29.95 (ISBN 0-85151-209-7). Banner of Truth.
Plumer, William, Jr. Life of William Plumer. LC 77-87384. (American History, Politics & Law Ser). 1969. Repr. of 1857 ed. lib. bdg. 69.50 (ISBN 0-306-71608-9). Da Capo.
--Missouri Compromises & Presidential Politics, 1820-1825: From the Letters of William Plumer. Jr. Brown, Everett S., ed. LC 76-103942. (American Constitutional & Legal History Ser). 1970. Repr. of 1926 ed. lib. bdg. 22.50 (ISBN 0-306-71869-3). Da Capo.
Plummer, Charles C. & McGeary, David. Physical Geology. 2nd ed. 528p. 1982. pap. text ed. write for info. (ISBN 0-697-05038-6); instrs.' manual avail. (ISBN 0-697-05021-1); study guide avail. (ISBN 0-697-05039-4); lab manual avail. (ISBN 0-697-05041-6); slides avail. (ISBN 0-697-05022-X). Wm C Brown.
Plummer, David. Introduction to Practical Biochemistry: The Greatest Adventure in Modern Archaeology. 2nd ed. 1978. pap. text ed. 32.50x (ISBN 0-07-084074-1, C). McGraw.
Plummer, Gail. The Business of Show Business. LC 72-6180. (Illus.). 238p. 1973. Repr. of 1961 ed. lib. bdg. 21.00x (ISBN 0-8371-6485-0, PLSB). Greenwood.
Plummer, James L., ed. Energy Vulnerability. 488p. 1982. prof ref 37.50x (ISBN 0-88410-871-6). Ballinger Pub.
Plummer, John. The Last Flowering: French Painting in Manuscripts, 1420-1530. (Illus.). 252p. 1982. 89.00 (ISBN 0-19-503262-4). Oxford U Pr.
Plummer, John, jt. auth. see Cockerell, Sydney C.
Plummer, Ken. Documents of Life: An Introduction to the Problems & Literature of a Humanistic Method. (Contemporary Social Research Ser.: No. 7). 208p. 1983. text ed. 28.50x (ISBN 0-04-321029-5); pap. text ed. 12.50x. Allen Unwin.
Plummer, L. Gordon. By the Holy Tetrakyts: Symbol & Reality in Man & Universe. (Study Ser.: No. 9). (Illus.). 96p. (Orig.). 1982. pap. 5.75 (ISBN 0-913004-44-8). Point Loma Pub.
Plumpp, Sterling. The Mojo Hands Call-I Must Go. LC 82-10360. 94p. 1982. 11.95 (ISBN 0-938410-05-9); pap. 5.95 (ISBN 0-938410-04-0). Thunder's Mouth.
Plumpton, C. & Tomkys, W. H. Theoretical Mechanics in SI Units: In SI Units, Vols. 1-2. 2nd ed. 1971. Vol. 1. pap. 9.25 (ISBN 0-08-016268-1); Vol. 2. pap. 11.25 (ISBN 0-08-016591-5). Pergamon.
Plumpton, C. A., jt. auth. see Chirgwin, B.
Plumstead, A. W. see Emerson, Ralph W.
Plung, D. L., jt. ed. see Harkins, C.
Plung, Daniel L., jt. auth. see Harkins, Craig.
Plunket, Robert. My Search for Warren Harding. LC 82-48742. 1983. 13.95 (ISBN 0-394-52981-2). Knopf.
Plunkett, James. Farewell Companions. LC 77-26829. 1978. 10.95 o.p. (ISBN 0-698-10901-5, Coward). Putnam Pub Group.
Plunkett, Lorne C. & Hale, Guy A. The Proactive Manager: The Complete Book of Problem-Solving & Decision-Making. LC 81-11382. 221p. 1982. 23.95x (ISBN 0-471-08509-X, Pub. by Wiley-Interscience). Wiley.
Plunkett, Orda A., jt. auth. see Wilson, J. Walter.
Plunkett, T. J., jt. auth. see Brownstone, Meyer.
Plunkett, W. Richard. Supervision: The Direction of People at Work. 3rd ed. 400p. 1983. text ed. write for info. (ISBN 0-697-08087-0); instrs.' manual avail. (ISBN 0-697-08095-1). Wm C Brown.
Plunkett, Warren R. Business. 2nd ed. 544p. 1982. text ed. write for info. (ISBN 0-697-08065-X); instrs.' manual avail. (ISBN 0-697-08078-1); student guide avail. (ISBN 0-697-08077-3); avail. Test Item File (ISBN 0-697-08083-8); avail. transparencies (ISBN 0-697-08082-X). Wm C Brown.
--Supervision: The Direction of People at Work. 2nd ed. 370p. 1979. text ed. write for info. o.p. (ISBN 0-697-08028-5); study guide avail. o.p. (ISBN 0-697-08029-3). Wm C Brown.
Plunkett, Warren R. & Attner, Raymond F. Introduction to Management. 544p. 1983. text ed. 22.95x (ISBN 0-534-01298-1). Kent Pub Co.
Pluscauskas, Martha, ed. Canadian Serials Directory 1976 (Repertorie Des Publications Seriees Canadiennes) LC 73-76123. 1977. Net. 75.00 o.p. (ISBN 0-8020-4507-3). U of Toronto Pr.
Pluszczewski, Stefan, tr. see Rozdzienski, Walenty.
Pluta, Joseph E. & Wright, Rita J. Texas Fact Book, 1984. (Illus.). 200p. 1983. pap. price not set. U of Tex Busn Res.
Plutarch. Plutarch's Lives. White, John S., ed. LC 66-28487. (Illus.). 468p. (gr. 7 up). 1900. 11.00x (ISBN 0-8196-0174-8). Biblo.
--Plutarch's Lives. Dryden, John, tr. 10.95 (ISBN 0-394-60407-5). Modern Lib.
--Plutarch's Themistocles & Aristides. Perrin, Bernadotte, ed. 1901. text ed. 65.00x (ISBN 0-686-83702-9). Elliots Bks.
Plutarchus. The Roman Questions of Plutarchus. Rose, H. J., tr. 1924. 11.00x (ISBN 0-8196-0284-1). Biblo.
Plutchik, Robert. Emotions: Facts. Theories & a New Model. (Orig.). 1962. pap. text ed. 2.95x (ISBN 0-685-19725-5). Phila Bk Co.
--Foundations of Experimental Research. 3rd ed. 272p. 1982. pap. text ed. 14.95 scp (ISBN 0-06-045265-X, HarpC). Har-Row.
--Fundamentos de Investigacion Experimental. rev. ed. 1975. pap. text ed. 10.30 o.p. (ISBN 0-06-316991-6, IntlDept). Har-Row.
Plutchik, Robert & Kellerman, Henry, eds. Emotion: Theory, Research & Experience, Vol. 2. 340p. 1983. price not set (ISBN 0-12-558702-3). Acad Pr.
Plutzik, Laghi M., jt. auth. see Plutzik, Roberta.

Plutzik, Roberta & Plutzik, Laghi M. The Private Life of Parents: How to Take Care of Yourself & Your Partner While Raising Happy, Healthy Children; A Complete Survival Guide. LC 82-11750. (Illus.). 320p. 1983. 15.95 (ISBN 0-89696-119-2, An Everest House Book). Dodd.

Plymell, Pamela B., ed. Blues Anthology. 1983. cancelled (ISBN 0-916156-50-8); pap. cancelled (ISBN 0-916156-49-4). Cherry Valley.

Plywood Clinic, 3rd, Portland, Mar.1975. Modern Plywood Techniques Vol. 3: Proceedings. Lambert, Herbert G., ed. LC 74-20159. (Plywood Clinic Library: A Forest Industries Book). (Illus.). 240p. 1976. pap. 29.50 o.p. (ISBN 0-87930-048-5). Miller Freeman.

Po, A. Li Wan see **Li Wan Po, A.**

Poag, C. Wylie. Ecologic Atlas of Benthic Foraminifera of the Gulf of Mexico. LC 81-3720. 192p. 1981. 27.50 (ISBN 0-87933-900-4). Hutchinson Ross.

Poag, James F. Wolfram Von Eschenbach. (World Authors Ser.). lib. bdg. 15.95 (ISBN 0-8057-2304-8, Twayne). G K Hall.

Poage, George R. Henry Clay & the Whig Party. 1965. 9.00 (ISBN 0-8446-1351-7). Peter Smith.

Poague, Leland, jt. auth. see **Cadbury, William.**

Poague, Leland A. Howard Hawks. (Filmmakers Ser.). 1982. lib. bdg. 15.95 (ISBN 0-8057-9285-6, Twayne). G K Hall.

Poate, J. M., et al, eds. Thin Films: Interdiffusion & Reactions. LC 77-25348. (Electrochemical Society Ser.). 1978. 54.95x (ISBN 0-471-02238-1, Pub. by Wiley-Interscience). Wiley.

Poate, John M. & Mayer, James W. Laser Annealing of Semiconductors. 1982. 67.00 (ISBN 0-12-558820-8). Acad Pr.

Pochedly. Neuroblastoma: Clinical & Biological Manifestations. 1982. 49.50 (ISBN 0-444-00702-4). Elsevier.

Pochedly, Carl. The Child with Leukemia. (Illus.). 312p. 1973. 15.25x o.p. (ISBN 0-398-02735-8). C C Thomas.

Pochin, Jean. Without a Wedding-Ring: Casework with Unmarried Parents. LC 72-84196. 1969. 5.00x o.p. (ISBN 0-8052-3292-3). Schocken.

Pochin-Mould, Daphne. Irish Pilgrimage. 1957. 7.95 (ISBN 0-8159-5816-1). Devin.

Pochman, Henry A. & Feltskog, E. N., eds. The Complete Works of Washington Irving: Mahomet & His Successors, 1850. (Critical Editions Program). 1970. lib. bdg. 25.00 (ISBN 0-8057-8505-1, Twayne). G K Hall.

Pochtrager, Frances P. Pizazz or Perish. (Illus.). 104p. 1982. 19.95 (ISBN 0-686-83079-2). Retail Report.

Pocketpac Bks. Promises for the Golden Years. 96p. 1983. pap. 1.95 (ISBN 0-87788-320-3). Shaw Pubs.

Pocock, Gordon. Boileau & the Nature of Neo-Classicism. LC 79-50885. (Major European Authors Ser.). 1980. 34.50 (ISBN 0-521-22772-0). Cambridge U Pr.

--Corneille & Racine. LC 72-97886. 352p. 1973. 49.50 (ISBN 0-521-20197-7); pap. 13.95x (ISBN 0-521-09814-9). Cambridge U Pr.

Pocock, J. G., ed. The Political Works of James Harrington. LC 75-41712. (Studies in the History and Theory of Politics: No. 27). 1977. 79.50 (ISBN 0-521-21161-1). Cambridge U Pr.

Pocock, M. A., jt. auth. see **Taylor, A. H.**

Pocock, Nick. Did W. D. Custead Fly First? The Story of W. D. Custead of Elm Mott - Waco, Texas - Airship Builder Before the Wrights Flew. LC 74-83996. (Illus.). 1974. pap. 5.00 (ISBN 0-915376-00-8); microfilm 20.00 (ISBN 0-915376-01-6). Spec Aviation.

Pocztar, Jerry. The Theory & Practice of Programmed Instruction: A Guide for Teachers. (Monographs on Education, No. 7). (Illus.). 179p. (Orig.). 1972. pap. 7.00 o.p. (ISBN 92-3-100936-2, U679, UNESCO). Unipub.

Podder, Arabinda, jt. auth. see **Vidyasagara, Isvarchandra.**

Podel & Stewart. Prevention of Coronary Heart Disease. 1982. text ed. 29.95 (ISBN 0-201-16300-4, Med-Nurse). A-W.

Podell, Joel, et al. Activity Guide for Salesmanship. 1979. pap. text ed. 11.00x (ISBN 0-394-32210-X). Random.

Podendorf, Illa. Animal Homes. LC 82-4466. (New True Bks.). (Illus.). 48p. (gr. k-4). 1982. PLB 9.25 (ISBN 0-516-01666-0). Childrens.

--Insects. LC 81-7689. (The New True Bks.). (Illus.). 48p. (gr. k-4). 1981. PLB 9.25 (ISBN 0-516-01627-X). Childrens.

--Jungles. LC 82-4454. (New True Bks.). (gr. k-4). 1982. 9.25 (ISBN 0-516-01631-8). Childrens.

--One Hundred One Science Experiments. LC 60-11157. (Illus.). 160p. (gr. 3-6). 1974. Repr. 4.95 o.p. (ISBN 0-448-11785-1, G&D). Putnam Pub Group.

--Pets. LC 81-7679. (The New True Bks.). (Illus.). 48p. (gr. k-4). 1981. PLB 9.25 (ISBN 0-516-01641-5). Childrens.

--Seasons. LC 81-7751. (The New True Bks.). (Illus.). 48p. (gr. k-4). 1981. PLB 9.25 (ISBN 0-516-01647-4). Childrens.

--Space. LC 82-4507. (New True Bks.). (gr. k-4). 1982. 9.25 (ISBN 0-516-01650-4). Childrens.

--Weeds & Wild Flowers. LC 81-7737. (The New True Bks.). (Illus.). 48p. (gr. k-4). 1981. PLB 9.25 (ISBN 0-516-01661-X). Childrens.

Podgorecki, Adam. Law & Society. 1974. 24.95x (ISBN 0-7100-7983-4); pap. 10.00 (ISBN 0-7100-8035-2). Routledge & Kegan.

Podhajsky, Alois. The Art of Dressage. LC 75-21241. 192p. 1976. 8.95 o.p. (ISBN 0-385-01552-6). Doubleday.

Podhoretz, Norman. The Present Danger. 1980. 7.95 o.s.i. (ISBN 0-671-41395-3); pap. 3.95 (ISBN 0-671-41328-7). S&S.

--Why We Were in Vietnam. 1982. 12.95 (ISBN 0-671-44578-2). S&S.

Podol, Peter L. Fernando Arrabal. (World Authors Ser.). 1978. lib. bdg. 15.95 (ISBN 0-8057-6340-6, Twayne). G K Hall.

Podolny, Walter & Muller, Jean M. Construction & Design of Prestressed Concrete Segmental Bridges. LC 81-13025. (Wiley Ser. of Practical Construction Guides). 561p. 1982. 68.95x (ISBN 0-471-05658-8, Pub. by Wiley Interscience). Wiley.

Podolny, Walter, Jr. & Scalzi, John B. Construction & Design of Cable-Stayed Bridges. LC 75-46578. (Practical Construction Guides Ser.). 506p. 1976. 54.00 o.p. (ISBN 0-471-75625-3, Pub. by Wiley-Interscience). Wiley.

Podolski, T. M. Socialist Banking & Monetary Control: The Experience of Poland. 49.50 (ISBN 0-521-08598-5). Cambridge U Pr.

Podolsky, Leo, ed. Guild Repertoire: Elementary A & B. 48p. (gr. 3-12). 1960. pap. text ed. 6.50 (ISBN 0-87487-639-7). Summy.

--Guild Repertoire: Elementary C & D. 48p. (gr. 3-12). 1961. pap. text ed. 6.40 (ISBN 0-87487-640-0). Summy.

--Guild Repertoire: Intermediate A. 32p. (gr. 3-12). 1959. pap. text ed. 4.95 (ISBN 0-87487-641-9). Summy.

--Guild Repertoire: Intermediate B. 32p. (gr. 3-12). 1959. pap. text ed. 4.95 (ISBN 0-87487-642-7). Summy.

--Guild Repertoire: Intermediate C & D. 64p. (gr. 3-12). 1959. pap. text ed. 8.60 (ISBN 0-87487-643-5). Summy.

Podolsky, Stephen & Viswanathan, M., eds. Secondary Diabetes: The Spectrum of the Diabetics Syndromes. (Illus.). 624p. 1980. 57.00 (ISBN 0-89004-372-8). Raven.

Podracky, John. Photographic Retouching & Airbrush Techniques. (Illus.). 1980. text ed. 16.95 (ISBN 0-13-665257-3). P-H.

Podrazik, Walter, jt. auth. see **Castleman, Harry.**

Podrazik, Walter J., jt. auth. see **Castleman, Harry.**

Poduska, Bernard. Understanding Psychology & Dimensions of Adjustment. (Illus.). 576p. 1980. text ed. 26.50 (ISBN 0-07-050365-6); instrs.' manual & test file 5.00 (ISBN 0-07-050366-4); test bank o.p. 2.95 (ISBN 0-07-050367-2). McGraw.

Podvesko, M. L. Ukrainian-English, English-Ukrainian Dictionary, 2 vols. 45.00 (ISBN 0-686-97885-4). Heinman.

Poe, Arthur, jt. auth. see **Lipschutz, Seymour.**

Poe, Edgar A. Eighteen Best Stories of Edgar Allan Poe. Wilbur, Richard, ed. (Orig.). pap. 2.95 (ISBN 0-440-32227-8, LE). Dell.

--Great Short Works of Edgar Allan Poe. Thompson, J. R., ed. 1970. pap. 3.37i (ISBN 0-06-083093-X, P3093, PL). Har-Row.

--Marginalia. LC 80-22585. 235p. 1981. 11.95x (ISBN 0-8139-0812-4). U Pr of Va.

--The Pit & the Pendulum. (Creative's Classics Ser.). (Illus.). 48p. (gr. 4-9). 1980. PLB 7.95 (ISBN 0-87191-771-8). Creative Ed.

--Portable Poe. Stern, Phillip V., ed. (Viking Portable Library: No. 12). 1977. pap. 6.95 (ISBN 0-14-015012-9). Penguin.

Poe, Edgar A see **Eyre, A. G.**

Poe, Edgar A see **Swan, D. K.**

Poe, Edgar Allan. Al Aaraaf. LC 73-13697. 1933. Repr. of 1829 ed. lib. bdg. 12.50 (ISBN 0-8414-6704-8). Folcroft.

--Anastatic Printing. LC 73-13697. 1973. lib. bdg. 10.00 (ISBN 0-8414-1481-5). Folcroft.

--The Best of Poe. new & abr. ed. Farr, Naunerle, ed. (Now Age Illustrated III Ser.). (Illus.). (gr. 4-12). 1977. text ed. 5.00 (ISBN 0-88301-281-2); pap. text ed. 1.95 (ISBN 0-88301-269-3). Pendulum Pr.

--The Cask of Amontillado. (Creative's Classics Ser.). (Illus.). 32p. (gr. 5-9). 1980. lib. bdg. 7.95 (ISBN 0-87191-773-4). Creative Ed.

--Complete Poetry & Selected Criticism of Edgar Allan Poe. Tate, Allen, ed. 1981. pap. 5.95 (ISBN 0-452-00548-5, F548, Mer). NAL.

--Complete Tales & Poems of Edgar Allan Poe. 9.95 (ISBN 0-394-60408-3). Modern Lib.

--The Complete Works of Edgar Allan Poe, 10 vols. 1981. Repr. of 1908 ed. Set. lib. bdg. 400.00 (ISBN 0-89987-660-9). Darby Bks.

--The Devil in the Belfry. LC 72-13328. (Seedling Bks.). (Illus.). 32p. (gr. 2-6). 1974. PLB 4.95g (ISBN 0-8225-0281-X). Lerner Pubns.

--Doings of Gotham. LC 74-26950. 1929. 25.00 (ISBN 0-8414-6707-2). Folcroft.

--Edgar Allan Poe, Stories & Poems. (Classics Ser). (gr. 9 up). pap. 1.50 (ISBN 0-8049-0008-6, CL-8). Airmont.

--Edgar Allan Poe's Contribution to Alexander's Weekly Messenger. 83p. 1980. Repr. of 1943 ed. lib. bdg. 17.50 (ISBN 0-8495-4383-5). Arden Lib.

--Fall of the House of Usher & Other Tales. (RL 7). pap. 2.75 (ISBN 0-451-51659-1, CE1659, Sig Classics). NAL.

--The Gold Bug. Harris, Raymond, ed. (Jamestown Classics Ser.). (Illus.). 48p. (Orig.). 1982. pap. text ed. 2.00x (ISBN 0-89061-268-4, 479); tchr's ed 3.00x (ISBN 0-89061-269-2, 481). Jamestown Pubs.

--Goldbug & Other Stories: The Black Cat, the Pit & the Pendulum. (Illus.). 1962. pap. 2.50 (ISBN 0-8283-1437-3, 22, IPL). Branden.

--Great Tales & Poems of Edgar Allan Poe. 448p. 1982. pap. 2.95 (ISBN 0-686-37067-8). WSP.

--Great Tales of Horror. Sohn, David A., ed. (gr. 7-9). pap. 1.95 (ISBN 0-553-13768-9, Y13768-9). Bantam.

--The Last Letters of Edgar Allan Poe to Sarah Helen Whitman. LC 74-26841. 1974. Repr. of 1909 ed. lib. bdg. 15.00 (ISBN 0-8414-4899-X). Folcroft.

--Masque of the Red Death. Harris, Raymond, ed. (Jamestown Classics Ser.). (Illus.). 48p. (Orig.). 1982. pap. text ed. 2.00x (ISBN 0-89061-271-4, 475); tchr's ed. 3.00x (ISBN 0-89061-272-2, 477). Jamestown Pubs.

--Merlin Baltimore: Eighteen Twenty-Seven. Mabbott, Thomas O., ed. Bd. with Recollections of Edgar Allan Poe. Wilmer, Lambert A. 1941. Repr. lib. bdg. 10.00 (ISBN 0-8414-9262-X). Folcroft.

--The Murders in the Rue Morgue. (Illus.). 1980. Repr. deluxe ed. 29.75 (ISBN 0-89901-011-3). Found Class Reprints.

--Murders in the Rue Morgue. rev. ed. Dixson, Robert J., ed. Bd. with The Gold Bug. (American Classics Ser.: Bk. 3). (gr. 9 up). 1973. pap. text ed. 3.25 (ISBN 0-88345-199-9, 18122); cassettes 40.00 (ISBN 0-685-38998-7); 40.00 o.p. tapes (ISBN 0-685-38999-5). Regents Pub.

--The Murders in the Rue Morgue & the Gold Bug. (American Classics Ser.). (gr. 9-12). 1977. pap. text ed. 3.20 (ISBN 0-88343-404-0); tchrs'. manual 1.50 (ISBN 0-88343-405-9); casettes 39.00 (ISBN 0-88343-421-0). McDougal-Littell.

--The Narrative of Arthur Gordon Pym. LC 72-75138. (Illus.). 190p. 1974. pap. 8.50 (ISBN 0-87923-147-5); 15.00. Godine.

--Oeuvres en Prose: Histoires Extraordinaires, Adventures d'Arthur Gordon Pym, Eureka, etc. Baudelaire, tr. 1184p. 41.50 (ISBN 0-686-56551-7). French & Eur.

--The Pit & the Pendulum. Harris, Raymond, ed. (The Jamestown Classics Ser.). (Illus.). 48p. (Orig.). 1982. pap. text ed. 2.00x (ISBN 0-89061-265-X, 471); tchr's ed. 3.00x (ISBN 0-89061-266-8, 473). Jamestown Pubs.

--Poems & Essays. 1975. 9.95x (ISBN 0-460-00791-2, Evman); pap. 4.50x (ISBN 0-460-01791-8, Evman). Biblio Dist.

--The Science Fiction of Edgar Allan Poe. Beaver, Harald, ed. (English Library Ser.). 1976. pap. 3.95 (ISBN 0-14-043106-3). Penguin.

--Selected Poetry & Prose. Mabott, T. O., ed. 1931. 3.95 (ISBN 0-394-60082-7, M82). Modern Lib.

--The Selected Poetry & Prose. Mabbott, T. O., ed. 1951. pap. 3.25 (ISBN 0-686-38911-5, Mod LibC). Modern Lib.

--Selected Writings of Edgar Allan Poe. Davidson, E. H., ed. LC 56-13895. 1956. pap. 4.95 (ISBN 0-395-05110-X, A11, RivEd, 3-47645). HM.

--Tales. (Great Ill, Classic Ser.). (gr. 9 up). 1979. 8.95 (ISBN 0-396-07759-5). Dodd.

--Tales & The Raven & Other Poems. LC 69-13800. 1975. 6.00 (ISBN 0-685-56443-6); pap. 4.00 (ISBN 0-675-09530-1). Brown Bk.

--Tales of Edgar Allan Poe. LC 80-14064. (Raintree Short Classics). (Illus.). 48p. (gr. 4 up). 1980. PLB 13.85 (ISBN 0-8172-1662-6). Raintree Pubs.

--Tales of Edgar Allan Poe. (gr. 3 up). 1979. 3.50 (ISBN 0-307-12227-1, Golden Pr). Western Pub.

--Tales of Mystery & Imagination. 1975. 8.95x (ISBN 0-460-00336-4, Evman); pap. 3.95x (ISBN 0-460-01336-X, Evman). Biblio Dist.

--Tales of Mystery & Imagination. 438p. 1981. Repr. lib. bdg. 14.95 (ISBN 0-89968-236-7). Lightyear.

--Tales of Mystery & Imagination. 1981. Repr. lib. bdg. 16.95x (ISBN 0-89966-434-2). Buccaneer Bks.

--The Tell-Tale Heart. (Creative's Classics Ser.). (Illus.). 32p. (gr. 4-9). 1980. PLB 7.95 (ISBN 0-87191-772-6). Creative Ed.

--The Tell-Tale Heart. Harris, Raymond, ed. (The Jamestown Classics). (Illus.). 48p. (Orig.). 1982. pap. text ed. 2.00x (ISBN 0-89061-262-5, 467); tchr's ed. 3.00x (ISBN 0-89061-263-3, 469). Jamestown Pubs.

--Works of Edgar Allan Poe, 10 vols. facsimile ed. Stedman, Edmund C. & Woodberry, George E., eds. LC 71-169773. (Select Bibliographies Reprint Ser). Repr. of 1895 ed. Set. 250.00 (ISBN 0-8369-5993-0). Ayer Co.

Poe, Edgar Allan & Foye, Raymond. The Unknown Poe. LC 80-2431. 1980. 10.95x (ISBN 0-87286-119-8); pap. 5.95x (ISBN 0-87286-110-4). City Lights.

Poe, Edgar Allan & Verne, Jules. Mystery of Arthur G. Pym. 3.95 (ISBN 0-685-06584-7). Assoc Bk.

Poe, Edgar Allen. Tales of Mystery & Imagination, Retold by Henniker-Major. (Oxford Progressive English Readers Ser.). (Illus.). (gr. 3 up). 1975. pap. text ed. 3.50x (ISBN 0-19-580511-9). Oxford U Pr.

Poe, Elizabeth W. From Poetry to Prose in Old Provencal. 1983. 16.00 (ISBN 0-917786-33-5). French Lit.

Poe, Roy, et al. Getting Involoved with Business. (Illus.). 576p. (gr. 9-10). 1980. text ed. 13.48 (ISBN 0-07-050335-4, G); learning activity kit I 5.12 (ISBN 0-07-050336-2); learning activity kit II 5.12 (ISBN 0-07-050337-0). McGraw.

Poe, Roy W. The McGraw-Hill Guide to Effective Business Reports. (Illus.). 192p. 1982. 21.95 (ISBN 0-07-050341-9). McGraw.

Poe, Roy W. & Fruehling, R. T. Business Communications: A Problem Solving Approach. (Illus.). 1978. text ed. 18.75 (ISBN 0-07-050362-1, G); wkbk 5.90 (ISBN 0-07-050363-X); instructor's manual & key 9.80 (ISBN 0-07-050364-8). McGraw.

Poe, Roy W. & Fruehling, Rosemary T. Business Communications: A Problem-Solving Approach. (Illus.). 384p. 1973. text ed. 16.35 o.p. (ISBN 0-07-050360-5, G). McGraw.

Poe, Tina, jt. auth. see **Barker, Louisa.**

Poedjosoedarmo, Soepomo, jt. auth. see **Wolff, John U.**

Poehlman, William R., tr. see **Lohse, Eduard.**

Poeldinger, W. & Taeuber, K., eds. Nomifensine-Clinical & Experimental Investigation. (Journal: Internatinal Pharmacopsychiatry, Vol.17, Suppl.1,1982). iv, 148p. 1982. pap. 28.75 (ISBN 3-8055-3585-6). S Karger.

Poellot, Luther, tr. see **Chemitz, Martin.**

Poelt, J. Bestimmungsschluessel Europaeischer Flechten. (Illus.). 1969. pap. 32.00 (ISBN 3-7682-0159-7). Lubrecht & Cramer.

Poelt, J. & Vezda, A. Bestimmungsschluessel Europaeischer Flechten, Suppl. II. (Bibliotheca Lichenologica: No. 16). 390p. (Ger.). 1981. text ed. 32.00x (ISBN 3-7682-1312-9). Lubrecht & Cramer.

--Bestimmungsschluessel Europaeischer Flechten. (Bibliotheca Lichenologica Ser.: No. 9, suppl. I). 1977. lib. bdg. 20.00x (ISBN 3-7682-1162-2). Lubrecht & Cramer.

Poelt, J., jt. auth. see **Mayrhofer, '.**

Poen, Monte M., ed. Strictly Personal & Confidential: The Letters Harry Truman Never Mailed. 224p. 1983. pap. 5.70i (ISBN 0-316-71222-1). Little.

Poeppig, E. & Endlicher, S. Nova Genera Ac Species Plantarum Quas in Regno Chilensi, Peruviano & in Terra Amazonica Annis 1827-32: 1835-45. 1968. 224.00 (ISBN 3-7682-0549-5). Lubrecht & Cramer.

Poerck, R. A. De see **Krug, C. A. & De Poerck, R. A.**

Poesse, Walter. Juan Ruiz de Alarcon. (World Authors Ser.). lib. bdg. 14.95 (ISBN 0-8057-2012-X, Twayne). G K Hall.

Po-Fei Huang, Parker, jt. auth. see **Stimson, Hugh M.**

Poffenberger, Thomas. Fertility & Family Life in an Indian Village. LC 75-9025. (Michigan Papers on South & Southeast Asia: No. 10). (Illus.). xii, 114p. (Orig.). 1975. pap. 6.00x (ISBN 0-89148-010-2). Ctr S&SE Asian.

Poffenberger, Thomas & Sebaly, Kim. The Socialization of Family Size Values: Youth & Family Planning in an Indian Village. LC 76-53996. (Michigan Papers on South and Southeast Asia: No. 12). (Illus.). xiv, 159p. (Orig.). 1976. pap. 6.00x (ISBN 0-89148-012-9). Ctr S&SE Asian.

Poggi, Gianfranco. The Development of the Modern State: A Sociological Introduction. LC 77-76148. 1978. 10.95x (ISBN 0-8047-0959-9); pap. 4.95 (ISBN 0-8047-1042-2, SP9). Stanford U Pr.

Poggie, J. J., Jr. & Pollnac, R. B., eds. Small Fishing Ports in Southern New England. (Marine Bulletin Ser.: No. 39). 125p. 1981. 3.00 o.p. (ISBN 0-686-36987-4, P873). URI Mas.

Poggie, John J., et al. The Evolution of Human Adaptations: Readings in Anthropology. (Illus.). 480p. 1976. pap. text ed. 14.95 (ISBN 0-02-396000-0). Macmillan.

Poggie, John J., Jr. & Lynch, Robert N., eds. Rethinking Modernization. LC 72-826. 352p. 1974. lib. bdg. 29.95 (ISBN 0-8371-6394-3, POM/). Greenwood.

Poggio, Tomaso, jt. ed. see **Reichardt, Werner E.**

Pogodeinski, Michael. How to Survive Nuclear War. (Illus.). 224p. (Orig.). 1982. pap. 7.95 (ISBN 0-89621-072-3). Thorndike Pr.

Pogonowski, Iwo. Concise Polish-English-English-Polish Dictionary. 436p. (Orig.). 1983. pap. 3.95 (ISBN 0-88254-799-2). Hippocrene Bks.

Pogorelov, A. V. Hilbert's Fourth Problem. (Scripa Series in Mathematics). 97p. 1979. 16.00x o.s.i. (ISBN 0-470-26735-6). Halsted Pr.

Pogorzelski, Henry A. & Ryan, William J. Foundations of Semiological Theory of Numbers. 350p. (Orig.). 1982. pap. text ed. 29.95 (ISBN 0-89101-053-X). U Maine Orono.

Pogrebin, L. C. Stories for Free Children. 144p. 1982. 14.95 (ISBN 0-07-050389-3, GB). McGraw.

Pogrebin, Lottie C. Growing up Free: Raising Your Kids in the 80's. LC 80-13054. 528p. 1980. 15.95 o.p. (ISBN 0-07-050370-2, GB). McGraw.

Pogrebin, Mark. Managing Scarce Resources for Jails. LC 82-13409. (Illus.). 144p. 1982. lib. bdg. 18.50 (ISBN 0-8191-2641-1); pap. text ed. 8.25 (ISBN 0-8191-2642-X). U Pr of Amer.

Pogson, C. I., jt. auth. see **Denton, R. M.**

Pogue, Forrest C. George C. Marshall: Ordeal & Hope, 1939-1943. 1966. 19.95 (ISBN 0-670-33686-6). Viking Pr.

Pogue, Thomas F. & Sgontz, Larry G. Government & Economic Choice: An Introduction to Public Finance. LC 77-75157. (Illus.). 1978. text ed. 23.95 (ISBN 0-395-25112-5). HM.

Pohier, Marie, jt. ed. see Mieth, Dietmar.

Pohl, A. Permutations & Combinations. (Finite Math Text Ser.). write for info. (ISBN 0-685-84480-3). J W Wills.

--Principles of Counting. (Finite Math Text Ser.). write for info. (ISBN 0-685-84479-X). J W Wills.

--Probability: A Set Theory Approach. (Finite Math Text Ser.). write for info. (ISBN 0-685-84478-1). J W Wills.

Pohl, C. F. Mozart & Haydn in London, 2 vols. in 1. LC 70-125059. (Music Ser). 1970. Repr. of 1867 ed. lib. bdg. 42.50 (ISBN 0-306-70024-7). Da Capo.

Pohl, Frederick. Frederick Pohl's Favorite Stories: Four Decades As a Science Fiction Editor. 504p. 1981. cancelled (ISBN 0-399-12592-2). Putnam Pub Group.

Pohl, Frederick & Williamson, Jack. Undersea Quest. 160p. 1982. pap. 1.95 (ISBN 0-345-30701-1, Del Rey). Ballantine.

--Wall Around a Star. 288p. (Orig.). 1983. pap. 2.95 (ISBN 0-345-28995-1, Del Rey). Ballantine.

Pohl, Frederick, ed. Nebula Winners Fourteen. LC 66-20974. (Harper Science Fiction Ser.). 240p. 1980. 13.41i (ISBN 0-06-013382-1, HarpT). Har-Row.

Pohl, Frederik, ed. Nebula Winners Fourteen. 240p. 1982. pap. 2.25 (ISBN 0-553-20931-0). Bantam.

Pohl, H., jt. ed. see Engels, W.

Pohl, H. A. Dielectrophoresis. LC 77-71421. (Cambridge Monographs on Physics). (Illus.). 1978. 112.50 (ISBN 0-521-21657-5). Cambridge U Pr.

Pohl, Ira & Shaw, Alan. The Nature of Computation: An Introduction to Computer Science. (Illus.). 1981. text ed. 22.95x (ISBN 0-914894-12-9). Computer Sci.

Pohl, James W., jt. auth. see Randolph, J. Ralph.

Pohl, Richard W. How to Know the Grasses. 3rd ed. (Pictured Key Nature Ser.). 250p. 1978. wire coil (ISBN 0-697-04876-4); text ed. avail. (ISBN 0-697-04877-2). Wm C Brown.

Pohl, Thomas W., jt. auth. see Bergman, Edward F.

Pohl, W. E., tr. see Draf, W.

Pohle, Robert W., Jr. & Hart, Douglas C. The Films of Christopher Lee. LC 82-10424. (Illus.). 249p. 1983. 32.50 (ISBN 0-8108-1573-7). Scarecrow.

Pohlmann, Lillian. Love Can Say No. LC 66-10140. (gr. 7-10). 1966. 5.50 o.s.i. (ISBN 0-664-32365-0). Westminster.

Pohlmeyer, J., jt. ed. see Honerkamp, J.

Pohorecky & Brick. Stress & Alcohol Use. Date not set. 74.00 (ISBN 0-444-00730-X). Elsevier.

Pohto, H. A., ed. High Pressure Engineering & Technology for Pressure Vessels & Piping Systems. (PVP Ser.: Vol. 61). 189p. 1982. 34.00. ASME.

Poinar, George O., Jr. Natural History of Nematodes. (Illus.). 320p. 1983. 34.95 (ISBN 0-13-609925-4). P-H.

Poincare, H. The Foundations of Science: Science & Hypothesis, the Value of Science, Science & Method. Halstead, George B., tr. from Fr. LC 81-48682. 568p. 1982. lib. bdg. 29.50 (ISBN 0-8191-2318-8); pap. text ed. 18.75 (ISBN 0-8191-2319-6). U Pr of Amer.

Poincelot, R. Horticulture: Principles & Practical Applications. 1980. 25.95 (ISBN 0-13-394809-9). P-H.

Poincelot, Raymond. Gardening Indoors with House Plants. LC 74-16238. (Illus.). 272p. 1974. 12.95 (ISBN 0-87857-085-3); pap. 6.95 (ISBN 0-87857-108-6). Rodale Pr Inc.

Poindexter, J. C. & Jones, Charles P. Money, Financial Markets & the Economy. 1979. text ed. 24.95 (ISBN 0-8299-0225-2); cancelled (ISBN 0-8299-0270-8). West Pub.

Poinsett, Brenda. When Jesus Prayed. LC 80-67896. 1981. pap. 3.95 (ISBN 0-8054-5179-X). Broadman.

Poinsett, Joel R. Calendar of the Joel R. Poinsett Papers. Heilman, Grace E., ed. 1941. 3.00 o.p. (ISBN 0-910732-02-7). Pa Hist Soc.

Pointer, Michael. The Sherlock Holmes File. (Illus.). 1976. 10.00 o.p. (ISBN 0-517-52560-7, C N Potter Bks). Crown.

Pointing, K. G., jt. auth. see Harte, N. B.

Pointon, ed. see Lennox-Kerr, P.

Points & Meridians & Worsley, J. R. Traditional Chinese Acupuncture, Vol. 1. 1982. 195.00x (ISBN 0-906540-03-8, Pub. by Element Bks). State Mutual Bk.

Poirer, Richard. Comic Sense of Henry James: A Study of the Early Novels. 1967. pap. 4.95 o.p. (ISBN 0-19-500438-8, GB). Oxford U Pr.

Poirier, D. J. The Econometrics of Structural Change. (Contributions to Economic Analysis: Vol. 97). 1976. 38.50 (ISBN 0-444-10966-8, North-Holland). Elsevier.

Poirier, Frank E. Fossil Evidence: The Human Evolutionary Journey. 3rd ed. LC 80-24939. (Illus.). 428p. 1981. pap. text ed. 17.95 (ISBN 0-8016-3952-2). Mosby.

--An Introduction to Physical Anthropology & the Archeological Record. LC 81-70138. 480p. (Orig.). 1982. pap. text ed. 17.95x. Burgess.

Poirier, J., ed. see Kirkwood, John G.

Poirier, J. P., jt. auth. see Nicolas, A.

Poirier, Louis J., et al, eds. see International Conference on Parkinson's Disease, No. 6.

Poirier, Richard. Robert Frost. LC 76-57259. (The Work of Knowing). 1977. 18.95x (ISBN 0-19-502216-5). Oxford U Pr.

--Robert Frost: The Work of Knowing. 1979. pap. 7.95 (ISBN 0-19-502615-2, GB 586, GB). Oxford U Pr.

Poirier, Richard, jt. ed. see Kermode, Frank.

Poirot, James & Groves, David. Computers & Mathematics. (Illus.). (gr. 11-12). 1979. text ed. 21.95 list price (ISBN 0-88408-119-2); pap. text ed. 16.95 o.p. (ISBN 0-686-86775-0). Sterling Swift.

Poirot, James L. & Retzlaff, Don A. Microcomputer Workbook: Apple II Ed. 2nd ed. 137p. (gr. 6 up). 1979. pap. text ed. 5.95 (ISBN 0-88408-139-7); tchr's. manual 5.95 (ISBN 0-88408-145-1). Sterling Swift.

Pois, Joseph. Watchdog on the Potomac: A Study of the Comptroller General of the United States. LC 78-66276. 1979. pap. text ed. 13.50 (ISBN 0-8191-0691-7). U Pr of Amer.

Pois, Robert. Emil Nolde. LC 81-43498. (Illus.). 310p. (Orig.). 1982. lib. bdg. 24.00 (ISBN 0-8191-2367-6); pap. text ed. 12.00 (ISBN 0-8191-2368-4). U Pr of Amer.

Pois, Robert A. Bourgeois Democrats of Weimar Germany. LC 76-3198. (Transactions Ser.: Vol. 66, Pt. 3). 1976. pap. 6.00 o.p. (ISBN 0-87169-664-9). Am Philos.

--Friedrich Meinecke & German Politics in the Twentieth Century. LC 70-157818. 192p. 1972. 32.50x (ISBN 0-520-02045-6). U of Cal Pr.

Poisner. Secretory Granule. (Secretory Process Ser.: Vol. 1). Date not set. 113.00 (ISBN 0-444-80383-1). Elsevier.

Poissonet, P., ed. Vegetation Dynamics in Grasslands, Heathlands & Mediterranean Ligneous Formations. 1982. lib. bdg. 85.00 (ISBN 0-686-36955-6, Pub. by Junk Pubs Netherlands). Kluwer Boston.

Poister, Theodore H. Performance Monitoring for Transportation Programs. LC 81-47574. 256p. 1982. 31.95x (ISBN 0-669-04683-3). Lexington Bks.

--Public Program Analysis. LC 77-27308. 640p. 1978. 22.50 (ISBN 0-8391-1190-8). Univ Park.

Poister, Theodore H., et al. Applied Program Evaluation in Local Government. LC 78-20374. 240p. 1979. 25.95 (ISBN 0-669-02731-6). Lexington Bks.

Poitras, G., jt. auth. see Adie, R.

Poitrass, Edward W., tr. see Hwang Sun-won.

Poix, Carol de see De Poix, Carol.

Pojasek, R. B. Impact of Legislation & Implementation on Disposal Management Practices. LC 79-56117. (Toxic & Hazardous Waste Disposal Ser.: Vol. 3). 1980. 49.95 (ISBN 0-250-40253-X). Ann Arbor Science.

--New & Promising Ultimate Disposal Options. LC 79-56116. (Toxic & Hazardous Waste Disposal Ser.: Vol. 4). 1980. 49.95 (ISBN 0-250-40265-3). Ann Arbor Science.

Pojasek, Robert B. Options for Stabilization-Solidification, Vol. 2. LC 78-50312. (Toxic & Hazardous Waste Disposal Ser.). 1979. 49.95 (ISBN 0-250-40252-1). Ann Arbor Science.

--Processes for Stabilization-Solidification, Vol. 1. LC 78-50312. (Toxic & Hazardous Waste Disposal Ser.). 1979. 49.95 (ISBN 0-250-40251-3). Ann Arbor Science.

Pojasek, Robert B., ed. Drinking Water Quality Enhancement Through Source Protection. LC 77-76913. 1977. 49.95 (ISBN 0-250-40188-6). Ann Arbor Science.

Pokladnik, Kathryn. Incl. The Legend of Crown Point. (ISBN 0-912854). Dist. by 412. GLA Pr.

Pokornowski, Ila M., jt. ed. see Creekmore, Anna M.

Pokress, E., jt. auth. see Sandri-White, Alex.

Pokrovsky, V. L. & Talapov, A. L. Theory of Incommensurate Crystals. (Soviet Scientific Reviews Supplement Ser. Physics: Vol. 1). 140p. 1983. 77.50 (ISBN 3-7186-0134-6). Harwood Academic.

Pol, Therese, tr. see Reich, Wilhelm.

Polackova, Kaca, tr. see Liehm, Antonin J.

Polak, Ada. Glass: Its Traditions & Its Makers. LC 74-25236. (Illus.). 226p. 1975. 15.95 o.p. (ISBN 0-399-11523-4). Putnam Pub Group.

Polak, H. S., et al. Mahatma Gandhi. 1966. pap. 3.00 o.s.i. (ISBN 0-88253-170-0). Ind-US Inc.

Polak, J. B. & Hupkes, G., eds. Vervoer Voor Gehandicapten: Illusie of Realiteit? 340p. (Dutch.). pap. 17.50x (ISBN 90-70176-62-9). Foris Pubns.

Polak, J. M., jt. ed. see Steward, P. J.

Polak, Johan, illus. True-To-Life ABC Book Including Numbers. rev. ed. (Nursery Treasure Bks). (Illus.). (ps). 1962. 2.50 (ISBN 0-448-04204-5, G&D). Putnam Pub Group.

Polakoff, Claire. Into Indigo: African Textiles & Dyeing Techniques. LC 77-76281. (Illus.). 1980. pap. 7.95 o.p. (ISBN 0-385-08504-4, Anch). Doubleday.

Polakoff, Keith I. American History of Political Parties. LC 80-21505. 480p. 1981. pap. text ed. 19.50x (ISBN 0-471-07747-X). Wiley.

Polakoff, Murray & Durkin, Thomas A. Financial Institutions & Markets. 2nd ed. LC 80-82758. (Illus.). 673p. 1981. text ed. 27.95 (ISBN 0-395-29191-7); instr's. manual 1.00 (ISBN 0-395-30055-X). HM.

Polakowski, N. H. & Ripling, E. Strength & Structure of Engineering Materials. 1965. text ed. 32.95 (ISBN 0-13-851790-8). P-H.

Poland Central Statistical Office. Concise Statistical Yearbook of Poland, 1982. 21st ed. LC 49-25078. (Illus.). 304p. (Orig.). 1982. pap. 35.00 (ISBN 0-8002-3025-6). Intl Pubns Serv.

Poland, Elizabeth Y., jt. auth. see Martin, Robert A.

Poland, James L., et al. Musculoskeletal System. 2nd ed. (Medical Outline Ser.). 1981. pap. 21.50 (ISBN 0-87488-667-8). Med Exam.

Poland, Larry W. Spirit Power: All You Need When You Need It! LC 77-91763. (Illus.). 1978. pap. 2.95 o.p. (ISBN 0-918956-39-0). Campus Crusade.

Poland, Michael D., jt. auth. see Livingston, James A.

Polano, Machiel K., jt. auth. see Fitzpatrick, Thomas B.

Polansky, Joseph, jt. auth. see Nielsen, Greg.

Polansky, Norman A., et al. Child Neglect: Understanding & Reaching the Parent. LC 72-83496. 1972. pap. 5.45 (ISBN 0-87868-097-7, G-18). Child Welfare.

Polanyi, Arensberg & Pearson, eds. Trade & Market in the Early Empires. LC 57-6745. 1971. pap. 5.95 (ISBN 0-89526-991-0). Regnery-Gateway.

Polanyi, George. What Price North Sea Gas. (Institute of Economic Affairs, Hobart Papers Ser.: No. 38). pap. 2.50 o.p. (ISBN 0-255-69556-X); 2.50 o.p. Transatlantic.

Polanyi, Karl. Great Transformation: The Political & Economic Origins of Our Time. 1957. pap. 7.95 (ISBN 0-8070-5679-0, BP45). Beacon Pr.

Polanyi, Livia. The American Story: From the Structure of Linguistic Texts to the Grammar of a Culture. (The Language & Being Ser.). 1983. write for info. (ISBN 0-89391-041-4). Ablex Pub.

Polanyi, Michael. Personal Knowledge: Towards a Post-Critical Philosophy. LC 58-5162. xiv, 428p. 1974. pap. 9.95 (ISBN 0-226-67288-3, P583, Phoen). U of Chicago Pr.

Polanyi, Michael & Prosch, Harry. Meaning. LC 75-5067. 1977. pap. 7.95 (ISBN 0-226-67295-6, P740, Phoen). U of Chicago Pr.

Polaroid Corporation Staff. Photomicrography with Polaroid Land Films. (Illus.). 54p. (Orig.). 1983. pap. 6.95 (ISBN 0-240-51703-2). Butterworth.

--Polaroid Black & White Land Films. (Illus.). 72p. (Orig.). 1983. pap. 6.95 (ISBN 0-240-51705-9). Butterworth.

--Polaroid Color Films. (Illus.). 56p. 1983. pap. 6.95 (ISBN 0-240-51706-7). Butterworth.

--Storing, Handling, & Preserving Polaroid Photographs. (Illus.). 64p. (Orig.). 1983. pap. 7.95 (ISBN 0-240-51704-0). Butterworth.

Polczak, Raymond F., Jr. Something for You. 1983. 4.95 (ISBN 0-8062-2139-9). Carlton.

Poldauf, J. Czech-English-Czech Dictionary. 4th ed. 1980. text ed. 20.00x (ISBN 0-89918-253-4, C253). Vanous.

Poldauf, J. & Osicka, A. Czechoslovakian Dictionary: "Anglicko-Cesky Slovnick". 640p. 1970. text ed. 25.00x o.p. (ISBN 0-89918-157-0, C157). Vanous.

Pole, J. R. The Gift of Government: Political Responsibility from the English Restoration to American Independence. LC 82-13533. (The Richard B. Russell Lecture Ser.: No. 1). 216p. 1983. 16.00 (ISBN 0-8203-0652-5). U of Ga Pr.

--Paths to the American Past. LC 79-830. 1979. 22.50x (ISBN 0-19-502579-2). Oxford U Pr.

--Political Representation in England & the Origins of the American Republic. 1966. 26.00 (ISBN 0-312-62440-9). St Martin.

--The Pursuit of Equality in American History. LC 76-20020. (Jefferson Memorial Lecture Ser.). 1978. 28.50x (ISBN 0-520-03286-1); pap. 5.95 (ISBN 0-520-03947-5). U of Cal Pr.

Poled, Mattityahu. The Literary Works of Najib Mahfuz. 168p. 1983. 39.95 (ISBN 0-87855-135-2). Transaction Bks.

Poleman, Horace I. Census of Indic Manuscripts in the United States & Canada. 1938. pap. 40.00 (ISBN 0-527-02686-7). Kraus Repr.

Polen, O. W. The Sunday School Teacher. 1956. pap. 4.95 (ISBN 0-87148-765-9). Pathway Pr.

Polenberg, Richard, jt. auth. see LaFeber, Walter.

Polenske, Karen, ed. see International Conference Sixth Vienna, 1974.

Polenske, Karen R. State Estimates of Technology, 1963. LC 73-1641. (Multiregional Input-Output Study: Vol. 4). (Illus.). 544p. 1974. 27.95 (ISBN 0-669-87007-2). Lexington Bks.

--State Estimates of the Gross National Product: 1947, 1958, & 1963. LC 79-145900. (Multiregional Input Output Study: Vol. 1). 488p. 1972. 32.95 (ISBN 0-669-62539-6). Lexington Bks.

--The United States Multiregional Input-Output Accounts & Model. LC 78-332. (Illus.). 384p. 1980. 37.95x (ISBN 0-669-02173-3). Lexington Bks.

Polentz, Lloyd M. Engineering Fundamentals for Professional Engineers Exams. 2nd ed. LC 78-21927. (Illus.). 1980. 27.95 (ISBN 0-07-050380-X); pap. 14.95 (ISBN 0-07-050381-8). McGraw.

Polese, Carolyn. Something About a Mermaid. LC 77-15585. (Illus.). (gr. 4-7). 1978. 6.95 o.p. (ISBN 0-525-39590-3). Dutton.

Polette, Nancy. E is for Everybody: A Manual for Bringing Fine Picture Books into the Hands & Hearts of Children. 2nd ed. LC 82-10508. 194p. 1982. 12.50 (ISBN 0-8108-1579-6). Scarecrow.

--Three R's for the Gifted: Reading, Writing, & Research. LC 82-31. 180p. 1982. lib. bdg. 18.50 (ISBN 0-87287-289-0). Libs Unl.

Polette, Nancy & Hamlin, Marjorie. Exploring Books with Gifted Children. LC 80-23721. 1980. lib. bdg. 18.50 (ISBN 0-87287-216-5). Libs Unl.

Poley, Wayne, et al. Alcoholism: A Treatment Manual. LC 78-13435. 1979. 14.95x o.s.i. (ISBN 0-470-26523-X). Halsted Pr.

Polezhaev, L. V. Organ Regeneration in Animals: Recovery of Organ Regeneration Ability in Animals. (Illus.). 200p. 1972. 19.75x o.p. (ISBN 0-398-02381-6). C C Thomas.

Polgreen, Cathleen, jt. auth. see Polgreen, John.

Polgreen, John & Polgreen, Cathleen. Earth in Space. Date not set. 2.95 (ISBN 0-394-80127-X, BYR); PLB 4.39 (ISBN 0-394-90127-4). Random.

Polhemus, Robert M. Comic Faith: The Great Tradition from Austen to Joyce. LC 79-24856. x, 398p. 1980. 25.00 (ISBN 0-226-67320-0, Phoen); pap. 9.95 (ISBN 0-226-67321-9). U of Chicago Pr.

Polhemus, Russell. Power for All Seasons. LC 80-84213. (Illus.). 192p. (Orig.). 1983. pap. text ed. 6.95 (ISBN 0-88011-003-1). Leisure Pr.

Polhill, R. M. & Raven, P. H., eds. Advances in Legume Systematics, 2 Pts. (Illus.). 1981. pap. 82.50 (ISBN 0-85521-224-1, Pub. by Brit Mus Nat Hist England). Sabbot-Natural Hist Bks.

Poliakoff, Stephen. American Days: A Play. 65p. 1979. pap. 5.95 (ISBN 0-413-46890-9). Methuen Inc.

--Hitting Town & City Sugar. 134p. 1978. pap. 7.50 (ISBN 0-413-38880-8). Methuen Inc.

Poliakov, Leon. Harvest of Hate: The Nazi Program for the Destruction of the Jews in Europe. LC 74-110836. 1971. Repr. of 1954 ed. lib. bdg. 19.00x (ISBN 0-8371-2635-5, POHH). Greenwood.

--Harvest of Hate: The Nazi Program for the Destruction of the Jews of Europe. rev. ed. LC 78-71294. 1979. pap. 4.95 (ISBN 0-8052-5006-9, Pub. by Holocaust Library). Schocken.

--The History of Anti-Semitism: From the Time of Christ to the Court Jews. Howard, Richard, tr. LC 65-10228. (Illus.). 340p. 1974. pap. 5.95 o.p. (ISBN 0-8052-0443-1). Schocken.

--The History of Anti-Semitism, Vol.IV: Suicidal Europe, Eighteen-Seventy-Nineteen Thirty-Three. (Anti-Semitism Ser.). 528p. 1983. 17.50 (ISBN 0-8149-0863-2). Vanguard.

Poliakov, Leon & Sabille, Jacques. Jews under the Italian Occupation. LC 81-22202. (Illus.). 208p. 1983. Repr. of 1955 ed. 23.50x (ISBN 0-86527-344-8). Fertig.

Poliakova, Liudmila V. Soviet Music. Shartse, Olga, ed. Danko, Xena, tr. LC 78-66920. (Encore Music Editions Ser.). (Illus.). 1980. Repr. of 1961 ed. cancelled o.p. (ISBN 0-88355-757-6). Hyperion Conn.

Policano, Dominick J. Letter of Credit Guidebook. LC 81-66568. (Illus., Orig.). 1983. pap. 38.00 (ISBN 0-9606022-0-8). Exec Ed Pr.

Policastro, N. C. The Passion, the Pathos, & the Romances of Dr. Annuziato. LC 79-62926. 96p. 1979. 6.95 o.p. (ISBN 0-533-04221-6). Vantage.

Police Foundation. Progress in Policing: Essays on Change. Staufenberger, Richard A., ed. 176p. 1980. prof ref 19.50x (ISBN 0-88410-843-0); pap. 9.95 (ISBN 0-88410-395-1). Ballinger Pub.

Polich, J. Michael & Armor, David J. The Course of Alcoholism: Four Years After Treatment. Braiker, Harriet B., ed. LC 80-24316. (Personality Processes Ser.). 334p. 1981. 31.95x (ISBN 0-471-08682-7, Pub. by Wiley-Interscience). Wiley.

Polikoff, Alexander. Housing the Poor: The Case for Heroism. LC 77-11869. 240p. 1977. prof ref 18.50x (ISBN 0-88410-665-9). Ballinger Pub.

Polikoff, Judy. Every Loving Gift: How a Family's Courage Saved a Special Child. 256p. 1983. 14.95 (ISBN 0-399-12783-6). Putnam.

Polimeni, Ralph S., jt. auth. see Cashin, James.

Polin, Claire C. Music of the Ancient Near East. LC 73-20879. (Illus.). 138p. 1974. Repr. of 1954 ed. lib. bdg. 16.00x (ISBN 0-8371-5796-X, PONE). Greenwood.

Polin, Glenn, ed. Will Someone Please Tell Me What an Apple Can Do. (Orig.). 1982. pap. text ed. 12.95 (ISBN 0-88408-152-4). Sterling Swift.

Poling, Carol. Apple II Word Processing. DeVoney, Chris & Hedrick, Marshall, eds. 250p. 1982. 19.95 (ISBN 0-88022-014-7). Que Corp.

Poling, Mitch. Electric Powered Model Aircraft Handbook. Angle, Burr, ed. (Illus., Orig.). 1983. pap. price not set (ISBN 0-89024-050-7). Kalmbach.

Polisensky, J. V. The Thirty Years War. Evans, Robert, tr. 1971. 36.50x (ISBN 0-520-01868-0). U of Cal Pr.

--War & Society in Europe, 1618-1648. LC 77-71423. (Illus.). 1978. 39.50 (ISBN 0-521-21659-1). Cambridge U Pr.

Polisensky, Josef. Aristocrats & the Crowd in the Revolutionary Year Eighteen Forty-Eight: A Contribution to the History of Revolution & Counter-Revolution. Snider, Frederick, tr. LC 79-14765. 1980. 44.50x (ISBN 0-87395-398-3); pap. 14.95x (ISBN 0-87395-424-6). State U NY Pr.

Polish Academy of Sciences, Institute of Mathematics, ed. Spectral Theory, Vol. 8. (Banach Center Publications). 603p. 1982. 55.00 (ISBN 83-01-01495-4). Intl Pubns Serv.

Polish, Daniel F., jt. ed. see Fisher, Eugene J.

Polisky, M. K. & Meehan, J. Solving Business Problems on the Electronic Calculator. 2nd ed. 256p. 1982. text ed. 8.96 (ISBN 0-07-041281-2); tchr's manual & key 3.00 (ISBN 0-07-041282-0). McGraw.

Polit, Denise & Hungler, Bernadette P. Nursing Research: Principles & Methods. LC 78-18493. 1978. text ed. 19.95 o.p. (ISBN 0-397-54220-8, Lippincott Nursing). Lippincott.

Politaske, Daniel. Music. 2nd ed. 1979. 21.95 (ISBN 0-13-607556-8); study guide & wkbk. 8.95 (ISBN 0-13-607564-9); records set 18.95 (ISBN 0-13-607580-0). P-H.

Politella, Dario. Directory of the College Student Press in America: 1977-78. 4th ed. 1978. 25.00 o.p. (ISBN 0-917460-02-2). Oxbridge Comm.

Politics & Power Editorial Board. Politics & Power Four: Law, Politics & Justice. (Politics & Power Ser.). 260p. (Orig.). 1982. pap. 17.50 (ISBN 0-7100-0984-4). Routledge & Kegan.

Politiek, R. D. & Bakker, J. J., eds. Livestock Production in Europe: Perspectives & Prospects. (Developments in Animal & Veterinary Sciences Ser.: No. 8). 354p. 1982. 58.25 (ISBN 0-444-42105-X). Elsevier.

Politz, Edward A., Jr. Empire State. 448p. 1983. 15.95 (ISBN 0-02-597960-4). Macmillan.

Politzer, Heinz. Franz Kafka: Parable & Paradox. rev. & enl. ed. LC 62-20733. (Illus.). 432p. (YA) (gr. 9-12). 1966. 25.00x o.p. (ISBN 0-8014-0341-3); pap. 6.95x (ISBN 0-8014-9022-7, CP22). Cornell U Pr.

Politzer, R., et al. France: une Tapisserie. 1965. text ed. 12.20 o.p. (ISBN 0-07-050382-6, W); tchrs' ed. 9.60 o.p. (ISBN 0-07-050383-4); tests 56.00 o.p. (ISBN 0-07-050391-5). McGraw.

Politzer, Robert, et al. La France: une Tapisserie. 2nd ed. (Illus.). 496p. 1972. text ed. 24.04 (ISBN 0-07-050384-2, W); instructor's manual 3.36 (ISBN 0-07-050385-0); tapes 491.08 (ISBN 0-07-097890-5); tests 85.76 (ISBN 0-07-050387-7). McGraw.

Politzer, Robert L. Active Review of German: A German Review Grammar. LC 82-15208. 240p. 1983. Repr. of 1971 ed. write for info. (ISBN 0-89874-496-2). Krieger.

--Teaching French: An Introduction to Applied Linguistics. 2nd ed. LC 65-14561. 1965. text ed. 20.95x (ISBN 0-471-00430-8). Wiley.

--Workbook to Accompany Active Review of German. 108p. pap. text ed. 7.95 (ISBN 0-686-84495-5). Krieger.

Politzer, Robert L. & Hagiwara, Michio P. Active Review of French: Selected Patterns, Vocabulary & Pronunciation Problems for Speakers of English. LC 63-155633. 1963. pap. 21.95x (ISBN 0-471-00438-3); tapes 3.00 (ISBN 0-471-00439-1). Wiley.

Polivka, Raymond P. & Pakin, Sandra. APL: The Language & Its Usage. (Illus.). 496p. 1975. 29.95 (ISBN 0-13-038885-8); solutions manual 4.95 (ISBN 0-13-039008-9). P-H.

Polivy, Janet & Herman, Peter. Breaking the Diet Habit: The Natural Weight Alternative. 256p. 1983. 16.50 (ISBN 0-465-00754-6). Basic.

Polk, Anthony, jt. auth. see Spence, Gerry L.

Polk, Cara S. Her Mother's Daughter. 544p. 1982. 13.95 (ISBN 0-517-54727-9). Crown.

Polk, Edwin, jt. auth. see Polk, Ralph W.

Polk, James K. The Camelia Caper. 1978. 7.95 o.p. (ISBN 0-533-03175-3). Vantage.

Polk, Mary. The Way We Were. LC 62-17309. 1962. 7.95 (ISBN 0-910244-28-6). Blair.

Polk, Noel, ed. see Faulkner, William.

Polk, Ralph W. & Polk, Edwin. Practice of Printing. rev. ed. (Illus.). (gr. 9-12). 1971. text ed. 17.28 (ISBN 0-87002-101-X); 4.12 (ISBN 0-87002-029-3). Bennett IL.

Polk, William R. The Elusive Peace: The Middle East in the Twentieth Century. LC 79-16393. 1979. 18.95x (ISBN 0-312-24383-9). St Martin.

Polking, Kirk. Let's Go on the Half Moon with Henry Hudson. (Building America Ser.). (Illus.). (gr. 3-7). 1964. PLB 4.29 o.p. (ISBN 0-399-60372-7). Putnam Pub Group.

Polking, Kirk, ed. The Writer's Encyclopedia. 480p. 1983. 19.95 (ISBN 0-89879-103-0). Writers Digest.

Polkingharn, Anne T. & Toohey, Catherine. Creative Encounters: Activities to Expand Children's Responses to Literature. 120p. 1983. lib. bdg. 15.00 (ISBN 0-87287-371-4). Libs Unl.

Polkinghorne, J. C. Models of High Energy Processes. LC 79-296. (Monographs on Mathematical Physics). (Illus.). 1980. 32.50 (ISBN 0-521-22369-5). Cambridge U Pr.

Polkinghorne, Ruby K. Weaving & Other Pleasant Occupations. LC 71-143640. 1971. Repr. of 1940 ed. 34.00x (ISBN 0-8103-3659-6). Gale.

Pollack, ed. Material Science & Metallurgy. 3rd ed. 1980. text ed. 22.95 (ISBN 0-8359-4280-5); solutions manual avail. (ISBN 0-8359-4282-1). Reston.

Pollack, Alan, jt. auth. see Guillemin, Victor.

Pollack, Ervin H., ed. The Brandeis Reader: The Life & Contributions of Mr. Justice Louis D. Brandeis. LC 56-12251. (Docket Ser.: Vol. 7). 256p. 1956. pap. 2.50 (ISBN 0-379-11307-4). Oceana.

Pollack, Erwin & Menacker, Julius. Spanish-Speaking Students & Guidance. (Guidance Monograph). 1971. pap. 2.40 o.p. (ISBN 0-395-12439-5). HM.

Pollack, Herman. Manufacturing & Machine Tool Operations. 2nd ed. (Illus.). 1979. ref. 24.95 (ISBN 0-13-555771-2). P-H.

--Tool Design. (Illus.). 528p. 1976. 22.95 (ISBN 0-87909-840-6); solutions manual o.p. avail. Reston.

Pollack, Irving M., jt. ed. see Fabozzi, Frank J.

Pollack, Jonathan. Security, Strategy, & the Logic of Chinese Foreign Policy. (Research Papers & Policy Studies (Rpps): No. 5). 80p. 1982. 5.00x (ISBN 0-912966-34-3). IEAS.

Pollack, Jonathan D., jt. ed. see Marwah, Onkar.

Pollack, Martin, ed. Illinois Media Directory. LC 82-71390. 150p. (Orig.). 1982. pap. 50.00 (ISBN 0-936836-04-0). Alliance Pubs.

Pollack, Martin, ed. see Danion, Boots.

Pollack, Morris & Geist, Harry. Structured COBOL Programming. 340p. (Orig.). 1982. pap. text ed. 19.95 (ISBN 0-672-97690-0). Bobbs.

Pollack, Oliver B. Empires in Collision: Anglo-Burmese Relations in the Mid-Nineteenth Century. LC 78-75239. (Contributions in Comparative Colonial Studies: No. 1). (Illus.). 1980. lib. bdg. 29.95 (ISBN 0-313-20824-7, PEC/). Greenwood.

Pollack, Rachel. Golden Vanity. (Orig.). 1980. pap. 1.95 o.p. (ISBN 0-425-04483-1). Berkley Pub.

Pollack, Richard & Sloane, Irving. Guitar Repair: A Manual of Repair for Guitars & Fretted Instruments. 1973. 17.95 (ISBN 0-525-12002-5, 01743-520). Dutton.

Pollack, Richard, ed. Stop the Presses, I Want to Get off. 337p. 1976. pap. 3.95 o.s.i. (ISBN 0-440-58051-X, Delta). Dell.

Pollack, Seymour, ed. Identifying Dangerous Persons for Legal Purposes. LC 81-48485. 1982. 7.95x (ISBN 0-87589-910-2, MHS-16). Jossey-Bass.

--Studies in Computer Science. (MAA Studies in Mathematics: No. 22). 200p. 1982. text ed. write for info. (ISBN 0-88385-124-5). Math Assn.

Pollack, Seymour V. Structured FORTRAN 77 Programming for Hewlett-Packard Computers. (Boyd & Fraser Computer Science Ser.). 512p. (Orig.). 1983. pap. text ed. 17.95 (ISBN 0-87835-130-2). Boyd & Fraser.

Pollack, Simon R. Jewish Wit for All Occasions. LC 79-65341. 192p. (Orig.). 1979. pap. 5.95 o.s.i. (ISBN 0-89104-153-2, A & W Visual Library). A & W Pubs.

Pollack-Latham, Christine L. & Canobbio, Mary M. Current Concepts in Cardiac Care. LC 82-6831. 234p. 1982. 28.50 (ISBN 0-89443-659-7). Aspen Systems.

Pollak, Felix. Say When. (Chapbk Ser.). 1979. pap. 3.00 (ISBN 0-685-84498-6). Juniper Pr WI.

--Subject to Change. (William N. Judson Ser: No. 8). 10.00 (ISBN 0-685-88250-0); pap. 4.50 (ISBN 0-685-88251-9). Juniper Pr WI.

Pollak, G., ed. Algebraic Theory of Semigroups. (Colloquia Mathematica Societatis Janos Bolyai Ser.: Vol. 20). 1979. 102.25 (ISBN 0-444-85282-4, North Holland). Elsevier.

Pollak, Karen, jt. auth. see Pollak, Oliver B.

Pollak, Margaret. Adaptive Development. (Studies in Developmental Pediatrics Ser: Vol. 3). 240p. 1981. text ed. cancelled (ISBN 0-88416-380-6). Wright-PSG.

--Nine Years Old. 196p. 1979. text ed. 29.95 o.p. (ISBN 0-8391-1490-7). Univ Park.

Pollak, Michael, jt. auth. see Nelkin, Dorothy.

Pollak, Oliver B. & Pollak, Karen. Theses & Dissertations on Southern Africa: An International Bibliography. (Ser. Seventy). 1976. lib. bdg. 18.00 o.p. (ISBN 0-8161-7863-1, Hall Reference). G K Hall.

Pollak, Otto & Kelley, Nancy L. The Challenges of Aging. LC 80-27600. 144p. 1982. 9.95 (ISBN 0-88427-045-9, Dist. by Everest Hse). North River.

Pollakowski, Henry O. Urban Housing Markets & Residential Location. LC 78-20609. 160p. 1981. 19.95x (ISBN 0-669-02773-1). Lexington Bks.

Polland. Sabrina. 1978. 9.95 o.s.i. (ISBN 0-440-07893-8). Delacorte.

Polland, Arthur, ed. Thackeray: Vanity Fair. 1981. pap. 20.00x (ISBN 0-686-97814-5, Pub. by Macmillan England). State Mutual Bk.

Polland, Barbara. Grandma & Grandpa Are Special People. 1983. pap. 7.95 (ISBN 0-89087-343-7). Celestial Arts.

Polland, Barbara K. The Sensible Book: A Celebration of Your Five Senses. LC 73-21782. (ps). 1973. pap. 5.95 o.s.i. (ISBN 0-912310-53-7). Celestial Arts.

Polland, Madeleine A. All Their Kingdoms. 1981. 11.95 o.s.i. (ISBN 0-440-00019-X). Delacorte.

Pollard, A. Process Control. 1971. pap. text ed. 17.50x o.p. (ISBN 0-435-72561-0). Heinemann Ed.

Pollard, A. H. An Introduction to the Mathematics of Finance. rev. ed. 1978. pap. 10.00 (ISBN 0-08-021796-6). Pergamon.

Pollard, A. H., et al. Demographic Techniques. 161p. 1974. 23.00 o.p. (ISBN 0-08-017378-0). Pergamon.

Pollard, A. W., ed. English Miracle Plays, Moralities & Interludes: Specimens of the Pre-Elizabethan Drama. 8th ed. 1979. pap. 15.95x o.p. (ISBN 0-19-871098-4). Oxford U Pr.

Pollard, Alfred W. Shakespeare Folios & Quartos: A Study in the Bibliography of Shakespeare's Plays, 1594-1685. LC 72-114087. (Illus.). 1970. Repr. of 1909 ed. 25.00x (ISBN 0-8154-0322-4). Cooper Sq.

Pollard, B. R., jt. auth. see Gibson, W. M.

Pollard, D. E., jt. auth. see Tung, P. C.

Pollard, David E. A Chinese Look at Literature: The Literary Values of Chou Tso-Jen in Relation to the Tradition. 1974. 30.00x (ISBN 0-520-02409-5). U of Cal Pr.

Pollard, Frank. Keeping Face. 1983. 3.25 (ISBN 0-8054-5216-8). Broadman.

Pollard, Harold R. Trends in Management Thinking, 1960-1970. 331p. 1978. 14.95 o.p. (ISBN 0-87201-880-6). Gulf Pub.

Pollard, Hugh M. Pioneers of Popular Education: 1760-1850. LC 73-20922. 297p. 1974. Repr. of 1956 ed. lib. bdg. 17.50x (ISBN 0-8371-5871-0, POPP). Greenwood.

Pollard, J. H. A Handbook of Numerical & Statistical Techniques. LC 76-27908. (Illus.). 1977. 49.50 (ISBN 0-521-21440-8); pap. 18.95 (ISBN 0-521-29750-8). Cambridge U Pr.

--Mathematical Models for the Growth of Human Populations. LC 72-91957. 204p. 1973. 32.50 (ISBN 0-521-20111-X); pap. 10.95x (ISBN 0-521-29442-8). Cambridge U Pr.

Pollard, J. H., jt. auth. see Benjamin, B.

Pollard, J. H., jt. auth. see Hossack, I. B.

Pollard, Jack. Lawn Bowls the Australian Way. (Illus.). 17.50x (ISBN 0-392-03677-0, ABC). Sportshelf.

Pollard, Marie B. Growing Child in Contemporary Society. 1969. text ed. 8.95 o.p. (ISBN 0-02-825900-9). Glencoe.

Pollard, Morris, ed. Perspectives in Virology: The Gustav Stern Symposium, Vol. 10. LC 77-84126. (The Gustav Stern Symposium Ser.). 276p. 1978. 34.50 (ISBN 0-89004-214-4). Raven.

Pollard, Sidney. Development of the British Economy: 1914-1967. 2nd ed. LC 71-82436. 1969. 17.95 o.p. (ISBN 0-312-19670-9). St Martin.

--European Economic Integration: 1815-1970. (Illus.). 180p. (Orig.). 1974. pap. text ed. 9.95 o.p. (ISBN 0-15-524743-3, HC). HarBraceJ.

--European Economic Integration 1815-1970. Barraclough, Geoffrey, ed. (Library of European Civilization Ser.). (Illus.). 180p. 1974. 8.75 o.s.i. (ISBN 0-500-32031-4). Transatlantic.

--Integration of the European Economy Since 1815. (Studies on Contemporary Europe: No. 4). 96p. 1981. text ed. 17.95x (ISBN 0-04-336069-6); pap. text ed. 6.95x (ISBN 0-04-336070-X). Allen Unwin.

Pollard, Sidney & Holmes, Colin. Documents of European Economic History, 3 vols. Incl. Vol. 1. Process of Industrialization: 1750-1870. 1969 (ISBN 0-312-21525-8); Vol. 2. Industrial Power & National Rivalry: 1870-1914. 1972 (ISBN 0-312-21560-6); Vol. 3. The End of the Old Europe: 1914-1939. 1973 (ISBN 0-312-21595-9). LC 68-10751. 32.50. St Martin.

Pollard, Sidney, ed. The Gold Standard & Employment Policies Between the Wars. (Debates in Economic History Ser.). 1970. pap. 9.95x (ISBN 0-416-29950-4). Methuen Inc.

Pollard, Spencer D., ed. see National Academy of Arbitrators-14th Annual Meeting.

Pollard, T. E. Fullness of Humanity: Christ's Humanness & Ours. 128p. 1982. text ed. 19.95x (ISBN 0-907459-10-2, Pub. by Almond Pr England); pap. text ed. 9.95x (ISBN 0-907459-11-0, Pub. by Almond Pr England). Eisenbrauns.

Pollay, Richard W., ed. Information Sources in Advertising History. LC 78-75259. 1979. lib. bdg. 35.00 (ISBN 0-313-21422-0, PIA/). Greenwood.

Poller, Nidra. Eggs As Usual Breakfast...Etc. (Illus.). 26p. (gr. 2 up). 1980. PLB 10.00 stiched binding (ISBN 0-686-68704-3). Lawrence Hill.

Pollet, J. V., ed. Julius Pflug: Correspondance. (Suppl.). (Illus.). vi, 316p. 1982. write for info (ISBN 90-04-06752-3). E J Brill.

Polletta, Gregory T. Intention & Choice: The Character of Prose. (Orig.). 1967. pap. text ed. 4.50 (ISBN 0-685-19736-0). Phila Bk Co.

Polley, Joseph. Applied Real Estate Math. 2nd ed. (Illus.). 256p. 1980. pap. text ed. 14.95 (ISBN 0-8359-0252-8); instrs.' manual avail. (ISBN 0-8359-0253-6). Reston.

Polley, Maxine. Dance Aerobics: Two. 160p. 1983. pap. 6.95 (ISBN 0-89037-256-X). Anderson World.

Polley, Rainer. Anton Friedrich Justus Thibaut (AD 1772-1840) In Seinen Selbstzeugnissen und Briefen. 1095p. (Ger.). 1982. write for info. (ISBN 3-8204-6039-X). P Lang Pubs.

Pollin, Burton. Music for Shelley's Poetry. LC 74-4446. (Music Reprint Ser.). 174p. 1974. lib. bdg. 22.50 (ISBN 0-306-70640-7). Da Capo.

Pollin, Burton R. Dictionary of Names & Titles in Poe's Collected Works. LC 68-28982. (Paperback Ser.). 1968. pap. 22.50 (ISBN 0-306-71154-0). Da Capo.

--Poe, Creator of Words. rev. & augmented ed. LC 80-51588. 96p. 1980. 11.00x (ISBN 0-935164-04-9). N T Smith.

Pollin, Burton R., ed. The Imaginary Voyages: In the Collected Works of Edgar Allen Poe. (Critical Editions Program). 1981. lib. bdg. 50.00 (ISBN 0-8057-8534-5, Twayne). G K Hall.

Pollin, Burton R., ed. see Godwin, William.

Pollio, H. R., et al. Psychology & the Poetics of Growth: Figurative Language in Psychology, Psychotherapy, & Education. LC 77-9880. 1977. 16.50x o.s.i. (ISBN 0-470-99158-5). Halsted Pr.

Pollio, Howard. Behavior & Existence: An Introduction to Empirical Humanistic Psychology. LC 81-1531. 512p. 1981. text ed. 21.95 (ISBN 0-8185-0425-0). Brooks-Cole.

Pollio, Howard R. The Psychology of Symbolic Activity. LC 72-1943. 1974. text ed. 22.95 (ISBN 0-201-05851-0). A-W.

Pollis, Adamantia & Schwab, Peter, eds. Human Rights: Cultural & Ideological Perspectives. LC 78-19771. (Praeger Special Studies). 1979. 25.95 o.p. (ISBN 0-03-046631-8); pap. 11.95 o.p. (ISBN 0-03-057717-9). Praeger.

Pollis, Adamantis, jt. auth. see Pinkele, Carl F.

Pollitt, Ernesto & Leibel, Rudolph, eds. Iron Deficiency, Brain Biochemistry & Behavior. 229p. 1982. text ed. 28.50 (ISBN 0-89004-690-5). Raven.

Pollitt, J. J. Art & Experience in Classical Greece. LC 74-160094. (Illus.). 1972. 34.50 (ISBN 0-521-08065-7); pap. 9.95x (ISBN 0-521-09662-6). Cambridge U Pr.

Pollitz, Edward. The Scorpion's Sting. (Orig.). 1983. pap. 3.50 (ISBN 0-440-17872-X). Dell.

Pollnac, R. B., jt. ed. see Poggie, J. J., Jr.

Pollnac, Richard B. Sociocultural Aspects of Developing Small-Scale Fisheries: Delivering Services to the Poor. (Working Paper: No. 490). iii, 61p. 1981. 5.00 (ISBN 0-686-36058-3, WP-0490). World Bank.

Pollock, Algernon J. La Paz Con Dios. 2nd ed. Mahecha, Alberto, ed. Bautista, SAra, tr. from Eng. (La Serie Diamante). 48p. (Span.). 1982. pap. 0.85 (ISBN 0-942504-09-7). Overcomer Pr.

Pollock, Algernon J. & Bennett, Gordon H. El Pecado Despues de la Conversion. 2nd ed. Bautista, Sara, tr. from Eng. (La Serie Diamante). 36p. (Span.). 1982. pap. 0.85 (ISBN 0-942504-04-6). Overcomer Pr.

Pollock, Bruce. A Man's Guide to Housework. (Illus.). 32p. 1982. pap. 1.25 (ISBN 0-88009-022-7). OUP.

Pollock, Carroll W. Communicate What You Mean: Grammar for High Level ESL. 224p. 1982. pap. text ed. 10.95 (ISBN 0-13-153486-6). P-H.

Pollock, D. J., jt. auth. see Fookes, P. J.

Pollock, D. S. The Algebra of Econometrics. 360p. 1979. 69.95 (ISBN 0-471-99753-6, Pub. by Wiley-Interscience). Wiley.

Pollock, Dale. George Lucas: A Biography. (Illus.). 1983. pap. 8.95 o.p. (ISBN 0-686-82045-2, Harmony). Crown.

--Skywalking: The Life & Films of George Lucas. 1983. 14.95 (ISBN 0-517-54677-9, Harmony). Crown.

Pollock, David A. Methods of Electronic Audio Surveillance. (Illus.). 418p. 1979. 28.00x (ISBN 0-398-02382-4). C C Thomas.

Pollock, David H., jt. ed. see Ritter, Archibald R.

Pollock, E. O., jt. auth. see Howard, B. D.

Pollock, Edward & Maitland, Frederic W. History of English Law Before the Time of Edward First, 2 vols. Vol. 1. pap. 29.95 (ISBN 0-521-09515-8); Vol. 1. 59.00 (ISBN 0-521-07062-7); Vol. 2. pap. 29.95x (ISBN 0-521-09516-6). Cambridge U Pr.

Pollock, Frederick. Expansion of the Common Law. vii, 164p. 1974. Repr. of 1904 ed. lib. bdg. 15.00x o.p. (ISBN 0-8377-2503-8). Rothman.

Pollock, George H., jt. ed. see Gedo, John E.

Pollock, Griselda. Mary Cassatt. LC 79-1914. (Illus.). 104p. 1980. 19.18i (ISBN 0-06-013348-1, HarpT). Har-Row.

Pollock, Ian. Beware of the Cat. LC 77-82688. (Illus.). 1977. pap. 2.95 o.p. (ISBN 0-8467-0385-8, Pub. by Two Continents). Hippocrene Bks.

--Unmarried Couples. (Illus., Orig.). 1978. pap. 3.95 o.p. (ISBN 0-8467-0521-4, Pub. by Two Continents). Hippocrene Bks.

Pollock, J. G. Topical Reviews in Vascular Surgery, Vol. 1. (Illus.). 240p. 1982. text ed. 32.50 (ISBN 0-7236-0575-0). Wright-PSG.

Pollock, Jackson. The Last Sketchbook. 1982. 500.00. Johnson Repr.

Pollock, John. Apostle. Orig. Title: Man Who Shook the World. 244p. 1972. pap. 5.95 (ISBN 0-88207-233-1). Victor Bks.

--Wilberforce. LC 77-86525. (Illus.). 1978. 22.50x (ISBN 0-312-87942-3). St Martin.

Pollock, M., ed. Common Denominators in Art & Science. 220p. 1983. 27.00 (ISBN 0-08-028457-4). Pergamon.

Pollock, Michael L. & Schmidt, Donald H. Heart Disease & Rehabilitation. 725p. 1979. 55.00 (ISBN 0-471-09492-7, Pub. by Wiley Med). Wiley.

Pollock, Michael L., et al. Health & Fitness Through Physical Activity. LC 78-495. (College of Sports Medicine Ser.). 1978. text ed. 22.95x (ISBN 0-471-69285-9). Wiley.

Pollock, Norman H. The Struggle Against Sleeping Sickness in Nyasaland & Northern Rhodesia. (Papers in International Studies: Africa: No. 5). 1969. pap. 3.00 (ISBN 0-89680-039-3, Ohio U Ctr Intl). Ohio U Pr.

Pollock, Penny. Ants Don't Get Sunday Off. LC 78-8283. (See & Read Storybooks). (Illus.). (gr. 1-4). 1978. PLB 6.99 (ISBN 0-399-61129-0). Putnam Pub Group.

--Garlanda: The Ups & Downs of an Uppity Teapot. (Illus.). 80p. (gr. 2-6). 1980. 7.95 o.p. (ISBN 0-399-20713-9). Putnam Pub Group.

--Keeping it Secret. (Illus.). 112p. 1982. 8.95 (ISBN 0-399-20934-4). Putnam Pub Group.

--The Slug Who Thought He Was a Snail. Cauley, Lorinda B., tr. (See & Read Bks.). (Illus.). 48p. (gr. 1-3). 1980. PLB 6.29 (ISBN 0-399-61147-9). Putnam Pub Group.

--The Spit Bug Who Couldn't Spit. (Illus.). 48p. 1982. PLB 6.99 (ISBN 0-399-61152-5). Putnam Pub Group.

Pollock, Robert W. The Education of a Country Doctor. 1978. 8.95 o.p. (ISBN 0-533-02996-1). Vantage.

Pollock, Ross, jt. auth. see David, Paul T.

Pollock, Sandy. Alternative Careers for Teachers. 128p. 1979. 8.95 (ISBN 0-916782-16-6). Impact VA.

Pollock, Susan, jt. auth. see Chamberlin, Susan.

Pollock, Ted. Managing Others Creatively. 1974. pap. 4.50 o.p. (ISBN 0-8015-4854-3, Hawthorn). Dutton.

--Managing Yourself Creatively. 1974. pap. 4.95 o.p. (ISBN 0-8015-4860-8, Hawthorn). Dutton.

Pollowy, Anne-Marie. The Urban Nest. LC 76-22583. (Community Development Ser: Vol. 26). (Illus.). 1977. 25.00 o.p. (ISBN 0-87933-235-2). Hutchinson Ross.

Polmar, Norman. Russian Bombers. (Illus.). 250p. Date not set. 19.95 (ISBN 0-933852-26-6). Nautical & Aviation. Postponed.

Polnac, Lennis R. & Wilkerson, Geroge J. Writing with Aims & Modes. 1978. pap. text ed. 5.95 (ISBN 0-88408-090-0). Sterling Swift.

Polnauer, Josef, ed. see Webern, Anton.

Polnay, Peter De see De Polnay, Peter.

Polner, Murray. American Jewish Biographies. (Illus.). 500p. 1982. 39.95x (ISBN 0-87196-462-7). Facts on File.

Polo, J. Regino Perez see Perez-Polo, J. Regino & De Vellis, Jean.

Polo, Marco. The Travels of Marco Polo. Latham, Ronald, tr. from Fr. (Illus.). 318p. 1982. 35.00x (ISBN 0-89835-058-1). Abaris Bks.

--The Travels of Marco Polo. 1982. Repr. lib. bdg. 18.95x (ISBN 0-89967-045-8). Harmony Raine.

Poloma, Margaret M. The Charismatic Movement: Is There a New Pentecost? (Social Movements: Past & Present Ser.). 1982. lib. bdg. 17.95 (ISBN 0-8057-9701-7, Twayne). G K Hall.

--Contemporary Sociological Theory. 1979. pap. 13.95 (ISBN 0-02-396100-7). Macmillan.

Polome, Edgar C. Language, Society, & Paleoculture. Dil, Anwar S., ed. LC 82-80925. (Language Science & National Development Ser.). 488p. 1982. 20.00x (ISBN 0-8047-1149-6). Stanford U Pr.

Polon, Linda & Cantwell, Aileen. Making Kids Click: Language Arts. LC 78-19203. 1979. pap. text ed. 11.95 o.p. (ISBN 0-673-16392-X). Scott F.

--The Whole Earth Holiday Book. 1983. pap. text ed. 12.95 (ISBN 0-673-16585-X). Scott F.

--Write Up a Storm. LC 78-18528. 1979. pap. text ed. 11.95x (ISBN 0-673-16154-4). Scott F.

Polonovski, J. Cholesterol Metabolism & Lipolytic Enzymes. (Illus.). 218p. 1977. 34.75x (ISBN 0-89352-010-1). Masson Pub.

Polonsky, Abraham. Zenia's Way. 1980. 12.45i (ISBN 0-690-01896-7). Har-Row.

--Zenia's Way. LC 79-24884. 288p. 1980. 12.45i (ISBN 0-690-01896-7). T Y Crowell.

Polos, Nicholas C. John Swett: California's Frontier Schoolmaster. LC 78-69836. (Illus.). 1978. pap. text ed. 11.25 (ISBN 0-8191-0580-5). U Pr of Amer.

Pols, Edward. The Acts of Our Being: A Reflection on Agency & Responsibility. LC 81-16319. 256p. 1982. lib. bdg. 20.00x (ISBN 0-87023-354-8). U of Mass Pr.

Polsby, N. W., jt. auth. see Greenstein, F. I.

Polsby, Nelson. Congress & the Presidency. 3rd ed. 192p. 1976. pap. text ed. 10.95 (ISBN 0-13-167692-X). P-H.

--Consequences of Party Reform. (Illus.). 275p. 1983. 24.95 (ISBN 0-19-503234-9, GB736, GB); pap. 8.95 (ISBN 0-19-503315-9). Oxford U Pr.

Polsby, Nelson W., ed. The Modern Presidency. LC 81-40776. 250p. 1981. pap. text ed. 10.75 (ISBN 0-8191-1822-2). U Pr of Amer.

--Reapportionment in the 1970s. LC 73-142046. (Institute of Governmental Studies, UC Berkely). 1971. 36.00x (ISBN 0-520-01885-0). U of Cal Pr.

--What If...? A Selection of Social-Science Fiction. 224p. 1982. 12.95 (ISBN 0-86616-018-3). Greene.

Polsky, Howard W. Cottage Six: Social System of Delinquent Boys in Residential Treatment. LC 76-50144. (Illus.). 192p. 1977. pap. text ed. 7.50 (ISBN 0-88275-475-0). Krieger.

Polsky, Howard W., jt. auth. see Bakal, Yitzhak.

Polsky, Samuel, ed. Medico-Legal Reader. LC 56-12250. (Temple University Studies in Law & Medicine). 256p. 1956. 15.00 (ISBN 0-379-11306-6); pap. 2.50 (ISBN 0-686-96822-0). Oceana.

Polson, Archer. Law & Lawyers or: Sketches & Illustrations of Legal History & Biography, 2 Vols. (Illus.). 1982. Repr. of 1840 ed. lib. bdg. 57.50x (ISBN 0-8377-1013-8). Rothman.

Polson, Jim G. Handbook of Farm & Ranch Estate Planning. 270p. 1982. 39.95 (ISBN 0-13-377952-1, Busn). P-H.

Polston, Don. Be More Than You Are. LC 77-75404. (Orig.). pap. 3.95 (ISBN 0-89081-071-0). Harvest Hse.

Polt, John H. Gaspar Melchor de Jovellanos. (World Authors Ser.). 1971. lib. bdg. 15.95 (ISBN 0-8057-2476-1, Twayne). G K Hall.

Poltarnees, Welleran. Further up & Further in. Date not set. pap. price not set o.s.i. (ISBN 0-914676-03-2, Star Eleph Bks). Green Tiger Pr.

--Kay Nielsen: An Appreciation. (Illus.). 40p. 1976. pap. 12.50 (ISBN 0-914676-02-4, Star & Eleph Bks). Green Tiger Pr.

Polti, Georges. Thirty-Six Dramatic Situations. 1921. 8.95 (ISBN 0-87116-109-5). Writer.

Poltrack, D. P. Television Marketing: Network, Local & Cable. 384p. 1983. 27.50 (ISBN 0-07-050406-7). McGraw.

Poluga, Charles, jt. auth. see Auvil, Daniel L.

Polunin, Nicholas, ed. see International Conference on Environment Future, 2nd.

Polunin, Oleg. Flowers of Europe: A Field Guide. 1969. 50.00x (ISBN 0-19-217621-8). Oxford U Pr.

Polvay, Marina. All Along the Danube: Classic Cookery from the Great Cuisines of Eastern Europe. (Creative Cooking Ser.). (Illus.). 1980. 19.95 o.p. (ISBN 0-13-022251-8, Spec); pap. 9.95 o.p. (ISBN 0-13-022244-5). P-H.

Polwhele, Eliz, jt. ed. see Milhous, Judith.

Polya, G. Vom Losen Mathematischer Aufgaben-Einsicht und Entdeckung, Lernen und Lehren, Vol. II. (Science & Civilization Ser.: No. 21). (Illus.). 286p. 1967. 39.05x (ISBN 3-7643-0298-4). Birkhauser.

Polya, G. & Szego, G. Isoperimetric Inequalities in Mathematical Physics. 1951. pap. 26.00 (ISBN 0-527-02743-X). Kraus Repr.

Polya, George. George Polya-Collected Papers, 2 vols. Boas, Ralph, ed. 1974. Vol. 1, Singularities Of Analytic Functions. 42.50x (ISBN 0-262-02104-8); Vol. 2, 1975 Location Of Zeros. 35.00x (ISBN 0-262-02103-X). MIT Pr.

--Mathematical Discovery: On Understanding, Learning, & Teaching Problem Solving. 448p. 1981. text ed. 22.95 (ISBN 0-471-08975-3). Wiley.

Polya, George & Kilpatrick, Jeremy. The Stanford Mathematics Problem Book: With Hints & Solutions. LC 73-86270. 1974. pap. text ed. 4.50x o.p. (ISBN 0-8077-2416-5). Tchrs Coll.

Polya, George & Latta, Gordon. Complex Variables. LC 73-14882. 352p. 1974. text ed. 30.50x o.p. (ISBN 0-471-69330-8). Wiley.

Polya, Gyorgy. Mathematical Discovery on Understanding, Learning & Teaching Problem Solving, 2 Vols. LC 62-8784. 1962. Vol. 1. 23.95x (ISBN 0-471-69333-2); Vol. 2. 16.95 o.p. (ISBN 0-471-69335-9). Wiley.

Polyakov, V. A., jt. auth. see Ferronsky, V. I.

Polybius. Polybius on Roman Imperialism. Bernstein, Alvin H., ed. Shuckburgh, Evelyn S., tr. LC 79-66479. 540p. (Orig.). 1980. pap. text ed. 8.50 (ISBN 0-89526-902-3). Regnery-Gateway.

Polymer Science Symposium, 67th. International Symposium on Marcomolecular Chemistry: Proceedings. Kabanov, V., ed. 207p. 1981. pap. 25.95 (ISBN 0-471-09013-1, Pub. by Wiley-Interscience). Wiley.

Polyviou, Polynos G. Equal Protection of the Laws. 759p. 1980. text ed. 55.00x (ISBN 0-7156-1399-5, Pub. by Duckworth England). Sheridan.

Polyviou, Polyvios G. Search & Seizure: Constitutional & Common Law. 391p. 1982. text ed. 55.00x (ISBN 0-7156-1592-0, Pub. by Duckworth England). Sheridan.

Polyzoides, G. History & Teachings of the Eastern Greek Orthodox Church. (Illus.). 96p. 3.20 (ISBN 0-686-83964-1). Divry.

--Stories from the New Testament. (Illus.). 112p. 3.20 (ISBN 0-686-83966-8). Divry.

--Stories from the Old Testament. (Illus.). 71p. (Gr.). 3.20 (ISBN 0-686-80434-1). Divry.

--What We See & Hear in a Greek Eastern Orthodox Church. 92p. 3.20 (ISBN 0-686-83965-X). Divry.

Polyzoides, Stefanos & Sherwood, Roger. Courtyard Housing in Los Angeles. LC 80-6057. (Illus.). 256p. 1982. 24.95 (ISBN 0-520-04251-4). U of Cal Pr.

Polzin, Robert & Rothman, Eugene, eds. The Biblical Mosaic. (Masoretic Studies). 6.75 (ISBN 0-686-96223-0, 06 06 10). Scholars Pr CA.

Polzin, Robert M. Biblical Structuralism: Method & Subjectivity in the Study of Ancient Texts. Beardslee, William A., ed. LC 76-15895. (Semeia Studies). 224p. 1977. pap. 5.95 o.p. (ISBN 0-8006-1506-9, 1-1506). Fortress.

Pomada, Elizabeth. Places to Go with Children in Northern California. rev. ed. LC 73-77335. (Illus.). 192p. 1980. pap. 4.95 o.p. (ISBN 0-87701-210-5). Chronicle Bks.

--Places to Go with Children in Northern California. LC 80-10140. (Illus.). 160p. (Orig.). 1981. pap. 5.95 (ISBN 0-87701-210-5). Chronicle Bks.

Pomaska, Anna. What's Wrong with This Picture Coloring Book. (Illus.). 48p. (Orig.). (gr. 2 up). 1983. pap. 2.25 (ISBN 0-486-24485-7). Dover.

Pomerance, Michla. Law of Self-Determination in Law & Practice. 1982. lib. bdg. 39.50 (ISBN 90-247-2594-1, Pub. by Martinus Nijhoff Netherlands). Kluwer Boston.

Pomerantz, Charlotte. Buffy & Albert. (Illus.). (gr. 1-4). 1982. 7.50 (ISBN 0-688-00920-4); PLB 6.67 (ISBN 0-688-00921-2). Greenwillow.

--If I Had a Paka: Poems in Eleven Languages. (Illus.). (ps-3). 1982. 9.50 (ISBN 0-688-00836-4); PLB 8.59 (ISBN 0-688-00837-2). Greenwillow.

Pomerantz, James, jt. ed. see Kubovy, Michael.

Pomerantz, Virginia & Schultz, Dodi. Mothers & Fathers Medical Encyclopedia. rev. ed. (Illus.). 1978. pap. 3.95 (ISBN 0-451-11798-0, AE1798, Sig). NAL.

Pomerantz, Virginia E. & Schultz, Dodie. The Mothers' & Fathers' Medical Encyclopedia. LC 76-48167. 1977. pap. 3.95 (ISBN 0-451-11798-0, Pub. by NAL). Formur Intl.

Pomeranz, F., et al. Pensions: An Accounting & Management Guide. 329p. 1976. 44.95x (ISBN 0-471-06548-X, Pub. by Wiley-Interscience). Wiley.

Pomeranz, Y. Advances in Cereal Science & Technology, Vol. II. LC 76-8695. 463p. 1978. text ed. 36.00 (ISBN 0-913250-08-2). Am Assn Cereal Chem.

Pomeranz, Y., ed. Advances in Cereal Science & Technology, Vol. IV. LC 76-615872. 352p. 1981. text ed. 36.00 (ISBN 0-913250-21-X). Am Assn Cereal Chem.

--Advances in Cereal Science & Technology, Vol. V. LC 76-645872. (Fifth Ser.). 294p. 1982. text ed. 36.00 (ISBN 0-913250-28-7). Am Assn Cereal Chem.

--Cereals: A Renewable Resource, Theory & Practice. LC 81-71369. 728p. 1982. text ed. 30.00 (ISBN 0-913250-22-8). Am Assn Cereal Chem.

Pomerleau, Cynthia S., jt. auth. see Pomerleau, Ovide F.

Pomerleau, Ovide F. & Brady, John P. Behavioral Medicine: Theory & Practice. (Illus.). 336p. 1979. 36.00 (ISBN 0-683-06957-8); pap. 22.00 (ISBN 0-683-06956-X). Williams & Wilkins.

Pomerleau, Ovide F. & Pomerleau, Cynthia S. Break the Smoking Habit: A Behavioral Program for Giving up Cigarettes. LC 77-81301. (Illus.). 1977. pap. 5.95 o.p. (ISBN 0-87822-136-0, 1360). Res Press.

Pomernacki, Charles, jt. auth. see Trost, Stanley R.

Pomernanz, Felix, et al. Auditing in the Public Sector. 1976. 54.00 (ISBN 0-88262-123-8, 75-22798). Warren.

Pomerol, Charles, et al. Geology of France. (Illus.). 256p. 1980. 28.75x (ISBN 2-225-67001-3). Masson Pub.

Pomeroy, Ruth F., ed. The Redbook Cookbook. rev. ed. LC 70-153965. (Illus.). 1050p. 1976. 12.95 o.p. (ISBN 0-448-12265-0, G&D). Putnam Pub Group.

--Redbook's Wise Woman's Diet Cookbook. 310p. 1983. 14.95 (ISBN 0-453-00436-9). NAL.

Pomeroy, Wardell B., et al. Taking a Sex History. 353p. 1982. text ed. 24.95 (ISBN 0-02-925370-5). Free Pr.

Pomiane, Edouard de. French Cooking in Ten Minutes. Hyman, Philip & Hyman, Mary, trs. (Illus.). 1978. pap. 2.95 o.p. (ISBN 0-07-016490-8, SP). McGraw.

Pomian-Srzednicki, Maciej. Religious Changes in Contemporary Poland: Secularization & Politics. (International Library of Sociology). 227p. 1982. 24.95 (ISBN 0-7100-9245-8). Routledge & Kegan.

Pommereul, Francois & Rene, Jean De. Recherches Sur L'origine De L'esclavage Religieux et Politique Du Peuple, En France. Repr. of 1783 ed. 9.50 o.p. (ISBN 0-8287-0696-4). Clearwater Pub.

Pomonis, Carolyn. Lord How Different. Hausman, Gerald, ed. LC 80-299. 128p. (Orig.). 1980. pap. 6.95 (ISBN 0-913270-85-7, Sundial Bks). Sunstone Pr.

Pompa, Leon. Vico: A Study of the New Science. LC 74-79140. 216p. 1975. 29.95 (ISBN 0-521-20584-0). Cambridge U Pr.

Pompeiano, O., jt. auth. see Brodal, A.

Pompeiano, O. & Ajmone-Marsan, C., eds. Brain Mechanisms of Perceptual Awareness & Purposeful Behavior. (IBRO Ser.: No. 8). 520p. 1982. text ed. 63.00 (ISBN 0-89004-603-4). Raven.

Pompeiano, O., ed. see IBRO Symposium, Italy, September 1978.

Pomper, Claude L. International Investment Planning: An Integrated Approach. (Studies in Mathematical & Managerial Economics: Vol. 22). 1976. 38.50 (ISBN 0-7204-0380-4, North-Holland). Elsevier.

Pomper, Gerald, jt. auth. see Baker, Ross.

Pomper, Gerald M., ed. see Kleppner, Paul.

Pomper, Gerald M., ed. see Smith, Paul A.

Pomper, Philip. Russian Revolutionary Intelligentsia. LC 75-107303. (Europe Since 1500 Ser.). 1970. pap. 7.95x (ISBN 0-88295-749-X). Harlan Davidson.

Pompilio, Raymond. Volunteers, a Portrait of Small-Town Firefighters. LC 79-11059. (Illus.). 1979. 17.95 (ISBN 0-89594-021-3); pap. 10.95 (ISBN 0-89594-018-3). Crossing Pr.

Pomraning, G. C. Radiation Hydrodynamics. 304p. 1973. text ed. write for info. (ISBN 0-08-016893-0). Pergamon.

Pomraning, Gerald C., jt. ed. see Goodjohn, Albert J.

Ponce, Charles. Papers Toward A Radical Metaphysics: Alchemy. 160p. (Orig.). 1983. 17.95 (ISBN 0-938190-02-4); pap. 8.95 (ISBN 0-938190-01-6). North Atlantic.

Pond, Grace. Cats & Kittens. 1976. pap. 5.50 o.p. (ISBN 0-7134-3247-0, Pub. by Batsford England). David & Charles.

--Persian Cats. Foyle, Christina, ed. (Foyle's Handbks). 1973. 3.95 (ISBN 0-685-55820-7). Palmetto Pub.

Pond, Grace & Sager, Angela. The Intelligent Cat. 1980. pap. 4.95 (ISBN 0-686-63017-3, Perige). Putnam Pub Group.

Pond, Grace, ed. The Complete Cat Encyclopedia. (Illus.). 352p. 1972. 20.00 (ISBN 0-517-50140-6). Crown.

Pond, Mimi. The Valley Girls Guide to Life. (Orig.). 1982. pap. 2.95 (ISBN 0-440-59334-4, Dell Trade Pbks). Dell.

Pond, Samuel A., ed. Bricker's International Directory of University Executive Development Programs: 1982. 13th ed. LC 73-110249. 1981. 90.00X (ISBN 0-9604804-1-2). Bricker's Intl.

--Bricker's International Directory of University Executive Development Programs: 1983. 14th ed. 1982. 90.00X (ISBN 0-9604804-2-0). Bricker's Intl.

Pond, Samuel A. & Bricker, George W., eds. Bricker's International Directory of University Executive Development Programs: 1981. LC 73-110249. 1980. 85.00x o.p. (ISBN 0-9604804-0-4). Bricker's Intl.

Pond, Wilson G., jt. auth. see Church, David B.

Pond, Wilson G. & Mumpton, Frederick A., eds. Zeo-Agriculture: The Use of Natural Zeolites in Agriculture & Aquaculture. 450p. 1983. lib. bdg. 50.00x (ISBN 0-86531-602-3). Westview.

Pond, Wilson G., et al, eds. Animal Agriculture: Human Needs in the 21st Century. 600p. 1980. lib. bdg. 25.00 (ISBN 0-86531-032-7). Westview.

Ponder, Catherine. Dare to Prosper. 80p. 1983. pap. 3.00 (ISBN 0-87516-511-7). De Vorss.

--The Millionaire from Nazareth. (The Millionaires of the Bible Ser.). 1979. pap. 5.50 (ISBN 0-87516-370-X). De Vorss.

--The Millionaire Joshua. LC 77-86719. (The Millionaires of the Bible Ser.). 1978. pap. 4.95 (ISBN 0-87516-253-3). De Vorss.

--The Millionaire Moses. LC 77-71459. (The Millionaires of the Bible Ser.). 1977. pap. 4.95 (ISBN 0-87516-232-0). De Vorss.

--The Millionaires of Genesis. (The Millionaires of the Bible Ser.). 1976. pap. 4.95 (ISBN 0-87516-215-0). De Vorss.

--Open your Mind to Receive. 128p. 1983. pap. 3.95 (ISBN 0-87516-507-9). De Vorss.

--The Secret of Unlimited Prosperity. 60p. 1981. pap. 3.00 (ISBN 0-87516-419-6). De Vorss.

Ponder, Winifred. Clara Butt: Her Life Story. LC 77-16530. (Music Reprint Ser.: 1978). (Illus.). 1978. Repr. of 1928 ed. lib. bdg. 29.50 (ISBN 0-306-77529-8). Da Capo.

Ponente, Nello, ed. see Modigliani, Amadeo.

Ponge, Francis. The Making of the Pre. Fahnestock, Lee, tr. from Fr. LC 77-25156. (Illus.). 240p. 1982. pap. 14.95 (ISBN 0-8262-0381-7). U of Mo Pr.

--Sun Placed in the Abyss & Other Texts. Gavronsky, Serge, tr. from Fr. LC 77-3631. 1977. pap. 5.00 (ISBN 0-915342-22-7). SUN.

Pongratz, G. Corvin Koz Nineteen Fifty-Six. 1982. 14.00 o.p. (ISBN 0-936398-14-0). Framo Pub.

Poniachek, Harvey A. Monetary Independence Under Flexible Exchange Rates. (Illus.). 224p. 1979. 21.95x (ISBN 0-669-02728-6). Lexington Bks.

Ponicsan, Darryl. An Unmarried Man. 1980. 9.95 o.s.i. (ISBN 0-440-00104-8). Delacorte.

Ponnamperuma, C., jt. ed. see Buvet, R.

Ponnamperuma, Cyril, ed. Chemical Evolution of the Early Precambrian. 1977. 26.50 (ISBN 0-12-561360-1). Acad Pr.

Ponnamperuma, Cyril & Cameron, A. G. W., eds. Interstellar Communication: Scientific Perspectives. (Illus.). 272p. 1974. pap. text ed. 15.50 (ISBN 0-395-17809-6). HM.

Ponnanbalam, Satchi. Dependent Capitalism in Crisis: The Sri Lankan Economy, 1948-1980. 233p. 1982. text ed. 37.50x (ISBN 0-7069-1837-1, Pub. by Vikas India). Advent NY.

Ponomareff, Constantin V. Sergey Esenin. (World Authors Ser.). 1978. lib. bdg. 15.95 (ISBN 0-8057-6319-8, Twayne). G K Hall.

Ponomarev, B. N., ed. International Working-Class Movement, Vol. 2. 654p. 1981. 11.50 (ISBN 0-8285-2295-2, Pub. by Progress Pubs USSR). Imported Pubns.

Ponomarev, B. N., jt. ed. see Gromyko, A. A.

Ponomarev, Boris N. Marxism-Leninism, a Flourishing Science: A Reply to Critics. Skvirsky, David & Schneierson, Vic, trs. from Rus. LC 79-14101. 1980. pap. text ed. 1.75 (ISBN 0-7178-0564-6). Intl Pub Co.

Pons, C., jt. auth. see Dechesne, B. H.

Pons, Valdo & Francis, Ray, eds. The Problems of the Contemporary City: Studies in Urban Sociology. (Sociological Review Monograph: No. 30). 1983. pap. price not set (ISBN 0-7100-9471-X). Routledge & Kegan.

Ponse, Barbara. Identities in the Lesbian World: The Social Construction of Self. LC 77-84763. (Contributions in Sociology: No. 28). 1978. lib. bdg. 25.00 (ISBN 0-8371-9889-5, PLW/). Greenwood.

Ponselle, Rosa & Drake, James A. Ponselle: A Singer's Life. LC 79-6628. (Illus.). 360p. 1982. 22.50 (ISBN 0-385-15641-3). Doubleday.

Ponsonby, Arthur. English Diaries: A Review of English Diaries from the Sixteenth to the Twentieth Century with an Introduction on Diary Writing. LC 75-152247. 1971. Repr. of 1923 ed. 38.00x (ISBN 0-8103-3711-8). Gale.

Ponsonby-Fane, Richard A. Collected Works, 6 vols. Incl. Vol. 1. Studies in Shinto & Shrines. 581p. 1954; Vol. 2. Kyoto, the Old Capital of Japan(794-1869) 465p. 1956 (ISBN 0-8002-1246-0); Vol. 3. The Imperial House of Japan. 479p. 1959 (ISBN 0-8002-1247-9); Vol. 4. Sovereign & Subject. 471p. 1962 (ISBN 0-8002-1248-7); Vol. 5. The Vicissitudes of Shinto. 436p. 1963 (ISBN 0-8002-1249-5); Vol. 6. Visiting Famous Shrines in Japan. 463p (ISBN 0-8002-1249-5). 1963. 45.00x ea. (ISBN 0-8002-2366-7). Intl Pubns Serv.

Ponsot, Marie & Deen, Rosemary. Beat Not the Poor Desk: Writing-What to Teach, How to Teach It, & Why. LC 81-15519. 224p. (Orig.). 1981. pap. text ed. 9.00 (ISBN 0-86709-009-X). Boynton Cook Pub.

Ponsot, Marie, tr. see Baudouy, Michel-Aime.

Ponssaid, J. P. Competitive Strategies: An Advanced Textbook in Game Theory for Business Students. 1982. 49.00 (ISBN 0-444-86230-7). Elsevier.

Ponstein, J. Approaches to the Theory of Optimization. LC 79-41419. (Cambridge Tracts in Mathematics: No. 77). (Illus.). 140p. 1980. 39.95 (ISBN 0-521-23155-8). Cambridge U Pr.

Ponterotto, I. L., jt. auth. see Mondelli, R. J.

Ponti & ASBO-ASFSA. A Guide for Financing School Food & Nutrition Services. (Research Bulletin: No. 10). pap. 0.69 (ISBN 0-685-57180-7). Assn Sch Busn.

Pontiero, Giovanni, ed. Duse on Tour: Guido Noccioli's Diaries, 1906-1907. LC 82-4751. (Illus.). 1982. lib. bdg. 32.00x (ISBN 0-87023-369-6). U of Mass Pr.

Pontifex. Lung Cancer: Proceedings of the Chalkidiki Meeting, Sept. 1981. (International Congress Ser.: Vol. 558). 1982. 83.00 (ISBN 0-444-90224-4). Elsevier.

Pontifical Academy of Sciences, 1975. Biological & Artificial Membranes & Desalination of Water: Proceedings. Passino, Roberto, ed. 1976. 127.50 (ISBN 0-444-99822-5). Elsevier.

Pontifical Institute of Mediaeval Studies, Toronto. Dictionary Catalog of the Library of the Pontifical Institute of Mediaeval Studies: First Supplement. 1979. lib. bdg. 125.00 (ISBN 0-8161-1061-1, Hall Library). G K Hall.

Pontifical Institute of Medieval Studies, Ontario. Dictionary Catalogue of the Library of the Pontifical Institute of Medieval Studies, 5 vols. 1972. Set. lib. bdg. 485.00 (ISBN 0-8161-0970-2, Hall Library). G K Hall.

Ponting. Beginners Guide to Weaving. 1982. text ed. write for info (ISBN 0-408-00574-2). Butterworth.

Ponting, K. G. & Jenkins, David. The British Wool Textile Industry 1770-1914. 384p. 1982. 80.00x (ISBN 0-435-32469-1, Pub. by Heinemann England). State Mutual Bk.

Ponting, K. G., jt. ed. see Harte, N. B.

Ponting, Ken. A Dictionary of Dyes & Dyeing. 216p. 1982. 35.00x (ISBN 0-7135-1311-X, Pub. by Bell & Hyman England). State Mutual Bk.

Ponting, Kenneth G. The Woollen Industry of South-West England. LC 77-78616. (Origins of Industry). (Illus.). 1971. lib. bdg. 25.00x (ISBN 0-678-07751-7). Kelley.

Ponton, Geoffrey & Gill, Peter. Introduction to Politics. 280p. 1982. 19.95x (ISBN 0-85520-466-4, Pub. by Martin Robertson England); pap. 9.95x (ISBN 0-85520-467-2, Pub. by Martin Robertson England). Biblio Dist.

Ponton, Melva. Syllabus for Applied Child Development. 112p. 1982. pap. text ed. 7.95 (ISBN 0-8403-2831-1). Kendall-Hunt.

Pooch, Udo W. & Chattergy, Rahul. Minicomputers: Hardware, Software, & Selection. (Illus.). 1980. text ed. 24.95 (ISBN 0-8299-0055-1). West Pub.

Pooch, Udo W., jt. auth. see Chattergy, Rahul.

Pool, Ethel, jt. auth. see Bailey, Henry T.

Pool, Ithiel D. Technologies of Freedom. (Illus.). 344p. 1983. 20.00 (ISBN 0-674-87232-0, Belknap Pr). Harvard U Pr.

Pool, Ithiel de Sola see De Sola Pool, Ithiel.

Pool, Ithiel Sola De see De Sola Pool, Ithiel.

Pool, Mary J., jt. ed. see Seebohm, Caroline.

Poole, Alan, jt. auth. see Makhijani, Arjun.

Poole, C. F., jt. ed. see Ziatkis, A.

Poole, Charles P. Electron Spin Resonance: A Comprehensive Treatise on Experimental Techniques. 2nd ed. 848p. 1983. 69.00 (ISBN 0-471-04678-7, Pub. by Wiley-Interscience). Wiley.

Poole, Charles P., et al. Relaxation in Magnetic Resonance: Dielectric & Mossbauer Applications. 1971. 58.50 (ISBN 0-12-561450-0). Acad Pr.

Poole, Ernest. His Family. new ed. LC 17-13623. 1974. Repr. of 1917 ed. 14.95 (ISBN 0-910220-64-6). Berg.

Poole, F., jt. ed. see Draffan, I. W.

Poole, Francis. Gestures. pap. 3.00 (ISBN 0-686-81813-X). Anhinga Pr.

Poole, Francis, jt. ed. see Brock, Van K.

Poole, Frazer G., ed. see Library Equipment Institute, New York, July 7-9, 1966.

Poole, Frederick K. Album of Modern China. LC 80-25081. (Picture Albums Ser.). (Illus.). (gr. 5 up). 1981. 9.60 (ISBN 0-531-01502-5). Watts.

--Jordan. rev. ed. O'Brien, Linda, ed. (First Bks.). (Illus.). (gr. 4-6). 1978. PLB 8.90 s&l (ISBN 0-531-02241-2). Watts.

Poole, Gray, jt. auth. see Poole, Lynn.

Poole, Gray J. Nuts from Forest, Orchard & Field. LC 74-7662. (Illus.). 80p. (gr. 5 up). 1974. 5.95 o.p. (ISBN 0-396-06993-2). Dodd.

Poole, James. Badminton. 3rd ed. 1982. pap. text ed. 7.95x (ISBN 0-673-16041-6). Scott F.

Poole, Lon. The Apple II User's Guide. 388p. 1981. pap. 16.95 (ISBN 0-931988-46-2). Osborne-McGraw.

--Some Common BASIC Programs: TSR-80 Level II Edition. 194p. pap. 14.99 (ISBN 0-931988-54-3). Osborne-McGraw.

Poole, Lon & Davidson, Gregory. Practical PASCAL Programs. (Orig.). 1982. pap. 15.99 (ISBN 0-931988-74-8). Osborne-McGraw.

Poole, Lynn & Poole, Gray. Scientists Who Work Outdoors. LC 63-15473. (Illus.). 1963. 3.50 o.p. (ISBN 0-396-04804-8). Dodd.

--Volcanoes in Action: Science & Legend. (gr. 5 up). 1962. PLB 7.95 (ISBN 0-07-050422-9, GB). McGraw.

Poole, M., ed. Creativity Across the Curriculum. (Classroom & Curriculum in Australia). 1980. text ed. 22.50x (ISBN 0-86861-177-8); pap. text ed. 9.95x (ISBN 0-86861-185-9). Allen Unwin.

Poole, M. J., jt. auth. see Egelstaff, P. A.

Poole, Micael, jt. auth. see Mansfield, Roger.

Poole, Michael & Mansfield, Roger. Managerial Roles in Industrial Relations: Towards a Definitive Survey of Research & Formulation of Models. 162p. 1980. text ed. 27.75x (ISBN 0-566-00377-5). Gower Pub Ltd.

Poole, Millicent E. Youth: Expectations & Transitions. 300p. Date not set. pap. 20.00 (ISBN 0-7100-9283-0). Routledge & Kegan.

Poole, Peter A. Profiles in American Foreign Policy: Stimson, Kennan, Acheson, Dulles, Rusk, Kissinger, & Vance. LC 80-5624. (Illus.). 154p. (Orig.). 1981. lib. bdg. 19.25 (ISBN 0-8191-1422-7); pap. text ed. 8.25 (ISBN 0-8191-1423-5). U Pr of Amer.

--The United States & Indochina from FDR to Nixon. LC 77-26285. (Orig.). 1978. pap. text ed. 6.50 o.p. (ISBN 0-88275-427-0). Krieger.

Poole, Peter A., ed. Indochina: Perspectives for Reconciliation. LC 75-62006. (Papers in International Studies: Southeast Asia: No. 36). (Illus.). 1975. pap. 6.00x (ISBN 0-89680-022-9, Ohio U Ctr Intl). Ohio U Pr.

Poole, R. S. see Hill, G. F.

Poole, Robert W. An Introduction to Quantitative Ecology. (Population Biology Ser). (Illus.). 480p. 1974. text ed. 24.50 o.p. (ISBN 0-07-050415-6, C). McGraw.

Poole, Robert W., Jr., ed. Instead of Regulation: Alternatives to Federal Regulatory Agencies. LC 81-47333. 416p. 1981. 26.95x (ISBN 0-669-04585-3). Lexington Bks.

Poole, Roger. The Unknown Virginia Woolf. 285p. 1982. pap. text ed. 10.95x (ISBN 0-391-02669-0). Humanities.

Poole, Rogers. The Unknown Virginia Woolf. LC 78-3458. 1978. 21.95 (ISBN 0-521-21987-6). Cambridge U Pr.

Poole, Trevor B. Social Behaviour in Mammals. (Tertiary Level Biology Ser.). 1982. 45.00x (ISBN 0-412-00101-2, Pub. by Chapman & Hall); pap. 19.95x (ISBN 0-412-00111-X). Methuen Inc.

Poole, William. Money & the Economy: A Monetarist View. LC 78-52499. (Perspectives on Economics). (Illus.). 1978. 8.95 (ISBN 0-201-08364-7). A-W.

Pooley, A. C., jt. auth. see Scott, H. B.

Pooley, Beverley J. The Evolution of British Planning Legislation. LC 63-63300. (Michigan Legal Publications Ser.). 100p. 1982. Repr. of 1960 ed. lib. bdg. 26.00 (ISBN 0-89941-173-8). W S Hein.

Pooley, Beverly J. Planning & Zoning in the United States. LC 61-63301. (Michigan Legal Publications Ser.). 123p. 1982. Repr. of 1961 ed. lib. bdg. 26.00 (ISBN 0-89941-173-8). W S Hein.

Pooley, James. Trade Secrets: How to Protect Your Ideas & Assets. 160p. 1982. pap. 11.95 (ISBN 0-931988-93-4). Osborne-McGraw.

Pooley, Roger, ed. see Gascoigne, George.

Poon, Eileen. Seeker of the Sun. 1983. 5.95 (ISBN 0-533-05605-5). Vantage.

Poon, Leonard, ed. Aging in the Nineteen-Eighties: Psychological Issues. LC 80-18515. 1980. 32.00 (ISBN 0-686-70082-1). Am Psychol.

Poor, Alfred E. Colonial Architecture of Cape Cod, Nantucket & Martha's Vineyard. (Illus.). 11.00 (ISBN 0-8446-0851-3). Peter Smith.

Poor, Henry V. Resumption & the Silver Question. Repr. of 1878 ed. lib. bdg. cancelled o.p. (ISBN 0-8371-0619-2, PORS). Greenwood.

Poor, Walter A. Differential Geometric Structures. (Illus.). 320p. 1981. text ed. 42.95 (ISBN 0-07-050435-0, C). McGraw.

Poore, Ben. Half-Breed in Johnsonville. 1981. 5.75 (ISBN 0-8062-1579-8). Carlton.

Poore, Dudley, tr. see Carneiro, Cecilio J.

Poorman, Berta & Poorman, Sonja. Spread a Little Christmas Cheer. 1982. pap. 3.50 (ISBN 0-686-38388-5). Eldridge Pub.

Poorman, Sonja, jt. auth. see Poorman, Berta.

Poortvliet, Rien & Huygen, Wil. Secrets of the Gnomes. LC 82-3948. (Illus.). 200p. 1982. 19.95 (ISBN 0-8109-1614-2). Abrams.

Poovey, W. A. Letting the Word Come Alive. (Preacher's Workshop Ser.). 48p. 1977. pap. text ed. 2.50 (ISBN 0-570-07401-0, 12-2673). Concordia.

--We Sing Your Praise, O Lord: Dramas & Meditations on Six Favorite Hymns. LC 80-67792. 128p. 1980. pap. 4.50 (ISBN 0-8066-1853-1, 10-7022); pap. 1.95 (ISBN 0-8066-1854-X, 10-7023). Augsburg.

Poovey, W. A., ed. Planning a Christian Funeral: A Minister's Guide. LC 78-52198. 1978. pap. 4.95 (ISBN 0-8066-1668-7, 10-4990). Augsburg.

Pop, Iggy & Wohrer, Anne. I Need More. (Illus.). 128p. 1982. pap. 9.95 (ISBN 0-943828-50-3). Karz-Cohl Pub.

Popa, Vasko. Vasko Popa: Collected Poems. Pennington, Anne, tr. LC 78-50706. 1979. o. p. 12.50 (ISBN 0-89255-033-3); pap. 7.95 (ISBN 0-89255-034-1). Persea Bks.

Pope, Alan & Goin, Kenneth L. High-Speed Wind Tunnel Testing. LC 78-15823. 486p. 1978. Repr. of 1965 ed. lib. bdg. 29.50 (ISBN 0-88275-727-X). Krieger.

Pope, Alan & Harper, J. J. Low-Speed Wind Tunnel Testing. LC 66-17619. 1966. 44.95x (ISBN 0-471-69392-8, Pub. by Wiley-Interscience). Wiley.

Pope, Alexander. Art of Sinking in Poetry: Martinus Scriblerus' Peri Bathous: A Critical Edition. Steeves, Edna L., ed. LC 68-15162. 1968. Repr. of 1952 ed. 10.00x o.p. (ISBN 0-8462-1179-3). Russell.

--An Essay on Man by Alexander Pope. Mack, Maynard, ed. (Library Reprints Ser.). 1982. 42.00x (ISBN 0-416-34010-5). Methuen Inc.

--Poems of Alexander Pope: A One-Vol. Ed. of the Twickenham Text with Selected Annotations. Butt, John, ed. (Illus.). 1963. 45.00x (ISBN 0-300-00340-4); pap. 13.95x 1966 (ISBN 0-300-00030-8, Y163). Yale U Pr.

Pope, Alexander, tr. Iliad of Homer, Vol. 1, Bks. 1-9, Vol. 2. Bks. 10-24. Mack, Maynard, et al, eds. (Illus.). 1967. Set. 75.00x o.p. (ISBN 0-300-00746-9). Yale U Pr.

Pope, Carl. Sahib: An American Misadventure in India. 192p. 1972. 6.95 o.s.i. (ISBN 0-87140-553-9). Liveright.

Pope, D. & Moss, R. L. Current Odour Problems & Control Techniques in the UK, 1980. 1981. 35.00x (ISBN 0-686-97053-5, Pub. by W Spring England). State Mutual Bk.

Pope, Daniel. The Making of Modern Advertising. 275p. 1983. 18.95 (ISBN 0-465-04325-9). Basic.

Pope, Diana, compiled by. Mobil New Zealand Travel Guide-North Island. (Illus.). 1973. pap. 14.65 (ISBN 0-589-00721-1, Pub. by Reed Books Australia). C E Tuttle.

--Mobil New Zealand Travel Guide: South Island. LC 74-76513. (Illus.). 1975. pap. 14.65 (ISBN 0-589-00861-7, Pub. by Reed Books Australia). C E Tuttle.

Pope, Dorothy. He Wanted to Die. 1972. pap. 1.50 (ISBN 0-85363-086-0). OMF Bks.

Pope, Gustavus W. Journey to Mars. LC 73-13262. (Classics of Science Fiction Ser). (Illus.). 551p. 1974. 16.50 (ISBN 0-88355-116-0); pap. 5.75 (ISBN 0-88355-145-4). Hyperion Conn.

Pope, Isabel, tr. see Salazar, Adolfo.

Pope, Jack, jt. ed. see Walker, Orville C.

Pope, John C., ed. Seven Old English Poems. 240p. 1981. pap. text ed. 8.95x (ISBN 0-686-86522-7). Norton.

Pope John XXIII. Journal of a Soul. White, Dorothy, tr. LC 79-7786. (Illus.). 504p. 1980. pap. 7.95 (ISBN 0-385-14842-9, Im). Doubleday.

Pope, Katherine, jt. auth. see Pearson, Carol.

Pope, Liston. Millhands & Preachers: A Study of Gastonia. (Studies in Religious Education Ser.: No. 15). (Illus.). 1965. pap. 10.95x (ISBN 0-300-00182-7). Yale U Pr.

Pope, M. I. & Judd, M. D. Differential Thermal Analysis. 1977. 42.95 (ISBN 0-471-25958-6, Pub. by Wiley Heyden). Wiley.

Pope, M. K. From Latin to Modern French. 600p. 1934. 20.00 (ISBN 0-7190-0176-5). Manchester.

Pope, M. T. Heteropoly & Isopoly Oxometalates. (Inorganic Chemistry Concepts Ser.: Vol. 8). (Illus.). 190p. 1983. 52.00 (ISBN 0-387-11889-6). Springer-Verlag.

Pope, Martin & Swenberg, Charles E. Electronic Processes in Organic Crystals. (Monographs on the Physics & Chemistry of Materials). (Illus.). 842p. 1982. 145.00x (ISBN 0-19-851334-8). Oxford U Pr.

Pope, Maurice. Aegean Writing & Linear A. (Studies in Mediterranean Archaeology Ser.: No. VIII). (Illus.). 1964. pap. text ed. 4.75x (ISBN 91-85058-07-6). Humanities.

Pope, Michael. Introducing Oil Painting. 1977. pap. 15.50 o.p. (ISBN 0-7134-0238-5, Pub. by Batsford England). David & Charles.

--Introducing Watercolour Painting. 1973. 17.50 (ISBN 0-7134-2434-6, Pub. by Batsford England). David & Charles.

Pope, Myrtle P. Critical Bibliography of Works by & About Francis Thompson. 1959. pap. 3.00 o.p. (ISBN 0-87104-058-1). NY Pub Lib.

Pope, Nolan F., jt. auth. see Woods, Lawrence A.

Pope, Randolph D., ed. The Analysis of Literary Texts: Current Trends in Methodology (Third & Fourth York College Colloquia) LC 79-54144. (Studies in Literary Analysis). 336p. 1980. lib. bdg. 16.95x (ISBN 0-916950-14-X); pap. text ed. 10.95x (ISBN 0-916950-13-1). Bilingual Pr.

Pope, Ronald R., annotations by. Soviet Views on the Cuban Missile Crisis: Myth & Reality in Foreign Policy Analysis. (Illus.). 298p. (Orig.). 1982. lib. bdg. 22.25 (ISBN 0-8191-2584-9); pap. text ed. 11.75 (ISBN 0-8191-2585-7). U Pr of Amer.

Pope, Saxton T. Bows & Arrows. (California Library Reprint). 1974. Repr. 18.00x (ISBN 0-520-02641-1). U of Cal Pr.

Pope, Virginia, tr. see Papini, Giovanni.

Pope-Hennessy, John. Fra Angelico. rev. ed. LC 74-9200. (Illus.). 296p. 1975. 64.50x (ISBN 0-8014-0855-5). Cornell U Pr.

Popejoy, Bill & Arcangeli, Gianfranco. Beni E Benignita. (Italian.). 1980. pap. 1.75 (ISBN 0-8297-0664-X). Life Pubs Intl.

Popelka, Jan, jt. auth. see Lineman, Rose.

Popenoe, Chris, ed. Books for Inner Development: The Yes! 1976. pap. 5.95 (ISBN 0-394-73544-7). Random.

Popenoe, David. Sociology. 4th ed. 1980. text ed. 22.95 (ISBN 0-13-820944-8); wkbk. 8.95 (ISBN 0-13-820977-4). P-H.

--Sociology. 5th ed. 640p. text ed. 22.95 (ISBN 0-686-92020-1); study guide 8.95 (ISBN 0-13-820779-8). P-H.

Popescu, Charlotte. Horses at Work. (History in Focus Ser.). (Illus.). 72p. (gr. 7-12). 1983. 14.95 (ISBN 0-7134-4451-7, Pub. by Batsford England). David & Charles.

Popescu, J. Italian for Commerce. 1968. 20.00 o.s.i. (ISBN 0-08-012454-2). Pergamon.

Popesko, Peter. Atlas of Topographical Anatomy of the Domestic Animals. LC 77-84681. 1978. 55.00 (ISBN 0-7216-7275-2). Saunders.

Popham, E., et al. A Teaching-Learning System for Business Education. 1975. 20.05 (ISBN 0-07-050504-7, G). McGraw.

Popham, E. L., jt. auth. see Place, Irene M.

Popham, G. T. Government in Britain. 1969. 24.00 o.p. (ISBN 0-08-013418-1); pap. 10.75 o.p. (ISBN 0-08-013417-3). Pergamon.

Popham, James & Baker, Eva. Establishing Instructional Goals. 1970. pap. text ed. 14.95 (ISBN 0-13-289256-1). P-H.

Popham, Peter. The Complete Guide to Japan. (The Complete Asian Guide Ser.). (Illus.). 144p. (Orig.). 1982. pap. 9.95 (ISBN 962-7031-17-8). C E Tuttle.

--Japan in Focus. (The "In Focus" Ser.). (Illus.). 64p. (Orig.). 1982. pap. 5.95 (ISBN 962-7031-20-8). C E Tuttle.

Popham, W. Educational Evaluation. 1975. 24.95 (ISBN 0-13-240515-6). P-H.

Popham, W. & Baker, Eva. Systematic Instruction. 1970. pap. text ed. 15.95 (ISBN 0-13-880690-X). P-H.

Popham, W. James. Criterion-Referenced Measurement. (Illus.). 1978. pap. 18.95 (ISBN 0-13-193607-7). P-H.

--Evaluation in Education. new ed. LC 74-12822. 601p. 1974. 26.00 (ISBN 0-8211-1512-X); text ed. 23.50 (ISBN 0-685-57220-X). McCutchan.

--Modern Educational Measurement. (Illus.). 496p. 1981. text ed. 25.95 (ISBN 0-13-591982-7). P-H.

Popic, R., et al. Scientific Technological Dictionary. 1140p. (Eng. & Serbocroatian.). 1980. 95.00 (ISBN 0-686-97432-8, M-9688). French & Eur.

Popkewitz, Thomas S & Tabachnick, B. Robert. The Study of Schooling: Field-Based Methodologies in Educational Research & Evaluation. 316p. 1981. 26.50 (ISBN 0-686-98366-1). Praeger.

Popkin, Gary. Introductory Structured Cobol Programming. (Orig.). 1980. pap. text ed. 16.95 (ISBN 0-442-23166-0); instr's. manual 4.95 (ISBN 0-442-26773-8). Van Nos Reinhold.

Popkin, Gary S. Advanced Structured COBOL. 512p. 1983. pap. text ed. 23.95x (ISBN 0-534-01394-5). Kent Pub Co.

--Introductory Structured Cobol Programming. LC 80-51061. 471p. 1981. pap. text ed. 17.95x (ISBN 0-442-23166-0); instr's manual avail. 0.00 (ISBN 0-442-26773-8). Kent Pub Co.

Popkin, Gary S. & Pike, Arthur M. Introduction to Data Processing. 2nd ed. (Illus.). 1981. 20.95 (ISBN 0-395-29483-5). HM.

--Introduction to Data Processing with BASIC. 2nd ed. (Illus.). 592p. 1981. text ed. 21.50 (ISBN 0-395-30091-6); study guide 7.95 (ISBN 0-395-29485-1). HM.

Popkin, Henry. Theatres of Europe: West & East. (Illus.). 330p. Date not set. 18.95 (ISBN 0-8180-0508-4). Horizon.

Popkin, Joel, ed. see National Bureau of Economic Research Conference on Income & Wealth.

Popkin, P. R., jt. auth. see Hill, Leslie A.

Popkin, Richard H. The History of Scepticism from Erasmus to Spinoza. LC 78-65469. 1979. 30.00x (ISBN 0-520-03827-4); pap. 8.50x (ISBN 0-520-03876-2, CAMPUS NO. 226). U of Cal Pr.

Popkin, Richard H. & Stroll, Avrum. Philosophy Made Simple. pap. 4.95 (ISBN 0-385-01217-9, Made). Doubleday.

Popkin, Richard H., ed. see Hume, David.

Popkin, Samuel. The Rational Peasant: The Political Economy of Rural Society in Vietnam. LC 77-83105. 1979. 23.50x (ISBN 0-520-03561-5); pap. 6.95x (ISBN 0-520-03954-8, CAMPUS NO. 236). U of Cal Pr.

Popkin, Zelda. Dear Once. 1977. pap. 1.95 o.p. (ISBN 0-451-07428-9, J7428, Sig). NAL.

Popko, Edward. Transitions: A Photographic Documentary of Squatter Settlements. LC 77-17777. (Community Development Ser.: Vol. 42). (Illus.). 1978. 32.00 (ISBN 0-87933-316-2). Hutchinson Ross.

Poplasen, Ilija. The New World Order. 250p. 1982. 20.00 (ISBN 0-935352-12-0). MIR PA.

Poplavskii, Boris I. V Venke Iz Voska; Dirizhabl' Neizvestnogo Napravleniia. 2nd ed. Karlinsky, Simon, ed. (Modern Russian Litrature & Culture Studies & Texts: Vol. 9). (Illus.). 123p. 1981. pap. 7.50 (ISBN 0-933884-19-2). Berkeley Slavic.

Pople, J. A. & Beveridge, D. L. Approximate Molecular Orbital Theory. 1970. text ed. 35.00 (ISBN 0-07-050512-8, C). McGraw.

Pople, J. A., et al. High Resolution Nuclear Magnetic Resonance. (Advanced Chemistry Ser.). 1959. text ed. 27.00 o.p. (ISBN 0-07-050516-0, C). McGraw.

Poplin, Dennis E. Communities: A Survey of Theories & Methods of Research. 2nd ed. 1979. text ed. 20.95x (ISBN 0-02-396160-0). Macmillan.

Popoff, Irmis B. Gurdjieff: His Work on Myself... with Others... for the Work. rev ed. LC 73-79122. 198p. 1982. pap. 4.95 (ISBN 0-87728-417-2). Weiser.

Popoff, Peter. America's Family Crisis. Tanner, Don, ed. LC 82-82843. 80p. 1982. pap. 2.00 (ISBN 0-938544-15-2). Faith Messenger.

--Demons At Your Doorstep. Tanner, Don, ed. LC 82-82842. (Illus.). 56p. 1982. pap. 1.50 (ISBN 0-938544-13-6). Faith Messenger.

--Set Free from Satan's Slavery. Tanner, Don, ed. LC 82-83455. 64p. 1982. pap. 2.00 (ISBN 0-938544-17-9). Faith Messenger.

--Ye Shall Recieve Power: The Amazing Miracle of Holy Spirit Baptism. Tanner, Don, ed. LC 82-71629. 96p. 1982. pap. 2.00 (ISBN 0-938544-14-4). Faith Messenger.

Popov, Egor O. Mechanics of Materials: SI Version. 2nd ed. (Illus.). 1978. 29.95 (ISBN 0-13-571299-8). P-H.

Popov, Egor P. & Medwadowski, Stefan J., eds. Concrete Shell Buckling. LC 80-69968. (SP-67). 240p. (Orig.). 1981. pap. 30.50 (ISBN 0-686-95244-8). ACI.

Popov, G. & Ratcliffe, M. The Sahelian Tree Locust Anacridium Melanorhodon Walker. 1968. 35.00x (ISBN 0-85135-044-5, Pub. by Centre Overseas Research). State Mutual Bk.

Popov, G., jt. auth. see Dill, William R.

Popov, G. B. Ecological Studies on Ovipostion by Swarms of the Desert Locust (Schistocerca Gregaria Forskal) in Eastern Africa. 1958. 35.00x (ISBN 0-85135-029-1, Pub. by Centre Overseas Research). State Mutual Bk.

--Studies on Oviposition, Egg Development & Mortality in Oedaleus Senegalenis: Krauss, Orthoptera, Acridoidea in the Sahel. 1980. 35.00x (ISBN 0-85135-111-5, Pub. by Centre Overseas Research). State Mutual Bk.

Popov, G. B., jt. auth. see Stower, W. J.

Popov, V. N., jt. auth. see Konopleva, N. P.

Popovic, Branko D. Introductory Engineering Electromagnetics. (Engineering Ser). 1971. text ed. 30.95 (ISBN 0-201-05871-5). A-W.

Popovich, jt. auth. see Moncrief.

Popovich, D. Prescriptive Behavior Checklist, Vol. I. (Illus.). 448p. 1977. pap. text ed. 12.95 (ISBN 0-8391-1100-2). Univ Park.

Popovich, Dorothy. A Prescriptive Behavioral Checklist for Severely & Profoundly Retarded, Vol. III. 416p. (Orig.). 1981. pap. text ed. 12.95 (ISBN 0-8391-4148-3). Univ Park.

--A Prescriptive Behavioral Checklist for the Severely & Profoundly Retarded, Vol. II. 352p. 1981. pap. text ed. 12.95 (ISBN 0-8391-4147-5). Univ Park.

Popovich, Richard E. The Measurement of Thought: A Heuristic Approach to This Development. 2nd ed. 180p. 1982. 7.95 (ISBN 0-9604876-0-3). REP Pubs.

Popovics, Sandor. Concrete Making Materials. LC 78-1111. (Illus.). 1979. text ed. 28.50 (ISBN 0-07-050505-5, C). McGraw.

Popovics, Sandor, ed. Fundamentals of Portland Cement Concrete: Vol. 1: Fresh Concrete. LC 81-16257. 477p. 1982. 56.95x (ISBN 0-471-86217-7, Pub. by Wiley-Interscience). Wiley.

Popovych, Orest & Tomkins, Reginald. Nonaqueous Solution Chemistry. LC 80-21693. 500p. 1981. 63.00 (ISBN 0-471-02673-5, Pub. by Wiley-Interscience). Wiley.

Popp, A. John, et al, eds. Neural Trauma. LC 78-24627. (Seminars in Neurological Surgery). 408p. 1979. text ed. 41.00 (ISBN 0-89004-257-8). Raven.

Popp, Dennis. Ice Racing. LC 72-5421. (Superwheels & Thrill Sports Bks.). (Illus.). 48p. (gr. 3-6). 1973. PLB 7.95g (ISBN 0-8225-0403-0). Lerner Pubns.

Popp, Lothar & Thomsen, Russel J. Ultrasound in Obstetrics & Gynecology. (Illus.). 1978. text ed. 18.95 o.p. (ISBN 0-07-050507-1, HP). McGraw.

Poppe, Nicholas. Reminiscences. Schwarz, Henry G., ed. LC 82-4544. (Studies on East Asia: Vol. 16). (Illus.). 331p. 1983. 30.00 (ISBN 0-914584-16-2). West Wash Univ.

Poppe, Nicholas, ed. The Twelve Deeds of Buddha: A Mongolian Version of the Lalitavistara & English Translation. (Asiatische Forschungen Ser.: Band 23). Orig. Title: Mongolian. 238p. 1967. pap. 25.00x (ISBN 3-447-00120-8). Intl Pubns Serv.

Poppenhagen, Brent W., jt. auth. see Schuttenberg, Ernest M.

Popper, Evelyn. Les Images et les Mots. rev ed. 1971. 4.80 o.p. (ISBN 0-02-826040-6). Glencoe.

Popper, Frank. The Politics of Land-Use Reform. 338p. 1981. 25.00 (ISBN 0-299-08530-9); pap. text ed. 8.50 (ISBN 0-299-08534-1). U of Wis Pr.

Popper, Frank, jt. auth. see Geisler, Charles.

Popper, H. Modern Cost Engineering Techniques: An Economic Analysis & Cost Estimation Manual, with Comprehensive Data on Plant & Equipment Costs in Processes Industries. 1970. 12.00 (ISBN 0-07-050530-6, P&RB). McGraw.

--Modern Technical Management Techniques: For Engineers in Management. 1971. 24.50 o.p. (ISBN 0-07-050529-2, P&RB). McGraw.

Popper, Hans & Schaffner, Fenton, eds. Progress in Liver Diseases, Vol. 7. 1982. 59.00 (ISBN 0-8089-1467-7). Grune.

Popper, Karl. Realism & the Aim of Science. Bartley, W. W., III, ed. LC 82-501. (Postscript to the Logic of Scientific Discovery). 432p. 1983. text ed. 35.00x (ISBN 0-8476-7015-5). Rowman.

--Unended Quest. LC 76-2155. 1976. 16.50x (ISBN 0-87548-366-6); pap. 6.50 o.p. (ISBN 0-87548-343-7). Open Court.

Popper, Karl R. Conjectures & Refutations: The Growth of Scientific Knowledge. 1968. pap. 7.95xi (ISBN 0-06-131376-9, TB1376, Torch). Har-Row.

--The Logic of Scientific Discovery. LC 59-8371. 1959. 10.75x o.s.i. (ISBN 0-465-04188-4). Basic.

Popper, P. Isostatic Pressing. 1976. 35.95 o.p. (ISBN 0-471-25959-4, Wiley Heyden). Wiley.

Poppino, Mary A., jt. auth. see Moore, David P.

Poppino, Rollie E. Brazil: The Land & People. 2nd ed. (Latin American Histories Ser.). (Illus.). 1973. 19.95x (ISBN 0-19-501696-3); pap. 5.95x (ISBN 0-19-501697-1). Oxford U Pr.

Poppy, Willard J. & Wilson, Leland L. Exploring the Physical Sciences. 2nd ed. (Illus.). 464p. 1973. text ed. 24.95 (ISBN 0-13-297457-6); study guide 2.95 (ISBN 0-13-297531-9). P-H.

Population Council. Catalogue of the Population Council Library. 1979. lib. bdg. 280.00 (ISBN 0-8161-0278-3, Hall Library). G K Hall.

Population Institute, Univ. of the Philippines. First Conference on Population, 1965. 1966. 4.50x (ISBN 0-8248-0435-X). UH Pr.

Popyk, M. K. Word Processing & Information Systems: A Practical Approach. 352p. 1983. 15.50 (ISBN 0-07-050574-8, G). McGraw.

--Word Processing: Essential Concepts. 240p. 1983. 11.95 (ISBN 0-07-048472-4, G). McGraw.

Popyk, M. K., jt. auth. see Boyce, B.

Poqueras-Mayo, A., jt. auth. see Laurenti, Joseph L.

Poquette, Radnor J., jt. auth. see Wright, P. H.

Porada, Edith & Dyson, R. H. Ancient Iran. (Art of the World Library). 6.95 o.p. (ISBN 0-517-50828-1). Crown.

Porat, Dan I. & Barna, Arpad. Introduction to Digital Techniques. LC 78-17696. (Electronic Technology Ser.). 1979. text ed. 28.95 (ISBN 0-471-02924-6); solutions manual 3.00 (ISBN 0-471-04351-6). Wiley.

Porat, Dan I., jt. auth. see Barna, Arpad.

Porat, Freida & Will, Mimi. The Dynamic Secretary. (Illus.). 240p. 1983. 14.95 (ISBN 0-13-221853-4); pap. 7.95 (ISBN 0-13-221846-1). P-H.

Porch, James M. Daybreak: Faith for Ordinary Days. 1983. 3.25 (ISBN 0-8054-5206-0). Broadman.

Porcino, Jane. Growing Older, Getting Better: A Handbook for Women in the Second Half of Life. (Illus.). 288p. 1983. 17.95 (ISBN 0-201-05593-7); pap. 8.95 (ISBN 0-201-05592-9). A-W.

Pordage, S., tr. see Willis, Thomas.

Pore, Renate. A Conflict of Interest: Women in German Social Democracy, 1919 to 1933. LC 80-27183. (Contributions in Women's Studies: No. 26). (Illus.). 152p. 1981. lib. bdg. 25.00 (ISBN 0-313-22856-6, PCW/). Greenwood.

Porell, Frank W. Models of Intra-Urban Relocation. (Studies in Applied Regional Science). 1982. lib. bdg. 35.00 (ISBN 0-686-97460-3). Kluwer-Nijhoff.

Porends, Norman J., jt. auth. see Benes, Vaclav.

Porizek, Radoslav, jt. auth. see Puzman, Josef.

Porkert, Manfred. The Theoretical Foundations of Chinese Medicine: Systems of Correspondence. LC 73-4960. (Asian Science Ser.: No. 3). 1974. pap. 12.50 (ISBN 0-262-66040-7). MIT Pr.

Pornschlegel, Hans. Job Evaluation & the Role of Trade Unions. 50p. 1982. write for info. Intl Labour Office.

Porochnia, Leonard. The Minicomputer: To Buy or Not to Buy. 122p. pap. 12.95 (ISBN 0-86641-085-6, 82134). Natl Assn Accts.

Porphyrios, Demetri, ed. Classicism Is Not a Style: An Architectural Design Profile. (Academy Architecture Ser.). (Illus.). 128p. 1982. pap. 19.95 (ISBN 0-312-14266-8). St Martin.

Porqueras-Mayo, Albert, et al. The New Catalan Short Story: An Anthology. LC 82-21927. 278p. (Orig.). 1983. lib. bdg. 22.50 (ISBN 0-8191-2899-6); pap. text ed. 11.75 (ISBN 0-8191-2900-3). U Pr of Amer.

Porro, Jeffrey D., jt. ed. see Olive, Marsha M.

Port Sines Investigating Panel. Failure of the Breakwater at Port Sines, Portugal. LC 82-70493. 296p. 1982. pap. text ed. 22.00 (ISBN 0-686-82486-5). Am Soc Civil Eng.

Porta, Giambattista Della see Della Porta, Giambattista.

Portal, Colette. The Beauty of Birth. (Illus.). (gr. 6 up). 1971. PLB 4.99 o.p. (ISBN 0-394-92287-5). Knopf.

Porte, J. F. Sir Charles V. Stanford. LC 76-12570. (Music Reprint Ser.). 1976. Repr. of 1921 ed. lib. bdg. 21.50 (ISBN 0-306-70790-X). Da Capo.

Porte, Joel. Emerson: Prospect & Retrospect, No. 10. (Harvard English Studies). 208p. 1982. text ed. 16.50x (ISBN 0-674-24915-1); pap. text ed. 5.95x (ISBN 0-674-24917-8). Harvard U Pr.

--Representative Man: Ralph Waldo Emerson in His Time. (Illus.). 1979. 22.50x (ISBN 0-19-502436-2). Oxford U Pr.

Porten, Bezalel. Archives from Elephantine: The Life of an Ancient Jewish Military Colony. (Illus.). 1968. 40.00x (ISBN 0-520-01028-0). U of Cal Pr.

Porteour. Desalination Techniques. Date not set. 53.50 (ISBN 0-85334-175-3, Pub. by Applied Sci England). Elsevier.

Porteous, A. J., et al, eds. see Smith, Norman K.

Porteous, Alexander. Forest Folklore, Mythology & Romance. LC 68-26597. 1968. Repr. of 1928 ed. 34.00x (ISBN 0-8103-3456-9). Gale.

Porteous, I. R. Topological Geometry. 2nd ed. LC 79-41611. 1981. 59.50 (ISBN 0-521-23160-4); pap. 24.95 (ISBN 0-521-29839-3). Cambridge U Pr.

Porteous, Norman W. Daniel, a Commentary. LC 65-21071. (Old Testament Library). 1965. 14.95 (ISBN 0-664-20663-8). Westminster.

Porter, A. N. The Origins of the South African War: Joseph Chamberlain & the Diplomacy of Imperialism 1895-1899. LC 79-28491. 320p. 1980. 26.00x (ISBN 0-312-58874-7). St Martin.

Porter, Alan L., jt. auth. see Rossini, Frederick A.

Porter, Albert W. Pattern: A Design Principle. LC 75-21118. (Concepts of Design Ser.). (Illus.). 80p. (gr. 7-12). 1975. 9.95 (ISBN 0-87192-077-8). Davis Mass.

--Shape & Form: Design Elements. LC 74-82681. (Concepts of Design Ser). (Illus.). 80p. (gr. 7up). 1974. 9.95 (ISBN 0-87192-064-6). Davis Mass.

Porter, Alyene. Papa Was a Preacher. 192p. 1979. 2.95 (ISBN 0-8007-8359-X, Spiro Bks). Revell.

Porter, B. & Moss, R. Memphis III, Part Two: Saqqara to Dahsur. (Topographical Bibliography of Ancient Egyptian Hieroglyphical Texts, Reliefs & Paintings: Fas. 3). 237p. 1981. pap. text ed. 90.00x (ISBN 0-900416-24-6, Pub. by Aris & Phillips England). Humanities.

Porter, Benjamin F. Reminiscences of Men & Things in Alabama. Walls, Sara, ed. (Illus.). 1983. 19.50 (ISBN 0-916620-56-5). Portals Pr.

Porter, Bern. Isla Vista. (Illus.). 36p. 1981. nps (ISBN 0-918824-31-1). Turkey Pr.

--The Wastemaker: Nineteen Twenty-Six to Nineteen Sixty-One. 300p. pap. 16.50 (ISBN 0-686-74432-2). Porter.

Porter, Bernard. Britain Europe & the World, 1850 to 1982: Illusions of Grandeur. 184p. text ed. 19.50x (ISBN 0-04-909011-9). Allen Unwin.

--The Refugee Question in Mid-Victorian Politics. LC 78-73947. (Illus.). 1980. 44.50 (ISBN 0-521-22638-4). Cambridge U Pr.

Porter, Bernard H. What Henry Miller Said & Why It Is Important. 2nd ed. (Illus.). 1972. 7.50 (ISBN 0-685-19458-2). Porter.

Porter, Brian. Stability Criteria for Linear Dynamical Systems. 1968. 34.50 o.s.i. (ISBN 0-12-562050-0). Acad Pr.

Porter, Bruce, jt. auth. see Curvin, Robert.

Porter, Burton F. The Good Life: Alternatives in Ethics. (Illus.). 1980. pap. text ed. 12.95x (ISBN 0-02-396120-1). Macmillan.

--Philosophy: A Literary & Conceptual Approach. 2nd ed. 496p. 1980. pap. text ed. 14.95 (ISBN 0-15-570553-9, HC). HarBraceJ.

Porter, Catherine, tr. see Todorov, Tzvetan.

Porter, Charlotte, et al, trs. see D'Annunzio, Gabriele.

Porter, Cyrus. If I Had a Bus. LC 73-19195. (Stretch Bks). (Illus.). 17p. (gr. k-3). 1974. 3.50 (ISBN 0-448-11737-1, G&D). Putnam Pub Group.

--If I Had a Dog. LC 73-19197. (Stretch Bks). (Illus.). 17p. (gr. k-3). 1974. 3.50 (ISBN 0-448-11739-8, G&D). Putnam Pub Group.

--If I Had a Farm. LC 73-19198. (Stretch Bks). (Illus.). 17p. (gr. k-3). 1974. 3.50 (ISBN 0-448-11740-1, G&D). Putnam Pub Group.

--If I Had a House. LC 73-19196. (Stretch Bks). (Illus.). 17p. (gr. k-3). 1974. 3.50 (ISBN 0-448-11738-X, G&D). Putnam Pub Group.

--If I Met Mother Goose. (Stretch Bks.). (Illus.). 17p. (ps-2). 1975. 3.50 (ISBN 0-448-12085-2, G&D). Putnam Pub Group.

--If I Say A B C. (Stretch Bks.). (Illus.). 17p. (ps-2). 1975. 3.50 (ISBN 0-448-12084-4, G&D). Putnam Pub Group.

Porter, D. & Padley, J. S. Training University Administrators in Europe: An OECD-IMHE Report. 137p. 1982. text ed. 29.00x (ISBN 0-566-00522-0). Gower Pub Ltd.

Porter, David, ed. Vision on Fire: Emma Goldman on the Spanish Revolution. LC 82-74015. (Illus.). 400p. (Orig.). 1983. pap. 7.50t (ISBN 0-9610348-2-3). Commonground Pr.

Porter, David L. Help! Let Me Out! (gr. k-3). 1982. PLB 8.95 (ISBN 0-395-32438-6); 8.70. HM.

--Seventy-Sixth Congress & World War II, 1939-1940. LC 79-4843. 256p. 1979. text ed. 19.50x (ISBN 0-8262-0281-0). U of Mo Pr.

Porter, Donald. Kiowa Fires. (American Indians Ser.: No. 11). (Orig.). 1983. pap. 3.50 (ISBN 0-440-04558-4). Dell.

Porter, Donald C. The Renegade. (Readers Request Ser.). 1983. lib. bdg. 19.95 (ISBN 0-8161-3447-2, Large Print Bks). G K Hall.

--Renno. (Readers Request Ser.). 1983. lib. bdg. 17.95 (ISBN 0-8161-3450-2, Large Print Bks). G K Hall.

--Tomahawk. (Readers Request Ser.). 1983. lib. bdg. 18.95 (ISBN 0-8161-3451-0, Large Print Bks). G K Hall.

--War Chief. (Readers Request Ser.). 1983. lib. bdg. 19.95 (ISBN 0-8161-3448-0, Large Print Bks). G K Hall.

--War Cry. 1983. pap. 3.50 (ISBN 0-686-42972-9). Bantam.

--White Indian. (Readers Request Ser.). 1983. lib. bdg. 19.95 (ISBN 0-8161-3446-4, Large Print Bks). G K Hall.

Porter, Donald P. The Sachem. (Readers Request Ser.). 1983. lib. bdg. 19.95 (ISBN 0-8161-3449-9, Large Print Bks). G K Hall.

Porter, Dorothy B., ed. Afro-Braziliana: A Working Bibliography. 1978. 46.50 (ISBN 0-8161-8016-4, Hall Reference). G K Hall.

Porter, Douglas R. & Cole, Susan. Affordable Housing: Twenty Examples from the Private Sector. LC 82-83409. (Illus.). 106p. 1982. pap. text ed. 18.00 (ISBN 0-87420-616-2, A13). Urban Land.

Porter, E. Pollyanna 'n' Hollywood. 1980. lib. bdg. 16.95 (ISBN 0-89968-252-9). Lightyear.

Porter, Earl. In the Wake of the Keel-Boats. 1978. 8.95 o.p. (ISBN 0-533-03256-3). Vantage.

Porter, Edward A., jt. auth. see Fitch, Richard D.

Porter, Eliot. The Greek World. (Illus.). 1980. 20.95 (ISBN 0-525-11812-8). Dutton.

--Intimate Landscapes. O'Neill, John P., et al, eds. (Illus.). 1979. 35.00 (ISBN 0-87099-209-0). Metro Mus Art.

Porter, Eliot & Harwood, Michael. Moments of Discovery: Adventures with American Birds. LC 76-10255. 1977. 29.95 o.p. (ISBN 0-525-15925-8). Dutton.

Porter, Elizabeth. Water Management in England & Wales. LC 77-83998. (Cambridge Geographical Studies: No. 10). (Illus.). 1979. 44.50 (ISBN 0-521-21865-9). Cambridge U Pr.

Porter, Ethel J. Skid Row Undaunted. 1983. 7.95 (ISBN 0-8062-2130-5). Carlton.

Porter, G. S. Song of the Cardinal. LC 79-89575. Date not set. 8.95 o.p. (ISBN 0-912728-29-9). Newbury Bks.

Porter, Gareth & Hildebrand, George C. Cambodia: Starvation & Revolution. LC 76-1646. (Illus.). 128p. 1976. 6.95 (ISBN 0-85345-382-9, CL3829). Monthly Rev.

Porter, Gareth, ed. Vietnam: A History in Documents. 1981. pap. 9.95 (ISBN 0-452-00637-6, F637, Mer). NAL.

Porter, Gene S. Freckles. 254p. 1980. Repr. PLB 15.95 (ISBN 0-89966-224-2). Buccaneer Bks.

--The Harvester. 560p. 1977. PLB 19.95 (ISBN 0-89966-225-0). Buccaneer Bks.

--Moths of the Limberlost. 1980. Repr. lib. bdg. 18.95 (ISBN 0-89967-042-3). Harmony Raine.

Porter, George, ed. Nephrotoxic Mechanisms of Drugs & Environmental Toxins. LC 82-13156. 486p. 1982. 49.50x (ISBN 0-306-40977-1, Plenum Med Bk). Plenum Pub.

Porter, George & Friday, James R., eds. Advice to Lectures: An Anthology Taken from the Writings of Michael Faraday & Lawrance Bragg. 1975. pap. 2.00x o.p. (ISBN 0-7201-0446-7, Pub. by Mansell England). Wilson.

Porter, George, jt. ed. see Bragg, William L.

Porter, George R. Progress of the Nation. new ed. Hirst, F. W., ed. LC 77-85189. Repr. of 1912 ed. 37.50x (ISBN 0-678-00538-9). Kelley.

Porter, Glenn. The Rise of Big Business. LC 73-632. (AHM American History Ser.). 1973. pap. 5.95x (ISBN 0-88295-750-3). Harlan Davidson.

Porter, Glenn & Cuff, Robert, eds. Enterprise & National Development: Essays in Canadian Business & Economic History. LC 73-84693. (Illus.). 1973. pap. 3.50 o.p. (ISBN 0-88866-532-6). Samuel Stevens.

Porter, Glenn, ed. see Giebelhaus, August W.

Porter, Glenn, ed. see Tedlow, Richard S.

Porter, Glenn, ed. see Yeager, Mary.

Porter, H. Boone. Keeping the Church Year. 1978. pap. 4.95 (ISBN 0-8164-2161-7). Seabury.

Porter, Horace. Campaigning with Grant. LC 81-14445. (Collector's Library of the Civil War). 26.60 (ISBN 0-8094-4200-0). Silver.
Porter, Ian H., jt. ed. see Vallet, H. Lawrence.
Porter, Ian H., et al, eds. see Symposium of the Birth Defects Institute of the New York State Dept. of Health, Second, October, 1971.
Porter, J. A. The Drama of Speech Acts: Shakespeare's Lancastrian Tetralogy. LC 78-57310. 1979. 19.50x (ISBN 0-520-03702-2). U of Cal Pr.
Porter, J. D., ed. Oman & the Persian Gulf, 1835-1949. 1982. Ltd. to 350 copies 34.95 (ISBN 0-89712-125-2). Documentary Pubns.
Porter, J. Marshall. Hallowed Be This Land. 1981. 6.50 (ISBN 0-87012-430-7). McClain.
Porter, Jack N. The Jew As Outsider: Historical & Contemporary Perspectives, Collected Essays, 1974-1980. LC 80-6247. 232p. (Orig.). 1982. lib. bdg. 20.50 (ISBN 0-8191-1638-6); pap. text ed. 10.50 (ISBN 0-8191-1639-4). U Pr of Amer.
--Jewish Partisans: A Documentary of Jewish Resistance in the Soviet Union During World War II, Vol. 1. LC 81-40258. (Illus.). 312p. (Orig.). 1982. lib. bdg. 25.25 (ISBN 0-8191-2179-7); pap. text ed. 12.75 (ISBN 0-8191-2180-0). U Pr of Amer.
Porter, Jack N., jt. auth. see Doress, Irvin.
Porter, Jack N., ed. Jewish Partisans: A Documentary of Jewish Resistance in the Soviet Union During World War II, Vol. II. LC 81-40258. 314p. (Orig.). 1982. lib. bdg. 24.25 (ISBN 0-8191-2537-7); pap. text ed. 12.75 (ISBN 0-8191-2538-5). U Pr of Amer.
--The Sociology of American Jews: A Critical Anthology. 2nd, rev. ed. LC 80-5760. 330p. 1980. pap. text ed. 12.75 (ISBN 0-8191-1236-4). U Pr of Amer.
Porter, Jack W. & Henrysson, Harald. A Jussi Bjoerling Discography. LC 82-81146. 192p. (Orig.). 1982. pap. 17.50 (ISBN 0-9608546-0-6). Jussi.
Porter, Jimathan & Chapple, Jonathan. Integrating the Computer with Your Business: Accounting for Computer Charges. LC 80-13930. 308p. 1980. pap. 34.95x (ISBN 0-470-26984-7). Halsted Pr.
Porter, John. If I Make My Bed in Hell. LC 79-84346. 1979. pap. 2.50 o.p. (ISBN 0-89877-005-X). Jeremy Bks.
Porter, John W. & Spurgeon, Sandra L. Biosynthesis of Isoprenoid Compounds, Vol. I. LC 80-28511. 558p. 1981. 66.95 (ISBN 0-471-04807-0, Pub. by Wiley-Interscience). Wiley.
--Biosynthesis of Isoprenoid Compounds, Vol. II. 550p. 1983. price not set (ISBN 0-471-09038-7, Pub. by Wiley-Interscience). Wiley.
Porter, Jonathan. Tseng Kuo-Fan's Private Bureaucracy. LC 72-619560. (China Research Monographs: No. 9). 1972. pap. 5.00x (ISBN 0-912966-10-6). IEAS.
Porter, Judith D. Black Child, White Child: The Development of Racial Attitudes. LC 76-133213. 1971. 14.00x o.p. (ISBN 0-674-07610-9); pap. 5.95x o.p. (ISBN 0-674-07611-7). Harvard U Pr.
Porter, K., jt. auth. see Ellinwood, L.
Porter, Katherine A. Pale Horse, Pale Rider. LC 67-62420. 12.95 (ISBN 0-15-170750-2). HarBraceJ.
--Ship of Fools. 1972. pap. 2.50 (ISBN 0-451-09272-4, E9272, Sig). NAL.
Porter, Kenneth R. Herpetology. 1972. text ed. 26.95 o.p. (ISBN 0-7216-7295-7, CBS C). SCP.
Porter, Kent. Building Model Ships from Scratch. LC 76-45071. (Illus.). 1977. 12.95 (ISBN 0-8306-7907-3); pap. 7.95 (ISBN 0-8306-6907-8, 907). TAB Bks.
Porter, Kingsley A. Construction of Lombard & Gothic Vaults. 1911. 65.00x (ISBN 0-685-69851-3). Elliots Bks.
Porter, Kirk H. History of Suffrage in the United States. LC 18-22279. 1969. Repr. of 1918 ed. lib. bdg. 18.50x (ISBN 0-8371-0620-6, POHS). Greenwood.
Porter, L., jt. auth. see Steers, R.
Porter, L. W., jt. ed. see Rosenzweig, M. R.
Porter, Laurence, tr. see De Maistre, Joseph.
Porter, Lindsay. MGB-Guide to Purchase & D.I.Y Restoration. (Illus.). 200p. 1982. write for info. (ISBN 0-85429-303-5). Haynes Pubns.
Porter, Lyman W., jt. auth. see Allen, Robert W.
Porter, Lyman W., jt. auth. see Steers, Richard M.
Porter, Lyman W., ed. see Hall, Douglas T.
Porter, Lyman W., ed. see Schneider, Benjamin.
Porter, Lyman W., et al. Behavior in Organizations. (Psychology & Management Ser.). (Illus.). 561p. 1974. text ed. 28.50 (ISBN 0-07-050527-6, C); exam questions 15.00 (ISBN 0-07-050528-4). McGraw.
Porter, M. Erin, jt. auth. see Gabbard-Alley, Anne.
Porter, M. Gilbert. The Art of Grit: Ken Kesey's Fiction. LC 81-69835. (Literary Frontiers Editions). 112p. pap. text ed. 8.00x (ISBN 0-8262-0368-X). U of Mo Pr.
Porter, Margaret, tr. see Vivien, Renee.
Porter, Marilyn. Home, Work, & Class Consciousness. 200p. 1983. 25.00 (ISBN 0-7190-0899-9). Manchester.
Porter, Mark. The Time of Your Life. 1983. pap. 4.95 (ISBN 0-88207-387-7). Victor Bks.
Porter, Mary, jt. auth. see Katsigris, Costas.
Porter, Michael E. Cases in Competitive Strategy. (Illus.). 400p. 1982. text ed. 22.50 (ISBN 0-02-925410-8). Free Pr.
Porter, Paul R. The Recovery of American Cities. LC 75-39090. (Illus.). 192p. 1976. 8.95 o.p. (ISBN 0-8467-0152-9, Pub. by Two Continents). Hippocrene Bks.
Porter, Penny. Howard's Monster. (gr. k-3). 1978. 4.50 o.p. (ISBN 0-682-49144-6). Exposition.
Porter, Peter & Sergeant, Howard. Gregory Awards. 1981. 11.50 (ISBN 0-436-37812-4, Pub. by Secker & Warburg). David & Charles.
Porter Productions. Fargo North's Decoder Game Book. (Electric Company Game Books). (Illus.). (ps-5). 1978. 2.95 o.s.i. (ISBN 0-448-14397-6, G&D). Putnam Pub Group.
--If I Met Raggedy Andy. LC 78-71510. (Stretch Bk.). (ps-k). 1979. 3.50 (ISBN 0-448-16364-0, G&D). Putnam Pub Group.
--If I Met Raggedy Ann. LC 78-71509. (Stretch Bk.). (Illus.). (ps-k). 1979. 3.50 (ISBN 0-448-16365-9, G&D). Putnam Pub Group.
--Stretch Books. Incl. If I Had a Parade. 3.50 (ISBN 0-448-12874-8); If I Met a Dinosaur. 2.50 o.s.i. (ISBN 0-448-12873-X). (Illus.). (ps-2). 1977 (G&D). Putnam Pub Group.
--Zig-Zag Color & Recolor Books. Incl. Dinosaurs. o.s.i. (ISBN 0-448-12187-5); Fairy Tale Parade (ISBN 0-448-12189-1); Animal Safari. o.s.i. (ISBN 0-448-12188-3); Where We Live (ISBN 0-448-12190-5). (Illus.). (gr. k-3). 1976. 1.95 (ISBN 0-685-61937-0, G&D). Putnam Pub Group.
Porter Productions, ed. Baby Animals. (Fold-A-Bks.). (Illus.). 16p. (ps). 1981. 2.95 (ISBN 0-448-11770-3, G&D). Putnam Pub Group.
--Everything on Wheels. (Fold-A-Bks.). (Illus.). 16p. (ps). 1981. 2.95 (ISBN 0-448-11771-1, G&D). Putnam Pub Group.
--The Little Engine That Could. (Stretch Bks.). (Illus.). 16p. (ps). 1981. 3.50 (ISBN 0-448-16266-0, G&D). Putnam Pub Group.
--One Nose, Ten Toes. (Stretch Bks.). (Illus.). 16p. (ps). 1981. 3.50 (ISBN 0-686-73576-5, G&D). Putnam Pub Group.
--Santa's Workshop. (Fold-A-Bks.). (Illus.). 16p. (ps). 1981. 2.95 (ISBN 0-448-11772-X, G&D). Putnam Pub Group.
--Up & Down & In & Out. (Fold-a-Bks.). (Illus.). 16p. (ps). 1981. 2.95 (ISBN 0-448-11773-8, G&D). Putnam Pub Group.
Porter, Q. N. & Baides, J. Mass Spectrometry of Heterocyclic Compounds. LC 70-123744. (General Heterocyclic Chemistry Ser.). 582p. (Orig.). 1971. 39.50 o.p. (ISBN 0-471-69504-1). Krieger.
Porter, R., ed. Neurophysiology III. (International Review of Physiology: Vol. 17). 320p. 1978. text ed. 24.50 o.p. (ISBN 0-8391-1067-7). Univ Park.
Porter, R., jt. ed. see Rousseau, G. S.
Porter, R. M., jt. ed. see Gallo, D. M.
Porter, Raymond J. P. H. Pearse. (English Authors Ser.: No. 154). 1973. lib. bdg. 10.95 o.p. (ISBN 0-8057-1434-0, Twayne). G K Hall.
Porter, Raymond J., jt. ed. see Brophy, James D.
Porter, Richard E., jt. auth. see Samovar, Larry A.
Porter, Richard N., tr. see Cizevskij, Dmitrij.
Porter, Robert. The Mushroom Hunt: How to Sharpen Your Eye for the Field & Find America's Choicest Mushrooms. (Illus.). 96p. 1983. 18.95 (ISBN 0-525-24137-X, 01840-550); pap. 11.95 (ISBN 0-525-48007-2, 01160-350). Dutton.
Porter, Robert, ed. Guide to Corporate Giving, No. 3. LC 82-20732. 592p. 1983. 39.95 (ISBN 0-915400-39-1). Am Council Arts.
--United Arts Fundraising, 1982. 64p. 1983. pap. 15.00 (ISBN 0-915400-42-1). Am Council Arts.
Porter, Roger. Presidential Decision Making. LC 80-10165. 272p. 1980. 24.95 (ISBN 0-521-23337-2). Cambridge U Pr.
--Presidential Decision Making: The Economic Policy Board. LC 80-10165. 272p. 1982. pap. 9.95 (ISBN 0-521-27112-6). Cambridge U Pr.
Porter, Roy. English Society in the Eighteenth Century. 416p. 1982. 40.00x o.p. (ISBN 0-7139-1417-3, Pub. by Penguin Bks). State Mutual Bk.
--English Society in the 18th Century. 1983. pap. 5.95 (ISBN 0-14-022099-2, Pelican). Penguin.
--The Making of Geology: Earth Science in Britain, 1660-1815. LC 76-56220. 1977. 39.50 (ISBN 0-521-21521-8). Cambridge U Pr.
Porter, Roy S. The History of the Earth Sciences: An Annotated Bibliography. LC 81-43367. 250p. 1983. lib. bdg. 30.00 (ISBN 0-8240-9267-8). Garland Pub.
Porter, Roze M. Thistle Hill, the Cattle Baron's Legacy. LC 80-67827. 456p. 1980. 19.95x o.p. (ISBN 0-87706-113-0). Branch-Smith.
Porter, Standish, jt. auth. see Ingamells, Lynn.
Porter, Stanley. Petroleum Accounting Practices. 1965. 44.50 (ISBN 0-07-050524-1, P&RB). McGraw.
Porter, Stephen C., ed. Late Quaternary Environments of the United States, Volume 1: The Late Pleistocene. (Illus.). 480p. 1983. 45.00x (ISBN 0-8166-1169-6). U of Minn Pr.
Porter, Stuart R., jt. auth. see Angel, Allen R.
Porter, Susan W., jt. auth. see Tinker, Jack.
Porter, Sylvia. Sylvia Porter's Financial Almanac for 1983. LC 82-72419. 160p. 1982. 8.95 (ISBN 0-8362-7908-5). Andrews & McMeel.
--Sylvia Porter's Financial Almanac for 1984. 160p. 1983. 8.95 (ISBN 0-8362-7913-1). Andrews & McMeel.
--Sylvia Porter's Income Tax Book, 1982. 184p. (Orig.). 1981. pap. 3.95 o.p. (ISBN 0-380-77925-0, 77925). Avon.
--Sylvia Porter's Income Tax Book, 1983. 176p. 1982. pap. 3.95 (ISBN 0-380-81687-3, 81687). Avon.
--Sylvia Porter's Nineteen Eighty-One Tax Book. 1981. pap. 3.95 o.p. (ISBN 0-380-76752-X, 76752). Avon.
--Sylvia Porter's Your Own Money. 768p. 1983. 12.95 (ISBN 0-380-83527-4). Avon.
Porter, T. & Durwood, A. Wealth: How to Achieve It! (Illus.). 352p. 1976. 19.95 (ISBN 0-87909-878-3); pap. 12.95 (ISBN 0-87909-877-5). Reston.
Porter, Tom. Architectural Color. (Illus.). 128p. 1982. 29.95 (ISBN 0-8230-7407-2, Whitney Lib). Watson-Guptill.
Porter, William E. The Italian Journalist. 256p. 1983. text ed. 18.00 (ISBN 0-472-10028-9). U of Mich Pr.
Porter, William S. see Henry, O., pseud.
Porterfield, Amanda. Feminine Spirituality in America: From Sarah Edwards to Martha Graham. 248p. 1980. 27.95 (ISBN 0-87722-175-8). Temple U Pr.
Porterfield, Austin. Cultures of Violence. 1965. 7.00 o.p. (ISBN 0-912646-36-5). Tex Christian.
--Mirror for Adjustment. 1967. 8.00 o.p. (ISBN 0-912646-35-7). Tex Christian.
--The Now Generation. 1971. 4.00 o.p. (ISBN 0-912646-33-0). Tex Christian.
--Wait the Withering Rain. 1953. 2.50 o.p. (ISBN 0-912646-37-3). Tex Christian.
Porterfield, Austin & Talbert, Robert. Crime, Suicide & Social Well-Being. 1948. 3.00 o.p. (ISBN 0-912646-38-1). Tex Christian.
Porterfield, Christopher, jt. auth. see Cavett, Dick.
Porterfield, James T. Investment Decisions & Capital Costs. (Illus.). 1965. pap. 11.95 ref. ed. o.p. (ISBN 0-13-502617-2). P-H.
Porterfield, William W. Advanced Inorganic Chemistry. (Illus.). 650p. Date not set. text ed. 30.00 (ISBN 0-686-82179-3). A-W.
--Inorganic Chemistry: A Unified Approach. (Illus.). 768p. Date not set. text ed. 30.00 (ISBN 0-201-05660-7). A-W.
Porteus, Geoff. Yesterday's Town: Dartford. 1981. 39.50x o.p. (ISBN 0-86023-135-6, Pub. by Barracuda England). State Mutual Bk.
Portgate & Firmin. Noggin & the Whale. 10.50x (ISBN 0-7182-0231-7, SpS). Sportshelf.
Porth, Carol. Pathophysiology: Concepts of Altered Health States. (Illus.). 608p. 1982. text ed. 23.75 (ISBN 0-397-54252-6, Lippincott Medical). Lippincott.
Porth, Jacquelyn S., ed. Defense & Foreign Affairs Handbook, 1983. 5th ed. (Illus.). 1982. 117.00x (ISBN 0-9605932-1-7). Defense & Foreign Aff.
Portillo, Alvaro del. Faithful & Laity in the Church. 200p. pap. 4.75 (ISBN 0-933932-40-5). Scepter Pubs.
--On Priesthood. 95p. 1974. 3.50 o.p. (ISBN 0-933932-46-4). Scepter Pubs.
Portis, Alan M. Electromagnetic Fields: Sources & Media. LC 78-7585. 1978. text ed. 37.95 (ISBN 0-471-01906-2); solutions manual o.p. (ISBN 0-471-03717-6). Wiley.
Portis, Charles. True Grit. (RL 8). pap. 1.75 (ISBN 0-451-11607-0, AE1607, Sig). NAL.
--True Grit. 1968. 9.95 o.p. (ISBN 0-671-76380-6); large type 6.95 o.p. (ISBN 0-671-20301-0). S&S.
Portland Cement Association Staff. Design & Construction of Large-Panel Concrete Structures (EBO96D) Methodology. Date not set. pap. 8.00 (ISBN 0-89312-036-7). Portland Cement.
--Design & Construction of Large-Panel Concrete Structures (EBO95D) Special Topics. Date not set. pap. 13.00 (ISBN 0-89312-037-5). Portland Cement.
Portman, Donald J. & Ryznar, Edward. An Investigation of Heat Exchange. (International Indian Ocean Expedition Meteorological Monographs: No. 5). 1971. 15.00x (ISBN 0-8248-0097-4, Eastwest Ctr). UH Pr.
Portman, John & Barnett, Jonathan. The Architect As Developer. (Illus.). 1976. 39.95 (ISBN 0-07-050536-5, P&RB). McGraw.
Portmann, Adolf. Animal Forms & Patterns: A Study of the Appearance of Animals. Czech, Hella, tr. from Ger. LC 67-14962. (Illus.). 1971. 6.00x o.p. (ISBN 0-8052-3003-3); pap. 3.95 (ISBN 0-8052-0309-5). Schocken.
Portmann, Michel, et al. The Ear & Temporal Bone. LC 78-61476. (Illus.). 464p. 1979. 82.50x (ISBN 0-89352-034-9). Masson Pub.
Portney, Paul R., ed. Current Issues in Natural Resource Policy. LC 82-47982. 272p. 1982. 27.50 (ISBN 0-8018-2916-X); pap. 9.50 (ISBN 0-8018-2917-8). Resources Future.
Portnoy, Dina. Women: The Recruiter's Last Resort. 40p. 1974. 2.00 (ISBN 0-686-43095-6). Recon Pubns.
Portnoy, Howard. Hot Rain. LC 77-6369. 1977. 8.95 o.p. (ISBN 0-399-11920-5). Putnam Pub Group.
Portnoy, Julius. Music in the Life of Man. LC 73-9265. (Illus.). 300p. 1973. Repr. of 1963 ed. lib. bdg. 20.25x (ISBN 0-8371-7000-1, POMU). Greenwood.
Portoghesi, Paolo. Postmodern: The Architecture of the Post-Industrial Society. (Illus.). 160p. 1983. 25.00 (ISBN 0-8478-0472-0). Rizzoli Intl.
Portoles, A., et al, eds. Modern Trends in Bacterial Transformation & Transfection: Proceedings of the Third European Meeting on Transformation & Transfection, Spain, Sept. 1976. 1977. 62.75 (ISBN 0-7204-0608-0, North-Holland). Elsevier.
Porton, Gary G. The Traditions of Rabbi Ishmael, Pt. IV: The Material as a Whole. (Studies in Judaism in Late Antiquity: Vol. 19). xiv, 261p. 1982. write for info. (ISBN 90-04-06414-1). E J Brill.
Portugal, Franklin H. & Cohen, Jack S. A Century of DNA. (Illus.). 400p. 1977. 25.00x (ISBN 0-262-16067-6); pap. 6.95 (ISBN 0-686-96796-8). MIT Pr.
Portugal, Nancy & Main, Jody. Potted Plant Organic Care. 3rd ed. LC 79-22173. (Living on This Planet Ser.). (Illus.). 80p. 1978. pap. 4.50 (ISBN 0-9601088-7-4). Wild Horses Potted Plant.
Portugal, Nancy, jt. auth. see Main, Jody.
Portugal, Pam. A Place for Human Beings. 2nd. ed. (Living on This Planet Ser.). (Illus.). 160p. 1978. pap. 6.95 (ISBN 0-9601088-5-8). Wild Horses Potted Plant.
Portuges, Paul, tr. Aztec Birth: Turquoise Mockingbird of Light. LC 79-114869. (Inklings Ser.: No. 2). (Nahuatl & English.). 1979. pap. 3.00 (ISBN 0-930012-32-1). Mudborn.
Portuges, Stephen H., jt. auth. see Jacobson, Gerald F.
Posa, John G., ed. see Electronics Magazine.
Posamentier, Alfred S., et al. Geometry: Its Elements & Structure. 2nd ed. 624p. (gr. 10). 1977. text ed. 17.64 (ISBN 0-07-050551-9, W); tchr's ed. 19.20 (ISBN 0-07-050552-7); tchr's manual 9.84 (ISBN 0-07-050554-3); tests 3.64 (ISBN 0-07-050553-5). McGraw.
Posavac, Emile J. & Carey, Raymond G. Program Evaluation: Methods & Case Studies. (Illus.). 1980. text ed. 23.95 (ISBN 0-13-729665-7). P-H.
Posell, Elsa. Dogs. LC 81-7742. (The New True Bks.). (Illus.). 48p. (gr. k-4). 1981. PLB 9.25 (ISBN 0-516-01614-8). Childrens.
--Elephants. LC 81-38470. (New True Bks.). (Illus.). 48p. (gr. k-4). 1982. PLB 9.25 (ISBN 0-686-97369-0). Childrens.
--Horses. LC 81-7741. (The New True Bks.). (Illus.). 48p. (gr. k-4). 1981. PLB 9.25 (ISBN 0-516-01623-7). Childrens.
--Whales & Other Sea Mammals. LC 82-4451. (New True Bks.). (gr. k-4). 1982. 9.25 (ISBN 0-516-01663-6). Childrens.
Posey, Carl A. Kiev Footprint. LC 82-22186. 1983. 12.95 (ISBN 0-396-08115-0). Dodd.
Posey, Kayte Lee, jt. auth. see Arnold, Dovie.
Posey, Rollin B. American Government. 11th ed. LC 77-11126. (Quality Paperbacks: No. 372). 352p. (Orig.). 1983. pap. 7.95 (ISBN 0-8226-0372-1). Littlefield.
Posgate, Helen B. Madame de Stael. (World Authors Ser.). 13.95 (ISBN 0-8057-6438-0, Twayne). G K Hall.
Poshek, Neila & De Tornya, Rheba. Teaching-Learning Strategies in Baccalaureate Nursing Education. 34p. 1976. 3.50 (ISBN 0-686-38280-3, 15-1622). Natl League Nurse.
Poslusney, Venard. Attaining Spiritual Maturity for Contemplation (According to St. John of the Cross) (Orig.). 1973. pap. 1.50 (ISBN 0-914544-04-7). Living Flame Pr.
--Prayer of Love: The Art of Aspiration. 128p. (Orig.). 1975. pap. 2.50 (ISBN 0-914544-07-1). Living Flame Pr.
--Union with the Lord in Prayer: Beyond Meditation to Affective Prayer, Aspiration & Contemplation. (Orig.). 1973. pap. 1.50 (ISBN 0-914544-03-9). Living Flame Pr.
Posnansky, Merrick, jt. auth. see Ehret, Christopher.
Posner, Barbara M. Nutrition & the Elderly: Policy Development, Program Planning, & Evaluation. LC 77-17683. 208p. 1979. 22.95 (ISBN 0-669-02085-0). Lexington Bks.
Posner, Donald, jt. auth. see Held, Julius.
Posner, Michael I. Cognition: An Introduction. 1974. pap. text ed. 9.95x (ISBN 0-673-07860-4). Scott F.
Posner, Michael I., jt. auth. see Fitts, Paul M.
Posner, Neil, ed. see Delson, Donn & Hurst, Walter E.
Posner, Neil, ed. see Michalove, Ed & Delson, Donn.
Posner, Neil, ed. see Paulson, Terry & Delson, Joyce.
Posner, R. The Romance Languages: A Linguistic Introduction. 8.50 (ISBN 0-8446-0853-X). Peter Smith.
Posner, Richard. The Impassioned. 352p. (Orig.). 1980. pap. 2.75 o.s.i. (ISBN 0-515-04624-8). Jove Pubns.
--Tort Law: Cases & Economic Analysis. LC 81-82981. 792p. 1982. text ed. 26.00 (ISBN 0-316-71436-4). Little.
--Tycoon. (Orig.). 1983. pap. price not set (ISBN 0-440-18856-3). Dell.
Posner, Richard, jt. auth. see Castoire, Marie.
Posner, Richard A. Economic Analysis of Law. 2nd ed. 1977. 19.95 (ISBN 0-316-71432-1). Little.

Posner, Richard A. & Easterbrook, Frank H. Antitrust-Cases, Economic Notes, & Other Materials. 2nd ed. LC 80-25590. (American Casebook Ser.). (Illus.). 1077p. 1980. text ed. 23.95 (ISBN 0-8299-2115-X); 1982 supplement avail. (ISBN 0-314-70608-9). West Pub.
Posner, Steve, jt. auth. see Sandler, Bernard.
Pospesel, Howard. Introduction to Logic: Predicate Logic. (Illus.). 224p. 1976. text ed. 13.95 (ISBN 0-13-486225-2). P-H.
Pospisil, Leopold J. The Ethnology of Law. 2nd ed. LC 77-75811. 1978. pap. text ed. 9.95 o.p. (ISBN 0-8465-5825-4). Benjamin-Cummings.
Possas, Mario L. & Coutinho, Mauricio. Multinational Enterprises, Technology & Employment in Brrazil: Three Case Studies. (Working Paper Ser.: No. 21). Date not set. price not set. Intl Labour Office.
Possehl, Gregory L. Indus Civilization in Saurashtra. 264p. 1981. text ed. 47.25x (ISBN 0-391-02260-1, Pub. by Concept India). Humanities.
Possehl, Gregory L., ed. Ancient Cities of the Indus. LC 78-54442. (Illus.). 438p. 1979. lib. bdg. 39.95 o.p. (ISBN 0-89089-093-5). Carolina Acad Pr.
Posserello, Jodie A. The Totally Awesome Val Guide. Black, Sue, as told to. (Illus.). 96p. pap. 2.95 (ISBN 0-8431-0621-2). Price Stern.
Possinger, Callie, ed. The Official Directory of Industrial & Commercial Traffic Executives-1983 Edition. LC 72-626342. (Illus.). 566p. 1982. 50.00 (ISBN 0-87408-023-1). Traffic Serv.
Post, C. R. History of Spanish Painting, Nineteen Thirty-Nineteen Sixty Six, Vols. 1-14. LC 30-7776. Repr. of 1938 ed. Set. 870.00 (ISBN 0-527-72000-3). Kraus Repr.
Post, Chandler R. Mediaeval Spanish Allegory. LC 73-137072. (Havard Studies in Comparative Lit: Vol. 4). (Illus.). 331p. 1974. Repr. of 1915 ed. lib. bdg. 17.00x (ISBN 0-8371-5535-5, POSA). Greenwood.
Post, Charles G., Jr. Supreme Court & Political Questions. LC 74-87386. (American History, Politics & Law Ser). 1969. Repr. of 1936 ed. lib. bdg. 25.00 (ISBN 0-306-71610-0). Da Capo.
Post, Dan R. Volkswagen: Nine Lives Later. 2nd ed. LC 82-173212. (Illus.). 320p. 1982. pap. 19.95 (ISBN 0-911160-42-6). Post-Era.
Post, Elizabeth. The New Emily Post's Etiquette. LC 74-14667. (Funk & W Bk.). (Illus.). 880p. 1975. 15.34i (ISBN 0-308-10167-7); thumb-indexed 16.30i (ISBN 0-308-10168-5). T y Crowell.
Post, Elizabeth & Staffieri, Anthony. The Complete Book of Entertaining From the Emily Post Institute. 1982. pap. 8.50 (ISBN 0-686-97246-5, Fireside). S&S.
Post, Elizabeth L. Emily Post's Complete Book of Wedding Etiquette. LC 81-48168. (Illus.). 224p. (Bound with Emily Post's Wedding Planner). 1981. 16.30i o.p. (ISBN 0-06-181682-5, HarpT). Har-Row.
--Emily Post's Complete Book of Wedding Etiquette. Bd. with Emily Post's Wedding Planner. 1982. 16.30i (ISBN 0-06-181682-5). Har-Row.
Post, Elizabeth L., ed. Emily Post's Wedding Etiquette: Wonderful World of Weddings. (Funk & W Bk.). (Illus.). 1970. 14.95i o.p. (ISBN 0-308-50005-9). T Y Crowell.
Post, Emil L. Two-Valued Iterative Systems of Mathematical Logic. 1941. pap. 10.00 (ISBN 0-527-02721-9). Kraus Repr.
Post, Emily & Staffieri, Anthony. The Complete Book of Entertaining from the Emily Post Institute. LC 80-7879. 320p. 1981. 15.34i (ISBN 0-690-01970-X). Har-Row.
Post, F., jt. auth. see Isaacs, A. D.
Post, Gaines, Jr. The Humanities: What is Their Place in American Education & Culture? (Vital Issues Ser.: Vol. XXXI, No. 9). 0.80 (ISBN 0-686-84149-2). Ctr Info Am.
Post, James. Corporate Behavior & Social Change. 300p. 1981. pap. text ed. 13.95 (ISBN 0-8359-1082-2); text ed. 18.00 (ISBN 0-8359-1083-0). Reston.
Post, James E., jt. auth. see Preston, Lee E.
Post, Jeremiah, jt. ed. see Post, Joyce.
Post, Jonathan F. Henry Vaughan: The Unfolding Vision. LC 82-47609. 264p. 1983. 22.50x (ISBN 0-691-06527-6). Princeton U Pr.
Post, Joyce & Post, Jeremiah, eds. Travel in the United States: A Guide to Information Sources. (Geography & Travel Information Guide Ser.: Vol. 3). 600p. 1981. 42.00x (ISBN 0-8103-1423-1). Gale.
Post, K. W. & Jenkins, G. D. The Price of Liberty: Personality & Politics in Colonial Nigeria. LC 70-186251. (African Studies, No. 7). (Illus.). 500p. 1973. 42.50 (ISBN 0-521-08503-9). Cambridge U Pr.
Post, Ken. Strike the Iron: A Colony at War: Jamaica 1939-1945, 2 vols. set. 567p. 1981. Vol. 1. text ed. 40.00x (ISBN 0-391-02390-X, Pub. by Inst Social Studies). Vol. 2 (ISBN 0-391-02454-X). Humanities.
Post, Kenneth & Vickers, Michael. Structure & Conflict in Nigeria 1960-1965. 256p. 1973. 27.50 (ISBN 0-299-06470-0). U of Wis Pr.
Post, Laurens van der see Van der Post, Laurens.
Post, Laurens van der see Van Der Post, Laurens.
Post, Laurens Van Der see Van Der Post, Laurens.
Post, Levi A. The Vatican Plato & Its Relations. (APA Philological Monographs). 22.50 (ISBN 0-686-95231-6, 40-00-04). Scholars Pr CA.
--The Vatican Plato & Its Relations. (Annual Publications Ser.). 15.00 o.p. (ISBN 0-686-96316-4, 40 00 03). Scholars Pr CA.
Post, Louis F. Deportations Delirium of Nineteen-Twenty. LC 73-114343. (Civil Liberties in American History Ser). 1970. Repr. of 1923 ed. lib. bdg. 42.50 (ISBN 0-306-71882-0). Da Capo.
Post Office Research Dept. London England. Human Factors in Telecommunications International Symposium, 5th. 1970. 75.00 (ISBN 0-686-37975-6). Info Gatekeepers.
Post, Thomas R., jt. auth. see Humphreys, Alan H.
Postal, Bernard & Koppman, Lionel. American Jewish Landmarks: A Travel Guide & History, Vol. 3, The Middle West. Schiff, Susan, ed. LC 76-27401. (Jewish Landmarks & History Ser.). 352p. (Orig.). 1983. 21.95 (ISBN 0-8303-0156-9); pap. 12.50 (ISBN 0-8303-0158-5). Fleet.
--American Jewish Landmarks: A Travel Guide & History, Vol. 4, The West. Schiff, Susan, ed. (Jewish Landmarks & History Ser.). 416p. (Orig.). 1983. 20.00 (ISBN 0-8303-0165-8); pap. 12.50 (ISBN 0-8303-0164-X). Fleet.
Postal, Paul M. On Raising: An Inquiry into One Rule of English Grammar & Its Theoretical Implications. LC 73-16482. (Current Studies in Linguistics: No. 5). 432p. 1974. 25.00x (ISBN 0-262-16057-9); pap. 6.95x (ISBN 0-262-66041-5). MIT Pr.
Postal, Paul M., jt. auth. see Katz, Jerrold J.
Postal, Paul M., jt. auth. see Keyser, Samuel J.
Postan, Elizabeth, jt. ed. see Holbrook, David.
Postan, M. M. Essays on Medieval Agriculture & General Problems of the Medieval Economy. (Illus.). 300p. 1973. 42.50 (ISBN 0-521-08744-9). Cambridge U Pr.
--Fact & Relevance: Essays on Historical Method. 1971. 29.95 (ISBN 0-521-07841-5). Cambridge U Pr.
--The Medieval Economy & Society: An Economic History of Britain, 1100-1500. LC 72-87202. 1973. 31.50x (ISBN 0-520-02325-0). U of Cal Pr.
--Medieval Trade & Finance. (Illus.). 350p. 1973. 49.50 (ISBN 0-521-08745-7). Cambridge U Pr.
Postan, M. M., jt. auth. see Brooke, C. N.
Postan, Michael, jt. ed. see Mathias, Peter.
Poste. Drawing Birds. 2nd ed. (The Grosset Art Instruction Ser.: No. 6). (Illus.). 48p. Date not set. pap. 1.95 (ISBN 0-448-00515-8, G&D). Putnam Pub Group.
Poste & Nicholson. Cytoskeletal Elements. (Cell Surface Reviews Ser.: Vol. 7). 1982. 99.75 (ISBN 0-444-80335-1). Elsevier.
--Membrane Reconstitution. (Cell Surface Reviews: Vol. 8). Date not set. 76.75 (ISBN 0-444-80391-2). Elsevier.
--The Synthesis, Assembly & Turnover of Cell Surface Components. (Cell Surface Reviews: Vol. 4). 1978. 131.00 (ISBN 0-444-00232-4, North-Holland). Elsevier.
Poste & Nicolson, eds. Dynamic Aspects of Cell Surface Organization. (Cell Surface Reviews Ser.: Vol. 3). 1977. 142.75 (ISBN 0-7204-0623-4, North-Holland). Elsevier.
Poste, jt. auth. see Cotman.
Poste, G. & Nicholson, G., eds. The Cell Surface in Animal Embryogenesis & Development. (Cell Surface Reviews: Vol. 1). 1977. 142.75 (ISBN 0-7204-0597-1, North-Holland). Elsevier.
--Virus Infection & the Cell Surface. (Cell Surface Reviews: Vol. 2). 1977. 92.00 (ISBN 0-7204-0598-X, North-Holland). Elsevier.
Postel, A. Williams. Mineral Resources of Africa. (African Handbooks Ser.: Vol. 2). (Illus.). 3.00x (ISBN 0-686-24091-X). Univ Mus of U.
Postel, G. De Originibus seu de Hebraicae Linguae et Gentis Antiquitate, Atque Variarum Linguarum Affinitate. (Linguistics 13th-18th Centuries). 60p. (Fr.). 1974. Repr. of 1538 ed. lib. bdg. 26.00 o.p. (ISBN 0-8287-0698-0, 71-5010). Clearwater Pub.
--Linguarum Douze Characteribus Differentium Introductio ac Legendi Methodus. (Linguistics 13th-18th Centuries). 180p. (Fr.). 1974. Repr. of 1538 ed. lib. bdg. 53.00x o.p. (ISBN 0-8287-0699-9, 71-5009). Clearwater Pub.
Postels, A. & Ruprecht, F. J. Illustrationes Algarum in Itinere Circa Orben...Collectarum. 1963. Repr. of 1840 ed. 80.00 (ISBN 3-7682-0158-9). Lubrecht & Cramer.
Poster, Amy G., et al. Japanese Paintings & Prints of the Shijo School. (Illus.). 48p. 1981. pap. 3.95 (ISBN 0-87273-085-9). Bklyn Mus.
Poster, Don S., et al, eds. Treatment of Cancer Chemotherapy Induced Nausea & Vomiting. LC 81-8217. (Illus.). 248p. 1981. 34.25x (ISBN 0-89352-153-1). Masson Pub.
Postgate. Nitrogen Fixation. (Studies in Biology: No. 92). 1978. 5.95 o.p. (ISBN 0-7131-2688-4). Univ Park.
Postgate, J. P., ed. see Propertius.
Postgate, J. R. Fundamentals of Nitrogen Fixation. LC 82-4182. (Illus.). 200p. Date not set. price not set (ISBN 0-521-24169-3); pap. price not set (ISBN 0-521-28494-5). Cambridge U Pr.
Postgate, Raymond. Story of a Year: 1848. LC 75-17508. (Illus.). 286p. 1975. Repr. of 1955 ed. lib. bdg. 18.00x (ISBN 0-8371-8249-2, POSY). Greenwood.
Postl, Anton. Laboratory Experiments in Physical Science. new ed. 1978. 6.95x o.s.i. (ISBN 0-88246-089-7). Oreg St U Bkstrs.
Postlethwayt, Malachy. Great Britain's True System. LC 67-18579. Repr. of 1757 ed. 35.00x (ISBN 0-678-00250-9). Kelley.
--Universal Dictionary of Trade & Commerce, 2 Vols. 4th ed. LC 67-29516. Repr. of 1774 ed. Set. 250.00x (ISBN 0-678-00551-6). Kelley.
Postlewait, Thomas, jt. ed. see Paradis, James.
Postlewaite, Philip F. Policy Readings in Individual Taxation. (Illus.). 364p. 1980. 20.00 (ISBN 0-07-050538-1). McGraw.
Postma, H. L. The Witch's Garden. LC 78-11414. (Illus.). (gr. k-3). 1979. 8.95 (ISBN 0-07-050535-7, GB). McGraw.
Postma, Lidia. The Stolen Mirror. LC 75-43888. (Illus.). 32p. (ps-3). 1976. 8.95 (ISBN 0-07-050533-0, GB); PLB 7.95 (ISBN 0-07-050534-9). McGraw.
Postma, Minnie. Tales from the Basotho: Fiction from the Oral Tradition of a Black South African People. McDermid, Susie, tr. from Afrikaans. (American Folklore Society Memoir Ser.: No. 59). 203p. 1974. 12.50x o.p. (ISBN 0-292-74608-3). U of Tex Pr.
Postma, Thijs. Fokker Aircraft. (Illus.). 160p. 1980. 19.95 (ISBN 0-86720-578-4). Sci Bks Intl.
Postman, Leo & Keppel, Geoffrey, eds. Norms of Word Association. 1970. 68.50 (ISBN 0-12-563050-6). Acad Pr.
Postman, Neil. Teaching As a Conserving Activity. 1979. 9.95 o.s.i. (ISBN 0-440-08651-5). Delacorte.
--Teaching As a Conserving Activity. pap. 7.00 (ISBN 0-686-84061-5). Intl Gen Semantics.
Postman, Neil & Weingartner, Charles. Linguistics. 1966. pap. 2.95 o.s.i. (ISBN 0-440-54844-6, Delta). Dell.
--The School Book: For People Who Want to Know What All the Hollaring Is About. 320p. 1974. 7.95 o.s.i. (ISBN 0-440-07649-8). Delacorte.
--Soft Revolution. 1971. pap. 2.35 o.s.i. (ISBN 0-440-58084-6, Delta). Dell.
--Teaching As a Subversive Activity. 1969. 9.95 o.s.i. (ISBN 0-440-08556-X). Delacorte.
Postman, Neil & Weingatner, Charles. The School Book. 320p. 1975. pap. 4.95 o.s.i. (ISBN 0-440-57642-3, Delta). Dell.
Postnikov, M. Lectures in Geometry: Linear Algebra & Differential Geometry. 319p. 1982. 8.45 (ISBN 0-8285-2461-0, Pub. by Mir Pubs USSR). Imported Pubns.
Postnikov, M. M. The Variational Theory of Geodesics. Scripta Technica Inc., tr. from Rus. 200p. 1983. pap. 4.50 (ISBN 0-486-63166-4). Dover.
Poston, Elizabeth & Arma, Paul. Gambit Book of French Folk Songs. LC 79-160414. (Illus.). 150p. (Eng. & Fr.). 1972. 11.95 (ISBN 0-87645-061-3). Gambit.
Poston, Elizabeth, tr. see Schneider, Marcel.
Poston, H. L. Surviving & Succeeding in Real Estate. (Illus.). 151p. 1982. 14.95 (ISBN 0-13-879148-1); pap. 7.95 (ISBN 0-13-879130-9). P-H.
Poston, John W., jt. auth. see Eichholz, Geoffrey G.
Poston, T. Catastrophe Theory & Its Applications. (Surveys & References Ser.: No. 2). 510p. 1979. text ed. 65.00 (ISBN 0-273-01029-8); pap. 28.50 (ISBN 0-273-08429-1). Pitman Pub MA.
Poston, T., jt. auth. see Dodson, C. T.
Postow, Elliot, jt. auth. see Takashima, Shiro.
Postuma, J. A. Manual of Planktonic Foraminifera. 1971. 98.00 (ISBN 0-444-40909-2). Elsevier.
Postyn, Jo K., jt. auth. see Postyn, Sol.
Postyn, Sol & Postyn, Jo K. Raising Cash: A Guide to Financing & Controlling Your Business. (Finance Ser.). (Illus.). 300p. 1981. 25.00 (ISBN 0-534-97966-1). Lifetime Learn.
Potapova, Nina. Russian Elementary Course, 2 Vols. 3rd ed. 1969. Vol. 1, 364p. 52.00x (ISBN 0-677-20890-1); Vol. 2, 488p. 64.00 (ISBN 0-677-20900-2). Gordon.
Potash, Robert A. Mexican Government & Industrial Development in the Early Republic: The Banco de Avio. Rev. ed. LC 82-15969. 264p. 1983. lib. bdg. 27.50x (ISBN 0-87023-382-3). U of Mass Pr.
Pote, Winston. Mountain Troops. (Illus.). 84p. 7.95 (ISBN 0-89272-150-2). Down East.
Poteet, David. How to Trace Your Family Tree. 2nd ed. LC 79-84344. (Illus.). 157p. 1979. pap. 2.95 (ISBN 0-89877-002-5). Jeremy Bks.
Poteet, G. Howard. Complete Illustrated Guide to Basic Carpentry. (Illus.). 256p. 1980. 12.95 o.p. (ISBN 0-13-161380-4, Parker). P-H.
--How to Treasure Hunt in the City. Nelson, Bettye, ed. LC 76-40846. (Illus., Orig.). pap. cancelled (ISBN 0-915920-27-1). Ram Pub.
Potega, Patrick H. Basics of R-C Scale. 80p. pap. 11.95 (ISBN 0-942794-00-1). Model Agency.
Potegal, Michael, ed. Spatial Abilities: Development & Physiological Foundations. rev. ed. (Developmental Psychology Ser.). 1982. 36.00 (ISBN 0-12-563080-8). Acad Pr.
Potel, Jean-Yves. The Promise of Solidarity. 256p. 1982. 26.95 (ISBN 0-03-061776-6); pap. 9.95 (ISBN 0-03-062364-2). Praeger.
Potgieter, P. J. Index to Literature on Race Relations in South Africa, 1910-1975. 1979. lib. bdg. 49.00 (ISBN 0-8161-8295-7, Hall Reference). G K Hall.
Potholm, C. The Theory & Practice of African Politics. 1979. pap. 13.95 (ISBN 0-13-913533-2). P-H.
Potholm, C. P. & Morgan, R. E., eds. Focus on Police: The Police in American Society. 1976. pap. text ed. 18.50 o.p. (ISBN 0-470-15075-0); pap. text ed. 6.95 o.p. (ISBN 0-470-15077-7). Halsted Pr.
Potholm, Christian P. Strategy & Conflict: The Search for Historical Malleability. LC 78-71368. (Illus.). 1979. pap. 8.25 (ISBN 0-8191-0668-2). U Pr of Amer.
Potholm, Christian P. & Fredland, Richard A., eds. Integration & Disintegration in East Africa. LC 80-5914. 229p. 1980. lib. bdg. 20.00 (ISBN 0-8191-1298-4); pap. text ed. 10.25 (ISBN 0-8191-1299-2). U Pr of Amer.
Poticha, Joseph S. & Southwood, Art. Use It or You'll Lose It. LC 78-13130. 1978. 8.95 o.p. (ISBN 0-399-90020-9, Marek). Putnam Pub Group.
Potichnyj, Peter J & Shapiro, Jane P., eds. From the Cold War to Detente. LC 75-19808. (Praeger Special Studies). 238p. 1976. 35.95 o.p. (ISBN 0-275-56200-X). Praeger.
Potichnyj, Peter J., jt. ed. see Shapiro, Jane P.
Potocki, Patricia A. & Miller, Barbara L. Hands On: A Manipulative Curriculum for Teaching Multiply Handicapped Hearing Impaired Students. 1980. 3-ring binder 39.00 (ISBN 0-88450-722-X, 3124-B). Communication Skill.
Potok, Chaim. The Book of Lights. large print ed. LC 82-3277. 660p. 1982. Repr. of 1981 ed. 13.95 (ISBN 0-89621-358-7). Thorndike Pr.
--Chosen. (gr. 7 up). 1967. 9.95 o.p. (ISBN 0-671-13674-7); large type 7.95 o.p. (ISBN 0-671-20302-9). S&S.
Pottebaum, G. A. Jesus: The Gift of Life. (Little People's Paperbacks Ser.). 1979. pap. 0.99 (ISBN 0-8164-2246-X). Seabury.
Potten, C. S., jt. ed. see Lord, B. I.
Pottenger, Francis M. & Bowes, Edwin E. Fundamentals of Chemistry. 1976. text ed. 19.95x (ISBN 0-673-07876-0). Scott F.
Pottenger, Francis M., et al. Fundamentals of Chemistry in the Laboratory. 1976. pap. 8.95x (ISBN 0-673-07877-9). Scott F.
Pottenger, Maritha. Healing & the Horoscope. 1982. pap. 9.95 (ISBN 0-686-96467-5, Pub. by Astro Comp Serv). Para Res.
Potter, A. M., jt. ed. see Chapman, B.
Potter, Alexander, jt. auth. see Potter, Margaret.
Potter, Beatrix. Jeannot Lapin: Benjamin Bunny. (gr. 3-7). bds. 4.50 (ISBN 0-7232-0651-1). Warne.
--Peter Rabbit. (Nursery Treasure Bks). (Illus.). (ps). 1962. 1.50 o.p. (ISBN 0-448-04203-7, G&D). Putnam Pub Group.
--Peter Rabbit Books, 23 Vols. (Illus.). (ps-2). Set. 79.95 (ISBN 0-7232-1374-7). Warne.
--The Peter Rabbit Diary. (Illus.). 90p. 1983. 3.95 (ISBN 0-7232-2982-1). Warne.
--Tale of Peter Rabbit. (Illus.). (ps-2). 1902. bds. 3.50 (ISBN 0-7232-0592-2); pap. 1.95 (ISBN 0-7232-6226-8). Warne.
--Tale of Peter Rabbit & Other Children's Favorites, 4 vols. Incl. The Tale of Peter Rabbit; The Tale of Benjamin Bunny; The Tale of Squirrel Nutkin; The Tale of Two Bad Mice. (Illus.). (gr. 3 up). 1975. 11.95 o.p. (ISBN 0-517-52464-3). Crown.
--The Tale of Peter Rabbit & Other Stories. LC 82-47808. 1982. 16.95 (ISBN 0-394-52845-X). Knopf.
--The Tale of Tom Kitten. (Illus.). 58p. (gr. k up). 1983. pap. 1.50 (ISBN 0-486-24502-0). Dover.
Potter, Beatrix & Stewart, Pat. The Tale of Two Bad Mice: A Coloring Book. (Illus.). 32p. (Orig.). (gr. 1 up). 1982. pap. 2.00 (ISBN 0-486-24385-0). Dover.
Potter, Burtt, Jr. The Church Reaching Out. LC 76-12219. 1976. 8.95 (ISBN 0-87716-062-7, Pub. by Moore Pub Co). F Apple.
Potter, C. W., et al. Introduction to Medical Microbiology. 1968. 8.95 o.p. (ISBN 0-407-56500-0). Butterworth.
Potter, Charles F. The Lost Years of Jesus Revealed. 160p. 1982. pap. 2.25 (ISBN 0-686-96933-2, GM). Fawcett.
Potter, Charles H. Perennials in the Garden. LC 59-6124. (Illus.). 1959. 12.95 (ISBN 0-87599-094-0). S G Phillips.
Potter, D. E. Computational Physics. LC 72-8613. 304p. 1973. 62.95 (ISBN 0-471-69555-6, Pub. by Wiley-Interscience). Wiley.
Potter, David A., jt. auth. see Sidar, Alexander G., Jr.
Potter, David M. Division & the Stresses of Reunion: 1845-1876. 240p. 1973. pap. 9.95x (ISBN 0-673-05786-0). Scott F.
--Impending Crises, Eighteen Forty-Eight to Eighteen Sixty-One. (New American Nation Ser.). 1976. pap. 9.95xi (ISBN 0-06-131929-5, TB1929, Torch). Har-Row.
--People of Plenty: Economic Abundance & the American Character. (Walgreen Foundation Lecutre Ser). 1954. pap. 5.95 (ISBN 0-226-67633-1, P28, Phoen). U of Chicago Pr.
Potter, Edgar R. Cowboy Slang. Rev. ed. 192p. 1983. pap. 9.95 (ISBN 0-87842-155-6). Mountain Pr.

Potter, Edward E., ed. Legal & Practical Alternatives to Employee Selection Compliance & Litigation Under Title Six. 320p. 1983. pap. 19.75 (ISBN 0-937856-07-X). Equal Employ.
--Legal & Practical Alternatives to Employee Selection Compliance & Litigation under Title VII. LC 83-80033. (EEAC Monograph Ser.: No. 2). 320p. (Orig.). 1983. pap. 19.75. Equal Employ.
Potter, Elmer B. Nimitz. LC 76-1056. 507p. 1976. 21.95 (ISBN 0-87021-492-6). Naval Inst Pr.
Potter, G. R., ed. Huldrych Zwingli. LC 78-5311. (Documents of Modern History Ser.). 1978. 23.00x (ISBN 0-312-39633-3). St Martin.
Potter, G. R., jt. ed. see Pipkin, H. Wayne.
Potter, George B. & Frates, Jeffrey E. Data Processing: An Introduction. (Illus.). 328p. 1982. pap. text ed. 13.95x (ISBN 0-941018-06-7). Martin Pr.
Potter, I. G., jt. ed. see Hardisty, M. W.
Potter, James L. & Fich, S. Theory of Networks & Lines. (Illus.). 1963. ref. ed. 31.95 (ISBN 0-13-913228-7). P-H.
Potter, Janice. The Liberty We Seek: Loyalist Ideology in Colonial New York & Massachusetts. 256p. 1983. text ed. 22.50x (ISBN 0-674-53026-8). Harvard U Pr.
Potter, Jeffrey. Men, Money & Magic: The Story of Dorothy Schiff. (Illus.). 416p. 1976. 9.95 o.p. (ISBN 0-698-10666-0, Coward). Putnam Pub Group.
--Men, Money & Magic: The Story of Dorothy Schiff. (Illus.). 1977. pap. 2.25 o.p. (ISBN 0-451-07691-5, E7691, Sig). NAL.
Potter, John. Yacht Survey Nineteen Seventy-Nine: A Consumer Guide to New Sailboats. 35.00 o.p. (ISBN 0-685-42971-7, 9330/79). Gaylord Prof Pubns.
Potter, Joseph, jt. auth. see Miro, Carmen.
Potter, Joy H. Elio Vittorini. (World Authors Ser.). 1979. lib. bdg. 15.95 (ISBN 0-8057-6359-7, Twayne). G K Hall.
Potter, Karl H. Presuppositions of India's Philosophies. LC 72-6843. 276p. 1973. Repr. of 1963 ed. lib. bdg. 19.75x o.p. (ISBN 0-8371-6497-4, POPI); pap. 4.95 o.p. (ISBN 0-8371-8958-6, POP). Greenwood.
Potter, Karl H., ed. The Encyclopedia of Indian Philosophies: Bibliography, Vol. 1. 2nd ed. 842p. Date not set. 27.00 (ISBN 0-89581-366-1). Lancaster-Miller.
Potter, Lillian F., jt. auth. see Schwartz, Estelle R.
Potter, Louis, Jr. The Art of Cello Playing. (Illus.). 236p. (Orig.). 1980. pap. text ed. 16.50 (ISBN 0-87487-071-2). Summy.
Potter, Margaret & Potter, Alexander. Houses. 48p. 1973. 12.95 o.p. (ISBN 0-7195-2812-7). Transatlantic.
Potter, Marian. Blatherskite. LC 80-18450. 192p. (gr. 4-6). 1980. 8.75 (ISBN 0-688-22249-8); PLB 8.40 (ISBN 0-688-32249-2). Morrow.
--The Shared Room. LC 79-18012. 192p. (gr. 7-9). 1979. 8.75 (ISBN 0-688-22209-9); PLB 8.40 (ISBN 0-688-32209-3). Morrow.
Potter, Maurice D. & Corbman, B. P. Textiles: Fiber to Fabric. 4th ed. 1967. text ed. 20.05 o.p. (ISBN 0-07-050542-X, G); instructors' key 5.00 o.p. (ISBN 0-07-050541-1). McGraw.
Potter, Merle C. Mathematical Methods in the Physical Sciences. (Illus.). 1978. ref. ed. 29.95 (ISBN 0-13-561134-2). P-H.
Potter, Neil. Oil. LC 80-50955. (New Reference Library Ser.). PLB 11.96 (ISBN 0-382-06396-1). Silver.
--Oil Rig. LC 78-61231. (Careers Ser.). (Illus.). 1978. PLB 11.96 (ISBN 0-382-06195-0). Silver.
Potter, Neil & Frost, Jack. The Queen Mary: Her Inception & History. LC 70-131366. (Illus.). 1971. 10.00 o.p. (ISBN 0-911302-14-X). San Francisco Pr.
Potter, P. D., jt. auth. see Rusch, W. V.
Potter, Patricia A., jt. auth. see Perry, Anne G.
Potter, Philip. Life in All Its Fullness. 183p. 1983. 5.95 (ISBN 0-8028-1938-9). Eerdmans.
Potter, Philip J. Power Plant Theory & Design. 2nd ed. (Illus.). 1959. 41.95 (ISBN 0-471-06689-3). Wiley.
Potter, R. William. Issues for the Eighties: Energy, 1981. 1982. 4.00 (ISBN 0-686-33164-8). Ctr Analysis Public Issues.
Potter, Ralph B. War & Moral Discourse. LC 69-18111. (Orig.). 1969. pap. 1.95 (ISBN 0-8042-0863-8). John Knox.
Potter, Robert B. The Urban Retailing System: Location, Cognition & Behaviour. 247p. 1982. text ed. 37.00x (ISBN 0-566-00458-5). Gower Pub Ltd.
Potter, Robert G., jt. ed. see Bongaarts, John.
Potter, Robert R. Making Sense: Exploring Semantics & Critical Thinking. 1983. 8.50 (ISBN 0-686-84072-0). Intl Gen Semantics.
Potter, Sulamith H. Family Life in a Northern Thai Village: A Study of the Structural Significance of Women. LC 76-52035. 1978. 17.50x (ISBN 0-520-03430-9); pap. 5.25x (ISBN 0-520-04044-9). U of Cal Pr.
Potter, T., jt. auth. see Rac, G.
Potter, T. W. The Changing Landscape of South Etruria. (Illus.). 1979. 30.00 (ISBN 0-312-12953-X). St Martin.
Potter, Van R. Bioethics: Bridge to the Future. (Illus.). 1971. pap. 12.95 ref. ed. (ISBN 0-13-076505-8). P-H.
Potter, William G. & Faber, Arlene. Serials Automation for Acquisition & Inventory Control. 192p. 1982. pap. text ed. 15.00 (ISBN 0-8389-3267-3). ALA.
Potterton, Homan & Keaveney, Raymond. National Gallery of Ireland: Fifty Pictures. (Illus.). 50p. pap. 9.95 (ISBN 0-903162-05-9, Pub. by Salem Hse Ltd.). Merrimack Bk Serv.
Potterton, Homan, intro. by. The National Gallery of Ireland Illustrated Summary Catalogue of Paintings. 1982. 125.00x (ISBN 0-7171-1144-X, Pub. by Gill & Macmillan Ireland). State Mutual Bk.
Pottinger, David. Quilts From the Indiana Amish: A Regional Collection. (Illus.). 80p. 1983. 22.95 (ISBN 0-525-93285-2, 02229-660); pap. 12.95 (ISBN 0-525-48043-9, 01258-370). Dutton.
Pottinger, Don. The Official Chart of the Tower of London. (Illus.). 1978. pap. 2.95 o.p. (ISBN 0-517-53412-6). Crown.
Pottinger, J. Stanley, jt. auth. see Dennis, Warren L.
Pottle, Frederick, jt. ed. see Reed, Joseph W.
Pottle, Frederick A., ed. see Boswell, James.
Potts, D. C. & Charlton, D. G., eds. French Thought since Sixteen Hundred. LC 75-2862. 96p. 1974. pap. 4.95x (ISBN 0-416-81630-4). Methuen Inc.
Potts, D. Gordon, jt. auth. see Newton, Thomas H.
Potts, D. M., jt. auth. see Peel, J.
Potts, Daniel L. International Metallic Materials Cross Reference. 2nd ed. 432p. 1982. 75.00x (ISBN 0-931690-16-1). GE Tech Market.
Potts, F. A., jt. auth. see Borradaile, L. A.
Potts, John. Beyond Initial Reading. LC 75-36499. 1976. 7.00x o.p. (ISBN 0-8052-3619-8). Schocken.
Potts, L. J., jt. auth. see White, T. H.
Potts, Malcolm, et al. Abortion. LC 76-27907. (Illus.). 1977. 70.00 (ISBN 0-521-21442-4); pap. 22.95x (ISBN 0-521-29150-X). Cambridge U Pr.
Potts, Phil. Survival is the Bottom Line. 58p. (Orig.). 1980. pap. 2.95 o.p. (ISBN 0-89260-182-5). Hwong Pub.
Potts, Stephen W. From Here to Absurdity: The Moral Battlefields of Joseph Heller. LC 81-21602. (The Milford Series: Popular Writers of Today: Vol. 36). 64p. 1982. lib. bdg. 9.95x (ISBN 0-89370-156-4); pap. 3.95x (ISBN 0-89370-256-0). Borgo Pr.
Potvin, Claude, tr. see Wade, Harlan.
Potvin, Denis & Fischler, Stan. Power on Ice. LC 76-9198. (Illus.). (YA) 1977. 12.45i (ISBN 0-06-013387-2, HarpT). Har-Row.
Potvin, Rose-Ella, tr. see Wade, Harlan.
Poucher, W. A. & Howard, G. M. Perfumes, Cosmetics & Soaps. Incl. Vol. 1. The Raw Materials of Perfumery. 7th ed. LC 74-8885. 381p. 1974. 52.00x (ISBN 0-412-10640-X); Vol. 2. Production, Manufacture & Application of Perfumes. 8th ed. LC 74-8883. 379p. 1974. 52.00x (ISBN 0-412-10650-7); Vol. 3. Modern Cosmetics. 8th ed. LC 74-8882. 465p. 1974. 52.00x (ISBN 0-412-10660-4). 1975 (Pub. by Chapman & Hall). Methuen Inc.
Poudyal, Sriram. Planned Development in Nepal. 1982. 14.00 (ISBN 0-8364-0917-5, Pub. by Sterling). South Asia Bks.
Pough, F. H., jt. ed. see Gans, C.
Pough, Frederick H. A Field Guide to Rocks & Minerals. 4th ed. (Peterson Field Guide Ser.). 1976. 12.95 (ISBN 0-395-24047-6); pap. 10.95 (ISBN 0-395-24049-2). HM.
Pough, Harvey, jt. auth. see Gans, Carl.
Poulantzas, Nicos. Classes in Contemporary Capitalism. (Illus.). 1978. pap. 6.75 (Pub by NLB); 22.50 (ISBN 0-8052-7041-8). Schocken.
--The Crisis of the Dictatorships: Portugal, Spain, Greece. 1976. 10.50 (ISBN 0-8052-7033-7, Pub. by NLB). Schocken.
--Fascism & Dictatorship. 1980. pap. 11.50 (ISBN 0-8052-7029-9, Pub. by Verso). Schocken.
--Fascism & Dictatorship. 1974. 18.50x (ISBN 0-902308-85-8, Pub by NLB); pap. 11.50 (ISBN 0-8052-7029-9). Schocken.
--State, Power, Socialism. 270p. 1980. pap. 8.75 (ISBN 0-86091-013-X, Pub. by NLB); 15.50x (ISBN 0-8052-7055-8). Schocken.
Poularikas, Alexander, jt. auth. see Seely, Samuel.
Poulet, Anne. Corot to Braque: French Paintings from the Museum of Fine Arts, Boston. Spear, Judy, ed. Murphy, Alexandra. LC 79-1719. (Illus.). 196p. 1979. 19.95 (ISBN 0-87846-151-5); pap. 13.95 (ISBN 0-686-96801-8). Mus Fine Arts Boston.
Poulet, Virginia. Blue Bug & the Bullies. LC 79-159789. (Blue Bug Bks.). (Illus.). 32p. (gr. k-3). 1971. PLB 9.25 (ISBN 0-516-03418-9); pap. 2.95 (ISBN 0-516-43418-7). Childrens.
--Blue Bug's Treasure. LC 75-40352. (Illus.). 32p. (gr. k-2). 1976. PLB 9.25 (ISBN 0-516-03424-3); pap. 2.95 (ISBN 0-516-43424-1). Childrens.
--Blue Bug's Vegetable Garden. LC 73-8896. (Illus.). 32p. (gr. k-3). 1973. PLB 9.25 (ISBN 0-516-03421-9); pap. 2.95 (ISBN 0-516-43421-7). Childrens.
Poulin, A., ed. see Logan, John, Jr.
Poulin, A., Jr. Contemporary American Poetry. 3rd ed. LC 79-91632. (Illus.). 1980. pap. text ed. 14.50 (ISBN 0-395-28635-2). HM.
Poulin, Clarence. Tailoring Suits the Professional Way. rev. ed. (Illus.). (gr. 9-12). 1973. text ed. 13.28 (ISBN 0-87002-128-1). Bennett IL.
Poull, Jean & Weber, C. A. Songs of the Cajean. 1979. 7.50 o.p. (ISBN 0-533-04065-5). Vantage.
Poulos, H. G. & Davis, E. H. Elastic Solutions for Soil & Rock Mechanics. LC 73-17171. (Soil Engineering Ser.). 424p. 1974. text ed. 54.50 (ISBN 0-471-69565-3). Wiley.
--Pile Foundation Analysis & Design. (Geotechnical Engineering Ser.). 1980. text ed. 44.95x (ISBN 0-471-02084-2). Wiley.
Poulos, Steve J., jt. auth. see Hirschfeld, Ronald C.
Poulson, Barry W. Economic History of the United States. 672p. 1981. text ed. 24.95 (ISBN 0-02-396220-8). Macmillan.
Poulson, Barry W., et al, eds. U. S. - Mexico Economic Relations. (Special Studies in International Economics & Business). 1979. lib. bdg. 40.00 (ISBN 0-89158-469-2). Westview.
Poulson, Doranne. Those Hilarious Years. 1979. 6.95 o.p. (ISBN 0-533-03916-9). Vantage.
Poulson, T., jt. auth. see Mohr, Charles E.
Poulsson, Emilie. Finger Plays for Nursery & Kindergarten. LC 74-165397. (Illus.). (ps-k). 1971. pap. 1.95 (ISBN 0-486-22588-7). Dover.
Poulter, Sebastian M., jt. auth. see Palmer, Vernon V.
Poulter, Virgil, ed. see Walrod, Michael R.
Poulter, Virgil L., ed. see Payne, David L.
Poultney, David. Studying Music History: Learning, Reasoning & Writing About Music History & Literature. 256p. 1983. pap. text ed. 9.95 (ISBN 0-13-858860-0). P-H.
Poulton, Diana. John Dowland. 2nd ed. (Illus.). 550p. 1982. 38.50x (ISBN 0-520-04687-0). U of Cal Pr.
Poulton, G. A. & James, Terry. Pre-Schooling in the Community. 160p. 1975. 14.95x (ISBN 0-7100-8245-2); pap. 7.95 (ISBN 0-7100-8246-0). Routledge & Kegan.
Poulton, Helen J. Nevada State Agencies. 47p. 1964. pap. 1.75x (ISBN 0-87417-009-5). U of Nev Pr.
Pouncey, Philip, jt. auth. see Gere, J. A.
Pound, Arthur. Lake Ontario. LC 70-118789. (Empire Historical Publications Ser: No. 87). 1970. Repr. of 1945 ed. 12.00 o.p. (ISBN 0-87198-087-8). Friedman.
Pound, Ezra. Antheil & the Treatise on Harmony. 2nd ed. LC 68-27463. (Music Ser). (gr. 9 up). 1968. Repr. of 1927 ed. lib. bdg. 21.50 (ISBN 0-306-70981-3). Da Capo.
--The Collected Early Poems of Ezra Pound. King, Michael, et al, eds. LC 76-7086. 352p. 1982. pap. 8.95 (ISBN 0-8112-0843-5, NDP540). New Directions.
Pound, Ezra & Ford, Ford Madox. Pound-Ford: The Story of a Literary Friendship. Seyersted, Brita L., ed. LC 82-2255. 384p. 1982. 22.95 (ISBN 0-8112-0833-8). New Directions.
Pound, Ezra, ed. see Fenollosa, Ernest.
Pound, Louise. Nebraska Folklore. LC 75-36101. 243p. 1976. Repr. of 1960 ed. lib. bdg. 17.75x (ISBN 0-8371-8616-1, PONF). Greenwood.
--Selected Writings. LC 79-139144. 1971. Repr. of 1949 ed. lib. bdg. 18.50x (ISBN 0-8371-5760-9, POWR). Greenwood.
Pound, Roscoe. Criminal Justice in America. LC 79-37841. (American Constitutional & Legal History Ser). 224p. 1972. Repr. of 1930 ed. lib. bdg. 27.50 (ISBN 0-306-70435-8). Da Capo.
Pound, Roscoe, ed. see Cleveland Foundation.
Pounds, N. J. An Historical Geography of Europe, Fifteen Hundred to Eighteen Forty. LC 78-18102. (Illus.). 1980. 52.50 (ISBN 0-521-22379-2). Cambridge U Pr.
Pounds, Norman J. Political Geography. 2nd ed. (Geography Ser.). (Illus.). 448p. 1972. text ed. 39.95 (ISBN 0-07-050566-7, C). McGraw.
--Ruhr: A Study in Historical & Economic Geography. LC 68-55636. (Illus.). 1968. Repr. of 1952 ed. lib. bdg. 15.75x (ISBN 0-8371-0621-4, POTR). Greenwood.
Pountney, Harold. Police Photography. (Illus.). 1971. 26.75 (ISBN 0-85334-621-6, Pub. by Applied Sci England). Elsevier.
Poupard, Dennis, ed. Literature Criticism from 1400 to 1800, Vol. 1. 1983. 55.00x (ISBN 0-686-96396-2). Gale.
Pournelle, J. E. There Will Be War. 320p. 1983. pap. 2.95 (ISBN 0-523-48555-7). Pinnacle Bks.
Pournelle, Jerry. King David's Spaceship. 1981. 11.95 o.p. (ISBN 0-671-25328-X). S&S.
Pournelle, Jerry & Green, Roland. Janissaries: Clan & Crown. (Illus.). 437p. 1982. pap. 5.95 (ISBN 0-441-38288-6, Pub. by Ace Science Fiction). Ace Bks.
Pournelle, Jerry, jt. auth. see Niven, Larry.
Pousada, Lidia, jt. auth. see Nahemow, Lucille.
Poussin, Charles D., jt. auth. see Bernstein, Serge.
Poutney, Ernie. For the Socialist Cause. 1973 ed. 80p. pap. 5.95 (ISBN 0-686-37392-8). Beekman Pubs.
Pouzin. The Cyclades Computer Network: Toward Layered Architectures. (International Council for Computer Communications Ser.: Vol. 2). 1982. 51.00 (ISBN 0-444-86482-2). Elsevier.
Povell, Roy A., jt. auth. see Langer, Marshall J.
Poverman, C. E. Solomon's Daughter. (Contemporary American Fiction Ser.). 1983. pap. 5.95 (ISBN 0-14-006280-7). Penguin.
Povey, John. Roy Campbell. (World Authors Ser.). 1977. lib. bdg. 15.95 (ISBN 0-8057-6277-9, Twayne). G K Hall.
Powanda, M. C. & Canonico, P. G., eds. Infection: The Physiologic & Metabolic Responses of the Host. 450p. 1982. 120.00 (ISBN 0-444-80336-X). Elsevier.
Powder Metallurgy Equipment Ass'n. Powder Metallurgy Equipment Manual, 4 parts. 161p. 1977. 18.00x (ISBN 0-918404-37-1); members 12.00 (ISBN 0-686-86346-1). Metal Powder.
Powdrrell, Fances D., jt. auth. see Malakoff, Anna.
Powell. Barclodiad y Gawres. 94p. 1982. 50.00x (ISBN 0-85323-400-0, Pub. by Liverpool Univ England). State Mutual Bk.
--Renaissance Italy. (Warwick Press Ser.). (gr. 5 up). 1980. PLB 9.90 (ISBN 0-531-09164-3, B34). Watts.
Powell, A. E. Causal Body. 1972. 18.95 (ISBN 0-8356-5034-0). Theos Pub Hse.
--Mental Body. 1975. 11.95 o.p. (ISBN 0-8356-5504-0). Theos Pub Hse.
Powell, A. W. B. New Zealand Mollusca. (Illus.). 532p. 1983. 60.00 (ISBN 0-00-216906-1, Pub. by W Collins Australia). Intl Schol Bk Serv.
Powell, Alan. Far Country: A Short History of the Northern Territory. (Illus.). 301p. 1982. pap. text ed. 19.95 (ISBN 0-522-84226-7, Pub. by Melbourne U Pr Australia). Intl Schol Bk Serv.
Powell, Anthony. The Strangers All Are Gone. (Anthony Powell's Memoirs Ser.). (Illus.). 212p. 1983. 18.50 (ISBN 0-03-063279-X). HR&W.
Powell, Anton. Rise of Islam. LC 79-89730. (Modern Knowledge Library). (gr. 5 up). 1980. 9.90 (ISBN 0-531-09165-1). Watts.
Powell, Arlyn. Nature Photography. (Illus.). 144p. 1983. pap. 14.95 o.p. (ISBN 0-930764-35-8). Curtin & London.
Powell, Arthur E. The Astral Body. LC 73-4775. (Classics Ser.). 280p. 1973. pap. 5.50 (ISBN 0-8356-0438-1, Quest). Theos Pub Hse.
Powell, Claire. The Meaning of Flowers: A Garland of Plant Lore & Symbolism from Popular Custom & Literature. LC 78-51422. (Illus.). 1979. o.p. (ISBN 0-394-50765-7); pap. 5.95 (ISBN 0-394-73730-X). Shambhala Pubns.
Powell, Conrad, jt. auth. see Winecoff, Larry.
Powell, D., jt. auth. see Skrabanek, P.
Powell, David. Look-Alike, Sound-Alike, Not-Alike Words: An Index of Confusables. LC 81-40715. 190p. (Orig.). 1982. lib. bdg. 20.75 (ISBN 0-8191-2564-4); pap. text ed. 9.75 (ISBN 0-8191-2565-2). U Pr of Amer.
Powell, David, jt. auth. see Skrabanek, Petr.
Powell, David, tr. see Carlson, G. Raymond.
Powell, David, tr. see Hook & Boren.
Powell, David E. Antireligious Propaganda in the Soviet Union: A Study of Mass Persuasion. LC 74-34127. 206p. 1975. 27.50x (ISBN 0-262-16061-7); pap. 5.95 (ISBN 0-262-66042-3). MIT Pr.
Powell, David R., tr. see Augsburger, David.
Powell, E. Naughty (Jokes) but Nice. (Illus.). 1955. 2.95 o.p. (ISBN 0-685-21997-6). Wehman.
Powell, Edward A. The Army Behind the Army. LC 74-75242. (The United States in World War 1 Ser). (Illus.). xiii, 470p. 1974. Repr. of 1919 ed. lib. bdg. 25.95x (ISBN 0-89198-107-1). Ozer.
Powell, Elizabeth A. Pennsylvania Butter: Tools & Processes. (Vol. I). (Illus.). 27p. 1974. pap. 3.00 (ISBN 0-910302-09-X). Bucks Co Hist.
--Pennsylvania Pottery: Tools & Processes. (Tools of the Nation Maker Ser.: Vol. II). (Illus.). 20p. 1972. pap. 3.00 (ISBN 0-910302-10-3). Bucks Co Hist.
Powell, Elsa A., tr. see Ekvall, Robert B.
Powell, Elsie R. de see Mayhall, Jack & Mayhall, Carole.
Powell, Enoch J. Saving in a Free Society. 2nd ed. (gr. 10-12). 1966. 4.25 (ISBN 0-685-29099-9). Transatlantic.
Powell, Eric F. The Natural Home Physician. LC 79-50415. Date not set. 8.95 (ISBN 0-448-16558-9, G&D); pap. 5.95 (ISBN 0-686-76823-X). Putnam Pub Group. Postponed.
Powell, Eustace G. The Dutch School of Historical & Portrait Painting, 2 vols. (The Art Library of the Great Masters of the World). (Illus.). 147p. 1983. Set. 137.50 (ISBN 0-86650-043-X). Gloucester Art.
Powell, Fred A. From My Front Porch. 53p. 1979. 3.50 o.p. (ISBN 0-8059-2684-4). Dorrance.
Powell, Fred W., ed. Hall J. Kelley on Oregon. LC 79-87635. (The American Scene Ser). (Illus.). 412p. 1972. Repr. of 1932 ed. lib. bdg. 49.50 (ISBN 0-306-71796-4). Da Capo.
Powell, G. Bingham, Jr., jt. auth. see Almond, Gabriel A.
Powell, G. M., jt. auth. see Russell, N. J.
Powell, G. S. The Green Howards. (Illus.). 250p. 1983. 21.50 (ISBN 0-436-37910-4, Pub by Secker & Warburg). David & Charles.
Powell, Geoffery & Fullick, Roy. Suez: The Double War. (Illus.). 240p. 1979. 24.00 o.p. (ISBN 0-241-10182-4, Pub. by Hamish Hamilton England). David & Charles.
Powell, Gloria J., ed. The Psychosocial Development of Minority Group Children. 600p. 1983. price not set (ISBN 0-87630-277-0). Brunner-Mazel.
Powell, Graham E. Brain Function Therapy. 326p. 1981. 23.95x (ISBN 0-566-00315-5, 04112-2, Pub. by Gower Pub Co England). Lexington Bks.

Powell, H. Benjamin. Philadelphia's First Fuel Crisis: Jacob Cist & the Developing Market for Pennsylvania Anthracite. LC 77-88471. (Illus.). 1978. 14.95x (ISBN 0-271-00533-5). Pa St U Pr.

Powell, H. M. The Santa Fe Trail. 1979. ltd. ed. cancelled 195.00 (ISBN 0-87140-634-9). Liveright.

Powell, Helen & Leatherbarrow, David, eds. Masterpieces of Architectural Drawing. (Illus.). 192p. 1983. 45.00 (ISBN 0-89659-326-6). Abbeville Pr.

Powell, Herb, jt. auth. see Pitcoff, Ramsey K.

Powell, Hollis C. The River Rat. 224p. 1982. 10.50 (ISBN 0-682-49891-2, Banner). Exposition.

Powell, Irena. Writers & Society in Modern Japan. LC 82-48432. 230p. 1983. 24.95 (ISBN 0-87011-558-8). Kodansha.

Powell, J. Aircraft Radio Systems. (Aerospace Engineering Ser.). 416p. 1981. text ed. 74.00 (ISBN 0-273-08444-5). Pitman Pub MA.

Powell, J. C. American Siberia or Fourteen Years' Experience in a Southern Convict Camp. LC 79-108222. (Criminology, Law Enforcement, & Social Problems Ser.: No. 105). (Illus., With intro. & index added). 1970. Repr. of 1891 ed. 12.50x (ISBN 0-87585-105-3). Patterson Smith.

--The American Siberia, or Fourteen Years' Experience in a Southern Convict Camp. LC 76-44514. (Floridiana Facsimile Ser). 1976. Repr. of 1891 ed. 12.00 (ISBN 0-8130-0372-5). U Presses Fla.

Powell, J. David, jt. auth. see Franklin, Gene F.

Powell, J. Lewis. Executive Speaking: An Acquired Skill. 2nd, rev. ed. 174p. 1980. 15.00 (ISBN 0-87179-321-0). BNA.

Powell, J. M. Environmental Management in Australia, 1788-1914: Guardians, Improvers & Profit: an Introductory Survey. 1977. 24.95x o.p. (ISBN 0-19-550478-X). Oxford U Pr.

Powell, J. M. & Williams, M., eds. Australian Space, Australian Time: Geographical Perspectives. (Illus.). 1975. 36.50x o.p. (ISBN 0-19-550456-9). Oxford U Pr.

Powell, J. P. Philosophy of Education. 3rd ed. 1974. pap. 8.50 (ISBN 0-7190-0597-3). Manchester.

Powell, J. U. & Barber, E. A., eds. New Chapters in the History of Greek Literature. 1921. 9.00x (ISBN 0-8196-0286-8). Biblo.

--New Chapters in the History of Greek Literature. (Second Ser). 1929. 9.00x (ISBN 0-8196-0287-6). Biblo.

Powell, James. Apache Moon. LC 82-48709. (DD Western Ser.). 192p. 1983. 11.95 (ISBN 0-385-18748-3). Doubleday.

Powell, James D., jt. auth. see Hicks, Herbert G.

Powell, James N. The Tao of Symbols. 1982. 11.50 (ISBN 0-688-01351-1, Quill); pap. 6.50 (ISBN 0-688-01354-6). Morrow.

Powell, Jocelyn. Restoration Theatre Production. (Theatre Production Studies). (Illus.). 240p. 1983. write for info. (ISBN 0-7100-9321-7). Routledge & Kegan.

Powell, John. Fully Human, Fully Alive. 2.95 o.p. (ISBN 0-686-92319-7, 6375). Hazelden.

--Fully Human, Fully Alive. pap. 2.95 (ISBN 0-686-36737-5). Inst Rat Liv.

--He Touched Me. 2.75 o.p. (ISBN 0-686-92339-1, 6450). Hazelden.

--Mystery of the Church. (Illus.). (gr. 7-9). 1967. pap. 4.95 o.p. (ISBN 0-02-826220-4). Glencoe.

--The Secret of Staying in Love. 3.95 o.p. (ISBN 0-686-92404-5, 6630). Hazelden.

--Why Am I Afraid to Love? 2.75 o.p. (ISBN 0-686-92417-7, 6660). Hazelden.

--Why Am I Afraid to Tell You Who I Am? 3.25 o.p. (ISBN 0-686-92418-5, 6670). Hazelden.

Powell, John B. My Twenty-Five Years in China. LC 76-27721. (China in the 20th Century Ser.). 1976. Repr. of 1945 ed. lib. bdg. 45.00 (ISBN 0-306-70761-6). Da Capo.

Powell, John W. Report on the Lands of the Arid Region of the U. S. 224p. 1983. pap. 9.95 (ISBN 0-916782-28-X). Harvard Common Pr.

Powell, Jonathan, jt. auth. see Champion, Bob.

Powell, Judith W. & LeLieuvre, Robert B. Peoplework: Communications Dynamics for Librarians. 152p. 1980. pap. 8.00 (ISBN 0-8389-0290-1). ALA.

Powell, Ken & Cook, Chris. English Historical Facts, 1485-1603. 228p. 1977. 21.50x o.p. (ISBN 0-87471-865-1). Rowman.

Powell, Lawrence C. The Blue Train. LC 76-54947. 128p. 1978. 10.00 (ISBN 0-88496-073-0); pap. 3.95 (ISBN 0-88496-105-2). Capra Pr.

--California Classics. (Illus.). 416p. 1983. pap. 9.95 (ISBN 0-88496-184-2). Capra Pr.

--From the Heartland: Profiles of People & Places of the Southwest & Beyond. LC 75-43347. (Illus.). 96p. 1976. 9.50 o.p. (ISBN 0-87358-155-5). Northland.

--Southwest Classics: The Creative Literature of the Arid Lands--Essays on the Books & Their Writers. 384p. 1982. pap. 9.95 (ISBN 0-8165-0795-3). U of Ariz Pr.

--Southwestern Book Trails. LC 82-82399. 1982. lib. bdg. 15.00x (ISBN 0-88307-657-8); pap. 7.95 (ISBN 0-88307-656-X). Gannon.

Powell, Lawrence N. New Masters: Northern Planters During the Civil War & Reconstruction. LC 79-64226. 1980. 22.50x (ISBN 0-300-02217-4); pap. 7.95x (ISBN 0-300-02882-2, Y-432). Yale U Pr.

Powell, M. J. Approximation Theory & Methods. (Illus.). 300p. 1981. 62.50 (ISBN 0-521-22472-1); pap. 22.95 (ISBN 0-521-29514-9). Cambridge U Pr.

Powell, M. J. V., ed. House Builders Reference Book. (Illus.). 1979. text ed. 89.95 (ISBN 0-408-00337-5). Butterworth.

Powell, Marcia, jt. auth. see Stallings, James O.

Powell, Mary Jo & Gold, Charlotte H., eds. A Manual of Style for the New York State School of Industrial & Labor Relations at Cornell University. 1973. pap. 2.00 o.s.i. (ISBN 0-87546-052-6). ILR Pr.

Powell, Neil. A Season of Calm Weather. 64p. 1982. pap. text ed. 7.00x (ISBN 0-85635-353-1, 80459, Pub. by Carcanet New Pr England). Humanities.

Powell, Nowland Van see Van Powell, Nowland.

Powell, P. & Timms, P. L. Chemistry of the Non-Metals. (Illus.). 1974. pap. 12.95x o.p. (ISBN 0-412-12200-6, Pub. by Chapman & Hall). Methuen Inc.

Powell, Paul W. The Complete Disciple. 120p. 1982. pap. 3.95 (ISBN 0-88207-307-9). Victor Bks.

Powell, Peter & Oddo, Sandra. Solar for Existing Houses: A Guide to Analysing, Designing & Constructing Solar Systems for Home Retrofit. LC 81-43372. (Illus.). 256p. 1983. pap. 12.95 (ISBN 0-385-17634-1). Doubleday.

Powell, Peter J. People of the Sacred Mountain: A History of the Northern Cheyenne Chiefs & Warrior Societies, 1830-1879, 2 vols. LC 76-50454. (Harper & Row Native American Publishing Program). (Illus.). 1376p. 1981. Set. 125.00i (ISBN 0-06-451550-8, HarpR). Har-Row.

Powell, R. B., tr. see Ruyslinck, Ward.

Powell, R. E., jt. auth. see Daugherty, J. S.

Powell, R. E., jt. auth. see Latimer, Wedall M.

Powell, Ralph A. Freely Chosen Reality. LC 82-21943. 194p. (Orig.). 1983. lib. bdg. 21.50 (ISBN 0-8191-2924-0); pap. text ed. 10.25 (ISBN 0-8191-2925-9). U Pr of Amer.

Powell, Richard. I Take This Land. 1982. pap. 2.95 (ISBN 0-89176-038-5, 6038). Mockingbird Bks.

--Pioneer, Go Home! new ed. 246p. 1976. pap. 1.75 o.s.i. (ISBN 0-89176-008-3, 6008). Mockingbird Bks.

Powell, Richard R. Compromises of Conflicting Claims: A Century of California Law in the Period 1760-1860. LC 76-54968. 332p. (Orig.). 1977. lib. bdg. 22.50 (ISBN 0-379-00655-3). Oceana.

Powell, Robert. Crisis in Consciousness. 200p. 1967. 12.00 (ISBN 0-227-67426-X). Attic Pr.

Powell, Russell H., ed. Handbooks & Tables in Science & Technology. 2nd ed. 384p. 1983. lib. bdg. 55.00 (ISBN 0-89774-039-4). Oryx Pr.

Powell, S., jt. auth. see Land, A. H.

Powell, Sheppard T. Water Conditioning for Industry. 1954. 27.50 o.p. (ISBN 0-07-050572-1, P&RB). McGraw.

Powell, Sherry, jt. ed. see Stern, Marilyn.

Powell, Shirley. Mobility & Adaptation: The Anasazi of Black Mesa, Arizona. (Publications in Archaeology Ser.). 1983. price not set (ISBN 0-8093-1107-0). S Ill U Pr.

Powell, T. G. The Celts. (Ancient Peoples & Places Ser.). (Illus.). 1983. pap. 9.95 (ISBN 0-500-27275-1). Thames Hudson.

Powell, Terry. Nobody's Perfect. 1979. pap. 3.50 (ISBN 0-88207-577-2). Victor Bks.

Powell, Thomas F. Josiah Royce. (World Leaders Ser.). lib. bdg. 12.95 (ISBN 0-8057-3713-8, Twayne). G K Hall.

Powell, Violet. Flora Annie Steele. (Illus.). 1981. 21.50 (ISBN 0-434-59957-3, Pub. by Heinemann). David & Charles.

Powell, W. R., jt. auth. see Berl, W. G.

Powell, Walbridge J. Art, Crafts, & Fine Arts Shows in Washington. 34p. (Orig.). 1982. pap. 2.50x (ISBN 0-686-37612-9). Searchers Pubns.

Powell, Wayne. Divorce Guide for British Columbia. 7th ed. 104p. 1981. 9.95 (ISBN 0-88908-142-5); forms 9.95 (ISBN 0-686-35994-1). Self Counsel Pr.

Powell, William S. John Pory, 1572-1636: The Life & Letters of a Man of Many Parts. LC 75-45074. (Illus.). 1977. incl. microfiche 19.00x (ISBN 0-8078-1270-6). U of NC Pr.

--North Carolina Gazetteer. LC 68-25916. xviii, 561p. (Maps). 1976. pap. 10.95 (ISBN 0-8078-1247-1). U of NC Pr.

Powell, William S., jt. auth. see Lefler, Hugh T.

Powell, William S., ed. Correspondence of William Tryon & Other Selected Papers, Vol. II: 1768-1818. (Illus.). xxxiii, 958p. 1981. 28.00 (ISBN 0-86526-147-4). NC Archives.

Powell de Lobo, Virginia, tr. see McManus, Una & Cooper, John C.

Powell-Smith, V. A Modern View of the Law for Builders & Surveyors. 1967. inquire for price (ISBN 0-08-012297-3). Pergamon.

Powelson, J., jt. auth. see Loehr, Wm.

Powelson, John P. A Select Bibliography on Economic Development: With Annotations. (Special Studies in Social, Political & Economic Development). 1979. lib. bdg. 35.50 (ISBN 0-89158-497-8). Westview.

Powelson, John P., jt. auth. see Loehr, William.

Power, Arthur. Conversations with James Joyce. Hart, Clive, ed. LC 82-1839. (Phoenix). 112p. 1983. pap. 4.95 (ISBN 0-226-67720-6). U of Chicago Pr.

Power, David, jt. ed. see Collins, Mary.

Power, David, jt. ed. see Maldonado, Luis.

Power, E. G. The Easter Rising & Irish Independence. Reeves, Marjorie, ed. (Then & There Ser.). (Illus.). 96p. (Orig.). (gr. 7-12). 1979. pap. text ed. 3.10 (ISBN 0-582-22120-X). Longman.

Power Editors. Plant Energy System: Energy Systems Engineering. 1967. 59.50 (ISBN 0-07-050588-8, P&RB). McGraw.

Power, Edward J. Main Currents in the History of Education. 2nd ed. 1970. text ed. 26.00 o.p. (ISBN 0-07-050581-0, C). McGraw.

--Philosophy of Education: Studies in Philosophies, Schooling & Educational Policies. 448p. 1982. text ed. 22.95 (ISBN 0-13-663252-1). P-H.

Power, Effie. Bag O' Tales. LC 68-26598. 1968. Repr. of 1934 ed. 34.00x (ISBN 0-8103-3486-0). Gale.

Power, Eileen, tr. see Boissonnade, Prosper.

Power, Elaine. Small Birds of the New Zealand Bush. (Illus.). 27p. 1983. pap. 8.95 (ISBN 0-00-216984-3, Pub. by W Collins Australia). Intl Schol Bk Serv.

Power, Fred B., jt. auth. see Miller, Roger L.

Power, Harry W. Foraging Behavior of Mountain Bluebirds with Emphasis on Sexual Foraging Differences. 72p. 1980. 8.50 (ISBN 0-943610-28-1). Am Ornithologists.

Power, Henry M. & Simpson, Robert J. Introduction to Dynamics & Control. (Illus.). 1978. pap. text ed. 29.95 (ISBN 0-07-084081-4, C). McGraw.

Power Instrumentation Symposium, 21st, Philadelphia, 1978. Instrumentation in the Power Industry: Proceedings, Vol. 21. LC 62-52679. 88p. 1978. pap. text ed. 12.00x o.p. (ISBN 0-87664-409-4). Instru Soc.

Power, Marjory W., jt. auth. see Haviland, William A.

Power, Sr. Mary J. In the Name of the Bee: The Significance of Emily Dickinson. LC 74-115690. (Illus.). 1970. Repr. of 1944 ed. 9.00x (ISBN 0-8196-0266-3). Biblo.

Power, Morgory W., jt. auth. see Haviland, William.

Power, P. The Role of the Family in the Rehabilitation of the Physically Disabled. 576p. 1980. pap. text ed. 14.95 (ISBN 0-8391-1549-0). Univ Park.

Power, P. B. A Book of Comfort. 1974. pap. 2.95 (ISBN 0-85151-203-8). Banner of Truth.

Power, Paul F., ed. The Meanings of Gandhi. (Illus.). 1971. 10.00x (ISBN 0-8248-0104-0, Eastwest Ctr). UH Pr.

Power, Paul W. A Guide to Vocational Assessment: A Practical Approach for Rehabilitation Professionals. 1983. pap. text ed. price not set (ISBN 0-8391-1718-3, 15865). Univ Park.

Power, S. Hankel Operators on Hilbert Space. (Research Notes in Mathematics Ser.: No. 64). 120p. 1982. pap. text ed. 15.50 (ISBN 0-273-08518-2). Pitman Pub MA.

Power, Thomas C. Practical Shop Mathematics. (Illus.). 1979. pap. text ed. 15.95 (ISBN 0-07-050591-8, G); ans. to even- numbered problems 4.00 (ISBN 0-07-050592-6). McGraw.

Powers, B. Ward. Learn to Read the Greek New Testament. 300p. 21.00 (ISBN 0-85364-291-5); pap. text ed. 13.95 (ISBN 0-85364-292-3). Attic Pr.

Powers, Bill. A Test of Love. LC 78-12913. (Triumph Ser.). (Illus.). 1979. lib. bdg. 8.90 s&l (ISBN 0-531-02888-7). Watts.

Powers, Bob. Kern River Country. (Illus.). 1982. 16.95 (ISBN 0-87026-052-9). Westernlore.

Powers, Charles F. A Matter of Honor. 176p. 1983. 12.99 (ISBN 0-910829-03-9); pap. 3.95 (ISBN 0-910829-04-7). First East.

Powers, David R. & Powers, Mary F. Making Participatory Management Work: Effective Participatory Decision Making in Academic Administration. (Higher Education Ser.). 1983. text ed. write for info. (ISBN 0-87589-567-0). Jossey-Bass.

Powers, Edward A. & Lees, Mary W. Encounter with Family Realities. (Illus.). 1977. pap. 16.95 (ISBN 0-8299-0051-9). West Pub.

--Process in Relationship: Marriage & Family. 2nd ed. (Illus.). 300p. 1976. pap. text ed. 9.50 (ISBN 0-8299-0082-9). West Pub.

Powers, Edwin & Witmer, Helen. Experiment in the Prevention of Delinquency: The Cambridge - Somerville Youth Study. LC 70-172573. (Criminology, Law Enforcement, & Social Problems Ser.: No. 159). 1972. Repr. of 1951 ed. 18.50x (ISBN 0-87585-159-2). Patterson Smith.

Powers, J. F. Look How the Fish Live. 1975. 6.95 o.p. (ISBN 0-394-49608-6). Knopf.

Powers, J. Patrick. Construction Dewatering: A Guide to Theory & Practice. LC 80-18851. (Wiley Ser. of Practical Construction Guides). 484p. 1981. 45.95 (ISBN 0-471-69591-2, Pub. by Wiley-Interscience). Wiley.

Powers, Jo Marie. Basics of Quantity Food Production. LC 78-23194. (Service Management Ser.). 514p. 1979. text ed. 27.95x (ISBN 0-471-03421-5). Wiley.

Powers, John M., ed. see Craig, Robert G. & O'Brien, William J.

Powers, John R. Do Black Patent Leather Shoes Really Reflect Up? 1982. pap. 2.95 (ISBN 0-446-31089-1). Warner Bks.

--The Last Catholic in America. 224p. 1982. pap. 2.75 (ISBN 0-446-31040-9). Warner Bks.

Powers, Lyall. Merrill Studies in the Portrait of a Lady. LC 75-116607. 1970. pap. text ed. 3.50x (ISBN 0-675-09357-0). Merrill.

Powers, Lyall H. Faulkner's Yoknapatawpha Comedy. 296p. 1980. 19.95 (ISBN 0-472-08727-4). U of Mich Pr.

Powers, Margaret. Gluten Free & Good. (Orig.). Date not set. pap. 7.95 (ISBN 0-9610140-0-8). Old Town Pr.

Powers, Mark J. & Vogel, David J. Inside the Financial Futures Markets. LC 80-23157. 320p. 1981. 24.95 (ISBN 0-471-08136-1). Ronald Pr.

--Inside the Financial Futures Markets. LC 80-23157. 320p. 1981. 24.95x (ISBN 0-471-08136-1). Wiley.

Powers, Mary F., jt. auth. see Powers, David R.

Powers, Mary G. Measures of Socio-Economic Status: Current Issues. (AAAS Selected Symposium 81). 205p. 1982. lib. bdg. 20.00x (ISBN 0-86531-395-4). Westview.

Powers, Mary G., jt. auth. see Nam, Charles B.

Powers, Nora. Affairs of the Heart. 192p. (Orig.). 1980. pap. 1.50 (ISBN 0-671-57003-X, Pub. by Silhouette Bks). S&S.

--Design for Love. 192p. (Orig.). 1980. pap. 1.50 (ISBN 0-671-57042-0, Pub. by Silhouette Bks). S&S.

Powers, Richard. The Dilemma of Education in a Democracy. LC 81-85568. 190p. Date not set. 14.95 (ISBN 0-89526-662-8). Regnery-Gateway. Postponed.

Powers, Richard & Osborne, James G. Fundamentals of Behavior. LC 75-40098. (Illus.). 200p. 1976. pap. text ed. 15.95 (ISBN 0-8299-0073-X). West Pub.

Powers, Richard, ed. see Davis, Mac.

Powers, Richard G. G-Men: Hoover's FBI in American Popular Culture. (Illus.). 320p. 1983. price not set (ISBN 0-8093-1096-1). S Ill U Pr.

Powers, Robert M. The Coattails of God. (Illus.). 400p. (Orig.). 1982. 15.95 (ISBN 0-446-51231-1); pap. 3.50 (ISBN 0-446-90092-3). Warner Bks.

Powers, Ron. The Newscasters: The News Business As Show Business. LC 76-62789. 256p. 1977. 8.95 o.p. (ISBN 0-312-57207-7). St Martin.

--Toot-Toot-Tootsie, Good-Bye. 1981. 10.95 o.s.i. (ISBN 0-440-08190-4). Delacorte.

Powers, Stephen. Tribes of California. LC 75-13150. 1977. 40.00x (ISBN 0-520-03023-0); pap. 10.95 (ISBN 0-520-03172-5, CAL 327). U of Cal Pr.

Powers, Thomas. Thinking about the Next War. LC 82-47930. 1982. 10.95 (ISBN 0-394-52831-X). Knopf.

Powers, Thomas F. Introduction to Management in the Hospitality Industry. LC 78-23205. (Service Management Ser.). 1979. text ed. 23.95x (ISBN 0-471-03128-3); tchrs.' manual 9.00 (ISBN 0-471-05355-4). Wiley.

Powers, Thomas F., ed. Educating for Careers: Policy Issues in a Time of Change. LC 77-1639. 1977. 18.95x (ISBN 0-271-00511-4). Pa St U Pr.

Powers, W. Robert. Electrical Fires in New York City - 1976. Date not set. 2.50 (ISBN 0-686-22739-5, TR 77-3). Society Fire Protect.

Powers, Ward. Learn to Read the Greek New Testament. 336p. 1983. 19.95 (ISBN 0-8028-3578-3). Eerdmans.

Powers, William G., jt. auth. see Scott, Michael D.

Powers, William K. Here Is Your Hobby: Indian Dancing & Costumes. (Here Is Your Hobby Ser.). (Illus.). (gr. 5-8). 1966. PLB 5.29 o.p. (ISBN 0-399-60249-6). Putnam Pub Group.

--Indians of the Northern Plains. (American Indians Then & Now Ser.). (Illus.). (gr. 8 up). 1969. 6.75 o.p. (ISBN 0-399-20103-3). Putnam Pub Group.

--Indians of the Southern Plains. (American Indians Then & Now Ser.). (Illus.). (gr. 8 up). 1971. 6.75 o.p. (ISBN 0-399-20104-1). Putnam Pub Group.

--Oglala Religion. LC 76-30614. (Illus.). xxii, 233p. 1977. 16.95x (ISBN 0-8032-0910-X, BB 802, Bison); pap. 5.95 (ISBN 0-8032-8706-2). U of Nebr Pr.

--Oglala Religion. LC 76-30614. 254p. 1982. pap. 5.95 (ISBN 0-8032-8706-2, BB 802, Bison). U of Nebr Pr.

Powers, William T., jt. auth. see Glasser, William.

Powicke, Frederick M. Modern Historians & the Study of History: Essays & Papers. LC 75-25496. 1976. Repr. of 1955 ed. lib. bdg. 18.25x (ISBN 0-8371-8428-2, POMH). Greenwood.

--Reformation in England. (Oxford Paperbacks Ser). 1961. pap. 4.95x o.p. (ISBN 0-19-285001-6). Oxford U Pr.

--Ways of Medieval Life & Thought. LC 64-13394. (Illus.). 1949. 9.00x (ISBN 0-8196-0137-3). Biblo.

Powis, Raymond L. & Powis, Wendy J. A Thinker's Guide to Ultrasonic Imaging. 1983. 32.50 (ISBN 0-8067-1581-2). Urban & S.

Powis, Wendy J., jt. auth. see Powis, Raymond L.

Powitt, A. H. Hair Structure & Chemistry Simplified. new ed. (Illus.). 300p. 1977. text ed. 19.40 (ISBN 0-87350-080-6). Milady.

Powledge, Fred. A Forgiving Wind: On Becoming a Sailor. LC 82-16867. (Illus.). 224p. 1983. 12.95 (ISBN 0-87156-330-4). Sierra.

--Model City. LC 75-130487. (Illus.). 1970. 7.95 o.p. (ISBN 0-671-20670-2). S&S.

Powley, A. E. Broadcast from the Front. (Canadian War Museum Historical Publications Ser.). (Illus.). 189p. 1975. 10.95 o.p. (ISBN 0-88866-565-2). Samuel Stevens.

Powlis, La Verne. The Black Woman's Beauty Book: A Complete Guide to Great Looks. LC 78-22349. (Illus.). 1979. 17.95 (ISBN 0-385-14450-4). Doubleday.

Powlison, Dave, jt. auth. see Tillman, Dick.

Powlison, Esther & Powlison, Paul. La Fiesta Yagua, Jina: Una Rica Herencia Cultural. (Comunidades y Culturas Peruanas: No. 8). 102p. 1976. pap. 4.00x o.s.i. (ISBN 0-88312-761-X); microfiche 2.25x (ISBN 0-686-77054-4). Summer Inst Ling.

Powlison, Paul, jt. auth. see Powlison, Esther.

Pownall, David E., compiled by. Articles on Twentieth Century Literature: An Annotated Bibliography 1954-1970, 8 vols. LC 73-6588. Set. lib. bdg. 480.00 (ISBN 0-527-72150-6). Kraus Intl.

Pownall, Glen. Perfumery. (New Crafts Books Ser.). 72p. 1980. 7.50 (ISBN 0-686-96753-4, Pub. by Viking Sevenseas New Zealand). Intl Schol Bk Serv.

Pownall, Malcolm. Functions & Graphs: Calculus Preparatory Mathematics. (Illus.). 592p. 1983. 24.95 (ISBN 0-13-332304-8). P-H.

Pownall, Thomas. Administration of the Colonies. LC 79-146155. (Era of the American Revolution Ser). 1971. Repr. of 1768 ed. lib. bdg. 49.50 (ISBN 0-306-70123-5). Da Capo.

Powne, Michael. Ethiopian Music, an Introduction: A Survey of Ecclesiastical & Secular Ethiopian Music & Instruments. LC 80-14087. (Illus.). xix, 160p. 1980. Repr. of 1966 ed. lib. bdg. 21.00x (ISBN 0-313-22161-8, POEM). Greenwood.

Powys, Marian. Lace & Lace Making. (Illus.). 219p. 1981. Repr. of 1955 ed. 42.00x (ISBN 0-8103-4312-6). Gale.

Poyer, D. C. White Continent. (Orig.). pap. 2.50 o.s.i. (ISBN 0-515-05479-8). Jove Pubns.

Poynter, Dan. Hang Gliding Manual with Log. 7th ed. LC 76-14105. (Illus.). 1982. pap. 1.50 (ISBN 0-915516-12-8). Para Pub.

--Parachuting: The Skydivers' Handbook. 4th ed. LC 77-83469. (Illus.). 1983. o. p. 11.95 (ISBN 0-915516-17-9); pap. 7.95 (ISBN 0-915516-16-0). Para Pub.

--Parascending, the Basic Handbook of Tow Launched Para-Gliding. LC 81-9596. (Illus.). 104p. (Orig.). Date not set. pap. 5.95 (ISBN 0-915516-30-6). Para Pub.

--Word Processors & Information Processing. 172p. 1983. 16.95 (ISBN 0-13-963553-X); pap. 11.95 (ISBN 0-13-963546-7). P-H.

Poynter, Dan & Danna, Mark. Frisbee Players' Handbook. 3rd ed. LC 77-79101. (Illus.). 1980. pap. text ed. 6.95 o. p. (ISBN 0-915516-20-9); pap. 9.95 with disc (ISBN 0-915516-15-2); pap. 6.95 without disc (ISBN 0-915516-19-5). Para Pub.

Poynter, Margaret. The Racquetball Book. LC 79-24534. (Illus.). 128p. (gr. 4 up). 1980. PLB 8.79 o.p. (ISBN 0-671-33014-4). Messner.

--Too Few Happy Endings: The Dilemma of the Humane Societies. LC 81-2239. (Illus.). 144p. (gr. 5 up). 1981. PLB 9.95 (ISBN 0-689-30864-7). Atheneum.

--Wildland Fire Fighting. LC 82-1735. (Illus.). 144p. (gr. 5-9). 1982. 9.95 (ISBN 0-689-30939-2). Atheneum.

Poynter, Margaret & Collins, Donald. Under the High Seas: New Frontiers in Oceanography. LC 82-16338. (Illus.). 160p. (gr. 5-9). 1983. 10.95 (ISBN 0-689-30977-5). Atheneum.

Poynton. Metering Pumps. (Chemical Industries Ser.). 216p. 1983. 29.75 (ISBN 0-8247-1759-7). Dekker.

Poyser, Norman L. Prostaglandins in Reproduction. (Prostaglandins Research Studies). 260p. 1981. 49.95 (ISBN 0-471-09986-4, Pub. by Res Stud Pr). Wiley.

Pozas, Ricardo. Juan the Chamula: An Ethnological Recreation of the Life of a Mexican Indian. Kemp, Lysander, tr. (Illus.). 123p. 1962. pap. 3.95x (ISBN 0-520-01027-2, CAMPUS 287). U of Cal Pr.

Pozen, Robert, jt. auth. see Phelan, James.

Pozgar, George D. Legal Aspects of Health Care Administration. LC 78-17276. 266p. 1979. text ed. 25.00 (ISBN 0-89443-044-0). Aspen Systems.

--Legal Aspects of Health Care Administration. 2nd ed. 250p. 1983. write for info (ISBN 0-89443-810-7). Aspen Systems.

Pozos, Robert S. & Wittmers, Lorentz E., Jr., eds. The Nature & Treatment of Hypothermia. LC 82-23909. (University of Minnesota Continuing Medical Education Ser.: Vol. 2). (Illus.). 288p. 1983. 35.00x (ISBN 0-8166-1154-8). U of Minn Pr.

Prabha, Krishna. Towns: A Structural Analysis. 1979. text ed. 14.25x (ISBN 0-391-01860-4). Humanities.

Prabhavananda, Swami. Upanishads: Breath of the Eternal. Manchester, Frederick, tr. pap. 1.95 (ISBN 0-451-62060-7, MJ2060, Ment). NAL.

Prabhavananda, Swami & Manchester, Frederick, trs. Upanishads: Breath of the Eternal. LC 48-5935. 11.00 (ISBN 0-87481-007-8); pap. 6.50 (ISBN 0-87481-040-X). Vedanta Pr.

Prabhavananda, Swami, tr. see Bhagavad-Gita.

Prabhu, R. K., compiled by. A Gandhian Rosary. 140p. pap. 0.95 (ISBN 0-686-95657-5, 1962). Self Realization.

Prabhudesai, R. K. & Das, D. K. Chemical Engineering for Professional Engineer's Examinations. 448p. 1983. 32.50 (ISBN 0-07-050640-X, P&RB). McGraw.

Practical Photography Magazine Editors. Practical Photography Yearbook. (Illus.). 1978. pap. 7.95 o.p. (ISBN 0-8174-2120-3, Amphoto). Watson-Guptill.

Practical Wireless Staff. Practical Wireless Circuits. 18th ed. 5.25x o.p. (ISBN 0-600-41244-X). Transatlantic.

Pracy, R., et al. Ear, Nose, Throat: Surgery & Nursing. LC 77-84317. 1977. 22.50 (ISBN 0-471-03918-7). Wiley.

Pradhan, Narindar S., jt. ed. see Chander, Jagdish.

Pradhan, Prakash C. Foreign Policy of Kampuchea. 400p. 1983. text ed. 30.00x (ISBN 0-391-02799-9, Pub. by Radiant Pub India). Humanities.

Pradhan, Suesh B. International Pharmaceutical Marketing. LC 82-15022. 352p. 1983. lib. bdg. 49.95 (ISBN 0-89930-009-X, PPH/, Quorum). Greenwood.

Pradl, Gordon M., ed. see Britton, James.

Prado, Caio, Jr. The Colonial Background of Modern Brazil. Macedo, Suzette, tr. LC 67-11849. 1967. pap. 5.50x o.s.i. (ISBN 0-520-01549-5, CAMPUS 18). U of Cal Pr.

Prado, Carlos G. Illusions of Faith: A Critique of Non-Credal Religion. (Orig.). 1980. pap. text ed. 6.95 (ISBN 0-8403-2176-7). Kendall-Hunt.

Prado, Marcial. Practical Spanish Grammar: A Self Teaching Guide. (Self Teaching Guides Ser.). 240p. 1983. pap. text ed. write for info. (ISBN 0-471-89893-7). Wiley.

--Practical Spanish Grammar: A Self Teaching Guide. (Self-Teaching Ser.). 240p. 1983. pap. text ed. 8.95 (ISBN 0-686-84630-3). Wiley.

Pradt. Parallele de la Puissance Anglaise et Russe Relativement a l'Europe, Suivi d'un Apercu sur la Grece. (Nineteenth Century Russia Ser.). 254p. (Fr.). 1974. Repr. of 1823 ed. lib. bdg. 69.50x o.p. (ISBN 0-8287-0701-4, R79). Clearwater Pub.

Praeger, R. L. An Account of the Genus Sedum As Found in Cultivation. (Illus.). 1967. pap. 18.40 (ISBN 3-7682-0446-4). Lubrecht & Cramer.

--An Account of the Sempervivum Group. 1967. pap. 16.00 (ISBN 3-7682-0445-6). Lubrecht & Cramer.

Praetorius, Michael. The Syntagma Musicum of Michael Praetorius, Vol. 2: De Organographica. Blumenfeld, Harold, tr. LC 72-14061. (Music Reprint Ser.). (Illus.). 1980. Repr. of 1962 ed. 22.50 (ISBN 0-306-70563-X). Da Capo.

Prag, A., jt. auth. see Lockwood, Edward H.

Prag, A. J. The Oresteia: Iconographic & Narrative Tradition. (Illus.). 210p. 1983. pap. text ed. 65.00x (ISBN 0-85668-134-2, 41065, Pub. by Aris & Phillips England). Humanities.

Prager, Arthur & Prager, Emily. World War II Resistance Stories. (Triumph Ser.). (gr. 5 up). 1979. PLB 8.90 s&l (ISBN 0-531-02296-X). Watts.

Prager, Emily. A Visit From the Footbinder: And Other Stories. 1982. 14.95 (ISBN 0-671-61013-9). S&S.

Prager, Emily, jt. auth. see Prager, Arthur.

Prager, Frank D. & Scaglia, Gustina. Brunelleschi: Studies of His Technology & Inventions. 1970. 15.00 (ISBN 0-262-16031-5). MIT Pr.

Prager, Frank D., jt. auth. see Scaglia, Gustina.

Pragg, H. M. van see Mendlewicz, J. & Van Pragg, H. M.

Prahalad, C. K., jt. auth. see Silvers, John B.

Prain, D. see Jackson, B. D., et al.

Prais, S. J. The Evolution of Giant Firms in Britain: A Study in the Growth of Concentration in Manufacturing Industry in Britain, 1909-1970. LC 76-18410. (National Institute of Economic & Social Research Economic & Social Studies: No. 30). (Illus.). 321p. 1981. pap. 17.95 (ISBN 0-521-28273-X). Cambridge U Pr.

Prajnanananda, Swami. Historical Development of Indian Music. 2nd. rev. ed. (Illus.). 495p. 1973. 15.00x o.p. (ISBN 0-88386-344-8). South Asia Bks.

Prakash, N. Differential Geometry: An Integrated Approach. 1982. write for info. (ISBN 0-07-096560-9). McGraw.

Prakash, O. Applied Physiology in Clinical Respiratory Care. 1982. 76.00 (ISBN 90-247-2662-X, Pub. by Martinus Nijhoff Netherlands). Kluwer Boston.

Prakash, Ram & Khanna, L. S. Theory & Practice of Silvicultural Systems. 263p. 1979. text ed. 10.00 (ISBN 0-686-38950-6, Pub. by Intl Bk Dist). Intl Schol Bk Serv.

Prakash, Shamsher. Soil Dynamics. (Illus.). 432p. 1981. text ed. 33.50 (ISBN 0-07-050658-2, C); student's manual 4.95 (ISBN 0-07-050659-0). McGraw.

Prakken, Sarah L., ed. Reader's Adviser: A Layman's Guide to Literature 1974-1977, 3 vols. 12th ed. Incl. The Best in American & British Fiction, Poetry, Essays, Literary Biography, Bibliography, & Reference: Vol. One. Prakken, Sarah L., ed. 808p. 1974 (ISBN 0-8352-0781-1); The Best in American & British Drama & World Literature in English Translation: Vol. Two. Sypher, F. J., ed. 774p. 1977 (ISBN 0-8352-0852-4); The Best in the Reference Literature of the World: Vol. Three. Clarke, Jack A., ed. 1977 (ISBN 0-8352-0853-2). LC 57-13277. 45.00 ea. (ISBN 0-8352-0982-2); 120.00 set (ISBN 0-685-85682-8). Bowker.

Prall, S. E. Puritan Revolution: A Documentary History. 9.50 (ISBN 0-8446-2756-9). Peter Smith.

Pramoedya, Ananta T. Heap of Ashes. (Asian & Pacific Writing Ser.). 1975. 14.95x (ISBN 0-7022-1060-9); pap. 8.50 (ISBN 0-7022-1071-4). U of Queensland Pr.

Prance, Claude A. A Companion to Charles Lamb. 416p. 1982. 24.00 (ISBN 0-7201-1657-0, Pub. by Mansell England). Wilson.

Prange, Arthur J., Jr. The Thyroid Axis, Drugs & Behavior. LC 73-90468. 213p. 1974. 27.00 (ISBN 0-911216-34-0). Raven.

Prange, G. W. Miracle at Midway. Goldstein, D. M. & Dillon, K. V., eds. (New Press Ser.). 416p. 1982. 24.95 (ISBN 0-07-050672-8). McGraw.

Praninskas, Jean. Rapid Review of English Grammar. 2nd ed. (Illus.). 352p. 1975. pap. 13.50 (ISBN 0-13-753145-1). P-H.

Prasad, Ananda S., ed. Clinical, Biochemical, & Nurtitional Aspects of Trace Elements. (Current Tropics in Nutrition & Disease Ser.: Vol. 6). 577p. 1982. 96.00 (ISBN 0-8451-1605-3). A R Liss.

Prasad, Ananda S. & Dreosti, Ivor E., eds. Clinical Applications of Recent Advances in Zinc Metabolism. LC 82-17294. (Current Topics in Nutrition & Disease Ser.: Vol. 7). 197p. 1982. 26.00 (ISBN 0-8451-1606-1). A R Liss.

Prasad, Bhrigunath. Structure of the Epididymis of Birds & the Seasonal Changes in the Epididymis of the Parrot. 1965. pap. 5.00x o.p. (ISBN 0-210-98100-8). Asia.

Prasad, C. V., jt. auth. see Khan, M. E.

Prasad, Kedar N. & Vernadakis, Antonia, eds. Mechanisms of Actions of Neurotoxic Substances. 236p. 1981. text ed. 29.00 (ISBN 0-89004-638-7). Raven.

Prasad, Madhusudan, ed. Indian English Novelists: An Anthology of Critical Essays. 240p. 1982. 34.95 (ISBN 0-940500-48-5, Pub. by Sterling India). Asia Bk Corp.

Prasad, Manchar, jt. auth. see Kadambi, V.

Prasad, N. J. The Language Issue in India. 1980. text ed. 11.75x (ISBN 0-391-01935-X). Humanities.

Prasad, Nageshwar. Ideology & Organization in Indian Politics. 304p. 1980. 29.95x (ISBN 0-940500-77-9, Pub by Allied Pubs India). Asia Bk Corp.

Prasad, Rajendra. At the Feet of Mahatma Gandhi. LC 79-156204. 1971. Repr. of 1961 ed. lib. bdg. 18.50x (ISBN 0-8371-6154-1, PRMG). Greenwood.

--Portrait of a President: Letters of Dr. Rajendra Prasad, 2 Vols. Darbar, Gyanvati, ed. 284p. 1976. 24.00x set (ISBN 0-7069-0289-0). Intl Pubns Serv.

Prasad, S. Benjamin & Shetty, Y. Krishna. An Introduction to Multinational Management. (Illus.). 256p. 1976. 16.95 (ISBN 0-13-489203-8). P-H.

Prasanna, A. R., et al, eds. Gravitation, Quanta & the Universe: Proceedings of the Einstein Centenary Symposium Held at Ahmedabad, India 29 January to 3 February, 1979. LC 80-17051. 326p. 1980. 49.95x (ISBN 0-470-27007-1). Halsted Pr.

Prasansuk, S. & Bunnag, C., eds. Aspects of Modern Otolaryngological Practice: First Congress of the Asian Otorhinolaringological Federation, Pattaya, 1981. (Advances in Oto-Rhino-Laryngology: Vol. 29). (Illus.). xii, 236p. 1983. 98.25 (ISBN 3-8055-3592-9). S Karger.

Prasow, Paul. Collective Bargaining & Civil Service in Public Employment: Conflict & Accommodation. (IPA Training Manual). 344p. 1976. 10.00 o.s.i. (ISBN 0-89215-068-8). U Cal LA Indus Rel.

Prasow, Paul & Peters, Edward. Abritration & Collective Bargaining. LC 78-89791. 1970. text ed. 27.50 (ISBN 0-07-050673-6, C). McGraw.

--Arbitration & Collective Bargaining. 2nd ed. 480p. 1983. 28.95 (ISBN 0-07-050674-4, C). McGraw.

Prasse, K. W., jt. auth. see Duncan, J. R.

Prassel, Frank R. Criminal Law, Justice & Society. LC 78-12980. 1979. 21.95x o.p. (ISBN 0-673-16297-4). Scott F.

Prast, William G. Securing U.S. Energy Supplies: The Private Sector As an Instrument of Public Policy. LC 79-2978. 128p. 18.95x (ISBN 0-669-03305-7). Lexington Bks.

Prast, William G. & Lax, Howard L. Oil-Futures Markets: An Introduction. LC 82-48622. 1983. write for info. (ISBN 0-669-06354-1). Lexington Bks.

Prasuhn, Alan L. Fundamentals of Fluid Mechanics. (Illus.). 1980. text ed. 31.95 (ISBN 0-13-339507-3). P-H.

Pratapaditya Pal. Nepal: Where the Gods Are Young. LC 75-769. (Illus.). 136p. 1975. 19.95 o.p. (ISBN 0-87848-045-5). Asia Soc.

Prater, Arnold. How to Beat the Blahs. LC 77-24827. 1977. pap. 1.95 o.p. (ISBN 0-89081-038-9, 0389). Harvest Hse.

Prather, Elizabeth, et al. Washington Speech Sound Discrimination Test. (Instruction bklt. 7 picture cards. 64 test forms). 1971. text ed. 11.95x (ISBN 0-8134-1222-6, 1222); test forms 2.50x (ISBN 0-8134-1223-4, 1223). Interstate.

Prather, Hugh. I Touch the Earth, the Earth Touches Me. LC 72-79420. 160p. 1972. pap. 6.95 (ISBN 0-385-05063-1). Doubleday.

--Notes on Love & Courage. LC 77-75873. 1977. pap. 6.95 (ISBN 0-385-12772-3). Doubleday.

Prather, Ronald E. Discrete Mathematical Structures for Computer Science. LC 75-25014. (Illus.). 680p. 1976. text ed. 28.95 (ISBN 0-395-20622-7); solutions manual 3.50 (ISBN 0-395-20623-5). HM.

Pratley, J. B. Study Notes for Technicians, Vol. 3. 148p. 1983. write for info. (ISBN 0-07-084663-4). McGraw.

--Study Notes for Technicians: Electrical & Electronic Principles, Vol. 1. 96p. 1982. 7.00 (ISBN 0-07-084661-8). McGraw.

Pratney, Winkey. El Joven y Su Dios. (El Joven y Sus Inquietudes Ser.). Date not set. 2.50 (ISBN 0-88113-163-6). Edit Betania.

--El Joven y Su Mundo. (El Joven y Sus Inquietudes). Date not set. 1.95 (ISBN 0-88113-164-4). Edit Betania.

--El Joven y Sus Amigos. (El Joven y Sus Inquietudes Ser). Date not set. 1.75 (ISBN 0-88113-162-8). Edit Betania.

--El Joven y Sus Dilemas. (El Joven y Sus Inquietudes). Date not set. 1.95 (ISBN 0-88113-165-2). Edit Betania.

--Youth Aflame. 448p. (Orig.). 1983. pap. 5.95 (ISBN 0-87123-659-1). Bethany Hse.

Praton, Clifford H., ed. see Christophe, Henri.

Prats, A. J. The Autonomous Image: Cinematic Narration & Humanism. LC 81-50182. 192p. 1981. 14.50x (ISBN 0-8131-1406-3). U Pr of Ky.

Pratt. The Caring Touch. 1981. 7.95 (ISBN 0-471-25960-8, Pub. by Wiley Heyden). Wiley.

Pratt & Brooks. Juvenile Hormone Biochemistry. (Developments in Endocrinology Ser.: Vol. 15). 1982. 79.75 (ISBN 0-444-80390-4). Elsevier.

Pratt, A. Bank Frauds: Their Detection & Prevention. 2nd ed. 276p. 1965. 33.95x o.p. (ISBN 0-471-06574-9). Wiley.

Pratt, A. W. Heat Transmission in Building. LC 80-42021. 308p. 1981. 51.95x (ISBN 0-471-27971-4, Pub. by Wiley-Interscience). Wiley.

Pratt, Alan, ed. Directory of Waste Disposal & Recovery. 232p. 1978. 60.00x (ISBN 0-686-99829-4, Pub. by Graham & Trotman England). State Mutual Bk.

Pratt, Allan D. The Information of the Image. (Libraries & Information Science Ser.). 118p. 1981. 17.50 (ISBN 0-89391-055-4). Ablex Pub.

Pratt, Arthur. How to Help & Understand the Alcoholic or Drug Addict. LC 80-82964. 127p. 1981. lib. bdg. 14.95 o.p. (ISBN 0-915216-62-0); pap. 4.95 (ISBN 0-915216-63-9). Love Street.

Pratt, C. Critical Phase in Tanzania, Nineteen Forty-Five to Nineteen Sixty-Eight. LC 75-22979. (Illus.). 360p. 1976. 44.50 (ISBN 0-521-20824-6). Cambridge U Pr.

Pratt, C., jt. auth. see Nesdale, A.

Pratt, David. Curriculum: Design & Development. 503p. 1980. text ed. 21.95 (ISBN 0-15-516735-9, HC). HarBraceJ.

Pratt, Ellen. Amy & the Cloudbasket. LC 75-25035. (Illus.). 38p. (Orig.). (ps-3). 1975. pap. 3.25 (ISBN 0-914996-08-8). Lollipop Power.

Pratt, Fletcher. Stanton, Lincoln's Secretary of War. Repr. of 1953 ed. lib. bdg. 20.50x o.p. (ISBN 0-8371-4000-5, PRST). Greenwood.

--War for the World. 1951. text ed. 8.50x (ISBN 0-686-83845-9). Elliots Bks.

Pratt, Francois. A Lantern in Lahore. 1983. 14.95x (ISBN 0-8290-1306-7). Irvington.

Pratt, Gerry. God Is Blue & Other Stories. 150p. 1978. 8.50 (ISBN 0-917304-38-1); pap. 7.50. Timber.

Pratt, Henry R. Countercurrent Separation Processes. 1967. 76.75 (ISBN 0-444-40461-9). Elsevier.

Pratt, James N. The Tea Lover's Treasury. LC 82-3472. (Illus.). 240p. (Orig.). 1982. pap. 7.95 (ISBN 0-89286-191-6). One Hund One Prods.

Pratt, James N. & De Caso, Jacques. The Wine Bibber's Bible. rev. ed. LC 79-177349. (Illus.). 1975. pap. 4.95 o.p. (ISBN 0-912238-71-2). One Hund One Prods.

Pratt, John C., ed. George Eliot's Middlemarch Notebooks: A Transcription. Neufeldt, Victor A. LC 74-16715. 1979. 42.50x (ISBN 0-520-02867-8). U of Cal Pr.

Pratt, Julius W. Cordell Hull: Nineteen Thirty Three to Nineteen Forty Four. LC 72-197305. (American Secretaries of State & Their Diplomacy, New Ser. 1925-1961: Vol. 12 & 13). 1964. 22.50x (ISBN 0-8154-0184-1). Cooper Sq.

Pratt, Julius W., et al. A History of United States Foreign Policy. 4th ed. 1980. text ed. 25.95 (ISBN 0-13-392282-0). P-H.

Pratt, L. R. East of Malta West of Suez. LC 75-23534. (Illus.). 224p. 1975. 34.50 (ISBN 0-521-20869-6). Cambridge U Pr.

Pratt, Lois. Family Structure & Effective Health Behavior: The Energized Family. LC 75-29817. (Illus.). 256p. 1976. pap. text ed. 13.95 (ISBN 0-395-18702-8). HM.

Pratt, Louis H. James Baldwin. (United States Authors Ser.). 1978. lib. bdg. 10.95 (ISBN 0-8057-7193-X, Twayne). G K Hall.

Pratt, Mary L. Toward a Speech Act Theory of Literary Discourse. LC 76-26424. (Midland Bks.: No. 264). 256p. 1977. 12.95 (ISBN 0-253-37006-X); pap. 7.95x (ISBN 0-253-20264-7). Ind U Pr.

Pratt, Noel. Homeopathic Prescribing. reprint ed. LC 82-84324. 1983. pap. 8.95 (ISBN 0-87983-325-4). Keats.

Pratt, Norma F. Morris Hillquit: A Political History of an American Jewish Socialist. LC 78-55349. (Illus.). 1979. lib. bdg. 29.95 (ISBN 0-313-20526-4, PMH/). Greenwood.

Pratt, Orson, ed. see Smith, Joseph.

Pratt, Parley P. Key to the Science of Theology. 5th ed. Repr. of 1891 ed. leatherette 5.00 o.p. (ISBN 0-914740-19-9). Western Epics.

Pratt, Richard. David Adler: The Architect & His Work. (Illus.). 1971. 20.00 o.p. (ISBN 0-87131-026-0). M Evans.

Pratt, Robert A., ed. see Chaucer, Geoffrey.

Pratt, Shannon. Valuing a Business: The Analysis & Appraisal of Closely Held Companies. LC 80-85475. 424p. 1981. 45.00 (ISBN 0-87094-205-0). Dow Jones-Irwin.

Pratt, Terence. Programming Languages: Design & Implementation. (Illus.). 496p. 1975. 29.95 (ISBN 0-13-730432-3). P-H.

Pratt, Vernon. The Philosophy of the Social Sciences. 1978. 17.95x o.p. (ISBN 0-416-76370-7); pap. 11.95x (ISBN 0-416-76380-4). Methuen Inc.

Pratt, William B. Chemotherapy of Infection. (Illus.). 1977. text ed. 24.95x (ISBN 0-19-502163-0); pap. text ed. 16.95x (ISBN 0-19-502162-2). Oxford U Pr.

Pratt, William B. & Ruddon, Raymond W. The Anticancer Drugs. (Illus.). 1979. text ed. 24.95x (ISBN 0-19-502565-2); pap. text ed. 15.95x (ISBN 0-19-502566-0). Oxford U Pr.

Pratt, William K. Digital Image Processing. LC 77-20888. 1978. 52.50 (ISBN 0-471-01888-0, Pub. by Wiley-Interscience). Wiley.

Pratt-Butler, Grace K. The Three, Four & Five Year Old in a School Setting. new ed. (Elementary Education Ser). 272p. 1975. text ed. 10.95 (ISBN 0-675-08724-4). Merrill.

Pratten, C. F. Comparisons of the Performance of Swedish & U.K. Companies. LC 76-19625. (Applied Economics Ser.: Occasional Papers, No. 47). (Illus.). 1976. pap. 18.95x (ISBN 0-521-29134-8). Cambridge U Pr.

--Labour Productivity Differentials Within International Companies. LC 76-8294. (Department of Applied Economics. Occasional Papers: No. 50). (Illus.). 1976. pap. 17.95x (ISBN 0-521-29102-X). Cambridge U Pr.

Prausnitz, Frederick. Score to Podium. 1982. 24.95x (ISBN 0-393-95154-5). Norton.

Prausnitz, J. M. Molecular Thermodynamics of Fluid-Phase Equilibria. LC 69-16866. 1969. ref. ed. 38.95 (ISBN 0-13-599639-2). P-H.

Pravitz, James, jt. auth. see Bennett, James.

Prawel, Sherwood, Jr., jt. auth. see Ketter, Robert L.

Prawer, S. S. Caligari's Children: The Film As Tale of Terror. 1980. 22.50x (ISBN 0-19-217584-X). Oxford U Pr.

--Heine: The Tragic Satirist. 1961. 55.00 (ISBN 0-521-05990-9). Cambridge U Pr.

--Karl Marx & World Literature. 1976. 29.95x o.p. (ISBN 0-19-815745-2). Oxford U Pr.

Prawer, S. S. & Riley, V. J. Theses in Germanic Studies, 1962-67. 18p. 1968. 25.00x (ISBN 0-85457-032-2, Pub. by Inst Germanic Stud England). State Mutual Bk.

Preaud, Tamara & Gauthier, Serge. Ceramics of the Twentieth Century. LC 82-50107. (Illus.). 224p. 1982. 80.00 (ISBN 0-8478-0436-4). Rizzoli Intl.

Prebble, John. The Lion in the North: A Personal View of Scotland's History. (Illus.). 344p. 1971. 22.50x o.p. (ISBN 0-436-38608-9). Intl Pubns Serv.

Prebish, Charles S. Buddhist Monastic Discipline: The Sanskrit Pratimoksa Sutras of the Mahasamghikas & Mulasarvastivadins. LC 74-10743. (Institute for Advanced Study of World Religions Ser.). 1975. 16.95x (ISBN 0-271-01171-8). Pa St U Pr.

Preble, Donna. Yamino-Kwiti. (Illus.). 256p. (gr. 4-10). 1983. pap. 5.95 (ISBN 0-930588-09-6). Heyday Bks.

Preble, Duane. Artforms. 2nd ed. (Orig.). 1978. pap. text ed. 24.95 scp (ISBN 0-06-386828-8, HarpC); instr's. manual avail. (ISBN 0-06-376077-0). Har-Row.

Preble, George H. The Symbols, Standards, Flags & Banners of Ancient & Modern Nations. 1980. lib. bdg. 12.00 (ISBN 0-8161-8476-3, Hall Reference). G K Hall.

Preda, I., ed. see Antaloczy, Z.

Predazzi, Enrico, jt. auth. see Leader, Elliot.

Pree, Gladis de see De Pree, Gordon & De Pree, Gladis.

Pree, Gordon De see De Pree, Gordon & De Pree, Gladis.

Preece & Light. Cell Electrophoresis in Cancer. (Developments in Cancer Research Ser.: Vol. 6). 1982. 53.75 (ISBN 0-444-80374-2). Elsevier.

Preece, A. W. & Sabolovic, D., eds. Cell Electrophoresis: Clinical Application & Methodology. (Inserm Symposium Ser.: Vol. 11). 496p. 1979. 74.50 (ISBN 0-7204-0674-9). Elsevier.

Preece, Warren E., ed. Encyclopaedia Britannica, 30 vols. 1983. per set 829.00 (ISBN 0-85229-400-X). Ency Brit Ed.

Preeg, Ernest H. The Evolution of a Revolution: Peru & Its Relations with the United States, 1968-1980. LC 81-85655. (Committee on Changing International Realities Ser.). 76p. 1981. pap. 7.00 (ISBN 0-686-36871-1). Natl Planning.

Preen, Brian S. Schooling for the Mentally Retarded: An Historical Perspective. LC 76-15867. 1977. 14.95x o.p. (ISBN 0-312-70175-6). St Martin.

Preer, Jean L. Lawyers vs. Educators: Black Colleges & Desegregation in Public Higher Education. LC 81-22567. (Contributions in American Studies: No. 61). 312p. 1982. lib. bdg. 29.95 (ISBN 0-313-23094-3, PLE/). Greenwood.

Preger, Paul D., Jr., jt. auth. see Lowenstein, Bertrand E.

Prehm, Herbert J., jt. auth. see Cegelka, Patricia T.

Preis, Art. Labor's Giant Step: Twenty Years of the CIO. LC 72-79771. cloth 30.00 (ISBN 0-87348-024-4). Path Pr NY.

Preis, Sandra & Cocks, George. Arithmetic. 2nd ed. (Illus.). 416p. 1980. pap. text ed. 19.95 (ISBN 0-13-046201-2). P-H.

Preiser, Wolfgang F., ed. Environmental Design Research Vol. 1: Selected Papers. LC 72-2010. (Community Development Ser: Vol. 3). 1973. 30.00 o.p. (ISBN 0-87933-029-5). Hutchinson Ross.

--Environmental Design Research, Vol. 2: Symposia & Workshops. LC 72-2010. (Community Development Ser.: Vol. 4). 1973. 30.00 o.p. (ISBN 0-87933-028-7). Hutchinson Ross.

--Facility Programming. LC 77-17881. (Community Development Ser.: Vol. 39). (Illus.). 1978. 40.00 (ISBN 0-87933-310-3). Hutchinson Ross.

Preisman, F. Robin Bright, Faiya Fredman, Reesey Shaw. (Illus.). 8p. 1974. 1.50x (ISBN 0-686-99818-9). La Jolla Mus Contemp Art.

Preiss, Byron. The Secret. 208p. 1982. pap. 9.95 (ISBN 0-553-01408-0). Bantam.

Preiss, Irene, ed. see Immerzeel, George & Ockenga, Earl.

Prejean, Blanche & Danielson, Wayne. Programmed News Style. (Basic Skills in Journalism Ser.). 1978. pap. text ed. 9.95 (ISBN 0-13-730655-5). P-H.

Prekopa, A., ed. Progress in Operations Research, 2 Vols. (Colloquia Mathematica Societatis Janos Bolyai: No. 12). 1976. Set. 95.75 (ISBN 0-7204-2836-X, North-Holland). Elsevier.

--Survey of Mathematical Programming, 3 vols. 1979. Set. 191.50 (ISBN 0-444-85033-3, North Holland). Elsevier.

Prekopa, A., ed. see Conference on Mathematical Programming, 3rd, Matrafured, Hungary, 1975.

Prelutsky, Jack, tr. see Lindgren, Barbro.

Prelutsky, James N. The Sheriff of Rottenshot. (ps-3). 1982. 8.50 (ISBN 0-688-00205-6); PLB 7.63 (ISBN 0-688-00198-X). Greenwillow.

Premack, Ann, jt. auth. see Premack, David.

Premack, David. Intelligence in Ape & Man. LC 76-26470. 370p. 1976. text ed. 24.95 (ISBN 0-89859-136-8). L Erlbaum Assocs.

Premack, David & Premack, Ann. The Mind of an Ape. (Illus.). 1983. 15.50 (ISBN 0-393-01581-5). Norton.

Premazon, Judith, jt. auth. see Sheppard, Valerie.

Preminger, Alex & Hardison, O. B., Jr., eds. Classical Literary Criticism: Translations & Interpretations, Vol. 1. LC 73-84722. (Classical & Medieval Literary Criticism Ser.). 300p. Date not set. pap. 10.95 (ISBN 0-8044-6664-5). Ungar. Postponed.

Preminger, Alex, Jr. & Hardison, O. B., eds. Medieval Literary Criticism: Translations & Interpretations, Vol. 2. LC 73-84722. (Classical & Medieval Literary Criticism). 250p. 1983. pap. 10.95 (ISBN 0-8044-6665-3). Ungar.

Prempree, Thongbliew, et al. Radiobiology Examination Review Book. 1975. spiral bdg. 14.75 (ISBN 0-87488-487-X). Med Exam.

Prendergast, C., jt. auth. see Crockett, James U.

Prendergast, Curtis. The First Aviators. LC 81-18209. (Epic of Flight Ser.). PLB 19.96 (ISBN 0-8094-3263-3). Silver.

Prendergast, E. D. & Boys, J. V. The Birds of Dorset. (Illus.). 304p. 1983. 43.00 (ISBN 0-7153-8380-9). David & Charles.

Prendergast, Roy M. Film Music: A Neglected Art. (Illus.). 1978. pap. 6.95 (ISBN 0-393-00862-2, N862, Norton Lib). Norton.

Prensky, Sol & Castellucis, Richard. Electronic Instrumentation. 3rd ed. (Illus.). 480p. 1982. 26.95 (ISBN 0-13-251611-X). P-H.

Prensky, Sol & Seidman, Arthur. Linear Integrated Circuits. 2nd ed. (Illus.). 1981. text ed. 22.95 (ISBN 0-8359-4084-5). Reston.

Prensky, Sol D. Manual of Linear Integrated Circuits. LC 73-15979. (Illus.). 240p. 1974. 22.95 (ISBN 0-87909-466-4). Reston.

Prenter, P. M. Splines & Variational Methods. LC 75-4689. (Pure & Applied Mathematics Ser). 323p. 1975. 36.95x (ISBN 0-471-69660-9, Pub. by Wiley-Interscience). Wiley.

Prentice, Ann E. Financial Planning for Libraries. LC 82-7330. 236p. 1983. 14.50 (ISBN 0-8108-1565-6). Scarecrow.

Prentice, Diana & Prentice, James. More Than Talking. 184p. (gr. 10-12). 1983. pap. 7.03 (ISBN 0-931054-12-5). Clark Pub.

Prentice, Diana, jt. auth. see Hensley, Dana.

Prentice-Hall Editorial Staff, ed. Legal Secretary's Encyclopedic Dictionary. 3rd ed. DeVries, Mary A. LC 81-8700. 445p. 1982. 24.95 (ISBN 0-13-528869-X, Busn). P-H.

Prentice, J. M. Dynamics of Mechanical Systems. 2nd ed. LC 79-41460. 486p. 1980. 79.95x (ISBN 0-470-26938-3). Halsted Pr.

Prentice, James, jt. auth. see Prentice, Diana.

Prentice, Richard, jt. auth. see Roberts, Arthur.

Prentice, Robert P. Psychology of Love According to St. Bonaventure. (Philosophy Ser). 1957. 7.00 o.p. (ISBN 0-686-11536-8). Franciscan Inst.

Prentice, Robin, ed. The National Trust for Scotland Guide. rev. ed. (Illus.). 1981. 19.95 (ISBN 0-393-01479-7). Norton.

Prentice, Sartell. The Heritage of the Cathedral. (Illus.). 1953. 6.00 (ISBN 0-688-01780-0). Morrow.

Prentis, James M. Engineering Mechanics. (Oxford Engineering Science Texts Ser.). (Illus.). 1979. text ed. 59.00x (ISBN 0-19-856205-5); pap. text ed. 18.50x (ISBN 0-19-856206-3). Oxford U Pr.

Prentiss, Charlotte. Love's Savage Embrace. 304p. (Orig.). 1981. pap. 2.75 o.s.i. (ISBN 0-515-05272-8). Jove Pubns.

Prentiss, Hervey Putnam. Timothy Pickering As the Leader of New England Federalism, 1800-1815. LC 71-124882. (American Scene Ser). (Illus.). 118p. 1972. Repr. of 1934 ed. lib. bdg. 22.50 (ISBN 0-306-71052-8). Da Capo.

Prentiss, Stan. Basic Color Television Course. LC 73-189960. (Basic Textbook Ser). (Illus.). 395p. 1972. 12.95 o.p. (ISBN 0-8306-2601-8); pap. 9.95 o.p. (ISBN 0-8306-1601-2, 601). TAB Bks.

--Japanese Color TV: Sony, Vol. 5. LC 70-152886. (Schematic Servicing Manual Ser). (Illus.). 1975. vinyl 8.95 (ISBN 0-8306-4700-7); pap. 5.95 o.p. (ISBN 0-8306-3700-1, 700). TAB Bks.

--Motorola Color TV Service Manual, Vol. 2. LC 76-91323. (Schematic-Servicing Manual Ser). 1972. vinyl o.p. 10.95 (ISBN 0-8306-2584-4); pap. 7.95 (ISBN 0-8306-1584-9, 584). TAB Bks.

--Servicing the New Modular Color TV Receivers, Vol. 1. LC 73-78195. (Schematic Servicing Manual Ser). (Illus.). 178p. 1973. 9.95 o.p. leatherette (ISBN 0-8306-3662-5); pap. 6.95 (ISBN 0-8306-2662-X, 662). TAB Bks.

Prentky, R. A. The Biological Aspects of Normal Personality. 400p. 1979. text ed. 32.95 (ISBN 0-8391-1462-1). Univ Park.

Preobrazhensky, E. A. The Crisis of Soviet Industrialization: Selected Essays. Filtzer, Donald A., ed. LC 78-73224. 1979. 30.00 (ISBN 0-87332-121-9). M E Sharpe.

Preparata, Franco P. & Yeh, Raymond T. Introduction to Discrete Structures. LC 72-3461. 1973. text ed. 27.95 (ISBN 0-201-05968-1). A-W.

Pres, Terrence Des see Des Pres, Terrence.

Presas, Remy A. Modern Arnis: For Self-Defense. (Illus.). 1983. pap. 6.95 (ISBN 0-89750-089-X, 426). Ohara Pubns.

Presch, William, jt. auth. see Weichert, Charles K.

Prescod, Suzanne. Current Research on Marriage, Families, & Divorce. 1979. looseleaf bdg. 25.00 (ISBN 0-915260-09-3). Atcom.

Prescot, Dary. Delia of Valla. 192p. 1982. pap. 2.35 (ISBN 0-87997-784-1, UE1784). DAW Bks.

Prescot, Dray. Fliers of Antares. 1982. pap. 2.25 (ISBN 0-87997-733-7, UE1733). DAW Bks.

--A Fortune for Kregan. (Science Fiction Ser.). (Illus., Orig.). 1979. pap. 1.95 o.p. (ISBN 0-87997-505-9, UJ1505). Daw Bks.

--Legions of Antares. (Science Fiction Ser.). 192p. 1981. pap. 2.25 (ISBN 0-87997-648-9, UE1648). DAW Bks.

--A Life for Kregen. (Science Fiction Ser). (Illus.). 1979. pap. 1.75 o.p. (ISBN 0-87997-456-7, UE1456). DAW Bks.

Prescott, Bryan. Effective Decision Making: A Self-Development Program. 100p. 1980. text ed. 22.25x (ISBN 0-566-02211-7). Gower Pub Ltd.

Prescott, David & Wilson, Leslie, eds. Methods in Cell Biology: Vol. 24A: The Cytoskeleton: Cytoskeletal Proteins, Isolation & Characterization. 464p. 1982. 49.00 (ISBN 0-12-564124-9). Acad Pr.

--Methods in Cell Biology: Vol. 25B: The Cytoskeleton: Biological Systems & in-Vitro Models. 448p. 1982. 47.00 (ISBN 0-12-564125-7). Acad Pr.

Prescott, David M., ed. Methods in Cell Physiology. Incl. Vol. 1. 1964. 58.50 (ISBN 0-12-564101-X); Vol. 2. 1966. 58.50 (ISBN 0-12-564102-8); Vol. 3. 1969. 58.50 (ISBN 0-12-564103-6); Vol. 4. 1970. 58.50 (ISBN 0-12-564104-4); Vol. 5. 1972. 58.50 (ISBN 0-12-564105-2); Vol. 6. 1973. 58.50 (ISBN 0-12-564106-0); Vol. 7. 1974. 58.50 (ISBN 0-12-564107-9); Vol. 8. 1974. 58.50 (ISBN 0-12-564108-7); Vol. 9. 1975. 58.50 (ISBN 0-12-564109-5); Vol. 10. 1975. 58.50 (ISBN 0-12-564110-9); Vol. 11. Yeast Cells. 1975. 58.50 (ISBN 0-12-564111-7); Vol. 12. 1975. 58.50 (ISBN 0-12-564112-5); Vol. 13. 1976. 58.50 (ISBN 0-12-564113-3); Vol. 14. 1976. 58.50 (ISBN 0-12-564114-1); Vol. 15. 1977. 58.50 (ISBN 0-12-564115-X); Vol. 16. Chromatin & Chromosomal Protein Research I. Stein, Gary & Stein, Janet, eds. 1977. 59.50 (ISBN 0-12-564116-8). Acad Pr.

Prescott, David M., et al, eds. Methods in Cell Biology, Vols. 17-20. 1978. Vol. 17. 55.00 (ISBN 0-12-564117-6); Vol. 18. 55.50 (ISBN 0-12-564118-4); Vol. 19. 50.50 (ISBN 0-12-564119-2); Vol. 20. 67.50 (ISBN 0-12-564120-6). Acad Pr.

Prescott, Evelyn, jt. tr. see Cavender, Elsie.

Prescott, Frank W. & Zimmerman, Joseph F. The Politics of the Veto of Legislation in New York State, 2 vols. LC 79-9696. 649p. 1980. Set. text ed. 59.50 (ISBN 0-8191-0984-3); softcover set 38.25 (ISBN 0-8191-0986-X). U Pr of Amer.

Prescott, G. W. A Contribution to a Bibliography of Antarctic & Subantarctic Algae Together with a Checklist of Freshwater Taxa Reported to 1977. (Bibliotheca Phycologica: No. 45). 1979. lib. bdg. 32.00 (ISBN 3-7682-1216-5). Lubrecht & Cramer.

Prescott, G. W. & Bicudo, Carlos E. A Synopsis of North American Desmids, Pt. II: Desmidiaceae; Placodermae, Section 4. LC 70-183418. x, 700p. 1982. 65.00x (ISBN 0-8032-3650-6). U of Nebr Pr.

Prescott, Gerald W. Algae of the Western Great Lakes Area: With Illustrated Key to the Genera of Desmids on Freshwater Diatoms. (Illus.). 977p. 1983. lib. bdg. 60.80X (ISBN 3-87429-206-1, Pub. by Koeltz Germany); pap. text ed. 28.00X (ISBN 3-87429-205-3). Lubrecht & Cramer.

--The Diatoms: A Photomicrographic Book. (Illus.). (gr. 4 up). 1977. PLB 5.99 o.p. (ISBN 0-698-30631-7, Coward). Putnam Pub Group.

Prescott, Gordon R., jt. auth. see Hudson, L. Frank.

Prescott, J. R. Political Geography. 1972. 18.95 (ISBN 0-312-62300-3). St Martin.

Prescott, James R. & Lewis, Cris W. Urban Regional Economic Growth & Policy. LC 74-83857. (Man, Community & Natural Resources Ser.). 1975. 12.50 o.p. (ISBN 0-250-40071-5). Ann Arbor Science.

Prescott, James R., jt. auth. see Fullerton, Herbert H.

Prescott, John. Directory of Shipowners, Shipbuilders & Marine Engineers, 1982. 80th ed. LC 35-4199. 1534p. 1982. 70.00x (ISBN 0-617-00277-0). Intl Pubns Serv.

Prescott, John, ed. Directory of Shipowners, Shipbuilders & Marine Engineers 1981. 79th ed. LC 25-4199. 1514p. 1981. 60.00x o.p. (ISBN 0-617-00319-X). Intl Pubns Serv.

Prescott, L. F. & Gibaldi, M., eds. Handbook of Clinical Pharmacokinetics. 1200p. text ed. write for info. (ISBN 0-86792-004-1, Pub by Adis Pr Australia). Wright-PSG.

Prescott, Mary A. How to Raise & Train a Bullmastiff. (Orig.). pap. 2.95 (ISBN 0-87666-260-2, DS1065). TFH Pubns.

Prescott, W. H. Correspondence of William Hickling Prescott, 1833-1847. Wolcott, Roger, ed. LC 76-112312. (American Public Figures Ser). 1970. Repr. of 1925 ed. lib. bdg. 49.50 (ISBN 0-306-71912-6). Da Capo.

Prescott, William H. The Conquest of Mexico. Bd. with The Conquest of Peru. 1931. 10.95 (ISBN 0-394-60471-7). Modern Lib.

--Conquest of Peru. abr ed. Von Hagen, Victor W., ed. pap. 1.50 o.p. (ISBN 0-451-61495-X, MW1495, Ment). NAL.

--History of the Conquest of Mexico, 2 vols. in 1. 1957. 14.95x o.p. (ISBN 0-460-10397-0, Evman). Biblio Dist.

Presidents Commission. The Electoral & Democratic Process in the Eighties. (Illus.). 107p. 1982. 12.95 (ISBN 0-13-247114-0); pap. 4.95 (ISBN 0-13-247106-X). P-H.

President's Commission. Urban America in the Eighties, Prospects & Perspectives. (Illus.). 116p. 1982. 12.95 (ISBN 0-13-939603-9); pap. 4.95 (ISBN 0-686-73243-X). P-H.

President's Commission for a National Agenda for the Eighties. A National Agenda for the Eighties. 1981. pap. 2.95 o.p. (ISBN 0-451-62011-9, ME2011, Ment). NAL.

President's Commission On Immigration & Naturalization. Whom We Shall Welcome. LC 73-146270. (Civil Liberties in American History Ser). 1971. Repr. of 1953 ed. lib. bdg. 45.00 (ISBN 0-306-70145-6). Da Capo.

President's Commission on National Goals. Goals for Americans. LC 60-53566. 3.50 o.p. (ISBN 0-936904-08-9); pap. 1.95 (ISBN 0-936904-09-7). Am Assembly.

Preslan, Kristina. Group Crafts for Teachers & Librarians on Limited Budgets. LC 80-13145. (Illus.). 105p. 1980. pap. 11.50 (ISBN 0-87287-218-1). Libs Unl.

Presles, Olivier. Encephalites Aigues Virales. (Illus.). viii, 464p. 1982. pap. 58.75 (ISBN 3-8055-3561-9). S Karger.

Presley, Bruce. A Guide to Programming IBM Personal Computer. 173p. 1982. pap. 16.95 (ISBN 0-442-26015-6). Van Nos Reinhold.

--A Guide to Programming in Level II BASIC. 190p. 1982. pap. 12.95 (ISBN 0-442-25892-5). Van Nos Reinhold.

Presley, Dee, et al. Elvis We Love You Tender. (Illus.). 1980. 14.95 o.s.i. (ISBN 0-440-02323-8). Delacorte.

Presley, J. R., jt. auth. see Coffey, P.

Presley, J. R., et al. Case Studies in Macro-Economics. Maunder, Peter, ed. (Case Studies in Economic Analysis). 1977. 5.00x o.p. (ISBN 0-435-84473-3); tchr's ed. 8.50x o.p. (ISBN 0-435-84474-1). Heinemann Ed.

Presley, James. A Saga of Wealth. LC 78-136. 1978. 14.95 (ISBN 0-399-11852-7). Putnam Pub Group.

Presley, James, jt. auth. see McCamy, John.

Presley, John W. To Be Exact: A Guide for Revision. 320p. 1982. pap. 11.95 (ISBN 0-13-922807-1). P-H.

Presley, M. W., jt. auth. see McGillis, K. A.

Presnall, Lewis F. Alcoholism: The Exposed Family. 3.25 o.p. (ISBN 0-686-92089-9). Hazelden.

--Search for Serenity. 4.95 o.p. (ISBN 0-686-92402-9, 6280); pap. 3.00 o.p. (ISBN 0-686-98516-8, 6620). Hazelden.

Presper, Mary. Joys of Woodstoves & Fireplaces. LC 78-73323. pap. 6.95 o.p. (ISBN 0-448-14847-1, G&D). Putnam Pub Group.

Press, C. & Verburg, K. American Policy Studies. LC 80-22992. 234p. 1981. pap. text ed. 12.95x (ISBN 0-471-07866-2). Wiley.

Press, C., jt. auth. see Adrian, C. R.

Press, Charles & VerBerg, Kenneth. State & Community Governments in the Federal System. LC 78-22064. 1979. text ed. 21.95x (ISBN 0-471-02725-1); tchrs.' manual 6.00 (ISBN 0-471-04909-3). Wiley.

Press, Charles & VerBurg, Kenneth. State & Community Governments in the Federal System. 2nd ed. 600p. 1983. text ed. write for info. (ISBN 0-471-86979-1); write for info. tchr's ed. (ISBN 0-471-87199-0). Wiley.

Press, Charles, jt. auth. see Adrian, Charles R.

Press, Hans J. Simple Science Experiments. 1974. 12.50 (ISBN 0-7134-2894-5, Pub. by Batsford England). David & Charles.

Press, Irwin. Tradition & Adaptation: Life in a Modern Yucatan Maya Village. LC 75-71. (Illus.). 288p. 1975. lib. bdg. 27.50 (ISBN 0-8371-7954-8, PYM/). Greenwood.

Press, Irwin & Smith, Estellie. Urban Place & Process: Readings in the Anthropology of Cities. (Illus.). 1980. pap. text ed. 14.95x (ISBN 0-02-396540-1). Macmillan.

Press, John. Rule & Energy: Trends in British Poetry Since Second World War. LC 76-10158. (George Elliston Poetry Foundation Lectures, University of Cincinnati). 1976. Repr. of 1963 ed. lib. bdg. 18.25x (ISBN 0-8371-8853-9, PRRE). Greenwood.

Press, Larry & Whittaker, Lou, eds. Personal Computing Digest. (Illus.). vi, 211p. 1980. pap. 14.00 (ISBN 0-88283-012-0). AFIPS Pr.

Press, Margaret L. Chemehuevi: A Grammar & Lexicon. (U. C. Publications in Linguistics Ser.: Vol. 92). 1980. pap. 16.50x (ISBN 0-520-09600-2). U of Cal Pr.

Pressat, Roland. Statistical Demography. Courtney, Damien A., tr. from Fr. LC 78-19251. 1978. 25.00x (ISBN 0-312-76134-1). St Martin.

--A Workbook in Demography. Grebenik, E. & Sym, C. A., trs. from Fr. (Illus.). 1974. pap. 16.95x (ISBN 0-416-78160-8). Methuen Inc.

Presseau, Jack R. I'm Saved, You're Saved--Maybe. LC 76-12401. 1977. 3.99 (ISBN 0-8042-0832-8). John Knox.

Presser, Janice & Brewer, Gail S. Breastfeeding. LC 82-48736. 1983. 14.95 (ISBN 0-394-52414-4). Knopf.

Pressman, Andy & Pressman, Peter. Integrated Space Systems: Vocabulary for Room Language. 128p. 1980. 16.95 (ISBN 0-442-23162-8); pap. 9.95 o.p. (ISBN 0-442-23167-9). Van Nos Reinhold.

Pressman, David R. Patent It Yourself! How to Protect, Patent & Market Your Inventions. LC 78-10232. 1979. 21.95 (ISBN 0-07-050780-5, P&RB). McGraw.

Pressman, Israel, jt. auth. see Gordon, Gilbert.

Pressman, Jeffrey L. Federal Programs & City Politics: The Dynamics of the Aid Process in Oakland. (Oakland Project Ser). 1975. 28.50x (ISBN 0-520-02749-3); pap. 6.50x (ISBN 0-520-03508-9). U of Cal Pr.

Pressman, Maurice J. Workmen's Compensation in Maryland. 2nd ed. 1977. with 1980 suppl. 50.00 (ISBN 0-87215-196-4); 1980 suppl. only 15.00 (ISBN 0-87215-435-1). Michie-Bobbs.

Pressman, Peter, jt. auth. see Pressman, Andy.

Pressman, R. S. Software Engineering: A Practitioner's Approach. (Software Engineering & Technology Ser.). 1982. 32.95 (ISBN 0-07-050781-3); instr's. manual 8.00 (ISBN 0-07-050782-1). McGraw.

Pressman, Robert M. & Siegler, Rodie. The Independent Practitioner: Practice Management for the Allied Health Profess onal. LC 82-73633. (Dorsey Professional Ser.). 250p. 1983. 19.95 (ISBN 0-87094-315-4). Dow Jones-Irwin.

Pressnell, S. L., ed. Money & Banking in Japan. LC 72-93885. 450p. 1974. 30.00 (ISBN 0-312-54460-X). St Martin.

Presson, Hazel. Student Journalist & Interviewing. rev. ed. LC 67-10292. (Student Journalist Ser). (gr. 7 up). 1982. PLB 7.97 (ISBN 0-8239-0488-1). Rosen Pr.

Prest, A. R. The Taxation of Urban Land. 208p. 1982. 25.00 (ISBN 0-7190-0817-4). Manchester.

Presthus, R. Elites in the Policy Process. LC 73-94135. 512p. 1974. 42.50 (ISBN 0-521-20344-9). Cambridge U Pr.

--Public Administration. 6th ed. 1975. text ed. 22.50 (ISBN 0-471-07058-0). Wiley.

Preston, jt. auth. see Hawkins.

Preston, A., jt. auth. see Mahan, A.

Preston, Adrian, ed. see Wolseley, Garnet.

Preston, Adrian, ed. see Wolseley, Gerald.

Preston, Anthony. Submarines. (Illus.). 220p. 1982. 24.95 (ISBN 0-312-77475-3). St Martin.

Preston, Anthony, ed. Camera at Sea Nineteen Thirty Nine-Nineteen Forty Five. LC 78-52367. (Illus.). 1978. 22.95 o.p. (ISBN 0-87021-823-9). Naval Inst Pr.

Preston, Antony. Super Destroyers. 72p. 1980. 11.50x o.p. (ISBN 0-85177-131-9, Pub. by Cornell England). State Mutual Bk.

--Warships of the World. (Illus.). 224p. 1981. 16.95 (ISBN 0-86720-580-6). Sci Bks Intl.

Preston, C. Trilogy of Christmas Plays for Children. LC 67-17157. (Illus.). (gr. 5 up). 1967. 5.95 o.p. (ISBN 0-15-290450-6, HJ). HarBraceJ.

Preston, Charles. Can Board Chairmen Get Measles? & Other Quandries of American Business & Industry. 1983. 9.95 (ISBN 0-517-54898-4). Crown.

--Crosswords for the Connoisseur, No. 27. 100p. Date not set. pap. price not set (ISBN 0-448-02095-5, G&D). Putnam Pub Group.

--Crosswords from the National Observer, No. 1. 64p. Date not set. pap. price not set (ISBN 0-448-00886-6, G&D). Putnam Pub Group.

--Dow Jones-Irwin Crosswords for the Serious. 1980. pap. 3.95 ea. Bk. 1 (ISBN 0-87128-585-1). Bk. 2 (ISBN 0-87128-586-X). Dow Jones-Irwin.

--Dow Jones-Irwin Crosswords for the Serious, Bk. 8. 60p. 1982. pap. 3.95 (ISBN 0-87094-296-4). Dow Jones-Irwin.

--Dow Jones-Irwin Crosswords for the Serious, Bk. 10. 60p. 1982. pap. 3.95 (ISBN 0-87094-344-8). Dow Jones-Irwin.

--Signet Crossword Puzzle Book, No. 1. 1980. pap. 1.50 o.p. (ISBN 0-451-09079-9, W9079, Sig). NAL.

--Signet Crossword Puzzle Book, No. 6. 1982. pap. 1.75 (ISBN 0-451-11473-6, AE1473, Sig). NAL.

--Superbrain Crosswords for the Connoisseur. 100p. Date not set. pap. price not set (ISBN 0-448-14686-X, G&D). Putnam Pub Group.

Preston, Charles, ed. Crossword Puzzles in Large Type, Bk. 1. 96p. 1973. pap. 2.95 (ISBN 0-448-01564-1, G&D). Putnam Pub Group.

--Crossword Puzzles in Large Type, Bk. 2. (Illus.). 96p. 1974. pap. 2.95 (ISBN 0-448-11648-0, G&D). Putnam Pub Group.

--Crossword Puzzles in Large Type, Bk. 3. 96p. 1975. pap. 2.95 (ISBN 0-448-11885-8, G&D). Putnam Pub Group.

--Crossword Puzzles in Large Type, Bk. 4. 96p. 1976. pap. 2.95 (ISBN 0-448-12571-4, G&D). Putnam Pub Group.

--Crosswords for the Connoisseur. Incl. Series 5 (ISBN 0-448-01595-1); Series 6 (ISBN 0-448-01567-6); Series 7 (ISBN 0-448-01524-2); Series 8 (ISBN 0-448-01528-5); Series 9 (ISBN 0-448-01530-7); Series 10 (ISBN 0-448-01535-8); Series 11 (ISBN 0-448-01538-2); Series 12 (ISBN 0-448-01546-3); Series 13 (ISBN 0-448-01529-3); Series 14 (ISBN 0-448-01719-9); Series 15 (ISBN 0-448-01722-9); Series 16 (ISBN 0-448-01834-9); Series 18 (ISBN 0-448-01791-1); Series 19 (ISBN 0-448-02092-0); Series 20 (ISBN 0-448-02088-2); Series 21 (ISBN 0-448-01561-7); Series 22 (ISBN 0-448-11549-2); Series 23 (ISBN 0-448-11730-4); Series 24 (ISBN 0-448-12229-4). pap. 2.95 ea. (G&D). Putnam Pub Group.

--Crosswords for the Connoisseur, Ser. 25. pap. 2.95 (ISBN 0-448-14048-9, G&D). Putnam Pub Group.

--Crosswords from the National Observer, No. 3. (Illus.). 64p. 1974. pap. 2.95 (ISBN 0-448-11799-1, G&D). Putnam Pub Group.

--Crosswords from the National Observer, No. 4. (Illus.). 64p. 1975. pap. 2.95 (ISBN 0-448-11999-4, G&D). Putnam Pub Group.

--Crosswords from the National Observer, No. 2. (Illus.). 64p. (Orig.). 1973. pap. 2.95 (ISBN 0-448-00888-2, G&D). Putnam Pub Group.

--Crosswords from the National Observer: No. 5. (Illus.). 64p. 1976. pap. 2.95 (ISBN 0-448-12492-0, G&D). Putnam Pub Group.

--Dow Jones-Irwin Crosswords for the Serious, Bk. 9. 60p. 1982. pap. 3.95 (ISBN 0-87094-343-X). Dow Jones-Irwin.

--Dow Jones-Irwin Crosswords for the Serious, Bk. 11. 48p. (Orig.). 1983. pap. 3.95 (ISBN 0-87094-372-3). Dow Jones-Irwin.

--Dow Jones-Irwin Crosswords for the Serious, Bk. 12. 48p. (Orig.). 1983. pap. 3.95 (ISBN 0-87094-373-1). Dow Jones-Irwin.

--Dow Jones-Irwin Crosswords for the Serious, Bk. 13. 48p. (Orig.). 1983. pap. 3.95 (ISBN 0-87094-407-X). Dow Jones-Irwin.

--Dow Jones-Irwin Crosswords for the Serious, Bk. 14. 48p. (Orig.). 1983. pap. 3.95 (ISBN 0-87094-408-8). Dow Jones-Irwin.

--Dow Jones-Irwin Crosswords for the Serious, Bk. 15. 48p. (Orig.). 1983. pap. 3.95 (ISBN 0-87094-409-6). Dow Jones-Irwin.

--Dow Jones-Irwin Crosswords for the Serious, Bk. 16. 48p. (Orig.). 1983. pap. 3.95 (ISBN 0-87094-410-X). Dow Jones-Irwin.

--Riddle & Fact Find Book, No. 1. (Basic Activity Bks.). (Illus.). 64p. (gr. 2-5). 1976. pap. 1.25 (ISBN 0-448-11964-1, G&D). Putnam Pub Group.

--Riddle & Fact Find Book, No. 2. (Basic Activity Bks.). (Illus.). 64p. (gr. 2-5). 1976. pap. 1.25 (ISBN 0-448-11965-X, G&D). Putnam Pub Group.

--Signet Crossword Puzzle Book, No. 7. 1982. pap. 1.75 (ISBN 0-451-11570-8, AE1570, Sig). NAL.

Preston, Charles G., jt. auth. see Place, Marian T.

Preston, Daniel D. The Life & Work of the Minister. 1968. 5.95 (ISBN 0-934942-11-0). White Wing Pub.

Preston, David A. Environment, Society & Rural Change in Latin America: The Past, Present & Future in the Country. LC 79-41481. 256p. 1980. 49.95 (ISBN 0-471-27713-4, Pub. by Wiley-Interscience). Wiley.

Preston, David A., jt. auth. see Odell, Peter R.

Preston, Dickson J. Young Frederick Douglass, The Maryland Years. 241p. 1980. 15.00 (ISBN 0-686-36710-3). Md Hist.

Preston, Don, jt. auth. see Warrick, Ruth.

Preston, Effa E. The Popular Commencement Book. LC 70-175776. 434p. 1975. Repr. of 1931 ed. 37.00x (ISBN 0-8103-4034-8). Gale.

Preston, Fayrene. Silver Miracles. (Loveswept Ser.: No. 4). 1983. pap. 1.95 (ISBN 0-686-43205-3). Bantam.

Preston, Frederick W., jt. auth. see Smith, Ronald W.

Preston, Geoff. Race Aurora AFX: A Guide to HO Model Racing Cars. (Illus.). 100p. (Orig.). 1982. pap. 12.50x (ISBN 0-85242-727-1). Intl Pubns Serv.

Preston, Geoffrey. God's Way to Be Human. LC 78-65902. 112p. 1978. 4.95 o.p. (ISBN 0-8091-0280-3). Paulist Pr.

--Hallowing the Time: Meditations on the Cycle of the Christian Liturgy. LC 80-82253. 176p. (Orig.). 1980. pap. 5.95 o.p. (ISBN 0-8091-2339-8). Paulist Pr.

Preston, George R., Jr. Thomas Wolfe: A Bibliography. LC 74-12760. (Illus.). 1979. Repr. of 1943 ed. lib. bdg. 15.75x (ISBN 0-8371-7750-2, PRTW). Greenwood.

Preston, Harriet W. & Dodge, Louise. The Private Life of the Romans. (Illus.). 167p. 1982. Repr. of 1896 ed. lib. bdg. 50.00 (ISBN 0-8495-4412-2). Arden Lib.

Preston, Hayter, jt. auth. see Brangwyn, Frank.

Preston, Howard H. History of Banking in Iowa. Bruchey, Stuart, ed. LC 80-1167. (The Rise of Commercial Banking Ser.). (Illus.). 1981. Repr. of 1922 ed. lib. bdg. 39.00x (ISBN 0-405-13677-3). Ayer Co.

Preston, Howard K. & Sollenberger, N. J. Modern Prestressed Concrete. (Illus.). 1967. 28.95 (ISBN 0-07-050823-2, P&RB). McGraw.

Preston, Ivan L. The Great American Blow-up: Puffery in Advertising & Selling. LC 74-27313. 384p. 1975. 27.50 (ISBN 0-299-06730-0); pap. 9.95 (ISBN 0-299-06734-3). U of Wis Pr.

Preston, J. Dennis, et al. Cancer Chemotherapeutic Agents: Handbook of Clinical Data, 8 vols. 2nd ed. 1982. Set. lib. bdg. 21.95 (ISBN 0-8161-2236-9, Hall Medical Bks). G K Hall.

Preston, Jack, jt. ed. see Carraher, Charles E., Jr.

Preston, Jack D. & Bergen, Stephen F. Color Science & Dental Art: A Self-Teaching Program. LC 80-17295. (Illus.). 88p. 1980. pap. 25.00 (ISBN 0-8016-4038-5). Mosby.

Preston, John. Franny: The Queen of Provincetown. 96p. (Orig.). 1983. pap. 4.95 (ISBN 0-932870-31-7). Alyson Pubns.

--Peter Bosten. 1977. Repr. of 1915 ed. pap. 8.00 o.p. (ISBN 0-8309-0200-7). Herald Hse.

Preston, Julia, jt. auth. see Byers, Patricia.

Preston, K. Blake & Rossetti. LC 73-117999. (Studies in Comparative Literature, No. 35). 1970. Repr. of 1944 ed. lib. bdg. 38.95x (ISBN 0-8383-1054-0). Haskell.

Preston, Kendall, Jr. Coherent Optical Computers. LC 73-152008. (Illus.). 336p. 1972. 36.50 o.p. (ISBN 0-07-050785-6, P&RB). McGraw.

Preston, Lee E. & Post, James E. Private Management & Public Policy: The Principle of Public Responsibility. (Illus.). 192p. 1975. pap. text ed. 13.95 (ISBN 0-13-710970-9). P-H.

Preston, Lee E., ed. Research in Corporate Social Performance, Vol. 1. 291p. 1978. 42.50 (ISBN 0-89232-069-9). Jai Pr.

--Research in Corporate Social Performance & Policy, Vol. 2. (Orig.). 1980. lib. bdg. 42.50 (ISBN 0-89232-133-4). Jai Pr.

--Research in Corporate Social Performance & Policy, Vol. 3. 325p. 1981. 42.50 (ISBN 0-89232-184-9). Jai Pr.

Preston, M. A. & Bhaduri, R. K. Structure of the Nucleus. 475p. 1975. 39.50 (ISBN 0-201-05976-2, Adv Bk Prog); pap. text ed. 25.50 (ISBN 0-201-05977-0, Adv Bk Prog). A-W.

Preston, Michael, jt. ed. see Palley, Marian.

Preston, Michael B., jt. ed. see Palley, Marian L.

Preston, P. N. Benzimidazoles & Congeneric Tricyclic Compounds, Pt. 1, Vol. 40. LC 80-17383. (Chemistry of Heterocyclic Compounds Ser.). 687p. 1981. 220.50 (ISBN 0-471-03792-3, Pub. by Wiley-Interscience). Wiley.

--Benzimidazoles & Congeneric Tricyclic Compounds, Vol. 40, Pt. 2. LC 80-17383. (Chemistry of Heterocyclic Compounds Ser.). 1200p. 1980. 220.50 (ISBN 0-471-08189-2, Pub. by Wiley-Interscience). Wiley.

Preston, P. W. Theories of Development. (International Library of Sociology). 300p. 1982. 27.95 (ISBN 0-7100-9055-2). Routledge & Kegan.

Preston, Paul & Nelson, Ralph. Salesmanship: A Contemporary Approach. 1981. 18.95 (ISBN 0-8359-6933-9); instr's manual free. Reston.

Preston, Paul, jt. auth. see Zimmerer, Thomas W.

Preston, R. D. The Physical Biology of Plant Cell Walls. (Illus.). 1974. 59.95x (ISBN 0-412-11600-6, Pub. by Chapman & Hall). Methuen Inc.

Preston, R. D., ed. Advances in Botanical Research. Incl. Vol. 1. 1963. 57.50 (ISBN 0-12-005901-0); Vol. 2. 1965. o.s. 57.00 (ISBN 0-12-005902-9); Vol. 3. 1970. 49.00 (ISBN 0-12-005903-7). Acad Pr.

--Advances in Botanical Research, Vol. 5. (Serial Publication). 1977. 40.50 (ISBN 0-12-005905-3). Acad Pr.

Preston, Ralph C. & Botel, Morton. How to Study. 4th ed. 176p. 1981. pap. 7.95 (ISBN 0-574-19625-0, 13-3625); instr's. guide avail. (ISBN 0-574-19626-9, 13-3626). SRA.

--How to Study. 1974. pap. text ed. 6.00 o.s.i. (ISBN 0-574-51295-0, 5-1295); instr's guide avail. o.s.i. (ISBN 0-574-51296-9, 5-1296); specimen set 7.47 o.s.i. (ISBN 0-574-51299-3, 5-1299). SRA.

Preston, Richard J., Jr. North American Trees. 3rd ed. (Illus.). 1977. pap. 5.95x (ISBN 0-262-66031-8). MIT Pr.

Preston, Samuel, et al. Causes of Death: Life Tables for National Populations. (Studies in Population). 800p. 1972. 54.50 (ISBN 0-12-785664-1). Acad Pr.

Preston, T. R. & Willis, M. B. Intensive Beef Production. 2nd ed. 1974. 26.00 o.p. (ISBN 0-08-018980-6); text ed. 43.00 o.p. (ISBN 0-08-017788-3). Pergamon.

Preston, Thomas A. Coronary Artery Surgery: A Critical Review. LC 76-51977. 278p. 1977. 17.00 (ISBN 0-89004-165-2). Raven.

Preston, Wheeler. American Biographies. LC 73-10407. x, 1147p. 1975. Repr. of 1940 ed. 77.00x (ISBN 0-8103-4054-2). Gale.

Preston, William. Cork & Wine. (Illus.). 64p. 1983. 12.00 (ISBN 0-937088-04-8). Illum Pr.

Preston-Dunlop, Valerie. A Handbook for Dance in Education. 256p. 1980. 29.00x (ISBN 0-7121-0815-7, Pub. by Macdonald & Evans). State Mutual Bk.

Preston-Mauks, Susan. Synchronized Swimming Is For Me. LC 82-17102. (Sports For Me Bks.). (Illus.). 48p. (gr. 2-5). 1983. PLB 6.95g (ISBN 0-8225-1139-8). Lerner Pubns.

Prestwich, Michael. The Three Edwards: War & State in England, 1272-1377. LC 80-5095. 1980. 26.00 (ISBN 0-312-80251-X). St Martin.

PreTest Service Inc. Family Practice: PreTest Self-Assessment & Review. Catlin, Robin J., ed. (Illus.). 250p. (Orig.). 1981. pap. 29.95 (ISBN 0-07-051652-9). McGraw.

Pretlow, Theresa, jt. auth. see Pretlow, Thomas G.

Pretlow, Thomas G. & Pretlow, Theresa. Cell Separation: Methods & Selected Applications, Vol. 1. 1982. 35.00 (ISBN 0-12-564501-5). Acad Pr.

Pretsch, E., jt. auth. see Clerc, J. T.

Pretschner, D. P. Engymetry & Personal Computing in Nuclear Medicine. (Lecture Notes in Medical Informatics: Vol. 18). 133p. 1983. pap. 11.50 (ISBN 0-387-11598-6). Springer-Verlag.

Pretto, G., et al. Life on Earth. Orlandi, Enzo & Marcolungo, G., eds. Pleasance, Simon, tr. from Ital. LC 77-78800. Orig. Title: Il Mondo Della Natura. 1977. 19.95 o.p. (ISBN 0-88225-251-8). Newsweek.

Pretty, Ronald T., ed. Jane's Weapon System, 1982-1983. (Jane's Yearbooks). (Illus.). 1000p. 1982. 140.00 (ISBN 0-86720-619-5). Sci Bks Intl.

Pretz, Bernhard. Dictionary of Military Technological Abbreviations & Acronyms. 450p. 1983. price not set. Routledge & Kegan.

Preucil, Doris. Suzuki Viola School: Piano Accompaniment, Vol. B. 64p. (gr. k-12). 1982. pap. text ed. write for info. (ISBN 0-87487-246-4). Summy.

Preus, J. A. It Is Written. LC 76-162532. (Contemporary Theology Ser.). (Orig.). 1971. pap. 3.50 (ISBN 0-570-06718-9, 12-2364). Concordia.

Preus, James S. Carlstadts Ordinaciones & Luther's Liberty. (Harvard Theological Review & Studies). 1974. pap. 9.00 (ISBN 0-89130-223-9, 020027). Scholars Pr Ca.

Preus, Robert. Getting into the Theology of Concord. 1978. pap. 3.50 (ISBN 0-570-03767-0, 12-2702). Concordia.

Preus, Robert D. Theology of Post-Reformation Lutheranism, Vol. 2. 350p. 1972. 16.50 (ISBN 0-570-03226-1, 15-2123). Concordia.

Preuss, Anne M., ed. see Bean, Jacob & Turcic, Lawrence.

Preuss, Arthur, ed. Dictionary of Secret & Other Societies. LC 66-21186. 1966. Repr. of 1924 ed. 45.00x (ISBN 0-8103-3083-0). Gale.

Preuss, Eduard. Laue Atlas. LC 73-10599. 432p. 1974. 52.95 o.p. (ISBN 0-470-69685-0, Pub. by Wiley). Krieger.

Prevention Magazine. The Complete Book of Vitamins. 1977. 19.95 (ISBN 0-87857-176-0). Rodale Pr Inc.

Prevention Magazine Editors, jt. auth. see Keough, Carol.

Prevention Magazine Editors, jt. auth. see Moyer, Anne.

Prevert, Jacques & Carne, Marcel. Jour Se Leve. (Film Scripts-Classic Ser.). 1970. pap. 2.25 o.p. (ISBN 0-671-20616-8, Touchstone Bks). S&S.

Prevette, Earl. How to Increase Your Sales by Telephone. 1958. 29.95 (ISBN 0-910140-12-X). Anthony.

Previero, A. & Coletti-Previero, M. A., eds. Solid Phase Methods in Protein Sequence Analysis: Proceedings of the 2nd Int'l Conference on Solid Phase Methods in Protein Sequence Analysis, Montpelier, France, September 1977. (Inserm Symposium: Vol. 5). 1978. 66.50 (ISBN 0-7204-0654-4, North-Holland). Elsevier.

Previews Staff. The New Previews Book of Dream Houses. 1979. 19.95 o.p. (ISBN 0-517-53711-7, Dist. by Crown); pap. 8.95 o.p. (ISBN 0-517-53712-5). Crown.

--The New Previews' Dream House Catalog. rev., 3rd ed. (Illus.). 192p. 1980. pap. 10.95 o.p. (ISBN 0-517-54083-5, Harmony). Crown.

--Previews Book of Dream Houses. (Illus.). 17.95 o.p. (ISBN 0-517-53341-3); pap. 8.95 o.p. (ISBN 0-517-53342-1). Crown.

Previte, Joseph J. Human Physiology. (Illus.). 736p. 1983. text ed. 29.95 (ISBN 0-07-050786-4, C); write for info instr's manual (ISBN 0-07-050787-2); write for info study guide (ISBN 0-07-050788-0). McGraw.

Previte-Orton, C. W. Outlines of Medieval History. 2nd ed. LC 64-25837. 1916. 10.00x (ISBN 0-8196-0147-0). Biblo.

--Political Satire in English Poetry. LC 68-749. (Studies in Poetry, No. 38). 1969. Repr. lib. bdg. 49.95x o.p. (ISBN 0-8383-0676-4). Haskell.

Previte-Orton, C. W., ed. The Shorter Cambridge Medieval History, 2 vols. Incl. Vol. 1. The Later Roman Empire to the Twelfth Century. (Illus.). 644p. pap. 67.50 (ISBN 0-521-20962-5); pap. (ISBN 0-521-09976-5); Vol. 2. The Twelfth Century to the Renaissance. (Illus.). 558p. 64.50 (ISBN 0-521-20963-3); pap. (ISBN 0-521-09977-3). (Medieval History Ser). 1975. pap. 18.95 ea. Set. 110.00 (ISBN 0-521-05993-3); Set. pap. 32.50 (ISBN 0-521-08758-9). Cambridge U Pr.

Previts, Gary J. & Merino, Barabara D. A History of Accounting in America: An Historical Interpretation of the Cultural Significance of Accounting. LC 79-616. 378p. 1979. 39.95 (ISBN 0-471-05172-1). Ronald Pr.

Previts, Gary J., ed. see Edwards, James D.

Prevo, Helen. Manners. 1970. pap. 2.75x (ISBN 0-88323-055-0, 153); tchr's. key 2.75x (ISBN 0-88323-056-9, 154). Richards Pub.

--Work for Everyone. 1971. pap. 2.50x o.p. (ISBN 0-88323-085-2, 189). Richards Pub.

Prevo, Helen, jt. auth. see Weaver, Martha.

Prevo, Helen R. English That We Need. 1965. pap. 2.75x (ISBN 0-88323-009-7, 109). Richards Pub.

--Family Life: Book One. 1967. pap. 3.00x (ISBN 0-88323-010-0, 110); wkbk. 2.75x (ISBN 0-88323-011-9, 111). Richards Pub.

--Family Life: Book Two. 1969. pap. 3.00x (ISBN 0-88323-012-7, 112); wkbk. 2.75x (ISBN 0-88323-013-5, 113). Richards Pub.

--More English That We Need. 1968. pap. 2.75x (ISBN 0-88323-057-7, 155). Richards Pub.

--My Language Arts Book. 1973. pap. 2.75x (ISBN 0-88323-113-1, 201). Richards Pub.

--The World Around Us. (Illus.). 1975. pap. 3.25x (ISBN 0-88323-121-2, 209); tchr's key 7.95 (ISBN 0-88323-130-1, 215). Richards Pub.

Prevost, Clovis, jt. auth. see Descharnes, Robert.

Prewitt, Kenneth & Verba, Sidney. An Introduction to American Government. 3rd ed. LC 78-12041. 1979. text ed. 22.50 scp o.p. (ISBN 0-06-045279-X, HarpC); instr's. manual avail. o.p. (ISBN 0-06-364576-9). Har-Row.

--An Introduction to American Government. 4th ed. 752p. 1983. text ed. 20.50 scp (ISBN 0-06-045277-3, HarpC); instr's. manual avail. (ISBN 0-06-365255-2); study guide 7.50 (ISBN 0-06-044857-1). Har-Row.

Prezbindowski, Kathleen. Guide to Learning Anatomy & Physiology. (Illus.). 362p. 1980. pap. text ed. 12.95 (ISBN 0-8016-4040-7). Mosby.

Prezzolini, Giuseppe see Marchione, Margherita & Scalia, S. Eugene.

Pribil, F. Analytical Application of EDTA & Related Compounds. 368p. 1972. text ed. 100.00 (ISBN 0-08-016363-7). Pergamon.

Pribil, R. Applied Complexometry, Vol.5. Stulikova, M., et al, trs. (Analytical Chemistry Ser.). (Illus.). 425p. 1982. 75.00 (ISBN 0-08-026277-5). Pergamon.

Pribor, Donald. Biology: Life Interactions. (Illus.). Date not set. text ed. 16.95 (ISBN 0-07-050827-5); 3.95 (ISBN 0-07-050828-3). McGraw.

Pribram, Henry W. Radiologic Diagnosis of the Sella Trucica. (Illus.). 244p. 1983. 16.50 (ISBN 0-87527-228-2). Green.

Pribram, Karl H. Languages of the Brain: Experimental Paradoxes & Principles in Neuropsychology. 5th ed. 432p. 1982. Repr. of 1971 ed. text ed. 19.95x (ISBN 0-913412-22-8). Brandon Hse.

Pribram, Karl H., ed. Central Processing of Sensory Input. 150p. 1976. pap. text ed. 4.95x o.p. (ISBN 0-262-66023-7). MIT Pr.

Price. Dynamic Mass Spectrometry, Vol. 6. 99.95 (ISBN 0-471-26191-2, Pub. by Wiley Heyden). Wiley.

--Sports Illustrated Golf. rev. ed. LC 72-4143. (Illus.). (gr. 7-9). 1972. 5.95i (ISBN 0-397-00937-2); pap. 2.95i (ISBN 0-397-00938-0, LP-068). Har-Row.

--The Unfortunate Comedy. 208p. 1982. 40.00x (ISBN 0-85323-000-5, Pub. by Liverpool Univ England). State Mutual Bk.

Price & Price. Homeowner's Guide to Saving Energy. rev. ed. 384p. 1981. 13.95 o.p. (ISBN 0-8306-9923-6); pap. 8.95 o.p. (ISBN 0-8306-9691-1, 1104). TAB Bks.

Price, A. Grenfell, ed. see Cook, James.

Price, A. Grenfell, tr. see British Australian & New Zealand Antarctic Research Expedition-1929-1931.

Price, Alan see Synge, John M.

Price, Alfred. The Spitfire Story. (Illus.). 256p. 1982. 29.95 (ISBN 0-86720-624-1). Sci Bks Intl.

Price, Alfred, jt. auth. see Ethell, Jeffrey.

Price, Anthony. Old Vengeful. LC 82-48710. (Crime Club Ser.). 192p. 1983. 11.95 (ISBN 0-385-18750-5). Doubleday.

Price, Barrie Jo, jt. auth. see Marsh, George E.

Price, Barry. The Lea-Francis Story. 1978. 24.95 (ISBN 0-7134-0785-9, Pub. by Batsford England). David & Charles.

Price, Belinda. Presents & Decorations on a Shoestring. (Illus.). 1972. 7.95 o.p. (ISBN 0-571-09762-6). Transatlantic.

Price, Bertram, jt. auth. see Chatterjee, Samprit.

Price, Bill, jt. auth. see Lemons, Wayne.

Price, Bren. Inside the Wind. Hausman, Gerald, ed. LC 82-19302. (Illus.). 64p. 1983. 37.95 (ISBN 0-86534-016-1). Sunstone Pr.

Price, Bren T. Basic Composition Activities Kit. 232p. 1982. comb-bound 22.50X (ISBN 0-87628-169-2). Ctr Appl Res.

Price, Brynmor F. & Nida, Eugene A. A Translator's Handbook on the Book of Jonah. (Helps for Translators Ser.). 1982. Repr. of 1978 ed. soft cover 2.80x (ISBN 0-8267-0199-X, 08552). United Bible.

Price, C. A. Centrifugation in Density Gradients. LC 81-12693. 1982. 59.50 (ISBN 0-12-564580-5). Acad Pr.

--Molecular Approaches to Plant Physiology. 1970. text ed. 42.95 (ISBN 0-07-050853-4, C). McGraw.

Price, C. C. Geometry of Molecules. 1971. 6.95 o.p. (ISBN 0-07-050866-6, C); pap. 12.95 (ISBN 0-07-050867-4). McGraw.

Price, C. J. & Reed, C. J. Practical Parasitology: General Laboratory Techniques & Parasitic Protozoa Notes for Students of Animal Husbandry. 112p. 1970. pap. 3.00 (ISBN 0-686-92905-5, F330, FAO). Unipub.

Price, Charles. Golfer at Large. LC 82-71259. 241p. 1982. 12.95 (ISBN 0-689-11334-X). Atheneum.

Price, Charles C., ed. Synthesis of Life. LC 74-3026. (Benchmark Papers in Organic Chemistry: Vol. 1). 391p. 1974. text ed. 52.50 (ISBN 0-87933-131-3). Hutchinson Ross.

Price, Charles C. & Vandenberg, Edwin J., eds. Coordination Polymerization. (Polymer Science & Technology Ser.). 342p. 1983. 42.50 (ISBN 0-306-41139-3, Plenum Pr). Plenum Pub.

Price, Charles P. & Weil, Louis. Liturgy for Living. (Church's Teaching Ser.: Vol. 5). 1979. 5.95 (ISBN 0-8164-0422-4); pap. 3.95 (ISBN 0-8164-2218-4); user guide .95 (ISBN 0-8164-2225-7). Seabury.

Price, Charles S. Real Faith: One of the Classic Faith-Builders. 1972. pap. 4.95 (ISBN 0-912106-82-4, Pub. by Logos). Bridge Pub.

Price, Christene, ed. Food for the Senses: Recipes & Artwork from the Esalen Community. (Illus.). 120p. (Orig.). 1982. pap. 5.95. C Price.

Price, Christopher P. & Spencer, Kevin, eds. Centrifugal Analysers in Clinical Chemistry. 520p. 1980. 75.00 (ISBN 0-03-058854-5). Praeger.

Price, Clement A. Freedom Not Far Distant: A Documentary History of Afro-Americans in New Jersey, Vol. 16. (Illus.). 334p. 1980. 17.95 (ISBN 0-911020-01-2). NJ Hist Soc.

Price, D., ed. Dynamic Mass Spectrometry, Vol. 2. 1971. 83.00 (ISBN 0-471-25962-4, Pub. by Wiley Heyden). Wiley.

--Dynamic Mass Spectrometry, Vol. 3. 1974. 83.00 (ISBN 0-471-25963-2, Pub. by Wiley Heyden). Wiley.

Price, D. & Todd, J. F., eds. Dynamic Mass Spectrometry, Vol. 4. 1976. 83.00 (ISBN 0-471-25964-0, Pub. by Wiley Heyden). Wiley.

--Dynamic Mass Spectrometry, Vol. 5. 1978. 83.00 (ISBN 0-471-25966-7, Pub. by Wiley Heyden). Wiley.

Price, D. & Williams, J. E., eds. Dynamic Mass Spectrometry, Vol. 1. 1970. 83.00 (ISBN 0-471-25961-6, Pub. by Wiley Heyden). Wiley.

Price, D. C. Patrons & Musicians of the English Renaissance. LC 80-40054. (Cambridge Studies in Music). (Illus.). 250p. 1981. 59.50 (ISBN 0-521-22806-9). Cambridge U Pr.

Price, D. Porter. Intelligent Dieting for Weight Loss & Prevention of Disease. (Illus.). 200p. 1982. 17.95 (ISBN 0-9606246-1-9); pap. 13.95 (ISBN 0-9606246-2-7). SW Sci Pub.

Price, David. Appeals Procedure. 1981. 100.00x (ISBN 0-686-97087-X, Pub. by Fourmat England). State Mutual Bk.

--UCSD Pascal. (Illus.). 192p. 1983. 19.95 (ISBN 0-13-935478-6); pap. 12.95 (ISBN 0-13-935460-3). P-H.

Price, David L. The Grimmetts of Virginia of the Revolutionary War Era & Their Descendents. LC 80-81609. 250p. 1980. pap. 10.00 (ISBN 0-9604482-0-9). D L Price.

--Magic: A Pictoral History of Conjurers in the Theater. LC 81-68623. 544p. 1982. 60.00 (ISBN 0-8453-4738-1). Cornwall Bks.

Price, Diana, ed. see Berger, Jason & Berger, Susanna.

Price, E. Hoffmann. Operation Longlife. 320p. 1983. pap. 2.75 (ISBN 0-345-30715-1, Del Rey). Ballantine.

Price, Eugenia. Beloved Invader. LC 65-20589. 1965. 12.45i (ISBN 0-397-10013-2). Har-Row.

--Burden Is Light. rev. ed. 1975. pap. write for info. Jove Pubns.

--Diary of a Novel: The Story of Writing Margaret's Story. LC 80-7869. 160p. 1980. 11.49i (ISBN 0-690-01937-8). Har-Row.

--Discoveries. 1979. pap. 3.95 (ISBN 0-310-31281-7). Zondervan.

--Just As I Am. (Trumpet Bks). 1976. pap. 1.75 o.p. (ISBN 0-87981-055-6). Holman.

--Just As I Am. 1982. pap. 1.75 o.p. (ISBN 0-8054-5911-1). Broadman.

--Learning to Live. (Trumpet Bks). 1976. pap. 1.95 o.p. (ISBN 0-87981-062-9). Holman.

--Learning to Live. (Orig.). pap. write for info (ISBN 0-515-09656-3). Jove Pubns.

--Leave Your Self Alone. 1979. 7.95 o.p. (ISBN 0-310-31430-5). Zondervan.

--Make Love Your Aim. 192p. 1972. pap. 2.95 o.p. (ISBN 0-310-31312-0). Zondervan.

--Make Love Your Aim. 192p. 1983. pap. 5.59 (ISBN 0-310-31311-2). Zondervan.

--Margaret's Story. 432p. 1982. pap. 3.50 (ISBN 0-553-22583-9). Bantam.

--No Pat Answers. pap. 2.95 o.p. (ISBN 0-310-31332-5); study guide o.p.o.p. 0.75 o.p. (ISBN 0-310-31333-3). Zondervan.

--No Pat Answers. 144p. 1983. pap. 4.95 (ISBN 0-310-31331-7). Zondervan.

--Savannah. LC 82-45572. 552p. 1983. 17.95 (ISBN 0-385-15274-4). Doubleday.

--Share My Pleasant Stones. 6.95 (ISBN 0-310-31341-4). Zondervan.

--The Unique World of Women. 248p. 1982. pap. 7.95 (ISBN 0-310-31351-1). Zondervan.

--A Woman's Choice. 192p. 1983. pap. 5.95 (ISBN 0-310-31381-3). Zondervan.

Price, F. W. Basic Molecular Biology. 497p. 1979. 33.95x (ISBN 0-471-69729-X). Wiley.

Price, Flo. Quick & Easy Casseroles. 1976. pap. 1.50 o.s.i. (ISBN 0-89129-158-X). Jove Pubns.

Price, Frederick K. Faith, Foolishness, or Presumption. 160p. (Orig.). 1979. pap. 4.95 (ISBN 0-89274-103-1). Harrison Hse.

--The Holy Spirit the Missing Ingredient. 1978. pap. text ed. 1.50 (ISBN 0-89274-081-7). Harrison Hse.

--How to Obtain Strong Faith: Six Principles. 184p. pap. 4.95 (ISBN 0-89274-042-6). Harrison Hse.

--Is Healing for All? (Orig.). 1976. pap. 3.95 (ISBN 0-89274-005-1). Harrison Hse.

Price, Glanville, tr. see Leroy, Maurice.

Price, H., tr. see Weil, Simone.

Price, J. & Urban, L. Definitive Word-Processing. 1983. pap. 8.95 (ISBN 0-14-046591-X). Penguin.

Price, J., jt. auth. see Flanders, H.

Price, J. H. Psychiatric Investigations. 1972. 14.95 o.p. (ISBN 0-407-36680-6). Butterworth.

Price, J. Harding. A Synopsis of Psychiatry. (Illus.). 312p. 1982. text ed. 27.50 (ISBN 0-7236-0611-0). Wright-PSG.

Price, J. M. Guia de Estudios Sobre Jesus el Maestro. 50p. 1982. pap. 4.50 (ISBN 0-311-43501-7). Casa Bautista.

Price, J. W. Tin & Tin-Alloy Plating. 1982. 159.00x (ISBN 0-686-81702-8, Pub. by Electrochemical Scotland). State Mutual Bk.

Price, Jacob M., ed. Joshua Johnson's Letterbook, 1771-4: Letters from a Merchant in London to His Partners in Maryland. 1979. 50.00x (ISBN 0-686-96606-6, Pub by London Rec Soc England). State Mutual Bk.

Price, James H., jt. auth. see Steen, Edwin B.

Price, James H., jt. ed. see Sims, Reginald W.

Price, Jane. You're Not Too Old to Have a Baby. 1978. pap. 3.95 (ISBN 0-14-004910-X). Penguin.

Price, Jerome B. The Antinuclear Movement. (Social Movements: Past & Present). 1982. lib. bdg. 15.95 (ISBN 0-8057-9705-X, Twayne). G K Hall.

Price, John. America at the Crossroads. 1979. 2.50 (ISBN 0-8423-0064-3). Tyndale.

--Contemporary Estate Planning: Text & Problems. LC 82-81493. 1982. text ed. 25.00 (ISBN 0-316-71856-4). Little.

Price, John A. Native Studies: American & Canadian Indians. 1978. pap. text ed. 23.50x (ISBN 0-07-082695-1, C). McGraw.

Price, John-Allen. Doomsday Ship. 1982. pap. 3.25 (ISBN 0-8217-1107-5). Zebra.

Price, John F. Lie Groups & Compact Groups. LC 76-14034. (London Mathematical Society Lecture Notes Ser.: No. 25). 1977. pap. 18.95x (ISBN 0-521-21340-1). Cambridge U Pr.

Price, John H., jt. auth. see Lovins, Amory B.

Price, John V. David Hume. LC 68-24287. (English Authors Ser.: No. 77). 1969. lib. bdg. 13.95 o.p. (ISBN 0-8057-1280-1, Twayne). G K Hall.

Price, Jonathan. How to Find Work. 267p. 1983. pap. 3.50 (ISBN 0-451-12070-1, Sig). NAL.

Price, Judith. Executive Style. 1980. 19.95 o.p. (ISBN 0-671-25354-9, Linden). S&S.

Price, Justin J., jt. auth. see Flanders, Harley.

Price, Karl F. & Walker, James W. Issues in Business: An Introduction to American Enterprise. 3rd ed. LC 76-30750. 1977. text ed. 28.95x (ISBN 0-471-69734-6); tchrs.' manual 5.00 (ISBN 0-471-02613-1). Wiley.

Price, Leonard & Ghilchik, Margaret. Safer Cancer Chemotherapy. (Illus.). 128p. 1981. text ed. 25.00 (ISBN 0-02-858880-0, Bailliere-Tindall). Saunders.

Price, Lorna. The Plan of St. Gall in Brief: An Overview Based on the Three-Volume Work by Walter Horn & Ernest Born. LC 82-70215. (Illus.). 120p. 1982. 55.00 (ISBN 0-520-04736-2); pap. 27.50 (ISBN 0-520-04334-0). U of Cal Pr.

Price, Marion, jt. auth. see Stacey, Margaret.

Price, Martin. Forms of Life: Character & Moral Imagination in the Novel. LC 82-16064. 400p. 1983. text ed. 27.50x (ISBN 0-300-02867-9). Yale U Pr.

Price, Martin, ed. Dickens: A Collection of Critical Essays. LC 67-25931. (Twentieth Century Views Ser). (Orig.). 1967. 12.95 o.p. (ISBN 0-13-208611-5, Spec). P-H.

--Selected Poetry of Alexander Pope. (Signet Classics). 1970. pap. 1.50 o.p. (ISBN 0-451-50853-X, CW853, Sig Classics). NAL.

Price, Martin, jt. auth. see Burnham, Patricia M.

Price, Mary. The Peasants' Revolt. Reeves, Marjorie, ed. (Then & There Ser.). (Illus.). 96p. (Orig.). (gr. 7-12). 1980. pap. text ed. 3.10 (ISBN 0-582-20164-0). Longman.

Price, Mary & Price, Vincent. A Treasury of Great Recipes. 39.50 (ISBN 0-448-11867-X, G&D). Putnam Pub Group.

Price, Mary R. A Portrait of Britain in the Middle Ages 1066-1485. 256p. 1982. Repr. of 1951 ed. lib. bdg. 30.00 (ISBN 0-8495-4413-0). Arden Lib.

Price, Mary R., jt. auth. see Lindsay, Donald.

Price, Melvia. The Drop-Out Epidemic: Discussion of Educational Problems, Particularly for Minorities. 1983. pap. 6.95 (ISBN 0-937196-04-5). Sunset Prods.

--New & Different Friends. (Illus.). 44p. (gr. k-8). 1980. 6.95 (ISBN 0-937196-06-1); wkbk. 3.95 (ISBN 0-937196-07-X); 8.95 set. Sunset Prods.

Price, Melvia, ed. & prologue by. Energy, Beauty & Spirit: An Anthology of Contemporary Poems by Numerous Poets. 1980. pap. 10.95 (ISBN 0-937196-00-2). Sunset Prods.

Price, Michael H. & Turner, George E. Human Monsters in the Cinema. LC 78-75327. (Illus.). write for info. (ISBN 0-498-02360-5). A S Barnes.

Price, Mila U., jt. auth. see Morrison, Eleanor S.

Price, Miles O., et al. Effective Legal Research. 4th ed. 501p. 1979. 19.95 (ISBN 0-316-71832-7); problems wkbk., 1979 8.95 (ISBN 0-316-71855-6). Little.

Price, Molly. The Iris Book. (Illus.). 224p. 1973. Repr. of 1966 ed. pap. 5.00 (ISBN 0-486-21522-9). Dover.

Price, Nancy. An Accomplished Woman. LC 78-12456. 1979. 8.95 (ISBN 0-698-10964-3, Coward). Putnam Pub Group.

--An Accomplished Woman. 1980. pap. 2.50 o.p. (ISBN 0-451-09115-9, E9115, Sig). NAL.

Price, Nancy W., jt. auth. see Van der Meulen, Jan.

Price, Nelson L. The Destruction of Death. 1983. 3.25 (ISBN 0-8054-1528-9). Broadman.

--Supreme Happiness. LC 78-67000. 1979. 3.95 o.p. (ISBN 0-8054-5269-9). Broadman.

Price, P. F. & Simon, L. M., eds. Miniconference on Partial Equations. new ed. 133p. (Orig.). pap. text ed. 13.95 (ISBN 0-86784-123-0, 1246, Pub. by ANUP Australia). Bks Australia.

Price, Pamela A. & Moore, Anne J. Strategies in Administration& Teaching in Associate Degree Nursing Education. 66p. 1976. 4.95 (ISBN 0-686-38278-1, 23-1630). Natl League Nurse.

Price, Pamela V. Monarch Guide to the Wines of Bordeaux. (Illus.). 1978. pap. 2.95 o.p. (ISBN 0-671-18360-5). Monarch Pr.

Price, Paxton P., ed. International Book & Library Activities: The History of a U. S. Foreign Policy. LC 82-3297. 264p. 1982. 15.00 (ISBN 0-8108-1545-1). Scarecrow.

Price, Peter W. Insect Ecology. LC 75-12720. 514p. 1975. 27.95 (ISBN 0-471-69721-4, Pub. by Wiley-Interscience). Wiley.

Price, R. Masters, Unions & Men. LC 79-21229. (Illus.). 1980. 42.50 (ISBN 0-521-22882-4). Cambridge U Pr.

Price, R. F. Reference Book of English Words & Phrases for Foreign Science Students. 1966. text ed. 20.00 (ISBN 0-08-011750-3); pap. text ed. 9.25 (ISBN 0-08-020381-7). Pergamon.

Price, Ray G., et al. General Business for Everyday Living. 4th ed. 1971. text ed. 13.96 o.p. (ISBN 0-07-050800-3, G); tchr's. source bk. & key 23.80 o.p. (ISBN 0-07-050805-4); student activity guides. bks. 1 & 2 5.40 ea. o.p.; tchr's. eds. activity guides 7.10 ea. o.p.; test bklts. 1 & 2 1.80 ea. o.p. McGraw.

--Business & You As a Consumer, Worker & Citizen. rev. 5th ed. (Illus.). (gr. 9-10). 1978. text ed. 16.00 (ISBN 0-07-050810-0, G); learning activity guides 1 & 2 5.40 ea.; 2 sets unit tests 1.80 ea.; source bk. & key 23.75 (ISBN 0-07-050811-9). McGraw.

Price, Reynolds. Mustian: Two Novels & a Story. LC 82-73009. 320p. 1983. 14.95 (ISBN 0-689-11377-3). Atheneum.

--Vital Provisions. LC 82-71255. 192p. 1982. 14.95 (ISBN 0-689-11322-6); pap. 7.95 (ISBN 0-689-11323-4). Atheneum.

--The Wings of the Dove: (Standard Ed.) LC 75-133743. 1970. pap. text ed. 3.50x (ISBN 0-675-09334-1). Merrill.

Price, Richard. The Breaks. 480p. 1983. 16.50 (ISBN 0-671-45236-3). S&S.

--Ladies' Man. 1978. 8.95 o.s.i. (ISBN 0-395-27082-0). HM.

--Two Tracts on Civil Liberties. LC 74-169641. (Era of the American Revolution Ser.). 1972. Repr. lib. bdg. 42.50 (ISBN 0-306-70233-9). Da Capo.

Price, Robert, jt. auth. see Bain, George S.

Price, Robert M. & Rosberg, Carl G., eds. The Apartheid Regime: Political Power & Racial Domination. LC 79-27269. (Research Ser.: No. 43). (Illus.). 1980. pap. 12.50x (ISBN 0-87725-143-6). U of Cal Intl St.

Price, Roger. Droodles. 1965. pap. 1.75 (ISBN 0-8431-0009-5). Price Stern.

--The Economic Modernization of France, 1730-1880. LC 75-14447. 1975. 31.95x o.p. (ISBN 0-470-69722-9). Halsted Pr.

--More World's Worst Elephant Jokes, Plus Grape & Pickle Jokes. rev. ed. 1972. pap. 1.50 o.s.i. (ISBN 0-8431-0011-7). Price Stern.

Price, Roger, et al. World's Worst Monster Jokes. 1965. pap. 1.50 o.s.i. (ISBN 0-8431-0035-4). Price Stern.

Price, Ronald, et al, eds. Digital Radiography: A Focus on Clinical Utility. 448p. Date not set. 39.50 (ISBN 0-8089-1544-4). Grune.

Price, Ronald R. & Croft, Barbara Y., eds. Single Photon Emission Computed Tomography & Other Selected Computer Topics. LC 80-52817. (Illus.). 252p. 1980. pap. 27.00 (ISBN 0-932004-06-7). Soc Nuclear Med.

Price, S. G. Preparing for Teletex. 100p. 1982. pap. 15.00x (ISBN 0-85012-372-0). Intl Pubns Serv.

Price, Seymour G. A Guide to Monitoring & Controlling Utility Costs. LC 73-88887. 108p. 1973. spiral 15.00 o.p. (ISBN 0-87179-192-7). BNA.

Price Stern Editors. World's Worst Jokes. 1969. pap. 1.75 (ISBN 0-8431-0068-0). Price Stern.

Price, Steven D. All the King's Horses: The Story of the Budweiser Clydesdales. (Illus.). 200p. 1983. 26.00 (ISBN 0-670-22588-6). Viking Pr.

--Panorama of American Horses. 1974. 12.50 o.p. (ISBN 0-517-51786-8). Crown.

Price, Sylvia & Wilson, Lorraine. Pathophysiology. 2nd ed. (Illus.). 1024p. 1982. 32.50x (ISBN 0-07-050863-1). McGraw.

Price, T. T., tr. see Maurer, H. A.

Price, Theodora H. Kourotrophos: Cults & Representations of the Greek Nursing Dieties. 1978. text ed. 54.00x o.p. (ISBN 90-04052-51-8). Humanities.

Price, Thomas R., ed. see Princeton Conference on Cerebrovascular Disease, 11th., Mar. 1978.

Price, V. B., jt. auth. see Price, Vincent.

Price, Vincent. Vincent Price: His Movies, His Plays, His Life. LC 77-16940. (gr. 3-7). 1978. 6.95a o.p. (ISBN 0-385-11594-6); PLB (ISBN 0-385-11595-4). Doubleday.

Price, Vincent & Price, V. B. Monsters. LC 77-94851. (Illus.). 192p. 1981. pap. 12.95 (ISBN 0-448-14305-4, G&D). Putnam Pub Group.

--Vincent Price's World of Monsters. (Illus.). 1981. cancelled (ISBN 0-686-78590-8, G&D); pap. 12.95 (ISBN 0-686-78591-6). Putnam Pub Group.

Price, Vincent, jt. auth. see Price, Mary.

Price, Vincent B. Semblances (1962-1971) 1976. pap. 4.95 (ISBN 0-913270-64-4). Sunstone Pr.

Price, Virginia A. The Type A Behavior Pattern: A Model for Research & Practice. 26.50 (ISBN 0-12-564680-1). Acad Pr.

Price, W. C. & Chissick, S. S. The Uncertainty Principle & Foundations of Quantum Mechanics: A Fifty Years' Survey. 1977. 119.95 (ISBN 0-471-99414-6). Wiley.

Price, W. G. & Bishop, R. E. Probabilistic Theory of Ship Dynamics. 1974. 45.00x (ISBN 0-412-12430-0, Pub. by Chapman & Hall). Methuen Inc.

Price, W. J. Nuclear Radiation Detection. 2nd ed. (Nuclear Engineering Ser.). 1964. text ed. 39.50 o.p. (ISBN 0-07-050860-7, P&RB). McGraw.

--Spectrochemical Analysis by Atomic Absorption. 1979. casebound 61.95 (ISBN 0-471-25967-5, Wiley Heyden). Wiley.

Price, W. V., jt. auth. see Van Slyke, L. L.

Price, Wendell W. Contemporary Problems of Evangelism. LC 76-12941. 1976. 3.95 (ISBN 0-87509-070-2); pap. 2.50 (ISBN 0-87509-071-0). Chr Pubns.

Price, Willard. Amazon Adventure. (Illus.). 256p. 1983. 9.95 (ISBN 0-224-60621-2, Pub by Jonathan Cape). Merrimack Bk Serv.

--Underwater Adventure. (Illus.). 208p. (gr. 3 up). 1983. 9.95 (ISBN 0-224-61180-1, Pub by Jonathan Cape). Merrimack Bk Serv.

--Volcano Adventure. (Illus.). 192p. (gr. 3 up). 1983. 9.95 (ISBN 0-224-60625-5, Pub by Jonathan Cape). Merrimack Bk Serv.

--Whale Adventure. (Illus.). 192p. (gr. 3 up). 1983. 9.95 (ISBN 0-224-60625-5, Pub by Jonathan Cape). Merrimack Bk Serv.

Price-Mars, Jean. So Spoke the Uncle. Shannon, Magdaline W., tr. from Fr. (Illus.). 240p. 1983. 16.00x (ISBN 0-89410-389-X); pap. 7.00x (ISBN 0-89410-390-3). Three Continents.

Prichard, Anita. Anita Prichard's Complete Candy Cookbook. (Illus.). 1978. 12.95 o.p. (ISBN 0-517-53245-X, Harmony). Crown.

--Back-to-Basics American Cooking. LC 82-82108. (Illus.). 480p. 1983. 18.95 (ISBN 0-448-16052-8, G&D). Putnam Pub Group.

Prichard, Doris, jt. auth. see Sicignano, Robert.

Prichard, Harold A. Moral Obligation. 1949. 29.50x (ISBN 0-19-824154-2). Oxford U Pr.

Prichard, Robert W. & Robinson, Robert E. Twenty Thousand Medical Words. 288p. 1972. 6.50 o.p. (ISBN 0-07-050873-9, HP); pap. 11.95 (ISBN 0-07-050874-7). McGraw.

Prickard, A. O., tr. see Longinus, Cassius.

Prickel, Donald, jt. auth. see Mitchell, Robert.

Pride & Ferrell. Marketing. 3rd ed. 1982. text ed. 27.95 (ISBN 0-686-84538-2, BS36); write for info. supplementary materials. HM.

Pride, Kitty. Chatino Syntax. (Publications in Linguistics & Related Fields Ser.: No. 12). pap. 2.50 o.p. (ISBN 0-88312-012-7); microfiche 3.00 (ISBN 0-88312-412-2). Summer Inst Ling.

Pride, Kitty, jt. auth. see Pride, Leslie.

Pride, Leslie & Pride, Kitty. Vocabulario Chatino de Tataltepec. (Vocabularios Indigenas Ser.: No. 15). 103p. 1970. pap. 3.00x (ISBN 0-88312-655-9); microfiche 2.25 (ISBN 0-88312-317-7). Summer Inst Ling.

Pride, William, jt. auth. see Ferrel, O. C.

Pride, William M. & Ferrell, O. C. Marketing: Basic Concepts & Decisions. 3rd ed. LC 82-83363. 784p. 25.95 (ISBN 0-395-32816-0); write for info. supplementary materials. HM.

Pride, William M. & Perrell, O. C. Marketing: Basic Concepts & Decisions. 2nd ed. LC 79-88040. 1980. text ed. 24.95 (ISBN 0-395-28059-1); study guide 9.50 (ISBN 0-395-28163-6); instr's. manual 4.00 (ISBN 0-395-28161-X); test bank 2.70 (ISBN 0-395-28162-8). HM.

Pride, William M., jt. auth. see Robicheaux, Robert A.

Prideaux, Gary D., ed. Perspectives in Experimental Linguistics: Papers from the University of Alberta Conference on Experimental Linguistics, Edmonton, 13-14 Oct. 1978. (Current Issues in Linguistic Theory Ser.: No. 24). xi, 176p. 1979. 21.00 (ISBN 90-272-3503-1, 10). Benjamins North Am.

Prideaux, Tom. World of Delacroix. LC 66-21130. (Library of Art Ser.). (Illus.). (gr. 6 up). 1966. 19.92 (ISBN 0-8094-0262-9, Pub. by Time-Life). Silver.

--World of Whistler. LC 70-116437. (Library of Art Ser.). (Illus.). (gr. 6 up). 1970. 19.92 (ISBN 0-8094-0285-8, Pub. by Time-Life). Silver.

Pridham, Geoffrey. Christian Democracy in Western Germany. LC 77-9235. 1978. 27.50x (ISBN 0-312-13396-0). St Martin.

--The Nature of the Italian Party System. 1981. 26.00x (ISBN 0-312-56194-6). St Martin.

Pridmore, F. Coins of the British Commonwealth of Nations to the End of the Reign of George VI, 4 vols. Incl. Vol. I. Europe. 16.00 (ISBN 0-686-52274-5); Vol. III. West Indies. 24.00 (ISBN 0-686-52275-3); Vol. IV, Part I. India. 80.00 (ISBN 0-686-52276-1); Vol. IV, Part II. 95.00. Pub. by Spink & Son England). S J Durst.

Priebe, Duane A., tr. see Pannenberg, Wolfhart.

Priede, J. G., jt. ed. see MacDonald, A. G.

Priehs, T. J., ed. see Arnberger, Leslie P.

Priehs, T. J., ed. see Trimble, Stephen.

Priehs, T. J., ed. see Lister, Robert H. & Lister, Florence C.

Prier, James E., jt. auth. see Oehme, Frederick W.

Pries, Nancy, jt. ed. see Arksey, Laura.

Priesing, Elwood R. Music & the Dance. 1978. 10.00 o.p. (ISBN 0-682-48957-3, Banner). Exposition.

Priest, E. Solar Magnetohydrodynamics. 1982. lib. bdg. 99.00 (ISBN 90-277-1374-X, Pub. by Reidel Holland). Kluwer Boston.

Priest, Harold M. Divine Comedy: Purgatorio Notes. (Illus., Orig.). 1971. pap. 2.95 (ISBN 0-8220-0394-5). Cliffs.

--Faerie Queene Notes. (Orig.). 1968. pap. 2.95 (ISBN 0-8220-0452-6). Cliffs.

--More's Utopia & Utopian Literature Notes. 64p. (Orig.). 1975. pap. text ed. 2.75 (ISBN 0-8220-1318-5). Cliffs.

Priest, Joseph. Problems of Our Physical Environment: Energy - Transportation - Pollution. LC 72-9317. 1973. text ed. 19.95 (ISBN 0-201-05972-X). A-W.

Priest, R. G. Psychiatry in Medical Practice. 500p. 1982. text ed. 58.00x (ISBN 0-7121-1672-9). Intl Ideas.

Priest, R. G., ed. Sleep Research. 240p. 1979. text ed. 32.50 o.p. (ISBN 0-8391-1430-3). Univ Park.

Priest, R. G., et al, eds. Benzodiazepines Today & Tomorrow. 312p. 1980. text ed. 44.50 (ISBN 0-8391-1659-4). Univ Park.

Priestland, Gerald. The Future of Violence. 174p. 1975. 12.50 (ISBN 0-241-02454-4). Transatlantic.

Priestley, F. E. Language & Structure in Tennyson's Poetry. (Andre Deutsch Language Library). 1977. lib. bdg. 18.50 o.p. (ISBN 0-233-96390-1). Westview.

Priestley, J. B. Angel Pavement. (Phoenix Fiction Ser.). iv, 494p. 1958. pap. 8.95 (ISBN 0-226-68210-2). U of Chicago Pr.

--Bright Day. (Phoenix Fiction Ser.). vi, 364p. 1974. pap. 7.95 (ISBN 0-226-68211-0). U of Chicago Pr.

--The Good Companions. 1980. lib. bdg. 21.95x (ISBN 0-89967-044-X). Harmony Raine.

--The Good Companions. (Phoenix Fiction Ser.). 640p. 1956. pap. 9.95 (ISBN 0-226-68223-4). U of Chicago Pr.

--Salt Is Leaving. Barzun, J. & Taylor, W. H., eds. LC 81-47381. (Crime Fiction 1950-1975 Ser.). 247p. 1982. lib. bdg. 14.95 (ISBN 0-8240-4988-8). Garland Pub.

Priestley, John B. They Walk in the City. LC 76-165447. 392p. 1972. Repr. of 1936 ed. lib. bdg. 19.00x (ISBN 0-8371-6224-6, PRWC). Greenwood.

Priestley, Joseph. Scientific Autobiography of Joseph Priestley, 1733-1804: Selected Scientific Correspondence, with Commentary. Schofield, Robert E., ed. 1967. 23.00x o.p. (ISBN 0-262-19035-4). MIT Pr.

Priestley, Lee. America's Space Shuttle. LC 78-15963. (Illus.). 96p. (gr. 4-6). 1978. PLB 7.29 o.p. (ISBN 0-671-32947-2). Messner.

--Tour to Romance. (YA) 1979. 6.95 (ISBN 0-685-59938-8, Avalon). Bouregy.

Priestley, M. B., ed. Spectral Analysis & the Time Series, 2 Vols. in 1, Vol. 1 & Vol.2. (Probability & Mathematical Statistics Ser.). 1983. 39.50 (ISBN 0-12-564922-3). Acad Pr.

Priestley, Philip, et al. Social Skills & Problem Solving: A Handbook of Methods. (Illus.). 1979. 29.95x (ISBN 0-422-76540-6, Pub. by Tavistock England). Methuen Inc.

Priestly, Harold E. Truly Bizarre. 1980. pap. 1.95 o.p. (ISBN 0-451-09207-4, J9207, Sig). NAL.

Priestly, J. The Theological & Miscellaneous Works, 25 vols. in 26. Repr. Set. 1206.00 (ISBN 0-527-72751-2). Kraus Repr.

Priestly, R. J., ed. Effects of Heating on Foodstuffs. (Illus.). 1979. 67.75x (ISBN 0-85334-797-2, Pub. by Applied Sci England). Elsevier.

Priestly, Tom M., jt. auth. see Derwing, Bruce L.

Prieto. Pablo's Petunias. LC 72-190269. (Illus.). (gr. 3-5). 1972. PLB 6.75x (ISBN 0-87783-058-4); pap. 2.95x deluxe ed. (ISBN 0-87783-102-5). Oddo.

Prieto, Carlos. Mining in the New World. (Illus.). 1973. 18.95 (ISBN 0-07-050862-3, P&RB). McGraw.

Prieto, Ignacio C., ed. see Institute of Judicial Investigations.

Prieto, Mariana. Fun Jewelry. Rahmas, D. Steve, ed. (Handicraft Ser.: No. 10). (Illus.). 32p. (Orig.). (gr. 7-12). 1973. lib. bdg. 2.45 incl. catalog cards o.p. (ISBN 0-87157-910-3); pap. 1.25 vinyl laminated covers o.p. (ISBN 0-87157-410-1). SamHar Pr.

Prifti, Peter R. Socialist Albania since 1944: Domestic & Foreign Developments. LC 78-1728. (MIT Studies in Communism, Revisionism, & Revolution Ser.: No. 22). 1978. 27.50x (ISBN 0-262-16070-6). MIT Pr.

Prigmore, Charles S. & Atherton, Charles P. Social Welfare Policy: Analysis & Formulation. 1979. text ed. 16.95 (ISBN 0-669-01425-7). Heath.

Prigogine, I. Advances in Chemical Physics, Vol. 54. Rice, Stuart A., ed. 352p. 1983. price not set (ISBN 0-471-89570-9, Pub. by Wiley-Interscience). Wiley.

--Introduction to Thermodynamics of Irreversible Processes. 3rd ed. LC 67-29540. 1968. 21.95x o.p. (ISBN 0-470-69928-0, Pub. by Wiley-Interscience). Wiley.

Prigogine, I. & Rice, S. A. Advances in Chemical Physics, Vol. 40. 504p. 1979. 75.00x (ISBN 0-471-03884-9, Pub. by Wiley-Interscience). Wiley.

--Advances in Chemical Physics, Vol. 41. 539p. 1980. 65.00x (ISBN 0-471-05742-8, Pub. by Wiley-Interscience). Wiley.

Prigogine, I. & Rice, Stuart A. Advances in Chemical Physics, Vol. 48. (Advances in Chemical Physics Ser.). 549p. 1981. 78.00x (ISBN 0-471-08294-5, Pub. by Wiley-Interscience). Wiley.

--Advances in Chemical Physics, Vol. 49. LC 58-9935. (Advances in Chemical Physics Ser.). 688p. 1982. 90.00x (ISBN 0-471-09361-0, Pub. by Wiley-Interscience). Wiley.

--Advances in Chemical Physics, Vol. 51. LC 53-9935. (Advances in Chemical Physics Ser.). 289p. 1982. text ed. 50.00 (ISBN 0-471-86439-0, Pub. by Wiley-Interscience). Wiley.

--Advances in Chemical Physics, Vol. 52. (Advances in Chemical Physics Ser.). 608p. 1982. 70.00x (ISBN 0-471-86845-0, Pub. by Wiley-Interscience). Wiley.

Prigogine, I., jt. auth. see Nicolis, G.

Prigogine, I., et al, eds. Advances in Chemical Physics, Vol. 17. 284p. 1970. 35.50 o.p. (ISBN 0-471-69922-5). Krieger.

Prillaman, Douglas & Abbott, John. Educational Diagnosis & Prescriptive Teaching: A Practical Approach to Special Education in the Least Restrictive Environment. 1982. pap. 0.21.50 write for info. (ISBN 0-8224-1951-3). Pitman Learning.

Primack, Mark. Greater Boston Park & Recreation Guide. (Illus.). 288p. 1983. pap. 9.95 (ISBN 0-87106-979-2). Globe Pequot.

Primack, Phil. The New England Fair. LC 81-86607. (Illus.). 286p. (Orig.). 1982. pap. 9.95 (ISBN 0-87106-970-9). Globe Pequot.

Primavera, Elise. Basil & Maggie. LC 82-48455. (Illus.). 32p. (gr. 1-3). 1983. 9.57i (ISBN 0-397-32027-2, JBL-J); PLB 9.89g (ISBN 0-397-32028-0). Har-Row.

Prime, Alfred C., ed. Arts & Crafts in Philadelphia, Maryland, & South Carolina, 1721-1785, 2 Vols. LC 79-75356. (Architecture & Decorative Art Ser). 1969. Repr. of 1929 ed. Set. lib. bdg. 55.00 (ISBN 0-306-71320-9). Da Capo.

Prime, C. T. Investigations in Woodland Ecology. (Investigations in Biology Ser.). 1970. pap. text ed. 3.95x (ISBN 0-435-60283-7). Heinemann Ed.

Prime, Derek. Baker's Bible Study Guide. (Baker's Paperback Reference Library). 296p. 1982. pap. 8.95 (ISBN 0-8010-7076-7). Baker Bk.

--Tell Me About the Bible, About God. (Illus., Orig.). (gr. 4-6). 1967. pap. 1.50 o.p. (ISBN 0-8024-3617-X). Moody.

--Tell Me About the Lord Jesus Christ. (Illus., Orig.). (gr. 4-6). 1967. pap. 1.50 o.p. (ISBN 0-8024-3618-8). Moody.

--Tell Me About the Lord's Prayer. (Illus., Orig.). (gr. 4-6). 1967. pap. 1.50 o.p. (ISBN 0-8024-3620-X). Moody.

--Tell Me About the Ten Commandments. (gr. 4-6). 1969. pap. 1.50 o.p. (ISBN 0-8024-3627-7). Moody.

Prime, Honor. Matthew's Ear. (Illus.). (ps-5). cancelled (ISBN 0-571-06063-3). Faber & Faber.

Primmer, Brian. The Berlioz Style. 1973. 16.50x o.p. (ISBN 0-19-713136-0). Oxford U Pr.

Primrose, S. B. & Dimmock, N. J. Introduction to Modern Virology. 2nd ed. (Basic Microbiology Ser.: Vol. 2). 251p. 1980. pap. text ed. 22.95x (ISBN 0-470-26941-3). Halsted Pr.

Primrose, S. B., jt. auth. see Old, R. W.

Primrose, S. B. & Wardlaw, Alastair, eds. Sourcebook of Experiments for the Teaching of Microbiology. (SGM Special Publications). 53.50 (ISBN 0-12-565680-7). Acad Pr.

Prince, A. Alloy Phase Equilibria. 1970. pap. 31.75 (ISBN 0-444-40462-7). Elsevier.

Prince, Alison. The Doubting Kind. 1979. pap. text ed. 1.95 o.p. (ISBN 0-448-16499-X, G&D). Putnam Pub Group.

--The Doubting Kind. (gr. 7 up). 1977. 9.95 (ISBN 0-688-22126-2); PLB 9.55 (ISBN 0-688-32126-7). Morrow.

--The Turkey's Nest. LC 79-28126. 224p. (gr. 7-9). 1980. 9.75 (ISBN 0-688-22224-2); PLB 9.36 (ISBN 0-688-32224-7). Morrow.

Prince, Derek. Faith to Live by. 1977. pap. 4.95 (ISBN 0-934920-25-7, B-29). Derek Prince.

--Last Word on the Middle East. 160p. 1982. 9.95 (ISBN 0-310-60040-5). Chosen Bks Pub.

--Shaping History Through Prayer & Fasting. 1973. 2.25 (ISBN 0-934920-23-0, B-25); pap. 1.25 (ISBN 0-686-12766-8, B-25). Derek Prince.

--Shaping History Through Prayer & Fasting. 1975. pap. 1.95 o.p. (ISBN 0-8007-8180-5, Spire Bks). Revell.

Prince, Derek, jt. auth. see Prince, Lydia.

Prince, Eleanor F., illus. Basic Training for Horses: English & Western. LC 76-42383. (Illus.). 1979. 17.95 (ISBN 0-385-03244-7). Doubleday.

Prince, F. T., ed. see Shakespeare, William.

Prince, Francine. Francine Prince's Vitamin Diet for Quick & Easy Weight Loss. 1982. 6.95 (ISBN 0-686-97447-6). Cornerstone.

Prince, J. H. A Better Life After Fifty. (Illus.). 200p. 1969. 1.25 o.p. (ISBN 0-589-07015-0, Pub. by Reed Books Australia). C E Tuttle.

--The Universal Urge: Courtship & Mating Among Animals. LC 72-6950. (Illus.). 160p. (gr. 6 up). 1972. 7.95 o.p. (ISBN 0-525-66234-0). Lodestar Bks.

Prince, Lydia. Appointment in Jerusalem. 1975. 7.95 (ISBN 0-934920-24-9, B-26). Derek Prince.

Prince, Lydia & Prince, Derek. Appointment in Jerusalem. 1981. pap. 5.95 (ISBN 0-912376-75-9, 4109-1). Chosen Bks Pub.

Prince, Marjorie M. The Cheese Stands Alone. LC 73-6737. (Illus.). 176p. (gr. 5 up). 1973. 7.95 o.s.i. (ISBN 0-395-17511-9). HM.

Prince, Melvin, jt. auth. see Bloch, Herbert A.

Prince, Morton, et al. Psychotherapeutics: A Symposium. LC 75-16728. (Classics in Psychiatry Ser.). 1976. Repr. of 1910 ed. 11.00x (ISBN 0-405-07451-4). Ayer Co.

Prince, Pamela. Secret World of Teddy Bears. 1983. 9.95 (ISBN 0-517-55022-9, Harmony). Crown.

Prince, Patricia. Contreras Clinic Laetrile Cookbook. 9.95x (ISBN 0-8159-5221-X). Cancer Control Soc.

Prince, Richard. Why I Go to the Movies Alone. (Illus.). 128p. (Orig.). 1982. 12.95 (ISBN 0-934378-37-1); pap. 5.95 (ISBN 0-934378-38-X). Tanam Pr.

Prince, Soledad G., tr. see Garbee, Ed & Van Dyke, Henry.

Prince De Monaco. Du Pauperisme en France et des Moyens de le Detruire. (Conditions of the 19th Century French Working Class Ser.). 260p. (Fr.). 1974. Repr. of 1839 ed. lib. bdg. 71.00x o.p. (ISBN 0-8287-0632-8, 1146). Clearwater Pub.

Prince of Wales, frwd. by. Castles in Wales. 192p. 1983. 24.95 (ISBN 0-86145-125-2, Pub. by Auto Assn-British Tourist Authority England). Merrimack Bk Serv.

Princeteau, T. Cornelie Ou la Pupille De Voltaire. Repr. of 1825 ed. 32.00 o.p. (ISBN 0-8287-0703-0). Clearwater Pub.

Princeton Center for Infancy. The Parenting Advisor. 1977. pap. 11.95 (ISBN 0-385-14330-3, Anch). Doubleday.

Princeton Center for Infancy & Early Childhood. First Twelve Months of Life. 14.95 o.p. (ISBN 0-448-02032-7, G&D); pap. 9.95 (ISBN 0-448-02149-8, Today Press). Putnam Pub Group.

Princeton Conference on Cerebrovascular Disease, 11th., Mar. 1978. Proceedings. Price, Thomas R. & Nelson, Erland, eds. LC 77-84127. 424p. 1979. text ed. 33.00 (ISBN 0-89004-292-6). Raven.

Princeton Conferences on Cerebrovascular Diseases, 10th. Cerebrovascular Diseases. Scheinberg, Peritz, ed. LC 75-25125. 408p. 1976. 30.00 (ISBN 0-89004-095-8). Raven.

Princeton University. Dictionary Catalog of the Princeton University Plasma Physics Laboratory Library, 4 vols. 1970. Set. lib. bdg. 380.00 (ISBN 0-8161-0881-1, Hal Library). G K Hall.

--Dictionary Catalog of the Princeton University Plasma Physics Laboratory Library, First Supplement. 1973. lib. bdg. 150.00 (ISBN 0-8161-1032-8, Hall Library). G K Hall.

Princeton University Office of Population Research. Population Index Bibliography Cumulated 1935-1968 by Authors & Geographical Areas, 9 vols. 1971. Set. lib. bdg. 855.00 (ISBN 0-8161-0880-3, Hall Library); lib. bdg. 415.00 By Author (ISBN 0-8161-0231-7); lib. bdg. 495.00 By Geogaphical Area (ISBN 0-8161-0116-7). G K Hall.

Prince Vajiranānavarorasa. Autobiography: The Life of Prince-Patriarch Vajiranana of Siam, 1860-1921. Reynolds, Craig J., tr. from Vietnamese. LC 79-9725. (Southeast Asia Translation Ser.: Vol. 3). (Illus.). liv, 88p. 1979. 15.95x (ISBN 0-8214-0376-1, 82-82733). Ohio U Pr.

Prindl, Andreas R. Foreign Exchange Risk. LC 75-37684. 168p. 1976. 32.95 (ISBN 0-471-01653-5, Pub. by Wiley-Interscience). Wiley.

Prindle, Paul W. Ancestry of Elizabeth Barrett Gillespie: Mrs. William Sperry Beinecke. LC 76-15134. (Illus.). 1976. 65.00 o.p. (ISBN 0-87104-271-1). NY Pub Lib.

--Ancestry of William Sperry Beinecke. LC 74-83343. (Illus.). 1974. 35.00 o.p. (ISBN 0-87104-270-3). NY Pub Lib.

--Descendants of John & Mary Jane (Cunningham) Gillespie. LC 73-85068. (Illus.). 1973. text ed. 20.00 o.p. (ISBN 0-87104-272-X). NY Pub Lib.

Prineas, et al. The Minnesota Code Manual of Electrocardiographic Findings. (Illus.). 240p. 1982. text ed. 29.50 (ISBN 0-7236-7053-6). Wright PSG.

Pring, J. T., ed. The Oxford Dictionary of Modern Greek: English-Greek. 1982. 14.95x (ISBN 0-19-864136-2). Oxford U Pr.

Pring, Julian T., ed. Oxford Dictionary of Modern Greek. Greek-English. 1965. 13.50x o.p. (ISBN 0-19-864207-5). Oxford U Pr.

Pring, M. J. Technical Analysis Explained: An Illustrated Guide for the Investor. 1980. 35.95 (ISBN 0-07-050871-2). McGraw.

Pring, Martin J. How to Forecast Interest Rates: A Guide to Profits for Consumers, Managers & Investors. 192p. 1981. 16.50 (ISBN 0-07-050865-8, P&RB). McGraw.

--International Investing Made Easy. new ed. 224p. 1980. 17.95 (ISBN 0-07-050872-0, P&RB). McGraw.

Pringle, Charles D., jt. auth. see Longenecker, Justin G.

Pringle, David. Earth Is the Alien Planet: J. G. Ballard's Four-Dimensional Nightmare. LC 79-13065. (The Milford Ser.: Popular Writers of Today: Vol. 26). 1979. lib. bdg. 9.95x (ISBN 0-89370-138-6); pap. 3.95 (ISBN 0-89370-238-2). Borgo Pr.

Pringle, Ian, jt. ed. see Freedman, Ariva.

Pringle, John J., jt. auth. see Solomon, Ezra.

Pringle, Laurence. Animals & Their Niches: How Species Share Resources. (Illus.). (gr. 3-7). 1977. 7.95 (ISBN 0-688-22127-0); PLB 7.63 (ISBN 0-688-32127-5). Morrow.

--Chains, Webs, & Pyramids: The Flow of Energy in Nature. LC 75-1084. (Illus.). (gr. 3-6). 1975. 7.95 o.p. (ISBN 0-690-00562-8, TYC-J); PLB 10.89 (ISBN 0-690-00563-6). Har-Row.

--Cockroaches: Here, There & Everywhere. LC 79-132301. (A Let's-Read & Find-Out Science Bk). (Illus.). (gr. k-3). 1971. PLB 9.89 o.p. (ISBN 0-690-19680-6, TYC-J). Har-Row.

--Dinosaurs & Their World. LC 68-11506. (Illus.). (gr. 2-5). 1976. pap. 2.95 (ISBN 0-15-626060-3, VoyB). HarBraceJ.

--Feral: Tame Animals Gone Wild. LC 82-60741. (Illus.). 96p. (gr. 5up). 1983. 9.95 (ISBN 0-02-775420-0). Macmillan.

--Listen to the Crows. LC 75-43535. (Illus.). 40p. (gr. 3-7). 1976. 10.89 (ISBN 0-690-01069-9, TYC-J). Har-Row.

--The Minnow Family. LC 75-28335. (Illus.). 64p. (gr. 3-7). 1976. 7.95 (ISBN 0-688-22060-6); PLB 7.63 (ISBN 0-688-32060-0). Morrow.

--Natural Fire, Its Ecology in Forests. LC 79-13606. (Illus.). 64p. (gr. 4-6). 1979. 6.48 o.s.i. (ISBN 0-688-22210-2); PLB 7.44 (ISBN 0-688-32210-7). Morrow.

--Radiation: Waves & Particles Benefits & Risks. LC 82-16721. (Illus.). 64p. (gr. 7-12). 1983. lib. bdg. 9.95 (ISBN 0-89490-054-4). Enslow Pubs.

--Twist, Wiggle, & Squirm: A Book About Earthworms. LC 74-184983. (A Let's-Read-&-Find-Out Science Bk). (Illus.). 33p. (gr. k-3). 1973. 9.57i o.p. (ISBN 0-690-84154-X, TYC-J); PLB 8.79 o.p. (ISBN 0-690-84155-8). Har-Row.

--Water Plants. LC 74-23942. (A Let's-Read & Find-Out Science Bk). (Illus.). 40p. (gr. k-3). 1975. 6.95 o.p. (ISBN 0-690-00737-X, TYC-J); PLB 10.89 (ISBN 0-690-00738-8). Har-Row.

--Wolfman: Exploring the World of Wolves. LC 82-19144. (Illus.). 96p. (gr. 6-8). 1983. 12.95 (ISBN 0-684-17832-X). Scribner.

Pringle, M. & Naidoo, S. Early Child Care in Britain. (International Monographs on Early Child Care). 186p. 1975. 24.00x (ISBN 0-677-05200-6). Gordon.

Pringle, M. L., ed. Caring for Children: A Symposium on Co-Operation in Child Care. (Studies in Child Development). (Orig.). 1969. pap. text ed. 4.50x o.p. (ISBN 0-582-32439-4). Humanities.

Pringle, Mia K. The Needs of Children. LC 75-10752. 192p. 1975. 8.00x o.p. (ISBN 0-8052-3598-1); pap. 2.95 o.p. (ISBN 0-8052-0502-0). Schocken.

Pringle, Peter & Spigelman, James. The Nuclear Barons. 592p. 1983. pap. 4.95 (ISBN 0-380-62364-1, 62364-1, Discus). Avon.

Pringle, R., tr. see Steuber, U.

Pringle, Robin. Banking in Britain. LC 75-3960. (Illus.). 1975. pap. 6.95x (ISBN 0-416-81220-1). Methuen Inc.

Pringle, Roger. Poems for Warwickshire. 1980. 18.00x o.p. (ISBN 0-906418-05-4, Pub. by Roundwood). State Mutual Bk.

Pringle, Terry. This Is the Child. LC 82-48876. 1983. 13.95 (ISBN 0-394-52921-9). Knopf.

Pringle, Thom, tr. see Ambrosi, Hans.

Pringle, W. S. Insect Flight. Head, J. J., ed. LC 78-53327. (Carolina Biology Readers Ser.). 16p. 1983. pap. text ed. 1.60 (ISBN 0-19-914167-3, 45-9652). Carolina Biological.

Pringsheim, Klaus H. Neighbors Across the Pacific: The Development of Economic & Political Relations Between Canada & Japan. LC 82-11713. (Contributions in Political Science Ser.: No. 90). 256p. 1983. lib. bdg. 29.95 (ISBN 0-313-23507-4, PRN/). Greenwood.

Prinol, Andreas R. Japanese Finance: A Guide to Banking in Japan. 137p. 1981. 21.50x (ISBN 0-471-09982-1, Pub. by Wiley-Interscience). Wiley.

Prins, Gwyn. The Hidden Hippopotamus: Reappraisal in African History, the Early Colonial Experience. LC 79-41658. (African Studies: No. 28). (Illus.). 320p. 1980. 49.50 (ISBN 0-521-22915-4). Cambridge U Pr.

Prins, Herschel. Offenders, Deviants, or Patients? 1980. 25.00x (ISBN 0-422-76800-6, Pub by Tavistock England); pap. 13.50x (ISBN 0-422-76810-3). Methuen Inc.

Print Project. The Unusual-by-Mail Catalog. (Illus.). 192p. 1980. 14.95 o.p. (ISBN 0-312-83374-1); pap. 7.95 (ISBN 0-312-83375-X). St Martin.

Printing, Lelli, ed. see Keim, Abe.

Printing Research Institutes. Advances in Printing Science & Technology: Proceedings of the 16th International Conference of Printing Research Institutes, Miami, Florida, June 1981, Vol. 16. 470p. 1982. 55.00 (ISBN 0-7273-0108-X). Bowker.

Printz-Pahlson, Goran, jt. tr. see Matthias, John.

Printz-Pahlson, Goran, tr. see Ostergren, Jan.

Printz-Pahlson, Ulla, tr. from Swedish. A Dreamed Life. Orig. Title: Dromen om ett liv. 220p. 1983. 16.95 (ISBN 0-8214-0710-4, 82-84796); pap. 8.95 (ISBN 0-8214-0711-2, 82-84804). Ohio U Pr.

Prinz, Joachim. Popes from the Ghetto: A View of Medieval Christendom. LC 66-16301. (Illus.). 1968. pap. 1.95 o.p. (ISBN 0-8052-0174-2). Schocken.

Prinz, Martin, et al, eds. Simon & Schuster's Guide to Rocks & Minerals. (Illus.). 1978. pap. 9.95 (ISBN 0-671-24396-9). S&S.

Prioleau, Elizabeth S. The Circle of Eros: Sexuality in the Work of William Dean Howells. LC 82-14788. 328p. 1983. text ed. 27.50 (ISBN 0-8223-0492-9). Duke.

Priolo, Joan. Decoupage: Simple & Sophisticated. LC 73-93597. (Little Craft Book Ser). (Illus.). 48p. (gr. 4 up). 1974. 5.95 o.p. (ISBN 0-8069-5300-4); PLB 6.69 o.p. (ISBN 0-8069-5301-2). Sterling.

Prior, Allan. A Cast of Stars. LC 82-1029. (A William Abrahams Bk.). 444p. Date not set. 16.95 (ISBN 0-03-061943-2). HR&W.

Prior, Arthur N. Objects of Thought. Geach, P., ed. 1971. 31.50x (ISBN 0-19-824354-5). Oxford U Pr.

--Time & Modality. LC 78-26696. (Illus.). 1979. Repr. of 1957 ed. lib. bdg. 18.50x (ISBN 0-313-20911-1, PRTI). Greenwood.

Prior, Brenda. Little Sleeping Beauty. (Arch Bks: Set 6). 1969. laminated bdg. 0.89 (ISBN 0-570-06041-9, 59-1156). Concordia.

Prior, Joanne. Soft Furnishing. (Leisure Time Bks). (Illus.). pap. 12.50x (ISBN 0-7135-1589-9, LTB). Sportshelf.

Prior, John A. & Silberstein, Jack S. Physical Diagnosis: The History & Examination of the Patient. 6th ed. LC 81-38432. (Illus.). 525p. 1981. text ed. 29.95 (ISBN 0-8016-4054-7). Mosby.

Prior, Mike, et al. Politics & Power I. Purdy, David, et al, eds. 240p. (Orig.). 1980. pap. 13.95 (ISBN 0-7100-0593-8). Routledge & Kegan.

Prior, Robin. The World Crisis as History. 288p. 1983. text ed. 31.00x (ISBN 0-7099-2011-3, Pub. by Croom Helm Ltd England). Biblio Dist.

Prior, Tom & Wannan, Bill. Plundering Sons. (Illus.). 20.00x (ISBN 0-392-04196-0, ABC). Sportshelf.

Prior, William W. Not Our House. 1979. 7.95 o.p. (ISBN 0-533-03842-1). Vantage.

Priovolos, Theophilos. Coffee & the Ivory Coast: An Econometric Study. LC 80-8630. (The Wharton Econometric Studies). (Illus.). 240p. 1981. 26.95 (ISBN 0-669-04331-1). Lexington Bks.

Prisco, Salvatore, III. An Introduction to Psychohistory: Theories & Case Studies. LC 80-8245. 190p. 1980. lib. bdg. 19.75 (ISBN 0-8191-1335-2); pap. text ed. 9.75 (ISBN 0-8191-1336-0). U Pr of Amer.

Prishvin, Mikhail. The Lake & the Woods: or, Nature's Calendar. Goodman, W. L., tr. from Russian. LC 75-27685. (Illus.). 258p. 1976. Repr. of 1951 ed. lib. bdg. 17.50x (ISBN 0-8371-8465-7, PRLW). Greenwood.

Prising, Robin. Manila Goodbye. LC 74-28236. 224p. 1975. 7.95 o.s.i. (ISBN 0-395-20432-1). HM.

Prison Discipline Society. Reports of the Prison Discipline Society, Boston: Reports 1-29, 1826-1854, 6 vols. LC 71-129322. (Criminology, Law Enforcement, & Social Problems Ser.: No. 155). (Illus.). 1972. Set. 170.00x (ISBN 0-87585-155-X). Patterson Smith.

Prista, Alexander R. Essential Portuguese Grammar. 114p. (Orig.). 1966. pap. 2.50 (ISBN 0-486-21650-0). Dover.

Pritchard. Environmental Science Four Checkbook. 1982. text ed. 22.50 (ISBN 0-408-00663-3); pap. text ed. 12.50 (ISBN 0-408-00608-0). Butterworth.

Pritchard, Anita. Fondue Magic: Fun, Flame & Saucery. (Illus.). 1969. 5.95 (ISBN 0-8208-0220-4). Hearthside.

Pritchard, D. B. Begin Chess: An Intro to the Game & to the Basics of Tactics & Strategy. 160p. (RL 7). 1973. pap. 1.75 (ISBN 0-451-11590-2, AE1590, Sig). NAL.

Pritchard, D. C., jt. ed. see Lynes, J. A.

Pritchard, David. Brain Games. 1982. pap. 3.95 (ISBN 0-14-005682-3). Penguin.

Pritchard, David A. Mental Health Law in Mississippi. LC 78-62247. 1978. pap. text ed. 12.50 (ISBN 0-8191-0568-6). U Pr of Amer.

Pritchard, Elaine. The Young Chess Player. (Illus.). 104p. 1976. 6.95 o.p. (ISBN 0-571-10567-X). Faber & Faber.

Pritchard, G., ed. Developments in Reinforced Plastics, No. 2. 196p. 1982. 43.00 (ISBN 0-85334-125-7, Pub. by Applied Sci England). Elsevier.

Pritchard, George. The Aggressions of the French at Tahiti & Other Islands in the Pacific. De Deckker, P. T., ed. (Illus.). 200p. 1982. 38.00x (ISBN 0-19-647994-0). Oxford U Pr.

Pritchard, H. Wayne, pref. by. Resource Conservation Glossary. 3rd ed. LC 82-5830. 193p. 1982. pap. 7.00 (ISBN 0-935734-09-0). Soil Conservation.

Pritchard, J. A. Planning Office Automation: Information Management Systems. 180p. 1982. pap. 27.50x (ISBN 0-85012-366-6). Intl Pubns Serv.

--Security in On-Line Systems. (Illus., Orig.). 1979. pap. 35.00x (ISBN 0-85012-211-2). Intl Pubns Serv.

--Selection & Use of Terminals in On-Line Systems. LC 74-76261. 120p. 1974. 30.00x (ISBN 0-85012-117-5). Intl Pubns Serv.

Pritchard, J. M. Africa: Geography of a Changing Continent. LC 71-145838. 1971. text ed. 22.50x (ISBN 0-8419-0071-X, Africana). Holmes & Meier.

Pritchard, James B. The Bronze Age Cemetery at Gibeon. (Museum Monographs). (Illus.). 123p. 1963. soft bound 3.50x (ISBN 0-934718-17-2). Univ Mus of U PA.

--The Cemetery at Tell es-Sa'idiyeh, Jordan. (University Museum Monographs: No. 41). (Illus., Orig.). 1980. pap. 12.50x (ISBN 0-934718-32-6). Univ Mus of U PA.

--Palestinian Figurines in Relation to Certain Goddesses Known Through Literature. 1943. pap. 12.00 (ISBN 0-527-02698-0). Kraus Repr.

--The Water System of Gibeon. (Museum Monograph). viii, 34p. 1961. 5.00x (ISBN 0-934718-14-8). Univ Mus of U PA.

Pritchard, James B., et al. Sarepta: A Preliminary Report on the Iron Age. (Museum Monographs). (Illus.). 114p. 1975. bound 12.50xsoft (ISBN 0-934718-24-5). Univ Mus of U Pa.

Pritchard, John P. Literary Wise Men of Gotham: Criticism in New York, 1815-1860. LC 77-7157. 1977. Repr. of 1963 ed. lib. bdg. 17.50x (ISBN 0-8371-9664-7, PRLI). Greenwood.

Pritchard, Mary H. & Kruse, Gunther O., eds. The Collection & Preservation of Animal Parasites. LC 81-19869. iv, 141p. (Orig.). 1982. pap. 10.95x (ISBN 0-8032-8704-6). U of Nebr Pr.

Pritchard, Michael S., jt. ed. see Ellin, Joseph.

Pritchard, Peter C. Encyclopedia of Turtles. (Illus.). 1979. 49.95 (ISBN 0-87666-918-6, H-1011). TFH Pubns.

Pritchard, R. M. Housing & the Spatial Structure of the City. LC 75-3859. (Cambridge Geographical Studies). (Illus.). 403p. 1976. 44.50 (ISBN 0-521-20882-3). Cambridge U Pr.

Pritchard, Robert. Operational Financial Management. LC 76-25062. (Illus.). 1977. text ed. 22.95 (ISBN 0-13-637827-7). P-H.

Pritchard, S., ed. Developments in Reinforced Plastics, Vol. 1. 1980. 67.75 (ISBN 0-85334-919-3, Pub. by Applied Sci England). Elsevier.

Pritchard, Violet. English Medieval Graffiti. 1967. 54.50 (ISBN 0-521-05998-4). Cambridge U Pr.

Pritchard, William. Seeing Through Everything: English Literature Between the Wars. LC 76-47434. 1977. 16.95 (ISBN 0-19-519951-0). Oxford U Pr.

Pritchard, William H. Lives of the Modern Poets. 1980. 19.95x (ISBN 0-19-502690-X). Oxford U Pr.

--Lives of the Modern Poets. 1981. pap. 7.95 (ISBN 0-19-502989-5, GB 652, GB). Oxford U Pr.

Pritchet, C. D. Iohannis Alexandrini Commentaria in Librum de Sectis Galeni. xxi, 108p. 1982. write for info. (ISBN 90-04-06566-0). E J Brill.

Pritchett, C. H. The American Constitutional System. 5th ed. Munson, Eric M., ed. (American Government Ser.). 160p. 1981. pap. text ed. 9.95 (ISBN 0-07-050893-3). McGraw.

Pritchett, C. Herman. Congress Versus the Supreme Court, Nineteen Fifty-Seven to Nineteen Sixty. LC 73-249. (American Constitutional & Legal History Ser.). 182p. 1973. Repr. of 1961 ed. lib. bdg. 25.00 (ISBN 0-306-70568-0). Da Capo.

Pritchett, C. W. Sicilian Scheveningen. 1977. 22.50 o.p. (ISBN 0-7134-0087-0, Pub. by Batsford England). David & Charles.

Pritchett, Charles H. The American Constitutional System. 4th ed. 1975. 13.95 (ISBN 0-07-050889-5, C). McGraw.

Pritchett, Craig. Nimzo-Indian: Nimzowitsch, (4e3) Hubner Taimanov Variations. (Algebraic Chess Openings Ser.). (Illus.). 144p. 1980. 22.50 (ISBN 0-7134-1446-4, Pub. by Batsford England); pap. 15.95 (ISBN 0-7134-1447-2). David & Charles.

Pritchett, G. Herman. The Federal System in Constitutional Law. (Illus.). 1978. pap. 15.95 ref. ed. (ISBN 0-13-308460-4). P-H.

Pritchett, Herman C., jt. ed. see Murphy, Walter F.

Pritchett, Kendrick W. Studies in Ancient Greek Topography. LC 65-65210. (Publications in Classical Studies: Vol. 28). 374p. 1982. pap. text ed. 30.00x (ISBN 0-520-09660-6), U of Cal Pr.

Pritchett, Morgan H. & Woodcock, Susan R. The Eastern Shore of Maryland. (Illus.). 233p. 1980. 29.95 (ISBN 0-686-36665-4). Md Hist.

Pritchett, S. Travis & Stinton, John E. Individual Annuities As a Source of Retirement Income. LC 75-32900. (FLMI Insurance Education Program Ser.). 1976. pap. 5.50 o.p. (ISBN 0-915322-17-X). LOMA.

--Individual Annuities As a Source of Retirement Income. rev. ed. (FLMI Insurance Education Program Ser.). 94p. 1982. pap. text ed. 9.00 (ISBN 0-915322-50-1). LOMA.

Pritchett, V. S. Collected Stories. LC 81-48279. 1982. 20.00 (ISBN 0-394-52417-9). Random.

--The Spanish Temper. LC 76-7943. 1976. Repr. of 1954 ed. lib. bdg. 21.00x (ISBN 0-8371-8862-8, PRSP). Greenwood.

--The Tale Bearers: Essays on English, American & Other Writers. 1980. 11.95 o.p. (ISBN 0-394-50486-0); pap. 4.95 (ISBN 0-394-74683-X). Random.

--The Turn of the Years. 1982. 10.00 (ISBN 0-394-52502-7). Random.

Pritchett, W. Kendrick. Dionysius of Halicarnassus: On Thucydides. 1975. 24.50x (ISBN 0-520-02922-4); pap. 9.50x (ISBN 0-520-02959-3). U of Cal Pr.

--The Greek State at War, Pt. 2. LC 74-77991. 1975. 30.00x (ISBN 0-520-02565-2). U of Cal Pr.

--The Greek State at War, Pt. 3. 1980. 35.75x (ISBN 0-520-03781-2). U of Cal Pr.

--Studies in Ancient Greek Topography: Part III (Roads) (U. C. Publications in Classical Studies: Vol. 22). 436p. 1981. 26.50x (ISBN 0-520-09635-5). U of Cal Pr.

Pritchett, William L. Properties & Management of Forest Soils. LC 78-23196. 1979. text ed. 33.95x (ISBN 0-471-03718-4). Wiley.

Prithipaul, K. Dad, jt. ed. see Waugh, Earle H.

Pritikin, Nathan. The Pritikin Permanent Weight-Loss Manual. LC 80-84945. (Illus.). 416p. 1981. 14.95 (ISBN 0-448-12437-8, G&D). Putnam Pub Group.

Pritikin, Roland I. & Grace, Eugene V. Essentials of Ophthalmology. 3rd ed. LC 71-99301. (Illus.). 1979. 25.00 (ISBN 0-87716-028-7, Pub. by Moore Pub Co). F Apple.

Pritkin, Nathan & McGrady, Patrick, Jr. Pritikin Program for Diet & Exercise. 1979. 14.95 (ISBN 0-448-14302-X, G&D). Putnam Pub Group.

Pritsker, A. Alan. The Gasp IV Simulation Language. LC 74-3281. 416p. 1974. 35.95x (ISBN 0-471-70045-2, Pub. by Wiley-Interscience). Wiley.

Pritt, D. N., ed. Law, Class & Society, 4 vols. 641p. 1970. 44.00x set (ISBN 0-8464-0547-4). Beekman Pubs.

Prittie, Terence. The Velvet Chancellors: A History of Post-War Germany. (Illus.). 286p. 1981. text ed. 24.00x (ISBN 0-8419-6750-4). Holmes & Meier.

Pritzel, G. A. Thesaurus Literature Botanicae. 2nd ed. 1972. 72.00 (ISBN 3-87429-035-2). Lubrecht & Cramer.

Pritzker, Alan B. & Young, Robert E. Simulation with Gasp PL-I: A PL-I Based Continuous Discrete Simulation Language. LC 75-23182. 335p. 1975. 32.50x o.s.i. (ISBN 0-471-70046-0, Pub. by Wiley-Interscience). Wiley.

Privett, Katherine H. The Dreams of Exiles. LC 82-2886. (Kestrel Chapbooks Ser.). 24p. 1982. pap. 3.00 (ISBN 0-914974-34-3). Holmgangers.

Proakis, John G. Digital Communications. (McGraw-Hill Series in Electrical Engineering). (Illus.). 688p. 1983. text ed. 37.5003876408x (ISBN 0-07-050927-1, C); solutions manual 14.95 (ISBN 0-07-050928-X). McGraw.

Proal, Louis. Political Crime. LC 70-172565. (Criminology, Law Enforcement, & Social Problems Ser.: No. 146). (With intro. & index added). 1973. Repr. of 1898 ed. 15.00x (ISBN 0-87585-146-0). Patterson Smith.

Probert, Belinda. Beyond Orange & Green: The Political Economy of the Northern Ireland Crisis. 176p. 1978. 25.00 (ISBN 0-905762-16-9, Pub. by Zed Pr England); pap. 8.50 (ISBN 0-905762-17-7, Pub. by Zed Pr England). Lawrence Hill.

Probert, Christina. Shoes in Vogue Since Nineteen Ten. LC 81-67880. (Accessories in Vogue Ser.). (Illus.). 96p. 1981. pap. 9.95 (ISBN 0-89659-241-3); 6-copy display 59.70 (ISBN 0-686-96633-3). Abbeville Pr.

Probst, Calvin, ed. HPG Hospital Purchasing Guide: Nineteen Eighty Two. 6th ed. (Annual Ser.). 1982. pap. text ed. 95.00 (ISBN 0-933916-06-X). IMS Pr.

--HPG Hospital Purchasing Guide, 1983. (Annual Ser.). 1983. pap. text ed. 110.00 (ISBN 0-910190-28-3). IMS Pr.

--LPG Laboratory Purchasing Guide. (Annual Ser.). 1982. pap. text ed. 35.00 (ISBN 0-933916-08-6). IMS Pr.

--LPG Laboratory Purchasing Guide. (Annual Ser.). 1983. pap. text ed. 35.00 (ISBN 0-910190-29-1). IMS Pr.

--RPG Rehab Purchasing Guide. (Annual Ser.). 1983. pap. text ed. 35.00 (ISBN 0-910190-22-4). IMS Pr.

Probst, Gerhard F. & Bodine, Jay F., eds. Perspectives on Max Frisch. LC 80-5181. 232p. 1982. 20.50x (ISBN 0-8131-1438-1). U Pr of Ky.

Probst, Raymond E., ed. Obstetrics & Gynecology Specialty Board Review. 6th ed. 1981. pap. 28.50 (ISBN 0-87488-304-0). Med Exam.

Probstein, R. F. & Hicks, R. E. Synthetic Fuels. (Chemical Engineering Ser.). 576p. 1982. 37.50x (ISBN 0-07-050908-5). McGraw.

Proby, Kathryn H. Mario Sanchez-Painter of Key West Memories. LC 81-50557. (Illus.). 64p. Date not set. pap. 14.95 (ISBN 0-686-84313-4). Banyan Bks.

Probyn, Peter, ed. The Complete Drawing Book. (Illus.). 400p. 1970. 25.00 (ISBN 0-8230-0780-4). Watson-Guptill.

Procaccini, Joseph & Kiefaber, Mark. Parent Burnout. LC 81-43593. (Illus.). 264p. 1983. 15.95 (ISBN 0-385-18041-1). Doubleday.

Prochasca, Alice. History of the General Federation of Trade Unions, 1899-1980. 350p. 1982. text ed. 35.00x (ISBN 0-686-95344-4). Allen Unwin.

Prochazka, A. see Taylor, A.

Prochnow, Herbert V. Thousand & One Ways to Improve Your Conversation & Speeches. LC 70-109301. 341p. 1972. Repr. of 1952 ed. lib. bdg. 17.25x (ISBN 0-8371-3844-2, PRWI). Greenwood.

--Toastmaster's Quips & Stories: & How to Use Them. LC 81-85040. 192p. 1982. 12.95 (ISBN 0-8069-0238-8); lib. bdg. 15.69 (ISBN 0-8069-0239-6). Sterling.

Prochnow, Herbert V. & Prochnow, Herbert V., Jr. The Toastmaster's Treasure Chest. LC 78-2161. 1979. 15.34i (ISBN 0-06-013447-X, HarpT). Har-Row.

--A Treasure Chest of Quotations for All Occasions. LC 82-48130. 480p. 1983. 17.95 (ISBN 0-06-015043-2, HarpT). Har-Row.

Prock, Alfred & McConkey, Gladys, eds. Topics in Chemical Physics. 1962. 17.00 (ISBN 0-444-40463-5). Elsevier.

Procko, Bohdan P. Ukrainian Catholics in America: A History. LC 81-43718. 184p. (Orig.). 1982. lib. bdg. 22.00 (ISBN 0-8191-2409-5); pap. text ed. 10.00 (ISBN 0-8191-2410-9). U Pr of Amer.

Procopio, Mariellen, jt. auth. see Perella, Frederick J.

Procopius. Secret History. Atwater, Richard, tr. 1961. pap. 4.95x (ISBN 0-472-08728-2, AA). U of Mich Pr.

Procter, Mary & Matuszeski, Bill. Gritty Cities: A Second Look at Allentown, Bethlehem, Bridgeport, Hoboken, Lancaster, Norwich, Paterson, Reading, Trenton, Troy, Waterbury, & Wilmington. LC 78-15149. (Illus.). 288p. 1978. lib. bdg. 24.95 (ISBN 0-87722-143-X); pap. 10.95 (ISBN 0-87722-144-8). Temple U Pr.

Proctor & Anderson. Nose: Upper Airway Phipiology. 1982. 132.00 (ISBN 0-444-80377-7). Elsevier.

Proctor, Alexander P. Alexander Phimister Proctor, Sculptor in Buckskin: An Autobiography. Proctor, Hester E., ed. LC 77-108803. (Illus.). 1971. 17.50 o.p. (ISBN 0-8061-0912-2). U of Okla Pr.

Proctor, C. R., jt. ed. see Loeffler, F. J.

Proctor, Charles W. Authorities & Rights of Interstate Truckers, 2 vols. 1958. with 1961 Cum. Suppl. 35.00 o.p. (ISBN 0-87215-044-5); 1961 cum. suppl. 10.00 o.p. (ISBN 0-87215-292-8). Michie-Bobbs.

Proctor, D. The Experience of Thucydides. 264p. 1981. text ed. 36.00x (ISBN 0-85668-153-9, Pub. by Aris & Phillips England); pap. text ed. 29.00x (ISBN 0-85668-206-3). Humanities.

Proctor, G. L. The Vikings. Reeves, Marjorie, ed. (Then & There Ser.). (Illus.). 112p. (gr. 7-12). pap. text ed. 3.10 (ISBN 0-582-20386-4). Longman.

Proctor, George W. Enemies. LC 82-45334. (Double D Western Ser.). 192p. 1983. 11.95 (ISBN 0-385-17654-6). Doubleday.

Proctor, Harvey W., et al, eds. Year Book of Cardiology, 1982. (Illus.). 480p. 1982. 37.95 (ISBN 0-8151-4174-2). Year Bk Med.

--Year Book of Cardiology 1983. 1983. 40.00 (ISBN 0-8151-4202-1). Year Bk Med.

Proctor, Hester E., ed. see Proctor, Alexander P.

Proctor, J. O. Techniques, Notes, Tips for Teachers. 1968. pap. text ed. 7.80 (ISBN 0-8273-0361-0). Delmar.

Proctor, John & Proctor, Susan. Color in Plants & Flowers. LC 78-56356. (Illus.). 1978. 11.95 (ISBN 0-89696-017-X, An Everest House Book). Dodd.

Proctor, Paul, ed. Longman Dictionary of Contemporary English. (Illus.). 1979. text ed. 14.95x (ISBN 0-582-52571-3); pap. text ed. 11.95x (ISBN 0-582-55608-2). Longman.

Proctor, Richard, jt. auth. see Lew, Jennifer.

Proctor, Richard W. The Barber's Shop. rev. & enl. ed. LC 74-79753. (Illus.). 1971. Repr. of 1883 ed. 30.00x (ISBN 0-8103-3036-9). Gale.

Proctor, Susan, jt. auth. see Proctor, John.

Proctor, Tony. Management: Theory & Principles. 250p. 1982. pap. text ed. 15.95 (ISBN 0-7121-1389-4). Intl Ideas.

Proctor, Wesley, tr. see Meredith, Howard & Milan, Virginia E.

Proctor, William. The Templeton Touch. LC 82-45873. 264p. 1983. 14.95 (ISBN 0-385-18302-X). Doubleday.

Proctor, William, jt. auth. see Boa, Kenneth.

Prodan, M. Forest Biometrics. 1968. inquire for price o.p. (ISBN 0-08-012441-0). Pergamon.

Proddow, Penelope. Art Tells a Story: The Bible. LC 76-18363. (Illus.). (gr. 4-6). 1979. 7.95a o.p. (ISBN 0-385-11113-4); PLB 7.95a (ISBN 0-385-11114-2). Doubleday.

Prod'Homme, J. G. Les Symphonies De Beethoven. 13th ed. LC 76-52485. (Music Reprint Ser.). (Illus., Fr.). 1977. Repr. of 1906 ed. lib. bdg. 45.00 (ISBN 0-306-70859-0). Da Capo.

Proehl, Stephen. Over New York: An Aerial View. 1980. 24.95 (ISBN 0-395-29096-1); pap. 12.95 (ISBN 0-395-29097-X). HM.

Proehl, Steven. Over Cape Cod & the Islands. 1979. o.s. 20.00 (ISBN 0-395-27064-2); pap. text ed. 11.95 (ISBN 0-395-27937-2). HM.

Proenneke, Richard, jt. auth. see Keith, Sam.

Professional Education Publications Staff, ed. Construction Contract Claims. LC 78-74032. 600p. 1978. softbound 15.00 (ISBN 0-686-96983-9). Amer Bar Assn.

Professional Photographers of America. Professional Photography Prophotos I. (Illus.). 1978. 10.95 o.p. (ISBN 0-8174-2446-6, Amphoto); pap. 4.95 o.p. (ISBN 0-8174-2119-X). Watson-Guptill.

Professional Research Publications, ed. ProSports Career Guide. 130p. 1983. pap. 15.00 (ISBN 0-931066-01-8). Prof Research.

Proffer, Carl & Proffer, Ellendea, eds. The Barsukov Triangle & the Two-Toned Blonde & Other Stories. 330p. 1983. 25.00 (ISBN 0-88233-805-6); pap. 8.50 (ISBN 0-88233-806-4). Ardis Pubs.

--The Twenties: An Anthology. 480p. 1983. 30.00 (ISBN 0-88233-820-X). Ardis Pubs.

Proffer, Carl R. Metropole Whitebook. 110p. 1983. 12.00 (ISBN 0-88233-816-1). Ardis Pubs.

Proffer, Carl R., ed. Russian Romantic Prose: An Anthology. (Illus.). 1979. 17.50x (ISBN 0-931556-00-7). Translation Pr.

Proffer, Ellendea. Mikhail Bulgakov. 1983. 30.00 (ISBN 0-88233-198-1). Ardis Pubs.

Proffer, Ellendea, ed. Bulgakov Photographic Bibliography. 140p. 1983. 22.50 (ISBN 0-88233-812-9); pap. 12.50 (ISBN 0-88233-813-7). Ardis Pubs.

Proffer, Ellendea, jt. ed. see Proffer, Carl.

Proffitt, Edward. Poetry: An Introduction & Anthology. LC 80-80842. 384p. 1981. pap. text ed. 10.95 (ISBN 0-395-29486-X); instr's. manual 0.50 (ISBN 0-395-29487-8). HM.

Profio, A. Edward. Experimental Reactor Physics. LC 75-35735. 832p. 1976. 55.95x (ISBN 0-471-70095-9, Pub. by Wiley-Interscience). Wiley.

--Radiation Shielding & Dosimetry. LC 78-15649. 1979. 54.95x (ISBN 0-471-04329-X, Pub. by Wiley-Interscience). Wiley.

Proft, Melanie De see De Proft, Melanie & Culinary Arts Institute Staff.

Progoff, Ira. At a Journal Workshop: The Basic Text & Guide for Using the Intensive Journal. LC 75-13932. 12.50 o.s.i. (ISBN 0-87941-003-5); pap. 7.95, 1977 (ISBN 0-87941-006-X). Dialogue Hse.

--Cloud of Unknowing. 1963. 5.00 o.p. (ISBN 0-517-52768-5). Crown.

--Jung, Synchronicity, & Human Destiny. LC 73-84937. 244p. 1975. 6.50 o.p. (ISBN 0-517-52767-7). Crown.

--Jung, Synchronicity, & Human Destiny. 192p. 1975. pap. 4.95 o.s.i. (ISBN 0-440-54375-4, Delta). Dell.

--The Star Cross. 2nd, enl. ed. LC 70-176111. (Entrance Meditation Ser.). 1981. pap. 3.95 (ISBN 0-87941-001-9). Dialogue Hse.

--The Well & the Cathedral: With an Introduction on Its Use in the Practice of Meditation. 2nd ed. LC 76-20823. (Entrance Meditation Ser.). 1977. 8.95 (ISBN 0-87941-004-3); pap. 3.95 2nd ed. rev. 1981 (ISBN 0-87941-005-1). Dialogue Hse.

Program of Policy Studies in Science & Technology, for National Science Foun. Legal-Institutional Implications of Wind Energy Conversion Systems (WECS) 320p. 1982. pap. 34.50x (ISBN 0-89934-170-5, W061). Solar Energy Info.

Progress Publishers, Moscow, ed. Contemporary Bourgeois Legal Thought: A Marxist Analysis. 311p. 1975. 16.00x o.p. (ISBN 0-8464-0277-7). Beekman Pubs.

Prohaska, Ray. A Basic Course in Design. rev. ed. LC 80-10766. 96p. 1980. pap. 12.50 (ISBN 0-89134-031-9). North Light Pub.

Prohaska, Steve. Little Known Secrets of Health & Long Life: Health - Long Life. 1.45x o.p. (ISBN 0-668-03315-0). Cancer Control Soc.

Prohias, Antonio. The Fourth Mad Declassified Papers on Spy Vs. Spy. (Illus.). 192p. 1974. pap. 1.95 (ISBN 0-446-94423-8). Warner Bks.

--Spy vs. Spy Follow-up File. (Illus.). 192p. 1975. pap. 1.95 (ISBN 0-446-30457-3). Warner Bks.

Proia, Nicholas C. Barron's Compact Guide to College Transfer. (Barron's Educational Ser.). 304p. 1983. pap. cancelled (ISBN 0-8120-2370-6). Barron.

Prokes, J. Hydraulic Mechanisms in Automation. 1977. 57.50 (ISBN 0-444-99829-2). Elsevier.

Prokopoff, Stephen S. & Siegfried, Joan C. The Nineteenth-Century Architecture of Saratoga Springs. (Illus.). 104p. 1970. pap. 3.50 o.p. (ISBN 0-89062-001-6). Pub Ctr Cult Res.

Prokopowicz, Sergey. Poems of Mhorka. 1980. 4.95 (ISBN 0-8062-1561-5). Carlton.

Prokosch, Frederic. The Asiatics. Van Doren, Carl, intro. by. 1982. pap. 8.25 (ISBN 0-374-51767-3). FS&G.

--The Asiatics: A Novel. LC 70-138620. (Illus.). 371p. Repr. of 1941 ed. lib. bdg. 19.75x (ISBN 0-8371-5732-3, PRAS). Greenwood.

--A Ballad of Love. LC 74-178787. 311p. 1972. Repr. of 1960 ed. lib. bdg. 16.25x (ISBN 0-8371-6287-4, PRBL). Greenwood.

--The Idols of the Cave. LC 78-178788. 373p. Repr. of 1946 ed. lib. bdg. 18.75x (ISBN 0-8371-6289-0, PRIC). Greenwood.

--Night of the Poor. LC 71-178789. 359p. Repr. of 1939 ed. lib. bdg. 18.25x (ISBN 0-8371-6288-2, PRNP). Greenwood.

--The Seven Sisters. LC 73-178792. 405p. Repr. of 1962 ed. lib. bdg. 20.50x (ISBN 0-8371-6286-6, PRSS). Greenwood.

--A Tale for Midnight. 354p. 1973. Repr. of 1955 ed. lib. bdg. 18.25x (ISBN 0-8371-6281-5, PRIM). Greenwood.

--Voices: A Memoir. 1982. 18.50 (ISBN 0-374-28509-8). FS&G.

Prolla, J. B. Approximation Theory & Functional Analysis. (Proceedings). 1979. 64.00 (ISBN 0-444-85264-6). Elsevier.

--Topics in Functional Analysis over Valued Decision Rings. (Mathematical Studies Ser.: Vol. 77). Date not set. 42.75 (ISBN 0-444-86535-7, North Holland). Elsevier.

Prombles, E. S. Flatulence Denied: Stalking the Fartological Imperative. (Orig.). 1983. pap. price not set (ISBN 0-941086-02-X). Melodious Pubns.

Promfret, John E. Colonial New Jersey: A History. LC 72-1228. (A History of the American Colonies Ser.). 1973. lib. bdg. 30.00 (ISBN 0-527-18716-X). Kraus Intl.

Pronay, Nicholas & Taylor, John. Parliamentary Texts of the Later Middle Ages. 1980. 49.50x (ISBN 0-19-822368-4). Oxford U Pr.

Pronay, Nicholas, jt. auth. see Thorpe, Frances.

Pronek, Neal. Land Hermit Crabs. (Illus.). 96p. 4.95 (ISBN 0-87666-932-1). TFH Pubns.

--Oscars. 1972. 5.95 (ISBN 0-87666-765-5, PS-687). TFH Pubns.

Pronikov, A. S. Dependability & Durability of Engineering Products. 1973. text ed. 32.50 (ISBN 0-408-70383-0). Butterworth.

Pronin, Barbara. Substitute Teaching: A Handbook for Hassle-Free Subbing. (Illus.). 190p. 1983. 12.95 (ISBN 0-312-77481-8). St Martin.

Pronin, Monica. Energy Index, 1978: Select Guide to Energy Documents, Laws, & Statistics, Vol. 6. LC 73-89098. 1978. 95.00 o.p. (ISBN 0-89947-001-7). EIC Intell.

Pronin, Monica, ed. Energy Index, 1979. LC 73-89098. 1980. 125.00 o.p. (ISBN 0-89947-006-8). EIC Intell.

--Energy Index, 1980: A Guide to Energy Documents, Laws & Statistics. LC 73-89098. 125.00 o.p. (ISBN 0-89947-010-6). EIC Intell.

--Environment Index 1979. LC 73-189498. 1980. 125.00 o.p. (ISBN 0-89947-005-X). EIC Intell.

--Environmental Index 1980: A Guide to the Key Literature of the Year. LC 73-189498. 135.00 o.p. (ISBN 0-89947-011-4). EIC Intell.

--Land Use Planning Abstracts, Seventy-Eight to Seventy-Nine: A Select Guide to Land & Water Resources Information. LC 74-28044. 1979. 95.00 o.p. (ISBN 0-89947-002-5). EIC Intell.

--Toxic Substance Sourcebook II. LC 77-28044. Orig. Title: Toxic Substance Sourcebook Series I. 560p. 1980. 95.00 o.p. (ISBN 0-89947-008-4). EIC Intell.

Pronin, Monica, jt. ed. see Ross, Steven.

Pronko, Leonard C. Georges Feydeau. LC 74-16788. (Literature & Life Ser.). (Illus.). 218p. 1975. 11.95 (ISBN 0-8044-2700-3). Ungar.

Pronzini, Bill. Case File: The Best of the "Nameless Dectective" Stories. 256p. 1983. 13.95 (ISBN 0-312-12338-8). St Martin.

--Dragonfire: A "Nameless Detective" Mystery. 208p. 1982. 10.95 (ISBN 0-312-21893-1). St Martin.

--The Gallows Land. 1983. 11.95 (ISBN 0-8027-4016-2). Walker & Co.

--Games. LC 76-25413. 1976. 7.95 o.p. (ISBN 0-399-11588-9). Putnam Pub Group.

--Gun in Cheek. 255p. 1982. 15.95 (ISBN 0-698-11180-X, Pub. by Coward). Putnam Pub Group.

--Masques. 224p. 1983. pap. 2.95 (ISBN 0-425-05936-7). Berkley Pub.

--Snowbound. LC 73-87200. 1974. 6.95 o.p. (ISBN 0-399-11264-2). Putnam Pub Group.

Pronzini, Bill & Malzberg, Barry N. Acts of Mercy. LC 77-88405. 1977. 8.95 o.p. (ISBN 0-399-11996-5). Putnam Pub Group.

Pronzini, Bill & Wilcox, Collin. Two-Spot. LC 78-1969. 1978. 8.95 o.p. (ISBN 0-399-12129-3). Putnam Pub Group.

Pronzini, Bill, jt. auth. see Anderson, Jack.

Pronzini, Bill, ed. The Arbor House Treasure of Detective & Mystery Stories from the Great Pulps. 1983. 15.95 (ISBN 0-87795-451-8). Arbor Hse.

--Midnight Specials. 1978. pap. 1.75 o.p. (ISBN 0-380-01941-8, 37903). Avon.

Proper, Churchill. Footwear: Leathercraft. LC 78-185669. (Handicraft Ser.: No. 1). (Illus.). 32p. (Orig.). (gr. 7-12). 1971. lib. bdg. 2.45 incl. catalog cards o.p. (ISBN 0-87157-901-4); pap. 1.25 vinyl laminated covers o.p. (ISBN 0-87157-401-2). SamHar Pr.

--Furniture & Accessories. new ed. LC 76-185671. (Handicraft Ser.: No. 3). (Illus.). 32p. (Orig.). (gr. 7-12). 1971. lib. bdg. 2.45 incl. catalog cards o.p. (ISBN 0-686-01112-0); pap. 1.25 vinyl laminated covers o.p. (ISBN 0-87157-403-9). SamHar Pr.

--Indian Crafts. LC 70-185672. (Handicraft Ser.: No. 4). (Illus.). 32p. (Orig.). (gr. 7-12). 1971. lib. bdg. 2.45 incl. catalog cards o.p. (ISBN 0-87157-904-9); pap. 1.25 vinyl laminated covers o.p. (ISBN 0-87157-404-7). SamHar Pr.

--Leathercraft: Bags, Cases, Purses. LC 72-185670. (Handicraft Ser.: No. 2). (Illus.). 32p. (Orig.). (gr. 7-12). 1971. lib. bdg. 2.45 incl. catalog cards o.p. (ISBN 0-87157-902-2); pap. 1.25 vinyl laminated covers o.p. (ISBN 0-87157-402-0). SamHar Pr.

Propertius. Elegies, 3 bks. Camps, W. A., ed. 1961-67. Bk. 1. text ed. 22.50 (ISBN 0-521-06000-1); pap. 9.95x (ISBN 0-521-29210-7); Bk. 2. text ed. 22.50 (ISBN 0-521-06001-X); Bk. 3. text ed. 17.95 (ISBN 0-521-06002-8). Cambridge U Pr.

--Select Elegies. Postgate, J. P., ed. (Latin). 1881. 5.95x o.p. (ISBN 0-312-65170-8). St Martin.

Propertius, Sextus. The Poems of Sextus Propertius. McCulloch, J. P., tr. LC 78-115490. (Bilingual ed.). 1975. 33.00x (ISBN 0-520-01714-5); pap. 2.95 (ISBN 0-520-02774-4). U of Cal Pr.

Prophet, John. Church Langton & William Hanbury. 1982. 125.00x (ISBN 0-686-99794-8, Pub. by Sycamore Pr England). State Mutual Bk.

Prophit, Penny, jt. auth. see Long, Lynette.

Proppe, Karl H., jt. auth. see Suit, Herman D.

Propper, Alice M. Prison Homosexuality: Myth & Reality. LC 79-48003. 256p. 1981. 24.95x (ISBN 0-669-03628-5). Lexington Bks.

Propper, Eugene M. & Branch, Taylor. Labyrinth. 1983. pap. 6.95 (ISBN 0-14-006683-7). Penguin.

Propst, Nell. Those Strenuous Dames of the Colorado Prairie. (Illus.). 1982. 16.95 (ISBN 0-87108-627-1). Pruett.

Prorr, Manfred & Limbrunner, Alfred. Breeding Birds of Europe: Vol. 1-Divers to Auks. Stoneman, Richard, ed. (Illus.). 327p. 1983. 24.00 (ISBN 0-88072-026-3). Tanager Bks.

Prosch, Harry, jt. auth. see Polanyi, Michael.

Proschan, Frank & Serfling, R. J., eds. Reliability & Biometry: Statistical Analysis of Lifelength. LC 74-78907. (Illus.). x, 815p. 1974. text ed. 38.00 (ISBN 0-89871-159-2). Soc Indus-Appl Math.

Prose, Francine. Animal Magnetism. LC 77-28220. 1978. 8.95 o.p. (ISBN 0-399-12160-9, Pub. by Berkley). Putnam Pub Group.

--Hungry Hearts. 210p. 1983. 12.95 (ISBN 0-686-38841-0). Pacific Search.

--Hungry Hearts. 1983. 12.95 (ISBN 0-394-52767-4). Pantheon.

Proskauer, Julien J. Spook Crooks: Exposing the Secrets of the Propheteers Who Conduct Our Wickedest Industry. LC 70-162517. (Illus.). 1971. Repr. of 1932 ed. 34.00x (ISBN 0-8103-3760-6). Gale.
Prosnak, J., jt. ed. see Muchenberg, B.
Prossdorf. Some Classes of Singular Equations. (North-Holland Mathematical Library: Vol. 17). 1978. 76.75 (ISBN 0-7204-0501-7, North-Holland). Elsevier.
Prosser, Albert L. Nasson: The First Seventy Years. (Illus.). 348p. Date not set. 17.50 (ISBN 0-914016-90-3). Phoenix Pub.
Prosser, David. Peel Your Own Onion. LC 78-65529. 1979. 10.95 o.p. (ISBN 0-89696-030-7, An Everest House Book). Dodd.
Prosser, Eleanor. Hamlet & Revenge. 2nd ed. LC 71-120745. 1971. 15.00x (ISBN 0-8047-0316-7); pap. 5.95x (ISBN 0-8047-0317-5). Stanford U Pr.
Prosser, H. J., jt. auth. see Wilson, A. D.
Prosser, Michael H. The Cultural Dialogue: An Introduction to Intercultural Communication. LC 77-89049. (Illus.). 1978. text ed. 17.95 (ISBN 0-395-24448-X). HM.
Prosser, William L. Selected Topics on the Law of Torts. LC 54-62473. (Thomas M. Cooley Lectures: No. 4). xi, 627p. 1982. Repr. of 1953 ed. lib. bdg. 35.00 (ISBN 0-89941-174-6). W S Hein.
Prosser, William L., et al. Cases & Materials on Torts. 7th Ed. ed. LC 82-7279. (University Casebook Ser.). 1350p. 1982. text ed. write for info. (ISBN 0-88277-066-7). Foundation Pr.
Prostano, Emanuel T. & Prostano, Joyce S. Case Studies in Library-Media Management. (Library Science Text). 100p. 1982. pap. text ed. 13.50x (ISBN 0-87287-344-7). Libs Unl.
--The School Library Media Center. 3rd ed. (Library Science Text Ser.). 200p. 1982. 28.00 (ISBN 0-87287-286-6); pap. text ed. 20.00 (ISBN 0-87287-334-X). Libs Unl.
Prostano, Joyce S., jt. auth. see Prostano, Emanuel T.
Protein Advisory Group of the United Nations System. Nutritional Improvement of Food Legumes by Breeding. Milner, Max, ed. LC 7-28198. 416p. 1975. 47.00 o.p. (ISBN 0-471-70112-2, Pub. by Wiley-Interscience). Wiley.
Proterra, Michael. Homo Spiritualis Nititur Fide: Martin Luther & Ignatius of Loyola, an Analytical & Comparative Study of a Hermeneutic Based on the Heuristic Structure of Discretio. LC 82-21837. 92p. (Orig.). 1983. lib. bdg. 17.50 (ISBN 0-8191-2938-0); pap. text ed. 7.25 (ISBN 0-8191-2939-9). U Pr of Amer.
Prothero, R. M. see Kosinski, L. A.
Prothero, R. Mansell, ed. People & Land in Africa South of the Sahara: Readings in Social Geography. (Illus.). 1972. pap. text ed. 9.95x o.p. (ISBN 0-19-501287-9). Oxford U Pr.
Protheroe, William, et al. Astronomy. (Physical Science Ser.). 464p. 1976. 17.95 (ISBN 0-675-08687-6). Additional supplements may be obtained from publisher. Merrill.
Protheroe, William M., et al. Exploring the Universe. 2nd ed. (Illus.). 480p. 1981. text ed. 25.95 (ISBN 0-675-08154-8). Additional supplements may be obtained from publisher. Merrill.
Prothro, James W. Dollar Decade: Business Ideas in the 1920's. Repr. of 1954 ed. lib. bdg. 15.50x (ISBN 0-8371-2299-6, PRDD). Greenwood.
Prothro, James W., jt. auth. see Matthews, Donald R.
Prottas, Jeffrey M. People-Processing. LC 78-19567. 192p. 1979. 21.95x (ISBN 0-669-02628-X). Lexington Bks.
Protter, M. H. & Morrey, C. B. A First Course in Real Analysis. LC 76-43978. (Undergraduate Texts in Mathematics Ser.). 1977. 26.00 (ISBN 0-387-90215-5). Springer-Verlag.
Protter, Murray H. & Morrey, Charles B., Jr. Analytic Geometry. 2nd ed. (Illus.). 432p. 1975. text ed. 19.95 (ISBN 0-201-05997-5). A-W.
--College Calculus with Analytic Geometry. 3rd ed. LC 76-12800. (Mathematics Ser.). 1977. text ed. 32.95 (ISBN 0-201-06030-2); study guide 4.95 (ISBN 0-201-06036-1); study supplemental 8.95 (ISBN 0-201-06032-9). A-W.
Protzman, John M. Confounded Interest. (Illus.). 44p. (Orig.). 1982. pap. 11.95 (ISBN 0-9608898-0-9, 2-EJD). JMP Mfg.
Proud, Franklin M. The Golden Triangle. LC 77-24120. 1978. 7.95 o.p. (ISBN 0-312-33785-X). St Martin.
Proudfoot, Alice B., ed. Patrick: Sixteen Centuries with Ireland's Patron Saint. (Illus.). 160p. 1983. 19.95 (ISBN 0-02-599280-5). Macmillan.
Proudhon, Pierre J. What Is Property. 1966. 20.00 (ISBN 0-86527-210-7). Fertig.
Proudley, Brian & Proudley, Valerie. Garden Flowers in Colors. (Illus.). 236p. 1980. pap. 6.95 o.p. (ISBN 0-7137-1120-5, Pub. by Blandford Pr England). Sterling.
--Heathers in Color. (Color Ser.). (Illus.). 1974. 9.95 o.p. (ISBN 0-7137-0635-X, Pub by Blandford Pr England). Sterling.
Proudley, Valerie, jt. auth. see Proudley, Brian.
Proulx, E. Annie. The Gardener's Journal & Record Book. Halpin, Anne, ed. (Illus.). 208p. 1983. 15.95 (ISBN 0-87857-461-1, 01-162-0); pap. 9.95 (ISBN 0-87857-462-X, 01-162-1). Rodale Pr Inc.
--Plan & Make Your Own Fences & Gates, Walkways, Walls & Drives. Halpin, Anne, ed. (Illus.). 224p. 1983. 16.95 (ISBN 0-87857-452-2, 14-048-0); pap. 11.95 (ISBN 0-87857-453-0, 14-048-1). Rodale Pr Inc.
Proum, Im, jt. auth. see Huffman, Franklin E.
Prouse, Robert. Ticket to Hell via Dieppe. 1982. 14.95 (ISBN 0-7706-0009-3). Van Nos Reinhold.
Proust, L., jt. auth. see Pitard, J.
Proust, Marcel. A L'Ombre Des Jeunes Filles En Fleurs. (Coll. Folio). 1965. pap. 4.50 (ISBN 0-685-23900-4, 1428). French & Eur.
--Marcel Proust: Selected Letters, 1880-1903. Kolb, Philip, ed. Manheim, Ralph, tr. LC 81-43567. 456p. 1983. 19.95 (ISBN 0-385-14394-X). Doubleday.
--Past Recaptured. Mayor, Andreas, tr. 1970. 10.00 o.p. (ISBN 0-394-43989-9); pap. 5.95 (ISBN 0-394-50649-9). Random.
--Remembrance of Things Past, 3 vols. Moncrieff, C. Scott & Kilmartin, Terence, trs. from Fr. LC 82-40052. Orig. Title: A La Recherche Du Temps Perdu. 1982. Set. pap. 40.00 (ISBN 0-394-71243-9, Vin); pap. 12.95 ea. Vol. 1, 1056p. Vol. 2, 1216p. Vol. 3, 1144p. Random.
--Sweet Cheat Gone. Moncrieff, C. Scott, tr. 1970. pap. 4.65 (ISBN 0-394-70599-8, Vin). Random.
Prout, jt. auth. see Smith.
Prout, George R., Jr., jt. auth. see Bonney, William W.
Prout, H. Thompson & Brown, Douglas T. Counseling & Psychotherapy with Children & Adolescents. 1983. 19.95 (ISBN 0-936166-13-4). Mariner Pub.
Prouty, C. T., ed. George Gascoigne's A Hundredth Sundrie Flowres. LC 43-52910. 304p. 1970. Repr. 18.00x (ISBN 0-8262-0591-7). U of Mo Pr.
Prouty, Charles T. Contention & Shakespeare's 2 Henry V. 1954. 34.50x (ISBN 0-685-69852-1). Elliots Bks.
Prouty, Charles T., ed. see Kyd, Thomas.
Provan, Jill & Glogowski, Maryruth P., eds. Management Media Directory: An Annotated Guide of Commercially Available Audiovisual Programs for Business & Management Schools, in-House Training & Development Programs, Management Consultants, & Human Resource Managers. (A Neal Schuman Book). 412p. 1982. 115.00x (ISBN 0-8103-0170-9). Gale.
Provence, Sally. Guide for the Care of Infants in Groups. LC 67-26025. 1967. pap. 5.75 (ISBN 0-87868-061-6, I-32). Child Welfare.
Provence, Sally & Naylor, Audrey. Early Intervention: Methods & Outcome in a Service-Centered Study. LC 82-48906. 192p. 1983. text ed. 20.00x (ISBN 0-300-02854-7). Yale U Pr.
Provencher, R. G. Arson 1976. 1976. 3.25 (ISBN 0-686-17605-7, TR 76-3). Society Fire Protect.
Provendie, Zina. The Royal Swedish Diet & Weight Control Program. LC 78-55541. (Illus.). 1978. pap. 3.95 o.p. (ISBN 0-448-16186-9, G&D). Putnam Pub Group.
Provensen, Alice & Provensen, Martin. A Book of Seasons. LC 75-36470. (Pictureback Ser). (Illus.). 32p. (ps-1). 1975. pap. 1.50 (ISBN 0-394-83242-6, BYR). Random.
--The Mother Goose Book. LC 76-8548. (Illus.). (gr. 1 up). 1976. 6.95 o.p. (ISBN 0-394-82122-X, BYR); PLB 7.99 (ISBN 0-394-92122-4). Random.
--Our Animal Friends at Maple Hill Farm. LC 74-828. (Illus.). 64p. (gr. k-3). 1974. 3.95 o.p. (ISBN 0-394-82123-8, BYR); PLB 8.99 (ISBN 0-394-92123-2). Random.
Provensen, Alice & Provensen, Martin, illus. Baby's Toys. (Golden Cloth Bks). (Illus.). 8p. (ps). 1972. 1.50 (ISBN 0-307-10747-7, Golden Pr). Western Pub.
--Old Mother Hubbard. LC 76-24176. (Picturebacks Ser.). (Illus.). 32p. (ps-2). 1982. PLB 4.99 (ISBN 0-394-93460-1); pap. 1.50 saddle stitched (ISBN 0-394-83460-7). Random.
Provensen, Martin, jt. auth. see Provensen, Alice.
Provenso, Asterie B., jt. auth. see Provenso, Eugene F., Jr.
Provenso, Eugene F., Jr. & Provenso, Asterie B. The Ford Trimotor. (Model Historic Aircraft Ser.). 1982. 6.95 o.p. (ISBN 0-517-54652-3). Crown.
Provenzano, J., jt. ed. see Bliss, Dorothy E.
Provenzano, Marian D., ed. see Stewart, Elbert.
Provenzano, Marian D., ed. see Wurtzel, Alan.
Provenzo, Asterie & Provenzo, Eugene. World War I: Fokker Triplane DR-1. (Model Aircraft Ser.). 1982. pap. 6.95 o.p. (ISBN 0-517-54731-7). Crown.
Provenzo, Asterie, jt. auth. see Provenzo, Eugene.
Provenzo, Eugene & Provenzo, Asterie. World War I: Spad XIII. 1982. pap. 6.95 o.p. (ISBN 0-517-54730-9). Crown.
Provenzo, Eugene, jt. auth. see Provenzo, Asterie.
Provenzo, Eugene F., Jr., jt. auth. see Button, H. Warren.
Province, Charles M. General Patton's Third Army Speech. (Illus.). 1979. pap. 0.50 o.p. (ISBN 0-932348-04-1). C M Province.
--General Patton's Third Army Speech, Vol. 5. (The Patton Ser.). (Illus.). 1980. pap. 1.00 (ISBN 0-932348-07-6). C M Province.
--Patton: Anatomy of a Warrior, Vol. 4. (The Patton Ser.). 1980. pap. 3.00 (ISBN 0-932348-09-2). C M Province.
--Patton: Anatomy of a Warrior (a Play) 1979. pap. 2.00 o.p. (ISBN 0-932348-06-8). C M Province.
--The Patton Myths. 1979. pap. 2.00 o.p. (ISBN 0-686-52685-6). C M Province.
--The Patton Myths, Vol. 3. (The Patton Ser.). (Illus.). 1980. pap. 3.00 (ISBN 0-932348-08-4). C M Province.
--Pure Patton. (The Patton Ser.: Vol. 2). (Illus.). 1979. pap. 3.00 (ISBN 0-932348-03-3). C M Province.
--The Unknown Patton. (Illus.). 224p. 1982. 20.00 (ISBN 0-686-86048-9). Hippocrene Bks.
Province, Charles M., ed. see Patton, George S., Jr.
Province, Lacy. Lacy's Quilting Design Book. (Illus.). 1978. 2.00 o.p. (ISBN 0-932348-02-5). C M Province.
--Mom's Eat-a Bite-a Pie Recipe Book. (Illus.). 1978. pap. 3.00 o.p. (ISBN 0-932348-01-7). C M Province.
Provincial Archives & Victoria, British Columbia. Dictionary Catalogue of the Library of the Provincial Archives of British Columbia, 8 vols. 1971. Set. lib. bdg. 760.00 (ISBN 0-8161-0912-5, Hall Library). G K Hall.
Provost, Gary. The Freelance Writer's Handbook. 1982. pap. 3.50 (ISBN 0-451-62124-7, Ment). NAL.
--The Pork Chop War. LC 82-9589. 192p. (gr. 6-8). 1982. 9.95 (ISBN 0-02-775180-5). Bradbury Pr.
Provost, James H., ed. Official Ministry in a New Age. 247p. 1981. pap. 8.00x (ISBN 0-943616-05-0). Canon Law Soc.
Provus, Malcolm M. Discrepancy Evaluation: For Educational Program Improvement & Assessment. LC 75-146312. 1971. 23.50 (ISBN 0-8211-1509-X); text ed. 21.25 (ISBN 0-685-04199-9). McCutchan.
Prowler, Don, ed. see National Passive Solar Conference, 2nd Conference, Philadelphia, 1978.
Prowler, Donald, jt. ed. see Cook, Jeffrey.
Prowse, Philip, et al. Exchanges. (Main Course English Ser.: Level 2). (Orig.). 1981. pap. text ed. 8.95x o.p. (ISBN 0-435-28470-3). Heinemann Ed.
Proxmire, William. Uncle Sam: Last of the Bigtime Spenders. 1972. 6.95 o.p. (ISBN 0-671-21432-2). S&S.
Prozesky. A Field Guide to the Birds of Southern Africa. 29.95 (ISBN 0-686-42762-9, Collins Pub England). Greene.
Prpic, George J. Croatia & the Croatians: An Annotated Bibliography. LC 80-66277. (Illus.). 315p. 1982. 16.95 (ISBN 0-910164-05-3); pap. 9.95 (ISBN 0-910164-02-9). Assoc Bk Pubs Guidance.
--South Slavic Immigration in America. (The Immigrant Heritage of America Ser.). 1978. lib. bdg. 13.95 (ISBN 0-8057-8413-6, Twayne). G K Hall.
Prucha, F. P. Broadax & Bayonet: The Role of the United States Army in the Development of the Northwest, 1815-1860. (Illus.). 6.50 (ISBN 0-8446-2760-7). Peter Smith.
Prucha, J., ed. Soviet Studies in Language & Language Behavior. (North-Holland Linguistics Ser.: Vol. 24). 1976. pap. 47.00 (ISBN 0-444-10990-0, North-Holland). Elsevier.
Prudden, B. Bonnie Prudden's Fitness Book: A Picture Guide with Exercise & Reducing Plans. (Illus.). 345p. 1959. 16.50 o.p. (ISBN 0-471-07214-1, Pub. by Wiley-Interscience). Wiley.
Prudden, Bonnie. Exer-Sex. (Illus.). 1980. pap. 4.50 (ISBN 0-553-10698-8). Aquarian Pr.
--How to Keep Your Family Fit & Healthy. (Illus.). 1975. 5.95 (ISBN 0-88349-041-2). Aquarian Pr.
--Teenage Fitness. LC 63-10628. (Illus.). 1965. 13.41i (ISBN 0-06-111380-8, HarpT). Har-Row.
Prudden, P. M. Further Study of Prehistoric Small House-Ruins in the San Juan Watershed. LC 18-15717. 1918. pap. 8.00 (ISBN 0-527-00520-7). Kraus Repr.
Prudden, Suzy. Exercise Program for Young Children. LC 82-40506. (Illus.). 192p. 1983. pap. 6.95 (ISBN 0-89480-371-9). Workman Pub.
--See How They Run: Suzy Prudden's Running Book for Kids. LC 78-71308. (Illus.). (gr. 3 up). 1979. lib. bdg. 5.99 (ISBN 0-448-13126-9, G&D); pap. 3.95 (ISBN 0-448-16828-6). Putnam Pub Group.
Prudden, Suzy & Sussman, Jeffrey. Suzy Prudden's Family Fitness Book. (Illus.). 1978. pap. 4.95 o.p. (ISBN 0-448-14502-2, G&D). Putnam Pub Group.
Prudden, T. M. About Lobsters. LC 62-21299. (Illus.). 1973. pap. 6.95 (ISBN 0-87027-127-X). Cumberland Pr.
Prudential Insurance Company of America. Health Insurance Fundamentals: To Prepare for the Health Insurance License Examination. LC 76-17650. 170p. pap. text ed. 4.95 (ISBN 0-471-01937-2). Krieger.
--Life Insurance Fundamentals: To Prepare for the Life Insurance Agents' License Examination. LC 76-17652. 314p. Repr. of 1976 ed. pap. text ed. 8.95 (ISBN 0-471-01938-0). Krieger.
Prudhoe, J., tr. see Goethe.
Prudhoe, J., tr. see Schiller.
Prudhoe, Stephen. British Polyclad Turbellarians. LC 82-4508. (Synopses of the British Fauna: No. 26). (Illus.). 64p. Date not set. pap. price not set (ISBN 0-521-27076-6). Cambridge U Pr.
Prudhoe, Stephen & Bray, Rodney A. Platyhelminth Parasites of the Amphibia. (Illus.). 218p. 1982. 87.00x (ISBN 0-19-858509-8). Oxford U Pr.
Prudhommeau, Germaine & Guillot, Genevieve. The Book of Ballet. (Illus.). 432p. 1980. 15.95 (ISBN 0-13-079905-X, Spec); pap. 8.95. P-H.
Prudhommeau, Germaine, jt. auth. see Guillot, Genevieve.
Prud'Homme Van Reine, W. F. see Van Reine, W. F. Prud'Homme.
Pruessen, Ronald W., jt. ed. see Miller, Lynn H.
Pruett, James W., compiled by. Studies in Musicology: Essays in History, Style & Bibliography of Music in Memory of Glenn Haydon. LC 76-7574. (Illus.). 1976. Repr. of 1969 ed. lib. bdg. 20.50x (ISBN 0-8371-8883-0, PRSM). Greenwood.
Prugh, Dane G. The Psychosocial Aspects of Pediatrics. LC 81-8289. 300p. 1983. text ed. write for info (ISBN 0-8121-0614-8). Lea & Febiger.
Pruginin, Yoel, jt. auth. see Hepher, Dalfour.
Pruitt. Boreal Ecology. (Studies in Biology: No. 91). 1978. 5.95 o.p. (ISBN 0-7131-2686-8). Univ Park.
Pruitt, Bettye, ed. The Massachusetts Tax Valuation List of, 1171. 1978. lib. bdg. 90.00 (ISBN 0-8161-0245-7, Hall Library). G K Hall.
Pruitt, Bill. Ravine Street. 1977. 1.50 o.p. (ISBN 0-934834-11-3). White Pine.
Pruitt, Fred. A Great Sacrifice. 31p. 1982. pap. 0.25 (ISBN 0-686-36262-4); pap. 1.00 5 copies (ISBN 0-686-37284-0). Faith Pub Hse.
Pruitt, Ida, ed. see T'ai-t'ai, Ning L.
Pruitt, Jim. Coaching Beginning Basketball. (Coaching Ser.). (Illus.). 1980. 12.95 (ISBN 0-8092-7089-7); pap. 7.95 (ISBN 0-8092-7088-9). Contemp Bks.
Pruitt, Raymond M. Fundamentals of the Faith. 1981. 16.95 (ISBN 0-934942-21-8). White Wing Pub.
Pruitt, Robert J. And Then Shall the End Come. 1979. pap. 1.75 (ISBN 0-934942-20-X). White Wing Pub.
--The Death of the Third Nature. 1975. pap. 1.60 (ISBN 0-934942-04-8). White Wing Pub.
--The Kingdom of God & the Church of God. 1977. pap. 1.75 (ISBN 0-934942-09-9). White Wing Pub.
Prunier, S. B. Madame Prunier's Fish Cookery Book. 1971. pap. 3.00 o.p. (ISBN 0-486-22679-4). Dover.
Prunieres, Henry. Monteverdi: His Life & Work. MacKie, Marie D., tr. LC 70-100830. (Illus.). 293p. 1973. Repr. of 1926 ed. lib. bdg. 15.50x (ISBN 0-8371-3996-1, PRMO). Greenwood.
--A New History of Music: The Middle Ages to Mozart. Lockspeiser, Edward, tr. & ed. LC 75-183327. 413p. Date not set. Repr. of 1943 ed. price not set. Vienna Hse.
Prus, Robert C. & Sharper, C. R. Road Hustler: The Career Contingencies of Professional Card & Dice Players. 192p. 1977. 18.95 o.p. (ISBN 0-669-00960-1). Lexington Bks.
Prussin, Labelle. Architecture in Northern Ghana: A Study of Forms & Functions. LC 75-84789. (Illus.). 1969. 30.00x (ISBN 0-520-01613-0). U of Cal Pr.
Prutsker, A., et al. Simulation with Gasp Two: A Fortran Based Simulation Language. (Automatic Computation Ser). 1969. pap. text ed. 19.95 (ISBN 0-13-810424-7). P-H.
Prutskov, Nikita I. Gleb Uspensky. (World Authors Ser.: Russia: No. 190). lib. bdg. 15.95 (ISBN 0-8057-2914-3, Twayne). G K Hall.
Pruyn, John V. Catalogue of Books Relating to the Literature of the Law. 300p. 1982. Repr. of 1901 ed. lib. bdg. 32.50x (ISBN 0-8377-1015-4). Rothman.
Pruyser, Paul W. The Minister As Diagnostician: Personal Problems in Pastoral Perspective. LC 76-8922. 1976. pap. 6.95 (ISBN 0-664-24123-9). Westminster.
--The Play of Imagination. 1983. write for info (ISBN 0-8236-4138-4). Intl Univs Pr.
Pruzham, I. & Kniazeva, V. The Russian Portrait of the Late Nineteenth-Early Twentieth Centuries. 294p. 1980. 90.00x (ISBN 0-686-97600-2, Pub. by Collet's). State Mutual Bk.
Pryce, Dick. Hunting for Beginners: An Introduction to Hunting Guns & Gun Safety. (Illus.). 1978. pap. 5.95 o.s.i. (ISBN 0-695-80931-8). Follett.
Pryce-Jones, David, et al. The World of the Public School. LC 77-72369. 1977. 10.00 o.p. (ISBN 0-312-89230-6). St Martin.
Pryde, A. & Gilbert, M. T. Application of High Performance Liquid Chromatography. 1979. 35.00x (ISBN 0-412-14220-1, Pub. by Chapman & Hall). Methuen Inc.
Pryde, George S., ed. see Scotland. Treaties.
Pryde, Philip R. Conservation in the Soviet Union. LC 72-182025. (Illus.). 325p. 1972. 42.50 (ISBN 0-521-08432-6). Cambridge U Pr.
Pryke, E. J. Redactional Style in the Marcan Gospel. LC 76-52184. (Society for New Testament Studies Monographs: No. 33). 1978. 39.50 (ISBN 0-521-21430-0). Cambridge U Pr.
Pryke, Richard. Public Enterprise in Practice. LC 71-187569. 1972. 32.50 (ISBN 0-312-65450-2). St Martin.
Pryke, Richard & Dodgson, John. The British Rail Problem: A Case Study in Economic Disaster. LC 75-30589. 288p. 1975. lib. bdg. 30.00 o.p. (ISBN 0-89158-521-4). Westview.
Pryor, Andrew J. Browns Ferry Nuclear Plant Fire. 1977. 4.25 (ISBN 0-686-22684-4, TR 77-2). Society Fire Protection.
Pryor, Anthony, jt. auth. see Pearson, Charles.

Pryor, E. Voyage en Provence. (Illus.). 1977. pap. text ed. 3.95x (ISBN 0-582-36038-2); cassette 10.50x (ISBN 0-582-37170-8). Longman.

Pryor, E. J. Mineral Processing. 3rd ed. (Illus.). 1974. Repr. of 1965 ed. 71.75 (ISBN 0-444-20010-X, Pub. by Applied Sci England). Elsevier.

Pryor, Fred. Balances. 224p. 1982. pap. 11.95 (ISBN 0-936602-70-8). Harbor Pub CA.

Pryor, Harold, ed. James K. Polk Cookbook. Armstrong, Emma P. LC 78-60329. (Illus.). 254p. 1978. pap. 7.95 (ISBN 0-9607668-0-4). James K Polk.

Pryor, Karen. Nursing Your Baby. rev. ed. LC 73-4116. (Illus.). 304p. 1973. 12.45i (ISBN 0-06-013443-7, HarpT). Har-Row.

Pryor, Lindsay D. Biology of Eucalyptus. (Studies in Biology: No. 61). 88p. 1976. pap. text ed. 8.95 (ISBN 0-7131-2543-8). E Arnold.

Pryor, Neale. You Can Trust Your Bible. 3.60 (ISBN 0-89137-524-4). Quality Pubns.

Pryor, Pauline. The Faint-Hearted Felon. (Candlelight Regency Ser.: No. 667). (Orig.). 1981. pap. 1.50 o.s.i. (ISBN 0-440-12506-5). Dell.

Pryor, Richard. Cactus Pryor Inside Texas. LC 82-62069. (Illus.). 194p. 1982. 13.95 (ISBN 0-88319-062-1); pap. 9.95 (ISBN 0-88319-063-X). Shoal Creek Pub.

Pryor, Sam & Burnett, John. All God's Creatures: The Autobiography of Sam Pryor. 1981. 10.00 o.p. (ISBN 0-533-04946-6). Vantage.

Pryse, Marjorie, ed. Selected Stories of Mary E. Wilkins Freeman. 1983. 27.50 (ISBN 0-393-01726-5); pap. 5.95 (ISBN 0-393-30106-0). Norton.

Pryse-Phillips, William & Murray, T. J. A Concise Textbook-Essential Neurology. 2nd ed. LC 77-91653. 1982. 32.50 (ISBN 0-87488-740-2). Med Exam.

Prys-Roberts, C. & Vickers, M. D., eds. Cardiovascular Measurement in Anaesthesiology: Proceedings. (European Academy of Anaesthesiology Ser.: Vol. 2). (Illus.). 326p. 1982. pap. 47.20 (ISBN 0-387-11719-9). Springer-Verlag.

Prytherch, R. J. Sources of Information in Librarianship & Information Science. 1983. write for info (ISBN 0-566-03436-0, 06087-9, Pub. by Gower Pub Co England). Lexington Bks.

Prywes, M., jt. ed. see Sela, M.

Przelecki, Marian. The Logic of Empirical Theories. (Monographs in Modern Logic). 1969. 12.50 o.p. (ISBN 0-7100-6230-3). Routledge & Kegan.

Przemieniecki, J. S. Theory of Matrix Structural Analysis. 1968. text ed. 34.00 (ISBN 0-07-050904-2, C). McGraw.

Przetak, Louis. Standard Details for Fire-Resistive Building Construction. (Illus.). 1977. 36.50 (ISBN 0-07-050910-7, P&RB). McGraw.

Przeworska-Rolewicz, D. Shifts & Periodicity for Right Invertible Operators. LC 80-467. (Research Notes in Mathematics Ser.: No. 43). 191p. (Orig.). 1980. pap. text ed. 21.95 (ISBN 0-273-08478-X). Pitman Pub MA.

Przeworski, Adam & Teune, Henry. Logic of Comparative Social Inquiry. (Comparative Studies in Behavioral Science Ser). 1970. 22.95 o.p. (ISBN 0-471-70142-4, Pub. by Wiley-Interscience). Wiley.

Przybylski, Benno. Righteousness in Matthew & His World of Thought. LC 79-41371. (Society for New Testament Studies Monographs: No. 41). 240p. 1981. 27.95 (ISBN 0-521-22566-3). Cambridge U Pr.

Psacharopoulos, George. Higher Education in Developing Countries: A Cost-Benefit Analysis. (Working Papers: No. 440). 129p. 1980. 5.00 (ISBN 0-686-36039-7, WP-0440). World Bank.

Psathas, George, ed. Phenomenological Sociology: Issues & Applications. LC 73-2805. 384p. 1973. 31.50 o.s.i. (ISBN 0-471-70152-1, Pub. by Wiley-Interscience). Wiley.

Psellus, Michael. Fourteen Byzantine Rulers. Sewter, E. R., tr. 1979. pap. 6.95 (ISBN 0-14-044169-7). Penguin.

Pshenichny, B. & Danikin, Y. Numerical Methods in Extremal Problems. 276p. 1978. 8.95 (ISBN 0-8285-0732-5, Pub. by MIR Pubs USSR). Imported Pubns.

Psia, jt. auth. see Abraham, Horst.

Ptacek, William, jt. auth. see Sullivan, Peggy.

Ptolemy, Claudius. Cosmography. 6000.00 (ISBN 0-384-48140-X). Johnson Repr.

Public Archives of Canada. Catalogue of the Public Archives Library of Canada: Collection of Published Material with a Chronological List of Pamphlets. 1979. lib. bdg. 1200.00 (ISBN 0-8161-0316-X, Hall Library). G K Hall.

Public Archives of Canada (Ottawa) Catalogue of the National Map Collection, 16 vols. 1976. Set. lib. bdg. 1490.00 (ISBN 0-8161-1215-0, Hall Library). G K Hall.

Public Citizen Health Research Group, jt. auth. see Laws, Priscilla W.

Public Citizen Litigation Group, jt. auth. see Lasson, Kenneth.

Public Interest Economics Foundation. Attacking Regulatory Problems: An Agenda for Research in the 1980's. Ferguson, Allen R., ed. 1981. prof ref 30.00x (ISBN 0-88410-598-9). Ballinger Pub.

Public Interest Economics Foundation, et al. Benefits of Health & Safety Regulation. Ferguson, Allen R. & Behn, Judith, eds. 296p. 1981. prof ref 30.00x (ISBN 0-88410-721-3). Ballinger Pub.

Public Library Association, jt. auth. see Goals, Guidelines & Standards Committee.

Public Management Institute Staff. Board Member Trustee Handbook. 47.50 (ISBN 0-686-82265-X, 53A). Public Management.

--Direct Mail Fund Raising. Date not set. price not set ring binder. Public Management.

--Grants Administration. 75.00 (ISBN 0-686-82261-7, 33A). Public Management.

--How to Get Better Results from Groups. Date not set. cancelled. Public Management.

--How to Get Corporate Grants. 47.50 (ISBN 0-686-82254-4, 80A). Public Management.

--New Grants Planner: The Four Steps to Funding. Date not set. price not set-ring binder. Public Management.

Public Management Institute Staff, jt. auth. see Conrad, Daniel L.

Public Management Institute Staff, jt. auth. see Gilman, Kenneth.

Public Service Co. of New Mexico for U. S. Department of Energy. Technical & Economic Assessment of Solar Hybrid Repowering: Final Report. 450p. 1981. pap. 49.50x (ISBN 0-89934-083-0, T-044). Solar Energy Info.

Public Service Materials Center, compiled by. Survey of Grant-Making Foundations, 1980-81. 10.00 (ISBN 0-686-37130-5). Public Serv Materials.

Public Service Materials Center, ed. The Survey of Grant-Making Foundations 1983-1984. 1982. 15.95 (ISBN 0-686-37910-1). Public Serv Materials.

Public Service Satellite Consortium. Teleguide: A Handbook for Video Teleconferencing. 92p. 1981. 34.50 (ISBN 0-686-98115-4). Telecom Lib.

Publication Associates, ed. see May, Julian.

Publications Department Staff. The Zoological Society of London 1826-1976 & Beyond: Symposia of the Zoological Society of London, No. 40. Zuckerman, Lord, ed. 1977. 40.00 (ISBN 0-12-613340-9). Acad Pr.

Publisher's Editorial Staff. District of Columbia Court Rules, 2 vols. 1981. 35.00 (ISBN 0-87215-414-9). Michie-Bobbs.

--Indiana Banking & Related Laws. 3rd ed. LC 78-15745. 1977. 50.00, with 1978 suppl o.p. (ISBN 0-672-83720-X, Bobbs-Merrill Law); 1978 suppl. 10.00 o.p. (ISBN 0-672-83721-8). Michie-Bobbs.

Puccini, Giacomo. La Boheme: Opera Guide & Libretto. Bleiler, Ellen, tr. (Illus., Orig.). 1962. pap. 2.75 (ISBN 0-486-20404-9). Dover.

--Puccini's Madama Butterfly. (Opera Libretto Ser.). 64p. (Orig.). 1983. pap. 1.95 (ISBN 0-486-24465-2). Dover.

Puccio, Denise, jt. auth. see Maricondo, Barbara.

Pucelik, R. Frank, jt. auth. see Lewis, Byron A.

Pucell. Matter of Time. 1975. pap. 5.95 (ISBN 0-686-84623-0, Nonpareil Bks). Godine.

Puchala, Donald J., jt. ed. see Hopkins, Raymond F.

Puchala, Donald J., ed. see United Nations Assn. of the U.S.A.

Pucillo, Gladys, compiled by. A Little Book About Baby. 1981. 3.95 (ISBN 0-8378-1932-6). Gibson.

--A Little Book of Friendship. 1981. 3.95 (ISBN 0-8378-1931-8). Gibson.

Puckett, Earl, jt. auth. see Palmer, Arnold.

Puckett, Newbell N. Folk Beliefs of the Southern Negro. LC 68-55780. (Criminology, Law Enforcement, & Social Problems Ser.: No. 22). (Illus.). 1968. Repr. of 1926 ed. 18.00x (ISBN 0-87585-022-7). Patterson Smith.

Puckett, Newbell N., compiled by. Popular Beliefs & Superstitions: A Compendium of American Folklore, 3 vols. 1903p. 1981. Set. lib. bdg. 110.00 (ISBN 0-8161-8585-9, Hall Reference). G K Hall.

Puckett, R. E., jt. auth. see Romanowitz, H. A.

Pudaite, Mawii. Beyond the Next Mountain. 160p. (Orig.). 1982. pap. 5.95 (ISBN 0-8423-0154-2). Tyndale.

Pudaite, Rochunga. My Billion Bible Dream. 1982. pap. 5.95 (ISBN 0-8407-5812-X). Nelson.

Puddepha, D. N. Coarse Fishing Is Easy. (Illus.). 160p. 1970. 2.50 o.p. (ISBN 0-7153-4750-0). David & Charles.

Puddephatt, R. J. The Chemistry of Gold. (Topics in Inorganic & General Chemistry: Vol. 16). 1978. 59.75 (ISBN 0-444-41624-2). Elsevier.

Puech, P. & Krebs, R., eds. International Adalst Symposium: Proceedings, Fourth Symposium. (International Congress Ser.: No. 516). 1981. 63.50 (ISBN 0-444-90154-X). Elsevier.

Pueschal, Siegfried M., jt. ed. see Sadick, Tamah L.

Pueschel, M., jt. auth. see Seigfried, F. R.

Pueschel, Siegfried M. The Young Child with Down Syndrome. 272p. 1983. 29.95x (ISBN 0-89885-120-3). Human Sci Pr.

Puett, jt. auth. see Roman.

Puetz, Belinda E. Networking for Nurses: Intra & Interprofessional Relations. LC 82-20669. 206p. 1982. 22.50 (ISBN 0-89443-670-8). Aspen Systems.

Puetz, Belinda E. & Peters, Faye L. Continuing Education for Nurses: A Complete Guide to Effective Programs. LC 81-2830. 269p. 1981. text ed. 26.95 (ISBN 0-89443-373-3). Aspen Systems.

Puff, C. Richard, ed. Memory Organization & Structure. LC 79-21039. 1979. 34.50 (ISBN 0-12-566750-7). Acad Pr.

Pugach, Noel H. Paul S. Reinsch: Open Door Diplomat in Action. LC 79-1503. (KTO Studies in American History Er.). 1979. lib. bdg. 30.00 (ISBN 0-527-73050-5). Kraus Intl.

Pugachev. Probablility Theory & Mathematical Statistics. Sinitsyna, I. V., tr. Eykhoff, P., ed. 450p. Date not set. 90.00 (ISBN 0-08-029148-1). Pergamon.

Pugel, Thomas A. International Market Linkages & U.S. Manufacturing: An International Perspective. LC 78-24108. 152p. 1979. prof ref 19.50x (ISBN 0-88410-490-7). Ballinger Pub.

Pugh, A., ed. Robot Vision. (International Trends in Manufacturing Technology Ser.). 356p. 1983. 47.50 (ISBN 0-387-12073-4). Springer-Verlag.

Pugh, C. E. & Wei, B. C., eds. Advances in Design & Analysis Methodology for Pressure Vessels & Piping. (PVP Ser.: Vol. 56). 142p. 1982. 34.00 (H00213). ASME.

Pugh, Cedric. Housing in Capitalist Societies. 300p. 1980. lib. bdg. 44.00 (ISBN 0-566-00336-8). Gower Pub Ltd.

Pugh, D., ed. see International Congress of Allergology.

Pugh, D. S., et al. Research in Organizational Behavior. pap. text ed. 6.50x o.p. (ISBN 0-435-82692-1). Heinemann Ed.

Pugh, Diana, jt. ed. see Feldman, Paula R.

Pugh, Eric. A Dictionary of Acronyms, & Abbreviations. rev. ed. pap. 8.95 o.p. (ISBN 0-915794-03-9). Gaylord Prof Pubns.

--Dictionary of Acronyms & Abbreviations, Third. pap. 9.95 o.p. (ISBN 0-915794-05-5). Gaylord Prof Pubns.

--Second Dictionary of Acronyms & Abbreviations: More Abbreviations in Management, Technology & Information Science. 400p. 1974. 20.00 o.p. (ISBN 0-208-01354-7, Archon). Shoe String.

Pugh, H. L., ed. Mechanical Behaviour of Materials Under Pressure. (Illus.). 1970. 112.75 (ISBN 0-444-20043-6, Pub. by Applied Sci England). Elsevier.

Pugh, J. W. & Hippaka, William H. California Real Estate Finance. 3rd ed. (Illus.). 1978. text ed. 24.95 (ISBN 0-13-112680-6). P-H.

Pugh, Meredith, jt. auth. see Perry, Joseph B., Jr.

Pugh, Meredith D. Collective Behavior: A Source Book. 1980. pap. 13.95 (ISBN 0-8299-0317-8). West Pub.

Pugh, Ralph B. Imprisonment in Medieval England. LC 68-12061. (Illus.). 59.50 (ISBN 0-521-06005-2). Cambridge U Pr.

Pugh, W., jt. ed. see Huth, H.

Pu Gill Gwon. The Dynamic Art of Breaking. LC 77-89191. (Ser. 128). 1977. pap. 6.95 (ISBN 0-89750-023-7). Ohara Pubns.

Pugmire, M. C. Experiences in Music for Young Children. LC 76-4304. (gr. 10-12). 1977. pap. text ed. 12.80 (ISBN 0-8273-0567-2); instructor's guide 3.75 (ISBN 0-8273-0568-0); tape cassette 5.95 (ISBN 0-8273-0566-4). Delmar.

Pugmire, Roger L. How to Use Your Dictionary. 88p. 1980. 15.00x (ISBN 0-7121-2163-3, Pub. by Macdonald & Evans). State Mutual Bk.

Pugsley, John A. The Alpha Strategy. 2nd ed. LC 81-50893. 1981. 13.95 (ISBN 0-936906-04-9). Stratford Pr.

Puhek, Ronald E. The Metaphysical Imperative: A Critique of the Modern Approach to Science. LC 82-40244. 166p. (Orig.). 1983. lib. bdg. 20.75 (ISBN 0-8191-2663-2); pap. text ed. 9.75 (ISBN 0-8191-2664-0). U Pr of Amer.

Puhn, Fred. How to Make Your Car Handle. LC 80-85270. 1976. pap. 9.95 (ISBN 0-912656-46-8). H P Bks.

Puhvel, Jaan, jt. ed. see Anderson, William S.

Puhvel, Jaan, ed. see Dumezil, Georges.

Puhvel, Martin. Beowulf & Celtic Tradition. 280p. 1977. text ed. 11.00x o. p. (ISBN 0-88920-043-2, Pub. by Wilfrid Laurier U Pr Canada); pap. text ed. 7.00x (ISBN 0-88920-042-4). Humanities.

Puiboube, Daniel. The Art of Making Miniature Models. LC 77-27999. (Illus.). 1979. 15.00 o.p. (ISBN 0-668-04564-7). Arco.

Puig, Manuel. Eternal Curse on the Reader of These Pages. 1982. 13.50 (ISBN 0-394-52151-X). Random.

--Eternal Curse on the Reader of These Pages. LC 82-40431. 240p. 1983. pap. 3.95 (ISBN 0-394-71384-2, Vin). Random.

--Heartbreak Tango: A Serial. Levine, Suzanne J., tr. from Span. LC 80-6124. Orig. Title: Boquitas Pintadas. 224p. 1981. pap. 3.50 (ISBN 0-394-74660-0, Vin). Random.

Pujadas, Guillermo. Coronary Angiography. (Illus.). 1980. text ed. 42.00 (ISBN 0-07-050912-3). McGraw.

Pujals, Josefina A. El Bosque Indomado...Donde Chilla el Obsceno Pajaro de la Noche. LC 81-69533. 134p. (Orig., Span.). 1982. pap. 15.95 (ISBN 0-89729-304-5). Ediciones.

Pujohn, G., ed. Performance Data Communication Systems & Their Applications. 1982. 55.50 (ISBN 0-444-86283-8). Elsevier.

Pukui, Mary K. & Elbert, Samuel H. Hawaiian Dictionary. rev. ed. Orig. Title: Hawaiian-English Dictionary English-Hawaiian Dictionary. 1971. 20.00 (ISBN 0-87022-662-2). UH Pr.

Pukui, Mary K., jt. auth. see Elbert, Samuel H.

Pukui, Mary K. & Korn, Alfons L., eds. The Echo of Our Song: Chants & Poems of the Hawaiians. Pukui, Mary K. & Korn, Alfons L., trs. from Hawaiian. LC 72-91620. 250p. 1973. 14.00 o.p. (ISBN 0-8248-0248-9); deluxe ed. 30.00 (ISBN 0-8248-0285-3). UH Pr.

Pukui, Mary K. & Korn, Alfons L., trs. The Echo of Our Song: Chants & Poems of the Hawaiians. LC 72-91620. 1979. pap. 4.95 (ISBN 0-8248-0668-9). UH Pr.

Pukui, Mary K., tr. see Kamakau, S. M.

Pukui, Mary K., tr. see Papa, John.

Pukui, Mary K., tr. see Pukui, Mary K. & Korn, Alfons L.

Pukui, Mary K., et al. Place Names of Hawaii. 2nd ed. LC 73-85582. 320p. 1974 (ISBN 0-8248-0208-X). pap. 5.95 (ISBN 0-8248-0524-0). UH Pr.

--The Pocket Hawaiian Dictionary: With a Concise Hawaiian Grammar. LC 74-78865. 280p. 1975. pap. 1.95 (ISBN 0-8248-0307-8). UH Pr.

Pula, Robert, ed. see Korzybski, Alfred.

Puleo, Nicole. Drag Racing. LC 72-5420. (Superwheels & Thrill Sports Bks.). (Illus.). 48p. (gr. 3-6). 1973. PLB 7.95g (ISBN 0-8225-0406-5). Lerner Pubns.

Puleston, Dennis E. The Settlement Survey of Tikal. (Tikal Reports Ser.: No. 13). 1983. write for info. Univ Mus of U PA.

Puleston, W. D. Armed Forces of the Pacific. 1941. text ed. 39.50x (ISBN 0-686-83478-X). Elliots Bks.

Puleston, William D. Influence of Sea Power in World War II. Repr. of 1947 ed. lib. bdg. 17.50x (ISBN 0-8371-3997-X, PUSP). Greenwood.

Pulgar, M., jt. auth. see Timms, W. W.

Pulitzer. The American City: An Urban Odyssey to 11 U. S. Cities. (Illus.). 192p. 1983. pap. 9.95 (ISBN 0-517-54591-8). Crown.

Pullan, Brian. A History of Early Renaissance Italy. LC 72-93030. 363p. 1973. 12.95 o.p. (ISBN 0-312-38290-1). St Martin.

Pullan, Brian, tr. see Tenenti, Alberto.

Pullan, Janet, tr. see Tenenti, Alberto.

Pullar, Philippa. The Shortest Journey. 256p. 1982. 19.95 (ISBN 0-686-83903-X, Pub by Hamish Hamilton England). David & Charles.

Pullein-Thompson, Josephine, et al. Black Beauty's Clan. (Illus.). 288p. (gr. 7-9). 1980. 8.95 (ISBN 0-07-050913-1). McGraw.

--Black Beauty's Family. (Illus.). 288p. (gr. 7-9). 1980. 8.95 (ISBN 0-07-050914-X). McGraw.

Pullen, Jo A., jt. auth. see Faiola, Theodora.

Pullen, Mary-Helen, jt. auth. see Swank, Roy L.

Pulleyblank, Edwin G. The Background of the Rebellion of An Lu-Shan. LC 82-6200. (London Oriental Ser.). (Illus.). x, 264p. Date not set. Repr. of 1955 ed. lib. bdg. 35.00x (ISBN 0-313-23549-X, PUBA). Greenwood.

Pulliam, John D. History of Education in America. 3rd ed. 288p. 1982. pap. text ed. 11.95 (ISBN 0-675-09820-3). Merrill.

Pulliam, William E., et al. America Rediscovered. Incl. Its Economic Life. 7.80 (ISBN 0-395-21949-3); Its Foreign Affairs. 7.80 (ISBN 0-395-21952-3); Its People. 7.80 (ISBN 0-395-21950-7); Its Political Life. 7.80 (ISBN 0-395-21951-5). LC 75-28704. 1976. tchr's guide 8.00 (ISBN 0-395-21948-5). HM.

Pullman, A., jt. ed. see Daudel, R.

Pullman, B. Intermolecular Interactions: From Diatomics to Biopolymers. LC 77-24278. (Perspectives in Quantum Chemistry). 1977. 104.95 (ISBN 0-471-99507-X). Wiley.

Pullman, Bernard, ed. Quantum Mechanics of Molecular Conformations. LC 75-43927. (Perspectives in Quantum Chemistry). 1976. 87.95 (ISBN 0-471-01489-3, Pub. by Wiley-Interscience). Wiley.

Pullon, Peter A. & Miller, Arthur S. Oral Pathology: An Independent Learning Program. 90p. 1974. pap. text ed. 4.75 (ISBN 0-7216-9867-0); filmstrips 250.00 (ISBN 0-7216-9866-2); slides o. p. 375.00 (ISBN 0-7216-9872-7). Saunders.

Pullum, Geoffrey, jt. ed. see Goyvaerts, Didier.

Pulman, Michael B. The Elizabethan Privy Council in the Fifteen Seventies. LC 73-115497. 1971. 34.50x (ISBN 0-520-01716-1). U of Cal Pr.

Pulmer, Karin. Die Dementierte Alternative. 241p. (Ger.). 1982. write for info. (ISBN 3-8204-6271-6). P Lang Pubs.

Pulos, Arthur J. American Design Ethic: A History of Industrial Design. (Illus.). 576p. 1983. 50.00 (ISBN 0-262-16085-4). MIT Pr.

Pulp & Paper Week Staff. Pulp & Paper North American Industry Factbook, 1980-81. (Illus.). 353p. 1980. pap. 135.00 o.p. (ISBN 0-87930-090-6). Miller Freeman.

--Pulp & Paper North American Industry Factbook, 1982-83. (Illus.). 392p. 1982. 145.00 (ISBN 0-87930-090-6). Miller Freeman.

Pulsinelli, Linda. Living Mathematics: A Survey. (Illus.). 576p. 1982. 21.95 (ISBN 0-13-538819-8). P-H.

Pulsinelli, Linda & Hooper, Patricia. Intermediate Algebra. 560p. 1983. pap. text ed. 21.95 (ISBN 0-02-357120-9). Macmillan.

Pulsinelli, Linda, jt. auth. see Hooper, Patricia.

Pulsinelli, Robert W., jt. auth. see Miller, Roger L.

Pulsipher, G., jt. auth. see Rosenow, J.

Pultr, A. & Trnkova, V. Combinatorial, Algebraic & Topological Representation of Categories. (Mathematical Library Ser.: Vol. 22). 1980. 59.75 (ISBN 0-444-85083-X). Elsevier.

Pulver, Harry E. Construction Estimates & Costs. 4th ed. LC 68-30565. (Modern Structure Ser.). (Illus.). 1969. 42.50 (ISBN 0-07-050931-X, P&RB). McGraw.

Pulver, Jeffery. A Biographical Dictionary of Old English Music. LC 69-16666. (Music Ser). 538p. 1973. Repr. of 1927 ed. lib. bdg. 47.50 (ISBN 0-306-71103-6). Da Capo.

Pulver, Jeffrey. Paganini: The Romantic Virtuoso. LC 69-11669. (Music Ser). 1970. Repr. of 1936 ed. lib. bdg. 29.50 (ISBN 0-306-71199-0). Da Capo.

Pulvertaft, R. G. Hand. 3rd ed. (Operative Surgery Ser.). 1977. 109.95 (ISBN 0-407-00618-4). Butterworth.

Pulvino, Charles, jt. ed. see Colangelo, Nicholas.

Pulvino, Charles J. & Colangelo, Nicholas. Exercises in Counseling the Elderly: A Manual to Accompany Counseling for the Growing Years-65 & Over. LC 81-71403. 120p. (Orig.). 1982. pap. 40.95 (ISBN 0-932796-11-7). Ed Media Corp.

Puma, Thomas. The Adventures of Tom & Fiore. 1983. 5.95 (ISBN 0-533-05384-6). Vantage.

Pummer, Reinhard, jt. ed. see Sethi, A. S.

Pun, L, et al. Integrated Automation Practice. LC 74-81330. 368p. 1976. 34.00 (ISBN 0-444-10709-6, North-Holland). Elsevier.

Pun, Pattle P. Evolution: Nature & Scripture in Conflict? 336p. (Orig.). 1982. pap. 9.95 (ISBN 0-310-42561-1). Zondervan.

Punch, M. Progressive Retreat. LC 75-41615. 182p. 1977. 21.95 (ISBN 0-521-21182-4). Cambridge U Pr.

Punch, Maurice, ed. Control in the Police Organization. (Organization Studies: No. 4). 368p. 1983. 30.00x (ISBN 0-262-16090-0). MIT Pr.

Puner, Morton. To the Good Long Life: What We Know About Growing Old. LC 73-80054. 320p. 1974. 10.00x o.p. (ISBN 0-87663-191-X). Universe.

--Vital Maturity: Living Longer & Better. LC 78-68919. 1979. 12.50x (ISBN 0-87663-232-0); pap. 6.95 (ISBN 0-87663-994-5). Universe.

Pungor, E. & Buzas, I., eds. Ion Selective Electrodes: Proceedings of the 3rd Symposium in 1981. (Analytical Chemistry Symposia Ser.: Vol. 8). 1982. 91.50 (ISBN 0-444-99714-8). Elsevier.

Punithalingham, E. Plant Diseases Attributed to Botryodiplodia Theobromae Pat. (Bibliotheca Mycologica: No. 71). (Illus.). 200p. 1980. lib. bdg. 16.00 (ISBN 3-7682-1256-4). Lubrecht & Cramer.

Punnett, Dick. Talk-Along--Count the Possums. LC 81-21773. (Talk Along Bks.). (ps-2). 1982. 9.25 (ISBN 0-516-06581-5). Childrens.

--Talk-Along--Help Jumbo Escape. LC 81-21667. (Talk-Along Bks.). (ps-2). 1982. 9.25 (ISBN 0-516-06584-X). Childrens.

--Talk-Along--Name Lizzy's Colors. LC 82-1172. (Talk-Along Bks.). (ps-2). 1982. 9.25 (ISBN 0-516-06582-3). Childrens.

--Talk-Along: Name Patty's Pets. LC 81-18056. (Illus.). (ps-2). 1982. PLB 9.25g (ISBN 0-516-06583-1). Childrens.

Punnett, R. M. Front Bench Opposition. LC 73-85300. 508p. 1973. 21.50 o.p. (ISBN 0-312-30905-8). St Martin.

Punt, W. & Clark, G. C. Northwest European Pollen Flora, No. 3. 1981. 47.00 (ISBN 0-444-41996-9). Elsevier.

Punt, W., ed. The Northwest European Pollen Flora, No. 1. 1976. 42.75 (ISBN 0-444-41421-5). Elsevier.

--The Northwest European Pollen Flora, No. 2. 1980. 61.75 (ISBN 0-444-41880-6). Elsevier.

Punter, David. Blake, Hegel & Dialectic. (Elementa Ser.: Band XXVI). 268p. 1982. pap. text ed. 23.00x (ISBN 90-6203-694-5, Pub. by Rodopi Holland). Humanities.

Pupo-Walker, Enrique, jt. auth. see Debicki, Andrew.

Puppi, Lionello. Andrea Palladio. LC 74-21496. (Illus.). 456p. 1975. 60.00 o.p. (ISBN 0-8212-0645-1, 039705). NYGS.

--The Villa Badoer at Fratta Polesine. Enggass, Catherine, tr. LC 75-19403. (Corpus Palladianum: Vol. 7). (Illus.). 1978. 42.50x (ISBN 0-271-01203-X). Pa St U Pr.

Puppi, Lionello, ed. Rembrandt. (Art Library Ser.: Vol. 27). 1968. pap. 2.95 o.p. (ISBN 0-448-00476-3, G&D). Putnam Pub Group.

Purcal, J. D. Rice Economy: Employment & Income in Malaysia. (Illus.). 1972. text ed. 12.00x (ISBN 0-8248-0103-2, Eastwest Ctr). UH Pr.

Purcell, Arthur H. The Waste Watchers: A Citizen's Handbook for Conserving Energy & Resources. LC 79-8438. (Illus.). 1980. pap. 5.50 o.p. (ISBN 0-385-14220-X, Anch). Doubleday.

Purcell, E. F., jt. ed. see Bradley, S. E.

Purcell, Edmund S. Life of Cardinal Manning, Archbishop of Westminster, 2 vols. LC 70-126605. (Europe 1815-1945 Ser.). 1534p. 1973. Repr. of 1896 ed. Set. lib. bdg. 115.00 (ISBN 0-306-70050-6). Da Capo.

Purcell, Edward L. The States & Energy Siting, Vol. I. 70p. 1982. pap. 8.00 (ISBN 0-87292-026-7). Coun State Govts.

Purcell, Edwin J. Calculus with Analytic Geometry. 3rd ed. LC 77-7977. (Illus.). 1978. 33.95 (ISBN 0-13-112052-2); solutions manual by patterson 6.95 (ISBN 0-13-112037-9); pap. text ed. 1.00 linear algebra suppl. (ISBN 0-13-112029-8). P-H.

Purcell, Elizabeth, jt. ed. see Bowers, John Z.

Purcell, Elizabeth, jt. ed. see Friedman, Charles P.

Purcell, Elizabeth F., ed. The Role of the University Teaching Hospital: An International Perspective. (Illus.). 258p. 1982. pap. 10.00 (ISBN 0-914362-39-9). J Macy Foun.

Purcell, Elizabeth F., jt. ed. see Bowers, John Z.

Purcell, Elizabeth F., jt. ed. see Bradley, Stanley E.

Purcell, Elizabeth F., jt. ed. see Dalrymple, Willard.

Purcell, Elizabeth F., jt. ed. see Warren, Kenneth S.

Purcell, H. J., jt. auth. see Rees, A. R.

Purcell, Henry, jt. auth. see Playford, John.

Purcell, Hugh. The Spanish Civil War. (Putnam Documentary History Ser.). (Illus.). 128p. 1973. 6.95 o.p. (ISBN 0-399-11238-3). Putnam Pub Group.

Purcell, John W. African Animals. LC 82-9541. (New True Bks.). (Illus.). (gr. k-4). 1982. 9.25g (ISBN 0-516-01665-2). Childrens.

Purcell, Julia A., et al. Heart Attack, What's Ahead? Hull, Nancy R., ed. (Illus.). 68p. (Orig.). 1980. pap. text ed. 5.00 (ISBN 0-939838-02-8). Pritchett & Hull.

Purcell, Julia Ann. Cardiac Catheterization. Hull, Nancy R., ed. (Illus.). 36p. 1982. 4.00 (ISBN 0-939838-10-9). Pritchett & Hull.

Purcell, Julia Ann & Johnston, Barbara. Angina de Pecho. Hull, Nancy R., ed. Gonzalez, Olimpia, tr. (Illus.). 24p. 1982. 3.50 (ISBN 0-686-83978-1). Pritchett & Hull.

Purcell, L. E., ed. Economic Recovery Tax Act: Implications for State Finances. 20p. 1982. pap. 5.00 (ISBN 0-87292-030-5). Coun State Govts.

--Forest Resource Management in the States. 112p. 1982. pap. 8.00 (ISBN 0-87292-028-3). Coun State Govts.

--The States & Energy Siting, Vol. II. 150p. 1982. pap. 8.00 (ISBN 0-87292-027-5). Coun State Govts.

Purcell, L. Edward, ed. State Water Quality Planning Issues. 64p. (Orig.). 1982. pap. 8.00 (ISBN 0-87292-031-3, RM 719). Coun State Govts.

--Suggested State Legislation, 1983, Vol. 42. 395p. (Orig.). 1982. pap. 15.00 (ISBN 0-87292-032-1). Coun State Govts.

Purcell, Sally, selected by. Charles of Orleans. 112p. 1979. text ed. 6.95x o.p. (ISBN 0-902145-68-1, Pub. by Carcanet New Pr England); pap. text ed. 4.95x (ISBN 0-902145-69-X). Humanities.

Purcell, Sally, ed. George Peele: Selected Works. (Fyfield Ser.). 1979. 7.95 o.p. (ISBN 0-902145-68-1, Pub. by Carcanet New Pr England); pap. 4.95 o.p. (ISBN 0-902145-69-X). Humanities.

Purcell, Sally, tr. see Dante.

Purcell, Susan K. The Mexican Profit-Sharing Decision. LC 74-84148. 224p. 1976. 38.50x (ISBN 0-520-02843-0). U of Cal Pr.

Purcell, Wayne. Agriculture Marketing: Systems, Coordination, Cash & Future Prices. (Illus.). 1979. text ed. 20.95 (ISBN 0-8359-0195-5); instrs'. manual avail. (ISBN 0-8359-0196-3). Reston.

Purcell, William P., et al. Strategy of Drug Design: A Guide to Biological Activity. LC 72-13240. 240p. 1973. 20.50 o.p. (ISBN 0-471-70236-6, Pub. by Wiley-Interscience). Wiley.

Purchase, I. F., ed. Mycotoxins. 443p. 1975. 137.00 (ISBN 0-444-41254-9, North Holland). Elsevier.

--Mycotoxins in Human Health: Symposium. LC 72-3778. 306p. 1971. 49.95 o.p. (ISBN 0-470-70232-X). Halsted Pr.

Purchon, R. D. The Biology of the Mollusca. 2nd ed. 1977. 60.00 (ISBN 0-08-021028-7). Pergamon.

Purdom, Charles B. Harley Granville Barker Man of the Theatre, Dramatist & Scholar. LC 72-156205. (Illus.). 1971. Repr. of 1956 ed. lib. bdg. 19.00x (ISBN 0-8371-6155-X, PUGB). Greenwood.

Purdom, P. Walton & Anderson, Stanley H. Ecosystems & Human Affairs. 1980. pap. text ed. 6.50 (ISBN 0-675-08035-5). Merrill.

--Environmental Science: Managing the Environment. (Physics & Physical Science Ser.). 536p. 1980. text ed. 24.95 (ISBN 0-675-08170-X). Additional supplements may be obtained from publisher. Merrill.

--Environmental Science: Managing the Environment. 1983. text ed. 23.95 (ISBN 0-675-20009-1). Additional supplements may be obtained from publisher. Merrill.

Purdue University Industrial Waste Conference, 35th. Proceedings. Bell, John M., ed. LC 77-84415. 994p. 1981. text ed. 69.95 (ISBN 0-250-40363-3). Ann Arbor Science.

Purdum, Jack. C Programming Guide. 1983. pap. 17.95 (ISBN 0-88022-022-8). Que Corp.

Purdy, David, et al, eds. see Prior, Mike, et al.

Purdy, J. M., jt. auth. see Edwards, R. G.

Purdy, James. Color of Darkness. LC 74-26739. 175p. 1975. Repr. lib. bdg. 19.25x (ISBN 0-8371-7874-6, PUCD). Greenwood.

Purdy, Richard Little & Millgate, Michael, eds. The Collected Letters of Thomas Hardy: Vol. 2 1893-1901. (Illus.). 1980. 49.50x o.p. (ISBN 0-19-812619-0). Oxford U Pr.

Purdy, Strother B. The Hole in the Fabric: Science, Contemporary Literature, & Henry James. LC 76-6667. (Critical Essays in Modern Literature Ser.). 1977. 12.95 (ISBN 0-686-31717-3). U of Pittsburgh Pr.

Purdy, Susan. Christmas Gifts Good Enough to Eat. LC 80-28510. (Holiday Cookbooks). (Illus.). 96p. (gr. 4 up). 1981. PLB 9.40 (ISBN 0-531-04314-2); pap. 3.95 (ISBN 0-531-03542-5). Watts.

--Halloween Cookbook. (Holidays Cookbooks Ser). (gr. 4 up). 1977. PLB 9.40 s&l (ISBN -0531-01320-0); 2.95 (ISBN 0-531-01340-5). Watts.

--Holiday Cards for You to Make. LC 67-10375. (Illus.). (gr. 4-9). 1967. 10.89 o.p. (ISBN 0-397-31574-0, JBL-J). Har-Row.

Purdy, Susan G. Jewish Holiday Cookbook. (Holiday Cookbook Ser.). (Illus.). (gr. 4 up). 1979. s&l 8.90 o.p. (ISBN 0-531-02281-1); pap. 2.95 o.p. (ISBN 0-531-03430-5). Watts.

Puri & Meher. Indian Forest Ecology. 2nd. Ed. ed. 179.00x (ISBN 0-686-84457-2, Pub. by Oxford & I B H India). State Mutual Bk.

Puri, Balraj. Jammu & Kasmir: Triumph & Tragedy of Indian Federalisation. 280p. 1981. 32.95x (ISBN 0-940500-47-7, Pub. by Sterling India). Asia Bk Corp.

Puri, G. S., et al. Research Methods in Plant Ecology. 1968. 15.95x (ISBN 0-210-26925-1). Asia.

Puri, M. L. & Sen, P. K. Nonparametric Methods in Multivariate Analysis. LC 79-129052. (Ser. in Probability & Mathematical Statistics). 1971. 53.95x (ISBN 0-471-70240-4, Pub. by Wiley-Interscience). Wiley.

Puri, M. L., ed. Nonparametric Techniques in Statistical Inference. LC 74-116750. (Illus.). 1970. 99.50 (ISBN 0-521-07817-2). Cambridge U Pr.

Puri, Mohinder, ed. see Singer, H. W.

Puri, S. P. Special Theory of Relativity. 1973. text ed. 15.00x o.p. (ISBN 0-210-22586-6). Asia.

Purich, Daniel L., ed. Contemporary Enzyme Kinetics & Mechanisms. LC 82-16265. Date not set. price not set (ISBN 0-12-568050-3). Acad Pr.

Purington, Robert C. Fire Fighting Hydraulics. Cleverdon, Ardelle, ed. (Illus.). 416p. (Orig.). 1974. pap. text ed. 21.95 (ISBN 0-07-050957-3, G); instructor's guide 4.00 (ISBN 0-07-050958-1). McGraw.

Purinton, Carl E. Troy State University Writings & Research, Vol. II, No. 2. 52p. 1971. pap. 1.95 (ISBN 0-686-97226-0). TSU Pr.

Purkart, Josef, ed. see Boncompagno da Signa.

Purkey, William W. Inviting School Success. 1978. pap. 9.95x (ISBN 0-534-00566-7). Wadsworth Pub.

Purkis, Andrew & Hodson, Paul. Housing & Community Care. 58p. 1982. pap. text ed. 9.75x (ISBN 0-7199-1076-5, Pub. by Bedford England). Renouf.

Purkis, Helen M. French Course for West Africa, 4 bks. 1962-65. Bk. 1. text ed. 6.95x (ISBN 0-521-06009-5); Bk. 2. text ed. 6.95x (ISBN 0-521-06010-9); Bk. 3. text ed. 6.95x (ISBN 0-521-06011-7); Bk. 4. text ed. 6.95x (ISBN 0-521-06012-5). Cambridge U Pr.

Purkiser, W. T. Hebrews, James, Peter. Greathouse, William M. & Taylor, Willard H., eds. (Beacon Bible Expositions: Vol. 11). 232p. 1974. 5.95 (ISBN 0-8341-0322-2). Beacon Hill.

--Interpreting Christian Holiness. (Orig.). 1971. pap. 1.25 (ISBN 0-8341-0221-8). Beacon Hill.

Purpel, David & Belanger, Maurice. Curriculum & the Cultural Revolution: A Book of Essays & Readings. LC 76-183259. 300p. 1972. 24.75x (ISBN 0-8211-1509-X); text ed. 22.25x (ISBN 0-686-82934-4). McCutchan.

Purpel, David E & Ryan, Kevin, eds. Moral Education: It Comes with the Territory. LC 76-18041. 1976. 24.75 (ISBN 0-8211-1516-2); text ed. 22.75x (ISBN 0-685-71410-1). McCutchan.

Purpel, David E., jt. ed. see Gress, James R.

Purpura, D. P., et al, eds. Experimental Models of Epilepsy: A Manual for the Laboratory Worker. LC 72-181308. (Illus.). 615p. 1972. 43.00 (ISBN 0-911216-26-X). Raven.

--Neurosurgical Management of the Epilepsies. LC 74-80533. (Advances in Neurology Ser: Vol. 8). 378p. 1975. 35.00 (ISBN 0-911216-88-X). Raven.

Purpura, Dominick & Schade, J., eds. Growth & Maturation of the Brain. (Progress in Brain Research: Vol. 4). (Illus.). 1964. 73.25 (ISBN 0-444-40460-0, North Holland). Elsevier.

Purpura, Dominick P., jt. ed. see Yahr, Melvin D.

Pursel, Margaret S. A Look at Birth. LC 77-13050. (Awareness Bks.). (Illus.). (gr. 3-6). 1977. PLB 4.95g (ISBN 0-8225-1307-2). Lerner Pubns.

Pursell, Carroll, ed. From Conservation to Ecology: The Development of Environmental Concern. LC 72-10945. (Problem Studies in American History Ser.). 1973. pap. 4.95x o.p. (ISBN 0-88295-751-1). Harlan Davidson.

Pursell, Carroll W., Jr., jt. ed. see Kranzberg, Melvin.

Pursell, Margaret S. A Look at Adoption. LC 17-13080. (Awareness Bks.). (Illus.). (gr. 3-6). 1977. PLB 4.95g (ISBN 0-8225-1310-2). Lerner Pubns.

--A Look at Divorce. LC 75-38464. (Awarness Bks.). (Illus.). 36p. (gr. 3-6). 1976. PLB 4.95g (ISBN 0-8225-1301-3). Lerner Pubns.

--A Look at Physical Handicaps. LC 75-38468. (Awareness Bks.). (Illus.). 36p. (gr. 3-6). 1976. PLB 4.95g (ISBN 0-8225-1305-6). Lerner Pubns.

--A Look at the Environment. LC 75-38465. (Awareness Bks.). (Illus.). 36p. (gr. 3-6). 1976. PLB 4.95g (ISBN 0-8225-1302-1). Lerner Pubns.

Pursell, Thomas. Making Fishing Tackle. LC 76-13065. (Early Craft Bks.). (Illus.). (gr. k-3). 1976. PLB 3.95g (ISBN 0-8225-0881-8). Lerner Pubns.

Purser, Harry. Psychology for Speech Therapists. Chapman, Antony & Gale, Anthony, eds. (Psychology for Professional Groups Ser.). 300p. 1982. 49.00x (ISBN 0-333-31855-2, Pub. by Macmillan England). State Mutual Bk.

--Psychology for Speech Therapists. (Psychology for Professional Groups Ser.). 300p. 1982. text ed. 22.25x (ISBN 0-333-31855-2, Pub. by Macmillan England); pap. text ed. 19.25x (ISBN 0-333-31885-4). Humanities.

Pursglove, D. M. Friend of the Great: A Life of D. V. Grigorovich, 1822-1899. 1981. 70.00x o.p. (ISBN 0-86127-218-8, Pub. by Avebury Pub England). State Mutual Bk.

Pursh, Frederick. Flora Americae Septentrionalis. (Historia Naturalis Classica Ser.: 104). 1979. Repr. of 1814 ed. lib. bdg. 48.00 (ISBN 3-7682-1242-4). Lubrecht & Cramer.

Pursley, Duane, jt. auth. see Deems, Eugene F., Jr.

Pursley, Robert D. Introduction to Criminal Justice. 2nd ed. 592p. 1980. text ed. 23.95 (ISBN 0-02-470700-7). Macmillan.

Pursuit, Dan G., jt. auth. see Kenney, John P.

Purta, Judith T. see Branson, Margaret S. & Torney-Purta, Judith.

Purtell, Joseph. The Tiffany Caper. LC 73-93770. 224p. 1974. 6.95 o.p. (ISBN 0-698-10596-6, Coward). Putnam Pub Group.

Purtill, Richard. Thinking About Ethics. 160p. 1976. pap. text ed. 10.95 (ISBN 0-13-917716-7). P-H.

--Thinking About Religion: A Philosophical Introduction to Religion. 1978. pap. text ed. 11.95 (ISBN 0-13-917724-8). P-H.

Purtill, Richard L. The Golden Gryphon Feather. (Science Fiction Ser.). (Illus., Orig.). 1979. pap. 1.75 o.p. (ISBN 0-87997-506-7, UE1506). Daw Bks.

--Philosophically Speaking. 256p. 1975. pap. text ed. 14.95 (ISBN 0-13-662551-7). P-H.

Purtscher, Nora. Rilke: Man & Poet. LC 71-169852. (Illus.). 373p. 1972. Repr. of 1950 ed. lib. bdg. 19.25x (ISBN 0-8371-6247-5, PURI). Greenwood.

Purucker, G. De see De Purucker, G.

Purucker, G. de see De Purucker, G.

Purucker, G. De see De Purucker, G. & Tingley, Katherine.

Purves, Alan C. & Rippere, Victoria. Elements of Writing about a Literary Work: A Study of Response to Literature. (Research Report: No. 9). 10p. (Orig.). 1968. pap. 4.20 (ISBN 0-8141-1316-8); pap. 3.00 members (ISBN 0-686-86408-5). NCTE.

Purves, Alan C., ed. How Porcupines Make Love. (Orig.). 1972. pap. text ed. 17.95 (ISBN 0-471-00694-7). Wiley.

Purves, Alan C., et al, eds. Educational Policy & International Assessment: Implications of the IEA Surveys of Achievement. LC 74-30962. (National Society for the Study of Education, Contemporary Educational Issues Ser). 250p. 1975. 19.00 (ISBN 0-8211-1515-4); pap. text ed. 16.95 (ISBN 0-685-52137-0). McCutchan.

Purves, Alec A. The Medals, Decorations & Orders of the Great War 1914-1918. 200p. 1982. 40.00 (ISBN 0-686-92024-4, Pub. by Picton England). State Mutual Bk.

Purves, D. Trace Element Contamination of the Environment. (Fundamental Aspects of Pollution Ser.: Vol. 1). 1977. 55.50 (ISBN 0-444-41570-X). Elsevier.

Purves, Jock. The Unlisted Legion. 1978. pap. 3.95 (ISBN 0-85151-245-3). Banner of Truth.

Purves, M. J. The Physiology of the Cerebral Circulation. LC 70-169577. (Physiological Society Monographs: No. 28). (Illus.). 40p. 1972. 85.00 (ISBN 0-521-08300-1). Cambridge U Pr.

Purves, M. J., ed. The Peripheral Arterial Chemoreceptors. LC 74-16996. (Illus.). 500p. 1975. 85.00 (ISBN 0-521-20522-0). Cambridge U Pr.

Purves, P. E. & Pilleri, G., eds. Echolocation in Whales & Dolphins. write for info. (ISBN 0-12-567960-2). Acad Pr.

Purves, William & Orians, Gordon. Life. 1000p. 1983. text ed. write for info. (ISBN 0-87150-768-4, 4521). Grant Pr.

Purvis, Arthur J., jt. auth. see Phillips, Donald A.

Purvis, Frederick. Power Tools for Home & Garden. 1973. pap. 4.50 o.p. (ISBN 0-7137-0561-2). Transatlantic.

Purvis, Hoyt. U. S. Policy & the Third World. LC 82-80498. (Policy Research Project Ser.: No. 47). 113p. 1982. 7.50 (ISBN 0-89940-649-1). LBJ Sch Public Affairs.

Purvis, Hoyt, jt. ed. see Weintraub, Sidney.

Purvis, Jennie & Samet, Shelly. Music in Developmental Therapy. (Illus.). 264p. 1976. pap. 19.95 (ISBN 0-8391-0895-8). Univ Park.

Purwin, Sig. The Roller Book. 128p. 1983. pap. 11.95 (ISBN 0-89134-056-4). North Light Pub.

Puryear, Douglas A. Helping People in Crisis: A Practical, Family-Oriented Approach to Effective Crisis Intervention. LC 79-88108. (Social & Behavioral Science Ser.). 1979. text ed. 16.95x (ISBN 0-87589-421-6). Jossey-Bass.

Puryear, Herbert B. The Edgar Cayce Primer: Discovering the Path to Psychic Power. 240p. 1982. pap. 2.95 (ISBN 0-553-22738-6). Bantam.

Puryear, Herbert B. & Thurston, Mark. Meditation & the Mind of Man. rev. ed. 1975. pap. 6.95 (ISBN 0-87604-105-5). ARE Pr.

Pusateri, C. Joseph. Enterprise in Radio: WWL & the Business of Broadcasting in America. LC 79-9598. 378p. 1980. text ed. 23.25 (ISBN 0-8191-0954-1); pap. text ed. 13.50 (ISBN 0-8191-0955-X). U Pr of Amer.

Pusch, Hans. Working Together on Rudolf Steiner's Mystery Dramas. LC 80-67024. (Steiner's Mystery Dramas Ser.). (Illus.). 144p. (Orig.). 1980. pap. text ed. 9.95 (ISBN 0-910142-91-2). Anthroposophic.

Pusch, Hans, tr. see Steiner, Rudolf.

Pusch, Margaret D., et al. Multicultural Education: A Cross-Cultural Training Approach. LC 79-92379. (Illus.). 276p. (Orig.). 1979. pap. text ed. 12.95x (ISBN 0-933662-06-8). Intercult Pr.

Pusch, Ruth, tr. see Steiner, Rudolf.

Pusey, E. B., tr. The Confessions of St Augustine. 379p. 1982. Repr. of 1982 ed. lib. bdg. 20.00 (ISBN 0-8495-0081-8). Arden Lib.

Pusey, Edward B. Daniel the Prophet. 1978. 19.50 (ISBN 0-86524-103-1, 2701). Klock & Klock.

Pusey, Edward B., tr. see Augustine, Saint.

Pusey, James R. China & Charles Darwin. (Harvard East Asian Monographs: No. 100). 543p. 1982. text ed. 25.00x (ISBN 0-674-11735-2). Harvard U Pr.

Pusey, William A. The History & Epidemiology of Syphilis. (Illus.). 110p. 1933. photocopy ed. spiral 10.75x (ISBN 0-398-04400-7). C C Thomas.

Pushkarev, Boris S. & Zupan, Jeffrey M. Urban Space for Pedestrians: A Quantitative Approach: a Report of the Regional Plan Association. LC 75-29242. 272p. 1975. text ed. 27.50x (ISBN 0-262-16063-3). MIT Pr.

Pushkariov, Vasily, jt. ed. see Laurina, Vera.

Pushkin, Alexander. Alexander Pushkin: Complete Prose Fiction. Debreczeny, Paul, tr. from Rus. LC 81-85450. (Illus.). 560p. 1983. 38.50x (ISBN 0-8047-1142-9). Stanford U Pr.

--Boris Godounov. Hayes, Alfred, tr. from Rus. LC 82-70183. (Illus.). 112p. 1982. 19.95 (ISBN 0-670-18198-6, Studio). Viking Pr.

--Boris Godunov. Barbour, Philip L., tr. LC 75-31441. (Columbia Slavic Studies). 1976. Repr. of 1953 ed. lib. bdg. 19.75x (ISBN 0-8371-8522-X, PUBG). Greenwood.

--The Bronze Horseman. Thomas, D. M., tr. from Rus. 1983. pap. 5.95 (ISBN 0-14-042309-5). Penguin.

--Collected Poetry. Arndt, Walter, tr. from Rus. 475p. 1983. 30.00 (ISBN 0-88233-825-0); pap. write for info. (ISBN 0-88233-826-9). Ardis Pubs.

--The Poems Prose & Plays of Pushkin. Yarmolinsky, Avrahm, ed. 1943. 5.95 o.s.i. (ISBN 0-394-60762-7, G62). Modern Lib.

Pushkin, Alexander see Bond, Otto F., et al.

Pushkin, Alexander S. Complete Prose Tales of Pushkin. 1968. pap. 8.95 (ISBN 0-393-00465-1, Norton Lib). Norton.

Pushpadanta. Siva-Mahimna Stotram (the Hymn on the Greatness of Siva) Pavitrananda, Swami, tr. pap. 1.50 (ISBN 0-87481-148-1). Vedanta Pr.

Puskar, A. The Use of High-Intensity Ultrasonics. (Materials Science Monographs: No. 13). 304p. 1982. 70.25 (ISBN 0-444-99690-7). Elsevier.

Puskin, Alexander. Letters of Alexander Pushkin, 3 Vols. in 1. Shaw, J. Thomas, tr. (Illus.). 880p. 1967. pap. 17.50x (ISBN 0-299-04644-3). U of Wis Pr.

Pustilnick, Robert A., jt. auth. see Samuel, Arthur F.

Putallaz, Ann, jt. auth. see Anderson, W. H.

Puterbaugh, Donald L., jt. auth. see Fling, Paul N.

Puth, Robert C. American Economic History. 485p. 1983. 25.95 (ISBN 0-03-050556-9). Dryden Pr.

Puth, Robert C., ed. Current Issues in American Economy, 1980-1981. (Orig.). 1980. pap. text ed. 11.95 (ISBN 0-669-02479-1). Heath.

Puthoff, H., jt. auth. see Torg, R.

Putigny, Bob. Easter Island. LC 75-39804. (Island Ser.). (Illus.). 128p. 1976. pap. 7.95 o.p. (ISBN 0-8467-0164-2, Pub. by Two Continents). Hippocrene Bks.

Putnam, et al. Major Systems of the Human Body. LC 70-128602. 1970. 5.95 o.p. (ISBN 0-913590-38-X). Slack Inc.

Putnam, D. F., jt. auth. see Chapman, L. J.

Putnam, George G. Salem Vessels & Their Voyages, 4 vols. Incl. A History of the Pepper Trade with the Island of Sumatra. Vol. 1 (ISBN 0-88389-105-0); A History of the "George", "Glide", "Taria Topan" & "St Paul", in Trade with Calcutta, East Coast of Africa, Madagascar, & the Philippine Islands. Vol. 2 (ISBN 0-88389-106-9); History of the 'Astrea', 'Mindoro', 'Sooloo', 'Panay', 'Dragon', 'Highlander', 'Shirley', & 'Formosa', with Some Account of Their Masters, & Other Reminiscences of Salem Shipmasters. Vol. 3 (ISBN 0-88389-107-7); A History of the European, African, Australian, & South Pacific Islands Trade As Carried on by Salem Merchants, Particularly the Firm of N. L. Rogers & Brothers. sold with set only 15.00 ea.. LC 30-1353. (Illus.). 680p. 1924-30. 55.00 set (ISBN 0-88389-017-8); 15.00 ea. Essex Inst.

Putnam, George H. Books & Their Makers During the Middle Ages, 2 Vols. 1962. Set. text ed. 50.00x (ISBN 0-391-01060-3). Humanities.

Putnam, H. Philosophical Papers, 2 vols. Incl. Vol. 1. Mathematics, Matter & Method. (Illus.). 32.95 o.p. (ISBN 0-521-20665-0); Vol. 2. Mind, Language & Reality. 39.50 (ISBN 0-521-20668-5); pap. 13.95x (ISBN 0-521-29551-3). 1975. Cambridge U Pr.

--Philosophical Papers: Mathematics, Matter & Methods, Vol. 1. 2nd ed. LC 75-8315. 1979. 39.50 (ISBN 0-521-22553-1); pap. 13.50 (ISBN 0-521-29550-5). Cambridge U Pr.

--Philosophical Papers: Reason, Truth & History, Vol. 3. LC 81-6126. 224p. 1981. 29.50 (ISBN 0-521-23035-7); pap. 9.95 (ISBN 0-521-29776-1). Cambridge U Pr.

--Philosophical Papers: Vol. 3, Realism & Reason. LC 82-12903. 250p. Date not set. price not set (ISBN 0-521-24672-5). Cambridge U Pr.

Putnam, Jackson K. Modern California Politics. Hundley, Norris, Jr. & Schutz, John A., eds. LC 80-80026. (Golden State Ser.). 112p. 1980. pap. text ed. 5.95x (ISBN 0-87835-096-9). Boyd & Fraser.

Putnam, Katherine & Comiskey, Kate, eds. Encyclopedia for the TRS-80, Vol. 4. (Illus.). 272p. (Orig.). 1981. 19.95 (ISBN 0-88006-033-6, EN8104); pap. 10.95 (ISBN 0-88006-034-4, EN8084). Green Pub Inc.

Putnam, Katherine, ed. see Domuret, Allan J., et al.

Putnam, Margaret, jt. auth. see McDannel, Kathleen H.

Putnam, Robert D., jt. auth. see Aberbach, Joel D.

Putnam, S., tr. see Pirandello, Luigi.

Putnam, Sallie. Richmond During War. LC 82-19154. (Collector's Library of the Civil War). 26.60 (ISBN 0-8094-4262-0). Silver.

Putnam, Samuel, ed. The Portable Cervantes. 1957. pap. 14.95 (ISBN 0-670-21012-9). Viking Pr.

Putnam, Samuel, ed. see Rabelais, Francois.

Putnam, Samuel, tr. & intro. by see Cervantes, Miguel.

Putney, Gail J., jt. auth. see Putney, Snell.

Putney, Snell. The Conquest of Society. 1972. pap. 5.95x o.p. (ISBN 0-534-00168-8). Wadsworth Pub.

Putney, Snell & Putney, Gail J. The Adjusted American: Normal Neuroses in the Individual & Society. Orig. Title: Normal Neurosis. 256p. 1972. pap. 1.95i o.p. (ISBN 0-06-080270-7, P270, PL). Har-Row.

Putnik, Edwin. Art of Flute Playing. LC 75-146521. (Illus.). 1970. pap. 10.95 (ISBN 0-87487-077-1). Summy.

Putsep, Ervin. Modern Hospital: International Planning Practices. 682p. 1980. text ed. 89.95 (ISBN 0-85324-141-4). Aspen Systems.

Putter, Irving, tr. see Chateaubriand, Francois-Rene de.

Putterill, Martin & Bloch, Cheree. Providing for Leisure for the City Dweller: A Review of Needs & Processes with Guidelines for Change. (Illus.). 141p. 1978. pap. 16.00x o.p. (ISBN 0-8476-3113-3). Rowman.

Putterman, Allen M., ed. Cosmetic Oculoplastic Surgery. 1982. 64.50 (793418). Grune.

Putterman, Jaydie & Lesur, Rosalynde. Police. (Illus.). 192p. 1983. 19.95 (ISBN 0-03-062429-0); pap. 11.95 (ISBN 0-03-059597-5). HR&W.

Putterman, S. J. Superfluid Hydrodynamics. LC 74-75578. (Low Temperature Physics Ser.: Vol. 3). 443p. 1974. 66.00 (ISBN 0-444-10681-2, North-Holland); pap. 27.75 (ISBN 0-444-10713-4). Elsevier.

Puttock, A. G. Trees & Shrubs for Small Gardens. (Illus.). 5.50x (ISBN 0-392-05056-0, LTB). Sportshelf.

Putz, George & Spectre, Peter. All About Maine. (Illus.). 1979. pap. 10.95 (ISBN 0-89272-060-3, PIC429). Down East.

Putzel, Max. The Man in the Mirror: William Marion Reedy & His Magazine. LC 72-6189. (Illus.). 351p. 1973. Repr. of 1963 ed. lib. bdg. 18.50x (ISBN 0-8371-6453-2, PUMM). Greenwood.

Putzell-Korah, S. The Evolving Consciousness: An Hegelian Reading of the Novels of George Eliot. (Salzburg-Romantic Reassessment Ser.: No. 29). 140p. 1982. pap. text ed. 25.00x (ISBN 0-391-02777-8, Pub. by Salzburg Austria). Humanities.

Puu, T. The Allocation of Road Capital in Two-Dimensional Space: A Continuous Approach. (Studies in Regional Science & Urban Economics: Vol. 5). 1979. 36.25 (ISBN 0-444-85324-3, North Holland). Elsevier.

Puu, Tonu & Wibe, Soren, eds. The Economics of Technological Progress. LC 79-24308. 400p. 1980. 37.50 (ISBN 0-312-23666-2). St Martin.

Puustinen, Toivo. Hello Kid. 1980. pap. 4.95 o.p. (ISBN 0-89260-144-2). Hwong Pub.

Puyana De Palacios, Alicia. The Economic Integration Among Unequal Partners: The Case of the Andean Group. (Pergamon Policy Studies on International Development). (Illus.). 300p. 1982. 40.00 (ISBN 0-08-028822-7). Pergamon.

Pu Yi, Aisin-Gioro. From Emperor to Citizen, Vol. I. 2nd ed. 1980. 7.95 (ISBN 0-8351-0619-5); pap. 6.95 o.p. (ISBN 0-8351-0621-7). China Bks.

--From Emperor to Citizen, Vol. II. 2nd ed. 1980. 7.95 o.p. (ISBN 0-8351-0620-9); pap. 6.95 o.p. (ISBN 0-8351-0622-5). China Bks.

Puynode, Gustave Du see Du Puynode, Gustave.

Puzman, Josef & Porizek, Radoslav. Communication Control in Computer Networks. LC 80-41259. (Wiley Series in Computing). 296p. 1981. 44.95 (ISBN 0-471-27894-7, Pub. by Wiley Interscience). Wiley.

Puzo. Las Vegas. 1977. 2.95 o.p. (ISBN 0-448-12462-9, G&D). Putnam Pub Group.

Puzo, Mario. Fools Die: A Novel. LC 78-9608. 1978. 12.50 o.s.i. (ISBN 0-399-12244-3). Putnam Pub Group.

--The Godfather. 1969. 14.95 (ISBN 0-399-10342-2). Putnam Pub Group.

--The Godfather Papers & Other Confessions. 224p. 1972. 6.95 o.s.i. (ISBN 0-399-10935-8). Putnam Pub Group.

Pyarelal. Mahatma Gandhi, 3 vols. Incl. Vol. I. The Early Phase (1869-96) 875p. cloth 17.00x o.p. (ISBN 0-686-87165-0); Vol. II. The Discovery of Satyagraha. 445p. 55.00x o.p. (ISBN 0-686-87166-9); Vol. V, pt. I. The Last Phase (1946-8) 742p. 13.00x o.p. (ISBN 0-686-87167-7); cloth 18.50x o.p. (ISBN 0-686-91561-5). Greenlf Bks.

Pyatt, G., et al. Social Accounting for Development Planning with Special Reference to Sri Lanka. LC 76-53523. 1978. 37.50 (ISBN 0-521-21578-1). Cambridge U Pr.

Pye, David. Nature & Aesthetics of Design. 160p. 1982. pap. 9.95 (ISBN 0-442-27379-7). Van Nos Reinhold.

--Nature & Art of Workmanship. LC 68-12062. (Illus.). 1968. 29.50 (ISBN 0-521-06016-8); pap. 10.95 (ISBN 0-521-29356-1). Cambridge U Pr.

Pye, K., jt. ed. see Goudie, A. S.

Pye, Lucian W. China: An Introduction. 2nd ed. 384p. 1978. pap. 10.95 (ISBN 0-316-72407-6). Little.

--Redefining American Policy in Southeast Asia. 1982. pap. 3.75 (ISBN 0-8447-1095-4). Am Enterprise.

--Southeast Asia's Political Systems. 2nd ed. (Comparative Asian Government Ser). (Illus.). 128p. 1974. 10.95 (ISBN 0-13-823690-9); pap. text ed. 7.95 (ISBN 0-13-823682-8). P-H.

Pye, Lucien W. Chinese Commercial Negotiating Style. LC 82-14228. (Rand Corporation Research Studies). 112p. 1982. text ed. 17.50 (ISBN 0-89946-168-9); pap. text ed. 6.95 (ISBN 0-89946-171-9). Oelgeschlager.

Pye, Michael. The Study of Kanji. 1971. pap. 24.50 (ISBN 0-89346-007-9, Pub. by Hokuseido Pr.). Heian Intl.

Pye, Michael, jt. ed. see Morgan, Robert.

Pyenson, Lewis. Mathematics, Physical Reality, & Neohumanism in Nineteenth & Early Twentieth Century German Education. LC 82-72156. (Memoirs Ser.: Vol. 150). 1983. pap. text ed. 10.00 (ISBN 0-87169-150-7). Am Philos.

Pyhrr, Stephen A. & Cooper, James R. Real Estate Investment. LC 81-24130. 798p. 1982. text ed. 28.50 (ISBN 0-471-87752-2). Wiley.

Pyk, Ann. The Hammer of Thunder. (Illus.). (gr. 4-9). 1972. PLB 4.86 o.p. (ISBN 0-399-60752-8). Putnam Pub Group.

Pykare, Nina. The Dazzled Heart. (Orig.). 1980. pap. 1.50 o.s.i. (ISBN 0-440-11919-7). Dell.

--The Innocent Heart. (Orig.). 1981. pap. 1.50 o.s.i. (ISBN 0-440-14475-2). Dell.

--Lady Incognita. (Orig.). 1980. pap. 1.50 o.s.i. (ISBN 0-440-14942-8). Dell.

--Love's Folly. (Orig.). 1980. pap. 1.50 o.s.i. (ISBN 0-440-14959-2). Dell.

--The Rake's Companion. (Orig.). 1980. pap. 1.50 o.s.i. (ISBN 0-440-17238-1). Dell.

--The Scandalous Season. (Candlelight Regency Ser.). 1979. pap. 1.50 o.s.i. (ISBN 0-440-18234-4). Dell.

Pyle. The ADA Programming Language. 1981. pap. 17.95 (ISBN 0-686-78673-4). P-H.

Pyle, Donna M. Sioux City. (Illus.). 32p. (Orig.). 1981. pap. 1.00 (ISBN 0-9606944-0-4). Pyle.

Pyle, Ernest W. New Techniques for Welding & Extending Sprinkler Pipes. 1976. 2.50 (ISBN 0-686-17608-1, TR 76-2). Society Fire Protect.

Pyle, Gerald F., ed. New Directions in Medical Geography. Medical Geography Papers from the 75th Anniversary Meeting of the Association of American Geographers, Philadelphia Pa., April 1979. (Illus.). 86p. 1980. 22.50 (ISBN 0-08-025817-4). Pergamon.

Pyle, Howard. Story of King Arthur & His Knights. (Companion Lib.). (Illus.). (gr. 7-9). 2.95 (ISBN 0-448-05472-8, G&D). Putnam Pub Group.

--The Story of the Champions of the Round Table. (Illus.). (ps-4). 1968. pap. 6.00 (ISBN 0-486-21883-X). Dover.

--The Wonder Clock or, Four & Twenty Marvelous Tales, Being One for Each Hour of the Day. (Illus.). (gr. 3-6). pap. 5.95 (ISBN 0-486-21446-X). Dover.

Pyle, Howard, ed. Buccaneers & Marooners of America. LC 78-142007. 1971. Repr. of 1891 ed. 38.00x (ISBN 0-8103-3620-0). Gale.

--Merry Adventures of Robin Hood. (Illus.). (gr. 4-6). Illus. Jr. Lib. 5.95 (ISBN 0-448-05820-0, G&D); Companion Lib. Ed. 2.95 (ISBN 0-448-05473-6); deluxe ed. 8.95 (ISBN 0-448-06020-5). Putnam Pub Group.

Pyle, Howard, ed. see Mallory, Thomas.

Pyle, L., jt. auth. see Barnett, A.

Pylee, M. V. Crisis, Conscience & the Constitution. viii, 175p. (Orig.). 1982. pap. text ed. 8.95x (ISBN 0-686-96961-8, Pub. by Jaisingh & Mehta India). Apt Bks.

Pym, Barbara. Excellent Women. LC 78-19877. 256p. 1980. pap. 3.50i (ISBN 0-06-080512-9, P 512, PL). Har-Row.

--No Fond Return of Love. 250p. 1983. 12.95 (ISBN 0-525-24145-0, 01258-370). Dutton.

--Some Tame Gazelle. 252p. 1983. 12.95 (ISBN 0-525-24178-7, 01258-370). Dutton.

--An Unsuitable Attachment. LC 82-48817. 256p. 1983. pap. 2.84i (ISBN 0-06-080653-2, P 653, PL). Har-Row.

Pym, J. S., ed. see Flett, T. M.

Pyne, Reginald H. Professional Discipline in Nursing. (Illus.). 172p. 1981. pap. text ed. 11.50 (ISBN 0-632-00728-1, B 4056-3). Mosby.

Pynn, Ronald. American Politics: Changing Expectations. 1981. text ed. write for info. (ISBN 0-442-25865-8). Van Nos Reinhold.

Pyrah, G. B. Imperial Policy & South Africa, 1902-1910. LC 74-9170. (Illus.). 272p. 1975. Repr. of 1955 ed. lib. bdg. 17.25x (ISBN 0-8371-7619-0, PYIP). Greenwood.

Pyre, James F. Formation of Tennyson's Style. LC 68-8979. 1968. Repr. of 1921 ed. 8.50x (ISBN 0-87753-033-5). Phaeton.

Pytel, Andrew, jt. auth. see Singer, Ferdinand L.

Q

Q, Mike & Q, Pat. Professional Portrait Photography. (Illus.). 1979. 19.95 (ISBN 0-8174-2457-1, Amphoto); pap. 12.95 o.p. (ISBN 0-8174-2131-9). Watson-Guptill.

Q, Mike, jt. auth. see Q, Pat.

Q, Pat & Q, Mike. The Manual of Slide Duplicating. (Illus.). 1978. 14.95 (ISBN 0-8174-2426-1, Amphoto). Watson-Guptill.

Q, Pat, jt. auth. see Q, Mike.

Qadri, A. A. Muslim Personal Law. pap. 6.50 (ISBN 0-686-18553-6). Kazi Pubns.

Qayyum, A. On Striving to Be a Muslim. pap. 7.50 (ISBN 0-686-63908-1). Kazi Pubns.

Qazi, M. A. ABC Islamic Reader. pap. 2.00 (ISBN 0-686-83566-2). Kazi Pubns.

--Alif Ba Ta Islamic Reader. pap. 2.00 (ISBN 0-686-83570-0). Kazi Pubns.

--Bilal in Hadith. pap. 1.25 (ISBN 0-686-18324-X). Kazi Pubns.

Qing, Ai. The Black Eel. Xianyi, Yang & Friend, Robert C., trs. from Chinese. (Illus.). 103p. (Orig.). 1982. pap. 2.95 (ISBN 0-8351-1043-5). China Bks.

--Selected Poems of Ai Qing. Eoyang, Eugene C., ed. LC 82-47956. 240p. (Orig., Chinese.). 1983. 25.00 (ISBN 0-253-34519-7); pap. 10.95 (ISBN 0-253-20302-3). Ind U Pr.

Qoyawayma, Elizabeth P. see White, Elizabeth, pseud.

Quackenbush, R. Piet Potter on the Run. 48p. 1982. 9.95 (ISBN 0-07-051029-6). McGraw.

--Piet Potter's Hot Clue. 48p. 1982. 9.95 (ISBN 0-07-051030-X). McGraw.

Quackenbush, Robert. The Boy Who Waited for Santa Claus. LC 80-22735. (Easy-Read Story Bks.). (Illus.). 32p. (gr. k-3). 1981. 3.95 (ISBN 0-531-02470-9); s&l 8.60 (ISBN 0-531-04189-1). Watts.

--I Don't Want to Go, I Don't Know How to Act. LC 82-48458. (Illus.). 32p. (gr. k-2). 1983. 7.93i (ISBN 0-397-32033-7, JBL-J); pap. 8.89g (ISBN 0-397-32034-5). Har-Row.

--The Man on the Flying Trapeze: The Circus Life of Emmett Kelly Sr. Told with Pictures & Song! LC 75-5614. (Illus.). 40p. (gr. k-2). 1975. 9.57i (ISBN 0-397-31643-7, JBL-J). Har-Row.

--No Mouse for Me! (Easy-Read Story Bks.). (Illus.). 32p. (gr. k-3). 1981. 3.95 (ISBN 0-531-03541-7); lib. bdg. 8.90 (ISBN 0-531-04303-7). Watts.

--Piet Potter Returns. (gr. 4-6). 1981. lib. bdg. 7.95 (ISBN 0-07-051022-9). McGraw.

--Piet Potter's First Case. (gr. 3-6). 7.95 (ISBN 0-07-051021-0, GB). McGraw.

--Pop! Goes the Weasel & Yankee Doodle: New York in 1776 & Today, with Songs & Pictures. LC 75-28312. (gr. k-3). 1976. 9.57i (ISBN 0-397-31675-5, JBL-J). Har-Row.

--Quick, Annie, Give Me a Catchy Line! (Illus.). 40p. (gr. 3-7). 1983. 8.95 (ISBN 0-13-749762-8). P-H.

--She'll Be Comin' 'round the Mountain. LC 73-2943. (Illus.). 40p. (gr. k-2). 1973. 9.95i (ISBN 0-397-31480-9, JBL-J). Har-Row.

--Stairway to Doom: A Miss Mallard Mystery. (Illus.). 48p. (ps-5). 1983. 8.95 (ISBN 0-686-83442-9). P-H.

--There'll Be a Hot Time in the Old Town Tonight. LC 74-4283. (Illus.). 32p. (gr. 3-7). 1974. 9.57i (ISBN 0-397-31585-6, JBL-J). Har-Row.

Quadagno, Jill S. Historical Perspectives on Aging & Social Policy: Work & Family in Nineteenth Century England. LC 82-11621. (Studies in Social Discontinuity). 1982. 24.50 (ISBN 0-12-569450-4). Acad Pr.

Quade, E. Analysis for Military Decisions. 1970. 34.25 (ISBN 0-444-10014-8). Elsevier.

Quade, Edward S., jt. auth. see Majone, Giandomenico.

Quade, Quentin L., ed. The Pope & Revolution: John Paul II Confronts Liberation Theology. LC 82-4971. xi, 195p. (Orig.). 1982. 11.50 (ISBN 0-89633-059-1); pap. 7.00 (ISBN 0-89633-054-0). Ethics & Public Policy.

Quadflieg, Josef. The Twelve Apostles. O'Connell, Matthew J., tr. from Ger. (Illus.). 156p. (Orig.). (gr. 5-6). 1982. 8.95 (ISBN 0-916134-49-0). Pueblo Pub CO.

Quagliano, James & Vallarino, L. Chemistry. 3rd ed. 1969. ref. ed. 29.95x (ISBN 0-13-128926-8); answers to selected problems 0.25 (ISBN 0-13-128934-9). P-H.

Quagliano, Tony. Fierce Meadows. 24p. 1981. pap. 2.50 (ISBN 0-932136-04-4). Petronium Pr.

Quaife, Milo M., et al. History of the United States Flag. LC 64-2613. (Illus.). 1961. 17.26i (ISBN 0-06-013455-0, HarpT). Har-Row.

Quak, A. Wordkonkordanz zu Denaltmittel und Altniederfrankischen Psalmen und Glossen. (Amsterdamer Publikationen zur Sprache und Literature: No. 22). (Ger.). 1973. pap. text ed. 17.00x o.p. (ISBN 90-6203-427-6). Humanities.

Quale, G. Robina. Eastern Civilizations. 2nd ed. (Illus., Orig.). 1975. 17.95 o.p. (ISBN 0-13-222976-5); pap. text ed. 18.95 (ISBN 0-13-222992-7). P-H.

Qualls, Barry. The Secular Pilgrims of Victorian Fiction: The Novel as Book of Life. LC 82-1165. (Illus.). 234p. 1982. 39.50 (ISBN 0-521-24409-9); pap. 11.95 (ISBN 0-521-27201-7). Cambridge U Pr.

Qualls, P. David, jt. ed. see Masson, Robert T.

Qualman, Al. Blood on the Half Shell. (Illus.). 1982. pap. 6.50 (ISBN 0-8323-0411-5). Binford.

Qualter, Terence H. Graham Wallas & the Great Society. LC 79-1374. 260p. 1980. 26.00 (ISBN 0-312-34213-6). St Martin.

Quammen, David. Zolta Configuration. LC 81-43729. 312p. 1983. 14.95 (ISBN 0-385-17899-9). Doubleday.

Quan, Robert S. & Roebuck, Julian B. Lotus among the Magnolias: The Mississippi Chinese. LC 81-7444. (Illus.). 192p. 1982. 15.00x (ISBN 0-87805-156-2). U Pr of Miss.

Quanbeck, Alton H. & Blechman, Barry M. Strategic Forces: Issues for the Mid-Seventies. (Studies in Defense Policy). 110p. 1973. pap. 4.95 (ISBN 0-8157-7283-1). Brookings.

Quanbeck, Alton H. & Woods, Archie L. Modernizing the Strategic Bomber Force. (Studies in Defense Policy). 1976. 3.95 o.p. (ISBN 0-8157-7281-5). Brookings.

Quandt, Ivan J. Teaching Reading. 1977. 20.50 (ISBN 0-395-30700-7). HM.

Quandt, Richard E. Economics Cumulative Index, Vol. 13. Date not set. 60.00 (ISBN 0-88274-012-1). R & D Pr.

Quandt, Richard E., jt. auth. see Henderson, James.

Quandt, Richard E., jt. auth. see Malkiel, Burton G.

Quandt, Richard E., jt. ed. see Goldfeld, Stephen M.

Quandt, William B. Decade of Decisions: American Policy Toward the Arab-Israeli Conflict, 1967-1976. LC 77-73499. 1977. 14.95 o.p. (ISBN 0-520-03469-4); pap. 8.95x (ISBN 0-520-03536-4). U of Cal Pr.

--Revolution & Political Leadership: Algeria 1954-1968. 1969. pap. text ed. 7.95x (ISBN 0-262-67002-X). MIT Pr.

--Saudi Arabia's Oil Policy. LC 82-73524. 65p. 1982. pap. 5.95 (ISBN 0-8157-7287-4). Brookings.

Quandt, William B., et al. The Politics of Palestinian Nationalism. 1973. 22.50x (ISBN 0-520-02336-6); pap. 4.95 (ISBN 0-520-02372-2, CAMPUS 93). U of Cal Pr.

Quang-Tho. Proton & Carbon NMR Spectra of Polymers, Vol. 1. 1981. 192.00 o.p. (ISBN 0-85501-671-X). Wiley.

Quante, Wolfgang. The Exodus of Corporate Headquarters from New York City. LC 75-19809. (Special Studies). (Illus.). 234p. 1976. 31.95 o.p. (ISBN 0-275-55770-7). Praeger.

Quantum Chemistry, International Congress, 3rd & Sabin, J. R. Proceedings, Pts. 1 & 2. 1004p. 1980. pap. text ed. 67.95x (ISBN 0-471-08810-2, Pub. by Wiley-Interscience). Wiley.

Quantz, Crawford. Methods of Psychic Development. LC 82-83876. 1983. pap. 6.95 (ISBN 0-87728-545-4). Weiser.

Quantz, Johann J. On Playing the Flute. Reilly, Edward R., tr. LC 75-10986. (Illus.). 1975. 23.95 (ISBN 0-02-871940-9); pap. 8.95 (ISBN 0-02-871930-1). Schirmer Bks.

Quaranta, Joseph J., jt. auth. see Riccio, Anthony C.

Quarantelli, E. L. Chemical Disasters: Preparations & Responses at the Local Level. 170p. 1983. text ed. 22.50x (ISBN 0-8290-1289-3). Irvington.

Quarles, J. C., tr. see Leavell, Marta B.

Quarles, J. C., tr. see Sullivan, James L.

Quarles, Jaime C., tr. see Brown, Jamieson-Fausett.

Quarles, Jaime C., tr. see Latourette, Kenneth S.

Quarles, Lemuel C., tr. see Brown, Jamieson-Fausett.

Quarles, Lemuel C., tr. see Latourette, Kenneth S.

Quarmby, F. Banknotes & Banking in the Isle of Man. 1971. 15.00 (ISBN 0-685-51509-5, Pub by Spink & Son England). S J Durst.

Quarrie, Bruce. Napoleon's Campaigns in Miniature: A Wargamer's Guide to the Napoleonic Wars 1796-1815. 1982. 24.95 (ISBN 0-85059-606-8). Aztex.

Quarrie, P. R., tr. see Alfonsi, Petrus.

Quarrington, Paul. Home Game. LC 82-45602. 450p. 1983. 17.95 (ISBN 0-385-18422-0). Doubleday.

Quarto, Charles J. Storytime Blue. 1982. write for info. (ISBN 0-9609344-0-5); pap. 9.95 (ISBN 0-9609344-1-3). G D Kieffer.

Quasem, M. A. Jewels of the Qur'an: Al-Ghazali's Theory. 240p. (Orig.). 1983. pap. 8.95 (ISBN 0-7103-0034-4). Routledge & Kegan.

--The Recitation & Interpretation of the Qur'an: Al-Gharzali's Theory. 124p. (Orig.). 1982. pap. 9.95 (ISBN 0-7103-0035-2). Routledge & Kegan.

--Salvation of the Soul & Islamic Devotions. 200p. (Orig.). 1983. pap. 8.95 (ISBN 0-7103-0033-6, Kegan Paul). Routledge & Kegan.

Quasem, Mohammad A. The Ethics of Al-Ghazali. LC 78-15259. (Monographs in Islamic Religion & Theology). 1978. 35.00x (ISBN 0-88206-021-X). Caravan Bks.

Quasha, George. Traveling in the Castle. (Illus.). 120p. (Orig.). 1983. ltd., signed ed. 20.00 (ISBN 0-930794-53-2); pap. 5.50 (ISBN 0-930794-54-0). Station Hill Pr.

Quasha, George & Rothenberg, Jerome, eds. America a Prophecy: A New Reading of American Poetry from Pre-Columbian Times to the Present. 1974. pap. 4.95 o.p. (ISBN 0-394-71976-X, Vin). Random.

Quastler, Henry, jt. ed. see Morowitz, H.

Quat, Helen. Wonderful World of Freezer Cooking. 5.95 (ISBN 0-8208-0217-4). Hearthside.

Quattlebaum, Julian K. The Great Savannah Races. (Brown Thrasher Ser.). (Illus.). 144p. 1983. 19.95 (ISBN 0-8203-0665-7). U of Ga Pr.

Quattrochi, Joseph. Federal Tax Research. 208p. 1982. pap. text ed. 11.95 (ISBN 0-15-527108-3). HarBraceJ.

Quattrochi, Judy, jt. auth. see Medlen, Lynn.

Quay, Effie A. And Now Infanticide. 2nd ed. 1980. pap. 1.00 (ISBN 0-937930-01-6). Sun Life.

Quay, Herbert C. & Werry, John S. Psychopathological Disorders of Childhood. 2nd ed. LC 78-24238. 1979. text ed. 30.95 (ISBN 0-471-04268-4). Wiley.

Quay, Richard H. & Olevnik, Peter P. The Financing of American Higher Education: A Bibliographic Handbook. price not set (ISBN 0-89774-047-5). Oryx Pr.

Quay, Richard H., compiled by. Index to Anthologies on Postsecondary Education, 1960-1978. LC 79-8286. 1980. lib. bdg. 35.00 (ISBN 0-313-21272-4, QPE/). Greenwood.

Quayle, A. Advances in Mass Spectrometry, Vol. 8. (Advances in Mass Spectrometry Ser.). 1200p. 1980. 428.00 (ISBN 0-471-25987-X, Pub. by Wiley Heyden). Wiley.

Quayle, Eric. Early Children's Books: A Collector's Guide. LC 82-13863. (Illus.). 256p. 1983. text ed. 28.50x (ISBN 0-389-20331-9). B&N Imports.

Quayle, J. R. & Bull, A. T., eds. New Dimensions in Microbiology. Mixed Substrates, Mixed Cultures, & Microbial Communities: Proceedings of a Royal Society Discussion Meeting, November 11-12, 1981. (RSL Philosophical Transactions of the Royal Society of London, Ser. B: Vol. 297, No. 1088). (Illus.). 200p. 1982. text ed. 63.00x (ISBN 0-85403-189-8, Pub. by Royal Soc London). Scholium Intl.

Qubein, Nido. Nido Qubein's Professional Selling Techniques. 1983. 14.95 (ISBN 0-910580-78-2). Farnswth Pub.

Quebedeaux, Ricahard. The New Charasmatics II: How a Christian Renewal Movement Became a Part of the American Religious Mainstream. LC 82-48417. 228p. 1983. pap. 8.95 (ISBN 0-06-066723-0, HarpR). Har-Row.

Quebedeaux, Richard. By What Authority: The Rise of Personality Cults in American Christianity. LC 81-47431. 192p. 1982. 11.95i (ISBN 0-06-066724-9, HarpR). Har-Row.

--I Found It: The Story of Bill Bright and the Campus Crusade. LC 78-20582. (Illus.). 1979. 8.95i o.p. (ISBN 0-06-066727-3, HarpR). Har-Row.

Quebedeaux, Richard, ed. Lifestyle: Conversations with Members of the Unification Church. LC 82-50799. (Conference Ser.: No. 13). (Orig.). 1982. 12.95 (ISBN 0-932894-18-6); pap. 9.95 (ISBN 0-932894-13-5). Unif Theol Seminary.

Queen, Ellery. Copper Frame. Bd. with A Room to Die in. 1981. pap. 2.75 (ISBN 0-451-09978-8, E9978, Sig). NAL.

--The Door Between. Bd. with The Devil to Pay. 1980. pap. 2.50 (ISBN 0-451-11309-8, AE1309, Sig). NAL.

--Double Ellery Queen. 1978. pap. 1.75 o.p. (ISBN 0-451-08025-4, E8025, Sig). NAL.

--Fine & Private Place: A Madman Theory. 1982. pap. 2.25 (ISBN 0-451-11855-3, AE1855, Sig). NAL.

--French Powder Mystery. pap. 2.50 (ISBN 0-451-11925-8, AE1925, Sig). NAL.

--The Killer Touch. Bd. with The Devil's Cook. 1982. pap. 2.75 (ISBN 0-451-11351-9, AE1351, Sig). NAL.

--Roman Hat Mystery. pap. 2.50 (ISBN 0-451-11836-7, AE1836, Sig). NAL.

--The Scarlet Letters. Bd. with The Glass Village. 1981. pap. 2.25 o.p. (ISBN 0-451-09675-4, E9675, Sig). NAL.

--The Siamese Twin Mystery: Special 50th Anniversary Edition. 1979. pap. 1.75 o.p. (ISBN 0-451-08664-3, E8664, Sig). NAL.

--The Spanish Cape Mystery. 1979. pap. 1.75 o.p. (ISBN 0-451-08864-6, E8864, Sig). NAL.

--Ten Days' Wonder. Bd. with The King Is Dead. 1980. pap. 2.25 o.p. (ISBN 0-451-09488-3, E9488, Sig). NAL.

--There Was an Old Woman. Bd. with The Origin of Evil. 1980. pap. 1.95 o.p. (ISBN 0-451-09306-2, J9306, Sig). NAL.

--Wife or Death & the Golden Goose. 1978. pap. 2.50 (ISBN 0-451-11305-5, AE1422, Sig). NAL.

Queen, Ellery, ed. Ellery Queen's A Multitude of Sins. 1978. 8.95 o.s.i. (ISBN 0-8037-2256-7). Davis Pubns.

--Ellery Queen's Circumstantial Evidence. 287p. 1980. 9.95 o.s.i. (ISBN 0-8037-2213-3). Davis Pubns.

--Ellery Queen's Cops & Capers. LC 77-81935. 1977. pap. 1.50 o.s.i. (ISBN 0-89559-001-8). Davis Pubns.

Queen, Ellery, ed. & intro. by. Ellery Queen's Crime Wave: 30th Mystery Annual. LC 75-43963. 1976. 8.95 o.p. (ISBN 0-399-11737-7). Putnam Pub Group.

Queen, Ellery, ed. Ellery Queen's Crimes & Consequences. LC 77-82626. 1977. pap. 1.50 o.s.i. (ISBN 0-89559-002-6). Davis Pubns.

--Ellery Queen's Doors to Mystery. 288p. 1981. 9.95 o.s.i. (ISBN 0-8037-2194-3). Davis Pubns.

--Ellery Queen's Eyewitnesses. 288p. 1983. 12.95 (ISBN 0-385-27911-6). Davis Pubns.

--Ellery Queen's Eyewitnesses. 288p. 1983. 12.95 (ISBN 0-686-84859-4). Dial.

--Ellery Queen's Lost Ladies. 288p. 1983. 12.95 (ISBN 0-385-27915-9). Davis Pubns.

--Ellery Queen's Masks of Mystery. 1978. 8.95 o.s.i. (ISBN 0-8037-2255-9). Davis Pubns.

--Ellery Queen's Scenes of the Crime. 1979. 8.95 o.s.i. (ISBN 0-8037-2301-6). Davis Pubns.

--Ellery Queen's Windows of Mystery. 288p. 1980. 9.95 o.s.i. (ISBN 0-8037-2368-7). Davis Pubns.

--Ellery Queen's Wings of Mystery. 1979. 8.95 o.s.i. (ISBN 0-8037-2300-8). Davis Pubns.

--Ellery Queen's X Marks the Plot. LC 77-81937. pap. 1.95 o.s.i. (ISBN 0-89559-004-2). Davis Pubns.

Queen, Ellery, ed. see Ellin, Stanley.

Queen, Ellery, intro. by see Gardner, Erle S.

Queen, Louise L., jt. ed. see Keller, Rosemary S.

Queen, Richard & Hass, Patricia. Inside & Out: Hostage to Iran, Hostage to Myself. (Illus.). 1981. 13.95 (ISBN 0-399-12645-7). Putnam Pub Group.

Queen, William H., jt. auth. see Reimold, Robert J.

Queens, Ellery. The Dragon's Teeth. Bd. with Calamity Town. 1980. pap. 2.50 (ISBN 0-451-11310-1, AE1310, Sig). NAL.

Quehen, Hugh de see Butler, Samuel.

Quellette, Fernand. A Biography of Edgard Varese. (Illus.). xiv, 270p. 1981. Repr. of 1968 ed. lib. bdg. 27.50 (ISBN 0-306-76103-3). Da Capo.

Queneau, Raymond. Exercises in Style. 2nd ed. Wright, Barbara, tr. from Fr. LC 80-26102. (Illus.). 208p. 1981. 12.95 (ISBN 0-686-86499-9); pap. 4.95 (ISBN 0-8112-0789-7, ND513). New Directions.

--Selected Poems. Savory, Teo, tr. LC 69-13017. (French Ser). (Eng. & Fr., Fr). 1970. 10.00 (ISBN 0-87775-084-X); pap. 4.00 (ISBN 0-686-96911-1). Unicorn Pr.

Quennell, Charles H., jt. auth. see Quennell, Marjorie.

Quennell, Marjorie & Quennell, Charles H. Everyday Things in Ancient Greece. (Illus.). (gr. 7-9). 1954. 6.75 o.p. (ISBN 0-399-20051-7). Putnam Pub Group.

Quennell, Peter. Affairs of the Mind: The Salon in Europe & America from the 18th to the 20th Century. (Illus.). 1980. 14.95 (ISBN 0-915220-57-1). New Republic.

--Customs & Characters: Contemporary Portraits. 1983. 16.00i (ISBN 0-686-82203-X). Little.

--The Profane Virtues: Four Studies of the Eighteenth Century. LC 78-11551. (Illus.). 1979. Repr. of 1945 ed. lib. bdg. 20.75x (ISBN 0-313-21039-X, QUPV). Greenwood.

Quennell, Peter, ed. Marcel Proust. LC 70-153473. 1971. 12.95 o.p. (ISBN 0-671-21013-0). S&S.

Quennell, Peter, ed. see Connolly, Cyril.

Quenzer, Linda F., jt. auth. see Feldman, Robert S.

Quere, Y., jt. auth. see Leteurtre, J.

Quereshi, M. Y. Statistics & Behavior: An Introduction. LC 79-5514. 1980. pap. text ed. 12.50 (ISBN 0-8191-0901-0). U Pr of Amer.

Quertermous, Russell & Quertermous, Steven. Modern Guns Identification & Values. (Illus.). pap. 11.95 (ISBN 0-89145-146-3). Wallace-Homestead.

Quertermous, Steve, ed. Flea Market Trader. 4th, rev. ed. 288p. Date not set. pap. 7.95 (ISBN 0-89145-212-5). Collector Bks.

Quertermous, Steven, jt. auth. see Quertermous, Russell.

Quesnel, Louis B., jt. ed. see Russell, A. D.

Quesnell, Quentin. Cycle A: The Commandments. (The Gospel in the Church). 210p. 1983. pap. 7.95 (ISBN 0-8245-0568-9). Crossroad NY.

--His Word Endures. LC 72-13196. 126p. 1974. pap. 0.95 o.p. (ISBN 0-8189-1111-5, Pub. by Alba Bks). Alba.

Quest, Eica. Design for Murder. LC 80-43004. 1981. 10.95 (ISBN 0-385-17671-6). Doubleday.

Questar, George D. American Foreign Policy: The Lost Consensus. 288p. 1982. 28.95 (ISBN 0-03-061666-2); pap. 12.95 (ISBN 0-03-061664-6). Praeger.

Quester, G. H. Offense & Defense in the International System. LC 76-28329. (Wiley Series in International Relations). 1977. pap. 14.95x (ISBN 0-471-70256-0). Wiley.

Quester, George H., ed. Nuclear Proliferation: Breaking the Chain. LC 80-53960. 258p. 1981. 22.50 (ISBN 0-299-08600-3); pap. text ed. 7.95x (ISBN 0-299-08604-6). U of Wis Pr.

Quiason, Serafin D. English "Country Trade" with the Philippines: 1644-1765. 1966. 4.00x o.p. (ISBN 0-8248-0437-6). UH Pr.

Quible & Johnson. Introduction to Word Processing. 277p. 1981. 16.95 (ISBN 0-686-98089-1). Telecom Lib.

Quible, Zane K. Introduction to Administrative Office Management. 2nd ed. 1980. 20.95 (ISBN 0-316-72884-5); tchr's ed. free (ISBN 0-316-72885-3); study guide 7.95 (ISBN 0-316-72886-1). Little.

Quible, Zane K. & Johnson, Margaret H. Introduction to Word Processing. 1980. text ed. 18.95 (ISBN 0-316-72888-8); tchr's ed. avail. (ISBN 0-316-72889-6). Little.

Quible, Zane K., et al. Introduction to Business Communication. (Illus.). 496p. 1981. text ed. 20.95 (ISBN 0-13-479055-3). P-H.

Quick, J. Fishing the Nymph. 139p. 1959. 17.95 o.s.i. (ISBN 0-471-07162-5, Pub. by Wiley-Interscience). Wiley.

Quick, John. Artist's & Illustrator's Encyclopedia. 2nd ed. LC 77-6700. (Handbook Ser). 1977. 27.95 (ISBN 0-07-051063-6, P&RB). McGraw.

--Dictionary of Weapons & Military Terms. (Illus.). 515p. 1973. 34.95 (ISBN 0-07-051057-1, P&RB). McGraw.

--A Short Book on the Subject of Speaking. (Illus.). 1978. 16.95 (ISBN 0-07-051050-4, P&RB). McGraw.

Quick, Joseph H., et al. Work-Factor Time Standards: Measurement of Manual & Mental Work. (Illus.). 1962. 6.95 o.p. (ISBN 0-07-051061-X). McGraw.

Quick, William D., jt. auth. see Wright, Mildred S.

Quie, Paul G., jt. ed. see Gallin, John I.

Quigley, D. T. National Malnutrition. 1981. 7.95x (ISBN 0-686-76743-8). Regent House.

Quigley, Edward J., jt. auth. see Marker, Carolyn G.

Quigley, Eileen E. Introduction to Home Economics. 2nd ed. (Illus.). 1974. text ed. 18.95x (ISBN 0-02-397200-9). Macmillan.

Quigley, Isabel, tr. see Cassola, Carlo.

Quigley, John. Queen's Royal. 1977. 10.95 o.p. (ISBN 0-698-10756-X, Coward). Putnam Pub Group.

Quigley, John M. & Kemper, Peter. The Economics of Refuse Collection. LC 75-38941. 204p. 1976. prof ref 22.50x (ISBN 0-88410-604-7). Ballinger Pub.

Quigley, John M., jt. ed. see Meyer, John R.

Quigley, Pat. Creative Writing: A Handbook for Teaching Classes Wherever Adults Gather. (Illus.). 98p. 1982. pap. 6.95 (ISBN 0-932910-40-8). Potentials Development.

Quigley, Stacy. Do I Have To? LC 79-23890. (Life & Living from a Child's Point of View Ser.). (Illus.). (gr. k-5). 1980. PLB 13.30 (ISBN 0-8172-1352-X). Raintree Pubs.

Quigley, Stephen P., ed. Language Acquisition. (The Volta Review: Jan. 1966). 2.95 o.p. (ISBN 0-88200-127-2, C2336). Alexander Graham.

Quignon-Fleuret, Dominique. Mathieu. (QLP Ser.). (Illus.). 1977. 7.95 (ISBN 0-517-53086-4). Crown.

Quilan, Hamid, ed. see Sabiq, Sayyed.

Quill, J. Michael. Prelude to the Radicals: The North & Reconstruction During 1865. LC 79-9674. 179p. 1980. text ed. 20.00 (ISBN 0-8191-0978-9); pap. text ed. 9.50 (ISBN 0-8191-0979-7). U Pr of Amer.

Quill, Lawrence L., ed. The Chemistry & Metallurgy of Miscellaneous Materials. (National Nuclear Energy Ser.: Division IV, Vol. 19c). 172p. 1955. pap. 16.00 (ISBN 0-87079-161-3, TID-5212); microfiche 4.50 (ISBN 0-87079-162-1, TID-5212). DOE.

Quiller, Stephen & Whipple, Barbara. Water Media Techniques: Fresh Ideas for Combining Watercolor, Acrylic, Gouache, & Casein. (Illus.). 144p. 1983. 22.50 (ISBN 0-8230-5671-6). Watson-Guptill.

Quiller-Couch, Arthur & Dumaurier, Daphne. Castle D'or. 274p. 1976. Repr. of 1962 ed. lib. bdg. 14.50x (ISBN 0-89244-091-0). Queens Hse.

Quiller-Couch, Arthur, et al, eds. see Shakespeare, William.

Quilligan, E. J. & Kretchmer, Norman, eds. Fetal & Maternal Medicine. LC 79-4345. 1979. 52.50 (ISBN 0-471-50737-7, Pub. by Wiley Medical). Wiley.

Quilligan, Edward J. Current Therapy in Obstetrics & Gynecology. LC 79-65461. (Illus.). 224p. 1980. text ed. 24.50 o.p. (ISBN 0-7216-7414-3). Saunders.

Quilligan, Edward J., jt. auth. see Zuspan, Frederick P.

Quillinan, Edward, jt. auth. see Brydges, Samuel E.

Quilling, Joan, jt. auth. see Martin, Betty B.

Quimby, Ernest. Black Political Dependency in Bedford-Stuyvesant. LC 81-84741. 144p. 1982. 15.00 o.p. (ISBN 0-85345-607-0, CL6070); pap. 5.95 o.p. (ISBN 0-85345-608-9, PB6089). Monthly Rev.

Quimby, Ian M. Material Culture & the Study of American Life. (A Winterthur Bk.). (Illus.). 1978. 12.95x o.p. (ISBN 0-393-05661-9); pap. 7.95x (ISBN 0-393-09037-X). Norton.

Quimby, Ian M., ed. Winterthur Portfolio No. 8: Thematic Issue on Religion in America. (A Winterthur Bk.). (Illus.). 1973. 15.00 (ISBN 0-226-92134-4). U of Chicago Pr.

Quimby, Myrtle. Cougar. LC 67-23452. (Illus.). (gr. 5-9). 1968. PLB 9.57i (ISBN 0-200-71993-9, 315770, AbS-J). Har-Row.

Quin, Louis D. & Verkade, John G., eds. Phosphorus Chemistry: Proceedings in the 1981 International Conference. (ACS Symposium Ser.: No. 171). 1981. write for info. (ISBN 0-8412-0663-5). Am Chemical.

Quinault, R. & Stevenson, J., eds. Popular Protest & Public Order: Six Studies in British History, 1790-1920. LC 74-26213. 256p. 1975. 25.00 (ISBN 0-312-63105-7). St Martin.

Quince, Thelma, jt. ed. see Webb, Terry.

Quincer, Sheldon B. Whitefield's Sermon Outlines. pap. 3.95 o.p. (ISBN 0-8028-1157-4). Eerdmans.

Quincey, Thomas De see De Quincy, Thomas.

Quincy, H. Keith. The Seamy Side of Government: Essays on Punishment & Coercion. LC 78-78400. 1979. pap. text ed. 8.00 (ISBN 0-8191-0707-7). U Pr of Amer.

Quine, W. V. Philosophy of Logic. 1970. pap. 10.95 ref. ed. (ISBN 0-13-663625-X). P-H.

Quine, W. V., ed. Selected Logic Papers. (Orig.). 1966. pap. text ed. 4.50 (ISBN 0-685-19766-2). Phila Bk Co.

Quine, Willard. From a Logical Point of View: Logico-Philosophical Essays. pap. 3.95xi o.p. (ISBN 0-06-130566-9, TB566, Torch). Har-Row.

Quine, Willard van Orman. The Roots of Reference. LC 73-86488. (Carus Lecture Ser.: Vol. 14). 163p. 1974. 16.00x (ISBN 0-87548-123-X). Open Court.

Quine, Willard van Orman see Quine, Willard van Orman.

Quin-Harkin, Janet. Ten-Bay Summer. 1982. pap. 1.95 (ISBN 0-553-22519-7). Bantam.

Quinitchette, Lucille. She. 16p. (Orig.). 1978. pap. 2.00 (ISBN 0-935252-17-7). Street Pr.

Quinlan, Charles, Jr. Orthographic Projection Simplified. rev. ed. (gr. 9-10). 1982. pap. text ed. 6.36 (ISBN 0-87345-057-4). McKnight.

Quinlan, Hamid, ed. see Ali-Nadawi, Abul H.

Quinlan, Hamid, ed. see Badawi, Gamal A.

Quinlan, Hamid, ed. see Boisard, Marcel.

Quinlan, Hamid, ed. see Choudhury, Masudul A.

Quinlan, Hamid, ed. see El Liwaru, Saidi J. & El Liwaru, Maisha Z.

Quinlan, Hamid, ed. see Hazm, Imam Ibn.

Quinlan, Hamid, ed. see Izzidien, Mouel Y.

Quinlan, Hamid, ed. see Sharif, Zeenat.

Quinlan, Hamid, ed. see Siddiqui, Zeba.

Quinlan, Hamid, ed. see Yadegari, Mohammad.

Quinlan, J. Industrial Publicity. Date not set. 19.95 (ISBN 0-442-27781-4). Van Nos Reinhold.

Quinlan, P. M. & Compton, W. V. Espanol Rapido. Hargreaves, P. H., ed. 1971. 6.50 o.p. (ISBN 0-249-44089-X). Transatlantic.

Quinlan, Richard M., jt. auth. see Tanford, J. Alexander.

Quinlan, Sterling. The Hundred Million Dollar Lunch. LC 73-20838. 256p. 1974. 6.95cancelled o.p. (ISBN 0-87955-310-3). O'Hara.

Quinley, Harold E. & Glock, Charles Y. Anti-Semitism in America. 225p. Repr. 9.95 (ISBN 0-686-95027-5). ADL.

Quinly, William J., jt. auth. see Tillin, Alma M.

Quinn, A. D. Design & Construction of Ports & Marine Structures. 2nd ed. 1971. 48.50 (ISBN 0-07-051064-4, P&RB). McGraw.

Quinn, A. James & Griffin, James A. Thoughts for Our Times. LC 79-107233. 1969. pap. 1.95 o.p. (ISBN 0-8189-0174-8). Alba.

Quinn, Alison M., jt. auth. see Quinn, David B.

Quinn, Arthur. The Confidence of British Philosophers: An Essay in Historical Narrative. (Studies in the History of Christian Thought: No. XVII). 1977. text ed. 45.75x o.p. (ISBN 9-0040-5397-2). Humanities.

Quinn, B. G., jt. auth. see Nicholls, D. F.

Quinn, Bernard, jt. auth. see Byers, David.

Quinn, Bernard, et al. Churches & Church Membership in the U. S. 1980: An Enumeration by Region, State & County Based on Data Reported by 111 Church Bodies. 1982. pap. 24.00x (ISBN 0-914422-12-X). Glenmary Res Ctr.

Quinn, Bernetta. Dancing in Stillness. 90p. (Orig.). 1983. pap. 4.95 (ISBN 0-932662-44-7). St Andrews NC.

Quinn, Betty N., jt. ed. see Lawall, Gilbert.

Quinn, Brian S., jt. auth. see Einzig, Paul.

Quinn, Carin. Your Career As a Physician. LC 79-802. 1979. pap. 7.95 (ISBN 0-668-04742-9, 4742); pap. 4.50 (ISBN 0-668-04753-4, 4753). Arco.

Quinn, David B. North America from Earliest Discovery to First Settlement: The Norse Voyages to 1612. (New American Nation Ser.). (Illus.). 1977. 18.22xi (ISBN 0-06-013458-5, HarpT). Har-Row.

Quinn, David B. & Quinn, Alison M. The First Colonists: Documents on the Planting of the First English Settlements in North America, 1584-1590. 199p. 1982. pap. 5.00 (ISBN 0-86526-195-4). NC Archives.

Quinn, Derry. The Limbo Connection. (Crime Ser). 1979. pap. 2.95 (ISBN 0-14-005118-X). Penguin.

--The Solstice Man. LC 77-16762. 1978. 7.95 o.p. (ISBN 0-312-74296-7). St Martin.

Quinn, Edward, jt. ed. see Gassner, John.

Quinn, Edward, tr. see Klein, Charlotte.

Quinn, Edward, tr. see Kung, Hans.

Quinn, James. But Never Eat on a Saturday Night: Behind the Scenes in All Kinds of Great American Restaurants. LC 82-45449. 216p. 1983. pap. 6.95 (ISBN 0-385-18220-1, Anch). Doubleday.

--The Literature of Thoroughbred Handicapping 1965-1982: A Selective Review for the Practioner. LC 82-84680. (Illus.). 176p. 1983. pap. 9.95 (ISBN 0-89650-794-7). Gamblers.

Quinn, Jane B. Everyone's Money Book. 1979. 14.95 o.s.i. (ISBN 0-440-05725-6). Delacorte.

Quinn, John J., jt. auth. see Houston, Neal B.

Quinn, John P. Gambling & Gambling Devices. LC 69-14942. (Criminology, Law Enforcement, & Social Problems Ser.: No. 48). (Illus.). 1969. Repr. of 1912 ed. 12.00x (ISBN 0-87585-048-0). Patterson Smith.

Quinn, John P., jt. auth. see Quinn, Zdenka.

Quinn, Michael A., jt. ed. see Mendelson, Robert E.

Quinn, Michelle. Katharine Gibbs Handbook of Business English. 352p. 1982. 14.95 (ISBN 0-02-911680-5). Free Pr.

Quinn, Mildred D., jt. ed. see Reinhardt, Adina M.

Quinn, Philip L. Divine Commands & Moral Requirements. (Clarendon Library of Logic & Philosophy). 1978. text ed. 33.00x (ISBN 0-19-824413-4). Oxford U Pr.

Quinn, R. J. Sacraments of Growth & Renewal. 1969. pap. 3.95 o.p. (ISBN 0-02-826250-6). Glencoe.

Quinn, Robert P. & Staines, Graham L. Quality of Employment Survey, 1977: Descriptive Statistics, with Comparison Data from the 1969-70 & 1972-73 Surveys. LC 78-71659. (Illus.). 364p. 1979. pap. text ed. 16.00x o.p. (ISBN 0-87944-231-X). Inst Soc. Res.

Quinn, Robert P., et al. The Chosen Few: A Study of Discrimination in Executive Selection. LC 68-64118. 50p. 1968. pap. 5.00 (ISBN 0-87944-058-9). Inst Soc Res.

--The Decision to Discriminate: A Study of Executive Selection. LC 68-65536. 162p. 1968. pap. 7.00x (ISBN 0-87944-062-7). Inst Soc Res.

Quinn, Sandra L. & Kanter, Sanford. America's Royalty: All the President's Children. LC 82-12006. 256p. 1983. lib. bdg. 35.00 (ISBN 0-313-23645-3, QUA/). Greenwood.

Quinn, Sandra L. & Kanter, Sanford B. How to Pass an Essay Examination. 48p. 1982. pap. text ed. 3.95 (ISBN 0-8403-2705-6). Kendall-Hunt.

Quinn, T. A. & Salzman, Ed. California Public Administration. LC 77-93787. 1978. pap. text ed. 4.95 (ISBN 0-930302-15-X). Cal Journal.

--California Public Administration. 2nd ed. (Illus.). 120p. 1982. pap. 4.95 (ISBN 0-930302-51-6). Cal Journal.

Quinn, T. J. Athens & Samos, Lesbos & Chios: 478-404 B. C. 11/1982 ed. 112p. 17.50 (ISBN 0-7190-1295-3). Manchester.

Quinn, T. J., ed. Temperature. (Monographs in Physical Measurement). write for info. (ISBN 0-12-569680-9). Acad Pr.

Quinn, Terence, jt. ed. see Pimsleur, Paul.

Quinn, Thomas. Dairy Farm Management. LC 77-90330. 1980. pap. text ed. 18.80 (ISBN 0-8273-1679-8); instructor's guide 4.25. Delmar.

Quinn, Thomas R. Old-Fashioned Homemade Ice Cream: With 58 Original Recipes. (Illus.). 48p. (Orig.). 1983. pap. 2.95 (ISBN 0-486-24495-4). Dover.

Quinn, Tom. The Working Retrievers: Being an Illustrated Discourse on Retrievers; Their Selection, Breeding, Care & Handling, & New Information on Training Dogs for Hunting & Field Training. (Illus.). 256p. 1983. 24.95 (ISBN 0-525-93287-9, 02423-720). Dutton.

Quinn, Vincent. Hart Crane. (U. S. Authors Ser.: No. 35). 1963. lib. bdg. 10.95 o.p. (ISBN 0-8057-0164-8, Twayne). G K Hall.

Quinn, William A. & Hall, Audley S. Jongleur: A Modified Theory of Oral Improvisation & Its Effects on the Performance & Transmission of Middle English Romance. LC 81-40643. 432p. 1982. lib. bdg. 27.75 (ISBN 0-8191-2320-X); pap. text ed. 15.50 (ISBN 0-8191-2321-8). U Pr of Amer.

Quinn, Zdenka & Quinn, John P. Water Sprite of the Golden Town: Folk Tales of Bohemia. LC 79-163290. (Illus.). (gr. 4 up). 1971. 6.25 (ISBN 0-8255-7537-0); PLB 6.47 (ISBN 0-8255-7538-9). Macrae.

Quinnell, A. J. The Mahdi. 320p. 1983. pap. 3.50 (ISBN 0-449-20168-6, Crest). Fawcett.

--The Snap. LC 82-20802. 272p. 1983. 14.95 (ISBN 0-688-01898-X). Morrow.

Quinney, Richard. Social Existence: Metaphysics, Marxism & the Social Sciences. (Sage Library of Social Research: Vol. 141). 194p. 1982. 22.00 (ISBN 0-8039-0830-X); pap. 10.95 (ISBN 0-8039-0831-8). Sage.

Quinney, Richard, jt. auth. see Beirne, Piers.

Quinn O. S. F., Sr. Bernetta. Randall Jarrell. (United States Authors Ser.). 1981. lib. bdg. 11.95 (ISBN 0-8057-7266-9, Twayne). G K Hall.

Quinones, Nathan, ed. see Silverstein, Ruth, et al.

Quinones, Ricardo J. Dante Alighieri. (World Authors Ser.). 1979. lib. bdg. 13.95 (ISBN 0-8057-6405-4, Twayne). G K Hall.

Quint, Howard H., et al, eds. Main Problems in American History, 1 Vol. 4th ed. 1978. Vol. 1, 382 pgs. text ed. 14.25x (ISBN 0-256-02051-5). Dorsey.

Quint, J. C. Nurse & the Dying Patient. 1973. 9.95x (ISBN 0-02-397230-0). Macmillan.

Quintana, Ricardo. Swift: An Introduction. LC 79-17607. 1979. Repr. of 1955 ed. lib. bdg. 18.50x (ISBN 0-313-22052-2, QUST). Greenwood.

Quintana, Ricardo, ed. & intro. by see Swift, Jonathan.

Quintana, Richard, intro. by see Swift, Jonathan.

Quintana, Richardo. The Mind & Art of Jonathan Swift. 10.50 (ISBN 0-8446-1370-3). Peter Smith.

Quintanilha, A. La Probleme De la Sexualite Chez les Champignons: Recherches Sur le Genre Coprinus. (Illus.). 1968. pap. 16.00 (ISBN 3-7682-0556-8). Lubrecht & Cramer.

Quintanilla, Guadalupe C. & Silman, James B. El Espiritu Siempre Eterno Del Mexico Americano. 1977. pap. text ed. 8.50 o.p. (ISBN 0-8191-0121-4). U Pr of Amer.

Quintas, Louis V., jt. ed. see Gewirtz, Allan.

Quinton, A., tr. see Ajdukiewicz, K.

Quinton, Anthony, ed. Political Philosophy. (Oxford Readings in Philosophy). (Orig.). 1967. pap. 6.95x (ISBN 0-19-875002-1). Oxford U Pr.

Quinton, P. M. & Martinez, J. R., eds. Fluid & Electrolyte Anormalities in Exocrine Glands in Cystic Fibrosis. (Illus.). 1982. 18.75 (ISBN 0-911302-45-X). San Francisco Pr.

Qui-Phiet, Tran. Faulkner & the French New Novelist. LC 80-66067. (Scholarly Monographs). 85p. 1980. pap. 7.50 o.p. (ISBN 0-8408-0503-9). Carrollton Pr.

Quiram, Jacquelyn F., ed. see Whitsitt, Robert E., II.

Quirk. Coal Models & Use in Government Planning. 288p. 1982. 29.95 (ISBN 0-03-061576-3). Praeger.

Quirk, Cathleen. Rue & Grace: Poems. 64p. 1981. 13.95 (ISBN 0-89594-054-X); pap. 3.95 (ISBN 0-89594-055-8). Crossing Pr.

Quirk, James & Saposnik, R. Introduction to General Equilibrium Theory & Welfare Economics. (Economics Handbook). 1968. text ed. 37.50 (ISBN 0-07-051076-8, C). McGraw.

Quirk, James, jt. auth. see McDougall, Duncan.

Quirk, James P. Intermediate Microeconomics. LC 75-34009. (Illus.). 448p. 1976. text ed. 21.95 (ISBN 0-574-19265-4, 13-2265); instr's guide avail. (ISBN 0-574-19266-2, 13-2266); mathematical notes 3.95 (ISBN 0-574-19267-0, 13-2267). SRA.

Quirk, James P. & McDougall, Duncan. Microeconomics. 1981. pap. text ed. 14.95 (ISBN 0-574-19410-X, 13-2410); instr's guide avail. (ISBN 0-574-19411-8, 13-2411). SRA.

Quirk, James P., jt. auth. see McDougall, Duncan.

Quirk, John E. No Red Ribbons. 1965. 5.95 (ISBN 0-8159-6306-8). Devin.

Quirk, John P. & Worzbyt, John C. The Assessment of Behavior Problem Children: A Systematic Behavioral Approach. (Illus.). 212p. 1983. 19.75x (ISBN 0-398-04790-1). C C Thomas.

Quirk, Lawrence J. The Films of Warren Beatty. (Illus.). 1979. 14.95 (ISBN 0-8065-0670-9); pap. 7.95 (ISBN 0-8065-0758-6). Citadel Pr.

Quirk, Leslie W. How to Write a Short Story. 77p. 1982. Repr. of 1911 ed. lib. bdg. 25.00 (ISBN 0-89987-675-7). Darby Bks.

Quirk, R., et al. Grammar of Contemporary English. 1120p. 1972. text ed. 49.00x (ISBN 0-582-52444-X). Longman.

Quirk, Randolph. Style & Communication in the English Language. 160p. 1982. pap. text ed. 12.95 (ISBN 0-7131-6260-0). E Arnold.

Quirk, Randolph & Greenbaum, Sidney. A Concise Grammar of Contemporary English. 484p. 1973. text ed. 21.95 (ISBN 0-15-512930-9, HC). HarBraceJ.

Quirk, Randolph & Wrenn, C. L. An Old English Grammar. 2nd ed. 166p. 1973. pap. 10.95x (ISBN 0-416-77240-4). Methuen Inc.

Quirk, Robert E. Affair of Honor: Woodrow Wilson & the Occupation of Vera Cruz. 1967. pap. 4.95 (ISBN 0-393-00390-6, Norton Lib). Norton.

Quirk, Thomas C., Jr. & Gundy, Samuel C. Reptiles & Amphibians Coloring Book. (Illus.). 48p. (Orig.). 1981. pap. 2.50 (ISBN 0-486-24111-4). Dover.

Quirk, Tom. Melville's Confidence Man: From Knave to Knight. LC 82-2824. 184p. 1982. 18.00 (ISBN 0-8262-0370-1). U of Mo Pr.

Quirke, Lillian M. The Rug Book: How to Make All Kinds of Rugs. (Creative Handcrafts Ser.). (Illus.). 1980. 16.95 o.p. (ISBN 0-13-783704-6, Spec); pap. 8.95 o.p. (ISBN 0-686-96842-5). P-H.

Quiroga, Horacio. The Decapitated Chicken & Other Stories. Peden, Margaret S., tr. from Sp. (Texas Pan American Ser). (Illus.). 213p. 1976. 12.95 o.p. (ISBN 0-292-77514-8). U of Tex Pr.

Quiros, T. E. Por Sendas Biblicas. 162p. (Span.). 1978. pap. 2.50 (ISBN 0-311-08753-1). Casa Bautista.

Quiroz, Adrian Gonzalez. Llegando Al Alcoholico. 1979. pap. 1.10 (ISBN 0-311-46077-1). Casa Bautista.

Quisenberry, James D., ed. & intro. by. Changing Family Lifestyles: Their Effect on Children. (Illus.). 64p. 1982. pap. 5.75 (ISBN 0-87173-100-2). ACEI.

Quisling, Ronald G. Correlative Neuroradiology. LC 79-26947. 1980. 65.00x (ISBN 0-471-05737-1, Pub. by Wiley Medical). Wiley.

Quispel, A. Biology of Nitrogen Fixation. (Frontiers of Biology Ser.: Vol. 33). 769p. 1974. 133.25 (ISBN 0-444-10630-8, North-Holland). Elsevier.

Quispel, Gilles. The Secret Book of Revelation: The Apocalypse of St. John The Divine. LC 78-6436. (Illus.). 1979. 39.95 o.p. (ISBN 0-07-051080-6). McGraw.

Quisumbing, Purificacion V., jt. ed. see Anand, R. P.

Quittner, Pal. Problems, Programs, Processing, Results. LC 77-70310. 381p. 1977. 35.00x o.s.i. (ISBN 0-8448-1085-1). Crane-Russak Co.

Quo, F. Q., ed. Politics of the Pacific Nations. (Replica Edition Ser.). 275p. 1983. softcover 20.00x (ISBN 0-86531-951-0). Westview.

Quo, James C. English-Chinese Dictionary, Romanized. 323p. 15.00 (ISBN 0-87557-008-9, 008-9). Saphrograph.

Quoist, Michel. I've Met Jesus Christ. LC 73-79643. 160p. 1975. pap. 3.50 (ISBN 0-385-02802-4, Im). Doubleday.

--With Open Heart. 264p. (Orig.). 1983. pap. 8.95 (ISBN 0-8245-0569-7). Crossroad NY.

Quraishi, M. Sayeed. Biochemical Insect Control: Its Impact on Economy, Environment & Natural Selection. LC 76-29701. 1977. 37.95x o.s.i. (ISBN 0-471-70275-7, Pub. by Wiley-Interscience). Wiley.

Quraishi, Salim, jt. ed. see Shaw, Graham W.

Qureishi, S. Aleem. Pakistan. (World Bibliographical Ser.: No. 10). 1982. write for info. (ISBN 0-903450-13-5). ABC-Clio.

Qureshi, A. I. Fiscal System of Islam. 1981. 6.95 (ISBN 0-686-97866-8). Kazi Pubns.

Qureshi, Z. H. Arabic for Beginners. pap. 2.00 (ISBN 0-686-83564-6). Kazi Pubns.

--Arabic Writing for Beginners: Part Two. pap. 2.00 (ISBN 0-686-83572-7). Kazi Pubns.

Qutb, M. Islam: The Misunderstood Religion. pap. 5.50 (ISBN 0-686-18500-5). Kazi Pubns.

Qutb, S. This Religion of Islam. pap. 3.00 o.p. (ISBN 0-686-18480-7). Kazi Pubns.

R

R. Hoe & Co. Catalogue of Printing Presses & Printers' Materials, Lithographic Presses, Stereotyping & Electrotyping Machinery, Binders' Presses & Materials. Bidwell, John, ed. LC 78-74397. (Nineteenth-Century Book Arts & Printing History Ser.: Vol. 11). (Illus.). 1980. lib. bdg. 22.00 o.s.i. (ISBN 0-8240-3885-1). Garland Pub.

R. R. Bowker Company, ed. Magazine Industry Market Place, 1983. new ed. 670p. 1983. pap. 39.95 (ISBN 0-8352-1579-2). Bowker.

--Publishers Weekly Yearbook, 1982. 300p. 29.95 (ISBN 0-8352-1689-6); pap. 19.95 (ISBN 0-8352-1691-8). Bowker.

R. R. Bowker Staff. Audiovisual Market Place, 1983. new ed. 470p. pap. 39.95 (ISBN 0-8352-1577-6). Bowker.

--International Literary Market Place, 1983-84. new ed. 530p. 1983. pap. 55.00 (ISBN 0-8352-1576-8). Bowker.

R. W. Norton Art Gallery. The Seasonal Transitions of Richard Earl Thompson. LC 82-12437. (Illus.). 76p. 1982. pap. 10.00x (ISBN 0-913060-20-8). Norton Art.

Raab, Earl, jt. auth. see Lipset, Seymour M.

Raab, Reginald, tr. see Wachsmuth, Guenther.

Raab, Rex & Klingborg, Arne. Eloquent Concrete: How Rudolf Steiner Employed Reinforced Concrete. (Illus.). 141p. 1979. pap. 19.95 (ISBN 0-85440-354-X, Pub. by Steinerbooks). Anthroposophic.

Raab, Robert A. Coping with Death. rev. ed. (Coping Ser.). 1982. lib. bdg. 7.97 (ISBN 0-8239-0421-0). Rosen Pr.

Raabe, Wilhelm. Else Von der Tanne: A Translation & Commentary with an Introduction to Wilhelm Raabe's Life & Work. O'Flaherty, James C. & King, Janet K., trs. LC 78-181895. 160p. 1972. 11.50 o.s.i. (ISBN 0-8173-8554-1); pap. 4.50 o.s.i. (ISBN 0-8173-8557-6). U of Ala Pr.

Raalte, Joan Van see Stewart, Arlene & Van Raalte, Joan.

Ra'anan, Gavriel. Factions & Their "Debates" Over International Policy During the Zhdanovschina. 1983. write for info. (Archon). Shoe String.

--International Policy Formation in the USSR: Factional "Debates" During the Zhdanoschina. 1983. price not set (ISBN 0-208-01976-6, Archon Bks). Shoe String.

Ra'Anan, Gavriel D. Yugoslavia After Tito: Scenarios & Implications. LC 77-4164. 200p. 1978. 25.00 (ISBN 0-89158-335-1). Westview.

Ra'anan, Uri, jt. auth. see Pfaltzgraff, Robert.

Ra'Anan, Uri, et al. Arms Transfer to the Third World: Problems & Policies. LC 77-17949. (Westview Special Studies in International Relations & U.S. Foreign Policy). 1978. lib. bdg. 40.00 (ISBN 0-89158-092-1). Westview.

Ra'anan, Uri, jt. ed. see Pfaltzgraff, Robert L., Jr.

Raarup, Peter, ed. see Transitour, Inc.

Raat, W. Dirk. The Mexican Revolution: An Annotated Guide to Recent Scholarship. 1982. lib. bdg. 39.95 (ISBN 0-8161-8352-X, Hall Reference). G K Hall.

Rabalais, J. Wayne. Principles of Ultraviolet Photoelectron Spectroscopy. LC 76-28413. (Wiley-Interscience Monographs in Chemical Physics). 1977. 58.50 o.s.i. (ISBN 0-471-70285-4, Pub. by Wiley-Interscience). Wiley.

Rabald, Erich. Corrosion Guide. 2nd rev. ed. 1968. 149.00 (ISBN 0-444-40465-1). Elsevier.

Raban, Avner, jt. auth. see Linder, Elisha.

Raban, Jonathan. Old Glory: Am American Voyage. 410p. 1982. pap. 6.95 (ISBN 0-14-006308-0). Penguin.

Raban, S. Mortmain Legislation & the English Church, 1279-1500. LC 81-21685. (Cambridge Studies in Medieval Life & Thought: No. 17). (Illus.). 244p. 1982. 39.50 (ISBN 0-521-24233-9). Cambridge U Pr.

Rabassa, Gregory, tr. see Benet, Juan.

Rabassa, Gregory, tr. see Cortazar, Julio.

Rabassa, Gregory, tr. see Garcia-Marquez, Gabriel.

Rabassa, Gregory, tr. see Garcia Marquez, Gabriel.

Rabassa, Gregory, tr. see Valenzuela, Luisa.

Rabassa, Gregory, tr. see Vargas Llosa, Mario.

Rabassa, Gregoy, tr. see Lins, Osman.

Rabat Seminar, 1962. The Teaching of Sciences in African Universities: Report. (The Development of Higher Education Ser.). 112p. 1964. pap. 4.00 (ISBN 0-686-94191-8, U659, UNESCO). Unipub.

Rabb, Theodore K., ed. The Thirty Years' War. 2nd ed. LC 80-6215. (Illus.). 190p. 1981. lib. bdg. 19.75 (ISBN 0-8191-1746-3); pap. text ed. 7.50 (ISBN 0-8191-1747-1). U Pr of Amer.

Rabe, Berniece. Naomi. LC 75-4599. 192p. (gr. 6 up). 1975. 9.95 o.p. (ISBN 0-525-66444-0). Lodestar Bks.

Rabe, David. Basic Training of Pavlo Hummel. 1978. pap. 3.95 o.p. (ISBN 0-14-048137-0). Penguin.

Rabe, Steven G., jt. ed. see Brown, Richard D.

Rabek, J. F., jt. ed. see Ranby, B.

Rabek, Jack, jt. auth. see Ranby, Bengt.

Rabek, Jan F. Experimental Methods in Polymer Chemistry: Physical Principles. LC 79-40511. 1980. 179.95 (ISBN 0-471-27604-9, Pub. by Wiley-Interscience). Wiley.

Rabelais, Francois. Gargantua & Pantagruel. 1980. Repr. of 1929 ed. 12.95x ea. (ISBN 0-686-34319-0, Evman). Vol. 1. Vol. 2 (ISBN 0-460-00827-7). Biblio Dist.

--The Portable Rabelais. Putnam, Samuel, ed. (Viking Portable Library: No. 21). 1977. pap. 6.95 (ISBN 0-14-015021-8). Penguin.

Raben, J. & Marks, G. Data Bases in the Humanities & the Social Sciences. 1980. 42.75 (ISBN 0-444-86220-X). Elsevier.

Rabenau, A., ed. Problems of Nonstoichiometry. 1970. 25.75 (ISBN 0-444-10047-4, North-Holland). Elsevier.

Rabenau, A., jt. ed. see Rodymans, C.

Rabens, Neil. One Happy Little Songbird. (A Happy Day Book). (Illus.). 24p. (gr. k-3). 1979. 1.29 (ISBN 0-87239-361-5, 3631). Standard Pub.

Rabenstein, Albert. Elementary Differential Equations with Linear Algebra. 3rd ed. 518p. 1982. text ed. 21.95 (ISBN 0-12-573945-1); avail. Instr's Manual 2.50 (ISBN 0-12-573946-X). Acad Pr.

--Introduction to Ordinary Differential Equations. 2nd ed. 538p. 1972. 20.00 (ISBN 0-12-573957-5). Acad Pr.

Raber, Dorothy A. Protestantism in Changing Taiwan: A Call to Creative Response. LC 78-61042. (Illus.). 1978. pap. 5.95 (ISBN 0-87808-329-4). William Carey Lib.

Rabianski, Joseph, jt. auth. see Epley, Donald R.

Rabichow, Helen G. & Sklansky, Morris A. Effective Counseling of Adolescents. 216p. 1980. 10.95 o.s.i. (ISBN 0-695-81340-4). Follett.

Rabie, J. Man Apart. 1969. 6.95 o.p. (ISBN 0-02-600290-6). Macmillan.

Rabier, Jacques-Rene. Euro-Barometer 4: Consumer Attitudes in Europe, October November 1975. LC 79-83752. 1979. write for info. codebk. (ISBN 0-89138-988-1). ICPSR.

Rabier, Jacques-Rene & Inglehart, Ronald. Euro-Barometer 10-A: Scientific Priorities in the European Community, October-November 1978. LC 81-84734. 1981. write for info. (ISBN 0-89138-944-X). ICPSR.

--Euro-Barometer 11: The Year of the Child in Europe, April 1979. LC 81-84735. 1981. write for info. (ISBN 0-89138-943-1). ICPSR.

--Euro-Barometer 12: European Parliamentary Elections, October-November 1979. LC 81-84736. 1981. write for info. (ISBN 0-89138-942-3). ICPSR.

--Euro-Barometer 13: Regional Development & Integration, April 1980. LC 82-81760. 1982. write for info. (ISBN 0-89138-937-7, ICPSR 7957). ICPSR.

--Euro-Barometer 14: Trust in the European Community, October 1980. LC 82-81761. write for info. (ISBN 0-89138-936-9, ICPSR 7958). ICPSR.

--Euro-Barometer 15: Membership in the European Community, April 1981. LC 82-81762. 1982. write for info. (ISBN 0-89138-935-0, ICPSR 7959). ICPSR.

--Euro-Barometer 3: European Men & Women, May 1975. LC 79-83750. 1979. codebk. write for info. (ISBN 0-89138-989-X). ICPSR.

--Euro-Barometer 5: Revenues, Satisfaction, & Poverty, May 1976. LC 79-83756. 1979. codebk. write for info. (ISBN 0-89138-987-3). ICPSR.

--Euro-Barometer 6: Twenty Years of the Common Market, October-November 1976. LC 79-83757. 1979. codebk. write for info. (ISBN 0-89138-986-5). ICPSR.

Rabii, S. Physics of Four-Six Compounds & Alloys. 264p. 1974. 60.00x (ISBN 0-677-05070-4). Gordon.

Rabil, Albert, Jr., jt. ed. see King, Margaret L.

Rabin. Handbook of Public Personnel. (Public Administration & Public Policies Ser.). 776p. 1983. write for info. (ISBN 0-8247-1318-4). Dekker.

Rabin, jt. auth. see Golembiewski.

Rabin, Alan A. & Yeager, Leland B. Monetary Approaches to the Balance of Payments & Exchange Rates. LC 82-15587. (Essays in International Finance Ser.: No. 148). 1982. pap. text ed. 2.50x (ISBN 0-88165-055-2). Princeton U Int Finan Econ.

Rabin, Albert I. Further Explorations in Personality. LC 80-19407. (Personality Processes Ser.). 281p. 1981. 32.50 (ISBN 0-471-07721-6, Pub. by Wiley-Interscience). Wiley.

Rabin, Carol. Guide to Music Festivals in North America. rev., enl. ed. LC 78-74201. 260p. 1981. 6.95 o.p. (ISBN 0-912944-67-6). Berkshire Traveller.

Rabin, Carol P. Music Festivals in America. Rev. ed. LC 78-73844. (Illus.). 286p. 1983. pap. 8.95 (ISBN 0-912944-74-9). Berkshire Traveller.

--Music Festivals in Europe. LC 79-55709. (Illus.). 1980. pap. 5.95 (ISBN 0-912944-59-5). Berkshire Traveller.

Rabin, Chaim. Qumran Studies. LC 74-26735. 151p. 1975. pap. 3.95 o.p. (ISBN 0-8052-0482-2). Schocken.

Rabin, David & McKenna, Terence, eds. Clinical Endocrinology & Metabolism. (The Science & Practice of Clinical Medicine Ser.). 1982. 69.50 (ISBN 0-8089-1394-8). Grune.

Rabin, Edward H. Fundamentals of Modern Real Property Law. 2nd ed. (University Casebook Ser.). 1982. write for info. tchrs. manual (ISBN 0-88277-106-X). Foundation Pr.

Rabin, Edward H. & Schwartz, Mortimer D. The Pollution Crisis: Official Documents, 1972-1976, 2 vols. LC 73-37009. 1976. lib. bdg. 46.00 ea. Vol. 1 (ISBN 0-379-00163-2). Vol. 2 (ISBN 0-379-00174-8). Oceana.

Rabin, Gil. Changes. LC 73-5492. 160p. (gr. 5 up). 1973. PLB 10.89 (ISBN 0-06-024827-0, HarpJ). Har-Row.

Rabin, Jack, jt. auth. see Vocino, Thomas.

Rabin, Jack, jt. ed. see Golembiewski, Robert T.

Rabin, Lucy F. Ford Madox Brown & the Pre-Raphaelite History-Picture. LC 77-94725. (Outstanding Dissertations in the Fine Arts Ser.). 1979. lib. bdg. 31.00 o.s.i. (ISBN 0-8240-3246-2). Garland Pub.

Rabin, Lynch. Handbook on Public Budgeting & Financial Management. (Public Adminstration & Public Policy Ser.). 720p. 1983. 99.75 (ISBN 0-8247-1253-6). Dekker.

Rabin, Pauline L., jt. ed. see Stone, William J.

Rabinbach, Anson. The Crisis of Austrian Socialism: From Red Vienna to Civil War, Nineteen Twenty Seven-Nineteen Thirty Four. LC 82-10919. (Illus.). 312p. 1983. lib. bdg. 22.00 (ISBN 0-226-70121-2). U of Chicago Pr.

Rabiner, L. R., jt. ed. see Flanagan, J. L.

Rabiner, Lawrence R. & Gold, Bernard. Theory & Application of Digital Signal Processing. (Illus.). 720p. 1975. ref. ed. 34.95 (ISBN 0-13-914101-4). P-H.

Rabiner, Lawrence R. & Schafer, Ronald W. Digital Processing of Speech Signals. (P-H Signal Processing Ser.). 1978. ref. ed. 37.00 (ISBN 0-13-213603-1). P-H.

Rabiner, Lawrence R. & Rader, Charles N., eds. Digital Signal Processing. LC 72-90358. (Illus.). 1972. 29.95 (ISBN 0-87942-017-0). Inst Electrical.

Rabinovitch, B. S., et al, eds. Annual Review of Physical Chemistry, Vol. 33. LC 51-1658. (Illus.). 1982. text ed. 22.00 (ISBN 0-8243-1033-0). Annual Reviews.

Rabinovitch, Sacha, tr. see Josipovici, Gabriel.

Rabinovitz, Frances F., jt. auth. see Fried, Robert C.

Rabinow, Paul. Reflections on Fieldwork in Morocco. LC 77-71066. (Quantum Ser.). 1977. 18.95x (ISBN 0-520-03450-3); pap. 6.50x (ISBN 0-520-03529-1). U of Cal Pr.

Rabinow, Paul & Sullivan, William M., eds. Interpretive Social Science: A Reader. LC 77-85743. 1979. 36.50x (ISBN 0-520-03588-7); pap. 8.95x (ISBN 0-520-03834-7). U of Cal Pr.

Rabinowich, Ellen. Horses & Foals. (Easy-Read Fact Bk.). (Illus.). (gr. 2-4). 1979. PLB 8.60 s&l (ISBN 0-531-02272-2). Watts.

--Kangaroos, Koalas, & Other Marsupials. LC 78-5805. (First Bks). (Illus.). (gr. 4-6). 1978. PLB 8.90 s&l (ISBN 0-531-01489-4). Watts.

--The Loch Ness Monster. (Easy-Read Fact Bks.). (Illus.). (gr. 2-4). 1979. PLB 8.60 s&l (ISBN 0-531-02274-9). Watts.

--Rock Fever. LC 78-12715. (Triumph Ser.). (Illus.). (gr. 6 up). 1979. PLB 8.90 s&l (ISBN 0-531-02889-5). Watts.

--Seals, Sea Lions, & Walruses. (gr. 4 up). 1980. PLB 8.90 (ISBN 0-531-04106-9). Watts.

--Underneath I'm Different. LC 82-14919. 192p. (gr. 7 up). 1983. 12.95 (ISBN 0-440-09253-1). Delacorte.

Rabinowitch, Alexander. The Bolsheviks Come to Power: The Revolution of 1917 in Petrograd. 1976. 14.95x (ISBN 0-393-05586-8, N893, Norton Lib); pap. 8.95 (ISBN 0-393-00893-2). Norton.

Rabinowitch, Eugene & Govindjee, G. Photosynthesis. LC 75-77830. 1969. pap. 17.95 (ISBN 0-471-70424-5). Wiley.

Rabinowitsch, Wolf Z. Lithuanian Hasidism. LC 72-148840. (Illus.). 1971. 7.00x o.p. (ISBN 0-8052-3402-0). Schocken.

Rabinowitz, Howard N. Race Relations in the Urban South 1865-1890. (Urban Life in America Ser.). (Illus.). 1978. 22.50x (ISBN 0-19-502283-1). Oxford U Pr.

Rabinowitz, Howard N., ed. Southern Black Leaders of the Reconstruction Era. LC 81-11372. (Blacks in the New World Ser.). (Illus.). 400p. 1982. 27.50 (ISBN 0-252-00929-0); pap. 9.95 (ISBN 0-252-00972-X). U of Ill Pr.

Rabinowitz, Isaac, ed. The Book of the Honeycomb's Flow: Sepher Nopheth Suphim by Judah Messer Leon. LC 81-15273. 792p. 1983. 48.50x (ISBN 0-8014-0870-9). Cornell U Pr.

Rabinowitz, Philip, jt. auth. see Ralston, A.

Rabinsky, Leatrice & Mann, Gertrude. Journey of Conscience: Young People Respond to the Holocaust. 112p. Repr. 1.50 (ISBN 0-686-95073-9). ADL.

Rabjohn, N. Organic Syntheses Collective Volumes, Vol. 4. 1036p. 1963. 49.50x (ISBN 0-471-70470-9, 2-203). Wiley.

Rabkin, Eric, jt. auth. see Scholes, Robert.

Rabkin, Eric S., jt. auth. see Hayman, David.

Rabkin, Eric S., ed. Fantastic Worlds: Myths, Tales, & Stories. 1979. 22.50x (ISBN 0-19-502542-3, GB 572); pap. 12.95 (ISBN 0-19-502541-5). Oxford U Pr.

--Science Fiction: An Historical Anthology. 496p. 1983. 19.95 (ISBN 0-19-503271-3). Oxford U Pr.

--Science Fiction: An Historical Anthology. 496p. 1983. pap. 9.95 (ISBN 0-19-503272-1, GB 729, GB). Oxford U Pr.

Rabkin, Eric S., et al, eds. The End of the World. 1983. price not set (ISBN 0-8093-1033-3). S Ill U Pr.

Rabkin, Jacob, jt. auth. see Rabkin, Richard.

Rabkin, Judith G., jt. ed. see Klein, Donald F.

Rabkin, Leo, jt. auth. see McDonald, Robert.

Rabkin, Norman. Shakespeare & the Problem of Meaning. LC 80-18538. 1981. lib. bdg. 16.00x (ISBN 0-226-70177-8, Phoen); pap. 4.95 (ISBN 0-226-70178-6). U of Chicago Pr.

Rabkin, Norman, jt. auth. see Fraser, Russel A.

Rabkin, Richard. Strategic Psychotherapy: Brief & Symptomatic Treatment. LC 76-43472. 1977. 12.95x o.s.i. (ISBN 0-465-08217-3). Basic.

Rabkin, Richard & Rabkin, Jacob. Nature Guide to Florida. LC 78-23491. (Illus.). 80p. 1978. pap. 9.95 (ISBN 0-916224-44-9). Banyan Bks.

Raboff, Ernest. Da Vinci. LC 78-139054. (gr. 3-7). PLB 8.95 o.p. (ISBN 0-385-07738-6). Doubleday.

--Pierre-Auguste Renoir. LC 72-93205. (gr. 3-7). 1970. 8.95 (ISBN 0-385-04929-3); PLB 8.95 (ISBN 0-385-03775-9). Doubleday.

--Rembrandt. LC 70-121782. (gr. 3-7). PLB 8.95a o.p. (ISBN 0-385-02402-9). Doubleday.

--Vincent Van Gogh. LC 73-75362. 36p. (gr. 3-7). 1975. 8.95 (ISBN 0-385-05009-7); PLB o.p. (ISBN 0-385-06999-5). Doubleday.

Rabold, J. Gregory, jt. auth. see Marshall, Daniel P.

Raboteau, Albert J. Slave Religion: The Invisible Institution in the Antebellum South. (Illus.). 1980. pap. 7.95 (ISBN 0-19-502705-1, GB 594, GB). Oxford U Pr.

Rabotnov, Y. N. Creep Problems in Structural Members. (Applied Mathematics & Mechanics Ser.: Vol. 7). 1969. 93.00 (ISBN 0-444-10259-0, North-Holland). Elsevier.

Rabow, Jerome, jt. auth. see Goldman, Marion S.

Raburn, Terry. Beirut, Ciudad En LLamas. Carrodeguas, Andy, et al, eds. Kjellgreen, Shily, tr. from Eng. Orig. Title: Under The Guns in Beirut. 235p. (Span.). 1981. pap. 2.50 (ISBN 0-8297-1133-3). Life Pubs Intl.

Rabushka, Alvin, jt. auth. see Hall, Robert F.

Raby, Frederick J., ed. Oxford Book of Medieval Latin Verse. (Lat). 1959. 19.95x (ISBN 0-19-812119-9). Oxford U Pr.

Raby, Julian. Venice, Durer & the Oriental Mode. (Hans Huth Memorial Studies: No. 1). (Illus.). 96p. 1983. text ed. 50.00x (ISBN 0-85667-162-2, Pub. by Sotheby Pubns England). Biblio Dist.

Raby, Peter. Fair Ophelia: A Life of Harriet Smithson Berlioz. (Illus.). 209p. 1983. 24.95 (ISBN 0-521-24421-8). Cambridge U Pr.

Raby, William & Tidwell, Victor H. Introduction to Federal Taxation, 1983. (Illus.). 240p. 1982. 24.95 (ISBN 0-13-483537-9); pap. 9.95 study guide (ISBN 0-13-483545-X). P-H.

Raby, William L. Income Tax & Business Decisions: An Introductory Tax Text. 4th ed. LC 77-25840. (Illus.). 1978. ref. ed. 25.95 (ISBN 0-13-454363-7). P-H.

Rac, G. & Potter, T. Informal Reading Diagnosis: A Practical Guide for the Classroom Teacher. 2nd ed. 1981. 18.95 (ISBN 0-13-464628-2); pap. 16.95 (ISBN 0-13-464610-X). P-H.

Racagni, jt. auth. see Brambilla.

Racagni, G., jt. ed. see Costa, E.

Race, George J., ed. see Loose Leaf References Services.

Race, William H. The Classical Priamel from Homer to Boethius. (Mnemosyne: Suppl. 74). xii, 171p. 1982. pap. write for info. (ISBN 90-04-06515-6). E J Brill.

Rachel, F., jt. auth. see Dunn, J. D.

Rachlin & Marriott. Plains Indian Mythology. (RL 7). 1977. pap. 2.50 (ISBN 0-451-62036-4, ME2036, Ment). NAL.

Rachlin, Carol, jt. auth. see Marriott, Alice.

Rachlin, Carol K., jt. auth. see Marriott, Alice.

Rachlin, Harvey. The Songwriter's Handbook. LC 77-2946. (Funk & W Bk.). (Illus.). 1977. 12.02i (ISBN 0-308-10321-1). T Y Crowell.

Rachlin, Howard. Behaviorism in Everyday Life. (Psychology in Action Ser.). (Illus.). 224p. 1980. 12.95 o.p. (ISBN 0-13-074583-9, Spec); pap. 4.95 o.p. (ISBN 0-13-074575-8). P-H.

Rachlin, Joseph W. & Tauber, Gilbert, eds. Papers of the Fifth Symposium on Hudson River Ecology 1980. 107p. (Orig.). 1981. pap. 15.00x (ISBN 0-89062-131-4, Pub. by HRES). Pub Ctr Cult Res.

Rachlin, Norman S. & Cerwinske, Laura. Eleven Steps to Building a Profitable Accounting Practice. LC 82-10106. (Illus.). 320p. 1983. 29.95 (ISBN 0-07-051103-9). McGraw.

Rachlin, Robert. Return on Investment: Strategies for Profit. (Illus.). 1979. text ed. 12.95t (ISBN 0-13-779116-X, Spec); pap. text ed. 4.95 o.p. (ISBN 0-13-779108-9). P-H.

Rachlis, Eugene. The Story of the U. S. Coast Guard. (Landmark Ser.: No. 97). (Illus.). (gr. 3-7). 1961. PLB 5.99 o.p. (ISBN 0-394-90397-8). Random.

Rachman, David. Marketing Strategy & Structure. LC 73-17352. (Illus.). 448p. 1974. text ed. 23.95 (ISBN 0-13-558338-1). P-H.

Rachman, David & Mescon, Michael. Business Today. 3rd ed. 512p. 1982. 22.00 (ISBN 0-394-32686-5); wkbk. 11.95 (ISBN 0-394-32900-7). Random.

Rachman, David J. & Mescon, Michael M. Business Today. 2nd ed. LC 78-20701. 1979. text ed. 18.95x o.p. (ISBN 0-394-32092-1); pap. text ed. 6.95 Student Course Mastery Guide by Dennis Guseman et al o.p. (ISBN 0-686-86677-0). Random.

Rachman, S. & Hodgson, R. Obsessions & Compulsions. 1980. 29.95 (ISBN 0-13-629139-2). P-H.

Rachman, S. J. & Philips, Clare. Psychology & Behavioral Medicine. LC 79-8589. (Illus.). 1980. 24.95 (ISBN 0-521-23178-7); pap. 7.95 (ISBN 0-521-29850-4). Cambridge U Pr.

Rachman, S. J. & Wilson, G. T. The Effects of Psychological Therapy. 2nd, enl. ed. (FEBS Ser.: Vol. 24). 400p. 1980. 25.00 (ISBN 0-08-024675-3); pap. 16.00 (ISBN 0-08-024674-5). Pergamon.

Rachman, S. J., ed. see Darwin, Charles.

Rachocki, A. J. Alluvial Fans: An Attempt at an Empirical Approach. LC 80-42061. 161p. 1981. 39.95 (ISBN 0-471-27999-4, Pub. by Wiley-Interscience). Wiley.

Rachow, Louis A., ed. Theatre & Performing Arts Collections. LC 81-6567. (Special Collections Ser.: Vol. 1, No. 1). 166p. 1981. text ed. 24.95 (ISBN 0-917724-47-X, B47). Haworth Pr.

Raciborski, M. Parasitische Algen und Pilze Javas, 3 pts. in 1. 1973. Repr. of 1900 ed. 20.00 (ISBN 3-7682-0855-9). Lubrecht & Cramer.

Racina, Thom. The Great Los Angeles Blizzard. LC 77-4156. 1977. 8.95 o.p. (ISBN 0-399-12033-5). Putnam Pub Group.

Racina, Thom & Johnson, Joe. The Gannon Girls. (Orig.). 1979. pap. 2.25 o.s.i. (ISBN 0-515-05384-8). Jove Pubns.

Racine, Daniel L. Leon-Gontran, Damas, 1912-1978. Founder of Negritude: A Memorial Casebook. LC 79-64101. 1979. pap. text ed. 12.50 (ISBN 0-8191-0727-1). U Pr of Amer.

Racine, Jean. Phedre. Rawlings, Margaret, tr. (Bilingual). 1962. pap. 4.95 (ISBN 0-525-47099-9, 0481-140). Dutton.

Racine, Phillip. Spartanburg: A Pictorial History. LC 80-20869. (Illus.). 192p. 1980. pap. 12.95 o.p. (ISBN 0-89865-051-8). Donning Co.

Racker, Darlene K. Transmission Electron Microscopy: Methods of Application. (Illus.). 192p. 1983. pap. 24.75x spiral (ISBN 0-398-04713-8). C C Thomas.

Rackham, Arthur, illus. Grimm Fairy Tales. (Illus.). 1982. 14.95 (ISBN 0-434-95862-X, Pub. by Heinemann). David & Charles.

Rackham, Jeff, jt. ed. see Bertagnolli, Olivia.

Rackham, Oliver. Ancient Woodland: Its History, Vegetation & Uses in England. 392p. 1980. text ed. 99.95 (ISBN 0-7131-2723-6). E Arnold.

--Trees & Woodland in the British Landscape. (Illus.). 176p. 1978. Repr. of 1976 ed. 15.75x o.p. (ISBN 0-460-04183-5, Pub. by J. M. Dent England). Biblio Dist.

Rackin, Phyllis. Shakespeare's Tragedies. LC 75-34216. (Literature and Life Ser.). (Illus.). 175p. 1978. 11.95 (ISBN 0-8044-2706-2). Ungar.

--Shakespeare's Tragedies. LC 75-34216. (Literature & Life Ser.). (Illus.). 192p. 1983. pap. 5.95 (ISBN 0-8044-6668-8). Ungar.

Rackley, Charles E., jt. ed. see Russell, Richard O., Jr.

Racle, Fred. Introduction to Evolution. (P-H Biology Ser.). (Illus.). 1979. pap. 12.95 ref. (ISBN 0-13-482869-0). P-H.

Racquet & Tennis Club New York. Dictionary Catalogue of the Library of Sports in the Racquet & Tennis Club with Special Collections on Tennis, Lawn Tennis, & Early American Sports, 2 vols. 1970. Set. lib. bdg. 190.00 (ISBN 0-8161-0916-8, Hall Library). G K Hall.

Raczkowski, George. Principles of Machine Dynamics. 104p. 1979. pap. 14.95 (ISBN 0-87201-440-1). Gulf Pub.

Rad, Gerhard Von see Von Rad, Gerhard.

Rada, jt. auth. see Warren, Mary P.

Radau, Hugo. Letters to the Cassite Kings, from the Temple Archives of Nippur. (Publications of the Babylonian Section, Ser. A: Vol. 17). (Illus.). 174p. 1908. soft bound 8.00 o.p. (ISBN 0-686-11915-0). Univ Mus of U PA.

--Ninib, the Determiner of Fates from the Temple Library of Nippur. (Publications of the Babylonian Section, Ser. D: Vol. 5-2). (Illus.). 73p. 1910. bound 2.00xsoft (ISBN 0-686-11919-3). Univ Mus of U PA.

Radcliff, Ruth K. & Ogden, Sheila J. Calculation of Drug Dosages: A Workbook. 2nd ed. 290p. 1980. pap. text ed. 13.95 (ISBN 0-8016-4067-9). Mosby.

Radcliffe, Alexander. Works of Capt. Alexander Radcliffe. LC 81-9003. 1981. Repr. of 1696 ed. 36.00x (ISBN 0-8201-1365-4). Schol Facsimiles.

Radcliffe, Ann. Italian, Or, the Confessional of the Black Penitents. Garber, Frederick, ed. (Oxford English Novels Ser). 1968. 17.95x o.p. (ISBN 0-19-255315-1). Oxford U Pr.

Radcliffe, C. W., jt. auth. see Suh, C. H.

Radcliffe College, the Arthur & Elizabeth Schlesinger Library on the History of Women in America. Manuscripts Inventory & the Catalogs of Manuscripts, Books & Pictures, 3 vols. 1973. lib. bdg. 285.00 book catalog (ISBN 0-8161-1053-0, Hall Library). G K Hall.

Radcliffe, George L. Governor T. L. H. Hicks of Maryland & the Civil War. 131p. 1965. 5.00 (ISBN 0-686-36834-7). Md Hist.

Radcliffe, Janette. American Baroness. (Orig.). 1980. pap. 2.50 o.s.i. (ISBN 0-440-10267-7). Dell.

--Gift of Violets. 1977. pap. 1.50 o.s.i. (ISBN 0-440-12891-9). Dell.

Radcliffe, Joe. This Business of Disco. 192p. 1980. 14.50 (ISBN 0-8230-7756-X, Billboard Bks). Watson-Guptill.

Radcliffe, P. Beethoven's String Quartets. LC 77-26271. (Illus.). 1978. 27.95 (ISBN 0-521-21963-9); pap. 8.95 (ISBN 0-521-29326-X). Cambridge U Pr.

Radcliffe, Talbot. Spaniels for Sport. 136p. 1983. text ed. 8.95 (ISBN 0-571-08772-8). Faber & Faber.

Radcliff-Umstead, Douglas, ed. Italian Culture One, Nineteen Seventy-Eight to Nineteen Seventy-Nine. 119p. Date not set. pap. 12.00 individual subscription (ISBN 0-686-91974-2); pap. 15.00 institutional subscription (ISBN 0-686-98428-5). Medieval & Renaissance NY.

--Italian Culture Three, Nineteen Eighty-One. 1982. individual subscription 12.00 (ISBN 0-686-91981-5); institutional subscription 15.00 (ISBN 0-686-98430-7). Medieval & Renaissance NY.

--Italian Culture Two, Nineteen Eighty. 126p. 1982. individual subscription 12.00 (ISBN 0-686-91978-5); institutional subscription 15.00 (ISBN 0-686-98429-3). MedievaL & Renaissance NY.

Raddatz, Fritz J., ed. Karl Marx-Friedrich Engels: Selected Letters. 1982. 13.95 o.p. (ISBN 0-316-73211-7). Little.

Radde, Ingeborg C., jt. auth. see MacLeod, Stuart M.

Radding, Charles. The Modern Presidency. (American Government Ser.). (gr. 7 up). 1979. PLB 8.90 s&l o.p. (ISBN 0-531-02266-8). Watts.

Raddon, Rosemary. The Framework of School Librarianship. 1982. write for info. (ISBN 0-566-03435-2, 06088-7, Pub. by Gower Pub Co England). Lexington Bks.

Rade, L. Statistics at the School Level. 242p. 1975. 26.25 (ISBN 0-470-70486-1). Krieger.

Radebaugh, Lee, jt. auth. see Arpan, Jeffrey.

Radebaugh, Lee H., jt. auth. see Arpan, Jeffrey S.

Radeker, Johannes. Korte Beschrijving Van Het Beroemde En Prachtige Orgel in De Groote of St. Bavooskerk Te Haerlem. (Bibliotheca Organologica: Vol. 14). 1974. Repr. of 1775 ed. wrappers 17.50 o.s.i. (ISBN 90-6027-323-0, Pub. by Frits/Netherlands). Pendragon NY.

Radelet, Louis A. The Police & the Community. 3rd ed. 627p. 1980. text ed. 23.95 (ISBN 0-02-470680-9). Macmillan.

Radeloff, D. J., jt. auth. see Charlesworth, R.

Radeloff, Deanna J. & Zechman, Roberta. Children in Your Life: A Guide to Child Care & Parenting. LC 80-67826. (Home Economics Ser.). 346p. 1981. pap. 15.20 (ISBN 0-8273-1748-4); instr's. guide 2.75 (ISBN 0-8273-1749-2). Delmar.

Rademacher, H. Topics in Analytic Number Theory. LC 72-79326. (Die Grundelehren der Mathematischen Wissenschaften: Vol. 169). (Illus.). 340p. 1973. 52.50 o.p. (ISBN 0-387-05447-2). Springer-Verlag.

Rademacher, Hans. Collected Papers of Hans Rademacher, 2 vols. Grosswald, Emil, ed. (Mathematicians of Our Time Ser.: Vols. 3 & 4). 1356p. 1974. 50.00x ea. Vol. 1 (ISBN 0-262-07054-5). Vol. 2 (ISBN 0-262-07055-3). Set. 95.00x (ISBN 0-686-31697-5). MIT Pr.

Rademacher, Susan C., jt. auth. see Klem, Joan R.

Rademacher, William J. Working with Parish Councils. LC 77-71024. (Orig.). 1977. pap. 1.75 o.p. (ISBN 0-8189-1149-2, 149, Pub. by Alba Bks). Alba.

Rademaker, Analie J. Technical Skills in Registered Nursing & Related Occupations. Kalisch, Philip & Kalisch, Beatrice, eds. LC 82-13520. (Studies in Nursing Management: No. 7). 120p. 1982. 34.95 (ISBN 0-8357-1370-9, Pub. by UMI Res Pr). Univ Microfilms.

Rademaker, O., et al. Dynamics & Control of Continuous Distillation Units. LC 74-83315. 726p. 1975. 117.00 (ISBN 0-444-41234-4). Elsevier.

Rader, Benjamin. American Sports: From the Age of Folk Games to the Age of Spectators. (Illus.). 384p. 1983. pap. 20.95 (ISBN 0-13-031369-6). P-H.

Rader, Charles M., jt. auth. see Gold, Bernard.

Rader, Charles N., jt. ed. see Rabiner, Lawrence R.

Rader, M., jt. auth. see Jessup, Bertram.

Rader, Melvin. Marx's Interpretation of History. 1979. 17.95x (ISBN 0-19-502474-5); pap. text ed. 6.95x (ISBN 0-19-502475-3). Oxford U Pr.

Rader, Ralph W. Tennyson's Maud: The Biographical Genesis. (Library Reprint Ser.: Vol. 90). 1978. 30.00x (ISBN 0-520-03617-4). U of Cal Pr.

Rader, Randall R., jt. ed. see McGuigan, Patrick B.

Rader, Robert J. Advanced Software Design Techniques. 1979. 15.00 o.p. (ISBN 0-07-091043-X, Petrocelli Bks). McGraw.

--Advanced Software Design Techniques. (Illus.). 172p. 1979. text ed. 17.50 (ISBN 0-89433-046-2). Petrocelli.

Rader, Rosemary. Breaking Boundaries: Male-Female Friendship in Early Christian Communities. (Theological Inquiries Ser.). 144p. 1983. pap. 6.95 (ISBN 0-8091-2506-4). Paulist Pr.

Rader, Stanley. Against the Gates of Hell. LC 80-16425. (Illus.). 320p. 1980. 12.00 o.p. (ISBN 0-89696-108-7, An Everest House Book). Dodd.

Radet & Barre. La Negresse ou le Pouvoir de la Reconnaissance. (Bibliotheque Africaine Ser.). 56p. (Fr.). 1974. Repr. of 1787 ed. lib. bdg. 25.50x o.p. (ISBN 0-8287-0708-1, 72-2151). Clearwater Pub.

Radetzki, Marian. Uranium: Economic & Political Instability in a Strategic Commodity Market. 1981. 32.50 (ISBN 0-312-83424-1). St Martin.

Radford, Albert E., ed. see Cronquist, Arthur.

Radford, Andrew. Transformational Syntax: A Student's Guide to Chomsky's Extended Standard Theory. LC 81-10025. (Cambridge Textbooks in Linguistics Ser.). 225p. 1982. 42.50 (ISBN 0-521-24274-6); pap. 13.95 (ISBN 0-521-28574-7). Cambridge U Pr.

Radford, Andrew, ed. Italian Syntax. LC 77-71424. (Cambridge Studies in Linguistics: No. 21). 1977. 44.50 (ISBN 0-521-21643-5). Cambridge U Pr.

Radford, Don. Changes: Stage 3. LC 77-83001. (Science 5-13 Ser.). (Illus.). 1977. pap. text ed. 12.85 (ISBN 0-356-04346-0). Raintree Pubs.

--Changes: Stages 1 & 2 & Background. LC 77-83001. (Science 5-13 Ser.). (Illus.). 1977. pap. text ed. 12.85 (ISBN 0-356-04105-0). Raintree Pubs.

--The Materials We Use. (Science in Today's World). (Illus.). 72p. (gr. 7-12). 1983. 14.95 (ISBN 0-7134-4073-2, Pub. by Batsford England). David & Charles.

--Metals: Background Information. LC 77-83004. (Science 5-13 Ser.). (Illus.). 1977. pap. text ed. 11.55 (ISBN 0-356-04104-2). Raintree Pubs.

--Metals: Stages 1 & 2. LC 77-83004. (Science 5-13). (Illus.). 1977. pap. text ed. 11.55 (ISBN 0-356-04103-4). Raintree Pubs.

--Science from Toys: Stages 1 & 2 & Background. LC 77-83000. (Science 5-13 Ser.). (Illus.). 1977. pap. text ed. 12.85 (ISBN 0-356-04006-2). Raintree Pubs.

--Science, Models & Toys: Stage 3. LC 77-82998. (Science 5-13 Ser.). (Illus.). 1977. pap. text ed. 12.85 (ISBN 0-356-04351-7). Raintree Pubs.

Radford, Georgia F. & Radford, Warren H. Sculpture in the Sun: Hawaii's Art for Open Spaces. LC 77-92972. 1978. pap. 7.95 (ISBN 0-8248-0526-7). UH Pr.

Radford, John & Burton, Andrew. Thinking: Its Nature & Development. LC 73-8197. 432p. 1974. pap. 23.95 (ISBN 0-471-70475-X, Pub. by Wiley-Interscience). Wiley.

Radford, John & Rose, David. The Teaching of Psychology: Method, Content, & Context. LC 79-40824. 362p. 1980. 47.95 (ISBN 0-471-27665-0, Pub. by Wiley-Interscience). Wiley.

Radford, K. J. Complex Decision Problems: An Integrated Strategy for Resolution. (Illus.). 224p. 1977. text ed. 17.95 (ISBN 0-87909-171-1). Reston.

--Information Systems for Strategic Decisions. (Illus.). 1978. ref. ed. 19.95 (ISBN 0-87909-389-7). Reston.

--Modern Managerial Decision Making. 1981. text ed. 19.95 (ISBN 0-8359-4571-5); instr's. manual avail. (ISBN 0-8359-4229-5). Reston.

Radford, Loren, jt. auth. see Haigh, Roger.

Radford, Loren, et al. Introduction to Technical Mathematics. (Math Ser.). 688p. 1982. text ed. write for info. (ISBN 0-87150-339-5, 2711). Prindle.

Radford, Penny. Rooms for Living. LC 77-78534. (Design Centre Books). (Illus.). 1977. pap. 4.95 o.p. (ISBN 0-8256-3077-0, 030077, Quick Fox). Putnam Pub Group.

Radford, Ruby L. Dwight D. Eisenhower. (See & Read Biographies). (Illus.). (gr. k-4). 1970. PLB 3.96 o.p. (ISBN 0-399-60142-2). Putnam Pub Group.

--Mary McLeod Bethune. new ed. (See & Read Biographies). (Illus.). 64p. (gr. k-4). 1973. PLB 4.49 o.p. (ISBN 0-399-60811-7). Putnam Pub Group.

--Robert Fulton. (See & Read Biographies). (Illus.). (gr. k-4). 1970. PLB 4.49 o.p. (ISBN 0-399-60537-1). Putnam Pub Group.

Radford, Warren H., jt. auth. see Radford, Georgia F.

Radford, William A. Old House Measured & Scaled Drawings for Builders & Carpenters: An Early 20th Century Pictorial Sourcebook, with 183 Detailed Plates. 2nd ed. (Illus.). 200p. 1983. pap. 7.95 (ISBN 0-486-24438-5). Dover.

Radha, Sivananda. Kundalini Yoga for the West. LC 81-40488. (Illus.). 379p. 1981. pap. 10.95 (ISBN 0-394-74884-0). Shambhala Pubns.

Radha, Swami S. The Divine Light Invocation. 54p. 1982. pap. 3.00 (ISBN 0-931454-08-5). Timeless Bks.

Radhakrishna, S., jt. auth. see Jain, S. C.

Radhakrishnan. Hindu Moral Life & Action. text ed. write for info (ISBN 0-391-02011-0). Humanities.

Radhakrishnan, S. Indian Religions. (Orient Paperbacks Ser.). 196p. 1981. pap. 3.95 (ISBN 0-86578-084-6); 8.95 (ISBN 0-86578-117-6). Ind-US Inc.

Radhakrishnan, T., jt. auth. see Rajaraman, V.

Radicchi, S., jt. ed. see Chandrasekaran, B.

Radice, Betty, tr. The Letters of the Younger Pliny. (Penguin Classics Ser.). 320p. 1975. pap. 3.95 (ISBN 0-14-044127-1). Penguin.

Radice, E. A., jt. ed. see Kaser, M. C.

Radiguet, Raymond. Le Diable au Corps. (Easy Reader, B). pap. 3.95 (ISBN 0-88436-059-8, 40273). EMC.

Radin, E. L., et al. Practical Biomechanics for the Orthopedic Surgeon. 168p. 1979. 31.50x (ISBN 0-471-02703-0, Pub. by Wiley Med). Wiley.

Radin, P., ed. see California State Library Sutro Branch San Francisco.

Radin, Paul. African Folktales. 344p. (Orig.). 1983. pap. 9.95 (ISBN 0-8052-0732-5). Schocken.

--Trickster: A Study in American Indian Mythology. Repr. of 1956 ed. lib. bdg. 22.50x (ISBN 0-8371-2112-4, RATT). Greenwood.

--The Trickster: A Study in American Indian Mythology. new ed. LC 74-88986. 223p. 1972. pap. 5.95 (ISBN 0-8052-0351-6). Schocken.

Radin, R. J. Full Potential: Your Career & Life Planning Workbook. 240p. 1983. pap. 7.95 (ISBN 0-07-051091-1, GB). McGraw.

Radin, Sheldon & Falk, Robert. Physics for Scientists & Engineers. 928p. 1982. 31.95 (ISBN 0-13-674002-2). P-H.

Radine, Lawrence B. The Taming of the Troops: Social Control in the United States Army. LC 76-5262. (Contributions in Sociology Ser.: No. 22). (Orig.). 1976. lib. bdg. 29.95 (ISBN 0-8371-8911-X, RTT/). Greenwood.

Radiopress (Japan), ed. China Directory, 1983. 11th ed. LC 79-642283. 578p. 1982. 85.00x (ISBN 0-8002-3072-8). Intl Pubns Serv.

Radius, Marianne. Ninety Story Sermons for Children's Church. 286p. 1976. pap. 6.95 (ISBN 0-8010-7641-2). Baker Bk.

Radke, Freida. Word Resources. 3rd ed. LC 78-16414. 1979. pap. 10.95 o.p. (ISBN 0-672-61439-1). Odyssey Pr.

Radke, Ken. The Race That is Set Before Us. 160p. 1982. pap. 3.95 (ISBN 0-8407-5816-2). Nelson.

Radl, Shirley, jt. auth. see Zimbardo, Philip G.

Radl, Shirley L. Money, Morals, & Motherhood: The Hidden Agenda of the Religious New Right. 1983. pap. 7.95 (ISBN 0-686-43193-6, Delta). Dell.

--Money, Morals, & Motherhood: The Hidden Agenda of the Religious New Right. 1983. 15.95 (ISBN 0-686-38881-X, Sey Lawr). Delacorte.

Radl, Shirley L., jt. auth. see Zimbardo, Philip G.

Radlaeur, Ruth. Carlsbad Caverns National Park. LC 81-4560. (Parks for People Ser.). (Illus.). 48p. (gr. 3 up). 1981. PLB 10.60 (ISBN 0-516-07742-2). Childrens.

Radlaner, Ed. Karting Winners. LC 82-1129. (Fact & Fiction Bks.). (Illus.). (gr. 3-6). 1982. PLB 9.95g (ISBN 0-516-07811-9); pap. 3.95 (ISBN 0-516-47811-7). Childrens.

Radlaner, Ed & Radlaner, Ruth. Minibike Mania. LC 82-4403. (Mania Bks.). (Illus.). (gr. k-5). 1982. PLB 9.25g (ISBN 0-516-07792-9); pap. 2.95 (ISBN 0-516-47792-7). Childrens.

--Minibike Winners. LC 82-1150. (Fact & Fiction Bks.). (Illus.). (gr. 3-6). 1982. PLB 9.95g (ISBN 0-516-07814-3); pap. 3.95 (ISBN 0-516-47814-1). Childrens.

--Motorcycle Winners. LC 82-1177. (Fact & Fiction Bks.). (Illus.). (gr. 3-6). 1982. PLB 9.95g (ISBN 0-516-07815-1); pap. 3.95 (ISBN 0-516-47815-X). Childrens.

--Parade Mania. LC 82-4133. (Mania Bks.). (Illus.). (gr. k-5). 1982. PLB 9.25g (ISBN 0-516-07793-7); pap. 2.95 (ISBN 0-516-47793-5). Childrens.

Radlaner, Ruth, jt. auth. see Radlaner, Ed.

Radlauer, E. & Radlauer, R. Reading Incentive Program Series, 20 bks. Incl. Bicycle Racing. (ISBN 0-8372-0782-7); Bicycles. (ISBN 0-8372-0785-1); Custom Cars (ISBN 0-8372-0388-0); Dogs (ISBN 0-8372-0787-8); Drag Racing (ISBN 0-8372-0275-2); Drag Racing-Funny Cars (ISBN 0-8372-0379-1); Dune Buggies (ISBN 0-8372-0382-1); Dune Buggy Racing (ISBN 0-8372-0385-6); Horses (ISBN 0-8372-0373-2); Hot Air Balloons (ISBN 0-8372-0784-3); Karting (ISBN 0-8372-0271-X); Mighty Midgets (ISBN 0-8372-0272-8); Minibikes (ISBN 0-8372-0696-0); Motorcycle Racing (ISBN 0-8372-0695-2); Motorcycles (ISBN 0-8372-0274-4); Slot Car Racing (ISBN 0-8372-0273-6); Snowmobiles (ISBN 0-8372-0698-7); Surfing (ISBN 0-8372-0376-7); Teen Fair (ISBN 0-8372-0276-0); VW-Bugs (ISBN 0-8372-0697-9). (Illus.). (gr. 3-12). 1968-71. pap. 2.88 ea.; Set. pap. 57.60 (ISBN 0-8372-0965-X); tchr's. manual 1.98 (ISBN 0-8372-0477-1); cassettes, records & spirit masters avail. Bowmar-Noble.

Radlauer, Ed. Contest Mania. LC 81-9975. (Mania Bks.). (Illus.). 32p. (gr. k-5). 1981. PLB 9.25 (ISBN 0-516-07786-4); pap. 2.95 (ISBN 0-516-47786-2). Childrens.

--Cowboy Mania. LC 89-9969. (Mania Bks.). (Illus.). 32p. (gr. k-5). 1981. PLB 9.25 (ISBN 0-516-07787-2); pap. 2.95 (ISBN 0-516-47787-0). Childrens.

--Some Basics About Corvettes. LC 81-3797. (Gemini Ser.). (Illus.). 32p. (gr. 3 up). 1981. PLB 9.25 (ISBN 0-516-07693-0); pap. 2.95 (ISBN 0-516-47693-9). Childrens.

--Some Basics About Karate. LC 81-2743. (Gemini Ser.). (Illus.). 32p. (gr. 3 up). 1981. PLB 9.25 (ISBN 0-516-07694-9); pap. 2.95 (ISBN 0-516-47694-7). Childrens.

--Volcano Mania. LC 81-9916. (Mania Bks.). (Illus.). 32p. (gr. k-5). 1981. PLB 9.25 (ISBN 0-516-07788-0); pap. 2.95 (ISBN 0-516-47788-9). Childrens.

Radlauer, Edward. Dinosaur Mania. LC 78-23914. (Ready, Get Set, Go). (Illus.). 32p. (gr. k-6). 1979. PLB 9.25 (ISBN 0-516-07470-9, Elk Grove Bks); pap. 2.95 (ISBN 0-516-47470-7). Childrens.

--Monkey Mania. LC 77-8820. (Ready, Get Set, Go Books). (Illus.). 32p. (gr. 1-4). 1977. PLB 9.25 (ISBN 0-516-07466-0, Elk Grove Bks); pap. 2.95 (ISBN 0-516-47466-9, Elk Grove Bks). Childrens.

--Motorcycle Mania. LC 73-6657. (Ready, Get Set, Go Ser.). (Illus.). 32p. (gr. 1-4). 1973. PLB 9.25 (ISBN 0-516-07421-0, Elk Grove Bks); pap. 2.95 (ISBN 0-516-47421-9). Childrens.

--Shark Mania. LC 76-13500. (Ready, Get Set, Go Ser.). (Illus.). (gr. 1-4). 1976. PLB 9.25 (ISBN 0-516-07410-5, Elk Grove Bks); pap. 2.95 (ISBN 0-516-47410-3). Childrens.

--Some Basics About Classic Cars. LC 80-12587. (Gemini Ser.). (Illus.). 32p. 1980. 9.25g (ISBN 0-516-07689-2); pap. 2.95 (ISBN 0-516-47689-0). Childrens.

--Wild Wheels. LC 74-8460. (Ready, Get Set, Go Ser.). (Illus.). 32p. (gr. 1-4). 1974. PLB 9.25 (ISBN 0-516-07419-9, Elk Grove Bks); pap. 2.95 (ISBN 0-516-47419-7). Childrens.

Radlauer, R., jt. auth. see Radlauer, E.

Radlauer, Ruth. Denali National Park. LC 81-3876. (Parks for People Ser.). (Illus.). 48p. (gr. 3 up). 1981. PLB 10.60 (ISBN 0-516-07743-0). Childrens.

Radler, Don H. & Kephart, Newell C. Success Through Play. LC 59-6316. (Illus.). 1960. 13.41i (ISBN 0-06-013465-8, HarpT). Har-Row.

Radley, Gail. Zahra's Search. LC 82-11583. (Illus.). 32p. (Orig.). (gr. 2-6). 1982. pap. 3.75 (ISBN 0-87743-161-2). Baha'i.

--Zaira et Amir. Monajem, Shohreh, tr. LC 82-16331. Orig. Title: Zahra's Search. (Illus.). 32p. (Orig., Fr.). (gr. 2-6). 1982. pap. write for info. (ISBN 0-87743-179-5). Baha'i.

Radley, J. A. Starch Production Technology. (Illus.). 1976. 131.25x (ISBN 0-85334-662-3, Pub. by Applied Sci England). Elsevier.

Radley, J. A., ed. Examination & Analysis of Starch & Starch Products. (Illus.). 1976. 63.75x (ISBN 0-85334-692-5, Pub. by Applied Sci England). Elsevier.

--Industrial Uses of Starch & Its Derivatives. 1976. 63.75 (ISBN 0-85334-691-7, Pub. by Applied Sci England). Elsevier.

Radley, Roger J., ed. I Find My Joy in the Lord. LC 76-24446. (Emmaus Book Ser.). 144p. 1977. pap. 1.95 o.p. (ISBN 0-8091-1990-0). Paulist Pr.

Radley, Sheila. A Talent for Destruction. 224p. 1982. 10.95 (ISBN 0-684-17663-7, ScribT). Scribner.

Radley, Virginia L. Elizabeth Barrett Browning. (English Authors Ser.). lib. bdg. 11.95 (ISBN 0-8057-1064-7, Twayne). G K Hall.

--Samuel Taylor Coleridge. (English Authors Ser.). 1966. lib. bdg. 11.95 (ISBN 0-8057-1100-7, Twayne). G K Hall.

Radloff, V. V. South-Siberian Oral Literature Turkic Texts, Vol. 1. LC 66-64926. (Uralic & Altaic Ser: Vol. 79, Bk. 1). (Repr of 1866 ed). 1967. pap. text ed. 18.00x o.p. (ISBN 0-87750-075-4). Res Ctr Lang Semiotic.

--South-Siberian Oral Literature: Turkic Texts, Vol. 2. LC 66-64926. (Uralic & Altaic Ser: Vol. 79, Bk. 2). (Repr. of 1866 ed). 1968. pap. text ed. 25.00x o.p. (ISBN 0-87750-076-2). Res Ctr Lang Semiotic.

Radnoti, Miklos. Forced March: Selected Poems. Wilmer, Clive & Gomori, George, trs. from Hungarian. 62p. (Orig.). 1980. pap. 6.95 o.p. (ISBN 0-85635-275-6, Pub. by Carcanet New Pr England). Humanities.

--Forced March: Selected Poems. Wilmer, Clive & Gomori, George, trs. 62p. 1979. pap. text ed. 6.95x (ISBN 0-85635-275-6, Pub. by Carcanet New Pr England). Humanities.

Radojcic, S., et al. Icons. (Illus.). 237p. 1980. 50.00 (ISBN 0-933516-07-X). Alpine Bk Co.

Radok, J. R., ed. Problems of Continuum Mechanics. (Illus.). xx, 601p. 1961. text ed. 42.50 (ISBN 0-89871-040-5). Soc Indus-Appl Math.

Radosh, Ronald. Prophets on the Right: Profiles of Conservative Critics of American Globalism. LC 74-20840. 1975. 9.95 o.p. (ISBN 0-671-21901-4). S&S.

Radosh, Ronald & Milton, Joyce. The Rosenberg File: A Search for the Truth. LC 82-15569. 656p. Date not set. 22.50 (ISBN 0-03-049036-7). HR&W.

Radtke, Georg A. Encyclopedia of Budgerigars. Friese, U. Erich, tr. from Ger. 320p. 1981. 19.95 (ISBN 0-87666-899-6, H-1027). TFH Pubns.

Radtke, George A. Budgerigars. Orig. Title: Wellensitticher-Mein Hobby. (Illus.). 1979. 4.95 (ISBN 0-87666-984-4, KW-011). TFH Pubns.

Radvanyi, Janos. Delusion & Reality: Gambits, Hoaxes, & Diplomatic One-Upmanship in Vietnam. LC 78-57066. 1978. 10.95 (ISBN 0-89526-693-8). Regnery-Gateway.

Radwan, Ann B. The Dutch in Western India, Sixteen Hundred One-Sixteen Thirty Two. 1979. 14.00 (ISBN 0-8364-0311-8). South Asia Bks.

Radwan, Samir, jt. ed. see Ghai, Dharam.

Radway, Jerrold E., ed. Corrosion & Deposits from Combustion Gases: Abstracts & Index 1982. 675p. 1983. text ed. 69.50 (ISBN 0-89116-301-8). Hemisphere Pub.

Radway, Laurence I. Foreign Policy & National Defense: The Liberal Democracy in World Affairs. 1969. pap. 6.95x o.p. (ISBN 0-673-05560-4). Scott F.

Radzinowicz, Leon & Hood, Roger. Criminology & the Administration of Criminal Justice: A Bibliography. LC 76-24998. (Orig.). 1976. lib. bdg. 35.00x (ISBN 0-8371-9068-1, RCA/). Greenwood.

Radzinowicz, Leon, ed. see Maguire, Mike & Bennett, Trevor.

Radzinowicz, Sir Leon & Wolfgang, Marvin E., eds. Crime & Justice, 3 vols. 2nd, rev. ed. LC 76-9403. 1977. Vol. 1. 25.00x o.p. (ISBN 0-465-01462-3); Vol. 2. 25.00x o.s.i. (ISBN 0-465-01463-1); Vol. 3. 25.00x (ISBN 0-465-01464-X); Set. 72.00x (ISBN 0-465-01469-0); Vol. 1. pap. 10.95x (ISBN 0-465-01465-8); Vol. 2. pap. 9.50x (ISBN 0-465-01466-6); Vol. 3. pap. 14.95x (ISBN 0-465-01467-4). Basic.

Rae, Allan N. Crop Management Economics. LC 76-55129. 1977. 17.95 o.p. (ISBN 0-312-17657-0). St Martin.

Rae, B. Bennet. The Lemon Sole. (Illus.). 108p. 13.25 (ISBN 0-85238-013-5, FN40, FNB). Unipub.

Rae, Daphne. Love Until It Hurts: The Work of Mother Teresa & Her Missionaries of Charity. LC 81-47424. (Illus., Orig.). 1981. pap. 9.57i (ISBN 0-06-066729-X, RD 368, HarpR). Har-Row.

Rae, Helen, jt. ed. see Lynch, Richard.

Rae, John. Life of Adam Smith. LC 63-23522. Repr. of 1895 ed. 35.00x (ISBN 0-678-00101-4). Kelley.

--The Third Twin. LC 80-16001. 128p. (gr. 5-9). 1981. 8.95 o.p. (ISBN 0-7232-6192-X). Warne.

Rae, John B. Datsun: A History of Nissan Motor Corporation in the U.S.A. 1960-1980. (Illus.). 1982. 22.50 (ISBN 0-07-051112-8). McGraw.

Rae, Patricia. Student Nurse. (Nurse Ser.). 1983. pap. 2.95 (ISBN 0-8217-1123-7). Zebra.

Rae, Wesley D. Thomas Lodge. (English Authors Ser.: No. 59). 12.95 o.p. (ISBN 0-686-78391-3, Twayne). G K Hall.

Raeburn, Ben, jt. ed. see Kaufman, Edgar.

Raeburn, Michael. Architecture of the Western World. LC 80-50659. (Illus.). 304p. 1982. 37.50 (ISBN 0-8478-0349-X); pap. 19.95 (ISBN 0-8478-0435-6). Rizzoli Intl.

Raedmacher, H. Higher Mathematics from an Elementary Point of View. Goldfeld, L., ed. 160p. Date not set. text ed. price not set (ISBN 3-7643-3064-3). Birkhauser.

Raef, Laura. Dangerous Designs. 1981. pap. 6.95 (ISBN 0-686-84690-7, Avalon). Bouregy.

--Target for Terror. 1980. 6.95 (ISBN 0-686-59803-2, Avalon). Bouregy.

Raeff, Marc. Origins of the Russian Intelligentsia: The Eighteenth-Century Nobility. LC 66-19152. (Orig.). 1966. pap. 4.95 (ISBN 0-15-670150-2, Harv). HarBraceJ.

--The Well-Ordered Police State: Social & Institutional Change Through Law in the Germanies & Russia, 1660-1800. LC 82-19980. 304p. 1983. text ed. 23.50x (ISBN 0-300-02869-5). Yale U Pr.

Raeff, Marc, ed. Peter the Great Changes Russia. 2nd ed. (Problems in European Civilization Ser.). 1972. pap. text ed. 5.95 (ISBN 0-669-82701-0). Heath.

Rae-Grant, Quentin, jt. ed. see Stienhauer, Paul D.

Raeithel, Gert. Awful America: A Dictionary of 200 Years of European Abuse. Aman, Reinhold, ed. Zohn, Harry, tr. from Ger, French, Italian, Russ. Polish. LC 76-5698. (Maledicta Press Publications, Ser.: Vol.7). 1983. 15.00 (ISBN 0-916500-07-1). Maledicta. Postponed.

Rael, Leyla & Rudhyar, Dane. Astrological Aspects. pap. 9.95 (ISBN 0-943358-00-0). Aurora Press.

Raelson, Jeffrey. Getting to Know German Wines. (Illus.). 80p. pap. 4.95 (ISBN 0-686-84222-7). Banyan Bks.

Raemsch, Dorothy C. October Dawn: Poems. 26p. 1980. 3.75 (ISBN 0-9605398-0-8). Raemsch Pubns.

Raese, Jon W. & Baughman, Gary L., eds. Oil Shale Symposium Proceedings Index 1964-82. 100p. 1982. pap. text ed. 30.00 (ISBN 0-918062-52-7). Colo Sch Mines.

Raese, Jon W., ed. see Clark, George B.

Raese, Jon W., ed. see Huber, G. C.

Raese, Jon W., ed. see Smith, Duane A.

Raese, Jon W., ed. see Willard, Beatrice L.

Raese, Jon Wl, ed. see McCalpin, James P.

Raethel, Heinz-Sigurd. Bird Diseases. Ahrens, Christa, tr. from Ger. (Illus.). 96p. 1981. 4.95 (ISBN 0-87666-897-X, KW-122). TFH Pubns.

Raevskaia-Hughes, jt. ed. see Fleishman, L.

Rafaelsen, Lise, jt. ed. see Pines, Malcolm.

Rafelson, M. E., ed. Cellular & Humoral Defense against Disease. (Journal: Clinical Physiology & Biochemistry: Vol. 1, No. 2-5, 1983). (Illus.). 200p. 1983. pap. price not set (ISBN 3-8055-3693-3). S Karger.

Rafelson, Max E., et al. Basic Biochemistry. 4th ed. (Illus.). 1979. pap. text ed. 19.95 o.p. (ISBN 0-02-397610-1). Macmillan.

Raff, Beverly & Boyle, Rena F. Evaluation of Teaching Effectiveness. 42p. 1977. 4.50 (ISBN 0-686-38298-6, 15-1680). Natl League Nurse.

Raff, Beverly, ed. see Friesner, Arlyne.

Raff, Ellison S., ed. Computers & Operations Research: Environmental Applications. 1977. pap. text ed. 34.50 (ISBN 0-08-021348-0). Pergamon.

Raff, Martin J. Infectious Diseases. 2nd ed. (Medical Examination Review Bks.: Vol. 30). 1982. pap. 27.50 (ISBN 0-87488-147-1). Med Exam.

Raff, Rudolf A. & Kaufman, Thomas C. Embryos, Genes, & Evolution. 352p. 1983. text ed. 35.95 (ISBN 0-02-397500-8). Macmillan.

Raffaele, J. A. System & Unsystem: How American Society Works. LC 74-5214. 1974. 11.95 o.s.i. (ISBN 0-470-70484-5); pap. 6.95x o.s.i. (ISBN 0-470-70483-7). Halsted Pr.

Raffaele, Joseph A. The Economic Development of Nations. 1971. text ed. 11.95 (ISBN 0-685-77207-1, 0-394-30456). Phila Bk Co.

--The Mafia Principle. LC 79-89994. 1979. pap. text ed. 10.75 (ISBN 0-8191-0856-1). U Pr of Amer.

--The Management of Technology: Change in a Society of Organized Advocacies. rev. ed. LC 79-63752. 1979. pap. text ed. 12.75 (ISBN 0-8191-0739-5). U Pr of Amer.

Raffat, Donne. The Caspian Circle. 1978. 10.00 o.s.i. (ISBN 0-395-25933-9). HM.

Raffauf, Robert F. Handbook of Alkaloids & Alkaloid-Containing Plants. LC 73-113713. 1970. 145.00 (ISBN 0-471-70478-4, Pub. by Wiley-Interscience). Wiley.

Raffe, Marjorie & Harwood, Cecil. Eurthmy & the Impulse of Dance. 63p. 1974. pap. 5.00 (ISBN 0-85440-278-0, Pub. by Steinerbooks). Anthroposophic.

Raffel, Burton. Development of Modern Indonesian Poetry. LC 67-63246. 1967. 34.50x (ISBN 0-87395-024-0). State U NY Pr.

--Robert Lowell. LC 81-40470. (Literature and Life Ser.). 160p. 1982. 11.95 (ISBN 0-8044-2707-0). Ungar.

--T. S. Eliot. LC 81-70119. (Literature and Life Ser.). 160p. 1982. 11.95 (ISBN 0-8044-2708-9). Ungar.

Raffel, Burton, ed. Anthology of Modern Indonesian Poetry. 2nd ed. LC 68-19044. 1968. pap. 12.95x (ISBN 0-87395-031-3). State U NY Pr.

Raffel, Burton & Burago, Alla, eds. Selected Works of Nikolai S. Gumilev. LC 74-161442. 1972. 29.50x (ISBN 0-87395-098-4). State U NY Pr.

Raffel, Burton, tr. see Anwar, Chairil.

Raffel, Burton, tr. see Horace.

Raffel, Burton, tr. & intro. by see Horatius Flaccus.

Raffel, Jeffrey A. The Politics of School Desegregation: The Metropolitan Remedy in Delaware. 312p. 1980. 29.95 (ISBN 0-87722-176-6). Temple U Pr.

Raffel, Jeffrey A. & Shisko, Robert. Systematic Analysis of University Libraries: Application of Cost-Benefit Analysis to the M. I. T. Libraries. 1969. 17.50x (ISBN 0-262-18037-5). MIT Pr.

Raffel, Marshall. The U. S. Health System: Origins & Functions. LC 80-86. 1980. 23.50x (ISBN 0-471-04512-8, Pub. by Wiley Med). Wiley.

Raffensperger, Ellen & Zusy, Mary J. Quick Reference to Medical-Surgical Nursing. (Illus.). 510p. 1982. pap. text ed. 13.75 (ISBN 0-397-54358-1, Lippincott Nursing). Lippincott.

Rafferty, Jean. The Cruel Game: The Inside Story of Snooker. (Illus.). 160p. 1983. 22.50 (ISBN 0-241-10950-7, Pub. by Hamish Hamilton England); pap. 14.95 (ISBN 0-241-10951-5). David & Charles.

Rafferty, Kathleen, ed. The Dell Crossword Dictionary. 1983. pap. 5.95 (ISBN 0-440-56314-3, Dell Trade Pbks). Dell.

--Dell Crossword Puzzle Dictionary. 1983. pap. 3.50 (ISBN 0-440-16314-5). Dell.

Rafferty, Milton D. Historical Atlas of Missouri. LC 81-675048. (Illus.). 272p. 1982. 22.50 (ISBN 0-8061-1663-3); pap. 11.95 (ISBN 0-8061-1732-X). U of Okla Pr.

--Missouri: A Geography. (Geographies of the United States). 250p. 1983. lib. bdg. 35.00 o.p. (ISBN 0-86531-068-8); text ed. 20.00x o.p. (ISBN 0-686-78096-5); pap. 18.00 o.p. (ISBN 0-86531-435-7). Westview.

Rafferty, Robert. Careers in the Military: Good Training for Civilian Life. 1980. 11.95 (ISBN 0-525-66668-0). Lodestar Bks.

--One Hundred & One Lists: How to Do Practically Everything Faster, Easier, & Cheaper. Foley, June, ed. 160p. (Orig.). 1982. pap. 4.95 o.p. (ISBN 0-911818-27-8). World Almanac.

--One Hundred-One Lists: How to Do Practically Everything Faster, Easier & Cheaper. 160p. 1982. pap. 4.95 o.p. (ISBN 0-686-82100-9). World Almanac.

Rafferty, Sadie, jt. auth. see Rossi, Nick.

Raffler-Engel, Walburga von. Nonverbal Behavior in the Career Interview. 120p. 1983. pap. 14.00 (ISBN 90-272-2517-6). Benjamins North Am.

Rafiquzzaman, Mohamed. Microprocessors & Microcomputer Development Systems: Designing Microprocessor-Based Systems. 640p. 1983. text ed. 26.50 scp (ISBN 0-06-045312-5, HarpC); instr's. manual avail. (ISBN 0-06-365303-6). Har-Row.

Rafla Demetrius, Sameer. Mucous & Salivary Gland Tumours. (Illus.). 296p. 1970. photocopy ed. spiral 29.75x (ISBN 0-398-01537-6). C C Thomas.

Rafter, Rosalie & Alaia, Cheri. Practice RCT Writing Exam, No. 3. of 20 5.50 set (ISBN 0-937820-24-5). Westsea Pub.

--Practice RCT Writing Exam, No. 4. 1982. of 20 5.50 set (ISBN 0-937820-29-6). Westsea Pub.

Ragan, David. Who's Who in Hollywood, 1900-1976. 1977. 30.00 o.p. (ISBN 0-517-54822-4, Arlington Hse). Crown.

Ragan, Donal M. Structural Geology: An Introduction to Geometrical Techniques. 2nd ed. LC 73-3335. (Illus.). 288p. 1973. pap. text ed. 20.95 (ISBN 0-471-70481-4). Wiley.

Ragan, James. In the Talking Hours. 1979. 7.95 (ISBN 0-933090-00-5); pap. text ed. 3.95 (ISBN 0-686-96709-7). Eden Hall Pr.

Ragan, Lawrence, ed. see Ragan Report Workshop.

Ragan, Lise B., ed. see Garcia, Mary H. & Gonzalez-Mena, Janet.

Ragan Report Editors. Organizational Communication: Questions & Answers. 124p. (Orig.). 1980. pap. 9.95 o.p. (ISBN 0-931368-04-9). Ragan Comm.

Ragan Report Workshop. Workshops Notebook. Ragan, Lawrence & Lange, Catherine, eds. (Communications Library). 78p. 1982. three-ring binder 25.00 (ISBN 0-931368-11-1). Ragan Comm.

Ragan, Robert. Step-by-Step Bookkeeping. rev. ed. LC 74-7814. (Illus.). 1979. pap. 5.95 (ISBN 0-8069-8690-5). Sterling.

Ragan, Sam. Journey into Morning. Bayes, Ronald H., ed. (Illus.). 54p. 1981. 8.95 (ISBN 0-932662-34-X); pap. 4.95 (ISBN 0-932662-35-8). St Andrews NC.

--To the Water's Edge. 50p. 1971. 7.95 (ISBN 0-87716-032-5, Pub. by Moore Pub Co). F Apple.

Ragan, Sam, ed. Poetry Under the Stars. LC 79-65627. 1979. 12.00 (ISBN 0-87716-106-2, Pub. by Moore Pub Co). F Apple.

Ragaway, Martin. How to Get a Teenager to Run Away from Home. (The Laughter Library). 1980. 1.95 (ISBN 0-8431-0537-2). Price Stern.

--You Don't Have to Count Your Birthdays Until... (Laughter Library). (Illus.). 1979. pap. 1.75 o.p. (ISBN 0-8431-0534-8). Price Stern.

Ragaway, Martin, jt. ed. see Sloan, L. L.

Ragaway, Martin A. World's Worst Doctor Jokes. rev. ed. (Illus.). 48p. (Orig.). 1979. pap. 1.50 o.s.i. (ISBN 0-8431-0202-0). Price Stern.

--The World's Worst Golf Jokes. (Gift Bks. Ser.). 1972. pap. 1.75 (ISBN 0-8431-0200-4). Price Stern.

Ragaz, Anna, jt. auth. see Ackerman, A. Bernard.

Ragazzini, Giuseppe & Biagi, Adele, eds. Concise English-Italian Italian-English Dictionary. LC 73-17088. 1214p. 1973. pap. text ed. 12.95x (ISBN 0-582-55505-1). Longman.

Ragbourne, Jo. Seed Collage. (Illus.). 1983. 16.95 (ISBN 0-85936-241-8, Pub. by Midas Bks England). Hippocrene Bks.

Ragen, Joseph E. & Finston, Charles. Inside the World's Toughest Prison. (Illus.). 944p. 1962. photocopy ed. spiral 93.75x (ISBN 0-398-01538-4). C C Thomas.

Ragette, Friedrich. Architecture in Lebanon: The Lebanese House During the 18th & 19th Centuries. LC 80-14121. 1980. Repr. of 1974 ed. 60.00x (ISBN 0-88206-041-4). Caravan Bks.

Raggett, R. J., ed. Jane's Military Communications, 1982. (Jane's Yearbooks). (Illus.). 650p. 1982. 140.00 (ISBN 0-86720-615-2). Sci Bks Intl.

--Jane's Military Communications, 1983. 4th ed. (Jane's Yearbooks). (Illus.). 720p. 1983. 140.00x (ISBN 0-86720-646-2). Sci Bks Intl.

Raghavan, T. E., jt. auth. see Parthasarathy, T.

Raghavan, V., ed. The Ramayana Tradition in Asia. 1982. 18.00x (ISBN 0-8364-0899-3, Pub. by National Sahitya Akademi). South Asia Bks.

Ragland, Kay. Guinea Pigs. (Illus.). 1979. 4.95 (ISBN 0-87666-925-9, KW-016). TFH Pubns.

--Kittens. (Illus.). 1979. 4.95 (ISBN 0-87666-857-0, KW-019). TFH Pubns.

Ragont, Joe. How to Witness Successfully - Leader's Guide. 1979. pap. 4.95 (ISBN 0-8024-3793-1). Moody.

Ragosta, Millie J. Dream Weaver. LC 82-45266. (Starlight Romance Ser.). 192p. 1983. 11.95 (ISBN 0-385-18077-2). Doubleday.

--The House on Curtin Street. LC 78-22539. (Romantic Suspense Ser.). 1979. 10.95 o.p. (ISBN 0-385-12255-1). Doubleday.

Ragsdell, K. M., jt. auth. see Ravindran, A.

Raguin, Yves. Attention to the Mystery: Entry into the Spiritual Life. LC 82-60595. 1983. pap. 5.95 (ISBN 0-8091-2494-7). Paulist Pr.

Ragusa, Olga. Say It in Italian. pap. 2.25 (ISBN 0-486-20806-0). Dover.

Rahamimoff, P. & Harell, Moshe. Appetite & Lack of Appetite in Infancy & Early Childhood. 179p. 1979. 15.00x (ISBN 0-87397-146-9). Strode.

Rahav, Giora, jt. auth. see Shoham, Giora S.

Rahbar, Muhammad D. Cup of Jamshid: A Collection of Original Ghazal Poetry. Rahbar, Muhammad D., tr. from Urdu. LC 74-76004. (World Culture Ser.: No. 901). 199p. 1974. 10.00 (ISBN 0-89007-002-4). C Stark.

Rahde, H. F., jt. auth. see Hepworth, J. B.

Rahe, Harves. Index to Research in Business & Office Education. 192p. 1974. pap. text ed. 12.40 (ISBN 0-07-051138-1, G). McGraw.

Rahe, J., jt. auth. see Kopal, Z.

Raheja, P. C., et al. Textbook of Crop Production. (Illus.). 550p. 1983. text ed. 40.00x (ISBN 0-210-22588-2). Asia.

Rahim, Syed A. & Middleton, John, eds. Perspectives in Communication Policy & Planning. (Communications Monographs: No.3). 1978. pap. text ed. 5.00x (ISBN 0-8248-0581-X, Eastwest Ctr). UH Pr.

Rahimtoola, Shahbudin H., ed. Controversies in Coronary Artery Disease. LC 82-7373. (Cardiovascular Clinics Ser.: Vol. 13, No. 1). (Illus.). 367p. 1982. 45.00 (ISBN 0-8036-7272-1). Davis Co.

Rahm, B., jt. auth. see Bechler, Leo.

Rahm, D. A. Slides for Geology: Study Guide. 1971. text ed. 3.95 o.p. (ISBN 0-07-075217-6, C); 450.00 o.p. (ISBN 0-07-075215-X). McGraw.

Rahman, Fazlur. Islam. 2nd ed. LC 78-68547. 1979. pap. 6.50 (ISBN 0-226-70280-4); pap. 7.95 (ISBN 0-226-70281-2, P806, Phoen). U of Chicago Pr.

--Islam & Modernity: Transformation of an Intellectual Tradition. LC 82-2720. (Publications of the Center for Middle Eastern Studies: No. 15). 176p. 1982. lib. bdg. 15.00x (ISBN 0-226-70283-9). U of Chicago Pr.

--The Philosophy of Mulla Sadra Shirazi. LC 75-31693. 1976. 34.50x (ISBN 0-87395-300-2). State U NY Pr.

Rahman, N. K. & Guidotti, C., eds. Photon-Assisted Collisions & Related Topics. 377p. 1982. 63.50 (ISBN 0-686-84008-9). Harwood Academic.

Rahmas, D. Steve. Karl Marx: Philosophical Father of Communism. new ed. (Outstanding Personalities Ser.). 32p. 1975. lib. bdg. 2.95 incl. catalog cards (ISBN 0-87157-579-5); pap. 1.95 vinyl laminated covers (ISBN 0-87157-079-3). SamHar Pr.

Rahmas, D. Steve, ed. see Abbazia, Patrick.

Rahmas, D. Steve, ed. see Badrig, Robert H.

Rahmas, D. Steve, ed. see Barger, James.

Rahmas, D. Steve, ed. see Buchanan, John G.

Rahmas, D. Steve, ed. see Cevasco, G. A.

Rahmas, D. Steve, ed. see Finke, Blythe F.

Rahmas, D. Steve, ed. see Foy, Elizabeth & Schurer, John.

Rahmas, D. Steve, ed. see Fredman, Lionel E.

Rahmas, D. Steve, ed. see Fredman, Lionel E. & Kurland, Gerald.

Rahmas, D. Steve, ed. see Hecht, Robert A.

Rahmas, D. Steve, ed. see Kurland, Gerald.

Rahmas, D. Steve, ed. see Mallin, Jay.

Rahmas, D. Steve, ed. see Mushkat, Jerome.

Rahmas, D. Steve, ed. see Musso, Louis.

Rahmas, D. Steve, ed. see Paley, Alan L.

Rahmas, D. Steve, ed. see Prieto, Mariana.

Rahmas, D. Steve, ed. see Roucek, Joseph.

Rahmas, D. Steve, ed. see Roucek, Joseph S.

Rahmas, D. Steve, ed. see Salsini, Paul.

Rahmas, D. Steve, ed. see Shivanandan, Mary.

Rahmas, D. Steve, ed. see Stillman, Peter.

Rahmas, D. Steve, ed. see Whitney, R. W.

Rahmas, Sigurd C., ed. see Finke, Blythe F.

Rahmas, Sigurd C., ed. see Green, Bill.

Rahmas, Sigurd C., ed. see Hecht, Robert A.

Rahmas, Sigurd C., ed. see Jones, William M.

Rahmas, Sigurd C., ed. see Kurland, Gerald R.

Rahmas, Sigurd C., ed. see Longo, Lucas.

Rahmas, Sigurd C., ed. see Musso, Louis, III.

Rahmas, Sigurd C., ed. see Paley, Alan.

Rahmas, Sigurd C., ed. see Reynolds, Moira D.

Rahmas, Sigurd C., ed. see Richie, Claude G.

Rahmas, Sigurd C., ed. see Westphal, Ethel.

Rahmas, Steve, ed. see Abbazia, Patrick.

Rahmato, Dessalegn, ed. see African Bibliographic Center.

Rahmel, A., jt. ed. see Holmes, D. R.

Rahmus, D. Steve, ed. see Paley, Alan L.

Rahn, Carl. Science & the Religious Life. 1928. 37.50x (ISBN 0-685-69853-X). Elliots Bks.

Rahn, James J. Making Weather Work for You: A Practical Guide for Gardener & Farmer. LC 79-15725. (Illus.). 1979. pap. 7.95 o.p. (ISBN 0-88266-159-0). Garden Way Pub.

Rahn, Jay. A Theory for All Music: Problems & Solutions in the Analysis of Non-Western Forms. 288p. 1983. 35.00x (ISBN 0-8020-5538-9). U of Toronto Pr.

Rahn, Joan E. Biology: The Science of Life. 2nd ed. (Illus.). 1980. text ed. 24.95x (ISBN 0-02-397620-9). Macmillan.

--Eyes & Seeing. LC 80-23988. (Illus.). 128p. (gr. 5-9). 1981. PLB 10.95 (ISBN 0-689-30828-0). Atheneum.

--Nature in the City: Plants. LC 76-44324. (Science Information Ser.). (Illus.). (gr. k-5). 1977. PLB 10.25 o.p. (ISBN 0-8172-0661-2). Raintree Pubs.

--Plants That Changed History. LC 82-1748. (Illus.). 160p. (gr. 4-8). 1982. 9.95 (ISBN 0-689-30940-6). Atheneum.

Rahner, Hugo. Greek Myths & Christian Mystery. LC 79-156736. (Illus.). 1971. Repr. of 1963 ed. 15.00x (ISBN 0-8196-0270-1). Biblo.

Rahner, Karl. Faith & Ministry. (Theological Investigations Ser.: Vol. 19). 352p. 1983. 19.50 (ISBN 0-686-83771-1). Crossroad NY.

--Free Speech in the Church. LC 79-8717. Orig. Title: Das Freie Wort in der Kirche. 112p. 1981. Repr. of 1959 ed. lib. bdg. 19.25x (ISBN 0-313-20849-2, RAFS). Greenwood.

--God & Revelation, Vol. 18. (Theological Investigations Ser.). 352p. 1983. 19.50 (ISBN 0-8245-0571-9). Crossroad NY.

--The Love of Jesus & the Love of Neighbor. 96p. 1983. pap. 5.95 (ISBN 0-8245-0570-0). Crossroad NY.

--Watch & Pray with Me: The Seven Last Words. 1977. pap. 4.95 o.p. (ISBN 0-8245-0402-X). Seabury.

Raho, Louis, jt. auth. see Mears, Peter.

Rahr, Virginia A., jt. auth. see Beare, Patricia G.

Rai, G. S. Databook on Geriatrics. 228p. 1980. text ed. 19.95 o.p. (ISBN 0-8391-4109-2). Univ Park.

Rai, Krishna P., et al. Kulung-Nepali-English Glossary. 84p. 1975. pap. 2.00x (ISBN 0-88312-780-6) (ISBN 0-88312-379-7). Summer Inst Ling.

Rai, Rajkumar. The Geomorphology of Sonar Basin. 1980. pap. text ed. 16.00x (ISBN 0-391-01835-3). Humanities.

Rai, Sudha. V. S. Naipaul: A Study in Expatriate Sensibility. 192p. 1982. text ed. 7.50x (ISBN 0-391-02696-8). Humanities.

Raia, A., jt. auth. see Margulies, N.

Raia, Anthony P. Managing by Objectives. 1974. pap. 10.95x (ISBN 0-673-07757-8). Scott F.

Raia, Anthony P., jt. auth. see Margulies, Newton.

Raiborn, Mitchell H., jt. auth. see Anderson, Henry R.

Raichle, Marcus E., et al, eds. Tenth International Symposiumon: Cerebral Blood Flow & Metabolism. 604p. 1981. text ed. 66.00 (ISBN 0-89004-666-2). Raven.

Raichur, S. & Liske, C. T., eds. The Politics of Aid, Trade & Investment. LC 75-31886. (Comparative Political Economics & Public Policy Ser.). 218p. 1976. 25.95 o.s.i. (ISBN 0-470-54117-2). Halsted Pr.

Raiffa, H., jt. auth. see Luce, Robert D.

Raiffa, Howard, jt. auth. see Keeney, Ralph L.

Raigan, E. F. The Saturday Evening Post Dried Foods Unlimited Cookbook. LC 80-67060. (Illus.). 208p. 1980. pap. 5.95 (ISBN 0-89387-041-2, Co-Pub. by Sat Eve Post). Curtis Pub Co.

Raim, Joan. Case Reports in Reading & Learning Disabilities: Psychoeducational Evaluation & Remedial Planning. (Illus.). 300p. 1982. pap. 17.75x (ISBN 0-398-04565-8). C C Thomas.

Raimes, Ann. Techniques in Teaching Writing. (Teaching Techniques in English as a Second or Foreign Language Ser.). (Illus.). 128p. (Orig.). 1983. pap. text ed. 3.95x (ISBN 0-19-503250-0). Oxford U Pr.

Raimes, S. Wave Mechanics of Electronics in Metals. 1961. 24.50 (ISBN 0-444-10037-7). Elsevier.

Raimi, Ralph A. Vested Interests. xiv, 209p. 1982. 12.95 (ISBN 0-9609370-0-5). Raimi.

Raimo, John, ed. Biographical Directory of the Governors of the United States, 1978-1982. 1983. 45.00X (ISBN 0-930466-62-4). Meckler Pub.

Raimondi, A. J., ed. Concepts in Pediatric Neurosurgery, No. 3. (Illus.). xxii, 226p. 1983. 118.75 (ISBN 3-8055-3580-5). S Karger.

Raimondi, Anthony J. Pediatric Neuroradiology. LC 74-186953. (Illus.). 1972. text ed. 45.00 o.p. (ISBN 0-7216-7438-0). Saunders.

Raimondi, Anthony J., et al. The Dandy-Walker Syndrome. (Illus.). vi, 80p. 1983. 34.75 (ISBN 3-8055-1722-X). S Karger.

Raine, James W. Land of Saddle-Bags: A Study of the Mountain People of Appalachia. LC 70-78223. (Illus.). 1969. Repr. of 1924 ed. 30.00x (ISBN 0-8103-0160-1). Gale.

Raine, Kathleen, ed. see Blake, William.

Raine, N. The Treatment of Inherited Metabolic Disease. LC 74-19903. 294p. 1975. 19.95 o.p. (ISBN 0-444-19516-5). Elsevier.

Raine, Norman R. Tugboat Annie, Great Stories from the Saturday Evening Post. LC 77-78985. 320p. 1977. 5.95 (ISBN 0-89387-010-2, Co-Pub. by Sat Eve Post). Curtis Pub Co.

Rainer, Werner, jt. ed. see Schneider-Cuvay, M. Michaela.

Raines, Howell. My Soul Is Rested: Movement Days in the Deep South Remembered. LC 76-51292. 1977. 12.95 (ISBN 0-399-11853-5). Putnam Pub Group.

Raines, John C. & Dean, Thomas, eds. Marxism & Radical Religion: Essays Toward a Revolutionary Humanism. LC 78-119903. 176p. 1970. 19.95 (ISBN 0-87722-002-6). Temple U Pr.

Raines, John C., et al, eds. Community & Capital in Conflict: Plant Closings & Job Loss. 318p. 1982. 22.95 (ISBN 0-87722-270-3). Temple U Pr.

Raines, Margaret. Consumers' Management. rev. ed. Orig. Title: Managing Livingtime. (Illus.). (gr. 9-12). 1973. text ed. 17.28 (ISBN 0-87002-123-0); tchr's guide avail. Bennett IL.

Raines, Robert A. A Faithing Oak: Meditations from the Mountain. 128p. 1982. 9.95 (ISBN 0-8245-0485-2). Crossroad NY.

Raines, Robert A., ed. see Wallis, Jim.

Raineval, Melville, jt. ed. see Ruvigny.

Rainey, Buck. Those Fabulous Serials: 1912-1956. (Illus.). Date not set. 30.00 (ISBN 0-498-02584-5). A S Barnes.

Rainey, Buck, jt. auth. see Adams, Les.

Rainey, Froelich G. & Lerici, Carlo M. The Search for Sybaris, 1960-1965. (Museum Monographs). (Illus.). 313p. 1967. bound 10.00xsoft (ISBN 0-934718-21-0). Univ Mus of U PA.

Rainey, Lee, jt. auth. see Kyper, Frank.

Rainey, Patricia A. Illusions: A Journey into Perception. (Illus.). 112p. (Orig.). 1973. pap. 9.50 o.p. (ISBN 0-208-01212-5, Linnet). Shoe String.

Rainey, R. C. Insect Flight. LC 75-22091. (Royal Entomological Society of London Symposium Ser.). 287p. 1976. 69.95 o.s.i. (ISBN 0-470-70550-7). Halsted Pr.

--Meteorology & the Migration of Desert Locusts: Applications of Synoptic Meteorology in Locust Control. 1963. 35.00 (ISBN 0-686-82414-8, Pub. by Centre Overseas Research). State Mutual Bk.

Rainey, R. C. & Aspilden, C. Meteorology & the Migration of Desert Locusts. (Technical Note Ser.). 1963. pap. 25.00 (ISBN 0-685-22324-8, W25, WMO). Unipub.

Rainey, R. C. & Waloff, Z. The Behavior of the Red Locust (Normadacris Septemfasciata Serville) in Relation to the Topography, Meteorology & Vegetatation of the Rukwa Rift Valley, Tanganyika. 1957. 35.00x (ISBN 0-85135-031-3, Pub. by Centre Overseas Research). State Mutual Bk.

Rainey, R. C., jt. auth. see Waloff, Z.

Rainford, Marcus. Our Lord Prays for His Own. 1978. pap. 8.95 o.p. (ISBN 0-8024-6195-6). Moody.

Rainier, Peter. My Vanished Africa. 1940. text ed. 29.50x (ISBN 0-686-83628-6). Elliots Bks.

Rains, Albert & Henderson, Laurance G., eds. With Heritage So Rich. Rev. ed. (Landmark Reprint Ser.). 200p. 1983. 12.95 (ISBN 0-89133-104-2). Preservation Pr.

Rains, John. Cruising Ports: California to Florida Via Panama. New ed. (Illus.). 208p. (Orig.). 1982. pap. 17.95 (ISBN 0-930030-27-3). Western Marine Ent.

Rains, Karen J. & Shugart, Cecil G. The Phenomena of Physics: A Conceptual Laboratory Program. 176p. 1982. pap. text ed. 14.95 (ISBN 0-8403-2771-4). Kendall-Hunt.

Rainsbury, Robert. Written English: An Introduction for Beginning Students of English As a Second Language. 1977. pap. 10.95 (ISBN 0-13-970673-9). P-H.

Rainsford, K. D. & Brune, K., eds. Symposium on Aspirin & Related Drugs: Their Actions & Uses. Whitehouse, M. W., tr. (Agents & Actions Suppl. Ser.: No. 1). 118p. 1977. pap. 24.20x (ISBN 3-7643-0902-4). Birkhauser.

Raintree, George P. The Prentice-Hall Great International Atlas. 416p. 1981. 69.95 (ISBN 0-13-695833-8). P-H.

Rainville, E. D. & Bedient, P. E. Elementary Differential Equations. 6th ed. 1981. 27.95x (ISBN 0-02-397770-1). Macmillan.

--Short Course in Differential Equations. 6th ed. 1981. 24.95x (ISBN 0-02-397760-4). Macmillan.

Rainville, Earl D. Special Functions. LC 70-172380. (Illus.). xii, 365p. 1972. Repr. of 1960 ed. text ed. 15.95 (ISBN 0-8284-0258-2). Chelsea Pub.

Rainwater, Clarence, jt. auth. see Walker, Sandy.

Rainwater, Dorothy T. Encyclopedia of American Silver Manufacturers. (Illus.). 222p. 1975. 8.95 (ISBN 0-686-36484-8). Md Hist.

Rainwater, Dorothy T. & Felger, Donna H. American Spoons: Souvenir & Historical with Prices. (Illus.). 9.95 (ISBN 0-8407-4308-4). Wallace-Homestead.

--A Collector's Guide to Spoons Around the World. 2nd ed. (Illus.). 19.95 (ISBN 0-686-84756-3). Schiffer.

Rainwater, Lee & Yancey, William L. Moynihan Report & the Politics of Controversy. (Illus.). 1967. pap. 11.50x (ISBN 0-262-68009-2). MIT Pr.

Raish, Peggy, jt. auth. see Klaus, Billie.

Raistrick, Arthur. Industrial Archaeology: An Historical Survey. (Illus.). 1972. text ed. 19.95x o.p. (ISBN 0-413-28050-0, Pub. by Eyre Methuen England). Methuen Inc.

Raistrick, Duncan & Davies, Ian. Dealing with Drink. 256p. 1981. 30.00x (ISBN 0-563-16489-1, BBC Pubns). State Mutual Bk.

Raitsin, V. I. Planning the Standard of Living According to Consumption Norms. Kirsch, Leonard J., ed. LC 68-14429. 1969. 22.50 (ISBN 0-87332-021-2). M E Sharpe.

Raitz, Karl B. & Ulack, Richard. Land, People, & Development in Appalachia. 375p. 1983. lib. bdg. 30.00x (ISBN 0-86531-075-0). Westview.

Raizis, M. Bryon. Dionysios Solomos. (World Authors Ser.). lib. bdg. 15.95 (ISBN 0-8057-2846-5, Twayne). G K Hall.

Raj, Des. Design of Sample Surveys. 1971. text ed. 22.50 o.p. (ISBN 0-07-051155-1, C). McGraw.

Raj, Deva, ed. see Experts Group Meeting, National Institute of Urban Affairs, & Town & Country Planning, India, April, 1977.

Rajaee, Farhang, ed. see Taleqani, Mahmood.

Rajaee, Farhang, jt. tr. see Taleqani, Mahmood.

Rajagapalachari, Chakravarti, tr. see Vyasa.

Rajagopal, D., ed. Commentaries on Living. 1956. 11.95 o.p. (ISBN 0-575-00415-0, Pub. by Gollancz England). David & Charles.

Rajagopalachari, Chakravarti, ed. & tr. see Valmiki.

Rajagopalachari, Chakravarti, ed. see Vyasa.

Rajan, B., ed. see Hawthorne, Nathaniel.

Rajan, Balachandra. Dark Dancer, a Novel. Repr. of 1958 ed. lib. bdg. 15.75x (ISBN 0-8371-3139-1, RADD). Greenwood.

Rajan, Bhalchandra. Too Long in the West. 1961. pap. 2.35 (ISBN 0-88253-175-1). Ind-US Inc.

Rajan, K. V. Invitation to Indian Architecture. (Heritage India Ser.). (Illus.). 100p. 1982. text ed. 27.00x (ISBN 0-391-02735-2). Humanities.

Rajan, M. S. Expanding Jurisdiction of the United Nations. LC 81-16985. 252p. 1982. 30.00 (ISBN 0-379-20727-3). Oceana.

--India in World Affairs 1954-56. 30.00x o.p. (ISBN 0-210-26916-2). Asia.

--Sovereignty Over Natural Resources. 1978. text ed. 15.00x (ISBN 0-391-00869-2). Humanities.

Rajan, Mohan S. Atoms of Hope. 155p. 1980. 14.95x (ISBN 0-940500-39-6, Pub by Allied Pubs India). Asia Bk Corp.

Rajan, Mohini, jt. auth. see Lynton, Harriet R.

Rajan, S. V. & Rao, H. G. Soil & Crop Productivity. 1973. 12.95x (ISBN 0-210-27100-0). Asia.

Rajan, V. N. Victimology in India. 176p. 1981. 14.95x (ISBN 0-940500-86-8, Pub by Allied Pubs India). Asia Bk Corp.

Rajana, C. The Chemical & Petro-Chemical Industries of Russia & Eastern Europe, 1960-1980. 100.00x (ISBN 0-686-96989-8, Pub. by Scottish Academic Pr Scotland). State Mutual Bk.

Rajaraman, R. Solitons & Instantons: An Introduction to Solitons & Instantons in Quantum Field Theory. 412p. 1982. 83.00 (ISBN 0-444-86229-3). Elsevier.

Rajaraman, V. & Radhakrishnan, T. An Introduction to Digital Computer Design. 2nd ed. (Illus.). 416p. 1983. pap. 19.95 (ISBN 0-13-480657-3). P-H.

Rajaratnam, N. Turbulent Jets. (Developments in Water Science: Vol. 5). 1976. 68.00 (ISBN 0-444-41372-3). Elsevier.

Rajasekaran, P. K., jt. auth. see Srinath, M. D.

Rajasekhara, S. Early Chalukya Art at Aihola. (Illus.). 1982. text ed. write for info. (ISBN 0-7069-1963-7, Pub. by Vikas India). Advent NY.

Rajbman, N. S. & Chadeev, V. M. Identification of Industrial Processes: The Application of Computers in Research & Production Control. 1978. 64.00 (ISBN 0-444-85181-X, North-Holland). Elsevier.

Rajbman, N. S., ed. Identification & System Parameter Estimation: Proceedings of the 4th IFAC Symposium, Tbilisi, USSR, September, 1976. 1978. 191.50 (ISBN 0-444-85096-1, North-Holland). Elsevier.

Rajecki, D. W. Comparing Behavior: Studying Man Studying Animals. 304p. 1983. write for info. (ISBN 0-89859-259-3). L Erlbaum Assocs.

Rajhans, Gyan S. & Bragg, Gordon M. Engineering Aspects of Asbestos Dust Control. LC 77-92598. (Illus.). 1978. 39.95 (ISBN 0-250-40227-0). Ann Arbor Science.

Rajhans, Gyan S. & Sullivan, John. Asbestos Sampling & Analysis. LC 80-65511. 1981. text ed. 39.95 (ISBN 0-250-40335-8). Ann Arbor Science.

Rajka, George. Atopic Dermatitis. LC 74-14868. (Major Problems in Dermatology Ser: No. 3). (Illus.). 165p. 1975. 10.00 (ISBN 0-7216-7448-8). Saunders.

Rajneesh, Acharya. The Mysteries of Life & Death. Bisen, Malini, tr. from Hindi. 1978. pap. 3.50 (ISBN 0-89684-045-X, Pub. by Motilal Banarsidass India). Orient Bk Dist.

Rajneesh, Bhagwan S. The Book of the Secrets. pap. 6.95i (ISBN 0-06-090564-6, CN 564, CN). Har-Row.

--I Am the Gate: Initiation & Discipleship. (Orig.). 1977. pap. 5.72i (ISBN 0-06-090573-5, CN-573, CN). Har-Row.

--I Say Unto You, 2 vols. (Jesus Ser.). (Illus.). 19.50 ea. (ISBN 0-88050-085-9). Vol. II o.p. Vol. I. pap. 15.95 ea. (ISBN 0-88050-585-0). Vol. II (ISBN 0-88050-586-9). Rajneesh Found Intl.

--Meditation: The Art of Ecstasy. Bharti, Ma S., ed. 1978. pap. 3.37i (ISBN 0-06-080394-0, P394, PL). Har-Row.

--The Psychology of the Esoteric. (Orig.). 1978. pap. 4.95i (ISBN 0-06-090616-2, CN 616, CN). Har-Row.

--Sex. Lear, Pat, ed. (Quotations from Bhagwan Shree Rajneesh: No. 1). 104p. 1981. pap. 3.95 (ISBN 0-941990-01-X). Lear.

--The Wisdom of the Sands, 2 vols. (Illus.). 1980. Vol. I, 349 pgs. 19.95 ea. (ISBN 0-88050-174-X). Vol. II, 366 pgs (ISBN 0-88050-175-8). Vol.1. pap. 15.95 ea. (ISBN 0-88050-674-1). Rajneesh Found Intl.

Rajneesh, Bhagwan Shree. Ah This! Rajneesh Foundation International, ed. (Illus.). 240p. 1982. pap. 8.95 (ISBN 0-88050-502-8). Rajneesh Found Intl.

--Book of Wisdom, Vol. I. Rajneesh Foundation International, ed. 385p. 1982. pap. 9.95 (ISBN 0-88050-530-3). Rajneesh Found Intl.

--Don't Bite My Finger, Look Where I Am Pointing. Rajneesh Foundation International, ed. 230p. 1982. pap. 14.95 (ISBN 0-88050-550-8). Rajneesh Found Intl.

--Don't Look Before You Leap. Rajneesh Foundation International, ed. 232p. 1983. pap. 12.95 (ISBN 0-88050-554-0). Rajneesh Found Intl.

--The Goose is Out. Rajneesh Foundation International, ed. 286p. 1982. pap. 10.95 (ISBN 0-88050-571-0). Rajneesh Found Intl.

--Love, Life, Laughter. Rajneesh Foundation International, ed. 64p. 1983. pap. 3.95 (ISBN 0-88050-696-2). Rajneesh Found Intl.

--The Orange Book. 2nd ed. Rajneesh Foundation International, ed. (Illus.). 227p. 1983. pap. 4.95 (ISBN 0-686-84534-X). Rajneesh Found Intl.

--The Secret of Secrets, Vol. 2. Rajneesh Foundation International, ed. 537p. 1983. pap. 16.95 (ISBN 0-88050-629-6). Rajneesh Found Intl.

--Walking in Zen, Sitting in Zen. Rajneesh Foundation International, ed. (Illus.). 450p. 1982. pap. 10.95 (ISBN 0-88050-668-7). Rajneesh Found Intl.

Rajneesh Foundation International, ed. see Rajneesh, Bhagwan Shree.

Rajneesh Foundation International, ed. see Rajneesh, Bhagwan shree.

Rajneesh Foundation International, ed. see Rajneesh, Bhagwan Shree.

Rajouane, Maggie. Loving the Single Man. 1977. Repr. text ed. 11.95 (ISBN 0-914094-05-X). Symphony.

Raju, K. Ranga, jt. auth. see Garde, R. J.

Raju, M. Bapi, jt. auth. see Raju, M. R.

Raju, M. R. & Raju, M. Bapi. Heavy Particple Radiotherapy. LC 79-27459. 1980. 42.00 (ISBN 0-12-576250-X). Acad Pr.

Raju, P. T. The Philosophical Traditions of India. LC 70-189859. 1972. 10.95x (ISBN 0-8229-1105-1). U of Pittsburgh Pr.

RAK Associates, jt. auth. see Kuehn, Dick.

Rakel, Robert E., ed. Year Book of Family Practice 1983. 1983. 41.00 (ISBN 0-8151-7024-6). Year Bk Med.

Rakes, Thomas A. & Choate, Joyce S. Individual Evaluation Procedures in Reading. 256p. 1983. 19.95 (ISBN 0-13-457226-2); pap. 14.95 (ISBN 0-13-457218-1). P-H.

Rakich, J. & Darr, K., eds. Hospital Organization & Management: Text & Readings. 3rd ed. LC 77-24710. (Health Systems Mgmt. Ser.: Vol. 11). 600p. 1983. text ed. 29.95 (ISBN 0-89335-176-8). SP Med & Sci Bks.

Rakosnik, J., jt. auth. see Tichy, M.

Rakove, Jack N. The Beginnings of National Politics: An Interpretive History of the Continental Congress. LC 82-15186. (Paperback Reprint Ser.). 512p. (Orig.). 1982. pap. text ed. 8.95 (ISBN 0-8018-2864-3). Johns Hopkins.
Rakovski, Marc. Towards an East European Marxism. LC 77-18171. 1978. 18.95 (ISBN 0-312-81048-2). St Martin.
Rakow, Sue F., jt. auth. see Carpenter, Carol B.
Rakowska-Harmstone, Teresa, ed. Perspectives for Change in Communist Societies. (Special Studies on the Soviet Union & Eastern Europe). 1979. lib. bdg. 25.00 (ISBN 0-89158-336-X). Westview.
Rakowski, James P., ed. Transportation Economics: A Guide to Information Sources. LC 73-17584. (Economics Information Guide Series: Vol. 5). 200p. 1976. 42.00x (ISBN 0-8103-1307-3). Gale.
Raktoe, B. L., et al. Factorial Designs. LC 80-28905. (Wiley Series in Probability & Mathematical Statistics). 209p. 1981. 31.95 (ISBN 0-471-09040-9, Pub. by Wiley-Interscience). Wiley.
Ralegh, Walter. A Choice of Sir Walter Ralegh's Verse. Nye, Robert, ed. 72p. 1972. pap. 3.95 (ISBN 0-571-08753-1). Faber & Faber.
Raleigh, Alexander. The Book of Esther. 1980. 9.75 (ISBN 0-86524-037-X, 1701). Klock & Klock.
Raleigh, John H. The Chronicle of Leopold & Molly Bloom: "Ulysses" As Narrative. LC 76-20025. 1978. 20.00x (ISBN 0-520-03301-9). U of Cal Pr.
Raleigh, Walter, et al, eds. Shakespeare's England: An Account of the Life & Manners of His Age, 2 Vols. (Illus.). 1916. 59.00x o.p. (ISBN 0-19-821252-6). Oxford U Pr.
Ralfs, J. British Desmidieae. (Illus.). 1962. 32.00 (ISBN 3-7682-0144-9). Lubrecht & Cramer.
Ralis, H. A., et al. Techniques in Neurohistology. 1973. 14.95 o.p. (ISBN 0-407-77400-9). Butterworth.
Rall, Eilene M., jt. auth. see Snyder, Karl E.
Rall, J. E. & Kopin, I. J. The Thyroid & Biogenic Amines. (Methods in Investigative & Diagnostic Endocrinology Ser.: Vol. 1). 1972. 155.50 (ISBN 0-444-10371-6, North-Holland). Elsevier.
Rall, L. B. Error in Digital Computation, Vol. II. 1965. 14.00 (ISBN 0-471-70653-1, Pub. by Wiley). Krieger.
Ralli, Mary P., jt. auth. see Ordman, Kathryn A.
Rallis, T. Intercity Transportation: Engineering & Planning. 1978. 54.95 o.s.i. (ISBN 0-470-01394-X). Halsted Pr.
Ralls, Kenneth, et al. Introduction to Materials Science & Engineering. LC 76-10813. 608p. 1976. text ed. 35.95x (ISBN 0-471-70665-5); solutions manual 10.00 (ISBN 0-471-02397-3). Wiley.
Ralov, Kirsten, ed. The Bournonville School, 4 Vols. Agersnap, Harald, et al. Incl. Vol. 1. Daily Classes. ix, 109p (ISBN 0-8247-6521-4); Vol. 3. Music. xiv, 133p (ISBN 0-8247-6522-2); Vol. 3. Benesh Notation. xiv, 133p. o.p. (ISBN 0-8247-6523-0); Vol. 4. Labanotation: Dance Program-Vol. 12. xxv, 105p. o.p. (ISBN 0-8247-6523-0). LC 78-9554. (The Dance Program: Vol. 12). (Illus.). xv, 187p. 1979. pap. 19.95 set (ISBN 0-8247-6520-6). Princeton Bk Co.
Ralph, C. H. Books in the Dock. 1970. 7.50 o.p. (ISBN 0-233-95901-7). Transatlantic.
Ralph, Charles L. Introductory Animal Physiology. (McGraw Hill Ser. in Organismic Biology). (Illus.). 1978. text ed. 29.95 (ISBN 0-07-051156-X, C). McGraw.
Ralph, Christine A., jt. auth. see Cetron, Marvin J.
Ralph, James. Case of Authors by Profession or Trade, 1758, Champion 1739. LC 66-10008. 1966. 31.00x (ISBN 0-8201-1037-X). Schol Facsimiles.
Ralph, L. Philip. The Renaissance in Perspective. 224p. 1973. o.p 13.95 (ISBN 0-312-67270-5); pap. text ed. 8.95 (ISBN 0-312-67235-7). St Martin.
Ralph McElroy Company, tr. see Chuang, Yao H.
Ralph, Margaret. Historias Que Jesus Conto. (Serie Jirafa). Orig. Title: Stories Jesus Told. 28p. 1979. 3.95 (ISBN 0-311-38537-0, Edit Mundo). Casa Bautista.
--Jesus: Historias de su Vida. LaValle, Teresa, tr. (Serie Jirafa). Orig. Title: The Life of Jesus. 28p. 1979. 3.95 (ISBN 0-311-38536-2, Edit Mundo). Casa Bautista.
--Personas Escogidas De Dios. (Serie Jirafa). Orig. Title: God's Special People. 28p. 1979. 3.95 (ISBN 0-311-38535-4, Edit Mundo). Casa Bautista.
Ralph, Philip L., jt. auth. see Burns, Edward M.
Ralphs, S. Dante's Journey to the Centre. 1972. 9.50 (ISBN 0-7190-1254-6). Manchester.
Ralston & Tarshis. Six Weeks to a Better Level of Tennis. LC 77-3289. 1977. 9.95 o.p. (ISBN 0-671-22580-4). S&S.
Ralston, A. & Rabinowitz, Philip. A First Course in Numerical Analysis. (McGraw Hill Intl. Ser. in Pure & Applied Mathematics). (Illus.). 1978. text ed. 32.50 (ISBN 0-07-051158-6, C); answer manual 31.00 (ISBN 0-07-051167-5). McGraw.
Ralston, Anthony. Introduction to Programming & Computer Science. LC 77-13034. 538p. 1978. Repr. of 1971 ed. lib. bdg. 28.00 (ISBN 0-88275-619-2). Krieger.
Ralston, Anthony, ed. Encyclopedia of Computer Science & Engineering. 2nd ed. 1700p. 1982. 87.50 (ISBN 0-442-24496-7). Van Nos Reinhold.
Ralston, Anthony & Wilf, H. S., eds. Mathematical Methods for Digital Computers, 2 Vols. LC 60-6509. 1960. Vol. 1. 42.50 o.s.i. (ISBN 0-471-70686-8); Vol. 2. 42.95 (ISBN 0-471-70689-2, Pub by Wiley-Interscience). Wiley.
Ralston, Caroline. Grass Huts & Warehouses: A Study of Five Pacific Beach Communities of the Nineteenth Century. LC 77-92406. 1978. text ed. 14.00x (ISBN 0-8248-0597-6). UH Pr.
Ralston, David B. Army of the Republic: The Place of the Military in the Political Evolution of France, 1871-1914. 1967. 20.00x (ISBN 0-262-18021-9). MIT Pr.
Ralston, John & White, Mike. Coaching Today's Athlete: A Football Textbook. LC 78-175727. (Illus.). 471p. 1971. text ed. 18.95 (ISBN 0-87484-193-3). Mayfield Pub.
Ram, James & Townshend, John N. A Treatise on Facts As Subjects of Inquiry by a Jury. 3rd ed. 486p. 1982. Repr. of 1873 ed. lib. bdg. 35.00x (ISBN 0-8377-1033-2). Rothman.
Ram, M. D. Surgery. 7th ed. (Medical Examination Review Book: Vol. 5). 1981. pap. 11.95 (ISBN 0-87488-105-6). Med Exam.
Ram, Michael. Essential Mathematics for College Physics: A Self Study Guide. 278p. 1982. pap. text ed. 10.95x (ISBN 0-471-86454-4). Wiley.
Rama, Frederick Lenz. The Wheel of Dharma. Blank, Nina, et al, eds. LC 82-83343. (Illus.). 112p. (Orig.). 1982. pap. text ed. 5.00 (ISBN 0-941868-01-X). Lakshmi.
Rama, Sarma. Things Unattempted: A Study of Milton. 154p. 1982. text ed. 16.25x (ISBN 0-7069-1393-0, Pub. by Vikas India). Humanities.
Rama, Swami. Enlightenment Without God (Mandukya Upanishad) LC 82-83391. 144p. (Orig.). 1982. pap. 4.95 (ISBN 0-89389-084-7). Himalayan Intl Inst.
--Lectures on Yoga. rev., 6th ed. LC 79-114571. (Illus.). 1979. 7.50 (ISBN 0-89389-050-2); pap. 5.95 (ISBN 0-89389-051-0). Himalayan Intl Inst.
Ramachandran, Gopalasamudram N., ed. Treatise on Collagen, 2 Vols. 1968. Vol. 2A. 68.50 (ISBN 0-12-576772-2); Vol. 2B. 77.00 (ISBN 0-12-576780-3). Acad Pr.
Ramachandran, H. Behaviour in Space: Rural Marketing in an Underdeveloped Economy. 121p. 1982. text ed. 14.50x (ISBN 0-391-02784-0, 40855, Pub. by Concept India). Humanities.
--Village Clusters & Rural Development. 140p. 1980. text ed. 15.00x (ISBN 0-391-02138-9). Humanities.
Ramachandran, L. Food Planning: Some Vital Aspects. 392p. 1982. 22.95x (ISBN 0-940500-68-X, Pub by Allied Pubs India). Asia Bk Corp.
Ramachandran, P. A. & Chaudhari, R. V. Three Phase Catalytic Reactors. (Topics in Chemical Engineering Ser.: Vol. 2). 530p. 1982. write for info. (ISBN 0-677-05650-8). Gordon.
Ramachandran, Srinivasa, jt. auth. see Finch, Christopher.
Ramachandran, V. S. Calcium Chloride in Concrete: Science & Technology. (Illus.). 1976. text ed. 57.50x (ISBN 0-85334-682-8, Pub. by Applied Sci England). Elsevier.
Ramage, Craufurd T. Familiar Quotations from German & Spanish Authors. LC 68-2043. (With English translations). Repr. of 1904 ed. 34.00x (ISBN 0-8103-3192-6). Gale.
--Familiar Quotations from Greek Authors. LC 68-22044. Orig. Title: Beautiful Thoughts from Greek Authors. 1968. Repr. of 1895 ed. 34.00x (ISBN 0-8103-3193-4). Gale.
Ramai, Raja V., ed. Longwall-Shortwall Mining: State-of-the-Art. LC 81-67436. (Illus.). 296p. 33.00x (ISBN 0-89520-288-3). Soc Mining Eng.
Ramakrishnananda, Swami. God & Divine Incarnations. pap. 3.00 (ISBN 0-87481-445-6). Vedanta Pr.
--Krishna: Pastoral & Kingmaker. pap. 2.25 (ISBN 0-87481-447-2). Vedanta Pr.
Ramakrisnananda, Swami. Life of Sri Ranauja. 1979. pap. 6.75 o.p. (ISBN 0-87481-446-4). Vedanta Pr.
Ramaley, Judith A., jt. auth. see Bevelander, Gerrit.
Ramaley, Judith A., ed. Covert Discrimination & Women in the Sciences. LC 77-18443. (AAAS Selected Symposium Ser: No. 14). (Illus.). 1978. lib. bdg. 15.00 o.p. (ISBN 0-89158-442-0). Westview.
Ramalho, R. S. Introduction to Wastewater Treatment Processes. 2nd ed. write for info. (ISBN 0-12-576560-6). Acad Pr.
Ramalingam, P. Systems Analysis for Managerial Decisions: A Computer Approach. LC 76-10534. 1976. 40.95x (ISBN 0-471-70710-4); tchr's. manual 13.00 (ISBN 0-471-01949-6). Wiley.
Ramalingham, R., jt. ed. see Kops, L.
Ramalingom, T. Dictionary of Instrument Science. LC 81-14724. 588p. 1982. 24.95 (ISBN 0-471-86396-3, Pub. by Wiley-Interscience). Wiley.
Ramamurti, C. C. Orthopaedics in Primary Care. Tinker, Richard, ed. 404p. 1979. pap. 39.00 (ISBN 0-683-07150-5). Williams & Wilkins.
Raman, M. Pattabhi see Pattabhi Raman, M.
Raman, T. A. India. rev. ed. LC 83-800522. (World Cultures Ser). (Illus.). (gr. 6 up). 1983. 1-4 copies 11.20 (ISBN 0-88296-128-4); 5 or more 8.96 (ISBN 0-686-96717-8); tchrs'. guide 8.96 (ISBN 0-88296-393-7). Fideler.
Ramanathan, K. V. Management Control in Nonprofit Organizations: Text & Cases. LC 82-8331. 611p. 1982. text ed. 29.95 (ISBN 0-471-06487-4). Wiley.
Ramanathan, R. Introduction to The Theory of Economic Growth. (Lecture Notes in Economics & Mathematical Systems: Vol. 205). (Illus.). 347p. 1983. pap. 23.00 (ISBN 0-387-11943-4). Springer-Verlag.
Ramani, R. V., ed. Proceedings: Fourteenth APCOM. LC 76-58570. 1977. 23.00x (ISBN 0-89520-047-3). Soc Mining Eng.
Ramani, S., ed. Data Communication & Computer Networks. 1981. 42.75 (ISBN 0-444-86220-X). Elsevier.
Ramanujachari, C., tr. see Tyagaraja.
Ramanujan, A. K., tr. Fifteen Poems from a Classical Tamil Anthology. (Translated from Tamil). 8.00 (ISBN 0-89253-774-4). Ind-US Inc.
Ramanujan, S. Collected Papers. LC 62-8326. 1962. 18.95 (ISBN 0-8284-0159-4). Chelsea Pub.
Ramanzani, R. K. The United States & Iran: The Patterns of Influence. 204p. 1982. 23.95 (ISBN 0-03-049001-4); pap. 11.95 (ISBN 0-03-048996-2). Praeger.
Ramaswami. English Critical Traditon, Vol. 1. 543p. 1979. pap. text ed. 6.75x (ISBN 0-391-01768-3). Humanities.
Ramaswami, S. & Seturaman, V. S. The English Critical Tradition: An Anthology of English Literary Criticism, Vol. 2. 746p. 1980. pap. text ed. 9.50x (ISBN 0-391-01769-1). Humanities.
Ramaswami, V. K. Trade & Development: Essays in Economics. 178p. 1972. 20.00x (ISBN 0-262-18053-7). MIT Pr.
Ramaswamy, G. S. Design & Construction of Concrete Shell Roofs. rev. ed. LC 81-19299. 640p. 1983. lib. bdg. write for info. (ISBN 0-89874-001-0). Krieger.
Ramaswamy, G. S. & Rao, V. V. S I Units: A Source Book. 1973. 15.00 o.p. (ISBN 0-07-096575-7, P&RB). McGraw.
Ramati, Alexander. The Assisi Underground: The Priest Who Rescued Jews. 224p. Repr. 8.95 (ISBN 0-686-95053-4). ADL.
Ramazani, Nesta. Persian Cooking: A Table of Exotic Delights. LC 73-90182. (Illus.). 296p. 1982. Repr. of 1974 ed. 12.95 (ISBN 0-8139-0962-7). U Pr of Va.
Ramazani, Rouhollah K. Foreign Policy of Iran, Fifteen Hundred to Nineteen Forty-One: A Developing Nation in World Affairs. LC 66-12469. 330p. 1966. 14.95x (ISBN 0-8139-0200-2). U Pr of Va.
Ramb, R., jt. auth. see Loose, S.
Rambeau & Rambeau. Guidebook to Better Reading. (gr. 5-12). pap. 2.97 (ISBN 0-8372-4200-2); tchr's manual 2.97 (ISBN 0-8372-4201-0); West Word Bound Bk. 1.98 (ISBN 0-8372-4202-9); tchr's ed. 1.98 (ISBN 0-8372-4203-7); suppl. reader set & dupl. masters avail. Bowmar-Noble.
Ramberg, Bennett. Destruction of Nuclear-Energy Facilities in War: The Problem & the Implications. LC 80-7691. 224p. 1980. 22.95x (ISBN 0-669-03767-2). Lexington Bks.
Ramberg, Bennett, jt. auth. see Maghroori, Ray.
Rambo, B. J. Ward Clerk Skills. LC 77-1819. (Nursing & Allied Health Ser.). 1977. pap. text ed. 10.50 (ISBN 0-07-051176-4, G); teacher's manual & key 4.00 (ISBN 0-07-051177-2). McGraw.
Rambo, Beverly J. & Watson, Diane. Your Career in Health Care. 1976. 13.95 (ISBN 0-07-051166-7, G); instr's. manual 5.00 (ISBN 0-07-051167-5). McGraw.
Rambo, Beverly J. & Wood, Lucile A. Nursing Skills for Clinical Practice. 3rd ed. (Illus.). 787p. 1982. 18.95 (ISBN 0-7216-7458-5). Saunders.
Rambo, Beverly J., jt. ed. see Wood, Lucile A.
Ramchandani, R. H. India & Africa. 314p. 1980. text ed. 17.25x (ISBN 0-391-01796-9). Humanities.
Ramchandani, R. R., jt. ed. see Ali, Shanti S.
Ramdas, V., jt. ed. see Chaney, J. F.
Ramden, H. JCL & Advanced FORTRAN Programming. (Methods in Geomathematics Ser.: Vol. 2). 1976. pap. 42.75 (ISBN 0-444-41415-0). Elsevier.
Ramdohr, P. The Ore Minerals & Their Intergrowths. 1980. 97.00 o.p. (ISBN 0-08-011635-3). Pergamon.
Ramee, Louise De La see De La Ramee, Louise.
Ramee, Marue C., jt. auth. see Carson, Byrta R.
Rameh, Clea, jt. auth. see Abreu, Maria I.
Ramella, Richard. Computer Carnival. McCarthy, Nan, ed. (Illus.). 218p. (Orig.). 1982. pap. 16.95 (ISBN 0-88006-055-7). Green Pub Inc.
Rameshwar Rao, S., tr. The Mahabharata. 2nd ed. Orig. Title: The Children's Mahabharata. 219p. 1976. pap. text ed. 3.95 (ISBN 0-89253-041-3). Ind-US Inc.
Ramey, Ardella & Mrozek, Ronald. A Company Policy & Personnel Workbook. (Successful Business Library). 300p. 1982. 33.95 (ISBN 0-916378-19-5). Pub Serv Inc.
Ramey, James W., jt. auth. see Calderone, Mary S.
Ramfjord, Sigurd P., jt. auth. see Ash, Major M., Jr.
Ramig, Christopher J., jt. auth. see Hall, Mary A.
Ramirez. Manual & Atlas of Penicillia. 1982. 149.00 (ISBN 0-444-80369-6). Elsevier.
Ramirez, Bruno. When Workers Fight: The Politics of Industrial Relations in the Progressive Era, 1898-1916. LC 77-83895. (Contributions in Labor History: No. 2). 1978. lib. bdg. 27.50 (ISBN 0-8371-9826-7, RAW/). Greenwood.
Ramirez, E. V. & Weiss, M. Microprocessing Fundamentals: Hardware & Software. 1980. 17.95 (ISBN 0-07-051172-1); instr's. manual 2.50 (ISBN 0-07-051173-X). McGraw.
Ramirez, Manuel, 3rd & Castandea, Alfredo. Cultural Democracy, Biocognitive Development & Education. 1974. 20.00 (ISBN 0-12-577250-5). Acad Pr.
Ramirez, Miguel, jt. ed. see Scheer, Linda.
Ramirez-Aranjo, Alejandro, jt. auth. see Eoff, Sherman H.
Ramirez-Araujo, Alejandro, ed. see Eoff, Sherman, et al.
Ramirez de Arellano, Annette B. & Seipp, Conrad. Colonialism, Catholicism, & Contraception: A History of Birth Control in Puerto Rico. LC 82-13646. 290p. 1983. 24.00x (ISBN 0-8078-1544-6). U of NC Pr.
Ramirez de Arellano, Annette B., jt. auth. see Arbona, Guillermo.
Ramirez-Munoz, J. Atomic Absorption Spectroscopy. 1968. 63.50 (ISBN 0-444-40468-6). Elsevier.
Ramirez-Vazquez, P. Industrial Design & Human Development, No. 510. Lazo-Margain, A., ed. (International Congress Ser.). 1982. 79.75 (ISBN 0-444-90170-1). Elsevier.
Ramm, Bernard. Diccionario de Teologia Contemporanea. Valle, Roger V., tr. 143p. Date not set. pap. price not set (ISBN 0-311-09064-8). Casa Bautista.
Ramm, Bernard L. After Fundamentalism: The Future of Evangelical Theology. LC 82-47792. 240p. 1982. 14.95 (ISBN 0-06-055789-3, HarpR). Har-Row.
--His Way Out. LC 73-87284. 240p. (Orig.). 1974. pap. 2.95 o.p. (ISBN 0-8307-0456-6, S282-1-27). Regal.
Ramm, E., ed. Buckling of Shells, Stuttgart, FRG 1982: Proceedings. (Illus.). 672p. 1982. 42.00 (ISBN 0-387-11785-7). Springer-Verlag.
Rammel, Hal. Aero Into the Aether. (Illus.). 28p. 1980. pap. 2.50 (ISBN 0-941194-14-0). Black Swan Pr.
Ramming, H. G. & Kowalik, Z. Numerical Modelling of Marine Hydrodynamics: Applications to Dynamic Physical Processes. (Oceanography Ser.: Vol. 26). 1980. 61.75 (ISBN 0-444-41849-0). Elsevier.
Ramo, Simon. America's Technology Slip. LC 80-21525. 297p. 1980. 19.95x (ISBN 0-471-05976-5, Pub. by Wiley-Interscience). Wiley.
--Extraordinary Tennis for the Ordinary Player. 1977. 5.95 o.p. (ISBN 0-517-53032-5); pap. 1.95 o.p. (ISBN 0-517-52987-4). Crown.
--The Management of Innovative Technological Corporations. LC 79-19460. 1980. 31.95 (ISBN 0-471-04436-9, Pub. by Wiley-Interscience). Wiley.
Ramo, Simon, et al. Fields & Waves in Communications Electronics. LC 65-19477. 1965. 40.95 (ISBN 0-471-70720-1). Wiley.
Ramond, Charles. The Art of Using Science in Marketing. (Sheth Ser.). 1974. pap. text ed. 17.50 scp o.p. (ISBN 0-06-045321-4, HarpC). Har-Row.
Ramondino, Salvatore, ed. New World Spanish-English, English-Spanish Dictionary. pap. 3.50 (ISBN 0-451-11312-8, E9043, Sig). NAL.
Ramondio, Salvatore, jt. auth. see Pei, Mario.
Ramon-Moliner, Enrique, tr. see Ramon y Cajal, Santiago.
Ramon Y Cajal, Santiago. Structure of the Retina. Thorpe, Sylvia A., tr. (Illus.). 224p. 1972. photocopy ed. spiral 22.50x (ISBN 0-398-02385-9). C C Thomas.
--Studies on the Diencephalon. Ramon-Moliner, Enrique, tr. (Illus.). 248p. 1966. photocopy ed. spiral 23.75x (ISBN 0-398-01542-2). C C Thomas.
--Studies on Vertebrate Neurogenesis. Guth, Lloyd, tr. (Illus.). 448p. 1960. photocopy ed. spiral 43.75x (ISBN 0-398-04401-5). C C Thomas.
Ramos, Gloria. Careers in Construction. LC 74-11903. (Early Career Bks.). (Illus.). 36p. (gr. 2-5). 1975. PLB 5.95g (ISBN 0-8225-0323-9). Lerner Pubns.
Ramos, Graciliano. Anguish. Kaplan, L. C., tr. from Port. LC 72-163539. 259p. 1972. Repr. of 1946 ed. lib. bdg. 18.00x (ISBN 0-8371-6203-3, RAAN). Greenwood.
--Childhood. Oliviera, Celso D., et al, trs. 174p. 1982. 14.95 (ISBN 0-7206-0531-8, Pub. by Peter Owen). Merrimack Bk Serv.
Ramos, Maximo D. Creatures of Philippine Lower Mythology. 1971. 10.00x o.p. (ISBN 0-8248-0440-6). UH Pr.
Ramos, Suzanne. The Complete Book of Child Custody. LC 78-26061. 1979. 10.95 (ISBN 0-399-12204-4). Putnam Pub Group.
Ramos, Teresita & Goulet, Rosalina M. Intermediate Tagalog: Developing Cultural Awareness Through Language. LC 81-16037. (Pali: Philippines Ser.). 542p. 1981. pap. text ed. 15.00x (ISBN 0-8248-0776-6). UH Pr.
Ramos, Teresita V. Tagalog Dictionary. McKaughan, Howard P., ed. LC 71-152471. (PALI Language Texts: Philippines). (Orig.). 1971. pap. text ed. 7.50x (ISBN 0-87022-676-2). UH Pr.

--Tagalog Structures. McKaughan, Howard P., ed. LC 75-152472. (PALI Language Texts: Philippines). (Orig.). 1971. pap. text ed. 5.50x (ISBN 0-87022-677-0). UH Pr.

Ramos, Teresita V. & De Guzman, Videa. Tagalog for Beginners. McKaughan, Howard P., ed. (PALI Language Texts: Philippines). (Orig.). 1971. pap. text ed. 12.00x (ISBN 0-87022-678-9). UH Pr.

Ramot, Bracha, ed. Genetic Polymorphisms & Diseases in Man. 1974. 43.50 (ISBN 0-12-577140-1). Acad Pr.

--Red Cell Structure & Metabolism: Proceedings. 1971. 43.50 (ISBN 0-12-577150-9). Acad Pr.

Ramous, Arthur. Applied Kinematics. 348p. 1972. text ed. 22.95 (ISBN 0-13-041202-3). P-H.

Ramp, Eugene & Semb, George. Behavior Analysis: Areas of Research & Application. LC 74-340095. (Illus.). 432p. 1975. ref. ed. 22.95 o.p. (ISBN 0-13-074195-7). P-H.

Ramp, Wilma, compiled by. Fantastic Oatmeal Recipes. 64p. pap. 3.75 (ISBN 0-9603858-3-5). Penfield.

Rampo, Edogawa. Japanese Tales of Mystery & Imagination. Harris, James B., tr. LC 56-6804. (Illus.). (gr. 9 up). 1956. pap. 5.25 (ISBN 0-8048-0319-6). C E Tuttle.

Rampp, Donald L., jt. auth. see Rampp, Lary C.

Rampp, Lary C. & Rampp, Donald L. The Civil War in the Indian Territory. (Illus.). 1975. 9.95 o.p. (ISBN 0-686-25783-9). Presidial.

Rampton, V. W., jt. auth. see Tucker, J. W.

Rampulla, Phyllis. Journey Beyond the Reflection. 1983. 5.95 (ISBN 0-533-05300-5). Vantage.

Ramquist, Grace. Complete Christmas Programs, No. 2. (Orig.). 1968. pap. 1.95 o.p. (ISBN 0-310-31521-2). Zondervan.

--Complete Christmas Programs, No. 4. 64p. 1972. pap. 1.95 o.p. (ISBN 0-310-31541-7). Zondervan.

--Complete Christmas Programs, No. 5. 64p. 1975. pap. 2.95 (ISBN 0-310-31551-4). Zondervan.

--Complete Christmas Programs, No. 6. 64p. 1980. pap. 2.95 (ISBN 0-310-31571-9, 10638P). Zondervan.

--Complete Christmas Programs, No. 7. 80p. 1980. pap. 2.95 (ISBN 0-310-31581-6, 10639P). Zondervan.

Rams, Edwin. Real Estate Consultant's Handbook. 1978. 22.95 (ISBN 0-87909-720-5). Reston.

Ramsay. Stereochemistry. 1981. 29.95 (ISBN 0-471-26103-3, Wiley Heyden); pap. 19.95 (ISBN 0-471-26104-1). Wiley.

--Synopsis of Endocrinology & Metabolism. 2nd ed. 224p. 1980. pap. 16.50 (ISBN 0-7236-0485-1). Wright-PSG.

Ramsay, George. Essay on the Distribution of Wealth. LC 72-179344. Repr. of 1836 ed. 30.00x (ISBN 0-678-00884-1). Kelley.

Ramsay, Jack & Strawn, John. The Coach's Art. LC 78-5458. 1978. 9.95 o.p. (ISBN 0-917304-36-5); pap. 6.95 o.p. (ISBN 0-917304-55-1, Pub. by Timber Pr). Timber.

Ramsay, James, tr. see Philippe, Robert.

Ramsay, James A. Physiological Approach to the Lower Animals. 2nd ed. LC 68-21398. (Illus.). 1968. text ed. 32.50 (ISBN 0-521-07185-2); pap. 10.95x (ISBN 0-521-09537-9). Cambridge U Pr.

Ramsay, James O. Multiscale: Four Programs for Multidimensional Scaling by the Method of Maximum Likelihood. pap. 10.50 (ISBN 0-89498-002-5). Natl Ed Res.

Ramsay, John G. Folding & Fracturing of Rocks. (International Ser. in Earth & Planetary Sciences). (Illus.). 1967. text ed. 55.00 (ISBN 0-07-051170-5, C). McGraw.

Ramsay, Laura. Food Processor Cooking-Naturally. (Illus.). 304p. 1983. 15.50 (ISBN 0-8092-5727-0); pap. 9.95 (ISBN 0-8092-5726-2). Contemp Bks.

--Food Processor Cooking-Naturally. (Illus.). 176p. 1983. pap. 8.95 (ISBN 0-686-38406-7). Contemp Bks.

Ramsay, Mark. The Falcon, No. 3: The Bloody Cross. 1982. pap. 2.50 (ISBN 0-451-11917-7, AE1917, Sig). NAL.

Ramsay, Robert. The Corsican Time-Bomb. 176p. 1982. 26.50 (ISBN 0-7190-0893-X). Manchester.

--Hawaiian Tramways. (Illus.). 36p. 1976. pap. 4.00 o.p. (ISBN 0-87095-062-2). Golden West.

Ramsay, Robert L. Our Storehouse of Missouri Place Names. LC 73-79512. 160p. 1952. pap. 5.00x (ISBN 0-8262-0586-0). U of Mo Pr.

Ramsay, W. M. & Bell, Gertrude L. One Thousand & One Churches. (Illus.). xvi, 580p. 1983. Repr. of 1905 ed. lib. bdg. 80.00x (ISBN 0-89241-121-X). Caratzas Bros.

Ramsay, W. M., ed. Studies in the History & Art of the Eastern Roman Provinces of the Roman Empire. (Illus.). xiii, 391p. 1983. Repr. of 1906 ed. lib. bdg. 60.00x (ISBN 0-89241-215-1). Caratzas Bros.

Ramsay, William. Unpaid Costs of Electrical Energy: Health & Environmental Impacts of Coal & Nuclear Power. LC 78-15668. 1979. 20.00x (ISBN 0-8018-2172-X); pap. 5.95x (ISBN 0-8018-2230-0). Johns Hopkins.

Ramsay, William H. Historical Commentary on the Epistle to the Galatians. 1978. 17.75 (ISBN 0-86524-107-4, 4801). Klock & Klock.

Ramsay, William M. Cities of St. Paul. pap. 6.95 o.p. (ISBN 0-8010-7601-3). Baker Bk.

Ramsbottom, T. Warp Sizing Mechanisms. 1964. 7.50 o.p. (ISBN 0-87245-262-X). Textile Bk.

Ramsdale, Jeanne. Persian Cats. (Orig.). 1962. pap. 2.50 o.p. (ISBN 0-87666-178-9, M507). TFH Pubns.

--Persian Cats & Other Longhairs. (Illus.). 1964. 14.95 (ISBN 0-87666-179-7, H918). TFH Pubns.

Ramsden, David. Peripheral Metabolism & Action of Thyroid Hormones, Vol. 1. 1977. 19.20 (ISBN 0-904406-54-7). Eden Pr.

Ramsden, David B. Peripheral Metabolism & Action of Thyroid Hormones, Vol. 2. (Annual Research Reviews). 1978. 28.80 (ISBN 0-88831-029-3). Eden Pr.

Ramsden, Evelyn, tr. see Senje, Sigurd.

Ramsden, H. Weak-Pronoun Position in the Early Romance Languages. 1963. 18.50 (ISBN 0-7190-1213-9). Manchester.

Ramsden, John, jt. ed. see Cook, Chris.

Ramseu, Marjorie, jt. ed. see Dittmann, Laura L.

Ramsey, Anne, compiled by. Eurostat Index. 156p. (Orig.). 1981. pap. text ed. 35.00x (ISBN 0-906011-15-9, Pub by Capital Plan Info). Oryx Pr.

Ramsey, Brian G. Electronic Transitions in Organometalloids. (Organometallic Chemistry Ser). 1969. 55.50 (ISBN 0-12-576950-4). Acad Pr.

Ramsey, Charles E., jt. auth. see McCarty, Donald J.

Ramsey, Dan. Budget Flying. (McGraw-Hill Series in Aviation). (Illus.). 176p. 1980. 18.05 (ISBN 0-07-051202-7). McGraw.

--How to Be a Disc Jockey. (Illus.). 224p. 1981. 19.95 (ISBN 0-8306-9661-X, 1263); pap. 8.95 (ISBN 0-8306-1263-7, 1263). TAB Bks.

--One Hundred & One Successful Ways to Turn Weekends into Wealth. 216p. 1980. 14.95 o.p. (ISBN 0-13-634808-4, Parker). P-H.

Ramsey, Elizabeth A. The Placenta: Human & Animal. 204p. 1982. 32.50 (ISBN 0-03-060292-0). Praeger.

Ramsey, Elizabeth M. & Donner, Martin W. Placental Vasculature & Circulation. LC 79-65527. (Illus.). 101p. 1980. text ed. 25.00 (ISBN 0-7216-7446-1). Saunders.

Ramsey, Eloise. Folklore for Children & Young People. LC 52-10251. Repr. of 1952 ed. 16.00 (ISBN 0-527-01127-4). Kraus Repr.

Ramsey, Evelyn. Show Me, Lord. 178p. pap. 4.95 (ISBN 0-8341-0781-3). Beacon Hill.

Ramsey, Frank C. Protein-Energy Malnutrition in Barbados: The Role of Continuity of Care. new ed. LC 79-88999. (Illus.). 1979. pap. 4.00 o.p. (ISBN 0-914362-28-3). J Macy Foun.

Ramsey, Frederic, Jr. Been Here & Gone. 1969. pap. 4.95x o.p. (ISBN 0-8135-0335-3). Rutgers U Pr.

Ramsey, Ian T. On Being Sure in Religion. 1963. text ed. 11.75x o.p. (ISBN 0-485-11063-6, Athlone Pr). Humanities.

Ramsey, J. B., jt. ed. see Kmenta, J.

Ramsey, James B. The Economics of Exploration for Energy Resources. Altman, Edward I. & Walter, Ingo, eds. LC 80-82477. (Contemporary Studies in Economic & Financial Analysis: Vol. 26). 400p. 1981. 45.00 (ISBN 0-89232-159-8). Jai Pr.

Ramsey, James B., ed. Bidding & Oil Leases, Vol. 25. Walter, Ingo I. LC 79-3169. (Contemporary Studies in Economic & Financial Analysis Monographs). 320p. (Orig.). 1980. lib. bdg. 36.00 (ISBN 0-89232-148-2). Jai Pr.

Ramsey, John. Concepts of Politics: A Working Book in American National Government. LC 73-76346. 1974. pap. 8.95 (ISBN 0-675-08941-7). Merrill.

--Spain: The Rise of the First World Power. LC 79-135705. (Mediterranean Europe Series: No. 1). 320p. 1973. 18.50 o.s.i. (ISBN 0-8173-5704-1). U of Ala Pr.

Ramsey, Johnny. Back to Bible Preaching. pap. 4.25 (ISBN 0-89137-007-2). Quality Pubns.

--Bible Treasures. pap. 8.50 (ISBN 0-89137-009-9). Quality Pubns.

--Search the Scriptures. pap. 5.35 (ISBN 0-89137-008-0). Quality Pubns.

Ramsey, Julian W. My Brother's Keeper. LC 79-66100. (Illus.). 1979. 5.50 (ISBN 0-911838-54-6). Windy Row.

Ramsey, Marjorie E. & Bayless, Kathleen M. Kindergarten: Programs & Practices. LC 80-11478. (Illus.). 324p. 1980. pap. text ed. 16.95 (ISBN 0-8016-4076-8). Mosby.

Ramsey, Marjorie E., jt. auth. see Bayless, Kathleen M.

Ramsey, Mark. The Falcon: Black Pope, No. 2. 1982. pap. 2.50 (ISBN 0-451-11771-9, AE1771, Sig). NAL.

--The Falcon, No. 1: The Falcon Strikes. 1982. pap. 2.50 (ISBN 0-451-11770-0, AE1770, Sig). NAL.

Ramsey, Michael. Jesus & the Living Past. 1980. 8.95x (ISBN 0-19-213963-0). Oxford U Pr.

Ramsey, P. A. Rome in the Renaissance: The City & the Myth. 464p. 1983. 22.00 (ISBN 0-86698-057-1). Medieval & Renaissance NY.

Ramsey, Peter. Tudor Economic Problems. 1963. 11.95 o.p. (ISBN 0-686-79188-6, Pub. by Gollancz England). David & Charles.

Ramsgard, William C. Making Systems Work: The Psychology of Business Systems. LC 77-5933. (Business Data Processing Ser.). 1977. 35.50 o.p. (ISBN 0-471-01522-9, Pub. by Wiley-Interscience). Wiley.

--Making Systems Work: The Psychology of Business Systems. LC 77-5933. 280p. Repr. of 1977 ed. text ed. 24.50 (ISBN 0-471-01522-9). Krieger.

Ramshaw, Mark, jt. auth. see Hartnell, Tim.

Ramshaw, R. S. Power Electronics: Thyristor Controlled Power For Electric Motors. (Modern Electrical Studies). 1975. pap. 15.95x (ISBN 0-412-14160-4, Pub. by Chapman & Hall). Methuen Inc.

Ramsland, Clement, jt. ed. see Bowditch, John.

Ramu, S. Anantha, jt. auth. see Iyengar, K. T.

Ramusack, Barbara N. The Princes of India in the Twilight of Empire: Dissolution of a Patron-Client System, 1914-1939. LC 78-18161. (Illus.). 1978. 20.00x (ISBN 0-8142-0272-1). Ohio St U Pr.

Ranald, Margaret L., et al. A Style Manual for College Students: A Guide to Written Assignments & Papers. rev ed. 1982. pap. 1.00 (ISBN 0-930146-07-7). Queens Coll Pr.

Ranby, B. & Rabek, J. F., eds. Singlet Oxygen: Reactions with Organic Compounds & Polymers. LC 77-2793. 1978. 71.95 (ISBN 0-471-99535-5, Pub. by Wiley-Interscience). Wiley.

Ranby, Bengt & Rabek, Jack. Photodegradation, Photo-Oxidation & Photostabilization of Polymers: Principles & Applications. LC 74-2498. 532p. 1975. 100.00 o.p. (ISBN 0-471-70788-0, Pub. by Wiley-Interscience). Wiley.

Rance, H. F. Raw Materials & Processing of Paper Making. (Handbook of Paper Science: Vol. 1). 1980. 68.00 (ISBN 0-444-41778-8). Elsevier.

--Structure & Physical Properties of Paper. (Handbook of Paper Science: Vol. 2). 1982. 85.00 (ISBN 0-444-41974-8). Elsevier.

Rancho Bernardo Junior Woman's Club. Serving the Good Life in Rancho Bernardo. (Illus.). 310p. 1982. Easel Binder 12.95 (ISBN 0-686-36317-5). Rancho Bern.

Ranck, Joyce H., ed. see Eddingfield, June.

Ranck, Katherine Q. Portrait of Dona Elena. LC 82-83842. 1982. pap. 4.00 (ISBN 0-686-84780-6). Tonatiuh-Quinto Sol Intl.

Rancourt, Karen L. Yeah, but Children Need.... 1978. 8.95 o.p. (ISBN 0-8467-0451-X, Pub. by Two Continents). Hippocrene Bks.

Rancurello, Antos C. A Study of Franz Brentano. LC 68-14641. 1968. 32.50 (ISBN 0-12-577050-2). Acad Pr.

Rand, A. Stanley see Burghardt, Gordon M.

Rand, Ann & Rand, Paul. Listen! Listen! LC 70-91011. (Illus.). (ps-3). 1970. 5.95 (ISBN 0-15-245580-9, HJ). HarBraceJ.

Rand, Ann, jt. auth. see Rand, Paul.

Rand, Ayn. Anthem. pap. 1.75 (ISBN 0-451-11712-3, AE1712, Sig). NAL.

--Atlas Shrugged. 1970. pap. 4.95 (ISBN 0-451-11676-3, AE1676, Sig). NAL.

--Atlas Shrugged. 1957. 22.95 (ISBN 0-394-41576-0). Random.

--Capitalism: The Unknown Ideal. 1967. pap. 2.95 (ISBN 0-451-11376-4, AE1376, Sig). NAL.

--For the New Intellectual. pap. 2.95 (ISBN 0-451-12189-9, AE2189, Sig). NAL.

--Fountainhead. pap. 3.95 (ISBN 0-451-11810-3, AE1810, Sig). NAL.

--New Left: The Anti-Industrial Revolution. (Orig.). 1971. pap. 2.75 (ISBN 0-451-11382-9, AE1382, Sig). NAL.

--Philosophy: Who Needs It? LC 82-4320. 288p. 1982. 15.95 (ISBN 0-672-52725-1). Bobbs.

--Romantic Manifesto. 1971. pap. 2.95 (ISBN 0-451-12374-3, AE2374, Sig). NAL.

--Virtue of Selfishness. pap. 2.50 (ISBN 0-451-12206-2, AE2206, Sig). NAL.

Rand, Clayton. Sons of the South. LC 61-8069. (Illus.). 212p. 1961. 7.95 (ISBN 0-911116-76-1). Pelican.

Rand Corporation & Elmore, Richard F. Reform & Retrenchment: The Politics of California School Finance Reform. (Rand Educational Policy Ser.). 480p. 1982. prof ref 26.00x (ISBN 0-88410-196-7). Ballinger Pub.

Rand, D., et al, eds. Progress in Electrochemistry. (Studies in Physical & Theoretical Chemistry). 1982. 95.75 (ISBN 0-444-41955-1). Elsevier.

Rand, David M. & Paynter, Raymond A., Jr. Ornithological Gazetteer of Uruguay. iv, 75p. 1981. 4.00 (ISBN 0-686-35832-5). Nuttall Ornithological.

Rand, Edward K. Cicero in the Courtroom of Saint Thomas Aquinas. (Aquinas Lecture Ser.). 1945. 7.95 (ISBN 0-87462-109-7). Marquette.

Rand, Elizabeth, ed. see Seales, John B.

Rand, James. The Great Sky & the Silence. LC 77-8341. 1978. 10.95 o.p. (ISBN 0-07-051175-6, GB). McGraw.

Rand, John. People's Lewiston - Auburn, Maine 1875-1975. LC 75-7980. (Illus.). 128p. 1975. 9.95 (ISBN 0-87027-164-4); pap. 7.95 (ISBN 0-87027-165-2). Cumberland Pr.

Rand, Ken. Point-Counterpoint. (gr. 3-8). 1979. 6.95 (ISBN 0-88488-125-3). Creative Pubns.

Rand, Ken, jt. auth. see Fair, Jan.

Rand McNally. Guide to Florida. 5th ed. LC 79-656302. (Illus.). 1979. pap. 4.95 o.p. (ISBN 0-528-84109-2). Rand.

--The New International Atlas. LC 80-51969. (Illus.). 568p. 1982. 100.00 (ISBN 0-528-83111-9); deluxe ed. 125.00 (ISBN 0-528-83112-7). Rand.

--Pocket Vacation Guide. 1983. pap. 3.95 (ISBN 0-528-84436-9). Rand.

--Pocket World Atlas. LC 80-83201. (Illus.). 160p. 1980. pap. 4.95 (ISBN 0-528-83097-X). Rand.

Rand McNally Editors. Rand McNally Handy Railroad Atlas of the United States. 1978. pap. 9.95 (ISBN 0-528-24147-8). Rand.

--Zip Code Atlas. 1975. pap. 17.95 (ISBN 0-528-21068-8). Rand.

Rand, Patricia. Land & Water Issues Related to Energy Development. LC 81-70868. 1982. 39.95 (ISBN 0-250-40538-5). Ann Arbor Science.

Rand, Paul & Rand, Ann. I Know a Lot of Things. LC 56-5576. (Illus.). 32p. (ps-1). 1973. pap. 1.35 (ISBN 0-15-644400-3, VoyB). HarBraceJ.

Rand, Paul, jt. auth. see Rand, Ann.

Rand, Suzanne. Ask Connie. 1982. pap. 1.95 (ISBN 0-553-11518-9). Bantam.

Randal, Jonathan. Book on Lebanon. 256p. 1983. 16.75 (ISBN 0-670-55186-4). Viking Pr.

Randal, Jonthan. The Tragedy of Lebanon. 1983. pap. 16.75 (ISBN 0-670-42259-2). Viking Pr.

Randal, Judith. All About Heredity. (Allabout Ser.: No. 48). (Illus.). (gr. 5-9). 1963. PLB 5.39 o.p. (ISBN 0-394-90248-3). Random.

Randall, Bob. The Calling. 256p. 1983. pap. 2.95 (ISBN 0-515-07102-1). Jove Pubns.

--The Next. 352p. (Orig.). 1981. pap. 2.75 o.p. (ISBN 0-446-95740-2). Warner Bks.

Randall, C. H., Jr. Medicolegal Problems in Blood Transfusion. 43p. 1969. 1.00 o.p. (ISBN 0-685-48757-1). Am Assn Blood.

Randall, Cher. Total Preparation for Childbirth. 1979. pap. 5.95 (ISBN 0-88270-331-5, Pub. by Logos). Bridge Pub.

Randall, Clifford W. & Benefield, Larry D. Biological Processes Design for Wastewater Treatment. (Environmental Sciences Ser.). (Illus.). 1980. text ed. 34.95 (ISBN 0-13-076406-X). P-H.

Randall, Clyde L., jt. auth. see Nichols, David H.

Randall, D. J., jt. ed. see Hoar, W. S.

Randall, D. J., et al. The Evolution of Air Breathing in Vertebrates. LC 80-462. (Illus.). 176p. 1981. 29.95 (ISBN 0-521-22259-1). Cambridge U Pr.

Randall, Dale B. Gentle Flame: The Life & Verse of Dudley Fourth Lord North. 300p. 1983. text ed. 30.00 (ISBN 0-8223-0491-0). Duke.

Randall, Diana. Dragon Lover. 320p. (Orig.). 1981. pap. write for info o.s.i. Jove Pubns.

Randall, Elinor, tr. see Marti, Jose.

Randall, Frances, jt. auth. see Whitcomb, Norma.

Randall, Frances, jt. auth. see Whitcomb, Norma A.

Randall, J. E. The Use of Microcomputers for Physiological Simulation. 1980. pap. 22.50 (ISBN 0-201-06128-7). A-W.

Randall, James C. Polymer Sequence Determinations from Plus One Plus Three C NMR. 1977. 27.50 (ISBN 0-12-578050-8). Acad Pr.

Randall, James G. & Donald, David. Civil War & Reconstruction. 2nd., rev. ed. 1969. text ed. 22.95 (ISBN 0-669-50831-4). Heath.

Randall, John. The Book of Revelation: What Does It Really Say. (Orig.). 1977. 2.50 (ISBN 0-914544-16-0). Living Flame Pr.

--In God's Providence: The Birth of a Catholic Charismatic Parish. (Orig.). 1973. 1.50 o.p. (ISBN 0-914544-01-2). Living Flame Pr.

--Wisdom Instructs Her Children: The Power of the Spirit & the Word. 128p. (Orig.). 1981. pap. 3.50 (ISBN 0-914544-36-5). Living Flame Pr.

Randall, John, et al. Mary: Pathway to Fruitfulness. (Orig.). 1978. pap. 2.50 (ISBN 0-914544-28-4). Living Flame Pr.

Randall, John C. How to Save Time... & Worry Less. LC 79-92477. (Illus.). 65p. (Orig.). 1980. pap. 10.00x (ISBN 0-935864-01-6, 804). Hotline Multi-Ent.

Randall, John E. Caribbean Reef Fishes. 29.95 (ISBN 0-87666-017-0, H932). TFH Pubns.

Randall, John H., Jr. & Buchler, Justus. Philosophy: An Introduction. rev. ed. 1971. pap. 5.50 (ISBN 0-06-460041-6, CO 41, COS). B&N NY.

Randall, John L. Parapsychology & the Nature of Life. 1977. pap. 3.95i o.p. (ISBN 0-06-090571-9, CN 571, CN). Har-Row.

Randall, Magaret. Sandino's Daughters. Yanz, Linda, ed. (Illus.). 220p. 1981. pap. 7.95 (ISBN 0-919888-33-X). Left Bank.

Randall, Margaret. Doris Tijerino: Inside the Nicaraguan Revolution. 176p. 1978. pap. 5.25 (ISBN 0-919888-83-6). Crossing Pr.

--Sandino's Daughters: Testimonies of Nicaraguan Women in Struggle. 220p. 1981. pap. 7.95 (ISBN 0-919888-33-X). Crossing Pr.

--Women in Cuba-Twenty Years Later. LC 80-54055. (Illus.). 182p. 1981. 19.95 (ISBN 0-918266-15-7); pap. 7.95 (ISBN 0-918266-14-9). Smyrna.

Randall, Paula. After the Big Bang. 105p. (Orig.). 1980. pap. 3.95 o.p. (ISBN 0-89260-186-8). Hwong Pub.

Randall, Peter. Newburyport & the Merrimack. LC 81-66562. (Illus.). 88p. 1981. pap. 6.95 (ISBN 0-89272-088-3, PIC427). Down East.

Randall, Peter, ed. see Vallier, Jane.

Randall, Peter, jt. ed. see Whitaker, Linton A.

Randall, Peter, tr. see Boesak, Allan.

Randall, Peter E. One Hundred Fifteen Country Inns of New Hampshire & Vermont. (Illus., Orig.). 1982. pap. 9.00 (ISBN 0-89272-141-3, PIC490). Down East.

--Salem & Marblehead. (Illus.). 88p. 1983. pap. 8.95t (ISBN 0-89272-163-4). Down East.

Randall, Richard S. Censorship of the Movies: The Social & Political Control of a Mass Medium. LC 68-14035. 296p. 1968. 22.50 (ISBN 0-299-04731-8); pap. 9.95x (ISBN 0-299-04734-2). U of Wis Pr.

Randall, Robert. The Dawning Light. 1982. pap. 2.50 (ISBN 0-441-13898-5, Pub. by Ace Science Fiction). Ace Bks.

--Microcomputers in Small Business: How to Select & Implement Microcomputer Hardware in Your Small Business. (Illus.). 134p. 1983. 16.95 (ISBN 0-13-580753-0); pap. 8.95 (ISBN 0-13-580746-8). P-H.

Randall, Rona. The Eagle at the Gate. 1978. pap. 2.25 o.p. (ISBN 0-380-42846-6, 42846). Avon.

--Eagle at the Gate. LC 77-10062. 1978. 8.95 (ISBN 0-698-10863-9, Coward). Putnam Pub Group.

--The Ladies of Hanover Square. 1981. 13.95 (ISBN 0-698-11067-6, Coward). Putnam Pub Group.

--The Mating Dance. 1980. pap. 2.75 o.p. (ISBN 0-380-50591-6, 50591). Avon.

--The Mating Dance. LC 78-31724. 1979. 10.95 o.p. (ISBN 0-698-10961-9, Coward). Putnam Pub Group.

Randall, Vicky. Women in Politics. LC 82-10657. 220p. 1982. 25.00x (ISBN 0-312-88729-9). St Martin.

Randall, Walter C. Neural Regulation of the Heart. (Illus.). 1976. 32.50x (ISBN 0-19-502080-4). Oxford U Pr.

Randall, Willard. A Little Revenge: Benjamin Franklin & His Son. 1983. 18.00i (ISBN 0-316-73364-4). Little.

Randall-MacIver, David. Greek Cities in Italy & Sicily. Repr. of 1931 ed. lib. bdg. 15.75x (ISBN 0-8371-4318-7, RAGC). Greenwood.

--Italy Before the Romans. LC 76-145874. (Illus.). 159p. 1972. Repr. of 1928 ed. lib. bdg. 18.50x o.p. (ISBN 0-8154-0426-3). Cooper Sq.

Randell, B. The Origins of Digital Computers. 3rd ed. (Texts & Mongraphs in Computer Science). (Illus.). 470p. 1982. 29.50 (ISBN 0-387-11319-3). Springer-Verlag.

Randell, B., jt. ed. see Anderson, T.

Randell, Brooke, et al. Adaptation Nursing: The Roy Conceptual Model Applied. LC 81-18844. (Illus.). 297p. 1982. pap. text ed. 13.95 (ISBN 0-8016-4024-5). Mosby.

RanDelle, B. J. & Marshbum, Sandra. Lessons in Love. LC 24-476. (Illus.). 64p. (gr. k-4). 1982. text ed. 5.95 (ISBN 0-910445-00-1). Randelle Pubns.

Randeraat, J. Van & Setterington, R. E., eds. Piezoelectric Ceramics. 2nd ed. (Mullard Publications Ser.). (Illus.). 211p. 1974. text ed. 29.50x (ISBN 0-901232-75-0). Scholium Intl.

Randers, Jorgen, ed. Elements of the System Dynamics Method. (Illus.). 1980. text ed. 37.50x (ISBN 0-262-18092-8). MIT Pr.

Randers-Pherson, Justine D. Barbarians & Romans: The Birth Struggle of Europe, A.D. 400-700. LC 82-20025. (Illus.). 416p. 1983. 29.50 (ISBN 0-8061-1818-0). U of Okla Pr.

Randhawa, Bikkar S. & Coffman, William E., eds. Visual Learning, Thinking, & Communication. (Cognition & Perception Ser.). 1978. 29.50 (ISBN 0-12-579450-9). Acad Pr.

Randhawa, G. S., jt. auth. see Chaddha, K. L.

Randhawa, G. S., jt. ed. see Chadha, K. L.

Randi, James. Flim Flam. LC 82-60953. (Illus.). 340p. 1982. pap. 9.95 (ISBN 0-87975-198-3). Prometheus Bks.

--The Truth About Uri Geller. rev. ed. LC 82-60951. (Illus.). 325p. 1982. 8.95 (ISBN 0-87975-199-1). Prometheus Bks.

Randisi, Jennifer L. A Tissue of Lies: Eudora Welty & the Southern Romance. LC 82-45042. 198p. (Orig.). 1982. PLB 22.00 (ISBN 0-8191-2451-6); pap. text ed. 10.25 (ISBN 0-8191-2452-4). U Pr of Amer.

Randisi, Robert J. Eye in the Ring. 256p. 1982. pap. 2.75 (ISBN 0-380-81455-2, 81455). Avon.

Randle, Gretchen R., ed. Electronic Industries Information Sources. LC 67-31262. (Management Information Guide Ser.: No. 13). 1968. 42.00x (ISBN 0-8103-0813-4). Gale.

Randle, P. J. & Denton, R. M. Hormones & Cells Metabolism. rev. ed. Head, J. J., ed. LC 78-69515. (Carolina Biology Readers Ser.). 16p. 1982. pap. 1.60 (ISBN 0-89278-279-X, 45-9679). Carolina Biological.

Randle, Paul A. & Swensen, Philip R. Managing Your Money: An Investment Guide for Professionals & Entrepreneurs. LC 79-12669. 1979. 21.50 (ISBN 0-534-97996-3); pap. 13.50 (ISBN 0-534-97994-7). Lifetime Learn.

--Personal Financial Planning for Executives. (Finance Ser.). (Illus.). 298p. 1981. 17.95 (ISBN 0-534-97996-3); pap. write for info. (ISBN 0-534-97994-7). Lifetime Learn.

Randles, Ronald H. & Wolfe, Douglas A. Introduction to the Theory of Nonparametric Statistics. LC 79-411. (Ser. in Probability & Mathematical Statistics). 1979. 41.95 (ISBN 0-471-04245-5, Pub. by Wiley-Interscience). Wiley.

Randolph, jt. auth. see Miles.

Randolph, Alan D. & Larson, Maurice A. Theory of Particulate Processes. 1971. 47.50 (ISBN 0-12-579650-1). Acad Pr.

Randolph, Daniel, et al. Counseling & Community Psychology: A Bibliography. 86p. 1979. softcover 5.95 (ISBN 0-932930-09-3). Pilgrimage Inc.

Randolph, Elise. Passionate Appeal. (Candlelight Ecstasy Ser.: No. 143). (Orig.). 1983. pap. 1.95 (ISBN 0-440-16670-5). Dell.

Randolph, Elizabeth. How to Be Your Cat's Best Friend. (Illus.). 224p. 1983. pap. 6.70y (ISBN 0-316-73377-6). Little.

Randolph, Elizabeth, ed. Baby Book. (Illus.). 72p. (Orig.). 1982. pap. 2.50 (ISBN 0-918178-30-4). Simplicity.

Randolph, Erwin P. William Law. (English Authors Ser.). 1980. lib. bdg. 14.95 (ISBN 0-8057-6765-7, Twayne). G K Hall.

Randolph, J. Ralph. British Travelers Among the Southern Indians, 1660-1763. LC 72-858. (American Exploration & Travel Ser.: Vol. 62). 350p. 1973. 14.50 o.p. (ISBN 0-8061-1019-8). U of Okla Pr.

Randolph, J. Ralph & Pohl, James W. People of America: They Came from Many Lands. (Illus.). (gr. 5). 1973. text ed. 9.60 (ISBN 0-87443-043-7); tchr's ed. 8.80 (ISBN 0-87443-044-5); preprinted masters 6.20 (ISBN 0-87443-045-3). Benson.

Randolph, Robert M. Thank God It's Monday: How to Turn Work Into an Adventure. LC 82-11926. (Illus.). 249p. 1982. 15.95 (ISBN 0-87624-623-4). Inst Busn Plan.

Randolph, Shirley L., jt. auth. see Heiniger, Margot C.

Randolph, Theron G. & Moss, Ralph W. An Alternative Approach to Allergies. 320p. 1982. pap. 3.95 (ISBN 0-553-20830-6). Bantam.

Randolph, Thomas. Poems & Amyntas of Thomas Randolph. Parry, John J., ed. 1917. text ed. 39.50x (ISBN 0-686-83704-5). Elliots Bks.

Randolph, Vance. Ozark Folksongs. Cohen, Norm, ed. LC 81-4403. (Music in American Life Ser.). 1982. cloth 35.00 (ISBN 0-252-00952-5); pap. 14.95 (ISBN 0-686-96904-9). U of Ill Pr.

--We Always Lie to Strangers. LC 74-12852. (Illus.). 309p. 1974. Repr. of 1951 ed. lib. bdg. 19.25x (ISBN 0-8371-7765-0, RAAL). Greenwood.

Randolph, Vance, ed. Who Blowed up the Church House? & Other Ozark Folk Tales. LC 75-31424. (Illus.). 232p. 1976. Repr. of 1952 ed. lib. bdg. 17.00x (ISBN 0-8371-8497-5, RACH). Greenwood.

Random, Michael. Mawlana Rumi: Sufism & Dance. (Illus.). 192p. Date not set. cancelled (ISBN 0-686-97714-9). Inner Tradit.

Raney, Dave, ed. The Goal & the Glory. (Orig.). Date not set. pap. 5.95 (ISBN 0-8007-5084-5, Power Bks). Revell.

Raney, R. Beverly, jt. auth. see Brashear, H. Robert.

Rang, Mary Lu. Manual of Newborn Care Plans. (Spiral Manual Ser. - Nursing: Nursing). 1981. spiral bdg. 11.95 (ISBN 0-316-73380-6). Little.

Rang, Mercer, ed. Children's Fractures. 2nd ed. (Illus.). 300p. 1982. text ed. 42.50 (ISBN 0-397-50476-4, Lippincott Medical). Lippincott.

Ranganathan, D. Challenging Problems in Organic Reaction Mechanisms. 1972. 24.00 (ISBN 0-12-580050-9). Acad Pr.

Rangarao, B. V. & Chaubey, N. P., eds. Social Perspective of Development of Science & Technology in India. 1983. 22.00x (ISBN 0-8364-0931-0, Pub. by Heritage India). South Asia Bks.

Range, Dale G., ed. Aspects of Early Childhood Education: Theory to Research to Practice. LC 79-28850. (Educational Psychology Ser.). 1980. 19.50 (ISBN 0-12-580150-5). Acad Pr.

Rangel-Ribeiro, Victor. Baroque Music: A Practical Guide for the Performer. LC 80-5222. (Illus.). 260p. 1981. 30.00 (ISBN 0-02-871980-8). Schirmer Bks.

Ranger, Robin. Arms & Politics: 1958-1978. (Illus.). 280p. (Orig.). 1979. pap. text ed. 14.50 (ISBN 0-7715-5677-2). Westview.

Ranger, T. O. Dance & Society in Eastern Africa 1890-1970: The Beni Ngoma. LC 74-76389. 1974. 30.00x (ISBN 0-520-02729-9). U of Cal Pr.

Ranger, T. O., ed. Aspects of Central African History. (Illus.). xiv, 290p. 1968. pap. text ed. 12.00x (ISBN 0-435-94800-8). Heinemann Ed.

Ranger, T. O. & Kimambo, Isaria, eds. The Historical Study of African Religion. (Library Reprint Ser.). 1976. 40.00x (ISBN 0-520-03179-2). U of Cal Pr.

Ranger, T. O. & Weller, John, eds. Themes in the Christian History of Central Africa. 1975. 39.00x (ISBN 0-520-02536-9). U of Cal Pr.

Ranger, T. O., jt. ed. see Peel, J. D. Y.

Rani, Osman, jt. ed. see Fisk, E. K.

Ranieri, Ralph F. What to Do When You Feel Depressed. (Illus.). 1978. pap. 0.50 o.p. (ISBN 0-89570-150-2). Claretian Pubns.

Ranis, Gustave, ed. The Gap Between Rich & Poor Nations. 1972. 32.50 (ISBN 0-312-31640-2). St Martin.

Ranis, P. Five Latin American Nations: A Comparative Political Study. 1971. pap. text ed. 8.95x (ISBN 0-02-398200-4). Macmillan.

Ranjhan, S. K. & Pathak, N. N. Management & Feeding of Buffaloes. 1979. pap. 7.95x (ISBN 0-7069-0778-7, Pub. by Vikas India). Advent NY.

Rank, Hugh. Edwin O'Connor. (United States Authors Ser.). 1974. lib. bdg. 12.95 (ISBN 0-8057-0555-4, Twayne). G K Hall.

Ranke, Hermann. Early Babylonian Personal Names from the Published Tablets of the So-Called Hammurabi Dynasty 2000 B. C. (Publications of the Babylonian Section, Ser. D: Vol. 3). 255p. 1905. soft bound 3.00x (ISBN 0-686-11916-9). Univ Mus of U PA.

Ranki, Gyorgy, jt. auth. see Berend, Ivan.

Rankilor, P. R. Membranes in Ground Engineering. LC 80-40504. 377p. 1981. 61.95 (ISBN 0-471-27808-4, Pub. by Wiley-Interscience). Wiley.

Rankin, Carroll W. Dandelion Cottage. 4th ed. 1977. Repr. of 1904 ed. 5.95 (ISBN 0-938746-00-6). Marquette Cnty Hist.

Rankin, Hugh F. North Carolina in the American Revolution. 5th ed. (Illus.). 1982. pap. 1.00 (ISBN 0-86526-091-5). NC Archives.

--Pirates of Colonial North Carolina. (Illus.). 1981. pap. 1.00 (ISBN 0-86526-100-8). NC Archives.

Rankin, Jake & Rankin, Marni. The Getaway Guide IV: Short Vacations in Southern California. LC 82-19060. (Illus.). 248p. (Orig.). 1983. pap. 9.95 (ISBN 0-686-43071-9). Pacific Search.

--The Getaway Guide 0778997xx: Short Vacations in the Pacific Northwest. revised ed. LC 82-18784. (2nd). 223p. 1983. pap. 9.95 (ISBN 0-686-43073-5). Pacific Search.

Rankin, Marni, jt. auth. see Rankin, Jake.

Rankin, Molly. When the Fuse is Lit. 128p. Date not set. pap. 4.95 (ISBN 0-686-43178-2). Pacific Pr Pub Assn.

Rankin, Paula. Augers. LC 80-70565. (Poetry Ser.). 1981. 12.95 (ISBN 0-915604-45-0); pap. 4.95 (ISBN 0-915604-46-9). Carnegie-Mellon.

--By the Wreckmaster's Cottage. LC 77-80343. (Poetry Ser). 1977. pap. 3.95 (ISBN 0-915604-13-2). Carnegie-Mellon.

Rankin, Perry E. O Mind, Be Still. LC 81-90522. 106p. 1982. 7.95 (ISBN 0-533-05222-X). Vantage.

Rankin, R. A. Modular Forms & Functions. LC 76-11089. (Illus.). 1977. 75.00 (ISBN 0-521-21212-X). Cambridge U Pr.

Rankin, Robert. Uniforms of the Marines. (Illus.). (gr. 6-8). 1970. PLB 5.86 o.p. (ISBN 0-399-60649-1). Putnam Pub Group.

Rankin, Robert H. Military Headdress: A Pictorial History of Military Headgear from 1660-1914. LC 75-43821. (Illus.). 1976. 14.95 o.p. (ISBN 0-88254-371-7). Hippocrene Bks.

--Official Price Guide to Military Collectibles. LC 78-72034. (Collector Ser.). (Illus.). 400p. 1981. pap. 9.95 o.p. (ISBN 0-87637-014-8, 014-08). Hse of Collectibles.

Rankin, Robert P., jt. auth. see Lowry, Ritchie P.

Rankin, Sally & Duffy, Karen L., eds. Patient Education: Issues, Principles & Guidelines. (Illus.). 328p. 1983. pap. text ed. price not set (ISBN 0-397-54398-0, Lippincott Medical). Lippincott.

Rankin, William P. Business Management of General Consumer Magazines. LC 80-12147. 216p. 1980. 26.95 (ISBN 0-03-056696-7). Praeger.

Ranlett, John G. Money & Banking: An Introduction to Analysis & Policy. 3rd ed. LC 77-23251. 1977. text ed. 32.95x (ISBN 0-471-70815-1); tchr's manual 4.50 (ISBN 0-471-02579-8). Wiley.

Rannells, John. The Core of the City. LC 74-12853. (Columbia Institute for Urban Land Use & Housing Studies Ser.). (Illus.). 233p. 1974. Repr. of 1956 ed. lib. bdg. 17.75x (ISBN 0-8371-7764-2, RACC). Greenwood.

Ranney, Austin. Curing the Mischiefs of Faction: Party Reform in America. (Jefferson Memorial Lectures). 1975. 24.50x (ISBN 0-520-02650-0); pap. 3.25 (ISBN 0-520-03215-2, CAL 335). U of Cal Pr.

--The Doctrine of Responsible Party Government, Its Origins & Present State. LC 82-15517. (Illus.). ix, 176p. 1982. Repr. of 1962 ed. lib. bdg. 22.50x (ISBN 0-313-22873-6, RADR). Greenwood.

Ranney, Austin, jt. auth. see Bone, Hugh A.

Ranney, M. W. Silicones, 2 vols. Incl; Vol. 2. Coatings, Printing Inks, Cellular Plastics, Textiles & Consumer Products (ISBN 0-8155-0669-4). LC 77-77019. (Chemical Technology Review Ser.: Vols. 91-92). (Illus.). 1977. 69.00 set o.p. (ISBN 0-686-77306-3). Noyes.

Rannie, David W. The Elements of Style: An Introduction to Literary Criticism. 312p. 1982. Repr. of 1960 ed. lib. bdg. 40.00 (ISBN 0-89760-775-9). Telegraph Bks.

Ransauer, jt. ed. see Boyd.

Ransford, Oliver. David Livingstone: The Dark Interior. LC 78-50673. 1978. 25.00 (ISBN 0-312-18379-8). St Martin.

Ransford, Pat, tr. see Melotti, Umberto.

Ransom, C. G. The Age of Velikowsky. 1978. pap. 3.95 o.s.i. (ISBN 0-440-50323-X, Delta). Dell.

Ransom, Donald. Nothin' but the 'Boo. (Illus.). 20p. (Orig.). 1981. pap. text ed. 2.50 (ISBN 0-686-32817-5). Skydog OR.

Ransom, Elizabeth, jt. auth. see Johnson, Daphne.

Ransom, Grayce A. & Stowe, Elaine. Crackerjacks. rev. ed. (Cornerstone Ser.). (gr. 4-5). 1978. pap. text ed. 5.32 (ISBN 0-201-41026-5, Sch Div); tchr's ed. 6.76 (ISBN 0-201-41027-3). A-W.

--Drumbeats. rev. ed. (Cornerstone Ser.). (gr. 4-5). 1978. pap. text ed. 5.32 (ISBN 0-201-41028-1, Sch Div); tchr's ed. 6.76 (ISBN 0-201-41029-X). A-W.

Ransom, Harry H. The Conscience of the University & Other Essays. Ransom, Hazel H., ed. 117p. 1982. text ed. 12.50 (ISBN 0-292-71078-X); Limited Ed. 125.00 (ISBN 0-292-71080-1). U of Tex Pr.

Ransom, Hazel H., ed. see Ransom, Harry H.

Ransom, Jay E., jt. ed. see Collins, Henry H., Jr.

Ransom, P. J. Archaeolgy of Railways. (Illus.). 1981. 31.50 (ISBN 0-437-14401-1, Pub. by Heinemann). David & Charles.

--Archaeology of Canals. (Illus.). 1979. 31.50 (ISBN 0-437-14400-3, Pub. by Heinemann). David & Charles.

--Holiday Cruising in Ireland: A Guide to Irish Inland Waterways. (Illus.). 152p. 1971. 4.50 o.p. (ISBN 0-7153-5003-X). David & Charles.

--Railways Revived. (Illus.). Date not set. 7.95 o.s.i. (ISBN 0-571-09972-6). Faber & Faber.

--Your Book of Steam Railway Preservation. (Your Book Of...Ser.). (Illus.). 112p. (gr. 5-8). 1983. 10.95 (ISBN 0-571-11931-X). Faber & Faber.

Ransom, R. Handbook of Drosophila Development. 1982. 106.50 (ISBN 0-444-80366-1); pap. 42.75 (ISBN 0-444-80418-8). Elsevier.

Ransom, R. & Sutch, R. One Kind of Freedom. LC 76-27909. 1978. 44.50 (ISBN 0-521-21450-5); pap. 13.95x (ISBN 0-521-29203-4). Cambridge U Pr.

Ransom, R. J. Computers & Embryos: Models in Developmental Biology. 224p. 1981. 39.95 (ISBN 0-471-09972-4, Pub. by Wiley-Interscience). Wiley.

Ransom, Roger L. Coping with Capitalism: The Economic Transformation of the United States 1776-1980. (Illus.). 224p. 1981. pap. text ed. 11.95 (ISBN 0-13-172288-3). P-H.

Ransom, W. H. Building Failures: Diagnosis & Avoidance. (Illus.). 176p. 1981. 19.95x (ISBN 0-419-11750-4, Pub. by E&FN Spon England); pap. 9.95x (ISBN 0-419-11760-1). Methuen Inc.

Ransom, W. M. Last Rites. 1978. 3.00 (ISBN 0-918116-13-9). Jawbone Pr.

Ransome, A. Edgar Allan Poe: A Critical Study. LC 72-3534. (Studies in Poe, No. 23). 1972. Repr. of 1910 ed. lib. bdg. 49.95x (ISBN 0-8383-1548-8). Haskell.

Ransome, Arthur. We Didn't Mean to Go to Sea. 1981. PLB 11.95 (ISBN 0-8398-2698-2, Gregg). G K Hall.

Ransome, Hilda M. The Sacred Bee in Ancient Times & Folklore. 1976. lib. bdg. 100.00 (ISBN 0-8490-2552-4). Gordon Pr.

Ransome-Wallis, P. The Last Steam Locomotive of British Railways. 27.50x (ISBN 0-392-15392-0, SpS). Sportshelf.

Rantz, Phillip, jt. auth. see Grinsell, Leslie.

Ranucci, E. R. & Teeters, J. L. Creating Escher-Type Drawings. (gr. 7-12). 1977. wkbk 11.50 (ISBN 0-88488-087-7). Creative Pubns.

Ranucci, Ernest. Seeing Shapes. 1973. pap. 7.25 wkbk. (ISBN 0-88488-038-9). Creative Pubns.

Ranwell, D. S. Ecology of Salt Marshes & Sand Dunes. (Illus.). 1972. 32.00x (ISBN 0-412-10500-4, Pub. by Chapman & Hall). Methuen Inc.

Ranzou, Marie-Louise & Applegate, Margaret. The Communtiy College & Continuing Education of Health Care Personnel. 66p. 1978. 5.50 (ISBN 0-686-38243-9, 23-1710). Natl League Nurse.

Rao, Adapa R. Emerson & Social Reform. 132p. 1981. text ed. 12.00x (ISBN 0-391-02199-0). Humanities.

Rao, Ashok. Capacity Management Training Aid. LC 82-72090. 39p. 1982. tchr's. ed 27.00 (ISBN 0-935406-18-2). Am Prod & Inventory.

Rao, B. Ramachandra. The American Fictional Hero: An Analysis of the Works of Fitzgerald, Wolfe, Farrell, Dos Passos & Steinbeck. (English Language & Literature Ser.: No. 4). 1979. text ed. 5.95x o.s.i. (ISBN 0-210-40620-8, Pub. by Bahri India). Asia.

Rao, Bhaskara K., ed. Theories of Charges: A Study of Finitely Additive Measures. (Pure & Applied Mathmatics Ser.). Date not set. price not set (ISBN 0-12-095780-9). Acad Pr.

Rao, C. N. Ultra-Violet & Visible Spectroscopy: Chemical Applications. 3rd ed. 256p. 1975. 45.95 o.p. (ISBN 0-408-70624-4). Butterworth.

Rao, C. N. & Ferraro, J. R. Spectroscopy in Inorganic Chemistry. 1970-1971. Vol. 1. 59.50 (ISBN 0-12-580201-3); Vol. 2. 59.50 (ISBN 0-12-580202-1). Acad Pr.

Rao, C. N. & Rao, K. J. Phase Transition in Solids: An Approach to the Study of Chemistry & Physics of Solids. (Illus.). 1978. text ed. 52.00x (ISBN 0-07-051185-3, C). McGraw.

Rao, C. R. Essays on Econometrics & Planning. 1965. 37.00 o.p. (ISBN 0-08-011025-8). Pergamon.

Rao, C. R. & Mitra, Sujit K. Generalized Inverse of Matrices & Its Applications. LC 74-158528. (Ser. in Probability & Statistics Section). 1971. 38.95 (ISBN 0-471-70821-6, Pub. by Wiley-Interscience). Wiley.

Rao, Chintamani N. Chemical Applications of Infrared Spectroscopy. 1964. 59.50 (ISBN 0-12-580250-1). Acad Pr.

Rao, D. V. Dimensions of Backwardness. 122p. 1981. text ed. 14.25x (ISBN 0-391-02277-6, Pub. by Concept India). Humanities.

Rao, G. Gopal, jt. auth. see Skelton, Mary L.

Rao, G. Lakshmana. Brain Drain & Foreign Students. LC 78-10903. (Illus.). 1979. 26.00 (ISBN 0-312-09437-X). St Martin.

Rao, H. G., jt. auth. see Rajan, S. V.

Rao, K. Bhaskara. Paul Scott. (English Authors Ser.). 1980. 14.95 (ISBN 0-8057-6773-8, Twayne). G K Hall.
Rao, K. J., jt. auth. see Rao, C. N.
Rao, K. K., jt. auth. see Hall, D. O.
Rao, K. N. Wavelength Standards in the Infrared. 1966. 44.00 (ISBN 0-12-580650-7). Acad Pr.
Rao, K. N. & Mathews, C. Weldon, eds. Molecular Spectroscopy: Modern Research. 1972. 62.50 (ISBN 0-12-580640-X). Acad Pr.
Rao, K. R., jt. auth. see Ahmed, N.
Rao, K. R., jt. auth. see Deepak, Adarsh.
Rao, K. Ramakrishna. J. B. Rhine: On the Frontiers of Science. LC 82-17206. (Illus.). 278p. 1982. lib. bdg. 19.95x (ISBN 0-89950-053-6). McFarland & Co.
Rao, K. Ramamohan, jt. auth. see Elliott, Douglas F.
Rao, K. V. Management Science. 552p. Date not set. 11.95x (ISBN 0-07-451975-1). McGraw.
Rao, Kamala. Studies in Family Planning: India. LC 75-901634. 1974. 22.50x o.p. (ISBN 0-88386-563-7). South Asia Bks.
Rao, Krishna. A Dictionary of Bharata Natya. (Illus.). 100p. 1980. text ed. 15.95x (ISBN 0-86131-155-8, Pub. by Orient Longman Ltd India). Apt Bks.
Rao, N. Narayana. Elements of Engineering Electromagnetics. (Illus.). 1977. 33.95 (ISBN 0-13-264150-X). P-H.
Rao, N. R., tr. see Vyasa.
Rao, Natti S. Design of Machine Elements for Polymer Processing with Computer Programs. 208p. 1981. text ed. 29.00x (ISBN 0-02-949630-6, Pub. by Hanser International). Macmillan.
Rao, P. Sreenivasa. The Public Order of Ocean Resources: A Critique of the Contemporary Law of the Sea. LC 75-12741. 336p. 1975. text ed. 30.00x (ISBN 0-262-18072-3). MIT Pr.
Rao, P. Syamasundar & Miller, Max D. Pediatric Cardiology. LC 61-66847. (Medical Examination Review Ser.: Vol. 37). 1980. pap. 25.00 (ISBN 0-87488-140-4). Med Exam.
Rao, P. V. Computer Programming in Fortran & Other Languages. 1982. write for info. (ISBN 0-07-096569-2). McGraw.
Rao, Poyu, et al, eds. Premature Chromosome Condensation: Application in Basic, Clinical & Mutation Research. (Cell Biology Ser.). 1982. 45.00 (ISBN 0-12-580450-4). Acad Pr.
Rao, Prakasa, jt. ed. see Basawa, Ishwar.
Rao, R. Growth of Cities. 176p. 1981. text ed. 14.25x (ISBN 0-391-02270-9, Pub. by Concept India). Humanities.
Rao, R. Ranga, jt. auth. see Bhattacharya, R. N.
Rao, R. V. Small Industries & a Developing Economy. 1979. text ed. 12.50x (ISBN 0-391-01829-9). Humanities.
Rao, Raja. Kanthapura. LC 63-18637. 1967. Repr. 5.95 (ISBN 0-8112-0168-6, NDP224). New Directions.
Rao, S. & Dawson, P. R. Investigations on the Use of Boron-Sodium Carbonate Fluxes in Secondary Brass Melting 1979. 1981. 40.00x (ISBN 0-686-97099-3, Pub. by W Spring England). State Mutual Bk.
--A State of the Art Report on Secondary Aluminum Production Processes with Particular Emphasis Fluxes & Emission Control, 1980. 1981. 90.00x (ISBN 0-686-97165-5, Pub. by W Spring England). State Mutual Bk.
Rao, S. R. The Decipherment of the Indus Script. (Illus.). xxxii, 456p. 1982. text ed. 75.00x (ISBN 0-210-40630-5, Pub. by Jaisingh & Mehta India). Apt Bks.
Rao, Sethu, jt. auth. see Bouvier, Leon.
Rao, Shanta R. Seethu: A Novel. 160p. 1980. pap. text ed. 3.95x (ISBN 0-86131-178-7, Pub. by Orient Longman Ltd India). Apt Bks.
Rao, Shanto R. The Children's Mahabharata. (Illus.). 350p. 1980. pap. text ed. 7.50x (ISBN 0-86131-266-X, Pub by Orient Longman Ltd India). Apt Bks.
Rao, T. R. Error Coding for Arithmetic Processors. 1974. 43.50 (ISBN 0-12-580750-3). Acad Pr.
Rao, V. G. The Corporation Income Tax in India. 240p. 1980. text ed. 14.25x (ISBN 0-391-02133-8). Humanities.
Rao, V. K. Food, Nutrition & Poverty. x, 154p. 1982. text ed. 22.50 (ISBN 0-7069-1886-X, Pub. by Vikas India). Advent NY.
--India's National Income 1950-1980: An Analysis of Economic Growth & Change. LC 82-22972. (Illus.). 224p. 1983. 20.00 (ISBN 0-8039-1950-6). Sage.
Rao, V. V., jt. auth. see Ramaswamy, G. S.
Rapaport, Diane S. How to Make & Sell Your Own Record. (Illus.). pap. cancelled o.p. (ISBN 0-517-53479-7, Dist. by Crown). Crown.
Rapaport, E. Cardiology Update, 1979: Reviews for Physicians. 1979. 32.50 (ISBN 0-444-00298-7). Elsevier.
--Cardiology Update, 1983. 1982. 39.50 (ISBN 0-444-00763-6). Elsevier.
Rapaport, Elizabeth, ed. see Mill, John S.
Rapaport, Samuel I. Introduction to Hematology. (Illus.). 1971. pap. 17.50x o.p. (ISBN 0-06-142232-0, Harper Medical). Lippincott.
Raper, Arthur F. Tragedy of Lynching. LC 69-14943. (Criminology, Law Enforcement, & Social Problems Ser.: No. 25). (With a new intro. by the author). 1969. Repr. of 1933 ed. 16.00x (ISBN 0-87585-025-1). Patterson Smith.
--The Tragedy of Lynching. 8.50 (ISBN 0-8446-0230-2). Peter Smith.
Raper, Arthur F; see Shay, Frank.
Raper, C. David & Kramer, Paul J. Crop Reactions to Water & Temperature Stresses in Humid, Temperate Climates. (Special Studies in Agricultural Science & Policy). 425p. 1982. lib. bdg. 30.00 (ISBN 0-86531-176-5). Westview.
Raper, J. R. Without Shelter: The Career of Ellen Glasgow. LC 82-15863. (Southern Literary Studies). xii, 273p. 1982. Repr. of 1971 ed. lib. bdg. 39.75x (ISBN 0-313-23742-5, RAWS). Greenwood.
--Without Shelter: The Early Career of Ellen Glasgow. LC 74-142337. (Southern Literary Studies). xiv, 274p. 1971. 22.50x o.p. (ISBN 0-8071-0904-5). La State U Pr.
Raper, Kenneth B. & Fennell, Dorothy I. The Genus Aspergillus. LC 65-21117. 704p. 1973. Repr. of 1965 ed. 35.50 (ISBN 0-88275-109-3). Krieger.
Raphael. Raphael: Tables of Houses. 4.95x o.p. (ISBN 0-685-38474-8). Wehman.
--Raphael's Astro Ephemeris (Any Year) pap. 3.95x (ISBN 0-685-22085-0). Wehman.
--Raphael's Key to Astrology. 118p. 6.50 (ISBN 0-686-38233-1). Sun Bks.
Raphael, Chaim. A Feast of History. (Illus.). 250p. Repr. of 1972 ed. 24.95 o.p. (ISBN 0-686-79546-6). Behrman.
--The Springs of Jewish Life. LC 82-70853. 1982. 16.50 (ISBN 0-465-08192-4). Basic.
Raphael, Chester M., ed. see Reich, Wilhelm.
Raphael, Coleman & Lindskog, Robert. Preparing for the Civil Engineering Professional Examination. LC 82-24270. (Civil Engineering Ser.). 248p. 1983. pap. 17.95 (ISBN 0-910554-41-2). Eng Pr.
Raphael, D. D. Moral Philosophy. (Oxford Paperbacks University Ser.). (Orig.). 1981. pap. text ed. 7.95x (ISBN 0-19-289136-7). Oxford U Pr.
Raphael, Dan. Matt. 1982. lib. bdg. 75.00 (ISBN 0-686-81931-4). Porter.
--Polymerge. 24p. (Orig.). 1979. pap. text ed. 2.00 (ISBN 0-686-35895-3). Skydog OR.
Raphael, Dana. Breast Feeding & Food Policy in a Hungry World. LC 78-27683. 1979. 26.00 (ISBN 0-12-580950-6). Acad Pr.
Raphael, Elaine & Bolognese, Don. Donkey, It's Snowing. LC 80-8449. (Illus.). 32p. (ps-3). 1981. 7.95i (ISBN 0-06-020554-7, HarpJ); PLB 8.89g (ISBN 0-06-020555-5). Har-Row.
--Turnabout. LC 80-11866. (Illus.). 32p. (gr. 1-3). 1980. 8.95 o.p. (ISBN 0-670-73281-8). Viking Pr.
Raphael, F. & McLeish, K., trs. Aeschylus: The Oresteia. LC 78-6013. (Greek & Roman Authors Ser.). 1979. 15.95 (ISBN 0-521-22060-2); pap. 4.95 (ISBN 0-521-29344-8). Cambridge U Pr.
Raphael, Frederic. Byron. LC 82-80493. (Illus.). 224p. 1982. 18.95 (ISBN 0-500-01278-4). Thames Hudson.
--The Graduate Wife. 1978. 15.00 o.p. (ISBN 0-86025-094-6). State Mutual Bk.
Raphael, Frederic, tr. see Catullus.
Raphael, Levine & Healy, Rett. The Ten Commandments of Marriage. (Illus.). 96p. 1983. pap. 7.95 (ISBN 0-914842-96-X). Madrona Pubs.
Raphael, Marc L., ed. Jews & Judaism in the United States: A Documentary History. 352p. 1983. pap. text ed. 9.95x (ISBN 0-87441-347-8). Behrman.
Raphael, Morris. The Battle in the Bayou Country. (Illus.). 199p. (gr. 5-12). 1976. 10.95 (ISBN 0-9608866-0-5). M Raphael.
--Weeks Hall: The Master of the Shadows. LC 81-90439. (Illus.). 207p. (gr. 5-12). 1981. 14.95 (ISBN 0-9608866-1-3). M Raphael.
Raphael, Rick. The Defector. LC 79-6887. 336p. 1980. 10.95 o.p. (ISBN 0-385-15916-1). Doubleday.
Raphael, Robert. Richard Wagner. (World Authors Ser.: Germany: No. 77). lib. bdg. 10.95 o.p. (ISBN 0-8057-2976-3, Twayne). G K Hall.
Raphael, Stanley S. Lynch's Medical Laboratory Technology, 2 vols. 3rd ed. LC 74-17761. (Illus.). 2080p. 1976. Vol. 1. text ed. 30.00 o. p. (ISBN 0-7216-7463-1); Vol. 2. text ed. 30.00 (ISBN 0-7216-7464-X). Saunders.
Raphaelson, Elliot. Planning Your Financial Future. LC 81-11629. 239p. 1982. 19.95x (ISBN 0-471-08134-5). Wiley.
Raphaelson, Joel, jt. auth. see Roman, Kenneth.
Raphaelson, Samson. Three Screen Comedies by Samson Raphaelson: Trouble in Paradise, The Shop Around the Corner, Heaven Can Wait. 512p. 1983. 19.95 (ISBN 0-299-08780-8). U of Wis Pr.
Raphalion, Robin, ed. see Nankin, Michael & Korvetz, Elliot.
Rapid Excavation & Tunneling Conference, 1979. R E T C Proceedings, 2 vols. Hustrulid, William A. & Maevis, Alfred C., eds. LC 79-52280. (Illus.). 1819p. 1979. 60.00x (ISBN 0-89520-266-2). Soc Mining Eng.
Rapin, Isabelle. Children with Brain Dysfunction: Neurology, Cognition, Language, & Behavior. (International Review of Child Neurology Ser.). 300p. 1982. text ed. 37.50 (ISBN 0-89004-844-4). Raven.
Rapin, M., jt. ed. see Tinker, J.
Rapolla, A. & Keller, G. V., eds. Geophysical Aspects of the Energy Problem. (Developments in Energy Research Ser.: Vol. 1). 1980. 64.00 (ISBN 0-444-41845-8). Elsevier.
Rapoport, Amos. House Form & Culture. LC 69-14550. (Geography Ser). 1969. pap. 12.95 ref. ed. (ISBN 0-13-395673-3). P-H.
--The Meaning of the Built Environment: A Non-Verbal Communication Approach. 200p. 1982. 25.00 (ISBN 0-8039-1892-5); pap. 12.50 (ISBN 0-8039-1893-3). Sage.
Rapoport, Anatol. Mathematical Models in the Social Behavioral Sciences. 450p. 1983. 37.50 (ISBN 0-471-86449-8, Pub. by Wiley-Interscience). Wiley.
--N-Person Game Theory: Concepts & Applications. (Ann Arbor Science Library). (Illus.). 348p. 1970. pap. 5.95 o.p. (ISBN 0-472-05017-6). U of Mich Pr.
--Operational Philosophy. LC 70-105277. 1969. pap. text ed. 5.50x o.p. (ISBN 0-918970-03-2). Intl Gen Semantics.
Rapoport, Bonnie. Dining in Baltimore. (Illus.). 195p. 1981. pap. 7.95 (ISBN 0-686-36739-1). Md Hist.
Rapoport, Henry, jt. auth. see Cason, James.
Rapoport, John, et al. Understanding Health Economics. LC 81-14987. 554p. 1982. text ed. 36.50 (ISBN 0-89443-380-6). Aspen Systems.
Rapoport, Louis. The Lost Jews: Last of the Ethiopian Falashas. LC 79-92340. (Illus.). 264p. 1980. 16.95 (ISBN 0-8128-2720-1). Stein & Day.
Rapoport, Rhona & Rapoport, Robert. Dual-Career Families Re-Examined. rev. ed. 1977. pap. 4.95i o.p. (ISBN 0-06-090521-2, CN 521, CN). Har-Row.
Rapoport, Rhona, jt. ed. see Rapoport, Robert.
Rapoport, Robert, jt. auth. see Rapoport, Rhona.
Rapoport, Robert & Rapoport, Rhona, eds. Working Couples. 1978. pap. 4.95i o.p. (ISBN 0-06-090594-8, CN 594, CN). Har-Row.
Rapoport, Roger. California Dreaming. 320p. (Orig.). 1982. pap. 9.95 (ISBN 0-917316-48-7). Nolo Pr.
Rapoport, Ron, ed. see Oliver, Chip.
Rapoport, Stanley I. Blood-Brain Barrier in Physiology & Medicine. LC 75-26280. 328p. 1976. 37.00 (ISBN 0-89004-079-6). Raven.
Rapp, Donald. Solar Energy. (Illus.). 576p. 1981. text ed. 35.95 (ISBN 0-13-822213-4). P-H.
Rapp, Doris J. Allergies & Your Family. LC 79-93250. (Illus.). 352p. 1980. 12.95 (ISBN 0-8069-5558-9); lib. bdg. 15.69 (ISBN 0-8069-5559-7); pap. 7.95 (ISBN 0-8069-8878-9). Sterling.
Rapp, Florence D. Love in Its Many Aspects: A Collection of Love Poems. 1978. 4.95 o.p. (ISBN 0-533-03626-7). Vantage.
Rapp, Georg, tr. see Fried, Erich.
Rapp, Helen, tr. see Solzhenitsyn, Alexander.
Rapp, Kenneth W. West Point: Whistler in Cadet Gray, & Other Stories About the United States Military Academy. LC 78-61828. (Illus.). 1978. 7.50 o.p. (ISBN 0-88427-031-9); pap. 3.95 o.p. (ISBN 0-88427-032-7, Dist. by Caroline House Pubs). North River.
Rapp, Lea B. Put Your Kid in Show Biz. LC 80-54346. (Illus.). 160p. 1981. 13.95 (ISBN 0-8069-7040-5); lib. bdg. 16.79 (ISBN 0-8069-7041-3); pap. 7.95 (ISBN 0-8069-7508-3). Sterling.
Rapp, William F., jt. auth. see Beranek, Susan K.
Rapp, William F., ed. Railway History Monograph, Vol. 7. (Railway History Monograph). (Illus.). 63p. 1979. 8.00 o.p. (ISBN 0-916170-17-9). J-B Pubs.
Rapp, William G. Construction of Structural Steel Building Frames. 2nd ed. LC 79-19146. (Wiley Ser. of Practical Construction Guides). 1980. 49.95 (ISBN 0-471-05603-0, Pub. by Wiley-Interscience). Wiley.
Rappaport, Alfred. Information for Decision-Making: Quantitative & Behavioral Dimensions. 2nd ed. (Illus.). 384p. 1975. ref. ed. 19.95 o.p. (ISBN 0-13-464388-7). P-H.
Rappaport, Alfred & Lerner, Eugene M. Segment Reporting for Managers & Investors. 7.95 (ISBN 0-86641-024-4, 7252). Natl Assn Accts.
Rappaport, Alfred, ed. Information for Decision Making: Readings in Cost & Managerial Accounting. 3rd ed. (Illus.). 416p. 1982. pap. 21.95 (ISBN 0-13-464354-2). P-H.
Rappaport, Armin & Traina, Richard. Source Problems in American History. 416p. 1972. pap. text ed. 10.95 (ISBN 0-02-398410-4). Macmillan.
Rappaport, Donald & Butler, Robert E. Money & Your Business. (Illus.). 673p. 1982. 135.00 set (ISBN 0-13-600023-1); Vol. 1 67.50 (ISBN 0-13-600007-X); Vol. 2 67.50 (ISBN 0-13-600015-0). NY Inst Finance.
Rappaport, Doreen, jt. auth. see Kempler, Susan.
Rappaport, H., jt. auth. see Mathe, G.
Rappaport, Julian, et al. Innovations in Helping Chronic Patients: College Students in a Mental Institution. 1971. 35.50 (ISBN 0-12-581150-0). Acad Pr.
Rappaport, L. H. SEC Accounting Practice & Procedure. 3rd ed. 1288p. 1972. 59.95x (ISBN 0-471-06550-1, Pub. by Wiley-Interscience). Wiley.
Rappaport, Roy A. Pigs for the Ancestors: Ritual in the Ecology of a New Guinea People. LC 68-13926. (Illus.). 1968. pap. 7.95x (ISBN 0-300-01378-7, Y230). Yale U Pr.
Rappaport, Stephen, jt. auth. see Lamb, Robert.
Rappaport, Steven see Devarahi, pseud.
Rappeport, Rhoda. Fred Shero: A Kaleidoscopic View of the Philadelphia Flyers' Coach. LC 77-76649. 1977. 7.95 o.p. (ISBN 0-312-30362-9). St Martin.
Rappolt, Hedwig, tr. see Buchner, Georg.
Rappoport, Angelo S. Folklore of the Jews. LC 71-167125. Repr. of 1937 ed. 34.00x (ISBN 0-8103-3864-5). Gale.
--Superstitions of Sailors. LC 71-158207. 1971. Repr. of 1928 ed. 37.00x (ISBN 0-8103-3739-8). Gale.
Rappoport, Angelo S., tr. see Coudenhove-Kalergi, Heinrich J.
Rappoport, L. & Summers, D. Human Judgement & Social Interaction. 416p. 1973. 13.50 (ISBN 0-03-085870-4, Pub. by HR&W). Krieger.
Rappoport, Leon, jt. auth. see Wertheimer, Michael.
Rappoport, Leon, jt. ed. see Kren, George.
Rapport, Diane S. How to Make & Sell Your Own Records (the Complete Guide to Independent Recording) 1980. pap. 9.95 (ISBN 0-8256-9932-0, Quick Fox). Putnam Pub Group.
Rapport, Maurice M. & Gorio, Alfredo, eds. Gangliosides in Neurological & Neuromuscular Function, Development, & Repair. 296p. 1981. text ed. 36.50 (ISBN 0-89004-660-3). Raven.
Rapson, Linda B. Kipper. LC 81-11175. 128p. 1981. pap. 3.50 (ISBN 0-8024-4558-6). Moody.
--Kipper Plays Cupid. LC 81-11294. 128p. 1981. pap. 3.50 (ISBN 0-8024-4559-4). Moody.
Rapson, Richard L. Denials of Doubt: An Interpretation of American History. LC 78-58595. 1978. pap. text ed. 14.75 (ISBN 0-8191-0541-4). U Pr of Amer.
--Fairly Lucky You Live Hawaii! LC 80-5530. 166p. 1980. lib. bdg. 15.50 (ISBN 0-8191-1167-8); pap. text ed. 6.75 (ISBN 0-8191-1168-6). U Pr of Amer.
Rapson, Richard L., ed. Cult of Youth in Middle-Class America. LC 74-146876. (Problems in American Civilization Ser.). 118p. pap. text ed. 5.50 o.p. (ISBN 0-669-73387-3). Heath.
Raptis, Michael. Revolution & Counter Revolution in Chile. LC 74-82175. 160p. 1945. 20.00 (ISBN 0-312-67970-X). St Martin.
Raptis, Michel. Socialism, Democracy & Selfmanagement: Political Essays. LC 79-56924. 172p. 1980. 26.00 (ISBN 0-312-73653-3). St Martin.
Rare Fruit Council International Staff. Tropical Fruit Recipes. (Illus.). 176p. Date not set. pap. 10.95 (ISBN 0-686-84236-7). Banyan Bks.
Rarey, George H., jt. auth. see Jones, Ralph E.
Rarey, Kaneut P., jt. auth. see Youtsey, John W.
Rarick, Carrie. Jeanies Valentines. (Beginning-to-Read Ser.). 32p. (gr. k-3). 1982. PLB 4.39 (ISBN 0-695-41674-X, Dist. by Caroline Hse); pap. 1.95 (ISBN 0-695-31674-5). Follett.
Rarick, G. Lawrence, ed. Physical Activity: Human Growth & Development. 1973. 48.50 (ISBN 0-12-581550-6). Acad Pr.
Rasband, Ester. Man & Woman: The Joy in Oneness. LC 82-70997. 54p. 1982. 5.95 (ISBN 0-87747-917-8). Deseret Bk.
Rasberry, Robert W. The Technique of Political Lying. LC 80-5976. 301p. 1981. 21.25 (ISBN 0-8191-1482-0); pap. text ed. 10.00 (ISBN 0-8191-1483-9). U Pr of Amer.
Rasberry, Robert W., jt. auth. see Flacks, Niki.
Rasch, G. Probalistic Models for Some Intelligence & Attainment Tests. LC 80-16546. 208p. 1980. lib. bdg. 21.00x o.s.i. (ISBN 0-226-70553-6); pap. 9.00x (ISBN 0-226-70554-4). U of Chicago Pr.
Raschke, Carl A. The Alchemy of the Word: Language & the End of Theology. LC 79-15490. (American Academy of Religion, Studies in Religion: No. 20). 1979. 14.00 (ISBN 0-89130-319-7, 01-00-20); pap. 9.95 (ISBN 0-89130-320-0). Scholars Pr Ca.
Raschke, Carl A., ed. New Dimensions in Philosophical Theology. (AAR Thematic Studies). 19.50 (ISBN 0-89130-577-7, 01-24-91). Scholars Pr CA.
--New Dimensions in Philosophical Theology. (Thematic Studies). 12.95 (ISBN 0-686-96217-6, 01 20 49:1). Scholars Pr CA.
Rase, H. F. & Barrow, M. H. Piping Design for Process Plants. LC 63-17483. 1963. 48.95 (ISBN 0-471-70920-4, Pub. by Wiley-Interscience). Wiley.
--Project Engineering of Process Plants. 1957. 53.50 (ISBN 0-471-70917-4, Pub. by Wiley-Interscience). Wiley.
Rase, Howard F. Chemical Reactor Design for Process Plants, 2 vols. Incl. Vol. 1. Principles & Techniques. 66.95 (ISBN 0-471-01891-0); Vol. 2. Case Studies & Design Data. 33.95 (ISBN 0-471-01890-2). LC 77-1285. 1977 (Pub. by Wiley-Interscience). Wiley.
Rash, J. E. & Hudson, C. S. Freeze-Fracture: Methods, Artifacts, & Interpretations. LC 79-109. (Illus.). 216p. 1979. text ed. 23.00 (ISBN 0-89004-386-8). Raven.
Rash, J. Keogh & Pigg, R. Morgan. Health Education Curriculum: A Guide for Curriculum Development in Health Education. LC 78-24493. 1979. text ed. 24.95x (ISBN 0-471-03765-6). Wiley.
Rashba, E. I. & Sturge, M. D. Excitons. (Modern Problems in Solid State Physics Ser.: Vol. 2). 1982. 181.00 (ISBN 0-444-86202-1). Elsevier.

Rashdall, Hastings. A Comparative Analysis of Psychological Hedonism & Rationalistic Utilitarianism. (Science of Man Library). (Illus.). 143p. 1983. 79.65 (ISBN 0-89266-385-5). Am Classical Coll Pr.

Rashid, Haroun Er. Geography of Bangladesh. (Illus.). 1978. lib. bdg. 35.00 (ISBN 0-89158-356-4). Westview.

Rashid, Jamil, jt. ed. see Gardezi, Hassan.

Rashiduzzaman, M. Rural Leadership & Population Control in Bangladesh. LC 82-40245. 110p. (Orig.). 1982. lib. bdg. 19.50 (ISBN 0-8191-2637-3); pap. text ed. 8.25 (ISBN 0-8191-2638-1). U Pr of Amer.

Rashkind, William J., ed. Congenital Heart Disease. LC 81-6979. (Benchmark Papers in Human Physiology: Vol. 16). 416p. 1982. 55.00 (ISBN 0-87933-414-2). Hutchinson Ross.

Rasic, J., jt. auth. see Kurmann, J.

Raskevics, J., et al. English-Latvian-Russian Dictionary. 718p. 1977. 50.00x (ISBN 0-686-82324-9, Pub. by Collets). State Mutual Bk.

Raskhodoff, Nickolas M. Electronic Drafting & Design. 4th ed. (Illus.). 576p. 1982. 23.95 (ISBN 0-13-250621-1). P-H.

Raskin, A. H. State of the Unions. Date not set. 16.95 (ISBN 0-393-01519-X). Norton.

Raskin, Allen, jt. ed. see Schulterbrandt, Joy G.

Raskin, Barbara. Out of Order. 1979. 9.95 o.p. (ISBN 0-671-24281-4). S&S.

Raskin, Ellen. Figgs & Phantoms. LC 73-17309. (Illus.). 160p. (gr. 4-7). 1974. 10.95 (ISBN 0-525-29680-8, 01063-320); pap. 1.95 (ISBN 0-525-45035-1, Anytime Bks). Dutton.

--Mysterious Disappearance of Leon: (I Mean Noel) (gr. 4-7). 1971. 9.95 o.p. (ISBN 0-525-35540-5); pap. 1.95 (ISBN 0-525-45010-6, 0461-140). Dutton.

--Spectacles. LC 68-12234. (Illus.). (gr. k-4). 1968. PLB 10.95 (ISBN 0-689-20352-7). Atheneum.

--Tattooed Potato & Other Clues. (gr. 4-7). 1975. 9.95 (ISBN 0-525-40805-3). Dutton.

Raskin, Eugene. Architecture & People. 192p. 1974. ref. ed. 21.95 (ISBN 0-13-044594-0). P-H.

--Citronella. 1980. 10.95 (ISBN 0-686-98251-7); pap. 4.95 (ISBN 0-8197-0483-0). Bloch.

--Sequel to Cities: What Happens When Cities Are Extinct. 1970. 3.95x o.p. (ISBN 0-685-03327-9, BPB10004); pap. 1.95x o.p. (ISBN 0-8197-0004-5). Bloch.

Raskin, Jonah. My Search for Traven. LC 79-50643. 1980. 10.00 o.p. (ISBN 0-448-15177-4, G&D). Putnam Pub Group.

Raskin, Marcus. Being & Doing. LC 72-8654. 1973. pap. 4.95 o.p. (ISBN 0-8070-4385-0, BP457). Beacon Pr.

Raskin, Neil H. & Appenzeller, Otto. Headache. LC 79-66042. (Monograph in Major Problems in Internal Medicine: No. 19). (Illus.). 244p. 1980. 22.50 (ISBN 0-7216-7467-4). Saunders.

Raskova, H., ed. Pharmacology & Toxicology of Naturally Occurring Toxins, 2 vols. LC 77-130797. 1971. Vol. 1. 65.00 (ISBN 0-08-016319-X); Vol. 2. 65.00 (ISBN 0-08-016798-5); Set. 100.00 (ISBN 0-08-016797-7). Pergamon.

Rasmus, Lucy. The Carrot Cookbook, 57 Recipes. (Illus.). 1982. pap. 2.50 (ISBN 0-933646-17-8). Aries Pr.

Rasmusen, Benjamin, jt. auth. see Hutt, Frederick B.

Rasmussen, Anne M., tr. see Willumsen, Dorrit.

Rasmussen, David W. Agriculture in the U. S. A Documentary History, 4 Vols. (Documentary Reference Collection Ser.). 1975. lib. bdg. 40.00 ea. Vol. 1 (ISBN 0-313-20148-X). Vol. 2 (ISBN 0-313-20149-8). Vol. 3 (ISBN 0-313-20150-1). Vol. 4 (ISBN 0-313-20151-X). Set. lib. bdg. 175.00 (ISBN 0-313-20147-1, RAAG/). Greenwood.

Rasmussen, David W. & Struyk, Raymond J. A Housing Strategy for the City of Detroit: Policy Perspectives Based on Economic Analysis. LC 81-51874. (Illus.). 81p. (Orig.). 1981. pap. text ed. 9.00 (ISBN 0-87766-300-9, URI 32500). Urban Inst.

Rasmussen, Eileen C. Of Lost Loves & Other People. 1979. 5.00 o.p. (ISBN 0-682-49473-9). Exposition.

Rasmussen, Howard. Calcium & Camp As Synarchic Messengers. LC 81-10482. 370p. 1981. 44.50 (ISBN 0-471-08396-8, Pub. by Wiley-Interscience). Wiley.

Rasmussen, Jorgen S. Retrenchment & Revival: A Study of the Contemporary British Liberal Party. LC 64-17263. 1964. 2.00 o.p. (ISBN 0-8165-0079-7). U of Ariz Pr.

Rasmussen, Knud. Beyond the High Hills: A Book of Eskimo Poems. LC 61-14072. (Illus.). (gr. 3 up). 1961. 6.95 o.p. (ISBN 0-529-03690-8, Philomel). Putnam Pub Group.

--The People of the Polar North. LC 75-167126. 1975. Repr. of 1908 ed. 34.00x (ISBN 0-685-52348-9). Gale.

Rasmussen, Linda, et al, eds. A Harvest Yet to Reap: A History of Prairie Women. 240p. 1976. pap. 13.95 (ISBN 0-8032-8907-3). U of Nebr Pr.

Rasmussen, M. L., jt. auth. see Reddy, J. N.

Rasmussen, N., jt. auth. see Oldenberg, Otto.

Rasmussen, S. E. Danish Textiles. (Illus.). 22.50 o.p. (ISBN 0-87245-324-3). Textile Bk.

Rasmussen, Steen E. Towns & Buildings. 1969. pap. 9.95x (ISBN 0-262-68011-4). MIT Pr.

Rasmussen, T. B. Bucchero Pottery from Southern Etruria. LC 78-13464. (Cambridge Classical Studies). (Illus.). 1979. 44.50 (ISBN 0-521-22316-4). Cambridge U Pr.

Rasmussen, Theodore & Marino, Raul, eds. Functional Neurosurgery. LC 77-85871. 288p. 1979. text ed. 38.00 (ISBN 0-89004-228-4). Raven.

Rasmussen, Wayne D., jt. ed. see Brewster, David E.

Rasor, Reba G., ed. see State Bar of Texas Council of the Family Law Section.

Raspail, F. V. Manual for Health with Domestic Medicine & Pharmacy. Mocq, Louis, tr. 1983. 10.00 (ISBN 0-533-05266-1). Vantage.

Raspall de Cauhe, Joana, et al. Diccionari Usual de Sinonims Catalans: Mots i Frases. 572p. (Cata.). 1975. 17.50 (ISBN 84-7211-111-3, S-50048). French & Eur.

Rasponi, Lanfranco. The Last Prima Donnas. 1982. 22.50 (ISBN 0-394-52153-6). Knopf.

Rassam, Amal, jt. auth. see Bates, Daniel.

Rassias, G. M., jt. auth. see Rassias, T. M.

Rassias, T. M. & Rassias, G. M. Albert Einstein, 1879-1955: Selected Topics: Physics, Astrophysics, Mathematics & History of Science. 1982. 83.00 (ISBN 0-444-86161-0). Elsevier.

Rassinier, Paul. The Drama of the European Jews. 3rd ed. (Illus.). 1976. pap. 9.95 (ISBN 0-918184-01-0). Bibliophile.

--The Real Eichmann Trial or the Incorrigible Victors. 2nd ed. LC 76-19192. (Illus.). 1979. 9.95 (ISBN 0-911038-48-5). Bibliophile.

Rassmussen, David & Haworth, Charles. Economics: Principles & Applications. LC 78-2245. 672p. 1979. text ed. 20.95 (ISBN 0-574-19280-8, 13-2280); instr's guide avail. (ISBN 0-574-19281-6, 13-2281); study guide 7.95 (ISBN 0-574-19282-4, 13-2282); lecture resource supplement 3.75 (ISBN 0-574-19284-0, 13-2284). SRA.

Rast, Walter E. Taanach I: Studies in the Iron Age Pottery. LC 76-5474. (American Schools of Oriental Research, Excavation Reports Ser.). 283p. 1978. text ed. 25.00x (ISBN 0-89757-201-7, Am Sch Orient Res). Eisenbrauns.

Rastetter, J., jt. auth. see Begemann, H.

Rastogi, B., jt. auth. see Gupta, H.

Rastoin, J. & Boley, B. A., eds. Transactions of the International Conference on Structural Mechanics & Reactor Technology: 116th Meeting, 13 Vols. 1982. Set. 298.00 (ISBN 0-444-86268-4). Elsevier.

Rastyannikov, V. G. Agrarian Evolution in a Multiform Structure Society: Experience of Independent India. Kostrov, Konstantin A., tr. from Rus. 373p. 1981. 29.95 (ISBN 0-7100-0755-8). Routledge & Kegan.

Rasula, Jed. Tabula Rasula. (Illus.). 96p. 1983. ltd., signed 20.00 (ISBN 0-930794-61-3); pap. 5.50 (ISBN 0-930794-62-1). Station Hill Pr.

Ratajczak, H. & Orville-Thomas, W. J. Molecular Interactions. Vol. 1, 448 Pp. 91.95 (ISBN 0-471-27664-2, 1-500); Vol. 2. 119.95 (ISBN 0-471-27681-2). Wiley.

--Molecular Interactions, Vol. 3. (Molecular Interactions Ser.). 656p. 1982. 123.95 (ISBN 0-471-10033-1, Pub. by Wiley-Interscience). Wiley.

Ratan, Jai, tr. see Chander, Krishan.

Ratcliff, Carter. Jean Dubuffet, Partitions 1980-1981; Psycho-Sites 1981. (Illus.). 36p. (Orig.). 1982. pap. text ed. 16.50 (ISBN 0-938608-10-X). Pace Gallery Pubns.

Ratcliff, Richard. Real Estate Analysis. 1961. text ed. 19.95 (ISBN 0-07-051197-7, C). McGraw.

Ratcliff, Ruth. German Tales & Legends. 144p. 1982. 29.00x (ISBN 0-584-62059-4, Pub. by Muller Ltd). State Mutual Bk.

Ratcliffe, D. A., ed. A Nature Conservation, 2 vols. Incl. Vol. 1. 125.00 (ISBN 0-521-21159-X); Vol. 2. 99.00 (ISBN 0-521-21403-3). LC 76-11065. (Illus.). 1977. Cambridge U Pr.

Ratcliffe, F. N., jt. auth. see Fenner, Frank.

Ratcliffe, L., ed. see Lack, David.

Ratcliffe, M., jt. auth. see Popov, G.

Ratcliffe, N. A. & Llewellyn, P. J. Practical Illustrated Histology. 246p. 1983. text ed. 21.95 (ISBN 0-02-398560-7). Macmillan.

Ratcliffe, N. A. & Llewllyn, P. J. Practical Illustrated Histology. 1982. 70.00x (ISBN 0-333-32653-9, Pub. by Macmillan England). State Mutual Bk.

Ratcliffe, THomas A. Introduction to Accounting. 1982. 17.00 (ISBN 0-89419-197-7). Inst Energy.

Rateaver, Gylver, ed. see Hainsworth, P. H.

Ratensky, Alexander. Drawing & Modelmaking: A Primer for Students of Architecture & Design. (Illus.). 144p. 1983. 17.50 (ISBN 0-8230-7369-6, Whitney Lib). Watson-Guptill.

Rath, Eric. Container Systems. LC 72-13139. (Materials Handling & Packaging Ser.). 608p. 1973. 69.95 (ISBN 0-471-70921-2, Pub. by Wiley-Interscience). Wiley.

Rath, Frederick L. & O'Connell, Merrilyn R. Administration: A Bibliography on Historical Organization Practices, Vol. 5. LC 75-26770. 250p. 1980. text ed. 14.95x (ISBN 0-910050-44-9). AASLH.

Rath, P. M., jt. auth. see Mason, R. E.

Rath, Patricia M. Succeeding on the Job: A Self-Study Guide for Students. 1970. pap. text ed. 7.25x (ISBN 0-8134-1167-X, 1167). Interstate.

Rath, Patricia M, et al. Supervising on the Job: A Self-Study Guide for Students. 1971. pap. text ed. 7.25x (ISBN 0-8134-1238-2, 1238). Interstate.

Rath, Patricia M., et al. Applying for a Job-a Self-Study Guide for Students. 1968. pap. text ed. 7.25x (ISBN 0-8134-0928-4, 928). Interstate.

Rath, Wilhelm. The Imagery of the Goetheanum Windows. Mann, William, tr. from German. (Illus.). 30p. 1976. 12.50 (ISBN 0-85440-300-0, Pub. by Steinerbooks). Anthroposophic.

Rathbone, Belinda, ed. One of a Kind: Recent Polaroid Color Photography. LC 79-50785. (Illus.). 80p. 1979. 40.00 (ISBN 0-87923-289-7). Godine.

Rathbone, E., jt. auth. see Rathbone, R. S.

Rathbone, Eleanor. The Disinherited Family. 360p. 1983. 19.95 (ISBN 0-905046-14-5); pap. 11.95 (ISBN 0-905046-13-7). Falling Wall.

Rathbone, Julian. A Raving Monarchist. LC 77-9127. 1978. 7.95 o.p. (ISBN 0-312-66412-5). St Martin.

Rathbone, Perry T., intro. by. Forsyth Wickes Collection. (Illus.). 1968. 8.50 (ISBN 0-87846-164-7); pap. 2.50 (ISBN 0-686-82944-1). Mus Fine Arts Boston.

Rathbone, Perry T., frwd. by. Great Museums: Museum of Fine Arts, Boston. (Illus.). 1969. 19.95 (ISBN 0-88225-205-4, Pub. by Newsweek). Mus Fine Arts Boston.

Rathbone, R., jt. ed. see Marks, S.

Rathbone, R. S. & Rathbone, E. Health & the Nature of Man. 1971. 19.95 (ISBN 0-07-051205-1, C); pap. 9.95 o.p. (ISBN 0-07-051206-X); 2.95 o.p. instructor's manual (ISBN 0-07-051207-8). McGraw.

Rathbun, Ivan T. Building Construction Specifications. 272p. 1972. text ed. 17.95 (ISBN 0-07-051209-4, G); instructor's manual 1.50 (ISBN 0-07-051210-8). McGraw.

Rathbun, John W. American Literary Criticism: Vol. I, 1800-1860. (United States Authors Ser.). 1979. lib. bdg. 12.95 (ISBN 0-8057-7263-4, Twayne). G K Hall.

Rathbun, John W. & Clark, Harry H. American Literary Criticism: Vol. II, 1860-1905. (United States Authors Ser.). 1979. lib. bdg. 12.95 (ISBN 0-8057-7264-2, Twayne). G K Hall.

Rathbun, Katharine C., jt. auth. see Richards, Edward P., III.

Rathbun, William, jt. auth. see Trunber, Henry.

Rathburn, Seward H. Background for Architecture. 1926. 49.50x (ISBN 0-685-69854-8). Elliots Bks.

Rathe, John C. Radiographic Tumor Localizer. 71p. 1982. 12.50 (ISBN 0-87527-249-5). Green.

Rather, L. J. Mind & Body in Eighteenth Century Medicine: A Study Based on Jerome Gaub's De Regimine Mentis. (Wellcome Institute of the History of Medicine). 1965. 31.00x (ISBN 0-520-01049-3). U of Cal Pr.

Rather, Lois. Bufano & the U. S. A. (Illus.). 1975. ltd. ed. 20.00 o.p. (ISBN 0-686-20623-1). Rather Pr.

--Dunsmuir House. (Illus.). 1982. limited ed. 25.00 (ISBN 0-686-37970-5). Rather Pr.

Rathi, M. L. & Kumar, S. Perinatal Medicine, 2 Vols. 1980-82. Vol. 1. text ed. 35.00 (ISBN 0-07-051204-3); Vol. 2. text ed. 39.50 (ISBN 0-07-051208-6). McGraw.

Rathje, William L. & Schiffer, Michael B. Archaeology. 434p. 1982. 19.95 (ISBN 0-15-502950-9, HC). HarBraceJ.

Rathkopf, Arden H., jt. auth. see Rathkopf, Charles A.

Rathkopf, Charles A. & Rathkopf, Arden H. The Law of Zoning & Planning, with Forms, 5 vols. LC 56-2013. 1977. Set. looseleaf with 1979 suppl. 275.00 (ISBN 0-87632-020-5). Boardman.

Rathlesberger, James, ed. Nixon & the Environment: The Politics of Devastation. (Illus.). 1972. pap. 2.45 o.p. (ISBN 0-686-01906-7, Dist. by Random). Village Voice.

Rathmore, Fateh S., et al. With Tigers in the Wild: An Experience in an Indian Forest. (Illus.). 196p. Date not set. text ed. 75.00x (ISBN 0-7069-1023-0, Pub. by Vikas India). Advent NY.

Raths, Louis, et al. Teaching for Learning. LC 79-95170. 1967. pap. text ed. 6.95 (ISBN 0-675-09417-8). Merrill.

--Values & Teaching. 2nd ed. (Educational Foundations Ser.). 1978. pap. text ed. 13.95 (ISBN 0-675-08514-4). Merrill.

Rathus, Spencer & Nevid, Jeffrey. BT--Behavior Therapy. 1978. pap. 2.98 (ISBN 0-451-09949-4, E9949, Sig). NAL.

Rational Dress Association. Exhibition Catalogue, 1883 & Gazette, 1888-1889. Stansky, Peter & Shewan, Rodney, eds. LC 76-18323. (Aesthetic Movement & the Arts & Crafts Movement Ser.). 1978. lib. bdg. 44.00x o.s.i. (ISBN 0-8240-2456-7). Garland Pub.

Ratkevich, Ronald P., jt. auth. see Casanova, Richard L.

Ratliff, Bascom W., et al. Social Work in Hospitals. 128p. 1982. 14.75x (ISBN 0-398-04699-9). C C Thomas.

Ratliff, Gerald L. The Theatre Student-Playscript Interpretation & Production. (Theatre Student Ser.). (Illus.). 160p. lib. bdg. 12.50 (ISBN 0-686-82646-9). Rosen Pr.

Ratnatunga, Manel. Syria: What Is She? (Illus.). 216p. 1983. pap. 9.95 (ISBN 9971-65-061-4). Hippocrene Bks.

Ratner, David L. Securities Regulation in a Nutshell. 2nd ed. LC 82-11108. (Nutshell Ser.). 312p. 1982. pap. text ed. 6.95 (ISBN 0-314-66864-0). West Pub.

Ratner, David L., jt. ed. see Painter, William H.

Ratner, Leonard G. Harmony: Structure & Style. (Music Ser.). 1962. text ed. 28.50 (ISBN 0-07-051213-2, C). McGraw.

--Music: The Listener's Art. 3rd ed. LC 76-23395. 1977. text ed. 25.00 (ISBN 0-07-051221-3, C); 7.95 (ISBN 0-07-051222-1). McGraw.

Ratner, Marc L. William Styron. (United States Authors Ser.). lib. bdg. 12.95 (ISBN 0-8057-0708-5, Twayne). G K Hall.

Ratner, Marilyn. Plenty of Patches: An Introduction to Patchwork, Quilting & Applique. LC 77-3401. (Illus.). (gr. 4 up). 1978. 9.95i o.p. (ISBN 0-690-01329-9, TYC-J); PLB 9.89 o.p. (ISBN 0-690-03836-4). Har-Row.

Ratner, Marilyn, jt. auth. see Cooper, Terry.

Ratner, Ronnie S., ed. Equal Employment Policy for Women: Strategies for Implementation in the United States, Canada & Western Europe. 544p. 1980. 34.95 (ISBN 0-87722-156-1). Temple U Pr.

Ratner, Sidney, et al. The Evolution of the American Economy: Growth, Welfare & Decision Making. LC 78-13838. 1980. 19.50x (ISBN 0-465-02127-1). Basic.

Ratnesar, Padnam. Problems in Otolarynology. Fry, J. & Williams, K., eds. (Problems in Practice Ser.: Vol. 8). 175p. 1982. text ed. 16.50 (ISBN 0-8036-7297-7). Davis Co.

Rattan, S. S. Resupinate Aphyllophorales of the Northwestern Himalayas. (Bibliotheca Mycologica Ser.: No. 60). (Illus.). 1977. lib. bdg. 48.00x (ISBN 3-7682-1172-X). Lubrecht & Cramer.

Rattan, S. S. & Khurana, I. P. S. The Clavaria of the Sikkim Himalayas. (Bibliotheca Mycologica Ser.: No. 66). (Illus.). 1978. pap. text ed. 10.00x (ISBN 3-7682-1212-2). Lubrecht & Cramer.

Rattazzi, Mario C. & Scandalios, John G., eds. Isozymes. LC 77-12288. (Current Topics in Biological & Medical Research Ser.: Vol. 6). 297p. 1982. 58.00 (ISBN 0-8451-0255-9). A R Liss.

Rattenbury, Judith. Introduction to the IBM 360 Computer & OS-JCL (Job Control Language) rev. ed. LC 73-620248. 103p. 1974. 8.00x (ISBN 0-87944-011-2). Inst Soc Res.

Rattenbury, Judith & Pelletier, Paula. Data Processing in the Social Sciences with OSIRIS. LC 74-620138. 245p. 1974. 15.00x (ISBN 0-87944-163-1); pap. 10.00x (ISBN 0-87944-162-3). Inst Soc Res.

Ratti, J. S. College Algebra. 1977. 23.95x (ISBN 0-02-398640-9, 39864). Macmillan.

--College Algebra & Trigonometry. (Illus.). 1977. 24.95x (ISBN 0-02-398530-5). Macmillan.

Ratti, J. S., jt. auth. see Goodman, A. W.

Rattner, Joseph. Alfred Adler. Zohn, Harry, tr. from Ger. LC 82-40251. (Literature & Life Ser.). 190p. 1983. 11.95 (ISBN 0-8044-5988-6). Ungar.

Rattray, J. M. Grass Cover of Africa. (FAO Agricultural Studies: No. 49). (Orig.). 1968. pap. 13.50 (ISBN 92-5-100386-6, F211, FAO). Unipub.

Rattray, R. S. Ashanti. (Illus.). 1981. Repr. of 1923 ed. 27.00x o.p. (ISBN 0-19-823149-0). Oxford U Pr.

--Ashanti Proverbs: The Primitive Ethics of a Savage People. 1981. 14.95x o.p. (ISBN 0-19-823147-4). Oxford U Pr.

Rattray, Robert S. Religion & Art in Ashanti. (Illus.). 1980. Repr. of 1970 ed. 29.00x o.p. (ISBN 0-19-823144-X). Oxford U Pr.

Ratyck, Joanna see Crean, John E., et al.

Ratzer, Gerald. A FORTRAN Seventy-Seven Course. 144p. 1981. pap. text ed. 9.95 (ISBN 0-8403-2427-8). Kendall-Hunt.

Ratzinger, Joseph C. Eschatology: Death & Eternal Life. Cunningham, Robert J., tr. 1983. 12.00 (ISBN 0-8199-0855-X). Franciscan Herald.

Rau, John G. & Wooten, David C. Environmental Impact Analysis Handbook. (Illus.). 1979. 44.50 (ISBN 0-07-051217-5, P&RB). McGraw.

Rau, Joseph L. & Rau, Mary Y. Fundamental Respiratory Therapy Equipment. (Illus.). 206p. 1978. pap. 15.00 (ISBN 0-8151-7080-7); instr's guide 2.50 (ISBN 0-8151-7082-3); slide tray set 197.50 (ISBN 0-686-94894-7). Year Bk Med.

Rau, Mary Y., jt. auth. see Rau, Joseph L.

Rau, Nicholas. Matrices & Mathematical Programming: An Introduction for Economists. 1981. 20.00x (ISBN 0-312-52299-1). St Martin.

Rau, Santha R. Cooking of India. LC 79-98164. (Foods of the World Ser.). (Illus.). (gr. 6 up). 1969. PLB 17.28 (ISBN 0-8094-0069-3, Pub. by Time-Life). Silver.

Rau, Santha R., tr. see Sivasankara, Pillai T.

Rau, William E. A Bibliography of Pre-Independence Zambia: The Social Sciences. 1978. lib. bdg. 49.00 (ISBN 0-8161-7872-0, Hall Reference). G K Hall.

Raubinger, Frederick M., et al. Leadership in the Secondary School. new ed. (Education-Administration Ser.). 464p. 1974. text ed. 22.95x (ISBN 0-675-08796-1). Merrill.

Rauch, Friedrich. Psychology; or, a View of the Human Soul, Including Anthropology. LC 74-22335. (Hist. of Psych. Ser.). 1975. 47.00x (ISBN 0-8201-1142-2). Schol Facsimiles.

Rauch, H. W., et al. Ceramic Fibers & Fibrous Composite Materials. (Refractory Materials Ser: Vol. 3). 1968. 56.00 (ISBN 0-12-582850-0). Acad Pr.

Rauch, Irmangard & Carr, Gerald F., eds. Language Change. LC 82-48626. 288p. 1983. 20.00x (ISBN 0-253-33196-X). Ind U Pr.

Rauch, James, ed. Guide to the Ink Industry. LC 81-84941. (Illus.). 140p. 1982. pap. 85.00 (ISBN 0-917148-18-5). Kline.

Rauch, James, jt. ed. see Deitsch, Maian.

Raucher, Herman. Maynard's House. 1980. 10.95 (ISBN 0-399-12508-6). Putnam Pub Group.

Raudive, Konstantin. Breakthrough: An Amazing Experiment in Electronic Communication with the Dead. Morton, J., ed. Fowler, N., tr. from Ger. 1971. text ed. 11.25x o.p. (ISBN 0-900675-54-3). Humanities.

Raudsepp. More Creative Growth Games. 1980. 4.95 (ISBN 0-399-50456-7, Perige). Putnam Pub Group.

Raudsepp, Eugene. How Creative Are You? 196p. 1981. pap. 4.95 (ISBN 0-399-50513-X, Perige). Putnam Pub Group.

Rauf, A. Story of Islamic Culture. 1981. 2.50 (ISBN 0-686-97868-4). Kazi Pubns.

Rauf, Abdur. West Pakistan: Rural Education & Development. LC 78-101087. 1970. 12.00x (ISBN 0-8248-0089-3, Eastwest Ctr). UH Pr.

Rauf, S. A. Advice to a Friend. pap. 2.00 (ISBN 0-686-18474-2). Kazi Pubns.

Rauh, Gisa, ed. Essays on Deixis. 200p. 1983. pap. write for info. (ISBN 3-87808-959-7). Benjamins North Am.

Raum, Hans, jt. ed. see Crouch, Milton.

Raumer, Frederick Von see Von Raumer, Frederick.

Raun, Donald L., jt. auth. see Anderson, Donald L.

Rauner, Judy A., jt. auth. see Trost, Arty.

Rauner, Yu. L. Heat Balance of the Plant Cover. 220p. 1977. 70.00x (ISBN 0-686-84456-4, Pub. by Oxford & I B H India). State Mutual Bk.

Raup, Omer B. & Earhart, Robert L. Geology Along Going-to-the-Sun Road Glacier National Park Montana. LC 82-84746. (Illus.). 64p. 1983. pap. 4.95 (ISBN 0-934318-11-5). Falcon Pr MT.

Rausa, Rosario. Skyraider: The Douglas A-1 "Flying Dump Truck". (Illus.). 224p. 1982. 17.95 (ISBN 0-933852-31-2). Nautical & Aviation.

Rausch, D. O., et al, eds. Lead-Zinc Update. LC 77-83619. (Illus.). 1977. text ed. 25.00x (ISBN 0-89520-250-6). Soc Mining Eng.

Rausch, David A. Messianic Judaism: Its History, Theology, & Polity. (Texts & Studies in Religion: Vol. 14). 304p. 1983. 39.95x (ISBN 0-88946-802-8). E Mellen.

Rausch, Edwin, ed. Management in Institutions of Higher Learning. LC 79-650. 320p. 1980. 28.95x (ISBN 0-669-02856-8). Lexington Bks.

Rausch, Erwin. Balancing Needs of People & Organizations: The Linking Elements Concept. LC 78-62297. 344p. 1978. 22.50 (ISBN 0-87179-274-5). BNA.

Rausch, Tondra S., jt. auth. see Rund, Douglas A.

Rauschenberg, Roy A. Daniel Carl Solander, Naturalist on the "Endeavour". LC 68-54560. (Transactions Ser.: Vol. 58, Pt. 8). (Illus.). 1968. pap. 1.00 o.p. (ISBN 0-87169-588-X). Am Philos.

Rauscher, William V. Church in Frenzy. 182p. 1980. 9.95 o.p. (ISBN 0-312-13478-9). St Martin.

Raushenbush, Richard. The Terrorist War in Guatemala. LC 82-14167. 82p. (Orig.). pap. 5.00 (ISBN 0-910637-05-9). Coun Inter Ed.

Raushenbush, Stephen. March of Fascism. 1939. text ed. 39.50x (ISBN 0-686-83616-2). Elliots Bks.

Rausser. New Directions in Econometric Modelling & Forecasting in U.S. Agriculture. Date not set. 85.00 (ISBN 0-444-00736-9). Elsevier.

Rauter, Rosemarie, compiled by. Printed for Children. 448p. 1978. pap. 28.00x (ISBN 0-89664-111-2, Pub. by K G Saur). Gale.

Ravage, John A. The Television: The Director's Viewpoint. (Westview Special Studies in Communications). 1978. lib. bdg. 20.00x o.p. (ISBN 0-89158-337-8); softcover 11.00 (ISBN 0-86531-229-X). Westview.

Ravasio, P. & Hopkins, G. Local Computer Networks. 1982. 59.75 (ISBN 0-444-86386-9). Elsevier.

Raveche, H. J. Perspectives in Statistical Physics. (Studies in Statistical Mechanics: Vol. 9). 1981. 64.00 (ISBN 0-444-86026-6). Elsevier.

Raveendran, Pottayil B. The Merger. Date not set. 6.95 (ISBN 0-533-04984-9). Vantage.

Raveling, George. A Rebounder's Workshop: A Drill Manual for Rebounding. LC 82-83922. (Illus.). 112p. (Orig.). 1983. pap. 5.95 (ISBN 0-88011-063-5). Leisure Pr.

--War on the Boards: A Rebounding Manual. LC 82-83921. (Illus.). 112p. (Orig.). 1983. pap. 5.95 (ISBN 0-88011-062-7). Leisure Pr.

Raven, Bertram H. & Rubin, Jeffrey Z. Social Psychology. 2nd ed. 650p. 1983. 15.95x (ISBN 0-471-06225-1); tchr's. ed. avail. (ISBN 0-471-87305-5). Wiley.

Raven, Bertran & Rubin, Jeffrey. Social Psychology: People in Groups. LC 75-32693. 592p. 1976. 29.95 (ISBN 0-471-70970-0). Wiley.

Raven, Charles. Underworld Nights: Tales of London Underworld. 9.50 (ISBN 0-392-16400-0, SpS). Sportshelf.

Raven, F. A. Die Schwachen Verben des Althochdeutschen, Vol. 2. LC 64-23934. 224p. 1967. 24.60 (ISBN 0-8173-0801-6). U of Ala Pr.

Raven, Francis. Automatic Control Engineering. 3rd ed. (Illus.). 1978. text ed. 34.50 (ISBN 0-07-051228-0, C); solutions manual 12.00 (ISBN 0-07-051229-9). McGraw.

Raven, Francis H. Mathematics of Engineering Systems. 1983. Repr. of 1966 ed. cancelled (ISBN 0-89874-411-3). Krieger.

--Mathematics of Engineering Systems. 1966. text ed. 39.50x (ISBN 0-07-051230-2, C). McGraw.

Raven, J., jt. auth. see Palmer, Roy.

Raven, John E., jt. auth. see Kirk, Geoffrey S.

Raven, Jon. The Folklore of Staffordshire. (Folklore of the British Isles Ser). (Illus.). 223p. 1978. 13.50x o.p. (ISBN 0-8476-6021-4). Rowman.

Raven, P. H., jt. ed. see Polhill, R. M.

Raven, Peter H. Native Shrubs of Southern California. (California Natural History Guides Ser.: No. 15). (Illus.). 1966. 14.95x o.p. (ISBN 0-520-03097-4); pap. 3.95 (ISBN 0-520-01050-7). U of Cal Pr.

Raven, Peter H., et al. Biology of Plants. 3rd ed. 1981. text ed. 27.95 (ISBN 0-87901-132-7); lab manual 11.95x (ISBN 0-87901-142-4); prep guide avail. (ISBN 0-87901-143-2). Worth.

Ravenal, Earl C. Never Again: Learning from America's Foreign Policy Failures. LC 77-91392. 176p. 1978. 24.95 (ISBN 0-87722-107-3). Temple U Pr.

Ravenhill, Leonard. Porque No Llega el Avivamiento. 144p. Date not set. 2.25 (ISBN 0-88113-250-0). Edit Betania.

Ravenlock, Constance. Rendezvous at Grammercy. (Candlelight Regency Special Ser.: No. 676). (Orig.). pap. 1.50 o.s.i. (ISBN 0-440-17289-6). Dell.

Ravenscroft, Trevor. The Cup of Destiny: The Quest for the Grail. 194p. 1982. pap. 6.95 (ISBN 0-87728-546-2). Weiser.

--The Spear of Destiny: The Occult Power Behind the Spear Which Pierced the Side of Christ... & How Hitler Inverted the Force in a Bid to Conquer the World. 384p. 1982. pap. 7.95 (ISBN 0-87728-547-0). Weiser.

Ravetz, Jerome R. Scientific Knowledge & Its Social Problems. 1973. pap. 9.95 (ISBN 0-19-519721-6, 388, GB). Oxford U Pr.

Ravi Dass & Aparna, eds. The Marriage & Family Book: A Spiritual Guide. LC 77-87862. (Illus., Orig.). 1978. pap. 5.95 o.p. (ISBN 0-8052-0582-9). Schocken.

Ravila, Paavo. Finnish Literary Reader. LC 65-63019. (Uralic & Altaic Ser.: Vol. 44). (Orig.). 1965. pap. text ed. 3.50x o.p. (ISBN 0-87750-012-6). Res Ctr Lang Semiotic.

Ravindran, A. & Ragsdell, K. M. Engineering Optimization: Methods & Application. 550p. 1983. 44.95 (ISBN 0-471-05579-4, Pub. by Wiley Interscience). Wiley.

Ravitch, Diane, jt. ed. see Goodenow, Ronald K.

Ravitch, Mark M. Congenital Deformities of the Chest Wall & Their Operative Correction. LC 76-54041. (Illus.). 1977. text ed. 23.50 o.p. (ISBN 0-7216-7479-8). Saunders.

--Intussusception in Infants & Children. (Illus.). 156p. 1983. 28.50 (ISBN 0-87527-169-3). Green.

Ravitch, Mark M., ed. Current Problems In Surgery: Bound Volume 1981. 1982. 42.00 (ISBN 0-8151-7106-4). Year Bk Med.

Ravitz, Abe C. David Graham Phillips. (United States Authors Ser.). 14.95 (ISBN 0-8057-0583-X, Twayne). G K Hall.

Raviv, J., ed. Uses of Computers in Aiding the Disabled: Proceedings of the IFIP-IMIA Working Conference, Haifa, Israel, November 3-5, 1981. 446p. 1982. 55.50 (ISBN 0-444-86436-9, North Holland). Elsevier.

Raviv, J., et al, eds. Computer Aided Tomography & Ultrasonics in Medicine. 1979. 42.75 (ISBN 0-444-85299-9, North Holland). Elsevier.

Raw, Barbara C. The Art & Background of Old English Poetry. LC 78-390. 1978. 22.50x (ISBN 0-312-04984-6). St Martin.

Rawcliffe, D. H. Occult & Supernatural Phenomena. Orig. Title: Psychology of the Occult. 1952. pap. 5.00 o.p. (ISBN 0-486-20503-7). Dover.

Rawding, F. W. The Buddha. LC 78-56789. (Cambridge Topic Bks). (Illus.). (gr. 5-10). PLB 6.95g (ISBN 0-8225-1212-2). Lerner Pubns.

--Gandhi & the Struggle for India's Independence. LC 81-14241. (Cambridge Topic Bks.). (Illus.). 52p. (gr. 6 up). 1982. PLB 6.95g (ISBN 0-8225-1225-4). Lerner Pubns.

Rawer, K., ed. Winds & Turbulence in Stratosphere, Mesosphere & Ionosphere. 1968. 49.00 (ISBN 0-444-10261-2). Elsevier.

Rawick, George P. From Sundown to Sunup. LC 71-105986. 1972. lib. bdg. 25.00x (ISBN 0-8371-6299-8, RSM&); pap. 4.45 (ISBN 0-8371-6747-7). Greenwood.

Rawitz, Helen. Don't Cry in Your Beer...Drink It. 1978. 4.95 o.p. (ISBN 0-533-03587-2). Vantage.

Rawlings, Eleanor H., ed. The Cornucopia of Design & Illustration for Decoupage & Other Arts & Crafts. (Illus.). 160p. (Orig.). 1983. pap. 6.95 (ISBN 0-486-24486-5). Dover.

Rawlings, Margaret, tr. see Racine, Jean.

Rawlings, Marjorie K. Cross Creek. LC 42-36118. 1975. Repr. of 1942 ed. 12.95 (ISBN 0-910220-67-0). Berg.

--Golden Apples. new ed. LC 35-18688. 1977. 12.95 (ISBN 0-910220-84-0). Berg.

--The Sojourner. new ed. LC 52-14613. 1977. 12.95 (ISBN 0-910220-82-4). Berg.

--South Moon Under. new ed. LC 33-5485. 1977. 12.95 (ISBN 0-910220-83-2). Berg.

--When the Whippoorwill-Short Stories. LC 40-27409. 1973. 12.95 (ISBN 0-910220-53-0). Berg.

Rawlings, Maurice. Mas Alla del Umbral de La Muerte. 160p. Date not set. 2.50 (ISBN 0-88113-300-0). Edit Betania.

Rawlings, Sandra, jt. auth. see Specht, Sally.

Rawlins, Jack. Demon Prince: The Dissonant Worlds of Jack Vance. LC 81-21600. (The Milford Series: Popular Writers of Today: Vol. 40). 64p. 1983. lib. bdg. 9.95x (ISBN 0-89370-163-7); pap. text ed. 3.95x (ISBN 0-89370-263-3). Borgo Pr.

Rawlins, Jack P. Thackeray's Novels: A Fiction That Is True. 1975. 28.50x (ISBN 0-520-02562-8). U of Cal Pr.

Rawlins, M. D., jt. auth. see Smith, S. E.

Rawlins, M. D. & Gever, G., eds. European Prazosin Symposium: 1978. 1980. 39.75 (ISBN 0-444-90090-X). Elsevier.

Rawlins, N. Omri. Introduction to Agribusiness. (Illus.). 1980. text ed. 16.95 (ISBN 0-13-477703-4). P-H.

Rawlinson, D. H. Practice of Criticism. 1968. 34.50 (ISBN 0-521-06045-1); pap. 10.50x (ISBN 0-521-09540-9). Cambridge U Pr.

Rawlinson, M. K., jt. auth. see Sanderson, M.

Rawls, Eugene. A Handbook of Yoga for Modern Living. (Orig.). pap. 1.50 o.s.i. (ISBN 0-515-00958-X). Jove Pubns.

Rawls, James J., jt. auth. see Bean, Walton.

Rawls, Walter, Jr. & Davis, Albert R. Magnetism & Its Effect on the Living System. 9.50x (ISBN 0-682-48087-8). Cancer Control Soc.

Rawls, Wendall, Jr. Cold Storage. 1980. 10.95 o.p. (ISBN 0-671-24287-3, 24287). S&S.

Rawls, Wilson. Summer of the Monkeys. LC 75-32295. 1977. 10.95a (ISBN 0-385-11450-8); PLB (ISBN 0-385-13004-X). Doubleday.

--Where the Red Fern Grows. LC 61-9201. 11.95a (ISBN 0-385-02059-7); PLB (ISBN 0-385-05619-2). Doubleday.

Rawlsinson, George. History of Ancient Egypt, 2 Vols. 312p. 1982. Repr. of 1876 ed. lib. bdg. 150.00 set (ISBN 0-89760-754-6). Telegraph Bks.

Rawn, J. David. Biochemistry. 976p. 1983. text ed. 37.95 scp (ISBN 0-06-045335-4, HarpC); scp study guide 11.50 (ISBN 0-06-045334-6). Har-Row.

Rawnsley, A. A Manual of Industrial Marketing Research. 196p. 1978. 53.95 (ISBN 0-471-99537-1, Pub. by Wiley-Interscience). Wiley.

Rawnsley, C. F. & Wright, Robert. Night Fighter. (War Library). 320p. 1983. pap. 2.95 (ISBN 0-345-31025-X). Ballantine.

Rawnsley, Howard M., jt. auth. see Mitruka, Brij M.

Rawson & Carlwright. Witches. (Story Book). (gr. k-4). 1979. 5.95 (ISBN 0-86020-341-7, Usborne-Hayes); PLB 8.95 (ISBN 0-88110-057-9); pap. 2.95 (ISBN 0-86020-340-9). EDC.

Rawson & Lloyd. The Miracles of Jesus. (Children's Picture Bible Ser.). (gr. 4-6). 1982. 6.95 (ISBN 0-86020-518-5, Usborne-Hayes); PLB 9.95 (ISBN 0-88110-099-4); pap. 3.95 (ISBN 0-86020-523-1). EDC.

Rawson & Spector. Riding & Pony Care. (Animal World Ser.). (gr. 4-6). 1978. 6.95 (ISBN 0-86020-153-8, Usborne-Hayes); PLB 9.95 (ISBN 0-88110-084-6); pap. 3.95 (ISBN 0-686-36302-7). EDC.

Rawson, jt. auth. see Cartwright.

Rawson, C. J. Henry Fielding & the Augustan Ideal Under Stress: Nature's Dance of Death & Other Studies. 280p. 1972. 20.00x (ISBN 0-7100-7454-9). Routledge & Kegan.

Rawson, Claude, ed. The Character of Swift's Satire: A Revised Focus. LC 81-72062. 265p. 1983. 27.50 (ISBN 0-87413-209-6). U Delaware Pr.

Rawson, Clayton. Death From a Top Hat. 1979. lib. bdg. 9.95 (ISBN 0-8398-2542-0, Gregg). G K Hall.

--The Footprints on the Ceiling. 1979. lib. bdg. 9.95 (ISBN 0-8398-2543-9, Gregg). G K Hall.

--The Great Merlini, 5 bks. 45.00 (ISBN 0-686-74236-2, Gregg). G K Hall.

--The Great Merlini: The Complete Stories of the Magician Detective. 1979. lib. bdg. 9.95 (ISBN 0-8398-2546-3, Gregg). G K Hall.

--The Headless Lady. 1979. lib. bdg. 9.95 (ISBN 0-8398-2544-7, Gregg). G K Hall.

--No Coffin for the Corpse. 1979. lib. bdg. 9.95 (ISBN 0-8398-2545-5, Gregg). G K Hall.

Rawson, H. Properties & Applications of Glass. (Glass Science & Technology Ser.: Vol. 3). 1980. 55.50 (ISBN 0-444-41922-5). Elsevier.

Rawson, Hugh. A Dictionary of Euphemisms & Other Double Talk. 320p. 1981. 15.95 (ISBN 0-517-54518-7). Crown.

Rawson, P. F., jt. auth. see Casey, R.

Rawson, Peter. Tantra: The Indian Cult of Ecstasy. (Illus.). 128p. 1974. 2.98 o.p. (ISBN 0-517-51710-8). Crown.

Rawson, Philip & Legeza, Laslo. Tao: The Eastern Philosophy of Time & Change. (Illus.). 128p. 1974. 2.98 o.p. (ISBN 0-517-51709-4). Crown.

Rawston, Yvonne. Oh, You Beautiful Doll! 1982. 8.95 (ISBN 0-399-50667-5, Perige). Putnam Pub Group.

Rawstron, E. M., jt. auth. see Wise, M. J.

Ray & Lewis. Exploring Professional Cooking. rev. ed. (gr. 9-12). 1980. text ed. 18.60 (ISBN 0-87002-315-2); student guide 8.16 (ISBN 0-87002-163-X); tchr's guide 11.00 (ISBN 0-87002-302-0); visual masters 15.96 (ISBN 0-87002-172-9). Bennett IL.

Ray, ed. Immunobiology & Transplantation, Cancer & Pregnancy. 500p. 1983. text ed. price not set (ISBN 0-08-025994-4). Pergamon.

Ray, Ann, ed. see Herzog, Stephanie.

Ray, B. Two-Six Compounds. LC 72-93126. 1969. 40.00 (ISBN 0-08-006624-0). Pergamon.

Ray, Barbara W. The Reiki Factor: A Guide to Physical & Spiritual Healing. 144p. 1983. 8.00 (ISBN 0-682-49935-8). Exposition.

Ray, Benjamin C. African Religions: Symbol, Ritual & Community. 1976. pap. 12.95 (ISBN 0-13-018622-8). P-H.

Ray, C. A. La Vida Responsable: Orientacion Biblica Sobre Nuestro Estilo De Vivir. Lopez, Albert C., tr. Orig. Title: Living the Responsible Life. 160p. 1982. Repr. of 1980 ed. 3.50 (ISBN 0-311-46079-8). Casa Bautista.

Ray, C. T., ed. see Walker, W. C., et al.

Ray, Charles M. & Elson, Charles L. Supervision. 496p. 1983. text ed. 26.95 (ISBN 0-03-054556-0). Dryden Pr.

Ray, Cyril. The Complete Book of Spirits & Liqueurs. 1978. 12.95 o.p. (ISBN 0-02-601150-6). Macmillan.

--Ray on Wine. 198p. 1979. 12.00x o.p. (ISBN 0-460-04387-0, Pub. by J. M. Dent England). Biblio Dist.

Ray, David. The Touched Life: Poems, Selected & New. LC 82-3371. (Poets Now: No. 4). 213p. 1982. 13.50 (ISBN 0-8108-1535-4). Scarecrow.

Ray, David, jt. auth. see Frank, Ted.

Ray, David, ed. From A to Z: 200 Contemporary American Poets, New Letters. LC 82-75174. xii, 259p. 1981. 18.95x (ISBN 0-8040-0369-6); pap. 9.95 (ISBN 0-8040-0370-X). Swallow.

Ray, David & Singh, Amritjit, eds. India. (New Letters Ser.). 272p. (Orig.). 1982. pap. 5.00 (ISBN 0-938652-05-2). Univ Missouri.

--India: A New Letters Book. 277p. 1983. pap. 10.95 (ISBN 0-8214-0736-8, 82-85058). Ohio U Pr.

Ray, G. F. & Uhlmann, L. The Innovation Process in the Energy Industry. LC 78-17064. (National Institute of Economic & Social Research, Occasional Papers Ser.: No. 30). 1979. 24.95 (ISBN 0-521-22371-7). Cambridge U Pr.

Ray, G. F., jt. auth. see Nabseth, L.

Ray, G. H. & Hutchinson, P. J. The Financing & Financial Control of Small Enterprise Development. 280p. 1983. 25.00 (ISBN 0-89397-154-5). Nichols Pub.

Ray, George. Incorporating the Professional Practice. 2nd ed. (Illus.). 1978. 32.95 o.p. (ISBN 0-13-455923-1, Busn). P-H.

Ray, Gordon N. The Art of the French Illustrated Book, 2 vols. LC 82-71590. (Illus.). 640p. 1982. 185.00x (ISBN 0-8014-1535-7). Cornell U Pr.

Ray, Graham H. & Smith, Joe. Hardy Developments Ltd. 412p. 1982. text ed. 42.00x (ISBN 0-566-02251-6). Gower Pub Ltd.

Ray, Grayce, jt. ed. see Vinz, Mark.

Ray, Hemen. China's Vietnam War. 150p. 1982. text ed. 12.00x (ISBN 0-391-02816-2, Pub. by Radiant Pub India). Humanities.

Ray, Isaac. Contributions to Mental Pathology (1873). LC 73-9908. (Hist. of Psych. Ser.). 450p. 1973. Repr. of 1873 ed. lib. bdg. 60.00x (ISBN 0-8201-1120-1). Schol Facsimiles.

--A Treatise on the Medical Jurisprudence of Insanity. (Historical Foundations of Forensic Psychiatry & Psychology Ser.). xvi, 480p. 1983. Repr. of 1838 ed. lib. bdg. 45.00 (ISBN 0-306-76181-5). Da Capo.

Ray, J. Methodus Plantarum Nova. (Illus.). 1962. Repr. of 1682 ed. 14.40 (ISBN 3-7682-0119-8). Lubrecht & Cramer.

Ray, J. Edgar. Art of Bricklaying. Johnson, Harold V., ed. (Illus.). (gr. 9-12). 1971. pap. text ed. 14.24 (ISBN 0-87002-271-7). Bennett IL.

Ray, J. P., compiled by. The Diary of a Dead Man: 1862-1864. LC 76-18627. (Illus.). 430p. 1979. pap. 3.00 (ISBN 0-89062-099-7). Eastern Acorn.

Ray, Jack H., jt. auth. see Schmits, Larry J.

Ray, James L. Global Politics. LC 78-69552. (Illus.). 1979. text ed. 19.50 (ISBN 0-395-26542-8); instr's. manual 1.00 (ISBN 0-395-26540-1). HM.

--Global Politics. 2nd ed. LC 82-81582. 416p. 1982. pap. text ed. 19.95 (ISBN 0-395-32781-4); write for info. instr's manual (ISBN 0-395-32782-2). Hm.

Ray, Janet. Towards Women's Rights. (Focus on Canadian History Ser.). 96p. (gr. 6-10). 1982. PLB 8.40 (ISBN 0-686-79027-8). Watts.

Ray, Jo A. Careers in Computers. LC 72-7647. (Early Career Bks.). (Illus.). 36p. (gr. 2-5). 1973. PLB 5.95g (ISBN 0-8225-0307-7). Lerner Pubns.

--Careers in Football. LC 72-7649. (Early Career Bks.). (Illus.). 36p. (gr. 2-5). 1973. PLB 5.95g (ISBN 0-8225-0314-X). Lerner Pubns.

--Careers in Hockey. LC 72-7650. (Early Career Bks.). (Illus.). 36p. (gr. 2-5). 1973. PLB 5.95g (ISBN 0-8225-0315-8). Lerner Pubns.

--Careers with a Police Department. LC 72-5415. (Early Career Bks.). (Illus.). 36p. (gr. 2-5). 1973. PLB 5.95g (ISBN 0-8225-0305-0). Lerner Pubns.

Ray, JoAnne. American Assassins. LC 72-8293. (Real World Bks. - Crisis & Conflict). (Illus.). 96p. (gr. 6-12). 1974. PLB 5.95g (ISBN 0-8225-0637-8). Lerner Pubns.

Ray, John. Cars. (Junior Reference Ser.). (Illus.). 96p. (gr. 7 up). 8.95 o.p. (ISBN 0-7136-1322-X). Dufour.

--Hitler & Mussolini. 1970. pap. text ed. 3.95x o.p. (ISBN 0-435-31755-5). Heinemann Ed.

--Lloyd George & Churchill. (Men Who Made History Ser.). 1970. pap. text ed. 3.95x o.p. (ISBN 0-435-31756-3). Heinemann Ed.

--Roosevelt & Kennedy. 1970. pap. text ed. 3.95x o.p. (ISBN 0-435-31757-1). Heinemann Ed.

Ray, John B., jt. auth. see Fullerton, Ralph O.

Ray, Keith, ed. see Architectural Record Magazine.

Ray, Marie B. The Importance of Feeling Inferior. LC 80-19319. 266p. 1980. Repr. of 1971 ed. lib. bdg. 12.95x (ISBN 0-89370-606-X). Borgo Pr.

--The Importance of Feeling Inferior. 1971. pap. 4.95 o.p. (ISBN 0-87877-006-2, G-6). Newcastle Pub.

Ray, Mary F. & Dondi, Beda. Professional Cooking & Baking. (Illus.). 450p. 1981. text ed. 15.32 (ISBN 0-87002-328-4); tchr's guide 6.60 (ISBN 0-87002-329-2); student guide 5.12 (ISBN 0-87002-330-6). Bennett IL.

Ray, Oakley. Drugs, Society & Human Behavior. 3rd ed. LC 82-8203. (Illus.). 512p. 1983. pap. text ed. 17.95 (ISBN 0-8016-4092-X). Mosby.

Ray, Robert D. & Barmada, Riad. Orthopedic Surgery Case Studies. 1976. spiral bdg. 17.50 (ISBN 0-87488-030-0). Med Exam.

Ray, Sibnarayan, ed. Gandhi, India & the World: An International Symposium. LC 78-135345. 336p. 1970. 29.95 (ISBN 0-87722-004-2). Temple U Pr.

--Vak: An Anthology of Australian, European & Indian Verse. 14.00 (ISBN 0-89253-623-3); pap. 8.00 (ISBN 0-86578-108-7). Ind-US Inc.

Ray, Sidney F. The Lens & All Its Jobs. (Media Manuals Ser.). (Illus.). 1977. pap. 10.95 o.s.i. (ISBN 0-240-50951-X). Focal Pr.

Ray, Sondra. Celebration of Breath. 192p. 1983. pap. 6.95 (ISBN 0-89087-355-0). Celestial Arts.

Ray, Syamal K. Indian Bureaucracy at the Crossroads. 407p. 1979. 34.95 (ISBN 0-686-42714-9, Pub. by Sterling India). Asia Bk Corp.

Ray, Talton F. The Politics of the Barrios of Venezuela. rev. ed. (Illus.). 1969. 33.00x (ISBN 0-520-01461-8). U of Cal Pr.

Ray, Ted. My Turn Next. (Illus.). 10.50 (ISBN 0-392-04036-0, SpS). Sportshelf.

Ray, Verne F., et al. Apache Indians X. Horr, David A., ed. (American Indian Ethnohistory Ser.). 1978. lib. bdg. 42.00 o.s.i. (ISBN 0-8240-0718-2). Garland Pub.

Ray, W. Harmon. Advanced Process Control. (Chemical Engineering Ser.). (Illus.). 1980. text ed. 33.50 (ISBN 0-07-051250-7, C); solutions manual 18.00 (ISBN 0-07-051251-5). McGraw.

Ray, William, ed. Conversations: Reynolds Price & William Ray. (Mississippi Collection Bulletin, No. 9). (Illus.). 82p. 1976. pap. 5.95x o.p. (ISBN 0-87870-086-2). Memphis St Univ.

Ray, Willis. Introduction to Manufacturing Careers. (gr. 7-10). 1975. pap. text ed. 7.33 activity ed. (ISBN 0-87345-177-5). McKnight.

Ray, Willis H. & Szekely, Julian. Process Optimization with Applications in Metallurgy & Chemical Engineering. LC 73-936. 371p. 1973. 46.95 (ISBN 0-471-71070-9, Pub. by Wiley-Interscience). Wiley.

Raya, Joseph. Acathist Hymn to the Name of Jesus. De Vinck, Jose M., ed. 40p. 1983. 5.00x (ISBN 0-911726-45-4); pap. 3.50x (ISBN 0-911726-46-2). Alleluia Pr.

Raya, Joseph & DeVinck, Jose. Apostolos: Byzantine Epistles Lectionary. 550p. 1981. 87.50x (ISBN 0-911726-37-3); folded sheets 67.50x (ISBN 0-911726-38-1). Alleluia Pr.

Raya, Joseph & De Vinck, Jose. Byzantine Daily Worship. (Illus.). 1036p. 1969. pap. 19.75 (ISBN 0-911726-07-1) (ISBN 0-911726-09-8) (ISBN 0-911726-00-4). Alleluia Pr.

Rayband, ed. Pediatric Oncology. (International Congress Ser.: Vol. 570). 1982. 81.00 (ISBN 0-444-90247-3). Elsevier.

Raybould, E. C., jt. auth. see Leach, D. J.

Rayburn, Carl B. Tuskeemah of the Desert: And Other Poems. 1978. 4.95 o.p. (ISBN 0-533-03625-9). Vantage.

Raychard, Al. Trout & Salmon Fishing in Northern New England. LC 82-5930. (Illus.). 208p. (Orig.). 1982. pap. 7.95 (ISBN 0-89621-068-5). Thorndike Pr.

Raychaudhuri, G. S., jt. auth. see Krishna, Raj.

Raychaudhuri, S. P., jt. ed. see Singh, B. P.

Raycraft, Carol, jt. auth. see Raycraft, Don.

Raycraft, Don & Raycraft, Carol. Early American Kitchen Antiques, Bk. 2. pap. 6.95 (ISBN 0-87069-180-5); price guide 1.50 (ISBN 0-87069-237-2). Wallace-Homestead.

Raye, David E., jt. auth. see Gaviglio, Glen.

Rayechaudhuri, S. P. & Nariani, T. K. Virus & Mycoplasm Diseases of Plants in India. 102p. 1977. 50.00x (ISBN 0-686-84449-1, Pub by Oxford & I B H India). State Mutual Bk.

Rayer. Beginners Guide to Amateur Radio. 1982. text ed. write for info (ISBN 0-408-01132-7). Butterworth.

--Beginner's Guide to Amateur Radio. (Illus.). 1982. pap. 9.95 (ISBN 0-408-01126-2). Focal Pr.

Rayfield, Donald. The Dream of Lhasa: The Life of Nikolay Przhevalsky (1839-88), Explorer of Central Asia. LC 76-20326. (Illus.). xii, 221p. 1976. 15.00x (ISBN 0-8214-0369-9, 82-82626). Ohio U Pr.

Rayfield, Joan, tr. see Maquet, Jacques.

Rayfield, Susan, jt. auth. see Guilfoyle, Ann.

Raygor. Reading for Significant Facts. (Basic Skills System). 1982. 11.95 (ISBN 0-07-051380-5). McGraw.

Raygor, A. & Scnmelzer, R. Word Attack & Spelling: An Audio Tutorial. 1981. 350.00 (ISBN 0-13-963215-8); student wkbk. 9.95 (ISBN 0-13-963223-9). P-H.

Raygor, Alton, ed. see Lewick-Wallace, Mary.

Raygor, Alton, ed. see Wallace, Mary L.

Raygor, Alton L. & Schick, George B. Reading at Efficient Rates. 2nd ed. (McGraw-Hill Basic Skills). (Illus.). 192p. 1980. pap. text ed. 13.50 (ISBN 0-07-044418-8, C). McGraw.

Raygor, Alton L. & Wark, David M. Systems for Study. 2nd ed. (McGraw-Hill Basic Skills Ser.). (Illus.). 1979. pap. text ed. 13.50 (ISBN 0-07-044419-6). McGraw.

Raygor, Alton L., ed. see Learning Technology Incorporated.

Raygor, Alton L., ed. see Shew-Pincar.

Rayman, A. A. High Speed Marine Steam Engine. rev. ed. (Illus.). 60p. 1978. pap. 5.00x (ISBN 0-85242-540-6). Intl Pubns Serv.

Rayman, Eric, ed. One Hundred Years of Harvard Lampoon Parodies: The Scourge of Better-Known Periodicals Since 1912. 1976. 6.95 o.p. (ISBN 0-517-52592-5, Harmony). Crown.

Raymo, Anne & Vose, Holly. Sew-up Art: How to Do It, 26 Applique Projects. LC 75-45768. (Illus.). 104p. (Orig.). 1976. pap. 4.95 o.p. (ISBN 0-8256-3065-7, Quick Fox). Putnam Pub Group.

Raymo, Chet. Geologic & Topographic Profile of the United States along Interstate 80. (Illus.). 21p. (Orig.). (gr. 6-12). 1982. pap. text ed. 6.95 (ISBN 0-8331-1714-9, 473). Hubbard Sci.

Raymond, Alex. Flash Gordon in the Planet Mongo. (Illus.). 160p. (YA) 1974. 14.95 o.p. (ISBN 0-517-51581-4). Crown.

--Flash Gordon in the Underwater World of Mongo. (Illus.). 160p. 1974. 14.95 o.p. (ISBN 0-517-51582-2). Crown.

--Flash Gordon Versus Frozen Horrors, Vol. 4. Kaler, David, ed. 1978. pap. 9.95 o.p. (ISBN 0-517-53360-X). Crown.

Raymond, Alex, jt. auth. see Hammett, Dashiell.

Raymond, Corey E., et al. Problems in Marketing. 6th ed. (Marketing Ser.). (Illus.). 832p. 1981. 27.95 (ISBN 0-07-013141-4); instructor's manual 20.00 (ISBN 0-07-013142-2). McGraw.

Raymond, Dick. Garden Way's Joy of Gardening. Thabault, George, ed. (Illus.). 384p. 1983. 25.00 (ISBN 0-88266-320-8); pap. 17.95 (ISBN 0-88266-319-4). Garden Way Pub.

Raymond, Dora N. Captain Lee Hall of Texas. (Illus.). 384p. 1982. 19.95 (ISBN 0-8061-0086-9). U of Okla Pr.

Raymond, E. T. Disraeli: Alien Patriot. 346p. 1982. Repr. of 1925 ed. lib. bdg. 50.00 (ISBN 0-89987-723-0). Darby Bks.

Raymond, Ernest. We, the Accused: T. V. edition. 1983. pap. 3.95 (ISBN 0-14-006220-3). Penguin.

Raymond, Gregory A., jt. auth. see Fry, Earl H.

Raymond, Irving W., jt. ed. see Lopez, Robert S.

Raymond, Jacque, jt. auth. see Banerji, Dilip.

Raymond, James, jt. auth. see Goldfarb, Ronald.

Raymond, James C., ed. Literacy as a Human Problem. LC 81-19757. 1982. 16.50 (ISBN 0-8173-0108-9); pap. 6.95 (ISBN 0-8173-0110-0). U of Ala Pr.

Raymond, Janice. Why Does the Willow Weep, I Wonder. 1982. 4.95 (ISBN 0-686-35736-1). D R Benbow.

Raymond, Joseph. The Paper Miners' Manual: Turning Paper to Gold. LC 82-81179. (Illus.). 106p. 1982. 19.95 (ISBN 0-686-37029-5); pap. 14.95 (ISBN 0-686-37030-9). Pegasus Van Nuys.

Raymond, Louise. Adoption & After. rev. ed. Dywasuk, Colette T., rev. by. LC 73-14285. 266p. 1974. 14.37i (ISBN 0-06-013531-X, HarpT). Har-Row.

Raymond, M. The Man Who Got Even with God. 174p. 1973. pap. 1.25 o.p. (ISBN 0-8189-1106-9, Pub. by Alba Bks). Alba.

--You: The Surprising Answer to the Question Who Are You? LC 57-13414. 312p. 1972. pap. 1.45 o.p. (ISBN 0-8189-1108-5, Pub. by Alba Bks). Alba.

Raymond, Stephen, jt. auth. see Gruberg, Edward.

Raymond, W. Merchants Tokens of the United States: An Anthology. Durst, S. J., ed. (Illus.). 1982. softcover 12.00 o.p. (ISBN 0-915262-81-9). S J Durst.

--Private Gold Coins Struck in the U. S. 1830-1861. (Illus.). 1983. Repr. of 1931 ed. softcover 6.00 (ISBN 0-915262-93-2). S J Durst.

Raymond, Walter J., ed. see Agyeman-Badu, Yaw & Osei-Hwedie, Kwaku.

Raymond, Wayne & Mulliner, K., eds. Southeast Asia, an Emerging Center of World Influence? Economic & Resource Considerations. LC 76-620090. (Papers in International Studies: Southeast Asia: No. 42). (Illus.). 1977. pap. 9.00 (ISBN 0-89680-028-8, Ohio U Ctr Intl). Ohio U Pr.

Raymont, J. E. Plankton & Productivity in the Oceans. 1963. pap. 36.00 o.p. (ISBN 0-08-010185-2); pap. 19.50 o.p. (ISBN 0-08-019009-X). Pergamon.

--Plankton & Productivity in the Oceans: Zooplankton, Vol. 2. 2nd ed. (Illus.). 700p. 1983. 75.00 (ISBN 0-08-024404-1); pap. 19.00 (ISBN 0-08-024403-3). Pergamon.

Raymont, Michael E., ed. Sulfur Recovery & Utilization. (ACS Symposium Ser.: No.183). 1982. write for info. (ISBN 0-8412-0713-5). Am Chemical.

Raynal, Francois, jt. auth. see Guyot, Jacqueline.

Raynaud, C., ed. Nuclear Medicine & Biology Advances: Proceedings of the Third World Congress on Nuclear Medicine & Biology, August 29 - September 2, 1982, Paris, France, 7 Vols. 3685p. 1982. Set. 300.00 (ISBN 0-08-029814-1). Pergamon.

Rayner, Claire. Bedford Row. (Orig.). 1979. pap. 2.50 o.p. (ISBN 0-451-08819-0, E8819, Sig). NAL.

--Bedford Row. LC 77-9360. 1977. 8.95 (ISBN 0-399-11997-3). Putnam Pub Group.

--Charing Cross. LC 79-13844. 1979. 10.95 (ISBN 0-399-12368-7). Putnam Pub Group.

--Covent Garden. 1980. pap. 2.25 o.p. (ISBN 0-451-09301-1, E9301, Sig). NAL.

--Covent Garden. LC 78-18439. 1978. 10.00 (ISBN 0-399-12205-2). Putnam Pub Group.

--The Enduring Years. 592p. 1982. 15.95 (ISBN 0-440-02460-9). Delacorte.

--Everything Your Doctor Would Tell You If He Had the Time. (Illus.). 1980. 14.95 (ISBN 0-399-12482-9). Putnam Pub Group.

--Everything Your Doctor Would Tell You If He Had the Time. 1983. pap. 7.95 (ISBN 0-399-50548-2, Perige). Putnam Pub Group.

--Soho Square. LC 76-42180. 1976. 8.95 o.p. (ISBN 0-399-11879-9). Putnam Pub Group.

--The Strand. (Performers Ser.). 300p. 1981. 11.95 (ISBN 0-399-12537-X). Putnam Pub Group.

--Trafalgar Square. Orig. Title: The Strand. 320p. 1982. pap. 3.25 o.s.i. (ISBN 0-8439-1152-2, Leisure Bks). Nordon Pubns.

Rayner, Dorothy H. Stratigraphy of the British Isles. 2nd ed. LC 79-8523. (Illus.). 400p. 1981. 69.50 (ISBN 0-521-23452-2). Cambridge U Pr.

Rayner, J. N. An Introduction to Spectral Analysis. (Monographs in Spatial & Environmental Systems Analysis). 174p. 1971. 15.50x (ISBN 0-85086-026-1, Pub. by Pion England). Methuen Inc.

Rayner, Keith, ed. Eye Movements in Reading: Perceptual & Language Processes. LC 82-11565. (Perspectives in Neurolinguistics, Neuropsychology & Psycholinguistics). Date not set. 52.00 (ISBN 0-12-583680-5). Acad Pr.

Rayner, Mary. The Witchfinder. LC 76-22600. (Illus.). (gr. 5-9). 1976. 8.95 (ISBN 0-688-22082-7); PLB 8.59 (ISBN 0-688-32082-1). Morrow.

Rayner, P. A., jt. auth. see Cope, G. M.

Rayner-Canham, Geoffrey & Last, Arthur. Foundations of Chemistry. (Illus.). 525p. 1983. text ed. 21.95 (ISBN 0-201-10284-6); Instrs' Manual avail. (ISBN 0-201-10414-8); Study Guide avail. (ISBN 0-201-10415-6); Laboratory Manual avail. (ISBN 0-201-10416-4). A-W.

Raynes, Anthony E., jt. auth. see Rosenberg, Chaim M.

Raynes, Jean. The Blood Carnelian. LC 79-7053. (Romantic Suspense Ser.). 1979. 10.95 o.p. (ISBN 0-385-15019-9). Doubleday.

Raynor, Dorka. This Is My Father & Me. LC 73-7320. (Concept Bks.). (Illus.). 40p. (ps up). 1973. 8.25g o.p. (ISBN 0-8075-7883-5). A Whitman.

Raynor, Henry. Music & Society Since Eighteen Fifteen. LC 76-1377. 1976. 15.00x o.p. (ISBN 0-8052-3626-0). Schocken.

Raynor, John. Anatomy & Physiology. 1977. text ed. 24.50 scp (ISBN 0-06-045339-7, HarpC); instructor's manual avail. (ISBN 0-06-365350-8); scp study guide 10.50 (ISBN 0-06-045338-9). Har-Row.

Raynor, Sherry & Drouillard, Richard. Get a Wiggle on. Alonso, Lou, ed. (Illus.). 80p. 1978. pap. 3.75 (ISBN 0-88314-077-2, 245-26174). AAHPERD.

--Move It!!! Alonso, Lou, ed. 96p. 1978. pap. 3.75 (ISBN 0-88314-132-9, 245-26176). AAHPERD.

Rayshich, Hale & McGuire. Blueprint Reading for Machine Technology. 1984. pap. text ed. 19.95 (ISBN 0-534-01383-X). Breton Pubs.

Rayson, Ann, ed. see Dunford, Elizabeth P.

Rayward-Smith. Combinatorial Optimization Two. (Mathematical Programming Studies: Vol. 13). 1980. 25.75 (ISBN 0-444-86040-1). Elsevier.

Raz, Joseph. The Authority of Law: Essays on Law & Morality. 1979. text ed. 24.95x (ISBN 0-19-825345-1). Oxford U Pr.

--The Concept of a Legal System: An Introduction to the Theory of a Legal System. 2nd ed. 1980. 24.95x o.p. (ISBN 0-19-825362-1); pap. 13.95 (ISBN 0-19-825363-X). Oxford U Pr.

Raz, Joseph, ed. Practical Reasoning. LC 78-40255. (Oxford Readings in Philosophy Ser.). 1979. pap. 7.95x (ISBN 0-19-875041-2). Oxford U Pr.

Raz, S. Tigre Grammar & Texts. LC 81-71735. (Afroasiatic Dialects Ser.: Vol. 4). 250p. 1983. pap. write for info (ISBN 0-89003-097-9). Undena Pubns.

Raza, Moonis, et al. The Valley of Kashmir: The Land, Vol. 1. LC 77-93391. 1978. 23.95 o.p. (ISBN 0-89089-058-7). Carolina Acad Pr.

Razi, Najm A. The Path of God's Bondsmen from Origin to Return. Algar, Hamid, tr. LC 81-21780. 1983. 60.00x (ISBN 0-88206-052-X). Caravan Bks.

Razi, Zvi. Life, Marriage & Death in a Medieval Parish. LC 79-8491. (Past & Present Publications). (Illus.). 1980. 29.95 (ISBN 0-521-23252-X). Cambridge U Pr.

Razin, Shmuel, ed. Methods in Mycoplasmology: Diagnostic Mycoplasmology, Vol. 2. Date not set. price not set (ISBN 0-12-583802-6). Acad Pr.

Raznjevic, Kuzman. Handbook of Thermodynamic Tables & Charts. 400p. 1976. 59.95 (ISBN 0-07-051270-1, P&RB). McGraw.

Razzi, James. The Christmas Book: A Punch-Out Book. (Illus.). 32p. (gr. 2-6). 1980. pap. 3.95 o.p. (ISBN 0-394-84406-8). Random.

--Star Wars: Artoo Detoo's Activity Book. (Illus.). 1979. pap. 1.50 (ISBN 0-394-84036-4, BYR). Random.

Razzoli, Guido, jt. auth. see Buonassisi, Vincenzo.

RCAF Exercise Plans Publishers. Wushu: The Official Chinese Family Exercise Book. (Illus.). 1981. 19.95 o.s.i. (ISBN 0-671-43887-5); pap. 9.95 o.s.i. (ISBN 0-671-42079-8). S&S.

Re, Edward D. Breif Writing & Oral Argument. 5th Rev. ed. 484p. 1983. lib. bdg. 17.50 (ISBN 0-379-01050-X). Oceana.

--Brief Writing & Oral Argument. 4th rev ed. LC 73-11059. 400p. 1977. 15.00 o.p. (ISBN 0-686-57657-8). Oceana.

--Freedom's Prophet. LC 81-85341. 401p. 1982. lib. bdg. 35.00 (ISBN 0-379-20061-9). Oceana.

Re, Joseph. Earn & Learn: Cooperative Education Opportunities Offered by the Federal Government,1982-1984. 4th ed. 1982. pap. 1.50 (ISBN 0-917760-34-4). Octameron Assocs.

Rea, Amadeo M. Once a River: Bird Life & Habitat Changes on the Middle Gila. 270p. 1983. 24.50 (ISBN 0-8165-0799-6). U of Ariz Pr.

Rea, C. British Basidomysetaceae: A Handbook to the Larger British Fungi. 1968. pap. 40.00 (ISBN 3-7682-0561-4). Lubrecht & Cramer.

Rea, Desmond. Political Co-operation in Divided Societies: A Series of Papers Relevant to the Conflict in Northern Ireland. 1982. 79.00x (ISBN 0-7171-1162-8, Pub. by Gill & Macmillan Ireland). State Mutual Bk.

Rea, Desmond, ed. Northern Ireland, the Republic of Ireland & Great Britain: Problems of Political Co-Operation. 300p. 1982. 50.00x (ISBN 0-7171-1162-8, Pub. by Macmillan England). State Mutual Bk.

Rea, Jesse R., jt. auth. see Kostiner, Edward.

Rea, John, et al. Building a Hospital: A Primer for Administrators. LC 77-18854. 88p. (Orig.). 1978. pap. 18.75 (ISBN 0-87258-210-8, AHA-043150). Am Hospital.

Rea, Kenneth. Canton in Revolution: The Collected Papers of Earl Swisher, 1925-1928. 1977. lib. bdg. 24.75x o.p. (ISBN 0-89158-304-1). Westview.

Rea, Kenneth W. & Brewer, John C., eds. The Forgotten Ambassador: The Reports of John Leighton Stuart, 1946-1949. (Replica Edition Ser.). 350p. 1981. lib. bdg. 30.00 (ISBN 0-86531-157-9). Westview.

Rea, R. Sam. The Tax & Estate Planner's Complete Guide for Servicing the Professional Client. 237p. 1982. 59.50 (ISBN 0-87624-566-1). Inst Busn Plan.

Rea, Richard, jt. auth. see Gray, John W.

Rea, Robert R., jt. ed. see Servies, James.

Read. Dictionary of Gemmology. 1982. text ed. 34.95 (ISBN 0-408-00571-8). Butterworth.

--Gemmological Instruments. 2nd ed. 1983. text ed. price not set (ISBN 0-408-01190-4). Butterworth.

Read, et al. Continuous Progress in Spelling. (gr. 4-12). pap. 3.18 activity bk. (ISBN 0-8372-4382-3); tchr's manual 5.28 (ISBN 0-8372-4381-5); suppl. materials avail. Bowmar-Noble.

Read, A. E. Modern Trends in Gastroenterology, Vol. 5. 1975. 44.95 o.p. (ISBN 0-407-00034-8). Butterworth.

Read, Ann K., jt. auth. see Garrison, Linda.

Read, Anthony & Fisher, David. Operation Lucy: The Most Secret Spy Ring of the Second World War. (Illus.). 1981. 14.95 (ISBN 0-698-11079-X, Coward). Putnam Pub Group.

Read, B., jt. auth. see Brinnin, J. M.

Read, B. E. & Dean, G. D. Determination of Dynamic Properties of Polymers & Composites. LC 78-12690. 1979. 69.95x o.s.i. (ISBN 0-470-26543-4). Halsted Pr.

Read, Beryl J. Pip's Mountain. (The Pathfinder Ser.). (Illus.). 96p. (Orig.). 1980. pap. 1.95 o.p. (ISBN 0-310-37901-6). Zondervan.

Read, D., et al. Health Education: The Search for Values. 1977. 15.95 (ISBN 0-13-384511-7). P-H.

Read, Danny L., jt. auth. see Kennington, Donald.

Read, David H. Unfinished Easter: Sermons on the Ministry. LC 77-20454. (Ministers Paperback Library). 1978. pap. 4.95i o.p. (ISBN 0-06-066812-1, RD 263, HarpR). Har-Row.

Read, Donald. Peterloo. LC 72-7212. Repr. of 1958 ed. 17.50x (ISBN 0-678-06791-0). Kelley.

Read, Donald A. Healthy Sexuality. 1979. pap. 7.95x (ISBN 0-02-398800-2); instrs'. manual avail. Macmillan.
--Looking in: Exploring One's Personal Health Values. (Health Education Ser.). (Illus.). 1977. pap. text ed. 10.95 (ISBN 0-13-540484-3). P-H.
Read, Donald A. & Greene, Walter H. Creative Teaching in Health. 3rd ed. (Illus.). 1980. text ed. 20.95x (ISBN 0-02-398700-6). Macmillan.
Read, Donald C. & Simon, Sidney B. Humanistic Education Sourcebook. (Illus.). 480p. 1975. ref. ed. 22.95 (ISBN 0-13-447714-6); pap. 16.95 (ISBN 0-13-447706-5). P-H.
Read, F. H. Electromagnetic Radiation. LC 79-41484. (Manchester Physics Ser.). 331p. 1980. 62.95 (ISBN 0-471-27718-5); pap. 27.95 (ISBN 0-471-27714-2). Wiley.
Read, F. H., jt. auth. see Harting, E.
Read, Gardner. Contemporary Instrumental Techniques. LC 75-27455. (Illus.). 1976. 21.00 (ISBN 0-02-872100-4). Schirmer Bks.
--Style & Orchestration. LC 77-15884. 1979. 23.95 (ISBN 0-02-872110-1). Schirmer Bks.
Read, H. H. & Watson, Janet. Introduction & Geology, 2 vols. Incl. Vol. 1. Principles. 2nd ed. LC 76-50637. 1977. 34.95 o.s.i. (ISBN 0-470-99031-7); Vol. 2, 2 pts. LC 75-501. 1975; Pt. 1. Early Stages of Earth History. 221p. 24.95 o.s.i. (ISBN 0-470-71165-5); Pt. 2. Later Stages of Earth History. 371p. 34.95 o.s.i. (ISBN 0-470-71166-3). Halsted Pr.
Read, Herbert. Art & Industry. LC 54-7895. (Midland Bks.: No. 32). (Illus.). 256p. 1961. pap. 2.75x o.p. (ISBN 0-253-20032-6). Ind U Pr.
--The Philosophy of Modern Art. 278p. 1964. pap. 7.95 (ISBN 0-571-06506-6). Faber & Faber.
--To Hell with Culture & Other Essays on Art & Society. LC 62-18153. 1963. pap. 3.95 o.p. (ISBN 0-8052-0081-9). Schocken.
Read, Herbert & Cassou, Jean. Jan Le Witt. 172p. 1972. 42.00 o.p. (ISBN 0-912050-17-9, Library Pr). Open Court.
Read, James & Yapp, Malcolm. Law. Killingray, Margaret & O'Connor, Edmund, eds. (World History Ser.). (Illus.). (gr. 10). 1980. Repr. of 1977 ed. lib. bdg. 6.95 (ISBN 0-89908-144-4); pap. text ed. 2.25 (ISBN 0-89908-119-3). Greenhaven.
Read, Jan. Monarch Guide to the Wines of Spain & Portugal. (Illus.). 1978. pap. 2.95 o.p. (ISBN 0-671-18359-1). Monarch Pr.
--The Wines of Portugal. (Books on Wine). 192p. 1983. 11.95 (ISBN 0-571-11951-4); pap. 5.95 (ISBN 0-571-11952-2). Faber & Faber.
--The Wines of Spain. (Books on Wine). (Illus.). 272p. 1983. 11.95 (ISBN 0-571-11937-9); pap. 6.95 (ISBN 0-571-11938-7). Faber & Faber.
--Wines of Spain & Portugal. (Illus.). 280p. 1980. 13.95 o.p. (ISBN 0-571-10266-2). Faber & Faber.
Read, Jenny. Jenny Read: In Pursuit of Art & Life. Johnson, Dallas & Heersoma, Kathleen, eds. LC 82-73449. (Illus., Orig.). 1982. 15.95 (ISBN 0-914064-17-7, Co. Pub with Antioch U Pr); pap. 10.95 (ISBN 0-914064-18-5). Celo Pr.
Read, Leonard E. How Do We Know? 128p. 1981. 3.00 (ISBN 0-910614-68-7). Foun Econ Ed.
Read, M. K. Juan Huarte de San Juan. (World Authors Ser.). 1981. lib. bdg. 15.95 (ISBN 0-8057-6461-5, Twayne). G K Hall.
Read, Maggie. Going to School. LC 81-52654. (Starters Ser.). PLB 8.00 (ISBN 0-382-06482-8). Silver.
Read, Miss Chronicles of Fairacre. 1977. 10.95 o.s.i. (ISBN 0-395-25181-8). HM.
Read, P. G. Gemmological Instruments. 1978. 29.95 o.p. (ISBN 0-408-00316-2). Butterworth.
Read, Piers P. Alive: The Story of the Andes Survivors. 1975. pap. 3.50 (ISBN 0-380-00321-X, 58826-9). Avon.
--The Villa Golitsyn. 208p. 1983. pap. 3.50 (ISBN 0-380-61929-6, Bard). Avon.
Read, Ronald C., ed. Graph Theory & Computing. 1972. 56.50 (ISBN 0-12-583850-6). Acad Pr.
Read, Stanley E. & Zabriskie, John B., eds. Streptococcal Diseases & the Immune Response. LC 79-26638. 1980. 50.00 (ISBN 0-12-583880-8). Acad Pr.
Read, Thomas. The Female Poets of America: With Portraits, Biographical Notices, & Specimens of Their Writings. LC 76-9777. (Illus.). 1978. Repr. of 1857 ed. 74.00x (ISBN 0-8103-4290-1). Gale.
Read, W. L., jt. auth. see Chappell, R. T.
Read, William R. & Ineson, Frank A. Brazil 1980: The Protestant Handbook. 1973. pap. 5.00 (ISBN 0-912552-04-2). MARC.
Reade, B. Ballet Designs & Illustrations. 240p. 1967. 60.00x (ISBN 0-686-98220-7, Pub. by HMSO). State Mutual Bk.
Readence, John E., et al. Content Area Reading: An Integrated Approach. 240p. 1981. text ed. 15.95 (ISBN 0-8403-2316-6). Kendall-Hunt.
Readence, John E., jt. auth. see Moore, David W.
Reader, C. T. & Hooper, C. Stirling Engines. 1982. 49.95x (ISBN 0-419-12400-4, Pub. by E & FN Spon). Methuen Inc.
Reader, Dennis J. Coming Back Alive. LC 79-5147. (Illus.). 256p. (gr. 7 up). 1981. 9.95 (ISBN 0-394-84359-2); PLB 9.99 (ISBN 0-394-94359-7). Random.
--Coming Back Alive. 256p. 1983. pap. 2.25 (ISBN 0-380-61416-2, Flare). Avon.
Reader, J. The Divine Mystery. 79p. pap. 3.95 (ISBN 0-88172-117-4). Believers Bkshelf.
Reader, W. R. Fifty Years of Unilever. (Illus.). 1980. 18.95 (ISBN 0-434-62501-9, Pub. by Heinemann). David & Charles.
Reader's Digest Editors. America From the Road: A Motorist's Guide to Our Country's Natural Wonders & Most Interesting Places. LC 81-50918. (Illus.). 448p. 1982. 25.50 (ISBN 0-89577-103-9, Pub. by RD Assn). Random.
--America the Beautiful. LC 73-103727. (Illus.). 352p. 1970. 18.50 (ISBN 0-686-84601-X, Pub. by RD Assn). Random.
--American Folklore & Legend. LC 77-80638. (Illus.). 448p. 1978. 21.50 (ISBN 0-89577-045-8, Pub. by RD Assn). Random.
--America's Fascinating Indian Heritage. LC 78-55614. (Illus.). 416p. 1978. 20.50 (ISBN 0-89577-019-9, Pub. by RD Assn). Random.
Readers Digest Editors. Animals Can Be Almost Human. LC 79-53750. (Illus.). 416p. 1979. 18.50 (ISBN 0-89577-069-5, Pub. by RD Assn). Random.
--Animals You Will Never Forget. LC 69-15867. (Illus.). 416p. 1969. 16.98 (ISBN 0-89577-049-0). RD Assn.
Reader's Digest Editors. At Home With French, 3 vols., 4 tapes. 666p. 1978. Set. pap. 42.50 (ISBN 0-89577-057-1, Pub. by RD Assn). Random.
--Atlas of the Bible: An Illustrated Guide to the Holy Land. LC 80-53426. (Illus.). 256p. 1981. 20.50 (ISBN 0-89577-097-0, Pub. by RD Assn). Random.
--Back to Basics: How to Learn & Enjoy Traditional American Skills. LC 80-50373. (Illus.). 456p. 1981. 20.50 (ISBN 0-89577-086-5, Pub. by RD Assn). Random.
--The Best of the West, 2 Vols. LC 75-10496. (Illus.). 1246p. 1976. 15.99 (ISBN 0-89577-027-X). RD Assn.
--The Book of Christmas. LC 73-84158. (Illus.). 304p. 1973. 14.98 (ISBN 0-89577-013-X). RD Assn.
--Complete Car Care Manual. LC 80-53207. (Illus.). 480p. 1981. 23.50 (ISBN 0-89577-088-1, Pub. by RD Assn). Random.
--Complete Do-It-Yourself Manual. LC 72-87867. (Illus.). 600p. 1973. 20.50 (ISBN 0-89577-010-5, Pub. by RD Assn). Random.
--Complete Guide to Needlework. LC 78-71704. (Illus.). 504p. 1979. 19.50 (ISBN 0-89577-059-8, Pub. by RD Assn). Random.
--Complete Guide to Sewing. LC 75-32106. (Illus.). 528p. 1976. 20.50 (ISBN 0-89577-026-1, Pub. by RD Assn). Random.
--Crafts & Hobbies. LC 79-63118. (Illus.). 456p. 1979. 20.50 (ISBN 0-89577-063-6, Pub. by RD Assn). Random.
--Creative Cooking. LC 76-24397. (Illus.). 432p. 1977. 16.50 (ISBN 0-89577-037-7, Pub. by RD Assn). Random.
--Drive America, 5 Vols. LC 80-53041. (Illus.). 236p. (Orig.). 1981. Set. pap. 24.00 (ISBN 0-89577-085-7, Pub. by RD Assn). Random.
--Eat Better, Live Better. LC 82-60100. (Illus.). 416p. 1982. 21.50 (ISBN 0-89577-141-1, Pub. by RD Assn). Random.
--Family Health Guide & Medical Encyclopedia. rev ed. LC 76-23541. (Illus.). 640p. 1976. 16.98 (ISBN 0-89577-032-6). RD Assn.
--Family Legal Guide: A Complete Encyclopedia of Law for the Layman. LC 81-50467. 1268p. 1981. 23.50 (ISBN 0-89577-100-4, Pub. by RD Assn). Random.
--Family Songbook. LC 70-84403. (Illus.). 252p. 1969. Lie-flat spiral bdg. 20.50 (ISBN 0-89577-002-4, Pub. by RD Assn). Random.
--Family Songbook of Faith & Joy: 129 All-Time Inspirational Favorites. LC 74-26223. 288p. 1975. Lie-flat spiral bdg. 20.50 (ISBN 0-89577-021-0, Pub. by RD Assn). Random.
Readers Digest Editors. Family Word Finder. LC 75-18006. 896p. 1975. 17.50 (ISBN 0-89577-023-7, Pub. by RD Assn). Random.
--Farmhouse Cookery: Recipes From the Country Kitchen. (Illus.). 400p. 1981. 24.95 o.p. (ISBN 0-686-92642-0). Readers Digest.
Reader's Digest Editors. Festival of Popular Songs. LC 77-24818. (Illus.). 288p. 1977. Lie-flat spiral bdg. 20.50 (ISBN 0-89577-035-0, Pub. by RD Assn). Random.
--The Fight for Life. LC 78-63130. 638p. 1981. 13.96 (ISBN 0-89577-163-2). RD Assn.
--Fireside Reader. LC 77-76319. (Illus.). 640p. 1978. 14.98 (ISBN 0-89577-099-7). RD Assn.
--Fix-It-Yourself Manual. LC 77-73634. (Illus.). 480p. 1977. 20.50 (ISBN 0-89577-040-7, Pub. by RD Assn). Random.
--Great Adventures That Changed Our World: The World's Great Explorers, Their Truiumphs & Tragedies. LC 78-52846. (Illus.). 384p. 1978. 17.50 (ISBN 0-89577-048-2, Pub. by RD Assn). Random.
--Great American Short Stories. LC 76-10933. 640p. 1977. 13.98 (ISBN 0-89577-033-4). RD Assn.
--Great Cases of Interpol. LC 81-50533. (Illus.). 560p. 1982. 16.50 (ISBN 0-89577-101-2, Pub. by RD Assn). Random.
--Great Cases of Scotland Yard. LC 77-86612. (Illus.). 692p. 1978. 16.50 (ISBN 0-89577-053-9, Pub. by RD Assn). Random.
--Great Events of the 20th Century. LC 76-23540. (Illus.). 544p. 1977. 19.50 (ISBN 0-89577-034-2, Pub. by RD Assn). Random.
--Great Music's Greatest Hits: 97 Unforgettable Classics for Piano & Organ. LC 79-53751. 252p. 1980. Lie-flat spiral bdg. 18.50 (ISBN 0-89577-066-0, Pub. by RD Assn). Random.
--Great People of the Bible & How They Lived. LC 73-86027. (Illus.). 432p. 1974. 19.50 (ISBN 0-89577-015-6, Pub. by RD Assn). Random.
--Great Short Stories of the World. LC 72-81158. 800p. 1972. 13.98 (ISBN 0-89577-008-3). RD Assn.
--Great Short Tales of Mystery & Terror. LC 80-52212. (Illus.). 640p. 1982. 14.98 (ISBN 0-89577-091-1). RD Assn.
--Great Stories of Mystery & Suspense, 2 Vols. LC 73-76284. (Open-ended Ser.). 1294p. 1981. Set. 15.99 (ISBN 0-89577-083-0). RD Assn.
--Great Stories of Mystery & Suspense, 2 vols. LC 73-76284. (Open-Ended Ser.). 1290p. 1977. 15.99 (ISBN 0-89577-136-5). RD Assn.
--Great Tales of the Sea. LC 77-81738. (Illus.). 640p. 1978. 14.98 (ISBN 0-89577-016-4). RD Assn.
--High Stakes & Desperate Men. LC 74-3808. (Illus.). 736p. 1974. 14.98 (ISBN 0-89577-017-2). RD Assn.
--Home Improvements Manual. LC 81-84488. (Illus.). 384p. 1982. 21.50 (ISBN 0-89577-132-2, Pub. by RD Assn). Random.
--Illustrated Guide to Gardening. LC 77-85145. (Illus.). 672p. 1978. 22.50 (ISBN 0-89577-046-6, Pub. by RD Assn). Random.
--Illustrated Story of World War II. LC 69-15868. (Illus.). 528p. 1969. 15.99 (ISBN 0-89577-029-6). RD Assn.
--Into the Unknown. LC 80-54189. (Illus.). 352p. 1981. 20.50 (ISBN 0-89577-098-9, Pub. by RD Assn). Random.
--Joy of Nature: How to Observe & Appreciate the Great Outdoors. LC 76-29320. (Illus.). 352p. 1977. 15.99 (ISBN 0-89577-036-9). RD Assn.
--The Last Two Million Years: Reader's Digest History of Man. LC 77-71204. (Illus.). 488p. 1973. 19.50 (ISBN 0-89577-018-0, Pub. by RD Assn). Random.
--Marvels & Mysteries of the World Around Us. LC 72-77610. (Illus.). 320p. 1972. 15.99 (ISBN 0-89577-012-1). RD Assn.
--Mysteries of the Unexplained. LC 82-60791. (Illus.). 320p. 1983. 21.50 (ISBN 0-89577-146-2, Pub. by RD Assn). Random.
--Natural Wonders of the World. LC 80-50353. (Illus.). 464p. 1980. 20.50 (ISBN 0-89577-087-3, Pub. by RD Assn). Random.
--North American Wildlife. LC 81-50919. (Illus.). 576p. 1982. 20.50 (ISBN 0-89577-102-0). RD Assn.
--Our Magnificent Wildlife. LC 74-30861. (Illus.). 352p. 1975. 16.98 (ISBN 0-393-21410-9). RD Assn.
--Our Magnificent Wildlife: How to Enjoy & Preserve It. LC 74-30861. (Illus.). 352p. 1975. 16.98 (ISBN 0-89577-022-9). RD Assn.
--People in Peril. LC 82-60965. (Illus.). 576p. 1983. 17.98 (ISBN 0-89577-154-3). RD Assn.
--Popular Songs That Will Live Forever. LC 81-8447. (Illus.). 252p. 1982. 20.50 (ISBN 0-89577-104-7, Pub. by RD Assn). Random.
--Practical Guide to Home Landscaping. LC 72-157525. (Illus.). 480p. 1972. 18.50 (ISBN 0-89577-005-9, Pub. by RD Assn). Random.
--Reader's Digest Almanac & Yearbook, 1983. LC 66-14383. (Illus.). 1024p. 1983. 7.50 (ISBN 0-89577-152-7, Pub. by RD Assn). Random.
--The Reader's Digest Country & Western Songbook. (Illus.). 252p. 1983. Lie-flat spiral bdg. 20.50 (ISBN 0-89577-147-0, Pub. by RD Assn). Random.
--The Reader's Digest Merry Christmas Songbook. LC 81-51285. (Illus.). 252p. 1981. Lie-flat spiral bdg. 20.50 (ISBN 0-89577-105-5, Pub. by RD Assn). Random.
--Scenic Wonders of America: An Illustrated Guide to Our Natural Splendors. LC 72-91832. (Illus.). 576p. 1973. 19.50 (ISBN 0-89577-009-1, Pub. by RD Assn). Random.
--Secrets of Better Cooking. LC 72-91833. (Illus.). 762p. 1973. 17.50 (ISBN 0-89577-011-3, Pub. by RD Assn). Random.
--Secrets of the Seas. LC 72-80582. (Illus.). 384p. 1972. 13.96 (ISBN 0-89577-051-2). RD Assn.
--Seventy Favorite Stories for Young Readers. LC 76-19444. (Illus.). 448p. 1976. 14.98 (ISBN 0-89577-031-8). RD Assn.
--Six Gothic Tales. LC 77-83406. (Illus.). 640p. 1979. 16.50 (ISBN 0-89577-060-1, Pub. by RD Assn). Random.
--Stories Behind Everyday Things. LC 79-88053. (Illus.). 416p. 1980. 20.50 (ISBN 0-89577-068-7, Pub. by RD Assn). Random.
Readers Digest Editors. The Story of America. LC 75-3837. (Illus.). 528p. 1975. 18.50 (ISBN 0-89577-024-5, Pub. by RD Assn). Random.
Reader's Digest Editors. Story of the Great American West. LC 76-23542. (Illus.). 384p. 1977. 19.50 (ISBN 0-89577-039-3). RD Assoc.
--Story of the Great American West. LC 76-23542. (Illus.). 384p. 1977. 19.50 (ISBN 0-89577-039-3, Pub. by RD Assn). Random.
--Storytime. LC 82-80898. (Illus.). 448p. (gr. 1-8). 1982. 15.99 (ISBN 0-89577-145-4). RD Assn.
--Strange Stories, Amazing Facts. LC 76-2966. (Illus.). 608p. 1976. 19.50 (ISBN 0-89577-028-8, Pub. by RD Assn). Random.
Readers Digest Editors. Success with House Plants. LC 78-59802. (Illus.). 480p. 1979. 20.50 (ISBN 0-89577-052-0, Pub. by Reader's Digest). Random.
Reader's Digest Editors. Success with Words. LC 82-62542. 704p. 1983. 20.97 (ISBN 0-89577-168-3, Pub. by RD Assn). Random.
--Treasures of America. LC 73-83812. (Illus.). 624p. 1974. 15.99 (ISBN 0-89577-014-8). RD Assn.
--Treasury of Best Loved Songs: 114 All-Time Family Favorites. LC 71-183858. 288p. 1972. 20.50 (ISBN 0-89577-007-5, Pub. by RD Assn). Random.
--Treasury of Great Books. LC 80-50421. (Illus.). 640p. 1980. 14.98 (ISBN 0-89577-084-9). RD Assn.
--True Stories of Great Escapes. LC 77-84357. (Illus.). 608p. 1977. 17.00 (ISBN 0-89577-041-5, Pub. by RD Assn). Random.
--True Stories of World War II. LC 79-66914. (Illus.). 448p. 1980. 14.98 (ISBN 0-89577-081-4). RD Assn.
--Use the Right Word. LC 72-8783. 726p. 1968. 14.98 (ISBN 0-89577-025-3). RD Assn.
--The World's Best Fairy Tales, 2 vols. LC 79-89496. (Illus.). 832p. 1967. Set. 17.50 (ISBN 0-89577-078-4, Pub. by RD Assn). Random.
--The World's Last Mysteries. LC 77-87127. (Illus.). 320p. 1978. 18.50 (ISBN 0-89577-044-X, Pub. by RD Assn). Random.
--Write Better, Speak Better. LC 75-183859. 730p. 1972. 17.50 (ISBN 0-89577-006-7, Pub. by RD Assn). Random.
--You & the Law. LC 77-75374. 864p. 1975. 18.50 (ISBN 0-89577-038-5, Pub. by RD Assn). Random.
--You & the Law. 3rd., rev. ed. LC 82-61749. 864p. 1983. 20.50 (ISBN 0-89577-164-0, Pub. by RD Assn). Random.
--You & Your Rights. LC 81-84665. 448p. 1982. 20.50 (ISBN 0-89577-137-3, Pub. by RD Assn). Random.
Reader's Digest Editors, selected by. More Tests & Teasers. 240p. 1982. pap. 2.75 (ISBN 0-425-05739-9). Berkley Pub.
--They Beat the Odds. 256p. 1983. pap. 2.75 (ISBN 0-425-05994-4). Berkley Pub.
--They Changed Our World. 1982. pap. 2.75 o.p. (ISBN 0-425-05607-4). Berkley Pub.
Reader's Digest Special. Curious Creatures. (Orig.). 1981. pap. 2.75 o.p. (ISBN 0-425-05156-0). Berkley Pub.
--Mind Power. (Orig.). 1981. pap. 2.75 o.p. (ISBN 0-425-05157-9). Berkley Pub.
Readett, Alan G., jt. auth. see Herbst, Robert.
Readett, Alan G., jt. ed. see Herbst, Robert.
Reading, H. G., jt. ed. see Ballance, P. F.
Reading, Hugo F. A Dictionary of the Social Sciences. 1977. 18.00 (ISBN 0-7100-8642-3); pap. 6.95 (ISBN 0-7100-8650-4). Routledge & Kegan.
Reading, Peter. Diplopic. 64p. 1983. 12.50 (ISBN 0-436-40983-6, Pub. by Secker & Warburg). David & Charles.
--Tom O'Bedlam's Beauties. 1981. 11.50 (ISBN 0-436-43900-X, Pub. by Secker & Warburg). David & Charles.
Readon, Betty. Discrimination, Vol. 2: No. 2. 111p. Date not set. 5.00 (ISBN 0-686-43044-1). Decade Media.
Ready, Barbara C., ed. Peterson's Annual Guides to Graduate Study: Engineering & Applied Sciences, 1983. 800p. 1982. pap. 17.95 (ISBN 0-87866-189-1). Petersons Guides.
--Peterson's Guides to Graduate Study: Physical Sciences & Mathematics, 1983. 650p. (Orig.). 1982. pap. 17.95 (ISBN 0-87866-188-3). Petersons Guides.
Ready, John, ed. Lasers in Modern Industry. LC 79-66705. (Manufacturing Update Ser.). (Illus.). 1979. 32.00 (ISBN 0-87263-052-8). SME.
Ready, John F. Effects of High-Power Laser Radiation. 1971. 58.50 (ISBN 0-12-583950-2). Acad Pr.
Ready, Kirk L. Custom Cars. LC 82-7757. (Superwheels & Thrill Sports Bks.). (Illus.). 48p. (gr. 4 up). 1982. PLB 7.95g (ISBN 0-8225-0508-8). Lerner Pubns.
Ready, Nigel, jt. auth. see Karatzas, Theodoros.
Ready, R. K. Administrator's Job: Issues & Dilemmas. 1967. pap. text ed. 7.50 o.p. (ISBN 0-07-051300-7, C). McGraw.
Reagan, Alice E. H. I. Kimball, Entrepreneur. (Illus.). 170p. 1983. 9.95 (ISBN 0-87797-064-5). Cherokee.
Reagan, Charles, ed. Studies in the Philosophy of Paul Ricoeur. LC 79-10343. xxvi, 194p. 1979. 16.00x (ISBN 0-8214-0223-4, 82-82287). Ohio U Pr.
Reagan, Charles A. The Reagan Story. (Illus.). 260p. 1981. pap. 4.95 o.p. (ISBN 0-89260-210-4). Hwong Pub.
Reagan, Christopher J., jt. ed. see Burns, Norman T.
Reagan, James W., jt. auth. see Keebler, Catherine M.
Reagan, James W., jt. ed. see Keebler, Catherine M.
Reagan, Michael D. & Sanzone, John G. The New Federalism. 2nd ed. 1981. pap. text ed. 5.95x (ISBN 0-19-502772-8). Oxford U Pr.

Reagan, Ron. Siamese Cats. (Illus.). 127p. 1981. 4.95 (ISBN 0-87666-860-0, KW-062). TFH Pubns.
Reagan, Ronald. From California to the Capital. LC 82-12822. 218p. 1983. pap. 7.95 (ISBN 0-8159-6720-9). Devin.
--Ronald Reagan Talks to America. 1983. 12.95 (ISBN 0-8159-6719-5); pap. 7.95. Devin.
Reage, Pauline. Istoriia O. Oguibenine, Boris, tr. from Fr. Orig. Title: Lhistoire d O. 350p. (Rus.). 1983. 18.50 (ISBN 0-88233-733-5); pap. 12.00 (ISBN 0-88233-734-3). Ardis Pubs.
Real Estate Education Co. & Grubb & Ellis Commercial Brokerage Co. Successful Leasing & Selling of Retail Property. 256p. 1980. binder 49.95 o.s.i. (ISBN 0-695-81503-2). Follett.
Real Estate Research Corporation. Infill Development Strategies. LC 82-50809. (Illus.). 132p. 1982. pap. 24.95 (ISBN 0-87420-613-8, 127). Urban Land.
Reale, Giovanni. The Concept of First Philosophy & the Unity of the Metaphysics of Aristotle. Catan, John R., tr. LC 79-13867. 1980. 58.50x (ISBN 0-87395-385-1); pap. 19.95x (ISBN 0-87395-443-2). State U NY Pr.
Realist. No Business Like God's Business. 239p. 1982. 10.95 (ISBN 0-533-04912-1). Vantage.
Ream, Glen O. Out of New Mexico's Past. LC 80-166. (Illus.). 160p. (Orig.). 1980. pap. 6.95 (ISBN 0-913270-86-5, Sundial Bks). Sunstone Pr.
Reamer, Frederic G. Ethical Dilemmas in Social Service. 304p. 1982. 17.50x (ISBN 0-231-05188-3). Columbia U Pr.
Reams, Bernard D., Jr. & Dunn, Donald J. Immigration & Nationality Law Review, 1976-1981: 1976-84, 5 vols. LC 76-43517. 1977. Vol. 1, 1976-77. lib. bdg. 32.50 (ISBN 0-930342-08-9); Vol. 2, 1978-79. lib. bdg. 32.50 (ISBN 0-930342-67-4); Vol. 3, 1979-80. lib. bdg. 32.50 (ISBN 0-89941-061-8); Vol. 4, 1980-81. lib. bdg. 35.00 (ISBN 0-89941-096-0); Vol. 5, 1981-82. lib. bdg. 35.00 (ISBN 0-930342-68-2). W S Hein.
Reams, Bernard D., Jr., ed. Education of the Handicapped: Legislative Histories & Administrative Documents, V.1-55, 55. LC 82-81360. (Legislative Histories of the Law of the Handicapped Ser.: Part two). 1982. lib. bdg. 1925.00x (ISBN 0-89941-157-6). W S Hein.
--Internal Revenue Acts of the United States: The Revenue Act of 1954 with Legislative Histories & Congressional Documents, 11. LC 82-83005. 8000p. 1982. lib. bdg. 440.00 (ISBN 0-89941-168-1). W S Hein.
--Internal Revenue Acts of the United States: 1950-1951 Legislative Histories, Laws & Administrative Documents, 7 vols. in 9. LC 82-81278. 1982. lib. bdg. 360.00 (ISBN 0-89941-155-X). W S Hein.
Reams, Bernard D., Jr., ed. see Ault, Warren O.
Reams, Bernard D., Jr., ed. see Burge, William.
Reams, Bernard D., Jr., ed. see Goffin, R. J.
Reams, Bernard D., Jr., ed. see Hughes, David.
Reams, Bernard D., Jr., ed. see Plucknett, Theodore F.
Reams, Bernard D., Jr., ed. see Street, Thomas A.
Reams, Bernard J., Jr. Federal Consumer Protection: Laws, Rules & Regulations, 5 bdrs. Ferguson, J. Ray, ed. LC 78-11285. 1979. looseleaf 85.00 ea. (ISBN 0-379-10025-8); Set. 425.00. Oceana.
Reamy, Lois. Travelability: A Guide for Physically Disabled Travelers in the United States. 1978. 13.95 (ISBN 0-02-601170-0). Macmillan.
Reamy, Tom. Blind Voices. LC 78-3817. 1978. 8.95 o.p. (ISBN 0-399-12240-0, Pub. by Berkley). Putnam Pub Group.
Reap, Charles A., Jr. Complete Handbook for Dental Auxiliaries. (Illus.). 150p. 1981. pap. 18.00 (ISBN 0-931386-44-6). Quint Pub Co.
Rearden, Jim, ed. Alaska Magazine's Alaska Hunting Guide. (Illus.). 1979. pap. 5.95 o.p. (ISBN 0-88240-127-0). Alaska Northwest.
Reardon, B. Liberalism & Tradition. LC 75-7214. 320p. 1975. 47.50 (ISBN 0-521-20776-2). Cambridge U Pr.
Reardon, Eugene F. & Jeakle, William T. How to College: A Humorous Guide to the Four Years. LC 82-99932. (Illus.). 208p. 1982. pap. 4.95x (ISBN 0-910617-00-7). Primer Pr CA.
Reardon, James J. & McMahon, Judi. Plastic Surgery for Men. 288p. 1981. 14.95 (ISBN 0-89696-069-2, An Everest House Book). Dodd.
Reardon, John J. Peyton Randolph, 1721-1775: One Who Presided. LC 81-70431. (Illus.). 112p. 1982. 12.95 (ISBN 0-89089-201-6). Carolina Acad Pr.
Reardon, Robert. The Early Morning Light. 1979. 3.50 o.p. (ISBN 0-87162-217-3, D3550). Warner Pr.
Reardon, Thomas, jt. auth. see Gambino, Anthony J.
Reardon, William R. & Pawley, Thomas D. Black Teacher & the Dramatic Arts: A Dialogue, Bibliography & Anthology. LC 73-90789. 1970. 29.95 (ISBN 0-8371-1850-6, Pub. by Negro U Pr). Greenwood.
Rearick, Ron, jt. auth. see Hanes, Mari.
Reaske, Christopher R. College Writer's Guide to the Study of Literature. (Orig.). 1970. pap. text ed. 2.95x (ISBN 0-685-19712-3). Phila Bk Co.
Reaske, Christopher R., jt. auth. see Arny, Mary T.
Reaske, Christopher R. & Willson, Robert F., Jr., eds. Student Voices. (Orig.). 1971. pap. text ed. 3.95 (ISBN 0-685-04769-5). Phila Bk Co.
Reason, James & Mycielska, Klara. Absent Minded? The Psychology of Mental Lapses & Everyday Errors. (Illus.). 263p. 1982. 13.95 (ISBN 0-13-001743-4); pap. 6.95 (ISBN 0-13-001735-3). P-H.
Reason, Peter & Rowan, John, eds. Human Inquiry: A Source Book of New Paradigm Research. LC 80-41585. 530p. 1981. 69.95 (ISBN 0-471-27935-8, Pub. by Wiley-Interscience); pap. 21.00 (ISBN 0-471-27936-6, Pub. by Wiley-Interscience). Wiley.
Reasoner, Charles F. Releasing Children to Literature: A Teacher's Guide to Yearling Books. pap. text ed. 2.00, free with order of 25 Yearling books o.s.i. (ISBN 0-685-29121-9). Dell.
Reasoner, Charles F., intro. by. For Kids Only. LC 76-28183. (Illus.). (gr. 1 up). 1977. 8.95 o.s.i. (ISBN 0-440-02738-1); pap. 4.95 o.s.i. (ISBN 0-440-02690-3). Delacorte.
Reasoner, Harry. Before the Colors Fade. LC 82-16685. 206p. 1983. pap. 5.95 (ISBN 0-688-01544-1). Quill NY.
Reaver, J. Russell. Moments of Transition: Processes of Structuring in Man, Society & Art. LC 82-40086. 130p. (Orig.). 1982. lib. bdg. 19.00 (ISBN 0-8191-2545-8); pap. text ed. 8.00 (ISBN 0-8191-2546-6). U Pr of Amer.
--O'Neill Concordance, 3 Vols. LC 73-75960. 1969. 140.00x (ISBN 0-8103-1001-5). Gale.
Reaves, Paul M., jt. auth. see Etgen, William M.
Reaves, V. Heading South. (Illus.). 152p. 1982. 5.95 (ISBN 0-9607036-0-8). Bradt Ent.
Reavey, George, tr. see Berdiaev, Nikolai.
Reavey, George, tr. see Gogol, Nicolai V.
Reavin, Sara. Elise. (Orig.). 1980. pap. 2.95 o.p. (ISBN 0-451-09483-2, E9483, Sig). NAL.
Reavis, Charles. Home Sausage Making. LC 80-39703. (Illus.). 128p. 1980. pap. 7.95 (ISBN 0-88266-246-5). Garden Way Pub.
Reay. The Biology of Aquaculture. (Studies in Biology: No. 106). 1979. 5.95 o.p. (ISBN 0-8391-0256-9). Univ Park.
Reay, D. A., jt. auth. see Dunn, P. D.
Reay, D. A., ed. Advances in Heat Pipe Technology: Proceedings of the IV International Heat Pipe Conference, September 7-10, 1981. LC 81-82554. (Illus.). 1982. 100.00 (ISBN 0-08-027284-3). Pergamon.
Reay, D. A., ed. see International Heat Pipe Conference, Iv, London, 7-10 Sepbember 1981.
Reay, David A. Heat Recovery Systems: A Directory of Equipment & Techniques. LC 79-10877. (Energy Ser.). 590p. 1979. 65.00x (ISBN 0-419-11400-9, Pub. by E & FN Spon England). Methuen Inc.
Reay, Lee. Incredible Passage: Through the Hole-in-the-Rock. Hechtle, Ranier, ed. (Illus.). 128p. (Orig.). 1981. 5.95 (ISBN 0-934826-05-6); pap. 4.50 (ISBN 0-934826-06-4). Meadow Lane.
--Lambs in the Meadow. LC 79-66222. (Illus.). 1979. 7.95 (ISBN 0-934826-00-5); pap. 5.95 (ISBN 0-934826-01-3). Meadow Lane.
Reay, P. J. Aquaculture. (Studies in Biology: No. 106). 64p. 1979. pap. text ed. 8.95 (ISBN 0-7131-2721-X). E Arnold.
Reba, Richard & Goodenough, David J. Diagnostic Imaging Medicine. 1983. 87.00 (ISBN 90-247-2798-7, Pub. by Martinus Nijhoff Netherlands). Kluwer Boston.
Rebecca S. Parkinson & Associates, et al. Managing Health Promotion in the Workplace: Guidelines for Implementation & Evaluation. LC 81-84693. 314p. 1982. 24.95 (ISBN 0-87484-567-X). Mayfield Pub.
Rebelo, Ivonia, jt. auth. see Cable, Vincent.
Reber, Arthur S. & Scarborough, Don L. Toward a Psychology of Reading: The Proceedings of the C. U. N. Y. Conferences. LC 76-47695. 352p. 1977. text ed. 24.95 (ISBN 0-89859-201-1). L Erlbaum Assocs.
Reber, Ralph W. & Terry, Gloria. Behavioral Insights for Supervision. 2nd ed. (Illus.). 240p. 1982. pap. 14.95 (ISBN 0-13-073114-5). P-H.
Rebeta-Burditt, Joyce. Triplets. 1981. 15.95 o.s.i. (ISBN 0-440-08943-3, Sey Lawr). Delacorte.
Rebhorn, Eldon. Woodturning. (gr. 9-12). 1970. text ed. 16.64 (ISBN 0-87345-047-7). McKnight.
Rebikoff, Dimitri & Cherney, Paul. Underwater Photography. 2nd ed. (Illus.). 144p. 1975. 8.95 o.p. (ISBN 0-8174-0490-2, Amphoto). Watson-Guptill.
Rebischung, James. Japan: The Facts of Modern Business & Social Life. LC 74-15653. (Illus.). 1975. pap. 4.75 (ISBN 0-8048-1147-4, Tut Bks). C E Tuttle.
Rebisz, Jacqueline, ed. see Metz, Mary S. & Helstrom, Jo.
Rebore, Ronald W. Personnel Administration in Education: A Management Approach for Educational Organizations. (Illus.). 336p. 1982. 25.95 (ISBN 0-13-657742-3). P-H.
Reboul, Antoine. Thou Shalt Not Kill. Craig, Stephanie, tr. LC 77-77312. Orig. Title: Tu Ne Tueras Point. (gr. 5-8). 1969. 10.95 (ISBN 0-87599-161-0). S G Phillips.
Reboullet, et al. Methode Orange-Workbook 1. (Methode Orange Ser.). (Illus., Fr.). (gr. 7-12). 1979. pap. text ed. 2.95 (ISBN 0-88345-408-4); tchrs' manual 6.25 (ISBN 0-88345-411-4); cassettes 80.00 (ISBN 0-686-60844-5); slides 120.00 (ISBN 0-686-60845-3). Regents Pub.
Rebrisz, J., ed. see Woodford, P. & Kernan, D.
Rebuffat, Gaston. Men & the Matterhorn. Brockett, Eleanor, tr. (Illus.). 1973. 22.50 o.p. (ISBN 0-19-519059-9). Oxford U Pr.
Reca, Lucio G. Argentina: Country Case Study of Agricultural Prices, Taxes & Subsidies. (Working Paper: No. 386). 72p. 1980. 5.00 (ISBN 0-686-36064-8, WP-0386). World Bank.
Recent & Fossil Marine Diatoms, 3rd Symposium, 1975. Proceedings. Simonsen, R., ed. 1975. 100.00 (ISBN 3-7682-5453-4). Lubrecht & Cramer.
Rech, R. & Moore, K. E., eds. Introduction to Psychopharmacology. LC 78-116995. 365p. 1971. 17.00 (ISBN 0-911216-12-X). Raven.
Rechcigl, Miloslav, Jr. Man, Food & Nutrition: Strategies & Technological Measures for Alleviating the World Food Problem. LC 82-6560. 352p. (Orig.). 1982. Repr. of 1973 ed. 44.95 (ISBN 0-89874-509-8). Krieger.
Rechenbach, Charles W. & Garnett, Eugene R. A Bibliography of Scientific, Technical, & Specialized Dictionaries. 1969. pap. 16.95 (ISBN 0-8132-0251-5). Cath U Pr.
Rechenberg, H., jt. auth. see Mehra, Jagdish.
Rechin, Bill & Wilder, Don. There's No Escape from the Legion. 128p. 1983. pap. 1.95 (ISBN 0-449-12461-4, GM). Fawcett.
Rechinger, K. H. Flora of Lowland Iraq. 1964. 60.00 (ISBN 3-7682-0217-8). Lubrecht & Cramer.
Rechs, James R., jt. auth. see Regestein, Quentin R.
Rechtschaffen, Bernard & Marck, Louis. Two Thousand & One German & English Idioms: 2001 Deutsche und Englische Idiome. 1984. pap. 9.95 (ISBN 0-8120-0474-4). Barron. Postponed.
Rechy, John. City of Night. 1962. pap. 3.95 (ISBN 0-394-17147-0, B213, BC). Grove.
--The Fourth Angel. 160p. Date not set. pap. 6.95. Seaver Bks.
Reckhow, Kenneth H. & Chapra, Steven. Engineering Approaches for Lake Management, 2 vols. LC 79-56115. 200p. 1983. Vol. 1: Data Analysis & Empirical Modeling. text ed. 37.50 (ISBN 0-250-40344-7); Vol. 2: Mechanistic Modeling. text ed. 37.50 (ISBN 0-250-40392-7); Set. text ed. 75.00 (ISBN 0-250-40516-4). Ann Arbor Science.
Reckless, Walter C. Vice in Chicago. LC 69-16243. (Criminology, Law Enforcement, & Social Problems Ser.: No. 84). 1969. Repr. of 1933 ed. 15.00x (ISBN 0-87585-084-7). Patterson Smith.
Recob, James B., jt. auth. see Amy, William O.
Recondo, A. M. de see De Recondo, A. M.
Reconstruction of the Globe Playhouse Symposium. The Third Globe. Hodges, C. Walter, et al, eds. (Illus.). 268p. 1981. 16.95 (ISBN 0-8143-1680-8). Wayne St. U Pr.
Record Controls, Inc., & H. F. M. A. Staff. A Guide to the Retention & Preservation of Records (with Destruction Schedules) 5th hospital ed. LC 77-94914. (Illus.). 1978. 15.00 (ISBN 0-930228-07-3). Healthcare Fin Man Assn.
Record, Jane C. Staffing Primary Care in Nineteen Ninety: Physician Replacement & Cost Savings. (Health Care & Society Ser.: No. 6). 1981. text ed. 26.50 (ISBN 0-8261-3370-3). Springer Pub.
Record, Jeffrey. Sizing up the Soviet Army. (Studies in Defense Policy). 51p. 1975. pap. 4.95 (ISBN 0-8157-7367-6). Brookings.
--U. S. Nuclear Weapons in Europe: Issues & Alternatives. (Studies in Defense Policy). 70p. 1974. pap. 4.95 (ISBN 0-8157-7365-X). Brookings.
Record, Jeffrey & Hanks, Robert J. U. S. Strategy at the Crossroads: Two Views. LC 82-82774. (Foreign Policy Ser.). 72p. 1982. 7.50 (ISBN 0-89549-044-7). Inst Foreign Policy Anal.
Record, Jeffrey, jt. auth. see Binkin, Martin.
Record, Jeffrey, jt. auth. see Lawrence, Richard D.
Record, Nancy. Bed for the Night. LC 68-56700. (People & Their Useful Things Ser.). (Illus.). (gr. 5-10). 1968. PLB 3.95g (ISBN 0-8225-0268-2). Lerner Pubns.
--On Top: The Story of Outer Garments. LC 77-128802. (People & Their Useful Things Ser.). (gr. 5-9). 1972. PLB 3.95g (ISBN 0-8225-0275-5). Lerner Pubns.
Record, Nancy A. Coffers & Cabinets. LC 68-56700. (People & Their Useful Things Ser.). (Illus.). (gr. 5-10). 1968. PLB 3.95g (ISBN 0-8225-0269-0). Lerner Pubns.
--Come to the Table. LC 73-128801. (People & Their Useful Things Ser.). (Illus.). (gr. 5-9). 1972. PLB 3.95g (ISBN 0-8225-0274-7). Lerner Pubns.
Recording for the Blind, Staff. A Cook's Tour. 241p. 1982. pap. 7.95x (ISBN 0-914091-19-0). Chicago Review.
Rector, Alan, jt. auth. see Zimmerman, Joan.
Rector, Barry M. & Rector, Floyd C., eds. The Kidney, 2 vols. 2nd ed. 1981. Vol. 1. text ed. write for info. o.p. (ISBN 0-7216-1967-3); Vol. 2. text ed. write for info. o.p. (ISBN 0-7216-1968-1); Set. text ed. write for info. o.p. (ISBN 0-7216-1969-X). Saunders.
Rector, Floyd C., jt. ed. see Brenner, Barry M.
Rector, Floyd C., jt. ed. see Rector, Barry M.
Rector, Justine J., jt. auth. see Tinney, James S.
Rector, Margaret, ed. Cowboy Life on the Texas Plains: The Photographs of Ray Rector. LC 82-40316. (The Centennial Series of the Association of Former Students: No. 12). (Illus.). 124p. (YA) 1982. 19.95 (ISBN 0-89096-131-X); special limited edition 50.00x (ISBN 0-89096-139-5). Tex A&M Univ Pr.
Rector, Robert E. & Zwick, Earl J. Finite Mathematics & Its Applications. LC 78-69547. (Illus.). 1979. text ed. 23.50 (ISBN 0-395-27206-8); instr's. manual 1.00 (ISBN 0-395-27207-6). HM.
Rector, William F., III, ed. Leadership in Space for Benefits on Earth. LC 57-43769. (Advances in the Astronautical Sciences Ser.: Vol. 47). (Illus.). 310p. 1982. lib. bdg. 45.00x (ISBN 0-87703-168-1); pap. text ed. 35.00x (ISBN 0-87703-169-X). Am Astronaut.
Redburn, F. Stevens & Buss, Terry. Public Policies for Communities in Economic Crisis. 1981. pap. 6.00 (ISBN 0-918592-54-2). Policy Studies.
Redburn, F. Stevens, jt. auth. see Buss, Terry F.
Redburn, F. Stevens & Buss, Terry F., eds. Public Policies for Distressed Communities. LC 80-8393. (A Policy Studies Organization Bk.). 288p. 1982. 28.95x (ISBN 0-669-04105-X). Lexington Bks.
Redcliff, M. R. Agrarian Reform & Peasant Organization on the Ecuadorian Coast. (Univ. of London Institute of Latin American Studies Monographs: No. 8). (Illus.). 1978. text ed. 38.00x (ISBN 0-485-17708-0, Athlone Pr). Humanities.
Redcliffe Press Ltd., ed. Skin for Skin. 152p. 1982. 25.00x (ISBN 0-686-82401-6, Pub. by Redcliffe England). State Mutual Bk.
--This is Bristol. 112p. 1982. 50.00x (ISBN 0-905459-28-8, Pub. by Redcliffe England). State Mutual Bk.
Redd, William H. & Sleator, William. Take Charge: A Personal Guide to Behavior Modification. 1977. 7.95 o.p. (ISBN 0-394-40910-8); pap. 2.45 (ISBN 0-394-72511-5). Random.
Redd, William H., et al. Behavior Modification: Behavioral Approaches to Human Problems. 1978. text ed. 20.00x (ISBN 0-394-32134-0). Random.
Reddall, Henry. Fact, Fancy & Fable. LC 68-25519. 1968. Repr. of 1889 ed. 34.00x (ISBN 0-8103-3093-8). Gale.
Reddding, S. G. The Working Class Manager. 1979. text ed. 31.25x (ISBN 0-566-00291-4). Gower Pub Ltd.
Redden, John D. Catholic Philosophy of Education. 1956. 5.95 o.p. (ISBN 0-02-826320-0). Glencoe.
Redden, Kenneth. Introductory Survey of the Place of Law in Our Civilization. 1946. 7.50 o.p. (ISBN 0-87215-071-2). Michie-Bobbs.
Redden, Kenneth L. Federal Regulation of Family Law. (Federal Law Library). 457p. 1982. 40.00 (ISBN 0-87215-558-7). Michie-Bobbs.
Redden, Kenneth R. Punitive Damages. 1000p. 1980. with 1982 suppl. 60.00 (ISBN 0-87215-303-7); 1982 suppl. only 17.50 (ISBN 0-87215-580-3). Michie-Bobbs.
Redden, Kenneth R. & McClellan, James. Federal Regulation of Consumer-Creditor Relations: Federal Law Library. 666p. 1982. 45.00 (ISBN 0-87215-441-6). Michie-Bobbs.
Redden, Kenneth R., jt. auth. see Saltzburg, Stephen A.
Redder, Ronald. Perforated Mood-Swing Book. LC 76-186644. (Illus.). 100p. (Orig.). (YA) 1972. pap. 2.95 o.p. (ISBN 0-570-03134-6, 12-2381). Concordia.
Reddig, Jill S., jt. auth. see Burke, John G.
Reddihough & Knight. Questions & Answers: Color TV. 2nd ed. (Illus.). 1975. pap. 4.95 (ISBN 0-408-00162-3). Focal Pr.
Reddin, W. J. Effective Management by Objectives: The 3-D Method of MBO. 1971. 26.50 (ISBN 0-07-051360-0, P&RB). McGraw.
--Managerial Effectiveness. 1970. 24.95 (ISBN 0-07-051358-9, C). McGraw.
Redding, Saunders, jt. ed. see Davis, Arthur P.
Redding, W. Charles. How to Conduct a Readership Survey: A Guide for Organizational Editors & Communications Managers. LC 81-86059. (The Ragan Communications Library). 152p. 1982. pap. 30.00 (ISBN 0-931368-08-1). Ragan Comm.
Reddish, V. C. Stellar Formation. 225p. 1978. text ed. 48.00 (ISBN 0-08-018062-0); pap. text ed. 21.00 (ISBN 0-08-023053-9). Pergamon.
Reddix, Valerie. The Claw & the Spiderweb. (Pennypincher Bks.). (gr. 3-6). 1982. pap. 1.75 (ISBN 0-89191-709-8). Cook.
Reddy, G. P. veer see Pardee, Arthur B. & Veer Reddy, G. P.
Reddy, G. Ram & Sharma, B. Regionalism in India: A Study of Telangana. 1980. text ed. 18.25x (ISBN 0-391-01868-X). Humanities.
Reddy, J. N. & Rasmussen, M. L. Advanced Engineering Analysis. LC 81-14730. 488p. 1982. 39.95 (ISBN 0-471-09349-1, Pub. by Wiley-Interscience). Wiley.
Reddy, J. N., jt. auth. see Oden, J. T.
Reddy, J. N., ed. Penalty-Finite Elements Mehtods In Mechanics. (AMD Ser.: Vol. 51). 1982. 40.00 (H00235). ASME.
Reddy, P. S., et al, eds. Pericardial Disease. (Illus.). 391p. 1982. text ed. 43.50 (ISBN 0-686-82957-3). Raven.
Rede, C. Van see Cocks, Leslie V. & Van Rede, C.
Redei, George P. Genetics. 1982. text ed. 27.95x (ISBN 0-02-398850-9). Macmillan.
Redei, L. Algebra, Vol. 1. 1967. 77.00 (ISBN 0-08-010954-3). Pergamon.
--Lacunary Polynomials Over Finite Fields. LC 72-88577. 250p. 1973. write for info. (ISBN 0-444-10400-3, North-Holland). Elsevier.

Redeker, James R. Discipline: Policies & Procedures. 250p. 1983. text ed. 20.00 (ISBN 0-87179-394-6); pap. text ed. 15.00 (ISBN 0-87179-399-7). BNA.

Redemptorist Pastoral Publication. Jesus Loves You. 80p. (gr. 1-3). 1983. 4.95 (ISBN 0-89243-175-X). Liguori Pubns.

--Manual Para el Catolico De Hoy. 1978. pap. 1.50 (ISBN 0-89243-091-5). Liguori Pubns.

--Questions People Ask. 80p. 1982. pap. 2.50 (ISBN 0-89243-167-9). Liguori Pubns.

Redfarn & Nelson. Nylon Plastics Technology. 1977. 19.95 o.p. (ISBN 0-408-00251-4). Butterworth.

Redfearn, David J. Predictors of Nurses' Compliance with Physicians' Inappropriate Orders. Kalisch, Philip & Kalisch, Beatrice, eds. LC 82-16119. (Studies in Nursing Management Ser.: No. 6). 134p. 1982. 34.95 (ISBN 0-8357-1372-5, Pub. by UMI Res Pr). Univ Microfilms.

Redfern, Barrie. Local Radio. (Media Manual Ser.). (Illus.). 1978. pap. 10.95 (ISBN 0-240-50980-3). Focal Pr.

Redfern, George B. Evaluating Teachers & Administrators: A Performance Objective Approach. (Westview Special Studies in Education). 186p. 1980. lib. bdg. 20.00 (ISBN 0-89158-760-8); pap. 9.50 (ISBN 0-89158-890-6). Westview.

Redfern, H. B., jt. auth. see Mauldon, E.

Redfield, Louise N., tr. see D'Olivet, Fabre.

Redford, jt. auth. see Mills.

Redford, A. & Chaloner, W. H., eds. Labour Migration in England, 1800-50. 1976. pap. 9.00 (ISBN 0-7190-0636-8). Manchester.

Redford, Lawrence H., ed. The Occupation of Japan: Economic Policy & Reform. 382p. 1980. pap. 6.00 (ISBN 0-9606418-2-3). MacArthur Memorial.

--The Occupation of Japan: Impact of Legal Reform. 212p. 1978. pap. 5.00 (ISBN 0-9606418-1-5). MacArthur Memorial.

Redford, Lora B. Getting to Know the Central Himalayas: Nepal, Sikkim, Bhutan. (Getting to Know Ser.). (Illus.). (gr. 3-5). 1964. PLB 3.97 o.p. (ISBN 0-698-30110-2, Coward). Putnam Pub Group.

Redford, Robert. The Outlaw Trail. LC 77-87795. (Illus.). 225p. 1981. 25.00 (ISBN 0-448-14590-1, G&D); pap. 14.95 (ISBN 0-448-12024-0). Putnam Pub Group.

Redgrave, Deirdre & Brook, Danae. To Be a Redgrave. 1982. 14.95 (ISBN 0-671-42429-7, Linden). S&S.

Redgrove, Peter. Cornwall in Verse. 96p. 1983. 13.95 (ISBN 0-436-40987-9, Pub. by Secker & Warburg). David & Charles.

--In the Country of the Skin. 1973. 14.95 (ISBN 0-7100-7514-6). Routledge & Kegan.

--Sons of My Skin. 1975. 14.95 (ISBN 0-7100-8073-5). Routledge & Kegan.

--Terrors of Dr. Treviles. 1974. 12.95 (ISBN 0-7100-7919-2). Routledge & Kegan.

Redgrove, Peter, jt. auth. see Shuttle, Penelope.

Redheffer, R. M., jt. auth. see Sokolnikoff, Ivan S.

Redheffer, Raymond, jt. auth. see Levinson, Norman.

Redinbaugh, L. D. Retailing Management: A Planning Approach. 1975. 24.95 (ISBN 0-07-051366-X, C); instr's. manual 16.50 (ISBN 0-07-051367-8). McGraw.

Redinbaugh, Larry D. & Neu, Clyde W. Small Business Management: A Planning Approach. (Illus.). 1980. pap. text ed. 22.95 (ISBN 0-8299-0307-0); instrs.' manual avail. (ISBN 0-8299-0569-3). West Pub.

Redinger, Reul O. Silver: An Instructional Guide to the Silversmith's Art. (Illus.). 144p. 1980. 14.95 o.p. (ISBN 0-13-810218-X, Spec); pap. 6.95 o.p. (ISBN 0-13-810200-7). P-H.

Redish, Martin H. Federal Courts: Cases, Comments & Questions. LC 82-24763. 871p. 1983. text ed. 24.95 (ISBN 0-314-71146-5). West Pub.

Redivo, Hugo. The Okanagan. (Illus.). 1978. 11.95x (ISBN 0-19-540286-3). Oxford U Pr.

Redland, A. & Leonard, B. Process in Clinical Nursing. 1981. pap. 16.95 (ISBN 0-13-723205-5). P-H.

Redleaf, Rhoda, ed. Field Trips: An Adventure in Learning. (Illus.). 75p. (Orig.). 1980. pap. text ed. 8.95 (ISBN 0-934140-14-6). Toys N Things.

Redlich, F. C., jt. auth. see Hollingshead, A. B.

Redlich, F. C., ed. Social Psychiatry. LC 68-27002. (ARNMD Research Publications Ser: Vol.47). 396p. 1969. 27.50 (ISBN 0-89004-159-8). Raven.

Redlich, Josef. Austrian War Government. (Economic & Social History of the World War Ser.). 1929. 49.50x (ISBN 0-685-69855-6). Elliots Bks.

Redlich, Josef & Hirst, Francis W. History of Local Government in England, Bk. 1. LC 71-110121. Repr. of 1903 ed. lib. bdg. 25.00x (ISBN 0-678-07005-9). Kelley.

Redlich, Norman. Professional Responsibility: A Problem Approach. 1976. pap. 8.95 o.p. (ISBN 0-316-73655-4). Little.

--Professional Responsibility: Problems & Other Materials. 2nd ed. 1983. write for info. (ISBN 0-316-73657-0). Little.

Redlich, Otto. Thermodynamics: Fundamentals, Applications. 1976. 57.50 (ISBN 0-444-41487-8). Elsevier.

Redlich, Shimon. Propaganda & Nationalism in Wartime Russia: The Jewish Anti-Fascist Committee in the USSR, 1941-1948. (East European Monographs: No. 108). 256p. 1982. 20.00x (ISBN 0-88033-001-5). East Eur Quarterly.

Redman see Borchardt, Jack A., et al.

Redman, C. L., ed. Social Archeology: Beyond Subsistence & Dating. (Studies in Archaeology Ser.). 1978. 39.50 (ISBN 0-12-585150-2). Acad Pr.

Redman, Charles L. Research & Theory in Current Archeology. LC 73-6717. 384p. 1973. pap. text ed. 20.00 (ISBN 0-471-71291-4, Pub. by Wiley-Interscience). Wiley.

Redman, Charles L., ed. Research & Theory in Current Archeology. 400p. 1983. Repr. of 1973 ed. lib. bdg. write for info. (ISBN 0-89874-226-9). Krieger.

Redman, Eric. The Dance of Legislation. 320p. 1973. 9.95 o.p. (ISBN 0-671-21494-2). S&S.

Redman, Helen C. & Fisch, Allan E. Computed Tomography of the Body. LC 78-64721. (Advanced Exercises in Diagnostic Radiology Ser.: Vol. 13). (Illus.). 263p. 1979. pap. text ed. 19.95 o.p. (ISBN 0-7216-7492-5). Saunders.

Redman, Helen C., jt. auth. see Reuter, Stewart R.

Redman, Joseph A. There Are Trees in the Forest. 1978. 4.50 o.p. (ISBN 0-533-03471-X). Vantage.

Redman, Scott. Real Men Don't Cook Quiche: The Real Man's Cookbook. Feirstein, Bruce, ed. (Illus., Orig.). 1982. pap. 3.95 (ISBN 0-671-46308-X). PB.

Redmayne, Paul, ed. see Insull, Thomas.

Redmond, C. F., jt. ed. see Lodge, H. C.

Redmond, Donald A. Sherlock Holmes, a Study in Sources. 375p. 1982. 24.95 (ISBN 0-7735-0391-9). McGill-Queens U Pr.

Redmond, Eugene. In a Time of Rain & Desire: New Love Poems. 5.50 (ISBN 0-916692-13-2); softcover 3.00 (ISBN 0-916692-05-1). Black River.

--River of Bones & Flesh & Blood: Poems, 1962-71. 1971. 3.95 (ISBN 0-916692-11-6); softcover 2.00 (ISBN 0-916692-03-5). Black River.

--Sentry of the Four Golden Pillars: Poems, 1963-70. 1970. 2.95 (ISBN 0-916692-10-8); softcover 1.00 (ISBN 0-916692-02-7). Black River.

--Songs from an Afro Phone: Poems, 1970-72. 1972. 4.95 (ISBN 0-916692-12-4); softcover 2.50 (ISBN 0-916692-04-3). Black River.

Redmond, Eugene, ed. Griefs of Joy: Selected Contemporary Afro-American Poetry for Students. 1976. pap. write for info (ISBN 0-916692-08-6). Black River.

--Sides of the River: A Mini-Anthology of Black Writings. 1969. pap. 1.50 (ISBN 0-916692-01-9). Black River.

Redmond, Geoffrey P., jt. ed. see Sokya, Lester F.

Redmond, Gertrude T. & Ouellette, Frances. Concept & Case Studies in Physical & Mental Health Nursing: A Life Cycle Approach. 1982. pap. 12.95 (ISBN 0-201-06207-0, Med-Nurse). A-W.

Redmond, J., et al, eds. Year's Work in English Studies 1979. (Year's Work in English Studies: Vol. 60). 519p. 1982. text ed. 43.75x (ISBN 0-391-02623-2, Pub. by Murray England). Humanities.

Redmond, James, ed. Drama & Nemesis. LC 79-9054. (Themes in Drama Ser.: No. 2). (Illus.). 1980. 37.50 (ISBN 0-521-22179-X). Cambridge U Pr.

--Drama, Dance & Music. (Themes in Drama Ser.: No. 3). (Illus.). 260p. 1981. 39.50 (ISBN 0-521-22180-3). Cambridge U Pr.

--Drama in Society. LC 77-54723. (Themes in Drama: No. 1). (Illus.). 1979. 37.50 (ISBN 0-521-22076-9). Cambridge U Pr.

Redmond, James, ed. see Morris, William.

Redmond, P. W. General Principles of English Law. 416p. 1979. 35.00x (ISBN 0-7121-0725-8, Pub. by Macdonald & Evans). State Mutual Bk.

Redmore, Fred H. Fundamentals of Chemistry. (Illus.). 1979. ref. ed. 29.95 (ISBN 0-13-335158-0); lab manual 14.95 (ISBN 0-13-335174-2); 9.95 (ISBN 0-13-335182-3); sol. manual 8.95 (ISBN 0-13-335166-1). P-H.

Redner, Harry. In the Beginning Was the Deed: Reflections on the Passage of Faust. LC 81-16090. 304p. 1982. 30.00x (ISBN 0-520-04435-5). U of Cal Pr.

Rednick, Herman. The Hidden Door to Reality: A Book of Mystical Experiences. LC 81-85124. 160p. (Orig.). 1982. 9.95 (ISBN 0-942184-00-9); pap. 6.00 (ISBN 0-942184-01-7). Open Door Pub.

--The Spiritual Principle in Art. 1978. 6.95 o.p. (ISBN 0-533-03457-4). Vantage.

Redpath, Alan. Making of a Man of God: Studies in the Life of David. 256p. 1962. 10.95 (ISBN 0-8007-0189-5). Revell.

Redpath, Ann. Jim Boen--a Man of Opposites: A Man of Opposites. 48p. (gr. 4-8). 1980. PLB 7.95 (ISBN 0-87191-744-0). Creative Ed.

Redpath, Ann, ed. see Frevert, Patricia D.

Redpath, Ann, ed. see Larson, Norita D.

Redpath, Henry A., jt. auth. see Hatch, Edwin.

Redpath, Peter A. A Simplified Introduction to the Wisdom of St. Thomas. LC 80-5230. 180p. 1980. lib. bdg. 18.75 (ISBN 0-8191-1058-2); pap. text ed. 9.50 (ISBN 0-8191-1059-0). U Pr of Amer.

Redpath, Theodore, ed. see Donne, John.

Redpath, Theodore, jt. ed. see Ingram, W. G.

Redshaw, S. C., jt. auth. see Rushton, K. R.

Redstone, L. G. Public Art: New Directions. 1981. 37.95 (ISBN 0-07-051345-7). McGraw.

Redstone, Louis G. Art in Architecture. LC 68-13098. (Illus.). 1968. 49.50 (ISBN 0-07-051365-1, P&RB). McGraw.

--The New Downtowns: Rebuilding Business Districts. (Illus.). 1976. 49.50 o.p. (ISBN 0-07-051369-4, P&RB). McGraw.

--The New Downtowns: Rebuilding Business Districts. LC 82-17111. 356p. 1983. Repr. of 1976 ed. lib. bdg. p.n.s. (ISBN 0-89874-560-8). Krieger.

Redwood, Alec. Deadline Moscow. 147p. 1980. 20.00 (ISBN 0-86116-012-6, Pub. by New Horizon England). State Mutual Bk.

Redwood, John & Hatch, John. Controlling Public Industries. 176p. 1982. text ed. 24.00x (ISBN 0-631-13017-9, Pub. by Basil Blackwell England); pap. text ed. 9.95x (ISBN 0-631-13078-0, Pub. by Basil Blackwell England). Biblio Dist.

Ree, J. M. Van see Van Ree, J. M. & Terenius, L.

Reece, B. & Manning, G. Wilson RV: An in-Basket Simulation. 1976. soft bdg. 7.75 (ISBN 0-07-051485-2, G); instructor's manual & key 5.50 (ISBN 0-07-051486-0). McGraw.

Reece, Barry & Brandt, Rhonda O. Effective Human Relations in Business. 1981. 22.95 (ISBN 0-395-30701-5); instr's manual 2.00 (ISBN 0-395-30702-3). HM.

Reece, Barry L., jt. auth. see Manning, Gerald L.

Reece, Colleen. The Calling of Elizabeth Courtland. 256p. 1982. pap. 4.50 (ISBN 0-8024-1145-2). Moody.

--Honor Bound. 176p. (gr. 3 up). 1983. 3.95 (ISBN 0-8024-0153-8). Moody.

--Mark of Our Moccasins. (Indian Culture Ser.). 1982. 2.95 (ISBN 0-686-81747-8). MT Coun Indian.

--Thank You. LC 82-9560. (What Does it Mean? Ser.). (Illus.). 32p. (gr. 1-2). 1982. PLB 4.95 (ISBN 0-89565-239-0, 4899, Pub. by Childs World). Standard Pub.

Reece, Colleen L. Alpine Meadows Nurse. (YA) 1980. 6.95 (ISBN 0-686-73939-6, Avalon). Bouregy.

--Ballad for Nurse Lark. (YA) 1979. 6.95 (ISBN 0-685-95868-X, Avalon). Bouregy.

--Come Home, Nurse Jenny. (YA) 1978. 6.95 (ISBN 0-685-19055-2, Avalon). Bouregy.

--Everlasting Melody. (YA) 1979. 6.95 (ISBN 0-685-90721-X, Avalon). Bouregy.

--In Search of Twilight. (YA) 1978. 6.95 (ISBN 0-685-84748-9, Avalon). Bouregy.

--Nurse Autumn's Secret Love. (YA) 1979. 6.95 (ISBN 0-686-52547-7, Avalon). Bouregy.

--Nurse Camilla's Love. (YA) 6.95 (ISBN 0-686-73925-6, Avalon). Bouregy.

--Nurse Julie's Sacrifice. (YA) 1980. 6.95 (ISBN 0-686-59797-4, Avalon). Bouregy.

Reece, Collen L. The Outsider. Schroeder, Howard, ed. Furan Illustrators. LC 81-3298. (Roundup Ser.). (Illus.). 48p. (Orig.). (gr. 3 up). 1981. PLB 7.95 (ISBN 0-89686-150-3); pap. text ed. 3.95 (ISBN 0-89686-158-9). Crestwood Hse.

Reece, Daphne. Historic Houses of California. (Illus.). 192p. (Orig.). 1983. pap. 7.95 (ISBN 0-87701-199-0). Chronicle Bks.

Reece, Daphne E., jt. auth. see Storey, Joan.

Reece, James S., jt. auth. see Goodman, Sam R.

Reece, Robert M. Reece & Chamberlain's Manual of Emergency Pediatrics. 2nd ed. LC 77-11352. (Illus.). 1978. pap. text ed. 24.50 o.p. (ISBN 0-7216-7498-4). Saunders.

Reed, A. W. Place Names of Australia. 1973. 8.75 o.p. (ISBN 0-589-07115-7, Pub. by Reed Books Australia). C E Tuttle.

Reed, Adele. Old Mammoth. Smith, Genny, ed. LC 82-60130. (Illus.). 200p. 1982. 25.00; pap. 14.50. Genny Smith Bks.

Reed, Anne. Starlit Seduction, No. 83. 1982. pap. 1.75 (ISBN 0-515-06694-X). Jove Pubns.

Reed, Arthur. Airport. LC 78-61230. (Careers Ser.). (Illus.). 1978. PLB 12.68 (ISBN 0-382-06196-9). Silver.

Reed, Barbara. Nutritional Guidelines For the Counselor. 1982. pap. 10.00 (ISBN 0-686-83743-6). Natural Pr.

Reed, Barry. The Verdict. 256p. 1983. pap. 2.95 (ISBN 0-553-23329-7). Bantam.

Reed, Betty J. Golfin' with a Dolphin. (Early Childhood Bk.). (Illus.). (ps-2). PLB 4.95 o.p. (ISBN 0-513-00447-5). Denison.

--Mouse in the House. (Illus.). (gr. k-3). PLB 4.95 o.p. (ISBN 0-513-01158-7). Denison.

Reed, Bika. The Fields of Transformation: Basic Principles of Evolution According to the Thought of Ancient Egypt. (Illus.). 256p. 1983. pap. 8.95 (ISBN 0-89281-016-5). Inner Tradit.

Reed, Bill. Mr. Siggie Morrison with His Comb & Paper. (Australian Theatre Workshop Ser.). 1972. pap. text ed. 4.50x o.p. (ISBN 0-85859-026-3, 00525). Heinemann Ed.

--Truganinni. (Austalian Theatre Workshop Ser.). 1977. pap. text ed. 4.50x o.p. (ISBN 0-85859-150-2, 00529). Heinemann Ed.

Reed, Bill, jt. auth. see Ehrenstein, David.

Reed, Bobbie. Prescription for a Broken Heart. 1982. pap. 4.95 (ISBN 0-8307-0856-1, 5416901). Regal.

Reed, Brian. Crewe Locomotive Works. (Illus.). 240p. 1982. 27.50 (ISBN 0-7153-8228-4). David & Charles.

Reed, C. B. The Coal Era in the U.S. A Study of Our Viable Alternatives. LC 81-68030. 1981. pap. text ed. 9.95 (ISBN 0-250-40484-2). Ann Arbor Science.

--Fuels, Minerals & Human Survival. LC 74-21575. 1975. softcover 16.50 (ISBN 0-250-40256-4). Ann Arbor Science.

Reed, C. J., jt. auth. see Price, C. J.

Reed, Charles E., jt. ed. see Dempsey, Jerome A.

Reed, Chester A. Bird Guide: Land Birds East of the Rockies. 7.95 (ISBN 0-385-04809-2). Doubleday.

--North American Birds Eggs. rev. ed. (Illus.). 1965. pap. 5.00 o.p. (ISBN 0-486-21361-7). Dover.

Reed, Dick A. The Complete Investor's Guide to Silver Dollar Investing. 1982. 18.95 (ISBN 0-911349-00-6). English Fact.

Reed, Douglas. Battle for Rhodesia. 1967. 8.95 (ISBN 0-8159-5102-7). Devin.

Reed, E. & Jones, R. Reasons for Realism: Selected Essays of James J. Gibson. (Illus.). 449p. 1982. text ed. 39.95 (ISBN 0-89859-207-0). L Erlbaum Assocs.

Reed, E., et al. Commercial Banking. 2nd ed. 1980. 23.95 (ISBN 0-13-152785-1). P-H.

Reed, Edward A., jt. auth. see Eary, Donald F.

Reed, Edward B. Lyra Levis. 1922. 19.50x (ISBN 0-686-51414-9). Elliots Bks.

Reed, Edward B., ed. Songs From the British Drama. 1925. text ed. 49.50x (ISBN 0-686-83775-4). Elliots Bks.

Reed, Edwin T. Bells of Long Ago. 1946. 3.95 (ISBN 0-8323-0147-7). Binford.

Reed, Evelyn. Sexism & Science. LC 77-92144. (Illus.). 1977. cloth 17.00 (ISBN 0-87348-540-8). Path Pr NY.

Reed, F. Morton. Odd & Curious, Vol. II. (Illus.). 1983, softcover 7.00 (ISBN 0-686-64440-9); lib. bdg. 12.50 (ISBN 0-915262-38-X). S J Durst.

Reed, Frank C., jt. auth. see Firestone, David B.

Reed, G. & Rehm, H. J., eds. Biotechnology: Volume 1: Microbial Fundamentals. (Illus.). 532p. 1981. 309.00x (ISBN 0-89573-041-3). Verlag Chemie.

Reed, G. A., jt. auth. see Sander, K. F.

Reed, G. H. Refrigeration: A Practical Manual for Apprentices. 3rd ed. (Illus.). 1974. 14.50 (ISBN 0-85334-605-4, Pub. by Applied Sci England). Elsevier.

Reed, G. M., ed. Set-Theoretic Topology. 1977. 34.50 (ISBN 0-12-584950-8). Acad Pr.

Reed, George M. Surveys in General Topology. LC 79-28483. 1980. 46.00 (ISBN 0-12-584960-5). Acad Pr.

Reed, Gerald. Enzymes in Food Processing. 2nd ed. 1975. 66.50 (ISBN 0-12-584852-8). Acad Pr.

Reed, Gervais, jt. auth. see Moseley, Spencer.

Reed, Graham. Magic for Every Occasion. (Illus.). 128p. (gr. 5 up). 1981. 9.25 (ISBN 0-525-66733-4, 0898-270). Lodestar Bks.

Reed, Gretchen M. & Sheppard, Vincent F. Basic Structures of the Head & Neck: A Programmed Instruction in Clinical Anatomy for Dental Professionals. LC 75-298. (Illus.). 640p. 1976. pap. text ed. 28.00 (ISBN 0-7216-7516-6). Saunders.

--Regulation of Fluid & Electrolyte Balance: A Programmed Instruction in Clinical Physiology. LC 76-20109. (Illus.). 1977. pap. text ed. 12.95 (ISBN 0-7216-7513-1). Saunders.

Reed, Harold W. The Dynamics of Leadership. 263p. 1982. pap. text ed. 12.95x (ISBN 0-8134-2261-2). Interstate.

Reed, Henry, tr. see De Balzac, Honore.

Reed, Henry H. & Duckworth, Sophia. Central Park: A History & a Guide. rev. ed. (Illus.). 184p. 1972. pap. 2.50 o.p. (ISBN 0-517-50082-5, C N Potter Bks). Crown.

Reed, Henry H., ed. see Small, Herbert.

Reed, Ione. Pioneering in Oregon's Coast Range: Surviving the Depression Years. (Illus.). 140p. (Orig.). 1983. pap. 7.95 (ISBN 0-934784-31-0). Calapooia Pubns.

Reed, Ishmael. Conjure: Selected Poems, Nineteen Sixty-Three to Nineteen Seventy. LC 72-77568. 106p. 1972. 8.00x (ISBN 0-87023-114-6); pap. 3.95 o.p. (ISBN 0-87023-115-4). U of Mass Pr.

Reed, Ishmael, ed. Quilt Three. 164p. (Orig.). 1982. pap. 4.95 (ISBN 0-931676-07-X). Reed & Youngs Quilt.

Reed, J., jt. ed. see Black, M.

Reed, J. J. Electron Microprobe Analysis. LC 74-94356. (Monographs on Physics). (Illus.). 350p. 1975. 62.50 (ISBN 0-521-20466-6). Cambridge U Pr.

Reed, James. The Missionary Mind & American East Asia Policy, 1911-1915. (Harvard East Asian Monographs: No. 104). 300p. 1983. text ed. 20.00x (ISBN 0-686-82629-9). Harvard U Pr.

Reed, Jeanne. Business English: A Gregg Text-Kit for Adult Education. 3rd ed. 1978. text ed. 14.65 (ISBN 0-07-051497-6, G); instructor's manual & key 5.10 (ISBN 0-07-051498-4). McGraw.

Reed, Jeanne & Finch, R. Business Writing, a Gregg Text-Kit in Adult Education. 1970. text ed. 14.40 (ISBN 0-07-051480-1, G); instructor's guide 6.15 (ISBN 0-07-051481-X). McGraw.

Reed, Jeremy. Bleecker Street. (Carcanet New Poetry Ser.). 61p. (Orig.). 1981. pap. 6.95 o.p. (ISBN 0-85635-328-0, Pub. by Carcanet New Pr England). Humanities.

Reed, John. Adventures of a Young Man: Short Stories from Life. LC 75-14275. 144p. pap. 3.00 o.s.i. (ISBN 0-87286-083-3). City Lights.

Reed, John, tr. see Oyono, Ferdinand.

Reed, John, tr. see Senglor, Leopold S.

Reed, John Q. Benjamin Penhallow Shillaber. (U. S. Authors Ser.). lib. bdg. 14.95 (ISBN 0-8057-0664-X, Twayne). G K Hall.

Reed, John R. A Gallery of Spiders: Poems. LC 80-81894. (Ontario Review Press Poetry Ser.). 72p. 1980. 10.95 (ISBN 0-86538-005-8); pap. 5.95 (ISBN 0-86538-006-6). Ontario Rev NJ.

--The Natural History of H. G. Wells. LC 81-11261. x, 294p. 1982. lib. bdg. 23.95x (ISBN 0-8214-0628-0, 82-84010). Ohio U Pr.

--Perception & Design in Tennyson's "Idylls of the King". LC 77-122100. 270p. 1969. 15.00x (ISBN 0-8214-0078-9, 82-80820). Ohio U Pr.

--Victorian Conventions. LC 73-92908. xiii, 561p. 1975. 20.00x (ISBN 0-8214-0147-5, 82-81503). Ohio U Pr.

Reed, John S. Southerners: The Social Psychology of Sectionalism. LC 82-13631. 170p. 1983. 17.00x (ISBN 0-8078-1542-X); pap. 5.95x (ISBN 0-8078-4098-X). U of NC Pr.

Reed, John T. Aggressive Tax Avoidance for Real Estate Investors. 2nd ed. 282p. 1982. pap. 15.00 (ISBN 0-686-86682-7). Real Estate Investor.

--Aggressive Tax Avoidance for Real Estate Investors. Rev. ed. 300p. 1983. pap. 19.95 (ISBN 0-939224-06-2). Real Estate Investor.

--Sensible Finance Techniques for Real Estate. 300p. 1983. pap. 19.95 (ISBN 0-939224-05-4). Real Estate Investor. Postponed.

Reed, Joseph W. & Pottle, Frederick, eds. Boswell: Laird of Auchinleck 1778-1782. 1977. 29.95 (ISBN 0-07-051520-4, P&RB). McGraw.

Reed, Joseph W., Jr., ed. see Walpole, Horace.

Reed, Karen L. The Chinese in Tehama County: 1860-1890. (ANCRR Research Paper: No. 6). 1980. 4.00 (ISBN 0-686-38938-7). Assn NC Records.

Reed, Kate. One Hundred & One Uses for a Dead Preppie. LC 81-84866. (Illus.). 112p. (Orig.). 1981. pap. 2.95 (ISBN 0-89815-059-0). Ten Speed Pr.

Reed, Kathlyn & Sanderson, Sharon. OTR Concepts of Occupational Therapy. 2nd ed. (Illus.). 312p. 1983. text ed. price not set (ISBN 0-683-07205-6). Williams & Wilkins.

Reed, Kenneth T. S. N. Behrman. (United States Authors Ser.: No. 256). 1975. lib. bdg. 14.95 (ISBN 0-8057-7154-9, Twayne). G K Hall.

--Truman Capote. (United States Authors Ser.). 1981. lib. bdg. 10.95 (ISBN 0-8057-7321-5, Twayne). G K Hall.

Reed, Kit. Magic Time. 240p. 1981. pap. 2.25 o.p. (ISBN 0-425-04745-8). Berkley Pub.

--Magic Time. LC 79-14129. 1980. 10.95 (ISBN 0-399-12423-3). Putnam Pub Group.

Reed, Langford. The Complete Limerick Book: The Origin, History & Achievements of the Limerick. LC 78-175778. (Illus.). 147p. 1974. Repr. of 1925 ed. 30.00x (ISBN 0-8103-3974-9). Gale.

Reed, Louis S., et al. Health Insurance & Psychiatric Care: Utilization & Cost. 412p. 1972. 8.00 o.p. (ISBN 0-685-31187-2, 217). Am Psychiatric.

Reed, M. A. Mapping the Landscape: Studies in the Interpretation of Historical Documents. 1982. 80.00x o.p. (ISBN 0-86127-307-9, Pub. by Avebury Pub England). State Mutual Bk.

Reed, M. P. Residential Carpentry. 705p. 1980. 23.95 (ISBN 0-471-03164-X); tchr's. manual 5.00 (ISBN 0-471-07784-4). Wiley.

Reed, Marshall J. Data for Geothermal Wells in The Geysers-Clear Lake Area of California As of November 1980. (Special Report Ser.: No. 11). (Illus.). 37p. 1982. pap. 6.50 (ISBN 0-934412-11-1). Geothermal.

Reed, Maxine K. & Reed, Robert M. Career Opportunites in Television & Video. 248p. 1982. 19.95x (ISBN 0-87196-613-1). Facts on File.

Reed, Merl E., jt. ed. see Fink, Gary.

Reed, Michael. The Georgian Triumph: Seventeen Hundred to Eighteen Thirty. (Making of Britain Ser.). (Illus.). 224p. 1983. 24.95 (ISBN 0-7100-9414-0). Routledge & Kegan.

Reed, Mort. Encyclopedia of U. S. Coins. 3rd ed. (Illus.). 1983. lib. bdg. 19.95 (ISBN 0-915262-79-7). S J Durst.

Reed, Mortimer. Complete Guide to Residential Remodeling. (Illus.). 320p. 1983. 28.95 (ISBN 0-13-160663-8); pap. 14.95 (ISBN 0-13-160671-9). P-H.

Reed, Pat B. Nutrition: An Applied Science. (Illus.). 650p. 1980. text ed. 25.95 (ISBN 0-8299-0311-9); instrs.' manual avail. (ISBN 0-8299-0570-7). West Pub.

Reed, Prentiss B., Sr., jt. auth. see Thomas, Paul I.

Reed, R. D., jt. auth. see Roy, R. R.

Reed, Rex. Travolta to Keaton. LC 78-27028. (Illus.). 1979. 9.95 o.p. (ISBN 0-688-03434-9). Morrow.

Reed, Richard J. Cutaneous Vasculitides: Immunologic & Histologic Correlations. LC 77-22502. (Illus.). 50p. 1978. text ed. 20.00 o.s.i. (ISBN 0-89189-033-5, 16-1-028-00); text & slides 58.00 o.s.i. (ISBN 0-89189-097-1, 15-1-028-00). Am Soc Clinical.

Reed, Robert, ed. Thirty-Two Picture Postcards of Old Washington D.C. 1977. pap. 2.95 (ISBN 0-486-23418-5). Dover.

Reed, Robert D. Furnace Operations. 3rd ed. 230p. 1981. 29.95x (ISBN 0-87201-301-4). Gulf Pub.

--How & Where to Research & Find Information about Child Abuse. LC 82-60571. 40p. (Orig.). 1983. pap. 4.50 (ISBN 0-88247-692-0). R & E Res Assoc.

--How & Where to Research & Find Information on Aging in America. LC 82-60572. 80p. (Orig.). 1983. pap. 4.50 (ISBN 0-686-81658-7). R & E Res Assoc.

Reed, Robert M., jt. auth. see Reed, Maxine K.

Reed, Robert R. Colonial Manila: The Context of Hispanic Urbanism & Process of Morphogenesis. (Publications in Geography Ser.: Vol. 22). 1978. pap. 16.50x (ISBN 0-520-09579-0). U of Cal Pr.

Reed, Robert R., Jr. Occult on the Tudor & Stuart Stage. 1965. 6.50 o.p. (ISBN 0-8158-0170-X). Chris Mass.

Reed, Sampson. Observations on the Growth of the Mind with Remarks on Other Subjects. LC 78-100126. 1970. Repr. of 1838 ed. 25.00x (ISBN 0-8201-1070-1). Schol Facsimiles.

Reed, Stephen K. Cognition: Theory & Applications. LC 81-3829. 448p. 1981. text ed. 22.95 (ISBN 0-8185-0462-5). Brooks-Cole.

Reed, Suellen B., jt. auth. see Anderson, Edith H.

Reed, T. J. Thomas Mann: The Uses of Tradition. 1974. pap. 11.95x (ISBN 0-19-815747-9). Oxford U Pr.

Reed, T. M. & Gubbins, K. E. Applied Statistical Mechanics. (Chemical Engineering Ser.). (Illus.). 496p. 1973. text ed. 25.95 o.p. (ISBN 0-07-051495-X, C); solutions manual o.p. 4.00 o.p. (ISBN 0-07-051496-8). McGraw.

Reed, Terry. Indy: Race & Ritual. LC 79-25342. (Illus.). 1980. pap. 8.95 o.p. (ISBN 0-89141-075-9). Presidio Pr.

Reed, Thomas B. Free Energy of Formation of Binary Compounds: An Atlas of Charts for High Temperature Chemical Calculations. 1972. 20.00x (ISBN 0-262-18051-0). MIT Pr.

Reed, Thomas B., ed. see Swedish Academy of Engineering.

Reed, Thomas S. A Profile of Brigadire General Alfred N. A. Duffie. 1982. 11.00 (ISBN 0-89126-109-5). MA AH Pub.

Reed, W. L., ed. see Shaw, Martin & Coleman, Henry.

Reed, Walt. Great American Illustrators. LC 79-5378. 160p. 1980. 19.95 o.p. (ISBN 0-89659-075-5). Abbeville Pr.

--John Clymer: An Artist's Rendezvous with the Frontier West. LC 75-11164. (Illus.). 1976. 40.00 o.p. (ISBN 0-87358-151-2). Northland.

Reed, Walt, ed. The Figure: An Artist's Approach to Drawing & Construction. (Illus.). 144p. 1976. 16.00 o.p. (ISBN 0-8230-1695-1). Watson-Guptill.

Reed, William. Who's Who in Black Corporate America. Doggett, Edna, ed. (Illus.). 268p. 1982. 65.00 (ISBN 0-686-43317-3). Whos Who Corp.

Reede, Rien D. Die Flote in der Allgemeine Musikelische Zeitung' (1798-1848) (The Flute Library: Vol. 18). 350p. 1981. write for info. o.s.i. (ISBN 90-6027-324-9, Pub by Frits Knuf Netherlands). Pendragon NY.

Reeder, Carolyn & Reeder, Jack. Shenandoah Heritage: The Story of the People Before the Park. LC 78-61240. 1978. 3.95 (ISBN 0-915746-10-7). Potomac Appalach.

Reeder, D. A., ed. Urban Education in the Nineteenth Century. LC 77-26280. 1978. 22.50x (ISBN 0-312-83446-2). St Martin.

Reeder, David, ed. see Dyos, H. J.

Reeder, Jack, jt. auth. see Reeder, Carolyn.

Reeder, Maurice M. & Palmer, Philip E. The Radiology of Tropical Disease with Epidemiological, Pathological & Clinical Correlation. (Illus.). 1080p. 1981. lib. bdg. 125.00 (ISBN 0-683-07199-8). Williams & Wilkins.

Reeder, Rachel, ed. Liturgy: Diakonia. (Journal of The Liturgical Conference: Vol. 2, No. 4). (Illus.). 84p. (Orig.). 1982. pap. 7.95 (ISBN 0-918208-28-9). Liturgical Conf.

--Liturgy: Easter's Fifty Days. (Journal of The Liturgical Conference: Vol. 3, No. 1). (Illus.). 72p. 1982. pap. text ed. 7.95 (ISBN 0-918208-29-7). Liturgical Conf.

--Liturgy: One Church, Many Churches. (Quarterly Journal of The Liturgical Conference: Vol. 3, No. 2). (Illus.). 80p. (Orig.). 1983. pap. text ed. 7.95 (ISBN 0-918208-30-0). Liturgical Conf.

--Liturgy: With Lyre & Harp. (Quarterly Journal of The Liturgical Conference: Vol. 3, No. 3). (Illus.). 80p. (Orig.). 1983. pap. text ed. 7.95 (ISBN 0-918208-31-9). Liturgical Conf.

Reeder, Robert H., jt. auth. see Fisher, Edward C.

Reeder, Roberta, tr. see Lezhnev, Abram.

Reeder, Sharon, et al. Maternity Nursing. 14th ed. LC 79-22993. 775p. 1980. text ed. 24.95x o.p. (ISBN 0-397-54253-4, Lippincott Nursing). Lippincott.

Reeder, Sharon R. & Mastroianni, Luigi, Jr. Maternity Nursing. 15th ed. (Illus.). 1200p. 1983. text ed. 29.95 (ISBN 0-397-54369-7, Lippincott Medical). Lippincott.

Reed-Flora, Rosalind & Lang, Thomas A. Health Behaviors: Concepts, Values, & Options. (Illus.). 1982. pap. text ed. 17.50 (ISBN 0-8299-0358-5). West Pub.

Reed-Hill, Robert E. Physical Metallurgy Principles. 2nd ed. (University Ser. in Basic Engineering). 1973. text ed. 19.95 (ISBN 0-442-26868-8). Van Nos Reinhold.

Reedman, J. H. Techniques in Mineral Exploration. (Illus.). 1979. text ed. 53.50 (ISBN 0-85334-851-0, Pub. by Applied Sci England). Elsevier.

--Techniques of Mineral Exploration. (Applied Research Ser.). 1979. 92.25 (ISBN 0-85334-817-0); pap. 53.50 (ISBN 0-85334-851-0). Elsevier.

Reedman, Keith. The Book of Long Eaton. 1981. 39.50x o.p. (ISBN 0-86023-078-3, Pub. by Barracuda England). State Mutual Bk.

Reedy, George. Lyndon B. Johnson: A Memoir. 176p. 1982. text ed. 12.95 (ISBN 0-8362-6610-2). Andrews & McMeel.

Reedy, Jeremiah, jt. ed. see Ronning, Ronald H.

Reedy, William J., ed. Becoming a Catholic Christian. 198p. pap. 5.95 (ISBN 0-8215-9326-9). Sadlier.

Reekie, W. D. & Allen, D. E. Economics of Modern Business. 300p. 1983. text ed. 29.50x (ISBN 0-631-13115-9, Pub. by Basil Blackwell England). Biblio Dist.

Reekie, W. Duncan, jt. ed. see Hirst, I. R.

Reel, Jerome V., Jr. Index to Biographies of Englishmen, 1000-1485: Found in Dissertations & Theses. LC 74-19807. 689p. 1975. lib. bdg. 49.95 (ISBN 0-8371-7846-0, RIB/). Greenwood.

Reel, Rita & Reel, Val. TLC (Two Thousand Tips on Dog Care) Rev. ed. (Illus.). 240p. 1982. 12.95 (ISBN 0-9607100-2-7); pap. 9.95 (ISBN 0-9607100-1-9). Rival Pubs.

Reel, Val, jt. auth. see Reel, Rita.

Reeman, Douglas. The Deep Silence. 1968. 5.95 (ISBN 0-399-10204-3). Putnam Pub Group.

--The Deep Silence. 320p. 1982. pap. 2.95 (ISBN 0-515-06733-4). Jove Pubns.

--The Destroyers. 288p. 1974. 7.95 (ISBN 0-399-11399-1). Putnam Pub Group.

--The Greatest Enemy. pap. 2.25 o.s.i. (ISBN 0-515-05448-8). Jove Pubns.

--The Greatest Enemy. 1971. 5.95 o.s.i. (ISBN 0-399-10360-0). Putnam Pub Group.

--His Majesty's U-Boat. 288p. 1983. pap. 2.95 (ISBN 0-515-06747-4). Jove Pubns.

--The Last Raider. pap. 2.25 o.s.i. (ISBN 0-515-05730-4). Jove Pubns.

--Path of the Storm. 352p. 1983. pap. 2.95 (ISBN 0-515-06884-5). Jove Pubns.

--A Prayer for the Ship. 256p. 1973. 6.95 (ISBN 0-399-11139-5). Putnam Pub Group.

--The Pride & the Anguish: Dark Days in Singapore! 320p. pap. 2.95 (ISBN 0-515-06805-5). Jove Pubns.

--Rendezvous-South Atlantic. 320p. 1972. 6.95 (ISBN 0-399-10936-6). Putnam Pub Group.

--Surface with Daring. LC 76-39920. 1977. 8.95 (ISBN 0-399-11891-8). Putnam Pub Group.

--To Risks Unknown. 304p. pap. 2.95 (ISBN 0-515-06893-4). Jove Pubns.

--Torpedo Run. 272p. 1982. pap. 2.95 (ISBN 0-515-06638-9). Jove Pubns.

--Winged Escort. 1975. 7.95 o.s.i. (ISBN 0-399-11635-4). Putnam Pub Group.

Reep, Diana. The Rescue & Romances: Popular Novels Before World War 1. LC 82-61169. 144p. 1982. 12.95 (ISBN 0-87972-211-8); pap. 6.95 (ISBN 0-87972-212-6). Bowling Green Univ.

Rees, ed. see Greville, Fulke.

Rees, A. R. & Purcell, H. J. Disease & the Environment: Proceedings of the Inaugural Conference of the Society for Environmental Therapy Held in Oxford March, 1981. 206p. 1982. 43.95x (ISBN 0-471-10203-2, Pub. by Wiley Med). Wiley.

Rees, Alan, ed. Contemporary Problems in Technical Library & Information Center Management: A State-of-the-Art. LC 74-14289. 1974. 18.50 (ISBN 0-87715-107-5). Am Soc Info Sci.

Rees, Alan M., ed. Consumer Health Information Service, 1982. 125p. reference bk. 25.00 (ISBN 0-686-84112-3). Microfilming Corp.

Rees, Albert. The Economics of Trade Unions. 2nd rev. ed. LC 77-1668. 1977. 12.50x o.s.i. (ISBN 0-226-70701-6); pap. 4.95x (ISBN 0-226-70702-4, P279). U of Chicago Pr.

--The Economics of Work & Pay. 2nd ed. (Illus.). 1979. text ed. 19.50 scp (ISBN 0-06-045354-0, HarpC). Har-Row.

Rees, Albert, jt. ed. see Watts, Harold W.

Rees, Barbara. Harriet Dark: Branwell Bronte's Lost Novel. 1980. pap. 1.95 o.p. (ISBN 0-446-90356-6). Warner Bks.

Rees, Charles S., jt. auth. see Rees, Paul K.

Rees, Charles S., jt. auth. see Sparks, Fred W.

Rees, Clair. Off Road Vehicle Digest. 1980. pap. 7.95 o.s.i. (ISBN 0-695-81271-8). Follett.

Rees, Clair, jt. auth. see Elman, Robert.

Rees, Clair F. Beginner's Guide to Guns & Shooting. 1978. pap. 6.95 o.s.i. (ISBN 0-695-80945-8). Follett.

--The Digest Book of Trap & Skeet Shooting. (The Sports & Leisure Library). (Illus.). 96p. Date not set. pap. 2.95 (ISBN 0-695-81319-6). Follett. Postponed.

Rees, D. A. Polysaccharide Shapes. (Outline Studies in Biology). 1977. pap. 6.50x (ISBN 0-412-13030-0, Pub. by Chapman & Hall). Methuen Inc.

Rees, Dafydd & Lazell, Barry. Chart File, Vol. 2. 192p. (Orig.). 1983. pap. 2.95 (ISBN 0-933328-68-0). Delilah Bks.

Rees, David. Silence. 128p. (gr. 7 up). 1981. 10.75 (ISBN 0-525-66756-3, 01044-330). Lodestar Bks.

Rees, E. G. Notes in Geometry. (Universitexts Ser.). (Illus.). 109p. 1983. pap. 14.00 (ISBN 0-387-12053-X). Springer-Verlag.

Rees, Ennis. Fables from Aesop. (Illus.). 1966. 19.95x (ISBN 0-19-500077-3). Oxford U Pr.

Rees, G. J., ed. Semi-Insulating III-V Materials Nottingham 1980. 367p. 42.50 (ISBN 0-906812-05-4, Pub. by Shiva Pub England). Imprint Edns.

Rees, Goronwy. Chapter of Accidents. LC 73-161407. 270p. 1972. 17.00x o.p. (ISBN 0-912050-08-X, Library Pr). Open Court.

Rees, H., jt. auth. see Jones, R. N.

Rees, H. H. Insect Biochemistry. 1977. pap. 6.50x (ISBN 0-412-13130-7, Pub. by Chapman & Hall). Methuen Inc.

Rees, Hedley, jt. auth. see Hughes-Hallett, Andrew.

Rees, Helen G. Shaniko People. (Illus.). 1982. 10.95 (ISBN 0-8323-0414-X); pap. 7.95 (ISBN 0-8323-0415-8). Binford.

Rees, Henry. Australasia. 464p. 1975. 35.00x (ISBN 0-7121-0134-9, Pub. by MacDonald & Evans). State Mutual Bk.

Rees, Hubert & Jones, Robert N. Chromosome Genetics, Vol. III. LC 77-16211. (Genetics - Principles & Perspectives). 160p. 1978. pap. 19.95 (ISBN 0-8391-1195-9). Univ Park.

Rees, Joan. Jane Austen: Woman & Writer. LC 76-2166. 1976. 8.95 o.p. (ISBN 0-312-44030-8). St Martin.

--Shakespeare & the Story: Aspects of the Creation. 1978. text ed. 35.75x (ISBN 0-485-11179-9, Athlone Pr). Humanities.

Rees, John, et al, eds. Industrial Location & Regional Systems: Spatial Organization in the Economic Sector. (Illus.). 260p. 1981. 25.95x (ISBN 0-89789-008-6). J F Bergin.

Rees, L., ed. Proceedings: Fifth International Conference on Zeolites. 1980. 99.95 (ISBN 0-471-25989-6, Wiley Heyden). Wiley.

Rees, M. & Stoneham, R. Supernovae: A Survey of Current Research. 1982. 69.00 (ISBN 90-277-1442-8, Pub. by Reidel Holland). Kluwer Boston.

Rees, Martin, et al. Black Holes, Gravitational Waves & Cosmology: Introduction to Current Research. (Topics in Astrophysics & Space Physics Ser.). 436p. 1974. 60.00x (ISBN 0-677-04580-8). Gordon.

Rees, Paul, et al. Intermediate Algebra. 1978. text ed. 22.50 (ISBN 0-07-051731-2, C); instr's. manual 14.00 (ISBN 0-07-051732-0). McGraw.

Rees, Paul K. Analytic Geometry. 3rd ed. 1970. text ed. 19.95 (ISBN 0-13-034264-5); ans. suppl. 0.50 (ISBN 0-13-034272-6). P-H.

Rees, Paul K. & Rees, Charles S. Principles of Mathematics. 4th ed. (Illus.). 512p. 1982. 23.95 (ISBN 0-13-709691-7). P-H.

Rees, Paul K. & Sparks, Fred W. Algebra, Trigonometry & Analytic Geometry. 2nd ed. (Illus.). 512p. 1975. text ed. 27.50 (ISBN 0-07-051720-7, C); instr's. manual 15.00 (ISBN 0-07-051719-3). McGraw.

--Calculus with Analytic Geometry. LC 68-17508. (Illus.). 1969. text ed. 34.95 (ISBN 0-07-051675-8, C); instr's manual 11.95 (ISBN 0-07-051674-X). McGraw.

Rees, Paul K., et al. Algebra & Trigonometry. 3rd ed. (Illus.). 576p. 1975. text ed. 27.50 (ISBN 0-07-051723-1, C); instr's. manual 15.00 (ISBN 0-07-051721-5). McGraw.

--College Algebra. 8th, rev. ed. (Illus.). 560p. 1981. text ed. 24.50 (ISBN 0-07-051733-9); instr's. manual 10.00 (ISBN 0-07-051734-7). McGraw.

Rees, Robert & Menikoff, Barry. The Short Story: An Introductory Anthology. 2nd ed. 666p. 1975. pap. text ed. 10.95 (ISBN 0-316-73704-6); pap. instructor's manual avail. (ISBN 0-316-73705-4). Little.

Rees, Robert A., ed. see Irving, Washington.

Rees, Russell E. Fire on the Earth. LC 79-65676. 1979. 7.95 o.s.i. (ISBN 0-932970-07-9). Prinit Pr.

Rees, S., jt. auth. see Jefferson, K.

Rees, Samuel. David Jones. (English Authors Ser.). 1978. 14.95 (ISBN 0-8057-6726-6, Twayne). G K Hall.

Rees, Stuart & Wallace, Alison. Verdicts on Social Work. 224p. 1982. pap. text ed. 14.95 (ISBN 0-7131-6279-1). E Arnold.

Rees, Teresa L. & Atkinson, Paul. Youth Unemployment & State Intervention. 160p. 1983. pap. 11.95 (ISBN 0-7100-9263-6). Routledge & Kegan.

Rees, Thomas. Reminiscences of Literary London from 1779 - 1853. LC 68-24476. 1969. Repr. of 1896 ed. 30.00x (ISBN 0-8103-3888-2). Gale.

Rees, Wilbur E. Three Dollars Worth of God. LC 77-151044. 1971. 2.95 o.p. (ISBN 0-8170-0505-6). Judson.

Reese, Becky D., jt. auth. see Goetzman, William H.

Reese, Bob. The Critter Race. LC 81-3874. (Critterland Adventures Ser.). (Illus.). 24p. (ps-2). 1981. PLB 7.35 (ISBN 0-516-02302-0); pap. 1.75 (ISBN 0-516-42302-9). Childrens.

--Huzzard Buzzard. LC 81-6118. (Critterland Adventures Ser.). (Illus.). 24p. (ps-2). 1981. PLB 7.35 (ISBN 0-516-02303-9); pap. 1.75 (ISBN 0-516-42303-7). Childrens.
--Lactus Cactus. LC 81-3866. (Critterland Adventures Ser.). (Illus.). 24p. (ps-2). 1981. PLB 7.35 (ISBN 0-516-02304-7); pap. 1.75 (ISBN 0-516-42304-5). Childrens.
--Rapid Robert Roadrunner. LC 81-6090. (Critterland Adventures Ser.). (Illus.). 24p. (ps-2). 1981. PLB 7.35 (ISBN 0-516-02305-5); pap. 1.75 (ISBN 0-516-42305-3). Childrens.
--Scary Larry the Very Very Hairy Tarantula. LC 81-3871. (Critterland Adventures Ser.). (Illus.). 24p. (ps-2). 1981. 7.35 (ISBN 0-516-02306-3); pap. 1.75 (ISBN 0-516-42306-1). Childrens.
--Tweedle-De-Dee Tumbleweed. LC 81-6155. (Critterland Adventures Ser.). (Illus.). 24p. (ps-2). 1981. PLB 7.35 (ISBN 0-516-02307-1); pap. 1.75 (ISBN 0-516-42307-X). Childrens.
Reese, Craig E. Deregulation & Environmental Quality: The Use of Tax Policy to Control Pollution in North America & Western Europe. LC 82-11266. (Illus.). 480p. 1983. lib. bdg. 45.00 (ISBN 0-89930-018-9, RDE/, Quorum). Greenwood.
Reese, Craig E., jt. auth. see Crumbley, D. Larry.
Reese, Ernst S. & Lighter, Frederick J. Contrasts in Behavior: Adaptations in the Aquatic & Terrestrial Environments. LC 78-8284. 1978. 42.50 (ISBN 0-471-71390-2, Pub. by Wiley-Interscience). Wiley.
Reese, Francesca G., jt. ed. see Gardner, John W.
Reese, George, ed. The Official Papers of Francis Fauquier, Lieutenant Governor of Virginia, 1761-1763: Vol. II, 1761-1763. LC 80-19866. (Virginia Historical Society Documents Ser.: Vol. 15). 1065p. 1981. 50.00x (ISBN 0-8139-0895-7). U Pr of Va.
--Proceedings in the Court of Vice-Admiralty of Virginia: 1698-1775. write for info (ISBN 0-88490-113-0). Va State Lib.
Reese, Hayne, ed. Advances in Child Development & Behavior. Incl. Vol. 1. 1964. 39.50 (ISBN 0-12-009701-X); Vol. 2. Lipsitt, Lewis P. & Spiker, Charles G, eds. 1965. 41.50 (ISBN 0-12-009702-8); Vol. 3. 1967. 41.50 (ISBN 0-12-009703-6); Vol. 4. Lipsitt, Lewis P & Reese, Hayne W., eds. 1969. 41.50 (ISBN 0-12-009704-4); Vol. 5. 1970. 41.00 (ISBN 0-12-009705-2); Vol. 6. 1971. 41.50 (ISBN 0-12-009706-0); Vol. 7. 1973. 37.50 (ISBN 0-12-009707-9); Vol. 8. 1974. 37.50 (ISBN 0-12-009708-7); Vol. 9. 1974. 37.50 (ISBN 0-12-009709-5); Vol. 10. 1975. 37.50 (ISBN 0-12-009710-9); lib. ed. 49.50 (ISBN 0-12-009774-5); microfiche 27.00 (ISBN 0-12-009775-3); Vol. 11. 1976. 37.50 (ISBN 0-12-009711-7); lib. ed. 49.50 (ISBN 0-12-009776-1); microfiche 27.00 (ISBN 0-12-009777-X); Vol. 12. 1978. 32.00 (ISBN 0-12-009712-5); lib ed. 41.50 (ISBN 0-12-009778-8); microfiche 22.50 (ISBN 0-12-009779-6); Vol. 13. 1979. 33.00 (ISBN 0-12-009713-3); lib ed. 42.00 (ISBN 0-12-009780-X); microfiche 24.50 (ISBN 0-12-009781-8). LC 63-23237. Acad Pr.
Reese, Hayne W. Perception of Stimulus Relations: Discrimination Learning & Transposition. (Child Psychology Ser.). 1968. 53.50 (ISBN 0-12-585550-8). Acad Pr.
Reese, Hayne W. & Lipsitt, Lewis P., eds. Advances in Child Development & Behavior Vol. 14. LC 63-23237. 1979. 38.00 (ISBN 0-12-009714-1); lib ed. 48.50 (ISBN 0-12-009782-6); microfiche 28.00 (ISBN 0-12-009783-4). Acad Pr.
Reese, Hayne W. see Reese, Hayne.
Reese, Hayne W., jt. ed. see Turner, Ralph R.
Reese, James V. & Kennamer, Lorrin. Texas - Land of Contrast: Its History & Geography. (Illus.). (gr. 7). 1978. text ed. 17.32 (ISBN 0-87443-046-1); tchr's ed. 17.32 (ISBN 0-87443-047-X); preprinted masters 44.00 (ISBN 0-87443-048-8). Benson.
Reese, John. A Pair of Deuces. large print ed. LC 81-4463. 242p. 1981. 8.95x o.p. (ISBN 0-89621-274-2). Thorndike Pr.
Reese, Karen J., ed. see North American Prairie Conference, 6th, Ohio State Univ., Columbus, Ohio, Aug. 12-17, 1978.
Reese, Loretta. Fifty-Four Crafts with Easy Patterns. LC 78-62788. (Illus.). 1979. pap. 3.95 (ISBN 0-87239-175-2, 2134). Standard Pub.
Reese, Loretta, jt. auth. see Graff, Michelle.
Reese, Lyn & Wilkinson, Jean. I'm on My Way Running. 384p. 4.95 (ISBN 0-380-83022-1, Discus). Avon.
Reese, M. M. Shakespeare: His World & His Work. 2nd ed. 1980. 29.95 (ISBN 0-312-71421-1). St Martin.
Reese, M. M., ed. Elizabethan Verse Romances. (Routledge English Texts). 1971. 7.95 o.p. (ISBN 0-7100-4517-4); pap. 2.95 o.p. (ISBN 0-7100-4518-2). Routledge & Kegan.
Reese, M. M., ed. see Gibbon, Edward.
Reese, Mary Ellen, jt. auth. see Gulley, Bill.
Reese, Michael, II. Autographs of the Confederacy. LC 81-68377. 250p. 47.95 (ISBN 0-940746-00-X); deluxe ed. 89.95 (ISBN 0-686-42866-8). Cohasco.
Reese, Ralph, ed. The Secret Life of Cats. 112p. 1982. 10.95 (ISBN 0-02-040580-4). Macmillan.
Reese, Ray. How Many Things Can You Do in the Nude? (Illus.). 176p. (Orig.). 1982. pap. 9.95 (ISBN 0-89696-116-8, An Everest House Book). Dodd.
Reese, Richard G. Pilot's Guide to Southwestern Airports. (Illus.). 1983. 3 ring binder 28.95b (ISBN 0-686-43374-2, Pub. by RGR Pubns.). Aviation.
Reese, T. & Trezel, S. Snares & Swindles in Bridge. 1981. pap. 15.00x (ISBN 0-686-97601-0, Pub. by Gollancz England). State Mutual Bk.
Reese, Terence. Begin Bridge with Reese. 1979. pap. 2.50 (ISBN 0-451-08478-0, W8478, Sig). NAL.
--Bridge Conventions, Finesses & Coups. (Illus.). 1970. pap. 3.50 (ISBN 0-486-22631-X). Dover.
--Winning at Casino Gambling. 1979. pap. 2.50 (ISBN 0-451-12335-2, AE2335, Sig). NAL.
--Your Book of Contract Bridge. (gr. 7 up). 1971. 5.50 o.p. (ISBN 0-571-06387-X). Transatlantic.
Reese, Terence & Bird, David. Bridge: The Modern Game. 256p. 1983. 15.95 (ISBN 0-571-13053-4). Faber & Faber.
--Miracles of Card Play. (Master Bridge Ser.). (Illus.). 128p. 1982. 15.95 (ISBN 0-575-03079-8, Pub. by Gollancz England). David & Charles.
Reese, Terence & Jourdain, Patrick. Squeeze Play Made Easy. LC 80-52344. (Illus.). 160p. 1980. 8.95 o.p. (ISBN 0-8069-4940-6); lib. bdg. 8.29 o.p. (ISBN 0-8069-4941-4). Sterling.
Reese, Terence & Trezel, Roger. Blocking & Unblocking Plays in Bridge. (Master Bridge Ser.). (Illus.). 128p. 1980. pap. 4.50 (ISBN 0-575-02749-5, Pub. by Gollancz England). David & Charles.
--Safety Plays in Bridge. (Master Bridge Ser.). (Illus.). 128p. 1976. pap. 4.50 (ISBN 0-575-02748-7, Pub. by Gollancz England). David & Charles.
--Those Extra Chances in Bridge. (Master Bridge Ser.). (Illus.). 128p. 1978. pap. 4.50 (ISBN 0-575-02634-0, Pub. by Gollancz England). David & Charles.
--When to Duck, WHen to Win in Bridge. (Master Bridge Ser.). (Illus.). 128p. 1978. pap. 4.50 (ISBN 0-575-02635-9, Pub. by Gollancz England). David & Charles.
Reese, Terence & Watkins, Anthony. Poker: Game of Skill. 176p. (Orig.). 1964. pap. 4.95 (ISBN 0-571-05869-8, +014). Faber & Faber.
Reese, Terence, tr. see Sharif, Omar.
Reese, Thomas J. The Politics of Taxation. LC 79-8413. (Illus.). xxv, 237p. 1980. lib. bdg. 25.00 (ISBN 0-89930-003-0, RPT/, Quorum). Greenwood.
Reese, William L. & Freeman, Eugene, eds. Process & Divinity: The Hartshorne Festschrift. LC 64-13547. 644p. 1964. 30.00x (ISBN 0-87548-054-3). Open Court.
Reeser, Clayton & Loper, Marvin. Management: The Key to Organizational Effectiveness. 1978. pap. 17.95x (ISBN 0-673-15077-1). Scott F.
Reesink, Marijke. The Princess Who Always Ran Away. (Illus.). 32p. (gr. k-4). 1981. 9.95 (ISBN 0-07-051714-2). McGraw.
Reetz, Elaine. Come Back in Time, Vol. 2. (Illus.). 240p. 1982. pap. 9.95 (ISBN 0-939398-03-6). Fox River.
Reeve, F. A. Victorian & Edwardian Cambridge. 1971. pap. 10.50 o.p. (ISBN 0-7134-0093-5, Pub. by Batsford England). David & Charles.
Reeve, F. D., tr. see Solzhenitsyn, Alexander.
Reeve, Kay A. Santa Fe & Taos, Eighteen Ninety Eight to Nineteen Forty-Two: An American Cultural Center. Treadwell, Hugh W., ed. (Southwestern Studies: No. 67). (Illus.). 72p. 1982. 10.00x (ISBN 0-87404-126-0); pap. 4.00x (ISBN 0-686-97220-1). Tex Western.
Reeve, Pamela. Faith Is. 1970. pap. 4.95 (ISBN 0-930014-05-7). Multnomah.
--La Fe Es. Orig. Title: Faith Is. 50p. (Span.). 1983. spiral bd 4.95 (ISBN 0-930014-96-0). Multnomah.
--Parables by the Sea. LC 77-6209. (Illus.). 1976. gift ed. o.p. 5.95 (ISBN 0-930014-10-3); pap. 5.95 (ISBN 0-930014-11-1). Multnomah.
--Parables by the Sea. pap. 4.95 (ISBN 0-8423-4798-4); pap. 5.95 deluxe ed. (ISBN 0-8423-4799-2). Tyndale.
Reeve, William C. Georg Buchner. LC 77-4599. (Literature and Life Ser.). (Illus.). 1979. 11.95 (ISBN 0-8044-2711-9). Ungar.
Reeves, jt. auth. see Tozzini.
Reeves, A. C. Lancastrian Englishmen. LC 81-40138. 432p. (Orig.). 1982. lib. bdg. 26.25 (ISBN 0-8191-1943-1); pap. text ed. 15.50 (ISBN 0-8191-1944-X). U Pr of Amer.
Reeves, A. Compton, ed. see Mudroch, Vaclav.
Reeves, Andrew L. Toxicology: Principles & Practice, Vol. 1. LC 80-19259. 224p. 1981. 32.00 (ISBN 0-471-71340-6, Pub. by Wiley-Interscience). Wiley.
Reeves, C. C., Jr. Introduction to Paleolimnology. (Developments in Sedimentology: Vol. 11). 1968. 60.50 (ISBN 0-444-40768-5). Elsevier.
Reeves, C. M. An Introduction to Logical Design of Digital Circuits. LC 77-182029. (Computer Science Texts Ser.: No. 1). (Illus.). 200p. 1972. text ed. 12.95 (ISBN 0-521-09705-3). Cambridge U Pr.
Reeves, Campbell. Coming Out Even. LC 73-77499. 1973. 9.95 (ISBN 0-87716-043-0, Pub. by Moore Pub Co). F Apple.
Reeves, Charles A. & Clark, Thom B. Mathematics for the Elementary School Teacher. 1982. text ed. 21.95x (ISBN 0-673-16051-3). Scott F.
Reeves, Clyde H. & Ellsworth, Scott, eds. The Role of the State in Property Taxation. LC 82-48536. (Lincoln Institute of Land Policy Books). 1983. write for info. (ISBN 0-669-06292-8). Lexington Bks.
Reeves, Dona B., jt. ed. see Lich, Glen E.
Reeves, Earl. Aviation's Place in Tomorrow's Business. (Airlines History Project Ser.). Date not set. price not set (ISBN 0-404-19331-5). AMS Pr.
Reeves, Earl, jt. ed. see Filipovitch, Anthony.
Reeves, Emma B. Reeves Review, Book II. LC 82-61874. (Illus.). 504p. 1982. lib. bdg. 30.00 (ISBN 0-911013-00-8). E B Reeves.
Reeves, Gearldine. Creating Japanese Floral Art. 96p. Date not set. 8.95 (ISBN 0-686-82962-X); pap. 5.95 (ISBN 0-89496-032-6). Ross Bks.
Reeves, George. Idioms in Action. 1975. pap. 8.95 (ISBN 0-912066-63-6). Newbury Hse.
Reeves, Henry. In a Meadow's Calm. LC 79-70025. 1971. 4.00 (ISBN 0-911838-13-9). Windy Row.
Reeves, Hubert. Evolution Stellaire et Nucleosynthese. (Cours & Documents de Mathematiques & de Physique Ser.). 114p. (Orig.). 1968. 26.00x (ISBN 0-677-50150-1). Gordon.
--Nuclear Reactions in Stellar Surfaces & Their Relations with Stellar Evolution. (Topics in Astrophysics & Space Physics Ser). (Illus.). 100p. 1971. 24.00x (ISBN 0-677-02960-8). Gordon.
Reeves, James. Collected Poems 1929-1974. 1974. text ed. 24.50x o.p. (ISBN 0-435-14770-6). Heinemann Ed.
--Commitment to Poetry. 1969. 10.00x o.p. (ISBN 0-435-18769-4). Heinemann Ed.
--The Critical Sense. 1956. text ed. 5.00x o.p. (ISBN 0-435-18765-1). Heinemann Ed.
--The Critical Sense: Practical Criticism of Prose & of Poetry. 159p. 1982. Repr. of 1956 ed. lib. bdg. 25.00 (ISBN 0-8495-4700-8). Arden Lib.
--Teaching Poetry. 1958. pap. text ed. 8.00x o.p. (ISBN 0-435-14762-5). Heinemann Ed.
Reeves, James & Culpan, Norman. Dialogue & Drama. 1950. pap. text ed. 4.00x o.p. (ISBN 0-435-23751-9). Heinemann Ed.
Reeves, James & Seymour-Smith, Martin. Inside Poetry. 1970. text ed. 9.50x o.p. (ISBN 0-435-18772-4). Heinemann Ed.
Reeves, James, retold by. Giants & Warriors. (Illus., Orig.). 1978. pap. 2.95 o.p. (ISBN 0-8467-0540-0, Pub. by Two Continents). Hippocrene Bks.
--Heroes & Monsters. (Illus., Orig.). 1978. pap. 2.95 o.p. (ISBN 0-8467-0539-7, Pub. by Two Continents). Hippocrene Bks.
Reeves, James, ed. see Sharp, Cecil J.
Reeves, John. Murder by Microphone. 224p. 1980. pap. 2.25 o.p. (ISBN 0-380-43729-5, 43729). Avon.
Reeves, John & Maibach, Howard. Clinical Dermatology Illustrated. 250p. 1983. text ed. write for info. (ISBN 0-86792-010-6, Pub by Adis Pr Australia). Wright-PSG.
Reeves, John A., jt. auth. see Freedley, George.
Reeves, John A., jt. auth. see Simon, J. Malcolm.
Reeves, John P., ed. Microbial Permeability. LC 73-4299. (Benchmark Papers in Microbiology Ser). 442p. 1973. 55.50 (ISBN 0-12-787320-1). Acad Pr.
Reeves, Lawrence. Mopeds: A Guide to Models, Maintenance, & Safety. (Illus.). 96p. (gr. 8-11). 1983. PLB 8.79 (ISBN 0-671-46100-1). Messner.
Reeves, Marjorie. Explorers of the Elizabethan Age. (Then & There Ser.). (Illus.). 96p. (gr. 7-12). 1977. pap. text ed. 3.10 (ISBN 0-582-21728-8). Longman.
--The Medieval Castle. (Then & There Ser.). 105p. (gr. 7-12). 1963. pap. text ed. 3.10 (ISBN 0-582-20392-9). Longman.
--The Medieval Monastery: Then & There Ser. (Illus.). 90p. (Orig.). (gr. 7-12). 1980. pap. text ed. 3.10 (ISBN 0-582-20372-4). Longman.
--The Medieval Town. (Then & There Ser.). (Illus.). 90p. (gr. 7-12). 1954. pap. text ed. 3.10 (ISBN 0-582-20374-0). Longman.
--The Medieval Village. (Then & There Ser.). (Illus.). 90p. (Orig.). (gr. 7-12). 1954. pap. text ed. 3.10 (ISBN 0-582-20375-9). Longman.
--The Norman Conquest. (Then & There Ser.). (Illus.). 60p. (Orig.). (gr. 7-12). 1959. pap. text ed. 3.10 (ISBN 0-582-20378-3). Longman.
Reeves, Marjorie, jt. auth. see Addy, John.
Reeves, Marjorie, jt. auth. see Longmate, Elizabeth.
Reeves, Marjorie, jt. auth. see Rosenthal, Miriam.
Reeves, Marjorie, jt. auth. see Stokes, Gweneth.
Reeves, Marjorie, jt. auth. see Taylor, Geoffrey.
Reeves, Marjorie, ed. see Barrett, G. W.
Reeves, Marjorie, ed. see Beacroft, B. W.
Reeves, Marjorie, ed. see Beacroft, Bernard.
Reeves, Marjorie, ed. see Bolton, James.
Reeves, Marjorie, ed. see Bradbury, Jim.
Reeves, Marjorie, ed. see Chamberlain, E. R.
Reeves, Marjorie, ed. see Cubitt, Heather.
Reeves, Marjorie, ed. see Currie, Barbara.
Reeves, Marjorie, ed. see Dorner, Jane.
Reeves, Marjorie, ed. see Evans, Gillian.
Reeves, Marjorie, ed. see Gill, W. J.
Reeves, Marjorie, ed. see Greenwood, Marjorie.
Reeves, Marjorie, ed. see Holt, J. C.
Reeves, Marjorie, ed. see Liversidge, Joan.
Reeves, Marjorie, ed. see Lonsdale, Anne.
Reeves, Marjorie, ed. see Mack, Donald W.
Reeves, Marjorie, ed. see McWilliam, H. O.
Reeves, Marjorie, ed. see Mitchell, R. J.
Reeves, Marjorie, ed. see Mitchison, Naomi.
Reeves, Marjorie, ed. see Power, E. G.
Reeves, Marjorie, ed. see Price, Mary.
Reeves, Marjorie, ed. see Proctor, G. L.
Reeves, Marjorie, ed. see Ritchie, W. K.
Reeves, Marjorie, ed. see Rithchie, W. K.
Reeves, Marjorie, ed. see Sheppard, E. J.
Reeves, Marjorie, ed. see Speed, P. F.
Reeves, Marjorie, ed. see Sylvester, David W.
Reeves, Marjorie, ed. see Tate, Nicholas.
Reeves, Marjorie, ed. see Turner, Derek.
Reeves, Marjorie, ed. see West, John.
Reeves, Marjorie, ed. see Williams, Ann.
Reeves, Maud P. Round about a Pound a Week. 234p. 1983. pap. 6.95 (ISBN 0-86068-066-5, Virago Pr). Merrimack Bk Serv.
Reeves, Michael. Travolta: A Photo Bio. (Illus.). 1978. pap. 1.95 o.s.i. (ISBN 0-515-04850-X). Jove Pubns.
Reeves, Nigel, jt. auth. see Dewhurst, Kenneth.
Reeves, Paschal. Merrill Studies in Look Homeward Angel. LC 70-119518. 1970. pap. text ed. 3.50x o.p. (ISBN 0-675-09354-6). Merrill.
Reeves, Perry B., jt. auth. see Lowman, Robert G.
Reeves, R. B., ed. Application of Walls to Landslide Control Problems. LC 82-70668. 144p. 1982. pap. text ed. 14.00 (ISBN 0-87262-302-5). Am SOc Civil Eng.
Reeves, R. D. & Brooks, R. R. Trace Element Analysis of Geological Materials. LC 78-8064. (Chemical Analysis: Monographs on Analytical Chemistry & Its Applications). 1978. 57.50 (ISBN 0-471-71338-4, Pub. by Wiley-Interscience). Wiley.
Reeves, Robert G. Flora of Central Texas. Orig. Title: Flora of South Central Texas. 1977. pap. text ed. 11.50x (ISBN 0-934786-00-3). G Davis.
Reeves, Robert G., ed. Manual of Remote Sensing, 2 vols. Incl. Vol. 1. Theory, Principles & Techniques; Vol. 2. Photographic Interpretation & Applications. LC 75-7552. (Illus.). 1975. 45.00 o.p. (ISBN 0-937294-04-7). ASP.
Reeves, Sally K. & Reeves, William D. Historic City Park: New Orleans. (Illus.). 256p. 1982. 24.95 (ISBN 0-9610062-0-X). Friends City Park.
Reeves, Thomas C. The Life & Times of Joe McCarthy. LC 79-3730. 1981. 19.95. Stein & Day.
--McCarthyism. 2nd ed. LC 81-18575. 1982. pap. text ed. 5.95 (ISBN 0-89874-426-1). Krieger.
Reeves, William D., jt. auth. see Reeves, Sally K.
Reeves, William J. Librarians As Professionals: The Occupation's Impact on Library Work Arrangements. LC 79-2389. (Illus.). 192p. 1980. 22.95x (ISBN 0-669-03163-1). Lexington Bks.
Reference International Publishers. Handbook of Architectural Technology. (Illus.). 1979. 32.50 (ISBN 0-07-051740-1, P&RB). McGraw.
Reff, Theodore. Manet & Modern Paris. 1982. pap. 17.50 (ISBN 0-89468-060-9). Natl Gallery Art.
--Manet & Modern Paris: One Hundred Paintings, Drawings, Prints, & Photographs by Manet & His Contemporaries. LC 82-18965. (Illus.). 280p. 1983. 39.95 (ISBN 0-226-70720-2); pap. write for info. U of Chicago Pr.
Refsum, S. & Bolis, C. L., eds. International Conference on Peripheral Neuropathies: Proceedings, International Conference, Madrid, June, 1981. (International Congress Ser.: No. 592). 210p. 1982. 62.75 (ISBN 0-444-90277-5, Excerpta Medica). Elsevier.
Regan, David. Evoked Potentials in Psychology, Sensory Physiology, & Clinical Medicine. 300p. 1972. 34.95x (ISBN 0-412-10920-4, Pub. by Chapman & Hall England). Methuen Inc.
Regan, J. Peter. Massachusetts Real Estate Principles & Practices. 1978. pap. text ed. 14.95 (ISBN 0-316-73844-1); tchr's. ed. avail. (ISBN 0-316-73846-8). Little.
Regan, Jane, jt. auth. see Cove, Mary.
Regan, Tom. Matters of Life & Death. 341p. 1980. pap. text ed. 10.00 (ISBN 0-394-32114-6). Random.
Regan, Tom, ed. Matters of Life & Death: New Introductory Essays in Moral Philosophy. 368p. 1980. 29.95 (ISBN 0-87722-181-2). Temple U Pr.
Regardie. Stress Control & Relaxation: A Bio-Holistic Approach to Self-Control & Health. 1983. pap. 7.95 (ISBN 0-686-43155-3). Falcon Pr Az.
--Wilhelm Reich: His Theory & Therapy. 1983. price not set. Falcon Pr Az.
Regardie & Hyatt. Liber Nuts. 1983. price not set. Falcon Pr Az.
Regardie, Israel. The Complete Golden Dawn System of Magic, 2 vols. 1200p. 1983. Vol. 1. 59.54 (ISBN 0-941404-12-9); Vol. 1. collector's ed. 150.00 (ISBN 0-941404-11-0); Vol. 2. 59.95 (ISBN 0-941404-14-5); Vol. 2. collector's ed. 150.00 (ISBN 0-941404-13-7). Falcon Pr Az.
--Energy, Prayer & Relaxation. 80p. 1982. pap. 6.95 (ISBN 0-941404-02-1). Falcon Pr Az.
--Eye in the Triangle. 523p. 1982. 49.95 (ISBN 0-941404-07-2); pap. 12.95 (ISBN 0-941404-08-0). Falcon Pr Az.
--Foundations of Practical Magic. 160p. 1983. pap. 6.95 (ISBN 0-85030-315-X). Newcastle Pub.
--Gems from the Equinox. 1100p. 1982. Repr. of 1974 ed. 39.95 (ISBN 0-941404-10-2). Falcon Pr Az.
--A Practical Guide to Geomantic Divination. pap. 2.50 (ISBN 0-87728-170-X). Weiser.
--What You Should Know About the Golden Dawn. 3rd, rev. ed. 220p. 1983. pap. 10.95 (ISBN 0-941404-15-3). Falcon Pr Az.
Regardie, Israel & Hyatt, Christopher S. The Regardie Tapes. 1982. pap. 49.95 set of 6 (ISBN 0-941404-05-6); pap. 11.95 each. Falcon Pr Az.

Regardie, Israel & Stephensen, P. R. The Legend of Aleister Crowley. 175p. 1983. pap. 9.95 (ISBN 0-941404-20-X). Falcon Pr Az.
Regardie, Israel, jt. auth. see Crowley, Aleister.
Regardie, Israel, ed. see Crowley, Aleister.
Regazzoni, Guido, jt. auth. see Bigon, Mario.
Regel, C. Von see Von Wiesner, J. & Von Regel, C.
Regelski, Thomas A. Arts Education & Brain Research. 32p. 1978. 2.00 (ISBN 0-940796-22-8, 1002). Music Ed.
--Principles & Problems of Music Education. (Illus.). 328p. 1975. ref. ed. o.p. 17.95 (ISBN 0-13-709840-5); pap. 18.95 ref. ed. (ISBN 0-13-709832-4). P-H.
--Teaching General Music: Action Learning for Middle & Secondary Schools. LC 80-5561. (Illus.). 448p. 1981. text ed. 14.95 (ISBN 0-02-872070-9). Schirmer Bks.
Regener, Eric. Pitch Notation & Equal Temperament: A Formal Study. (U. C. Publ: Occasional Papers: No. 6). pap. 19.50x (ISBN 0-520-09453-0). U of Cal Pr.
Regensteiner, Else. The Art of Weaving. 1982. 20.95x (ISBN 0-87245-455-X). Textile Bk.
Regent House, ed. Sugarless Recipes Cookbook. 88p. 1983. pap. 7.95 (ISBN 0-911238-71-9). Regent House.
Reger, Roger, et al. Special Education: Children with Learning Problems. (Illus.). 1968. 9.95x (ISBN 0-19-501031-0). Oxford U Pr.
Regestein, Quentin R. & Rechs, James R. Sound Sleep. 1980. 10.95 o.p. (ISBN 0-671-24960-6). S&S.
Regester, Seeley. The Dead Letter. 1979. lib. bdg. 9.95 (ISBN 0-8398-2534-X, Gregg). G K Hall.
Reggie the Retiree, pseud. Laughs & Limericks on Aging. large print ed. (Illus.). 96p. 1982. pap. 4.95 (ISBN 0-9609960-0-1). Reggie the Retiree.
Reggio, Kathryn & Davidson, Josephine. Individualized Health Incentive Program Modules For Physically Disabled Students, 5 Vols. Shooltz, Danna, ed. Incl. Vol. 1. Safety & Survival Education. 336p. 1976; Vol. 2. Environmental & Community Health. 62p; Vol. 3. Sociological Health Problems. 56p. 1977; Vol. 4. Mental Health & Family Life Education. (Illus.). 138p. 1977; Vol. 5. Physical Health. (Illus.). 138p. 1977. 4.50 ea.; 17.50 set (ISBN 0-686-38806-2). Human Res Ctr.
Regier, Margaret I. You Don't Like Me Anymore. (Illus.). 109p. (Orig.). 1979. pap. 3.50 o.p. (ISBN 0-940644-01-0). River Hse.
Regier, Marilyn C. Social Policy in Action: Perspectives on the Implementation of Alcoholism Reforms. LC 78-20274. 208p. 1979. 23.95x (ISBN 0-669-02716-2). Lexington Bks.
Regier, Mary H. & Mohapatra, Ram N. Biomedical Statistics with Computing. (Medical Computing Ser.). 309p. 1982. 34.95 (ISBN 0-471-10449-3, Pub. by REs Stud Pr). Wiley.
Reginald, R. By Any Other Name: A Comprehensive Checklist of Science Fiction & Fantasy Pseudonyms. LC 80-10924. (Reference Library: Vol. 9). 128p. 1983. lib. bdg. 9.95x (ISBN 0-89370-805-4); pap. 3.95x (ISBN 0-89370-905-0). Borgo Pr.
--A Guide to Science Fiction & Fantasy in the Library of Congress Classification Scheme. LC 80-11418. (Borgo Reference Library: Vol. 8). 64p. 1983. lib. bdg. 9.95x (ISBN 0-89370-807-0); pap. 3.95x (ISBN 0-89370-907-7). Borgo Pr.
--Science Fiction & Fantasy Awards. LC 80-10788. (Borgo Reference Library: Vol. 2). 64p. 1981. lib. bdg. 9.95x (ISBN 0-89370-806-2); pap. text ed. 3.95x (ISBN 0-89370-906-9). Borgo Pr.
--To Be Continued... An Annotated Bibliography of Science Fiction & Fantasy Series & Sequels. LC 80-11206. (Borgo Reference Library: Vol. 11). 64p. 1983. lib. bdg. 9.95x (ISBN 0-89370-808-9); pap. 3.95x (ISBN 0-89370-908-5). Borgo Pr.
--X, Y & Z: A List of Those Books Examined in the Course of Compiling Science Fiction & Fantasy Literature, a Checklist, 1700 to 1974, with Contemporary Science Fiction Authors II, Which Were Judged to Fall Outside the Genre of Fantastic Literature; an Anti-Bibliography. LC 80-11697. (Borgo Reference Library: Vol. 10). 160p. 1983. lib. bdg. 19.95x (ISBN 0-89370-809-7); pap. 9.95x (ISBN 0-89370-909-3). Borgo Pr.
Reginald, R. & Burgess, Mary A. The Milford Series: Popular Writers of Today; an Index to Volumes 1 to 40. LC 80-15340. (Borgo Reference Library: Vol. 5). 64p. 1983. lib. bdg. 9.95x (ISBN 0-89370-803-8); pap. 3.95x (ISBN 0-89370-903-4). Borgo Pr.
Reginald, R. & Currey, L. W. Science-Fiction Price Guide. LC 80-22693. (Borgo Reference Library: Vol. 7). 256p. (Orig.). 1983. lib. bdg. 29.95x (ISBN 0-89370-150-5); pap. text ed. 19.95x (ISBN 0-89370-250-1). Borgo Pr.
Reginald, R. & Elliot, Jeffrey M. Tempest in a Teapot: The Falkland Islands War. (Stokvis Studies in Historical Chronology & Thought: Vol. 3). 128p. 1983. lib. bdg. 11.95x (ISBN 0-89370-167-X); pap. text ed. 5.95x (ISBN 0-89370-267-6). Borgo Pr.
Reginald, R. & Lewis, Dan. In His Native Habitat: Characteristics of the Science-Fiction Writer. LC 80-11207. (Borgo Reference Library: Vol. 1). 64p. 1983. lib. bdg. 9.95x (ISBN 0-89370-810-0); pap. text ed. 3.95x (ISBN 0-89370-910-7). Borgo Pr.
--Science Fiction & Fantasy Statistics. LC 80-10690. (Borgo Reference Library: Vol. 3). 64p. 1983. lib. bdg. 9.95x (ISBN 0-89370-804-6); pap. 3.95x (ISBN 0-89370-904-2). Borgo Pr.
Reginald, R., jt. auth. see Currey, L. W.
Reginald, R., jt. auth. see Elliot, Jeffrey M.
Reginald, R., jt. auth. see Hancer, Kevin B.
Reginald, R., jt. auth. see Menville, Douglas A.
Reginald, R., ed. see Morris, Kenneth.
Reginald, Robert, ed. Science Fiction & Fantasy Literature: A Checklist from 1700 to 1974...with Contemporary Science Fiction Authors II, 2 vols. LC 76-46130. 1979. 145.00x set (ISBN 0-8103-1051-1). Gale.
Reginald, Robert & Burgess, M. R., eds. Cumulative Paperback Index, Nineteen Thirty-Nine to Nineteen Fifty-Nine: A Comprehensive Bibliographic Guide to 14,000 Mass-Market Paperback Books of 33 Publishers Issued Under 69 Imprints. LC 73-6866. 375p. 1973. 40.00x (ISBN 0-8103-1050-3). Gale.
Regino, Thomas, jt. auth. see Cheremisinoff, Paul N.
Regional Conference for Asia & the Far East, 3rd, Bandung, 1956. Report. 94p. 1957. pap. 4.25 (ISBN 0-686-92902-0, F390, FAO). Unipub.
Regional Conference for Latin America, 4th, Santiago, 1956. Report. 89p. 1957. pap. 4.75 (ISBN 0-686-92898-9, F378, FAO). Unipub.
Regional Conference on Water Resources Development in Asia & the Far East, 9th Session. Proceedings. (Water Resources Development Ser.: No. 40). pap. 6.00 (ISBN 0-686-92926-8, UN72/2F20, UN). Unipub.
Regional Conference on Water Resources Development in Asia & the Far East, 10th Session. Proceedings. (Water Resources Development Ser.: No. 44). pap. 8.50 (ISBN 0-686-92936-5, UN74/2F10, UN). Unipub.
Regional Fisheries Advisory Commission for the Southwest Atlantic, 6th Session, Montevideo, 1974. Report. (FAO Fisheries Reports: No. 159). 65p. 1975. pap. 7.50 (ISBN 0-686-93982-4, F861, FAO). Unipub.
Regional Plan Association. Office Industry: Patterns of Growth & Location. Armstrong, R. B., ed. 1972. 25.00x (ISBN 0-262-18052-9). MIT Pr.
Regional Seminar on Community Preparedness & Disaster Prevention. Proceedings. (Water Resources Development Ser.: No. 49). pap. 10.00 (ISBN 0-686-92999-3, UN78/2F13, UN). Unipub.
Regional Seminar on Methods of Amelioration of Saline & Waterlogged Soils, Baghdad, 1970. Salinity Seminar: Report. (Irrigation & Drainage Papers: No. 7). 260p. 1969. pap. 17.00 (ISBN 0-686-92708-7, F976, FAO). Unipub.
Regional Seminar on Synoptic Analysis & Forecasting in the Tropics of Asia & the South-West Pacific, Singapore, 1970. Proceedings. (WMO Pubns. Ser.: No. 321). 552p. 1972. pap. 55.00 (ISBN 0-686-93906-9, WMO). Unipub.
Regional Symposium on the Development of Deltaic Areas, 3rd. Proceedings. (Water Resources Development Ser.: No. 50). pap. 17.00 (ISBN 0-686-92995-0, UN78/2F10, UN). Unipub.
Regional Technical Conference on Flood Control in Asia & the Far East, 1951. Proceedings. (Water Resources Development Ser.: No. 3). pap. 5.00 (ISBN 0-686-92923-3, UN53/2F1, UN). Unipub.
Regional Workshops on Aqualculture Planning in Asia, Bangkok, 1975. Aquaculture Planning in Asia: Report. (Fisheries Papers: No. 1). 157p. 1976. pap. 10.50 o.p. (ISBN 92-5-100010-7, F718, FAO). Unipub.
Regis, Louis-Marie. Saint Thomas & Epistemology. (Aquinas Lecture Ser.). 1946. 7.95 (ISBN 0-87462-110-0). Marquette.
Register, W. Raymond. Discovery by Lamplight. 64p. 1972. 4.00 o.p. (ISBN 0-685-25029-6). Golden Quill.
Regmi, Mahesh C. Landownership in Nepal. LC 74-77734. 1976. 38.50x (ISBN 0-520-02750-7). U of Cal Pr.
Regnault, F. Aging of the Lens: Cellular & Biochemical Aspects. 1980. 62.50 (ISBN 0-444-80217-7). Elsevier.
Regnault, F. & Duhault, J., eds. Cellular & Biochemical Aspects in Diabetic Retinopathy. (Inserm Symposium Ser.: Vol. 7). 1978. 61.50 (ISBN 0-7204-0661-7, ISY 7, Biomedical Pr). Elsevier.
Regnault-Warin, Jean-Joseph. Elements De Politique. (Rousseauism: 1788-1797 Ser.). (Fr.). 1978. Repr. of 1792 ed. lib. bdg. 63.50x o.p. (ISBN 0-8287-0711-1). Clearwater Pub.
Regner, Hermann, ed. Music for Children. (Orff-Schulwerk: Vol. 2). 1977. pap. 22.50 (ISBN 0-930448-00-6). Eur-Am Music.
Regnery, Henry. Memoirs of a Dissident Publisher. LC 78-22269. 260p. 1979. 12.95 (ISBN 0-15-173752-5). Regnery-Gateway.
Regniers, Beatrice S. De see De Regniers, Beatrice S.
Regniers, Beatrice S. De see De Regniers, Beatrice S. & Haas, Irene.
Regniers, Beatrice S. De see De Regniers, Beatrice S. & Pierce, Leona.
Regniers, Beatrice Schenk de. Going for a Walk. LC 81-48065. (Illus.). 32p. (ps-1). 1982. Repr. of 1961 ed. 7.64 (ISBN 0-06-024851-3, HarpJ); PLB 7.89g (ISBN 0-06-024852-1). Har-Row.
Regosin, Richard. The Matter of My Book: Montaigne's "Essais" As the Book of the Self. LC 77-75398. 1977. 18.95x (ISBN 0-520-03476-7). U of Cal Pr.
Regush, June & Regush, Nicholas. Dream Worlds, the Complete Guide to Dreams & Dreaming. (Orig.). 1977. pap. 1.75 o.p. (ISBN 0-451-07400-9, E7400, Sig). NAL.
Regush, June, jt. auth. see Regush, Nicholas.
Regush, Nicholas & Merta, Jan. Exploring the Human Aura. LC 75-2304. 180p. 1975. 6.95 o.p. (ISBN 0-13-297036-8). P-H.
Regush, Nicholas & Regush, June. The New Consciousness Catalog. LC 79-87. (Illus.). 1979. pap. 6.95 o.p. (ISBN 0-399-11923-X). Putnam Pub Group.
Regush, Nicholas, jt. auth. see Regush, June.
Reh, A. M. Continuing German: A Bridge to Literature. 1971. text ed. 28.50 (ISBN 0-07-051698-7, C); tchr's. manual 10.95 (ISBN 0-07-051711-8); tapes 225.00 (ISBN 0-07-051699-5); demonstration tape o.p. 3.95 (ISBN 0-07-051712-6). McGraw.
Reh, Emma, et al, eds. see United States Institute of Inter-American Affairs.
Rehabilitation International Vocational Commission. Rehabilitation International Vocational Seminar, Toronto, Canada, 1980. 9.00 (ISBN 0-686-94892-0). Rehab Intl.
Rehbein, Jochen, jt. auth. see Ehlich, Konrad.
Rehder, A. The Bradley Bibliography: A Guide to the Literature of the Woody Plants of the World, Published Before the Beginning of the 20th Century, 5 vols. Sargent, C. S., ed. 3895p. 1976. Repr. Set. lib. bdg. 552.00x. Vol. I. Vol. II (ISBN 3-87429-107-3). Vol. III (ISBN 3-87429-108-1). Vol. IV (ISBN 3-87429-109-X). Vol. V (ISBN 3-87429-110-3). Lubrecht & Cramer.
Rehder, Alfred. Bibliography of Cultivated Trees & Shrubs Hardy in the Cooler Temperature Regions of the Northern Hemisphere. (Collectanea Bibliographica Ser.: No. 9). 1978. lib. bdg. 96.00x (ISBN 3-87429-128-6). Lubrecht & Cramer.
Rehder, Harrold A. The Audubon Society Field Guide to North American Seashells. LC 80-84239. 1981. 12.50 (ISBN 0-394-51913-2). Knopf.
Reher, Charles A., ed. Settlement & Subsistence Along the Lower Chaco River: The CGP Survey. LC 77-71906. (Illus.). 614p. 1977. pap. 15.00x o.p. (ISBN 0-8263-0449-4). U of NM Pr.
Rehfeld, W. German Narrative Prose, Vol. 3. 1967. 13.50 (ISBN 0-85496-024-4). Dufour.
Rehg, Kenneth L. & Sohl, Damian G. Ponapean-English Dictionary. LC 79-19451. (Pali Language Texts: Micronesia). 1979. pap. text ed. 9.00x (ISBN 0-8248-0562-3). UH Pr.
--Ponapean Reference Grammar. LC 80-13276. (Pali Language Texts: Micronesia). 1981. pap. text ed. 16.00x (ISBN 0-8248-0718-9). UH Pr.
Rehkopf, Donald C., ed. Portraits in Words: An Introduction to the Study of Biography. 1962. write for info. o.p.; write for info. o.p. Odyssey Pr.
Rehm, H. J., jt. ed. see Reed, G.
Rehm, J., jt. auth. see Winold, A.
Rehm, Karl M. Basic Black & White Photography. LC 75-42568. (Illus.). 192p. 1977. pap. 9.95 (ISBN 0-8174-2403-2, Amphoto); Spanish Ed. pap. 9.95 o.p. (ISBN 0-686-67405-7). Watson-Guptill.
Rehm, Lynn P., ed. Behavior Therapy for Depression: Present Status & Future Directions. 1980. 32.50 (ISBN 0-12-585880-9). Acad Pr.
Rehman, Z. Payamber: The Messenger, Vol. I, II, III. 7.50 ea. Kazi Pubns.
Rehmus, Charles M., ed. see National Academy of Arbitrators-21st Annnual Meeting.
Rehr, Helen, jt. auth. see Miller, Rosalind.
Rehr, Helen, jt. ed. see Rosenberg, Gary.
Rehr, Paula B. Why Is Everyone Growing up & I'm Still in the 8th Grade? Poems about School Life Today. (Illus.). 48p. 1980. pap. 3.50 (ISBN 0-912048-10-7). Garrett Pk.
Rehrauer, George. Macmillan Film Bibliography, 2 vols. 1982. Set. lib. bdg. 120.00x (ISBN 0-02-696400-7); Vol. 1. lib. bdg. 90.00x (ISBN 0-02-696410-4); Vol. 2. lib. bdg. 50.00x (ISBN 0-02-696420-1). Macmillan.
Reibel, Daniel B. Registration Methods for the Small Museum. LC 78-15994. (Illus.). 1978. pap. 8.95 (ISBN 0-910050-37-6). AASLH.
Reibsamen, Gary G., jt. auth. see Christian, Jeffrey M.
Reich, Ali. Jump Rope Jingles. LC 82-13317. (Annie Hummingbird Bks.). (Illus.). 16p. (ps-8). 1983. pap. 1.25 saddle-wire (ISBN 0-394-85674-0). Random.
--Meet the Care Bears. LC 82-61672. (Care Bear Mini-Storybooks). (Illus.). 32p. (gr. 1-6). 1983. pap. 1.25 saddle-stitched (ISBN 0-394-85844-1). Random.
Reich, Bernard. The Quest for Peace: U. S. - Israeli Relations & the Arab-Israeli Conflict. LC 76-45940. 495p. 1977. text ed. 24.95 o.p. (ISBN 0-87855-226-X). Transaction Bks.
Reich, Bernard, jt. ed. see Long, David E.
Reich, Hanns, ed. see Held, Heinz.
Reich, Hanns, ed. see Roth, Eugene.
Reich, J. G. & Selkov, E. Energy Metabolism of the Cell: A Theoretical Treatise. LC 81-66389. 352p. 1982. 74.00 (ISBN 0-12-585920-1). Acad Pr.
Reich, John W. Experimenting in Society: Issues & Examples in Applied Social Psychology. 1981. pap. text ed. 13.50x (ISBN 0-673-15457-2). Scott F.
Reich, Lilly J. The Viennese Pastry Cookbook. 1978. pap. 8.95 o.p. (ISBN 0-02-010110-4). Macmillan.
Reich, Naomi, et al. Essentials of Clothing Construction. 2nd ed. (Illus.). 1978. pap. 13.95 (ISBN 0-13-284398-6). P-H.
Reich, Peter A., ed. see Linguistic Association of Canada & the U.S.
Reich, Robert, jt. auth. see Magaziner, Ira.
Reich, Robert B., jt. auth. see Magaziner, Ira C.
Reich, Sheldon, jt. auth. see Brewer, Donald J.
Reich, Steve. Writings About Music. 1974. pap. 9.75 (ISBN 0-686-67541-X, 50-26921). Eur-Am Music.
Reich, Warren T., ed. Encyclopedia of Bioethics, 2 vols. 1982. Set. lib. bdg. 125.00X (ISBN 0-02-925910-X). Macmillan.
Reich, Wilhelm. The Bioelectrical Investigation of Sexuality & Anxiety. Faber, Marion, et al, trs. from Ger. Higgins, Mary & Raphael, Chester M., eds. 172p. 1982. 15.00 (ISBN 0-374-28843-7); pap. 7.95 (ISBN 0-374-51728-2). FS&G.
--Children of the Future: On the Prevention of Sexual Pathology. Jordan, Inge, et al, trs. from Ger. 1982. 15.50 (ISBN 0-374-12173-7). FS&G.
--Ether, God & Devil & Cosmic Superimposition. Pol, Therese, tr. (Illus.). 260p. 1972. 10.00 o.p. (ISBN 0-374-14907-0); pap. 5.95 (ISBN 0-374-50991-3). FS&G.
--The Invasion of Compulsory Sex-Morality. xxix, 215p. 1971. 10.00 (ISBN 0-374-17707-4); pap. 3.45 o.p. (ISBN 0-374-50939-5). FS&G.
--Listen, Little Man! Manheim, Ralph, tr. (Illus.). 144p. 1974. pap. 4.95 (ISBN 0-374-50401-6). FS&G.
--The Mass Psychology of Fascism. 1974. pap. 3.95 o.p. (ISBN 0-671-21790-9, Touchstone Bks). S&S.
--The Murder of Christ. 1974. pap. 5.95 o.p. (ISBN 0-671-21912-X, Touchstone Bks). S&S.
--The Murder of Christ: The Emotional Plague of Mankind. 228p. 1953. o. p. 5.95 o.p. (ISBN 0-374-21625-8); pap. 5.95 o.p. (ISBN 0-374-50476-8, N290). FS&G.
--Orgonomischer Funktionalismus. 110p. 1973. 35.00 o.p. (ISBN 0-374-22724-1). FS&G.
--Record of a Friendship: The Correspondence of Wilhelm Reich & A. S. Neill. Placzek, Beverley, ed. 1981. 20.00 (ISBN 0-374-24807-9). FS&G.
--The Sexual Revolution: Toward a Self Regulating Character Structure. Pol, Therese, tr. from Ger. LC 73-76780. 273p. (Orig.). 1974. 12.95 (ISBN 0-374-26172-5); pap. 4.95 o.p. (ISBN 0-374-50269-2). FS&G.
Reich, Willi, ed. see Webern, Anton.
Reichard, Gary W. The Reaffirmation of Republicanism: Eisenhower & the Eighty-Third Congress. LC 75-1017. (Twentieth Century America Ser.). 320p. 1975. 19.95x (ISBN 0-87049-167-9). U of Tenn Pr.
Reichard, Gary W., jt. ed. see Bremner, Robert H.
Reichard, Gladys A. Weaving a Navajo Blanket. 1974. pap. 3.00 (ISBN 0-686-95796-2). Jefferson Natl.
Reichard, Gladys A., jt. auth. see Newcomb, Franc J.
Reichard, Richard W. Crippled from Birth: German Social Democracy 1844-1870. (Illus.). 1969. 10.50 (ISBN 0-8138-0372-1). Iowa St U Pr.
Reichard, Robert. Figure Finaglers. (Illus.). 228p. 1974. 5.75 o.p. (ISBN 0-07-051777-0, P&RB). McGraw.
Reichard, Robert S. The Numbers Game: Uses & Abuses of Managerial Statistics. LC 77-172032. (Illus.). 384p. 1972. 19.50 o.p. (ISBN 0-07-051776-2, P&RB). McGraw.
Reichardt, Arthur C. Knickerbocker Barber. 1983. 8.95 (ISBN 0-533-05335-8). Vantage.
Reichardt, Jasia & Abakanowicz, Magdalena. Magdalena Abakanowicz. LC 82-11511. (Illus.). 192p. (Orig.). 1983. pap. 24.95 (ISBN 0-89659-323-1). Abbeville Pr.
Reichardt, W. Dictionary of Acoustics: English-German-French-Russian-Spanish-Polish-Madarsko-Slovene. 267p. (Eng., Ger., Fr., Rus., Span., Pol., Madarsko & Slovene.). 1978. 95.00 (ISBN 0-686-92601-3, M-9897). French & Eur.
Reichardt, W., ed. Processing of Optical Data by Organisms & by Machines. (Italian Physical Society: Course No. 43). 1970. 87.50 (ISBN 0-12-368843-4). Acad Pr.
Reichardt, Werner E. & Poggio, Tomaso, eds. Theoretical Approaches in Neurobiology. (Illus.). 208p. 1980. text ed. 22.50x (ISBN 0-262-18100-2). MIT Pr.
Reichart, Walter A., ed. The Complete Works of Washington Irving, Journals & Notebooks, Vol. 3: 1819-1827. (Critical Editions Program). 1970. lib. bdg. 32.00 (ISBN 0-8057-8502-7, Twayne). G K Hall.
Reichart, Walter A., ed. see Irving, Washington.
Reichel, Aaron. The Jewish Billy Sunday. Friedman, Robert S., ed. LC 82-9664. 256p. 12.95 (ISBN 0-89865-174-3); pap. 6.95 (ISBN 0-89865-299-5). Donning Co.
Reichel, E., jt. auth. see Baumgartner, A.
Reichel, Jocelyn. I Seen a Million Sparrows. (Illus.). 144p. 1983. pap. 5.95 (ISBN 0-8024-0185-6). Moody.
--Old Age Is Not for Sissies. 144p. 1981. pap. 5.95 (ISBN 0-8024-9311-4). Moody.

--Retirement Is for the Birds. LC 81-18982. 160p. 1982. pap. 5.95 (ISBN 0-8024-7295-8). Moody.

Reichel, Norbert. Der Dichter In der Stadt. 205p. (Ger.). 1982. write for info. (ISBN 3-8204-5815-8). P Lang Pubs.

Reichel, William. Clinical Aspects of Aging. 2nd ed. (Illus.). 553p. 1983. lib. bdg. price not set (ISBN 0-683-07203-X). Williams & Wilkins.

Reichel-Dolmatoff, G. The Shaman & the Jaguar: A Study of Narcotic Drugs Among the Indians of Colombia. LC 74-83672. 301p. 1975. 29.95 (ISBN 0-87722-038-7). Temple U Pr.

Reichenbach, Bruce. Evil & a Good God. xviii, 198p. 1982. 22.50 (ISBN 0-8232-1080-4); pap. 9.00 (ISBN 0-8232-1081-2). Fordham.

--Is Man the Phoenix? A Study of Immortality. LC 82-21905. 198p. 1983. pap. text ed. 9.50 (ISBN 0-8191-2672-1). U Pr of Amer.

Reichenbach, Hans. Axiomatization of the Theory of Relativity. Reichenbach, Maria, ed. & tr. LC 68-21540. 1968. 28.50x (ISBN 0-520-01525-8). U of Cal Pr.

--Laws, Modalities, & Counterfactuals. LC 74-29798. Orig. Title: Nomological Statements & Admissible Operations. 1977. 28.50x (ISBN 0-520-02966-6). U of Cal Pr.

--Philosophy of Space & Time. Reichenbach, Maria, tr. 1957. pap. text ed. 4.75 (ISBN 0-486-60443-8). Dover.

--The Rise of Scientific Philosophy. 1951. 28.50x (ISBN 0-520-01053-1); pap. 4.95 (ISBN 0-520-01055-8, CAL3). U of Cal Pr.

--The Theory of Probability: An Inquiry into the Logical & Mathematical Foundations of the Calculus of Probability. (California Library Reprint Series: No. 23). 1971. 39.50x (ISBN 0-520-01929-6). U of Cal Pr.

--The Theory of Relativity & A Priori Knowledge. 1965. 30.00x (ISBN 0-520-01059-0). U of Cal Pr.

Reichenbach, Hans & Reichenbach, Maria. The Direction of Time. LC 55-9883. (California Library Reprint Ser.: No. 26). 292p. 1972. 28.50x (ISBN 0-520-04764-8). U of Cal Pr.

Reichenbach, Maria, jt. auth. see Reichenbach, Hans.

Reichenbach, Maria, ed. & tr. see Reichenbach, Hans.

Reichenbach, Maria, tr. see Reichenbach, Hans.

Reichenbach-Klinke, H. & Elkan, E. Principal Diseases of Lower Vertebrates. Incl. Book 1. Diseases of Fishes. (Illus.). pap. 19.95 (ISBN 0-87666-042-1, PS-205); Book 2. Diseases of Amphibians. pap. 12.95 (ISBN 0-87666-044-8, PS-206); Book 3. Diseases of Reptiles. pap. 19.95 (ISBN 0-87666-045-6, PS-207). 1972. TFH Pubns.

Reichenbach-Klinke, H., jt. auth. see Elkan, E.

Reichenbach-Klinke, H. H. Fish Pathology. (Illus.). 512p. (Orig.). 1973. pap. text ed. 29.95 (ISBN 0-87666-074-X, PS-204). TFH Pubns.

Reichert, Richard. Born in the Spirit of Jesus. 84p. (Orig.). 1980. pap. text ed. 2.95 (ISBN 0-697-01725-7); tchr's manual 3.50 (ISBN 0-697-01726-5); spirit masters 10.95 (ISBN 0-697-01727-3). Wm C Brown.

--Community of the Spirit. 120p. 1982. pap. 3.60 (ISBN 0-697-01796-6); tchr's manual 3.50 (ISBN 0-697-01797-4). Wm C Brown.

Reichert, Richard, jt. auth. see Reichert, Sara.

Reichert, Sara & Reichert, Richard. In Wisdom & the Spirit: A Religious Education Program for Those Over 65. pap. 3.95 o.p. (ISBN 0-8091-1969-2). Paulist Pr.

Reichle, D. E., ed. Dynamic Properties of Forest Ecosystems. LC 78-72093. (International Biological Programme Ser.: No. 23). (Illus.). 850p. 1981. 115.00 (ISBN 0-521-22508-6). Cambridge U Pr.

Reichler, Joseph. The World Series: Seventy-Sixth Anniversity Edition. 1979. 17.95 o.s.i. (ISBN 0-671-25152-X). S&S.

Reichler, Joseph L. The Great All-Time Baseball Record Book. LC 81-182. (Illus.). 544p. 1981. 19.95 (ISBN 0-02-603100-0); prepack(12) 95.40. Macmillan.

Reichlin, Seymour, et al, eds. The Hypothalamus, Vol. 56. LC 77-83691. (Association for Research in Nervous & Mental Disease Research Publications). 504p. 1978. 48.00 (ISBN 0-89004-167-9). Raven.

Reichman, C., et al. Knitted Fabric Primer. 20.00 o.p. (ISBN 0-87245-269-7). Textile Bk.

Reichman, Charles. Guide to the Manufacture of Sweaters, Knit Shirts & Swimwear. (Illus.). 1963. 10.00 o.p. (ISBN 0-87245-266-2). Textile Bk.

--Knitted Stretch Technology. (Knitting Production Ser). 10.00 o.p. (ISBN 0-87245-268-9). Textile Bk.

--Wool & Synthetic Knitwear Handbook. (Knitting Production Ser). 12.00 o.p. (ISBN 0-87245-272-7). Textile Bk.

Reichman, Louis C., jt. auth. see Wishart, Barry J.

Reichman, Stella J. Great Big Beautiful Doll. 1978. pap. 1.95 o.p. (ISBN 0-451-08047-5, J8047, Sig). NAL.

Reichmann, Felix. The Sources of Western Literacy: The Middle Eastern Civilizations. LC 79-8292. (Contributions in Librarianship & Information Science: No. 29). 274p. 1980. lib. bdg. 29.95 (ISBN 0-313-20948-0, RWL/). Greenwood.

Reichmann, Felix & Tharpe, Josephine M. Bibliographic Control of Microforms. LC 72-2463. 256p. 1972. lib. bdg. 27.50 (ISBN 0-8371-6423-0, RCM/). Greenwood.

Reichmann, W. J. The Spell of Mathematics. 1967. 7.95x o.p. (ISBN 0-416-46440-8). Methuen Inc.

Reichs, Kathleen J., ed. Hominid Origins: Inquiries Past & Present. LC 82-20161. (Illus.). 278p. (Orig.). 1983. lib. bdg. 22.50 (ISBN 0-8191-2864-3); pap. text ed. 11.75 (ISBN 0-8191-2865-1). U Pr of Amer.

Reid. Appropriate Methods of Treating Water & Wastewater in Developing Countries. LC 81-67513. 392p. 1982. 27.50 (ISBN 0-250-40413-3). Ann Arbor Science.

--A Surgeon's Management of Gangrene. 240p. 1978. text ed. 19.50 o.p. (ISBN 0-8391-1297-1). Univ Park.

Reid, et al. Diccionario Totonaco de Xicotepec de Juarez. (Vocabularios Indigenas Ser.: No. 17). 1974. pap. 12.00x (ISBN 0-88312-752-0); microfiche 4.50 (ISBN 0-88312-552-8). Summer Inst Ling.

Reid, Adrian. Confessions of a Hitchhiker. (Orig.). 1970. pap. 0.95 o.p. (ISBN 0-451-06700-2, Q6700, Sig). NAL.

--The Goddaughter. 1980. pap. 2.25 o.p. (ISBN 0-380-47571-5, 47571, 47571). Avon.

Reid, Alan. Discovery & Exploration: A Concise History. (Illus.). 328p. 1982. 19.95 (ISBN 0-85614-071-6, 5402-6). Arco.

Reid, Alastair. Ounce, Dice, Trice. 1980. lib. bdg. 6.95 (ISBN 0-8398-2612-5, Gregg). G K Hall.

Reid, Alastair, tr. see Neruda, Pablo.

Reid, Alastair, et al, trs. see Neruda, Pablo.

Reid, Alastair, et al, trs. see Padilla, Herberto.

Reid, Allan. Modern Applied Selling. 3rd ed. 1981. text ed. 23.50x (ISBN 0-673-16113-7). Scott F.

Reid, Allan, ed. Readings in Modern Applied Salesmanship. LC 76-11367. (Illus.). 1976. pap. text ed. 10.95 o.p. (ISBN 0-87620-579-1). Scott F.

Reid, B. L. Art by Subtraction: A Dissenting Opinion of Gertrude Stein. (Illus.). 1958. 12.95x o.p. (ISBN 0-8061-0404-X). U of Okla Pr.

Reid, C. N. Deformation Geometry for Material Scientists. LC 73-4716. 220p. 1971. text ed. 27.00 (ISBN 0-08-017237-7); pap. text ed. 13.25 (ISBN 0-08-017745-X). Pergamon.

Reid, Charles. Choice & Action: An Introduction to Ethics. 1981. pap. text ed. 15.95 (ISBN 0-02-399180-1). Macmillan.

--Painting What You Want to See: Forty-Six Lessons, Assignments, & Painting Critiques on Watercolor & Oil. (Illus.). 144p. 1983. 22.50 (ISBN 0-8230-3878-5). Watson-Guptill.

Reid, Charles F., III. Guide to Residential Financing. 2nd ed. Mascari, Claude J., et al, eds. LC 81-51990. 256p. 1981. 12.75 (ISBN 0-9603790-2-9). Rouse Real Estate.

Reid, Charles, 3rd. Guide to Residential Financing. Mascari, Claude J., et al, eds. LC 79-92645. 225p. 1979. pap. text ed. cancelled o.p. (ISBN 0-9603790-1-0); 12.50 o.p. three-ring loose-leaf binder (ISBN 0-9603790-0-2). Rouse Real Estate.

Reid, Christopher. Pea Soup. 64p. 1983. pap. 11.95 (ISBN 0-19-211952-4). Oxford U Pr.

Reid, Clyde H. Dreams: Discovering Your Inner Teacher. 144p. 1983. pap. 7.95 (ISBN 0-86683-703-5). Winston Pr.

Reid, Constance. Jerzy Neyman-From Life. (Illus.). 320p. 1982. 19.80 (ISBN 0-387-90747-5). Springer-Verlag.

Reid, Cornelius L. A Dictionary of Vocal Terminology: An Analysis. LC 81-86074. 500p. 1983. 37.50 (ISBN 0-915282-07-0). J Patelson Music.

Reid, Cynthia. A Primer of Human Neuroanatomy. 1978. pap. text ed. 10.00 o.p. (ISBN 0-397-58237-4, Lippincott Nursing). Lippincott.

Reid, D. K. & Hresko, W. P. A Cognitive Approach to Learning Disabilities. 1981. 22.50 (ISBN 0-07-051768-1). McGraw.

Reid, D. Kim, jt. auth. see Gallagher, Jeanette.

Reid, Daniel P. The Complete Guide to China. (The Complete Asian Guide Ser.). (Illus.). 126p. 1981. pap. 6.95 (ISBN 962-7031-03-8, Pub. by CFW Pubns Hong Kong). C E Tuttle.

--The Complete Guide to Korea. (The Complete Asian Guide Ser.). (Illus.). 128p. (Orig.). 1982. pap. 9.95 (ISBN 962-7031-18-6). C E Tuttle.

--The Complete Guide to Taiwan. (The Complete Asian Guide Ser.). (Illus., Orig.). 1983. pap. 9.95 (ISBN 962-7031-19-4, Pub. by CFW Pubns Hong Kong). C E Tuttle.

--Korea in Focus. (The "In Focus" Ser.). (Illus.). 64p. (Orig.). 1982. pap. 5.95 (ISBN 962-7031-21-6). C E Tuttle.

--Taiwan in Focus. (The "In Focus" Ser.). (Illus.). 64p. (Orig.). 1983. pap. 5.95 (ISBN 962-7031-22-4). C E Tuttle.

Reid, David R. Thoughts for Growing Christians. LC 82-7913. 160p. 1982. pap. 3.95 (ISBN 0-8024-2200-4). Moody.

Reid, Derek A. A Monograph of the Stipitate Steroid Fungi. (Illus.). 1965. pap. 64.00 (ISBN 3-7682-5418-6). Lubrecht & Cramer.

Reid, Donald M. Lawyers & Politics in the Arab World, 1880-1960. LC 80-71053. (Studies in Middle Eastern History: No. 5). 435p. 1981. 35.00x (ISBN 0-88297-028-3). Bibliotheca.

Reid, Duncan E., et al. Principles & Management of Human Reproduction. LC 70-118593. (Illus.). 1972. 30.00 o.p. (ISBN 0-7216-7532-8). Saunders.

Reid, E. Cell Populations. LC 79-40729. (Methodological Surveys in Biochemistry Ser.: Vol. 8). 1979. 69.95x o.s.i. (ISBN 0-470-26809-3). Halsted Pr.

Reid, Elmer T. Practical Guide for Royal Arch Chapter Officers & Companions. (Illus.). 1980. Repr. of 1970 ed. 3.95 (ISBN 0-686-43318-1). Macoy Pub.

Reid, Eric, ed. Membranous Elements & Movement of Molecules. LC 77-77378. (Methodological Surveys Ser: Vol. 6). 1977. 66.95 o.s.i. (ISBN 0-470-99186-0). Halsted Pr.

Reid, F. H. & Goldie, W. Gold Plating Technology. 630p. 1980. 160.00x (ISBN 0-901150-02-9, Pub. by Electrochemical Scotland). State Mutual Bk.

Reid, Gary. Linear System Fundamentals: Continuous, Discrete & Modern. (McGraw-Hill Series in Electrical Engineering). (Illus.). 512p. 1983. text ed. 36.00x (ISBN 0-07-051808-4, C); solutions manual 8.00 (ISBN 0-07-051809-2). McGraw.

Reid, George K. Pond Life. Zim, Herbert S., ed. (Golden Guide Ser). (Illus.). (gr. 7 up). 1967. PLB 11.54 (ISBN 0-307-63535-X, Golden Pr); pap. 2.95 (ISBN 0-307-24017-7). Western Pub.

Reid, Gordon. A Nest of Hornets. (Illus.). 249p. 1982. 36.95 (ISBN 0-19-554358-0). Oxford U Pr.

Reid, Helen E. From the Vaults. 83p. (Orig.). 1982. pap. text ed. 4.95. Metzger Pr.

Reid, Howard, jt. auth. see Croucher, Michael.

Reid, Ian. The Short Story. (Critical Idiom Ser.). 1977. 9.95x (ISBN 0-416-56060-1); pap. 4.95x (ISBN 0-416-56070-9). Methuen Inc.

Reid, Inez S. Together Black Women. 2nd ed. LC 73-83156. 348p. 1974. 12.95 o.s.i. (ISBN 0-89388-114-7); pap. 6.95 (ISBN 0-89388-115-5). Okpaku Communications.

Reid, Ivan. Social Class Differences in Britain: A Sourcebook. (Illus.). 1977. text ed. 15.00x o.p. (ISBN 0-7291-0165-7); pap. text ed. 7.75x o.p. (ISBN 0-7291-0160-6). Humanities.

Reid, J. C. & Cape, Peter. A Book of New Zealand. Rev. ed. (Illus.). 291p. 1979. 15.95 (ISBN 0-00-216942-8, Pub. by W Collins Australia). Intl Schol Bk Serv.

Reid, J. C., jt. auth. see Wilkes, G. A.

Reid, J. Gavin, jt. auth. see Hay, James G.

Reid, J. K., tr. see Calvin, John.

Reid, James. The Offering. LC 77-11632. 1978. 8.95 o.p. (ISBN 0-399-12074-2). Putnam Pub Group.

Reid, James J. Trebalism & Society in Islamic Iran 1500-1629. (Studies in Near Eastern Culture & Society Ser.: Vol. 4). 220p. 1983. pap. write for info. (82-50984); write for info. (ISBN 0-89003-125-8). Undena Pubns.

Reid, James M. & Wendlinger, Robert M. Effective Letters: A Program for Self-Instruction. 3rd ed. (Illus.). 1978. pap. text ed. 15.95 (ISBN 0-07-051817-3, C); instructor's manual 16.00 (ISBN 0-07-051818-1). McGraw.

Reid, James M., jt. auth. see Bossone, Richard M.

Reid, James M., Jr., jt. auth. see Bossone, Richard M.

Reid, Jane. Metrics for Everyday Use. new ed. LC 74-24660. 24p. (gr. 7-12). 1975. pap. text ed. 3.96 (ISBN 0-87002-216-4). Bennett IL.

Reid, John P. A Better Kind of Hatchet: Law, Trade, Diplomacy in the Cherokee Nation. LC 75-15544. 262p. 1975. 20.00x (ISBN 0-271-01197-1). Pa St U Pr.

--In a Defiant Stance: The Conditions of Law in Massachusetts Bay, the Irish Comparison, & the Coming of the American Revolution. LC 76-42453. 1977. 20.00x (ISBN 0-271-01240-4). Pa St U Pr.

--In a Rebellious Spirit: The Argument of Facts, the Liberty Riot, & the Coming of the American Revolution. LC 78-50065. 1979. 18.95x (ISBN 0-271-00202-6). Pa St U Pr.

Reid, John T. & Hunter, J. R. Humbolt County Nevada. facs. ed. (Shorey Historical Ser.). 70p. Repr. of 1913 ed. pap. 3.95 (ISBN 0-8466-0174-5, SJS174). Shorey.

Reid, Joseph L., ed. Antarctic Oceanology One. LC 78-151300. (Antarctic Research Ser.: Vol. 15). (Illus.). 1971. 28.50 (ISBN 0-87590-115-8). Am Geophysical.

Reid, Joseph L., jt. ed. see Capurro, L. R.

Reid, Joy M. The Process of Composition. (Illus.). 224p. 1982. pap. text ed. 10.95 (ISBN 0-13-723015-X). P-H.

Reid, Joyce M. The Concise Oxford Dictionary of French Literature. rev. abr. ed. Orig. Title: The Oxford Companion to French Literature. 1976. 18.95x (ISBN 0-19-866118-5). Oxford U Pr.

Reid, K. Relationship Between Numerical Computation & Programming Language. Date not set. 32.00 (ISBN 0-444-86377-X). Elsevier.

Reid, Kenneth C. Watermills of London Countryside: Their Place in English Landscape & Life, 2 vols. 1982. Vol. 1. 50.00 ea. (ISBN 0-284-39165-4, Pub. by C Skilton Scotland). Vol. II (ISBN 0-284-98584-8). State Mutual Bk.

Reid, Lawrence A. Central Bontoc: Sentence, Paragraph & Discourse. (Publications in Linguistics & Related Fields Ser.: No. 27). 185p. 1970. pap. 3.25x (ISBN 0-88312-029-1); microfiche 2.25 (ISBN 0-88312-429-7). Summer Inst Ling.

--An Ivatan Syntax. (Oceanic Linguistics Special Publication Ser.: No. 2). (Orig.). 1966. pap. text ed. 6.00x (ISBN 0-87022-690-8). UH Pr.

--Philippine Minor Languages: Word Lists & Phonologies. LC 70-150659. (Oceanic Linguistics Special Publication Ser: No. 8). (Orig.). 1971. pap. text ed. 7.00x (ISBN 0-87022-691-6). UH Pr.

Reid, Loren. Speaking Well. 3rd ed. (McGraw-Hill Speech Ser.). (Illus.). 1977. pap. text ed. 19.95 (ISBN 0-07-051783-5, C). McGraw.

--Teaching Speech. 4th ed. (Speech Ser.). 1971. 13.95 o.p. (ISBN 0-07-051785-1, C). McGraw.

Reid, Loretta G. Control & Communication in Programs. Stone, Harold, ed. LC 82-6893. (Computer Science: Systems Programming Ser.: No. 13). 176p. 1982. 39.95 (ISBN 0-8357-1349-0). Univ Microfilms.

Reid, Louis A. A Study in Aesthetics. LC 70-114546. 415p. 1973. Repr. of 1954 ed. lib. bdg. 29.75x (ISBN 0-8371-4794-8, RESA). Greenwood.

Reid, Mehry M. Persian Ceramic Designs. (The International Design Library). (Illus.). 48p. (Orig.). 1983. pap. 2.95 (ISBN 0-88045-024-X). Stemmer Hse.

Reid, Norma, ed. Ultramicrotomy. (Practical Methods in Electron Microscopy Ser.: Vol. 3, Pt. 2). 353p. 1975. pap. 17.50 (ISBN 0-444-10667-7, North-Holland). Elsevier.

Reid, Paul E. A Model of Interpersonal Speech Communication. LC 79-64197. 1979. pap. text ed. 6.75 (ISBN 0-8191-0755-7). U Pr of Amer.

Reid, R. Problems of Russian Romantic Literature. 1982. 60.00x o.p. (ISBN 0-86127-206-4, Pub. by Avebury Pub England). State Mutual Bk.

Reid, R. J. Law of Moses & Its Lesson. pap. 0.30 o.p. (ISBN 0-87213-693-0). Loizeaux.

Reid, Robert. A Treasury of the Sierra Nevada. Winnett, Thomas, ed. (Illus.). 256p. pap. 7.95 (ISBN 0-89997-023-0). Wilderness Pr.

Reid, Robert, ed. Country Inns of America Cookbook. (Illus.). 180p. 1982. 24.95 (ISBN 0-686-82288-9). HR&W.

Reid, Robert A. & Leech, Rachel M. Biochemistry & Structure of Cell Organelles. (Tertiary Level Biology Series). 176p. 1980. 39.95x o.s.i. (ISBN 0-470-26980-4); pap. text ed. 21.95x o.s.i. (ISBN 0-470-26981-2). Halsted Pr.

Reid, Robert C., jt. auth. see Modell, Michael.

Reid, Ronald F., et al. Introduction to the Field of Speech. 1965. pap. 8.95x o.p. (ISBN 0-673-05712-7). Scott F.

Reid, S. W., ed. see Brown, Charles B.

Reid, Samuel R. Merger, Managers & the Economy. 1968. 23.95 (ISBN 0-07-051787-8, C). McGraw.

--The New Industrial Order: Concentration, Regulation & Public Policy. 1976. text ed. 16.50 o.p. (ISBN 0-07-051779-7, C); pap. text ed. 15.95 o.p. (ISBN 0-07-051780-0). McGraw.

Reid, Susan. Femininity & the American Dream. 1978. 5.95 o.p. (ISBN 0-533-03050-1). Vantage.

Reid, Susan, ed. The Black Experience: A Manual for Students in the Helping Professions. 1976. pap. text ed. 6.75 o.p. (ISBN 0-8191-0001-3). U Pr of Amer.

Reid, Thomas. Thomas Reid's Inquiry & Essays. Lehrer, Keith & Beanblossom, Ronald E., eds. LC 75-1197. (LLA Ser: No. 156). 431p. 1975. pap. 9.25 (ISBN 0-672-61173-2). Bobbs.

--Thomas Reid's Lectures on Natural Theology (1780) Duncan, Elmer H., ed. LC 80-5964. 177p. 1981. lib. bdg. 21.50 (ISBN 0-8191-1354-9); pap. text ed. 9.75 (ISBN 0-8191-1355-7). U Pr of Amer.

Reid, Virginia. Reading Ladders for Human Relations. 5th ed. LC 72-87462. 1972. 10.50 o.p. (ISBN 0-8268-1375-5); pap. 4.50 o.p. (ISBN 0-8268-1373-9). ACE.

Reid, W., jt. auth. see Drazin, P.

Reid, W. A., jt. auth. see Taylor, Philip H.

Reid, W. A., jt. ed. see Taylor, P. H.

Reid, W. H., jt. auth. see Drazin, P. G.

Reid, W. Max. The Mohawk Valley: Its Legends & Its History. (Illus.). 1979. Repr. of 1901 ed. 22.50 o.p. (ISBN 0-916346-32-3). Harbor Hill Bks.

Reid, W. T. Riccati Differential Equations. (Mathematics in Science & Engineering Ser.: Vol. 86). 1972. 42.00 (ISBN 0-12-586250-4). Acad Pr.

Reid, Walter & Myddleton, D. R. The Meaning of Company Acounts. 3rd ed. 354p. 1982. text ed. 47.50x (ISBN 0-566-02284-2). Gower Pub Ltd.

Reid, William. Arms Through the Ages. (Illus.). 15.95 o.p. (ISBN 0-517-29855-4). Crown.

Reid, William D. Death Notices of Ontario. 417p. 1980. 20.00 (ISBN 0-912606-06-1). Hunterdon Hse.

--The Loyalists in Ontario: The Sons & Daughters of the American Loyalists of Upper Canada. 1973. 18.00 (ISBN 0-912606-02-9). Hunterdon Hse.

--Marriage Notices of Ontario. 1980. 25.00 (ISBN 0-912606-05-3). Hunterdon Hse.

Reid, William H. Basic Intensive Psychotherapy. LC 79-24337. 1980. 15.00 o.p. (ISBN 0-87630-227-4). Brunner-Mazel.

Reid, William H., jt. auth. see Lion, John R.

Reid, William T. Ordinary Differential Equations. LC 74-123745. 553p. 1971. 31.00 (ISBN 0-471-71499-2, Pub. by Wiley). Krieger.

Reidel, Carl H., ed. New England Prospects: Critical Choices in a Time of Change. LC 81-51604. (Futures of New England Ser.). (Illus.). 220p. 1982. text ed. 18.00x (ISBN 0-87451-213-1); pap. 9.00x (ISBN 0-87451-220-4). U Pr of New Eng.

Reidel, Marlene. From Egg to Bird. LC 81-56. (Carolrhoda Start to Finish Bks.). (Illus.). 24p. (ps-3). 1981. PLB 5.95g (ISBN 0-87614-159-9). Carolrhoda Bks.

Reidemeister, Kurt. Kombinatorische Topologie. (Ger). 14.95 (ISBN 0-8284-0076-8). Chelsea Pub.

Reider, Frederic. Order of the S. S. & How Did It Happen? LC 81-52162. (Illus.). 256p. 1981. 24.95 (ISBN 0-89404-061-8). Aztex.

Reidl, John O. A Catalogue of Renaissance Philosphers. 192p. 29.95 (ISBN 0-87462-433-9). Marquette.

Reidy, John, ed. see Derby, Harry L.

Reidy, M. J. Mirror of Truth. 1982. 7.95 (ISBN 0-686-97948-6). Vantage.

Reif, Daniel K. The Passive Solar Water Heaters: How to Design & Build a Batch System. (Illus.). 188p. (Orig.). 1983. pap. 23.95 (ISBN 0-471-88650-5). Wiley.

Reif, F., jt. ed. see Tuma, David T.

Reif, Frederick. Fundamentals of Statistical & Thermal Physics. (Fundamentals of Physics Ser.). (Illus.). 1965. text ed. 36.50 (ISBN 0-07-051800-9, C); solutions manual 25.00 (ISBN 0-07-035077-9). McGraw.

Reif, Stefan C., jt. ed. see Emerton, J. A.

Reiff, Robert F. A Stylistic Analysis of Arshile Gorky's Art from 1943-1948. LC 76-23679. (Outstanding Dissertations in the Fine Arts - American). (Illus.). 1977. Repr. of 1961 ed. lib. bdg. 52.00 o.s.i. (ISBN 0-8240-2719-1). Garland Pub.

Reiffenstuhl, Gunther & Platzer, Werner. Atlas of Vaginal Surgery Technique & Surgical Anatomy, 2 vols. Friedman, Judith & Friedman, Emanuel, trs. LC 74-9437. (Illus.). 733p. 1975. Set. text ed. 44.00 (ISBN 0-7216-7542-5); Vol. 1. text ed. 24.50 (ISBN 0-7216-7543-3); Vol. 2. text ed. 24.50 (ISBN 0-7216-7544-1). Saunders.

Reif-Lehrer, Liane. Writing a Successful Grant Application. 106p. 1982. pap. text ed. 9.50 (ISBN 0-86720-007-3); 16.00 (ISBN 0-86720-009-X). Sci Bks Intl.

Reifsnider, Elizabeth G., ed. California Water Resources Directory: A Guide to Organizations & Information Resources. LC 82-70810. (California Information Guides Ser.). (Illus., Orig.). 1983. pap. 20.00x (ISBN 0-912102-60-8). Cal Inst Public.

Reigel, C. E. & Perkins, E. A. Executive Typewriting. 1966. text ed. 16.50 (ISBN 0-07-051089-X, G); instructor's guide & key 5.90 (ISBN 0-07-051812-2). McGraw.

Reigel, Charles E. & Perkins, Edward A. Executive Typewriting. 2nd ed. (Illus.). 256p. (gr. 12 up). 1980. practice set in envelope container 14.00 (ISBN 0-07-051826-2); instrs'. guide & visual key 4.95 (ISBN 0-07-051827-0). McGraw.

Reigel, Stanley & Owen, P. John. Administrative Law: The Law of Government Agencies. LC 81-67512. 1982. 15.95 (ISBN 0-250-40451-6). Ann Arbor Science.

Reigeluth, Charles M. Instructional Design Theories & Models: An Overview of Their Current Status. 432p. 1983. text ed. write for info. (ISBN 0-89859-275-5). L Erlbaum Assocs.

Reiger, George. Wanderer on My Native Shore. 1983. price not set (ISBN 0-671-25423-5). S&S.

Reiger, George, jt. auth. see Line, Les.

Reigh, Mildred & Hauck, William. Algebra Review Manual: Program for Self Instruction. 1967. pap. 15.00 o.p. (ISBN 0-07-051805-X, C); tchr's manual 14.50 o.p. (ISBN 0-07-051804-1). McGraw.

Reigh, Mildred, et al. Brief Algebra Review Manual: A Program for Self-Instruction. (gr. 9 up). 1966. text ed. 18.95 (ISBN 0-07-051811-4, C); pap. text ed. 14.95 (ISBN 0-07-051807-6); instr's. manual 14.50 (ISBN 0-07-051804-1). McGraw.

Reigle, David. The Books of Kiu-Te in the Tibetan Buddhist Tantras. (Secret Doctrine Reference Ser.). (Illus.). 80p. (Orig.). 1983. pap. 3.50 (ISBN 0-913510-49-1). Wizards.

Reihlen, H., intro. by. Export Directory of German Industries, 1980. 27th ed. LC 57-16210. 1332p. (Orig.). 1980. pap. 55.00x o.p. (ISBN 0-8002-2695-X). Intl Pubns Serv.

Reiitsu, Kojima. China's Economy & Technology. Selden, Mark, ed. Selden, Kyoko, tr. 400p. 1982. write for info. (ISBN 0-87332-211-8). M E Sharpe.

Reijnen, G. C. Utilization of Outer Space & International Law. 1981. 64.00 (ISBN 0-444-41965-9). Elsevier.

Reiley, H. Edward & Shry, Carroll L., Jr. Introductory Horticulture. 2nd ed. 640p. 1983. text ed. write for info. (ISBN 0-8273-2198-8); instr's guide 3.75 (ISBN 0-8273-2199-6). Delmar.

Reiling, Henry B., et al. Business Law: Text & Cases. 1216p. 1982. text ed. 26.95x (ISBN 0-534-01131-4). Kent Pub Co.

Reiling, J. & Swellengrebel, J. L. Translator's Handbook on the Gospel of Luke. (Helps for Translators Ser.). 1982. Repr. of 1971 ed. 8.40x (ISBN 0-8267-0136-1, 08512). United Bible.

Reill, Peter H. The German Enlightenment & the Rise of Historicism. LC 73-87244. 318p. 1975. 39.50x (ISBN 0-520-02594-6). U of Cal Pr.

Reilly, C. Metal Contamination of Food. (Applied Science Ser.). 1980. 43.00 (ISBN 0-85334-905-3, Pub. by Applied Sci England). Elsevier.

Reilly, Cari, jt. auth. see Hall, Maureen.

Reilly, Catherine. Scars upon My Heart: Women's Poetry & Verse of the First World War. 144p. 1983. pap. 7.50 (ISBN 0-86068-226-9, Virago pr). Merrimack Bk Serv.

Reilly, Catherine W. & Cotterell, Laurence. English Poetry of the First World War: A Bibliography. LC 77-95261. 1978. 32.50x (ISBN 0-312-25517-9). St Martin.

Reilly, Cyril A. Song of Creation. 64p. 1983. pap. 9.95 (ISBN 0-86683-710-8). Winston Pr.

Reilly, Edward R., tr. see Quantz, Johann J.

Reilly, Elizabeth C. Dictionary of Colonial American Printers' Ornaments & Illustrations. LC 75-5023. (Illus.). xxxvi, 514p. 1975. 45.00x (ISBN 0-912296-06-2, Dist. by U Pr of Va). Am Antiquarian.

Reilly, Eugene J. The Complete Guide to Telephone System Evaluation. 300p. 1980. 175.00 (ISBN 0-686-98041-7). Telecom Lib.

Reilly, Harold J. & Brod, Ruth H. Edgar Cayce Handbook for Health Through Drugless Therapy. 1977. pap. 3.95 (ISBN 0-515-07250-8). Jove Pubns.

Reilly, John C., Jr. United States Navy Destroyers of World War II. (Illus.). 160p. 1983. 16.95 (ISBN 0-7137-1026-8, Pub. by Blandford Pr England). Sterling.

Reilly, John H. Arthur Adamov. LC 74-2162. (World Authors Ser.). 1974. lib. bdg. 14.95 (ISBN 0-8057-2005-7, Twayne). G K Hall.

--Jean Giraudoux. (World Authors Ser.). 1978. lib. bdg. 9.95 (ISBN 0-8057-6354-6, Twayne). G K Hall.

Reilly, John W. The Language of Real Estate in Michigan. 1979. pap. 18.95 o.s.i. (ISBN 0-695-81251-3). Follett.

Reilly, Marta T., et al. Guide to Resource Organizations Serving Minority Language Groups. LC 81-149654. (Resources in Bilingual Education Ser.). 186p. (Orig.). 1981. pap. 8.00 (ISBN 0-89763-053-X). Natl Clearinghse Bilingual Ed.

Reilly, Mary V., et al. Wait in Joyful Hope! (Illus., Orig.). 1980. pap. 4.95 (ISBN 0-8192-1275-X). Morehouse.

Reilly, Patrick. Jonathan Swift: The Brave Desponder. 287p. 1982. 20.00x (ISBN 0-8093-1075-9). S Ill U Pr.

Reilly, R. Public Relations in Action. 1981. 23.95 (ISBN 0-13-738526-9). P-H.

Reilly, Robin. William Pitt the Younger. LC 78-13050. (Illus.). 1979. 19.95 (ISBN 0-399-12130-7). Putnam Pub Group.

Reilly, Thomas C., jt. auth. see Brown, Michael D.

Reilly, William J. Successful Human Relations: In Business, in the Home, in Government. 1952. 13.41i (ISBN 0-06-035520-4, HarpT). Har-Row.

Reim, G. Studien zum Altestamentlichen Hintergrund Des Johannesevangeliums. LC 72-76086. (New Testament Studies Monograph, No. 22). 280p. (Ger.). 1973. 54.50 (ISBN 0-521-08630-2). Cambridge U Pr.

Reiman, Donald, ed. English Romantic Poetry, Eighteen Hundred-Eighteen Thirty-Five: A Guide to Information Sources. LC 74-11527. (American Literature, English Literature, & World Literatures in English Information Guide Ser.: Vol. 27). 1979. 42.00x (ISBN 0-8103-1231-X). Gale.

Reiman, Donald, ed. see Dacre, Charlotte.

Reiman, Donald H. Percy Bysshe Shelley. LC 74-80028. (Griffin Authors Ser). 188p. 1975. pap. 4.95 (ISBN 0-312-60060-7). St Martin.

--Percy Bysshe Shelley. (English Authors Ser.). lib. bdg. 11.95 (ISBN 0-8057-1488-X, Twayne). G K Hall.

Reiman, Donald H., ed. Dramatic Scenes & Other Poems 1819; Marcian Colonna, 1820: Proctor Bryan Waller ("Barry Cornwall") (1787-1874) LC 75-31246. (Romantic Context Ser.: Poetry 1789-1830). 1978. lib. bdg. 47.00 o.s.i. (ISBN 0-8240-2194-0). Garland Pub.

--The Flood of Thessaly: Proctor Bryan Waller. LC 75-31248. (Romantic Context Ser.: Poetry 1789-1830). 1978. Repr. of 1823 ed. lib. bdg. 47.00 o.s.i. (ISBN 0-8240-2196-7). Garland Pub.

Reiman, Donald H., ed. see Barrett, Eaton S.

Reiman, Donald H., ed. see Bland, Robert.

Reiman, Donald H., ed. see Darwin, Erasmus.

Reiman, Donald H., ed. see Elliott, Ebenezer.

Reiman, Donald H., ed. see Frere, John H.

Reiman, Donald H., ed. see Gent, Thomas.

Reiman, Donald H., ed. see Hayley, William.

Reiman, Donald H., ed. see Heber, Reginald.

Reiman, Donald H., ed. see Hemans, Felicia D.

Reiman, Donald H., ed. see Lloyd, Charles.

Reiman, Donald H., ed. see Mant, Richard.

Reiman, Donald H., ed. see Merivale, John H.

Reiman, Donald H., ed. see Montgomery, James.

Reiman, Donald H., ed. see Opie, Amelia.

Reiman, Donald H., ed. see Sotheby, William.

Reiman, Donald H., ed. see Thelwall, John.

Reiman, Donald H., ed. see Thurlow, Edward.

Reiman, Jeffrey H. The Rich Get Richer & the Poor Get Prison: Ideology, Class & Criminal Justice. LC 78-23986. 1979. pap. text ed. 10.95x (ISBN 0-471-04726-0). Wiley.

Reimann see Weyl, Hermann, et al.

Reimann, Charles. Incredible Seney. 1982. 5.95 (ISBN 0-932212-26-3). Avery Color.

Reimers, David M. White Protestantism & the Negro. 1965. 13.95x (ISBN 0-19-501195-3). Oxford U Pr.

Reimers, Henry L. The Abrams Story. 1977. 7.50 (ISBN 0-87770-181-4). Ye Galleon.

Reimold, Orlando S. One Mind's Eye-View of the Mind. 1979. 9.50 o.p. (ISBN 0-8022-2231-5). Philos Lib.

Reimold, Robert J. & Queen, William H. Ecology of Halophytes. 1974. 49.50 (ISBN 0-12-586450-7). Acad Pr.

Rein. Dilemmas of Welfare Policy. 190p. 1982. 23.95 (ISBN 0-03-056137-X). Praeger.

Rein, G. A. Sir John Robert Seeley: A Study of the Historian. Herkless, John L., ed. 1983. 25.00 (ISBN 0-89341-550-2). Longwood Pr.

Rein, Gerhard, ed. New Look at the Apostles Creed. LeFort, David, tr. LC 72-75401. 1969. pap. 2.95 o.p. (ISBN 0-8066-0915-X, 10-4646). Augsburg.

Rein, Irving J. The Great American Communication Catalogue. (Speech Communications Ser.). (Illus.). 160p. 1975. pap. 14.95 (ISBN 0-13-363580-5). P-H.

--The Public Speaking Book. 1981. pap. text ed. 10.95x (ISBN 0-673-15188-3). Scott F.

--Rudy's Red Wagon: Communication Strategies in Contemporary Society. 1972. pap. 8.95x (ISBN 0-673-07623-7). Scott F.

Rein, Martin. From Policy to Practice. 384p. 1983. 17.50 (ISBN 0-87332-194-4); pap. price not set (ISBN 0-87332-219-3). M E Sharpe.

--Social Policy: Issues of Choice & Change. 392p. 1983. pap. text ed. 14.95 (ISBN 0-87332-235-5). M E Sharpe.

Reinach, Jacquelyn. Carefree Cooking. LC 71-113261. 1970. 5.95 (ISBN 0-8208-0222-0). Hearthside.

Reinach, Jacquelyn, jt. auth. see Lewis, Shari.

Reinders Folmer, A. N. & Shouten, J. Geriatrics for the Practitioner. (International Congress Ser.: No. 554). 1981. 48.00 (ISBN 0-444-90223-6). Elsevier.

Reine, W. F. Prud'Homme Van see Van Reine, W. F. Prud'Homme.

Reineck, H. E. & Singh, I. B. Depositional Sedimentary Environments-with Reference to Terrigenous Classics. (Illus.). 439p. 1974. 29.80 (ISBN 0-387-10189-6). Springer-Verlag.

Reinecke, John E., jt. auth. see Tsuzaki, Stanley M.

Reinecke, John E., et al. A Bibliography of Pidgin & Creole Languages. LC 73-91459. (Oceanic Linguistics Special Publication Ser.: No. 14). 860p. (Orig.). 1975. pap. 27.50x (ISBN 0-8248-0306-X). UH Pr.

Reinecker, Herbert. Der Kommissar Lasst Bitten. (Easy Readers, B). 1976. pap. text ed. 3.95 (ISBN 0-88436-291-4). EMC.

Reiner, Beatrice S. & Kaufman, Irving. Character Disorders in Parents of Delinquents. LC 59-15631. 1959. pap. 5.50 (ISBN 0-87304-089-9). Family Serv.

Reiner, Erica & Pingree, D. Babylonian Planetary Omens, Enuma Anu Enlil, Tablet 50-51. LC 79-67168. (Bibliotheca Mesopotamica Ser.: Vol. 2, Pt. 2). 100p. (Orig.). 1980. pap. 12.75x (ISBN 0-89003-049-9). Undena Pubns.

Reiner, Erica & Pingree, David. The Venus Tablet of Ammisaduqa. LC 75-26241. (Bibliotheca Mesopotamica Ser: Vol. 2, Pt. 1). 60p. 1975. pap. 6.75x o.p. (ISBN 0-89003-010-3). Undena Pubns.

Reiner, Irving, jt. auth. see Curtis, Charles W.

Reiner, Laurence E. Methods & Materials of Residential Construction. (Illus.). 336p. 1981. text ed. 25.95 (ISBN 0-13-578864-1). P-H.

Reiner, Lawrence E. Manual of Light Construction & Speculative Building. (Illus.). 1978. 27.95 (ISBN 0-07-051837-8, P&RB). McGraw.

Reiner, M. Selected Papers on Rheology. 463p. 1975. 72.50 (ISBN 0-444-41301-4). Elsevier.

Reiner, Miriam, et al, eds. Standard Methods of Clinical Chemistry. Incl. Vol. 1. Reiner, Miriam, ed. 1953. 30.00 (ISBN 0-12-609101-3); Vol. 2. Seligson, David, ed. 1958. 32.50 (ISBN 0-12-609102-1); Vol. 3. 1961. 32.50 o.p. (ISBN 0-12-609103-X); Vol. 4. 1964. 32.50 (ISBN 0-12-609104-8); Vol. 5. Meites, S., ed. 1965. 32.50 (ISBN 0-12-609105-6); Vol. 6. MacDonald, R. P., ed. 1970. 42.00 (ISBN 0-12-609106-4); Vol. 7. 1972. 48.50 (ISBN 0-12-609107-2). Acad Pr.

Reiner, R. The Blue-Coated Worker. LC 77-85695. (Cambridge Studies in Sociology: No. 10). (Illus.). 1978. 42.50 (ISBN 0-521-21889-6); pap. 13.95 (ISBN 0-521-29482-7). Cambridge U Pr.

Reinert, jt. auth. see Jacobson.

Reinert, Henry R. Children in Conflict: Educational Strategies for the Emotionally Distrubed & Behaviorally Disordered. 2nd ed. LC 79-22526. (Illus.). 256p. 1980. 19.95 (ISBN 0-8016-4109-8). Mosby.

Reinert, Henry R., jt. auth. see Swanson, H. Lee.

Reinert, Otto & Arnott, Peter. Twenty Three Plays: An Introductory Anthology. 1978. pap. text ed. 14.95 (ISBN 0-316-73950-2). Little.

Reinert, Otto, ed. Six Plays: An Introductory Anthology. 416p. 1973. pap. text ed. 8.95 (ISBN 0-316-73948-0). Little.

Reinert, Otto & Arnott, Peter, eds. Thirteen Plays: An Introduction. 1978. pap. text ed. 11.95 (ISBN 0-316-73949-9). Little.

Reinert, Rick. The Tooth Chicken. (Good Friends Ser.). (Illus.). 16p. (gr. k-6). 1982. pap. 1.25 (ISBN 0-686-84018-6). Ideals.

Reinertsen, Lauren. Clipart Book of Promotional & Program Artwork. 2nd ed. LC 74-84398. (Illus.). 64p. 1974. pap. 11.95 (ISBN 0-87874-013-9). Galloway.

Reinfeld, Fred. Attack & Counterattack in Chess. 1970. pap. 3.80i (ISBN 0-06-463204-0, EH 204, EH). B&N NY.

--Better Chess. (Better Ser.). (Illus.). (gr. 7 up). 1976. 16.95x o.p. (ISBN 0-7182-0149-3, SpS). Sportshelf.

--Chess for Children. rev. ed. LC 58-7612. (Illus.). 72p. (gr. 3-12). 1980. 7.95 (ISBN 0-8069-4904-X); PLB 9.99 (ISBN 0-8069-4905-8). Sterling.

--Chess Is an Easy Game. LC 61-18952. (gr. 5 up). 1962. 7.95 (ISBN 0-8069-4906-6); PLB 9.99 (ISBN 0-8069-4907-4). Sterling.

--Chess: Win in Twenty Moves or Less. pap. 3.50 (ISBN 0-06-463358-6, EH 358, EH). B&N NY.

--Hypermodern Chess. 1948. pap. 4.50 (ISBN 0-486-20448-0). Dover.

--Winning Chess Openings. (Illus.). 296p. 1973. pap. 6.95 (ISBN 0-02-029760-2, Collier). Macmillan.

Reinfeld, Fred & Hobson, Burton. Catalogue of the World's Most Popular Coins. 10th ed. LC 78-66299. (Illus.). 1979. 19.95 (ISBN 0-8069-6070-1); lib. bdg. 17.59 o.p. (ISBN 0-8069-6071-X). Sterling.

--Catalogue of the World's Most Popular Coins. 11th ed. (Illus.). 544p. 1983. 24.95 (ISBN 0-8069-6078-7); lib. bdg. 29.49 (ISBN 0-8069-6079-5); pap. 16.95 (ISBN 0-8069-7708-6). Sterling.

Reinfeld, Fred & Hobson, Burton H. How to Build a Coin Collection. LC 58-12544. (Illus.). (gr. 3 up). 1977. 8.95 (ISBN 0-8069-6068-X); PLB 10.99 (ISBN 0-8069-6069-8). Sterling.

Reinfeld, Fred & Obojska, Robert. The Stamp Collector's Handbook. LC 80-945. 1980. 7.95 (ISBN 0-385-17077-7). Doubleday.

Reinfeld, Fred & Obojski, Robert. Coin Collector's Handbook. rev. ed. LC 80-946. 160p. 1980. 7.95 (ISBN 0-385-17078-5). Doubleday.

Reinfeld, Fred, jt. auth. see Horowitz, I. A.

Reinfeld, Fred & Fine, Reuben, eds. Lasker's Greatest Chess Games, 1889-1914. 1965. pap. 3.95 (ISBN 0-486-21450-8). Dover.

Reinfeld, Nyles. Survival Management for Industry. 1981. text ed. 21.95 (ISBN 0-8359-7410-3); instr's. manual free (ISBN 0-8359-7411-1). Reston.

Reinfeld, Nyles V. Open Heart Surgery: A Second Chance. 192p. 1983. 14.00 (ISBN 0-13-637520-0); pap. 6.95 (ISBN 0-13-637512-X). P-H.

--Production & Inventory Control. 1981. text ed. 22.95 (ISBN 0-8359-5629-6). Reston.

Reingold, et al. Combinatorial Algorithms: Theory & Practice. 1977. text ed. 27.95 (ISBN 0-13-152447-X). P-H.

Reingold, Carmel B. California Cuisine. 192p. 1983. pap. 5.95 (ISBN 0-380-82156-7, 82156). Avon.

--The Crockery Pot Cookbook. (Orig.). 1975. pap. 1.50 o.s.i. (ISBN 0-515-03950-0). Jove Pubns.

--Cuisinart: Food Processing Cooking. 1976. pap. 5.95 o.s.i. (ISBN 0-440-51604-8, Delta). Dell.

--Cuisinart Food Processor Cookbook. rev. ed. 1981. pap. 9.95 (Delta). Dell.

--The Lifelong Anti-Cancer Diet. 1982. pap. 3.50 (ISBN 0-451-12220-8, AE2220, Sig). NAL.

Reingold, Edward & Hansen, Wilfred J. Data Structures. (Computer Systems Ser.). (Illus.). 450p. text ed. 28.95 (ISBN 0-316-73951-0); solutions manual avail. (ISBN 0-316-73930-8). Little.

Reinhard, David W. The Republic Right Since 1945. LC 82-40460. 304p. 1983. 25.00x (ISBN 0-8131-1484-5). U Pr of Ky.

Reinhard, P. G., jt. auth. see Goeke, K.

Reinhardt, Adina M., jt. auth. see Faber, Marilyn M.

Reinhardt, Adina M. & Quinn, Mildred D., eds. Family Centered Community Nursing: A Sociocultural Framework. LC 73-8681. 304p. 1973. pap. text ed. 13.50 o.p. (ISBN 0-8016-4102-0). Mosby.

Reinhardt, Howard E. & Loftsgaarden, Don O. Elementary Probability & Statistical Reasoning. 1977. text ed. 19.95 (ISBN 0-669-08300-3); o.p. (ISBN 0-669-00241-0). Heath.

Reinhardt, Jon M. Foreign Policy & National Integration: The Case of Indonesia. LC 70-175548. (Monograph: No. 17). (Illus.). vi, 230p. 1971. 8.50x (ISBN 0-686-30901-4). Yale U SE Asia.

--Foreign Policy & National Integration: The Case of Indonesia. (Illus.). 230p. 1971. 8.50 (ISBN 0-686-38048-7). Yale U SE Asia.

Reinhardt, Kurt F., tr. see Landgrebe, Ludwig.

Reinhardt, Richard W., jt. auth. see Johnson, Paul C.

Reinhart, Charles. You Can't Do That: Beatles Bootlegs & Novelty Records, 1963-1980. (Rock & Roll Reference Ser.: No. 5). 450p. 1981. individuals 14.95 (ISBN 0-87650-128-5); 17.95institutions. Pierian.

Reinharz, Jehuda, jt. auth. see Mendes-Flohr, Paul R.

Reinharz, Shulamit. On Becoming a Social Scientist: From Survey Research & Participent Observation to Experiental Analysis. LC 79-83577. (Social & Behavioral Science Ser.). 1979. 22.95x (ISBN 0-87589-409-7). Jossey-Bass.

Reinhoff & Abrams, eds. Computer in the Doctor's Office. 1980. 42.75 (ISBN 0-444-86051-7). Elsevier.

Reinhold, Meyer. Diaspora: The Jews Among the Greeks & Romans. (Illus.). 192p. 1983. 24.95 (ISBN 0-88866-619-5). Samuel Stevens.

Reinhold, Meyer, ed. The Classic Pages: Classical Reading of Eighteenth-Century Americans. (APA Special Publications Ser.). 12.00 (ISBN 0-686-95209-X, 40-05-03). Scholars Pr CA.

Reinhold, Meyer, jt. ed. see Lewis, Naphtali.

Reinhold, Susan, jt. auth. see Brown, Robert.

Reinhold, Timothy A., ed. Wind Tunnel Modeling for Civil Engineering Applications. LC 82-14594. (Illus.). 704p. 1982. 55.00 (ISBN 0-521-25278-4). Cambridge U Pr.

Reinhoudt, D. N. Structure & Activity of Anti-Tumour Agents. 1983. 47.50 (ISBN 90-247-2783-9, Pub. by Martinus Nijhoff Netherlands). Kluwer Boston.

Reinig, William C. Enviromental Surveillance in the Vicinity of Nuclear Facilities. (Illus.). 480p. 1970. photocopy ed. spiral 47.50x (ISBN 0-398-01568-6). C C Thomas.

Reining, Priscilla. Challenging Desertification in West Africa: Insights from Landsat into Carrying Capacity, Cultivation & Settlement Site Identification in Upper Volta & Niger. LC 79-21120. (Papers in International Studies: African Ser.: No. 39). (Orig.). 1980. 15.00 (ISBN 0-89680-102-0, Ohio U Ctr Intl). Ohio U Pr.

Reining, Priscilla & Lenkerd, Barbara, eds. Village Viability in Contemporary Society. (AAAS Selected Symposium: No. 34). 1979. lib. bdg. 29.00 (ISBN 0-89158-472-2). Westview.

Reinis, Stanislav & Goldman, Jerome M. The Chemistry of Behavior: A Molecular Approach to Neuronal Plasticity. LC 82-13294. 622p. 1982. 55.00 (ISBN 0-306-41161-X, Plenum Pr). Plenum Pub.

Reinisch, Edith H. & Minear, Ralph E. Health of the Preschool Child. LC 78-8743. 1978. text ed. 22.95x (ISBN 0-471-60800-9); test manual 3.00 (ISBN 0-471-06310-X). Wiley.

Reinitz, R. Tensions in American Puritanism. (Problems in American History Ser.). 1970. pap. 10.50x o.p. (ISBN 0-471-71561-1). Wiley.

Reinius, Trish. The Planet of Tears. (Illus.). 1979. pap. 6.95 (ISBN 0-89742-016-0, Dawne-Leigh, Dawne-Leigh). Celestial Arts.

Reinking, James A., et al. Improving College Writing: A Book of Exercises. 300p. 1981. pap. 9.95x (ISBN 0-312-41060-3); instr's. manual avail. (ISBN 0-312-41061-1). St Martin.

Reinl, Edda. The Little Snake. (Picture Book Studio Ser.). (Illus.). 28p. (Eng.). 1982. 9.95 (ISBN 0-907234-15-1). Neugebauer Pr.

Reino, Joseph. Karl Shapiro. (United States Authors Ser.). 1981. lib. bdg. 12.95 (ISBN 0-8057-7333-9, Twayne). G K Hall.

Reinold, E., jt. ed. see Gitsch, E.

Reinprecht, Hansheinz. The Hermann Gmeiner Book: The Story of the S O S -Children's Villages & Their Founder. 1978. pap. 4.95 o.p. (ISBN 0-533-03453-1). Vantage.

Reinsch, Lamar & Stano, Michael. Communications in Interviews. 256p. 1982. pap. 13.95 (ISBN 0-13-153502-1). P-H.

Reinsmith, Richard. Somebody to Kill. (Bodyguard Ser.: No. 4). 224p. (Orig.). Date not set. pap. cancelled o.p. (ISBN 0-505-51798-1). Tower Bks.

--Somebody to Kill. (Bodyguard Ser.: No. 4). 224p. (Orig.). 1982. pap. 2.50 o.s.i. (ISBN 0-8439-1177-8, Leisure Bks). Nordon Pubns.

Reinstedt, Randall A. Incredible Ghosts of Old Monterey's Hotel Del Monte. LC 80-131190. (Illus.). 48p. 1980. pap. 2.95 (ISBN 0-933818-07-6). Ghost Town.

--Incredible Ghosts of the Big Sur Coast. LC 82-164106. (Illus.). 52p. 1981. pap. 2.95 (ISBN 0-933818-08-4). Ghost Town.

--Mysterious Sea Monsters of California's Central Coast. LC 80-114610. (Illus.). 68p. (Orig.). 1979. pap. 4.50 (ISBN 0-933818-06-8). Ghost Town.

Reinstein, Cary E. HP-41-HP-IL System Dictionary. 96p. 1982. pap. 12.00 o.p. (ISBN 0-942358-01-5). Corvallis Software.

Reintjes, John F., ed. Nonlinear Optical Parametric Processes in Liquids & Gases. LC 82-11603. Date not set. price not set (ISBN 0-12-585980-5). Acad Pr.

Reis, Mary. Batik. LC 72-13334. (Early Craft Bks.). (Illus.). 36p. (gr. 1-4). 1973. PLB 3.95g (ISBN 0-8225-0852-4). Lerner Pubns.

Reis, Roberto, jt. ed. see Foster, David W.

Reisberg, Ken. Card Games. LC 78-11646. (First Bks.). (Illus.). (gr. 4 up). 1979. PLB 8.90s&l (ISBN 0-531-02253-6). Watts.

--Card Tricks. LC 80-11111. (gr. 1-3). 1980. PLB 8.90 (ISBN 0-531-04137-9). Watts.

--Coin Fun. LC 81-22. (Easy-Read Activity Bks.). (Illus.). 32p. (gr. 1-3). 1981. PLB 8.90 (ISBN 0-686-86862-5). Watts.

--Martial Arts. (First Bks.). (Illus.). (gr. 4 up). 1979. s&l 8.90 (ISBN 0-531-04077-1). Watts.

Reisch, Kenneth, et al. Woody Ornamentals for the Midwest. (Illus.). 1975. wire coil bdg. 10.95 (ISBN 0-8403-1265-2). Kendall-Hunt.

Reischauer, Edwin O. & Craig, Albert M. Japan: Tradition & Transformation. LC 77-77979. (Illus.). 1978. text ed. 18.95 (ISBN 0-395-25814-6). HM.

Reischauer, Edwin O., jt. auth. see Fairbank, John K.

Reischauer, Robert D., et al. Reforming School Finance. (Studies in Social Economics). 1973. 12.95 (ISBN 0-8157-7396-X); pap. 6.95 (ISBN 0-8157-7395-1). Brookings.

Reische, Diana, ed. see Simon, Anne, et al.

Reisdorff, James J. & Bartels, Michael M. Railroad Stations in Nebraska: An Era of Use & Reuse. LC 82-61823. (Illus.). 112p. 1982. text ed. 23.50 (ISBN 0-9609568-0-8). South Platte.

Reiser, Howard. Skateboarding. (First Bks.). (Illus.). (gr. 4 up). 1978. PLB 8.90 s&l (ISBN 0-531-01412-6). Watts.

Reiser, Oliver L. This Holyest Erthe. (Illus., Orig.). 1983. pap. 5.95 (ISBN 0-89407-022-3). Strawberry Hill.

Reiser, Stanley J. Medicine & the Reign of Technology. LC 77-87389. (Illus.). 317p. (Orig.). 1981. pap. 10.95 (ISBN 0-521-28223-3). Cambridge U Pr.

--Medicine & the Reign of Technology. LC 77-87389. (Illus.). 1978. 29.95 (ISBN 0-521-21907-8). Cambridge U Pr.

Reiser, Stanley J., et al, eds. Ethics in Medicine: Historical Perspectives and Contemporary Concerns. 1977. text ed. 49.50x (ISBN 0-262-18081-2); pap. 21.95x (ISBN 0-262-68029-7). MIT Pr.

Reiser, Virginia, ed. Favorite Short Stories in Large Print. 720p. 1982. lib. bdg. 17.95 (ISBN 0-8161-3434-0, Large Print Bks). G K Hall.

Reisfeld, A. Warp Knit Engineering. 1966. 24.00 o.p. (ISBN 0-87245-275-1). Textile Bk.

Reisfeld, A., et al. Fundamentals of Raschel Knitting. (Illus.). 1958. 5.75 o.p. (ISBN 0-87245-274-3). Textile Bk.

Reisig, W., jt. ed. see Girault, C.

Reisinger, Ernest C. The Carnal Christian: What Should We Think of the Carnal Christian? 75p. 0.95 (ISBN 0-686-77770-0). Banner of Truth.

Reisler, Mark. By the Sweat of Their Brow: Mexican Immigrant Labor in the United States, 1900-1940. LC 76-5329. 304p. (Orig.). 1976. lib. bdg. 27.50x (ISBN 0-8371-8894-6, RPE/). Greenwood.

--By the Sweat of Their Brow: Mexican Immigrant Labor in the United States, 1900-1940. LC 76-5329. xi, 298p. 1977. pap. text ed. 5.95 (ISBN 0-313-20160-9, RPE/). Greenwood.

Reisman, A., jt. auth. see Mesarovic, M.

Reisman, Albert F., ed. Business Loan Workouts: A Course Handbook. 699p. 1981. 30.00 (ISBN 0-686-43272-X, A4-4039). PLI.

Reisman, Arnold. Materials Management for Health Services. LC 79-3524. 512p. 1981. 37.95x (ISBN 0-669-03458-4). Lexington Bks.

--Phase Equilibria. (Physical Chemistry Ser: Vol. 19). 1970. 69.00 (ISBN 0-12-586350-0). Acad Pr.

--Systems Analysis in Health-Care Delivery. LC 79-3907. 336p. 1979. 26.95x (ISBN 0-669-02855-X). Lexington Bks.

Reisman, D. A. Richard Titmuss: Welfare & Society. (Heinemann Educational Bks). 1977. text ed. 18.00x (ISBN 0-435-82749-9); pap. text ed. 10.00x (ISBN 0-435-82750-2). Heinemann Ed.

Reisman, Daniel & Durst, Sanford J. Buying & Selling Country Land. (Illus.). 1981. lib. bdg. 24.95 (ISBN 0-915262-40-1). S J Durst.

Reisman, Fredericka K. Teaching Mathematics: Methods & Content. 2nd ed. 1981. 19.50 (ISBN 0-395-30706-6); Instr's manual 1.25 (ISBN 0-395-30707-4). HM.

Reisman, Fredericka K. & Kauffman, Samuel H. Teaching Mathematics to Children with Special Needs. (Special Education Ser.). 336p. 1980. text ed. 21.95x (ISBN 0-675-08175-0). Merrill.

Reisman, Fredricka. A Guide to the Diagnostic Teaching of Arithmetic. 3rd ed. 184p. 1982. pap. text ed. 9.95 (ISBN 0-675-09879-3). Merrill.

Reisman, John M. A History of Clinical Psychology: Enlarged Edition of the Development of Clinical Psychology. LC 75-40102. (Century Psychology Ser.). 430p. 1976. pap. text ed. 10.95x (ISBN 0-8290-0873-X); 29.50x (ISBN 0-686-96755-0). Irvington.

Reismann, Herbert & Pawlik, Peter S. Elasticity, Theory & Applications. LC 80-10145. 1980. 49.95 (ISBN 0-471-03165-8, Pub. by Wiley-Interscience). Wiley.

Reisner, Barbara, tr. see Salmen, Walter.

Reisner, K. & Gosepath, J. Craniotomography: An Atlas & Guide. Michaelis, L. S., tr. from Ger. LC 75-16102. (Illus.). 208p. 1977. 54.50 o.p. (ISBN 0-88416-244-3). Wright-PSG.

Reiss, Bob. Night Landings. 228p. 1983. 14.45i (ISBN 0-316-73965-0). Little.

Reiss, David. M A S H. rev. ed. 160p. 1983. pap. 9.95 (ISBN 0-672-52762-6). Bobbs.

Reiss, Edmund. Boethius. (Twayne's World Authors Ser.). 1982. lib. bdg. 18.95 (ISBN 0-8057-6519-0, Twayne). G K Hall.

--William Dunbar. (English Authors Ser.). 1979. lib. bdg. 14.95 (ISBN 0-8057-6750-9, Twayne). G K Hall.

Reiss, Ellen, intro. by see Siegel, Eli.

Reiss, James. Express. LC 82-13504. (Pitt Poetry Ser.). 74p. 1983. 10.95 (ISBN 0-8229-3474-4); pap. 4.95 (ISBN 0-8229-5346-3). U of Pittsburgh Pr.

Reiss, John J. Colors. LC 69-13653. (Illus.). 32p. (ps-2). 1969. 10.95 (ISBN 0-02-776130-4). Bradbury Pr.

--Numbers. LC 76-151313. (Illus.). 32p. (ps-1). 1971. 10.95 (ISBN 0-02-776150-9). Bradbury Pr.

--Shapes. LC 73-76545. (Illus.). 32p. (ps-2). 1974. 10.95 (ISBN 0-02-776190-8). Bradbury Pr.

Reiss, S., et al. Abnormality: Experimental & Clinical Approach. 1977. 25.95x (ISBN 0-02-399300-6, 39930). Macmillan.

Reiss, Wilhelm, jt. auth. see Morrison, Cathryn.

Reisser, Marsha J., jt. auth. see Floyd, Samuel A., Jr.

Reissig, J. L., ed. Microbial Interactions. (Receptors & Recognition Series B: Vol. 3). 1977. 49.95x (ISBN 0-412-14310-0, Pub. by Chapman & Hall). Methuen Inc.

Reissman, L., jt. auth. see Silvert, K. H.

Reissman, Leonard. Inequality in American Society: Social Stratification. 1973. pap. 6.95x o.p. (ISBN 0-673-05921-9). Scott F.

Reister, Floyd N., ed. Private Aviation: A Guide to Information Sources. LC 79-84660. (Sports, Games, & Pastimes Information Guide Ser.: Vol. 3). 1979. 42.00x (ISBN 0-8103-1440-1). Gale.

Reistroffer, Mary. Conversations: Foster Parents & Social Workers: on the Jobs, No. 3. LC 73-93881. 1974. pap. 3.00 (ISBN 0-87868-111-6, F-50). Child Welfare.

Reit, Seymour. All Kinds of Planes. (Golden Look-Look Bks.). (ps-3). 1978. PLB 6.08 (ISBN 0-307-61853-6, Golden Pr); pap. 1.25 (ISBN 0-307-11853-3). Western Pub.

--Bugs Bunny Goes to the Dentist. (Look-Look Bks.). (Illus.). 1978. PLB 6.08 (ISBN 0-307-61843-9, Golden Pr); pap. 1.25 (ISBN 0-307-11843-6). Western Pub.

--Child of the Navajos. LC 74-162608. (Illus.). (gr. 2-5). 1971. PLB 5.95 o.p. (ISBN 0-396-06414-0). Dodd.

--The Fox & the Hound Storybook. (Specials Ser.). 40p. (ps-3). 1981. 5.95 (ISBN 0-307-16802-6, Golden Pr); Golden Pr. PLB 10.69 (ISBN 0-307-66802-9). Western Pub.

Reite, Martin & Caine, Nancy, eds. Child Abuse: The Nonhuman Primate Data. (Monographs in Primatology: Vol. 1). 200p. 1983. write for info. (ISBN 0-8451-3400-0). A R Liss.

Reiter, B. P. The Saturday Night Knife & Gun Club. 240p. 1982. 2.95 (ISBN 0-553-11332-1). Bantam.

Reiter, Elmar R. Atmospheric Transport Processes, Pt. 2: Chemical Tracers. LC 76-603262. (DOE Critical Review Ser.). 382p. 1971. pap. 17.50 (ISBN 0-87079-140-0, TID-25314); microfiche 4.50 (ISBN 0-87079-141-9, TID-25314). DOE.

--Atmospheric Transport Processes, Pt. 3: Hydrodynamic Tracers. LC 76-603262. (DOE Critical Review Ser.). 212p. 1972. pap. 13.25 (ISBN 0-87079-142-7, TID-25731); microfiche 4.50 (ISBN 0-87079-143-5, TID-25731). DOE.

--Atmospheric Transport Processes, Pt. 4: Radioactive Tracers. LC 76-603262. (DOE Critical Review Ser.). 620p. 1978. 23.50 (ISBN 0-87079-114-1, TID-27114); microfiche 4.50 (ISBN 0-87079-145-1, TID-27114). DOE.

Reiter, J. The Women. LC 78-1346. (The Old West Ser.). (Illus.). 1978. 17.28 (ISBN 0-8094-1514-3). Silver.

Reiter, Russel. The Pineal, Vol. 2. 1977. 21.60 (ISBN 0-88831-006-4). Eden Pr.

Reiter, Russel J. The Pineal, Vol. 3. Horrobin, D. F., ed. 1979. 28.80 (ISBN 0-88831-039-0). Eden Pr.

--The Pineal, Vol. 4. Horrobin, D. F., ed. (Annual Research Reviews). 1979. 24.00 (ISBN 0-88831-066-8). Eden Pr.

--The Pineal, Vol. 5. David, J. & Horrobin, F., eds. (Annual Research Reviews). 236p. 1980. 30.00 (ISBN 0-88831-084-6). Eden Pr.

--The Pineal, Vol. 6. Horrobin, David, ed. (Annual Research Reviews Ser.). 265p. 1981. 32.00 (ISBN 0-88831-116-8). Eden Pr.

--The Pineal & Its Hormones, Vol.92. LC 82-7154. (Progress in Clinical & Biological Research Ser.). 310p. 1982. 30.00 (ISBN 0-8451-0092-0). A R Liss.

Reith, Alma C., et al, eds. see Writers' Group of the Dearborn Branch of the American Association of University Women.

Reith, Charles. The Blind Eye of History: A Study of the Origins of the Present Police Era. LC 74-26636. (Criminology, Law Enforcement, & Social Problems Ser.: No. 203). 1975. Repr. of 1952 ed. 14.00x (ISBN 0-87585-203-3). Patterson Smith.

Reith, Edward J., jt. auth. see Ross, Michael H.

Reith, Edward J., et al. Textbook of Anatomy & Physiology. 2nd ed. (Illus.). 1978. pap. text ed. 25.50 (ISBN 0-07-051873-4, HP); instr's guide 10.95 (ISBN 0-07-051877-7); study guide 10.95 (ISBN 0-07-051876-9). McGraw.

Reith, Karl F. Mikrologie. 126p. (Ger.). 1982. write for info. (ISBN 3-8204-5817-4). P Lang Pubs.

Reithmaier, L. W. Instrument Pilot's Guide. 1982. pap. write for info. (ISBN 0-8168-6463-2). Aero.

--Private Pilot's Guide. 3rd ed. 1982. pap. write for info. (ISBN 0-8168-7602-9). Aero.

Reitlinger, Gerald. The Economics of Taste, 3 Vols. LC 82-80311. (Illus.). 1959p. 1982. Repr. of 1907 ed. 100.00 (ISBN 0-87817-288-2). Hacker.

Reitman, A. The Election Process. 2nd ed. LC 80-14986. (Legal Almanac Ser.: No. 24). 122p. 1980. 5.95. Oceana.

Reitz, H. Joseph, jt. auth. see Jewell, Linda N.

Reitz, John R., et al. Foundations of Electromagnetic Theory. 3rd ed. LC 78-18649. (Physics Ser.). (Illus.). 1979. text ed. 28.95 (ISBN 0-201-06332-8); answer bk. 1.00 (ISBN 0-201-06333-6). A-W.

Rejaunier, Jeanne. Affair in Rome. 352p. (Orig.). 1981. pap. 2.50 o.p. (ISBN 0-523-41005-0). Pinnacle Bks.

Rejda, George E. Principles of Insurance. 1982. text ed. 24.50x (ISBN 0-673-15344-4). Scott F.

--Social Insurance & Economic Security. (Illus.). 528p. 1976. 23.95 (ISBN 0-13-815779-0). P-H.

Rejda, George E. & Ginsberg, Ralph B., eds. Risk & Its Treatment: Changing Societal Consequences. LC 78-72994. (Annals: No. 443). 1979. 15.00 (ISBN 0-87761-238-2); pap. 7.95 (ISBN 0-87761-239-0). Am Acad Pol Soc Sci.

Rejnis, Ruth. A Woman's Guide to New Careers in Real Estate. 1978. pap. 5.95 o.p. (ISBN 0-8092-7403-5). Contemp Bks.

Rekers, George A. Growing up Straight. LC 82-8197. 1982. pap. 5.95 (ISBN 0-8024-0156-2). Moody.

Rekker, R. F. The Hydrophobic Fragmental Constant: Its Derivation & Application with a Means of Characterizing Membrane Systems. (Pharmacochemistry Library: Vol. 1). 1977. 64.00 (ISBN 0-444-41548-3). Elsevier.

Rekker, R. F., jt. ed. see Nauta, W. T.

Rekosh, Lois. Basic Social Studies Skills. 1979. pap. 5.95 (ISBN 0-07-051171-3, Trafalgar Hse Pub). McGraw.

Rele, J. R. & Kanitkar, Tara. Fertility & Family Planning in Greater Bombay. 217p. 1980. 22.95x (ISBN 0-940500-87-6, Pub by Popular Prakashan India). Asia Bk Corp.

Relf, Patricia. The First Day of School. (Golden Storytime Bks.). (Illus.). 24p. (ps). 1981. 1.95 (ISBN 0-307-11957-2, Golden Pr); 6.08 (ISBN 0-307-61957-5). Western Pub.

Relier, J. P., jt. ed. see Minkowski, A.

Religious Education Staff. Insights: Spirit Masters for Reading the New Testament. (To Live Is Christ Ser.). 1978. 12.95 (ISBN 0-697-01674-9). Wm C Brown.

--Lord & Savior: Friend & Brother, Spirit Masters for The Jesus Book. (To Live Is Christ Ser.). 1979. 10.95 (ISBN 0-697-01692-7). Wm C Brown.

--Man & Woman Spirit Masters. (To Live Is Christ Ser.). 1980. 10.95 (ISBN 0-697-01752-4). Wm C Brown.

--Mystery, Value, & Awareness: Spirit Masters for Religions of the World. (To Live Is Christ Ser.). 1979. 10.95 (ISBN 0-697-01730-3). Wm C Brown.

--Pluralism, Similarities, & Contrast: Spirit Masters for Religion in North America. (To Live Is Christ Ser.). 1979. 10.95 (ISBN 0-697-01735-4). Wm C Brown.

--The Spirit Alive in Prayer: Spirit Masters. 1979. 9.95 (ISBN 0-697-01699-4). Wm C Brown.

--The Spirit Alive in Service: Spirit Masters. 1979. 9.95 (ISBN 0-697-01712-5). Wm C Brown.

--The Spirit Alive in Vocations: Spirit Masters. 1980. 9.95 (ISBN 0-697-01755-9). Wm C Brown.

Religous Education Staff. The Spirit Alive in Liturgy: Spirit Masters. 1981. 9.95 (ISBN 0-686-84105-0). Wm C Brown.

--The Spirit Alive in You: Spirit Masters. 1982. 9.95 (ISBN 0-697-01805-9). Wm C Brown.

Relis, Nurie & Strauss, Gail. Sewing for Fashion Design. (Illus.). 1978. ref. 18.95 (ISBN 0-87909-755-8). Reston.

Relis, Nurie, jt. auth. see Jaffe, Hilde.

Relkin, R. The Pineal Gland: Current Endocrinology-Basic & clinical Aspects. 320p. 1982. 45.00 (ISBN 0-444-00714-8). Elsevier.

Relkin, Richard. The Pineal, Vol. 1. 1976. 21.60 (ISBN 0-904406-26-1). Eden Pr.

Reller, Theodore L., jt. ed. see Erickson, Donald A.

Relman, Arnold S., intro. by. Current Concepts in Nutrition. (Illus.). 131p. (Orig.). 1979. pap. text ed. 6.00 (ISBN 0-910133-01-8). MA Med Soc.

Relph, E. Place & Placelessness. (Research in Planning & Design Ser.). 156p. 1976. 15.50x (ISBN 0-85086-055-5, Pub. by Pion England). Methuen Inc.

Rels, Herbert. Rules of Printed English. 1980. 25.00x o.p. (ISBN 0-232-51038-5, Pub. by Darton-Longman-Todd England). State Mutual Bk.

Relyea, Harold C., jt. ed. see Riley, Tom.

Rembar, Charles. The Law of the Land. 1980. 15.00 o.p. (ISBN 0-671-24322-5). S&S.

Rembold & Armbruster. Inter, Technology for Computer: Controlled Manufacturing Processes. (Manufacturing Engineering & Materials Processing Ser.). 360p. 1983. not set 48.50 (ISBN 0-8247-1836-4). Dekker.

Rementeria, Jose L., ed. Drug Abuse in Pregnancy & Neonatal Effects. LC 77-3541. (Illus.). 300p. 1977. text ed. 23.50 o.p. (ISBN 0-8016-4108-X). Mosby.

Remer, J. Changing Schools Through the Arts. 160p. 1982. 15.95 (ISBN 0-07-051847-5). McGraw.

Remer, Rory, ed. Counselor & Research. 1981. Part I. 2.00 (ISBN 0-686-36396-5); nonmembers 2.50 (ISBN 0-686-37304-9); Part II. 2.00 (ISBN 0-686-37305-7); nonmembers 2.50 (ISBN 0-686-37306-5). Am Personnel.

Remers, H. Lee, jt. auth. see Brooke, Michael Z.

Remers, William A. The Chemistry of Antitumor Antibiotics, Vol. 1. LC 78-12436. 1979. 43.95 (ISBN 0-471-01791-4, Pub. by Wiley-Interscience). Wiley.

Remington, et al. Criminal Justice Administration. rev. ed. (Contemporary Legal Education Ser.). 1982. 26.00 (ISBN 0-87215-406-8, Bobbs-Merrill Law). Michie-Bobbs.

Remington, Frederic. Frederic Remington: One Hundred Seventy-Three Drawings & Illustrations. Pitz, Henry C., ed. & intro. by. LC 78-158963. (Illus.). 160p. (Orig.). 1972. pap. 7.00 (ISBN 0-486-20714-5). Dover.

--Illustrations of Frederic Remington. (Bounty Bks.). (Illus.). 1970. 5.98 o.p. (ISBN 0-517-00243-4); deluxe ed. 10.00 o.p. (ISBN 0-517-51106-1). Crown.

Remington, Jack S. & Swartz, Morton N. Current Clinical Topics in Infectious Diseases, No. 1. (Illus.). 1980. text ed. 35.00 (ISBN 0-07-051850-5). McGraw.

--Current Clinical Topics in Infectious Diseases, No. 2. (Illus.). 304p. 1981. text ed. 35.00 (ISBN 0-07-051851-3, HP). McGraw.

--Current Clinical Topics in Infectious Diseases, No. 3. (Illus.). 304p. 1982. text ed. 35.00 (ISBN 0-07-051852-1). McGraw.

Remington, R. & Schork, M. A. Statistics with Applications to the Biological & Health Sciences. 1970. 28.95 (ISBN 0-13-846188-0). P-H.

Remington, Robin A., ed. The International Relations of Eastern Europe: A Guide to Information Sources. LC 73-17512. (International Relations Information Guide Ser.: Vol. 8). 1978. 42.00x (ISBN 0-8103-1320-0). Gale.

Remini, Robert V. Andrew Jackson. (World Leaders Ser). 1966. lib. bdg. 8.95 o.p. (ISBN 0-8057-3048-6, G K Hall). G K Hall.

--The Revolutionary Age of Andrew Jackson. LC 74-2623. (gr. 7 up). 1976. 10.95i o.p. (ISBN 0-06-024856-4, HarpJ); PLB 10.89 (ISBN 0-06-024857-2). Har-Row.

Remini, Robert V. & Miles, Edwin A., eds. The Era of Good Feelings & the Age of Jackson, 1816-1841. LC 79-84211. (Goldentree Bibliographies in American History). 1979. text ed. 23.95x (ISBN 0-88295-578-0); pap. text ed. 18.95x (ISBN 0-88295-579-9). Harlan Davidson.

Remini, William C., ed. Evaluation of Current Developments in Municipal Waste Treatment: Proceedings. LC 77-10538. (ERDA Symposium Ser.). 128p. 1977. pap. 11.25 (ISBN 0-87079-201-6, CONF-770108); microfiche 4.50 (ISBN 0-87079-205-9, CONF-770108). DOE.

Remizovich, V. S., jt. auth. see Kalashnikov, N. P.

Remler, P. Ascomyceten auf Ericaceen in den Ostalpen. (Bibliotheca Mycologica: No. 68). (Illus., Ger.). 1980. lib. bdg. 32.00x (ISBN 3-7682-1248-3). Lubrecht & Cramer.

Remley, Mary L., ed. Women in Sport: A Guide to Information Sources. LC 80-14773. (Sports, Games, & Pastimes Information Guide Ser.: Vol. 10). 140p. 1980. 42.00x (ISBN 0-8103-1461-4). Gale.

Remling, John. Brakes. LC 77-7262. (Automotive Mechanics Ser.). 1978. text ed. 19.95x (ISBN 0-471-71645-6); tchrs.' manual 3.00 (ISBN 0-471-03764-8). Wiley.

--Steering & Suspension. LC 77-10529. (Automotive Ser.). 1978. 19.95x (ISBN 0-471-71646-4); tchrs.' manual avail. (ISBN 0-471-03763-X). Wiley.

Remmers, H. Lee, jt. auth. see Brooke, Michael Z.

Remmington, Patricia W. Policing: The Occupation & the Introduction of Female Officers--an Anthropologist's Study. LC 80-6291. (Illus.). 227p. (Orig.). 1981. lib. bdg. 19.75 (ISBN 0-8191-1646-7); pap. text ed. 10.25 (ISBN 0-8191-1647-5). U Pr of Amer.

Remmling, Gunter W. & Campbell, Robert B. Basic Sociology. (Quality Paperback: No. 229). 1976. pap. 4.95 (ISBN 0-8226-0229-6). Littlefield.

Remmling, Gunter W., ed. Towards the Sociology of Knowledge: Origin & Development of a Sociological Thought Style. (International Library of Sociology). (Illus.). 463p. 1974. text ed. 25.00x (ISBN 0-391-00291-0). Humanities.

Remnant, Mary. Musical Instruments of the West. LC 77-20880. 1978. 25.00x (ISBN 0-312-55583-0). St Martin.

Remnant, Peter, ed. see Leibniz, G. W.

Remnant, Peter, tr. see Leibniz, G. W.

Remond, Rene & Bourdin, Janine, eds. Edouard Daladier, Chef de Gouvernement avril 1938-septembre 1939. 1977. lib. bdg. 31.25x o.p. (ISBN 2-7246-0378-8); pap. text ed. 23.75x o.p. (ISBN 2-7246-0377-X). Clearwater Pub.

Remoussin, Philippe, tr. see Lindsey, Hal.

Remp, Richard, jt. auth. see Etzioni, Amitai.

Rempel, S. & Schulze, B. W. Index Theory of Elliptic Boundary Problems. 394p. 1982. text ed. 48.95. Birkhauser.

Remson, Irwin, jt. auth. see Howard, Arthur D.

Remson, Irwin, et al. Numerical Methods in Subsurface Hydrology. LC 75-142139. 1971. 50.50 (ISBN 0-471-71650-2, Pub. by Wiley-Interscience). Wiley.

Remuzzi, Giuseppe, et al, eds. Hemostasis, Prostaglandins & Renal Disease. (Monographs of the Mario Negri Institute for Pharmacological Research). 475p. 1980. text ed. 58.00 (ISBN 0-89004-484-8). Raven.

Remy. The Eighteenth Day. LC 78-74577. 1979. 10.00 o.p. (ISBN 0-89696-042-0, An Everest House Book). Dodd.

Remy, Pierre-Jean. Compartment East: Love & Adventure on the Orient Express. 1980. 13.95 o.p. (ISBN 0-688-03739-9). Morrow.

--Maria Callas. 1980. 12.95 o.p. (ISBN 0-312-51448-4). St Martin.

Remy, Richard, jt. auth. see LaRaus, Roger.

Remy, Richard C., et al. International Learning & International Education in a Global Age. LC 75-7588. 1975. pap. 6.95 (ISBN 0-87986-003-0, 498-15252). Coun Soc Studies.

Renard. Poil de Carotte. (Easy Reader, A). pap. 2.95 (ISBN 0-88436-046-6, 40264). EMC.

Renard, G. & Weulersee, G. Life & Work in Modern Europe: Fifteenth to Eighteenth Century. Richards, Margaret, tr. 1968. text ed. 13.00x o.p. (ISBN 0-391-02004-8). Humanities.

Renauld, Ron. Table for Five. 224p. (Orig.). 1983. pap. 2.50 (ISBN 0-523-42062-5). Pinnacle Bks.

--Times Change. 288p. (Orig.). 1981. pap. 2.75 o.p. (ISBN 0-523-41107-3). Pinnacle Bks.

Renault, Mary. Kind Are Her Answers. 287p. 1976. Repr. of 1940 ed. lib. bdg. 16.95x (ISBN 0-89244-078-3). Queens Hse.

--The Middle Mist. 288p. 1976. Repr. of 1945 ed. lib. bdg. 15.95x (ISBN 0-89244-080-5). Queens Hse.

--North Face. 286p. 1976. Repr. of 1948 ed. lib. bdg. 16.95x (ISBN 0-89244-081-3). Queens Hse.

--Promise of Love. 1974. pap. 2.25 o.s.i. (ISBN 0-515-05147-0, A3422). Jove Pubns.

--Promise of Love. 382p. 1976. Repr. of 1939 ed. lib. bdg. 17.95x (ISBN 0-89244-079-1). Queens Hse.

--Return to Night. 303p. 1976. Repr. of 1947 ed. lib. bdg. 16.95x (ISBN 0-89244-082-1). Queens Hse.

Rendall, Jane. The Origins of the Scottish Enlightenment: 1707-1776. 1979. 26.00x (ISBN 0-312-58866-6). St Martin.

Rendel, James M. Canalisation & Gene Control. LC 67-28421. (Illus.). 1968. 34.50 (ISBN 0-12-586950-9). Acad Pr.

Rendell, D. A., jt. auth. see Hill, R. R.

Rendell, Ruth. The Fever Tree & Other Stories. 191p. 1983. 11.95 (ISBN 0-686-37690-0). Pantheon.

--A Judgement in Stone. 1978. lib. bdg. 11.50 o.p. (ISBN 0-8161-6604-8, Large Print Bks). G K Hall.

--Master of the Moor. (General Ser.). 1982. lib. bdg. 13.95 (ISBN 0-8161-3437-5, Large Print Bks). G K Hall.

Render, Sylvia L. Charles W. Chesnutt. (United States Authors Ser.). 1980. lib. bdg. 12.95 (ISBN 0-8057-7272-3, Twayne). G K Hall.

Render, Sylvia L., ed. The Short Fiction of Charles W. Chesnutt. LC 73-88973. 436p. 1974. 15.00 (ISBN 0-88258-012-4). Howard U Pr.

Rendle, Alfred B. Classification of Flowering Plants, 2 bks. Incl. Bk. 1. Gymnosperms & Monocotyledons. 75.00 (ISBN 0-521-06056-7); Bk. 2. Dicotyledons. 90.00 (ISBN 0-521-06057-5). Cambridge U Pr.

Rendleman, Danny. The Winter Rooms. 65p. 1975. 3.50 (ISBN 0-87886-061-4). Ithaca Hse.

Rendleman, Danny L. Signals to the Blind. 50p. 1972. 2.95 (ISBN 0-87886-015-0). Ithaca Hse.

Rendleman, Doug, ed. Enforcement of Judgements & Liens in Virginia. 433p. 1982. 35.00 (ISBN 0-87215-419-X). Michie-Bobbs.

Rendleman, Ron. Tears for a King. 1979. pap. 2.95 (ISBN 0-89877-003-3). Omega Pubns Or.

Rendler, Elaine, ed. see Bauman, William A.

Rendra, Willibordus S. The Struggles of the Naga Tribe. Lane, Max, tr. from Indonesian. LC 79-16537. Orig. Title: Kisah Perjuangan Suku Naga. 1979. 20.00x (ISBN 0-312-76876-1). St Martin.

Rendu, Jo M. Introduction to Geostatistical Methods of Mineral Evaluation. 84p. 1980. 30.00x (ISBN 0-620-03313-4, Pub. by Mining Journal England). State Mutual Bk.

Rene, Jean De, jt. auth. see Pommereul, Francois.

Reneman, Robert S. & Hoeks, Arnold P. Doppler Ultrasound in the Diagnosis of Cerebrovascular. (Ultrasound in Biomedicine Research Ser.). 320p. 1982. 46.00 (ISBN 0-471-10165-6, Pub. by Res Stud Pr). Wiley.

Renfield, Richard. If Teachers Were Free. 1971. pap. 2.75 o.s.i. (ISBN 0-440-53971-4, Delta). Dell.

Renford, Raymond K. The Non-Official British in India to 1920. 400p. 1982. 34.00x (ISBN 0-19-561388-0). Oxford U Pr.

Renfrew, Colin. Before Civilization. 1979. pap. 6.95 (ISBN 0-521-29643-9). Cambridge U Pr.

--The Emergence of Civilisation, the Cyclades & the Aegean in the Third Millennium. (Illus.). 1972. 89.95x (ISBN 0-416-16480-3). Methuen Inc.

Renfrew, Colin, ed. Problems in European Prehistory. LC 79-87702. (Illus.). 1979. 27.95 (ISBN 0-521-22938-3). Cambridge U Pr.

Renfrew, Colin & Shennan, Stephen, eds. Ranking, Resource & Exchange: Aspects of the Archaeology of Early European Society. LC 81-21611. (New Directions in Archaeology Ser.). 168p. 1982. 42.50 (ISBN 0-521-24282-7). Cambridge U Pr.

Renfrew, Colin, et al. Theory & Explanation in Archaeology: The Southampton Conference. 1982. 49.50 (ISBN 0-12-586960-6). Acad Pr.

Renfro, Nancy. Puppet Corner in Every Library. Schwalb, Ann W., ed. (Illus.). 110p. 1977. pap. 8.95 (ISBN 0-931044-01-4). Renfro Studios.

--Puppetry & the Art of Story Creation. Schwalb, Ann W., ed. (Puppetry in Education Ser.). (Illus.). 164p. (Orig.). 1979. pap. 12.50 (ISBN 0-931044-02-2). Renfro Studios.

Renfro, Nancy, jt. auth. see Hunt, Tamara.

Renfroe, Walter J., Jr., tr. see Delbruck, Hans.

Renich, Fred. When Chisel Hits the Rock. 132p. 1980. pap. 4.50 (ISBN 0-88207-218-8). Victor Bks.

Renick, Marion. Ohio. (States of the Nation Ser). (Illus.). (gr. 6-8). 1970. PLB 5.99 o.p. (ISBN 0-698-30267-2, Coward). Putnam Pub Group.

Renier, Dominique, jt. auth. see Marchac, Daniel.

Renier, Gustaaf J. History: Its Purpose & Method. LC 82-3522. (Reprints of Scholarly Excellence Ser.). 272p. 1982. 14.95x (ISBN 0-86554-036-5). Mercer Univ Pr.

Renier, Judith, jt. auth. see Curtis, Eileen.

Renkema, Jan, ed. Taalschat. 108p. (Dutch.). pap. 8.60x (ISBN 0-686-37588-2). Foris Pubns.

Renken, Aleda. Trouble at Briden High. (Midwestern Memories Ser.). (Illus.). (gr. 5-9). 1978. o. p 4.95 (ISBN 0-570-07808-3, 39-1003); pap. 3.50 (ISBN 0-570-07803-2, 39-1013). Concordia.

Renkin, Eugene, ed. see American Physiological Society.

Renkin, Eugene M., jt. ed. see Fishman, Alfred P.

Renn, Ludwig. War. Muir, Willa & Muir, Edwin, trs. from Ger. 1983. 21.00 (ISBN 0-86527-324-3). Fertig.

Renna, Thomas J. The West in the Early Middle Ages: Three Hundred to Ten Fifty. 150p. 1977. pap. text ed. 7.75 o.p. (ISBN 0-8191-0238-5). U Pr of Amer.

Renner. Complete Dentures: A Guide for Patient Treatment. LC 80-28018. (Monographs in Dentristy: Vol. 3). 1981. 43.25x (ISBN 0-89352-123-X). Masson Pub.

Renner, Adrienne G., jt. auth. see Layman, N. Kathryn.

Renner, Al G. How to Make & Use a Microlab. LC 71-121383. (Illus.). (gr. 6-9). 1971. PLB 5.49 o.p. (ISBN 0-399-60269-0). Putnam Pub Group.

--How to Make & Use Electric Motors. new ed. LC 73-77421. 129p. (gr. 6-10). 1974. PLB 6.69 (ISBN 0-399-60858-3). Putnam Pub Group.

Renner, Beverly H. The Hideaway Summer. LC 77-11848. (Illus.). 1978. 8.95i o.p. (ISBN 0-06-024862-9, HarpJ); PLB 9.89 (ISBN 0-06-024863-7). Har-Row.

Renner, Frederic G. Charles Russell. (Art Bks.). 1976. pap. 7.95 o.p. (ISBN 0-451-79973-9, G9973, Sig). NAL.

Renner, John W. & Stafford, Don G. Teaching Science in the Elementary School. 3rd ed. (Illus.). 1979. text ed. 20.95 scp o.p. (ISBN 0-06-045381-8, HarpC). Har-Row.

Renner, John W., jt. ed. see Saterstrom, Mary H.

Renner, Robert P., jt. auth. see Boucher, Louis J.

Renner, Susanne, jt. auth. see Kubitzki, Klaus.

Rennert, Amy. Making It in Photography. (Illus.). 128p. (gr. 6-8). 1980. 7.95 (ISBN 0-399-20691-4). Putnam Pub Group.

Rennert, Hugo A. Spanish Pastoral Romances. LC 67-29552. 1968. Repr. of 1912 ed. 10.00x (ISBN 0-8196-0214-0). Biblo.

Rennie, Dorothy A., jt. auth. see Isaacson, Martin J.

Rennie, Susan & Grimstad, Kirsten, eds. The New Woman's Survival Sourcebook. 1975. pap. 6.95 o.p. (ISBN 0-394-73035-6). Knopf.

Rennie, W. see Demosthenes.

Rennie, Ysabel. The Search for Criminal Man. LC 77-3109. (Dangerous Offenders Project Ser.). 368p. 1978. 23.95x (ISBN 0-669-01480-X). Lexington Bks.

Reno, Marie R. When the Music Changed. 1980. pap. 12.95 o.p. (ISBN 0-453-00384-2, H384). NAL.

Reno, Philip. Navajo Resources & Economic Develpoment: Navajo Resources & Their Use. (Illus.). 183p. 1983. pap. 7.95x (ISBN 0-8263-0653-5). U of NM Pr.

Reno, Phillip. Taos Pueblo. 2nd rev ed. LC 72-78538. 36p. 1972. pap. 2.95 o.p. (ISBN 0-8040-0329-7, SB). Swallow.

Renoir, Jean. La Grande Illusion. (Bibliotheque des Classiques du Cinema Ser.). (Illus.). 260p. (Fr.). 1981. cancelled (ISBN 0-8044-2720-8); pap. 4.95 (ISBN 0-686-86829-3). Ungar.

Renold, Albert E. & Cahill, George F., Jr., eds. Handbook of Physiology: Sec. 5: Adipose Tissue. (American Physiological Society Ser.). (Illus.). 832p. 1965. 28.00 o.p. (ISBN 0-683-07232-3). Williams & Wilkins.

Renold, Albert E., ed. see American Physiological Society.

Renold, Edward, jt. auth. see Fuller, John.

Renolds, Clark. Carrier War. LC 81-18209. (Epic of Flight Ser.). PLB 19.96 (ISBN 0-686-79793-0). Silver.

Renouvin, Pierre. Forms of War Government in France. (Economic & Social History of the World War Ser.). 1927. 49.50x (ISBN 0-685-69856-4). Elliots Bks.

Renowden, Gareth. Video. (Inside Story Ser.). (Illus.). 40p. (gr. 4 up). 1983. PLB 9.90 (ISBN 0-531-04584-6). Watts.

Rensch, Calvin, jt. auth. see Oltrogge, David.

Rensch, Calvin R. Proto Chinantec Phonology. 122p. 1968. pap. 2.00x (ISBN 0-88312-797-0); microfiche 2.25 (ISBN 0-88312-490-4). Summer Inst Ling.

Rensch, Gary D. The Hidden Treasure Game. (Illus.). 1982. pap. 9.45 (ISBN 0-941508-02-1); deluxe ed. 19.00 (ISBN 0-941508-03-X). Gold Star Pubns.

Renshaw, Domeena C. Incest: Understanding & Treatment. 1982. text ed. 17.95 (ISBN 0-316-74031-4). Little.

Rensselaer, John K. Van see Van Rensselaer, Mrs. John K.

Rensselaer, Mariana G. Van see Rensselaer Van, Mariana G.

Rensselaer, Phillip Van see Van Rensselaer, Phillip.

Rensselaer Van, Mariana G. Henry Hobson Richardson & His Works. 12.50 (ISBN 0-8446-5843-X). Peter Smith.

Renstrom, Arthur G. Wilbur & Orville Wright: Pictorial Materials. LC 82-600194. (Illus.). xxi, 201p. 1982. 6.00 (ISBN 0-8444-0399-7). Lib Congress.

Renton, Alexander W., et al, eds. see Burge, William.

Rentoul, J. N. Growing Orchids. (Illus.). 218p. 1982. 14.95 (ISBN 0-85091-147-8). Timber.

--Growing Orchids Book Three: Vandas, Denrobiums & Others. (Illus.). 241p. 1983. 26.95 (ISBN 0-917304-22-5); pap. 19.95 (ISBN 0-917304-32-2). Timber.

Renty. The Businessman's Everyday English-French Dictionary. pap. 7.95 o.p. (ISBN 0-686-66992-4, 4100). Larousse.

Rentz, George, jt. auth. see Anderson, Norman.

Renu, Ma, ed. see Dass, Baba Hari.

Renvoize, Jean. Children in Danger. 1975. 13.00 o.p. (ISBN 0-7100-7892-7). Routledge & Kegan.

--Incest: A Family Pattern. 224p. 1983. 15.95 (ISBN 0-7100-9073-0). Routledge & Kegan.

Renwick, jt. auth. see George.

Renwick, George W. InterAct: Australia-U. S. LC 80-83910. (Country Orientation Ser.). 61p. 1980. pap. text ed. 10.00x (ISBN 0-933662-16-5). Intercult Pr.

Renwick, George W., ed. see Fieg, John.

Renwick, George W., ed. see Haws, Frank.

Renyi, A. Probability Theory. Lauwerier, H. A. & Koiter, W. T., eds. (Applied Mathematics & Mechanics Ser.: Vol. 10). 1970. 85.00 (ISBN 0-444-10015-6, North-Holland). Elsevier.

Renyi, Alfred. Dialogues on Mathematics. LC 67-13839. 1967. (ISBN 0-8162-7124-0); pap. (ISBN 0-8162-7134-8). Holden-Day.

Renyong, Wu & Enguang, Wang, eds. Directory of Chinese Libraries. (World Books Reference Guide: No. 3). 500p. (Chinese & Eng.). 1982. 48.00x (ISBN 0-686-81685-4). Gale.

Renz, O. The Cretaceous Amonites of Venezuela. (Illus.). 216p. 1982. 69.95x (ISBN 3-7643-1364-1). Birkhauser.

Renzglia, Karen S. Comparative Developmental Investigation of the Gametophyte Generation in the Metzgeriales (Hepatophyta) (Bryophytorum Bibliotheca Ser.: 24). (Illus.). 253p. (Orig.). 1982. text ed. 54.00x (ISBN 3-7682-1336-6). Lubrecht & Cramer.

Renzo, D. J. De see De Renzo, D. J.

Renzulli, Joseph S. The Enrichment Triad Model: A Guide for Developing Defensible Programs for the Gifted & Talented. (Illus.). 89p. 1977. pap. 8.95 (ISBN 0-936386-01-0). Creative Learning.

Renzulli, Joseph S. & Smith, Linda H. A Guidebook for Developing Individualized Educational Programs for Gifted & Talented Students. 51p. 1979. pap. 8.95 (ISBN 0-936386-13-4). Creative Learning.

Repak, T. A., jt. auth. see Levin, Murray B.

Report of a Conference Held in January 1979. The Chronic Mental Patient: Problems, Solutions, & Recommendations for a Public Policy. Talbott, John A., ed. LC 78-73984. 259p. 1979. pap. 11.00x (ISBN 0-89042-141-2, P242-0). Am Psychiatric.

Report of the AFIPS Panel on Transborder Data Flow. Proceedings. Turn, Rein, ed. LC 79-93002. (Transborder Data Flow: Concerns in Privacy Protection & Free Flow of Information: Vol. 1). (Illus.). xviii, 186p. 1979. pap. 17.25 (ISBN 0-88283-004-X). AFIPS Pr.

Repp, Gloria. Secret of the Sleeping Otter. (Voyager Ser.). (Orig.). 1983. pap. 3.50 (ISBN 0-8010-7721-4). Baker Bk.

Repp, Victor, jt. auth. see McCarthy, Willard J.

Reppy, Alison. Ordinance of William the Conqueror, 1072: Its Implication in the Modern Law of Succession. LC 55-5962. 122p. 1954. 15.00 (ISBN 0-379-00101-2). Oceana.

Reppy, William A. & Samuel, Cynthia A. Community Property in the U. S. A Comparative Study by Cases, Materials & Problems. 2nd ed. (Contemporary Legal Education Ser). 1982. 25.00 (ISBN 0-87215-492-0, Bobbs Merrill Law); 1979 suppl. 4.00 (ISBN 0-672-83855-9). Michie-Bobbs.

Reps, Paul. Zen Telegrams: Seventy-Nine Picture Poems. LC 59-8189. (Illus.). 1959. pap. 7.95 (ISBN 0-8048-0645-4). C E Tuttle.

Requa, Barbara & Holroyd, Sam V. Applied Pharmacology for the Dental Hygienist. LC 81-14168. 348p. 1982. pap. 18.95 (ISBN 0-8016-2239-5). Mosby.

ReQua, Eloise & Statham, Jane, eds. Developing Nations: A Guide to Information Sources. LC 65-17576. (Management Information Guide Ser.: No. 5). 1965. 42.00x (ISBN 0-8103-0805-3). Gale.

Requin, J., jt. auth. see Stelmach, G. A.

Reres, Mary, jt. auth. see Robinson, Alice.

Reres, Mary E. Stress in Patient Care. 1983. pap. price not set (ISBN 0-8391-1815-5, 16608). Univ Park.

Resch, K. & Kirchner, H. Mechanics of Lymphocyte Activation. 1982. 109.00 (ISBN 0-444-80376-9). Elsevier.

Rescher, Nicholas. Cognitive Systematization: A Systems-Theoretic Approach to a Coherentist Theory of Knowledge. LC 78-18317. 211p. 1979. 21.50x (ISBN 0-8476-6094-X). Rowman.
--Dialectics: A Controversy-Oriented Approach to the Theory of Knowledge. LC 77-9542. 1977. 34.50x (ISBN 0-87395-372-X). State U NY Pr.
--Distributive Justice: A Constructive Critique of the Utilitarian Theory of Distribution. LC 82-45162. (The Nicholas Rescher Ser.). 182p. 1982. pap. text ed. 9.25 (ISBN 0-8191-2686-1). U Pr of Amer.
--Introduction to Value Theory. LC 82-45292. (UPA-Rescher Ser.). 200p. 1982. pap. 10.25 (ISBN 0-8191-2474-5). U Pr of Amer.
--Kant's Theory of Knowledge & Reality: A Group of Essays. LC 82-21817. (Nicholas Rescher Ser.). 160p. (Orig.). 1983. lib. bdg. 20.75 (ISBN 0-8191-2960-7); pap. text ed. 9.75 (ISBN 0-8191-2961-5). U Pr of Amer.
--Many-Valued Logic. LC 69-11708. 1969. text ed. 17.50 o.p. (ISBN 0-07-051893-9, C). McGraw.
--Mid-Journey: An Unfinished Autobiography. LC 82-45083. (Illus.). 204p. (Orig.). 1983. lib. bdg. 21.50 (ISBN 0-8191-2522-9); pap. text ed. 10.25 (ISBN 0-8191-2523-7). U Pr of Amer.
--Risk: A Philosophical Introduction to the Theory of Risk Evaluation & Management. LC 82-21970. (Nicholas Rescher Ser.). 218p. (Orig.). 1983, lib. bdg. 23.50 (ISBN 0-8191-2269-6); pap. text ed. 10.75 (ISBN 0-8191-2270-X). U Pr of Amer.
--Scepticism: A Critical Reappraisal. LC 79-22990. 265p. 1980. 30.00x (ISBN 0-8476-6240-3). Rowman.
Rescher, Nicholas & Brandom, Robert. The Logic of Inconsistency: A Study in Nonstandard Possible-World Semantics & Ontology. LC 80-11638. (American Philosophical Quarterly Library of Philosophy). 174p. 1979. 22.50x (ISBN 0-8476-6248-9). Rowman.
Reschke, R. C., jt. auth. see Lytle, R. J.
Reschovsky, Andrew, et al. The Massachusetts State Tax System: Options for Reform. (Illus.). 300p. 1983. pap. write for info. (ISBN 0-943142-04-0). Joint Cen Urban.
Research & Education Association Staff, ed. Advanced Methods for Solving Differential Equations. LC 82-80750. (Illus.). 352p. (Orig.). 1982. pap. text ed. 12.30x (ISBN 0-87891-541-9). Res & Educ.
--Behavioral Genetics. LC 82-80748. (Illus.). 224p. 1982. text ed. 12.30x (ISBN 0-87891-537-0). Res & Educ.
--Handbook of Economic Analysis. LC 81-86217. (Illus.). 224p. (Orig.). 1982. pap. text ed. 13.50x (ISBN 0-87891-535-4). Res & Educ.
--Handbook of Museum Technology. LC 82-80747. (Illus.). 416p. (Orig.). 1982. pap. text ed. 12.30x (ISBN 0-87891-540-0). Res & Educ.
--Human Aging. LC 82-80749. (Illus.). 544p. (Orig.). 1982. pap. text ed. 13.50x (ISBN 0-87891-536-2). Res & Educ.
--Mathematical Modeling. LC 82-80745. (Illus.). 384p. (Orig.). 1982. pap. text ed. 12.30x (ISBN 0-87891-538-9). Res & Educ.
--Technical Design Graphics Problem Solver. LC 81-86648. (Illus.). 832p. (Orig.). 1981. 18.85x (ISBN 0-87891-534-6). Res & Educ.
--Theory of Linear Systems. LC 82-80746. (Illus.). 224p. (Orig.). 1982. pap. text ed. 9.70x (ISBN 0-87891-539-7). Res & Educ.
Research & Forecasts, Inc. & Friedberg, Ardy. America Afraid: How Fear of Crime Changes the Way We Live. 256p. 1983. 15.95 (ISBN 0-453-00425-3, H425). NAL.
Research Committee on the Study of Honolulu Residents, compiled by. Honolulu Residents in Multi-Ethnic Perspective: Toward a Theory of the American National Character. 1980. pap. text ed. 7.50x (ISBN 0-8248-0717-0). UH Pr.
Research Developments in Drug & Alcohol Use. Proceedings, Vol. 362. 244p. 1981. 49.00 (ISBN 0-89766-117-6, Millman Pub); pap. write for info. (ISBN 0-89766-118-4). NY Acad Sci.
Research Libraries of New York Public Library & Library of Congress. Bibliographic Guide to Technology: 1982. 1983. lib. bdg. 250.00 (ISBN 0-8161-6981-0, Biblio Guides). G K Hall.
Research Libraries of the New York Public Library & the Library of Congress. Bibliographic Guide to Art & Architecture: 1979. (Library Catalogs-Bib. Guides). 1980. lib. bdg. 135.00 o.p. (ISBN 0-8161-6863-6, BBiblio Guides). G K Hall.
Research Libraries of the New York Public Library & Library of Congress. Bibliographic Guide to Art & Architecture: 1982. 1983. lib. bdg. 125.00 (ISBN 0-8161-6967-5, Biblio Guides). G K Hall.
--Bibliographic Guide to Black Stuides: 1982. 1983. lib. bdg. 85.00 (ISBN 0-8161-6968-3, Biblio Guides). G K Hall.
--Bibliographic Guide to Business & Economics: 1982. 1983. lib. bdg. 335.00 (ISBN 0-8161-6983-7, Biblio Guides). G K Hall.
--Bibliographic Guide to Conference Publications: 1982. 1983. lib. bdg. 180.00 (ISBN 0-8161-6969-1, Biblio Guides). G K Hall.
Research Libraries of the New York Public Library. Bibliographic Guide to Dance: 1977. 1978. lib. bdg. 95.00 o.p. (ISBN 0-8161-6837-7, Biblio Guides). G K Hall.
Research Libraries of the New York Public Library, ed. Bibliographic Guide to Dance: 1978. (Library Catalogs Bib.Guides). 1979. lib. bdg. 125.00 o.p. (ISBN 0-8161-6851-2, Pub. by Biblio Guides). G K Hall.
Research Libraries of the New york Public Library & Library of Congress. Bibliographic Guide to Dance: 1982. 1983. lib. bdg. 195.00 (ISBN 0-8161-6970-5, Biblio Guides). G K Hall.
--Bibliographic Guide to Education: 1982. 1983. lib. bdg. 135.00 (ISBN 0-8161-6971-3, Biblio Guides). G K Hall.
--Bibliographic Guide to Government Publications-Foriegn: 1982. 1983. lib. bdg. 295.00 (ISBN 0-8161-6972-1, Biblio Guides). G K Hall.
--Bibliographic Guide to Government Publications-U. S. 1982. 1983. lib. bdg. 295.00 (ISBN 0-8161-6973-X, Biblio Guides). G K Hall.
Research Libraries of the New York Public Libraries & Library of Congress. Bibliographic Guide to Latin American Studies: 1982. 1983. lib. bdg. 350.00 (ISBN 0-8161-6974-8, Biblio Guides). G K Hall.
Research Libraries of the New York Public Library & Library of Congress. Bibliographic Guide to Law: 1982. 1983. lib. bdg. 225.00 (ISBN 0-8161-6975-6, Biblio Guides). G K Hall.
--Bibliographic Guide to Maps & Atlases: 1982. 1983. lib. bdg. 150.00 (ISBN 0-8161-6976-4, Biblio Guides). G K Hall.
--Bibliographic Guide to Music: 1982. 1983. lib. bdg. 125.00 (ISBN 0-8161-6977-2, Biblio Guides). G K Hall.
--Bibliographic Guide to North American History: 1982. 1983. lib. bdg. 150.00 (ISBN 0-8161-6978-0, Biblio Guides). G K Hall.
--Bibliographic Guide to Psychology: 1982. 1983. lib. bdg. 95.00 (ISBN 0-8161-6979-9, Biblio Guides). G K Hall.
Research Libraries of the New York Public Library & the Library of Congress. Bibliographic Guide to Soviet & East European Studies: 1979. 1980. lib. bdg. 295.00 (ISBN 0-8161-6877-6, Pub. by Hall Biblio Guides). G K Hall.
Research Libraries of the New York Public Library & Library of Congress. Bibliographic Guide to Soviet & East European Studies: 1982. 1983. lib. bdg. 350.00 (ISBN 0-8161-6980-2, Biblio Guides). G K Hall.
--Bibliographic Guide to Theatre Arts: 1982. 1983. lib. bdg. 125.00 (ISBN 0-8161-6982-9, Biblio Guides). G K Hall.
Research Libraries of the New York Public Library. Catalog of Government Publications, Supplement 1974. 1976. lib. bdg. 210.00 (ISBN 0-8161-0060-8, Hall Library). G K Hall.
--Catalog of the Theatre & Drama Collections, Supplement 1974. 1976. lib. bdg. 105.00 (ISBN 0-8161-0058-6, Hall Library). G K Hall.
--Dictionary Catalog of Materials on New York City. 1977. lib. bdg. 285.00 (ISBN 0-8161-0079-9, Hall Library). G K Hall.
--Dictionary Catalog of the Art & Architecture Division, Supplement 1974. 1976. lib. bdg. 80.00 (ISBN 0-8161-0061-6, Hall Library). G K Hall.
--Dictionary Catalog of the Music Collection. 2nd ed. 1983. lib. bdg. 6000.00 (ISBN 0-8161-0374-7, Hall Library). G K Hall.
--Dictionary Catalog of the Music Collection, Supplement 1974. 1976. lib. bdg. 80.00 (ISBN 0-8161-0059-4, Hall Library). G K Hall.
Research Publications Editors. The Washington Post Index: January-December 1981. LC 75-642739. 771p. 1982. 200.00. Res Pubns Conn.
Research Publications Inc. History of Photography: Bibliography & Reel Guide to the Microfilm Collection. LC 82-15002. 91p. 1982. text ed. 55.00 (ISBN 0-89235-058-X). Res Pubns Conn.
Research Symposia-53rd Conference, 80. Proceedings. Water Pollution Control Federation, ed. Date not set. pap. 20.00 (ISBN 0-686-30424-1). Water Pollution.
Research 7 Education Association Staff. Advanced Calculus Problem Solver: A Supplement to Any Class Text. (Illus.). 1088p. 1981. pap. text ed. 22.85x (ISBN 0-87891-533-8). Res & Educ.
Resenberg, Richard & Kelly, John D. Shortcuts & Strategies for the SAT. (Shortcuts Ser.). 192p. (Orig.). 1982. pap. 6.95 (ISBN 0-671-46906-1). Monarch Pr.
Reser, Margie, et al, eds. Symposium on Nucleation & Crystallization in Glasses & Melts. 15.00 o.p. (ISBN 0-916094-15-4). Am Ceramic.
Reshetar, John S., Jr. The Ukrainian Revolution, 1917-1920: A Study in Nationalism. LC 72-4292. (World Affairs Ser.: National & International Viewpoints). 376p. 1972. Repr. of 1952 ed. 22.00 (ISBN 0-405-04584-0). Ayer Co.
Reshetar, John S., Jr., ed. see Meissner, Boris.
Reshevsky. Art of Positional Play. 1980. pap. 7.95 (ISBN 0-679-14101-4). McKay.
Resibois, P. & De Leener, M. F. Classical Kinetic Theory of Fluids. LC 76-58852. 1977. 54.95 (ISBN 0-471-71694-4, Pub. by Wiley-Interscience). Wiley.
Residence Lighting Committee. Design Criteria for Lighting Interior Living Spaces. rev. ed. (Illus.). 52p. 1980. 13.50 (ISBN 0-87995-006-4, RP-11); 8.00. Illum Eng.
Resnekov, Leon & Julian, Desmond, eds. Friedberg's: Diseases of the Heart. 4th ed. (Illus.). Date not set. price not set (ISBN 0-443-08003-8). Churchill.
Resnick & Sanders. Ultrasound in Urology. (Illus.). 1979. 43.00 o.p. (ISBN 0-683-07217-X). Williams & Wilkins.
Resnick, Alan N., jt. auth. see Weintraub, Benjamin.
Resnick, David, jt. auth. see Halliday, Robert.
Resnick, Donald & Niwayama, Gen. Diagnosis of Bone & Joint Disorders with Emphasis on Articlar Abnormalities. (Illus.). 2200p. 1981. Vol. 1. 100.00 (ISBN 0-7216-7561-1); Vol. Ii. 120.00 (ISBN 0-686-86723-8); Vol. Iii. 120.00 (ISBN 0-686-91540-2); Set. 325.00 (ISBN 0-7216-7564-6). Saunders.
Resnick, Herman & Patti, Rino, eds. Change from Within: Humanizing Social Welfare Organizations. 344p. 1980. 29.50x (ISBN 0-87722-173-1); pap. 12.95 (ISBN 0-87722-200-2). Temple U Pr.
Resnick, Idrian. The Long Transition: Building Socialism in Tanzania. LC 80-8089. 416p. 1982. 18.50 (ISBN 0-85345-554-6, CL5546); pap. 10.00 (ISBN 0-85345-555-4, PB5554). Monthly Rev.
Resnick, Lauren B. & Weaver, Phyllis A. Theory & Practice of Early Reading, Vol. 2. LC 79-23784. 368p. 1980. text ed. 24.95x (ISBN 0-89859-010-8). L Erlbaum Assocs.
Resnick, Martin I. Current Trends in Urology, Vol. 1. (Illus.). 178p. 1981. 26.00 (ISBN 0-686-77756-5, 7216-1). Williams & Wilkins.
--Current Trends in Urology, Vol. 2. (Illus.). 184p. 1982. 28.00 (ISBN 0-683-07218-8). Williams & Wilkins.
Resnick, Martin I. & Older, Robert A. Diagnosis of Genitourinary Disorders. LC 81-65551. (Illus.). 1982. text ed. 79.00 (ISBN 0-86577-015-8). Thieme-Stratton.
Resnick, Michael. Walpurgis II. (Orig.). 1982. pap. 2.25 o.p. (ISBN 0-686-91637-9, Sig). NAL.
Resnick, Mike. Birthright: The Book of Man. (Orig.). 1982. pap. 2.75 (ISBN 0-451-11358-6, AE1358, Sig). NAL.
--Sideshow. (Tales of the Galactic Midway Ser.: No. 1). 160p. 1982. pap. 2.50 (ISBN 0-451-11848-0, AE1848, Sig). NAL.
--Tales of the Galactic Midway, No. 1: Sideshow. 1982. pap. 2.50 (ISBN 0-451-11848-0, AE1848, Sig). NAL.
--Tales of the Galactic Midway, No. 2: The Three-Legged Hootch Dancer. (No. 2). 155p. 1983. pap. 2.50 (Sig). NAL.
--Walpurgis III. 166p. 1982. pap. 2.25 (ISBN 0-451-11572-4, AE1572, Sig). NAL.
Resnick, R. Basic Concepts in Relativity & Early Quantum Theory. 1972. pap. 15.50 (ISBN 0-471-71703-7). Wiley.
--Introduction to Special Relativity. 1972. pap. 15.50 (ISBN 0-471-71725-8). Wiley.
Resnick, Robert & Halliday, David. Physics, Pt. 1. 3rd ed. LC 77-1295. 1977. text ed. 27.50x (ISBN 0-471-71716-9); write for info Arabic Translation avail. (ISBN 0-471-04506-3). Wiley.
Resnick, Robert, jt. auth. see Eisberg, Robert.
Resnick, Robert, jt. auth. see Halliday, David.
Resnick, Seymour. Essential French Grammar. (Orig.). 1963. pap. 2.75 (ISBN 0-486-20419-7). Dover.
Resnick, Susan, tr. see Schwaller de Lubicz, Isha.
Resnick, Sylvia. Burt Reynolds: An Unauthorized Biography. (Illus.). 160p. 1983. 10.95 (ISBN 0-312-10876-1). St Martin.
Resnick, W. Process Analysis & Design for Chemical Engineers. 1980. text ed. 29.95 (ISBN 0-07-051887-4); solutions manual avail. McGraw.
Resnik, H. L. & Hathorne, B. C. Teaching Outlines in Suicide Studies & Crisis Intervention. (Illus.). 1974. pap. 7.50 o.p. (ISBN 0-87618-017-9). R J Brady.
Resnik, H. L., jt. auth. see Mitchell, Jeffrey.
Resource Systems International. Arc Welding: Equipment. 1982. pap. text ed. 15.00 (ISBN 0-686-86698-3). Reston.
--Boilermaker Hand Tools. 1982. pap. text ed. 15.00 (ISBN 0-686-32045-X). Reston.
--Welding & Cutting Safety. 1982. pap. text ed. 15.00 (ISBN 0-686-32085-9). Reston.
Resources & Technical Div., Resources Section Bookdealer-Library Relations Committee. Guidelines for Handling Library Orders for Serials & Periodicals. LC 74-11137. (Acquisitons Guidelines: No. 2). 16p. 74. pap. text ed. 3.00 (ISBN 0-8389-3158-8). ALA.
Ress, D. A., jt. ed. see LLoyd, C.
Ressler, Pauline. Poems for Praise & Power. pap. 2.90 (ISBN 0-686-24053-7). Rod & Staff.
Ressner, Phillip. Dudley Pippin's Summer. LC 78-19831. (Illus.). (gr. 2-5). 1979. 6.95i o.p. (ISBN 0-06-024887-4, HarpJ); PLB 8.89 (ISBN 0-06-024888-2). Har-Row.
Restarick, Henry B. Sun Yat Sen, Liberator of China. 1931. text ed. 14.50x (ISBN 0-686-83796-7). Elliots Bks.
Restaurant Business Inc. Menu Planning & Foods Merchandising. 1st ed. LC 73-163322. 1971. 17.50 o.p. (ISBN 0-672-96092-3); tchrs' manual 6.67 (ISBN 0-672-96094-X); wkbk. 7.50 (ISBN 0-672-96093-1). Bobbs.
Restino, Susan. Mrs. Restino's Country Kitchen. LC 74-28704. (Illus.). 304p. (Orig.). 1976. pap. 7.95 o.p. (ISBN 0-8256-3060-6, Quick Fox). Putnam Pub Group.
Restle, Frank. Learning: Animal Behavior & Human Cognition. (Psychology Ser.). (Illus.). 330p. 1975. text ed. 19.00 o.p. (ISBN 0-07-051910-2, C). McGraw.
Resume Service Staff. Resumes That Get Jobs. 3rd ed. LC 80-26456. 192p. 1981. 10.00 (ISBN 0-668-05202-3); pap. 3.95 (ISBN 0-668-05210-4). Arco.
Retey, James & Robinson, John A. Stereospecificity in Organic Chemistry & Enzymology. (Monographs in Modern Chemistry: Vol. 13). (Illus.). 336p. 1982. 86.30x (ISBN 0-89573-038-3). Verlag Chemie.
Rethacker, J. P., jt. auth. see Herbin, Robert.
Rethans, Arno J., jt. auth. see Goslin, Lewis N.
Retherford, Robert D. The Changing Sex Differential in Mortality. LC 74-19808. (Studies in Demography & Urban Population). (Illus.). 1975. lib. bdg. 25.00x (ISBN 0-8371-7848-7, RSX/). Greenwood.
Retif De La Bretonne, Nicolas E. Le Thesmographe. (Utopias in the Enlightenment Ser.). 590p. (Fr.). 1974. Repr. of 1789 ed. lib. bdg. 144.00x o.p. (ISBN 0-8287-0721-9, 033). Clearwater Pub.
Retinger, J. Conrad & His Contemporaries. LC 72-6504. (Studies in Conrad, No. 8). 156p. 1972. Repr. of 1941 ed. lib. bdg. 31.95x (ISBN 0-8383-1621-2). Haskell.
Retor, Georges. L' Agni: Variete Dialectale Sanvi. (Black Africa Ser.). 229p. (Fr.). 1974. Repr. of 1970 ed. lib. bdg. 64.00 o.p. (ISBN 0-8287-0722-7, 71-2003). Clearwater Pub.
Rettich, Judi. Pennsylvania Dutch Designs for Hand Coloring: Create Your Own Decorative Awards, Certificates & Notepaper. (Illus.). 48p. (Orig.). 1983. pap. 2.25 (ISBN 0-486-24496-2). Dover.
Rettich, Margaret. The Silver Touch & Other Family Christmas Stories. Crawford, Elizabeth D., tr. (Illus.). (gr. 4-6). 1978. 7.50 o.p. (ISBN 0-688-22164-5); PLB 9.36 (ISBN 0-688-32164-X). Morrow.
Rettich, Margret. The Tightwad's Curse & Other Pleasantly Chilling Stories. Crawford, Elizabeth D., tr. from Ger. LC 79-17832. (Illus.). 192p. (gr. 4-6). 1979. 8.75 (ISBN 0-688-22211-0); PLB 8.40 (ISBN 0-688-32211-5). Morrow.
--The Voyage of the Jolly Boat. Jones, Olive, tr. from Ger. (Illus.). 32p. (gr. k-4). 1981. 9.95 (ISBN 0-416-30791-4). Methuen Inc.
Rettig, Jack L. Careers: Exploration & Decision. LC 74-611. (gr. 7-12). 1974. text ed. 7.64 o.p. (ISBN 0-8224-4686-3); pap. text ed. 5.20 (ISBN 0-8224-4678-2); tchrs' guide 1.60 (ISBN 0-8224-4694-4). Pitman Learning.
Rettig, Richard P. Father's Love & Father's Law: The Disciplined Life. 1980. 7.95 o.p. (ISBN 0-8062-1339-6). Carlton.
Rettig, Richard P., et al. Manny: A Criminal-Addict's Story. 1977. pap. text ed. 12.50 (ISBN 0-395-24838-8). HM.
Rettig, Robert B. Guide to Cambridge Architecture: Ten Walking Tours. 1969. pap. 6.95 (ISBN 0-262-68017-3). MIT Pr.
Rettke, Marion P. Highland Rapture. (Orig.). 1979. pap. 1.75 o.s.i. (ISBN 0-515-05318-X). Jove Pubns.
Retzlaff, Don A., jt. auth. see Poirot, James L.
Reuben, Bryan G., jt. auth. see Wittcoff, Harold.
Reuben, Bryan G., jt. auth. see Wittcoff, Harold A.
Reuben, David. Dr. David Reuben's Mental First-Aid Manual: Instant Relief From 25 of Life's Worst Problems. (Illus.). 256p. 1982. 13.50 (ISBN 0-02-605730-1). Macmillan.
--Save Your Life Diet. pap. 2.50x (ISBN 0-345-28579-4); 7.95x (ISBN 0-394-49880-1). Cancer Control Soc.
Reuben, John P., et al, eds. Electrobiology of Nerve, Synapse & Muscle. LC 75-14587. 405p. 1976. 38.00 (ISBN 0-89004-030-3). Raven.
Reuben, Liz. Trading Secrets. (Hi-Lo Ser.). (Illus.). 96p. (Orig.). (YA) (gr. 7-12). 1983. pap. 1.75 (ISBN 0-440-98834-9, LFL). Dell.
Reuben, Ruth, tr. see Sheldon, Charles M.
Reubens, Beatrice G. Preparation for Work: A Cross-Country Analysis. LC 77-84454. (Conservation of Human Resources Ser.: Vol. 4). Date not set. text ed. 25.00x (ISBN 0-86598-028-4). Allanheld.
Reubens, E. M. Chess-Trick & Treat. (Illus., Orig.). 1962. pap. 3.00 (ISBN 0-8283-1431-4, 37, IPL). Branden.
Reubens, Edwin P., ed. The Challenge of the New International Economic Order. (Westview Special Studies in International Economics & Business). 220p. 1981. lib. bdg. 30.00 (ISBN 0-89158-762-4); pap. 12.50 (ISBN 0-86531-078-5). Westview.
Reuijl, Jan C. On the Determination of Advertising Effectiveness: An Empirical Study of the German Cigarette Market. 1982. lib. bdg. 30.00 (ISBN 0-89838-125-8). Kluwer-Nijhoff.
Reukauf, Diane & Trause, Mary Anne. Some Days Are Better Than Others: A Book About Breastfeeding. 1982. text ed. 14.95 (ISBN 0-8359-7054-X); pap. text ed. 9.95 (ISBN 0-686-96872-7). Reston.
Reumann, John. Righteousness in the New Testament: Justification in Lutheran-Catholic Dialogue. LC 81-43086. 320p. 1982. pap. 13.95 (ISBN 0-8006-1616-2, 1-1616). Fortress.
--Righteousness in the New Testament: Justification in Lutheran-Catholic Dialogue. LC 81-85385. 320p. (Orig.). 1982. pap. 13.95 (ISBN 0-8091-2436-X). Paulist Pr.

Reumann, John, ed. see Ellis, E. Earle.

Reumann, John, ed. see Harner, Philip B.

Reumann, John, ed. see Wolff, Hans W.

Reumert, Elith. Hans Andersen the Man. Brochner, Jessie, tr. from Danish. LC 71-110811. (Tower Bks). (Illus.). 1971. Repr. of 1927 ed. 37.00x (ISBN 0-8103-3902-1). Gale.

Reusch, William. An Introduction to Organic Chemistry. LC 76-50855. 1977. text ed. 34.50 (ISBN 0-8162-7161-5). Holden Day.

Reuscher, John A. Essays on the Metaphysical Foundation of Personal Identity. LC 80-6067. 111p. 1981. lib. bdg. 17.75 (ISBN 0-8191-1471-5); pap. text ed. 8.00 (ISBN 0-8191-1472-3). U Pr of Amer.

Reuss-Ianni, Elizabeth. Two Cultures of Policing: Street Cops & Management Officers. 175p. 1983. 24.95 (ISBN 0-87855-469-6). Transaction Bks.

Reuss-Ianni, Elizabeth, jt. auth. see Ianni, Francis A.

Reute, H., jt. auth. see Baker, P. F.

Reutemann, Charles. Let's Pray Two. LC 82-60612. (Illus.). 224p. (Orig.). 1982. pap. 6.95 (ISBN 0-88489-148-8). St Mary's.

Reuter, Fritz. Seven Years of My Life. Bayerschmidt, Carl F., tr. (International Studies & Translations). 1975. lib. bdg. 12.95 (ISBN 0-8057-5740-6, Twayne). G K Hall.

Reuter, Helmut H. Der Intellektuelle und die Politik. 234p. (Ger.). 1982. write for info. (ISBN 3-8204-5769-0). P Lang Pubs.

Reuter, Margaret. Earthquakes: Our Restless Planet. LC 76-45653. (Science Information Ser.). (Illus.). (gr. 4-6). 1977. PLB 12.50 o.p. (ISBN 0-8172-0352-4). Raintree Pubs.

--Two Thousand Plus Index & Glossary. (gr. k-3). 1977. PLB 10.25 o.p. (ISBN 0-8172-1025-3). Raintree Pubs.

Reuter, Peter. Monopoly & the Mafia. 228p. 1983. 17.50 (ISBN 0-262-18107-X). MIT Pr.

Reuter, Stewart R. & Redman, Helen C. Gastrointestinal Angiography. 2nd ed. LC 76-50156. (Monographs in Clinical Radiology: Vol. 1). (Illus.). 1977. text ed. 35.00 o.p. (ISBN 0-7216-7566-2). Saunders.

Reuter, T. The Medieval Nobility: Studies in the Ruling Class of France & Germany from the 6th to the 12th Centuries. (Europe in the Middle Ages Ser.: Vol 14). 1978. 61.75 (ISBN 0-444-85136-4, North Holland). Elsevier.

Reuter, Timothy, ed. The Greatest Englishman: Essays on St. Boniface & the Church at Crediton. 140p. 1980. text ed. 15.00 (ISBN 0-85364-277-X). Attic Pr.

Reuters Ltd. Reuters Glossary of International Economic & Financial Terms. 224p. 1983. 11.95 (ISBN 0-698-11205-9, Coward). Putnam Pub Group.

Reuterskiold, Alex de see Mirabaud, Paul & De Reuterskiold, Alex.

Reuther, David, jt. auth. see Doty, Roy.

Reuther, Victor. Brothers Reuther & the Story of the U.A.W. A Memoir. 1976. 16.95 o.s.i. (ISBN 0-395-24304-1). HM.

Reuther, Victor G. The Brothers Reuther & the Story of the U.A.W. A Memoir. 1979. pap. 8.95 o.s.i. (ISBN 0-395-27515-6). HM.

Reutter, E. E., Jr. The Supreme Court's Impact on Public Education. 200p. 1982. 9.00 (ISBN 0-87367-783-8); pap. 7.00 (ISBN 0-87367-784-6). Phi Delta Kappa.

Reutter, E. F., Jr. Schools & the Laws. 5th ed. LC 70-12249. (Legal Almanac Ser.: No.17). 118p. 1981. 5.95 (ISBN 0-379-11139-X); pap. write for info. (ISBN 0-379-11141-1). Oceana.

Reutter, J., jt. auth. see Verzello, J. R.

Reveal, Betsy, jt. auth. see Chase, Gordon.

Revel, Jean-Francois. On Proust. Turnell, Martin, tr. from Fr. LC 70-161409. 193p. 1972. 15.50x (ISBN 0-912050-10-1); pap. 6.00x (ISBN 0-87548-326-7). Open Court.

Reveley, Edith. A Pause for Breath. LC 82-22293. 210p. 1983. 14.95 (ISBN 0-87951-165-6). Overlook Pr.

Reveley, W. Taylor. War Powers of the President & Congress: Who Holds the Arrow & Olive Branch? LC 80-29046. 394p. 1981. 15.95x (ISBN 0-8139-0808-6). U Pr of Va.

Revelis, B. G. Greek-English Letterwriting. 6.00 (ISBN 0-685-09036-1). Divry.

Revell. Strabismus: A History of Orthoptic Technique. (Illus.). 1973. 23.95 o.p. (ISBN 0-407-93262-3). Butterworth.

Revell, Donald. From the Abandoned Cities. LC 82-48677. (National Poetry Ser.). 64p. 1983. 9.57i (ISBN 0-06-015167-6, HarpT); pap. 9.95 (ISBN 0-06-091058-5). Har-Row.

Revell, Peter. James Whitcomb Riley. (United States Authors Ser). lib. bdg. 11.95 (ISBN 0-8057-0624-0, Twayne). G K Hall.

--Paul Laurence Dunbar. (United States Authors Ser.). 1979. lib. bdg. 12.95 (ISBN 0-8057-7213-8, Twayne). G K Hall.

ReVelle. Environmental Studies: Issues & Choices for Society. 1980. text ed. 18.95 (ISBN 0-442-22069-3); instr's. manual 3.95 (ISBN 0-442-25753-8). Van Nos Reinhold.

ReVelle, Charles & ReVelle, Penny. The Environment: Issues & Choices. 762p. 1981. text ed. write for info (ISBN 0-87150-758-7). Grant Pr.

ReVelle, Charles S. & ReVelle, Penelope L. Sourcebook on the Environment: The Scientific Perspective. 1974. pap. text ed. 13.50 (ISBN 0-395-17018-4). HM.

ReVelle, Jack B., jt. auth. see Brown, Kenneth S.

ReVelle, Penelope L., jt. auth. see ReVelle, Charles S.

ReVelle, Penny, jt. auth. see ReVelle, Charles.

Revelli, Clare. Color & You. (Illus., Orig.). 1982. 4.95 (ISBN 0-9608092-0-1). Just Clare.

Revens, Lee, ed. The Graphic Work of Felicien Rops. (Illus.). 1975. 14.95 o.p. (ISBN 0-685-59185-9). L Amiel Pub.

Reverby, Susan & Rosner, David, eds. Health Care in America: Essays in Social History. (Illus.). 288p. 1979. 29.95 (ISBN 0-87722-153-7); pap. 9.95x (ISBN 0-87722-171-5). Temple U Pr.

Revere, John D. The Assassin. (Justin Perry Ser.: No. 1). 208p. 1983. pap. 2.25 (ISBN 0-523-41732-2). Pinnacle Bks.

Revesz, G. E. Introduction to Formal Languages. 256p. 1983. 25.95x (ISBN 0-07-051916-1). McGraw.

Revesz, P., ed. Limit Theorems of Probability Theory. (Colloquia Mathematica Societatis Janos Bolyai: Vol. 11). 1975. 83.75 (ISBN 0-444-11010-0, North-Holland). Elsevier.

Revilla. Gramatica Espanola Moderna. rev. ed. 1975. text ed. 8.95 (ISBN 0-07-090830-3, W). McGraw.

Reville, Albert. Jesus De Nazareth: Etudes Critiques Sur les Antecedents de L'histoire Evangelique et la Vie de Jesus. (Fr.). 1981. Repr. of 1906 ed. Set. lib. bdg. 325.00 o.p. (ISBN 0-8287-0014-1); Vol. 1, 454 Pgs. lib bdg. avail. o.p. (ISBN 0-8287-0015-X); Vol. 2, 476 Pgs. lib. bdg. write for info. o.p. (ISBN 0-8287-0016-8). Clearwater Pub.

--The Native Religions of Mexico & Peru: Hibbert Lectures. Wicksteed, Phillip H., tr. LC 77-27167. 224p. 1983. Repr. of 1884 ed. 29.50 (ISBN 0-404-60405-6). Ams Pr.

Revilo. Pigs in Love. (Illus.). 96p. 1982. pap. 3.95 (ISBN 0-517-54707-4, C N Potter Bks). Crown.

Revis, Alesia, jt. auth. see Greenfield, Eloise.

Revitch, Eugene & Schlesinger, Louis B. Psychopathology of Homicide. (Illus.). 272p. 1981. 27.50x (ISBN 0-398-04178-4). C C Thomas.

Revlon. Revlon Art of Beauty. LC 81-43587. (Illus.). 128p. 1982. 14.95 (ISBN 0-385-17871-9, Dolp). Doubleday.

Revoir, Trudie W. Christmas Workshop for the Church Family. 96p. 1982. pap. 6.95 (ISBN 0-8170-0963-9). Judson.

Revoltella, Roberto, et al, eds. Expression of Differentiated Function in Cancer Cells. 542p. 1982. text ed. 63.50 (ISBN 0-89004-693-X). Raven.

Revsine, Lawrence. Replacement Cost Accounting. (Contemporary Topics in Accounting Ser). (Illus.). 224p. (Ref. ed). 1973. pap. 11.95 (ISBN 0-13-773630-4). P-H.

Revue Musicale. Wagner et la France. LC 77-4006. (Music Reprint Ser., 1977). (Illus.). 1977. Repr. of 1923 ed. lib. bdg. 27.50 (ISBN 0-306-70889-2). Da Capo.

Revuz, D. Markov Chains. LC 74-80112. (Mathematical Library: Vol. 11). 336p. 1975. 55.50 (ISBN 0-444-10752-5, North-Holland). Elsevier.

Rew, Alan. Social Images & Process in Urban New Guinea: A Study of Port Moresby. LC 74-17389. (AES Ser). 262p. 1974. text ed. 23.95 (ISBN 0-8299-0024-1). West Pub.

Rew, Lois J., ed. see Shannon, Foster.

Rew, Lois J., ed. see Shannon, Foster H.

Rewald, John. The History of Impressionism. (Illus.). 1980. 40.00 (ISBN 0-686-86526-X, 365149); pap. 22.50 (ISBN 0-87070-369-2). NYGS.

Rex, D. F., ed. Climate of the Free Atmosphere. (World Survey of Climatology: Vol. 4). 1969. 121.50 (ISBN 0-444-40703-0). Elsevier.

Rex, Erna. The Lengthening Shadow. 1962. 4.50x (ISBN 0-87315-020-1). Golden Bell.

Rex, John. Discovering Sociology: Studies in Sociological Theory & Method. 288p. 1973. 25.95x (ISBN 0-7100-7411-5). Routledge & Kegan.

--Key Problems of Sociological Theory. (International Library of Sociology & Social Reconstruction). 1976. text ed. 11.25x o. p. (ISBN 0-7100-3409-1); pap. text ed. 8.50x (ISBN 0-7100-6903-0). Humanities.

--Race, Colonialism & the City. 324p. 1973. 27.50x (ISBN 0-7100-7412-3). Routledge & Kegan.

--Race Relations in Sociological Theory. 180p. (Orig.). 1983. pap. 10.95 (ISBN 0-7100-9299-7). Routledge & Kegan.

--Sociology & the Demystification of the Modern World. (International Library of Sociology Ser.). 1974. 23.95x (ISBN 0-7100-7858-7). Routledge & Kegan.

Rex, John & Moore, Robert. Race, Community, & Conflict: A Study of Sparkbrook. 1967. pap. 6.50x o.p. (ISBN 0-19-218162-9). Oxford U Pr.

Rex, John, ed. Approaches to Sociology: An Introduction to the Major Trends in British Sociology. (International Library of Sociology Ser.). 1974. 25.00x (ISBN 0-7100-7824-2); pap. 10.00 (ISBN 0-7100-7825-0). Routledge & Kegan.

Rex, Walter, tr. see D'Alembert, Jean L.

Rexford, Kenneth. Electrical Control for Machines. 2nd ed. 384p. 1983. pap. text ed. 24.00 (ISBN 0-8273-2175-9); lab manual 8.00 (ISBN 0-8273-2177-5); write for info. instr's guide (ISBN 0-8273-2176-7). Delmar.

Rexroat, Stephen. L' Esprit de l'Ecole du Dimanche. Cosson, Annie, ed. DeJonj, Marie-Christine, tr. Orig. Title: The Sunday School Spirit. 158p. 1982. pap. 1.60 (ISBN 0-8297-1026-4). Life Pubs Intl.

Rexroth, Kenneth. Collected Shorter Poems. LC 66-17818. 1967. 12.75 o.p. (ISBN 0-8112-0367-0); pap. 7.95 (ISBN 0-8112-0178-3, NDP243). New Directions.

Rey, Greta. Good Morning, Lord: Devotions for Young Teens. (Good Morning, Lord Ser.). 96p. 1983. 4.95 (ISBN 0-8010-7719-2). Baker Bk.

Rey, H. A. Cecily G. & the Nine Monkeys. (Illus.). (gr. 1-3). 1942. reinforced bdg. 10.95 (ISBN 0-395-18430-4). HM.

--Curious George. (Illus.). (gr. k-3). 1941. reinforced bdg. 8.95 (ISBN 0-395-15993-8). HM.

--Jorge el Curioso. (Illus., Span.). (ps-3). pap. 4.95 (ISBN 0-395-24909-0, Sandpiper). HM.

Rey, H. A. & Rey, Margaret. Curious George Paper Dolls in Full Color. (Toy Bks., Paper Dolls). (Illus.). 32p. (Orig.). (gr. 1 up). 1983. pap. 3.00 (ISBN 0-486-24386-9). Dover.

Rey, H. A., jt. auth. see Rey, Margaret.

Rey, Jack, jt. auth. see Basch, Peter.

Rey, Jean-Noel & Santoni, Georges. Quand les Francais Parlent. 1975. text ed. 13.95 (ISBN 0-88377-042-3). Newbury Hse.

Rey, Lester del see Beresford, J. D.

Rey, Lester del see Delaney, Samuel R.

Rey, Lester Del see Del Rey, Lester.

Rey, Lester del see Hubbard, L. Ron.

Rey, Lester del see Smith, Edward E.

Rey, Lester del see Van Vogt, A. E.

Rey, Lester del see Williamson, Jack.

Rey, Louis & Stonehouse, Bernard. The Arctic Ocean: The Hydrographic Environment & the Fate of Pollutants. 400p. 1982. 89.95 (ISBN 0-471-87464-7, Pub. by Wiley-Interscience). Wiley.

Rey, Margaret & Rey, H. A. Billy's Picture. LC 48-7829. (Illus.). (ps-1). 1948. PLB 12.89 (ISBN 0-06-024906-4, HarpJ). Har-Row.

--Curious George Flies a Kite. (Illus.). (gr. k-3). 1958. reinforced bdg. 9.95 (ISBN 0-395-16965-8). HM.

--Curious George Flies a Kite. (Illus.). (gr. k-3). 1977. pap. 3.95 (ISBN 0-395-25937-1). HM.

--Pretzel. LC 44-9584. (Illus.). (ps-1). 1944. PLB 12.89 (ISBN 0-06-024911-0, HarpJ). Har-Row.

--Spotty. LC 45-9836. (Illus.). (ps-1). 1945. PLB 12.89 (ISBN 0-06-024921-8, HarpJ). Har-Row.

Rey, Margaret, jt. auth. see Rey, H. A.

Rey, Pierre. The Widow. LC 77-8995. 1977. 9.95 o.p. (ISBN 0-399-12075-0). Putnam Pub Group.

Rey, Robert. Manet. (Q L P Art Ser). (Illus.). 7.95 (ISBN 0-517-03722-X). Crown.

Rey, William H. Georg Buchners "Dantons Tod". 121p. (Ger.). 1982. write for info. (ISBN 3-261-04933-2). P Lang Pubs.

Reybaud, Louis. Le Coton, Son Regime, Ses Problemes, Son Influence En Europe. (Conditions of the 19th Century French Working Class Ser.). 480p. (Fr.). 1974. Repr. of 1863 ed. lib. bdg. 120.00 o.p. (ISBN 0-8287-0727-8, 1173). Clearwater Pub.

--Etudes sur le Regime des Manufactures. (Conditions of the 19th Century French Working Class Ser.). 427p. (Fr.). 1974. Repr. of 1859 ed. lib. bdg. 108.00 o.p. (ISBN 0-8287-0728-6, 1033). Clearwater Pub.

--Le Fer et la Houille. (Conditions of the 19th Century French Working Class Ser.). 454p. (Fr.). 1974. Repr. of 1874 ed. lib. bdg. 114.00 o.p. (ISBN 0-8287-0729-4, 1175). Clearwater Pub.

--La Laine. (Conditions of the 19th Century French Working Class Ser.). 466p. (Fr.). 1974. Repr. of 1867 ed. lib. bdg. 116.50 o.p. (ISBN 0-8287-0730-8, 1174). Clearwater Pub.

Reychler, Luc. Patterns of Diplomatic Thinking: A Cross National Study of Structural & Social-Psychological Determinants. LC 78-19774. (Praeger Special Studies). 1979. 28.50 o.p. (ISBN 0-03-046636-9). Praeger.

Reyes, Benito F. Scientific Evidence of the Existence of the Soul. rev. ed. LC 70-122432. 1970. 6.95 (ISBN 0-8356-0192-7, Quest); pap. 2.45 o.p. (ISBN 0-8356-0404-7). Theos Pub Hse.

Reyes, M. Philomene de los. The Biblical Theme in Modern Drama. 1979. text ed. 12.50x (ISBN 0-8248-0633-6, Pub. by U of Philippines Pr); pap. text ed. 8.50x (ISBN 0-8248-0644-1, Pub. by U of Philippines Pr). UH Pr.

Reyment, R. A., jt. auth. see Cubitt, J. M.

Reymond, Arnold. History of the Sciences in Greco-Roman Antiquity. Bray, Ruth G. De, tr. LC 63-18046. 1963. 10.00x (ISBN 0-8196-0128-4). Biblo.

Reyna, Rudy de see De Reyna, Rudy.

Reyna, Ruth. Philosophy of Matter in the Atomic Era. 6.95x o.p. (ISBN 0-210-34021-5). Asia.

Reynaud, Joyce. Samoyeds. (Illus.). 128p. 1980. 4.95 (ISBN 0-87666-680-2, KW-072). TFH Pubns.

Reynertson, A. J. Work of the Film Director. (Library of Film & Television Practice). (Illus.). 272p. 1970. 23.95 (ISBN 0-240-50712-6). Focal Pr.

Reynoldds, James J., jt. auth. see Harshbarger, Ronald J.

Reynolds, A. J. Turbulent Flows in Engineering. LC 73-8464. (Illus.). 1974. 87.50 o.p. (ISBN 0-471-71782-7, Pub. by Wiley-Interscience). Wiley.

Reynolds, Amy, ed. see Lewis, Helen C.

Reynolds, B. The Material Culture of the Peoples of the Gwembe Valley. (Kariba Studies: Vol. 3). 276p. 1968. 22.50 (ISBN 0-7190-1241-4). Manchester.

Reynolds, Barbara. Cambridge Italian Dictionary, 2 vols. LC 74-77384. 1962. Vol. 1. Italian-English 1962. 175.00 (ISBN 0-521-06059-1); Vol. 2, English-italian 1981. 225.00 (ISBN 0-521-08708-2). Cambridge U Pr.

--The Concise Cambridge Italian Dictionary. 792p. 1975. pap. 8.95 (ISBN 0-14-051064-8). Penguin.

Reynolds, Barbara, tr. see Ariosto, Ludovico.

Reynolds, Bede. Draw Your Strength from the Lord. LC 76-7102. 1976. pap. 1.75 o.p. (ISBN 0-8189-1133-6, Pub. by Alba Bks). Alba.

--Project Sainthood: Your Business. LC 75-9275. 186p. 1975. pap. 1.65 o.p. (ISBN 0-8189-1125-5, Pub. by Alba Bks). Alba.

--A Rebel from Riches. 2nd ed. LC 74-27608. (Illus.). 150p. 1975. pap. 1.65 o.p. (ISBN 0-8189-1122-0, Pub. by Alba Bks). Alba.

Reynolds, Ben, tr. see Le Roy-Ladurie, Emmanuel.

Reynolds, Bertha C. Social Work & Social Living. LC 75-29534. (Classics Ser.). 176p. 1975. pap. 5.00 (ISBN 0-87101-071-2, CBC-071-I). Natl Assn Soc Wkrs.

Reynolds, Bill & Ferrigno, Lou. Weight Training for Beginners. (Illus.). 96p. 1982. 10.50 (ISBN 0-8092-5729-7); pap. 5.95 (ISBN 0-8092-5728-9). Contemp Bks.

Reynolds, Bill, jt. auth. see Sprague, Ken.

Reynolds, Bill, ed. see Combes, Laura.

Reynolds, Bill, ed. see Weider, Joe.

Reynolds, Brenda, et al. Psychological Improvements for Corporate Management with High Impact Foreign Words & Phrases. Bartone, J. C., ed. 120p. 1982. 26.00 (ISBN 0-941864-38-3); pap. 18.00 (ISBN 0-941864-39-1). ABBE Pubs Assn.

Reynolds, Cecil R. The Handbook of School Psychology. 1304p. 1982. text ed. 54.95x (ISBN 0-471-05869-6). Wiley.

Reynolds, Charles E. & Steedman, James C. Examples of the Design of Buildings to CP 110 & Allied Codes. rev. ed. (Viewpoint Publications Ser.). (Illus.). 1978. pap. 45.00x (ISBN 0-7210-1091-1). Scholium Intl.

--Reinforced Concrete Designer's Handbook. 9th ed. (Viewpoint Ser.). 506p. 1981. text ed. 54.00x (ISBN 0-7210-1198-5, Pub. by C & CA London); pap. text ed. 42.00x (ISBN 0-7210-1199-3). Scholium Intl.

Reynolds, Clark G. The Fast Carriers: The Forging of an Air Navy. LC 77-10914. 522p. 1978. Repr. of 1968 ed. 25.50 (ISBN 0-88275-608-7). Krieger.

Reynolds, Clark W. & Tello, Carlos, eds. U. S. - Mexico Relations: Economic & Social Aspects. LC 81-86450. 400p. 1983. 25.00x (ISBN 0-8047-1163-1). Stanford U Pr.

Reynolds, Clifford S. Polly Hill. LC 82-5509. (Illus.). 104p. 1982. pap. 4.95 (ISBN 0-89621-067-7). Thorndike Pr.

Reynolds, Clyde. Asahi Pentax M Series Book. (Camera Bks). (Illus.). 1983. pap. 9.95x (ISBN 0-240-51194-8). Focal Pr.

--Camera Movements. (Illus.). 1983. 21.95x (ISBN 0-240-51143-3). Focal Pr.

--Focalguide to Cameras. (Focalguide Ser.). (Illus.). 1976. pap. 7.95 (ISBN 0-240-50963-3). Focal Pr.

--Lenses. (Photographer's Library). (Illus.). 1983. pap. 12.95x (ISBN 0-240-51120-4). Focal Pr.

--Mamiya Twin Lens Book. (Camera Books). 1977. 9.95 o.p. (ISBN 0-240-51102-6); pap. 7.95 (ISBN 0-240-50974-9). Focal Pr.

--Minolta XE-1 and SR-T Book. (Camera Book Ser.). (Illus.). 1975. pap. 9.95 (ISBN 0-240-50907-2). Focal Pr.

--Nikkormat Book. (Camera Books). (Illus.). 1976. 11.95 o.p. (ISBN 0-240-51103-4); pap. 9.95 (ISBN 0-240-50908-0). Focal Pr.

--The Nikon Book. (Camera Books). 1977. pap. 9.95 (ISBN 0-240-50905-6). Focal Pr.

--Nikon FE FM EM Book. (Camera Book Ser.). (Illus.). 128p. 1980. pap. 9.95 (ISBN 0-240-51034-8). Focal Pr.

Reynolds, Clyde, ed. Newnes Book of Photography. 144p. 1982. pap. 11.95 (ISBN 0-408-01162-9). Focal Pr.

Reynolds, Craig J., tr. see Prince Vajirananavarorasa.

Reynolds, D. R., jt. auth. see Riley, J. R.

Reynolds, David. The Creation of the Anglo-American Alliance: A Study in Competitive Cooperation. LC 81-16503. xiii, 397p. 1982. 28.00x (ISBN 0-8078-1507-1). U of NC Pr.

Reynolds, David K. Morita Psychotherapy. LC 74-30530. 200p. 1976. 19.95 (ISBN 0-520-02937-2). U of Cal Pr.

--Naikin Psychotherapy: Meditation for Self-Development. LC 82-21862. 184p. 1983. 15.00x (ISBN 0-226-71029-7). U of Chicago Pr.

--The Quiet Therapies: Japanese Pathways to Personal Growth. LC 80-17611. 143p. 1982. pap. 4.95 (ISBN 0-8248-0801-0). UH Pr.

--The Quiet Therapies: Japanese Pathways to Personal Growth. LC 80-17611. 144p. 1980. 8.95 (ISBN 0-8248-0690-5). UH Pr.

Reynolds, David K. & Farberow, Norman L. Endangered Hope: Experiences in Psychiatric Aftercare Facilities. LC 77-73500. 1978. 18.95x (ISBN 0-520-03457-0). U of Cal Pr.

Reynolds, David S. George Lippard. (United States Authors Ser.). 1982. lib. bdg. 15.95 (ISBN 0-8057-7350-9, Twayne). G K Hall.

Reynolds, E. Field Is Won. (Illus.). 1969. 6.50 o.p. (ISBN 0-685-07631-8, 80622). Glencoe.

Reynolds, E. H., jt. ed. see Botez, M. I.

Reynolds, Edward. Treatise of the Passions & Faculties of the Soule of Man. LC 79-161935. (Hist. of Psych. Ser.). 1971. 59.00x (ISBN 0-8201-1095-7). Schol Facsimiles.

Reynolds, Erma. Bible People Quiz Book. (Quiz & Puzzle Books). 1979. pap. 2.50 (ISBN 0-8010-7692-7). Baker Bk.

--Bible Sayings Quiz Book. (Quiz & Puzzle Bks.). 96p. (Orig.). 1983. pap. 2.95 (ISBN 0-8010-7720-6). Baker Bk.

Reynolds, Frank E., et al. Guide to Buddhist Religion. 440p. 1981. lib. bdg. 55.00 (ISBN 0-8161-7900-X, Hall Reference). G K Hall.

Reynolds, Fred D. & Wells, William D. Consumer Behavior. (Marketing Ser.). (Illus.). 1976. text ed. 26.50 (ISBN 0-07-052031-3, C); instr's manual 5.50 (ISBN 0-07-052032-1). McGraw.

Reynolds, G., tr. see Birkmayer, W. & Riederer, P.

Reynolds, G. J. Lymphoid Tissue: Institute of Medical Laboratory Sciences Monographs. (Illus.). 128p. 1982. pap. 10.00 (ISBN 0-7236-0645-5). Wright-PSG.

Reynolds, George S. A Primer of Operant Conditioning. 2nd ed. 1975. text ed. 13.50x (ISBN 0-673-07964-3). Scott F.

Reynolds, George W., jt. auth. see Bigge, Morris L.

Reynolds, George W., jt. auth. see Thierauf, Robert J.

Reynolds, Gordon. Oxford School Music Books, Beginners' Series, 3 bks. (gr. 1-3). 1961. text ed. 1.00 ea. o.p.; Vol. 1. (ISBN 0-19-321531-4); Vol. 2. (ISBN 0-19-321532-2); Vol. 3. (ISBN 0-19-321533-0); tchrs' manual 2.90 o.p. (ISBN 0-19-321525-X). Oxford U Pr.

Reynolds, Hazel W. Flower of Caroon Manor. 438p. 1982. 16.50 (ISBN 0-9608106-0-9). H W Reynolds.

--Flower of Caroone Manor: A History of Eastern Kent County, Delaware. (Illus.). 464p. 1982. 16.50 (ISBN 0-686-97717-3). Gateway Pr.

Reynolds, Helen. Cops & Dollars: The Economics of Criminal Law & Justice. (Illus.). 280p. 1981. pap. 15.75x (ISBN 0-398-04115-6). C C Thomas.

Reynolds, Howard, jt. auth. see Whiddon, N. Susan.

Reynolds, Iona D. Yellow Is the Corn. 1978. 3.95 o.p. (ISBN 0-533-01845-5). Vantage.

Reynolds, J., jt. auth. see Badcock, W.

Reynolds, J. W., jt. auth. see Hepburn, C.

Reynolds, James F., jt. auth. see Paris, David C.

Reynolds, Jan. Williams Family of Painters. (Illus.). 331p. 1977. 44.50 o.p. (ISBN 0-902028-41-3). Antique Collect.

Reynolds, Jane. Cosmobiology, Vol. 1: Natal Chart Principles. (Illus.). 1977. pap. 7.95 (ISBN 0-930114-00-0). Darin Devel.

--Cosmobiology, Vol. 2: The Life Blueprint. LC 77-86688. (Illus.). 1978. pap. text ed. 12.50 (ISBN 0-930114-01-9). Darin Devel.

Reynolds, John C., Jr., jt. auth. see Wootton, Lutian R.

Reynolds, John I. Indian-American Joint Ventures: Business Policy Relationships. LC 77-18587. 1978. pap. text ed. 11.50 o.p. (ISBN 0-8191-0403-5). U Pr of Amer.

Reynolds, John J. Juan Timoneda. (World Author Ser.). 1975. lib. bdg. 15.95 (ISBN 0-8057-6205-1, Twayne). G K Hall.

Reynolds, Joseph P., et al. Environmental & Economic Considerations in Energy Utilization. LC 81-66619. 595p. 1981. text ed. 59.95 (ISBN 0-250-40468-0); pap. 9.95 o.p. (ISBN 0-250-40482-6). Ann Arbor Science.

Reynolds, Julie, ed. see Dranow, Ralph.

Reynolds, Kay, ed. see Pini, Wendy & Pini, Richard.

Reynolds, L. & Simmonds, D. Presentation of Data in Science. rev. ed. 1982. 37.00 (ISBN 90-247-2398-1, Pub. by Martinus Nijhoff Netherlands). Kluwer Boston.

Reynolds, Leighton D., ed. see Seneca.

Reynolds, Lloyd, et al. Readings in Labor Economics & Labor Relations. 3rd ed. 496p. 1982. pap. text ed. 16.95 (ISBN 0-13-761577-9). P-H.

Reynolds, Lloyd G. The American Economy in Perspective. Brooks, Barbara & Lieberman, Bonnie, eds. (Illus.). 480p. 1981. pap. text ed. 16.95x (ISBN 0-07-052028-3, C); instr's. manual 16.95 (ISBN 0-07-052030-5). McGraw.

--Image & Reality in Economic Development. LC 77-76312. 1977. 35.00x (ISBN 0-300-02088-0). Yale U Pr.

--Labor Economics & Labor Relations. 8th ed. (Illus.). 656p. 24.95 (ISBN 0-13-517680-8). P-H.

Reynolds, Lloyd G., et al. Evolution of Wage Structure. LC 56-5945. Repr. of 1956 ed. 21.00 o.p. (ISBN 0-08-022308-7). Pergamon.

--Readings in Labor Economics & Labor Relations. 2nd ed. (Illus.). 1978. pap. text ed. 16.95 (ISBN 0-13-761569-8). P-H.

Reynolds, Lloyd J. My Dear Runemeister: A Voyage Through the Alphabet. LC 81-51920. (Illus.). 72p. (Orig.). 1982. pap. 6.95 (ISBN 0-8008-5452-7, Pentalic). Taplinger.

Reynolds, Lorna, jt. ed. see O'Driscoll, Robert.

Reynolds, Mack. Compounded Interests. (Boskone Bks.). (Illus.). xii, 164p. 1983. 13.00 (ISBN 0-915368-20-X); deluxe ed. 25.00 (ISBN 0-915368-82-X). NESFA Pr.

Reynolds, Mary. Italian Family Cooking. 1976. 7.50 o.p. (ISBN 0-600-38092-0). Transatlantic.

Reynolds, Maureen. Convection Oven Cook Book. Bobet, Bonnie, ed. LC 79-92455. (Illus., Orig.). 1980. pap. 4.95 o.p. (ISBN 0-911954-53-8). Nitty Gritty.

Reynolds, Maureen, ed. see Kyte, Barbara & Greenberg, Kathy.

Reynolds, Maureen, ed. see Pappas, Lou S.

Reynolds, Maureen, ed. see Wolf, Stanley.

Reynolds, Max, jt. auth. see Ilfrey, Jack.

Reynolds, Michael M., ed. Guide to Theses & Dissertations: An Annotated, International Bibliography of Bibliographies. LC 74-11184. 600p. 1975. 48.00x (ISBN 0-8103-0976-9). Gale.

Reynolds, Michael S. Critical Essays on Ernest Hemingway's "In Our Time". (Critical Essays in American Literature Ser.). 330p. 1983. lib. bdg. 32.00 (ISBN 0-8161-8637-5). G K Hall.

Reynolds, Moira D. Margaret Sanger, Leader for Birth Control. Rahmas, Sigurd C., ed. (Outstanding Personalities Ser.: No. 93). 32p. (gr. 9-12). 1982. 2.95 (ISBN 0-87157-593-0); pap. text ed. 1.95 (ISBN 0-87157-093-9). SamHar Pr.

Reynolds, Morgan. Unions & the Economy. 1983. 15.00 (ISBN 0-89526-626-1). Regnery-Gateway.

Reynolds, Patrick M. History & Mystery of Pennsylvania. (Pennsylvania Profiles Ser.: Vol. V). (Illus.). 56p. 1981. pap. 3.65 (ISBN 0-932514-05-7). Red Rose Studio.

--Pennsylvania Profiles. 1978. pap. 3.65 (ISBN 0-932514-01-4). Red Rose Studio.

--Startling Stories About Pennsylvania. (Pennsylvania Profiles Ser.: Vol. IV). (Illus.). 56p. (Orig.). 1980. pap. 3.65 (ISBN 0-932514-04-9). Red Rose Studio.

--Strange but True. 1978. pap. 3.65 (ISBN 0-932514-00-6). Red Rose Studio.

--Weird Things & Other Oddities. (Pennsylvania Profiles Ser.: Vol. 3). (Illus.). 1979. pap. 3.65 (ISBN 0-932514-03-0). Red Rose Studio.

Reynolds, Patrick M., et al. Pennsylvania's Hectic Heritage. (Pennsylvania Profiles Ser.: Vol. VI). (Illus.). 56p. (gr. 7-12). 1982. pap. 3.65 (ISBN 0-932514-06-5). Red Rose Studi.

Reynolds, Paul. International Commodity Agreements & the Common Fund: A Legal & Financial Analysis. LC 78-16265. (Praeger Special Studies). 1978. 29.95 o.p. (ISBN 0-03-044266-4). Praeger.

Reynolds, Paul D. China's International Banking & Financial System. 240p. 1982. 25.95 (ISBN 0-03-056971-0). Praeger.

--Ethics & Social Science Research. 250p. (Orig.). 1982. pap. 12.95 reference (ISBN 0-13-290965-0). P-H.

Reynolds, Peter J. Life in the Iron Age. LC 78-56800. (Cambridge Topic Bks). (Illus.). (gr. 5-10). 1978. PLB 6.95g (ISBN 0-8225-1214-9). Lerner Pubns.

Reynolds, R. Gene. Assurance. 128p. 1982. pap. 3.95 (ISBN 0-8423-0088-0). Tyndale.

Reynolds, Ray P., ed. Bookhunter's Guide to the West & Southwest, 1980-1982. (Bookhunter's Guides Ser.). 130p. (Orig.). 1980. pap. 6.60 o.p. (ISBN 0-934792-01-1). Ephemera.

Reynolds, Rebecca, jt. auth. see Hanson, Richard.

Reynolds, Rebecca, jt. auth. see Strong, Bryan.

Reynolds, Sian, tr. see Braudel, Fernand.

Reynolds, Sian, tr. see Le Roy-Ladurie, Emmanuel.

Reynolds, Susan. An Introduction to the History of English Medieval Towns. (Illus.). 1971. pap. 13.95 (ISBN 0-19-822697-7). Oxford U Pr.

Reynolds, Thomas L., Jr. Youth's Search for Self. LC 82-70866. (gr. 7-12). 1983. pap. 4.50 (ISBN 0-8054-5338-5). Broadman.

Reynolds, Tim. Dawn Chorus. LC 80-24377. 42p. 1980. 4.00 (ISBN 0-87886-111-4). Ithaca Hse.

Reynolds, Tom D. Unit Operations & Processes in Environmental Engineering. LC 81-12308. (Civil Engineering Ser.). 670p. 1982. text ed. 34.95 (ISBN 0-8185-0493-5). Brooks-Cole.

Reynolds, W. N. Physical Properties of Graphite. (Illus.). 1968. 33.00 (ISBN 0-444-20012-6, Pub. by Applied Sci England). Elsevier.

Reynolds, Walter F. Commercially Available Chemical Agents for Paper & Board Manufacture. 3rd ed. (TAPPI PRESS Reports). 74p. 1980. pap. 44.95 (ISBN 0-89852-383-4, 01-01-R083). TAPPI.

--Dry Strength Additives. LC 79-67261. (TAPPI PRESS Books). 204p. 1980. 29.95 (ISBN 0-89852-044-4, 01-02-B044). TAPPI.

Reynolds, William. The Theory of the Law of Evidence as Established in the United States & of the Conduct of the Examination of Witnesses. 3rd ed. xix, 206p. 1983. Repr. of 1897 ed. lib. bdg. 22.50x (ISBN 0-8377-1039-1). Rothman.

Reynolds, William C. Thermodynamics. 2nd ed. LC 68-20722. 1968. text ed. 34.00 (ISBN 0-07-052039-9, C). McGraw.

Reynolds, William C. & Perkins, Henry C. Engineering Thermodynamics. 2nd ed. 1977. text ed. 33.50 (ISBN 0-07-052046-1, C); solutions manual 25.00 (ISBN 0-07-052047-X). McGraw.

Reynolds, William J. Hymns of Our Faith. LC 64-14049. 1964. 16.95 (ISBN 0-8054-6805-6). Broadman.

Reys, et al. Keystrokes: Calculator Activities for Young Students, Addition & Subtraction. (gr. 2-6). 1979. 7.95 (ISBN 0-88488-129-6). Creative Pubns.

--Keystrokes: Calculator Activities for Young Students, Multiplication & Division. (gr. 2-6). 1979. 7.95 (ISBN 0-88488-130-X). Creative Pubns.

Reys, Barbara. Elementary School Mathematics: What Parents Should Know About Estimation. (Illus.). 16p. 1982. pap. 2.50 (ISBN 0-87353-202-3). NCTM.

--Elementary School Mathematics: What Parents Should Know About Problem Solving. (Illus.). 16p. 1982. pap. 2.50 (ISBN 0-87353-203-1). NCTM.

Rezak, Richard & Henry, Vernon J., eds. Contributions on the Geological & Geophysical Oceanography of the Gulf of Mexico. LC 73-149761. (Texas A&M University Oceanographic Studies on the Gulf of Mexico: Vol. 3). 303p. 1972. 29.95x (ISBN 0-87201-348-0). Gulf Pub.

Rezits, Joseph. Guitar Music in Print. LC 80-84548. 500p. (Orig.). 1983. pap. 65.00 (ISBN 0-8497-7802-6, PM9, Pub. by Pallma). Kjos.

Rezler, Agnes & Stevens, Barbara. The Nurse Evaluator in Education & Service. 1978. text ed. 27.50 (ISBN 0-07-052060-7, HP). McGraw.

Rezler, Julius. Automation & Industrial Labor. 1969. text ed. 6.95x (ISBN 0-685-19708-5). Phila Bk Co.

Rezmerski, John C. Held for Questioning: Poems. LC 70-99191. (Breakthrough Bks). 72p. 1969. 6.95 (ISBN 0-8262-0086-9); pap. 5.95 (ISBN 0-686-76909-0). U of Mo Pr.

Rezneck, Samuel. Business Depressions & Financial Panics: Collected Essays in American Business & Economic History. 1968. lib. bdg. 25.00x (ISBN 0-8371-1501-9, REB/). Greenwood.

--The Saga of an American Jewish Family Since the Revolution: A History of the Family of Jonas Phillips. LC 79-6725. 1980. text ed. 20.00 (ISBN 0-8191-0939-8); pap. text ed. 10.50 (ISBN 0-8191-0940-1). U Pr of Amer.

--Unrecognized Patriots: The Jews in the American Revolution. LC 74-15160. (Illus.). 1975. lib. bdg. 29.95x (ISBN 0-8371-7803-7, RRJ/). Greenwood.

Reznik, John W. Racquetball. LC 80-66320. (Illus.). 192p. 1980. pap. 6.95 (ISBN 0-8069-8928-9). Sterling.

--Racquetball. LC 78-66320. 1979. 10.95 (ISBN 0-8069-4138-3); lib. bdg. 13.29 (ISBN 0-8069-4139-1). Sterling.

Reznik, John W., jt. auth. see Mueller, Pat.

Reznikoff, Marvin, jt. ed. see Aronow, edward.

Reznikoff, S. C. Specifications for Commercial Interiors: Professional Liabilities, Regulations, & Performance Criteria. (Illus.). 1979. 32.50 (ISBN 0-8230-7353-X, Whitney Lib). Watson-Guptill.

Rezny, Arthur A. & Sales, M. Vance. The Educator in the Law Library. 3rd ed. 1982. pap. 3.95x (ISBN 0-8134-2221-3). Interstate.

Rezzuto, Thomas, jt. auth. see Selden, Samuel, Jr.

Rhea, Carolyn. My Heart Kneels, Too. 1965. 2.95 o.p. (ISBN 0-448-01665-6, G&D). Putnam Pub Group.

--Such Is My Confidence. 1961. 2.50 o.p. (ISBN 0-448-01660-5, G&D). Putnam Pub Group.

Rhea, Nicholas. Constable Around the Village. 1982. 11.95 (ISBN 0-312-16441-6). St Martin.

--Constable on the Hill. LC 79-83824. 1979. 8.95 o.p. (ISBN 0-312-16439-4). St Martin.

Rhee, Jhoon. Tan-Gun & To-San of Tae Kwon Do Hyung. LC 71-150320. (Ser.: No. 106). (Illus.). 1971. pap. text ed. 7.50 (ISBN 0-89750-001-6). Ohara Pubns.

Rhee, Kyu-Ho. To the Young Korean Intellectuals. LC 81-84201. (Illus.). 200p. 1980. 14.95 (ISBN 0-930878-24-8). Hollym Intl.

Rhee, Yung W., jt. auth. see Westphal, Larry E.

Rhees, R., ed. see Wittgenstein, Ludwig.

Rhees, R., tr. see Wittgenstein, Ludwig.

Rhein, Phillip H. Albert Camus. (World Authors Ser.). 1969. lib. bdg. 11.95 (ISBN 0-8057-2196-7, Twayne). G K Hall.

Rheinboldt, Cornelie J., tr. see Burger, Dionys.

Rheinboldt, W. C., tr. see Stiefel, E. L.

Rheinboldt, Werner C. Methods for Solving Systems of Nonlinear Equations: Proceedings. (CBMS Regional Conference Ser.: Vol. 14). ix, 104p. (Orig.). 1974. pap. text ed. 11.00 (ISBN 0-89871-011-1). Soc Indus-Appl Math.

Rheinboldt, Werner C., jt. ed. see Ortega, James M.

Rheinfelder, William A. CATV Circuit Engineering. LC 74-25566. (Illus.). 1975. 14.95 (ISBN 0-8306-4798-8, 798). TAB Bks.

Rheingold, A. L., ed. see Hudson Symposium, 9th, Plattsburgh, N.Y., Apr. 1976.

Rheingold, Howard & Levine, Howard. Talking Tech: A Conversational Guide to Science & Technology. (Illus.). 324p. 1983. pap. 6.95 (ISBN 0-688-01603-0). Quill NY.

Rheinheimer, G. Aquatic Microbiology. 2nd ed. LC 79-40645. 235p. 1981. 31.95 (ISBN 0-471-27643-X, Pub. by Wiley-Interscience). Wiley.

Rhine, J. B. Extra-Sensory Perception. 1983. pap. 8.00 (ISBN 0-8283-1464-0). Branden.

Rhine, J. B., et al. ESP after Sixty Years. 15.00 (ISBN 0-8283-1409-8). Branden.

Rhine, Joseph B. New Frontiers of the Mind: The Story of the Duke Experiments. LC 71-178080. (Illus.). 275p. 1972. Repr. of 1937 ed. lib. bdg. 27.50x (ISBN 0-8371-6279-3, RHNF). Greenwood.

Rhine, Louisa E. Mind Over Matter. 1972. pap. 2.95 o.p. (ISBN 0-02-077690-X, Collier). Macmillan.

Rhine, W. Ray, ed. Making Schools More Effective: New Directions from Follow Through. LC 81-4901. (Educational Psychology Ser.). 1981. 29.50 (ISBN 0-12-587060-4). Acad Pr.

Rhinehart, Luke. The Dice Man. 1983. pap. 4.95 (ISBN 0-440-31966-8, LE). Dell.

--Long Voyage Back. 416p. 1983. 15.95 (ISBN 0-440-04617-3). Delacorte.

Rhines, Frederick N. Phase Diagrams in Metallurgy: Their Development & Applications. 1956. text ed. 37.50 (ISBN 0-07-052070-4, C). McGraw.

Rho, M. & Wilkinson, D., eds. Mesons in Nuclei, 3 vols. 1979. Set. 238.50 (ISBN 0-444-85052-X, North Holland); Vol. 1. 93.75 (ISBN 0-444-85255-7); Vol. 2. 93.75 (ISBN 0-444-85256-5); Vol. 3. 93.75 (ISBN 0-444-85257-3). Elsevier.

Rhoades, Chuck, jt. auth. see Cooperman, Carolyn.

Rhoades, Gale R. Waybill to Lost Spanish Signs & Symbols. (Illus., Orig.). 1982. pap. 6.00 (ISBN 0-942688-02-3). Dream Garden.

Rhoads, David M. Israel in Revolution, 6-74 C.E. A Political History Based on the Writings of Josephus. LC 75-36452. 208p. 1976. 5.00 o.p. (ISBN 0-8006-0442-3, 1-442); pap. 3.00 o.p. (ISBN 0-8006-1442-9, 1-1442). Fortress.

Rhoads, Mary L., jt. auth. see Bower, Cynthia E.

Rhoads, RRalph F. Oh Youth of Mine. LC 81-86211. 64p. pap. 2.95 (ISBN 0-686-42884-6). GWP.

Rhoads, Steven E. Valuing Life: Public Policy Dilemmas. (Special Studies in Public Policy & Public Systems Management). 1979. lib. bdg. 29.50 (ISBN 0-89158-650-4); pap. 15.00 (ISBN 0-86531-341-5). Westview.

Rhoda, Richard. Urban & Regional Analysis for Development Planning. (Replica Edition). 200p. 1982. softcover 18.75 (ISBN 0-86531-916-2). Westview.

Rhode, Bill. The Flying Devils: A True Story of Aerial Barnstorming. 1983. 10.95 (ISBN 0-533-05554-7). Vantage.

Rhode, Grant F. & Whitlock, Reid E. Treaties of the People's Republic of China, 1949-1978: An Annotated Compilation. (Westview Special Studies on China & East Asia). (Illus.). 208p. 1980. lib. bdg. 27.50 (ISBN 0-89158-761-6). Westview.

Rhode Island Historical Preservation Commission. Downtown Providence. (Statewide Historical Preservation Report Ser.). (Illus.). 74p. 1981. pap. 4.50 (ISBN 0-917012-25-9). RI Pubns Soc.

Rhode, John G., jt. auth. see Lawler, Edward E.

Rhoden, Chris C. Economics: Facts, Theory & Policy. LC 75-35954. 1976. text ed. 21.95 o.p. (ISBN 0-471-71802-5); tchrs.' manual 7.50 (ISBN 0-471-71801-7). Wiley.

Rhoden, Harold. High Stakes: The Gamble for the Howard Hughes Will. 416p. 1980. 12.95 o.p. (ISBN 0-517-54067-3). Crown.

Rhodes & Walker, eds. Developments in Thin-Walled Structures, Vol. 1. 1982. 67.75 (ISBN 0-85334-123-0, Pub. by Applied Sci England). Elsevier.

Rhodes, A. & Fletcher, D. L. Principles of Industrial Microbiology. 1966. inquire for price o.p. (ISBN 0-08-011906-9); pap. 15.00 o.p. (ISBN 0-08-011905-0). Pergamon.

Rhodes, Arnold B. Mighty Acts of God. (Orig.). 1964. pap. 6.50 (ISBN 0-8042-9010-5); tchrs' ed. 3.45 (ISBN 0-8042-9012-1). John Knox.

Rhodes, Buck A., jt. ed. see Subramanian, Gopal.

Rhodes, Dallas D., ed. Adjustments of the Fluvial System. Williams, Garnett P. (Binghamton Symposia in Geomorphology International Ser.: No. 10). (Illus.). 372p. 1982. Repr. of 1979 ed. text ed. 35.00x (ISBN 0-04-551059-8). Allen Unwin.

Rhodes, Ellen. Dermatology for the Physician. (Illus.). 1980. text ed. 21.00 o.p. (ISBN 0-02-858930-0, Pub. by Bailliere-Tindall). Saunders.

Rhodes, Emma. The Legend of Innislite. 1979. 4.50 o.p. (ISBN 0-533-03890-1). Vantage.

Rhodes, George F., jt. ed. see Basmann, R. L.

Rhodes, J. D. Theory of Electrical Filters. LC 75-30767. 1976. 67.95 (ISBN 0-471-71806-8, Pub. by Wiley-Interscience). Wiley.

Rhodes, J. H. The Crying Winds. (YA) 1980. 6.95 (ISBN 0-686-73942-6, Avalon). Bouregy.

--Dangerous Summer. (YA) 1980. 6.95 (ISBN 0-686-73928-0, Avalon). Bouregy.

--Evil at Sunfire. (YA) 1981. 6.95 (ISBN 0-686-74800-X, Avalon). Bouregy.

--Fear Island. 1981. pap. 6.95 (ISBN 0-686-84707-5, Avalon). Bouregy.

--Legacy of Greenbrier. (YA) 1981. 6.95 (ISBN 0-686-74793-3, Avalon). Bouregy.

--The Watcher of Windcliff. (YA) 1980. 6.95 (ISBN 0-686-76781-0, Avalon). Bouregy.

Rhodes, James. The Agricultural Marketing System. 2nd ed. LC 77-95339. (Agricultural Economics Ser.). 446p. 1978. text ed. 28.95x (ISBN 0-471-86991-0). Wiley.

Rhodes, James M. The Hitler Movement: A Modern Millenarian Revolution. LC 78-70391. (Publications Ser.: 213). 263p. 1980. 15.95x o.p. (ISBN 0-8179-7131-9). Hoover Inst Pr.

Rhodes, James R. James R. Rhodes' Poems. LC 82-20374. 112p. 1982. 8.00x (ISBN 0-88946-999-7). E Mellen.

Rhodes, Janis. Nutrition Mission. (ps-2). 1982. 4.95 (ISBN 0-86653-092-4, GA 443). Good Apple.

Rhodes, Joan, jt. auth. see Kutie, Rita C.

Rhodes, Jodie. Winners & Losers. 1982. pap. 2.95 (ISBN 0-515-06420-3). Jove Pubns.

Rhodes, Lucien, jt. auth. see Little, Jeffrey B.

Rhodes, Lynette I. Science within Art. LC 79-93193. (Themes in Art Ser.). (Illus.). 72p. 1980. pap. 7.95x o.p. (ISBN 0-910386-57-9, Pub. by Cleveland Mus Art). Ind U Pr.

Rhodes, Mitchell L., jt. auth. see Brashear, Richard E.

Rhodes, Neil S., jt. auth. see Lieberman, Jethro K.

Rhodes, Philip. Childbirth. Head, J. J., ed. LC 45-9711. (Carolina Biology Reader Ser.). (Illus.). 16p. (gr. 11-12). 1980. pap. 1.60 (ISBN 0-89278-311-7, 45-9411). Carolina Biological.

Rhodes, R. A. Public Administration & Policy Analysis. 1979. text ed. 28.50x (ISBN 0-566-00239-6). Gower Pub Ltd.

Rhodes, R. A. & Hull, C. Intergovernmental Relations in the European Community. 96p. 1977. text ed. 28.00x (ISBN 0-566-00191-8). Gower Pub Ltd.

Rhodes, R. A. W. Control & Power in Central-Local Government Relations. 194p. 1981. text ed. 34.25x (ISBN 0-566-00333-3). Gower Pub Ltd.

Rhodes, R. G. & Mulhall, B. E. Magnetic Levitation for Rail Transport. (Monographs on Cryogenics). 114p. 1981. 37.50x (ISBN 0-19-854802-8). Oxford U Pr.

Rhodes, R. S. & Cook, L. B. Basic Engineering Drawing. (Illus.). 192p. (Orig.). 1975. pap. text ed. 12.95x o.p. (ISBN 0-8464-0176-2). Beekman Pubs.

Rhodes, Richard. Holy Secrets. LC 76-56329. 1978. 8.95 o.p. (ISBN 0-385-02565-3). Doubleday.

--The Ozarks. LC 73-90480. (American Wilderness Ser). (Illus.). (gr. 6 up). 1974. lib. bdg. 15.96 (ISBN 0-8094-1197-0, Pub. by Time-Life). Silver.

--Sons of Earth. 1981. 13.95 (ISBN 0-698-11055-2, Coward). Putnam Pub Group.

Rhodes, Robert E. & Janik, Del Ivan, eds. Studies in Ruskin: Essays in Honor of Van Akin Burd. LC 81-16883. (Illus.). xx, 244p. 1982. lib. bdg. 20.95x (ISBN 0-8214-0627-2, 82-84002). Ohio U Pr.

Rhodes, Robert E., jt. ed. see Casey, Daniel J.

Rhodes, Robert I., ed. Imperialism & Underdevelopment: A Reader. LC 70-122736. 1971. pap. 7.95 (ISBN 0-85345-155-9, PB-1559). Monthly Rev.

Rhodes, Robert P. The Insoluble Problems of Crime. LC 76-46275. 1977. text ed. 16.95x (ISBN 0-471-71799-1). Wiley.

Rhodes, Susan R., jt. auth. see Doering, Mildred.

Rhodes, Tonya S. Color Related Decorating Textiles. LC 76-24006. (Shuttle Craft Guild Monograph: No. 14). (Illus.). 35p. 1965. pap. 7.45 (ISBN 0-916658-14-7). HTH Pubs.

Rhodes, William & Paul, James L. Emotionally Disturbed & Deviant Children: New Views & Approaches. LC 77-17630. 1978. ref. ed. 23.95 (ISBN 0-13-274662-X). P-H.

Rhodes, William C. Emotionally Disturbed Student & Guidance. (Guidance Monograph). 1970. pap. 2.40 o.p. (ISBN 0-395-09947-1). HM.

Rhodin, Johannes A. An Atlas of Histology. (Illus.). 1975. text ed. 24.00x (ISBN 0-19-501944-X). Oxford U Pr.

Rhodius, Hans & Darling, John. Walter Spies & Balinese Art. Stowell, John, ed. (Illus.). 96p. 1980. 25.00 (ISBN 0-686-43012-3, Tropical Mus Amsterdam Netherlands). Heinman.

Rhone. Wage & Salary Admininistration for Classified School Employees. (Bulletin 25). 1976. 10.00 (ISBN 0-685-05650-3). Assn Sch Busn.

--A Wage & Salary Program Based on Position Evaluation for Administrative & Supervisory Staff. 1980. 8.95 (ISBN 0-910170-15-0). Assn Sch Busn.

Rhone, L. C. & Yates, H. David. Total Auto Body Repair. 2nd ed. 464p. 1982. text ed. 23.95t (ISBN 0-672-97967-5); instr's. guide 3.33 (ISBN 0-672-97969-1); wkbk. 9.95t (ISBN 0-672-97968-3). Bobbs.

Rhoodie, Nic. Intergroup Accommodation in Plural Societies. 1979. 26.00x (ISBN 0-312-41921-X). St Martin.

Rhymes, I. L., jt. auth. see Austen, D. E.

Rhyne, C. Thomas. Faith Establishes the Law. Kee, Howard, ed. LC 81-1794. (Society of Biblical Literature Dissertation Ser.). 1981. pap. text ed. 13.50 (ISBN 0-89130-483-5, 06-01-55); pap. 13.50 (ISBN 0-686-96881-6). Scholars Pr CA.

Rhyne, Nancy. The Grand Strand: An Uncommon Guide to Myrtle Beach & Its Surroundings. LC 80-39647. (Illus.). 128p. (Orig.). 1981. pap. 4.95 (ISBN 0-914788-36-1). East Woods.

Rhyne, T. L. Acoustic Instrumentation & Characterisation of Lung Tissue. 109p. 1980. pap. 37.95 (ISBN 0-471-27884-X, Pub. by Wiley-Interscience). Wiley.

Rhyne, V. Thomas. Fundamentals of Digital Systems Design. LC 72-6903. (Illus.). 560p. 1973. 31.95 (ISBN 0-13-336156-X). P-H.

Rhys, Chris, jt. auth. see Godwin, Terry.

Rhys, John. Celtic Folklore, 2 vols. 1981. Vol. I. pap. 25.00x (ISBN 0-7045-0405-7, Pub. by Wildwood House); Vol. II. pap. 25.00 (ISBN 0-7045-0406-5). State Mutual Bk.

Riain, Maire Ni. The Sex Trade. LC 80-54360. 76p. 1982. 6.95 (ISBN 0-533-04928-8). Vantage.

Riasanovsky, Nicholas V. A History of Russia. 3rd ed. LC 76-42634. (Illus.). 1977. 35.00 (ISBN 0-19-502129-0); text ed. 20.95x (ISBN 0-19-502128-2). Oxford U Pr.

--Nicholas I & Official Nationality in Russia, 1825-1855. (Russian & East European Studies). 1959. 23.50 o.p. (ISBN 0-520-01064-7); pap. 7.95x (ISBN 0-520-01065-5, CAMPUS 120). U of Cal Pr.

--The Teaching of Charles Fourier. LC 77-84043. 1969. 32.50x (ISBN 0-520-01405-7). U of Cal Pr.

Riasanovsky, Nicholas V. & Struve, Gleb, eds. California Slavic Studies. Incl. Vol. I. 1960 (ISBN 0-520-09037-3); Vol. II. 1963 (ISBN 0-520-09038-1); Vol. V. 1970 (ISBN 0-520-09043-8); Vol. VII. 1974 (ISBN 0-520-09485-9); Vol. VIII. 1975 (ISBN 0-520-09519-7); Vol. IX. 1976 (ISBN 0-520-09541-3); Vol. X. 1977 (ISBN 0-520-09564-2). (Vols. I, II pap. only). 19.95x ea. o.p. (ISBN 0-686-63969-3). U of Cal Pr.

Ribalta, Marta. Habitat: Areas of Communication, No. 3. (Illus.). 264p. 1982. pap. 9.95 (ISBN 84-7031-447-5, Pub. by Editorial Blume Spain). Intl Schol Bk Serv.

--Habitat Four: Living in the City. (Illus., Orig., Eng., Fr. & Span.). 1977. pap. 5.95 o.p. (ISBN 0-87663-965-1, Editorial Blume). Universe.

--Habitat One: The Living Room. 1976. pap. 5.95 o.p. (ISBN 0-87663-938-4, Editorial Blume). Universe.

--Habitat: The Living Room, No. 1. (Illus.). 86p. 1982. pap. 9.95 (ISBN 84-7031-229-4, Pub. by Editorial Blume Spain). Intl Schol Bk Serv.

--Habitat Three: Halls, Staircases. (Illus.). 96p. 1976. pap. 5.95 o.p. (ISBN 0-87663-942-2, Editorial Blume). Universe.

--Habitat V: Living in the Country. (Illus.). 1978. pap. 5.95 o.p. (ISBN 0-87663-973-2, Editorial Blume). Universe.

--Habitat VI: Contemporary Furniture. (Illus.). 1978. pap. 5.95 o.p. (ISBN 0-87663-974-0, Editorial Blume). Universe.

--New Interiors, No. 2. (Illus.). 300p. 1982. 9.95 (ISBN 84-7031-226-X, Pub. by Editorial Blume Spain). Intl Schol Bk Serv.

--New Interiors, No. 3. (Illus.). 262p. 1982. 9.95 (ISBN 84-7031-227-8, Pub. by Editorial Blume Spain). Intl Schol Bk Serv.

Ribalta, Marta, ed. Habitat, No. 2. (Illus.). 176p. 1982. pap. 9.95 (ISBN 84-7031-437-8, Pub. by Editorial Blume Spain). Intl Schol Bk Serv.

--Habitat: City Living, No. 4. (Illus.). 91p. 1982. pap. 9.95 (ISBN 84-7031-035-6, Pub. by Editorial Blume Spain). Intl Schol Bk Serv.

--Habitat: Furniture, No. 6. (Illus.). 269p. 1982. pap. 9.95 (ISBN 84-7031-059-3, Pub. by Editorial Blume Spain). Intl Schol Bk Serv.

--Habitat: Lanscape Gardening, No. 7. (Illus.). 94p. 1982. pap. 14.95 (ISBN 84-7031-089-5, Pub. by Editorial Blume Spain). Intl Schol Bk Serv.

--Habitat: Living in the Country, No. 5. (Illus.). 181p. 1982. pap. 9.95 (ISBN 84-7031-046-1, Pub. by Editorial Blume Spain). Intl Schol Bk Serv.

Ribalta, Marta, ed. see Martinell, Cesar.

Riban, David M. Introduction to Physical Science. (Illus.). 656p. 1981. text ed. 25.50 (ISBN 0-07-052140-9, C); instr's manual 8.95 (ISBN 0-07-052141-7). McGraw.

Ribbens, William B. & Mansour, Norman. Understanding Automotive Electronics. LC 81-51952. (Understanding Ser.). (Illus.). 256p. (Orig.). 1982. pap. 6.95 (ISBN 0-89512-044-5, LCB5771). Tex Instr Inc.

Ribbinck, Tony, jt. auth. see Jackson, P. B.

Ribble, Margaret A. The Rights of Infants. 128p. 1973. pap. 1.25 o.p. (ISBN 0-451-07735-0, Y7735, Sig). NAL.

Ribbons, D. W., jt. ed. see Norris, J. R.

Ribbons, D. W., jt. ed. see Smith, E. E.

Ribeiro, Alvaro, jt. ed. see Wellek, Rene.

Ribeiro, O. K. A Source Book of the Genus Phytophtora. (Illus.). 1978. lib. bdg. 32.00 (ISBN 3-7682-1200-9). Lubrecht & Cramer.

Ribeiro, Victor R. see Rangel-Ribeiro, Victor.

Ribel, A. Biology of Normal & Cancerous Exocrine Pancreatic Cells. (INSERM Symposia Ser.: Vol. 15). 1980. 56.25 (ISBN 0-444-80269-X). Elsevier.

Ribenboim, P. Algebraic Numbers. LC 74-37174. (Pure & Applied Mathematics Ser.). 360p. 1972. 45.95 (ISBN 0-471-71804-1, Pub. by Wiley-Interscience). Wiley.

Ribera, Gilbert J. Machine Calculation for Business & Personal Use. 2nd ed. LC 79-83523. 1979. pap. text ed. 15.95x (ISBN 0-8162-7180-1); solutions manual 2.50x (ISBN 0-8162-7181-X). Holden-Day.

Riberner, Irving, jt. ed. see Kittredge, George L.

Ribner, Irving & Huffman, Clifford C. Tudor & Stuart Drama. 2nd ed. LC 76-5215. (Goldentree Bibliographies in Language & Literature). 1978. text ed. 22.50x (ISBN 0-88295-572-1); pap. text ed. 13.95x (ISBN 0-88295-554-3). Harlan Davidson.

Ribner, Irving, jt. ed. see Kittredge, George L.

Ribner, Irving, ed. see Shakespeare, William.

Ribner, Richard & Cherian, Thyparambil C. Living Without Fatigue. 1983. pap. 7.95 (ISBN 0-8159-6117-0). Devin.

Ribock, J. J. Bemerkungen Uber Die Flote, und Versuch Einer Kurzen Anleitung Zur Bessern Einrichtung und Behandlung Derselben. (The Flute Library: Vol. 13). 1980. Repr. of 1782 ed. 40.00 o.s.i. (ISBN 0-686-30868-9, Pub. by Frits Knuf Netherlands); 32.50 o.s.i. (ISBN 90-6027-325-7). Pendragon NY.

Riboud, Jacques. The Mechanics of Money. 1980. 20.00x (ISBN 0-312-52455-2). St Martin.

Ribton-Turner, C. J. A History of Vagrants & Vagrancy, & Beggars & Begging. LC 75-129315. (Criminology, Law Enforcement, & Social Problems Ser.: No. 138). (Illus.). 780p. 1972. Repr. of 1887 ed. lib. bdg. 45.00x (ISBN 0-87585-138-X). Patterson Smith.

Ribuffo, Leo. The Old Christian Right: The Protestant Far Right from the Great Depression to the Cold War. 1983. write for info. (ISBN 0-87722-297-5). Temple U Pr.

Ricard, Robert. The Spiritual Conquest of Mexico: An Essay on the Apostolate & the Evangelizing Methods of the Mendicant Orders in New Spain, 1523-1572. Simpson, Lesley B., tr. from Sp. (California Library Reprint Ser.: No. 57). (Illus.). 435p. 1974. 34.50x (ISBN 0-520-02760-4); pap. 9.95 (ISBN 0-520-04784-2). U of Cal Pr.

Ricardo, David. Works & Correspondence of David Ricardo, 11 vols. Sraffa, P., ed. 1951. Vols. 1-11. 49.50 ea.; 54.50 ea. Cambridge U Pr.

--The Works & Correspondence of David Ricardo: Index, Vol. 14. Sraffa, P. & Dobb, M. H., eds. 1973. 54.50 (ISBN 0-521-20039-3). Cambridge U Pr.

--The Works & Correspondence of David Ricardo, Vol. 1: Principles of Political Economy. Sraffa, P., ed. 437p. 1981. pap. 15.95 (ISBN 0-521-28505-4). Cambridge U Pr.

Ricardo, Ilona, jt. auth. see Richter, Peyton.

Ricca, A. B., jt. auth. see Maglis, J. V.

Riccardi, Vincent M. The Genetic Approach to Human Disease. (Illus.). 1977. text ed. 23.95x (ISBN 0-19-502175-4); pap. text ed. 13.95x (ISBN 0-19-502176-2). Oxford U Pr.

Riccardi, Vincent M. & Kurtz, Susanne M. Communication & Counseling in Health Care. 1983. pap. text ed. 14.75x (ISBN 0-398-04825-8). C C Thomas.

Riccardi, Vincent M. & Mulvihill, John J., eds. Neurofibromatosis (von Recklinghausen Disease) (Advances in Neurology Ser.: Vol. 29). 304p. 1981. text ed. 32.50 (ISBN 0-686-64310-0). Raven.

Ricchiuti, Paul. Elijah Jeremiah Phillips' Great Journey. (Hello World Ser.). 1975. pap. 1.65 o.p. (ISBN 0-8163-0185-9, 05303-3). Pacific Pr Pub Assn.

Ricci, Benjamin. Physical & Physiological Conditioning for Men. 2nd ed. (Physical Education Activities Ser). 56p. 1972. pap. text ed. write for info. (ISBN 0-697-07114-6); tchrs.' manual avail. (ISBN 0-697-07228-2). Wm C Brown.

Ricci, Edward M., jt. ed. see Hare, Francis H., Jr.

Ricci, Goirgoi, et al, eds. Therapeutic Selectivity & Risk-Benefit Assessment of Hypolipidemic Drugs. 351p. 1982. text ed. 43.00 (ISBN 0-89004-649-2). Raven.

Ricci, Isolina. Mom's House, Dad's House: Making Shared Custody Work. 224p. 1980. 12.95 (ISBN 0-02-602550-7); pap. 5.95. Macmillan.

Ricci, J. Elsevier's Banking Dictionary. 2nd ed. (Eng., Fr., Ital., Span., Dutch & Ger.). 1980. 64.00 (ISBN 0-444-41834-2). Elsevier.

Ricci, Jay, ed. see Waser, Jurg, et al.

Ricci, M. & Marone, G., eds. Progress in Clinical Immunology. (Monographs in Allergy: Vol. 18). (Illus.). viii, 222p. 1983. 90.00 (ISBN 3-8055-3697-6). S Karger.

Ricci, R. A., jt. auth. see Broglia, R. A.

Ricci, R. A., jt. auth. see Faraggi, H.

Ricci, R. A., jt. ed. see Cindro, N.

Ricci, Robert, jt. auth. see Fink, Robert R.

Ricci, Robert, jt. auth. see Kynaston, Trent.

Ricciardi, Antonio. St. Maximilian Kolbe. Daughters of St. Paul, tr. from Ital. (Illus.). 314p. 1982. 7.95 (ISBN 0-8198-6838-8, ST0283); pap. 6.50 (ISBN 0-8198-6837-X). Dghtrs St Paul.

Ricciardi, L. & Scott, A., eds. Biomathematics in Nineteen Eighty. (North-Holland Mathematics Studies: Vol. 58). 298p. 1982. 51.00 (ISBN 0-444-86355-9). Elsevier.

Riccio, Anthony C. & Quaranta, Joseph J. Establishing Guidance Programs in Secondary Schools. (Guidance Monograph). 1968. pap. 2.40 o.p. (ISBN 0-395-09905-6). HM.

Riccio, Dolores & Bingham, Joan. The Complete All-In-The-Oven Cookbook. LC 80-5712. 396p. 1982. 14.95 (ISBN 0-8128-2699-X); pap. 9.95 (ISBN 0-8128-6165-5). Stein & Day.

Riccio, Dolores, jt. auth. see Bingham, Joan.

Ricciuti, Edward. Older Than the Dinosaurs: The Origin & Rise of the Mammals. LC 77-26606. (Illus.). 96p. (gr. 5-12). 1980. 7.95i (ISBN 0-690-01328-0, TYC-J); PLB 9.89 (ISBN 0-690-03879-8). Har-Row.

Ricciuti, Edward, jt. auth. see Line, Les.

Ricciuti, Edward R. Killers of the Seas. (Illus.). 308p. 1975. pap. 7.95 (ISBN 0-02-063650-4, Collier). Macmillan.

--Shelf Pets. LC 76-135782. (Illus.). (gr. 5 up). 1971. PLB 10.89 (ISBN 0-06-024994-3, HarpJ). Har-Row.

--Sounds of Animals at Night. LC 76-3843. (Illus.). (gr. 3-7). 1977. 10.89 (ISBN 0-06-024980-3, HarpJ); PLB 8.79 (ISBN 0-06-024981-1). Har-Row.

--To the Brink of Extinction. LC 73-14341. (Illus.). 160p. (gr. 5 up). 1974. PLB 10.89 (ISBN 0-06-024983-8, HarpJ). Har-Row.

--The Wild Cats. LC 78-24725. (Illus.). 1979. 24.95 o.p. (ISBN 0-88225-270-4). Newsweek.

Ricciuti, Henry N., jt. auth. see Caldwell, Bettye.

Rice & Netzer. Handbook of Ozone Technology & Applications, Vol. 1. LC 81-70869. 386p. 1982. 49.95 (ISBN 0-250-40324-2). Ann Arbor Science.

Rice, Alan, tr. see Koster, Hans-Curt, ed.

Rice, Alice N. Kids Are Sense-Ational. (gr. 3-6). 1981. 3.95 (ISBN 0-86653-011-8, GA 239). Good Apple.

Rice, Alice R. The Goodship Friendship. (gr. 3-6). 1981. 3.95 (ISBN 0-86653-031-2, GA 259). Good Apple.

Rice, Allan L., tr. see Semm, K.

Rice, Anne. The Feast of All Saints. 1980. 14.95 o.p. (ISBN 0-671-24755-7). S&S.

Rice, Arnold, ed. Herbert Hoover, 1874-1964: Chronology, Documents, Bibliographical Aids. LC 78-111215. (Presidential Chronology Ser.). 114p. 1971. 8.00 (ISBN 0-379-12071-2). Oceana.

Rice, Arnold S. American Civilization. 256p. (Orig.). (gr. 11-12). 1983. pap. 6.68i (ISBN 0-06-460145-5, COS CO 145). B&N NY.

Rice, Arnold S., jt. auth. see Krout, John A.

Rice, B. J. & Strange, Jerry D. Applied Analysis for Physicists & Engineers. 1972. write for info. (ISBN 0-87150-137-6, PWS 1051). Prindle.

Rice, Barbara. The Power of a Woman's Love. 160p. 1982. 8.95 (ISBN 0-8007-1342-7). Revell.

Rice, Berkeley, et al. The Psychology Primer. 1975. 5.28 o.p. (ISBN 0-02-647180-9, 64718); familytree (poster) 3.36 o.p. (ISBN 0-02-647150-7, 64715). Glencoe.

Rice, Bernard & Strange, Jerry. Technical Math with Calculus. 1983. text ed. write for info. (ISBN 0-87150-376-X, 2801). Prindle.

Rice, Bernard J. & Strange, Jerry D. Technical Math. (Math Ser.). 672p. 1982. text ed. write for info. (ISBN 0-87150-327-1, 2611). Prindle.

Rice, Bernard J., jt. auth. see Strange, Jerry D.

Rice, Betty. Public Relations for Public Libraries. 133p. 1972. lib. bdg. 10.00 (ISBN 0-8242-0476-X). Wilson.

Rice, Brian & Evans, Tony. The English Sunrise. LC 73-177658. 1972. pap. 5.95 (ISBN 0-8256-3900-X, 030900, Quick Fox). Putnam Pub Group.

Rice, C. B., jt. auth. see Stock, R.

Rice, C. Duncan. The Rise & Fall of Black Slavery. LC 72-9149. (Illus.). 448p. 1975. 17.26xi (ISBN 0-06-013552-2, HarpT). Har-Row.

Rice, Dale. Classroom Behavior from A to Z. LC 73-86804. 1974. pap. 5.50 o.p. (ISBN 0-8224-1375-2). Pitman Learning.

--Energy from Fossil Fuels. (A Look Inside Ser.). (Illus.). 48p. (gr. 4 up). 1983. PLB 14.25 (ISBN 0-8172-1417-8). Raintree Pubs.

Rice, Dale H., ed. Surgery of the Salivary Glands. 155p. 1982. 20.00 (ISBN 0-941158-03-9, D4120-9). Mosby.

Rice, David, jt. ed. see Botein, Michael.

Rice, E. B. Extension in the Andes. LC 74-12334. (Economic Monograph Ser.: No. 13). 554p. 1975. 25.00x (ISBN 0-262-18071-5). MIT Pr.

Rice, Earle, Jr. Fear on Ice. LC 80-82984. (SporTellers Ser.). (Illus.). 64p. (gr. 4 up). 1981. PLB 8.65 (ISBN 0-516-02262-8). Childrens.

--Tiger, Lion, Hawk. LC 77-81595. (Pacesetters Ser.). (Illus.). 64p. (gr. 4 up). 1978. PLB 8.65 (ISBN 0-516-02173-7). Childrens.

Rice, Edward. Eastern Definitions. LC 77-19359. (Illus.). 1980. pap. 8.95 (ISBN 0-385-15631-6, Anch). Doubleday.

Rice, Edward E. Mao's Way. LC 70-186116. (Center for Chinese Studies, Uc Berkeley). 600p. 1972. 40.00x (ISBN 0-520-02199-1); pap. 4.95 (ISBN 0-520-02623-3). U of Cal Pr.

Rice, Emmett A., et al. A Brief History of Physical Education. 5th ed. (Illus.). 1969. 27.95 o.s.i. (ISBN 0-471-07082-3). Wiley.

Rice, Eve. Goodnight, Goodnight. LC 79-17253. (Illus.). (gr. k-1). 1980. 8.75 (ISBN 0-688-80254-0); PLB 8.88 (ISBN 0-688-84254-2). Greenwillow.

--Sam Who Never Forgets. LC 76-30370. 32p. (ps-3). 1977. 9.36 o.p. (ISBN 0-688-80088-2); PLB 9.36 (ISBN 0-688-84088-4). Greenwillow.

Rice, F. Philip. Morality & Youth: A Guide for Christian Parents. LC 80-11433. 1980. pap. 10.95 (ISBN 0-664-24315-0). Westminster.

Rice, Frank A. Eastern Arabic: An Introduction to the Spoken Arabic of Palestine, Syria & Lebanon. pap. 12.00x (ISBN 0-86685-049-X). Intl Bk Ctr.

Rice, Gail. Preparing Your Own ABE Reading Materials. 48p. 1981. pap. 5.95 o.s.i. (ISBN 0-686-79149-5). Follett.

Rice, Gini. Relics of the Road. Incl. GMC Truck Gems, 1900-1950 (ISBN 0-8038-6326-8). 9.50 ea. Hastings.

Rice, Harold S. & Knight, Raymond M. Technical Mathematics. 3rd ed. 1972. text ed. 21.50 (ISBN 0-07-052200-6, G); instructor's manual 3.00 (ISBN 0-07-052201-4); answer key 3.00 (ISBN 0-07-052202-2). McGraw.

--Technical Mathematics with Calculus. 3rd ed. (Illus.). 704p. 1974. text ed. 25.95 (ISBN 0-07-052205-7, G); tchrs manual 4.00 (ISBN 0-07-052206-5); answer key 3.00 (ISBN 0-07-052207-3). McGraw.

Rice, Hazel V. Gastrointestinal Nursing. (Nursing Outline Ser.). 1978. pap. 12.75 (ISBN 0-87488-392-X). Med Exam.

Rice, Helen S. Everyone Needs Someone. (Geneal Ser.). 1979. lib. bdg. 7.95 (ISBN 0-8161-6772-9, Large Print Bks). G K Hall.

--Just for You: A Special Collection of Inspirational Verses. LC 67-10385. 1967. 6.95 (ISBN 0-385-07721-1). Doubleday.

--Love. (Illus.). 128p. 1980. 10.95 (ISBN 0-8007-1072-X); Keepsake ed. 13.95 (ISBN 0-8007-1073-8). Revell.

--Loving Promises. (Illus.). 128p. 1975. 10.95 (ISBN 0-8007-0736-2); boxed keepsake ed 13.95 (ISBN 0-8007-0737-0). Revell.

--The Story of the Christmas Guest. (Illus.). 32p. 1972. 5.95 o.p. (ISBN 0-8007-0544-0). Revell.

Rice, Helen S., jt. auth. see Allen, Charles L.

Rice, Herman. True Flight. 1974. pap. 5.00x cancelled o.p. (ISBN 0-911720-80-4, Pub. by True Flight). Aviation.

Rice, Hugh A. L. Thomas Ken: Bishop & Non-Juror. LC 58-4172. 1958. 7.50x (ISBN 0-8401-2008-7). Allenson-Breckinridge.

Rice, James. Gaston Drills an Offshore Oil Well. LC 82-11240. (Gaston Ser.). (Illus.). 48p. (gr. 4 up). 1982. 9.95 (ISBN 0-88289-289-4). Pelican.

--Gaston Lays an Offshore Pipeline. LC 79-20335. (Illus.). 1979. 8.95 (ISBN 0-88289-177-4). Pelican.

--Lyn & the Fuzzy. LC 75-19096. (Illus.). 32p. (gr. 2-6). 1975. 8.95 (ISBN 0-88289-087-5). Pelican.

--Nashville Ninety Eight. LC 76-59113. 10.95 (ISBN 0-87716-089-9, Pub. by Moore Pub Co). F Apple.

Rice, James, jt. auth. see Durio, Alice.

Rice, James see Trosclair.

Rice, James O. & Rosaler, Bob. Standard Handbook of Plant Engineering. (Illus.). 1280p. 1982. 79.50 (ISBN 0-07-052160-3). McGraw.

Rice, John R. Matrix Computation & Mathematical Software. Stewart, Charles E., ed. (Computer Science Ser.). (Illus.). 288p. 1981. text ed. 29.95 (ISBN 0-07-052145-X); solutions manual o.p. 5.95 (ISBN 0-07-052146-8). McGraw.

--Numerical Methods, Software & Analysis. 800p. 1983. text ed. 34.95 (ISBN 0-07-052209-X); pap. text ed. 19.95 (ISBN 0-07-052208-1). McGraw.

--When a Christian Sins. 1954. pap. 2.95 (ISBN 0-8024-9434-X). Moody.

Rice, John W. Successful Selling from A to Dollars: The Professional's Guide to Money-Making Sales Techniques. (Illus.). 216p. 1983. 15.95 (ISBN 0-13-872069-X); pap. 6.95 (ISBN 0-13-872051-7). P-H.

Rice, Keith A. Out of Canaan. 192p. 1983. 12.95 (ISBN 0-684-17857-5, ScribT). Scribner.

Rice, Kym. Early American Taverns: For the Entertainment of Friends & Strangers. LC 82-42786. 1983. pap. 12.95. Regnery-Gateway.

Rice, Laura N., jt. auth. see Wexler, David A.

Rice, Mabel. Cognition to Language. 242p. 1979. pap. text ed. 12.95 (ISBN 0-8391-1548-2). Univ Park.

Rice, Mac M. & Rice, Vivian B. When Can I Say, "I Love You"? LC 76-54926. 1977. pap. 2.95 (ISBN 0-8024-9436-6). Moody.

Rice, Margery S. Working Class Wives: The Classic Account of Women's Lives in the 1930's. 212p. pap. 5.95 (ISBN 0-686-38947-6, Virago Pr). Merrimack Bk Serv.

Rice, Mary F. & Flatter, Charles H. Help Me Learn: A Handbook for Teaching Young Children. 192p. 1979. 13.95 (ISBN 0-13-386292-5); pap. 6.95 (ISBN 0-13-386284-4). P-H.

Rice, Otis K. The Hatfields & the McCoys. LC 78-57388. (Kentucky Bicentennial Bookshelf Ser.). (Illus.). 160p. 1978. 6.95 o.p. (ISBN 0-8131-0235-9). U Pr of Ky.

Rice, Paul & Rice, Valeta. Aquarius: Through the Numbers. 48p. 1983. pap. 2.50 (ISBN 0-87728-575-6). Weiser.

--Aries: Through the Numbers. 48p. 1983. pap. 2.50 (ISBN 0-87728-565-9). Weiser.

--Cancer: Through the Numbers. 48p. 1983. pap. 2.50 (ISBN 0-87728-568-3). Weiser.

--Capricorn: Through the Numbers. 48p. 1983. pap. 2.50 (ISBN 0-87728-574-8). Weiser.

--Gemini: Through the Numbers. 48p. 1983. pap. 2.50 (ISBN 0-87728-567-5). Weiser.

--Leo: Through the Numbers. 48p. 1983. pap. 2.50 (ISBN 0-87728-569-1). Weiser.

--Libra: Through the Numbers. 48p. 1983. pap. 2.50 (ISBN 0-87728-571-3). Weiser.

--Pisces: Through the Numbers. 48p. 1983. pap. 2.50 (ISBN 0-87728-576-4). Weiser.

--Sagittarius: Through the Numbers. 48p. 1983. pap. 2.50 (ISBN 0-87728-573-X). Weiser.

--Scorpio: Through the Numbers. 48p. 1983. pap. 2.50 (ISBN 0-87728-572-1). Weiser.

--Taurus: Through the Numbers. 48p. 1983. pap. 2.50 (ISBN 0-87728-566-7). Weiser.

--Virgo: Through the Numbers. 48p. 1983. pap. 2.50 (ISBN 0-87728-570-5). Weiser.

Rice, Philip F. Getting Rich with Rental Property: A Guide for Today's Economy. 167p. 1982. 12.95 (ISBN 0-13-369645-6); pap. 6.95 (ISBN 0-13-369637-5). P-H.

Rice, Rip C., ed. see Masschelein, Willy J.

Rice, Rip G. Biological Activated Carbon. LC 81-69256. 611p. 1982. text ed. 47.50 (ISBN 0-250-40427-3). Ann Arbor Science.

Rice, Rip G. & Netzer, Aharon, eds. Handbook of Ozone Technology & Applications, Vol. 2. LC 81-70869. (Illus.). 325p. 1983. 49.95 (ISBN 0-250-40577-6). Ann Arbor Science.

--Handbook of Ozone Technology & Applications, Vol. 3. LC 81-70869. (Illus.). 325p. 1983. 49.95 (ISBN 0-250-40578-4). Ann Arbor Science.

--Handbook of Ozone Technology & Applications, Vol. 4. LC 81-70869. (Illus.). 325p. 1983. 49.95 (ISBN 0-250-40579-2). Ann Arbor Science.

Rice, Robert M. American Family Policy: Content & Context. LC 77-15664. 1977. pap. 6.95 o.p. (ISBN 0-87304-160-7). Family Serv.

Rice, Russ. Kentucky Basketball. LC 75-32110. (College Sports Ser.). 1980. 11.95 o.p. (ISBN 0-87397-078-0). Strode.

Rice, Russell. Kentucky Basketball: Big Blue Machine. 1982. 11.95 (ISBN 0-87397-240-6). Strode.

--The Wildcat Legacy: A Pictorial History of Kentucky Basketball. LC 82-80433. (Illus.). 184p. 1982. 19.95 (ISBN 0-938694-09-X). JCP Corp VA.

Rice, S. Getting Started in Prints & Patterns. 1971. pap. 2.95 o.p. (ISBN 0-685-01115-1, 80623). Glencoe.

Rice, S. A., jt. auth. see Prigogine, I.

Rice, Stan. Body of Work. LC 82-84377. (Lost Roads Poetry Ser.: No. 21). 63p. 1983. pap. 5.95 (ISBN 0-918786-24-X). Lost Roads.

Rice, Stanley. CRT Typesetting Handbook. 415p. 1981. 35.00 o.p. (ISBN 0-442-23889-4). Van Nos Reinhold.

Rice, Stuart A. For Ilya Prigogine. LC 58-9935. (Advances in Chemical Physics Ser.: Vol. 38). 1978. 72.00 o.s.i. (ISBN 0-471-03883-0, Pub. by Wiley-Interscience). Wiley.

--Polyelectrolyte Solutions: A Theoretical Introduction. (Molecular Biology Ser.). 1961. 69.50 (ISBN 0-12-587350-6). Acad Pr.

Rice, Stuart A., jt. auth. see Prigogine, I.

Rice, Stuart A., ed. see Prigogine, I.

Rice, Tamara T. A Concise History of Russian Art. (World of Art). (Illus.). 1963. pap. text ed. 9.95 o.p. (ISBN 0-19-520002-0). Oxford U Pr.

--Finding Out About the Early Russians. (Illus.). (gr. 7 up). 12.75x (ISBN 0-392-02903-0, SpS). Sportshelf.

Rice, Thomas J., ed. English Fiction, Nineteen Hundred to Nineteen Fifty: A Guide to Information Sources. LC 73-16989. (American Literature, English Literature, and World Literatures in English Information Guide Ser.: Vol. 20). 680p. 1979. 42.00x (ISBN 0-8103-1217-4). Gale.

--English Fiction, 1900-1950: A Guide to Information Sources, Vol. 2. (American Literature, English Literature, & World Literature in English Information Guide Ser.: Vol. 21). 627p. 1983. 42.00x (ISBN 0-8103-1505-X). Gale.

Rice, Timothy, jt. ed. see Falck, Robert.

Rice, Tom. Beach Banquet. Swant, Dale, ed. (Illus.). 64p. (Orig.). 1983. pap. 2.95 (ISBN 0-943470-01-3). Daisy Pub WA.

Rice, Valeta, jt. auth. see Rice, Paul.

Rice, Victor A., et al. Breeding & Improvement of Farm Animals. 6th ed. (Agricultural Science Ser.). 1967. text ed. 19.50 o.p. (ISBN 0-07-052179-4, C). McGraw.

Rice, Vivian B., jt. auth. see Rice, Mac M.

Rice, Wayne & Yaconelli, Mike. Far Out Ideas for Young Groups. 96p. 1975. pap. 5.95 (ISBN 0-310-34941-9). Zondervan.

--Holiday Ideas for Youth Groups. (Ideas for Youth Groups Ser.). 160p. (Orig.). 1981. pap. 7.95 (ISBN 0-310-34991-5). Zondervan.

--Right-on Ideas for Youth Groups. (Illus.). 96p. 1973. pap. 5.95 (ISBN 0-310-34951-6). Zondervan.

--Super Ideas for Youth Groups. (Orig.). 1979. pap. 5.95 (ISBN 0-310-34981-8). Zondervan.

--Way Out Ideas for Youth Groups. pap. 5.95 (ISBN 0-310-34961-3). Zondervan.

Rice, William & Wolf, Burton. Where to Eat in America. 1977. pap. 7.95 (ISBN 0-394-73728-8). Random.

Rice, Wlliam Hyde. Hawaiian Legends. LC 77-83648. (Special Publication Ser.: No. 63). (Illus.). 162p. 1977. pap. 25.00 (ISBN 0-910240-21-3). Bishop Mus.

Rich, Adrienne. Sources. 60p. 1983. 160.00 (ISBN 0-940592-15-0). Heyeck Pr.

Rich, Adrienne & Gelpi, Barbara, eds. Adrienne Rich's Poetry. (Critical Editions Ser). 150p. 1975. 7.95 (ISBN 0-393-04399-1); pap. text ed. 5.95x (ISBN 0-393-09241-0). Norton.

Rich, Alan, et al. Dancin' Disco Your Way to Health. (Illus.). cancelled (ISBN 0-89169-533-8). Reed Bks.

Rich, Allan. Listeners Guide to Opera. 1980. 9.95 o.p. (ISBN 0-671-25442-1). S&S.

--Listeners Guide to Classical Music. 1980. 9.95 o.p. (ISBN 0-671-25440-5). S&S.

Rich, Andrea & Smith, Arthur L. Rhetoric of Revolution. LC 79-99291. 12.00 (ISBN 0-87716-010-4, Pub. by Moore Pub Co). F Apple.

Rich, Avery E., ed. Potato Diseases. LC 82-24290. (Monograph). Date not set. price not set. Acad Pr.

Rich, Barbara. Let's Go to a Jetport. (Let's Go Ser.). (Illus.). 48p. (gr. 3-5). 1973. PLB 4.29 o.p. (ISBN 0-399-60788-9). Putnam Pub Group.

Rich, Barnabe. Faultes, Faults, & Nothing Else but Faultes. LC 65-10396. Repr. of 1606 ed. 32.00x (ISBN 0-8201-1266-6). Schol Facsimiles.

Rich, Barnett. Elementary Algebra. (Orig.). 1960. pap. 5.95 (ISBN 0-07-052244-8, SP). McGraw.

--Modern Elementary Algebra. (Schaum Outline Ser). 1973. pap. 5.95 (ISBN 0-07-052247-2, SP). McGraw.

--Review of Elementary Mathematics. (Schaum's Outline Ser). (Orig.). 1977. pap. 5.95 (ISBN 0-07-052260-X, SP). McGraw.

Rich, Barnett, jt. auth. see Dressler, Isidore.

Rich, Daniel, jt. auth. see Lakoff, Sanford A.

Rich, Daniel & Veigel, Jon M., eds. The Solar Energy Transition: Implementation & Policy Implications. 205p. 1983. lib. bdg. 23.00x (ISBN 0-86531-603-1). Westview.

Rich, E. Artificial Intelligence. 480p. 1982. 24.95x (ISBN 0-07-052261-8). McGraw.

Rich, Elaine S., ed. Breaking Bread Together: A Devotional Book for Women. 1958. 3.95 o.p. (ISBN 0-8361-1323-3). Herald Pr.

Rich, Harry. Mutatis Alphonsus. LC 76-29271. (Illus.). 48p. 1977. pap. 6.95 (ISBN 0-685-91112-8, Hog Hill Pr.). Globe Pequot.

Rich, Harvey E. & Jolicoeur, Pamela M. Student Attitudes & Academic Environments: A Study of California Higher Education. LC 78-2953. (Praeger Special Studies). 1978. 21.95 o.p. (ISBN 0-03-041431-8). Praeger.

Rich, Hobart L. Disturbed Students: Characteristics & Educational Strategies. (Illus.). 368p. 1982. pap. text ed. 19.95 (ISBN 0-8391-1708-6). Univ Park.

Rich, Jack C. Materials & Methods of Sculpture. (Illus.). 1947. 25.00x (ISBN 0-19-500080-3). Oxford U Pr.

Rich, Jane K. & Blake, Nelson M., eds. A Lasting Spring: Jessie Catherine Kinsley, Daughter of the Oneida Community. LC 82-19200. (York State Bks.). (Illus.). 300p. (Orig.). 1983. 32.00x (ISBN 0-8156-0183-2); pap. 14.95 (ISBN 0-8156-0176-X). Syracuse U Pr.

Rich, Jay, jt. auth. see Eyde, Donna R.

Rich, Linvil G. Environmental Systems Engineering. (Illus.). 468p. 1973. text ed. 37.00 (ISBN 0-07-052250-2, C). McGraw.

--Low-Maintenance, Mechanically-Simple Wastewater Treatment Systems. (Water Resources & Environmental Engineering). (Illus.). 1980. text ed. 28.50 (ISBN 0-07-052252-9). McGraw.

--Unit Operations of Sanitary Engineering. LC 61-15410. soft bdg. 15.00 (ISBN 0-686-11818-9). Rich SC.

--Unit Processes of Sanitary Engineering. LC 63-14067. soft bdg. 15.00 (ISBN 0-686-15000-7). Rich SC.

Rich, Louise D. The Coast of Maine. rev ed. LC 75-6662. (Illus.). 385p. 1975. 9.95i (ISBN 0-690-00698-5, TYC-T); pap. 6.95i o.p. (ISBN 0-690-00957-7, TYC-T). T Y Crowell.

--We Took to the Woods. (Illus.). 1975. pap. 5.95 (ISBN 0-89272-016-6). Down East.

Rich, Norman. Friedrich Von Holstein: Politics & Diplomacy in the Era of Bismarck & Wilhelm. 1965. 145.00 (ISBN 0-521-06077-X). Cambridge U Pr.

--Hitler's War Aims: Ideology, the Nazi State, & the Course of Expansion. 400p. 1976. pap. 8.95 (ISBN 0-393-00802-9, Norton Lib). Norton.

Rich, Norman, jt. auth. see Wind, Gary.

Rich, R. A., et al. Hydrothermal Uranium Deposits. (Developments in Economic Geology: Vol. 6). 1977. 40.50 (ISBN 0-444-41551-3). Elsevier.

Rich, Richard, ed. Urban Service Distributions. (Orig.). 1981. pap. 6.00 (ISBN 0-918592-46-1). Policy Studies.

Rich, Richard C., jt. auth. see Manheim, Jarol B.

Rich, Richard C., ed. Analyzing Urban Service Distributions: New Concepts & New Measures. LC 80-7690. (A Policy Studies Organization Bk.). 272p. 1982. 28.95x (ISBN 0-669-03766-4). Lexington Bks.

--The Politics of Urban Public Services. LC 80-7689. (A Policy Studies Organization Book Ser.). (Illus.). 288p. 1981. 26.95x (ISBN 0-669-03765-6). Lexington Bks.

Rich, Robert F. Social Science Information & Public Policy Making: The Interaction Between Bureaucratic Politics & the Use of Survey Data. LC 79-92468. (Social & Behavioral Science Ser.). 1981. text ed. 22.95x (ISBN 0-87589-497-6). Jossey-Bass.

Rich, Robert M. Crimes Without Victims: Deviance & the Criminal Law. LC 78-63258. 1978. pap. text ed. 11.50 (ISBN 0-8191-0618-6). U Pr of Amer.

--Essays on the Theory & Practice of Criminal Justice. 319p. 1977. pap. text ed. 12.75 (ISBN 0-8191-0235-0). U Pr of Amer.

--Juvenile Delinquency: A Paradigmatic Perspective. LC 78-53025. 1978. pap. text ed. 10.75x o.p. (ISBN 0-8191-0493-0). U Pr of Amer.

Rich, Shelley, illus. The Family Bond: A Woman's Place. 72p. 1977. pap. text ed. 3.00 (ISBN 0-686-43396-3). N Grey Inc.

Rich, Susan see Deitsch, Marian.

Rich, Susan, ed. Kline Guide to the Paint Industry. 6th ed. LC 81-84942. (Illus.). 200p. 1981. pap. 97.00 (ISBN 0-917148-01-0). Kline.

--Profiles of U.S. Chemical Distributors. LC 81-83812. 265p. 1981. pap. 277.00 (ISBN 0-917148-77-0). Kline.

Rich, Susan, jt. ed. see Currry, Susan.

Rich, Vernon. Law & the Administration of Justice. 2nd ed. LC 78-31516. 1979. text ed. 22.95x (ISBN 0-471-04961-1). Wiley.

Rich, Virginia. The Baked Bean Supper Murders. 288p. 1983. 13.95 (ISBN 0-525-24185-X, 01354-410). Dutton.

Rich, William D. & Sutton, L. Paul. Sentencing by Mathematics: An Evaluation of the Early Attempts to Develop & Implement Sentencing Guidelines. LC 82-42713. 239p. pap. 20.00 (ISBN 0-89656-057-0, R 071). Natl Ctr St Courts.

Richan, Willard C. Social Service Politics in the United States & Britain. 290p. 1981. 27.95 (ISBN 0-87722-216-9). Temple U Pr.

Richard, jt. auth. see Frankel.

Richard, Alison F. Primate Ecology & Social Organization. Head, J. J., ed. LC 80-66617. (Carolina Biology Readers Ser.). (Illus.). 16p. (gr. 10 up). 1982. pap. 1.60 (ISBN 0-89278-308-7, 45-9708). Carolina Biological.

Richard, Earl. Acts Six: One to Eight: Four: The Authors Method of Composition. LC 78-12926. (Society of Biblical Literature. Dissertation Ser.: No. 41). (Orig.). 1978. pap. 10.95 (ISBN 0-89130-261-1, 06-01-41). Scholars Pr Ca.

Richard, Frederic M., jt. ed. see Tometsko, Andrew M.

Richard, Glasstone. Dancing As a Career for Men. LC 80-54339. (Illus.). 120p. (gr. 10 up). 1981. 10.95 (ISBN 0-8069-4640-7); lib. bdg. 13.29 (ISBN 0-8069-4641-5). Sterling.

Richard, Graham. Great Press Barons. LC 81-86274. (In Profile Ser.). PLB 12.68 (ISBN 0-382-06636-7). Silver.

Richard, Ivor. We, the British. LC 80-2623. 264p. 1983. 16.95 (ISBN 0-385-14531-4). Doubleday.

Richard, J. The Latin Kingdom of Jerusalem, 2 Pts. (Europe in the Middle Ages Selected Studies: Vol. 11). 1978. Set. 91.50 (ISBN 0-444-85092-9, North-Holland). Elsevier.

Richard, L. E., ed. see Grant, Ruthie.

Richard, L. S. Whaling Trade in Old New Zealand. 16.50x (ISBN 0-392-07499-0, ABC). Sportshelf.

Richard, Lucien J. A Kenotic Christology: In the Humanity of Jesus the Christ, the Compassion of Our God. LC 80-40915. 342p. (Orig.). 1982. lib. bdg. 25.25 (ISBN 0-8191-2199-1); pap. text ed. 12.75 (ISBN 0-8191-2200-9). U Pr of Amer.

Richard, Nancy, jt. auth. see Carll, Barbara.

Richard, Olga, jt. auth. see MacCann, Donnarae.

Richard, Rich. How to BS Effectively. (Illus.). 64p. (Orig.). 1981. pap. 4.94 o.s.i. (ISBN 0-9606784-0-9). IBS Pub Co.

Richards, A. I. & Kuper, Adam, eds. Councils in Action: Comparative Studies. LC 76-160101. (Cambridge Papers in Social Anthropology: No. 6). (Illus.). 1971. 24.95 (ISBN 0-521-08240-4). Cambridge U Pr.

Richards, Alun. Barque Whisper. 1980. 10.00 o.p. (ISBN 0-312-06707-0). St Martin.

Richards, Arlene & Wills, Irene. How to Get It Together When Your Parents Are Coming Apart. LC 76-12746. (gr. 7 up). 1976. 7.95 o.p. (ISBN 0-679-20322-2). McKay.

Richards, Arlene K. & Willis, Irene. Leaving Home. LC 80-12721. 195p. (gr. 7 up). 1980. 8.95 (ISBN 0-689-30757-8). Atheneum.

--What to Do if You or Someone You Know Is under 18 & Pregnant. LC 82-12698. (Illus.). 256p. 1983. 9.55 (ISBN 0-688-51961-X); pap. 7.00 (ISBN 0-688-01044-X). Lothrop.

Richards, Audrey. Chisungu: A Girls Initiation Ceremony Among the Bemba. 1982. pap. 10.95 (ISBN 0-422-78070-7, Pub. by Tavistock). Methuen Inc.

Richards, Audrey I. The Multicultural States of East Africa. (Keith Callard Lectures Ser). 1969. 5.00 o.p. (ISBN 0-7735-0067-7); pap. 4.25 (ISBN 0-7735-0077-4). McGill-Queens U Pr.

Richards, Aurelia. The Mormon Trail: In Story Form. pap. 4.95 o.p. (ISBN 0-89036-137-1). Hawkes Pub Inc.

Richards, Barbara. Sydney: More Than a Harbor. (Illus.). 14.50x (ISBN 0-392-05493-0, ABC). Sportshelf.

Richards, Bartlett, Jr. & Van Ackeren, Ruth. Bartlett Richards: Nebraska Sandhills Cattleman. LC 79-92129. (Illus.). 289p. (Orig.). 1980. 12.00 (ISBN 0-686-31143-4). Nebraska Hist.

Richards, Bernard, ed. see James, Henry.

Richards, Bertrand F. Gene Stratton Porter. (United States Author Ser.). 1980. lib. bdg. 11.95 (ISBN 0-8057-7304-5, Twayne). G K Hall.

Richards, Carl, jt. auth. see Swisher, Doug.

Richards, Charles & Richards, Janet. Classic Chinese & Japanese Cooking. 2nd rev. ed. LC 58-11331. 1972. pap. 1.50 o.p. (ISBN 0-87286-068-X). City Lights.

Richards, Charlie R., jt. auth. see Badalato, Billy.

Richards, Curtis. Halloween. 176p. 1982. pap. write for info. (ISBN 0-553-22740-8). Bantam.

Richards, D. L. Telecommunication by Speech: A Transmission Performance-of-Telephone Networks. 1973. 65.95 o.s.i. (ISBN 0-470-71949-4). Halsted Pr.
Richards, Dennis L., ed. Montana's Genealogical Records. (The Gale Genealogy & Local History Ser.: Vol. 11). 330p. 1981. 42.00x (ISBN 0-8103-1487-8). Gale.
Richards, Derek, jt. auth. see Percival, Ian C
Richards, Dorothy F. Marty Finds a Treasure. LC 82-7425. (Illus.). 32p. (gr. 3-4). 1982. lib. bdg. 4.95 (ISBN 0-686-83154-3). Dandelion Hse.
--Wise Owl ABC Book. LC 81-6187. (The Wise Owl Ser.). (Illus.). 32p. (ps-2). 1981. 9.25 (ISBN 0-516-06561-0). Childrens.
--Wise Owl's Birthday Colors. LC 81-10144. (Wise Owl Plus Ser.). (Illus.). 32p. (ps-2). 1981. PLB 9.25 (ISBN 0-516-06562-9). Childrens.
--Wise Owl's Counting Book. LC 81-2399. (The Wise Owl Ser.). (Illus.). 32p. (ps-2). 1981. 9.25 (ISBN 0-516-06565-3). Childrens.
Richards, E. J., tr. see De Pizan, Christine.
Richards, Edward P., III & Rathbun, Katharine C. Medical Risk Management: Preventive Legal Strategies for Health Care Providers. LC 82-16346. 311p. 1982. 29.95 (ISBN 0-89443-840-9). Aspen Systems.
Richards, Eugene. Few Comforts or Surprises: The Arkansas Delta. 1973. 15.00 o.p. (ISBN 0-262-18062-6); pap. 4.95 (ISBN 0-262-68024-6). MIT Pr.
Richards, Francis A., ed. Coastal Upwelling Ecosystems Analysis Program. 1977. pap. text ed. 19.50 (ISBN 0-08-021375-8). Pergamon.
Richards, H. E., jt. auth. see Lawrence, Ralph R.
Richards, Herbert. Dog Breeding for Professionals. (Illus.). 1978. 12.95 (ISBN 0-87666-659-4, H969). TFH Pubns.
--The T. F. H. Book of Puppies. (Illus.). 96p. 6.95 (ISBN 0-686-97807-2, HP-013). TFH Pubns.
Richards, Hubert. Reading Paul Today: A New Introduction to the Man & His Letters. LC 79-26287. (Biblical Foundations Ser.). (Illus.). 152p. 1980. pap. 2.49 (ISBN 0-8042-0392-X). John Knox.
--What Happens When You Pray? (Student Christian Movement Press Ser.). (Orig.). 1980. pap. 6.95x (ISBN 0-19-520335-6). Oxford U Pr.
Richards, Hubert J. ABC of the Bible. 1967. 3.95 o.p. (ISBN 0-685-07604-0, 80628). Glencoe.
Richards, Hubert J., jt. auth. see De Rosa, Peter.
Richards, I. A. New & Selected Poems. 1979. pap. 6.95 o.p. (ISBN 0-85635-241-1, Pub. by Carcanet New Pr England). Humanities.
--The Portable Coleridge. 1961. pap. 14.95 (ISBN 0-670-22708-0). Viking Pr.
--Science & Poetry. LC 74-6484. (Studies in Poetry, No. 38). 1974. lib. bdg. 29.95x o.p. (ISBN 0-8383-1916-5). Haskell.
Richards, Ivor A. Plato's Republic. (Orig.). 24.50 (ISBN 0-521-05965-8); pap. 6.95x (ISBN 0-521-09359-7). Cambridge U Pr.
Richards, Ivor A., jt. auth. see Ogden, Charles K.
Richards, J. Swordsmen of the Screen. (Cinema & Society Ser.). (Illus.). 1977. 25.00 (ISBN 0-7100-8478-1). Routledge & Kegan.
Richards, J. A. Analysis of Periodically Time-Varying Systems. (Communications & Control Engineering Ser.). (Illus.). 173p. 1983. 29.50 (ISBN 0-387-11689-3). Springer-Verlag.
Richards, J. C. Words in Action One: A Basic Illustrated English Vocabulary. (Illus.). 102p. (Orig.). 1978. pap. 6.50x (ISBN 0-19-581666-8). Oxford U Pr.
--Words in Action Three: A Basic Illustrated English Vocabulary. (Illus.). 132p. (Orig.). 1978. pap. 6.50x. Oxford U Pr.
--Words in Action Two: A Basic Illustrated English Vocabulary. (Illus.). 110p. (Orig.). 1978. pap. 6.50x (ISBN 0-19-581698-6). Oxford U Pr.
Richards, J. M. Eight-Hundred Years of Finnish Architecture. (Illus.). 1978. 37.50 (ISBN 0-7153-7512-1). David & Charles.
Richards, J. T. The Firebrands. 272p. 1982. pap. 2.95 (ISBN 0-515-05633-2). Jove Pubns.
Richards, Jack. Error Analysis: Perspectives on Second Language Acquisition. (Applied Linguistics & Language Study). 1974. pap. text ed. 10.75 (ISBN 0-582-55044-0). Longman.
Richards, Jack C., ed. Understanding Second & Foreign Language Learning. LC 78-24457. 1978. pap. text ed. 12.95 (ISBN 0-88377-124-1). Newbury Hse.
Richards, Jack R., jt. ed. see Oller, John W., Jr.
Richards, James. PASCAL. 1982. 13.75 (ISBN 0-12-587520-7). Acad Pr.
Richards, Janet, jt. auth. see Richards, Charles.
Richards, Jean H. Jesus Went About Doing Good. LC 80-70475. (gr. 1-4). 1983. 5.95 (ISBN 0-8054-4289-8). Broadman.
Richards, Jeffrey. Swordsmen of the Screen: From Douglas Fairbanks to Michael York. (Cinema & Society Ser.). (Illus.). 312p. 1980. pap. 9.95 (ISBN 0-7100-0681-0). Routledge & Kegan.
Richards, Jessica. Mistress of the Western Wind. 208p. (Orig.). 1980. pap. 2.50 o.s.i. (ISBN 0-515-04755-4). Jove Pubns.
--Tularosa. 336p. (Orig.). pap. 2.25 o.s.i. (ISBN 0-515-04761-9). Jove Pubns.
Richards, John. Hidden Country: Nature on Your Doorstep. LC 72-12745. (Illus.). 144p. (gr. 5-8). 1973. PLB 10.95 (ISBN 0-87599-195-5). S G Phillips.
Richards, John & Richards, Mary. Experiencing Self-Mastery. 64p. (Orig.). 1983. pap. 3.95 (ISBN 0-942044-02-9). Polestar.
Richards, John F. & Tucker, Richard P. Global Deforestation & the Nineteenth Century World Economy. (Duke Press Policy Studies). 300p. 1983. 25.00 (ISBN 0-8223-0482-1). Duke.
Richards, John F., ed. Precious Metals in the Later Medieval & Early Modern World. LC 82-73059. (Illus.). 500p. 1982. 39.95 (ISBN 0-89089-224-5). Carolina Acad Pr.
Richards, Judith. The Sounds of Silence. 1977. 8.95 (ISBN 0-399-11950-7). Putnam Pub Group.
Richards, Judith W. Fundamentals of Development Finance: A Practitioner's Guide. 224p. 1983. 31.95 (ISBN 0-03-062191-7). Praeger.
Richards, Katharine L. How Christmas Came to the Sunday-Schools: The Observance of Christmas in the Protestant Church Schools of the United States. LC 70-159860. 1971. Repr. of 1934 ed. 34.00x (ISBN 0-8103-3793-2). Gale.
Richards, Keith. Rivers: Form & Process in Alluvial Channels. 1982. 35.00x (ISBN 0-416-74900-3); pap. 17.95x (ISBN 0-416-74910-0). Methuen Inc.
Richards, Kenneth, jt. ed. see Mayer, David.
Richards, Kent, ed. Society of Biblical Literature: Seminar Papers 1982. (SBL Ser.). 574p. 1982. pap. text ed. 15.00 (ISBN 0-89130-607-2, 06-09-21). Scholars Pr CA.
--Society of Biblical Literature 1981: Seminar Papers. (SBL Seminar Papers). 6.00 o.p. (ISBN 0-686-96233-8, 06 09 20). Scholars Pr CA.
Richards, Larry. Born to Grow. LC 74-92603. 1974. pap. 3.95 (ISBN 0-88207-708-2). Victor Bks.
--Let Day Begin. LC 75-36697. (Bible Alive Ser.). 252p. pap. text ed. 2.95 o.p. (ISBN 0-912692-87-1); tchrs' ed. 3.95 (ISBN 0-912692-86-3). Cook.
--Lift High the Torch. LC 77-78498. (Bible Alive Ser.). (Illus.). 1978. pap. text ed. 2.95 o.p. (ISBN 0-89191-086-7); tchr's ed. 3.95 (ISBN 0-89191-087-5). Cook.
--The Servant King. LC 76-6581. (Bible Alive Ser). (Illus.). 1976. pap. text ed. 2.95 (ISBN 0-912692-99-5); tchr's. ed. o.p. __. 3.95 (ISBN 0-912692-98-7). Cook.
--Teaching Youth. 1982. pap. 4.95 (ISBN 0-8341-0776-7). Beacon Hill.
--Years of Darkness, Days of Glory. LC 76-6582. (Bible Alive Ser). (Illus.). 1977. pap. text ed. 2.95 (ISBN 0-912692-97-9); tchr's. ed. o.p. 3.95 (ISBN 0-912692-96-0). Cook.
Richards, Larry & Johnson, Paul. Death & the Caring Community. LC 80-19752. (Critical Concern Bks.). 1981. 9.95 o.p. (ISBN 0-930014-45-6). Multnomah.
--Death & the Caring Community. LC 80-19752. (Critical Concern Ser.). 210p. 1982. pap. 5.95 (ISBN 0-88070-006-8). Multnomah.
Richards, Larry E. & LaCava, Jerry J. Business Statistics: Why & When. 2nd ed. (Illus.). 512p. 1983. text ed. 24.95 (ISBN 0-07-052276-6, C); wkbk. 15.00 (ISBN 0-07-052278-2); write for info. instr's manual (ISBN 0-07-052277-4). McGraw.
Richards, Larry E., et al. Business Statistics: Why & When. (Illus.). 1978. text ed. 23.95 (ISBN 0-07-052273-1, C); wkbk. 9.95 (ISBN 0-07-052275-8); instructor's manual 10.00 (ISBN 0-07-052274-X). McGraw.
Richards, Laura E. Abigail Adams & Her Times. LC 78-143631. 1971. Repr. of 1917 ed. 34.00x (ISBN 0-8103-3640-5). Gale.
Richards, Laura E. & Elliott, Maude H. Julia Ward Howe, 2 Vols in One. LC 16-694. 1970. 14.95 (ISBN 0-910220-24-7). Berg.
Richards, Lawrence O. Believer's Promise Book: Seven Hundred Prayers & Promises from the NIV. 80p. (Orig.). 1982. pap. 1.75 (ISBN 0-310-43462-9). Zondervan.
--Creative Bible Teaching. LC 74-104830. 1970. 9.95 (ISBN 0-8024-1640-3). Moody.
--Our Life Together: A Woman's Workshop on Fellowship. (Woman's Workshop Ser.). 160p. (Orig.). 1981. pap. 3.95 (ISBN 0-310-43451-3). Zondervan.
--The Word Bible Handbook. 1982. 10.95 (ISBN 0-8499-0279-7). Word Pub.
--The Word Parents Handbook. 1983. 8.95 (ISBN 0-8499-0328-9). Word Bks.
Richards, Lawrence O. & Hoeldtke, Clyde. A Theology of Church Leadership. (Illus.). 352p. 1980. 15.95 (ISBN 0-310-31960-9). Zondervan.
Richards, Lawrence P. & Bock, Walter J. Functional Anatomy & Adaptive Evolution of the Feeding Apparatus in the Hawaiian Honeycreeper Genus Loxops (Drepanidae) 173p. 1973. 9.00. Am Ornithologists.
Richards, Leonard L. The Advent of American Democracy. 1977. pap. 9.95x (ISBN 0-673-07904-X). Scott F.
--Gentlemen of Property and Standing: Anti-Abolition Mobs in Jacksonian America. 1970. pap. 5.95 (ISBN 0-19-501351-4, 347, GB). Oxford U Pr.
Richards, Lockie. Dressage: Begin the Right Way. LC 75-6. (Illus.). 96p. 1975. 13.95 (ISBN 0-7153-6926-1). David & Charles.
Richards, M. & Whitby-Strevens, C. BCPL-The Language & Its Compiler. LC 77-71098. (Illus.). 1981. 26.50 (ISBN 0-521-21965-5); pap. 29.95 (ISBN 0-521-28681-6). Cambridge U Pr.
Richards, M. Innocentia, tr. see Guillet, J.
Richards, M. P., ed. The Integration of the Child into a Social World. LC 73-82464. 320p. 1974. 44.50 (ISBN 0-521-20306-6); pap. 14.95x (ISBN 0-521-09830-0). Cambridge U Pr.
Richards, Margaret, tr. see Renard, G. & Weulersee, G.
Richards, Mary, jt. auth. see Richards, John.
Richards, Mary C. Toward Wholeness: Rudolf Steiner Education in America. LC 80-14905, 1980. 18.95 (ISBN 0-686-94086-5); pap. 7.95 (ISBN 0-8195-6062-6). Wesleyan U Pr.
Richards, Max. Organizational Goal Structures. (West Series in Business Policy & Planning). (Illus.). 1978. pap. text ed. 12.50 (ISBN 0-8299-0210-4). West Pub.
Richards, Norman. Dreamers & Doers: Inventors Who Changed the World. LC 81-21029. 156p. (gr. 5 up). 1983. 8.95 (ISBN 0-689-30914-7). Atheneum.
--Story of Old Ironsides. LC 67-20099. (Cornerstones of Freedom Ser). (Illus.). 32p. (gr. 2-5). 1967. PLB 7.95 (ISBN 0-516-04628-4); pap. 2.50 (ISBN 0-516-44628-2). Childrens.
--The Story of the Alamo: (Cornerstones of Freedom) LC 70-100698. (Illus.). 32p. (gr. 4-8). 1970. 7.95 (ISBN 0-516-04601-2); pap. 2.50 (ISBN 0-516-44601-0). Childrens.
--The Story of the Bonhomme Richard: (Cornerstones of Freedom) LC 76-82961. (Illus.). 32p. (gr. 3-5). 1969. 7.95 (ISBN 0-516-04602-0); pap. 2.50 (ISBN 0-516-44602-9). Childrens.
--Tractors, Plows & Harvesters: A Book About Farm Machines. LC 77-83821. (gr. 1-3). 1978. 8.95 o.p. (ISBN 0-385-12347-7); PLB 8.95 (ISBN 0-385-12348-5). Doubleday.
Richards, O. W. A Revisional Study of the Masarid Wasps (Hymenoptera, Vespoidea) (Illus.). 294p. 1962. 31.00x (ISBN 0-565-00697-5, Pub. by Brit Mus Nat Hist England). Sabbot-Natural Hist Bks.
--The Social Wasps of the Americas Excluding the Vespinae. (Illus.). 1978. 95.00x (ISBN 0-565-00785-8, Pub. by Brit Mus Nat Hist). Sabbot-Natural Hist Bks.
--The Study of the Numbers of the Red Locust (Nomadacris Septemfasciata Serville) 1953. 35.00x (ISBN 0-85135-032-1, Pub. by Centre Overseas Research). State Mutual Bk.
Richards, O. W. & Davies, R. G. Imm's Outline of Entomology. 6th ed. 1978. 24.95x (ISBN 0-412-21660-4, Pub. by Chapman & Hall England); pap. 12.95x (ISBN 0-412-21670-1). Methuen Inc.
Richards, O. W. & Waloff, N. Studies on the Biology & Population Dynamics of British Grasshoppers. 1954. 35.00x (ISBN 0-85135-034-8, Pub. by Centre Overseas Research). State Mutual Bk.
Richards, P. J., jt. ed. see Leonor, M. D.
Richards, P. W. Life of the Jungle. 1970. 14.95 (ISBN 0-07-052265-0, P&RB); by subscription 12.95 (ISBN 0-07-046012-4). McGraw.
Richards, Pamela, et al. Crime As Play: Delinquency in a Middle Class Suburb. LC 79-12772. 280p. 1979. prof ref 22.50x (ISBN 0-88410-798-1). Ballinger Pub.
Richards, Paul A., jt. ed. see Simpson, David W.
Richards, Paul W. Tropical Rain Forest. LC 79-50507. (Illus.). 1952. 75.00 (ISBN 0-521-06079-6); pap. 27.95 (ISBN 0-521-29658-7). Cambridge U Pr.
Richards, Peter, ed. see New York City Planning Commission.
Richards, R. K. Electronic Digital Components & Circuits. 520p. 1967. 25.50 (ISBN 0-442-36912-3, Pub. by Van Nos Reinhold). Krieger.
Richards, R. Michael, jt. auth. see Lawson, David H.
Richards, R. W., jt. auth. see Pethrick, R. A.
Richards, Renee & Ames, John. Second Serve: The Renee Richards Story. LC 82-48510. (Illus.). 420p. 1983. 16.95 (ISBN 0-8128-2897-6). Stein & Day.
Richards, Roy. Early Experiences. LC 77-82994. (Science 5-13 Ser.). (Illus.). 1977. pap. text ed. 12.85 (ISBN 0-356-04005-4). Raintree Pubs.
--Holes, Gaps & Cavities: Stages 1 & 2. LC 77-82990. (Science 5-13 Ser.). (Illus.). 1977. pap. text ed. 12.85 (ISBN 0-356-04108-5). Raintree Pubs.
--Ourselves: Stages 1 & 2. LC 77-83006. (Science 5-13 Ser.). (Illus.). 1977. pap. text ed. 12.85 (ISBN 0-356-04349-5). Raintree Pubs.
--Time: Stages 1 & 2 & Background. LC 77-82997. (Science 5-13 Ser.). (Illus.). 1977. pap. text ed. 11.55 (ISBN 0-356-04008-9). Raintree Pubs.
Richards, Ruth M. Text & Concordance of Isaac Israeli's Tratado de las Fiebres. 1982. 5.00 (ISBN 0-942260-19-8). Hispanic Seminary.
Richards, Stanley, ed. Best Short Plays of the World Theater: 1968-1973. 1973. 7.95 o.p. (ISBN 0-517-50589-4). Crown.
Richards, T. H. Energy Methods in Stress Analysis with an Introduction to Finite Element Techniques. LC 79-29647. (Engineering Science Ser.). 410p. 1980. pap. 39.95x o.p. (ISBN 0-470-27068-3). Halsted Pr.
Richards, T. H. & Stanley., P., eds. Stability Problems in Engineering Structures & Components. (Illus.). 1979. 80.00x (ISBN 0-85334-836-7, Pub. by Applied Sci England). Elsevier.
Richards, T. H., jt. ed. see Gibbs, H. G.
Richards, Ted, jt. auth. see Shelton, Gilbert.
Richards, Thomas C. Cobol: An Introduction. (Data Processing Ser.). 350p. 1981. pap. text ed. 16.95 (ISBN 0-675-08041-X). Additional supplements may be obtained from publisher. Merrill.
Richards, Thomas J., jt. auth. see Kempf, Albert F.
Richards, Vernon. Impossiblities of Social Democracy. 142p. 1978. pap. 2.25 (ISBN 0-900384-16-6). Left Bank.
--Protest Without Illusions. 168p. 1981. pap. 4.25 (ISBN 0-900384-19-0). Left Bank.
Richards, Vernon, ed. see Malatesta, Errico.
Richards, Vernon, tr. see Leval, Gaston.
Richards, Viv & Foot, David. Viv Richards. 1979. 11.50 (ISBN 0-437-14470-4, Pub. by World's Work). David & Charles.
Richards, W. G. & Horsley, J. A. Ab Initio Molecular Orbital Calculations for Chemists. (Oxford Science Research Papers Ser). 1970. 22.50x (ISBN 0-19-855348-X). Oxford U Pr.
Richards, W. Graham & Cooper, David L. Ab Initio Molecular Orbital Calculations for Chemists. 2nd ed. (Illus.). 1982. pap. 17.95 (ISBN 0-19-855369-2). Oxford U Pr.
Richardson. Laboratory Operations for Rotating Electric Machinery & Transformer Technology. 256p. 1980. pap. text ed. 9.95 (ISBN 0-8359-3925-1). Reston.
Richardson & Peterson. Systematic Materials Analysis. 1974. Vol. 2. 54.00 (ISBN 0-12-587802-8); Vol. 3. 63.00 (ISBN 0-12-587803-6). Acad Pr.
Richardson, jt. auth. see Fitter.
Richardson, jt. ed. see Stangos, Nikos.
Richardson, jt. auth. see White.
Richardson, A., jt. auth. see Carter, G. W.
Richardson, Alan. Genesis One & Two. (Student Christian Movement Press-Torch Bible Ser.). (Orig.). 1953. pap. 7.95x (ISBN 0-19-520302-X). Oxford U Pr.
--The Gospel According to St. John. (Student Christian Movement Press-Torch Bible Ser.). (Orig.). 1959. pap. 7.95x (ISBN 0-19-520303-8). Oxford U Pr.
--An Introduction to the Theology of the New Testament. (Student Christian Movement Press Ser.). (Orig.). 1958. pap. 10.95x (ISBN 0-19-520336-4). Oxford U Pr.
Richardson, Alan, ed. Dictionary of Christian Theology. LC 69-19153. 1969. 13.95 (ISBN 0-664-20860-6). Westminster.
Richardson, Allen G. Polecat Bench. Jones, Jean, ed. LC 82-84447. (Illus.). 220p. 1983. 12.95 (ISBN 0-936204-40-0); pap. 7.95 (ISBN 0-936204-39-7). Jelm Mtn.
Richardson, Arleta. More Stories from Grandma's Attic. LC 78-73125. (Illus.). (gr. 1-4). 1979. pap. 2.50 (ISBN 0-89191-131-6). Cook.
Richardson, Ben & Fahey, William A. Great Black Americans. 2nd. rev. ed. LC 75-12841. (Illus.). 352p. (gr. 5 up). 1976. 14.38i (ISBN 0-690-00994-1, TYC-J). Har-Row.
Richardson, Bill & Richardson, Dana. Appaloosa Horse. pap. 5.00 (ISBN 0-87980-182-4). Wilshire.
Richardson, Bob. The Gunnpiexer Cookbook. LC 81-80617. (Illus.). 1981. pap. 9.95 (ISBN 0-686-95503-X). Comm Tech.
Richardson, Bonham C. Carribean Migrants: Environment & Human Survival on St. Kitts & Nevis. LC 82-7078. (Illus.). 224p. 1983. text ed. 19.95x (ISBN 0-87049-360-4); pap. text ed. 12.50x (ISBN 0-87049-361-2). U of Tenn Pr.
Richardson, Brian, ed. & intro. by see Machiavelli, Niccolo.
Richardson, C. J., jt. auth. see Himelfarb, A.
Richardson, C. James, jt. auth. see Himelfarb, Alexander.
Richardson, Curtis J., ed. Pocosin Wetlands: An Integrated Analysis of Coastal Plain Freshwater Bogs in North Carolina. LC 81-7158. 1982. 25.00 (ISBN 0-87933-414-2). Hutchinson Ross.
Richardson, D. G. & Meheriuk, M. Third National Controlled Atmosphere Research Committee. 1982. 39.95 (ISBN 0-917304-26-8). Timber.
Richardson, Dana, jt. auth. see Richardson, Bill.
Richardson, Dana R., jt. auth. see Haidinger, Timothy P.
Richardson, David, jt. auth. see Katona, Steve.
Richardson, Don. Il Figlio Della Pace. Arcangeli, Gianfranco, ed. 230p. (Ital.). 1981. pap. 2.00 (ISBN 0-8297-0940-1). Life Pubs Intl.
Richardson, Donald. Knocking Them Dead. (Illus.). 50p. 1982. pap. 2.95 (ISBN 0-686-82300-1). New Poets.
--Rotating Electric Machines & Transformers. 2nd ed. 1982. text ed. 23.95 (ISBN 0-8359-6750-6); instrs'. manual avail. (ISBN 0-8359-6751-4). Reston.
Richardson, Donald W. The Revelation of Jesus Christ. 1977. pap. 0.75 (ISBN 0-8042-3597-X). John Knox.
Richardson, Doug. Naval Armament. (Illus.). 160p. 1982. 19.95 (ISBN 0-86720-553-9). Sci Bks Intl.
Richardson, E. L., jt. ed. see Starika, W. A.
Richardson, Edgar P. & Hindle, Brooke. Charles Willson Peale & His World. 1983. 40.00 (ISBN 0-8109-1478-6). Abrams.
Richardson, Ellis & Freeman, Harold, Jr. Reading Progress Feedback System (RFFS) 86p. (Orig.). 1981. pap. 7.00 (ISBN 0-939632-32-2). ILM.
Richardson, Ernie, jt. auth. see Mulvoy, Mark.
Richardson, Frank C., jt. auth. see Woolfolk, Robert L.

Richardson, Frank H. Solo para Muchachos. 112p. 1967. pap. 1.95 (ISBN 0-311-46929-9). Casa Bautista.

Richardson, Frank M. Mars Without Venus: Study of Some Homosexual Generals. 188p. 1982. 14.95 (ISBN 0-85158-148-X, Pub. by Salem Hse Ltd.). Merrimack Bk Serv.

Richardson, G. & Fletcher, W. Illustrierte Geschichten: Free Composition in German. (Illus., Ger.). 1969. pap. text ed. 5.95x (ISBN 0-312-40880-3). St Martin.

--Petites Histoires: Free Composition for Junior Forms. (Illus., Fr.). (gr. 7-9). 1952. pap. 6.95 o.p. (ISBN 0-312-60375-4). St Martin.

Richardson, Gary L. & Birkin, Stanley J. Problem Solving Using PLIC: An Introduction for Business and the Social Sciences. LC 75-4724. 358p. pap. text ed. 21.95 (ISBN 0-686-84497-1). Krieger.

Richardson, Genevra, et al. Policing Pollution: A Study of Regulation & Enforcement. (Oxford Socio-Legal Studies). 250p. 1983. 34.95 (ISBN 0-19-827510-2); pap. 15.95 (ISBN 0-19-827512-9). Oxford U Pr.

Richardson, George. Iconology, 2 vols. Orgel, Stephen, ed. LC 78-68201. (Philosophy of Images Ser.: Vol. 20). (Illus.). 1980. Set. lib. bdg. 132.00 o.s.i. (ISBN 0-8240-3694-8). Garland Pub.

Richardson, H. D. & Baron, Mary. Developmental Counseling in Education. 1975. pap. 2.40 o.p. (ISBN 0-395-20034-2). HM.

Richardson, H. E., ed. Best Loved Short Stories of Jesse Stewart. 448p. 1982. 14.95 (ISBN 0-07-062305-8). McGraw.

Richardson, H. Edward. How to Think & Write. 1970. pap. 10.95x (ISBN 0-673-05289-3). Scott F.

Richardson, H. L. & Wood, Wallis W. Firearms & Freedom. Date not set. pap. cancelled o.p. (ISBN 0-89245-010-X). Seventy Six.

Richardson, H. W. The New Urban Economics, & Alternatives. (Research in Planning & Design Ser.). 266p. 1977. 23.50x (ISBN 0-85086-058-X, Pub. by Pion England). Methuen Inc.

Richardson, Harry W. Economic Aspects of the Energy Crisis. LC 75-8360. 256p. 1975. 22.95x (ISBN 0-669-03327-8). Lexington Bks.

--Regional Development Policy & Planning in Spain. (Illus.). 268p. 1975. 24.95x o.p. (ISBN 0-347-01091-1, 99440-5, Pub. by Saxon Hse). Lexington Bks.

Richardson, Herbert W., jt. ed. see Clark, Elizabeth.

Richardson, I. M. The Adventures of Eros & Psyche. LC 82-16057. (Illus.). 32p. (gr. 4-8). 1983. PLB 8.79 (ISBN 0-89375-861-2); pap. text ed. 2.50 (ISBN 0-89375-862-0). Troll Assocs.

--The Adventures of Hercules. LC 82-16557. (Illus.). 32p. (gr. 4-8). 1983. PLB 8.79 (ISBN 0-89375-865-5); pap. text ed. 2.50 (ISBN 0-89375-866-3). Troll Assocs.

--Demeter & Persephone: The Seasons of Time. LC 82-16023. (Illus.). 32p. (gr. 4-8). 1983. PLB 8.79 (ISBN 0-89375-863-9); pap. text ed. 2.50 (ISBN 0-89375-864-7). Troll Assocs.

--Prometheus & the Story of Fire. LC 82-15979. (Illus.). 32p. (gr. 4-8). 1983. PLB 8.79 (ISBN 0-89375-859-0); pap. text ed. 2.50 (ISBN 0-89375-860-4). Troll Assocs.

Richardson, I. M., ed. see Sewell, Anna.

Richardson, J., jt. auth. see Corlett, E. N.

Richardson, J. David. Understanding International Economics: Theory & Practice. (Illus.). 506p. 1980. text ed. 19.95 (ISBN 0-316-74429-8). Little.

Richardson, J. G. Precast Concrete Production. 1977. pap. 32.50 (ISBN 0-7210-0912-3). Scholium Intl.

Richardson, J. H. & Peterson, R. V., eds. Systematic Materials Analysis. (Materials Science Ser.: Vol. 1). 1974. 59.50 (ISBN 0-12-587801-X). Acad Pr.

--Systematic Materials Analysis, Vol. 4. (Materials Science & Technology Ser). 1978. 64.00 (ISBN 0-12-587804-4). Acad Pr.

Richardson, J. T. The Grammar of Justification: An Interpretation of Wittgenstein's Philosophy of Language. 39.00x (ISBN 0-686-97001-2, Pub. by Scottish Academic Pr Scotland). State Mutual Bk.

Richardson, J. T., ed. Practical Formwork & Mould Construction. 2nd ed. (Illus.). xv, 294p. 1976. 43.00 (ISBN 0-85334-629-1, Pub. by Applied Sci England). Elsevier.

Richardson, Jean, tr. see De Carli, Franco.

Richardson, Jeanne M., jt. auth. see Malinowsky, H. Robert.

Richardson, Joanna. Sarah Bernhardt & Her World. LC 76-29164. (Illus.). 1977. 15.95 o.p. (ISBN 0-399-11887-X). Putnam Pub Group.

Richardson, John. Manet. (Phaidon Color Library). (Illus.). 1983. 27.50 (ISBN 0-7148-2233-7, Pub. by Salem Hse Ltd); pap. 18.95 (ISBN 0-7148-2243-4). Merrimack Bk Serv.

Richardson, John A. Art: The Way It Is. 2nd ed. (Illus.). 368p. 1980. pap. text ed. 18.95 (ISBN 0-13-049148-9). P-H.

Richardson, John G. Formwork Construction & Practice. (Viewpoint Publication Ser.). (Illus.). 1978. pap. text ed. 50.00x (ISBN 0-7210-1058-X). Scholium Intl.

Richardson, John, Jr. Graduate Research in Government Information, 1928-1982. Date not set. write for info. (ISBN 0-89774-063-7). Oryx Pr.

Richardson, John, Jr. & Ginsberg, Ralph B., eds. The Human Dimension of Foreign Policy: An American Perspective. LC 78-62597. (Annals: No. 442). 1979. 15.00 (ISBN 0-87761-234-X); pap. 7.95 (ISBN 0-87761-235-8). Am Acad Pol Soc Sci.

Richardson, John T. The Grammar of Justification: An Interpretation of Wittgenstein's Philosophy of Language. LC 75-37303. 160p. 1976. 25.00 (ISBN 0-312-34230-6). St Martin.

--Mental Imagery & Human Memory. LC 79-26849. 180p. 1980. 25.00 (ISBN 0-312-52975-9). St Martin.

Richardson, Joseph A. & Matheny, Kenneth B. Concepts & Components of Effective Teaching. 94p. 1978. 5.95 (ISBN 0-686-38285-4, 16-1750). Natl League Nurse.

Richardson, Judith, jt. auth. see Richardson, Lloyd.

Richardson, Kay. A Heart Surrendered. (YA) 1978. 6.95 (ISBN 0-685-05588-4, Avalon). Bouregy.

Richardson, L. F., jt. auth. see Richardson, M.

Richardson, L., Jr., ed. Propertius: Elegies I-IV. LC 76-26153. (American Philological Association Ser.: Vol. 5). 1977. 13.95x o.p. (ISBN 0-8061-1371-5). U of Okla Pr.

Richardson, Larry L. & Richardson, Peter N. Library Research in German Studies. (Language, Literature, & Civilization). 1984. price not set (ISBN 0-86531-195-1). Westview.

Richardson, Laurel W. & Taylor, Verta. Feminist Frontiers: Rethinking Sex, Gender, & Society. LC 82-11396. 416p. 1983. pap. text ed. 11.95 (ISBN 0-201-06197-X). A-W.

Richardson, Leonard F., jt. auth. see Richardson, M.

Richardson, Linda. Bankers in the Selling Role: A Consultative Guide to Cross-Selling Financial Services. LC 80-28804. 168p. 1981. 24.95 (ISBN 0-471-09010-7, Pub. by Wiley-Interscience). Wiley.

Richardson, Lloyd & Richardson, Judith. The Mathematics of Drugs & Solutions with Clinical Applications. 2nd rev. ed. (Illus.). 1980. pap. text ed. 12.95 (ISBN 0-07-052311-8); instr's manual 8.95 (ISBN 0-07-052312-6). McGraw.

Richardson, Lloyd I., et al. A Mathematics Activity Curriculum for Early Childhood & Special Education. (Illus.). 1980. pap. text ed. 13.95x (ISBN 0-02-399710-9). Macmillan.

Richardson, M. Translocation in Plants. (Studies in Biology: No. 10). 68p. 1975. pap. text ed. 8.95 (ISBN 0-7131-2497-0). E Arnold.

Richardson, M. & Richardson, L. F. Fundamentals of Mathematics. 4th ed. 1973. 19.95x (ISBN 0-02-399690-0). Macmillan.

Richardson, M. & Richardson, Leonard F. College Algebra. 4th ed. (Illus.). 464p. 1973. text ed. 21.95 o.p. (ISBN 0-13-141762-2). P-H.

Richardson, M. O., ed. Polymer Engineering Composites. (Illus.). 1977. 90.25 (ISBN 0-85334-722-0, Pub. by Applied Sci England). Elsevier.

Richardson, Margaret. The Craft Architects. (Illus.). 160p. 1983. 25.00 (ISBN 0-8478-0483-6); pap. 15.00 (ISBN 0-686-84064-X). Rizzoli Intl.

Richardson, Margaret, jt. auth. see Lever, Jill.

Richardson, Nigel. Martin Luther King. (Profiles Ser.). (Illus.). 64p. (gr. 4-6). 1983. 7.95 (ISBN 0-241-10931-0, Pub. by Hamish Hamilton England). David & Charles.

Richardson, Peter. Chinese Mine Labour in the Transvaal. 287p. 1982. text ed. 31.50x (ISBN 0-333-27222-6, Pub. by Macmillan England). Humanities.

Richardson, Peter N., jt. auth. see Richardson, Larry L.

Richardson, R. C. The Debate on the English Revolution. LC 77-73803. 1977. 25.00 (ISBN 0-312-18890-0). St Martin.

Richardson, R. C. & James, T. B., eds. The Urban Experience: A Sourcebook. 224p. 1983. 25.00 (ISBN 0-7190-0900-6). Manchester.

Richardson, Ralph W. The Hudson River Basin, Vol. 2. 1979. 28.50 (ISBN 0-12-588402-8). Acad Pr.

--The Hudson River Basin: Environmental Problems & Instititional Response, Vol. 1. 1979. 29.50 (ISBN 0-12-588401-X). Acad Pr.

Richardson, Richard E. & Barton, Roger E. The Dental Assistant. 5th ed. (Illus.). 1978. text ed. 31.50 (ISBN 0-07-052301-0, HP). McGraw.

Richardson, Robert A., jt. auth. see Davis, Ann N.

Richardson, Robert O. How to Get Your Own Patent. LC 80-54340. (Illus.). 128p. 1981. 16.95 (ISBN 0-8069-5564-3); lib. bdg. 19.99 (ISBN 0-8069-5565-1); pap. 8.95 (ISBN 0-8069-8990-4). Sterling.

Richardson, Robin & Chapman, John. Images of Life: Problems of Religious Belief & Human Relations in Schools. LC 73-180621. (Report of Bloxham Project Research Unit). 1973. text ed. 15.00x o.p. (ISBN 0-8401-2012-5). Allenson-Breckinridge.

Richardson, Rosamond, jt. auth. see Doeser, Linda.

Richardson, Rupert N., et al. Texas: The Lone Star State. 4th ed. (Illus.). 464p. 1981. text ed. 22.95 (ISBN 0-13-912444-6). P-H.

Richardson, Samuel. Pamela; or, Virtue Rewarded, 1801, 4 vols. Shugrue, Michael F., ed. (The Flowering of the Novel, 1740-1775 Ser: Vol. 1). 1974. lib. bdg. 50.00 ea. o.s.i. (ISBN 0-8240-1100-7). Garland Pub.

Richardson, Susan M., jt. auth. see Merrill, Virginia.

Richardson, T. D. Your Book of Skating. 6.50 o.p. (ISBN 0-571-05602-4). Transatlantic.

Richardson, Terry. Modern Industrial Plastics. LC 72-92621. 1974. 21.95 (ISBN 0-672-97657-9). Bobbs.

Richardson, Tony, jt. ed. see Stangos, Niko.

Richardson, W. Christian Doctrine: The Faith...Once Delivered. LC 82-25598. (Christian Activities Ser.). 448p. 1983. pap. 9.95 (ISBN 0-87239-610-X). Standard Pub.

Richardson, W. J. Cost Improvement, Work Sampling & Short Interval Scheduling. 1976. 21.95 o.p. (ISBN 0-87909-139-8). Reston.

Richardson, William. Zolotoe Runo & Russian Modernism. 200p. Date not set. 27.50 (ISBN 0-88233-795-5). Ardis Pubs.

Richardson, William B. & Moore, Gary. Working in Horticulture. (Career Preparations for Agricultural-Agribusiness Ser.). (Illus.). 1980. text ed. 18.96 (ISBN 0-07-052285-5); tchr's. manual & key 4.00 (ISBN 0-07-052287-1); activity guide 7.96 (ISBN 0-07-052286-3). McGraw.

Richardson Woman's Club. The Texas Experience: Friendship & Food Texas Style, A Cookbook from the Richardson Woman's Club. Dennis, Ivanette, ed. (Illus.). 373p. 1982. lib. bdg. 12.95 (ISBN 0-9609416-0-6). Hart Graphics.

Richart, F. E., Jr., et al. Vibrations of Soils & Foundations. (Civil Engineering Ser). 1970. ref. ed. 33.95 (ISBN 0-13-941716-8). P-H.

Richart, Ralph M., jt. auth. see Ferenczy, Alex.

Richarz, Sherrill. Understanding Children Through Obeservation. 200p. 1980. pap. text ed. 10.50 (ISBN 0-8299-0337-2). West Pub.

Richason, Benjamin F. Introduction to Remote Sensing of the Environment. (National Council for Geography Education Pacesetter Ser.). (Illus.). 1978. text ed. 32.95 (ISBN 0-8403-2834-6). Kendall-Hunt.

Richason, Benjamin F., Jr., ed. Laboratory Manual for Introduction to Remote Sensing of the Environment. (Pacesetter Ser). (Illus.). 1978. pap. text ed. 10.95 (ISBN 0-8403-1898-7). Kendall Hunt.

Riche. Daily Life in the World of Charlemagne. 368p. 1982. 70.00x (ISBN 0-85323-124-9, Pub. by Liverpool Univ England); 39.00x (ISBN 0-85323-174-5). State Mutual Bk.

Richens, A. & Woodford, F. P. Anticonvulsant Drugs & Enzyme Induction. (Institute for Research into Mental & Multiple Handicap Study Group: Vol. 9). 1976. 45.00 (ISBN 90-219-5002-2, Excerpta Medica). Elsevier.

Richert, et al. Retailing Principles & Practices. 6th ed. (Illus.). 592p. (gr. 11-12). 1974. text ed. 15.48 (ISBN 0-07-052325-8, G); tchr's manual & key 6.50 (ISBN 0-07-052329-0); 2 sets of problems & projects 5.72 ea.; tests 3.88 (ISBN 0-07-052328-2). McGraw.

Richert, John P. German Lay Judges: Recruitment & Representativeness. 1982. 25.00 (ISBN 0-8130-0701-1). U Presses Fla.

Riches, John, ed. see Theissen, Gerd.

Riches, Phyllis M., ed. Analytical Bibliography of Universal Collected Biography. 1980. Repr. 99.00x (ISBN 0-8103-0168-7). Gale.

Riches, Robert J. Breeding Snakes in Captivity. LC 76-6930. (Pet Reference Ser.). (Illus.). 96p. 1976. pap. 5.95 (ISBN 0-915096-01-3). Palmetto Pub.

Richey, C. B., et al. Agricultural Engineers' Handbook. 1961. 55.00 (ISBN 0-07-052617-6, P&RB). McGraw.

Richey, David, ed. Trout Fishermen's Digest. (Digest Bks). 288p. (Orig.). 1976. pap. 7.95 o.s.i. (ISBN 0-695-80641-6). Follett.

Richey, Hursty. Near Fatal Attraction. LC 76-26783. 1977. 12.95 o.s.i. (ISBN 0-87949-076-4). Ashley Bks.

Richey, Jane. Fundamentals of Organic Chemistry: Solutions Manual. 136p. 1983. pap. 7.95 (ISBN 0-686-38831-3). P H.

Richey, Robert. Planning for Teaching: An Introduction to Education. 6th ed. (Illus.). 1979. text ed. 23.50 (ISBN 0-07-052360-6, C); instructor's manual 15.00 (ISBN 0-07-052361-4). McGraw.

Richey, Robert W. Planning for Teaching. 5th ed. (Foundation in Education Ser.). (Illus.). 608p. 1972. text ed. 15.95 o.p. (ISBN 0-07-052342-8, C); instructor's resources bk. 3.95 o.p. (ISBN 0-07-052343-6). McGraw.

--Preparing for a Career in Education: Challenges, Changes, & Issues. (Illus.). 288p. 1974. pap. text ed. 16.95 (ISBN 0-07-052346-0, C). McGraw.

Richie, Claude G. Kemal Ataturk, Father of the Turkish Republic. Rahmas, Sigurd C., ed. (Outstanding Personalities Ser.: No. 92). 32p. (gr. 9-12). 1982. 2.95 (ISBN 0-87157-592-2); pap. text ed. 1.95 (ISBN 0-87157-092-0). SamHar Pr.

Richler, Mordecai. Images of Spain. (Illus.). 1977. 27.50 o.p. (ISBN 0-393-08792-1). Norton.

--The Street. 1977. pap. 1.95 o.p. (ISBN 0-14-004418-3). Penguin.

Rich-McCoy, Lois. Late Bloomer: Profiles of Women Who Found Their True Callings. LC 79-1679. (Illus.). 224p. 1980. 13.41i (ISBN 0-06-013593-X, HarpT). Har-Row.

--Millionairess: Self-Made Women in America. LC 78-2142. 1978. 11.49i (ISBN 0-06-012852-6, HarpT). Har-Row.

Richman, Barry M. & Copen, Melvyn R. International Management & Economic Development. LC 77-24758. 692p. 1978. Repr. of 1972 ed. lib. bdg. 28.50 (ISBN 0-88275-597-8). Krieger.

Richman, Irving B. Spanish Conquerors. 1919. text ed. 8.50x (ISBN 0-686-83782-7). Elliots Bks.

Richman, Larry L., ed. Prominent Men & Women of Provo, Utah 1982. 500p. 1982. 39.95 (ISBN 0-941846-00-8). Richman Pub.

Richman, Leon H., jt. auth. see Mayer, Morris F.

Richman, Michael. Daniel Chester French: An American Sculptor. LC 76-40897. (Illus.). 1976. pap. 5.95 o.p. (ISBN 0-87099-153-1). Metro Mus Art.

--Daniel Chester French: An American Sculptor. (Landmark Reprint Ser.). (Illus.). 208p. 1983. pap. 15.95 (ISBN 0-89133-048-8). Preservation Pr.

Richman, Michael, ed. Outdoor Sculpture in the Berkshires. LC 80-82444. (Illus.). 80p. 1980. pap. 6.95 (ISBN 0-89133-091-7). Preservation Pr.

Richman, N., et al. Pre-School to School: A Behavioural Study. (Behavioural Development: Monographs). 1982. 25.00 (ISBN 0-12-587940-7). Acad Pr.

Richman, Paul. Characteristics & Operations. 1967. 24.50 o.p. (ISBN 0-07-052340-1, P&RB). McGraw.

--MOS Field-Effect Transistors & Integrated Circuits. LC 73-9892. 259p. 1973. pap. text ed. 34.95 (ISBN 0-471-72030-5, Pub. by Wiley-Interscience). Wiley.

Richman, Phyllis C. Best Restaurants & Others: Washington, D. C. rev. ed. LC 82-18897. (Best Restaurants Ser.). (Illus.). 272p. (Orig.). 1982. pap. 4.95 (ISBN 0-89286-200-9). One Hund One Prods.

--Best Restaurants Washington D. C. & Environs. LC 80-11923. 256p. (Orig.). 1980. pap. 3.95 o.p. (ISBN 0-89286-166-5). One Hund One Prods.

Richman, Saul. Guy: The Life & Times of Guy Lombardo. (Illus.). 192p. 1980. 10.00 o.p. (ISBN 0-517-54000-2). Crown.

Richman, Sidney. Bernard Malamud. (United States Authors Ser.: No. 109). 1966. lib. bdg. 11.95 (ISBN 0-8057-0472-8, Twayne). G K Hall.

Richmann, D. L., jt. auth. see Loucks, R. G.

Richmind, Robert W., jt. ed. see Ripley, John W.

Richmond, A. E. Calculus for Electronics. 2nd ed. 1971. text ed. 24.95 (ISBN 0-07-052351-7, G); answer key 1.50 (ISBN 0-07-052352-5). McGraw.

--Calculus for Electronics. 3rd ed. 512p. 1982. text ed. 24.95x (ISBN 0-07-052353-3, C); instr's manual & key 1.50 (ISBN 0-07-052354-1). McGraw.

Richmond, Bert O. & Kicklighter, Richard H. Childrens Adaptive Behavior Report. 16p. (Orig.). 1982. pap. 0.75 (ISBN 0-89334-030-8). Humanics Ltd.

--Children's Adaptive Behavior Scale: Administrator's Manual. rev. ed. (Orig.). 1983. pap. 14.95 (ISBN 0-89334-040-5). Humanics Ltd.

Richmond, C. R., jt. ed. see Cowser, K. E.

Richmond, C. R., et al, eds. Mammalian Cells: Probes & Problems, Proceedings. LC 75-600009. (ERDA Symposium Ser.). 324p. 1975. pap. 17.00 (CONF-731007); microfiche 4.50 (ISBN 0-87079-267-9, CONF-731007). DOE.

Richmond, Colin. John Hopton: A Fifteenth-Century Suffolk Gentleman. (Illus.). 280p. 1981. 42.50 (ISBN 0-521-23434-4). Cambridge U Pr.

Richmond, Doug. Trail Bike: How to Select Ride & Maintain. LC 72-91687. (Illus.). 160p. 1972. pap. cancelled (ISBN 0-912656-08-5). H P Bks.

Richmond, Edmun B. New Directions in Language Teaching in Sub-Saharan Africa: A Seven-Country Study of Current Policies & Programs for Teaching Official & National Languages & Adult Functional Literacy. LC 82-23831. (Illus.). 74p. (Orig.). 1983. pap. text ed. 6.50 (ISBN 0-8191-2980-1, Co-pub. by Ctr Applied Ling). U Pr of Amer.

Richmond, Garland & Kirby, George. Auslese. (Illus., Ger.). 1968. pap. text ed. 22.50 (ISBN 0-07-052627-3, C). McGraw.

Richmond, Hugh M. The Christian Revolutionary: John Milton. 1975. 26.50x (ISBN 0-520-02443-5). U of Cal Pr.

Richmond, Ian, jt. auth. see Collingwood, R. G.

Richmond, John. Resources of Classroom Language. 224p. 1982. pap. text ed. 14.95 (ISBN 0-7131-6234-1). E Arnold.

Richmond, Legh see Trimmer, Sarah.

Richmond, Leonard. Landscape Painting in Oils. (The Grosset Art Instruction Ser.: No. 37). (Illus.). 48p. Date not set. pap. 2.95 (ISBN 0-448-00546-8, G&D). Putnam Pub Group.

--Oil Painting. (Grosset Art Instruction Ser.: Vol. 33). 1966. pap. 1.95 (ISBN 0-448-00542-5, G&D). Putnam Pub Group.

--Sketching Out of Doors. (Grosset Art Instruction Ser.: Vol. 26). (Illus.). 48p. pap. 2.95 (ISBN 0-448-00535-2, G&D). Putnam Pub Group.

Richmond, Leonard & Littlejohns, J. Fundamentals of Pastel Painting. (Illus.). pap. 9.95 o.p. (ISBN 0-8230-2051-7). Watson-Guptill.

--Fundamentals of Watercolor Painting. (Illus.). 1978. pap. 10.95 (ISBN 0-8230-2076-2). Watson-Guptill.

Richmond, M. Barrie. Total Tennis: The Mind Body Method. 1980. 11.95 o.p. (ISBN 0-02-603180-9). Macmillan.

Richmond, M. H., jt. auth. see Norris, J. R.

Richmond, M. H., jt. ed. see Clarke, P. H.

Richmond, M. S. Prison Profiles. 1965. 9.00 o.p. (ISBN 0-379-00238-8). Oceana.

Richmond, Mary E. Friendly Visiting among the Poor, a Handbook for Charity Workers. LC 69-16244. (Criminology, Law Enforcement, & Social Problems Ser.: No. 92). (With intro. added). 1969. Repr. of 1899 ed. 10.00x (ISBN 0-87585-092-8). Patterson Smith.
--Social Diagnosis. 512p. 1917. 9.95x (ISBN 0-87154-703-1). Russell Sage.
Richmond, Mary L., ed. see Filley, Dorothy M.
Richmond, Mossie J. Issues in Year-Round Education. (Illus.). 1977. 8.95 o.p. (ISBN 0-8158-0345-1). Chris Mass.
Richmond, Olney H. The Mystic Test Book. (Orig.). 1983. pap. 9.95 (ISBN 0-87877-064-X). Newcastle Pub.
--The Mystic Test Book. 1983. lib. bdg. 17.95x (ISBN 0-89370-664-7). Borgo Pr.
Richmond, P. G. Introduction to Piaget. LC 73-116854. 1971. pap. 5.95x o.p. (ISBN 0-465-09514-3, TB5015). Basic.
Richmond, Phyllis A. Introduction to PRECIS for North American Usage. LC 80-25977. 321p. 1981. lib. bdg. 27.50 (ISBN 0-87287-240-8). Libs Unl.
Richmond, R. A. Viscometric Testing of Barley-Meal Water Mixture for Pipeline Design, 1977. 1981. 40.00x (ISBN 0-686-97161-2, Pub. by W Spring England). State Mutual Bk.
Richmond, Robert. Kansas a Land of Contrast. rev. ed. LC 79-53861. 1979. pap. text ed. 13.95x (ISBN 0-88273-026-6). Forum Pr IL.
Richmond, Robert W., ed. see Bird, Roy D. & Wallace, Douglass W.
Richmond, Roe. Guns at Goliad. (Lashtrow Ser.: No. 4). 1980. pap. 1.75 (ISBN 0-8439-0796-7). Nordon Pubns.
Richmond, Samuel B. Operations Research for Management Decisions. LC 68-20552. (Illus.). 600p. 1968. 32.95 (ISBN 0-471-06620-6); manual o.p. (ISBN 0-471-07476-4). Wiley.
--Statistical Analysis. 2nd ed. (Illus.). 1964. 32.50 (ISBN 0-471-06621-4); manual o.p. (ISBN 0-471-07477-2). Wiley.
Richmond, Stanley. Clarinet & Saxophone Experience. 1980. 30.00x o.p. (ISBN 0-686-75607-X, Pub. by Darton-Longman-Todd England). State Mutual Bk.
Richmond, Virginia P., jt. auth. see McCroskey, James C.
Richmond, W. Kenneth. The School Curriculum. 1971. pap. 8.95x (ISBN 0-416-65760-5). Methuen Inc.
Richmond-Abbot, Marie. Masculine & Feminine: Sex Roles Over the Life Cycle. LC 82-11400. 384p. Date not set. pap. text ed. 11.95 (ISBN 0-201-06194-5). A-W.
Richmond-Watson, Angela, tr. see Mery, Fernand.
Richow, Harold E. Encyclopedia of R. F. D. Cancels. (Illus.). 289p. 1983. 26.00 (ISBN 0-916170-21-7). J-B Pubs.
Richstad, Jim & McMillan, Michael, eds. Mass Communication & Journalism in the Pacific Islands: A Bibliography. LC 77-20795. 1978. text ed. 15.00x (ISBN 0-8248-0497-X, Eastwest Ctr). UH Pr.
Richstad, Jim, jt. ed. see Harms, L. S.
Richstad, Jim, et al. The Pacific Islands Press: A Directory. LC 73-83935. 96p. (Orig.). 1973. pap. text ed. 3.95x (ISBN 0-8248-0291-8, Eastwest Ctr). UH Pr.
Richter, A. J., Jr. Vacation Timesharing. 1982. 20.00 (ISBN 0-914434-23-3). Atcom.
Richter, Anton H., tr. see Eisenberg, C. G.
Richter, Conrad. Early Americana & Other Stories. 1978. lib. bdg. 10.95 (ISBN 0-8398-2468-8, Gregg). G K Hall.
--Light in the Forest. (YA) 1953. 10.95 (ISBN 0-394-43314-9). Knopf.
--The Town. 1981. lib. bdg. 17.95x (ISBN 0-89967-048-2). Harmony Raine.
--The Trees. (YA) 1940. 12.95 (ISBN 0-394-44951-7). Knopf.
Richter, D. Women Scientists: The Road to Liberation. 1982. 50.00x (ISBN 0-686-42942-7, Pub. by Macmillan England). State Mutual Bk.
Richter, Daniel K. Rediscovered Links in the Covenant Chain: Previously Unpublished Transcripts of New York Indian Treaty Minutes, 1677-1691. 40p. 1982. pap. 4.50 (ISBN 0-912296-56-9, Dist. by U Pr of VA). Am Antiquarian.
Richter, Daniel K., jt. auth. see Vaughan, Alden T.
Richter, Donald C. Riotous Victorians. LC 80-25055. (Illus.). xii, 185p. 1981. text ed. 14.95x (ISBN 0-8214-0571-3, 82-83632); pap. 5.95x (ISBN 0-8214-0618-3, 82-83640). Ohio U Pr.
Richter, Elizabeth. The Teenage Hospital Experience: You Can Handle it. (gr. 11 up). 1982. 11.95 (ISBN 0-698-20554-5, Coward). Putnam Pub Group.
Richter, G. W. & Epstein, M. A., eds. International Review of Experimental Pathology. Incl. Vol. 1. 1962. 68.00 (ISBN 0-12-364901-3); Vol. 2. 1963. 68.00 (ISBN 0-12-364902-1); Vol. 3. 1965. 68.00 (ISBN 0-12-364903-X); Vol. 4. 1965. 68.00 (ISBN 0-12-364904-8); Vol. 5. 1967. 68.00 (ISBN 0-12-364905-6); Vol. 6. 1968. 68.00 (ISBN 0-12-364906-4); Vol. 7. 1969. 68.00 (ISBN 0-12-364907-2); Vol. 8. 1969. 68.00 (ISBN 0-12-364908-0); Vol. 9. 1971. 68.00 (ISBN 0-12-364909-9); Vol. 10. 1972. 68.00 (ISBN 0-12-364910-2); Vol. 11. 1972. 68.00 (ISBN 0-12-364911-0); Vol. 12. 1973. 68.00 (ISBN 0-12-364912-9); Vol. 17. 1977. 57.00 (ISBN 0-12-364917-X); Vol. 18. 1978. 60.00 (ISBN 0-12-364918-8); Vol. 19. 1979. 34.00 (ISBN 0-12-364919-6). Acad Pr.
--International Review of Experimental Pathology. LC 62-21145. (Serial Publication). 1982. Vol. 23. 34.50 (ISBN 0-12-364923-4); Vol. 24. write for info. (ISBN 0-12-364924-2). Acad Pr.
--International Review of Experimental Pathology, Vol. 20. (Serial Publication). 1979. 39.50 (ISBN 0-12-364920-X). Acad Pr.
--International Review of Experimental Pathology, Vol. 21. 1980. 39.50 (ISBN 0-12-364921-8). Acad Pr.
--International Review of Experimental Pathology, Vol. 22. 1980. 34.00 (ISBN 0-12-364922-6). Acad Pr.
Richter, Gisela. A Handbook of Greek Art: A Survey of the Visual Arts of Ancient Greece. (Illus.). 432p. 1980. pap. 13.50 (ISBN 0-525-47651-2, 01311-390). Dutton.
Richter, H. V., jt. auth. see Jones, G. W.
Richter, Herbert P. Practical Electrical Wiring, Residential, Farm & Industrial. 8th ed. 1972. 12.50 o.p. (ISBN 0-07-052385-1, P&RB). McGraw.
Richter, Herbert P. & Schwan, W. Creighton. Practical Electrical Wiring. 12th ed. (Illus.). 672p. 1982. 27.95 (ISBN 0-07-052389-4). McGraw.
--Practical Electrical Wiring: Residential, Farm, & Industrial. 11th ed. (Illus.). 1978. 19.75 o.p. (ISBN 0-07-052388-6, P&RB). McGraw.
Richter, Herbert W. Electrical & Electronic Drafting. LC 76-20506. (Electronic Technology Ser). 1977. text ed. 26.95x (ISBN 0-471-72035-6); solutions manual 3.00 (ISBN 0-471-02541-0). Wiley.
Richter, Horst E. All Mighty. Van Heurck, Jan, tr. LC 80-80649. 256p. 1983. 19.95 (ISBN 0-89793-028-2). Hunter Hse.
Richter, J. Yurao Janka. (Illus.). 180p. 1982. 15.95 (ISBN 0-930410-05-X). Bradt Ent.
Richter, Jean P., ed. see Leonardo Da Vinci.
Richter, Judy. Horse & Rider: From Basics to Show Competition. LC 82-11670. (Illus.). 160p. (Orig.). 1982. pap. 6.95 (ISBN 0-668-05569-3, 5569). Arco.
Richter, Konrad. Simple Stephen & the Magic Fish. LC 82-15489. (Illus.). 24p. (gr. 1-6). 1983. PLB 10.95 (ISBN 0-686-84506-4). Faber & Faber.
Richter, L. & Le Beux, P., eds. Implementing Functions: Microprocessing & Firmware. 1982. 74.50 (ISBN 0-444-86282-X). Elsevier.
Richter, L., ed. see EUROMICRO Symposium on Microprocessing & Microprogramming, 8th, 1982.
Richter, M., ed. Political Theory of Montesquieu. LC 76-4753. 400p. 1977. 39.50 (ISBN 0-521-21156-5); pap. 11.95 (ISBN 0-521-29061-9). Cambridge U Pr.
Richter, Manfred. Internationale Bibliographic der Farbenlehre und Ihrer Grenzgebiete (International Bibliography on Color Science & Related Fields) annotated ed. Incl. Vol. 1. 1940-49. 257p. 1952. 25.00x o.p. (ISBN 3-7881-4015-1); Vol. 2. 1950-54. 846p. 1963. 47.50x o.p. (ISBN 3-7881-4015-1). LC 62-28957. Intl Pubns Serv.
Richter, Maurice N., Jr. Science As a Cultural Process. 160p. 1972. pap. text ed. 6.95 (ISBN 0-87073-073-8). Schenkman.
--Society: A Macroscopic View. 1980. lib. bdg. 15.95 (ISBN 0-8161-8415-1, Univ Bks). G K Hall.
--Technology & Social Complexity. 160p. 1982. 34.50x (ISBN 0-87395-644-3); pap. 10.95x (ISBN 0-87395-645-1). State U NY Pr.
Richter, Maxwell. Clinical Immunology-A Physician's Guide. 2nd. ed. (Illus.). 344p. 1981. lib. bdg. 14.95 (ISBN 0-683-07255-2). Williams & Wilkins.
Richter, Mischa. Quack? LC 77-11828. (Illus.). 1978. 5.95 o.p. (ISBN 0-06-025020-8, HarpJ); PLB 7.89 o.p. (ISBN 0-06-025021-6). Har-Row.
Richter, N., jt. auth. see Hoegner, W.
Richter, P., jt. auth. see La Fauci, H. M.
Richter, Peyton & Ricardo, Ilona. Voltaire. (World Authors Ser.). 1980. cloth 11.95 (ISBN 0-8057-6425-9, Twayne). G K Hall.
Richter, Robert. Windfall Journal. 83p. 1980. pap. 4.50 (ISBN 0-936204-10-9). Jelm Mtn.
Richter, S., jt. auth. see Forcese, D.
Richter-Heinrich, E. & Miller, N. E. Biofeedback: Basic Problems in Clinical Applications. Date not set. 34.00 (ISBN 0-444-86345-1). Elsevier.
Richterich, R. Clinical Chemistry: Theory, Practice & Interpretation. Colombo, J. P., ed. LC 80-40286. 766p. 1981. 94.25 (ISBN 0-471-27809-2, Pub. by Wiley-Interscience). Wiley.
Richtmyer, Floyd K., et al. Introduction to Modern Physics. 6th ed. LC 69-13213. (Illus.). 1969. text ed. 42.50 (ISBN 0-07-052506-4, C). McGraw.
Richtmyer, Robert D. & Morton, K. W. Difference Methods for Initial-Value Problems. 2nd ed. LC 67-13959. (Pure & Applied Mathematics Ser.). (Illus.). 1967. 46.50 (ISBN 0-470-72040-9, Pub. by Wiley-Interscience). Wiley.
Ricigliano, Daniel A. Melody & Harmony in Contemporary Songwriting. LC 78-51645. 1978. pap. text ed. 12.50 (ISBN 0-935058-01-X); wrbk. 8.50 (ISBN 0-935058-02-8). Donato Music.
--Popular & Jazz Harmony. LC 66-26789. 1967. pap. 9.95 (ISBN 0-935058-03-6). Donato Music.
Rick, John W. Prehistoric Hunters of the High Andes. LC 79-28090. (Studies in Archaeology Ser.). 1980. 31.50 (ISBN 0-12-587760-9). Acad Pr.
Rickard, Henry C., ed. Behavioral Intervention in Human Problems. LC 76-112398. 434p. 1972. 33.00 (ISBN 0-08-016327-0); pap. 14.00 (ISBN 0-08-017737-9). Pergamon.
Rickard, J. A. & Martin, Clyde I. Call of the Southwest. (Illus.). (gr. 5). 1955. text ed. 6.84 (ISBN 0-87443-037-2). Benson.
--From Old Lands to New. (Illus.). (gr. 6). 1955. text ed. 6.84 (ISBN 0-87443-015-1). Benson.
--Under Texas Skies. (Illus.). (gr. 4). 1964. text ed. 6.84 (ISBN 0-87443-035-6); tchr's ed. 3.12 (ISBN 0-87443-036-4). Benson.
Rickard, J. M., jt. auth. see Michell, John.
Rickard, Jack, jt. auth. see Silverstone, Lou.
Rickard, Peter. Langue Francaise au Seizieme Siecle. (Illus., Fr.). 1968. 75.00 (ISBN 0-521-06921-1). Cambridge U Pr.
Rickard, Peter, ed. & tr. see Pessoa, Fernando.
Rickard, T. A. Across the San Juan Mountains. Benham, Jack L., ed. (Illus.). 178p. (Orig.). 1980. pap. 7.95 (ISBN 0-941026-03-5). Bear Creek Pub.
Rickards, T., jt. auth. see Carson, J. W.
Rickart, Charles E. General Theory of Banach Algebras. LC 74-143. 406p. 1974. Repr. of 1960 ed. 23.00 (ISBN 0-88275-091-7). Krieger.
Rickels, Milton. George Washington Harris. (United States Authors Ser.). 13.95 (ISBN 0-8057-0344-6, Twayne). G K Hall.
Rickels, Milton & Rickels, Patricia. Seba Smith. (United States Authors Ser.). 1977. lib. bdg. 13.95 (ISBN 0-8057-7185-9, Twayne). G K Hall.
Rickels, Patricia, jt. auth. see Rickels, Milton.
Ricken, H. Vademecum Fuer Pilzfreunde: Taschenbuch Zur Bequemen Bestimmung Aller in Mittel-Europa Vorkommenden Ansehnlichen Pilzkoerper. 1969. Repr. of 1920 ed. pap. 16.00 (ISBN 3-7682-0603-3). Lubrecht & Cramer.
Rickenbacker, Edward V. Rickenbacker. (Airlines History Project Ser.). (Illus.). Date not set. price not set (ISBN 0-404-19332-3). AMS Pr.
Rickenbacker, William F., ed. The Twelve Year Sentence: Radical Views of Compulsory Schooling. LC 73-23107. 236p. 1974. 16.00x (ISBN 0-87548-152-3). Open Court.
Ricker, N. H. Transient Waves in Visco-Elastic Media. (Developments in Solid-Earth Geophysics: Vol. 10). 1977. 72.50 (ISBN 0-444-41526-2). Elsevier.
Rickerson, Wayne. Christian Family Activities for Families with Preschoolers. LC 82-5583. (Illus.). 96p. (Orig.). 1982. pap. 4.95 (ISBN 0-87239-568-5, 2963). Standard Pub.
Rickers-Ovsiankina, M. Rorschach Psychology. 2nd ed. LC 74-2666. 672p. 1977. Repr. of 1960 ed. 32.50 (ISBN 0-88275-168-9). Krieger.
Rickert, Edith, jt. auth. see Manly, John M.
Rickert, Jessica A., ed. Exploring Careers in Dentistry. (Careers in Depth Ser.). 140p. 1983. lib. bdg. 7.97 (ISBN 0-8239-0604-3). Rosen Pr.
Ricketson, William F., jt. auth. see Wilson, Jerome D.
Rickett, Frances. Stalked. 240p. 1983. pap. 2.95 (ISBN 0-380-81463-3). Avon.
Rickett, H. W. Wild Flowers of the United States, Index. LC 66-17920. 160p. 1975. 39.95 (ISBN 0-07-052647-8, P&RB). McGraw.
Rickett, H. W., ed. Wild Flowers of America. 1963. 15.00 o.p. (ISBN 0-517-02682-1). Crown.
Rickett, Harold W. The New Field Book of American Wild Flowers. LC 63-14464. (Putnam's Nature Field Bks.). (Illus.). 1963. 7.95 o.p. (ISBN 0-399-10283-3). Putnam Pub Group.
--The New Field Book of American Wild Flowers. LC 63-14464. (Putnam's Nature Field Bks.). (Illus.). (YA) 1978. pap. 4.50 o.p. (ISBN 0-399-12157-9). Putnam Pub Group.
--Wildflowers of the United States, 6 vols. Incl. Vol. 1. Northeastern States. 1966. 69.50 (ISBN 0-07-052614-1); Vol. 2. Southeastern States. 1967. 99.50 (ISBN 0-07-052630-3); Vol. 3. Texas. 1969. 79.50 (ISBN 0-07-052633-8); Vol. 4. Southwestern States. 1970. 99.95 (ISBN 0-07-052636-2); Vol. 5. Northeastern States. 96.95 (ISBN 0-07-052640-0); Vol. 6. The Central Mountains & Plains. 96.95 (ISBN 0-07-052643-5). P&RB). McGraw.
Rickett, Richard, tr. see Harrer, Heinrich.
Ricketts, D. E., jt. auth. see Gray, J.
Ricketts, David, jt. auth. see Sax, Richard.
Ricketts, Edward F. & Calvin, Jack. Between Pacific Tides. 4th rev. ed. LC 68-17140. (Illus.). 1968. 15.95 (ISBN 0-8047-0641-7); hardbound 11.95x (ISBN 0-8047-0642-5). Stanford U Pr.
Ricketts, Edward F., jt. auth. see Steinbeck, John.
Ricketts, Howard. Objects of Virtue. (Illus.). 20.00 o.p. (ISBN 0-87556-266-3). Saifer.
Ricketts, L. W. Fundamentals of Nuclear Hardening of Electronic Equipment. LC 72-1479. (Illus.). 576p. 1972. 64.95 (ISBN 0-471-72100-X, Pub. by Wiley-Interscience). Wiley.
Ricketts, Sarah, jt. auth. see Bubna, Donald.
Ricketts, Viva L., jt. auth. see Pisano, Beverly.
Rickey, Don. Ten-Dollar Horse, Forty-Dollar Saddle. 1976. 10.95 (ISBN 0-686-95763-6). Jefferson Natl.
Rickey, Don, Jr. Forty Miles a Day on Beans & Hay: The Enlisted Soldier Fighting the Indian Wars. (Illus.). 1977. pap. 9.95 (ISBN 0-8061-1113-5). U of Okla Pr.
Rickford, H. Dieter. Showcase Quarterly. 144p. (Orig.). 1983. 8.95 (ISBN 0-942098-03-X). Class Media Prod.
Rickford, H. Dieter, ed. Showcase Oregon Restaurants. 168p. (Orig.). 1982. pap. 4.95 (ISBN 0-942098-02-1). Class Media Prod.
Rickham, P. P., ed. Pediatric Surgery in Tropical Countries. LC 81-24085. (Progress in Pediatric Surgery Ser.: Vol. 15). (Illus.). 311p. 1982. text ed. 32.00 (ISBN 0-8067-1515-4). Urban & S.
Ricklefs, Robert E. Ecology. 2nd ed. LC 78-60315. (Illus.). 966p. 1979. text ed. 29.95x (ISBN 0-913462-07-1). Chiron Pr.
--The Economy of Nature. LC 82-83643. (Illus.). 576p. 1983. 21.95x (ISBN 0-913462-09-8). Chiron Pr.
Ricklin. Meniscus Lesions. 1983. write for info. (ISBN 0-86577-094-8). Thieme-Stratton.
Rickman, H. P. Wilhelm Dilthey: Pioneer of the Human Sciences. LC 78-68828. 1980. 26.50x (ISBN 0-520-03879-7). U of Cal Pr.
Rickman, H. P., ed. W. Dilthey Selected Writings. LC 75-23530. 280p. 1976. 39.50 (ISBN 0-521-20966-8); pap. 12.95x (ISBN 0-521-29588-2). Cambridge U Pr.
Rickman, John. Eight Flat-Racing Stables. (Illus.). 1979. 14.95 (ISBN 0-434-63710-6, Pub. by Heinemann). David & Charles.
Rickmers, A. D. & Todd, H. N. Statistics: An Introduction. 1967. 32.50 (ISBN 0-07-052616-8, C); ans. 25.00 (ISBN 0-07-052622-2). McGraw.
Ricks, Christopher, ed. Tennyson: Poems of 1842. 384p. 1981. 29.00x (ISBN 0-7121-0151-9, Pub. by Macdonald & Evans). State Mutual Bk.
Ricks, Christopher, ed. see Milton, John.
Ricks, David. Big Business Blunders. LC 82-71900. 200p. 1982. 11.95 (ISBN 0-87094-290-5). Dow Jones-Irwin.
Ricks, David A. International Dimensions of Corporate Finance. LC 77-22693. (Foundations of Finance Ser.). (Illus.). 1978. pap. text ed. 12.95 (ISBN 0-13-471706-6). P-H.
Ricks, David A., ed. International Dimensions of Accounting. (International Dimensions of Business Ser.). 200p. 1982. text ed. cancelled. Kent Pub Co.
Ricks, David A., ed. see Kujawa, Duane.
Ricks, David A., ed. see Schellhammer, Hans.
Ricks, Davis A., ed. see Phatak, Arvind.
Ricks, Eldin. Book of Mormon Study Guide. 1976. pap. 4.95 (ISBN 0-87747-038-3). Deseret Bk.
Ricks, George. Pistol Packin' Parson. 1979. pap. 5.95 o.p. (ISBN 0-89036-118-5). Hawkes Pub Inc.
Ricks, Truett A., jt. auth. see Gaines, Larry K.
Rickwood, D., jt. auth. see Birnie, G. D.
Rickwood, D. & Hames, B., eds. Gel Electrophoresis of Nucleic Acids: A Practical Approach. 200p. 1981. 18.00 (ISBN 0-904147-24-X). IRL Pr.
Rickword, Edgell. Behind the Eyes: Collected Poems & Translations. (Poetry Ser.). 1979. 8.95 o.p. (ISBN 0-85635-075-3, Pub. by Carcanet New Pr England). Humanities.
--Essays & Opinions Nineteen Hundred Twenty One to Nineteen Hundred Thirty One. Young, Alan, ed. 326p. 1974. text ed. 14.75x (ISBN 0-85635-071-0, Pub. by Carcanet New Pr England); pap. text ed. 10.95x (ISBN 0-85635-293-4). Humanities.
--Essays & Opinions Nineteen Twenty-One to Nineteen Thirty-One. Young, Alan, ed. 326p. (Orig.). 1980. pap. 10.95 o.p. (ISBN 0-85635-293-4, Pub. by Carcanet New Pr England). Humanities.
Rico, Don, ed. see Hurst, Walter E.
Rico, Gabriele L. Writing the Natural Way: Using Right-Brain Techniques to Release Your Expressive Powers. (Illus.). 272p. 1983. 15.95 (ISBN 0-87477-186-2); pap. 9.95 (ISBN 0-87477-236-2). J P Tarcher.
Rico, Ul De see De Rico, Ul.
Ricoeur, Paul. Interpretation Theory: Discourse & the Surplus of Meaning. LC 76-29604. 1976. pap. 8.00x (ISBN 0-912646-59-4). Tex Christian.
--Political & Social Essays. Stewart, David & Bien, Joseph, eds. LC 74-82500. ix, 293p. 1974. 17.00x (ISBN 0-8214-0169-6, 82-81685). Ohio U Pr.
Ricouard, M. J. Formwork for Concrete Construction. 1982. 60.00x (ISBN 0-686-42939-7, Pub. by Macmillan England). State Mutual Bk.
Riddel, Joseph N. C. Day Lewis. (English Authors Ser.: No. 124). 1971. lib. bdg. 10.95 o.p. (ISBN 0-8057-1336-0, Twayne). G K Hall.
Riddell see Bleiler, E. F.
Riddell, C., jt. auth. see Coulson, Margaret A.
Riddell, Carol, jt. auth. see Coulson, Margaret.
Riddell, Tom, et al. Economics: A Tool for Understanding Society. 2nd ed. (Economics Ser.). (Illus.). 512p. 1982. pap. text ed. 15.95 (ISBN 0-201-06354-9); write for info. instr's manual (ISBN 0-201-06355-7). A-W.
Riddering, David, tr. see Lin, Yi.

Riddick, John A. see Weissberger, A.

Riddick, Walter E. & Stewart, Eva M. Workbook for Program Evaluation in the Human Services. 196p. (Orig.). 1981. lib. bdg. 20.75 (ISBN 0-8191-1782-X); pap. text ed. 10.00 (ISBN 0-8191-1783-8). U Pr of Amer.

Riddle, Douglas F. Analytic Geometry with Vectors. 3rd ed. 1978. 22.95x (ISBN 0-534-01030-X). Wadsworth Pub.

Riddle, G. W. Accounting Level III. 272p. 1982. pap. text ed. 17.50 (ISBN 0-7121-0175-6). Intl Ideas.

Riddle, Maxwell. The Complete Book of Puppy Training & Care. rev. ed. 1971. 6.95 o.p. (ISBN 0-698-10079-4, Coward). Putnam Pub Group.

--This Is the Chihuahua. (Illus.). 1959. 12.95 (ISBN 0-87666-267-X, PS611). TFH Pubns.

Riddle, Ronald. Flying Dragons, Flowing Streams: Music in the Life of San Fancisco's Chinese. LC 82-12005. (Contributions in Intercultural & Comparative Studies: No. 7). xiv, 249p. 1983. lib. bdg. 29.95 (ISBN 0-313-23682-8, RIF/). Greenwood.

Ride, W. D. Guide to the Native Mammals of Australia. (Illus.). 1970. 42.00x (ISBN 0-19-550252-3). Oxford U Pr.

Ridenour, Crea. Ocupate en Ensenar. 1981. pap. 1.35 (ISBN 0-311-11031-2). Casa Bautista.

Ridenour, Dian M. & Johnston, Jane. A Guide to Post-Secondary Educational Opportunities for the Learning Disabled. 183p. 1981. pap. 12.00 (ISBN 0-9608010-0-6). Time Out.

Ridenour, Fritz. How to Be a Christian Without Being Religious. pap. 2.95 (ISBN 0-8423-1450-4). Tyndale.

Ridenour, George, ed. see Browning, Robert.

Ridenour, Marcella V., et al. Motor Development: Issues & Applications. Ridenour, Marcella V., ed. LC 77-92489. (Illus.). 240p. 1978. text ed. 13.95x (ISBN 0-916622-06-1). Princeton Bk Co.

Rideout, Edward H. & Isacson, Orjan, eds. Energy Systems Handbook, 1982. rev., 3rd ed. LC 81-52535. 320p. 1982. pap. 9.95 (ISBN 0-941114-00-7). Tech Handbk.

Rideout, Walter B., ed. see Anderson, Sherwood.

Rider, Alex. A la Ferme - At the Farm. LC 62-12923. (gr. 3-5). PLB 2.50 o.p. (ISBN 0-385-06520-5). Doubleday.

Rider, C. C. & Taylor, C. B. Isoenzymes. 1981. pap. 6.50x (ISBN 0-412-15640-7, Pub. by Chapman & Hall England). Methuen Inc.

Rider, David, ed. Frankenstein. pap. 1.99 o.p. (ISBN 0-448-12638-9, G&D). Putnam Pub Group.

Rider, Don K. Energy: Hydrocarbon Fuels & Chemical Resources. LC 81-196. 493p. 1981. 39.95 (ISBN 0-471-05915-3, Pub. by Wiley-Interscience). Wiley.

Rider, J. A. see Zeman, W.

Rider, John R. Your Future in Broadcasting. LC 70-146047. (Career Guidance Ser). 125p. 1974. pap. 4.50 (ISBN 0-668-03427-0). Arco.

Rider, R., jt. auth. see Rose, T.

Rider, R. L., jt. auth. see Abbott, Waldo M.

Rider, Robin E., compiled by. A Bibliography of Early Modern Algebra, Fifteen Hundred to Eighteen Hundred. LC 81-51030. (Berkeley Papers in History of Science: No. 7). 150p. (Orig.). 1982. pap. 5.00x (ISBN 0-918102-08-1). U Cal Hist Sci Tech.

Ridge, John R. Life & Adventures of Joaquin Murieta, the Celebrated California Bandit. (Western Frontier Library: No. 4). (Illus.). 1977. 10.95 (ISBN 0-8061-0312-4); pap. 6.95 (ISBN 0-8061-1429-0). U of Okla Pr.

Ridge, Martin. The New Bilingualism: An American Dilemma. 272p. 1982. 20.00 (ISBN 0-88474-104-4). Transaction Bks.

Ridge, Martin & Billington, Ray A., eds. America's Frontier Story: A Documentary History of Westward Expansion. LC 79-28118. 668p. 1980. pap. text ed. 16.00 (ISBN 0-89874-090-8). Krieger.

Ridge, Martin, et al. Liberty & Union, 2 vols. 2nd ed. (Illus.). 525p. (gr. 7-12). 1973. Vol. 1. pap. 22.64 (ISBN 0-395-14395-0); Vol. 2. pap. 22.64 (ISBN 0-395-14379-9); tchr's ed., vols. 1 & 2 23.12 ea.; student's wkguide, vols. 1 & 2 5.88 ea.; tchr's ed. student's wkguide, vols. 1 & 2 6.44 ea.; progress tests, vols. 1 & 2 52.24 ea.; sample tests, vol. 1 o.p. 0.56 (ISBN 0-685-38964-2); sample tests, vol. 2 o.p. 1.00 (ISBN 0-685-38965-0). HM.

Ridgeway, Donald G. The Healthy Peasant Gourmet. LC 82-90747. (Illus.). 220p. 1983. 12.95 (ISBN 0-910361-01-0); pap. 7.95 (ISBN 0-910361-00-2). Earth Basics.

Ridgeway, James & Conner, Bettina. New Energy: Understanding the Crisis & a Guide to an Alternative Energy System. LC 74-16669. (Institute for Policy Studies Ser.). 228p. 1975. 7.93 (ISBN 0-8070-0504-5). Beacon Pr.

Ridgeway, James, ed. Powering Civilization: The Complete Energy Reader. LC 82-47878. 416p. 1983. 22.50 (ISBN 0-394-51471-8); pap. 12.95 (ISBN 0-394-71129-7). Pantheon.

Ridgeway, Julie, ed. see Bailey, Adrian.

Ridgeway, Steve, ed. see Bailey, Adrian.

Ridgley, Marlene. Folk Tales: Geting to Know Southeast Asia. Kim, Carolynn & Schanzenbach, Gordon, eds. LC 78-64448. (Papers in International Studies: Southeast Asia: No. 1.). 1978. pap. text ed. 8.00 (ISBN 0-89680-074-1, Ohio U Ctr Intl). Ohio U Pr.

Ridgway, Whitman H. Community Leadership in Maryland, 1790-1840. 414p. 1979. 22.50 (ISBN 0-686-36835-5). Md Hist.

Riding, R. J. School Learning: Mechanisms & Processes. (Psychology & Education Ser.). 1977. text ed. 11.25x o.p. (ISBN 0-7291-0066-9); pap. text ed. 5.25x o.p. (ISBN 0-7291-0061-8). Humanities.

Ridler, E., jt. auth. see Holloway, A.

Ridler, P. Pocket Guide to...FORTRAN. 64p. spiral bdg. 6.95 (ISBN 0-201-07746-9). A-W.

Ridley, A. & Williams, D. L. Simple Experiments in Textile Science. 1974. pap. text ed. 5.00x o.p. (ISBN 0-435-42235-9). Heinemann Ed.

Ridley, C. M. The Vulva. LC 75-19852. (Major Problems in Dermatology Ser.: No. 5). (Illus.). 275p. 1975. text ed. 10.00 (ISBN 0-7216-7582-4). Saunders.

Ridley, F. & Blondel, J. Public Administration in France. new ed. 1969. 27.50x (ISBN 0-7100-2037-6). Routledge & Kegan.

Ridley, F. F. Revolutionary Syndicalism in France. LC 73-123663. 1971. 42.50 (ISBN 0-521-07907-1). Cambridge U Pr.

Ridley, F. F., ed. Government & Administration in Western Europe. LC 79-13518. 1979. 26.00x (ISBN 0-312-34113-X). St Martin.

Ridley, Gustave. From Boredom to Bliss. Campbell, Jean, ed. (Illus.). 24p. (Orig.). 1983. pap. 6.95 (ISBN 0-9610544-0-9). Harmonious Pr.

Ridley, Jasper. Statesman & Saint: Wosley & More, a Study in Contrast. 384p. 1983. 20.75 (ISBN 0-670-48905-0). Viking Pr.

Ridley, John H. Gynecologic Surgery: Errors, Safeguards & Salvage. 2nd. ed. (Illus.). 397p. 1981. lib. bdg. 41.00 (ISBN 0-683-07277-3). Williams & Wilkins.

--Gynecologic Surgery: Errors, Safeguards, & Salvage. 430p. 1974. 27.00 o.p. (ISBN 0-683-07276-5). Williams & Wilkins.

Ridley, M. R., ed. see Shakespeare, William.

Ridley, Michael. Oriental Antiques. LC 77-26876. (Arco Color Ser.). (Illus.). 1978. 8.95 o.p. (ISBN 0-668-04474-8); pap. 5.95 o.p. (ISBN 0-668-04485-3). Arco.

Ridley, Nancy. Nancy Ridley's Love Affair with History. 1982. pap. 15.95 o.p. (ISBN 0-85362-191-8). Routledge & Kegan.

Ridlon, G. T. The Gookin & Googin Family. LC 70-94961. (Saco Valley Settlements Ser). 1970. pap. 1.50 (ISBN 0-8048-0771-X). C E Tuttle.

--The Thompson Family. LC 79-142775. (Saco Valley Settlements Ser). 1970. pap. 2.00 (ISBN 0-8048-0845-7). C E Tuttle.

Ridlon, Marci. A Frog Sandwich. LC 73-81994. (Beginning to Read Ser.). (Illus.). 32p. (gr. 1-3). 1973. 2.50 o.s.i. (ISBN 0-695-80417-0). Follett.

--Kittens & More Kittens. (Beginning-to-Read Ser.). (Illus.). (gr. 2-4). 1967. pap. 1.50 o.s.i. (ISBN 0-695-34868-X). Follett.

Ridout, J. Water Weed Problems: Potential Utilisation & Control. 1980. 35.00x (ISBN 0-85135-112-3, Pub. by Centre Overseas Research). State Mutual Bk.

Ridout, S. King Saul, Man After the Flesh. 5.75 (ISBN 0-88172-118-2). Believers Bkshelf.

Ridpath, Iran, jt. auth. see Ardley, Neil.

Ridsdale, R. E. Electric Circuits. 2nd ed. 736p. 1983. 24.95x (ISBN 0-07-052948-5, G). McGraw.

--Electric Circuits for Engineering Technology. 1975. 23.95 (ISBN 0-07-052937-X, G); instructor's manual 2.50 (ISBN 0-07-052938-8). McGraw.

Rie, Ellen D., jt. ed. see Rie, Herbert E.

Rie, Herbert E. & Rie, Ellen D., eds. Handbook of Minimal Brain Dysfunctions: A Critical View. LC 78-25656. (Personality Processes Ser.). 1980. 54.95 (ISBN 0-471-02959-9, Pub. by Wiley-Interscience). Wiley.

Riebel, John P. How to Write Reports, Papers, Theses Articles. 128p. 1972. lib. bdg. 8.00 o.p. (ISBN 0-668-02392-9); pap. 6.00 o.p. (ISBN 0-668-02391-0). Arco.

--How to Write Successful Business Letters. LC 71-112737. 1971. lib. bdg. 6.95 o.p. (ISBN 0-668-02483-6); pap. 5.00 o.p. (ISBN 0-668-02290-6). Arco.

Rieber, R. W. & Salzinger, Kurt, eds. The Roots of American Psychology: Historical Influences & Implications for the Future, Vol. 291. (Annals of the New York Academy of Sciences). 394p. 1977. 22.00x (ISBN 0-89072-037-1). NY Acad Sci.

Rieber, Robert W., ed. Dialogues on the Psychology of Language & Thought: Conversations with Noam Chomsky, Charles Osgood, Jean Piaget, Ulric Neisser & Marcel Kinsbourne. (Cognition & Language Ser.). 174p. 1983. 19.50x (ISBN 0-306-41185-7, Plenum Pr). Plenum Pub.

Rieber, Robert W. & Jay, John, eds. Body & Mind: Past, Present & Future. LC 79-6777. 1980. 22.50 (ISBN 0-12-588260-2). Acad Pr.

Rieber, Robert W., jt. ed. see Aaronson, Doris.

Rieber, W., ed. Language Development & Aphasia in Children: New Essays & a Translation of "Kindersprache und Aphasie". LC 79-26057. (Perspectives in Neurolinguistics & Psycholinguistics Ser.). 1980. 18.50 (ISBN 0-12-588280-7). Acad Pr.

Riechel, Klaus-Walter. Economic Effects of Exchange-Rate Changes. LC 78-58926. 176p. 1978. 19.95x (ISBN 0-669-02376-0). Lexington Bks.

Riecken, Henry W., ed. see Social Science Research Council Conference on Social Experiments.

Riecken, Susan. A Baker's Dozen: A Sampler of Early American Cookie Cut-Outs with Recipes. (Illus.). 1982. pap. 3.95 (ISBN 0-942820-01-0). Steam Pr MA.

Riecker, R. E., ed. Rio Grande Rift: Tectonics & Magmatism. (Special Publication Ser.). 1979. 25.00 (ISBN 0-87590-214-6, SP0023). Am Geophysical.

Riedel, Marc & Vales, Pedro A., eds. Treating the Offender: Problems & Issues. LC 76-12870. 192p. 1977. 26.95 o.p. (ISBN 0-275-56350-2). Praeger.

Riedel, W. R. & Saito, T., eds. Marine Plankton & Sediments: Kiel Symposium. (Micropaleontology Special Publications Ser.: No. 3). 235p. 1980. 20.00 (ISBN 0-686-84254-5). Am Mus Natl Hist.

Riederer, P., jt. auth. see Birkmayer, W.

Riedesel, C. Alan. Teaching Elementary School Mathematics. 3rd ed. (Illus.). 1980. text ed. 25.95 (ISBN 0-13-892549-6). P-H.

Riedesel, C. Alan & Callahan, Leroy G. Elementary School Mathematics for Teachers. 1977. pap. text ed. 14.95x (ISBN 0-06-045412-1, HarpC). Har-Row.

Riedesel, Marvin L., jt. ed. see Hoff, C. Clayton.

Riedl, Frederick. History of Hungarian Literature. Ginever, C. A., tr. LC 68-26602. 1968. Repr. of 1906 ed. 34.00x (ISBN 0-8103-3221-3). Gale.

Riedl, John C., tr. see Giles Of Rome.

Riedl, John O. University in Process. (Aquinas Lecture Ser.). 1965. 7.95 (ISBN 0-87462-130-5). Marquette.

Riedl, R. Order in Living Organisms: A Systems Analysis of Evolution. LC 77-28245. 1979. 64.95 (ISBN 0-471-99635-1, Pub. by Wiley-Interscience). Wiley.

Riedler, W., ed. Scientific Ballooning: Proceedings of a Symposium of the 21st Plenary Meeting of the Committee on Space Research, Innsbruck, Austria, May 29-June 10 1978. LC 78-41182. (Illus.). 226p. 1979. 63.00 (ISBN 0-08-023420-8). Pergamon.

Riedman, Sarah. Allergies. (First Books Ser.). (Illus.). (gr. 4-6). 1978. PLB 8.90 s&l (ISBN 0-531-01352-9). Watts.

Riedman, Sarah R. Biological Clocks. LC 81-43873. (Illus.). 128p. (gr. 5 up). 1982. 10.10i (ISBN 0-690-04182-9, TYC-J); PLB 10.89g (ISBN 0-690-04183-7). Har-Row.

--Diabetes. LC 80-14473. (gr. 4 up). 1980. PLB 8.90 (ISBN 0-531-04107-7). Watts.

--Gardening Without Soil. LC 78-13088. (First Bks.). (Illus.). (gr. 4-6). 1979. PLB 8.90 s&l (ISBN 0-531-02256-0). Watts.

--Naming Living Things: The Grouping of Plants & Animals. LC 63-8619. (Illus.). (gr. 4-6). 1963. 3.79 o.p. (ISBN 0-528-80069-8). Rand.

--Sharks. (Easy-Read Fact Bks.). (Illus.). (gr. 2-4). 1977. PLB 8.60 (ISBN 0-531-01314-6). Watts.

--Spiders. (Easy-Read Fact Bks.). (Illus.). (gr. 2-4). 1979. PLB 8.60 s&l (ISBN 0-531-02853-4). Watts.

Riedmann, Agnes, jt. auth. see Lamanna, Mary A.

Riefenstahl, Leni. Vanishing Africa. Talbot, Kathrine, tr. from Ger. 1982. 30.00x (ISBN 0-517-54914-X, Harmony Bks). Crown.

Rieff, Philip. Fellow Teachers. 256p. 1975. pap. 3.25 o.s.i. (ISBN 0-440-54730-X, Delta). Dell.

Riefler, Winfield W. Money Rates & Money Markets in the U. S. (Illus.). Repr. of 1930 ed. lib. bdg. 19.50x o.p. (ISBN 0-678-01242-3). Kelley.

Riegel, E. C. Flight from Inflation: The Monetary Alternative. MacCallum, Spencer H. & Morton, George, eds. LC 76-25381. (Illus.). 1978. 13.95 (ISBN 0-9600300-9-3); pap. 5.95 (ISBN 0-686-67492-8). Heather Foun.

--The New Approach to Freedom. new, rev. ed. MacCallum, Spencer H., ed. LC 76-24987. (Illus.). 1977. 14.95 (ISBN 0-9600300-7-7). Heather Foun.

Riegel, Garland T. The American Species of Dacnusinae Hymenoptera-Braconidae. (Novitates Arthropodae Ser.). (Illus.). 200p. (Orig.). 1982. pap. 12.00x (ISBN 0-916170-19-5). J-B Pubs.

Riegel, K. F. see Lewis, M. & Rosenblum, L. A.

Riegel, Klaus F. Foundations of Dialectical Psychology. LC 79-6943. 1979. 18.50 (ISBN 0-12-588080-4). Acad Pr.

--Psychology, Mon Amour: A Countertext. LC 77-89422. (Illus.). 1978. pap. text ed. 11.50 o.p. (ISBN 0-395-25748-4). HM.

Riegel, O. U. Crown of Glory: Life of J. J. Strang, Moses of the Mormons. 1935. 49.50x (ISBN 0-685-69857-2). Elliots Bks.

Riegel, Oscar W. Mobilizing For Chaos: Story of the New Propaganda. 1934. text ed. 14.50x (ISBN 0-686-83627-8). Elliots Bks.

Riegel, R. & Miller, J. Insurance Principles & Practices: Property & Liability. 6th ed. 1976. text ed. 24.95 (ISBN 0-13-468868-6). P-H.

Rieger, Samuel, ed. The Genesis & Classification of Cold Soils: Monographs. 206p. Date not set. price not set (ISBN 0-12-588120-7). Acad Pr.

Riehl, C. Luise. Family Nursing. (Illus.). 384p. 1974. text ed. 19.96 (ISBN 0-87002-154-0). Bennett IL.

Riehl, Heinz & Rodriquez, Rita M. Foreign Exchange Markets. (Illus.). 1977. 34.95 (ISBN 0-07-052670-2, P&RB). McGraw.

Riehl, Herbert. Introduction to the Atmosphere. 3rd ed. (Illus.). 1978. text ed. 29.95 (ISBN 0-07-052656-7, C). McGraw.

Rieke, H. H. & Chilingarian, G. V. Compaction of Argillaceous Sediments. LC 74-190682. (Developments in Sedimentology Ser.: Vol. 16). 350p. 1974. 68.00 (ISBN 0-444-41054-6). Elsevier.

Riekes, Linda & Ackerly, Salley M. Lawmaking. 2nd ed. (Law in Action Ser.). (Illus.). (gr. 5-9). 1980. pap. 4.95 o.s.i. (ISBN 0-8299-1023-9); tchrs.' ed. 4.95 o.s.i. (ISBN 0-8299-1024-7). West Pub.

Riemann, Hans & Bryan, Frank L., eds. Food-Borne Infections & Intoxication. 2nd ed. LC 79-14935. (Food Science & Technology Ser.). 1979. 74.00 (ISBN 0-12-588360-9). Acad Pr.

Riemenschneider, Dieter, ed. The History & Historiography of Commonwealth Literature. 260p. 1983. pap. 24.00 (ISBN 3-87808-941-4). Benjamins North Am.

Riemer, A. P. Antic Fables: Patterns of Evasion in Shakespeare's Comedies. LC 80-13330. 1980. 22.50 (ISBN 0-312-04369-4). St Martin.

Riemer, Eleanor S. & Fout, John C., eds. European Women: A Documentary History, Seventeen Eighty-Nine to Nineteen Forty-Five. LC 79-26373. (Illus.). 1980. text ed. 17.50x (ISBN 0-8052-3737-2); pap. 7.95 (ISBN 0-8052-0644-2). Schocken.

Riemer, Jack, ed. Jewish Reflections on Death. LC 74-18242. 192p. 1976. 7.95x o.p. (ISBN 0-8052-3560-4); pap. 5.95 (ISBN 0-8052-0516-0). Schocken.

Riemer, Jeffrey W. & Brooks, Nancy A. Framing the Artist: A Social Portrait of Mid-American Artists. LC 82-13514. 98p. 1982. 18.25 (ISBN 0-8191-2675-6); pap. text ed. 7.00 (ISBN 0-8191-2676-4). U Pr of Amer.

Riemersma, R. A. & Oliver, M. F., eds. Catecholamines in the Non-Ischaemic & Ischaemic Myocardium: Proceedings of the Sixth Argenteuil Symposiym, Waterloo, Belgium, 1981. 260p. 1982. 89.00 (ISBN 0-444-80439-0, Biomedical Pr). Elsevier.

Riencourt, Amaury de. Sex & Power in History. 480p. 1975. pap. 3.95 o.s.i. (ISBN 0-440-55948-0, Delta). Dell.

Riendeau, Albert J. Advisory Committees for Occupational Education: A Guide to Organization & Operation. (Illus.). 1976. pap. text ed. 8.95 (ISBN 0-07-052680-X, G). McGraw.

Rieppel, Oliver. The Phylogeny of Anguinomorph Lizards. 88p. 1980. pap. text ed. 41.80 (ISBN 3-7643-1224-6). Birkhauser.

Ries. Marketing Warfare. 1983. write for info. (ISBN 0-07-052730-X). McGraw.

Ries, Al & Trout, Jack. Positioning: The Battle for Your Mind. 224p. 1980. 14.95 (ISBN 0-07-065263-5, P&RB). McGraw.

Ries, Al, jt. auth. see Trout, Jack.

Riesbeck, Christopher K., jt. auth. see Schank, Roger C.

Rieselbach, Leroy, ed. Legislative Reform. new ed. 1977. pap. 6.00 (ISBN 0-918592-21-6). Policy Studies.

Rieselbach, Leroy N. Legislative Reform: The Policy Impact. LC 77-223. (Policy Studies Organization Ser.). (Illus.). 272p. 1978. 19.95x o.p. (ISBN 0-669-01436-2, Dist. by Transaction Bks). Lexington Bks.

--Roots of Isolationism: Congressional Voting & Presidential Leadership in Foreign Policy. (Orig.). 1966. 10.25 (ISBN 0-672-51169-X); pap. 4.35 o.p. (ISBN 0-672-60770-0). Bobbs.

Rieselbach, Richard E. & Garnick, Marc B., eds. Cancer & the Kidney. LC 81-8277. (Illus.). 1982. text ed. 96.00 (ISBN 0-8121-0804-3). Lea & Febiger.

Riesen, Austin H. Developmental Neuropsychology of Sensory Deprivation. 1975. 36.50 (ISBN 0-12-588550-4). Acad Pr.

Riesen, Austin H. & Kinder, E. F. Postural Development of Infant Chimpanzees. 1952. 49.50x (ISBN 0-685-69858-0). Elliots Bks.

Riesen, Austin H., jt. auth. see Newton, Grant.

Riess, Fred, jt. auth. see Lucas, Ted.

Riess, R. Dean, jt. auth. see Johnson, Lee W.

Riess, Steven A. Touching Base: Professional Baseball & American Culture in the Progressive Era. LC 79-6570. (Contributions in American Studies: No. 48). (Illus.). xv, 268p. 1980. lib. bdg. 27.50x (ISBN 0-313-20671-6, RTB/). Greenwood.

Riesser, Paul C. & Riesser, Teri K. The Holistic Healers. 168p. (Orig.). 1983. pap. 5.95 (ISBN 0-87784-814-9). Inter-Varsity.

Riesser, Teri K., jt. auth. see Riesser, Paul C.

Riessman, Frank. Blueprint for the Disadvantaged. 48p. 0.75 o.p. (ISBN 0-686-74910-3). ADL.

--The Inner City Child. LC 76-8414. 160p. 1976. 11.49i (ISBN 0-06-013567-0, HarpT). Har-Row.

Riessman, Frank, jt. ed. see Gartner, Alan.

Rieter, Russel J., ed. The Pineal Gland: Extra-Reproductive Effects. 248p. 1982. 74.00 (ISBN 0-8493-5717-9). CRC Pr.

Riethmuller, Gert, et al, eds. Natural & Induced Cell-Mediated Cytotoxicity: Effector & Regulatory Mechanisms. LC 79-14162. (Perspectives in Immunology Ser.). 1979. 22.50 (ISBN 0-12-584650-9). Acad Pr.

Rietschel, Georg. Die Aufgabe der Orgel Im Gottesdienst Bis in das 18. (Bibliotheca Organologica: Vol. 53). iv, 72p. 1979. Repr. of 1893 ed. 36.50 o.s.i. (ISBN 90-6027-329-X, Pub. by Frits Knuf Netherlands); wrappers 24.00 o.s.i. (ISBN 90-6027-328-1). Pendragon NY.

Rietsma, W. D. Atherosclerosis. (Jonxis Lectures Ser.: Vol. 2). 1979. 34.50 (ISBN 0-444-90075-6). Elsevier.

Rietveld, Gordon & Rietveld, Jane. Greece: Aegean Island Guide. (Illus.). 247p. 1982. 18.95 (ISBN 0-13-365015-4); pap. 8.95 (ISBN 0-13-365007-3). P-H.

Rietveld, Jane, jt. auth. see Rietveld, Gordon.

Rietveld, P. Multiple Objective Decision Methods & Regional Planning. (Studies in Regional Science & Urban Economics: Vol. 7). 1980. 47.00 (ISBN 0-444-86001-0). Elsevier.

Rietz, Henry L. Mathematical Statistics. (Carus Monograph: No. 3). 181p. 1927. 16.50 o.s.i. (ISBN 0-88385-003-6). Math Assn.

Rieupeyrant, Jean L. The American West. LC 80-54636. (Picture Histories Ser.). PLB 12.68 (ISBN 0-382-06586-7). Silver.

Riewald, J. G. & Bakker, J. The Critical Reception of American Literature in the Netherlands 1824-1900: A Documentary Conspectus from Contemporary Periodicals. (Costerus Ser.: Vol. XXXIII). 349p. 1982. pap. text ed. 32.25x (ISBN 90-6203-544-2, Pub. by Rudopi Holland). Humanities.

Rifbjerg, Klaus. Anna, I, Anna. Taylor, Alexander, tr. from Danish. 250p. (Orig.). 1982. pap. 9.95 (ISBN 0-915306-30-1). Curbstone.

Rifenbark, Richard K. & Johnson, D. How to Beat the Salary Trap: Eight Steps to Financial Independence. 1978. 11.95 (ISBN 0-07-052810-1, GB). McGraw.

Riffaterre, Hermine, jt. ed. see Caws, Mary A.

Riffaterre, Michael. Languages of Knowledge & Inquiry. 192p. 1982. 25.00x (ISBN 0-231-05518-8); pap. 12.50 (ISBN 0-231-05519-6). Columbia U Pr.

Rifkin, Bernard. American Labor Sourcebook. 1980. 59.50 (ISBN 0-07-052830-6, P&RB). McGraw.

Rifkin, Erik, jt. auth. see Sheridan, David.

Rifkin, Harold, jt. auth. see Ellenberg, Max.

Rifkin, Jeremy. Algeny. 288p. 1983. 14.75 (ISBN 0-670-10885-5). Viking Pr.

Rifkin, Jeremy & Howard, Ted. The Emerging Order: God in the Age of Scarcity. LC 79-10612. 1979. 10.00 (ISBN 0-399-12319-9). Putnam Pub Group.

--The Emerging Order: God in the Age of Scarcity. (Epiphany Bks.). 1983. pap. 2.95 (ISBN 0-345-30464-0). Ballantine.

Rifkin, Morris W., jt. auth. see Zoubek, Charles E.

Rifkin, Shepard. The Snow Rattlers. LC 76-23311. 1977. 7.95 o.p. (ISBN 0-399-11880-2). Putnam Pub Group.

Rifkind, Carole. Field Guide to American Architecture. (Illus.). 1980. 19.95 (ISBN 0-453-00375-3, H375). NAL.

--Main Street: The Face of Urban America. LC 76-5527. (Illus.). 1979. pap. 8.95i o.p. (ISBN 0-06-090663-4, CN 663, CN). Har-Row.

Riga, Peter J. Church & Revolution. 1967. 5.95 o.p. (ISBN 0-685-07619-9, 80640). Glencoe.

--Human Rights as Human Realities. LC 81-69244. (New Studies on Law & Society). 170p. (Orig.). 1982. text ed. 24.00x (ISBN 0-86733-016-3). Assoc Faculty Pr.

Rigamonti, A., ed. see International School of Physics "Enrico Fermi" Course LIX, Varenna on Lake Como, July 9-21 1973.

Rigaudy, J. & Klesney, S. P., eds. Nomenclature of Organic Chemistry: The Blue Book: 1978 Ed. Sections A-F & H. 1979. text ed. 39.00 (ISBN 0-08-022369-9). Pergamon.

Rigault, George. St. Louis De Montfort. 2.50 o.s.i. (ISBN 0-910984-06-9). Montfort Pubns.

Rigby, Andrew. Alternative Realities: A Study of Communes & Their Members. (International Library of Sociology). 1974. 27.50 (ISBN 0-7100-7715-7). Routledge & Kegan.

Rigby, D. S. & Hanson, R. N. Production Typing Projects. 1980. text ed. 5.96 (ISBN 0-07-052836-5); tchr's manual & key avail. McGraw.

Rigby, D. S., jt. auth. see Hanson, R. N.

Rigby, D. Sue, jt. auth. see Hanson, Robert N.

Rigby, G. R., intro. by. Expanding Horizons in Chemical Engineering. (Chemeca Ser.). 241p. (Orig.). 1979. pap. text ed. 54.00x (ISBN 0-85825-116-7, Pub. by Inst Engineering Australia). Renouf.

Rigby, George. Lulu & Archie, Their Life & Times. (Illus.). 150p. 1983. 20.00x (ISBN 0-939518-03-1). Tortoise Pr.

Rigby, Ida K. Karl Hofer. LC 75-23811. (Outstanding Dissertations in the Fine Arts - 20th Century). (Illus.). 1976. lib. bdg. 45.00 o.s.i. (ISBN 0-8240-2005-7). Garland Pub.

Rigby, J. Keith, jt. auth. see Petersen, Morris S.

Rigby, T. H. Lenin's Government. LC 78-18754. (Soviet & East European Studies). 1979. 52.50 (ISBN 0-521-22281-8). Cambridge U Pr.

Rigby, T. H., jt. auth. see Miller, Robert F.

Rigby, T. H., et al. Authority, Power & Policy in the USSR: Essays Dedicated to Leonard Schapiro. LC 79-27750. 192p. 1980. 26.00 (ISBN 0-312-06122-6). St Martin.

Rigden, B., jt. auth. see Kavanagh, B.

Rigden, John S. Physics & the Sound of Music. LC 77-5638. 1977. 20.50x (ISBN 0-471-02433-3). Wiley.

Rigdon, jt. auth. see Brunworth.

Rigdon, Charles. The Caramour Woman. 448p. 1983. pap. 2.95 (ISBN 0-446-90227-6). Warner Bks.

Rigdon, Robert. Discovering Yourself. 1982. pap. 4.95 (ISBN 0-8423-0617-X). Tyndale.

Rigdon, Walter, ed. Biographical Encyclopaedia & Who's Who of the American Theatre. 1966. 82.50 o.p. (ISBN 0-685-11949-1). Heineman.

Riger, Robert. The Athlete: Writings, Drawings, Photographs & Television Sports; an Original Collection of 25 Years of Work. 1980. 24.95 o.p. (ISBN 0-671-24940-1). S&S.

Rigg, Donald C., jt. auth. see Kramer, Melinda G.

Rigg, George, ed. Editing Medieval Texts. LC 76-52722. (Conference on Editorial Problems Ser.: Vol. 12). 1977. lib. bdg. 16.50 o.s.i. (ISBN 0-8240-2426-5). Garland Pub.

Rigg, Peter W. Words of Still Waters. 68p. 1980. pap. 4.00 (ISBN 0-910477-00-0). LoonBooks.

Riggans, Walter. Numbers. Gibson, John C., ed. (Daily Study Bible-Old Testament). 300p. (Orig.). 1983. price not set (ISBN 0-664-21393-6); pap. price not set (ISBN 0-664-24474-2). Westminster.

Riggar, T. F. Utilizing Community Resources: An Overview for the Human Services. (Illus.). 1983. pap. text ed. price not set (ISBN 0-8391-1796-5, 17655). Univ Park.

Riggle, H. M., jt. auth. see Speck, Von S.

Riggs, Charles, jt. auth. see Johnson, Dewayne J.

Riggs, Donald A., tr. see Cheng, Francois.

Riggs, Donald E. Strategic Planning for Library Managers. 1983. write for info. (ISBN 0-89774-049-1). Oryx Pr.

Riggs, Douglas S. Mathematical Approach to Physiological Problems: A Critical Primer. 1970. pap. 7.95x o.p. (ISBN 0-262-68018-1). MIT Pr.

Riggs, Fred W. Thailand: The Modernization of a Bureaucratic Polity. (Illus.). 1966. text ed. 17.50x (ISBN 0-8248-0034-6, Eastwest Ctr). UH Pr.

Riggs, Henry E. Accounting: A Survey. 1981. text ed. 23.95 (ISBN 0-07-052851-9, C); instr's. manual 29.95 (ISBN 0-07-052852-7). McGraw.

Riggs, J. L. Production Systems: Planning, Analysis, & Control. (Wiley Series in Management). 649p. 1981. text ed. 33.95x (ISBN 0-471-05946-3); p.n.s. (ISBN 0-471-08940-0). Wiley.

Riggs, James L. Economic Decision Models for Engineers & Managers. 414p. Date not set. Repr. of 1968 ed. lib. bdg. (ISBN 0-89874-448-2). Krieger.

--Engineering Economics. 2nd ed. (Industrial Engineering & Management Science Ser.). (Illus.). 672p. 1982. 32.95x (ISBN 0-07-052862-4); instr's. manual 13.50 (ISBN 0-07-052863-2); tax supplement avail. McGraw.

--Engineering Economics. (McGraw-Hill Ser. in Industrial Engineering & Management Science). (Illus.). 1977. text ed. 32.50 (ISBN 0-07-052860-8, C); solns. manual 14.00 (ISBN 0-07-052861-6). McGraw.

--Essentials of Engineering Economics. (Industrial Engineering & Management Science Ser.). (Illus.). 528p. 1982. 24.95x (ISBN 0-07-052864-0). McGraw.

Riggs, James L. & Felix, Glenn H. Productivity by Objectives. (Illus.). 272p. 1983. text ed. 23.95 (ISBN 0-13-725374-5). P-H.

Riggs, James L., et al. Industrial Organization & Management. 6th ed. (Illus.). 1979. text ed. 31.50 (ISBN 0-07-052854-3, C); solutions manual 10.00 (ISBN 0-07-052855-1). McGraw.

Riggs, John B. Guide to Manuscripts in the Eleutharian Mills Historical Library, Supplement Containing Acessions for Years 1966 through 1975. 293p. 1978. cloth 15.00x (ISBN 0-914650-15-7). Eleutharian Mills-Hagley.

Riggs, Karen B. The Preppy Chef. (Illus.). 237p. 1982. 7.00 (ISBN 0-686-37893-8). Riggs.

Riggs, Lynne E., jt. auth. see Ashihara, Yoshinobu.

Riggs, Maida L. Jump to Joy: Helping Children Grow Through Active Play. (Illus.). 208p. 1980. 12.95 o.p. (ISBN 0-13-512343-7, Spec); pap. 6.95 o.p. (ISBN 0-13-512335-6). P-H.

Riggs, Maida L., et al. Early Childhood. Kneer, Marian, ed. (Basic Stuff Ser.: No. II, 1 of 3). 108p. (Orig.). 1981. pap. text ed. 6.25 (ISBN 0-88314-021-7). AAHPERD.

Riggs, Ralph M. The Spirit Himself. 1949. 4.95 (ISBN 0-88243-590-6, 02-0590). Gospel Pub.

Riggs, Timothy A. The Print Council Index to Oeuvre-Catalogues of Prints by European & American Artists. (Orig.). 1983. lib. bdg. 105.00 (ISBN 0-527-75346-7). Kraus Intl.

Riggs, William G. The Christian Poet in Paradise Lost. 1972. 27.50x (ISBN 0-520-02081-2). U of Cal Pr.

Righetti, P. J., et al, eds. Isoelectric Focusing: Lab Techniques in Biochemistry & Molecular Biology, Vol. 5, Pt. 2. 1976. pap. 21.75 (ISBN 0-444-11215-4, North-Holland). Elsevier.

Righter, William. Myth & Literature. (Concepts of Literature Ser.). 1975. 15.00x (ISBN 0-7100-8137-5). Routledge & Kegan.

Rights, R., jt. auth. see Ketzner, R.

Rigler, Leo G., tr. see Hoeffken, Walther & Lanyi, Marton.

Rigney, Barbara H. Madness & Sexual Politics in the Feminist Novel: Studies in Bronte, Woolf, Lessing & Atwood. LC 78-53291. 158p. 1978. 20.00 (ISBN 0-299-07710-1); pap. 7.95t (ISBN 0-299-07714-4). U of Wis Pr.

Rigney, D. A. Fundamentals of Friction & Wear of Materials. 1980. 79.00 (ISBN 0-87170-115-4). ASM.

Rigney, D. A. & Glaeser, W. A., eds. Source Book on Wear Control Technology. 1978. 46.00 (ISBN 0-87170-028-X). ASM.

Rigter, H. & Crabbe, J. C. Alcohol Tolerance & Dependence. 1981. 96.75 (ISBN 0-444-80212-6). Elsevier.

Riha, L., jt. ed. see Sterzl, J.

Riha, Thomas, ed. Readings in Russian Civilization, 3 vols. rev. ed. Incl. Vol. 1. Russia Before Peter the Great, 900-1700. 8.75x o.s.i. (ISBN 0-226-71852-2); pap. 6.50 (ISBN 0-226-71853-0); Vol. 2. Imperial Russia, 1700-1917. o.s.i. (ISBN 0-226-71854-9); pap. 7.50x (ISBN 0-226-71855-7); Vol. 3. Soviet Russia, 1917-Present. 9.50x (ISBN 0-226-71856-5); pap. 9.00x (ISBN 0-226-71857-3). LC 69-14825. 1969. U of Chicago Pr.

Rihani, Ameen. Arabian Peak & Desert. LC 82-4457. 1983. 40.00x (ISBN 0-88206-055-4). Caravan Bks.

--Around the Coasts of Arabia. LC 82-4462. 1983. 45.00x (ISBN 0-88206-056-2). Caravan Bks.

--Ibn Sa'oud of Arabia. LC 82-4573. 1983. 45.00x (ISBN 0-88206-057-0). Caravan Bks.

Riis, Jacob. How the Other Half Lives. 231p. 1957. pap. 6.25 (ISBN 0-8090-0012-1, AmCen). Hill & Wang.

Riis, Jacob A. Battle with the Slum. LC 69-16245. (Criminology, Law Enforcement, & Social Problems Ser.: No. 77). (Illus.). 1969. Repr. of 1902 ed. 15.00x (ISBN 0-87585-077-4). Patterson Smith.

--The Battle with the Slum: A Ten Years War Rewritten. 1972. 29.00 (ISBN 0-8290-0653-2); pap. text ed. 12.95x (ISBN 0-686-96754-2). Irvington.

--How the Other Half Lives: Studies Among the Tenements of New York. (Illus.). 12.50 (ISBN 0-8446-0233-7). Peter Smith.

Rijn, Rembrandt Van see Van Rijn, Rembrandt.

Rijnsdorp, John E., jt. auth. see Roffel, Brian.

Riker. Finding My Way. (gr. 9-12). 1979. pap. 9.28 (ISBN 0-87002-304-7); student guide 3.00 (ISBN 0-87002-309-8); tchr's guide 3.92 (ISBN 0-87002-311-X). Bennett IL.

Riker, A. J., jt. ed. see Kozlowski, T. T.

Riker, Audrey. Me: Understanding Myself & Others. 1982. 12.60 (ISBN 0-87002-367-5); student guide 3.96 (ISBN 0-87002-190-7); tchr's guide 3.96 (ISBN 0-87002-188-5). Bennett IL.

Riker, Audrey, jt. auth. see Riker, Charles.

Riker, Audrey, et al. Married Life. rev. ed. (gr. 10-12). 1976. text ed. 16.64 (ISBN 0-87002-071-4); student guide 3.24 (ISBN 0-87002-208-3). tchr's guide free. Bennett IL.

Riker, Charles & Riker, Audrey. Understanding Parenthood. pap. 2.45 o.p. (ISBN 0-8091-1707-X). Paulist Pr.

Riker, James, Jr. Annals of Newton, Queens County, New York. 448p. 1982. Repr. of 1852 ed. lib. bdg. 25.00 (ISBN 0-912606-08-8). Hunterdon Hse.

Riker, John H. The Art of Ethical Thinking. LC 78-66415. 1978. pap. text ed. 8.25 (ISBN 0-8191-0481-7). U Pr of Amer.

Riker, Tom & Roberts, Richard. The First Directory of Natural & Health Foods. LC 79-13757. 1979. 17.95 (ISBN 0-399-12419-5, Perigee); pap. 8.95 (ISBN 0-399-50399-4). Putnam Pub Group.

Riker, William H. Study of Local Politics. (Orig.). 1959. pap. text ed. 2.35 (ISBN 0-685-19773-5). Phila Bk Co.

Rikhoff, Jean. Robert E. Lee: Soldier of the South. (American Hero Biographies). (Illus.). (gr. 3-5). 1968. PLB 4.49 o.p. (ISBN 0-399-60539-8). Putnam Pub Group.

--Where Were You in '76. LC 78-7955. 1978. 9.95 o.p. (ISBN 0-399-90021-7, Marek). Putnam Pub Group.

Rikhye, Bhalinder L. Negotiating the End of Conflicts II: Namibia & Zimbabwe. (IPA Reports Ser.: No. 9). 128p. 1980. 3.00x (ISBN 0-686-36946-7). Intl Peace.

Rikhye, Indar J. & Volkmar, John. The Middle East & the New Realism. (IPA Reports Ser.: No. 4). 99p. 1975. 2.65x (ISBN 0-686-36941-6). Intl Peace.

Rikitake, T. Earthquake Prediction. (Developments in Solid Earth Geophysics: Vol. 9). 1976. 64.00 (ISBN 0-444-41373-1). Elsevier.

Rikki. Secrets of the Children of Og, 1st Part. (The Story of Og & Man Ser.). (Illus.). 220p. (Orig.). 1982. pap. 10.00 (ISBN 0-910149-01-1). Missing Link.

Rikko, Fritz, jt. auth. see Newman, Joel.

Riland, George. New Steinerbooks Dictionary of the Paranormal. 368p. (Orig.). 1982. pap. 7.95 (ISBN 0-446-97010-7). Warner Bks.

--The New Steinerbooks Dictionary of the Paranormal. LC 79-93353. (Steinerbks Spiritual Science Library). 370p. 1980. lib. bdg. 20.00 (ISBN 0-89345-028-6). Garber Comm.

Rile, Karen. Afternoon of a Faun. 256p. 1983. 14.45i (ISBN 0-316-74657-6). Little.

Riley. A Field Guide to the Butterflies of the West Indies. 27.95 (0686427866, Collins Pub England). Greene.

Riley, jt. auth. see Higgins.

Riley, A. & Symonds, E. M. Investigation of Labetatol in the Management of Hypertension in Pregnancy. (International Congress Ser.: Vol. 591). 1982. 53.25 (ISBN 0-444-90272-4). Elsevier.

Riley, Alan & Riley, Joann. Camping & Backpacking with Your Dog. (Illus.). 1979. 4.95 (ISBN 0-87666-675-6, KW-013). TFH Pubns.

Riley, Carroll L. The Frontier People: The Greater Southwest in the Protohistoric Period. LC 82-50284. (Occasional Paper Ser.: No. 1). Date not set. price not set (ISBN 0-88104-000-2). S Ill U Pr.

Riley, Charles M. Our Mineral Resources: An Elementary Textbook in Economic Geology. 4th ed. LC 76-57669. (Illus.). 348p. 1977. Repr. of 1967 ed. lib. bdg. 18.50 (ISBN 0-88275-530-7). Krieger.

Riley, Clayton, jt. auth. see King, The Reverend Martin Luther.

Riley, Daniel, ed. Strength Training by the Experts. LC 76-62810. (Illus.). 1977. pap. text ed. 6.95 cancelled o.p. (ISBN 0-918438-02-0). Leisure Pr.

Riley, Daniel P. Strength Training for Football: The Penn State Way. (Illus.). 1978. pap. text ed. 4.95 cancelled o.p. (ISBN 0-918438-42-X). Leisure Pr.

Riley, Denis R. & Young, Anthony. World Vegetation. 1967. 7.95x (ISBN 0-521-06083-4). Cambridge U Pr.

Riley, Don, jt. auth. see Selvig, Dick.

Riley, Donald P., et al. Parent-Child Communication. LC 77-13652. (Workshop Models for Family Life Education Ser.). 1977. plastic comb 12.95 (ISBN 0-87304-157-7). Family Serv.

Riley, Donald P., jt. auth. see Apgar, Kathryn.

Riley, E. M., tr. see Glotz, G.

Riley, Edith M., tr. see Beguin, Albert.

Riley, Eldon H. Guidebook to Security Interests in Personal Property. LC 80-19223. 1981. 55.00 (ISBN 0-87632-312-3). Boardman.

Riley, Eugene W. & Acuna, Victor E. Transmission Systems, Vol. VIII. 1976. 7.95 (ISBN 0-686-98064-6). Telecom Lib.

--Understanding Transmission, Vol. VII. 1976. 7.95 (ISBN 0-686-98063-8). Telecom Lib.

Riley, Gary L. & Baldridge, Victor J., eds. Governing Academic Organizations: New Problems, New Perspectives. LC 76-56995. 1977. 24.75x (ISBN 0-8211-1715-7); text ed. 22.25x (ISBN 0-685-75001-9). McCutchan.

Riley, Glenda. Frontierswomen, the Iowa Experience. LC 80-28298. (Illus.). 211p. 1981. 7.50x (ISBN 0-8138-1471-5). Iowa St U Pr.

Riley, J. P. & Chester, R., eds. Chemical Oceanography, Vol. 8. write for info. (ISBN 0-12-588608-X). Acad Pr.

Riley, J. R. & Reynolds, D. R. Radar Observations of Spodoptera Exempta Kenya: March-April 1979. 1981. 35.00x (ISBN 0-85135-115-8, Pub. by Centre Overseas Research). State Mutual Bk.

Riley, James C. International Government Finance & the Amsterdam Capital Market: 1740-1815. LC 79-152. (Illus.). 1980. 47.50 (ISBN 0-521-22677-5). Cambridge U Pr.

Riley, James W. Best Loved Poems of James Whitcomb Riley. 1960. 3.95 o.p. (ISBN 0-448-01261-8, G&D). Putnam Pub Group.

--Complete Poetical Works of James Whitcomb Riley. 1963. 8.95 o.p. (ISBN 0-448-01272-3, G&D). Putnam Pub Group.

--The Complete Works of James Whitcomb Riley, 10 Vols. 1983. Repr. of 1916 ed. lib. bdg. 400.00 Set (ISBN 0-89984-846-X). Century Bookbindery.

--The Hoosier Book Containing Poems in Dialect. 1911. Repr. lib. bdg. 20.00 (ISBN 0-8414-7436-2). Folcroft.

Riley, Jeannie C. & Buckingham, Jamie. From Harper Valley to the Mountain Top. 1981. PLB 10.95 o.p. (ISBN 0-912376-63-5). Chosen Bks Pub.

--From Harper Valley to the Mountain Top. (Epiphany Bks.). (Illus.). 1983. pap. 2.75 (ISBN 0-345-30481-0). Ballantine.

Riley, Joann, jt. auth. see Riley, Alan.

Riley, John W., Jr. see Riley, Matilda W., et al.

Riley, K. F. Mathematical Methods for the Physical Sciences. LC 73-89765. 512p. (Orig.). 1974. 63.50 (ISBN 0-521-20390-2); pap. 24.95x (ISBN 0-521-09839-4). Cambridge U Pr.

--Problems for Physics Students: With Hints & Answers. LC 82-4575. 100p. 1982. 24.95 (ISBN 0-521-24921-X); pap. 11.95 (ISBN 0-521-27073-1). Cambridge U Pr.

Riley, Kastinger. Weibliche Muse: Sechs Essays Uber Kunstlerisch Schaffende Frauen der Goethezeit. LC 81-69883. (Studies in German Literature, Linguistics, & Culture: Vol. 8). (Illus.). 300p. 1983. 25.00x (ISBN 0-938100-05-X). Camden Hse.

Riley, Mary Ann K. Case Studies in Nursing Fundamentals. 1979. pap. text ed. 9.95 (ISBN 0-02-401400-1). Macmillan.

Riley, Mary T. Laton: The Parent Book. new ed. LC 77-79313. (Illus.). 150p. 1978. pap. 14.95 (ISBN 0-89334-012-X). Humanics Ltd.

Riley, Matilda W. & Foner, Anne. Aging & Society, Vol. One: An Inventory of Research Findings. LC 68-54406. 636p. 1968. 25.00x (ISBN 0-87154-718-X). Russell Sage.

Riley, Matilda W., ed. Aging from Birth to Death: Interdisciplinary Perspectives. (AAAS Selected Symposium: No. 30). (Illus.). 1979. lib. bdg. 22.50 (ISBN 0-89158-363-7). Westview.

Riley, Matilda W. & Abeles, Ronald P., eds. Aging from Birth to Death: Sociotemporal Perspectives, Vol. 2. (AAAS Selected Symposium Ser.: No. 79). 240p. 1982. lib. bdg. 20.00 (ISBN 0-86531-382-2). Westview.

Riley, Matilda W. & Merton, Robert K., eds. Sociological Research, Vol. 2. 195p. 1963. pap. text ed. 13.95 (ISBN 0-15-582313-2). HarBraceJ.

Riley, Matilda W., et al. Aging & Society, Vol. Three: A Sociology of Age Stratification. LC 68-54406. 652p. 1972. 20.00x (ISBN 0-87154-720-1). Russell Sage.

Riley, Matilda W., et al, eds. Aging & Society, Vol. Two: Aging & the Professions. Riley, John W., Jr. & Johnson, Marilyn E. LC 68-54406. 410p. 1969. 11.50x (ISBN 0-87154-719-8). Russell Sage.

--Aging in Society. 288p. 1982. text ed. write for info. (ISBN 0-89859-267-4). L Erlbaum Assocs.

Riley, Michael. Massachusetts Legal Forms-Probate. 175p. 1983. write for info. looseleaf binder (ISBN 0-88063-013-2). Butterworth Legal Pubs.

Riley, Michael J., jt. auth. see Crane, Dwight D.

Riley, Patrick. Kant's Political Philosophy. LC 82-573. (Philosophy & Society Ser.). 224p. 1983. text ed. 28.95x (ISBN 0-8476-6763-4). Rowman.

Riley, Patrick, ed. The Political Writings of Leibniz. LC 78-171681. (Cambridge Studies in the History & Theory of Politics). 214p. 1981. pap. 13.95 (ISBN 0-521-28585-2). Cambridge U Pr.

Riley, R. C. Great Western Album. 16.50x (ISBN 0-392-07860-0, SpS). Sportshelf.

Riley, R. C. & Ashworth, Gregory. Benelux: An Economic Geography of Belgium, the Netherlands, & Luxembourg. LC 74-84586. (Illus.). 256p. 1975. text ed. 30.00 (ISBN 0-8419-0174-0). Holmes & Meier.

Riley, Raymond C. Belgium. new ed. LC 76-18938. (Westview Special Studies in Industrial Geography). (Illus.). 1976. lib. bdg. 27.50 o.p. (ISBN 0-89158-625-3). Westview.

Riley, Rebecca R. & Ohrn, Steven G., eds. South African Politics: A Film Guide. (Occasional Papers on Visual Communication). 25p. (Orig.). 1975. pap. text ed. 2.00 (ISBN 0-941934-17-9). Ind U Afro-Amer Arts.

Riley, Robert A., jt. ed. see Guthrie, David L.

Riley, Roger D. Poetry from Life. 1978. 4.55 o.p. (ISBN 0-533-03689-5). Vantage.

Riley, S. P. & Skirrow, G., eds. Chemical Oceanography, 6 vols. 2nd ed. Vol. 1. 1975. 95.50 (ISBN 0-12-588601-2); Vol. 2. 1975. 103.00 (ISBN 0-12-588602-0); Vol. 3. 1975. 90.00 (ISBN 0-12-588603-9); Vol. 4. 1975. 57.50 (ISBN 0-12-588604-7); Vol. 5. 1976. 66.00 (ISBN 0-12-588605-5); Vol. 6. 1976. 66.00 (ISBN 0-12-588606-3). Acad Pr.

Riley, Sue. Afraid. LC 77-15627. (What Does It Mean Ser.). (Illus.). (gr. k-2). 1978. PLB 5.95 (ISBN 0-89565-011-8). Childs World.

--Angry. LC 77-16791. (What Does It Mean Ser.). (Illus.). (ps-2). 1978. PLB 5.95 (ISBN 0-89565-014-2). Childs World.

--Help! LC 77-16030. (What Does It Mean Ser.). (Illus.). (ps-2). 1978. PLB 5.95 (ISBN 0-89565-012-6). Childs World.

--Sorry. LC 77-16811. (What Does It Mean Ser.). (Illus.). (ps-2). 1978. PLB 5.95 (ISBN 0-89565-013-4). Childs World.

--Success. LC 77-20992. (What Does It Mean Ser.). (Illus.). (ps-2). 1978. PLB 5.95 (ISBN 0-89565-016-9). Childs World.

Riley, Terrence L. & Roy, Alec. Pseudoseizures. (Illus.). 240p. 1982. lib. bdg. 34.00 (ISBN 0-683-07280-3). Williams & Wilkins.

Riley, Thomas J. Noteven, the Mouse: A Christmas Story. LC 82-61683. (Illus.). 32p. 1982. pap. 3.00 (ISBN 0-933050-13-5). New Eng Pr VT.

Riley, Tom, jt. auth. see Kohl, Sam.

Riley, Tom & Relyea, Harold C., eds. Freedom of Information Trends in the Information Age. 180p. 1983. text ed. 27.50x (ISBN 0-7146-3221-X, F Cass Co). Biblio Dist.

Riley, V. J., jt. auth. see Bock, C. V.

Riley, V. J., jt. auth. see Prawer, S. S.

Riley, V. J., jt. auth. see Robson-Scott, W. D.

Riley, W. B. Investpak for TRS-80 Model I. 1982. Set. 200.00 (ISBN 0-07-079513-4). McGraw.

Riley, W. B. & Montgomery, A. Guide to Computer Assisted Investment Analysis. 1982. 19.95 (ISBN 0-07-052916-7); pap. 14.95 (ISBN 0-07-052917-5). McGraw.

Riley, W. B. & Montgomery, A. H. Investpak for Apple II Version. 1982. Set. 200.00 (ISBN 0-07-079512-6). McGraw.

--Investpak for TRS-80 Model III. 1982. 200.00 (ISBN 0-07-079514-2). McGraw.

Riley, William F., jt. auth. see Dally, James W.

Riley-Smith, J. Knights of St. John in Jerusalem & Cyprus: 1050-1310. (Illus.). 1967. 26.00 (ISBN 0-312-45850-9, K83500). St Martin.

Rilke, Rainer M. For the Sake of a Single Verse. (Illus.). 64p. 1974. pap. 12.95 o.p. (ISBN 0-517-51205-X, C N Potter Bks). Crown.

--Letters of Rainer Maria Rilke, 2 vols. Greene, Jane B. & Norton, M. D., trs. Incl. Vol. 1. 1892-1910; Vol. 2. 1910-1926. (Illus.). Set. 24.00 (ISBN 0-8446-2809-3). Peter Smith.

--New Poems. Leishman, J. B., tr. LC 64-19422. (Bilingual). 1964. 16.50 o.s.i. (ISBN 0-8112-0376-X). New Directions.

--Poems. McKay, G. W., ed. (Clarendon German Ser). (gr. 9 up). 1965. pap. 4.95x (ISBN 0-19-500366-7). Oxford U Pr.

--Requiem for a Woman & Selected Lyric Poems. Gaus, Andy, tr. from Ger. LC 80-65910. 56p. (Orig.). 1981. pap. 6.00 (ISBN 0-939660-00-8). Threshold VT.

--Selected Poems. bilingual ed. MacIntyre, C. F., tr. 1941. pap. 4.95 (ISBN 0-520-01070-1, CAL4). U of Cal Pr.

--The Sonnets to Orpheus. Pitchford, Kenneth, tr. from Ger. LC 81-84492. (Illus.). 68p. (Orig.). 1982. pap. 7.95 (ISBN 0-938266-01-2). Purchase Pr.

--Visions of Christ: A Posthumous Cycle of Poems. Mandel, Siegfried, ed. Kramer, Aaron, tr. from Ger. LC 67-23560. (Illus.). 1967. 13.50x (ISBN 0-87081-021-9). Colo Assoc.

--Where Silence Reigns: Selected Prose. LC 78-9079. 1978. 4.95 (ISBN 0-8112-0703-X); pap. 3.95 o.s. (ISBN 0-8112-0697-1, NDP464). New Directions.

Rilke, Rainer Maria. Selected Poetry of Rainer Maria Rilke. Mitchell, Stephen, ed. 315p. 1982. 25.00 (ISBN 0-394-52434-9). Random.

Rilla, Wolf. The Chinese Consortium. (Orig.). 1980. pap. 2.25 o.p. (ISBN 0-451-09298-8, E9298, Sig). NAL.

--The Illusionists. 1977. 8.95 o.p. (ISBN 0-312-40670-3). St Martin.

Rima, Ingrid. Labor Markets, Wages, & Employment. (Illus.). 1980. 14.95x (ISBN 0-393-95058-1). Norton.

Rimbaud, Arthur. Complete Works. Schmidt, Paul, tr. 1976. pap. 5.95i (ISBN 0-06-090490-9, CN490, CN). Har-Row.

--A Season in Hell. Peschel, Enid R., tr. Bd. with Illuminations. (Illus., Engl. & Fre.). 1974. pap. 7.95 (ISBN 0-19-501760-9, 403, GB). Oxford U Pr.

Rimbault, E. F. London Eighteen Seventy-Seven. (Auction Catalogues of Music Ser.: Vol. 6). 1975. wrappers 42.50 o.s.i. (ISBN 90-6027-330-3, Pub. by Frits Knuf Netherlands). Pendragon NY.

Rimbault, Edward F., jt. auth. see Hopkins, Edward J.

Rimer, J. Thomas. Mori Ogai. LC 74-28163. (World Authors Ser.: No. 355). 1975. lib. bdg. 10.95 o.p. (ISBN 0-8057-2636-5, Twayne). G K Hall.

Rimer, J. Thomas, ed, see Ogai, Mori.

Rimer, J. Thomas, tr. see Ogai, Mori.

Rimkunas, Richard, jt. auth. see Phillips, Warren R.

Rimm, David C. & Masters, John C. Behavior Therapy: Techniques & Empirical Findings. 2nd ed. 538p. 1979. 26.00 (ISBN 0-12-588860-0). Acad Pr.

Rimmer, Bob. The Harrad Experiment. pap. cancelled (ISBN 0-686-98247-9, E823, Ever). Grove.

Rimmer, Bob & Matthews, Allayne. The Harrad Game. pap. cancelled (ISBN 0-686-98246-0, E824, Ever). Grove.

Rimmer, C. B. The Dirks Escape. (Illus.). 191p. 1979. pap. 2.25 o.p. (ISBN 0-686-65430-7). Jeremy Bks.

Rimmer, J. G., jt. auth. see Titherington, D.

Rimmer, Joan, tr. see Dunning, Albert.

Rimmer, Robert. The Premar Experiments. 1976. pap. 1.95 o.p. (ISBN 0-451-07515-3, J7515, Sig). NAL.

--The Rebellion of Yale Marratt. 1979. pap. 2.50 o.p. (ISBN 0-451-08851-4, E8851, Sig). NAL.

Rimmer, Robert H. Gold Lovers. 1974. pap. 1.25 o.p. (ISBN 0-451-06970-6, Y6970, Sig). NAL.

--The Love Explosion. 1980. pap. 2.75 o.p. (ISBN 0-451-09519-7, E9519, Sig). NAL.

--Proposition Thirty-One. 1971. pap. 1.95 o.p. (ISBN 0-451-07514-5, J7514, Sig). NAL.

--Thursday, My Love. 1972. pap. 1.75 o.p. (ISBN 0-451-07109-3, E7109, Sig). NAL.

Rimmer, Russell J. Generic Bifurications for Involutary Area Preserving Maps. LC 82-20615. (Memoirs of the American Mathematical Society Ser.: No. 272). 10.50 (ISBN 0-8218-2272-1, MEMO/272). Am Math.

Rimms, F. V., ed. Brother Earth, Sister Sky. 1981. 1.50 (ISBN 0-942582-03-9). Erie St Pr.

Rimpoche, Kunga & Cutillo, Brian, trs. from Tibetan. Drinking the Mountain Stream. LC 78-61174. (Illus.). 191p. (Orig.). 1982. pap. 7.95 (ISBN 0-87773-784-3). Great Eastern.

Rimrott, F. P. & Tabarrok, B., eds. Theoretical & Applied Mechanics. 1981. 85.00 (ISBN 0-444-85411-8). Elsevier.

Rinaldi, S. Environmental Systems Analysis & Management. 1982. 85.00 (ISBN 0-444-86406-7). Elsevier.

Rinaker, Clarissa, jt. ed. see Zeitlin, Jacob.

Rinaldi, Augusto & Tyndalo, Vassili. The Complete Book of Mushrooms: Over 1,000 Species & Varieties of American, European, & Asiatic Mushrooms. (Illus.). 330p. 1974. 17.95 o.p. (ISBN 0-517-51493-1). Crown.

Rinaldi, Sergio, et al. Modeling & Control of River Quality. LC 77-30475. (Illus.). 1978. text ed. 75.00 (ISBN 0-07-052925-6, C). McGraw.

Rinbochay, Lati. Mind in Tibetan Buddhism. Napper, Elizabeth, ed. LC 80-84848. 172p. (Orig.). 1980. 12.95 (ISBN 0-937938-03-3, Pub. by Snow Lion); pap. 7.95 (ISBN 0-937938-02-5). Gabriel Pr.

Rinbochy, Khetsun S. Tantric Practice in Nying-ma. Hopkins, Jeffery & Klein, Anne, eds. 238p. (Orig.). 1983. 16.00 (ISBN 0-937938-13-0); pap. text ed. 10.95 (ISBN 0-937938-14-9). Gabriel Pr.

Rinden, Robert & Witke, Roxane. The Red Flag Waves: A Guide to the Hung-Ch'i P'iao-P'iao Collection. LC 68-65796. (China Research Monographs: No. 3). 159p. 1968. pap. 4.50x (ISBN 0-912966-04-1). IEAS.

Rinder, Robert M. A Practical Guide to Small Computers for Business & Professional Use. rev. ed. 288p. 1983. pap. 9.95 (ISBN 0-671-47091-4). Monarch Pr.

Rindfleisch, D. Utilizing System Three Sixty - Three Seventy OS & VS Job Control Language & Utility Programs. 1979. 27.95 (ISBN 0-13-939793-0). P-H.

Rindfleisch, Norval. In Loveless Clarity & Other Stories. (Ithaca House Fiction Ser.). 141p. 1972. 3.95 o.p. (ISBN 0-87886-017-7). Ithaca Hse.

Rindfuss, R. R. & Sweet, James, eds. Postwar Fertility Trends & Differentials in the United States. (Studies in Population Ser.). 1977. 22.50 (ISBN 0-12-589250-0). Acad Pr.

Rindzinsky, Milka, tr. from English. Confesion de fe las Iglesias Menonitas. 32p. (Orig.). 1983. pap. 0.60x (ISBN 0-8361-1258-X). Herald Pr.

Rinehart, C. Dean & Smith, Ward C. Earthquakes & Young Volcanoes Along the Eastern Sierra Nevada: At Mammoth Lakes 1980, Lone Pine 1872, & Inyo & Mono Craters. Smith, Genny, ed. LC 81-51293. (Illus., Orig.). 1982. pap. 5.95 (ISBN 0-931378-02-8, Dist. by W. Kaufmann Inc.). Genny Smith Bks.

Rinehart, Constance, jt. ed. see Magrill, Rose Mary.

Rinehart, Dean, et al. Mammoth Lakes Sierra: A Handbook for Roadside & Trail. rev ed. Smith, Genny S., ed. LC 76-7970. (Illus.). 1976. pap. 7.95 (ISBN 0-931378-00-1, Dist. by W. Kaufmann Inc.). Genny Smith Bks.

Rinehart, Jeanne B., jt. ed. see Hektoen, Faith H.

Rinehart, Paula, jt. auth. see Rinehart, Stacy.

Rinehart, Stacy & Rinehart, Paula. Choices: Finding God's Way in Dating, Sex, Singleness & Marriage. LC 82-62071. 1983. pap. 3.95 (ISBN 0-89109-494-6). NavPress.

Rines, Alice R., jt. auth. see DeChow, Georgeen H.

Rines, Michael. Marketing Handbook. 2nd ed. 372p. 1981. text ed. 57.00x (ISBN 0-566-02200-1). Gower Pub Ltd.

Ring, et al. The Early Virtuoso. 64p. (gr. 3-12). 1974. pap. text ed. 7.95 (ISBN 0-87487-630-3). Summy.

Ring, Alfred A. Valuation of Real Estate. 2nd ed. 1970. ref. ed. 23.95 (ISBN 0-13-939892-9). P-H.

Ring, Alfred A. & Dasso, Jerome. Real Estate Principles & Practices. 9th ed. (Illus.). 752p. 1981. text ed. 31.95 (ISBN 0-13-765958-X); pap. text ed. 24.95 (ISBN 0-686-96837-9). P-H.

Ring, Alvin M. Laboratory Assistants Examination Review Book, Vol. 1. 3rd ed. 1979. 12.75 (ISBN 0-87488-455-1). Med Exam.

Ring, Constance, tr. see Wrasman, Marilyn W. & Haag, Diana B.

Ring, Daniel F., ed. Studies in Creative Partnership: Federal Aid to Public Libraries During the New Deal. LC 80-15762. 154p. 1980. 11.00 (ISBN 0-8108-1319-X). Scarecrow.

Ring, Jeanne & Graeser, Kathi, eds. Who's Who in Electronics, 1982. rev. ed. 912p. (Annual). 1983. 75.00 (ISBN 0-916512-69-X). Harris Pub.

Ring, Kathryn, ed. see Lansky, Vicki.

Ring, Kenneth. Life at Death: A Scientific Investigation of the Near Death Experience. 1980. 11.95 o.p. (ISBN 0-698-11032-3, Coward). Putnam Pub Group.

--Life at Death: A Scientific Investigation of the Near-Death Experience. LC 82-5427. 310p. (Orig.). 1982. pap. 7.50 (ISBN 0-688-01253-1). Quill NY.

--Life at Death: A Scientific Investigation of the Near-Death Experience. 1982. pap. 7.50 (ISBN 0-688-01253-1). Morrow.

Ringe, Donald A. American Gothic: Imagination & Reason in Nineteenth-Century Fiction. LC 82-4877. 224p. 1982. 17.00x (ISBN 0-8131-1464-0). U Pr of Ky.

--Charles Brockden Brown. (United States Authors Ser.). 13.95 (ISBN 0-8057-0100-1, Twayne). G K Hall.

--James Fenimore Cooper. (United States Authors Ser.). 10.95 (ISBN 0-8057-0156-7, Twayne). G K Hall.

Ringe, Donald A., ed. see Cooper, James F., et al.

Ringelblum, Emmanuel. Notes from the Warsaw Ghetto: The Journal of Emmanuel Ringelblum. Sloan, Jacob, ed. & tr. LC 74-10147. 389p. 1974. pap. 8.95 (ISBN 0-8052-0460-1). Schocken.

--Polish-Jewish Relations During the Second World War. Allon, Dafna, et al, trs. LC 76-1394. 330p. 1976. 20.00 (ISBN 0-86527-155-0). Fertig.

Ringenbach, Paul T. Tramps & Reformers, 1873-1916: The Discovery of Unemployment in New York. LC 77-175610. (Contributions in American History: No. 27). (Illus.). 224p. 1973. lib. bdg. 27.50x (ISBN 0-8371-6266-1, RAT/). Greenwood.

Ringenberg, Lawrence A. College Geometry. LC 77-2631. (Illus.). 320p. 1977. Repr. of 1968 ed. lib. bdg. 16.50 (ISBN 0-88275-545-5). Krieger.

Ringer, Gordon, tr. see Marcel, Gabriel.

Ringer, Virginia, tr. see Marcel, Gabriel.

Ringler, Karin E. Coping with Chemotherapy. Nathan, Peter E., ed. (Research in Clinical Psychology Ser.: No. 6). 1983. price not set (ISBN 0-8357-1389-X). Univ Microfilms.

Ringness, Thomas A. The Affective Domain in Education. 184p. 1975. pap. text ed. 8.95 (ISBN 0-316-74660-6). Little.

Ringold, Fran, ed. Awards III. (Nimrod Ser.). 109p. (Orig.). 1981. pap. text ed. 5.50 (ISBN 0-942374-06-1). Art & Human Council Tulsa.

Ringold, Fran & Allen, Roger, eds. Arabic Literature: Then & Now. (Nimrod Ser.). (Illus.). 149p. 1981. pap. text ed. 5.50 (ISBN 0-942374-07-X). Art & Human Council Tulsa.

Ringold, Francine, ed. Awards IV. (Nimrod Ser.). (Illus.). 112p. (Orig.). 1982. pap. 5.50 (ISBN 0-942374-09-6). Art & Human Council Tulsa.

--Frontiers: Land, Space, & Mind. (Nimrod Ser.). 96p. 1982. pap. text ed. 5.50 (ISBN 0-942374-08-8). Art & Human Council Tulsa.

Ringrose, Douglas. The Manger Dogs. (Illus.). 1977. 4.95 o.p. (ISBN 0-533-02746-2). Vantage.

Ringrose, John R., jt. ed. see Kadison, Richard V.

Ringsdorf, jt. auth. see Cheraksin.

Ringsdorf, W., jt. auth. see Cheraskin, E.

Ringstad, M. Adventures on Library Shelves. LC 68-16398. (Illus.). (gr. 2 up). 1967. PLB 7.99x prebound (ISBN 0-87783-001-0); pap. 2.95x deluxe ed. (ISBN 0-87783-156-4). Oddo.

Rinhart, Floyd & Rinhart, Marion. The Good Old Summertime: Americans at Play 1830-1900. 1977. 14.95 o.p. (ISBN 0-685-76361-7, C N Potter Bks). Crown.

--Summertime. (Illus.). 1978. pap. 7.95 o.p. (ISBN 0-517-52015-X, C N Potter Bks). Crown.

Rinhart, Marion, jt. auth. see Rinhart, Floyd.

Rini, Lisa, jt. auth. see Werner, Peter H.

Rink, Evald. Technical Americana: A Checklist of Technical Publications Printed Before 1831. LC 81-4036. 1981. lib. bdg. 70.00 (ISBN 0-527-75447-1). Kraus Intl.

Rinker, Harry L., ed. Warman's Antiques & Their Prices. 16th ed. LC 79-4331. (Illus.). 680p. 1982. pap. 10.95 o.p. (ISBN 0-911594-02-7). Warman.

--Warman's Antiques & Their Prices. 17th ed. LC 79-4331. (Illus.). 712p. 1983. pap. 10.95 (ISBN 0-911594-03-5). Warman.

Rinker, Rosalind. Conversational Prayer. 1976. pap. write for info (ISBN 0-89129-210-1). Jove Pubns.

--How to Have Family Prayers. 1977. 5.95 o.p. (ISBN 0-310-32160-3); pap. 4.95 (ISBN 0-310-32161-1). Zondervan.

Rinkoff, Barbara. Harry's Homemade Robot. (gr. 5-7). 1969. 3.50 o.p. (ISBN 0-517-50236-4). Crown.

Rinn, L. A., jt. ed. see Scharer, Peter.

Rinn, Roger C., jt. ed. see Markle, Allan.

Rinne, U. K. & Klinger, M. Parkinson's Disease: Current Progress, Problems & Management. 1980. 74.00 (ISBN 0-444-80263-0). Elsevier.

Rinpoche, Namgyal. The Song of Awakening: A Guide to Liberation Through Maranussati, Mindfulness of Death. Wongmo, Karma C., ed. LC 79-65090. 108p. (Orig.). 1979. pap. 7.50 o.p. (ISBN 0-9602722-0-8). Open Path.

Rinsky, Lee A. Teaching Word Attack Skills. 2nd ed. 174p. 1981. pap. text ed. 9.95 (ISBN 0-89787-511-7). Gorsuch Scarisbrick.

Rinsky, Lee A. & Fossard, Esta de. The Contemporary Classroom Reading Inventory. 166p. (Orig.). 1980. pap. text ed. 8.95 (ISBN 0-89787-510-9). Gorsuch Scarisbrick.

Rinsler, Norma, ed. see De Nerval, Gerard.

Rinsley, Donald B. Borderline & Other Self Disorders. LC 81-20538. 1982. 27.50 (ISBN 0-87668-447-9). Aronson.

Rintala, Marvin. The Constitution of Silence: Essays on Generational Themes. LC 78-20018. (Contributions in Political Science: No. 25). 1979. lib. bdg. 25.00x (ISBN 0-313-20723-2, RCS/). Greenwood.

Rintelmann, W. Hearing Assessment. 640p. 1979. text ed. 24.95 (ISBN 0-8391-1448-6). Univ Park.

Rinzler, Carol. The Girl Who Had All the Breaks. 1980. 9.95 (ISBN 0-399-12352-0). Putnam Pub Group.

Rinzler, Carol A. The Dictionary of Medical Folklore. LC 78-69518. 1979. 14.37i (ISBN 0-690-01704-9). T Y Crowell.

--The Signet Book of Chocolate. 1978. pap. 1.95 o.p. (ISBN 0-451-08395-4, J8395, Sig). NAL.

--Strictly Female: An Evaluation of Brand-Name Health & Hygiene Products for Women. 1981. pap. 7.95 (ISBN 0-452-25370-5, Z5370, Plume). NAL.

Rinzler, Carol Ann. Strictly Female: The Brand-Name Guide to Women's Health & Hygiene Products. (Medical Library). 304p. 1982. pap. 7.95 (ISBN 0-686-84851-9, 4138-7). Mosby.

Rinzler, Carol E. The Girl Who Got All the Breaks. 176p. 1981. pap. 2.25 o.p. (ISBN 0-380-56077-1, 56077). Avon.

Riofrancos, Maro, tr. see Vazquez, Adolfo Sanchez.

Riordan, Brendan P., jt. auth. see Placa, Alan.

Riordan, J. Sport in Soviet Society. LC 76-9729. (Soviet & East European Studies). (Illus.). 1977. 49.50 (ISBN 0-521-21284-7); pap. 15.95 (ISBN 0-521-28023-0). Cambridge U Pr.

Riordan, James. Flight into Danger. LC 80-52522. (Starters Ser.). PLB 8.00 (ISBN 0-382-06506-9). Silver.

--Tales of King Arthur. (Illus.). 128p. (gr. 4-7). 1982. 11.95 (ISBN 0-528-82383-3). Rand.

Riordan, James, ed. Sport Under Communism: A Comparative Study. 1978. 17.95 o.p. (ISBN 0-7735-0505-9). McGill-Queens U Pr.

Riordan, James, tr. The Three Magic Gifts. (Illus.). (gr. k-4). 1980. 11.95 (ISBN 0-19-520194-9). Oxford U Pr.

Riordan, Jan. A Practical Guide to Breastfeeding. (Illus.). 370p. 1983. pap. text ed. 15.95 (ISBN 0-8016-4230-2). Mosby.

Riordan, John C. The Art Collection at Potsdam. (Illus.). 118p. (Orig.). 1982. pap. 10.00 (ISBN 0-942746-04-X). Brainerd.

Riordan, John J. & Cotliar, William. How to Develop Your GMP-QC Manual. 96p. 1977. pap. 30.00 (ISBN 0-914176-20-X). Wash Busn Info.

Riordon, James. The Secert Castle. LC 80-52524. (Starters Ser.). PLB 8.00 (ISBN 0-382-06508-5). Silver.

Riordon, P. H. & Hollister, V. F., eds. Geology of Asbestos Deposits. LC 80-52898. (Illus.). 118p. (Orig.). 1981. pap. 32.00x (ISBN 0-89520-277-8, 277-8). Soc Mining Eng.

Riordon, William L. Plunkitt of Tammany Hall. 1969. pap. 2.25 (ISBN 0-525-47118-9, 0218-070). Dutton.

Rios, Alberto. Sleeping on Fists. 36p. 1981. pap. 5.00 o.p. (ISBN 0-937160-02-4). Dooryard.

Riotte, Louise. Nuts for the Food Gardener: Growing Quick Crops Anywhere. LC 74-83146. (Illus.). 144p. 1975. pap. 5.95 o.p. (ISBN 0-88266-043-8). Garden Way Pub.

--Planetary Planting. 1982. pap. 9.95 (ISBN 0-917086-38-4, Pub. by Astro Comp Serv). Para Res.

--Planetary Planting: A Guide to Organic Gardening by the Signs of the Zodiac. LC 74-32481. 1976. 9.95 o.p. (ISBN 0-671-21953-7). S&S.

--Roses Love Garlic: Secrets of Companion Planting with Flowers. (Illus.). 224p. (Orig.). 1982. pap. 6.95 (ISBN 0-88266-331-3). Garden Way Pub.

Riotton, C. & Christopherson, William. Cytology of the Female Genital Tract Tumours. (World Health Organization: International Histological Classification of Tumours Ser.: No. 8). (Illus.). 1977. 69.50 (ISBN 0-89189-108-0, 70-0-008-20); incl. slides 168.50 (ISBN 0-89189-109-9, 70-1-008-00). Am Soc Clinical.

Riotton, G. & Christopherson, W. M. Cytology of Non-Gynaecological Sites. (World Health Organization: International Histological Classification of Tumours Ser.: No. 17). (Illus.). 1977. text ed. 69.50 o.p. (ISBN 92-4-176017-6, 70-1-017-20); with slides 205.00 o.p. (ISBN 0-89189-125-0, 70-1-017-00). Am Soc Clinical.

Rioux, William. You Can Improve Your Child's School. 1980. 12.95 o.p. (ISBN 0-671-25116-3). S&S.

Ripa, Cesare. Iconologia. LC 75-27865. (Renaissance & the Gods Ser.: Vol. 21). (Illus.). 1976. Repr. of 1611 ed. lib. bdg. 66.00 o.s.i. (ISBN 0-8240-2070-7). Garland Pub.

--Iconologie. Baudouin, Jean, tr. LC 75-27874. (Renaissance & the Gods Ser.: Vol. 29). (Illus., Fr.). 1976. Repr. of 1644 ed. lib. bdg. 73.00 o.s.i. (ISBN 0-8240-2078-2). Garland Pub.

Ripa, Louis C. Surveying Manual. 1964. 27.50 (ISBN 0-07-052935-3, P&RB). McGraw.

Riper, Charles van see Van Riper, Charles.

Riper, Charles Van see Van Riper, Charles.

Riper, Guernsey Van see Van Riper, Guernsey, Jr.

Riper, Guernsey Van Jr. see Van Riper, Guernsey, Jr.

Riper, Peter van see Van Riper, Peter.

Ripin, Edwin M. The Instrument Catalogs of Leopoldo Franciolini. (Music Indexes & Bibliographies: No. 9). 1974. pap. 17.00 (ISBN 0-913574-09-0). Eur-Am Music.

Ripin, Edwin M., ed. Keyboard Instruments: Studies in Keyboard Organology, 1500-1800. (Illus.). 84p. 1977. pap. 3.50 (ISBN 0-486-23363-4). Dover.

Ripin, Rowena, tr. see Buhler, Charlotte.

Ripley, Brian D. Spatial Statistics. LC 80-26104. (Probability & Mathematical Statistics Ser.: Applied Probability & Statistics). 352p. 1981. 31.95 (ISBN 0-471-08367-4, Pub. by Wiley-Interscience). Wiley.

Ripley, Dillon, jt. auth. see Ali, Salim.

Ripley, J. A., Jr. & Whitten, R. C. The Elements & Structure of the Physical Sciences. 2nd ed. 1969. text ed. 13.50 o.p. (ISBN 0-471-72322-3, Pub. by Wiley). Krieger.

Ripley, John W. & Richmind, Robert W., eds. A Century of Healing Arts-Eighteen Fifty to Nineteen Fifty. (Illus.). 176p. 1980. pap. 6.25 (ISBN 0-686-70064-3). Shawnee County Hist.

Ripley, Randall. Congress: Process & Policy. 3d ed. 1983. text ed. write for info (ISBN 0-393-95291-6). Norton.

Ripley, Randall B. The Politics of Economic & Human Resource Development. LC 79-173977. (Policy Analysis Ser). 1972. 10.95 o.p. (ISBN 0-672-51479-6); pap. 4.35 o.p. (ISBN 0-672-61070-1). Bobbs.

Ripley, Randall B. & Franklin, Grace A., eds. National Government & Policy in the United States. LC 76-41997. 1977. pap. text ed. 9.95 (ISBN 0-87581-212-0, 212). Peacock Pubs.

Ripley, S. Dillon. The Land & Wildlife of Tropical Asia. rev. ed. LC 80-52261. (Life Nature Library). PLB 13.40 (ISBN 0-8094-3867-4). Silver.

Ripley, S. Dillon, jt. auth. see Ali, Salim.

Ripley, Theresa M., jt. auth. see Loughary, John W.

Ripley's Believe It Or Not Staff. Ripley's Believe It Or Not Book of Chance. 352p. 1982. 14.95 (ISBN 0-698-11197-4, Coward). Putnam Pub Group.

Ripling, E., jt. auth. see Polakowski, N. H.

Ripnen, Kenneth H. Office Space Administration. (Illus.). 224p. 1974. 23.50 o.p. (ISBN 0-07-052936-1, P&RB). McGraw.

Rippere, Victoria, jt. auth. see Purves, Alan C.

Ripperger, Eugene A., jt. auth. see Oden, John T.

Rippery, Elizabeth, jt. auth. see Kelburn, Richard.

Rippetoe, Leaman. Words of Praise & Hope. 1982. 6.95 (ISBN 0-533-05438-9). Vantage.

Ripple, Paula. Walking with Loneliness. LC 82-73048. 176p. (Orig.). 1982. pap. 4.95 (ISBN 0-87793-259-X). Ave Maria.

Ripple, Richard E., et al. Human Development. LC 81-81703. (Illus.). 640p. 1982. text ed. 22.95 (ISBN 0-686-86051-9); Instr's manual 1.00 (ISBN 0-395-28755-3); study guide 8.50 (ISBN 0-686-91514-3). HM.

Rippley, La Vern J. The German-Americans. (Immigrant Heritage of America Ser.). 1976. lib. bdg. 12.95 (ISBN 0-8057-8405-5, Twayne). G K Hall.

Rippley, La Vern J., tr. see Sallet, Richard.

Rippley, Lavern. Of German Ways. (BN 4000 Ser.). pap. 5.95 (ISBN 0-06-464036-1, BN). B&N NY.

Rippon, Angela. Mark Phillips: The Man & His Horses. LC 82-81008. (Illus.). 320p. 1982. 19.95 (ISBN 0-688-01519-0). Morrow.

Rippon, Anton. Classic Moments of the Ashes. 144p. 1982. 35.00x (ISBN 0-86190-051-0, Pub. by Moorland). State Mutual Bk.

--Cricket Around the World. 144p. 1982. 35.00x (ISBN 0-86190-055-3, Pub. by Moorland). State Mutual Bk.

Rippon, Michelle & Meyers, Walter E. Combining Sentences. 201p. 1979. pap. text ed. 10.95 (ISBN 0-15-512250-9, HC); instructor's manual avail. (ISBN 0-15-512251-7). HarBraceJ.

Rippon, W. B., jt. auth. see Jamieson, A. M.

Rippy, James F. Joel R. Poinsett, Versatile American. LC 68-30826. (Illus.). 1968. Repr. of 1935 ed. lib. bdg. 15.75x o.p. (ISBN 0-8371-0200-6, RIVA). Greenwood.

Rippy, Susan, jt. auth. see Brinkerhoff, Donna.

Rips, Geoffrey. Unamerican Activities: The Campaign Against the Underground Press in the United States, 1960-1979. 160p. 1981. pap. 7.95 (ISBN 0-87286-127-9). City Lights.

Ris, Thomas F. The Neat Stuff Something-to-Do Book. LC 79-16632. (Illus.). 96p. (gr. 3 up). 1979. PLB 7.29 o.p. (ISBN 0-671-33078-0). Messner.

Rischer, Carl E., jt. auth. see Easton, Thomas A.

Rischin, Moses, ed. see Dillon, Merton L.

Rischin, Moses, ed. see Hapgood, Hutchins.

Risdon, D. H. Color Treasury of Songbirds. (Bounty Bk. Ser.). (Illus.). 64p. 1974. pap. 1.98 o.p. (ISBN 0-517-51431-1). Crown.

Risdon, Donald H. Your Book of Pet Keeping. (Illus.). (gr. 3-7). 1964. 6.75 o.p. (ISBN 0-571-05771-3). Transatlantic.

Risdon, R. A. & Turner, D. R. Atlas of Renal Pathology. (Current Histopathology Ser.: Vol. 2). (Illus.). 150p. 1981. text ed. 43.50 (ISBN 0-397-50452-7, Lippincott Medical). Lippincott.

Risebero, Bill. Modern Architecture & Design. 256p. 1982. 50.00x (ISBN 0-906969-18-2, Pub. by Benn Pubns). State Mutual Bk.

Riser, Wayne H. Your Future in Veterinary Medicine. LC 75-29656. 160p. (YA) 1976. pap. 4.50 (ISBN 0-668-03916-7). Arco.

Rishel, R. W., jt. auth. see Fleming, W. H.

Rishoi, Don C. Food Store Sanitation. LC 75-35904. 302p. 1976. text ed. 21.95 (ISBN 0-86730-305-0). Lebhar Friedman.

Rising, Edward. Ambulatory Care Systems, Vol. 1: Design of Ambulatory Care Systems for Improved Patient Flow. LC 76-55865. 160p. 1977. 19.95x (ISBN 0-669-01323-4). Lexington Bks.

Rising, Gerald R., jt. auth. see Johnson, Donovan A.

Risinger, Hettie. Innovative Machine Quilting. LC 79-91393. (Illus.). 164p. 1980. 16.95 (ISBN 0-8069-5398-5). Sterling.

--Innovative Machine Quilting. LC 79-91393. (Illus.). 164p. 1982. pap. 8.95 (ISBN 0-8069-7566-0). Sterling.

--Innovative Patchwork Piecing. (Illus.). 160p. 1983. 16.95 (ISBN 0-8069-5486-8); lib. bdg. 19.99 (ISBN 0-8069-5487-6); pap. 8.95 (ISBN 0-8069-7700-0). Sterling.

Risjord, Norman. Representative Americans: The Revolutionary Generation, Vol. 2. 1980. pap. text ed. 8.95x (ISBN 0-669-02710-3). Heath.

Risjord, Norman K. Representative Americans: The Colonists, Vol. I. (Representative Americans Ser.). 272p. 1981. pap. text ed. 8.95 (ISBN 0-669-02831-2). Heath.

Risk, Paul H. Outdoor Safety & Survival. 300p. 1983. write for info. (ISBN 0-471-03891-1). Wiley.

Riskel, R. W., jt. auth. see Fleming, W. H.

Riskind, Mary. Apple Is My Sign. (gr. 5-8). 1981. 8.95 (ISBN 0-395-30852-6). HM.

Risko, Victoria. Testing-Teaching Module of Auditory Discrimination. 1975. pap. 13.50x manual & 25 recording forms (ISBN 0-87879-099-3); Set. 25 diagnostic tests o.p. 6.00 (ISBN 0-686-96645-7). Acad Therapy.

Risley, Curtis. Ayer Public Relations & Publicity Stylebook: 1983. rev. ed. 1983. pap. text ed. 12.95 (ISBN 0-910190-27-5). IMS Pr.

Riso, Ovid. Advertising Cost Control Handbook. LC 72-10036. 387p. 1973. 22.00 (ISBN 0-442-26954-4). Krieger.

Risom, Ole. I Am a Mouse. (Golden Sturdy Bk.). 1974. 3.95 (ISBN 0-307-12126-7, Golden Pr). Western Pub.

Rison, Laverne. Sing Long & Loud of Leafy Trees. (Illus.). 37p. 1979. pap. 3.00 (ISBN 0-934040-04-4). Quality Ohio.

Risse, Joe. Electronic Test Equipment & How to Use It. LC 74-79581. (Illus.). 204p. 1974. 7.95 (ISBN 0-8306-4723-6); pap. 4.95 o.p. (ISBN 0-8306-3723-0, 723). TAB Bks.

Risser, Joy. OJT Traffic Clerk Resource Materials. 2nd ed. (Gregg Office Job Training Program). (Illus.). 112p. (gr. 11-12). 1980. soft cover 5.60 (ISBN 0-07-052960-4); training manual 4.16 (ISBN 0-07-052961-2). McGraw.

Risser, P. G. The True Prairie Ecosystem. LC 79-19857. (The US-IBP Synthesis Ser.: Vol. 16). 544p. 1981. 31.50 (ISBN 0-87933-361-8). Hutchinson Ross.

Risser, P. G., et al. The True Prairie Ecosystem. (US-IBP Synthesis Ser.: Vol. 16). 1981. 31.50 (ISBN 0-12-787330-9). Acad Pr.

Rissover, F. & Birch, D. Mass Media & the Popular Arts. 13.95x (ISBN 0-07-052950-7, C); pap. 8.95 o.p. (ISBN 0-07-052944-2). McGraw.

--Mass Media & the Popular Arts. 3rd ed. 496p. 1983. 15.95x (ISBN 0-07-052956-6, C). McGraw.

Rist, J. M. On the Independence of Matthew & Mark. LC 76-40840. (Society for New Testament Studies Monographs: No. 22). 1978. 22.95 (ISBN 0-521-21476-9). Cambridge U Pr.

--Plotinus: The Road to Reality. 1977. 39.50 (ISBN 0-521-06085-0); pap. 10.95 (ISBN 0-521-29202-6). Cambridge U Pr.

--Stoic Philosophy. LC 79-85736. 1969. 39.50 (ISBN 0-521-07620-X); pap. 10.95 (ISBN 0-521-29201-8). Cambridge U Pr.

Rist, John M. Human Value: A Study in Ancient Philosophical Ethics. (Philosophia Antiqua Ser.: Vol. 40). v, 175p. 1982. pap. write for info. (ISBN 90-04-06757-4). E J Brill.

Rist, Ray C. Guestworkers in Germany: Prospects for Pluralism. LC 78-6282. (Praeger Special Studies). 1978. 30.50 o.p. (ISBN 0-03-040766-4). Praeger.

Rist, Ray C. & Anson, Ronald J. Education, Social Science, & the Judicial Process. LC 77-962. 1977. pap. text ed. 8.95x (ISBN 0-8077-2532-3). Tchrs Coll.

Rist, Ray C., ed. Confronting Youth Unemployment in the Nineteen Eighties: Rhetoric Versus Reality. LC 80-19730. (Pergamon Policy Studies on Social Issues). 236p. 1980. 33.00 (ISBN 0-08-026077-2). Pergamon.

--Desegregated Schools: Appraisals of an American Experiment. LC 79-6958. 1979. 21.00 (ISBN 0-12-588980-1). Acad Pr.

Ristic, M. Momcilo, ed. Sintering-New Developments. (Materials Science Monographs: Vol. 4). 1979. 72.50 (ISBN 0-444-41796-6). Elsevier.

Ristic, Miodrag, jt. auth. see Weinman, David.

Ristic, Miodrag & Kreier, Julius P., eds. Babesiosis. 1981. 51.50 (ISBN 0-12-588950-X). Acad Pr.

Ristic, Velimir M. Principles of Acoustic Devices. 325p. 1983. 37.50 (ISBN 0-471-09153-7, Pub. by Wiley-Interscience). Wiley.

Risvold, Floyd E., ed. see Weichmann, Louis J.

Ritcey, G. M. & Ashbrook, A. W. Solvent Extraction, Pt. 2: Principles & Applications to Process Metallurgy. (Process Metallurgy Ser.: Vol. 1, Pt. 2). 1979. 98.00 (ISBN 0-444-41771-0). Elsevier.

Ritcey, G. M. & Ashbrook, A. W., eds. Solvent Extraction, Pt. 1. (Process Metallurgy Ser.: Vol. 1, Pt. 1). Date not set. 64.00 (ISBN 0-686-95178-6). Elsevier.

Ritche, James. Homeowner's Tools. rev. ed. (Successful Home Improvement Ser.). 96p. 1981. pap. 3.95 (ISBN 0-8249-6101-3). Ideals.

Ritchen, Ralph. Motor's Auto Troubleshooter. 6.95x o.p. (ISBN 0-685-22053-2). Wehman.

Ritchey, John A., jt. auth. see Amrine, Harold.

Ritchey, S. J. & Taper, L. J. Maternal & Child Nutrition. 432p. 1983. text ed. 22.95 scp (ISBN 0-06-453519-3, HarpC). Har-Row.

Ritchie, Andrew. King of the Road. 200p. 1975. 12.95 o.s.i. (ISBN 0-913668-42-7); pap. 7.95 o.s.i. (ISBN 0-913668-41-9). Ten Speed Pr.

Ritchie, Anne T. Records of Tennyson, Ruskin & Browning. LC 70-172549. Repr. of 1892 ed. 15.00 (ISBN 0-405-08893-0, Pub. by Blom). Ayer Co.

Ritchie, D. A., jt. auth. see Pennington, T. H.

Ritchie, D. A., jt. auth. see Smith, K. M.

Ritchie, Dennis M., jt. auth. see Kernighan, Brian W.

Ritchie, Donald. Biology. (College Outlines Ser.). pap. 4.95 o.p. (ISBN 0-671-08016-4). Monarch Pr.

Ritchie, Donald & Carola, Robert. Biology. LC 78-67450. (Life Sciences Ser.). 1979. text ed. 25.95 (ISBN 0-201-06335-2); inst. manual avail. (ISBN 0-201-06336-0); study guide 9.95 (ISBN 0-201-06337-9). A-W.

Ritchie, Donald D. & Carola, Robert. Biology. 2nd ed. LC 82-11318. (Biology Ser.). (Illus.). 672p. Date not set. text ed. 25.95 (ISBN 0-201-06356-5); Instrs' Manual avail. (ISBN 0-201-06357-3); Study Guide avail. (ISBN 0-201-06358-1); Transparencies avail. (ISBN 0-201-06394-8); Slides avail. (ISBN 0-201-06393-X); Test Bank avail. (ISBN 0-201-06359-X). A-W.

Ritchie, Donald D., jt. auth. see Fuller, Harry J.

Ritchie, F. Fabulae Faciles. Kirtland, John C., ed. (Illus.). 1931. pap. text ed. 6.95x (ISBN 0-582-35954-6). Longman.

Ritchie, G. Admiralty Chart or Harvest of Soundings. 1967. 17.50 (ISBN 0-444-19830-X). Elsevier.

Ritchie, Gary A., ed. New Agricultural Crops. (AAAS Selected Symposium: No. 38). 1979. lib. bdg. 26.00 (ISBN 0-89158-473-0). Westview.

Ritchie, George. Electronics Construction & Assembly. (Illus.). 1980. lib. bdg. 18.95 (ISBN 0-13-250472-3). P-H.

Ritchie, J. B. & Thompson, Paul H. Organization & People: Readings, Cases & Exercises in Organizational Behavior. LC 76-3566. (Management Ser.). (Illus.). 400p. 1976. pap. text ed. 12.50 o.s.i. (ISBN 0-8299-0103-5). West Pub.

--Organization & People: Readings, Cases & Exercises in Organizational Behavior. 2nd ed. (Ser. in Management). 1980. pap. 16.95 (ISBN 0-8299-0274-0); instrs.' manual avail. (ISBN 0-8299-0571-5). West Pub.

Ritchie, J. M. German Expressionist Drama. (World Author Ser.). 1977. lib. bdg. 13.95 (ISBN 0-8057-6261-2, Twayne). G K Hall.

Ritchie, James D. Sourcebook of Farm Energy Alternatives. 384p. 1983. 32.50 (ISBN 0-07-052951-5). McGraw.

Ritchie, James L., et al. Thallium--201 Myocardial Imaging. LC 78-3004. 166p. 1978. 20.50 (ISBN 0-89004-274-8). Raven.

Ritchie, Jean A. Learning Better Nutrition: A Second Study of Approaches & Techniques. (FAO Nutritional Studies: No. 20). (Orig.). 1973. pap. 15.50 (ISBN 0-685-09392-1, F254, FAO). Unipub.

Ritchie, John. Australia As Once We Were. (Illus.). 1977. text ed. 24.50x (ISBN 0-8419-6102-6). Holmes & Meier.

Ritchie, Oscar W., jt. auth. see Koller, Marvin R.

Ritchie, Robert L. & Simons, C. J. Essays in Translation from French. text ed. 29.95x (ISBN 0-521-06092-3); pap. 10.95x (ISBN 0-521-09205-1). Cambridge U Pr.

Ritchie, W. K. The France of Louis XIV. Reeves, Marjorie, ed. (Then & There Ser.). (Illus.). 96p. (Orig.). (gr. 7-12). 1977. pap. text ed. 3.10 (ISBN 0-582-20540-9). Longman.

Ritchie, William A. Archaeology of New York State. rev ed. LC 80-13378. (Illus.). 1980. Repr. of 1969 ed. 22.50 (ISBN 0-916346-41-2). Harbor Hill Bks.

Ritchie-Calder. Leonardo. LC 70-130350. 1970. 12.95 o.p. (ISBN 0-671-20713-X). S&S.

Ritelbaum, Harry. How To Write a Thesis. (How To Write Ser.). 144p. (Orig.). 1982. pap. 4.95 (ISBN 0-671-18726-0). Monarch Pr.

Ritger, Dick, jt. auth. see Allen, George.

Ritger, Paul D. & Rose, Nicholas J. Differential Equations with Applications. (International Ser. in Pure & Applied Physics). 1968. text ed. 32.50 (ISBN 0-07-052945-0, C). McGraw.

Rithchie, W. K. Russia under Peter the Great. Reeves, Marjorie, ed. (Then & There Ser.). (Illus.). 96p. (Orig.). (gr. 7-12). 1979. pap. text ed. 3.10 (ISBN 0-582-22161-7). Longman.

Rithye, Indar J. The Sinai Blunder. 200p. 1978. 24.00x (ISBN 0-686-36949-1). Intl Peace.

Ritota, Michael C., jt. auth. see Mangiola, Stelio.

Ritson, Christopher. Agricultural Economics: Principles & Policy. LC 77-73600. 1977. 27.50 (ISBN 0-312-01460-0). St Martin.

--Agricultural Economics: Principles & Policy. 409p. 1982. pap. text ed. 14.95x (ISBN 0-86531-453-5). Westview.

Ritson, Joseph. Ancient Songs & Ballads, from the Reign of King Henry 2nd to the Revolution. LC 67-23930. 1968. Repr. of 1877 ed. 37.00x (ISBN 0-8103-3417-8). Gale.

Ritsos, Yannis. Erotica. Friar, Kimon, tr. from Gr. LC 82-17018. 80p. 1982. 13.50 (ISBN 0-937584-05-3); pap. 6.95 (ISBN 0-937584-06-1). Sachem Pr.

--The Fourth Dimension: Selected Poems of Yannis Ritsos. Dalven, Rae, tr. from Greek. LC 75-01463. 184p. 1977. 15.00x (ISBN 0-87923-181-5); pap. 6.95 o.p. (ISBN 0-87923-182-3). Godine.

--Selected Poems. Keeley, Edmund, tr. 1983. write for info (ISBN 0-88001-017-7). Ecco Pr.

--Subterranean Horses. Savvas, Minas, tr. from Greek. LC 80-83220. (International Poetry: Vol. 3). (Illus.). xii, 63p. 1980. 12.95x (ISBN 0-8214-0579-9, 82-83673); pap. 6.95 (ISBN 0-8214-0580-2, 82-83681). Ohio U Pr.

Ritter, Archibald R. The Economic Development of Revolutionary Cuba: Strategy & Performance. LC 73-3670. (Special Studies). (Illus.). 394p. 1974. 36.95 o.p. (ISBN 0-275-28727-0). Praeger.

Ritter, Archibald R. & Pollock, David H., eds. Latin American Prospects for the 1980's: Equity, Democratization & Development. 344p. 1983. 29.95 (ISBN 0-03-061363-9). Praeger.

Ritter, Betsy. Life in the Ghost City of Rhyolite, Nevada. (Illus.). 1982. 7.50 (ISBN 0-930704-12-6). Sagebrush Pr.

Ritter, Collett. Men of the Machine. (Illus.). 254p. 1977. 8.95 (ISBN 0-913428-28-0). Landfall Pr.

Ritter, David R. Consultation, Education & Prevention in Community Mental Health. (Illus.). 206p. 1982. 19.50x (ISBN 0-398-04717-0). C C Thomas.

Ritter, Dian, compiled by. Gingersnaps. LC 76-15809. 1976. boxed 5.50 (ISBN 0-8378-1747-1). Gibson.

--Spice of Life. LC 71-148612. (Illus.). 1971. boxed 5.50 (ISBN 0-8378-1788-9). Gibson.

Ritter, F. J. Chemical Ecology: Odour Communication in Animals. 1979. 71.00 (ISBN 0-444-80103-0). Elsevier.

Ritter, Gerhard. Frederick the Great: A Historical Profile. Paret, Peter, tr. & intro. by. 1968. 26.50x (ISBN 0-520-01074-4); pap. 5.95x (ISBN 0-520-02775-2). U of Cal Pr.

Ritter, Lawrence & Silber, William L. Money. rev., 3rd ed. LC 76-43483. 1977. 11.95 o.p. (ISBN 0-465-04714-9); pap. 4.95x o.p. (ISBN 0-465-04716-5). Basic.

Ritter, Lawrence S. & Honig, Donald. One Hundred Greatest Baseball Players of All Time. Thomas, Pamela, ed. 288p. 1981. 14.95 o.p. (ISBN 0-517-54300-1). Crown.

Ritter, Lawrence S. & Silber, William L. Principles of Money, Banking, & Financial Markets. 1983. text ed. 23.95x (ISBN 0-686-82533-0); write for info. (ISBN 0-465-06345-4); wkbk. 10.00. Basic.

Ritter, Margaret. The Burning Woman. LC 78-23850. 1979. 10.00 (ISBN 0-399-12310-5). Putnam Pub Group.

Ritter, Paul. Educreation: Education for Creation, Growth & Change. 2nd ed. 1979. text ed. 55.00 (ISBN 0-08-021475-4); pap. text ed. 26.00 (ISBN 0-08-021476-2). Pergamon.

Ritterband, P. Education, Employment & Migration. LC 76-62584. (American Sociological Association Rose Monographs). (Illus.). 1978. 24.95 (ISBN 0-521-21586-2); pap. 8.95x (ISBN 0-521-29192-5). Cambridge U Pr.

Ritterband, Paul. Modern Jewish Fertility. (Studies in Judaism in Modern Times: Vol. 1). 293p. 1981. text ed. 38.75x (ISBN 0-686-86102-7, Pub. by Brill Holland). Humanities.

Ritterbush, Philip. Overtures to Biology: Speculations of Eighteenth Century Naturalists. 1964. 49.50x (ISBN 0-685-69859-9). Elliots Bks.

Ritterbush, Philip C. The Built Environment: Ideas in Engineering for Human Adaptive Potential. (Illus.). 150p. (Orig.). 1983. pap. 27.00x (ISBN 0-942776-04-6). Inst Cult Prog.

--The Institutional Innovations Our Society Requires: A Recoconniassance Paper for the Academy for Contemporary Problems. 2nd ed. 148p. 1980. pap. 21.00 (ISBN 0-942776-00-3, Pub by I.C.P.). Pub Ctr Cult Res.

--The Propagation of Science Into Wider Culture. 139p. 1980. pap. 24.00 (ISBN 0-942776-02-X, Pub by I.C.P.). Pub Ctr Cult Res.

Ritterbush, Philip C., jt. ed. see Starr, Chauncey.

Rittereiser, Robert. Margin Regulations & Practices. 2nd ed. 1982-83. Repr. of 1973 ed. 25.00 (ISBN 0-13-557041-7). NY Inst Finance.

Ritter-Sanders, M. Handbook of Advanced Solid-State Troubleshooting. 1977. 19.95 (ISBN 0-87909-321-8). Reston.

Rittershausen, Brian & Rittershausen, Wilma. Orchids As Indoor Plants. (Illus.). 90p. 1983. pap. 7.95 (ISBN 0-7137-1303-8, Pub. by Blandford Pr England). Sterling.

Rittershausen, Wilma, jt. auth. see Rittershausen, Brian.

Ritti, Richard R., jt. auth. see Klein, Stuart M.

Rittlemeyer, Friedrich. Meditation: Guidance of the Inner Life. 1981. pap. 10.95 (ISBN 0-903540-45-2, Pub. by Floris Books). St George Bk Serv.

Rittman, A. & Rittman, L. Volcanoes. LC 76-6035. (Illus.). 1976. 12.95 o.p. (ISBN 0-399-11725-3). Putnam Pub Group.

Rittman, L., jt. auth. see Rittman, A.

Rittof, David J., jt. auth. see Baird, John E., Jr.

Ritums, John, ed. see Martin, Philip R.

Ritvo, Edward, jt. auth. see Conroy, Mary.

Ritz, David. The Man Who Brought the Dodgers Back to Brooklyn. 1981. 12.95 o.p. (ISBN 0-671-25356-5). S&S.

--Search for Happiness. 1980. 12.95 o.p. (ISBN 0-671-25233-X, 25233). S&S.

Ritzen, Martin, et al, eds. Biology of Normal Human Growth: Transactions of the First Karolinska Institute Nobel Conference. 350p. 1981. 42.50 (ISBN 0-686-77676-3). Raven.

Ritzer, George. Working: Conflict & Change. 2nd ed. (Illus.). 1977. text ed. 23.95 (ISBN 0-13-967638-4). P-H.

Ritzer, George & Trice, Harrison M. An Occupation in Conflict: A Study of the Personnel Manager. LC 76-627591. 140p. 1969. 5.00 (ISBN 0-87546-033-X). ILR Pr.

Ritzmann, Stephan E., ed. Pathology of Immunoglobulins: Diagnostic & Clinical Aspects. LC 82-18021. (Protein Abnormalities Ser.: Vol. 2). 396p. 1982. 38.00 (ISBN 0-8451-2801-9). A R Liss.

Ritzmann, Stephan E. & Daniels, Jerry C., eds. Serum Protein Abnormalities: Diagnostic & Clinical Aspects. LC 82-18001. 550p. 1982. 60.00 (ISBN 0-8451-2799-3). A R Liss.

Ritzmann, Stephen E., ed. Physiology of Immunoglobulins: Diagnostic & Clinical Aspects. LC 82-13101. (Protein Abornormalities Ser.: Vol. 1). 372p. 1982. 38.00 (ISBN 0-686-43002-6). A R Liss.

Riva, Anna. Candle Burning Magic. 96p. 1980. pap. 3.50 (ISBN 0-943832-06-3). Intl Imports.

--Devotions to the Saints. 112p. 1982. pap. 3.50 (ISBN 0-943832-08-X). Intl Imports.

--Golden Secrets of Mystic Oils. 64p. 1978. pap. 3.50 (ISBN 0-943832-05-5). Intl Imports.

--Modern Herbal Spellbook. (Illus.). 1974. pap. 3.00 (ISBN 0-943832-03-9). Intl Imports.

--Modern Witchcraft Spellbook. (Illus.). 64p. (Orig.). 1973. pap. 3.00 (ISBN 0-943832-02-0). Intl Imports.

--Secrets of Magical Seals. (Illus.). 64p. 1975. pap. 3.50 (ISBN 0-943832-04-7). Intl Imports.

--Voodoo Handbook of Cult Secrets. (Illus.). 48p. 1974. pap. 2.00 (ISBN 0-943832-01-2). Intl Imports.

Riva, Joseph P., Jr. World Petroleum Resources & Reserves. (Special Study). (Illus.). 250p. 1983. lib. bdg. 45.00 (ISBN 0-86531-446-2). Westview.

Rivas, Daniel, tr. see Milady Staff.

Rivas, Jose G., tr. see Routh, E. C.

Rivas, Jose G., tr. see Torrey, R. A.

Rive, Anna. Powers of the Psalms. 128p. (Orig.). 1982. pap. 3.95 (ISBN 0-943832-07-1). Intl Imports.

Rivello, Robert M. Theory & Analysis of Flight Structures. LC 68-25662. 1968. text ed. 40.50 (ISBN 0-07-052985-X, C). McGraw.

Rivenes, Richard, et al. Foundations of Physical Education. LC 77-75155. (Illus.). 1978. text ed. 19.95 (ISBN 0-395-25389-6). HM.

River, I. Night Rained Her. 1976. 5.00 (ISBN 0-686-15292-1). Merging Media.

River Oaks Garden Club, ed. Garden Book for Houston & the Gulf Coast. LC 75-5316. (Illus.). 191p. (Includes planting calendar). 1975. 10.95 (ISBN 0-88415-350-9). Pacesetter Pr.

Rivera, Carlos, tr. see Gurney, Nancy & Gurney, Eric.

Rivera, Evelyn, tr. see Garcia, Connie & Medina, Arthur.

Rivera, Feliciano, jt. ed. see Meier, Matt S.

Rivera, Francisco P. & Hurtado, Mario. Introduccion a la Literatura Espanola. (gr. 11-12). 1976. pap. text ed. 9.25 (ISBN 0-88345-437-8). Regents Pub.

Rivera, Jose E. The Vortex. James, E. K., tr. from Span. LC 75-44095. 1979. Repr. of 1935 ed. 19.50 (ISBN 0-685-64299-2). Fertig.

Rivera, Joseph De see De Rivera, Joseph.

Rivera, Joseph de see De Rivera, Joseph.

Rivera, Julius. Latin America: A Sociocultural Interpretation. rev. ed. LC 77-27271. 268p. 1980. pap. text ed. 9.95x (ISBN 0-8290-0444-0); pap. text ed. 8.95x (ISBN 0-686-96757-7). Irvington.

Rivero, Mariano E. & Von-Tschudi, John J. Peruvian Antiquities. Hawks, Francis L., tr. (The Americas Collection Ser.). (Illus.). 306p. 1982. pap. 24.95 (ISBN 0-936332-15-8). Falcon Hill Pr.

Riverol, Armando. The Action Reporter. Olsen, Roger E., ed. (ESL Teacher Reference-Resource Ser.). 1983. pap. write for info (ISBN 0-88084-003-X). Alemany pr.

Rivers, Caryl & Baruch, Grace. Beyond Sugar & Spice: How Women Grow, Learn, & Thrive. LC 79-12516. 1979. 10.95 (ISBN 0-399-12164-1). Putnam Pub Group.

Rivers, Elias L., tr. see Zaldivar, Gladys.

Rivers, Francine. Kathleen. 1979. pap. 2.25 o.s.i. (ISBN 0-515-04726-0). Jove Pubns.

--Sycamore Hill. 288p. (Orig.). 1981. pap. 2.75 o.p. (ISBN 0-523-41324-6). Pinnacle Bks.

--This Golden Valley. 416p. 1983. pap. text ed. 3.50 (ISBN 0-515-06823-3). Jove Pubns.

Rivers, Gayle & Hudson, James. The Teheran Contract. LC 80-1850. (Illus.). 1981. 12.95 (ISBN 0-385-17200-1). Doubleday.

Rivers, Isabel, ed. Books & their Readers in Eighteenth-Century England. LC 82-7317. 1982. 30.00x (ISBN 0-312-09248-2). St Martin.

Rivers, J. W. Proud & On My Feet: Poems by J. W. Rivers. (Contemporary Poetry Ser.). 96p. 1983. 8.95x (ISBN 0-8203-0632-0); pap. 4.95x (ISBN 0-8203-0633-9). U of Ga Pr.

Rivers, Joan. A Funny Thing Happened to Me While I Was in Las Vegas. (Illus.). 14.95 (ISBN 0-685-79810-0, G&D); pap. 6.95 (ISBN 0-448-12855-1, G&D). Putnam Pub Group.

Rivers, Kay M. Jill Wins a Friend. LC 76-16021. (Early Sports Ser.). (Illus.). (gr. 1-3). 1976. PLB 5.95 (ISBN 0-913778-59-1); pap. 2.75 (ISBN 0-89565-123-8). Childs World.

Rivers, Kendall. Master of Hearts. (Adventures in Love Ser.: No. 33). 1982. pap. 1.95 (ISBN 0-451-11840-5, AJ1840, Sig). NAL.

Rivers, Larry & Brightman, Carol. Larry Rivers: Drawings & Digressions. (Illus.). 1979. 35.00 (ISBN 0-517-53430-4, C N Potter Bks). Crown.

Rivers, W. H. Instinct & the Unconscious: A Contribution to a Biological Theory of the Psycho-Neuroses. 252p. 1982. Repr. of 1920 ed. lib. bdg. 50.00 (ISBN 0-89984-849-4). Century Bookbindery.

Rivers, Wilga. A Practical Guide to the Teaching of French. 1975. pap. text ed. 9.95x (ISBN 0-19-501911-3). Oxford U Pr.

Rivers, Wilga, et al. A Practical Guide to the Teaching of German. 1975. pap. text ed. 9.95x (ISBN 0-19-501910-5). Oxford U Pr.

Rivers, Wilga M. Psychologist & the Foreign-Language Teacher. 1964. 12.00x o.s.i. (ISBN 0-226-72095-0). U of Chicago Pr.

Rivers, Wilga M. & Temperley, Mary S. A Practical Guide to the Teaching of English: As a Second or Foreign Language. 1977. pap. 9.50x (ISBN 0-19-502210-6). Oxford U Pr.

Rivers, William, jt. ed. see Brenner, Daniel.

Rivers, William E. Business Reports: Samples from the "Real World". (Illus.). 272p. 1981. pap. 11.95 (ISBN 0-13-107656-6). P-H.

Rivers, William H. History of Melanesian Society, 2 Vols. (Illus.). 1968. Repr. of 1914 ed. Set. text ed. 38.50x o.p. (ISBN 90-62340-56-3). Humanities.

Rivers, William L. Writing: Craft & Art. 256p. 1975. pap. text ed. 9.95 (ISBN 0-13-970202-4). P-H.

Rivers, William L. & Schramm, Wilbur. Responsibility in Mass Communication. 3rd ed. LC 68-28216. 1969. 15.34i (ISBN 0-06-013594-8, HarpT); pap. 6.01i (ISBN 0-06-090832-7, CN-832). Har-Row.

Rivers, William R., jt. auth. see Sellers, Leonard.

Rives, Margaret R. Blue Ridge Parkway. LC 82-82578. (The Story Behind the Scenery Ser.). (Illus.). 48p. (Orig.). 1982. 7.95 (ISBN 0-916122-82-4); pap. 3.00 (ISBN 0-916122-81-6). KC Pubns.

Rivett, Patrick. Model Building for Decision Analysis. LC 79-40739. 1980. 29.95 (ISBN 0-471-27654-5, Pub. by Wiley-Interscience). Wiley.

Rivett, Patrick, jt. auth. see Ackoff, R. L.

Riviere, Bill. The Gunner's Bible. rev ed. LC 73-77415. 192p. 1973. pap. 4.95 (ISBN 0-385-02423-1). Doubleday.

Riviere, Joan, tr. see Freud, Sigmund.

Riviere, Marie-Claude. Pin Pictures with Wire & Thread. Egan, E. W., tr. from Fr. LC 75-14521. (Little Craft Book Ser.). (Illus.). 48p. 1975. 6.95 (ISBN 0-8069-5340-3); PLB 8.99 (ISBN 0-8069-5341-1). Sterling.

Riviere, William & L. L. Bean Staff. The L. L. Bean Guide to the Outdoors. LC 81-6009. (Illus.). 384p. 1981. 15.50 (ISBN 0-394-51928-0). Random.

Rivin, Zelma, jt. auth. see Clark, Anne.

Rivise, Charles W. & Caesar, A. D. Interference Law & Practice with Forms, 4 Vols. 1940. 75.00 o.p. (ISBN 0-87215-111-5). Michie-Bobbs.

Rivkin, Robert S. The Rights of Servicemen. (ACLU Handbook Ser). (Orig.). 1972. pap. 1.50 o.p. (ISBN 0-380-01526-9, 33365, Discus). Avon.

Rivkin, Robert S. & Stichman, Barton F. The Rights of Military Personnel. 1977. pap. 1.50 o.p. (ISBN 0-380-01668-0, 33365, Discus). Avon.

Rivkin, S. Technology Unbound. 1969. 12.25 o.p. (ISBN 0-08-006424-8); pap. 6.25 o.p. (ISBN 0-08-006391-8). Pergamon.

Rivkin, Steven R. A New Guide to Federal Cable Television Regulation. LC 77-28389. 1978. text ed. 35.00x (ISBN 0-262-18089-8). MIT Pr.

Rivlin, Alice M. Systematic Thinking for Social Action. LC 74-161600. 1971. 14.95 (ISBN 0-8157-7478-8); pap. 5.95 (ISBN 0-8157-7477-X). Brookings.

Rivlin, Alice M. & Timpane, P. Michael, eds. Ethical & Legal Issues of Social Experimentation. (Studies in Social Experimentation). 180p. 1975. 15.95 (ISBN 0-8157-7482-6); pap. 6.95 (ISBN 0-8157-7481-8). Brookings.

--Planned Variation in Education: Should We Give up or Try Harder? (Studies in Social Experimentation). 184p. 1975. 12.95 (ISBN 0-8157-7480-X); pap. 5.95 (ISBN 0-8157-7479-6). Brookings.

Rivlin, Theodore J. The Chebyshev Polynomials. LC 74-10876. (Pure & Applied Mathematics Ser). 192p. 1974. 34.95 (ISBN 0-471-72470-X, Pub. by Wiley-Interscience). Wiley.

Rix, Alan G. Japan's Economic Aid: Policy-Making & Politics. 1980. 32.50 (ISBN 0-312-44063-4). St Martin.

Rix, David, jt. tr. see King, Donald.

Rizer, Arden, Jr. Catalogue of Numbers. LC 74-3486. 120p. 1981. pap. text ed. 7.50 (ISBN 0-941762-04-1). Psychic Forum.

Rizvi, S. F. Multivariate Control System Design in the Presence of Interaction. 1978. 1981. 50.00x (ISBN 0-686-97119-1, Pub. by W Spring England). State Mutual Bk.

Rizzi, Joseph N. Joe's War: The Memoirs of a Doughboy. Baumgartner, Richard A., ed. & intro. by. (Illus.). 170p. 1983. 11.95 (ISBN 0-9604770-1-2). Der Angriff.

Rizzi, Luigi. Issues in Italian Syntax. 240p. 1981. 36.00x (ISBN 0-686-32121-9); pap. 21.00x (ISBN 0-686-32122-7). Foris Pubns.

Rizzo, Joseph V., jt. auth. see Suran, Bernard G.

Rizzo, Mario J., ed. Time, Uncertainty & Disequilibrium: Exploration of Austrian Themes. LC 78-13872. 256p. 1979. 23.95x (ISBN 0-669-02698-0). Lexington Bks.

Rizzo, N. D., jt. ed. see Gray, W.

Rizzo, Tania, jt. ed. see Kuhner, David.

Rizzoli, Hugo V., jt. auth. see Horwitz, Norman H.

Rizzoli, P. M., jt. ed. see Osborne, A. R.

Rizzuto, Jim. Modern Hawaiian Gamefishing. LC 76-58414. (Orig.). 1977. pap. 8.50 (ISBN 0-8248-0481-3). UH Pr.

Rjndt, Philippe Van see Van Rjndt, Philippe.

Roa, Annia. Peter Pelican-Pedro Pelicano. LC 64-22715. (Illus., Sp. & Eng.). (gr. k-4). 1974. 4.95 (ISBN 0-87208-006-4). Island Pr.

Roach, A. S. The Theory of Random Clumping. 94p. 1968. text ed. 5.95x o.p. (ISBN 0-416-42790-1, Pub. by Chapman & Hall England). Methuen Inc.

Roach, Don & Loddy, Edmund J., Jr. Basic College Chemistry. 1979. text ed. 25.00 (ISBN 0-07-052987-6); instructor's manual 19.95 (ISBN 0-07-052988-4); lab manual 13.95 (ISBN 0-07-052991-4); study guide 10.95 (ISBN 0-07-052990-6). McGraw.

Roach, Donald, ed. Music for Children's Choirs: A Selective Graded Listing. 44p. 1977. 3.50 (ISBN 0-940796-08-2, 1024). Music Ed.

Roach, G. F., tr. see Jorgens, K.

Roach, Hildred. Black American Music: Past & Present. 208p. 1983. Repr. of 1973 ed. text ed. price not set (ISBN 0-89874-610-8). Krieger.

Roach, John. Public Examinations in England, 1850-1900. LC 71-123668. (Cambridge Texts & Studies in the History of Education). 1971. 39.95 (ISBN 0-521-07931-4). Cambridge U Pr.

--Social Reform in England Seventeen Eighty to Eighteen Eighty. LC 78-6384. 1978. 26.00x (ISBN 0-312-73481-6). St Martin.

Roach, Penelope. Political Socialization in the New Nations of Africa. LC 66-24873. (Orig.). 1967. pap. text ed. 3.50x (ISBN 0-8077-2042-9). Tchrs Coll.

Roach, Peter. The Eight Fifteen to War: The Memories of a Desert Rat. (Illus.). 156p. 1982. 22.50 (ISBN 0-436-41700-6, Pub. by Secker & Warburg). David & Charles.

Roach, William, ed. Continuations of the Old French Perceval of Chretien De Troyes, 4 vols. Incl. Vol. 1. The First Continuation: Redaction of Manuscripts T V D. 1949. 7.50 (ISBN 0-87169-999-0); Vol. 2. The First Continuation: Redaction of Manuscripts E M Q U. Ivy, Robert H., Jr., ed. 1950. 7.50 (ISBN 0-87169-998-2); Vol. 3, Pt. 1. The First Continuation: Redaction of Manuscripts A L P R S. 1952. 7.50 (ISBN 0-87169-997-4); Vol. 3 Pt. 2. The First Continuation: Glossary to Vols. 1-3. Foulet, Lucien, ed. 1955. 5.00 (ISBN 0-87169-996-6); Vol. 4. The Second Continuation. 1971. 10.00 (ISBN 0-87169-995-8); The Third Continuation. 1983. 40.00 (ISBN 0-87169-994-X). Am Philos.

Roache, Patrick J. Computational Fluid Dynamics. rev. ed. 1982. 22.50 (ISBN 0-913478-05-9). Hermosa.

Roache-Selk, Evelyn. From the Womb of Earth: An Appreciation of Yoruba Bronze Art. LC 78-56919. (Illus.). 1978. pap. text ed. 7.00 (ISBN 0-8191-0521-X). U Pr of Amer.

Roadarmel, Gordon, ed. & tr. Death in Delhi: Modern Hindi Short Stories. LC 74-187871. 1973. 18.95x (ISBN 0-520-02220-3). U of Cal Pr.

Roaf, John, jt. auth. see Kalman, Harold.

Roald, Albert & Harry, Hahnewald, eds. Dictionary of Medical Technology: English, German, Spanish, French, Russian, Polish, Hungarian, Czechoslovakian, Technik-Woerterbuch. 1978. 81.00x (ISBN 0-8002-0410-7). Intl Pubns Serv.

Roalson, Louise, ed. Notably Norwegian: Recipes, Festivals, Folk Arts. LC 82-81569. (Illus.). 88p. 1982. pap. 5.95 (ISBN 0-941016-05-6). Penfield.

Roark, James L. Masters Without Slaves. 1977. 12.95 o.p. (ISBN 0-393-05562-0); pap. 5.95x (ISBN 0-393-00901-7). Norton.

Roark, Raymond J. & Young, Warren C. Formulas for Stress & Strain. 5th ed. (Illus.). 512p. 1976. 39.00 (ISBN 0-07-053031-9, P&RB). McGraw.

Roath, S., ed. Topical Reviews in Haematology, Vol. 2. (Illus.). 240p. 1982. text ed. 32.50 (ISBN 0-7236-0615-3). Wright-PSG.

Rob, ed. see Ballantyne, J.

Rob, ed. see Dudley, H.

Rob, C., ed. Vascular Surgery. 3rd ed. (Operative Surgery Ser.). 1976. 99.95 (ISBN 0-407-00644-3). Butterworth.

Rob, Charles, ed. see London, P. S.

Rob, Charles, ed. see Symon, Lindsay.

Roback, A. A. A Bibliography of Character & Personality. 340p. 1982. Repr. of 1927 ed. lib. bdg. 85.00 (ISBN 0-89984-847-8). Century Bookbindery.

Roback, Abraham A. History of Psychology & Psychiatry. Repr. of 1961 ed. lib. bdg. 19.75x (ISBN 0-8371-2104-3, ROHP). Greenwood.

Robana, A., jt. auth. see Gitman, L. J.

Robards, Terry. The New York Times Book of Wine. 480p. 1977. pap. 7.95 (ISBN 0-380-01720-2, 60467). Avon.

Robarts, Edward. The Marquesan Journal of Edward Robarts: 1797-1824. Dening, Greg, ed. (Pacific History Ser.: No. 6). 350p. 1974. text ed. 15.00x (ISBN 0-8248-0297-7). UH Pr.

Robb. Fundamentals of Evidence & Argument. new ed. Applbaum, Ronald & Hart, Roderick, eds. (MODCOM Modules in Speech Communication Ser.). 1976. pap. text ed. 2.75 (ISBN 0-574-22517-X, 13-5517). SRA.

--Lifestyle: The Autobiography of Robb. (Illus.). 1979. 19.95 o.p. (ISBN 0-241-10169-7, Pub. by Hamish Hamilton England). David & Charles.

Robb, Allan P., jt. ed. see McElrath, Joseph R., Jr.

Robb, D. A. & Pierpoint, S. Metals & micronutrients: Uptake & Utilization by Plants. write for info. (ISBN 0-12-589580-1). Acad Pr.

Robb, David M., ed. see Kimbell Art Museum.

Robb, George P., jt. auth. see Kooker, Earl W.

Robb, George P., et al. Assessment of Individual Mental Ability. LC 73-177298. 354p. 1972. text ed. 19.95 scp (ISBN 0-7002-2357-6, HarpC). Har-Row.

Robb, James H. Man As Infinite Spirit. (Aquinas Lecture). 1974. 7.95 (ISBN 0-87462-139-9). Marquette.

Robb, Joan. School Certificate Biology. 14.50x (ISBN 0-392-08362-0, ABC). Sportshelf.

Robb, John S. Streaks of Squatter Life & Far-West Scenes. LC 62-7018. 1978. Repr. of 1847 ed. 30.00x (ISBN 0-8201-1038-8). Schol Facsimiles.

Robb, Louis. Dictionary of Modern Business. (Span. - Eng. & Eng. -Span.). 1960. 30.00 (ISBN 0-910136-00-9). Anderson Kramer.

Robb, Louis A. Dictionary of Legal Terms, Spanish-English & English-Spanish. 1955. 25.00 (ISBN 0-471-72534-X, Pub. by Wiley-Interscience). Wiley.

--Engineers' Dictionary, Spanish-English, English-Spanish. 2nd ed. 1949. 47.50 (ISBN 0-471-72501-3, Pub. by Wiley-Interscience). Wiley.

Robb, Margaret D. Dynamics of Motor-Skill Acquisition. (Illus.). 192p. 1972. pap. text ed. 11.95 (ISBN 0-13-222059-8). P-H.

Robb, William, jt. auth. see Hamilton, Douglas M.

Robbe-Grillet, Alain. The Erasers. Howard, Richard, tr. from Fr. 1964. pap. 9.95 (ISBN 0-394-17118-7, E691, Ever). Grove.

--Snapshots. Morissette, Bruce, tr. pap. 2.95 o.s.i. (ISBN 0-394-17784-3, E435, Ever). Grove.

Robbert, G. S. Luther as Interpreter of Scripture. LC 12-2960. 1982. pap. 8.95 (ISBN 0-570-03867-7). Concordia.

Robbie, Dorothy. Ribbon with Gold. (Lost Play Ser.). pap. 1.25x (ISBN 0-912262-41-9). Proscenium.

Robbin, Edward, ed. Thursday's Child, No. 3. 200p. (Orig.). 1982. pap. 4.95x (ISBN 0-9603518-3-3). Glen Pr.

Robbin, Irving. Basic Inventions. (How & Why Wonder Books Ser.). (gr. 4-6). deluxe ed. 1.95 o.p. (ISBN 0-448-04058-1, G&D). Putnam Pub Group.

--Explorations & Discoveries. (How & Why Wonder Books Ser.). (gr. 4-6). deluxe ed. 1.95 o.p. (ISBN 0-448-04019-0, G&D). Putnam Pub Group.

Robbins, jt. auth. see Nordoff.

Robbins, jt. auth. see Sackheim.

Robbins, Alan S., et al. Geriatric Medicine: An Education Resource Guide. 448p. 1981. prof ref 37.50x (ISBN 0-88410-728-0). Ballinger Pub.

Robbins, Allan. Sixty-Eight Zero Nine Microcomputer Design Guide. 750p. (Orig.). Date not set. pap. 19.95 o.p. (ISBN 0-931988-52-7). Osborne-McGraw.

Robbins, Arthur, jt. auth. see Mayle, Peter.

Robbins, Arthur, et al. Expressive Therapy: A Creative Arts Approach to Depth-Oriented Treatment. LC 80-13005. 319p. 1980. text ed. 29.95 (ISBN 0-87705-101-1). Human Sci Pr.

Robbins, Carol T. & Wolff, Herbert. The Very Best: Ice Cream & Where to Find It. LC 82-91069. (Illus.). 252p. (Orig.). 1982. pap. 8.95 (ISBN 0-911729-00-3). Very Best.

Robbins, Chandler, et al. Birds of North America: A Guide to Field Identification. (Golden Field Guide Ser). (Illus.). (gr. 7 up). 1966. 9.95 (ISBN 0-307-47002-4, Golden Pr); PLB 13.08 (ISBN 0-307-63656-9); pap. 6.95 (ISBN 0-307-13656-6). Western Pub.

Robbins, Charles. Harry Truman: Last of His Kind, an Informal Portrait. (Illus.). 1979. 14.95 (ISBN 0-688-03447-0). Morrow.

Robbins, Charles T., ed. Wildlife Feeding & Nutrition. LC 82-13720. Date not set. price not set (ISBN 0-12-589380-9). Acad Pr.

Robbins, Christopher. Air America. LC 78-9861. 1979. 10.95 o.p. (ISBN 0-399-12207-9). Putnam Pub Group.

Robbins, Claude L. & Hunter, Kerri C. Daylighting Availability Data for Selected Cities in the United States. (Progress in Solar Energy Ser.: Suppl.). 275p. 1983. pap. text ed. 21.00 (ISBN 0-89553-140-2). Am Solar Energy.

--Hourly Availability of Sunlight in the United States. 150p. 1983. pap. text ed. 13.50 (ISBN 0-89553-141-0). Am Solar Energy.

--A Method for Predicting Energy Savings Attributed to Daylighting. (Progress in Solar Energy Ser.: Suppl.). 225p. 1983. pap. text ed. 18.00 (ISBN 0-89553-139-9). Am Solar Energy.

Robbins, Clive, jt. auth. see Nordoff, Paul.

Robbins, Clive E., jt. auth. see Nordoff, Paul.

Robbins, Daniel. Edward Koren: Prints & Drawings, 1959-1981. Littlefield, Thomson, ed. (Illus.). 56p. (Orig.). 1982. pap. 10.00x (ISBN 0-910763-00-3). SUNY Albany U Art.

Robbins, Daniel & Bourdon, David. Raid the Icebox with Andy Warhol. (Illus.). 104p. 1970. pap. 4.00 o.p. (ISBN 0-913456-94-2). Interbk Inc.

Robbins, David, jt. auth. see Brown, Richard.

Robbins, David & Caldwell, Lesley, eds. Rethinking Social Inequality. 263p. 1982. text ed. 36.50x (ISBN 0-566-00557-3). Gower Pub Ltd.

Robbins, Dick L., jt. ed. see Gershwin, M. Eric.

Robbins, Edwin. Psychiatric Technician's Handbook. (Allied Health Professions Monograph). 1983. 16.00 (ISBN 0-87527-285-1). Green.

Robbins, Frank. Under the Starry Plough: Recollections of the Irish Citizen Army. (Illus.). 251p. (Orig.). 1977. pap. text ed. 5.95x o.p. (ISBN 0-906187-00-1, Pub. by Acad Pr Ireland). Facsimile Bk.

Robbins, Frank E. Defense of Prior Invention Patent Infringement Litigation. LC 77-84298. 1977. 20.00 (ISBN 0-685-86093-0, G1-0645). PLI.

--Quiotepec Chinantec Grammar. 150p. 1968. pap. 1.50x (ISBN 0-88312-799-7); microfiche 2.25 (ISBN 0-88312-492-0). Summer Inst Ling.

Robbins, Franklyn A., jt. auth. see Mancini, Janet K.

Robbins, Harold. Goodbye, Janette. 1981. 14.95 o.p. (ISBN 0-671-22593-6). S&S.

--Spellbinder. 320p. 1982. 14.50 (ISBN 0-671-41634-0). S&S.

Robbins, Harry W., tr. see De Lorris, Guillaume & De Meun, Jean.

Robbins, Herbert & Van Ryzin, John. Introduction to Statistics. LC 75-1005. (Illus.). 416p. 1975. text ed. 22.95 (ISBN 0-574-18132-6, 13-2200); solutions manual 3.25 (ISBN 0-574-18133-4, 13-2201). SRA.

Robbins, Herbert, jt. auth. see Courant, Richard.

Robbins, Ira P. Comparative Post-Conviction Remedies. LC 79-4751. 128p. 1980. 16.95x (ISBN 0-669-03023-6). Lexington Bks.

--Prisoners' Rights Sourcebook, II, Vol. 2. 1980. cancelled (ISBN 0-87632-111-2). Boardman.

Robbins, J. Albert, ed. American Literary Scholarship, 1980. LC 65-1950. 592p. 1982. 37.75 (ISBN 0-8223-0464-3). Duke.

Robbins, Jack A., ed. The Complete Poetry of John Reed. LC 82-21915. 102p. (Orig.). 1983. lib. bdg. 16.75 (ISBN 0-8191-2931-3); pap. text ed. 6.75 (ISBN 0-8191-2932-1). U Pr of Amer.

Robbins, James G. & Jones, Barbara S. Effective Communication for Today's Manager. LC 74-79216. (Illus.). 240p. 1974. 15.95 (ISBN 0-86730-512-6). Lebhar Friedman.

Robbins, Jane. Citizen Participation & Public Library Policy. LC 74-34248. 191p. 1975. 11.00 o.p. (ISBN 0-8108-0796-3). Scarecrow.

Robbins, Jhan. Anatomy of a Prostitute. 1974. pap. 1.50 o.p. (ISBN 0-451-06028-8, W6028, Sig). NAL.

--Bess & Harry. 1980. 10.95 (ISBN 0-399-12443-8). Putnam Pub Group.

--Front Page Marriage: Helen Hayes & Charles MacArthur. (Illus.). 224p. 1982. 12.95 (ISBN 0-399-12691-0). Putnam Pub Group.

Robbins, Johnny. You Can Be A Country Music Songwriter. (Illus.). 84p. 1982. pap. 4.95 (ISBN 0-9609748-0-6). Green Block.

Robbins, Kay. Return Engagement, No. 73. 1982. pap. 1.75 (ISBN 0-515-06684-2). Jove Pubns.

--Taken by Storm. (Second Chance at Love Ser.: No. 110). pap. 1.75 (ISBN 0-515-06874-8). Jove Pubns.

Robbins, Keith. The Eclipse of a Great Power: Modern Britain 1870-1975. LC 81-18608. (Illus.). 304p. 1983. text ed. 33.00x (ISBN 0-582-48971-7); pap. text ed. 14.95x (ISBN 0-582-48972-5). Longman.

Robbins, Keith, ed. Religion & Humanism: Papers Read at the Eighteenth Summer Meeting & the Nineteenth Winter Meeting of the Ecclesiastical History Society. (Studies in Church History: Vol. 17). (Illus.). 378p. 1981. 36.00x (ISBN 0-631-19270-0, Pub. by Basil Blackwell). Biblio Dist.

Robbins, Kenneth. A Good & Dandy World. 1980. pap. 1.50 (ISBN 0-686-38380-X). Eldridge Pub.

Robbins, Lionel C. Essay on the Nature & Significance of Economic Science. 2nd ed. 1969. 17.95 o.p. (ISBN 0-312-26320-1). St Martin.

Robbins, Maria P., ed. The Cook's Quotation Book. 88p. 1983. 8.95 (ISBN 0-916366-19-7). Pushcart Pr.

Robbins, Martin. Reply to the Headlines: Poems 1965-1970. LC 73-115028. 70p. 1970. 6.00 o.p. (ISBN 0-8040-0260-6). Swallow.

Robbins, Martin D., et al. Who Runs the Computer? Strategies for the Management of Computers in Higher Education. LC 75-19416. 102p. 1975. lib. bdg. 19.75 o.p. (ISBN 0-89158-000-X). Westview.

Robbins, Maurice & Irving, Mary B. The Amateur Archaeologist's Handbook. 3rd ed. LC 80-7901. (Illus.). 304p. 13.41i (ISBN 0-690-01976-9, HarpT). Har-Row.

Robbins, Naomi, jt. auth. see Herstein, Sheila.

Robbins, Paul. Medieval Romance. 1983. pap. 4.95 (ISBN 0-8283-1881-6). Branden.

Robbins, Paul R. Marijuana: A Short Course Updated for the Eighties. LC 75-22753. 80p. 1983. pap. 4.95 (ISBN 0-8283-1856-5). Branden.

Robbins, Ralph, jt. auth. see Jefferys, William H.

Robbins, Roland W. Pilgrim John Alden's Progress: Archaeological Excavations in Duxbury. 1969. 2.00 (ISBN 0-686-38916-6). Pilgrim Hall.

Robbins, Rossell H. Encyclopedia of Witchcraft & Demonology. (Illus.). 1959. 12.95 o.p. (ISBN 0-517-00053-9). Crown.

Robbins, Roy M. Our Landed Heritage: The Public Domain, 1776-1970. 2nd rev. ed. LC 75-3569. (Illus.). xii, 503p. (A Bicentennial Edition). 1976. pap. 5.95x o.p. (ISBN 0-8032-5803-8, BB 588, Bison). U of Nebr Pr.

Robbins, Sidney M. Securities Market. LC 66-15499. 1966. 12.95 (ISBN 0-02-926570-3). Free Pr.

Robbins, Stanley L. & Angell, Marcia. Basic Pathology. 2nd ed. LC 75-19853. (Illus.). 800p. 1976. text ed. 21.95 o.p. (ISBN 0-7216-7599-9). Saunders.

Robbins, Stanley L., et al. Basic Pathology. 3rd ed. LC 80-54854. (Illus.). 694p. text ed. 29.50 (ISBN 0-7216-7600-6). Saunders.

Robbins, Stephen P. The Administrative Process. 2nd ed. (Illus.). 1980. text ed. 23.95 (ISBN 0-13-007385-7); study guide 9.95 (ISBN 0-13-007369-5). P-H.

--Organization Theory: The Structure & Design of Organizations. (Illus.). 432p. 1983. text ed. 23.95 (ISBN 0-13-641910-0). P-H.

--Organizational Behavior: Concepts, Controversies & Applications. 2nd ed. (Illus.). 608p. 1983. 22.95 (ISBN 0-686-92017-1). P-H.

--Personnel: The Management of Human Resources. LC 77-23046. (Illus.). 1978. text ed. 23.95 (ISBN 0-13-657833-0). P-H.

Robbins, William G. Lumberjacks & Legislators: Political Economy of the U.S. Lumber Industry, 1890-1941. LC 81-48375. (Environmental History Ser.: No. 5). (Illus.). 284p. 1982. 22.50x (ISBN 0-89096-129-8). Tex A&M Univ Pr.

Robbins, William J., et al. Growth. 1928. 39.50x (ISBN 0-685-89755-9). Elliots Bks.

Robboy, Howard, et al, eds. Social Interaction: Introductory Readings in Sociology. LC 78-65244. 1979. 18.95 o.p. (ISBN 0-312-73296-1); pap. text ed. 9.95 (ISBN 0-312-73297-X); instr's. manual avail. (ISBN 0-312-73298-8). St Martin.

Robe, Lucy B. Just So It's Healthy: Drinking & Drugs Can Harm Your Unborn Baby. rev. ed. LC 77-87742. 1982. pap. 6.95 (ISBN 0-89638-062-9). CompCare.

Robe, Stanley L. Azuela & the Mexican Underdogs. LC 76-20031. 1979. 28.50x (ISBN 0-520-03293-4). U of Cal Pr.

Robe, Stanley L., ed. Hispanic Legends from New Mexico: Narratives from the R. D. Jameson Collection. (U. C. Publications in Folkore & Mythology Studies: Vol. 31). pap. 30.00x o.s.i. (ISBN 0-520-09614-2). U of Cal Pr.

Robeck, Bruce W. Legislators & Party Loyalty: The Impact of Reapportionment in California. LC 77-18634. 1978. pap. text ed. 8.25 (ISBN 0-8191-0424-8). U Pr of Amer.

Robeck, Mildred C. & Wilson, John A. Psychology of Reading: Foundations of Instruction. LC 73-13797. 600p. 1974. text ed. 29.95x (ISBN 0-471-72580-3). Wiley.

Robeck, Nesta De see De Robeck, Nesta.

Roberg, Roy R. Police Management & Organizational Behavior: A Contingency Approach. (Criminal Justice Ser.). (Illus.). 1979. text ed. 22.50 (ISBN 0-8299-0275-9); instrs.' manual avail. (ISBN 0-8299-0599-5). West Pub.

Roberg, Roy R. & Webb, Vincent J. Critical Issues in Corrections: Problems, Trends, & Prospects. 390p. 1981. pap. text ed. 17.50 (ISBN 0-8299-0405-0). West Pub.

Roberg, Roy R., ed. The Changing Police Role: New Dimensions & New Issues. LC 75-41541. (Administration of Justice Ser.: Vol. 3). 308p. 1976. pap. text ed. 8.95 (ISBN 0-914526-03-0). Justice Sys.

Roberge, James K. Operational Amplifiers: Theory & Practice. LC 75-2309. 656p. 1975. text ed. 38.50x (ISBN 0-471-72585-4). Wiley.

Roberge, James K., jt. auth. see Wedlock, Bruce D.

Roberson, E. C. Atomic Energy. 12.75x (ISBN 0-392-07602-0, SpS). Sportshelf.

Roberson, G. Gale, jt. auth. see Hodes, Barnet.

Roberson, G. Gale, jt. auth. see Smith, Len Y.

Roberson, James O., jt. auth. see Browning, Jon E.

Roberson, John A. & Crowe, Clayton T. Engineering Fluid Mechanics. 2nd ed. LC 79-87855. (Illus.). 1980. text ed. 32.95 (ISBN 0-395-28357-4); solutions manual 7.50 (ISBN 0-395-28358-2). HM.

Roberson, William H. Louis Simpson: A Reference Guide. 1980. lib. bdg. 20.00 (ISBN 0-8161-8494-1, Hall Reference). G K Hall.

Robert. Robert & Signorelly. French-Italian. 3008p. (Fr. & Ital.). 1981. 75.00 (ISBN 0-686-97412-3, M-9403). French & Eur.

Robert Bentley, Inc. Toyota Celica Service Manual: 1978-1983. (Illus.). 576p. (Orig.). 1983. pap. 21.95 (ISBN 0-8376-0255-6). Bentley.

--Toyota Corolla Tercel Service Manual 1980-1983. 3rd, rev. ed. (Illus.). 485p. (Orig.). 1983. pap. 21.95 (ISBN 0-8376-0348-X). Bentley.

--Toyota Corolla 1600 Service Manual, 1975, 1976, 1977, 1978, 1979. LC 79-53189. (Illus.). 1979. pap. 21.95 (ISBN 0-8376-0242-4). Bentley.

--Toyota Pickup Truck Service Manual, 1978-1982. (Illus.). 480p. (Orig.). 1982. pap. 21.95 (ISBN 0-8376-0251-3). Bentley.

--Volkswagen Dasher Service Manual, 1974-1981, Including Diesel. rev. ed. LC 81-66944. (Illus.). 692p. (Orig.). 1981. pap. 24.95 (ISBN 0-8376-0083-9). Bentley.

--Volkswagen Rabbit-Jetta Diesel Service Manual: 1977-83 Including Pickup Truck & Turbo-Diesel. 4th, rev. ed. LC 82-74510. (Illus.). 600p. (Orig.). 1983. pap. 21.95 (ISBN 0-8376-0109-6). Bentley.

--Volkswagen Rabbit-Scirocco-Jetta Service Manual: 1980-83 Gasoline Models Including Pickup Truck & Convertible. 4th, rev. ed. LC 82-74511. (Illus.). 600p. (Orig.). 1983. pap. 21.95 (ISBN 0-8376-0113-4). Bentley.

--Volkswagen Rabbit-Scirocco Service Manual, Gasoline Models, 1975, 1976, 1977, 1978, 1979. rev. ed. LC 79-57170. (Illus.). 628p. (Orig.). 1980. pap. 21.95 (ISBN 0-8376-0098-7). Bentley.

Robert, Henry M. Parliamentary Law: Bicentennial Edition. LC 75-9940. 590p. 1975. 14.95x o.p. (ISBN 0-470-72592-3). Halsted Pr.

--Robert's Rules of Order. Vixman, Rachel, ed. (YA) (gr. 9-12). 1982. pap. 2.75 (ISBN 0-515-06648-6). Jove Pubns.

Robert Lang Adams & Associates. The Metropolitan Washington Job Bank including Baltimore & Northern Virginia: A Comprehensive Guide to Major Employers Throughout the Greater D. C.-Baltimore Area. (Job Bank Ser.). 300p. 1982. pap. 9.95 (ISBN 0-937860-10-7). Adams Inc MA.

--The New England Job Bank. (Job Bank Ser.). 300p. 1982. pap. cancelled o.p. (ISBN 0-937860-11-5). Adams Inc MA.

--The Northern California Job Bank: A Comprehensive Guide to Major Employers Throughout North California. (Job Bank Ser.). 300p. 1982. pap. 9.95 (ISBN 0-937860-12-3). Adams Inc MA.

--The Pennsylvania Job Bank: A Comprehensive Guide to Major Employers Throughout Pennsylvania. (Job Bank Ser.). 300p. 1983. pap. 9.95 (ISBN 0-937860-09-3). Adams Inc MA.

--The Southwest Job Bank: A Comprehensive Guide to Major Employers Throughout Colorado, Arizona, New Mexico & Utah. (Job Bank Ser.). 300p. 1983. pap. 9.95 o.p. (ISBN 0-937860-15-8). Adams Inc MA.

Robert Long Adams & Associates & Noble, John H., eds. The Texas Job Bank: A Comprehensive Guide to Major Employers Throughout Texas. (Job Bank Ser.). 252p. 1982. pap. 9.95 (ISBN 0-937860-06-9). Adams Inc MA.

Robert Long Adams Associates. The Mid-Atlantic Job Bank. 400p. 1981. pap. cancelled o.p. (ISBN 0-686-30615-5). Adams Inc MA.

--The Northwest Job Bank. 400p. Date not set. pap. 9.95 o.p. (ISBN 0-686-30614-7). Adams Inc MA. Postponed.

--The Sun Belt Job Bank. 400p. 1981. pap. cancelled o.p. (ISBN 0-686-30617-1). Adams Inc MA.

Robert, Michael, ed. The Faber Book of Modern Verse. 3rd ed. 416p. 1962. pap. 6.95 o.p. (ISBN 0-571-06348-9). Faber & Faber.

Robert Morris Associates. Incentive Compensation Systems for Commercial Loan Officers: State of the Art. LC 82-25913. (Illus.). 48p. (Orig.). 1983. pap. text ed. 19.50 (ISBN 0-936742-07-0). Robt Morris Assocs.

--Information on Deteriorating Accounts: Handle With Care. (Illus.). 96p. (Orig.). 1982. pap. 31.50 NACM & RMA members (ISBN 0-936742-05-4); pap. 45.00 nonmembers. Robt Morris Assocs.

--An Integrated Approach to Foreign Bank Analysis. LC 81-84671. (Illus.). 48p. (Orig.). 1981. pap. 11.50 (ISBN 0-936742-04-6). Robt Morris Assocs.

Robert, William J., jt. auth. see Corley, Robert N.

Robert, Williar & Houdin, William J. Card Sharper-Their Tricks Exposed or the Art of Always Winning. 158p. 1982. pap. 3.95 (ISBN 0-686-42831-5). Gamblers.

Robertiello, Richard C. A Man in the Making: Grandfathers, Fathers, & Sons. LC 79-15709. 1979. 9.95 o.p. (ISBN 0-399-90056-X, Marek). Putnam Pub Group.

--Your Own True Love: The New Positive View of Narcissism, the Person You Love the Most Should Be...You. LC 78-6051. 1978. 8.95 o.p. (ISBN 0-399-90022-5, Marek). Putnam Pub Group.

Robertis, E. D. De see De Robertis, E. D. & Carrea, R.

Robertis, Eduardo De see DeRobertis, Eduardo & Schacht, Jochen.

Robert Mannyng of Brunne. The Works of Robert Mannyng of Brunne, 1303-1338: Volume 1: Handlyng Synne. Sullens, Idelle, ed. 1983. 25.00 (ISBN 0-86698-052-0). Medieval & Renaissance NY.

Roberto, John, ed. Creative Communication & Community Building. LC 81-83635. (Creative Resources for Youth Ministry Ser.: Vol. 1). (Illus.). 108p. (Orig.). 1981. pap. 8.95 (ISBN 0-88489-135-6). St Mary's.

Roberts. The Complete Handbook of Stone Masonry...with Projects. 416p. 1981. 16.95 o.p. (ISBN 0-8306-9642-3); pap. 10.95 o.p. (ISBN 0-8306-1264-5, 1264). TAB Bks.

--Hot Rolling of Steel. (Manufacturing Engineering Ser.). 700p. 1983. write for info. (ISBN 0-8247-1345-1). Dekker.

--Pictorial History of the Automobile. 1977. 7.95 o.p. (ISBN 0-448-12592-7, G&D). Putnam Pub Group.

Roberts & Sharp. Civilian Defence. 280p. Repr. of 1967 ed. cloth 11.00 (ISBN 0-686-87174-X). Greenlf Bks.

Roberts, jt. auth. see Evans.

Roberts, jt. auth. see Hill.

Roberts, et al. Audio-Active Italian, 2 vols. 1980. Vol. 1, 135 Pgs. 79.00x o.p. (ISBN 0-88432-055-3, 1101-1102). Vol. 2, 142 Pgs. J Norton Pubs.

Roberts, A. Applied Geotechnology: A Text for Students & Engineers on Rock Excavation & Related Topics. (Illus.). 416p. 1982. 50.00 (ISBN 0-08-024015-1); pap. 25.00 (ISBN 0-08-024014-3). Pergamon.

Roberts, A. & Bush, B. M., eds. Neurones Without Impulses. LC 79-42572. (Society for Experimental Biology Seminar Ser.: No. 6). (Illus.). 250p. 1981. 59.50 (ISBN 0-521-23364-X); pap. 22.95 (ISBN 0-521-29935-7). Cambridge U Pr.

Roberts, A., ed. see Ante-Nicene Fathers.

Roberts, A. Lorean. Transactional Analysis Approaches to Counseling. 1975. pap. 2.40 o.p. (ISBN 0-395-20035-0). HM.

Roberts, A. W. Breeze for a Bargeman. 144p. 1982. 25.00x (ISBN 0-86138-007-X, Pub. by Terence Dalton England). State Mutual Bk.

--Elementary Linear Algebra. 1982. text ed. 19.95 (ISBN 0-8053-8302-6); write for info. instr's guide (ISBN 0-8053-8303-4); student solution manual 4.95 (ISBN 0-686-83170-5). A-W.

Roberts, Adam & Guelff, Richard, eds. Documents on the Laws of War. 1982. 29.95x (ISBN 0-19-876117-1); pap. 17.95x (ISBN 0-19-876118-X). Oxford U Pr.

Roberts, Alan P., jt. auth. see Allen, T. O.

Roberts, Albert R. Correctional Treatment of the Offender: A Book of Readings. (Illus.). 350p. 1974. pap. 12.75x (ISBN 0-398-03085-5). C C Thomas.

--Self-Destructive Behavior. (Illus.). 232p. 1975. photocopy ed. spiral 22.75x (ISBN 0-398-03290-4). C C Thomas.

--Sheltering Battered Women: A National Study & Service Guide. (Focus on Women Ser.: No. 3). 1981. pap. text ed. 17.95 (ISBN 0-8261-2691-X). Springer Pub.

Roberts, Alexander, tr. see Irenaeus, St.

Roberts, Allen. Web of Intrigue. 1979. 12.95 (ISBN 0-87716-104-6, Pub. by Moore Pub Co). F Apple.

Roberts, Allen E. House Undivided: The Story of Freemasonry & the Civil War. 1982. Repr. of 1976 ed. 12.50 (ISBN 0-686-43324-6). Macoy Pub.

Roberts, Allen P., jt. auth. see Allen, T. O.

Roberts, Andrew D. A History of the Bemba: Political Growth & Change in North-Eastern Zambia Before 1900. LC 73-5813. 454p. 1973. 35.00 (ISBN 0-299-06450-6). U of Wis Pr.

Roberts, Anne F. Library Instruction for Librarians. (Library Science Text Ser.). 200p. 1982. 26.00 (ISBN 0-87287-298-X); pap. text ed. 18.50 (ISBN 0-87287-331-5). Libs Unl.

Roberts, Arthur & Prentice, Richard. Programming for Numerical Control Machines. 2nd ed. (Illus.). 1978. text ed. 22.50 (ISBN 0-07-053156-0, G). McGraw.

Roberts, B. H. Joseph Smith, the Prophet Teacher. Repr. leatherette 5.00 o.p. (ISBN 0-914740-18-0). Western Epics.

Roberts, B. M., jt. auth. see Croome, D. J.

Roberts, Barbara D., jt. auth. see Tier, Lynne L.

Roberts, Benjamin C. Industrial Relations: Contemporary Issues. LC 68-23089. (International Institute of Labor Studies). 1969. 25.00 (ISBN 0-312-41440-4). St Martin.

Roberts, Benjamin C. & De Bellecombe, L. Greyfie. Collective Bargaining in African Countries. (International Institute for Labor Studies Ser). 1967. 27.50 (ISBN 0-312-14980-8). St Martin.

Roberts, Benjamin C., ed. Towards Industrial Democracy: Europe, Japan & the United States. LC 78-71100. (Atlantic Institute for International Affairs Research Ser.: No. 2). 300p. 1979. text ed. 23.00x (ISBN 0-916672-20-4). Allanheld.

Roberts, Bob. Last of the Sailormen. 12.00 (ISBN 0-7100-2042-2). Routledge & Kegan.

Roberts, Bobby, II, ed. see Williams, Hobie L.

Roberts, Bobby, III. Once Upon a Midnight. White, Mosezelle & Morant, Mack B., eds. 30p. (Orig.). pap. text ed. 2.95 o.s.i. (ISBN 0-936026-01-4). R&M Pub Co.

Roberts, Brian R., jt. auth. see Buckley, Peter J.

Roberts, Bruce & Roberts, Nancy. America's Most Haunted Places. LC 75-23188. 96p. (gr. 6-7). 1976. 8.95 o.p. (ISBN 0-385-09965-7). Doubleday.

Roberts, Carey & Seely, Rebecca. Tidewater Dynasty: The Lees of Stratford Hall. LC 80-8758. 1981. 14.95 (ISBN 0-15-190294-1). HarBraceJ.

Roberts, Catherine. Science, Animals & Evolution: Reflections on Some Unrealized Potentials of Biology & Medicine. LC 79-52322. (Contributions in Philosophy: No. 14). 1980. lib. bdg. 25.00x (ISBN 0-313-21479-4, RSA/). Greenwood.

Roberts, Charles E., Jr. Ordinary Differential Equations: A Computational Approach. LC 78-13023. 1979. 26.95 (ISBN 0-13-639757-3). P-H.

Roberts, Clayton, jt. auth. see Roberts, David.

Roberts, D. F. & Thomson, A. M. The Biology of Human Fetal Growth. LC 75-28154. (Study of Human Biology Ser: Vol. 15). 1976. 34.95x o.s.i. (ISBN 0-470-72584-2). Halsted Pr.

Roberts, D. F., ed. Human Variation & Natural Selection, Vol. 13. 220p. 1975. write for info. (ISBN 0-85066-080-7, Pub. by Taylor & Francis). Intl Pubns Serv.

Roberts, D. F. & Sunderland, E., eds. Genetic Variation in Britain, Vol. 12. 314p. 1973. write for info. (ISBN 0-85066-062-9, Pub. by Taylor & Francis). Intl Pubns Serv.

Roberts, D. H. Coronary Artery Bypass Patient. 1983. 59.50 (ISBN 0-8151-7303-2). Year Bk Med.

Roberts, D. S. Faith, Hope & Love: Learning about I Corinthians 13. (Concept Bks.: Ser. 4). (gr. 1-4). 1983. pap. 3.50 (ISBN 0-570-08526-8). Concordia.

Roberts, D. V., ed. Enzyme Kinetics. LC 76-11091. (Cambridge Chemistry Texts Ser.). (Illus.). 1977. 60.00 (ISBN 0-521-21274-X); pap. 21.95x (ISBN 0-521-29080-5). Cambridge U Pr.

Roberts, D. W. Gynecology & Obstetrics. (Operative Surgery Ser.). 1977. 69.95 (ISBN 0-407-00615-X). Butterworth.

Roberts, Darrah L. Art Glass Shades. (Illus.). 4.95 (ISBN 0-686-51485-8, 99004); price guide 1.50 (ISBN 0-686-51486-6). Wallace-Homestead.

Roberts, David. Animals & Their Babies. Duenwald, Doris, ed. LC 78-52829. (Illus.). (gr. k-3). 1978. 2.95 o.s.i. (ISBN 0-448-16064-1, G&D). Putnam Pub Group.

--Great Exploration Hoaxes. Michaelman, Herbert, ed. 192p. 1981. 10.95 o.p. (ISBN 0-517-54075-4, Michaelman Books). Crown.

--Yesterday the Holy Land. Van der Mass, Ed, tr. from Dutch. (Illus.). 144p. (Eng.). 1982. 16.95 (ISBN 0-310-45620-7). Zondervan.

Roberts, David & Roberts, Clayton. History of England, 2 vols. (Illus.). 1980. Vol. I To 1714. pap. text ed. 18.95 (ISBN 0-13-390005-3); Vol. II 1688 To Present. pap. text ed. 18.95 (ISBN 0-13-390013-4). P-H.

Roberts, Dennis M. Descriptive & Inferential Statistical Topics. 2nd ed. 1979. pap. text ed. 19.95 (ISBN 0-8403-2071-X). Kendall-Hunt.

Roberts, Don. Prayers for the Young Child. 1981. pap. 6.95 (ISBN 0-570-04051-5, 56-1717). Concordia.

Roberts, Don, ed. Mediamobiles. (PLR Ser.: No. 19). 124p. (Orig.). Date not set. pap. text ed. 7.00 (ISBN 0-8389-3232-0). ALA.

Roberts, Donald L. The Perfect Church. LC 79-56331. 95p. (Orig.). 1980. pap. 2.25 (ISBN 0-87509-267-5). Chr Pubns.

--The Practicing Church. LC 1-67318. 100p. (Orig.). 1981. pap. 2.95 (ISBN 0-87509-303-5). Chr Pubns.

Roberts, Doreen. Teaching Art. 1978. 19.95 o.p. (ISBN 0-686-82895-X, Pub. by Batsford England); pap. 12.95 (ISBN 0-7134-2314-5). David & Charles.

Roberts, Douglas. To Adam with Love. 1975. pap. 1.50 o.s.i. (ISBN 0-89129-009-5). Jove Pubns.

Roberts, Duane F. Marketing & Leasing of Office Space. Schleker, Peggy J., ed. LC 79-89774. 289p. 1979. 21.95 (ISBN 0-912104-42-2). Inst Real Estate.

Roberts, E., et al, eds. GABA in Nervous System Function. LC 74-21983. 576p. 1976. 40.00 (ISBN 0-89004-043-5). Raven.

Roberts, E. F. The Law & the Preservation of Agricultural Land. LC 82-12616. 145p. 1982. pap. 6.95 (ISBN 0-9609010-0-0). NE Regional Ctr.

Roberts, Edgar. Writing Themes About Literature. 5th ed. 352p. 1983. pap. 9.95 (ISBN 0-13-971655-6). P H.

Roberts, Edgar V. Writing Themes About Literature. 4th ed. 1977. pap. text ed. 9.95 (ISBN 0-13-970582-1). P-H.

--Writing Themes About Literature (Brief Edition) (Illus.). 224p. 1982. pap. 7.95 ref. ed. (ISBN 0-13-970566-X). P-H.

Roberts, Edgar V., ed. see Gay, John.

Roberts, Edith T., tr. see Erhard, Ludwig.

Roberts, Edward, et al, eds. Biomedical Innovation. (Illus.). 368p. 1982. 30.00x (ISBN 0-262-18103-7). MIT Pr.

Roberts, Edward B., ed. Managerial Applications of System Dynamics. LC 77-26952. (MIT Press Wright-Allen Ser. in System Dynamics). 1978. 50.00x (ISBN 0-262-18088-X); pap. text ed. 17.50x (ISBN 0-262-68035-1). MIT Pr.

Roberts, Elizabeth, ed. Childhood Sexual Learning: The Unwritten Curriculum. 304p. 1980. prof ref 25.00x (ISBN 0-88410-374-9). Ballinger Pub.

Roberts, Ernie. Spring Prairie. 255p. 1981. pap. 5.95 o.p. (ISBN 0-89260-199-X). Hwong Pub.

Roberts, F. H. Australian Ticks. 1982. 30.00x (ISBN 0-686-97917-6, Pub. by CSIRO Australia). State Mutual Bk.

Roberts, F. S. Measurement Theory. (Encyclopedia of Mathematics & Its Applications: Vol. 7). 1979. text ed. 29.50 (ISBN 0-201-13506-X, Adv Bk Prog). A-W.

Roberts, F. S., ed. Energy Mathematics & Models: Proceedings. LC 75-41915. (SIAM-SIMS Conference Ser.: No. 3). xxiv, 276p. 1976. pap. 24.00 (ISBN 0-89871-029-4). Soc Indus-Appl Math.

Roberts, Florence B. Perinatal Nursing: Care of Newborns & Their Families. (Illus.). 1976. pap. text ed. 14.95 (ISBN 0-07-053125-0, HP). McGraw.

Roberts, Florence B., jt. auth. see Clements, Imelda W.

Roberts, Frances J. Dialogues with God. 1968. 4.95 (ISBN 0-932814-07-7); pap. 3.50 (ISBN 0-932814-08-5). Kings Farspan.

Roberts, Fred M. Guide to the Ricoh Hi-Color 35 & Marine Capsule. (Illus., Orig.). 1972. pap. 3.50 (ISBN 0-912746-05-X). F M Roberts.

--Nikonos Photography: The Camera & the System. 3rd ed. LC 77-80027. 1977. pap. 7.50 (ISBN 0-912746-00-9). F M Roberts.

Roberts, Fred S. Graph Theory & Its Applications to Problems of Society. LC 78-6277. (CBMS-NSF Regional Conference Ser.: Vol. 29). (Illus.). v, 122p. (Orig.). 1978. pap. text ed. 15.50 (ISBN 0-89871-026-X). Soc Indus-Appl Math.

Roberts, Frederick. An Introduction to Everyday Science. (Illus.). (gr. 9 up). 14.50x (ISBN 0-392-03551-0, SpS). Sportshelf.

Roberts, G. & Cary, R. Tool Steels. 4th ed. 1980. 90.00 (ISBN 0-87170-096-4). ASM.

--Wear & Fracture Prevention. 1981. 44.00 (ISBN 0-87170-110-3). ASM.

Roberts, G. C., jt. ed. see Burgen, A. S.

Roberts, G. K. Dictionary of Political Analysis. LC 70-151309. 1971. text ed. 22.50 (ISBN 0-312-20930-4). St Martin.

Roberts, Gene, Jr., jt. auth. see Nelson, Jack.

Roberts, Geoffrey K. Political Parties & Pressure Groups in Britain. LC 73-175009. 198p. 1972. 16.95 o.p. (ISBN 0-312-62335-6). St Martin.

Roberts, Geoffrey R. English in Primary Schools. 1972. 12.00x o.p. (ISBN 0-7100-7308-9); pap. 5.00 (ISBN 0-7100-7309-7). Routledge & Kegan.

Roberts, George. Scrut. LC 82-81349. 72p. 1983. pap. 4.00 (ISBN 0-930100-10-7). Holy Cow.

Roberts, Glenys. Metropolitan Myths. 176p. 1982. 16.95 (ISBN 0-575-03154-9, Pub by Gollancz England); pap. 12.50 (ISBN 0-575-03232-4, Pub. by Gollancz England). David & Charles.

Roberts, Gloria A. & Horowitz, Blanche. A Family Planning Library Manual. rev., 4th ed. LC 82-119. 100p. (Orig.). 1975. 7.50 (ISBN 0-934586-08-X). Plan Parent.

Roberts, H. V. Forecasting. Date not set. price not set (ISBN 0-07-053136-6). McGraw.

Roberts, Harold S. Labor-Management Relations in the Public Service. rev. ed. LC 70-98135. 1970. text ed. 35.00x (ISBN 0-87022-710-6). UH Pr.

--Roberts' Dictionary of Industrial Relations. rev. ed. LC 78-175029. 616p. 1971. 22.00 (ISBN 0-87179-135-8). BNA.

Roberts, Harry V. Conversational Statistics. (Data Analysis Ser.). 256p. 1981. pap. text ed. 18.95 o.p. (ISBN 0-07-053135-8, C). McGraw.

--Interactive Data Analysis. Date not set. text ed. price not set (ISBN 0-8162-7206-9). Holden-Day.

Roberts, Helen H. Basketry of the San Carlos Apache Indians. LC 72-10331. (Beautiful Rio Grande Classics Ser). Repr. of 1929 ed. lib. bdg. 12.00 o.s.i. (ISBN 0-87380-096-6); pap. 8.00 o.s.i. (ISBN 0-87380-134-2). Rio Grande.

--Concow-Maidu Indians of Round Valley. Mill, Dorothy, ed. (ANCRR Occasional Publication Ser.: No. 5). 1980. 6.00 (ISBN 0-686-38939-5). Assn NC Records.

Roberts, Helen R. Come Spring, Summer, Fall or Winter. 1978. pap. 3.00 (ISBN 0-932044-20-4). M O Pub Co.

Roberts, Henry C., tr. The Complete Prophecies of Nostradamus. (Illus.). 352p. 1983. 10.95 (ISBN 0-517-54956-5). Crown.

Roberts, Henry D., jt. auth. see Thomson, James.

Roberts, Howard R. Food Safety. LC 80-25335. 339p. 1981. 49.95 (ISBN 0-471-06458-0, Pub. by Wiley-Interscience). Wiley.

Roberts, Hugh. An Urban Profile of the Middle East. LC 78-27185. 1979. 40.00x (ISBN 0-312-83467-5). St Martin.

Roberts, I. F., jt. auth. see Cantor, Leonard M.

Roberts, J. C., jt. auth. see Lynch, M.

Roberts, J. Fraser. Introduction to Medical Genetics. 7th ed. (Illus.). 1978. pap. text ed. 19.95x (ISBN 0-19-261214-X). Oxford U Pr.

Roberts, J. M. The French Revolution. 1979. text ed. 12.95 o.p. (ISBN 0-19-215822-8); pap. text ed. 6.95x (ISBN 0-19-289069-7). Oxford U Pr.

Roberts, J. M., jt. ed. see Taylor, A. J.

Roberts, J. R. Gunsmith, No. 11: One-Handed Gun. 224p. 1982. pap. 2.25 (ISBN 0-441-30866-X, Pub. by Charter Bks). Ace Bks.

--The Gunsmith, No. 4: The Guns of Abilene. 224p. 1982. pap. 2.25 (ISBN 0-441-30859-7, Pub. by Charter Bks). Ace Bks.

--The Gunsmith. No. 5: Three Guns for Glory. 224p. 1982. pap. 2.25 (ISBN 0-441-30860-0, Pub. by Charter Bks). Ace Bks.

Roberts, J. W. Acts, 2 Pts. (Living Word Paperback Ser.). (Orig.). 1967. pap. 2.95 ea.; Pt. 1. (ISBN 0-8344-0030-8); Pt. 2. (ISBN 0-8344-0031-6). Sweet.

Roberts, James C. The Conservative Decade. 1980. 12.95 o.p. (ISBN 0-87000-462-X, Arlington Hse). Crown.

Roberts, James L. Absalom, Absalom Notes. rev. ed. (Orig.). 1970. pap. 2.50 (ISBN 0-8220-0110-1). Cliffs.

--As I Lay Dying Notes. (Orig.). 1969. pap. 2.95 (ISBN 0-8220-0210-8). Cliffs.

--Crime & Punishment Notes. (Orig.). (YA) 1963. pap. 2.50 (ISBN 0-8220-0328-7). Cliffs.

--Death of a Salesman Notes. (Orig.). 1964. pap. 2.50 (ISBN 0-8220-0382-1). Cliffs.

--Farewell to Arms Notes. (Orig.). 1966. pap. 2.50 (ISBN 0-8220-0461-5). Cliffs.

--Grapes of Wrath Notes. (Orig.). 1965. pap. 2.25 (ISBN 0-8220-0542-5). Cliffs.

--Light in August Notes. rev. ed. (Orig.). 1968. pap. 2.95 (ISBN 0-8220-0744-4). Cliffs.

--Madame Bovary Notes. (Orig.). 1964. pap. 2.75 (ISBN 0-8220-0780-0). Cliffs.

--Notes from Underground Notes. (Orig.). 1970. pap. 2.75 (ISBN 0-8220-0900-5). Cliffs.

--Portrait of a Lady Notes. (Orig.). 1965. pap. 2.50 (ISBN 0-8220-1066-6). Cliffs.

Roberts, James L. & Calandra, Denis M. Tartuffe Notes, Misanthrope Notes & Bourgeois Gentleman Notes. (Orig.). 1968. pap. 2.95 (ISBN 0-8220-1265-0). Cliffs.

Roberts, James T., ed. Fundamentals of Tracheal Intubation. Date not set. price not set (ISBN 0-8089-1546-0). Grune.

Roberts, Jane. Emir's Education in the Proper Use of Magical Powers. (Illus.). 1979. 7.95 o.s.i. (ISBN 0-440-02275-4, E Friede). Delacorte.

--The Guthlac Poems of the Exeter Book. 1979. text ed. 38.00x (ISBN 0-19-812462-7). Oxford U Pr.

--How to Develop Your ESP Power. new ed. LC 66-17331. 264p. 1980. pap. 7.95 (ISBN 0-8119-0379-6). Fell.

Roberts, Jane & Butts, Robert F. The Individual & the Nature of Mass Events: A Seth Book. LC 80-22600. 336p. 1981. 10.95 (ISBN 0-13-457259-9). P-H.

Roberts, Janet L. Forget-Me-Not. 432p. (Orig.). 1983. pap. 3.50 o.p. (ISBN 0-446-30715-7). Warner Bks.

--Love Song. 1980. pap. 1.95 o.p. (ISBN 0-523-40842-0). Pinnacle Bks.

--Scarlet Poppies. 480p. 1983. pap. 3.50 (ISBN 0-446-30211-2). Warner Bks.

--Silver Jasmine. 480p. 1980. pap. 2.95 o.p. (ISBN 0-446-30224-4). Warner Bks.

Roberts, January & Robie, Diane C. Open Adoption & Open Placement. 100p. 1981. 3.95 (ISBN 0-941976-00-9). Adoption Pr.

Roberts, Jean & Ahuja, Elizabeth M. Hearing Sensitivity & Related Medical Findings among Youths Twelve to Seventeen Years: U.S. Stevenson, Taloria, ed. LC 75-619079. (Data from the Health Examination Survey Series 11: No. 154). 51p. 1975. pap. text ed. 1.50 (ISBN 0-8406-0043-7). Natl Ctr Health Stats.

Roberts, Jean, jt. auth. see Ganley, James P.

Roberts, Jennifer T. Accountability in Athenian Government. 288p. 1982. text ed. 30.00 (ISBN 0-299-08680-1). U of Wis Pr.

Roberts, Jim. Jesus Calms the Storm. 16p. 1978. 2.49 o.p. (ISBN 0-8307-0614-3, 56-057-09). Regal.

--Jonah. 16p. 1978. pap. 2.49 o.p. (ISBN 0-8307-0612-7, 56-055-04). Regal.

--Three Men in a Furnace. 16p. 1978. 2.49 o.p. (ISBN 0-8307-0613-5, 56-056-01). Regal.

Roberts, John. Anatomy of the Ship: Battlecruiser Hood. LC 81-85587. (Illus.). 96p. 1982. 19.95 (ISBN 0-87021-078-5). Naval Inst Pr.

--Anatomy of the Ship: The Aircraft Carrier Intrepid. LC 82-81105. (Illus.). 128p. 1982. text ed. 21.95 (ISBN 0-87021-901-4). Naval Inst Pr.

--The Battlecruiser Hood. 128p. 1982. 50.00x (ISBN 0-85177-250-1, Pub. by Conway Maritime England). State Mutual Bk.

--Warship, Vol. 5. LC 78-55455. (Illus.). 288p. 1982. 23.95 (ISBN 0-87021-980-4). Naval Inst Pr.

Roberts, John D. & Caserio, M. C. Basic Principles of Organic Chemistry. 2nd ed. LC 77-76749. 1977. 34.95 (ISBN 0-8053-8329-8); student supplement 11.95 (ISBN 0-8053-8327-1). Benjamin-Cummings.

Roberts, John M. The Building Site: Planning & Practice. 288p. 1983. write for info. (ISBN 0-471-08868-4, Pub. by Wiley-Interscience). Wiley.

Roberts, John R. John Donne: An Annotated Bibliography of Modern Criticism, 1968-1978. LC 82-1849. 448p. 1982. 32.00 (ISBN 0-8262-0364-7). U of Mo Pr.

Roberts, John S. The Latin Tinge: The Impact of Latin American Music on the United States. LC 78-26534. (Illus.). 1979. 16.95x (ISBN 0-19-502564-4). Oxford U Pr.

--Oxytocin: Vol. 1. 1977. 14.40 (ISBN 0-88831-010-2). Eden Pr.

Roberts, Joseph, jt. auth. see Holcenberg, John C.

Roberts, Joseph B., Jr. & Ciardi, John. Troy State University Writings & Research, Vol. II, No. 1. 64p. 1971. pap. 1.95 (ISBN 0-686-97225-2). TSU Pr.

Roberts, Joseph F., Jr., ed. Working Press of the Nation, 5 vols. LC 46-7041. 1982. 241.00 (ISBN 0-686-15351-0). Working Pr.

Roberts, Joseph M., Sr. Construction Management: An Effective Approach. (Illus.). 368p. 1980. 22.95 (ISBN 0-8359-0927-1); text ed. 17.95 (ISBN 0-686-96863-8). Reston.

Roberts, Julian L., Jr., jt. auth. see Sawyer, Donald T.

Roberts, June C. Born in the Spring: A Collection of Spring Wildflowers. LC 75-36979. (Illus.). 160p. 1976. 15.00 (ISBN 0-8214-0195-5, 82-81982); pap. 8.50 (ISBN 0-8214-0226-9, 82-81990). Ohio U Pr.

Roberts, Karlene H., et al. Developing an Interdisciplinary Science of Organizations. LC 78-62568. (Social & Behavioral Science Ser.). (Illus.). 1978. text ed. 19.95x (ISBN 0-87589-393-7). Jossey-Bass.

Roberts, Kate. Feet in Chains. Walters, Idwal & Jones, John I., trs. from Welsh. 1977. 3.50 (ISBN 0-89733-005-6). Academy Chi Ltd.

--The Living Sleep. Griffith, Wyn, tr. from Welsh. 1976. 3.50 (ISBN 0-902375-14-8). Academy Chi Ltd.

Roberts, Keith. Bruegel. (Phaidon Color Library). (Illus.). 84p. 1983. 27.50 (ISBN 0-7148-2225-6, Pub. by Salem Hse Ltd); pap. 18.95 (ISBN 0-7148-2239-6). Merrimack Bk Serv.
--Degas. (Phaidon Color Library). (Illus.). 84p. 1983. 27.50 (ISBN 0-7148-2226-4, Pub. by Salem Hse Ltd); pap. 18.95 (ISBN 0-7148-2240-X). Merrimack Bk Serv.
--Pavane. 288p. 1982. pap. 2.75 (ISBN 0-441-65431-2, Pub. by Ace Science Fiction). Ace Bks.
Roberts, Kenneth. The Battle of Cowpens. LC 58-8107. 3.50 o.p. (ISBN 0-686-67647-5). Doubleday.
--The Northwest Passage. 1983. write for info. Haas Ent NH.
Roberts, Kenneth D. Introduction to Rule Collecting. (Illus.). 22p. (Orig.). 1982. pap. text ed. 2.00 (ISBN 0-913602-52-3). K Roberts.
--Tools for the Trades & Crafts. 1976. 22.00 (ISBN 0-913602-18-3). K Roberts.
--Wooden Planes in Nineteenth Century America. 2nd ed. (Illus.). 324p. Repr. of 1978 ed. 30.00x (ISBN 0-913602-53-1). K Roberts.
Roberts, Kenneth D., ed. Belcher Brothers & Co.'s Eighteen Sixty Price List of Boxwood & Ivory Rules. (Illus.). 40p. 1982. pap. text ed. 5.00 (ISBN 0-913602-51-5). K Roberts.
--The Carpenter's Slide Rule: Its History & Use. 32p. (Orig.). 1982. pap. text ed. 4.00 (ISBN 0-913602-50-7). K Roberts.
--John Rabone & Sons Eighteen Ninety-Two Catalogue of Rules, Tapes, Spirit Levels, etc. (Illus.). 96p. 1982. pap. 20.00X (ISBN 0-913602-49-3). K Roberts.
Roberts, Kenneth D., ed. see Greenfield Tool Company.
Roberts, L. W. Cytodifferentiation in Plants. LC 75-10041. (Developmental & Cell Biology Ser.: No. 2). (Illus.). 250p. 1976. 37.50 (ISBN 0-521-20804-1). Cambridge U Pr.
Roberts, Larry S., jt. auth. see Schmidt, Gerald D.
Roberts, Lawrence D. Approaches to Nature in the Middle Ages. 1983. 15.00 (ISBN 0-86698-051-2). Medieval & Renaissance NY.
Roberts, Leslie. The Mackenzie. LC 73-20906. 276p. 1974. Repr. of 1949 ed. lib. bdg. 15.75x (ISBN 0-8371-5864-8, ROMR). Greenwood.
Roberts, Lois H. Now It Is Time. LC 82-71221. 1983. 5.95 (ISBN 0-8054-7228-2). Broadman.
Roberts, Lois W., ed. Anacapa Island. 1982. pap. 7.50 (ISBN 0-87461-040-0). McNally.
Roberts, M. J. British Spiders. write for info. (ISBN 0-12-589680-8). Acad Pr.
Roberts, Marc J., jt. ed. see Caves, Richard E.
Roberts, Margaret. California Pioneers: Tales of Explorers, Indians, & Settlers. LC 81-22543. (Illus.). 296p. (gr. 6 up). 1982. 12.95 (ISBN 0-914598-42-2); pap. text ed. 9.95 student ed. (ISBN 0-914598-43-0). Padre Prods.
Roberts, Mark K. Soldier for Hire, No. 1: Commando Squad. 1982. pap. 2.50 (ISBN 0-8217-1094-X). Zebra.
--Soldier for Hire, No. 7: Pathet Vengeance. 1983. pap. 2.50 (ISBN 0-8217-1140-7). Zebra.
Roberts, Martha D., jt. auth. see Roberts, Mervin F.
Roberts, Martha G. Honeymaid: The Story of Silver Dollar Tabor. new ed. 1977. pap. 3.95x (ISBN 0-87315-064-3). Golden Bell.
Roberts, Mervin. Tropical Fish. (Illus.). pap. 6.95 (ISBN 0-87666-780-9, H915). TFH Pubns.
Roberts, Mervin F. All About Boas & Other Snakes. (Illus.). 96p. (Orig.). 1975. 6.95 (ISBN 0-87666-763-9, PS-313). TFH Pubns.
--All About Breeding Canaries. (Illus.). 128p. 1982. 8.95 (ISBN 0-87666-821-X, PS-790). TFH Pubns.
--All About Chameleons & Anoles. (Illus.). 1977. pap. 3.95 (ISBN 0-87666-772-8, PS-310). TFH Pubns.
--All About Ferrets. (Illus.). 1977. pap. 3.95 (ISBN 0-87666-914-3, PS-754). TFH Pubns.
--All About Land Hermit Crabs. new ed. (Illus.). 1978. pap. text ed. 2.95 (ISBN 0-87666-920-8, PS-767). TFH Pubns.
--All About Salamanders. 96p. (Orig.). 1976. pap. 3.95 (ISBN 0-87666-901-1, PS-312). TFH Pubns.
--Breeding Zebra Finches. (Illus.). 96p. 1980. 4.95 (ISBN 0-87666-883-X, KW-056). TFH Pubns.
--Guinea Pigs for Beginners. (Illus.). 1972. pap. 2.95 (ISBN 0-87666-198-3, M-541). TFH Pubns.
--How to Raise Hamsters. pap. 2.50 o.p. (ISBN 0-87666-205-X, M508). TFH Pubns.
--Pigeons. (Orig.). pap. 2.95 (ISBN 0-87666-432-X, M512). TFH Pubns.
--Society Finches, Breeding. (Illus.). 1979. 4.95 (ISBN 0-87666-991-7, KW-030). TFH Pubns.
--Teddy Bear Hamsters. (Illus.). 96p. (Orig.). 1974. 4.95 (ISBN 0-87666-776-0, PS710). TFH Pubns.
--Turtles. (Illus.). 96p. 1980. 4.95 (ISBN 0-87666-928-3, KWO51). TFH Pubns.
--Zebra Finches. (Illus.). 1981. 4.95 (ISBN 0-87666-882-1, KW-055). TFH Pubns.
Roberts, Mervin F. & Roberts, Martha D. All About Iguanas. (Orig.). 1976. 3.95 (ISBN 0-87666-774-4, PS311). TFH Pubns.
Roberts, Mervin F., Jr. Your Terrarium. (Orig.). pap. 2.95 o.p. (ISBN 0-87666-225-4, M511). TFH Pubns.
Roberts, Michael. Early Vasas. (Illus.). 1968. 64.50 (ISBN 0-521-06930-0). Cambridge U Pr.
--Fans: How We Go Crazy Over Sports. LC 76-26880. 1978. 8.95 o.s.i. (ISBN 0-915220-20-2); pap. 3.95 (ISBN 0-915220-46-6). New Republic.
--Selected Poems & Prose. Grubb, Frederick, ed. 205p. 1980. 18.95x (ISBN 0-85635-263-2, Pub. by Carcanet New Pr England). Humanities.
--The Swedish Imperial Experience: Fifteen Sixty to Seventeen Eighteen. LC 78-58799. (Illus.). 1979. 27.95 (ISBN 0-521-22502-7). Cambridge U Pr.
--T. E. Hulme. 356p. 1982. Repr. of 1938 ed. text ed. 21.00x (ISBN 0-85635-411-2, 61258, Pub. by Carcanet New Pr England). Humanities.
Roberts, Michael, ed. Sweden's Age of Greatness: Sixteen Thirty-Two to Seventeen-Eighteen. LC 73-77736. (Problems in Focus Ser.). 288p. 1973. 25.00 (ISBN 0-312-78015-X). St Martin.
Roberts, Michael C., jt. auth. see Walker, C. Eugene.
Roberts, Michael C. & Lyman, Robert D., eds. Publishing Child-Oriented Articles in Pyschology: A Compendium of Publication Outlets. LC 82-45067. 178p. (Orig.). 1982. lib. bdg. 22.00 (ISBN 0-8191-2660-8); pap. text ed. 10.00 (ISBN 0-8191-2661-6). U Pr of Amer.
Roberts, N. Use of Social Science Literature. (Information Sources in Sciences & Technology Ser.). 1976. 34.95 o.p. (ISBN 0-408-10602-6). Butterworth.
Roberts, N. J., jt. auth. see Townroe, P. M.
Roberts, Nancy. Appalachian Ghosts. LC 77-76263. (gr. 3-7). 1978. 7.95a o.p. (ISBN 0-385-12294-2); PLB 7.95a (ISBN 0-385-12295-0). Doubleday.
--Southern Ghosts. LC 77-82962. (Illus.). 1979. 7.95a o.p. (ISBN 0-385-12813-4); PLB 7.95a (ISBN 0-385-12814-2). Doubleday.
Roberts, Nancy & Andersen, David. Introduction To Computer Simulation: The System Dynamics Approach. (Illus.). Date not set. text ed. 18.95 (ISBN 0-201-06414-6). A-W.
Roberts, Nancy, jt. auth. see Roberts, Bruce.
Roberts, Nesta. Companion Guide to Normandy. (Illus.). 336p. 1983. 15.95 (ISBN 0-13-154583-3); pap. 7.95 (ISBN 0-13-154575-2). P-H.
Roberts, Nesta, jt. auth. see Hale, Geoffrey.
Roberts, Newton. The Cyclical Theories of Stock Market Action. (The Recondite Sources of Stock Market Action Library). (Illus.). 129p. 1983. 47.55 (ISBN 0-86654-052-0). Inst Econ Finan.
Roberts, Oral. Classic Sermons. (Orig.). Date not set. pap. price not set o.s.i. (ISBN 0-89274-190-2, HH-190). Harrison Hse.
--Flood Tide. 143p. 1981. pap. 3.95 o.s.i. (ISBN 0-89274-191-0). Harrison Hse.
--The Miracle of Seed Faith. 172p. 1977. pap. 1.50 o.p. (ISBN 0-8007-8299-2, Spire Bks). Revell.
--Three Most Important Steps to Your Better Health & Miracle Living. pap. 1.95 o.p. (ISBN 0-8007-8313-1, Spire Bks). Revell.
Roberts, P. & Shaw, T. Mineral Resources in Regional & Strategic Planning. 165p. 1982. text ed. 37.25x (ISBN 0-566-00395-3). Gower Pub Ltd.
Roberts, P. H., ed. see Specialist Symposium on Geophysical Fluid Dynamics, European Geophysical Society, Fourth Meeting, Munich September, 1977.
Roberts, P. J. Biochemistry of Dementia. LC 79-42895. 1980. 54.95x (ISBN 0-471-27698-7, Pub. by Wiley-Interscience). Wiley.
Roberts, Pamela. Teaching the Child Rider. 7.50x o.p. (ISBN 0-87556-302-3). Saifer.
Roberts, Patricia. Tender Prey. LC 82-45562. (Illus.). 240p. 1983. 13.95 (ISBN 0-385-18392-5). Doubleday.
Roberts, Patrick. Psychology of Tragic Drama. 1975. 27.50x (ISBN 0-7100-8034-4). Routledge & Kegan.
Roberts, Patsy. Versatility, Poems of Sunshine & Shadows. 1982. 5.95 (ISBN 0-533-05326-9). Vantage.
Roberts, Pattie & Andrews, Sherry. Patti Roberts. 1983. 8.95 (ISBN 0-8499-0346-7). Word Bks.
Roberts, Peter. Anthracite Coal Communities. (Illus.). xiii, 387p. Repr. of 1904 ed. lib. bdg. 20.00x (ISBN 0-8371-4965-7, ROAC). Greenwood.
--The New Immigration: A Study of the Industrial & Social Life of Southeastern Europeans in America. LC 78-145490. (American Immigration Library). xxii, 418p. 1971. Repr. of 1912 ed. lib. bdg. 21.95x (ISBN 0-89198-023-7). Ozer.
Roberts, Peter C. Modelling Large Systems: Limits to Growth Revisited. LC 78-13339. (Orasa Text). 1978. pap. 27.95x o.s.i. (ISBN 0-470-26528-0); write for info. tchr's manual avail. o.s.i. Halsted Pr.
Roberts, Philip, jt. auth. see Hay, Malcolm.
Roberts, R. The Classic Slum. 1978. 14.00 (ISBN 0-7190-0453-5). Manchester.
--Imprisoned Tongues. 1968. pap. 5.00 (ISBN 0-7190-0596-5). Manchester.
Roberts, R. & Linn, S., eds. Nucleases. LC 82-71651. (Cold Spring Harbor Monograph: Vol. 14). 450p. 1982. 45.00X (ISBN 0-87969-155-7). Cold Spring Harbor.
Roberts, R. J. Microbial Diseases of Fish, Vol. 9. 40.50 (ISBN 0-12-589660-3). Acad Pr.
Roberts, Ralph & Ouellette, Robert B. Industrial Applications of Electroorganic Synthesis. LC 82-71530. (Illus.). 205p. 1982. 29.95 (ISBN 0-250-40585-7). Ann Arbor Science.
Roberts, Randy. Papa Jack: Jack Johnson & the Era of White Hopes. LC 82-49017. 288p. 1983. 14.95 (ISBN 0-686-84093-3). Free Pr.
Roberts, Ransom. How to Have a Happier Year: Take a Number (Nonsense Numerology) LC 81-90709. (Illus.). 128p. (Orig.). 1982. pap. write for info. (ISBN 0-9607834-0-7). R Roberts.
Roberts, Ray. John Updike: A Biographical Checklist. Date not set. 12.50 (ISBN 0-89679-011-8); pap. text ed. 4.50 (ISBN 0-89679-010-X). Moretus Pr.
Roberts, Richard. Tales for Jung Folk: Original Fairytales for All Ages Illustrating C. G. Jung's Archetypes of the Collective Unconscious. (Illus.). 175p. (Orig.). 1983. pap. 9.95 (ISBN 0-942380-01-0). Vernal Equinox.
Roberts, Richard, jt. auth. see Riker, Tom.
Roberts, Richard A., jt. auth. see Gabel, Robert A.
Roberts, Richard B., ed. Studies in Macromolecular Biosynthesis. (Illus.). 702p. 1964. 29.00 o.p. (ISBN 0-87279-635-3, 624). Carnegie Inst.
Roberts, Richard B., et al. Studies of Biosynthesis in Escherichia Coli. (Illus.). 521p. 1958. pap. 21.50 o.p. (ISBN 0-87279-618-3, 607). Carnegie Inst.
Roberts, Richard O. Revival. 186p. 1982. pap. 5.95 (ISBN 0-8423-5575-8). Tyndale.
Roberts, Robert. The Social Laws of the Quran: Considered, & Compared with Those of the Hebrew & Other Ancient Codes. 1971. Repr. of 1925 ed. text ed. 8.00x o.p. (ISBN 0-7007-0009-9). Humanities.
Roberts, Robert C. Spirituality & Human Emotion. 128p. 1983. pap. 7.95 (ISBN 0-8028-1939-7). Eerdmans.
Roberts, Roger L., ed. see Julian of Norwich.
Roberts, Ron E. Social Problems: Human Possibilities. LC 78-163. (Illus.). 310p. 1978. pap. text ed. 13.95 o.p. (ISBN 0-8016-4143-8). Mosby.
Roberts, Ron E. & Brintnall, Douglas. Reinventing Social Inequality. 320p. 1982. text ed. 19.95x (ISBN 0-87073-793-7); pap. text ed. 11.95x (ISBN 0-87073-794-5). Schenkman.
Roberts, Ronald. Making a Simple Violin & Viola. 1976. 12.95 o.p. (ISBN 0-7153-6964-4); plans 3.95 (ISBN 0-686-77112-5). David & Charles.
Roberts, Ronald J., jt. ed. see Muir, James F.
Roberts, S. & Lajtha, A., eds. Mechanisms, Regulation & Special Functions of Protein Synthesis in the Brain. (Developments in Neuro-Science: Vol. 2). 1978. 84.75 (ISBN 0-444-80030-1, Biomedical Pr). Elsevier.
Roberts, S. M. & Scheinmann, F., eds. Chemistry, Biochemistry & Pharmacology of Prostanoids. 1979. text ed. 97.00 (ISBN 0-08-023799-1). Pergamon.
Roberts, Sanford M. Dynamic Programming in Chemical Engineering & Process Control. (Mathematics in Science & Engineering Ser.: Vol. 12). 1964. 58.00 (ISBN 0-12-589450-3). Acad Pr.
Roberts, Shannon, ed. Rocky Mountain Diamonds '82: A Gentleman's Guide to the Best Single Women in the Rockies. (Illus.). 432p. 1982. pap. 14.95x (ISBN 0-941258-02-5). Shannon Pubns.
Roberts, Sharon, jt. auth. see Roy, Callista.
Roberts, Simon. Order & Dispute: An Introduction to Legal Anthropology. LC 78-24778. 1979. 20.00 (ISBN 0-312-58713-9). St Martin.
Roberts, Spencer E., tr. see Shestov, Lev.
Roberts, Stanley. Gambling Times Guide to Blackjack. (Illus., Orig.). 1983. pap. text ed. 5.95 (ISBN 0-89746-014-6). Lyle Stuart.
Roberts, Stephen D. & England, William L., eds. Survey of the Application of Simulation to Health Care. (SCS Simulation Ser.: Vol. 10, No. 1). 30.00 (ISBN 0-686-36678-6). Soc Computer Sim.
Roberts, Suzanne. Danger in Paradise. (YA) 6.95 (ISBN 0-685-07427-7, Avalon). Bouregy.
--Farewell to Alexandria. (Orig.). 1980. pap. 1.25 o.s.i. (ISBN 0-440-12587-1). Dell.
--Love in the Wilds. (Orig.). 1980. pap. 1.50 o.s.i. (ISBN 0-440-14837-5). Dell.
Roberts, T., jt. auth. see Hendricks, G.
Roberts, T. A., et al, eds. Psychrotrophic Microorganisms in Spoilage & Pathogenicity. LC 81-67902. 552p. 1982. 49.50 (ISBN 0-12-589720-0). Acad Pr.
Roberts, T. D. M. Neurophysiology of Postural Mechanisms. 2nd ed. 1978. text ed. 105.00 (ISBN 0-408-70808-5). Butterworth.
Roberts, T. R. Radiochromatography: The Chromatography & Electrophoresis of Radiolabelled Compounds. (Journal of Chromatography Library: Vol. 14). 1978. 42.75 (ISBN 0-444-41656-0). Elsevier.
Roberts, T. R., jt. auth. see Hutson, D. H.
Roberts, Tom. Developing Effective Managers. LC 75-318208. (Management in Perspective Ser.). 168p. 1974. pap. 7.50x o.p. (ISBN 0-85292-100-4). Intl Pubns Serv.
Roberts, Ursula. The Mystery of the Human Aura. pap. 1.95 (ISBN 0-87728-331-1). Weiser.
Roberts, W. The Reproductive System: Disease, Diagnosis, Treatment. (Clinical Monographs Ser.). (Illus.). 1974. pap. 7.95 o.p. (ISBN 0-87618-062-4). R J Brady.
Roberts, Warren. A Bibliography of D. H. Lawrence. 2nd ed. LC 81-10149. (Illus.). 475p. 1982. 79.50 (ISBN 0-521-22295-8). Cambridge U Pr.
--Jane Austen & the French Revolution. LC 79-19838. 1979. 21.00x (ISBN 0-312-43993-8). St Martin.
Roberts, Wayne, jt. auth. see Gretler, Kathryn.
Roberts, Wayne A. Linear Algebra. 1982. 19.95 (ISBN 0-8053-8302-6); instr's guide avail. (ISBN 0-8053-8303-4); solns. manual 5.95 (ISBN 0-8053-8304-2). Benjamin-Cummings.
Roberts, William. Earlier History of English Bookselling. LC 66-28043. 1967. Repr. of 1889 ed. 30.00x (ISBN 0-8103-3314-7). Gale.
Roberts, Willo D. The Face at the Window. (Raven House Mysteries Ser.). 224p. 1983. pap. cancelled (ISBN 0-373-63054-9, Pub. by Worldwide). Harlequin Bks.
--The Girl with the Silver Eyes. LC 80-12391. 192p. (gr. 4-6). 1980. 10.95 (ISBN 0-689-30786-1). Atheneum.
--The Pet-Sitting Peril. LC 82-13757. 192p. (gr. 4-6). 1983. 10.95 (ISBN 0-689-30963-5). Atheneum.
Robertshaw, Joseph E. & Mecca, Stephen J. Problem Solving: A Systems Approach. (Illus.). 1979. text ed. 24.00 (ISBN 0-89433-075-6). Petrocelli.
Robertshaw, Joseph E., jt. auth. see Mecca, Stephen J.
Robertson & Cassidy. Development of Modern English. 2nd ed. 1953. 18.95 (ISBN 0-13-208330-2). P-H.
Robertson, A. F., jt. auth. see Dunn, J.
Robertson, A. H. Human Rights in the World: An Introduction to the International Protection of Human Rights. LC 82-10238. 1982. 22.50x (ISBN 0-312-39961-8). St Martin.
Robertson, A. M., jt. auth. see Hobson, P. N.
Robertson, A. P. & Robertson, Wendy. Topological Vector Spaces. 2nd ed. LC 72-89805. (Cambridge Tracts in Mathematics Ser: No. 53). 1980. 21.50 (ISBN 0-521-20124-1); pap. 11.95 (ISBN 0-521-29882-2). Cambridge U Pr.
Robertson, A. T. Una Armonia De los Cuatro Evangelios. Patterson, W. F., tr. from Eng. Orig. Title: Harmony of the Four Gospels. 259p. (Sp.). 1981. pap. 4.95 (ISBN 0-311-04302-X). Casa Bautista.
--Estudios en el Nuevo Testamento. Hale, Sara A., tr. from Eng. Orig. Title: Studies in the New Testament. 224p. (Span.). 1981. pap. 3.50 (ISBN 0-311-03629-5). Casa Bautista.
--A Harmony of the Gospels. 1932. 11.59i (ISBN 0-06-066890-3, HarpR). Har-Row.
--Paul's Joy in Christ. 1979. pap. 5.95 (ISBN 0-8054-1380-4). Broadman.
--Studies in Mark's Gospel. LC 78-57212. 1978. pap. 2.95 o.p. (ISBN 0-8054-1373-1). Broadman.
Robertson, A. T. & Davis, W. Hersey. New Short Grammar of the Greek New Testament. 10th ed. 1977. pap. 10.95 (ISBN 0-8010-7656-0). Baker Bk.
Robertson, Alan, ed. Selected Experiments in Laboratory & Domestic Animals: Proceedings. 245p. 1980. pap. 37.25 o.p. (ISBN 0-85198-461-4, CAB). Unipub.
Robertson, Andrew. Strategic Marketing: A Business Response to Consumerism. LC 78-3. 34.95x o.p. (ISBN 0-470-26313-X). Halsted Pr.
Robertson, Arlene, ed. see Linares, Enrique.
Robertson, Arlene, ed. see Merriman, Raymond.
Robertson, Arlene, ed. see Starck, Marcia.
Robertson, Arthur. Matthew. (Everyman's Bible Commentary Ser.). (Orig.). 1983. pap. 4.50 (ISBN 0-8024-0233-X). Moody.
Robertson, Arthur H. The Law of International Institutions in Europe. LC 61-13627. (Melland Schill Lecture Ser.). 140p. 1961. 10.00 (ISBN 0-379-11901-3). Oceana.
Robertson, Audrey. Health, Safety & First Aid: A Guide for Training Child Care Workers. 115p. (Orig.). 1980. pap. 11.95 (ISBN 0-934140-04-9). Toys N Things.
Robertson, Audrey, ed. Infant-Toddler Growth & Development: A Guide for Training Child Care Workers. 26p. (Orig.). 1979. GBC Binding 8.95 (ISBN 0-934140-10-3). Toys N Things.
--New Parents: Guidelines for Teaching Infant-Toddler Growth & Development - Birth - 24 Months. (Illus.). 300p. (Orig.). 1982. pap. text ed. 18.95 (ISBN 0-934140-11-1). Toys N Things.
Robertson, Barry C. Modern Physics for Applied Science. LC 80-21884. 464p. 1981. text ed. 25.50x (ISBN 0-471-05343-0). Wiley.
Robertson, C. Grant. Bismarck. LC 68-9604. 1969. Repr. of 1918 ed. 28.50x (ISBN 0-86527-008-2). Fertig.
Robertson, C. J. The Origins of the Scottish Railway System, 1722-1844. 450p. 1983. text ed. 42.00x (ISBN 0-85976-088-X, Pub. by Donald England). Humanities.
Robertson, C. P. & Herrera, R. Nitrogen Cycling in Ecosystems of Latin America & the Caribbean. 1982. 65.00 (ISBN 0-686-38400-8, Pub. by Martinus Nijhoff Netherlands). Kluwer Boston.
Robertson, Caroline E. Neurological-Neurosurgical Nursing Handbook. Gardner, Alvin F., ed. (Allied Health Professions Monograph Ser.). 434p. 1983. 40.00 (ISBN 0-87527-322-X). Green.
Robertson, Charles. The Children. 384p. 1982. pap. 3.50 (ISBN 0-553-20920-5). Bantam.
Robertson, Christina. Divorce & Decision-Making: A Woman's Guide. 220p. 1980. pap. 7.95 o.p. (ISBN 0-695-81343-9). Follett.
Robertson, D. W., Jr. Literature of Medieval England. LC 75-95827. 1970. text ed. 37.50 (ISBN 0-07-053158-7, C). McGraw.

Robertson, Dan H. & Bellenger, Danny N. Sales Management: Decision Making for Improved Profitability. (Illus.). 1980. text ed. 23.95x (ISBN 0-02-402180-6). Macmillan.

Robertson, David. The Old Testament & the Literary Critic. Tucker, Gene M., ed. LC 76-62620. (Guides to Biblical Scholarship Ser). 96p. (Orig.). 1977. pap. 4.25 (ISBN 0-8006-0463-6, 1-463). Fortress.

--A Theory of Party Competition. LC 74-23542. 232p. 1975. 38.95 (ISBN 0-471-72737-7, Pub. by Wiley-Interscience). Wiley.

Robertson, David, jt. ed. see Freemand, Michael.

Robertson, David, jt. ed. see Greene, Bruce M.

Robertson, David H. & Smith, Craig R. Manual of Clinical Pharmacology. (Illus.). 368p. 1981. soft cover 19.00 (ISBN 0-683-07300-1). Williams & Wilkins.

Robertson, Sir Dennis H. Economic Commentaries. LC 77-27311. (Illus.). 1978. Repr. of 1956 ed. lib. bdg. 18.25x (ISBN 0-313-20216-8, ROECC). Greenwood.

Robertson, Don. Make a Wish. LC 77-14531. 1978. 8.95 o.p. (ISBN 0-399-12043-2). Putnam Pub Group.

--Miss Margaret Ridpath & the Dismantling of the Universe. 1977. 10.00 o.p. (ISBN 0-399-11925-6). Putnam Pub Group.

--Mystical Union. LC 78-2895. 1978. 8.95 (ISBN 0-399-12237-0). Putnam Pub Group.

--Praise the Human Season. 544p. 1983. pap. 3.95 (ISBN 0-345-29528-5). Ballantine.

Robertson, Donald S. Greek & Roman Architecture. 2nd ed. (Illus.). 1969. 54.50 (ISBN 0-521-06104-0); pap. 14.95 (ISBN 0-521-09452-6). Cambridge U Pr.

Robertson, Dorothy L. Fairy Tales from the Philippines. LC 76-132626. (Illus.). (gr. 3-7). 1971. 5.95 o.p. (ISBN 0-396-07170-8). Dodd.

Robertson, Douglas see Allen, W. S.

Robertson, E. F., jt. ed. see Campbell, C. M.

Robertson, E. Graeme & Robertson, Joan. Cast Iron Decoration: A World Survey. (Illus.). 1977. 27.50 o.p. (ISBN 0-8230-7122-7). Watson-Guptill.

Robertson, E. H., ed. see Thomas, J. Heywood.

Robertson, E. H., ed. see Towers, Bernard.

Robertson, Eric S., ed. see Browning, Oscar.

Robertson, Esmonde M. Mussolini As Empire-Builder: Europe & Africa, 1932-36. LC 77-79016. (The Making of the 20th Century Ser.). 1978. 25.00x (ISBN 0-312-55589-X). St Martin.

Robertson, F. E. A Practical Treatise on Organ Building, 2 vols. (Bibliotheca Organologica: Vol. 46). Repr. of 1972 ed. wrappers 22.50 o.s.i. (ISBN 90-6027-331-1, Pub. by Frits Knuf Netherlands); Vol. 1, Text. Vol. 2, Plates. Pendragon NY.

Robertson, G., jt. auth. see Kuske, A.

Robertson, G. W. Standardization of the Measurement of Evaporation as a Climatic Factor. (Technical Notes Ser.: No. 11). 10p. 1956. pap. write for info. o.p. (WMO). Unipub.

Robertson, George. Port. (Faber Wine Books Ser.). 192p. 1982. pap. 7.95 (ISBN 0-571-11766-X). Faber & Faber.

Robertson, Hector M. Aspects of the Rise of Economic Individualism. LC 73-17059. Repr. of 1933 ed. 19.50x (ISBN 0-678-00867-1). Kelley.

Robertson, Ian. Loire Valley, Normandy, Brittany. (Blue Guides Ser.). Date not set. 24.95 (ISBN 0-393-01542-4); pap. 15.95 (ISBN 0-393-00095-8). Norton.

--Paris & Environs. 5th ed. (Blue Guides Ser.). 1983. 25.00x (ISBN 0-393-01561-0); pap. 14.70x (ISBN 0-393-30013-7). Norton.

--Sociology. 2nd ed. 1981. text ed. 21.95 (ISBN 0-87901-134-3); study guide 7.95 (ISBN 0-87901-144-0); reader 12.95x (ISBN 0-87901-168-8). Worth.

Robertson, Ian, jt. auth. see Heather, Nick.

Robertson, Ian, ed. The Social World. 2nd ed. x, 396p. 1981. pap. text ed. 12.95x (ISBN 0-87901-168-8). Worth.

Robertson, Jian, ed. see Pforr, Manfred & Limbrunner, Alfred.

Robertson, Irvine G. What the Cults Believe. 1966. pap. 5.95 (ISBN 0-8024-9409-9). Moody.

Robertson, J. A. List of Documents in Spanish Archives Relating to the History of the United States. 1910. pap. 32.00 (ISBN 0-527-00699-8). Kraus Repr.

Robertson, J. C. The Basic Principles of Architectural Design. (Illus.). 127p. 1983. 47.25 (ISBN 0-86650-058-8). Gloucester Art.

Robertson, J. D., jt. auth. see Grillo, John P.

Robertson, J. M. & Wislicenus, G. F., eds. Cavitation State of Knowledge. 1969. 18.50 o.p. (ISBN 0-685-06523-5, I00013). ASME.

Robertson, J. M., jt. ed. see Dummer, Geoffrey W.

Robertson, Jack. Selling to the Federal Government: A Guide for Business. 1978. 17.95 o.p. (ISBN 0-07-053170-6, P&RB). McGraw.

Robertson, James. Young Children in Hospital. 2nd ed. 1970. pap. 9.95x (ISBN 0-422-75060-3, Pub. by Tavistock England). Methuen Inc.

Robertson, James & Robertson, Joyce. A Baby in the Family. 1983. pap. 6.95 (ISBN 0-14-046499-9). Penguin.

Robertson, James I., Jr., compiled by. An Index-Guide to the Southern Historical Society Papers, 1876-1959, 2 vols. LC 79-24910. 1980. Set. lib. bdg. 125.00 (ISBN 0-527-75516-8). Kraus Intl.

Robertson, James I., Jr. & McMurry, Richard M., eds. Rank & File: Civil War Essays in Honor of Bell Irvin Wiley. LC 76-48787. (Illus.). 1977. 8.95 o.p. (ISBN 0-89141-011-2). Presidio Pr.

Robertson, Jenny. King in a Stable. (Illus.). (gr. 2-5). 1977. pap. 4.95 (ISBN 0-87239-123-X, 2990). Standard Pub.

Robertson, Joan, jt. auth. see Robertson, E. Graeme.

Robertson, John. Australia at War Nineteen Thirty-Nine to Nineteen Forty-Five. (Illus.). 288p. (Orig.). 1982. 31.50 (ISBN 0-434-63800-5, Pub. by W Heinemann). David & Charles.

--Here I Am, God, Where Are You? 1975. pap. 2.50 (ISBN 0-8423-1416-4). Tyndale.

Robertson, John A. & American Civil Liberties Union. Rights of the Critically Ill. 200p. 1983. prof ref 19.95x (ISBN 0-88410-733-7). Ballinger Pub.

Robertson, John M. Comfort. 1977. pap. 2.50 (ISBN 0-8423-0432-0). Tyndale.

--Introduction to the Study of the Shakespeare Canon, Proceeding on Problem of Titus Andronicus. Repr. of 1924 ed. lib. bdg. 18.75x (ISBN 0-8371-3744-6, ROSH). Greenwood.

--Roots & Wings: Prayers & Promises for Parents. 84p. 1983. pap. 2.50 (ISBN 0-8423-5712-2). Tyndale.

--Together: Prayers & Promises for Newlyweds. 64p. 1982. pap. 2.50 (ISBN 0-8423-7282-2). Tyndale.

Robertson, John W. Edgar A. Pe: A Study of a Psychopathic. 331p. 1982. Repr. of 1943 ed. lib. bdg. 45.00 (ISBN 0-89987-728-1). Darby Bks.

Robertson, Joyce, jt. auth. see Robertson, James.

Robertson, K. G. Public Secrets: A Study in the Development of Government Secrets. 224p. 1982. 50.00x (ISBN 0-333-32008-5, Pub. by Macmillan England). State Mutual Bk.

Robertson, Kirk. CETA & the Arts in Santa Barbara. 1978. pap. 3.00x (ISBN 0-916918-10-6). Duck Down.

Robertson, Kirk, ed. see Wagner, D. R.

Robertson, Martha O., jt. ed. see Klaus, Marshall.

Robertson, Martin. History of Greek Art, 2 vols. LC 73-79317. 1976. Set. 125.00 (ISBN 0-521-20277-9). Cambridge U Pr.

--A Shorter History of Greek Art. (Illus.). 256p. 1981. 64.50 (ISBN 0-521-23629-0); pap. 19.95 (ISBN 0-521-28084-2). Cambridge U Pr.

Robertson, Mary E. After Freud. LC 80-20497. 230p. 1981. pap. 10.95 cloth (ISBN 0-87395-462-9). State U NY Pr.

--Speak, Angel. LC 82-73015. 256p. 1983. 12.95 (ISBN 0-689-11362-5). Atheneum.

Robertson, Mary Ella. Guide for Board Organization in Social Agencies. rev. ed. 1975. pap. 4.25 (ISBN 0-87868-176-0, AM-21). Child Welfare.

Robertson, Merle G. The Sculpture of Palenque, Vol. 1: The Temple of the Inscriptions. LC 82-341. (Illus.). 350p. 1983. 125.00 (ISBN 0-691-03560-1). Princeton U Pr.

Robertson, P. J. The Leavies on Fiction: A Historic Partnership. LC 80-5099. 172p. 1981. 22.50x (ISBN 0-312-47731-7). St Martin.

Robertson, Patricia & Bounds, Barbara. Sunshine Math Addition & Subtraction. (Illus.). (gr. k-3). 1977. wkbk. 8.25 (ISBN 0-88488-067-2). Creative Pubns.

--Sunshine Math Numeration. (gr. k-3). 1977. wkbk. 8.25 (ISBN 0-88488-066-4). Creative Pubns.

Robertson, Patrick. Movie Facts & Feats. LC 80-52340. (Illus.). 272p. 1980. 19.95 (ISBN 0-8069-0204-3); lib. bdg. 23.59 (ISBN 0-8069-0205-1). Sterling.

Robertson, Priscilla. An Experience of Women: Pattern & Change in Nineteenth-Century Europe. LC 81-9315. 673p. 1982. 34.95 (ISBN 0-87722-234-7). Temple U Pr.

Robertson, Richard T., ed. Neuroanatomical Research Technique. (Methods in Physiological Psych. Ser.: Vol. 2). 1978. 47.50 (ISBN 0-12-590350-2). Acad Pr.

Robertson, Roland. The Sociological Interpretation of Religion. LC 77-79214. (Introductions to Sociology Ser.). 264p. 1972. Repr. of 1970 ed. 6.50x o.p. (ISBN 0-8052-3347-4). Schocken.

Robertson, Seonaid. Dyes from Plants. 1978. pap. 8.95 o.p. (ISBN 0-442-26975-7). Van Nos Reinhold.

Robertson, Seonaid M. Creative Crafts in Education. (Illus.). 1967. Repr. of 1952 ed. 22.50x (ISBN 0-7100-2045-7). Routledge & Kegan.

--Rosegarden & Labyrinth: A Study in Art Education. (Illus.). 1963. 16.95x o.p. (ISBN 0-7100-2046-5). Routledge & Kegan.

Robertson, Thomas, jt. auth. see Kassarjian, Harold.

Robertson, Thomas S. Consumer Behavior. 1970. pap. 8.95x (ISBN 0-673-07553-2). Scott F.

Robertson, W. B. The Endometrium. (Postgraduate Pathology Ser.). 1981. text ed. 65.95 (ISBN 0-407-00171-9). Butterworth.

Robertson, Warren. Free to Act: How to Star in Your Own Life. LC 77-3616. (N/F). 1978. 8.95 o.p. (ISBN 0-399-11961-2). Putnam Pub Group.

Robertson, Wendy, jt. auth. see Robertson, A. P.

Robertson, Wilmont, ed. Best of Instauration 1977. 127p. 1982. pap. 15.00 (ISBN 0-914576-19-4). Howard Allen.

Robertson, Wilmot. Ventilations. Rev. ed. LC 74-20120. 113p. 1982. pap. 4.95 (ISBN 0-914576-06-2). Howard Allen.

Robertson-Nicoll, W., ed. The Expositor's Bible, 6 Vols. 1982. 195.00 (ISBN 0-8010-6685-9). Baker Bk.

Roberval, Gilles. Aristarchi Samii De Mundi Systemate, Partibus et Motibus Eiusdem Libellus: Adjectae Sunt Ae De Roverval... Repr. of 1644 ed. 49.00 o.p. (ISBN 0-8287-0734-0). Clearwater Pub.

--Divers Ouvrages De Mathematique et De Physique Par Messieurs De L'academie Royale Des Sciences. Repr. of 1693 ed. 72.00 o.p. (ISBN 0-8287-0735-9). Clearwater Pub.

--Traite de Mecanique des Poids Soutenus Par des Puissances Sur les Plans Inclines. Repr. of 1636 ed. 20.00 o.p. (ISBN 0-8287-0736-7). Clearwater Pub.

Robeson, Eslanda. African Journey. LC 73-164468. (Illus.). 154p. 1972. Repr. of 1945 ed. lib. bdg. 17.50x (ISBN 0-8371-6222-X, ROAJ). Greenwood.

Robey, Cora L. & Morgan, Ethelyn H. Basic Communication Skills: Writing, Speaking, Listening. 272p. 1983. pap. text ed. 13.50 scp (ISBN 0-06-045498-9, HarpC). Har-Row.

Robey, David, ed. Structuralism: An Introduction-Wolfson College Lectures 1972. 1973. pap. text ed. 12.95x (ISBN 0-19-874017-4). Oxford U Pr.

Robey, Harriet. There's a Dance in the Old Dame Yet. (General Ser.). 1982. lib. bdg. 14.95 (ISBN 0-8161-3478-2, Large Print Bks). G K Hall.

Robichaud, Beryl & Buell, Murray F. Vegetation of New Jersey: A Study of Landscape Diversity. (Illus.). 352p. 1973. 25.00x (ISBN 0-8135-0745-6); pap. 9.95 (ISBN 0-8135-0795-2). Rutgers U Pr.

Robichaud, Beryl & Muscat, Eugene. Data Processing Work Kit. 2nd ed. 96p. (gr. 9-12). 1983. practice set 7.96 (ISBN 0-07-053207-9, C); instr's manual & key 2.50 (ISBN 0-07-053206-0). McGraw.

Robichaud, Beryl, et al. Introduction to Data Processing. 2nd ed. Orig. Title: Understanding Modern Business Data Processing. (Illus.). (gr. 9-12). 1976. text ed. 13.12 (ISBN 0-07-053190-0, G); tchr's manual & key 3.95 (ISBN 0-07-053191-9); activities 9.60 (ISBN 0-07-053192-7); instructor's manual & key to work kit 2.55 (ISBN 0-07-053193-5). McGraw.

Robicheaux, Robert. Marketing: Contemporary Dimensions. 3rd ed. LC 82-82470. 432p. 1982. pap. text ed. 13.95 (ISBN 0-395-33166-8). HM.

Robicheaux, Robert A. & Pride, William M. Marketing: Contemporary Dimensions. 2nd ed. LC 79-89125. 1980. pap. text ed. 12.50 (ISBN 0-395-28500-3). HM.

Robichek, Alexander A. & Myers, Stewart C. Optimal Financing Decisions. (Illus.). 1966. pap. 11.95x ref. ed. o.p. (ISBN 0-13-638114-6). P-H.

Robicsek, Francis. A Study in Maya Art & History: The Mat Symbol. LC 75-18351. (Illus.). 1975. o. p. 22.00x (ISBN 0-934490-25-2); soft cover 5.00x (ISBN 0-934490-26-0). Mus Am Ind.

Robicsek, Francis & Hale, Donald. The Maya Book of the Dead: The Ceramic Codex. (Illus.). 288p. 48.50 (ISBN 0-686-87499-4). U of Okla Pr.

Robie, Diane C., jt. auth. see Roberts, January.

Robiette, A. G. Electric Melting Practice. 412p. 1972. 64.95x o.s.i. (ISBN 0-470-72787-X). Halsted Pr.

--Electric Smelting Processes. LC 73-2039. (Illus.). 276p. 1973. 49.95x o.p. (ISBN 0-470-72786-1). Halsted Pr.

Robigne, Bennel De see De Robigne, Bennett M.

Robillard, Raymond A. Interdependence of Free Enterprise & Governments in the Global Marketplace. LC 79-66832. 1979. pap. text ed. 9.75 (ISBN 0-8191-0852-9). U Pr of Amer.

Robiller, Franz. Birds Throughout the World. (Illus.). 218p. 1980. 17.50 (ISBN 0-88254-577-9). Hippocrene Bks.

Robin. Higher Excited States of Polyatomic Molecules. Vol. 1. 1974. 48.50 (ISBN 0-12-589901-7); Vol. 2. 1975. 63.00 (ISBN 0-12-589902-5). Acad Pr.

--How to Get the Most Out of Your Audio Recording & Playback. (Illus.). 128p. 1980. pap. 7.95 (ISBN 0-8359-2957-4). Reston.

Robin, Christopher. How to Build Your Own Stereo Speakers: Construction, Applications, Circuits & Characteristics. (Illus.). 1978. ref. ed. 16.95 (ISBN 0-87909-374-9); pap. 8.95 (ISBN 0-8359-2936-1). Reston.

Robin, Donald, jt. auth. see Walters, Glenn.

Robin, Eddie. Position Play in Three Cushion Billiards. (Three Cushion Billiards Ser.: Vol. III). (Illus.). 431p. 1980. 28.00 o.p. (ISBN 0-936362-00-6). E Robin Pub.

--Position Play in Three Cushion Billiards. (Three Cushion Billiards Ser.: Vol. III). (Illus.). 431p. 1983. 36.00. E Robin Pub.

Robin, Gerald D. Introduction to the Criminal Justice System: Principles, Procedures, Practice. (Illus.). 1980. text ed. 20.95 scp o.p. (ISBN 0-06-045504-7, HarpC); instrs.' manual avail. o.p. (ISBN 0-06-365513-6). Har-Row.

--Introduction to the Criminal Justice System: Principles, Procedures, Practice. 2nd ed. 550p. 1983. text ed. 21.50 scp (ISBN 0-06-045512-8, HarpC); instr's. manual avail. (ISBN 0-06-365524-1). Har-Row.

Robin, Gordon C. Scoliosis & Neurological Disease. LC 75-19283. 1975. 44.95 o.s.i. (ISBN 0-470-72795-0). Halsted Pr.

Robin, Jean. Elmdon, Continuity & Change in a Northwest Essex Village. LC 79-12964. (Illus.). 1980. 47.50 (ISBN 0-521-22820-4). Cambridge U Pr.

Robin, Leon. Greek Thought & the Origins of the Scientific Spirit. Dobie, Marryat R., tr. LC 66-27142. 1967. Repr. of 1928 ed. 18.00x o.p. (ISBN 0-8462-0906-3). Russell.

Robin, M. Canadian Provincial Politics. 2nd ed. 1978. pap. 13.25 (ISBN 0-13-113233-4). P-H.

Robin, Stanley & Wagenfeld, Morton, eds. Paraprofessionals in the Human Services. LC 80-18011. (Community Psychology Ser.: Vol. VI). 368p. 1981. 34.95 (ISBN 0-87705-490-8). Human Sci Pr.

Robin, Stanley S., jt. auth. see Bosco, James J.

Robinet, B., ed. see Colloque Sur la Programmation, Paris, 9-11 April, 1974.

Robinett. Teaching English to Speakers of Other Languages: Substance & Technique. 1979. 8.95 (ISBN 0-07-053179-X). McGraw.

Robinett, Betty W. & Schachter, Jacqueline. Second Language Learning: Contrastive Analysis, Error Analysis & Related Aspects. 432p. 1983. text ed. 30.00x (ISBN 0-472-10027-0); pap. text ed. 14.95x (ISBN 0-472-08033-4). U of Mich Pr.

Robins, Adrienne, ed. The Writer's Practical Rhetoric. 1980. text ed. 16.50x (ISBN 0-673-15694-X). Scott F.

Robins, Arthur J., jt. auth. see Katahn, Martin.

Robins, Corinne, intro. by. A. I. R. Overview: An Exhibition in Two Parts, 1971 to 1977. (Illus.). 43p. 1978. pap. 3.00 (ISBN 0-89062-126-8, Pub by A.I.R. Gallery). Pub Ctr Cult Res.

Robins, Denise. Desert Rapture. 1978. pap. 1.75 o.p. (ISBN 0-380-42416-9, 42416). Avon.

--The Feast Is Finished. 1979. pap. 1.75 o.p. (ISBN 0-380-45096-8, 45096). Avon.

--Life & Love. 1978. pap. 1.75 o.p. (ISBN 0-380-41384-1, 41384). Avon.

--The Long Shadow. 1979. pap. 1.75 o.p. (ISBN 0-380-47167-1, 47167). Avon.

--Love Me No More. 1976. pap. 1.25 o.p. (ISBN 0-380-00825-4, 30916). Avon.

--Meet Me in Monte Carlo. 1979. pap. 1.75 o.p. (ISBN 0-380-43620-5, 43620). Avon.

--My Lady Destiny. 1978. pap. 1.95 o.p. (ISBN 0-380-38372-1, 38372). Avon.

--My True Love. 1977. pap. 1.25 o.p. (ISBN 0-380-01643-5, 33001). Avon.

--The Tiger in Men. 1979. pap. 1.75 o.s.i. (ISBN 0-380-45005-4, 45005). Avon.

--Venetian Rhapsody. 1979. pap. 1.75 o.p. (ISBN 0-380-44255-8, 44255). Avon.

--Winged Love. 1978. pap. 1.95 o.p. (ISBN 0-380-39909-1, 39909). Avon.

Robins, Eli. The Final Months: A Study of the Lives of 134 Persons Who Committed Suicide. 1981. text ed. 35.00x (ISBN 0-19-502911-9). Oxford U Pr.

Robins, G. V. Food Science in Catering. 1980. pap. 21.50 (ISBN 0-434-90297-7, Pub. by Heinemann). David & Charles.

Robins, Kaylyn, jt. auth. see Schnexaydre, Linda.

Robins, Lee N. Deviant Children Grown up: A Sociological & Psychiatric Study of Sociopathic Personality. LC 74-9671. 366p. 1974. Repr. of 1966 ed. 17.50 o.p. (ISBN 0-88275-183-2). Krieger.

Robins, Lee N., et al, eds. The Social Consequences of Psychiatric Illness. LC 80-11090. 1980. 25.00 o.p. (ISBN 0-87630-226-6). Brunner-Mazel.

Robins, Natalie. Eclipse. LC 82-75158. viii, 64p. 1981. 12.95x (ISBN 0-8040-0367-X); pap. 5.95 (ISBN 0-8040-0368-8). Swallow.

Robins, Perry & Bennett, Richard G., eds. Current Concepts in the Management of Skin Cancer. (Illus.). 68p. 1978. pap. 10.50x (ISBN 0-9602346-0-8). Masson Pub.

Robins, Peter. The Gay Touch. LC 82-12704. 96p. 1982. 12.95 (ISBN 0-89594-085-X); pap. 4.95 (ISBN 0-89594-084-1). Crossing Pr.

Robins, Philip K. & Weiner, Samuel, eds. Child Care & Public Policy. LC 77-17724. (Studies of the Economic Issues). (Illus.). 256p. 1978. 21.95x o.p. (ISBN 0-669-02088-5). Lexington Bks.

Robins-Mowry, Dorothy. The Hidden Sun: Women of Modern Japan. 370p. 1983. lib. bdg. 30.00 (ISBN 0-86531-421-7); pap. text ed. 11.95 (ISBN 0-86531-437-3). Westview.

Robinson. Advanced Cobol. 1976. 27.50 (ISBN 0-444-19453-3). Elsevier.

--American Education: Its Organization & Control. 1968. pap. text ed. 12.95 (ISBN 0-675-09823-8). Merrill.

--Beginners Guide to Fabric Printing & Dyeing. 1982. text ed. 9.95 (ISBN 0-408-00575-0). Butterworth.

--Selected Papers of Abraham Robinson, 3 vols. Korner, S., et al, eds. LC 77-92395. 1979. Vol. 2. text ed. 50.00x (ISBN 0-300-02072-4); Vol. 3. text ed. 40.00x (ISBN 0-300-02073-2); Vol. 3. text ed. 55.00x (ISBN 0-300-02071-6). Yale U Pr.

Robinson, A. Complete Theories. 2nd rev. ed. (Studies in Logic & the Foundations of Mathematics: Vol. 46). 1977. text ed. 38.50 (ISBN 0-7204-0690-0, North-Holland). Elsevier.

--The Repair of Vehicle Bodies. 1973. text ed. 16.50x o.p. (ISBN 0-435-72054-6). Heinemann Ed.

Robinson, A. N. Mechanics of Independence: A Study in Political & Economic Transformation. 1971. 20.00x (ISBN 0-262-18044-8). MIT Pr.

Robinson, Adele J., ed. Portland Symphony Cookbook. 5th ed. LC 74-84052. 1974. 9.95 (ISBN 0-9601266-1-9). Portland Symphony.

Robinson, Adjai. Femi & Old Grandaddie. (Illus.). 48p. (gr. k-3). 1972. PLB 4.69 o.p. (ISBN 0-698-30453-5, Coward). Putnam Pub Group.

--Kasho & the Twin Flutes. (Illus.). 48p. (gr. k-3). 1973. PLB 4.97 o.p. (ISBN 0-698-30517-5, Coward). Putnam Pub Group.

--Three African Tales. LC 78-13927. (Illus.). (gr. 3-7). 1979. 6.95 (ISBN 0-399-20656-6). Putnam Pub Group.

Robinson, Adrian & Millward, Roy. The Shell Book of the British Coast. (Illus.). 496p. (Orig.). 1983. 31.50 (ISBN 0-7153-8150-4). David & Charles.

Robinson, Alice & Reres, Mary. Your Future in Nursing Careers. LC 72-75218. (Illus.). 128p. 1975. pap. 4.50 (ISBN 0-668-03429-7). Arco.

Robinson, Anthony, ed. Air Power: Three World's Air Forces. (Illus.). 312p. Date not set. 29.95 o.p. (ISBN 0-87165-080-0, ZD Bks). Ziff-Davis Pub.

Robinson, Archie. George Meany & His Times. 1982. 17.95 (ISBN 0-671-42163-8). S&S.

Robinson, Arthur, jt. ed. see Kaplan, Nathan O.

Robinson, Arthur, et al. Elements of Cartography. 4th ed. LC 78-1670. 1978. 31.50x (ISBN 0-471-01781-7). Wiley.

Robinson, Arthur H., et al. Atlas of Wisconsin. LC 73-15262. 126p. 1974. 27.50 (ISBN 0-299-06530-8); pap. 15.00 (ISBN 0-299-06534-0). U of Wis Pr.

Robinson, Arthur W. The Personal Life of the Christian. 1981. pap. 7.95 (ISBN 0-19-213427-2). Oxford U Pr.

Robinson, Austin. Appropriate Technologies for Third World Development. LC 26-416. 1979. 35.00 (ISBN 0-312-04672-3). St Martin.

Robinson, B. W. Japanese Sword-Fittings & Associated Metalwork. (Baur Collection Geneva: Vol. 7). (Illus.). 448p. 1981. 250.00 (ISBN 2-88031-003-2, Pub. by Baur Foundation Switzerland). Routledge & Kegan.

--Kuniyoshi: The Warrior Prints. LC 81-70706. (Illus.). 240p. 1982. 55.00x (ISBN 0-8014-1488-1). Cornell U Pr.

Robinson, Barbara. The Best Christmas Pageant Ever. 80p. 1982. pap. 2.50 (ISBN 0-8423-0137-2). Tyndale.

Robinson, Barbara & Wolfson, Evelyn. Environmental Education Manual. LC 82-741. 1982. pap. text ed. 15.95x (ISBN 0-8077-2715-6). Tchrs Coll.

Robinson, Barbara J. & Robinson, J. Cordell. The Mexican American: A Critical Guide to Research Aids, Vol. 1. Stueart, Robert D., ed. LC 76-5643. (Foundations in Library & Information Science Ser). 1980. lib. bdg. 42.50 (ISBN 0-89232-006-0). Jai Pr.

Robinson, Bernard. Peter First & John First. (Scripture Discussion Outlines Ser). 1968. pap. 0.75 o.p. (ISBN 0-685-07659-8, 80648). Glencoe.

Robinson, Blackwell. The North Carolina Adventure. (Illus.). (gr. 3-6). 1969. text ed. 9.95 (ISBN 0-87716-017-1, Pub. by Moore Pub Co). F Apple.

Robinson, Brian. The Fischer Indole Synthesis. 928p. 1983. 131.00 (ISBN 0-471-10009-9, Pub. by Wiley-Interscience). Wiley.

Robinson, Bryan E., jt. auth. see Flake-Hobson, Carol.

Robinson, Cedric J. The Terms of Order: Political Science & the Myth of Leadership. LC 79-15023. 1980. 39.50x (ISBN 0-87395-411-4); pap. 13.95x (ISBN 0-87395-453-X). State U NY Pr.

Robinson, Charles A., Jr. First Book of Ancient Egypt. LC 77-20858. (First Bks). (Illus.). (gr. 4-6). 1960. PLB 7.90 (ISBN 0-531-00462-7). Watts.

Robinson, Charles N. British Tar in Fact & Fiction. LC 68-26601. (Illus.). 1968. Repr. of 1909 ed. 37.00x (ISBN 0-8103-3514-X). Gale.

Robinson, Christopher. French Literature in the Twentieth Century. (Comparative Literature Ser.). 288p. 1980. 15.00x (ISBN 0-389-20121-9). B&N Imports.

Robinson, Clayton, jt. ed. see Kalin, Berkeley.

Robinson, Corinne H. & Weigley, Emma S. Fundamentals of Normal Nutrition. 3rd ed. (Illus.). 1978. 24.95x (ISBN 0-02-402330-2). Macmillan.

Robinson, Corrine H. Basic Nutrition & Diet Therapy. 4th ed. (Illus.). 1980. pap. text ed. 13.95x (ISBN 0-02-402450-3). Macmillan.

Robinson, D. M., jt. ed. see Jamieson, G. A.

Robinson, D. W., jt. ed. see Bratteli, O.

Robinson, D. Z., et al. Nuclear Energy Today & Tomorrow. 1971. 9.95x o.p. (ISBN 0-435-68280-6). Heinemann Ed.

Robinson, Daniel. Psychology: Traditions & Perspectives. 1976. 14.95x (ISBN 0-442-26969-2); instructor's manual 1.00x (ISBN 0-442-26968-4). Van Nos Reinhold.

Robinson, Daniel N. Psychology & Law: Can Justice Survive the Social Sciences? 1980. text ed. 14.95x o.p. (ISBN 0-19-502725-6); pap. text ed. 7.95x (ISBN 0-19-502726-4). Oxford U Pr.

--Toward a Science of Human Nature: Aspirations of Nineteenth Century Psychology. LC 81-38458. 256p. 1982. 27.50x (ISBN 0-231-05174-3); pap. 15.50x (ISBN 0-231-05175-1). Columbia U Pr.

Robinson, Darline, jt. auth. see Robison, James.

Robinson, David. The Book of Lincolnshire Seaside. 1981. 39.50x o.p. (ISBN 0-86023-122-4, Pub. by Barracuda England). State Mutual Bk.

--Encyclopedia of Gerbils. 224p. 1980. 12.95 (ISBN 0-87666-915-1, H-974). TFH Pubns.

--Encyclopedia of Pet Rabbits. (Illus.). 320p. 1979. 14.95 (ISBN 0-87666-911-9, H-984). TFH Pubns.

--From Drinking to Alcoholism: A Sociological Commentary. LC 75-26597. 224p. 1976. 39.95x (ISBN 0-471-01357-9); pap. text ed. 11.95 o.p. (ISBN 0-471-01358-7, Pub. by Wiley-Interscience). Wiley.

--Gerbils. LC 76-9037. (Illus.). (YA) 1976. bds. 2.25 o.p. (ISBN 0-668-03987-6). Arco.

--The Process of Becoming Ill. (Medicine, Illness & Society Ser). 1971. 18.00x o.p. (ISBN 0-7100-7096-9). Routledge & Kegan.

--Writing Reports for Management Decisions. LC 79-75628. 1969. text ed. 15.95x o.p. (ISBN 0-675-09504-2). Merrill.

Robinson, David, ed. see Aranda, Francisco.

Robinson, David A. Accounts Receivable & Inventory Lending: How to Establish & Operate a Department. LC 77-5322. (Illus.). 1977. 36.00 o.p. (ISBN 0-87267-029-5). Bankers.

Robinson, Dennis, jt. auth. see Robinson, Jacqueline.

Robinson, Dennis M., jt. auth. see Robinson, Jacqueline.

Robinson, Doane. History of the Dakota or Sioux Indians. 1967. Repr. 15.00 o.p. (ISBN 0-87018-053-3). Ross.

Robinson, Dorothy N. The Official Price Guide to American Silver & Silverplate 1982. (Illus.). 400p. 1981. pap. 9.95 o.p. (ISBN 0-87637-184-5). Hse of Collectibles.

Robinson, Dorothy N. & Feeny, Bill. Official Price Guide to American Pottery & Porcelain. LC 78-72031. (Collector Ser.). (Illus.). 400p. 1980. pap. 9.95 o.p. (ISBN 0-87637-013-X, 013-0X). Hse of Collectibles.

Robinson, Douglas. Act Two Beginners Please. Incl. Melody. 72p. 2.95 o.p. (ISBN 0-521-07417-7); Piano. 112p. 9.95 (ISBN 0-521-07416-9). LC 69-16285. 1970. Cambridge U Pr.

--All Beginners Please. 1967. Melody. 3.95 (ISBN 0-521-06111-3); Piano. o.p. (ISBN 0-521-06110-5). Cambridge U Pr.

Robinson, Douglas, ed. see Starr, Walter A., Jr.

Robinson, Douglas H., jt. auth. see Keller, Charles L.

Robinson, Dow F. Aztec Studies Two: Sierra Nahuat Word Structure. (Publications in Linguistics & Related Fields Ser.: No. 22). 186p. 1970. pap. 3.50x (ISBN 0-88312-024-0); microfiche 2.25 (ISBN 0-88312-424-6). Summer Inst Ling.

--Manual for Bilingual Dictionaries, 3 vols. 1969. o. p. 5.00 (ISBN 0-685-40975-9); Set. microfiche 9.00; Vol. I. microfiche 3.00 (ISBN 0-88312-327-4); Vol. II. microfiche 3.00 (ISBN 0-88312-328-2); Vol. III. microfiche 3.00 (ISBN 0-88312-329-0). Summer Inst Ling.

Robinson, Duncan. William Morris, Edward Burne-Jones & the Kelmscott Chaucer. 160p. 1982. 95.00x (ISBN 0-86092-038-0, Pub. by Fraser Bks). State Mutual Bk.

Robinson, E., jt. auth. see Bate, R. H.

Robinson, E. A., jt. auth. see Silvia, M. T.

Robinson, E. A. & Griffin, Keith, eds. The Economic Development of Bangladesh Within a Socialist Framework: Proceedings of a Conference Held by the International Economic Association at Daca. LC 74-8438. (International Economic Assoc. Ser.). 1974. 59.95 o.s.i. (ISBN 0-470-72803-5). Halsted Pr.

Robinson, E. A., ed. see American Economic Association & Royal Economic Society.

Robinson, E. John. The Seascape Painter's Problem Book. (Illus., Orig.). 1976. 19.50 (ISBN 0-8230-4737-7). Watson-Guptill.

Robinson, E. R. Time Dependent Chemical Processes. LC 75-1124. 370p. 1975. 54.95x o.s.i. (ISBN 0-470-72802-7). Halsted Pr.

Robinson, Edward. The Original Vision: A Study of the Religious Experience of Childhood. 192p. (Orig.). 1983. pap. 7.95 (ISBN 0-8164-2439-X). Seabury.

Robinson, Edward, tr. see Gesenius, William.

Robinson, Edward S. & Robinson, Florence R. Readings in General Psychology. 812p. 1982. Repr. of 1923 ed. lib. bdg. 85.00 (ISBN 0-89984-848-6). Century Bookbindery.

Robinson, Edwin A. Selected Letters of Edwin Arlington Robinson. LC 79-15514. (Illus.). 1980. Repr. of 1940 ed. lib. bdg. 20.25x (ISBN 0-313-21266-X, ROSL). Greenwood.

--Untriangulated Stars: Letters of Edwin Arlington Robinson to Harry de Forest Smith, 1890-1905. Sutcliffe, Denham, ed. LC 76-113064. (Illus.). xxvii, 348p. Repr. of 1947 ed. lib. bdg. 20.75x (ISBN 0-8371-4704-2, ROUS). Greenwood.

Robinson, Edwin S. Basic Physical Geology. 686p. 1982. text ed. 26.95x (ISBN 0-471-72809-8); tchr's. manual 7.50 (ISBN 0-471-86926-0). Wiley.

Robinson, Elwyn B. History of North Dakota. LC 66-10877. (Illus.). xiv, 599p. 1966. 25.00x (ISBN 0-8032-0155-9, BB 811, Bison); 13.95x (ISBN 0-8032-8909-X). U of Nebr Pr.

Robinson, Enders A. Least Squares Regression Analysis in Terms of Linear Algebra. LC 81-82322. (Illus.). 520p. 1981. 25.00 (ISBN 0-910835-01-2). Goose Pond Pr.

--Migration of Geophysical Data. LC 82-82537. (Illus.). 224p. 1982. text ed. 34.00 (ISBN 0-934634-14-9). Intl Human Res.

--Statistical Reasoning & Decision Making. LC 81-85240. (Illus.). 200p. 1981. 12.00 (ISBN 0-910835-02-0). Goose Pond Pr.

--Times Series Analysis & Applications. LC 81-81825. (Illus.). 628p. 1981. 25.00 (ISBN 0-910835-00-4). Goose Pond Pr.

Robinson, Enders A. & Silvia, Manual T. Digital Foundations of Time Series Analysis: Wave-Equation Space-Time Processing, Vol. II. 450p. 1981. text ed. 37.00 (ISBN 0-8162-7271-9). Holden-Day.

Robinson, Enders A. & Treitel, Sven. Geophysical Signal Analysis. (Signal Processing Ser.). (Illus.). 1980. text ed. 40.00 (ISBN 0-13-352658-5). P-H.

Robinson, Eric & Fitter, Richard, eds. John Clare's Birds. (Illus.). 1982. 16.50x (ISBN 0-19-212977-5). Oxford U Pr.

Robinson, F. Separatism among Indian Muslims. (South Asian Studies: No. 16). 400p. 1975. 49.50 (ISBN 0-521-20432-1). Cambridge U Pr.

Robinson, Florence R., jt. auth. see Robinson, Edward S.

Robinson, Forrest G. & Robinson, Margaret G. Wallace Stegner. (U.S. Authors Ser.: No. 282). 1977. lib. bdg. 10.95 o.p. (ISBN 0-8057-7182-4, Twayne). G K Hall.

Robinson, Francis. Atlas of the Islamic World: Since 1500. (Illus.). 240p. 1982. 35.00 (ISBN 0-87196-629-8). Facts on File.

Robinson, Frank E., jt. auth. see Gerbracht, Carl.

Robinson, Franklin W. One Hundred Master Drawings from New England Private Collections. LC 73-85877. (Illus.). 221p. 1973. pap. 10.00x o.p. (ISBN 0-87451-087-2). U Pr of New Eng.

Robinson, Fred C., jt. auth. see Greenfield, Stanley B.

Robinson, Fred C., jt. auth. see Mitchell, Bruce.

Robinson, Frederick W. Church & Chapel, 1863, 3 vols. in 1. Wolff, Robert L., ed. LC 75-1500. (Victorian Fiction Ser.). 1975. lib. bdg. 66.00 o.s.i. (ISBN 0-8240-1575-4). Garland Pub.

Robinson, G. N. & Watson, A. Augmentin: Clavulanate Potentiated Amoxycillin. (International Congress Ser.: Vol. 544). 1981. 61.00 (ISBN 0-444-90188-4). Elsevier.

Robinson, G. W., tr. see Wang-Wei.

Robinson, Gail. Raven the Trickster: Legends of the North American Indians. LC 82-4017. (Illus.). 128p. (gr. 3-7). 1982. 8.95 (ISBN 0-689-50247-8, McElderry Bk). Atheneum.

Robinson, Gary W. What Is the Future? 1983. 5.95 (ISBN 0-533-05568-7). Vantage.

Robinson, Geoffrey C. & Clarke, Heather F. The Hospital Care of Children: A Review of Contemporary Issues. 1980. 24.95x (ISBN 0-19-502673-X). Oxford U Pr.

Robinson, George M., jt. auth. see Moulton, Janice.

Robinson, Gerald G., jt. auth. see Nelson, Gideon E.

Robinson, Geroid T. Rural Russia under the Old Regime: A History of the Landlord-Peasant World & a Prologue to the Peasant Revolution of 1917. 1967. pap. 9.95x (ISBN 0-520-01075-2). U of Cal Pr.

Robinson, Glen O., et al. The Administrative Process: Supplement. 2nd ed. (American Casebook Ser.). 182p. 1983. pap. text ed. write for info. (ISBN 0-314-72079-0). West Pub.

Robinson, Gwen R. Skiing: Conditioning & Technique. LC 73-91389. (Illus.). 99p. 1974. pap. 4.95 (ISBN 0-87484-278-6). Mayfield Pub.

Robinson, H. & Bamford, C. G. Geography of the EEC. 288p. 1983. pap. 16.95x (ISBN 0-7121-0732-0). Intl Ideas.

Robinson, H. & Smith, N. Reading Instruction for Today's Children. 1980. 24.95 (ISBN 0-13-755157-6). P-H.

Robinson, H. Alan, jt. ed. see Berger, Allen.

Robinson, H. S. & Wilson, K. The Encyclopedia of Myths & Legends of All Nations. rev. ed. Picard, Barbara L., ed. 1978. Repr. of 1974 ed. text ed. 23.50x (ISBN 0-7182-0561-8, LTB). Sportshelf.

Robinson, Haddon. Biblical Preaching. LC 80-66776. 1980. 10.95 (ISBN 0-8010-7700-1). Baker Bk.

Robinson, Haddon, jt. ed. see Litfin, Duane.

Robinson, Haddon W. Grief. 24p. 1976. Repr. pap. 1.50 (ISBN 0-310-32261-8). Zondervan.

--Psalm Twenty-Three. (Illus., Orig.). 1968. pap. 2.95 (ISBN 0-8024-6935-3); pap. 3.95 large print o.p. (ISBN 0-8024-6934-5). Moody.

Robinson, Halbert B. & Robinson, Nancy M. The Mentally Retarded Child. 2nd ed. (Psychology Ser.). (Illus.). 672p. 1976. text ed. 28.50 (ISBN 0-07-053202-8, C); instructor's manual 15.00 (ISBN 0-07-053203-6). McGraw.

Robinson, Hamilton B. G. & Miller, Arthur S. Colby, Kerr, & Robinson's Color Atlas of Oral Pathology. 4th ed. (Illus.). 288p. 1982. text ed. 32.50 (ISBN 0-397-50563-9, Lippincott Medical). Lippincott.

Robinson, Helene. Basic Piano for Adults. 1967 pap. 11.95x (ISBN 0-534-00065-7). Wadsworth Pub.

Robinson, Henry, et al. Certain Considerations in Order to a More Speedy, Cheap, & Equal Distribution of Justice Throughout the Nation. Berkowitz, David S. & Thorne, Samuel E., eds. LC 77-86668. (Classics of English Legal History in the Modern Era Ser.: Vol. 49). 317p. 1979. lib. bdg. 55.00 o.s.i. (ISBN 0-8240-3098-2). Garland Pub.

Robinson, Henry H. Negotiability in the Federal Sector. LC 80-28672. 232p. 1981. 22.50 (ISBN 0-87546-080-1); pap. 14.95 (ISBN 0-87546-081-X). ILR Pr.

Robinson, Herbert S. English Shakespearian Criticism in the Eighteenth Century. LC 66-24445. 1968. Repr. of 1932 ed. 10.00x (ISBN 0-87752-094-1). Gordian.

Robinson, Hilary. Somerville & Ross: A Critical Appreciation. 220p. 1980. 26.00x (ISBN 0-312-74426-9). St Martin.

Robinson, Howard. Matter & Sense: A Critique of Contemporary Materialism. LC 82-1176. (Cambridge Studies in Philosophy). 160p. 1982. 19.95 (ISBN 0-521-24471-4). Cambridge U Pr.

Robinson, Hugh. Database Analysis & Design. 375p. 1981. pap. text ed. 26.50x (ISBN 0-686-81668-4, Pub. by Studentlitteratur). Renouf.

Robinson, Ian. Chaucer & the English Tradition. LC 79-163179. 1972. 44.50 (ISBN 0-521-08231-5); pap. o.p. (ISBN 0-521-09899-8). Cambridge U Pr.

--The New Grammarian's Funeral. LC 75-6009. (Illus.). 225p. 1975. 29.95 (ISBN 0-521-20856-4); pap. 11.95 (ISBN 0-521-29316-2). Cambridge U Pr.

Robinson, Ian, jt. auth. see Horowitz, Paul.

Robinson, Ira M., jt. ed. see Perks, William T.

Robinson, J. Highways & Our Environment. 1971. 51.50 (ISBN 0-07-053315-6, P&RB). McGraw.

--Integrated Theory of Finite Element Methods. LC 73-2792. 428p. 1973. 67.50 o.p. (ISBN 0-471-72807-1, Pub. by Wiley-Interscience). Wiley.

--Pesticides & Ecosystems. 1982. 6.95x o.p. (ISBN 0-412-11860-2, Pub. by Chapman & Hall). Methuen Inc.

Robinson, J., ed. Shuttle Propulsion Systems. (AD-05 Ser.). 1982. 24.00 (H00243). ASME.

Robinson, J. A. Looking at Language. (Local Search Ser.). (Illus.). 1974. 7.95 (ISBN 0-7100-7589-8). Routledge & Kegan.

Robinson, J. Armitage, tr. see Irenaeus, St.

Robinson, J. Cordell, jt. auth. see Robinson, Barbara J.

Robinson, J. Hedley. Using the Telescope: A Handbook for Astronomers. LC 78-10759. 1979. 12.95x o.p. (ISBN 0-470-26514-0). Halsted Pr.

Robinson, J. Hedley & Muirden, James. Astronomy Data Book. 2nd ed. LC 78-21698. 1979. 24.95x (ISBN 0-470-26594-9). Halsted Pr.

Robinson, J. Lister. Mechanics of Materials. LC 68-55336. 345p. 1969. text ed. 16.00 (ISBN 0-471-72810-1, Pub. by Wiley). Krieger.

Robinson, J. P. The Effects of Weapons on Ecosystems. LC 79-41226. (Illus.). 76p. 1979. 12.25 o.s.i. (ISBN 0-08-025656-2). Pergamon.

Robinson, J. S. Corrosion Inhibitors: Recent Developments. LC 79-14637. (Chemical Technology Review Ser.: No. 132). (Illus.). 1979. 42.00 o.p. (ISBN 0-8155-0757-7). Noyes.

Robinson, J. S., ed. Extrusion of Plastics. LC 82-62311. 270p. (Orig.). 1982. pap. 45.00 (ISBN 0-942378-01-6). Polymers & Plastics Tech Pub Hse.

Robinson, J. W. & Dowling, R. H. Intestinal Adaptation & Its Mechanisms. (Illus.). 646p. 1982. text ed. 75.00 (ISBN 0-85200-442-7, Pub. by MTP Pr England). Kluwer Boston.

Robinson, Jackie & Duckett, Al. I Never Had It Made. (Illus.). 230p. 1972. 7.95 o.p. (ISBN 0-399-11021-6). Putnam Pub Group.

Robinson, Jacqueline & Robinson, Dennis. Complete Preparation for High School Entrance Examinations for Special Private & Parochial High Schools. 1981. pap. 7.95 (ISBN 0-668-05155-8, 5155). Arco.

Robinson, Jacqueline & Robinson, Dennis M. High School Entrance Examinations. LC 80-22278. 538p. 1981. lib. bdg. 12.00 (ISBN 0-668-05149-3); pap. 7.95 (ISBN 0-668-05155-8). Arco.

Robinson, James. Pornography: The Polluting of America. Date not set. pap. 2.50 (ISBN 0-8423-4858-1). Tyndale.

Robinson, James & Cox, Jimmie. In Search of a Father. 1979. pap. 1.95 (ISBN 0-8423-1634-5). Tyndale.

Robinson, James & Mino, Yutaka. A Collector's Choices: Asian Art from the Collection of Dr. Walter Compton. LC 82-84073. (Illus.). 64p. (Orig.). 1983. pap. text ed. price not set. Ind Mus Art.

Robinson, James D. How to Use The Bible. 1982. pap. 2.95 (ISBN 0-570-03853-7, 12-2808). Concordia.

Robinson, James H. New History. 1965. pap. text ed. 3.50 (ISBN 0-02-926610-6). Free Pr.

Robinson, James M. A New Quest of the Historical Jesus & Other Essays. LC 82-48586. 224p. 1983. pap. text ed. 11.95 (ISBN 0-8006-1698-7). Fortress.

--The Problem of History in Mark. LC 57-857. (Scholars Press Reprint Ser.). pap. 6.00 (ISBN 0-89130-334-0, 00-07-03). Scholars Pr CA.

Robinson, James M. & Cobb, John B., Jr., eds. The Later Heidegger & Theology. LC 78-23619. 1979. Repr. of 1963 ed. lib. bdg. 19.75x (ISBN 0-313-20783-6, ROLH). Greenwood.

Robinson, James W. & Dernoncourt, Wayne L. The Grievance Procedure & Arbitration: Text & Cases. LC 77-18573. 1978. pap. text ed. 12.50 (ISBN 0-8191-0411-6). U Pr of Amer.

Robinson, James W., et al, eds. Introduction to Labor. 1975. pap. 13.95 (ISBN 0-13-485490-X). P-H.

Robinson, Jancis. The Great Wine Book: The Finest Wines from the Most Renowned Vineyards of France, the United States, Germany, Italy, Spain, & Australia. LC 82-6427. (Illus.). 240p. 1982. 24.95 (ISBN 0-688-00727-9). Morrow.

Robinson, Jay & Hardiman, Jim. The Comeback. 1983. pap. 2.95 (ISBN 0-8423-0401-0). Tyndale.

Robinson, Jay L., jt. auth. see Bailey, Richard W.

Robinson, Jean. The Mystery of Lincoln Detweiler & the Dog Who Barked Spanish. (gr. 3-8). 1977. PLB 3.96 (ISBN 0-695-40713-9); trade ed. 3.00 (ISBN 0-695-80713-7). Follett.

Robinson, Jeff, ed. CZ Service-Repair Handbook: Single Exhaust Models-Through 1978. (Illus.). pap. text ed. 10.95 o.p. (ISBN 0-89287-102-4, M425). Clymer Pubns.

--Datsun Service-Repair Handbook 2W Pickups, 1970-1982. (Illus.). pap. 11.95 (ISBN 0-89287-151-2, A-148). Clymer Pubns.

--Volkswagen Service--Repair Handbook: Dasher, 1974-1980. (Illus.). pap. 11.95 o.p. (ISBN 0-89287-154-7, A121). Clymer Pubns.

Robinson, Jeffrey C., ed. see Van Ghent, Dorothy.

Robinson, Jeri. Activities for Anyone, Anytime, Anywhere. LC 82-15353. 96p. 1983. 13.51 (ISBN 0-316-75144-8); pap. 5.25 (ISBN 0-316-75145-6). Little.

Robinson, Jerry. The Comics: An Illustrated History of Comic Strip Art. (Illus.). 256p. 1974. 15.00 o.p. (ISBN 0-399-10937-4). Putnam Pub Group.

--The Nineteen Seventies: Best Editorial Cartoons of the Decade. (McGraw-Hill Paperbacks Ser.). (Illus.). 192p. (Orig.). 1980. pap. 8.95 (ISBN 0-07-053281-8). McGraw.

Robinson, Jill. Bed-Time-Story. LC 74-8578. 1974. 7.95 o.p. (ISBN 0-394-48803-2, BYR); pap. 1.95 (ISBN 0-449-24064-9). Random.

Robinson, Jo, jt. auth. see Staeheli, Jean.

Robinson, Jo Ann O. Abraham Went Out: A Biography of A. J. Muste. LC 81-14492. 341p. 1982. 24.95 (ISBN 0-87722-231-2). Temple U Pr.

Robinson, Joan. Aspects of Development & Underdevelopment. LC 78-25610. (Modern Economics Ser.). 1979. 24.95 (ISBN 0-521-22637-6); pap. 8.95 (ISBN 0-521-29589-0). Cambridge U Pr.

--Collected Economic Papers of Joan Robinson, 5 vols. 1980. Set. text ed. 145.00x (ISBN 0-262-18099-5); 27.50x ea. Vol. 1 (ISBN 0-262-18093-6). Vol. 2 (ISBN 0-262-18094-4). Vol. 3 (ISBN 0-262-18095-2). Vol. 4 (ISBN 0-262-18096-0). Vol. 5 (ISBN 0-262-18097-9). Index. text ed. 15.00x (ISBN 0-262-18098-7). MIT Pr.

--The Dark House of the Sea Witch. LC 79-10845. (gr. 3-6). 1979. 7.95 (ISBN 0-698-20494-8, Coward). Putnam Pub Group.

--Economics: An Awkward Corner. 1965. pap. text ed. 4.95x (ISBN 0-04-330080-4). Allen Unwin.

--Essays in the Theory of Economic Growth. 1962. 20.00 (ISBN 0-312-26390-2). St Martin.

--The Generalization of the General Theory & Other Essays. LC 79-15275. 1979. 22.50x (ISBN 0-312-31963-0). St Martin.

--Introduction to the Theory of Employment. 2nd ed. 1969. 16.95 (ISBN 0-312-43435-9). St Martin.

--What Are the Questions? & Other Essays: Further Contributions to Economics. LC 80-28062. 214p. 1981. 22.50 (ISBN 0-87332-199-5); pap. 7.95 (ISBN 0-87332-200-2). M E Sharpe.

Robinson, Joan & Eatwell, John. An Introduction to Modern Economics. (Illus.). 368p. 1974. text ed. 13.00 o.p. (ISBN 0-07-084024-5, C); pap. text ed. 11.50 o.p. (ISBN 0-07-084025-3). McGraw.

Robinson, John. In Extremity. LC 77-77725. 176p. 1980. 27.50 (ISBN 0-521-21690-7); pap. 8.50 (ISBN 0-521-29730-3). Cambridge U Pr.

--The San Gabriels: Southern California Mountain Country. LC 77-24507. (Illus.). 200p. 1977. 23.95 (ISBN 0-87095-061-4). Golden West.

Robinson, John A. Honest to God. 1963. pap. 3.95 (ISBN 0-664-24465-3). Westminster.

Robinson, John A., jt. auth. see Retey, James.

Robinson, John L. Living Hard: Southern Americans in the Great Depression. LC 80-5817. 272p. 1981. lib. bdg. 22.25 (ISBN 0-8191-1379-4); pap. text ed. 11.50 (ISBN 0-8191-1380-8). U Pr of Amer.

Robinson, John M. The Dukes of Norfolk. (Illus.). 288p. 1983. 29.95 (ISBN 0-19-215869-4). Oxford U Pr.

--Introduction to Early Greek Philosophy. LC 68-1065. 1968. pap. text ed. 14.95 (ISBN 0-395-05316-1). HM.

Robinson, John P. & Shaver, Phillip R. Measures of Social Psychological Attitudes. rev. ed. LC 79-627967. 750p. 1973. 30.00x (ISBN 0-87944-069-4); pap. 24.00x (ISBN 0-87944-130-5). Inst Soc Res.

Robinson, John W. Southern California's First Railroad: L.A. & San Pedro Railroad, 1869-1873. (Los Angeles Miscellany Ser.: No. 10). 1978. 20.00 (ISBN 0-87093-310-8). Dawsons.

Robinson, Joseph E., ed. Computer Applications in Petroleum Geology. LC 82-3113. (Computer Methods in the Geosciences Ser.). 176p. 1982. 26.95 (ISBN 0-87933-432-0); pap. 16.95 (ISBN 0-87933-444-4). Hutchinson Ross.

Robinson, Joseph F. Using Videotape. 2nd ed. Beards, P. H., ed. (Media Manual Ser.). (Illus.). 1981. pap. 10.95 (ISBN 0-240-51107-7). Focal Pr.

Robinson, Joseph R., jt. auth. see Elonka, Stephen M.

Robinson, Julian & Robinson, Renee. Instant Dress Making: The Three-in-One Guide. (Illus.). 293p. 1974. 7.50 o.p. (ISBN 0-370-10298-3). Transatlantic.

Robinson, Keith & Wilson, Robert, eds. Extending Economics Within the Curriculum. (Direct Editions Ser). (Orig.). 1978. pap. 18.95 (ISBN 0-7100-8629-6). Routledge & Kegan.

Robinson, Ken, ed. see Cotton, Charles.

Robinson, Kenneth A., jt. auth. see Carrick, Alice V.

Robinson, Kitty K. & Greene, Ethel J. Putting It All Together: Skills & Activities for the Elementary Child. 1978. pap. text ed. 10.50 (ISBN 0-8191-0362-4). U Pr of Amer.

Robinson, L. H., ed. Mud Cleaners & Combination Separators. (Mud Equipment Manual Ser.: No. 7). 1982. pap. text ed. 10.75 (ISBN 0-87201-619-6). Gulf Pub.

Robinson, Larry M., jt. auth. see Cooper, Philip D.

Robinson, Lawrence L. From the Dark Side to the Bright Side. 1978. 5.95 o.p. (ISBN 0-533-03718-2). Vantage.

Robinson, Leigh. The Eviction Book for California. 2nd ed. LC 79-57254. (Illus.). 170p. (Orig.). 1982. pap. text ed. 13.50 (ISBN 0-932956-02-5). Express.

--Landlording: A Handy Manual for Scrupulous Landlords & Landladies Who Do It Themselves. Rev. ed. LC 79-57253. 272p. 1981. pap. text ed. 15.00 (ISBN 0-932956-01-7); pap. text ed. 17.50 Canadian edition (ISBN 0-932956-03-3). Express.

Robinson, Lennox, jt. ed. see Macdonagh, Donagh.

Robinson, Leonard W. In the Whale. 64p. 1983. pap. 6.95 (ISBN 0-935306-21-8). Barnwood Pr.

Robinson, Lisa. Walk on Glass. 1983. pap. 3.50 (ISBN 0-441-87127-5, Pub. by Charter Bks). Ace Bks.

Robinson, Louis N. History & Organization of Criminal Statistics in the United States. LC 69-16246. (Criminology, Law Enforcement, & Social Problems Ser.: No. 83). 1969. Repr. of 1911 ed. 6.50x (ISBN 0-87585-083-9). Patterson Smith.

Robinson, Lydia J., tr. see Garbe, Richard.

Robinson, M. Political Structure in a Changing Sinhalese Village. LC 74-31806. (South Asian Studies: No. 15). (Illus.). 368p. 1975. 44.50 (ISBN 0-521-20374-0). Cambridge U Pr.

Robinson, M. S. Catalogue of Drawings of Willem Van de Velde Senior & Junior, 2 vols. (Illus.). 240p. 1958. Vol. 1. 119.00 (ISBN 0-521-06114-8); Vol. 2, 1974. 110.00 (ISBN 0-521-06115-6). Cambridge U Pr.

Robinson, Mabel L. Runner of the Mountain Tops: The Life of Louis Agassiz. LC 73-167139. 1971. Repr. of 1939 ed. 34.00x (ISBN 0-8103-3806-8). Gale.

Robinson, Margaret. Schools & Social Work. 1978. 25.00x (ISBN 0-7100-0004-9); pap. 12.95 (ISBN 0-7100-0005-7). Routledge & Kegan.

Robinson, Margaret, tr. see Van Eeden, Frederik.

Robinson, Margaret G., jt. auth. see Robinson, Forrest G.

Robinson, Marilyn & Bisignano, Judith. Creating Your Future: Level 2. (Illus.). 72p. 1982. 6.95g (ISBN 0-9607366-8-9, KP108). Kino Pubns.

Robinson, Marilynne. Housekeeping. 219p. 1980. 10.95 (ISBN 0-374-17313-3). FS&G.

Robinson, Marion S. Moon Light My Way from This Dead Room. 1978. 8.95 o.p. (ISBN 0-533-03113-3). Vantage.

Robinson, Mary E. Jemimalee. (Illus.). (gr. 5 up). 1979. pap. 1.50 (ISBN 0-380-45849-7, 45849-7, Camelot). Avon.

Robinson, Michael C., jt. ed. see Hoy, Suellen M.

Robinson, Michael F. Opera Before Mozart. 2nd ed. 1972. text ed. 8.25x o. p. (ISBN 0-09-080421-X, Hutchinson U Lib); pap. text ed. 9.00x (ISBN 0-09-080422-8). Humanities.

Robinson, Michael J. Over the Wire & on TV: CBS and UPI in Campaign '80. 350p. 1983. 17.50x (ISBN 0-87154-722-8). Russell Sage.

Robinson, Michael J., jt. auth. see Sheehan, Margaret A.

Robinson, Nancy M., jt. auth. see Robinson, Halbert B.

Robinson, Nancy M., et al. A World of Children: Daycare & Preschool Institutions. LC 78-11601. (Psychology Ser.). (Illus.). 1979. pap. text ed. 13.95 (ISBN 0-8185-0288-6). Brooks-Cole.

Robinson, Nicholas A. Historic Preservation Law. LC 79-89326. (Real Estate Law & Practice Course Handbook Ser.: 1978-1979). 1979. pap. 20.00 o.p. (ISBN 0-686-59546-7, N4-4338). PLI.

--Historic Preservation Law Nineteen Eighty. LC 80-81531. (Nineteen Eighty-Nineteen Eighty-One Real Estate Law & Practice Course Handbook Ser. Subscription). 840p. 1980. pap. text ed. 30.00 (ISBN 0-686-75082-9, N4-4357). PLI.

Robinson, O. P., jt. auth. see Leigh, D. A.

Robinson, P., ed. Fundamentals of Experimental Psychology: A Comparative Approach. 2nd ed. 1981. 23.95 (ISBN 0-13-339135-3); pap. 8.95 wkbk (ISBN 0-13-339127-2). P-H.

Robinson, P. J. & Holbrook, K. A. Unimolecular Reactions. LC 70-161690. 1972. 50.95 o.p. (ISBN 0-471-72814-4, Pub. by Wiley-Interscience). Wiley.

Robinson, Paul. The Art of the Conductor: Bernstein. 1982. 10.95 (ISBN 0-8149-0865-9). Vanguard.

--Modernization of Sex. 1977. pap. 2.95i o.p. (ISBN 0-06-090548-4, CN 548, CN). Har-Row.

Robinson, Pauline. Using English: International Edition. (Illus.). 224p. 1983. pap. text ed. 10.00x (ISBN 0-631-12953-7, Pub. by Basil Blackwell England). Biblio Dist.

--Using English Today: Teacher's Book. (Illus.). 224p. 1983. pap. text ed. 7.95x (ISBN 0-631-12585-X, Pub. by Basil Blackwell). Biblio Dist.

Robinson, Pearl T. & Skinner, Elliot P., eds. Transformation & Resiliency in Africa. 336p. 1983. 14.95 (ISBN 0-88258-054-X). Howard U Pr.

Robinson, Peter M. Practical Fungal Physiology. LC 78-4243. 1978. pap. 15.95 (ISBN 0-471-99656-4, Pub. by Wiley-Interscience). Wiley.

Robinson-Pforzheimer Collection. Old-Fashioned Type Specimens. 5th ed. 1969. 2.00 o.p. (ISBN 0-87104-136-7). NY Pub Lib.

Robinson, Phyliss C. The Life of Willa Cather. 1983. 17.95 (ISBN 0-686-43267-3). Doubleday.

Robinson, Phyllis C. Willa: The Life of Willa Cather. 1983. 17.95. Doubleday.

Robinson, R. Ways to Move. (Topics in Geography Ser.). (Illus.). 1977. 17.95 (ISBN 0-521-21271-5); pap. 9.95 (ISBN 0-521-29081-3). Cambridge U Pr.

Robinson, R. K. Dairy Microbiology, Vol. 1: The Microbiology of Milk. 1981. 43.00 (ISBN 0-85334-948-7, Pub. by Applied Sci England). Elsevier.

--Dairy Microbiology, Vol. 2: The Microbiology of Milk Products. 1981. 51.25 (ISBN 0-85334-961-4 Pub. by Applied Sci England). Elsevier.

--The Vanishing Harvest: A Study of Food & its Conservation. (Illus.). 1982. 35.00x (ISBN 0-19-854713-7). Oxford U Pr.

Robinson, Ras. A New You. 67p. (Orig.). 1982. pap. 2.00 (ISBN 0-937778-06-0, MB 21). Fulness Hse.

Robinson, Ras & McElreath, Jesse. Spiritual Daybook. (Illus.). 1980. 7.00 (ISBN 0-937778-04-4). Fulness Hse.

Robinson, Ras, jt. auth. see Beasley, Manley.

Robinson, Ras, ed. The Finest of Fulness. 192p. 1979. pap. 4.00 (ISBN 0-937778-00-1). Fulness Hse.

--Prayer. 48p. (Orig.). 1983. pap. 2.00 (ISBN 0-937778-07-9). Fulness Hse.

Robinson, Ray. Baseball's Most Colorful Managers. (Putnam Sports Shelf). (Illus.). (gr. 5-9). 1969. PLB 4.97 o.p. (ISBN 0-399-60044-2). Putnam Pub Group.

--Greatest World Series Thrillers. (Major League Baseball Library). (Illus.). (gr. 4-7). 1965. 2.50 o.p. (ISBN 0-394-80181-4, BYR); PLB 3.69 (ISBN 0-394-90181-9). Random.

Robinson, Ray, jt. auth. see LeGrand, Julian.

Robinson, Raymond. The Growing of America: Seventeen Eighty-Nine to Eighteen Forty-Eight. LC 78-67275. 1979. pap. text ed. 10.95x (ISBN 0-88273-112-2). Forum Pr IL.

Robinson, Renee, jt. auth. see Robinson, Julian.

Robinson, Richard. Definition. 1950. 32.50x (ISBN 0-19-824160-7). Oxford U Pr.

--How to Save Tax Dollars When You Sell Your House. 1979. pap. 3.95 o.s.i. (ISBN 0-695-81290-4). Follett.

--Video Primer. rev. & updated ed. (Illus.). 400p. 1981. pap. 8.95 (ISBN 0-8256-3131-9, Quick Fox). Putnam Pub Group.

--The Video Primer. rev. ed. (Illus.). 432p. 1982. pap. 9.95 (ISBN 0-399-50698-5, Perige). Putnam Pub Group.

--The Video Primer: Equipment, Production & Concepts. LC 73-89670. 1974. pap. 8.95 (ISBN 0-8256-3139-4, 030033, Quick Fox). Putnam Pub Group.

Robinson, Richard & Johnson, Willard L. The Buddhist Religion. 2nd ed. (Religious Life of Man Ser.). 1977. pap. 8.95x o.p. (ISBN 0-8221-0193-9). Dickenson.

Robinson, Richard D. National Control of Foreign Business: A Survey of Fifteen Countries. LC 75-44938. (Special Studies). (Illus.). 1976. 48.95 o.p. (ISBN 0-275-56500-9). Praeger.

Robinson, Robert. Landscape with Dead Dons. 1983. pap. 2.95 (ISBN 0-14-001831-X). Penguin.

Robinson, Robert E., jt. auth. see Prichard, Robert W.

Robinson, Robert H. The Craft of Dismantling a Crab. (Illus.). 96p. 1977. pap. 4.95 (ISBN 0-686-36742-1). Md Hist.

--The Essential Book of Shellfish. LC 82-184274. (Illus.). 160p. 1983. pap. 6.95 (ISBN 0-89709-040-3). Liberty Pub.

Robinson, Roland & Wrightman, Dwayne. Financial Markets: The Accumulation & Allocation of Wealth. 2nd ed. (Illus.). 1980. text ed. 24.95 (ISBN 0-07-053274-5); instrs'. manual 18.95 (ISBN 0-07-053275-3). McGraw.

Robinson, Roland I. Management of Bank Funds. 2nd ed. (Illus.). 1962. text ed. 26.50 (ISBN 0-07-053279-6, C). McGraw.

Robinson, Ronald. Tumors That Secrete Catecholamines: A Study of Their Natural History & Their Diagnosis. LC 79-41731. 132p. 1980. 47.95x (ISBN 0-471-27748-7). Wiley.

Robinson, Russell D. Introduction to Helping Adults Learn & Change. 1979. pap. 9.95 (ISBN 0-9600154-9-3). Bible Study Pr.

--Teaching the Scriptures: A Syllabus for Bible Study. (Illus.). 156p. 1977. 10.95 (ISBN 0-9600154-3-4); pap. 8.95 (ISBN 0-9600154-4-2). Bible Study Pr.

Robinson, Ruth E. & Farudi, Daryush. Buy Books Where-Sell Books Where: A Directory of Out of Print Booksellers & Their Author-Subject Specialties. 3rd ed. (Orig.). 1982. pap. 3.95 (ISBN 0-9603556-4-2). Robinson Bks.

Robinson, Sandra J., jt. auth. see Besner, Hilda F.

Robinson, Sandra T., jt. auth. see Goldberg, Lucianne.

Robinson, Sharon. Contemporary Quilting. LC 81-66572. (Illus.). 120p. 1982. 15.95 (ISBN 0-87192-134-0). Davis Mass.

Robinson, Sherman, jt. auth. see Melo, Jaime de.

Robinson, Sondra T., jt. auth. see Lee, Susan.

Robinson, Spider. Antinomy. (Orig.). 1980. pap. 2.25 o.s.i. (ISBN 0-440-10235-9). Dell.

Robinson, Stearn. Dreamer's Dictionary. 1975. pap. 3.96 (ISBN 0-446-30610-X). Warner Bks.

Robinson, Stephan M., jt. ed. see Day, Richard H.

Robinson, Stephen E. The Testament of Adam: An Examination of the Syriac & Greek Traditions. LC 80-12209. (Society of Biblical Literature Dissertation Ser.: No. 52). pap. 13.50 (ISBN 0-89130-399-5, 06-01-52). Scholars Pr CA.

Robinson, T., jt. auth. see Hammond, J., Jr.

Robinson, T. H. & Brockington, L. H., eds. Paradigms & Exercises in Syriac Grammar. 4th ed. 1962. pap. 13.50x (ISBN 0-19-815458-5). Oxford U Pr.

Robinson, Terry, jt. auth. see Strait, Raymond.

Robinson, Thomas W., ed. The Cultural Revolution in China. LC 77-129609. 1971. 39.00x (ISBN 0-520-01811-7). U of Cal Pr.

Robinson, Tom. An Eskimo Birthday. LC 74-23750. (Illus.). (gr. 2-5). 1975. 5.25 o.p. (ISBN 0-396-07065-5). Dodd.

Robinson, Trevor. Organic Constituents of Higher Plants. 4th ed. 1980. 13.75x o.p. (ISBN 0-935118-01-2). Cordus Pr.

Robinson, Vester. Manual of Solid State Circuit Design & Troubleshooting. (Illus.). 1977. 22.95 (ISBN 0-87909-464-8). Reston.

Robinson, Vinnie. Devil in Disguise. 145p. 1982. 9.95 (ISBN 0-9610404-0-8). Mogul Bk.

Robinson, W. Stitt. The Southern Colonial Frontier: 1607-1763. LC 78-21432. (Histories of the American Frontier Ser). 1979. 14.95x (ISBN 0-8263-0502-4); pap. 9.95x (ISBN 0-8263-0503-2). U of NM Pr.

Robinson, W. Stitt, Jr. Mother Earth: Land Grants in Virginia, 1607-1699. (Illus.). 77p. 1957. pap. 2.95 (ISBN 0-8139-0136-7). U Pr of Va.

Robinson, W. W. Los Angeles from the Days of the Pueblo. Nunis, Doyce B., Jr., ed. LC 81-68447. (Orig.). 1982. pap. 7.95 (ISBN 0-87701-242-3). Chronicle Bks.

Robinson, Wayne. I Once Spoke in Tongues. pap. 1.50 o.p. (ISBN 0-89129-013-3). Jove Pubns.

Robinson, William A. Best Sales Promotions, Vol. 5. LC 77-80156. 160p. 1982. 27.95 (ISBN 0-87251-070-0). Crain Bks.

Robinson, William A. & Schultz, Don E. Sales Promotion Management. LC 82-70974. 512p. 1982. 27.95 (ISBN 0-87251-072-7). Crain Bks.

Robinson, William C. Law of Patents, 3 vols. 1971. Repr. of 1890 ed. Set. 125.00 o.p. (ISBN 0-87632-039-6). Boardman.

Robinson, William H. Phillis Wheatley: A Bio-Bibliography. 1981. 19.00 (ISBN 0-8161-8318-X, Hall Reference). G K Hall.

--Phyllis Wheatly & Her Writings. LC 82-21027. 300p. 1983. lib. bdg. 36.00 (ISBN 0-8240-9346-1). Garland Pub.

Robinson, William H., ed. Critical Essays on Phillis Wheatley. (Critical Essays on American Literature Ser.). 1982. lib. bdg. 32.50 (ISBN 0-8161-8336-8). G K Hall.

Robinson, William L. Fool Hen: The Spruce Grouse on the Yellow Dog Plains. LC 79-3962. (Illus.). 242p. 1980. 19.50 (ISBN 0-299-07960-0). U of Wis Pr.

Robinson-Treiman, Robert, ed. Research in Social Stratification & Mobility: An Annual Compilation of Research, Vol. 1. 1980. lib. bdg. 42.50 (ISBN 0-89232-067-2). Jai Pr.

Robischon, Paulette & Lange, Crystal M. Utilization of the Clinical Laboratory in Baccalaureate Nursing Programs. 33p. 1978. 3.95 (ISBN 0-686-38283-8, 15-1726). Natl League Nurse.

Robison, Alan, jt. ed. see Greengard, Paul.

Robison, Bonnie & Sports Illustrated Editors. Sports Illustrated Volleyball. LC 72-3880. (Sports Illustrated Library Ser). 1970. 5.95i (ISBN 0-397-00842-2, LP-71); pap. 2.95i o.p. (ISBN 0-397-00905-4). Har-Row.

Robison, G. A., jt. ed. see Greengard, P.

Robison, G. Alan. Cyclic AMP. 528p. 1971. 59.50 (ISBN 0-12-590450-9). Acad Pr.

Robison, G. Alan, jt. ed. see Greengard, Paul.

Robison, J. Vincent. Modern Algebra & Trigonometry. 2nd ed. (Illus.). 448p. 1972. text ed. 27.00 (ISBN 0-07-053330-X, C); instructor's manual 15.00 (ISBN 0-07-053331-8). McGraw.

Robison, James. Attack on the Family. pap. 2.95 (ISBN 0-8423-0092-9). Tyndale.

Robison, James & Cox, Jim. Save America to Save the World. pap. 1.95 (ISBN 0-8423-5823-4). Tyndale.

Robison, James & Robinson, Darline. Children's Travel Guide. (Activities Bk.: Vol. I-Colo., Utah, N.M.). pap. 5.95 (ISBN 0-89051-079-2). CLP Pubs.

Robison, Nancy. Nancy Lopez: Wonder Woman of Golf. LC 78-23931. (Sports Stars Ser.). (Illus.). 48p. (gr. 2-8). 1979. PLB 7.95 (ISBN 0-516-04302-1); pap. 2.50 (ISBN 0-516-44302-X). Childrens.

--U. & M.E. Schroeder, Howard, ed. LC 81-3200. (Roundup Ser.). (Illus.). 48p. (gr. 3 up). 1981. lib. bdg. 7.95 (ISBN 0-89686-151-1); pap. 3.95 (ISBN 0-89686-159-7). Crestwood Hse.

Robison, Nancy L. The Missing Ball of String. LC 77-8709. (For Real Ser.). (Illus.). (gr. k-4). 1977. PLB 6.69 (ISBN 0-8116-4306-9). Garrard.

--The Mystery at Hilltop Camp. LC 78-21523. (Mystery Ser.). (gr. k-3). 1979. PLB 6.79 (ISBN 0-8116-6407-4). Garrard.

--Where Did My Little Fox Go? LC 76-47543. (Imagination Ser.). (Illus.). (gr. k-3). 1977. lib. bdg. 6.69 (ISBN 0-8116-4405-7). Garrard.

Robison, R. A., ed. Treatise on Invertebrate Paleontology, Pt. F, Suppl. 1: Coelenterata (Anthozoa: Rugosa & Tabulata) LC 53-12913. (Illus.). 1981. 38.00x (ISBN 0-8137-3029-5). Geol Soc.

--Treatise on Invertebrate Paleontology, Pt. W, Suppl. 2: Conodonta. LC 53-12913. (Illus.). 1981. 18.00x (ISBN 0-8137-3028-7). Geol Soc.

Robison, Richard A. & Tiechert, Curt, eds. Treatise on Invertebrate Paleontology, Pt. A: Introduction (Fossilization, Biogeography & Biostratigraphy) LC 53-12913. 1979. 25.00x (ISBN 0-8137-3001-5). Geol Soc.

Robison, S., tr. see Juvenal.

Robison, Sophia Moses. Can Delinquency Be Measured? LC 75-129307. (Criminology, Law Enforcement, & Social Problems Ser.: No. 129). (Illus.). 312p. (With intro. added). 1972. Repr. of 1936 ed. 15.00x (ISBN 0-87585-129-0). Patterson Smith.

Robl, Tom & Koppenaal, Dave. The Chemical & Engineering Properties of Eastern Oil Shale. Pettit, Rhonda, ed. 303p. (Orig.). 1982. pap. text ed. 10.00 (ISBN 0-86607-014-1). Inst Mining & Minerals.

Robledo, Anthony, IV. Of Verse & Vision. 1983. 5.95 (ISBN 0-533-05622-5). Vantage.

Roblee, C. & McKechnie, A. Investigation of Fires. 1981. 18.95 (ISBN 0-13-503169-9). P-H.

Robleto, Adolfo. Amor, Fe y Esperanza. (No. 2). 96p. 1980. pap. 2.25 (ISBN 0-311-08757-4). Casa Bautista.

--Catecismo Biblico y Doctrinal Para el Nuevo Creyente. 1979. pap. 1.50 (ISBN 0-311-09088-5). Casa Bautista.

--Dramas y Poemas Para Dias Especiales, No. 1. 94p. (Span.). 1980. pap. 2.50 (ISBN 0-311-07004-3, Edit Mundo). Casa Bautista.

--Dramas y Poemas Para Dias Especiales, No. 2. 1981. Repr. of 1979 ed. 2.50 (ISBN 0-311-07008-6, Edit Mundo). Casa Bautista.

--Sermones para Dias Especiales, Toma II. 96p. 1981. Repr. of 1979 ed. 2.75 (ISBN 0-311-07011-6). Casa Bautista.

--Sermones para Dias Especiales, Toma I. 112p. (Span.). 1980. Repr. of 1973 ed. 2.50 (ISBN 0-311-07009-4). Casa Bautista.

Robleto, Adolfo, compiled by. Five-Hundred & One Ilustraciones Nuevas. 320p. pap. 8.25 (ISBN 0-311-42062-1). Casa Bautista.

Robleto, Adolfo, tr. see Conner, T.

Robleto, Adolfo, tr. see Cowman, Mrs. Charles E.

Robleto, Adolfo, tr. see Dana, H. E. & Mantey, J. R.

Robleto, Un Adolfo. Un Vistazo a la Doctrina Romana. 128p. 1980. pap. 2.75 (ISBN 0-311-05319-X). Casa Bautista.

Robotham, John & Shields, Gerald. Freedom of Access to Library Materials. 1982. 22.95 (ISBN 0-918212-31-6). Neal-Schuman.

Robotti, Frances D. Whaling & Old Salem: A Chronicle of the Sea. (Illus.). 292p. 1983. Repr. 17.95x (ISBN 0-685-41738-7). Fountainhead.

Robottom, John. Modern Russia. (Illus.). (gr. 7 up). 1971. PLB 5.72 o.p. (ISBN 0-07-053343-1, GB). McGraw.

Roboz, Steven & Steiner, Rudolf. Islam: Study Notes. Roboz, Steven, ed. 33p. 1980. pap. 2.95 (ISBN 0-88010-050-8, Pub. by Steiner Book Centre Canada). Anthroposophic.

Roboz, Steven, ed. see Roboz, Steven & Steiner, Rudolf.

Roboz, Steven, ed. see Steiner, Rudolf.

Robson. Mishkat-Ul-Masabih, 2 vols. 29.50 (ISBN 0-686-18348-7). Kazi Pubns.

Robson, Adam. The Education of Children Engaged in Industry in England Eighteen Thirty-Three to Eighteen Seventy-Six. Repr. of 1931 ed. lib. bdg. 19.50x (ISBN 0-87991-816-0). Porcupine Pr.

Robson, Bonnie. My Parents Are Divorced, Too: Teenagers Talk About Their Experiences & How They Cope. LC 79-91417. 1980. 10.95 (ISBN 0-89696-091-9, An Everest House Book); pap. 6.95 (ISBN 0-89696-083-8). Dodd.

Robson, Brian T. Urban Growth: An Approach. (Illus.). 320p. 1973. pap. 11.95x (ISBN 0-416-78710-X). Methuen Inc.

Robson, Clifford B. Ngugi Wa Thiong'o. LC 79-53096. 1979. 18.95x (ISBN 0-312-57245-X). St Martin.

Robson, D. & Fox, J. D., eds. Nuclear Analogue States. LC 76-17849. (Benchmark Papers in Nuclear Physics Ser.: Vol. 1). 1976. 60.50 (ISBN 0-12-787356-2). Acad Pr.

Robson, David, jt. auth. see Goldberg, Adele.

Robson, Ernest & Wendt, Larry. Phonetic Music with Electronic Music. LC 81-90189. 1981. bk. only 19.45 (ISBN 0-934982-02-3); with book & cassette 23.45 (ISBN 0-686-31759-9); cass. only 12.00 (ISBN 0-686-34446-4). Primary Pr.

Robson, Graham. The Range Rover - Land Rover. (Illus.). 1979. 19.95 o.p. (ISBN 0-7153-7707-8). David & Charles.

--Rover Story: A Century of Success. (Illus.). 1981. 24.95 (ISBN 0-85059-543-6). Aztex.

Robson, Graham, jt. auth. see Jackson, Judith, II.

Robson, J. M., ed. see Mill, John S.

Robson, J. R. Famine: Its Causes Effects & Management. (Food & Nutrition in History & Anthropology Ser.). 180p. 1981. 28.00 (ISBN 0-677-16180-8). Gordon.

Robson, Jeremy. Poetry Dimension One. 1975. 10.00 o.p. (ISBN 0-312-61810-7). St Martin.

Robson, John M., ed. see Mill, John S.

Robson, John R., et al. Malnutrition, Its Causation & Control. 632p. 1972. Set. 70.00x (ISBN 0-677-03140-8). Gordon.

Robson, Kenneth S. The Borderline Child: Approaches to Etiology, Diagnosis & Treatment. (Illus.). 320p. 1983. 24.95 (ISBN 0-07-053346-6, P&RB). McGraw.

Robson, P. D., jt. auth. see Harris, D. J.

Robson, Peter. Economics of International Integration. (Studies in Economics). (Illus.). 1980. text ed. 25.00x (ISBN 0-04-338090-5); pap. text ed. 11.50x (ISBN 0-04-338091-3). Allen Unwin.

Robson, Peter & Watchman, Paul, eds. Justice, Lord Denning & the Constitution. 272p. 1981. text ed. 31.25x (ISBN 0-566-00399-6); pap. text ed. 18.00x (ISBN 0-566-00454-2). Gower Pub Ltd.

Robson, Sherry, ed. see Manning, Barbara S.

Robson, T. B. Consolidated & Other Group Accounts. 2nd ed. LC 82-48381. (Accountancy in Transition Ser.). 156p. 1982. lib. bdg. 20.00 (ISBN 0-8240-5326-5). Garland Pub.

Robson, Vivian E. A Beginners Guide to Practical Astrology. 184p. 9.00 (ISBN 0-686-38212-9). Sun Bks.

Robson, W. W. The Definition of Literature & Other Essays. LC 82-4196. 220p. 1983. 37.50 (ISBN 0-521-24495-1). Cambridge U Pr.

Robson, W. W., ed. Essays & Studies-1978. (Essays & Studies: Vol. 31). 130p. 1978. text ed. 18.00x (ISBN 0-391-00838-2). Humanities.

Robson-Scott, W. D. & Riley, V. J. Theses in Germanic Studies, 1967-72. 18p. 1973. 20.00x (ISBN 0-85457-055-1, Pub. by Inst Germanic Stud England). State Mutual Bk.

Roby, Mary L. Afraid of the Dark. 1978. pap. 1.50 o.p. (ISBN 0-523-40330-5). Pinnacle Bks.

--The Broken Key. 224p. 1974. pap. 1.25 o.p. (ISBN 0-451-06766-5, Y6766, Sig). NAL.

--This Land Turns Evil Slowly. Bd. with Dig a Narrow Grave. 1978. pap. 2.50 (ISBN 0-451-11696-8, AE1696, Sig). NAL.

--White Peacock. Incl. Shadow Over Grove House. 1978. pap. 2.75 (ISBN 0-451-11952-5, AE1952, Sig). NAL.

Roca, F. Catala, jt. auth. see Pelauzy, M. A.

Roca, Nancy. House Plants: A Primer For Simple Care. rev. ed. LC 73-87672. (Orig.). 1979. pap. 4.95 (ISBN 0-89815-006-X). Ten Speed Pr.

Roca, Paul M. Spanish Jesuit Churches in Mexico's Tarahumara. LC 78-14467. 1979. 18.50x o.s.i. (ISBN 0-8165-0651-5); pap. 11.50 (ISBN 0-8165-0572-1). U of Ariz Pr.

Roca, Ruben A., ed. Market Research for Shopping Centers. 1980. 35.00 (ISBN 0-913598-11-9). Intl Coun Shop.

Rocco, Sha. Sex Mythology. (Illus.). 55p. 1982. pap. 3.00 (ISBN 0-686-83041-5). Am Atheist.

Rocek, Martin, jt. ed. see Hawking, Stephen.

Roch, John, jt. tr. see Yannela, Donald.

Rocha e Silva, Mauricio. Rational Frontiers of Science. LC 82-46. 1982. pap. 7.50 (ISBN 0-89874-190-4). Krieger.

Rochard, Henri. For the Love of Kate. 1977. Repr. 9.00 (ISBN 0-686-21177-4). Maple Mont.

Roche, Alex F., jt. ed. see Malina, Robert M.

Roche, Alphonse V. Alphonse Daudet. LC 75-25549. (World Authors Ser.). 1976. lib. bdg. 12.95 (ISBN 0-8057-6223-X, Twayne). G K Hall.

Roche, Charles. Football's Stunting Defenses. LC 82-6321. 181p. 1982. 14.95 (ISBN 0-13-324020-7, Parker). P-H.

Roche, Douglas & Deroo, Remi. Man to Man. 1969. 6.95 o.p. (ISBN 0-685-07654-7, 80168). Glencoe.

Roche, G. The Balancing Act: Quota Hiring in Higher Education. LC 74-11130. 1974. pap. 4.00x (ISBN 0-87548-305-4). Open Court.

Roche, G., et al. The Balancing Act: Black Studies Revisited. LC 75-11131. 1974. 17.00x (ISBN 0-87548-295-3). Open Court.

Roche, George, III. Swarms of Officers: America's Bureaucracy. 1982. 14.95 (ISBN 0-686-81784-2). Devin.

Roche, Jerome. Lassus. 1982. pap. 9.95x (ISBN 0-19-315237-1). Oxford U Pr.

Roche, Paul, tr. Oedipus Plays of Sophocles. 1971. pap. 2.95 (ISBN 0-451-62160-3, MJ2160, Ment). NAL.

Roche, Philip. Criminal Mind: A Study of Communication Between the Criminal Law & Psychiatry. LC 76-28524. 1976. Repr. of 1958 ed. lib. bdg. 27.50x (ISBN 0-8371-9056-8, ROCM). Greenwood.

Roche, R. L., jt. ed. see Yamada, Y.

Roche, Richard. Egyptian Myths & the Ra Ta Story: Based on the Edgar Cayce Readings. 1975. pap. 1.95 o.p. (ISBN 0-87604-084-9). ARE Pr.

Roche, Thomas P., ed. see Spenser, Edmund.

Roche, Thomas P., Jr., jt. ed. see Cullen, Patrick.

Roche De Coppens, Peter. The Spiritual Perspective I: Key Issues & Themes Interpreted from the Standpoint of Spiritual Consciousness. LC 80-487. 163p. 1980. text ed. 20.00 (ISBN 0-8191-1017-5); pap. text ed. 9.50 (ISBN 0-8191-1018-3). U Pr of Amer.

Rochefort, Christiane. Les Petits Enfants Du Siecle. (Easy Readers, Ser. A). 80p. 1976. pap. text ed. 3.95 (ISBN 0-88436-226-4, 40267). EMC.

Rochefoucauld, La Duc De. Maxims of la Rochefoucauld. Heard, John, tr. pap. 3.00 (ISBN 0-8283-1448-9, IPL). Branden.

Rochell, Carlton, ed. Wheeler & Goldhor's Practical Administration of Public Libraries. rev. ed. LC 79-3401. (Illus.). 480p. 1981. 28.80i (ISBN 0-06-013601-4, HarpT). Har-Row.

Rochell, Carlton, ed. see Colloquium, June 27-28, 1980.

Rochelle, Gary T., jt. ed. see Hudson, John L.

Rochelle, Pierre Drieu la see La Rochelle, Pierre Drieu.

Rocher, Ludo, intro. by see Paulinus & Bartholomaeo, S.

Rocher, Rosane. Orientalism, Poetry & Millenium. 1983. 34.00x (ISBN 0-8364-0870-5). South Asia Bks.

Rochester, J. Martin, jt. auth. see Coplin, William D.

Rochester, Stuart I. American Liberal Disillusionment in the Wake of World War I. LC 76-47613. 1977. 18.95x (ISBN 0-271-01233-1). Pa St U Pr.

Rochford, Thomas, jt. auth. see Gorer, Richard.

Rochlin, Gene I. Plutonium, Power, & Politics: International Arrangements for the Disposition of Spent Nuclear Fuel. LC 78-68833. 1979. 34.50x (ISBN 0-520-03887-8). U of Cal Pr.

Rochlin, Gregory. Man's Aggression: The Defense of the Self. LC 73-144339. 299p. 1973. 12.95 (ISBN 0-87645-068-0). Gambit.

Rochow, Eugene G. Inorganic Syntheses, Vol. 6. 284p. 1983. Repr. of 1960 ed. lib. bdg. price not set (ISBN 0-89874-539-X). Krieger.

Rock & McIntosh, eds. Deviance & Social Control. 1974. pap. 7.95x o.p. (ISBN 0-422-75620-2, Pub. by Tavistock). Methuen Inc.

Rock, D. Politics in Argentina 1890-1930. LC 74-12974. (Latin American Studies: No. 19). 304p. 1975. 32.50 (ISBN 0-521-20663-4). Cambridge U Pr.

Rock, Gail. Addie & the King of Hearts. LC 75-35776. 96p. (gr. 4-6). 1976. 4.95 o.p. (ISBN 0-394-83228-0); PLB 5.99 (ISBN 0-394-93228-5). Knopf.

--The House Without a Christmas Tree. 96p. (gr. 4-6). 1982. pap. 1.95 (Skylark). Bantam.

--The House Without a Christmas Tree. LC 74-162. (Illus.). 96p. (gr. 2 up). 1974. 4.95 (ISBN 0-394-82833-X); PLB 6.99 (ISBN 0-394-92833-4). Knopf.

--The Thanksgiving Treasure. LC 74-163. (Illus.). 96p. (gr. 2 up). 1974. 4.95 o.p. (ISBN 0-394-82834-8); PLB 6.99 (ISBN 0-394-92834-2). Knopf.

Rock, Irvin. An Introduction to Perception. (Illus.). 576p. 1975. text ed. 25.95x (ISBN 0-02-402490-2). Macmillan.

--Orientation & Form. 1974. 26.00 (ISBN 0-12-591250-1). Acad Pr.

Rock, James M., ed. Money, Banking & Macroeconomics: A Guide to Information Sources. LC 73-17585. (Economics Information Guide Ser.: Vol. 11). 1977. 42.00x (ISBN 0-8103-1300-6). Gale.

Rock, John A., jt. auth. see Jones, Howard W., Jr.

Rock, Judith. Theology in the Shape of Dance: Using Dance in Worship & Theological Process. 1977. 2.50 (ISBN 0-941500-16-0). Sharing Co.

Rock, M. L. Handbook of Wage & Salary Administration. 1972. 49.95 (ISBN 0-07-053348-2, P&RB). McGraw.

Rock, Maxine, jt. auth. see Taylor, David M.

Rock Mechanics International Society & the U. S. National Committee, 16th. Design Methods in Rock Mechanics: Proceedings. American Society of Civil Engineers, et al, eds. 432p. 1977. text ed. 31.00 o.p. (ISBN 0-87262-080-8). Am Soc Civil Eng.

Rock, Paul. Making People Pay. (International Library of Sociology). 1973. 27.95x (ISBN 0-7100-7684-3). Routledge & Kegan.

Rock, Paul, ed. Drugs & Politics. LC 76-1766. (Society Bk.). 333p. 1977. 12.95 (ISBN 0-87855-076-3); pap. text ed. 3.95 o. p. (ISBN 0-87855-572-2). Transaction Bks.

Rock, Peter A. Chemical Thermodynamics. McQuarrie, Donald A., ed. LC 82-51233. (Physical Chemistry Ser.). (Illus.). 553p. 1983. 24.00x (ISBN 0-935702-10-5). Univ Sci Bks.

Rockafellar, R. Tyrrell. Conjugate Duality & Optimization. (CBMS Regional Conference Ser.: Vol. 16). 74p. (Orig.). 1974. pap. text ed. 9.00 (ISBN 0-89871-013-8). Soc Indus-Appl Math.

Rockcastle, Verne, et al. Addison-Wesley Science Experience Records Books, Gr. 3-6. (Addison-Wesley Science Program Ser.). (gr. 1-6). 1980. 3.12 o.p. (ISBN 0-686-77685-2, Sch Div); Gr. 3. 3.80 (ISBN 0-201-05383-7); Gr. 4. l.p. 4.80 (ISBN 0-201-05384-5); Gr. 5. l.p. 5.72 (ISBN 0-201-05385-3); Gr. 6. l.p. 5.72 (ISBN 0-201-05386-1). A-W.

Rockcastle, Verne N., jt. auth. see Schmidt, Victor E.

Rockdale Temple Sisterhood. In the Beginning: A Collection of Hors D'oeuvres. rev. ed. Bd. with And Beginning Again: More Hors D'oeuvres for Cooks Who Love in the Beginning. 1982. pap. 13.95 slipcased (ISBN 0-9602338-2-2). Rockdale Ridge.

Rockefeller, Edwin S. Antitrust Questions & Answers. LC 73-93042. 704p. 1974. 18.50 o.p. (ISBN 0-87179-183-8). BNA.

--Desk Book of FTC Practice & Procedure. 3rd ed. LC 79-91002. 1979. text ed. 20.00 (ISBN 0-686-58547-X, A1-1270). PLI.

Rockefeller University & State University of New York, Nov. 26-27, 1965. The Future of Biology. Bronk, Detev W., ed. LC 67-63223. 1966. pap. 18.00x (ISBN 0-87395-268-5). State U NY Pr.

Rockel, Eric G., jt. auth. see Brooks, Neal A.

Rocker & Laurence. Fetoscopy. 1981. 93.75 (ISBN 0-444-80337-8). Elsevier.

Rockey, D. Phonetic Lexicon of Monosyllabic & Some Disyllabic Words, with Homophones, Arranged According to Their Phonetic Structure. 1973. 47.95 (ISBN 0-471-26113-0, Wiley Heyden). Wiley.

Rockland, Louis B. & Stewart, George F., eds. Water Activity: Influences on Food Quality: Proceedings of Second International Symposium on Properties of Water Affecting Food Quality. LC 79-26632. 1980. 68.50 (ISBN 0-12-591350-8). Acad Pr.

Rockland, Mae S. The Hanukkah Book. LC 75-10609. (Illus.). 160p. 1975. 4.95 o.p. (ISBN 0-8052-3590-6). Schocken.

--The Work of Our Hands: Jewish Needlecraft for Today. LC 72-91608. (Illus.). 250p. 1975. 10.00 o.p. (ISBN 0-8052-3502-7); pap. 5.95 o.p. (ISBN 0-8052-0489-X). Schocken.

Rockland, Mae S. & Rockland, Michael A. The Jewish Yellow Pages: A Directory of Goods & Services. LC 76-26524. (Illus.). 1976. pap. 7.95 o.p. (ISBN 0-8052-0554-3). Schocken.

Rockland, Michael A., jt. auth. see Rockland, Mae S.

Rockley, Alicia A. History of Gardening in England. LC 68-21522. 1969. Repr. of 1896 ed. 34.00x (ISBN 0-8103-3845-9). Gale.

Rockne, Jon, tr. see Alefeld, Gotz & Herzberger, Jurgen.

Rockne, Knute. The Four Winners. 1980. 10.00 (ISBN 0-8159-5509-X). Devin.

Rockness, Miriam H. A Time to Play: On Childhood & Creativity. 192p. 1983. pap. 5.95 (ISBN 0-310-45871-4). Zondervan.

Rockowitz, et al. Barron's How to Prepare for the High School Equivalency Exam (GED) rev. 5th ed. LC 78-16766. (gr. 10-12). 1978. 21.95 (ISBN 0-8120-5306-0); pap. text ed. 7.95 (ISBN 0-8120-0645-3). Barron.

Rocks, Lawrence. Developing Your Chemistry Fundamentals. 564p. 1979. 19.95x (ISBN 0-87814-041-7). Pennwell Books Division.

--Fuels for Tomorrow. 190p. 1980. 29.95x (ISBN 0-87814-135-9). Pennwell Pub.

Rocks, Lawrence E. & Runyon, Richard. The Energy Crisis. 224p. 1972. 5.95 o.p. (ISBN 0-517-50164-3). Crown.

Rockstein. Physiology of the Insecta. 2nd ed. 1974. Vol. 1, 1973. 69.50 (ISBN 0-12-591601-9); Vol. 2, 1974. 69.50 (ISBN 0-12-591602-7); Vol. 3, 1974. 69.50 (ISBN 0-12-591603-5); Vol. 4, 1974. 64.50 (ISBN 0-12-591604-3); Vol. 5, 1974. 74.50 (ISBN 0-12-591605-1); Vol. 6, 1974. 72.50 (ISBN 0-12-591606-X); 316.00 set (ISBN 0-686-67021-3). Acad Pr.

Rockstein, Morris & Sussman, Marvin. Biology of Aging. 1979. pap. text ed. 11.95x (ISBN 0-534-00687-6). Wadsworth Pub.

Rockstein, Morris, ed. Biochemistry of Insects. LC 77-1121. 1978. 45.50 (ISBN 0-12-591640-X). Acad Pr.

Rockstein, Morris & Baker, George T., eds. Molecular Genetic Mechanisms in Aging & Development. 1972. 27.00 (ISBN 0-12-591550-0). Acad Pr.

Rockstein, Morris & Sussman, Marvin L., eds. Development & Aging in the Nervous System. 1973. 25.00 (ISBN 0-12-591650-7). Acad Pr.

Rockstroh, et al. Slow Brain Potentials & Behavior. LC 82-1939. 271p. 1982. text ed. 39.00 (ISBN 0-8067-0291-5). Urban & S.

Rockswold, E. P., ed. Pre-Immigrant & Pioneer. 1982. pap. 5.95 (ISBN 0-934860-22-X). Adventure Pubns.

Rockwell, Anne. The Girl with a Donkey Tail. LC 78-12823. (Illus.). (gr. 1-4). 1979. 6.95 o.p. (ISBN 0-525-30661-7). Dutton.

--I Like the Library. LC 77-6365. (ps-4). 1977. 9.95 (ISBN 0-525-32528-X, 0966-290). Dutton.

--No More Work. (Greenwillow Read-Alone Bks.). (Illus.). 56p. (gr. 1-4). 1976. 9.55; PLB 5.71 (ISBN 0-688-84021-3). Greenwillow.

--Up a Tall Tree. LC 79-7695. (Reading-on-My-Own Bks.). (Illus.). 64p. (gr. 2). 1981. 6.95a o.p. (ISBN 0-385-15556-5); PLB 6.95a (ISBN 0-385-15557-3). Doubleday.

--Walking Shoes. LC 79-7696. (Reading on My Own Ser.). (Illus.). (ps-3). 1980. PLB 6.95a (ISBN 0-385-14731-7). Doubleday.

--Willy Runs Away. (gr. 4-7). 1978. 6.95 o.p. (ISBN 0-525-42795-3). Dutton.

Rockwell, Anne & Rockwell, Harlow. Can I Help? LC 82-15375. (My World Ser.). (Illus.). 24p. (ps-k). 1982. 7.95 (ISBN 0-02-777720-0). Macmillan.

--I Love My Pets. LC 82-15188. (My World Ser.). (Illus.). 24p. (ps-k). 1982. 7.95 (ISBN 0-02-777710-3). Macmillan.

--The Night We Slept Outside. LC 82-17963. (Ready-to-Read Ser.). (Illus.). 48p. (gr. 1-4). 1983. 8.95 (ISBN 0-02-777450-3). Macmillan.

Rockwell, F. A. How to Write Plots That Sell. LC 74-23408. 288p. 1975. 10.00 o.p. (ISBN 0-8092-8350-6); pap. 8.95 (ISBN 0-8092-8249-6). Contemp Bks.

Rockwell, Frances. Graphology for Lovers. (Orig.). 1979. pap. 1.75 o.p. (ISBN 0-451-08854-9, E8854, Sig). NAL.

Rockwell, Harlow. My Dentist. LC 75-6974. (Illus.). 32p. (ps-3). 1975. 9.75 (ISBN 0-688-80011-4); PLB 9.36 (ISBN 0-688-84011-6). Greenwillow.

Rockwell, Harlow, jt. auth. see Rockwell, Anne.

Rockwell, James R., Jr., jt. auth. see Goldman, Leon.

Rockwell, Jane. Cats & Kittens. LC 73-14560. (First Bks). (Illus.). 72p. (gr. 4-7). 1974. PLB 8.90 (ISBN 0-531-00812-6). Watts.

Rockwell, Joan. Fact in Fiction: The Use of Literature in the Systematic Study of Society. 211p. 1974. 18.95 (ISBN 0-7100-7877-3). Routledge & Kegan.

Rockwell, John. All American Music: Composition in the Late Twentieth Century. LC 82-48885. 288p. 1983. 15.95 (ISBN 0-394-51163-8). Knopf.

Rockwell, Kiffin A., jt. auth. see McQueen, William A.

Rockwell, Nancy. Hardy Boys Code Activity Book. (Elephant Books Ser.). (Illus.). (gr. 3-7). 1978. pap. 1.50 o.s.i. (ISBN 0-448-14771-8, G&D). Putnam Pub Group.

--The Nancy Drew Code Activity Book. (Elephant Books Ser.). (Illus.). (gr. 3-7). 1978. pap. 1.50 o.s.i. (ISBN 0-448-14781-5, G&D). Putnam Pub Group.

Rockwell, Norman. Norman Rockwell--My Adventures As an Illustrator. LC 79-55715. (Illus.). 256p. 1979. 15.95 (ISBN 0-89387-034-X, Co. Pub. by Sat Eve Post). Curtis Pub Co.

Rockwell, Robert E. & Williams, Robert A. Hug a Tree & Other Things to Do Outdoors with Young Children. 112p. 1983. pap. 7.95 (ISBN 0-87659-105-5). Gryphon Hse.

Rockwell, Robert E., jt. auth. see Endres, Jeannette.

Rockwell, Theodore, 3rd, ed. Reactor Shielding Design Manual. 478p. 1956. hardbound 35.50 (ISBN 0-87079-338-1, TID-7004). DOE.

Rockwell, Thomas. How to Eat Fried Worms. 128p. 1975. pap. 1.95 (ISBN 0-440-44545-0, YB). Dell.

--How to Eat Fried Worms. LC 73-4262. (gr. 4-6). 1973. PLB 8.90 (ISBN 0-531-02631-0). Watts.

Rockwell, Wilson, ed. Memoirs of a Lawman. LC 82-71330. 378p. 1962. 12.95 (ISBN 0-8040-0200-2). Swallow.

Rockwood, Charles E., jt. ed. see Gapinski, James.

Rockwood, Irving, ed. see Elder, Charles D. & Cobb, Roger W.

Rockwood, Irving, ed. see Paris, David C. & Reynolds, James F.

Rockwood, Jerome. Craftsmen of Dionysus: An Approach to Acting. 1966. pap. 10.95x (ISBN 0-673-05719-4). Scott F.

Rockwood, Roy. Bomba, the Jungle Boy. LC 77-84109. (Bomba Books Ser.: Vol. 1). (Illus.). (gr. 4-9). 1978. 2.95 o.s.i. (ISBN 0-448-14701-7, G&D). Putnam Pub Group.

--Bomba, the Jungle Boy: At the Moving Mountain. (Bomba Books Ser.: Vol. 2). (Illus.). (gr. 4-9). 1978. 2.95 o.s.i. (ISBN 0-448-14702-5, G&D). Putnam Pub Group.

Roda, E., ed. Bile Acids in Gastroenterology. 250p. 1983. text ed. 45.00 (ISBN 0-85200-488-5, Pub. by MTP Pr England). Kluwer Boston.

Roda, Janet. No-Sew Decorating. (Orig.). 1981. pap. 9.95 o.s.i. (ISBN 0-440-56207-4, Delta). Dell.

Rodahl, Kaare, jt. auth. see Astrand, Per-Olof.

Rodahl, Karre. Akiviak. 1979. 9.95 (ISBN 0-393-01181-X). Norton.

Rodale, Jerome I. Natural Way to Better Eyesight. (Orig.). 1968. pap. 1.50 o.s.i. (ISBN 0-515-01827-9, V1827). Jove Pubns.

Rodale Press, ed. see Smyser, Carol.

Rodale Press Editors. Bicycling & Photography. 96p. 1982. pap. 3.95 (ISBN 0-87857-282-1, 12-677-1). Rodale Pr Inc.

--The Organic Gardeners Complete Guide to Vegetables & Fruits. Halpin, Anne, ed. (Illus.). 528p. 1982. 21.95 (ISBN 0-87857-386-0, 01-025-0). Rodale Pr Inc.

--Solar Food Dryer. (Illus.). 64p. 1982. pap. 14.95 (ISBN 0-87857-333-X, 15-000-0). Rodale Pr Inc.

Rodale, Robert. Sane Living in a Mad World. pap. 1.25 o.p. (ISBN 0-451-05385-0, Y5385, Sig). NAL.

Rodaniche, A. F., jt. ed. see Moynihan, Martin.

Rodd, Laurel R. Nichiren: A Biography. (Occasional Paper; Arizona State Univ., Center for Asian Studies: No. 11). 86p. 1978. pap. text ed. 3.00 (ISBN 0-939252-07-4). ASU Ctr Asian.

--Nichiren: Selected Readings. LC 79-17054. (Asian Studies in Hawaii: No. 26). 224p. 1980. pap. text ed. 10.75x o.p. (ISBN 0-8248-0682-4). UH Pr.

Rodda & Trieschmann. Commercial Property Risk Management & Insurance, 2 vols. 1978. 18.00 ea. o.p. IIA.

Rodda, J. C., et al. Systematic Hydrology. 1976. 49.95 o.p. (ISBN 0-408-00234-4). Butterworth.

Rodda, John C. Facets of Hydrology. LC 75-26568. 1976. 106.95 (ISBN 0-471-01359-5, Pub. by Wiley-Interscience). Wiley.

Rodda, P. U., jt. ed. see Leviton, A. E.

Rodda, William H., et al. Commercial Property Risk Management & Insurance, 2 vols. 1980. write for info. o.p. (CPCU 3). IIA.

Rodda, Williams H. & Trieschmann, James S. Commercial Property Risk Management & Insurance, 2 Vols. LC 78-52690. 1982. Vol. 1. text ed. 18.00 (ISBN 0-89463-004-0); Vol. 2. text ed. 18.00 (ISBN 0-89463-005-9). Am Inst Property.

Rodden, C. J., ed. Analysis of Essential Nuclear Reactor Materials. LC 64-60035. (AEC Technical Information Center Ser.). 1291p. 1964. pap. 83.50 microfiche (ISBN 0-87079-393-4, TID-21384); microfiche 4.50 (ISBN 0-87079-136-2, TID-21384). DOE.

Rodden, Clement J., ed. Selected Measurement Methods for Plutonium & Uranium in the Nuclear Fuel Cycle. 2nd ed. LC 72-600015. (AEC Technical Information Center Ser.). 440p. 1972. pap. 19.00 (ISBN 0-87079-354-3, TID-7029 (2ND ED.)); microfiche 4.50 (ISBN 0-87079-355-1, TID-7029 (2ND ED.)). DOE.

Roddenberry, Gene, jt. auth. see Sackett, Susan.

Roddick, Dan, jt. auth. see Tips, Charles.

Roddick, Ellen. Holding Patterns. 224p. 1981. 10.95 o.p. (ISBN 0-312-38833-0). St Martin.

Roddy & Coolen. Electronic Communications. 2nd ed. (Illus.). 640p. 1980. text ed. 24.95 (ISBN 0-8359-1631-6); solns manual avail. (ISBN 0-8359-1632-4). Reston.

Roddy, D. J., et al, eds. see Lunar Science Symposium on Planetary Cratering Mechanics, Flagstaff, Ariz., 1976.

Rodean, Howard C. Nuclear-Explosion Seismology. LC 73-170333. (AEC Critical Review Ser.). 164p. 1971. pap. 12.00 (ISBN 0-87079-288-1, TID-25572); microfiche 4.00 (ISBN 0-87079-289-X, TID-25572). DOE.

Rodee, Carlton C. & Anderson, Totten J. Introduction to Political Science. 4th ed. (Illus.). 544p. 1983. text ed. 23.95 (ISBN 0-07-053386-5, C); write for info. (ISBN 0-07-053387-3). McGraw.

Rodee, Marian E. Old Navajo Rugs: Their Development from 1900 to 1940. LC 80-54560. (Illus.). 96p. 1981. 25.00 (ISBN 0-8263-0566-0); pap. 15.95 (ISBN 0-8263-0567-9). U of NM Pr.

--Southwestern Weaving: The Collection of the Maxwell Museum. rev. ed. 1981. write for info (ISBN 0-8263-0587-3); pap. 14.95. U of NM Pr.

Rodefeld, Richard D., et al. Change in Rural America: Causes, Consequences & Alternatives. LC 78-4644. (Illus.). 1978. pap. text ed. 17.95 o.p. (ISBN 0-8016-4145-4). Mosby.

Rodehaver, Gladys K., jt. ed. see Easu.

Rodemacher, P. G., jt. auth. see Klem, Joan R.

Roden, Martin. Analog & Digital Communication Systems. 1979. 32.95 (ISBN 0-13-032722-0). P-H.

Roden, Martin S. Digital & Data Communications Systems. (Illus.). 416p. 1982. 32.95 (ISBN 0-13-212142-5). P-H.

Rodenberger, Lou H., ed. Her Work: Stories by Texas Women. LC 82-60562. 347p. 1982. 16.95 (ISBN 0-940672-05-7); pap. 8.95 (ISBN 0-940672-04-9). Shearer Pub.

Rodenborg, L. Epilithische Vegetation in Einem Alten Waldgebiet auf Mittel-Oeland, Schweden. (Bibliotheca Lichenologica Ser.: No. 8). (Illus.). 1977. pap. text ed. 12.00x (ISBN 3-7682-1151-7). Lubrecht & Cramer.

Rodenmayer, Robert N. Thanks Be to God. 126p. 1960. 7.50 (ISBN 0-227-67615-7). Attic Pr.

Roderick, G. & Stephens, M., eds. Higher Education for All? 206p. 1979. write for info. (ISBN 0-905273-10-9, Pub. by Taylor & Francis). Intl Pubns Serv.

Roderick, Jessie A., jt. auth. see Berman, Louise M.

Roderick, Marilyn, ed. Infection Control in Critical Care. LC 82-13951. 184p. 1982. 26.95 (ISBN 0-89443-844-1). Aspen Systems.

Roderick, Samuel D. The Fully Colored Art Quaderno of the Best Paintings by Francisco Goya. (Illus.). 1979. deluxe ed. 28.50 (ISBN 0-930582-45-4). Gloucester Art.

Roderus, Frank. Duster: The Story of a Texas Cattle Drive. LC 77-2218. 1977. 8.50 (ISBN 0-8309-0164-7). Ind Pr MO.

--Jason Evers, His Own Story. LC 79-6888. (Double D Western Ser.). 192p. 1980. 10.95 o.p. (ISBN 0-385-15755-X). Doubleday.

--Ordeal of Hogue Bynell. LC 82-45303. (Double D Western Ser.). 192p. 1982. 11.95 (ISBN 0-385-18029-2). Doubleday.

Rodes, David S., ed. see Shadwell, Thomas.

Rodes, J. H. Shadow over Hawkhaven. 1982. 6.95 (ISBN 0-686-84176-X, Avalon). Bouregy.

Rodes, Robert E., Jr. The Legal Enterprise. 1983. price not set. U of Notre Dame Pr.

Rodger, William. Official Price Guide to Old Books & Autographs. 2nd ed. (Collector Ser.). (Illus.). 400p. 1980. pap. 8.95 o.p. (ISBN 0-87637-113-6, 113-06). Hse of Collectibles.

Rodgers, Allan G. Resource Material for Handling Unemployment Cases in Massachusetts. Spriggs, Marshall T., ed. (Tools of the Trade for Massachusetts Lawyers Ser.). (Orig.). 1983. pap. price not set (ISBN 0-910001-04-9). MA Poverty Law.

Rodgers, Audrey T. The Universal Drum: Dance Imagery in the Poetry of Eliot, Crane, Roethke & Williams. LC 79-12480. 1979. 16.95x (ISBN 0-271-00220-4). Pa St U Pr.

Rodgers, Bill. One for the Road: The Marathon & Me. 1981. 10.95 o.p. (ISBN 0-671-25087-6). S&S.

Rodgers, Bill & Concannon, Joe. Marathoning. 1980. 11.95 o.p. (ISBN 0-671-25087-6). S&S.

Rodgers, Brian. Battle Against Poverty: Vol. 1 & 2, Towards a Welfare State. (Library of Social Policy & Administration). 1969. Vol. 1. pap. text ed. 3.00x (ISBN 0-7100-4027-X); Vol. 2. pap. text ed. 3.00x (ISBN 0-7100-6451-9). Humanities.

Rodgers, Bruce. Gay Talk: A (Sometimes Outrageous) Dictionary of Gay Slang. LC 79-13972. 1979. pap. 4.95 (ISBN 0-399-50392-7, Perige). Putnam Pub Group.

Rodgers, Charles A., jt. auth. see Juszli, Frank L.

Rodgers, David L. & Whetten, David A. Interorganizational Coordination: Theory, Research, & Implementation. 176p. 1982. pap. text ed. 12.50x (ISBN 0-8138-0986-X). Iowa St U Pr.

Rodgers, Diane, jt. auth. see Miller, Lani.

Rodgers, Eamon J., ed. Benito Perez Galdos: Tormento. 1978. text ed. 29.00 (ISBN 0-08-018089-2); pap. text ed. 14.00 (ISBN 0-08-018088-4). Pergamon.

Rodgers, Frank. A Guide to British Government Publications. 750p. 1980. 40.00 (ISBN 0-8242-0617-7). Wilson.

Rodgers, Frederick A. Curriculum & Instruction in the Elementary School. (Illus.). 320p. 1975. text ed. 18.95x (ISBN 0-02-402610-7). Macmillan.

Rodgers, Gerry, et al. Population, Employment, & Inequality: The Bachue Model Applied to the Philippines. LC 78-60535. (Praeger Special Studies). 1978. 34.95 o.p. (ISBN 0-03-047216-4). Praeger.

Rodgers, Harrell R. Cost of Human Neglect: America's Welfare Failure. LC 82-10390. 192p. 1982. 25.00 (ISBN 0-686-97716-5); pap. 12.95 (ISBN 0-87332-238-X). M E Sharpe.

Rodgers, Harrell R. & Bullock, Charles S. Law & Social Change: Civil Rights Laws & Their Consequences. (Illus.). 160p. 1972. pap. text ed. 18.50 (ISBN 0-07-053378-4, C). McGraw.

Rodgers, Harrell R. & Harrington, Michael. Unfinished Democracy: The American Political System. 1981. text ed. 21.95x (ISBN 0-673-15458-0); pap. text ed. 19.95x (ISBN 0-673-15415-7). Scott F.

Rodgers, Harrell R., Jr. & Bullock, Charles S., 3rd. Coercion to Compliance. (Politics of Education Ser.). (Illus.). 208p. 1976. 18.95x o.p. (ISBN 0-669-00691-2); pap. 11.95 o.p. (ISBN 0-669-00965-2). Lexington Bks.

Rodgers, John M. State Estimates of Interegional Commodity Trade Flows, 1963. LC 73-8811. (Multiregional Input-Output Study: Vol. 5). (Illus.). 480p. 1973. 28.95x (ISBN 0-669-89227-0). Lexington Bks.

--State Estimates of Outputs, Employment & Payrolls: 1947, 1958, & 1963. LC 72-5759. (Multiregional Input-Output Study: Vol. 2). (Illus.). 320p. 1972. 28.95x (ISBN 0-669-73494-2). Lexington Bks.

Rodgers, Joseph L., Jr. Citizen Committees: A Guide to Their Use in Local Government. LC 76-56193. 120p. 1977. prof ref 15.00x (ISBN 0-88410-654-3). Ballinger Pub.

Rodgers, Joseph Lee, Jr. Environmental Impact Assessment: Growth Management, & the Comprehensive Plan. LC 76-16844. 208p. 1976. prof ref 19.50x (ISBN 0-88410-447-8). Ballinger Pub.

Rodgers, Leland. Barron's How to Prepare for the Graduate Record Examination - Advanced Biology. LC 74-10918. 1975. pap. 5.50 (ISBN 0-8120-2072-3). Barron.

Rodgers, Mary. Summer Switch. LC 79-2690. (A Charlotte Zolotow Bk.). 192p. (gr. 5 up). 1982. 9.13i (ISBN 0-06-025058-5, HarpJ); PLB 9.89g (ISBN 0-06-025059-3). Har-Row.

Rodgers, Peter. Knowing Jesus. LC 82-14832. 64p. (Orig.). pap. 1.95 (ISBN 0-87784-383-X). Inter-Varsity.

Rodgers, Richard. Musical Stages. 1978. pap. 2.95 o.s.i. (ISBN 0-515-04647-7). Jove Pubns.

Rodgers, Richard & Hammerstein, Oscar. Six Plays. 1959. 3.95 o.s.i. (ISBN 0-394-60200-5, M200). Modern Lib.

Rodgers, Stanley F., jt. auth. see Schultz, David A.

Rodgers, Susan S., jt. auth. see Good, Shirley R.

Rodgers, Willard L., jt. auth. see Herzog, A. Reguls.

Rodgon, M. Single-Word Usage, Cognitive Development & the Beginnings of Combinatorial Speech. LC 75-7211. (Illus.). 192p. 1976. 29.95 (ISBN 0-521-20884-X). Cambridge U Pr.

Rodi, Stephen. Complete Solutions Manual to Accompany Swokowski's Calculus: Alternate Ed. (Math Ser.). 750p. 1982. pap. text ed. write for info. (ISBN 0-87150-342-5, 2733). Prindle.

Rodieck, Jorma. The Little Bitty Snake. Burnett, Yumiko M. & Contreras, Moyra, trs. (Illus.). 24p. 1983. English - Japanese. PLB 9.50 (ISBN 0-940880-06-7); English - Spanish. PLB 9.50 (ISBN 0-940880-02-4); English - French. PLB 9.50 (ISBN 0-940880-04-0); English - Japanese. pap. 4.00 (ISBN 0-940880-07-5); English - Spanish. pap. 4.00 (ISBN 0-940880-03-2); English - French. pap. 4.00 (ISBN 0-940880-05-9). Open Hand.

Rodin. Rodin on Art & Artists: With Sixty Illustrations of His Work. 2nd ed. (Fine Art Ser.). (Illus.). 160p. 1983. pap. 6.95 (ISBN 0-486-24487-3). Dover.

Rodin, Burt. Calculus with Analytic Geometry. 1969. ref. ed. 33.95 (ISBN 0-13-112060-3). P-H.

Rodin, Burton. Basic Calculus with Applications. 1978. 25.50x (ISBN 0-673-16224-9); o.p. incl. solutions manual (ISBN 0-87620-098-6). Scott F.

Rodin, Judith, jt. auth. see Schachter, Stanley.

Rodino, Walter, jt. auth. see Durante, Francesco.

Rodis-Jamero, Nilo, jt. auth. see Johnston, Joe.

Roditi, Edouard. The Disorderly Poet. (Capra Chapbook Ser.: No. 29). 56p. (Orig.). 1975. pap. 4.00 (ISBN 0-88496-026-9). Capra Pr.

--More Dialogues on Art. (Illus.). 250p. (Orig.). 1983. pap. 10.95 (ISBN 0-915520-57-5). Ross Erikson.

Roditi, Edouard, tr. see Emre, Yunus.

Rodman, George. Mass Media Issues: Analysis & Debate. 320p. 1981. pap. text ed. 13.95 (ISBN 0-574-22570-6, 13-5570). SRA.

Rodman, Hyman. Lower-Class Families: The Culture of Poverty in Negro Trinidad. 1971. 10.95x o.p. (ISBN 0-19-501379-4); pap. 7.95x (ISBN 0-19-501378-6). Oxford U Pr.

Rodman, Hyman, ed. Marriage, Family & Society: A Reader. 1965. pap. text ed. 4.95x (ISBN 0-685-69597-2). Phila Bk Co.

Rodman, Selden. Artists in Tune with Their World. (Illus.). 1982. 19.95 (ISBN 0-671-25611-4). S&S.

--The Brazil Traveler. LC 75-13350. (Illus.). 104p. 1975. pap. 7.95 (ISBN 0-8159-5113-2). Devin.

Rodman, Selden & Kearns, James. The Heart of Beethoven. LC 76-51291. (Illus.). 1977. Repr. of 1962 ed. lib. bdg. 20.50x (ISBN 0-8371-9441-5, ROHE). Greenwood.

Rodman, Selden, ed. One Hundred American Poems. rev. ed. 367p. 1972. pap. 1.50 o.p. (ISBN 0-451-61666-9, MW1666, Ment). NAL.

--One-Hundred British Poets. pap. 2.25 o.p. (ISBN 0-451-61308-2, ME1308, Ment). NAL.

Rodman, Selden, jt. ed. see Eberhart, Richard.

Rodna, N., jt. auth. see Petrescu, P.

Rodna, Nicolae, jt. auth. see Peterscu, Paul.

Rodney, Lynn S. & Ford, Phyllis M. Camp Administration: Schools, Communities, Organizations. LC 74-155211. (Illus.). 410p. 1971. 25.50 o.s.i. (ISBN 0-471-07107-2). Wiley.

Rodney, Lynn S. & Toalson, Robert F. The Administration of Recreation, Parks, & Leisure Services. 2nd ed. LC 80-17723. 486p. 1981. text ed. 24.95x (ISBN 0-471-05806-8). Wiley.

Rodney, Walter. A History of the Upper Guinea Coast, 1545-1800. LC 79-48070. 1980. pap. 7.95 (ISBN 0-85345-546-5). Monthly Rev.

--How Europe Underdeveloped Africa. Rev. ed. LC 81-6240. 302p. 1982. 12.95 (ISBN 0-88258-105-8). Howard U Pr.

Rodnick, David. Postwar Germans. 1948. 42.50x (ISBN 0-685-89773-7). Elliots Bks.

Rodonvilliers, Le P., jt. auth. see Ducis, V.

Rodowski, Colby. What about Me. (YA) 1978. pap. 1.50 (ISBN 0-440-99692-9, LFL). Dell.

Rodowsky. A Summer's Worth of Shame. (gr. 7 up). 1980. PLB 8.90 (ISBN 0-531-04110-7, B50). Watts.

Rodowsky, Colby. Evy-Ivy-Over. LC 78-6989. (gr. 5 up). 1978. PLB 8.90 s&l (ISBN 0-531-02245-5). Watts.

--H, My Name is Henley. 192p. (gr. 6 up). 1982. 10.95 (ISBN 0-374-32831-5). FS&G.

Rodrigo, R., jt. ed. see Manske, R.

Rodrigue, Garry. Parallel Computations, Vol. 1. (Computational Techniques Ser.). 1982. 59.00 (ISBN 0-12-592101-2). Acad Pr.

Rodrigues, Jose H. Brazil & Africa. Mazzara, Richard A. & Hileman, Sam, trs. 1965. 37.50x (ISBN 0-520-01076-0). U of Cal Pr.

Rodrigues, Otilio, jt. tr. see Kavanaugh, Kieran.

Rodriguez, Angel M. Substitution in the Hebrew Cultus. (Andrews University Seminary Doctoral Dissertation Ser.). xiv, 339p. (Orig.). 1982. pap. 8.95 (ISBN 0-943872-35-9). Andrews Univ Pr.

Rodriguez, Cookie. Larmes de Delivrance. Cosson, Annie, ed. Luc-Barbier, Jean, tr. from Eng. Orig. Title: Please Make Me Cry. 234p. (Fr.). 1982. pap. 2.50 (ISBN 0-8297-1109-0). Life Pubs Intl.

Rodriguez, Edward J. & Santoro, Anthony. The Law of Doing Business in Connecticut. 320p. 1983. write for info. (ISBN 0-88063-011-6). Butterworth Legal Pubs.

Rodriguez, F. Principles of Polymer Systems. 1970. text ed. 33.00 (ISBN 0-07-053380-6, C); solutions manual 7.95 (ISBN 0-07-053381-4). McGraw.

Rodriguez, Fred. Education in a Multicultural Society. LC 82-23755. 172p. (Orig.). 1983. lib. bdg. 21.75 (ISBN 0-8191-2977-1); pap. text ed. 10.50 (ISBN 0-8191-2978-X). U Pr of Amer.

--Mainstreaming a Multicultural Concept into Teacher Education Guidelines for Teacher Trainers. LC 82-60529. 125p. (Orig.). 1983. pap. 12.95 (ISBN 0-88247-688-2). R & E Res Assoc.

Rodriguez, J. G., ed. Recent Advances in Acarology. LC 79-17386. 1979. Vol. 1. 46.00 (ISBN 0-12-592201-9); Vol. 2. 42.00 (ISBN 0-12-592202-7). Acad Pr.

Rodriguez, Jorge A., tr. see Westberg, Granger.

Rodriguez, Jose M., tr. see Campbell, Doak S.

Rodriguez, Mario. The Cadiz Experiment in Central America, 1808-1826. LC 76-50256. 1978. 34.50x (ISBN 0-520-03394-9). U of Cal Pr.

Rodriguez, Mario B. Cuentistas de Hoy. LC 52-14409. (Span). 1952. pap. text ed. 10.50 (ISBN 0-395-05317-X). HM.

Rodriguez, O. Jaime. The Emergence of Spanish America: Vincente Rocafuerte & Spanish Americanism, 1808-1832. LC 74-22972. 392p. 1976. 38.50x (ISBN 0-520-02875-9). U of Cal Pr.

Rodriguez, Raymond L. Promoters: Structure & Function. Chamberlin, Michael J., ed. 540p. 1982. 41.50 (ISBN 0-03-059919-9). Praeger.

Rodriguez, Richard. Hunger of Memory: The Education of Richard Rodriguez, An Autobiography. 1981. 13.95 (ISBN 0-686-96533-7). Godine.

Rodriguez, Rita M. Foreign-Exchange Management in U.S. Multinationals. LC 78-54703. 144p. 1980. 19.95x (ISBN 0-669-02330-2). Lexington Bks.

Rodriguez, Rita M., jt. auth. see Carter, E. Eugene.

Rodriguez-Castellano, Juan. Introduccion a la Historia De Espana. 1956. 7.95x o.p. (ISBN 0-19-501037-X). Oxford U Pr.

Rodriguez-Novas, J., jt. auth. see De Vries, H. P.

Rodriguez-Novas, Jose, jt. auth. see Goldschmidt, Werner.

Rodriquez, F. Principles of Polymer Systems. 2nd ed. 1982. 34.95 (ISBN 0-07-053382-2); solutions manual 15.00 (ISBN 0-07-053383-0). McGraw.

Rodriquez, Mary D. Hawaiian Spelling Bee. (Illus.). (gr. 1-5). PLB 6.19 (ISBN 0-8313-0084-1). Lantern.

Rodriquez, Raphael, jt. ed. see Zavala, Iris M.

Rodriquez, Rita M., jt. auth. see Riehl, Heinz.

Rodriquez-Nieto, Catherine, tr. see Corpi, Lucha.

Rodriruez, Mario B., et al. Cuentos De Ambos Mundos. Eoff, S. H., ed. (Graded Spanish Readers: Bk. 2). 1950. pap. text ed. 4.95 (ISBN 0-395-04125-2). HM.

Roduner, Edna, jt. auth. see Roduner, Robert S.

Roduner, Robert S. & Roduner, Edna. The Amazing Twentieth Century. 1979. 6.95 o.p. (ISBN 0-533-04168-6). Vantage.

Rodway, Allan. The Craft of Criticism. LC 82-4499. 192p. 1982. 32.50 (ISBN 0-521-23320-8); pap. 9.95 (ISBN 0-521-29909-8). Cambridge U Pr.

--English Comedy. LC 74-25377. 1975. 30.00x (ISBN 0-520-02935-6). U of Cal Pr.

Rodway, Avril. Fairies. (Leprechaun Library). (Illus.). 64p. 1981. 4.95 (ISBN 0-399-12610-4). Putnam Pub Group.

--A Literary Herbal. (The Leprechaun Library). (Illus.). 64p. 1980. 3.95 (ISBN 0-399-12545-0). Putnam Pub Group.

Rodwell, J. M., ed. & tr. Koran. 1978. pap. 3.50x (ISBN 0-460-01380-7, Evman). Biblio Dist.

Rodwell, Robert R. Your Book of Aeromodelling. (Illus.). 4.25 o.p. (ISBN 0-571-04644-4). Transatlantic.

Rodwin, Lloyd, et al. Planning Urban Growth & Regional Development: The Experience of the Guayana Program in Venezuela. LC 68-18240. (MIT-Harvard Joint Center for Urban Studies Ser). (Illus.). 1969. 23.00x o.p. (ISBN 0-262-18028-6). MIT Pr.

Rodwin, Victor G. The Health Planning Predicament: France, Quebec, England, & the United States. Leslie, Charles, ed. LC 82-45910. (Comparative Studies of Health Systems & Medical Care Ser.). 160p. 1983. 16.50x (ISBN 0-520-04446-0). U of Cal Pr.

Rodymans, C. & Rabenau, A., eds. Crystal Structure & Chemical Bonding in Inorganic Chemistry. 1975. 42.75 (ISBN 0-444-10961-7). Elsevier.

Rodzinski, Witold. History of China, Vol. 1. 1979. text ed. 56.00 (ISBN 0-08-021806-7). Pergamon.

Rodziszewski, Audrey Korwin see Konwicki, Tadeusz.

Rodziszewski, George Korwin see Konwicki, Tadeusz.

Roe & Stoodt. Secondary School Reading Instruction: The Content Areas. 2d ed. 1983. text ed. 22.95 (ISBN 0-686-84558-7, ET02); instr's manual avail. (ET03). HM.

Roe, A. C., jt. auth. see Braymer, Daniel H.

Roe, Alan R., jt. auth. see Bhatt, Vinayak V.

Roe, Betty D. & Ross, Elinor P. Developing Power in Reading. 2nd ed. 1977. pap. text ed. 9.95 (ISBN 0-8403-1042-0). Kendall-Hunt.

Roe, Betty D. & Stoodt, Barbara D. Secondary School Reading Instruction: The Content Areas. 2d ed. LC 82-83290. 1983. 21.95 (ISBN 0-395-32783-0); write for info. instr's. manual (ISBN 0-395-32784-9). HM.

Roe, Betty D., jt. auth. see Burns, Paul C.

Roe, Betty D., et al. Reading Instruction in the Secondary School. Rev. ed. 1978. 21.95 (ISBN 0-395-30710-4). HM.

Roe, Daphne A. Geriatric Nutrition. (Illus.). 304p. 1983. 22.95 (ISBN 0-13-354035-9). P-H.

Roe, Derek. Prehistory: An Introduction. LC 70-81799. 1970. 28.50x (ISBN 0-520-01406-5); pap. 3.25 (ISBN 0-520-02252-1). U of Cal Pr.

Roe, F. J. C., jt. ed. see Ambrose, E. J.

Roe, Francis J., ed. Metabolic Aspects of Food Safety. LC 72-142181. 1971. 63.50 (ISBN 0-12-592550-6). Acad Pr.

Roe, Graham, ed. Seminar on AACR2. 98p. 1981. pap. 17.50 (ISBN 0-85365-593-6, Pub. by Lib Assn England). Oryx Pr.

Roe, John, jt. auth. see Collison, Robert.

Roe, Joseph W. English & American Tool Builders. (Illus.). Repr. of 1916 ed. lib. bdg. 15.00x o.p. (ISBN 0-678-01246-6). Kelley.

Roe, L. B. Practical Electrical Project Engineering. 1978. 30.25 (ISBN 0-07-053392-X). McGraw.

--Practices & Procedures of Industrial Electrical Design. LC 70-168754. (Illus.). 288p. 1972. 41.95 (ISBN 0-07-053390-3, P&RB). McGraw.

Roe, P. L. Numerical Methods in Aeronautical Fluid Dynamics. (IMA Conference Ser.). Date not set. 55.50 (ISBN 0-12-592520-4). Acad Pr.

Roe, Paul F. Choral Music Education. LC 77-100403. (Music Ser). 1970. ref. ed. 21.95 (ISBN 0-13-133348-8). P-H.

--Choral Music Education. 2nd ed. (Illus.). 352p. 1983. text ed. 21.95 (ISBN 0-13-133322-4). P-H.

Roe, Richard, jt. ed. see Wilson, Samuel.

Roe, Shirley A. Matter, Life & Generation: Eighteenth Century Embryology & the Haller-Wolff Debate. LC 80-19611. (Illus.). 216p. 1981. 34.50 (ISBN 0-521-23540-5). Cambridge U Pr.

Roe, William H. & Drake, Thelbert L. The Principalship. 2nd ed. (Illus.). 1980. text ed. 22.95x (ISBN 0-02-402680-8). Macmillan.

Roeber, Edward. Interpreting Guidance Programs to School Personnel. (Guidance Monograph). 1968. pap. 2.40 o.p. (ISBN 0-395-09911-0). HM.

Roeber, Edward C., jt. auth. see Baer, Max F.

Roeber, Johanna, jt. auth. see Dale, Barbara.

Roebuck, Carl, ed. Muses at Work: Arts, Crafts, & Professions in Ancient Greece & Rome. 1969. 12.50 o.p. (ISBN 0-262-18034-0). MIT Pr.

Roebuck, E. M., jt. auth. see Sherlock, A. J.

Roebuck, Field, Jr. Applied Petroleum Resevoir Technology. 1979. 38.00 (ISBN 0-89931-002-8). Inst Energy.

--Economic Analysis of Petroleum Ventures. 1979. 31.00 (ISBN 0-89419-038-5). Inst Energy.

Roebuck, J. A., Jr., et al. Engineering Anthropometry Methods. LC 74-34272. (Human Factors Ser). 459p. 1975. 49.50 o.p. (ISBN 0-471-72975-2, Pub. by Wiley-Interscience). Wiley.

Roebuck, Julian. The Southern Redneck. 222p. 1982. 25.95 (ISBN 0-03-059803-6). Praeger.

Roebuck, Julian & Weeber, Stanley C. Political Crime in the United States: Analyzing Crimes by & Against Government. LC 78-19463. (Praeger Special Studies). 1978. 29.95 o.p. (ISBN 0-03-044241-9). Praeger.

Roebuck, Julian B., jt. auth. see Quan, Robert S.

Roebuck, Kenneth C. Gun-Dog Training Spaniels & Retrievers. LC 82-5667. (Illus.). 160p. 1982. 12.95 (ISBN 0-686-91943-2). Stackpole.

Roedell, Wendy C., et al. Gifted Young Children. Tannenbaum, Abraham J., ed. LC 80-10707. (Perspectives on Gifted & Talented Education Ser.). (Orig.). 1980. pap. text ed. 6.95x (ISBN 0-8077-2587-0). Tchrs Coll.

Roeder, Edward. PACs Americana: A Directory of Political Action Committees & Their Interests. LC 81-85581. 1982. lib. bdg. 200.00 (ISBN 0-942236-00-9); pap. 200.00. Sunshine Serv.

Roeder, Ralph. Man of the Renaissance: Four Law Givers - Savonarola, Machiavelli, Castiglione, Aretino. LC 78-122059. (Illus.). Repr. of 1933 ed. 35.00x (ISBN 0-678-03171-1). Kelley.

Roeder, Ralph, tr. see Goncourt, Edmond L.

Roeder, S. B. W., jt. auth. see Fukushima, E.

Roederer, J. G. Introduction to the Physics & Psychophysics of Music. LC 72-97698. (Heidelberg Science Library: Vol. 16). (Illus.). xii, 164p. 1973. pap. 8.70 (ISBN 0-387-90116-7). Springer-Verlag.

Roediger, Henry L., III, jt. auth. see Kantowitz, Barry H.

Roekaerts, D., jt. auth. see Langouche, F.

Roelandt, J. Practical Echocardiology. 1977. 49.95x (ISBN 0-471-27891-2). Res Stud Pr.

--The Practice of M-Mode & Two-Dimensional Echocardiagraphy. 1983. 59.00 (ISBN 90-247-2745-6, Pub. by Martinus Nijhoff Netherlands). Kluwer Boston.

Roelandt, J. & Hugenholtz, P. G. Long-Term Ambulatory Electrocardiography. 1982. text ed. 39.50 (ISBN 90-247-2664-6, Pub. by Martinus Nijhoff Netherlands). Kluwer Boston.

Roelandt, J., jt. auth. see Meltzer, R. S.

Roelants, G. E., jt. ed. see Loor, F.

Roelli, H. J. see Anderhalden, A.

Roelofs. Astronomy & Land Surveying. 1950. 11.50 (ISBN 0-444-40771-5). Elsevier.

Roelofs, Robert, et al. Environment & Society: A Book of Readings on Environmental Policy, Attitudes & Values. 448p. 1974. pap. text ed. 17.95 (ISBN 0-13-283374-3). P-H.

Roels, Oswald A., ed. Hudson River Colloquium, Vol. 250. (Annals of the New York Academy of Sciences). 185p. 1974. 29.00x (ISBN 0-89072-764-3). NY Acad Sci.

Roemer, John. Analytical Foundations of Marxian Economic Theory. LC 80-22646. (Illus.). 224p. 1981. 39.50 (ISBN 0-521-23047-0). Cambridge U Pr.

Roemer, Michael & Stern, Joseph J. Cases in Economic Development Projects: Policies & Statistics. 1981. text ed. 34.95 (ISBN 0-408-10730-8); pap. text ed. 14.95 (ISBN 0-408-10729-4). Butterworth.

Roemer, Milton. Ambulatory Health Services in America: Past, Present & Future. LC 81-8554. 452p. 1981. text ed. 38.50 (ISBN 0-89443-388-1). Aspen Systems.

Roemer, Milton I. Social Medicine: The Advance of Organized Health Services in America. LC 78-17621. (Health Care & Society Ser.: Vol. 3). 1978. text ed. 36.50 (ISBN 0-8261-2600-6). Springer Pub.

--Systems of Health Care. LC 77-85142. (International Health Perspectives Ser.: Vol. 5 of 5). 1977. pap. text ed. 8.00 o.s.i. (ISBN 0-8261-2495-X). Springer Pub.

Roemer, Tamise. Gestalt Astrology. 320p. (Orig.). 1983. pap. 14.95 (ISBN 0-914918-33-8). Para Res.

Roemheld, Lutz. Bernard Voyenne: Der Foderalismus Pierre-Joseph Proudhons. 197p. (Ger.). 1982. write for info. (ISBN 3-8204-7023-9). P Lang Pubs.

Roener. Short-Circuit Currents in Three Phase Networks. 1972. 16.95 (ISBN 0-471-25991-8, Wiley Heyden). Wiley.

Roes, Carol. Four Negro Spirituals. Date not set. pap. 3.75 (ISBN 0-930932-24-2); record incl. M Loke.

--Hula Book, No. 10. 1982. pap. 4.50 (ISBN 0-930932-23-4); record incl. M Loke.

--Hula Book: The Governor's Waltz & The Steersman, No. 9. 1982. pap. 4.50 (ISBN 0-686-43079-4); record incl. M Loke.

--Hula Book: Twelve Little Letters & Plus & Minus, No. 8. 1982. pap. 4.50 (ISBN 0-930932-21-8); record incl. M Loke.

Roes, Carol & Loke, M. Three Hulas from Hawaii. (Hula Book Ser.: Bk. 6). 1968. pap. 4.50 with record (ISBN 0-930932-11-0). M Loke.

Roesdahl, Else. Viking Age Denmark. 272p. 1982. 60.00x (ISBN 0-7141-8027-0, Pub. by Brit Mus Pubns England). State Mutual Bk.

Roesel, Catherine E. Immunology: A Self-Instructional Approach. 1978. pap. text ed. 18.50 (ISBN 0-07-053411-X, HP). McGraw.

Roeseler, W. G. Successful American Urban Plans. LC 81-47028. 224p. 1981. 27.95x (ISBN 0-669-04540-3). Lexington Bks.

Roesler. Gansebraten. (Easy Reader, A). pap. 2.95 (ISBN 0-88436-109-8, 45262). EMC.

Roesner, Raymond E., jt. ed. see Huttrer, Gerald W.

Roessel, Ruth. Women in Navajo Society. LC 81-1293. (Illus.). 184p. 1981. 15.00x (ISBN 0-936008-01-6). Navajo Curr.

Roesser, Robert P., jt. auth. see Givone, Donald D.

Roessler, Robert, ed. see Interdisciplinary Research Conference - 1961.

Roethel, Hans K. & Benjamin, Jean K. Kandinsky: Catalogue Raisonne of the Oil Paintings, Vol. I, 1900-1915. LC 81-69483. (Illus.). 1982. 135.00x (ISBN 0-8014-1478-4). Cornell U Pr.

Roethke, Theodore. Roethke: Collected Poems. LC 65-23785. 11.95 o.p. (ISBN 0-385-05557-9). Doubleday.

Roethlisberger, Fritz J. The Elusive Phenomena: An Autobiographical Account of My Work in the Field of Organizational Behavior at the Harvard Business School. Lombard, George F., ed. 1978. 20.00x (ISBN 0-87584-116-3). Harvard Busn.

--Man-In-Organization: Essays of F. J. Roethlisberger. LC 68-28695. (Illus.). 1968. 17.50x (ISBN 0-674-54500-1, Belknap Pr). Harvard U Pr.

Roethlisberger, Marcel. Claude Lorrain: The Drawings, 2 vols., boxed. Incl. Vol. 1. Catalogue (ISBN 0-520-01458-8); Vol. 2. Plates (ISBN 0-520-01805-2). LC 66-24050. (Studies in the History of Art: No. 8). (Illus.). 1969. 110.00x ea. U of Cal Pr.

Roets, Lois. Basic Skills Reading Workbook: Grade 1. (Basic Skills Workbooks). 32p. (gr. 1). 1982. tchrs' ed. 0.99 (ISBN 0-8209-0363-9, RW-B). ESP.

Roets, Lois F. Jumbo Reading Yearbook: Grade 1. (Jumbo Reading Ser.). 96p. (gr. 1). 1979. 14.00 (ISBN 0-8209-0012-5, JRY 1). ESP.

Roets, Perry J. The Economic Order. 1969. pap. 7.95 o.p. (ISBN 0-87462-457-6). Marquette.

--Managerial Responsibility. 312p. 9.95 o.p. (ISBN 0-87462-459-2). Marquette.

--The Person in the Social Order. 1970. pap. 8.95 o.p. (ISBN 0-87462-458-4). Marquette.

Roett, Riordan. Paraguay. 135p. 1983. lib. bdg. 16.50x (ISBN 0-86531-272-9). Westview.

Roetzel, Calvin J. The Letters of Paul: Conversations in Context. LC 74-21901. (Biblical Foundations Ser.). 160p. (Orig.). 1975. pap. 5.95 o.p. (ISBN 0-8042-0208-7). John Knox.

Rofes, Eric E. I Thought People Like That Killed Themselves: Lesbians, Gay Men & Suicide. LC 82-9301. 186p. 1983. 12.00 (ISBN 0-912516-70-4); pap. 6.95 (ISBN 0-912516-69-0). Grey Fox.

Roff, William R., tr. see Boestamam, Ahmad.

Roffel, Brian & Rijnsdorp, John E. Process Dynamics, Control & Protection. LC 81-68029. (Illus.). 415p. 1982. text ed. 59.95 (ISBN 0-250-40483-4). Ann Arbor Science.

Roffey, C. G. Photopolymerization of Surface Coatings. LC 81-12916. 320p. 1982. 54.95 (ISBN 0-471-10063-3, Pub. by Wiley-Interscience). Wiley.

Roffey, J. Locusts & Grasshoppers of Economic Importance in Thailand. 1979. 75.00x (ISBN 0-686-82431-8, Pub. by Centre Overseas Research). State Mutual Bk.

--Observations on Night Flight on the Desert Locust (Schistocerca Gregaria Forskal) 1963. 35.00x (ISBN 0-85135-033-X, Pub. by Centre Overseas Research). State Mutual Bk.

Roffman, Arlyn J. The Classroom Teacher's Guide to Mainstreaming. (Illus.). 112p. 1983. 14.75x (ISBN 0-398-04786-3). C C Thomas.

Rofheart, Martha. Lionheart! 1982. pap. 3.50 (ISBN 0-451-11617-8, AE1617, Sig). NAL.

Rogal, Samuel J. A Chronological Outline of British Literature. LC 79-8577. 1980. lib. bdg. 29.95x (ISBN 0-313-21477-8, ROB/). Greenwood.

Rogan, Barbara. Changing States. LC 80-2061. 192p. 1981. 11.95 (ISBN 0-385-17373-3). Doubleday.

--Changing States. 256p. 1983. pap. 3.50 (ISBN 0-440-11049-1). Dell.

Rogan, Helen. Mixed Company: Women in the Modern Army. 336p. 1981. 14.95 (ISBN 0-399-12654-6). Putnam Pub Group.

--Mixed Company: Women in the Modern Army. LC 82-70570. 334p. 1982. pap. 8.95 (ISBN 0-8070-6707-5, BP642). Beacon Pr.

Rogasky, Barbara, retold by see Grimm Brothers.

Rogbinson, Jeff. Audi Service-Repair Handbook: Fox--1973-1979. (Illus.). pap. 11.95 o.p. (ISBN 0-89287-155-5, A132). Clymer Pubns.

Roger, E. H., jt. auth. see Lambert, P. M.

Rogers. Issues in Adolescent Psychology. 3rd ed. 1977. pap. 15.95 (ISBN 0-13-506428-7). P-H.

Rogers, A. Statistical Analysis of Spatial Dispersion. (Monographs in Spatial & Environmental Systems Analysis). 164p. 1980. 17.00x (ISBN 0-85086-045-8, Pub. by Pion England). Methuen Inc.

Rogers, A. C., jt. auth. see Cohen, Leon J.

Rogers, A. P., jt. auth. see Biggs, A. K.

Rogers, A. Robert. The Humanities: A Selective Guide to Information Sources. 2nd ed. LC 79-25335. (Library Science Text Ser.). 1980. lib. bdg. 33.00x (ISBN 0-87287-206-8); pap. text ed. 21.00x (ISBN 0-87287-222-X). Libs Unl.

Rogers, A. W. Techniques of Autoradiography. 3rd, rev. & enl. ed. LC 78-16861. 1979. 87.25 (ISBN 0-444-80063-8, North Holland). Elsevier.

Rogers, Adrian. The Secret of Supernatural Living. 144p. 1982. 7.95 (ISBN 0-8407-5270-9). Nelson.

Rogers, Alan. Empire & Liberty: American Resistance to British Authority, 1755-1763. 1975. 28.50x (ISBN 0-520-02275-0). U of Cal Pr.

Rogers, Alan W., jt. auth. see Best, Robin H.

Rogers, Andrei, jt. ed. see Land, Kenneth C.

Rogers, Archibald C. Monticello Fault. LC 79-63913. 1979. 14.95 (ISBN 0-87716-098-8, Pub. by Moore Pub Co). F Apple.

Rogers, Barbara. The Domestication of Women: Discrimination in Developing Societies. LC 79-26691. 1980. 26.00 (ISBN 0-312-21627-0). St Martin.

--In the Center: The Story of a Retreat. LC 82-84468. 145p. (Orig.). 1983. pap. 4.95 (ISBN 0-87793-267-0). Ave Maria.

--White Wealth & Black Poverty: American Investments in Southern Africa. LC 75-35353. (Studies in Human Rights: No. 2). 288p. 1976. lib. bdg. 29.95x (ISBN 0-8371-8277-8, RWW/). Greenwood.

Rogers, Bernard. Art of Orchestration: Principles of Tone Color in Modern Scoring. Repr. of 1951 ed. lib. bdg. 25.00x (ISBN 0-8371-2969-9, ROAO). Greenwood.

Rogers, Betty. Will Rogers. (Illus.). 312p. (YA) 1982. 16.95 (ISBN 0-8061-1526-2). U of Okla Pr.

Rogers, Carl. Freedom to Learn: A View of What Education Might Become. LC 72-75629. 1969. text ed. 11.95 o.s.i. (ISBN 0-675-09519-0); pap. text ed. 8.95 (ISBN 0-675-09579-4). Merrill.

Rogers, Carl R. Client Centered Therapy. LC 51-9139. 1951. pap. text ed. 16.95 (ISBN 0-395-05322-6). HM.

--Counseling & Psychotherapy. LC 42-24693. 1942. text ed. 18.95 o.p. (ISBN 0-395-05321-8). HM.

--Freedom to Learn. 448p. 1982. text ed. 9.95 (ISBN 0-675-20012-1). Merrill.

Rogers, Charles R. Joy. 1979. pap. 1.00 (ISBN 0-89841-001-0). Zoe Pubns.

Rogers, Chris. Honda GL Eleven Hundred Goldwing. 180p. 1982. pap. 9.50 (ISBN 0-85696-669-X). Haynes Pubns.

Rogers, Cornwell B. Spirit of Revolution in Seventeen Eighty Nine: A Study of Public Opinion As Revealed in the Political Songs & Other Popular Literature. Repr. of 1949 ed. lib. bdg. 12.50x (ISBN 0-8371-1632-5, ROSR). Greenwood.

Rogers, Cyril. Budgerigars. (Illus.). 93p. 1976. 3.95 (ISBN 0-7028-1051-7). Avian Pubns.

--How to Keep Seed Eating Birds. 1974. pap. 2.50 (ISBN 0-7028-1068-1). Palmetto Pub.

--How to Keep Seedeating Birds in Cage & Aviary. (Illus.). 96p. 1978. 3.95 (ISBN 0-7028-1068-1). Avian Pubns.

--Seed Eating Birds As Pets. (Illus.). 105p. 1974. 8.95 (ISBN 0-85152-940-2). Palmetto Pub.

--Zebra Finches. (Illus.). 94p. 1977. pap. 3.95 (ISBN 0-7028-1085-1). Avian Pubns.

Rogers, Cyril H. Budgerigars. Foyle, Christina, ed. (Foyle's Handbooks). 1973. 3.95 (ISBN 0-685-55808-8). Palmetto Pub.

--Canaries. Foyle, Christina, ed. (Foyle's Handbks). (Illus.). 1973. 3.95 (ISBN 0-685-55797-9). Palmetto Pub.

--Foreign Birds. LC 76-8861. (Illus.). 1976. bds. 2.25 o.p. (ISBN 0-668-03986-8). Arco.

--Foreign Birds. Foyle, Christina, ed. (Foyle's Handbks). 1973. 3.95 (ISBN 0-685-55809-6). Palmetto Pub.

--Parrot Guide. 2nd ed. (Illus.). 256p. 14.95 (ISBN 0-87666-546-6, PL-2984). TFH Pubns.

--Parrots. LC 76-10771. (Illus.). 1976. bds. 2.25 o.p. (ISBN 0-668-03990-6). Arco.

Rogers, D. & Ruchlin, H. Economics & Education: Principles & Applications. LC 74-143519. 1971. text ed. 14.95 (ISBN 0-02-926690-4). Free Pr.

Rogers, D. F., jt. auth. see Adams, J. A.

Rogers, D. F., ed. Computer Applications in the Automation of Shipyard Operation & Ship Design, Vol. 4. 1982. 53.25 (ISBN 0-444-86408-3). Elsevier.

--Computer Graphics in Engineering Education. 136p. 1982. 33.00 (ISBN 0-08-028949-5). Pergamon.

Rogers, Dale E. Angel Unaware. (Orig.). 1982. pap. 2.25 (ISBN 0-515-06076-3). Jove Pubns.

--Angel Unaware. 1975. pap. 2.25 o.p. (ISBN 0-685-84180-4, PV091). Jove Pubns.

--Dearest Debbie. 1966. pap. write for info o.s.i. (ISBN 0-515-09028-X). Jove Pubns.

--Let Us Love. 1982. 7.95 (ISBN 0-8499-0298-3). Word Pub.

--Where He Leads. 1975. pap. 1.50 o.s.i. (ISBN 0-89129-002-8). Jove Pubns.

--Woman at the Well. 192p. 1970. pap. 3.95 (ISBN 0-8007-5023-3, Power Bks); pap. 1.95 o.p. (ISBN 0-8007-8090-6, Spire Bks). Revell.

Rogers, Dale E. & Carlson, Carole C. Grandparents Can. 128p. 1983. 7.95 (ISBN 0-8007-1343-5). Revell.

Rogers, David. Inventory of Educational Improvement Efforts in the New York City Public Schools. LC 77-10481. 1977. pap. text ed. 14.50x (ISBN 0-8077-2531-5). Tchrs Coll.

Rogers, David, jt. ed. see Whiting, Larry.

Rogers, David C. Accounting for Managers: The Non-Accountant's Guide to the Language of Business. 136p. 1971. 17.50x o.p. (ISBN 0-85227-003-8). Intl Pubns Serv.

Rogers, David E. American Medicine: Challenges for the 1980's. LC 78-16183. 160p. 1978. prof ref 19.00x (ISBN 0-88410-530-X). Ballinger Pub.

Rogers, David E., et al, eds. Year Book of Medicine, 1982. (Illus.). 640p. 1982. 37.00 (ISBN 0-8151-7445-4). Year Bk Med.

Rogers, David F. & Adams, J. Alan. Mathematical Elements for Computer Graphics. 1976. 18.95 (ISBN 0-07-053527-2, C). McGraw.

Rogers, Deborah W. & Rogers, Ivor A. J. R. R. Tolkien. (English Authors Ser.). 1980. lib. bdg. 11.95 (ISBN 0-8057-6796-7, Twayne). G K Hall.

Rogers, Dexter, jt. auth. see Touchstone, Joseph C.

Rogers, Dilwyn J., ed. A Bibliography of African Ecology: A Geographically & Topically Classified List of Books & Articles. LC 78-19935. (Special Bibliographic Ser: No. 6). 1979. lib. bdg. 45.00x (ISBN 0-313-20552-3, RAE/). Greenwood.

Rogers, Dorothy. Adolescence: A Psychological Perspective. 2nd ed. LC 77-16639. (Illus.). 1978. pap. text ed. 12.95 (ISBN 0-8185-0249-5); test items upon adoption of text free (ISBN 0-685-85040-4). Brooks-Cole.

--Adolescents & Youth. 4th ed. (Illus.). 544p. 1981. text ed. 23.95 (ISBN 0-13-008748-3). P-H.

--The Adult Years: An Introduction to Aging. 2nd ed. (Illus.). 496p. 1982. 23.95 (ISBN 0-13-008961-3). P-H.

--Issues in Adult Development. LC 79-26993. 1980. pap. text ed. 13.95 (ISBN 0-8185-0385-8). Brooks-Cole.

--Issues in Life-Span Human Development. LC 79-27550. 1980. pap. text ed. 13.95 (ISBN 0-8185-0390-4). Brooks-Cole.

--Life-Span Human Development. LC 80-25158. 512p. 1981. text ed. 22.95 (ISBN 0-8185-0389-0). Brooks-Cole.

Rogers, Edgar. A Handy Guide to Jewish Coins. LC 77-77252. (Illus.). 1977. Repr. of 1915 ed. lib. bdg. 15.00 (ISBN 0-915262-14-2). S J Durst.

Rogers, Elizabeth P., jt. auth. see Brown, William H.

Rogers, Elliott C., jt. auth. see Copeland, Melvin T.

Rogers, Everett M. Diffusion of Innovations. 3rd ed. (Illus.). 512p. 1982. text ed. 18.95 (ISBN 0-02-926650-5). Free Pr.

Rogers, Everett M. & Burdge, Rabel J. Social Change in Rural Society. 2nd ed. (Illus.). 1972. text ed. 22.95 (ISBN 0-13-815464-3). P-H.

Rogers, Ferial & Minter, Phyllis V. Goats: Their Care & Breeding. (Illus.). 100p. 1980. 3.95 (ISBN 0-686-85660-0, 4948-0, Pub. by K & R Bks England). Arco.

Rogers, Frances A. Comparative Vertebrate Anatomy: An Outline Text. (Illus.). 122p. 1983. spiral 12.75x (ISBN 0-398-04756-1). C C Thomas.

Rogers, Frank & Sharp, Andrew. The Road to Maturity. (Studies in 20th Century History Ser.). 1977. pap. text ed. 4.50x o.p. (ISBN 0-86863-544-8, 00548). Heinemann Ed.

Rogers, Franklin R., ed. see Twain, Mark.

Rogers, Fred. Josephine, The Short-Neck Giraffe. (I Am, I Can, I Will Ser.). 32p. pap. 3.95 (ISBN 0-8331-0036-X). Hubbard Sci.

--Speedy Delivery. LC 73-15437. (I Am, I Can, I Will Ser.). 44p. 1979. pap. 3.95 (ISBN 0-8331-0037-8). Hubbard Sci.

Rogers, Fred & Head, Barry. Mister Rogers Talks with Parents. (Illus.). 1983. pap. 5.95 (ISBN 0-425-05883-2). Berkley Pub.

Rogers, Fred B. Your Body Is Wonderfully Made. (Illus.). 1974. PLB 4.29 o.p. (ISBN 0-399-60834-6). Putnam Pub Group.

Rogers, G. F. & Mayhem, Y. R. Thermodynamic & Transport Properties of Fluids SI Units. 3rd. ed. 24p. (Orig.). 1980. pap. 2.50x o.p. (ISBN 0-631-12891-3, Pub. by Basil Blackwell England). Biblio Dist.

Rogers, G. L. Noncoherent Optical Processing. LC 77-5453. 192p. Repr. of 1977 ed. text ed. 33.95 (ISBN 0-471-73055-6). Krieger.

Rogers, G. R. & Mayhem, Y. R. Diagram of Temperature Rise v. Fuel-Air Ratio: For the Combustion of a Gas Turbine Fuel of Nominal Composition. (Illus.). 1980. pap. 2.50x o.p. (ISBN 0-631-12581-7, Pub. by Basil Blackwell England). Biblio Dist.

Rogers, George W., ed. see Alaska Scinece Conference, 20th, University of Alaska, 1969.

Rogers, H. C. Napoleon's Army. (Illus.). 192p. 1982. pap. 8.95 (ISBN 0-88254-709-7). Hippocrene Bks.

Rogers, Harold. On the Other Side of Tomorrow. 1974. 1.75x o.p. (ISBN 0-8358-0299-X). Upper Room.

Rogers, Harry E. The Debt Relief Kit. 200p. (Orig.). 1983. pap. 9.95 (ISBN 0-937464-04-X). Lawkits.

Rogers, Hartley, Jr. Theory of Recursive Functions & Effective Computability. (Higher Mathematics Ser.). 1967. text ed. 44.95 (ISBN 0-07-053522-1, C). McGraw.

Rogers, Horatio. World War I through My Sights. LC 74-31941. (Illus.). 268p. 1976. 10.95 o.p. (ISBN 0-89141-004-X). Presidio Pr.

Rogers, Ivor A., jt. auth. see Rogers, Deborah W.

Rogers, J. A. From "Superman to Man". rev. ed. 132p. 1941. 6.95 (ISBN 0-9602294-4-2). H M Rogers.

Rogers, J. W. & Millan, W. H. Coil Slitting. LC 73-7903. 127p. 1974. pap. text ed. 10.00 (ISBN 0-08-017696-8). Pergamon.

Rogers, Jack. Confessions of a Conservative Evangelical. LC 74-12249. 1974. pap. 2.65 o.s.i. (ISBN 0-664-24996-5). Westminster.

Rogers, James H. America Weighs Her Gold. 1931. text ed. 29.50x (ISBN 0-686-83460-7). Elliots Bks.

--Capitalism in Crisis. 1938. text ed. 29.50x (ISBN 0-686-83499-2). Elliots Bks.

Rogers, Jane & Long, Jeremy. The Vowel Crowd. (Orig.). 1980. pap. text ed. 2.50x o.p. (ISBN 0-435-10761-5); tchrs ed 7.50x o.p. (ISBN 0-435-10762-3). Heinemann Ed.

Rogers, Janice L., ed. see Dittman, Richard & Schmieg, Glenn.

Rogers, Jean. Goodbye, My Island. LC 82-15816. (Illus.). 96p. (gr. 5-7). 1983. 9.00 (ISBN 0-688-01964-1); PLB 8.59 (ISBN 0-688-01965-X). Greenwillow.

Rogers, JoAnn V. Nonprint Cataloging for Multimedia Collections: A Guide Based on AACR 2. (Library Science Text Ser.). 230p. 1982. 21.00 (ISBN 0-87287-284-X). Libs Unl.

Rogers, Katharine M. William Wycherley. (English Authors Ser.: No. 127). lib. bdg. 7.95 o.p. (ISBN 0-8057-1584-3, Twayne). G K Hall.

Rogers, Katherine, ed. The Signet Classic Book of Eighteenth & Nineteenth Century British Drama. (Orig.). 1979. pap. 2.95 (ISBN 0-451-51265-0, CE1265, Sig Classics). NAL.

Rogers, Kenneth. Advanced Calculus. (Mathematics Ser.). 384p. 1976. text ed. 23.95x (ISBN 0-675-08651-5). Additional supplements may be obtained from publisher. Merrill.

Rogers, Lou. First Thanksgiving. (Beginning-to-Read Ser.). (Illus.). (gr. 2-4). 1962. PLB 4.39 (ISBN 0-695-42884-5, Dist. by Caroline Hse); pap. 1.95 (ISBN 0-695-32884-0). Follett.

Rogers, Maggie & Hawkins, Judith. Glass Christmas Ornament: Old & New. A Collector's Compendium & Price Guide. LC 77-16741. (Illus.). 1977. pap. 9.95 (ISBN 0-917304-07-1). Timber.

Rogers, Malcolm. Museums & Galleries of London. (Blue Guides Ser.). (Illus.). 1983. 22.50 (ISBN 0-393-01657-9); pap. 12.95 (ISBN 0-393-30064-1). Norton.

Rogers, Malcolm, jt. ed. see Ormond, Richard.

Rogers, Marc & Griffith, Roger. Getting a Roof over Your Head: Affordable Housing Alternatives. (Illus.). 167p. 1982. pap. 9.95 (ISBN 0-88266-317-8). Garden Way Pub.

Rogers, Mark E., ed. Waiting for Godot. (Illus., Orig.). 1980. pap. 2.00 ltd. (ISBN 0-937528-01-3). Burning Bush.

Rogers, Mary. Women, Divorce & Money. 1982. pap. 4.95 (ISBN 0-07-053497-7). McGraw.

Rogers, Mary B. & Smith, Sherry A. We Can Fly: Stories of Katherine Stinson & Other Gutsy Texas Women. LC 82-80441. (Illus.). 184p. (Orig.). (gr. 7). 1983. 24.95 (ISBN 0-936650-02-8); pap. 12.95 (ISBN 0-936650-03-6). E C Temple.

Rogers, Matilda. First Book of Tree Identification. (Illus.). Date not set. 4.50 (ISBN 0-394-85706-2, BYR). Random.

Rogers, May. Waverly Dictionary. 2nd ed. LC 66-27850. 1967. Repr. of 1885 ed. 37.00x (ISBN 0-8103-3222-1). Gale.

Rogers, Michael. How to Overcome Nervousness. 22p. 1973. pap. 1.95 (ISBN 0-88010-051-6, Pub. by New Knowledge Bks England). Anthroposophic.

Rogers, Natalie. Emerging Woman: A Decade of Midlife Transitions. LC 79-92627. 1980. 8.50 (ISBN 0-9605634-0-7). Personal Press.

Rogers, Natalie H. Talk-Power: How to Speak Without Fear. LC 82-5174. 1982. 12.95 (ISBN 0-396-08080-4). Dodd.

Rogers, P. P. & Lapuente, F. A. Diccionario De Seudonimos Literarios Espanoles, Con Algunas Iniciales. 610p. 1977. 38.95 (ISBN 84-249-1352-3, S-50152). French & Eur.

Rogers, Pat. The Augustan Vision. 318p. 1978. 10.95x (ISBN 0-416-70970-2). Methuen Inc.

--Eighteenth-Century Encounters: Essays on Literature & Society in the Age of Walpole. 220p. 1983. 21.00x (ISBN 0-389-20090-5). B&N Imports.

Rogers, Pat, ed. see Swift, Jonathan.

Rogers, Paul. Tables & Formulas for Fixed End Moments of Members of Constant Moment of Inertia & for Simply Supported Beams. 2nd ed. LC 65-28016. 1965. 10.50 (ISBN 0-8044-4850-7). Ungar.

--Things Surely Believed among Us. Date not set. 2.00 (ISBN 0-89225-181-6). Gospel Advocate.

Rogers, Paul, jt. auth. see Skellern, Claire.

Rogers, Paul T. Saul's Book. 350p. 1982. 15.95 (ISBN 0-916366-04-9); pap. 14.95 o.p. (ISBN 0-916366-13-8). Godine.

--Saul's Book. 1983. 15.95 (ISBN 0-916366-16-2). Pushcart Pr.

Rogers, Peter. What Becomes a Legend Most. 1979. 12.95 o.s.i. (ISBN 0-671-25077-9). S&S.

Rogers, Peter, jt. auth. see Steinitz, Carl.

Rogers, Rex, ed. Sex Education: Rationale & Reaction. LC 73-89764. (Illus.). 320p. 1974. 34.50x (ISBN 0-521-20477-1); pap. 10.95 (ISBN 0-521-09858-0). Cambridge U Pr.

Rogers, Robert. Metaphor: A Psychoanalytic View. LC 77-80477. 1978. 17.95x (ISBN 0-520-03548-8). U of Cal Pr.

Rogers, Robert M. Respiratory Intensive Care. (Illus.). 448p. 1977. photocopy ed. spiral 45.00x (ISBN 0-398-03601-2). C C Thomas.

Rogers, Rolf E. & McIntire, Robert H. Organization & Management Theory. (Management Ser.). 448p. 1983. text ed. 26.95x (ISBN 0-471-87697-6); tchr's. ed. avail. (ISBN 0-471-87209-1). Wiley.

Rogers, Rosemary. The Crowd Pleasers. 528p. 1978. pap. 3.50 (ISBN 0-380-75622-6, 82412-4). Avon.

--The Insiders. 1978. pap. 2.95 (ISBN 0-380-40576-8, 81885). Avon.

--Love Play. 384p. 1981. pap. 4.95 (ISBN 0-380-77917-X, 77917). Avon.

--Sweet Savage Love. 640p. 1979. pap. 3.95 (ISBN 0-380-00815-7, 81877-9). Avon.

--Wicked Loving Lies. 1976. pap. 3.95 (ISBN 0-380-00776-2, 81893-0). Avon.

Rogers, Rutherford D. & Weber, David C. University Library Administration. (Illus.). 454p. 1971. 23.00 (ISBN 0-8242-0417-4). Wilson.

Rogers, Spencer. The Shamans Healing Way. 1976. pap. 4.95 (ISBN 0-916552-06-3). Acoma Bks.

Rogers, Spencer L. The Aging Skeleton: Aspects of Human Bone Involution. (Illus.). 120p. 1982. 14.75x (ISBN 0-398-04710-3). C C Thomas.

Rogers, Stanley F., jt. auth. see Schulz, David A.

Rogers, T. Howard. Marine Corrosion. 1968. text ed. 34.95 o.p. (ISBN 0-600-41190-7). Butterworth.

Rogers, Theresa F. & Friedman, Nathalie S. Printers Face Automation: The Impact of Technology on Work & Retirement Among Skilled Craftsmen. LC 79-3047. 208p. 1980. 23.95x (ISBN 0-669-03310-3). Lexington Bks.

Rogers, Thomas. The Confession of a Child of the Century. LC 78-189740. 1972. 7.95 o.p. (ISBN 0-671-21266-4). S&S.

Rogers, Timothy, ed. School for the Community: A Grammar School Reorganizes. 1971. 14.00x o.p. (ISBN 0-7100-7134-5). Routledge & Kegan.

--Those First Affections: An Anthology of Poems Composed Between the Ages of 2 & 8. 1979. 17.95 (ISBN 0-7100-0303-X); pap. 7.50 (ISBN 0-7100-0304-8). Routledge & Kegan.

Rogers, Wallace, jt. auth. see Wiebers, Jacob.

Rogers, Walter R., jt. auth. see Bracey, Lucius H.

Rogers, Walter T. Dictionary of Abbreviations. LC 68-30662. 1969. Repr. of 1913 ed. 37.00x (ISBN 0-8103-3338-4). Gale.

Rogers, Will. The Cowboy Philosopher on Prohibition. Stout, Joseph A., Jr. & Rollins, Peter C., eds. LC 75-21295. (The Writings of Will Rogers Ser.: Ser. I, Vol. 5). (Illus.). 52p. 1975. 6.95 (ISBN 0-914956-06-X). Okla State Univ Pr.

--How to Be Funny & Other Writings of Will Rogers. Gragert, Steven K., ed. LC 82-80505. (The Writings of Will Rogers Ser.: No. 5). (Illus.). 185p. 1982. Vol. 3. 10.95 (ISBN 0-914956-23-X). Okla State Univ Pr.

--The Illiterate Digest. LC 77-145720. (Illus.). 351p. 1975. Repr. of 1924 ed. 42.00x (ISBN 0-8103-3975-7). Gale.

--The Illiterate Digest. Stout, Joseph A., Jr., ed. LC 74-82796. (The Writings of Will Rogers Ser.: Ser. I, Vol. 3). (Illus.). 230p. 1974. 10.50 (ISBN 0-914956-04-3). Okla State Univ Pr.

--More Letters of a Self-Made Diplomat. Gragert, Steven K., ed. LC 82-80504. (The Writings of Will Rogers Ser.: Ser. V, Vol. 2). (Illus.). 200p. 1982. 10.95 (ISBN 0-914956-22-1). Okla State Univ Pr.

--Radio Broadcasts of Will Rogers. Gragert, Steven K., ed. LC 82-61001. (The Writings of Will Rogers Ser.: VI, Vol. I). (Illus.). 200p. 1983. price not set (ISBN 0-914956-24-8). Okla State Univ Pr.

--Will Rogers' Daily Telegrams: The Hoover Years, 1931-1933, Vol. 3. Smallwood, James M. & Gragert, Steven K., eds. LC 78-78290. (The Writings of Will Rogers Ser., Series III: Vol. 3). (Illus.). 389p. 1979. 19.95 (ISBN 0-914956-12-4). Okla State Univ Pr.

--Will Rogers' Weekly Articles: The Coolidge Years, 1925-1927, Vol. 2. Smallwood, James M. & Gragert, Steven K., eds. LC 79-57650. (The Writings of Will Rogers Ser., Series IV: Vol. 2). (Illus.). 368p. 1980. 19.95 (ISBN 0-914956-16-7). Okla State Univ Pr.

--Will Rogers' Weekly Articles: The Harding-Coolidge Years, 1922-1925, Vol. 1. Smallwood, James M. & Gragert, Steven K., eds. LC 79-57650. (The Writings of Will Rogers Ser., Series IV: Vol. 1). (Illus.). 431p. 1980. 19.95 (ISBN 0-914956-15-9). Okla State Univ Pr.

--Will Roger's Weekly Articles: The Hoover Years 1931-1933. Gragert, Steven K., ed. LC 79-57650. (Writings of Will Rogers Ser.: No. 4). (Illus.). 280p. 1982. 17.95 (ISBN 0-914956-19-1). Okla State Univ Pr.

--Will Rogers' Weekly Articles: The Roosevelt Years: 1933-1935. Gragert, Steven K., ed. LC 79-57650. (The Writings of Will Rogers Ser.: Ser. IV, Vol. 6). (Illus.). 309p. 1982. 17.95 (ISBN 0-914956-21-3). Okla State Univ Pr.

Rogers, Will, Jr. Convention Articles of Will Rogers, Ser.II, Vol.I. Stout, Joseph A. & Rollins, Peter C., eds. LC 76-5609. (The Writings of Will Rogers Ser.: No. 2). 174p. 1976. 10.50 (ISBN 0-914956-08-6). Okla State Univ Pr.

--The Cowboy Philosopher on the Peace Conference. Stout, Joseph A. & Rollins, Peter C., eds. LC 75-8471. (The Writings of Will Rogers Ser., Series I: Vol. 4). (Illus.). 47p. 1975. 6.95 (ISBN 0-914956-05-1). Okla State Univ Pr.

Rogers, William, jt. auth. see Hammond, Robert.

Rogers, William Elford. The Three Genres & the Interpretation of Lyric. LC 82-12293. 280p. 1983. pap. 23.50 (ISBN 0-691-06554-3). Princeton U Pr.

Rogers, Wynn. Advanced Badminton. (Physical Education Activities Ser). 74p. 1970. pap. text ed. write for info. (ISBN 0-697-07002-6); tchrs.' manual avail. (ISBN 0-697-07214-2). Wm C Brown.

Rogerson, Alan, jt. auth. see Sondheimer, Ernst.

Rogerson, John. Beginning Old Testament Study. LC 82-20210. 160p. 1983. pap. price not set (ISBN 0-664-24451-3). Westminster.

Rogers-Warren, A. Ecological Perspectives in Behavior Analysis. 264p. 1977. text ed. 24.95 (ISBN 0-8391-1148-7). Univ Park.

Rogers-Warren, Ann & Warren, Steven F., eds. Teaching Functional Language. (Language Intervention Ser.). (Illus.). 1983. price not set (ISBN 0-8391-1798-1, 15660). Univ Park.

Roget, Peter M. Roget's International Thesaurus. 4th ed. LC 62-12806. 1977. 12.50i (ISBN 0-690-00010-3); thumb indexed 13.95i (ISBN 0-690-00011-1). T y Crowell.

--Roget's Thesaurus of English Words & Phrases. Dutch, R. A., ed. 1965. 11.95 (ISBN 0-312-68880-6); thumb indexed 13.50 (ISBN 0-312-68845-8). St Martin.

--Roget's Thesaurus of Words & Phrases. 1960. 6.95 (ISBN 0-448-01607-9, G&D). Putnam Pub Group.

--Roget's University Thesaurus. Mawson, C. O., ed. (Apollo Eds.). (YA) (gr. 9-12). pap. 6.95i o.p. (ISBN 0-8152-0062-5, A62). T Y Crowell.

Rogge, jt. ed. see Haggarty.

Roggenkamp. Stave Churches in Norway. 17.95 (ISBN 0-85440-205-5). Anthroposophic.

Rogger, Hans & Weber, Eugen, eds. The European Right: A Historical Profile. 1965. pap. 9.75x (ISBN 0-520-01080-9, CAL124). U of Cal Pr.

Roggwiller, P. & Sittig, Roland, eds. Semiconductor Devices for Power Conditioning. (Brown Boveri Symposia Ser.). 386p. 1982. 49.50x (ISBN 0-306-41131-8, Plenum Pr). Plenum Pub.

Roghair, Gene H., tr. The Epic of Palnadu: A Study & Translation of Palnati Virula Katha, a Telegu Oral Tradition from Andhra Pradesh, India. (Illus.). 1982. 49.95x (ISBN 0-19-815456-9). Oxford U Pr.

Rogin, Michael P. Fathers & Children: Andrew Jackson & the Subjugation of the American Indian. LC 76-10814. 1976. Repr. of 1975 ed. 13.95 (ISBN 0-394-71881-X, Vin). Random.

--The Intellectuals & McCarthy: The Radical Specter. (Illus.). 366p. 1967. pap. 7.95x (ISBN 0-262-68015-7). MIT Pr.

--Subversive Genealogy: Politics & Art in Herman Melville. LC 82-48743. 363p. 1983. 20.00 (ISBN 0-394-50609-X). Knopf.

Rogin, Michael P. & Shover, John L. Political Change in California: Critical Elections & Social Movements, 1890-1966. LC 72-95506. (Contributions in American History: No. 5). 1970. lib. bdg. 25.00x (ISBN 0-8371-2346-1, ROP/). Greenwood.

Rogler, L. H. & Hollingshead, A. B. Trapped: Families & Schizophrenia. LC 75-14043. 452p. 1975. Repr. of 1965 ed. 21.00 (ISBN 0-88275-302-9). Krieger.

Rogler, LLoyd H., jt. auth. see Farber, Anne.

Rogliatti, G. Leica: The First Fifty Years. 2nd ed. 1975. 25.95 (ISBN 0-85242-416-7). Hove Camera.

Rogliatti, Gianni. Great Collectors' Cars. LC 72-79968. (Illus.). 320p. 1973. 8.95 (ISBN 0-448-01914-0, G&D). Putnam Pub Group.

Rognebakke, M. & Driessle, H. Warum Nicht Auf Deutsch, Vol. 1. rev. ed. 1970. 7.24 o.p. (ISBN 0-685-65902-X); tchr's ed. 8.80 o.p. (ISBN 0-02-826960-8). Glencoe.

Rognebakke, Myrtle & Driessle, Hannelore. Warum Nicht Auf Deutsch, Vol. 2. 1969. 7.24 o.p. (ISBN 0-685-07674-1, 82691); tchr's ed. 8.80 o.p. (ISBN 0-685-07675-X). Glencoe.

Rogness, Alvin N. The Story of the American Lutheran Church. LC 80-65555. 96p. (Orig.). 1980. pap. 3.95 (ISBN 0-8066-1800-0, 10-6038). Augsburg.

--Table of the Lord: Holy Communion in the Life of the Church. LC 82-72640. 96p. (Orig.). 1983. pap. 4.50 (ISBN 0-8066-1946-5, 10-6182). Augsburg.

Rogo, D. Scott. Leaving the Body: A Practical Guide to Astral Projection. (Illus.). 190p. 1983. 14.95 (ISBN 0-13-528034-6); pap. 5.95 (ISBN 0-13-528026-5). P-H.

Rogo, Scott. UFO Abductions: True Cases of Alien Kidnappings. (Orig.). 1980. pap. 2.25 (ISBN 0-451-09472-7, E9472, Sig). NAL.

Rogo, Scott D. Miracles: A Parascientific Inquiry into Wondrous Phenomena. (Illus.). 352p. 1982. pap. 9.95 (ISBN 0-8092-5596-0). Contemp Bks.

Rogoff, Abraham M. Formative Years of the Jewish Labor Movement in the United States: (1890-1900) LC 78-21163. 1979. Repr. of 1945 ed. lib. bdg. 16.25x (ISBN 0-313-20881-6, ROFJ). Greenwood.

Rogoff, Martin. Daddy Cooks. 240p. (Orig.). Date not set. pap. cancelled o.p. (ISBN 0-505-51737-X). Tower Bks.

Rogosin, Donn. Invisible Men: Life in Baseball's Negro Leagues. LC 82-73026. (Illus.). 320p. 1983. 14.95 (ISBN 0-689-11363-3). Atheneum.

Rogosin, Elinor. The Dance Makers: Conversations with American Choreographers. (Illus.). 192p. 1980. 14.95 o.s.i. (ISBN 0-8027-0648-7). Walker & Co.

Rogosinski, Werner. Fourier Series. 2nd ed. LC 50-6214. 7.95 (ISBN 0-8284-0067-9). Chelsea Pub.

Rogovin. What's the Hurry. 208p. 1982. text ed. 15.95 (ISBN 0-8391-1761-2). Univ Park.

Rogovin, Anne. Let Me Do It! LC 78-3316. (Illus.). 1980. 14.95i (ISBN 0-381-98300-5); pap. 7.95i (ISBN 0-381-98301-3). T Y Crowell.

Rogovin, Charles, jt. ed. see Edelhertz, Herbert.

Rogow, Arnold. The Dying of the Light: A Searching Look at America Today. LC 75-15762. 1975. 10.00 o.p. (ISBN 0-399-11509-9). Putnam Pub Group.

Rogowski, Augustus R. Elements of Internal Combustion Engines. (Illus.). 1953. text ed. 34.00 (ISBN 0-07-053575-2, C). McGraw.

Rogowsky, Edward T., jt. auth. see Abbot, David W.

Rohani, S. Hazrat. The Universal Players. 1979. 4.95 o.p. (ISBN 0-533-03897-9). Vantage.

Rohatgi, V. K., jt. auth. see Laha, R. G.

Rohatgi, Vijay K. An Introduction to Probability Theory & Mathematical Statistics. LC 75-14378. (Series in Probability & Mathematical Statistics: Probability & Mathematical Statistics Section). 704p. 1976. 41.95 (ISBN 0-471-73135-8, Pub by Wiley-Interscience). Wiley.

Rohatgi-Mukherjee, K. K. Fundamentals of Photochemistry. LC 78-12088. 1979. 16.95x o.s.i. (ISBN 0-470-26547-7). Halsted Pr.

Rohberger, Mary. Story to Anti-Story. LC 78-69581. 1978. pap. text ed. 11.50 (ISBN 0-395-26387-5); instr's. manual 0.50 (ISBN 0-395-26388-3). HM.

Rohde, Eleanour S. Herbs & Herb Gardening. LC 70-180975. (Illus.). 1976. Repr. of 1936 ed. 42.00x (ISBN 0-8103-4303-7). Gale.

--Rose Recipes from Olden Times. (Illus.). 8.00 (ISBN 0-8446-4804-3). Peter Smith.

--The Scented Garden. LC 70-175781. 1974. Repr. of 1931 ed. 40.00x (ISBN 0-8103-3874-2). Gale.

Rohde, Jill & Rohde, Ron. The New Good (but Cheap) Chicago Restaurant Book: Where to Find Great Meals at Little Neighborhood Restaurants from 1.50 to 4.95. rev & enl ed. LC 82-73872. 250p. 1977. pap. 4.95 (ISBN 0-8040-0698-9). Swallow.

Rohde, Richard A., jt. auth. see Zuckerman, Bert M.

Rohde, Ron, jt. auth. see Rohde, Jill.

Rohde, S. M., et al, eds. Topics in Fluid Film Bearing & Rotor Bearing Systems Design & Optimization. (Bk. No. 100118). 1978. 30.00 o.p. (ISBN 0-685-37588-9). ASME.

Rohde, Ulrich L. Digital PLL Frequency Synthesizers: Theory & Design. (Illus.). 608p. 1983. text ed. 49.95 (ISBN 0-13-214239-2). P-H.

Rohe, Fred. Fred Rohe's Complete Book of Natural Foods. LC 82-50282. (Illus.). 448p. (Orig.). 1983. pap. 10.95 (ISBN 0-394-71240-4). Shambhala Pubns.

--Metabolic Ecology. 1982. 5.95x (ISBN 0-686-37598-X). Cancer Control Soc.

Roheim, Geza. Australian Totemism: A Psycho-Analytic Study in Anthropology. 487p. 1971. Repr. of 1925 ed. text ed. 28.50x o.p. (ISBN 0-391-00196-5). Humanities.

Rohl. An Introduction to Compiler Writing. (Computer Monograph Ser: No. 22). 1975. 25.95 (ISBN 0-444-19523-8). Elsevier.

Rohl, J. S. Writing PASCAL Programs. LC 82-14591. (Cambridge Computer Science Texts Ser.: No. 16). 250p. Date not set. 24.95 (ISBN 0-521-25077-3); pap. 11.95 (ISBN 0-521-27196-7). Cambridge U Pr.

Rohl, J. S. & Barrett, H. J. Programming Via Pascal. LC 79-17433. (Cambridge Computer Science Texts Ser.: No. 12). 300p. 1980. 38.50 (ISBN 0-521-22628-7); pap. 16.95 (ISBN 0-521-29583-1). Cambridge U Pr.

Rohlen, Thomas P. For Harmony & Strength: Japanese White-Collar Organization in Anthropological Perspective. LC 73-91668. 1974. 36.50x (ISBN 0-520-02674-8); pap. 7.95x (ISBN 0-520-03849-5). U of Cal Pr.

Rohlich, Gerard & Howe, Richard. The Toxic Substances Control Act: Overview & Evaluation. (Policy Research Project Ser.: No. 50). 247p. 1982. 7.50 (ISBN 0-89940-650-5). LBJ Sch Public Affairs.

Rohlich, Thomas H., tr. A Tale of Eleventh-Century Japan: Hamamatsu Chunagon Monogatari. LC 82-61380. (Princeton Library of Asian Translations). 256p. 1983. 30.00x (ISBN 0-691-05377-4). Princeton U Pr.

Rohlmeier, Charles. Residential Construction: Blueprint Reading & Practices. 1983. pap. 19.95 (ISBN 0-534-01387-2, Breton). Wadsworth Pub.

Rohmer, Harriet. The Legend of Food Mountain: La Montana del Alimento. Ada, Alama F., tr. LC 81-71634. (Illus.). 24p. (gr. k-8). 1982. 8.95 (ISBN 0-89239-022-0). Childrens Book Pr.

Rohmer, Sax. The Dream-Detective. LC 77-77454. 1977. pap. 3.50 (ISBN 0-486-23504-1). Dover.

--The Romance of Sorcery. 1973. Repr. of 1914 ed. 34.00x (ISBN 0-685-70657-5). Gale.

Rohn, Peter H. Treaty Profiles. new ed. LC 73-83352. 300p. 1974. text ed. 35.00 o.p. (ISBN 0-87436-131-1). ABC-Clio.

--World Treaty Index. 2nd ed. 4386p. 1983. Set. lib. bdg. 850.00 (ISBN 0-87436-329-2). ABC-Clio.

--World Treaty Index & Treaty Profiles, 6 vols. LC 73-83352. 3300p. 1974. text ed. 510.00 o.p. (ISBN 0-87436-132-X). ABC-Clio.

Rohr, Donald G., jt. auth. see Ergang, Robert.

Rohr, Jean-Geoffroy. Un Missionnaire Republicain en Russie, 3 vols. (Nineteenth Century Russia Ser.). (Fr.). 1974. Repr. of 1852 ed. Set. lib. bdg. 290.00x o.p. (ISBN 0-8287-0737-5). Clearwater Pub.

Rohr, Michael S., jt. auth. see McDonald, John C.

Rohrbach, Jerry, jt. auth. see Heiderbrecht, Paul.

Rohrbach, Peter T., jt. auth. see Holmes, Oliver W.

Rohrer, jt. auth. see Guenthner.

Rohrer, jt. auth. see Morris.

Rohrer, Daniel M. Freedom of Speech & Human Rights: An International Perspective. 1979. pap. text ed. 10.95 (ISBN 0-8403-1987-8, 40198701). Kendall-Hunt.

--Mass Media, Freedom of Speech, & Advertising: A Study in Communication Law. 1979. text ed. 29.95 (ISBN 0-8403-1988-6, 40198801). Kendall-Hunt.

Rohrer, Norman B. Leighton Ford: A Life Surprised. 1981. pap. 5.95 (ISBN 0-8423-2133-0). Tyndale.

Rohrer, R., ed. see Motil, John M.

Rohrer, R. A., jt. auth. see Director, S. W.

Rohrkemper, John C. John Dos Passos: A Reference Guide. 1980. lib. bdg. 22.00 (ISBN 0-8161-8105-5, Hall Reference). G K Hall.

Rohrlich, Chester. Law & Practice in Corporate Control. vii, 268p. 1982. Repr. of 1933 ed. lib. bdg. 30.00 (ISBN 0-89941-184-3). W S Hein.

Rohrlich, George F., ed. Environmental Management: Economic & Social Dimensions. LC 76-2355. 360p. 1976. prof ref 22.50x (ISBN 0-88410-421-4). Ballinger Pub.

Rohrlick, Paula. Exploring the Arts: Films & Videotapes for Young Viewers. LC 82-9588. (Illus.). 181p. 1982. 24.95 (ISBN 0-8352-1515-6). Bowker.

Rohrman, N., jt. auth. see Smith, Wendell.

Rohrs, M., jt. auth. see Petzold, A.

Rohsenow, Warren & Hartnett, J. P. Handbook of Heat Transfer. 1504p. 1973. 72.00 (ISBN 0-07-053576-0, P&RB). McGraw.

Rohsenow, Warren M. & Choi, H. Heat, Mass & Momentum Transfer. (Illus.). 1961. text ed. 33.95 (ISBN 0-13-385187-7). P-H.

Roiphe, Anne. Generation Without Memory. 1981. 11.95 o.s.i. (ISBN 0-671-41455-0, Linden). S&S.

--Generation Without Memory: A Jewish Journey in Christian America. LC 82-70567. 294p. 1982. pap. 7.64 (ISBN 0-8070-3601-3, BP645). Beacon Pr.

Roisen, Fred J. & Hsu, Linda. Histology. 2nd ed. (Medical Examination Review Ser.). 1982. pap. text ed. 12.95 (ISBN 0-87488-219-2). Med Exam.

--Histology Review. (Basic Science Review Bks.). 1975. write for info o.p. (ISBN 0-87488-219-2). Med Exam.

Roizin, L. & Shiraki, H., eds. Neurotoxicology, Vol. 1. LC 77-4632. 686p. 1977. 75.50 (ISBN 0-89004-148-2). Raven.

Roizman, Bernard, ed. The Herpes Viruses. LC 82-15034. (The Viruses: Vol.1). 1982. 39.50x (ISBN 0-686-83976-5, Plenum Pr). Plenum Pub.

Roizman, Bernard, ed. see New York Academy of Sciences, Nov. 28-30, 1979.

Rojankovsky, Feodor. Tall Book of Mother Goose. (Tall Book Ser.). (Illus.). (ps-1). 1942. 6.95 (ISBN 0-06-025055-0, HarpJ); PLB 7.89 (ISBN 0-06-025056-9). Har-Row.

--Tall Book of Nursery Tales. LC 44-3881. (Tall Book Ser.). (Illus.). (ps-1). 1944. 6.95i (ISBN 0-06-025065-8, HarpJ); PLB 7.89 (ISBN 0-06-025066-6). Har-Row.

Rojankovsky, Feodor, jt. auth. see Langstaff, John.

Rojas. Redaccion Comercial Estructurada. 2nd ed. 200p. 1982. 9.12 (ISBN 0-07-053566-3). McGraw.

Rojas Zorrilla, Francisco de see MacCurdy, Raymond R. & De Rojas Zorrilla, Francisco.

Rojek, Dean G., jt. auth. see Jensen, Gary F.

Rojo, J. P. Pterocarpus (Leguminosae-Papilionaceae) Revised for the World. 1971. 24.00 (ISBN 3-7682-0726-9). Lubrecht & Cramer.

Rokeah, David. Eyes in the Rock: Selected Poems. LC 82-70654. (Poetry in Europe Ser.: No. 7). 78p. 1968. 6.95 (ISBN 0-8040-0106-5). Swallow.

Rokkan, Elizabeth, jt. auth. see Vesaas, Tarjei.

Rokkan, S., jt. auth. see Lipset, Seymour M.

Rokkan, Stein, ed. A Quarter Century of International Social Science: International Social Science Council. 1979. text ed. 59.00x (ISBN 0-391-01930-9). Humanities.

Rokkan, Stein, jt. ed. see Dogan, Mattei.

Rokosz, Francis M. Administrative Procedures for Conducting Recreational Sports Tournaments: From Archery to Wrestling. (Illus.). 268p. 1982. spiral 24.75x (ISBN 0-398-04722-7). C C Thomas.

--Structured Intramurals. LC 81-40765. (Illus.). 317p. 1982. pap. text ed. 13.25 (ISBN 0-8191-1942-3). U Pr of Amer.

Rola, Stanislas Klossowski De see Klossowski de Rola, Stanislas.

Roland, Betty. L'Envers du Reve. (Collection Colombine). 192p. 1983. pap. 1.95 (ISBN 0-373-48058-X). Harlequin Bks.

Roland, Charles P., jt. auth. see Simkins, Francis B.

Roland, Charles P., ed. see Cowdrey, Albert E.

Roland, Donna. Grandfather's Stories. (Orig.). (gr. 2-4). 1982. pap. 2.75 (ISBN 0-686-36144-X). Open My World.

Roland, Harold E. & Moriarty, Brian. System Safety Engineering & Management. (Systems Engineering & Analysis Ser.). 320p. 1983. 34.95x (ISBN 0-471-09695-4, Pub. by Wiley-Interscience). Wiley.

Roland, Jacquie. I Drive People Crazy Too. LC 82-99890. (Illus.). 96p. 1982. pap. text ed. 3.95 (ISBN 0-910403-00-7). Parrish Art.

Roland, Maxwell. Response to Contraception. LC 72-93120. (Major Problems in Obstetrics & Gynecology Ser.: No. 5). (Illus.). 162p. 1973. text ed. 9.00 o.p. (ISBN 0-7216-7640-5). Saunders.

Roland, Michelle. Beloved Stranger. (Second Chance at Love Ser.: No. 102). Date not set. pap. 1.75 (ISBN 0-515-06866-7). Jove Pubns.

Rolde, Neil. Sir William Pepperrell of Colonial New England. (Illus.). xi, 221p. 1982. 12.95 (ISBN 0-88448-048-8); pap. 8.95 (ISBN 0-88448-047-X). Harpswell Pr.

Rolen, Pierre L., jt. auth. see Lengstrand, Rolf.

Roley, B. A., jt. ed. see Jaeger, T. A.

Roleyr, B. A., jt. ed. see Jaeger, T. A.

Rolf, Ida P. Rolfing: The Integration of Human Structures. (Illus.). 304p. 1978. pap. 11.95 (ISBN 0-06-465096-0, PBN 5096, BN). B&N NY.

Rolf, Jon E., jt. ed. see Kent, Martha W.

Rolf, Robert. Masamune Hakucho. (World Authors Ser.). 1979. lib. bdg. 15.95 (ISBN 0-8057-6375-9, Twayne). G K Hall.

Rolfe & Lennon. The Heal Yourself Home Handbook of Unusual Remedies. LC 82-14274. 205p. 1983. 14.95 (ISBN 0-13-384685-7, Parker); pap. 4.95 (ISBN 0-13-384677-6). P-H.

Rolfe, Fr. Hadrian the Seventh. 1982. pap. 4.95 (ISBN 0-14-002031-4). Penguin.

Rolfe, Frederick C. Nicholas Crabbe: Or, The One & the Many, a Romance. LC 77-11680. 1977. Repr. of 1958 ed. lib. bdg. 20.50x (ISBN 0-8371-9816-X, RONC). Greenwood.

Rolfe, John. True Relation of the State of Virginia Lefte by Sir Thomas Dale, Knight, in May Last 1616. LC 78-157111. (Jamestown Documents Ser). 240p. 1971. pap. 2.95 (ISBN 0-8139-0368-8). U Pr of Va.

Rolfe, Lionel & Lennon, Nigey. Natures Twelve Magic Healers: The Amazing Secrets of Cell Salts. 1978. 14.95 o.p. (ISBN 0-13-610519-X, Parker). P-H.

Rolih, Susan & Albietz, Carol, eds. Enzymes, Inhibitions & Absorptions. (Illus.). 72p. 1981. 13.00 (ISBN 0-914404-67-9). Am Assn Blood.

Roll, Charles R., Jr. The Distribution of Rural Incomes in China: A Comparison of the 1930's & 1950's. LC 78-74301. (The Modern Chinese Economy Ser.: Vol. 13). 223p. 1980. lib. bdg. 22.00 o.s.i. (ISBN 0-8240-4288-3). Garland Pub.

Roll, Hans U. Physics of the Marine Atmosphere. (International Geophysics Ser.: Vol. 7). 1965. 57.00 (ISBN 0-12-593650-8). Acad Pr.

Roll, Richard J. & Young, G. Douglas. Getting Yours. 1983. pap. 6.95 (ISBN 0-440-53005-9, Delta). Dell.

--Getting Yours: Financial Success Strategies for Young Professionals in a Tougher Era. 204p. 1982. 12.95 (ISBN 0-399-12583-3). Putnam Pub Group.

Roll, Richard J., jt. auth. see Downs, Hugh.

Roll, William. Poltergeist. pap. 2.50 (ISBN 0-451-12110-4, AE2110, Sig). NAL.

Roll, William G., et al, eds. Research in Parapsychology 1981: Abstracts & Papers from the Twenty-Fourth Annual Convention of the Parapsychological Association, 1981. LC 66-28580. 252p. 1982. 15.00 (ISBN 0-8108-1550-8). Scarecrow.

Rolla, G., ed. Tooth Surface Interactions & Preventive Dentistry: Proceedings. (Illus.). 217p. 1980. pap. 36.00 (ISBN 0-904147-29-0). IRL Pr.

Rollain, jt. auth. see Kraus.

Rolland. Follicular Maturation & Ovulation. (International Congress Ser.: Vol. 560). 1982. 83.00 (ISBN 0-444-90231-7). Elsevier.

Rolland, Alvin E. & Wineinger, Tom. Elementary Algebra. 320p. 1982. text ed. 20.95X (ISBN 0-534-01142-X). Wadsworth Pub.

Rolland, Barbara, et al. Le Francais: Langue & Culture. 2nd ed. 1979. text ed. 13.95x (ISBN 0-442-27040-2). Van Nos Reinhold.

Rolland, Romain. The Living Thoughts of Rousseau. 159p. 1982. Repr. of 1939 ed. lib. bdg. 20.00 (ISBN 0-8495-4649-4). Arden Lib.

Rolland, Solange C., jt. auth. see Graham, Gwethalyn.

Rollband, Jim. The Long & the Short of Chinese Cooking. LC 76-17271. (Illus.). 200p. 1976. 15.95 (ISBN 0-912278-83-8); pap. 6.95 (ISBN 0-912278-78-1). Crossing Pr.

Rolle, Andrew F. California: A History. 3rd ed. LC 77-90674. (Illus.). 1978. text ed. 24.95x (ISBN 0-88295-776-7). Harlan Davidson.

Rolle, Andrew, Jr. Los Angeles. Hundley, Norris, Jr. & Schutz, John A., eds. LC 81-67252. (Golden State Ser.). (Illus.). 120p. 1981. pap. text ed. 5.95x (ISBN 0-87835-119-1). Boyd & Fraser.

Rolle, Denys. The Humble Petition of Denys Rolle, Esq., Setting Forth the Hardships, Inconveniences, & Grievances Which Have Attended Him in His Attempts to Make a Settlement in East Florida, Humbly Praying Such Relief. Sturgill, Claude C., ed. LC 77-5133. (Bicentennial Floridiana Facsimile Ser.). 1977. Repr. of 1765 ed. 6.50 (ISBN 0-8130-0417-9). U Presses Fla.

Rolle, Kurt A. Introduction to Thermodynamics. 2nd ed. LC 79-90390. 1980. text ed. 26.95 (ISBN 0-675-08268-4). Additional supplements may be obtained from publisher. Merrill.

Roller, Douglas. Richardson-De Priest Family. LC 75-36488. Repr. of 1905 ed. write for info (ISBN 0-685-89827-X). Va Bk.

Roller, Duane & Blum, Ronald. Physics, 2 vols. Incl. Vol. 1. Mechanics, Waves & Thermodynamics. 26.95; Vol. 2. Electricity, Magnetism & Light. 28.95. LC 81-81011. (Illus.). 1981. wkbk.& sol. manual avail. Holden-Day.

Roller, Duane, jt. auth. see Blum, Ronald.

Roller-Massar, Ann. Discovering the Basis of Life: An Introduction to Molecular Biology. (Illus.). 320p. 1973. pap. text ed. 19.95 (ISBN 0-07-053564-7, C). McGraw.

Rollett, A. P., jt. auth. see Cundy, Henry M.

Rollett, R., et al. Fertilizers & Soil Amendments. 1981. 27.95 (ISBN 0-13-314336-8). P-H.

Rollin, Betty. Am I Getting Paid for This? 1982. 14.95 (ISBN 0-316-75454-4). Little.

--First You Cry. 1977. pap. 2.50 (J8534, Sig). NAL.

Rollin, Sue. Illustrated Atlas of Archaeology. (Illustrated Atlas Ser.). (Illus.). 48p. (gr. 4 up). 1982. PLB 12.90 (ISBN 0-531-09207-0). Watts.

Rolling, L., jt. auth. see Goetschalckx, J.

Rollins, Alden. The Fall of Rome: A Reference Guide. LC 82-23918. 144p. 1983. lib. bdg. 15.95x (ISBN 0-89950-034-X). McFarland & Co.

Rollins, Charlemae. Christmas Gif' (Illus.). 1963. 7.95 o.s.i. (ISBN 0-695-81190-8). Follett.

Rollins, Frances. Getting to Know Canada. (Getting to Know Ser.). (Illus.). (gr. 3-5). 1966. PLB 3.97 o.p. (ISBN 0-698-30109-9, Coward). Putnam Pub Group.

Rollins, Hyder E., ed. see Pepys, Samuel.

Rollins, Hyder E., ed. see Shakespeare, William.

Rollins, Hyder E., ed. see Tottel, R.

Rollins, Joan H., ed. Hidden Minorities: The Persistence of Ethnicity in American Life. LC 81-40137. 268p. (Orig.). 1982. lib. bdg. 22.75 (ISBN 0-8191-2052-9); pap. text ed. 11.50 (ISBN 0-8191-2053-7). U Pr of Amer.

Rollins, Patrick, tr. see Oldenburg, S. S.

Rollins, Peter C., ed. Hollywood as Historian: American Film in a Cultural Context. LC 82-49118. 288p. 1983. 26.00 (ISBN 0-8131-1486-1); pap. 10.00 (ISBN 0-8131-0154-9). U Pr of Ky.

Rollins, Peter C., ed. see Rogers, Will.

Rollins, Peter C., ed. see Rogers, Will, Jr.

Rollins, Wayne G. Jung & The Bible. LC 82-48091. 156p. 1983. pap. 9.50 (ISBN 0-8042-1117-5). John Knox.

Rollins-Griffin, Ramona. Chaco Canyon Ruins: Ancient Spirits Were Our Neighbors. LC 79-150688. 1971. 8.50 o.p. (ISBN 0-87358-070-2). Northland.

Rollo, F. David, jt. ed. see Erickson, Jon J.

Rollo, Vera F. Ask Me: About Maryland Geography. new ed. (Illus., With time line chart of Maryland history). (gr. 4-5). 1980. pap. 4.50 ea. (ISBN 0-917882-04-0); pap. 39.75 for 10 bks with chart (ISBN 0-686-96785-2). Maryland Hist Pr.

--A Geography of Maryland: Ask Me! (About Maryland) 200p. (gr. k-6). 1981. casebnd. 10.50 (ISBN 0-917882-10-5); tchrs. handbk. 6.00 (ISBN 0-686-96786-0). Maryland Hist Pr.

--Your Maryland. rev. ed. (Illus.). 414p. 1976. 9.75 (ISBN 0-686-36836-3). Md Hist.

Rolls, E. T., jt. ed. see Wauquier, A.

Rolls, Maurice J., jt. auth. see Jones, Gwyn E.

Rolls, T. B. Power Distribution in Industrial Installations, VIII. rev. ed. (IEE Monograph Ser.: No. 10). (Illus.). 100p. 1972. pap. 21.75 (ISBN 0-906048-29-X). Inst Elect Eng.

Rolo, P. J. Entente Cordiale: The Origins & Negotiations of the Anglo-French Agreements of April 8, 1904. LC 77-86588. 1970. 22.50 (ISBN 0-312-25690-6). St Martin.

Roloff, Joan G. Encounter: Readings for Thinking, Talking, Writing. 2nd ed. LC 73-7356. (Illus.). 416p. 1974. pap. text ed. 11.95x (ISBN 0-02-477150-3). Macmillan.

Roloff, Leland H. The Perception & Evocation of Literature. 1973. text ed. 16.95x (ISBN 0-673-07550-8). Scott F.

Roloff, Michael, tr. see Hesse, Hermann.

Roloff, Michael E. & Berger, Charles R. Social Cognition & Communication. 352p. 1982. 29.95 (ISBN 0-8039-1898-4); pap. 14.95 (ISBN 0-8039-1899-2). Sage.

Roloff-Stoddard, Joan & Wylder, Robert C. The Writing Book. 2nd ed. 1981. pap. text ed. 13.95x (ISBN 0-02-472090-9). Macmillan.

Roloff-Stoddard, Joan, et al. Vocabulary: The Words Used to Express Ideas & Feelings. 1980. pap. text ed. 11.95x (ISBN 0-02-477440-5). Macmillan.

Rolph, C. H. Mr. Prone: A Week in the Life of an Ignorant Man. (Illus.). 1977. 6.95x o.p. (ISBN 0-19-212966-X). Oxford U Pr.

Rolph, Earl R. Theory of Fiscal Economics. LC 76-156206. (Illus.). 1971. Repr. of 1954 ed. lib. bdg. 18.75x (ISBN 0-8371-6156-8, ROFE). Greenwood.

--The Theory of Fiscal Economics. (California Library Reprint Series: No. 21). 1971. 30.00x (ISBN 0-520-01926-1). U of Cal Pr.

Rolph, Elizabeth S. Nuclear Power & the Public Safety: A Study in Regulation. LC 78-24795. (Illus.). 240p. 1979. 18.95x (ISBN 0-669-02822-3). Lexington Bks.

Rolph, John, jt. auth. see Morris, Carl.

Rolphe, Douglas, et al. Airplanes of the World, Fourteen Ninety to Nineteen Seventy-Six. enlarged ed. (Illus.). 1978. 11.95 o.s.i. (ISBN 0-671-22684-3). S&S.

Rolshoven, Juergen, jt. ed. see Knabe, Peter E.

Rolshoven, Jurgen, jt. ed. see Knabe, Peter E.

Rolstadas, A., jt. ed. see Falster, P.

Rolston, Holmes. First Thessalonians-Philemon. LC 59-10454. (Layman's Bible Commentary Ser: Vol. 23). pap. 3.95 (ISBN 0-8042-3083-8). John Knox.

Rolt, L. T. From Sea to Sea: The Canal du Midi. LC 73-92899. (Illus.). ix, 198p. 1973. 12.00x (ISBN 0-8214-0152-1, 82-81552). Ohio U Pr.

Rolvaag, O. E. The Boat of Longing, a Novel. Solum, Nora O., tr. LC 73-11844. 304p. 1974. Repr. of 1933 ed. lib. bdg. 25.00x (ISBN 0-8371-7069-9, ROBL). Greenwood.

--Giants in the Earth. 1965. pap. 2.95i (ISBN 0-06-083047-6, P3047, PL). Har-Row.

--Giants in the Earth: A Saga of the Prairie. LC 27-12513. 1927. 16.30i (ISBN 0-06-013595-6, HarpT). Har-Row.

--Their Father's God. Ager, Trygve M., tr. LC 82-17636. x, 338p. 1983. pap. 7.95 (ISBN 0-8032-8911-1, BB 824, Bison). U of Nebr Pr.

Rolvaag, Ole E. Pure Gold. Erdahl, Sivert, tr. LC 73-11846. 346p. 1973. Repr. of 1930 ed. lib. bdg. 25.00x (ISBN 0-8371-7070-2, ROPG). Greenwood.

--Their Fathers' God: A Novel. Ager, Trygve M., tr. LC 73-11847. 338p. 1974. Repr. of 1931 ed. lib. bdg. 25.00x (ISBN 0-8371-7068-0, ROFG). Greenwood.

Rolwing, Richard J. A Philosophy of Revelation: According to Karl Rahner. LC 78-63067. 1978. pap. text ed. 7.25 (ISBN 0-8191-0609-7). U Pr of Amer.

Rom, jt. auth. see Lee, J. S.

Rom, J., ed. see International Symposium on Modern Developments in Fluid Dynamics.

Rom, William N., ed. Environmental & Occupational Medicine. 1982. text ed. 68.50 (ISBN 0-316-75560-5). Little.

Rom, William N. & Archer, Victor E., eds. Health Implications of New Energy Technologies. LC 80-68824. (Illus.). 785p. 1980. 49.95 (ISBN 0-250-40361-7). Ann Arbor Science.

Romagnesi, H. & Gilles, G. Les Rhodophylles des Forets Cotieres du Gabon et de la Cote d'ivoire. (Nova Hedwigia Beiheft: No. 59). (Illus.). lib. bdg. 100.00 (ISBN 3-7682-5459-3). Lubrecht & Cramer.

Romagnesi, H., jt. auth. see Kuehner, R.

Romagnoli, Robert. What's So Funny: A Witty Wacky Laugh Book. Duenewald, Doris, ed. LC 78-58210. (Electric Co. Bks.). (Illus.). (gr. 3-7). pap. 2.95 (ISBN 0-448-16400-0, G&D). Putnam Pub Group.

Romain, Elizabeth. Popular Variations in Latin-American Dancing. rev. ed. 68p. (gr. 10 up). 1983. pap. text ed. 10.50x (ISBN 0-392-16896-0, SpS). Sportshelf.

Romaine, Suzanne, ed. Sociolinguistic Variation in Speech Communities. 224p. 1982. pap. text ed. 18.95 (ISBN 0-7131-6355-0). E Arnold.

Romaine, William. Life, Walk & Triumph of Faith: With an Account of His Life and Work by Peter Toon. 439p. 1970. 14.00 (ISBN 0-227-67744-7). Attic Pr.

Roman & Puett. International Business & Technological Innovation. 1982. 35.00 (ISBN 0-444-00715-6). Elsevier.

Roman, A. Between War & Peace. 1983. 13.95 (ISBN 0-686-84434-3). Vantage.

Roman, Beverly. Infant Stimulation Training Skills. 1978. bound 12.95spiral (ISBN 0-87804-316-0). Mafex.

Roman, Herschel L., et al, eds. Annual Review of Genetics, Vol. 16. LC 67-298891. (Illus.). 1982. text ed. 22.00 (ISBN 0-8243-1216-3). Annual Reviews.

Roman, J. F., et al. The Luxor Museum of Ancient Egyptian Art. (Vol. 1). (Illus.). xv, 219p. 1979. 20.00 (ISBN 0-913696-30-7, Pub by Am Res Ctr Egypt). Undena Pubns.

Roman, James. Cablemania: The Cable Television Source Book. (Illus.). 240p. 1983. 18.95 (ISBN 0-13-110106-4); pap. 9.95 (ISBN 0-13-110098-X). P-H.

Roman, Kenneth & Raphaelson, Joel. Writing That Works. LC 80-8695. 160p. 1981. 11.49i (ISBN 0-06-014843-8, HarpT). Har-Row.

Roman, Murray. Telemarketing Campaigns that Work! (Illus.). 320p. 1983. 29.95 (ISBN 0-07-053598-1, P&RB). McGraw.

--Telephone Marketing: How to Build Business by Telephone. new ed. (Illus.). 1976. 35.95 (ISBN 0-07-053595-7, P&RB). McGraw.

Roman, Paul. Some Modern Mathematics for Physicists & Other Outsiders. LC 74-1385. 1975. Vol. 1. text ed. 43.00 o.p. (ISBN 0-08-018097-3). Vol. 2. Vol. 2. pap. text ed. 28.00 (ISBN 0-686-96850-6). Pergamon.

Roman, Paul M. & Trice, Harrison M. Explorations in Psychiatric Sociology. LC 74-8345. 200p. 1974. text ed. 11.95 o.p. (ISBN 0-8036-7550-X). Davis Co.

--Schizophrenia & the Poor. LC 67-63483. (ILR Paperback Ser.: No. 3). 96p. 1967. pap. 3.00 (ISBN 0-87546-028-3); pap. 6.00 special hard bdg. (ISBN 0-87546-270-7). ILR Pr.

Roman, Paul M., jt. auth. see Trice, Harrison M.

Roman, Zoltan. Productivity & Economic Growth. Lukacs, Laszlo, tr. from Hungarian. LC 82-173070. (Illus.). 276p. 1982. 30.00x (ISBN 963-05-2786-3). Intl Pubns Serv.

Romand, R., ed. Development of Auditory & Vestibular Systems. Date not set. price not set (ISBN 0-12-594450-0). Acad Pr.

Romanenghi de Powell, Elsa, tr. see Kerstan, Reinhold.

Romanenghi de Powell, Elsa R., tr. see Charles, J. Norman & Charles, Sharon.

Romanenghi de Powell, Elsie, tr. see Eareckson, Joni & Estes, Steve.

Romanes, G. J., ed. see Cunningham.

Romani, George T. The Neopolitan Revolution of Eighteen Twenty to Eighteen Twenty-One. LC 78-6235. (Illus.). 1978. Repr. of 1950 ed. lib. bdg. 20.75x (ISBN 0-313-20395-4, RONE). Greenwood.

Roman-Lopez, Carmen & Litoff, Carol. Diet Modification. (Illus.). 312p. 1983. pap. 22.95 looseleaf (ISBN 0-89313-030-3). G F Stickley.

Romanne-James, Constance. Herb-Lore for Housewives. LC 71-180978. (Illus.). 264p. 1974. Repr. of 1938 ed. 34.00x (ISBN 0-8103-3976-5). Gale.

Romano, Branko E. Chicken Toons. LC 82-83844. 1982. pap. 4.00 (ISBN 0-89229-010-2). Tonatiuh-Quinto Sol Intl.

Romano, Joseph A. & Wiener, Matthew B. Mill's Pharmacy State Board Review. 29th ed. LC 76-14721. 1977. pap. 16.50 o.p. (ISBN 0-87488-430-6). Med Exam.

--Mill's Pharmacy State Board Review. 30th ed. 1983. pap. text ed. 16.50 (ISBN 0-87488-430-6). Med Exam.

Romano, Octavio I. Word Toons. LC 82-83843. 1982. pap. 3.50 (ISBN 0-89229-011-0). Tonatiuh-Quinto Sol Intl.

Romano, R. & Leiman, M. Views on Capitalism. 1970. pap. 6.95x o.p. (ISBN 0-02-477210-0, 47721). Glencoe.

Romano, Ronald R. The Super Five Hundred Rapid Weight Loss Program. LC 80-29466. 228p. 1981. 14.95 o.p. (ISBN 0-13-875930-8, Parker). P-H.

Romanofsky, Peter, ed. Social Service Organizations, 2 vols. LC 77-84754. (Greenwood Encyclopedia of American Institutions: No. 2). 1978. lib. bdg. 75.00x (ISBN 0-8371-9829-1, RSS/). Greenwood.

Romanos, Michael C., ed. Western European Cities in Crisis. LC 78-21445. (Illus.). 272p. 1979. 26.95x (ISBN 0-669-02800-2). Lexington Bks.

Romanowitz, H. A. & Puckett, R. E. Introduction to Electronics. 2nd ed. LC 75-23060. 531p. 1976. text ed. 30.95 (ISBN 0-471-73264-8); tchrs.' manual 4.00 (ISBN 0-471-01509-1). Wiley.

Romantowski, Jane, jt. auth. see Lipson, Greta.

Romanucci-Ross, Lola. Conflict, Violence, & Morality in a Mexican Village. LC 73-77391. 202p. 1973. pap. text ed. 7.95 o.p. (ISBN 0-87484-276-X). Mayfield Pub.

Romanucci-Ross, Lola, jt. auth. see De Vos, George.

Romanucci-Ross, Lola, et al, eds. The Anthropology of Medicine: From Culture to Method. (Illus.). 416p. 1983. text ed. 29.95x (ISBN 0-686-78905-9); pap. text ed. 14.95x (ISBN 0-89789-013-2). J F Bergin.

Romanyshyn, John. Social Welfare: Charity to Justice. 1971. 17.95 o.p. (ISBN 0-394-31026-8). Random.

Romasco, Albert U. The Politics of Recovery: Roosevelt's New Deal. LC 82-14499. 270p. 1983. 17.95 (ISBN 0-19-503248-9). Oxford U Pr.

--Poverty of Abundance: Hoover, the Nation, the Depression. LC 65-26565. 1968. pap. 6.95 (ISBN 0-19-500760-3, 231, GB). Oxford U Pr.

Romashko, Sandra. Birds of the Water, Sea & Shore. LC 77-81169. (Illus.). 1983. pap. 3.25 (ISBN 0-89317-016-X). Windward Pub.

Romashko, Sandra D. Shell Book: A Complete Guide to Collecting & Identifying. 3rd ed. LC 76-360976. (Illus.). 64p. 1982. pap. 3.50 (ISBN 0-686-98131-6). Windward Pub.

--The Sportsfisherman's Handbook: Where, When & How to Catch & Identify All the Recognized Gamefish of the World. LC 76-379974. (Illus.). 64p. (Orig.). 1975. pap. 2.75 o.p. (ISBN 0-89317-003-8). Windward Pub.

Rombauer, Irma & Becker, Marion R. Joy of Cooking. pap. 7.95 (ISBN 0-452-25309-8, 25309, Plume). NAL.

Rombauer, Irma, jt. auth. see Becker, Marion R.

Rombauer, Irma S. & Becker, Marion R. Joy of Cooking. rev. ed. LC 75-10772. (Illus.). 930p. 1975. 15.95 (ISBN 0-672-51831-7); deluxe ed. 22.95 (ISBN 0-672-52385-X). Bobbs.

--The Joy of Cooking. pap. 5.95 o.p. (ISBN 0-451-07166-2, E8978, Sig). NAL.

Romberg, Bertil. Carl Jonas Love Almquist. LC 76-16859. (World Authors Ser). 1977. lib. bdg. 15.95 (ISBN 0-8057-6241-8, Twayne). G K Hall.

Romberg, Jenean & Rutz, Miriam E. Art Today & Every Day: Classroom Activities for the Elementary School Year. (Illus.). 272p. 1972. 16.50 (ISBN 0-13-049056-3, Parker). P-H.

Romberger, J. A. & Mikola, P., eds. International Review of Forestry Research, Vols. 1-3. 1964-70. 50.00 ea. Vol. 1 (ISBN 0-12-365501-3). Vol. 2 o.p (ISBN 0-12-365502-1). Vol. 3 (ISBN 0-12-365503-X). Acad Pr.

Romberger, John A., ed. Biosystematics in Agriculture. LC 77-84408. (Beltsville Symposia in Agricultural Research Ser.: No. 2). 352p. 1978. text ed. 24.00x o.p. (ISBN 0-470-26416-0). Allanheld.

Romberger, John A., ed. see Beltsville Symposia in Agricultural Research.

Romberger, Judy. Lolly. LC 80-2062. 264p. 1981. 12.95 o.p. (ISBN 0-385-15860-2). Doubleday.

Rome, Adam see Weaver, Glenn.

Rome, Carol C. A New Look at Bargello: The Florentine Needlepoint Stitch Book. LC 72-84322. (Arts & Crafts Ser). (Illus.). 96p. 1973. 5.95 o.p. (ISBN 0-517-50055-8). Crown.

Rome, Margaret. Une Fleur Dans le desert. (Harlequin Romantique Ser.). 192p. 1983. pap. 1.95 (ISBN 0-373-41181-2). Harlequin Bks.

--Le Lion De Venise. (Harlequin Romantique). 192p. 1983. pap. 1.95 (ISBN 0-373-41193-6). Harlequin Bks.

--Rapture of the Deep. (Harlequin Romances Ser.). 192p. 1983. pap. 1.75 (ISBN 0-373-02553-X). Harlequin Bks.

Romen, A. S. Self-Suggestion & Its Influence on the Human Organism. Lewis, A. S. & Forsky, V., eds. LC 80-28703. Orig. Title: Samovnushenie I Ego Vliianie Na Organizm Cheloveka. (Illus.). 220p. 1980. 25.00 (ISBN 0-87332-195-2). M E Sharpe.

Romer, Stephen, tr. see Baghio'o, Jean-Louis.

Romero, Adrian, jt. auth. see Browne, Louis.

Romero, Carlos, jt. auth. see Romero, Mary A.

Romero, Felix, jt. auth. see Hoffman, Edward G.

Romero, Jose & Guzman, Betty. Two Hundred & Fifty Conjugated Spanish Verbs. 264p. (Orig.). 1981. pap. 2.95 (ISBN 0-8092-5845-5). Contemp Bks.

Romero, Jose M. Un Psicologo Puertorriqueno Entrevista a Albert Ellis. pap. 3.50 (ISBN 0-686-36790-1). Inst Rat Liv.

Romero, Juan. Los Himnos De Juan Romero. (Spanish Bks.). (Span.). 1978. 2.00 (ISBN 0-8297-0886-3). Life Pubs Intl.

Romero, Mary A. & Romero, Carlos. Los Bilingos. Smith, James C., Jr., ed. LC 77-25364. (Illus.). 1978. pap. 3.95 (ISBN 0-913270-70-9). Sunstone Pr.

Romero, Orlando. Nambe-Year One. LC 76-13385. (Illus.). 1976. 4.95 o.p. (ISBN 0-89229-004-8); pap. 6.50 (ISBN 0-89229-003-X). Tonatiuh-Quinto Sol Intl.

Romfh, Richard F. Patients' Guide to Doctors: How to Hire & Fire Your Doctor. LC 81-17665. 1983. 19.95 (ISBN 0-87949-199-X). Ashley Bks.

Romig, Harry G., jt. auth. see Dodge, Harold F.

Romig, Harry G., jt. auth. see Hayes, Glenn E.

Romig, Ralph. Sacred Refuge. LC 80-14984. 1983. 14.95 (ISBN 0-87949-189-2). Ashley Bks.

Romine, Jack S. Sentence Mastery. 2nd ed. 1966. text ed. 11.95 (ISBN 0-13-806695-7). P-H.

Romine, Jack S., et al. College Business English. 3rd ed. (Illus.). 400p. 1981. text ed. 16.95 (ISBN 0-13-141960-9). P-H.

Romiszowski, A. J. Producing Instructional Systems. 350p. 1983. 33.50 (ISBN 0-89397-085-9). Nichols Pub.

--The Selection & Use of Instructional Media: A Systems Approach. LC 74-2120. 360p. 1974. 29.95 o.p. (ISBN 0-470-73290-3). Halsted Pr.

Rommetviet, Ragnar. On Message Structure: A Framework for the Study of Language & Communication. LC 74-174. 143p. 1974. 27.95 o.p. (ISBN 0-471-73295-8, Pub. by Wiley-Interscience). Wiley.

Romney, C. Park. Raising Rabbits at Home. (Illus.). 92p. 1981. pap. 2.95 (ISBN 0-940986-01-9). ValuWrite.

Romney, Marion G. Learning for the Eternities. LC 77-22135. 1977. 6.95 o.p. (ISBN 0-87747-676-4). Deseret Bk.

Romney, S., et al. Gynecology & Obstetrics: The Health Care of Women. 1975. 37.00 o.p. (ISBN 0-07-053581-7, HP). McGraw.

Romney, Seymour, et al, eds. Gynecology & Obstetrics: The Health Care of Women. 2nd ed. (Illus.). 1980. text ed. 55.00 (ISBN 0-07-053582-5, HP). McGraw.

Romo, Ricardo. East Los Angeles: History of a Barrio. LC 82-10891. 232p. 1983. 22.50x (ISBN 0-292-72040-8); pap. 8.95 (ISBN 0-292-72041-6). U of Tex Pr.

Romo, Richard & Brinson, Bonne. How to Make & Use Your Own Visual Delights. 96p. 1982. pap. text ed. 6.95 (ISBN 0-86158-185-7). Newbury Hse.

Romoser, William S. The Science of Entomology. 2nd ed. (Illus.). 544p. 1981. 25.95x (ISBN 0-02-403410-X). Macmillan.

Romsdahl, Marvin M., jt. ed. see Stroehlein, John R.

Romtvedt, David. Moon. 1983. 60.00 (ISBN 0-931460-14-X); pap. 5.95 (ISBN 0-931460-16-6). Bieler.

Rona, D. C. Guide to Professional Records. (Illus.). 50p. (Orig.). 1982. pap. 8.50 (ISBN 0-911127-00-3). CRS Con.

Rona, P. A. & Lowell, R. P. Seafloor Spreading Centers: Hydrothermal Systems. LC 79-18265. (Bench Papers in Geology: Vol. 56). 424p. 1980. 51.50 (ISBN 0-87933-363-4). Hutchinson Ross.

Ronai, Lili. Corals. LC 75-6865. (A Let's Read & Find Out Science Bk). (Illus.). 40p. (gr. k-3). 1976. 10.89 (ISBN 0-690-00921-6, TYC-J). Har-Row.

Ronald, Ann. The New West of Edward Abbey. 272p. 1982. 19.95x (ISBN 0-8263-0635-7). U of NM Pr.

Ronaldson, Dolores, ed. see Witter, Evelyn.

Ronan, C. A. Isaac Newton. (Clarendon Biography Ser.). (Illus.). 1976. pap. 3.50 o.s.i. (ISBN 0-912728-05-1). Newbury Bks.

Ronan, Colin. Deep Space: A Guide to the Cosmos. LC 82-9966. 208p. 1982. 25.95 (ISBN 0-02-604510-9). Macmillan.

--Galileo. LC 74-76233. (Illus.). 264p. 1974. 14.95 o.p. (ISBN 0-399-11364-9). Putnam Pub Group.

Ronan, Colin A. The Shorter Science & Civilisation in China, Vol. 1. LC 77-82513. (Illus.). 1978. 34.50 (ISBN 0-521-21821-7). Cambridge U Pr.

--Shorter Science & Civilization in China, Vol. 2. LC 77-82513. (Illus.). 250p. 1982. 34.50 (ISBN 0-521-23582-0); pap. cancelled (ISBN 0-521-28053-2). Cambridge U Pr.

--Shorter Science & Civilization in China, Vol. 1. LC 77-82513. (Illus.). 337p. 1980. pap. 15.95 (ISBN 0-521-29286-7). Cambridge U Pr.

Rona-Tas, A., ed. Studies in Chuvash Etymology I. 240p. 1982. 20.00 (ISBN 0-686-36268-3). Benjamins North Am.

Ronay, Egon. Egon Ronay's Lucas Guide to Hotels, Restaurants & Inns in Great Britain & Ireland, 1983. LC 74-644899. (Illus.). 862p. 1983. pap. 13.95 (ISBN 0-03-063331-1). HR&W.

--Egon Ronay's TWA Guide Nineteen Eighty Three to Good Restaurants in 35 European Cities. 1983. pap. 6.95 (ISBN 0-517-54877-1, Harmony Bks). Crown.

Ronay, Nadja. Ginger. LC 82-170230. 62p. 1981. 17.95 (ISBN 0-943516-00-5). Magnolia Pubns Inc.

Roncaglia, Alessandro. Sraffa & the Theory of Prices. LC 77-7241. 1978. 41.25 o.p. (ISBN 0-471-99538-X, Pub. by Wiley-Interscience). Wiley.
Ronck, Ronn, ed. see Baker, Ray J.
Roncucci, R. & Van Peteghem, C. Quantitative Mass Spectrometry in Life Sciences, Vol. II. 1979. 81.00 (ISBN 0-444-41760-5). Elsevier.
Roncucci, Romeo R, ed. see International Symposium on Quantitative Mass Spectrometry in Life Sciences, 1st, State University of Ghent Belgium June 16-18 1976.
Ronda, James P., ed. see Eliot, John.
Rondebush, Jay. Mary Cassatt. (Q. L. P. Ser.). (Illus.). 1979. 7.95 (ISBN 0-517-53740-0). Crown.
Rondinelli, Dennis A. Secondary Cities in Developing Countries: Policies for Diffusing Urbanization. (Sage Library of Social Research). (Illus.). 256p. 1983. 25.00 (ISBN 0-8039-1945-X); pap. 12.50 (ISBN 0-8039-1946-8). Sage.
Rondinelli, Dennis A. & Ruddle, Kenneth. Urbanization & Rural Development: A Spatial Policy for Equitable Growth. LC 78-17790. (Special Studies). 1978. 27.95 o.p. (ISBN 0-03-043111-5). Praeger.
Rondle, C. J., ed. Disease Eradication. 270p. 1981. 60.00x (ISBN 0-333-31188-4, Pub. by Macmillan England). State Mutual Bk.
Rondthaler, Edward. Traveler's Instant Money Converter. rev. ed. 64p. 1974. pap. 1.95 (ISBN 0-448-11729-0, G&D). Putnam Pub Group.
Ronen. The Quest for Self-Determination. 1979. text ed. 20.00x (ISBN 0-300-02364-2); pap. 5.95x (ISBN 0-300-02840-7, Y-416). Yale U Pr.
Ronen, Avraham. Introducing Prehistory. LC 72-10803. (Lerner Archaeology Ser.: Digging up the Past). (Illus.). (gr. 5 up). 1976. PLB 7.95g (ISBN 0-8225-0833-8). Lerner Pubns.
Ronen, Joshua. Entrepreneurship. LC 82-47950. 336p. 1982. 33.95x (ISBN 0-669-05715-0). Lexington Bks.
Ronen, Simcha. The Flexible Work Schedule: An Innovation in the Quality of Work Life. (Illus.). 352p. 1980. 22.95 (ISBN 0-07-053607-4). McGraw.
Roney, Raymond G., jt. auth. see Casciero, Albert J.
Rong, Kuang, ed. Fifteen Strings of Cash. (Illus., Orig.). 1982. pap. 4.95 (ISBN 0-8351-1103-2). China Bks.
Ronken, Harriet O. & Lawrence, Paul R. Administering Changes: A Case Study of Human Relations in a Factory. LC 72-5458. 324p. 1972. Repr. of 1952 ed. lib. bdg. 12.50x (ISBN 0-8371-6437-0, ROAD). Greenwood.
Ronning, Ronald H. & Reedy, Jeremiah, eds. Articulating the Ineffable: Approaches to the Teaching of Humanities. LC 81-43697. 130p. 1983. pap. text ed. 8.25 (ISBN 0-8191-2702-7). U Pr of Amer.
Ronnow, Robert. Janie Huzzie Bows. 64p. (Orig.). 1983. pap. 6.95 (ISBN 0-935306-18-8). Barnwood Pr.
Ronsard, Pierre De. Poems of Pierre De Ronsard. Kilmer, Nicholas, ed. LC 75-17287. (Illus.). 1979. 19.95x (ISBN 0-520-03078-8). U of Cal Pr.
Ronsard, Pierre de see Ronsard, Pierre De.
Ronsley, Joseph, ed. Selected Plays of Denis Johnston. (Irish Drama Selections Ser.: No. 2). 1982. 33.50 (ISBN 0-8132-0576-X); pap. 7.95x (ISBN 0-8132-0577-8). Cath U Pr.
Ronson, Mavis. We Never Meant to Go So Far. (Illus.). 6.95 o.p. (ISBN 0-685-20650-5). Transatlantic.
Ronstadt, Robert. Research & Development Abroad by U. S. Multinationals. LC 77-10672. (Praeger Special Studies). 1977. 24.95 o.p. (ISBN 0-03-022661-9). Praeger.
Ronstadt, Robert C., ed. Entrepreneurship: Bibliography 1982. 1982. pap. 3.95 (ISBN 0-686-91855-X). Lord Pub.
Ronte, Dieter, et al. Batuz. (Illus.). 176p. 1981. 45.00 (ISBN 0-8478-0386-4). Rizzoli Intl.
Rony, A. Kohar, ed. Vietnamese Holdings in the Library of Congress: A Bibliography. LC 81-2847. v, 224p. 1982. 12.00 (ISBN 0-8444-0362-8). Lib Congress.
Rony, Peter. Microcomputer Interfacing & Programming. 2nd ed. Date not set. pap. 17.95 (ISBN 0-672-21933-6). Sams.
Roocek, Joseph S., ed. Programmed Teaching: A Symposium on Automation in Education. LC 65-14265. 1965. 10.00 o.p. (ISBN 0-685-91413-5). Philos Lib.
Rood, H. W. Kingdoms of the Blind. LC 79-54442. (Illus.). 295p. 1980. lib. bdg. 19.95 (ISBN 0-89089-121-4). Carolina Acad Pr.
Rood, Karen L., ed. American Writers in Paris, Nineteen Twenty to Nineteen Thirty-Nine. LC 79-26101. (Dictionary of Literary Biography Ser.: Vol. 4). (Illus.). 1980. 74.00x (ISBN 0-8103-0916-5, Bruccoli Clark Book). Gale.
Rood, Karen L., et al, eds. Dictionary of Literary Biography Yearbook: 1980. LC 81-4188. 368p. 1981. 74.00x (ISBN 0-8103-1600-5). Gale.
Rood, Robert T. & Trefil, James S. Are We Alone? (Illus.). 272p. 1983. pap. 6.95 (ISBN 0-686-83774-6, ScribT). Scribner.
Roody, Peter, et al. Medical Abbreviations & Acronyms. 1976. pap. text ed. 12.95 (ISBN 0-07-053604-X, HP). McGraw.
Roodyn, D. B. Automated Enzyme Assays, Vol. 2, Pt. 1. (Laboratory Techniques in Biochemistry & Molecular Biology Ser.). 1970. pap. 18.50 (ISBN 0-444-10056-3, North-Holland). Elsevier.
Roodyn, Donald B., ed. Subcellular Biochemistry, Vol. 9. 425p. 1983. 52.50x (ISBN 0-306-41091-5, Plenum Pr). Plenum Pub.
Roof, Wade C. Community & Commitment: Religious Plausibility in a Liberal Protestant Church. 1978. 24.00 (ISBN 0-444-99038-0). Elsevier.
--Community & Commitment: Religious Plausibility in a Liberal Protestant Church. LC 77-16329. 288p. pap. 10.95 (ISBN 0-8298-0669-5). Pilgrim NY.
Roof, Wade C. & Ginsberg, Ralph B., eds. Race & Residence in American Cities. LC 78-72993. (Annals: No. 441). 1979. 15.00 (ISBN 0-87761-236-6); pap. 6.00 o.p. (ISBN 0-87761-237-4). Am Acad-Pol Soc Sci.
Rook, Douglas N. & Rook, Pearl L. The Sound of Thought. LC 76-42355. (Illus.). 53p. 1977. 5.50 (ISBN 0-911838-48-1). Windy Row.
Rook, Pearl L., jt. auth. see Rook, Douglas N.
Rooke, Leon. Shakespeare's Dog. LC 82-48889. 1983. 10.95 (ISBN 0-394-53031-4). Knopf.
Rooke, M. Leigh & Wingrove, C. Ray. Benefaction or Bondage? Social Policy & the Aged. LC 79-5437. 1980. pap. text ed. 8.25 (ISBN 0-8191-0885-5); text ed. 18.50 (ISBN 0-8191-1037-X). U Pr of Amer.
Rooke, Patrick, et al. The Normans. LC 78-56586. (Peoples of the Past Ser.). (Illus.). 1978. lib. bdg. 12.68 (ISBN 0-382-06184-5). Silver.
Rooks, Charles S. The Atlanta Elections of Nineteen Sixty-nine. 1970. 4.00 (ISBN 0-686-37998-5). Voter Ed Proj.
Rooks, George. Conversations sans Fin. 136p. 1983. pap. text ed. 7.95 (ISBN 0-88377-278-7). Newbury Hse.
--Non-Stop Discussion Workbook! Problems for Intermediate & Advanced Students of English. (Orig.). 1981. pap. text ed. 7.95 (ISBN 0-88377-171-3). Newbury Hse.
Rooks, George & Scholberg, Kenneth R. Conversar Sin Parar. 136p. 1982. pap. text ed. 8.95 (ISBN 0-88377-222-1). Newbury Hse.
Room, Adrian. Dictionary of Cryptic Crossword Clues. 288p. 1983. price not set (ISBN 0-7100-9415-9). Routledge & Kegan.
--Dictionary of the Origins of Names in Classical Mythology: Mythonoma. 320p. 1983. 18.95 (ISBN 0-7100-9262-8). Routledge & Kegan.
--Room's Dictionary of Differences. (Illus.). 132p. 1982. pap. 5.95 (ISBN 0-89696-178-8, An Everest House Book). Dodd.
--Room's Dictionary of Distinguishables & Confusibles, 2 vols. 1981. 19.95 (ISBN 0-7100-9472-8). Routledge & Kegan.
Room, Adrian, compiled by. Place-Name Changes Since Nineteen Hundred: A World Gazetteer. LC 79-4300. 1979. 12.00 (ISBN 0-8108-1210-X). Scarecrow.
Room, Graham. The Sociology of Welfare: Social Policy, Stratification & Political Order. 1979. 30.00x (ISBN 0-312-74080-8). St Martin.
Room, M. B. Wanted Your Daily Life. 1976. pap. 1.75 (ISBN 0-87508-011-1). Chr Lit.
Roomkin, Myron, jt. ed. see Juris, Hervey A.
Rooney, Andrew A. And More By Andy Rooney. LC 82-45183. 256p. 1982. 12.95 (ISBN 0-689-11316-1). Atheneum.
--A Few Minutes with Andy Rooney. (General Ser.). 1982. lib. bdg. 13.95 (ISBN 0-8161-3421-9, Large Print Bks). G K Hall.
Rooney, David. Sir Charles Arden-Clarke. 236p. 1982. text ed. 22.50 (ISBN 0-89874-598-5). Krieger.
Rooney, James R. Autopsy of the Horse: Technique & Interpretation. LC 75-11887. 164p. 1976. Repr. of 1970 ed. 16.50 (ISBN 0-88275-329-0). Krieger.
--Biomechanics of Lameness in Horses. LC 76-18771. (Illus.). 272p. 1977. Repr. of 1969 ed. 19.50 (ISBN 0-88275-447-5). Krieger.
--Mechanics of the Horse. LC 78-8774. 104p. 1980. lib. bdg. 14.50 (ISBN 0-88275-693-1). Krieger.
Roos, Bernard W. Analytic Functions & Distributions in Physics & Engineering. LC 69-19241. 521p. 1969. text ed. 28.50 (ISBN 0-471-73334-2, Pub. by Wiley). Krieger.
Roos, Stephen. My Horrible Secret. (Orig.). (gr. k-6). 1983. pap. 2.25 (ISBN 0-440-43956-6, YB). Dell.
--My Horrible Secret. LC 82-14954. (Illus.). 128p. (gr. 4-7). 1983. 10.95 (ISBN 0-440-03788-3). Delacorte.
Roose-Evans, James. Experimental Theatre: From Stanislavsky to Today. LC 73-81311. pap. 8.95 o.p. (ISBN 0-87663-961-9). Universe.
Roosevelt, Anna C. & Smith, J. G., eds. The Ancestors: Native Artisans of the Americas. LC 79-89536. (Illus.). 1979. pap. 17.50 (ISBN 0-934490-00-7). Mus Am Ind.
Roosevelt, Eleanor. Autobiography of Eleanor Roosevelt. LC 61-12222. pap. 6.95 o.p. (ISBN 0-06-465094-4, P/BN 5094, BN). B&N NY.
--Autobiography of Eleanor Roosevelt. LC 61-12222. (Illus.). 1961. 21.10i (ISBN 0-06-013615-4, HarpT). Har-Row.
Roosevelt, Elliott. The Conservators. 1983. 16.95 (ISBN 0-87795-456-9). Arbor Hse.
Roosevelt, Elliott & Brough, James. Mother R: Eleanor Roosevelt's Untold Story. LC 77-7281. (Illus.). 1977. 8.95 o.p. (ISBN 0-399-11998-1). Putnam Pub Group.
--Rendezvous with Destiny: The Roosevelts of the White House. (Illus.). 384p. 1975. 10.00 o.p. (ISBN 0-399-11545-5). Putnam Pub Group.
--An Untold Story: The Roosevelts of Hyde Park. (Illus.). 320p. 1973. 7.95 o.p. (ISBN 0-399-11127-1). Putnam Pub Group.
Roosevelt, Hilborne. Manufacturer of Church, Chapel, Concert & Chamber Organs. (Bibliotheca Organologica: Vol. 37). 117p. 22.50 o.s.i. (ISBN 90-6027-332-X, Pub. by Frits Knuf Netherlands). Pendragon NY.
Roosevelt, Kermit. Memories of My Father. (Illus.). 98p. Date not set. Repr. of 1920 ed. 54.85 (ISBN 0-89901-026-1). Found Class Reprints.
Roosevelt, Michele C. Animals in the Woods. LC 80-54770. (Board Bks.). (Illus.). 14p. (ps). 1981. bds. 3.50 (ISBN 0-394-84810-1). Random.
Roosevelt, Michele C., illus. Zoo Animals. LC 82-15003. (Board Bks.). (Illus.). 12p. (ps). 1983. 3.50 (ISBN 0-394-85285-0). Random.
Roosevelt, Ruth. Living in Step. (Paperbacks Ser.). 1977. Repr. of 1976 ed. pap. 5.95 (ISBN 0-07-053596-5, SP). McGraw.
Roosevelt, Theodore. Ranch Life & the Hunting Trail. LC 81-13521. (Classics of the Old West Ser.). PLB 17.28 (ISBN 0-8094-3983-2). Silver.
--Ranch Life & the Hunting Trail. LC 82-20091. (Illus.). 196p. 1983. 19.95x (ISBN 0-8032-3865-7, BB 833); pap. 8.95 (ISBN 0-8032-8913-8, Bison). U of Nebr Pr.
Root, Bailey S. & Root, Lillian D. Sexy Cooking: A Cookbook for Lovers. LC 82-72720. (Illus.). 320p. 1982. cancelled 15.95 o.p. (ISBN 0-931494-24-9); pap. 8.95 cancelled o.p. (ISBN 0-931494-25-7). Brunswick Pub.
Root, E. Merrill. America's Steadfast Dream. 1971. pap. 4.95 (ISBN 0-88279-117-6). Western Islands.
Root, Kathleen B. & Byers, E. E. Medical Secretary: Terminology & Transcription. 3rd ed. 1967. 21.95 (ISBN 0-07-053586-8, G); student transcript 7.15 (ISBN 0-07-053589-2). McGraw.
--Medical Typing Practice. 2nd ed. 1967. 9.95 (ISBN 0-07-053585-X, G). McGraw.
Root, Leon & Kiernan, Thomas. Oh, My Aching Back! 1975. pap. 3.50 (ISBN 0-451-12174-0, AE2174, Sig). NAL.
Root, Lillian D., jt. auth. see Root, Bailey S.
Root, Marcus A. The Camera & the Pencil. 1971. 13.25 (ISBN 0-87931-400-1). Helios Vt.
Root, Orrin. Training for Service: a Survey of the Bible: Instructor's Edition. (Illus.). 128p. (Orig.). 1964. pap. 2.95 (ISBN 0-87239-325-9, 3219). Standard Pub.
--Training for Service: a Survey of the Bible: Pupil's Edition. (Illus.). 96p. (Orig.). 1964. pap. 2.50 (ISBN 0-87239-326-7, 3220). Standard Pub.
Root, Orrin, ed. see McCord, David.
Root, Orrin, ed. see Staton, Knofel.
Root, Robert, jt. auth. see Gilmore, Gene.
Root, Robert K. The Poetical Career of Alexander Pope. 8.00 (ISBN 0-8446-1392-4). Peter Smith.
Root, Robert L. Thomas Southerne. (English Authors Ser.). 13.95 (ISBN 0-8057-6727-4, Twayne). G K Hall.
Root, Shelton L., Jr., jt. auth. see Arbuthnot, May H.
Root, Vella M., et al. Official Book of the Schipperke. 2nd ed. LC 75-39181. (Complete Breed Bk.). (Illus.). 14.95 o.p. (ISBN 0-87605-301-0). Howell Bk.
Root, W. S. & Hoffman, F. G., eds. Physiological Pharmacology: A Comprehensive Treatise, 4 vols. Incl. Vol. 1. The Nervous System, Part A. 1963. 82.00 (ISBN 0-12-595701-7); Vol. 2. The Nervous System, Part B. 1965. 64.50 (ISBN 0-12-595702-5); Vol. 3. The Nervous System, Part C. 1967. 67.00 (ISBN 0-12-595703-3); Vol. 4. The Nervous System, Part D. 1967. 67.00 (ISBN 0-12-595704-1); Vol. 5. The Nervous System, Part E. 1974. 82.00 (ISBN 0-12-595705-X). Acad Pr.
Root, Waverley. The Best of Italian Cooking. (Illus.). 272p. 1982. 13.95 (ISBN 0-448-16063-3, G&D). Putnam Pub Group.
--Cooking of Italy. LC 68-19230. (Foods of the World Ser.). (Illus.). (gr. 6 up). 1968. PLB 17.28 (ISBN 0-8094-0057-X, Pub. by Time-Life). Silver.
--Food: An Informal Dictionary. (Illus.). 1980. 24.95 o.p. (ISBN 0-671-22589-8). S&S.
Root, Waverly, et al. Herbs & Spices: The Pursuit of Flavor. LC 80-18563. (Illus.). 1980. 19.95 o.p. (ISBN 0-07-053591-4). McGraw.
Root, William S. New Contract Bridge Outlines on Standard Bidding. 64p. (YA) 1971. pap. 1.50 o.p. (ISBN 0-517-50213-5). Crown.
Rootes, Nina, tr. see Cendrars, Blaise.
Rooth, Anne R. & White, James P. The Ninth Car. LC 78-9515. 1978. 8.95 o.p. (ISBN 0-399-12284-2). Putnam Pub Group.
Roots, Ivan A. Commonwealth & Protectorate: The English Civil War & Its Aftermath. LC 76-8164. 1976. Repr. of 1966 ed. lib. bdg. 29.75x (ISBN 0-8371-8854-7, ROCP). Greenwood.
Roper, Alan see Dryden, John.
Roper, Ann. Metric Recipes for the Classroom. 1977. 4.50 (ISBN 0-88488-084-2). Creative Pubns.
Roper, Ann & Harvey, Linda. Dots Math Too! (gr. 3-6). 1978. 6.25 (ISBN 0-88488-118-0). Creative Pubns.
Roper, Ann, jt. auth. see Harvey, Linda.
Roper, Christopher, jt. ed. see Harding, Colin.
Roper, Daniel C. Fifty Years of Public Life. LC 68-29747. (Illus.). 1968. Repr. of 1941 ed. lib. bdg. 18.75x o.p. (ISBN 0-8371-0205-7, ROFY). Greenwood.
Roper, Derek, ed. Wordsworth & Coleridge: Lyrical Ballads 1805. 432p. 1979. 29.00x (ISBN 0-7121-0140-3, Pub. by Macdonald & Evans). State Mutual Bk.
Roper, Donna C. Archeological Survey & Settlement Pattern Models in Central Illinois. (Scientific Papers Ser.: Vol. XVI). (Illus.). 156p. 1979. pap. 4.50 (ISBN 0-87338-230-7). Ill St Museum.
Roper, Elmo B. You & Your Leaders, Their Actions & Your Reactions 1936-1956. LC 76-29698. 1976. Repr. of 1957 ed. lib. bdg. 20.50x (ISBN 0-8371-9273-0, ROYO). Greenwood.
Roper, Gayle G. New Program Ideas for Women's Groups. (Paperback Program Ser). 1978. pap. 2.75 (ISBN 0-8010-7662-5). Baker Bk.
Roper, Lester. Love's Captive. 1979. pap. 1.50 o.s.i. (ISBN 0-440-14756-5). Dell.
Roper, R. G., jt. auth. see Kato, S.
Roper, Steve. Climber's Guide to the High Sierra. rev. ed. LC 75-45108. (Totebk Ser). (Illus.). 384p. 1976. pap. 8.95 (ISBN 0-87156-147-6). Sierra.
Roper, Steve & Steck, Allen. Fifty Classic Climbs of North America. LC 79-13001. (Paperback Library). (Illus.). 336p. 1981. pap. 10.95 (ISBN 0-87156-292-8). Sierra.
Roper, Steve, jt. ed. see Steck, Allen.
Roper, Susan. Shadows on the Tor. 1977. 7.95 o.p. (ISBN 0-671-22748-3). S&S.
Roper, William. A Life of Sir Thomas More. (Illus.). 128p. (Orig.). 1983. pap. 6.95 (ISBN 0-87243-118-5). Templegate.
Roper, William L. Sequoyah & His Miracle. (Indian Culture Ser.). (gr. 6-12). 1972. 1.95 o.p. (ISBN 0-89992-056-X). MT Coun Indian.
Ropiequet, Suzanne, tr. see Boisgontier, Jacques.
Ropke, John C. Concrete Problems: Causes & Cures. (Illus.). 192p. 1982. 26.50 (ISBN 0-07-053609-0). McGraw.
Ropke, Wilhelm T. Economics of the Free Society. Boarman, Patrick M., tr. LC 81-52210. 290p. 1963. 7.95x o.p. (ISBN 0-89526-679-2). Regnery-Gateway.
--Humane Economy: The Social Framework of a Free Society. Henderson, Elizabeth, tr. 1960. pap. 6.95 (ISBN 0-89526-988-0). Regnery-Gateway.
Ropp, Robert De see De Ropp, Robert.
Ropp, Robert S. De see De Ropp, Robert S.
Ropp, Theodore. War in the Modern World. rev. ed. 1962. pap. 4.95 (ISBN 0-02-036400-8, Collier). Macmillan.
Ropper. Neurological & Neurosurgical Intensive Care. 304p. 1982. text ed. 37.50 (ISBN 0-8391-1759-0). Univ Park.
Roppolo, J. P. Philip Barry. (United States Authors Ser.). 12.95 (ISBN 0-8057-0040-4, Twayne). G K Hall.
Roquelaure, A. N. The Claiming of Sleeping Beauty. 288p. 1983. pap. 6.95 (ISBN 0-525-48054-4, 0869-260). Dutton.
Roquemore, Kathleen. It's All in Your Numbers: The Secrets of Numerology. LC 74-20411. (Illus.). 320p. (YA) 1975. 15.34i (ISBN 0-06-013597-2, HarpT). Har-Row.
Roquette-Buisson, Odile de see De Roquette-Buisson, Odile.
Rorabacher, Louise & Dunbar, Georgia. Assignments in Exposition. 7th ed. 355p. 1982. pap. text ed. 9.95 scp (ISBN 0-06-045576-4, HarpC); instr's. manual avail. (ISBN 0-06-365567-5). Har-Row.
Rorabacher, Louise E. Frank Dalby Davison. (World Authors Ser.). 1979. lib. bdg. 15.95 (ISBN 0-8057-6355-4, Twayne). G K Hall.
Rorabaugh, W. J. The Alcoholic Republic: An American Tradition. (Illus.). 1979. 18.95x (ISBN 0-19-502584-9). Oxford U Pr.
--The Alcoholic Republic: An American Tradition. (Illus.). 1981. pap. 7.95 (ISBN 0-19-502990-9, GB 653). Oxford U Pr.
Rordorf, Willy & Schneider, Andre. L'Evolution Du Concept De Tradition Dans l'Englise Ancienne. xxxii, 208p. (Fr.). 1982. write for info. P Lang Pubs.
Rordorf, Willy, et al. The Eucharist of the Early Christians. O'Connell, Matthew J., tr. from Fr. 1978. pap. 9.95 (ISBN 0-916134-33-4). Pueblo Pub Co.
Rorem, C. Rufus. Accounting Method. LC 82-48382. (Accountancy in Transition Ser.). 613p. 1982. lib. bdg. 60.00 (ISBN 0-8240-5327-3). Garland Pub.
Rorem, Ned. An Absolute Gift: A New Diary. 1978. 9.95 o.p. (ISBN 0-671-22666-5). S&S.
--The Paris & New York Diaries of Ned Rorem. LC 82-73718. 464p. 1983. pap. 15.00 (ISBN 0-86547-109-6). N Point Pr.
--Setting the Tone: Essays & Diary. LC 82-14427. 384p. 1983. 17.95 (ISBN 0-698-11234-2, Coward). Putnam Pub Group.
Rorer, David. American Inter-State Law. Mayer, Levy, ed. lvii, 400p. 1983. Repr. of 1879 ed. lib. bdg. 35.00x (ISBN 0-8377-1038-3). Rothman.

Rorex, Robert A. & Wen Fong, trs. Eighteen Songs of a Nomad Flute: The Story of Lady Wen-Chi. LC 74-11140. (Illus.). 1974. 18.50 (ISBN 0-87099-095-0). Metro Mus Art.

Rorimer, Anne, jt. auth. see Speyer, A. James.

Rorison, I. & Hunt, R. Amenity Grassland: An Ecological Perspective. 261p. 1980. 69.95 (ISBN 0-471-27666-9, Pub. by Wiley-Interscience). Wiley.

Rorke, Lucy B. Pathology of Perinatal Brain Injury. 159p. 1982. text ed. 16.50 (ISBN 0-89004-688-3). Raven.

Rorres, Chris, jt. auth. see Anton, Howard.

Rorty, Amelie O., ed. Essays on Aristotle's Ethics. LC 78-62858. (Major Thinkers Ser.). 1981. 37.50x (ISBN 0-520-03773-1); pap. 9.95 (ISBN 0-520-04041-4, CAMPUS 245). U of Cal Pr.

--Explaining Emotions. LC 78-62859. 1980. 40.00x (ISBN 0-520-03775-8); pap. 9.95x (ISBN 0-520-03921-1, CAMPUS NO. 232). U of Cal Pr.

Rorvig, Mark, et al. Changing Information Concepts & Technologies: A Reader for the Professional Librarian. LC 82-166. (Professional Librarian Ser.). 179p. 1982. text ed. 34.50 (ISBN 0-86729-028-5); pap. text ed. 27.50 (ISBN 0-86729-027-7). Knowledge Indus.

Rorvik, David. Good Housekeeping Woman's Medical Guide. 1976. pap. 1.95 o.p. (ISBN 0-380-00566-2, 28886). Avon.

Ros, Herbert S. It's So Nice to Remember: The Recollection of an Italian Diplomat. 1978. 8.95 o.p. (ISBN 0-533-03151-6). Vantage.

Rosa, A., jt. auth. see Lindner, C. C.

Rosa, Alfred & Eschholz, Paul, eds. Models for Writers: Short Essays for Composition. LC 81-51841. 358p. 1982. pap. text ed. 8.95 (ISBN 0-312-53590-2); Instr's. manual avail. St Martin.

Rosa, Alfred, jt. ed. see Eschholz, Paul.

Rosa, Alfred F., jt. auth. see Escholz, Paul A.

Rosa, Alfred F. & Eschholz, Paul A., eds. Contemporary Fiction in America & England, 1950-1970: A Guide to Information Sources. LC 73-16990. (American Literature, English Literature, & World Literatures in English Information Guide Series: Vol. 10). 220p. 1976. 42.00x (ISBN 0-8103-1219-0). Gale.

Rosa, J., et al, eds. Development of Therapeutic Agents for Sickle Cell Disease. (INSERM Symposium: Vol. 9). 1979. 58.75 (ISBN 0-7204-0671-4, North Holland). Elsevier.

Rosa, Jean J., ed. World Crisis in Social Security. 245p. (Orig.). 1982. pap. text ed. 9.95 (ISBN 0-917616-44-8). ICS Pr.

Rosa, Joseph G. The West of Wild Bill Hickok. (Illus.). 201p. 1982. 24.95 (ISBN 0-8061-1604-8). U of Okla Pr.

Rosa, Manuel A., ed. Corrugating Defect Terminology: Fabrication Manuel for Corrugated Box Plants. 4th, rev. ed. (Illus.). 236p. 1982. pap. 49.95 (ISBN 0-89852-403-2, 01 01R 103). TAPPI.

Rosa, Mathilde La see Boni, Ada.

Rosa, N., jt. auth. see McCombs, L.

Rosa, Nicholas. Desktop Computing for Managers. Miller, Merl, ed. 250p. Date not set. pap. 12.95 (ISBN 0-88056-062-2). Dilithium Pr.

Rosa, Peter De see De Rosa, Peter.

Rosado, Puig. Animal Life. (Illus.). 64p. 1982. pap. 8.95 (ISBN 0-312-03781-3). St Martin.

Rosage, David E. Discovering Pathways to Prayer. 160p. (Orig.). 1975. pap. 2.95 (ISBN 0-914544-08-X). Living Flame Pr.

--Follow Me: A Pocket Guide to Daily Scriptural Prayer. 1982. pap. 3.95 (ISBN 0-89283-168-5). Servant.

--Linger with Me: Moments Aside with Jesus. (Orig.). 1979. 3.50 (ISBN 0-914544-24-1). Living Flame Pr.

--Praying with Mary. 128p. (Orig.). 1980. pap. 2.95 (ISBN 0-914544-31-4). Living Flame Pr.

--Praying with Scripture in the Holy Land: Daily Meditations with the Risen Jesus. (Orig.). 1977. pap. 2.95 (ISBN 0-914544-14-4). Living Flame Pr.

Rosaldo, Michael Z. Knowledge & Passion. LC 79-12632. (Cambridge Studies in Cultural Systems). (Illus.). 1980. 29.95 (ISBN 0-521-22582-5); pap. 8.95 (ISBN 0-521-29562-9). Cambridge U Pr.

Rosaldo, Michelle Z. & Lamphere, Louise, eds. Woman, Culture & Society. LC 73-89861. 368p. 1974. 17.50x (ISBN 0-8047-0850-9); pap. 6.95 (ISBN 0-8047-0851-7, SP133). Stanford U Pr.

Rosaldo, Michelle Z., jt. ed. see Keohane, Nannerl O.

Rosaldo, R., et al. Chicano: The Evolution of a People. rev. ed. LC 76-46344. 478p. 1981. pap. text ed. 17.50 o.p. (ISBN 0-88275-467-X). Krieger.

Rosaldo, Renato & Calvert, Robert A. Chicano: The Evolution of a People. 2nd ed. LC 82-10091. 428p. 1982. lib. bdg. 17.50 (ISBN 0-89874-151-3). Krieger.

Rosaler, Bob, jt. auth. see Rice, James O.

Rosaluk, Warren. Throw Away Your Resume & Get That Job. (Illus.). 132p. 1983. 12.95 (ISBN 0-13-920587-X); pap. 5.95 (ISBN 0-13-920595-0). P-H.

Rosand, David, jt. auth. see Hanning, Robert W.

Rosberg, Carl G., jt. auth. see Jackson, Robert H.

Rosberg, Carl G. & Callaghy, Thomas M., eds. Socialism in Sub-Saharan Africa: A New Assessment. LC 79-84635. (Research Ser.: No. 38). (Illus.). 1979. pap. 12.95x (ISBN 0-87725-138-X). U of Cal Intl St.

Rosberg, Carl G., jt. ed. see Price, Robert M.

Rosberg, Robert. Game of Thieves. (Illus.). 272p. 1982. 12.95 (An Everest House Book). Dodd.

Rosbotham, Lyle. Kew, The Royal Botanic Gardens. (Illus.). 52p. 1982. pap. 30.00 (ISBN 0-917796-02-0). Press Four Fifty One.

Rosbottom, Ronald C. Choderlos de Laclos. (World Authors Ser.). 1978. 15.95 (ISBN 0-8057-6343-0, Twayne). G K Hall.

Roscher, Wilhelm & Hillman, James, eds. Pan & the Nightmare: Two Essays. (Dunquin Ser.: No. 4). 151p. 1972. pap. text ed. 7.50 (ISBN 0-88214-204-6). Spring Pubns.

Roscoe, Adrian A. Uhuru's Fires: African Literature East to South. LC 76-3038. 280p. 1977. 42.50 (ISBN 0-521-21295-2); pap. 12.95 (ISBN 0-521-29089-9). Cambridge U Pr.

Roscoe, Henry. Lives of Eminent British Lawyers. 428p. 1982. Repr. of 1830 ed. lib. bdg. 35.00x (ISBN 0-8377-1037-5). Rothman.

Roscow, Judith, jt. auth. see Klein, Barbara.

Rosdahl, Caroline B., jt. auth. see Story, Donna K.

Rose. Build Your Own Eiffel Tower. 1982. 7.95 (ISBN 0-399-50535-0). Putnam Pub Group.

--Invasive Radiology. 1983. 17.50 (ISBN 0-8151-7394-6). Year Bk Med.

Rose, A. H. & Harrison, J. S., eds. The Yeasts. Incl. Vol. 1. 1969. 80.50 o.p. (ISBN 0-12-596401-3); Vol. 2. Physiology & Biochemistry of Yeasts. 1971. 91.00 (ISBN 0-12-596402-1); Vol. 3. 1970. o.s. 94.00 (ISBN 0-12-596403-X). Acad Pr.

Rose, A. H. & Morris, J. Gareth, eds. Advances in Microbial Physiology, Vol. 23. (Serial Publication). 268p. 1982. 43.50 (ISBN 0-12-027723-9). Acad Pr.

Rose, A. H., jt. ed. see Hughes, D. E.

Rose, A. H., et al, eds. Advances in Microbial Physiology. Incl. Vol. 1. 1967. o.p. (ISBN 0-12-027701-8); Vol. 2. 1968. 34.50 (ISBN 0-12-027702-6); Vol. 3. 1969. 40.00 (ISBN 0-12-027703-4); Vol. 4. 1970. 56.50 (ISBN 0-12-027704-2); Vol. 5. 1970. 45.00 (ISBN 0-12-027705-0); Vol. 6. 1971. 58.50 (ISBN 0-12-027706-9); Vol. 7. Rose, A. H. & Tempest, D. W., eds. 1972. 49.50 (ISBN 0-12-027707-7); Vol. 8. 1972. 43.50 (ISBN 0-12-027708-5); Vol. 9. 1973. 40.50 (ISBN 0-12-027709-3); Vol. 10. 1973. 48.00 (ISBN 0-12-027710-7); Vol. 14. 1977. 66.00 (ISBN 0-12-027714-X); Vol. 15. 1977. 71.00 (ISBN 0-12-027715-8); Vol. 16. 1978. 60.00 (ISBN 0-12-027716-6); Vol. 17. 1978. 63.50 (ISBN 0-12-027717-4). Acad Pr.

Rose, A. W. Geochemical Exploration Nineteen Eighty. Gundlach, H., ed. (Developments in Economic Geology Ser.: Vol. 15). 1981. 153.25 (ISBN 0-444-42012-6). Elsevier.

Rose, Al. Born in New Orleans. (Illus.). 1983. 14.50 (ISBN 0-916620-68-9). Portals Pr.

Rose, Alan. B. Y. O. Japanese Pagoda. 1982. 8.95 (ISBN 0-686-98329-7, Perige). Putnam Pub Group.

--Build Your Own Brooklyn Bridge. (The World at Your Feet Ser.). 40p. (gr. 10 up). 1980. pap. 7.95 (ISBN 0-399-50504-0, Perige). Putnam Pub Group.

--Build Your Own Cable Car. (The World on the Move Ser.). 40p. 1982. pap. 8.95 (ISBN 0-399-50558-X, Perige). Putnam Pub Group.

--Build Your Own Chrysler Building. (The World at Your Feet Ser.). 40p. (gr. 10 up). 1980. pap. 7.95 (ISBN 0-399-50505-9, Perige). Putnam Pub Group.

--Build Your Own Empire State Building. (The World at Your Feet Ser.). 40p. (gr. 10 up). 1980. pap. 7.95 (ISBN 0-399-50506-7, Perige). Putnam Pub Group.

--Build Your Own Japanese Pagoda. 40p. 1982. pap. 8.95 (ISBN 0-399-50679-9, Perige). Putnam Pub Group.

--Build Your Own Saturn V. (The World on the Move Ser.). 40p. 1982. pap. 8.95 (ISBN 0-399-50681-0, Perige). Putnam Pub Group.

--Build Your Own Taj Mahal. (The World at Your Feet Ser.). 1981. pap. 7.95 (ISBN 0-399-50562-8, Perige). Putnam Pub Group.

--Build Your Own Titanic. (The World on the Move Ser.). 40p. 1982. pap. 8.95 (ISBN 0-399-50564-4, Perige). Putnam Pub Group.

--Build Your Own Tower of London & Tower Bridge. (The World at Your Feet Ser.). 1982. pap. 8.95 (ISBN 0-399-50566-0, Perige). Putnam Pub Group.

Rose, Albert. Governing Metropolitan Toronto: A Social & Political Analysis 1953-1971. LC 72-157821. (Institute of Governmental Studies, U. C. Berkeley & Lane Studies in Regional Government). 1973. 33.00x (ISBN 0-520-02041-3). U of Cal Pr.

Rose, Allen J. & Schick, Barbara A. APL in Practice. LC 80-5351. 374p. 1980. 32.95 (ISBN 0-471-08275-9, Pub. by Wiley-Interscienc). Wiley.

Rose, Allen J., jt. auth. see Gilman, Leonard.

Rose, Andrew. The Pre-Raphaelites. (Phaidon Color Library). (Illus.). 84p. 1983. 25.00 (ISBN 0-7148-2180-2, Pub. by Salem Hse Ltd); pap. 17.95 (ISBN 0-7148-2166-7). Merrimack Bk Serv.

Rose, Ann. Pot Full of Luck. (Illus.). (ps-3). 1982. 9.50 (ISBN 0-688-00392-3); PLB 8.59 (ISBN 0-688-00393-1). Lothrop.

Rose, Anne. Pot Full of Luck. LC 81-5750. (Illus.). 32p. (ps-3). 1982. cancelled 9.00 (ISBN 0-688-00392-3); PLB 8.59 cancelled (ISBN 0-688-00393-1). Longman.

Rose, Arnold M. Theory & Method in Social Sciences. LC 73-17922. 351p. 1974. Repr. of 1954 ed. lib. bdg. 18.50x (ISBN 0-8371-7277-2, ROSS). Greenwood.

Rose, Bernice. A Century of Modern Drawing. 160p. 1982. 40.00x (ISBN 0-7141-0791-3, Pub. by Brit Mus Pubns England). State Mutual Bk.

Rose, Brian, ed. Modern Trends in Education. LC 79-174706. 1972. 22.50 (ISBN 0-312-54250-X). St Martin.

Rose, Burton D. Clinical Physiology of Acid Base & Electrolyte Disorders. 1st ed. (Illus.). 1977. pap. text ed. 19.95 (ISBN 0-07-053621-X, HP). McGraw.

--Pathophysiology of Renal Disease. (Illus.). 1981. 29.95 (ISBN 0-07-053616-3); pap. text ed. 19.95 (ISBN 0-07-053615-5). McGraw.

Rose, C. W. Agricultural Physics. 1966. 17.75 o.s.i. (ISBN 0-08-011885-2); pap. 12.00 o.p. (ISBN 0-08-011884-4). Pergamon.

Rose, Carol. Teaching Language Arts to Children. 510p. 1982. text ed. 21.95 (ISBN 0-15-588808-0, HC). HarBraceJ.

Rose, Carol M. Some Emerging Issues in Legal Liability of Children's Agencies. LC 77-88236. 1978. pap. 6.90 (ISBN 0-87868-173-6, AM-30). Child Welfare.

Rose, Christina. Astrological Counseling. 128p. 1983. pap. 7.95 (ISBN 0-85030-301-X). Newcastle Pub.

Rose, Cissy. Willie & Billie & Other Tales for Children. 1980. 4.50 o.p. (ISBN 0-8062-1343-4). Carlton.

Rose, Clifford & Capildeo, Rudy. Stroke: The Facts. (The Facts Ser.). (Illus.). 1981. text ed. 12.95x (ISBN 0-19-261170-4, GB701); pap. 6.95. Oxford U Pr.

Rose, Clifford F. & Gawel, M. Migraine: The Facts. (Illus.). 1980. text ed. 12.95x (ISBN 0-19-261161-5). Oxford U Pr.

Rose, Clifford F., ed. Advances in Stroke Therapy. 405p. Date not set. text ed. 44.50 (ISBN 0-89004-847-9). Raven.

Rose, Clifford F. & Bynum, W. F., eds. Historical Aspects of the Neurosciences: A Festschrift for Macdonald Critchley. 564p. 1982. text ed. 64.00 (ISBN 0-89004-661-1). Raven.

Rose, Darrell E. Audiological Assessment. 2nd ed. 1978. 25.95 (ISBN 0-13-050815-2). P-H.

Rose, David, jt. auth. see Radford, John.

Rose, Dorothy. Really Big Shoe. Klimo, Kate, ed. (Playboards Ser.). (Illus.). 5p. (ps-1). Date not set. bds. 3.95 (ISBN 0-671-45309-2, Little Simon). S&S. Postponed.

Rose, E. Cases of Conscience. LC 74-76947. 272p. 1975. 42.50 (ISBN 0-521-20462-3). Cambridge U Pr.

Rose, Earlene. Rose's for You: Poems. 1982. 4.95 (ISBN 0-916620-66-2). Portals Pr.

Rose, Edgar & Bozeat, Nicholas. Communal Facilities in Sheltered Housing. 1980. text ed. 29.50x (ISBN 0-566-00354-6). Gower Pub Ltd.

Rose, Elizabeth & Rose, Gerald. How St. Francis Tamed the Wolf. (ps-1). 1983. 8.95 (ISBN 0-686-38879-8, Pub. by Chatto & Windus). Merrimack Bk Serv.

Rose, Elizabeth, jt. auth. see Rose, Gerald.

Rose, Elizabeth A. The Lizzie's Own Journal La Vie Heureuse. Carson, Robert R., ed. 1983. 10.00 (ISBN 0-686-84439-4). Vantage.

Rose, Elizabeth A. & Carson, Robert R. Lizzie's Own Journal: La Vie Heureuse. 1983. 10.00 (ISBN 0-533-05628-4). Vantage.

Rose, Ellen C. The Tree Outside the Window: Doris Lessing's "Children of Violence". LC 76-44671. 94p. 1976. text ed. 11.00x (ISBN 0-8357-0189-1, Pub. by Univ. Microfilms Intl. Order form). U Pr of New Eng.

Rose, Ernst. A History of German Literature. LC 60-9405. (Gotham Library). (Orig.). 1960. 12.00x o.p. (ISBN 0-8147-0362-3); pap. 9.50x o.p. (ISBN 0-8147-0363-1). NYU Pr.

Rose, F. Clifford, jt. auth. see Perkin, G. D.

Rose, F. Clifford & Capildeo, Rudy, eds. Research Progress in Parkinson's Disease. 448p. 1981. pap. text ed. 54.50 (ISBN 0-272-79601-8). Pitman Pub MA.

Rose, Francis. Lichens as Pollution Monitors. (Studies in Biology: No. 66). 64p. 1976. pap. text ed. 8.95 (ISBN 0-7131-2555-1). E Arnold.

Rose, George & Rose, Margaret, eds. Letters of General Peleg Wadsworth to His Son John, Student at Harvard College, 1796-1798. 1961. pap. 3.00 o.p. (ISBN 0-915592-05-3). Maine Hist.

Rose, George G. My Three Voyages in a Square-Rigged Sailing Ship. 1982. 9.00 (ISBN 0-533-05437-0). Vantage.

Rose, Gerald. How George Lost His Voice. (Illus.). 32p. (ps). 1983. bds. 8.95 (ISBN 0-370-30435-7, Pub by The Bodley Head). Merrimack Bk Serv.

--Intellectual Property Law Review, 1982. LC 79-88703. 1982. 57.50 (ISBN 0-87632-148-1). Boardman.

--Patent Law Handbook, 1982-83. LC 78-17713. 1982. 27.50 (ISBN 0-87632-253-4). Boardman.

--PB on Ice. (Illus.). 32p. (ps). 1983. bds. 8.95 (ISBN 0-370-30464-0, Pub by The Bodley Head). Merrimack Bk Serv.

Rose, Gerald & Rose, Elizabeth. Lucky Hans. (Illus.). 32p. (ps-5). 1976. 8.95 o.p. (ISBN 0-571-10905-5). Faber & Faber.

--Punch & Judy Carry on. (Illus.). (ps-5). Date not set. cancelled o.s.i. (ISBN 0-571-05161-8). Faber & Faber.

Rose, Gerald, jt. auth. see Rose, Elizabeth.

Rose, Gordon & Marshall, Tony M. Counselling & School Social Work: An Experimental Study. LC 74-1752. 345p. 1975. 33.95 o.p. (ISBN 0-471-73549-3, Pub. by Wiley-Interscience). Wiley.

Rose, H. J., tr. see Plutarchus.

Rose, Harold. Your Guide to Northern Italy. LC 65-50296. (Your Guide Ser). (Illus.). 1965. 5.25x o.p. (ISBN 0-8002-0783-1). Intl Pubns Serv.

Rose, Harold M. Black Suburbanization: Access to Improved Quality of Life or Maintenance of the Status Quo. LC 76-49004. 304p. 1976. prof ref 20.00x (ISBN 0-88410-445-1). Ballinger Pub.

Rose, Harold M., ed. Lethal Aspects of Urban Violence. LC 77-18680. (Illus.). 128p. 1979. 16.95x (ISBN 0-669-02117-2). Lexington Bks.

Rose, Harvey. Solar Energy Now. LC 81-70870. 222p. 1982. 19.95 (ISBN 0-250-40537-7). Ann Arbor Science.

Rose, Harvey & Pinkerton, Amy. The Energy Crisis, Conservation & Solar. LC 81-66619. 210p. 1981. text ed. 14.95 (ISBN 0-250-40460-5); pap. 9.95 (ISBN 0-250-40482-6). Ann Arbor Science.

Rose, Helen W. Quilting with Strips & Strings: Full with Complete Instructions for Making 12 Patchwork Quiltblocks. (Quilting Ser.). (Illus.). 48p. (Orig.). 1983. pap. 3.25 (ISBN 0-486-24357-5). Dover.

Rose, Herbert J. Handbook of Greek Mythology. 1959. pap. 5.50 (ISBN 0-525-47041-7, 0534-160). Dutton.

Rose, Hilary & Rose, Steven. Ideology of-In the Natural Sciences. 363p. 1980. pap. text ed. 11.95x (ISBN 0-87073-881-X). Schenkman.

Rose, Howard N. A Thesaurus of Slang. LC 72-167144. xii, 120p. Repr. of 1934 ed. 34.00x (ISBN 0-8103-3115-2). Gale.

Rose, I. H. Elementary Functions: A Precalculus Primer. 1973. text ed. 16.50x (ISBN 0-673-07625-3). Scott F.

Rose, Irene B., jt. auth. see Conger, Flora S.

Rose, Israel H. & Phillips, Esther R. Elementary Functions for Precalculus Mathematics. 1978. text ed. 17.95x (ISBN 0-673-15069-0). Scott F.

Rose, J. Progress of Cybernetics, 3 vols. 1406p. 1970. Set. 255.00 (ISBN 0-677-14190-4). Gordon.

Rose, J., ed. Advances in Cybernetics & Systems, 3 vols. 1728p. 1974. Set. 257.00x (ISBN 0-677-15650-2). Gordon.

Rose, J., ed. see Hutchins, John G. B.

Rose, J., ed. see Lacan, J.

Rose, J. J., jt. auth. see Bowcock, Philip.

Rose, J. W. & Cooper, J., eds. Technical Data on Fuel: S. I. Units. 7th rev. ed. LC 77-24872. 1978. 99.95 o.s.i. (ISBN 0-470-99239-5). Halsted Pr.

Rose, Jacqueline, tr. see Lacan, Jacques & Ecole Freudienne.

Rose, James H., jt. auth. see Lee, Ruth W.

Rose, James M. & Eichholz, Alice, eds. Black Genesis: An Annotated Bibliography for Black Genealogical Research. LC 77-74819. (Genealogy & Local History Ser.: Vol. 1). (Illus.). 1978. 42.00x (ISBN 0-8103-1400-2). Gale.

Rose, James M., jt. ed. see Eichholz, Alice.

Rose, Jeanne. Ask Jeanne Rose About Herbs. Passwater, Richard & Mindell, Earl, eds. (Good Health Guide Ser.). 36p. (Orig.). 1983. pap. text ed. 1.45 (ISBN 0-87983-315-7). Keats.

--Herbs & Things: Jeanne Rose's Herbal. 1972. 5.95 (ISBN 0-448-01139-5, G&D). Putnam Pub Group.

--Jeanne Rose's Herbal Body Book. (Illus.). 400p. Date not set. pap. price not set (ISBN 0-448-12242-1, G&D). Putnam Pub Group.

--Jeanne Rose's Herbal Guide to Inner Health. (Illus.). 1978. 10.00 o.p. (ISBN 0-448-14555-3, G&D); pap. 6.95 1980 (ISBN 0-448-14522-7). Putnam Pub Group.

--Kitchen Cosmetics: Using Plants & Herbs in Cosmetics. LC 77-17077. 1978. 9.95 (ISBN 0-915572-25-7); pap. 5.95 (ISBN 0-915572-24-9). Panjandrum.

Rose, Jennifer. Out of a Dream. (Second Chance at Love, Contemporary Ser.: No. 4). 192p. (Orig.). 1981. pap. 1.75 o.s.i. (ISBN 0-515-05777-0). Jove Pubns.

--Twilight Embrace, No. 86. 1982. pap. 1.75 (ISBN 0-515-06697-4). Jove Pubns.

Rose, Jerome G. Legal Foundations of Environmental Planning. 488p. 1983. text ed. 22.95x (ISBN 0-88285-090-3, Dist. by Transaction Bks). Ctr Urban Pol Res.

--Tax Expenditure Limitations: How to Implement & Live Within Them. 255p. 1982. 20.00 (ISBN 0-88285-078-4). Transaction Bks.

Rose, Jerry. Outbreaks. 256p. 1981. 9.95 (ISBN 0-02-926790-0). Free Pr.

Rose, Jerry D. Introduction to Sociology. 4th ed. 1980. pap. 16.50 (ISBN 0-395-30714-7); Tchrs Manual 1.00 (ISBN 0-395-30715-5). HM.

--Peoples. 1976. pap. 15.00 (ISBN 0-395-30716-3). HM.

Rose, Jerry G., ed. Proceedings: Fifth Kentucky Coal Refuse Disposal & Utilization Seminar & Stability Analysis of Refuse Dams Workshop. 75p. 1980. pap. text ed. 10.00 (ISBN 0-686-94732-0). Inst Mining & Minerals.

Rose, John E., Jr. Big Words for Big Shooters. 272p. (Orig.). 1982. pap. 6.95 (ISBN 0-89696-151-6, An Everest House Book). Dodd.

Rose, John S. A Course on Group Theory. LC 76-22984. (Illus.). 1978. 57.50 (ISBN 0-521-21409-2); pap. 19.95x (ISBN 0-521-29142-9). Cambridge U Pr.

Rose, Joseph. They Called Him Wild Bill. 1974. 7.95 (ISBN 0-8061-1217-4). Jefferson Natl.

Rose, Joseph L., et al. Basic Physics in Diagnostic Ultrasound. LC 79-14932. 1979. 38.50 (ISBN 0-471-05735-5, Pub. by Wiley Medical). Wiley.

Rose, June. Elizabeth Fry: A Biography. 1980. 25.00 (ISBN 0-312-24248-4). St Martin.

Rose, Karen. There Is a Season. 1969. pap. 1.25 o.p. (ISBN 0-380-01517-X, 39537). Avon.

Rose, Kenneth J. Classification of the Animal Kingdom. 1980. 8.95 o.s.i. (ISBN 0-679-20508-X). McKay.

Rose, L. M. Application of Mathematical Modelling to Process Development & Design. 1974. 53.50 (ISBN 0-85334-584-8). Elsevier.

--Engineering Investment Decisions. 1976. 40.50 (ISBN 0-444-41522-X). Elsevier.

Rose, L. M., ed. Chemical Reactor Design in Practice. (Chemical Engineering Monographs: Vol. 13). 1981. 70.25 (ISBN 0-444-42018-5). Elsevier.

Rose, Larry L. & Hadaway, C. Kirk, eds. The Urban Challenge. LC 82-71026. 1982. pap. 5.95 (ISBN 0-8054-6238-4). Broadman.

Rose, Leo E. Nepal: Strategy for Survival. LC 75-100022. (Center of South & Southeast Asia Studies, UC Berkeley). 1971. 36.50x (ISBN 0-520-01643-2). U of Cal Pr.

Rose, Leo E. & Scholz, John T. Nepal: Profile of a Himalayan Kingdom. LC 79-17857. (Nations of Contemporary Asia Ser.). (Illus.). 150p. 1980. lib. bdg. 16.50 (ISBN 0-89158-651-2). Westview.

Rose, Linda. Hands. 1980. 14.95 o.s.i. (ISBN 0-671-24944-4). S&S.

Rose, Lisle A. The Long Shadow: Reflections on the Second World War Era. LC 77-84760. (Contributions in American History: No.70). 1978. lib. bdg. 27.50x (ISBN 0-8371-9892-5, ROL/). Greenwood.

--The Roots of Tragedy: The United States & the Struggle for Asia, 1945-1953. LC 75-35354. (Contributions in American History: No. 48). 352p. 1976. lib. bdg. 29.95x (ISBN 0-8371-8592-0, RRT/). Greenwood.

Rose, Louis F. & Kaye, Donald. Internal Medicine for Dentistry. (Illus.). 1408p. 1983. text ed. 41.50 (ISBN 0-8016-4200-0). Mosby.

Rose, Louis F., jt. auth. see Kaye, Donald.

Rose, Louisa, ed. see Anderson, Barrie, et al.

Rose, M. A., jt. auth. see Jaswon, M. A.

Rose, M. E. & Johnstone, R. A. Mass Spectrometry for Chemists & Biochemists. LC 81-10122. (Cambridge Texts in Chemistry & Biochemistry). 275p. 1982. 49.50 (ISBN 0-521-23729-7); pap. 19.95 (ISBN 0-521-28184-9). Cambridge U Pr.

Rose, Margaret, jt. ed. see Rose, George.

Rose, Marilyn. Translation Spectrum: Essays in Theory & Practice. 1980. 33.50x (ISBN 0-87395-436-X); pap. 8.95x (ISBN 0-87395-437-8). State U NY Pr.

Rose, Mark. Alien Encounters: Anatomy of Science Fiction. LC 81-683. 224p. 1981. 12.95x (ISBN 0-674-01565-7); pap. 4.95. Harvard U Pr.

Rose, Mark H., jt. ed. see Daniels, George H.

Rose, Martial, ed. Wakefield Mystery Plays. 1969. pap. 8.95x (ISBN 0-393-00483-X, Norton Lib). Norton.

Rose, Martin R., et al. The Past Climate of Arroyo Hondo, New Mexico, Reconstructed from Tree Rings. LC 80-21834. (Arroyo Hondo Archaeological Ser.: Vol. 4). (Illus., Orig.). 1981. pap. 7.50 (ISBN 0-933452-05-5). Schol Am Res.

Rose, Mary C. Clara Barton: Soldier of Mercy. LC 60-7080. (Discovery Books Ser). (Illus.). (gr. 2-5). 1960. PLB 6.69 (ISBN 0-8116-6250-0). Garrard.

Rose, Michael. French Industrial Studies. 148p. 1977. text ed. 25.50x (ISBN 0-566-00207-8). Gower Pub Ltd.

--Servants of Post-Industrial Power: Sociologie Du Travail in Modern France. LC 78-65594. 1979. 27.50 (ISBN 0-87332-130-8). M E Sharpe.

Rose, Michael D. Selected Federal Taxation Statutes & Regulations, 1981. 1264p. 1982. pap. 12.95 (ISBN 0-314-68630-4); 1983 supplement avail. (ISBN 0-314-72244-0). West Pub.

Rose, Mitchel D., jt. auth. see Luria, Zella.

Rose, Nicholas J., jt. auth. see Ritger, Paul D.

Rose, Noel & Bigazzi, Pierluigi E. Methods in Immunodiagnosis. 2nd ed. LC 80-15273. (Techniques in Pure & Applied Microbiology). 269p. 1980. 27.50 (ISBN 0-471-02208-X, Pub. by Wiley Med). Wiley.

Rose, Noel R. & Milgrom, Felix, eds. Principles of Immunology. 2nd ed. (Illus.). 1979. pap. text ed. 19.95 (ISBN 0-02-403610-2). Macmillan.

Rose, Noel R. & Siegel, Benjamin, eds. The Reticuloendothelial System: A Comprehensive Treatise, Immunopathology, Vol. 4. 430p. 1982. 55.00x (ISBN 0-306-40979-8, Plenum Pr). Plenum Pub.

Rose, Pat R. The Solar Boat Book. rev. ed. 266p. 1983. 14.95 (ISBN 0-89815-089-2); pap. 8.95 (ISBN 0-89815-086-8). Ten Speed Pr.

Rose, Peter I. Mainstream & Margins: Jews, Blacks, & Other Americans. 241p. 1983. 24.95 (ISBN 0-87855-473-4). Transaction Bks.

Rose, Peter I., ed. Nation of Nations: The Ethnic Experience & the Racial Crisis. LC 81-40797. 366p. 1981. pap. text ed. 13.50 (ISBN 0-8191-1801-X). U Pr of Amer.

--The Study of Society: An Integrated Anthology. 4th ed. 1977. pap. text ed. 11.95x (ISBN 0-394-31229-5). Random.

Rose, Peter J. They & We. 190p. pap. 7.95 (ISBN 0-686-95008-9). ADL.

Rose, Peter L. De see De Rose, Peter L.

Rose, Phyllis. Woman of Letters: A Life of Virginia Woolf. (Illus.). 1978. 18.95x (ISBN 0-19-502370-6). Oxford U Pr.

--Woman of Letters: A Life of Virginia Woolf. (Illus.). 1979. pap. 6.95 (ISBN 0-19-502621-7, GB 589, GB). Oxford U Pr.

Rose, R. B. The Making of the Sans-Culottes: Democratic Ideas & Institutions in Paris 1789-92. 224p. 1982. 22.50 (ISBN 0-7190-0879-4). Manchester.

Rose, R. M., et al. Electronic Properties. LC 66-16132. (Structure & Properties of Materials, Vol. 4). 1966. pap. text ed. 18.95 (ISBN 0-471-73548-5). Wiley.

Rose, R. M., et al see Wulff, J.

Rose, Richard. Politics in England. 3rd ed. 392p. 1980. pap. text ed. 10.95 (ISBN 0-316-75641-5). Little.

--The Territorial Dimension in Government: Understanding the United Kingdom. 1982. pap. 12.95x (ISBN 0-934540-16-0). Chatham Hse Pubs.

Rose, Richard & McAllister, Ian. United Kingdom Facts. 160p. 1982. 80.00x (ISBN 0-333-25341-8, Pub. by Macmillan England). State Mutual Bk.

Rose, Richard, ed. Studies in British Politics. 3rd. ed. LC 76-11279. 1977. 25.00x (ISBN 0-312-77070-7). St Martin.

Rose, Richard & Page, Edward C., eds. Fiscal Stress in Cities. LC 82-9500. (Illus.). 256p. Date not set. 29.95 (ISBN 0-521-24607-5). Cambridge U Pr.

Rose, Richard, jt. ed. see Madgwick, Peter.

Rose, Sheldon D. A Casebook in Group Therapy: A Behavioral-Cognitive Approach. (Social Work Practice Ser.). (Illus.). 1979. text ed. 18.95 (ISBN 0-13-117408-8). P-H.

--Group Therapy: A Behavioral Approach. (Illus.). 1977. 23.95 (ISBN 0-13-365239-4). P-H.

Rose, Stanley F. The Peruvian Revolution's Approach: Investment Policy & Investor Climate 1968-Present. LC 81-80767. xiii, 518p. 1981. lib. bdg. 32.50 (ISBN 0-89941-097-9). W S Hein.

Rose, Steven. The Conscious Brain. 1976. pap. 6.95 (ISBN 0-394-71146-7, Vin). Random.

Rose, Steven, jt. auth. see Rose, Hilary.

Rose, Stuart. Royal Mail Stamps. 29.95. StanGib Ltd.

Rose, T. & Rider, R. Corrosion of Metals in Concrete. (Technical Report Ser.: No. 58). 142p. 1977. 2.00 (ISBN 0-938412-28-0, P629). URI Mas.

Rose, Warren. Logistics Management: Systems & Components. 650p. 1979. text ed. write for info. (ISBN 0-697-08026-9); instrs.' manual avail. (ISBN 0-697-08199-0). Wm C Brown.

Rose, Wendy. What Happened When the Hopi Hit New York. (Contact II Chapbook Ser.). (Illus.). 56p. (Orig.). 1982. pap. 3.50 (ISBN 0-936556-08-0, Pub. by Inland Book Co). Contact Two.

Rose, William, ed. The History of the Damnable Life & Deserved Death of Doctor John Faustus: Together with the Second Report of Faustus Containing His Appearances and the Deeds of Wagner, 1592. 327p. 1982. Repr. of 1982 ed. lib. bdg. 40.00 (ISBN 0-8495-1717-6). Arden Lib.

Rose, Willie L. A Documentary History of Slavery in North America. LC 75-16906. 1976. 35.00x (ISBN 0-19-501976-8); pap. text ed. 14.95x (ISBN 0-19-501978-4). Oxford U Pr.

--Rehearsal for Reconstruction: The Port Royal Experiment. LC 76-9266. (Illus.). 1976. 22.50x (ISBN 0-19-519881-6). Oxford U Pr.

--Rehearsal for Reconstruction: The Port Royal Experiment. 1976. pap. 10.95x (ISBN 0-19-519882-4, GB). Oxford U Pr.

--Slavery & Freedom. Freehling, William H., ed. 1982. 17.95x (ISBN 0-19-502969-0). Oxford U Pr.

--Slavery & Freedom. expanded ed. Freehling, William W., ed. 272p. 1983. pap. 7.95 (ISBN 0-19-503266-7, GB 723, GB). Oxford U Pr.

Rose-Ackerman, Susan. Corruption: A Study in Political Economy. 1978. 27.00 (ISBN 0-12-596350-5). Acad Pr.

Roseau, M. Asymptotic Wave Theory. LC 74-26167. (Applied Mathematics & Mechanics Ser.: Vol. 20). 349p. 1976. 68.00 (ISBN 0-444-10798-3, North-Holland). Elsevier.

Rosebaum, Robert A., ed. see Neumann, Inge S.

Roseberry, C. R. From Niagara to Montauk: The Scenic Pleasures of New York State. LC 81-5640. (Illus.). 242p. 1981. 34.50x (ISBN 0-87395-496-3); pap. 10.95 (ISBN 0-87395-497-1). State U NY Pr.

Roseberry, Eric, ed. Faber Book of Carols & Christmas Songs. Date not set. pap. price not set. Faber & Faber.

Roseboro, John & Libby, Bill. Glory Days with the Dodgers: And Other Days with Others. LC 77-23697. 1978. 9.95 o.p. (ISBN 0-689-10864-8). Atheneum.

Rosebush, Waldo E. American Firearms & the Changing Frontier. 1962. pap. 4.50 (ISBN 0-910524-01-7). Eastern Wash.

Rosecrance, Barbara. Voice & Vision. LC 23-71598. 248p. 1982. 22.50x (ISBN 0-8014-1502-0). Cornell U Pr.

Rosecrance, Richard. International Relations: Peace or War. (Illus.). 288p. (Orig.). 1972. pap. text ed. 18.95 (ISBN 0-07-053698-8, C). McGraw.

Rosefielde, Steven. False Science: Underestimating the Soviet Threat. LC 81-1050. 300p. 1982. text ed. 14.95 (ISBN 0-87855-868-3). Transaction Bk.

Rosefsky, Robert. The Ins & Outs of Moving. 288p. 1972. pap. 2.45 o.s.i. (ISBN 0-695-80342-5). Follett.

--Personal Finance: Television Course. 2nd ed. 736p. 1982. text ed. 19.95 (ISBN 0-471-09201-0); study guide avail. (ISBN 0-471-86818-3). Wiley.

--Rosefsky's Guide to Financial Security for the Mature Family. (Deluxe ed). 1977. pap. 7.95 o.s.i. (ISBN 0-695-80549-5). Follett.

Rosefsky, Robert S. Money Talks: Bob Rosefsky's Complete Program for Financial Success. LC 82-8561. 687p. 1982. 14.95 (ISBN 0-471-87330-6); study guide avail. (ISBN 0-471-87103-6). Wiley.

--Personal Finance & Money Management. LC 77-20283. 1978. text ed. 19.95 o.p. (ISBN 0-471-01740-X); tchr.'s manual 4.00 o.p. (ISBN 0-471-03762-1); study guide by M. H. Ivener avail. o.p.; supple. 8.00 o.p. (ISBN 0-471-08563-4). Wiley.

Rosefsky, Robert S., jt. auth. see Ivener, Martin H.

Rose-Hancock, Marga, jt. ed. see McCrone, Carole N.

Rose-Innes, A. C. Introduction to Superconductivity. 244p. 1969. text ed. 26.40 o.p. (ISBN 0-08-013469-6); pap. 18.15 o.p. (ISBN 0-08-019011-1). Pergamon.

Roseliep, Raymond. Listen to Light: Haiku. LC 80-39854. (Illus.). 128p. 1980. 10.00 (ISBN 0-934184-05-4); pap. 5.00 o. p. (ISBN 0-934184-06-2). Alembic Pr.

--Sky in My Legs. (Haiku Ser.: No. 7). 1980. pap. 3.00 (ISBN 0-686-61809-2). Juniper Pr WI.

--Wake to the Bell: A Garland of Christmas Poems. 1977. pap. 1.75 o.p. (ISBN 0-916684-20-2). Rook Pr.

Roseliep, Raymond, ed. Ino the Round Air. 1977. pap. 3.50 o.p. (ISBN 0-916684-08-3). Rook Pr.

Roselip, Raymond. Step on the Rain: Haiku. 1977. pap. 2.95 o.p. (ISBN 0-916684-23-7). Rook Pr.

Roselle, Daniel. Samuel Griswold Goodrich, Creator of Peter Parley. LC 68-19534. 1968. 27.50x (ISBN 0-87395-033-X). State U Ny Pr.

Roselle, William C., jt. auth. see Gabriel, Michael R.

Roseman, Ed. Casebook for Sales Managers. 1975. pap. 24.95 plastic spiral binder (ISBN 0-686-98293-2). Sales & Mktg.

--Salesman to Sales Manager. 1975. pap. 24.95 plastic spiral binder (ISBN 0-686-98292-4). Sales & Mktg.

Roseman, Mansdorf. Controlled Released Delivery Systems. 400p. 1983. 57.50 (ISBN 0-8247-1728-7). Dekker.

Rosemont, Henry & Schwartz, Benjamin, eds. Studies in Classical Chinese Thought. (AAR Thematic Studies). pap. 8.95 (ISBN 0-686-95077-1, 01-24-73). Scholars Pr CA.

--Studies in Classical Chinese Thought. (Thematic Studies). 5.95 o.p. (ISBN 0-686-96206-0, 01-20 47:4). Scholars Pr CA.

Rosemont, Henry, Jr., tr. see Leibniz, Gottfried W.

Rosemont, Henry P. Benjamin Franklin & the Philadelphia Typographical Strikers of 1786. (UPHS Monograph: No. 1). 32p. 5.00 (ISBN 0-686-37775-3). Union Printers Hist Soc.

Rosen. Philosophic Systems & Education. 1968. pap. text ed. 9.50 (ISBN 0-675-09592-1). Merrill.

Rosen, A. & Freiden, R. Word Processing. 2nd ed. 1981. 20.95 (ISBN 0-13-963488-6). P-H.

Rosen, A. & Hubbard, W. Word Processing Keyboarding Applications & Exercises. 291p. 1981. pap. text ed. 19.95 (ISBN 0-471-08700-9); Working Papers 6.95 (ISBN 0-471-09790-X); tchr's. manual 8.00 (ISBN 0-471-07734-8). Wiley.

Rosen, Andrew. Rise up, Women! The Militant Campaign of the Women's Social & Political Union, 1903-1914. (Illus.). 1974. 27.50 (ISBN 0-7100-7934-6). Routledge & Kegan.

Rosen, Arnold & Fielden, Rosemary. Word Processing. 2nd ed. 430p. 1981. 18.95 (ISBN 0-686-98087-5). Telecom Lib.

Rosen, Arnold, et al. Administrative Procedures for the Electronic Office. LC 81-11431. 520p. 1982. text ed. 19.95 (ISBN 0-471-08700-9); study guide 8.95 (ISBN 0-471-86469-2); tchrs. manual avail. (ISBN 0-471-86579-6). Wiley.

Rosen, Bernard. Strategies of Ethics. LC 77-77431. (Illus.). 1978. text ed. 17.95 (ISBN 0-395-25077-3); instr's. manual 0.65 (ISBN 0-395-25078-1). HM.

Rosen, Carol. Plays of Impasse: The Institutional Setting in Contemporary Drama. LC 82-61381. (Illus.). 304p. 1983. 20.00x (ISBN 0-691-06565-9). Princeton U Pr.

Rosen, Ceil & Rosen, Moishe. Christ in the Passover. LC 77-10689. 1978. pap. 3.95 (ISBN 0-8024-1392-7). Moody.

Rosen, David, ed. Verdi's Macbeth: A Source Book. (Illus.). 700p. 1981. text ed. 29.95x (ISBN 0-393-95073-5). Norton.

Rosen, Doris B. Employment Testing & Minority Groups. (Key Issues Ser.: No. 6). 36p. 1970. pap. 2.00 o.s.i. (ISBN 0-87546-239-1). ILR Pr.

Rosen, F., ed. see Bentham, Jeremy.

Rosen, George. Democracy & Economic Change in India. rev. ed. 1966. 32.50x (ISBN 0-520-01089-2). U of Cal Pr.

Rosen, Gerald. The Relaxation Book: An Illustrated Self-Help Program. (Psychology Today Book Club). (Illus.). 1977. 10.95 (ISBN 0-13-772210-9, Spec); pap. 4.95 (ISBN 0-13-772202-8, Spec). P-H.

Rosen, Gerald M. The Relaxation Book: An Illustrated Self-Help Program. 4.95 o.p. (ISBN 0-686-92399-5, 6611). Hazelden.

Rosen, Haiim B. A Textbook of Israeli Hebrew: With an Introduction to the Classical Language. 2nd ed. LC 62-9116. 1976. pap. text ed. 12.00x (ISBN 0-226-72603-7, P689, Phoen, P684). U of Chicago Pr.

Rosen, Harold. Language & Class: A Critcal Look at the Theories of Basil Bernstein. 3rd ed. 23p. 1974. pap. 1.75 (ISBN 0-9502702-1-0). Falling Wall.

Rosen, Harold J. Construction Specifications Writing. 2nd ed. LC 81-5001. (Practical Construction Guides Ser.). 240p. 1981. 27.95 (ISBN 0-471-08328-3, Pub. by Wiley-Interscience). Wiley.

--Construction Specifications Writing: Principles & Procedures. LC 73-16138. (Practical Construction Guides Ser). 256p. 1974. 24.95 o.p. (ISBN 0-471-73551-5, Pub. by Wiley-Interscience). Wiley.

Rosen, Harold J. & Bennett, Philip M. Construction Materials Evaluation & Selection: A Systematic Approach. LC 79-15885. (Wiley Series of Practical Construction Guides). 1979. 29.95 (ISBN 0-471-73565-5, Pub. by Wiley-Interscience). Wiley.

Rosen, Harry, et al, eds. The Consumer & the Health Care Systems: Social & Managerial Perspectives. (Health Systems Management Ser.: Vol. 9). 1977. 17.95x o.p. (ISBN 0-470-99112-7). Halsted Pr.

Rosen, Hjalmar, jt. auth. see Stagner, Ross.

Rosen, Ira, jt. auth. see Gray, Mike.

Rosen, J. Symmetry Discovered. LC 75-6006. (Illus.). 150p. 1975. 21.95 (ISBN 0-521-20695-2). Cambridge U Pr.

Rosen, James C., jt. ed. see Bond, Lynne A.

Rosen, Joe. A Symmetry Primer for Scientists. 208p. 1983. 26.95 (ISBN 0-471-87672-0, Pub. by Wiley-Interscience). Wiley.

Rosen, Kenneth. A Regional Effects of Residential Construction. 220p. 1983. cancelled (ISBN 0-88410-618-7). Ballinger Pub.

--Seasonal Cycles in the Housing Market: Patterns, Costs & Policies. (Illus.). 1979. text ed. 22.50x (ISBN 0-262-18091-X). MIT Pr.

Rosen, Kenneth D. Condominium Conversions: Ken Rosen's Success Formula for Big Profits. LC 82-11251. 233p. 1983. 19.95 (ISBN 0-13-167049-2, Busn). P-H.

Rosen, Kenneth T., jt. ed. see Kaufman, George.

Rosen, L. S. Topics in Managerial Accounting. 2nd ed. 412p. 1974. text ed. 22.00 o.p. (ISBN 0-07-077690-3, C). McGraw.

Rosen, Laura. Top of the City: New York's Hidden Rooftop World. (Illus.). 1982. 24.95 (ISBN 0-500-01288-1). Thames Hudson.

Rosen, Lawrence R. The Dow Jones-Irwin Guide to Interest. rev. ed. LC 81-67119. 1981. 15.95 (ISBN 0-87094-260-3). Dow Jones-Irwin.

Rosen, Leonard, jt. auth. see Behrens, Laurence.

Rosen, M. & Mitchell, S., eds. The Need for Interpretation: Contemporary Conceptions of the Philospher's Task. 192p. 1982. text ed. 29.50x (ISBN 0-485-11224-8, Althlone Pr). Humanities.

Rosen, M., et al, eds. Habilitation of the Handicapped. 390p. 1977. text ed. 22.95 (ISBN 0-8391-1137-1). Univ Park.

Rosen, M. J. Introduction to Photography: A Self Directing Approach. 2nd ed. LC 81-82564. 1982. 18.50 (ISBN 0-395-29765-6); instr's manual 1.50 (ISBN 0-395-29766-4). HM.

Rosen, Marjorie. Popcorn Venus. (Illus.). 1974. pap. 1.95 o.p. (ISBN 0-380-00177-2, 21410). Avon.

Rosen, Mel, jt. auth. see Kurzban, Stan.

Rosen, Mel, ed. Crosswords: From the Nation's Expert Puzzle Constructors, Fifty Stimulating Stumpers Guaranteed to Challenge & Tantalize any Crossword Connoisseur. 122p. (Orig.). 1983. lib. bdg. 12.90 (ISBN 0-89471-197-0); pap. 4.95 (ISBN 0-89471-196-2). Running Pr.

Rosen, Michael. Hegel's Dialectic & Its Criticism. LC 81-24211. 210p. 1982. 24.95 (ISBN 0-521-24484-6). Cambridge U Pr.

--Mind Your Own Business. LC 74-9969. (Illus.). 96p. (gr. 3 up). 1974. 10.95 (ISBN 0-87599-209-9). S G Phillips.

--You Can't Catch Me. (Illus.). (gr. 2 up). 1983. 9.95 (ISBN 0-233-97345-1). Andre Deutsch.

Rosen, Milton J. Surfactants & Interfacial Phenomena. LC 77-19092. 1978. 36.95 (ISBN 0-471-73600-7, Pub. by Wiley-Interscience). Wiley.

Rosen, Milton J. & Goldsmith, Henry A., eds. Systematic Analysis of Surface-Active Agents. 2nd ed. LC 78-173678. (Chemical Analysis, Vol. 12). 1972. 75.00 (ISBN 0-471-73595-7). Wiley.

Rosen, Moishe. Share the New Life with a Jew. LC 76-7627. 1976. pap. 2.95 (ISBN 0-8024-7898-0). Moody.

--Y'shua. 128p. (Orig.). 1983. pap. 2.95 (ISBN 0-8024-9842-6). Moody.

Rosen, Moishe, jt. auth. see Rosen, Ceil.

Rosen, Peter & Baker, Frank J. Emergency Medicine: Concepts & Clinical Practice, 2 vols. (Illus.). 2016p. 1983. text ed. 99.95 (ISBN 0-8016-3057-6). Mosby.

Rosen, Philip T. The Modern Stentors: Radio Broadcasters & the Federal Government,1920-1934. LC 79-8952. (Contributions in Economics & Economic History: No. 31). (Illus.). 267p. 1980. lib. bdg. 29.95x (ISBN 0-313-21231-7, RMS/). Greenwood.

Rosen, R. D. Psychobabble. LC 77-76465. 1977. 8.95 o.p. (ISBN 0-689-10775-7). Atheneum.

Rosen, Robert. Dynamical Systems Theory in Biology: Stability Theory & Its Applications, Vol. 1. LC 74-126231. (Biomedical Engineering Ser.). 1970. 43.50 o.p. (ISBN 0-471-73550-7, Pub. by Wiley-Interscience). Wiley.

Rosen, Robert, ed. Foundations of Mathematical Biology, 3 vols. Incl. Vol. 1. Subcellular Systems. 1972. 46.50 (ISBN 0-12-597201-6); Vol. 2. Cellular Systems. 1972. 49.50 (ISBN 0-12-597202-4); Vol. 3. 1973. 62.00 (ISBN 0-12-597203-2). 118.00 set (ISBN 0-686-66889-8). Acad Pr.

Rosen, Robert N. A Short History of Charleston. (Illus.). 160p. (Orig.). 1982. pap. 8.95 (ISBN 0-938530-04-6). Lexikos.

Rosen, Ruth. The Lost Sisterhood: Prostitution in America, 1900-1918. LC 81-23678. 245p. 1982. 18.50 (ISBN 0-8018-2664-0). Johns Hopkins.

Rosen, Saul. Lectures on the Measurement & Evaluation of the Performance of Computing Systems. (CBMS Regional Conference Ser.: Vol. 23). (Illus.). vii, 138p. (Orig.). 1976. pap. text ed. 12.00 (ISBN 0-89871-020-0). Soc Indus-Appl Math.

Rosen, Selma. Children's Clothing: Designing, Selecting Fabrics, Patternmaking, Sewing. (Illus.). 150p. 1983. text ed. 15.00 (ISBN 0-87005-430-9). Fairchild.

Rosen, Sidney. Galileo & the Magic Numbers. (Illus.). (gr. 7 up). 1958. 9.95 (ISBN 0-316-75704-7). Little.

Rosen, Stanley. The Role of Sent-Down Youth in the Chinese Cultural Revolution: The Case of Guangzhow. LC 81-80848. (China Research Monographs: No. 19). 112p. 1981. pap. 8.00x (ISBN 0-912966-29-7). IEAS.

Rosen, Stephen L. Fundamental Principles of Polymeric Materials. LC 81-10320. (Society of Plastics Engineers Monographs Ser.). 346p. 1982. 32.50 (ISBN 0-471-08704-1, Pub. by Wiley-Interscience). Wiley.

Rosen, Theodore A. & Daniels, Aubrey C. Performance Management: Improving Quality & Productivity Through Positive Reinforcement. (Illus.). 1982. write for info. (ISBN 0-937100-01-3). Perf Manage.

Rosen, Trix. Strong & Sexy: The New Body Beautiful. (Illus.). 144p. (Orig.). 1983. pap. 9.95 (ISBN 0-933328-59-1). Delilah Bks.

Rosen, Victor J., jt. auth. see Mix, Terence J.

Rosen, Winifred, jt. auth. see Weil, Andrew.

Rosenau, Fred. S. & Chase, Leslie, eds. Business Realities in the Information Industry. 100p. 1983. 39.95 (ISBN 0-942774-10-8). Info Indus.

Rosenau, Fred S., jt. ed. see Henderson, Faye.

Rosenau, Helen. Boullee & Visionary Architecture. 1976. 25.00 o.p. (ISBN 0-517-52569-0, Harmony). Crown.

Rosenau, James N. Public Opinion & Foreign Policy. (Orig.). 1961. pap. text ed. 2.75 (ISBN 0-685-19758-1). Phila Bk Co.

Rosenau, James N., ed. Comparing Foreign Policies: Theories, Findings, & Methods. LC 72-98047. 442p. 1974. 21.50x o.p. (ISBN 0-470-73613-5). Halsted Pr.

Rosenau, Milton D., Jr. Successful Project Management: A Step-by-Step Approach with Practical Examples. LC 80-24720. 266p. 1981. text ed. 25.95 (ISBN 0-534-97977-7). Lifetime Learn.

Rosenau, William. Jewish Ceremonial Institutions & Customs. rev. ed. 3rd. ed. LC 70-78222. (Illus.). 1971. Repr. of 1925 ed. 30.00x (ISBN 0-8103-3402-X). Gale.

Rosenav, Milton D., Jr. Innovation: Managing the Development of Profitable New Products. (Engineering Ser.). 182p. 1982. 25.00 (ISBN 0-534-97934-3). Lifetime Learn.

Rosenbach, A. S. American Jewish Bibliography. 1977. Set. 25.00x (ISBN 0-939084-11-2, BRCB, Pub. by Rosenbach Mus & Lib). U Pr of Va.

Rosenbach, Joseph B., et al. College Algebra. 5th ed. LC 79-135634. 1971. text ed. 25.95 (ISBN 0-471-00473-1); solutions manual avail. (ISBN 0-471-00474-X). Wiley.

--Essentials of Trigonometry. 2nd rev. ed. 1974. text ed. 27.95 (ISBN 0-471-01104-5). Wiley.

Rosenbaum, Bernard L., ed. How to Motivate Today's Workers: Motivational Models for Managers & Supervisors. (Illus.). 192p. 1981. 17.95 (ISBN 0-07-053711-9, P&RB). McGraw.

Rosenbaum, C. Peter & Beebe, John E., III, eds. Psychiatric Treatment: Crisis, Clinic & Consultation. (Illus.). 624p. 1975. text ed. 33.95 (ISBN 0-07-053710-0, HP). McGraw.

Rosenbaum, Edward E. Rheumatology. (New Directions in Therapy Ser.). 1980. pap. 21.50 (ISBN 0-87488-683-X). Med Exam.

Rosenbaum, Ernest H. Living with Cancer. LC 82-2125. (Medical Library). 293p. 1982. pap. 7.95 (ISBN 0-452-25340-3, 4165-9). Mosby.

Rosenbaum, Fred. Architects of Reform: Congregation & Community Leadership, Emanuel of San Francisco. 1849-1980. LC 80-54032. 241p. 1980. 19.95 (ISBN 0-686-30818-2); pap. 9.95 (ISBN 0-686-30819-0). Magnes Mus.

Rosenbaum, H. J., jt. auth. see Hellman, R. G.

Rosenbaum, Helen. Teen Superstar Trivia Quiz Book. (Illus.). 1979. pap. 1.75 o.p. (ISBN 0-451-08899-9, E8899, Sig). NAL.

Rosenbaum, Helen, ed. Beatle's Trivia Quiz Book. (Illus., Orig.). 1978. pap. 1.75 o.p. (ISBN 0-451-08225-7, E8225, Sig). NAL.

Rosenbaum, Jonathan, jt. auth. see Hoberman, J.

Rosenbaum, Judith, ed. Judicial Discipline & Disability Digest. LC 81-65601. 600p. 1981. 400.00; lib. bdg. 200.00. Am Judicature.

Rosenbaum, Judith, jt. ed. see Stewart, Tamara.

Rosenbaum, Kurt. Community of Fate: German-Soviet Diplomatic Relations, 1922-1928. LC 65-18573. 1965. 18.95x (ISBN 0-8156-2079-9). Syracuse U Pr.

Rosenbaum, Lee. The Complete Guide to Collecting Art. LC 82-47837. 1982. 17.50 (ISBN 0-394-51347-9). Knopf.

Rosenbaum, Marsha. Women on Heroin. (Crime, Law & Deviance Ser.). 205p. (Orig.). 1981. 20.00x (ISBN 0-8135-0921-1); pap. 8.95x (ISBN 0-8135-0946-7). Rutgers U Pr.

Rosenbaum, Maurice, tr. see Mehnert, Klaus.

Rosenbaum, Max, ed. Compliant Behavior: Beyond Obedience to Authority. 224p. 1982. 24.95x (ISBN 0-89885-115-7). Human Sci Pr.

--Handbook of Short-Term Therapy Groups. 448p. 1983. 34.95 (ISBN 0-07-053712-7, P&RB). McGraw.

Rosenbaum, Michael, ed. Perspectives on Behavior Therapy in the Eighties. (Springer Ser. in Behavior Therapy & Behavioral Medicine: Vol. 9). 480p. 1983. text ed. 37.95 (ISBN 0-8261-4070-X). Springer Pub.

Rosenbaum, Peter S., jt. auth. see Jacobs, Roderick A.

Rosenbaum, Peter S., jt. ed. see Jacobs, Roderick A.

Rosenbaum, Robert A. The Public Issues Handbook: A Guide for the Concerned Citizen. LC 82-15812. (Illus.). 416p. 1983. lib. bdg. 35.00 (ISBN 0-313-23504-X, RPI/). Greenwood.

Rosenbaum, Robert J. History of Mexican Americans in Texas. (Texas History Ser.). (Illus.). 38p. 1981. pap. text ed. 1.95x (ISBN 0-686-43253-3). American Pr.

--Mexicano Resistance in the Southwest: "The Sacred Right of Self-Preservation". (Illus.). 253p. 1981. 17.95 (ISBN 0-292-77562-8). U of Tex Pr.

Rosenbaum, Robert J., ed. see Davis, Ronald L.

Rosenbaum, Robert J., ed. see Green, George N.

Rosenbaum, Robert J., ed. see Henson, Margaret S.

Rosenbaum, Robert J., ed. see Jordan, Terry G.

Rosenbaum, Robert J., ed. see McDonald, Archie P.

Rosenbaum, Robert J., ed. see Maxwell, Robert S.

Rosenbaum, Robert J., ed. see Myres, Sandra L.

Rosenbaum, Robert J., ed. see Pilkington, William T.

Rosenbaum, Robert J., ed. see Whisenhunt, Donald W.

Rosenbaum, Ron. Rebirth of the Salesman: Tales of the Song & Dance Seventies. 1979. pap. 4.95 o.s.i. (ISBN 0-440-57226-6, Delta). Dell.

Rosenbaum, Samuel, tr. see Gerstinger, Heinz.

Rosenbaum, Samuel, tr. see Melchinger, Siegfried.

Rosenbaum, Walter A. Coal & Crisis: The Political Dilemma of Energy Management. LC 78-8606. (Praeger Special Studies). 1978. 23.95 o.p. (ISBN 0-03-042596-4). Praeger.

--Energy, Politics & Public Policy. LC 80-29273. 240p. 1981. pap. 8.95 (ISBN 0-87187-166-1). Congr Quarterly.

Rosenberg. Tropical Fish. 1977. pap. text ed. 5.50x (ISBN 0-582-35902-3). Longman.

Rosenberg, Aimee, illus. Look in the Yard. (Illus.). 14p. (ps). 1982. 2.95 (ISBN 0-448-12311-8, G&D). Putnam Pub Group.

Rosenberg, Alan L., ed. Living with Your Arthritis: A Home Program for Arthritis Management. LC 77-17572. (Illus.). 1979. lib. bdg. 8.95 o.p. (ISBN 0-668-04519-1); pap. 3.95 o.p. (ISBN 0-668-04522-1). Arco.

Rosenberg, Alexander, jt. auth. see Beauchamp, Tom L.

Rosenberg, Amye. Sam the Detective's Reading Readiness Book. (Illus.). 63p. (ps). 1982. pap. text ed. 3.50 (ISBN 0-87441-361-3). Behrman.

Rosenberg, Amye, illus. My Telephone Book. (Softies Ser.). (Illus.). 12p. (ps-2). 1981. vinyl 5.95 o.p. (ISBN 0-671-42526-9, Little Simon). S&S.

Rosenberg, B. G., jt. auth. see Hyde, Janet.

Rosenberg, B. G., jt. auth. see Hyde, Janet S.

Rosenberg, Bernard & Silverstein, Harry. The Varieties of Delinquent Experience. LC 82-10576. 192p. pap. 6.95 (ISBN 0-8052-0736-8). Schocken.

Rosenberg, Betty. Genreflecting: A Guide to Reading Interests in Genre Fiction. LC 82-14067. 260p. 1982. 23.50 (ISBN 0-87287-333-1). Libs Unl.

Rosenberg, Bruce A. Custer & the Epic of Defeat. LC 74-14631. 352p. 1974. 22.50x (ISBN 0-271-01172-6). Pa St U Pr.

Rosenberg, Chaim M. & Raynes, Anthony E. Keeping Patients in Psychiatric Treatment. LC 76-10184. 1976. prof ref 18.50x (ISBN 0-88410-504-0). Ballinger Pub.

Rosenberg, Charles E. Cholera Years: The United States in 1832, 1849, & 1866. LC 62-18121. 1968. pap. 6.95 (ISBN 0-226-72679-7, P320, Phoen). U of Chicago Pr.

Rosenberg, Claude N., Jr. The Common Sense Way to Stock Market Profits. rev. ed. 1978. pap. 1.95 o.p. (ISBN 0-451-08397-0, J8397, Sig). NAL.

--Stock Market Primer. 1982. 14.95 (ISBN 0-446-51226-5); pap. 3.50 (ISBN 0-446-90679-4). Warner Bks.

Rosenberg, David. Blues of the Sky: Interpreted from the Original Hebrew Book of Psalms. LC 76-9991. 53p. 1976. 4.00 (ISBN 0-06-067009-6). SUN.

--Chosen Days: Celebrating Jewish Festivals in Poetry & Art. LC 79-7906. (Illus.). 224p. 1980. 14.95 o.p. (ISBN 0-385-14365-6). Doubleday.

--Job Speaks. 101p. 1980. Repr. of 1977 ed. 4.95 (ISBN 0-934450-09-9). Unmuzzled Ox.

--Lightworks: Interpreted from the Original Hebrew Book of Isaiah. LC 78-3356. 78p. 1978. 4.00 (ISBN 0-686-81738-9). SUN.

Rosenberg, E. & Rosenberg, N. Postwar America: Readings & Reminiscences. 336p. 1976. pap. 13.95 (ISBN 0-13-685495-8). P-H.

Rosenberg, Emily S., jt. auth. see Rosenberg, Norman L.

Rosenberg, Eugene & Cohen, Irun. Microbial Biology. 1983. text ed. 25.95 (ISBN 0-686-37624-2, CBS C). SCP.

Rosenberg, G. D. & Runcorn, S. K. Growth Rhythms & the History of the Earth's Rotation. LC 74-18096. 559p. 1975. 132.95 (ISBN 0-471-73616-3, Pub. by Wiley-Interscience). Wiley.

Rosenberg, Gary & Rehr, Helen, eds. Advancing Social Work Practice in the Health Care Field: Emerging Issues & New Perspectives. LC 82-9249. (Social Work in Health Care Ser.: Vol. 8, No. 3). 176p. 1983. text ed. 29.95 (ISBN 0-917724-91-7, B91). Haworth Pr.

Rosenberg, Gary, jt. ed. see Lurie, Abraham.

Rosenberg, Harold. The Act & the Actor: Making the Self. 238p. pap. 7.95 (ISBN 0-226-72675-4). U of Chicago Pr.

--Arshile Gorky: The Man, the Times, the Idea. (Illus.). 144p. 1981. pap. 7.95 (ISBN 0-935296-20-4). Sheep Meadow.

--Art on the Edge: Creators & Situations. LC 82-24807. (Illus.). xiv, 304p. 1983. pap. 8.95 (ISBN 0-226-72674-6). U of Chicago Pr.

--Artworks & Packages. LC 82-13406. (Illus.). 232p. 1983. pap. 7.95 (ISBN 0-226-72683-5). U of Chicago Pr.

--Barnett Newman. LC 77-25433. (Contemporary Artist Ser.). (Illus.). 1978. 75.00 (ISBN 0-8109-1360-7). Abrams.

--The De-Definition of Art. LC 83-1101. (Illus.). 256p. 1983. pap. 8.95 (ISBN 0-226-72673-8). U of Chicago Pr.

--The Tradition of the New. LC 82-13509. 286p. 1983. pap. 7.95 (ISBN 0-226-72684-3). U of chicago Pr.

--Willem De Kooning. LC 73-15620. (Illus.). 296p. 1974. 75.00 o.p. (ISBN 0-8109-0123-4). Abrams.

Rosenberg, Harold & Feldzaman, A. N. The Doctor's Book of Vitamin Therapy: Megavitamins for Health. 320p. 1974. 7.95 o.p. (ISBN 0-399-11350-9). Putnam Pub Group.

Rosenberg, Harvey S. & Bernstein, Jay, eds. Perspective in Pediatric Pathology, Vol. 6. LC 72-88828. (Illus.). 296p. 1981. 60.50x (ISBN 0-89352-152-3). Masson Pub.

--Perspectives in Pediatric Pathology, Vol. 7. (Illus.). 340p. 1982. 67.50x (ISBN 0-89352-183-3). Masson Pub.

Rosenberg, Harvey S. & Bolande, Robert P., eds. Perspectives in Pediatric Pathology, Vol. 5. LC 72-88828. (Illus.). 309p. 1979. 50.00x (ISBN 0-89352-061-6). Masson Pub.

Rosenberg, I., jt. ed. see Csakany, B.

Rosenberg, I. G., jt. ed. see Deza, M.

Rosenberg, Isaac. Collected Poems. Bottomley, Denys & Harding, Gordon, eds. LC 73-91125. 1974. 6.00x o.p. (ISBN 0-8052-3036-X). Schocken.

Rosenberg, Jay. The Practice of Philosophy: A Handbook for Beginners. 1978. pap. text ed. 9.95 (ISBN 0-13-687178-X). P-H.

Rosenberg, Jay F. Thinking Clearly about Death. 256p. 1983. pap. 10.95 (ISBN 0-13-917559-8). P-H.

Rosenberg, Jay F. & Travis, Charles. Readings in the Philosophy of Language. LC 70-132170. 1971. text ed. 27.95 (ISBN 0-13-759332-5). P-H.

Rosenberg, Jeff & Charlsen, David. Jeff Rosenberg on Rollerskating. (Paragon). 1979. pap. cancelled (ISBN 0-399-50390-0). Putnam Pub Group.

Rosenberg, Jerome J. Student Manual Curriculum. 368p. 1977. pap. text ed. 14.25 (ISBN 0-8191-0233-4). U Pr of Amer.

Rosenberg, Jerome L. College Chemistry. 5th ed. (Orig.). 1964. pap. 3.95 o.p. (ISBN 0-07-053713-5, SP). McGraw.

--Schaum's Outline of College Chemistry. 6th ed. (Schaum's Outline Ser.). (Illus.). 1980. pap. 6.95 (ISBN 0-07-053706-2). McGraw.

Rosenberg, Jerry M. Dictionary of Banking & Finance. LC 81-21961. 690p. 1982. 24.95 (ISBN 0-471-08096-9, Pub. by Wiley-Interscience). Wiley.

--Dictionary of Business & Management. 2nd. ed. 600p. 1983. 29.95 (ISBN 0-471-86730-6, Pub. by Wiley-Interscience). Wiley.

--Inside the Wall Street Journal: The History & the Power of Dow Jones & Company & America's Most Influential Newspaper. 352p. 1982. 16.95 (ISBN 0-02-604860-4). Macmillan.

Rosenberg, John, ed. The Question of Intervention. 200p. 1983. 18.50x (ISBN 0-8419-0641-6). Holmes & Meier.

Rosenberg, Jon M. The Story of Baseball. rev. ed. (Landmark Giant Ser.: No. 4). (Illus.). (gr. 7 up). 1964. 4.95 o.p. (ISBN 0-394-81677-3); PLB 5.99 o.p. (ISBN 0-394-91677-8). Random.

Rosenberg, Kenyon C. & Doskey, John S. Media Equipment: A Guide & Dictionary. LC 76-25554. (Illus.). 190p. 1976. lib. bdg. 18.50 (ISBN 0-87287-155-X). Libs Unl.

Rosenberg, L., jt. auth. see Mandell, M.

Rosenberg, Leon E., jt. auth. see Bondy, Philip K.

Rosenberg, Lesley. Child Star & the Sun Cakes. LC 78-31409. (Illus.). (ps-4). 1979. 6.95 o.p. (ISBN 0-89742-020-9, Dawne-Leigh); pap. 4.95 o.p. (ISBN 0-89742-007-1). Celestial Arts.

Rosenberg, M. B. English-Russian Dictionary of Refrigerating & Cryogenic Engineering. 467p. 1978. Leatherette 15.95 (ISBN 0-686-92382-0, M-9063). French & Eur.

Rosenberg, M. J. The Cybernetics of Art. (Studies in Cybernetics: Vol. 4). 206p. 1982. 42.50 (ISBN 0-677-05970-1). Gordon.

Rosenberg, Marshall B. Diagnostic Teaching. LC 68-57927. (Orig.). 1968. pap. 7.00x o.p. (ISBN 0-87562-013-2). Spec Child.

--From Now on. 2nd ed. 149p. 1977. pap. 3.50 (ISBN 0-686-16825-9). Community Psychol.

--Mutual Education: Toward Autonomy & Interdependence. LC 72-86807. 159p. (Orig.). 1972. pap. 5.50x o.p. (ISBN 0-87562-040-X). Spec Child.

Rosenberg, Marshall B., ed. Educational Therapy, Vol. 3: Educational Programs. LC 67-8807. 437p. (Orig.). 1973. text ed. 10.50 o.p. (ISBN 0-87562-026-4); pap. 9.00 o.p. (ISBN 0-87562-027-2). Spec Child.

Rosenberg, Martin E. Sound & Hearing. (Studies in Biology: No. 145). 64p. 1983. pap. text ed. 8.95 (ISBN 0-7131-2850-X). E Arnold.

Rosenberg, Marvin. The Masks of King Lear. LC 74-115492. 448p. 1972. 37.50x (ISBN 0-520-01718-8). U of Cal Pr.

--The Masks of Macbeth. LC 76-14295. 1978. 48.50x (ISBN 0-520-03262-4). U of Cal Pr.

Rosenberg, Maurice, et al. Elements of Civil Procedure, Cases & Materials: 1982 Supplement. 3rd ed. (University Casebook Ser.). 157p. 1982. pap. text ed. write for info. (ISBN 0-88277-082-9). Foundation Pr.

Rosenberg, Maxine. My Friend Leslie: The Story of a Handicapped Child. LC 82-12734. (Illus.). (gr. 1-3). 1983. 9.00 (ISBN 0-688-01690-1); PLB 8.59 (ISBN 0-688-01691-X). Lothrop.

Rosenberg, Meir. The Jewish Cat Book: A Different Breed! LC 82-62085. (Illus.). 50p. (gr. 8-12). 1982. pap. 4.50 (ISBN 0-916288-15-3). Micah Pubns.

Rosenberg, Morris & Turner, Ralph H. Social Psychology: Sociological Perspectives. LC 81-66976. 720p. 1981. text ed. 28.85 (ISBN 0-465-07904-0); pap. text ed. 17.95 (ISBN 0-465-07905-9). Basic.

Rosenberg, N., jt. auth. see Rosenberg, E.

Rosenberg, Nathan. Inside the Black Box: Technology & Economics. LC 82-4563. 304p. 1983. 29.95 (ISBN 0-521-24808-6); pap. 12.95 (ISBN 0-521-27367-6). Cambridge U Pr.

--Perspectives on Technology. LC 75-14623. 336p. 1976. 47.50 (ISBN 0-521-20957-9); pap. 14.95x (ISBN 0-521-29011-2). Cambridge U Pr.

--Technology & American Economic Growth. LC 76-52621. 224p. 1972. pap. 7.95 (ISBN 0-87332-104-9). M E Sharpe.

Rosenberg, Nathan & Vincenti, Walter G. The Britannia Bridge: Generation & Diffusion of Technological Knowledge. (Illus.). 1978. text ed. 12.50x o.p. (ISBN 0-262-18087-1). MIT Pr.

Rosenberg, Norman J. Microclimate: The Biological Environment. LC 74-8952. 336p. 1974. 26.50 (ISBN 0-471-73615-5, Pub. by Wiley-Interscience). Wiley.

Rosenberg, Norman J., ed. Drought in the Great Plains: Research on Impacts & Strategies. LC 80-8425. 1980. 18.00 (ISBN 0-918334-34-9). WRP.

--North American Droughts. LC 78-52024. (AAAS Selected Symposium Ser.). (Illus.). 1978. lib. bdg. 20.00 o.p. (ISBN 0-89158-443-9). Westview.

Rosenberg, Norman L. & Rosenberg, Emily S. In Our Times. 2nd ed. (Illus.). 336p. 1982. pap. 15.95 reference (ISBN 0-13-453787-4). P-H.

Rosenberg, Paul, ed. The Urban Information Thesaurus: A Vocabulary for Social Documentation. LC 76-52604. 1977. lib. bdg. 35.00x (ISBN 0-8371-9483-0, UTH). Greenwood.

Rosenberg, Peter D. Patent Law Fundamentals. 2nd ed. LC 80-10710. 1980. 65.00 (ISBN 0-87632-098-1). Boardman.

Rosenberg, Philip, jt. auth. see Grosso, Sonny.

Rosenberg, R. & Karnopp, D. Introduction to Physical Systems Dynamics. 512p. 1983. 32.95x (ISBN 0-07-053905-7, C); solutions manual 9.95 (ISBN 0-07-053906-5). McGraw.

Rosenberg, R., jt. auth. see Bonnice, J. G.

Rosenberg, R., et al. Business Law: UCC Applications. 6th ed. LC 82-13001. 640p. 1983. text ed. 17.25x (ISBN 0-07-053901-4, C); write for info instr's guide & key (ISBN 0-07-053903-0); study guide 7.55 (ISBN 0-07-053902-2). Mcgraw.

Rosenberg, R. M., jt. auth. see Klotz, Irving M.

Rosenberg, R. Robert. Business Math-Thirty. 1968. pap. text ed. 5.52 o.p. (ISBN 0-07-053800-X, G). McGraw.

--Business Mathematics, Exercises, Problems, & Tests. 7th, rev. ed. 1970. text ed. 9.28 (ISBN 0-07-053772-0, G); tchr's key 5.50 (ISBN 0-07-053774-7); tests free (ISBN 0-07-053773-9). McGraw.

--College Business Mathematics. 5th ed. (Illus.). 384p. 1973. text ed. 16.95 o.p. (ISBN 0-07-053797-6, G); tchr's manual & key 7.50 o.p. (ISBN 0-07-053799-2); activity guide 7.25 o.p. (ISBN 0-07-053798-4). McGraw.

--College Mathematics. 4th ed. 1967. text ed. 14.05 o.p. (ISBN 0-07-053790-9, G); problem-solution guide 7.25 o.p. (ISBN 0-07-053792-5); problem-solution guide instructor's edn. 6.75 o.p. (ISBN 0-07-053791-7). McGraw.

--Mathematicas Para Contabilidad y Administracion. (Span). 1972. text ed. 12.35 (ISBN 0-07-053722-4, G). McGraw.

--Schaum's Outline of College Business Law. LC 77-940. (Schaum's Outline Ser.). 1977. pap. 6.95 (ISBN 0-07-053805-0, SP). McGraw.

Rosenberg, R. Robert & Alvey, C. George. Business Math Thirty. 2nd ed. (Illus.). (gr. 9-12). 1976. pap. text ed. 7.36 (ISBN 0-07-053802-6, G); tchr's manual & key 4.95 (ISBN 0-07-053803-4). McGraw.

Rosenberg, R. Robert & Bonnice, Joseph G. Business Law-Thirty. 2nd ed. 1976. 7.72 (ISBN 0-07-053670-8, G); tchr's manual & key 6.20 (ISBN 0-07-053672-4). McGraw.

Rosenberg, R. Robert & Lewis, H. Business Mathematics. 7th ed. 1968. text ed. 15.96 (ISBN 0-07-053775-5, G); tchr's ed. 15.95 (ISBN 0-07-053778-X); wkbk. 6.56 (ISBN 0-07-053776-3); key to wkbk. & tests 4.50 (ISBN 0-07-053784-4); tests 2.24 (ISBN 0-07-053777-1). McGraw.

Rosenberg, R. Robert & Naples, Ralph V. Outline of Personal Finance. (Schaum's Outline Ser.). (Orig.). 1976. pap. 4.95 (ISBN 0-07-053834-4, SP). McGraw.

Rosenberg, R. Robert & Ott, William G. College Business Law. 4th ed. 1972. text ed. 13.95 o.p. (ISBN 0-07-053785-2, G); instructor's manual & key 5.20 o.p. (ISBN 0-07-053787-9); study guide o.p. 5.65 o.p. (ISBN 0-07-053786-0). McGraw.

Rosenberg, R. Robert & Sexton, J. E. Business Math on the Job: Practice Set. 1969. text ed. 7.40 (ISBN 0-07-053770-4, G); tchr's manual 4.50 (ISBN 0-07-053771-2). McGraw.

Rosenberg, R. Robert & Whitcraft, John E. Understanding Business & Consumer Law. 6th ed. (Illus.). (YA) (gr. 11-12). 1978. text ed. 15.48 (ISBN 0-07-053631-7, G); test 1.00 (ISBN 0-07-053633-3); perf. guide 5.12 (ISBN 0-07-053632-5); tchr's. manual 8.90 (ISBN 0-07-053634-1). McGraw.

Rosenberg, R. Robert, jt. auth. see Brown, Gordon W.

Rosenberg, R. Robert, et al. Business Mathematics. 8th ed. (Illus.). 576p. (gr. 9-10). 1975. text ed. 15.96 (ISBN 0-07-053700-3, G); tchr's ed. 16.50 (ISBN 0-07-053703-8); wkbk. 6.52 (ISBN 0-07-053701-1); tchr's key to wkbk. & tests 3.95 (ISBN 0-07-053704-6); tests 2.24 (ISBN 0-07-053702-X). McGraw.

--College Business Law. 5th ed. Byers, Edward E., ed. 1978. text ed. 17.10 (ISBN 0-07-053885-9, G); instructor's manual & key 6.60 (ISBN 0-07-053887-5); individual performance guide 7.85 (ISBN 0-07-053886-7). McGraw.

--Consumer Math & You: Activity Guide. (Illus.). 1978. 14.36 (ISBN 0-07-053641-4, G); tchrs manual & key 5.50 (ISBN 0-07-053642-2); activity guide 4.96 (ISBN 0-07-053643-0). McGraw.

Rosenberg, Richard. Competence in Mathematics, Bk. I. (Mathematic Ser.). 96p. 1981. wkbk. 4.50 (ISBN 0-9602800-4-9). Comp Pr.

--Competence in Mathematics, Bk. II. (Mathematics Ser.). 90p. 1981. wkbk. 4.50 (ISBN 0-9602800-5-7). Comp Pr.

--Lovejoy's Math Review for the SAT. Levy, Valerie, ed. (Exam Preparation Guides). (Orig.). 1983. pap. 7.95 (ISBN 0-671-47150-3). Monarch Pr.

Rosenberg, Robert, et al. Business Mathematics. 9th, rev. ed. LC 80-18533. 576p. (gr. 9-12). 1981. text ed. 15.48 (ISBN 0-07-053726-7, G); wkbk. 6.36 (ISBN 0-07-053727-5); manual & key for workbook 16.50tchr's. (ISBN 0-07-053729-1). McGraw.

Rosenberg, Roberta, ed. Wolfert's Roost: The Complete Works of W. Irving. (Critical Editions Program). 1979. lib. bdg. 25.00 (ISBN 0-8057-8519-1, Twayne). G K Hall.

Rosenberg, Rutger, ed. see Barrett, Gary W.

Rosenberg, Samuel N. Harper's Grammar of French. 384p. 1983. text ed. 14.50 scp (ISBN 0-06-045581-0, HarpC); scp wkbk. 5.00 (ISBN 0-06-045583-7). Har-Row.

Rosenberg, Stanley, jt. auth. see Lawrence, Ronald M.

Rosenberg, Stephen N. The Brenda Maneuver. LC 82-12601. 224p. 1982. 13.95 (ISBN 0-937858-12-9). Newmarket.

Rosenberg, Steven A., ed. Serologic Analysis of Human Cancer Antigens. LC 79-19361. 1980. 51.50 (ISBN 0-12-597160-5). Acad Pr.

Rosenberg, Stuart E. Judaism. 159p. pap. 2.45 (ISBN 0-686-95139-5). ADL.

Rosenberg, Ted. Minolta Sixteen Guide. (Illus.). 1973. 4.95 o.p. (ISBN 0-8174-0464-3, Amphoto). Watson-Guptill.

Rosenberg, William G. Bolshevik Visions: First Phase of the Cultural Revolution in Soviet Russia. 350p. 1983. 27.00 (ISBN 0-88233-650-9). Ardis Pubs.

Rosenberg, William G. & Young, Marilyn B. Transforming Russia & China: Revolutionary Struggle in the Twentieth Century. 1982. 19.95x (ISBN 0-19-502965-8); pap. text ed. 6.95x (ISBN 0-19-502966-6). Oxford U Pr.

Rosenberger, F. Fundamentals of Crystal Growth I: Macroscopic Equilibrium & Transport Concepts. 2nd ed. (Springer Series in Solid-State Sciences: Vol. 5). (Illus.). 530p. 1982. 35.00 (ISBN 0-387-09023-1). Springer-Verlag.

Rosenberger, Gustav. Clinical Examination of Cattle. (Illus.). 469p. 1980. 47.00 (ISBN 0-7216-7705-3). Saunders.

Rosenberger, Homer T. The Pennsylvania Germans, 1890 to 1965, Vol. 63. 1966. 20.00 o.p. (ISBN 0-911122-17-6). Penn German Soc.

--The Philadelphia & Erie Railroad: Its Place in American Economic History. LC 74-75110. (Illus.). 748p. 1975. lib. bdg. 22.50 (ISBN 0-914932-02-0). Rose Hill.

Rosenberger, Joseph. Apocalypse U. S. A.! (Death Merchant Ser.: No. 54). 224p. (Orig.). 1983. pap. 2.25 (ISBN 0-523-41998-8). Pinnacle Bks.

--Armageddon, U.S.A. (Death Merchant Ser.: No. 19). 1976. pap. 1.50 o.p. (ISBN 0-523-40460-3). Pinnacle Bks.

--The Bermuda Triangle Action. (Death Merchant Ser.: No. 37). (Orig.). 1980. pap. 1.75 o.p. (ISBN 0-523-40701-7). Pinnacle Bks.

--Blood Bath. (Death Merchant Ser.: No. 46). 192p. (Orig.). 1981. pap. 1.95 o.p. (ISBN 0-523-41327-0). Pinnacle Bks.

--Blueprint Invisibility. (Death Merchant Ser.: No. 40). 192p. (Orig.). 1980. pap. 1.75 o.p. (ISBN 0-523-41018-2). Pinnacle Bks.

--The Budapest Action, No. 23. (Death Merchant Ser.). 1977. pap. 1.25 o.p. (ISBN 0-523-40078-0). Pinnacle Bks.

--Deadly Manhunt. (Death Merchant Ser.: No. 32). 1979. pap. 1.50 o.p. (ISBN 0-523-40475-1). Pinnacle Bks.

--The Death Merchant: Chinese Conspiracy. (Death Merchant Ser., No. 4). 192p. (Orig.). 1973. pap. 1.95 (ISBN 0-523-41348-3). Pinnacle Bks.

--Death Merchant, No. 10: Mainline Plot. (Orig.). 1974. pap. 1.95 (ISBN 0-523-41354-8). Pinnacle Bks.

--Death Merchant, No. 11: Manhattan Wipeout. 192p. (Orig.). 1975. pap. 1.75 o.p. (ISBN 0-523-40816-1). Pinnacle Bks.

--Death Merchant No. 21: The Pole Star Secret. (The Death Merchant Ser). (Orig.). 1977. pap. 1.75 o.p. (ISBN 0-523-40826-9). Pinnacle Bks.

--Death Merchant, No. 3: The Psychotron Plot. 192p. (Orig.). 1972. pap. 1.95 (ISBN 0-523-41347-5). Pinnacle Bks.

--The Death Merchant, No. 5: Satan Strike. 1972. pap. 1.95 (ISBN 0-523-41349-1). Pinnacle Bks.

--The Death Merchant, No. 6: The Albanian Connection. 192p. (Orig.). 1973. pap. 1.95 (ISBN 0-523-41350-5). Pinnacle Bks.

--The Death Merchant, No. 7: The Castro File. 192p. (Orig.). 1974. pap. 1.95 (ISBN 0-523-41351-3). Pinnacle Bks.

--The Death Merchant, No. 8: Billionaire Mission. (Orig.). 1974. pap. 1.95 (ISBN 0-523-41352-1). Pinnacle Bks.

--The Death Merchant, No. 9: The Laser War. 192p. (Orig.). 1974. pap. 1.95 (ISBN 0-523-41353-X). Pinnacle Bks.

--The Enigma Project: Death Merchant No. 25. (Death Merchant Ser.). 1977. pap. 1.25 o.p. (ISBN 0-523-40117-5). Pinnacle Bks.

--Fatal Formula. (Death Merchant Ser.: No. 29). (Orig.). 1978. pap. 1.50 o.p. (ISBN 0-523-40272-4). Pinnacle Bks.

--Hell in Hindu Land. (Death Merchant Ser.: No. 20). 1977. pap. 1.50 o.p. (ISBN 0-523-40256-2). Pinnacle Bks.

--Invasion of the Clones. (Death Merchant Ser.: No. 16). 192p. 1976. pap. 1.75 o.p. (ISBN 0-523-40821-8). Pinnacle Bks.

--The Iron Swastika Plot. (Death Merchant Ser.: No. 15). 192p. (Orig.). 1976. pap. 1.25 o.p. (ISBN 0-523-22823-6). Pinnacle Bks.

--The KGB Frame. (Death Merchant Ser., No. 12). 192p. 1975. pap. 1.75 o.p. (ISBN 0-523-40817-X). Pinnacle Bks.

--The Kronos Plot: Death Merchant No. 24. (Death Merchant Ser.). 1977. pap. 1.50 o.p. (ISBN 0-523-40352-6). Pinnacle Bks.

--Massacre in Rome. (Death Merchang Ser: No. 35). (Orig.). 1979. pap. 1.50 o.p. (ISBN 0-523-40478-6). Pinnacle Bks.

--The Mato Grosso Horror. (Death Merchant Ser.: No. 13). 192p. (Orig.). 1975. pap. 1.50 o.p. (ISBN 0-523-40497-2). Pinnacle Bks.

--The Mexican Hit. (Death Merchant: No. 26). 1978. pap. 1.50 o.p. (ISBN 0-523-40118-3). Pinnacle Bks.

--Nightmare in Algeria. (Death Merchant Ser.: No.18). (Orig.). 1976. pap. 1.25 o.p. (ISBN 0-523-22911-9). Pinnacle Bks.

--Nipponese Nightmare. (Death Merchant Ser.: No. 28). 1978. pap. 1.75 o.p. (ISBN 0-523-40833-1). Pinnacle Bks.

--Operation Thunderbolt. (Death Merchant: No. 31). 1978. pap. 1.50 o.p. (ISBN 0-523-40392-5). Pinnacle Bks.

--The Shambhala Strike. (Death Merchant Ser.: No. 30). 1978. pap. 1.50 o.p. (ISBN 0-523-40385-2). Pinnacle Bks.

--The Surinam Affair. (The Death Merchant Ser.: No. 27). 1978. pap. 1.50 o.p. (ISBN 0-523-40119-1). Pinnacle Bks.

--Vengeance of the Golden Hawk. (Death Merchant Ser.: No. 14). 192p. (Orig.). 1976. pap. 1.75 o.p. (ISBN 0-523-40819-6). Pinnacle Bks.

--The Zemlya Expedition. (Death Merchant: No. 17). (Orig.). 1976. pap. 1.75 o.p. (ISBN 0-523-40822-6). Pinnacle Bks.

Rosenberger, Joseph N. Death Merchant, No. 2: Operation Overkill. (Orig.). 1972. pap. 1.95 (ISBN 0-523-41346-7). Pinnacle Bks.

Rosenberry, Edward H. Melville. (Illus.). 1979. 18.00 (ISBN 0-7100-8989-9). Routledge & Kegan.

Rosenblatt, Aaron & Waldfogel, Diana, eds. Handbook of Clinical Social Work. LC 82-49042. (Social & Behavioral Science Ser.). 1983. text ed. 65.00x (ISBN 0-87589-562-X). Jossey-Bass.

Rosenblatt, G. M. & Worrell, W. L., eds. Progress in Solid State Chemistry, Vol. 13. (Illus.). 376p. 1982. 112.00 (ISBN 0-08-029712-9). Pergamon.

Rosenblatt, Jay, et al, eds. Advances in the Study of Behavior, Vol. 13. (Serial Publication). Date not set. price not set (ISBN 0-12-004513-3). Acad Pr.

Rosenblatt, Jay S., ed. Advances in the Study of Behavior, Vol. 12. 263p. 1982. 27.00 (ISBN 0-12-004512-5). Acad Pr.

Rosenblatt, Louise M. The Reader, the Text, the Poem: The Transactional Theory of the Literary Work. LC 78-16335. 214p. 1978. 13.50x (ISBN 0-8093-0883-5). S Ill U Pr.

Rosenblatt, R. A. & Moscovice, I. S. Rural Health Care. (Health Services Ser.). 301p. 1982. text ed. 19.95 (ISBN 0-471-05419-4, Pub. by Wiley Med). Wiley.

Rosenblatt, Roger. Children of War. LC 82-45366. 216p. 1983. 14.95 (ISBN 0-385-18250-3, Anchor Pr). Doubleday.

Rosenblatt, S. Bernard, et al. Modern Business: A Systems Approach. 2nd ed. LC 76-13803. (Illus.). 1977. text ed. 23.50 (ISBN 0-395-21381-9); instr's. manual 1.00 (ISBN 0-395-21391-6); study guide 10.50 (ISBN 0-395-21390-8); test bank 1.00 (ISBN 0-395-21392-4); transparencies 15.95 set (ISBN 0-395-21393-2). HM.

--Communication in Business. 2nd ed. (Illus.). 368p. 1982. text ed. 21.95 (ISBN 0-13-153478-5). P-H.

Rosenblatt, Samuel M., ed. Technology & Economic Development: A Realistic Perspective. (Special Studies in Social, Political & Economic Development). 1979. lib. bdg. 25.00 (ISBN 0-89158-474-9). Westview.

Rosenblatt, Seymour & Dodson, Reynolds. Beyond Valium: The Brave New World of Psychochemistry. 316p. 1981. 13.95 (ISBN 0-399-12577-9). Putnam Pub Group.

Rosenbloom. Centenary Issues of the Civil Service Act of 1883. (Annuals of Public Administration Ser.). 152p. 1982. 19.50 (ISBN 0-8247-1704-X). Dekker.

--Marketing Channels. 2nd ed. 480p. 1983. 27.95 (ISBN 0-03-058996-7). Dryden Pr.

--Public Adminstration & Law. (Public Adminstration Public Policy Ser.). 280p. 1983. 27.50 (ISBN 0-8247-1791-0). Dekker.

Rosenbloom, Arthur H., jt. auth. see Bishop, John A.

Rosenbloom, Bert. Retail Marketing. 470p. 1981. text ed. 25.95 (ISBN 0-394-32192-8). Random.

Rosenbloom, D. L., ed. see Twentieth Century Fund. Task Force on Financing Congressional Campaigns.

Rosenbloom, David, ed. Public Personnel Policy in a Political Environment: A Symposium. (Orig.). 1982. pap. 6.00 (ISBN 0-918592-59-3). Policy Studies.

Rosenbloom, David H. Federal Equal Employment Opportunity: Politics & Public Personnel Administration. LC 77-954. (Special Studies). 1976. 27.50 o.p. (ISBN 0-275-24420-2). Praeger.

Rosenbloom, David H., jt. auth. see Nachmias, David.

Rosenbloom, J. S., jt. auth. see Hallman, G. V.

Rosenbloom, Jerry & Hallman, G. Victor. Employee Benefit Planning. (Series in Risk, Insurance & Security). (Illus.). 544p. 1981. text ed. 27.95 (ISBN 0-13-274811-8). P-H.

Rosenbloom, Jerry, jt. auth. see Hallman, G. Victor.

Rosenbloom, Jonathan. Blue Jeans. LC 76-20739. (Illus.). 64p. (gr. 3-5). 1976. 6.64 o.p. (ISBN 0-671-32798-4). Messner.

Rosenbloom, Joseph. Bananas Don't Grow on Trees: A Guide to Popular Misconceptions. LC 78-57783. (Illus.). (gr. 6 up). 1978. 8.95 (ISBN 0-8069-3100-0); PLB 10.99 (ISBN 0-8069-3101-9). Sterling.

--Biggest Riddle Book in the World. LC 76-1165. (Illus.). 320p. (gr. 2 up). 1976. 8.95 (ISBN 0-8069-4532-X); PLB 10.99 (ISBN 0-8069-4533-8). Sterling.

--Daffy Definitions. LC 82-19323. (Illus.). 128p. (gr. 4 up). 1983. 7.95 (ISBN 0-8069-4668-7); PLB 9.99 (ISBN 0-8069-4669-5); pap. 2.95 (ISBN 0-8069-7704-3). Sterling.

--Daffy Dictionary: Funabridged Definitions from Aardvark to Zuider Zee. LC 76-51173. (Illus.). (gr. 3 up). 1977. 7.95 o.p. (ISBN 0-8069-4542-7); PLB 8.29 o.p. (ISBN 0-8069-4543-5). Sterling.

--Doctor Knock-Knock's Official Knock-Knock Dictionary. LC 76-19796. (Illus.). (gr. 3 up). 1976. 7.95 (ISBN 0-8069-4536-2); PLB 9.99 (ISBN 0-8069-4537-0). Sterling.

--Gigantic Joke Book. LC 77-93310. (Illus.). (gr. 2 up). 1978. 8.95 (ISBN 0-8069-4590-7); PLB 10.99 (ISBN 0-8069-4591-5). Sterling.

--How Do You Make an Elephant Laugh? & Six Hundred Ninety-Nine Other Zany Riddles. LC 79-65074. (Illus.). (gr. 3 up). 1979. 7.95 (ISBN 0-8069-4604-0); PLB 9.99 (ISBN 0-8069-4605-9). Sterling.

--The Looniest Limerick Book in the World. LC 81-85034. (Illus.). 128p. (gr. 3 up). 1982. 7.95 (ISBN 0-8069-4660-1); PLB 9.99 (ISBN 0-8069-4661-X). Sterling.

--Mad Scientist: Riddle-Jokes-Fun. LC 82-50555. (Illus.). 128p. (gr. 5 up). 1982. 7.95 (ISBN 0-8069-4662-8); lib. bdg. 9.99 (ISBN 0-8069-4663-6). Sterling.

--Maximillian You're the Greatest. (gr. 3-6). 1979. pap. 1.50 (ISBN 0-448-17023-X, G&D). Putnam Pub Group.

--Monster Madness: Riddles, Jokes, & Fun. LC 80-52339. (Illus.). 128p. (gr. 2 up). 1980. 7.95 (ISBN 0-8069-4634-2); PLB 9.99 (ISBN 0-8069-4635-0); pap. 2.95 (ISBN 0-8069-7562-8). Sterling.

--The Official Wild West Joke Book. LC 82-19537. (Illus.). 128p. (gr. 3 up). 1983. 7.95 (ISBN 0-8069-4666-0); PLB 9.99 (ISBN 0-8069-4667-9). Sterling.

--Polar Bears Like It Hot: A Guide to Popular Misconceptions. LC 79-91397. (Illus.). 160p. (gr. 8 up). 1980. 8.95 (ISBN 0-8069-4612-1); PLB 8.29 (ISBN 0-8069-4613-X). Sterling.

--Ridiculous Nicholas Pet Riddles. LC 81-8744. (Illus.). 64p. (gr. 1 up). 1981. 7.95 (ISBN 0-8069-4654-7); lib. bdg. 9.99g (ISBN 0-8069-4655-5). Sterling.

--Ridiculous Nicholas Riddle Book. LC 81-50988. (Illus.). 64p. (gr. 2 up). 1981. 7.95 (ISBN 0-8069-4652-0); lib. bdg. 9.99g (ISBN 0-8069-4653-9). Sterling.

--Silly Verse (and Even Worse) LC 78-66322. (gr. 1 up). 1979. 7.95 (ISBN 0-8069-4600-8); PLB 9.99 (ISBN 0-8069-4601-6). Sterling.

--Snappy Put-Downs & Funny Insults. LC 80-54348. (Illus.). 128p. (gr. 3-6). 1981. 7.95 (ISBN 0-8069-4646-6); lib. bdg. 9.99 (ISBN 0-8069-4647-4). Sterling.

Rosenbloom, P. C., ed. Modern Viewpoints in the Curriculum. 1964. text ed. 15.95 o.p. (ISBN 0-07-053849-2, C). McGraw.

Rosenbloom, Richard S. & Russell, John R. New Tools for Urban Management: Studies in Systems & Organizational Analysis. LC 73-168850. (Illus.). 1971. 16.50x (ISBN 0-87584-093-0). Harvard Busn.

Rosenblueth, E., jt. auth. see Lomnitz, C.

Rosenblueth, E., jt. auth. see Newmark, N. M.

Rosenblum, Art. The Natural Birth Control Book. LC 82-72903. 1982. pap. 6.00 (ISBN 0-916726-02-9). Aquarian Res.

Rosenblum, Edwin E. How to Raise & Train a Brittany Spaniel. (Orig.). pap. 2.95 (ISBN 0-87666-257-2, DS1063). TFH Pubns.

--How to Raise & Train a Bull Terrier. (Orig.). pap. 2.95 (ISBN 0-87666-261-0, DS1066). TFH Pubns.

--How to Raise & Train a Staffordshire Terrier. (Orig.). pap. 2.95 (ISBN 0-87666-399-4, DS1123). TFH Pubns.

Rosenblum, Helen F. Minerva's Turn. 1980. 12.95 (ISBN 0-399-12532-9). Putnam Pub Group.

Rosenblum, L. A., jt. auth. see Lewis, M.

Rosenblum, Leonard, jt. ed. see Lewis, Michael.

Rosenblum, Leonard A. & Cooper, Robert W. Squirrel Monkey. 1968. 63.00 (ISBN 0-12-597150-8). Acad Pr.

Rosenblum, Leonard A., jt. auth. see Lewis, Michael.

Rosenblum, Leonard A., ed. Primate Behavior: Developments in Field & Laboratory Research, 4 vols. Vol. 2, 1971. 46.50 (ISBN 0-12-534002-8); Vol. 3, 1974. 37.50 (ISBN 0-12-534003-6); Vol. 4, 1975. 56.00 (ISBN 0-12-534004-4). Acad Pr.

Rosenblum, M. L. & Wilson, C. B., eds. Brain Tumor Biology. (Progress in Experimental Tumor Research Ser.: Vol. 27). (Illus.). viii, 250p. 1983. bound 100.75 (ISBN 3-8055-3698-4). S Karger.

--Brain Tumor Therapy. (Progress in Experimental Tumor Research: Vol. 28). (Illus.). viii, 250p. 1983. 100.75 (ISBN 3-8055-3699-2). S Karger.

Rosenblum, Marc. Economics of the Consumer. LC 72-84425. (Real World of Economics Ser). Orig. Title: Consumer Economics. (Illus.). (gr. 5-11). 1970. PLB 4.95g (ISBN 0-8225-0622-X). Lerner Pubns.

--How a Market Economy Works. LC 71-84414. (Real World of Economics Ser). Orig. Title: Economics. (Illus.). (gr. 5-11). 1970. PLB 4.95g (ISBN 0-8225-0611-4). Lerner Pubns.

--Stock Market. LC 76-84418. (Real World of Economics Ser). (Illus.). (gr. 5-11). 1970. PLB 4.95g (ISBN 0-8225-0615-7). Lerner Pubns.

Rosenblum, Martin J. Protractive Verse: Movement for Free Verse Prosody. 50p. (Orig.). 1976. pap. text ed. 4.00 o.p. (ISBN 0-89018-001-6). Lionhead Pub.

--Still Life. LC 82-83128. 40p. (Orig.). 1982. 10.00 (ISBN 0-89018-010-5); pap. 5.00 (ISBN 0-89018-009-1). Lionhead Pub.

--The Werewolf Sequence (a Poem in 100 Sequences) 150p. (Orig.). 1974. pap. 10.00 (ISBN 0-87924-029-6). Membrane Pr.

Rosenblum, Morris, jt. auth. see Nurnberg, Maxwell.

Rosenblum, Ralph & Karen, Robert. When the Shooting Stops...the Cutting Begins: A Film Editor's Story. (Illus.). 1979. 12.95 o.p. (ISBN 0-670-75991-0). Viking Pr.

Rosenblum, Robert. Cubism & Twentieth Century Art. 1976. pap. 17.95 (ISBN 0-13-195065-7). P-H.

--The International Style of Eighteen Hundred: A Study in Linear Abstraction. LC 75-23813. (Outstanding Dissertations in the Fine Arts - 18th Century). (Illus.). 1976. lib. bdg. 37.50 o.s.i. (ISBN 0-8240-2006-5). Garland Pub.

--The Sculpture of Picasso. (Illus.). 72p. (Orig.). 1982. pap. 16.00 (ISBN 0-938608-08-8). Pace Gallery Pubns.

--The Sweetheart Deal. LC 75-34329. 1976. 8.95 o.p. (ISBN 0-399-11727-X). Putnam Pub Group.

Rosenblum, Robert, intro. by. Mark Rothko: The Surrealist Years. (Illus.). 40p. 1981. pap. 15.00 (ISBN 0-938608-03-7). Pace Gallery Pubns.

Rosenblum, Robert, ed. see De La Chavignerie, Emile B. & Auvray, Louis.

Rosenbluth, M. N., ed. Advanced Plasma Theory. (Italian Physical Society: Course 25). 1964. 56.50 (ISBN 0-12-368825-6). Acad Pr.

Rosenbluth, Rosalyn. Why Won't the Dragon Roar? LC 76-30610. (Imagination Ser.). (Illus.). (gr. 1-4). 1977. PLB 6.69 (ISBN 0-8116-4407-3). Garrard.

Rosenburg, Harold S. Nutrition & Stress. Passwater, Richard A. & Mindell, Earl, eds. (Good Health Guide Ser.). 32p. (Orig.). 1983. pap. 1.45 (ISBN 0-87983-298-3). Keats.

Rosenburg, Samuel N., jt. tr. see Danon, Samuel.

Rosenbusch, Maria H. & Graber, Ana M. Converstional Spanish for Children: A Curriculum Guide. 160p. 1982. pap. text ed. 8.95x (ISBN 0-8138-0336-5). Iowa St U Pr.

Rosencrans, Joyce. A Cook for All Seasons. (Illus.). 320p. (Orig.). 1982. pap. 7.95x (ISBN 0-933002-02-5). Cin Post.

Rosencwaig, Allan. Photoacoustics & Photoacoustic Spectroscopy, Vol. 57. LC 80-17286. (Chemical Analysis Ser.). 309p. 1980. 50.95 (ISBN 0-471-04495-4, Pub. by Wiley-Interscience). Wiley.

Rosendorff, Clive. Clinical Cardiovascular & Pulmonary Physiology. 1982. text ed. write for info. (ISBN 0-89004-866-5). Raven.

Rosenfeld, jt. auth. see Zirkel, G.

Rosenfeld, A., jt. ed. see Kanal, L. N.

Rosenfeld, Albert, jt. auth. see Kliman, Gilbert W.

Rosenfeld, Alvin. The Plot to Destroy Israel: The Road to Armageddon. 1977. 8.95 o.p. (ISBN 0-399-11854-3). Putnam Pub Group.

Rosenfeld, Alvin H., ed. see Wheelwright, John.

Rosenfeld, Anne H. Psychiatric Education: Prologue to the 1980's. Busse, Ewald W., et al, eds. 544p. 1976. 15.00 o.p. (ISBN 0-685-84651-2, P235-0). Am Psychiatric.

Rosenfeld, Azriel. Picture Languages: Formal Models for Picture Recognition. (Computer Science & Applied Mathematics Ser.). 1979. 32.50 (ISBN 0-12-597340-3). Acad Pr.

Rosenfeld, C., jt. ed. see Serrou, B.

Rosenfeld, Charles & Cooke, Robert. The Eruption of Mount St. Helens. 1982. 25.00 (ISBN 0-262-18106-1). MIT Pr.

Rosenfeld, Helen, et al. Comprehensive Social Studies. (Arco's Regents Review Ser.). 288p. 1983. pap. 3.95 (ISBN 0-668-05699-1, 5699). Arco.

Rosenfeld, Irene & Beath, O. A. Selenium. 2nd ed. 1964. 55.50 (ISBN 0-12-597550-3). Acad Pr.

Rosenfeld, Isadore. The Complete Medical Exam. 1978. 11.95 o.p. (ISBN 0-671-22844-7). S&S.

--Second Opinion. 1981. 15.95 (ISBN 0-671-25242-9, Linden). S&S.

Rosenfeld, J. L., ed. Information Processing Seventy-Four. LC 74-76063. 1107p. 1975. 106.50 (ISBN 0-444-10689-8, North-Holland). Elsevier.

Rosenfeld, Jeffrey P. Relationships: The Marriage & Family Reader. 1981. pap. text ed. 10.95x o.p. (ISBN 0-673-15267-7). Scott F.

Rosenfeld, Joseph, jt. auth. see Klotter, John C.

Rosenfeld, Joseph G., jt. auth. see Blanco, Ralph F.

Rosenfeld, Lawrence. Human Interaction in the Small Group Setting. LC 72-92860. 1973. text ed. 15.95x (ISBN 0-675-08997-2). Merrill.

--Now That We're All Here...Relations in Small Groups. (Interpersonal Communication Ser.). (Illus.). 1976. pap. text ed. 6.95x (ISBN 0-675-08642-6). Merrill.

Rosenfeld, Lulla. Death & I Ching: A Mystery Novel. Southern, Carol, ed. 192p. 1981. 9.95 (ISBN 0-517-54029-0, C N Potter Bks). Crown.

Rosenfeld, Paul. Discoveries of a Music Critic. LC 79-183510. 402p. Date not set. Repr. of 1936 ed. price not set. Vienna Hse.

--Musical Impressions: Selections from Paul Rosenfeld's Criticism. Leibowitz, Herbert A., ed. LC 76-75252. 334p. 1969. 7.95 o.p. (ISBN 0-8090-7172-X). Hill & Wang.

Rosenfeld, Robert, jt. auth. see Naiman, Arnold.

Rosenfeld, S., jt. ed. see Serrou, B.

Rosenfeldt, Diane. Ken Russell: A Guide to Reference & Resources. 1978. lib. bdg. 17.50 (ISBN 0-8161-7881-X, Hall Reference). G K Hall.

--Richard Lester: A Guide to References & Resources. 1978. lib. bdg. 18.50 (ISBN 0-8161-8185-3, Hall Reference). G K Hall.

Rosenfelt, W. E., ed. Spirit of Seventy Six. 1976. lib. bdg. 9.95 o.p. (ISBN 0-513-01493-4). Denison.

Rosenfield, A. R., et al, eds. Dislocation Dynamics. LC 68-11937. (Series in Materials Science & Engineering). (Illus.). 1968. text ed. 62.00 o.p. (ISBN 0-07-053807-7, P&RB). McGraw.

--What Does the Charpy Test Really Tell Us? 1978. 6.00 o.p. (ISBN 0-87170-027-1). ASM.

Rosenfield, Alvin H. A Double Dying: Reflections on Holocaust Literature. 210p. Repr. 17.50 (ISBN 0-686-95050-X). ADL.

Rosenfield, Bernard. Let's Go to the F.B.I. (Lets Go Ser.). (Illus.). (gr. 4-6). 1960. PLB 4.29 o.p. (ISBN 0-399-60369-7). Putnam Pub Group.

Rosenfield, John M., ed. Song of the Brush: Japanese Paintings from the Sanso Collection. LC 79-19922. (Seattle Art Museum Ser.). (Illus.). 172p. 1979. 35.00 o.p. (ISBN 0-295-95867-7); pap. 22.95 o.p. (ISBN 0-295-95868-5). U of Wash Pr.

Rosenfield, Nancy S. The Radiology of Childhood Leukemia & Its Therapy. 124p. 1982. pap. text ed. 22.50 (ISBN 0-87527-173-1). Green.

Rosenfield, Stanley B. Labor Protective Provisions in Airline Mergers. LC 80-70478. (New Studies on Law & Society). 308p. 1981. 34.00x (ISBN 0-86733-004-X); pap. 19.50x (ISBN 0-686-96664-3). Assoc Faculty Pr.

--Regulation of International Commercial Aviation. 1982. looseleaf binder 85.00 o.p. (ISBN 0-379-11818-1). Oceana.

Rosengarten, A. A Handbook of Architectural Styles. Smith, Roger T., ed. 532p. 1983. pap. 12.50 (ISBN 0-88072-011-5). Tanager Bks.

Rosengarten, Andrew. The Illustrated Book of Indian, Egyptian & West Asiatic Architecture. (The Masterpieces of World Architecture Library). (Illus.). 120p. 1983. Repr. of 1878 ed. 97.85 (ISBN 0-89901-082-2). Found Class Reprints.

Rosengarten, Frederick. The Book of Spices. rev. ed. 1973. pap. 3.95 (ISBN 0-515-06490-4, Y3220). Jove Pubns.

Rosengarten, Theodore. All God's Dangers: The Life of Nate Shaw. 1975. pap. 2.95 (ISBN 0-380-00508-5, 56333-9). Avon.

Rosengrant, R. J., et al, trs. see Izerghina, A.

Rosengren, William & Lefton, Mark. Organization & Clients: Essays in the Sociology of Service. LC 72-122308. 1970. text ed. 11.95x (ISBN 0-675-09313-9). Merrill.

Rosenhan, David L., jt. auth. see Seligman, Martin E.

Rosenkrantz, Linda. Talk. 1968. 4.95 o.p. (ISBN 0-399-10788-6). Putnam Pub Group.

Rosenkrantz, Roger D. Foundations & Applications of Inductive Probability. xiv, 326p. (Orig.). 1981. lib. bdg. 29.00x (ISBN 0-917930-23-1); pap. text ed. 15.00x (ISBN 0-917930-03-7). Ridgeview.

Rosenkranz, George. Bid Your Way to the Top. Hirsch, Tannah, ed. 1978. 5.95 (ISBN 0-87643-026-4). Barclay Bridge.

--Win with Romex: The Key to Accurate Bidding. (Illus.). 384p. 1975. 9.95 o.p. (ISBN 0-517-52445-7). Crown.

Rosenman, Jane, ed. see Slavitt, David.

Rosenman, John B. The Best Laugh Last. LC 81-12990. 224p. 1981. 12.95 (ISBN 0-914232-44-4). Treacle.

Rosenmeyer, Thomas G. The Art of Aeschylus. (Illus.). 393p. 1983. pap. 12.95 (ISBN 0-520-04608-0, CAL 541). U of Cal Pr.

--The Green Cabinet: Theocritus & the European Pastoral Lyric. LC 78-82376. 1969. 30.00x (ISBN 0-520-01381-6); pap. 7.50x (ISBN 0-520-02362-5, CAMPUS90). U of Cal Pr.

Rosenmeyer, Thomas G., ed. see Johnson, W. R.

Rosenmuller, J. The Theory of Games & Markets: An Introduction to Game Theory & Related Topics. 1981. 74.50 (ISBN 0-444-85482-7). Elsevier.

Rosenn, K. S. Law & Inflation. 1978. write for info. o.p. (ISBN 0-685-81205-7, North-Holland). Elsevier.

Rosenne, S. Documents on the International Court of Justice. 2nd ed. LC 73-91985. 497p. 1979. 50.00 (ISBN 0-379-20460-6). Oceana.

Rosenne, Shabtai, ed. League of Nations Committee of Experts for the Progressive Codification of International Law (1925-1928) LC 77-165998. 1972. Set. lib. bdg. 75.00 (ISBN 0-379-00147-0). Oceana.

--League of Nations Conference for the Codification of International Law (1930, 4 vols. LC 74-23544. 1975. Set. lib. bdg. 200.00 (ISBN 0-379-10100-9); lib. bdg. 50.00 ea.; Vol. 1. lib. bdg. (ISBN 0-379-10101-7); Vol. 2. lib. bdg. (ISBN 0-379-10102-5); Vol. 3. lib. bdg. (ISBN 0-379-10103-3); Vol. 4. lib. bdg. (ISBN 0-379-10104-1). Oceana.

Rosenoer, V. & Rothschild, M. A., eds. Controversies in Clinical Care. LC 80-21593. (Illus.). 312p. 1981. text ed. 30.00 (ISBN 0-89335-121-0). Spectrum Pub.

Rosenow, J. & Pulsipher, G. Tourism: The Business & History of Tourism in the U. S. LC 78-65964. (Illus.). 264p. 19.95 (ISBN 0-933400-44-6); pap. 12.95 (ISBN 0-686-96026-2). Dill Ent.

Rosenqvist, T. Principles of Extractive Metallurgy. 2nd ed. 608p. 1983. 42.95x (ISBN 0-07-053910-3, C). McGraw.

Rosenqvist, Terkel. Principles of Extractive Metallurgy. (Illus.). 576p. 1974. text ed. 38.00 (ISBN 0-07-053847-6, C); solutions manual 7.95 (ISBN 0-07-053848-4). McGraw.

Rosensfiel, Leonie, ed. see Rosenstiel, Leonie, et al.

Rosensfit, Gail R. Huckleberry Finn. (Living Literature Workbook Ser.). (Orig.). (gr. 7). pap. 1.50 cancelled o.p. (ISBN 0-671-09248-0). Monarch Pr.

Rosenstein, Ira. Left on the Field to Die, Part 2: Yehudi Weismann. 42p. (Orig.). 1982. pap. 3.00 (ISBN 0-9605438-1-3). Starlight Pr.

Rosenstein, Joseph G. Linear Orderings. LC 80-2341. (Pure & Applied Mathematics Ser.). 1982. 64.00 (ISBN 0-12-597680-1). Acad Pr.

Rosenstein, Nicholas R. The Diseases of Children & Their Remedies. (Nutrition Foundation Reprint Ser.). 1982. 43.00 (ISBN 0-12-727550-9). Acad Pr.

Rosenstiel, Annette, ed. Red & White: Indian Views of the White Man, 1492-1982. LC 82-23901. (Illus.). 192p. 1983. 14.95 (ISBN 0-87663-373-4). Universe.

Rosenstiel, Leonie, et al. Schirmer History of Music. Rosensfiel, Leonie, ed. 1982. text ed. 19.95x (ISBN 0-02-872190-X). Schirmer Bks.

Rosenstock, Gershon G. F. A. Trendelenburg: Forerunner to John Dewey. LC 64-11167. (Philosophical Explorations Ser). 188p. 1964. 6.95x o.p. (ISBN 0-8093-0144-X). S Ill U Pr.

Rosenstock, Janet, jt. auth. see Adair, Dennis.

Rosenstock, Laura, jt. auth. see Lanchner, Carolyn.

Rosenstock-Huessy, Eugen, ed. Judaism Despite Christianity: The "Letters on Christianity & Judaism " Between Eugen Rosenstock-Huessy & Franz Rosenzweig. LC 68-10993. 1971. pap. 2.45 o.p. (ISBN 0-8052-0315-X). Schocken.

Rosenstone, Robert. Romantic Revolutionary: A Biography of John Reed. 1975. 17.95 (ISBN 0-394-46103-7). Knopf.

Rosenstone, Robert A. Crusade of the Left: The Lincoln Battalion in the Spanish Civil War. LC 80-5703. 435p. lib. bdg. 24.50 (ISBN 0-8191-1159-7); pap. text ed. 14.75 (ISBN 0-8191-1160-0). U Pr of Amer.

Rosenstone, Robert A., jt. ed. see Boskin, Joseph.

Rosenstone, Steven J., jt. auth. see Wolfinger, Raymond E.

Rosenstreich, D. L., jt. ed. see Oppenhiem, J. J.

Rosenthal, Alan S., jt. ed. see Unanue, Emil R.

Rosenthal, Barbara. Sensations. LC 81-70287. (Illus.). 48p. 1983. pap. 5.95 (ISBN 0-89822-022-X). Visual Studies.

Rosenthal, Barbara & Rosenthal, Nadia. Christmas: New Ideas for an Old-Fashioned Celebration. (Illus.). 192p. 1980. 12.95 (ISBN 0-517-53695-1, C N Potter Bks). Crown.

Rosenthal, Bernard. Critical Essays on Charles Brockden Brown. (Critical Essays on American Literature). 1981. lib. bdg. 25.00 (ISBN 0-8161-8255-8, Twayne). G K Hall.

Rosenthal, Bert. Marques Johnson: Nobody Does it Better. LC 82-4459. (Sports Stars Ser.). (Illus.). (gr. 2-8). 1982. PLB 7.95g (ISBN 0-516-04325-0); pap. 2.50 (ISBN 0-516-44325-9). Childrens.

--Sugar Ray Leonard: The Baby-Faced Boxer. LC 82-4472. (Sports Stars Ser.). (Illus.). (gr. 2-8). 1982. PLB 7.95g (ISBN 0-516-04326-9); pap. 2.50 (ISBN 0-516-44326-7). Childrens.

Rosenthal, Beth E., jt. auth. see Naxon, Jan L.

Rosenthal, Clifford N., jt. ed. see Engel, Barbara A.

Rosenthal, Constance, jt. auth. see Coplan, Kate.

Rosenthal, D. Genetic Theory & Abnormal Behavior. 1970. text ed. 22.00 o.p. (ISBN 0-07-053864-6, C). McGraw.

Rosenthal, Daniel. Resistance & Deformation of Solid Media. LC 72-10583. 372p. 1974. text ed. 25.00 (ISBN 0-08-017100-1). Pergamon.

Rosenthal, David. Materialism & the Mind-Body Problem. LC 77-157186. (Central Issues in Philosophy Ser.). (Illus.). 1971. pap. 13.95 ref. ed. (ISBN 0-13-560177-0). P-H.

Rosenthal, Donald, ed. The City in Indian Politics. LC 76-900868. 1976. 14.00x o.p. (ISBN 0-88386-859-8). South Asia Bks.

Rosenthal, Donald B. The Expansive Elite: District Politics & State Policy-Making in India. 1977. 36.50x (ISBN 0-520-03160-1). U of Cal Pr.

Rosenthal, Douglas E. Lawyer & Client: Who's in Charge? LC 73-83891. 230p. 1974. 10.50x (ISBN 0-87154-725-2). Russell Sage.

Rosenthal, Douglas E. & Knighton, William M. National Laws & International Commerce: The Problem of Extraterritoriality. (Chatham House Papers Ser.: No. 17). 96p. (Orig.). 1982. pap. 10.00 (ISBN 0-7100-9338-1). Routledge & Kegan.

Rosenthal, Ed, jt. auth. see Frank, Mel.

Rosenthal, Erwin I. Islam in the Modern National State. 1966. 44.50 (ISBN 0-521-06134-2). Cambridge U Pr.

Rosenthal, Franz. The Classical Heritage in Islam. Marmorstein, Emile, tr. LC 69-12476. 1975. 39.00x (ISBN 0-520-01997-0). U of Cal Pr.

Rosenthal, G. Herbiovores. 1982. pap. 32.00 (ISBN 0-12-597182-6). Acad Pr.

Rosenthal, Gary. Volleyball: The Game & How to Play It. (Illus.). 256p. 1983. 12.95 (ISBN 0-686-83674-X, ScribT). Scribner.

Rosenthal, Glenda G. The Mediterranean Basin. new ed. 224p. 1982. text ed. 39.95 (ISBN 0-408-10711-1). Butterworth.

Rosenthal, Harold. Annals of Opera 1940-1981. 520p. 1983. 55.00x (ISBN 0-8476-7108-9). Rowman.

--Fifty Faces of Football: The American Game & What has Made it Great. LC 81-66009. (Illus.). 320p. 1981. 12.95 (ISBN 0-689-11218-1). Atheneum.

--My Mad World of Opera: The Autobiography of the Editor of Opera Magazine. (Illus.). 234p. 1982. text ed. 29.75x (ISBN 0-8419-6305-3). Holmes & Meier.

--The Ten Best Years of Baseball: An Informal History of the Fifties. 184p. 1981. pap. 5.95 o.p. (ISBN 0-442-27063-1). Van Nos Reinhold.

Rosenthal, Irving & Rudman, Harry W. Business Letter Writing Made Simple. rev. ed. pap. 4.95 (ISBN 0-385-01206-3, Made). Doubleday.

Rosenthal, Joan. Lord Is My Strength. 1976. pap. 1.25 o.s.i. (ISBN 0-89129-086-9). Jove Pubns.

Rosenthal, Joseph A., jt. ed. see Di Roma, Edward.

Rosenthal, Linda, jt. auth. see McKay, Sandra.

Rosenthal, M. L. Poetry & the Common Life. LC 82-16913. 176p. 1983. 15.00x (ISBN 0-8052-3851-4); pap. 6.95x (ISBN 0-8052-0738-4). Schocken.

--Sailing into the Unknown: Yeats, Pound, & Eliot. 1978. 15.95x (ISBN 0-19-502318-8). Oxford U Pr.

Rosenthal, M. L. & Gall, Sally M. The Modern Poetic Sequence: The Genius of Modern Poetry. 544p. 1983. 29.95 (ISBN 0-19-503170-9). Oxford U Pr.

Rosenthal, Macha L. Modern Poets: A Critical Introduction. (YA) (gr. 9 up). 1965. pap. 7.95 (ISBN 0-19-500718-2, GB). Oxford U Pr.

Rosenthal, Marvin J. Not Without Design. LC 80-81031. 1980. pap. 3.50 (ISBN 0-915540-27-4). Friends Israel-Spearhead Pr.

Rosenthal, Michael. Constable: The East Anglian Landscapes. LC 82-48908. (Illus.). 240p. 1983. 29.95 (ISBN 0-300-03014-2). Yale U Pr.

Rosenthal, Miriam & Reeves, Marjorie. The French Revolution. (Then & There Ser.). (Illus.). 106p. (Orig.). (gr. 7-12). 1965. pap. text ed. 3.10 (ISBN 0-582-20403-8). Longman.

Rosenthal, Mitchell, et al. Rehabilitation of the Head-Injured Adult. 400p. 1983. 29.95 (ISBN 0-8036-7625-5). Davis Co.

Rosenthal, Nadia, jt. auth. see Rosenthal, Barbara.

Rosenthal, R. The Sign of the Ivory Horn: Eastern African Civilizations. LC 70-132279. (gr. 9 up). 1971. PLB 7.50 (ISBN 0-379-00449-6). Oceana.

Rosenthal, Renate. Jewelry of the Ancient World. LC 72-10797. (Lerner Archaeology Series: Digging up the Past). (gr. 5 up). 1975. PLB 7.95g (ISBN 0-8225-0830-3). Lerner Pubns.

Rosenthal, Richard. The Hearing-Loss Handbook. LC 75-9496. (Illus.). 225p. 1975. 8.95 o.p. (ISBN 0-312-36540-3). St Martin.

Rosenthal, Robert. Experimenter Effects in Behavior Research. enlarged ed. LC 75-37669. (Century Psychology Ser.). 1976. 15.95x o.p. (ISBN 0-470-01391-5). Halsted Pr.

Rosenthal, Robert & Jacobson, Lenore. Pygmalion in the Classroom: Teacher Expectation & Pupils' Intellectual Development. enl. ed. 265p. 1983. pap. text ed. 10.95 (ISBN 0-8290-1265-6). Irvington.

Rosenthal, Robert & Kazanjian, Gary. How to Design for Stained Glass: Even If You Think You Don't Know How to Draw. (Illus.). 84p. (Orig.). 1982. pap. 4.95 (ISBN 0-941170-00-4, 740000-5, Quick Fox). Putnam Pub Group.

Rosenthal, Robert & Rosnow, Ralph L. Primer of Methods for the Behavioral Sciences. LC 74-18295. 1975. text ed. 24.50 o.s.i. (ISBN 0-471-73676-7); pap. text ed. 13.95x o.p. (ISBN 0-471-73675-9). Wiley.

--The Volunteer Subject. LC 74-16378. (Personality Processes Ser). 288p. 1975. 27.50 o.p. (ISBN 0-471-73670-8, Pub. by Wiley-Interscience). Wiley.

Rosenthal, Robert, jt. ed. see Sebeok, Thomas A.

Rosenthal, Robert, et al. Different Strokes: Pathways to Maturity in the Boston Ghetto. LC 76-7952. 1976. lib. bdg. 30.50 o.p. (ISBN 0-89158-036-0); pap. 11.50 o.p. (ISBN 0-89158-047-6). Westview.

Rosenthal, Stanley. One God or Three? 1978. pap. text ed. 1.75 (ISBN 0-87508-464-8). Chr Lit.

Rosenthal, Stephen R. Managing Government Operations. 1982. pap. text ed. 13.50x (ISBN 0-673-16462-4). Scott F.

Rosenthal, Steven T. The Politics of Dependency: Urban Reform in Istanbul. LC 79-7588. (Contributions in Comparative Colonial Studies: No. 3). (Illus.). 1980. lib. bdg. 29.95 (ISBN 0-313-20927-8, RPO/). Greenwood.
Rosenthal, Susan N. & Bennet, John M. Practical Cancer Chemotherapy. (Medical Outline Ser.). 1981. pap. text ed. 22.50 (ISBN 0-87488-848-4). Med Exam.
Rosenthal, Ted. How Could I Not Be Among You? LC 73-80922. 80p. 1973. 6.95 o.p. (ISBN 0-8076-0713-4); pap. 3.95 o.p. (ISBN 0-8076-0714-2). Persea Bks.
Rosenthal-Schneider, Ilse. Reality & Scientific Truth: Discussions with Einstein, von Laue, & Planck. Braun, Thomas, ed. (Illus.). 150p. 1981. 13.95 (ISBN 0-8143-1650-6). Wayne St U Pr.
Rosenwald, G. C. see Lewis, M. & Rosenblum, L. A.
Rosenzweig, jt. auth. see Sinz.
Rosenzweig, James, jt. auth. see Kast, Fremont.
Rosenzweig, James E., jt. auth. see Kast, Fremont E.
Rosenzweig, Linda E., jt. ed. see Copus, David A.
Rosenzweig, M. R. & Porter, L. W., eds. Annual Review of Psychology, Vol. 34. LC 50-13143. (Illus.). 1983. text ed. 27.00 (ISBN 0-8243-0234-6). Annual Reviews.
Rosenzweig, Mark, jt. auth. see Mussen, Paul.
Rosenzweig, Mark R. & Leiman, Arnold L. Physiological Psychology. (Illus.). 736p. 1982. text ed. 24.95 (ISBN 0-669-02901-7). Heath.
Rosenzweig, Mark R. & Bennett, Edward L., eds. Neural Mechanisms of Learning & Memory. LC 75-35780. 1000p. 1976. text ed. 42.50x (ISBN 0-262-18076-6). MIT Pr.
Rosenzweig, Norman & Griscom, Hilda. Psychopharmacology & Psychotherapy: Synthesis or Antithesis? LC 78-4088. 224p. 1978. text ed. 22.95 (ISBN 0-87705-354-5). Human Sci Pr.
Rosenzweig, Robert M., jt. auth. see Babbidge, Homer D.
Rosenzweig, Saul. Aggressive Behavior & the Rosenzweig Picture-Frustration Study. LC 78-18200. (Praeger Special Studies). 1978. 25.95 o.p. (ISBN 0-03-045656-8). Praeger.
--Freud, Jung & the Kingmaker: The Visit to America-The Letters of Sigmund Freud & G. S. Hall, 1908 to 1923 & Freud's Five Lectures at Clark University. LC 78-65156. 1983. 17.50 (ISBN 0-930172-03-5). Rana Hse.
Roser, Wiltrud. Everything about Easter Rabbits. Mayer, Eva L., tr. from Ger. LC 72-7430. (Trophy Picture Bk.). (Illus.). 32p. (ps-2). 1983. pap. 3.13i (ISBN 0-06-443038-3, Trophy). Har-Row.
Rosetti, Rick & Stone, Phil. Rick Rosetti's Baseball Book. (Illus.). 96p. (Orig.). 1980. pap. 5.95 (ISBN 0-920510-09-4, Pub. by Personal Lib). Dodd.
Rosevear, D. R. Carnivores of West Africa. (Illus.). 1974. text ed. 81.00x (ISBN 0-565-00723-8, Pub. by Brit Mus Nat Hist). Sabbot-Natural Hist Bks.
--The Rodents of West Africa. (Illus.). 1969. text ed. 71.50x (ISBN 0-565-00677-0, Pub. by Brit Mus Nat Hist). Sabbot-Natural Hist Bks.
Roseveare, Helen. Living Faith. LC 80-27923. (Orig.). 1981. pap. 4.95 (ISBN 0-8024-4941-7). Moody.
--Living Sacrifice. 1979. pap. 5.95 (ISBN 0-8024-4943-3). Moody.
Roseveare, N. T. Mercury's Perihelion from Le Verrier to Einstein. (Illus.). 216p. 1982. 49.00x (ISBN 0-19-858174-2). Oxford U Pr.
Rosevelt, Fran van see Nieuwenhuys, Rob.
Rosevelt, Frans van see Van Schendel, Arthur.
Rosher, Grace. Beyond the Horizon: Being New Evidence from the Other Side of Life. 154p. 1961. 9.95 (ISBN 0-227-67412-X). Attic Pr.
Roshier, Bob & Teff, Harvey. Law & Society in England. 1980. 25.00x (ISBN 0-422-76720-4, Pub by Tavistock England); pap. 11.95x (ISBN 0-422-76730-1). Methuen Inc.
Roshko, A., jt. auth. see Liepmann, Hans W.
Roshko, Anatol, et al see Heat Transfer & Fluid Mechanics Institute.
Rosholt, Malcolm. Lumbermen On the Chippewa. LC 82-60957. (Illus.). 304p. 1982. 24.95 (ISBN 0-910417-00-8). Rosholt Hse.
--The Wisconsin Logging Book Eighteen Thirty-Nine to Nineteen Thirty-Nine. 3rd. ed. LC 80-53389. (Illus.). 304p. 1983. Repr. of 1980 ed. lib. bdg. 24.95 (ISBN 0-910417-01-6). Rosholt Hse.
Rosholt, Malcolm, tr. see Nelson, E. Clifford.
Rosier, Lydia. Biography of a Bald Eagle. (Nature Biography Ser.). (Illus.). 64p. (gr. 2-5). 1973. PLB 5.49 o.p. (ISBN 0-399-60783-8). Putnam Pub Group.
Rosignoli, Guido. Ribbons of Orders, Decorations, & Medals. LC 76-28307. (Arco Color Books). 1977. 7.95 o.p. (ISBN 0-668-04104-8, 4104); pap. 5.95 (ISBN 0-668-04253-2, 4253). Arco.
Rosin, H. The Lord Is God. 1956. pap. 2.00 o.p. (ISBN 0-686-14409-0, 08643). Am Bible.
Rosing, Kenneth E., jt. auth. see Odell, Peter R.
Rosinger. Nonlinear Partial Differential Equations: Sequential & Weak Solutions. (Mathematical Studies: Vol. 44). 1980. 47.00 (ISBN 0-444-86055-X, North Holland). Elsevier.
Rosinger, E. E. Nonlinear Equivalence: Reduction of Pde's to Ode's & Fast Convergent Numerical Methods. (Research Notes in Mathematics: No. 77). 200p. 1983. pap. text ed. 21.95 (ISBN 0-273-08570-0). Pitman Pub MA.
Rosinski, Richard R. The Development of Visual Perception. LC 76-21558. (Goodyear Developmental Psychology Ser.). 1977. text ed. 17.95x (ISBN 0-673-16186-2). Scott F.
Rosis, Helen De see De Rosis, Helen.
Roskam, William E, jt. ed. see Nichols, Egbert R.
Roskamp, Karl W. Capital Formation in West Germany. LC 64-22331. (Center for Economic Studies Monographs: No. 3). 1965. 13.95x o.p. (ISBN 0-8143-1247-0). Wayne St U Pr.
Roskamp, Karl W., ed. see International Institute of Public Finance, 35th Congress, 1979.
Roske, Ralph J. & Van Doren, Charles. Lincoln's Commando: The Biography of Commander W. B. Cushing, U.S.N. LC 73-7311. (Illus.). 310p. 1973. Repr. of 1957 ed. lib. bdg. 17.25x (ISBN 0-8371-6923-2, ROLC). Greenwood.
Roskill, Stephen. Hankey: Man of Secrets 1919-1931, Vol. 2. LC 75-156341. (Illus.). 576p. 1972. 15.00 o.p. (ISBN 0-312-36015-0, H03270). St Martin.
Roskind, Robert & Owner - Builder Center. Before You Build. LC 81-51897. 192p. (Orig.). 1981. pap. 7.95 (ISBN 0-89815-036-1). Ten Speed Pr.
Roskos, Roland. Problem Solving in Physical Chemistry. LC 74-24649. 1974. pap. text ed. 12.50 (ISBN 0-8299-0028-4). West Pub.
Roslansky, J. Uniqueness of Man. LC 69-18385. (Nobel Conference Lectures Ser.). 9.50x o.p. (ISBN 0-8303-0092-9, Acad Edns). Fleet.
Roslansky, J., ed. Nobel Conference Lectures. Incl. 1966: The Control of the Environment. 1967 (ISBN 0-7204-4029-7); 1967: The Human Mind. 1967 (ISBN 0-7204-4037-8); 1969: Communication. 1969 (ISBN 0-7204-4053-X); 1971: Shaping the Future. 1972 (ISBN 0-7204-4096-3); 1972: The End of Life. 1973 (ISBN 0-7204-6035-2). 12.25 ea. (North Holland). Elsevier.
Rosler, Lee. Opportunities in Life Insurance Sales. Rev. ed. LC 65-19433. 1983. pap. 4.95 (ISBN 0-910580-54-5). Farnswth Pub.
Rosman, Abraham & Rubel, Paula G. The Tapestry of Culture. 1981. pap. text ed. 11.95x o.p. (ISBN 0-673-15281-2). Scott F.
Rosman, N. Paul, jt. auth. see Herskowitz, Joel.
Rosmond, Babette. Monarch. LC 77-27299. 1978. 9.95 o.p. (ISBN 0-399-90009-8, Marek). Putnam Pub Group.
Rosner, Bernard & Beckerman, Jay. Inside the World of Miniatures & Dollhouses: A Comprehensive Guide to Collecting & Creating. LC 76-16458. (Illus.). 256p. 1976. pap. 9.95 o.p. (ISBN 0-679-50620-9). McKay.
Rosner, David. A Once Charitable Enterprise: Hospitals & Health Care in Brooklyn & New York, 1855-1915. LC 81-21725. (Interdisciplinary Perspectives on Modern History Ser.). 288p. 1982. 29.50 (ISBN 0-521-24217-7). Cambridge U Pr.
Rosner, David, jt. ed. see Reverby, Susan.
Rosner, Hilda, tr. see Hesse, Hermann.
Rosner, Joseph. Myths of Child Rearing. LC 82-19924. 1983. 15.50 (ISBN 0-934878-23-4); pap. 8.95 (ISBN 0-934878-29-3). Dembner Bks.
--The Story of the Writings. Borowitz, Eugene B., ed. LC 78-116680. (Illus.). 159p. (gr. 6-7). 1975. pap. text ed. 5.95x o.p. (ISBN 0-87441-229-3). Behrman.
Rosner, Lynn. Let's Go to a Horse Show. LC 74-78641. (Let's Go Ser.). (Illus.). 48p. (gr. 2-6). 1975. PLB 4.29 o.p. (ISBN 0-399-60912-1). Putnam Pub Group.
Rosner, Menachem, jt. auth. see Palgi, Michal.
Rosner, Roy D. Distributed Telecommunications Networks via Satellites & Packet Switching. (Engineering Ser.). 235p. 1982. 31.50 (ISBN 0-534-97933-5). Lifetime Learn.
Rosner, Stanley & Abt, Lawrence E. The Creative Expression. LC 75-37977. (Illus.). 384p. 1976. 18.00 (ISBN 0-88427-015-7). North River.
Rosnow, Ralph, ed. see Goldstein, Jeffrey H.
Rosnow, Ralph L. Paradigms in Transition: The Methodology of Social Inquiry. 176p. 1981. text ed. 18.95x (ISBN 0-19-502876-7); pap. text ed. 8.95x (ISBN 0-19-502877-5). Oxford U Pr.
Rosnow, Ralph L., jt. auth. see Rosenthal, Robert.
Rosof, Patricia, et al, eds. Ethnic & Immigration Groups: Twentieth-Century History & Comparative Analysis. LC 82-23323. (Trends in History Ser.: Vol. 2, No. 4). 1983. text ed. 20.00 (ISBN 0-917724-46-1, B46). Haworth Pr.
--The Middle East & North Africa: Medieval & Modern History. LC 82-11931. (Trends in History Ser.: Vol. 2, No. 3). 128p. 1983. text ed. 20.00 (ISBN 0-917724-45-3, B45). Haworth Pr.
Rosof, Patricia J. & Zeisel, William. Black History. (Trends in History, Vol. 3, No. 1). 128p. 1983. text ed. 20.00 (ISBN 0-86656-135-8, B135). Haworth Pr.
Rosof, Patricia J. & Zeisel, William, eds. The Military & Society. LC 81-20073. (Trends in History: Vol. 2, No. 2). 128p. 1982. text ed. 20.00 (ISBN 0-917724-44-5, B44). Haworth Pr.
--Urban History: Reviews of Recent Research. LC 80-27903. (Trends in History Ser.: Vol. 2, No. 1). 103p. 1982. text ed. 20.00 (ISBN 0-917724-26-7, B26). Haworth Pr.
Rosoff, Arnold J. Informed Consent: A Guide for Health Care Providers. LC 80-23886. 520p. 1981. text ed. 49.50 (ISBN 0-89443-293-1). Aspen Systems.
Rosoff, Iris, ed. see Shyne, Kevin.
Rosolack, Stephen, jt. auth. see Haberlen, John.
Rosovsky, H., ed. Industralization in Two Systems: Essays in Honor of Alexander Gerschenkron, 2 pts. Incl. Pt. I. Capitalism; Pt. II. Society Socialism. 289p. 1966. 14.00 (ISBN 0-471-73674-0). Krieger.
Rosovsky, Henry, jt. ed. see Patrick, Hugh.
Rosow, Jerome M. & Zager, Robert. The Future of Older Workers in America: New Options for an Extended Working Life. 135p. softcover 9.95 (ISBN 0-686-84776-8). Work in Amer.
--Job Strategies for Urban Youth. 102p. softcover 7.95 (ISBN 0-686-84777-6); softcover summary 3.95 (ISBN 0-686-84778-4). Work in Amer.
--New Work Schedules for A Changing Society. 128p. 10.95 (ISBN 0-686-84774-1); softcover summary 4.95 (ISBN 0-686-84775-X). Work in Amer.
--Productivity Through Work Innovations. 176p. 1982. 15.00 (ISBN 0-686-84772-5); softcover summary 6.50 (ISBN 0-686-84773-3). Work in Amer.
Rosow, Michael P. see Zager, Robert.
Rosow, Michael P., jt. ed. see Zager, Robert.
Rosowsky, Andre. Azepines, Pt. 2. (Chemistry of Heterocyclic Compounds). 850p. 1983. 175.00 (ISBN 0-471-89592-X, Pub. by Wiley-Interscience). Wiley.
--Azepines: Heterocyclic Compounds. (Series of Monographs: Pt. 1). 700p. 1983. 150.00 (ISBN 0-471-01878-3, Pub. by Wiley-Interscience). Wiley.
Ross, jt. auth. see Best.
Ross, jt. auth. see Greenwood.
Ross, A. & Sabidussi, G. Theory & Practice of Combinations. (Mathematics Studies Ser.: Vol. 60). 1982. 68.00 (ISBN 0-444-86318-4, North Holland). Elsevier.
Ross, A. M., ed. Industrial Relations & Economic Development. (International Institute for Labor Studies). 1967. 22.50 o.p. (ISBN 0-312-41510-9). St Martin.
Ross, Alan. Bill Brandt: Portraits. 120p. 1982. 80.00x (ISBN 0-86092-062-3, Pub. by Fraser Bks). State Mutual Bk.
Ross, Alan O. Child Behavior Therapy: Principles, Procedures & Empirical Basis. LC 80-24109. 425p. 1981. text ed. 28.50 (ISBN 0-471-02981-5). Wiley.
--Learning Disability: The Unrealized Potential. 1977. 21.95 (ISBN 0-07-053875-1, P&RB). McGraw.
--Psychological Aspects of Learning Disorders of Children. (Special Education Ser.). (Illus.). 320p. 1976. text ed. 22.50 (ISBN 0-07-053845-X, C). McGraw.
--Psychological Disorders of Children: A Behavioral Approach to Theory, Research & Therapy. (Psychology Ser.). (Illus.). 1979. text ed. 27.50 (ISBN 0-07-053883-2). McGraw.
Ross, Alec. Words for Work: Writing Fundamentals for Vocational-Technical Students. (Illus., Orig.). 1970. pap. text ed. 11.95 (ISBN 0-395-05333-1). HM.
Ross, Alec, jt. auth. see Kocher, Helen R.
Ross, Alf. On Guilt, Responsibility & Punishment. LC 73-94446. 1975. 27.50x (ISBN 0-520-02717-5). U of Cal Pr.
--On Law & Justice. (California Library Repr). 1975. Repr. of 1959 ed. 36.50x (ISBN 0-520-02851-1). U of Cal Pr.
Ross, Angus, ed. see Smollett, Tobias.
Ross, Ann, jt. auth. see Supree, Burton.
Ross, Anne. Everyday Life of the Pagan Celts. (Everyday Life Ser.). (Illus.). (gr. 7-11). 1970. 6.75 o.p. (ISBN 0-399-20068-1). Putnam Pub Group.
--Teenage Mothers-Teenage Fathers. 128p. 1982. 10.95 (ISBN 0-920510-53-1, Pub. by Personal Lib). Dodd.
Ross, Anne, jt. auth. see Place, Robin.
Ross, Arnold, jt. ed. see Newman, William A.
Ross, B. Joyce. J. E. Spingarn & the Rise of the NAACP. LC 78-139326. (Studies in American Negro Life). 1972. 10.00 o.p. (ISBN 0-689-10531-2); pap. text ed. 3.95x o.p. (ISBN 0-689-70337-6, NL32). Atheneum.
Ross, Barry & Tarr, William. The Second Now You See It, Now You Don't: More Lessons in Sleight of Hand. (Illus.). 1978. 10.95 o.p. (ISBN 0-394-50036-9); pap. 6.95 (ISBN 0-394-72766-5). Random.
Ross, Bernard H., jt. auth. see Fritschler, A. Lee.
Ross, Bernard H., ed. Urban Management: A Guide to Information Sources. LC 78-10310. (The Urban Studies Information Guide Ser.: Vol. 8). 1979. 42.00x (ISBN 0-8103-1430-4). Gale.
Ross, Bette M. Gennie, the Huguenot Woman. (Illus.). 192p. 1983. 10.95 (ISBN 0-8007-1358-3). Revell.
--Song of Deborah. 256p. 1981. 10.95 (ISBN 0-8007-1263-3). Revell.
Ross, Beverly & Durgin, Jean. Junior Broadway. LC 82-23983. (Illus.). 225p. (Orig.). 1983. pap. 13.95x (ISBN 0-89950-033-1). McFarland & Co.
Ross, Bob, jt. auth. see Fletcher, Mike.
Ross, Bob L. The Restoration Movement. 1981. pap. 1.95 (ISBN 0-686-35837-6). Pilgrim pubns.
--Salvation by Grace Through Faith in Contrast to the Restorationist Doctrine. 1979. pap. 1.00 (ISBN 0-686-35836-8). Pilgrim Pubns.
Ross, Bow. Cooking Amid Chaos. 1983. pap. 7.95 (ISBN 0-89272-168-5). Down East.
Ross, C. A., ed. Paleobiogeography. LC 76-12969. (Benchmark Papers in Geology Ser.: Vol. 31). 1976. 56.50 (ISBN 0-12-787365-1). Acad Pr.
Ross, C. T. & Johns, T. Computer Analysis of Skeletal Structures. 1981. 26.00x (ISBN 0-419-11970-1, Pub. by E & Fn Spon England). Methuen Inc.
Ross, Caroline. Miss Nobody. 256p. 1981. 11.95 (ISBN 0-312-92536-0). Congdon & Weed.
Ross, Cathy R. & Beggs, Denise M. The Whole Baby Catalogue. LC 76-43410. (Illus.). 224p. 1977. pap. 6.95 o.p. (ISBN 0-8069-8774-X). Sterling.
Ross, Charles. Edward Fourth. LC 74-79771. (English Monarchs Ser). (Illus.). 1975. 48.50x (ISBN 0-520-02781-7). U of Cal Pr.
--The Inner Sanctuary. 1967. pap. 2.95 (ISBN 0-686-12520-7). Banner of Truth.
Ross, Charles, ed. see Vale, M. G.
Ross, Charles L. The Composition of The Rainbow & Women in Love: A History. LC 79-1422. (Illus.). 168p. 1979. 13.50x (ISBN 0-8139-0704-7). U Pr of Va.
Ross, Charlotte. Who Is the Minister's Wife? A Search for Personal Fulfillment. LC 79-24027. 1980. pap. 6.95 (ISBN 0-664-24302-9). Westminster.
Ross, Clarissa. Eternal Desire. 1979. pap. 2.50 o.s.i. (ISBN 0-515-04818-6). Jove Pubns.
--Moscow Mists. 1977. pap. 1.95 (ISBN 0-380-00912-9, 32011). Avon.
--Summer of the Shaman. 240p. (Orig.). 1982. pap. 1.95 (ISBN 0-446-90796-0). Warner Bks.
--Tangier Nights. 304p. (Orig.). 1981. pap. 2.75 o.s.i. (ISBN 0-515-05368-6). Jove Pubns.
Ross, Clarkson. Beside the Seaside. 13.50x (ISBN 0-392-02254-0, SpS). Sportshelf.
Ross, Cleon W., jt. ed. see Salisbury, Frank B.
Ross, Corinne. Christmas in Britain. Lopez, Jadwiga, ed. LC 78-58921. (Round the World Christmas Program Ser.). (Illus.). 1978. write for info. o.p. (ISBN 0-7166-2007-3). World Bk.
--Christmas in Italy. Lopez, Jadwiga, ed. LC 79-65246. (Round the World Christmas Program Ser.). 1979. write for info. (ISBN 0-7166-2008-1). World Bk.
--Christmas in Mexico. Lopez, Jadwiga, ed. LC 76-21970. (Round the World Christmas Program Ser.). (Illus.). 1976. 7.95 (ISBN 0-7166-2002-2). World Bk.
--Christmas in Scandinavia. Lopez, Jadwiga, ed. LC 77-80352. (Rounc the World Christmas Program Ser.). (Illus.). 1977. 7.95 o.p. (ISBN 0-7166-2003-0). World Bk.
Ross, Corinne M. Mid-Atlantic Guest House Book. (Illus.). 192p. 1983. pap. 7.95 (ISBN 0-914788-62-0). East Woods.
--The New England Guest House Book. LC 79-4899. (Illus.). 192p. 1979. pap. 6.95 o.p. (ISBN 0-914788-15-9). East Woods.
--The Southern Guest House Book. rev. ed. 192p. 1983. pap. 7.95 (ISBN 0-914788-71-X). East Woods.
Ross, D. Aristote. (Publications Gramma Ser.). 436p. 1971. 32.00x (ISBN 0-685-33030-3). Gordon.
--Energy from the Waves. 2nd ed. (Illus.). 1979. text ed. 23.00 o.p. (ISBN 0-08-023271-X); pap. text ed. 8.25 (ISBN 0-08-023272-8). Pergamon.
Ross, D. N. A Surgeon's Guide to Cardiac Diagnosis: Pt. 1, The Diagnostic Approach. (Illus.). viii, 72p. 1962. pap. 21.30 (ISBN 0-387-03967-8). Springer-Verlag.
Ross, Dana F. Nevada! (General Ser.). 1982. lib. bdg. 15.95 (ISBN 0-8161-3396-4, Large Print Bks). G K Hall.
--Washington! (Wagons West Ser.). 1982. pap. 3.50 (ISBN 0-553-20919-1). Bantam.
--Washington. (General Ser.). 1983. price not set (Large Print Bks). G K Hall.
Ross, Dave. Mummy Madness. (Illus.). (gr. 3 up). 1979. PLB 6.90 s&l (ISBN 0-531-04094-1). Watts.
Ross, David. Aristotle. 5th ed. 312p. 1964. pap. 12.50x (ISBN 0-416-68150-6). Methuen Inc.
--Introduction to Oceanography. 2nd ed. LC 76-17838. (Illus.). 1977. text ed. 26.95 (ISBN 0-13-491332-9). P-H.
Ross, David, ed. Illustrated Treasury of Poetry for Children. LC 76-86680. (Illus.). (gr. 4 up). 1970. 12.95 (ISBN 0-448-02828-X, G&D). Putnam Pub Group.
Ross, David A. Introduction to Oceanography. 3rd ed. (Illus.). 528p. 1982. 26.95 (ISBN 0-13-491357-4). P-H.
Ross, David A., jt. auth. see Simon, Andrew L.
Ross, David P., Jr., ed. see Adams, Russell L.
Ross, Diana. Little Red Engine Goes to Market. (Illus.). (gr. k-2). 7.95 o.p. (ISBN 0-571-06330-6). Transatlantic.
Ross, Diane & Schaffer, Elyse. The Birthday Party Book. (Illus., Orig.). 1979. spiral bdg. 6.95 (ISBN 0-8437-2803-5). Hammond Inc.
Ross, Donald. A Public Citizen's Action Manual. 238p. Date not set. pap. 1.95 (ISBN 0-686-36537-2). Ctr Responsive Law.
Ross, Donald, jt. auth. see Nader, Ralph.
Ross, Donald K. Newspaper Correspondent's Manual. 1962. pap. 1.95 o.p. (ISBN 0-87462-425-8). Marquette.
Ross, Donald M., jt. auth. see Sutton, George A.

Ross, Dorothea M. & Ross, Sheila A. Hyperactivity: Research, Theory & Action. LC 76-5227. (Personality Processes Ser.). 480p. 1976. 33.95 o.p. (ISBN 0-471-73678-3, Pub. by Wiley-Interscience). Wiley.
Ross, Dorothea M. & Ross, Shella A. Hyperactivity: Current Issues, Research & Theory. 2nd ed. 500p. 1982. 36.95 (ISBN 0-471-06331-2, Pub. by Wiley-Interscience). Wiley.
Ross, Douglas A. Optoelectronic Devices & Optical Imaging Techniques. (Electrical & Electronic Engineering Ser.). (Illus.). 137p. 1979. text ed. 27.50x (ISBN 0-333-24292-0, Pub. by MacMillan London); pap. text ed. 18.50x (ISBN 0-333-25335-3, Pub. by MacMillan London). Scholium Intl.
Ross, Douglas A., jt. auth. see Mueller, Peter G.
Ross, E. Denison. This English Language. LC 73-167147. 266p. 1973. Repr. of 1939 ed. 34.00x (ISBN 0-8103-3184-5). Gale.
Ross, E. K. On Death & Dying. 1969. 11.95; pap. 3.95 (ISBN 0-02-089130-X, 08913). Macmillan.
Ross, Ed. Professional Electrical-Electronic Engineers License Study Guide. LC 77-7495. (Illus.). 1977. 13.95 o.p. (ISBN 0-8306-7742-9); pap. 7.95 o.p. (ISBN 0-8306-6742-3, 742). TAB Bks.
Ross, Edward A. The Old World in the New: The Significance of Past & Present Immigration to the American People. LC 77-145491. (American Immigration Library). x, 327p. 1971. Repr. of 1914 ed. lib. bdg. 17.95x (ISBN 0-89198-024-5). Ozer.
Ross, Elinor P., jt. auth. see Roe, Betty D.
Ross, Elizabeth & Ross, Gerald. How St. Francis Tamed the Wolf. (Illus.). 32p. (ps). 1983. bds. 8.95 (ISBN 0-370-30506-X, Pub by The Bodley Head). Merrimack Bk Serv.
Ross, Elizabeth D. The Kindergarten Crusade: The Establishment of Preschool Education in the United States. LC 75-36986. ix, 119p. 1976. 9.00x (ISBN 0-8214-0206-4, 82-82139); pap. 4.25 o.s.i. (ISBN 0-8214-0228-5). Ohio U Pr.
Ross, Eric B., ed. Beyond the Myths of Culture: Essays in Cultural Materialism. LC 79-6772. (Studies in Anthropology Ser.). 1980. 32.50 (ISBN 0-12-598180-5). Acad Pr.
Ross, Eva J. Living in Society. 1966. 4.96 o.p. (ISBN 0-02-827000-2); teachers' manual 2.32 o.p. (ISBN 0-02-827020-7). Glencoe.
Ross, F. G. M., jt. auth. see Gordon, I. R. S.
Ross, Frank. Dead Runner. LC 76-44499. 1977. 8.95 o.p. (ISBN 0-689-10774-9). Atheneum.
Ross, Frank, Jr. The Metric System: Measures for All Mankind. LC 74-14503. (Illus.). 128p. (gr. 7-10). 1974. 12.95 (ISBN 0-87599-198-X). S G Phillips.
--Undersea Vechicles & Habitats: The Peaceful Uses of the Ocean. LC 76-106577. (Illus.). (gr. 5-8). 1970. 10.95i o.p. (ISBN 0-690-84416-6, TYC-J). Har-Row.
Ross, Frederick C. Introduction to Microbiology. 1983. text ed. 22.95 (ISBN 0-675-20003-2); student guide 6.95 (ISBN 0-675-20066-0). Additional supplements may be obtained from publisher. Merrill.
Ross, G. R., ed. see Descartes, Rene.
Ross, George, jt. auth. see Lange, Peter.
Ross, Gerald, jt. auth. see Ross, Elizabeth.
Ross, Gordon, et al. Pathophysiology of the Heart. LC 81-23603. (Illus.). 320p. 1982. flexi-cover 17.50x (ISBN 0-89352-149-3). Masson Pub.
Ross, Gregory A. Grounds for Grammar. 1976. pap. text ed. 8.25 (ISBN 0-8191-0063-3). U Pr of Amer.
Ross, H. John. Technique of Systems & Procedures. (Illus.). 19.50 (ISBN 0-911056-01-7). Office Res.
Ross, H. Laurence, ed. Perspectives on the Social Order. 3rd ed. (Illus.). 608p. 1973. pap. 16.95 (ISBN 0-07-053872-7, C). McGraw.
Ross, Harvey. Fighting Depression. 221p. (Orig.). 1975. pap. 3.25 (ISBN 0-686-71005-3). Larchmont Bks.
--Fighting Depression. 2.25x (ISBN 0-686-36347-7). Cancer Control Soc.
Ross, Harvey, jt. auth. see Saunders, Jeraldine.
Ross, Heather C. The Art of Arabian Costume. 1982. 59.00x (ISBN 0-907513-00-X, Pub. by Cave Pubns England). State Mutual Bk.
--The Art of Arabian Costume: A Saudi Arabian Profile. (Illus.). 188p. 1982. 50.00 (ISBN 0-7103-0031-X, Kegan Paul). Routledge & Kegan.
--The Art of Bedouin Jewellery. 1982. 59.00x (ISBN 0-907513-01-8, Pub. by Cave Pubns England). State Mutual Bk.
--The Art of Bedouin Jewellery: A Saudi Arabian Profile. (Illus.). 132p. 1982. 45.00 (ISBN 0-7103-0032-8, Kegan Paul). Routledge & Kegan.
Ross, Herbert H. Textbook of Entomology. 3rd ed. LC 65-16424. 1965. 27.95x o.p. (ISBN 0-471-73692-9). Wiley.
Ross, Herbert H., et al. A Textbook of Entomology. 4th ed. LC 81-16097. 696p. 1982. text ed. 27.95 (ISBN 0-471-73694-5). Wiley.
Ross, I. K. Biology of the Fungi. 1979. 28.50 (ISBN 0-07-053870-0). McGraw.
Ross, Ian C., ed. see Sterne, Lawrence.
Ross, Ian S. William Dunbar. xiv, 284p. 1981. text ed. 24.00x (ISBN 0-686-87023-9, Pub. by E J Brill England). Humanities.
Ross, J. & O'Rourke, R. A. Understanding the Heart & Its Disease. 1975. 16.95 (ISBN 0-07-053861-1, C); pap. 14.95 (ISBN 0-07-053862-X). McGraw.
Ross, J. M. & Chanan, G. Comprehensive Schools in Focus. (Exploring Education Ser.). 1972. pap. text ed. 3.00x o.p. (ISBN 0-85633-014-0, NFER). Humanities.
Ross, J. Michael & Berg, William M. I Respectfully Disagree with the Judge's Order: The Boston School Desegregation Controversy. LC 80-5818. 782p. (Orig.). 1981. lib. bdg. 31.75 (ISBN 0-8191-1657-2); pap. text ed. 22.50 (ISBN 0-8191-1658-0). U Pr of Amer.
Ross, Jack C. An Assembly of Good Fellows: Voluntary Associations in History. LC 75-35355. 320p. 1976. lib. bdg. 29.95x (ISBN 0-8371-8586-6, RGF/). Greenwood.
Ross, Jack C. & Wheeler, Raymond H. Black Belonging: A Study of the Social Correlates of Work Relations Among Negroes. LC 77-105974. (Contributions in Sociology: No. 7). 1971. lib. bdg. 29.95x (ISBN 0-8371-3298-3, RBB/); pap. 4.95 (ISBN 0-8371-5962-8). Greenwood.
Ross, Jack C., ed. Participation, Associations, & Change: Essays from Albert Meister. 325p. 1982. cancelled 19.95 (ISBN 0-87855-423-8). Transaction Bks.
Ross, James. Whisky. (Illus.). 1970. 12.00 o.p. (ISBN 0-7100-6685-6). Routledge & Kegan.
Ross, James, jt. auth. see Forbes, Jean.
Ross, James F. Portraying Analogy. LC 81-15463. (Cambridge Studies in Philosophy). (Illus.). 280p. 1982. 29.50 (ISBN 0-521-23805-6). Cambridge U Pr.
Ross, James F., ed. Inquiries into Medieval Philosophy: A Collection in Honor of Francis P. Clarke. LC 74-105984. (Contributions in Philosophy: No. 4). 1971. lib. bdg. 29.95x (ISBN 0-8371-3311-4, RMP/). Greenwood.
Ross, James F., tr. Suarez: Disputation Six, on Formal & Universal Unity. (Medieval Philosophical Texts in Translation: No. 15). 1965. pap. 7.95 (ISBN 0-87462-215-8). Marquette.
Ross, Jeffrey A., et al. The Mobilization of Collective Identity: Comparative Perspectives. LC 80-5439. 373p. 1980. lib. bdg. 21.00 o.p. (ISBN 0-8191-1100-7); pap. text ed. 13.75 (ISBN 0-8191-1101-5). U Pr of Amer.
Ross, Jeffrey S., jt. auth. see Ross, Martin J.
Ross, Joel E. Modern Management & Information Systems. (Illus.). 288p. 1976. 19.95 (ISBN 0-87909-499-0). Reston.
Ross, Joel E., jt. auth. see Murdick, Robert C.
Ross, Joel E., jt. auth. see Murdick, Robert G.
Ross, John B. The Economic System of Mexico. 130p. 1971. 5.00 o.p. (ISBN 0-912098-09-0). Cal Inst Intl St.
Ross, John F. Handbook for Radio Engineering Managers. 1000p. 1980. text ed. 89.95 (ISBN 0-408-00424-X). Butterworth.
Ross, John M. Trials in Collections: An Index to Famous Trials Throughout the World. LC 82-21635. 218p. 1983. 16.00 (ISBN 0-8108-1603-2). Scarecrow.
Ross, John R., ed. see Borkin, Ann.
Ross, Jonathan. Death's Head. 256p. 1983. 11.95 (ISBN 0-312-18882-X). St Martin.
Ross, Joseph A., jt. auth. see Pessin, Allan H.
Ross, Josephine. The Monarchy of Britain. LC 82-81952. (Illus.). 192p. 1982. 17.50 (ISBN 0-688-00949-2). Morrow.
--Suitors to the Queen: The Men in the Life of Elizabeth I of England. LC 75-31864. (Illus.). 208p. 1975. 8.95 o.p. (ISBN 0-698-10698-9, Coward). Putnam Pub Group.
--The Tudors: England's Golden Age. LC 79-84036. (Illus.). 1979. 15.95 o.p. (ISBN 0-399-12417-9). Putnam Pub Group.
--The Winter Queen: A Biography of Elizabeth of Bohemia. 1979. 18.95x (ISBN 0-312-88232-7). St Martin.
Ross, Judith W., jt. auth. see Winslade, William J.
Ross, K. F. Phase Contrast & Interference Microscopy. 1967. 26.00 (ISBN 0-312-60410-6). St Martin.
Ross, Lanson. Total Life Prosperity. 170p. (Orig.). 1982. pap. 4.95 (ISBN 0-8423-7293-8). Tyndale.
Ross, Lee, jt. auth. see Nisbett, Richard.
Ross, Lee, jt. ed. see Flavell, John.
Ross, Leonard Q. Education of Hyman Kaplan. LC 38-6588. (gr. 10 up). 1968. pap. 2.95 (ISBN 0-15-627811-1, Harv). HarBraceJ.
Ross, Lola Romanucci see Romanucci-Ross, Lola.
Ross, Lydia. Cycles: In Universe & Man. rev. ed. Small, W. Emmett & Todd, Helen, eds. (Theosophical Manual: No. 8). 92p. 1975. pap. 2.50 (ISBN 0-913004-19-7, 913004-19). Point Loma Pub.
Ross, Lydia & Ryan, Charles J. Theosophia: An Introduction. 1974. pap. 1.75 (ISBN 0-913004-13-8). Point Loma Pub.
Ross, Maggie. Fire of Your Life. LC 82-61420. 128p. 1983. pap. 4.95 (ISBN 0-8091-2513-7). Paulist Pr.
Ross, Malcolm. The Dukes. 1981. 14.95 o.s.i. (ISBN 0-671-25111-2). S&S.
Ross, Marc H. Grass Roots in an African City: Political Behavior in Nairobi. LC 74-34263. 192p. 1975. text ed. 25.00x (ISBN 0-262-18074-X). MIT Pr.
Ross, Marc H. & Williams, Robert H. Our Energy-Regaining Control. (Illus.). 320p. 1980. 19.95 (ISBN 0-07-053894-8, P&RB). McGraw.
Ross, Marilyn. Britannia: The Dancing Years. 288p. (Orig.). 1982. pap. 2.95 (ISBN 0-523-41183-9). Pinnacle Bks.
Ross, Mark. Auditory Management of Hearing-Impaired Children. (Perspectives in Audiology Ser.). 392p. 1978. text ed. 19.95 (ISBN 0-8391-1246-7). Univ Park.
--Hard of Hearing Children in Regular Schools. (Illus.). 272p. 1982. 20.95 (ISBN 0-13-383802-1). P-H.
Ross, Mark, jt. auth. see Ross, Ray.
Ross, Mark, jt. auth. see Ross, Raymond S.
Ross, Martin J. & Ross, Jeffrey S. Handbook of Everyday Law. 4th, rev. ed. LC 80-8216. (Illus.). 384p. 1981. 15.30i (ISBN 0-06-013659-6, HarpT). Har-Row.
Ross, Mary C., jt. auth. see Collier, Kathleen W.
Ross, Michael, ed. see Wilson, Arthur N.
Ross, Michael F. Beyond Metabolism: The New Japanese Architecture. LC 77-13696. (Illus.). 1978. 24.75 (ISBN 0-07-053893-X, Architectural Rec Bks). McGraw.
Ross, Michael H. & Reith, Edward J. Histology: A Text & Atlas. 352p. 1983. text ed. 25.50 scp (ISBN 0-06-045602-7, HarpC). Har-Row.
Ross, Michael J., jt. auth. see Goldbach, John.
Ross, Monte, ed. Laser Applications, 3 vols. Vol. 1, 1971. 57.00 (ISBN 0-12-431901-7); Vol. 2, 1974. 57.00 (ISBN 0-12-431902-5); Vol. 3, 1977. 46.00 (ISBN 0-12-431903-3). Acad Pr.
Ross, Murray G. The University: The Anatomy of Academe. LC 75-43957. 1976. 13.50 o.p. (ISBN 0-07-053876-X, P&RB). McGraw.
Ross, N. W., jt. auth. see Chmura, G. L.
Ross, N. W. & Nixon, D. W., eds. Boat & Marine Equipment Theft: Summary Report of a 1979 National Workshop. (Marine Memo Ser.: No. 64). 48p. 1980. 2.00 o.p. (ISBN 0-686-36981-5, P838). URI Mas.
Ross, Nancy W. Joan of Arc. (World Landmark Ser: No. 4). (Illus.). (gr. 7-9). Date not set. PLB price not set (ISBN 0-394-85339-3, BYR). Random.
--Three Ways of Asian Wisdom. 1978. 14.95 o.p. (ISBN 0-671-24231-8). S&S.
--Three Ways of Asian Wisdom: Hinduism, Buddhism, Zen. (Illus.). 1978. pap. 10.50 (ISBN 0-671-24230-X, Touchstone Bks). S&S.
Ross, Nina, ed. Directory of U.S. Toy Lending Libraries. 123p. (Orig.). pap. 24.00 (ISBN 0-934140-19-7). Toys N Things.
Ross, Novelene. Manet's "Bar at the Folies-Bergere" & the Myths of Popular Illustration. Foster, Stephen C., ed. LC 82-8430. (Studies in Fine Arts: The Avant-Garde: No. 34). 186p. 1982. 39.95 (ISBN 0-8357-1357-1, Pub. by UMI Res Pr). Univ Microfilms.
Ross, Pat. M & M & the Bad News Babies. LC 81-18714. (I Am Reading Bk.). (Illus.). 48p. (gr. 1-4). 1983. 6.95 (ISBN 0-686-37683-8); PLB 7.99 (ISBN 0-394-94532-8). Pantheon.
--M & M & the Haunted House. (gr. k-6). 1982. pap. 1.75 (ISBN 0-440-45544-8, YB). Dell.
--Meet M & M. (gr. k-6). 1982. pap. 1.75 (ISBN 0-440-45546-4, YB). Dell.
Ross, Penina S. VIP Visitors at the Israeli President's House. (Illus.). 1982. 0.00 (ISBN 0-86628-024-3). Ridgefield Pub.
Ross, R. Adam Kok's Griquas. (African Studies: No. 21). (Illus.). 1977. 27.50 (ISBN 0-521-21199-9). Cambridge U Pr.
--Essentials of Speech Communication. 1979. pap. 14.95 (ISBN 0-13-289314-2). P-H.
Ross, R., ed. Symposium on Recent & Fossil Diatoms Proceedings Budapest Sept. 1980, Taxonomy, Morphology, Ecology, Biology, 6th. (Illus.). 500p. 1982. text ed. 100.00x (ISBN 3-87429-192-8). Lubrecht & Cramer.
Ross, R. B. Handbook of Metal Treatments & Testing. 1977. 49.95x (ISBN 0-419-10960-9, Pub. by E & FN Spon). Methuen Inc.
--Metallic Materials Specification Handbook. 3rd ed. 1980. 95.00x (ISBN 0-419-11360-6, Pub. E & FN Spon England). Methuen Inc.
Ross, R. N., jt. auth. see Cohen, S. I.
Ross, Ralph. Symbols & Civilization: Science, Morals, Religion, Art. LC 62-21848. 1963. pap. 3.25 (ISBN 0-15-687605-1, Harv). HarBraceJ.
Ross, Ralph see Dewey, John.
Ross, Ramon R. Storyteller. 2nd ed. (Elementary Education Ser.: No. C22). 240p. 1980. pap. text ed. 9.95 (ISBN 0-675-08169-6). Additional supplements may be obtained from publisher. Merrill.
Ross, Ray & Ross, Mark. Relating & Interacting: An Introduction to Interpersonal Communication. (Illus.). 320p. 1981. pap. text ed. 16.95 (ISBN 0-13-771923-X). P-H.
Ross, Raymond S. & Ross, Mark. Understanding Persuasion. (P-H Speech Communication Ser.). (Illus.). 224p. 1981. pap. text ed. 13.95 (ISBN 0-13-936484-6). P-H.
Ross, Robert. The Apartment Finder's Handbook. 1971. pap. 3.95 o.p. (ISBN 0-686-02010-3, Dist. by Random). Village Voice.
--Cape of Torments: Slavery & Resistance in South Africa. (International Library of Anthropology). 176p. 1983. price not set (ISBN 0-7100-9407-8). Routledge & Kegan.
--A French Finish. LC 76-48309. 1977. 7.95 o.p. (ISBN 0-399-11884-5). Putnam Pub Group.
--Research: An Introduction. pap. 4.95 (ISBN 0-06-460141-2, CO 141, COS). B&N NY.
Ross, Robert, jt. auth. see Daubitz, Paul.
Ross, Robert D. The Management of Public Relations: Analysis & Planning External Relations. LC 77-9288. (Marketing Management Ser.). 1977. 37.50 (ISBN 0-471-03109-7). Ronald Pr.
Ross, Robert H. Ancient Persians Designs for Needlepoint. LC 82-5716. (Illus.). 96p. 1982. 19.95 (ISBN 0-312-03583-7). St Martin.
--The Georgian Revolt: Rise & Fall of a Poetic Ideal 1910-1922. 296p. 1982. Repr. of 1965 ed. lib. bdg. 30.00 (ISBN 0-8495-4701-6). Arden Lib.
Ross, Robert J. Infinite Syntax. (Language & Being Ser.). 1983. write for info (ISBN 0-89391-042-2). Ablex Pub.
Ross, Robert R. & McKay, Hugh B. Self-Mutilation. (Illus.). 208p. 1979. 22.95 (ISBN 0-669-02116-4). Lexington Bks.
Ross, Robert S. American National Government. 3rd ed. 1981. pap. 12.95 (ISBN 0-395-30717-1); Tchrs Manual 1.25 (ISBN 0-395-31248-5). HM.
Ross, Rockford, jt. auth. see Starkey, J. Denbigh.
Ross, Ruth. Prospering Woman. 224p. 1982. pap. 7.95 (ISBN 0-931432-09-X). Whatever Pub.
Ross, S. An Introduction to Ordinary Differential Equations. 3rd ed. 503p. 1980. text ed. 25.95 (ISBN 0-471-03295-6); solutions manual avail. (ISBN 0-471-05775-4). Wiley.
--The Seafood Cookbook. 1978. 12.95 (ISBN 0-07-053881-6). McGraw.
Ross, S. D., jt. auth. see Considine, Douglas M.
Ross, S. L., jt. auth. see Best, G. A.
Ross, Sam. Windy City. 1979. 12.50 o.p. (ISBN 0-399-12335-0). Putnam Pub Group.
Ross, Sheila A., jt. auth. see Ross, Dorothea M.
Ross, Sheldon. A First Course in Probability. (Illus.). 416p. 1976. text ed. 26.95x (ISBN 0-02-403880-6). Macmillan.
--Introduction to Probability Models. 2nd ed. (Probability & Mathematical Statistics Ser.). 1980. 26.00 (ISBN 0-12-598460-X); solutions manual 2.00 (ISBN 0-12-598462-6). Acad Pr.
Ross, Sheldon, ed. Introduction to Stochastic Dynamic Programming: Probability & Mathematical. LC 82-18163. Date not set. price not set (ISBN 0-12-598420-0). Acad Pr.
Ross, Sheldon M. Applied Probability Models with Optimization Applications. LC 73-111376. 1970. write for info. Holden-Day.
--Stochastic Processes. LC 82-8619. (Probability & Mathematical Statistics Ser.). 309p. 1983. text ed. 29.95 (ISBN 0-471-09942-2); solutions manual avail. (ISBN 0-471-87236-9). Wiley.
Ross, Shella A., jt. auth. see Ross, Dorothea M.
Ross, Shepley L. Differential Equations. 2nd ed. LC 73-84447. 1974. text ed. 29.95 (ISBN 0-471-00930-X). Wiley.
Ross, Shirley. The Complex Carbohydrate Handbook. 192p. 1981. pap. 6.95 (ISBN 0-688-00593-4). Quill NY.
--First Aid for House Plants. LC 75-37763. 175p. 1976. 9.95 o.p. (ISBN 0-07-053869-7, GB); pap. 6.95 o.p. (ISBN 0-07-053868-9). McGraw.
Ross, Sidney, et al. Anodic Oxidation. (Organic Chemistry Ser.). 1975. 63.00 (ISBN 0-12-597650-X). Acad Pr.
Ross, Skip & Carlson, Carole. Say Yes to Your Potential. 1983. 8.95 (ISBN 0-8499-0309-2). Word Pub.
Ross, Stan. World of Drafting. (gr. 7-9). 1971. text ed. 18.64 (ISBN 0-87345-078-7). McKnight.
Ross, Stanely R., jt. ed. see Erb, Richard D.
Ross, Stanley R., ed. Is the Mexican Revolution Dead? 2nd ed. LC 75-14017. 377p. 1971. 24.95 (ISBN 0-87722-075-1); pap. 8.95 (ISBN 0-87722-047-6). Temple U Pr.
--Latin America in Transition: Problems in Training & Research. LC 71-112607. 1970. 24.50x (ISBN 0-87395-068-2). State U NY Pr.
Ross, Stephen D. Learning & Discovery. 148p. 1981. 30.00 (ISBN 0-677-05110-7). Gordon.
--Philosophical Mysteries. LC 80-26837. (Ser. in Philosophy). 160p. 1981. 39.50x (ISBN 0-87395-524-2); pap. 12.95x (ISBN 0-87395-525-0). State U NY Pr.
--Transition to an Ordinal Metaphysics. 162p. 1980. 39.50x (ISBN 0-87395-434-3); pap. 12.95x (ISBN 0-87395-435-1). State U NY Pr.
Ross, Stephen David. A Theory of Art: Inexhaustibility by Contrast. LC 81-9027. (SUNY Ser. in Systematic Philosophy). 246p. 1982. 39.50x (ISBN 0-87395-554-4); pap. 11.95x (ISBN 0-87395-555-2). State U NY Pr.
Ross, Stephen V. Spelling Made Simple. rev. ed. LC 80-2624. (Illus.). 192p. 1981. pap. 4.50 (ISBN 0-385-17482-9, Made). Doubleday.
Ross, Steve, ed. Environment Regulation Handbook, Nineteen Eighty. 295.00 o.p. (ISBN 0-89947-013-0). EIC Intell.
Ross, Steven. European Diplomatic History Seventeen Eighty-Nine to Eighteen Fifteen: France Against Europe. LC 81-8242. 436p. 1981. Repr. of 1969 ed. lib. bdg. 14.50 (ISBN 0-89874-369-9). Krieger.
Ross, Steven & Pronin, Monica, eds. Toxic Substances Sourcebook: The Professional's Guide to the Information Sources, Key Literature & Laws of a Critical New Field. LC 77-84943. 1978. 95.00 o.p. (ISBN 0-686-05537-3, 5977). EIC Intell.

Ross, Steven M. Introductory Statistics: A Conceptual Approach. 1982. 14.50x (ISBN 0-8134-2248-5). Interstate.

Ross, Steven S., jt. auth. see Kolb, John.

Ross, Steven S., ed. Toxic Substances Sourcebook: The Professional's Guide to Information Sources, Key Literature, & Laws. LC 77-28044. (Series 1). 1978. 95.00 o.p. (ISBN 0-89947-004-1). EIC Intell.

Ross, Thomas W., ed. see Chaucer, Geoffrey.

Ross, Timothy A. Chiang Kuei. LC 74-2172. (World Authors Ser.: China: No. 320). 1974. lib. bdg. 15.95 o.p. (ISBN 0-8057-2214-9, Twayne). G K Hall.

Ross, Timothy L., jt. auth. see Moore, Brian E.

Ross, Tony. Hugo & Oddsock. (Illus.). (gr. 1-3). 1978. 6.95 (ISBN 0-695-80959-8); PLB 4.65 trade ed. (ISBN 0-695-40959-X). Follett.

--Hugo & the Man Who Stole Colors. (Picture Bk). (Illus.). (gr. 1-3). 1977. 6.95 o.s.i. (ISBN 0-695-80774-9); lib. ed. 6.99 o.s.i. (ISBN 0-695-40774-0). Follett.

--Naughty Nicky. (Illus.). 24p. (gr. k-3). 1983. 11.95 (ISBN 0-03-063522-5). HR&W.

Ross, Tony, adapted by. & illus. Puss in Boots: The Story of A Sneaky Cat. LC 81-2181. (Illus.). 32p. (gr. k-2). 1981. 8.95 o.s.i. (ISBN 0-440-07122-4); PLB 8.89 o.s.i. (ISBN 0-440-07157-7). Delacorte.

Ross, W. Phantom of Edgewater Hall. (YA) 1980. 6.95 (ISBN 0-686-59799-0, Avalon). Bouregy.

Ross, W. David, ed. see Aristotle.

Ross, W. E. Nurse Grace's Dilemma. 1982. pap. 6.95 (ISBN 0-686-84735-0, Avalon). Bouregy.

--One Louisburg Square. (Inflation Fighter Ser.). 192p. 1982. pap. 1.50 o.s.i. (ISBN 0-8439-1148-4, Leisure Bks). Nordon Pubns.

--Phantom in Red. 1982. pap. 6.95 (ISBN 0-686-84713-X, Avalon). Bouregy.

--This Uncertain Love. 1982. 6.95 (ISBN 0-686-84186-7, Avalon). Bouregy.

Ross, W. E. D. The Dark Lane. (YA) 1979. 6.95 (ISBN 0-685-65268-8, Avalon). Bouregy.

--Hospital Crisis. (YA) 1979. 6.95 (ISBN 0-685-93875-1, Avalon). Bouregy.

--Magic of Love. (YA) 1980. 6.95 (ISBN 0-686-73917-5, Avalon). Bouregy.

--Onstage for Love. (YA) 1981. 6.95 (ISBN 0-686-73955-8, Avalon). Bouregy.

--The Queen's Stairway. (YA) 1978. 6.95 (ISBN 0-685-19063-3, Avalon). Bouregy.

--Return to Barton. (YA) 1978. 6.95 (ISBN 0-685-86411-1, Avalon). Bouregy.

Ross, W. Ogden. Marketing in Commercial Banks. LC 68-579749. 1968. 13.50 (ISBN 0-912164-07-7). Masterco Pr.

Ross, W. S. The Life-Death Ratio. 1977. 10.00 (ISBN 0-07-053874-3). McGraw.

Ross, Wilda. Can You Find the Animal? LC 73-88024. (Science Is What & Why Ser.). (Illus.). 48p. (gr. 2-3). 1974. PLB 5.99 o.p. (ISBN 0-698-30539-6, Coward). Putnam Pub Group.

--Cracks & Crannies. LC 75-7528. (What Lives There Ser.). (Illus.). 32p. (gr. 2-6). 1975. PLB 4.99 o.p. (ISBN 0-698-30598-1, Coward). Putnam Pub Group.

--The Rain Forest. (What Lives There Ser.). (Illus.). (gr. 3-5). 1977. PLB 5.99 o.p. (ISBN 0-698-30641-4, Coward). Putnam Pub Group.

--What Did the Dinosaurs Eat? (Science Is What & Why Ser.). (Illus.). 48p. (gr. 2-3). 1972. PLB 5.99 o.p. (ISBN 0-698-30443-8, Coward). Putnam Pub Group.

--Who Lives in This Log? (Science Is What & Why Ser). (Illus.). (gr. 2-3). 1971. PLB 4.49 o.p. (ISBN 0-698-30405-5, Coward). Putnam Pub Group.

Ross, Sir William D. Kant's Ethical Theory: A Commentary on the Grundlegung zur Metaphysid ser Sitten. LC 78-6730. 1978. Repr. of 1954 ed. lib. bdg. 18.25x (ISBN 0-8371-9059-2, ROKE). Greenwood.

Rossabi, Morris, ed. China among Equals: The Middle Kingdom & Its Neighbors, 10th-14th Centuries. LC 81-11486. 400p. 1983. text ed. 28.50x (ISBN 0-520-04383-9); pap. text ed. 12.50x (ISBN 0-520-04562-9). U of Cal Pr.

Rossano, A. T., jt. auth. see Cooper, H. B.

Rossant, Colette. Colette Rossant's After-Five Gourmet. LC 80-6014. (Illus.). 320p. 1981. 15.50 (ISBN 0-394-50506-9). Random.

--Colette's Slim Cuisine. (Illus.). 256p. 1983. 14.95 (ISBN 0-688-01937-4). Morrow.

Rossant, Colette & Herman, Jill. A Mostly French Food Processor Cookbook. (Illus., Orig.). 1977. pap. 4.95 (ISBN 0-452-25238-5, Z5238, Plume). NAL.

Rossbach, Jeffey. Ambivalent Conspirators: John Brown, the Secret Six, & a Theory of Slave Violence. LC 82-60303. 312p. 1983. 23.50x (ISBN 0-8122-7859-3). U of Pa Pr.

Rossbacher, Lisa A. Career Opportunities in Geology & the Earth Sciences. LC 82-1799. 192p. 1982. 12.95 (ISBN 0-668-05205-8); pap. 7.95 (ISBN 0-668-05220-1). Arco.

Rossdale, Peter. Horse Ailments Explained. LC 78-8941. (Horseman's Handbook Ser.). (Illus.). 1979. 7.95 o.p. (ISBN 0-668-04582-5); pap. 3.95 (ISBN 0-668-04586-8). Arco.

--Seeing Equine Practice. (Illus.). 1976. pap. 14.95i o.p. (ISBN 0-397-58208-0, Heinemann). Har-Row.

Rossel, Seymour. Family. LC 79-26227. (gr. 4 up). 1980. PLB 8.90 (ISBN 0-531-04102-6). Watts.

--Journey Through Jewish History, Vol. II. (Illus.). 128p. (gr. 6). 1983. pap. text ed. 4.95 (ISBN 0-87441-366-4). Behrman.

Rossel, Seymour, jt. ed. see Zisenwine, David.

Rosselet-Christ, Claudine. Les Perceptions De Soi, De l'Ideal et D'Autrui Dans les Relations D'Autorite et De Subordination. 183p. (Fr.). 1982. write for info. (ISBN 3-261-04995-2). P Lang Pubs.

Rossell, James H. & Frasure, William W. Managerial Accounting: An Introduction. 3rd ed. Date not set. text ed. 22.95 (ISBN 0-675-08420-2); wkbk. 7.95 (ISBN 0-675-08107-6). Additional supplements may be obtained from publisher. Merrill.

Rosselli, John. Lord William Bentinck: The Making of a Liberal Imperialist, 1774-1839. 1974. 31.50x (ISBN 0-520-02299-8). U of Cal Pr.

Rosser, Barkley J. Simplified Independence Proofs: Boolean Valued Models of Set Theory. (Pure & Applied Mathematics Ser: Vol. 31). 1969. 43.50 (ISBN 0-12-598050-7). Acad Pr.

Rosser, Colin & Harris, C. C. The Family & Social Change: A Study of Family & Kinship in a South Wales Town. (International Library of Sociology). 256p. 1983. pap. 10.95 (ISBN 0-7100-9434-5). Routledge & Kegan.

Rosser, James M. & Mossberg, Howard E. An Analysis of Health Care Delivery. LC 80-11611. 188p. 1983. Repr. of 1977 ed. lib. bdg. write for info. (ISBN 0-89874-158-0). Krieger.

Rosset, Hannelore, ed. see Batchelor, Stephen.

Rossetti, Dante G. The Best Poems by Dante Gabriele Rossetti. (The Most Meaningful Classics in World Culture Ser.). (Illus.). 108p. Date not set. Repr. of 1881 ed. 66.45 (ISBN 0-86650-055-3). Gloucester Art.

--Jan Van Hunks. Wahl, John R., ed. (Arents Tobacco Pub. Ser., No. 3). 1952. 10.00 o.p. (ISBN 0-87104-098-0). NY Pub Lib.

Rossetti, W. M. The Diary of W. M. Rossetti 1870-1873. Bornand, Odette, ed. 1978. 42.00x (ISBN 0-19-812458-9). Oxford U Pr.

Rossetti, William M. The P. R. B. Journal: William Michel Rossetti's Diary of the Pre-Raphaelite Brotherhood 1849-1853, Together with the Other Pre-Raphaelite Documents. Fredeman, William D., ed. (Illus., Ed. from the original manuscript with an introduction and notes.). 1975. 34.50x (ISBN 0-19-812505-4). Oxford U Pr.

Rossetto, L. Major-General Orde Charles Wingate & the Development of Long-Range Penetration. 1982. 54.00 (ISBN 0-89126-107-9). MA-AH Pub.

Rossettos, John N., jt. auth. see Tong, Pin.

Rossi, Aldo, jt. auth. see Eisenman, Peter.

Rossi, Alfred. Minneapolis Rehearsals: Tyrone Guthrie Directs Hamlet. LC 70-115496. 1970. 34.50x (ISBN 0-520-01719-6). U of Cal Pr.

Rossi, Alice. Feminists in Politics: A Panel Analysis of the First National Women's Conference. 1982. 29.50 (ISBN 0-12-598280-1). Acad Pr.

Rossi, Alice S. & Calderwood, Ann, eds. Academic Women on the Move. LC 73-76761. 576p. 1973. 15.00x (ISBN 0-87154-752-X). Russell Sage.

Rossi, B., ed. Space Exploration & the Solar System. (Italian Physical Society: Course 24). 1964. 56.50 (ISBN 0-12-368824-8). Acad Pr.

Rossi, Boniface E. Welding Engineering. (Illus.). 1974. text ed. 14.50 o.p. (ISBN 0-07-053895-6, G). McGraw.

Rossi, Claude J. De see De Rossi, Claude J.

Rossi, Emilio, et al. Lipizzaner: The Story of the Horses Lipica: Commemorating the 400th Anniversary of the Lippizaner. Espeland, Pamela, ed. LC 80-28576. (Illus.). 215p. 1981. 18.95 (ISBN 0-89893-172-X). CDP.

Rossi, Ernest E. & Plano, Jack C. The Latin American Political Dictionary. LC 79-27128. (Clio Dictionaries in Political Science Ser.: No. 1). 261p. 1981. 19.75 (ISBN 0-87436-324-1); pap. 9.75 (ISBN 0-87436-327-6). ABC-Clio.

Rossi, Ernest L., ed. see Erickson, Milton H.

Rossi, G. B. In-Vivo & In-Vitro Erythropoiesis: Friend System. (Giovanni Lorrenzini Foundation Symposium Ser.: Vol. 5). 1980. 96.75 (ISBN 0-444-80229-0). Elsevier.

Rossi, H. H., jt. auth. see Hall, E. J.

Rossi, Ino, ed. People in Culture: A Survey of Cultural Anthropology. (Illus.). 640p. 1980. 33.95x (ISBN 0-686-75100-0); pap. 15.95x (ISBN 0-686-75101-9). J F Bergin.

Rossi, John, jt. ed. see Davidoff, Frank.

Rossi, Lee D. & Gasser, Michael. Academic English for International Students. 300p. 1983. pap. text ed. 9.95 (ISBN 0-13-000950-4); tapes 90.00. P-H.

Rossi, Michael. The Wisest Fools. 168p. 1983. 9.95 (ISBN 0-8407-5285-7); pap. 4.95 (ISBN 0-8407-5842-1). Nelson.

Rossi, Nick & Rafferty, Sadie. Music Through the Centuries. LC 80-9066. (Illus.). 760p. 1981. lib. bdg. 30.00 (ISBN 0-8191-1498-7); pap. text ed. 17.50 (ISBN 0-8191-1499-5). U Pr of Amer.

Rossi, Nicki. Hearing Music: An Introduction. 428p. (Orig.). pap. text ed. 16.95 (ISBN 0-15-535597-X); instructors manual 1.95 (ISBN 0-15-535598-8); records 20.95 (ISBN 0-15-535599-6). HarBraceJ.

Rossi, Peter H. & Lyall, Katharine C. Reforming Public Welfare: A Critique of the Negative Income Tax Experiment. LC 75-41509. 208p. 1976. 11.95x (ISBN 0-87154-754-6). Russell Sage.

Rossi, Peter H., jt. auth. see Berk, Richard A.

Rossi, Peter H., ed. Standards for Evaluation Practice. LC 81-48579. 1982. 7.95x (ISBN 0-87589-917-X, PE-15). Jossey-Bass.

Rossi, Peter H., et al. Money, Work & Crime: A Field Experiment in Reducing Recidivism Through Postrelease Financial Aid to Prisoners. LC 80-512. (Quantitative Studies in Social Relations Ser.). 1980. 29.50 (ISBN 0-12-598240-2). Acad Pr.

Rossi, Philip. Together Toward Hope: A Journey to Moral Theology. 1983. price not set. U of Notre Dame Pr.

Rossi, Robert J. & Gilmartin, Kevin J. Agencies Working Together: A Guide to Interagency Coordination & Planning. (Sage Human Service Guides: Vol. 28). 120p. 1982. pap. 7.50 (ISBN 0-8039-0973-X). Sage.

--Handbook of Social Indicators. LC 79-12540. 216p. 1979. lib. bdg. 25.00 o.s.i. (ISBN 0-8240-7135-2). Garland Pub.

Rossi, Sheila I. & Pam, Leslie. Hypnotic Experiences: A Medley of Inductions (includes 60-mintue audiotape) 400p. 1983. text ed. 29.50x (ISBN 0-8290-1314-8). Irvington.

Rossides, Daniel. The History & Nature of Sociological Theory. (Illus., LC 77-074382). 1978. text ed. 24.50 (ISBN 0-395-25059-5). HM.

Rossides, Daniel W. The American Class System: An Introduction to Social Stratification. LC 80-5856. 505p. 1980. lib. bdg. 26.25 (ISBN 0-8191-1252-6); pap. text ed. 15.75 (ISBN 0-8191-1253-4). U Pr of Amer.

Rossides, Eugene T. U. S. Customs, Tariffs & Trade. LC 77-7647. 844p. 1977. 55.00 (ISBN 0-87179-241-9). BNA.

Rossier, H. Meditations on Joshua. 5.75 (ISBN 0-88172-119-0). Believers Bkshelf.

--Que Pasa Despues de la Muerte? 2nd ed. Bennett, Gordon H., ed. Bautista, Sara, tr. from Eng. (La Serie Diamante). (Illus.). 36p. (Span.). 1982. pap. 0.85 (ISBN 0-942504-07-0). Overcomer Pr.

Rossi-Landi, Ferruccio. Language As Work & Trade: A Semiotic Homology for Linguistics & Economics. 192p. 1983. 25.95x (ISBN 0-89789-022-1). J F Bergin.

Rossing, Thomas D. Science of Sound: Musical, Electronic, Environmental. LC 80-12028. (Chemistry Ser.). (Illus.). 512p. 1981. text ed. 26.95 (ISBN 0-201-06505-3). A-W.

Rossini, Frederick A. & Porter, Alan L. Integrated Impact Assessment. (Social Impact Assessment Series: No. 8). 300p. 1983. softcover 22.50x (ISBN 0-86531-623-6). Westview.

Rossini, Frederick D. Fundamental Measures & Constants for Science & Technology. LC 74-14759. 142p. Repr. of 1974 ed. text ed. 34.50 (ISBN 0-8493-5079-4). Krieger.

Rossiter, B. see Weissberger, A.

Rossiter, B. W. Techniques of Chemistry: Vol. 9, Chemical Experimentation Under Extreme Conditions. 369p. 1980. 46.50 (ISBN 0-471-93269-8). Wiley.

Rossiter, B. W., jt. ed. see Weissberger, A.

Rossiter, Clinton. American Presidency. rev. ed. pap. 1.75 o.p. (ISBN 0-451-61514-X, ME1514, Ment). NAL.

Rossiter, Elizabeth. Some Pleasure There to Find. LC 75-34383. 1976. 7.95 o.p. (ISBN 0-399-11728-8). Putnam Pub Group.

Rossiter, John. The Man Who Came Back. 1979. 8.95 o.s.i. (ISBN 0-395-27216-5). HM.

--The Manipulators. 1974. 6.95 o.p. (ISBN 0-671-21679-1). S&S.

Rossiter, Margaret W. Women Scientists in America: Struggles & Strategies to 1940. LC 81-20902. (Illus.). 448p. 1982. text ed. 27.50x (ISBN 0-8018-2443-5). Johns Hopkins.

Rossiter, V. Electromagnetism. 29.95 (ISBN 0-471-25992-6, Pub. by Wiley Heyden). Wiley.

Ross-Larson, Bruce, ed. Edit Yourself: A Manual for Everyone Who Works With Words. 1982. 11.95 (ISBN 0-393-01640-4). Norton.

Rossler, Otto E. see Gurel, Okan.

Rossman, Antonio, jt. auth. see Lane, Paul H.

Rossman, Parker. Sexual Experience Between Men & Boys. 1976. 10.95 o.s.i. (ISBN 0-8096-1911-3, Assn Pr). Follett.

Rossnagel, W. E. Handbook of Rigging: In Construction & Industrial Operations. 3rd ed. 1964. 34.50 (ISBN 0-07-053940-5, P&RB). McGraw.

Rossner, John. Toward Recovery of the Primordial Tradition: Ancient Insights & Modern Discoveries, 2 bks, Vol. 1. Incl. Bk. 1. From Ancient Magic to Future Technology. LC 79-66892. 12.50 (ISBN 0-8191-0861-8); Bk. 2. Toward a Parapsychology of Religion: from Ancient Religion to Future Science. LC 79-66893. 12.00 (ISBN 0-8191-0862-6). 1979. 13.25. U Pr of Amer.

Rossner, Judith. Emmeline. 1980. 12.95 o.s.i. (ISBN 0-671-22938-9). S&S.

Rossum, Rex Van see Van Rossum, Rex.

Rost, Leonhard. The Succession to the Throne of David. (Bible & Literature Ser.: No. 7). Orig. Title: Die Uberlieferung von derThronnachfolge Davids. 160p. 1982. text ed. 25.95x (ISBN 0-686-42728-9, Pub. by Almond Pr England); pap. text ed. 12.95x (ISBN 0-686-42729-7, Pub. by Almond Pr England). Eisenbrauns.

Rost, Michael & Stratton, Robert. Listening Transitions: From Listening to Speaking. 2d ed. 72p. pap. text ed. 5.00 (ISBN 0-940264-16-1); 3 cassettes 25.00 (ISBN 0-940264-17-X); transcripts 3.50 (ISBN 0-940264-28-5). Lingual Hse Pub.

Rost, Michael, ed. see Griffee, Dale.

Rost, Michael A. Listening Contours. 2nd ed. (Lingual House Listening Skills Ser.). 1981. pap. text ed. 5.95 (ISBN 0-940264-10-2); tchrs'. manual 7.95 (ISBN 0-940264-12-9); three cassettes. set 29.50 (ISBN 0-940264-11-0). Lingual Hse Pub.

Rost, Michael A. & Stratton, Robert K. Listening Transitions. (Lingual House Listening Skills Ser.). (Illus.). 144p. 1980. pap. text ed. 6.50 o.p. (ISBN 0-940264-08-0); three cassettes. set 29.50 o.p. (ISBN 0-940264-09-9). Lingual Hse Pub.

Rost, Thomas L. & Gifford, Ernest M., eds. Mechanisms & Control of Cell Division. 1977. 46.00 (ISBN 0-12-787370-8). Acad Pr.

Rost, Thomas L., et al. Botany: A Brief Introduction to Plant Biology. LC 78-5433. 1979. text ed. 24.95 (ISBN 0-471-02114-8); tchrs. manual 6.00 (ISBN 0-471-03758-3). Wiley.

Rostand, Edmond. Cyrano de Begerac. Hooker, Brian, tr. from Fr. (Bantam Classic Ser.). 196p. (Orig.). (gr. 9-12). 1981. pap. 1.50 (ISBN 0-553-21030-0). Bantam.

--Cyrano De Bergerac. Blair, Lowell, tr. (RL 9). 1972. pap. 1.75 (ISBN 0-451-51656-7, CE1656, Sig Classics). NAL.

Rostand, Jean. The Substance of Man. Brandeis, Irma, tr. LC 72-7509. 298p. 1973. Repr. of 1962 ed. lib. bdg. 15.50x (ISBN 0-8371-6517-2, ROSM). Greenwood.

Rosten, Leo. Joys of Yiddish. 1968. 19.95 (ISBN 0-07-053975-8, GB). McGraw.

--King Silky! LC 79-3413. 352p. 1980. 13.41i (ISBN 0-06-013684-7, HarpT). Har-Row.

--O Kaplan! My Kaplan! LC 74-15891. 384p. 13.41i (ISBN 0-06-013676-6, HarpT). Har-Row.

--People I Have Loved, Known or Admired. 1970. 8.95 o.p. (ISBN 0-07-053976-6, GB). McGraw.

--The Power of Positive Nonsense. 1977. 9.95 (ISBN 0-07-053985-5, GB). McGraw.

Rosten, Leo, ed. Religions of America. LC 74-11705. 1975. 15.95 o.p. (ISBN 0-671-21970-7, Touchstone Bks); pap. 9.95 (ISBN 0-671-21971-5, Touchstone Bks). S&S.

Rosten, Norman. Marilyn: An Untold Story. pap. 1.50 o.p. (ISBN 0-451-08880-8, W8880, Sig). NAL.

Rostoker, William & Dvorak, J. R. Interpretation of Metallographic Structures. 1964. 54.00 o.p. (ISBN 0-12-598250-X). Acad Pr.

Roston, Murray. Sixteenth-Century English Literature. (History of Literature Ser.). (Illus.). 235p. 1983. 28.50 (ISBN 0-8052-3825-5). Schocken.

--The Soul of Wit: A Study of John Donne. 1974. text ed. 34.00x (ISBN 0-19-812053-2). Oxford U Pr.

Roston, Ruth. I Live in the Watchmakers Town. LC 81-83880. (Minnesota Voices Project Ser.: No. 4). (Illus.). 76p. 1981. pap. 3.00 (ISBN 0-89823-028-4). New Rivers Pr.

Rostov, Mara. Eroica. 1978. pap. 1.95 o.s.i. (ISBN 0-515-04469-5). Jove Pubns.

--Eroica. LC 76-30824. 1977. 8.95 (ISBN 0-399-11926-4). Putnam Pub Group.

--Night Hunt. LC 78-24034. 1979. 10.95 (ISBN 0-399-12311-3). Putnam Pub Group.

Rostovtsow, J. N., tr. see Berg, Leo S.

Rostovtzeff, Michail I. Animal Style in South Russia & China. LC 75-143361. (Illus.). 1973. Repr. of 1929 ed. 25.00 o.p. (ISBN 0-87817-080-4). Hacker.

Rostovtzeff, Mikhail I. Greece. Bickerman, Elias J., ed. Duff, J. D., tr. (Illus.). 1963. pap. 7.95x (ISBN 0-19-500368-3). Oxford U Pr.

--Rome. Bickerman, Elias J., ed. Duff, J. D., tr. 1960. pap. 7.95x (ISBN 0-19-500224-5). Oxford U Pr.

Rostow, Eugene V. A National Policy for the Oil Industry. 1948. 39.50x (ISBN 0-686-51421-1). Elliots Bks.

--The Sovereign Prerogative. LC 73-17923. 318p. 1974. Repr. of 1962 ed. lib. bdg. 18.25x (ISBN 0-8371-7276-4, RSOP). Greenwood.

Rostow, W. W. How It All Began: The Origins of Modern Economic Growth. LC 74-18062. 276p. 1975. 11.50 o.p. (ISBN 0-07-053897-2, GB). McGraw.

--Open Skies: Eisenhower's Proposal of July 21, 1955. (Ideas & Action Ser.: No. 4). 238p. 1983. text ed. 25.00x (ISBN 0-292-76023-X); pap. 10.95 (ISBN 0-292-76024-8). U of Tex Pr.

--Politics & the Stages of Growth. LC 70-149440. 1971. 42.50 (ISBN 0-521-08197-1); pap. 11.95 (ISBN 0-521-09653-7). Cambridge U Pr.

--Stages of Economic Growth. 2nd ed. (Illus.). 1971. 37.50 (ISBN 0-521-08100-9); pap. 10.95x (ISBN 0-521-09650-2). Cambridge U Pr.

Rostow, W. W., jt. auth. see Millikan, Max F.

Rostow, Walt W. Economics of Take-off into Sustained Growth. (International Economic Assn. Ser). (Illus.). 1963. 32.50 (ISBN 0-312-23555-0). St Martin.

Rostron, M., jt. auth. see Hutton, G.

Roswell, Florence & Natchez, Gladys. Reading Disability: A Human Approach. 3rd rev. ed. LC 76-55874. 1977. 16.95x (ISBN 0-465-06849-9). Basic.

Roszak, Betty & Roszak, Theodore, eds. Masculine-Feminine: Readings in Sexual Mythology & the Liberation of Women. (Orig.). 1970. pap. 6.95xi (ISBN 0-06-131952-X, TB 1952, Torch). Har-Row.

Roszak, Theodore. Making of a Counter Culture. LC 69-15215. pap. 6.50 o.p. (ISBN 0-385-07329-1, A697, Anch). Doubleday.

--Person Planet: The Creative Disintegration of Industrial Society. LC 75-6165. (Illus.). 1978. pap. 7.95 (ISBN 0-385-00082-0, Anch). Doubleday.

Roszak, Theodore, jt. ed. see Roszak, Betty.

Roszel, Renee. Hostage Heart. (Harlequin American Romance Ser.). 256p. 1983. pap. 2.50 (ISBN 0-373-16010-0). Harlequin Bks.

Rota, Gian-Carlo, jt. auth. see Crapo, Henry H.

Rota, Gian-Carlo, ed. Studies in Algebra & Number Theory. LC 79-4638. (Advances in Mathematics Supplementary Studies Ser.: Vol. 6). 1979. (ISBN 0-12-599153-3). Acad Pr.

--Studies in Algebraic Topology. (Advances in Mathematics Supplementary Studies Ser.: Vol. 5). 1979. 46.50 (ISBN 0-12-599152-5). Acad Pr.

--Studies in Analysis. (Advances in Mathematics Supplementary Studies Ser.: Vol. 4). 1979. 52.50 (ISBN 0-12-599150-9). Acad Pr.

--Studies in Foundations & Combinatorics: Advances in Mathematics Supplementary Studies, Vol. 1. 1978. 48.00 (ISBN 0-12-599101-0). Acad Pr.

--Studies in Probability & Ergodic Theory: Advances in Mathematics Supplementary Studies, Vol. 2. 1978. 52.50 (ISBN 0-12-599102-9). Acad Pr.

Rotar, Peter P. Grasses of Hawaii. (Illus.). 1968. text ed. 17.50x (ISBN 0-87022-715-7). UH Pr.

Rotatori, Anthony F. & Fox, Robert. Behavioral Weight Reduction Program for Mentally Handicapped Persons. 232p. (Orig.). 1981. pap. text ed. 14.95 (ISBN 0-8391-1661-6). Univ Park.

Rotberg, Robert I. Black Heart: Gore-Browne & the Politics of Multiracial Zambia. (Perspectives on Southern Africa Ser: Vol. 20). 1978. 30.00x (ISBN 0-520-03164-4). U of Cal Pr.

--Imperialism, Colonialism, & Hunger: East & Central Africa. LC 82-48009. 288p. 1982. 28.95x (ISBN 0-669-05871-8). Lexington Bks.

Rotberg, Robert I. & Overholt, William H. Zimbabwe's Economic Prospects. (Seven Springs Reports). 1980. pap. 2.00 (ISBN 0-943006-10-4). Seven Springs.

Rotberg, Robert I., ed. Namibia: Political & Economic Prospects. LC 81-48672. 144p. 1982. 18.95 (ISBN 0-669-05531-X). Lexington Bks.

Rotberg, Robert I. & Barratt, John, eds. Conflict & Compromise in South Africa. LC 79-7712. 244p. 1980. 25.95x (ISBN 0-669-03205-0). Lexington Bks.

Rotberg, Robert I., jt. ed. see Chittick, H. Neville.

Rotch, William, et al. The Executive's Guide to Management Accounting & Control Systems, Vol. 1. rev. ed. LC 81-70861. (Illus.). 183p. 1982. text ed. 16.95x (ISBN 0-931920-35-3). Dame Pubns.

Rotchstein, Janice, jt. auth. see Ebert, Alan.

Rote, Kyle, Jr. & Kane, Basil. Kyle Rote, Jr.'s Complete Book of Soccer. (Illus.). 1978. 10.95 o.p. (ISBN 0-671-22714-9). S&S.

Rotella, Alexis K. Clouds in My Teacup. 40p. 1983. pap. 3.00 (ISBN 0-941190-04-8). Wind Chimes.

Rotella, Guy. Three Contemporary Poets of New England. (United States Authors Ser.). 200p. 1983. lib. bdg. 16.95 (ISBN 0-8057-7377-0, Twayne). G K Hall.

Rotella, Guy, jt. ed. see Blessington, Francis C.

Rotella, Guy L. E. E. Cummings: A Reference Guide. 1979. lib. bdg. 26.00 (ISBN 0-8161-8079-2, Hall Reference). G K Hall.

Rotenberg, M., ed. Biomathematics & Cell Kinetics. (Developments in Cell Biology Ser.: Vol. 8). 1981. 70.25 (ISBN 0-444-80371-8). Elsevier.

Rotenberg, Mordechai. Dialogue with Deviance: The Hasidic Ethic & the Theory of Social Contraction. LC 81-13309. 224p. 1983. text ed. 25.00x (ISBN 0-89727-031-2). Inst Study Human.

Rotenstein, C. Lace Manufacturing on Raschel Machines. 7.95 o.p. (ISBN 0-87245-284-0). Textile Bk.

Rotenstein, Charles. Manufacture of Raschel Wool & Cotton Outerwear. 1969. 8.50 o.p. (ISBN 0-87245-285-9). Textile Bk.

Rotenstreich, Nathan. Between Past & Present: An Essay On History. 1958. text ed. 13.50x (ISBN 0-686-83489-5). Elliots Bks.

Rotenstreich, Nathan, jt. ed. see Bauer, Yehuda.

Roters, Eberhard. Berlin Nineteen Ten to Nineteen Thirty-Three. LC 82-50423. (Illus.). 268p. 1982. 60.00 (ISBN 0-8478-0439-9). Rizzoli Intl.

Roth. Collins Guide to the Water. 29.95 (ISBN 0-686-42791-2, Collins Pub England). Greene.

Roth, A. Vacuum Sealing Techniques. 1966. inquire for price o.p. (ISBN 0-08-011587-X). Pergamon.

--Vacuum Technology. 1982. 64.00 (ISBN 0-444-86027-4). Elsevier.

Roth, Alexander, ed. Allergy in the World: A Guide for Physicians & Travelers. LC 77-11666. 1978. text ed. 12.00x (ISBN 0-8248-0521-6). UH Pr.

Roth, Alexander D., jt. ed. see Turn, Rein.

Roth, Alfred C. & Baird, Ronald J. Small Gas Engines. rev. ed. LC 81-6209. (Illus.). 232p. text ed. 12.00 (ISBN 0-87006-326-X). Goodheart.

Roth, Arthur. The Yucky Monster. LC 78-72112. (Illus.). (gr. k-4). 1979. 6.75 (ISBN 0-89799-148-6); pap. 3.50 (ISBN 0-89799-066-8). Dandelion Pr.

Roth, Audrey & Camacho, Oliver. Words People Use. (Orig.). 1972. pap. text ed. 10.95 (ISBN 0-316-75764-0). Little.

Roth, Bernhard A. Here Is Your Hobby: Archery. (Here Is Your Hobby Ser.). (Illus.). (gr. 5 up). 1962. PLB 5.29 o.p. (ISBN 0-399-60242-9). Putnam Pub Group.

Roth, Beth N., ed. see Winterborn, Benjamin.

Roth, Bette, jt. auth. see Grad, Eli.

Roth, Cecil. A History of the Marranos. LC 74-10149. 448p. 1974. pap. 10.95 (ISBN 0-8052-0463-6). Schocken.

--House of Nasi: The Duke of Naxos. Repr. of 1948 ed. lib. bdg. 16.25x (ISBN 0-8371-2387-9, ROHN). Greenwood.

--Short History of the Jewish People. rev. ed. LC 70-107212. (Illus.). 1970. 14.95 (ISBN 0-87677-004-9); pap. 6.95 (ISBN 0-87677-183-5). Hartmore.

--Spanish Inquisition. (Orig.). 1964. pap. 5.95 (ISBN 0-393-00255-1, Norton Lib). Norton.

Roth, Charlene D. Making Dollhouse Accessories. (Illus.). 1977. 8.95 o.p. (ISBN 0-517-52878-9); pap. 4.95 o.p. (ISBN 0-517-52879-7). Crown.

--Making Original Dolls of Composition, Bisque & Porcelain. (Illus.). 192p. 1980. 12.95 o.p. (ISBN 0-517-53717-6). Crown.

Roth, Charles. More Power to You! LC 82-50122. 158p. 1982. 4.95 (ISBN 0-87159-093-X). Unity Bks.

Roth, Charles B. Secrets of Closing Sales. 4th ed. LC 75-98967. 1970. 10.95 o.p. (ISBN 0-13-797969-X, Busn). P-H.

Roth, Charles B. & Alexander, Roy. Secrets of Closing Sales. 5th ed. LC 82-12312. 276p. 1982. 14.95 (ISBN 0-13-797910-X, Busn). P-H.

Roth, Charles H. Fundamentals of Logic Design. 2nd ed. (Electrical Engineering Ser.). (Illus.). 1979. pap. 25.95 (ISBN 0-8299-0226-0); instrs. manual avail. (ISBN 0-8299-0572-3). West Pub.

Roth, Charles H., Jr. Use of the Dual-Trace Oscilloscope: A Programmed Text. rev. ed. 256p. 1982. 20.95 (ISBN 0-13-940031-1); pap. text ed. 16.95 (ISBN 0-13-940023-0). P-H.

Roth, David. Best of Friends. LC 82-23378. 208p. (gr. 7 up). 1983. 10.95 (ISBN 0-395-33889-1). HM.

Roth, David & Wilson, Frank L. The Comparative Study of Politics. 2nd ed. (Illus.). 1980. text ed. 22.95 (ISBN 0-13-154237-0). P-H.

Roth, David M; see Weaver, Glenn.

Roth, Dennis M. The Friar Estates of the Philippines. LC 76-21550. 1977. 12.00x o.p. (ISBN 0-8263-0429-X). U of NM Pr.

Roth, Edward S., ed. Gaging: Practical Design & Application. LC 80-53424. (Manufacturing Update Ser.). (Illus.). 289p. 1981. 32.00 (ISBN 0-87263-064-1). SME.

Roth, Ernest, ed. Plants for the Home. LC 77-82737. (Illus.). 1977. 7.95 o.p. (ISBN 0-8467-0370-X, Pub. by Two Continents). Hippocrene Bks.

Roth, Ernst, tr. Composers' Autographs, 2 vols. Incl. Vol. 1. Palestrina to Beethoven. Gerstenberg, Walter, ed. & annotations by. 30.00 (ISBN 0-8386-3105-3); Vol. 2. Schubert to Stravinsky. Hurlimann, Martin, ed. 25.00 (ISBN 0-8386-7344-9). LC 68-9354. (Illus.). 175p. 1968. 50.00 (ISBN 0-686-96712-7). Fairleigh Dickinson.

Roth, Eugene. Children & Their Fathers. Reich, Hanns, ed. (Illus.). 1983. pap. 4.95 (ISBN 0-8090-1505-6, Terra Magica). Hill & Wang.

Roth, Filibert. Forest Regulation. 1925. 4.95x (ISBN 0-685-21784-1). Wahr.

--Forest Valuation. 1926. 4.95x (ISBN 0-685-21785-X). Wahr.

Roth, Gabriel & Wynne, George W. Free Enterprise Urban Transportation. (Learning From Abroad Ser.: Vol. 5). 48p. (Orig.). 1982. pap. 4.95 (ISBN 0-87855-914-0). Transaction Bks.

Roth, Geneen. Feeding the Hungry Heart. LC 82-4137. 1982. 12.95 (ISBN 0-672-52731-6). Bobbs.

Roth, Grace M. Tobacco & the Cardiovascular System: The Effects of Smoking & of Nicotine on Normal Persons. (Illus.). 72p. 1951. photocopy ed. spiral 9.75x (ISBN 0-398-04408-2). C C Thomas.

Roth, Guenther & Schluchter, Wolfgang. Max Weber's Vision of History: Ethics & Methods. LC 77-20328. 1979. 28.50x (ISBN 0-520-03604-2). U of Cal Pr.

Roth, H. Ling. Aborigines of Tasmania. 3rd ed. 1969. Repr. of 1899 ed. text ed. 21.50x o.p. (ISBN 0-391-01940-6). Humanities.

Roth, Hal. The Longest Race. (Illus.). 1983. 19.50 (ISBN 0-393-03278-7). Norton.

Roth, Harold. First Class! The Postal System in Action. LC 82-14520. (Illus.). 56p. (gr. 3-7). 1983. 10.95 (ISBN 0-394-85384-9); PLB 10.99 (ISBN 0-394-95384-3). Pantheon.

Roth, Henry. Call It Sleep. 1964. pap. 3.95 (ISBN 0-380-00755-X, 60764-6, Bard). Avon.

--Master Violinists in Performance. (Illus.). 320p. 1982. 14.95 (ISBN 0-87666-594-6). Paganiniana Pubns.

Roth, Henry, jt. auth. see Applebaum, Samuel.

Roth, Henry H. In Empty Rooms: Tales of Love. LC 79-50422. (Illus.). 102p. 1980. pap. 5.95x (ISBN 0-913204-11-0). December Pr.

Roth, Hy, jt. auth. see Cromie, Robert.

Roth, Ira. Smile of Destiny. 1982. 9.95 (ISBN 0-8062-1727-8). Carlton.

Roth, Irene. Cecil Roth, Historian Without Tears: A Memoir. (Illus.). 288p. 1982. 14.95 (ISBN 0-87203-103-9). Hermon.

Roth, Jane, jt. auth. see Mannerberg, Donald.

Roth, Jordan T., jt. auth. see Downey, Robert J.

Roth, Jordon T., jt. auth. see Downey, Robert J.

Roth, Joseph. Flight Without End. Le Vay, David, tr. LC 76-47077. 144p. 1977. 15.00 (ISBN 0-87951-057-9). Overlook Pr.

--The Silent Prophet. Le Vay, David, tr. from Ger. LC 79-67676. 216p. 1980. 15.00 (ISBN 0-87951-110-9). Overlook Pr.

Roth, Julius A., ed. Research in Sociology of Health Care, Vol. 1. 400p. 1980. lib. bdg. 47.50 (ISBN 0-89232-145-8). Jai Pr.

--Research in the Sociology of Health Care, Vol. 2. 400p. 1981. 47.50 (ISBN 0-89232-199-7). Jai Pr.

Roth, Julius A., ed. see Byrd, Doris Elaine.

Roth, June. The Allergic Gourmet. (Illus.). 288p. 1983. 14.95 (ISBN 0-8092-5612-6). Contemp Bks.

--The Bagel Book. Shaw, Grace, ed. (Illus.). 1978. 12.95 o.p. (ISBN 0-448-16382-9, G&D); pap. 3.95 o.p. (ISBN 0-448-16384-5). Putnam Pub Group.

--June Roth's Thousand Calorie Cook Book. LC 68-19158. (Illus.). 1968. Repr. of 1967 ed. lib. bdg. 2.95 (ISBN 0-668-01740-6). Arco.

--Living Better with a Special Diet. LC 82-11652. 276p. 1983. lib. bdg. 12.95 (ISBN 0-668-05718-1); pap. 7.95 (ISBN 0-668-05651-7). Arco.

--Low-Cholesterol Jewish Cookery: The Unsaturated Fat Way. LC 77-13968. 1978. pap. 2.95 (ISBN 0-668-04420-9). Arco.

--Salt-Free Cooking with Herbs & Spices. LC 77-81178. 1977. pap. 7.95 (ISBN 0-8092-7722-0). Contemp Bks.

Roth, K., jt. auth. see Halberstam, H.

Roth, L. O., et al. Introduction to Agricultural Engineering. (Illus.). 1975. pap. text ed. 22.50 (ISBN 0-87055-302-X). AVI.

Roth, Leland M. The Architecture of McKim, Mead & White, 1870-1920: A Building List. LC 77-83368. (Library of Humanities Reference Bks.: No. 114). lib. bdg. 54.00 o.s.i. (ISBN 0-8240-9850-1). Garland Pub.

--A Concise History of American Architecture. LC 78-2169. (Icon Editions). (Illus.). 1979. 25.00i (ISBN 0-06-438490-X, HarpT); pap. 11.95i (ISBN 0-06-430086-2, IN-86). Har-Row.

Roth, Leon. Judaism, a Portrait. LC 61-5918. 240p. 1972. pap. 4.95 (ISBN 0-8052-0344-3). Schocken.

Roth, Lillian. I'll Cry Tomorrow. 320p. 1977. pap. 5.95 (ISBN 0-8119-0385-0). Fell.

Roth, Lloyd J. & Stumpf, Walter, eds. Autoradiography of Diffusible Substances. 1969. 60.00 (ISBN 0-12-598550-9). Acad Pr.

Roth, Mark & Walters, Sally. Twenty Bicycle Tours in the Finger Lakes: Scenic Route to Central New York's Best Waterfalls, Wineries, Beacher & Parks. (Twenty Bicycle Tours Ser.). (Illus.). 160p. (Orig.). 1983. pap. 6.95 (ISBN 0-942440-09-9). Backcountry Pubns.

Roth, Moira, ed. The Amazing Decade-Women's Performance Art in America 1970-1980. (Illus.). 250p. 1983. pap. 10.00 (ISBN 0-937122-09-2). Astro Artz.

Roth, Oscar. Heart Attack! A Question & Answer Book. 1979. lib. bdg. 14.50 o.p. (ISBN 0-8161-6688-9, Large Print Bks). G K Hall.

Roth, Oscar & Galton, Lawrence. Heart Attack: A Question & Answer Book. 1980. pap. 4.95 o.p. (ISBN 0-8092-7054-4). Contemp Bks.

Roth, Philip. The Ghost Writer. 1980. lib. bdg. 10.95 o.p. (ISBN 0-8161-3069-8, Large Print Bks). G K Hall.

--Goodbye Columbus & Five Short Stories. 5.95 (ISBN 0-394-60374-5). Modern Lib.

--The Great American Novel. 1973. pap. 7.95 (ISBN 0-374-51584-0). FS&G.

--Letting Go. 1962. pap. 9.95 (ISBN 0-374-51701-0). FS&G.

--Portnoy's Complaint. LC 69-16414. 1969. 15.00 (ISBN 0-394-44198-2). Random.

--Portnoy's Complaint. 288p. 6.95 (ISBN 0-394-60810-0). Modern Lib.

Roth, Phyllis A. Bram Stoker. (English Authors Ser.). 1982. lib. bdg. 13.95 (ISBN 0-8057-6828-9, Twayne). G K Hall.

Roth, Robert. Sand in the Wind. 640p. 1983. pap. 3.50 (ISBN 0-523-41954-6). Pinnacle Bks.

Roth, Robert A. How to Conduct Surveys, Follow-up Studies, & Basic Data Collection in Evaluation Studies. (Illus.). 132p. (Orig.). 1981. pap. text ed. 9.25 (ISBN 0-8191-1650-5). U Pr of Amer.

--Individualized Staff Development Programs for Competency Development: A Systematic Approach. LC 80-8258. 123p. 1980. pap. text ed. 7.75 o.p. (ISBN 0-8191-1326-3). U Pr of Amer.

--The Program Evaluation Instruction Series, Bks. I, II, III. (Illus.). 180p. (Orig.). 1982. Set. pap. 11.25 wkbk. (ISBN 0-8191-2057-X). U Pr of Amer.

--The Program Evaluation Instructional Series, Bks. V, VI. (Illus.). 122p. (Orig.). 1982. Set. pap. 9.25 wkbk. (ISBN 0-8191-2206-8). U Pr of Amer.

Roth, Robert A. & Finlayson, Birdwell. Stones: Clinical Management of Urolithiasis, Vol. 6. (International Perspectives in Urology Ser.). (Illus.). 485p. 1982. lib. bdg. 48.00 (ISBN 0-683-07388-5). Williams & Wilkins.

Roth, Robert F. International Marketing Communications. LC 81-66513. 1982. 22.95 (ISBN 0-87251-058-1). Crain Bks.

Roth, Robert J. John Dewey & Self Realization. LC 77-26178. 1978. Repr. of 1963 ed. lib. bdg. 17.00x (ISBN 0-313-20088-2, ROJD). Greenwood.

Roth, Robert M. Underachieving Students & Guidance. (Guidance Monograph). 1970. pap. 2.40 o.p. (ISBN 0-395-09951-X). HM.

Roth, Sandra & Bieker, Beverly. Creative Gift Wrapping. LC 82-11345. (Illus.). 112p. (Orig.). 1982. pap. 6.95 (ISBN 0-914788-63-9). East Woods.

Roth, Sanford H. New Directions in Arthritis Therapy. LC 79-24449. (Illus.). 196p. 1980. 21.50 (ISBN 0-88416-188-9). Wright-PSG.

Roth, Walton T., jt. auth. see Insel, Paul M.

Roth, William, jt. auth. see Gliedman, John.

Rothacker, Viola. Precious Jewels. 1979. 6.50 o.p. (ISBN 0-533-03832-4). Vantage.

--Walking with the Master. 3.95 o.p. (ISBN 0-533-00948-0). Vantage.

Rothafel, Roxy. Roxy's Ski Guide to New England. LC 78-61682. (Illus.). 192p. 1978. pap. 5.95 o.p. (ISBN 0-914788-08-6). East Woods.

Rothaus, Barbara, jt. auth. see Silberman, Leonard.

Rothaus, James. The Detroit Lions. (The NFL Today Ser.). (Illus.). 48p. (gr. 4-12). 1982. PLB 7.95 (ISBN 0-87191-811-0); pap. 3.75 (ISBN 0-89812-257-0). Creative Ed.

Rothbard, Murray N. America's Great Depression. rev. ed. (Studies in Economic Theory). 361p. 1975. 12.00x o.p. (ISBN 0-8362-0634-7); pap. 5.00x o.p. (ISBN 0-8362-0647-9). NYU Pr.

--Conceived in Liberty, Vol. 1. 1975. 15.00 o.p. (ISBN 0-87000-262-7, Arlington Hse). Crown.

--Conceived in Liberty: The Revolutionary War, 1775-1784. (Illus.). 1979. 14.95 o.p. (ISBN 0-87000-352-6, Arlington Hse). Crown.

--Conceived in Liberty, Vol.3: Advance to Revolution, 1760-1775. 1976. 12.95 o.p. (ISBN 0-87000-343-7, Arlington Hse). Crown.

Rothbart, Harold A. Mechanical Design & Systems Handbook. 1964. 69.50 (ISBN 0-07-054019-5, P&RB). McGraw.

Rothberg, Abraham. The Great Waltz. LC 77-9576. 1978. 8.95 o.p. (ISBN 0-399-12076-9). Putnam Pub Group.

Rothberg, David L., ed. Variations in Hospital Use: Geographic & Temporal Patterns of Care in the United States. LC 81-47027. (The University Health Policy Consortium Ser.). 272p. 1982. 29.95x (ISBN 0-669-04545-4). Lexington Bks.

Rothberg, Gabriel B. Structured EDP Auditing. (Data Processing Ser.). (Illus.). 302p. 1982. 30.00 (ISBN 0-534-97931-9). Lifetime Learn.

Rothblat, George H. & Christofalo, Vincent J., eds. Growth, Nutrition & Metabolism of Cells in Culture. Vol. 1, 1972. 59.00 (ISBN 0-12-598301-8); Vol. 2, 1972. 59.00 (ISBN 0-12-598302-6); Vol. 3, 1977. 51.00 (ISBN 0-12-598303-4); Set. 140.50 (ISBN 0-686-76964-3). Acad Pr.

Rothblatt, Donald N., ed. National Policy for Urban & Regional Development. LC 73-11672. (Illus.). 368p. 1974. 22.95x o.p. (ISBN 0-669-85043-8). Lexington Bks.

Rothblatt, Henry B. That Damned Lawyer. 1983. 14.95 (ISBN 0-89696-198-2). Dodd.

Rothblatt, Sheldon. The Revolution of the Dons: Cambridge & Society in Victorian England. 320p. 1981. 47.50 (ISBN 0-521-23958-3); pap. 15.95 (ISBN 0-521-28370-1). Cambridge U Pr.

Rothblum, Lawrence, jt. auth. see Busch, Harris.

Rothblum, Lawrence, jt. ed. see Busch, Harris.

Rothchild, Donald & Curry, Robert L., Jr. Scarcity, Choice, & Public Policy in Middle Africa. LC 76-50255. 1978. 30.00x (ISBN 0-520-03378-7); pap. 8.50x (ISBN 0-520-03534-8). U of Cal Pr.

Rothchild, Donald & Olorunsola, Victor A., eds. State vs Ethnic Claims: African Policy Dilemmas. (Special Studies on Africa). 1982. lib. bdg. 25.00 (ISBN 0-86531-503-5); pap. text ed. 11.95 (ISBN 0-86531-504-3). Westview.

Rothchild, John. Stop Burning Your Money: The Intelligent Homeowner's Guide to Household Energy Savings. LC 81-5271. (Illus.). 1981. 15.50 (ISBN 0-394-51366-5). Random.

Rothchild, Sylvia, ed. Voices from the Holocaust. 1982. pap. 7.95 (ISBN 0-452-00603-1, Mer). NAL.

Rothe, Bertha, ed. Daniel Webster Reader. LC 56-7268. (Docket Ser.: No. 5). 255p. (Orig.). 1956. 15.00 (ISBN 0-379-11305-8); pap. 2.50 (ISBN 0-379-11305-8). Oceana.

Rothe, Jean-Pierre. The Seismicity of the Earth, 1953-1965. (Earth Sciences Ser.: No. 1). (Illus.). 336p. (Eng. & Fr.). 1969. pap. 26.50 o.p. (ISBN 0-686-94183-7, UNESCO). Unipub.

Rothenberg, et al. Voice of Blood: Interspecies Communication. Guss, David, ed. (Illus.). 150p. (Orig.). cancelled (ISBN 0-915572-66-4); pap. cancelled (ISBN 0-915572-65-6). Panjandrum.

Rothenberg, Albert. The Emerging Goddess: The Creative Process in Art, Science, & other Fields. LC 78-26486. (Illus.). 440p. 1982. pap. 10.95 (ISBN 0-226-72949-4). U of Chicago Pr.

Rothenberg, Dianne, compiled by. Directory of Educational Programs for Adults Who Work with Children. LC 79-64954. 104p. 1979. pap. 3.00 (ISBN 0-912674-66-0, NAEYC #314). Natl Assn Child.

Rothenberg, Eleanore. Regulation & Expansion of Health Facilities. LC 76-7381. (Special Studies). (Illus.). 144p. 1976. 25.95 o.p. (ISBN 0-275-23080-5). Praeger.
Rothenberg, G. B. Specialty Steels-Recent Developments. LC 76-47275. (Chemical Technology Review Ser.: No. 83). (Illus.). 1977. 39.00 o.p. (ISBN 0-8155-0649-X). Noyes.
Rothenberg, Gunther E. Napoleon's Great Adversaries: The Archduke Charles & the Austrian Army, 1792-1814. LC 82-47512. 224p. 1982. 18.95 (ISBN 0-253-33969-3). Ind U Pr.
Rothenberg, Gunther E. & Kiraly, Bela K. East Central European Society & War in Pre-Revolutionary Eighteenth Century. (Brooklyn College Studies on Society in Change). 574p. 1982. 35.00x (ISBN 0-686-82237-4). East Eur Quarterly.
Rothenberg, J. & Heggie, I. G. Transport & the Urban Environment: Proceedings of a Conference Held by the International Economic Assoc. at Lyngby. LC 73-15142. (International Economic Association Ser.). 273p. 1974. 26.95x o.s.i. (ISBN 0-470-73969-X). Halsted Pr.
Rothenberg, J. G. & Heggie, I. G., eds. The Management of Water Quality & the Environment: Proceedings of a Conference Held by the International Economic Assoc. at Lyngby. LC 74-7584. (International Economic Association Ser.). 1974. 49.95x o.s.i. (ISBN 0-470-73960-6). Halsted Pr.
Rothenberg, Jerome. Altar Pieces. (Illus.). 1982. portfolio ed., signed 50.00 (ISBN 0-930794-47-8); pap. 5.50 (ISBN 0-930794-48-6). Station Hill Pr.
--Economic Evaluation of Urban Renewal. LC 67-19190. (Studies of Government Finance). 1967. 14.95 (ISBN 0-8157-7592-X). Brookings.
--That Dada Strain. LC 82-18827. 96p. 1983. pap. 7.25 (ISBN 0-8112-0860-5, NDP550). New Directions.
Rothenberg, Jerome & Lenowitz, Harris. Gematria Twenty-Seven. (Illus.). 1977. pap. 3.00 (ISBN 0-87924-047-4). Membrane Pr.
Rothenberg, Jerome, jt. auth. see Edel, Matthew.
Rothenberg, Jerome, ed. Shaking the Pumpkin: Traditional Poetry of the Indian North Americas. LC 74-171317. 1972. pap. 6.95 o.p. (ISBN 0-385-01296-9, Anch). Doubleday.
Rothenberg, Jerome, jt. ed. see Quasha, George.
Rothenberg, Polly. Creative Stained Glass. (Arts & Crafts Ser.). (Illus.). 96p. 1973. 7.95 o.p. (ISBN 0-517-50581-9); pap. 3.95 (ISBN 0-517-50582-7). Crown.
Rothenberg, Robert. Health in the Later Years. 1972. pap. 2.25 o.p. (ISBN 0-451-08073-4, E8073, Sig). NAL.
--New American Medical Dictionary & Health Manual. rev. ed. pap. 4.50 (ISBN 0-451-12027-2, AE2027, Sig). NAL.
Rothenberg, Robert E., ed. The New Illustrated Medical Encyclopedia for Home Use: A Practical Guide to Good Health. 7th ed. (Illus.). 752p. 1982. 27.50 (ISBN 0-8109-1334-8). Abrams.
Rothenbuehler, Mary L., ed. Family Secrets: Recipes from Grandma Fowler's Kitchen. (Illus.). 1981. pap. 2.25 (ISBN 0-939010-00-3). Zephyr Pr.
Rothenstein, John, ed. see Spencer, Stanley.
Rother, K., jt. ed. see Opferkuch, W.
Rotherham, Edward R., jt. auth. see Cady, Leo.
Rothermich, John A., ed. see Carlsen, G. Robert.
Rothermich, John A., jt. ed. see Howe, Florence.
Rothermich, John A., ed. see Schanker, Harry H.
Rothermund, D. & Wadhwa, D. C. Zamindars, Mines & Peasants: Studies in the History of an Indian Coalfield. 1979. 16.50x o.p. (ISBN 0-8364-0331-2). South Asia Bks.
Rothermund, Dietmar. India. 224p. 1982. 75.00x (ISBN 0-584-11021-9, Pub. by Muller Ltd). State Mutual Bk.
Rothermund, Dietmar & Dolder, Willi. India. LC 82-50540. (Illus.). 224p. 1982. 29.95 (ISBN 0-312-41329-7). St Martin.
Rothfeld, Benjamin, et al, eds. Nuclear Medicine in Vitro. 2nd ed. (Illus.). 420p. 1983. text ed. 50.00 (ISBN 0-397-50505-1, Lippincott Medical). Lippincott.
Rothfield, Lawrence I., ed. Structure & Function of Biological Membranes. (Molecular Biology Ser.). 1971. 64.50 (ISBN 0-12-598650-5). Acad Pr.
Rothfleisch, Sheldon. The No-Nonsense Guide to Cosmetic Surgery. LC 78-73318. (Illus.). 1979. pap. 5.95 o.p. (ISBN 0-448-16417-5, G&D). Putnam Pub Group.
Rothgiesser, Ruben. Well of Gerar. Schneiderman, Harry, tr. from Ger. LC 53-7603. 1953. 3.00 o.p. (ISBN 0-8276-0165-4, 259). Jewish Pubn.
Rothkirchen, Livia, jt. ed. see Sandberg, Moshe.
Rothman, Alan. You Can Ski Like a Skater. LC 82-81809. (Illus.). 160p. (Orig.). 1983. pap. 6.95 (ISBN 0-88011-061-9). Leisure Pr.
Rothman, Beulah, jt. ed. see Papell, Catherine P.
Rothman, David J. Conscience & Convenience: The Asylum & Its Alternatives in Progressive America. 1980. 17.50 (ISBN 0-316-75774-8); pap. 10.95 (ISBN 0-316-75775-6). Little.
--The Discovery of the Asylum: Social Order & Disorder in the New Republic. LC 71-143711. (Illus.). 1971. 12.50 (ISBN 0-316-75770-5); pap. 9.95 (ISBN 0-316-75771-3). Little.
Rothman, Eugene, jt. ed. see Polzin, Robert.
Rothman, Harry & Greenshields, Roderick. Energy from Alcohol: The Brazilian Experience. LC 82-21956. 200p. 1983. 20.00x (ISBN 0-8131-1479-9). U Pr of Ky.
Rothman, J. Social R & D: Research & Development in the Human Services. 1980. pap. text ed. 16.95 (ISBN 0-13-818112-8). P-H.
Rothman, Jack, ed. Issues in Race & Ethnic Relations. LC 76-9544. 1977. pap. text ed. 11.95 (ISBN 0-87581-193-0). Peacock Pubs.
Rothman, Joel. The Compleat Jazz Drummer. new ed. 512p. 1974. 30.00x o.p. (ISBN 0-913952-03-6). J R Pubns.
--The Compleat Rock Drummer. 518p. 1973. 30.00x o.p. (ISBN 0-913952-01-X). J R Pubns.
--I Can Be Anything You Can Be. LC 72-90694. (Illus.). 32p. (gr. k-4). 1973. 6.50 (ISBN 0-87592-024-1). Scroll Pr.
--Night Lights. LC 74-188434. (Illus.). 40p. (ps-3). 1972. 5.95g o.p. (ISBN 0-8075-5628-9). A Whitman.
Rothman, Richard H. & Simeone, Frederick A., eds. The Spine, 2 vols. LC 74-4584. (Illus.). 922p. 1975. Vol. 1. 60.00 (ISBN 0-7216-7719-3); Vol. 2. 60.00 (ISBN 0-7216-7720-7); Set. 120.00 (ISBN 0-686-67075-2). Saunders.
Rothman, Robert A. Inequality & Stratification in the U. S. (P-H Ser. in Sociology). (Illus.). 1978. pap. 13.95 ref. ed. (ISBN 0-13-464305-4). P-H.
Rothman, Sheila. Woman's Proper Place: A History of Changing Ideals & Practices, 1870 to the Present. LC 78-55000. 1978. 15.00x o.s.i. (ISBN 0-465-09203-9). Basic.
Rothman, Stanley & Breslauer, George. Soviet Politics & Society. (Illus.). 1978. pap. text ed. 15.95 (ISBN 0-8299-0146-9). West Pub.
Rothman, Stanley & Licther, Robert S. Roots of Radicalism: Jews, Christians & the New Left. (Illus.). 1982. 27.95x (ISBN 0-19-503125-3). Oxford U Pr.
Rothman, Stanley & Mosmann, Charles. Computers & Society. 2nd ed. LC 75-31622. (Illus.). 416p. 1976. text ed. 19.95 (ISBN 0-574-21055-5, 13-4055); instr's guide avail. (ISBN 0-574-21056-3, 13-4056). SRA.
Rothman, Stanley, et al. European Society & Politics: Britain, France & Germany. LC 75-43682. (Illus.). 600p. 1976. pap. text ed. 15.95 (ISBN 0-8299-0068-3). West Pub.
Rothman, William. Hitchcock: The Muderous Gaze. 27.50 (ISBN 0-686-36002-8). Harvard Film Studies.
Rothman, William A. Bibliography of Collective Bargaining in Hospitals & Related Facilities, 1972-1974. LC 76-21690. (ILR Bibliography Ser.: No. 14). 164p. 1976. pap. 4.25 (ISBN 0-87546-060-7); pap. 7.25 special hard bdg. (ISBN 0-87546-287-1). ILR Pr.
--Interviewing for a Career in Health Care. 148p. 1983. pap. 6.95 (ISBN 0-938352-51-2). Hampton Pr MI.
Rothrock, George A. & Jones, Tom B. Europe; a Brief History, Vol. I: Prehistory to 1815. rev. & expanded 2nd ed. LC 81-43503. (Illus.). 410p. lib. bdg. 23.25 (ISBN 0-8191-2069-3); pap. text ed. 11.50 (ISBN 0-8191-2070-7). U Pr of Amer.
--Europe; a Brief History, Vol. II: Renaissance to the Present, 2 vols. rev. & expanded 2nd ed. LC 81-43503. (Illus.). 276p. 1982. Vol. 2. PLB 23.00 (ISBN 0-8191-2071-5); pap. text ed. 11.50 (ISBN 0-8191-2072-3). U Pr of Amer.
Rothschild, Bernard B. Construction Bonds & Insurance Guide. rev. ed. 1979. loose leaf binder 22.50x (ISBN 0-913962-09-0). Am Inst Arch.
Rothschild, Bruce M. Rheumatology: A Primary Care Approach. (Illus.). 430p. 1982. text ed. 39.50 (ISBN 0-914316-33-8). Yorke Med.
Rothschild, Donald P. & Koch, Charles H. Fundamentals of Administrative Practice & Procedure. (Contemporary Legal Education Ser.). 954p. 1981. text ed. 27.00 (ISBN 0-87215-412-2). Michie-Bobbs.
Rothschild, Dorothy de. The Rothschilds at Waddesdon Manor. (Illus.). 1979. 20.00 (ISBN 0-670-60854-8, The Vendome Pr.). Viking Pr.
Rothschild, Eric, ed. Documentary Sources of Western Civilization: Subject Index. 116p. (gr. 7-12). 1977. pap. 10.00 (ISBN 0-686-96792-5). Microfilming Corp.
Rothschild, Joan, ed. Machina ex Dea: Feminist Perspectives on Technology. (Athene Ser.). 250p. 1983. 27.50 (ISBN 0-08-029404-9); pap. 10.95 (ISBN 0-08-029403-0). Pergamon.
--Women, Technology & Innovation. (Journal of Women's Studies International Quarterly 4(Si)). 88p. 1982. 19.00 (ISBN 0-08-028943-6). Pergamon.
Rothschild, Kurt. The Theory of Wages. 2nd ed. (Illus.). viii, 178p. Repr. of 1954 ed. pap. 8.95x (ISBN 0-87991-848-9). Porcupine Pr.
Rothschild, Loren R., ed. The Letters of William Somerset Maugham to Lady Juliet Duff. (Illus.). 112p. write for info. limited ed. 300 copies. Rassela Pr.
Rothschild, M. The Life & Art of Thomas Gainsborough. (The Great Art Masters of the World). (Illus.). 102p. 1983. 97.75 (ISBN 0-86650-044-8). Gloucester Art.
Rothschild, M., jt. auth. see Hopkins, G. H.
Rothschild, M. A., jt. ed. see Rosenoer, V.
Rothschild, M. A., et al, eds. Alcohol & Abnormal Protein Biosynthesis, Biochemical & Clinical. 550p. 1975. text ed. 49.00 (ISBN 0-08-017708-5). Pergamon.
Rothschild, Marcus A. & Waldmann, Thomas, eds. Plasma Protein Metabolism: Regulation of Synthesis, Distribution & Degradation. 1970. 60.00 (ISBN 0-12-598750-1). Acad Pr.
Rothschild, Mary A. A Case of Black & White: Northern Volunteers & the Southern Freedom Summers, 1964-1965. LC 82-6175. (Contributions in Afro-American & African Studies: No. 69). 288p. 1982. lib. bdg. 29.95 (ISBN 0-313-23430-2, RBL/). Greenwood.
Rothschild, Miriam. Dear Lord Rothschild: Birds, Butterflies & History. (Illus.). 500p. 1983. 30.00 (ISBN 0-86689-019-X). Balaban Intl Sci Serv.
Rothschild, Miriam, jt. auth. see Hopkins, G. H.
Rothschild, Norman. Making Slide Duplicates, Titles, & Filmstrips. (Illus.). 1973. 11.95 o.p. (ISBN 0-8174-0553-4, Amphoto). Watson-Guptill.
Rothschild, W. G., jt. auth. see Moller, K. D.
Rothschild-Whitt, Joyce, jt. ed. see Lindenfeld, Frank.
Rothstein, Anne, et al. Motor Learning. Kneer, Marian, ed. (Basic Stuff Ser.: No. I, 3 of 6). (Illus.). 109p. (Orig.). 1981. pap. text ed. 6.25 (ISBN 0-88314-026-8). AAHPERD.
Rothstein, Arnold. The Structural Hypothesis. 1983. write for info (ISBN 0-8236-6175-X). Intl Univs Pr.
Rothstein, Arthur. Photojournalism. 3rd ed. (Illus.). 224p. 1973. 13.95 o.p. (ISBN 0-8174-0484-8, Amphoto). Watson-Guptill.
--Photojournalism. 4th ed. (Illus.). 1979. 15.95 o.p. (ISBN 0-8174-2469-5, Amphoto); pap. 9.95 o.p. (ISBN 0-8174-2137-8). Watson-Guptill.
Rothstein, Eric. George Farquhar. (English Authors Ser.). 14.95 (ISBN 0-8057-1188-0, Twayne). G K Hall.
--Restoration Tragedy: Form & the Process of Change. LC 78-5529. 1978. Repr. of 1967 ed. lib. bdg. 18.75x (ISBN 0-313-20472-1, RORET). Greenwood.
--Systems of Order & Inquiry in Later Eighteenth-Century Fiction. LC 74-16716. 284p. 1975. 30.00x (ISBN 0-520-02862-7). U of Cal Pr.
Rothstein, Eric & Wittreich, Joseph A., Jr., eds. Literary Monographs, Vol. 6 & 7. LC 66-25869. 1975. 20.00 ea.; Vol. 6, 192p. (ISBN 0-299-06610-X); Vol. 7, 172p. (ISBN 0-299-06620-7). U of Wis Pr.
--Literary Monographs, Vol. 8: George Eliot, De Quincey, & Emerson. LC 66-25869. 224p. 1976. 20.00 (ISBN 0-299-06950-8). U of Wis Pr.
Rothstein, Evelyn. Easy Student Writer Worksheets. Gess, Diane, ed. (The Write Track T. M. Ser.). (Illus., Each level 35p.). 1982. 9.95 ea. Level 2-3 (ISBN 0-9606172-1-3). Level 3-4 (ISBN 0-9606172-2-1). Level 4-5 (ISBN 0-9606172-3-X). Level 5-6 (ISBN 0-9606172-4-8). E Rothstein Assoc.
Rothstein, Frances, jt. ed. see Leons, Madeline B.
Rothstein, Frances A. Three Different Worlds: Women, Men, & Children in an Industrializing Community. LC 82-6216. (Contributions in Family Studies: No. 7). (Illus.). 176p. 1982. lib. bdg. 27.50 (ISBN 0-313-22594-X, RTW/). Greenwood.
Rothstein, Marian, tr. see Walzer, M.
Rothstein, Morton. Biochemical Approaches to Aging. 1982. 39.50. Acad Pr.
Rothweiler, Paul R. Blood Sports. (Orig.). pap. 2.25 o.s.i. (ISBN 0-515-05410-0). Jove Pubns.
--Blood Sports. (Orig.). 1980. write for info (ISBN 0-515-05410-0). Jove Pubns.
Rothwell, John C., jt. auth. see Hailstones, Thomas J.
Rothwell, Kenneth J., jt. auth. see Gordon, Bernard K.
Rothwell, Kenneth S. Questions of Rhetoric & Usage. 2nd ed. 304p. 1974. pap. text ed. 10.95 (ISBN 0-316-75801-9); instructor's manual avail. (ISBN 0-316-75802-7). Little.
Rothwell, Mel-Thomas. Preaching Holiness Effectively. 160p. 1982. pap. 4.95 (ISBN 0-8341-0784-8). Beacon Hill.
Rothwell, Norman V. Human Genetics. (Illus.). 1977. text ed. 21.95 o.p. (ISBN 0-13-445080-9). P-H.
--Understanding Genetics. 3rd ed. (Illus.). 1983. text ed. 28.95x (ISBN 0-19-503123-7). Oxford U Pr.
Rothwell, Roy & Zegveld, Walter. Technical Change & Employment. 1979. 20.00x (ISBN 0-312-78770-7). St Martin.
Rothwell, W. & Barron, W. R. Studies in Medieval Literature & Languages. Blamires, D. M. & Thorpe, L., eds. 404p. 1973. 29.00 (ISBN 0-7190-0550-7). Manchester.
Rotkiewiez, W., ed. Electromagnetic Compatibility in Radio Engineering. (Studies in Electrical & Electronic Engineering: Vol. 6). 1982. 61.75 (ISBN 0-444-99722-9). Elsevier.
Rotkin, Charles E. Photographer's Survival Guide: The Insider's View of Professionalism. 320p. 1982. 17.50 (ISBN 0-8174-5409-8, Amphoto); pap. 10.95 (ISBN 0-8174-5410-1). Watson-Guptill.
Rotkovich, Rachel, ed. Quality Patient Care & the Role of the Clinical Nurse Specialist. LC 76-5393. 189p. 1976. 24.95 o.p. (ISBN 0-471-74015-2, Pub. by Wiley Medical). Wiley.
Rotman, A., et al. Platelets: Cellular Response Mechanisms & Their Biological Significance: Proceedings. LC 80-4127. 327p. 1980. 59.95 (ISBN 0-471-27896-3, Pub. by Wiley-Interscience). Wiley.
Rotmans, Elmer A., et al. Basic Drafting Technology. 2nd ed. LC 78-50424. (gr. 8). 1980. pap. text ed. 20.80 (ISBN 0-8273-1293-8); instr's. guide 2.40 (ISBN 0-8273-1294-6). Delmar.
Rotondi, M. Aims & Methods of Comparative Law, 2 vols. LC 72-181274. 1973. 18.00 ea. (ISBN 0-379-00026-1). Oceana.
Rotovision. Art Directors' Index to Photographers, No. 7. (Illus.). 1981. 80.00 (ISBN 2-88046-005-0); pap. 17.50 (ISBN 2-88046-010-7). Norton.
--Jan Saudek-Photographs. 1982. 40.00 (ISBN 2-88046-028-X). Norton.
Rotrosen, John, jt. ed. see Stanley, Michael.
Rotsler, William. The Hidden Worlds of Zandra. (Science Fiction Ser.). 192p. 1983. 11.95 (ISBN 0-385-14614-0). Doubleday.
--Joanie Loves Chachi: A Test of Hearts, No. 2. Schneider, Meg, ed. 160p. (gr. 3-7). 1982. pap. 2.95 (ISBN 0-671-46011-0). Wanderer Bks.
--Joanie Loves Chachi: Secrets, No. 1. Barish, Wendy, ed. 160p. (gr. 3-7). 1982. pap. 2.95 (ISBN 0-671-46010-2). Wanderer Bks.
--Mr. Merlin: Episode No. 2. 160p. (gr. 3-7). 1981. pap. 2.95 o.p. (ISBN 0-671-44480-8). Wanderer Bks.
--The Pirate Movie. Schneider, Meg, ed. (Illus.). 192p. (gr. 3 up). 1982. pap. 2.95 (ISBN 0-671-45999-6). Wanderer Bks.
--Plot-Your-Own-Adventure TM: Distress Call. Barish, Wendy, ed. (Star Trek II). (Illus., Orig.). (gr. 3-7). 1982. pap. 2.95 (ISBN 0-671-46389-6). Wanderer Bks.
--Vice Squad. 240p. (Orig.). 1982. pap. 2.50 o.p. (ISBN 0-523-41779-9). Pinnacle Bks.
Rotsler, William & Barish, Wendy. Star Trek II: Biographies. 160p. (gr. 3-7). 1982. pap. 3.95 (ISBN 0-671-46391-8). Wanderer Bks.
--Star Trek II: Short Stories. 160p. (gr. 3-7). 1982. pap. 2.95 (ISBN 0-671-46390-X). Wanderer Bks.
Rotsstein, Aaron. Judgement in St. Peter's. LC 79-16951. 1980. 9.95 (ISBN 0-399-12444-6). Putnam Pub Group.
Rottenberg, David. Fire of Knowledge. (Orig.). 1983. pap. 3.95 (ISBN 0-910291-01-2). Cedar Crest Bks.
--A Windless Place. 1982. pap. 3.95 (ISBN 0-910291-00-4). Cedar Crest Bks.
Rottenberg, Dorian, tr. see Marshak, Samuil & Harms, David.
Rotter, Hans-August. Growing Plants Without Soil. (Illus.). 120p. 1983. 15.95 (ISBN 0-7158-0797-8, Pub. by EP Publishing England). Sterling.
Rotter, Jerome I., et al, eds. The Genetics & Heterogeneity of Common Gastrointestinal Disorders. 1980. 40.00 (ISBN 0-12-598760-9). Acad Pr.
Rotter, Pat, ed. Last Night's Stranger: One Night Stands & Other Staples of Modern Life. 284p. 1983. 17.95 (ISBN 0-89479-104-4). A & W Pubs.
Rotterdam, Heidrun Z. & Sommers, Sheldon C. Biopsy Diagnosis of the Digestive Tract. (Biopsy Interpretation Ser.). 490p. 1981. text ed. 49.50 (ISBN 0-89004-541-0). Raven.
Rottgen, Steffi, et al. The Art of Mosaics: Selections from the Gilbert Collection. rev. ed. Hall, Alla T., tr. from German. (Illus.). 224p. (Orig.). 1982. 27.50 (ISBN 0-87587-109-7); pap. 17.50. LA Co Art Mus.
Rotunda, Ronald D. Modern Constitutional Law, Cases & Notes, 1982 Supplement. (American Casebook Ser.). 167p. 1982. pap. text ed. 4.95 (ISBN 0-314-69922-8). West Pub.
--Six Justices on Civil Rights. 1983. lib. bdg. 22.50 (ISBN 0-379-20044-9). Oceana.
Rotunda, Ronald D., jt. auth. see Hay, Peter.
Rotzler, W. Photography As Artistic Experiment: From Fox Talbot to Moholy-Nagy. (Illus.). 1976. pap. 6.95 o.p. (ISBN 0-8174-0317-5, Amphoto). Watson-Guptill.
Rouard, Marguerite & Simon, Jacques. Children's Play Spaces: From Sandbox to Adventure Playground. (Illus.). 160p. 1983. 37.95 (ISBN 0-87951-056-0); pap. 13.95 (ISBN 0-87951-166-4). Overlook Pr.
Rouault, Georges. The Passion. (Fine Art Ser.). (Illus.). 80p. 1983. pap. 7.95 (ISBN 0-486-24370-2). Dover.
Rouault, Olivier. Terga Final Reports, No. 1: L'Archive de Puzurum. (Bibliotheca Mesopotamica Ser.: Vol. 15). 110p. (Fr. & Akkadian.). 1983. write for info. (ISBN 0-89003-103-7); pap. write for info. (ISBN 0-89003-102-9). Undena Pubns.
Roubiczek, Paul. Existentialism: for & Against. (Orig.). 34.50x (ISBN 0-521-06140-7); pap. 9.95 (ISBN 0-521-09243-4). Cambridge U Pr.
Roucek, Joseph. Tito: Modern Leader of Yugoslavia. Rahmas, D. Steve, ed. LC 73-87625. (Outstanding Personalities Ser.: No. 62). 32p. (Orig.). (gr. 7-12). 1973. lib. bdg. 2.95 incl. catalog cards (ISBN 0-87157-562-0); pap. 1.95 vinyl laminated covers (ISBN 0-87157-062-9). SamHar Pr.
Roucek, Joseph S. Balkan Politics: International Relations in No Man's Land. LC 75-106696. (Illus.). 1971. Repr. of 1948 ed. lib. bdg. 15.75x (ISBN 0-8371-3370-X, ROBP). Greenwood.

--Capital Punishment. new ed. Rahmas, D. Steve, ed. (Topics of Our Times Ser.). 32p. 1975. lib. bdg. 2.95 incl. catalog cards (ISBN 0-87157-816-6); pap. 1.95 vinyl laminated covers (ISBN 0-686-11242-3). SamHar Pr.

--Sexual Attack & the Crime of Rape. rev. ed. Rahmas, D. Steve, ed. (Topics of Our Times Ser.). 32p. 1980. lib. bdg. 2.95 incl. catalog cards (ISBN 0-87157-814-X); pap. 1.95 vinyl laminated covers (ISBN 0-87157-314-8). SamHar Pr.

--Social Control for the Nineteen Eighties: A Handbook for Order in a Democratic Society. LC 77-91112. (Contributions in Sociology: No. 31). 1978. lib. bdg. 35.00x (ISBN 0-313-20048-3, RSC/). Greenwood.

Rouche, N. & Mawhin, J. Ordinary Differential Equations: Stability & Periodic Solutions. LC 80-13039. (Surveys & References Ser.: No. 5). 208p. 1980. text ed. 58.00 (ISBN 0-273-08419-4). Pitman Pub MA.

Roucheux, Nicole. Practical Guide to the South Pacific. rev. ed. (Illus.). 1980. pap. 6.95 (ISBN 0-8048-1341-8). C E Tuttle.

Roucoux, A. & Crommelinck, M. Physiological & Pathological Aspects of Eye Movements. 1983. 76.00 (ISBN 90-619-3730-2, Pub. by Junk Pubs Netherlands). Kluwer Boston.

Roud, Richard. A Passion for Films. 1983. pap. 15.75 (ISBN 0-670-36687-0). Viking Pr.

Rouder, Susan. American Politics: Playing the Game. LC 76-13962. Orig. Title: Game of American Politics: How to Play. (Illus.). 1977. pap. text ed. 15.95 o.p. (ISBN 0-395-24971-6); instr. manual 1.10 o.p. (ISBN 0-395-24972-4). HM.

Roueche, Berton. What's Left. 8.95 (ISBN 0-911660-21-6). Yankee Peddler.

Roueche, James R. Dysphagia: An Assessment & Management Program for the Adult. 56p. 1980. 15.00 (ISBN 0-686-95725-3, 706). Sis Kenny Inst.

Roueche, N. E. & Mink, B. Washburn. The Language of Mathematics: An Individualized Introduction. LC 78-13397. 1979. 22.95 (ISBN 0-13-522920-0). P-H.

Roueche, Nelda. Business Mathematics: A Collegiate Approach. 3rd ed. LC 78-16746. 1978. text ed. 19.95 o.p. (ISBN 0-13-105007-9). P-H.

Roueche, Nelda W. Fundamentals of Business Mathematics. (Illus.). 1979. pap. 15.95 (ISBN 0-13-334441-X). P-H.

Rouge Et Noir. Gambling World. LC 68-22047. 1968. Repr. of 1898 ed. 37.00x (ISBN 0-8103-3551-4). Gale.

Rougement, D. de see De Rougemont, D.

Rougemont, Denis De see De Rougemont, Denis.

Rougeul-Buser, A., jt. auth. see Buser, P. A.

Rough, Robert H. Art History. (College Outlines Ser.). pap. 4.95 o.p. (ISBN 0-671-08038-5, 08038). Monarch Pr.

Roughgarden, Jonathan. Theory of Population Genetics & Evolutionary Ecology: An Introduction. 1979. text ed. 31.95x (ISBN 0-02-403180-1). Macmillan.

Rougier, J. Paul. Les Associations Ouvrieres. (Conditions of the 19th Century French Working Class Ser.). 472p. (Fr.). 1974. Repr. of 1864 ed. lib. bdg. 118.00 o.p. (ISBN 0-8287-0740-5, 1149). Clearwater Pub.

Rouiller, C., ed. The Liver: Morphology, Biochemistry, Physiology, 2 vols. 1963-64. 91.00 set (ISBN 0-686-66624-0); Vol. 1. 73.00 (ISBN 0-12-598901-6); Vol. 2. 73.00 (ISBN 0-12-598902-4). Acad Pr.

Rouiller, C. & Muller, A., eds. The Kidney: Morphology, Biochemistry, Physiology. Incl. Vols. 1-2. 1969. 89.00 (ISBN 0-686-76968-6). Vol. 1 (ISBN 0-12-598801-X). Vol. 2. 89.00 (ISBN 0-12-598802-8); Vols. 3-4. 1971. 68.00 ea. Vol. 3 (ISBN 0-12-598803-6). Vol. 4 (ISBN 0-12-598804-4). Set. 225.00 (ISBN 0-686-66787-5). Acad Pr.

Roukis, George S., jt. ed. see Montana, Patrick J.

Roulac, Stephen E. Tax Shelter Sale-Leaseback Financing: The Economic Realities. LC 76-14389. 176p. 1976. prof ref 25.00x (ISBN 0-88410-446-X). Ballinger Pub.

Roulac, Stephen E., jt. auth. see Maisel, Sherman J.

Roulston, Robert. James Norman Hall. (United States Authors Ser.). 1978. lib. bdg. 12.95 (ISBN 0-8057-7255-3, Twayne). G K Hall.

Roulstone, Michael. Taverns in Town. (Travel in England Ser.). (Illus.). 96p. 1975. 7.95 o.p. (ISBN 0-85944-001-X). Transatlantic.

Rounce, John F. Science for Beauty Therapists. 272p. 1982. 33.00x (ISBN 0-85950-331-3, Pub. by Thornes England). State Mutual Bk.

Round, F. E. The Biology of the Algae. 2nd ed. LC 73-89991. 288p. 1974. 19.95 o.p. (ISBN 0-312-07875-7); pap. 18.95 (ISBN 0-312-07910-9). St Martin.

Round, F. E. & Chapman, D. J., eds. Progress in Psychological Research, Vol. 1. 1982. 108.50 (ISBN 0-444-80396-3). Elsevier.

Round, Gilbert F., ed. Solid-Liquid Flow Abstracts, 3 Vols. 1969. Set. 245.00x (ISBN 0-677-40120-5); Vol. 1, 448p. 110.00x (ISBN 0-677-40080-2); Vol. 2, 458p. 113.00 (ISBN 0-677-40090-X); Vol. 3. 54.00x (ISBN 0-677-40100-0). Gordon.

Roundhill, Kenneth. Prescription for Today's Disciple. 1979. pap. 3.50 (ISBN 0-87508-466-4). Chr Lit.

Rounds, Glen. Blind Colt. (Illus.). 78p. (gr. 4-6). 1960. 10.95 (ISBN 0-8234-0010-7). Holiday.

--The Cowboy Trade. LC 73-119804. (Illus.). 96p. (gr. 4-8). 1972. 10.95 (ISBN 0-8234-0206-1). Holiday.

--The Day the Circus Came to Lone Tree. LC 73-78458. (Illus.). 40p. (gr. k-3). 1973. PLB 8.95 (ISBN 0-8234-0232-0). Holiday.

--Mr. Yowder & the Giant Bull Snake. LC 77-24136. (Illus.). 48p. (gr. 2-5). 1978. PLB 8.95 (ISBN 0-8234-0311-4). Holiday.

--Ol' Paul the Mighty Logger. (Illus.). 1978. pap. 1.25 o.p. (ISBN 0-380-40295-5, 40295, Camelot). Avon.

--The Prairie Schooners. (Illus.). 96p. (gr. 4-6). 1968. 10.95 (ISBN 0-8234-0088-3). Holiday.

--Stolen Pony. rev. ed. (Illus.). 96p. (gr. 4-6). 1969. 10.95 (ISBN 0-8234-0110-3). Holiday.

--The Treeless Plains. (Illus.). 96p. (gr. 4-6). 1967. 10.95 (ISBN 0-8234-0122-7). Holiday.

--Whitey & the Wild Horse. (gr. 4 up). 1977. pap. 0.95 o.p. (ISBN 0-440-49620-9, YB). Dell.

--Wild Appaloosa. LC 82-48751. (Illus.). 96p. (gr. 3-7). 1983. 10.95 (ISBN 0-8234-0482-X). Holiday.

--Wild Horses of the Red Desert. (Illus.). 48p. (gr. 4-6). 1969. PLB 7.95 (ISBN 0-8234-0146-4). Holiday.

--Wild Orphan. (Illus.). 84p. (gr. 4-6). 1961. 10.95 (ISBN 0-8234-0147-2). Holiday.

--Witney's First Round-Up. (gr. 2-5). 1982. pap. 1.95 (ISBN 0-380-57141-2, 57141-2). Avon.

Rouner, Leroy, jt. ed. see Howie, John.

Rountree, Moses. Henry Belk-Son of Sweet Union. LC 75-4487. 1975. 10.95 (ISBN 0-87716-058-9, Pub. by Moore Pub Co). F Apple.

Rountree, Owen. The Black Hills Duel. 160p. (Orig.). 1983. pap. 1.95 (ISBN 0-345-30758-5). Ballantine.

Rouquerol, J. & Sing, K. S. Adsorption at the Gas-Solid Interface: Proceedings of the International Symposium at Aux-en - Provence, Sept. 1981. (Studies in Surface Science & Catalysis: Vol. 10). 1982. 93.75 (ISBN 0-444-42087-8). Elsevier.

Rourke, C. P. & Sanderson, B. J. Introduction to Piecewise-Linear Topology. (Springer Study Edition Ser.). (Illus.). 130p. 1982. pap. 10.00 (ISBN 0-387-11102-6). Springer-Verlag.

Rourke, Francis E., ed. Bureaucratic Power in National Politics: Introductory Readings in American Politics. 3rd ed. 1978. pap. 10.95 (ISBN 0-316-75953-8). Little.

Rourke, Margaret. Lampshades. 5.50 o.p. (ISBN 0-392-12444-0, SpS). Sportshelf.

Rourke, Margaret V. & Gentry, Christine A. So You Want a Successful HERO Program. Simpson, Elizabeth, ed. (Careers in Home Economics Ser.). 1979. pap. text ed. 10.95 (ISBN 0-07-023176-1, G). McGraw.

Rourke, Robert E., jt. auth. see Mosteller, F. R.

Rouse, tr. Great Dialogues of Plato. pap. 3.95 (ISBN 0-451-62122-0, ME2122, Ment). NAL.

--Great Dialogues of Plato. pap. 9.95 (ISBN 0-452-25392-6, Z5392, Plume). NAL.

Rouse, Hunter, ed. Engineering Hydraulics. 1950. 69.95x (ISBN 0-471-74283-X, Pub. by Wiley-Interscience). Wiley.

Rouse, Irving. Introduction to Prehistory. LC 71-173715. (Illus.). 256p. 1972. text ed. 12.95 o.p. (ISBN 0-07-054100-0, C). McGraw.

Rouse, John E., Jr., ed. Public Administration in American Society: A Guide to Information Sources. (American Government & History Information Guide Ser.: Vol. 11). 300p. 1980. 42.00x (ISBN 0-8103-1424-X). Gale.

--Urban Housing--Public & Private: A Guide to Information Sources. LC 79-100279. (Urban Studies Information Guide Ser.: Vol. 5). 1978. 42.00x (ISBN 0-8103-1398-7). Gale.

Rouse, Mary & Kennedy, George A., eds. Stories from Ancient China. 3.75 (ISBN 0-686-09968-0). Far Eastern Pubns.

Rouse, Mary, ed. see Hu Shih.

Rouse, Parke, Jr. Planters & Pioneers. (Illus.). 216p. 1983. pap. 12.95 (ISBN 0-8038-5900-7). Hastings.

--Planters & Pioneers: Life in Colonial Virginia. LC 68-17650. (gr. 8 up). 1968. 10.95 o.s.i. (ISBN 0-8038-5713-6). Hastings.

Rouse, Richard H., ed. Serial Bibliographies for Medieval Studies. LC 68-31637. (UCLA Center for Medieval & Renaissance Studies). 1969. 30.00x (ISBN 0-520-01456-1). U of Cal Pr.

Rouse, Robert S. & Smith, Robert O. Energy: Resource, Slave, Pollutant; a Physical Science Text. 1975. 22.95x (ISBN 0-02-404000-2). Macmillan.

Rouse, Sandra H., jt. auth. see Rouse, William B.

Rouse, Sandra H., jt. ed. see Williams, Martha E.

Rouse, W. H. Gods, Heroes & Men of Ancient Greece. (RL 5). 1971. pap. 2.50 (ISBN 0-451-62207-3, ME2207, Ment). NAL.

Rouse, W. H., tr. see Homer.

Rouse, W. H., tr. see Xenophon.

Rouse, William B. & Rouse, Sandra H. Management of Library Networks: Policy Analysis, Implementation, & Control. LC 80-12644. (Information Sciences Ser.). 288p. 1980. 36.95 (ISBN 0-471-05534-4, Pub. by Wiley Interscience). Wiley.

Rouse, William H., tr. see Homer.

Rousey, Clyde L. Psychiatric Assessment by Speech & Hearing Behavior. (Illus.). 392p. 1974. photocopy ed.spiral 39.50x (ISBN 0-398-03034-0). C C Thomas.

Roush, Barbara. Labor of Love. 1982. pap. 2.50 (ISBN 0-380-80879-X, 80879). Avon.

Rouslin, Sheila, jt. ed. see Smoyak, Shirley A.

Rousmaniere, John. The Luxury Yachts. (Seafarers Ser.). 19.92 (ISBN 0-8094-2735-4). Silver.

Roussakis, Emmanuel N. International Banking: Principles & Practices. 556p. 1983. 39.95 (ISBN 0-03-062387-1). Praeger.

Rousseas, S. Capitalism & Catastrophe. LC 78-11996. (Illus.). 1979. 24.95 (ISBN 0-521-22333-4). Cambridge U Pr.

Rousseas, Stephen. The Political Economy of Reaganomics: A Critique. LC 82-10659. 1982. 20.00 (ISBN 0-87332-227-4); pap. 8.95 (ISBN 0-87332-239-8). M E Sharpe.

Rousseas, Stephen W. Monetary Theory. LC 81-40789. 302p. 1981. pap. text ed. 11.25 (ISBN 0-8191-1815-X). U Pr of Amer.

Rousseau, D. L. Vibrational Models & Point Groups in Crystals. 40p. 1982. text ed. 21.95 (ISBN 0-471-26143-2). Wiley.

Rousseau, G. S. Organic Form: The Life of an Idea. 1972. 8.00x o.p. (ISBN 0-7100-7246-5). Routledge & Kegan.

Rousseau, G. S. & Porter, R., eds. The Ferment of Knowledge: Studies in the Historiography of Eighteenth-Century Science. LC 80-40001. 550p. 1980. 49.50 (ISBN 0-521-22599-X). Cambridge U Pr.

Rousseau, Jean J. Annotated Social Contract. Sheroner, Charles M., ed. pap. 3.95 o.p. (ISBN 0-452-00369-5, FM369, Mer). NAL.

--Les Reveries du Promeneur Solitaire. 2nd ed. Niklaus, R., ed. (Modern French Text Ser.). 1946. pap. write for info. (ISBN 0-7190-0160-9). Manchester.

Rousseau, Jean-Jacques. Emile. Bloom, Allan, tr. LC 78-73765. 1979. o.s. 18.50 (ISBN 0-465-01930-7); pap. 9.95x (ISBN 0-465-01931-5). Basic.

--The Government of Poland. Kendall, Willmoore, tr. LC 70-165184. 1972. pap. text ed. 4.50 o.p. (ISBN 0-672-60391-8, LLA165). Bobbs.

--Of the Social Contract & Discourse on the Origin of Inequality & Discourse on Political Economy. Cress, Donald A., tr. from Fr. (HPC Philosophical Classics Ser.). 288p. 1983. lib. bdg. 15.95 (ISBN 0-915145-57-X); pap. text ed. 4.95 (ISBN 0-915145-56-1). Hackett Pub.

--On the Social Contract. Masters, Roger D., ed. Masters, Judith R., tr. LC 77-86291. 1978. text ed. 17.95x (ISBN 0-312-69445-8); pap. text ed. 8.95 (ISBN 0-312-69446-6). St Martin.

Rousseau, Jean Jacques. The Social Contract. Kendall, Willmore, tr. LC 54-8139. 1954. pap. 4.95 (ISBN 0-89526-917-1). Regnery-Gateway.

Rousseau, Jeanne, jt. auth. see Claessens, Bob.

Rousseau, Mary F., tr. Liber De Pomo: The Apple or Aristotle's Death. (Medieval Philosophical Texts in Translation: No. 18). 1968. pap. 7.95 (ISBN 0-87462-218-2). Marquette.

Rousseau, Richard W. Disclosure of the Ultimate: Fundamental Theology Reconsidered. LC 80-8259. 399p. 1980. lib. bdg. 24.25 (ISBN 0-8191-1284-4); pap. 14.50 (ISBN 0-8191-1285-2). U Pr of Amer.

Rousseau, Richard W., ed. Christianity & the Religions of the East: Models for a Dynamic Relationship. (Modern Theological Themes: Selections from the Literature Ser.: Vol. 2). 174p. (Orig.). 1982. pap. 15.00x (ISBN 0-940866-01-3). Ridge Row.

Rousseau, Richard W., ed. see Curtis, Charles J.

Rousseau, Ronald W., jt. auth. see Felder, Richard M.

Rousseau, Viateur, jt. auth. see Murphy, Daniel B.

Roussel, Hubert. The Houston Symphony Orchestra, 1913-1971. (Illus.). 257p. 1972. 15.95 (ISBN 0-292-73000-4). U of Tex Pr.

Roussel, Raymond. How I Wrote Certain of My Books. 2nd rev. ed. Winkfield, Trevor & Koch, Kenneth, trs. from Fr. LC 77-3630. 1977. pap. 5.00 (ISBN 0-915342-05-7). SUN.

Rousselet, Blanc P. Dictionnaire des Animaux. 250p. (Fr.). 1981. 12.95 (ISBN 0-686-97634-7, M-9771). French & Eur.

Rousset, David. The Legacy of the Bolshevik Revolution: A Critical History of the USSR, Vol. 1. 1982. 27.50x (ISBN 0-312-47802-X). St Martin.

--The Other Kingdom. Guthrie, Ramon, tr. from Fr. LC 81-12572. 173p. 1982. Repr. of 1947 ed. lib. bdg. 19.75 (ISBN 0-86527-339-1). Fertig.

Rout, L. B. The African Experience in Spanish America: 1502 to the Present Day. LC 75-9280. (Latin American Studies: No. 23). (Illus.). 276p. 1976. 47.50 (ISBN 0-521-20805-X); pap. 10.95x (ISBN 0-521-29010-4). Cambridge U Pr.

Routh, Donald K., ed. Learning, Speech, & the Complex Effects of Punishment: Essays Honoring George J. Wischner. 238p. 1982. 25.00 (ISBN 0-306-40960-7, Plenum Pr). Plenum Pub.

Routh, E. C. Quienes Son. Rivas, Jose G., tr. from Eng. Orig. Title: Who Are They? 80p. 1981. pap. 1.95 (ISBN 0-311-05756-X). Casa Bautista.

Routh, Guy. The Origin of Economic Ideas. LC 75-10791. 325p. 1975. 27.50 (ISBN 0-87332-071-9). M E Sharpe.

Routh, Jonathan. The Secret Life of Queen Victoria. LC 79-7320. 128p. 1980. 20.00 o.p. (ISBN 0-385-15353-8). Doubleday.

Routley, Erik. Church Music & the Christian Faith. LC 78-110219. 156p. 1978. pap. 5.95 (ISBN 0-916642-10-0). Agape IL.

--Exploring the Psalms. LC 74-20674. 1975. pap. 3.95 (ISBN 0-664-24999-X). Westminster.

--Man for Others. (Orig.). 1964. pap. 5.95x (ISBN 0-19-500463-9). Oxford U Pr.

Routley, Richard. Exploring Meinong's Jungle & Beyond. (Monograph Ser.: No. 3). xx, 1036p. 1980. pap. 18.00x (ISBN 0-909596-36-0). Ridgeview.

Routtenberg, Aryeh, ed. Biology of Reinforcement: Facet of Brain Stimulation Reward. (Behavioral Biology Ser.). 1980. 18.50 (ISBN 0-12-599350-1). Acad Pr.

Routtenberg, Lilly S. & Seldin, Ruth R. The Jewish Wedding Book: A Practical Guide to the Traditions & Social Customs of the Jewish Wedding. LC 67-13723. (Illus.). 1969. pap. 4.95 (ISBN 0-8052-0186-6). Schocken.

Rouvellat de Cussac. Situation des Esclaves dans les Colonies Francaises. (Slave Trade in France Ser., 1744-1848). 256p. (Fr.). 1974. Repr. of 1845 ed. lib. bdg. 70.00x o.p. (ISBN 0-8287-0741-3, TN 136). Clearwater Pub.

Rouverol, Jean. Harriet Beecher Stowe: Woman Crusader. (American Hero Biographies). (Illus.). (gr. 3-5). 1968. PLB 4.49 o.p. (ISBN 0-399-60226-7). Putnam Pub Group.

Rouvray, D. H., tr. see Mentwig, Joachim & Kreuder, Manfred.

Roux, Claude. Etude Ecologique et Phytosociologique des Peuplements Licheniques Saxicoles-Calcicoles du Sud-Est de la France. (Bibliotheca Lichenologica: Vol. 15). (Illus.). 558p. (Fr.). 1981. text ed. 60.00x (ISBN 3-7682-1301-3). Lubrecht & Cramer.

Roux, E., ed. see Societe de Chimie Physique, International Meeting, 29th, Orsay, Oct. 1976.

Roux, H. see Serratrice, G.

Roux, J. H. Le see Coetzer, P. W. & Le Roux, J. H.

Rovee-Collier, Carolyn see Lipsitt, Lewis P.

Rovee-Collier, Carolyn E. see Lipsitt, Lewis P.

Rover, Michelle. French for Business Studies. 95p. (Fr.). 1979. pap. text ed. 4.95x (ISBN 0-582-35900-7). Longman.

Rovere, Richard. Senator Joe McCarthy. 1973. pap. 3.95xi (ISBN 0-06-131970-8, TB1970, Torch). Har-Row.

Rovetch, Emily, ed. Like It Is: Arthur E. Thomas Interviews Leaders on Black America. 1981. text ed. 10.25 (ISBN 0-525-93193-7, 0995-200); pap. 6.25 (ISBN 0-525-93194-5, 0607-180); tchr's. guide 2.50 (ISBN 0-525-93195-3, 0240-100). Dutton.

Rovin, jt. auth. see Pero.

Rovin, Jeff. The Complete Guide to Conquering Video Games: How to Win Every Game in the Galaxy. Du Bay, Bill, tr. (Illus.). 407p. (Orig.). 1982. pap. 5.95 (ISBN 0-02-029970-2, Collier); pap. 59.50 prepack(10). Macmillan.

--Count Dracula Vampire Quiz Book. 1979. pap. 1.75 o.p. (ISBN 0-451-08710-0, E8710, Sig). NAL.

--The Second Signet Book of Movie Lists. 1982. pap. 1.95 (ISBN 0-451-11516-3, AJ1516, Sig). NAL.

--Signet Book of Movie Lists. (Illus., Orig.). 1979. pap. 1.75 o.p. (ISBN 0-451-08929-4, E8929, Sig). NAL.

--The Signet Book of T. V. Lists. 1982. pap. 2.25 (ISBN 0-451-11742-5, AE1742, Sig). NAL.

--The Super Hero Movie & TV Trivia Quiz Book. (Orig.). 1979. pap. 1.75 o.p. (ISBN 0-451-08474-8, E8474, Sig). NAL.

--The Transatlantic Guide to Solar System M-Seventeen. (Illus.). 288p. 1981. pap. 6.95 (ISBN 0-399-50492-3, Perige). Putnam Pub Group.

--The UFO Movie Quiz Book. (Illus., Orig.). 1978. pap. 1.50 o.p. (ISBN 0-451-08258-3, W8258, Sig). NAL.

Rovit, Earl, ed. Saul Bellow: A Collection of Critical Essays. (Twentieth Century Views Ser). (Illus.). 192p. 1975. 12.95 o.p. (ISBN 0-13-074872-2, Spec); pap. 2.45 o.p. (ISBN 0-13-074864-1, Spec). P-H.

Rovit, Earl H. Ernest Hemingway. (United States Authors Ser.). 1963. lib. bdg. 10.95 (ISBN 0-8057-0364-0, Twayne). G K Hall.

Rowan, Andrew N. Use of Alternatives in Drug Research. 208p. 1980. pap. text ed. 24.95 o.p. (ISBN 0-333-27014-2). Univ Park.

Rowan, Betty, et al. The Learning Match: A Developmental Guide to Teaching Young Children. (Ser. in Early Childhood). (Illus.). 1980. text ed. 22.95 (ISBN 0-13-527044-8). P-H.

Rowan, Ford. Technospies. LC 77-28067. 1978. 10.95 o.p. (ISBN 0-399-11855-1). Putnam Pub Group.

Rowan, James. I. W. W. in the Lumber Industry. (Shorey Historical Ser.). Repr. pap. 5.95 (ISBN 0-8466-0196-6, SJS196). Shorey.

Rowan, John, jt. ed. see Reason, Peter.

Rowan, Lilian & Laiken, D. S. Speedwalking: The Exercise Alternative. 1980. 9.95 (ISBN 0-686-68357-9). Putnam Pub Group.

Rowan, Richard L., jt. auth. see Campbell, Duncan C.

Rowan, Richard L., et al. Multinational Union Organizations in the Public Service, White-Collar, & Entertainment Industries. LC 81-52616. 1983. pap. 25.00 (ISBN 0-89546-022-X). Indus Res Unit-Wharton.

Rowat, Donald C., ed. International Handbook on Local Government Reorganization: Contemporary Developments. LC 79-54063. (Illus.). xv, 626p. 1980. lib. bdg. 55.00x (ISBN 0-313-21269-4, RHL/). Greenwood.
Rowatt, Wade, jt. auth. see Oates, Wayne E.
Rowbotham, John L., jt. auth. see Lenneberg, Edith.
Rowbotham, John R. Troubadours & Courts of Love. LC 68-22048. 1969. Repr. of 1895 ed. 30.00x (ISBN 0-8103-3840-8). Gale.
Rowbotham, Sheila. Woman's Consciousness, Man's World. 1974. pap. 3.95 (ISBN 0-14-021717-7, Pelican). Penguin.
Rowbottom, Ralph. Social Analysis. LC 78-306628. (Heinemann Educational Books). 1977. text ed. 19.00x (ISBN 0-435-82772-3); pap. text ed. 11.00x (ISBN 0-435-82773-1). Heinemann Ed.
Rowden, Harold H., ed. Christ the Lord: Studies in Christology Presented to Donald Guthrie. LC 82-171. 1982. 19.95 (ISBN 0-87784-955-2). Inter-Varsity.
Rowdon, Maurice. Elke & Belam. LC 77-21323. 1978. 9.95 o.p. (ISBN 0-399-12077-7). Putnam Pub Group.
Rowe. The Hard-Rock Men. 344p. 1982. 49.00x (ISBN 0-85323-120-6, Pub. by Liverpool Univ England). State Mutual Bk.
Rowe, A. H. & Johns, R. B. A Companion to Dental Studies, Vol. 2: Clinical Medical Sciences. (Illus.). 416p. 1982. text ed. 44.50 (ISBN 0-632-00802-4, B4222-1). Mosby.
Rowe, A. J. & Mason, R. O. Strategic Management & Business Planning: A Methodological Approach. 1982. text ed. 17.95 (ISBN 0-201-06387-5). A-W.
Rowe, A. J., jt. auth. see Patz, Alan L.
Rowe, Alan R. Social Physics & Cultural Sociology: A Primer of Two Typologies for Masters of Sociological Thought. LC 81-43803. 42p. (Orig.). 1982. pap. text ed. 4.75 (ISBN 0-8191-2307-2). U Pr of Amer.
Rowe, Basil. Under My Wings. (Airlines History Project Ser.). Date not set. price not set (ISBN 0-404-19333-1). AMS Pr.
Rowe, Bruce M., jt. auth. see Stein, Philip.
Rowe, Bruce M., jt. auth. see Stein, Philip L.
Rowe, Colin. The Mathematics of the Ideal Villa & Other Essays. LC 75-33908. 200p. 1976. 20.00x (ISBN 0-262-18077-4). MIT Pr.
Rowe, Colin & Koetter, Fred. Collage City. 1978. 27.50 (ISBN 0-262-18086-3). MIT Pr.
Rowe, D. The Experience of Depression. 275p. 1978. text ed. 49.95x (ISBN 0-471-99554-1, Pub. by Wiley-Interscience). Wiley.
Rowe, D. J., ed. London Radictism, Eighteen-Thirty-Eighteen-Fortythree: A Selection from the Papers of Francis Place. 1970. 50.00x (ISBN 0-686-96615-5, Pub by London Rec Soc England). State Mutual Bk.
Rowe, Diane, jt. auth. see Lindsay, Rae.
Rowe, Dorothy. Construction of Life & Death. 224p. 1982. 29.95x (ISBN 0-471-10064-1, Pub. by Wiley-Interscience). Wiley.
Rowe, G. S. Thomas McKean: The Shaping of an American Republicanism. LC 77-94085. (Illus.). 1978. text ed. 17.50x (ISBN 0-87081-100-2). Colo Assoc.
Rowe, Geoffrey W. Introduction to the Principles of Metalworking. (Illus.). 1955. 10.00 o.p. (ISBN 0-312-43225-9). St Martin.
Rowe, George. George Rowe's Illustrated Cheltenham Guide Eighteen Forty-five. 103p. 1981. pap. text ed. 8.25x (ISBN 0-904387-95-X, Pub. by Sutton England). Humanities.
Rowe, Gilbert T. The Sea: Deep-Sea Biology. (Ideas & Observations on Progress in the Study of the Seas: Vol. 8). 525p. 1983. 65.00x (ISBN 0-471-04402-4, Pub. by Wiley-Interscience). Wiley.
Rowe, H. Edward. Save America! 160p. 1976. pap. 1.95 (ISBN 0-8007-8396-4, Spire Bks). Revell.
Rowe, Jane. Yours by Choice: A Guide for Adoptive Parents. rev ed. 1982. pap. 6.95 (ISBN 0-7100-9035-8). Routledge & Kegan.
Rowe, John Carlos. Through the Custom House: Nineteenth Century American Fiction & Modern Theory. LC 81-20866. 256p. 1982. text ed. 18.95x (ISBN 0-8018-2677-2). Johns Hopkins.
Rowe, John L. & Etier, F. Typewriting Drills for Speed & Accuracy. 3rd ed. 1966. text ed. 7.96 (ISBN 0-07-054147-7, G). McGraw.
Rowe, John L. & Etier, Faborn. Typewriting Drills for Speed & Accuracy. 4th ed. 1977. text ed. 7.96 (ISBN 0-07-054151-5, G). McGraw.
Rowe, John L., et al. Gregg Typing, One Ninety-One Series. 2nd ed. Incl. Book 1, General Typing. text ed. 11.76 (ISBN 0-07-054105-1). learning guides pts. 1-6 3.24 (ISBN 0-07-054107-8); learning guides pts. 7-12 3.96 (ISBN 0-07-054108-6); Book 2, Vocational Office Typing. text ed. 13.20 (ISBN 0-07-054109-4). learning guides pts. 1-6 5.20 (ISBN 0-07-054111-6); learning guides pts. 7-12 5.40 (ISBN 0-07-054112-4). 1967 (G). McGraw.
Rowe, John R. & Pasch, Marvin. The New Model Me. (gr. 8-12). 1983. price not set (ISBN 0-8077-2733-4). Tchrs Coll.
Rowe, John W. Primary Commodities in International Trade. (Orig.). 1966. 42.50 (ISBN 0-521-06144-X); pap. 17.95x (ISBN 0-521-09277-9). Cambridge U Pr.
Rowe, John W. & Besdime, Richard W. Health & Disease in Old Age. 1982. text ed. 27.50 (ISBN 0-316-75967-8). Little.
Rowe, K. Management Techniques for Civil Engineering Construction. (Illus.). x, 268p. 1975. 39.00 (ISBN 0-85334-613-5, Pub. by Applied Sci England). Elsevier.
Rowe, K. L. & Jimerson, H. C. Communications in Marketing. 1971. 6.56 (ISBN 0-07-054156-6, G); tchr's manual & key 4.55 (ISBN 0-07-054157-4). McGraw.
Rowe, Kenneth L. Communications in Marketing. (Occupational Manuals & Projects in Marketing Ser.). (Illus.). (gr. 11-12). 1978. pap. text ed. 7.32 (ISBN 0-07-054154-X, G); tchr's manual & key 4.50 (ISBN 0-07-054155-8). McGraw.
Rowe, Mary B. Teaching Science As Continuous Inquiry: A Basic 2-E. 2nd ed. (Illus.). 1978. text ed. 27.50 (ISBN 0-07-054116-7, C); instructor's manual 15.00 (ISBN 0-07-054117-5). McGraw.
Rowe, P. L. Shorthand Fashion Sketching. 17.95x (ISBN 0-87245-286-7). Textile Bk.
Rowe, R. E. Concrete Bridge Design. 1972. Repr. of 1966 ed. text ed. 55.50x (ISBN 0-85334-110-9, Pub. by Applied Sci England). Elsevier.
Rowe, R. G. & Brewer, W. Hospital Activity Analysis. (Computers in Medicine Ser.). (Illus.). 112p. 1972. 15.95 o.p. (ISBN 0-407-55000-3). Butterworth.
Rowe, Robert D & Chestnut, Lauraline G., eds. Managing Air Quality & Scenic Resources at National Parks & Wilderness Areas. (Replica Edition). 310p. 1982. softcover 20.00x (ISBN 0-86531-941-3). Westview.
Rowe, William. Exotic Alphabets & Ornaments. (Illus.). 80p. (Orig.). 1974. pap. 4.50 (ISBN 0-486-22989-0). Dover.
--Goods & Merchandise: A Cornucopia of Nineteenth Century Cuts. (Pictorial Archive Ser.). (Illus.). 64p. (Orig.). 1982. pap. 4.00 (ISBN 0-486-24410-5). Dover.
--Surreal Stickers & Unreal Stamps. (Illus.). 16p. (Orig.). 1983. pap. 3.50 (ISBN 0-486-24371-0). Dover.
Rowe, William D. An Anatomy of Risk. LC 77-5048. (Systems Engineering & Analysis Ser.). 1977. 44.95x (ISBN 0-471-01994-1, Pub. by Wiley-Interscience). Wiley.
Rowe, William H. Ancient North Yarmouth & Yarmouth, Maine, Sixteen Thirty-Six to Nineteen Thirty-Six: A History. LC 79-57067. (Illus.). 1980. Repr. of 1937 ed. 28.50x (ISBN 0-89725-016-8). NH Pub Co.
Rowe, William L., ed. Studies in Labor Theory & Practice: Papers from the Fifth Midwest Marxist Scholars Conference. LC 81-82455. (Studies in Marxism: Vol. 12). 100p. 1982. 10.50x (ISBN 0-930656-23-7); pap. 3.95 (ISBN 0-930656-24-5). MEP Pubns.
Rowe, William L. & Wainwright, William J., eds. Philosophy of Religion: Selected Readings. 489p. 1973. pap. text ed. 15.95 (ISBN 0-15-570580-6, HC). HarBraceJ.
Rowe, William T., jt. ed. see Fogel, Joshua A.
Roweck, Hartmut. Die Gefaesspflanzen Von Schwedisch-Lappland: Beitrag Zu Ihrer Standortsoekologie und Verbreitung. (Flora et Vegetatio Mundi Ser.: Vol. 8). (Illus.). 804p. (Ger.). 1981. lib. bdg. 80.00x (ISBN 3-7682-1321-8, Pub. by Cramer Germany). Lubrecht & Cramer.
Rowell, C. Fraser. Environmental Control of Colouration in an Acridid, Gastrimargus Africanus (Saussure) 1970. 35.00x (ISBN 0-85135-000-3, Pub. by Centre Overseas Research). State Mutual Bk.
Rowell, G. The Victorian Theatre: 1792-1914. 2nd ed. LC 78-2900. (Illus.). 1979. 37.50 (ISBN 0-521-22070-X); pap. 12.50 (ISBN 0-521-29346-4). Cambridge U Pr.
Rowell, Galen & McPhee, John. Alaska: Images of the Country. LC 81-5265. (Illus.). 160p. 1981. 37.50 (ISBN 0-87156-290-1); limited ed. 100.00 (ISBN 0-87156-293-6). Sierra.
Rowell, George, adapted by. The Lyons Mail. 1969. pap. text ed. 2.50x o.p. (ISBN 0-435-23775-6). Heinemann Ed.
Rowell, Henry T., ed. see Carcopino, Jerome.
Rowell, Lewis. Thinking about Music: An Introduction to the Philosophy of Music. LC 82-21979. 308p. 1983. lib. bdg. 25.00x (ISBN 0-87023-386-6). U of Mass Pr.
Rowell, Lois. American Organ Music on Records. (Bibliotheca Organologica: Vol. 71). 17.50 o.s.i. (ISBN 90-6027-333-8, Pub. by Frits Knuf Netherlands). Pendragon NY.
Rowell, R. M. & Youngs, R. Modified Cellulosics. 1978. 37.50 (ISBN 0-12-599750-7). Acad Pr.
Rowell, Thelma. Social Behaviour of Monkeys. lib. bdg. 9.50x o.p. (ISBN 0-88307-442-7). Gannon.
Rowen, jt. ed. see Brunt.
Rowen, Betty. Learning Through Movement: Activities for the Preschool & Elementary Grades. 2nd, Rev. ed. LC 82-3317. 1982. pap. text ed. 7.95x (ISBN 0-8077-2720-2). Tchrs Coll.
Rowen, Harry, et al. Options for U. S. Energy. LC 77-89094. pap. 6.95 o.p. (ISBN 0-917616-20-0). ICS Pr.
Rowen, Henry S., jt. auth. see Imai, Ryukichi.
Rowen, Herbert H. History of Early Modern Europe, 1500-1815. 1960. pap. 15.95 o.p. (ISBN 0-672-60697-6). Bobbs.
Rowen, Herbert H., ed. From Absolutism to Revolution: 1648-1848. 2nd ed. (Ideas & Institutions in Western Civilization, Vol. 4). 1968. pap. text ed. 6.95x (ISBN 0-02-404110-6). Macmillan.
Rowen, Herbert H., tr. see Schulte Nordholt, Jan W.
Rowen, Herbert H., jt. auth. see Lyon, Bruce.
Rowen, Lilian. No More Headaches. 1982. 1.95 (ISBN 0-686-98334-3, Perige). Putnam Pub Group.
--No More Headaches: An Exercise Program for Tension Relief. 06/1982 ed. 32p. pap. 1.95 (ISBN 0-399-50614-4, Perige); pap. 46.80 24-copy counterpack (ISBN 0-399-50628-4). Putnam Pub Group.
Rowen, Louis H. Polynomial Identities in Ring Theory. (Pure & Applied Mathematics Ser.). 1980. 45.50 (ISBN 0-12-599850-3). Acad Pr.
Rowen, R. Music Through Sources & Documents. 1979. pap. 18.95 (ISBN 0-13-608331-5). P-H.
Rower, K. see Fluegge, E.
Rowers, Anne. The Young Empress. 1979. pap. 2.25 o.p. (ISBN 0-523-40482-4). Pinnacle Bks.
Rowes, Barbara. Grace Slick: The Biography. LC 78-22351. (Illus.). 1980. 10.95 o.p. (ISBN 0-385-13390-1). Doubleday.
Roweton, William E. My Reflections on Educational Psychology, Science & American Schools. LC 80-8262. 124p. 1980. lib. bdg. 18.00 (ISBN 0-8191-1329-8); pap. text ed. 8.25 (ISBN 0-8191-1330-1). U Pr of Amer.
Rowland, A. Westley, ed. Handbook of Institutional Advancement: A Practical Guide to College & University Relations, Fund Raising, Alumni Relations, Government Relations, Publications, & Executive Management for Continued Advancement. LC 76-50722. (Higher Education Ser.). (Illus.). 1977. text ed. 27.95x (ISBN 0-87589-313-9). Jossey-Bass.
Rowland, Amy Z. Handcrafted Doors & Windows. (Illus.). 1982. 19.95 (ISBN 0-87857-423-9, 14-757-0); pap. 12.95 (ISBN 0-87857-424-7, 14-757-1). Rodale Pr Inc.
Rowland, Beatrice & Rowland, Howard. In Celebration of Marriage. 288p. 1982. 21.95 (ISBN 0-698-11066-8, Coward); pap. 10.95 (ISBN 0-698-11065-X). Putnam Pub Group.
Rowland, Beatrice L., jt. auth. see Rowland, Howard S.
Rowland, Benjamin. Jaume Huguet: A Study of Late Gothic Painting in Catalonia. (Illus.). 1932. 59.50x (ISBN 0-686-51408-4). Elliots Bks.
Rowland, C. K., jt. auth. see Carp, Robert A.
Rowland, Daniel B. Mannerism - Style & Mood. 1964. 32.50x (ISBN 0-685-69860-2). Elliots Bks.
Rowland, Florence W. Let's Go to a Hospital. (Let's Go Ser.). (Illus.). (gr. 5-7). 1968. PLB 4.29 o.p. (ISBN 0-399-60374-3). Putnam Pub Group.
Rowland, Herbert. Matthias Claudius. (World Author Ser.). 146p. 1983. lib. bdg. 18.95 (ISBN 0-8057-6538-7, Twayne). G K Hall.
Rowland, Howard, jt. auth. see Rowland, Beatrice.
Rowland, Howard, jt. ed. see Lawrence, Kenneth.
Rowland, Howard S. & Rowland, Beatrice L. The Nurse's Almanac. LC 78-311. 860p. 1978. 45.00 (ISBN 0-89443-031-9); pap. 29.75 (ISBN 0-89443-040-8). Aspen Systems.
Rowland, John. A History of Sino-Indian Relations: Hostile Co-Existence. LC 66-29857. 304p. 1966. pap. 8.50 o.p. (ISBN 0-442-07085-3, Pub. by Van Nos Reinhold). Krieger.
Rowland, John H., jt. auth. see Jensen, Jens A.
Rowland, Lewis P., ed. Human Motor Neuron Diseases. 715p. 1982. text ed. 95.00 (ISBN 0-89004-737-5). Raven.
--Immunological Disorders of the Nervous System. LC 72-139827. (ARNMD Research Publications Ser: Vol. 49). 482p. 1971. 34.50 (ISBN 0-683-00243-0). Raven.
Rowland, Pleasant. Addison-Wesley Reading Program: Placement Tests. (Addison-Wesley Reading Program Ser.). (gr. k-6). 1982. 17.60 (ISBN 0-201-22655-3, Sch Div). A-W.
--Adventures of the Superkids, Bk. 1. (Addison-Wesley Reading Program). (gr. 1). 1979. pap. text ed. 7.76 (ISBN 0-201-20600-5, Sch Div); six skill-bks 5.48 (ISBN 0-201-21701-5); tchr. guides in binder 44.00 (ISBN 0-201-21702-3); skills sheets 24.96 (ISBN 0-686-77116-8). A-W.
--Happily Ever After Readiness Program. (Addison-Wesley Reading Program Ser.). 1982. pap. text ed. 157.48 (ISBN 0-201-21551-9, Sch Div); tchr's. ed. 52.00 (ISBN 0-201-21564-0). A-W.
--Happily Ever After: Readiness Teacher's Guide (Visual, Listening, Conceptual Development) rev. ed. (Addison-Wesley Reading Program Ser.). (ps-1). 1979. pap. text ed. 52.00 (ISBN 0-201-20389-8, Sch Div); dupe masters 25.76 (ISBN 0-201-20399-5). A-W.
--Meet the Superkids, 13 bklts. rev. ed. (Addison-Wesley Reading Program). (preprimer). 1979. Set. pap. text ed. 6.28 (ISBN 0-201-20400-2, Sch Div); tchr. guides with binder 44.00 (ISBN 0-201-20425-8); skills sheets & cassettes avail. A-W.
--Meet the Superkids Summer Preprimer Review. rev. ed. (The Addison-Wesley Reading Program Ser.). (gr. 1). 1980. pap. text ed. 13.32 (ISBN 0-201-20464-9, Sch Div). A-W.
--More Adventures of the Superkids, Bk. 2. rev. ed. (Addison-Wesley Reading Program). (gr. 1). 1979. pap. text ed. 8.28 (ISBN 0-201-20650-1, Sch Div); reader, 3 skills bks. 3.60 (ISBN 0-201-20651-X); binder with 3 tchr. guides, tape incl. 40.00 (ISBN 0-201-20652-8); pretest pkg. of dup. masters, gr. 1 44.00 (ISBN 0-201-20657-9); dupe masters avail. A-W.
--The Nitty Gritty, Rather Pretty, City. rev. ed. (Addison-Wesley Reading Program). (gr. 2). 1979. test package 34.48 (ISBN 0-201-20770-2, Sch Div); avail. tchr's man. progress & pretests 1.64 (ISBN 0-201-20760-5); pretest pkg. 34.48 (ISBN 0-201-20758-3); class record form & ans. key 1.64 (ISBN 0-201-20768-0). A-W.
--The Nitty-Gritty, Rather Pretty, City, 1st to 12th Streets. rev. ed. (Addison-Wesley Reading Program). (gr. 2). 1979. text ed. 8.76 (ISBN 0-201-20700-1, Sch Div); tchr's. guides in binder (6 booklets) 28.00 (ISBN 0-201-20702-8); student skills bks 2-1 3.12 (ISBN 0-201-20701-X); tchr. skills bks. 4.04 (ISBN 0-201-20709-5); skills sheets avail. A-W.
--The Nitty Gritty, Rather Pretty, City: 13th-24th Streets. rev. ed. (Addison-Wesley Reading Program). (gr. 2). 1979. text ed. 8.76 (ISBN 0-201-20750-8, Sch Div); skills bk., s.e. 3.12 (ISBN 0-201-20751-6); tchr's. guides in binder (6 booklets) 28.00 (ISBN 0-201-20752-4); skills sheets & tchrs.' ed. avail. A-W.
--The Superkids Club, 5 bklts. rev. ed. (Addison-Wesley Reading Program). (primer). 1979. Set. pap. text ed. 4.32 (ISBN 0-201-20500-9, Sch Div); tchr's guide in binder 44.00 (ISBN 0-201-20517-3); cassettes avail. A-W.
Rowland, Willard D., Jr. The Politics of T. V. Violence: Policy Uses of Communication Research. (People & Communication Ser.: Vol. 16). (Illus.). 320p. 1983. 25.00 (ISBN 0-8039-1952-2); pap. 12.50 (ISBN 0-8039-1953-0). Sage.
Rowland-Entwistle, Theodore. Exploring Animal Homes. LC 78-51052. (Explorer Bks). (Illus.). (gr. 3-5). 1978. 2.95 (ISBN 0-531-09093-0, Warwick Press); PLB 7.90 s&l (ISBN 0-531-09106-6). Watts.
--Exploring Animal Journeys. LC 78-51048. (Explorer Bks.). (Illus.). (gr. 3-5). 1978. 2.95 (ISBN 0-531-09094-9, Warwick Press); PLB 7.90 s&l (ISBN 0-531-09100-7). Watts.
--Illustrated Facts & Records Book of Animals. LC 82-18406. (Illus.). 236p. 1983. 9.95 (ISBN 0-668-05730-0, 5730). Arco.
Rowlands, Avril. Script Continuity & the Production Secretary. (Media Manual Ser.). (Illus.). 160p. 1977. pap. 10.95 (ISBN 0-240-50949-8). Focal Pr.
Rowlands, Gerald. How to Be Alive in the Spirit. (Aglow Cornerstone Ser.). 38p. 1982. pap. 2.00 (ISBN 0-930756-69-X). Women's Aglow.
--How to Know the Fullness of the Spirit. (Cornerstone Ser.). 32p. 1982. pap. 1.50 (ISBN 0-930756-68-1). Women's Aglow.
Rowlands, Samuel. Uncollected Poems, 1604-1617. Incl. Humors Ordinairie; Theater of Delightful Recreation; Humors Antique Faces; The Bride. LC 78-119867. 210p. 1970. 26.00x (ISBN 0-8201-1074-1). Schol Facsimiles.
Rowles, Graham D. Prisoners of Space? Exploring the Geographical Experience of Older People. LC 77-18655. 1978. lib. bdg. 27.00 o.p. (ISBN 0-89158-069-7); pap. 11.00 o.p. (ISBN 0-86531-072-6). Westview.
Rowles, Graham D., ed. Aging & Milieu: Enviromental Perspectives On Growing Old. 1982. 24.00 (ISBN 0-12-599950-X). Acad Pr.
Rowlett, Martha G. In Spirit & In Truth: A Guide to Praying. 112p. 1983. pap. 4.95 (ISBN 0-8358-0448-8). Upper Room.
Rowley, Anthony, ed. The Barons of European Industry. LC 74-11193. 1974. text ed. 24.50x (ISBN 0-8419-0171-6). Holmes & Meier.
Rowley, C. K. & Peacock, A. T. Welfare Economics: A Liberal Restatement. LC 75-22430. 198p. 1975. 29.95x o.s.i. (ISBN 0-470-74362-X). Halsted Pr.
Rowley, H. H. The Faith of Israel. (Student Christian Movement Press Ser.). (Orig.). 1956. pap. 6.95x o.p. (ISBN 0-19-520337-2). Oxford U Pr.
--Rediscovery of the Old Testament. 224p. 1946. 14.00 (ISBN 0-227-67576-2). Attic Pr.
Rowley, Ian. Bird Life. (Illus.). 284p. 1983. pap. 12.50 (ISBN 0-00-216436-1, Pub. by W Collins Australia). Intl Schol Bk Serv.
Rowley, J. C. & Trivedi, P. K. Econometrics of Investment. LC 74-32176. (Monographs on Applied Econometrics). 1975. 45.95 (ISBN 0-471-74361-5, Pub. by Wiley-Interscience). Wiley.
Rowley, J. E. & Turner, C. M. The Dissemination of Information. 356p. 1978. 30.30 (ISBN 0-233-96919-5, 05814-9, Pub. by Gower Pub Co England). Lexington Bks.
Rowley, J. E. & Turner, C. M. D. The Dissemination of Information. (Grafton Library of Information Science). 353p. 1978. lib. bdg. 32.50x (ISBN 0-89158-830-2). Westview.
Rowley, Jennifer E. Abstracting & Indexing. 155p. 1982. 15.00 (ISBN 0-85157-336-3, Pub. by Bingley England). Shoe String.
Rowley, Jenny E. & Rowley, Peter J. Operations Research. 152p. (Orig.). Date not set. pap. text ed. 10.00 (ISBN 0-8389-0337-1). ALA.
Rowley, Peter J., jt. auth. see Rowley, Jenny E.

Rowley, R., ed. see Rowley, Scott.
Rowley, Scott. Rowley on Partnership, 2 vols. 2nd ed. Rowley, R., ed. 1960. 60.00 set o.p. (ISBN 0-672-82380-2, Bobbs-Merrill Law). Michie-Bobbs.
Rowley, Trevor. Villages in the Landscape. (Archaeology in the Field Ser.). (Illus.). 211p. 1978. 15.75x o.p. (ISBN 0-460-04166-5, Pub by J. M. Dent England). Biblio Dist.
Rowley, William D. American West. LC 73-81060. 1980. pap. text ed. 6.95x (ISBN 0-88273-021-5). Forum Pr IL.
Rowlinson, J. & Swinton, F. L. Liquids & Liquid Mixtures. 3rd ed. 320p. 1982. text ed. 69.95 (ISBN 0-408-24192-6); pap. text ed. 34.95 (ISBN 0-408-24193-4). Butterworth.
Rowlinson, J. S. & Widom, B. Molecular Theory of Capillarity. (International Ser. of Monographs on Chemistry). (Illus.). 340p. 1982. 59.00x (ISBN 0-19-855612-8). Oxford U Pr.
Rowlinson, Pat & Jenkins, Morton. Human Biology: An Activity Approach. (Illus.). 304p. 1982. pap. text ed. 9.95 (ISBN 0-521-28200-4). Cambridge U Pr.
Rowlison, Bruce A. Creative Hospitality As a Means of Evangelism. rev. ed. LC 81-84182. (Illus.). 144p. 1982. pap. 5.95 (ISBN 0-938462-03-2). Green Leaf CA.
Rowlison, Bruce A., jt. auth. see Wiebe, Ronald W.
Rowntree, Derek. Probability. 160p. 1983. pap. text ed. 19.95 (ISBN 0-7131-2787-2). E Arnold.
Rowntree, Lester, jt. auth. see Jordan, Terry G.
Rowse, A. L. A Cornish Childhood: Autobiography of a Cornishman. 1979. 10.95 o.p. (ISBN 0-517-53845-8, C N Potter Bks). Crown.
--Eminent Elizabethans. LC 82-13484. (Illus.). 240p. 1983. 19.00 (ISBN 0-8203-0649-5). U of Ga Pr.
--England of Elizabeth. LC 78-53293. 562p. 1978. 25.00 (ISBN 0-299-07720-9); pap. 12.50 (ISBN 0-299-07724-1). U of Wis Pr.
--The Heritage of Britain. LC 77-74776. (Illus.). 1977. 14.95 o.p. (ISBN 0-399-12012-2). Putnam Pub Group.
--Oxford: In the History of England. LC 75-816. (Illus.). 256p. 1975. 15.95 o.p. (ISBN 0-399-11570-6). Putnam Pub Group.
--What Shakespeare Read & Thought. 1981. 12.95 (ISBN 0-698-11077-3, Coward). Putnam Pub Group.
Rowse, A. L., ed. The Annotated Shakespeare, 3 vols. 1978. Set. 75.00 (ISBN 0-517-53509-2, C N Potter Bks). Crown.
Rowse, Arthur, ed. Help: The Indispensable Almanac of Consumer Information, 1981. LC 76-11318. pap. 9.95 (ISBN 0-89696-109-5, An Everest House Book). Dodd.
Rowse, Arthur C. Help: The Consumer Almanac. 1979. pap. 8.95 o.p. (ISBN 0-89696-071-4, An Everest House Book). Dodd.
Rowse, Arthur E., ed. Help Nineteen Eighty-One. 648p. 1980. 15.00 o.p. (ISBN 0-686-65898-1, An Everest House Book); pap. 9.95 o.p. (ISBN 0-89696-109-5). Dodd.
Rowthorn, Anne. Samuel Seabury: A Bicentennial Biography. 160p. 1983. 14.95 (ISBN 0-8164-0517-4). Seabury.
Rowthorn, Bob. Capitalism, Conflict & Inflation: Essays in Political Economy. 1980. text ed. 21.50x (ISBN 0-85315-501-1); pap. text ed. 8.50x. Humanities.
Roxburgh, Nigel. Policy Responses to Resource Depletion: A Case of Mercury, Vol. 21. Walter, Ingo & Altman, Edward I., eds. (Contemporary Studies in Economic & Financial Analysis Ser.). 1980. lib. bdg. 36.00 (ISBN 0-89232-093-1). Jai Pr.
Roxon, Lillian. Rock Encyclopedia. 1971. pap. 9.95 (ISBN 0-448-14572-3, G&D). Putnam Pub Group.
Roy, A. B. & Trudinger, P. Biochemistry of Inorganic Compounds of Sulphur. LC 78-79056. (Illus.). 1970. 67.50 (ISBN 0-521-07581-5). Cambridge U Pr.
Roy, Alec. Hysteria. 304p. 1982. 39.95x (ISBN 0-471-28033-X, Pub. by Wiley-Interscience). Wiley.
Roy, Alec, jt. auth. see Riley, Terrence L.
Roy, Ashim K. & Gidwani, N. W. Indus Valley Civilization: A Bibliographic Essay. 264p. 1982. text ed. 21.00x (ISBN 0-391-02562-7). Humanities.
Roy, B. Modern Algebra & Graph Theory Applied to Management. LC 77-724. (Universitext). (Illus.). 1978. 24.70 o.p. (ISBN 0-387-08006-6). Springer-Verlag.
Roy, Callista & Roberts, Sharon. Theory Construction in Nursing: An Adaptation Model. (Illus.). 352p. 1981. text ed. 19.95 (ISBN 0-13-913657-6). P-H.
Roy, Claude C., jt. auth. see Silverman, Arnold.
Roy, Cristina. En El Pais Del Sol. 160p. (Span.). 1982. pap. 3.10 (ISBN 0-686-35757-4). Rod & Staff.
--Das Land des Sonnenscheins. 167p. (Ger.). 1982. pap. 3.10 (ISBN 0-686-35759-0). Rod & Staff.
--Sunshine Country. 160p. (YA) 5.40 (ISBN 0-686-05594-2); pap. 3.00 (ISBN 0-686-05595-0). Rod & Staff.
Roy, David T. & Tsien, Tsuen-hsuin, eds. Ancient China: Studies in Early Civilization. LC 79-4924. (Illus.). 382p. 1979. 16.50 o.p. (ISBN 0-295-95682-8, Pub. by Chinese Univ Hong Kong). U of Wash Pr.
Roy, Dilipkumar. Bhagavad Gita, a Revelation. 190p. 1975. 9.95 (ISBN 0-88253-698-2). Ind-US Inc.
Roy, Emil & Roy, Sandra. Literature One. 768p. 1976. pap. text ed. 13.95x (ISBN 0-02-404160-2). Macmillan.
Roy, Ewell P. Cooperatives: Development, Principles & Management. 4th ed. 1981. 15.95 (ISBN 0-8134-2143-8, 2143); text ed. 11.95x. Interstate.
Roy, F. Hampton, jt. auth. see Fraunfelder, F. T.
Roy, G. J. Notes on Instrumentation & Control. (Marine Engineering Ser.). 144p. 1978. pap. 9.95x (ISBN 0-540-07344-X). Sheridan.
--Steam Turbines & Gearing: Questions & Answers. (Marine Engineering Ser.). 96p. 1975. pap. 9.95x (ISBN 0-540-07338-5). Sheridan.
Roy, Joaquin & Staczer, John J. Lecturas De Prensa. 256p. (Orig.). 1982. pap. text ed. 10.95 (ISBN 0-15-550455-X, HC). HarBraceJ.
Roy, Kristina. The Heiress. Tenjack, Martha, tr. LC 79-56301. 1979. pap. 4.95 (ISBN 0-89107-176-8). Good News.
Roy, M. N. Fragments of a Prisioner's Diary: India's Message. Repr. of 1950 ed. 18.00 (ISBN 0-8364-0912-4, Pub. by Ajanta). South Asia Bks.
--Materialism. 1982. Repr. of 1951 ed. 18.50 (ISBN 0-8364-0914-0, Pub. by Ajanta). South Asia Bks.
--New Orientation. 1982. 18.00 (ISBN 0-8364-0910-8, Pub. by Ajanta). South Asia Bks.
Roy, Maria, ed. Battered Women: A Psychosociological Study of Domestic Violence. 1977. 10.95 (ISBN 0-686-35971-2); pap. 7.95 (ISBN 0-686-37230-1). AWAIC.
Roy, Mike. The Best of Mike Roy: From His CBS Radio Show. pap. 5.95 o.p. (ISBN 0-517-53755-9, Pub. by Ward Ritchie). Crown.
Roy, Mike & Fitzgerald, Don. Mike Roy's Crock Cookery. pap. 3.95 o.p. (ISBN 0-517-53762-1, Pub. by Ward Ritchie). Crown.
Roy, R., jt. auth. see Henisch, H. K.
Roy, R. R. & Reed, R. D. Interactions of Photons & Leptons with Matter. LC 68-23487. 1969. 50.50 (ISBN 0-12-601350-0). Acad Pr.
Roy, Ramashray. The Uncertain Verdict: A Study of the 1969 Elections in Four Indian States. (Illus.). 1975. 30.00x (ISBN 0-520-02475-3). U of Cal Pr.
Roy, Ranjan & Tucks, E. Chronic Pain: Psychosocial Factors in Rehabilitation. Basmajian, John V., ed. (Rehabilitation Medicine Library). (Illus.). 222p. 1982. 30.00 (ISBN 0-683-07394-X). Williams & Wilkins.
Roy, Robert L. Money-Saving Strategies for the Owner-Builder. LC 81-8843. (Illus.). 160p. (Orig.). 1981. pap. 7.95 (ISBN 0-8069-7548-2). Sterling.
--Underground Houses: How to Build a Low-Cost Home. LC 79-64505. (Illus.). 1979. pap. 6.95 (ISBN 0-8069-8856-8). Sterling.
Roy, Ron. Million Dollar Jeans. LC 82-18320. (Illus.). 96p. (gr. 4-7). 1983. 9.75 (ISBN 0-525-44047-X, 0947-280). Dutton.
Roy, Ronald. A Thousand Pails of Water. LC 78-3275. (Illus.). (gr. 1-3). 1978. 4.95 o.p. (ISBN 0-394-83752-5); PLB 5.99 (ISBN 0-394-93752-X). Knopf.
Roy, Ronald, jt. auth. see Graham, Robin.
Roy, S. The Restless Brahmin: Early Life of M. N. Roy. 148p. 1970. 4.00x o.p. (ISBN 0-8188-1161-7). Paragon.
Roy, Sander, jt. auth. see Berson, Dvera.
Roy, Sandra. Josephine Tey. (English Authors Ser.). 1980. lib. bdg. 12.95 (ISBN 0-8057-6776-2, Twayne). G K Hall.
Roy, Sandra, jt. auth. see Roy, Emil.
Roy, Shyamal, jt. auth. see Sanderson, Fred H.
Roy, Steven P. & Irvin, Richard F. Sports Medicine for the Athletic Trainer. (Illus.). 560p. 1983. text ed. 23.95 (ISBN 0-13-837807-X). P-H.
Roy, Subodh, ed. Communism in India: Unpublished Documents, 1925-1934. ix, 476p. 1972. 11.50x o.p. (ISBN 0-88386-247-6). South Asia Bks.
Roy, Subodh, ed. see Kaye, Cecil.
Roy, Thomas. The Curse of the Turtle. LC 78-6413. (gr. 5 up). 1978. 6.95 o.p. (ISBN 0-529-05502-3, Philomel). Putnam Pub Group.
Roy, Willy & Walker, Jim. Coaching Winning Soccer. 1979. 12.95 o.p. (ISBN 0-8092-7458-2); pap. 7.95 (ISBN 0-8092-7457-4). Contemp Bks.
Royal Automobile Club. Guide & Handbook to Great Britain - 1980. LC 51-34691. (Royal Automobile Club Guides Ser.). (Illus.). 608p. 1980. 15.00x o.p. (ISBN 0-902628-90-9). Intl Pubns Serv.
Royal Automobile Club, ed. RAC Continental Motoring Guide. (Illus.). 207p. (Orig.). 1982. pap. 7.50x (ISBN 0-86211-031-9). Intl Pubns Serv.
Royal Automobile Club (Great Britain), ed. RAC Continental Handbook. 42nd ed. (Illus.). 624p. 1981. 15.00x (ISBN 0-86211-022-X). Intl Pubns Serv.
--RAC Guide & Handbook 1982. 78th ed. (Illus.). 623p. 1982. 15.00x (ISBN 0-86211-032-7). Intl Pubns Serv.
Royal Botanic Gardens Library, Kew, England. Author & Classified Catalogues of the Royal Botanic Gardens Library, 9 vols. 1974. lib. bdg. 475.00 author 5 vols. (ISBN 0-8161-1086-7, Hall Library); lib. bdg. 395.00 4 vols. (ISBN 0-8161-1087-5). G K Hall.
Royal, Boyce. The Great Game of Buying Selling or Merging Lease-Rental Operations. 1976. 27.00 (ISBN 0-915260-02-6). Atcom.
Royal College of Psychiatrists. Alcohol & Alcoholism. LC 79-20712. 1979. 17.95 (ISBN 0-02-927510-5). Free Pr.
Royal Commonwealth Society, London. Subject Catalogue of the Royal Commonwealth Society, 7 vols. 1971. Set. 695.00 (ISBN 0-8161-0885-4, Hall Library). G K Hall.
Royal Economic Society, jt. auth. see American Economic Association.
Royal Economic Society & the Social Studies Research Council, ed. Surveys of Applied Economics, Vol. 2. LC 73-82638. 1977. 26.00x (ISBN 0-312-77770-1). St Martin.
Royal Entomological Society of London. Catalog of the Library of the Royal Entomological Society of London. (Printed Book Catalogs). 1980. lib. bdg. 495.00 (ISBN 0-8161-0315-1, Hall Library). G K Hall.
Royal Institute of International Affairs. British Yearbook of International Law. Incl. Vol. 3. 1965. o.p. (ISBN 0-19-214625-4); Vol. 7. 1965. o.p. (ISBN 0-19-214629-7); Vol. 39, 1963. Waldock, H. & Jennings, R. Y., eds. 1965. o.p. (ISBN 0-19-214622-X); Vol. 40, 1964. Waldock, H. & Jennings, R. Y., eds. 1966. o.p. (ISBN 0-19-214623-8); Vol. 41, 1965-66. Waldock, H. & Jennings, R. Y., eds. 1968. o.p. (ISBN 0-19-214657-2); Vol. 42, 1967. Waldock, H. & Jennings, R. Y., eds. 386p. 1969. 24.95x (ISBN 0-19-214658-0); Vol. 44. Waldcock, H. & Jennings, R. Y., eds. 1971. text ed. 24.95x o.p. (ISBN 0-19-214660-2); Vol. 45, 1971. Waldock, H. & Jennings, R. Y., eds. 1973. 94.00x (ISBN 0-19-214661-0). (Royal Institute of International Affairs Ser.). Oxford U Pr.
Royal Institute Of International Affairs London. Index to Periodical Articles, 1950-1964, 2 Vols. 1964. Set. 150.00 (ISBN 0-8161-0711-4, Hall Library). G K Hall.
Royal Institute of International Affairs-London. Index to Periodical Articles, 1965-1972. 1974. lib. bdg. 115.00 (ISBN 0-8161-1062-X, Hall Library). G K Hall.
Royal Institute of International Affairs, London. Index to Periodical Articles, 1973-1978. (Library Catalogs-Bib. Guides). 1979. lib. bdg. 125.00 (ISBN 0-8161-0281-3, Hall Library). G K Hall.
Royal Institute Of International Affairs. Problem of International Investment. LC 67-55858. Repr. of 1937 ed. 30.00x o.p. (ISBN 0-678-05195-X). Kelley.
Royal Institution Library of Science. Earth Sciences, 3 Vols. Bragg, W. L. & Runcorn, S. K., eds. LC 74-169065. 1592p. 1971. Set. 98.95 o.p. (ISBN 0-470-74389-1). Halsted Pr.
Royal National Foundation. Athens Civilization: The Past & the Future. 1968. 6.50 (ISBN 0-444-40747-2). Elsevier.
Royal Soc. of Chemistry, ed. The Periodic Table of the Elements. 1982. 30.00x (ISBN 0-686-81713-3, Pub. by Royal Soc Chem England). State Mutual Bk.
Royal Society, ed. The Emergence of Man. 216p. 1981. text ed. 49.50x (ISBN 0-686-96972-3, Pub. by British Acad England). Humanities.
Royal Society Discussion Meeting, January 27-28, 1982, Proceedings. The Earth's Core: Its Structure, Evolution & Magnetic Field. Runcorn, S. K. & Creer, K. M., eds. (Illus.). 289p. 1982. text ed. 87.00x (ISBN 0-85403-192-8, Pub. by Royal Soc London). Scholium Intl.
Royal Society of London. The Evolution of Sedimentary Basins: Proceedings of a Royal Society Discussion Meeting held on 3 & 4 June 1981. Kent, Peter & McKenzie, D. P., eds. (Illus.). 338p. 1982. text ed. 112.00x (ISBN 0-85403-184-7, Pub. by Royal Soc London). Scholium Intl.
--Recent Advances in Analytical Chemistry: Proceedings of a Royal Society Discussion Meeting held on 9 & 10 December 1981. Thomas, J. M., et al, eds. (Illus.). 219p. 1982. text ed. 70.00x (ISBN 0-85403-191-X, Pub. by Royal Soc London). Scholium Intl.
Royal Society of Medicine. Family Matters-Perspectives on the Family & Social Policy: Proceedings of the Symposium on Priority for the Family, Royal Society of Medicine, London, November 3-5, 1981. Franklin, A. White, ed. 160p. 1983. 19.95 (ISBN 0-08-028928-2). Pergamon.
Royal United Services Institute for Defence Studies, London & Marriott, John, eds. International Weapon Developments: A Survey of Current Developments in Weapons Systems. 3rd ed. LC 78-31785. (Illus.). 1979. pap. 7.95 o.p. (ISBN 0-89141-089-9). Presidio Pr.
Royal United Services Institute for Defence Studies, London. Nuclear Attack-Civil Defense: Aspects of Civil Defence in the Nuclear Age. (Illus.). 292p. 1982. 19.00 (ISBN 0-08-027041-7); pap. 11.50 (ISBN 0-08-027042-5). Pergamon.
Royal United Services Institute for Defence Studies (Rusi), Whitehall, London, UK. Rusi & Brassey's Defence Yearbook Nineteen Hundred-Eighty-Three. 93rd ed. (Rusi & Brassey's Defence Yearbook Ser.). 400p. 1983. 50.00 (ISBN 0-08-028346-2); pap. 20.00 (ISBN 0-08-028347-0). Pergamon.
Royal United Services Institute for Defense Studies, ed. Rusi & Brassey's Defence Yearbook, 1977-78. LC 75-29923. 1978. lib. bdg. 40.00 (ISBN 0-89158-823-X). Westview.
Royal-Dawson, Warren, compiled by. Miscellaneous Papers by or Concerning John Ruskin, 2 Vols. 80p. 1982. Repr. of 1918 ed. Set. lib. bdg. 200.00 (ISBN 0-89987-722-2). DarbyBks.
Royall, Anne N. Letters from Alabama, 1817-1822. Griffith, Lucille, ed. LC 70-76584. (Southern Historical Ser: Vol. 14). 233p. 1969. 11.50 o.p. (ISBN 0-8173-5219-8). U of Ala Pr.
Royall, Nicki. You Don't Need to Have a Repeat Cesarean. LC 82-83775. 192p. 1983. 14.95 (ISBN 0-8119-0487-3). Fell.
Royall, Vanessa. Come Faith Come Fire. 1979. pap. 2.95 (ISBN 0-440-12170-1). Dell.
--Flames of Desire. 1978. pap. 2.95 (ISBN 0-440-14637-2). Dell.
--Seize the Dawn. (Orig.). 1983. pap. 3.50 (ISBN 0-440-17335-3). Dell.
Royan, P. Van see Van Royen, P.
Royan, Van P. see Van Royen, P.
Royce. Channel Assault. LC 82-7132. 1983. 13.95 (ISBN 0-07-054172-8). McGraw.
Royce, James. Man & Meaning. LC 68-31664. Orig. Title: Man & His Nature. 1968. text ed. 29.00 (ISBN 0-07-054167-1, C). McGraw.
Royce, James E. Alcohol & Responsibility. 1979. pap. 1.95 (ISBN 0-89486-062-3). Hazelden.
--Alcohol Problems & Alcoholism: A Comprehensive Survey. 334p. 1981. 19.95 (ISBN 0-02-927540-7). Free Pr.
--Personality & Mental Health. rev. ed. 1964. 5.95 o.p. (ISBN 0-02-827200-5). Glencoe.
Royce, Joseph R., ed. Multivariate Analysis & Psychological Theory. 1973. 84.50 (ISBN 0-12-600750-0). Acad Pr.
Royce, Josiah. The Religious Philosophy of Josiah Royce. Brown, Stuart G., ed. LC 76-4496. 239p. 1976. Repr. of 1952 ed. lib. bdg. 17.00x (ISBN 0-8371-8810-5, RORP). Greenwood.
--The Spirit of Modern Philosophy. 519p. 1983. pap. 8.95 (ISBN 0-486-24432-6). Dover.
Royce, Katherine, tr. see Enriques, Federigo.
Royce, Kenneth. Bustillo. LC 76-26907. 256p. 1976. 7.95 o.p. (ISBN 0-698-10762-4, Coward). Putnam Pub Group.
--The Woodcutter Operation. LC 74-19462. 1975. 7.95 o.p. (ISBN 0-671-21916-2). S&S.
Royce, Kenneth, ed. The Third Arm. 300p. 1980. 9.95 (ISBN 0-07-054169-8, GB). McGraw.
Royce, Pat. Sailing Illustrated: The Sailor's Bible Since '56. 8th, rev. ed. LC 82-6925. (Illus.). 352p. 1982. pap. 8.95 (ISBN 0-930030-25-7). Western Marine Int.
Royce, Patrick M. Sailing Illustrated: The Sailor's Bible Since '56. 7th, rev. ed. (Illus.). 352p. 1979. pap. 7.95 o.p. (ISBN 0-930030-14-1). Western Marine Ent.
Royce, Sarah. A Frontier Lady: Recollections of the Gold Rush & Early California. Gabriel, Ralph H., ed. LC 76-44263. (Illus.). xvi, 144p. 1977. 12.50x (ISBN 0-8032-0909-6); pap. 4.95 (ISBN 0-8032-5856-9, BB 634, Bison). U of Nebr Pr.
Royden, H. L. Real Analysis. 2nd ed. 1968. text ed. 27.95x (ISBN 0-02-404150-5). Macmillan.
Royen, P. Van. The Genus Rubus (Rosaceae) in New Guinea. (Monographiae Phanerogamarum). 1969. 20.00 (ISBN 3-7682-0612-2). Lubrecht & C.
Royen, P. Van see Van Royen, P.
Royer, G. P. Fundamentals of Enzymology: Rate Enhancement, Specificity, Control & Applications. LC 81-11359. 232p. 1982. 27.50x (ISBN 0-471-04675-2, Pub. by Wiley-Interscience). Wiley.
Royer, James M. & Allan, Richard G. Psychology of Learning: Educational Applications. LC 77-12390. (Self-Teaching Guide Ser.). 1978. pap. text ed. 4.95 o.p. (ISBN 0-471-02270-5). Wiley.
Royer, Katherine. Nursery Happy Times Book. (Illus.). (ps). 1957. pap. 1.95 (ISBN 0-8361-1405-1). Herald Pr.
--Nursery Home Books. (Illus.). (ps). 1957. pap. 4.95 (ISBN 0-8361-1002-1). Herald Pr.
--Nursery Stories of Jesus. (Illus.). (ps). 1957. pap. 1.95 (ISBN 0-8361-1408-6). Herald Pr.
Royer, Katherine, ed. Nursery Songbook. (Illus.). (ps). 1957. pap. 1.95 (ISBN 0-8361-1407-8). Herald Pr.
Royer, King. Applied Field Surveying. LC 70-106014. 1970. 19.95 (ISBN 0-471-74395-X). Wiley.
--The Construction Manager in the Nineteen Eighties. (Illus.). 496p. 1981. text ed. 34.00 (ISBN 0-13-168690-9). P-H.
--Desk Book for Construction Superintendents. 2nd ed. (Illus.). 1980. text ed. 23.95 (ISBN 0-13-202028-9). P-H.
Royer, Pierre, et al. Pediatric Nephrology. LC 74-4585. (Major Problem in Clinical Pediatrics Ser.: Vol. 11). (Illus.). 415p. 1974. text ed. 25.00 o.p. (ISBN 0-7216-7776-2). Saunders.
Royko, Mike. Boss: Richard J. Daley of Chicago. 1971. pap. 2.95 (ISBN 0-451-12309-3, AE2309, Sig). NAL.
Roylance, Ward J. UTAH: A Guide to the State. Revised ed. 844p. 1982. Repr. of 1940 ed. 22.50 (ISBN 0-914740-25-3). Western Epics.
--UTAH: A Guide to the State, Tour Section Only. Revised ed. (Part 2). 400p. 1982. pap. 8.95. Western Epics.
Royle, Edward & Walvin, James. English Radicals & Reformers, 1760-1848. LC 82-40179. 232p. 1982. 18.50x (ISBN 0-8131-1471-3). U Pr of Ky.

Royle, Trevor. Death Before Dishonor: The True Story of Fighting Mac. 176p. 1983. 14.95 (ISBN 0-312-18605-3). St Martin.

Roys, H. E., ed. Disc Recording & Reproduction. LC 77-17927. (Benchmark Papers in Acoustic Ser.: Vol. 12). 416p. 1978. 48.50 (ISBN 0-87933-309-X). Hutchinson Ross.

Royster, Charles. Light-Horse Harry Lee & the Legacy of the American Revolution. LC 82-9620. (Illus.). 304p. 1982. pap. 7.95x (ISBN 0-521-27065-0). Cambridge U Pr.

Royster, Larry H., et al, eds. Noise-Control 81: Proceedings. (National Conference on Noise Control Engineering Ser.). 488p. 1981. 42.00 (ISBN 0-931784-04-2). Noise Control.

Royster, Salibelle. Arrowsmith Notes. (Orig.). 1964. pap. 2.50 (ISBN 0-8220-0201-9). Cliffs.

Rozakis, C. L. The Concept of Jus Cogens in the Law of Treaties. 1976. 36.25 (ISBN 0-7204-0485-1, North-Holland). Elsevier.

Rozanov, Vasilii V. Solitaria. Koteliansky, S. S., tr. from Rus. LC 79-13120. 1980. Repr. of 1927 ed. lib. bdg. 18.50x (ISBN 0-313-22004-2, ROSA). Greenwood.

Rozanov, Y. A. Innovation Processes. (Scripta Ser. in Mathematics). 1977. 14.50x o.p. (ISBN 0-470-99127-5). Halsted Pr.

--Markov Random Fields. Elson, C. M., tr. from Rus. (Illus.). 201p. 1983. 42.00 (ISBN 0-387-90708-4). Springer-Verlag.

Rozanow, Gora Z. Cultural Heritage of Jasna Gora. (Illus.). 1977. 13.00 (ISBN 0-912728-44-2). Newbury Bks.

Rozanski, Waclaw, ed. see Rozdzienski, Walenty.

Rozazza, John P., ed. Microbial Transformations of Bioactive Compounds, Vols. I & II. 1982. Vol. I, 144 pgs. 46.00 (ISBN 0-8493-6065-X); Vol. II, 200 pgs. 64.00 (ISBN 0-8493-6066-8). CRC Pr.

Rozdzienski, Walenty. Officina Ferraria: A Polish Poem of 1612 Describing the Noble Craft of Ironwork. Rozanski, Waclaw & Smith, Cyril S., eds. Pluszczewski, Stefan, tr. LC 76-26592. (SHOT Monograph Ser.: No. 9). 1977. text ed. 15.00x (ISBN 0-262-18079-0). MIT Pr.

Rozee, K. R., jt. ed. see Stuttard, Colins.

Rozenberg, G., jt. auth. see Herman, G. T.

Rozenberg, Grzegorz & Salomaa, Arto. The Mathematical Theory of L Systems. LC 79-25254. (Pure & Applied Mathematics Ser.). 1980. 50.00 (ISBN 0-12-597140-0). Acad Pr.

Rozencweig, M., jt. ed. see Cortes, Funes H.

Rozencweig, Marcel, jt. ed. see Muggia, Franco.

Rozier, R. G., jt. auth. see Hughes, John T.

Rozin, Elisabeth. Ethnic Cuisine: The Flavor-Principle Cookbook. 320p. 1983. 14.95 (ISBN 0-8289-0497-9). Greene.

Rozsa. Numerical Methods. (Colloquia Mathematica Ser.: Vol. 22). 1980. 85.00 (ISBN 0-444-85111-9). Elsevier.

Rozwenc, Edwin C. & Martin, Edward C. The Restless Americans: The Challenge of Change in American History, Vol.1. LC 76-180833. 336p. pap. text ed. 16.95 (ISBN 0-536-00734-9). Krieger.

--The Restless Americans: The Challenge of Change in American History, Vol.2. LC 76-180833. 368p. pap. text ed. 16.95 (ISBN 0-536-00735-7). Krieger.

Rozwenc, Edwin C., ed. Causes of the American Civil War. 2nd ed. (Problems in American Civilization Ser.). 1972. pap. text ed. 6.95 (ISBN 0-669-82727-4). Heath.

--New Deal: Revolution or Evolution. rev. ed. (Problems in American Civilization Ser.). 1959. pap. text ed. 5.95 (ISBN 0-669-23838-4). Heath.

--Reconstruction in the South. 2nd ed. (Problems in American Civilization Ser.). 1973. pap. text ed. 5.95x o.p. (ISBN 0-669-82735-5). Heath.

RSBR Committee. Purchasing an Encyclopedia. 24p. 1982. pap. text ed. 3.00 (ISBN 0-8389-3236-3). ALA.

--Reference & Subscription Books Reviews, 1981-1982. (RSBR Ser.). 240p. 1982. pap. text ed. 20.00 (ISBN 0-8389-0380-0). ALA.

RSBR Committee, ed. Reference & Subscription Book Reviews, 1980-81. 148p. Date not set. pap. text ed. 20.00 (ISBN 0-8389-3269-X). ALA.

Rua, Pedro J., ed. Introduccion a las Ciencias Sociales. LC 81-69790. 432p. 1982. pap. 8.50 (ISBN 0-940238-64-0). Ediciones Huracan.

Ruark, Gibbons. Program for Survival: Poems. LC 74-151089. 1971. pap. 3.95x o.p. (ISBN 0-8139-0325-4). U Pr of Va.

Ruault, Nicolas. Eloge De Marie-Francois De Voltaire. Repr. of 1788 ed. 34.00 o.p. (ISBN 0-8287-0744-8). Clearwater Pub.

Ruback, R. Barry, jt. auth. see Greenberg, Martin S.

Rubadeau, Duane O., jt. ed. see Athey, Irene J.

Rubano, Judith. Culture & Behavior in Hawaii: An Annotated Bibliography. (Social Science & Linguistics Institute Publications). 147p. 1971. pap. 6.00x (ISBN 0-8248-0242-X). UH Pr.

Rubanowice, Robert J. Crisis in Consciousness: The Thought of Ernst Troeltsch. LC 81-16085. xvi, 178p. 1982. 20.00 (ISBN 0-8130-0721-6). U Presses Fla.

Rubel, Mary. Double Happiness: Getting More from Chinese Popular Art. (Illus.). 172p. (Orig.). 1981. pap. 6.98 (ISBN 0-9609154-0-0). Magaru Enterprises.

Rubel, Nicole. Bruno Brontosaurus. 32p. pap. 2.25 (ISBN 0-380-83535-5, Camelot). Avon.

--Me & My Kitty. LC 82-21695. (Illus.). 24p. (ps-1). 1983. 7.95 (ISBN 0-02-777880-0). Macmillan.

Rubel, Nicole, jt. auth. see Gantos, Jack.

Rubel, Paula G., jt. auth. see Rosman, Abraham.

Rubel, Robert J. The Unruly School: Disorders, Disruptions, & Crimes. LC 77-3837. (Illus.). 208p. 1977. 21.95x (ISBN 0-669-01668-3). Lexington Bks.

Rubel, Tobert J., jt. auth. see Baker, Keith.

Ruben, Ann M. The CAMM Program: Creating A Mature Marriage. 162p. 1980. 29.95 (ISBN 0-9608400-0-1). Camm Pub.

Ruben, Brent D., ed. Communication Yearbook, Vol. 1. LC 76-45943. 656p. 1977. text ed. 29.95 (ISBN 0-87855-206-5). Transaction Bks.

--Communication Yearbook, Vol. 2. 587p. 1978. 29.95 (ISBN 0-87855-282-0). Transaction Bks.

Ruben, M. & Woodward, E. G. Revision Clinical Optics. 1982. 60.00x (ISBN 0-333-26107-0, Pub. by Macmillan England). State Mutual Bk.

Ruben, Montague. Soft Contact Lenses: Clinical & Applied Technology. LC 77-26918. (Clinical Ophthalmology Ser.). 1978. 65.95 (ISBN 0-471-74430-1, Pub. by Wiley Medical). Wiley.

Ruben, Patricia. What Is New? What Is Missing? What Is Different? LC 78-8109. (Illus.). (gr. k-2). 1978. 9.95i o.p. (ISBN 0-397-31816-2, JBL-J). Har-Row.

Ruben, Paula, jt. auth. see Dodson, Fitzhugh.

Rubens, Bernice. Favours. LC 78-32086. 1979. 8.95 o.p. (ISBN 0-671-40080-0). Summit Bks.

--Madame Sousatzka. 224p. 1982. 16.95 (ISBN 0-241-10844-6, Pub. by Hamish Hamilton England). David & Charles.

Rubens, Jeff, jt. auth. see Lukacs, Paul.

Rubens, Peter P. Rubens. Micheletti, Emma, ed. (Art Library Ser: No. 15). (Illus.). 1968. pap. 3.50 (ISBN 0-448-00464-X, G&D). Putnam Pub Group.

Rubens, Yvonne A., jt. auth. see Garfinkel, Robin.

Rubenstein, Alvin Z. Foreign Policy of the Soviet Union. 3rd ed. 448p. 1972. pap. text ed. 18.00 (ISBN 0-394-31699-1). Random.

Rubenstein, Bob. Best Restaurants of the Pacific Northwest: Pacific Northwest. LC 76-15698. (Best Restaurants Ser.). (Illus.). 204p. 1976. pap. 2.95 o.p. (ISBN 0-912238-85-2). One Hund One Prods.

Rubenstein, Bonnie, jt. auth. see Rubenstein, Mary.

Rubenstein, Bruce & Ziewacz, Lawrence. Michigan: A History of the Great Lakes State. (Orig.). 1981. pap. text ed. 14.95x (ISBN 0-88273-232-3). Forum Pr IL.

Rubenstein, Harvey M. Central City Malls. LC 78-7536. 1978. 42.50 (ISBN 0-471-03098-8, Pub. by Wiley-Interscience). Wiley.

--A Guide to Site & Environmental Planning. 2nd ed. LC 79-16142. 1980. 36.95 (ISBN 0-471-04729-5, Pub. by Wiley-Interscience). Wiley.

Rubenstein, Hymie. It's Getting Gooder & Gooder. (Orig.). 1976. pap. 4.95 (ISBN 0-89350-006-2). Fountain Pr.

Rubenstein, Irwin, et al, eds. Molecular Biology of Plants. LC 79-18510. 1979. 34.00 (ISBN 0-12-601950-9). Acad Pr.

--The Plant Seed: Development, Preservation & Germination. 1979. 26.00 (ISBN 0-12-602050-7). Acad Pr.

Rubenstein, James. The Cultural Landscape: An Introduction to Human Geography. (Illus.). 500p. 1983. text ed. 19.95 (ISBN 0-314-69674-1); instrs. manual avail. (ISBN 0-314-71118-X). West Pub.

Rubenstein, Jill. Sir Walter Scott: A Reference Guide. 1978. lib. bdg. 35.00 (ISBN 0-8161-7868-2, Hall Reference). G K Hall.

Rubenstein, Joshua, ed. see Marchenko, Anatoly.

Rubenstein, Leonard, jt. ed. see Georgakas, Dan.

Rubenstein, Mala. The Mala Rubenstein Complete Beauty & Diet Book. LC 82-82314. (Illus.). 256p. 1983. pap. 7.95 (ISBN 0-448-16611-9, G&D). Putnam Pub Group.

Rubenstein, Mary & Rubenstein, Bonnie. Will the Real Teacher Please Stand Up? 2nd ed. 1977. pap. text ed. 11.95x (ISBN 0-673-16153-6). Scott F.

Rubenstein, Paul M., jt. auth. see Maloney, Martin.

Rubenstein, Reuven Y. Simulation & the Monte Carlo Method. LC 81-1873. (Probability & Mathematical Statistics Ser.). 300p. 1981. 36.95x (ISBN 0-471-08917-6, Pub. by Wiley-Interscience). Wiley.

Rubenstein, Richard L. The Age of Triage: Fear & Hope in an Overcrowded World. LC 81-70487. 300p. 1983. 14.90 (ISBN 0-8070-4376-1). Beacon Pr.

Rubenstein, Richard L., ed. Modernization: The Humanist Response to Its Promise & Problems. LC 82-83241. 400p. 1982. 24.95 (ISBN 0-89226-015-7). ICF Pr.

Rubenstein, Ruth, jt. auth. see Bober, Phyllis P.

Rubenstein, W. D. Wealth & the Wealthy in the Modern World. LC 80-14632. 1980. 27.50 (ISBN 0-312-85936-8). St Martin.

Rubey, Jane A. & Franklin, Carolyn. Nutrition for Everybody: An Annotated List of Resources. rev. ed. (Nutrition Information Resource Ser.). (Illus.). 24p. 1981. pap. 2.00 (ISBN 0-910869-10-3). Soc Nutrition Ed.

Rubiano, Alfonso, tr. see Ferguson, Charles W., et al.

Rubiao, Murilo. The Ex-Magician & Other Stories. Colchie, Thomas, tr. from Portuguese. LC 78-2064. 1979. 13.41i (ISBN 0-06-013708-8, HarpT). Har-Row.

Rubin. Foundations of the Vocational Rehabilitation Process. 296p. 1978. pap. text ed. 18.95 (ISBN 0-8391-1301-3). Univ Park.

Rubin, jt. auth. see Blair.

Rubin, A., jt. auth. see Lemberger, L.

Rubin, A. J. Aqueous-Environmental Chemistry of Metals. LC 74-78805. (Illus.). 400p. 1976. 36.00 o.p. (ISBN 0-250-40060-X). Ann Arbor Science.

Rubin, Alan. Gopher Broke: And 59 other Sight Gags. (Illus.). 64p. 1983. pap. 2.95 (ISBN 0-517-54778-3). Crown.

--Punjabs. 1983. pap. 5.95 o.p. (ISBN 0-517-54778-3). Crown.

Rubin, Alan, jt. auth. see Anderson, Marc.

Rubin, Alan J., ed. Chemistry of Wastewater Technology. LC 76-50991. 1978. 49.95 (ISBN 0-250-40185-1). Ann Arbor Science.

Rubin, Arnold. Black Nanban: Africans in Japan During the Sixteenth Century. (African Humanities Ser.). (Illus., Orig.). 1974. pap. text ed. 2.00 (ISBN 0-941934-11-X). Ind U Afro-Amer Arts.

Rubin, Arnold P. The Youngest Outlaws: Runaways in America. LC 76-188. 192p. (gr. 7 up). 1976. PLB 7.79 o.p. (ISBN 0-671-32781-X). Messner.

Rubin, Audrey, ed. Gregg Typing for Colleges: Complete Course. (Gregg College Typing Ser.: Series 4). 1979. pap. text ed. 19.85 (ISBN 0-07-038251-4, G). McGraw.

Rubin, Audrey, ed. see Heller, Jack.

Rubin, Audrey, ed. see Liles, Parker, et al.

Rubin, B. L., jt. ed. see Crosignani, P. G.

Rubin, Barry. Paved with Good Intentions: The American Experience & Iran. (Illus.). 1980. 22.50 (ISBN 0-19-502805-8). Oxford U Pr.

Rubin, Barry, jt. ed. see Laqueur, Walter.

Rubin, Barry, jt. auth. see Greene, Owne.

Rubin, Bernard. Media, Politics, & Democracy. (Reconstruction of Society Ser.). (Illus.). 1977. pap. text ed. 7.95x (ISBN 0-19-502008-1). Oxford U Pr.

Rubin, Bob. All-Stars of the NFL. LC 76-8133. (Punt Pass & Kick Library Ser.: No. 24). (Illus.). (gr. 5 up). 1976. 2.50 (ISBN 0-394-83258-2, BYR); PLB 3.69 (ISBN 0-394-93258-7). Random.

Rubin, C., et al. Junk Food. (Orig.). 1980. pap. 9.95 o.s.i. (ISBN 0-440-54276-6, Delta). Dell.

Rubin, Caroline, ed. see Neigoff, Anne.

Rubin, Charles G. How to Win Your Case in Small Claims Court. 28p. pap. 1.95 (ISBN 0-686-36141-5). Legal Pubns CA.

--How to Win Your Case in Traffic Court. 66p. pap. 2.95 (ISBN 0-686-36140-7). Legal Pubns CA.

Rubin, Cynthia & Rubin, Jerome. The Oster Every Day a Gourmet Cookbook. 7.95 o.p. (ISBN 0-916752-29-1). Green Hill.

Rubin, D., jt. auth. see Levin, R.

Rubin, David. The Rights of Teachers. (ACLU Handbook Ser). (Orig.). 1972. pap. 1.50 o.p. (ISBN 0-380-00940-4, 25049, Discus). Avon.

Rubin, David, jt. auth. see Levin, Richard I.

Rubin, David L. Higher, Hidden Order: Design & Meaning in the Odes of Malherbe. (Studies in the Romance Languages & Literatures: No. 117). 124p. 1972. pap. 7.50x (ISBN 0-686-77166-4). U of NC Pr.

Rubin, Dorothy. Gaining Sentence Power. 1981. 12.95x (ISBN 0-02-404190-4). Macmillan.

--Reading & Learning Power. (Illus.). 1980. pap. text ed. 12.95x (ISBN 0-02-404290-0). Macmillan.

--The Vital Arts: Reading & Writing. 1978. pap. text ed. 11.95x (ISBN 0-02-404320-6); instrs'. manual avail. Macmillan.

--Vocabulary Expansion I. 416p. 1982. pap. text ed. 9.95 (ISBN 0-02-404220-X). Macmillan.

--Vocabulary Expansion II. 288p. 1982. pap. text ed. 9.95 (ISBN 0-02-404240-4). Macmillan.

Rubin, Gail. Psalmist with a Camera. LC 79-5086. (Illus.). 116p. 1979. 19.95 (ISBN 0-89659-076-3); pap. 12.95 (ISBN 0-89659-071-2). Abbeville Pr.

Rubin, H. Pensions & Employee Mobility in the Public Service. (Twentieth Century Fund Ser.). 1965. Repr. of 1965 ed. pap. 5.00 (ISBN 0-527-02834-7). Kraus Repr.

Rubin, H. Ted. The Courts: Fulcrum of the Justice System. 1976. pap. text ed. 12.95x o.p. (ISBN 0-673-16327-X). Scott F.

--Juvenile Justice: Policy Practice & Law. new ed. 1979. pap. text ed. 12.95x o.p. (ISBN 0-673-16315-6). Scott F.

--Juveniles in Justice. 1980. pap. text ed. 11.95x o.p. (ISBN 0-673-16314-8). Scott F.

Rubin, Herbert. Applied Social Research. 384p. 1983. text ed. 21.95 (ISBN 0-675-09793-2); student guide 7.95 (ISBN 0-675-20048-2). Additional supplements may be obtained from publisher. Merrill.

Rubin, Irene. Running in the Red: The Political Dynamics of Urban Fiscal Stress. LC 81-9329. 184p. 1982. 30.50x (ISBN 0-87395-564-1); pap. 9.95x (ISBN 0-87395-565-X). State U NY Pr.

Rubin, Irvin I. Injection Molding: Theory & Practice. LC 73-5. (S P E Monographs: Vol. 1). 887p. 1973. 58.95x (ISBN 0-471-74445-X, Pub. by Wiley-Interscience). Wiley.

Rubin, Irwin, et al. Improving the Coordination of Care: A Program for Health Team Development. LC 75-22431. 96p. 1975. prof ref 18.50x (ISBN 0-88410-120-7). Ballinger Pub.

Rubin, Irwin M., et al. Task-Oriented Team Development. (Illus.). 1978. 3 ring binder 80.00 (ISBN 0-07-054197-3, T&D); facilitator manual 15.00. McGraw.

Rubin, Jay, tr. see Soseki, Natsume.

Rubin, Jeffrey, jt. auth. see Raven, Bertran.

Rubin, Jeffrey & LaPorte, Valerie, eds. Alternatives in Rehabilitating the Handicapped: A Policy Analysis. LC 81-4144. 244p. 1982. 29.95 (ISBN 0-89885-010-X). Human Sci Pr.

Rubin, Jeffrey Z., jt. auth. see Raven, Bertram H.

Rubin, Jeffrey Z., ed. Dynamics of Third-Party Intervention: Kissinger in the Middle East. 328p. 1981. 27.95 (ISBN 0-03-051061-9). Praeger.

Rubin, Jerome, jt. auth. see Rubin, Cynthia.

Rubin, Jerry & Leonard, Mimi. The War Between the Sheets: What's Happening with Men in Bed Today-& What Men & Women Are Doing About It. 324p. 1980. 11.95 o.s.i. (ISBN 0-399-90093-4, Marek). Putnam Pub Group.

Rubin, Joan. Directory of Language Planning Organizations. LC 79-22330. 1980. pap. text ed. 4.50x (ISBN 0-8248-0687-5, Eastwest Ctr). UH Pr.

Rubin, Joan & Jernudd, Bjorn H. References for Students of Language Planning. LC 79-17656. 1979. pap. text ed. 4.50x (ISBN 0-8248-0686-7, Eastwest Ctr). UH Pr.

Rubin, Joan & Jernudd, Bjorn H., eds. Can Language Be Planned: Sociolinguistic Theory & Practice for Developing Nations. LC 70-129618. (Illus.). 1971. pap. text ed. 5.95x (ISBN 0-8248-0358-2). UH Pr.

Rubin, Jonathan. The Barking Deer. 336p. 1982. pap. 3.25 (ISBN 0-380-61135-X, 61135). Avon.

Rubin, Joseph B., jt. auth. see Lee, Dorris.

Rubin, Joseph J., ed. see De Forest, John W.

Rubin, K. H., jt. ed. see Pepler, D. J.

Rubin, Ken. Drop Coin Here. (Illus.). 1978. 12.95 o.p. (ISBN 0-517-53298-0). Crown.

Rubin, L. Optometry Handbook. 1975. 17.95 o.p. (ISBN 0-407-98500-X). Butterworth.

Rubin, Leon. The Nicholas Nickleby Story. 192p. 1981. 25.00x o.p. (ISBN 0-434-65530-9, Pub. by Heinemann England). State Mutual Bk.

Rubin, Lillian B. Intimate Strangers. LC 82-48678. 256p. 1983. 13.95 (ISBN 0-06-014922-1, HarpT). Har-Row.

--Women of a Certain Age: The Midlife Search for Self. LC 79-1681. 1979. 13.45i (ISBN 0-06-013706-1, HarpT). Har-Row.

Rubin, Louis D., Jr. The Literary South. LC 78-24221. 1979. text ed. 25.50x (ISBN 0-673-15695-8). Scott F.

Rubin, Louis D., Jr., ed. The Comic Imagination in American Literature. (Illus.). 448p. 1973. 35.00x o.p. (ISBN 0-8135-0758-8). Rutgers U Pr.

Rubin, Lucille S., ed. Movement for the Actor. LC 79-10461. (Illus.). 132p. 1980. pap. 7.95x (ISBN 0-89676-010-3). Drama Bk.

Rubin, M. J., ed. Studies in Antarctic Meteorology. LC 66-6578. (Antarctic Research Ser.: Vol. 9). 1966. 18.00 (ISBN 0-87590-109-3). Am Geophysical.

Rubin, Martin L., ed. see Conference on Computer Technology in Education for 1985 at Arlie House, Warrenton, Va., Sept. 15-18, 1975.

Rubin, Mary. How to Get Money for Research. 96p. 1983. 5.95 (ISBN 0-935312-18-8). Feminist Pr.

Rubin, Michael, jt. auth. see Olivieri, Peter.

Rubin, Michael, ed. Defending the Galaxy: The Complete Handbook of Videogaming. (Illus.). 224p. (Orig.). (gr. 8-12). pap. 4.95 (ISBN 0-937404-17-9). Triad Pub FL.

Rubin, Michael R. Information Economics & Policy in the United States. 1983. lib. bdg. price not set. Libs Unl.

Rubin, Murry & Haller, C. E. Communication Switching Systems. LC 74-22069. 400p. 1974. 23.50 (ISBN 0-88275-232-4). Krieger.

Rubin, Nancy. The New Suburban Woman. 1982. 13.95 (ISBN 0-686-91897-5, Coward). Putnam Pub Group.

--The New Suburban Woman: Beyond Myth & Motherhood. LC 81-19622. 352p. 1982. 13.95 (ISBN 0-698-11133-8, Coward). Putnam Pub Group.

Rubin, Neville & Warren, William M., eds. Dams in Africa. LC 68-19216. 1968. 25.00x o.p. (ISBN 0-678-05196-8). Kelley.

Rubin, R. D. & Franks, C. M., eds. Advances in Behavior Therapy: Proceedings. Incl. 1969 (ISBN 0-12-601450-7); 1969. 1971 (ISBN 0-12-601452-3); 1970. 1972 (ISBN 0-12-601453-1); 1971. 1973 (ISBN 0-12-601454-X). 49.50 ea. Acad Pr.

Rubin, Richard, jt. auth. see Goldberg, Philip.

Rubin, Richard L. Press, Party, & Presidency. 1981. pap. text ed. 6.95x (ISBN 0-393-95206-1). Norton.

--Press, Party, & Presidency. (Illus.). 1982. 18.95 (ISBN 0-393-01497-5). Norton.

Rubin, Richard R. & Fisher, John J., III. Your Preschooler. (Illus.). 320p. 1982. 23.95 (ISBN 0-02-605710-7); pap. 10.95 (ISBN 0-02-077830-9). Macmillan.

Rubin, Rick, jt. auth. see Byerly, Greg.

Rubin, Robert. Lou Gehrig: Courageous Star. LC 78-31604. (Sports Shelf Ser.). (Illus.). (gr. 5 up). 1979. PLB 6.99 (ISBN 0-399-61135-5). Putnam Pub Group.

--Satchel Paige: All-Time Baseball Great. LC 73-87215. (Putnam Sports Shelf). 160p. (gr. 5 up). 1974. PLB 6.29 o.p. (ISBN 0-399-60876-1). Putnam Pub Group.

--Tony Conigliaro: Up from Despair. (Putnam Sports Shelf). (gr. 5 up). 1971. PLB 5.29 o.p. (ISBN 0-399-60639-4). Putnam Pub Group.

--Ty Cobb: The Greatest. (Putnam Sports Shelf). (gr. 5 up). 1978. PLB 6.99 (ISBN 0-399-61110-X). Putnam Pub Group.

Rubin, Roger H., jt. auth. see Macklin, Eleanor D.

Rubin, Ruth. Voices of a People: The Story of Yiddish Folksong. 2nd rev. ed. LC 73-6983. (Illus.). 558p. 1973. Repr. of 1963 ed. 9.95 o.p. (ISBN 0-07-054194-9, P&RB). McGraw.

Rubin, S., jt. auth. see Bozarth, J.

Rubin, Sol. United States Prison Law: Sentencing to Prison, Prison Conditions, & Release - the Court Decisions - Prisoners' Rights, 7 bdrs. LC 74-23142. 1975. lib. bdg. 50.00 ea. (ISBN 0-379-10051-7). Oceana.

Rubin, Steven J. The James Bond Films. (Illus.). 224p. 1981. o. p 19.95 (ISBN 0-517-54813-5, Arlington Hse); pap. 10.95 (ISBN 0-517-54824-0). Crown.

--Meyer Levin. (United States Authors Ser.). 1982. lib. bdg. 13.95 (ISBN 0-8057-7335-5, Twayne). G K Hall.

Rubin, Susan, jt. auth. see Ilyin, Donna.

Rubin, Ted. Standards Relating to Court Organization & Administration. LC 76-14413. (IJA-ABA Juvenile Justice Standards Project Ser.). 224p. 1980. prof ref 20.00x (ISBN 0-88410-231-9); pap. 10.00x prof ref (ISBN 0-88410-820-1). Ballinger Pub.

Rubin, Theodore I. Alive & Fat & Thinning in America. LC 78-2006. (Illus.). 1978. 8.95 o.p. (ISBN 0-698-10915-5, Coward). Putnam Pub Group.

--The Angry Book. 3.95 o.p. (ISBN 0-686-92292-1, 6320). Hazelden.

--One to One: Understanding Human Relationships. Orig. Title: Locks. 256p. 1983. 15.75 (ISBN 0-670-43596-1). Viking Pr.

--Reflections in a Goldfish Tank: A Distinguished Psychiatrist, Novelist & Bestselling Author Meditates on Friends, Loved Ones, Patients, & Himself. 1977. 7.95 o.p. (ISBN 0-698-10807-8, Coward). Putman Pub.

Rubin, Vera & Zavalloni, Marisa. We Wish to Be Looked Upon. LC 69-19415. 1969. text ed. 10.95x (ISBN 0-8077-2067-4). Tchrs Coll.

Rubin, Vera & Schaedel, Richard, eds. The Haitian Potential: Research & Resources of Haiti. LC 73-78672. 1975. text ed. 16.95x (ISBN 0-8077-2377-0). Tchrs Coll.

Rubin, Vera & Tuden, Arthur, eds. Comparative Perspectives on Slavery in New World Plantation Societies, Vol. 292. (Annals of the New York Academy of Sciences). 1977. 42.00x (ISBN 0-89072-038-X). NY Acad Sci.

Rubin, William. Anthony Caro. LC 74-21725. (Illus.). 1975. 17.50 o.p. (ISBN 0-686-67781-1, 043729, Pub by Museum of Modern Art). NYGS.

Rubin, William, ed. De Chirico. (Illus.). 208p. 1982. 35.00 o.p. (ISBN 0-87070-290-4); pap. 17.50 (ISBN 0-87070-291-2). Museum Mod Art.

--De Chirico. (Illus.). 216p. 1982. 35.00 (ISBN 0-87070-290-4); pap. 17.50 (ISBN 0-686-98320-3). Macmillan.

Rubin, William S. Dada, Surrealism & Their Heritage. LC 68-17466. (Illus., Orig.). 1968. pap. 12.50 (ISBN 0-87070-284-X). Museum Mod Art.

--Picasso in the Collection of the Museum of Modern Art. LC 70-164877. (Illus.). 1972. 35.00 (ISBN 0-87070-537-7); pap. 17.50 (ISBN 0-87070-538-5). Museum Mod Art.

Rubin, Zick & McNeil, Elton B. The Psychology of Being Human. 3rd ed. 656p. 1981. text ed. 24.50 scp (ISBN 0-06-044383-9, HarpC); scp study guide 8.50 (ISBN 0-06-044307-3); scp activities manual 10.50 (ISBN 0-06-042471-0); instrs' manual avail. (ISBN 0-06-364211-5); test item avail. (ISBN 0-06-364210-7); instrs' manual test to accompany activity manual avail. (ISBN 0-06-362480-X). Har-Row.

--The Psychology of Being Human. 3rd, brief update ed. 544p. 1983. pap. text ed. 18.95 scp (ISBN 0-06-045649-3, HarpC); instr's manual avail. (ISBN 0-06-364212-3); test bank avail. (ISBN 0-06-364213-1); scp study guide 6.00 (ISBN 0-06-044308-1). Har-Row.

--Psychology of Being Human: Brief Update Edition. 504p. 1979. pap. text ed. 19.95 scp o.p. (ISBN 0-06-044386-3, HarpC); scp study guide 8.95 o.p. (ISBN 0-06-044385-5); instr's. manual avail. o.p. (ISBN 0-06-364241-7). Har-Row.

Rubincam, David P. & Rubincam, John. Diet the Natural Vitamin Way. LC 79-6558. Orig. Title: Diet with Vitamins. 288p. 1980. pap. 4.95 o.s.i. (ISBN 0-89104-177-X, A & W Visual Library). A & W Pubs.

Rubincam, John, jt. auth. see Rubincam, David P.

Rubinfeld, Daniel, jt. auth. see Pindyck, Robert S.

Rubinger, Michael. I Know an Astronaut. (Community Helper Bks.). (Illus.). 48p. (gr. 1-3). 1972. PLB 4.29 o.p. (ISBN 0-399-60713-7). Putnam Pub Group.

Rubington, Earl & Weinberg, Martin. Deviance: The Interactionist Perspective. 4th ed. 1981. pap. text ed. 13.95x (ISBN 0-02-404380-X). Macmillan.

Rubinow, S. I. Introduction to Mathematical Biology. LC 75-12520. 386p. 1975. 47.95 (ISBN 0-471-74446-8, Pub. by Wiley-Interscience). Wiley.

Rubinow, Sol I. Mathematical Problems in the Biological Sciences. (CBMS Regional Conference Ser.: Vol. 10). (Illus.). ix, 90p. (Orig.). 1973. pap. text ed. 9.00 (ISBN 0-89871-008-1). Soc Indus-Appl Math.

Rubinowicz, A. Quantum Mechanics. 2nd ed. 1968. 32.00 (ISBN 0-444-40741-3). Elsevier.

Rubin-Rabson, Grace, tr. see Sechehaye, Marguerite.

Rubins, A. Alfred. History of Jewish Costume. 1973. 15.00 o.p. (ISBN 0-517-50392-1). Crown.

Rubins, Harriet. Guinea Pigs: An Owner's Guide to Choosing, Raising, Breeding, & Showing. (Illus.). (gr. 5 up). 1982. 9.50 (ISBN 0-688-01430-5). Lothrop.

Rubinsky, Yuri & Wiseman, Ian. History of the End of the World. 1982. 13.50 (ISBN 0-688-01392-9); pap. 6.00 (ISBN 0-688-01388-0). Morrow.

Rubinstein, Alvin Z. Soviet Foreign Policy Since World War II: Imperial & Global. (Orig.). 1981. text ed. 16.95 (ISBN 0-316-76084-6); pap. text ed. 11.95 (ISBN 0-316-76085-4). Little.

--Soviet Policy Toward Turkey, Iran & Afghanistan. 218p. 1982. 25.95 (ISBN 0-03-052506-3); pap. 11.95 (ISBN 0-03-052511-X). Praeger.

Rubinstein, Alvin Z, ed. see Ginsburgs, George.

Rubinstein, Aryeh, ed. Hasidism. 128p. pap. 4.50 (ISBN 0-686-95129-8). ADL.

Rubinstein, Charlotte S. American Women Artists: From Early Indian Times to the Present. 1982. lib. bdg. 39.95 (ISBN 0-8161-8535-2, Hall Reference). G K Hall.

Rubinstein, David. School Attendance in London 1870-1904. LC 75-86243. 1969. 15.00x (ISBN 0-678-08000-3). Kelley.

Rubinstein, David & Simon, Brian. Evolution of the Comprehensive School: 1926-1972. 2nd ed. (Students Library of Education). 148p. 1973. 9.95x (ISBN 0-7100-7654-1); pap. 4.95 (ISBN 0-7100-7655-X). Routledge & Kegan.

Rubinstein, Donna. I Am the Only Survivor of Krasnostav. LC 82-61794. (Illus.). 1983. 10.00 (ISBN 0-88400-093-1). Shengold.

Rubinstein, Helge. The Ultimate Chocolate Cake: One Hundred Eleven Other Chocolate Indulgences. (Illus.). 336p. 1983. 14.95 (ISBN 0-312-92851-3). Congdon & Weed.

Rubinstein, Hilary. Europe's Wonderful Little Hotels & Inns. 5th ed. (Illus.). 608p. 1983. pap. 14.95 (ISBN 0-312-92193-4). Congdon & Weed.

Rubinstein, Israel, ed. see Gerson, Joel & Madry, Bobbi R.

Rubinstein, Lucien J., jt. auth. see Earle, Kenneth M.

Rubinstein, M. F., jt. auth. see Hurty, Walter C.

Rubinstein, Mark & Cox, John J. Options Markets. (Illus.). 432p. 1982. 29.95 o.p. (ISBN 0-13-638205-3). P-H.

Rubinstein, Morton K. A Doctor's Guide to Non-Prescription Drugs. 1977. pap. 2.25 (ISBN 0-451-09506-5, E9506, Sig). NAL.

Rubinstein, Moshe F. Matrix Computer Analysis of Structures. (Illus.). 1966. 34.95 (ISBN 0-13-565481-5). P-H.

Rubinstein, Ronald A., jt. auth. see Fry, Patricia B.

Rubio. Atlas of Angioacess Surgery. 1983. 95.00 (ISBN 0-8151-7451-9). Year Bk Med.

Rubio, Antonio, jt. auth. see Jackson, Eugene.

Rubio, J. E. Theory of Linear Systems. (Electrical Science Ser). 1971. 45.50 (ISBN 0-12-601650-X). Acad Pr.

Rubio, Pascal O., 3rd, ed. see Unibook Staff.

Ruble, Blair A. Soviet Trade Unions: Their Development in the 1970's. LC 80-29646. (Soviet & East European Studies). (Illus.). 160p. 1981. 32.50 (ISBN 0-521-23704-1). Cambridge U Pr.

Ruble, Shirley, ed. A Long-Term Underground Plan: An Anthology of Poems About the Eruption of Mount St. Helens. 3rd ed. 140p. 1982. pap. 5.00x (ISBN 0-9605952-0-1). Raindance.

Rublowsky, John. The Stoned Age: A History of Drugs in America. LC 73-93744. 160p. 1974. 6.95 o.p. (ISBN 0-399-11306-1). Putnam Pub Group.

Rubner, Max. The Laws of Energy Conservation in Nutrition. 1982. 42.50 (ISBN 0-12-602150-3). Acad Pr.

Rubright, Bob & MacDonald, Dan. Marketing Health & Human Services. LC 81-737. 248p. 1981. text ed. 28.95 (ISBN 0-89443-338-5). Aspen Systems.

Rubulis, Aleksis, ed. & tr. Latvian Folktales. 1982. 8.50 (ISBN 0-89023-020-X). Forrest Printing.

Ruby, Lois. Arriving at a Place You Never Left. (YA) (gr. 7-12). 1980. pap. 1.50 o.p. (ISBN 0-440-90254-1, LFL). Dell.

Ruby, Michael G., jt. auth. see Halvorsen, Robert.

Ruch, Theodore C. & Patton, Harry D., eds. Physiology & Biophysics. Incl. Vol. 1. The Nervous System. text ed. 38.00 (ISBN 0-7216-7821-1); Vol. 2. Circulation, Respiration & Fluid Balance. 495p. text ed. 30.00 (ISBN 0-7216-7818-1); Vol. 3. Digestion, Metabolism, Endocrine Function & Reproduction. 20th ed. 1973. text ed. 30.00 (ISBN 0-7216-7819-X). LC 73-180188. (Illus.). 1974. Saunders.

Ruch, Walter E. Chemical Detection of Gaseous Pollutants: An Annotated Bibliography. LC 66-29577. 180p. 1982. 24.00 (ISBN 0-250-40099-5). Ann Arbor Science.

Ruch, Walter E. & Held, Bruce. Respiratory Protection: OSHA & the Small Businessman. LC 75-7955. (Illus.). 1975. 15.00 o.p. (ISBN 0-250-40101-0). Ann Arbor Science.

Ruchin, T., jt. auth. see Olsen, L.

Ruchlin, H., jt. auth. see Rogers, D.

Ruchlis, Hyman. Orbit: Picture Story of Force & Motion. LC 58-5290. (Illus.). (gr. 5 up). 1958. PLB 8.79 o.p. (ISBN 0-06-025111-5, HarpJ). Har-Row.

Ruck, Carl A. Ancient Greek: A New Approach. 2nd ed. 1979. pap. text ed. 17.50x (ISBN 0-262-68031-9). MIT Pr.

Ruck, Heribert, jt. auth. see Deluc, Yves.

Ruck, Wolfgang E. Canoeing & Kayaking. (Illus.). 96p. 1974. 6.95 o.p. (ISBN 0-07-077761-6, GB). McGraw.

Ruckdeschel, Fred. Basic Scientific Subroutines, 2 vols. 1981. Vol. 1. 21.95 (ISBN 0-07-054201-5, P&RB); Vol. 2. 23.95 (ISBN 0-07-054202-3). McGraw.

Rucker, Rudy. The Fifty-Seventh Franz Kafka. 1983. pap. 2.50 (ISBN 0-441-23516-6, Pub. by Ace Science Fiction). Ace Bks.

--Infinity & the Mind: The Science & Philosophy of the Infinite. (Illus.). 342p. 1982. 15.95 (ISBN 3-7643-3034-1). Birkhauser.

Rucker, Walter E., jt. auth. see Dilley, Clyde A.

Ruckers Colloquium. Restauratieproblemen Van Antwerpse Klavecimbels: Lectures in English, French, German & Dutch by Ripin, Schutze, Skowroneck. (Keyboard Studies: Vol. 3). 85p. 1971. wrappers 20.00 o.s.i. (ISBN 90-6027-334-6, Pub. by Frits Knuf Netherlands). Pendragon NY.

Ruckers Colloquium 1977. Antwerpen, Museum Vleeshuis. (Brussels Museum of Musical Instruments Bulletin Ser.: Vol. 7). (Illus.). 130p. wrappers 20.00 o.p. (ISBN 90-6027-184-X, Pub. by Frits Knuf Netherlands). Pendragon NY.

Ruckle, W. H. Sequence Spaces. LC 80-22969. (Research Notes in Mathematics Ser.: No. 49). 224p. (Orig.). 1981. pap. text ed. 25.50 (ISBN 0-273-08507-7). Pitman Pub MA.

Ruckman, Ivy. Encounter. LC 77-26519. (gr. 7 up). 1978. PLB 7.95a o.p. (ISBN 0-385-14151-3). Doubleday.

--In a Class By Herself. LC 82-48759. 208p. (gr. 12 up). 12.95 (ISBN 0-15-238242-9, HJ). HarBraceJ.

--Melba the Brain. LC 79-19326. (Illus.). (gr. 3-5). 1979. 8.95 (ISBN 0-664-32655-2). Westminster.

--What's an Average Kid Like Me Doing Way up Here? LC 82-72820. 144p. (gr. 5-8). 1983. 11.95 (ISBN 0-440-08892-5). Delacorte.

Ruckman, Paul, jt. auth. see Lavely, Joe.

Ruck-Pauquet, Gina. Mumble Bear. (Illus.). 24p. (gr. 4-7). 1980. 7.95 o.p. (ISBN 0-399-20712-0). Putnam Pub Group.

Ruda, Jeffrey. Filipo Lippi Studies: Naturalism Style Anticonography in Early Renaissance Art. LC 79-57498. (Outstanding Dissertations in the Fine Arts Ser.: No. 5). 235p. 1982. lib. bdg. 33.50 o.s.i. (ISBN 0-8240-3940-8). Garland Pub.

Ruda, Jeffrey, et al. Studies in the History of Art 1975, Vol. 7. (Illus.). pap. 9.95 (ISBN 0-89468-049-8). Natl Gallery Art.

Rudd, Andrew & Clasing, Henry K., Jr. Modern Portfolio Theory: Principles of Investment Management. LC 81-71910. 430p. 1982. 42.50 (ISBN 0-87094-191-7). Dow Jones-Irwin.

Rudd, Dale F. & Watson, Charles C. Strategy of Process Engineering. 1968. 46.50 (ISBN 0-471-74455-7). Wiley.

Rudd, Dale F., jt. auth. see Berthouex, P. Mac.

Rudd, Dale F., et al. Petrochemical Technology Assessment. LC 81-3031. 370p. 1981. 46.95 (ISBN 0-471-08912-5, Pub. by Wiley-Interscience). Wiley.

--Process Synthesis. LC 73-3331. (International Ser. in Physical & Chemical Engineering). (Illus.). 320p. 1973. ref. ed. 33.95 (ISBN 0-13-723353-1). P-H.

Rudd, Ernest. The Highest Education: A Study of Graduate Education in Britain. 1975. 16.95x (ISBN 0-7100-8307-6). Routledge & Kegan.

Rudd, Kenneth D., et al. Dental Laboratory Procedures: Removable Partial Dentures, Vol. III. LC 79-16785. (Illus.). 675p. 1981. text ed. 54.95 (ISBN 0-8016-3516-0). Mosby.

Rudd, M. J., jt. auth. see Watrasiewicz, B. M.

Rudd, Margaret. Organized Innocence: The Story of Blake's Prophetic Books. LC 72-6209. (Illus.). 266p. 1973. Repr. of 1956 ed. lib. bdg. 17.50x (ISBN 0-8371-6458-3, RUOI). Greenwood.

Rudd, Niall. The Satires of Horace. 318p. Date not set. pap. 9.95x (ISBN 0-520-04718-4). U of Cal Pr. Postponed.

Rudd, Robert L. Environmental Toxicology: A Guide to Information Sources. LC 73-17540. (Man & the Environmrnt Information Guide Ser.: Vol. 7). 1977. 42.00x (ISBN 0-8103-1342-1). Gale.

--Pesticides & the Living Landscape. 334p. 1964. pap. 7.95x o.p. (ISBN 0-299-03214-0). U of Wis Pr.

Rudd, Steele. Me An' the Son. 1973. 2.25x o.p. (ISBN 0-7022-0821-3). U of Queensland Pr.

Rudd, Walter G. Assembly Language Programming & the IBM 360 & 370 Computers. 1976. 24.95 (ISBN 0-13-049536-0); wkbk. 10.95 (ISBN 0-13-049510-7). P-H.

Rudden, Bernard, jt. auth. see Lawson, Frederick H.

Rudden, M. N. & Wilson, J. Elements of Solid State Physics. LC 79-41730. 186p. 1980. 49.95 (ISBN 0-471-27750-9, Pub. by Wiley-Interscience); pap. 19.95 (ISBN 0-471-27749-5). Wiley.

Rudder, Robert S., tr. see Serrano-Plaja, Arturo.

Ruddick, Bob, jt. auth. see Greer, Gery.

Ruddick, William, ed. Sheridan: The Rivals, The School for Scandal & the Critic. 1981. pap. 25.00x (ISBN 0-686-97833-1, Pub. by Macmillan England). State Mutual Bk.

Ruddick, William, jt. ed. see O'Neill, Onora.

Ruddle, Kenneth. The Yukpa Cultivation System: A Study of Shifting Cultivation in Columbia & Venezuela. (Publications in Ibero-Americana Ser: Vol. 52). 1976. pap. 21.00x (ISBN 0-520-09497-2). U of Cal Pr.

Ruddle, Kenneth & Chesterfield, Ray. Education for Traditional Food Procurement in the Orinoco Delta. (University of California Publications in Ibero-Americana Ser.: Vol. 53). 1977. pap. 21.00x (ISBN 0-520-09551-0). U of Cal Pr.

Ruddle, Kenneth & Johnson, Dennis. Palm Sago: A Tropical Starch from Marginal Lands. LC 77-28981. 1978. pap. text ed. 7.50x (ISBN 0-8248-0577-1, Eastwest Ctr). UH Pr.

Ruddle, Kenneth, jt. auth. see Rondinelli, Dennis A.

Ruddle, R. W. Difficulties Encountered in Smelting in the Lead Blast Furnace. 56p. 1957. 11.50 (ISBN 0-686-38297-8). IMM North Am.

Ruddock, E. C. Arch Bridges & Their Builders, 1735-1835. LC 77-82514. (Illus.). 1979. 90.00 (ISBN 0-521-21816-0). Cambridge U Pr.

Ruddock, Ralph, ed. & pref. by. Six Approaches to the Person. 224p. 1972. 20.00x (ISBN 0-7100-7335-6); pap. 8.95 (ISBN 0-7100-7382-8). Routledge & Kegan.

Ruddon, R. W. Biological Markers of Neoplasia: Basic & Applied Aspects. 1978. 76.95 (ISBN 0-444-00292-8). Elsevier.

Ruddon, Raymond W. Cancer Biology. (Illus.). 1981. text ed. 24.95x (ISBN 0-19-502942-9); pap. text ed. 16.95x (ISBN 0-19-502943-7). Oxford U Pr.

Ruddon, Raymond W., jt. auth. see Pratt, William B.

Ruddy, F. see Francis, Deak.

Ruddy, Frank, ed. American International Law Cases, 1769-1978, 3 vols. LC 78-140621. (American International Law Cases Ser). 1977. lib. bdg. 45.00 ea. o.p. Oceana.

Rude, George. Crowd in the French Revolution. (Illus.). 1959. pap. text ed. 6.95x (ISBN 0-19-500370-5). Oxford U Pr.

--Hanoverian London, 1714-1808. LC 69-10590. (History of London Series). (Illus.). 1971. 33.00x (ISBN 0-520-01778-1). U of Cal Pr.

--Protest & Punishment: The Story of the Social & Political Protesters Transported to Australia, 1788-1868. 1978. 34.50x (ISBN 0-19-822430-3). Oxford U Pr.

--Revolutionary Europe 1783-1815. (History of Europe Ser.). pap. 5.50xi o.p. (ISBN 0-06-131272-X, TB1272, Torch). Har-Row.

Rudeanu, S. Boolean Functions & Equations. 1975. 42.75 (ISBN 0-444-10520-4). Elsevier.

Rudeanu, S., tr. see Tomescu, Ioan.

Rudeen, Kenneth. Jackie Robinson. LC 75-139100. (Biography Ser.). (Illus.). (gr. 2-5). 1971. PLB 10.89 (ISBN 0-690-45650-6, TYC-J); pap. 2.95 crocodile paperback ser. (ISBN 0-690-00208-4). Har-Row.

--Muhammad Ali. LC 76-12093. (Biography Ser.). (Illus.). 40p. (gr. 1-4). 1976. 10.89 (ISBN 0-690-01128-8, TYC-J). Har-Row.

--Roberto Clemente. LC 73-12794. (Biography Ser.). (Illus.). (gr. 1-5). 1974. PLB 10.89 (ISBN 0-690-00322-6, TYC-J). Har-Row.

--Wilt Chamberlain. LC 74-94800. (Biography Ser.). (Illus.). (gr. 2-5). 1970. 9.57i (ISBN 0-690-89458-9, TYC-J); PLB 10.89 (ISBN 0-690-01134-2). Har-Row.

Rudel, Joan, tr. see Steiner, Rudolf.

Rudelius, William, et al. An Introduction to Contemporary Business. 3rd ed. 560p. 1981. text ed. 21.95 (ISBN 0-15-541655-3, HC); tests 12.95 (ISBN 0-15-541658-8); study guide 7.95 (ISBN 0-15-541656-1); instructors manual 60.00 (ISBN 0-15-541657-X). HarBraceJ.

Rudenko, Mykola. Eagle's Ravine. (Ukrainian Ser.). 454p. 1982. 16.95 (ISBN 0-914834-34-7). Smoloskyp.

--On the Sea Floor. LC 81-50857. (Ukrainian Ser.). 74p. 1981. pap. 4.75 (ISBN 0-914834-32-0). Smoloskyp.

Ruder, Avima, jt. auth. see O'Neil, Carol L.

Ruderman, Jerome L. Jews in American History: A Teacher's Guide. 244p. 7.95 (ISBN 0-686-95134-4); pap. 3.95 (ISBN 0-686-99466-3). ADL.

Rudestam, Kjell E. Experiential Groups in Theory & Practice. LC 81-38555. (Psychology Ser.). 514p. 1982. text ed. 19.95 (ISBN 0-8185-0470-6). Brooks-Cole.

Rudestam, Kjell E. & Frankel, Mark. Treating the Multiproblem Family: A Casebook. LC 82-19739. (Psychology Ser.). 320p. 1983. pap. text ed. 12.95 (ISBN 0-534-01300-7). Brooks-Cole.

Rudhyar, Dane. The Astrological Houses: The Spectrum of Individual Experience. LC 74-180105. 1972. pap. 6.95 (ISBN 0-385-03827-5). Doubleday.

--Astrological Insights Into the Spiritual Life. pap. 7.95 (ISBN 0-686-36358-2). Aurora Press.

--Astrological Mandala: The Cycle of Transformations & Its 360 Symbolic Phases. 1974. pap. 4.95 (ISBN 0-394-71992-1, Vin). Random.

--An Astrological Study of Psychological Complexes. LC 75-10324. (Illus.). 156p. (Orig.). 1976. pap. 7.95 (ISBN 0-394-73174-3). Shambhala Pubns.

--An Astrological Tryptich. pap. 8.95 (ISBN 0-686-36355-8). Aurora Press.

--Fire out of the Stone. 2nd ed. LC 79-89943. Date not set. cancelled (ISBN 0-89793-020-7). Hunter Hse.

--The Galactic Dimension of Astrology. pap. 7.95 (ISBN 0-686-36356-6). Aurora Press.

--The Planetarization of Consciousness. pap. 9.95 (ISBN 0-686-36357-4). Aurora Press.

Rudhyar, Dane, jt. auth. see Rael, Leyla.

Rudhyar, Leyla Rael. The Lunation Process. pap. 3.95 (ISBN 0-686-36353-1). Aurora Press.

Rudiak, Il'ia, ed. Our Age: Photographs. 144p. 1983. 25.00 (ISBN 0-88233-814-5); pap. 10.00 (ISBN 0-88233-815-3). Ardis Pubs.

Rudick, Elliott, jt. auth. see Meier, August.

Rudin, Alfred. The Elements of Polymer Science & Engineering: An Introductory Text for Engineers & Chemists. 1982. 29.95 (ISBN 0-12-601680-1); solutions manual 4.00 (ISBN 0-12-601682-8). Acad Pr.

Rudin, Harry R. Germans in the Cameroons, Eighteen Eighty-Four to Nineteen Fourteen: A Case Study in Modern Imperialism. LC 39-5914. (Illus.). 1969. Repr. of 1938 ed. lib. bdg. 21.00x (ISBN 0-8371-0640-0, RUGC). Greenwood.

Rudin, Walter. Functional Analysis. LC 71-39686. (McGraw-Hill Series in Higher Mathematics). 1972. text ed. 37.50 (ISBN 0-07-054225-2, C). McGraw.

--Principles of Mathematical Analysis. (International Series in Pure & Applied Mathematics). 1976. text ed. 30.00 (ISBN 0-07-054235-X). McGraw.

--Real & Complex Analysis. 2nd ed. (Higher Mathematics Ser.). 416p. 1973. text ed. 37.50 (ISBN 0-07-054233-3, C). McGraw.

Rudinger, Joel. Poetry Project Three: Cambridge Poetry Projects. (Orig.). 1983. pap. 7.95 (ISBN 0-918342-16-3). Cambridge U Pr.

Rudinger, Joel, ed. Firelands Review: 1980. (Cambric Press Anthology of the Arts: No. AA-5). 1980. pap. 3.00 o.p. (ISBN 0-918342-13-9). Cambric.

Rudisill, Marie & Simmons, James C. Truman Capote. (Illus.). 224p. 1983. 11.95 (ISBN 0-686-84633-8). Morrow.

Rudiwger, Joel, ed. Cambric Poetry Project Two. 1980. pap. 8.00 (ISBN 0-918342-12-0). Cambric.

Rudkin, Anthony & Butcher, Irene, eds. Book World Directory of the Arab Countries, Turkey & Iran. 1981. 98.00x (ISBN 0-8103-1185-2, Pub. by Mansell England). Gale.

Rudkin, David. The Sons of Light. 1982. pap. 7.50 (ISBN 0-413-49120-X). Methuen Inc.

Rudkin, Margaret. The Margaret Rudkin Pepperidge Farm Cookbook. (Illus.). 440p. 1981. 15.95 (ISBN 0-448-01382-7, G&D). Putnam Pub Group.

--Pepperidge Farm Cookbook. 15.95 (ISBN 0-448-01382-7, G&D). Putnam Pub Group.

Rudler, G., ed. see Constant, Benjamin.

Rudler, Gustave, et al, eds. Putnam's Contemporary French Dictionary. LC 72-88105. (Fr. & Eng.). 1972. 2.95 o.p. (ISBN 0-399-11042-9). Putnam Pub Group.

Rudley, Stephen. The Abominable Snowcreature. (Illus.). (gr. 5 up). 1978. PLB 8.90 s&l (ISBN 0-531-02212-9). Watts.

--Psychic Detectives. (gr. 7 up). 1979. PLB 7.90 s&l (ISBN 0-531-02928-X). Watts.

Rudloe, Jack. The Living Dock at Panacea. 1977. 10.00 o.p. (ISBN 0-394-48855-5). Knopf.

Rudman, Harry W., jt. auth. see Rosenthal, Irving.

Rudman, Jack. Able Seaman. (Career Examination Ser.: C-1). (Cloth bdg. avail. on request). pap. 10.00 (ISBN 0-8373-0001-0). Natl Learning.

--Academic Subjects Chairman (English & Social Studies) (Teachers License Examination Ser.: CH-1). (Cloth bdg. avail. on request). pap. 15.95 (ISBN 0-8373-8151-7). Natl Learning.

--Account Clerk. (Career Examination Ser.: C-2). (Cloth bdg. avail. on request). pap. 10.00 (ISBN 0-8373-0003-7). Natl Learning.

--Accounting & Auditing Clerk. (Career Examination Ser.: C-5). (Cloth bdg. avail. on request). pap. 10.00 (ISBN 0-8373-0005-3). Natl Learning.

--Accounting & Business Practice Chairman. (Teachers License Examination Ser.: CH-2). (Cloth bdg. avail. on request). pap. 15.95 (ISBN 0-8373-8152-5). Natl Learning.

--Accounting & Business Practice, Sr. H.S. (Teachers License Examination Ser.: T-1). (Cloth bdg. avail. on request). pap. 13.95 (ISBN 0-8373-8001-4). Natl Learning.

--Accounting Assistant. (Career Examination Ser.: C-1071). (Cloth bdg. avail. on request). pap. 10.00 (ISBN 0-8373-1071-7). Natl Learning.

--Accounts Investigator. (Career Examination Ser.: C-1862). (Cloth bdg. avail. on request). pap. 10.00 (ISBN 0-8373-1862-9). Natl Learning.

--ACT Assessment Examination for College Entrance. (Admission Test Ser.: ATS-44). (Cloth bdg. avail. on request). pap. 13.95 (ISBN 0-8373-5044-1). Natl Learning.

--Activities Director. (Career Examination Ser.: C-2949). (Cloth bdg. avail. on request). pap. 12.00 (ISBN 0-8373-2949-3). Natl Learning.

--Activities Specialist. (Career Examination Ser.: C-1074). (Cloth bdg. avail. on request). pap. 10.00 (ISBN 0-8373-1074-1). Natl Learning.

--Actuarial Clerk. (Career Examination Ser.: C-2417). (Cloth bdg. avail. on request). pap. 10.00 (ISBN 0-686-67755-2). Natl Learning.

--Actuary. (Career Examination Ser.: C-7). (Cloth bdg. avail. on request). pap. 12.00 (ISBN 0-8373-0007-X). Natl Learning.

--Addressing Machine Operator. (Career Examination Ser.: C-1892). (Cloth bdg. avail. on request). pap. 8.00 (ISBN 0-8373-1892-0). Natl Learning.

--Addressograph Machine Operator. (Career Examination Ser.: C-1076). (Cloth bdg. avail on request). pap. 8.00 (ISBN 0-8373-1076-8). Natl Learning.

--Administrative Aide. (Career Examination Ser.: C-8). (Cloth bdg. avail on request). pap. 10.00 (ISBN 0-8373-0008-8). Natl Learning.

--Administrative Analyst. (Career Examination Ser.: C-2144). (Cloth bdg. avail. on request). 1977. pap. 12.00 (ISBN 0-8373-2144-1). Natl Learning.

--Administrative Assessor. (Career Examination Ser.: C-2596). (Cloth bdg. avail. on request). pap. 12.00 (ISBN 0-8373-2596-X). Natl Learning.

--Administrative Assistant. (Career Examination Ser.: C-9). (Cloth bdg. avail. on request). pap. 10.00 (ISBN 0-8373-0009-6). Natl Learning.

--Administrative Assistant, One. (Career Examination Ser.: C-1848). (Cloth bdg. avail. on request). pap. 10.00 (ISBN 0-8373-1848-3). Natl Learning.

--Administrative Assistant, Two. (Career Examination Ser.: C-1849). (Cloth bdg. avail. on request). pap. 12.00 (ISBN 0-8373-1849-1). Natl Learning.

--Administrative Auditor of Accounts. (Career Examination Ser.: C-2598). pap. 12.00 (ISBN 0-8373-2598-6); avail. Natl Learning.

--Administrative Business Promotion Coordinator. (Career Examination Ser.: C-2599). (Cloth bdg. avail. on request). pap. 12.00 (ISBN 0-8373-2599-4). Natl Learning.

--Administrative Careers Examination. (Career Examination Ser.: C-69). (Cloth bdg. avail. on request). pap. 10.00 (ISBN 0-8373-0069-X). Natl Learning.

--Administrative Claim Examiner. (Career Examination Ser.: C-2600). (Cloth bdg. avail. on request). pap. 12.00 (ISBN 0-8373-2600-1). Natl Learning.

--Administrative Clerk. (Career Examination Ser.: C-2014). (Cloth bdg. avail. on request). pap. 10.00 (ISBN 0-8373-2014-3). Natl Learning.

--Administrative Clerk (U.S.P.S.) (Career Examination Ser.: C-2101). (Cloth bdg. avail. on request). 1977. pap. 10.00 (ISBN 0-8373-2101-8). Natl Learning.

--Administrative Engineer. (Career Examination Ser.: C-2601). (Cloth bdg. avail. on request). pap. 12.00 (ISBN 0-8373-2601-X). Natl Learning.

--Administrative Fire Alarm Dispatcher. (Career Examination Ser.: C-2602). (Cloth bdg. avail. on request). pap. 12.00 (ISBN 0-8373-2602-8). Natl Learning.

--Administrative Fire Marshall (Uniformed) (Career Examination Ser.: C-2603). (Cloth bdg. avail. on request). pap. 12.00 (ISBN 0-8373-2603-6). Natl Learning.

--Administrative Housing Inspector. (Career Examination Ser.: C-2604). (Cloth bdg. avail. on request). pap. 12.00 (ISBN 0-8373-2604-4). Natl Learning.

--Administrative Housing Manager. (Career Examination Ser.: C-1799). (Cloth bdg. avail. on request). pap. 12.00 (ISBN 0-8373-1799-1). Natl Learning.

--Administrative Housing Superintendent. (Career Examination Ser.: C-1800). (Cloth bdg. avail. on request). pap. 12.00 (ISBN 0-8373-1800-9). Natl Learning.

--Administrative Investigator. (Career Examination Ser.: C-1924). (Cloth bdg. avail. on request). pap. 12.00 (ISBN 0-8373-1924-2). Natl Learning.

--Administrative Park & Recreation Manager. (Career Examination Ser.: C-2606). (Cloth bdg. avail. on request). pap. 12.00 (ISBN 0-8373-2606-0). Natl Learning.

--Administrative Project Coordinator. (Career Examination Ser.: C-1080). (Cloth bdg. avail. on request). pap. 12.00 (ISBN 0-8373-1080-6). Natl Learning.

--Administrative Public Information Specialist. (Career Examination Ser.: C-2607). (Cloth bdg. avail. on request). pap. 12.00 (ISBN 0-8373-2607-9). Natl Learning.

--Administrative Services Clerk. (Career Examination Ser.: C-2869). (Cloth bdg. avail. on request). pap. 10.00 (ISBN 0-8373-2869-1). Natl Learning.

--Administrative Superintendent of Highway Operations. (Career Examination Ser.: C-2608). (Cloth bdg. avail. on request). pap. 12.00 (ISBN 0-8373-2608-7). Natl Learning.

--Adminstrative Attorney. (Career Examination Ser.: C-2597). (Cloth bdg. avail. on request). pap. 12.00 (ISBN 0-8373-2597-8). Natl Learning.

--Admissions Officer. (Career Examination Ser.: C-1083). (Cloth bdg. avail. on request). pap. 12.00 (ISBN 0-8373-1083-0). Natl Learning.

--Adult APL Survey (APL-A) (Admission Test Ser.: ATS-60B). (Cloth bdg. avail. on request). pap. 11.95 (ISBN 0-8373-5060-3). Natl Learning.

--Adult Nurse Practitioner. (Certified Nurse Examination Ser.: CN-1). 21.95 (ISBN 0-8373-6151-6); pap. 13.95 (ISBN 0-8373-6101-X). Natl Learning.

--Affirmative Action Officer. (Career Examination Ser.: C-2647). (Cloth bdg. avail. on request). pap. 10.00 (ISBN 0-8373-2647-8). Natl Learning.

--Affirmative Action Specialist. (Career Examination Ser.: C-2581). (Cloth bdg. avail. on request). pap. 10.00 (ISBN 0-8373-2581-1). Natl Learning.

--Aging Services Representative. (Career Examination Ser.: C-2880). (Cloth bdg. avail. on request). pap. 12.00 (ISBN 0-8373-2880-2). Natl Learning.

--Agriculture. (National Teachers Examination Ser.: NT-20). (Cloth bdg. avail. on request). pap. 11.95 (ISBN 0-8373-8430-3). Natl Learning.

--Air Conditioning & Refrigeration. (Occupational Competency Examination Ser.: OCE-1). (Cloth bdg. avail. on request). pap. 13.95 (ISBN 0-8373-5701-2). Natl Learning.

--Air Pollution Control Engineering Trainee. (Career Examination Ser.: C-1926). (Cloth bdg. avail. on request). pap. 10.00 (ISBN 0-8373-1926-9). Natl Learning.

--Air Traffic Control Specialist - ATCS. (Career Examination Ser.: C-68). (Cloth bdg. avail. on request). pap. 10.00 (ISBN 0-8373-0068-1). Natl Learning.

--Airframe or Powerplant Mechanics. (Occupational Competency Examination Ser.: OCE-2). (Cloth bdg. avail. on request). pap. 13.95 (ISBN 0-8373-5702-0). Natl Learning.

--Airport Attendant. (Career Examination Ser.: C-306). (Cloth bdg. avail. on request). pap. 10.00 (ISBN 0-8373-0306-0). Natl Learning.

--Airport Security Guard. (Career Examination Ser.: C-456). (Cloth bdg. avail. on request). pap. 10.00 (ISBN 0-8373-0456-3). Natl Learning.

--Airport Security Supervisor. (Career Examination Ser.: C-2153). (Cloth bdg. avail. on request). 1976. 10.00 (ISBN 0-8373-2153-0). Natl Learning.

--Alcoholism Counselor. (Career Examination Ser.: C-2145). (Cloth bdg. avail. on request). 1976. pap. 12.00 (ISBN 0-8373-2145-X). Natl Learning.

--Ambulance Attendant. (Career Examination Ser.: C-1088). (Cloth bdg. avail. on request). pap. 10.00 (ISBN 0-8373-1088-1). Natl Learning.

--Ambulance Corpsman. (Career Examination Ser.: C-2650). (Cloth bdg. avail. upon request). pap. 10.00 (ISBN 0-8373-2650-8). Natl Learning.

--AMRA Medical Record Administrator National Registration Examination (RRA) (Admission Test Ser.: ATS-84). (Cloth bdg. avail. on request). pap. 13.95 (ISBN 0-8373-5084-0). Natl Learning.

--Anatomy, Physiology & Microbiology. (College Level Examination Ser.: CLEP-38). (Cloth bdg. avail. on request). 1977. pap. 11.95 (ISBN 0-8373-5388-2). Natl Learning.

--Animal Shelter Supervisor. (Career Examination Ser.: C-2263). (Cloth bdg. avail. on request). pap. 10.00 (ISBN 0-8373-2363-0). Natl Learning.

--Appliance Repair. (Occupational Competency Examination Ser.: OCE-3). (Cloth bdg. avail. on request). pap. 13.95 (ISBN 0-8373-5703-9). Natl Learning.

--Appraisal Investigator. (Career Examination Ser.: C-452). (Cloth bdg. avail. on request). pap. 12.00 (ISBN 0-8373-0452-0). Natl Learning.

--Architect. (Career Examination Ser.: C-17). (Cloth bdg. avail. on request). pap. 12.00 (ISBN 0-8373-0017-7). Natl Learning.

--Architectural Drafting. (Occupational Competency Examination Ser.: OCE-4). 21.95 (ISBN 0-8373-5754-3); pap. 13.95 (ISBN 0-8373-5704-7). Natl Learning.

--Architectural Draftsman. (Career Examination Ser.: C-1092). (Cloth bdg. avail. on request). pap. 10.00 (ISBN 0-8373-1092-X). Natl Learning.

--Area Services Coordinator. (Career Examination Ser.: C-18). (Cloth bdg. avail. on request). pap. 10.00 (ISBN 0-8373-0018-5). Natl Learning.

--Armature Winder. (Career Examination Ser.: C-2481). (Cloth bdg. avail. on request). pap. 10.00 (ISBN 0-8373-2481-5). Natl Learning.

--Art Education. (National Teachers Examination Ser.: NT-13). (Cloth bdg. avail. on request). pap. 11.95 (ISBN 0-8373-8423-0). Natl Learning.

--Assessment Assistant. (Career Examination Ser.: C-2181). (Cloth bdg. avail. on request). pap. 10.00 (ISBN 0-8373-2181-6). Natl Learning.

--Assessment Clerk. (Career Examination Ser.: C-2920). (Cloth bdg. avail. on request). pap. 10.00 (ISBN 0-8373-2920-5). Natl Learning.

--Assistant Accountant. (Career Examination Ser.: C-21). (Cloth bdg. avail. on request). pap. 10.00 (ISBN 0-8373-0021-5). Natl Learning.

--Assistant Accountant-Auditor. (Career Examination Ser.: C-2077). (Cloth bdg. avail. on request). 1977. pap. 10.00 (ISBN 0-8373-2077-1). Natl Learning.

--Assistant Actuary. (Career Examination Ser.: C-22). (Cloth bdg. avail. on request). pap. 10.00 (ISBN 0-8373-0022-3). Natl Learning.

--Assistant Administrator. (Career Examination Ser.: C-1093). (Cloth bdg. avail. on request). pap. 10.00 (ISBN 0-8373-1093-8). Natl Learning.

--Assistant Air Pollution Control Engineer. (Career Examination Ser.: C-1094). (Cloth bdg. avail on request). pap. 10.00 (ISBN 0-8373-1094-6). Natl Learning.

--Assistant Architectural Draftsman. (Career Examination Ser.: C-1095). (Cloth bdg. avail. on request). pap. 10.00 (ISBN 0-8373-1095-4). Natl Learning.

--Assistant Area Manager. (Career Examination Ser.: C-1096). (Cloth bdg. avail. on request). pap. 10.00 (ISBN 0-8373-1096-2). Natl Learning.

--Assistant Area Services Coordinator. (Career Examination Ser.: C-78). (Cloth bdg. avail. on request). pap. 10.00 (ISBN 0-8373-0078-9). Natl Learning.

--Assistant Assessor. (Career Examination Ser.: C-23). (Cloth bdg. avail. on request). pap. 10.00 (ISBN 0-8373-0023-1). Natl Learning.

--Assistant Automotive Shop Supervisor. (Career Examination Ser.: C-529). (Cloth bdg. avail. on request). pap. 12.00 (ISBN 0-8373-0529-2). Natl Learning.

--Assistant Bridge & Tunnel Maintainer. (Career Examination Ser.: C-27). (Cloth bdg. avail. on request). pap. 8.00 (ISBN 0-8373-0027-4). Natl Learning.

--Assistant Bridge Operator Trainee. (Career Examination Ser.: C-79). (Cloth bdg. avail. on request). pap. 8.00 (ISBN 0-8373-0079-7). Natl Learning.

--Assistant Budget Analyst. (Career Examination Ser.: C-1736). (Cloth bdg. avail on request). pap. 10.00 (ISBN 0-8373-1736-3). Natl Learning.

--Assistant Budget Examiner. (Career Examination Ser.: C-28). (Cloth bdg. avail. on request). pap. 10.00 (ISBN 0-8373-0028-2). Natl Learning.

--Assistant Building Custodian. (Career Examination Ser.: C-66). (Cloth bdg. avail. on request). pap. 10.00 (ISBN 0-8373-0066-5). Natl Learning.

--Assistant Building Electrical Engineer. (Career Examination Ser.: C-1909). (Cloth bdg. avail. on request). 1977. pap. 10.00 (ISBN 0-8373-1909-9). Natl Learning.

--Assistant Buildings Superintendent. (Career Examination Ser.: C-1097). (Cloth bdg. avail. on request). pap. 10.00 (ISBN 0-8373-0071-1). Natl Learning.

--Assistant Business Manager. (Career Examination Ser.: C-528). (Cloth bdg. avail. on request). pap. 12.00 (ISBN 0-8373-0528-4). Natl Learning.

--Assistant Business Officer. (Career Examination Ser.: C-2075). (Cloth bdg. avail. on request). 1977. pap. 12.00 (ISBN 0-8373-2075-5). Natl Learning.

--Assistant Cashier. (Career Examination Ser.: C-30). (Cloth bdg. avail. on request). pap. 8.00 (ISBN 0-8373-0030-4). Natl Learning.

--Assistant Clerk. (Career Examination Ser.: C-1099). (Cloth bdg. avail. on request). pap. 8.00 (ISBN 0-8373-1099-7). Natl Learning.

--Assistant Community Development Project Supervisor. (Career Examination Ser.: C-907). (Cloth bdg. avail. on request). pap. 12.00 (ISBN 0-8373-0907-7). Natl Learning.

--Assistant Community Organization Specialist: Urban Renewal. (Career Examination Ser.: C-1100). (Cloth bdg. avail. on request). pap. 10.00 (ISBN 0-8373-1100-4). Natl Learning.

--Assistant Court Clerk. (Career Examination Ser.: C-34). (Cloth bdg. avail. on request). pap. 10.00 (ISBN 0-8373-0034-7). Natl Learning.

--Assistant Custodial Work Supervisor. (Career Examination Ser.: C-2916). (Cloth bdg. avail. on request). pap. 10.00 (ISBN 0-8373-2916-7). Natl Learning.

--Assistant Custodian-Engineer. (Career Examination Ser.: C-36). (Cloth bdg. avail. on request). pap. 10.00 (ISBN 0-8373-0036-3). Natl Learning.

--Assistant Deputy Superintendent of Women's Prisons. (Career Examination Ser.: C-1697). (Cloth bdg. avail on request). pap. 12.00 (ISBN 0-8373-1697-9). Natl Learning.

--Assistant Deputy Warden. (Career Examination Ser.: C-1698). (Cloth bdg. avail on request). pap. 12.00 (ISBN 0-8373-1698-7). Natl Learning.

--Assistant Director (Child Welfare) (Career Examination Ser.: C-1809). (Cloth bdg. avail. on request). pap. 12.00 (ISBN 0-8373-1809-2). Natl Learning.

--Assistant Director of Custodial & Security Services. (Career Examination Ser.: C-2922). (Cloth bdg. avail. on request). pap. 14.00 (ISBN 0-8373-2922-1). Natl Learning.

--Assistant Director of Maintenance (Sewer District) (Career Examination Ser.: C-2908). (Cloth bdg. avail. on request). pap. 14.00 (ISBN 0-8373-2908-6). Natl Learning.

--Assistant Director of Nursing Care. (Career Examination Ser.: C-2858). (Cloth bdg. avail. on request). 1980. pap. 12.00 (ISBN 0-8373-2858-6). Natl Learning.

--Assistant Director of Traffic Control. (Career Examination Ser.: C-1876). (Cloth bdg. avail. on request). pap. 12.00 (ISBN 0-8373-1876-9). Natl Learning.

--Assistant Director of Traffic Safety. (Career Examination Ser.: C-458). (Cloth bdg. avail. on request). pap. 14.00 (ISBN 0-8373-0458-X). Natl Learning.

--Assistant Director (Welfare) (Career Examination Ser.: C-1802). (Cloth bdg. avail. on request). pap. 12.00 (ISBN 0-8373-1802-5). Natl Learning.
--Assistant Electrical Engineer. (Career Examination Ser.: C-37). (Cloth bdg. avail. on request). pap. 10.00 (ISBN 0-8373-0037-1). Natl Learning.
--Assistant Electronic Technician. (Career Examination Ser.: C-1982). (Cloth bdg. avail. on request). pap. 10.00 (ISBN 0-8373-1982-X). Natl Learning.
--Assistant Engineering Technician. (Career Examination Ser.: C-931). (Cloth bdg. avail. on request). pap. 10.00 (ISBN 0-8373-0931-X). Natl Learning.
--Assistant Federal & State Aid Coordinator. (Career Examination Ser.: C-1104). (Cloth bdg. avail. on request). pap. 10.00 (ISBN 0-8373-1104-7). Natl Learning.
--Assistant Fire Marshall. (Career Examination Ser.: C-1105). (Cloth bdg. avail on request). pap. 10.00 (ISBN 0-8373-1105-5). Natl Learning.
--Assistant Foreman. (Career Examination Ser.: C-38). (Cloth bdg. avail. on request). pap. 10.00 (ISBN 0-8373-0038-X). Natl Learning.
--Assistant Foreman (Department of Sanitation) (Career Examination Ser.: C-39). (Cloth bdg. avail. on request). pap. 10.00 (ISBN 0-8373-0039-8). Natl Learning.
--Assistant Gardener. (Career Examination Ser.: C-40). (Cloth bdg. avail. on request). pap. 8.00 (ISBN 0-8373-0040-1). Natl Learning.
--Assistant Head Custodian. (Career Examination Ser.: C-1822). (Cloth bdg. avail. on request). pap. 10.00 (ISBN 0-8373-1822-X). Natl Learning.
--Assistant Health Insurance Administrator. (Career Examination Ser.: C-358). (Cloth bdg. avail. on request). pap. 12.00 (ISBN 0-686-84412-2). Natl Learning.
--Assistant Heating & Ventilating Engineer. (Career Examination Ser.: C-1912). (Cloth bdg. avail. on request). pap. 10.00 (ISBN 0-8373-1912-9). Natl Learning.
--Assistant Hospital Administrator. (Career Examination Ser.: C-1107). (Cloth bdg. avail. on request). pap. 10.00 (ISBN 0-8373-1107-1). Natl Learning.
--Assistant Housing Manager. (Career Examination Ser.: C-41). (Cloth bdg. avail. on request). pap. 10.00 (ISBN 0-8373-0041-X). Natl Learning.
--Assistant Landscape Architect. (Career Examination Ser.: C-42). (Cloth bdg. avail. on request). pap. 10.00 (ISBN 0-8373-0042-8). Natl Learning.
--Assistant Landscape Engineer. (Career Examination Ser.: C-43). (Cloth bdg. avail. on request). pap. 10.00 (ISBN 0-8373-0043-6). Natl Learning.
--Assistant Library Director. (Career Examination Ser.: C-1108). (Cloth bdg. avail. on request). pap. 12.00 (ISBN 0-8373-1108-X). Natl Learning.
--Assistant Library Director 3. (Career Examination Ser.: C-2785). (Cloth bdg. avail. on request). 1980. pap. 12.00 (ISBN 0-8373-2785-7). Natl Learning.
--Assistant Library Director 4. (Career Examination Ser.: C-2786). (Cloth bdg. avail. on request). 1980. pap. 12.00 (ISBN 0-8373-2786-5). Natl Learning.
--Assistant Library Director 5. (Career Examination Ser.: C-2787). (Cloth bdg. avail. on request). 1980. pap. 12.00 (ISBN 0-8373-2787-3). Natl Learning.
--Assistant Park Supervisor. (Career Examination Ser.: C-1564). (Cloth bdg. avail. on request). pap. 10.00 (ISBN 0-8373-1564-6). Natl Learning.
--Assistant Payroll Supervisor. (Career Examination Ser.: C-1110). (Cloth bdg. avail. on request). pap. 10.00 (ISBN 0-8373-1110-1). Natl Learning.
--Assistant Plan Examiner. (Career Examination Ser.: C-932). (Cloth bdg. avail. on request). pap. 10.00 (ISBN 0-8373-0932-8). Natl Learning.
--Assistant Planner. (Career Examination Ser.: C-933). (Cloth bdg. avail. on request). pap. 10.00 (ISBN 0-8373-0933-6). Natl Learning.
--Assistant Power Plant Operator. (Career Examination Ser.: C-1905). (Cloth bdg. avail. on request). 1977. pap. 10.00 (ISBN 0-8373-1905-6). Natl Learning.
--Assistant Press Secretary. (Career Examination Ser.: C-1111). (Cloth bdg. avail. on request). pap. 10.00 (ISBN 0-8373-1111-X). Natl Learning.
--Assistant Principal: Elementary School. (Teachers License Examination Ser.: S-1). (Cloth bdg. avail. on request). pap. 17.95 (ISBN 0-8373-8101-0). Natl Learning.
--Assistant Principal: Jr. H.S. (Teachers License Examination Ser.: S-2). (Cloth bdg. avail. on request). pap. 17.95 (ISBN 0-8373-8102-9). Natl Learning.
--Assistant Procurement Coordinator. (Career Examination Ser.: C-916). (Cloth bdg. avail. on request). pap. 12.00 (ISBN 0-8373-0916-6). Natl Learning.
--Assistant Program Manager. (Career Examination Ser.: C-934). (Cloth bdg. avail. on request). pap. 10.00 (ISBN 0-8373-0934-4). Natl Learning.
--Assistant Project Coordinator. (Career Examination Ser.). (Cloth bdg. avail. on request). pap. 10.00 (ISBN 0-8373-2590-0). Natl Learning.
--Assistant Public Health Engineer. (Career Examination Ser.: C-2232). (Cloth bdg. avail. on request). pap. 10.00 (ISBN 0-8373-2232-4). Natl Learning.
--Assistant Radiologist. (Career Examination Ser.: C-1112). (Cloth bdg. avail. on request). pap. 12.00 (ISBN 0-8373-1112-8). Natl Learning.
--Assistant Recreation Supervisor. (Career Examination Ser.: C-45). (Cloth bdg. avail on request). pap. 10.00 (ISBN 0-8373-0045-2). Natl Learning.
--Assistant Resident Buildings Superintendent. (Career Examination Ser.: C-1058). (Cloth bdg. avail. on request). pap. 10.00 (ISBN 0-8373-1058-X). Natl Learning.
--Assistant Retirement Benefits Examiner. (Career Examination Ser.: C-1557). (Cloth bdg. avail on request). pap. 10.00 (ISBN 0-8373-1557-3). Natl Learning.
--Assistant Sanitary Engineer. (Career Examination Ser.: C-1969). (Cloth bdg. avail. on request). pap. 10.00 (ISBN 0-8373-1969-2). Natl Learning.
--Assistant School Custodian-Engineer. (Career Examination Ser.: C-46). (Cloth bdg. avail. on request). pap. 10.00 (ISBN 0-8373-0046-0). Natl Learning.
--Assistant School Transportation Supervisor. (Career Examination Ser.: C-112). (Cloth bdg. avail. on request). pap. 12.00 (ISBN 0-8373-0112-2). Natl Learning.
--Assistant Signal Circuit Engineer. (Career Examination Ser.: C-47). (Cloth bdg. avail. on request). pap. 10.00 (ISBN 0-8373-0047-9). Natl Learning.
--Assistant Social Worker. (Career Examination Ser.: C-1113). (Cloth bdg. avail. on request). 8.00 (ISBN 0-8373-1113-6). Natl Learning.
--Assistant Statistician. (Career Examination Ser.: C-49). (Cloth bdg. avail. on request). pap. 10.00 (ISBN 0-8373-0049-5). Natl Learning.
--Assistant Surveyor. (Career Examination Ser.: C-1972). (Cloth bdg. avail. on request). pap. 10.00 (ISBN 0-8373-1792-4). Natl Learning.
--Assistant Teacher. (Career Examination Ser.: C-1118). (Cloth bdg. avail. on request). pap. 10.00 (ISBN 0-8373-1118-7). Natl Learning.
--Assistant Tenant Supervisor. (Career Examination Ser.: C-542). (Cloth bdg. avail. on request). pap. 10.00 (ISBN 0-8373-0542-X). Natl Learning.
--Assistant to Assessor. (Career Examination Ser.: C-2182). (Cloth bdg. avail. on request). pap. 10.00 (ISBN 0-8373-2182-4). Natl Learning.
--Assistant to Commissioner. (Career Examination Ser.: C-1119). (Cloth bdg. avail. on request). pap. 12.00 (ISBN 0-8373-1119-5). Natl Learning.
--Assistant to Superintendent. (Career Examination Ser.: C-2210). (Cloth bdg. avail on request). pap. 12.00 (ISBN 0-8373-2210-3). Natl Learning.
--Assistant Tower Engineer. (Career Examination Ser.: C-211). (Cloth bdg. avail. on request). pap. 12.00 (ISBN 0-8373-0211-0). Natl Learning.
--Assistant Urban Designer. (Career Examination Ser.: C-1120). (Cloth bdg. avail. on request). pap. 10.00 (ISBN 0-8373-1120-9). Natl Learning.
--Assistant Water Maintenance Foreman. (Career Examination Ser.: C-2919). (Cloth bdg. avail. on request). pap. 12.00 (ISBN 0-8373-2919-1). Natl Learning.
--Assistant Water Service Foreman. (Career Examination Ser.: C-2924). (Cloth bdg. avail. on request). pap. 12.00 (ISBN 0-8373-2924-8). Natl Learning.
--Assistant Workmen's Compensation Examiner. (Career Examination Ser.: C-1643). (Cloth bdg. avail. on request). pap. 10.00 (ISBN 0-8373-1643-X). Natl Learning.
--Assistant Youth Guidance Technician. (Career Examination Ser.: C-938). (Cloth bdg. avail. on request). pap. 10.00 (ISBN 0-8373-0938-7). Natl Learning.
--Associate Accountant. (Career Examination Ser.: C-1798). (Cloth bdg. avail. on request). pap. 12.00 (ISBN 0-8373-1798-3). Natl Learning.
--Associate Attorney. (Career Examination Ser.: C-2269). (Cloth bdg. avail. on request). 1977. pap. 12.00 (ISBN 0-8373-2269-3). Natl Learning.
--Associate Biostatistician. (Career Examination Ser.: C-2292). (Cloth bdg. avail. on request). 1977. pap. 12.00 (ISBN 0-8373-2292-8). Natl Learning.
--Associate Capital Program Analyst. (Career Examination Ser.: C-2039). (Cloth bdg. avail. on request). pap. 12.00 (ISBN 0-8373-2039-9). Natl Learning.
--Associate Computer Programmer. (Career Examination Ser.: C-2206). (Cloth bdg. avail. on request). pap. 12.00 (ISBN 0-8373-2206-5). Natl Learning.
--Associate Computer Systems Analyst. (Career Examination Ser.: C-939). (Cloth bdg. avail. on request). pap. 12.00 (ISBN 0-685-17477-8). Natl Learning.
--Associate Court Clerk. (Career Examination Ser.: C-2587). (Cloth bdg. avail. on request). pap. 12.00 (ISBN 0-8373-2587-0). Natl Learning.
--Associate Information & Referral Coordinator. (Career Examination Ser.: C-2926). (Cloth bdg. avail. on request). pap. 12.00 (ISBN 0-8373-2926-4). Natl Learning.
--Associate Occupational Analyst. (Career Examination Ser.: C-2550). (Cloth bdg. avail. on request). pap. 12.00 (ISBN 0-8373-2550-1). Natl Learning.
--Associate Park Service Worker. (Career Examination Ser.). (Cloth bdg. avail. on request). pap. 10.00 (ISBN 0-8373-2469-6). Natl Learning.
--Associate Real Property Manager. (Career Examination Ser.: C-2890). (Cloth bdg. avail. on request). pap. 14.00 (ISBN 0-8373-2890-X). Natl Learning.
--Associate Social Services Management Specialist. (Career Examination Ser.: C-454). (Cloth bdg. avail. on request). pap. 14.00 (ISBN 0-8373-0454-7). Natl Learning.
--Associate Traffic Enforcement Agent. (Career Examination Ser.: C-215). (Cloth bdg. avail. on request). pap. 12.00 (ISBN 0-8373-0215-3). Natl Learning.
--Associate Worker's Compensation Review Analyst. (Career Examination Ser.: C-309). (Cloth bdg. avail. on request). pap. 12.00 (ISBN 0-8373-0309-5). Natl Learning.
--Attendance Teacher. (Teachers License Examination Ser.: T-2a). (Cloth bdg. avail. on request). pap. 13.95 (ISBN 0-8373-8002-2). Natl Learning.
--Attendance Teacher (Spanish) (Teachers License Examination Ser.: T-2b). (Span., Cloth bdg. avail. on request). pap. 13.95 (ISBN 0-686-66501-5). Natl Learning.
--Attorney. (Career Examination Ser.: C-56). (Cloth bdg. avail. on request). pap. 12.00 (ISBN 0-8373-0056-8). Natl Learning.
--Attorney-Departmental. (Career Examination Ser.: C-2234). (Cloth bdg. avail. on request). pap. 12.00 (ISBN 0-8373-2234-0). Natl Learning.
--Attorney Trainee. (Career Examination Ser.: C-57). (Cloth bdg. avail. on request). pap. 10.00 (ISBN 0-8373-0057-6). Natl Learning.
--Audio-Visual Aide. (Career Examination Ser.: C-2903). (Cloth bdg. avail. on request). pap. 12.00 (ISBN 0-8373-2903-5). Natl Learning.
--Audio-Visual Specialist. (Career Examination Ser.: C-1826). (Cloth bdg. avail. on request). pap. 12.00 (ISBN 0-8373-1826-2). Natl Learning.
--Audio-Visual Technician. (Career Examination Ser.: C-1894). (Cloth bdg. avail. on request). 1977. pap. 10.00 (ISBN 0-8373-1894-7). Natl Learning.
--Audiology. (National Teachers Examination Ser.: NT-34). (Cloth bdg. avail. on request). pap. 11.95 (ISBN 0-8373-8444-3). Natl Learning.
--Audit Clerk. (Career Examination Ser.: C-1907). (Cloth bdg. avail. on request). pap. 10.00 (ISBN 0-8373-1907-2). Natl Learning.
--Auditing Assistant. (Career Examination Ser.: C-2092). (Cloth bdg. avail. on request). 1977. pap. 10.00 (ISBN 0-8373-2092-5). Natl Learning.
--Auditor Trainee. (Career Examination Ser.: C-2404). (Cloth bdg. avail. on request). pap. 10.00 (ISBN 0-8373-2404-1). Natl Learning.
--Auto Body Repair. (Occupational Competency Examination Ser.: OCE-5). (Cloth bdg. avail. on request). 13.95 (ISBN 0-8373-5705-5). Natl Learning.
--Auto Body Repairman. (Career Examination Ser.: C-1125). (Cloth bdg. avail. on request). pap. 10.00 (ISBN 0-8373-1125-X). Natl Learning.
--Auto Engineman. (Career Examination Ser.: C-61). (Cloth bdg. avail. on request). pap. 10.00 (ISBN 0-8373-0061-4). Natl Learning.
--Auto Equipment Inspector. (Career Examination Ser.: C-1126). (Cloth bdg. avail. on request). pap. 10.00 (ISBN 0-8373-1126-8). Natl Learning.
--Auto Machinist. (Career Examination Ser.: C-62). (Cloth bdg. avail. on request). pap. 10.00 (ISBN 0-8373-0062-2). Natl Learning.
--Auto Maintenance Coordinator. (Career Examination Ser.: C-1127). (Cloth bdg. avail. on request). pap. 10.00 (ISBN 0-8373-1127-6). Natl Learning.
--Auto Mechanic. (Career Examination Ser.: C-63). (Cloth bdg. avail. on request). pap. 10.00 (ISBN 0-8373-0063-0). Natl Learning.
--Auto Mechanic (Diesel) (Career Examination Ser.: C-64). (Cloth bdg. avail. on request). pap. 10.00 (ISBN 0-8373-0064-9). Natl Learning.
--Auto Mechanics. (Occupational Competency Examination Ser.: OCE-7). (Cloth bdg. avail. on request). 13.95 (ISBN 0-8373-5707-1). Natl Learning.
--Auto Parts Storekeeper. (Career Examination Ser.: C-1128). (Cloth bdg. avail. on request). pap. 10.00 (ISBN 0-8373-1128-4). Natl Learning.
--Auto Shop Foreman. (Career Examination Ser.: C-1129). (Cloth bdg. avail. on request). pap. 10.00 (ISBN 0-8373-1129-2). Natl Learning.
--Auto Shop Supervisor. (Career Examination Ser.: C-1130). (Cloth bdg. avail. on request). pap. 10.00 (ISBN 0-8373-0048-7). Natl Learning.
--Automatic Heating. (Occupational Competency Examination Ser.: OCE-6). 21.95 (ISBN 0-8373-5756-X); pap. 13.95 (ISBN 0-8373-5706-3). Natl Learning.
--Automotive Facilities Inspector. (Career Examination Ser.: C-2213). (Cloth bdg. avail. on request). pap. 10.00 (ISBN 0-685-60478-0). Natl Learning.
--Automotive Maintenance Supervisor. (Career Examination Ser.: C-2096). (Cloth bdg. avail. on request). 1977. pap. 10.00 (ISBN 0-8373-2096-8). Natl Learning.
--Automotive Mechanic. (Career Examination Ser.: C-1131). (Cloth bdg. avail. on request). pap. 10.00 (ISBN 0-8373-1131-4). Natl Learning.
--Automotive Serviceman. (Career Examination Ser.: C-65). (Cloth bdg. avail. on request). pap. 10.00 (ISBN 0-8373-0065-7). Natl Learning.
--Auxiliary Teacher - Elementary School. (Teachers License Examination Ser.: T-3). (Cloth bdg. avail. on request). pap. 13.95 (ISBN 0-8373-8003-0). Natl Learning.
--Bank Examiner. (Career Examination Ser.: C-105). (Cloth bdg. avail. on request). pap. 12.00 (ISBN 0-8373-0105-X). Natl Learning.
--Basic Skills Assessment Program (BSAP) (Admission Test Ser.: ATS-59). (Cloth bdg. avail. on request). pap. 11.95 (ISBN 0-8373-5059-X). Natl Learning.
--Bay Constable I. (Career Examination Ser.: C-2524). (Cloth bdg. avail. on request). pap. 10.00 (ISBN 0-8373-2524-2). Natl Learning.
--Bay Constable II. (Career Examination Ser.: C-885). (Cloth bdg. avail. on request). pap. 12.00 (ISBN 0-8373-0885-2). Natl Learning.
--Beach Supervisor. (Career Examination Ser.: C-836). (Cloth bdg. avail. on request). pap. 10.00 (ISBN 0-8373-0836-4). Natl Learning.
--Behavioral Sciences for Nurses. (College Level Examination Ser.: CLEP-39). (Cloth bdg. avail. on request). 1977. pap. 11.95 (ISBN 0-8373-5389-0). Natl Learning.
--Beverage Control Investigator. (Career Examination Ser.: C-918). (Cloth bdg. avail. on request). pap. 10.00 (ISBN 0-8373-0918-2). Natl Learning.
--Bilingual Common Branches (1-6) (Spanish) Elementary School. (Teachers License Examination Ser.: T-68). (Cloth bdg. avail. on request). pap. 13.95 (ISBN 0-686-60486-5). Natl Learning.
--Bilingual Teacher in School & Community Relations. (Teachers License Examination Ser.: T-66). (Cloth bdg. avail. on request). pap. 13.95 (ISBN 0-8373-8086-3). Natl Learning.
--Bindery Worker. (Career Examination Ser.: C-84). (Cloth bdg. avail. on request). pap. 8.00 (ISBN 0-8373-0084-3). Natl Learning.
--Bingo Control Investigator. (Career Examination Ser.: C-106). (Cloth bdg. avail. on request). pap. 10.00 (ISBN 0-8373-0106-8). Natl Learning.
--Bingo Inspector. (Career Examination Ser.: C-846). (Cloth bdg. avail. on request). pap. 10.00 (ISBN 0-8373-0846-1). Natl Learning.
--Biological Aide. (Career Examination Ser.: C-86). (Cloth bdg. avail. on request). pap. 10.00 (ISBN 0-8373-0086-X). Natl Learning.
--Biological Sciences. (Graduate Record Area Examination Ser.: GRE-41). (Cloth bdg. avail. on request). pap. 13.95 (ISBN 0-8373-5241-X). Natl Learning.
--Biology. (Graduate Record Examination Ser.: GRE-1). (Cloth bdg. avail. on request). pap. 13.95 (ISBN 0-8373-5201-0). Natl Learning.
--Biology & General Science. (National Teachers Examination Ser.: NT-3). (Cloth bdg. avail. on request). pap. 11.95 (ISBN 0-8373-8413-3). Natl Learning.
--Biology & General Science - Sr. H.S. (Teachers License Examination Ser.: T-4). (Cloth bdg. avail. on request). pap. 13.95 (ISBN 0-8373-8004-9). Natl Learning.
--Biostatistician. (Career Examination Ser.: C-1135). (Cloth bdg. avail. on request). pap. 12.00 (ISBN 0-8373-1135-7). Natl Learning.
--Blacksmith's Helper. (Career Examination Ser.: C-108). (Cloth bdg. avail. on request). pap. 8.00 (ISBN 0-8373-0108-4). Natl Learning.
--Blind. (Teachers License Examination Ser.: T-5). (Cloth bdg. avail. on request). pap. 13.95 (ISBN 0-8373-8005-7). Natl Learning.
--Boiler Inspector. (Career Examination Ser.: C-87). (Cloth bdg. avail. on request). pap. 10.00 (ISBN 0-8373-0087-8). Natl Learning.
--Boiler Room Helper. (Career Examination Ser.: C-1138). (Cloth bdg. avail. on request). pap. 8.00 (ISBN 0-8373-1138-1). Natl Learning.
--Boilermaker. (Career Examination Ser.: C-109). (Cloth bdg. avail. on request). pap. 10.00 (ISBN 0-8373-0109-2). Natl Learning.
--Bookbinder. (Career Examination Ser.: C-88). (Cloth bdg. avail. on request). pap. 8.00 (ISBN 0-8373-0088-6). Natl Learning.
--Bookkeeping Machine Supervisor. (Career Examination Ser.: C-1140). (Cloth bdg. avail. on request). pap. 10.00 (ISBN 0-8373-1140-3). Natl Learning.
--Border Patrol Agent. (Career Examination Ser.: C-115). (Cloth bdg. avail. on request). pap. 10.00 (ISBN 0-8373-0115-7). Natl Learning.
--Border Patrol Inspector. (Career Examination Ser.: C-90). (Cloth bdg. avail. on request). pap. 10.00 (ISBN 0-8373-0090-8). Natl Learning.
--Border Patrolman. (Career Examination Ser.: C-1973). (Cloth bdg. avail. on request). pap. 10.00 (ISBN 0-8373-1973-0). Natl Learning.
--Bricklayer. (Career Examination Ser.: C-110). (Cloth bdg. avail. on request). pap. 10.00 (ISBN 0-8373-0110-6). Natl Learning.
--Bridge & Tunnel Lieutenant. (Career Examination Ser.: C-111). (Cloth bdg. avail. on request). pap. 10.00 (ISBN 0-8373-0111-4). Natl Learning.
--Bridge & Tunnel Officer. (Career Examination Ser.: C-95). (Cloth bdg. avail. on request). pap. 10.00 (ISBN 0-8373-0095-9). Natl Learning.

--Bridge & Tunnel Supervisor. (Career Examination Ser.: C-2222). (Cloth bdg. avail. on request). pap. 10.00 (ISBN 0-8373-2222-7). Natl Learning.

--Bridge Maintenance Supervisor. (Career Examination Ser.: C-2289). (Cloth bdg. avail. on request). 1977. pap. 10.00 (ISBN 0-8373-2289-8). Natl Learning.

--Bridge Maintenance Supervisor I. (Career Examination Ser.: C-855). (Cloth bdg. avail. on request). pap. 12.00 (ISBN 0-8373-0855-0). Natl Learning.

--Bridge Maintenance Supervisor II. (Career Examination Ser.: C-856). (Cloth bdg. avail. on request). pap. 12.00 (ISBN 0-8373-0856-9). Natl Learning.

--Bridge Maintenance Supervisor III. (Career Examination Ser.: C-857). (Cloth bdg. avil. on request). pap. 14.00 (ISBN 0-8373-0857-7). Natl Learning.

--Bridge Mechanic. (Career Examination Ser.: C-1141). (Cloth bdg. avail. on request). pap. 8.00 (ISBN 0-8373-1141-1). Natl Learning.

--Bridge Operations Supervisor. (Career Examination Ser.: C-1142). (Cloth bdg. avail. on request). pap. 10.00 (ISBN 0-8373-1142-X). Natl Learning.

--Bridge Repair Supervisor. (Career Examination Ser.: C-2288). (Cloth bdg. avail. on request). 1977. pap. 10.00 (ISBN 0-8373-2288-X). Natl Learning.

--Budget Assistant (USPS) (Career Examination Ser.: C-848). (Cloth bdg. avail. on reqest). pap. 10.00 (ISBN 0-8373-0848-8). Natl Learning.

--Budget Director. (Career Examination Ser.: C-2648). (Cloth bdg. avail. on request). pap. 12.00 (ISBN 0-8373-2648-6). Natl Learning.

--Budget Supervisor. (Career Examination Ser.: C-2684). (Cloth bdg. avail. on request). pap. 12.00 (ISBN 0-8373-2684-2). Natl Learning.

--Budget Technician. (Career Examination Ser.: C-2170). (Cloth bdg. avail. on request). 1976. pap. 10.00 (ISBN 0-8373-2170-0). Natl Learning.

--Building & Zone Administrator. (Career Examination Ser.: C-2342). (Cloth bdg. avail. on request). pap. 12.00 (ISBN 0-8373-2342-8). Natl Learning.

--Building Construction Estimator. (Career Examination Ser.: C-1145). (Cloth bdg. avail. on request). pap. 10.00 (ISBN 0-8373-1145-4). Natl Learning.

--Building Custodian. (Career Examination Ser.: C-99). (Cloth bdg. avail. on request). pap. 10.00 (ISBN 0-8373-0099-1). Natl Learning.

--Building Maintenance. (Occupational Competency Examination Ser.: OCE-8). (Cloth bdg. avail. on request). pap. 13.95 (ISBN 0-8373-5708-X). Natl Learning.

--Building Maintenance Foreman. (Career Examination Ser.: C-1147). (Cloth bdg. avail. on request). pap. 10.00 (ISBN 0-8373-1147-0). Natl Learning.

--Building Maintenance Supervisor. (Career Examination Ser.: C-1148). (Cloth bdg. avail. on request). pap. 10.00 (ISBN 0-8373-1148-9). Natl Learning.

--Building Mechanical Engineer. (Career Examination Ser.: C-2571). (Cloth bdg. avail. on request). pap. 12.00 (ISBN 0-8373-2571-4). Natl Learning.

--Building Plan Examiner. (Career Examination Ser.: C-1150). (Cloth bdg. avail. on request). pap. 10.00 (ISBN 0-8373-1150-0). Natl Learning.

--Building Structural Engineer. (Career Examination Ser.: C-2568). (Cloth bdg. avail. on request). pap. 12.00 (ISBN 0-8373-2568-4). Natl Learning.

--Business Assistant. (Career Examination Ser.: C-2885). (Cloth bdg. avail. on request). pap. 10.00 (ISBN 0-8373-2885-3). Natl Learning.

--Business Education. (National Teachers Examination Ser.: NT-10). (Cloth bdg. avail. on request). pap. 11.95 (ISBN 0-8373-8420-6). Natl Learning.

--Business Machine Maintainer & Repairer. (Career Examination Ser.: C-1155). (Cloth bdg. avail. on request). pap. 8.00 (ISBN 0-8373-1155-1). Natl Learning.

--Business Machine Supervisor. (Career Examination Ser.: C-1897). (Cloth bdg. avail. on request). pap. 10.00 (ISBN 0-8373-1897-1). Natl Learning.

--Business Manager. (Career Examination Ser.: C-1898). (Cloth bdg. avail. on request). pap. 12.00 (ISBN 0-8373-1898-X). Natl Learning.

--Cabinetmaking & Millwork. (Occupational Competency Examination Ser.: OCE-9). (Cloth bdg. avail. on request). pap. 13.95 (ISBN 0-8373-5709-8). Natl Learning.

--Cable Slicer. (Career Examination Ser.: C-1624). (Cloth bdg. avail. on request). pap. 8.00 (ISBN 0-8373-1624-3). Natl Learning.

--Cafeteria Supervisor. (Career Examination Ser.: C-1157). (Cloth bdg. avail. on request). pap. 10.00 (ISBN 0-8373-1157-8). Natl Learning.

--California High School Proficiency Examination. (Admission Test Ser.: ATS-39). (Cloth bdg. avail. on request). pap. 11.95 (ISBN 0-8373-5039-5). Natl Learning.

--Campus Public Safety Officer I. (Career Examination Ser.: C-881). (Cloth bdg. avail. on request). pap. 10.00 (ISBN 0-8373-0881-X). Natl Learning.

--Campus Public Safety Officer II. (Career Examination Ser.: C-882). (Cloth bdg. avail. on request). pap. 12.00 (ISBN 0-8373-0882-8). Natl Learning.

--Campus Security Guard I. (Career Examination Ser.: C-565). (Cloth bdg. avail. on request). pap. 10.00 (ISBN 0-8373-0565-9). Natl Learning.

--Campus Security Guard II. (Career Examination Ser.: C-566). (Cloth bdg. avail. on request). pap. 12.00 (ISBN 0-8373-0566-7). Natl Learning.

--Campus Security Guard III. (Career Examination Ser.: C-567). (Cloth bdg. avail. on request). pap. 12.00 (ISBN 0-8373-0567-5). Natl Learning.

--Campus Security Officer. (Career Examination Ser.: C-2260). (Cloth bdg. avail. on request). 1977. pap. 10.00 (ISBN 0-8373-2260-X). Natl Learning.

--Campus Security Officer One. (Career Examination Ser.: C-2261). (Cloth bdg. avail. on request). pap. 10.00 (ISBN 0-8373-2261-8). Natl Learning.

--Campus Security Officer Trainee. (Career Examination Ser.: C-2081). (Cloth bdg. avail. on request). 1977. pap. 10.00 (ISBN 0-8373-2081-X). Natl Learning.

--Capital Police Officer. (Career Examination Ser.: C-2264). (Cloth bdg. avail. on request). 1977. pap. 10.00 (ISBN 0-8373-2264-2). Natl Learning.

--Car Cleaner. (Career Examination Ser.: C-181). (Cloth bdg. avail. on request). pap. 8.00 (ISBN 0-8373-0181-5). Natl Learning.

--Car Maintainer - Group A. (Career Examination Ser.: C-122). (Cloth bdg. avail. on request). pap. 8.00 (ISBN 0-8373-0122-X). Natl Learning.

--Car Maintainer - Group B. (Career Examination Ser.: C-123). (Cloth bdg. avail. on request). pap. 8.00 (ISBN 0-8373-0123-8). Natl Learning.

--Car Maintainer - Group C. (Career Examination Ser.: C-182). (Cloth bdg. avail. on request). pap. 8.00 (ISBN 0-8373-0182-3). Natl Learning.

--Car Maintainer - Group D. (Career Examination Ser.: C-183). (Cloth bdg. avail. on request4). pap. 8.00 (ISBN 0-8373-0183-1). Natl Learning.

--Car Maintainer - Group E. (Career Examination Ser.: C-184). (Cloth bdg. avail. on request). pap. 8.00 (ISBN 0-8373-0184-X). Natl Learning.

--Car Maintainer - Group F. (Career Examination Ser.: C-185). (Cloth bdg. avail. on request). pap. 8.00 (ISBN 0-8373-0185-8). Natl Learning.

--Carpentry. (Occupational Competency Examination Ser.: OCE-10). (Cloth bdg. avail. on request). pap. 13.95 (ISBN 0-8373-5710-1). Natl Learning.

--Cartographer-Draftsman. (Career Examination Ser.: C-1160). (Cloth bdg. avail. on request). pap. 10.00 (ISBN 0-8373-1160-8). Natl Learning.

--Casework Supervisor. (Career Examination Ser.: C-2932). (Cloth bdg. avail. on request). pap. 12.00 (ISBN 0-8373-2932-9). Natl Learning.

--Caseworker Aide. (Career Examination Ser.: C-419). (Cloth bdg. avail. on request). pap. 10.00 (ISBN 0-8373-0419-9). Natl Learning.

--Caseworker One. (Career Examination Ser.: C-129). (Cloth bdg. avail. on request). pap. 10.00 (ISBN 0-8373-0129-7). Natl Learning.

--Cashier. (Career Examination Ser.: C-131). (Cloth bdg. avail. on request). pap. 10.00 (ISBN 0-8373-0131-9). Natl Learning.

--Cashier - Cashier I. (Career Examination Ser.: C-1327). (Cloth bdg. avail. on request). pap. 10.00 (ISBN 0-8373-1327-9). Natl Learning.

--Cashier II. (Career Examination Ser.: C-2899). (Cloth bdg. avail. on request). pap. 12.00 (ISBN 0-8373-2899-3). Natl Learning.

--Cashier-Transit Authority. (Career Examination Ser.: C-1787). (Cloth bdg. avail. on request). 1977. pap. 8.00 (ISBN 0-8373-1787-8). Natl Learning.

--Certified Electronic Technician. (Admission Test Ser.: ATS-38). (Cloth bdg. avail. on request). 1977. pap. 11.95 (ISBN 0-8373-5038-7). Natl Learning.

--Certified Laboratory Assistant. (Career Examination Ser.: C-179). (Cloth bdg. avail. on request). pap. 10.00 (ISBN 0-8373-0179-3). Natl Learning.

--Certified Public Accountant Examination (CPA) (Admission Test Ser.: ATS-71). (Cloth bdg. avail. on request). pap. 19.95 (ISBN 0-8373-5071-9). Natl Learning.

--Certified Safety Professional Examination (CSP) (Admission Test Ser.: ATS-72). (Cloth bdg. avail. on request). pap. 17.95 (ISBN 0-8373-5072-7). Natl Learning.

--Certified Shorthand Reporter. (Career Examination Ser.: C-133). (Cloth bdg. avail. on request). pap. 10.00 (ISBN 0-8373-0133-5). Natl Learning.

--Chemical Specialist in Adult Psychiatric & Mental Health Nursing. (Certified Nurse Examination Ser.: CN-14). 21.95 (ISBN 0-8373-6164-8); pap. 13.95 (ISBN 0-8373-6114-1). Natl Learning.

--Chemical Specialist in Medical-Surgical Nursery. (Certified Nurse Examination Ser.: CN-13). 21.95 (ISBN 0-8373-6163-X); pap. 13.95 (ISBN 0-8373-6113-3). Natl Learning.

--Chemistry. (Graduate Record Examination Ser.: GRE-2). (Cloth bdg. avail. on request). pap. 13.95 (ISBN 0-8373-5202-9). Natl Learning.

--Chemistry & General Sciences - Sr. H.S. (Teachers License Examination Ser.: T-6). (Cloth bdg. avail. on request). pap. 13.95 (ISBN 0-686-66502-3). Natl Learning.

--Chemistry, Physics & General Science. (National Teachers Examination Ser.: NT-7). (Cloth bdg. avail. on request). pap. 11.95 (ISBN 0-8373-8417-6). Natl Learning.

--Chief Account Clerk. (Career Examination Ser.: C-2707). (Cloth bdg. avail. on request). 1980. pap. 12.00 (ISBN 0-8373-2707-5). Natl Learning.

--Chief Accountant. (Career Examination Ser.: C-1565). (Cloth bdg. avail. on request). pap. 14.00 (ISBN 0-8373-1565-4). Natl Learning.

--Chief Beverage Control Investigator. (Career Examination Ser.: C-2825). (Cloth bdg. avail. on request). 1980. pap. 12.00 (ISBN 0-8373-2825-X). Natl Learning.

--Chief Budget Examiner. (Career Examination Ser.: C-2667). (Cloth bdg. avail. on request). pap. 14.00 (ISBN 0-8373-2667-2). Natl Learning.

--Chief Buildings Engineer. (Career Examination Ser.: C-1168). (Cloth bdg. avail. on request). pap. 14.00 (ISBN 0-8373-1168-3). Natl Learning.

--Chief Clerk. (Career Examination Ser.: C-189). (Cloth bdg. avail. on request). pap. 12.00 (ISBN 0-8373-0189-0). Natl Learning.

--Chief Deputy County Attorney. (Career Examination Ser.: C-1172). (Cloth bdg. avail. on request). pap. 12.00 (ISBN 0-8373-1172-1). Natl Learning.

--Chief Deputy Sheriff. (Career Examination Ser.: C-1173). (Cloth bdg. avail. on request). pap. 12.00 (ISBN 0-8373-1173-X). Natl Learning.

--Chief Excise Tax Investigator. (Career Examination Ser.: C-2420). (Cloth bdg. avail. on request). pap. 12.00 (ISBN 0-8373-2420-3). Natl Learning.

--Chief File Clerk. (Career Examination Ser.: C-453). (Cloth bdg. avail. on request). pap. 12.00 (ISBN 0-8373-0453-9). Natl Learning.

--Chief Marine Engineer. (Career Examination Ser.: C-1794). (Cloth bdg. avail. on request). pap. 12.00 (ISBN 0-8373-1794-0). Natl Learning.

--Chief of Stenographic Services. (Career Examination Ser.: C-943). (Cloth bdg. avail. on request). pap. 12.00 (ISBN 0-8373-0943-3). Natl Learning.

--Chief Probation Officer. (Career Examination Ser.: C-1593). (Cloth bdg. avail. on request). pap. 12.00 (ISBN 0-8373-1593-X). Natl Learning.

--Chief Process Server. (Career Examination Ser.: C-1182). (Cloth bdg. avail. on request). pap. 10.00 (ISBN 0-8373-1182-9). Natl Learning.

--Chief Public Health Nutritionist. (Career Examination Ser.). (Cloth bdg. avail. on request). pap. 12.00 (ISBN 0-8373-3156-0). Natl Learning.

--Chief Registrar. (Career Examination Ser.: C-1183). (Cloth bdg. avail. on request). pap. 10.00 (ISBN 0-8373-1183-7). Natl Learning.

--Chief Schedule Maker. (Career Examination Ser.: C-1729). (Cloth bdg. avail. on request). pap. 10.00 (ISBN 0-8373-1729-0); pap. 8.00 (ISBN 0-686-66837-5). Natl Learning.

--Chief Supervisor of Mechanical Installations. (Career Examination Ser.: C-2482). (Cloth bdg. avail. on request). pap. 12.00 (ISBN 0-8373-2482-3). Natl Learning.

--Chief Water Pollution Control Inspector. (Career Examination Ser.: C-1187). (Cloth bdg. avail. on request). pap. 12.00 (ISBN 0-8373-1187-X). Natl Learning.

--Chief Water Treatment Plant Operator. (Career Examination Ser.: C-2149). (Cloth bdg. avail. on request). 1976. pap. 12.00 (ISBN 0-8373-2149-2). Natl Learning.

--Child & Adolescent Nurse. (Certified Nurse Examination Ser.: CN-7). 21.95 (ISBN 0-8373-6157-5); pap. 13.95 (ISBN 0-8373-6107-9). Natl Learning.

--Children with Limited Vision. (Teachers License Examination Ser.: T-7). (Cloth bdg. avail. on request). pap. 13.95 (ISBN 0-8373-8007-3). Natl Learning.

--Children with Retarded Mental Development (C.R. M. D.) (Teachers License Examination Ser.: T-8). (Cloth bdg. avail. on request). pap. 13.95 (ISBN 0-8373-8008-1). Natl Learning.

--Civil Engineer: One to Five. (Career Examination Ser.: C-2000). (Cloth bdg. avail. on request). pap. 14.00 (ISBN 0-8373-2000-3). Natl Learning.

--Civil Engineering Trainee. (Career Examination Ser.: C-945). (Cloth bdg. avail. on request). pap. 10.00 (ISBN 0-8373-0945-X). Natl Learning.

--Civil Service Arithmetic. (Career Examination Ser.: CS-6). (Cloth bdg. avail. on request). pap. 8.00 (ISBN 0-8373-3706-2). Natl Learning.

--Civil Service General & Mental Abilities. (Career Examination Ser.: CS-16). (Cloth bdg. avail. on request). pap. 8.00 (ISBN 0-8373-3766-6). Natl Learning.

--Civil Service Grammar & Usage. (Career Examination Ser.: CS-7). (Cloth bdg. avail. on request). pap. 8.00 (ISBN 0-8373-3757-7). Natl Learning.

--Civil Service Graphs, Charts & Tables. (Career Examination Ser.: CS-11). (Cloth bdg. avail. on request). pap. 8.00 (ISBN 0-8373-3761-5). Natl Learning.

--Civil Service Home Study Course. (Career Examination Ser.: CS-1). (Cloth bdg. avail. on request). pap. 8.00 (ISBN 0-8373-3751-8). Natl Learning.

--Civil Service Mechanical Aptitude. (Career Examination Ser.: CS-15). (Cloth bdg. avail. on request). pap. 8.00 (ISBN 0-8373-3765-8). Natl Learning.

--Civil Service Reading Comprehension. (Career Examination Ser.: CS-8). (Cloth bdg. avail. on request). pap. 8.00 (ISBN 0-8373-3758-5). Natl Learning.

--Civil Service Spelling. (Career Examination Ser.: CS-9). (Cloth bdg. avail. on request). pap. 8.00 (ISBN 0-8373-3759-3). Natl Learning.

--Cleaner (Men) (Career Examination Ser.: C-946A). (Cloth bdg. avail. on request). pap. 8.00 (ISBN 0-8373-0946-8). Natl Learning.

--Cleaner (Women) (Career Examination Ser.: C-946B). (Cloth bdg. avail. on request). pap. 8.00 (ISBN 0-8373-0946-8). Natl Learning.

--Clerical Positions G-5. (Career Examination Ser.: C-1943). (Cloth bdg. avail. on request). pap. 10.00 (ISBN 0-8373-1943-9). Natl Learning.

--Clerical Training Supervisor. (Career Examination Ser.: C-1194). (Cloth bdg. avail. on request). pap. 10.00 (ISBN 0-8373-1194-2). Natl Learning.

--Clerk. (Career Examination Ser.: C-142). (Cloth bdg. avail. on request). pap. 8.00 (ISBN 0-8373-0142-4). Natl Learning.

--Clerk - Part-Time. (Career Examination Ser.: C-1191). (Cloth bdg. avail on request). pap. 8.00 (ISBN 0-8373-1191-8). Natl Learning.

--Clerk-Carrier (U.S.P.S.) (Career Examination Ser.: C-143). (Cloth bdg. avail. on request). pap. 8.00 (ISBN 0-8373-0143-2). Natl Learning.

--Clerk-Laborer. (Career Examination Ser.: C-1190). (Cloth bfg. aval. on request). 8.00 (ISBN 0-8373-1190-X). Natl Learning.

--Clerk-Seasonal. (Career Examination Ser.: C-1192). (Cloth bdg. avail. on request). pap. 8.00 (ISBN 0-8373-1192-6). Natl Learning.

--Clerk-Stenographer 2. (Career Examination Ser.: C-1650). (Cloth bdg. avail. on request). 1977. pap. 8.00 (ISBN 0-8373-1650-2); pap. 10.00 (ISBN 0-686-67793-5). Natl Learning.

--Clerk-Stenographer 3. (Career Examination Ser.: C-1651). (Cloth bdg. avail. on request). 1977. pap. 10.00 (ISBN 0-8373-1651-0). Natl Learning.

--Clerk-Stenographer 4. (Career Examination Ser.: C-1652). (Cloth bdg. avail on request). 1977. pap. 10.00 (ISBN 0-8373-1652-9). Natl Learning.

--Clerk-Technician (U.S.P.S.) (Career Examination Ser.: C-1633). (Cloth bdg. avail on request). 1977. pap. 10.00 (ISBN 0-8373-1633-2). Natl Learning.

--Clerk-Typist. (Career Examination Ser.: C-147). (Cloth bdg. avail. on request). pap. 8.00 (ISBN 0-8373-0147-5). Natl Learning.

--Clerk-Typist Trainee. (Career Examination Ser.: C-1193). (Cloth bdg. avail. on request). pap. 8.00 (ISBN 0-8373-1193-4). Natl Learning.

--Climber & Pruner. (Career Examination Ser.: C-148). (Cloth bdg. avail. on request). pap. 8.00 (ISBN 0-8373-0148-3). Natl Learning.

--Clinic Administrator. (Career Examination Ser.: C-915). (Cloth bdg. avail. on request). pap. 12.00 (ISBN 0-8373-0915-8). Natl Learning.

--Clinical Chemistry. (College Level Examination Ser.: CLEP-32). (Cloth bdg. avail. on request). pap. 11.95 (ISBN 0-8373-5332-7). Natl Learning.

--Clinical Laboratory Investigator. (Career Examination Ser.: C-2098). (Cloth bdg. avail. on request). 1976. pap. 10.00 (ISBN 0-8373-1196-9). Natl Learning.

--Clinical Nurse. (Career Examination Ser.: C-947). (Cloth bdg. avail. on request). pap. 10.00 (ISBN 0-8373-0947-6). Natl Learning.

--Clinical Psychologist Intern. (Career Examination Ser.: C-1196). (Cloth bdg. avail. on request). pap. 10.00 (ISBN 0-8373-1196-9). Natl Learning.

--Clinical Specialist in Child & Adolescent Psychiatric & Mental Health Nursing. (Certified Nurse Examination Ser.: CN-15). 21.95 (ISBN 0-8373-6165-6); pap. 13.95 (ISBN 0-8373-6115-X). Natl Learning.

--Clinician. (Career Examination Ser.: C-150). (Cloth bdg. avail. on request). pap. 10.00 (ISBN 0-8373-1197-7). Natl Learning.

--Clinician, Part-Time. (Career Examination Ser.: C-1197). (Cloth bdg. avail. on request). pap. 10.00 (ISBN 0-8373-1197-7). Natl Learning.

--Clock Repairer. (Career Examination Ser.: C-151). (Cloth bdg. avail on request). pap. 10.00 (ISBN 0-8373-0151-3). Natl Learning.

--College Administrative Assistant. (Career Examination Ser.: C-152). (Cloth bdg. avail. on request). pap. 10.00 (ISBN 0-8373-0152-1). Natl Learning.

--College Administrative Associate. (Career Examination Ser.: C-2658). (Cloth bdg. avail. on request). pap. 10.00 (ISBN 0-8373-2658-3). Natl Learning.

--College Algebra-Trigonometry. (College Level Examination Ser.: CLEP-7). (Cloth bdg. avail. on request). pap. 9.95 (ISBN 0-8373-5311-4). Natl Learning.

--College & University Basic Competency Tests (BCT-C&U) (Admission Test Ser.: ATS-58). (Cloth bdg. avail. on request). pap. 11.95 (ISBN 0-8373-5158-8). Natl Learning.

--College Real Estate. (Admission Test Ser.: ATS-7). (Cloth bdg. avail. on request). pap. 13.95 (ISBN 0-8373-5007-7). Natl Learning.

--Colleges of Podiatry Admission Test. (Admission Test Ser.: ATS-37). (Cloth bdg. avail. on request). 1976. pap. 11.95 (ISBN 0-8373-5037-9). Natl Learning.

--Commercial & Advertising Art. (Occupational Competency Examination Ser.: OCE-11). (Cloth bdg. avail. on request). pap. 13.95 (ISBN 0-8373-5711-X). Natl Learning.

--Commercial Photography. (Occupational Competency Examination Ser.: OCE-12). (Cloth bdg. avail. on request). pap. 13.95 (ISBN 0-8373-5712-8). Natl Learning.

--Commissary Clerk I. (Career Examination Ser.: C-216). (Cloth bdg. avail. on request). pap. 8.00 (ISBN 0-8373-0216-1). Natl Learning.

--Commissary Clerk II. (Career Examination Ser.: C-217). (Cloth bdg. avail. on request). pap. 8.00 (ISBN 0-8373-0217-X). Natl Learning.

--Commissary Clerk III. (Career Examination Ser.: C-218). (Cloth bdg. avail. on request). pap. 10.00 (ISBN 0-8373-0218-8). Natl Learning.

--Commissary Clerk IV. (Career Examination Ser.: C-219). (Cloth bdg. avail. on request). pap. 10.00 (ISBN 0-8373-0219-6). Natl Learning.

--Commission on Graduates of Foreign Nursing Schools Qualifying Examinations (CGFNS) (Admission Test Ser.: ATS-90). 25.95 (ISBN 0-8373-5190-1); pap. 17.95 (ISBN 0-8373-5090-5). Natl Learning.

--Commissioner of Correction. (Career Examination Ser.: C-1203). (Cloth bdg. avail. on request). pap. 12.00 (ISBN 0-8373-1858-0). Natl Learning.

--Commissioner of Deeds. (Career Examination Ser.: C-157). (Cloth bdg. avail. on reqqest). pap. 10.00 (ISBN 0-8373-0157-2). Natl Learning.

--Commissioner of General Services. (Career Examination Ser.: C-1858). (Cloth bdg. avail. on request). 1976. pap. 12.00 (ISBN 0-8373-1858-0). Natl Learning.

--Commissioner of Police. (Career Examination Ser.: C-1200). (Cloth bdg. avail. on request). pap. 12.00 (ISBN 0-8373-1200-0). Natl Learning.

--Commissioner of Recreation & Community Services. (Career Examination Ser.: C-1890). (Cloth bdg. avail. on request). pap. 12.00 (ISBN 0-8373-1890-4). Natl Learning.

--Commissioner of Social Services. (Career Examination Ser.: C-1205). (Cloth bdg. avail. on request). pap. 12.00 (ISBN 0-8373-1205-1). Natl Learning.

--Common Branches (1-6) Elementary School. (Teachers License Examinations Ser.: T-9). (Cloth bdg. avail. on request). 1976. pap. 13.95 (ISBN 0-8373-8009-X). Natl Learning.

--Communications Analyst. (Career Examination Ser.: C-1202). (Cloth bdg. avail. on request). pap. 10.00 (ISBN 0-8373-1202-7). Natl Learning.

--Communications Technician. (Career Examination Ser.: C-2186). (Cloth bdg. avail. on request). pap. 10.00 (ISBN 0-686-53317-8). Natl Learning.

--Community Centers (Physical Education) (Teachers License Examination Ser.: T-10). (Cloth bdg. avail. on request). pap. 13.95 (ISBN 0-8373-8010-3). Natl Learning.

--Community Development Assistant. (Career Examination Ser.: C-904). (Cloth bdg. avail. on request). pap. 10.00 (ISBN 0-8373-0904-2). Natl Learning.

--Community Development Housing Analyst. (Career Examination Ser.: C-905). (Cloth bdg. avail. on request). pap. 12.00 (ISBN 0-8373-0905-0). Natl Learning.

--Community Development Program Analyst. (Career Examination Ser.: C-903). (Cloth bdg. avail. on request). pap. 12.00 (ISBN 0-8373-0903-4). Natl Learning.

--Community Development Program Technician. (Career Examination Ser.: C-902). (Cloth bdg. avail. on request). pap. 10.00 (ISBN 0-8373-0902-6). Natl Learning.

--Community Development Project Director. (Career Examination Ser.: C-909). (Cloth bdg. avail. on request). pap. 14.00 (ISBN 0-8373-0909-3). Natl Learning.

--Community Development Project Supervisor. (Career Examination Ser.: C-908). (Cloth bdg. avail. on request). pap. 12.00 (ISBN 0-8373-0908-5). Natl Learning.

--Community Health Nurse. (Certified Nurse Examination Ser.: CN-4). 21.95 (ISBN 0-8373-6154-0); pap. 13.95 (ISBN 0-8373-6104-4). Natl Learning.

--Community Improvement Coordinator. (Career Examination Ser.: C-906). (Cloth bdg. avail. on request). pap. 12.00 (ISBN 0-8373-0906-9). Natl Learning.

--Community Relations Assistant. (Career Examination Ser.: C-1207). (Cloth bdg. avail. on request). pap. 10.00 (ISBN 0-8373-1207-8). Natl Learning.

--Community Service Aide. (Career Examination Ser.: C-1402). (Cloth bdg. avail. on request). pap. 10.00 (ISBN 0-8373-1402-X). Natl Learning.

--Community Service Worker. (Career Examination Ser.: C-2675). (Cloth bdg. avail. on request). pap. 10.00 (ISBN 0-8373-2675-3). Natl Learning.

--Community Services Assistant. (Career Examination Ser.: C-1403). (Cloth bdg. avail. on request). pap. 10.00 (ISBN 0-8373-1403-8). Natl Learning.

--Compensation Claims Auditor. (Career Examination Ser.: C-2126). (Cloth bdg. avail. on request). 1977. pap. 10.00 (ISBN 0-8373-2126-3). Natl Learning.

--Compensation Claims Clerk. (Career Examination Ser.: C-866). (Cloth bdg. avail. on request). pap. 8.00 (ISBN 0-8373-0866-6). Natl Learning.

--Compensation Claims Examiner. (Career Examination Ser.: C-2133). (Cloth bdg. avail. on request). 1977. pap. 10.00 (ISBN 0-8373-2133-6). Natl Learning.

--Compensation Claims Examiner Trainee. (Career Examination Ser.: C-879). (Cloth bdg. avail. on request). pap. 10.00 (ISBN 0-8373-0879-8). Natl Learning.

--Compensation Claims Investigator. (Career Examination Ser.: C-949). (Cloth bdg. avail. on request). pap. 10.00 (ISBN 0-8373-0949-2). Natl Learning.

--Compensation Claims Legal Investigator. (Career Examination Ser.: C-2100). (Cloth bdg. avail. on request). 1977. pap. 10.00 (ISBN 0-8373-2100-X). Natl Learning.

--Compensation Investigator. (Career Examination Ser.: C-950). (Cloth bdg. avail. on request). pap. 10.00 (ISBN 0-8373-0950-6). Natl Learning.

--Complaint Investigator. (Career Examination Ser.: C-1863). (Cloth bdg. avail. on request). pap. 10.00 (ISBN 0-8373-0950-6). Natl Learning.

--Compliance Investigator. (Career Examination Ser.: C-2421). (Cloth bdg. avail. on request). pap. 10.00 (ISBN 0-8373-2421-1). Natl Learning.

--Compositor (Job) (Career Examination Ser.: C-26497). (Cloth bdg. avail. on request). pap. 10.00 (ISBN 0-8373-2649-4). Natl Learning.

--Comprehensive High School. (Teachers License Examination Ser.: S-11). (Cloth bdg. avail. on request). pap. 17.95 (ISBN 0-686-66069-2). Natl Learning.

--Computer Aptitude Test-CAT. (Career Examination Ser.: C-180). (Cloth bdg. avail. on request). pap. 10.00 (ISBN 0-8373-0180-7). Natl Learning.

--Computer Associate (Applications Programming) (Career Examination Ser.: C-2470). (Cloth bdg. avail. on request). pap. 12.00 (ISBN 0-8373-2470-X). Natl Learning.

--Computer Associate (Operations) (Career Examination Ser.: C-2471). (Cloth bdg. avail. on request). pap. 12.00 (ISBN 0-8373-2471-8). Natl Learning.

--Computer Associate (Systems Programming) (Career Examination Ser.). (Cloth bdg. avail. on request). pap. 12.00 (ISBN 0-8373-2472-6). Natl Learning.

--Computer Associate (Technical Support) (Career Examination Ser.: C-2473). (Cloth bdg. avail. on request). pap. 12.00 (ISBN 0-8373-2473-4). Natl Learning.

--Computer Equipment Analyst. (Career Examination Ser.: C-1209). (Cloth bdg. avail. on request). pap. 10.00 (ISBN 0-8373-1209-4). Natl Learning.

--Computer Operator Trainee. (Career Examination Ser.: C-878). (Cloth bdg. avail. on request). pap. 10.00 (ISBN 0-8373-0878-X). Natl Learning.

--Computer Programmer Analyst Trainee. (Career Examination Ser.: C-2475). (Cloth bdg. avail. on request). pap. 8.00 (ISBN 0-8373-2475-0). Natl Learning.

--Computer Programming Supervisor. (Career Examination Ser.: C-1961). (Cloth bdg. avail. on request). pap. 12.00 (ISBN 0-8373-1961-7). Natl Learning.

--Computer Science. (Graduate Record Examination Ser.). 21.95 (ISBN 0-8373-5271-1); pap. 13.95 (ISBN 0-8373-5221-5). Natl Learning.

--Computer Specialist. (Career Examination Ser.: C-161). (Cloth bdg. avail. on request). pap. 12.00 (ISBN 0-8373-0161-0). Natl Learning.

--Computer Specialist (Applications Programming) (Career Examination Ser.: C-2871). (Cloth bdg. avail. on request). pap. 12.00 (ISBN 0-8373-2874-8). Natl Learning.

--Computer Specialist (Data Base Administration) (Career Examination Ser.: C-2876). (Cloth bdg. avail. on request). pap. 12.00 (ISBN 0-8373-2876-4). Natl Learning.

--Computer Specialist (Systems Programming) (Career Examination Ser.: C-2875). (Cloth bdg. avail. on request). pap. write for info. (ISBN 0-8373-2875-6). Natl Learning.

--Computer Systems Analyst. (Career Examination Ser.: C-162). (Coth bdg. avail. on request). pap. 12.00 (ISBN 0-8373-5221-5). Natl Learning.

--Computer Systems Analyst Trainee. (Career Examination Ser.: C-951). (Cloth bdg. avail. on). pap. 10.00 (ISBN 0-8373-0951-4). Natl Learning.

--Computer Systems Manager. (Career Examination Ser.: C-1668). (Cloth bdg. avail. on request). pap. 12.00 (ISBN 0-8373-1668-5). Natl Learning.

--Computer Technical Assistant. (Career Examination Ser.: C-1210). (Cloth bdg. avail on request). pap. 10.00 (ISBN 0-8373-1210-8). Natl Learning.

--Computer Technician. (Teachers License Examination Ser.: T-67). (Cloth bdg. avail. on request). pap. 13.95 (ISBN 0-8373-8087-1). Natl Learning.

--Consumer Affairs Inspector. (Career Examination Ser.: C-1655). (Cloth bdg. avail on request). pap. 10.00 (ISBN 0-8373-1655-3). Natl Learning.

--Consumer Affairs Investigator. (Career Examination Ser.: C-1214). (Cloth bdg. avail on request). pap. 10.00 (ISBN 0-8373-1214-0). Natl Learning.

--Consumer Affairs Research Assistant. (Career Examination Ser.: C-1215). (Cloth bdg. avail on request). pap. 10.00 (ISBN 0-8373-1215-9). Natl Learning.

--Consumer Affairs Specialist. (Career Examination Ser.: C-1864). (Cloth bdg. avail on request). 1977. pap. 10.00 (ISBN 0-8373-0955-7). Natl Learning.

--Consumer Frauds Representative. (Career Examination Ser.: C-876). (Cloth bdg. avail. on request). pap. 10.00 (ISBN 0-8373-0876-3). Natl Learning.

--Contract Specialist. (Career Examination Ser.: C-955). (Cloth bdg. avail on request). pap. 10.00 (ISBN 0-8373-0955-7). Natl Learning.

--Contracts Examiner. (Career Examination Ser.: C-888). (Cloth bdg. avail. on request). pap. 10.00 (ISBN 0-8373-0888-7). Natl Learning.

--Contracts Technician. (Career Examination Ser.: C-834). (Cloth bdg. avail. on request). pap. 10.00 (ISBN 0-8373-0834-8). Natl Learning.

--Coordinator of Child Support Enforcement. (Career Examination Ser.: C-927). (Cloth bdg. avail. on request). pap. 14.00 (ISBN 0-8373-0927-1). Natl Learning.

--Coordinator of Drug Abuse Educational Programs. (Career Examination Ser.: C-1767). (Cloth bdg. avail on request). 1976. pap. 12.00 (ISBN 0-8373-1767-3). Natl Learning.

--Coordinator of Educational Affairs. (Career Examination Ser.: C-2209). (Cloth bdg. avail on request). pap. 12.00 (ISBN 0-8373-2209-X). Natl Learning.

--Coordinator of Nursing Education. (Career Examination Ser.: C-1843). (Cloth bdg. avail on request). pap. 12.00 (ISBN 0-8373-1843-2). Natl Learning.

--Correction Captain. (Career Examination Ser.: C-165). (Cloth bdg. avail. on request). pap. 12.00 (ISBN 0-8373-0165-3). Natl Learning.

--Correction Counselor. (Career Examination Ser.: C-2593). (Cloth bdg. avail. on request). pap. 12.00 (ISBN 0-8373-2593-5). Natl Learning.

--Correction Hospital Officer (Men) (Career Examination Ser.: C-956A). (Cloth bdg. avail on request). pap. 10.00 (ISBN 0-686-82946-8). Natl Learning.

--Correction Hospital Officer (Women) (Career Examination Ser.: C-956b). (Cloth bdg. avail on request). pap. 10.00 (ISBN 0-686-82947-6). Natl Learning.

--Correction Lieutenant. (Career Examination Ser.: C-166). (Cloth bdg. avail on request). pap. 12.00 (ISBN 0-8373-0166-1). Natl Learning.

--Correction Matron. (Career Examination Ser.: C-1219). (Cloth bdg. avail on request). pap. 10.00 (ISBN 0-8373-1219-1). Natl Learning.

--Correction Officer I. (Career Examination Ser.: C-837). (Cloth bdg. avail. on request). pap. 10.00 (ISBN 0-8373-0837-2). Natl Learning.

--Correction Officer II. (Career Examination Ser.: C-838). (Cloth bdg. avail. on request). pap. 10.00 (ISBN 0-686-84416-5). Natl Learning.

--Correction Officer III. (Career Examination Ser.: C-839). (Cloth bdg. avail. on request). pap. 12.00 (ISBN 0-8373-0839-9). Natl Learning.

--Correction Officer IV. (Career Examination Ser.: C-840). (Cloth bdg. avail. on request). pap. 12.00 (ISBN 0-8373-0840-2). Natl Learning.

--Correction Officer (Men) (Career Examination Ser.: C-167). (Cloth bdg. avail on request). pap. 10.00 (ISBN 0-8373-0167-X). Natl Learning.

--Correction Officer Trainee. (Career Examination Ser.: C-957). (Cloth bdg. avail on request). pap. 10.00 (ISBN 0-8373-0957-3). Natl Learning.

--Correction Officer (Women) (Career Examination Ser.: C-168). (Cloth bdg. avail on request). pap. 10.00 (ISBN 0-8373-0168-8). Natl Learning.

--Correction Sergeant. (Career Examination Ser.: C-169). (Cloth bdg. avail on request). pap. 12.00 (ISBN 0-8373-0169-6). Natl Learning.

--Correction Youth Camp Officer (Men) (Career Examination Ser.: C-958A). (Cloth bdg. avail on request). pap. 10.00 (ISBN 0-8373-0958-1). Natl Learning.

--Correction Youth Camp Officer (Women) (Career Examination Ser.: C-958B). (Cloth bdg. avail on equest). pap. 10.00 (ISBN 0-8373-0958-1). Natl Learning.

--Correctional Treatment Specialist. (Career Examination Ser.: C-959). (Cloth bdg. avail on request). pap. 12.00 (ISBN 0-8373-0959-X). Natl Learning.

--Corrective Therapist. (Career Examination Ser.: C-960). (Cloth bdg. avail on request). pap. 10.00 (ISBN 0-8373-0960-3). Natl Learning.

--Cosmetologist. (Career Examination Ser.: C-22511). (Cloth bdg. avail on request). 1977. pap. 10.00 (ISBN 0-8373-2251-0). Natl Learning.

--Cosmetology. (Occupational Competency Examination Ser.: OCE-13). (Cloth bdg. avail. on request). pap. 13.95 (ISBN 0-8373-5713-6). Natl Learning.

--County Attorney. (Career Examination Ser.: C-1220). (Cloth bdg. avail on request). pap. 12.00 (ISBN 0-8373-1220-5). Natl Learning.

--County Clerk. (Career Examination Ser.: C-2114). (Cloth bdg. avail on request). 1977. pap. 12.00 (ISBN 0-8373-2114-X). Natl Learning.

--County Comptroller. (Career Examination Ser.: C-1222). (Cloth bdg. avail on request). pap. 12.00 (ISBN 0-8373-1222-1). Natl Learning.

--County Director of Accounting. (Career Examination Ser.: C-1960). (Cloth bdg. avail on request). pap. 12.00 (ISBN 0-8373-1960-9). Natl Learning.

--County Treasurer. (Career Examination Ser.: C-1255). (Cloth bdg. avail on request). pap. 12.00 (ISBN 0-8373-1225-6). Natl Learning.

--Court Clerk. (Career Examination Ser.: C-171). (Cloth bdg. avail on request). pap. 10.00 (ISBN 0-8373-0171-8). Natl Learning.

--Court Clerk One. (Career Examination Ser.: C-963). (Cloth bdg. avail on request). pap. 10.00 (ISBN 0-8373-0963-8). Natl Learning.

--Court Clerk Two. (Career Examination Ser.: C-964). (Cloth bdg. avail. on request). pap. 12.00 (ISBN 0-8373-0964-6). Natl Learning.

--Court Hearing Reporter. (Career Examination Ser.: C-172). (Cloth bdg. avail on request). pap. 10.00 (ISBN 0-8373-0172-6). Natl Learning.

--Court Law Stenographer. (Career Examination Ser.: C-173). (Cloth bdg. avail on request). pap. 10.00 (ISBN 0-8373-0173-4). Natl Learning.

--Court Officer. (Career Examination Ser.: C-966). (Cloth bdg. avail on request). pap. 10.00 (ISBN 0-8373-0966-2). Natl Learning.

--Court Reporter. (Career Examination Ser.: C-174). (Cloth bdg. avail on request). pap. 10.00 (ISBN 0-8373-0174-2). Natl Learning.

--Court Reporter One. (Career Examination Ser.: C-967). (Cloth bdg. avail on request). pap. 10.00 (ISBN 0-686-66499-X). Natl Learning.

--Court Reporter Two. (Career Examination Ser.: C-968). (Cloth bdg. avail on request). pap. 10.00 (ISBN 0-8373-0968-9). Natl Learning.

--Criminal Investigator. (Career Examination Ser.: C-1229). (Cloth bdg. avail on request). pap. 10.00 (ISBN 0-8373-1229-9). Natl Learning.

--Criminal Law Investigator. (Career Examination Ser.: C-969). (Cloth bdg. avail on request). pap. 10.00 (ISBN 0-8373-0969-7). Natl Learning.

--Custodial Assistant (Men) (Career Examination Ser.: C-141a). (Cloth bdg. avail on request). pap. 8.00 (ISBN 0-8373-0141-6). Natl Learning.

--Custodial Assistant (Women) (Career Examination Ser.: C-1418). (Cloth bdg. avail on request). pap. 8.00 (ISBN 0-8373-1418-6). Natl Learning.

--Custodial Foreman. (Career Examination Ser.: C-970). (Cloth bdg. avail on request). pap. 10.00 (ISBN 0-8373-0970-0). Natl Learning.

--Custodial Work Supervisor. (Career Examination Ser.: C-1231). (Cloth bdg. avail on request). pap. 10.00 (ISBN 0-8373-1231-0). Natl Learning.

--Custodian. (Career Examination Ser.: C-175). (Cloth bdg. avail on request). pap. 10.00 (ISBN 0-8373-0175-0). Natl Learning.

--Custodian-Engineer. (Career Examination Ser.: C-176). (Cloth bdg. avail on request). pap. 12.00 (ISBN 0-8373-0176-9). Natl Learning.

--Customs Inspector. (Career Examination Ser.: C-177). (Cloth bdg. avail on request). pap. 10.00 (ISBN 0-8373-0177-7). Natl Learning.

--Dance - Jr. H.S. (Teachers License Examination Ser.: T-64). (Cloth bdg. avail on request). pap. 13.95 (ISBN 0-8373-8084-7). Natl Learning.

--Data Base Manager. (Career Examination Ser.: C-2873). (Cloth bdg. avail. on request). pap. 14.00 (ISBN 0-8373-2873-X). Natl Learning.

--Data Collection Clerk. (Career Examination Ser.: C-1234). (Cloth bdg. avail on request). pap. 10.00 (ISBN 0-8373-1234-5). Natl Learning.

--Data Control Assistant. (Career Examination Ser.: C-2889). (Cloth bdg. avail. on request). pap. 10.00 (ISBN 0-8373-2889-6). Natl Learning.

--Data Control Specialist. (Career Examination Ser.: C-901). (Cloth bdg. avail. on request). pap. 12.00 (ISBN 0-8373-0901-8). Natl Learning.

--Data Entry Machine Operator. (Career Examination Ser.: C-2409). (Cloth bdg. avail. on request). pap. 10.00 (ISBN 0-8373-2409-2). Natl Learning.

--Data Processing. (Occupational Competency Examination Ser.: OCE-14). (Cloth bdg. avail. on request). pap. 13.95 (ISBN 0-8373-5714-4). Natl Learning.

--Data Processing Clerk I. (Career Examination Ser.: C-536). (Cloth bdg. avail. on request). pap. 10.00 (ISBN 0-8373-0536-5). Natl Learning.

--Data Processing Clerk II. (Career Examination Ser.: C-537). (Cloth bdg. avail. on request). pap. 12.00 (ISBN 0-8373-0537-3). Natl Learning.

--Data Processing Clerk III. (Career Examination Ser.: C-538). (Cloth bdg. avail. on request). pap. 12.00 (ISBN 0-8373-0538-1). Natl Learning.

--Data Processing Control Clerk. (Career Examination Ser.: C-2483). (Cloth bdg. avail. on request). pap. 10.00 (ISBN 0-8373-2483-1). Natl Learning.

--Data Processing Equipment Operator. (Career Examination Ser.: C-2301). (Cloth bdg. avail. on request). 1977. pap. 10.00 (ISBN 0-8373-2301-0). Natl Learning.

--Data Processing Operations Supervisor. (Career Examination Ser.: C-2347). (Cloth bdg. avail. on request). pap. 10.00 (ISBN 0-8373-2347-9). Natl Learning.

--Deaf & Hard of Hearing. (Teachers License Examination Ser.: T-11). (Cloth bdg. avail. on request). pap. 13.95 (ISBN 0-8373-8011-1). Natl Learning.

--Demolition Inspector. (Career Examination Ser.: C-191). (Cloth bdg. avail. on request). pap. 10.00 (ISBN 0-8373-0191-2). Natl Learning.

--Dental Admission Test (DAT) (Admission Test Ser.: ATS-12). 300p. (Cloth bdg. avail. on request). pap. 13.95 (ISBN 0-8373-5012-3). Natl Learning.

--Dental Assistant. (Career Examination Ser.: C-205). (Cloth bdg. avail. on request). pap. 10.00 (ISBN 0-8373-0205-6). Natl Learning.

--Dental Assisting. (Occupational Competency Examination Ser.: OCE-15). (Cloth bdg. avail. on request). pap. 13.95 (ISBN 0-8373-5715-2). Natl Learning.

--Dental Auxiliary Education Examination in Dental Materials. (College Level Examination Ser.: CLEP-47). (Cloth bdg. avail. on request). pap. 11.95 (ISBN 0-8373-5347-5). Natl Learning.

--Dental Auxiliary Education Examination in Head, Neck & Oral Anatomy. (College Level Examination Ser.: CLEP-48). (Cloth bdg. avail. on request). pap. 11.95 (ISBN 0-8373-5348-3). Natl Learning.

--Dental Auxiliary Education Examination in Oral Radiography. (College Level Examination Ser.: CLEP-49). (Cloth bdg. avail. on request). pap. 11.95 (ISBN 0-8373-5349-1). Natl Learning.

--Dental Auxiliary Education Examination in Tooth Morphology & Function. (College Level Examination Ser.: CLEP-50). (Cloth bdg. avail. on request). pap. 11.95 (ISBN 0-8373-5800-0). Natl Learning.

--Dental Hygiene Aptitude Test (DHAT) (Admission Test Ser.: ATS-32). (Cloth bdg. avail. on request). pap. 11.95 (ISBN 0-8373-5032-8). Natl Learning.

--Dental Hygienist. (Career Examination Ser.: C-192). (Cloth bdg. avail. on request). pap. 10.00 (ISBN 0-8373-0192-0). Natl Learning.

--Denver Proficiency & Review Program (PRP) (Admission Test Ser.: ATS-66). (Cloth bdg. avail. on request). pap. 11.95 (ISBN 0-8373-5066-2). Natl Learning.

--Department Librarian. (Career Examination Ser.: C-194). (Cloth bdg. avail. on request). pap. 12.00 (ISBN 0-8373-0194-7). Natl Learning.

--Department Library Aide. (Career Examination Ser.: C-206). (Cloth bdg. avail. on request). pap. 10.00 (ISBN 0-8373-0206-4). Natl Learning.

--Department Senior Librarian. (Career Examination Ser.: C-1622). (Cloth bdg. avail. on request). pap. 12.00 (ISBN 0-8373-1622-7, C-1622). Natl Learning.

--Deputy Assessor. (Career Examination Ser.: C-1237). (Cloth bdg. avail. on request). pap. 10.00 (ISBN 0-8373-1237-X). Natl Learning.

--Deputy Chief Clerk. (Career Examination Ser.: C-1238). (Cloth bdg. avail. on request). pap. 12.00 (ISBN 0-8373-1238-8). Natl Learning.

--Deputy Chief, Fire Department. (Career Examination Ser.: C-195). (Cloth bdg. avail. on request). pap. 12.00 (ISBN 0-8373-0195-5). Natl Learning.

--Deputy Chief Fire Marshall (Uniformed) (Career Examination Ser.: C-2169). (Cloth bdg. avail. on request). 1976. pap. 12.00 (ISBN 0-8373-2169-7). Natl Learning.

--Deputy Chief Marshall. (Career Examination Ser.: C-1239). (Cloth bdg. avail. on request). pap. 10.00 (ISBN 0-8373-1239-6). Natl Learning.

--Deputy Chief Registrar. (Career Examination Ser.: C-1240). (Cloth bdg. avail. on request). pap. 10.00 (ISBN 0-8373-1240-X). Natl Learning.

--Deputy Commissioner. (Career Examination Ser.: C-1241). (Cloth bdg. avail. on request). pap. 12.00 (ISBN 0-8373-1241-8). Natl Learning.

--Deputy Commissioner of Commerce & Industry. (Career Examination Ser.: C-1990). (Cloth bdg. avail. on request). pap. 12.00 (ISBN 0-8373-1990-0). Natl Learning.

--Deputy Commissioner of General Services. (Career Examination Ser.: C-1859). (Cloth bdg. avail. on request). pap. 12.00 (ISBN 0-8373-1859-9). Natl Learning.

--Deputy Commissioner of Jurors. (Career Examination Ser.: C-1242). (Cloth bdg. avail. on request). pap. 10.00 (ISBN 0-8373-1242-6). Natl Learning.

--Deputy Commissioner of Recreation & Community Services. (Career Examination Ser.: C-1891). (Cloth bdg. avail. on request). pap. 12.00 (ISBN 0-8373-1891-2). Natl Learning.

--Deputy County Attorney. (Career Examination Ser.: C-1244). (Cloth bdg. avail. on request). pap. 12.00 (ISBN 0-8373-1244-2). Natl Learning.

--Deputy County Clerk. (Career Examination Ser.: C-1772). (Cloth bdg. avail. on request). pap. 10.00 (ISBN 0-8373-1772-X). Natl Learning.

--Deputy Director of Administration. (Career Examination Ser.: C-1853). (Cloth bdg. avail. on request). pap. 12.00 (ISBN 0-8373-1853-X). Natl Learning.

--Deputy Director of Planning. (Career Examination Ser.: C-1708). (Cloth bdg. avail. on request). pap. 12.00 (ISBN 0-8373-1708-8). Natl Learning.

--Deputy Medical Examiner. (Career Examination Ser.: C-1245). (Cloth bdg. avail. on request). pap. 14.00 (ISBN 0-8373-1245-0). Natl Learning.

--Deputy Probation Director 4. (Career Examination Ser.: C-1900). (Cloth bdg. avail. on request). pap. 12.00 (ISBN 0-8373-1900-5). Natl Learning.

--Deputy Sheriff. (Career Examination Ser.: C-204). (Cloth bdg. avail. on request). pap. 10.00 (ISBN 0-8373-0204-8). Natl Learning.

--Deputy Superintendent of Women's Prisons. (Career Examination Ser.: C-1763). (Cloth bdg. avail. on request). 1977. pap. 12.00 (ISBN 0-8373-1763-0). Natl Learning.

--Deputy Town Clerk. (Career Examination Ser.: C-1855). (Cloth bdg. avail. on request). 1977. pap. 10.00 (ISBN 0-8373-1855-6). Natl Learning.

--Deputy United States Marshall. (Career Examination Ser.: C-1620). (Cloth bdg. avail. on request). pap. 10.00 (ISBN 0-8373-1620-0, C-1620). Natl Learning.

--Deputy Warden. (Career Examination Ser.: C-1762). (Cloth bdg. avail. on request). 1977. pap. 12.00 (ISBN 0-8373-1762-2). Natl Learning.

--Development Specialist. (Career Examination Ser.: C-923). (Cloth bdg. avail. on request). pap. 12.00 (ISBN 0-8373-0923-9). Natl Learning.

--Developmental Disabilities Program Aide. (Career Examination Ser.: C-864). (Cloth bdg. avail. on request). pap. 10.00 (ISBN 0-8373-0864-X). Natl Learning.

--Diesel Engine Repair. (Occupational Competency Examination Ser.: OCE-16). (Cloth bdg. avail. on request). pap. 13.95 (ISBN 0-8373-5716-0). Natl Learning.

--Dietician. (Career Examination Ser.: C-196). (Cloth bdg. avail. on request). pap. 10.00 (ISBN 0-8373-0196-3). Natl Learning.

--Differences in Nursing Care: Area 3. (ACT Proficiency Examination Program: PEP-45). (Cloth bdg. avail. on request). pap. 9.95 (ISBN 0-8373-5545-1). Natl Learning.

--Director of Administration. (Career Examination Ser.: C-1852). (Cloth bdg. avail. on request). pap. 12.00 (ISBN 0-8373-1852-1). Natl Learning.

--Director of Administrative Services. (Career Examination Ser.: C-1865). (Cloth bdg. avail. on request). pap. 12.00 (ISBN 0-8373-1865-3). Natl Learning.

--Director of Child Support Enforcement Bureau. (Career Examination Ser.: C-928). (Cloth bdg. avail. on request). pap. 14.00 (ISBN 0-8373-0928-X). Natl Learning.

--Director of Custodial & Security Services. (Career Examination Ser.: C-2923). (Cloth bdg. avail. on request). pap. 14.00 (ISBN 0-8373-2923-X). Natl Learning.

--Director of Drug Treatment Services. (Career Examination Ser.: C-2821). (Cloth bdg. avail. on request). 1980. pap. 14.00 (ISBN 0-8373-2821-7). Natl Learning.

--Director of Engineering, Building & Housing. (Career Examination Ser.: C-2391). (Cloth bdg. avail. on request). pap. 12.00 (ISBN 0-8373-2391-6). Natl Learning.

--Director of Fire Safety. (Career Examination Ser.: C-2396). (Cloth bdg. avail. on request). pap. 12.00 (ISBN 0-8373-2396-7). Natl Learning.

--Director of Graphics & Production. (Career Examination Ser.: C-1795). (Cloth bdg. avail. on request). pap. 12.00 (ISBN 0-8373-1795-9). Natl Learning.

--Director of Library. (Career Examination Ser.: C-1254). (Cloth bdg. avail. on request). pap. 12.00 (ISBN 0-8373-1254-X). Natl Learning.

--Director of Office Services. (Career Examination Ser.: C-1857). (Cloth bdg. avail. on request). pap. 12.00 (ISBN 0-8373-1857-2). Natl Learning.

--Director of Operations. (Career Examination Ser.: C-1827). (Cloth bdg. avail. on request). pap. 12.00 (ISBN 0-8373-1827-0). Natl Learning.

--Director of Patient Services. (Career Examination Ser.: C-2724). (Cloth bdg. avail. on request). 1980. pap. 14.00 (ISBN 0-8373-2724-5). Natl Learning.

--Director of Personnel. (Career Examination Ser.: C-2083). (Cloth bdg. avail. on request). 1977. pap. 12.00 (ISBN 0-8373-2083-6). Natl Learning.

--Director of Physical Development. (Career Examination Ser.: C-914). (Cloth bdg. avail. on request). pap. 14.00 (ISBN 0-8373-0914-X). Natl Learning.

--Director of Public Information. (Career Examination Ser.: C-1866). (Cloth bdg. avail. on request). pap. 12.00 (ISBN 0-8373-1866-1). Natl Learning.

--Director of Registrants. (Career Examination Ser.: C-1255). (Cloth bdg. avail. on request). pap. 10.00 (ISBN 0-8373-1255-8). Natl Learning.

--Director of Research & Evaluation. (Career Examination Ser.: C-2891). (Cloth bdg. avail. on request). pap. 14.00 (ISBN 0-8373-2891-8). Natl learning.

--Director of Security. (Career Examination Ser.: C-2444). (Cloth bdg. avail. on request). pap. 12.00 (ISBN 0-8373-2444-0). Natl Learning.

--Director of Social Services. (Career Examination Ser.: C-2666). (Cloth bdg. avail. on request). pap. 14.00 (ISBN 0-8373-2666-4). Natl Learning.

--Director of Traffic Control. (Career Examination Ser.: C-1877). (Cloth bdg. avail. on request). pap. 12.00 (ISBN 0-8373-1877-7). Natl Learning.

--Director of Traffic Safety. (Career Examination Ser.: C-527). (Cloth bdg. avail. on request). pap. 14.00 (ISBN 0-8373-0527-6). Natl Learning.

--Director of Transportation Operations. (Career Examination Ser.: C-114). (Cloth bdg. avail. on request). pap. 14.00 (ISBN 0-8373-0114-9). Natl Learning.

--Director of Youth Bureau. (Career Examination Ser.: C-2325). (Cloth bdg. avail. on request). pap. 12.00 (ISBN 0-8373-2325-8). Natl Learning.

--Dispatcher. (Career Examination Ser.: C-213). (Cloth bdg. avail. on request). pap. 12.00 (ISBN 0-8373-0213-7). Natl Learning.

--Distribution Clerk - Machine (U.S.P.S.) (Career Examination Ser.: C-2255). (Cloth bdg. avail. on request). 1977. pap. 8.00 (ISBN 0-8373-2255-3). Natl Learning.

--Distributive Education (Merchandising & Salesmanship) Chairman Sr. H.S. (Teachers License Examination Ser.: CH-3). (Cloth bdg. avail. on request). pap. 15.95 (ISBN 0-8373-8153-3). Natl Learning.

--Distributive Education (Merchandising & Salesmanship) Sr. H. S. (Teachers License Examination Ser.: T-12). (Cloth bdg. avail. on request). pap. 13.95 (ISBN 0-8373-8012-X). Natl Learning.

--District Attorney. (Career Examination Ser.: C-1257). (Cloth bdg. avail. on request). pap. 12.00 (ISBN 0-8373-1257-4). Natl Learning.

--District Business Officer. (Career Examination Ser.: C-1726). (Cloth bdg. avail. on request). pap. 12.00 (ISBN 0-8373-1726-6). Natl Learning.

--District Foreman (Department of Sanitation) (Career Examination Ser.: C-207). (Cloth bdg. avail. on request). pap. 10.00 (ISBN 0-8373-0207-2). Natl Learning.

--District Foreman (Highway Maintenance) (Career Examination Ser.: C-1978). (Cloth bdg. avail. on request). pap. 10.00 (ISBN 0-8373-1978-1). Natl Learning.

--District Foreman (Sewer Maintenance) (Career Examination Ser.: C-1815). (Cloth bdg. avail. on request). pap. 10.00 (ISBN 0-8373-1815-7). Natl Learning.

--District Foreman (Water Supply) (Career Examination Ser.: C-2037). (Cloth bdg. avail. on request). pap. 10.00 (ISBN 0-8373-2037-2). Natl Learning.

--District Foreman (Watershed Maintenance) (Career Examination Ser.: C-428). (Cloth bdg. avail. on request). pap. 12.00 (ISBN 0-8373-0428-8). Natl Learning.

--District Superintendent (Department of Sanitation) (Career Examination Ser.: C-201). (Cloth bdg. avail. on request). pap. 12.00 (ISBN 0-8373-0201-3). Natl Learning.

--District Supervisor of School Custodians. (Career Examination Ser.: C-2349). (Cloth bdg. avail. on request). pap. 12.00 (ISBN 0-8373-2349-5). Natl Learning.

--Dockbuilder. (Career Examination Ser.: C-1696). (Cloth bdg. avail. on request). pap. 10.00 (ISBN 0-8373-1696-0). Natl Learning.

--Dog Warden. (Career Examination Ser.: C-2645). (Cloth bdg. avail. on request). pap. 10.00 (ISBN 0-8373-2645-1). Natl Learning.

--Domestic Worker. (Career Examination Ser.: C-1258). (Cloth bdg. avail. on request). pap. 8.00 (ISBN 0-8373-1258-2). Natl Learning.

--Drafting Technician. (Career Examination Ser.: C-2678). (Cloth bdg. avail. on request). pap. 10.00 (ISBN 0-8373-2678-8). Natl Learning.

--Draftsman. (Career Examination Ser.: C-203). (Cloth bdg. avail. on request). pap. 10.00 (ISBN 0-8373-0203-X). Natl Learning.

--Dressmaking. (Occupational Competency Examination Ser.: OCE-17). (Cloth bdg. avail. on request). pap. 13.95 (ISBN 0-8373-5717-9). Natl Learning.

--Driver License Written Examination. (Career Examination Ser.: C-1635). (Cloth bdg. avail. on request). pap. 10.00 (ISBN 0-8373-1635-9). Natl Learning.

--Drug Abuse Education Group Leader. (Career Examination Ser.: C-1259). (Cloth bdg. avail. on request). pap. 12.00 (ISBN 0-8373-1259-0). Natl Learning.

--Drug Abuse Educator. (Career Examination Ser.: C-1597). (Cloth bdg. avail. on request). pap. 12.00 (ISBN 0-8373-1597-2). Natl Learning.

--Drug Abuse Group Worker. (Career Examination Ser.: C-1260). (Cloth bdg. avail. on request). pap. 10.00 (ISBN 0-8373-1260-4). Natl Learning.

--Drug Abuse Rehabilitation Counselor. (Career Examination Ser.: C-2929). (Cloth bdg. avail. on request). pap. 12.00 (ISBN 0-8373-2929-9). Natl Learning.

--Drug Abuse Technician. (Career Examination Ser.: C-1405). (Cloth bdg. avail. on request). pap. 10.00 (ISBN 0-8373-1405-4). Natl Learning.

--Drug Abuse Technician Trainee. (Career Examination Ser.: C-1406). (Cloth bdg. avail. on request). pap. 10.00 (ISBN 0-8373-1406-2). Natl Learning.

--Duplicating Machine Supervisor. (Career Examination Ser.: C-1408). (Cloth bdg. avail. on request). pap. 10.00 (ISBN 0-8373-1408-9). Natl Learning.

--Early Childhood - Elementary School (Pre-Kg.-2) (Teachers License Examination Ser.: T-13). (Cloth bdg. avail. on request). pap. 13.95 (ISBN 0-8373-8013-8). Natl Learning.

--Early Childhood Education - Kindergarten-Grade 3. (National Teachers Examination Ser.: NT-2). (Cloth bdg. avail. on request). pap. 11.95 (ISBN 0-8373-8412-5). Natl Learning.

--Earth Science & General Science - Sr. H.S. (Teachers License Examination Ser.: T-14). (Cloth bdg. avail. on request). pap. 13.95 (ISBN 0-8373-8014-6). Natl Learning.

--Economic Opportunity Program Specialist. (Career Examination Ser.: C-2545). (Cloth bdg. avail. on request). pap. 12.00 (ISBN 0-8373-2545-5). Natl Learning.

--Economics. (Graduate Record Examination Ser.: GRE-3). (Cloth bdg. avail. on request). pap. 13.95 (ISBN 0-8373-5203-7). Natl Learning.

--Editorial Assistant. (Career Examination Ser.: C-220). (Cloth bdg. avail. on request). pap. 10.00 (ISBN 0-8373-0220-X). Natl Learning.

--Editorial Clerk. (Career Examination Ser.: C-2564). (Cloth bdg. avail. on request). pap. 10.00 (ISBN 0-8373-2564-1). Natl Learning.

--Education. (Graduate Record Examination Ser.: GRE-4). (Cloth bdg. avail. on request). pap. 13.95 (ISBN 0-8373-5204-5). Natl Learning.

--Education. (Teachers License Examination Ser.: G-1). (Cloth bdg. avail. on request). pap. 10.00 (ISBN 0-8373-8191-6). Natl Learning.

--Education in an Urban Setting. (National Teachers Examination Ser.: NT-31). (Cloth bdg. avail. on request). pap. 11.95 (ISBN 0-8373-8441-9). Natl Learning.

--Education in the Elementary School - Grades 3-8. (National Teachers Examination Ser.: NT-1). (Cloth bdg. avail. on request). pap. 11.95 (ISBN 0-8373-8411-7). Natl Learning.

--Education of the Mentally Retarded. (National Teacher Examination Ser.: NT-24). (Cloth bdg. avail. on request). pap. 11.95 (ISBN 0-686-53780-7). Natl Learning.

--Education Program Assistant. (Career Examination Ser.: C-865). (Cloth bdg. avail. on request). pap. 12.00 (ISBN 0-8373-0865-8). Natl Learning.

--Education Supervisor. (Career Examination Ser.: C-2508). (Cloth bdg. avail. on request). pap. 12.00 (ISBN 0-8373-2508-0). Natl Learning.

--Education Supervisor (Developmental Disabilities) (Career Examination Ser.: C-2511). (Cloth bdg. avail. on request). pap. 12.00 (ISBN 0-8373-2511-0). Natl Learning.

--Education Supervisor (Special Subjects) (Career Examination Ser.: C-2509). pap. 12.00 (ISBN 0-8373-2509-9); avail. Natl Learning.

--Education Supervisor (Vocational) (Career Examination Ser.: C-2510). (Cloth bdg. avail. on request). pap. 12.00 (ISBN 0-8373-2510-2). Natl Learning.

--Educational Administration & Supervision. (National Teachers Examination Ser.: NT-15). (Cloth bdg. avail. on request). pap. 11.95 (ISBN 0-8373-8425-7). Natl Learning.

--Educational Commission for Foreign Medical Graduates Examination (ECFMG) (Admission Test Ser.: ATS-24). (Cloth bdg. avail. on request). pap. 19.95 (ISBN 0-8373-5024-7). Natl Learning.

--Educational Commission for Foreign Medical Graduates English Test (ECFMG-ET) (Admission Test Ser.: ATS-43). (Cloth bdg. avail. on request). pap. 13.95 (ISBN 0-8373-5043-3). Natl Learning.

--Educational Commission for Foreign Veterinary Graduates Examination (ECFVG) (Admission Test Ser.: ATS-49). (Cloth bdg. avail. on request). pap. 19.95 (ISBN 0-8373-5049-2). Natl Learning.

--Election Registrar. (Career Examination Ser.: C-1266). (Cloth bdg. avail. on request). pap. 10.00 (ISBN 0-8373-1266-3). Natl Learning.

--Electrical Engineering Trainee. (Career Examination Ser.: C-239). (Cloth bdg. avail. on request). pap. 10.00 (ISBN 0-8373-0239-0). Natl Learning.

--Electrical Inspector. (Career Examination Ser.: C-223). (Cloth bdg. avail. on request). pap. 10.00 (ISBN 0-8373-0223-4). Natl Learning.

--Electrical Installation. (Occupational Competency Examination Ser.: OCE-18). (Cloth bdg. avail. on request). pap. 13.95 (ISBN 0-8373-5718-7). Natl Learning.

--Electrician. (Career Examination Ser.: C-224). (Cloth bdg. avail. on request). pap. 10.00 (ISBN 0-8373-0224-2). Natl Learning.

--Electrician (Automobile) (Career Examination Ser.: C-1268). (Cloth bdg. avail. on request). pap. 10.00 (ISBN 0-8373-1268-X). Natl Learning.

--Electrician's Helper. (Career Examination Ser.: C-225). (Cloth bdg. avail. on request). pap. 10.00 (ISBN 0-8373-0225-0). Natl Learning.

--Electronic Computer Operator Trainee. (Career Examination Ser.: C-242). (Cloth bdg. avail. on request). pap. 8.00 (ISBN 0-8373-0242-0). Natl Learning.

--Electronic Equipment Maintainer. (Career Examination Ser.: C-227). (Cloth bdg. avail. on request). pap. 10.00 (ISBN 0-8373-0227-7). Natl Learning.

--Electronic Equipment Repairer. (Career Examination Ser.: C-243). (Cloth bdg. avail. on request). pap. 10.00 (ISBN 0-8373-0243-9). Natl Learning.

--Electronic Mechanic. (Career Examination Ser.: C-228). (Cloth bdg. avail. on request). pap. 10.00 (ISBN 0-8373-0228-5). Natl Learning.

--Electronic Technician. (Career Examination Ser.: C-229). (Cloth bdg. avail. on request). pap. 10.00 (ISBN 0-8373-0229-3). Natl Learning.

--Electronics Communication. (Occupational Competency Examination Ser.: OCE-19). (Cloth bdg. avail. on request). pap. 13.95 (ISBN 0-8373-5719-5). Natl Learning.
--Elementary School Basic Competency Tests (BCT-ES) (Admission Test Ser.: ATS-56). (Cloth bdg. avail. on request). pap. 11.95 (ISBN 0-8373-5056-5). Natl Learning.
--Elementary Schools. (Teachers Lesson Plan Bk.: E-1). (ps-6). pap. 3.95 (ISBN 0-686-84418-1). Natl Learning A.
--Elevator Inspector. (Career Examination Ser.: C-244). (Cloth bdg. avail. on request). pap. 10.00 (ISBN 0-8373-0244-7). Natl Learning.
--Elevator Mechanic. (Career Examination Ser.: C-1056). (Cloth bdg. avail. on request). pap. 10.00 (ISBN 0-8373-1056-3). Natl Learning.
--Elevator Operator. (Career Examination Ser.: C-230). (Cloth bdg. avail. on request). pap. 8.00 (ISBN 0-8373-0230-7). Natl Learning.
--Elevator Starter. (Career Examination Ser.: C-1270). (Cloth bdg. avail. on request). pap. 8.00 (ISBN 0-8373-1270-1). Natl Learning.
--Eligibility Specialist. (Career Examination Ser.: C-2958). (Cloth bdg. avail. on request). pap. 10.00 (ISBN 0-8373-2958-2). Natl Learning.
--Emergency Communications Specialist. (Career Examination Ser.: C-2878). (Cloth bdg. avail. on request). pap. 12.00 (ISBN 0-8373-2878-0). Natl Learning.
--Employment Counselor. (Career Examination Ser.: C-245). (Cloth bdg. avail. on request). pap. 12.00 (ISBN 0-8373-0245-5). Natl Learning.
--Employment Counselor Trainee. (Career Examination Ser.: C-246). (Cloth bdg. avail. on request). pap. 10.00 (ISBN 0-8373-0246-3). Natl Learning.
--Employment Security Placement Trainee. (Career Examination Ser.: C-2229). (Cloth bdg. avail. on request). pap. 10.00 (ISBN 0-8373-2229-4). Natl Learning.
--Engineering. (Graduate Record Examination Ser.: GRE-5). (Cloth bdg. avail. on request). pap. 13.95 (ISBN 0-8373-5205-3). Natl Learning.
--Engineering Aide. (Career Examination Ser.: C-233). (Cloth bdg. avail. on request). pap. 10.00 (ISBN 0-8373-0233-1). Natl Learning.
--Engineering Aide & Science Assistant. (Career Examination Ser.: C-232). (Cloth bdg. avail. on request). pap. 10.00 (ISBN 0-8373-0232-3). Natl Learning.
--Engineering Assistant. (Career Examination Ser.: C-234). (Cloth bdg. avail. on request). pap. 10.00 (ISBN 0-8373-0234-X). Natl Learning.
--Engineering Draftsman. (Career Examination Ser.: C-247). (Cloth bdg. avail. on request). pap. 10.00 (ISBN 0-8373-0247-1). Natl Learning.
--Engineering Materials Technician. (Career Examination Ser.: C-315). (Cloth bdg. avail. on request). pap. 10.00 (ISBN 0-8373-0315-X). Natl Learning.
--Engineering Technician (Drafting) (Career Examination Ser.: C-991). (Cloth bdg. avail. on request). pap. 10.00 (ISBN 0-8373-0991-3). Natl Learning.
--Engineering Technician Trainee. (Career Examination Ser.: C-248). (Cloth bdg. avail. on request). pap. 10.00 (ISBN 0-8373-0248-X). Natl Learning.
--English & Citizenship. (Teachers License Examination Ser.: T-17). (Cloth bdg. avail. on reqiest). pap. 13.95 (ISBN 0-8373-8017-0). Natl Learning.
--English As a Secondary Language (Day Elementary Schools) (Teachers License Examination Ser.: T-65a). (Cloth bdg. avail. on request). pap. 13.95 (ISBN 0-8373-8085-5). Natl Learning.
--English As a Secondary Language (Secondary Schools) (Teachers License Examination Ser.: T-65b). (Cloth bdg. avail. on request). pap. 13.95 (ISBN 0-685-18722-5). Natl Learning.
--English Chairman: Junior High School. (Teachers License Examination Ser.: CH-4). (Cloth bdg. avail. on request). pap. 15.95 (ISBN 0-8373-8154-1). Natl Learning.
--English Chairman: Senior High School. (Teachers License Examination Ser.: CH-5). (Cloth bdg. avail. on request). pap. 15.95 (ISBN 0-8373-8155-X). Natl Learning.
--English: Junior High School. (Teachers License Examination Ser.: T-15). (Cloth bdg. avail. on request). pap. 13.95 (ISBN 0-685-18728-4). Natl Learning.
--English Language & Literature. (National Teachers Examination Ser.: NT-4). (Cloth bdg. avail. on request). pap. 11.95 (ISBN 0-8373-8414-1). Natl Learning.
--English: Senior High School. (Teachers License Examination Ser.: T-16). (Cloth bdg. avail. on request). pap. 13.95 (ISBN 0-8373-8016-2). Natl Learning.
--Environmental Analyst. (Career Examination Ser.: C-2659). (Cloth bdg. avail. on request). pap. 10.00 (ISBN 0-8373-2659-1). Natl Learning.
--Environmental Assistant. (Career Examination Ser.: C-1583). (Cloth bdg. avail on request). pap. 10.00 (ISBN 0-8373-1583-2). Natl Learning.
--Environmental Control Specialist Trainee. (Career Examination Ser.: C-2067). (Cloth bdg. avail on request). 1977. pap. 10.00 (ISBN 0-8373-2067-4). Natl Learning.
--Environmental Health Aide. (Career Examination Ser.: C-1959). (Cloth bdg. avail. on request). pap. 10.00 (ISBN 0-8373-1959-5). Natl Learning.
--Environmental Health Technician. (Career Examination Ser.: C-2652). (Cloth bdg. avail. on request). pap. 10.00 (ISBN 0-8373-2652-4). Natl Learning.
--Environmental Planner. (Career Examination Ser.: C-2662). (Cloth bdg. avail. on request). pap. 10.00 (ISBN 0-8373-2662-1). Natl Learning.
--Environmentalist. (Career Examination Ser.: C-1584). (Cloth bdg. avail. on request). pap. 10.00 (ISBN 0-8373-1584-0). Natl Learning.
--Equipment Foreman. (Career Examination Ser.: C-1273). (Cloth bdg. avail. on request). pap. 10.00 (ISBN 0-8373-1273-6). Natl Learning.
--Equipment Operator. (Career Examination Ser.: C-1274). (Cloth bdg. avail. on request). pap. 10.00 (ISBN 0-8373-1274-4). Natl Learning.
--Equipment Specialist. (Career Examination Ser.: C-971). (Cloth bdg. avail. on request). pap. 10.00 (ISBN 0-8373-0971-9). Natl Learning.
--Estimator. (Career Examination Ser.: C-1275). (Cloth bdg. avail. on request). pap. 10.00 (ISBN 0-8373-1275-2). Natl Learning.
--Examen De Equivalencia Para el Diploma De Escuela Superior (EEE) (Admission Test Ser.: ATS-22). (Cloth bdg. avail. on request). 1977. pap. 17.95 (ISBN 0-8373-5022-0). Natl Learning.
--Examiner - Board of Examiners. (Teachers License Examination Ser.: GT-10). (Cloth bdg. avail. on request). pap. 17.95 (ISBN 0-8373-8130-4). Natl Learning.
--Examiner, Social Services. (Career Examination Ser.: C-2138). (Cloth bdg. avail. on request). 1977. pap. 8.00 (ISBN 0-8373-2138-7). Natl Learning.
--Excise Tax Investigator. (Career Examination Ser.: C-972). (Cloth bdg. avail. on request). pap. 8.00 (ISBN 0-8373-0972-7). Natl Learning.
--Executive Assistant. (Career Examination Ser.: C-1276). (Cloth bdg. avail. on request). pap. 10.00 (ISBN 0-8373-1276-0). Natl Learning.
--Executive Director. (Career Examination Ser.: C-1277). (Cloth bdg. avail. on request). 12.00 (ISBN 0-8373-1277-9). Natl Learning.
--Executive Director of Youth Bureau. (Career Examination Ser.: C-416). (Cloth bdg. avail. on request). pap. 14.00 (ISBN 0-8373-0416-4). Natl Learning.
--Executive Officer. (Career Examination Ser.: C-1278). (Cloth bdg. avail. on request). pap. 10.00 (ISBN 0-8373-1278-7). Natl Learning.
--Executive Secretary. (Career Examination Ser.: C-1279). (Cloth bdg. avail. on request). pap. 10.00 (ISBN 0-8373-1279-5). Natl Learning.
--Executive Staff Assistant. (Career Examination Ser.: C-1280). (Cloth bdg. avail. on request). pap. 10.00 (ISBN 0-8373-1280-9). Natl Learning.
--Exhibits Technician. (Career Examination Ser.: C-1281). (Cloth bdg. avail. on request). pap. 10.00 (ISBN 0-8373-1281-7). Natl Learning.
--Facility Management Assistant. (Career Examination Ser.: C-387). (Cloth bdg. avail. on request). pap. 10.00 (ISBN 0-8373-0387-7). Natl Learning.
--Factory Inspector. (Career Examination Ser.: C-283). (Cloth bdg. avail. on request). pap. 10.00 (ISBN 0-8373-0283-8). Natl Learning.
--Family Nurse Practitioner. (Certified Nurse Examination Ser.: CN-2). 21.95 (ISBN 0-8373-6152-4); pap. 13.95 (ISBN 0-8373-6102-8). Natl Learning.
--F.C.C. Aircraft Radiotelegraph Endorsement Examination (AR) (Admission Test Ser.: ATS-82). (Cloth bdg. avail. on request). pap. 13.95 o.p. (ISBN 0-8373-5082-4). Natl Learning.
--F.C.C. Amateur License Examination (AL) (Admission Test Ser.: ATS-83). (Cloth bdg. avail. on request). pap. 13.95 (ISBN 0-8373-5083-2). Natl Learning.
--F.C.C. Broadcast Station Operator Endorsement Examination (BSO) (Admission Test Ser.: ATS-80). (Cloth bdg. avail. on request). pap. 13.95 o.p. (ISBN 0-8373-5080-8). Natl Learning.
--F.C.C. Commmercial Radio Operator License Examination (CRO) (Admission Test Ser.: ATS-73). (Cloth bdg avail. on request). pap. 13.95 (ISBN 0-8373-5073-5). Natl Learning.
--F.C.C. Radiotelegraph First Class Operator License Examination (RTg-1) (Admission Test Ser.: ATS-79). (Cloth bdg. avail. on request). pap. 17.95 o.p. (ISBN 0-8373-5179-0). Natl Learning.
--F.C.C. Radiotelegraph Second Class Operator License Examination (RTg-2) (Admission Test Ser.: ATS-78). (Cloth bdg. avail on request). pap. 15.95 o.p. (ISBN 0-8373-5178-2). Natl Learning.
--F.C.C. Radiotelegraph Third Class Operator License Examination (RTg-3) (Admission Test Ser.: ATS-77). (Cloth bdg. avail on request). pap. 13.95 o.p. (ISBN 0-8373-5177-4). Natl Learning.
--F.C.C. Radiotelephone First Class Operator License Examination (RT-1) (Admission Test Ser.: ATS-76). (Cloth bdg. avail. on request). 27.95 o.p. (ISBN 0-8373-5176-6). Natl Learning.
--F.C.C. Radiotelephone Second Class Operator License Examination (RT-2) (Admission Test Ser.: ATS-75). (Cloth bdg. avail. on request). pap. 15.95 o.p. (ISBN 0-8373-5175-8). Natl Learning.
--F.C.C. Radiotelephone Third Class Operator License Examination (RT-3) (Admission Test Ser.: ATS-74). (Cloth bdg. avail. on request). 13.95 o.p. (ISBN 0-8373-5174-X). Natl Learning.
--F.C.C. Ship Radar Endorsement Examination (SR) (Admission Test Ser.: ATS-81). (Cloth bdg. avail. on request). pap. 13.95 o.p. (ISBN 0-8373-5181-2). Natl Learning.
--Federal Administrative & Management Examination. (Career Examination Ser.: C-250). (Cloth bdg. avail. on request). pap. 10.00 (ISBN 0-8373-0250-1). Natl Learning.
--Federal & State Aid Coordinator. (Career Examination Ser.: C-1282). (Cloth bdg. avail. on request). pap. 10.00 (ISBN 0-8373-1282-5). Natl Learning.
--Federal Construction Project Coordinator. (Career Examination Ser.: C-2879). (Cloth bdg. avail. on request). pap. 14.00 (ISBN 0-8373-2879-9). Natl Learning.
--Federal Mine Inspector. (Career Examination Ser.: C-1283). (Cloth bdg. avail. on request). pap. 10.00 (ISBN 0-8373-1283-3). Natl Learning.
--Federal Service Entrance Examination (FSEE) (Admission Test Ser.: ATS-16). (Cloth bdg. avail on request). 11.95 (ISBN 0-8373-5116-2). Natl Learning.
--Federal Service Management Intern Examination. (Career Examination Ser.: C-285). (Cloth bdg. avail. on request). pap. 10.00 (ISBN 0-8373-0285-4). Natl Learning.
--Federation Licensing Examination (FLEX) (Admission Test Ser.: ATS-31). (Cloth bdg. avail. on request). pap. 19.95 (ISBN 0-8373-5131-6). Natl Learning.
--Ferry Terminal Supervisor. (Career Examination Ser.: C-2142). (Cloth bdg. avail. on request). 1977. pap. 10.00 (ISBN 0-8373-2142-5). Natl Learning.
--Field Accountant. (Career Examination Ser.: C-1568). (Cloth bdg. avail. on request). pap. 10.00 (ISBN 0-8373-1568-9). Natl Learning.
--Field Investigator. (Career Examination Ser.: C-1285). (Cloth bdg. avail. on request). pap. 8.00 (ISBN 0-8373-1285-X). Natl Learning.
--Field Representative. (Career Examination Ser.: C-2115). (Cloth bdg. avail. on request). 1977. pap. 10.00 (ISBN 0-685-78607-2). Natl Learning.
--Field Representative, Senior Citizen Services Project. (Career Examination Ser.: C-2948). (Cloth bdg. avail. on request). pap. 12.00 (ISBN 0-8373-2948-5). Natl learning.
--Financial Analyst. (Career Examination Ser.: C-2642). (Cloth bdg. avail. on request). pap. 10.00 (ISBN 0-8373-2642-7). Natl Learning.
--Fine Arts Chairman Jr. H.S. (Questions Only) (Teachers License Examination Ser.: CH-6). (Cloth bdg. avail. on request). pap. 15.95 (ISBN 0-8373-8156-8). Natl Learning.
--Fine Arts Chairman Sr. H.S. (Teachers License Examination Ser.: CH-7). (Cloth bdg. avail. on request). pap. 15.95 (ISBN 0-8373-8157-6). Natl Learning.
--Fine Arts Jr. H.S. (Teachers License Examination Ser.: T-18). (Cloth bdg. avail. on request). pap. 13.95 (ISBN 0-8373-8018-9). Natl Learning.
--Fine Arts Sr. H.S. (Teachers License Examination Ser.: T-19). (Cloth bdg. avail. on request). pap. 13.95 (ISBN 0-8373-8019-7). Natl Learning.
--Fingerprint Technician. (Career Examination Ser.: C-255). (Cloth bdg. avail. on request). pap. 10.00 (ISBN 0-8373-0255-2). Natl Learning.
--Fingerprint Technician Trainee. (Career Examination Ser.: C-286). (Cloth bdg. avail. on request). pap. 10.00 (ISBN 0-8373-0286-2). Natl Learning.
--Fire Administration & Supervision. (Career Examination Ser.: CS-38). (Cloth bdg. avail. on request). pap. 10.00 (ISBN 0-8373-0038-X). Natl Learning.
--Fire Alarm Dispatcher. (Career Examination Ser.: C-256). (Cloth bdg. avail. on request). pap. 10.00 (ISBN 0-8373-0256-0). Natl Learning.
--Fire Inspector. (Career Examination Ser.: C-1288). (Cloth bdg. avail. on request). pap. 10.00 (ISBN 0-8373-1288-4). Natl Learning.
--Fire Officer. (Career Examination Ser.: C-1578). (Cloth bdg. avail. on request). pap. 10.00 (ISBN 0-8373-1578-6). Natl Learning.
--Fire Prevention Inspector. (Career Examination Ser.: C-287). (Cloth bdg. avail. on request). pap. 10.00 (ISBN 0-8373-0287-0). Natl Learning.
--Fire Safety Officer. (Career Examination Ser.: C-2230). (Cloth bdg. avail. on request). pap. 10.00 (ISBN 0-8373-2230-8). Natl Learning.
--Fireman Examinations - All States. (Career Examination Ser.: C-258). (Cloth bdg. avail. on request). pap. 10.00 (ISBN 0-8373-0258-7). Natl Learning.
--Fireman, Fire Department. (Career Examination Ser.: C-259). (Cloth bdg. avail. on request). pap. 10.00 (ISBN 0-8373-0259-5). Natl Learning.
--Fiscal Director. (Career Examination Ser.: C-1290). (Cloth bdg. avail. on request). pap. 14.00 (ISBN 0-8373-1290-6). Natl Learning.
--Fiscal Manager. (Career Examination Ser.: C-2686). (Cloth bdg. avail. on request). pap. 12.00 (ISBN 0-8373-2686-9). Natl Learning.
--Florida Functional Literacy Test (FLT) (Admission Test Ser.: ATS-54). (Cloth bdg. avail. on request). pap. 11.95 (ISBN 0-8373-5054-9). Natl Learning.
--Food Inspector. (Career Examination Ser.: C-2543). (Cloth bdg. avail. on request). pap. 8.00 (ISBN 0-8373-2543-9). Natl Learning.
--Food Service Supervisor. (Career Examination Ser.: C-1411). (Cloth bdg. avail. on request). pap. 10.00 (ISBN 0-8373-1411-9). Natl Learning.
--Foreign Language: French. (Regents External Degree Ser.: REDP-27). 17.95 (ISBN 0-8373-5677-6); pap. 9.95 (ISBN 0-8373-5627-X). Natl Learning.
--Foreign Language: German. (Regents External Degree Ser.: REDP-28). 17.95 (ISBN 0-8373-5678-4); pap. 9.95 (ISBN 0-8373-5628-8). Natl Learning.
--Foreign Language: Italian. (Regents External Degree Ser.: REDP-29). 17.95 (ISBN 0-8373-5679-2); pap. 9.95 (ISBN 0-8373-5629-6). Natl Learning.
--Foreign Language: Spanish. (Regents External Degree Ser.: REDP-30). 17.95 (ISBN 0-8373-5680-6); pap. 9.95 (ISBN 0-8373-5630-X). Natl Learning.
--Foreign Languages Chairman-Jr. H.S. (Teachers License Examination Ser.: CH-8). (Cloth bdg. avail. on request). pap. 15.95 (ISBN 0-8373-8158-4). Natl Learning.
--Foreign Languages Chairman-Sr. H.S. (Teachers License Examination Ser.: CH-9). (Cloth bdg. avail. on request). pap. 15.95 (ISBN 0-8373-8159-2). Natl Learning.
--Foreman. (Career Examination Ser.: C-262). (Cloth bdg. avail. on request). pap. 10.00 (ISBN 0-8373-0262-5). Natl Learning.
--Foreman Asphalt Worker. (Career Examination Ser.: C-2080). (Cloth bdg. avail. on request). 1977. pap. 10.00 (ISBN 0-8373-2080-1). Natl Learning.
--Foreman Auto Mechanic. (Career Examination Ser.: C-263). (Cloth bdg. avail. on request). pap. 10.00 (ISBN 0-8373-0263-3). Natl Learning.
--Foreman Blacksmith. (Career Examination Ser.: C-1709). (Cloth bdg. avail. on request). pap. 10.00 (ISBN 0-8373-1709-6). Natl Learning.
--Foreman Bricklayer. (Career Examination Ser.: C-2020). (Cloth bdg. avail. on request). pap. 10.00 (ISBN 0-8373-2020-8). Natl Learning.
--Foreman Bridge Painter. (Career Examination Ser.: C-1412). (Cloth bdg. avail. on request). pap. 10.00 (ISBN 0-8373-1412-7). Natl Learning.
--Foreman (Buses & Shops) (Career Examination Ser.: C-264). (Cloth bdg. avail. on request). pap. 10.00 (ISBN 0-8373-0264-1). Natl Learning.
--Foreman Cable Splicer. (Career Examination Ser.: C-2021). (Cloth bdg. avail. on request). pap. 10.00 (ISBN 0-8373-2021-6). Natl Learning.
--Foreman Carpenter. (Career Examination Ser.: C-1779). (Cloth bdg. avail. on request). pap. 10.00 (ISBN 0-8373-1779-7). Natl Learning.
--Foreman (Cars & Shops) (Career Examination Ser.: C-265). (Cloth bdg. avail. on request). pap. 10.00 (ISBN 0-8373-0265-X). Natl Learning.
--Foreman (Department of Sanitation) (Career Examination Ser.: C-266). (Cloth bdg. avail. on request). pap. 10.00 (ISBN 0-8373-0266-8). Natl Learning.
--Foreman Dockbuilder. (Career Examination Ser.: C 2022). (Cloth bdg. avail. on request). pap. 10.00 (ISBN 0-8373-2022-4). Natl Learning.
--Foreman (Electrical Power) (Career Examination Ser.: C-267). (Cloth bdg. avail. on request). pap. 10.00 (ISBN 0-8373-0267-6). Natl Learning.
--Foreman Electrician. (Career Examination Ser.: C-1710). (Cloth bdg. avail. on request). pap. 10.00 (ISBN 0-8373-1710-X). Natl Learning.
--Foreman (Electronic Equipment) (Career Examination Ser.: C-2032). (Cloth bdg. avail. on request). pap. 10.00 (ISBN 0-8373-2032-1). Natl Learning.
--Foreman Elevator Mechanic. (Career Examination Ser.: C-2165). (Cloth bdg. avail. on request). 1976. pap. 10.00 (ISBN 0-8373-2165-4). Natl Learning.
--Foreman (Elevators & Escalators) (Career Examination Ser.: C-1413). (Cloth bdg. avail. on request). pap. 10.00 (ISBN 0-8373-1413-5). Natl Learning.
--Foreman Furniture Maintainer. (Career Examination Ser.: C-2023). (Cloth bdg. avail. on request). pap. 10.00 (ISBN 0-8373-2023-2). Natl Learning.
--Foreman (Highways & Sewers) (Career Examination Ser.: C-2190). (Cloth bdg. avail. on request). pap. 10.00 (ISBN 0-8373-2190-5). Natl Learning.
--Foreman, Laborer-Janitor (U.S.P.S.) (Career Examination Ser.: C-1686). (Cloth bdg. avail. on request). pap. 10.00 (ISBN 0-8373-1686-3). Natl Learning.
--Foreman Lineman. (Career Examination Ser.: C-2024). (Cloth bdg. avail. on request). pap. 10.00 (ISBN 0-8373-2024-0). Natl Learning.
--Foreman Locksmith. (Career Examination Ser.: C-2223). (Cloth bdg. avail. on request). pap. 10.00 (ISBN 0-8373-2223-5). Natl Learning.
--Foreman Machinist. (Career Examination Ser.: C-1414). (Cloth bdg. avail. on request). pap. 10.00 (ISBN 0-8373-1414-3). Natl Learning.

--Foreman of Housing Caretakers. (Career Examination Ser.: C-269). (Cloth bdg. avail. on request). pap. 10.00 (ISBN 0-8373-0269-2). Natl Learning.

--Foreman of Housing Exterminators. (Career Examination Ser.: C-2514). (Cloth bdg. avail. on request). pap. 12.00 (ISBN 0-686-53718-1). Natl Learning.

--Foreman of Laborers. (Career Examination Ser.: C-270). (Cloth bdg. avail. on request). pap. 10.00 (ISBN 0-8373-0270-6). Natl Learning.

--Foreman of Lighting. (Career Examination Ser.: C-271). (Cloth bdg. avail. on request). pap. 10.00 (ISBN 0-8373-0271-4). Natl Learning.

--Foreman of Mechanics. (Career Examination Ser.: C-1605). (Cloth bdg. avail. on request). 1977. pap. 10.00 (ISBN 0-8373-1605-7). Natl Learning.

--Foreman of Mechanics (Motor Vehicles) (Career Examination Ser.: C-272). (Cloth bdg. avail. on request). pap. 10.00 (ISBN 0-8373-0272-2). Natl Learning.

--Foreman Painter. (Career Examination Ser.: C-273). (Cloth bdg. avail. on request). text ed. 10.00 (ISBN 0-8373-0273-0). Natl Learning.

--Foreman Plasterer. (Career Examination Ser.: C-2270). (Cloth bdg. avail. on request). 1977. pap. 10.00 (ISBN 0-8373-2270-7). Natl Learning.

--Foreman Plumber. (Career Examination Ser.: C-1415). (Cloth bdg. avail. on request). pap. 10.00 (ISBN 0-8373-1415-1). Natl Learning.

--Foreman (Power Cables) (Career Examination Ser.: C-2034). (Cloth bdg. avail. on request). pap. 10.00 (ISBN 0-8373-2034-8). Natl Learning.

--Foreman (Power Distribution) (Career Examination Ser.: C-274). (Cloth bdg. avail. on request). pap. 10.00 (ISBN 0-8373-0274-9). Natl Learning.

--Foreman (Railroad Watchman) (Career Examination Ser.: C-275). (Cloth bdg. avail. on request). pap. 10.00 (ISBN 0-8373-0275-7). Natl Learning.

--Foreman Roofer. (Career Examination Ser.: C-1416). (Cloth bdg. avail. on request). pap. 10.00 (ISBN 0-8373-1416-X). Natl Learning.

--Foreman (Sewer Maintenance) (Career Examination Ser.: C-1816). (Cloth bdg. avail. on request). pap. 10.00 (ISBN 0-8373-1816-5). Natl Learning.

--Foreman Sheet Metal Worker. (Career Examination Ser.: C-1711). (Cloth bdg. avail. on request). pap. 10.00 (ISBN 0-8373-1711-8). Natl Learning.

--Foreman (Signals) (Career Examination Ser.: C-276). (Cloth bdg. avail. on request). pap. 10.00 (ISBN 0-8373-0276-5). Natl Learning.

--Foreman Steamfitter. (Career Examination Ser.: C-2025). (Cloth bdg. avail. on request). pap. 10.00 (ISBN 0-8373-2025-9). Natl Learning.

--Foreman (Stores, Materials & Supplies) (Career Examination Ser.: C-1625). (Cloth bdg. avail. on request). pap. 10.00 (ISBN 0-8373-1625-1). Natl Learning.

--Foreman (Structures - Group A) (Carpentry) (Career Examination Ser.: C-1322). (Cloth bdg. avail. on request). pap. 12.00 (ISBN 0-8373-1322-8). Natl Learning.

--Foreman (Structures - Group B) (Masonry) (Career Examination Ser.: C-1323). (Cloth bdg. avail. on request). pap. 12.00 (ISBN 0-8373-1323-6). Natl Learning.

--Foreman (Structures - Group C) (Iron Work) (Career Examination Ser.: C-1324). (Cloth bdg. avail. on request). pap. 12.00 (ISBN 0-8373-1324-4). Natl Learning.

--Foreman (Structures - Group D) (Sheet Metal) (Career Examination Ser.: C-2777). (Cloth bdg. avail. on request). 1977. pap. 12.00 (ISBN 0-8373-2277-4). Natl Learning.

--Foreman (Structures - Group E (Plumbing) (Career Examination Ser.: C-2278). (Cloth bdg. avail. on request). 1977. text ed. 12.00 (ISBN 0-8373-2278-2). Natl Learning.

--Foreman (Structures - Group F) (Painting) (Career Examination Ser.: C-1325). (Cloth bdg. avail. on request). pap. 12.00 (ISBN 0-8373-1325-2). Natl Learning.

--Foreman (Telephones) (Career Examination Ser.: C-1970). (Cloth bdg. avail. on request). pap. 10.00 (ISBN 0-8373-1970-6). Natl Learning.

--Foreman (Track) (Career Examination Ser.: C-277). (Cloth bdg. avail. on request). pap. 10.00 (ISBN 0-8373-0277-3). Natl Learning.

--Foreman Traffic Device Maintenance. (Career Examination Ser.: C-1712). (Cloth bdg. avail. on request). pap. 10.00 (ISBN 0-8373-1712-6). Natl Learning.

--Foreman (Turnstiles) (Career Examination Ser.: C-2033). (Cloth bdg. avail. on request). pap. 10.00 (ISBN 0-8373-2033-X). Natl Learning.

--Foreman (Ventilation & Drainage) (Career Examination Ser.: C-278). (Cloth bdg. avail. on request). pap. 10.00 (ISBN 0-8373-0278-1). Natl Learning.

--Foreman (Water Supply) (Career Examination Ser.: C-279). (Cloth bdg. avail. on request). pap. 10.00 (ISBN 0-8373-0279-X). Natl Learning.

--Foreman (Watershed Maintenance) (Career Examination Ser.: C-280). (Cloth bdg. avail. on request). pap. 10.00 (ISBN 0-8373-0280-3). Natl Learning.

--Forensic Medicine Investigator. (Career Examination Ser.: C-2936). (Cloth bdg. avail. on request). pap. 12.00 (ISBN 0-8373-2936-1). Natl Learning.

--Forensic Scientist I (Toxicology) (Career Examination Ser.: C-2937). (Cloth bdg. avail. on request). pap. 14.00 (ISBN 0-8373-2937-X). Natl Learning.

--Forensic Scientist II (Toxicology) (Career Examination Ser.: C-2938). (Cloth bdg. avail. on request). pap. 14.00 (ISBN 0-8373-2938-8). Natl Learning.

--Forest Ranger. (Career Examination Ser.: C-281). (Cloth bdg. avail. on request). 10.00 (ISBN 0-8373-0281-1). Natl Learning.

--Forester. (Career Examination Ser.: C-289). (Cloth bdg. avail. on request). pap. 10.00 (ISBN 0-8373-0289-7). Natl Learning.

--Forestry Technician. (Career Examination Ser.: C-1424). (Cloth bdg. avail. on request). pap. 10.00 (ISBN 0-8373-1424-0). Natl Learning.

--Freight Rate Specialist. (Career Examination Ser.: C-973). (Cloth bdg. avail.on request). pap. 8.00 (ISBN 0-8373-0973-5). Natl Learning.

--French. (National Teachers Examination Ser.: NT-19). (Cloth bdg. avail. on request). pap. 11.95 (ISBN 0-8373-8429-X). Natl Learning.

--French. (Graduate Record Examination Ser.: GRE-6). (Cloth bdg. avail. on request). 13.95 (ISBN 0-8373-5206-1). Natl Learning.

--French. (College Level Examination Ser.: CLEP-44). 1976. 14.95 (ISBN 0-8373-5394-7); pap. 17.95 (ISBN 0-8373-5344-0). Natl Learning.

--French-Jr. H.S. (Teachers License Examination Ser.: T-20). (Cloth bdg. avail. on request). pap. 13.95 (ISBN 0-8373-8020-0). Natl Learning.

--French-Sr. H.S. (Teachers License Examination Ser.: T-21). (Cloth bdg. avail. on request). pap. 13.95 (ISBN 0-8373-8021-9). Natl Learning.

--Fundamentals of Nursing. (ACT Proficiency Examination Program: PEP-36). (Cloth bdg. avail. on request). pap. 9.95 (ISBN 0-8373-5536-2). Natl Learning.

--Game Management. (Career Examination Ser.: C-1291). (Cloth bdg. avail. on request). pap. 10.00 (ISBN 0-8373-1291-4). Natl Learning.

--Game Warden. (Career Examination Ser.: C-2012). (Cloth bdg. avail. on request). pap. 10.00 (ISBN 0-8373-2012-7). Natl Learning.

--Gang Foreman (Structures-Group A) (Carpentry) (Career Examination Ser.: C-290). (Cloth bdg. avail. on request). pap. 10.00 (ISBN 0-8373-0290-0). Natl Learning.

--Gang Foreman (Structures-Group B) (Masonry) (Career Examination Ser.: C-291). (Cloth bdg. avail. on request). pap. 10.00 (ISBN 0-8373-0291-9). Natl Learning.

--Gang Foreman (Structures-Group C) (Iron Woorks) (Career Examination Ser.: C-292). (Cloth bdg. avail. on request). pap. 10.00 (ISBN 0-8373-0292-7). Natl Learning.

--Gang Foreman (Structures-Group D) (Sheet Metal) (Career Examination Ser.: C-293). (Cloth bdg. avail. on request). pap. 10.00 (ISBN 0-8373-0293-5). Natl Learning.

--Gang Foreman (Structures-Group E) (Plumbing) (Career Examination Ser.: C-29a). (Cloth bdg. avail. on request). pap. 10.00 (ISBN 0-8373-0294-3). Natl Learning.

--Gang Foreman (Structures-Group F) (Painting) (Career Examination Ser.: C-295). (Cloth bdg. avail. on request). pap. 10.00 (ISBN 0-8373-0295-1). Natl Learning.

--Gang Foreman (Track) (Career Examination Ser.: C-296). (Cloth bdg. avail. on request). pap. 10.00 (ISBN 0-8373-0296-X). Natl Learning.

--Garage Foreman. (Career Examination Ser.: C-1603). (Cloth bdg. avail. on request). pap. 10.00 (ISBN 0-8373-1603-0). Natl Learning.

--General Aptitude Test. (Career Examination Ser.: CS-29). (Cloth bdg. avail. on request). pap. 8.00 (ISBN 0-8373-3779-8). Natl Learning.

--General Industrial Training Supervisor. (Career Examination Ser.: C-2893). (Cloth bdg. avail. on request). pap. 14.00 (ISBN 0-8373-2893-4). Natl Learning.

--General Mathematical Ability (G.E.D.) (Career Examination Ser.: CS-33). (Cloth bdg. avail. on request). pap. 8.00 (ISBN 0-8373-3733-X). Natl Learning.

--General Mechanic (USPS) (Career Examination Ser.: C-835). (Cloth bdg. avail. on request). pap. 10.00 (ISBN 0-8373-0835-6). Natl Learning.

--General Park Foreman. (Career Examination Ser.: C-299). (Cloth bdg. avail. on request). pap. 10.00 (ISBN 0-8373-0299-4). Natl Learning.

--General Park Manager. (Career Examination Ser.: C-386). (Cloth bdg. avail. on request). pap. 14.00 (ISBN 0-8373-0386-9). Natl Learning.

--General Printing. (Occupational Competency Examination Ser.: OCE-20). (Cloth bdg. avail. on request). pap. 13.95 (ISBN 0-8373-5720-9). Natl Learning.

--General Science-Jr. H.S. (Teachers License Examination Ser.: T-22). (Cloth bdg. avail. on request). pap. 13.95 (ISBN 0-8373-8022-7). Natl Learning.

--General Supervisor. (Career Examination Ser.: C-1295). (Cloth bdg. avail. on request). pap. 10.00 (ISBN 0-8373-1295-7). Natl Learning.

--Geography. (Graduate Record Examination Ser.: GRE-7). (Cloth bdg. avail. on request). 13.95 (ISBN 0-8373-5207-X). Natl Learning.

--Geologist. (Career Examination Ser.: C-301). (Cloth bdg. avail. on request). pap. 10.00 (ISBN 0-8373-0301-X). Natl Learning.

--Geology. (Graduate Record Examination Ser.: GRE-8). (Cloth bdg. avail. on request). pap. 13.95 (ISBN 0-8373-5208-8). Natl Learning.

--German. (Graduate-Record Examination Ser.: GRE-9). (Cloth bdg. avail. on request). pap. 13.95 (ISBN 0-8373-5209-6). Natl Learning.

--German. (National Teachers Examination Ser.: NT-32). (Cloth bdg. avail. on request). pap. 11.95 (ISBN 0-8373-8442-7). Natl Learning.

--Gerontological Nurse. (Certified Nurse Examination Ser.: CN-5). 21.95 (ISBN 0-8373-6155-9); pap. 13.95 (ISBN 0-8373-6105-2). Natl Learning.

--Gerontological Nurse Practitioner. (Certified Nurse Examination Ser.: CN-6). 21.95 (ISBN 0-8373-6156-7); pap. 13.95 (ISBN 0-8373-6106-0). Natl Learning.

--Golf Course Supervisor. (Career Examination Ser.: C-2774). (Cloth bdg. avail. on request). 1980. pap. 10.00 (ISBN 0-8373-2774-1). Natl Learning.

--Graduate Management Admission Test (GMAT) (Admission Test Ser.: ATS-14). 300p. (Cloth bdg. avail. on request). pap. 13.95 (ISBN 0-8373-5014-X). Natl Learning.

--Graduate Record Examination Aptitude Test. (Admission Test Ser.: ATS-10). 300p. (Cloth bdg. avail. on request). 13.95 (ISBN 0-8373-5010-7). Natl Learning.

--Grammar. (Teachers License Examination Ser.: G-2). (Cloth bdg. avail. on request). pap. 10.00 (ISBN 0-8373-8192-4). Natl Learning.

--Graphic Arts Specialist. (Career Examination Ser.: C-2672). (Cloth bdg. avail. on request). pap. 10.00 (ISBN 0-8373-2672-9). Natl Learning.

--Greenskeeper. (Career Examination Ser.: C-2656). (Cloth bdg. avail. on request). pap. 10.00 (ISBN 0-8373-2656-7). Natl Learning.

--Guidance Counselor - Elementary School. (Teachers License Examination Ser.: GT-1). (Cloth bdg. avail. on request). pap. 13.95 (ISBN 0-8373-8121-5). Natl Learning.

--Guidance Counselor - Jr. H.S. (Teachers License Examination Ser.: GT-2). (Cloth bdg. avail. on request). pap. 13.95 (ISBN 0-8373-8122-3). Natl Learning.

--Guidance Counselor - Sr. H.S. (Teachers License Examination Ser.: GT-3). (Cloth bdg. avail. on request). pap. 13.95 (ISBN 0-8373-8123-1). Natl Learning.

--Guidance Counselor, Elementary School. (National Teachers Examination Ser.: NT-16a). (Cloth bdg. avail. on request). pap. 11.95 (ISBN 0-8373-8426-5). Natl Learning.

--Guidance Counselor, Junior H.S. (National Teachers Examination Ser.: NT-16b). (Cloth bdg. avail. on request). pap. 11.95 (ISBN 0-8373-8427-3). Natl Learning.

--Guidance Counselor, Senior H.S. (National Teachers Examination Ser.: NT-16c). (Cloth bdg. avail. on request). pap. 11.95 (ISBN 0-8373-8428-1). Natl Learning.

--Habitation Specialist. (Career Examination Ser.: C-2900). (Cloth bdg avail. on request). pap. 12.00 (ISBN 0-8373-2900-0). Natl Learning.

--Handbook of Real Estate (HRE) (Admission Test Ser.: ATS-5). 300p. (Cloth bdg. avail. on request). 13.95 (ISBN 0-8373-5005-0). Natl Learning.

--Handbook of the Stock Market (HOS) (Admission Test Ser.: ATS-2). 300p. (Cloth bdg. avail. on request). pap. 7.50 (ISBN 0-8373-5005-0). Natl Learning.

--Hawaii Credit-by-Examination Program (CEP) (Admission Test Ser.: ATS-62). (Cloth bdg. avail on request). pap. 11.95 (ISBN 0-8373-5062-X). Natl Learning.

--Head Accountant-Audit Clerk. (Career Examination Ser.: C-2009). (Cloth bdg. avail. on request). pap. 12.00 (ISBN 0-8373-1654-5). Natl Learning.

--Head Bus Driver. (Career Examination Ser.: C-2198). (Cloth bdg. avail. on request). pap. 10.00 (ISBN 0-8373-2198-0). Natl Learning.

--Head Clerk. (Career Examination Ser.: C-347). (Cloth bdg. avail. on request). pap. 12.00 (ISBN 0-8373-0347-8). Natl Learning.

--Head Custodian. (Career Examination Ser.: C-1958). (Cloth bdg. avail. on request). pap. 12.00 (ISBN 0-8373-1958-7). Natl Learning.

--Head Custodian 1. (Career Examination Ser.: C-1823). (Cloth bdg. avail. on request). pap. 12.00 (ISBN 0-8373-1823-8). Natl Learning.

--Head Custodian 2. (Career Examination Ser.: C-1824). (Cloth bdg. avail. on request). pap. 12.00 (ISBN 0-8373-1824-6). Natl Learning.

--Head Nurse. (Career Examination Ser.: C-321). (Cloth bdg. avail. on request). pap. 12.00 (ISBN 0-8373-0321-4). Natl Learning.

--Head Process Server. (Career Examination Ser.: C-348). (Cloth bdg. avail. on request). 10.00 (ISBN 0-8373-0348-6). Natl Learning.

--Head Process Server & Court Aide. (Career Examination Ser.: C-349). (Cloth bdg. avail. on request). pap. 10.00 (ISBN 0-8373-0349-4). Natl Learning.

--Head Stationary Engineer. (Career Examination Ser.: C-1720). (Cloth bdg. avail on request). pap. 12.00 (ISBN 0-8373-1720-7). Natl Learning.

--Health - Jr. H.S. (Teachers License Examination Ser.: T-24a). (Cloth bdg. avail on request). pap. 13.95 (ISBN 0-8373-8024-3). Natl Learning.

--Health - Sr. H.S. (Teachers License Examination Ser.: T-24b). (Cloth bdg. avail. on request). pap. 13.95 (ISBN 0-685-18755-1). Natl Learning.

--Health & Physical Education - Jr. H.S. (Teachers License Examination Ser.: T-24). (Cloth bdg. avail. on request). pap. 13.95 (ISBN 0-8373-8025-1). Natl Learning.

--Health & Physical Education - Sr. H.S. (Teachers License Examination Ser.: T-25). (Cloth bdg. avail. on request). pap. 13.95 (ISBN 0-685-18748-9). Natl Learning.

--Health & Physical Education Chairman - Jr. H.S. (Teachers License Examination Ser.: CH-10). (Cloth bdg. avail. on request). pap. 15.95 (ISBN 0-8373-8160-6). Natl Learning.

--Health & Physical Education Chairman - Sr. H.S. (Teachers License Examination Ser.: CH-11). (Cloth bdg. avail. on request). pap. 15.95 (ISBN 0-685-18752-7). Natl Learning.

--Health Conservation. (Teachers License Examination Ser.: T-23). (Cloth bdg. avail. on request). pap. 13.95 (ISBN 0-8373-8023-5). Natl Learning.

--Health Insurance Administrator. (Career Examination Ser.: C-2687). (Cloth bdg. avail. on request). pap. 12.00 (ISBN 0-8373-2687-7). Natl Learning.

--Health One. (College Proficiency Examination Ser.: CPEP-17). 17.95 (ISBN 0-8373-5467-6); pap. 9.95 (ISBN 0-8373-5417-X). Natl Learning.

--Health One: Personal Health, Physical Aspects. (ACT Proficiency Examination Program Ser.: PEP-33). 17.95 (ISBN 0-8373-5583-4); pap. 9.95 (ISBN 0-8373-5533-8). Natl Learning.

--Health Support: Area I. (ACT Proficiency Examination Program: PEP-48). 17.95 (ISBN 0-8373-5598-2); pap. 9.95 (ISBN 0-8373-5548-6). Natl Learning.

--Health Support: Area I. (Regents External Degree Ser.: REDP-24). 17.95 (ISBN 0-8373-5674-1); pap. 9.95 (ISBN 0-8373-5624-5). Natl Learning.

--Health Support: Area II. (ACT Proficiency Examination Program: PEP-49). 17.95 (ISBN 0-8373-5599-0); pap. 9.95 (ISBN 0-8373-5549-4). Natl Learning.

--Health Support: Area II. (Regents External Degree Ser.: REDP-25). 17.95 (ISBN 0-8373-5675-X); pap. 9.95 (ISBN 0-8373-5625-3). Natl Learning.

--Health Three. (College Proficiency Examination Ser.: CPEP-19). 17.95 (ISBN 0-8373-5469-2); pap. 9.95 (ISBN 0-8373-5419-6). Natl Learning.

--Health Three: Public & Environmental Health. (ACT Proficiency Examination Program Ser.: PEP-35). 17.95 (ISBN 0-8373-5585-0); pap. 9.95 (ISBN 0-8373-5535-4). Natl Learning.

--Health Two. (College Proficiency Examination Ser.: CPEP-18). 17.95 (ISBN 0-8373-5468-4); pap. 9.95 (ISBN 0-8373-5418-8). Natl Learning.

--Health Two: Personal Health, Emotional-Social Aspects. (ACT Proficiency Examination Program Ser.: PEP-34). 17.95 (ISBN 0-8373-5584-2); pap. 9.95 (ISBN 0-8373-5534-6). Natl Learning.

--Heavy Equipment Repair Supervisor. (Career Examination Ser.: C-2614). (Cloth bdg. avail. on request). pap. 12.00 (ISBN 0-8373-2614-1). Natl Learning.

--Hebrew - Jr. & Sr. H.S. (Teachers License Examination Ser.: T-26). (Cloth bdg. avail. on request). pap. 13.95 (ISBN 0-8373-8026-X). Natl Learning.

--Hematology. (College Level Examination Ser.: CLEP-33). 19.95 (ISBN 0-8373-5383-1); pap. 11.95 (ISBN 0-8373-5333-5). Natl Learning.

--High Risk Perinatal Nurse. (Certified Nurse Examination Ser.: CN-10). 21.95 (ISBN 0-8373-6160-5); pap. 13.95 (ISBN 0-8373-6110-9). Natl Learning.

--High School APL Survey (APL-HS) (Admission Test Ser.: ATS-60A). 19.95 (ISBN 0-8373-5160-X); pap. 11.95 (ISBN 0-8373-5060-3). Natl Learning.

--High School Basic Competency Tests (BCT-HS) (Admission Test Ser.: ATS-57). 19.95 (ISBN 0-8373-5157-X); pap. 11.95 (ISBN 0-8373-5057-3). Natl Learning.

--High School Equivalency Diploma Examination (EE) (Admission Test Ser.: ATS-17). 21.95 (ISBN 0-8373-5117-0); pap. 13.95 (ISBN 0-8373-5017-4). Natl Learning.

--High School Equivalency Diplomacy Examination. (Career Examination Ser.: CS-50). (Cloth bdg. avail. on request). pap. 13.95 (ISBN 0-686-84423-8). Natl Learning.

--History. (Graduate Record Examination Ser.: GRE-10). 21.95 (ISBN 0-8373-5260-6); pap. 13.95 (ISBN 0-8373-5210-X). Natl Learning.

--History of American Education. (College Level Examination Ser.: CLEP-16). 17.95 (ISBN 0-8373-5366-1); pap. 9.95 (ISBN 0-8373-5316-5). Natl Learning.

--History of American Education. (College Proficiency Examination Ser.: CPEP-21). 17.95 (ISBN 0-8373-5471-4); pap. 9.95 (ISBN 0-8373-5421-8). Natl Learning.

--History of American Education. (ACT Proficiency Examination Program Ser.: PEP-29). 17.95 (ISBN 0-8373-5579-6); pap. 9.95 (ISBN 0-8373-5529-X). Natl Learning.
--Hoisting Machine Operator. (Career Examination Ser.: C-2257). (Cloth bdg. avail. on request). 1977. pap. 10.00 (ISBN 0-8373-2257-X). Natl Learning.
--Hoists & Rigging Inspector. (Career Examination Ser.: C-323). (Cloth bdg. avail. on request). pap. 10.00 (ISBN 0-8373-0323-0). Natl Learning.
--Home Economics - Jr. H.S. (Teachers License Examination Ser.: T-28). (Cloth bdg. avail. on request). pap. 13.95 (ISBN 0-8373-8028-6). Natl Learning.
--Home Economics - Sr. H.S. (Teachers License Examination Ser.: T-29). (Cloth bdg. avail. on request). pap. 13.95 (ISBN 0-8373-8029-4). Natl Learning.
--Home Economics Chairman - Jr. H.S. (Questions Only) (Teachers License Examination Ser.: CH-12). (Cloth bdg. avail on request). pap. 15.95 (ISBN 0-8373-8162-2). Natl Learning.
--Home Economics Chairman - Sr. H.S. (Questions Only) (Teachers License Examination Ser.: CH-13). (Cloth bdg. avail on request). pap. 15.95 (ISBN 0-8373-8163-0). Natl Learning.
--Home Economics Education. (National Teachers Examination Ser.: NT-12). (Cloth bdg. avail. on request). pap. 11.95 (ISBN 0-8373-8422-2). Natl Learning.
--Homebound. (Teachers License Examination Ser.: T-27). (Cloth bdg. avail. on request). pap. 13.95 (ISBN 0-8373-8027-8). Natl Learning.
--Hospital Administration Intern. (Career Examination Ser.: C-1967). (Cloth bdg. avail. on request). pap. 10.00 (ISBN 0-8373-1967-6). Natl Learning.
--Hospital Administrator. (Career Examination Ser.: C-1743). (Cloth bdg. avail. on request). 1977. pap. 12.00 (ISBN 0-685-78613-7). Natl Learning.
--Hospital Attendant. (Career Examination Ser.: C-325). (Cloth bdg. avail. on request). 10.00 (ISBN 0-8373-0325-7). Natl Learning.
--Hospital Care Investigator. (Career Examination Ser.: C-326). (Cloth bdg. avail. on request). pap. 10.00 (ISBN 0-8373-0326-5). Natl Learning.
--Hospital Care Investigator Trainee. (Career Examination Ser.: C-327). (Cloth bdg. avail. on request). pap. 10.00 (ISBN 0-8373-0327-3). Natl Learning.
--Hospital Case Investigator. (Career Examination Ser.: C-1889). (Cloth bdg. avail. on request). pap. 10.00 (ISBN 0-8373-1889-0). Natl Learning.
--Hospital Clerk. (Career Examination Ser.: C-328). (Cloth bdg. avail. on request). pap. 10.00 (ISBN 0-8373-0328-1). Natl Learning.
--Hospital Controller. (Career Examination Ser.: C-1760). (Cloth bdg. avail. on request). 1977. pap. 12.00 (ISBN 0-8373-1760-6). Natl Learning.
--Hospital Safety Officer. (Career Examination Ser.: C-118). (Cloth bdg. avail. on request). pap. 10.00 (ISBN 0-8373-0118-1). Natl Learning.
--Hospital Safety Officer Trainee. (Career Examination Ser.: C-119). (Cloth bdg. avail. on request). pap. 10.00 (ISBN 0-8373-0119-X). Natl Learning.
--Hospital Security Officer. (Career Examination Ser.: C-353). (Cloth bdg. avail. on request). pap. 10.00 (ISBN 0-8373-0353-2). Natl Learning.
--House Painter. (Career Examination Ser.: C-354). (Cloth bdg. avail. on request). pap. 10.00 (ISBN 0-8373-0354-0). Natl Learning.
--Housemother. (Career Examination Ser.: C-1306). (Cloth bdg. avail. on request). pap. 8.00 (ISBN 0-8373-1306-6). Natl Learning.
--Housing Assistant. (Career Examination Ser.: C-331). (Cloth bdg. avail. on request). pap. 10.00 (ISBN 0-685-17935-4). Natl Learning.
--Housing Captain. (Career Examination Ser.: C-332). (Cloth bdg. avail. on request). pap. 12.00 (ISBN 0-8373-0332-X). Natl Learning.
--Housing Community Activities Coordinator. (Career Examination Ser.: C-334). (Cloth bdg. avail. on request). pap. 10.00 (ISBN 0-8373-0334-6). Natl Learning.
--How to Get a Summer Job. (Career Examination Ser.: CS-23). (Cloth bdg. avail. on request). pap. 2.00 o.p. (ISBN 0-8373-4002-0). Natl Learning.
--Human Growth & Development. (College Level Examination Ser.: CLEP-17). 17.95 (ISBN 0-8373-5367-X); pap. 9.95 (ISBN 0-8373-5317-3). Natl Learning.
--Humanities. (Graduate Record Area Examination Ser.: GRE-42). 21.95 (ISBN 0-8373-5292-4); pap. 13.95 (ISBN 0-8373-5242-8). Natl Learning.
--Humanities. (College-Level Examination Ser.: ATS-9B). 17.95 (ISBN 0-8373-5109-X); pap. 9.95 (ISBN 0-8373-5009-3). Natl Learning.
--Identification Officer. (Career Examination Ser.: C-1986). (Cloth bdg. avail. on request). pap. 10.00 (ISBN 0-8373-1986-2). Natl Learning.
--Identification Specialist. (Career Examination Ser.: C-2294). (Cloth bdg. avail. on request). 1977. pap. 10.00 (ISBN 0-8373-2294-4). Natl Learning.
--Illustrator. (Career Examination Ser.: C-379). (Cloth bdg. avail. on request). pap. 11.00 (ISBN 0-8373-0379-6). Natl Learning.
--Illustrator Aide. (Career Examination Ser.: C-2930). (Cloth bdg. avail. on request). pap. 10.00 (ISBN 0-8373-2930-2). Natl Learning.
--Immigration Patrol Inspector. (Career Examination Ser.: C-362). (Cloth bdg. avail. on request). pap. 10.00 (ISBN 0-8373-0362-1). Natl Learning.
--Immunohematology & Blood Banking. (College Level Examination Ser.: CLEP-34). 19.95 (ISBN 0-8373-5384-X); pap. 11.95 (ISBN 0-8373-5334-3). Natl Learning.
--Incinerator Plant Foreman. (Career Examination Ser.: C-2163). (Cloth bdg. avail. on request). 1976. pap. 10.00 (ISBN 0-8373-0362-1). Natl Learning.
--Incinerator Plant Maintenance Foreman. (Career Examination Ser.: C-2773). (Cloth bdg. avail. on request). 1980. pap. 10.00 (ISBN 0-8373-2773-3). Natl Learning.
--Incinerator Plant Supervisor. (Career Examination Ser.: C-2164). (Cloth bdg. avail. on request). 1976. pap. 10.00 (ISBN 0-8373-2164-6). Natl Learning.
--Incinerator Stationary Engineer. (Career Examination Ser.: C-2636). (Cloth bdg. avail. on request). pap. 10.00 (ISBN 0-8373-2636-2). Natl Learning.
--Industrial Arts Chairman: Junior High School. (Teachers License Examination Ser.: CH-14). (Cloth bdg. avail. on request). pap. 15.95 (ISBN 0-8373-8164-9). Natl Learning.
--Industrial Arts Chairman: Senior High School. (Teachers License Examination Ser.: CH-15). (Cloth bdg. avail. on request). pap. 15.95 (ISBN 0-8373-8165-7). Natl Learning.
--Industrial Arts Education. (National Teachers Examination Ser.: NT-5). (Cloth bdg. avail. on request). pap. 11.95 (ISBN 0-8373-8415-X). Natl Learning.
--Industrial Arts: Junior High School. (Teachers License Examination Ser.: T-30). (Cloth bdg. avail. on request). pap. 13.95 (ISBN 0-8373-8030-8). Natl Learning.
--Industrial Arts: Senior High School. (Teachers License Examination Ser.: T-31). (Cloth bdg. avail on request). pap. 13.95 (ISBN 0-8373-8031-6). Natl Learning.
--Industrial Development Assistant. (Career Examination Ser.: C-2848). (Cloth bdg. avail. on request). 1980. pap. 10.00 (ISBN 0-8373-2848-9). Natl Learning.
--Industrial Electronics. (Occupational Competency Examination Ser.: OCE-21). 13.95 (ISBN 0-8373-5771-3); pap. 9.95 (ISBN 0-8373-5721-7). Natl Learning.
--Industrial Foreman. (Career Examination Ser.: C-1956). (Cloth bdg. avail. on request). pap. 10.00 (ISBN 0-8373-1956-0). Natl Learning.
--Industrial Hygienist. (Career Examination Ser.: C-381). (Cloth bdg. avail. on request). pap. 10.00 (ISBN 0-8373-0381-8). Natl Learning.
--Information & Referral Aide. (Career Examination Ser.: C-2892). (Cloth bdg. avail. on request). pap. 10.00 (ISBN 0-8373-2892-6). Natl Learning.
--Information & Referral Coordinator. (Career Examination Ser.: C-2927). (Cloth bdg. avail. on request). pap. 12.00 (ISBN 0-8373-2927-2). Natl Learning.
--Information Media Specialist. (Career Examination Ser.: C-1315). (Cloth bdg. avail. on request). pap. 10.00 (ISBN 0-8373-1315-5). Natl Learning.
--Information Specialist. (Career Examination Ser.: C-1316). (Cloth bdg. avail. on request). pap. 10.00 (ISBN 0-8373-1316-3). Natl Learning.
--Information Specialist 1. (Career Examination Ser.: C-1867). (Cloth bdg. avail. on request). pap. 10.00 (ISBN 0-8373-1867-X). Natl Learning.
--Information Specialist 2. (Career Examination Ser.: C-1868). (Cloth bdg. avail. on request). 12.00 (ISBN 0-8373-1868-8). Natl Learning.
--Initial-Level Supervisor Examination (U.S.P.S.) (Career Examination Ser.: C-1788). pap. 10.00 (ISBN 0-8373-1788-6). Natl Learning.
--Inspector. (Career Examination Ser.: C-364). (Cloth bdg. avail. on request). pap. 10.00 (ISBN 0-8373-0364-8). Natl Learning.
--Inspector of Markets, Weights, & Measures. (Career Examination Ser.: C-368). (Cloth bdg. avail. on request). pap. 10.00 (ISBN 0-8373-0368-0). Natl Learning.
--Institution Safety Officer. (Career Examination Ser.: C-370). (Cloth bdg. avail. on request). pap. 10.00 (ISBN 0-8373-0370-2). Natl Learning.
--Institution Steward. (Career Examination Ser.: C-2626). (Cloth bdg. avail. on request). pap. 10.00 (ISBN 0-8373-2626-5). Natl Learning.
--Institutional Inspector. (Career Examination Ser.: C-382). (Cloth bdg. avail. on request). pap. 10.00 (ISBN 0-8373-0382-6). Natl Learning.
--Insurance Agent - Insurance Broker. (Career Examination Ser.: C-373). (Cloth bdg. avail. on request). pap. 10.00 (ISBN 0-685-60430-6). Natl Learning.
--Insurance Broker. (Career Examination Ser.: C-373). (Cloth bdg. avail. on request). pap. 10.00 (ISBN 0-8373-0373-7). Natl Learning.
--Insurance Examiner. (Career Examination Ser.: C-2694). (Cloth bdg. avail. on request). pap. 10.00 (ISBN 0-8373-2694-X). Natl Learning.
--Insurance Fund Hearing Representative Trainee. (Career Examination Ser.: C-880). (Cloth bdg. avail. on request). pap. 10.00 (ISBN 0-8373-0880-1). Natl Learning.
--Insurance Salesman. (Career Examination Ser.: C-389). (Cloth bdg. avail. on request). pap. 10.00 (ISBN 0-8373-0374-5). Natl Learning.
--Intermediate Schools. (Teachers Lesson Plan Bk.: IS-1). (gr. 5-8). pap. 3.95 (ISBN 0-686-84419-X). Natl Learning.
--Introduction to Anatomy & Physiology. (College Proficiency Examination Ser.: CPEP-28). 1977. 17.95 (ISBN 0-8373-5478-1); pap. 9.95 (ISBN 0-8373-5428-5). Natl Learning.
--Introduction to Business Management. (College Level Examination Ser.: CLEP-18). 17.95 (ISBN 0-8373-5368-8); pap. 9.95 (ISBN 0-8373-5318-1). Natl Learning.
--Introduction to Criminal Justice. (ACT Proficiency Examination Program: PEP-8). 17.95 (ISBN 0-8373-5558-3); pap. 9.95 (ISBN 0-8373-5508-7). Natl Learning.
--Introduction to Criminal Justice. (College Proficiency Examination Ser.: CPEP-29). 1977. 17.95 (ISBN 0-8373-5479-X); pap. 9.95 (ISBN 0-8373-5429-3). Natl Learning.
--Introduction to the Teaching of Reading. (National Teacher Examination Ser.: NT-39). (Cloth bdg. avail. on request). pap. 11.95 (ISBN 0-686-53781-5). Natl Learning.
--Introductory Accounting. (College Level Examination Ser.: CLEP-19). 17.95 (ISBN 0-8373-5369-6); pap. 9.95 (ISBN 0-8373-5319-X). Natl Learning.
--Introductory Business Law. (College Level Examination Ser.: CLEP-20). 17.95 (ISBN 0-8373-5370-X); pap. 9.95 (ISBN 0-8373-5320-3). Natl Learning.
--Introductory Calculus. (College Level Examination Ser.: CLEP-21). 17.95 (ISBN 0-8373-5371-8); pap. 9.95 (ISBN 0-8373-5321-1). Natl Learning.
--Introductory Economics. (College Level Examination Ser.: CLEP-22). 17.95 (ISBN 0-8373-5372-6); pap. 9.95 (ISBN 0-8373-5322-X). Natl Learning.
--Introductory Macroeconomics. (College Level Examination Ser.: CLEP-41). 17.95 (ISBN 0-8373-5391-2); pap. 9.95 (ISBN 0-8373-5341-6). Natl Learning.
--Introductory Marketing. (College Level Examination Ser.: CLEP-23). 17.95 (ISBN 0-8373-5373-4); pap. 9.95 (ISBN 0-8373-5323-8). Natl Learning.
--Introductory Micro- & Macroeconomics. (College Level Examination Ser.: CLEP-42). 1977. 17.95 (ISBN 0-8373-5342-4); pap. 9.95 (ISBN 0-8373-5392-0). Natl Learning.
--Introductory Microeconomics. (College Level Examination Ser.: CLEP-40). 1977. 17.95 (ISBN 0-8373-5340-8); pap. 9.95 (ISBN 0-686-67795-1). Natl Learning.
--Introductory Sociology. (College Level Examination Ser.: CLEP-24). 17.95 (ISBN 0-8373-5374-2); pap. 9.95 (ISBN 0-8373-5324-6). Natl Learning.
--Inventory Control Clerk. (Career Examination Ser.: C-2616). (Cloth bdg. avail. on request). pap. 8.00 (ISBN 0-8373-2616-8). Natl Learning.
--Investigator. (Career Examination Ser.: C-377). (Cloth bdg. avail. on request). pap. 10.00 (ISBN 0-8373-0377-X). Natl Learning.
--Investigator-Inspector. (Career Examination Ser.: C-378). (Cloth bdg. avail. on request). pap. 10.00 (ISBN 0-8373-0378-8). Natl Learning.
--Italian: Junior High School. (Teachers License Examination Ser.: T-32a). (Cloth bdg. avail. on request). pap. 13.95 (ISBN 0-8373-8032-4). Natl Learning.
--Italian: Senior High School. (Teachers License Examination Ser.: T-32B). (Cloth bdg. avail. on request). pap. 13.95 (ISBN 0-686-84417-3). Natl Learning.
--Job Training Specialist. (Career Examination Ser.: C-02697). (Cloth bdg. avail. on request). pap. 10.00 (ISBN 0-8373-2697-4). Natl Learning.
--Journeyman. (Career Examination Ser.: C-409). (Cloth bdg. avail. on request). pap. 10.00 (ISBN 0-8373-0409-1). Natl Learning.
--Journeyman in the Printing Crafts. (Career Examination Ser.: C-410). (Cloth bdg. avail. on request). pap. 10.00 (ISBN 0-8373-0410-5). Natl Learning.
--Junior Account Clerk. (Career Examination Ser.: C-515). (Cloth bdg. avail. on request). pap. 10.00 (ISBN 0-8373-0515-2). Natl Learning.
--Junior Administration Assistant. (Career Examination Ser.: C-832). (Cloth bdg. avail. on request). pap. 8.00 (ISBN 0-8373-0832-1). Natl Learning.
--Junior Air Pollution Control Engineer. (Career Examination Ser.: C-1334). (Cloth bdg. avail. on request). pap. 10.00 (ISBN 0-8373-1334-1). Natl Learning.
--Junior Architect. (Career Examination Ser.: C-411). (Cloth bdg. avail on request). pap. 10.00 (ISBN 0-8373-0411-3). Natl Learning.
--Junior Area Services Coordinator. (Career Examination Ser.: C-390). (Cloth bdg. avail. on request). pap. 8.00 (ISBN 0-8373-0390-7). Natl Learning.
--Junior Building Custodian. (Career Examination Ser.: C-412). (Cloth bdg. avail. on request). pap. 10.00 (ISBN 0-8373-0412-1). Natl Learning.
--Junior Civil Engineer Trainee. (Career Examination Ser.: C-212). (Cloth bdg. avail. on request). pap. 10.00 (ISBN 0-8373-0212-9). Natl Learning.
--Junior Draftsman. (Career Examination Ser.: C-396). (Cloth bdg. avail. on request). pap. 8.00 (ISBN 0-8373-0396-6). Natl Learning.
--Junior Electrical Engineer. (Career Examination Ser.: C-397). (Cloth bdg. avail. on request). pap. 10.00 (ISBN 0-8373-0397-4). Natl Learning.
--Junior Geologist. (Career Examination Ser.: C-414). (Cloth bdg. avail. on request). pap. 10.00 (ISBN 0-8373-0414-8). Natl Learning.
--Junior High School. (Teachers Lesson Plan Bk.: J-1). (gr. 7-9). pap. 3.95 (ISBN 0-686-84420-3). Natl Learning.
--Junior Hospital Administrator. (Career Examination Ser.: C-400). (Cloth bdg. avail. on request). pap. 10.00 (ISBN 0-8373-0400-8). Natl Learning.
--Junior Planner. (Career Examination Ser.: C-415). (Cloth bdg. avail. on request). pap. 10.00 (ISBN 0-8373-0415-6). Natl Learning.
--Kitchen Supervisor. (Career Examination Ser.: C-1336). (Cloth bdg. avail. on request). pap. 10.00 (ISBN 0-8373-1336-8). Natl Learning.
--Labor Mediator. (Career Examination Ser.: C-2850). (Cloth bdg. avail. on request). 1980. pap. 10.00 (ISBN 0-8373-2850-0). Natl Learning.
--Labor Technician. (Career Examination Ser.: C-1587). (Cloth bdg. avail. on request). pap. 10.00 (ISBN 0-686-53357-7). Natl Learning.
--Laboratory Aide. (Career Examination Ser.: C-430). (Cloth bdg. avail. on request). pap. 10.00 (ISBN 0-8373-0430-X). Natl Learning.
--Laboratory Equipment Specialist. (Career Examination Ser.: C-2297). (Cloth bdg. avail. on request). 1977. pap. 10.00 (ISBN 0-8373-2297-9). Natl Learning.
--Laboratory Specialist - Jr. H.S. (Teachers License Examination Ser.: T-33). (Cloth bdg. avail. on request). pap. 13.95 (ISBN 0-8373-8033-2). Natl Learning.
--Laboratory Specialist (Biology) Sr. H.S. (Teachers License Examination Ser.: T-34). (Cloth bdg. avail. on request). pap. 13.95 (ISBN 0-8373-8034-0). Natl Learning.
--Laboratory Specialist (Physical Sciences) Sr. H.S. (Teachers License Examination Ser.: T-35). (Cloth bdg. avail. on request). pap. 13.95 (ISBN 0-8373-8035-9). Natl Learning.
--Laboratory Technician - Secondary Schools. (Teachers License Examination Ser.: T-36). (Cloth bdg. avail. on request). pap. 13.95- (ISBN 0-8373-8036-7). Natl Learning.
--Laboratory Technician Trainee. (Career Examination Ser.: C-2909). (Cloth bdg. avail on request). pap. 10.00 (ISBN 0-8373-2909-4). Natl Learning.
--Laborer. (Career Examination Ser.: C-434). (Cloth bdg. avail. on request). pap. 8.00 (ISBN 0-8373-0434-2). Natl Learning.
--Laborer Foreman. (Career Examination Ser.: C-1337). (Cloth bdg. avail. on request). pap. 10.00 (ISBN 0-8373-1337-6). Natl Learning.
--Land Management Specialist. (Career Examination Ser.: C-2618). (Cloth bdg. avail. on request). pap. 10.00 (ISBN 0-8373-2618-4). Natl Learning.
--Latin. (National Teachers Examination Ser.: NT-18). (Cloth bdg. avail. on request). pap. 11.95 (ISBN 0-8373-8408-7). Natl Learning.
--Latin Sr. H. S. (Teachers License Examination Ser.: T-37). (Cloth bng. avail. on request). pap. 13.95 (ISBN 0-8373-8037-5). Natl Learning.
--Laundry Foreman. (Career Examination Ser.: C-2244). (Cloth bdg. avail. on request). pap. 10.00 (ISBN 0-8373-2244-8). Natl Learning.
--Laundry Supervisor. (Career Examination Ser.: C-1339). (Cloth bdg. avail. on request). pap. 10.00 (ISBN 0-8373-1339-2). Natl Learning.
--Laundry Washman. (Career Examination Ser.: C-1340). (Cloth bdg. avail. on request). pap. 8.00 (ISBN 0-8373-1340-6). Natl Learning.
--Laundry Worker. (Career Examination Ser.: C-435). (Cloth bdg. avail. on request). pap. 8.00 (ISBN 0-8373-0435-0). Natl Learning.
--Law Department Investigator. (Career Examination Ser.: C-849). (Cloth bdg. avail. on request). pap. 10.00 (ISBN 0-8373-0849-6). Natl Learning.
--Law Library Clerk. (Career Examination Ser.: C-2888). (Cloth bdg. avail. on request). pap. 10.00 (ISBN 0-8373-2888-8). Natl Learning.
--Law School Admission Test (LSAT) (Admission Test Ser.: ATS-13). 300p. (Cloth bdg. avail. on request). pap. 13.95 (ISBN 0-8373-5013-1). Natl Learning.
--Law Stenographer. (Career Examination Ser.: C-436). (Cloth bdg. avail. on request). pap. 10.00 (ISBN 0-8373-0436-9). Natl Learning.
--Legal Coordinator. (Career Examination Ser.: C-2651). (Cloth bdg. avail. on request). pap. 12.00 (ISBN 0-8373-2651-6). Natl Learning.
--Legal Secretary. (Career Examination Ser.: C-1343). (Cloth bdg. avail. on request). pap. 10.00 (ISBN 0-8373-1343-0). Natl Learning.
--Legal Stenographer. (Career Examination Ser.: C-1344). (Cloth bdg. avail. on request). pap. 10.00 (ISBN 0-8373-1344-9). Natl Learning.
--Letterpress Pressman. (Career Examination Ser.: C-437). (Cloth bdg. avail. on request). pap. 8.00 (ISBN 0-8373-0437-7). Natl Learning.
--Librarian. (Career Examination Ser.: C-438). (Cloth bdg. avail. on request). pap. 10.00 (ISBN 0-8373-0438-5). Natl Learning.
--Librarian Trainee. (Career Examination Ser.: C-2864). (Cloth bdg. avail. on request). 1980. pap. 10.00 (ISBN 0-8373-2864-0). Natl Learning.

--Librarian 5. (Career Examination Ser.: C-2792). (Cloth bdg. avail. on request). 1980. pap. 14.00 (ISBN 0-8373-2792-X). Natl Learning.
--Library. (National Teachers Examination Ser.: NT-17). (Cloth bdg. avail. on request). pap. 11.95 (ISBN 0-8373-8407-9). Natl Learning.
--Library Assistant. (Career Examination Ser.: C-1345). (Cloth bdg. avail. on request). pap. 10.00 (ISBN 0-8373-1345-7). Natl Learning.
--Library Clerk. (Career Examination Ser.: C-1931). (Cloth bdg. avail. on request). pap. 10.00 (ISBN 0-8373-1931-5). Natl Learning.
--Library Director 3. (Career Examination Ser.: C-2780). (Cloth bdg. avail. on request). 1980. pap. 12.00 (ISBN 0-8373-2780-6). Natl Learning.
--Library Director 4. (Career Examination Ser.: C-2781). (Cloth bdg. avail. on request). 1980. pap. 14.00 (ISBN 0-8373-2781-4). Natl Learning.
--Library Director 5. (Career Examination Ser.: C-2782). (cloth bdg. avail. on request). 1980. pap. 14.00 (ISBN 0-8373-2782-2). Natl Learning.
--Library, Elementary School. (Teachers License Examination Ser.: T-38). (Cloth bdg. avail. on request). pap. 13.95 (ISBN 0-8373-8038-3). Natl Learning.
--Library, Secondary School. (Teachers License Examination Ser.: T-39). (Cloth bdg. avail. on request). pap. 13.95 (ISBN 0-8373-8039-1). Natl Learning.
--Library Technician. (Career Examination Ser.: C-2544). (Cloth bdg. avail. on request). pap. 10.00 (ISBN 0-8373-2544-7). Natl Learning.
--License Inspector. (Career Examination Ser.: C-439). (Cloth bdg. avail. on request). pap. 10.00 (ISBN 0-8373-0439-3). Natl Learning.
--License Investigator. (Career Examination Ser.: C-449). (Cloth bdg. avail. on request). pap. 10.00 (ISBN 0-8373-0449-0). Natl Learning.
--License Investigator (Spanish Speaking) (Career Examination Ser.: C-2286). (Cloth bdg. avail. on request). 1977. pap. 12.00 (ISBN 0-8373-2286-3). Natl Learning.
--Licensed Practical Nurse. (Career Examination Ser.: C-440). (Cloth bdg. avail. on request). pap. 10.00 (ISBN 0-8373-0440-7). Natl Learning.
--Life Skills Counselor. (Career Examination Ser.: C-2917). (Cloth bdg. avail. on request). pap. 12.00 (ISBN 0-8373-2917-5). Natl Learning.
--Lifeguard. (Career Examination Ser.: C-2300). (Cloth bdg. avail. on request). 1977. pap. 10.00 (ISBN 0-8373-2300-2). Natl Learning.
--Lighting Inspector. (Career Examination Ser.: C-2134). (Cloth bdg. avail. on request). 1977. pap. 10.00 (ISBN 0-8373-2134-4). Natl Learning.
--Literature. (Teachers License Examination Ser.: G-3). (Cloth bdg. avail. on request). pap. 10.00 (ISBN 0-685-18739-X). Natl Learning.
--Literature in English. (Graduate Record Examination Ser.: GRE-11). 21.95 (ISBN 0-8373-5261-4); pap. 13.95 (ISBN 0-8373-5211-8). Natl Learning.
--Lithographic Pressman. (Career Examination Ser.: C-445). (Cloth bdg. avail. on request). pap. 10.00 (ISBN 0-8373-0445-8). Natl Learning.
--Loan Advisor. (Career Examination Ser.: C-1321). (Cloth bdg. avail. on request). pap. 12.00 (ISBN 0-8373-1321-X). Natl Learning.
--Locksmith. (Career Examination Ser.: C-1348). (Cloth bdg. avail. on request). pap. 10.00 (ISBN 0-8373-1348-1). Natl Learning.
--Lottery Inspector. (Career Examination Ser.: C-451). (Cloth bdg. avail. on request). pap. 8.00 (ISBN 0-8373-0451-2). Natl Learning.
--Machine Drafting. (Occupational Competency Examination Ser.: OCE-24). 14.95 (ISBN 0-8373-5774-8); pap. 13.95 (ISBN 0-8373-5724-1). Natl Learning.
--Machine Trades. (Occupational Competency Examination Ser.: OCE-22). 21.95 (ISBN 0-8373-5772-1); pap. 13.95 (ISBN 0-8373-5722-5). Natl Learning.
--Machinist. (Career Examination Ser.: C-460). (Cloth bdg. avail. on request). pap. 10.00 (ISBN 0-8373-0460-1). Natl Learning.
--Machinist's Helper. (Career Examination Ser.: C-461). (Cloth bdg. avail. on request). pap. 10.00 (ISBN 0-8373-0461-X). Natl Learning.
--Magnetic Tape Librarian. (Career Examination Ser.: C-2872). (Cloth bdg. avail. on request). pap. 10.00 (ISBN 0-8373-2872-1). Natl Learning.
--Mail Division Supervisor. (Career Examination Ser.: C-2624). (Cloth bdg. avail. on request). pap. 10.00 (ISBN 0-8373-2624-9). Natl Learning.
--Mail Handler (U.S.P.S.) (Career Examination Ser.: C-462). (Cloth bdg. avail. on request). pap. 8.00 (ISBN 0-8373-0462-8). Natl Learning.
--Maintainer's Helper - Group A. (Career Examination Ser.: C-465). (Cloth bdg. avail. on request). pap. 10.00 (ISBN 0-8373-0465-2). Natl Learning.
--Maintainer's Helper - Group B. (Career Examination Ser.: C-466). (Cloth bdg. avail. on request). pap. 10.00 (ISBN 0-8373-0466-0). Natl Learning.
--Maintainer's Helper - Group C. (Career Examination Ser.: C-467). (Cloth bdg. avail. on request). pap. 10.00 (ISBN 0-8373-0467-9). Natl Learning.
--Maintainer's Helper - Group D. (Career Examination Ser.: C-468). (Cloth bdg. avail. on request). pap. 10.00 (ISBN 0-8373-0468-7). Natl Learning.
--Maintainer's Helper - Group E. (Career Examination Ser.: C-469). (Cloth bdg. avail. on request). 10.00 (ISBN 0-8373-0469-5). Natl Learning.
--Maintenance Carpenter. (Career Examination Ser.: C-1349). (Cloth bdg. avail. on request). pap. 10.00 (ISBN 0-8373-1349-X). Natl Learning.
--Maintenance Carpenter Foreman. (Career Examination Ser.: C-1350). (Cloth bdg. avail. on request). pap. 12.00 (ISBN 0-8373-1350-3). Natl Learning.
--Maintenance (Custodial) Branch Initial-Level Supervisor Examination (U.S.P.S.) (Career Examination Ser.: C-1775). (Cloth bdg. avail. on request). 10.00 (ISBN 0-8373-1775-4). Natl Learning.
--Maintenance Electrician. (Career Examination Ser.: C-1351). (Cloth bdg. avail. on request). pap. 10.00 (ISBN 0-685-18064-6). Natl Learning.
--Maintenance Locksmith. (Career Examination Ser.: C-1353). (Cloth bdg. avail. on request). pap. 10.00 (ISBN 0-8373-1353-8). Natl Learning.
--Maintenance Machinist. (Career Examination Ser.: C-1354). (Cloth bdg. avail. on request). pap. 10.00 (ISBN 0-8373-1354-6). Natl Learning.
--Maintenance Man. (Career Examination Ser.: C-463). (Cloth bdg. avail. on request). pap. 10.00 (ISBN 0-8373-0463-6). Natl Learning.
--Maintenance Man Trainee. (Career Examination Ser.: C-464). (Cloth bdg. avail. on request). pap. 10.00 (ISBN 0-8373-0464-4). Natl Learning.
--Maintenance Mason. (Career Examination Ser.: C-1355). (Cloth bdg. avail. on request). pap. 10.00 (ISBN 0-8373-1355-4). Natl Learning.
--Maintenance Mason Foreman. (Career Examination Ser.: C-1356). (Cloth bdg. avail. on request). pap. 12.00 (ISBN 0-8373-1356-2). Natl Learning.
--Maintenance Mechanic. (Career Examination Ser.: C-1357). (Cloth bdg. avail. on request). pap. 10.00 (ISBN 0-8373-1357-0). Natl Learning.
--Maintenance Painter. (Career Examination Ser.: C-1358). (Cloth bdg. avail. on request). pap. 10.00 (ISBN 0-8373-1358-9). Natl Learning.
--Maintenance Painter Foreman. (Career Examination Ser.: C-1359). (Cloth bdg. avail. on request). pap. 12.00 (ISBN 0-8373-1359-7). Natl Learning.
--Maintenance Plumber. (Career Examination Ser.: C-1360). (Cloth bdg. avail. on request). pap. 12.00 (ISBN 0-8373-1360-0). Natl Learning.
--Maintenance Plumber Foreman. (Career Examination Ser.: C-1361). (Cloth bdg. avail. on request). pap. 12.00 (ISBN 0-8373-1361-9). Natl Learning.
--Maintenance Supervisor. (Career Examination Ser.: C-2044). (Cloth bdg. avail. on request). pap. 12.00 (ISBN 0-8373-2044-5). Natl Learning.
--Maintenance Welder. (Career Examination Ser.: C-1362). (Cloth bdg. avail. on request). pap. 10.00 (ISBN 0-685-18078-6). Natl Learning.
--Management Analysis Trainee. (Career Examination Ser.: C-470). (Cloth bdg. avail. on request). pap. 10.00 (ISBN 0-8373-0470-9). Natl Learning.
--Management Analyst. (Career Examination Ser.: C-1061). (Cloth bdg. avail. on request). pap. 12.00 (ISBN 0-8373-1061-X). Natl Learning.
--Management Analyst Aide. (Career Examination Ser.: C-1721). (Cloth bdg. avail. on request). 1977. pap. 10.00 (ISBN 0-8373-1721-5). Natl Learning.
--Management Intern. (Career Examination Ser.: C-1927). (Cloth bdg. avail. on request). 1977. pap. 10.00 (ISBN 0-8373-1927-7). Natl Learning.
--Management Technician. (Career Examination Ser.: C-2751). (Cloth bdg. avail. on request). 1980. pap. 12.00 (ISBN 0-8373-2751-2). Natl Learning.
--Management Trainee (U.S.P.S.) (Career Examination Ser.: C-1690). (Cloth bdg. avail. on request). pap. 10.00 (ISBN 0-8373-1690-1). Natl Learning.
--Manager Computer Operations. (Career Examination Ser.: C-2241). (Cloth bdg. avail. on request). pap. 12.00 (ISBN 0-8373-2241-3). Natl Learning.
--Manpower Development Specialist. (Career Examination Ser.: C-2688). (Cloth bdg. avail. on request). pap. 12.00 (ISBN 0-8373-2688-5). Natl Learning.
--Manpower Program Administrator. (Career Examination Ser.: C-2671). (Cloth bdg. avail. on request). pap. 12.00 (ISBN 0-8373-2671-0). Natl Learning.
--Marketing Representative. (Career Examination Ser.: C-2465). (Cloth bdg. avail. on request). pap. 10.00 (ISBN 0-8373-2465-3). Natl Learning.
--Maryland Basic Mastery Test for Reading (BMT-R) (Admission Test Ser.: ATS-63). (Cloth bdg. avail. on request). pap. 11.95 (ISBN 0-8373-5063-8). Natl Learning.
--Mason. (Career Examination Ser.: C-473). (Cloth bdg. avail. on request). pap. 10.00 (ISBN 0-8373-0473-3). Natl Learning.
--Masonry. (Occupational Competency Examination Ser.: OCE-23). (Cloth bdg. avail. on request). pap. 13.95 (ISBN 0-8373-5723-3). Natl Learning.
--Mason's Helper. (Career Examination Ser.: C-474). (Cloth bdg. avail. on request) (ISBN 0-8373-0474-1). pap. 10.00 (ISBN 0-686-66500-7). Natl Learning.
--Master Electrician. (Career Examination Ser.: C-475). (Cloth bdg. avail. on request). pap. 12.00 (ISBN 0-8373-0475-X). Natl Learning.
--Master Plumber. (Career Examination Ser.: C-476). (Cloth bdg. avail. on request). pap. 12.00 (ISBN 0-8373-0476-8). Natl Learning.
--Master Rigger. (Career Examination Ser.: C-477). (Cloth bdg. avail. on request). pap. 10.00 (ISBN 0-8373-0477-6). Natl Learning.
--Master Sign Hanger. (Career Examination Ser.: C-478). (Cloth bdg. avail. on request). pap. 10.00 (ISBN 0-8373-0478-4). Natl Learning.
--Materials Testing Technician. (Career Examination Ser.: C-1834). (Cloth bdg. avail. on request). pap. 10.00 (ISBN 0-8373-1834-3). Natl Learning.
--Maternal & Child Health Nurse. (Certified Nurse Examination Ser.: CN-9). 21.95 (ISBN 0-8373-6159-1); pap. 13.95 (ISBN 0-8373-6109-5). Natl Learning.
--Mathematics. (Teachers License Examination Ser.: G-4). (Cloth bdg. avail. on request). pap. 10.00 (ISBN 0-8373-8194-0). Natl Learning.
--Mathematics. (National Teachers Examination Ser.: NT-6). (Cloth bdg. avail. on request). pap. 11.95 (ISBN 0-8373-8416-8). Natl Learning.
--Mathematics. (Graduate Record Examination Ser.: GRE-12). (Cloth bdg. avail. on request). pap. 13.95 (ISBN 0-8373-5212-6). Natl Learning.
--Mathematics Chairman-Jr. H.S. (Teachers License Examination Ser.: CH-16). (Cloth bdg. avail. on request). pap. 15.95 (ISBN 0-8373-8166-5). Natl Learning.
--Mathematics Chairman-Sr. H.S. (Teachers License Examination Ser.: CH-17). (Cloth bdg. avail. on request). pap. 15.95 (ISBN 0-8373-8167-3). Natl Learning.
--Mathematics-Jr. H.S. (Teachers License Examination Ser.: T-40). (Cloth bdg. avail. on request). pap. 13.95 (ISBN 0-8373-8040-5). Natl Learning.
--Mathematics-Sr. H.S. (Teachers License Examination Ser.: T-41). (Cloth bdg. avail. on request). pap. 13.95 (ISBN 0-8373-8041-3). Natl Learning.
--Meat Inspector - Poultry Inspector. (Career Examination Ser.: C-513). (Cloth bdg. avail. on request). pap. 10.00 (ISBN 0-8373-0513-6). Natl Learning.
--Meat Inspector Trainee. (Career Examination Ser.: C-518). (Cloth bdg. avail. on request). pap. 8.00 (ISBN 0-8373-0518-7). Natl Learning.
--Mechanical Technology. (Occupational Competency Examination Ser.: OCE-25). (Cloth bdg. avail. on request). pap. 13.95 (ISBN 0-8373-5725-X). Natl Learning.
--Media Specialist. (Career Examination Ser.: C-2894). (Cloth bdg. avail. on request). pap. 12.00 (ISBN 0-8373-2894-2). Natl Learning.
--Media Specialist - Library & Audio-Visual Services. (National Teachers Examination Ser.: NT-29). (Cloth bdg. avail. on request). pap. 11.95 (ISBN 0-8373-8439-7). Natl Learning.
--Medical Aide. (Career Examination Ser.: C-1364). (Cloth bdg. avail. on request). pap. 10.00 (ISBN 0-8373-1364-3). Natl Learning.
--Medical Assistant. (Career Examination Ser.: C-1365). (Cloth bdg. avail. on request). pap. 10.00 (ISBN 0-8373-1365-1). Natl Learning.
--Medical Assisting. (Occupational Competency Examination Ser.: OCE-26). (Cloth bdg. avail. on request). pap. 13.95 (ISBN 0-8373-5726-8). Natl Learning.
--Medical Claims Examiner. (Career Examination Ser.: C-2691). (Cloth bdg. avail. on request). pap. 10.00 (ISBN 0-8373-2691-5). Natl Learning.
--Medical Clerk. (Career Examination Ser.: C-1796). (Cloth bdg. avail. on request). pap. 10.00 (ISBN 0-8373-1796-7). Natl Learning.
--Medical College Admission Test (MCAT) (Admission Test Ser.: ATS-11). 300p. (Cloth bdg. avail. on request). pap. 13.95 (ISBN 0-8373-5011-5). Natl Learning.
--Medical Conduct Investigator. (Career Examination Ser.: C-2287). (Cloth bdg. avail. on request). 1977. pap. 10.00 (ISBN 0-8373-2287-1). Natl Learning.
--Medical Equipment Technician. (Career Examination Ser.: C-2654). (Cloth bdg. avail. on request). pap. 10.00 (ISBN 0-8373-2654-0). Natl Learning.
--Medical Officer (Departmental) (Career Examination Ser.: C-489). (Cloth bdg. avail. on request). pap. 14.00 (ISBN 0-8373-0489-X). Natl Learning.
--Medical Record Librarian. (Career Examination Ser.: C-491). (Cloth bdg. avail. on request). pap. 10.00 (ISBN 0-8373-0491-1). Natl Learning.
--Medical Record Technician. (Career Examination Ser.: C-2329). (Cloth bdg. avail. on request). pap. 10.00 (ISBN 0-8373-2329-0). Natl Learning.
--Medical Records Assistant. (Career Examination Ser.: C-2952). (Cloth bdg. avail. on request). pap. 10.00 (ISBN 0-8373-2952-3). Natl Learning.
--Medical Records Clerk. (Career Examination Ser.: C-2309). (Cloth bdg. avail. on request). 1977. pap. 10.00 (ISBN 0-8373-2309-6). Natl Learning.
--Medical Sciences Knowledge Profile Examination (MSKP) (Admission Test Ser.: AT-86). (Cloth bdg. avail. on request). pap. 19.95 (ISBN 0-8373-5086-7). Natl Learning.
--Medical Specialist. (Career Examination Ser.: C-1965). (Cloth bdg. avail. on request). 1977. pap. 14.00 (ISBN 0-8373-1965-X). Natl Learning.
--Medical Stenographer. (Career Examination Ser.: C-1368). (Cloth bdg. avail. on request). text ed. 10.00 (ISBN 0-8373-1368-6). Natl Learning.
--Medical Surgical Nursing. (College Proficiency Examination Ser.: CPEP-24). 19.95 (ISBN 0-8373-5474-9); pap. 11.95 (ISBN 0-8373-5424-2). Natl Learning.
--Men's Physical Education. (National Teachers Examination Ser.: NT-36). (Cloth bdg. avail. on request). pap. 11.95 (ISBN 0-8373-8446-X). Natl Learning.
--Mental Hygiene Nursing Program Coordinator. (Career Examination Ser.: C-2665). (Cloth bdg. avail. on request). pap. 12.00 (ISBN 0-8373-2665-6). Natl Learning.
--Metallurgist. (Career Examination Ser.: C-496). (Cloth bdg. avail. on request). pap. 10.00 (ISBN 0-8373-0496-2). Natl Learning.
--Microbiology. (College Level Examination Ser.: CLEP-35). (Cloth bdg. avail. on request). 11.95 (ISBN 0-8373-5335-1). Natl Learning.
--Middle Level Positions. (Career Examination Ser.: C-511). (Cloth bdg. avail. on request). pap. 10.00 (ISBN 0-8373-0511-X). Natl Learning.
--Miller Analogies Test (MAT) (Admission Test Ser.: ATS-18). 300p. 21.95 (ISBN 0-8373-5118-9); pap. 13.95 (ISBN 0-8373-5018-2). Natl Learning.
--Missouri Basic Essential Skills Test (BEST) (Admission Test Ser.: ATS-64). 19.95 (ISBN 0-8373-5164-2); pap. 11.95 (ISBN 0-8373-5064-6). Natl Learning.
--Mortgage Analyst. (Career Examination Ser.: C-2653). (Cloth bdg. avail. on request). pap. 10.00 (ISBN 0-8373-2653-2). Natl Learning.
--Mortgage Tax Clerk. (Career Examination Ser.: C-929). (Cloth bdg. avail. on request). pap. 10.00 (ISBN 0-8373-0929-8). Natl Learning.
--Mortuary Technician. (Career Examination Ser.: C-514). (Cloth bdg. avail. on request). pap. 10.00 (ISBN 0-8373-0514-4). Natl Learning.
--Mosquito Control Inspector. (Career Examination Ser.: C-2912). (Cloth bdg. avail. on request). pap. 10.00 (ISBN 0-8373-2912-4). Natl Learning.
--Motion Picture Operator. (Career Examination Ser.: C-501). (Cloth bdg. avail. on request). pap. 10.00 (ISBN 0-8373-0501-2). Natl Learning.
--Motor Carrier Investigator. (Career Examination Ser.: C-523). (Cloth bdg. avail. on request). pap. 10.00 (ISBN 0-8373-0523-3). Natl Learning.
--Motor Equipment Maintenance Foreman. (Career Examination Ser.: C-2084). (Cloth bdg. avail. on request). 1977. pap. 10.00 (ISBN 0-8373-2084-4). Natl Learning.
--Motor Equipment Manager. (Career Examination Ser.: C-359). (Cloth bdg. avail. on request). pap. 14.00 (ISBN 0-686-84424-6). Natl Learning.
--Motor Equipment Mechanic. (Career Examination Ser.: C-459). (Cloth bdg. avail. on request). pap. 12.00 (ISBN 0-8373-0459-8). Natl Learning.
--Motor Grader Operator. (Career Examination Ser.: C-502). (Cloth bdg. avail. on request). pap. 10.00 (ISBN 0-8373-0502-0). Natl Learning.
--Motor Vehicle Cashier. (Career Examination Ser.: C-1722). (Cloth bdg. avail. on request). pap. 10.00 (ISBN 0-8373-1722-3). Natl Learning.
--Motor Vehicle Dispatcher. (Career Examination Ser.: C-503). (Cloth bdg. avail. on request). pap. 10.00 (ISBN 0-8373-0503-9). Natl Learning.
--Motor Vehicle Foreman. (Career Examination Ser.: C-1781). (Cloth bdg. avail. on request). pap. 10.00 (ISBN 0-8373-1781-9). Natl Learning.
--Motor Vehicle Inspector. (Career Examination Ser.: C-2384). (Cloth bdg. avail. on request). pap. 10.00 (ISBN 0-8373-2384-3). Natl Learning.
--Motor Vehicle Investigator. (Career Examination Ser.: C-504). (Cloth avail. on request). pap. 10.00 (ISBN 0-8373-0504-7). Natl Learning.
--Motor Vehicle License Clerk. (Career Examination Ser.: C-505). (Cloth bdg. avail. on request). pap. 10.00 (ISBN 0-8373-0505-5). Natl Learning.
--Motor Vehicle License Examiner. (Career Examination Ser.: C-506). (Cloth bdg. avail. on request). pap. 10.00 (ISBN 0-8373-0506-3). Natl Learning.
--Motor Vehicle License Examiner 1. (Career Examination Ser.: C-1937). (Cloth bdg. avail. on request). pap. 10.00 (ISBN 0-8373-1937-4). Natl Learning.
--Motor Vehicle Officer. (Career Examination Ser.: C-2031). (Cloth bdg. avail. on request). pap. 10.00 (ISBN 0-8373-2031-3). Natl Learning.
--Motor Vehicle Operator. (Career Examination Ser.: C-507). (Cloth bdg. avail. on request). pap. 10.00 (ISBN 0-8373-0507-1). Natl Learning.
--Motor Vehicle Operator (U.S.P.S.) (Career Examination Ser.: C-508). (Cloth bdg. avail on request). pap. 10.00 (ISBN 0-8373-0508-X). Natl Learning.
--Motor Vehicle Program Manager. (Career Examination Ser.: C-311). (Cloth bdg. avail. on request). pap. 12.00 (ISBN 0-8373-0311-7). Natl Learning.

--Motor Vehicle Program Manager I. (Career Examination Ser.: C-312). (Cloth bdg. avail. on request). pap. 12.00 (ISBN 0-8373-0312-5). Natl Learning.

--Motor Vehicle Program Manager II. (Career Examination Ser.: C-313). (Cloth bdg. avail. on request). pap. 14.00 (ISBN 0-8373-0313-3). Natl Learning.

--Motor Vehicle Program Manager III. (Career Examination Ser.: C-314). (Cloth bdg. avail. on request). pap. 14.00 (ISBN 0-8373-0314-1). Natl Learning.

--Motor Vehicle Referee. (Career Examination Ser.: C-2330). (Cloth bdg. avail. on request). pap. 12.00 (ISBN 0-8373-2330-4). Natl Learning.

--Motorman. (Career Examination Ser.: C-509). (Cloth bdg. avail. on request). pap. 10.00 (ISBN 0-8373-0509-8). Natl Learning.

--Motorman Instructor. (Career Examination Ser.: C-510). (Cloth bdg. avail. on request). pap. 10.00 (ISBN 0-8373-0510-1). Natl Learning.

--Mower Maintenance Mechanic. (Career Examination Ser.: C-1373). (Cloth bdg. avail. on request). pap. 8.00 (ISBN 0-8373-1373-2). Natl Learning.

--Multi-Keyboard Operator. (Career Examination Ser.: C-455). (Cloth bdg. avail. on request). pap. 10.00 (ISBN 0-8373-0455-5). Natl Learning.

--Multistate Bar Examination (MBE) (Admission Test Ser.: ATS-8). 300p. 21.95 (ISBN 0-8373-5108-1); pap. 13.95 (ISBN 0-8373-5008-5). Natl Learning.

--Museum Laboratory Technician. (Career Examination Ser.: C-1377). (Cloth bdg. avail. on request). pap. 10.00 (ISBN 0-8373-1377-5). Natl Learning.

--Museum Supervisor. (Career Examination Ser.: C-2941). (Cloth bdg. avail. on request). pap. 10.00 (ISBN 0-8373-2941-8). Natl Learning.

--Music. (Graduate Record Examination Ser.: GRE-13). 21.95 (ISBN 0-8373-5263-0); pap. 13.95 (ISBN 0-8373-5213-4). Natl Learning.

--Music - Jr. H.S. (Teachers License Examination Ser.: T-42). (Cloth bdg. avail. on request). pap. 13.95 (ISBN 0-8373-8042-1). Natl Learning.

--Music - Sr. H.S. (Teachers License Examination Ser.: T-43). (Cloth bdg. avail. on request). pap. 13.95 (ISBN 0-8373-8043-X). Natl Learning.

--Music Chairman - Jr. H.S. (Teachers License Examination Ser.: CH-18). (Cloth bdg. avail. on request). pap. 15.95 (ISBN 0-8373-8168-1). Natl Learning.

--Music Chairman - Sr. H.S. (Teachers License Examination Ser.: CH-19). (Cloth bdg. avail. on request). pap. 15.95 (ISBN 0-8373-8169-X). Natl Learning.

--Music Education. (National Teachers Examination Ser.: NT-11). (Cloth bdg. avail. on request). pap. 11.95 (ISBN 0-8373-8421-4). Natl Learning.

--National Certifying Examination for Physician's Assistants (PA) (Admission Test Ser.: ATS-91). 25.95 (ISBN 0-8373-5191-X); pap. 17.95 (ISBN 0-8373-5091-3). Natl Learning.

--National Dental Boards. (Admission Test Ser.: ATS-36). (Cloth bdg. avail. on request). pap. 19.95 (ISBN 0-8373-5036-0). Natl Learning.

--National Dental Boards (NDB) Pt. 1, Pt. 1. (Admission Test Ser.: ATS-36A). (Cloth bdg. avail. on request). pap. 15.95 (ISBN 0-8373-5036-0). Natl Learning.

--National Dental Boards (NDB) Pt. 2, Pt. 2. (Admission Test Ser.: ATS-36B). (Cloth bdg. avail. on request). pap. 15.95 (ISBN 0-8373-5036-0). Natl Learning.

--National Medical Boards (NMB) (Admission Test Ser.: ATS-23). (Cloth bdg. avail. on request). pap. 19.95 (ISBN 0-8373-5023-9). Natl Learning.

--National Medical Boards (NMB) Pt. 1, Pt. 1. (Admission Test Ser.: ATS-23A). (Cloth bdg. avail. on request). pap. 15.95 (ISBN 0-8373-5023-9). Natl Learning.

--National Medical Boards (NMB) Pt. 2, Pt. 2. (Admission Test Ser.: ATS-23B). (Cloth bdg. avail. on request). pap. 15.95 (ISBN 0-8373-5023-9). Natl Learning.

--National Pharmacy Boards (NPB) (Admission Test Ser.: ATS-47). (Cloth bdg. avail. on request). pap. 19.95 (ISBN 0-8373-5047-6). Natl Learning.

--National Registry of Emergency Medical Technicians-Paramedic Examination (EMT) (Admission Test Ser.: ATS-70). (Cloth bdg. avail. on request). pap. 19.95 (ISBN 0-8373-5070-0). Natl Learning.

--National Teacher Examination - Common Examination (NTE) (Admission Test Ser.: ATS-15). 300p. (Cloth bdg. avail. on request). pap. 15.95 (ISBN 0-8373-5015-8). Natl Learning.

--National Veterinary Boards (NVB) (Admission Test Ser.: ATS-50). (Cloth bdg. avail. on request). pap. 19.95 (ISBN 0-8373-5050-6). Natl Learning.

--Naturalist. (Career Examination Ser.: C-1379). (Cloth bdg. avail. on request). pap. 10.00 (ISBN 0-8373-1379-1). Natl Learning.

--Nebraska Assessment Battery of Essential Learning Skills (N-ABELS) (Admission Test Ser.: ATS-65). (Cloth bdg. avail. on request). pap. 11.95 (ISBN 0-8373-5065-4). Natl Learning.

--Neighborhood Aide. (Career Examination Ser.: C-2910). (Cloth bdg. avail. on request). pap. 10.00 (ISBN 0-8373-2910-8). Natl Learning.

--Nevada Competency-Based High School Diploma Program (CHSD) (Admission Test Ser.: ATS-67). (Cloth bdg. avail. on request). pap. 11.95 (ISBN 0-8373-5167-7). Natl Learning.

--New York Basic Competency Tests (BCT-NY) (Admission Test Ser.: ATS-55). (Cloth bdg. avail. on request). pap. 11.95 (ISBN 0-8373-5055-7). Natl Learning.

--New York State Bar Examination (NYBE) (Admission Test Ser.: ATS-25). (Cloth bdg. avail. on request). pap. 21.95 (ISBN 0-8373-5125-1); pap. 13.95 (ISBN 0-8373-5025-5). Natl Learning.

--Notary Public. (Career Examination Ser.: C-531). (Cloth bdg. avail. on request). pap. 8.00 (ISBN 0-8373-0531-4). Natl Learning.

--Nurse. (Career Examination Ser.: C-532). (Cloth bdg. avail. on request). pap. 10.00 (ISBN 0-8373-0532-2). Natl Learning.

--Nurse Administrator. (Career Examination Ser.: C-2913). (Cloth bdg. avail. on request). pap. 12.00 (ISBN 0-8373-2913-2). Natl Learning.

--Nurse GS4-GS7. (Career Examination Ser.: C-533). (Cloth bdg. avail. on request). pap. 10.00 (ISBN 0-8373-0533-0). Natl Learning.

--Nurse's Aide. (Career Examination Ser.: C-535). (Cloth bdg. avail. on request). pap. 8.00 (ISBN 0-8373-0535-7). Natl Learning.

--Nursing Administration. (Certified Nurse Examination Ser.: CN-16). 21.95 (ISBN 0-8373-6166-4); pap. 13.95 (ISBN 0-8373-6116-8). Natl Learning.

--Nursing Administration (Advanced) (Certified Nurse Examination Ser.: CN-17). 21.95 (ISBN 0-8373-6167-2); pap. 13.95 (ISBN 0-8373-6117-6). Natl Learning.

--Nursing Assistant. (Career Examination Ser.: C-534). (Cloth bdg. avail. on request). pap. 10.00 (ISBN 0-8373-0534-9). Natl Learning.

--Nursing Chairman (Questions Only) (Teachers License Examination Ser.: CH-31). (Cloth bdg. avail. on request). pap. 15.95 (ISBN 0-8373-8181-9). Natl Learning.

--Nursing School Entrance Examinations for Practical Nurse. (Admission Test Ser.: ATS-20). 300p. (Cloth bdg. avail. on request). pap. 13.95 (ISBN 0-8373-5020-4). Natl Learning.

--Nursing School Entrance Examinations for Registered and Graduate Nurses (RN) (Admission Test Ser.: ATS-19). 21.95 (ISBN 0-8373-5119-7); pap. 13.95 (ISBN 0-8373-5019-0). Natl Learning.

--Nursing: Senior H.S. (Teachers License Examination Ser.: T-44). (Cloth bdg. avail. on request). pap. 13.95 (ISBN 0-8373-8044-8). Natl Learning.

--Occupational Competency Examination: General Examination. (Admission Test Ser.: ATS-33). (Cloth bdg. avail. on request). 15.95 (ISBN 0-8373-5033-6). Natl Learning.

--Office & Science Assistant. (Career Examination Ser.: C-552). (Cloth bdg. avail. on request). pap. 10.00 (ISBN 0-8373-0552-7). Natl Learning.

--Office Associate. (Career Examination Ser.: C-2450). (Cloth bdg. avail. on request). pap. 10.00 (ISBN 0-8373-2450-5). Natl Learning.

--Office Machine Operating-Sr. H.S. (Teachers License Examination Ser.: T-45). (Cloth bdg. avail. on request). pap. 13.95 (ISBN 0-8373-8045-6). Natl Learning.

--Offset Lithography. (Occupational Competency Examination Ser.: OCE-27). (Cloth bdg. avail. on request). pap. 13.95 (ISBN 0-8373-5727-6). Natl Learning.

--Offset Photographer. (Career Examination Ser.: C-560). (Cloth bdg. avail. on request). pap. 10.00 (ISBN 0-8373-0560-8). Natl Learning.

--Offset Pressman. (Career Examination Ser.: C-561). (Cloth bdg. avail. on request). pap. 10.00 (ISBN 0-8373-0561-6). Natl Learning.

--Offset Printing Machine Operator. (Career Examination Ser.: C-562). (Cloth bdg. avail. on request). pap. 10.00 (ISBN 0-8373-0562-4). Natl Learning.

--Oiler. (Career Examination Ser.: C-553). (Cloth bdg. avail. on request). 10.00 (ISBN 0-8373-1065-2). Natl Learning.

--Operations Research Analyst. (Career Examination Ser.: C-556). (Cloth bdg. avail. on request). pap. 10.00 (ISBN 0-8373-0556-X). Natl Learning.

--Optometry College Admission Test (OCAT) (Admission Test Ser.: ATS-27). (Cloth bdg. avail. on request). 1975. pap. 13.95 (ISBN 0-8373-5027-1). Natl Learning.

--Ornamental Horticulture. (Occupational Competency Examination Ser.: OCE-28). (Cloth bdg. avail. on request). pap. 13.95 (ISBN 0-8373-5728-4). Natl Learning.

--Packer. (Career Examination Ser.: C-1647). (Cloth bdg. avail. on request). 1977. pap. 8.00 (ISBN 0-8373-1647-2). Natl Learning.

--Painter. (Career Examination Ser.: C-570). (Cloth bdg. avail. on request). pap. 10.00 (ISBN 0-8373-0570-5). Natl Learning.

--Painting Inspector. (Career Examination Ser.: C-1778). (Cloth bdg. avail. on request). pap. 10.00 (ISBN 0-8373-1778-9). Natl Learning.

--Park Foreman. (Career Examination Ser.: C-571). (Cloth bdg. avail. on request). pap. 10.00 (ISBN 0-8373-0571-3). Natl Learning.

--Park Maintenance Supervisor. (Career Examination Ser.: C-2942). (Cloth bdg. avail. on request). pap. 12.00 (ISBN 0-8373-2942-6). Natl Learning.

--Park Manager I. (Career Examination Ser.: C-383). (Cloth bdg. avail. on request). pap. 12.00 (ISBN 0-8373-0383-4). Natl Learning.

--Park Manager II. (Career Examination Ser.: C-384). (Cloth bdg. avail. on request). pap. 12.00 (ISBN 0-8373-0384-2). Natl Learning.

--Park Manager III. (Career Examination Ser.: C-385). (Cloth bdg. avail. on request). pap. 14.00 (ISBN 0-8373-0385-0). Natl Learning.

--Park Supervisor. (Career Examination Ser.: C-1563). (Cloth bdg. avail. on request). pap. 10.00 (ISBN 0-8373-1563-8). Natl Learning.

--Parking Meter Attendant. (Career Examination Ser.: C-1063). (Cloth bdg. avail. on request). pap. 10.00 (ISBN 0-8373-1063-6). Natl Learning.

--Parking Meter Supervisor. (Career Examination Ser.: C-2592). (Cloth bdg. avail. on request). pap. 10.00 (ISBN 0-8373-2592-7). Natl Learning.

--Patrolman - Police Department. (Career Examination Ser.: C-576). (Cloth bdg. avail. on request). pap. 10.00 (ISBN 0-8373-0576-4). Natl Learning.

--Patrolman - Policewoman. (Career Examination Ser.: C-1922). (Cloth bdg. avail. on request). pap. 10.00 (ISBN 0-8373-1922-6). Natl Learning.

--Patrolman Examinations - All States. (Career Examination Ser.: C-575). (Cloth bdg. avail. on request). pap. 10.00 (ISBN 0-8373-0575-6). Natl Learning.

--Payroll Auditor. (Career Examination Ser.: C-2074). (Cloth bdg. avail. on request). 1977. pap. 10.00 (ISBN 0-8373-2074-7). Natl Learning.

--Payroll Clerk. (Career Examination Ser.: C-1596). (Cloth bdg. avail. on request). pap. 10.00 (ISBN 0-8373-1596-4). Natl Learning.

--Peace Corps Examination. (Career Examination Ser.: C-646). (Cloth bdg. avail. on request). pap. 10.00 (ISBN 0-8373-0646-9). Natl Learning.

--Pediatric Nurse Practitioner. (Certified Nurse Examination Ser.: CN-8). 21.95 (ISBN 0-8373-6158-3); pap. 13.95 (ISBN 0-8373-6108-7). Natl Learning.

--Personnel Administrator. (Career Examination Ser.: C-647). (Cloth bdg. avail. on request). pap. 12.00 (ISBN 0-8373-0647-7). Natl Learning.

--Personnel Analyst Trainee. (Career Examination Ser.: C-2395). (Cloth bdg. avail. on request). pap. 10.00 (ISBN 0-686-53383-6). Natl Learning.

--Personnel Assistant. (Career Examination Ser.: C-577). (Cloth bdg. avail. on request). pap. 10.00 (ISBN 0-8373-0577-2). Natl Learning.

--Personnel Associate. (Career Examination Ser.: C-648). (Cloth bdg. avail. on request). pap. 12.00 (ISBN 0-8373-0648-5). Natl Learning.

--Personnel Examiner. (Career Examination Ser.: C-578). (Cloth bdg. avail. on request). pap. 12.00 (ISBN 0-8373-0578-0). Natl Learning.

--Personnel Examining Trainee. (Career Examination Ser.: C-579). (Cloth bdg. avail. on request). pap. 10.00 (ISBN 0-8373-0579-9). Natl Learning.

--Personnel Manager. (Career Examination Ser.: C-2112). (Cloth bdg. avail. on request). 1977. pap. 12.00 (ISBN 0-8373-2112-3). Natl Learning.

--Personnel Specialist. (Career Examination Ser.: C-1386). (Cloth bdg. avail. on request). pap. 12.00 (ISBN 0-8373-1386-4). Natl Learning.

--Personnel Systems Analyst. (Career Examination Ser.: C-1387). (Cloth bdg. avail. on request). pap. 12.00 (ISBN 0-8373-1387-2). Natl Learning.

--Personnel Technician. (Career Examination Ser.: C-1944). (Cloth bdg. avail. on request). pap. 12.00 (ISBN 0-8373-1944-7). Natl Learning.

--Personnel Technician Trainee. (Career Examination Ser.: C-2274). (Cloth bdg. avail. on request). pap. 10.00 (ISBN 0-8373-2274-X). Natl Learning.

--Pharmacy Assistant II. (Career Examination Ser.: C-2943). (Cloth bdg. avail. on request). pap. 12.00 (ISBN 0-8373-2943-4). Natl Learning.

--Pharmacy Assistant 1. (Career Examination Ser.: C-1388). (Cloth bdg. avail. on request). pap. 10.00 (ISBN 0-8373-1388-0). Natl Learning.

--Pharmacy College Admission Test (PCAT) (Admission Test Ser.: ATS-52). (Cloth bdg. avail. on request). pap. 13.95 (ISBN 0-8373-5052-2). Natl Learning.

--Philosophy. (Graduate Record Examination Ser.: GRE-14). (Cloth bdg. avail. on request). pap. 13.95 (ISBN 0-8373-5214-2). Natl Learning.

--Photo Specialist. (Career Examination Ser.: C-1391). (Cloth bdg. avail. on request). pap. 10.00 (ISBN 0-8373-1391-0). Natl Learning.

--Photographer. (Career Examination Ser.: C-582). (Cloth bdg. avail. on request). pap. 10.00 (ISBN 0-8373-0582-9). Natl Learning.

--Photographic Specialist 1. (Career Examination Ser.: C-1870). (Cloth bdg. avail. on request). pap. 10.00 (ISBN 0-8373-1870-X). Natl Learning.

--Photographic Technician. (Career Examination Ser.: C-1872). (Cloth bdg. avail. on request). pap. 10.00 (ISBN 0-8373-1872-6). Natl Learning.

--Physical Education. (National Teachers Examination Ser.: NT-9). (Cloth bdg. avail. on request). pap. 11.95 (ISBN 0-8373-8419-2). Natl Learning.

--Physical Education. (Graduate Record Examination Ser.: GRE-20). (Cloth bdg. avail. on request). pap. 13.95 (ISBN 0-8373-5220-7). Natl Learning.

--Physical Science Aide. (Career Examination Ser.: C-583). (Cloth bdg. avail. on request). pap. 10.00 (ISBN 0-8373-0583-7). Natl Learning.

--Physical Science Technician. (Career Examination Ser.: C-584). (Cloth bdg. avail. on request). pap. 10.00 (ISBN 0-8373-0584-5). Natl Learning.

--Physical Sciences. (Graduate Record Area Examination Ser.: GRE-43). 21.95 (ISBN 0-8373-5293-2); pap. 13.95 (ISBN 0-8373-5243-6). Natl Learning.

--Physician's Assistant. (Career Examination Ser.: C-2557). (Cloth bdg. avail. on request). pap. 12.00 (ISBN 0-8373-2557-9). Natl Learning.

--Physics. (Graduate Record Examination Ser.: GRE-15). (Cloth bdg. avail. on request). pap. 13.95 (ISBN 0-8373-5215-0). Natl Learning.

--Physics & General Science - Sr. H.S. (Teachers License Examination Ser.: T-46). (Cloth bdg. avail. on request). pap. 13.95 (ISBN 0-8373-8046-4). Natl Learning.

--Placement Representative. (Career Examination Ser.: C-869). (Cloth bdg. avail. on request). pap. 12.00 (ISBN 0-8373-0869-0). Natl Learning.

--Placement Representative I. (Career Examination Ser.: C-868). (Cloth bdg. avail. on request). pap. 10.00 (ISBN 0-8373-0868-2). Natl Learning.

--Plan Examiner. (Career Examination Ser.: C-651). (Cloth bdg. avail. on request). pap. 10.00 (ISBN 0-8373-0651-5). Natl Learning.

--Planner. (Career Examination Ser.: C-588). (Cloth bdg. avail. on request). pap. 10.00 (ISBN 0-8373-0588-8). Natl Learning.

--Planning Aide. (Career Examination Ser.: C-2770). (Cloth bdg. avail. on request). 1980. pap. 10.00 (ISBN 0-8373-2770-9). Natl Learning.

--Planning & Evaluation Assistant. (Career Examination Ser.: C-549). (Cloth bdg. avail. on request). pap. 12.00 (ISBN 0-8373-0549-7). Natl Learning.

--Plant Maintenance Engineer. (Career Examination Ser.: C-2480). (Cloth bdg. avail. on request). pap. 10.00 (ISBN 0-8373-2480-7). Natl Learning.

--Plasterer. (Career Examination Ser.: C-589). (Cloth bdg. avail. on request). pap. 8.00 (ISBN 0-8373-0589-6). Natl Learning.

--Playgrounds (Health Education) Men. (Teachers License Examination Ser.: T-47a). (Cloth bdg. avail. on request). pap. 13.95 (ISBN 0-8373-8047-2). Natl Learning.

--Playgrounds (Health Education) Women. (Teachers License Examination Ser.: T-47b). (Cloth bdg. avail. on request). pap. 13.95 (ISBN 0-8373-8047-2). Natl Learning.

--Playgrounds (Kindergarten) (Teachers License Examination Ser.: T-48). (Cloth bdg. avail. on request). pap. 13.95 (ISBN 0-8373-8048-0). Natl Learning.

--Playgrounds (Swimming) (Teachers License Examination Ser.: T-49). (Cloth bdg. avail. on request). pap. 13.95 (ISBN 0-8373-8049-9). Natl Learning.

--Plumber. (Career Examination Ser.: C-591). (Cloth bdg. avail. on request). pap. 10.00 (ISBN 0-8373-0591-8). Natl Learning.

--Plumbing. (Occupational Competency Examination Ser.: OCE-29). (Cloth bdg. avail. on request). pap. 13.95 (ISBN 0-8373-5729-2). Natl Learning.

--Plumbing Engineer. (Career Examination Ser.: C-2713). (Cloth bdg. avail. on request). 1980. pap. 12.00 (ISBN 0-8373-2713-X). Natl Learning.

--Plumbing Inspector. (Career Examination Ser.: C-593). (Cloth bdg. avail. on request). pap. 10.00 (ISBN 0-8373-0593-4). Natl Learning.

--Police Administration & Supervision. (Career Examination Ser.: CS-32). (Cloth bdg. avail. on request). pap. 10.00 (ISBN 0-8373-3732-1). Natl Learning.

--Police Administrative Aide. (Career Examination Ser.: C-640). (Cloth bdg. avail. on request). pap. 10.00 (ISBN 0-8373-0640-X). Natl Learning.

--Police Captain. (Career Examination Ser.: C-121). (Cloth bdg. avail. on request). 1980. pap. 12.00 (ISBN 0-8373-2803-9). Natl Learning.

--Police Chief. (Career Examination Ser.: C-2754). (Cloth bdg. avail. on request). 1980. pap. 12.00 (ISBN 0-8373-2754-7). Natl Learning.

--Police Communications & Teletype Operator. (Career Examination Ser.: C-1847). (Cloth bdg. avail. on request). pap. 10.00 (ISBN 0-8373-1847-5). Natl Learning.

--Police Dispatcher. (Career Examination Ser.: C-2256). (Cloth bdg. avail. on request). 1977. pap. 10.00 (ISBN 0-8373-2256-1). Natl Learning.

--Police Officer. (Career Examination Ser.: C-1939). (Cloth bdg. avail. on request). 1977. pap. 10.00 (ISBN 0-8373-1939-0). Natl Learning.

--Police Officer - Los Angeles Police Department (LAPD) (Career Examination Ser.: C-2441). (Cloth bdg. avail. on request). pap. 10.00 (ISBN 0-8373-2441-6). Natl Learning.

--Police Officer - Nassau County Police Dept. (NCPD) (Career Examination Ser.: C-1755). (Cloth bdg. avail. on request). pap. 10.00 (ISBN 0-8373-1755-X). Natl Learning.

--Police Officer - New York Police Dept. (NYPD) (Career Examination Ser.: C-1739). (Cloth bdg. avail. on request). 1977. pap. 10.00 (ISBN 0-8373-1739-8). Natl Learning.

--Police Officer - Suffolk County Police Dept. (SCPD) (Career Examination Ser.: C-1741). (Cloth bdg. avail. on request). 1977. pap. 10.00 (ISBN 0-8373-1741-X). Natl Learning.

--Police Patrolman. (Career Examination Ser.: C-595). (Cloth bdg. avail. on request). pap. 10.00 (ISBN 0-8373-0595-0). Natl Learning.

--Police Trainee. (Career Examination Ser.: C-597). (Cloth bdg. avail. on request). pap. 10.00 (ISBN 0-8373-0597-7). Natl Learning.

--Policewoman. (Career Examination Ser.: C-598). (Cloth bdg. avail. on request). pap. 10.00 (ISBN 0-8373-0598-5). Natl Learning.

--Political Science. (Graduate Record Examination Ser.: GRE-16). (Cloth bdg. avail. on request). pap. 13.95 (ISBN 0-8373-5216-9). Natl Learning.

--Position Classification Specialist. (Career Examination Ser.: C-601). (Cloth bdg. avail. on request). pap. 12.00 (ISBN 0-8373-0601-9). Natl Learning.

--Postal Inspector (U.S.P.S.) (Career Examination Ser.: C-602). (Cloth bdg. avail. on request). pap. 10.00 (ISBN 0-8373-0602-7). Natl Learning.

--Power Cable Maintainer. (Career Examination Ser.: C-653). (Cloth bdg. avail. on request). pap. 10.00 (ISBN 0-8373-0653-1). Natl Learning.

--Power Distribution Maintainer. (Career Examination Ser.: C-1394). (Cloth bdg. avail. on request). pap. 10.00 (ISBN 0-8373-1394-5). Natl Learning.

--Power Maintainer - Group A. (Career Examination Ser.: C-607). (Cloth bdg. avail. on request). pap. 10.00 (ISBN 0-8373-0607-8). Natl Learning.

--Power Maintainer - Group B. (Career Examination Ser.: C-608). (Cloth bdg. avail. on request). pap. 10.00 (ISBN 0-8373-0608-6). Natl Learning.

--Power Maintainer - Group C. (Career Examination Ser.: C-609). (Cloth bdg. avail. on request). pap. 10.00 (ISBN 0-8373-0609-4). Natl Learning.

--Practical Nurse. (Career Examination Ser.: C-642). (Cloth bdg. avail. on request). pap. 10.00 (ISBN 0-8373-0642-6). Natl Learning.

--Pre-Employment Counselor. (Career Examination Ser.: C-1396). (Cloth bdg. avail. on request). pap. 10.00 (ISBN 0-8373-1396-1). Natl Learning.

--Pre-Law Equivalency Examination. (Admission Test Ser.: ATS-40). (Cloth bdg. avail. on request). pap. 13.95 (ISBN 0-8373-5040-9). Natl Learning.

--Preparing Written Material. (Career Examination Ser.: CS-37). (Cloth bdg. avail. on request). pap. 8.00 (ISBN 0-8373-3737-2). Natl Learning.

--Presser. (Career Examination Ser.: C-1397). (Cloth bdg. avail. on request). pap. 8.00 (ISBN 0-8373-1397-X). Natl Learning.

--Principal-Academic High School. (Teachers License Examination Ser.: S-5). (Cloth bdg. avail. on request). pap. 17.95 (ISBN 0-8373-8105-3). Natl Learning.

--Principal Account-Audit Clerk. (Career Examination Ser.: C-2008). (Cloth bdg. avail. on request). pap. 12.00 (ISBN 0-8373-2008-9). Natl Learning.

--Principal Account Clerk. (Career Examination Ser.: C-655). (Cloth bdg. avail. on request). pap. 12.00 (ISBN 0-8373-0655-8). Natl Learning.

--Principal Accountant. (Career Examination Ser.: C-654). (Cloth bdg. avail. on request). pap. 14.00 (ISBN 0-8373-0654-X). Natl Learning.

--Principal Actuarial Clerk. (Career Examination Ser.: C-2424). (Cloth bdg. avail. on request). pap. 12.00 (ISBN 0-8373-2424-6). Natl Learning.

--Principal Actuary. (Career Examination Ser.: C-610). (Cloth bdg. avail. on request). pap. 14.00 (ISBN 0-8373-0610-8). Natl Learning.

--Principal Addiction Specialist. (Career Examination Ser.: C-1398). (Cloth bdg. avail. on request). pap. 12.00 (ISBN 0-8373-2167-0). Natl Learning.

--Principal Administrative Services Clerk. (Career Examination Ser.: C-2871). (Cloth bdg. avail. on request). pap. 12.00 (ISBN 0-8373-2871-3). Natl Learning.

--Principal Admitting Clerk. (Career Examination Ser.: C-656). (Cloth bdg. avail. on request). pap. 12.00 (ISBN 0-8373-0656-6). Natl Learning.

--Principal Affirmative Action Officer. (Career Examination Ser.: C-2689). (Cloth bdg. avail. on request). pap. 12.00 (ISBN 0-8373-2689-3). Natl Learning.

--Principal Attorney. (Career Examination Ser.: C-1913). (Cloth bdg. avail. on request). pap. 14.00 (ISBN 0-8373-1913-7). Natl Learning.

--Principal Audit Clerk. (Career Examination Ser.: C-657). (Cloth bdg. avail. on request). pap. 12.00 (ISBN 0-8373-0657-4). Natl Learning.

--Principal Auditor. (Career Examination Ser.: C-2405). (Cloth bdg. avail. on request). pap. 12.00 (ISBN 0-8373-2405-X). Natl Learning.

--Principal Bookkeeper. (Career Examination Ser.: C-1756). (Cloth bdg. avail. on request). 1977. pap. 12.00 (ISBN 0-8373-1756-8). Natl Learning.

--Principal Budget Officer. (Career Examination Ser.: C-2685). (Cloth bdg. avail. on request). pap. 12.00 (ISBN 0-8373-2685-0). Natl Learning.

--Principal Building Inspector. (Career Examination Ser.: C-2853). (Cloth bdg. avail. on request). 1980. pap. 12.00 (ISBN 0-8373-2853-5). Natl Learning.

--Principal Buildings Manager. (Career Examination Ser.: C-2719). (Cloth bdg. avail. on request). pap. 12.00 (ISBN 0-8373-2719-9). Natl Learning.

--Principal Cashier. (Career Examination Ser.: C-1974). (Cloth bdg. avail. on request). pap. 12.00 (ISBN 0-8373-1974-9). Natl Learning.

--Principal Children's Counselor. (Career Examination Ser.: C-1602). (Cloth bdg. avail. on request). pap. 12.00 (ISBN 0-8373-1602-2). Natl Learning.

--Principal Clerk (Personnel) (Career Examination Ser.: C-1399). (Cloth bdg. avail. on request). pap. 12.00 (ISBN 0-8373-1399-6). Natl Learning.

--Principal Clerk Surrogate. (Career Examination Ser.: C-2129). (Cloth bdg. avail. on request). 1977. pap. 12.00 (ISBN 0-8373-2129-8). Natl Learning.

--Principal Communications Technician. (Career Examination Ser.: C-2413). (Cloth bdg. avail. on request). pap. 12.00 (ISBN 0-8373-2413-0). Natl Learning.

--Principal-Comprehensive High School. (Teachers License Examination Ser.: S-11). (Cloth bdg. avail. on request). pap. 17.95 (ISBN 0-8373-8111-8). Natl Learning.

--Principal Consumer Affairs Inspector. (Career Examination Ser.: C-1658). (Cloth bdg. avail. on request). 1977. pap. 12.00 (ISBN 0-8373-1658-8). Natl Learning.

--Principal Consumer Affairs Investigator. (Career Examination Ser.: C-2377). (Cloth bdg. avail. on request). pap. 12.00 (ISBN 0-8373-2377-0). Natl Learning.

--Principal Court Clerk. (Career Examination Ser.: C-2588). (Cloth bdg. avail. on request). pap. 12.00 (ISBN 0-8373-2588-9). Natl Learning.

--Principal Data Entry Machine Operator. (Career Examination Ser.: C-2866). (Cloth bdg. avail. on request). pap. 12.00 (ISBN 0-8373-2866-7). Natl Learning.

--Principal Data Processing Control Clerk. (Career Examination Ser.: C-2485). (Cloth bdg. avail. on request). pap. 12.00 (ISBN 0-8373-2485-8). Natl Learning.

--Principal Data Processing Equipment Operator. (Career Examination Ser.: C-2303). (Cloth bdg. avail. on request). 1977. pap. 12.00 (ISBN 0-8373-2303-7). Natl Learning.

--Principal Developmental Specialist. (Career Examination Ser.: C-925). (Cloth bdg. avail. on request). pap. 14.00 (ISBN 0-8373-0925-5). Natl Learning.

--Principal Drafting Technician. (Career Examination Ser.: C-2680). (Cloth bdg. avail. on request). pap. 12.00 (ISBN 0-8373-2680-X). Natl Learning.

--Principal Draftsman. (Career Examination Ser.: C-1576). (Cloth bdg. avail. on request). pap. 12.00 (ISBN 0-8373-1576-X). Natl Learning.

--Principal Drug & Alcohol Counselor. (Career Examination Ser.: C-2743). (Cloth bdg. avail. on request). 1980. pap. 12.00 (ISBN 0-8373-2743-1). Natl Learning.

--Principal-Elementary School. (Teachers License Examination Ser.: S-3). (Cloth bdg. avail. on request). pap. 17.95 (ISBN 0-8373-8103-7). Natl Learning.

--Principal Employment Security Clerk. (Career Examination Ser.: C-2352). (Cloth bdg. avail. on request). pap. 12.00 (ISBN 0-8373-2352-5). Natl Learning.

--Principal Engineering Aide. (Career Examination Ser.: C-1561). (Cloth bdg. avail. on request). pap. 12.00 (ISBN 0-8373-1561-1). Natl Learning.

--Principal Engineering Inspector. (Career Examination Ser.: C-911). (Cloth bdg. avail. on request). pap. 14.00 (ISBN 0-8373-0911-5). Natl Learning.

--Principal Engineering Technician. (Career Examination Ser.: C-1425). (Cloth bdg. avail. on request). pap. 12.00 (ISBN 0-8373-1425-9). Natl Learning.

--Principal Engineering Technician (Drafting) (Career Examination Ser.: C-1954). (Cloth bdg. avail. on request). pap. 12.00 (ISBN 0-8373-1954-4). Natl Learning.

--Principal Environmental Analyst. (Career Examination Ser.: C-2661). (Cloth bdg. avail. on request). pap. 12.00 (ISBN 0-8373-2661-3). Natl Learning.

--Principal Environmental Planner. (Career Examination Ser.: C-2664). (Cloth bdg. avail. on request). pap. 12.00 (ISBN 0-8373-2664-8). Natl Learning.

--Principal Evidence Technician. (Career Examination Ser.: C-2750). (Cloth bdg. avail. on request). 1980. pap. 12.00 (ISBN 0-8373-2750-4). Natl Learning.

--Principal Financial Analyst. (Career Examination Ser.: C-2644). (Cloth bdg. avail. on request). pap. 12.00 (ISBN 0-8373-2644-3). Natl Learning.

--Principal Forestry Technician. (Career Examination Ser.: C-2716). (Cloth bdg. avail. on request). 1980. pap. 12.00 (ISBN 0-8373-2716-4). Natl Learning.

--Principal Grants Anaylyst. (Career Examination Ser.: C-2835). (Cloth bdg. avail. on request). 1980. pap. 12.00 (ISBN 0-8373-2835-7). Natl Learning.

--Principal Groundskeeper. (Career Examination Ser.: C-1573). (Cloth bdg. avail. on request). pap. 12.00 (ISBN 0-8373-1573-5). Natl Learning.

--Principal Home Economist. (Career Examination Ser.: C-1627). (Cloth bdg. avail. on request). pap. 12.00 (ISBN 0-8373-1627-8). Natl Learning.

--Principal Hospital Care Investigator. (Career Examination Ser.: C-612). (Cloth bdg. avail. on request). pap. 12.00 (ISBN 0-8373-0612-4). Natl Learning.

--Principal Housing Inspector. (Career Examination Ser.: C-1753). (Cloth bdg. avail. on request). 1977. pap. 12.00 (ISBN 0-8373-1753-3). Natl Learning.

--Principal Human Resources Specialist. (Career Examination Ser.: C-974). (Cloth bdg. avail. on request). pap. 12.00 (ISBN 0-8373-0974-3). Natl Learning.

--Principal Illustrator. (Career Examination Ser.: C-1713). (Cloth bdg. avail. on request). pap. 12.00 (ISBN 0-8373-1713-4). Natl Learning.

--Principal Insurance Examiner. (Career Examination Ser.: C-2696). (Cloth bdg. avail. on request). pap. 12.00 (ISBN 0-8373-2696-6). Natl Learning.

--Principal Investigator. (Career Examination Ser.: C-1791). (Cloth bdg. avail. on request). pap. 12.00 (ISBN 0-8373-1791-6). Natl Learning.

--Principal-Junior H.S. (Teachers License Examination Ser.: S-4). (Cloth bdg. avail. on request). pap. 17.95 (ISBN 0-8373-8104-5). Natl Learning.

--Principal Juvenile Counselor. (Career Examination Ser.: C-422). (Cloth bdg. avail. on request). pap. 12.00 (ISBN 0-8373-0422-9). Natl Learning.

--Principal Key Punch Operator. (Career Examination Ser.: C-2103). (Cloth bdg. avail. on request). 1977. pap. 12.00 (ISBN 0-8373-2103-4). Natl Learning.

--Principal Labor Specialist. (Career Examination Ser.: C-2670). (Cloth bdg. avail. on request). pap. 12.00 (ISBN 0-8373-2670-2). Natl Learning.

--Principal Land Management Specialist. (Career Examination Ser.: C-2620). (Cloth bdg. avail. on request). pap. 12.00 (ISBN 0-8373-2620-6). Natl Learning.

--Principal Librarian. (Career Examination Ser.: C-2915). (Cloth bdg. avail. on request). pap. 14.00 (ISBN 0-8373-2915-9). Natl Learning.

--Principal Library Clerk. (Career Examination Ser.: C-1932). (Cloth bdg. avail. on request). pap. 12.00 (ISBN 0-8373-1932-3). Natl Learning.

--Principal Management Technician. (Career Examination Ser.: C-2753). (Cloth bdg. avail. on request). 1980. pap. 12.00 (ISBN 0-8373-2753-9). Natl Learning.

--Principal Manpower Development Specialist. (Career Examination Ser.: C-2819). (Cloth bdg. avail. on request). 1980. pap. 12.00 (ISBN 0-8373-2819-5). Natl Learning.

--Principal Occupational Analyst. (Career Examination Ser.: C-2535). (Cloth bdg. avail. on request). pap. 12.00 (ISBN 0-8373-2535-8). Natl Learning.

--Principal Office Assistant. (Career Examination Ser.: C-2595). pap. 12.00 (ISBN 0-8373-2595-1); avail. Natl Learning.

--Principal Park Supervisor. (Career Examination Ser.: C-2355). (Cloth bdg. avail. on request). pap. 12.00 (ISBN 0-8373-2355-X). Natl Learning.

--Principal Personnel Clerk. (Career Examination Ser.: C-2944). (Cloth bdg. avail. on request). pap. 12.00 (ISBN 0-8373-2944-2). Natl Learning.

--Principal Planner. (Career Examination Ser.: C-1764). (Cloth bdg. avail on request). 1973. pap. 12.00 (ISBN 0-8373-1764-9). Natl Learning.

--Principal Planner (Education) (Career Examination Ser.: C-1669). (Cloth bdg. avail. on request). pap. 12.00 (ISBN 0-8373-1669-3). Natl Learning.

--Principal Planner (Manpower) (Career Examination Ser.: C-1599). (Cloth bdg. avail. on request). pap. 12.00 (ISBN 0-8373-1599-9). Natl Learning.

--Principal Probation Officer. (Career Examination Ser.: C-1427). (Cloth bdg. avail. on request). pap. 12.00 (ISBN 0-8373-1427-5). Natl Learning.

--Principal Program Evaluation Specialist. (Career Examination Ser.: C-2701). (Cloth bdg. avail. on request). 1980. pap. 14.00 (ISBN 0-8373-2701-6). Natl Learning.

--Principal Program Examiner. (Career Examination Ser.: C-2756). (Cloth bdg. avail. on request). 1980. pap. 12.00 (ISBN 0-8373-2756-3). Natl Learning.

--Principal Program Specialist. (Career Examination Ser.: C-2863). (Cloth bdg. avail. on request). 1980. pap. 12.00 (ISBN 0-8373-2863-2). Natl Learning.

--Principal Public Health Nutritionist. (Career Examination Ser.: C-1566). (Cloth bdg. avail. on request). pap. 12.00 (ISBN 0-8373-1566-2). Natl Learning.

--Principal Purchase Inspector. (Career Examination Ser.: C-1747). (Cloth bdg. avail. on request). 1977. pap. 12.00 (ISBN 0-8373-1747-9). Natl Learning.

--Principal Purchasing Agent. (Career Examination Ser.: C-912). (Cloth bdg. avail. on request). pap. 12.00 (ISBN 0-8373-0912-3). Natl Learning.

--Principal Quantitative Analyst. (Career Examination Ser.: C-1715). (Cloth bdg. avail. on request). pap. 14.00 (ISBN 0-8373-1715-0). Natl Learning.

--Principal Real Estate Manager. (Career Examination Ser.: C-1628). (Cloth bdg. avail. on request). pap. 12.0004286595x (ISBN 0-8373-1628-6). Natl Learning.

--Principal Records Center Assistant. (Career Examination Ser.: C-1914). (Cloth bdg. avail. on request). pap. 12.00 (ISBN 0-8373-1914-5). Natl Learning.

--Principal Rent Examiner. (Career Examination Ser.: C-2093). (Cloth bdg. avail. on request). 1977. pap. 12.00 (ISBN 0-8373-2093-3). Natl Learning.

--Principal Right-Of-Way Aide. (Career Examination Ser.: C-2737). (Cloth bdg. avail. on request). 1980. pap. 12.00 (ISBN 0-8373-2737-7). Natl Learning.

--Principal Safety Coordinator. (Career Examination Ser.: C-2669). (Cloth bdg. avail. on request). pap. 12.00 (ISBN 0-8373-2669-9). Natl Learning.

--Principal Senior Citizens Program Coordinator. (Career Examination Ser.: C-2799). (Cloth bdg. avail. on request). 1980. pap. 12.00 (ISBN 0-8373-2799-7). Natl Learning.

--Principal-Six Hundred School. (Teachers License Examination Ser.: S-7). (Cloth bdg. avail. on request). pap. 17.95 (ISBN 0-8373-8107-X). Natl Learning.

--Principal Special Investigator. (Career Examination Ser.: C-1590). (Cloth bdg. avail. on request). pap. 12.00 (ISBN 0-8373-1590-5). Natl Learning.

--Principal Staff Development Specialist. (Career Examimation Ser.: C-2703). (Cloth bdg. avail. on request). 1980. pap. 14.00 (ISBN 0-8373-2703-2). Natl Learning.

--Principal Statistics Clerk. (Career Examination Ser.: C-977). (Cloth bdg. avail. on request). pap. 12.00 (ISBN 0-8373-0977-8). Natl Learning.

--Principal Stenographer. (Career Examination Ser.: C-614). (Cloth bdg. avail. on request). pap. 12.00 (ISBN 0-8373-0614-0). Natl Learning.

--Principal Stores Clerk. (Career Examination Ser.: C-978). (Cloth bdg. avail. on request). pap. 12.00 (ISBN 0-8373-0978-6). Natl Learning.

--Principal Tax Compliance Agent. (Career Examination Ser.: C-2954). (Cloth bdg. avail. on request). pap. 14.00 (ISBN 0-8373-2954-X). Natl Learning.

--Principal Telephone Operator. (Career Examination Ser.: C-2493). (Cloth bdg. avail. on request). pap. 12.00 (ISBN 0-8373-2493-9). Natl Learning.

--Principal Typist. (Career Examination Ser.: C-615). (Cloth bdg. avail. on request). pap. 12.00 (ISBN 0-8373-0615-9). Natl Learning.

--Principal-Vocational H.S. (Teachers License Examination Ser.: S-6). (Cloth bdg. avail. on request). pap. 17.95 (ISBN 0-8373-8106-1). Natl Learning.

--Principal Worker's Compensation Review Analyst. (Career Examination Ser.: C-310). (Cloth bdg. avail. on request). pap. 14.00 (ISBN 0-8373-0310-9). Natl Learning.

--Principal-Youth & Adult Center (Questions Only) (Teachers License Examination Ser.: S-8). (Cloth bdg. avail. on request). pap. 17.95 (ISBN 0-8373-8108-8). Natl Learning.

--Printer. (Career Examination Ser.: C-C16). (Cloth bdg. avail. on request). pap. 10.00 (ISBN 0-8373-0616-7). Natl Learning.

--Printer-Proofreader. (Career Examination Ser.: C-617). (Cloth bdg. avail. on request). pap. 10.00 (ISBN 0-8373-0617-5). Natl Learning.

--Private Investigator. (Career Examination Ser.: C-2462). (Cloth bdg. avail. on request). pap. 12.00 (ISBN 0-8373-2462-9). Natl Learning.

--Probation Director. (Career Examination Ser.: C-2266). (Cloth bdg. avail. on request). 1977. pap. 12.00 (ISBN 0-8373-2266-9). Natl Learning.

--Probation Investigator. (Career Examination Ser.: C-981). (Cloth bdg. avail. on request). pap. 10.00 (ISBN 0-8373-0981-6). Natl Learning.

--Probation Officer. (Career Examination Ser.: C-619). (Cloth bdg. avail. on request). pap. 10.00 (ISBN 0-8373-0619-1). Natl Learning.

--Process Server. (Career Examination Ser.: C-620). (Cloth bdg. avail. on request). pap. 8.00 (ISBN 0-8373-0620-5). Natl Learning.

--Procurement Clerk. (Career Examination Ser.: C-2623). (Cloth bdg. avail. on request). pap. 8.00 (ISBN 0-8373-2623-0). Natl Learning.

--Professional & Administrative Career Examination (PACE) (Career Examination Ser.: CS-28). (Cloth bdg. avail. on request). pap. 13.95 (ISBN 0-8373-5026-3). Natl Learning.

--Professional & Administrative Career Examination (PACE) (Admission Test Ser.: ATS-26). (Cloth bdg. avail. on request). pap. 13.95 (ISBN 0-8373-5026-3). Natl Learning.

--Professional Careers Test (PCT) (Career Examination Ser.: C-622). (Cloth bdg. avail. on request). pap. 10.00 (ISBN 0-8373-0622-1). Natl Learning.

--Professional Engineer. (Admission Test Ser.: ATS-35). (Cloth bdg. avail. on request). 19.95 (ISBN 0-8373-5035-2). Natl Learning.

--Professional Nurse. (Career Examination Ser.: C-624). (Cloth bdg. avail. on request). pap. 10.00 (ISBN 0-8373-0624-8). Natl Learning.

--Professional Strategies, Nursing. (ACT Proficiency Examination Program: PEP-50). (Cloth bdg. avail. on request). pap. 9.95 (ISBN 0-8373-5900-7). Natl Learning.

--Professional Strategies, Nursing. (Regents External Degree Ser.: REDP-26). (Cloth bdg. avail. on request). pap. 9.95 (ISBN 0-8373-5626-1). Natl Learning.

--Program Administrator. (Career Examination Ser.: C-2868). (Cloth bdg. avail. on request). pap. 14.00 (ISBN 0-8373-2868-3). Natl Learning.

--Program Examiner. (Career Examination Ser.: C-2655). (Cloth bdg. avail. on request). pap. 10.00 (ISBN 0-8373-2655-9). Natl Learning.

--Program Manager. (Career Examination Ser.: C-985). (Cloth bdg. avail. on request). pap. 10.00 (ISBN 0-8373-0985-9). Natl Learning.

--Programmer Aptitude Test (PAT) (Career Examination Ser.: C-643). (Cloth bdg. avail. on request). pap. 10.00 (ISBN 0-8373-0643-4). Natl Learning.

--Project Coordinator. (Career Examination Ser.: C-2589). (Cloth bdg. avail. on request). pap. 12.00 (ISBN 0-8373-2589-7). Natl Learning.

--Project Development Coordinator. (Career Examination Ser.: C-1432). (Cloth bdg. avail. on request). pap. 10.00 (ISBN 0-8373-1432-1). Natl Learning.

--Project Manager. (Career Examination Ser.: C-1433). (Cloth bdg. avail. on request). pap. 10.00 (ISBN 0-8373-1433-X). Natl Learning.

--Project Services Specialist. (Career Examination Ser.: C-1660). (Cloth bdg. avail. on request). pap. 10.00 (ISBN 0-8373-1660-X). Natl Learning.

--Psychiatric & Mental Health Nurse. (Certified Nurse Examination Ser.: CN-12). 21.95 (ISBN 0-8373-6162-1); pap. 13.95 (ISBN 0-8373-6112-5). Natl Learning.

--Psychiatric Nurse. (Career Examination Ser.: C-986). (Cloth bdg. avail. on request). pap. 10.00 (ISBN 0-8373-0986-7). Natl Learning.

--Psychiatric Senior Attendant. (Career Examination Ser.: C-1435). (Cloth bdg. avail. on request). pap. 10.00 (ISBN 0-8373-1435-6). Natl Learning.

--Psychiatric Social Work Assistant. (Career Examination Ser.: C-2414). (Cloth bdg. avail. on request). pap. 10.00 (ISBN 0-8373-2414-9). Natl Learning.

--Psychiatric Social Work Supervisor. (Career Examination Ser.: C-2357). (Cloth bdg. avail. on request). pap. 12.00 (ISBN 0-8373-2357-6). Natl Learning.

--Psychiatric Social Worker Trainee. (Career Examination Ser.: C-988). (Cloth bdg. avail. on request). pap. 10.00 (ISBN 0-8373-0988-3). Natl Learning.

--Psychiatric Staff Attendant. (Career Examination Ser.: C-1436). (Cloth bdg. avail. on request). pap. 10.00 (ISBN 0-8373-1436-4). Natl Learning.

--Psychological Foundations & Education. (National Teachers Examination Ser.: NC-1). (Cloth bdg. avail. on request). pap. 11.95 (ISBN 0-8373-8401-X). Natl Learning.

--Psychologist Trainee. (Career Examination Ser.: C-2621). (Cloth bdg. avail. on request). pap. 10.00 (ISBN 0-8373-2621-4). Natl Learning.

--Psychology. (Graduate Record Examination Ser.: GRE-17). (Cloth bdg. avail. on request). pap. 13.95 (ISBN 0-8373-5217-7). Natl Learning.

--Psychology Assistant. (Career Examination Ser.: C-1774). (Cloth bdg. avail. on request). pap. 10.00 (ISBN 0-8373-1774-6). Natl Learning.

--Psychology Assistant I. (Career Examination Ser.: C-919). (Cloth bdg. avail. on request). pap. 10.00 (ISBN 0-8373-0919-0). Natl Learning.

--Psychology Assistant II. (Career Examination Ser.: C-921). (Cloth bdg. avail. on request). pap. 12.00 (ISBN 0-8373-0921-2). Natl Learning.

--Psychology Assistant III. (Career Examination Ser.: C-933). (Cloth bdg. avail. on request). pap. 14.00 (ISBN 0-8373-0922-0). Natl Learning.

--Public Administrator. (Career Examination Ser.: C-1440). (Cloth bdg. avail. on request). pap. 12.00 (ISBN 0-8373-1440-2). Natl Learning.

--Public Buildings Manager. (Career Examination Ser.: C-2719). (Cloth bdg. avail. on request). 1980. pap. 12.00 (ISBN 0-8373-2719-9). Natl Learning.

--Public Health Administrator. (Career Examination Ser.: C-2082). (Cloth bdg. avail. on request). 1977. pap. 12.00 (ISBN 0-8373-2082-8). Natl Learning.

--Public Health Nurse. (Career Examination Ser.: C-631). (Cloth bdg. avail. on request). pap. 10.00 (ISBN 0-8373-0631-0). Natl Learning.

--Public Health Nutritionist. (Career Examination Ser.: C-632). (Cloth bdg. avail. on request). pap. 10.00 (ISBN 0-8373-0632-9). Natl Learning.

--Public Health Representative. (Career Examination Ser.: C-2369). (Cloth bdg. avail. on request). pap. 10.00 (ISBN 0-8373-2369-X). Natl Learning.

--Public Health Sanitarian. (Career Examination Ser.: C-633). (Cloth bdg. avail. on request). pap. 12.00 (ISBN 0-8373-0633-7). Natl Learning.

--Public Health Sanitarian Trainee. (Career Examination Ser.: C-984). (Cloth bdg. avail. on request). pap. 10.00 (ISBN 0-8373-0984-0). Natl Learning.

--Public Health Technician. (Career Examination Ser.: C-2226). (Cloth bdg. avail. on request). pap. 10.00 (ISBN 0-8373-2226-X). Natl Learning.

--Public Information Assistant. (Career Examination Ser.: C-2956). (Cloth bdg. avail. on request). pap. 10.00 (ISBN 0-8373-2956-6). Natl Learning.

--Public Information Officer. (Career Examination Ser.: C-2950). (Cloth bdg. avail. on request). pap. 12.00 (ISBN 0-8373-2950-7). Natl Learning.

--Public Information Specialist. (Career Examination Ser.: C-2103). (Cloth bdg. avail. on request). 1977. pap. 10.00 (ISBN 0-8373-2103-4). Natl Learning.

--Public Librarian. (Career Examination Ser.: C-989). (Cloth bdg. avail. on request). pap. 10.00 (ISBN 0-8373-0989-1). Natl Learning.

--Public Relations Assistant. (Career Examination Ser.: C-635). (Cloth bdg. avail. on request). pap. 10.00 (ISBN 0-8373-0635-3). Natl Learning.

--Public Relations Director. (Career Examination Ser.: C-1901). (Cloth bdg. avail. on request). pap. 12.00 (ISBN 0-8373-1901-3); pap. 10.00 (ISBN 0-686-66982-7). Natl Learning.

--Public Relations Specialist. (Career Examination Ser.: C-2934). (Cloth bdg. avail. on request). pap. 12.00 (ISBN 0-8373-2934-5). Natl Learning.

--Public Safety Dispatcher I. (Career Examination Ser.: C-116). (Cloth bdg. avail. on request). pap. 12.00 (ISBN 0-8373-0116-5). Natl Learning.

--Public Safety Dispatcher II. (Career Examination Ser.: C-117). (Cloth bdg. avail. on request). pap. 12.00 (ISBN 0-8373-0117-3). Natl Learning.

--Public Safety Officer I. (Career Examination Ser.: C-2895). (Cloth bdg. avail. on request). pap. 10.00 (ISBN 0-8373-2895-0). Natl Learning.

--Public Safety Officer II. (Career Examination Ser.: C-2896). (Cloth bdg. avail. on request). pap. 12.00 (ISBN 0-8373-2896-9). Natl Learning.

--Public Safety Officer III. (Career Examination Ser.: C-2897). (Cloth bdg. avail. on request). pap. 12.00 (ISBN 0-8373-2897-7). Natl Learning.

--Public Services Officer. (Career Examination Ser.: C-636). (Cloth bdg. avail. on request). pap. 10.00 (ISBN 0-8373-0636-1). Natl Learning.

--Public Work Wage Investigator. (Career Examination Ser.: C-990). (Cloth bdg. avail. on request). pap. 10.00 (ISBN 0-8373-0990-5). Natl Learning.

--Pump Station Operator. (Career Examination Ser.: C-2442). (Cloth bdg. avail. on request). pap. 10.00 (ISBN 0-8373-2442-4). Natl Learning.

--Purchase Inspector. (Career Examination Ser.: C-637). (Cloth bdg. avail. on request). pap. 10.00 (ISBN 0-8373-0637-X). Natl Learning.

--Purchase Inspector (Shop Steel) (Career Examination Ser.: C-2258). (Cloth bdg. avail. on request). 1977. pap. 10.00 (ISBN 0-8373-2258-8). Natl Learning.

--Purchasing Agent. (Career Examination Ser.: C-638). (Cloth bdg. avail. on request). pap. 10.00 (ISBN 0-8373-0638-8). Natl Learning.

--Purchasing Agent: Food. (Career Examination Ser.: C-2731). (Cloth bdg. avail. on request). 1980. pap. 12.00 (ISBN 0-8373-2731-8). Natl Learning.

--Purchasing Agent: Lumber. (Career Examination Ser.: C-2732). (Cloth bdg. avail. on request). 1980. pap. 12.00 (ISBN 0-8373-2732-6). Natl Learning.

--Purchasing Agent: Medical. (Career Examination Ser.: C-2733). (Cloth bdg. avail. on request). 1980. pap. 12.00 (ISBN 0-8373-2733-4). Natl Learning.

--Purchasing Agent: Printing. (Career Examination Ser.: C-2734). (Cloth bdg. avail. on request). 1980. pap. 12.00 (ISBN 0-8373-2734-2). Natl Learning.

--Purchasing Technician. (Career Examination Ser.: C-913). (Cloth bdg. avail. on request). pap. 10.00 (ISBN 0-8373-0913-1). Natl Learning.

--Qualifying Examination: Management Service. (Career Examination Ser.: CS-39). (Cloth bdg. avail. on request). pap. 12.00 (ISBN 0-686-84422-X). Natl Learning.

--Quality Control Investigator. (Career Examination Ser.: C-2137). (Cloth bdg. avail. on request). pap. 12.00 (ISBN 0-686-53443-3). Natl Learning.

--Quality Control Specialist. (Career Examination Ser.: C-1618). (Cloth bdg. avail. on request). pap. 12.00 (ISBN 0-8373-1618-9). Natl Learning.

--Quantity Food Preparation. (Occupational Competency Examination Ser.: OCE-30). (Cloth bdg. avail. on request). pap. 13.95 (ISBN 0-8373-5730-6). Natl Learning.

--Questions & Answers on Drug Education. (Career Examination Ser.: CS-24). (Cloth bdg. avail. on request). pap. 10.00 (ISBN 0-8373-4001-2). Natl Learning.

--Questions & Answers on the Real Estate License Examinations. (Admission Test Ser.: ATS-6). 300p. (Cloth bdg. avail. on request). pap. 13.95 (ISBN 0-8373-5006-9). Natl Learning.

--Radio & Telegraph Operator. (Career Examination Ser.: C-1443). (Cloth bdg. avail. on request). pap. 10.00 (ISBN 0-8373-1443-7). Natl Learning.

--Radio & Television Mechanic. (Career Examination Ser.: C-1445). (Cloth bdg. avail. on request). pap. 10.00 (ISBN 0-8373-1445-3). Natl Learning.

--Radio & Television Technician. (Career Examination Ser.: C-1446). (Cloth bdg. avail. on request). pap. 10.00 (ISBN 0-8373-1446-1). Natl Learning.

--Radio Broadcast Technician. (Career Examination Ser.: C-682). (Cloth bdg. avail. on request). pap. 10.00 (ISBN 0-8373-0682-5). Natl Learning.

--Radio Dispatcher. (Career Examination Ser.: C-540). (Cloth bdg. avail. on request). pap. 12.00 (ISBN 0-8373-0540-3). Natl Learning.

--Radio Mechanic. (Career Examination Ser.: C-660). (Cloth bdg. avail. on request). pap. 10.00 (ISBN 0-8373-0660-4). Natl Learning.

--Radio Operator. (Career Examination Ser.: C-683). (Cloth bdg. avail. on request). pap. 10.00 (ISBN 0-8373-0683-3). Natl Learning.

--Radio Station Manager. (Career Examination Ser.: C-2935). (Cloth bdg. avail. on request). pap. 12.00 (ISBN 0-8373-2935-3). Natl Learning.

--Radio Technologist. (Career Examination Ser.: C-1957). (Cloth bdg. avail. on request). pap. 10.00 (ISBN 0-8373-1957-9). Natl Learning.

--Radio Telephone Operator. (Career Examination Ser.: C-2883). (Cloth bdg. avail. on request). pap. 10.00 (ISBN 0-8373-2883-7). Natl Learning.

--Railroad Equipment Inspector. (Career Examination Ser.: C-210). (Cloth bdg. avail. on request). pap. 12.00 (ISBN 0-8373-0210-2). Natl Learning.

--Railroad Track & Structure Inspector. (Career Examination Ser.: C-209). (Cloth bdg. avail. on request). pap. 12.00 (ISBN 0-8373-0209-9). Natl Learning.

--Range Conservationist. (Career Examination Ser.: C-686). (Cloth bdg. avail. on request). pap. 10.00 (ISBN 0-8373-0686-8). Natl Learning.

--Ranger - U.S. Park Service. (Career Examination Ser.: C-665). (Cloth bdg. avail. on request). pap. 10.00 (ISBN 0-8373-0665-5). Natl Learning.

--Reading Interpretation in Social Studies, Natural Sciences & Literature (G.E.D.) (Career Examination Ser.: CS-34). (Cloth bdg. avail. on request). pap. 8.00 (ISBN 0-8373-3734-8). Natl Learning.

--Reading Specialist. (National Teachers Examination Ser.: NT-30). (Cloth bdg. avail. on request). pap. 11.95 (ISBN 0-8373-8440-0). Natl Learning.

--Real Estate Agent. (Career Examination Ser.: C-2179). (Cloth bdg. avail. on request). pap. 10.00 (ISBN 0-8373-2179-4). Natl Learning.

--Real Estate Broker. (Career Examination Ser.: C-666). (Cloth bdg. avail. on request). pap. 13.95 (ISBN 0-8373-0666-3). Natl Learning.

--Real Estate Broker (REB) (Admission Test Ser.: ATS-3). 300p. (Cloth bdg. avail. on request). pap. 13.95 (ISBN 0-8373-5003-4). Natl Learning.

--Real Estate Manager. (Career Examination Ser.: C-689). (Cloth bdg. avail. on request). pap. 10.00 (ISBN 0-8373-0689-2). Natl Learning.

--Real Estate Salesman. (Career Examination Ser.: C-668). (Cloth bdg. avail. on request). pap. 13.95 (ISBN 0-8373-0668-X). Natl Learning.

--Real Estate Salesman (RES) (Admission Test Ser.: ATS-4). 300p. (Cloth bdg. avail. on request). pap. 13.95 (ISBN 0-8373-5004-2). Natl Learning.

--Real Property Appraisal Technician. (Career Examination Ser.: C-2185). (Cloth bdg. avail. on request). pap. 10.00 (ISBN 0-8373-2185-9). Natl Learning.

--Real Property Appraiser. (Career Examination Ser.: C-841). (Cloth bdg. avail. on request). pap. 10.00 (ISBN 0-8373-0841-0). Natl learning.

--Real Property Appraiser I. (Career Examination Ser.: C-842). (Cloth bdg. avail. on request). pap. 10.00 (ISBN 0-8373-0842-9). Natl Learning.

--Real Property Appraiser II. (Career Examination Ser.: C-843). (Cloth bdg. avail. on request). pap. 10.00 (ISBN 0-8373-0843-7). Natl Learning.

--Real Property Appraiser III. (Career Examination Ser.: C-844). (Cloth bdg. avail. on request). pap. 12.00 (ISBN 0-8373-0844-5). Natl Learning.

--Real Property Appraiser IV. (Career Examination Ser.: C-845). (Cloth bdg. avail. on request). pap. 14.00 (ISBN 0-8373-0845-3). Natl Learning.

--Recording Clerk. (Career Examination Ser.: C-2914). (Cloth bdg. avail. on request). pap. 10.00 (ISBN 0-8373-2914-0). Natl Learning.

--Recreation Assistant. (Career Examination Ser.: C-526). (Cloth bdg. avail. on request). pap. 10.00 (ISBN 0-8373-0526-8). Natl Learning.

--Recreation Therapist. (Career Examination Ser.: C-2698). (Cloth bdg. avail. on request). pap. 12.00 (ISBN 0-8373-2698-2). Natl Learning.

--Recreation Worker. (Career Examination Ser.: C-429). (Cloth bdg. avail. on request). pap. 12.00 (ISBN 0-8373-0429-6). Natl Learning.

--Refrigerating Machine Mechanic. (Career Examination Ser.: C-1451). (Cloth bdg. avail. on request). pap. 10.00 (ISBN 0-8373-1451-8). Natl Learning.

--Refrigerating Machine Operator. (Career Examination Ser.: C-670). (Cloth bdg. avail. on request). pap. 10.00 (ISBN 0-8373-0670-1). Natl Learning.

--Regents Scholarship & College Qualification Test (RSE) (Admission Test Ser.: ATS-42). (Cloth bdg. avail. on request). pap. 13.95 (ISBN 0-8373-5042-5). Natl Learning.

--Regional Planner. (Career Examination Ser.: C-694). (Cloth bdg. avail. on request). pap. 10.00 (ISBN 0-8373-0694-9). Natl Learning.

--Registered Representative. (Admission Test Ser.: ATS-1). 300p. (Cloth bdg. avail. on request). pap. 13.95 (ISBN 0-8373-5001-8). Natl Learning.

--Registrar. (Career Examination Ser.: C-1452). (Cloth bdg. avail. on request). pap. 10.00 (ISBN 0-8373-1452-6). Natl Learning.

--Registration Examination for Dieticians (RED) (Admission Test Ser.: ATS-41). (Cloth bdg. avail. on request). pap. 13.95 (ISBN 0-8373-5041-7). Natl Learning.

--Rehabilitation Assistant. (Career Examination Ser.: C-545). (Cloth bdg. available on request). pap. 12.00 (ISBN 0-8373-0545-4). Natl Learning.

--Rehabilitation Counselor. (Career Examination Ser.: C-672). (Cloth bdg. avail. on request). pap. 12.00 (ISBN 0-8373-0672-8). Natl Learning.

--Rehabilitation Counselor Supervisor. (Career Examination Ser.: C-1980). (Cloth bdg. avail. on request). pap. 12.00 (ISBN 0-8373-1980-3). Natl Learning.

--Rehabilitation Counselor Trainee. (Career Examination Ser.: C-1783). (Cloth bdg. avail. on request). pap. 12.00 (ISBN 0-8373-1783-5). Natl Learning.

--Rehabilitation Inspector. (Career Examination Ser.: C-2639). (Cloth bldg. avail. on request). pap. 10.00 (ISBN 0-8373-2639-7). Natl Learning.

--Rehabilitation Interviewer. (Career Examination Ser.: C-2708). (Cloth bdg. avail. on request). 1980. pap. 10.00 (ISBN 0-8373-2708-3). Natl Learning.

--Related Technical Subjects (Biological & Chemical) Chairman - Sr. H.S. (Teachers License Examination Ser.: CH-20). (Cloth bdg. avail. on request). pap. 15.95 (ISBN 0-8373-8170-3). Natl Learning.

--Related Technical Subjects (Biological & Chemical) Sr. H.S. (Teachers License Examination Ser.: T-50). (Cloth bdg. avail. on request). pap. 13.95 (ISBN 0-8373-8050-2). Natl Learning.

--Related Technical Subjects (Mechanical, Structural, Electrical) Chairman - Sr. H.S. (Teachers License Examination Ser.: CH-21). (Cloth bdg. avail. on request). pap. 15.95 (ISBN 0-8373-8171-1). Natl Learning.

--Related Technical Subjects (Mechanical, Structural, Electrical) Sr. H.S. (Teachers License Examination Ser.: T-51). (Cloth bdg. avail. on request). pap. 13.95 (ISBN 0-8373-8051-0). Natl Learning.

--Repair Crew Chief. (Career Examination Ser.: C-1454). (Cloth bdg. avail. on request). pap. 10.00 (ISBN 0-8373-1453-4). Natl Learning.

--Repair Crew Worker. (Career Examination Ser.: C-2004). (Cloth bdg. avail. on request). pap. 8.00 (ISBN 0-8373-2004-6). Natl Learning.

--Repair Shop Manager. (Career Examination Ser.: C-1801). (Cloth bdg. avail. on request). pap. 10.00 (ISBN 0-8373-1801-7). Natl Learning.

--Repair Supervisor. (Career Examination Ser.: C-2615). pap. 10.00 (ISBN 0-8373-2615-X); avail. Natl Learning.

--Reporting Stenographer. (Career Examination Ser.: C-2125). (Cloth bdg. avail. on request). 1976. pap. 10.00 (ISBN 0-8373-2125-5). Natl Learning.

--Research Aide. (Career Examination Ser.: C-1580). (Cloth bdg. avail. on request). pap. 10.00 (ISBN 0-8373-1580-8). Natl Learning.

--Research Analyst. (Career Examination Ser.: C-1949). (Cloth bdg. avail. on request). pap. 12.00 (ISBN 0-8373-1949-8). Natl Learning.

--Research Assistant. (Career Examination Ser.: C-674). (Cloth bdg. avail. on request). pap. 12.00 (ISBN 0-8373-0674-4). Natl Learning.

--Research Technician. (Career Examination Ser.: C-1948). (Cloth bdg. avail. on request). pap. 12.00 (ISBN 0-8373-1948-X). Natl Learning.

--Research Worker. (Career Examination Ser.: C-546). (Cloth bdg. avail. on request). pap. 10.00 (ISBN 0-8373-0546-2). Natl Learning.

--Retirement Benefits Examiner. (Career Examination Ser.: C-1558). (Cloth bdg. avail. on request). pap. 10.00 (ISBN 0-685-60351-2). Natl Learning.

--Roofer. (Career Examination Ser.: C-677). (Cloth bdg. avail. on request). pap. 8.00 (ISBN 0-8373-0677-9). Natl Learning.

--Rural Carrier (U.S.P.S.) (Career Examination Ser.: C-678). (Cloth bdg. avail. on request). pap. 8.00 (ISBN 0-8373-0678-7). Natl Learning.

--Safety Consultant. (Career Examination Ser.: C-2540). (Cloth bdg. avail. on request). pap. 10.00 (ISBN 0-8373-2640-0). Natl Learning.

--Safety Coordinator. (Career Examination Ser.: C-1921). (Cloth bdg. avail. on request). pap. 10.00 (ISBN 0-8373-1921-8). Natl Learning.

--Safety Engineer. (Career Examination Ser.: C-797). (Cloth bdg. avail. on request). pap. 10.00 (ISBN 0-8373-0797-X). Natl Learning.

--Safety Supervisor. (Career Examination Ser.: C-2641). (Cloth bdg. avail. on request). pap. 10.00 (ISBN 0-8373-2641-9). Natl Learning.

--Sales Store Worker. (Career Examination Ser.: C-1460). (Cloth bdg. avail. on request). pap. 8.00 (ISBN 0-8373-1460-7). Natl Learning.

--Sandblaster. (Career Examination Ser.: C-1461). (Cloth bdg. avail. on request). pap. 8.00 (ISBN 0-8373-1461-5). Natl Learning.

--Sanitary Engineer II. (Career Examination Ser.: C-2945). (Cloth bdg. avail. on request). pap. 12.00 (ISBN 0-8373-2945-0). Natl Learning.

--Sanitary Engineer III. (Career Examination Ser.: C-2946). (Cloth bdg. avail. on request). pap. 14.00 (ISBN 0-8373-2946-9). Natl Learning.

--Sanitary Engineer IV. (Career Examination Ser.: C-2947). (Cloth bdg. avail. on request). pap. 14.00 (ISBN 0-8373-2947-7). Natl Learning.

--Sanitary Engineer 1. (Career Examination Ser.: C-798). (Cloth bdg. avail. on request). pap. 12.00 (ISBN 0-8373-0798-8). Natl Learning.

--Sanitation & Parking Violation Inspector. (Career Examination Ser.: C-1873). (Cloth bdg. avail. on request). pap. 10.00 (ISBN 0-8373-1873-4). Natl Learning.

--Sanitation Dispatcher. (Career Examination Ser.: C-2881). (Cloth bdg. avail. on request). pap. 10.00 (ISBN 0-8373-2881-0). Natl Learning.

--Scholastic Aptitude Test. (Admission Test Ser.: ATS-21). 300p. (Cloth bdg. avail. on request). pap. 11.95 (ISBN 0-8373-5021-2). Natl Learning.

--School Bus Executive. (Career Examination Ser.: C-2887). (Cloth bdg. avail. on request). pap. 14.00 (ISBN 0-8373-2887-X). Natl Learning.

--School Crossing Guard. (Career Examination Ser.: C-702). (Cloth bdg. avail. on request). pap. 8.00 (ISBN 0-8373-0702-3). Natl Learning.

--School Custodian-Engineer. (Career Examination Ser.: C-701). (Cloth bdg. avail. on request). pap. 10.00 (ISBN 0-8373-0701-5). Natl Learning.

--School Finance Manager. (Career Examination Ser.: C-2886). (Cloth bdg. avail. on request). pap. 12.00 (ISBN 0-8373-2886-1). Natl Learning.

--School Lunch Coordinator: C-317. (Career Examination Ser.). (Cloth bdg. avail. on request). pap. 10.00 (ISBN 0-8373-0317-6). Natl Learning.

--School Nurse Practitioner. (Certified Nurse Examination Ser.: CN-3). 21.95 (ISBN 0-8373-6153-2); pap. 13.95 (ISBN 0-8373-6103-6). Natl Learning.

--School Psychologist. (Teachers License Examination Ser.: GT-4). (Cloth bdg. avail. on request). pap. 13.95 (ISBN 0-8373-8124-X). Natl Learning.

--School Psychologist-in-Training. (Teachers License Examination Ser.: GT-5). (Cloth bdg. avail. on request). pap. 13.95 (ISBN 0-8373-8125-8). Natl Learning.

--School Psychology. (National Teacher Examination Ser.: NT-40). (Cloth bdg. avail. on request). pap. 11.95 (ISBN 0-8373-8500-8). Natl Learning.

--School Purchasing Agent. (Career Examination Ser.: C-863). (Cloth bdg. avail. on request). pap. 12.00 (ISBN 0-8373-0863-1). Natl Learning.

--School Research Assistant. (Teachers License Examination Ser.: GT-6). (Cloth bdg. avail. on request). pap. 13.95 (ISBN 0-8373-8126-6). Natl Learning.

--School Research Associate. (Teachers License Examination Ser.: GT-7). (Cloth bdg. avail. on request). pap. 13.95 (ISBN 0-8373-8127-4). Natl Learning.

--School Research Technician. (Teachers License Examination Ser.: GT-8). (Cloth bdg. avail. on request). pap. 13.95 (ISBN 0-8373-8128-2). Natl Learning.

--School Secretary. (Teachers License Examination Ser.: T-52). (Cloth bdg. avail. on request). pap. 13.95 (ISBN 0-8373-8052-9). Natl Learning.

--School Social Worker. (Teachers License Examination Ser.: GT-9). (Cloth bdg. avail. on request). pap. 13.95 (ISBN 0-8373-8129-0). Natl Learning.

--School Transportation Supervisor. (Career Examination Ser.: C-113). (Cloth bdg. avail. on request). pap. 12.00 (ISBN 0-8373-0113-0). Natl Learning.

--Science & Mathematics. (National Teachers Examination Ser.: NC-5). (Cloth bdg. avail. on request). pap. 11.95 (ISBN 0-8373-8405-2). Natl Learning.

--Sciences Chairman - Jr. H.S. (Teachers License Examination Ser.: CH-22). (Cloth bdg. avail. on request). pap. 15.95 (ISBN 0-8373-8172-X). Natl Learning.

--Sciences Chairman - Sr. H.S. (Teachers License Examination Ser.: CH-23). (Cloth bdg. avail. on request). pap. 15.95 (ISBN 0-8373-8173-8). Natl Learning.

--Seasonal Assistant. (Career Examination Ser.: C-704). (Cloth bdg. avail. on request). pap. 8.00 (ISBN 0-8373-0704-X). Natl Learning.

--Secretarial Assistant. (Career Examination Ser.: C-1464). (Cloth bdg. avail. on request). pap. 10.00 (ISBN 0-8373-1464-X). Natl Learning.

--Senior Accountant. (Career Examination Ser.: C-992). (Cloth bdg. avail. on request). pap. 12.00 (ISBN 0-8373-0992-1). Natl Learning.

--Senior Actuarial Clerk. (Career Examination Ser.: C-2418). (Cloth bdg. avail. on request). pap. 10.00 (ISBN 0-8373-2418-1). Natl Learning.

--Senior Administrative Assistant. (Career Examination Ser.: C-1468). (Cloth bdg. avail. on request). pap. 12.00 (ISBN 0-8373-1468-2). Natl Learning.

--Senior Administrative Associate. (Career Examination Ser.: C-2393). (Cloth bdg. avail. on request). pap. 12.00 (ISBN 0-8373-2393-2). Natl Learning.

--Senior Admitting Clerk. (Career Examination Ser.: C-994). (Cloth bdg. avail. on request). pap. 10.00 (ISBN 0-8373-0994-8). Natl Learning.

--Senior Airport Attendant. (Career Examination Ser.: C-307). (Cloth bdg. avail. on request). pap. 12.00 (ISBN 0-8373-0307-9). Natl Learning.

--Senior Airport Security Guard. (Career Examination Ser.: C-457). (Cloth bdg. avail. on request). pap. 12.00 (ISBN 0-8373-0457-1). Natl Learning.

--Senior Animal Shelter Officer. (Career Examination Ser.: C-2362). (Cloth bdg. avail. on request). pap. 10.00 (ISBN 0-8373-2362-2). Natl Learning.

--Senior Architect. (Career Examination Ser.: C-1326). (Cloth bdg. avail. on request). pap. 12.00 (ISBN 0-8373-1326-0). Natl Learning.

--Senior Assessment Clerk. (Career Examination Ser.: C-2921). (Cloth bdg. avail. on request). pap. 12.00 (ISBN 0-8373-2921-3). Natl Learning.

--Senior Attorney. (Career Examination Ser.: C-996). (Cloth bdg. avail. on request). pap. 12.00 (ISBN 0-8373-0996-4). Natl Learning.

--Senior Attorney (Realty) (Career Examination Ser.: C-568). (Cloth bdg. avail. on request). pap. 14.00 (ISBN 0-8373-0568-3). Natl Learning.

--Senior Bay Constable. (Career Examination Ser.: C-2525). (Cloth bdg. avail. on request). pap. 10.00 (ISBN 0-8373-2525-0). Natl Learning.

--Senior Bridge & Tunnel Maintainer. (Career Examination Ser.: C-1472). (Cloth bdg. avail. on request). pap. 10.00 (ISBN 0-8373-1472-0). Natl Learning.

--Senior Budget Analyst. (Career Examination Ser.: C-2415). (Cloth bdg. avail. on request). pap. 12.00 (ISBN 0-8373-2415-7). Natl Learning.

--Senior Budget Officer. (Career Examination Ser.: C-2683). (Cloth bdg. avail. on request). pap. 12.00 (ISBN 0-8373-2683-4). Natl Learning.

--Senior Building Guard. (Career Examination Ser.: C-2529). (Cloth bdg. avail. on request). pap. 10.00 (ISBN 0-8373-2529-3). Natl Learning.

--Senior Building Inspector. (Career Examination Ser.: C-2113). (Cloth bdg. avail. on request). 1977. pap. 12.00 (ISBN 0-8373-2113-1). Natl Learning.

--Senior Building Mechanical Engineer. (Career Examination Ser.: C-2572). (Cloth bdg. avail. on request). pap. 12.00 (ISBN 0-8373-2572-2). Natl Learning.

--Senior Building Structural Engineer. (Career Examination Ser.: C-2569). (Cloth bdg. avail. on request). pap. 12.00 (ISBN 0-8373-2569-2). Natl Learning.

--Senior Business Consultant. (Career Examination Ser.: C-1983). (Cloth bdg. avail. on request). pap. 12.00 (ISBN 0-8373-1983-8). Natl Learning.

--Senior Business Manager. (Career Examination Ser.: C-2359). (Cloth bdg. avail. on request). pap. 12.00 (ISBN 0-8373-2359-2). Natl Learning.

--Senior Caseworker. (Career Examination Ser.: C-2931). (Cloth bdg. avail. on request). pap. 12.00 (ISBN 0-8373-2931-0). Natl Learning.

--Senior Chemist. (Career Examination Ser.: C-2402). (Cloth bdg. avail. on request). pap. 12.00 (ISBN 0-8373-2402-5). Natl Learning.

--Senior Citizens' Activities Specialist. (Career Examination Ser.: C-900). (Cloth bdg. avail. on request). pap. 12.00 (ISBN 0-8373-0900-X). Natl Learning.

--Senior Citizens Program Coordinator. (Career Examination Ser.: C-2811). (Cloth bdg. avail. on request). 1980. pap. 12.00 (ISBN 0-8373-2811-X). Natl Learning.

--Senior Citizens Program Supervisor. (Career Examination Ser.: C-2360). (Cloth bdg. avail. on request). pap. 10.00 (ISBN 0-8373-2360-6). Natl Learning.

--Senior Citizens Service Coordinator. (Career Examination Ser.: C-2117). (Cloth bdg. avail. on request). 1977. pap. 10.00 (ISBN 0-8373-2117-4). Natl Learning.

--Senior Civil Engineer (Structures) (Career Examination Ser.: C-1917). (Cloth bdg. avail. on request). pap. 12.00 (ISBN 0-8373-1917-X). Natl Learning.

--Senior Claim Examiner. (Career Examination Ser.: C-1716). (Cloth bdg. avail. on request). pap. 10.00 (ISBN 0-8373-1716-9). Natl Learning.

--Senior Clerk. (Career Examination Ser.: C-707). (Cloth bdg. avail. on request). pap. 10.00 (ISBN 0-8373-0707-4). Natl Learning.

--Senior Clerk-Stenographer. (Career Examination Ser.: C-2633). (Cloth bdg. avail. on request). pap. 10.00 (ISBN 0-8373-2633-8). Natl Learning.

--Senior Clerk Surrogate. (Career Examination Ser.: C-2128). (Cloth bdg. avail. on request). 1977. pap. 10.00 (ISBN 0-8373-2128-X). Natl Learning.

--Senior Clerk-Typist. (Career Examination Ser.: C-1936). (Cloth bdg. avail. on request). pap. 10.00 (ISBN 0-8373-1936-6). Natl Learning.

--Senior Community Service Worker. (Career Examination Ser.: C-2676). (Cloth bdg. avail. on request). pap. 10.00 (ISBN 0-8373-2676-1). Natl Learning.

--Senior Compensation Claims Clerk. (Career Examination Ser.: C-867). (Cloth bdg. avail. on request). pap. 10.00 (ISBN 0-8373-0867-4). Natl Learning.

--Senior Compliance Investigator. (Career Examination Ser.: C-2422). (Cloth bdg. avail. on request). pap. 12.00 (ISBN 0-8373-2422-X). Natl Learning.

--Senior Computer Programmer. (Career Examination Ser.: C-1630). (Cloth bdg. avail. on request). pap. 12.00 (ISBN 0-8373-1630-8). Natl Learning.

--Senior Computer Systems Analyst. (Career Examination Ser.: C-999). (Cloth bdg. avail. on request). pap. 12.00 (ISBN 0-8373-0999-9). Natl Learning.

--Senior Construction Inspector. (Career Examination Ser.: C-709). (Cloth bdg. avail. on reqeust). pap. 10.00 (ISBN 0-8373-0709-0). Natl Learning.

--Senior Consumer Affairs Inspector. (Career Examination Ser.: C-1656). (Cloth bdg. avail. on reqeust). pap. 12.00 (ISBN 0-8373-1656-1). Natl Learning.

--Senior Consumer Affairs Investigator. Career Examination Ser.: (C-2376). (Cloth bdg. avail. on request). pap. 12.00 (ISBN 0-8373-2376-2). Natl Learning.

--Senior Consumer Frauds Representative. (Career Examination Ser.: C-877). (Cloth bdg. avail. on request). pap. 12.00 (ISBN 0-8373-0877-1). Natl Learning.

--Senior Demolition Inspector. (Career Examination Ser.: C-1475). (Cloth bdg. avail. on request). pap. 10.00 (ISBN 0-8373-1475-5). Natl Learning.

--Senior Deputy Sheriff. (Career Examination Ser.: C-1665). (Cloth bdg. avail. on request). pap. 12.00 (ISBN 0-8373-1665-0). Natl Learning.

--Senior Detective Investigator. (Career Examination Ser.: C-2038). (Cloth bdg. avail. on request). pap. 12.00 (ISBN 0-8373-2038-0). Natl Learning.

--Senior Dog Warden. (Career Examination Ser.: C-2646). (Cloth bdg. avail. on request). pap. 12.00 (ISBN 0-8373-2646-X). Natl Learning.

--Senior Drafting Technician. (Career Examination Ser.: C-2679). (Cloth bdg. avail. on request). pap. 10.00 (ISBN 0-8373-2679-6). Natl Learning.

--Senior Drug Abuse Educator. (Career Examination Ser.: C-2520). (Cloth bdg. avail. on request). pap. 12.00 (ISBN 0-8373-2520-X). Natl Learning.

--Senior Drug Abuse Rehabilitation Counselor. (Career Examination Ser.: C-2928). (Cloth bdg. avail. on request). pap. 12.00 (ISBN 0-8373-2928-0). Natl Learning.

--Senior Drug & Alcohol Counselor. (Career Examination Ser.: C-2742). (Cloth bdg. avail. on request). 1980. pap. 12.00 (ISBN 0-8373-2742-3). Natl Learning.

--Senior Duplicating Machine Operator. (Career Examination Ser.: C-1899). (Cloth bdg. avail. on request). pap. 10.00 (ISBN 0-8373-1899-8). Natl Learning.

--Senior Electrical Engineer. (Career Examination Ser.: C-1631). (Cloth bdg. avail. on request). pap. 12.00 (ISBN 0-8373-1631-6). Natl Learning.

--Senior Electrical Inspector. (Career Examination Ser.: C-712). (Cloth bdg. avail. on request). pap. 12.00 (ISBN 0-8373-0712-0). Natl Learning.

--Senior Employment Counselor. (Career Examination Ser.: C-1003). (Cloth bdg. avail. on request). pap. 12.00 (ISBN 0-8373-1003-2). Natl Learning.

--Senior Employment Interviewer. (Career Examination Ser.: C-2284). (Cloth bdg. avail. on request). 1977. pap. 12.00 (ISBN 0-8373-2284-7). Natl Learning.

--Senior Engineer. (Career Examination Ser.: C-1476). (Cloth bdg. avail. on request). pap. 12.00 (ISBN 0-8373-1476-3). Natl Learning.

--Senior Engineering Materials Technician. (Career Examination Ser.: C-316). (Cloth bdg. avail. on request). pap. 12.00 (ISBN 0-8373-0316-8). Natl Learning.

--Senior Environmental Analyst. (Career Examination Ser.: C-2660). (Cloth bdg. avail. on request). pap. 12.00 (ISBN 0-8373-2660-5). Natl Learning.

--Senior Environmental Planner. (Career Examination Ser.: C-2663). (Cloth bdg. avail. on request). pap. 12.00 (ISBN 0-8373-2663-X). Natl Learning.

--Senior Excise Tax Investigator. (Career Examination Ser.: C-2419). (Cloth bdg. avail. on request). pap. 10.00 (ISBN 0-8373-2419-X). Natl Learning.

--Senior File Clerk. (Career Examination Ser.: C-713). (Cloth bdg. avail. on request). pap. 10.00 (ISBN 0-8373-0713-9). Natl Learning.

--Senior Financial Analyst. (Career Examination Ser.: C-2643). (Cloth bdg. avail. on request). pap. 12.00 (ISBN 0-8373-2643-5). Natl Learning.

--Senior Grants Analyst. (Career Examination Ser.: C-2833). (Cloth bdg. avail. on request). 1980. pap. 12.00 (ISBN 0-8373-2833-0). Natl Learning.

--Senior Groundskeeper. (Career Examination Ser.: C-1572). (Cloth bdg. avail. on request). pap. 10.00 (ISBN 0-8373-1572-7). Natl Learning.

--Senior High School. (Teachers Lesson Plan Bk.: S-I). (gr. 9-12). pap. 3.95 (ISBN 0-686-84421-1). Natl Learning.

--Senior Highway Maintenance Supervisor. (Career Examination Ser.: C-2631). (Cloth bdg. avail. on request). pap. 12.00 (ISBN 0-8373-2631-1). Natl Learning.

--Senior Hospital Administration Consultant. (Career Examination Ser.: C-2769). (Cloth bdg. avail. on request). 1980. pap. 12.00 (ISBN 0-8373-2769-5). Natl Learning.

--Senior Housekeeper. (Career Examination Ser.: C-1007). (Cloth bdg. avail. on request). pap. 10.00 (ISBN 0-8373-1007-5). Natl Learning.

--Senior Illustrator. (Career Examination Ser.: C-1008). (Cloth bdg. avail. on request). pap. 12.00 (ISBN 0-8373-1008-3). Natl Learning.

--Senior Incinerator Stationary Engineer. (Career Examination Ser.: C-2637). (Cloth bdg. avail. on request). pap. 10.00 (ISBN 0-8373-2637-0). Natl Learning.

--Senior Insurance Examiner. (Career Examination Ser.: C-2685). (Cloth bdg. avail. on request). pap. 12.00 (ISBN 0-8373-2685-0). Natl Learning.

--Senior Internal Auditor. (Career Examination Ser.: C-1009). (Cloth bdg. avail. on request). pap. 12.00 (ISBN 0-8373-1009-1). Natl Learning.

--Senior Investment Analyst. (Career Examination Ser.: C-1623). (Cloth bdg. avail. on request). pap. 10.00 (ISBN 0-8373-1623-5). Natl Learning.

--Senior Juvenile Counselor. (Career Examination Ser.: C-421). (Cloth bdg. avail. on request). pap. 12.00 (ISBN 0-8373-0421-0). Natl Learning.

--Senior Labor-Management Practices Adjuster. (Career Examination Ser.: C-718). (Cloth bdg. avail. on request). pap. 12.00 (ISBN 0-8373-0789-9). Natl Learning.

--Senior Land Management Specialist. (Career Examination Ser.: C-2619). (Cloth bdg. avail. on request). pap. 12.00 (ISBN 0-8373-2619-2). Natl Learning.

--Senior Laundry Worker. (Career Examination Ser.: C-719). (Cloth bdg. avail. on request). pap. 10.00 (ISBN 0-8373-0719-8). Natl Learning.

--Senior Legal Stenographer. (Career Examination ser.: C-2634). (Cloth bdg. avail. on request). pap. 10.00 (ISBN 0-8373-2634-6). Natl Learning.

--Senior License Investigator. (Career Examination Ser.: C-2530). (Cloth bdg. avail). pap. 10.00 (ISBN 0-8373-2530-7). Natl Learning.

--Senior Management Analyst. (Career Examination Ser.: C-1782). (Cloth bdg. avail. on request). pap. 12.00 (ISBN 0-8373-1782-7). Natl Learning.

--Senior Manpower Counselor. (Career Examination Ser.: C-2436). (Cloth bdg. avail. on request). pap. 12.00 (ISBN 0-8373-2436-X). Natl Learning.

--Senior Marketing Representative. (Career Examination Ser.: C-2053). (Cloth bdg. avail. on request). 1977. pap. 10.00 (ISBN 0-8373-2053-4). Natl Learning.

--Senior Meat Inspector. (Career Examination Ser.: C-2054). (Cloth bdg. avail. on request). pap. 10.00 (ISBN 0-8373-2054-2). Natl Learning.

--Senior Mechanical Engineer. (Career Examination Ser.: C-1648). (Cloth bdg. avail on request). 1977. pap. 12.00 (ISBN 0-8373-1648-0). Natl Learning.

--Senior Medicaid Claims Examiner. (Career Examination Ser.: C-2692). (Cloth bdg. avail. on request). pap. 10.00 (ISBN 0-8373-2692-3). Natl Learning.

--Senior Medical Conduct Investigator. (Career Examination Ser.: X-2610). (Cloth bdg. avail. on request). pap. 10.00 (ISBN 0-8373-2610-9). Natl Learning.

--Senior Medical Emergency Dispatcher. (Career Examination Ser.: C-2332). (Cloth bdg. avail. on request). pap. 10.00 (ISBN 0-8373-2332-0). Natl Learning.

--Senior Medical Services Specialist. (Career Examination Ser.: C-2747). (Cloth bdg. avail. on request). 1980. pap. 12.00 (ISBN 0-8373-2747-4). Natl Learning.

--Senior Medical Social Worker. (Career Examination Ser.: C-2629). (Cloth bdg. avail. on request). pap. 12.00 (ISBN 0-8373-2629-X). Natl Learning.

--Senior Medical Stenographer. (Career Examination Ser.: C-2940). (Cloth bdg. avail. on request). pap. 12.00 (ISBN 0-8373-2940-X). Natl Learning.

--Senior Menagerie Keeper. (Career Examination Ser.: C-1971). (Cloth bdg. avail. on request). pap. 10.00 (ISBN 0-8373-1971-4). Natl Learning.

--Senior Methods Analyst. (Career Examination Ser.: C-1014). (Cloth bdg. avail. on request). pap. 12.00 (ISBN 0-8373-1014-8). Natl Learning.

--Senior Microbiologist. (Career Examination Ser.: C-1945). (Cloth bdg. avail. on request). pap. 12.00 (ISBN 0-8373-1945-5). Natl Learning.

--Senior Micrographics Operator. (Career Examination Ser.: C-2760). (Cloth bdg. avail. on request). 1980. pap. 10.00 (ISBN 0-8373-2760-1). Natl Learning.

--Senior Micrographics Technician. (Career Examination Ser.: C-2762). (Cloth bdg. avail. on request). 1980. pap. 10.00 (ISBN 0-8373-2762-8). Natl Learning.

--Senior Motor Vehicle License Clerk. (Career Examination Ser.: C-2611). (Cloth bdg. avail. on request). pap. 10.00 (ISBN 0-8373-2611-7). Natl Learning.

--Senior Museum Curator. (Career Examination Ser.: C-2374). (Cloth bdg. avail. on request). pap. 12.00 (ISBN 0-8373-2374-6). Natl Learning.

--Senior Neighborhood Aide. (Career Examination Ser.: C-2911). (Cloth bdg. avail. on request). pap. 12.00 (ISBN 0-8373-2911-6). Natl Learning.

--Senior Occupational Therapist. (Career Examination Ser.: C-2174). (Cloth bdg. avail. on request). pap. 12.00 (ISBN 0-8373-2174-3). Natl Learning.

--Senior Office Appliance Operator. (Career Examination Ser.: C-1677). (Cloth bdg. avail. on request). pap. 10.00 (ISBN 0-8373-1677-4). Natl Learning.

--Senior Office Assistant. (Career Examination Ser.: C-2594). (Cloth bdg. avail. on request). pap. 10.00 (ISBN 0-8373-2594-3). Natl Learning.

--Senior Office Machine Operator. (Career Examination Ser.: C-1480). (Cloth bdg. avail. on request). pap. 10.00 (ISBN 0-8373-1480-1). Natl Learning.

--Senior Office Worker. (Career Examination Ser.: C-2519). (Cloth bdg. avail. on request). pap. 10.00 (ISBN 0-8373-2519-6). Natl Learning.

--Senior Park Attendant. (Career Examination Ser.: C-1542). (Cloth bdg. avail. on request). pap. 10.00 (ISBN 0-8373-1542-5). Natl Learning.

--Senior Park Foreman. (Career Examination Ser.: C-1562). (Cloth bdg. avail. on request). pap. 10.00 (ISBN 0-8373-1562-X). Natl Learning.

--Senior Personnel Administrator. (Career Examination Ser.: C-2410). (Cloth bdg. avail. on request). pap. 12.00 (ISBN 0-8373-2410-6). Natl Learning.

--Senior Personnel Analyst. (Career Examination Ser.: C-2345). (Cloth bdg. avail. on request). pap. 12.00 (ISBN 0-8373-2345-2). Natl Learning.

--Senior Personnel Clerk. (Career Examination Ser.: C-2867). (Cloth bdg. avail. on request). pap. 10.00 (ISBN 0-8373-2867-5). Natl Learning.

--Senior Photographic Machine Operator. (Career Examination Ser.: C-2882). (Cloth bdg. avail. on request). pap. 10.00 (ISBN 0-8373-2882-9). Natl Learning.

--Senior Plumbing Inspector. (Career Examination Ser.: C-1740). (Cloth bdg. avail. on request). 12.00 (ISBN 0-8373-1740-1). Natl Learning.

--Senior Professional Conduct Investigator. (Career Examination Ser.: C-2298). (Cloth bdg. avail. on request). 1977. pap. 10.00 (ISBN 0-8373-2298-7). Natl Learning.

--Senior Program Specialist. (Career Examination Ser.: C-2862). (Cloth bdg. avail. on request). 1980. pap. 12.00 (ISBN 0-8373-2862-4). Natl Learning.
--Senior Project Coordinator. (Career Examination Ser.: C-1482). (Cloth bdg. avail. on request). pap. 12.00 (ISBN 0-8373-1482-8). Natl Learning.
--Senior Project Development Coordinator. (Career Examination Ser.: C-2898). (Cloth bdg. avail. on request). pap. 12.00 (ISBN 0-8373-2898-5). Natl Learning.
--Senior Project Services Specialist. (Career Examination Ser.: C-1662). (Cloth bdg. avail. on request). pap. 10.00 (ISBN 0-8373-1662-6). Natl Learning.
--Senior Public Information Assistant. (Career Examination Ser.: C-2957). (Cloth bdg. avail. on reques). pap. 12.00 (ISBN 0-8373-2957-4). Natl Learning.
--Senior Pump Operator. (Career Examination Ser.: C-2951). (Cloth bdg. avail. on request). pap. 12.00 (ISBN 0-8373-2951-5). Natl Learning.
--Senior Purchase Inspector. (Career Examination Ser.: C-1483). (Cloth bdg. avail. on request). pap. 10.00 (ISBN 0-8373-1483-6). Natl Learning.
--Senior Real Estate Appraiser. (Career Examination Ser.: C-569). (Cloth bdg. avail. on request). pap. 12.00 (ISBN 0-8373-0569-1). Natl Learning.
--Senior Records Center Assistant. (Career Examination Ser.: C-1919). (Cloth bdg. avail. on request). pap. 10.00 (ISBN 0-8373-1919-6). Natl Learning.
--Senior Rent Research Associate. (Career Examination Ser.: C-1023). (Cloth bdg. avail. on request). pap. 10.00 (ISBN 0-8373-1023-7). Natl Learning.
--Senior Research Assistant. (Career Examination Ser.: C-2717). (Cloth bdg. avail. on request). 1980. pap. 12.00 (ISBN 0-8373-2717-2). Natl Learning.
--Senior Safety Coordinator. (Career Examination Ser.: C-2668). (Cloth bdg. avail. on request). pap. 10.00 (ISBN 0-8373-2668-0). Natl Learning.
--Senior Sanitarian. (Career Examination Ser.: C-2430). (Cloth bdg. avail. on request). pap. 12.00 (ISBN 0-8373-2430-0). Natl Learning.
--Senior Security Officer. (Career Examination Ser.: C-2449). (Cloth bdg. avail. on request). pap. 10.00 (ISBN 0-8373-2449-1). Natl Learning.
--Senior Services Disability Analyst. (Career Examination Ser.: C-859). (Cloth bdg. avail. on request). pap. 10.00 (ISBN 0-8373-0859-3). Natl Learning.
--Senior Shorthand Reporter. (Career Examination Ser.: C-724). (Cloth bdg. avail. on request). pap. 10.00 (ISBN 0-8373-0724-4). Natl Learning.
--Senior Social Case Worker. (Career Examination Ser.: C-1555). (Cloth bdg. avail. on request). pap. 12.00 (ISBN 0-8373-1555-7). Natl Learning.
--Senior Social Services Employment Specialist. (Career Examination Ser.: C-2817). (Cloth bdg. avail. on request). 1980. pap. 12.00 (ISBN 0-8373-2817-9). Natl Learning.
--Senior Special Officer. (Career Examination Ser.: C-725). (Cloth bdg. avail. on request). pap. 10.00 (ISBN 0-8373-0725-2). Natl Learning.
--Senior Staff Development Specialist. (Career Examinatin Ser.: C-2702). (Cloth bdg. avail. on request). 1980. pap. 12.00 (ISBN 0-8373-2702-4). Natl Learning.
--Senior Statistician. (Career Examination Ser.: C-1025). (Cloth bdg. avail. on request). pap. 12.00 (ISBN 0-8373-1025-3). Natl Learning.
--Senior Stenographer. (Career Examination Ser.: C-726). (Cloth bdg. avail. on request). pap. 10.00 (ISBN 0-8373-0726-0). Natl Learning.
--Senior Stores Clerk. (Career Examination Ser.: C-2383). (Cloth bdg. avail. on request). 10.00 (ISBN 0-8373-2383-5). Natl Learning.
--Senior Street Club Worker. (Career Examination Ser.: C-727). (Cloth bdg. avail. on request). pap. 10.00 (ISBN 0-8373-0727-9). Natl Learning.
--Senior Superintendent of Construction. (Career Examination Ser.). (Cloth bdg. avail. on request). pap. 12.00 (ISBN 0-8373-0541-1). Natl Learning.
--Senior Systems Analyst. (Career Examination Ser.: C-2389). (Cloth bdg. avail. on request). pap. 12.00 (ISBN 0-8373-2389-4). Natl Learning.
--Senior Tax Compliance Agent. (Career Examination Ser.: C-2953). (Cloth bdg. avail. on request). pap. 12.00 (ISBN 0-8373-2953-1). Natl Learning.
--Senior Telephone Inspector. (Career Examination Ser.: C-2217). (Cloth bdg. avail. on request). 1977. pap. 10.00 (ISBN 0-8373-2217-0). Natl Learning.
--Senior Telephone Operator. (Career Examination Ser.: C-1027). (Cloth bdg. avail. on request). pap. 10.00 (ISBN 0-8373-1027-X). Natl Learning.
--Senior Tenant Supervisor. (Career Examination Ser.: C-544). (Cloth bdg. avail. on request). pap. 12.00 (ISBN 0-8373-0544-6). Natl Learning.
--Senior Title Searcher. (Career Examination Ser.: C-2086). (Cloth bdg. avail. on request). 1977. pap. 10.00 (ISBN 0-8373-2086-0). Natl Learning.
--Senior Traffic Supervisor. (Career Examination Ser.: C-2628). (Cloth bdg. avail. on request). pap. 12.00 (ISBN 0-8373-2628-1). Natl Learning.
--Senior Training Officer. (Career Examination Ser.: C-1485). (Cloth bdg. avail. on request). pap. 10.00 (ISBN 0-8373-1485-2). Natl Learning.
--Senior Training Technician (Police) (Career Examination Ser.: C-418). (Cloth bdg. avail. on request). pap. 14.09 (ISBN 0-8373-0418-0). Natl Learning.
--Senior Transportation Inspector. (Career Examination Ser.: C-1487). (Cloth bdg. avail. on request). pap. 10.00 (ISBN 0-8373-1487-9). Natl Learning.
--Senior Typist. (Career Examination Ser.: C-730). (Cloth bdg. avail. on request). pap. 10.00 (ISBN 0-8373-0730-9). Natl Learning.
--Senior Unemployment Insurance Claims Examiner. (Career Examination Ser.: C-2285). (Cloth bdg. avail. on request). 1977. pap. 12.00 (ISBN 0-8373-2285-5). Natl Learning.
--Senior Vocational Counselor. (Career Examination Ser.: C-2438). (Cloth bdg. avail. on request). pap. 12.00 (ISBN 0-8373-2438-6). Natl Learning.
--Senior Water Use Inspector. (Career Examination Ser.: C-1639). (Cloth bdg. avail. on request). pap. 10.00 (ISBN 0-8373-1639-1). Natl Learning.
--Senior Zoning Inspector. (Career Examination Ser.: C-2341). (Cloth bdg. avail. on request). pap. 12.00 (ISBN 0-8373-2341-X). Natl Learning.
--Sergeant-Bridge & Tunnel Authority. (Career Examination Ser.: C-732). (Cloth bdg. avail. on request). pap. 12.00 (ISBN 0-8373-0732-5). Natl Learning.
--Sergeant-Police Department. (Career Examination Ser.: C-733). (Cloth bdg. avail. on request). pap. 12.00 (ISBN 0-8373-0733-3). Natl Learning.
--Service Operations Supervisor. (Career Examination Ser.: C-1880). (Cloth bdg. avail. on request). pap. 10.00 (ISBN 0-8373-1880-7). Natl Learning.
--Sewage Plant Operator. (Career Examination Ser.: C-2443). (Cloth bdg. avail. on request). pap. 10.00 (ISBN 0-8373-1880-7). Natl Learning.
--Sewage Plant Operator Trainee. (Career Examination Ser.: C-2281). (Cloth bdg. avail. on request). 1977. pap. 10.00 (ISBN 0-8373-2281-2). Natl Learning.
--Sewage Treatment Operator. (Career Examination Ser.: C-1488). (Cloth bdg. avail. on request). pap. 10.00 (ISBN 0-8373-1488-7). Natl Learning.
--Sewage Treatment Operator Trainee. (Career Examination Ser.: C-1489). (Cloth bdg. avail. on request). pap. 10.00 (ISBN 0-8373-1489-5). Natl Learning.
--Sewage Treatment Worker. (Career Examination Ser.: C-734). (Cloth bdg. avail. on request). pap. 10.00 (ISBN 0-8373-0734-1). Natl Learning.
--Sewage Treatment Worker Trainee. (Career Examination Ser.: C-735). (Cloth bdg. avail. on request). pap. 10.00 (ISBN 0-8373-0735-X). Natl Learning.
--Sheet Metal Fabrication. (Occupational Competency Examination Ser.: OCE-31). (Cloth bdg. avail. on request). 13.95 (ISBN 0-8373-5731-4). Natl Learning.
--Sheet Metal Worker. (Career Examination Ser.: C-736). (Cloth bdg. avail. on request). pap. 10.00 (ISBN 0-8373-0736-8). Natl Learning.
--Sheriff. (Career Examination Ser.: C-794). (Cloth bdg. avail. on request). pap. 10.00 (ISBN 0-8373-0794-5). Natl Learning.
--Shop Carpenter. (Career Examination Ser.: C-739). (Cloth bdg. avail. on request). pap. 10.00 (ISBN 0-8373-0739-2). Natl Learning.
--Shop Subjects. (Teachers License Examination Ser.: T-53). (Cloth bdg. avail. on request). pap. 13.95 (ISBN 0-8373-8053-7). Natl Learning.
--Shop Subjects Chairman - Sr. H.S. (Teachers License Examination Ser.: CH-24). (Cloth bdg. avail. on request). pap. 15.95 (ISBN 0-8373-8174-6). Natl Learning.
--Sign Painter. (Career Examination Ser.: C-2090). (Cloth bdg. avail. on request). 1977. pap. 10.00 (ISBN 0-8373-2090-9). Natl Learning.
--Signal Maintainer. (Career Examination Ser.: C-742). (Cloth bdg. avail. on request). pap. 10.00 (ISBN 0-8373-0742-2). Natl Learning.
--Small Engine Repair. (Occupational Competency Examination Ser.: OCE-32). (Cloth bdg. avail. on request). pap. 13.95 (ISBN 0-8373-5732-2). Natl Learning.
--Social Investigator. (Career Examination Ser.: C-743). (Cloth bdg. avail. on request). pap. 10.00 (ISBN 0-8373-0743-0). Natl Learning.
--Social Sciences. (Graduate Record Area Examination Ser.: GRE-44). 21.95 (ISBN 0-8373-5294-0); pap. 13.95 (ISBN 0-8373-5244-4). Natl Learning.
--Social Service Representative. (Career Examination Ser.: C-745). (Cloth bdg. avail. on request). pap. 10.00 (ISBN 0-8373-0745-7). Natl Learning.
--Social Services Management Trainee. (Career Examination Ser.: C-1993). (Cloth bdg. avail. on request). pap. 10.00 (ISBN 0-8373-1993-5). Natl Learning.
--Social Studies. (National Teachers Examination Ser.: NT-8). (Cloth bdg. avail. on request). pap. 11.95 (ISBN 0-8373-8418-4). Natl Learning.
--Social Studies Chairman-Jr. H.S. (Teachers License Examination Ser.: CH-25). (Cloth bdg. avail. on request). pap. 15.95 (ISBN 0-8373-8175-4). Natl Learning.
--Social Studies Chairman-Sr. H.S. (Teachers License Examination Ser.: CH-26). (Cloth bdg. avail. on request). pap. 15.95 (ISBN 0-8373-8176-2). Natl Learning.
--Social Studies-Jr. H.S. (Teachers License Examination Ser.: T-54). (Cloth bdg. avail. on request). pap. 13.95 (ISBN 0-8373-8054-5). Natl Learning.
--Social Studies, Literature & the Fine Arts. (National Teachers Examination Ser.: NC-4). (Cloth bdg. avail. on request). pap. 11.95 (ISBN 0-8373-8404-4). Natl Learning.
--Social Studies-Sr. H.S. (Teachers License Examination Ser.: T-55). (Cloth bdg. avail. on request). pap. 13.95 (ISBN 0-8373-8055-3). Natl Learning.
--Societal Foundations of Education. (National Teachers Examination Ser.: NC-2). (Cloth bdg. avail. on request). pap. 11.95 (ISBN 0-8373-8402-8). Natl Learning.
--Sociology. (Graduate Record Examination Ser.: GRE-18). (Cloth bdg. avail. on request). pap. 13.95 (ISBN 0-8373-5218-5). Natl Learning.
--Soil Conservationist. (Career Examination Ser.: C-1032). (Cloth bdg. avail. on request). pap. 10.00 (ISBN 0-8373-1032-6). Natl Learning.
--Soil Scientist. (Career Examination Ser.: C-1033). (Cloth bdg. avail. on request). 10.00 (ISBN 0-8373-1033-4). Natl Learning.
--Spanish. (National Teachers Examination Ser.: NT-14). (Cloth bdg. avail. on request). pap. 11.95 (ISBN 0-8373-8424-9). Natl Learning.
--Spanish, Jr. H.S. (Teachers License Examination Ser.: T-56). (Cloth bdg. avail. on request). pap. 13.95 (ISBN 0-8373-8056-1). Natl Learning.
--Spanish, Sr. H.S. (Teachers License Examination Ser.: T-57). (Cloth bdg. avail. on request). pap. 13.95- (ISBN 0-8373-8057-X). Natl Learning.
--Special Investigations Inspector. (Career Examination Ser.: C-748). (Cloth bdg. avail. on request). 10.00 (ISBN 0-8373-0748-1). Natl Learning.
--Special Investigator. (Career Examination Ser.: C-1588). (Cloth bdg. avail. on request). pap. 10.00 (ISBN 0-8373-1588-3). Natl Learning.
--Special Officer. (Career Examination Ser.: C-749). (Cloth bdg. avail. on request). pap. 10.00 (ISBN 0-8373-0749-X). Natl Learning.
--Special Projects Coordinator. (Career Examination Ser.: C-2933). (Cloth bdg. avail. on request). pap. 12.00 (ISBN 0-8373-2933-7). Natl Learning.
--Special Rigger. (Career Examination Ser.: C-750). (Cloth bdg. avail. on request). pap. 10.00 (ISBN 0-8373-0750-3). Natl Learning.
--Special Service Manager. (Career Examination Ser.: C-2147). (Cloth bdg. avail. on request). 1976. pap. 12.00 (ISBN 0-8373-2147-6). Natl Learning.
--Special Sign Hanger. (Career Examination Ser.: C-751). (Cloth bdg. avail. on request). pap. 10.00 (ISBN 0-8373-0751-1). Natl Learning.
--Speech Chairman - Sr. H.S. (Teachers License Examination Ser.: CH-27). (Cloth bdg. avail. on request). pap. 15.95 (ISBN 0-8373-8177-0). Natl Learning.
--Speech Communication & Theatre. (National Teachers Examination Ser.: NT-35). (Cloth bdg. avail. on request). pap. 11.95 (ISBN 0-8373-8445-1). Natl Learning.
--Speech Improvement. (Teachers License Examination Ser.: T-59). (Cloth bdg. avail. on request). pap. 13.95 (ISBN 0-8373-8059-6). Natl Learning.
--Speech Pathology. (National Teachers Examination Ser.: NT-33). (Cloth bdg. avail. on request). pap. 11.95 (ISBN 0-8373-8443-5). Natl Learning.
--Speech, Sr. H.S. (Teachers License Examination Ser.: T-58). (Cloth bdg. avail. on request). pap. 13.95 (ISBN 0-685-18804-3). Natl Learning.
--Staff Analyst. (Career Examination Ser.: C-1551). (Cloth bdg. avail. on request). pap. 12.00 (ISBN 0-8373-1551-4). Natl Learning.
--Staff Development Coordinator. (Career Examination Ser.: C-2171). (Cloth bdg. avail. on request). 1976. pap. 12.00 (ISBN 0-8373-2171-9). Natl Learning.
--Staff Nurse. (Career Examination Ser.: C-756). (Cloth bdg. avail. on request). pap. 10.00 (ISBN 0-8373-0756-2). Natl Learning.
--State Accounts Auditor-Examiner of Municipal Affairs. (Career Examination Ser.: C-2367). (Bdg. avail. on request). pap. 12.00 (ISBN 0-8373-2367-3). Natl Learning.
--State Nursing Boards for Practical Nurse. (Admission Test Ser.: ATS-46). (Cloth bdg. avail. on request). pap. 13.95 (ISBN 0-8373-5046-8). Natl Learning.
--State Nursing Boards for Registered Nurse. (Admission Test Ser.: ATS-45). (Cloth bdg. avail. on request). pap. 13.95 (ISBN 0-8373-5045-X). Natl Learning.
--State Policewoman. (Career Examination Ser.: C-1692). (Cloth bdg. avail. on request). pap. 10.00 (ISBN 0-8373-1692-8). Natl Learning.
--State Trooper. (Career Examination Ser.: C-757). (Cloth bdg. avail. on request). pap. 10.00 (ISBN 0-8373-0757-0). Natl Learning.
--Stationary Engineer. (Career Examination Ser.: C-758). (Cloth bdg. avail. on request). pap. 10.00 (ISBN 0-8373-0758-9). Natl Learning.
--Stationary Engineer 1. (Career Examination Ser.: C-1903). (Cloth bdg. avail. on request). pap. 10.00 (ISBN 0-8373-1903-X). Natl Learning.
--Stationary Engineer 2. (Career Examination Ser.: C-1904). (Cloth bdg. avail. on request). pap. 12.00 (ISBN 0-8373-1904-8). Natl Learning.
--Stationary Fireman. (Career Examination Ser.: C-760). (Cloth bdg. avail. on request). pap. 10.00 (ISBN 0-8373-0760-0). Natl Learning.
--Statistician. (Career Examination Ser.: C-761). (Cloth bdg. avail. on request). pap. 10.00 (ISBN 0-8373-0761-9). Natl Learning.
--Statistics. (College Proficiency Examination Ser.: CPEP-15). 17.95 (ISBN 0-8373-5465-X); pap. 9.95 (ISBN 0-8373-5415-3). Natl Learning.
--Steam Fireman. (Career Examination Ser.: C-1035). (Cloth bdg. avail. on request). pap. 10.00 (ISBN 0-8373-1035-0). Natl Learning.
--Steam Fireman - Stationary Fireman. (Career Examination Ser.: C-1902). (Cloth bdg. avail. on request). pap. 10.00 (ISBN 0-8373-1902-1). Natl Learning.
--Steam Fitter. (Career Examination Ser.: C-763). (Cloth bdg. avail. on request). pap. 10.00 (ISBN 0-8373-0763-5). Natl Learning.
--Steel Construction Inspector. (Career Examination Ser.: C-765). (Cloth bdg. avail. on request). pap. 10.00 (ISBN 0-8373-0765-1). Natl Learning.
--Stenographer (Law) (Career Examination Ser.: C-1036). (Cloth bdg. avail. on request). pap. 10.00 (ISBN 0-8373-1036-9). Natl Learning.
--Stenography & Typewriting (Gregg & Pitman) Chairman - Sr. H.S. (Teachers License Examination Ser.: CH-28). (Cloth bdg. avail. on request). pap. 15.95 (ISBN 0-8373-8178-9). Natl Learning.
--Stenography & Typewriting (Gregg & Pitman) Sr. H.S. (Teachers License Examination Ser.: T-60). (Cloth bdg. avail. on request). pap. 13.95 (ISBN 0-8373-8060-X). Natl Learning.
--Stock Clerk. (Career Examination Ser.: C-2617). (Cloth bdg. avail. on request). pap. 8.00 (ISBN 0-8373-2617-6). Natl Learning.
--Storekeeper I. (Career Examination Ser.: C-2901). (Cloth bdg. avail. on request). pap. 10.00 (ISBN 0-8373-2901-9). Natl Learning.
--Storekeeper II. (Career Examination Ser.: C-2902). (Cloth bdg. avail. on request). pap. 12.00 (ISBN 0-8373-2902-7). Natl Learning.
--Student Aide. (Career Examination Ser.: C-1496). (Cloth bdg. avail. on request). pap. 8.00 (ISBN 0-8373-1496-8). Natl Learning.
--Student Trainee. (Career Examination Ser.: C-1039). (Cloth bdg. avail. on request). pap. 8.00 (ISBN 0-8373-1039-3). Natl Learning.
--Summer Aide. (Career Examination Ser.: C-1498). (Cloth bdg. avail. on request). pap. 8.00 (ISBN 0-8373-1498-4). Natl Learning.
--Summer Employment Examination. (Career Examination Ser.: C-1663). (Cloth bdg. avail. on request). 1977. pap. 8.00 (ISBN 0-8373-1663-4). Natl Learning.
--Summer Intern. (Career Examination Ser.: C-1499). (Cloth bdg. avail. on request). pap. 8.00 (ISBN 0-8373-1499-2). Natl Learning.
--Superintendent Building Service (U.S.P.S.) (Career Examination Ser.: C-1685). (Cloth bdg. avail. on request). pap. 10.00 (ISBN 0-8373-1685-5). Natl Learning.
--Superintendent for Administrative Services. (Career Examination Ser.: C-2815). (Cloth bdg. avail. on request). 1980. pap. 14.00 (ISBN 0-8373-2815-2) Natl Learning.
--Superintendent of Building Inspection. (Career Examination Ser.: C-2282). (Cloth bdg. avail. on request). 1977. pap. 12.00 (ISBN 0-8373-2282-0). Natl Learning.
--Superintendent of Buildings & Grounds. (Career Examination Ser.: C-1773). (Cloth bdg. avail. on request). pap. 12.00 (ISBN 0-8373-1773-8). Natl Learning.
--Superintendent of Construction. (Career Examination Ser.: C-1500). (Cloth bdg. avail. on request). pap. 12.00 (ISBN 0-8373-1500-X). Natl Learning.
--Superintendent of Heating & Ventilation. (Career Examination Ser.: C-2380). (Cloth bdg. avail. on request). pap. 12.00 (ISBN 0-8373-2380-0). Natl Learning.
--Superintendent of Highways. (Career Examination Ser.: C-2318). (Cloth bdg. avail. on request). pap. 12.00 (ISBN 0-8373-2318-5). Natl Learning.
--Superintendent of Public Works. (Career Examination Ser.: C-2305). (Cloth bdg. avail. on request). 1977. pap. 12.00 (ISBN 0-8373-2305-3). Natl Learning.
--Superintendent of Sanitation. (Career Examination Ser.: C-2457). (Cloth bdg. avail. on request). pap. 12.00 (ISBN 0-8373-2457-2). Natl Learning.
--Superintendent of Sewer Service. (Career Examination Ser.: C-2141). (Cloth bdg. avail. on request). 1977. pap. 12.00 (ISBN 0-8373-2141-7). Natl Learning.
--Superintendent of Sewers. (Career Examination Ser.: C-2276). (Cloth bdg. avail. on request). 1977. pap. 12.00 (ISBN 0-8373-2276-6). Natl Learning.
--Supervising Accountant. (Career Examination Ser.: C-1040). (Cloth bdg. avail. on request). pap. 12.00 (ISBN 0-8373-1040-7). Natl Learning.
--Supervising Addiction Specialist. (Career Examination Ser.: C-1501). (Cloth bdg. avail. on request). pap. 12.00 (ISBN 0-8373-1501-8). Natl Learning.

--Supervising Audiologist. (Career Examination Ser.: C-2237). (Cloth bdg. avail. on request). pap. 12.00 (ISBN 0-8373-2237-5). Natl Learning.
--Supervising Audit Clerk. (Career Examination Ser.: C-887). (Cloth bdg. avail. on request). pap. 10.00 (ISBN 0-8373-0887-9). Natl Learning.
--Supervising Auditor. (Career Examination Ser.: C-2681). (Cloth bdg. avail. on request). pap. 12.00 (ISBN 0-8373-2681-8). Natl Learning.
--Supervising Automotive Mechanic. (Career Examination Ser.: C-2575). (Cloth bdg. avail. on request). pap. 10.00 (ISBN 0-8373-2575-7). Natl Learning.
--Supervising Bookkeeper. (Career Examination Ser.: C-2682). (Cloth bdg. avail. on request). pap. 12.00 (ISBN 0-8373-2682-6). Natl Learning.
--Supervising Building Inspector. (Career Examination Ser.: C-2840). (Cloth bdg. avail. on request). 1980. pap. 12.00 (ISBN 0-8373-2840-3). Natl Learning.
--Supervising Building Plan Examiner. (Career Examination Ser.: C-862). (Cloth bdg. avail. on request). pap. 12.00 (ISBN 0-8373-0862-3). Natl Learning.
--Supervising Cashier. (Career Examination Ser.: C-774). (Cloth bdg. avail. on request). pap. 10.00 (ISBN 0-8373-0774-0). Natl Learning.
--Supervising Children's Counselor. (Career Examination Ser.: C-2010). (Cloth bdg. avail. on request). pap. 12.00 (ISBN 0-8373-2010-0). Natl Learning.
--Supervising Claim Examiner. (Career Examination Ser.: C-2322). (Cloth bdg. avail. on request). pap. 10.00 (ISBN 0-686-53581-2). Natl Learning.
--Supervising Community Service Worker. (Career Examination Ser.: C-2677). (Cloth bdg. avail. on request). pap. 12.00 (ISBN 0-8373-2677-X). Natl Learning.
--Supervising Construction Inspector. (Career Examination Ser.: C-1043). (Cloth bdg. avail. on request). pap. 12.00 (ISBN 0-8373-1043-1). Natl Learning.
--Supervising Consumer Affairs Inspector. (Career Examination Ser.: C-1657). (Cloth bdg. avail. on request). pap. 12.00 (ISBN 0-8373-1657-X). Natl Learning.
--Supervising Departmental Specialist. (Career Examination Ser.: C-935). (Cloth bdg. avail. on request). pap. 14.00 (ISBN 0-8373-0924-7). Natl Learning.
--Supervising Drug & Alcohol Community Coordinator. (Career Examination Ser.: C-2777). (Cloth bdg. avail. on request). 1980. pap. 12.00 (ISBN 0-8373-2777-6). Natl Learning.
--Supervising Electrical Inspector. (Career Examination Ser.: C-778). (Cloth bdg. avail. on request). pap. 12.00 (ISBN 0-8373-0778-3). Natl Learning.
--Supervising Grants Analyst. (Career Examination Ser.: C-2834). (Cloth bdg. avail. on request). 1980. pap. 12.00 (ISBN 0-8373-2834-9). Natl Learning.
--Supervising Highway Engineer. (Career Examination Ser.: C-2523). (Cloth bdg. avail. on request). pap. 10.00 (ISBN 0-8373-2523-4). Natl Learning.
--Supervising Highway Maintenance Supervisor. (Career Examination Ser.: C-2632). (Cloth bdg. avail. on request). pap. 12.00 (ISBN 0-8373-2632-X). Natl Learning.
--Supervising Incinerator Stationary Engineer. (Career Examination Ser.: C-2638). pap. 12.00 (ISBN 0-8373-2638-9). Natl Learning.
--Supervising Legal Stenographer. (Career Examination Ser.: C-2635). (Cloth bdg. avail. on request). pap. 12.00 (ISBN 0-8373-2635-4). Natl Learning.
--Supervising Medicaid Claims Examiner. (Career Examination Ser.: C-2693). (Cloth bdg. avail. on request). pap. 12.00 (ISBN 0-8373-2693-1). Natl Learning.
--Supervising Medical Social Worker. (Career Examination Ser.: C-2630). (Cloth bdg. avail. on request). pap. 12.00 (ISBN 0-8373-2630-3). Natl Learning.
--Supervising Nurse. (Career Examination Ser.: C-1883). (Cloth bdg. avail. on request). pap. 12.00 (ISBN 0-8373-1883-1). Natl Learning.
--Supervising Photographer. (Career Examination Ser.: C-2504). (Cloth bdg. avail. on request). pap. 12.00 (ISBN 0-8373-2504-8). Natl Learning.
--Supervising Physical Therapist. (Career Examination Ser.: C-2904). (Cloth bdg. avail. on request). pap. 12.00 (ISBN 0-8373-2904-3). Natl Learning.
--Supervising Probation Officer. (Career Examination Ser.: C-2591). (Cloth bdg. avail. on request). pap. 10.00 (ISBN 0-8373-2591-9). Natl Learning.
--Supervising Senior Citizens Club Leader. (Career Examination Ser.: C-2829). (Cloth bdg. avail. on request). pap. 12.00 (ISBN 0-8373-2829-2). Natl Learning.
--Supervising Storekeeper. (Career Examination Ser.: C-861). (Cloth bdg. avail. on request). pap. 10.00 (ISBN 0-8373-0861-5). Natl Learning.
--Supervising Systems Analyst. (Career Examination Ser.: C-2387). (Cloth bdg. avail. on request). pap. 12.00 (ISBN 0-8373-2387-8). Natl Learning.
--Supervising Taxi & Limosine Inspector. (Career Examination Ser.: C-2554). (Cloth bdg. avail. on request). pap. 10.00 (ISBN 0-8373-2554-4). Natl Learning.
--Supervising Therapist. (Career Examination Ser.: C-2253). (Cloth bdg. avail. on request). 1977. pap. 10.00 (ISBN 0-8373-2253-7). Natl Learning.
--Supervising Typist. (Career Examination Ser.: C-1928). (Cloth bdg. avail. on request). pap. 10.00 (ISBN 0-8373-1928-5). Natl Learning.
--Supervising Water Use Inspector. (Career Examination Ser.: C-1051). (Cloth bdg. avail. on request). pap. 10.00 (ISBN 0-8373-1051-2). Natl Learning.
--Supervision Test. (Teachers License Examination Ser.: S-9). (Cloth bdg. avail. on request). pap. 17.95 (ISBN 0-8373-8109-6). Natl Learning.
--Supervisor of Menagerie. (Career Examination Ser.: C-1792). (Cloth bdg. avail. on request). pap. 10.00 (ISBN 0-8373-1792-4). Natl Learning.
--Supervisor of Motor Repair. (Career Examination Ser.: C-1875). (Cloth bdg. avail. on request). pap. 10.00 (ISBN 0-8373-1875-0). Natl Learning.
--Supervisor of Motor Transport. (Career Examination Ser.: C-1509). (Cloth bdg. avail. on request). pap. 10.00 (ISBN 0-8373-1509-3). Natl Learning.
--Supervisor of Office Services. (Career Examination Ser.: C-2533). (Cloth bdg. avail. on request). pap. 10.00 (ISBN 0-8373-2533-1). Natl Learning.
--Supervisor of Professional Licensing. (Career Examination Ser.: C-1029). (Cloth bdg. avail. on request). pap. 10.00 (ISBN 0-8373-1029-6). Natl Learning.
--Supervisor of Tax Compliance Field Operations. (Career Examination Ser.: C-2955). (Cloth bdg. avail. on request). pap. 14.00 (ISBN 0-8373-2955-8). Natl Learning.
--Supervisor of Transportation. (Career Examination Ser.: C-1813). (Cloth bdg. avail. on request). pap. 10.00 (ISBN 0-8373-1813-0). Natl Learning.
--Supervisor (Power Distributor) (Career Examination Ser.: C-423). (Cloth bdg. avail. on request). pap. 12.00 (ISBN 0-8373-0423-7). Natl Learning.
--Supervisor (Structures) (Career Examination Ser.: C-424). (Cloth bdg. avail. on request). pap. 12.00 (ISBN 0-8373-0424-5). Natl Learning.
--Supervisor (Structures - Group C) (Iron Work) (Career Examination Ser.: C-425). (Cloth bdg. avail. on request). pap. 12.00 (ISBN 0-8373-0425-3). Natl Learning.
--Supervisor (Telephones) (Career Examination Ser.: C-426). (Cloth bdg. avail. on request). pap. 12.00 (ISBN 0-8373-0426-1). Natl Learning.
--Supervisor (Turnstiles) (Career Examination Ser.: C-427). (Cloth bdg. avail. on request). pap. 12.00 (ISBN 0-8373-0427-X). Natl Learning.
--Supervisor (Water & Sewer Systems) (Career Examination Ser.: C-2907). (Cloth bdg. avail. on request). pap. 10.00 (ISBN 0-8373-2907-8). Natl Learning.
--Supervisor 3 (Child Welfare) (Career Examination Ser.: C-1808). (Cloth bdg. avail. on request). pap. 12.00 (ISBN 0-8373-1808-4). Natl Learning.
--Supervisor 3 (Social Service) (Career Examination Ser.: C-1951). (Cloth bdg. avail. on request). pap. 12.00 (ISBN 0-8373-1951-X). Natl Learning.
--Supervisor 3 (Welfare) (Career Examination Ser.: C-1805). (Cloth bdg. avail. on request). pap. 12.00 (ISBN 0-8373-1805-X). Natl Learning.
--Supervisor's Handbook of Mnemonic Devices. (Teachers License Examination Ser.: S-10). (Cloth bdg. avail. on request). pap. 17.95 (ISBN 0-8373-8110-X). Natl Learning.
--Surgeon. (Career Examination Ser.: C-790). (Cloth bdg. avail. on request). pap. 16.00 (ISBN 0-8373-0790-2). Natl Learning.
--Swimming & Health Instructors - Sr. H.S. (Teachers License Examination Ser.: T-62). (Cloth bdg. avail. on request). pap. 13.95 (ISBN 0-8373-8062-6). Natl Learning.
--Switchboard Operator. (Career Examination Ser.: C-883). (Cloth bdg. avail. on request). pap. 10.00 (ISBN 0-8373-0883-6). Natl Learning.
--Switchboard Supervisor. (Career Examination Ser.: C-884). (Cloth bdg. avail. on request). pap. 10.00 (ISBN 0-8373-0884-4). Natl Learning.
--Tariff Examiner. (Career Examination Ser.: C-828). (Cloth bdg. avail. on request). pap. 8.00 (ISBN 0-8373-0828-3). Natl Learning.
--Tax Compliance Agent. (Career Examination Ser.: C-2122). (Cloth bdg. avail. on request). 1977. pap. 10.00 (ISBN 0-8373-2122-0). Natl Learning.
--Tax Examiner. (Career Examination Ser.: C-802). (Cloth bdg. avail. on request). pap. 10.00 (ISBN 0-8373-0802-X). Natl Learning.
--Tax Examiner Trainee. (Career Examination Ser.: C-803). (Cloth bdg. avail. on request). pap. 10.00 (ISBN 0-8373-0803-8). Natl Learning.
--Tax Technician. (Career Examination Ser.: C-2370). (Cloth bdg. avail. on request). pap. 10.00 (ISBN 0-8373-2370-3). Natl Learning.
--Tax Technician Trainee. (Career Examination Ser.: C-214). (Cloth bdg. avail. on request). pap. 10.00 (ISBN 0-8373-0214-5). Natl Learning.
--Taxpayer Service Representative. (Career Examination Ser.: C-833). (Cloth bdg. avail. on request). pap. 10.00 (ISBN 0-8373-0833-X). Natl Learning.
--Teacher-Trainer Chairman - Language Arts & Social Studies - I.S. & Jr. H.S. (Teachers License Examination Ser.: CH-30). (Cloth bdg. avail. on request). pap. 15.95 (ISBN 0-8373-8180-0). Natl Learning.
--Teacher-Trainer Chairman - Math & Science - I.S. & Jr. H.S. (Teachers License Examination Ser.: CH-29). (Cloth bdg. avail. on request). pap. 15.95 (ISBN 0-8373-8179-7). Natl Learning.
--Teaching Health Conservation. (National Teachers Examination Ser.: NT-23). (Cloth bdg. avail. on request). pap. 11.95 (ISBN 0-8373-8433-8). Natl Learning.
--Teaching Hearing Handicapped. (National Teachers Examination Ser.: NT-28). (Cloth bdg. avail. on request). pap. 11.95 (ISBN 0-8373-8438-9). Natl Learning.
--Teaching Orthopedically Handicapped. (National Teachers Examination Ser.: NT-25). (Cloth bdg. avail. on request). pap. 11.95 (ISBN 0-8373-8435-4). Natl Learning.
--Teaching Principles & Practices. (National Teachers Examination Ser.: NC-3). (Cloth bdg. avail. on request). pap. 11.95 (ISBN 0-8373-8403-6). Natl Learning.
--Teaching Speech Handicapped. (Teachers License Examination Ser.: NT-26). (Cloth bdg. avail. on request). pap. 11.95 (ISBN 0-8373-8436-2). Natl Learning.
--Teaching Visually Handicapped. (Teachers License Examination Ser.: NT-27). (Cloth bdg. avail. on request). pap. 11.95 (ISBN 0-8373-8437-0). Natl Learning.
--Technical Aide in Science & Engineering. (Career Examination Ser.: C-829). (Cloth bdg. avail. on request). pap. 10.00 (ISBN 0-8373-0829-1). Natl Learning.
--Technical & Professional Assistant. (Career Examination Ser.: C-805). (Cloth bdg. avail. on request). pap. 10.00 (ISBN 0-8373-0805-4). Natl Learning.
--Technical Assistant. (Career Examination Ser.: C-1515). 14.00 (ISBN 0-685-18570-2); pap. 10.00 (ISBN 0-8373-1515-8). Natl Learning.
--Technical Careers Test. (Career Examination Ser.: C-804). (Cloth bdg. avail. on request). pap. 10.00 (ISBN 0-8373-0804-6). Natl Learning.
--Telecommunications Aide. (Career Examination Ser.: C-2877). (Cloth bdg. avail. on request). pap. 10.00 (ISBN 0-8373-2877-2). Natl Learning.
--Telemetric Systems Specialist. (Career Examination Ser.: C-1940). (Cloth bdg. avail. on request). pap. 12.00 (ISBN 0-8373-1940-4). Natl Learning.
--Telephone Services Operator. (Career Examination Ser.: C-2586). (Cloth bdg. avail. on request). pap. 10.00 (ISBN 0-8373-2586-2). Natl Learning.
--Tenant Supervisor. (Career Examination Ser.: C-543). (Cloth bdg. avail. on request). pap. 10.00 (ISBN 0-8373-0543-8). Natl Learning.
--Test of English As a Foreign Language (TOEFL) (Admission Test Ser.: ATS-30). 21.95 (ISBN 0-8373-5130-8); pap. 13.95 (ISBN 0-8373-5030-1). Natl Learning.
--Test of General Educational Development (GED) (Admission Test Ser.: ATS-61). 21.95 (ISBN 0-8373-5161-8); pap. 13.95 (ISBN 0-8373-5061-1). Natl Learning.
--Tests & Measurements. (College Level Examination Ser.: CLEP-27). 17.95 (ISBN 0-8373-5377-7); pap. 9.95 (ISBN 0-8373-5327-0). Natl Learning.
--Texas Government. (National Teachers Examination Ser.: NT-38). (Cloth bdg. avail. on request). pap. 11.95 (ISBN 0-8373-8448-6). Natl Learning.
--Therapeutic Activities Specialist. (Career Examination Ser.: C-889). (Cloth bdg. avail. on request). pap. 12.00 (ISBN 0-8373-0889-5). Natl Learning.
--Ticket Agent. (Career Examination Ser.: C-808). (Cloth bdg. avail. on request). pap. 8.00 (ISBN 0-8373-0808-9). Natl Learning.
--Toll Equipment Maintenance Supervisor. (Career Examination Ser.: C-2547). (Cloth bdg. avail. on request). pap. 10.00 (ISBN 0-8373-2547-1). Natl Learning.
--Toll Equipment Mechanic. (Career Examination Ser.: C-2546). (Cloth bdg. avail. on request). pap. 8.00 (ISBN 0-8373-2546-3). Natl Learning.
--Toll Section Supervisor. (Career Examination Ser.: C-1947). (Cloth bdg. avail. on request). pap. 10.00 (ISBN 0-8373-1947-1). Natl Learning.
--Toolmaker. (Career Examination Ser.: C-1517). (Cloth bdg. avail. on request). pap. 10.00 (ISBN 0-8373-1517-4). Natl Learning.
--Towerman. (Career Examination Ser.: C-811). (Cloth bdg. avail. on request). pap. 10.00 (ISBN 0-8373-0811-9). Natl Learning.
--Town Clerk. (Career Examination Ser.: C-1854). (Cloth bdg. avail. on request). pap. 10.00 (ISBN 0-8373-2001-1). Natl Learning.
--Town Engineer. (Career Examination Ser.: C-2001). (Cloth bdg. avail. on request). pap. 12.00 (ISBN 0-8373-2001-1). Natl Learning.
--Trackman. (Career Examination Ser.: C-1066). (Cloth bdg. avail. on request). pap. 10.00 (ISBN 0-8373-1066-0). Natl Learning.
--Tractor Operator. (Career Examination Ser.: C-827). (Cloth bdg. avail. on request). pap. 10.00 (ISBN 0-8373-0827-5). Natl Learning.
--Tractor-Trailer Operator. (Career Examination Ser.: C-1519). (Cloth bdg. avail. on request). pap. 10.00 (ISBN 0-8373-1519-0). Natl Learning.
--Trades & Industrial Education. (National Teachers Examination Ser.: NT-22). (Cloth bdg. avail. on request). pap. 11.95 (ISBN 0-8373-8432-X). Natl Learning.
--Traffic Device Maintainer. (Career Examination Ser.: C-813). (Cloth bdg. avail. on request). pap. 10.00 (ISBN 0-8373-0813-5). Natl Learning.
--Traffic Device Maintainer Trainee. (Career Examination Ser.: C-814). (Cloth bdg. avail. on request). pap. 10.00 (ISBN 0-8373-0814-3). Natl Learning.
--Traffic Engineer. (Career Examination Ser.: C-1520). (Cloth bdg. avail. on request). pap. 10.00 (ISBN 0-8373-1520-4). Natl Learning.
--Traffic Engineer 1. (Career Examination Ser.: C-803). (Cloth bdg. avail. on request). pap. 10.00 (ISBN 0-8373-1886-6). Natl Learning.
--Traffic Supervisor. (Career Examination Ser.: C-2627). (Cloth bdg. avail. on request). pap. 10.00 (ISBN 0-8373-2627-3). Natl Learning.
--Traffic Technician. (Career Examination Ser.: C-1522). (Cloth bdg. avail. on request). pap. 10.00 (ISBN 0-8373-1522-0). Natl Learning.
--Traffic Technician 1. (Career Examination Ser.: C-2335). (Cloth bdg. avail. on request). pap. 10.00 (ISBN 0-8373-2335-5). Natl Learning.
--Traffic Technician 2. (Career Examination Ser.: C-2336). (Cloth bdg. avail. on request). pap. 12.00 (ISBN 0-8373-2336-3). Natl Learning.
--Traffic Technician 3. (Career Examination Ser.: C-1887). (Cloth bdg. avail. on request). pap. 12.00 (ISBN 0-8373-1887-4). Natl Learning.
--Train Dispatcher. (Career Examination Ser.: C-815). (Cloth bdg. avail. on request). pap. 10.00 (ISBN 0-8373-0815-1). Natl Learning.
--Trainee. (Career Examination Ser.: C-816). (Cloth bdg. avail. on request). pap. 8.00 (ISBN 0-8373-0816-X). Natl Learning.
--Training Specialist 2. (Career Examination Ser.: C-1768). (Cloth bdg. avail. on request). 1977. pap. 12.00 (ISBN 0-8373-1768-1). Natl Learning.
--Training Technician. (Career Examination Ser.: C-1524). (Cloth bdg. avail. on request). pap. 10.00 (ISBN 0-8373-1524-7). Natl Learning.
--Training Technician (Police) (Career Examination Ser.: C-417). (Cloth bdg. avail. on request). pap. 12.00 (ISBN 0-8373-0417-2). Natl Learning.
--Trainmaster. (Career Examination Ser.: C-817). (Cloth bdg. avail. on request). pap. 10.00 (ISBN 0-8373-0817-8). Natl Learning.
--Transit Electrical Helpers Series. (Career Examination Ser.: C-1963). (Cloth bdg. avail. on request). pap. 10.00 (ISBN 0-8373-1963-3). Natl Learning.
--Transit Management Analyst Trainee. (Career Examination Ser.: C-2095). (Cloth bdg. avail. on request). 1977. pap. 10.00 (ISBN 0-8373-2095-X). Natl Learning.
--Transit System Manager. (Career Examination Ser.: C-539). (Cloth bdg. avail. on request). pap. 12.00 (ISBN 0-8373-0539-X). Natl Learning.
--Transportation Assistant. (Career Examination Ser.: C-2358). (Cloth bdg. avail. on request). pap. 10.00 (ISBN 0-8373-2358-4). Natl Learning.
--Treasury Enforcement Agent. (Career Examination Ser.: C-823). (Cloth bdg. avail. on request). pap. 10.00 (ISBN 0-8373-0823-2). Natl Learning.
--Treatment Unit Clerk. (Career Examination Ser.: C-319). (Cloth bdg. avail. on request). pap. 10.00 (ISBN 0-8373-0319-2). Natl Learning.
--Tree Trimmer. (Career Examination Ser.: C-1526). (Cloth bdg. avail. on request). pap. 8.00 (ISBN 0-8373-1526-3). Natl Learning.
--Typewriting-Jr. H. S. (Teachers License Examination Ser.: T-63). (Cloth bdg. avail. on request). pap. 13.95 (ISBN 0-8373-8063-4). Natl Learning.
--Underwriter. (Career Examination Ser.: C-2011). (Cloth bdg. avail. on request). pap. 10.00 (ISBN 0-8373-2011-9). Natl Learning.
--Unemployment Insurance Claims Examiner. (Career Examination Ser.: C-851). (Cloth bdg. avail. on request). pap. 10.00 (ISBN 0-8373-0851-8). Natl Learning.
--Unemployment Insurance Hearing Representative. (Career Examination Ser.: C-2728). (Cloth bdg. avail. on request). 1980. pap. 12.00 (ISBN 0-8373-2728-8). Natl Learning.
--Unemployment Insurance Investigator. (Career Examination Ser.: C-2364). (Cloth bdg. avail. on request). pap. 10.00 (ISBN 0-8373-2364-9). Natl Learning.
--Unemployment Insurance Referee. (Career Examination Ser.: C-917). (Cloth bdg. avail. on request). pap. 14.00 (ISBN 0-8373-0917-4). Natl Learning.
--United States Marshall. (Career Examination Ser.: C-853). (Cloth bdg. avail. on request). pap. 10.00 (ISBN 0-8373-0853-4). Natl Learning.
--United States Park Police Officer. (Career Examination Ser.: C-1989). (Cloth bdg. avail. on request). pap. 10.00 (ISBN 0-8373-1989-7). Natl Learning.
--Urban Designer. (Career Examination Ser.). (Cloth bdg. avail. on request). pap. 10.00 (ISBN 0-8373-1527-1, C-1527). Natl Learning.
--Urban Forester. (Career Examination Ser.: C-2905). (Cloth bdg. avail. on request). pap. 12.00 (ISBN 0-8373-2905-1). Natl Learning.
--Urban Park Patrol Sergeant. (Career Examination Ser.). (Cloth bdg. avail. on request). pap. 10.00 (ISBN 0-8373-2541-2, C-2541). Natl Learning.

--Urban Planner. (Career Examination Ser.: C-854). (Cloth bdg. avail. on request). pap. 10.00 (ISBN 0-8373-0854-2). Natl Learning.
--Veteran Counselor. (Career Examination Ser.: C-2690). (Cloth bdg. avail. on request). pap. 12.00 (ISBN 0-8373-2690-7). Natl Learning.
--Veterinarian. (Career Examination Ser.: C-870). (Cloth bdg. avail. on request). pap. 14.00 (ISBN 0-8373-0870-4). Natl Learning.
--Veterinarian Trainee. (Career Examination Ser.: C-1529). (Cloth bdg. avail. on request). pap. 10.00 (ISBN 0-8373-1529-8). Natl Learning.
--Veterinary Aptitude Test (VAT) (Admission Test Ser.: ATS-29). 21.95 (ISBN 0-8373-5129-4); pap. 13.95 (ISBN 0-8373-5029-8). Natl Learning.
--Veterinary Medical Officer. (Career Examination Ser.: C-873). (Cloth bdg. avail. on request). pap. 12.00 (ISBN 0-8373-0873-9). Natl Learning.
--Veterinary Science Officer. (Career Examination Ser.: C-871). (Cloth bdg. avail. on request). pap. 12.00 (ISBN 0-8373-0871-2). Natl Learning.
--Visa Qualifying Examination (VQE) (Admission Test Ser.: ATS-48). 22.95 (ISBN 0-8373-5148-0); pap. 19.95 (ISBN 0-8373-5048-4). Natl Learning.
--Visiting Teacher. (Teachers License Examination Ser.: NT-21). (Cloth bdg. avail. on request). pap. 11.95 (ISBN 0-8373-8431-1). Natl Learning.
--Vocabulary. (Teachers License Examination Ser.: G-5). (Cloth bdg. avail. on request). pap. 10.00 (ISBN 0-8373-8195-9). Natl Learning.
--Vocational Counselor Trainee. (Career Examination Ser.: C-1531). (Cloth bdg. avail. on request). pap. 10.00 (ISBN 0-8373-1531-X). Natl Learning.
--Vocational Rehabilitation Counselor. (Career Examination Ser.: C-858). (Cloth bdg. avail. on request). pap. 10.00 (ISBN 0-8373-0858-5). Natl Learning.
--Vocational Training Supervisor. (Career Examination Ser.: C-2673). (Cloth bdg. avail. on request). pap. 12.00 (ISBN 0-8373-2673-7). Natl Learning.
--Warehouse Supervisor. (Career Examination Ser.: C-926). (Cloth bdg. avail. on request). pap. 10.00 (ISBN 0-8373-0926-3). Natl Learning.
--Water District Supervisor. (Career Examination Ser.: C-2625). (Cloth bdg. avail. on request). pap. 12.00 (ISBN 0-8373-2625-7). Natl Learning.
--Water Maintainance Foreman. (Career Examination Ser.: C-2925). (Cloth bdg. avail. on request). pap. 12.00 (ISBN 0-8373-2925-6). Natl Learning.
--Water Maintainance Man. (Career Examination Ser.: C-2657). (Cloth bdg. avail. on request). pap. 10.00 (ISBN 0-8373-2657-5). Natl Learning.
--Water Plant Operator. (Career Examination Ser.: C-897). (Cloth bdg. avail. on request). pap. 10.00 (ISBN 0-8373-0897-6). Natl Learning.
--Water Plant Operator Trainee. (Career Examination Ser.: C-886). (Cloth bdg. avail. on request). pap. 10.00 (ISBN 0-8373-0886-0). Natl Learning.
--Water Service Foreman. (Career Examination Ser.: C-2918). (Cloth bdg. avail. on request). pap. 12.00 (ISBN 0-686-84406-8). Natl Learning.
--Weigher. (Career Examination Ser.: C-2674). (Cloth bdg. avail. on request). pap. 8.00 (ISBN 0-8373-2674-5). Natl Learning.
--Welding. (Occupational Competency Examination Ser.: OCE-33). 21.95 (ISBN 0-8373-5783-7); pap. 13.95 (ISBN 0-8373-5733-0). Natl Learning.
--Welding Engineer. (Career Examination Ser.: C-1533). (Cloth bdg. avail. on request). pap. 10.00 (ISBN 0-8373-1533-6). Natl Learning.
--Western Civilization. (College Proficiency Examination Ser.: CPEP-16). 17.95 (ISBN 0-8373-5466-8); pap. 9.95 (ISBN 0-8373-5416-1). Natl Learning.
--Wiper (Uniformed) (Career Examination Ser.: C-1632). (Cloth bdg. avail. on request). pap. 8.00 (ISBN 0-8373-1632-4). Natl Learning.
--Women's Physical Education. (Teachers License Examination Ser.: NT-37). (Cloth bdg. avail. on request). pap. 11.95 (ISBN 0-8373-1632-4). Natl Learning.
--Worker's Compensation Review Analyst. (Career Examination Ser.: C-308). (Cloth bdg. avail. on request). pap. 10.00 (ISBN 0-8373-0308-7). Natl Learning.
--Workmen's Compensation Examiner. (Career Examination Ser.: C-1644). (Cloth bd. avail. on request). 1977. pap. 10.00 (ISBN 0-8373-1644-8). Natl Learning.
--Written English Expression. (National Teachers Examination Ser.: NC-6). (Cloth bdg. avail. on request). pap. 11.95 (ISBN 0-8373-8406-0). Natl Learning.
--Youth Corps Recruiter. (Career Examination Ser.: C-1537). (Cloth bdg. avail. on request). pap. 8.00 (ISBN 0-8373-1540-9). Natl Learning.
--Youth Counselor. (Career Examination Ser.: C-2906). (Cloth bdg. avail. on request). pap. 10.00 (ISBN 0-8373-2906-X). Natl Learning.
Rudman, Jack q. Senior Audio-Visual Aid Technician. (Career Examination Ser.: C-1471). (Cloth bdg. avail. on request). pap. 10.00 (ISBN 0-8373-1471-2). Natl Learning.
Rudman, Mark, tr. see Pasternak, Boris.
Rudman, Masha. Children's Literature: An Issues Approach. 1976. pap. text ed. 13.95. (ISBN 0-669-02270-5). Heath.
Rudman, Masha K., jt. auth. see Lee, Barbara.
Rudman, Reuben, ed. Diffraction Aspects of Orientationally Disordered (Plastic) Crystals. Date not set. pap. 10.00 (ISBN 0-937140-26-0). Polycrystal Bk Serv.
Rudner, Richard S. Philosophy of Social Science. (Orig.). 1966. pap. 10.95x ref. ed. (ISBN 0-13-664300-0). P-H.
Rudner, Richard S. & Scheffler, Israel, eds. Logic & Art: Essays in Honor of Nelson Goodman. LC 76-140799. 1972. 16.50 o.p. (ISBN 0-672-51639-X). Bobbs.
Rudnick, Dorothea, tr. see Baltzer, Fritz.
Rudnicki, Stefan, ed. Classical Monologues 3: The Age of Style. 192p. (Orig.). 1983. pap. 4.95x (ISBN 0-89676-036-7). Drama Bk.
--Classical Monologues 4: Shakespeare & Friends Encore. 144p. (Orig.). 1983. pap. text ed. 4.95x (ISBN 0-89676-037-5). Drama Bk.
--Classical Monologues 5: Warhorses. 96p. (Orig.). 1983. pap. text ed. 4.95x (ISBN 0-89676-038-3). Drama Bk.
Rudnik, Maryka, tr. see Pelgrom, Els.
Rudnik, Raphael. Frank Two Hundred Seven Poems. LC 81-16914. 70p. 1982. 14.95 (ISBN 0-8214-0634-5, 82-84077); pap. 7.95 (ISBN 0-8214-0635-3, 82-84085). Ohio U Pr.
Rudnik, Raphael, tr. see Pelgrom, Els.
Rudoff, Arnold G. Rudoff's Tax Shelter Directory. (Nineteen Eighty-Three Edition). 476p. 1982. 87.00 (ISBN 0-911711-00-7). Spectrum Fin Pr.
Rudoff, Carol. The Allergy Gourmet. (Illus.). 1983. pap. 9.95 (ISBN 0-930048-11-3). Prologue.
Rudoff, Harvey. Practically Complete Guide to Almost Real Musical Instruments for Nearly Everyone. LC 64-25637. (General Juvenile Bks.). (Illus.). (gr. k-5). 1964. PLB 3.95g (ISBN 0-8225-0252-6). Lerner Pubns.
Rudolf, Anthony, tr. see Tvardovsky, Alexander.
Rudolf, Anthony, tr. see Vinokurov, Evgeny.
Rudolph, B. Freddie. Bahamian Delights. 1979. 4.50 o.p. (ISBN 0-533-03386-1). Vantage.
Rudolph, Frederick. Mark Hopkins & the Log: Williams College, 1836-1872. 1956. text ed. 39.50x (ISBN 0-686-83618-9). Elliots Bks.
Rudolph, L. C. Francis Asbury. 240p. (Orig.). 1983. pap. 7.95 (ISBN 0-687-13461-7). Abingdon.
Rudolph, Lloyd & Rudolph, Susanne. The Regional Imperative (U. S. Foreign Policy Towards South Asian States) 465p. 1981. text ed. 17.25x (ISBN 0-391-02178-8, Pub. by Concept India). Humanities.
Rudolph, Lloyd I. & Rudolph, Susanne H. Modernity of Tradition: Political Development in India. LC 67-25527. 1967. 8.00x (ISBN 0-226-73134-0). U of Chicago Pr.
Rudolph, Marguerita. From Hand to Head: A Handbook for Teachers of Preschool Programs. LC 76-39624. 1977. pap. 4.95 (ISBN 0-8052-0564-0). Schocken.
--Should the Children Know? Encounters with Death in the Lives of Children. LC 77-73974. 1978. 8.95 (ISBN 0-8052-3684-8); pap. 5.95 (ISBN 0-8052-0662-0). Schocken.
Rudolph, Marguerita, tr. see Zakhoder, Boris.
Rudolph, R. L. Finance & Industrialization in the Austro-Hungarian Empire, 1873-1914. LC 75-2736. (Illus.). 350p. 1976. 49.50 (ISBN 0-521-20878-5). Cambridge U Pr.
Rudolph, Richard C., ed. Chinese Archaeological Abstracts. LC 77-620059. (Monumenta Archaeologica Ser.: No. 6). (Illus.). 1978. 35.00 (ISBN 0-917956-05-2). UCLA Arch.
Rudolph, Ross & Noe, Joel M. Chronic Problem Wounds. 1983. text ed. write for info. (ISBN 0-316-76110-9). Little.
Rudolph, Susanne, jt. auth. see Rudolph, Lloyd.
Rudolph, Susanne H., jt. auth. see Rudolph, Lloyd I.
Rudolph, Thomas D., ed. The Enterprise, Wisconsin, Radiation Forest: Preirradiation Ecological Studies, Pt. 1. LC 74-600049. (ERDA Technical Information Center Ser.). 155p. 1974. pap. 12.00 (TID-26113-PT. 1); microfiche 4.50 (ISBN 0-87079-193-1, TID-26113-PT. 1). DOE.
Rudolph, Valerie C. & Backscheider, P. R., eds. The Plays of Samuel Johnson of Cheshire. LC 78-66642. (Eighteenth Century English Drama Ser.). lib. bdg. 50.00 (ISBN 0-8240-3599-2). Garland Pub.
Rudolph, William B., jt. auth. see Bittinger, Marvin L.
Rudolph, Wolfgang. Harbor & Town: A Maritime Cultural History. Feininger, T. Lux, tr. from Ger. (Illus.). 231p. 1983. 22.50 (ISBN 0-686-84698-2). Hippocrene Bks.
Rudorf, E. Hugh, jt. auth. see Hodges, R. E.
Rudovsky, David, et al. The Rights of Prisoners. 1972. pap. 2.50 o.p. (ISBN 0-380-01387-8, 77016, Discus). Avon.
Rudow, Martin, jt. auth. see McCausland, Bob.
Rudoy, Marion, jt. auth. see Cordwell, Miriam.
Rudstrom, Lennart. A Family. (Illus.). 32p. (gr. 1-12). 1980. 9.95 (ISBN 0-399-20700-7). Putnam Pub Group.
Rudstrom, Lennart & Larsson, Carl. A Farm. LC 76-2130. (Illus.). (gr. 3 up). 1976. 9.95 (ISBN 0-399-20541-1). Putnam Pub Group.
--A Home. (Illus.). 32p. (gr. 3-5). 1974. 9.95 (ISBN 0-399-20400-8). Putnam Pub Group.
Rudwick, Bernard. Solving Management Problems: A Systems Approach to Planning & Control. LC 78-23266. (Systems Engineering & Analysis Ser.). 1979. 44.95x (ISBN 0-471-04246-3, Pub. by Wiley-Interscience). Wiley.
Rudwick, Bernard H. Systems Analysis for Effective Planning: Principles & Cases. (Systems Engineering & Analysis Ser). 1969. 49.95x (ISBN 0-471-74486-7, Pub. by Wiley-Interscience). Wiley.
Rudwick, Elliot. W. E. B. Du Bois: Propagandist of the Negro Protest. LC 68-16418. (Studies in American Negro Life). 1968. pap. text ed. 6.95x (ISBN 0-689-70169-1, NL6). Atheneum.
Rudwick, Elliott, jt. auth. see Meier, August.
Rudwin, Maximilian. The Devil in Legend & Literature. LC 73-85284. (Illus.). 365p. 1970. 21.00x (ISBN 0-87548-247-3); pap. 9.00x (ISBN 0-87548-248-1). Open Court.
Rudy, Ann. Mom Spelled Backwards Is Tired. LC 79-55442. 190p. 1980. 9.95 o.p. (ISBN 0-672-52627-1). Bobbs.
Rudy, Peter, et al. Russian: A Complete Elementary Course. 1970. 15.95x o.p. (ISBN 0-393-09871-0, NortonC); text & tape set o.p. 90.00 o.p. (ISBN 0-686-66509-0); tapes for duplication by school free o.p. (ISBN 0-393-99126-1). Norton.
Rudy, Stephan, ed. see Jakobson, Roman.
Rudy, Willis, jt. auth. see Brubacher, John S.
Rudzitis, Gundars. Residential Location Determinants of the Older Population. LC 82-10966. (Research Papers Ser.: No. 202). (Illus.). 117p. 1982. pap. text ed. 8.00 (ISBN 0-89065-107-8). U Chicago Dept Geog.
Rue, jt. auth. see Terry.
Rue, James & Shanahan, Louise. Daddy's Girl, Mama's Boy. 1979. pap. 2.25 o.p. (ISBN 0-451-08822-0, E8822, Sig). NAL.
Rue, James J. & Shanahan, Louise. A Catechism for Divorced Catholics. rev. ed. 1978. pap. 2.95 o.p. (ISBN 0-8199-0754-5). Franciscan Herald.
--Daddy's Girl, Mama's Boy. LC 77-15435. 1978. 8.95 o.p. (ISBN 0-672-52348-5). Bobbs.
Rue, Leonard L. World of the White-Tailed Deer. LC 62-11348. (Living World Book Ser). 1962. 12.45i (ISBN 0-397-00254-8). Har-Row.
Rue, Leonard L., III. Pictorial Guide to the Mammals of North America. (Apollo Eds.). (Illus.). 1977. pap. 7.95i (ISBN 0-8152-0420-5, A-420). T Y Crowell.
Rue, Leonard L., 3rd. Pictorial Guide to the Birds of North America. LC 73-109905. 1970. 14.37i (ISBN 0-690-62158-2). T Y Crowell.
--The World of the Ruffled Grouse. Terres, John, ed. LC 72-748. (Living World Bks). (Illus.). 291p. 1972. 11.49i (ISBN 0-397-00817-1). Har-Row.
Rue, Leslie W., jt. auth. see Terry, George R.
Rue, Roger L. Circumnavigating Vancouver Island. 1982. pap. 10.00 (ISBN 0-9609036-0-7). Evergreen Pacific.
Ruebner, Boris H. & Montgomery, Carolyn K. Pathology of the Liver & Biliary Tract. (Surgical Pathology Monograph Ser.). 368p. 1982. 39.50x (ISBN 0-471-02453-8, Pub. by Wiley Med). Wiley.
Ruecker, Norbert & Siedhoff, Thomas. Subject Catalog Film. 385p. 1983. price not set (ISBN 3-598-10414-6). K G Saur.
Rueckert, William H. Kenneth Burke & the Drama of Human Relations. 2nd ed. 310p. 1982. 14.95x (ISBN 0-520-03199-7); pap. 5.95 (ISBN 0-520-04417-7, CAL 514). U of Cal Pr.
Rueda, Enrique. Homosexual Network: Private Lives & Public Policy. 740p. 1983. 24.95 (ISBN 0-8159-5715-7); pap. 11.95 (ISBN 0-8159-5714-9). Devin.
Ruedisili, Lon C. & Firebaugh, Morris, eds. Perspectives on Energy: Issues, Ideas, & Environmental Dilemmas. 3rd ed. (Illus.). 1982. pap. text ed. 16.95x (ISBN 0-19-503038-9); cloth 24.95x (ISBN 0-19-503289-6). Oxford U Pr.
Ruedisili, Lon C. & Firebaugh, Morris W., eds. Perspectives on Energy: Issues, Ideas, & Environmental Dilemmas. 2nd ed. (Illus.). 1978. pap. text ed. 12.95x o.p. (ISBN 0-19-502341-2). Oxford U Pr.
Ruedisueli, Kevin. Making Your Place a Home. LC 76-56574. (Orig.). 1977. pap. 6.95 o.p. (ISBN 0-8256-3068-1, Quick Fox). Putnam Pub Group.
Rueff, Marcel & Jeger, Max. Sets & Boolean Algebra. (Mathematical Studies: Vol. 4). 1971. 19.95 o.p. (ISBN 0-444-19751-6). Elsevier.
Ruehl, Lothar. La Politique Militaire De la Cinquieme Republique. (Cahiers Ser.: No. 193). (Fr.). 1977. lib. bdg. 27.50x o.p. (ISBN 2-7246-0351-6, Pub by Presses de la Fondation Nationale des Sciences Politiques); pap. text ed. 19.00 o.p. (ISBN 2-7246-0328-1). Clearwater Pub.
Ruehl, P. W., jt. auth. see Tustison, F. E.
Ruehlmann, William. Stalking the Feature Story: How to Get & Write the Facts on the People, Places & Events that Make the News. LC 78-11265. pap. 5.95 (ISBN 0-394-72849-1, Vin). Random.
Ruel, O. J., ed. see National Radio Institute Staff.
Ruel, Oliver J., jt. auth. see Nolte, Robert C.
Ruelle, David. Thermodynamic Formalism: The Mathematical Structures of Classical Equilibrium Statistical Mechanics. LC 78-6756. (Encyclopedia of Mathematics & Its Applications: Vol. 5). (Illus.). 1978. text ed. 28.50 (ISBN 0-201-13504-3, Adv Bk Prog). A-W.
Ruesch, Hans. Naked Empress: Or the Great Medical Fraud. (Illus.). 202p. 1983. 9.95 (ISBN 0-686-38944-1, Pub. by Civis Switzerland). Civitas.
Ruesch, Jurgen & Kees, Weldon. Nonverbal Communication: Notes on the Visual Perception of Human Relations. 1956. 19.95x o.p. (ISBN 0-520-01100-7); pap. 6.95 (ISBN 0-520-02162-2, CAL243). U of Cal Pr.
Rueschhoff, Phil H. & Swartz, M. Evelyn. Teaching Art in the Elementary School: Enhancing Visual Perception. (Illus.). 1969. 26.95 (ISBN 0-471-06879-9). Wiley.
Ruesck, H., et al. Creep & Shrinkage: Their Effect on the Behavior of Concrete Structures. (Illus.). 304p. 1983. 60.00 (ISBN 0-387-90669-X). Springer-Verlag.
Rueter, Theodore, jt. auth. see Bitzer, Lloyd.
Ruether, Rosemary & McLaughlin, Eleanor. Women of Spirit. 1979. pap. 9.50 (ISBN 0-671-24805-7, Touchstone Bks). S&S.
Ruether, Rosemary R. Mary--the Feminine Face of the Church. LC 77-7652. (Illus.). 1977. pap. 4.50 (ISBN 0-664-24759-8). Westminster.
--New Woman-New Earth: Sexist Ideologies & Human Liberation. 255p. 1978. pap. 7.95 (ISBN 0-8164-2185-4). Seabury.
--Sexism & God Talk: Toward a Feminist Theology. LC 82-72502. 192p. 1983. 12.98 (ISBN 0-8070-1104-5). Beacon Pr.
--To Change the World: Christology & Cultural Criticism. 96p. 1983. pap. 5.95 (ISBN 0-8245-0573-5). Crossroad NY.
Ruettgers, H., ed. Trichomoniasis. (Journal: Gynaekologische Rundschau: Vol. 22, Supplement 2). (Illus.). iv, 88p. 1983. pap. 17.00 (ISBN 3-8055-3646-1). S Karger.
Ruey, M. J. A La Carte Enterprises: Office Manual. 1976. text ed. 6.40 (ISBN 0-07-054266-X, G); instr's manual 7.15 (ISBN 0-07-054267-8). McGraw.
Ruf, Henry L. Moral Investigations: An Introduction to Current Moral Problems. 1977. pap. text ed. 9.75 (ISBN 0-8191-0300-4). U Pr of Amer.
Rufer, Joseph. Composition with Twelve Notes Related Only to One Another. rev. ed. LC 78-9838. (Illus.). 1979. Repr. of 1954 ed. lib. bdg. 18.75x (ISBN 0-313-21236-8, RUCT). Greenwood.
Ruff, Loren K. Edward Sheldon. (United States Authors Ser.). 1982. lib. bdg. 14.95 (ISBN 0-8057-7331-2, Twayne). G K Hall.
Ruff, Peter. Olivia Newton-John. 1979. pap. 4.95 (ISBN 0-8256-3934-4, Quick Fox). Putnam Pub Group.
Ruffa, Anthony. Darwinism & Determinism: The Role of Direction in Evolution. 1983. 15.50 (ISBN 0-8283-1732-1); pap. 9.50 (ISBN 0-8283-1877-8). Branden.
Ruffell, Ann. Blood Brothers. LC 80-80538. (gr. 7 up). 1980. PLB 7.90 (ISBN 0-531-04177-8). Watts.
Ruffin, Roy J & Gregory, Paul. Principles of Economics. 1983. text ed. 25.95x (ISBN 0-673-15508-0). Scott F.
--Principles of Macroeconomics. 1982. pap. text ed. 15.95x (ISBN 0-673-15856-X). Scott F.
--Principles of Microeconomics. 1982. pap. text ed. 15.95x (ISBN 0-673-15857-8). Scott F.
Ruffini, Julio L., jt. ed. see Todd, Harry F.
Ruffini, R., jt. auth. see Giacconi.
Ruffini, R., ed. General Relativity. Date not set. 136.50 (ISBN 0-444-86357-5). Elsevier.
Ruffner, Budge, jt. auth. see Weiner, Melissa R.
Ruffner, Frederick G., Jr. & Thomas, Robert C., eds. Code Names Dictionary: A Guide to Code Names, Slang, Nicknames, Journalese, & Similar Terms. LC 63-21847. 1963. 38.00x (ISBN 0-8103-0685-9). Gale.
Ruffner, James & Bair, Frank, eds. Weather Almanac: A Reference Guide to Weather & Climate of the United States & Its Key Cities. 3rd ed. (Illus.). 700p. 1981. 65.00x (ISBN 0-8103-1053-8). Gale.
Ruffner, James, et al, eds. Eponyms Dictionaries Index: A Compilation of Terms Based on Names of Actual or Legendary Persons. LC 76-20341. 1977. 98.00x (ISBN 0-8103-0688-3). Gale.
Ruffner, James A., ed. Climates of the States, 2 vols. 2nd ed. LC 76-11672. (Illus.). 1200p. 1980. 128.00x (ISBN 0-8103-1036-8). Gale.
Ruffner, James A. & Bair, Frank E., eds. Weather of the United States Cities, 2 vols. LC 80-22694. (Illus.). 1100p. 1981. 95.00x set (ISBN 0-8103-1034-1). Gale.
Ruffner, James A., jt. ed. see Thomas, Robert C.
Ruffner, Tacey. Americana Articles. (Illus.). 138p. 1983. pap. 9.95 (ISBN 0-9610424-0-0). T Ruffner.
Ruffo-Fiore, Silvia. Niccolo Machiavelli. (World Authors Ser.). 1982. lib. bdg. 14.95 (ISBN 0-8057-6499-2, Twayne). G K Hall.
Rufsuold, Margaret. Guides to Educational Media. 4th ed. LC 77-5058. 1977. 6.00 (ISBN 0-8389-0232-4). ALA.
Rugg, Donald D. & Hale, Norman B. The Dow Jones-Irwin Guide to Mutual Funds. Rev. ed. LC 82-71381. 1982. 17.50 (ISBN 0-87094-352-9). Dow Jones-Irwin.
Rugg, Frederick E. Rugg's Recommendations on the Colleges. 2nd ed. LC 80-112292. 60p. 1984. pap. 6.95 (ISBN 0-686-32945-7). Whitebrook Bks.
Rugg, Tom & Feldman, Phil. Thirty Two Basic Programs for the TRS-80: Level II. 1980. write for info. Dilithium Pr.

Rugg, Tom, et al. More Than Thirty-Two BASIC Programs for the VIC Computer. 270p. 1983. pap. 19.95 (ISBN 0-88056-059-2). Dilithium Pr.

Rugge, John, jt. auth. see Davidson, James W.

Rugg-Gunn, A. J., jt. auth. see Murray, J. J.

Ruggieri, George D., jt. ed. see Baiardi, John C.

Ruggiero, Guido. Violence in Early Renaissance Venice. 1980. 25.00 (ISBN 0-8135-0894-0). Rutgers U Pr.

Ruggles, Joanne, jt. auth. see Ruggles, Philip.

Ruggles, Philip & Ruggles, Joanne. Darkroom Graphics. 1975. 14.95 o.p. (ISBN 0-8174-0573-9, Amphoto). Watson-Guptill.

Ruggles, Philip K. Printing Estimating. LC 79-13008. 1979. text ed. 23.95 (ISBN 0-534-00747-3, Breton Pubs). Wadsworth Pub.

Rugh, Roberts, et al. From Conception to Birth: The Drama of Life's Beginnings. LC 77-96803. (Illus.). 1971. 20.14i (ISBN 0-06-013728-2, HarpT). Har-Row.

Rugheimer, E. & Wawersik, J., eds. Anaesthesiology: Abstracts of Hamburg Meeting, Sept. 1980. (International Congress Ser.: No. 533). 1980. 79.75 (ISBN 0-444-90176-0). Elsevier.

Rugman, Alan M., ed. New Theories of the Multinational Enterprise. LC 82-6003. 1982. 27.50x (ISBN 0-312-57245-X). St Martin.

Ruhe, Robert. Geomorphology: Geomorphic Processor & Surficial Geology. 1975. text ed. 27.95 (ISBN 0-395-18553-X). HM.

Ruhl, Kathleen. Universal Supplementary Exercisebook. 1981. pap. text ed. 8.95x (ISBN 0-673-15453-X). Scott F.

--Universal Supplementary Exercisebook (U. S. E.) Form B. 1983. pap. text ed. 10.95x (ISBN 0-673-15619-2). Scott F.

Ruhloff, Jorg. Aufwachsen Im Fremden Land. 209p. (Ger.). 1982. write for info. (ISBN 3-8204-5847-6). P Lang Pubs.

Ruhm, Herbert, ed. see James, Henry.

Ruhm von Oppen, Beate, tr. see Adenauer, Konrad.

Ruhnau, Helen E. Drama of Patmos Initiations of John. LC 82-71052. 1982. pap. 10.95 soft cover (ISBN 0-941036-07-3). Colleasius Pr.

Ruhnau, Helena E. Journeys into the Fifth Dimension. LC 75-149286. (Illus.). 1975. 9.95 (ISBN 0-941036-02-2). Colleasius Pr.

--Key to the Golden Door. LC 81-90336. (Illus.). 1982. softcover 7.95 (ISBN 0-941036-06-5). Colleasius Pr.

--Light from the Fifth Dimension. LC 79-149287. (Illus.). 1981. softcover 9.95 (ISBN 0-941036-05-7). Colleasius Pr.

--Light on a Mountain. (Illus.). 1975. 8.95 (ISBN 0-941036-00-6); pap. 5.50 (ISBN 0-941036-01-4). Colleasius Pr.

--Mirror of a Soul. LC 81-67864. (Illus.). 1981. pap. 5.95x (ISBN 0-941036-04-9). Colleasius Pr.

--Reappearance of the Dove. LC 75-27625. (Illus.). 1978. 9.95 (ISBN 0-941036-03-0). Colleasius Pr.

Ruhnke, L. H. & Deepak, A. Hygroscopic Aerosols in the Planetary Boundary Layer. (Illus.). Date not set. price not set (ISBN 0-937194-02-6). Spectrum Pr.

Ruivo, Mario, ed. Marine Pollution & Sea Life. (Illus.). 624p. 1973. 75.00 (ISBN 0-85238-021-6, FN57, FNB). Unipub.

Ruiz, H. & Pavon, J. Florae Peruvianae & Chilensis Prodromus. (Illus.). 1965. Repr. of 1794 ed. 80.00 (ISBN 3-7682-0282-8). Lubrecht & Cramer.

--Prodromus et Flora Peruviana et Chilensis, 4 vols. in 1. (Illus.). 1965. Repr. of 1802 ed. 240.00 (ISBN 3-7682-0283-6). Lubrecht & Cramer.

Ruiz, Hugo. Hermanos, Ahora Cartas del Diablo. 64p. 1981. pap. 1.35 (ISBN 0-311-46045-3). Casa Bautista.

Ruiz, Juan. The Book of the Archpriest of Hita (Libo de buen amor) Singleton, Mack, tr. x, 182p. 1975. 7.50 (ISBN 0-942260-06-6). Hispanic Seminary.

--The Book of True Love: Bilingual Edition. Zahareas, Anthony N., ed. Daly, Saralyn R., tr. from Span. & intro. by. LC 77-12820. 1978. 22.50 (ISBN 0-271-00523-8); pap. text ed. 12.00x (ISBN 0-271-00545-9). Pa St U Pr.

Ruiz, Pedro, jt. auth. see Lowinson, Joyce.

Ruiz, Ramon E. Cuba: The Making of a Revolution. 1970. pap. 4.95x (ISBN 0-393-00513-5, N513, Norton Lib). Norton.

Ruiz, Stacey L., jt. ed. see Anderson, Kenneth R.

Ruiz-Fornells, Enrique, jt. auth. see Chatham, James R.

Ruiz-Salvador, Antonio, jt. auth. see Jones, Sonia.

Rukert, Norman G. The Fells Point Story. LC 75-40655. (Illus.). 1976. 8.95 o.p. (ISBN 0-910254-11-7). Bodine.

--Historic Canton. (Illus.). 103p. 1978. pap. 4.95 (ISBN 0-686-36509-7). Md Hist.

--The Port: Pride of Baltimore History. (Illus.). 192p. 1982. 16.95 (ISBN 0-910254-17-6); pap. 9.95. Bodine.

Rukeyser, Louis. How to Make Money in Wall Street. LC 73-14055. 288p. 1974. 7.95 (ISBN 0-385-07505-7); pap. 6.95 (ISBN 0-385-04652-9, Dolp). Doubleday.

Rukeyser, Muriel. Gates. LC 76-20738. 1976. 7.95 (ISBN 0-07-054268-6, GB); pap. 4.95 (ISBN 0-07-054269-4). McGraw.

--More Night. LC 79-2680. (Illus.). 32p. (gr. k-3). 1981. 8.95i o.p. (ISBN 0-06-025127-1, HarpJ); PLB 8.79g (ISBN 0-06-025128-X). Har-Row.

Rukowski, George B., jt. auth. see Oleksy, Jerome E.

Rule, Ann. Possession: A Novel. 1983. 15.50 (ISBN 0-393-01641-2). Norton.

--The Stranger Beside Me. (Illus.). 1981. pap. 3.95 (ISBN 0-451-12169-4, AE2169, Sig). NAL.

Rule, James, et al. The Politics of Privacy. (Orig.). 1980. pap. 2.50 o.p. (ISBN 0-451-61829-7, ME, Ment). NAL.

Rule, James B. Insight & Social Betterment: A Preface to Applied Social Science. 1978. text ed. 13.95x (ISBN 0-19-502392-7); pap. text ed. 6.95x (ISBN 0-19-502393-5). Oxford U Pr.

Rule, Jane. Lesbian Images. 250p. 1982. 15.95 (ISBN 0-89594-089-2); pap. 6.95 (ISBN 0-89594-088-4). Crossing Pr.

Rule, John. The Experience of Labour in Eighteenth Century Industry. 1980. 26.00 (ISBN 0-312-27664-8). St Martin.

Rule, Wilfred P. FORTRAN Seventy-Seven: A Practical Approach. 448p. 1983. text ed. write for info. (ISBN 0-87150-390-5, 8030). Prindle.

--Programcion FORTRAN IV. (Orig.). 1976. text ed. 10.50x o.p. (ISBN 0-06-316996-7, IntlDept). Har-Row.

Ruley, M. J. Practical Metal Projects. (gr. 9 up). text ed. 15.28 (ISBN 0-87345-137-6). McKnight.

--Projects in General Metalwork. (gr. 9 up). 1969. text ed. 15.28 (ISBN 0-87345-135-X). McKnight.

Ruley, M. J., jt. auth. see McGinnis, Harry.

Rulfo, Juan. The Burning Plain & Other Stories. Schade, George D., tr. from Sp. LC 67-25698. (Texas Pan American Ser.). (Illus.). 191p. 1967. 10.00x (ISBN 0-292-73685-1); pap. 6.95x (ISBN 0-292-70132-2). U of Tex Pr.

--Pedro Paramo: A Novel of Mexico. Kemp, Lysander, tr. from Spanish. 1959. pap. 2.45 (ISBN 0-394-17446-1, B207, BC). Grove.

Rullo. Standard Mangers Manual. Date not set. cancelled (ISBN 0-89433-000-4); pap. cancelled (ISBN 0-89433-018-7). Petrocelli.

Rullo, Thomas A., ed. Advances in Computer Programming Management, Vol. 1. 238p. 1980. 29.95 (ISBN 0-471-25995-0, Pub. by Wiley Heyden). Wiley.

--Advances in Computer Security Management, Vol. 1. 225p. 1980. 29.95 (ISBN 0-471-25999-3, Pub. by Wiley Heyden). Wiley.

--Advances in Data Base Management, Vol. 1. 230p. 1980. 29.95 (ISBN 0-471-25994-2, Pub. by Wiley Heyden). Wiley.

--Advances in Data Communications Management, Vol. 1. 225p. 1980. 29.95 (ISBN 0-471-25998-5, Pub. by Wiley Heyden). Wiley.

--Advances in Distributed Processing Management, Vol. 1. 225p. 1980. 29.95 (ISBN 0-471-25997-7, Pub. by Wiley Heyden). Wiley.

Ruloff, Dieter, jt. auth. see Frei, Daniel.

Rumack, Barry H., jt. ed. see Bayer, Marc J.

Rumaker, Michael. My First Satyrnalia. LC 81-1489. 200p. 1981. 12.95 o.p. (ISBN 0-912516-51-8); pap. 6.95 (ISBN 0-912516-50-X). Grey Fox.

Rumbelow, Donald. The Complete Jack the Ripper. 1976. pap. 1.95 o.p. (ISBN 0-451-07148-4, J7148, Sig). NAL.

Rumbelow, Donald, jt. auth. see Hindley, Judy.

Rumble, Greville & Harry, Keith, eds. The Distance Teaching University. LC 82-42559. 1982. 25.00x (ISBN 0-312-21323-9). St Martin.

Rumelhart, D. E. Introduction to Human Information Processing. 306p. 1977. text ed. 24.50 (ISBN 0-471-74500-6). Wiley.

Rumens, Carol. Star Whisper. 72p. 1983. 13.95 (ISBN 0-436-43901-8, Pub. by Secker & Warburg). David & Charles.

--Unplayed Music. 1981. 11.50 (ISBN 0-436-43900-X, Pub. by Secker & Warburg). David & Charles.

Rumford, Beatrix T., ed. The Abby Aldrich Rockefeller Art Collection. LC 75-36926. (Illus.). 31p. (Orig.). 1975. pap. 2.00 (ISBN 0-87935-033-4). Williamsburg.

Rumford, Benjamin T. Collected Works of Count Rumford, 5 vols. Brown, Sanborn C., ed. Incl. Vol. 1. Nature of Heat. (Illus.). xiv, 507p. 1968 (ISBN 0-674-13951-8); Vol. 2. Practical Applications of Heat. (Illus.). x, 533p. 1969 (ISBN 0-674-13952-6); Vol. 3. Devices & Techniques. (Illus.). x, 514p. 1969. o.p. (ISBN 0-674-13953-4); Vol. 4. Light & Armament. (Illus.). viii, 511p. 1970 (ISBN 0-674-13954-2); Vol. 5. Public Institutions. (Illus.). xii, 524p. 1970 (ISBN 0-674-13955-0). LC 68-17633. 25.00x ea. (Belknap Pr). Harvard U Pr.

--Memoires Sur la Chaleur. Repr. of 1804 ed. 71.00 o.p. (ISBN 0-8287-0745-6). Clearwater Pub.

--Recherches Sur la Chaleur Developpee Dans la Combustion, et Dans la Condensation Des Vapeurs. Repr. of 1812 ed. 38.00 o.p. (ISBN 0-8287-0746-4). Clearwater Pub.

Rumi. Night & Sleep. Barks, Coleman & Bly, Robert, trs. from Persian. (Illus.). 48p. 1981. signed handsewn edition 35.00 (ISBN 0-938756-01-X); pap. 6.00 (ISBN 0-938756-02-8). Yellow Moon.

Rumi, Jalal A. Mystical Poems of Rumi: Second Selection, Poems 201-400, Vol.34. Arberry, A. J., tr. LC 79-5101. (Persian Heritage Ser.). 200p. 1983. 25.00x (ISBN 0-89158-477-3). Caravan Bks.

Rumi, Jalal Al-Din. Rumi: Mystical Poems: Poems 201-400. Arberry, A. J., tr. (Bibliotheca Persica: Persian Heritage Ser.: No. 23). 1979. lib. bdg. 23.75x o.p. (ISBN 0-89158-477-3). Westview.

Rumke, Ph, jt. ed. see Boclima, E.

Rummel, W., jt. ed. see Forth, W.

Rump, Ariane & Wing-Tsit Chan, trs. Commentary on the Lao Tzu by Wang Pi. LC 79-11212. (Society for Asian & Comparative Philosophy Monograph: No. 6). 1979. pap. text ed. 6.00x (ISBN 0-8248-0677-8). UH Pr.

Rumpf, Betty. Papier Mache. LC 72-13343. (Early Craft Bks.). (Illus.). 36p. (gr. 1-4). 1974. PLB 3.95g (ISBN 0-8225-0858-3). Lerner Pubns.

Rumscheidt, Martin, ed. Footnotes to a Theology: The Karl Barth Colloquim of 1972. 151p. 1974. pap. text ed. 5.25x (ISBN 0-919812-02-3, Pub. by Laurier U Pr). Humanities.

Rumsey, Helen, jt. auth. see Clure, Beth.

Rumsey, Marian. Carolina Hurricane. LC 77-5622. (Illus.). (gr. 3-7). 1977. 9.50 (ISBN 0-688-22128-9); PLB 9.12 (ISBN 0-688-32128-3). Morrow.

--Lion on the Run. LC 72-7880. (Illus.). 160p. (gr. 3-7). 1973. 9.50 (ISBN 0-688-21770-2); PLB 9.12 (ISBN 0-688-31770-7). Morrow.

Runciman, S. The Byzantine Theocracy. LC 76-47405. (Weil Lectures Ser.). 1977. 27.95 (ISBN 0-521-21401-7). Cambridge U Pr.

Runciman, Steven. Byzantine Civilization. 1933. 18.75 o.p. (ISBN 0-312-11165-7). St Martin.

--Fall of Constantinople, Fourteen Fifty-Three. LC 65-10383. (Illus.). 1969. 32.50 o.p. (ISBN 0-521-06165-2); pap. 11.95 (ISBN 0-521-09573-5). Cambridge U Pr.

--Great Church in Captivity. LC 68-29330. 1968. 47.50 (ISBN 0-521-07188-7). Cambridge U Pr.

--History of the Crusades, 3 vols. 69.50 (ISBN 0-521-06161-X); Vol. 2. 74.50 (ISBN 0-521-06162-8); Vol. 3. 74.50 (ISBN 0-521-06163-6); 190.00 (ISBN 0-521-20554-9). Cambridge U Pr.

--The Medieval Manichee: A Study of the Christian Dualist Heresy. LC 82-4123. 224p. 1982. 34.50 (ISBN 0-521-06166-0); pap. 10.95 (ISBN 0-521-28926-2). Cambridge U Pr.

--Sicilian Vespers. 1958. 42.50 (ISBN 0-521-06167-9). Cambridge U Pr.

Runciman, W. G. Relative Deprivation & Social Justice. (Reports of the Institute of Community Studies). 1980. Repr. pap. 38.50x (ISBN 0-7100-3923-9). Routledge & Kegan.

--A Treatise on Social Theory, Vol. 1. LC 82-4493. (Illus.). 400p. Date not set. price not set (ISBN 0-521-24906-6). Cambridge U Pr.

Runciman, Walter G. A Critique of Max Weber's Philosophy of Social Science. LC 78-174257. 96p. 1972. 13.95 (ISBN 0-521-08411-3). Cambridge U Pr.

--Social Science & Political Theory. 1963. 19.95 o.p. (ISBN 0-521-07474-6); pap. 8.95x (ISBN 0-521-09562-X, 562). Cambridge U Pr.

--Sociology in Its Place & Other Essays. 1970. 24.95 (ISBN 0-521-07905-5). Cambridge U Pr.

Runciman, Walter G., ed. Max Weber: Selections in Translation. Matthews, E., tr. LC 77-80846. 1978. 42.50 (ISBN 0-521-21757-1); pap. 10.95 (ISBN 0-521-29268-9). Cambridge U Pr.

Runck, Bette, et al. Families Today: A Research Sampler on Families & Children, 2 vols. LC 79-66976. (Science Monographs: No. 1). (Illus., Orig.). 1980. Vol. 1. pap. 10.00 (ISBN 0-686-27076-2); Vol. 2. pap. 9.50 (ISBN 0-686-27077-0). Gov Printing Office.

Runcorn, S. K., jt. auth. see Rosenberg, G. D.

Runcorn, S. K., ed. Continental Drift. (International Geophysics Ser: Vol. 3). 1962. 61.00 (ISBN 0-12-602450-2). Acad Pr.

Runcorn, S. K., ed. see Royal Institution Library of Science.

Runcorn, S. K., ed. see Royal Society Discussion Meeting, January 27-28, 1982, Proceedings.

Runcorn, S. K., jt. ed. see Tarling, D. H.

Rund, Douglas A. & Rausch, Tondra S. Triage. LC 80-26477. (Illus.). 255p. 1981. pap. text ed. 15.95 (ISBN 0-8016-4221-3). Mosby.

Rund, Douglas A., jt. auth. see Mueller, Charles F.

Rund, Hanno. The Hamilton-Jacobi Theory in the Calculus of Variations: Its Role in Mathematics Theory & Application. LC 66-13030. 452p. 1973. Repr. of 1966 ed. 25.00 (ISBN 0-88275-063-1). Krieger.

Rundall, Thomas G., jt. ed. see Battistella, Roger M.

Rundback, Betty & Ackerman, Nancy. Bed & Breakfast U. S. A. A Guide to Tourist Homes & Guest Houses. rev. ed. (Illus.). 256p. 1983. pap. 5.95 (ISBN 0-525-93277-1, 0577-180). Dutton.

Rundell, Walter, Jr. Black-Market Money: The Collapse of U. S. Military Currency Control in World War 2. LC 64-15879. 1964. 10.00x o.p. (ISBN 0-8071-0725-5). La State U Pr.

Rundle, Paul A. & Swenson, Philip R. Personal Financial Planning for Physicians & Dentists. (Fin. Ser.). (Illus.). 268p. 1982. 27.50 (ISBN 0-534-97944-0). Lifetime Learn.

Rundle, R. N. International Affairs, Nineteen Thirty-Nine to Nineteen Seventy-Nine. (Illus.). 192p. 1982. pap. text ed. 14.50x (ISBN 0-8419-0678-5); 22.50x. Holmes & Meier.

Rundquist, Barry S., ed. Political Benefits: Empirical Studies of American Public Programs. LC 78-19542. 288p. 1980. 28.95x (ISBN 0-669-02509-7). Lexington Bks.

Runes, Dagobert & Schrickey, Harry G., eds. Encyclopedia of the Arts, 2 vols. 1982. Repr. of 1946 ed. Set. 68.00x (ISBN 0-8103-4162-X). Gale.

Runes, Dagobert D. Bible for the Liberal. 1946. 3.50 o.p. (ISBN 0-8022-1424-X). Philos Lib.

Runes, Dagobert D., ed. Dictionary of Philosophy. rev., enl. ed. LC 81-80240. 400p. 1983. Repr. 25.00 (ISBN 0-8022-2388-5). Philos Lib.

--Lost Legends of Israel. LC 61-7749. 1961. 4.75 o.p. (ISBN 0-8022-1443-6). Philos Lib.

Runge, Senta M. Face Lifting by Exercise. 9th ed. LC 56-6321. (Illus.). 1977. Repr. of 1961 ed. 18.00 (ISBN 0-9601042-1-6). Allegro Pub.

Runge, William, ed. see Berkeley, Henry R.

Rungeling, Brian, et al. Employment, Income, & Welfare in the Rural South. LC 77-10612. (Praeger Special Studies). 1977. 38.95 o.p. (ISBN 0-03-023041-1). Praeger.

Rungta, Radhe S. Rise of Business Corporations in India, 1851-1900. LC 69-10573. (South Asian Studies: No. 8). (Illus.). 1970. 37.50 (ISBN 0-521-07354-5). Cambridge U Pr.

Runk, Wesley T. Object Lessons for Christian Growth. (Object Lessons Ser.). Orig. Title: Growing up in God. 104p. 1974. pap. 2.50 o.p. (ISBN 0-8010-7629-3). Baker Bk.

Runkel, Sylvian, jt. auth. see Bull, Alvin.

Runkle, Gerald. A History of Western Political Theory. LC 68-21652. 668p. 1968. 27.50 (ISBN 0-471-07060-2). Wiley.

Runkle, Sylvian, jt. auth. see Bull, Alvin.

Runner Magazine. The Runners: How the Champions Train, Race & Persevered-a Success Formula for All Runners. (Orig.). 1979. pap. 2.75 o.s.i. (ISBN 0-515-05857-2). Jove Pubns.

Running Press. A Woman's Notebook III: Being a Blank Book with Quotes by Women. (Illus.). 96p. (Orig.). 1983. lib. bdg. 12.90 (ISBN 0-89471-211-X); pap. 4.95 (ISBN 0-89471-210-1). Running Pr.

Runser, Dennis J. Maintaining & Troubleshooting HPLC Systems: A Users Guide. LC 80-25444. 163p. 1981. 33.00 (ISBN 0-471-06479-3, Pub. by Wiley-Interscience). Wiley.

Runswick, H. Health Education: Practical Teaching Techniques. (Topics in Community Health). 120p. 1975. text ed. 9.95 (ISBN 0-471-26003-7, Pub. by Wiley Med). Wiley.

Runte, Hans, jt. ed. see Niedzielski, Henri.

Runyan, John W. Problem Oriented Primary Care. 2nd ed. (Illus.). 358p. 1982. pap. text ed. 17.50 (ISBN 0-06-142305-X, Harper Medical). Lippincott.

Runyan, Walter R. Semiconductor Measurements & Instrumentation. (Texas Instruments Electronics Ser.). (Illus.). 320p. 1975. 49.50 (ISBN 0-07-054273-2, P&RB). McGraw.

Runyan, William M. Life Histories & Psychobiography: Explorations in Theory & Method. (Illus.). 304p. 1982. 19.95 (ISBN 0-19-503189-X). Oxford U Pr.

Runyon. Consumer Behavior. 2nd ed. (Marketing & Management Ser.). 504p. 1980. text ed. 23.95 (ISBN 0-675-08159-9). Additional supplements may be obtained from publisher. Merrill.

Runyon, Catherine. All Wrong Mrs. Bear. (Illus.). (ps-2). 1972. pap. 2.50 (ISBN 0-8024-0140-6). Moody.

--Too Soon, Mr. Bear. LC 79-23404. (ps-5). 1979. pap. 1.95 (ISBN 0-8024-8788-2). Moody.

Runyon, Catherine, jt. auth. see Cohen, Gary G.

Runyon, Charles W. Soulmate. 1974. pap. 0.95 o.p. (ISBN 0-380-01560-9, 180286). Avon.

Runyon, Damon. A Treasury of Damon Runyon. LC 58-6363. Date not set. 6.95 (ISBN 0-394-60444-X). Modern Lib.

Runyon, Kenneth. The Practice of Marketing. 608p. 1982. text ed. 24.95 (ISBN 0-675-09886-6); study guide 9.95 (ISBN 0-675-09865-3). Additional supplements may be obtained from publisher. Merrill.

Runyon, Kenneth E. Advertising & the Practice of Marketing. (Marketing & Management Ser.). 1979. text ed. 26.95 (ISBN 0-675-08311-7). Additional supplements may be obtained from publisher. Merrill.

Runyon, R. & Haber, A. Fundamentals of Behavioral Statistics. 4th ed. 1980. 19.95 (ISBN 0-201-06375-1); write for info. (ISBN 0-201-06378-6); students' wkbk. 5.95 (ISBN 0-201-06376-X); test item booklet 2.50 (ISBN 0-201-06377-8); PSI study guide 6.95 (ISBN 0-201-06633-5); PSI instrs manual 2.75 (ISBN 0-201-06632-7). A-W.

Runyon, Richard, jt. auth. see Rocks, Lawrence E.

Runyon, Richard P. How Numbers Lie: A Consumer's Guide to the Fine Art of Numerical Deception. (Illus.). 192p. 1981. 12.95 o.s.i. (ISBN 0-86616-000-0); pap. 7.95 (ISBN 0-86616-001-9). Lewis Pub Co.

Runyon, Richard P., jt. auth. see Haber, Audrey.

Ruocchio, Albert C. & Klein, Maury D. Track Layout & Accessory Manual for Lionel Trains. (Illus.). 1979. pap. 2.60 saddle-stitched (ISBN 0-934580-08-1, K-4). MDK Inc.

Ruoff, Arthur L. Introduction to Materials Science. LC 79-4668. 718p. 1979. Repr. of 1972 ed. lib. bdg. 33.00 (ISBN 0-88275-960-4). Krieger.

Ruoslahti, E. Immunoadsorbents in Protein Purification. (Illus.). 96p. 1976. text ed. 29.50 o.p. (ISBN 0-8391-0924-5). Univ Park.

Ruotolo, Andrew K. Once Upon a Murder. (Illus.). 1979. 10.00 o.p. (ISBN 0-448-14652-5, G&D). Putnam Pub Group.

Ruo-Wang, Bao & Chelminski, Rudolph. Prisoner of Mao. 1976. pap. 3.95 (ISBN 0-14-004112-5). Penguin.

Ruoxi, Chen, jt. auth. see Dittmer, Lowell.

Rupen, Robert A. Mongols of the Twentieth Century. LC 63-64522. (Uralic & Altaic Ser: Vol. 37-Pt. 2). (Orig.). 1964. Pt. 2. pap. text ed. 6.00x o.p. (ISBN 0-87750-062-2). Res Ctr Lang Semiotic.

Ruperti, Alexander. Cycles of Becoming: The Planetary Pattern of Growth. LC 77-84029. 1978. pap. 9.95 (ISBN 0-916360-07-5). CRCS Pubns NV.

Rupley & Blair. Reading Diagnosis & Direct Instruction: A Guide for the Classroom. pap. text ed. 10.95 (ISBN 0-686-84560-9, ET07). HM.

--Reading Diagnosis & Remediation: Classroom & Clinic. 1982. text ed. 24.95 (ISBN 0-686-84559-5, ET05). HM.

Rupley, William H. & Blair, Timothy R. Reading Diagnosis & Remediation. 1979. 30.95 (ISBN 0-395-30720-1); Tchrs Manual o.s. 0.65 (ISBN 0-395-30721-X). HM.

--Reading Diagnosis & Remediation: Classroom & Clinic. 2d ed. LC 82-83365. 496p. 1983. text ed. 23.95 (ISBN 0-395-32785-7); write for info. instr's. manual (ISBN 0-395-32786-5). HM.

Rupp, E. Gordon & Watson, Philip S., eds. Luther & Erasmus: Free Will & Salvation. LC 76-79870. (Library of Christian Classics). 1978. softcover 8.95 (ISBN 0-664-24158-1). Westminster.

Rupp, George H. A Wavering Friendship: Russia & Austria 1876-1878. LC 76-8455. (Perspectives in European History: No. 11). Repr. of 1941 ed. lib. bdg. 35.00x (ISBN 0-87991-617-6). Porcupine Pr.

Rupp, Kalman. Entrepreneurs in Red: Structure & Organizational Innovation in the Centrally Planned Economy. 288p. 1982. 39.50x (ISBN 0-87395-635-4); pap. 14.95x (ISBN 0-87395-636-2). State U NY Pr.

Rupp, R. F., jt. auth. see Wujek, E. D.

Ruppe, Harry O. Introduction to Astronautics, 2 Vols. 1967-68. 67.00 ea. Vol. 1 (ISBN 0-12-603101-0). Vol. 2 (ISBN 0-12-603102-9). 103.00 set (ISBN 0-686-57486-9). Acad Pr.

Ruppel, Gregg. Manual of Pulmonary Function Testing. 2nd ed. LC 78-21100. (Illus.). 162p. 1979. pap. text ed. 13.95 o.p. (ISBN 0-8016-4209-4). Mosby.

--Manual of Pulmonary Function Testing. 3rd ed. LC 82-6399. (Illus.). 198p. 1982. pap. text ed. 14.50 (ISBN 0-8016-4215-9). Mosby.

Ruppersburg, Hugh M. Voice & Eye in Faulkner's Fiction. LC 82-17347. 200p. 1983. text ed. 16.00x (ISBN 0-8203-0627-4). U of Ga Pr.

Ruppin, Arthur. The Jewish Fate & Future. Dickes, E. W., tr. LC 76-97300. (Illus.). 386p. 1972. Repr. of 1940 ed. lib. bdg. 17.75x (ISBN 0-8371-2628-2, RUJF). Greenwood.

--Three Decades of Palestine: Speeches & Papers on the Upbuilding of the Jewish National Home. LC 70-97301. (Illus.). 342p. 1975. Repr. of 1936 ed. lib. bdg. 17.75x (ISBN 0-8371-2629-0, RUPA). Greenwood.

Ruppli, Michel. The Savoy Label: A Discography. LC 79-7727. (Discographies: No. 2). (Illus.). 1980. lib. bdg. 35.00x (ISBN 0-313-21199-X, RUS/). Greenwood.

Ruppli, Michel, compiled by. Atlantic Records: A Discography, 4 vols. LC 78-75237. (Discographies: No. 1). 1979. lib. bdg. 125.00x set (ISBN 0-313-21170-1, RAL/). Greenwood.

--The Prestige Label: A Discography. LC 79-8294. (Discographies: No. 3). 1980. lib. bdg. 35.00x (ISBN 0-313-22019-0, RPL/). Greenwood.

Ruprecht, F. J. Phycologia Ochotiensis. Tange des ochotskischen Meeres, (from Middendorff's Sibirische Reise) (Illus.). 1978. Repr. of 1851 ed. lib. bdg. 60.00 (ISBN 3-7682-1184-3). Lubrecht & Cramer.

Ruprecht, F. J., jt. auth. see Postels, A.

Ruprecht, Theodore K. & Jewett, Frank I. The Micro-Economics of Demographic Change: Family Planning & Economic Well Being. LC 75-57. (Illus.). 176p. 1975. 29.95 o.p. (ISBN 0-275-05530-2). Praeger.

Rus, Teodor. Data Structures & Operating Systems. LC 77-3262. (Wiley Series in Computing). 1979. 53.95 (ISBN 0-471-99517-7, Pub. by Wiley-Interscience). Wiley.

Rusalem, Herbert. Coping with the Unseen Environment: An Introduction to the Vocational Rehabilitation of Blind Persons. LC 71-154476. 1972. text ed. 17.95x (ISBN 0-8077-2072-0). Tchrs Coll.

--Guiding the Physically Handicapped College Student. LC 62-14646. (Orig.). 1962. pap. text ed. 4.95x o.p. (ISBN 0-8077-2071-2). Tchrs Coll.

Rusbuldt, Richard E. Evangelism on Purpose. 48p. 1980. pap. 3.95 (ISBN 0-8170-0894-2). Judson.

Ruscello, Dennis M., jt. auth. see St. Louis, Kenneth O.

Rusch, W. V. & Potter, P. D. Analysis of Reflector Antennas. (Electrical Science Ser). 1970. 42.00 (ISBN 0-12-603450-8). Acad Pr.

Rusche, Larry. Popcorn. 5.95 (ISBN 0-89586-139-9). H P Bks.

Rusco, Elmer R. Good Time Coming? Black Nevadans in the Nineteenth Century. LC 75-16969. (Contributions in Afro-American & African Studies: No. 15). (Illus.). 230p. 1975. lib. bdg. 25.00x (ISBN 0-8371-8286-7, RGT/). Greenwood.

Ruscoe, James. On the Threshold of Government: The Italian Communist 1976-1981. LC 81-14622. 304p. 1982. 27.50x (ISBN 0-312-58457-1). St Martin.

Ruse, Michael. Nature Animated. 1983. 49.50 (ISBN 90-277-1403-7, Pub. by Reidel Holland). Kluwer Boston.

--The Philosophy of Biology. 231p. 1973. pap. text ed. 8.95x (ISBN 0-09-115220-8, Hutchinson U Lib); text ed. 7.50x o. p. (ISBN 0-09-115221-6). Humanities.

Rush, Allison. The Last of Danu's Children. (gr. 7 up). 1982. PLB 9.95 (ISBN 0-395-32270-7); 9.70. HM.

Rush, Anne K. The Basic Back Book. LC 79-15651. (Illus.). 1979. 17.95 o.p. (ISBN 0-671-40055-X); pap. 8.95 (ISBN 0-671-40086-X). Summit Bks.

--Getting Clear. 1973. pap. 7.95 (ISBN 0-394-70970-5). Random.

Rush, Anne K., jt. auth. see Mander, Anica V.

Rush, Benjamin. The Autobiography of Benjamin Rush: His Travels Through Life. Corner, George W., ed. Repr. of 1948 ed. lib. bdg. 20.75x (ISBN 0-8371-3037-9, RUAR). Greenwood.

Rush, Cathy & Mifflin, Lawrie. Women's Basketball. 1976. pap. 4.95 o.p. (ISBN 0-8015-8794-8, Hawthorn). Dutton.

Rush, Elizabeth. House at the End of the Lane. (Illus., Orig.). 1982. pap. 10.00 o.s.i. (ISBN 0-914676-64-4, Star & Eleph Bks). Green Tiger Pr.

Rush, James E. Toward a General Theory of Healing. LC 80-8264. (Illus.). 314p. (Orig.). 1982. lib. bdg. 24.00 (ISBN 0-8191-1880-X); pap. text ed. 12.75 (ISBN 0-8191-1881-8). U Pr of Amer.

Rush, James E., jt. auth. see Davis, Charles H.

Rush, Kenneth, ed. see Atlantic Council.

Rush, Michael. Parliamentary Government in Britain. LC 80-25804. 260p. 1981. text ed. 35.00x (ISBN 0-8419-0680-7). Holmes & Meier.

Rush, Myron D. Management: A Biblical Approach. 1983. pap. 7.95 (ISBN 0-88207-607-8). Victor Bks.

--Richer Relationships. 180p. 1983. pap. 4.95 (ISBN 0-88207-399-0). Victor Bks.

Rush, N. Orwin. Diversions of a Westerner: With Emphasis Upon Owen Wister & Frederic Remington Books & Libraries. LC 78-53134. (Illus.). 224p. 1979. 10.00 o.p. (ISBN 0-932068-05-7). South Pass Pr.

Rush, Ralph E., jt. auth. see Matesky, Ralph.

Rush, Sarah. Hucket-A-Bucket Again. LC 67-15702. (General Juvenile Bks). (Illus.). (gr. k-3). 1967. PLB 3.95g (ISBN 0-8225-0266-6). Lerner Pubns.

--Hucket-A-Bucket Down the Street. LC 67-8403. (General Juvenile Bks). (Illus.). (gr. k-3). 1965. PLB 3.95g (ISBN 0-8225-0254-2). Lerner Pubns.

Rush, Sheila, jt. auth. see Clark, Chris.

Rushbrook, Frank. Fire Aboard: The Problems of Prevention & Control in Ships, Port Installations & Offshore Structures. 2nd ed. 638p. 1979. 65.00x (ISBN 0-85174-331-5). Sheridan.

Rushdie, Salman. Grimus. LC 78-65232. 320p. 1979. 16.95 (ISBN 0-87951-093-5); pap. 5.95 (ISBN 0-87951-138-9). Overlook Pr.

Rushford, Patricia H. Have You Hugged Your Teenager Today? 160p. 1982. pap. 5.95 (ISBN 0-8007-5098-5, PowerBks). Revell.

Rushforth, S. R., jt. auth. see Clark, R. L.

Rushforth, S. R., jt. auth. see Grimes, Judith A.

Rushforth, S. R., jt. auth. see Lawson, L. L.

Rushing, T. Benny. Topological Embeddings. (Pure & Applied Mathematics Ser., Vol. 52). 1973. 60.00 (ISBN 0-12-603550-4). Acad Pr.

Rushman, G. B., jt. auth. see Atkinson, R. S.

Rushmer, R. F. National Priorities for Health: Past, Present, & Projected. LC 79-25313. (Wiley Series in Health Service). 1980. 38.95 (ISBN 0-471-06472-6, Pub. by Wiley Med). Wiley.

Rushmer, Robert F. Humanizing Health Care: Alternative Futures for Medicine. LC 75-1399. (Illus.). 211p. 1975. 17.00x (ISBN 0-262-18075-8); pap. 5.95x (ISBN 0-262-68032-7). MIT Pr.

--Medical Engineering: Projections for Health Care Delivery. 1972. 63.00 (ISBN 0-12-603650-0). Acad Pr.

Rushmore, Helen. Cowboy Joe of the Circle S. LC 50-9425. (Illus.). (gr. 4-6). 1950. pap. 3.95 (ISBN 0-15-220548-9, VoyB). HarBraceJ.

--Old Billy Solves a Mystery. LC 73-17101. (American Folktales). (Illus.). 64p. (gr. 3-6). 1974. PLB 6.69 (ISBN 0-8116-4041-8). Garrard.

Rushnell, Elaine. My Mom's Having a Baby. Duenewald, Doris, ed. LC 77-95422. (Illus.). (gr. k-7). 1978. 5.95 (ISBN 0-448-16057-9, G&D). Putnam Pub Group.

Rushton. Visual Pigments in Man. 48p. 1982. 50.00x (ISBN 0-85323-223-7, Pub. by Liverpool Univ England). State Mutual Bk.

Rushton, J. & Turner, J. D., eds. Education & Deprivation. 1975. 12.00 (ISBN 0-7190-0624-4). Manchester.

Rushton, J., jt. ed. see Turner, J. D.

Rushton, J. Philippe. Altruism, Socialization, & Society. (P-H Ser. in Social Learning Theory). (Illus.). 1980. text ed. 22.95 (ISBN 0-13-023408-7). P-H.

Rushton, K. R. & Redshaw, S. C. Seepage & Groundwater Flow: Numerical Analysis by Analog & Digital Methods. LC 38-23359. (Series in Geotechnical Engineering). 1979. 69.95 (ISBN 0-471-99754-4, Pub. by Wiley-Interscience). Wiley.

Rusinow, Dennison. The Yugoslav Experiment 1948-1974. LC 76-20032. 1978. 38.50x (ISBN 0-520-03304-3); pap. 9.50x (ISBN 0-520-03730-8). U of Cal Pr.

Rusk, Gae. Umbrage. LC 81-85569. 192p. 1983. pap. 4.95 (ISBN 0-86666-053-4). GWP.

Rusk, Katherine. Renovating the Victorian House: A Guide for Aficionados of Old Houses. LC 82-12397. (Illus.). 200p. (Orig.). 1983. 24.95 (ISBN 0-89286-217-3); pap. 12.95 (ISBN 0-89286-187-8). One Hund One Prods.

Rusk, Robert R. & Scotland, James. Doctrines of the Great Educators. 5th ed. LC 78-12874. 1979. 22.50 (ISBN 0-312-21491-X); pap. text ed. 10.95x (ISBN 0-312-21492-8). St Martin.

Ruskin, Ariane. Art of the High Renaissance. (Discovering Art Ser). (Illus.). (gr. 7 up). 1972. 11.95 (ISBN 0-07-054288-0, GB). McGraw.

--History of Art. LC 73-5673. (Illus.). 320p. (gr. 7 up). 1974. PLB 15.90 (ISBN 0-531-01988-8). Watts.

--Nineteenth Century Art. (Discovering Art Ser). (Illus.). (gr. 5 up). 1969. 11.95 o.p. (ISBN 0-07-054292-9, GB); pap. 4.95 o.p. (ISBN 0-07-054293-7). McGraw.

Ruskin, Ariane, jt. auth. see Batterberry, Michael.

Ruskin, John. Letters from the Continent, 1858. Hayman, John, ed. 216p. 1982. 29.50x (ISBN 0-8020-5583-4). U of Toronto Pr.

--Ruskin As Literary Critic: Selections. Ball, A. H., ed. Repr. of 1928 ed. lib. bdg. 15.75x (ISBN 0-8371-1149-8, RULC). Greenwood.

--Sesame & Lilies. Incl. Two Paths; King of the Golden River. 1974. Repr. of 1907 ed. 8.95x (ISBN 0-460-00219-8, Evman). Biblio Dist.

--Unto This Last: Four Essays on the First Principles of Political Economy. new ed. Hubenka, Lloyd J., ed. LC 67-12118. xliv, 97p. 1967. 10.95x (ISBN 0-8032-0157-5). U of Nebr Pr.

Rusmore, Jean, jt. auth. see Spangle, Francis.

Rusnak, Robert J. Walter Hines Page & the World's Work: 1900-1913. LC 81-40929. 154p. (Orig.). 1982. lib. bdg. 19.00 (ISBN 0-8191-2604-7); pap. text ed. 8.25 (ISBN 0-8191-2605-5). U Pr of Amer.

Russ, C. A., ed. see Lenz, Siegfried.

Russ, Colin. Miniature Chess Problems. (Illus.). 262p. 1982. pap. 6.95 (ISBN 0-312-53370-5). St Martin.

Russ, Frederick A. & Kirkpatrick, Charles A. Marketing. 1982. 23.95 (ISBN 0-316-76272-5); tchrs' manual avail. (ISBN 0-316-76273-3); student's guide 8.95 (ISBN 0-316-76276-8); master transparencies avail. (ISBN 0-316-76271-7); test bank avail. (ISBN 0-316-76274-1). Little.

Russ, Frederick A., jt. auth. see Kirkpatrick, Charles A.

Russ, J. German Festivals & Customs. 180p. 1982. pap. text ed. 16.75x (ISBN 0-85496-365-0, 41266, Pub. by Wolff Pubs England). Humanities.

Russ, Joanna. Alyx. (Science Fiction Ser.). 288p. 1976. lib. bdg. 12.50 o.p. (ISBN 0-8398-2337-1, Gregg). G K Hall.

--And Chaos Died. (Science Fiction Ser.). 1978. lib. bdg. 10.00 o.p. (ISBN 0-8398-2410-6, Gregg). G K Hall.

--The Female Man. 1977. Repr. of 1975 ed. lib. bdg. 11.00 o.p. (ISBN 0-8398-2351-7, Gregg). G K Hall.

--We Who Are About to... 12.50 (ISBN 0-8398-2495-5, Gregg). G K Hall.

Russ, Martin. The Last Parallel. LC 73-438. (Illus.). 333p. 1973. Repr. of 1957 ed. lib. bdg. 19.75x (ISBN 0-8371-6770-1, RULP). Greenwood.

Russel, J. P. The Beatles on Record: A Listeners Guide. (Illus.). 256p. 14.95 (ISBN 0-684-17783-8, ScribT); pap. 9.95 (ISBN 0-686-95447-5). Scribner.

Russel, Joan, jt. auth. see Gregg, Joan Y.

Russel, John, intro. by. Jennifer Bartlett: In the Garden. (Illus.). 208p. 1982. 35.00 (ISBN 0-8109-0709-7). Abrams.

Russel, Robert. Estudios Panos IV: Una Gramatica Transformacional Del Amahuaca. (Serie Linguistica Peruana: No. 13). 1975. pap. 3.15 o.p. (ISBN 0-685-51591-5); microfiche 2.25x (ISBN 0-88312-344-4). Summer Inst Ling.

Russel, Robert R. Critical Studies in Antebellum Sectionalism: Essays in American Political & Economic History. LC 78-105977. (Contributions in American History: No. 7). 1972. lib. bdg. 25.00x (ISBN 0-8371-3304-1, RAS/). Greenwood.

Russel, Rosalie M. Deutsch-Lernen Macht Spass. LC 81-16184. 461p. (Orig., Ger.). 1982. text ed. 24.50x (ISBN 0-7022-1639-9). U of Queensland Pr.

Russell & Eschenburg. Contemporary Letter Writing. (Illus.). 5.95 (ISBN 0-8208-0336-7). Hearthside.

Russell, A. Clear Thinking for All. 1967. pap. text ed. 7.00 o.p. (ISBN 0-08-012281-7). Pergamon.

Russell, A. D. The Destruction of Bacterial Spores. 1982. 36.00 (ISBN 0-12-604060-5). Acad Pr.

Russell, A. D. & Quesnel, Louis B., eds. Antibiotics: Assessment of Antimicrobial Activity & Resistance. (Society for Applied Bacteriology Tech. Ser.: No. 18). Date not set. price not set (ISBN 0-12-604480-5). Acad Pr.

Russell, A. J. God at Eventide. 1975. pap. 1.25 o.p. (ISBN 0-89129-069-9, PV069). Jove Pubns.

Russell, A. J., ed. God Calling. 1972. pap. 2.95 (ISBN 0-515-06489-0). Jove Pubns.

--God Calling. 5.95 o.p. (ISBN 0-686-92323-5, 6060). Hazelden.

--God Calling: Large-Print Ed. 192p. 1981. 12.95 (ISBN 0-8007-1264-1); pap. 2.95 (ISBN 0-8007-8096-5, Spire Bks). Revell.

Russell, A. Lewis. Corporate & Industrial Security. 276p. 1980. 16.95 (ISBN 0-87201-796-6). Gulf Pub.

Russell, Amanda. A Woman Once Loved. (Orig.). 1979. pap. 2.50 o.s.i. (ISBN 0-515-04598-5). Jove Pubns.

Russell, Andy. Horns in the High Country. 1973. 15.50 (ISBN 0-394-47221-7). Knopf.

Russell, Arthur. The Machine Gunner. 1980. 15.00x o.p. (ISBN 0-900093-44-7, Pub. by Roundwood). State Mutual Bk.

Russell, B. La Philosophie De Leibniz. (Reimpressions G & B Ser.). 246p. 1971. 32.00x (ISBN 0-685-33031-1). Gordon.

Russell, Barry. Building Systems: Industrialization & Architecture. LC 80-41692. 758p. 1981. 71.00 (ISBN 0-471-27952-8, Pub. by Wiley-Interscience). Wiley.

Russell, Bert. Calked Boots & Other Northwest Writings. 4th ed. (Folklore). 1979. pap. 5.95 (ISBN 0-930344-00-6); 8.95 (ISBN 0-930344-03-0). Lacon Pubs.

--Hardships & Happy Times. 2nd ed. (Oral History Ser.: No. 1). 1978. pap. 6.95 (ISBN 0-930344-01-4); 9.95 (ISBN 0-930344-04-9). Lacon Pubs.

--Swiftwater People. 1st ed. (Oral History Ser.: No. 2). 1979. pap. 7.95 (ISBN 0-930344-02-2); 10.95 (ISBN 0-930344-05-7). Lacon Pubs.

Russell, Bertrand. Am I an Atheist of Agnostic. 32p. pap. 3.00. Am Atheist.

--Basic Writings of Bertrand Russell. Denonn, Lester E. & Egner, Robert E., eds. 1961. 12.50 o.p. (ISBN 0-671-06835-0). S&S.

--Bertrand Russell Speaks His Mind. LC 74-3626. (Illus.). 173p. 1974. Repr. of 1960 ed. lib. bdg. 19.25x (ISBN 0-8371-7445-7, RUBR). Greenwood.

--Education & the Good Life. new ed. LC 73-114378. 1970. pap. 5.95 (ISBN 0-87140-212-2). Liveright.

--The Good Citizen's Alphabet. 128p. 1970. 10.00x o.p. (ISBN 0-85247-064-9, Pub. by Baberbocchus). State Mutual Bk.

--History of Western Philosophy. 1945. 19.95 o.p. (ISBN 0-671-31400-9). S&S.

--Human Knowledge: Its Scope & Limits. (Orig.). (YA) (gr. 9 up). 1962. pap. 6.95 o.p. (ISBN 0-671-20145-X, Touchstone Bks). S&S.

--In Praise of Idleness. 1972. 7.95 o.p. (ISBN 0-671-21379-2). S&S.

--Introduction to Mathematical Philosophy. (Muirhead Library of Philoaophy Ser.). Repr. of 1963 ed. text ed. 21.00x (ISBN 0-04-510020-9). Humanities.

--Marriage & Morals. new ed. LC 70-114377. 1970. pap. 6.95 (ISBN 0-87140-211-4). Liveright.

--Outline of Philosophy. pap. 6.95 (ISBN 0-452-00576-0, F576, Mer). NAL.

--Problems of Philosophy. 1959. pap. 4.95 (ISBN 0-19-500212-1, GB). Oxford U Pr.

--Religion & Science. 1961. pap. 6.95 (ISBN 0-19-500228-8, GB). Oxford U Pr.

--Scientific Outlook. 1962. pap. 6.95 (ISBN 0-393-00137-7, Norton Lib). Norton.

--Unpopular Essays. 1951. pap. 5.95 (ISBN 0-671-20253-7, Touchstone Bks). S&S.

--Why I Am Not a Christian & Other Essays on Religion & Related Subjects. 1967. pap. 5.95 (ISBN 0-671-20323-1, Touchstone Bks). S&S.

Russell, Bertrand, jt. auth. see Whitehead, Alfred N.

Russell, Bertrand, ed. History of Western Philosophy. (gr. 12). 1967. pap. text ed. 12.95 (ISBN 0-671-20158-1, Touchstone Bks). S&S.

Russell, Betrand. The Collected Stories of Betrand Russell. Feinberg, Barry, ed. 1974. pap. 5.95 o.p. (ISBN 0-671-21673-2, Touchstone Bks). S&S.

Russell, Beverly. Designers' Workplaces: Thirty-Three Offices by Designers for Designers. (Illus.). 144p. 1983. 27.50 (ISBN 0-8230-7492-7, Whitney Lib). Watson-Guptill.

Russell, C. V. & Willig, P. L. German Tests Without Translation. 1965. 3.15 o.p. (ISBN 0-08-011248-X); pap. 2.70 o.p. (ISBN 0-08-011247-1). Pergamon.

Russell, Charles. Five on the Black Hand Side: A Play. LC 73-82643. 1973. 6.95 (ISBN 0-89388-092-2). Okpaku Communications.

Russell, Charles M. Trails Plowed Under. 1953. 19.95 (ISBN 0-385-04494-1). Doubleday.

Russell, Conrad. Crisis of Parliaments: English History 1509-1660. (Short Oxford History of the Modern World Ser.). 1971. pap. 9.95x (ISBN 0-19-501442-1). Oxford U Pr.

Russell County Historical Commission. The History of Russell County, Alabama. (Illus.). 500p. 1982. 50.00 (ISBN 0-686-97744-0). Natl ShareGraphics.

Russell, D. H. & Durie, G. M. Polyamines As Biochemical Markers of Normal & Malignant Growth. LC 75-43340. (Progress in Cancer Research & Therapy Ser.: Vol. 8). 192p. 1978. 23.50 (ISBN 0-89004-116-4). Raven.

Russell, D. S. Daniel. LC 81-1777. (The Daily Study Bible Ser.). 1981. 12.95 (ISBN 0-664-21800-8); pap. 6.95 (ISBN 0-664-24567-6). Westminster.

--The Jews from Alexander to Herod. 1967. pap. 12.50x (ISBN 0-19-836913-1). Oxford U Pr.

--Method & Message of Jewish Apocalyptic. LC 64-18683. (Old Testament Library). 1964. 14.95 (ISBN 0-664-20543-7). Westminster.

Russell, Dale & Harrington, Dick. Natural History Notebook, No. 5. 54p. 1982. pap. 2.50 (ISBN 0-686-97830-7, 56446-0, Pub. by Natl Mus Canada). U of Chicago Pr.

Russell, David, et al. Reading Aids Through the Grades: A Guide to Materials & 501 Activities for Individualizing Reading Instruction. 4th rev. ed. Mueser, Anne M., ed. LC 75-15639. 320p. 1981. pap. text ed. 11.95x (ISBN 0-8077-2609-5). Tchrs Coll.

Russell, Delbert W. Anne Herbert. (World Authors Ser.). 170p. 1983. lib. bdg. 18.95 (ISBN 0-8057-6531-X, Twayne). G K Hall.

Russell, Diana E. Rape in Marriage. 384p. 1982. 16.95 (ISBN 0-02-606190-2). Macmillan.

Russell, Diana E. & Van de Ven, Nicole, eds. Crimes Against Women. LC 76-25356. 1977. 6.95 o.p. (ISBN 0-89087-921-4). Les Femmes Pub.

Russell, Diane. Claude Lorrain: Sixteen Hundred to Sixteen Eighty-Two. LC 82-14250. (Illus.). 480p. 1982. 60.00 (ISBN 0-8076-1055-0). Braziller.

Russell, Diane H., ed. Polyamines in Normal & Neoplastic Growth. LC 72-96336. (Illus.). 441p. 1973. 38.00 (ISBN 0-911216-44-8). Raven.

Russell, Dora. The Tamarisk Tree. pap. (ISBN 0-86068-001-0). Academy Chi Ltd.

--The Tamarisk Tree: My Quest for Liberty & Love, Vol. 1. (Illus.). 304p. 1983. pap. 7.50 (ISBN 0-86068-001-0, Virago Pr). Merrimack Bk Serv.

Russell, Douglas A. Stage Costume Design: Theory, Technique & Style. 1973. 26.95 (ISBN 0-13-840322-8). P-H.

Russell, E. S. Form & Function: A Contribution to the History of Animal Morphology. LC 82-8575. (Phoenix). xlii, 384p. 1982. pap. 10.95 (ISBN 0-226-73173-1). U of Chicago Pr.

Russell, E. W., jt. ed. see Lal, R.

Russell, Elbert W., et al. Assessment of Brain Damage: A Neuropsychological Key Approach. LC 73-121914. (Personality Disorders Ser). 1970. 31.95 o.p. (ISBN 0-471-74550-2, Pub. by Wiley-Interscience). Wiley.

Russell, F. The Secret War. (World War II Ser.). PLB 19.92 (ISBN 0-8094-2547-5). Silver.

Russell, F. H. The Just War in the Middle Ages. LC 74-25655. (Studies in Medieval Life & Thought). 360p. 1975. 54.50 (ISBN 0-521-20690-1); pap. 17.95 (ISBN 0-521-29276-X). Cambridge U Pr.

Russell, F. S., ed. Advances in Marine Biology. Incl. Vol. 1. 1963. o.s. 64.50 (ISBN 0-12-026101-4); Vol. 2. 1964. 44.00 (ISBN 0-12-026102-2); Vol. 3. 1966. o.p. (ISBN 0-12-026103-0); Vol. 4. 1966. 51.50 (ISBN 0-12-026104-9); Vol. 5. 1968. 66.00 (ISBN 0-12-026105-7); Vol. 6. Yonge, Maurice, ed. 1969. 64.50 (ISBN 0-12-026106-5); Vol. 7. 1969. 60.00 (ISBN 0-12-026107-3); Vol. 8. 1970. 55.00 (ISBN 0-12-026108-1); Vol. 9. 1971. 88.50 (ISBN 0-12-026109-X); Vol. 10. 1972. 81.00 (ISBN 0-12-026110-3); Vol. 11. 1973. 49.50 (ISBN 0-12-026111-1); Vol. 15. 1978. 91.00 (ISBN 0-12-026115-4). Acad Pr.

Russell, Findlay. Snake Venom Poisoning. LC 83-3134. (Illus.). 576p. 1983. Repr. of 1980 ed. text ed. 57.50x (ISBN 0-87936-015-1). Scholium Intl.

Russell, Findlay E. Snake Venom Poisoning. 1980. text ed. 35.00i o.p. (ISBN 0-397-50472-1). Har-Row.

Russell, Francis. Lexington, Concord & Bunker Hill. LC 63-10834. (American Heritage Junior Library). 154p. (YA) (gr. 7 up). 1963. 12.95 o.p. (ISBN 0-06-024975-7, HarpJ). Har-Row.

--The Okefenokee Swamp. LC 73-78582. (American Wilderness Ser). (Illus.). (gr. 6 up). 1973. lib. bdg. 15.96 (ISBN 0-8094-1181-4, Pub. by Time-Life). Silver.

--World of Durer. LC 67-29856. (Library of Art Ser.). (Illus.). (gr. 6 up). 1967. 19.92 (ISBN 0-8094-0270-X, Pub. by Time-Life). Silver.

Russell, Franklin. Watchers at the Pond. LC 80-83963. 1981. 17.95 o.p. (ISBN 0-686-85998-7); pap. 7.95 (ISBN 0-87923-390-7). Godine.

Russell, Frederic, et al. Textbook of Salesmanship. 9th ed. (Illus.). 608p. 1973. text ed. 14.50 o.p. (ISBN 0-07-054334-8, C). McGraw.

--Textbook of Salesmanship. 10th ed. (Marketing Ser.). 1977. text ed. 24.95 (ISBN 0-07-054336-4, C). McGraw.

Russell, Frederic A., et al. Selling: Principles & Practices. (Illus.). 1982. 24.95x (ISBN 0-07-054353-4); instr's manual 20.95 (ISBN 0-07-054354-2). McGraw.

Russell, George K. Laboratory Investigations in Human Physiology. (Illus.). 1978. pap. text ed. 13.95x (ISBN 0-02-404680-9). Macmillan.

Russell, George W. E. Sydney Smith. LC 79-156929. 1971. Repr. of 1905 ed. 30.00x (ISBN 0-8103-3720-7). Gale.

Russell, Gillean, jt. auth. see Cyriax, James.

Russell, Glenn, jt. ed. see Meighan, Clement W.

Russell, Gordon E. Plant Breeding for Pest & Disease Resistance. 1978. 79.95 (ISBN 0-408-10613-1). Butterworth.

Russell, Grace. Rings & Things. pap. 1.50x o.p. (ISBN 0-8358-0243-4). Upper Room.

Russell, H. Diane. Claude Lorrain: A Tercentery Exhibition. 1982. pap. 29.95 (ISBN 0-89468-057-9). Natl Gallery Art.

Russell, Mrs. Hal. Settler Mac & the Charmed Quarter-Section. LC 82-71900. 159p. 1956. 6.95 (ISBN 0-8040-0271-1, SB). Swallow.

Russell, Helen. Pediatric Drugs & Nursing Intervention. (Illus.). 1979. pap. text ed. 11.95 (ISBN 0-07-054298-8). McGraw.

Russell, Henry N. Fate & Freedom. 1927. text ed. 29.50x (ISBN 0-686-83544-1). Elliots Bks.

Russell, Howard S. Indian New England Before the Mayflower. LC 79-63082. (Illus.). 296p. 1983. pap. 11.50 (ISBN 0-87451-255-7). U Pr of New Eng.

--A Long, Deep Furrow: Three Centuries of Farming in New England. Abr. ed. LC 81-51605. (Illus.). 394p. 1982. pap. 15.00 (ISBN 0-87451-214-X). U Pr of New Eng.

--A Long, Deep Furrow: Three Centuries of Farming in New England. LC 73-91314. (Illus.). 688p. 1976. text ed. 35.00x (ISBN 0-87451-093-7). U Pr of New Eng.

Russell, Hugh & Black, Kenneth. Understanding & Influencing Human Behavior. (Illus.). 240p. 1981. text ed. 16.95 (ISBN 0-13-936674-1, Spec). P-H.

Russell, I. Steele. Structure & Function of Cerebral Commissures. 520p. 1979. text ed. 49.50 o.p. (ISBN 0-8391-1391-9). Univ Park.

Russell, Ian & Major, Alan. Watching Wildlife. (Illus.). 192p. 1982. 17.50 (ISBN 0-7153-8469-4). David & Charles.

Russell, J. G. Radiology in Obstetrics & Antenatal Paediatrics. Trapnell, David H., ed. (Radiology in Clinical Diagnosis Ser.: Vol. 8). (Illus.). 1973. 18.95 o.p. (ISBN 0-407-38410-3). Butterworth.

Russell, J. G. B. & Fisher, A. S. Radiography in Obstetrics. 1975. 7.95 o.p. (ISBN 0-407-00009-7). Butterworth.

Russell, James. The Acquisition of Knowledge. LC 78-6881. 1978. 23.50x (ISBN 0-312-00273-4). St Martin.

--Marx-Engels Dictionary. LC 80-786. (Illus.). xxv, 140p. 1981. lib. bdg. 22.50x (ISBN 0-313-22035-2, RME/). Greenwood.

Russell, James R., ed. Madean Voghberkowtean: The Book of Lamentations, Gregory Narekatzi. LC 81-6177. 1981. 50.00x (ISBN 0-88206-029-5). Caravan Bks.

Russell, Jeremy L. Geopolitics of Natural Gas. 176p. 1983. prof ref 24.50x (ISBN 0-88410-610-1). Ballinger Pub.

Russell, Jim, ed. Murphy's Law. LC 77-90023. 1978. pap. 4.95 (ISBN 0-89087-224-4). Celestial Arts.

Russell, Joan. Creative Movement & Dance for Children. (Illus.). 1975. 10.95 (ISBN 0-8238-0183-7). Plays.

--The Woman's Day Book of Soft Toys & Dolls. (Illus.). 256p. 1975. 12.50 o.p. (ISBN 0-671-22085-3). S&S.

Russell, Joe W., Jr. Economic Disincentives for Energy Conservation. LC 79-13170. (Environmental Law Institute State & Local Energy Conservation Project Ser.). 176p. 1979. prof ref 22.50x (ISBN 0-88410-060-X). Ballinger Pub.

Russell, John. Erich Kleiber: A Memoir. (Illus.). ix, 256p. 1981. Repr. of 1957 ed. lib. bdg. 27.00 (ISBN 0-686-42958-3). Da Capo.

--The Meanings of Modern Art. LC 80-8217. (Illus.). 430p. 1981. 35.00i (ISBN 0-06-013701-0, IN-110, HarpT); pap. 16.95ix (ISBN 0-06-430110-9, HarpT). Har-Row.

--World of Matisse. LC 69-19503. (Library of Art Ser.). (Illus.). (gr. 6 up). 1969. 19.92 (ISBN 0-8094-0278-5, Pub. by Time-Life). Silver.

Russell, John B. General Chemistry. (McGraw-Hill Series in Chemistry). (Illus.). 832p. 1980. text ed. 27.50 (ISBN 0-07-054310-0); instr's manual 19.00 (ISBN 0-07-054312-7); study guide 16.50 (ISBN 0-07-054313-5); study guide 11.95 (ISBN 0-07-054311-9); solutions manual 9.95 (ISBN 0-07-054314-3). McGraw.

Russell, John R. Cases in Urban Management. 552p. 1974. text ed. 25.00x (ISBN 0-262-18066-9). MIT Pr.

Russell, John R., jt. auth. see Rosenbloom, Richard S.

Russell, Keith P. Eastman's Expectant Motherhood. 7th, Rev. ed. 1983. 6.95i (ISBN 0-316-20396-3). Little.

--Eastman's Expectant Motherhood Seventh Edition Revisied. (Illus.). 1970. 6.95 o.p. (ISBN 0-316-20395-5). Little.

Russell, Laura, jt. auth. see Channing, Marion L.

Russell, Leslie T., jt. auth. see Bowes, W. H.

Russell, Letty M. The Future of Partnership. LC 78-20805. 1979. pap. 7.95 (ISBN 0-664-24240-5). Westminster.

--Human Liberation in a Feminist Perspective-A Theology. LC 74-10613. 1974. pap. 6.95 (ISBN 0-664-24991-4). Westminster.

Russell, Letty M., ed. The Liberating Word: A Guide to Non-Sexist Interpretation of the Bible. LC 76-18689. 1976. pap. 4.95 (ISBN 0-664-24751-2). Westminster.

Russell, Louise. Technology in Hospitals: Medical Advances & Their Diffusion. (Studies in Social Economics). 1979. 18.95 (ISBN 0-8157-7630-6); pap. 7.95 (ISBN 0-8157-7629-2). Brookings.

Russell, Louise B. The Baby Boom Generation & the Economy. (Studies in Social Economics). 183p. 1982. 19.95 (ISBN 0-8157-7628-4); pap. 7.95 (ISBN 0-8157-7627-6). Brookings.

Russell, M., jt. auth. see Russell, Margo.

Russell, Margo & Russell, M. Afrikaners of the Kalahari. LC 77-85693. (African Studies: No. 24). (Illus.). 1979. 27.95 (ISBN 0-521-21897-7). Cambridge U Pr.

Russell, Marjorie H. Handbook of Christian Meditation. 1978. pap. 5.95 (ISBN 0-8159-5713-0). Devin.

Russell, Mark. Presenting Mark Russell. LC 80-13197. 192p. 1980. 10.95 (ISBN 0-89696-059-5, An Everest House Book). Dodd.

Russell, Martin. Backlash. 176p. 1983. 12.95 (ISBN 0-8027-5493-7). Walker & Co.

--Death Fuse. 196p. 1981. 9.95 o.p. (ISBN 0-312-18698-3). St Martin.

--The Man Without a Name. 1977. 7.95 o.p. (ISBN 0-698-10853-1, Coward). Putnam Pub Group.

Russell, Michel. Then Came Gantry. 1983. 6.95 (ISBN 0-686-84430-0). Vantage.

Russell, N. J. & Powell, G. M. Blood Biochemistry. (Biology in Medicine Ser.). 128p. 1983. text ed. 27.25x (ISBN 0-7099-0003-1, Pub. by Croom Helm Ltd England). Biblio Dist.

Russell, Nick. Poets by Appointment: Britain's Laureates. 192p. 1981. 17.50 o.p. (ISBN 0-7137-1161-2, Pub. by Blandford Pr England). Sterling.

Russell, Norman. Introduction to Plant Science: A Humanistic & Ecological Approach. LC 75-1445. (Illus.). 302p. 1975. pap. text ed. 15.95 (ISBN 0-8299-0043-8); instrs.' manual avail. (ISBN 0-8299-0603-7). West Pub.

Russell, Oland D. House of Mitsui. Repr. of 1939 ed. lib. bdg. 19.00x (ISBN 0-8371-4327-6, RUHM). Greenwood.

Russell, Osborne. Journal of a Trapper. Haines, Aubrey L., ed. LC 56-52. (Illus.). xxii, 241p. 1965. 16.50x (ISBN 0-8032-0897-9); pap. 4.95 (ISBN 0-8032-5166-1, BB 316, Bison). U of Nebr Pr.

Russell, P., ed. Electron Microscopy & X-Ray Applications to Environmental & Occupational Health Analysis, Vol.2. LC 80-68825. 248p. 1981. text ed. 49.95 (ISBN 0-250-40379-X). Ann Arbor Science.

Russell, Pamela R. The Woman Who Loved John Wilkes Booth. 1979. pap. 2.25 o.s.i. (ISBN 0-515-04869-0). Jove Pubns.

--The Woman Who Loved John Wilkes Booth. LC 77-18047. 1978. 10.95 o.p. (ISBN 0-399-12132-3). Putnam Pub Group.

Russell, Peggy, jt. auth. see Haggard, Merle.

Russell, Peter. Elemental Discourses. (Salzburg - Poetic Drama Ser.: No. 63). 212p. 1981. pap. text ed. 25.00x (ISBN 0-391-02774-3, Pub. by Salzburg Austria). Humanities.

--The Global Brain. (Illus.). 252p. 1983. 12.95 (ISBN 0-87477-210-9); pap. 7.95 (ISBN 0-87477-248-6). J P Tarcher.

--Malice Aforethought or the Tumor in the Brain. (Salzburg - Poetic Drama Ser.: No. 62). 97p. 1981. pap. text ed. 25.00x (ISBN 0-391-02775-1, Pub. by Salzburg Austria). Humanities.

--The TM Technique: A Skeptic's Guide to the TM Program. 1977. 9.75 (ISBN 0-7100-8345-9); pap. 7.95 (ISBN 0-7100-8672-5). Routledge & Kegan.

Russell, Peter & Shearer, Alistair. The Upanishads. (Orig.). 1978. pap. 5.95i o.p. (ISBN 0-06-090615-4, CN 615, CN). Har-Row.

Russell, Philip A. & Hutchings, Alan E., eds. Electron Microscopy & X-Ray Applications to Environmental & Occupational Health Analysis, Vol. 1. LC 77-92592. 1978. 49.95 (ISBN 0-250-40222-X). Ann Arbor Science.

Russell, R. R. & Wilkinson, M. Microeconomics: A Synthesis of Modern & Neoclassical Theory. (Economics Ser.). 1979. text ed. 35.95 (ISBN 0-471-94652-4). Wiley.

Russell, Ray. Incubus. 1981. pap. 3.25 (ISBN 0-440-14129-X). Dell.

Russell, Raymond M., jt. auth. see Coleman, Ronny J.

Russell, Richard O., Jr. & Rackley, Charles E., eds. Hemodynamic Monitoring in a Coronary Intensive Care Unit. 2nd-rev. ed. LC 81-68271. (Illus.). 416p. 1981. 39.00 o.p. (ISBN 0-87993-090-X). Futura Pub.

Russell, Robert. Act of Loving. LC 67-19287. 1967. 9.95 o.s.i. (ISBN 0-8149-0195-6). Vanguard.

--Electronic Troubleshooting with the Oscilloscope. (Illus.). 1979. text ed. 19.95 (ISBN 0-8359-1656-1). Reston.

Russell, Robert, jt. auth. see Pease, Jack G.

Russell, Robert A. Dry Those Tears. 133p. 1975. pap. 3.95 (ISBN 0-87516-203-7). De Vorss.

--God Works Through Faith. 1957. pap. 3.95 (ISBN 0-87516-325-4). De Vorss.

--Making the Contact. 90p. 1980. Repr. of 1956 ed. lexitone cover 3.00 (ISBN 0-87516-391-2). De Vorss.

--You Too Can Be Prosperous. 162p. 1975. pap. 3.50 (ISBN 0-87516-205-3). De Vorss.

Russell, Robert A., jt. auth. see Cook, Thomas M.

Russell, Robert C. Waves & Tides. LC 73-135252. (Illus.). 348p. Repr. of 1953 ed. lib. bdg. 17.75x (ISBN 0-8371-5171-6, RUWT). Greenwood.

Russell, Roger W., ed. Frontiers in Physiological Psychology. 1967. 39.00 (ISBN 0-12-604250-0). Acad Pr.

Russell, Ronald. Guide to British Topographical Prints. LC 79-53737. (Illus.). 1979. 32.00 o.p. (ISBN 0-7153-7810-4). David & Charles.

--Waterside Pubs: Pubs of the (British) Inland Waterways. LC 74-81057. 1975. 10.50 o.p. (ISBN 0-7153-6743-9). David & Charles.

Russell, Ross. Jazz Style in Kansas City & the Southwest. LC 72-138507. (California Library Reprint Ser.: No. 120). (Illus.). 344p. 1982. 22.50x (ISBN 0-520-04767-2); pap. 8.95 (ISBN 0-520-04785-0). U of Cal Pr.

Russell, S. P. Animales Que Ayudan. Orig. Title: Four Legged Helpers. 1979. 1.10 (ISBN 0-311-38510-9). Casa Bautista.

Russell, Solveig P. One, Two, Three, & More. LC 66-18230. (ps). 1966. bds. 5.95 laminated (ISBN 0-570-03410-8, 56-1062). Concordia.

--This Home is for Me. (Illus.). (gr. k-2). 1962. 1.35 o.p. (ISBN 0-8054-4125-5); bds. 0.60 (ISBN 0-8054-4124-7). Broadman.

--What's Under the Sea? LC 81-20521. (Illus.). 48p. (gr. 2-4). 1982. 8.95 (ISBN 0-687-44913-8). Abingdon.

Russell, Stuart H. Resource Recovery Economics: Methods for Feasibility Analysis. (Pollution Engineering & Technology Ser.: Vol. 22). (Illus.). 312p. 1982. 39.75 (ISBN 0-8247-1726-0). Dekker.

Russell, Susan, jt. auth. see Herbert, Cindy.

Russell, T. Fraser & Denn, Morton M. Introduction to Chemical Engineering Analysis. LC 72-2172. 480p. 1972. text ed. 44.95 (ISBN 0-471-74545-6); solution manual avail. (ISBN 0-471-74546-4). Wiley.

Russell, Thomas R., et al, eds. From Gene to Protein: Information Transfer in Normal & Abnormal Cells. (Miami Winter Symposia: Vol. 16). 1979. 42.50 (ISBN 0-12-604450-3). Acad Pr.

Russell, Tom. How to Use New Age Principles For Successful Selling. 30p. 1982. 2.00 (ISBN 0-911201-01-7). New Age Bus Bks.

Russell, W. Ritchie. Traumatic Amnesias. (Oxford Neurological Monographs). (Illus.). 1971. text ed. 14.95x (ISBN 0-19-857204-2). Oxford U Pr.

Russell, W. Ritchie & Dewar, A. J. Explaining the Brain. (Illus.). 1975. 14.95x (ISBN 0-19-217650-1); pap. text ed. 5.95x (ISBN 0-19-289079-4). Oxford U Pr.

Russell-Hunter, W. D. A Life of Invertebrates. 1979. text ed. 26.95x (ISBN 0-02-404620-5). Macmillan.

Russell-Wood, A. J. Fidalgos & Philanthropists: The Santa Casa de Misericordia of Bahia, 1550-1755. 1968. 42.50x (ISBN 0-520-01108-2). U of Cal Pr.

Russen, David. Iter Lunare. 168p. 1976. Repr. of 1703 ed. lib. bdg. 10.00 (ISBN 0-8398-2343-6, Gregg). G K Hall.

Russett, Bruce M. Community & Contention: Britain & America in the Twentieth Century. LC 82-20952. xii, 252p. 1983. Repr. of 1963 ed. lib. bdg. 29.75x (ISBN 0-313-23792-1, RUCC). Greenwood.

--International Regions & the International System. LC 73-16608. (Illus.). 252p. 1975. Repr. of 1967 ed. lib. bdg. 18.50x (ISBN 0-8371-7191-1, RUIR). Greenwood.

Russianoff, Leon. Clarinet Method, Bk. II. 1982. pap. 14.95 (ISBN 0-02-872250-7). Schirmer Bks.

--Clarinet Method, Bk. I. 1982. pap. 14.95 (ISBN 0-02-872230-2). Schirmer Bks.

Russianoff, Penelope. Why Do I Think I am Nothing Without a Man? 1982. 10.95 (ISBN 0-686-97770-X). Bantam.

Russianoff, Penelope, ed. Women in Crisis. LC 80-29492. 319p. 1981. 29.95 o.p. (ISBN 0-89885-051-7). Human Sci Pr.

Russo, Barbara A. Gastroenterology Nursing Continuing Education Review. 1976. pap. 12.75 (ISBN 0-87488-373-3). Med Exam.

Russo, David J. Families & Communities: A New View of American History. LC 74-11389. 1974. 9.00x (ISBN 0-910050-29-5). AASLH.

Russo, Eva M. & Shyne, Ann W. Coping with Disruptive Behavior in Group Care. LC 79-23739. 74p. (Orig.). 1980. 6.95 (ISBN 0-87868-137-X, GC-13). Child Welfare.

Russo, J. Robert. Serving & Surviving As a Human Service Worker. LC 80-18016. 170p. (Orig.). 1980. pap. text ed. 9.95 (ISBN 0-8185-0383-1). Brooks-Cole.

Russo, Joseph S. The Immaculate Conception Incarnate: Betrayal of Innocence. LC 82-90565. 1982. pap. 5.95 (ISBN 0-932742-02-5). World Action.

Russo, Monica & Dewire, Robert. The Complete Book of Bird Houses & Feeders. LC 75-36155. (Illus.). 1976. pap. 6.95 (ISBN 0-8069-8224-1). Sterling.

Russo, Raymond M., jt. auth. see Laude, Theresita.

Russo, Raymond M., et al. Advanced Textbook of Sexual Development & Disorders in Childhood & Adolescence. (Advances Textbook Ser.). 1983. pap. text ed. price not set (ISBN 0-87488-485-3). Med Exam.

Russo, Thomas A. Commodities Futures Trading Commission. 600p. 1982. 80.00x o.p. (ISBN 0-07-054348-8). McGraw.

Russo-Alesi, Anthony I. Martyrology Pronouncing Dictionary. LC 79-167151. 1973. Repr. of 1939 ed. 30.00x (ISBN 0-8103-3272-8). Gale.
Russon, A. & Russon, L. J. German Vocabulary in Context. 1977. pap. text ed. 3.25x (ISBN 0-582-36167-2). Longman.
Russon, L. J., jt. auth. see Russon, A.
Russon, S., jt. auth. see Kershaw, F.
Russsell, Robert. Valentin Kataev. (World Authors Ser.). 1981. 15.95 (ISBN 0-8057-6423-2, Twayne). G K Hall.
Rust, Brian. The American Dance Band Discography 1917-1942, 2 vols. 1976. 35.00 o.p. (ISBN 0-87000-248-1, Arlington Hse). Crown.
--The American Record Label Book: From the Mid-19th Century Through 1942. (Roots of Jazz Ser.). 1983. Repr. of 1978 ed. lib. bdg. 29.50 (ISBN 0-306-76211-0). Da Capo.
--Brian Rust's Guide to Discography. LC 79-6827. (Discographies: No. 4). (Illus.). x, 133p. 1980. lib. bdg. 22.50x (ISBN 0-313-22086-7, RGD/). Greenwood.
--Jazz Records 1897-1942. 4th ed. 1978. 60.00 o.p. (ISBN 0-87000-404-2, Arlington Hse). Crown.
Rust, Brian A. & Debus, Allen G. The Complete Entertainment Discography: From the Mid - 1897 to 1942. 1000p. 1973. 14.95 o.p. (ISBN 0-87000-150-7, Arlington Hse). Crown.
Rust, David E. Small French Paintings from the Bequest of Ailsa Mellon Bruce. LC 78-606019. (Illus.). pap. 2.00 (ISBN 0-89468-048-X). Natl Gallery Art.
Rust, Eric C. Judges, Ruth, First & Second Samuel. LC 59-10454. (Layman's Bible Commentary Ser: Vol. 6). 1961. pap. 3.95 (ISBN 0-8042-3066-8). John Knox.
--The Word & Words: Towards a Theology of Preaching. LC 82-8032. 128p. 1982. 10.95x (ISBN 0-86554-055-1). Mercer Univ Pr.
Rust, Kenn C. The Ninth Air Force Story. (WW-II Air Forces History Ser.). (Illus.). 64p. 1983. pap. 7.95 (ISBN 0-911852-93-X). Hist Aviation.
--Twelfth Air Force Story. LC 75-20996. (World War II Forces History). (Illus.). 64p. 1975. pap. 7.95 (ISBN 0-911852-77-8). Hist Aviation.
--Twentieth Air Force Story. LC 79-83637. (World War II History). (Illus.). 64p. 1979. pap. 7.95 (ISBN 0-911852-85-9). Hist Aviation.
Rust, Kenn C., ed. see Matt, Paul R.
Rust, Richard D., ed. see Irving, Washington.
Rust, Shirley J., ed. Consolidated Handicapper's. 1979. 9.95 o.p. (ISBN 0-89260-133-7). Hwong Pub.
Rust, Thomas, ed. see Matt, Paul, et al.
Rustad. Women in Khaki. 304p. 1982. 24.95 (ISBN 0-03-060149-5); pap. 12.95 (ISBN 0-03-062193-3). Praeger.
Rustagi, Jaggish S., ed. Optimizing Methods in Statistics: Proceedings. 1971. 63.00 (ISBN 0-12-604550-X). Acad Pr.
Rustaing De Saint-Jory, Louis. Les Femmes Militaires. (Utopias in the Enlightenment Ser.). 326p. (Fr.). 1974. Repr. of 1735 ed. lib. bdg. 85.50x o.p. (ISBN 0-8287-0751-0, 018). Clearwater Pub.
Rustaveli, Shota. The Lord of the Panther-Skin. Stevenson, R. H., tr. from Georgian. LC 76-13225. 1977. 29.50x (ISBN 0-87395-320-7). State U NY Pr.
Rustebakke, Homer M. Electric Utility Systems & Practices. 375p. 1983. 44.95 (ISBN 0-471-04890-9, Pub. by Wiley-Interscience). Wiley.
Rustemeyer, Ruth. Wahrnehmung Eigener Fahigkeit Bei Jungen und Madchen. 213p. (Ger.). 1982. write for info. (ISBN 3-8204-5755-0). P Lang Pubs.
Ruster, Bernd & Simma, Bruno. International Protection of the Environment: Treaties & Related Documents, 30 vols. 1975. text ed. 50.00x ea. (ISBN 0-379-10087-8). Oceana.
Rusti, Renee K. Ladybug Smiled. 32p. 1983. 5.95 (ISBN 0-89962-310-7). Todd & Honeywell.
--Truly a Lady Bug. 64p. 1983. 5.95 (ISBN 0-89962-311-5). Todd & Honeywell.
Rustin, Randall, ed. Courant Computer Science, Symposium 7: Computational Complexity. (Illus.). 268p. 1973. 25.00x (ISBN 0-917448-01-4). Algorithmics.
--Courant Computer Science, Symposium 8: Natural Language Processing. (Illus.). 350p. 1973. 30.00x (ISBN 0-917448-02-2). Algorithmics.
--Courant Computer Science Symposium 9: Combinatorial Algorithms. (Illus.). 126p. 1973. 20.00x (ISBN 0-917448-03-0). Algorithmics.
Ruston, H. & Bordogna, J. Electric Networks: Functions, Filters, Analysis. (Electrical & Electronic Engineering Ser.). 1965. text ed. 41.00 o.p. (ISBN 0-07-054343-7, C). McGraw.
Ruston, Henry. Programming with PL-1. (Illus.). 1978. text ed. 23.95 (ISBN 0-07-054350-X, C). McGraw.
Rustow, Dankwart A. Oil & Turmoil: America Faces OPEC & the Middle East. 320p. 1982. 15.95x (ISBN 0-393-01597-1). Norton.
--Oil & Turmoil: American Faces OPEC & the Middle East. 1982. pap. text ed. 5.95x (ISBN 0-393-95233-9). Norton.
Rustow, Dankwart A., jt. ed. see Czempiel, Ernst-Otto.
Ruszkiewicz, John J. Well-Bound Words: A Rhetoric. 1981. text ed. 15.50x (ISBN 0-673-15355-X). Scott F.
Rutan, Catherine. Changes in Position. 1983. pap. text ed. 3.50 (ISBN 0-911623-00-0). I Klang.
Rutenber, Culbert G. Reconciling Gospel. pap. 1.95 o.p. (ISBN 0-8170-0243-X). Judson.
Rutenberg, David. Multinational Management. 1982. text ed. 24.95 (ISBN 0-316-76365-9); solutions manual avail. (ISBN 0-316-76366-7). Little.
Rutenfranz, J., jt. ed. see Colquhoun, W. P.
Rutford, Robert H., jt. auth. see Zumberge, James H.
Rutgers, A. & Norris, K. A. Encyclopedia of Aviculture, 3 vols. (Illus.). 900p. 1982. boxed set 99.95 (ISBN 0-7137-1295-3, Pub. by Blandford Pr England). Sterling.
Ruth see Bellairs, Ruth, et al.
Ruth, Larry. M I Carbine. pap. 15.00 (ISBN 0-686-43086-7). Gun Room.
Ruth, Margaret. The Invisible You. LC 82-70544. (Orig.). 1982. pap. 5.95 (ISBN 0-9608130-0-4). Broome Closet.
Ruth, Merle. The Significance of the Christian Woman's Veiling. 1980. 1.00 (ISBN 0-686-30769-0). Rod & Staff.
Ruth, R. M., ed. see Nicholas, James.
Ruth, Sheila. Issues in Feminism: A First Course in Women's Studies. LC 79-88795. (Illus.). 1980. text ed. 14.50 (ISBN 0-395-28691-3). HM.
Ruth, V., jt. ed. see Parvez, H.
Ruth, W., jt. auth. see Stidger, Howe C.
Rutherford, Andrew & Cohen, Fred. Standards Relating to Corrections Administration. LC 77-3375. (IJA-ABA Juvenile Justice Sta ndards Project Ser.). 224p. 1980. prof ref 20.00x (ISBN 0-88410-750-7); pap. 10.00x prof ref (ISBN 0-88410-821-X). Ballinger Pub.
Rutherford, Anna & Hannah, Donald, eds. Commonwealth Short Stories. 245p. 1980. text ed. 19.50x (ISBN 0-8419-5075-X); pap. text ed. 9.50x (ISBN 0-686-96739-9). Holmes & Meier.
Rutherford, Constance. The Art of Making Paper Flowers: Full Size Patterns & Instructions for 16 Realistic Blossoms. (Illus.). 48p. (Orig.). 1983. pap. 2.95 (ISBN 0-486-24378-8). Dover.
Rutherford, Don. International Rugby. (Illus.). 192p. (Orig.). 1983. 17.50 (ISBN 0-434-65915-0, Pub. by W Heinemann). David & Charles.
Rutherford, Frederick. You & Your Baby. (Orig.). 1971. pap. 3.95 (ISBN 0-451-12177-5, AE2177, Sig). NAL.
Rutherford, Frederick W. You & Your Baby. LC 73-169831. 1971. 3.95x (ISBN 0-451-12177-5, Pub. by NAL). Formur Intl.
Rutherford, G. K. The Physical Environment of the Faeroe Islands. 1982. 39.50 (ISBN 90-6193-099-5, Pub. by Junk Pubs Netherlands). Kluwer Boston.
Rutherford, Jean, jt. auth. see Rutherford, Robert.
Rutherford, Phillip R. Dictionary of Maine Place-Names. LC 70-132915. 1971. 9.95 o.p. (ISBN 0-87027-121-0). Cumberland Pr.
Rutherford, Robert & Rutherford, Jean. Doctor Discusses Family Problems. (Illus.). 1969. pap. 2.50 o.p. (ISBN 0-910304-17-3). Budlong.
Rutherford, Robert D. Administrative Time Power. LC 78-61464. 111p. 1978. pap. text ed. 14.95 (ISBN 0-686-91717-0). Learning Concepts.
--Just in Time: The Inner Game of Time Management. LC 80-22409. 201p. 1981. 14.95 (ISBN 0-471-08434-4, Pub. by Wiley-Interscience). Wiley.
Rutherford, Ward. The Biography of Field Marshall Erwin Rommel. (The Commanders Ser.). (Illus.). 160p. 1981. 9.98 o.p. (ISBN 0-89196-104-6, Bk Value Intl). Quality Bks IL.
--Blitzkrieg Nineteen Forty. (Illus.). 1980. 16.95 (ISBN 0-399-12391-1). Putnam Pub Group.
--Hitler's Propoganda Machine. LC 77-87810. 1978. Repr. 9.95 o.p. (ISBN 0-448-14627-4, G&D). Putnam Pub Group.
Ruthledge, Mildred. Singing in the Kitchen. (Illus.). 1974. pap. 7.95 incl. record (ISBN 0-913270-23-7). Sunstone Pr.
Ruthmann, Daniele. Vers Une Nouvelle Culture Social-Democrate? 266p. (Ger.). 1982. Vol. 4, Germanus Legens. write for info (ISBN 3-8204-5970-7); Vol. 468, Langue et Litterature Allemandes, Vol. 468. write for info (ISBN 3-8204-5971-5). P Lang Pubs.
Ruthren, Malise. Cairo. (Great Cities Ser.). PLB 12.00 (ISBN 0-8094-3113-0). Silver.
Ruthven. From Down under. Date not set. 2.45 (ISBN 0-89989-027-X). Cross Roads.
Ruthven, K. K. Critical Assumptions. LC 78-57760. 1979. 29.95 (ISBN 0-521-22257-5). Cambridge U Pr.
--A Guide to Ezra Pound's "Personae" 1926. 1969. 35.75x (ISBN 0-520-01526-6). U of Cal Pr.
--A Guide to Pound's Personae (1926) 291p. 1983. pap. 7.95 (ISBN 0-520-04960-8, CAL 628). U of Cal Pr.
--Myth. LC 76-17221. (Critical Idiom Ser.: Vol. 31). 96p. 1976. 10.00x (ISBN 0-416-78990-0); pap. 4.95x (ISBN 0-416-79000-3). Methuen Inc.
Rutishauser, Rolf. Blattstellung und Sprossentwicklung bei Bluetenpflanzen unter Besonderer Beruecksichtigung der Nelkengewaechse. (Dissertatones Botanica: Vol. 62). (Illus.). 200p. (Ger.). pap. text ed. 20.00x (ISBN 3-7682-1304-8). Lubrecht & Cramer.
Rutkevich, M. N., ed. The Career Plans of Youth. Yanowitch, Murray, tr. LC 69-18828. (Orig.). 1969. 17.50 (ISBN 0-87332-027-1). M E Sharpe.
Rutkoff, Peter M. Revanche & Revision: The Ligue des Patriotes & the Origins of the Radical Right in France, 1882-1900. LC 80-39575. x, 182p. 1981. text ed. 16.50x (ISBN 0-8214-0589-6, 82-83780). Ohio U Pr.
Rutkoskie, Alice E. & Murphree, Carolyn T. Effective Writing for Business: An Analytical Approach. 1983. 15.95 (ISBN 0-675-20049-0). Additional supplements may be obtained from publisher. Merrill.
Rutkovsky, Paul. Commodity Character. LC 82-51222. (Artists' Bk.). 72p. (Orig.). 1982. pap. 7.50 (ISBN 0-89822-030-0). Visual Studies.
Rutkowski, ed. Advances in Smoking of Foods. 1978. text ed. 29.00 (ISBN 0-08-022002-9). Pergamon.
Rutkowski, Katherine, ed. Cable, Nineteen Eighty-One: The Future of Communications. (Technical Papers Ser.). (Illus.). 151p. (Orig.). 1981. 25.00 (ISBN 0-940272-01-6). Natl Cable.
--Videotex Services. (NCTA Executive Seminar Ser.: No. 1). (Orig.). 1980. pap. 40.00 o.p. (ISBN 0-940272-00-8). Natl Cable.
Rutland, jt. auth. see Chapman.
Rutland, J. P. The Amazing Fact Book of Cars, Vol. 1. LC 80-65591. (Illus., Orig.). (gr. 4). 1980. 5.95 (ISBN 0-86550-000-2); lib. bdg. 8.95 (ISBN 0-686-96962-6); pap. 2.95 (ISBN 0-86550-001-0). A & P Bks.
--The Amazing Fact Book of Ships & Boats, Vol. 3. LC 80-80618. (Illus.). 32p. (Orig.). (gr. 4 up). 1980. 5.95 (ISBN 0-86550-004-5); lib. bdg. 8.95 (ISBN 0-686-96965-0); pap. 2.95 (ISBN 0-86550-005-3). A & P Bks.
Rutland, Jonathan. Exploring the Violent Earth. LC 79-55265. (gr. 3-5). 1980. 2.95 (ISBN 0-531-09177-5, Warwick Press); PLB 7.90 (ISBN 0-531-09167-8). Watts.
--Exploring the World of Robots. LC 78-67836. (Explorer Books). (Illus.). (gr. 3-5). 1979. 2.95 o.p. (ISBN 0-531-09130-9, Warwick Press); PLB 7.90 s&l (ISBN 0-531-09115-5). Watts.
--Exploring the World of Speed. LC 78-67835. (Explorer Books). (Illus.). (gr. 3-5). 1979. 2.95 (ISBN 0-531-09129-5, Warwick Press); PLB 7.90 s&l (ISBN 0-531-09114-7). Watts.
--Exploring UFO's. LC 79-55264. (gr. 3-5). 1980. 2.95 (ISBN 0-531-09176-7, Warwick Press); PLB 7.90 (ISBN 0-531-09166-X). Watts.
--Photography & Film. LC 78-64659. (Fact Finders Ser.). (Illus.). 1979. PLB 8.00 (ISBN 0-382-06241-8). Silver.
--See Inside an Ancient Greek Town. LC 79-63368. (See Inside Bks.). (Illus.). (gr. 5 up). 1979. PLB 9.40 s&l (ISBN 0-531-09159-7, Warwick Press). Watts.
--See Inside an Oil Rig & Tanker. LC 78-66167. (See Inside Bks.). (Illus.). (gr. 5 up). 1979. PLB 9.40 (ISBN 0-531-09121-X, Warwick Press). Watts.
--Ships. LC 76-15007. (Modern Knowledge Library). (Illus.). 48p. (gr. 5 up). 1976. 9.90 (ISBN 0-531-01199-2). Watts.
--Take a Trip to France. LC 80-52720. (Take a Trip Ser.). (gr. 1-3). 1981. PLB 8.40 (ISBN 0-531-00989-0). Watts.
--Take a Trip to Israel. (Take a Trip to Ser.). (Illus.). 32p. (gr. 1-3). 1981. lib. bdg. 8.40 (ISBN 0-531-04318-5). Watts.
--Take a Trip to Spain. LC 80-52718. (Take a Trip Ser.). (gr. 1-3). 1981. PLB 8.40 (ISBN 0-531-00991-2). Watts.
Rutland, Robert A. The Birth of the Bill of Rights, 1776-1791. 243p. 1983. 24.95X (ISBN 0-930350-41-3); pap. text ed. 9.95X (ISBN 0-930350-40-5). NE U Pr.
Rutland, Robert A. & Mason, Thomas A., eds. The Papers of James Madison, Vol. 14: April 6, 1791 to March 16, 1793. LC 62-9144. 576p. 1982. 27.50x (ISBN 0-8139-0955-4). U Pr of Va.
Rutledge, A. J. Anatomy of a Park Plan: The Essentials of Recreation Area Design. 1971. 36.50 (ISBN 0-07-054347-X, P&RB). McGraw.
Rutledge, Archibald. Home by the River. 1976. Repr. 10.00 (ISBN 0-87844-032-1). Sandlapper Pub Co.
Rutledge, Dennis, jt. auth. see Jarmon, Charles.
Rutledge, Felix, et al. Gynecologic Oncology. LC 75-30951. 272p. 1976. 47.95 (ISBN 0-471-74720-3, Pub. by Wiley Medical). Wiley.
Rutledge, Harley D. Project Identification: The First Scientific Field Study of UFO Phenomena. (Illus.). 1981. 10.95 (ISBN 0-13-730713-6); pap. 6.95 (ISBN 0-13-730705-5). P-H.
Rutledge, Howard, et al. In the Presence of Mine Enemies. (Illus.). 128p. 1973. pap. 1.50 o.p. (ISBN 0-8007-8176-7, Spire Bks); Spire Comics Ser. 0.69 o.p. (ISBN 0-8007-8506-1, Spire Bks). Revell.
Rutledge, I., jt. ed. see Duncan, K.
Rutledge, Kenneth R. The Thoughts of Robert Jacques Turgot As They Apply to the Economic Complexities of Our Present Age. (The Living Thoughts of the Great Economists Ser.). (Illus.). 131p. 1981. 53.85 (ISBN 0-918968-86-0). Inst Econ Finan.
Rutman, Darrett B. Morning of America: 1603-1789. LC 77-131289. (Illus., Orig.). 1971. pap. text ed. 10.50 (ISBN 0-395-04333-6). HM.
Rutman, Roanne. Transfusion Therapy: Principles & Procedures. Miller, William V., ed. LC 81-12765. 402p. 1982. text ed. 39.50 (ISBN 0-89443-385-7). Aspen Systems.
Rutsala, Vern. Walking Home from the Ice-House. LC 80-70566. (Poetry Ser.). 1980. 12.95 (ISBN 0-915604-47-7); pap. 4.95 (ISBN 0-915604-48-5). Carnegie-Mellon.
Rutstein, David D. A Blueprint for Medical Care. 245p. 1974. 12.00x o.p. (ISBN 0-262-18065-0); pap. 5.95x (ISBN 0-262-68033-5). MIT Pr.
Rutstein, David D. & Eden, Murray. Engineering & Living Systems. 1970. 17.50x (ISBN 0-262-18048-0). MIT Pr.
Rutstrum, Calvin. Wilderness Cabin. (Illus.). 1961. 5.95 o.p. (ISBN 0-02-606350-6); rev. ed. 1972 o.p. 5.95 (ISBN 0-686-66488-4). Macmillan.
Rutt. Surgery of the Leg & Foot. (Hackenbroch Ser.). 1980. text ed. 65.00 (ISBN 0-7216-4446-5). Saunders.
Rutt, Richard. The Bamboo Grove: An Introduction to Sijo. LC 70-84785. (Center for Japanese & Korean Studies, UC Berkeley). 1971. 21.50x (ISBN 0-520-01611-4). U of Cal Pr.
Ruttenberg, Harold J., jt. auth. see Golden, Clinton S.
Ruttenberg, S., jt. ed. see Odishaw, H.
Ruttencutter, Helen D. Pianist's Progress. LC 78-22464. 1979. 11.49i (ISBN 0-690-01761-8). T Y Crowell.
Rutter, Andy, jt. auth. see Banahan, Mark.
Rutter, Barbara A. A Way of Caring: The Parents Guide to Foster Family Care. LC 78-51720. 1978. pap. text ed. 4.95 (ISBN 0-87868-127-2, F-55). Child Welfare.
Rutter, Michael, jt. ed. see Garmezy, Norman.
Rutter, Michael, et al, eds. Education, Health & Behaviour. LC 80-22639. 496p. 1981. Repr. of 1970 ed. text ed. 21.00 (ISBN 0-89874-268-4). Krieger.
Rutter, Russell J. & Pimlott, Douglas H. World of the Wolf. LC 67-16919. (Living World Books Ser). (gr. 4-9). 1968. 12.45i (ISBN 0-397-00570-9). Har-Row.
Ruttner, John, jt. ed. see Willcocks, David.
Rutz, Miriam E., jt. auth. see Romberg, Jenean.
Ruud, J. Teaching for Changed Attitudes & Values. LC 71-187577. 1972. pap. 1.50 (ISBN 0-686-14993-9, 265-08378). Home Econ Educ.
Ruud, Josephine B. & Hall, Olive A. Adult Education for Home & Family Life. LC 73-15684. 272p. 1974. text ed. 25.95 (ISBN 0-471-74780-7). Wiley.
Ruvigny & Raineval, Melville, eds. Ruvigny's Titled Nobility of Europe: An International Peerage, or "Who's Who" of the Sovereigns, Princes & Nobles of Europe. 1605p. 1980. Repr. of 1914 ed. 112.50x (ISBN 0-85011-028-9). Intl Pubns Serv.
Ruxin, Robert H. An Athlete's Guide to Agents. LC 82-47781. (Midland Bks.: No. 290). 176p. 1983. 18.75x (ISBN 0-253-10400-9); pap. 6.95 (ISBN 0-253-20290-6). Ind U Pr.
Ruxton, George. Life in the Far West. (Classics of the Old West). 1983. lib. bdg. 17.28 (ISBN 0-8094-4046-6). Silver.
Ruxton, George F. Life in the Far West. Hafen, LeRoy R., ed. (AET Ser.: Vol. 14). (Illus.). 1951. 6.95 o.p. (ISBN 0-8061-0221-7); pap. 6.95 (ISBN 0-8061-1534-3). U of Okla Pr.
Ruyle, Gene. Making a Life: Career Choices & the Life Process. 128p. (Orig.). 1983. pap. price not set (ISBN 0-8164-2408-X). Seabury.
Ruysch, W. A. Elsevier's Multilingual Dictionary of Insurance Technology. (Eng. & Dutch & Fr. & Ger. & Span. & Ital.). write for info (ISBN 0-685-82355-5). Elsevier.
Ruyslinck, Ward. The Depraved Sleepers & Golden Ophelia. Powell, R. B. & Smith, David, trs. (International Studies & Translations Program). 1978. lib. bdg. 10.95 (ISBN 0-8057-8158-7, Twayne). G K Hall.
Ruzicka, Jaromir & Hansen, Elo H. Flow Injection Analysis. LC 75-4460. (Analytical Chemistry & Its Applications Monographs). 207p. 1981. 44.00 (ISBN 0-471-08192-2, Pub. by Wiley-Interscience). Wiley.
Rweyemamu, J. F., ed. Industrialization & Income Distribution in Africa. 240p. 1981. 30.00 (ISBN 0-905762-55-X, Pub. by Zed Pr England); pap. 9.95 (ISBN 0-905762-84-3, Pub. by Zed Pr England). Lawrence Hill.
Ryal, Tim & Jappinen, Roe. Whole Again Resource Guide: An Annual Periodical & Resource Directory. (Illus.). 315p. 1983. pap. 12.95 (ISBN 0-88496-193-1). Capra Pr.
Ryall, A. Lloyd & Pentzer, W. T. Handling, Transportation & Storage of Fruits & Vegetables: Fruits & Tree Nuts, Vol. 2. 2nd ed. (Illus.). 1982. lib. bdg. 55.00 (ISBN 0-87055-410-7). AVI.
Ryall, R. W. Mechanisms of Drug Action on the Nervous System. LC 78-5965. (Cambridge Texts in the Physiological Sciences Ser.: No. 1). (Illus.). 1979. 29.95 (ISBN 0-521-22125-0); pap. 8.95x (ISBN 0-521-29364-2). Cambridge U Pr.
Ryals, Clyde de L. Becoming Browning: The Poems & Plays of Robert Browning, 1833-1846. 350p. 1983. price not set (ISBN 0-8142-0352-3). Ohio St U Pr.
Ryan & Rycroft. Kirstenbosch. (Illus.). 137p. 1981. 47.50x (ISBN 0-86978-174-X, Pub. by Timmins Africa). Intl Schol Bk Serv.

Ryan, Abram. The Conquered Banner & Selected Poems of the Confederate Priest-Poet. Liederbach, Robert J., ed. (Illus.). 50p. 1983. pap. 3.95x (ISBN 0-934906-05-X). R J Liederbach.
Ryan, Alan. J. S. Mill. (Routledge Author Guides). 1974. 20.00x (ISBN 0-7100-7954-0); pap. 10.95 (ISBN 0-7100-7955-9). Routledge & Kegan.
--John Stuart Mill. (Orig.). 1969. pap. text ed. 3.95 (ISBN 0-685-19693-3). Phila Bk Co.
--Panther! 1981. pap. 2.25 o.p. (ISBN 0-451-09726-2, E9726, Sig). NAL.
Ryan, Alan, ed. Perpetual Light. 512p. (Orig.). 1982. pap. 3.95 o.p. (ISBN 0-446-30013-6). Warner Bks.
--The Philosophy of Social Explanation. (Oxford Readings in Philosophy). 1973. pap. text ed. 6.95x (ISBN 0-19-875025-0). Oxford U Pr.
Ryan, Allan J. & Allman, Fred L. Sports Medicine. 1974. 74.50 (ISBN 0-12-605060-0). Acad Pr.
Ryan, Angela P., ed. Reading for Comprehension, 2 bks. Bk. 1. pap. text ed. 4.33 (ISBN 0-8428-0010-7); Bk. 2. pap. text ed. 4.33 (ISBN 0-8428-0011-5); Key Bk. 1. pap. text ed. 2.00 (ISBN 0-8428-0074-3); Key Bk. 2. 2.00 (ISBN 0-8428-0075-1). Cambridge Bk.
Ryan, Bernard. How to Help Your Child Start School. 1980. 9.95 o.p. (ISBN 0-934924-01-5). Caroline Hse.
Ryan, Bernard, Jr. How to Help Your Child Start School: A Practical Guide for Parents & Teachers of Four to Six Year Olds. 166p. 1981. pap. 4.95 (ISBN 0-399-50539-3, Perige). Putnam Pub Group.
Ryan, Bruce, ed. Program Abstracts 1980: AAG Louisville Meeting. 248p. (Orig.). 1980. pap. 3.00 (ISBN 0-89291-150-6). Assn Am Geographers.
Ryan, Charles J. H. P. Blavatsky & the Theosophical Movement: With 7 Appendixes. Small, W. Emmett & Todd, Helen, eds. (Illus.). 484p. 1975. pap. 7.00x (ISBN 0-913004-25-1). Point Loma Pub.
--What Is Theosophy? A General View of Occult Doctrine. rev. ed. Small, W. Emmett & Todd, Helen, eds. (Theosophical Manual: No. 1). 92p. 1975. pap. 2.25 (913004-18). Point Loma Pub.
Ryan, Charles J., jt. auth. see Ross, Lydia.
Ryan, Charles W. Basic Electricity. LC 76-4031. (Self-Teaching Guides Ser.). 1976. pap. text ed. 9.95 (ISBN 0-471-74787-4). Wiley.
Ryan, Daniel L. Computer Graphics Problems Manual. LC 82-19740. (Graphics Ser.). 125p. 1983. pap. text ed. 15.95 (ISBN 0-534-01293-0). Brooks-Cole.
--Computer Programming for Graphical Displays. LC 82-22624. 300p. 1983. pap. text ed. 18.95 (ISBN 0-534-01357-0). Brooks-Cole.
Ryan, Dennis. The Religious Element in Life. LC 77-18568. 1978. pap. text ed. 8.25 (ISBN 0-8191-0405-1). U Pr of Amer.
Ryan, Desmond. Deadlines. 288p. 1983. 15.00x (ISBN 0-393-01642-0). Norton.
Ryan, Desmond, ed. The Nineteen Sixteen Poets. LC 79-18768. 224p. 1980. Repr. of 1963 ed. lib. bdg. 19.25x (ISBN 0-313-22100-6, RYNI). Greenwood.
Ryan, Dixie. Stories of Champions: And the National Arabian Shows, Vol. 1. (Illus.). 1975. 13.95 (ISBN 0-912830-25-5). Printed Horse.
Ryan, Dorothy, jt. auth. see Ryan, George.
Ryan, E. P. Optimal Relay & Saturating Control Systems Synthesis. (IEE Control Engineering Ser.: No. 14). 352p. 1982. casebound 94.00 (ISBN 0-906048-56-7). Inst Elect Eng.
Ryan, Edward S. A Multi-Dimensional Analysis of Conflict in the Criminal Justice System. 331p. 1981. casebound 22.85 (ISBN 0-932930-34-4); softcover 16.95 (ISBN 0-686-33183-4). Pilgrimage Inc.
Ryan, Ellen B. & Giles, Howard. Attitudes Towards Language Variation Social & Applied Contexts. 304p. 1982. pap. text ed. 18.95 (ISBN 0-7131-6195-7). E Arnold.
Ryan, Fortune, jt. auth. see Dixon, Penelope.
Ryan, Frank. Sprint. (Library of Sports Skills). (Illus.). 1972. 9.95 (ISBN 0-670-66571-1). Viking Pr.
--Swimming Skills: Freestyle, Butterfly, Backstroke, Breaststroke, 4 vols. in 1. (Illus.). 1978. pap. 7.95 (ISBN 0-14-046338-0). Penguin.
Ryan, Frank L. Exemplars for the New Social Studies: Instruction in the Elementary Schools. LC 70-137484. (Illus.). 1971. pap. text ed. 16.95 (ISBN 0-13-294686-6). P-H.
--The Immediate Critical Reception of Ernest Hemingway. LC 79-6026. 77p. 1980. text ed. 14.75 (ISBN 0-8191-0970-3); pap. text ed. 7.00 (ISBN 0-8191-0971-1). U Pr of Amer.
Ryan, Frank L., jt. ed. see Joyce, William W.
Ryan, George & Ryan, Dorothy. Picture Postcards in the United States, 1893-1918. (Illus.). 1976. 24.95 (ISBN 0-517-52400-7, C N Potter Bks); pap. 10.95 (ISBN 0-517-54588-8). Crown.
Ryan, Gerard R., jt. auth. see House, Peter W.
Ryan, Halford. American Rhetoric from Roosevelt to Reagan: A Collection of Speeches & Critical Essays. 310p. (Orig.). 1983. pap. text ed. 10.95x (ISBN 0-88133-015-9). Waveland Pr.
Ryan, Herbert F., jt. auth. see D'Auria, Michael.
Ryan, J. A. The Physician & Sportsmedicine Guide to Running. 1980. pap. 7.95 (ISBN 0-07-054358-5). McGraw.
Ryan, James E. The Investor's Guide to U. S. Silver Stocks. Sarnoff, Paul, frwd. by. (Illus.). 240p. (Orig.). 1983. pap. 19.95 (ISBN 0-9610202-0-2). N W Silver Pr.
Ryan, Jeremy. Electronic Assembly. (Illus.). 1979. text ed. 18.95 (ISBN 0-8359-1639-1); pap. text ed. 13.95 (ISBN 0-8359-1638-3). Reston.
Ryan, Joanne E., jt. auth. see Gunter, Laurie M.
Ryan, Joanne W., jt. ed. see Kline, Mary-Jo.
Ryan, John. Pugwash & the Ghost Ship. LC 68-23218. (Illus.). (gr. k-3). 1968. 10.95 (ISBN 0-87599-146-7). S G Phillips.
--Pugwash in the Pacific. LC 73-929. (Illus.). 32p. (gr. k-3). 1973. 10.95 (ISBN 0-87599-199-8). S G Phillips.
Ryan, John P., et al. American Trial Judges: Their Work Styles & Performance. LC 80-756. (Illus.). 1980. 19.95 (ISBN 0-02-927620-9). Free Pr.
Ryan, Joseph. Stating Your Case-How to Interview for a Job as a Lawyer. LC 82-10996. 188p. 1982. pap. text ed. 7.95 (ISBN 0-314-67111-0). West Pub.
Ryan, Judith. The Uncompleted Past: Postwar German Novels & the Third Reich. 272p. 1983. 24.00 (ISBN 0-8143-1728-6). Wayne St U Pr.
Ryan, Kenneth. What More Would You Like to Know about the Church? LC 78-59318. 1978. 8.95 (ISBN 0-89310-043-9); pap. 4.95 o.p. (ISBN 0-89310-044-7). Carillon Bks.
Ryan, Kenneth, ed. The Catholic Digest Christmas Book. LC 77-82809. 1977. 7.95 (ISBN 0-89310-026-9); pap. 3.95 o.p. (ISBN 0-89310-027-7). Carillon Bks.
--The Fulton Sheen Reader. LC 78-57596. 1979. 10.00 (ISBN 0-89310-037-4); pap. 5.95 o.p. (ISBN 0-89310-038-2). Carillon Bks.
--What Would You Like to Know About the Catholic Church. 1977. 7.95 (ISBN 0-89310-010-2); pap. 1.95 o.p. (ISBN 0-89310-004-8). Carillon Bks.
--You & Your Mind. LC 77-72770. 1977. 6.95 (ISBN 0-89310-012-9); pap. 3.95 o.p. (ISBN 0-89310-019-6). Carillon Bks.
Ryan, Kevin & Cooper, James M. Kaleidoscope: Readings in Education. 3rd ed. LC 79-90056. (Illus.). 1980. pap. text ed. 12.50 (ISBN 0-395-28498-8). HM.
--Those Who Can, Teach. 3rd ed. LC 79-89788. (Illus.). 1980. text ed. 20.95 (ISBN 0-395-28495-3); instr's. manual 1.00 (ISBN 0-395-28496-1); learning guide 8.50 (ISBN 0-395-28497-X). HM.
Ryan, Kevin & Phillips, Debra H. The Workbook: Exploring a Career in Teaching. 350p. 1983. pap. text ed. 11.95 (ISBN 0-675-20057-1). Additional supplements may be obtained from publisher. Merrill.
Ryan, Kevin & Ryan, Marilyn. Making a Marriage: A Personal Book of Love, Marriage & Family. 224p. 1983. pap. 5.95 (ISBN 0-312-50663-5). St Martin.
Ryan, Kevin, jt. ed. see Purpel, David E.
Ryan, L., jt. auth. see Schubert, R.
Ryan, Lawrence V., ed. see Shakespeare, William.
Ryan, Margaret. Filling Out a Life. LC 82-71503. (Pine Street Poetry Ser.). 66p. (Orig.). 1982. pap. 10.95 (ISBN 0-931502-01-2). Front St.
Ryan, Marilyn, jt. auth. see Ryan, Kevin.
Ryan, Mary. The Empire of the Mother: American Writings on Women & the Family, 1830-1860. LC 82-15631. (Women & History Ser.: Nos. 2 & 3). 176p. 1982. text ed. 24.95 (ISBN 0-86656-133-1, B133). Haworth Pr.
Ryan, Mary P., ed. see Hill, Marie & Hill, Brennan.
Ryan, Michael & Norman, Marty. Bar-B-Que Your Boss. 1982. 3.95 (ISBN 0-399-50651-9, Perige). Putnam Pub Group.
Ryan, Michael A. The Pet Index. 194p. 1982. text ed. 32.00x (ISBN 0-686-42829-3). Gower Pub Ltd.
Ryan, Michael D., jt. auth. see Fernando, Quintas.
Ryan, Mick. Radical Alternatives to Prison & the Penal Lobby. LC 78-58895. 1978. 24.95 o.p. (ISBN 0-03-046351-3). Praeger.
Ryan, Mildred G. The Complete Encyclopedia of Stitchery: More Than 1400 Illustrations & 1000 Entries. LC 77-16942. (Illus.). 1979. 16.95 o.p. (ISBN 0-385-12385-X). Doubleday.
Ryan, Nancy H. Kathleen's Surrender. 1983. pap. 3.50 (ISBN 0-8217-1139-3). Zebra.
Ryan, Nolan, jt. auth. see Torre, Joe.
Ryan, Nolan, et al. Pitching & Hitting. 213p. 1982. pap. 5.95 (ISBN 0-13-676197-6). P-H.
Ryan, Patrick J. Imale: Yoruba Participation in the Muslim Tradition. LC 76-57774. 1978. pap. 9.00 (ISBN 0-89130-132-1, 02-01-11). Scholars Pr Ca.
Ryan, Peter J., jt. auth. see Henin, Claude G.
Ryan, Rachel. Prime Time. (Candlelight Ecstasy Ser.: No. 151). (Orig.). 1983. pap. 1.95 (ISBN 0-440-17040-0). Dell.
Ryan, Robert E. & Ryan, Robert E., Jr., eds. Headache & Head Pain: Diagnosis & Treatment. LC 78-8973. 428p. 1978. text ed. 54.50 (ISBN 0-8016-4242-6). Mosby.
Ryan, Robert M., jt. auth. see Klenk, Robert W.
Ryan, Roderick T. A History of Motion Picture Color Technology. (Illus.). 1977. 49.95 (ISBN 0-240-50953-6). Focal Pr.
Ryan, Sheila A. & Clayton, Bruce D. Handbook of Practical Pharmacology. 2nd ed. LC 79-26035. (Illus.). 358p. 1980. pap. text ed. 13.95 (ISBN 0-8016-4240-X). Mosby.
Ryan, T. F. Gunite, a Handbook for Engineers. 1973. pap. 14.50 (ISBN 0-7210-0820-8). Scholium Intl.
Ryan, Thomas P. Tales of Christian Unity: The Adventures of an Ecumenical Pilgrim. LC 82-60748. 224p. 1983. pap. 8.95 (ISBN 0-8091-2502-1). Paulist Pr.
Ryan, Thomas R. Orestes A. Brownson: The Pope's Champion in America. 1983. 8.50 (ISBN 0-8199-0857-6). Franciscan Herald.
Ryan, Tim & Jappinen, Rae. The Whole Again Resources Guide. LC 82-61917. (Illus.). 315p. 1982. pap. 12.95 (ISBN 0-88496-193-1). SourceNet.
Ryan, Tom. The Savage. 1979. pap. 2.95 (ISBN 0-451-11981-9, AE1981, Sig). NAL.
Ryan, Tom K. Sound off, Tumbleweeds! 128p. 1983. pap. 1.95 (ISBN 0-449-12386-3, GM). Fawcett.
Ryan, Victoria, jt. auth. see Marsh, Arthur.
Ryan, W. Non-Ferrous Extractive Metallurgy in the United Kingdom. 234p. 1968. 34.50x (ISBN 0-686-97550-2). IMM North Am.
Ryan, W. & Pedder, M. Basic Science for Nurses. 2nd ed. 256p. 1981. 17.50 (ISBN 0-07-072939-5). McGraw.
Ryan, W. J. & Pearce, D. W. Price Theory. 2nd ed. LC 76-19227. 1977. 22.50 (ISBN 0-312-64400-0). St Martin.
Ryan, Will G., jt. ed. see Schwartz, Theodore B.
Ryan, William. Blaming the Victim. 320p. 1972. pap. 2.45 (ISBN 0-394-72226-4, Vin). Random.
--Equality. LC 81-52258. 256p. 1982. pap. 6.95 (ISBN 0-394-71185-8). Random.
Ryan, William, jt. auth. see Guinness, Desmond.
Ryan, William, jt. auth. see Wiles, Cheryl.
Ryan, William J., jt. auth. see Pogorzelski, Henry A.
Ryavec, Karl W. Implementation of Soviet Economic Reforms: Political, Organizational & Social Processes. LC 75-3627. (Special Studies). (Illus.). 380p. 1975. 38.95 o.p. (ISBN 0-275-05240-0). Praeger.
Rybach, L. & Muffler, L. J., eds. Geothermal Systems: Principles & Case Histories. LC 80-40290. 359p. 1981. 69.95 (ISBN 0-471-27811-4, Pub. by Wiley-Interscience). Wiley.
Rybach, Ladislaus & Stegena, Lajos, eds. Geothermics & Geothermal Energy. (Contributions to Current Research in Geophysics Ser.: Vol. 7). 1979. text ed. 65.00x (ISBN 0-686-96860-3). Renouf.
Rybczynski, Witold. Paper Heroes: A Review of Appropriate Technology. LC 79-7055. (Illus.). 1980. pap. 4.95 o.p. (ISBN 0-385-14305-2, Anch). Doubleday.
Rybicki, George B. & Lightman, Alan P. Radiative Processes in Astrophysics. LC 79-15531. 1979. 44.95 (ISBN 0-471-04815-1, Pub by Wiley-Interscience). Wiley.
Rychener, Hans. Freude Am Wort Gutes Deutsch: Guter Stil. 282p. (Ger.). 1982. write for info. (ISBN 3-261-04984-7). P Lang Pubs.
Rychlak, Joseph. Personality & Lifestyle of Young Male Managers: A Logical Learning Theory Analysis. 29.50 (ISBN 0-12-605120-8). Acad Pr.
Rychlak, Joseph F. Discovering Free Will & Personal Responsibility. LC 78-31709. 1979. 17.95x (ISBN 0-19-502580-6); pap. text ed. 7.95x (ISBN 0-19-502687-X). Oxford U Pr.
--Introduction to Personality & Psychotherapy. 2nd ed. LC 80-68141. (Illus.). 800p. 1981. text ed. 28.95 (ISBN 0-395-29736-2); instr's manual 1.25 (ISBN 0-395-29737-0). HM.
--The Psychology of Rigorous Humanism. LC 76-54838. 547p. 1977. 37.50 (ISBN 0-471-74796-3, Pub. by Wiley-Interscience). Wiley.
Rychtman, Allen C., jt. auth. see Finston, Harmon L.
Ryck, Frances. The Sern Charter. LC 75-45249. 192p. 1976. 7.95 o.p. (ISBN 0-698-10740-3, Coward). Putnam Pub Group.
Ryckman, John. Ginger's Upstairs Pet. LC 78-161025. (Venture Ser). (Illus.). (gr. 1). 1971. PLB 6.69 (ISBN 0-8116-6717-0). Garrard.
Ryckman, John & McInnes, John. Wish Me Well. LC 72-157848. (Venture Ser). (Illus.). (gr. 1). 1971. PLB 6.69 (ISBN 0-8116-6714-6). Garrard.
Ryckman, Lucile D. Paid in Full: The Story of Harold Rykman, Missionary Pioneer to Paraguay & Brazil. (Illus.). 1979. pap. 3.75 o.p. (ISBN 0-89367-033-2). Light & Life.
Ryckman, W. G. The Art of Speaking Effectively. (Plaid Ser.). 90p. 1983. pap. 7.95 (ISBN 0-87094-387-1). Dow Jones-Irwin.
--The Art of Writing Clearly. (Plaid Ser.). 90p. 1983. pap. 7.95 (ISBN 0-87094-388-X). Dow Jones-Irwin.
--How to Pass the Employment Interview (With Flying Colors) LC 82-70157. 1982. 12.95 (ISBN 0-87094-291-3). Dow Jones-Irwin.
Rycroft, jt. auth. see Ryan.
Rycus, Judith S., jt. auth. see Hughes, Ronald C.
Rydberg, Viktor. The Christmas Tomten. (Illus.). 1981. 9.95 (ISBN 0-698-20528-6, Coward). Putnam Pub Group.
Rydel, Christine. A Nabokov's Who's Who: A Complete Guide to Character Names & Other Proper Names in the Works of Vladimir Nabokov. 200p. 1983. 20.00 (ISBN 0-686-82857-7); pap. 12.50 (ISBN 0-686-82858-5). Ardis Pubs.
Rydel, Christine, ed. An Anthology of Russian Romanticism. 1983. 25.00 (ISBN 0-88233-741-6). Ardis Pubs.
Ryden, Hope. The Little Deer of the Florida Keys. LC 77-20884. (Illus.). (gr. 3 up). 1978. 7.95 o.p. (ISBN 0-399-20635-3). Putnam Pub Group.
--The Wild Colt: The Life of a Young Mustang. (Illus.). (gr. 3 up). 1972. 6.95 o.p. (ISBN 0-698-20178-7, Coward). Putnam Pub Group.
--The Wild Pups: The True Story of a Coyote Family. (Illus.). (gr. 4 up). 1975. 6.95 o.p. (ISBN 0-399-20476-8). Putnam Pub Group.
Ryder. Picture Framing. (The Grosset Art Instruction Ser.: No. 43). 48p. Date not set. pap. price not set (ISBN 0-448-00552-2, G&D). Putnam Pub Group.
Ryder, A. J. German Revolution of Nineteen Eighteen. 1967. 47.50 (ISBN 0-521-06176-8). Cambridge U Pr.
Ryder, F. G. & McCormick, E. A. Lebendige Literatur: Deutsches Lesebuch Fur Anfanger. 2nd ed. 1974. pap. text ed. 12.50 (ISBN 0-395-13826-4). HM.
Ryder, G. H. Jigs, Fixtures, Tools & Gauges. 6th ed. Orig. Title: Jigs, Tools & Fixtures. (Illus.). 176p. 1973. text ed. 14.00x (ISBN 0-291-39432-9). Scholium Intl.
Ryder, George E., jt. auth. see Aldridge, Alan.
Ryder, Harriette. How to Get Married Again. (YA) 1978. text ed. 10.95 (ISBN 0-914094-18-1). Symphony.
Ryder, Hillyer. Colonial Coins of Vermont. updated ed. Bd. with Vermont Coinage. Slafter, Edmund. Repr. of 1870 ed. 1982. softcover 10.00 (ISBN 0-915262-65-7). S J Durst.
--Copper Coins of Massachusetts. 1981. Repr. of 1920 ed. softcover 6.00 (ISBN 0-915262-66-5). S J Durst.
Ryder, Joanne. C-3PO's Book About Robots. LC 82-20424. (Illus.). 32p. (gr. 3-8). 1983. pap. 1.25 saddle-stitched (ISBN 0-394-85690-2). Random.
--Fog in the Meadow. LC 77-25650. (Illus.). 1979. 9.57i (ISBN 0-06-025148-4, HarpJ); PLB 9.89 (ISBN 0-06-025149-2). Har-Row.
--The Incredible Space Machines. (A Three-Two-One Contact Bk.). (Illus.). 32p. (gr. 4-7). 1982. pap. 4.95 (ISBN 0-394-85201-X). Random.
--A Wet & Sandy Day. LC 76-18401. (Illus.). (gr. k-3). 1977. 6.95 o.p. (ISBN 0-06-025158-1, HarpJ); PLB 8.89 (ISBN 0-06-025159-X). Har-Row.
Ryder, Joanne & Feinberg, Harold S. Snail in the Woods. LC 78-22157. (Nature I Can Read Bks.). (Illus.). 64p. (gr. k-3). 1979. 7.64i o.p. (ISBN 0-06-025168-9, HarpJ); PLB 8.89 (ISBN 0-06-025169-7). Har-Row.
Ryder, John D. Electronic Fundamentals & Applications: Integrated & Discrete Systems. 5th ed. (Illus.). 640p. 1975. 31.95 (ISBN 0-13-251371-4). P-H.
Ryder, Judith & Silver, Harold. Modern English Society. 2nd ed. LC 77-8049. 1977. 24.00x (ISBN 0-416-55490-3); pap. 10.95x (ISBN 0-416-55500-4). Methuen Inc.
Ryder, Nicholas G. Ryder's Standard Geographic Reference: The United States of America. LC 81-90461. (Satellite Photo Maps of the World Ser.). (Illus.). 223p. 1981. 75.00 (ISBN 0-941784-00-2). Ryder Geo.
Ryder, Verdene. Contemporary Living. LC 80-28224. (Illus.). 352p. 1981. text ed. 14.64 (ISBN 0-87006-319-7); wkbk. 3.80 (ISBN 0-87006-410-X). Goodheart.
Ryder, Virginia P. Cormorants Landing: How to Do Your Own Condo-Conversion Plus Secrets of City Hall. LC 82-90719. (Illus.). 130p. 1983. pap. 10.00 (ISBN 0-935098-02-X). Amigo Pr.
Rydholm, Sven A. Pulping Processes. LC 65-18412. 1269p. 1965. 123.00 (ISBN 0-471-74793-9, Pub. by Wiley-Interscience). Wiley.
Ryding, William, jt. auth. see Sareil, Jean.
Ryding, William W. Petite Revision de Grammaire Francaise. 247p. 1975. text ed. 20.50 scp (ISBN 0-06-045686-8, HarpC). Har-Row.
Rydjord, John. Indian Place Names: Their Origin, Evolution, & Meanings Collected in Kansas from the Siouian, Alogonguin, Shoshonean, Caddoan, Iroquoian, & Other Tongues. LC 68-10303. (Illus.). 380p. 1982. 22.50 (ISBN 0-8061-0801-0); pap. 10.95 (ISBN 0-8061-1763-X). U of Okla Pr.
--Who Wants War? 272p. 1983. 12.00 (ISBN 0-682-49972-2). Exposition.
Rydzewski, Pamela. Art & Human Experience. 1967. 27.00 (ISBN 0-08-012136-5). Pergamon.
Rye, Bjorn R. The Expatriate. LC 74-17681. 224p. 1975. 7.95 o.p. (ISBN 0-672-52006-0). Bobbs.
Rye, James. Cloze Procedure & the Teaching of Reading. 144p. (Orig.). 1982. pap. text ed. 6.50x (ISBN 0-435-10781-X). Heinemann Ed.
Rye, Walter. Records & Record Searching. LC 68-30663. 1969. Repr. of 1897 ed. 34.00x (ISBN 0-8103-3133-0). Gale.
Ryeah, Ann. Australian Adventure: Girl Guides Under the Southern Cross. 8.50 (ISBN 0-392-14730-0, ABC). Sportshelf.
Ryel, D., jt. auth. see Dahlstrom, J.
Ryerse, Phyllis. A Guide to the History & Restoration of Antique Trunks. (Illus.). 34p. 1974. pap. 2.50 (ISBN 0-9603388-0-2). Ryerse.
Ryerson, Albert W. The Ryerson Genealogy: Genealogy & History of the Knickerbocker Families of Ryerson, Ryerse, Ryerss, Also Adriane & Martense Families All Descendants of Martin & Adriane Reyersz (Reyerszen) of Amsterdam, Holland. Holman, Alfred L., ed. 95.00x (ISBN 0-685-88555-0). Elliots Bks.
Ryerson, Margery A., ed. see Henri, Robert.
Ryge, Gunnary, jt. auth. see O'Brien, William.
Rykwert, Joseph. The First Moderns: The Architects of the Eighteenth Century. (Illus.). 1980. 55.00x (ISBN 0-262-18090-1). MIT Pr.

Rylaarsdam, J. Coert. Proverbs, Ecclesiastes, Song of Solomon. LC 59-10454. (Layman's Bible Commentary Ser: Vol. 10). 1964. 4.25 o.p. (ISBN 0-8042-3010-2); pap. 3.95 (ISBN 0-8042-3070-6). John Knox.

Ryland, Frederick. Chronological Outlines of English Literature. LC 68-30587. 1968. Repr. of 1914 ed. 32.00x (ISBN 0-8103-3223-X). Gale.

Ryland, J., jt. auth. see Hayward, R. J.

Ryland, J. S. & Hayward, P. J. A Synopsis of the British Marine Bryozoa. 1978. 15.00 o.s.i. (ISBN 0-12-605250-6). Acad Pr.

Rylander, Paul N. Catalytic Hydrogenation Over Platinum Metals. 1967. 67.50 (ISBN 0-12-605350-2). Acad Pr.

Rylant, Cynthia. Miss Maggie. LC 82-18206, (Illus.). 32p. 1983. 8.95 (ISBN 0-525-44048-8, 0869-260). Dutton.

Ryle, Anthony. Psychotherapy: A Cognitive Integration of Theory & Practice. 196p. 1982. 22.00 (ISBN 0-8089-1488-X). Grune.

Ryle, Gilbert. Dilemmas. 1954-1960. 19.95 o.p. (ISBN 0-521-06177-6); pap. 7.95x (ISBN 0-521-09115-2). Cambridge U Pr.

Ryle, J. Warriors of the White Nile: The Dinka. (Peoples of the Wild Ser.). 1982. 15.96 (ISBN 0-7054-0700-4, Pub. by Time-Life). Silver.

Ryle, J. C. Call to Holiness. (Summit Books). 1976. pap. 2.45 o.p. (ISBN 0-8010-7649-8). Baker Bk.

--Christian Leaders of the Eighteenth Century: Includes Whitefield, Wesley, Grimshaw, Romaine, Rowlands, Berridge, Venn, Walker, Harvey, Toplady, & Fletcher. 1978. pap. 6.45 (ISBN 0-85151-268-2). Banner of Truth.

--Expository Thoughts on the Gospels, 7 vols. Incl. St. Matthew. 426p. 1974. Repr (ISBN 0-227-67697-1); St. Mark. 384p. 1973. Repr (ISBN 0-227-67698-X); St. Luke, 2 vols. 978p. 1976. Repr. Vol. 1 (ISBN 0-227-67451-0). Vol. 2. 9.95 (ISBN 0-227-67452-9). 8.75 ea.; Set. 65.00 (ISBN 0-686-66964-9). Attic Pr.

--Holiness. 352p. 1977. Repr. of 1959 ed. 10.95 (ISBN 0-227-67482-0). Attic Pr.

--Practical Religion. 344p. 1977. Repr. of 1959 ed. 10.95 (ISBN 0-227-67569-X). Attic Pr.

Ryle, John C. Charges & Addresses. 1978. 15.95 (ISBN 0-85151-267-4). Banner of Truth.

--Old Paths: Being Plain Statements on Some of the Weightier Matters of Christianity. 1977. 10.95 (ISBN 0-227-67821-4). Attic Pr.

Ryle, John Charles. Knots Untied. 342p. 1977. Repr. of 1964 ed. 10.95 (ISBN 0-227-67511-8). Attic Pr.

Ryles, A. P. & Smith, K. Worked Examples in Essential Organic Chemistry. 161p. 1981. text ed. 26.95x (ISBN 0-471-27972-2, Pub. by Wiley-Interscience); pap. text ed. 10.95x (ISBN 0-471-27975-7). Wiley.

Ryles, A. P., et al. Essential Organic Chemistry for Students of the Life Sciences. LC 78-31504. 306p. 1980. 51.95 (ISBN 0-471-27582-4, Pub. by Wiley-Interscience); pap. 19.95 (ISBN 0-471-27581-6, Pub. by Wiley-Interscience). Wiley.

Rymer, Alta M. Beep-Bap-Zap-Jack. LC 74-20428. (Tales of Planet Artembo Ser.: Bk. 1). (Illus.). (gr. 4-7). 1974. 6.95 (ISBN 0-9600792-0-3). Rymer Bks.

--Captain Zomo. LC 79-67651. (Tales of Planet Artembo Ser.: Bk. 2). (Illus.). 48p. (Orig.). (gr. 4-6). Date not set. pap. text ed. 6.95 (ISBN 0-9600792-2-X). Rymer Bks.

--Stars of Obron: Chambo Returns. (Tales of Planet Artembo: Bk. 3). (Illus.). 48p. (Orig.). (gr. 4-6). Date not set. pap. text ed. 6.95 (ISBN 0-9600792-3-8). Rymer Bks.

Rymer, Marilyn P., et al. Medicaid Eligibility: Problems & Solutions. (Westview Replica Edition: an Urban Systems Research Report). 1979. lib. bdg. 35.00 (ISBN 0-89158-478-1). Westview.

Rymer, Thomas. Critical Works. Zimansky, Curt A., ed. LC 70-156207. 1971. Repr. of 1956 ed. lib. bdg. 18.00x (ISBN 0-8371-6157-6, RYCW). Greenwood.

Ryn, August Van see Van Ryn, August.

Rynberg, Elbert. God's New Job: An Exploration of the Roads of Love. limited ed. 160p. 1983. 8.50 (ISBN 0-682-49970-6). Exposition.

Ryner, Peter, jt. auth. see Armstrong, John M.

Ryner, Peter C., jt. auth. see Armstrong, John M.

Ryoichi, jt. ed. see Naito.

Ryrie, Charles. Acts of the Apostles. (Everyman's Bible Commentary Ser.). 1967. pap. 4.50 (ISBN 0-8024-2044-3). Moody.

--Survey of Bible Doctrine. LC 72-77958. 192p. 1972. pap. 5.95 (ISBN 0-8024-8435-2). Moody.

--We Believe in Biblical Inerrancy. 1976. pap. 0.50 (ISBN 0-937396-53-2). Walterick Pubs.

Ryrie, Charles C. Balancing the Christian Life. 1969. pap. 5.95 (ISBN 0-8024-0452-9). Moody.

--The Best Is Yet to Come. 128p. 1981. pap. 5.95 (ISBN 0-8024-4938-7). Moody.

--Biblical Theology of the New Testament. LC 59-11468. 1959. 9.95 (ISBN 0-8024-0712-9). Moody.

--Dispensationalism Today. LC 65-14611. 211p. 1973. pap. 5.95 (ISBN 0-8024-2256-X). Moody.

--Equilibrio Cristiana--Balancing the Christian Life. pap. 3.95 (ISBN 0-8024-2362-0). Moody.

--First & Second Thessalonians. (Everyman's Bible Commentary). 1968. pap. 4.50 (ISBN 0-8024-2052-4). Moody.

--The Grace of God. rev., new ed. 128p. 1975. pap. 4.95 (ISBN 0-8024-3251-4). Moody.

--Holy Spirit. LC 65-14610. (Orig.). 1965. pap. 3.95 (ISBN 0-8024-3565-3); pap. 4.95 leader's guide (ISBN 0-8024-3564-5). Moody.

--Making the Most of Life. (gr. 9-12). 1983. pap. 3.95 (ISBN 0-88207-587-X). SP Pubns.

--Psalms & Proverbs. 1978. pap. 2.50 o.p. (ISBN 0-8024-7437-3). Moody.

--The Role of Women in Church. LC 58-8329. 1979. pap. 5.95 (ISBN 0-8024-7371-7). Moody.

--What You Should Know About Social Responsibility. LC 81-16804. (Current Christian Issues Ser.). 1982. pap. 3.95 (ISBN 0-8024-9417-X). Moody.

--What You Should Know About the Rapture. LC 81-4019. (Current Christian Issues Ser.). 128p. 1981. pap. 3.95 (ISBN 0-8024-9416-1). Moody.

--You Mean the Bible Teaches That. 1974. pap. 4.95 (ISBN 0-8024-9828-0). Moody.

Rys, John. Celtic Folklore: Welsh & Manx, Vol. II. 317p. 1982. pap. 8.95 (ISBN 0-7045-0410-3, Pub. by Salem Hse Ltd.). Merrimack Bk Serv.

--Celtic Folklore: Welsh & Manx, Vol. I. 400p. 1982. pap. 9.95 (ISBN 0-7045-0405-7, Pub. by Salem Hse Ltd.). Merrimack Bk Serv.

Rys, P. & Zollinger, H. Fundamentals of the Chemistry & Application of Dyes. LC 78-37108. 1972. 34.95 o.p. (ISBN 0-471-74795-5, Pub by Wiley Interscience). Wiley.

Ryskamp, C. A., ed. see Boswell, James.

Ryskamp, Charles, ed. see Collins, William.

Ryskamp, Charles, ed. see Cowper, William.

Ryssel, H. & Glawischnig, H. Ion Implantation Techniques, Berchtesgaden, FRG, 1982. (Springer Series in Electrophysics: Vol. 10). (Illus.). 372p. 1983. 30.00 (ISBN 0-387-11878-0). Springer-Verlag.

Rystad, G., ed. Congress & American Foreign Policy. (Lund Studies in International History: No. 13). 156p. 1982. text ed. 18.00x (ISBN 91-24-31480-3, Pub. by Almquist & Wiksell Sweden). Humanities.

Ryther, Thomas E., jt. auth. see Chambliss, William J.

Ryu, Chi Sik, jt. auth. see Lee, Pong K.

Ryuk, Yi, jt. auth. see Bang, Im.

Ryusen, Miyahara, illus. Buddhist Paintings-Japanese National Treasures: Restored Copies. (Illus.). 127p. 1981. 65.00 (ISBN 4-333-01039-X, Pub. by Kosei Publishing Co). C E Tuttle.

Ryzin, John Van see Robbins, Herbert & Van Ryzin, John.

Ryzin, Lani Van see Van Ryzin, Lani.

Ryznar, Edward, jt. auth. see Portman, Donald J.

Rzhevsky, Nicholas. Russian Literature & Ideology: Herzen, Dostoevsky, Leontiev, Tolstoy, & Fadeyev. LC 82-1977. 224p. 1983. 18.95 (ISBN 0-252-00964-9). U of Ill Pr.

S

S. D. Myers, Inc. Accident Prevention Bulletin, No. 17.01. (Illus.). 97p. 1977. 15.00 (ISBN 0-939320-04-5). Myers Inc.

--TMI Evaluates Series, 10 bks. Date not set. write for info. (ISBN 0-939320-04-5). Myers Inc.

S M I C. Inadvertent Climate Modification. 1971. 20.00x (ISBN 0-262-19101-6); pap. 4.95 (ISBN 0-262-69033-0). MIT Pr.

SAA Business Archives Committee, ed. Directory of Business Archives in the United States & Canada. 56p. (Orig.). 1980. pap. 6.00 o.p. (ISBN 0-931828-24-4). Soc Am Archivists.

SAA College & University Archives Committee, ed. Directory of College & University Archives in the United States & Canada. LC 80-50627. 80p. 1980. pap. 10.00 o.p. (ISBN 0-931828-21-X). Soc Am Archivists.

SAA Committee on College & University Archives, ed. College & University Archives: Selected Readings. LC 79-19917. 234p. 1979. pap. 12.00 (ISBN 0-931828-16-3). Soc Am Archivists.

SAA Forms Manual Task Force. Archival Forms Manual. 100p. 1982. pap. 10.00 (ISBN 0-931828-53-8). Soc Am Archivists.

SAA State & Local Records Committee. Records Retention & Disposition Schedules: A Survey Report. 30p. 1977. pap. 5.00 (ISBN 0-931828-11-2). Soc Am Archivists.

Saab, Ann P., tr. The Peace of Paris Eighteen Fifty Six: Studies in War, Diplomacy, & Peacemaking. Baumgart, Winfried, ed. LC 79-27128. 230p. 1981. 29.75 (ISBN 0-87436-309-8); pap. 10.85 (ISBN 0-87436-334-9). ABC-Clio.

Saad, George N. Transitivity, Causation & Passivization: A Semantic-Syntatic Study of the Verb in Classical Arabic. (Library of Arab Linguistics). 136p. 1982. 50.00 (ISBN 0-7103-0037-9). Routledge & Kegan.

Saad, Michel A. see Heat Transfer & Fluid Mechanics Institute.

Saada, Adel S. Elasticity Theory & Applications. LC 82-17171. 660p. 1983. Repr. of 1974 ed. lib. bdg. write for info. (ISBN 0-89874-559-4). Krieger.

Saagpakk, Paul F. Estonian-English Dictionary. LC 81-43606. (Yale Linguistic Ser.). 1216p. 1982. 150.00x (ISBN 0-300-02849-0). Yale U Pr.

Saake, Thomas F. Business & Consumer Mathematics. (gr. 9-12). 1977. text ed. 17.76 (ISBN 0-201-06775-7, Sch Div); tchr's ed. 22.56 (ISBN 0-201-06776-5); dupl. masters avail. A-W.

Saal, Jocelyn. Dance of Love. 1982. pap. 1.95 (ISBN 0-553-20790-3). Bantam.

Saalman, Howard. Medieval Architecture. LC 68-24702. (Great Ages of World Architecture Ser). 128p. 1963. 7.95 o.s.i. (ISBN 0-8076-0174-8); pap. 5.95 o.s.i. (ISBN 0-8076-0336-8). Braziller.

Saalman, Howard, ed. see Manetti, Antonio.

Saam, Joseph. Zur Geschichte Des Klavierquartetts Bis in Die Romantik. 174p. 35.00 o.s.i. (ISBN 90-6027-335-4, Pub. by Frits Knuf Netherlands). Pendragon NY.

Saari, David J. American Court Management: Theories & Practices. LC 82-371. (Qurom Books Ser.). (Illus.). 1982. lib. bdg. 27.50 (ISBN 0-89930-006-5, SCR/, Quorum). Greenwood.

Saarikoski, Pentti. Poems Nineteen Fifty-Eight to Nineteen Eighty. Hollo, Anselm, tr. 120p. (Orig.). 1982. pap. 10.00 o.p. (ISBN 0-915124-76-9); 50.00 (ISBN 0-915124-78-5). Toothpaste.

Saarinen, Thomas. Environmental Planning: Perception & Behavior. LC 75-19533. (Illus.). 288p. 1976. pap. text ed. 13.95 (ISBN 0-395-20618-9). HM.

Saaty, T., jt. auth. see Busacker, Robert G.

Saaty, Thomas L. The Analytic Hierarchy Process. (Illus.). 296p. 1980. text ed. 39.50 (ISBN 0-07-054371-2). McGraw.

--Elements of Queueing Theory. (Illus.). 1961. text ed. 22.50 o.p. (ISBN 0-07-054370-4, C). McGraw.

Saaty, Thomas L. & Kainen, Paul C. The Four-Color Problem: Assaults & Conquest. (Illus.). 1977. text ed. 36.50x (ISBN 0-07-054382-8, C). McGraw.

Saba, Bonaventure. The Sinful, Intimate & Mysterious Life of Mary Magdalene, 2 vols. (A Significant Historical Personalities Library Bk.). (Illus.). 316p. 1983. 98.75 (ISBN 0-89266-397-9). Am Classical Coll Pr.

Saba, Thomas M., jt. ed. see Altura, Burton M.

Sabakian, William, et al. Logotherapy. LC 79-51917. 1979. 30.00x o.s.i. (ISBN 0-87668-302-2). Aronson.

Sabanes De Plou, Dafne, tr. see Simmons, Paul D. & Crawford, Kenneth.

Sabath, Barry, jt. ed. see Carringer, Robert L.

Sabath, L. D. Action of Antibiotics in Patients. (Illus.). 250p. (Orig.). 1982. pap. text ed. 25.50 (ISBN 3-456-81228-0, Pub by Hans Huber Switzerland). J K Burgess.

Sabath, L. D., jt. ed. see Neu, H. C.

Sabath, L. J., jt. ed. see Grassi, G. G.

Sabatier, Ernest. Astride the Equator. Nixon, Ursula, tr. 1978. 34.50x o.p. (ISBN 0-19-550520-4). Oxford U Pr.

Sabatier, Paul, jt. ed. see Mazmanian, Daniel.

Sabatier, Paul A., jt. ed. see Mazmanian, Daniel.

Sabatini, Rafael. Captain Blood. new ed. LC 22-16175. (Illus.). 1977. Repr. of 1922 ed. 13.95 (ISBN 0-910220-87-5). Berg.

Sabatino, David & Mann, Lester. Discipline & Behavioral Management: A Handbook of Tactics, Strategies & Programs. 300p. 1983. price not set (ISBN 0-89443-933-2). Aspen Systems.

Sabato, Ernesto. Tunel. Perez, Louis C., ed. (Span). 1965. pap. text ed. 7.95x (ISBN 0-02-404950-6). Macmillan.

Sabato, Larry. The Democratic Party Primary in Virginia: Tantamount to Election No Longer. LC 77-9615. 1977. 9.95x (ISBN 0-8139-0726-8). U Pr of Va.

--Goodbye to Good-Time Charlie. LC 78-333. (Illus.). 304p. 1978. 22.95x o.p. (ISBN 0-669-02161-X). Lexington Bks.

--Goodbye to Goodtime Charlie: American Governorship Transformed. LC 82-22033. 250p. 1983. pap. 8.95 (ISBN 0-87187-249-8). Congr Quarterly.

Sabato, Larry J. The Rise of Political Consultants: New Ways of Winning Elections. LC 81-66104. 288p. 1981. 20.95 (ISBN 0-465-07040-X). Basic.

--The Rise of Political Consultants: New Ways of Winning Elections. 1983. pap. 9.95 (ISBN 0-465-07041-8). Basic.

Sabbagh, Miiam. Silent Echoes. LC 81-86429. 64p. 1983. pap. 4.95 (ISBN 0-86666-107-7). GWP.

Sabek, Jerwan. English-French-Arabic Trilingual Dictionary. 35.00x (ISBN 0-86685-116-X). Intl Bk Ctr.

Saberhagen, Fred. Earth Descended. 288p. (Orig.). 1981. pap. 2.95 (ISBN 0-523-48564-6). Pinnacle Bks.

Saberhagen, Fred, jt. auth. see Zelazny, Roger.

Saberi, Reza. The Labyrinth. 246p. 1982. pap. 7.95 (ISBN 0-682-49898-X). Exposition.

Sabersky, Rolf H., et al. Fluid Flow: First Course in Fluid Mechanics. 2nd ed. 1971. text ed. 32.95x (ISBN 0-02-404970-0). Macmillan.

Saberwal, Satish, ed. Towards a Cultural Policy. 1974. 15.00x o.p. (ISBN 0-7069-0342-0, Pub. by Vikas India). Advent NY.

Sabey, B. R. Introductory Experimental Soil Science. 1969. spiral bdg. 5.40x (ISBN 0-87563-025-1). Stipes.

Sabidussi, G., jt. auth. see Ross, A.

Sabille, Jacques, jt. auth. see Poliakov, Leon.

Sabin, A. Ross, ed. Automatic Dryers. (Illus.). 182p. (gr. 11). 1982. 20.00 (ISBN 0-938336-05-3). Whirlpool.

--Range Service (Gas, Electric, Microwave) (Illus.). 254p. (gr. 11). 1980. 20.00 (ISBN 0-938336-06-1). Whirlpool.

--Refrigeration, Pt. I. (Illus.). 144p. (gr. 11). 1974. 20.00 (ISBN 0-938336-01-0). Whirlpool.

--Refrigeration, Pt. II. (Illus.). 208p. (gr. 11). 1974. 20.00 (ISBN 0-938336-02-9). Whirlpool.

Sabin, Francene. Amelia Earhart: Adventure in the Sky. LC 82-15987. (Illus.). 48p. (gr. 4-6). 1983. PLB 6.89 (ISBN 0-89375-839-6); pap. text ed. 1.95 (ISBN 0-89375-840-X). Troll Assocs.

--Jimmy Connors: King of the Courts. LC 77-11688. (Putnam Sports Shelf). (Illus.). (gr. 5 up). 1978. PLB 6.27 o.p. (ISBN 0-399-61115-0). Putnam Pub Group.

--Louis Pasteur: Young Scientist. LC 82-15924. (Illus.). 48p. (gr. 4-6). 1983. PLB 6.89 (ISBN 0-89375-853-1); pap. text ed. 1.95 (ISBN 0-89375-854-X). Troll Assocs.

--Set Point: The Story of Chris Evert. LC 76-41819. (Putnam Sports Shelf). (Illus.). (gr. 6-8). 1977. PLB 6.29 o.p. (ISBN 0-399-61073-1). Putnam Pub Group.

Sabin, Francene & Sabin, Louis. Dogs of America. (Illus.). (gr. 6 up). 1967. PLB 5.99 (ISBN 0-399-60131-7). Putnam Pub Group.

--Perfect Pets. LC 77-12598. (Illus.). (gr. 5 up). 1978. 7.95 (ISBN 0-399-20626-4). Putnam Pub Group.

Sabin, J. R., jt. auth. see Quantum Chemistry, International Congress, 3rd.

Sabin, John R., ed. see International Symposium on Quantum Biology & Quantum Pharmacology.

Sabin, Lou & Sendler, Dave. Stars of Pro Basketball. LC 73-117546. (Pro Basketball Library: No. 4). (Illus.). (gr. 5-9). 1970. PLB 3.69 o.p. (ISBN 0-394-90621-7); pap. 0.95 (ISBN 0-394-82203-X). Random.

Sabin, Louis. The Fabulous Dr. J: All-Time All-Star. (Putnam Sports Shelf). (Illus.). (gr. 5 up). 1976. PLB 6.99 (ISBN 0-399-61042-1). Putnam Pub Group.

--Johnny Bench: King of Catchers. LC 76-41906. (Putnam Sports Shelf). (Illus.). (gr. 6-8). 1977. PLB 6.29 o.p. (ISBN 0-399-61072-3). Putnam Pub Group.

--One Hundred Great Moments in Sports. LC 78-16034. (Putnam Sports Shelf). (Illus.). (gr. 6-8). 1979. PLB 6.99 (ISBN 0-399-61126-6). Putnam Pub Group.

--Pele: Soccer Superstar. (Putnam Sports Shelf). (Illus.). (gr. 5 up). 1976. PLB 6.29 o.p. (ISBN 0-399-61034-0). Putnam Pub Group.

--Pro Basketball's Greatest: Selected All-Star Offensive & Defensive Teams. LC 75-45485. (Putnam Sports Shelf). 128p. (gr. 5 up). 1976. PLB 5.29 o.p. (ISBN 0-399-60999-7). Putnam Pub Group.

--Thomas Alva Edison: Young Inventor. LC 82-15889. (Illus.). 48p. (gr. 4-6). 1983. PLB 6.89 (ISBN 0-89375-841-8); pap. text ed. 1.95 (ISBN 0-89375-842-6). Troll Assocs.

--Walt Frazier: No. 1 Guard of the NBA. LC 75-23458. (Putnam Sports Shelf). 128p. (gr. 5 up). 1976. PLB 5.49 o.p. (ISBN 0-399-60975-X). Putnam Pub Group.

--Wilbur & Orville Wright: The Flight to Adventure. LC 82-15879. (Illus.). 48p. (gr. 4-6). 1983. PLB 6.89 (ISBN 0-89375-851-5); pap. text ed. 1.95 (ISBN 0-89375-852-3). Troll Assocs.

Sabin, Louis, jt. auth. see Sabin, Francene.

Sabin, M. A., ed. Programming Techniques in Computer Aided Design. LC 73-92431. 200p. 1974. 57.50x (ISBN 0-85012-112-4). Intl Pubns Serv.

Sabin, William A. The Gregg Reference Manual. 5th ed. Tinervia, Joseph, ed. (gr. 9-12). 1977. 14.00 (ISBN 0-07-054388-7, G); minature ed. 8.20 (ISBN 0-07-054389-5); pap. text ed. 6.68 (ISBN 0-07-054387-9); key 2.05 (ISBN 0-07-054396-8); wkshts. 1.96 (ISBN 0-07-054395-X). McGraw.

Sabine, George H., ed. see Milton, John.

Sabine, Gordon & Sabine, Patricia. Books That Made a Difference. 1983. 18.50 (ISBN 0-208-02021-7, Lib Prof Pubns); pap. 13.50x (ISBN 0-208-02022-5, Lib Prof Pubns). Shoe String.

Sabine, Patricia, jt. auth. see Sabine, Gordon.

Sabini, Jon & Silver, Maury. Moralities of Everyday Life. (256). 1982. 19.95 (ISBN 0-19-503016-8, GB691); pap. 6.95 (ISBN 0-19-503017-6). Oxford U Pr.

Sabiq, Sayyed. Figh Al Sunnah. Quilan, Hamid, ed. Izzidien, Movel Y., tr. from Arabic. LC 82-70450. 1700p. (Orig.). 1983. text ed. 30.00 (ISBN 0-89259-033-5); pap. 20.00 (ISBN 0-686-81828-8). Am Trust Pubns.

Sabisch, Christian, jt. ed. see Galloway, David.

Sabiston, David C. & Spencer, Frank C., eds. Gibbon's Surgery of the Chest. 3rd ed. LC 74-25481. (Illus.). 1976. 105.00 o.p. (ISBN 0-7216-7872-6). Saunders.

Sabiston, David C., Jr. Davis-Christopher Textbook of Surgery, 2 vol. set. (Illus.). 2481p. 1981. Set. 89.00 (ISBN 0-7216-7878-5); Single Volume. 72.00 (ISBN 0-7216-7875-0); 42.50 o.p. (ISBN 0-686-79891-0). Saunders.

Sabiston, David C., Jr., ed. Davis-Christopher: Textbook of Surgery - the Biological Basis of Modern Surgical Practice, 2 vols. in 1. 11th ed. LC 76-4287. (Illus.). 1977. text ed. 49.00 o.p. (ISBN 0-7216-7868-8). Saunders.

Sabki, Hisham M. The United Nations & the Pacific Settlement of Disputes: A Case Study of Lybia. LC 77-962867. 207p. 1973. 15.00x (ISBN 0-8002-2122-2). Intl Pubns Serv.

Sable, Barbara K. The Vocal Sound. (Illus.). 224p. 1982. pap. 15.95 ref. ed. (ISBN 0-13-942979-4). P-H.

Sabloff, Jeremy A., jt. ed. see Bricker, Victoria R.

Sabnis, Gajanan M., ed. Handbook of Composite Construction Engineering. 1979. text ed. 27.50x o.p. (ISBN 0-442-27735-0). Van Nos Reinhold.

Sabol & Bender. A Concordance to Bronte's Jane Eyre. 1981. lib. bdg. 80.00 o.s.i. (ISBN 0-8240-9339-9). Garland Pub.

Sabol, Andrew J., ed. see Jonson, Ben.

Sabolovic, D., jt. ed. see Preece, A. W.

Sabourud, J. A., jt. auth. see Duconte, C. M.

Sabre, Ru Michael, jt. auth. see Vallance, Theodore.

Sabrosky, Alan N., et al. Blue-Collar Soldiers? Unionization & the U. S. Military. 166p. (Orig.). 1977. pap. 5.95 (ISBN 0-910191-03-4). For Policy Res.

Sabrosky, Judith A. From Rationality to Liberation: The Evolution of Feminist Ideology. LC 79-7065. (Contributions in Political Science: No. 32). 1980. lib. bdg. 25.00x (ISBN 0-313-20672-4, SRA/). Greenwood.

Sabry, Z., jt. auth. see Fremes, Ruth.

Sabzavari, Hadi Ibn Mahdi. The Metaphysics of Haji Mulla Hadi Sabzavari. Izutsu, Toshihiku & Mohaghegh, Mehdi, trs. from Persian. LC 76-18174. 248p. 1977. lib. bdg. 35.00x (ISBN 0-88206-011-2). Caravan Bks.

Saccheri, Girolamo. Euclides Vindicatus. 2nd ed. Halstead, George B., tr. from Lat. 1980. text ed. 16.95 (ISBN 0-8284-0289-2). Chelsea Pub.

Sacchi, Louise. Ocean Flying. (McGraw-Hill Ser. in Aviation). (Illus.). 240p. 1979. 19.95 (ISBN 0-07-054405-0). McGraw.

Saccio, Peter. Shakespeare's English Kings: History, Chronicle & Drama. 1977. pap. 7.95 (ISBN 0-19-502156-8, 508, GB). Oxford U Pr.

Sacco, W. J., jt. auth. see Berman, L. I.

Saccone, C., jt. auth. see Kroon, A. M.

Saccuzzo, Dennis P., jt. auth. see Kaplan, Robert M.

Sachar, A. L. History of the Jews. rev. ed. (gr. 6 up). 1967. 20.00 (ISBN 0-394-42871-4); pap. text ed. 17.00 (ISBN 0-394-30482-9). Knopf.

Sachar, Abram. The Redemption of the Unwanted. 1983. 19.95 (ISBN 0-312-66729-9, Pub. by Marek). St Martin.

Sachar, Edward J., ed. Hormones, Behavior, & Psychopathology. LC 75-16660. (American Psychopathological Association Ser.). 325p. 1976. 35.00 (ISBN 0-89004-094-X). Raven.

Sachar, Howard M. Course of Modern Jewish History. rev ed. 1977. pap. 10.95 (ISBN 0-440-51538-6, Delta). Dell.

--Egypt & Israel. 1981. 19.95 o.p. (ISBN 0-399-90124-8, Marek). Putnam Pub Group.

Sachar, Louis. Sideways Stories from Wayside School. LC 78-3213. (Illus.). 1978. trade ed. 3.96 (ISBN 0-695-80964-4); lib. bdg. 5.31 (ISBN 0-695-40964-6). Follett.

--Someday Angeline. 144p. 1983. pap. 2.25 (ISBN 0-380-83444-8, Camelot). Avon.

Sacharoff, Shanta N. The Flavors of India. LC 79-182418. (Illus.). 192p. (Orig.). 1972. pap. 6.95 (ISBN 0-912238-16-X). One Hund One Prods.

Sacharow, Stanley. Packaging Design. (Illus.). 256p. 1982. 45.00 (ISBN 0-86636-000-X). Photo Bk Co.

Sachchidananda. The Changing Munda. 1979. text ed. 26.25x (ISBN 0-391-01932-5). Humanities.

Sachchidananda & Lal. Elite & Development. 286p. 1980. text ed. 16.50x (ISBN 0-391-02129-X). Humanities.

Sachedina, Abdulaziz A. Islamic Messianism: The Idea of Mahdi in Twelver Shi'ism. LC 80-16767. 1980. text ed. 44.50x (ISBN 0-87395-442-4); pap. text ed. 16.95x (ISBN 0-87395-458-0). State U NY Pr.

Sacher, Jack & Eversole, James. The Art of Sound: An Introduction to Music. 2nd ed. (Illus.). 1977. pap. text ed. 17.95 (ISBN 0-13-048744-9); records 11.95 (ISBN 0-13-048660-4). P-H.

Sachithanandan, V. Whitman & Bharati: Comparative Study. 242p. 1980. pap. text ed. 7.25x (ISBN 0-391-01740-3). Humanities.

Sachs. The U F O Encyclopedia. 1980. 14.95 (ISBN 0-399-12365-2). Putnam Pub Group.

Sachs, A., jt. auth. see Neugebauer, O.

Sachs, Albie, jt. auth. see Naidoo, Indres.

Sachs, B. K., ed. General Relativity & Cosmology. (Italian Physical Society: Course 47). 1971. 70.00 (ISBN 0-12-368847-7). Acad Pr.

Sachs, Bernard J. & Nixon, George F. Balitimore Streetcars 1905-1963: The Semi-Convertible Era. (Orig.). 1982. pap. 14.95 (ISBN 0-9609638-0-4). Baltimore Streetcar.

Sachs, Carolyn E. Invisible Farmers: Women in Agricultural Production. 180p. 1983. text ed. 22.50x (ISBN 0-86598-094-2). Allanheld.

Sachs, Curt. Geist und Werden Des Musikinstrumente. 1975. 35.00 o.s.i. (ISBN 90-6027-336-2, Pub. by Frits Knuf Netherlands); wrappers 22.50 o.s.i. (ISBN 90-6027-023-1). Pendragon NY.

Sachs, E., jt. auth. see Gruver, W. A.

Sachs, G. & Voegeli, H. E. Principles & Methods of Sheet Metal Fabricating. 2nd ed. LC 66-26501. 576p. 1966. 28.50 (ISBN 0-442-15171-3, Pub. by Van Nos Reinhold). Krieger.

Sachs, G., jt. auth. see Schultz, I.

Sachs, George, ed. see Symposium on Gastric Secretion, Frankfurt Am Main, 1971.

Sachs, Harvey. Toscanini. (Illus.). 1978. 17.26i (ISBN 0-397-01320-5). Har-Row.

--Virtuoso: The Instrumentalist as Superstar. LC 82-80491. 1982. 17.95 (ISBN 0-500-01286-5). Thames Hudson.

Sachs, Jonathan & Meyer, Rick. The HHC User Guide. 200p. (Orig.). 1983. pap. 14.95 (ISBN 0-931988-87-X). Osborne-McGraw.

Sachs, Julius Von. History of Botany, 1530-1860. rev. ed. Balfour, Isaac B., ed. Garnsey, Henry E., tr. LC 66-24753. 1967. Repr. of 1890 ed. 11.00x (ISBN 0-8462-1797-X). Russell.

Sachs, Lorraine P. & Kane, Michael T. Measurement & Evaluation in Nursing Education. 106p. 1980. 5.50 (ISBN 0-686-38304-4, 17-1807). Natl League Nurse.

Sachs, M. General Relativity & Matter. 1982. 39.00 (ISBN 90-277-1381-2, Pub. by Reidel Holland). Kluwer Boston.

Sachs, Marianne. Leonardo & His World. LC 80-68208. (Great Masters Ser.). PLB 13.00 (ISBN 0-382-06374-0). Silver.

Sachs, Marilyn. Beach Towels. (Illus.). 80p. (gr. 7-11). 1982. 9.95 (ISBN 0-525-44003-8, 0966-290, Skinny Bk). Dutton.

--Bears' House. LC 76-157621. (gr. 4-7). 1971. 7.95a o.p. (ISBN 0-385-03363-X); PLB 7.95a (ISBN 0-385-06632-5). Doubleday.

--Bus Ride. LC 79-23596. (Illus.). (gr. 7 up). 1980. 9.25 (ISBN 0-525-27325-5, 0898-270, Skinny Book); pap. 2.50 (ISBN 0-525-45048-3, Skinny Book). Dutton.

--Call Me Ruth. LC 82-45208. 128p. 1982. 11.95 (ISBN 0-385-17607-4). Doubleday.

--Class Pictures. 144p. 1982. pap. 1.95 o.p. (ISBN 0-380-61408-1, 61408, Flare). Avon.

--Fleet Footed Florence. LC 76-56330. (Illus.). 48p. (gr. 2). 1981. 8.95 (ISBN 0-385-12745-6); PLB o.p. (ISBN 0-385-12746-4). Doubleday.

--Fourteen. LC 82-18209. 128p. (gr. 4-9). 1983. 9.95 (ISBN 0-525-44044-5, 0966-290). Dutton.

--A Secret Friend. LC 77-25606. (gr. 4-7). 1978. 8.95a o.p. (ISBN 0-385-13569-6); PLB 8.95a (ISBN 0-385-13570-X). Doubleday.

--A Summer's Lease. LC 78-12486. (gr. 5 up). 1979. 9.25 (ISBN 0-525-40480-5, 0898-270). Dutton.

--Veronica Ganz. LC 68-11813. (gr. 4-7). 1968. PLB 8.95 (ISBN 0-385-01436-8). Doubleday.

Sachs, Maurice. Witches' Sabbath. Howard, Richard, tr. 316p. 1982. pap. 9.95 (ISBN 0-8128-6155-8). Stein & Day.

Sachs, Mendel. Ideas of Matter: From Ancient Times to Bohr & Einstein. LC 80-6069. 334p. 1981. lib. bdg. 22.00 (ISBN 0-8191-1615-7); pap. text ed. 12.25 (ISBN 0-8191-1616-5). U Pr of Amer.

Sachs, Michael L., jt. ed. see Sacks, Michael H.

Sachs, Robert G., ed. National Energy Issues: How Do We Decide? Plutonium As a Test Case. LC 79-18341. (American Academy of Arts & Sciences Ser.). 360p. 1980. prof ref 27.50x (ISBN 0-88410-620-9). Ballinger Pub.

Sachs, Rudolf. British & American Business Terms. 144p. 1975. 20.00x (ISBN 0-7121-0242-6, Pub. by Macdonald & Evans). State Mutual Bk.

Sachs, Samuel, II. Favorite Paintings from the Minneapolis Institute of Arts. LC 80-70412. (Illus.). 1981. 14.95 (ISBN 0-89659-224-3); pap. write for info. (ISBN 0-89659-189-1). Minneapolis Inst Arts.

Sachs, Stephen, jt. ed. see Goldstein, Richard.

Sachs, William & Benson, George. Product Planning & Management. 376p. 1981. 22.95 (ISBN 0-87814-149-9). Pennwell Pub.

Sachs, Wulf. Black Anger. LC 68-23323. 1968. Repr. of 1947 ed. lib. bdg. 18.50x (ISBN 0-8371-0244-8, SABA). Greenwood.

Sachse, Herbert B. Semiconducting Temperature Sensors & Their Application. LC 75-2017. 380p. 1975. 34.50 o.p. (ISBN 0-471-74835-8, Pub. by Wiley-interscience). Wiley.

Sachse, Julius F. The Braddock Exhibition: Conditions of Pennsylvania During the Year 1775. a Translation of a French Pamphlet Found in the Ducal Library at Gotha, Germany, Vol. 25. Repr. of 1917 ed. 25.00 (ISBN 0-911122-04-4). Penn German Soc.

--Quaint Old Germantown in Philadelphia, Vol. 23. 30.00 (ISBN 0-911122-02-8). Penn German Soc.

Sachse, Julius F. & Nead, Daniel W. The Wayside Inns on the Lancaster Roadside Between Philadelphia & Lancaster: Bd. with The Pennsylvania German in the Settlement of Maryland, Vol. 22. Repr. of 1913 ed. 20.00 o.p. (ISBN 0-911122-01-X). Penn German Soc.

Sachse L. & Co. Full-Color Uniforms of the Prussian Army: 72 Plates From 1830. (Illus.). 80p. 1981. pap. 10.00 (ISBN 0-486-24085-1). Dover.

Sachse, William L. English History in the Making: Readings from the Sources from 1689, 2 vols. LC 67-10154. 1970. Vol. 1. pap. text ed. 18.50 o.p. (ISBN 0-471-00494-4); Vol. 2. pap. text ed. 12.95 o.p. (ISBN 0-471-00497-9). Wiley.

Sachse, William L., jt. auth. see Green, Eugene.

Sack, John. Fingerprint: The Autobiography of An American Man. Date not set. 13.95 (ISBN 0-394-50197-7). Random.

Sack, John & Gabriel, Judy M. Entering BASIC. 2nd ed. 160p. 1980. pap. text ed. 10.95 (ISBN 0-574-21270-1, 13-4270). SRA.

Sack, W. O. & Habel, R. E. Rooney's Guide to the Dissection of the Horse. LC 76-56521. (Illus.). 1979. with 10 microfiches 23.50x (ISBN 0-9601152-1-8). Veterinary Textbks.

Sackett, Gene P., ed. Observing Behavior, Vol. 1. LC 77-25276. 432p. 1977. text ed. 19.95 (ISBN 0-8391-1167-3). Univ Park.

--Observing Behavior, Vol. 2. LC 77-25276. 128p. 1977. text ed. 19.95 (ISBN 0-8391-1168-1). Univ Park.

Sackett, Robert E. Popular Entertainment, Class & Politics in Munich, 1900-1923. 208p. 1982. text ed. 20.00x (ISBN 0-674-69885-2). Harvard U Pr.

Sackett, S. J. Edgar Watson Howe. (United States Authors Ser.). lib. bdg. 13.95 (ISBN 0-8057-0383-7, Twayne). G K Hall.

Sackett, Susan & Roddenberry, Gene. The Making of Star Trek: The Motion Picture. 1980. 14.95 o.p. (ISBN 0-671-25181-3); pap. 7.95 o.p. (ISBN 0-671-79109-5). S&S.

Sackheim & Robbins. Programmed Mathematics for Nurses. 1983. 14.95 (ISBN 0-02-405170-5). Macmillan.

Sackheim, George & Lehman, Dennis. Chemistry for the Health Sciences. 4th ed. 1981. text ed. 23.95x (ISBN 0-02-405030-X); lab. manual 11.95x (ISBN 0-686-72523-9). Macmillan.

Sackheim, George I. Atomic & Molecular Orbitals. 1965. pap. 2.40x (ISBN 0-87563-002-2). Stipes.

--Chemical Calculations. 1983. 4.80x (ISBN 0-87563-228-9). Ser. B. Stipes.

Sackheim, George I., et al. Programmed Mathematics for Nursing. 4th ed. 1979. pap. text ed. 14.95x (ISBN 0-02-405190-X). Macmillan.

Sackman, H., ed. see IFIP Conference on Human Choice & Computers Apr. 1-5, 1974.

Sackman, Harold & Boehm, Barry W., eds. Planning Community Information Utilities. LC 72-83727. (Illus.). viii, 501p. 1972. 17.25 (ISBN 0-88283-000-7). AFIPS Pr.

Sackman, Harold & Nie, Norman, eds. The Information Utility & Social Choice. LC 78-129364. (Illus.). 310p. 1970. 10.50 (ISBN 0-88283-019-8). AFIPS Pr.

Sacks. Essentials of Welding. 1983. text ed. price not set (ISBN 0-87002-385-3). Bennett IL.

Sacks, Elizabeth. Shakespeare's Images of Pregnancy. 1980. 22.50x (ISBN 0-312-71595-1). St Martin.

Sacks, Florence, jt. auth. see Immel, Constance.

Sacks, Howard R., jt. auth. see Silver, Theodore.

Sacks, Karen. Sisters & Wives: The Past & Future of Sexual Equality. LC 78-75241. (Contributions in Women's Studies: No. 10). 1979. lib. bdg. 27.50x (ISBN 0-313-20983-9, SPA/). Greenwood.

--Sisters & Wives: The Past & Future of Sexual Equality. LC 82-13491. 288p. 1982. pap. 7.95 (ISBN 0-252-01004-3). U of Ill Pr.

Sacks, Kenneth. Polybius on the Writing of History. (U.C. Publications in Classical Studies: Vol. 24). 233p. 1981. 23.00x (ISBN 0-520-09633-9). U of Cal Pr.

Sacks, Mason J. Modern Tax Planning Checklists. 1977. 55.00 (ISBN 0-88262-158-0, 77-23758). Warren.

Sacks, Michael H. & Sachs, Michael L., eds. Psychology of Running. LC 81-82450. (Illus.). 295p. 1981. text ed. 15.95x (ISBN 0-931250-23-4). Human Kinetics.

Sacks, Oliver. Awakenings. (Illus.). 353p. 1983. pap. 7.95 (ISBN 0-525-48028-5, 0772-230, Obelisk). Dutton.

Sacks, Oliver W. Migraine: The Evolution of a Common Disorder. 1973. 22.50x (ISBN 0-520-01802-8); pap. 2.95 (ISBN 0-520-02484-2). U of Cal Pr.

Sacks, Raymond. Welding: Principles & Practice. (gr. 10-12). 1981. text ed. 26.00 (ISBN 0-87002-321-7); student guide 5.28 (ISBN 0-87002-193-1); tchr's guide 4.64 (ISBN 0-87002-198-2). Bennett IL.

Sacks, Richard S., jt. auth. see Brown, William E.

Sackson, Marian, jt. auth. see Gustavson, Frances.

Sackville-West, V. V. Sackville-West's Garden Book. LC 68-8261. (Illus.). 256p. 1983. pap. 9.95 (ISBN 0-689-70647-2, 295). Atheneum.

Saco, Don, ed. see Senter, Sylvia & Howe, Marguerite.

Sacy, L. Sylvestre De. Principe de Grammaire Generale Mis a la Portee des Enfants. (Linguistics 13th-18th Centuries Ser.). 197p. (Fr.). 1974. Repr. of 1799 ed. lib. bdg. 57.00x o.p. (ISBN 0-8287-0747-2, 5049). Clearwater Pub.

Sadamoto, Kuni, ed. Breaking the Barriers. (Illus.). 264p. 1982. pap. 50.00 (ISBN 4-915568-00-8, Pub. by Survey Japan). Intl Schol Bk Serv.

Sadananda. Vedantasara of Sadananda. pap. 3.00 (ISBN 0-87481-073-6). Vedanta Pr.

Sadat, Anwar El. In Search of Identity: An Autobiography. LC 77-3767. (Illus.). 1978. 13.41i (ISBN 0-06-013742-8, HarpT); pap. 6.95xi (ISBN 0-06-090705-3, CN-705). Har-Row.

Saddlemyer, Ann, ed. see Gregory, Isabella A.

Saddlemyer, Ann see Synge, John M.

Saddler, Allen. The Archery Contest. (King & Queen Ser.). (Illus.). 32p. (ps). 1983. bds. 3.95 (ISBN 0-19-279760-3, Pub by Oxford U Pr Childrens). Merrimack Bk Serv.

--The King Gets Fit. (King & Queen Ser.). (Illus.). 32p. (ps). 1983. bds. 3.95 (ISBN 0-19-279761-1, Pub by Oxford U Pr Childrens). Merrimack Bk Serv.

Saddy, Fehmy, ed. Arab-Latin American Relations: Energy, Trade & Investment. 205p. 1983. 29.95 (ISBN 0-87855-475-0). Transaction Bks.

Sade, Marquis De. Justine. Seaver, Richard & Wainhouse, Austryn, trs. from Fr. Bd. with Philosophy in the Bedroom; Eugenie De Franval; Other Writings. (Illus.). 1965. pap. 12.50 (ISBN 0-394-17123-3, B148, BC). Grove.

--One Hundred Twenty Days of Sodom & Other Writings. Wainhouse, Austryn & Seaver, Richard, eds. (Illus.). 1966. pap. 12.50 (ISBN 0-394-17119-5, B138, BC). Grove.

Sade, Marquis De see Sade, Marquis De.

Sadee, Wolfgang & Beelen, Geertruida C. Drug Level Monitoring: Analytical Techniques, Metabolism, & Pharmacokinetics. LC 79-22652. 495p. 1980. 48.95 (ISBN 0-471-04881-X, Pub. by Wiley-Interscience). Wiley.

Sadfie, Robert, jt. auth. see Peterson, Keith.

Sadhu, M. Concentration: A Guide to Mental Mastery. pap. 4.00 (ISBN 0-87980-023-2). Wilshire.

Sadick, Tamah L. & Pueschal, Siegfried M., eds. Genetic Diseases & Developmental Disabilities: Aspects of Detection & Prevention. (AAAS Selected Symposium: No. 33). 1979. lib. bdg. 16.50 (ISBN 0-89158-367-X). Westview.

Sadie, Stanley. The New Grove Mozart. (New Grove Composer Biography Ser.). (Illus.). 1983. 16.50 (ISBN 0-393-01680-3); pap. 7.95 (ISBN 0-393-30084-6). Norton.

Sadker, David M., jt. auth. see Sadker, Myra P.

Sadker, Myra P. & Sadker, David M. Now upon a Time: A Contemporary View of Children's Literature. 1977. text ed. 22.50 scp o.p. (ISBN 0-06-045693-0, HarpC). Har-Row.

Sadlack, Janet L. Enjoying Microwave Cooking. LC 75-3715. (Illus.). 1975. 5.45 (ISBN 0-918620-02-3); pap. 4.45 (ISBN 0-918620-01-5). Recipes Unltd.

--Microwave Meals Made Easy. LC 76-45673. (Illus.). 1976. 5.45 (ISBN 0-918620-12-0); pap. 4.45 (ISBN 0-918620-11-2). Recipes Unltd.

Sadlej, Joanna. Semi-Empirical Methods of Quantum Chemistry. (Chemical Science Ser.). 416p. 1982. 89.95x (ISBN 0-470-27547-2). Halsted Pr.

Sadler, jt. auth. see Anderson.

Sadler, Alfred M., Jr. & Sadler, Blair. Emergency Medical Care: The Neglected Public Service. LC 76-27275. 376p. 1977. prof ref 22.50x (ISBN 0-88410-126-6). Ballinger Pub.

Sadler, Alfred M., Jr. & Sadler, Blair L. Physician's Assistant: Today & Tomorrow: Issues Confronting New Health Practitioners. LC 75-22407. 280p. 1975. pap. 10.95x prof ref (ISBN 0-88410-124-X). Ballinger Pub.

Sadler, Blair, jt. auth. see Sadler, Alfred M., Jr.

Sadler, Blair L., jt. auth. see Sadler, Alfred M., Jr.

Sadler, Catherine E. Sasha: The Life of Alexandra Tolstoy. (Illus.). 160p. 1982. 9.95 (ISBN 0-399-20857-7). Putnam Pub Group.

--Treasure Mountain: Folktales From Southern China. LC 82-1805. (Illus.). 80p. (gr. 4-6). 1982. 11.95 (ISBN 0-689-30941-4). Atheneum.

Sadler, J. D. Modern Latin, Bk. I. 1978. 16.95x (ISBN 0-8061-1026-0); pap. 10.95x (ISBN 0-8061-1046-5). U of Okla Pr.

Sadler, Jacqueline D., jt. auth. see Sadler, Julius T., Jr.

Sadler, James C. Average Cloudiness in the Tropics from Satellite Observations. LC 69-17880. (International Indian Ocean Expedition Meteorological Monographs: No. 2). (Illus.). 1969. 12.00x (ISBN 0-8248-0081-8, Eastwest Ctr). UH Pr.

Sadler, Julius T., Jr. & Sadler, Jacqueline D. American Stables: An Architectural Tour. 1981. 29.95 (ISBN 0-8212-1105-6, 036676). NYGS.

Sadler, Lynn. Thomas Carew. (English Authors Ser.). 1979. lib. bdg. 14.95 (ISBN 0-8057-6683-9, Twayne); 9.95. G K Hall.

Sadler, Lynn V. John Bunyan. (English Authors Ser.). 1979. lib. bdg. 11.95 (ISBN 0-8057-6757-6, Twayne). G K Hall.

Sadlier, Paul & Sadlier, Ruth. Fifty Hikes in Vermont. LC 73-90338. (Illus.). 176p. 1974. pap. 6.95 (ISBN 0-912274-38-7). Backcountry Pubns.

Sadlier, Paul, jt. auth. see Sadlier, Ruth.

Sadlier, Ruth & Sadlier, Paul. Fifty Hikes in Vermont. rev. ed. LC 79-92572. (Fifty Hike Ser.). (Illus.). 1981. pap. 7.95 (ISBN 0-89725-013-3). Backcountry Pubns.

--Fifty Hikes in Vermont: Walks, Day Hikes & Backpacking Trips in the Green Mountain State. 2nd ed. LC 79-92572. (Fifty Hikes Ser.). (Illus.). 184p. 1983. pap. 7.95 (ISBN 0-942440-08-0). Backcountry Pubns.

--Short Walks on Cape Cod & the Vineyard. LC 75-34252. (Illus.). 96p. 1976. pap. 4.95 (ISBN 0-87106-066-3). Globe Pequot.

Sadlier, Ruth, jt. auth. see Sadlier, Paul.

Sadock, Benjamin J., jt. auth. see Kaplan, Harold I.

Sadoff, Ira. Palm Reading in Winter. LC 77-17147. 1978. 6.95 (ISBN 0-395-25766-2); pap. 4.50 o. s. (ISBN 0-395-26285-2). HM.

Sadoff, Robert. Legal Issues in the Care of Psychiatric Patients: A Guide for the Mental Health Professional. LC 82-5946. 144p. 1982. text ed. 15.95 (ISBN 0-8261-3650-8). Springer Pub.

Sadoff, Robert L. Violence & Responsibility: The Individual, Family & Society. 1978. 14.95x o.s.i. (ISBN 0-470-26422-5). Halsted Pr.

Sadoul & Milic-Emili. Small Airways in Health & Disease. (International Congress Ser.: Vol. 485). 1980. 50.25 (ISBN 0-444-90131-0). Elsevier.

Sadoul, Georges. Dictionary of Film Makers. Morris, Peter, tr. from Fr. LC 78-136028. 1972. 34.50x (ISBN 0-520-01862-1); pap. 5.95 (ISBN 0-520-02151-7, CAL241). U of Cal Pr.

--Dictionary of Films. Morris, Peter, tr. from Fr. LC 78-136028. 1972. 34.50x (ISBN 0-520-01864-8); pap. 8.95 (ISBN 0-520-02152-5, CAL240). U of Cal Pr.

Sadovsky, A. D., ed. see ISSS Working Group on Soil Information Systems 2nd Varna-Sofia, Bulgaria, 30 May - 4 June, 1977.

Sadowski, Zdzislaw, tr. see Kalecki, Michal.

Sadtler Research Laboratories, Inc. The Sadtler Handbooks. Incl. Sadtler Handbook of Proton NMR Spectra. 245.00 (ISBN 0-685-51845-0); Sadtler Handbook of Ultraviolet Spectra. 245.00 (ISBN 0-685-51846-9); Sadtler Handbook of Infrared Spectra. 245.00 (ISBN 0-685-93054-8). 1978. Set. 660.00 (ISBN 0-685-51844-2). Sadtler Res.

Saeed, M. Studies in Muslim Philosophy. 6.75 (ISBN 0-686-18601-X). Kazi Pubns.

Saeger, Glen. String Designs. LC 74-31703. (Little Craft Book Ser.). (Illus.). 48p. (gr. 5 up). 1975. 6.95 (ISBN 0-8069-5320-9); PLB 8.99 (ISBN 0-8069-5321-7). Sterling.

Saeger, Richard T. American Government & Politics: A Neoconservative Perspective. 1982. pap. text ed. 17.95x (ISBN 0-673-15360-6). Scott F.

Saeks, R., jt. auth. see Feintuch, Abraham.

Saeks, R., jt. auth. see Palmer, James D.

Saenger, Eugene L. Medical Aspects of Radiation Accidents. (AEC Technical Information Center Ser.). 376p. 1963. pap. 29.50 (ISBN 0-87079-268-7, TID-18867); microfiche 4.50 (ISBN 0-87079-388-8, TID-18867). DOE.

Saerchinger, Cesar. Artur Schnabel, a Biography. LC 73-7101. (Illus.). 354p. 1973. Repr. of 1958 ed. lib. bdg. 20.50x (ISBN 0-8371-6910-0, SASC). Greenwood.

Safa, Helen I., jt. ed. see Nash, June.

Safadi, Yasin H., jt. ed. see Auchterlonie, Paul.

Safanda, Elizabeth, jt. auth. see Bishop, Robert.

Safar. Cardiopulmonary Cerebral Resuscitation. 1981. text ed. 17.50 (ISBN 0-7216-7892-0). Saunders.

Safar, P. & Elam, J. O., eds. Advances in Cardiopulmonary Resuscitation. 1977. 26.10 (ISBN 0-387-90234-1). Springer-Verlag.

Safer, jt. auth. see Grunberg-Manago.

Safer, Arnold E. International Oil Policy. LC 79-7185. 192p. 1979. 17.95x (ISBN 0-669-02959-9). Lexington Bks.

Safer, Daniel J. School Programs for Disruptive Adolescents. (Illus.). 384p. 1982. 29.95 (ISBN 0-8391-1698-5). Univ Park.

Safer, Daniel J. & Allen, Richard P. Hyperactive Children: Diagnosis & Management. (Illus.). 256p. 1976. pap. text ed. 14.95 (ISBN 0-8391-0757-9). Univ Park.

Safer, Jane F. Spirals from the Sea: An Anthropological Look at Shells. (Illus.). 1982. 35.00 (ISBN 0-517-54036-3, C N Potter Bks). Crown.

Saferstein, Richard. Criminalistics: An Introduction to Forensic Science. 2nd ed. (Criminal Justice Ser.). 1981. 24.95 (ISBN 0-13-193300-0). P-H.

Saff, E. B. & Varga, R. S., eds. Pade & Rational Approximation: Theory & Applications. 1977. 36.50 (ISBN 0-12-614150-9). Acad Pr.

Saff, Edward, jt. auth. see Goodman, A. W.

Saffady, William. Computer-Output Microfilm: Its Library Applications. LC 78-18416. 1978. pap. 12.00 (ISBN 0-8389-3217-7). ALA.

--Micrographics. LC 78-1309. (Library Science Text Ser.). 1978. 28.00 (ISBN 0-87287-175-4). Libs Unl.

Saffar, Ruth E., jt. auth. see Lohman, Lou.

Saffell, David C. State & Local Government: Politics & Public Policies. 2nd ed. (Political Science Ser.). 384p. 1981. pap. text ed. 12.95 (ISBN 0-201-06568-1). A-W.

Saffell, David C., et al. The Politics of American National Government. 4th ed. 1981. pap. text ed. 13.95 (ISBN 0-316-76641-0); tchr's ed. avail. (ISBN 0-316-76642-9); study guide 6.95 (ISBN 0-316-76643-7). Little.

Saffer, T. H. & Kelly, O. Countdown Zero. 1983. pap. 5.95 (ISBN 0-14-006724-8). Penguin.

Saffer, Thomas H. & Kelly, Orville E. Countdown Zero. 336p. 1982. 15.95 (ISBN 0-399-12685-6). Putnam Pub Group.

Saffioti, Heleieth. Women in Class Society. Vale, Michael, tr. from Portugese. LC 77-76170. 1978. 16.50 (ISBN 0-85345-415-9, CL415-9); pap. 6.95 (ISBN 0-85345-530-9, PB530-9). Monthly Rev.

Saffon, M. J. M. J. Saffon's Youthlift. (Illus.). 128p. (Orig.). 1981. 12.50 (ISBN 0-446-51230-3); pap. 4.95 (ISBN 0-446-97816-7). Warner Bks.

Safford, Carleton L. & Bishop, Robert. America's Quilts & Coverlets. (Illus.). 320p. 1980. pap. 16.50 (ISBN 0-525-47566-4, 01602-480). Dutton.

Safford, Edward L., Jr. Model Radio Control. 3rd ed. (Illus.). 1979. 12.95 (ISBN 0-8306-9762-4); pap. 6.95 o.p. (ISBN 0-8306-1174-6, 1174). TAB Bks.

Safford, Edward L. Handbook of Marine Electronic & Electrical Systems. (Illus.). 1978. 14.95 o.p. (ISBN 0-8306-8939-7); pap. 9.95 o.p. (ISBN 0-8306-7939-1, 939). TAB Bks.

Safford, Edward L., Jr. Advanced Radio Control, Including Rockets & Robots. 2nd ed. 1980. 12.95 o.p. (ISBN 0-8306-9948-1); pap. 7.95 (ISBN 0-8306-1222-X, 1222). TAB Bks.

--Electrical Wiring Handbook. (Illus.). 434p. (Orig.). 1980. 17.95 o.p. (ISBN 0-8306-9932-5); pap. 15.95 (ISBN 0-8306-1245-9, 1245). Tab Bks.

Saffotti, Umberto & Wagoner, Joseph K., eds. Occupational Carcinogenesis, Vol. 271. (Annals of the New York Academy of Sciences). 516p. 1976. 41.00x (ISBN 0-89072-050-9). NY Acad Sci.

Saffron, Robert. The Demon Device. Doyle, Arthur C., as told to. LC 78-9836. 1979. 10.95 (ISBN 0-399-12285-0). Putnam Pub Group.

Saffron, Robert, jt. auth. see Merrill, Robert.

Safian, Louis A. Two Thousand Insults for All Occasions. 1965. pap. 4.95 (ISBN 0-8065-0039-5, C276). Citadel Pr.

Safian, Louis H. Two Thousand More Insults. 224p. 1976. pap. 4.95 (ISBN 0-8065-0521-4). Citadel Pr.

Safilios-Rothschild, Constantina. The Sociology & Social Psychology of Disability & Rehabilitation. LC 81-40787. 348p. 1981. pap. text ed. 11.25 (ISBN 0-8191-1817-6). U Pr of Amer.

Safonov, jt. auth. see Dodge.

Safonov, Michael G. Stability & Robustness of Multivariable Feedback Systems. (Signal Processing, Optimization & Control Ser.). 171p. 1980. 30.00x (ISBN 0-262-19180-6). MIT Pr.

Safouan, Moustafa. Pleasure & Being: Hedonism from a Psychoanalytic Point of View. Thom, Martin, tr. LC 82-16819. 150p. 1982. 20.00x (ISBN 0-312-61700-3). St Martin.

Safran, William, jt. auth. see Codding, George A., Jr.

Safran, Yehuda, tr. see Tammuz, Benjamin.

Safrit, Margaret J. Evaluation in Physical Education. 2nd ed. (Illus.). 1980. text ed. 20.95 (ISBN 0-13-292250-9). P-H.

Sagal, Paul T. Mind, Man & Machine. LC 81-23739. (Dialogue Ser.). 48p. (Orig.). 1982. pap. text ed. 2.50 (ISBN 0-915145-32-4). Hackett Pub.

--Skinner's Philosophy. LC 80-5737. 132p. 1981. lib. bdg. 18.00 (ISBN 0-8191-1432-4); pap. text ed. 8.25 (ISBN 0-8191-1433-2). U Pr of Amer.

Sagan, Carl. The Cosmic Connection: An Extraterrestrial Perspective. LC 73-81117. 288p. 1973. 8.95 o.p. (ISBN 0-385-00457-5, Anch). Doubleday.

--Cosmic Connection: An Extraterrestrial Perspective. LC 80-1867. (Illus.). 288p. 1980. pap. 7.95 (ISBN 0-385-17365-2, Anch). Doubleday.

--The Dragons of Eden. 1977. 10.95 (ISBN 0-394-41045-9). Random.

Sagan, Carl, ed. Communication with Extraterrestrial Intelligence. 1973. pap. 7.95 (ISBN 0-262-69037-3). MIT Pr.

Sagan, Eli. Cannibalism: Human Agression & Cultural Form. 148p. pap. 6.95 (ISBN 0-914434-24-1). Psychohistory Pr.

Sagan, Francoise. Bonjour Tristesse. 128p. 1983. pap. 4.95 (ISBN 0-525-48040-4, 0481-140). Dutton.

--Nightbird: Conversations with Francoise Sagan. (Clarkson N. Potter Bks.). 1980. 9.95 (ISBN 0-517-54224-2, C N Potter Bks). Crown.

--The Painted Lady: A Novel. 448p. 1983. 15.95 (ISBN 0-525-24148-5, 01505-450). Dutton.

Sagar, K. The Art of D. H. Lawrence. 279p. 1976. 42.50 (ISBN 0-521-06181-4); pap. 11.95 (ISBN 0-521-09387-2). Cambridge U Pr.

--The Art of Ted Hughes. 2nd ed. LC 77-90217. 1978. 44.50 (ISBN 0-521-21954-X); pap. 12.95 (ISBN 0-521-29321-9). Cambridge U Pr.

Sagar, Keith & Tabor, Stephen. Ted Hughes: A Bibliography, 1945-1980. 300p. 1982. 32.00 (ISBN 0-7201-1654-6, Pub. by Mansell England). Wilson.

Sagar, Keith, ed. A. D. H. Lawrence Handbook. LC 82-11569. (Illus.). 460p. 1982. text ed. 28.50x (ISBN 0-389-20312-2). B&N Imports.

Sagar, Keith, ed. see Lawrence, D. H.

Sagarin, Edward, jt. ed. see Balsam, M. S.

Sagarin, Edward, ed. see Ellis, Albert.

Sagarin, Edward, jt. ed. see Henslin, James M.

Sagarin, Edward, jt. ed. see Thornberry, Terence P.

Sagasti, F. Science et Technologie pour le Developpement: Rapport Comparatif Principal du Project "Instruments de Politique Scientifique et Technique". 124p. 1979. pap. 8.50 o.p. (ISBN 0-88936-218-1, IDRC-109F, IDRC). Unipub.

Sagay, Esi. African Hair Sculpture: A Manual. LC 74-82731. 1977. cancelled 0.00 o.p. (ISBN 0-89388-187-2). Okpaku Communications.

Sage, A. P. Systems Engineering: Methodology & Applications. (IEEE Press Reprint Ser.). 1977. 44.00 (ISBN 0-471-03746-X); pap. 25.95 (ISBN 0-471-03747-8). Wiley.

Sage, Andrew P. Methodology for Large Scale Systems. (Illus.). 1977. text ed. 39.95 (ISBN 0-07-054438-7, C); solutions manual 8.50 (ISBN 0-07-054439-5). McGraw.

Sage, Andrew P. & Melsa, James L. Estimation Theory with Applications to Communications & Control. LC 79-4648. 542p. 1979. Repr. of 1971 ed. lib. bdg. 28.50 (ISBN 0-88275-920-5). Krieger.

--System Identification. (Mathematics in Science & Engineering Ser: Vol. 80). 1971. 43.50 (ISBN 0-12-614450-8). Acad Pr.

Sage, Andrew P. & White, Chelsea C. Optimum Systems Control. 2nd ed. (Illus.). 1977. ref. ed. 34.00 (ISBN 0-13-638296-7). P-H.

Sage, Andrew P., jt. auth. see Melsa, James L.

Sage, Andrew P., ed. Systems Engineering: Methodology & Applications. LC 77-82294. 1977. 21.95 (ISBN 0-87942-098-7). Inst Electrical.

Sage, Daniel D., jt. auth. see Burrello, Leonard C.

Sage, Rufus B. Rocky Mountain Life: Or, Startling Scenes & Perilous Adventures in the Far West During an Expedition of Three Years. LC 82-20165. (Illus.). 351p. 1983. 23.50x (ISBN 0-8032-4142-9); pap. 7.50 (ISBN 0-8032-9137-X, BB 835, Bison). U of Nebr Pr.

Sagel, Stuart S. Special Procedures in Chest Radiology. LC 75-19855. (Monographs in Clinical Radiology: Vol. 8). (Illus.). 255p. 1976. text ed. 18.50 o.p. (ISBN 0-7216-7897-1). Saunders.

Sager & Bomar. Intravenous Medication: A Guide to Preparation Administration & Nursing Management. text ed. 17.50 (Lippincott Nursing). Lippincott.

Sager, A. W. Speak Your Way to Success. 1968. 15.95 o.p. (ISBN 0-07-054432-8, P&RB). McGraw.

Sager, Alan. Planning Home Care with the Elderly. 320p. 1983. prof ref 32.50x (ISBN 0-88410-725-6). Ballinger Pub.

Sager, Angela, jt. auth. see Pond, Grace.

Sager, Clifford J. & Kaplan, Helen S. Progress in Group & Family Therapy. LC 72-153376. 960p. 1972. 35.00 o.p. (ISBN 0-87630-048-4); pap. 17.95 o.p. (ISBN 0-87630-073-5). Brunner-Mazel.

Sager, Clifford J., et al. Treating the Remarried Family. LC 82-17811. 450p. 1983. 35.00 (ISBN 0-87630-323-8). Brunner-Mazel.

Sager, Diane P. & Bomar, Suzanne K. Quick Reference to Intravenous Drugs. (Quick References for Nurses Ser.). 375p. 1982. pap. text ed. 14.00 (Lippincott Nursing). Lippincott.

Sager, Donald J. Participatory Management in Libraries. LC 82-783. (Library Administration Ser.: No. 3). 216p. 1982. 14.50 (ISBN 0-8108-1530-3). Scarecrow.

Sager, Esther. From Moment to Moment. 1983. pap. 3.50 (ISBN 0-515-06221-9). Jove Pubns.

Sager, G. R., jt. ed. see Cherrett, J. M.

Sager, Harold G. Rebel for God. 1983. 5.75 (ISBN 0-8062-1868-1). Carlton.

Sager, Jeffrey, jt. auth. see Jason, Paul.

Sager, Juan. German Structure Drills. 16.50x (ISBN 0-392-08460-0, SpS). Sportshelf.

Sager, Keith, ed. The Achievement of Ted Hughes. LC 82-13522. 240p. 1983. text ed. 25.00x (ISBN 0-8203-0650-9). U of Ga Pr.

Sager, Naomi. Natural Language Information Processing: A Computer Grammmar of English & Its Applications. 1980. text ed. 39.50 (ISBN 0-201-06769-2). A-W.

Sagerman, Robert H. & Abramson, David H. Tumors of the Eye & Ocular Adnexae. (Illus.). 242p. 1982. pap. 100.00 (ISBN 0-08-027467-6, H230). Pergamon.

Saggittarus. Before the Setting Sun. LC 74-77416. 206p. Repr. of 1974 ed. 5.95 (ISBN 0-912444-17-7). Gaus.

--Countdown to Black Genocide. LC 73-78108. 128p. Repr. of 1973 ed. 4.95 (ISBN 0-912444-14-2). Gaus.

--I Am Ishmael, Son of a Blackamoor. LC 74-24547. 80p. 3.50 (ISBN 0-912444-19-3). Gaus.

--Neggar Journeys into Nightmares. LC 72-96167. 144p. 4.50 (ISBN 0-912444-18-5). Gaus.

Sagi, Abraham, jt. ed. see Lamb, Michael E.

Sagnier, Thierry. Bike! Motorcycles & the People Who Ride Them. LC 72-9151. (Illus.). 208p. 1974. 10.95 o.p. (ISBN 0-06-013736-3, HarpT); pap. 3.95i (ISBN 0-06-013743-6, TD-199, HarpT). Har-Row.

Sagnier, Thierry J. The IFO Report. 336p. 1983. pap. 2.95 (ISBN 0-380-83337-9). Avon.

Sagola, Mario J. The Naked Bishop. LC 79-21270. 1980. 10.95 (ISBN 0-698-11017-X, Coward). Putnam Pub Group.

Sagstetter, Karen. Lobbying. (American Government Ser.). (Illus.). (gr. 7 up). 1978. PLB 8.90 s&l (ISBN 0-531-01413-4). Watts.

Saguy. Applications of Computers in Food Research & Food Industry. (Food Science Ser.). 504p. 1983. price not set (ISBN 0-8247-1383-4). Dekker.

Sagvall Hein, A. -L., jt. ed. see Schneider, W.

Sagvari, Agnes, ed. Capitals of Europe: A Guide to the Sources for the History of Their Architecture & Construction. (Illus.). 359p. 1981. 80.00x (ISBN 0-686-72832-7, Pub. by K G Saur). Gale.

Sah, C. H. Hilbert's Third Problem. new ed. (Research Notes in Mathematics Ser.). 1979. pap. cancelled o.p. (ISBN 0-8224-8426-9). Pitman Pub MA.

Sah, Chin-Han. Hilbert's Third Problem: Congruence. (Research Notes in Mathematics Ser.: No. 33). 188p. (Orig.). 1979. pap. text ed. 23.00 (ISBN 0-273-08426-7). Pitman Pub MA.

Saha, Arthur W. The Year's Best Fantasy Stories, No. 8. 192p. 1982. pap. 2.50 (ISBN 0-686-95152-2). DAW Bks.

Saha, J., jt. ed. see Salkin, H. M.

Saha, L., jt. auth. see Fagerlind, I.

Saha, Lawrence J., jt. auth. see Husen, Torsten.

Saha, Suranjit K. & Barrow, Christopher J. River Basin Planning: Theory & Practice. 380p. 1981. 51.95 (ISBN 0-471-09977-5, Pub. by Wiley-Interscience). Wiley.

Sahad, Lou. The Forty-Niners: Super Champs of Pro Football. 1982. pap. 9.95 (ISBN 0-688-01309-0). Morrow.

--The L. A. Dodgers: The World Champions of Baseball. (Illus.). 1982. pap. 12.50 (ISBN 0-688-01236-1). Morrow.

Sahadi, Lou. Super Sundays One-Sixteen. (Illus.). 224p. 1982. pap. 10.95 (ISBN 0-8092-5623-1). Contemp Bks.

--Year of the Yankees. 1979. pap. 7.95 o.p. (ISBN 0-8092-7212-1); 14.95 o.p. (ISBN 0-8092-7214-8). Contemp Bks.

Sahadi, Lou & Palmer, Mickey. The Complete Book of Sports Photography: How to Take Quality, Action-Packed Pictures of Amateur & Pro Sports. (Illus.). 160p. (Orig.). 1982. 21.95 (ISBN 0-8174-3694-4, Amphoto); pap. 14.95 (ISBN 0-8174-3695-2). Watson-Guptill.

Sahakian, Mabel, jt. auth. see Sahakian, William S.

Sahakian, Mabel L. & Sahakian, William S. John Locke. (World Leaders Ser.). 1975. lib. bdg. 11.95 (ISBN 0-8057-3539-9, Twayne). G K Hall.

Sahakian, W. S. History & Systems of Social Psychology. 1981. 24.50 (ISBN 0-07-054425-5). McGraw.

Sahakian, William S. History of Philosophy. (Orig.). 1968. pap. 5.95 (ISBN 0-06-460002-5, CO2, COS). B&N NY.

--An Introduction to the Psychology of Learning. LC 82-81418. 526p. 1983. text ed. 19.95 (ISBN 0-87581-284-8). Peacock Pubs.

--Learning. 2nd ed. 1976. pap. 16.95 (ISBN 0-395-30832-1). HM.

--Psychology of Personality. 3rd ed. 1977. 17.95 (ISBN 0-395-30833-X). HM.

--Psychopathology Today: The Current Status of Abnormal Psychology. 2nd ed. LC 78-61875. 1979. pap. text ed. 16.50 (ISBN 0-87581-213-9). Peacock Pubs.

--Psychotherapy & Counseling. 2nd ed. 1976. 18.95 (ISBN 0-395-30834-8). HM.

Sahakian, William S. & Sahakian, Mabel. Plato. (World Leaders Ser.). 1977. lib. bdg. 11.95 (ISBN 0-8057-7690-7, Twayne). G K Hall.

Sahakian, William S., jt. auth. see Sahakian, Mabel L.

Sahal, D. Patterns of Technological Innovation. 1981. 36.50 (ISBN 0-201-06630-0). A-W.

Sahal, Devendra, ed. Research, Development, & Technological Innovation. LC 79-3095. 288p. 1980. 28.95x (ISBN 0-669-03377-4). Lexington Bks.

--The Transfer & Utilization of Technical Knowledge. LC 81-47708. 288p. 1982. 30.95X (ISBN 0-669-04722-8). Lexington Bks.

Sahay, Arun. Sociological Analysis. (International Library of Sociology). 220p. 1972. 18.95x (ISBN 0-7100-7363-1). Routledge & Kegan.

Sahler, Olle J. The Child from Three to Eighteen. LC 80-27126. (Illus.). 233p. 1981. softcover 18.95 (ISBN 0-8016-4290-6). Mosby.

Sahlin, Harry L., jt. ed. see Marshall, Lauriston C.

Sahlins, Marshall D. Tribesmen. (Illus., Orig.). 1968. pap. 9.95 ref. ed. (ISBN 0-13-930925-X). P-H.

Sahn, David J. & Anderson, Fred. Two Dimensional Anatomy of the Heart: An Atlas for Echocardiographers. LC 82-7108. 461p. 1982. 39.50 (ISBN 0-471-08246-5, Pub. by Wiley Med). Wiley.

Sahn, Seung. The Bone of Space. LC 82-2476. (Wheel Ser.: No. 2). (Illus.). 88p. (Orig.). 1982. pap. 4.95 (ISBN 0-87704-053-2). Four Seasons Foun.

--Only Don't Know: The Teaching Letters of Zen Master Seung Sahn, No. 3. (Wheel Ser.). 206p. (Orig.). 1982. pap. 6.95 (ISBN 0-87704-054-0). Four Seasons Foun.

Sahney, Vinod K. & May, James L. Scheduling Computer Operations. 1972. pap. text ed. 12.00 (ISBN 0-89806-017-6, 126); pap. text ed. 6.00 members. Inst Indus Eng.

Sahni, Chaman L. E. M. Forster: The Religious Dimension. 160p. 1981. text ed. 10.75 (ISBN 0-391-02201-6). Humanities.

Sahni, Sartaj, jt. auth. see Horowitz, Ellis.

Sahovic, Milan, ed. Principles of International Law Concerning Friendly Relations & Cooperation. LC 73-8985. 450p. 1972. lib. bdg. 17.50 (ISBN 0-379-00020-2). Oceana.

Sahs, Adolph L., et al. Aneurysmal Subarachnoid Hemorrhage: Report of the Cooperative Study. LC 81-2354. (Illus.). 388p. 1981. text ed. 35.00 (ISBN 0-8067-1861-7). Urban & S.

Sahtain Arab Women's Union. Middle East Cookbook: Middle East Cookbook. 10.00x (ISBN 0-86685-036-8). Intl Bk Ctr.

Sahula-Dycke, Ignatz. The God Fixation. 77p. 1976. 4.00 o.p. (ISBN 0-682-48504-7). Am Atheist.

Sai, F. A., jt. auth. see Tindall, H. D.

Said, Abdul A. & Lerche, Charles Q. Concepts of International Politics: A Global Perspective. 3rd ed. 1979. text ed. 22.95 (ISBN 0-13-166033-0). P-H.

Said, Ali A., pseud. The Blood of Adonis: Selected Poems. Hazo, Samuel, tr. from Ara. LC 70-134490. (Pitt Poetry Ser). 1971. 10.95 o.p. (ISBN 0-8229-3213-X); pap. 4.95 o.p. (ISBN 0-8229-5220-3). U of Pittsburgh Pr.

Said, Edward W. Orientalism. LC 79-10497. 1979. pap. 5.95 (ISBN 0-394-74067-X, Vin). Random.

--The World, the Text, & the Critic. 352p. 1983. 20.00x (ISBN 0-674-96186-2). Harvard U Pr.

Said, Rafik. Cultural Policy in Tunisia. (Studies & Documents on Cultural Policies). 56p. 1970. pap. 5.00 (ISBN 92-3-100850-1, U752, UNESCO). Unipub.

Said, Sami I., ed. Vasoactive Intestinal Peptide. (Advances in Peptide Hormone Research Ser.). 528p. 1982. text ed. 57.00 (ISBN 0-89004-443-0). Raven.

Saidi, F. Surgery of Hydatid Disease. LC 74-4587. (Illus.). 1976. text ed. 28.00 (ISBN 0-7216-7900-5). Saunders.

Saidman, Lawrence J. & Smith, N. Ty. Monitoring in Anesthesia. LC 77-12506. (Anesthesiology Ser.). 1977. 33.50 o.p. (ISBN 0-471-74980-X, Pub. by Wiley Medical). Wiley.

Saiga Editors. Incubation & Chick Rearing. 1981. 10.00x o.p. (ISBN 0-86230-018-5, Pub. by Saiga Pub). State Mutual Bk.

--Pheasant Keeping. 1981. 10.00x o.p. (ISBN 0-86230-015-0, Pub. by Saiga Pub). State Mutual Bk.

Saiga Editors, ed. Animals in the Garden. 1981. 10.00x (ISBN 0-86230-027-4, Pub. by Saiga Pub). State Mutual Bk.

--Fossils. 1981. 10.00x o.p. (ISBN 0-86230-028-2, Pub. by Saiga Pub). State Mutual Bk.

--Heavy Horses. 1981. 10.00x o.p. (ISBN 0-86230-025-8, Pub. by Saiga Pub). State Mutual Bk.

--Taxidermy. 1981. 10.00x o.p. (ISBN 0-86230-032-0, Pub. by Saiga Pub). State Mutual Bk.

Saige, Joseph. Voyage a la Nouvelle Philadelphie. (Utopias in the Enlightenment Ser.). 110p. (Fr.). 1974. Repr. of 1803 ed. lib. bdg. 37.50x o.p. (ISBN 0-8287-0749-9, 006). Clearwater Pub.

Saiger, Lydia. The Junk Food Cookbook. (Orig.). 1979. pap. 2.50 o.s.i. (ISBN 0-515-05740-1). Jove Pubns.

Saigi, Robert. Are We Sure There Is a Universe. 1983. 8.95 (ISBN 0-533-05319-6). Vantage.

Saigo, Barbara W., jt. auth. see Saigo, Roy H.

Saigo, Roy H. & Saigo, Barbara W. Botany: Principles & Applications. (Illus.). 560p. 1983. 27.95 (ISBN 0-13-080234-4). P-H.

Saik, Richard P. Vagotomy Testing. LC 82-83471. (Illus.). 176p. 1983. monograph 22.50 (ISBN 0-87993-189-2). Futura Pub.

Sailer, H. F. Transplantation of Lyophilized Cartilage in Maxillo-Facial Surgery. (Illus.). x, 138p. 1983. 69.00 (ISBN 3-8055-3570-8). S Karger.

Sailhamer, John. First & Second Chronicles. (Everyman's Bible Commentary Ser.). (Orig.). 1983. pap. 4.50 (ISBN 0-8024-2012-5). Moody.

Sailor & Guess. Severely Handicapped Students: An Instructional Design. 1982. text ed. 24.95 (ISBN 0-686-84566-8). HM.

Sailor, Wayne & Guess, Doug. Severely Handicapped Students: An Instructional design. LC 82-83289. 448p. 1982. text ed. 24.95 (ISBN 0-395-32788-1). HM.

Sailors, Ruth A., jt. auth. see Junior Welfare League of Enid, OK., Inc.

Saine, Thomas, jt. auth. see Burgoon, Judee K.

Saine, Thomas P. Georg Forster. (World Authors Ser.). lib. bdg. 15.95 (ISBN 0-8057-2316-1, Twayne). G K Hall.

Sainer, Arthur. The Radical Theater Notebook. 1975. pap. 2.65 o.p. (ISBN 0-380-00287-6, 22442, Discus). Avon.

Sainer, Elliot A., ed. Who's Who in Health Care. 2nd ed. LC 77-79993. 612p. 1982. text ed. 69.95 (ISBN 0-89443-092-0). Aspen Systems.

Saini, Balwant S. Building in Hot Dry Climates. LC 79-41777. 176p. 1980. 47.95 (ISBN 0-471-27764-9, Pub. by Wiley-Interscience). Wiley.

Sainsaulieu, Renaud. L' Identite au Travail: Les effets culturels de l'organisation. 1977. lib. bdg. 40.00x o.p. (ISBN 2-7246-0386-9); pap. text ed. 32.50x o.p. (ISBN 2-7246-0385-0). Clearwater Pub.

Sainsbury, David. Poultry Health & Management. 168p. 1980. text ed. 22.00x (ISBN 0-246-11173-9, Pub. by Granada England); pap. text ed. 12.25x (ISBN 0-246-11350-2). Renouf.

Sainsbury, Diana, jt. auth. see Singleton, Paul.

Sainsbury, Eric. Social Work with Families. (Library of Social Work). 1975. 16.95x (ISBN 0-7100-8039-5); pap. 8.95 (ISBN 0-7100-8040-9). Routledge & Kegan.

Sainsbury, Eric & Phillips, David. Social Work in Focus: Clinet' & Social Workers' Perception in Long Term Social Work. (Library of Social Work). 220p. (Orig.). 1982. pap. 10.95 (ISBN 0-7100-9068-4). Routledge & Kegan.

Sainsbury, Geoffrey, tr. see Simenon, Georges.

Sainsbury, I. E., jt. auth. see Creyke, W. E.

Sainsbury, John. Sainsbury's Woodturning Projects for Dining. LC 80-54347. (Illus.). 160p. 1981. 16.95 (ISBN 0-8069-5436-1); PLB 19.99 (ISBN 0-686-77380-2). Sterling.

--Sainsbury's Woodturning Projects for Dining. LC 80-54347. (Illus.). 160p. 1983. pap. 9.95 (ISBN 0-8069-7694-2). Sterling.

Sainsbury, M. J. Key to Psychiatry: A Textbook for Students. 3rd ed. 426p. 1980. text ed. 22.95 (ISBN 0-471-26009-6, Pub. by Wiley Med). Wiley.

Sainsbury, P. & Kreitman, N., eds. Methods of Psychiatric Research. 2nd ed. (Illus.). pap. text ed. 29.95x (ISBN 0-19-264419-X). Oxford U Pr.

St. Albans, Suzanne. Magic of a Mystic: Stories of Padre Pio. 1983. 5.95 (ISBN 0-517-54847-X, C N Potter Bks). Crown.

Saint, Andrew. The Image of the Architect. LC 82-48909. (Illus.). 192p. 1983. 19.95 (ISBN 0-300-03013-4). Yale Univ Pr.

St. Aubin de Teran, Lisa. The Long Way Home. LC 82-48149. (Fiction Ser.). 192p. 1983. 12.95 (ISBN 0-06-015124-2, HarpT). Har-Row.

St. Aubyn, Frederic C. Arthur Rimbaud. (World Authors Ser.). 1975. lib. bdg. 12.50 (ISBN 0-8057-6192-6, Twayne). G K Hall.

St. Aubyn, Fredric C. Stephane Mallarme. (World Authors Ser.: No. 52). 10.95 o.p. (ISBN 0-8057-2568-7, Twayne). G K Hall.

St. Augustine. The City of God. LC 58-5717. pap. 5.95 (ISBN 0-385-02910-1, Im). Doubleday.

--The City of God. 7.95 (ISBN 0-394-60397-4). Modern Lib.

St. Barbe, Richard. Caravan Story & Country Notebook. pap. 5.00. Friends Nature.

--Land of Tane: New Zealand Forests. 1956. 10.00 (ISBN 0-686-00581-3). Wellington.

--Sahara Challenge: Reclamation Plan. (Illus.). 1954. 10.00 (ISBN 0-686-00582-1). Wellington.

St. Barbe, Richard & Barbe. Kamiti: A Forester's Dream. (Illus.). 8.00 (ISBN 0-686-05049-5). Wellington.

St. Clair, Alexandrine N. The Image of the Turk in Europe. LC 73-18358. (Illus.). 72p. 1973. pap. 3.95 o.p. (ISBN 0-87099-085-3). Metro Mus Art.

St. Clair, Barry. Hey, Who Is That Man? (YA) (gr. 9-12). pap. 3.50 (ISBN 0-88207-583-7). Victor Bks.

St. Clair, David. David St. Clair's Lessons in Instant ESP. 1979. pap. 2.50 (ISBN 0-451-11713-1, AE1713, Sig). NAL.

St. Clair, Joy. Un Bonheur au Passe. (Harlequin Romantique Ser.). 192p. 1983. pap. 1.95 (ISBN 0-373-41182-0). Harlequin Bks.

--Heart under Siege. (Harlequin Romances Ser.). 192p. 1982. pap. 1.50 (ISBN 0-373-02472-X). Harlequin Bks.

St. Clair, Robert, ed. Teacher Attitudes in a Multicultural Setting. (Language & Literacy Ser.). 128p. (Orig.). 1983. pap. text ed. 14.95 (ISBN 0-88499-605-0). Inst Mod Lang.

St. Clair, Robert, et al, eds. Social & Educational Issues in Bilingualism & Biculturalism. LC 80-5700. (Illus.). 174p. (Orig.). 1982. lib. bdg. 20.75 (ISBN 0-8191-1939-3); pap. text ed. 10.00 (ISBN 0-8191-1940-7). U Pr of Amer.

St. Clair, Robert N. The Politics of Failure in Bilingual Education. (Language & Literacy Monograph Ser.). 1983. pap. text ed. 14.95 (ISBN 0-88499-600-X). Inst Mod Lang.

St. Clair, Robert N. & Giles, Howard, eds. The Social & Psychological Contexts of Language. LC 79-28232. 352p. 1980. text ed. 29.95x (ISBN 0-89859-021-3). L Erlbaum Assocs.

St. Clair, Robert N. & Leap, William L., eds. Language Renewal Among American Indian Tribes. LC 81-82493. (Orig.). 1982. pap. 8.95 (ISBN 0-89763-059-9). Natl Clearinghse Bilingual Ed.

St. Cyr, Albert N. And Cross the Rivers of My Mind. 1983. 6.95 (ISBN 0-533-05603-9). Vantage.

St. George, Edith. West of the Moon. 192p. 1981. pap. 1.50 o.s.i. (ISBN 0-671-57069-2). S&S.

St. George, George. Soviet Deserts & Mountains. (The World's Wild Places Ser.). (Illus.). 1978. lib. bdg. 15.96 (ISBN 0-8094-2014-7). Silver.

St. George, Judith. The Amazing Voyage of the New Orleans. (Illus.). 64p. (gr. 7-11). 1980. 6.95 (ISBN 0-399-20697-3). Putnam Pub Group.

--The Brooklyn Bridge: They Said It Couldn't Be Built. LC 81-22755. (Illus.). 128p. 1982. 10.95 (ISBN 0-399-20873-9). Putnam Pub Group.

--By George, Bloomers! LC 75-22005. (Break-of-Day Ser.). (Illus.). 48p. (gr. k-2). 1976. PLB 6.59 o.p. (ISBN 0-698-30601-5, Coward). Putnam Pub Group.

--Call Me Margo. 156p. (gr. 10 up). 1981. 8.95 (ISBN 0-399-20790-2). Putnam Pub Group.

--Call Me Margo. Date not set. pap. 2.25 (ISBN 0-451-11850-2, AE1850, Sig). NAL.

--The Chinese Puzzle of Shag Island. LC 75-43900. 160p. (gr. 5-10). 1976. 7.95 (ISBN 0-399-20491-1). Putnam Pub Group.

--The Girl with Spunk. (Illus.). 128p. (gr. 6-8). 1975. 6.95 o.p. (ISBN 0-399-20473-3). Putnam Pub Group.

--The Halloween Pumpkin Smasher. LC 77-26294. (Illus.). (gr. k-3). 1978. 8.95 (ISBN 0-399-20617-5). Putnam Pub Group.

--The Halo Wind. LC 78-16640. (gr. 6-8). 1978. 7.95 (ISBN 0-399-20651-5). Putnam Pub Group.

--Haunted. 156p. (YA) (gr. 7-12). 1980. 7.95 (ISBN 0-399-20736-8). Putnam Pub Group.

--Haunted. pap. 1.95 (ISBN 0-686-96949-9). Bantam.

--The Mysterious Girl in the Garden. (Illus.). 64p. 1981. 7.95 (ISBN 0-399-20822-4). Putnam Pub Group.

--Mystery at St. Martin's. new ed. LC 79-17547. (gr. 5 up). 1979. 7.95 (ISBN 0-399-20702-3). Putnam Pub Group.

--The Shad Are Running. LC 76-25208. (Illus.). (gr. 3-6). 1977. PLB 5.29 o.p. (ISBN 0-399-61045-6). Putnam Pub Group.

--The Shadow of the Shaman. LC 77-5161. (gr. 6-8). 1978. 7.95 o.p. (ISBN 0-399-20592-6). Putnam Pub Group.

St. Germain, Gregory. Resistance, No. 1: Night & Fog. 192p. Date not set. pap. 2.50 (ISBN 0-451-11827-8, Sig). NAL.

--Resistance, No. 2: Magyar Massacre. 192p. Date not set. pap. 2.50 (ISBN 0-451-11828-6, Sig). NAL.

St. Jacques, Elizabeth. Canadian Poets & Friends. new ed. (Illus.). 1977. pap. 3.00 (ISBN 0-932044-05-0). M O Pub Co.

--Canadian Poets & Friends. new ed. (Illus.). 1978. pap. 4.00 (ISBN 0-932044-18-2). M O Pub Co.

--Silver Sigh & Shadows Blue. (Illus.). 1978. pap. 3.50 (ISBN 0-932044-13-1). M O Pub Co.

St. James, Blakely. Christina's Awakening. 256p. (Orig.). 1983. pap. 2.95 (ISBN 0-425-05997-9). Berkley Pub.

--Christina's Conquest. LC 82-81386. (Christina Van Bell Ser.). 256p. 1982. pap. 2.95 (ISBN 0-86721-202-0). Playboy Pbks.

--Christina's Fantasy. 256p. (Orig.). 1983. pap. 2.95 (ISBN 0-425-06131-0). Berkley Pub.

--Christina's Need. 256p. (Orig.). 1983. pap. 2.95 (ISBN 0-425-06134-5). Berkley Pub.

--A Diamond for Christina. 240p. (Orig.). 1983. pap. 2.95 (ISBN 0-425-06069-1). Berkley Pub.

--A Festival for Christina. LC 82-60694. 1983. pap. 2.95 (ISBN 0-86721-240-3). Playboy Pbks.

St. John, Adela R. Affirmative Prayer in Action. 1977. pap. 2.50 (ISBN 0-451-11627-5, AE1627, Sig). NAL.

--Love, Laughter & Tears. 1979. pap. 2.50 o.p. (ISBN 0-451-08752-6, E8752, Sig). NAL.

--Some Are Born Great. (RL 10). 1975. pap. 1.95 o.p. (ISBN 0-451-06707-X, J6707, Sig). NAL.

St. John, J. A. Education of the People. LC 78-78982. (Social History of Education). Repr. of 1858 ed. 22.50x o.p. (ISBN 0-678-08458-0). Kelley.

St. John, Michael. From Arithmetic to Algebra. 132p. (Orig.). 1980. pap. text ed. 2.95 (ISBN 0-937354-00-7, TX-334-207). Delta Systems.

St. John, P. Infant & Junior Scripture Lesson. 274p. 1956. 5.00 (ISBN 0-227-67493-6). Attic Pr.

St. John, Patricia. The Secret at Pheasant Cottage. LC 78-24384. (gr. 6-8). 1979. pap. text ed. 2.95 (ISBN 0-8024-7683-X). Moody.

--Treasures of the Snow. (gr. 5-8). 1950. pap. 3.95 (ISBN 0-8024-0008-6). Moody.

--Where the River Begins. LC 80-12304. 128p. (Orig.). (gr. 5-8). pap. 2.95 (ISBN 0-8024-8124-8). Moody.

St. John, Patricia M. Star of Light. (gr. 5-8). 1953. pap. 3.95 (ISBN 0-8024-0004-3). Moody.

--The Tanglewoods' Secret. (gr. 5-8). 1951. pap. 3.95 (ISBN 0-8024-0007-8). Moody.

St. John, Primus. Love is Not a Consolation: It is a Light. LC 82-71661. 1982. 12.95 (ISBN 0-915604-74-4); pap. 5.95 (ISBN 0-915604-75-2). Carnegie-Mellon.

St. John, Robert. Tongue of the Prophets: The Life Story of Eliezer Ben Yehuda. LC 77-97303. 377p. 1972. Repr. of 1952 ed. lib. bdg. 20.75x (ISBN 0-8371-2631-2, STTP). Greenwood.

St. John, Wylly F. The Christmas Tree Mystery. (Illus.). (gr. 3-7). 1976. pap. 1.50 o.p. (ISBN 0-380-00767-3, 46300, Camelot). Avon.

--The Mystery of the Other Girl. 1977. pap. 1.50 o.p. (ISBN 0-380-01926-4, 48207, Camelot). Avon.

--The Secrets of Hidden Creek. (Illus.). 1976. pap. 1.75 o.p. (ISBN 0-380-00746-0, 51359, Camelot). Avon.

--Wylly Folk St. John. (gr. 5 up). 1979. pap. 9.00 o.p. (ISBN 0-380-46730-5, 46730, Camelot). Avon.

St. John Barclay, Glen. Anatomy of Horror: The Masters of Occult Fiction. LC 78-70899. 1979. 8.95 o.p. (ISBN 0-312-03408-3). St. Martin.

St. John Chrysostom. Sermon on the Decollation of St. John the Baptist, & on Herodias, & on Good & Evil Women. (Early Slavic Literatures, Studies, Texts, & Seminar Materials: Vol. 3). Orig. Title: V 29 den' mesiatsa avgusta slovo Ioanna Zlatoustogo na useknovenie glavy. 45p. (Church Slavic & Gr.). 1982. pap. 4.00 (ISBN 0-933884-23-0). Berkeley Slavic.

St. Johns, Adela R. Final Verdict. pap. 2.50 o.p. (ISBN 0-451-07994-9, E7994, Sig). NAL.

--No Good-Byes. 1982. pap. 3.50 (ISBN 0-451-11740-9, AE1740, Sig). NAL.

St. Johns, Adela Rogers. The Honeycomb. LC 69-15885. 1969. 8.95 (ISBN 0-385-02094-5). Doubleday.

St. John Thomas, David. A Regional History of the Railways of Great Britain: The West Country, Vol. 1. LC 80-70296. (Illus.). 256p. 1981. 23.95 (ISBN 0-7153-8152-0). David & Charles.

St. Jorre, John De. The Nigerian Civil War. (Illus.). 437p. 1972. 17.50x o.p. (ISBN 0-340-12640-X). Intl Pubns Serv.

St. Lawrence County Municipal Historians. Name Index to the Eighteen Seventy-Eight of Saint Lawrence County, NY. 76p. 1983. 10.00x (ISBN 0-932334-53-9). Heart of the Lakes.

St. Louis Board Of Education. Missouri: The Simplified Constitution. 2nd ed. 1965. 4.32 (ISBN 0-07-054452-2, W); tests 0.44 (ISBN 0-07-026220-9). McGraw.

St. Louis, Kenneth O. & Ruscello, Dennis M. Oral Speech Mechanism Screening Examination. 48p. 1981. pap. 14.95 (ISBN 0-8391-1665-9). Univ Park.

St. Louis Public Library. Heraldry Index of the St. Louis Public Library. 1980. lib. bdg. 475.00 (ISBN 0-8161-0311-9, Hall Library). G K Hall.

St. Marie, Satenig S. Homes Are for People. LC 72-10244. (Illus.). 400p. 1973. text ed. 24.95 o.s.i. (ISBN 0-471-82635-9); tchr's. manual avail. Wiley.

St. Martin, Hardie, ed. Roots & Wings: Poetry from Spain 1900-1975. LC 73-14293. 384p. (YA) 1976. 19.18i (ISBN 0-06-013976-5, HarpT); pap. 10.95i (ISBN 0-06-013981-1, TD-236, HarpT). Har-Row.

St. Maur, Suzan & Streep, Norbert. The Jewelry Book. (Illus.). 198p. 1981. 9.95 o.p. (ISBN 0-312-44230-0). St Martin.

St. Maximus the Confessor. The Church, the Liturgy & the Soul of Man. Stead, Dom J., tr. from Gr. LC 82-10545. 1982. pap. 6.95 (ISBN 0-932506-23-2). St Bedes Pubns.

St. Michel, Morgan. Nicole, No. 5. 256p. 1983. pap. 2.95 (ISBN 0-515-06647-8). Jove Pubns.

--Nicole Around the World. 256p. 2.95 (ISBN 0-515-06824-1). Jove Pubns.

--Nicole Down Under. 240p. 1983. pap. 2.95 (ISBN 0-515-06886-1). Jove Pubns.

--Nicole in Captivity. 240p. 1982. pap. 2.95 (ISBN 0-515-06347-9). Jove Pubns.

--Nicole's Love Cruise, No. 6. 256p. 1983. pap. 2.95 (ISBN 0-515-06800-4). Jove Pubns.

--Nicole's Pleasure Hunt. 256p. 1982. pap. 2.25 (ISBN 0-515-06348-7). Jove Pubns.

--Nicole's Summer Pleasures. 256p. 1983. pap. 2.95 (ISBN 0-515-06891-8). Jove Pubns.

Saint Paul Technical Vocational Institute Curriculum Committee. Mathematics for Careers: Adding & Subtracting Whole Numbers. LC 80-70486. (General Mathematics Ser.). 106p. (Orig.). 1981. pap. text ed. 7.00 (ISBN 0-8273-1590-2); instr's. guide 4.75 (ISBN 0-8273-1595-3). Delmar.

--Mathematics for Careers: Decimals. LC 80-70487. (General Mathematics Ser.). 103p. (Orig.). 1981. pap. text ed. 7.00 (ISBN 0-8273-1592-9); instr's. guide 4.75 (ISBN 0-8273-1595-3). Delmar.

--Mathematics for Careers: Fractions. LC 80-70485. (General Mathematics Ser.). 159p. (Orig.). 1981. pap. text ed. 7.00 (ISBN 0-8273-1593-7); instr's. guide 4.75 (ISBN 0-8273-1595-3). Delmar.

St. Paul Technical Vocational Institute Curriculum Committee. Mathematics for Careers: Measurement & Geometry. LC 80-67549. (General Mathematics Ser.). 161p. 1981. pap. text ed. 7.00 (ISBN 0-8273-2058-2); instr's. guide 3.25 (ISBN 0-8273-1881-2). Delmar.

Saint Paul Technical Vocational Institute Curriculum Committee. Mathematics for Careers: Mixed Numbers. LC 80-70488. (General Mathematics Ser.). 94p. pap. text ed. 7.00 (ISBN 0-8273-1594-5); instr's. guide 4.75 (ISBN 0-8273-1595-3). Delmar.

--Mathematics for Careers: Multiplying & Dividing Whole Numbers. LC 80-70489. (General Mathematics Ser.). 192p. (Orig.). 1981. pap. text ed. 7.00 (ISBN 0-8273-1591-0); instr's. guide 4.75 (ISBN 0-8273-1595-3). Delmar.

--Mathematics for Careers: Percents. LC 79-51557. (General Mathematics Ser.). 165p. 1981. pap. text ed. 7.00 (ISBN 0-8273-1880-4); instructor's guide 3.25 (ISBN 0-8273-1881-2). Delmar.

St. Peter, Joyce. Always Abigail. LC 81-47103. (Illus.). 128p. (gr. 3-5). 1981. 9.13i (ISBN 0-397-31934-7, JBL-J); PLB 9.89g (ISBN 0-397-31935-5). Har-Row.

St. Pierre, Brian & Low, Jennie. The Flavor of Chinatown. LC 82-14556. 160p. (Orig.). 1982. pap. 5.95 (ISBN 0-87701-261-X). Chronicle Bks.

St. Pierre, Paul. Smith & Other Events. LC 79-6167. 240p. 1983. 17.95 (ISBN 0-385-15990-0). Doubleday.

St. Sauver, Dennis. Lightening Round. (Tromp It Ser.). (gr. 4-8). 1973. PLB 4.95 o.p. (ISBN 0-912022-47-7); pap. 3.95 (ISBN 0-912022-40-X). EMC.

--Montana Adventure. LC 72-13919. (Tromp It Ser.). (gr. 4-8). 1972. 4.95 o.p. (ISBN 0-912022-50-7); pap. 3.95 (ISBN 0-912022-41-8). EMC.

--Pro Fever. LC 73-23112. (Four Seasons at Lakeview Ser.). 1974. 4.95 o.p. (ISBN 0-88436-069-5); pap. 3.95 (ISBN 0-88436-068-7). EMC.

--Rescue by Fire. LC 73-396. (Tromp It Ser.). 1973. 4.95 o.p. (ISBN 0-912022-61-2); pap. 3.95 (ISBN 0-912022-60-4). EMC.

--Ride to Remember. LC 72-13770. (Tromp It Ser.). (gr. 4-8). 1976. PLB 4.95 o.p. (ISBN 0-912022-51-5); pap. 3.95 (ISBN 0-912022-42-6). EMC.

--Rip's Ups & Downs. LC 74-550. (His Four Seasons at Lakeview Ser). 1974. 4.95 o.p. (ISBN 0-88436-073-3); pap. 3.95 (ISBN 0-88436-072-5). EMC.

--The Unlikely Hero. LC 73-23065. (Four Seasons at Lakeview Ser.). 1974. 4.95 o.p. (ISBN 0-88436-071-7); pap. 3.95 (ISBN 0-88436-070-9). EMC.

St. Vincent Hospital Staff & Peck, Theresa. Wellness: Extending the Health Care Mission. Date not set. pap. price not set (ISBN 0-87125-079-9). Cath Health.

St. Amant, Kristi, ed. see Arrants, Cheryl.

St. Clair, Robert N., ed. see Chew, Charles & Schlawin, Sheila.

St. Clair, Robert N., jt. ed. see Hoffer, Bates L.

St. Clair, Robert N., ed. see McCoy, Ingeborg & Ginsburg, Harvey.

St. Cyr, Napoleon, ed. see Coursen, H. R.

Saint-Denys, Hervey de see De Saint-Denys, Hervey.

Sainte-Beuve, C. A. Portraits of the Eighteenth Century: Historic & Literary, 2 Vols. Wormeley, Katherine P., tr. LC 64-15699. (Illus.). 1964. 40.00 o.p. (ISBN 0-8044-2759-3). Ungar.

--Portraits of the Seventeenth Century: Historic & Literary, 2 Vols. Wormeley, Katherine P., tr. (Illus.). 1964. Set. 40.00 o.p. (ISBN 0-8044-2756-9). Ungar.

Sainte-Beuve, Charles-Augustin. Chateaubriand et son groupe litteraire. (Classiques Larousse). (Fr). pap. 1.95 o.p. (ISBN 0-685-13825-9, 302). Larousse.

Sainte-Marie, Jean De. Les Etranges Evenements du Voyage de Son Altesse du Grand Empire des Abyssins. (Bibliotheque Africaine Ser.). 72p. (Fr.). 1974. Repr. of 1635 ed. lib. bdg. 29.00x o.p. (ISBN 0-8287-0750-2, 71-2163). Clearwater Pub.

Saint-Exupery, Antione De. El Principito. Del Carril, Bonifacio, tr. from Fr. LC 73-5511. (Illus.). 113p. (Span.). 1973. pap. 2.50 (ISBN 0-15-628450-2, Harv). HarBraceJ.

Saint-Exupery, Antoine De. Flight to Arras. Galantiere, Lewis, tr. LC 43-12440. 1969. pap. 3.50 (ISBN 0-15-631880-6, Harv). HarBraceJ.

--Der Kleine Prinz. Leitgeb, Grete & Leitgeb, Josef, trs. from Fr. LC 73-4886. (Illus.). 111p. (Ger.). 1973. pap. 2.50 (ISBN 0-15-625285-6, Harv). HarBraceJ.

--Little Prince. Woods, Katherine, tr. LC 67-1144. (Illus.). (gr. 3-7). 1968. pap. 1.95 (ISBN 0-15-652820-7, Harv). HarBraceJ.

--The Little Prince. Woods, Katherine, tr. from Fr. LC 67-1144. (Illus.). 95p. (gr. 4-6). 1943. pap. 1.95 (ISBN 0-15-652820-7, VoyB). HarBraceJ.

--The Little Prince. Woods, Katherine, tr. (Illus.). 1982. Repr. of 1943 ed. write for info. (Harv). HarBraceJ.

--Night Flight. Gilbert, Stuart, tr. from Fr. LC 73-16016. Orig. Title: Vol De Nuit. 87p. 1974. pap. 2.95 (ISBN 0-15-665605-1, Harv). HarBraceJ.

--Le Petit Prince. LC 43-5812. (Illus., Fr.). (gr. 3-7). 1943. 9.95 (ISBN 0-15-243818-1, HJ); pap. 1.95 (ISBN 0-15-650300-X, VoyB). HarBraceJ.

--Southern Mail. Cate, Curtis, tr. LC 79-182749. 1972. pap. 2.50 (ISBN 0-15-683901-6, Harv). HarBraceJ.

--Wind, Sand & Stars. LC 65-35872. 1967. pap. 3.50 (ISBN 0-15-697090-2, Harv). HarBraceJ.

Saint-Exupery, Antoine De see De Saint-Exupery, Antoine.

Saint-Foix, G. de see De Wyzewa, T. & De Saint-Foix, G.

St. Geme, Joseph W., Jr., ed. see Greenberg, Henry F., et al.

Saint-Germaine, Comte C. Practice of Palmistry. LC 76-16445. (Illus.). 1982. Repr. of 1897 ed. 9.50 (ISBN 0-87728-022-3). Weiser.

Saint-James, D., et al. Type Two Superconductivity. LC 67-27491. 1970. 42.00 o.p. (ISBN 0-08-012392-9); write for info. xerox copyflo avail. o.p. Pergamon.

St. John, Joanne, jt. auth. see Coombs, Robert H.

St. John, Judith B., jt. ed. see Moreland, Donald E.

St. Johns, Elaine, jt. auth. see Parker, William.

St. Jorre, John de see De St. Jorre, John.

St. Joseph, J. K., jt. auth. see Beresford, M. W.

St. Martin, Hardie, tr. see Donoso, Jose.

Saint-Martin, Louis Claude de. Theosophic Correspondence between Louis Claude de Saint-Martin & Kirchberger, Baron de Liebistorf. Penny, Edward B., tr. from Fr. LC 82-61304. xxxii, 326p. Repr. of 1949 ed. 13.75 (ISBN 0-911500-62-6). Theos U Pr.

St. More, Thomas see More, Thomas St., et al.

St. Peter, Charles, jt. auth. see Wejman, Jacqueline.

St. Peter, Genevieve, jt. auth. see Wejman, Jacqueline.

Saint-Pierre, Gaston & Boater, Debbie. The Metamorphic Technique. 1982. 25.00x (ISBN 0-686-99809-X, Pub. by Element Bks). State Mutual Bk.

Saint-Pierre, Jacques-Henri Bernardin de see Bernardin de Saint-Pierre, Jacques-Henri.

Saintsbury, George, tr. see Scherer, Edmond.

Saintsbury, George E. Dryden. LC 67-23875. 1968. Repr. of 1881 ed. 37.00x (ISBN 0-8103-3053-9). Gale.

--French Literature & Its Masters. Cairns, Huntington, ed. LC 77-163540. (Illus.). 326p. 1946. Repr. lib. bdg. 20.75x (ISBN 0-8371-6202-5, SAFL). Greenwood.

--History of English Prosody from the 12th Century to the Present Day, 3 Vols. 2nd ed. LC 60-10708. 1961. Repr. of 1923 ed. Set. 40.00x o.p. (ISBN 0-8462-0269-7). Russell.

--Prefaces & Essays. LC 77-100202. 446p. Repr. of 1933 ed. lib. bdg. 20.50x (ISBN 0-8371-4011-0, SAPE). Greenwood.

Saint-Simon, Claude-Henri De see De Saint-Simon, Claude-Henri.

St. Thomas Aquinas, see Thomas Aquinas, St.

Saint-Val, Alix. A L'Ombre De Tes Soleils. (Collection Colombine). 192p. 1983. pap. 1.95 (ISBN 0-373-48066-0). Harlequin Bks.

St. Vincent, Edna Millay see Millay, Edna St. Vincent.

Saissenlin, Remy, ed. see Lee, Sherman E.

Saito, Shiro. Philippine Ethnography: A Critically Annotated & Selected Bibliography. LC 72-92068. (East-West Bibliographic Ser.: No. 2). 512p. (Orig.). 1973. pap. text ed. 17.50x (ISBN 0-8248-0258-6). UH Pr.

Saito, Shiro, ed. Phillipine-American Relations: A Guide to Manuscript Sources in the United States. LC 82-12140. 280p. 1982. lib. bdg. 45.00 (ISBN 0-313-23632-1, SPH/). Greenwood.

Saito, T. & Burckle, L. H., eds. Late Neogene Epoch Boundaries. (Micropaleontology Special Publications Ser.: No. 1). 224p. 1975. 20.00 (ISBN 0-686-84248-0). Am Mus Natl Hist.

Saito, T., jt. ed. see Riedel, W. R.

Saito, T., jt. ed. see Takayanagi, T.

Saito, Tetsuo, jt. ed. see Georghiou, G. P.

Saka, Nannaji, jt. ed. see Suh, Nam P.

Sakai, A., jt. ed. see Li, P. H.

Sakai, Hikoichi & Mohri, Hideo, eds. Biological Functions of Microtubules & Related Structure: Proceedings, 13th Oji International Seminar, Tokyo, Japan, December, 1981. LC 82-11609. 1982. 32.00 (ISBN 0-12-615080-X). Acad Pr.

Sakai, Tune, jt. ed. see Biological Laboratory, Imperial Household.

Sakala, Carol. Women of South Asia: A Guide to Resources. LC 79-28191. 1980. lib. bdg. 30.00 (ISBN 0-527-78574-1); pap. 20.00 (ISBN 0-527-78575-X). Kraus Intl.

Sakamaki, Shunzo. Ryukyu: A Bibliographical Guide to Okinawan Studies. LC 63-14336. (Orig.). 1963. pap. text ed. 10.00x o.p. (ISBN 0-87022-724-6). UH Pr.

Sakamoto, Reiko. Hyperbolic Boundary-Value Problems. LC 81-3865. 230p. 1982. 34.50 (ISBN 0-521-23568-5). Cambridge U Pr.

Sakano, Theodore & Gregory, Stephen. Basic Physical Chemistry: Solutions Manual. 192p. 1983. pap. 11.95 (ISBN 0-686-38829-1). P H.

Sakata, Hiromi L. Music in the Mind: The Concepts of Music & Musician in Afghanistan. LC 82-23296. (Illus.). 250p. 1983. 32.50 (ISBN 0-87338-287-0). Kent St U Pr.

Sakers, George. Bowen's Ark. 1982. 14.95 (ISBN 0-671-43635-X). S&S.

Sakharov. Collected Scientific Works. 240p. 1982. 27.50 (ISBN 0-8247-1714-7). Dekker.

Sakharov, Andrei D. My Country & the World. 1975. pap. 1.95 (ISBN 0-394-72067-9, Vin). Random.

--Progress, Coexistence & Intellectual Freedom. rev. ed. 1970. 5.95 o.p. (ISBN 0-393-05428-4). Norton.

Sakhorov, Valdimir & Tosi, Umberto. High Treason. 1980. 11.95 (ISBN 0-399-12324-5). Putnam Pub Group.

Saki. The Short Stories of Saki. Date not set. 7.95 (ISBN 0-394-60428-8). Modern Lib.

Sakiey, Elizabeth & Fry, Edward. Three Thousand Instant Words. 1979. pap. text ed. 6.00x (ISBN 0-89061-249-8, 753S). Jamestown Pubs.

Sakkas, Basile. The Calendar Question. Holy Transfiguration Monastery, tr. from Fr. 96p. Date not set. pap. cancelled (ISBN 0-913026-24-7). St Nectarios.

Saklatvala, Beram. Sappho of Lesbos. 208p. 1982. 30.00x (ISBN 0-284-39146-8, Pub. by C Skilton Scotland). State Mutual Bk.

Sako, Sydney, jt. auth. see Finocchiaro, Mary.

Sakoian, Frances & Acker, Louis S. The Astrologer's Handbook. LC 78-160647. (Illus.). 480p. (YA) 1973. 15.34i (ISBN 0-06-013734-7, HarpT). Har-Row.

--Predictive Astrology: Understanding Transits As the Key to the Future. LC 77-3768. (Illus.). 1977. 16.30i (ISBN 0-06-013744-4, HarpT). Har-Row.

Sakoian, Frances & Caulfield, Betty. Astrological Patterns: Key to Self-Discovery. LC 79-2734. (Illus.). 1980. 15.34i (ISBN 0-06-013779-7, HarpT). Har-Row.

Sakol. Wonderful World of Country Music & Dance. 16.95 o.p. (ISBN 0-448-14392-5, G&D); pap. 9.95 (ISBN 0-448-14393-3). Putnam Pub Group.

Sakol, Jeannie. Hot Thirty. 1980. 9.95 o.s.i. (ISBN 0-440-03394-2). Delacorte.

Sakomoto. Gynecology & Obstetrics. (International Congress Ser.: Vol. 512). 1980. 220.50 (ISBN 0-444-90139-6). Elsevier.

Saks, Mark. The Calculator Cookbook: Maximizing the Computational Power of Your Hand-Held Calculator. 320p. 1983. 22.95 (ISBN 0-13-110395-4); pap. 10.95 (ISBN 0-13-110387-3). P-H.

Saks, S. & Zygmund, A. Analytic Functions. 3rd ed. 1971. text ed. 34.00 (ISBN 0-444-40873-8). Elsevier.

Saksena, Anuradha. Topics in the Analysis of Causatives with an Account of Hindi Paradigms. LC 82-40098. (University of California Publications in Linguistics: Vol. 98). 192p. Date not set. 13.50x (ISBN 0-520-09659-2). U of Cal Pr. Postponed.

Saksena, R. N., ed. see All India Sociological Conference.

Sakurai, J. J. Advanced Quantum Mechanics. 336p. 1967. text ed. 29.50 (ISBN 0-201-06710-2, Adv Bk Prog). A-W.

Sal, Eugene W. New York Court Forms. (Updated annually). loose-leaf bdg. 15.00 (ISBN 0-87526-250-3). Gould.

Sala, Andre. Take Heart. pap. 2.95 (ISBN 0-399-50468-0, Perige); 14 copy counterpack 41.30 (ISBN 0-399-50469-9). Putnam Pub Group.

Sala, Andre & Duxler, Margot. Expectations: A Completely Unexpected Guide to Planned & Unplanned Parenthood. (Illus.). 100p. 1981. pap. 3.95 (ISBN 0-399-50516-4, Perige). Putnam Pub Group.

Sala, F. & Barisi, B. Plant Cell Cultures: Result & Perspectives. (Developments in Plant Biology Ser.: Vol. 5). 1980. 76.25 (ISBN 0-444-80204-5). Elsevier.

Sala, Harold J. The Power of Persuasive Parenting. 111p. (Orig.). 1982. pap. 5.75x (ISBN 0-686-37686-2, Pub. by New Day Philippines). Cellar.

Salad, Mohamed K., ed. Somalia: A Bibliographical Survey. LC 76-51925. (Special Bibliographical Ser: No. 4). 1977. lib. bdg. 35.00x (ISBN 0-8371-9480-6, SSO/). Greenwood.

Saladin, Thomas A., jt. auth. see Sodeman, William A., Jr.

Saladino, Salvatore. Italy from Unification to 1919: Growth & Decay of a Liberal Regime. LC 75-101945. (AHM Europe Since 1500 Ser.). 1970. pap. text ed. 6.95x (ISBN 0-88295-762-7). Harlan Davidson.

Salaff, Janet W. Working Daughters of Hong Kong: Female Piety or Power in the Family? LC 80-23909. (American Sociological Association Rose Monographs). (Illus.). 304p. 1981. 29.95 (ISBN 0-521-23679-7); pap. 10.95 (ISBN 0-521-28148-2). Cambridge U Pr.

Salak, John S., ed. Dictionary of American Sports. LC 60-13658. 1961. 6.00 o.p. (ISBN 0-8022-1469-X). Philos Lib.

Salam, A. & Wigner, E. P., eds. Aspects of Quantum Theory. LC 72-75298. (Illus.). 300p. 1972. 42.50 (ISBN 0-521-08600-0). Cambridge U Pr.

Salaman, G. Community & Occupation. LC 73-92781. (Papers in Sociology: No. 4). (Illus.). 176p. 1974. pap. 10.95x (ISBN 0-521-09852-1). Cambridge U Pr.

Salaman, Graeme, jt. ed. see Dunkerley, David.

Salaman, Malcolm C. British Book Illustration Yesterday & Today, with Commentary. Holme, Geoffrey, ed. LC 73-175758. (Illus.). viii, 175p. 1974. Repr. of 1923 ed. 45.00x (ISBN 0-8103-3977-3). Gale.

Salamon, G., ed. see International Symposium of the French Institute for Health & Medical Research (Neurosciences), Marseilles, May 13-16, 1975.

Salamon, George. Arnold Zweig. (World Author Ser.). 1975. lib. bdg. 13.95 (ISBN 0-8057-6212-4, Twayne). G K Hall.

Salamon, Lester M. Welfare the Elusive Consensus: Where We Are, How We Got There, & What's Ahead. LC 78-12163. (Praeger Special Studies). 1978. 28.95 o.p. (ISBN 0-03-045601-0). Praeger.

Salamon, Lester M. & Abramson, Alan J. The Federal Budget & the Nonprofit Sector. (The Nonprofit Sector Ser.). 116p. (Orig.). 1982. pap. text ed. 11.50 (ISBN 0-87766-318-1, 34400). Urban Inst.

Salamon, Linda & Kinney, Arthur, eds. Nicholas Hilliard's Arte of Limning. (Illus.). 150p. 1983. 25.00 (ISBN 0-930350-31-6). NE U Pr.

Salamone, Rosa Maria, jt. ed. see Oberto, Martino.

Salancik, Gerald R., jt. auth. see Staw, Barry M.

Salant, Michael A. Post Keynesian Macrodynamics: A More General Theory. LC 82-99901. (Illus.). 170p. 1982. write for info. (ISBN 0-9609288-1-2); pap. write for info. (ISBN 0-9609288-0-4). M A Salant.

Salant, R. F., jt. ed. see Gopalkrishnan, S.

Salant, Stephen W. Imperfect Competition in the World Oil Market: A Computerized Nash-Cournot Model. LC 80-8737. 192p. 1981. 24.95x (ISBN 0-669-04344-3). Lexington Bks.

Salant, Walter S., jt. ed. see Krause, Lawrence B.

Salas, Charles G., jt. auth. see Salas, Saturnino L.

Salas, Floyd. Lay My Body on the Line. LC 78-53969. 1978. pap. 4.95 o.s.i. (ISBN 0-931676-02-9). Reed & Youngs Quilt.

Salas, S. L. & Hille, E. Calculus: One & Several Variables with Analytic Geometry, Pt. 1 & 2. 4th ed. 671p. 1982. text ed. 26.95 (ISBN 0-471-08055-1); student supp. 12.95 (ISBN 0-471-05383-X). Wiley.

Salas, S. L. & Hille, Einar. Calculus: One & Several Variables Combined. 4th ed. LC 81-19847. 1136p. 1982. 34.95 (ISBN 0-471-04660-4); avail. transparency; supplement avail. Wiley.

Salas, Saturnino L. & Salas, Charles G. Precalculus. 2nd ed. LC 78-23236. 1979. text ed. 24.95 (ISBN 0-471-03124-0); solutions manual 9.95 (ISBN 0-471-05515-8). Wiley.

Salaville, Jean-Babtise. De l'Organisation d'un Etat Monarchique ou Considerations sur les Vices de la Monarchie Francaise et sur la Necessite de Lui Donner une Constitution. (Rousseauism: 1788-1797). (Fr.). 1978. Repr. of 1789 ed. lib. bdg. 49.00x o.p. (ISBN 0-8287-0756-1). Clearwater Pub.

Salazar, A. C. Digital Signal Computers & Processors. (IEEE Press Selected Reprint Ser.). 690p. 1977. 37.95 o.p. (ISBN 0-471-03968-3, Pub. by Wiley-Interscience); pap. 24.95 o.p. (ISBN 0-471-03969-1). Wiley.

Salazar, Adolfo. Music in Our Time: Trends in Music Since the Romantic Era. Pope, Isabel, tr. Repr. of 1946 ed. lib. bdg. 16.00x (ISBN 0-8371-3014-X, SAMT). Greenwood.

Salazar, Andres C., ed. Digital Signal Computers & Processors. LC 77-82295. 1977. 37.95 (ISBN 0-87942-099-5). Inst Electrical.

Salazar, Nelia P., jt. auth. see Baltazar, Clare R.

Salazar, Omar M., et al. Bronchogenic Carcinoma. (Onclogic Division of Radiation Oncology Ser.: Vol. 13). (Illus.). 384p. 1981. pap. 100.00 (ISBN 0-08-027464-1). Pergamon.

Salazar, Tristan. The Complete Book of Furniture Restoration. (Illus.). 160p. 1982. 20.00 (ISBN 0-312-15630-8). St Martin.

Salber, Eva. Don't Send Me Flowers When I'm Dead: Voices of Rural Elderly. (Illus.). 180p. 1983. 25.00 (ISBN 0-8223-0529-1); pap. 12.50 (ISBN 0-8223-0565-8). Duke.

Salcman, Michael. Neurologic Emergencies: Recognition & Management. 266p. 1980. text ed. 30.00 (ISBN 0-89004-409-0). Raven.

Saldanha, C. J. & Nicolson, D. H. Flora of Hasson District Karnataka India. 1978p. 79.00x (ISBN 0-686-84452-1, Pub. by Oxford & I B H India). State Mutual Bk.

Sale, J. Kirk. The Land & People of Ghana. rev. ed. LC 74-377734. (Portraits of the Nations Ser.). (Illus.). (gr. 6 up). 1972. 9.57i o.p. (ISBN 0-397-31298-9, JBL-J). Har-Row.

Sale, Kirkpatrick. Human Scale. (Illus.). 1980. 15.95 o.p. (ISBN 0-698-11013-7, Coward). Putnam Pub Group.

--Human Scale. (Illus.). 540p. 1982. pap. 8.95 (ISBN 0-399-50621-7, Perige). Putnam Pub Group.

--Power Shift: The Rise of the Southern Rim & Its Challenge to the Eastern Establishment. 1975. 12.95 o.p. (ISBN 0-394-48947-0); pap. 4.95 (ISBN 0-394-72130-6). Random.

Sale, Larry L. Introduction to Middle School Teaching. 1979. text ed. 18.95 (ISBN 0-675-08279-X). Merrill.

Sale, Roger. Modern Heroism: Essays on D. H. Lawrence, William Empson, & J. R. R. Tolkien. LC 73-186106. 1973. 32.50x (ISBN 0-520-02208-4). U of Cal Pr.

--On Not Being Good Enough: Writings of a Working Critic. 1979. 17.95x (ISBN 0-19-502559-8). Oxford U Pr.

--On Writing. (Orig.). 1969. pap. text ed. 8.95 (ISBN 0-394-30254-0, RanC). Random.

--Reading Spenser: An Introduction to the Faeri Queene. (Orig.). pap. text ed. 3.95 (ISBN 0-685-19759-X). Phila Bk Co.

Saleeb, S. F., jt. auth. see Chen, W. F.

Saleeby, Najeeb M. Studies in Moro History, Law & Religion, Vol. 24. (Filipiniana Book Guild Ser.). 1977. wrps. 16.50 (ISBN 0-686-09463-8). Cellar.

Saleev. Basic Plasma Physics I. (Handbook of Plasma Physics: Vol. 1). Date not set. price not set (ISBN 0-444-86427-X). Elsevier.

Saleh, Dennis. First Z Poems. 1980. 18.50 (ISBN 0-931460-08-5). Bieler.

--Palmway. 67p. 1975. 3.50 (ISBN 0-87886-065-7). Ithaca Hse.

Saleilles, Raymond. Individualization of Punishment. Jastrow, Rachel S., tr. LC 68-55781. (Criminology, Law Enforcement, & Social Problems Ser.: No. 15). 1968. Repr. of 1911 ed. 20.00x (ISBN 0-87585-015-4). Patterson Smith.

Salem, Lionel. Electrons in Chemical Reactions: First Principles. LC 81-19833. 260p. 1982. 35.00x (ISBN 0-471-08474-3, Pub. by Wiley-Interscience). Wiley.

Salem, Raphael & Carleson, Lennart. Algebraic Numbers & Fourier Analysis & Selected Problems on Exceptional Set. LC 82-20053. (Wadsworth Mathematics Ser.). 224p. Repr. 29.95 (ISBN 0-534-98049-X). Wadsworth Pub.

Salem, Richard. New Blood. 1982. pap. 2.50 (ISBN 0-451-11615-1; AE1615, Sig). NAL.

Salemme, Lucia A. The Complete Book of Painting Techniques. 1982. 35.00 (ISBN 0-02-927910-0). Free Pr.

Salemson, Harold J., tr. see Cabanne, Pierre.

Salemson, Harold J., tr. see Dali, Salvador.

Salemson, Harold J., tr. see Diop, Cheikh A.

Salemson, Harold J., tr. see Perrin, Elula.

Salencon, J. Applications of the Theory of Plasticity in Soil Mechanics. (Ser. in Geotechnical Engineering). 158p. 1977. 53.95 (ISBN 0-471-74984-2). Wiley.

Salenius, Elmer W. Harley Granville-Barker. (English Authors Ser.). 1982. lib. bdg. 17.95 (ISBN 0-8057-6801-7, Twayne). G K Hall.

Salerni. Natural & Synthetic Organic Medicinal Compounds. LC 75-29249. (Illus.). 316p. 1976. pap. text ed. 14.95 o.p. (ISBN 0-8016-4303-1). Mosby.

Salerno, M. Constance, jt. auth. see Ingalls, A. Joy.

Salerno, Nan F. & Vanderburgh, Rosamond M. Shaman's Daughter. LC 79-20280. 334p. 1980. 12.50 o.p. (ISBN 0-13-807768-1). P-H.

Salerno, Nicolas A. & Hawkey, Nancy J. Composition & Literary Form: An Anthology. 2nd ed. (Orig.). 1978. pap. text ed. 12.95 (ISBN 0-316-76743-3); tchr's ed. avail. (ISBN 0-316-76742-5). Little.

Sales, Bruce D., jt. auth. see Elwork, Amiram.

Sales, John. West Country Gardens. 269p. 1980. text ed. 18.00x (ISBN 0-904387-55-0, Pub. by Sutton England); pap. text ed. 8.25x. Humanities.

Sales, M. Vance, jt. auth. see Rezny, Arthur A.

Saleska, Edward J., jt. ed. see Gockel, Herman W.

Saletore, R. N. Encyclopaedia of Indian Culture, Vol. I. 425p. 1981. text ed. 40.00x (ISBN 0-391-02282-2). Humanities.

--Indian Pirates. 200p. 1980. pap. text ed. 11.75x (ISBN 0-391-02183-4, Pub. by Concept India). Humanities.

Salevouris, Michael J., jt. auth. see Furay, Conal.

Salfelder, Karlhanns. Atlas of Deep Mycoses. LC 79-67221. (Illus.). 140p. 1980. text ed. 20.00 (ISBN 0-7216-7898-X). Saunders.

Salgado, G. Eyewitnesses of Shakespeare: First Hand Accounts of Performances, 1590-1890. 49.00x (ISBN 0-686-96997-9, Pub. by Scottish Academic Pr Scotland). State Mutual Bk.

Salgado, Gamini. English Drama: A Critical Introduction. 1980. 26.00 (ISBN 0-312-25429-6). St Martin.

Salgado, Maria A. Rafael Arevalo Martinez. (World Authors Ser.). 1979. lib. bdg. 15.95 (ISBN 0-8057-6387-2, Twayne). G K Hall.

Salgues de Cargill, Maruxa, jt. auth. see Terrell, Tracy D.

Saliba, David R. A Psychology of Fear: The Nightmare Formula of Edgar Allan Poe. LC 80-8267. 277p. 1980. lib. bdg. 21.25 (ISBN 0-8191-1269-0); pap. text ed. 11.50 (ISBN 0-8191-1270-4). U Pr of Amer.

Salibi, Kamal, jt. auth. see Grassmuck, George.

Salibi, Kamal S. The Modern History of Lebanon. LC 77-15054. 1977. Repr. 25.00x (ISBN 0-88206-015-5). Caravan Bks.

Saliga, Pauline. Chicago-Chicago. (Illus.). 1980. pap. 5.00 (ISBN 0-917562-15-1). Contemp Arts.

Salih, K., jt. ed. see Lo Fu-Chen.

Salin, ed. see Dauphine Conference on Money & International Money Problems, 3rd, Paris.

Salin, Lothar, jt. auth. see Fort, Joel.

Salin, P., ed. see Paris-Dauphine Conference on Money & International Monetary Problems, 5th, 1981.

Salinas, Carlos F., jt. auth. see Symposium Society of Craniofacial Genetics, 4th, San Diego. Ca., June, 1981.

Salinas, Pedro. Reality & the Poet in Spanish Poetry. Helman, Edith F., tr. from Span. LC 80-12201. xxx, 165p. 1980. Repr. of 1966 ed. lib. bdg. 19.00x (ISBN 0-313-22436-6, SARP). Greenwood.

Salinas, Wilson, jt. auth. see Moulaert, Frank.

Saling, Ann. Article Writing: A Creative Challenge. 208p. 1982. pap. 7.50 (ISBN 0-910455-00-7). ANSAL Pr.

Salingar, L. G. Shakespeare & the Traditions of Comedy. LC 73-91617. 368p. 1974. 60.00 (ISBN 0-521-20384-8); pap. 15.95x (ISBN 0-521-29113-5). Cambridge U Pr.

Salinger, Florence & Zagon, Eileen. Monograph Cataloging Notes. LC 81-12322. (Professional Librarian Ser.). 84p. 1981. pap. 12.95 (ISBN 0-914236-84-9). Knowledge Indus.

Salinger, Gerhard L., jt. auth. see Sears, Francis W.

Salinger, John. P. Burgundy Cherry. Brewer, John E. & Barrett, Benjamin, eds. 512p. 1983. pap. 8.95 (ISBN 0-939502-06-2). St Luke Pub.

Salinger, John P. The Naked Snow. Dickerman, Sherwood E. & Barrett, Benjamin, eds. 210p. 1983. 13.95 (ISBN 0-939502-01-1). St Luke Pub.

Salinger, Margaretta, jt. auth. see Sterling, Charles.

Salisbury, jt. auth. see Dorin.

Salisbury, Carola. Autumn in Araby. LC 82-45501. 288p. 1983. 14.95 (ISBN 0-385-17881-6). Doubleday.

Salisbury, Charlotte Y. Russian Diary. LC 73-9221. (Illus.). 192p. 1974. 6.95 o.s.i. (ISBN 0-8027-0450-6). Walker & Co.

Salisbury, Dallas L., ed. Economic Survival in Retirement: Which Pension is for You? LC 82-13857. 148p. (Orig.). 1982. pap. 10.00 (ISBN 0-86643-027-X). Employee Benefit.

--Retirement Income & the Economy: Policy Directions for the 80's. LC 81-12632. 1981. 18.00 (ISBN 0-86643-025-3); pap. 10.00 (ISBN 0-86643-023-7). Employee Benefit.

Salisbury, David F. Money Matters: Personal Financial Decision-Making with a Pocket Calculator. 228p. 1982. pap. 18.95 (ISBN 0-13-600528-4); pap. 9.95 (ISBN 0-13-600510-1). P-H.

Salisbury, E. J. see Jackson, B. D., et al.

Salisbury, Eugene W. New York Courts Manual of Procedure, 2 vols. (Both volumes supplemented annually). Vol. 1, 192 pp. looseleaf 13.50 (ISBN 0-87526-180-9); Vol. 2, 200 pp. looseleaf 12.50 (ISBN 0-87526-181-7). Gould.

Salisbury, Frank B. & Ross, Cleon W., eds. Plant Physiology. 2nd ed. 1978. text ed. 29.95x (ISBN 0-534-00562-4). Wadsworth Pub.

Salisbury, Gregorius. The Essence of the Supply-Side Economics for the Benefit of Politicians & Businessmen. (Research Center for Economic Psychology Library). (Illus.). 121p. 1983. 39.75 (ISBN 0-86654-060-1). Inst Econ Finan.

Salisbury, Harrison. Journey for Our Times: A Memoir. LC 81-47904. (Bessie Bks.). 416p. 1983. 18.75i (ISBN 0-06-039006-9, HarpT). Har-Row.

Salisbury, Harrison E. Black Night, White Snow: Russia's Revolutions 1905-1917. LC 74-18830. 1978. 17.95 (ISBN 0-385-00844-9). Doubleday.

Salisbury, J. K. see Kent, R. T.

Salisbury, Joan Curlee see Curlee-Salisbury, Joan.

Salisbury, John. The Baby Sitters. LC 77-88910. 1978. 9.95 o.p. (ISBN 0-689-10852-4). Atheneum.

Salisbury, John W. & Glaser, Peter E., eds. Lunar Surface Layer: Materials & Characteristics: Proceedings. 1964. 47.50 (ISBN 0-12-615450-3). Acad Pr.

Salisbury, Ray. Close the Door Behind You. 240p. 1983. 11.95 (ISBN 0-312-14484-9). St Martin.

Salisbury, Richard F. Vunamami: Economic Transformation in a Traditional Society. LC 70-79062. 1970. 34.50x (ISBN 0-520-01647-5). U of Cal Pr.

Salisbury, Robert H. Citizen Participation in the Public Schools. LC 79-7710. (Illus.). 240p. 1980. 25.95x (ISBN 0-669-03198-4). Lexington Bks.

Salisbury, William T. & Theberge, James D., eds. Spain in the 1970s: Economics, Social Structure, Foreign Policy. LC 75-19816. (Special Studies). 208p. 1976. text ed. 34.95 o.p. (ISBN 0-275-55800-2). Praeger.

Saliwanchik, R. Legal Protection for Microbiology & Genetic Engineering Inventions. (Biotechnology Ser.: No. 2). 1982. text ed. 34.95 (ISBN 0-201-10938-7, Adv Bk Prog). A-W.

Saljo, Roger. Learning & Understanding. (Goteborg Studies in Educational Sciences: No. 41). 212p. 1982. pap. text ed. 17.25x (ISBN 91-7346-106-7, Pub. by Acta-Universitatis Sweden). Humanities.

Salk, L., frwd. by. Your Child from One to Twelve. (Orig.). 1970. pap. 2.75 (ISBN 0-451-11659-3, AE1659, Sig). NAL.

Salk, Lee. Ask Dr. Salk. LC 81-66313. 1981. 10.95 (ISBN 0-672-52677-8). Bobbs.

--My Father, My Son: An Intimate Relationship. 276p. 1982. 13.95 (ISBN 0-399-12636-8). Putnam Pub Group.

--What Every Child Would Like Parents to Know About Divorce. 1979. pap. 2.25 o.p. (ISBN 0-446-92107-6). Warner Bks.

--Your Child's First Year. (Orig.). 1983. pap. 7.95 (ISBN 0-346-12581-2). Cornerstone.

Salkever, David. Hospital Sector Inflation. (Illus.). 208p. 1979. 24.95x (ISBN 0-669-00704-8). Lexington Bks.

Salkin, H. M. & Saha, J., eds. Studies in Linear Programming. LC 74-28998. (Studies in Management Science & Systems: Vol. 2). 322p. 1975. 49.00 (ISBN 0-444-10884-X, North-Holland). Elsevier.

Salkin, Harvey M. Integer Programming. (Illus.). 450p. 1975. text ed. 28.95 (ISBN 0-201-06841-9). A-W.

Salkind, A. J., jt. auth. see Falk, S. Uno.

Salkind, Alvin J., jt. ed. see Yeager, Ernest.

Salkind, C. T., ed. The Contest Problem Book. LC 61-13843. (New Mathematical Library: No. 5). 1975. pap. 7.50 o.s.i. (ISBN 0-88385-605-0). Math Assn.

--The Contest Problem Book 11: Annual High School Contests of the MAA. LC 66-15479. (New Mathematical Library: No. 17). 1975. pap. 7.50 (ISBN 0-88385-617-4). Math Assn.

Salkind, Neal. Theories of Human Development. (Orig.). 1980. pap. text ed. 13.95 (ISBN 0-442-25859-3). Van Nos Reinhold.

Salkman, Victoria. There Is a Child for You. 1972. 6.50 o.p. (ISBN 0-671-21443-8). S&S.

Sall, Dallas A. Inside Out. (Illus.). 80p. (Orig.). 1978. pap. 4.95 (ISBN 0-9604344-0-2). Sunrise Pub OR.

Sall, Millard. Faith, Psychology & Christian Maturity. 1977. pap. 5.95 o.p. (ISBN 0-310-32431-9). Zondervan.

Salle, Anthony J. Fundamental Principles of Bacteriology. 7th ed. (Illus.). 800p. 1973. text ed. 47.50 (ISBN 0-07-054480-8, C). McGraw.

Sallee, Susan, tr. see Farrokhzad, Forugh.

Salleh, Muhammad Haji. Time & Its People. (Writing in Asia Ser.). 1978. pap. text ed. 4.50x (ISBN 0-686-77466-3, 00237). Heinemann Ed.

Sallenave, Jean-Paul. Experience Analysis for Industrial Planning. LC 76-7164. (Illus.). 176p. 1976. 19.95x o.p. (ISBN 0-669-00658-0). Lexington Bks.

Sallese, Nicholas F. & Fernandez, Laura B. Pan y Mantequilla. 2nd ed. 1979. text ed. 9.95 (ISBN 0-442-25076-2); instructor's manual 2.00x (ISBN 0-442-25133-5); cassettes 59.95 (ISBN 0-442-25134-3); tapes 59.95x (ISBN 0-442-25135-1). Van Nos Reinhold.

Salles Gomes, P. E. Jean Vigo. Francovich, Allan, tr. LC 72-104102. 1972. 28.50x (ISBN 0-520-01676-9); pap. 5.95 (ISBN 0-520-02332-3, CAL252). U of Cal Pr.

Sallet, Richard. Russian-German Settlements in the United States. Rippley, La Vern J. & Bauer, Armand, trs. 9.50 (ISBN 0-686-95246-4). N Dak Inst.

Sallis, James. Teh Guitar Players: One Instrument & its Masters in American Music. LC 82-6403. (Illus.). 256p. 1982. 12.50 (ISBN 0-688-01375-9); pap. 6.50 (ISBN 0-688-01538-7). Morrow.

Sallis, John. The Gathering of Reason. LC 80-14485. (Continental Thought Ser.: Vol. 2). xii, 196p. 1981. 16.95x (ISBN 0-8214-0439-3, 82-83251). Ohio U Pr.

--Research in Phenomenology, Vol. 2. 263p. 1981. pap. text ed. 10.00x. Humanities.

Sallis, John, ed. Philosophy & Archaic Experience, Vol. 38. (Duquesne Studies: Philosophical). 225p. 1981. text ed. 19.50x (ISBN 0-8207-0152-1). Duquesne.

Sallis, John & Silverman, Hugh, eds. Continental Philosophy in America. 272p. 1982. pap. 23.50x (ISBN 0-8207-0160-2). Duquesne.

Sallis, Susan. Only Love. LC 79-2686. 256p. (YA) (gr. 7 up). 1980. 9.57i (ISBN 0-06-025174-3, HarpJ); PLB 10.89 (ISBN 0-06-025175-1). Har-Row.

--An Open Mind. LC 77-25678. (gr. 7 up). 1978. 8.95i (ISBN 0-06-025162-X, HarpJ); PLB 8.89 o.p. (ISBN 0-06-025163-8). Har-Row.

Sal Mani Joshi. God's Alternative: Swami Vivekenanda & His Band of Merry Shoeshine Boys. (God Ser.: No. 841). Date not set. cancelled (ISBN 0-89007-841-6). C Stark.

Salmanzadeh, Cyrus. Agricultural Change & Rural Society in Southern Iran. 274p. 1981. lib. bdg. 30.00 (ISBN 0-906559-03-0). Westview.

Salmen, Walter, ed. The Social Status of the Professional Musician from the 17th to the 19th Century. Kaufman, Herbert & Reisner, Barbara, trs. from Ger. Orig. Title: Der Sozialstatus des Berufsmusikers vom 17. bis 19. Jahrhundert. (Illus.). 332p. 1983. lib. bdg. 36.00 (ISBN 0-918728-16-9). Pendragon NY.

Salmi, Ella. Southwestern Soap. (Reading Books for College Students, or Adult School Students in Grade levels). (Illus.). 50p. 1983. pap. text ed. 4.00 (ISBN 0-686-38860-7); tchr's. guide 7.50 (ISBN 0-686-38861-5); Apple II discs 25.00 (ISBN 0-686-38862-3). Mentors.

Salmi, Ellablanche. Building Blocks of Reading Power-A. (Illus.). 150p. pap. 7.00 o.p. (ISBN 0-686-97356-9). Burgess.

--Building Blocks of Reading Power-B. (Illus.). 75p. pap. 5.00 o.p. (ISBN 0-686-97357-7). Burgess.

--Instructor's Guide for Building Blocks of Reading Power, A & B. 15.00 ea.; with game suppl. 25.00 ea. Mentors.

Salmi, Mario. Michelangelo: His Life. His Art. His Thought. (The Great Art Masters of the World Ser.). (Illus.). 615p. 1983. 245.25 (ISBN 0-86650-047-2). Gloucester Art.

Salmon. Fire Insurance Principles & Practices. (Research Bulletin: No. 18). pap. 0.50 o.p. (ISBN 0-685-57190-4). Assn Sch Busn.

Salmon, Arthur E. Alex Comfort. (English Authors Ser.). 1978. lib. bdg. 13.95 (ISBN 0-8057-6708-8, Twayne). G K Hall.

--Poets of the Apocalypse. (English Authors Ser.). 158p. 1983. lib. bdg. 16.95 (ISBN 0-8057-6846-7, Twayne). G K Hall.

Salmon, Charles, ed. Blood Groups & Other Red Cell Surface Markers in Health & Disease. LC 82-13096. (Illus.). 150p. 1982. 37.50 (ISBN 0-89352-193-0). Masson Pub.

Salmon, Charles G. & Johnson, John E. Steel Structures: Design & Behavior. 2nd ed. (Illus.). 1007p. 1980. text ed. 37.95 scp (ISBN 0-06-045694-9, HarpC); solutions manual avail. (ISBN 0-06-365805-4). Har-Row.

Salmon, Charles G., jt. auth. see Chu-Kia Wang.

Salmon, Charles G., jt. auth. see Wang, Chu-Kia.

Salmon, E. T. A History of the Roman World from 30 B.C. to A.D. 138. 6th ed. 368p. 1968. pap. 14.95x (ISBN 0-416-29570-3). Methuen Inc.

Salmon, Edward T. Augustus the Patrician. 1974. 2.00 o.p. (ISBN 0-88866-564-4). Samuel Stevens.

Salmon, Eliah J., jt. auth. see Bentz, Edward J., Jr.

Salmon, Elizabeth G. Good in Existential Metaphysics. (Aquinas Lecture). 1952. 7.95 (ISBN 0-87462-117-8). Marquette.

Salmon, Emily J., pref. by. A Hornbook of Virginia History. 3rd ed. (Illus.). Date not set. price not set (ISBN 0-88490-095-9); pap. price not set (ISBN 0-88490-094-0). Va State Lib.

Salmon, Geoffrey. The Working Office. (Illus.). 1978. pap. 16.95 o.p. (ISBN 0-8256-3138-6, Quick Fox). Putnam Pub Group.

Salmon, George. Conic Sections. 6th ed. LC 55-3390. 12.95 (ISBN 0-8284-0099-7); pap. 6.95 (ISBN 0-8284-0098-9). Chelsea Pub.

--Modern Higher Algebra. 5th ed. LC 64-13786. 12.95 (ISBN 0-8284-0150-0). Chelsea Pub.

Salmon, J. H. Society in Crisis: France in the Sixteenth Century. LC 75-5141. (Illus.). 300p. 1975. 30.00 (ISBN 0-312-73815-3). St Martin.

Salmon, J. H., ed. see Hotman, Francis.

Salmon, J. T. New Zealand Flowers & Plants in Colour. (Illus.). 1963. 32.95 (ISBN 0-589-00253-8, Pub. by Reed Books Australia). C E Tuttle.

Salmon, James F., jt. ed. see King, Thomas M.

Salmon, Jaslin U. Black Executives in White Businesses. LC 79-66859. 1979. pap. text ed. 8.25 (ISBN 0-8191-0860-X). U Pr of Amer.

Salmon, Margaret B. Diabetic Diet Exchanging Lists. (Illus.). 1977. pap. 1.50 (ISBN 0-918662-02-8). Techkits.

--Joy of Breastfeeding. LC 77-73690. (Illus.). 1977. write for info. o.p. (ISBN 0-918662-01-X); pap. 5.95 o.p. (ISBN 0-918662-00-1). Techkits.

--A Professional Dietitian's Natural Fiber Diet. (Illus.). 1979. 14.95 o.p. (ISBN 0-13-725333-8, Parker). P-H.

Salmon, Marilee H. Philosophy & Archaeology. (Studies in Archaeology Ser.). 20.00 (ISBN 0-12-615650-6). Acad Pr.

Salmon, P. R. Fibre-Optic Endoscopy. (Illus.). 237p. 1975. 32.00 o.p. (ISBN 0-8089-0862-6); pap. 23.25 o.p. (ISBN 0-686-77075-7). Grune.

Salmon, Raymond, jt. auth. see Masterton, Thomas.

Salmon, Richard D. The Job Hunter's Guide to the Rocky Mountain West. LC 78-74738. 1983. 13.95 (ISBN 0-918938-02-3). Brattle.

--The Job Hunter's Guide to the Sunbelt. LC 77-83139. 1982. 12.50x (ISBN 0-918938-01-5). Brattle.

Salmon, Vivian. The Study of Language in 17th-Century England. (Studies in the History of Linguistics Ser.). x, 218p. 1979. 30.00 (ISBN 90-272-0958-8, 17). Benjamins North Am.

Salmon, Wesley C. Logic. 2nd ed. (Foundations of Philosophy Ser). (Illus.). 160p. 1973. pap. 8.95 ref. ed. (ISBN 0-13-540104-6). P-H.

Salmona, M., et al, eds. Insolubilized Enzymes. LC 74-80537. 236p. 1974. 30.00 (ISBN 0-911216-60-X). Raven.

Salmond, Anne, ed. see Stirling, Eruera.

Salmond, John A. A Southern Rebel: The Life & Times of Aubrey Willis Williams, 1890-1965. LC 81-23087. (Fred W. Morrison Ser. in Southern Studies). xiv, 337p. 1983. 25.00x (ISBN 0-8078-1521-7). U of NC Pr.

Salmonson, Jessica A., ed. Amazons II. 240p. 1982. pap. 2.95 (ISBN 0-87997-736-1, UE1736). DAW Bks.

--Heroic Visions. pap. 2.95 (ISBN 0-441-32821-0, Pub. by Ace Science Fiction). Ace Bks.

Saloff-Astakhoff, N. I. Judith. 160p. Date not set. 2.25 (ISBN 0-88113-290-X). Edit Betania.

Salom, Georgine S., jt. auth. see Aaron, Jan.

Salomaa, Arto. Formal Languages. (ACM Monograph Ser). 1973. 49.50 (ISBN 0-12-615750-2). Acad Pr.

--Jewels of Formal Language Theory. (Illus.). 1981. text ed. 28.95x (ISBN 0-914894-69-2). Computer Sci.

Salomaa, Arto, jt. auth. see Rozenberg, Grzegorz.

Salomon, Allyn. Advertising Photography. (Illus.). 176p. 1982. 24.95 (ISBN 0-8174-3503-4, Amphoto). Watson-Guptill.

Salomon, Allyn & Lewin, Elyse. Child Photography. (Illus.). 176p. 1981. 19.95 o.p. (ISBN 0-8174-3665-0). Watson-Guptill.

Salomon, Jean-Jacques. Science & Politics: An Essay on the Scientific Situation in the Modern World. 1973. 22.50x (ISBN 0-262-19111-3). MIT Pr.

Salomon, Michel. Future Life. 384p. 1983. 17.75 (ISBN 0-02-606770-6). Macmillan.

Salomonsky, Verna C. Masterpieces of Furniture in Photographs & Measured Drawings. rev. ed. (Illus.). 1953. pap. 6.00 (ISBN 0-486-21381-1). Dover.

Saloom, Pamela, jt. auth. see Stoltz, Berdine.

Salop, L. J. Precambrian of the Northern Hemisphere. (Developments in Paleontology & Stratigraphy: Vol. 3). 1977. 85.00 (ISBN 0-444-41510-6). Elsevier.

Salottolo, A. Lawrence. Modern Police Service Encyclopedia. 2nd ed. LC 70-125939. (Illus.). 1970. pap. 8.00 o.p. (ISBN 0-668-02389-9). Arco.

Salper, Roberta L., ed. Female Liberation: History & Current Politics. 1971. pap. text ed. 4.50x (ISBN 0-394-31528-6). Phila Bk Co.

Salsburg, Z. W., ed. see Kirkwood, John G.

Salsbury, Barbara & Loveless, Cheri. Cut Your Grocery Bills in Half! Supermarket Survival. 250p. 1983. 14.95 (ISBN 0-87491-533-3); pap. 7.95 (ISBN 0-87491-531-7). Acropolis.

Salsini, Paul. Cole Porter, Twentieth Century Composer of Popular Songs. Rahmas, D. Steve, ed. LC 72-89206. (Outstanding Personalities Ser.: No. 41). 32p. 1972. lib. bdg. 2.95 incl. catalog cards (ISBN 0-87157-538-8); pap. 1.95 vinyl laminated covers (ISBN 0-87157-038-6). SamHar Pr.

Salstad, M. Louise. The Presentation of Women in Spanish Golden Age Literature: An Annotated Bibliography. 1980. lib. bdg. 27.00 (ISBN 0-8161-8505-0, Hall Reference). G K Hall.

Salstrom, Paul. Manual on Peace Walks. 27p. 1967. pap. 1.50 (ISBN 0-934676-11-9). Greenlf Bks.

Salt, E. Benton, et al. Teaching Physical Education in the Elementary School. 2nd ed. (Illus.). 1960. 17.50x o.p. (ISBN 0-471-07083-1). Wiley.

Salt, George. Cellular Defence Reactions of Insects. LC 71-118067. (Monographs in Experimental Biology: No. 16). (Illus.). 1970. 27.95 (ISBN 0-521-07936-5). Cambridge U Pr.

Salt, H. S. Richard Jefferies: A Study. 128p. 1982. Repr. of 1894 ed. lib. bdg. 25.00 (ISBN 0-89984-610-6). Century Bookbindery.
--Richard Jefferies: A Study. 128p. 1982. Repr. of 1894 ed. lib. bdg. 25.00 (ISBN 0-89760-851-8). Telegraph Bks.
Salt, J., jt. auth. see Lambert, David.
Salt, John & Clout, Hugh, eds. Migration in Post-War Europe: Geographical Essays. (Illus.). 1976. 29.95x o.p. (ISBN 0-19-874027-1). Oxford U Pr.
Salten, David G., et al. Mathematics-a Basic Course. (Illus.). pap. text ed. 5.73 (ISBN 0-8428-2013-2); key 2.00 (ISBN 0-8428-2036-1). Cambridge Bk.
Salten, Felix. Bambi. (Thrushwood Bks.). (Illus.). (gr. k-3). 1969. 3.95 (ISBN 0-448-02518-3, G&D). Putnam Pub Group.
--Bambi: A Life in the Woods. LC 74-124383. (Illus.). (gr. 4 up). 1970. 8.95 o.p. (ISBN 0-671-65136-6); pap. 4.95 o.p. (ISBN 0-671-79053-6). Wanderer Bks.
--Bambi: A Life in the Woods. (Illus.). 1982. pap. 2.95 (ISBN 0-671-46138-9). Archway.
Salter. Synopsis of Gastroenterology. 176p. 1980. pap. 25.00 (ISBN 0-686-36867-3). Wright-PSG.
Salter, Andrew. What Is Hypnosis? 106p. 1973. pap. 3.95 o.p. (ISBN 0-374-51038-5, N439). FS&G.
Salter, Cedric. Northern Spain. (Illus.). 1975. 10.95 o.s.i. (ISBN 0-8038-5041-7). Hastings.
Salter, Debbie. One Is More Than UN. 111p. 1978. pap. 2.50 (ISBN 0-8341-0548-9). Beacon Hill.
Salter, J., jt. auth. see British Computer Society.
Salter, James. Light Years. LC 81-83966. 320p. 1982. pap. 12.50x (ISBN 0-86547-064-2). N Point Pr.
--Solo Faces. (Contemporary American Fiction Ser.). 1980. pap. 3.95 (ISBN 0-14-005564-9). Penguin.
Salter, John T. The American Politician. LC 75-17541. (Illus.). 412p. 1975. Repr. of 1938 ed. lib. bdg. 23.25x o.p. (ISBN 0-8371-8239-5, SAAP). Greenwood.
Salter, Leonard A., Jr. Critical Review of Research in Land Economics. 280p. 1967. pap. 9.95 (ISBN 0-299-04424-6). U of Wis Pr.
Salter, Lionel, tr. see Schwendowius, Barbara & Domling, Wolfgang.
Salter, Thomas, ed. see Vernon, Sidney.
Salter, W. E. Productivity & Technical Change. (Cambridge Department of Applied Economics Monographs: No. 6). (Illus.). 1969. 35.50 o.p. (ISBN 0-521-06186-5); pap. 15.95x (ISBN 0-521-09568-9). Cambridge U Pr.
Salthouse, J. A. & Ware, M. J. Point Group Character Tables & Related Data. (Illus.). 64p. 1972. 11.95 (ISBN 0-521-08139-4). Cambridge U Pr.
Salthouse, Timothy A. Adult Cognition: An Experimental Psychology of Human Aging. (Springer Series in Cognitive Development). (Illus.). 253p. 1982. 24.90 o.p. (ISBN 0-387-90728-9). Springer-Verlag.
Salti, Danielle, tr. see Cueva, Agustin.
Saltkill, Sue. Country Christmas. (Illus.). 48p. 1983. 6.00 (ISBN 0-943574-21-8). That Patchwork.
--Log Cabin Constructions. (Favorite Patchwork Blocks Ser.). (Illus.). 30p. 1982. pap. 6.00 (ISBN 0-943574-11-0). That Patchwork.
Saltman, Benjamin. Deck. LC 79-22756. 63p. 1979. 4.00 (ISBN 0-87886-107-6). Ithaca Hse.
Saltman, D. J., jt. ed. see Amitsur, S. A.
Saltman, Jules & Zimering, Stanley. Abortion Today. 192p. 1973. pap. 10.50x o.p. (ISBN 0-398-02672-6). C C Thomas.
Saltman, Juliet. Open Housing. LC 78-19464. 1978. 36.95 o.p. (ISBN 0-03-022376-8). Praeger.
Saltman, Richard B. The Social & Political Thought of Michael Bakunin. LC 82-9348. (Contributions in Political Science Ser.: No. 88). 256p. 1983. lib. bdg. 35.00 (ISBN 0-313-23378-0, SPB/). Greenwood.
Saltman, William M., ed. The Stereo Rubbers. LC 76-45612. 1977. 78.50 o.p. (ISBN 0-471-74993-1, Pub. by Wiley-Interscience). Wiley.
Salton, G. & McGill, M. Introduction to Modern Information Retrieval. (Computer Science Ser.). 400p. 1983. 32.95 (ISBN 0-07-054484-0). McGraw.
Salton, G. & Schneider, H. J., eds. Research & Development in Information Retrieval: Proceedings, Berlin, 1982. (Lecture Notes in Computer Science Ser.: Vol. 146). 311p. 1983. pap. 14.50 (ISBN 0-387-11978-7). Springer-Verlag.
Salton, Gerard. Dynamic Information & Library Processing. (Illus.). 416p. 1975. ref. ed. 29.95 (ISBN 0-13-221325-7). P-H.
--A Theory of Indexing. (CBMS Regional Conference Ser.: Vol. 18). (Illus.). v, 56p. (Orig.). 1975. pap. text ed. 8.00 (ISBN 0-89871-015-4). Soc Indus-Appl Math.
Salton, Milton R., ed. Immunochemistry of Enzymes & Their Antibodies. LC 80-12475. 240p. 1983. Repr. of 1977 ed. lib. bdg. write for info. (ISBN 0-89874-165-3). Krieger.
Saltsburg, Howard, et al, eds. Fundamentals of Gas-Surface Interactions: Proceedings. 1967. 60.00 (ISBN 0-12-616950-0). Acad Pr.
Saltykov, Mikhail E. Fables. Volkhovsky, Vera, tr. from Rus. LC 74-14115. 257p. 1976. Repr. of 1941 ed. lib. bdg. 19.25x (ISBN 0-8371-7790-1, SAFA). Greenwood.
Saltykov-Shchedrin, M. E. Selected Satirical Writings. Foote, I. P., ed. 1977. text ed. 21.00x o.p. (ISBN 0-19-815641-3). Oxford U Pr.
Saltykov-Shchedrin, Mikhail. The Pompadours. Magarshack, David, tr. from Rus. & intro. by. Orig. Title: Pompadury. 300p. 1983. 20.00 (ISBN 0-88233-743-2). Ardis Pubs.
Saltz. Lifetime Family Record Book. 9.95 o.p. (ISBN 0-448-14658-4, G&D). Putnam Pub Group.
Saltz, Daniel. A Short Calculus. 3rd ed. 1980. text ed. 25.50x (ISBN 0-673-16060-2); o.p. answers to even-numbered problems (ISBN 0-8302-8201-7). Scott F.
Saltz, Daniel, jt. auth. see Bryant, Steven.
Saltzburg, Stephen A. & Redden, Kenneth R. Federal Rules of Evidence Manual. 3rd ed. 1982. 50.00 (ISBN 0-87215-500-5); 1981 suppl. o.p. 25.00 (ISBN 0-87215-391-6). Michie-Bobbs.
Saltzburg, Stephen A., jt. auth. see Lempert, Richard O.
Saltzburg, Stephen A., et al. Military Rules of Evidence Manual. 500p. 1981. with 1982 suppl. 40.00 (ISBN 0-87215-351-7); 1982 suppl. only 10.00 (ISBN 0-87215-474-2). Michie-Bobbs.
Saltzer, Joseph. Zone System Calibration Manual. 64p. 1979. mechanical binding 14.95 (ISBN 0-8174-2421-0, Amphoto). Watson-Guptill.
--A Zone System for All Formats. (Illus.). 1979. 25.00 (ISBN 0-8174-2419-9, Amphoto). Watson-Guptill.
Saltzgaber, Jan M., jt. auth. see Altschuler, Glenn C.
Saltzman, Barry, ed. Advances in Geophysics, Vol. 21. LC 52-12266. (Serial Publication). 1979. 55.50 (ISBN 0-12-018821-X); lib. ed. 67.50 (ISBN 0-12-018878-3); microfiche 36.00 (ISBN 0-12-018879-1). Acad Pr.
--Advances in Geophysics, Vol. 24. 312p. 1982. 46.00 (ISBN 0-12-018824-4); lib ed. 60.00 (ISBN 0-12-018884-8); microfiche 32.50. Acad Pr.
--Advances in Geophysics, Vol. 25. (Serial Publication). Date not set. price not set (ISBN 0-12-018825-2); price not set lib. ed. (ISBN 0-12-018886-4) (ISBN 0-12-018887-2). Acad Pr.
--Advances in Geophysics: Vol. 22 Estuarine Physics & Chemistry-Studies in Long Island Sound. 1980. 47.00 (ISBN 0-12-018822-8); lib. ed. 61.00 (ISBN 0-12-018880-5); microfiche 34.00 (ISBN 0-12-018881-3). Acad Pr.
Saltzman, Elliot, jt. ed. see Pick, Herbert L., Jr.
Saltzman, M., jt. auth. see Billmeyer, F. W., Jr.
Saltzman, Marvin L., jt. auth. see Muileman, Kathryn S.
Saltzman, Max, jt. auth. see Billmeyer, Fred W., Jr.
Saluga, Bill. Bill Saluga's Name Game Book. 1982. pap. 2.95 (ISBN 0-686-96946-4). Bantam.
Salukvadze, M. Vector-Valued Optimization Problems in Control Theory. Casti, John, tr. LC 79-23364. (Mathematics in Science & Engineering Ser.). 1979. 40.00 (ISBN 0-12-616750-8). Acad Pr.
Salustri, Carlo A. Roman Satirical Poems & Their Translation. Showerman, Grant, tr. from Ital. LC 78-21559. 1979. Repr. of 1945 ed. lib. bdg. 17.00x (ISBN 0-313-20745-3, SARS). Greenwood.
Salvador-Burris, Juanita, jt. ed. see Murata, Alice K.
Salvadori, B., jt. auth. see Luzzatti, G.
Salvadori, B. A. & Merialdi, A., eds. Fetal & Postnatal Outcome in EPH-Gestosis: Proceedings 13th International Meeting of the Organization Gestosis, Venice, 1981. (International Congress Ser.: No. 583). 320p. 1982. 74.50 (ISBN 0-444-90263-5, Excerpta Medica). Elsevier.
Salvadori, F. B. & Florio, P. L. Rare & Beautiful Animals. LC 78-55595. (Illus.). 1978. 12.95 (ISBN 0-88225-260-7). Newsweek.
Salvadori, Giuseppina, jt. auth. see Madrigal, Margarita.
Salvadori, Mario. Why Buildings Stand Up: The Stength of Architecture. (Illus.). 1982. pap. 6.95 (ISBN 0-07-054482-4). Mcgraw.
Salvadori, Mario & Levy, M. Structural Design in Architecture. 2nd ed. 1981. 31.95 (ISBN 0-13-853473-X). P-H.
Salvadori, Mario G. Statics & Strength of Structures. LC 70-138821. 1971. 29.95 (ISBN 0-13-844548-6). P-H.
Salvadori, Mario G. & Heller, Robert. Structure in Architecture: Building of Buildings. 2nd ed. (Illus.). 336p. 1975. 25.95 (ISBN 0-13-854109-4). P-H.
Salvadori, Massimo. The Liberal Heresy: Origins & Historical Development. LC 77-82859. 1978. 25.00 (ISBN 0-312-48250-7). St Martin.
Salvadori, P., jt. ed. see Ciardelli, F.
Salvaggio, Jerry L. Telecommunications: Issues & Choices for Society. Anderson, Gordon T., ed. (Annenberg-Longman Communication Ser.). (Illus.). 259p. 1983. text ed. 24.95x (ISBN 0-686-37900-4). Longman.
Salvatierra, Juan M. De see De Salvatierra, Juan M.
Salvato, Joseph A. Environmental Engineering & Sanitation. 3rd ed. LC 81-11509. (Environmental Science & Technology Ser.). 1163p. 1982. 55.00x (ISBN 0-471-04942-5, Pub. by Wiley-Interscience). Wiley.
Salvato, Joseph A., Jr. Environmental Engineering & Sanitation. 2nd ed. LC 79-37924. (Environmental Science & Technology Ser.). (Illus.). 1972. 42.00x o.p. (ISBN 0-471-75077-8, Pub. by Wiley-Interscience). Wiley.
Salvato, Sharon. The Fires of July, Bk. 1. (Orig.). 1983. pap. 5.95 (ISBN 0-440-52680-9, Dell Trade Pbks). Dell.
Salvatore, D. Schaum's Outline of International Economics. 2nd ed. 256p. 1983. 7.95 (ISBN 0-07-050640-X, P&RB). McGraw.
--Schaum's Outline of Microeconomic Theory. 2nd ed. 336p. 1983. 7.95 (ISBN 0-07-054514-6). McGraw.
Salvatore, Dominick. Internal Migration & Economic Development: A Theoretical & Empirical Study. LC 81-40066. 74p. 1981. lib. bdg. 16.75 (ISBN 0-8191-1640-8); pap. text ed. 7.00 (ISBN 0-8191-1641-6). U Pr of Amer.
--International Economics. 576p. 1983. text ed. 25.95 (ISBN 0-02-405300-7). Macmillan.
--Microeconomic Theory. 256p. (Orig.). 1974. pap. text ed. 6.95 (ISBN 0-07-054495-6, SP). McGraw.
--Theory & Problems of International Economics. (Schaum's Outline Ser). (Illus.). 224p. (Orig.). 1975. pap. 5.95 o.p. (ISBN 0-07-054496-4, SP). McGraw.
Salvatore, Dominick & Dowling, Edward T. Schaum's Outline of Development Economics. (Schaum's Outline Ser.). 1977. pap. 5.95 (ISBN 0-07-054494-8, SP). McGraw.
Salvatore, Dominick, jt. auth. see Berliner, Herman.
Salvemini, Gaetano. French Revolution. 1962. pap. 2.25x o.p. (ISBN 0-393-00179-2, Norton Lib). Norton.
Salvendy, Gavriel. Handbook of Industrial Engineering. LC 81-23059. 2086p. 1982. 64.95x (ISBN 0-471-05841-6, Pub. by Wiley-Interscience). Wiley.
Salvia, John & Ysseldyke, James E. Assessment in Special & Remedial Education. 2nd ed. (Illus.). 576p. 1981. text ed. 24.50 (ISBN 0-395-29694-3); instr's manual 1.00 (ISBN 0-395-29695-1). HM.
Salvin, Osbert, ed. see Maudslay, A. P.
Salvo, Louis J. De see De Salvo, Louis J.
Salwak, Dale. A. J. Cronin: A Reference Guide. 1983. lib. bdg. 28.00 (ISBN 0-8161-8595-6, Hall Reference). G K Hall.
--John Braine & John Wain: A Reference Guide. 1979. lib. bdg. 30.00 (ISBN 0-8161-8232-9, Hall Reference). G K Hall.
--John Wain. (English Authors Ser.). 1981. lib. bdg. 12.95 (ISBN 0-8057-6806-8, Twayne). G K Hall.
--Kingsley Amis: A Reference Guide. 1978. lib. bdg. 21.00 (ISBN 0-8161-8062-8, Hall Reference). G K Hall.
--Literary Voices Two: Interviews with Britain's "Angry Young Men". LC 81-21686. (The Milford Ser.: Popular Writers of Today: Vol. 39). (Illus.). 64p. 1983. lib. bdg. 9.95x (ISBN 0-89370-159-9); pap. 3.95x (ISBN 0-89370-259-5). Borgo Pr.
Salwen, Bert S., jt. ed. see Newman, Walter S.
Salyers, Paul. The Passing Day. LC 73-181457. 64p. 1972. 4.00 (ISBN 0-911838-16-3). Windy Row.
Salz, J., jt. auth. see Lucky, R. W.
Salzberger-Wittenberg, Isca. Psycho-Analytic Insight & Relationships: A Kleinian Approach. (Library of Social Work). 1970. cased 16.95x (ISBN 0-7100-6835-2). Routledge & Kegan.
Salzer, F. & Schacheter, C. Counterpoint in Composition: The Study of Voice Leading. (Music Ser.). 1969. text ed. 43.00 (ISBN 0-07-054497-2, C). McGraw.
Salzer, Felix. Structural Hearing: Tonal Coherence in Music, 2 Vols. (Illus.). 1952. text ed. 10.00 (ISBN 0-686-85909-X); Vol. 1. text ed. (ISBN 0-486-22275-6); Vol. 2. text ed. cancelled (ISBN 0-486-22276-4). Dover.
Salzer, I. E. Haunted House Mysteries. LC 78-10951. (Unsolved Mysteries of the World Ser.). PLB 11.96 (ISBN 0-89547-070-5). Silver.
Salzinger, Kurt. Psychology in Progress: An Interim Report, Vol. 270. (Annals of the New York Academy of Sciences). 1976. 9.50x (ISBN 0-89072-024-X). NY Acad Sci.
--Schizophrenia: Behavioral Aspects. LC 73-1276. (Approaches to Behavior Pathology Ser.). 181p. 1973. pap. text ed. 15.95 (ISBN 0-471-75090-5). Wiley.
Salzinger, Kurt & Feldman, Richard S. Studies in Verbal Behavior: An Empirical Approach. LC 76-179073. 474p. 1973. 28.00 (ISBN 0-08-016926-0). Pergamon.
Salzinger, Kurt & Denmark, Florence L., eds. Psychology: The State of the Art, Vol. 309. (Annals of the New York Academy of Sciences). 1978. 12.00x (ISBN 0-89072-065-7); pap. 12.00x (ISBN 0-89072-075-4). NY Acad Sci.
Salzinger, Kurt & Salzinger, Suzanne, eds. Research in Verbal Behavior & Some Neuro-Physiological Implications. 1967. 58.50 (ISBN 0-12-617150-5). Acad Pr.
Salzinger, Kurt, jt. ed. see Rieber, R. W.
Salzinger, Suzanne, jt. ed. see Salzinger, Kurt.
Salzinger, Suzanne, et al, eds. The Ecosystem of the "Sick" Child: Implications for Classification & Intervention for Disturbed & Mentally Retarded Children. 1980. 26.50 (ISBN 0-12-617250-1). Acad Pr.
Salzman, Ed, jt. auth. see Quinn, T. A.
Salzman, Jack. Albert Maltz. (United States Authors Ser.). 1978. lib. bdg. 13.95 (ISBN 0-8057-7228-6, Twayne). G K Hall.
--Merrill Studies in an American Tragedy. LC 70-150995. 1971. pap. text ed. 3.50x (ISBN 0-675-09205-1). Merrill.
Salzman, Jack, ed. see Dreiser, Theodore.
Salzman, Leon. Developments in Psychoanalysis. LC 61-18258. 314p. 1962. 44.00 (ISBN 0-8089-0395-0). Grune.
Salzman, Philip C., jt. ed. see Galaty, John G.
Salzman, Stanley A., jt. auth. see Miller, Charles D.
Salzmann, Zdenek, jt. auth. see Pi-Sunyer, Oriol.
Salztman, Barry, ed. Advances in Geophysics, Vol. 20. 48.50 (ISBN 0-12-018820-1); lib. ed. 62.50 (ISBN 0-12-018876-7); microfiche 35.50 (ISBN 0-12-018877-5). Acad Pr.
Samaan, Anne J., jt. auth. see Samaan, Sadek H.
Samaan, Sadek H. & Samaan, Anne J. Fears & Worries of Nigerian Igbo Secondary School Students: An Empirical Psychocultural Study. LC 76-620061. (Papers in International Studies: Africa: No. 30). (Illus.). 1976. pap. 6.00 (ISBN 0-89680-062-8, Ohio U Ctr Intl). Ohio U Pr.
Samaha, Joel. Criminal Law. (Illus.). 466p. 1982. text ed. 15.95 (ISBN 0-314-69675-X). West Pub.
Samaha, Joel B. Law & Order in Historical Perspective: The Case of Elizabethan Essex. LC 73-812. 1974. 25.00 (ISBN 0-12-785756-7). Acad Pr.
Samake, F., jt. auth. see Laplante, A.
Samal, Babrubahan. Transcription of the Eukaryotic Genome, Vol. 1. Horrobin, D. F., ed. (Annual Research Reviews). 1980. 38.00 (ISBN 0-88831-063-3, Dist. by Pergamon). Eden Pr.
--Transcription of the Eukaryotic Genome, Vol. 2. Horrobin, D. F., ed. LC 80-482436. (Annual Research Reviews Ser.). 237p. 1980. 30.00 (ISBN 0-88831-071-4). Eden Pr.
Samanin, R., jt. ed. see Garattini, S.
Samanin, Rosario, jt. ed. see Garattini, Silvio.
Samantha, Lester. The Brash American. (Orig.). 1981. pap. 1.50 o.s.i. (ISBN 0-440-10945-0). Dell.
Samaras, Lucas. Crude Delights. 96p. (Orig.). 1980. pap. 5.95 (ISBN 0-938608-00-2). Pace Gallery Pubns.
Samaras, Thomas T. Industrial Manager's Desk Handbook. (Illus.). 1980. 34.95 o.p. (ISBN 0-13-461491-7, Busn). P-H.
Samaras, Thomas T. & Czerwinski, Frank L. Fundamentals of Configuration Management. LC 75-127668. 371p. 1971. 44.95x o.p. (ISBN 0-471-75100-6, Pub. by Wiley-Interscience). Wiley.
Samaroff Stokowski, Olga S. The Listener's Music Book. rev. ed. LC 72-164473. 293p. Repr. of 1947 ed. lib. bdg. 15.50x (ISBN 0-8371-6217-3, STLM). Greenwood.
Samatar, Said. Oral Poetry & Somali Nationalism: The Case of Sayyid Mahammad Abdille Hasan. LC 81-18072. (African Studies: No. 32). (Illus.). 264p. 1982. 34.50 (ISBN 0-521-23833-1). Cambridge U Pr.
Samayoa, ed. Anaesthesiology. (International Congress Ser.: No. 490). (Abstracts). 1979. 30.75 (ISBN 0-444-90100-0). Elsevier.
Sambhi, ed. Heterogeneity of Renin & Renin Substrate. 1981. 72.00 (ISBN 0-444-00618-4). Elsevier.
Sambridge, Edward R. Purchasing Computers. 156p. 1979. text ed. 37.25x (ISBN 0-566-02193-5). Gower Pub Ltd.
Sambrook, A. J. English Pastoral Poetry. (English Authors Ser.). 163p. 1983. lib. bdg. 16.95 (ISBN 0-8057-6834-3, Twayne). G K Hall.
Sambrooke-Sturgess, Gerald. The Rules in Action. (Illus.). 138p. 1982. 12.95 (ISBN 0-914814-39-7). Sail Bks.
Sambrooke-Sturgess, Gerald, ed. see Twiname, Eric.
Sambursky, Shmuel, ed. Physical Thought from the Pre-Socratics to the Quantum Physicists. LC 74-12946. 584p. 1975. 25.00x (ISBN 0-87663-712-8, Pica Pr). Universe.
Samecl, E. see Von Wiesner, J. & Von Regel, C.
Samelson. English As a Second Language: Phase Zero Plus, Let's Begin. (Illus.). 288p. 1980. text ed. 17.95 (ISBN 0-8359-1725-8); pap. text ed. 14.95 (ISBN 0-8359-1724-X). Reston.
Samelson, Hans. Introduction to Linear Algebra. LC 74-17001. (Pure & Applied Mathematics Ser). 265p. 1974. 34.95x (ISBN 0-471-75170-7, Pub. by Wiley-Interscience). Wiley.
Samelson, William. English As a Second Language: Phase II-Let's Read. 1982. text ed. 17.00 (ISBN 0-8359-1736-3); pap. text ed. 13.00 (ISBN 0-8359-1735-5). Reston.
--English As a Second Language: Phase III-Let's Write. 2nd ed. 1982. text ed. 17.00 (ISBN 0-8359-1734-7); pap. text ed. 13.00 (ISBN 0-8359-1733-9). Reston.
--English As a Second Language: Phase IV: Let's Continue. (Illus.). 1979. text ed. 17.95 (ISBN 0-8359-1727-4); pap. text ed. 14.95 (ISBN 0-8359-1726-6); instrs'. manual avail. (ISBN 0-8359-1728-2). Reston.
--English As a Second Language Phase I: Phase I-Let's Converse. 2nd ed. (Illus.). 1980. text ed. 17.95 (ISBN 0-8359-1730-4); pap. text ed. 14.95 (ISBN 0-8359-1729-0). Reston.
Samet, P. A., ed. Euro IFIP, 1979. 1980. 95.75 (ISBN 0-444-85370-7). Elsevier.
Samet, Shelly, jt. auth. see Purvis, Jennie.

Sametz, Arnold, ed. Securities Activities of Commercial Banks. LC 80-8339. 208p. 1981. 24.95x (ISBN 0-669-04031-2). Lexington Bks.

Sametz, Arnold W. Prospects for Capital Formation & Capital Markets. LC 76-55113. (Illus.). 160p. 1978. 16.95x o.p. (ISBN 0-669-01505-9). Lexington Bks.

Sametz, Arnold W., jt. auth. see Altman, Edward I.

Sami, A. Intra Urban Market Geography: A Case Study of Patna. 219p. 1980. text ed. 16.50x (ISBN 0-391-02121-4). Humanities.

Sami, M. & Mezzalira, L., eds. Microprocessor Systems Software: Firmware & Hardware. 1981. 64.00 (ISBN 0-444-86098-3). Elsevier.

Sami, M., jt. ed. see Wilmink, J.

Samiy, A. H., et al, eds. see Braude, Abraham I.

Samli, A. Coskun. Marketing & Distribution Systems in Eastern Europe. LC 78-19754. 156p. 1978. 26.95 o.p. (ISBN 0-03-046486-2). Praeger.

Sammartino, Peter. The President of a Small College. 162p. 1982. 9.95 (ISBN 0-8453-4757-8). Cornwall Bks.

Sammes. Topics in Antibiotic Chemistry: Aminoglyosides & Ansamycins, Vol. I. 217p. 1977. pap. 49.95x (ISBN 0-470-99066-X). Halsted Pr.

Sammes, P. G. Topics in Antibiotic Chemistry, Vol. 6. 290p. 1982. 74.95X (ISBN 0-470-27517-0). Halsted Pr.

--Topics in Antibiotic Chemistry: Mechanisms of Action of Nalidixic Acid & Its Cogeners & New Synthetic B-Lactam Antibiotics, Vol. 3. LC 79-42955. 203p. 1980. 79.95x o.s.i. (ISBN 0-470-26882-4). Halsted Pr.

Sammet, Jean E. Programming Languages: History & Fundamentals. Forsythe, George, ed. (Automatic Computation Ser). 1969. ref. ed. 34.50 (ISBN 0-13-729988-5). P-H.

Sammon, Rick. Minolta SRT's. (Amphoto Pocket Companion Ser.). (Illus.). 1980. pap. 4.95 (ISBN 0-8174-4584-6, Amphoto). Watson-Guptill.

--Minolta XD's. (Amphoto Pocket Companion Ser.). (Illus.). 1980. pap. 4.95 (ISBN 0-8174-4584-6, Amphoto). Watson-Guptill.

--Minolta XG's. (Amphoto Pocket Companion Ser.). (Illus.). 1980. pap. 4.95 (ISBN 0-8174-4583-8, Amphoto). Watson-Guptill.

Sammons, Martha C. A Guide Through C. S. Lewis' Space Trilogy. LC 80-68329. 1980. pap. 5.95 (ISBN 0-89107-185-7, Crossway Bks). Good News.

Samois. Coming to Power: Writings & Graphics on Lesbian S/M. rev. ed. (Illus.). 288p. 1983. pap. 7.95 (ISBN 0-932870-28-7). Alyson Pubns.

Samovar, Larry & Mills, Jack. Oral Communication: Message & Response. 4th ed. 310p. 1980. pap. text ed. write for info. o.p. (ISBN 0-697-04165-4); instr's. manual avail. o.p. (ISBN 0-697-04175-1). Wm C Brown.

Samovar, Larry A. & King, Stephen W. Communication & Discussion in Small Groups. (Comm Comp Ser.). (Illus.). 48p. 1981. pap. text ed. 2.95 (ISBN 0-89787-308-4). Gorsuch Scarisbrick.

Samovar, Larry A. & Mills, Jack. Oral Communication: Message & Response. 5th ed. 320p. 1983. pap. text ed. write for info. (ISBN 0-697-04217-0); instr's. manual avail. (ISBN 0-697-04228-6). Wm C Brown.

Samovar, Larry A. & Porter, Richard E. Intercultural Communication: A Reader. 2nd ed. 1976. pap. 10.95x o.p. (ISBN 0-534-00448-2). Wadsworth Pub.

Samovar, Larry A., jt. auth. see Hellweg, Susan A.

Samovar, Larry A., et al. Understanding Intercultural Communication. 240p. 1980. pap. text ed. 41.95x (ISBN 0-534-00862-3). Wadsworth Pub.

Sampath, S. G, jt. ed. see Palusamy, S. S.

Sampey, R. Estudios Sobre el Antiguo Testamento. 1981. pap. 3.50 (ISBN 0-311-03627-9). Casa Bautista.

Samph, Thomas & Templeton, Bryce, eds. Evaluation in Medical Education: Past, Present, Future. LC 79-1163. (Illus.). 352p. 1979. prof ref 25.00x (ISBN 0-88410-522-9). Ballinger Pub.

Sample, Mike. Angler's Guide to Montana. (Illus.). 256p. (Orig.). 1983. pap. 8.95 (ISBN 0-934318-13-1). Falcon Pr MT.

Sample, W. Frederick, jt. auth. see Sarti, Dennis A.

Sampley, J. Paul. And the Two Shall Become One Flesh, a Study of Traditions in Ephesians 5: 1-33. LC 77-152644. (New Testament Studies: No. 16). 1971. 29.95 (ISBN 0-521-08131-9). Cambridge U Pr.

Sampliner, Richard E. Preventing Viral Hepatitis. 300p. 1983. 27.50 (ISBN 0-87527-229-0). Green.

Sampson, Anthony. The Money Lenders: The People & Politics of International Banking. 336p. 1983. pap. 6.95 (ISBN 0-14-006485-0). Penguin.

Sampson, Anthony, jt. ed. see Brandt, Willy.

Sampson, C. Garth. The Stone Age Archaeology of Southern Africa. 1974. 49.50 (ISBN 0-12-785759-1). Acad Pr.

Sampson, Earl D. Nikolay Gumilev. (World Authors Ser.). 14.95 (ISBN 0-8057-6341-4, Twayne). G K Hall.

Sampson, Edward C. E. B. White. (United States Authors Ser.). 1974. lib. bdg. 11.95 (ISBN 0-8057-0787-5, Twayne). G K Hall.

Sampson, Edward E. Social Psychology & Contemporary Society. 2nd ed. LC 75-30225. 567p. 1976. text ed. 29.95 (ISBN 0-471-75116-2); avail. tchr's manual (ISBN 0-471-01609-8). Wiley.

Sampson, Edward E. & Sampson, Marya. Group Process for the Health Professions. 2nd ed. LC 80-26487. 320p. 1981. pap. 14.95 (ISBN 0-471-08279-1, Pub. by Wiley Med). Wiley.

Sampson, Geoffrey. The Form of Language. (Illus.). 236p. 1980. 14.95x o.p. (ISBN 0-8464-0987-9). Beekman Pubs.

--Making Sense. 1980. text ed. 22.50x (ISBN 0-19-215950-X). Oxford U Pr.

Sampson, George. Concise Cambridge History of English Literature. rev. 3rd ed. LC 69-16287. 1970. 44.50 (ISBN 0-521-07385-5); pap. 18.95x (ISBN 0-521-09581-6). Cambridge U Pr.

--English for the English. Thompson, D., ed. LC 70-108111. (Studies in the Tests & History of Education). 1970. 14.95 o.p. (ISBN 0-521-07848-2); pap. 6.95 (ISBN 0-521-09964-1). Cambridge U Pr.

Sampson, Henry. History of Advertising from the Earliest Times. LC 68-22049. 1974. Repr. of 1874 ed. 54.00x (ISBN 0-8103-3515-8). Gale.

Sampson, Marmaduke B. Rationale of Crime & Its Appropriate Treatment: Being a Treatise on Criminal Jurisprudence Considered in Relation to Cerebral Organization. 2nd ed. (Criminology, Law Enforcement, & Social Problems Ser.: No. 174). (Illus., With index & intro. added & notes & ils. by Eliza W. Farnham). 1973. Repr. of 1846 ed. 12.00x (ISBN 0-87585-174-6). Patterson Smith.

Sampson, Martin W., III. International Policy Coordination: Issues in OPEC & EACM. (Monograph Series in World Affairs: Vol. 19, Bk. 4). 100p. (Orig.). 1983. pap. 5.00 (ISBN 0-87940-071-4). U of Denver Intl.

Sampson, Marya, jt. auth. see Sampson, Edward E.

Sampson, Olive. Remedial Education. (Special Needs in Education Ser.). 1975. 14.00x (ISBN 0-7100-8141-3); pap. 6.95 (ISBN 0-7100-8142-1). Routledge & Kegan.

Sampson, Pamela. The Incredible Invention of Alexander Woodmouse. (Illus.). 64p. (gr. 3 up). 1982. 8.95 (ISBN 0-528-82412-0). Rand.

Sampson, R. J., et al. The American Economy. 1975. 18.00 (ISBN 0-395-19780-5); instr's. guide 7.16 (ISBN 0-395-20467-4). HM.

Sampson, Robert C. Managing the Managers: A Realistic Approach to Applying the Behavioral Sciences. 1965. 22.95 (ISBN 0-07-054509-X, P&RB). McGraw.

Sampson, Roy & Farris, Martin T. Domestic Transportation: Practice, Theory, & Policy. 4th ed. LC 78-69576. (Illus.). 1979. text ed. 24.50 (ISBN 0-395-26793-5); instr's. manual 1.00 (ISBN 0-395-26794-3). HM.

Sampson, Roy J. & Calmus, Thomas W. Economics: Concepts, Applications, Analysis. 425p. 1974. text ed. 24.95 (ISBN 0-395-17812-6); instr's. manual 1.35 (ISBN 0-395-17856-8); study guide 9.50 (ISBN 0-395-17804-5). HM.

Sampson, Roy J., jt. auth. see Farris, Martin T.

Sams, Eric, jt. auth. see Brown, Maurice J.

Samskrti & Veda. Hatha Yoga Manual I. 2nd ed. (Illus., Orig.). 1979. spiral bdg. 5.95 (ISBN 0-89389-053-7). Himalayan Intl Inst.

Samson, Harold E. Tug Hill Country. 6th ed. 1982. 11.95 (ISBN 0-932052-13-4). North Country.

Samson, P. Glossary of Hematological & Seriological Terms. (Illus.). 128p. 1973. text ed. 13.95 (ISBN 0-407-72720-5). Butterworth.

Samson, R. W. Problem Solving Improvement. (Basic Skills System). 1970. text ed. 13.50 (ISBN 0-07-051372-4); tape 1 30.00 (ISBN 0-07-051373-2); tape 2 31.50 (ISBN 0-07-051459-3). McGraw.

Samsonov, G. V., ed. Refractory Transition Metal Compounds: High Temperature Cermets. 1964. 43.50 (ISBN 0-12-617550-0). Acad Pr.

Samsour, Roberta F., tr. see Sourek, Otakar.

Samstag, Nicholas. Bamboozled: How Business Is, by the Ad Boys. (Illus.). 1966. 5.50 o.p. (ISBN 0-685-11948-3). Heineman.

Samtur, Susan & Tuleja, Tad. Cashing in at the Checkout. LC 79-51120. (Illus.). 1979. 6.95 o.p. (ISBN 0-448-15704-7, G&D). Putnam Pub Group.

Samuel, Alan E., ed. Essays in Honor of C. Bradford Welles. (American Society of Papyrology Ser.). 30.00 (ISBN 0-686-95220-0, 31-00-01). Scholars Pr CA.

Samuel, Alan E., jt. auth. see Oates, John F.

Samuel, Arthur F. & Pustilnick, Robert A. Collections: A Virginia Law Practice Systems. 657p. 1982. looseleaf with forms 75.00 (ISBN 0-87215-506-4). Michie-Bobbs.

Samuel, Cynthia A., jt. auth. see Reppy, William A.

Samuel, D. N., ed. The Evangelical Succession. 144p. 1979. pap. 7.95 (ISBN 0-227-67834-6). Attic Pr.

Samuel, E. Introducing Batik. (Illus.). 1969. 14.50x (ISBN 0-87245-290-5). Textile Bk.

Samuel, Edwin, jt. ed. see Kamrat, Mordechai.

Samuel, Evelyn. Introducing Batik. LC 68-16174. (Introducing Ser). (Illus.). 1968. 9.95 o.p. (ISBN 0-8230-6120-5). Watson-Guptill.

Samuel, G. H. Cases in Consumer Law. 312p. 1979. 29.00x (ISBN 0-7121-0377-5, Pub. by Macdonald & Evans). State Mutual Bk.

Samuel, G. H., jt. auth. see Armour, L. A.

Samuel, Geoffrey, tr. see Heissig, Walther.

Samuel, Harold E. The Cantata in Nuremburg during the 17th Century. Buelow, George, ed. LC 82-1856. (Studies in Musicology: No. 56). 548p. 1982. 59.95 (ISBN 0-8357-1305-9, Pub. by UMI Res Pr). Univ Microfilms.

Samuel, Horace B. Shareholders Money. LC 82-48371. (Accountancy in Transition Ser.). 410p. 1982. lib. bdg. 40.00 (ISBN 0-8240-5328-1). Garland Pub.

Samuel, Leith. There Is an Answer. pap. 1.95 (ISBN 0-87508-469-9). Chr Lit.

Samuel, Mark A., jt. auth. see Swamy, N. V.

Samuel, Maurice. The Gentleman & the Jew. LC 70-163541. 325p. Repr. of 1950 ed. lib. bdg. 17.25x (ISBN 0-8371-6201-7, SAGJ). Greenwood.

Samuel, Maurice, tr. see Fleg, Edmond.

Samuel, Raphael, ed. Miners, Quarrymen & Saltworkers. (History Workshop Ser.). (Illus.). 1977. 24.00x (ISBN 0-7100-8353-X); pap. 12.50 (ISBN 0-7100-8354-8). Routledge & Kegan.

Samuel, Raphael & Stedman-Jones, Gareth, eds. Culture, Ideology & Politics: Essays for Eric Hobsbawn. (History Workshop Ser.). 320p. (Orig.). 1983. pap. 14.95 (ISBN 0-7100-9433-7). Routledge & Kegan.

Samuel, William S. Personality: Searching for the Sources of Human Behavior. (Illus.). 544p. 1981. 23.50 (ISBN 0-07-054520-0); instr's. manual 5.95 (ISBN 0-07-054521-9). McGraw.

Samuels, Alan R., jt. auth. see McClure, Charles R.

Samuels, C. L., jt. auth. see Brejcha, M. F.

Samuels, Charles, jt. auth. see Keaton, Buster.

Samuels, Clifford L. Automotive Air Conditioning. (Illus.). 288p. 1981. text ed. 18.95 (ISBN 0-13-054213-X); pap. text ed. 14.95 (ISBN 0-13-054205-9). P-H.

Samuels, Don, jt. auth. see Samuels, Mimi.

Samuels, Edward. Biotutorial: A Modular Program for Introductory Biology. Student Laboratory Guide. 1974. pap. 12.25 o.p. (ISBN 0-395-17855-X); Tchrs Manual 5.30 o.p. (ISBN 0-395-17789-8). HM.

Samuels, Ernest, ed. see Adams, Henry.

Samuels, Frederick. The Durable Group: Thoughts on Human Identity. 1977. pap. text ed. 8.25 (ISBN 0-8191-0207-5). U Pr of Amer.

Samuels, Gertrude. Adam's Daughter. (YA) (RL 6). 1979. pap. 1.75 (ISBN 0-451-11486-8, AE1486, Sig). NAL.

--Run, Shelley, Run. (YA) (RL 7). 1975. pap. 1.95 (ISBN 0-451-12051-5, AJ2051, Sig). NAL.

Samuels, Herbert, jt. ed. see Oppenheimer, Jack.

Samuels, Jay S., jt. ed. see Laberge, David.

Samuels, L. E. Optical Microscopy of Carbon Steels. 1980. 92.00 (ISBN 0-87170-082-4). ASM.

Samuels, Linda B., jt. auth. see Coffinberger, Richard L.

Samuels, M., jt. auth. see Ley, David.

Samuels, M. L. Linguistic Evolution with Special Reference to English. LC 72-176255. (Cambridge Studies in Linguistics: No. 5). (Illus.). 256p. 1973. 34.50 (ISBN 0-521-08385-0); pap. 11.95 (ISBN 0-521-09913-7). Cambridge U Pr.

Samuels, M. R., jt. auth. see Balzhiser, R. E.

Samuels, Martin A. Manual of Neurologic Therapeutics. 1978. spiral bound 14.95 o.p. (ISBN 0-316-76990-8). Little.

--Manual of Neurologic Therapeutics: With Essentials of Diagnosis. (Spiral Manual Ser.). 1982. spiralbound 15.95 (ISBN 0-316-76991-6). Little.

Samuels, Marwyn S., jt. ed. see Ley, David.

Samuels, Melvin L., jt. ed. see Johnson, Douglas E.

Samuels, Michael A. Education in Angola 1878-1914. LC 70-122747. (Illus.). 1970. pap. text ed. 10.50x (ISBN 0-8077-2087-9). Tchrs Coll.

Samuels, Mike & Samuels, Nancy. Seeing with the Mind's Eye. 1975. pap. 11.95 (ISBN 0-394-73113-1). Random.

--The Well Child Book. 480p. (Orig.). 1982. 22.50 (ISBN 0-671-40063-0); pap. 10.95 (ISBN 0-671-43893-X); coloring book 4.95 (ISBN 0-671-45466-8). Summit Bks.

Samuels, Mimi & Samuels, Don. The Complete Handbook of Peer Counseling. 5.95 o.p. (ISBN 0-686-92182-8, 4233). Hazelden.

Samuels, Nancy, jt. auth. see Samuels, Mike.

Samuels, Robert J. Structured Polymer Properties. LC 73-21781. 251p. 1974. 34.00 o.p. (ISBN 0-471-75155-3, Pub. by Wiley-Interscience). Wiley.

Samuels, S. Jay, ed. What Research Has to Say About Reading Instruction. 1978. pap. text ed. 6.25 (ISBN 0-685-59434-3). Intl Reading.

Samuels, Shirley. Disturbed Exceptional Children: An Integrated Approach. LC 80-22597. 366p. 1981. text ed. 29.95 (ISBN 0-89885-025-8). Human Sci Pr.

Samuels, Stuart. Midnight Movies. 224p. 1983. 9.95 (ISBN 0-02-081450-X). Macmillan.

Samuels, Warren & Wade, Larry, eds. Taxing & Spending Policy. (Orig.). 1980. pap. 6.00 (ISBN 0-918592-41-0). Policy Studies.

Samuels, Warren J., ed. The Methodology of Economic Thought. LC 78-62900. 603p. 1980. pap. text ed. 12.95 (ISBN 0-87855-645-1). Transaction Bks.

Samuels, Warren J. & Wade, Larry L., eds. Taxing & Spending Policy. LC 79-3689. (A Policy Studies Organization Book). 208p. 1980. 22.95x (ISBN 0-669-03469-X). Lexington Bks.

Samuelson, Paul. Economics from the Heart: A Samuelson Sampler. 320p. cloth 19.95 (ISBN 0-15-127487-8). HarBraceJ.

--Economics from the Heart: A Samuelson Sampler. 320p. pap. 6.95 (ISBN 0-15-627551-1, Harv). HarBraceJ.

Samuelson, Paul, ed. International Economic Relations. (International Economics Association Ser). 1969. lib. bdg. 19.95 o.p. (ISBN 0-312-42175-3). St Martin.

Samuelson, Paul A. Collected Scientific Papers of Paul Samuelson, 4 vols. Incl. Vol. 1. 1966. 55.00x (ISBN 0-262-19021-4); Vol. 2. 1966. 45.00x (ISBN 0-262-19080-X); Vol. 3. 1972. 45.00x (ISBN 0-262-19022-2); Vol. 4. 1978. 45.00x (ISBN 0-262-19167-9). MIT Pr.

--Economics. 11th ed. (Illus.). 1980. text ed. 25.95 (ISBN 0-07-054595-2); instructor's manual 19.50 (ISBN 0-07-054596-0); study guide 10.95 (ISBN 0-07-053271-0); test bank o.p. 10.95; transparency masters 25.00 (ISBN 0-07-054598-7); overhead transparencies 300.00 (ISBN 0-07-075000-9). McGraw.

--Economics. 9th ed. (Illus.). 928p. 1973. text ed. 24.95 (ISBN 0-07-054561-8, C). test bank 19.95 (ISBN 0-07-054563-4). McGraw.

--Economics. 10th ed. (Illus.). 1976. text ed. 17.95 o.p. (ISBN 0-07-054590-1, C); instructors manual 7.95 o.p. (ISBN 0-07-054591-X). test bank 9.95 o.p. (ISBN 0-07-054592-8). overhead transparencies 225.00 o.p. (ISBN 0-07-075000-9). McGraw.

--Foundations of Economic Analysis. Enl. ed. 544p. 1983. text ed. 25.00x (ISBN 0-674-31301-1); pap. 9.95 (ISBN 0-674-31303-8). Harvard U Pr.

--Readings in Economics. 7th ed. 1973. 15.00 (ISBN 0-07-054542-1, C); pap. 15.00 (ISBN 0-07-054543-X). McGraw.

Samuelson, Paul A., jt. ed. see Bicksler, James L.

Samuelson, Sue. Christmas: An Annotated Bibliography of Analytical Scholarship. Dundes, Alan, ed. LC 82-48083. (Garland Folklore Bibliographies Ser.). 200p. 1982. lib. bdg. 25.00 (ISBN 0-8240-9263-5). Garland Pub.

Samuelsson, B. & Paoletti, R., eds. Advances in Prostaglandin & Thromboxane Research, 2 vols. LC 75-14588. 1976. Vol. 1, 522 p. 57.00 (ISBN 0-89004-050-8); Vol. 2, 535 p. 59.00 (ISBN 0-89004-074-5). Raven.

Samuelsson, Bengt & Paoletti, Rodolfo, eds. Leukotrienes & Other Lipoxygenase Products. (Advances in Prostaglandin, Thromboxane, & Leukotriene Research Ser.: Vol. 9). 355p. 1982. text ed. 48.50 (ISBN 0-89004-741-3). Raven.

Samuelsson, Bengt, et al, eds. Advances in Prostaglandin & Thromboxane Research: Forth International Prostaglandin Conference, Washington, D. C, Vols. 6-8. 1980. Set. text ed. 190.50 (ISBN 0-89004-452-X); text ed. 65.50 ea. Vol. 6, 646 p. Vol. 7, 656 p (ISBN 0-89004-513-5). Vol. 8, 693 p (ISBN 0-89004-514-3). Raven.

Samways, Michael J. Biological Control of Pests & Weeds. (Studies in Biology: No. 132). 64p. 1981. pap. text ed. 8.95 (ISBN 0-7131-2822-4). E Arnold.

San Diego Police Dept. Police Tactics in Hazardous Situations. (Criminal Justice Ser.). 1976. pap. text ed. 9.95 o.p. (ISBN 0-8299-0628-2). West Pub.

San Francisco Mime Troupe. By Popular Demand: Plays & Other Works by the San Francisco Mime Troupe. LC 79-93008. Date not set. pap. cancelled (ISBN 0-686-32340-8). Performing Arts.

San, Kim, jt. auth. see Wales, Nym.

Sanabria, Sergio & Southard, Edna C. Portsmouth: Architecture in an Ohio River Town. LC 82-82114. (Illus., Orig.). 1982. pap. 7.50 (ISBN 0-940784-01-7). Miami Univ Art.

Sanadi, D. Rao, ed. Current Topics in Bioenergetics, Vol. II. (Serial Publications). 1981. 44.50 (ISBN 0-12-152511-2). Acad Pr.

Sanadi, Lalita. Mantra Meditation. rev. ed. D'Auri, Laura, ed. (Illus.). 160p. 1983. pap. 4.95 (ISBN 0-87407-204-2, FP-4). Thor.

Sanadi, R. D., ed. Current Topics in Bioenergetics, 8 vols. 1966-78. Vol. 1. 47.00 (ISBN 0-12-152501-5); Vol. 2. 47.00 (ISBN 0-12-152502-3); Vol. 3. 55.00 (ISBN 0-12-152503-1); Vol. 4. 55.00 (ISBN 0-12-152504-X); Vol. 5. 50.00 (ISBN 0-12-152505-8); Vol. 6. 60.00 (ISBN 0-12-152506-6); Vol. 7. 45.00 (ISBN 0-12-152507-4); Vol. 8. 45.00 (ISBN 0-12-152508-2). Acad Pr.

Sanadi, Rao, ed. Current Topics in Bioenergetics, Vol. 9. LC 66-28678. 1979. 49.50 (ISBN 0-12-152509-0). Acad Pr.

Sanadi, S. Rao. Current Topics in Bioenergetics, Vol. 10. LC 66-28678. (Serial Pub). 1980. 39.50 (ISBN 0-12-152510-4). Acad Pr.

Sanadon, David Duval see Duval Sanadon, David.

Sanasarian. Iranian Women's Movement. 190p. 1982. 23.95 (ISBN 0-03-059632-7). Praeger.

Sanazaro, Paul J., jt. ed. see Flook, E. Evelyn.

Sanborn, Charlotte J., ed. Case Management in Mental Health Services. LC 82-15495. 200p. 1983. text ed. 24.95 (ISBN 0-86656-109-9, B109). Haworth Pr.

Sanborn, Franklin. Personality of Emerson. LC 72-156911. (Studies in Emerson, No. 12). 1971. Repr. of 1903 ed. lib. bdg. 32.95x (ISBN 0-8383-1290-X). Haskell.

Sanborn, Franklin B. Recollections of Seventy Years. LC 67-23889. 1967. Repr. of 1909 ed. 42.00x (ISBN 0-8103-3045-8). Gale.
Sanborn, Franklin B., ed. Life of Henry David Thoreau, Including Many Essays Hitherto Unpublished & Some Accounts of His Family & Friends. LC 67-23890. 1968. Repr. of 1917 ed. 37.00x (ISBN 0-8103-3047-4). Gale.
Sanborn, Jane, jt. auth. see Sanborn, Laura.
Sanborn, Jane, ed. Bag of Tricks. (Illus.). 87p. (Orig.). 1983. pap. 6.95 (ISBN 0-910715-02-5). Search Public.
Sanborn, Laura & Eberhardt, Lorraine. Swim Free. 32p. (gr. 6-12). 1982. pap. 6.95 (ISBN 0-910715-00-9). Search Public.
Sanborn, Laura & Sanborn, Jane. The Mystery of Horseshoe Mountain. (Illus.). 92p. (Orig.). (gr. 4-12). 1983. pap. 5.95 (ISBN 0-910715-01-7). Search Public.
Sanborn, Margaret. The American River of El Dorado. LC 73-15160. 354p. 1982. pap. cancelled (ISBN 0-934136-23-8). Western Tanager.
--The Grand Tetons: The Story of the Men Who Tamed the Western Wilderness. LC 78-15287. 1978. 10.95 (ISBN 0-399-12045-9). Putnam Pub Group.
--Yosemite: Its Discovery, Its Wonders & Its People. LC 81-40237. (Illus.). 288p. 1981. 17.50 (ISBN 0-394-51794-6). Random.
Sanborn, Marion A. & Hartman, Betty G. Issues in Physical Education. 3rd ed. LC 81-20926. 271p. 1982. text ed. 17.00 (ISBN 0-8121-0848-5). Lea & Febiger.
Sanbrook, James, ed. see Thomson, James.
Sanburg, Carl. Rainbows Are Made: Poems by Carl Sandburg. Hopkins, Lee B., ed. (Illus.). (gr. 4 up). Date not set. 12.95 (ISBN 0-15-265480-1). HarBraceJ.
Sanburg, Delmer E., Jr. & Mulligan, F. K. The Archaeology of Two Northern California Sites. (Monograph Ser.: No. XXII). (Illus.). 90p. 1982. pap. 8.50 (ISBN 0-917956-41-9). UCLA Arch.
Sancha, Sheila. The Castle Story. LC 82-48802. (Illus.). 224p. 1983. pap. 8.61i (ISBN 0-06-091049-6, CN 1049, CN). Har-Row.
--The Luttrell Village: Country Life in the Middle Ages. LC 82-45585. (Illus.). 64p. (gr. 6-9). 1983. 12.45i (ISBN 0-690-04323-6, TYC-J); PLB 12.89g (ISBN 0-690-04324-4). Har-Row.
Sanchamau, J. B. L' Ecole des Peuples et des Rois. (Slave Trade in France Ser., 1744-1848). 170p. (Fr.). 1974. Repr. of 1790 ed. lib. bdg. 50.50x o.p. (ISBN 0-8287-0757-X, TN114). Clearwater Pub.
Sanches, Mary & Blount, Ben G. Sociocultural Dimensions of Language Use. (Language, Thought & Culture Ser.). 1975. 49.50 (ISBN 0-12-617850-X). Acad Pr.
Sanchez, jt. auth. see Bejarano.
Sanchez, A. E., jt. auth. see Angulo, D.
Sanchez, Augustin R., jt. auth. see Delgaty, Alfa.
Sanchez, David A. & Allen, Richard C., Jr. Differential Equations: An Introduction. LC 82-16326. (Illus.). 512p. Date not set. text ed. 22.95 (ISBN 0-201-07760-4). A-W.
Sanchez, David A., jt. auth. see Laken, William D.
Sanchez, E., jt. ed. see Gupta, M. M.
Sanchez, Gomez, jt. auth. see Bray, J.
Sanchez, Irene & Workman, E. L. The California Workers' Compensation Rehabilitation System: Supplement I. 1982. 9.95 (ISBN 0-686-83889-0). Macmillan.
Sanchez, Irene B. & Yund, Gloria S. Comida Sabrosa: Home-Style Southwestern Cooking. (Illus.). 128p. 1982. 14.95 (ISBN 0-8263-0636-5). U of NM Pr.
Sanchez, John. Blade Master: Advanced Survival Skills for Knife Fighters. (Illus.). 96p. 1982. pap. 10.00 (ISBN 0-87364-259-7). Paladin Ent.
Sanchez, Jorge, tr. see Smedes, Lewis.
Sanchez, Jose M., tr. see Kerfoot, H. F.
Sanchez, Juan B., jt. auth. see Branks, Judith.
Sanchez, Pedro A. Properties & Management of Soils in the Tropics. LC 76-22761. 618p. 1976. 48.50x (ISBN 0-471-75200-2, Pub. by Wiley-Interscience). Wiley.
Sanchez, Pedro C., jt. auth. see Carano, Paul.
Sanchez, Ray A., ed. see De Ford, Tamara.
Sanchez, Roberto G., ed. see Sanchez-Silva, Jose M.
Sanchez, Rosaura. Chicano Discourse: Socio-Historic Perspectives. 224p. 1983. pap. text ed. 15.95 (ISBN 0-88377-215-9). Newbury Hse.
Sanchez, Sonia. Love Poems. LC 73-83168. 208p. (Orig.). pap. 5.95 (ISBN 0-89388-104-X). Okpaku Communications.
Sanchez, Tony. Up & Down with the Rolling Stones. 1980. pap. 3.50 (ISBN 0-451-11933-9, AE1933, Sig). NAL.
--Up & Down with the Rolling Stones. (Illus.). 1979. pap. 8.95 (ISBN 0-688-08515-6). Quill NY.
Sanchez-Albornoz, Nicolas. The Population of Latin America. 1974. 42.50x (ISBN 0-520-01766-8); pap. 8.25x (ISBN 0-520-02745-0). U of Cal Pr.
Sanchez de Las Brozas, F. Minerva, Sive de Causis Linguae Latinae. (Linguistics 13th-18th Centuries). 588p. (Fr.). 1974. Repr. of 1587 ed. lib. bdg. 144.00x o.p. (ISBN 0-8287-0758-8, 71-5011). Clearwater Pub.
Sanchez Korrol, Virginia E. From Colonia to Community: The History of Puerto Ricans in New York City, 1917-1948. LC 82-18691. (Contributions in Ethnic Studies: No. 9). (Illus.). 256p. 1983. lib. bdg. 29.95 (ISBN 0-313-23458-2, F128). Greenwood.
Sanchez-Ocejo, Virgilio & Stevens, Wendelle C. UFO Contact from Undersea. (UFO Factbooks). (Illus.). 190p. 1982. lib. bdg. 14.95 (ISBN 0-9608558-0-7). UFO Photo.
Sanchez-Silva, Jose M. Marcelino Pan y Vino. (Easy Readers, Ser. A). 48p. (Span.). 1976. pap. text ed. 2.95 (ISBN 0-88436-280-9, 70263). EMC.
--Marcelino Pan y Vino. Mulvihill, Edward R. & Sanchez, Roberto G., eds. 1961. pap. 5.95x (ISBN 0-19-501043-4). Oxford U Pr.
Sanchez-Vazquez, Adolfo see Vazquez, Adolfo Sanchez.
Sanchez-Zarazua, J. R. The Theory of the Integration of Matter. 1978. 10.00 o.p. (ISBN 0-533-02685-7). Vantage.
Sanchis, Frank E. American Architecture: Westchester County, New York: Colonial to Contemporary. LC 77-21642. (Illus.). 1977. 45.00 (ISBN 0-88427-026-2). North River.
Sancho, Pedro. Account of the Conquest of Peru. Means, Philip A., tr. 1917. 20.00 (ISBN 0-527-19722-X). Kraus Repr.
Sanctuary, E. N. An Answer to the Voice for Human Rights. 1982. lib. bdg. 69.95 (ISBN 0-87700-417-X). Revisionist Pr.
Sand, George. The Bagpipers. LC 77-15563. (Illus.). 1977. lib. bdg. 14.95 o.p. (ISBN 0-915864-46-0); pap. 5.95 (ISBN 0-915864-45-2). Academy Chi Ltd.
Sand, Margaret. The Chanting of Children. LC 77-1014. 1978. 8.95 o.p. (ISBN 0-698-10859-0, Coward). Putnam Pub Group.
Sandage, Allan & Sandage, Mary, eds. Galaxies & the Universe, Vol. IX. LC 74-7559. (Stars & Stellar Systems Midway Reprint Ser.). (Illus.). 818p. 1983. pap. text ed. 40.00x (ISBN 0-226-45970-5). U of Chicago Pr.
Sandage, Mary, jt. ed. see Sandage, Allan.
Sandak, Cass R. Baseball & Softball. (Easy-Read Sports Bks.). (Illus.). 48p. (gr. 1-3). 1982. PLB 8.60 (ISBN 0-531-04374-6). Watts.
--Christmas. LC 80-11114. (gr. 2-4). 1980. PLB 8.90 (ISBN 0-531-04147-6). Watts.
--Easter. LC 80-10510. (gr. 2-4). 1980. PLB 8.90 (ISBN 0-531-04148-4). Watts.
--Explorers & Discovery. (A Reference First Bk.). (Illus.). 96p. (gr. 4 up). 1983. PLB 8.90 (ISBN 0-531-04537-4). Watts.
--Football. (Easy-Read Sports Bks). (Illus.). 48p. (gr. 1-3). 1982. PLB 8.60 (ISBN 0-531-04376-2). Watts.
--Museums: What They Are & How They Work. (First Bks.). (Illus.). 72p. (gr. 4 up). 1981. lib. bdg. 8.90 (ISBN 0-531-04348-7). Watts.
Sandalow, Terrance & Stein, Eric. Courts & Free Markets: Perspectives from the United States & Europe, 2 vols. 1982. Vol. 1. 39.50x (ISBN 0-19-825366-4); Vol. 2. pap. 39.50x (ISBN 0-19-825392-3). Oxford U Pr.
Sanday, Peggy R. Female Power & Male Dominance: On the Origins of Sexual Inequality. LC 80-18461. (Illus.). 256p. 1981. text ed. 37.50 (ISBN 0-521-23618-5); pap. text ed. 10.95 (ISBN 0-521-28075-3). Cambridge U Pr.
Sandbank, C. P. Optical Fiber Communication Systems. LC 79-40822. 347p. 1980. 59.95x (ISBN 0-471-27667-7, Pub. by Wiley-Interscience). Wiley.
Sandbauch, John. Astrology, Alchemy & Tarot. 307p. 1982. pap. 4.95 (ISBN 0-930706-08-0). Seek-It Pubns.
Sandberg, jt. auth. see Fawcett.
Sandberg, Alvin, jt. auth. see Fawcett, Susan.
Sandberg, Alvin, jt. auth. see Fawcett, Susan C.
Sandberg, Anne. Seeing the Invisible. 1977. pap. 4.95 (ISBN 0-88270-246-7, Pub. by Logos). Bridge Pub.
Sandberg, Berent. Brass Diamonds. 1980. 8.95 o.p. (ISBN 0-453-00383-4, H383). NAL.
--Brass Diamonds. 1981. pap. 2.50 o.p. (ISBN 0-451-09665-7, E9665, Sig). NAL.
--The Honeycomb Bid. (Orig.). 1981. pap. 2.95 o.p. (ISBN 0-451-11069-2, AE1069, Sig). NAL.
Sandberg, E. W., jt. auth. see Fowler, Frank P.
Sandberg, John E. Career Opportunities. LC 82-83779. 350p. text ed. 17.95x (ISBN 0-918452-37-6). Learning Pubns.
Sandberg, K. & Steinmetz, D. Creative English: The Basics for Comprehension & Expression, Bk. 1. (English As a Second Language Ser.). 1980. pap. 10.95 (ISBN 0-13-189555-9). P-H.
Sandberg, Karl C. & Tatham, Eddison C. French for Reading: A Programmed Approach for Graduate Degree Requirements. 1972. text ed. 17.95 (ISBN 0-13-331603-3). P-H.
Sandberg, Karl C. & Wende, John R. German for Reading: A Programmed Approach. 1973. pap. text ed. 18.95 (ISBN 0-13-354019-7). P-H.
Sandberg, Karl C., jt. auth. see Brown, Thomas H.
Sandberg, Moshe & Rothkirchen, Livia, eds. My Longest Year. 114p. 6.00 o.s.i. (ISBN 0-686-74945-6). ADL.
Sandberg, Neil C. Identity & Assimilation: The Welsh-English Dichotomy, a Case Study. LC 81-40717. (Illus.). 154p. (Orig.). 1982. lib. bdg. 21.25 (ISBN 0-8191-1968-7); pap. text ed. 9.25 (ISBN 0-8191-1969-5). U Pr of Amer.
Sandberg, Peter L. Stubb's Run. 1979. 7.95 o.p. (ISBN 0-395-28423-6). HM.
Sandblom, Philip. Creativity & Disease. (Illus.). 139p. 1982. 12.50 (ISBN 0-89313-066-4). G F Stickley.
Sandborn, E. B. Cells & Tissues by Light & Electron Microscopy. 1970. Vol. 1. 56.50 (ISBN 0-12-617901-8); Vol. 2. 56.50 (ISBN 0-12-617902-6). Acad Pr.
Sandbrook, R. Proletarians & African Capitalism: The Kenyan Case, 1960-1972. LC 73-91818. (Perspectives on Development: No. 4). 288p. 1975. 37.50 (ISBN 0-521-20428-3). Cambridge U Pr.
Sandburg, Carl. Abe Lincoln Grows up. LC 74-17180. (Illus.). 222p. (gr. 7 up). 1975. pap. 1.95 (ISBN 0-15-602615-5, VoyB). HarBraceJ.
--Abraham Lincoln: The Prairie Years & the War Years. rev. ed. LC 74-122389. (Illus.). 640p. (1 Vol.). Repr. of 1954 ed. 17.95 (ISBN 0-15-100640-7). HarBraceJ.
--The Complete Poems of Carl Sandburg. rev ed. LC 76-78865. 1970. 19.95 (ISBN 0-15-120773-9). HarBraceJ.
--Early Moon. LC 77-16488. (Illus.). (gr. 5 up). 1978. pap. 1.95 (ISBN 0-15-627326-8, VoyB). HarBraceJ.
--Honey & Salt. LC 63-9836. 1963. 11.95 (ISBN 0-15-142170-6). HarBraceJ.
--Honey & Salt. LC 63-9836. 1967. pap. 2.95 (ISBN 0-15-642165-8, Harv). HarBraceJ.
--Prairie-Town Boy. LC 77-4647. (Illus.). (gr. 9-12). 1977. pap. 1.75 (ISBN 0-15-673700-0, VoyB). HarBraceJ.
--Rootabaga Stories, Pt. 1. LC 73-13875. (Illus.). 230p. (gr. 4-6). 1974. pap. 2.25 (ISBN 0-15-678900-0, VoyB). HarBraceJ.
--The Wedding Procession of the Rag Doll & the Broom Handle & Who Was in It. LC 78-7912. (Illus.). (ps-3). 1978. pap. 2.25 (ISBN 0-15-695487-7, VoyB). HarBraceJ.
--Wind Song. LC 60-10248. (Illus.). (gr. 5 up). 1965. pap. 1.50 (ISBN 0-15-697096-1, VoyB). HarBraceJ.
Sandeen, Ernest R. & Hale, Frederick, eds. American Religion & Philosophy: A Guide to Information Sources. LC 73-17562. (American Studies Information Guide Ser.: Vol. 5). 1978. 42.00x (ISBN 0-8103-1262-X). Gale.
Sandefur, Charles R. Volleyball. LC 70-103063. (Phys. Ed. Ser.). 1970. pap. text ed. 7.95x (ISBN 0-673-16212-5). Scott F.
Sandel, Michael J. Liberalism & the Limits of Justice. LC 82-4394. 200p. 1982. 29.50 (ISBN 0-521-24501-X); pap. 9.95 (ISBN 0-521-27077-4). Cambridge U Pr.
Sandelin, Clarence K. Robert Nathan. (United States Authors Ser.). 14.95 (ISBN 0-8057-0548-1, Twayne). G K Hall.
Sandell, E. B. & Onishi, Hiroshi. Photometric Determination of Traces of Metals: General Aspects, Vol. 3. 4th ed. LC 77-18937. (Chemical Analysis Ser.). 1085p. 1978. 96.00 (ISBN 0-471-03094-5, Pub. by Wiley-Interscience). Wiley.
Sandelowski, Margarete. Women, Health, & Choice. (Illus.). 288p. 1981. pap. text ed. 13.95 (ISBN 0-13-962183-0). P-H.
Sandemose, Aksel. Werewolf. Lannestock, Gustaf, tr. (Nordic Translation Ser.). 1966. pap. 6.00 o.p. (ISBN 0-299-03744-4). U of Wis Pr.
Sander, J. Oswald. Satan Is No Myth. 141p. 1983. pap. 5.95 (ISBN 0-686-84263-4). Moody.
Sander, K. F. & Reed, G. A. Transmission & Propagation of Electromagnetic Waves. LC 77-87390. (Illus.). 1978. 87.50 (ISBN 0-521-21924-8); pap. 21.95x (ISBN 0-521-29312-X). Cambridge U Pr.
Sander, Volkmar, ed. see Brecht, Bertolt.
Sanderlin. Bartolome De las Casas: A Selection of His Writings. pap. text ed. 3.95x (ISBN 0-685-39883-8). Phila Bk Co.
Sanderlin, George. Eastward to India: Vasco Da Gama's Voyage. LC 65-20247. (Illus.). (gr. 5 up). 1965. PLB 12.89 (ISBN 0-06-025171-9, HarpJ). Har-Row.
--A Hoop to the Barrel: The Making of the American Constitution. (Illus.). 224p. (gr. 7 up). 1974. PLB 6.19 o.p. (ISBN 0-698-30511-6, Coward). Putnam Pub Group.
--Mark Twain: As Others Saw Him. LC 77-23897. (Illus.). (gr. 6-8). 1978. PLB 5.99 o.p. (ISBN 0-698-30686-4, Coward). Putnam Pub Group.
--The Settlement of California. (Illus.). 224p. (gr. 7 up). 1972. PLB 5.86 o.p. (ISBN 0-698-30456-X, Coward). Putnam Pub Group.
--Washington Irving: As Others Saw Him. LC 74-79701. (Illus.). 128p. (gr. 7 up). 1975. 5.95 o.p. (ISBN 0-698-20296-1, Coward). Putnam Pub Group.
Sanderlin, Owenita. Match Point. (gr. 3 up). 1979. pap. 1.50 (ISBN 0-307-21518-0, Golden Pr). Western Pub.
--Tennis Rebel. (Triumph Bks.). (Illus.). (gr. 5 up). 1978. PLB 8.90 s&l (ISBN 0-531-01466-5). Watts.
Sanders, jt. auth. see Resnick.
Sanders, Andrew. Victorian Historical Novel Eighteen Forty to Eighteen Eighty. LC 78-26592. 1979. 24.00 (ISBN 0-312-84293-7). St Martin.
Sanders, Buck. Ben Slayton, T-Man, No. 1: A Clear & Present Danger. (Men of Action Ser.). 160p. (Orig.). 1981. pap. 1.95 (ISBN 0-446-30020-9). Warner Bks.
--Ben Slayton, T-Man, No. 2: Star of Egypt. (Men of Action Ser.). 160p. (Orig.). 1981. pap. 1.95 (ISBN 0-446-30017-9). Warner Bks.
--Ben Slayton, T-Man, No. 3: Trail of the Twisted Cross. (Men of Acton Ser.). 160p. (Orig.). 1982. pap. 1.95 (ISBN 0-446-30131-0). Warner Bks.
--Ben Slayton, T-Man, No. 4. (Men of Action Ser.). 160p. (Orig.). 1982. pap. 1.95 o.s.i. (ISBN 0-446-30122-1). Warner Bks.
--Ben Slayton, T-Man, No. 5: Bayou Brigade. (Men of Action Ser.). 176p. (Orig.). 1982. pap. 1.95 (ISBN 0-446-30200-7). Warner Bks.
Sanders, C. L. & Bush, R. H., eds. Radionuclide Carcinogenesis: Proceedings. LC 73-600127. (AEC Symposium Ser.). 506p. 1973. pap. 20.75 (ISBN 0-87079-329-2, CONF-720505); microfiche 4.50 (ISBN 0-87079-330-6, CONF-720505). DOE.
Sanders, Charles. Synthesis: Responses to Literature. text ed. write for info. (ISBN 0-685-55635-2, 31044). Phila Bk Co.
Sanders, Charles L. & Schneider, Richard P., eds. Pulmonary Macrophage & Epithelial Cells: Proceedings. LC 77-12024. (ERDA Symposium Ser.). 628p. 1977. pap. 23.75 (ISBN 0-87079-204-0, CONF-760927); microfiche 4.50 (ISBN 0-87079-316-0, CONF-760927). DOE.
Sanders, Charles L., et al, eds. Pulmonary Toxicology of Respirable Particles: Proceedings. (DOE Symposium Ser.). 688p. 1980. pap. 25.25 (ISBN 0-87079-121-4, CONF-791002); microfiche 4.50 (ISBN 0-87079-404-3, CONF-791002). DOE.
Sanders, Coyne s., jt. auth. see Wiessman, Ginny.
Sanders, David. John Hersey. (United States Authors Ser.). lib. bdg. 11.95 (ISBN 0-8057-0376-4, Twayne). G K Hall.
--Patterns of Political Instability. LC 79-21422. 1980. 27.50x (ISBN 0-312-59808-4). St Martin.
Sanders, Dennis. The First of Everything. 1981. 13.95 o.s.i. (ISBN 0-440-02576-1). Delacorte.
--Gay Source: A Catalog for Men. LC 77-1896. (Illus.). 288p. 1977. pap. 6.95 (ISBN 0-698-10809-4, Coward). Putnam Pub Group.
Sanders, Derek A. Auditory Perception of Speech: An Introduction to Principles & Problems. LC 76-27320. (Illus.). 1977. text ed. 21.95 (ISBN 0-13-052787-4). P-H.
--Aural Rehabilitation: A Management Model. 2nd ed. (Illus.). 464p. 1982. 25.95 (ISBN 0-13-053215-0). P-H.
Sanders, Donald. Computer Essentials for Business. (Illus.). 1978. text ed. 19.95 (ISBN 0-07-054647-9, C); instructors manual 9.00 (ISBN 0-07-054649-5); study guide 9.95 (ISBN 0-07-054648-7). McGraw.
Sanders, Donald H. Computers in Business. 3rd ed. (Illus.). 576p. 1975. text ed. 21.95 (ISBN 0-07-054640-1, C); instructors' manual 7.95 (ISBN 0-07-054634-7). McGraw.
--Computers in Business. 4th ed. (Illus.). 1979. text ed. 15.95 (ISBN 0-07-054645-2, C); study guide 10.95 (ISBN 0-07-054646-0); instructor's manual 18.50 (ISBN 0-07-054652-5). McGraw.
--Computers in Society. 3rd ed. 536p. 1981. text ed. 21.95 (ISBN 0-07-054672-X, C); instructor's manual 9.95 (ISBN 0-07-054673-8); study guide 9.95 (ISBN 0-07-054674-6); test bank 9.95 (ISBN 0-07-054675-4). McGraw.
--Computers Today. Vastyan, James E., ed. (Illus.). 1982. text ed. 22.95 (ISBN 0-07-054681-9, C); study guide 7.95 (ISBN 0-07-054682-7). Mcgraw.
Sanders, Donald H. & Birkin, Stanley J. Computers & Management: In a Changing Society. 2nd ed. 1980. pap. text ed. 18.95 (ISBN 0-07-054627-4). McGraw.
Sanders, Donald H., et al. Statistics: A Fresh Approach. 2nd ed. (Illus.). 1979. text ed. 20.95 (ISBN 0-07-054667-3); wkbk. 8.95 (ISBN 0-07-054669-X); instructors manual 17.00 (ISBN 0-07-054668-1). McGraw.
Sanders, E. Dale, tr. see Abe, Kobo.
Sanders, E. P. Paul, the Law & the Jewish People. LC 82-17487. 240p. 1983. 19.95 (ISBN 0-8006-0698-1, 1-698). Fortress.
Sanders, Ed. The Family. 1972. pap. 1.95 o.p. (ISBN 0-380-00771-1, 24802). Avon.
Sanders, F. Kingsley. Interferons: An Example of Communication. Head, J. J., ed. LC 78-58639. (Carolina Biology Reader Ser.). (Illus.). 16p. (gr. 11 up). pap. 1.60 (ISBN 0-89278-288-9, 45-9688). Carolina Biological.
Sanders, G. D., et al. Chief Modern Poets of Britain & America, 2 Vols. in One. 5th ed. 1970. text ed. 23.95x (ISBN 0-02-405880-7). Macmillan.
--Chief Modern Poets of Britain & America, 2 vols. 5th ed. 1970. pap. 13.95x (ISBN 0-686-96783-6). Vol. 1 (ISBN 0-02-405890-4). Vol. 2 (ISBN 0-02-405900-5). Macmillan.
Sanders, Gerald H. Introduction to Contemporary Academic Debate. 2nd ed. LC 82-50791. 157p. 1983. pap. 7.95x (ISBN 0-917974-94-8). Waveland Pr.
Sanders, Gloria. Lower Limb Prosthetics: A Guide to Rehabilitation. (Illus.). 350p. 1983. 25.00 (ISBN 0-8036-7723-5). Davis Co.

Sanders, Gordon, jt. auth. see Wass, Alonzo.

Sanders, Harold H. Conversations with Harold H. Sanders: U. S. Policy for the Middle East in the 1980's. 1982. pap. 5.25 (ISBN 0-8447-3473-X). Am Enterprise.

Sanders, Herbert H. & Tomimoto, Kenkichi. The World of Japanese Ceramics. LC 67-16771. (Illus.). 267p. 1983. pap. 16.95 (ISBN 0-87011-557-X). Kodansha.

Sanders, I. T. The Community. 3rd ed. 526p. 1975. 23.50 (ISBN 0-471-06946-9). Wiley.

Sanders, Irwin & Whittaker, Roger. East European Peasantries: Social Relations; an Annotated Index of Periodical Articles. 1976. lib. bdg. 15.00 (ISBN 0-8161-7860-7, Hall Reference). G K Hall.

Sanders, Irwin T. Rural Society. (Illus.). 192p. 1977. text ed. 11.95 op (ISBN 0-13-784447-6); pap. text ed. 9.95 (ISBN 0-13-784439-5). P-H.

Sanders, Irwin T. & Bisselle, Walter C. East European Peasantries: Social Relations: An Annotated Bibliography of Periodical Articles, Vol. II. 1981. lib. bdg. 17.00 (ISBN 0-8161-8488-7, Hall Reference). G K Hall.

Sanders, Ivan, tr. see Konrad, George.

Sanders, J. Oswald. Enjoying Intimacy with God. LC 80-21398. 218p. 1980. pap. 5.95 (ISBN 0-8024-2346-9). Moody.

--The Incomparable Christ. LC 82-8183. 1982. pap. 6.95 (ISBN 0-8024-4081-9). Moody.

--Prayer Power Unlimited. LC 77-23472. 1977. 5.95 o.p. (ISBN 0-8024-6808-X); pap. 3.95 (ISBN 0-8024-6809-8). Moody.

--Satan Is No Myth. LC 74-15358. 1975. pap. 5.95 (ISBN 0-8024-7525-6). Moody.

--Spiritual Clinic. (J. Oswald Saunders Ser.). (Span). 1958. pap. 3.95 eng. ed. (ISBN 0-8024-0070-1). Moody.

--Spiritual Leadership. LC 67-14387. (J. Oswald Saunders Ser.). 160p. 1974. pap. 3.95 (ISBN 0-8024-8221-X). Moody.

--Your Best Years. 1982. pap. 5.95 (ISBN 0-8024-0455-3). Moody.

Sanders, J. T., jt. ed. see Irvine, S. H.

Sanders, James L., jt. ed. see Johannsen, Chris J.

Sanders, Jerry. Peddlars of Crisis. 340p. 1983. 20.00 (ISBN 0-89608-182-6); pap. 8.00 (ISBN 0-89608-181-8). South End Pr.

Sanders, John. A Firework for Oliver. 1979. 15.00x o.p. (ISBN 0-86025-090-3, Pub. by Ian Henry Pubns England). State Mutual Bk.

Sanders, John E. Principles of Physical Geology. 624p. 1981. text ed. 28.50 (ISBN 0-471-08424-7); tchr's manual avail. (ISBN 0-471-09378-5). Wiley.

Sanders, John E., jt. auth. see Friedman, Gerald M.

Sanders, John T. The Ethical Argument Against Government. LC 80-488. 271p. 1980. text ed. 20.75 (ISBN 0-8191-1015-9); pap. text ed. 10.50 (ISBN 0-8191-1016-7). U Pr of Amer.

Sanders, Joseph L. Roger Zelazny: A Primary & Secondary Bibliography. 1980. lib. bdg. 16.00 (ISBN 0-8161-8081-4, Hall Reference). G K Hall.

Sanders, Katherine C. Life Time System for Personal Effectiveness. 300p. 1983. 30.00 (ISBN 0-939344-02-5). Eupsychian.

Sanders, Lawrence. The Case of Lucy Bending. 480p. 1982. 14.95 (ISBN 0-399-12724-0). Putnam Pub Group.

--The Case of Lucy Bending. 1983. pap. 3.95 (ISBN 0-425-06077-2). Berkley Pub.

--The Marlow Chronicles. 1979. pap. text ed. 2.95 (ISBN 0-425-04390-8). Berkley Pub.

--Marlow Chronicles. LC 76-48891. 1977. 8.95 (ISBN 0-399-11927-2). Putnam Pub Group.

--The Second Deadly Sin. LC 77-3652. 1977. 9.95 (ISBN 0-399-12023-8). Putnam Pub Group.

--The Sixth Commandment. LC 78-13158. 1979. 10.95 (ISBN 0-399-12305-9). Putnam Pub Group.

--The Tangent Factor. LC 77-21173. 1978. 9.95 (ISBN 0-399-12133-1). Putnam Pub Group.

--The Tangent Objective. LC 76-930. 1976. 8.95 (ISBN 0-399-11750-4). Putnam Pub Group.

--The Tenth Commandment. 1980. 12.95 (ISBN 0-686-64422-0). Putnam Pub Group.

--The Third Deadly Sin. 480p. 1981. 13.95 (ISBN 0-399-12614-7). Putnam Pub Group.

--The Tomorrow File. LC 75-13994. 1975. 9.95 (ISBN 0-399-11687-7). Putnam Pub Group.

Sanders, Leonard. Act of War: A Novel of Love & Treason. 1982. 15.50 (ISBN 0-671-25610-6). S&S.

--Sonoma. 351p. 1981. 12.95 o.s.i. (ISBN 0-440-08111-4). Delacorte.

Sanders, Lloyd C. Celebrities of the Century: Being a Dictionary of Men & Women of the Nineteenth Century. LC 68-27185. 1971. Repr. of 1887 ed. 85.00x (ISBN 0-8103-3774-6). Gale.

Sanders, M. Elizabeth. The Regulation of Natural Gas: Policy & Politics, 1938-1978. 254p. 1981. 29.95 (ISBN 0-87722-221-5). Temple U Pr.

Sanders, M. S., jt. auth. see McCormick, E. J.

Sanders, Margaret M., jt. auth. see Wood, Merle.

Sanders, P. F. Bridge with a Perfect Partner. 1976. 8.50 (ISBN 0-575-02746-0, Pub. by Gollancz England). David & Charles.

Sanders, Patricia. The Search Consultant's Handbook. 32p. (Orig.). 1983. pap. 3.00 (ISBN 0-942916-02-6). ISC Pubns.

Sanders, Phronie, jt. auth. see Shertenlieb, Bill.

Sanders, Ralph. International Dynamics of Technology. LC 82-9220. (Contributions in Political Science Ser.: No. 87). 352p. 1983. lib. bdg. 35.00 (ISBN 0-313-23401-9, SAD/). Greenwood.

Sanders, Roger C., ed. Ultrasound Annual, 1982. 290p. 1982. text ed. 48.00 (ISBN 0-89004-861-4). Raven.

Sanders, Ron. Broadcasting in Guyana. (Case Studies on Broadcasting Systems). (Orig.). 1978. pap. 16.95 (ISBN 0-7100-0025-1). Routledge & Kegan.

Sanders, Ronald. The Downtown Jews: Portrait of an Immigrant Generation. 1977. pap. 2.50 o.p. (ISBN 0-451-07284-7, E7284, Sig). NAL.

Sanders, Rosanne. The Remembering Garden. (Clarkson N. Potter Bks.). (Illus.). 1980. 17.95 o.p. (ISBN 0-517-54169-6, C N Potter). Crown.

Sanders, Rostelle. When the Working Men Rise & Shine. 1984. 4.95 (ISBN 0-8062-2136-4). Carlton.

Sanders, Shirley F. Search for Enchantment. (YA) 1978. 6.95 (ISBN 0-685-86142-2, Avalon). Bouregy.

Sanders, Steven & Cheny, David. The Meaning of Life: Questions, Answers & Analysis. 1980. pap. text ed. 9.95 (ISBN 0-13-567438-7). P-H.

Sanders, Sylvia, jt. auth. see Bennett, Marilyn.

Sanders, Thomas E. & Peek, Walter W. Literature of the American Indian. LC 72-89050. 480p. 1973. text ed. 19.95x (ISBN 0-02-477640-8). Macmillan.

--Literature of the American Indian. abridged ed. 1976. pap. 14.95x (ISBN 0-02-477650-5). Macmillan.

Sanders, Wilbur. Dramatist & the Received Idea. 1968. 59.50 (ISBN 0-521-06924-6). Cambridge U Pr.

--John Donne's Poetry. LC 75-149436. 1971. 32.50 (ISBN 0-521-07968-3); pap. 9.95x (ISBN 0-521-09909-9). Cambridge U Pr.

Sanders, Wiley B. Negro Child Welfare in North Carolina. LC 68-55782. (Criminology, Law Enforcement, & Social Problems Ser.: No. 18). (Illus.). 1968. Repr. of 1933 ed. 15.00x (ISBN 0-87585-018-9). Patterson Smith.

Sanders, Wiley B., ed. Juvenile Offenders for a Thousand Years: Selected Readings from Anglo-Saxon Times to 1900. LC 76-97012. xx, 453p. 1969. 26.00x (ISBN 0-8078-1127-0). U of NC Pr.

Sanders, William. Backcountry Bikepacking: Everybody's Guide to Bicycle Camping. Wallace, Dan, ed. (Illus.). 300p. 1982. pap. 9.95 o.p. (ISBN 0-87857-371-2, 12-016-1). Rodale Pr Inc.

Sanders, William B. Criminology. LC 82-11332. 512p. 1983. text ed. write for info. (ISBN 0-201-07765-5). A-W.

Sanderson, Allen R., ed. DRI-McGraw-Hill Readings in Macroeconomics. (Illus.). 480p. 1981. pap. text ed. 11.95 (ISBN 0-07-054659-2). McGraw.

Sanderson, B. J., jt. auth. see Rourke, C. P.

Sanderson, Conner, ed. see Conner, Terri & Sanderson, Joyce.

Sanderson, Fred H. Japan's Food Prospects & Policies. 1978. pap. 4.95 (ISBN 0-8157-7701-9). Brookings.

Sanderson, Fred H. & Roy, Shyamal. Food Trends & Prospects in India. 1979. pap. 5.95 (ISBN 0-8157-7703-5). Brookings.

Sanderson, Gretchen & Shelton, Alphonse. Mixed Media & Watercolor. (Grosset Art Instruction Ser.: Vol. 73). pap. 2.95 (ISBN 0-448-00586-7, G&D). Putnam Pub Group.

Sanderson, J. D. Tennis Hacker's Handbook: How to Survive the Game & Learn to Love It. LC 77-7646. (Illus.). 128p. 1977. 5.95 o.s.i. (ISBN 0-89479-003-X). A & W Pubs.

Sanderson, J. H. & Phillips, Christine E. An Atlas of Laboratory Animal Haematology. (Illus.). 1981. text ed. 175.00x (ISBN 0-19-857520-3). Oxford U Pr.

Sanderson, James L. Sir John Davies. (English Authors Ser.: No. 175). 1975. lib. bdg. 10.95 o.p. (ISBN 0-8057-1141-4, Twayne). G K Hall.

Sanderson, James L. & Gordon, Walter K., eds. Exposition & the English Language: Introductory Studies. 2nd ed. (Orig.). 1969. pap. text ed. 18.95 (ISBN 0-13-298026-6). P-H.

Sanderson, James L., ed. see Shakespeare, William.

Sanderson, Joyce. Why Are You Here Now? 83p. (Orig.). 1981. pap. 6.95 (ISBN 0-942494-10-5). Coleman Graphics.

Sanderson, Joyce, jt. auth. see Conner, Terri.

Sanderson, Joyce, jt. auth. see Kinsthita, Louise.

Sanderson, Kenneth M, ed. see Blair, Walter.

Sanderson, M. & Rawlinson, M. K. Word Processing Manual. 200p. 1982. pap. text ed. 11.00x (ISBN 0-7121-2323-7). Intl Ideas.

Sanderson, Michael. Education, Economic Change & Society in England, 1780-1870. (Studies in Economic & Social Theory). 88p. 1983. pap. text ed. 6.25x (ISBN 0-333-32569-9, Pub. by Macmillan England). Humanities.

--Sucessful Problem Management. LC 78-21050. 227p. 1979. 30.50 (ISBN 0-471-04871-2, Pub. by Wiley-Interscience). Wiley.

Sanderson, R. T., ed. Polar Convalense. Date not set. 19.50 (ISBN 0-12-618080-6). Acad Pr.

Sanderson, R. Thomas. Principles of Chemistry. LC 63-11447. 626p. 1963. text ed. 18.00 (ISBN 0-471-75250-9, Pub. by Wiley). Krieger.

Sanderson, Samuel L. Science in Culture: A Study of Values & Institutions. LC 79-57289. 1980. 10.95 (ISBN 0-89754-007-7); pap. 3.50 (ISBN 0-89754-006-9). Dan River Pr.

Sanderson, Sharon, jt. auth. see Reed, Kathlyn.

Sanderson, Steven E. Agrarian Populism & the Mexican State: The Struggle for Land in Sonora. LC 80-14262. 1981. 24.50x (ISBN 0-520-04056-2). U of Cal Pr.

Sanderson, T. K. Communications Directory: Supplement. 72p. 1983. pap. 25.00 (ISBN 0-911304-03-7). T K Sanderson.

--Directory of American Savings & Loan Associations. 29th ed. 480p. 1983. 50.00 (ISBN 0-911304-02-9). T K Sanderson.

Sanderson, Virginia S. The Living Past. LC 82-1371. 1982. pap. 18.00 o.s.i. (ISBN 0-933786-06-9); 25.00 o.s.i. (ISBN 0-933786-05-0). Beech Hill.

Sandford, C. T. Economics of Public Finance. 1969. text ed. 13.20 o.p. (ISBN 0-08-013468-8); pap. 7.70 o.p. (ISBN 0-08-013467-X). Pergamon.

Sandford, Cedric. The Economic Structure. LC 81-20751. (Aspects of Modern Sociology Ser.). (Illus.). 128p. (Orig.). 1982. pap. text ed. 7.95x (ISBN 0-582-29544-0). Longman.

--Taxation & Social Policy. 1981. text ed. 28.00x (ISBN 0-435-82789-8). Heinemann Ed.

Sandford, Cedric T. Social Economics. 1977. text ed. 27.00x (ISBN 0-435-84780-5); pap. text ed. 11.00x (ISBN 0-435-84781-3). Heinemann Ed.

Sandford, John. The Mass Media of the German Speaking Countries. 1976. pap. text ed. 7.50x (ISBN 0-8138-0085-4). Iowa St U Pr.

--The New German Cinema. (Quality Paperbacks Ser.). (Illus.). 180p. 1982. pap. 10.95. Da Capo.

Sandford, John & Sandford, Paula. Restoring the Christian Family. 1979. 7.95 (ISBN 0-88270-347-1, Pub. by Logos). Bridge Pub.

--Transformation of the Inner Man. 1982. pap. 5.95 (ISBN 0-88270-539-3). Bridge Pub.

Sandford, Paula, jt. auth. see Sandford, John.

Sandhu, Harjit. Juvenile Delinquency-Causes, Control & Prevention. (Illus.). 1977. text ed. 21.95 (ISBN 0-07-054650-9, G); instructor's manual 4.50 (ISBN 0-07-054651-7). McGraw.

Sandhu, Harpreet & Bukkila, Laura. Guide to Publishers & Distributors Serving Minority Languages. rev. ed. LC 80-110698. 176p. 1980. pap. 7.50 (ISBN 0-89763-051-3). Natl Clearinghse Bilingual Ed.

Sandhu, Kernial S. Indians in Malaya, Seventeen Eighty-Six - Nineteen Fifty-Seven. (Illus.). 1969. 44.50 (ISBN 0-521-07274-3). Cambridge U Pr.

Sandifar, Larry L. Real Estate Sales Manager's Desk Book. LC 82-7696. 280p. 1982. 29.95 (ISBN 0-13-766352-8, Busn). P-H.

Sandifer, Frank H., jt. auth. see Mushkin, Selma J.

Sandifer, Kevin W. A Layman's Look at Starting a Religious Archives. Hall, Renee, et al, eds. 48p. (Orig.). 1982. pap. text ed. 7.50 (ISBN 0-910653-00-3). K W Sandifer.

Sandige, Richard. Digital Concepts Using Standard Integrated Circuits. (Illus.). 1978. text ed. 29.95 (ISBN 0-07-054653-3, C); instructor's manual 20.00 (ISBN 0-07-054654-1). McGraw.

Sandilands, Roger J. Monetary Correction & Housing Finance in Colombia, Brazil & Chile. 182p. 1980. text ed. 41.00x (ISBN 0-566-00355-4). Gower Pub Ltd.

Sandin, Robert T. The Search for Excellence: The Christian College in an Age of Educational Competition. LC 82-12482. 188p. 1982. text ed. 13.50x (ISBN 0-86554-037-3). Mercer Univ Pr.

Sandison, A. T., jt. auth. see Brothwell, Don.

Sandkowsky, Suzanne H., jt. auth. see Live, Anna H.

Sandler, Bernard & Posner, Steve. In Front of the Camera: How to Make It & Survive in Movies & Television. 1981. 13.50 o.p. (ISBN 0-525-93176-7, 01311-339); pap. 8.25 o.p. (ISBN 0-525-93177-5, 0801-240). Dutton.

Sandler, Gilbert. The Neighborhood: The Story of Baltimore's Little Italy. (Illus.). 93p. 1974. 5.95 (ISBN 0-686-36698-0). Md Hist.

Sandler, Irving. The New York School: The Painters & Sculptors of the Fifties. LC 77-82357. (Icon Editions). (Illus.). 1978. 35.00i (ISBN 0-06-438505-1, HarpT); pap. 15.95xi (ISBN 0-06-430094-3, IN-94, HarpT). Har-Row.

--The Triumph of American Painting: A History of Abstract Expressionism. (Icon Editions). (Illus.). 302p. 1976. pap. 12.95i (ISBN 0-06-430075-7, IN-75, HarpT). Har-Row.

Sandler, Lucy F. The Psalter of Robert de Lisle. (Illus.). 160p. 1982. 98.00x (ISBN 0-19-921028-4). Oxford U Pr.

Sandler, M., jt. auth. see Jeffcoate, S. L.

Sandler, M., jt. ed. see Costa, E.

Sandler, Martin W. As New Englanders Played. LC 79-55211. (Illus.). 96p. 1979. pap. 5.95 (ISBN 0-87106-034-5). Globe Pequot.

Sandler, Martin W., jt. auth. see Charren, Peggy.

Sandler, Maurice & Bourne, Geoffrey H., eds. Atherosclerosis & Its Origin. 1963. 67.00 (ISBN 0-12-618250-7). Acad Pr.

Sandler, Merton, ed. Mental Illness in Pregnancy & the Puerperium. (Illus.). 1979. text ed. 21.95x o.p. (ISBN 0-19-261150-X). Oxford U Pr.

--Psychopharmacology of Aggression. 247p. 1979. 27.00 (ISBN 0-89004-392-2). Raven.

--The Psychopharmacology of Alcohol. 293p. 1980. text ed. 35.00 (ISBN 0-89004-506-2). Raven.

--Psychopharmacology of Anticonvulsants. (Illus.). 1982. text ed. 29.50x (ISBN 0-19-261341-3). Oxford U Pr.

Sandler, P. L., jt. auth. see Bolitho, A. R.

Sandler, Reuben & Foster, L. Sheila. Modern Algebra. 1978. text ed. 24.50 scp o.p. (ISBN 0-06-045718-X, HarpC). Har-Row.

Sandler, Stanley I. Chemical & Engineering Thermodynamics. LC 77-1312. 587p. 1977. text ed. 40.95 (ISBN 0-471-01774-4); avail. sol. manual (ISBN 0-471-02736-7). Wiley.

Sandler, Stanley R. & Karo, Wolf. Organic Functional Group Preparations, 4 vols. (Organic Chemistry Ser.: Vol. 12). Vol.1. 1969. 61.00 (ISBN 0-12-618550-6); Vol.2. 1971. 59.00 (ISBN 0-12-618552-2); Vol. 3. 1972. 59.00 (ISBN 0-12-618553-0); 157.50 set (ISBN 0-686-66355-1). Acad Pr.

--Polymer Synthesis, Vol. 1. 1974. 61.00 (ISBN 0-12-618560-3). Acad Pr.

Sandler, Todd, ed. The Theory & Structures of International Political Economy. (Westview Special Studies in International Economics & Business). 280p. 1980. lib. bdg. 28.50 (ISBN 0-89158-765-9); pap. 12.50 (ISBN 0-86531-330-X). Westview.

Sandmaier, Marian. Alcohol Abuse & Women: A Guide to Getting Help. 1.75 o.p. (ISBN 0-686-92060-0). Hazelden.

--Hidden Alcoholic: Women & Alcholic Abuse in America. LC 79-17819. 1980. 12.95 o.p. (ISBN 0-07-054660-6). McGraw.

Sandman, Peter M., et al. Media: An Introductory Analysis of American Mass Communication. 3rd ed. 520p. 1982. 18.95 (ISBN 0-13-572545-3). P-H.

Sandman, Peter S., et al. Media Casebook: An Introductory Reader in American Mass Communications. 2nd ed. 1977. pap. text ed. 11.95 o.p. (ISBN 0-13-572453-8). P-H.

Sandmel, Samuel. A Jewish Understanding of the New Testament. 356p. pap. 6.95 (ISBN 0-686-95179-4). ADL.

--Judaism & Christian Beginnings. 29.95x (ISBN 0-19-502281-5); pap. 9.95x (ISBN 0-19-502282-3). Oxford U Pr.

--Philo of Alexandria: An Introduction. 1979. 15.95x (ISBN 0-19-502514-8); pap. 7.95 (ISBN 0-19-502515-6). Oxford U Pr.

--We Jews & Jesus. LC 65-11529. 1973. pap. 5.95 (ISBN 0-19-501676-9, GB). Oxford U Pr.

Sandmeyer, Elmer C. The Anti-Chinese Movement in California. LC 73-81137. 136p. 1973. 10.00 o.p. (ISBN 0-252-00338-1); pap. 3.95 o.p. (ISBN 0-252-00339-X). U of Ill Pr.

Sandmeyer, Louise, jt. auth. see Bartsch, Karl.

Sandmo, Agnar, ed. Essays in Public Economics: The Kiryat Anavim Papers. LC 77-7. 384p. 1978. 32.95x o.p. (ISBN 0-669-01424-9). Lexington Bks.

Sandon, Henry. Royal Worcester Porcelain: From Eighteen Sixty-Two to the Present Day. (Illus.). 288p. 1975. 17.50 o.p. (ISBN 0-517-52002-8, C N Potter Bks). Crown.

Sandor, Bela I. Experiments in Strengths of Materials. (Illus.). 1980. pap. text ed. 12.95 (ISBN 0-13-295329-3). P-H.

--Fundamentals of Cyclic Stress & Strain. LC 70-176415. (Illus.). 184p. 1972. text ed. 22.50 (ISBN 0-299-06100-0). U of Wis Pr.

--Strength of Materials. (Illus.). 1978. ref. ed. 31.95 (ISBN 0-13-852418-1). P-H.

Sandor, Bela I. & Schlack, A. L. Learning & Review Aid for Dynamics: To Go With Engineering Mechanics. 144p. (Orig.). 1983. pap. 9.95 (ISBN 0-13-278952-3). P-H.

--Learning & Review Aid for Statics: To Go With Engineering Mechanics. 176p. 1983. pap. 9.95 (ISBN 0-13-278903-5). P-H.

Sandor, Gyorgy. On Piano Playing: Motion, Sound, & Expression. (Illus.). 176p. 1981. 20.00 (ISBN 0-02-872280-9). Schirmer Bks.

Sandorf, Paul, ed. see MIT Students' System Project.

Sandori, Paul. The Logic of Machines & Structures. LC 81-19743. 180p. 1982. 29.95x (ISBN 0-471-86397-1; Pub. by Wiley-Interscience); pap. 19.95 (ISBN 0-471-86193-6, Pub. by Wiley-Interscience). Wiley.

Sandow, Stuart. Durations: The Encyclopedia of How Long Things Take. 1978. pap. 2.25 o.p. (ISBN 0-380-39859-1, 39859). Avon.

Sandoz, Ellis & Crabb, Cecil V., eds. A Tide of Discontent: The Nineteen-Eighty Elections & Their Meaning. LC 81-4586. 272p. 1981. pap. 8.95 (ISBN 0-87187-205-6). Congr Quarterly.

Sandoz, Mari. Cheyenne Autumn. 1975. Repr. 12.95 (ISBN 0-8038-1094-6). Hastings.

--Crazy Horse. Date not set. pap. 4.50 o.p. (ISBN 0-686-95772-5). Jefferson Natl.

--Love Song to the Plains. LC 61-6441. (Illus.). x, 305p. 1966. pap. 6.95 (ISBN 0-8032-5172-6, BB 349, Bison). U of Nebr Pr.

--Old Jules Country. LC 82-16041. 320p. 1983. pap. 6.50 (ISBN 0-8032-9136-1, BB 829, Bison). U of Nebr Pr.

Sandrea, Rafael & Nielsen, Ralph. Dynamics of Petroleum Reservoirs Under Gas Injection. 180p. 1974. 18.95x (ISBN 0-87201-219-0). Gulf Pub.

Sandreuter, William O. Whitewater Canoeing. (Illus.). 1978. pap. 5.95 o.s.i. (ISBN 0-695-80932-6). Follett.

Sandri, C. & Van Buren, J. M., eds. Membrane Morphology of the Vertebrate Nervous System: A Study with Freeze-etch Technique. 2nd, rev. ed. (Progress in Brain Research Ser.: Vol. 46). 370p. 1982. 90.75 (ISBN 0-444-80393-9). Elsevier.

Sandri, C., et al. Membrane Morphology of the Vertebrate Nervous System: A Study with Freeze Etch Technique. (Progress in Brain Research: Vol. 46). 1977. 101.50 (ISBN 0-444-41479-7, North Holland). Elsevier.

Sandri-White, Alex. Boobytraps of the Italian Language. 6.95 o.p. (ISBN 0-685-22760-X). Aurea.

--Dictionary of French Slang. 7.95 o.p. (ISBN 0-685-22763-4). Aurea.

--Dictionary of German Slang. 9.85 o.p. (ISBN 0-685-22758-8). Aurea.

--Dictionary of Italian Slang. 7.95 o.p. (ISBN 0-685-22761-8). Aurea.

--Worldwide Register of Adult Education. 1973. incl. supplement 8.95 (ISBN 0-685-22747-2); supplement only 4.95 (ISBN 0-686-76917-1). Aurea.

Sandri-White, Alex & Pokress, E. New Directory of Medical Schools. 1983. 11.95 (ISBN 0-685-22749-9). Aurea.

Sandri-White, Alex, ed. Directory of Educational Franchises. 2.00 o.p. (ISBN 0-685-31527-4). Aurea.

--Special Graduating Opportunities. 8.50 (ISBN 0-685-22756-1). Aurea.

Sands, Frederick & Broman, Sven. The Divine Garbo. LC 78-58096. (Illus.). 1979. 17.95 o.p. (ISBN 0-448-16245-8, G&D). Putnam Pub Group.

Sands, Gary. Land-Office Business: Land & Housing Prices in Rapidly Growing Metropolitan Areas. 179p. 1981. 22.95x (ISBN 0-669-04859-3). Lexington Bks.

Sands, Howard, jt. ed. see Hamet, Pavel.

Sands, John O. Yorktown's Captive Fleet. (Illus.). 1983. price not set (ISBN 0-917376-38-2). U Pr of Va.

Sands, Leo G. Marine Electronics Handbook. LC 72-97209. (Illus.). 192p. 1973. 7.95 o.p. (ISBN 0-8306-3638-2); pap. 4.95 o.p. (ISBN 0-8306-2638-7, 638). TAB Bks.

Sands, Melissa. The Passion Factor. 272p. 1983. pap. 2.95 (ISBN 0-425-05855-7). Berkley Pub.

Sands, William A. Modern Women's Gymnastics. (Illus.). 104p. (Orig.). 1983. pap. 6.95 (ISBN 0-8069-7686-1). Sterling.

Sandstede, G., ed. From Electrocatalysis to Fuel Cells. LC 79-38116. (Illus.). 441p. 1972. 25.00 (ISBN 0-295-95178-8). U of Wash Pr.

Sandstroem, Yvonne L., tr. see Gustafsson, Lars.

Sandstrom, A., jt. auth. see Nygard, F.

Sandulescu, Jacques & Gottlieb, Annie. The Carpathian Caper. LC 74-30584. 1975. 8.95 o.p. (ISBN 0-399-11511-0). Putnam Pub Group.

Sandum, Howard, ed. see Jones-Griffith, Philip.

Sandweiss, Martha A., ed. Masterworks of American Photography: The Amon Carter Museum Collection. LC 82-80594. (Illus.). 160p. 1982. 48.03i (ISBN 0-8487-0540-8). Oxmoor Hse.

Sandy, Alan, ed. see Irving, Washington.

Sandy, Gerald N. Heliodorus. (World Authors Ser.). 1982. lib. bdg. 15.95 (ISBN 0-8057-6490-9, Twayne). G K Hall.

Sandy, Stephen. Chapter & Verse. Hettich, Michael & Ahern, Colleen, eds. (Moonsquilt Press Poetry Chapbook). 25p. (Orig.). 1982. pap. 3.50 (ISBN 0-943216-00-1). Moons Quilt Pr.

--Riding to Greylock. LC 82-48741. 1983. 11.95 (ISBN 0-394-52819-0); pap. 6.95 (ISBN 0-394-71314-1). Knopf.

Sandzen, S. C. Color Atlas of Acute Hand Injuries. 1980. 115.00 (ISBN 0-07-054671-1). McGraw.

Sanes, Samuel. A Physician Faces Cancer in Himself. LC 79-13124. 1979. 14.95x (ISBN 0-87395-395-9); pap. 8.95x (ISBN 0-87395-449-1). State U NY Pr.

Sanfilippo, Rose E., ed. see Clark, Charlie, III.

Sanford. Digestive System Physiology. (Physical Principles in Medicine Ser.). 160p. 1982. pap. text ed. 14.95 (ISBN 0-8391-1751-5). Univ Park.

Sanford, A. J. & Garrod, S. C. Understanding Written Language: Explorations of Comprehension Beyond the Sentence. LC 80-40849. 224p. 1981. 35.95 (ISBN 0-471-27842-4, Pub. by Wiley-Interscience). Wiley.

Sanford, Adrian B. Using English: Grammar & Writing Skills. 420p. 1979. pap. text ed. 9.74 o.p. (ISBN 0-15-594481-9, HC). HarBraceJ.

Sanford, Agnes. The Healing Gifts of the Spirit. (Trumpet Bks). 1976. pap. 1.75 o.p. (ISBN 0-87981-056-4). Holman.

--Healing Gifts of the Spirit. 1976. pap. 2.50 (ISBN 0-515-06724-5). Jove Pubns.

--Healing Power of the Bible. 1969. 6.95i (ISBN 0-397-10103-1, Holman). Har-Row.

--The Healing Power of the Bible. (Trumpet Bks). 1976. pap. 1.95 o.p. (ISBN 0-87981-059-9). Holman.

--Healing Power of the Bible. 224p. 1983. pap. 2.50 o.p. (ISBN 0-515-07104-8). Jove Pubns.

--The Healing Touch of God. (Epiphany Ser.). 224p. 1983. pap. 2.50 (ISBN 0-345-30661-9). Ballantine.

--Sealed Orders: The Autobiography of a Christian Mystic. LC 72-76592. 312p. 1972. 6.95 o.p. (ISBN 0-912106-37-9, Pub. by Logos); pap. 7.95 (ISBN 0-88270-048-0). Bridge Pub.

Sanford, Aubrey. Human Relations: The Theory & Practice of Organizational Behavior. 2nd ed. (Business Ser.). 1977. text ed. 19.95 (ISBN 0-675-08505-5). Additional supplements may be obtained from publisher. Merrill.

Sanford, Cedric. National Economic Planning. 2nd ed. 1976. pap. text ed. 4.00x o.p. (ISBN 0-435-84569-1). Heinemann Ed.

Sanford, Dan C. The Future Association of Taiwan with the People's Republic of China. (China Research Monographs: No. 22). 155p. 1982. 8.00x (ISBN 0-912966-41-6). IEAS.

Sanford, Edward & Adelman, Harvey. Management Decisions: A Behavioral Approach. (Illus.). 1977. pap. text ed. 7.95 (ISBN 0-316-77046-9). Little.

Sanford, John A. Dreams: God's Forgotten Language. LC 60-29727. 1968. 10.10i (ISBN 0-397-10056-6). Har-Row.

--Kingdom Within: A Study of the Inner Meaning of Jesus' Sayings. LC 77-105548. 1970. 12.45i (ISBN 0-397-10101-5). Har-Row.

--The Man Who Lost His Shadow. LC 82-62414. 1983. 5.95 (ISBN 0-8091-0337-0). Paulist Pr.

--Ministry Burnout. 144p. 1982. 5.95 (ISBN 0-8091-0333-8). Paulist Pr.

Sanford, Linda T. The Silent Children: A Parents Guide to the Prevention of Child Sexual Abuse. 1982. pap. 7.95 (ISBN 0-07-054662-2). Mcgraw.

Sanford, Peter W., et al, eds. Galactic X-Ray Sources. 450p. 1982. 45.00x (ISBN 0-471-27963-3, Pub. by Wiley-Interscience). Wiley.

Sanford, Sara L. Jake's Late. (Illus.). 32p. (gr. 1-3). 1983. pap. 1.98 (ISBN 0-943944-01-5). Sneak-A-Peek Bks.

--Smirk Smiles. LC 50-332. (Illus.). 24p. 1983. pap. 1.98 (ISBN 0-943944-00-7, 950-333). Sneak-A-Peek Bks.

Sanford, William R. & Green, Carl R. Psychology: A Way to Grow. (Orig.). (gr. 10-12). 1982. text ed. 32.83 (ISBN 0-87720-637-6); pap. text ed. 19.58 (ISBN 0-87720-636-8). AMSCO Sch.

Sangduk Kim, jt. auth. see Paik, Woon Ki.

Sanger, jt. auth. see Petrillo.

Sanger, Gary C. Stock Exchange Listings, Firm Value & Market Efficiency. Dufey, Gunter, ed. LC 82-6936. (Research for Business Decisions Ser.: No. 51). 236p. 1982. 39.95 (ISBN 0-8357-1338-5). Univ Microfilms.

Sanger, Joan, jt. auth. see Hislop, Helen J.

Sanger, Margaret. Works, 8 vols. Incl. Vol. 1. Margaret Sanger, an Autobiography. Guttmacher, A., intro. by. 33.00 (ISBN 0-08-018730-7); Vol. 2. Happiness in Marriage. 18.00 (ISBN 0-08-018731-5); Vol. 3. Motherhood in Bondage. 33.00 (ISBN 0-08-018732-3); Vol. 4. My Fight for Birth Control. 24.00 (ISBN 0-08-018733-1); Vol. 5. The New Motherhood. 18.00 (ISBN 0-08-018734-X); Vol. 6. The Pivot of Civilization. 21.00 (ISBN 0-08-018735-8); Vol. 7. What Every Boy & Girl Should Know. 13.50 (ISBN 0-08-018736-6); Vol. 8. Woman & the New Race. 18.00 (ISBN 0-08-018737-4). 1976. Repr. 215.00 set (ISBN 0-08-020244-6). Pergamon.

Sanger, Marjory B. Forest in the Sand. LC 82-4076. (Illus.). 160p. (gr. 7 up). 1983. 10.95 (ISBN 0-689-50248-6, McElderry Bk). Atheneum.

--World of the Great White Heron. LC 67-18236. (Illus.). 1967. 14.95 (ISBN 0-8159-7214-8). Devin.

Sanger, Mary B. Welfare of the Poor. LC 79-20923. 1979. 17.50 (ISBN 0-12-618650-2). Acad Pr.

Sangharakshita. Survey of Buddhism. LC 79-2149. 1980. pap. 8.95 o.p. (ISBN 0-394-73732-6). Shambhala Pubns.

SanGiovanni, Lucinda F., jt. auth. see Boutilier, Mary A.

Sang Kyu Shim. The Making of a Martial Artist. (Illus.). 1980. 9.95 (ISBN 0-942062-01-9); pap. 6.95 (ISBN 0-942062-02-7). S K Shim Pub.

Sangrey, Dawn. Wifestyles: Women Talk about Marriage. 1983. 16.95 (ISBN 0-440-09721-5). Delacorte.

Sangrey, Dawn, jt. auth. see Bard, Morton.

Sanguily, Manuel. Nobles Memorias. 2nd ed. LC 80-67889. 246p. (Orig., Span.). pap. 12.00 (ISBN 0-89729-262-6). Ediciones.

Sani, Guelfo & Kos, Leon. Atlas of Vaginal Surgery. LC 76-55407. 1977. 66.50 o.p. (ISBN 0-471-02275-6, Pub. by Wiley Medical). Wiley.

Sanjdorj, M. Manchu Chinese Colonial Rule in Northern Mongolia. LC 80-17449. 1980. 26.00 (ISBN 0-312-51249-X). St Martin.

Sanjian, Avedis K., ed. see Eghishe.

Sanjian, Avedis K., ed. see Komurjian, Eremya.

San Juan, E., Jr., ed. Marxism & Human Liberation. (Orig.). 1973. pap. 3.95 o.s.i. (ISBN 0-440-55473-X, Delta). Dell.

San Juan, Huarte De see Huarte de San Juan, Juan.

San Juan, P. & Chiswick, Barry. The Dilemma of American Immigration: Beyond the Golden Door. 212p. 1983. 19.95 (ISBN 0-87855-481-5); pap. 8.95 (ISBN 0-87855-935-3). Transaction Bks.

Sanjur, Diva. Social & Cultural Perspectives in Nutrition. (Illus.). 352p. 1982. text ed. 21.95 (ISBN 0-13-815647-6). P-H.

Sankalia, H. D. Pre History of India. 1977. 12.50x o.p. (ISBN 0-8364-0101-8). South Asia Bks.

--Prehistory of India. (Illus.). 1977. text ed. 11.50x (ISBN 0-686-86107-8). Humanities.

Sankaracharya. Self Knowledge: Atma-Bodhi. Mahadevan, T. M., tr. lib. bdg. 8.50 (ISBN 0-89253-043-X); pap. text ed. 3.00 (ISBN 0-89253-044-8). Ind-US Inc.

Sankaranarayanan, K. Genetic Effects of Ionizing Radiation in Multicellular Eukaryotes & the Assessment of Genetic Radiation Hazards in Man. 385p. 1982. 81.00 (ISBN 0-444-80379-3). Elsevier.

Sankaranasayanan, N., ed. Book Distribution & Promotion Problems in South Asia. 1964. pap. 6.50 o.p. (ISBN 92-3-100539-1, U55, UNESCO). Unipub.

Sanker, Joyce, jt. auth. see Coates, Gary.

Sankey, Benjamin. A Companion to William Carlos Williams' Paterson. LC 72-121193. (Illus.). 1971. 38.50x (ISBN 0-520-01742-0). U of Cal Pr.

Sankey, J. P. & Savory, T. H. British Harvestment: Arachniad: Opilidnes: Keip and Notes for the Indentification of the Species. 1974. 10.00 o.s.i. (ISBN 0-12-619050-X). Acad Pr.

Sankhala, Kailash. Gardens of God: The Brid Sancuary at Bharatpur. 200p. 1982. 52.00x (ISBN 0-686-94077-6, Pub. By Garlandfold England). State Mutual Bk.

Sankovitch, Tilde. Jodelle et la Creation du Masque: Etude Structurale et Normative de l'Eugene. (Fr.). 15.00 (ISBN 0-917786-11-4). French Lit.

Sanks, Robert L., ed. Water Treatment Plant Design for the Practicing Engineer. LC 77-76914. 1978. 49.95 (ISBN 0-250-40183-5). Ann Arbor Science.

San Luis, Edward. Office & Office Building Security. LC 73-85627. (Illus.). 320p. 1973. 19.95 (ISBN 0-913708-12-7). Butterworth.

Sann, Paul. American Panorama: Fads, Follies, & Delusions of the American People. rev. ed. (Illus.). 1979. 17.95 o.p. (ISBN 0-517-53773-7). Crown.

--Trial in the Upper Room: A Heavenly Novel by the Defendent. Michaelman, Herbert, ed. 1981. 12.95 o.p. (ISBN 0-517-54284-6, Michelman Books). Crown.

Sannella, Lucia. The Female Pentecost. LC 75-16565. 1976. 13.95 (ISBN 0-87949-043-8). Ashley Bks.

Sanner, A. Elwood & Greathouse, William M. Beacon Bible Expositions, Vol. 2. 1978. 6.95 (ISBN 0-8341-0313-3). Beacon Hill.

Sanny, Lorne C. Art of Personal Witnessing. 1957. pap. 2.50 o.p. (ISBN 0-8024-0304-2). Moody.

Sano, Emily J., jt. auth. see Nishikawa, Kyotaro.

Sano, Roy see McDonald, Durstan R., et al.

Sano, T., jt. ed. see Lieberman, M.

Sanoff, Henry. Methods of Architectural Programming. LC 76-13231. (Community Development Ser: Vol. 29). (Illus.). 1977. 33.00 (ISBN 0-87933-253-0). Hutchinson Ross.

Sanoff, Henry & Sanoff, Joan. Learning Environments for Young Children. LC 81-81659. 100p. (Orig.). 1981. pap. 12.95 (ISBN 0-89334-065-0). Humanics Ltd.

Sanoff, Joan, jt. auth. see Sanoff, Henry.

Sanowski, Robert A., jt. auth. see Kovac, Alexander.

San Pedro, Diego de. The Castle of Love. LC 51-634. Repr. of 1549 ed. 29.00x (ISBN 0-8201-1217-8). Schol Facsimiles.

San Pedro, Diego De see San Pedro, Diego de.

Sanpete County Commission. The Other Forty Niners: A Topical History of Sanpete Country, Utah. Antrei, Albert C., et al, eds. 1982. write for info. (ISBN 0-914740-26-1). Western Epics.

San Pietro, Anthony, et al, eds. Regulatory Mechanisms for Protein Synthesis in Mammalian Cells. 1968. 54.50 (ISBN 0-12-618960-9). Acad Pr.

Sanrilippo, Leonardo. The Philosophical Essence of Man. (Illus.). 104p. 1983. 29.95 (ISBN 0-89266-400-2). Am Classical Coll Pr.

Sansom, Basil. The Camp at Wallaby Cross: Aboriginal Fringe Dwellers in Darwin. (Australian Inst Australia Ser.: No. 18). 280p. 1980. text ed. 17.75x o. p. (ISBN 0-391-01696-2, Pub. by Australian Inst Australia); pap. text ed. 10.25x (ISBN 0-391-01697-0). Humanities.

Sansom, Robert L. Economics of Insurgency in the Mekong Delta of Vietnam. 1970. 17.50x (ISBN 0-262-19064-8). MIT Pr.

Sansom, W. M. & Chapman, Harold. Victorian Life in Photographs. (Illus.). 1977. 15.95 o.p. (ISBN 0-500-25042-1). Thames Hudson.

Sanson, Riley W. Bible Crossword Fun. 48p. 1983. pap. 1.50 (ISBN 0-87239-588-X). Standard Pub.

Sansone, G., et al. Orthogonal Functions, Vol. 9. rev. ed. LC 75-11888. 424p. 1977. Repr. of 1959 ed. 23.50 (ISBN 0-88275-303-7). Krieger.

Santa Ana, Julio De see De Santa Ana, Julio.

Santa Barbara, Anthony A. Internal Revenue Service Practice & Procedure. LC 77-24829. 1977. text ed. 35.00 (ISBN 0-685-88299-3, J1-1415). PLI.

Santa Cruz, Mercedes. La Habana. Bacardi, Amalia E., tr. from Fr. 403p. (Orig., Span.). 1982. pap. 12.95 (ISBN 84-499-5244-1). Ediciones.

Santagata, Kenneth V., jt. auth. see Murphy, Arthur W.

Santa Lucas, A. P. The Ngandong Fossil Hominids: A Comparative Study of a Far Eastern Homo Erectus Group. LC 80-52035. (Publications in Anthropology: No. 78). 1980. pap. 13.50 (ISBN 0-913516-11-2). Yale U Anthro.

Santa Maria, Jack. Traditional Indian Cookery. LC 78-58227. (Illus.). 1978. pap. 4.95 o.p. (ISBN 0-394-73547-1). Shambhala Pubns.

Santamore, William P. & Bove, Alfred A., eds. Coronary Artery Disease: Etiology, Hemodynamic Consequences, Drug Therapy & Clinical Implications. LC 81-19731. 308p. 1982. 39.50 (ISBN 0-8067-1761-0). Urban & S.

Santareno, Bernardo. The Promise. Vieira, Nelson H., tr. from Portuguese. LC 81-84499. 107p. (Orig.). 1981. pap. 4.00 (ISBN 0-686-37031-7). Gavea-Brown.

Santas, Constantine. Aristotelis Valaoritis. LC 76-10673. (World Author Ser). 1976. lib. bdg. 15.95 (ISBN 0-8057-6246-9, Twayne). G K Hall.

Santas, Gerasimos X. Socrates. 1982. pap. 10.00 (ISBN 0-7100-9327-6). Routledge & Kegan.

Santayana, George. The Life of Reason: Vol. 3, Reason in Religion. 288p. 1982. pap. 4.50 (ISBN 0-486-24253-6). Dover.

--Reason in Art: Vol. 4, The Life of Reason. 230p. 1982. pap. 4.50 (ISBN 0-486-24358-3). Dover.

--Reason in Science: Volume Five of "The Life of Reason". 320p. 1983. pap. 5.00 (ISBN 0-486-24439-3). Dover.

Sante, Daniel P. Automatic Control System Technology. (Illus.). 1980. text ed. 21.95 (ISBN 0-13-054627-5). P-H.

Santer, M., jt. ed. see Wiles, Maurice.

Santer, Richard A. Michigan: Heart of the Great Lakes. LC 76-53268. (Illus.). 1977. pap. text ed. 10.50 (ISBN 0-8403-1698-4). Kendall-Hunt.

Santerre, Richard. Litterature Franco-Americaine de la Nouvelle: Angle Terre. (Anthologie Tome Ser.: No. 4). (Illus.). 215p. (Fr.). (gr. 10 up). 1980. pap. text ed. 5.50x (ISBN 0-911409-28-9). Natl Mat Dev.

Santerre, Richard, ed. Anthologie, 9 Vols. (Litterature Franco-Americaine de la Nouvelle-Angle Terre Ser.). (Fr.). (gr. 10 up). 1981. pap. text ed. 49.50x (ISBN 0-911409-24-6). Natl Mat Dev.

--Litterature Franco-Americaine de la Nouvelle: Angle Terre. (Anthologie Tome Ser.: No. 9). (Illus.). 365p. (Fr.). (gr. 10 up). 1981. pap. text ed. 5.50x (ISBN 0-911409-33-5). Natl Mat Dev.

--Litterature Franco-Americaine de la Nouvelle: Angle Terre. (Anthologie Tome Ser.: No. 1). (Illus.). 320p. (Fr.). (gr. 10 up). 1980. pap. text ed. 5.50x (ISBN 0-911409-25-4). Natl Mat Dev.

--Litterature Franco-Americaine de la Nouvelle: Angle Terre. (Anthologie Tome Ser.: No. 2). (Illus.). 250p. (Fr.). (gr. 10 up). 1980. pap. text ed. 5.50x (ISBN 0-911409-26-2). Natl Mat Dev.

--Litterature Franco-Americaine de la Nouvelle: Angle Terre. (Anthologie Tome Ser.: No. 3). (Illus.). 260p. (Fr.). (gr. 10 up). 1980. pap. text ed. 5.50x (ISBN 0-911409-27-0). Natl Mat Dev.

--Litterature Franco-Americaine de la Nouvelle: Angle Terre. (Anthologie Tome Ser.: No. 5). (Illus.). 378p. (Fr.). (gr. 10 up). 1981. pap. text ed. 5.50x (ISBN 0-911409-29-7). Natl Mat Dev.

--Litterature Franco-Americaine de la Nouvelle: Angle Terre. (Anthologie Tome Ser.: No. 6). (Illus.). 328p. (Fr.). (gr. 10 up). 1981. pap. text ed. 5.50x (ISBN 0-911409-30-0). Natl Mat Dev.

--Litterature Franco-Americaine de la Nouvelle: Angle Terre. (Anthologie Tome Ser.: No. 7). (Illus.). 294p. (Fr.). (gr. 10 up). 1981. pap. text ed. 5.50x (ISBN 0-911409-31-9). Natl Mat Dev.

--Litterature Franco-Americaine de la Nouvelle: Angle Terre. (Anthologie Tome Ser.: No. 8). (Illus.). 360p. (Fr.). (gr. 10 up). 1981. pap. text ed. 5.50 (ISBN 0-911409-32-7). Natl Mat Dev.

Santeusanio, Joan, jt. auth. see Hyman, Jane.

Santi. Botticelli. pap. 12.50 (ISBN 0-935748-41-5). ScalaBooks.

--Leonardo Da Vinci. pap. 12.50 (ISBN 0-935748-19-9). ScalaBooks.

--Raphael. pap. 12.50 (ISBN 0-935748-21-0). ScalaBooks.

Santi, Enrico M. Pablo Neruda: The Politics of Prophecy. 256p. 1982. 19.50x (ISBN 0-8014-1472-5). Cornell U Pr.

Santi, Roger De see De Santi, Roger.

Santiago, Danny. Famous All Over Town. 288p. 1983. 14.95 (ISBN 0-671-43249-4). S&S.

Santillana, Giorgio. The Crime of Galileo. LC 55-7400. (Midway Reprint Ser). (Illus.). xvi, 339p. 1955. pap. 11.00x (ISBN 0-226-73481-1). U of Chicago Pr.

Santillana, Giorgio De see De Santillana, Giorgio.

Santillana, Giorgio De see Santillana, Giorgio.

Santilli, R. M. Foundations of Theoretical Mechanics II: Birkhoffian Generalization of Hamiltonian Mechanics. (Texts & Monographs in Physics). 370p. 1983. 66.00 (ISBN 0-387-09482-2). Springer-Verlag.

Santini, Maurizo, ed. see Golgi Centennial Symposium, September 1973.

Santini, Rosmarie. Agnes Nixon's All My Children: Tara & Philip, Bk. 1. 256p. (Orig.). 1980. pap. 2.50 o.s.i. (ISBN 0-515-06058-5). Jove Pubns.

Santocki, J. Case Studies in Auditing. 288p. 1978. 30.00x (ISBN 0-7121-0373-2, Pub. by Macdonald & Evans). State Mutual Bk.

Santomasso, Eugene A. Origins & Aims of German Expressionist Architecture. Foster, Stephen, ed. LC 82-1925. (Studies in Fine Arts: The Avant-Garde: No. 24). 1983. write for info. (ISBN 0-8357-1306-7, Pub. by UMI Res Pr). Univ Microfilms.

Santoni, Georges, jt. auth. see Rey, Jean-Noel.

Santoni, Georges, ed. Contemporary French Culture & Society (Societe et Culture de la France Contemporaine) LC 80-25773. 270p. 1981. 34.50x (ISBN 0-87395-514-5); pap. 9.95x (ISBN 0-87395-515-3). State U NY Pr.

Santora, Charles G. Mr. Monk. LC 81-90511. 231p. 1981. velo-bind 9.00 (ISBN 0-686-37018-X). C G Santora.

Santora, Dolores. Conceptual Frameworks Used in Baccalaureate & Master's Degree Curricula. (League Exchange Ser.: No. 126). 49p. 1980. 4.95 (ISBN 0-686-38247-1, 15-1828). Natl League Nurse.

Santoro, Anthony, jt. auth. see Rodriguez, Edward J.

Santoro, Christopher, jt. auth. see Johnson, Evelyne.

Santos, Bienvenido N. The Praying Man. 172p. (Orig.). 1982. pap. 9.50x (ISBN 971-10-0002-4, Pub. by New Day Philippines). Cellar.

Santos, Jean Dos. Histoire de l'Ethiope Orientale Composee en Portugais. (Bibliotheque Africaine Ser.). 250p. (Fr.). 1974. Repr. of 1684 ed. lib. bdg. 68.50x o.p. (ISBN 0-8287-0759-6, 72-2104). Clearwater Pub.

Santos, Milton. The Shared Space: The Two Circuits of the Urban Economy in Underdeveloped Countries. xii, 266p. 1979. 13.95x (ISBN 0-416-79660-5); pap. 13.95x (ISBN 0-416-79670-2). Methuen Inc.

Santos, S. M. dos see Barney, G. C. & Dos Santos, S. M.

Santostefano, Sebastiano. A Biodevelopmental Approach to Clinical Child Psychology: Cognitive Controls & Cognitive Control Therapy. LC 78-18485. (Wiley Ser. on Personality Processes). 833p. 1978. 64.95 (ISBN 0-471-75380-7, Pub. by Wiley-Interscience). Wiley.

Santrey, Laurence. Davy Crockett: Young Pioneer. LC 82-16040. (Illus.). 48p. (gr. 4-6). 1983. PLB 6.89 (ISBN 0-89375-847-7); pap. text ed. 1.95 (ISBN 0-89375-848-5). Troll Assocs.

--Jim Thorpe: Young Athlete. LC 82-15982. (Illus.). 48p. (gr. 4-6). 1983. PLB 6.89 (ISBN 0-89375-845-0); pap. text ed. 1.95 (ISBN 0-89375-846-9). Troll Assocs.

--Young Frederick Douglass: Fight for Freedom. LC 82-15993. (Illus.). 48p. (gr. 4-6). 1983. PLB 6.89 (ISBN 0-89375-857-4); pap. text ed. 1.95 (ISBN 0-89375-858-2). Troll Assocs.

Santrey, Louis. Autumn. LC 82-19396. (Discovering the Seasons Ser.). (Illus.). 32p. (gr. 4-6). 1982. lib. bdg. 8.79 (ISBN 0-89375-905-8); pap. text ed. 2.50 (ISBN 0-89375-906-6). Troll Assocs.

--Spring: Discovering the Seasons Ser. LC 82-19381. (Illus.). 32p. (gr. 4-6). 1982. lib. bdg. 8.79 (ISBN 0-89375-909-0); pap. text ed. 2.50 (ISBN 0-89375-910-4). Troll Assocs.

--Summer. LC 82-19384. (Discovering the Seasons Ser.). (Illus.). 32p. (gr. 4-6). 1982. lib. bdg. 8.79 (ISBN 0-89375-911-2); pap. text ed. 2.50 (ISBN 0-89375-912-0). Troll Assocs.

--Winter. LC 82-19353. (Discovering the Seasons Ser.). (Illus.). 32p. (gr. 4-6). 1982. lib. bdg. 8.79 (ISBN 0-89375-907-4); pap. text ed. 2.50 (ISBN 0-89375-908-2). Troll Assocs.

Santrock, John W. Life-Span Development. 864p. 1983. text ed. write for info. (ISBN 0-697-06556-1); pap. text ed. avail.; instr's manual avail. (ISBN 0-697-06558-8); study guide avail. (ISBN 0-697-06557-X). Wm C Brown.

Santuccio, Mario, jt. auth. see Acquaviva, Sabino.

Santuci, Richard. Fine Figure Photography. 1970. 16.95 o.p. (ISBN 0-8174-0526-7, Amphoto). Watson-Guptill.

Sant-Vallier, Joly De. Reflexions Sur L'eloge De M. De Voltaire Par M. D'alembert. Repr. of 1780 ed. 32.00 o.p. (ISBN 0-8287-0760-X). Clearwater Pub.

Santvoord, George Van see Van Santvoord, George.

Sanusi, I. Daniel, jt. auth. see Misra, Raghunath P.

Sanzone, John G., jt. auth. see Reagan, Michael D.

Saornetti, C. The Middle Assyrian Laws. (Cybertica Mesopotomica Graphemic Categorizations Cuneiform Texts Ser.). 1982. pap. 11.00x (ISBN 0-89003-119-3). Undena Pubns.

Sao Saimong Mangrai. The Padaeng Chronicle & the Jengtung State Chronicle Translated. LC 80-67342. (Michigan Papers on South & Southeast Asia: No. 19). (Illus.). xxiv, 301p. 1981. 21.00x (ISBN 0-89148-020-X); pap. 11.50x (ISBN 0-89148-021-8). Ctr S&SE Asian.

Saotome, Mitsugi. Aikido & the Harmony of Nature. (Illus.). 330p. (Orig.). 1983. 25.75 (ISBN 0-8038-0487-3); pap. 17.95 (ISBN 0-8038-0403-2). Hastings.

Saper, Joel R. Headache Disorders: Current Concepts & Treatment Strategies. Orig. Title: Migraines. 320p. 1982. casebound 24.50 (ISBN 0-7236-7010-2). Wright-PSG.

Saperetti, Claudio. Assur 14446: Le Altre Famiglie. LC 82-50981. (Cuneiform Texas Ser.: Vol. 3). 196p. 1982. pap. 13.50 (ISBN 0-89003-118-5). Undena Pubns.

Saphier, M. Office Planning & Design. LC 68-11237. (Illus.). 1968. 39.95 (ISBN 0-07-054720-3, P&RB). McGraw.

Sapir, Andre & Lutz, Ernst. Trade in Non-Factor Services: Past Trends & Current Issues. (Workign Paper: No. 410). iii, 137p. 1980. 5.00 (ISBN 0-686-36210-1, WP-0410). World Bank.

Sapir, E. Notes on Chasta Costa Phonology & Morphology. (Anthropological Publications Ser.: Vol. 2-2). (Illus.). 1914. 2.00x (ISBN 0-686-24092-8). Univ Mus of U.

--Takelma Texts. (Anthropological Publications Ser.: Vol. 2-1). 1909. 3.50x (ISBN 0-686-24096-0). Univ Mus of U.

Sapir, Edward. Selected Writings of Edward Sapir in Language, Culture, & Personality. Mandelbaum, David G., ed. 1949. 37.50x (ISBN 0-520-01115-5). U of Cal Pr.

Sapir, Edward & Swadesh, Morris. Yana Dictionary. (U. C. Publ. in Linguistics: Vol. 22). 1960. pap. 14.00x (ISBN 0-520-09219-8). U of Cal Pr.

Sapir, Richard & Murphy, Warren. The Destroyer, No. 11: Kill or Cure. (Orig.). 1974. pap. 2.25 (ISBN 0-523-41856-6). Pinnacle Bks.

Sapir, Richard B. The Body. LC 82-45209. 352p. 1983. 16.95 (ISBN 0-385-18017-9). Doubleday.

Sapiro, Virginia. The Political Integration of Women. LC 82-2672. 248p. 1983. text ed. 16.95 (ISBN 0-252-00920-7). U of Ill Pr.

Sapolsky, Harvey M., jt. ed. see Altman, Stuart.

Saporetti, C. Assur. LC 82-50981. (Cybernetica Mesopotomia Data Sets, Cuneiform Texts Ser.: Vol. 3). 196p. 1982. pap. 13.50 (ISBN 0-89003-118-5). Undena Pubns.

--Assur 14446: la famiglia "A". (Cybernetica Mesopotamia, Data Sets: Cuneiform Texts Ser.: Vol. 1). 139p. 1979. pap. 11.00x soft only (ISBN 0-89003-036-7). Undena Pubns.

Saporetti, Claudio. Glieponimi medio-assiri. LC 79-63267. (Bibliotheca Mesopotamica Ser.: Vol. 9). viii, 184p. (Eng.). 1979. 24.50x (ISBN 0-89003-046-4); pap. 20.50x (ISBN 0-89003-037-5). Undena Pubns.

--Le Leggi medioassire. (Cybernetica Mesopotamia, Data Sets Ser.: Vol. 2). (Illus.). 181p. (Orig., Ital.). 1979. pap. 9.50x (ISBN 0-89003-036-7). Undena Pubns.

Saporta, Raphael. Basket in the Reeds. LC 64-25640. (Foreign Land Bks). (gr. k-7). 1965. PLB 5.95g (ISBN 0-8225-0352-2). Lerner Pubns.

Saposnik, Irving S. Robert Louis Stevenson. (English Authors Ser.: No. 167). 168p. 1974. lib. bdg. 11.95 (ISBN 0-8057-1517-7, Twayne). G K Hall.

Saposnik, R., jt. auth. see Quirk, James.

Saposs, David. Communism in American Unions. LC 75-40930. 1976. Repr. of 1959 ed. lib. bdg. 20.75x (ISBN 0-8371-8687-0, SACAU). Greenwood.

Sapp, Jacqueline W. Comprehensive Review of Dental Assisting. LC 81-1381. 228p. 1981. pap. 13.95 (ISBN 0-471-05728-2, Pub. by Wiley Med). Wiley.

Sapp, Stephen. Sexuality, the Bible & Science. LC 76-62617. 160p. 1977. 4.00 o.p. (ISBN 0-8006-0503-9, 1-503). Fortress.

Sappenfield, James, jt. ed. see Guttmann, Allen.

Sappenfield, James A., ed. see Cooper, James Fenimore.

Sappho. Memoir. 4th ed. Wharton, H. T., tr. 217p. 1974. Repr. of 1898 ed. text ed. 21.75x o.p. (ISBN 90-6090-002-2). Humanities.

--Sappho: A New Translation. Barnard, Mary, tr. 1958. pap. 2.95 (ISBN 0-520-01117-1, CAL16). U of Cal Pr.

Sapriel, J. Acousto-Optics. LC 78-16173. 126p. 1979. 33.95 (ISBN 0-471-99700-5, Pub. by Wiley-Interscience). Wiley.

Sapunov, Valentin N., jt. auth. see Schmid, Roland.

Saqr, A. Islamic Fundamentalism. 5.95 (ISBN 0-686-83888-2). Kazi Pubns.

Sarabyanov, Dmitry & Arbuzou, Grigory. Valentine Serov: Paintings, Graphic Works, Stage Designs. LC 80-68475. (Illus.). 328p. 1983. 45.00 (ISBN 0-8109-1605-3). Abrams.

Saracho, Olivia N. & Spodek, Bernard, eds. Understanding the Multicultural Experience in Early Childhood Education. 1983. pap. text ed. write for info. Natl Assn Child Ed.

Saradananda, Swami. Garland of Guidance: Intimate Answers to Important Questions. Aseshananda, Swami, tr. (God Ser.: No. 112). (Illus.). 1978. pap. 2.00 o.p. (ISBN 0-89007-112-8). C Stark.

Sarafino, Edward P. & Armstrong, James W. Child & Adolescent Development. 1980. text ed. 21.95x (ISBN 0-673-15103-4). Scott F.

Sarafinski, Dolores J., jt. auth. see Lehrman, Walter D.

Sarah, Elizabeth, jt. auth. see Friedman, Scarlet.

Saran, Parmatma & Eames, Edwin, eds. New Ethnics: Asian Indians in the U. S. 416p. 1980. 32.95 (ISBN 0-03-051121-6). Praeger.

Sarason, Barbara R., jt. auth. see Sarason, Irwin G.

Sarason, Bertram D. Hemingway & The Sun Set. 1972. 10.00 (ISBN 0-910972-06-0). Bruccoli.

Sarason, Irwin G. & Sarason, Barbara R. Abnormal Psychology: The Problem of Maladaptive Behavior. 3rd ed. (Century Psychology Ser.). (Illus.). 1980. text ed. 26.95 (ISBN 0-13-001107-X). P-H.

Sarason, Seymour B. Clinical Interaction with Special Reference to the Rorschach. Repr. of 1954 ed. lib. bdg. 17.75x (ISBN 0-8371-2258-9, SACI). Greenwood.

--The Creation of Settings & the Future Societies. LC 72-83964. (Social & Behavioral Science Ser.). 1972. 19.95x (ISBN 0-87589-146-2). Jossey-Bass.

--The Psychological Sense of Community: Prospects for a Community Psychology. LC 73-20962. (Social & Behavioral Science Ser.). 1974. 21.95x (ISBN 0-87589-216-7). Jossey-Bass.

Sarason, Seymour B., et al. Human Services & Resource Networks: Rationale, Possibilities, & Public Policy. LC 76-57307. (Social & Behavioral Science Ser.). 1977. text ed. 19.95x (ISBN 0-87589-309-0). Jossey-Bass.

Saraswathi, S. Minorities in Madras State: Group Interests in Modern Politics. LC 75-903357. 1974. 14.00x o.p. (ISBN 0-8364-0432-7). South Asia Bks.

Saraswati, Baidyanath. Pottery-Making Cultures & Indian Civilization. 1979. 27.50x o.p. (ISBN 0-8364-0321-5). South Asia Bks.

Saraswati, Dayanand. Yadav: Autobiography of Dayanand Saraswati. rev. ed. Yadav, K. C., ed. 1979. 10.00x o.p. (ISBN 0-8364-0372-X). South Asia Bks.

Saraydarian, Torkom. The Spring of Prosperity. 1982. 7.00 (ISBN 0-911794-12-3); pap. 5.00 (ISBN 0-911794-13-1). Aqua Educ.

Sarbaugh, Larry E. Teaching Speech Communication. (General Education Ser.). 1979. text ed. 16.95 (ISBN 0-675-08300-1). Merrill.

Sarbin, Hershel, jt. auth. see Chernoff, George.

Sarbin, Theodore R. & Mancuso, James C. Schizophrenia: Medical Diagnosis or Moral Verdict? (Pergamon General Psychology Ser.). 1981. 25.00 (ISBN 0-08-024613-3); pap. 9.50 (ISBN 0-08-024612-5). Pergamon.

Sarbin, Theodore R. & Scheibe, Karl. Studies in Social Identity. 416p. 1983. 15.00 (ISBN 0-03-059542-8). Praeger.

Sarchet, Bernard R., jt. auth. see Amos, John M.

Sardell, William. Modern Corporation Checklists. 1982. 56.00 (ISBN 0-88262-797-X). Warren.

Sardesai, D. R. Trade & Empire in Malaya & Singapore, 1869-1874. LC 75-632948. (Illus.). 22p. 1970. pap. 1.75x o.s.i. (ISBN 0-89680-009-1, Ohio U Ctr Intl). Ohio U Pr.

Sardinas, Joseph & Burch, John G. EDP Auditing: A Primer. LC 80-25981. 209p. 1981. pap. text ed. 16.50 (ISBN 0-471-12305-6); avail. tchr's manual (ISBN 0-471-09792-6). Wiley.

Sardinas, Joseph L., Jr. Computing Today: An Introduction to Business Data Processing. 485p. 1981. 17.95 (ISBN 0-686-98051-4). Telecom Lib.

Sardinas, Joseph L., Jr., jt. auth. see Burch, John G., Jr.

Sardinias, Joseph L., Jr. Computing Today: An Introduction to Business Data Processing. 512p. 1981. text ed. 19.95 (ISBN 0-13-165092-0); pap. 7.95 student guide (ISBN 0-13-165100-5). P-H.

Sareil, Jean & Ryding, William. Au Jour le Jour: A French Review. 2nd ed. LC 73-18083. 240p. 1974. text ed. 15.95 (ISBN 0-13-052977-X). P-H.

Sarel, Eimerl & Devore, Irven. The Primates. rev. ed. LC 80-52263. (Life Nature Library). PLB 13.40 (ISBN 0-8094-3915-8). Silver.

Sarf, Wayne. God Bless You, Buffalo Bill: A Layman's Guide to History & the Western Film. LC 80-71118. (Illus.). 280p. 1983. 27.50 (ISBN 0-8386-3089-8). Fairleigh Dickinson.

Sarfaty, Gordon A., et al, eds. Estrogen Receptor Assays in Breast Cancer: Laboratory Discrepancies & Quality Control. LC 81-8253. (Illus.). 248p. 1981. 31.00x (ISBN 0-89352-159-0). Masson Pub.

Sargeant, Howard & Fuller, John, eds. Gregory Awards Anthology 1982. 128p. 1982. pap. text ed. 8.50x (ISBN 0-85635-437-6, 51480, Pub. by Carcanet New Pr England). Humanities.

Sargent, Alice G. Beyond Sex Roles. (Illus.). 1977. pap. text ed. 16.50 (ISBN 0-8299-0104-3). West Pub.

Sargent, B. Minstrels. LC 73-80470. (Resources of Music Ser.: No. 8). (Illus.). 64p. 1974. pap. text ed. 4.95 (ISBN 0-521-20166-7). Cambridge U Pr.

--Minstrels II. LC 73-80470. (Resources of Music Ser.: No. 16). (Illus.). 1979. 5.95 (ISBN 0-521-21551-X). Cambridge U Pr.

--Troubadours. LC 73-93396. (Resources of Music Ser.: No. 7). (Illus.). 400p. 1974. pap. text ed. 5.95 (ISBN 0-521-20471-2); record 6.95 (ISBN 0-521-20476-3). Cambridge U Pr.

Sargent, Betsye. The Integrated Day in an American School. (Illus.). 1972. pap. 5.75 o.p. (ISBN 0-934338-25-6). NAIS.

Sargent, C. S., ed. see Rehder, A.

Sargent, Frederick, II, ed. Human Ecology: A Guide to Information Sources. (Health Affairs Information Guide Series, Gale Information Guide Library: Vol. 10). 300p. 1982. 42.00x (ISBN 0-8103-1504-1). Gale.

Sargent, Howard. Fishbowl Management: A Paricipative Approach to Systematic Management. LC 77-27924. 383p. 1978. 31.50 (ISBN 0-471-03574-2, Pub. by Wiley-Interscience). Wiley.

Sargent, J. Society, Schools & Progress in India. LC 68-21106. 1968. 24.00 o.s.i. (ISBN 0-08-012840-8); pap. 12.00 (ISBN 0-08-012839-4). Pergamon.

Sargent, Katherine. The Rose & the Sword. 256p. (Orig.). 1983. pap. 2.75 (ISBN 0-449-12379-0, GM). Fawcett.

Sargent, Lyman T., ed. Man Abroad: A Yarn of Some Other Century. (Science Fiction Ser.). 80p. 1976. Repr. of 1887 ed. lib. bdg. cancelled o.s.i. (ISBN 0-8398-2349-5, Gregg). G K Hall.

Sargent, Lynda. Judith Duchesne. 1979. 8.95 o.p. (ISBN 0-517-53905-5). Crown.

Sargent, Michael. Mycenae. McLeish, Kenneth & McLeish, Valerie, eds. (Aspects of Greek Life Ser.). (Illus.). 64p. (Orig.). (gr. 7-12). 1972. pap. text ed. 3.50 (ISBN 0-582-34401-8). Longman.

Sargent, Murray, III, et al. Laser Physics. LC 74-5049. (Illus.). 1974. text ed. 30.50 (ISBN 0-201-06912-1, Adv Bk Prog); pap. text ed. 15.50 (ISBN 0-201-06913-X, Adv Bk Prog). A-W.

Sargent, Pamela. The Alien Upstairs. LC 82-45271. (Science Fiction Ser.). 192p. 1983. 11.95 (ISBN 0-385-17803-4). Doubleday.

--Earthseed. LC 79-2666. 280p. (YA) (gr. 7 up). 1983. PLB 10.89g (ISBN 0-06-025188-3, HarpJ); pap. 6.68i (ISBN 0-06-025187-5). Har-Row.

Sargent, Pamela, ed. Women of Wonder: Science Fiction Stories by Women About Women. LC 74-8583. 1975. pap. 4.95 (ISBN 0-394-71041-X, Vin). Random.

Sargent, Robert. Aspects of A Southern Story. LC 82-51069. 72p. 1983. pap. text ed. 5.95 (ISBN 0-915380-15-3). Word Works.

--The Burning Heart: Foundational Experiences of Jesus & His Call. LC 82-15250. 64p. 1982. pap. 2.50 (ISBN 0-8146-1274-1). Liturgical Pr.

Sargent, S. Stansfeld. Nontraditional Therapy & Counseling with the Aging. LC 80-11303. (Adulthood & Aging Ser.). 256p. 1980. text ed. 19.95 o.p. (ISBN 0-8261-2800-9); pap. 14.95 (ISBN 0-8261-2801-7). Springer Pub.

Sargent, Sarah. Edge of Darkness. 128p. (gr. 7 up). 1982. 8.95 o.p. (ISBN 0-517-54539-X). Crown.

Sargent, Thelma, tr. from Gr. & The Homeric Hymns. 96p. 1973. 5.95x o.p. (ISBN 0-393-04369-X); pap. 4.95 (ISBN 0-393-00788-X). Norton.

Sargent, Thelma, tr. The Homeric Hymns: A Verse Translation. 96p. 1975. pap. 4.95 (ISBN 0-393-00788-X, Norton Lib). Norton.

Sargent, Thomas. Macroeconomic Theory. LC 78-4803. (Economic Theory, Econometrics & Mathematical Economics Ser.). 1979. 26.50 (ISBN 0-12-619750-4). Acad Pr.

Sarginson, Wes, jt. auth. see Bayne, Neil.

Sarhan, Samir, ed. Who's Who in Saudi Arabia: Nineteen Seventy-Eight - Seventy-Nine. 2nd ed. 1978. 54.00x (ISBN 0-685-59596-X, Europa/Tihama). Gale.

Sarig. Diseases of Fishes, Book 3: Warmwater Fishing. 19.95 (ISBN 0-87666-040-5, P5203). TFH Pubns.

Sarigny, Rudi. How to Make & Design Stuffed Toys. LC 77-92482. (Illus.). 1978. pap. 5.95 (ISBN 0-486-23625-0). Dover.

Sarin, Madhu. Urban Planning in the Third World: The Chandigarh Experience. 240p. 1982. 31.00 (ISBN 0-7201-1637-6, Pub. by Mansell England). Wilson.

Sariti, Anthony W., tr. see Li, Jui.

Sarju, Sawak. Gems for Living. 1983. 5.95 (ISBN 0-533-05491-5). Vantage.

Sarkadi, K. & Vincze, I. Mathematical Methods of Statistical Quality Control. 1974. 57.00 (ISBN 0-12-619250-2). Acad Pr.

Sarkanen, K. V. & Ludwig, Charles H. Lignins: Occurrence, Formation, Structure & Reactions. LC 79-148456. (Illus.). 916p. 1971. 99.00 (ISBN 0-471-75422-6, Pub. by Wiley-Interscience). Wiley.

Sarkanen, Kyosti V. & Tillman, David, eds. Progress in Biomass Conversion, Vol. 1. (Serial Publication). 1979. 26.00 (ISBN 0-12-535901-2). Acad Pr.

Sarkanen, Kyosti V. & Tillman, David A., eds. Progress in Biomass Conversion, Vol. 3. (Serial Publication). 304p. 1982. 24.50 (ISBN 0-12-535903-9). Acad Pr.

Sarkany, Pal & Ocsag, Imre. Dogs of Hungary. White, Kay, tr. from Hungarian. (Illus.). 141p. 1977. 17.50x o.p. (ISBN 963-13-3715-4). Intl Pubns Serv.

Sarkar, A. D. Mould & Core Material for the Steel Industry. 1967. 24.00 o.s.i. (ISBN 0-08-012486-0); pap. 10.75 (ISBN 0-08-012487-9). Pergamon.

Sarkar, Amal. Siva in Medieval Indian Literature. LC 75-901322. 1974. 13.75x o.p. (ISBN 0-8364-0467-X). South Asia Bks.

Sarkar, K. R. Public Finance in Ancient India. 1978. 14.00x o.p. (ISBN 0-8364-0155-7). South Asia Bks.

Sarkar, S., ed. Hindustan Year-Book & Who's Who in 1981. 49th ed. 212p. 1981. pap. 12.50x (ISBN 0-8002-3054-X, SA64-762). Intl Pubns Serv.

--Hindustan Yearbook & Who's Who, 1980. 48th ed. LC 64-762. 136p. (Orig.). 1980. pap. 12.50 o.p. (ISBN 0-8002-2766-2). Intl Pubns Serv.

Sarkar, Shukla. Epistemology & Ethics of G. E. Moore: A Critical Evaluation. 202p. 1981. text ed. 15.75x (ISBN 0-391-02266-0, Pub. by Concept Pub. Co. India). Humanities.

Sarker, A. K. Fluorescent Whitening Agents. 1970. 16.50x (ISBN 0-87245-411-8). Textile Bk.

Sarkesian, Sam C., ed. Non-Nuclear Conflicts in the Nuclear Age. 416p. 1980. 33.95 (ISBN 0-03-056138-8). Praeger.

--U. S. Policy & Low-Intensity Conflict: Potentials for Military Struggles in the 1980s. LC 80-24071. 224p. (Orig.). 1981. pap. 14.95 (ISBN 0-87855-851-9). Transaction Bks.

Sarkissian, Adele. Writers for Young Adults: Biographies Master Index. LC 79-13228. (Gale Biographical Index Ser.: Vol. 6). 1979. 52.00x (ISBN 0-8103-1083-X). Gale.

Satir, Virginia M. Peoplemaking. LC 73-188143. 1972. 9.95 (ISBN 0-8314-0031-5); pap. 7.95. Sci & Behavior.

Satkowski, Leon. Studies on Vasari's Architecture. LC 78-74377. (Fine Arts Dissertations, Fourth Ser.). 1980. lib. bdg. 38.00 o.s.i. (ISBN 0-8240-3964-5). Garland Pub.

Satnick, Shelly de see De Satnick, Shelly.

Sato, Esther M., et al. Japanese Now: Text, Vol. 2. 208p. 1983. text ed. 20.00x (ISBN 0-8248-0795-2); tchrs. ed. 15.00x (ISBN 0-8248-0796-0); wkbk. 4.00x (ISBN 0-8248-0797-9). UH Pr.

--Japanese Now, Vol. 1: Text, Vol. 7. LC 81-23142. 120p. 1982. pap. text ed. 15.00x (ISBN 0-8248-0773-1). UH Pr.

Sato, Giei & Nishimura, Eshin. Unsui: A Diary of Zen Monastic Life. Smith, Bardwell, ed. LC 73-78112. (Illus.). 125p. 1973. text ed. 12.00x (ISBN 0-8248-0277-2, Eastwest Ctr); pap. 8.95 (ISBN 0-8248-0272-1). UH Pr.

Sato, Gordon H., et al, eds. Growth of Cell in Hormonally Defined Media. LC 82-71652. (Cold Spring Harbor Conferences on Cell Proliferation Ser.: Vol. 9). 1213p. 1982. 2 bk set 140.00x (ISBN 0-87969-156-5). Cold Spring Harbor.

Sato, Hideo, jt. ed. see Destler, I. M.

Sato, Hiroaki, tr. see Takamura, Kotaro.

Sato, Hirosaki. One Hundred Frogs: From Renga to Haiku to English. LC 82-17505. (Illus.). 300p. 1983. pap. 12.50 (ISBN 0-8348-0176-0). Weatherhill.

Sato, Kazuo, ed. Industry & Business in Japan: An Anthology. LC 79-91904. 1980. text ed. 35.00 (ISBN 0-87332-152-9). M E Sharpe.

Sato, Ryo & Kato, Ryuichi. Microsomes, Drug Oxidations & Drug Toxicology. 636p. 1982. 59.95 (ISBN 0-471-87285-7, Pub. by Wiley-Interscience). Wiley.

Sato, Ryo & Kagawa, Yasuo, eds. Transport & Bioenergetics in Bimembranes. 261p. 1983. 45.00x (ISBN 0-306-41282-9, Plenum Pr). Plenum Pub.

Sato, Ryo & Shun-Ichi Ohnishi, eds. Structure, Dynamics & Biogenesis of Biomembranes. 187p. 1983. 39.50x (ISBN 0-306-41283-7, Plenum Pr). Plenum Pub.

Sato, Ryuzo & Suzawa, Gilbert. Research & Productivity: The Study of Endogenous Technical Change. 224p. 1983. 21.95 (ISBN 0-86569-068-5). Auburn Hse.

Sato, Sho. State & Local Government Law. 2nd ed. 1165p. 1977. 27.50 (ISBN 0-316-77116-3). Little.

Sato, T., jt. auth. see Okano, I.

Sato, Takashi. Field Crops in Thailand. (Southeast Asian Studies Monographs). 164p. 1966. boxed 10.00x o.p. (ISBN 0-8248-0370-1, Eastwest Ctr). UH Pr.

Satow, Ernest. A Diplomat in Japan. LC 82-50326. (Illus.). 432p. 1983. pap. 7.95 (ISBN 0-8048-1447-3). C E Tuttle.

Satow, Y. Ernest. Thirty-Five Millimeter Negs & Prints: And How to Get the Most from Them. (Illus.). 1969. 9.95 o.p. (ISBN 0-8174-0494-5, Amphoto). Watson-Guptill.

Satprakashananda, Swami. Swami Vivekananda's Contribution to the Present Age. LC 77-91628. (Illus.). 249p. 1978. 9.50 (ISBN 0-916356-58-2, 77-91628). Vedanta Soc St Louis.

SATPREM. The Mind of the Cells. Mahak, Francine & Venet, Luc, trs. from Fr. LC 82-15659. 215p. 1982. pap. 6.95 (ISBN 0-938710-06-0). Inst Evolutionary.

--Mother's Agenda Nineteen Seventy-one, Vol. 12. LC 80-472990. (Mother's Agenda Ser.). Orig. Title: L'Agenda De Mere, Vol. 12. 400p. (Orig.). 1983. pap. text ed. 12.50 (ISBN 0-938710-05-2). Inst Evolutionary.

Satran, Paul R. Balancing Act. (Finding Mr. Right Ser.). 1983. pap. 2.75 (ISBN 0-380-83659-9, 83659-9). Avon.

Satre, Lowell J., ed. see Melanchthon, Philipp.

Satriana, M. J., ed. Insecticide Manufacturing: Recent Processes & Applications. LC 82-19092. (Chemical Technology Review: No. 214). (Illus.). 332p. 1983. 45.00 (ISBN 0-8155-0920-0). Noyes.

Sattelle, D. B. & Hall, L. M., eds. Receptors for Neurotransmitters, Hormones & Pheromones in Insects. 1980. 54.00 (ISBN 0-444-80231-2). Elsevier.

Sattelmeyer, Robert, ed. see Thoreau, Henry D.

Sattenfield, Charles L. Let's Grow & Make Disciples! 92p. (Orig.). 1980. 2.50 (ISBN 0-88027-080-2). Firm Foun Pub.

Satter, Ellyn. Child of Mine: Feeding with Love & Good Sense. 300p. (Orig.). 1982. pap. 9.95 (ISBN 0-915950-54-5). Bull Pub.

Satterfield, Archie. Pacific Sea & Shore, Bk. 1. (Panorama Collection Ser.). (Illus.). 136p. 1982. 35.00 (ISBN 0-916076-53-9). Writing.

Satterfield, Archie & Bauer, Eddie. The Eddie Bauer Guide to Cross-Country Skiing. (Illus.). 256p. 1982. 17.95 (ISBN 0-201-07774-4); pap. 8.95 (ISBN 0-201-07775-2). A-W.

Satterfield, Archie, Sr. & Bauer, Eddie, Sr. The Eddie Bauer Guide to Family Camping. LC 82-13923. (Illus.). 320p. 1983. 17.95 (ISBN 0-201-07776-0); pap. 8.95 (ISBN 0-201-07777-9). A-W.

Satterfield, Charles. Heterogenous Catalysis in Practice. (Chemical Engineering Ser.). (Illus.). 464p. 1980. text ed. 37.50 (ISBN 0-07-054875-7); student manual 14.95 (ISBN 0-07-054876-5). McGraw.

Satterlee, Sarah & Auerbach, Debbie, eds. The Goodfellow Catalog of Wonderful Things, No. 3: A Mail Order Treasury of America's Finest Crafts. LC 81-1144. (Illus.). 720p. 1982. cancelled (ISBN 0-936016-25-6); pap. 19.95 (ISBN 0-936016-00-0). Goodfellow.

Satterlund, Donald R. Wildland Watershed Management. 400p. 1972. 27.95x (ISBN 0-471-06840-3). Wiley.

Satterthwaite, David, jt. auth. see Hardoy, Jorge E.

Satterthwaite, Edwin H., Jr. Source Language Debugging Tools. LC 79-50820. (Outstanding Dissertations in the Computer Sciences). 1980. lib. bdg. 32.00 o.s.i. (ISBN 0-8240-4416-9). Garland Pub.

Satterthwaite, Les. Television: Planning, Design, & Production. (Orig.). 1980. pap. text ed. 11.95 (ISBN 0-8403-2153-8). Kendall-Hunt.

Satterthwaite, Linton. Stone Artifacts at & Near the Finley Site, Near Eden, Wyoming. (Museum Monograph). (Illus.). iv, 22p. 1957. 1.50x (ISBN 0-934718-06-7). Univ Mus of U PA.

Satterthwaite, Linton, jt. auth. see Beetz, Carl P.

Satterthwaite, Linton, jt. auth. see Jones, Christopher.

Sattinger, M. J. Capital & Distribution of Labour Earnings. (Contributions to Economic Analysis Ser.: Vol. 126). 1980. 47.00 (ISBN 0-444-85397-9). Elsevier.

Sattler, Helen R. No Place for A Goat. LC 80-26558. (Illus.). 32p. (ps-3). 1982. 5.95 (ISBN 0-525-66723-7). Dandelion Pr.

--Noses Are Special. LC 81-20648. (Illus.). 32p. (gr. k-2). 1982. 7.95 (ISBN 0-687-28120-2). Abingdon.

--The Smallest Witch. LC 81-2202. (Illus.). 32p. (gr. k-4). 1982. 6.75 (ISBN 0-525-66747-4). Dandelion Pr.

Sattler, Henry V. Sex Is Alive & Well & Flourishing Among Christians. LC 79-88031. 1980. pap. 3.95 o.p. (ISBN 0-87973-523-6). Our Sunday Visitor.

Sattler, William M. & Miller, W. Discussion & Conference. 2nd ed. 1968. text ed. 20.95 (ISBN 0-13-216135-4). P-H.

Sattoo, T. & Madgwick, H. I. Forest Biomass. 1982. 35.00 (ISBN 90-247-2710-3, Pub. by Martinus Nijhoff Netherlands). Kluwer Boston.

Satty, Wilfried, illus. The Illustrated Edgar Allan Poe. (Illus.). 1976. 15.00 (ISBN 0-517-52742-1, C N Potter Bks). Crown.

Satullo, Steven A., jt. ed. see Bittman, Sam.

Saturday Evening Post Editors. The American Story. LC 75-16576. (Illus.). 320p. 1975. 9.95 o.p. (ISBN 0-89387-000-5, Co-Pub by Sat Eve Post). Curtis Pub Co.

--Fantasy Voyages--Great Science Fiction from the Saturday Evening Post. LC 79-55717. 300p. 1979. 7.95 (ISBN 0-89387-036-6, Co-Pub by Sat Eve Post). Curtis Pub Co.

--Norman Rockwell Review. LC 79-90499. (Illus.). 144p. 1979. 13.95 (ISBN 0-89387-033-1, Co-Pub. by Sat Eve Post). Curtis Pub Co.

--The Perfect Squelch, Last Laughs from the Saturday Evening Post. LC 80-67061. (Illus.). 112p. 1980. 6.50 (ISBN 0-89387-042-0, Co-Pub. by Sat Eve Post). Curtis Pub Co.

--Post Scripts Humor from the Saturday Evening Post. LC 78-53039. (Illus.). 112p. 1978. 6.50 (ISBN 0-89387-022-6, Co-Pub. by Sat Eve Post). Curtis Pub Co.

--The Presidents. rev. ed. LC 79-57491. (Illus.). 160p. 1981. pap. 8.50 (ISBN 0-89387-061-7, Co-Pub. by Sat Eve Post). Curtis Pub Co.

--The Presidents, with a Special Ronald Reagan Supplement. LC 79-57491. (Illus.). 160p. 1980. 13.95 (ISBN 0-89387-038-2, Co-Pub. by Sat Eve Post). Curtis Pub Co.

--The Saturday Evening Post Animal Book. LC 78-5308. (Illus.). 160p. 1978. 13.95 (ISBN 0-89387-019-6, Co-Pub. by Sat Eve Post). Curtis Pub Co.

--The Saturday Evening Post Automobile Book. LC 77-9002. (Illus.). 160p. 1977. 13.95 (ISBN 0-89387-012-9, Co-Pub by Sat Eve Post). Curtis Pub Co.

--The Saturday Evening Post Book of the Sea & Ships. LC 78-61519. (Illus.). 160p. 1978. 13.95 (ISBN 0-89387-023-4, Co-Pub by Sat Eve Post). Curtis Pub Co.

--The Saturday Evening Post Christmas Book. LC 76-24034. (Illus.). 160p. 1976. 13.95 (ISBN 0-89387-001-3, Co-Pub by Sat Eve Post). Curtis Pub Co.

--The Saturday Evening Post Christmas for Children Book. LC 81-65816. (Illus.). 112p. (ps up). 1981. 9.95 (ISBN 0-89387-056-0, Co-Pub by Sat Eve Post). Curtis Pub Co.

--The Saturday Evening Post Christmas Stories. LC 80-67058. (Illus.). 144p. 1980. 13.95 (ISBN 0-89387-046-3, Co-Pub by Sat Eve Post). Curtis Pub Co.

--The Saturday Evening Post Family Album. LC 80-67059. (Illus.). 144p. 1980. padded leatherette with 4-color onlay 15.95 (ISBN 0-89387-047-1, Co-Pub. by Sat Eve Post). Curtis Pub Co.

--The Saturday Evening Post Family Cookbook. LC 74-18928. (Illus.). 160p. 1979. pap. 5.95 (ISBN 0-89387-030-7, Co-Pub. by Sat Eve Post). Curtis Pub Co.

--The Saturday Evening Post Family Dictionary. LC 81-65812. (Illus.). 1500p. Date not set. cancelled o.p. (ISBN 0-89387-057-9, Co-Pub. by Sat Eve Post). Curtis Pub Co.

--The Saturday Evening Post Family Records Book. LC 81-65815. (Illus.). 144p. 1981. padded leatherette with 4-color onlay 15.95 (ISBN 0-89387-055-2, Co-Pub. by Sat Eve Post). Curtis Pub Co.

--The Saturday Evening Post Movie Book. LC 77-85389. (Illus.). 160p. 1977. 13.95 (ISBN 0-89387-013-7, Co-Pub by Sat Eve Post); pap. 7.95 (ISBN 0-686-30102-1). Curtis Pub Co.

--The Saturday Evening Post Norman Rockwell Book. LC 77-12286. (Illus.). 160p. 1977. 13.95 (ISBN 0-89387-007-2, Co-Pub. by Sat Eve Post). Curtis Pub Co.

--The Saturday Evening Post Reflections of a Decade 1901-1910. LC 80-67053. (Illus.). 144p. 1980. 15.95 (ISBN 0-89387-044-7, Co-Pub. by Sat Eve Post). Curtis Pub Co.

--The Saturday Evening Post Reflections of a Decade 1911-1920. LC 81-65811. (Illus.). 144p. 1983. 15.95 (ISBN 0-89387-059-5, Co-Pub. by Sat Eve Post). Curtis Pub Co.

--The Saturday Evening Post Saga of the American West. LC 80-67057. (Illus.). 144p. 1980. 15.95 (ISBN 0-89387-043-9, Co-Pub. by Sat Eve Post). Curtis Pub Co.

--The Saturday Evening Post Vegetable Primer. Saturday Evening Post Editors, ed. LC 80-70885. (Illus.). 144p. (Orig.). 1982. pap. 5.95 (ISBN 0-89387-045-5, Co-Pub. by Sat Eve Post). Curtis Pub Co.

--A Treasury of the Saturday Evening Post. LC 75-16576. (Illus.). 320p. 1979. pap. 7.95 (ISBN 0-89387-029-3, Co-Pub. by Sat Eve Post). Curtis Pub Co.

--Where Do You Think You Are? Map Mysteries from the Saturday Evening Post. LC 80-70989. (Illus.). 96p. Date not set. cancelled o.p. (ISBN 0-89387-054-4, Co-Pub. by Sat Eve Post). Curtis Pub Co.

--You Be the Judge from the Saturday Evening Post. LC 79-53768. (Illus.). 112p. 1979. 6.50 (ISBN 0-89387-035-8, Co-Pub. by Sat Eve Post). Curtis Pub Co.

Saturday Evening Post Editors, jt. auth. see Turgeon, Charlotte.

Satyamurti, T. The Nataraja Temple: History, Art & Architecture. 1978. 10.00x o.p. (ISBN 0-8364-0234-0). South Asia Bks.

Satyanarayanan, M. Multiprocessors: A Comparative Study. (Illus.). 208p. 1980. text ed. 27.00 (ISBN 0-13-605154-5). P-H.

Satyaprakash. Guide to Indian Periodical Literature: 1969, Vol. 6. 1975. 45.00x o.p. (ISBN 0-88386-390-1). South Asia Bks.

Satz, H. Statistical Mechanics of Quarks & Hadrons. 1981. 68.00 (ISBN 0-444-86227-7). Elsevier.

Sau, Ranjit. Trade, Capital & Underdevelopment: Towards a Marxist Theory. (Illus.). 1982. 15.00x (ISBN 0-19-561209-4). Oxford U Pr.

Saucier, Gene A. Woodwinds: Fundamental Performance Techniques. LC 80-5223. (Illus.). 300p. 1981. pap. text ed. 15.95 (ISBN 0-02-872300-7). Schirmer Bks.

Saucier, Weems A. & Wendel, Robert L. Toward Humanistic Teaching in High School. 384p. 1975. pap. text ed. 8.95x o.p. (ISBN 0-669-90381-7). Heath.

Saucy, Robert L. Is the Bible Reliable? 1983. pap. 4.50 (ISBN 0-88207-106-8). Victor Bks.

Sauer, Barbara. Walk the Dinosaur Trial. LC 81-68314. 1981. pap. 3.95x (ISBN 0-89051-078-4); tchr's guide 2.95x (ISBN 0-686-33035-8). CLP Pubs.

Sauer, Carl O. Geography of the Ozark Highland of Missouri. LC 20-4650. (Illus.). 1969. Repr. of 1920 ed. lib. bdg. 21.00x (ISBN 0-8371-0644-3, SAOH). Greenwood.

--Land & Life: A Selection from the Writings of Carl Ortwin Sauer. Leighly, John, ed. LC 63-21069. (California Library Reprint Ser.). 1974. 37.50x (ISBN 0-520-02633-0); pap. 3.95 (ISBN 0-520-01124-4, CAL 132). U of Cal Pr.

--Land & Life: A Selection from the Writing of Carl Ortwin Sauer. Leighly, John, ed. LC 63-21069. (California Library Reprint Ser.: No. 117). 441p. 1982. 20.00x (ISBN 0-520-04762-1). U of Cal Pr.

--Northern Mists. LC 68-16757. (Illus.). 1968. 19.95 o.p. (ISBN 0-520-01126-0). U of Cal Pr.

--Sixteenth-Century North America: The Land & People As Seen by Europeans. LC 75-138635. 1971. 30.00x (ISBN 0-520-01854-0); pap. 4.95 (ISBN 0-520-02777-9). U of Cal Pr.

Sauer, Charles & Chandy, Mani K. Computer Systems Performance Modeling. (Illus.). 384p. 1981. text ed. 27.95 (ISBN 0-13-165175-7). P-H.

Sauer, Erich. Dawn of World Redemption. 1951. pap. 3.95 o.p. (ISBN 0-8028-1174-4). Eerdmans.

--In the Arena of Faith. 1955. pap. 3.95 o.p. (ISBN 0-8028-1173-6). Eerdmans.

Sauer, Gordon C. John Gould, the Bird Man: A Chronology & Bibliography. (Illus.). 416p. 1982. 65.00 (ISBN 0-7006-0230-5). Univ Pr KS.

Sauer, Harry, Jr., jt. auth. see Look, Dwight C., Jr.

Sauer, Helmut. Developmental Biology of Physarum. LC 81-21682. (Developmental & Cell Biology Ser.: No. 11). 250p. 1982. 59.50 (ISBN 0-521-22703-8). Cambridge U Pr.

Sauer, I. Eve's Little Friends. 1981. 8.95 (ISBN 0-07-054830-7). McGraw.

Sauer, J. J. & Howell, R. H. Heat Pumps Systems. 384p. 1983. 39.95 (ISBN 0-471-08178-7, Pub. by Wiley-Interscience). Wiley.

Sauer, Jonathan D. Cayman Islands Seashore Vegetation: A Study in Comparative Biogeography. LC 82-2608. (Publications in Geographical Sciences: Vol. 25). 166p. 1983. pap. 16.00x (ISBN 0-520-09656-8). U of Cal Pr.

--Plants & Man on the Seychelles Coast: A Study in Historical Biogeography. (Illus.). 148p. 1967. 21.50 o.p. (ISBN 0-299-04300-2). U of Wis Pr.

Sauer, Val J., Jr. The Eschatology Handbook: The Bible Speaks to Us about Endtimes. (Illus.). 180p. (Orig.). 1981. pap. 7.95 (ISBN 0-8042-0066-1). John Knox.

Sauerbeck, F., jt. auth. see Jaeger, A.

Sauerbier, Charles L. Marine Cargo Operations. (Materials Handling & Packaging Ser.). 548p. 1956. 49.95x (ISBN 0-471-75504-4, Pub. by Wiley-Interscience). Wiley.

Sauerbrey, W., jt. auth. see Nasemann, T.

Sauers, Richard A., compiled by. The Gettysburg Campaign, June Third to August First, Eighteen Sixty-Three: A Comprehensive, Selectively Annotated Bibliography. LC 82-6099. 288p. 1982. lib. bdg. 35.00 (ISBN 0-313-23231-8, SAG/). Greenwood.

Saugnier. Relations de Plusieurs Voyages a la Cote d'Afrique, au Maroc, au Senegal, en Goree, Galam, etc. avec des Details Interessants pour Ceux Qui Se Destinent a la Traite des Negres. l'Or, et de l'Ivoire etc. (Bibliotheque Africaine Ser.). 350p. (Fr.). 1974. Repr. of 1791 ed. lib. bdg. 91.00x o.p. (ISBN 0-8287-0761-8, 72-2118). Clearwater Pub.

Saul, Arthur K. One Hundred & Twenty One Ways Toward a More Effective Church Library. 204p. 1980. pap. 4.95 (ISBN 0-88207-171-8). Victor Bks.

Saul, George B. Winter's Many Minds. 1983. pap. 2.95 (ISBN 0-939736-41-1). Wings ME.

Saul, John. Punish the Sinners. 1978. pap. 3.95 (ISBN 0-440-17084-2). Dell.

Saul, John S., ed. The Transition to Socialism in Mozambique. 416p. 1983. 18.00 (ISBN 0-85345-591-0, CL5910). Monthly Rev.

Saul, LouElla. The North Pacific Cretaceous Trigoniid Genus Yaadia. (Publications in Geological Science Ser.: Vol. 119). 1978. pap. 15.00x (ISBN 0-520-09582-0). U of Cal Pr.

Saul, Nigel. A Companion to Medieval England. (Illus.). 320p. 1983. text ed. 27.50x (ISBN 0-389-20359-9). B&N Imports.

--Knights & Esquires: The Gloucestershire Gentry in the Fourteenth Century. (Oxford Historical Monographs). (Illus.). 1981. 44.00x (ISBN 0-19-821883-4). Oxford U Pr.

Saul, S. Aging: An Album of People Growing Old. 2nd ed. 200p. 1983. text ed. 12.50 (ISBN 0-471-87331-4). Wiley.

Saul, S. B., jt. auth. see Milward, Alan S.

Saul, Shura. Aging: An Album of People Growing Old. LC 73-21973. 174p. 1974. pap. text ed. 12.95 o.p. (ISBN 0-471-75506-0). Wiley.

Saul, Shura, ed. Groupwork with the Frail Elderly. LC 82-15600. (Social Work with Groups Ser.: Vol. 5, No. 2). 181p. 1983. text ed. 14.95 (ISBN 0-917724-77-1, B77). Haworth Pr.

Sauldie, Madan M. Ethiopia: The Dawn of the Red Star. 300p. 1983. text ed. 37.50 (ISBN 0-86590-093-0). Apt Bks.

--Foreign Powers in the Horn of Africa. 300p. 1983. text ed. 40.00 (ISBN 0-86590-092-2). Apt Bks.

Sauli, Judith P. Giovanni Boccaccio. (Twayne's World Authors Ser.: No. 644). 1982. lib. bdg. 15.95 (ISBN 0-8057-6487-9, Twayne). G K Hall.

Saulle, Maria R. NATO & Its Activities: A Political & Juridical Approach on Consultation. LC 78-68924. 1979. lib. bdg. 16.00 (ISBN 0-379-20459-2). Oceana.

Saulnier, Karen L., jt. ed. see Bornstein, Harry.

Saunders. Edible & Useful Wild Plants of the United States & Canada. LC 75-46193. (Illus.). 320p. 1976. pap. 4.50 (ISBN 0-486-23310-3). Dover.

--The Political Economy of New & Old Countries. 1981. text ed. 39.95 (ISBN 0-408-10774-X). Butterworth.

Saunders, jt. auth. see Moseley.

Saunders, A. E. Small Craft Piloting & Coastal Navigation. LC 81-71657. (Illus.). 287p. 1982. 19.95 (ISBN 0-686-82298-6). Van Nos Reinhold.

Saunders, Alta. The Literature of Business: Contemporary. 5th ed. LC 77-109303. xii, 453p. Repr. of 1946 ed. lib. bdg. 20.50x (ISBN 0-8371-3846-9, SALB). Greenwood.

Saunders, B. John Evelyn & His Times. 1970. 23.00 (ISBN 0-08-007118-X). Pergamon.

Saunders, Beatrice. Portraits of Genius. (Illus.). (YA) (gr. 10 up). 1959. 8.95 o.p. (ISBN 0-7195-1215-8). Transatlantic.

Saunders, Blanche. Training You to Train Your Dog. rev. ed. LC 65-15553. (Illus.). 1952. 14.95 (ISBN 0-385-04264-7). Doubleday.

Saunders, Boyd & Saunders, Stephanie, eds. The Etchings of James Fowler Cooper. (Illus.). 196p. 1982. 70.00 (ISBN 0-686-82615-9). U of SC Pr.

Saunders, Brigitte, jt. auth. see Erdsneker, Barbara.

Saunders, C. T. East & West in the Energy Squeeze. 1980. 36.00 (ISBN 0-312-22473-7). St Martin.

Saunders, C. T., ed. Industrial Policies & Technology Transfers Between East & West. (East-West European Economic Interaction,Workshop Paper: Vol 3). (Illus.). 1978. pap. 31.40 (ISBN 0-387-81456-6). Springer-Verlag.

Saunders, Charles, ed. How to Live & Die with Texas Probate. 4th ed. 1983. pap. 9.95 (ISBN 0-87201-835-0). Gulf Pub.

Saunders, Charles A., ed. see State Bar of Texas Real Estate, Probate & Trust Law Sec.

Saunders, Charles R. Imaro. 1981. pap. 2.50 (ISBN 0-87997-667-5, UE 1667). DAW Bks.

Saunders, Diro A., ed. Decline & Fall of the Roman Empire. Date not set. pap. price not set (ISBN 0-14-043189-6). Penguin.

Saunders, E. D., tr. see Abe, Kobo.

Saunders, E. Dale, tr. see Abe, Kobo.

Saunders, Ernest W. Searching the Scriptures: A History of the Society of Biblical Literature 1880-1980. LC 82-10818. (Society of Biblical Literature - Biblical Scholarship in North America Ser.). pap. 15.00 (ISBN 0-89130-591-2, 06-11-08). Scholars Pr CA.

Saunders, Frank & Southwood, James. Torn Lace Curtains. LC 82-9194. 1982. 13.45 (ISBN 0-03-060046-4). HR&W.

Saunders, George H. Dynamics of Helicopter Flight. LC 74-30261. (Illus.). 304p. 1975. 35.95 (ISBN 0-471-75509-5, Pub. by Wiley-Interscience). Wiley.

Saunders, Hal M., jt. auth. see Carman, Robert A.

Saunders, Harry, tr. see Beckenbauer, Franz.

Saunders, J. B., tr. see Da Vinci, Leonardo.

Saunders, J. H. & Frisch, K. C. High Polymers, Part 2, Vol.16. (Polyurethanes, Chemistry & Technology Ser.). 896p. 1982. Repr. of 1964 ed. lib. bdg. 62.50 (ISBN 0-89874-561-6). Krieger.

Saunders, J. V., tr. see Pirenne, Henri.

Saunders, Jeraldine. Cruise Diary. (Illus.). 1982. 9.95 (ISBN 0-686-84160-3). J P Tarcher.

--Frisco Lady. (Orig.). 1979. pap. 2.50 o.p. (ISBN 0-523-40408-5). Pinnacle Bks.

Saunders, Jeraldine & Ross, Harvey. Hypoglycemia: The Disease Your Doctor Won't Treat. 256p. (Orig.). 1980. pap. 3.50 (ISBN 0-523-41778-0). Pinnacle Bks.

Saunders, John, tr. see Pereira, Antonio O.

Saunders, John, et al. Rural Electrification & Development: Social & Economic Impact in Costa Rica & Columbia. 1978. lib. bdg. 25.00 (ISBN 0-89158-274-6). Westview.

Saunders, John T. & Henze, Donald F. Private-Language Problem: A Philosophical Dialogue. (Orig.). 1967. pap. text ed. 3.25 (ISBN 0-685-19755-7). Phila Bk Co.

Saunders, K. C. Social Stigma of Occupations. 240p. 1981. text ed. 31.25x (ISBN 0-566-00334-1). Gower Pub Ltd.

Saunders, K. J. Organic Polymer Chemistry. 1973. 32.00x (ISBN 0-412-10580-2, Pub. by Chapman & Hall). Methuen Inc.

Saunders, Laura. Strange Exile. (YA) 1972. 6.95 (ISBN 0-685-28624-X, Avalon). Bouregy.

Saunders, Leonard & Fleming, Robert. Mathematics & Statistics-for Use in the Biological & Pharmaceutical Science. 2nd ed. 320p. 1971. 12.50 o.p. (ISBN 0-85369-077-4, Pub. by Pharmaceutical). Rittenhouse.

Saunders, M. Health Visiting Practice. 1968. 12.00 o.p. (ISBN 0-08-012899-8); pap. 5.75 o.p. (ISBN 0-08-012898-X). Pergamon.

--Multicultural Teaching: A Guide for the Classroom. 192p. Date not set. 10.50 (ISBN 0-07-084133-0). McGraw.

--The Mystery in the Drood Family. LC 74-6448. (Studies in Dickens, No. 52). 1974. lib. bdg. 48.95x (ISBN 0-8383-1973-4). Haskell.

Saunders, M., tr. see Vercel, Roger.

Saunders, Michael. Developments in English Teaching. (Changing Classroom). 1976. text ed. 9.00x o.p. (ISBN 0-7291-0036-7); pap. text ed. 3.75x o.p. (ISBN 0-7291-0031-6). Humanities.

Saunders, N. F. Factory Organization & Management. 5th ed. 1973. 14.95x o.p. (ISBN 0-8464-0399-4). Beekman Pubs.

Saunders, P. F. Bridge with a Perfect Partner. 1976. pap. 7.95x (ISBN 0-87643-022-1). Barclay Bridge.

Saunders, P. J. Estimation of Pollution Damage. 1976. 21.50 (ISBN 0-7190-0629-5). Manchester.

Saunders, P. T. An Introduction to Catastrophe Theory. LC 79-54172. (Illus.). 1980. 27.50 (ISBN 0-521-23042-X); pap. 9.95 (ISBN 0-521-29782-6). Cambridge U Pr.

Saunders, Paul L. Edward Jenner: The Cheltenham Years, Seventeen Ninety-Five to Eighteen Twenty-Three; Being a Chronicle of the Vaccination Campaign. LC 81-51607. (Illus.). 489p. 1982. 27.50x (ISBN 0-87451-215-8). U Pr of New England.

Saunders, Peter E. & David, Michael, eds. Tribal Visions. (Illus.). 1981. pap. 35.00 (ISBN 0-686-95100-X). Museum Bks.

Saunders, Ray. Horsekeeping: Management, Ailments & Injuries. (Illus.). 116p. 1983. 12.95 (ISBN 0-8069-3750-5); pap. 6.95 (ISBN 0-8069-7626-8). Sterling.

--Horsekeeping: Ownership, Stabling & Feeding. (Illus.). 120p. 1982. 12.95 (ISBN 0-8069-3748-3); pap. 6.95 (ISBN 0-8069-7616-0). Sterling.

Saunders, Richard. The Railroad Mergers & the Coming of Conrail. LC 77-91095. (Contributions in Economics & Economic History Ser.: No. 19). (Illus.). 1978. lib. bdg. 29.95x (ISBN 0-313-20049-1, SRM/). Greenwood.

Saunders, Robert J. & Miernyk, William H. Programmed Review Guide & Workbook. 1971. pap. text ed. 4.50 (ISBN 0-685-55636-0, 31538). Phila Bk Co.

Saunders, Ronald. Read English, Bk. 6. (Speak English Ser.). (Illus.). 80p. (Orig.). 1983. pap. text ed. 4.95 (ISBN 0-88499-680-8). Inst Mod Lang.

Saunders, Rubie. Baby-Sitting: A Concise Guide. (Illus.). (gr. 7-9). 1974. pap. 1.50 (ISBN 0-671-56012-3). Archway.

--The Beauty Book. Barish, Wendy, ed. (Just for Teens). 160p. (gr. 10 up). 1983. pap. 3.50 (ISBN 0-671-46271-7). Wanderer Bks.

--The Beauty Book. (Teen Survival Library). (Illus.). 160p. (gr. 9-12). 1983. PLB 9.79 (ISBN 0-671-46743-3). Messner.

Saunders, Stephanie, jt. ed. see Saunders, Boyd.

Saunders, Susan. The Green Slime. (Choose Your Own Adventure Ser.: No. 6). 64p. (gr. 1-8). 1982. pap. 7.95 (ISBN 0-553-05032-X). Bantam.

--Wale's Tale. LC 79-21985. (Illus.). (gr. k-3). 1980. 8.95 o.p. (ISBN 0-670-74870-6). Viking Pr.

Saunders, Susan & Anderson, Ann M. Violent Individuals & Families: A Handbook for Practitioners. (Illus.). 256p. 1983. text ed. write for info (ISBN 0-398-04833-9). C C Thomas.

Saunders, W. L., ed. British Librarianship Today. 1978. pap. 12.50 o.p. (ISBN 0-85365-498-0, 6506). Gaylord Prof Pubns.

Saunders, William H., jt. auth. see DeWesse, David F.

Saunders, William H., et al. Atlas of Ear Surgery. 3rd ed. LC 79-5235. (Illus.). 436p. 1979. text ed. 64.50 (ISBN 0-8016-4318-X). Mosby.

Saunders, William H., Jr., jt. auth. see Melander, Lars.

Saunt. Revision Notes on Building Measurement. 1981. text ed. 9.95 o.p. (ISBN 0-686-31753-X). Butterworth.

Saunt, T. J. Revision Notes on Building Economics. text ed. 4.95 o.p. (ISBN 0-408-00163-1). Butterworth.

Saurat, D. Milton, Man & Thinker. LC 76-121151. (Studies in Milton, No. 22). 1970. Repr. of 1925 ed. lib. bdg. 39.95x (ISBN 0-8383-1093-1). Haskell.

Sauser, Jean & Shay, Arthur. Racquetball Strategy. 1979. pap. 6.95 (ISBN 0-8092-7365-9). Contemp Bks.

Sausmarez, Maurice de see De Sausmarez, Maurice.

Sauvage, Pierre, jt. auth. see Coursodon, J. P.

Sauvageau, C. Remarques Sur les Spacelariacees. 1971. Repr. of 1904 ed. 60.00 (ISBN 3-7682-0717-X). Lubrecht & Cramer.

--Sur Quelques Myrionemacees. 1897. Repr. 16.00 (ISBN 3-7682-0705-6). Lubrecht & Cramer.

Sauvageau, Juan. Stories That Must Not Die, Vol. 1. LC 75-36692. (Illus., Eng. & Span.). 1975. pap. 3.50 (ISBN 0-916378-00-4). PSI Res.

--Stories That Must Not Die, Vol. 2. LC 76-13770. (Illus., Eng. & Span.). 1976. pap. 3.50 (ISBN 0-916378-01-2). PSI Res.

--Stories That Must Not Die, Vol. 3. (Illus.). 1976. pap. 3.50 (ISBN 0-916378-02-0). PSI Res.

--Stories That Must Not Die, Vol. 4. (Illus.). (gr. k-12). 1978. pap. text ed. 3.50 (ISBN 0-916378-11-X). PSI Res.

Sauvain, Philip. Britain's Living Heritage. (Illus.). 128p. 1982. 19.95 (ISBN 0-7134-3813-4, Pub. by Batsford England). David & Charles.

Sauvani, Karl P. The Group of Seventy-Seven: Evolution, Structure, Organization. LC 81-3998. 232p. 1981. 22.50 (ISBN 0-379-00964-1); pap. 10.00 (ISBN 0-686-84382-7). Oceana.

Sauvant, K. & Hasenpflug, H. The New International Economic Order: Conflict or Cooperation Between North & South? LC 76-26623. 1977. lib. bdg. 28.75x o.p. (ISBN 0-89158-139-1); pap. 16.50 o.p. (ISBN 0-89158-288-6). Westview.

Sauvant, Karl P. The Third World Without Superpowers: The Collected Documents of the Group of 77, 6 vols. LC 80-29266. 1981. Vol. 1-6. lib. bdg. 50.00 ea. (ISBN 0-379-00969-2). Oceana.

Sauvant, Karl P. & Lavipour, Farid G., eds. Controlling Multinational Enterprises: Problems, Strategies, Counterstrategies. (Special Studies in International Economics). 335p. 1982. softcover 25.00x (ISBN 0-89158-020-4). Westview.

Sauve, Mary J. & Pecherer, Angela. Concepts & Skills in Physical Assessment. LC 76-20120. 1977. pap. text ed. 16.95 o.p. (ISBN 0-7216-7939-0). Saunders.

Sauver, Dennis St. see St. Sauver, Dennis.

Sauvigny, G. de Bertier de see De Bertier de Sauvigny, G. & Pinkney, David H.

Sauvy, Alfred. Les Principaux Demographes Francais Au XVIII Siecle, 12 vols. (Principal French Demographic Works of the 18th Century Ser.). (Fr.). 1976. Repr. of 1682 ed. lib. bdg. 295.00x set o.p. (ISBN 0-8287-1399-5). Clearwater Pub.

Sauzey, Francois, jt. auth. see Basagni, Fabio.

Sava, Samuel G. Learning Through Discovery for Young Children. 1975. 12.95 o.p. (ISBN 0-07-054963-X, P&RB). McGraw.

Savacool, John K., jt. auth. see Smith, Eunice C.

Savacool, John K., jt. ed. see Smith, Eunice C.

Savage, Beth, jt. auth. see Marzollo, Jean.

Savage, David. Education Laws Nineteen Seventy-Eight: A Guide to New Directions in Federal Aid. 120p. 1979. pap. 11.95 o.p. (ISBN 0-87545-015-6). Natl Sch PR.

Savage, Donald T. Money & Banking. LC 76-56134. 491p. 1977. text ed. 32.95 (ISBN 0-471-75519-2); tchr's manual 4.00 (ISBN 0-471-02578-X). Wiley.

Savage, Edward H. Police Records & Recollections or Boston by Daylight & Gaslight for Two Hundred & Forty Years. LC 74-154048. (Criminology, Law Enforcement, & Social Problems Ser.: No. 123). (Illus., With intro. & index added). 1970. Repr. of 1873 ed. 15.00x (ISBN 0-87585-123-1). Patterson Smith.

Savage, Elizabeth. Willowood. LC 78-7866. 1978. 7.95 o.p. (ISBN 0-316-77138-4). Little.

Savage, Eric, jt. auth. see Wallace, Frank R.

Savage, Ernest A. Old English Libraries. LC 68-26177. (Illus.). 1968. Repr. of 1912 ed. 40.00x (ISBN 0-8103-3179-9). Gale.

Savage, Gail, et al. Three New England Watercolor Painters. LC 74-21601. (Illus.). 72p. (Orig.). 1974. pap. 4.75x (ISBN 0-86559-016-8). Art Inst Chi.

Savage, George. Dictionary of Nineteenth Century Antiques & Later Objets D'art. LC 78-53435. (Illus.). 1979. 22.50 (ISBN 0-399-12209-5). Putnam Pub Group.

Savage, Helen, ed. Library of Congress Cataloging Service: Bulletins 1-125 with Index, 2 vols. LC 79-25343. 1980. 130.00x set (ISBN 0-8103-1103-8). Gale.

--Library of Congress Classification Schedules: Indexes to Class P Subclasses & to Their Additions & Changes Through 1978, 10 pts. 1700p. 1982. Set. pap. 500.00x (ISBN 0-8103-1607-2); Avail. individually. pap. write for info. Gale.

Savage, Henry, Jr. Discovering America, Seventeen Hundred to Eighteen Seventy-Five. Morris, Richard B. & Commager, Henry S., eds. LC 78-20113. (New American Nation Ser.). (Illus.). 1979. 21.10i (ISBN 0-06-013782-7, HarpT). Har-Row.

Savage, J. A. The Scroll of Time. 6.50 (ISBN 0-88172-120-4). Believers Bkshelf.

Savage, J. E. The Complexity of Computing. LC 76-27733. 391p. 1976. 39.95 (ISBN 0-471-75517-6). Wiley.

Savage, James E., ed. see Overbury, Thomas.

Savage, John. The Gay Astrologer. LC 80-10483. 1982. pap. 9.95 (ISBN 0-87949-184-1). Ashley Bks.

Savage, John, jt. auth. see Jenkins, Carol.

Savage, John F. Effective Communication: Language Arts in the Elementary School. LC 76-47700. 448p. 1977. text ed. 17.95 (ISBN 0-574-23090-4, 13-6090). SRA.

--Linguistics for Teachers. LC 72-97928. 1973. pap. text ed. 12.95 (ISBN 0-574-17965-8, 13-0965). SRA.

Savage, John H. Bank Audits & Examinations: A Detailed Step-by-Step Program for CPA's Bank Internal Auditors, Bank Directors & Bank Examiners. LC 72-97346. (Illus.). 206p. 1973. 32.00 o.p. (ISBN 0-87267-018-X). Bankers.

--Bank Audits & Examinations: A Detailed, Step-by-Step Program for CPA's, Bank Internal Auditor's, Bank Directors & Bank Examiners. 2nd ed. LC 79-17701. 1980. text ed. 43.00 (ISBN 0-87267-033-3). Bankers.

Savage, Lee. Aldo's Dog House: Drawing in Perspective. LC 78-8580. (Illus.). (gr. 2-6). 1978. 5.95 o.p. (ISBN 0-698-20458-1, Coward). Putnam Pub Group.

Savage, Lyn, ed. see Balka, Don.

Savage, Lyn, ed. see Bezuszka, Stanley, et al.

Savage, N. E. & Wood, R. S. Man & His Environment: General Science, Bk. 2. (Secondary Science Ser.). (Illus., Orig.). (gr. 8-11). 1972. pap. text ed. 7.95 (ISBN 0-7100-7209-0). Routledge & Kegan.

--Matter & Energy: General Science, Bk. 1. (Secondary Science Ser.). (gr. 8-11). 1972. pap. text ed. 7.95 (ISBN 0-7100-7076-4). Routledge & Kegan.

Savage, Paul L., jt. auth. see Gabriel, Richard A.

Savage, Robert C. Pocket Prayers: Seven Hundred & Seventy-Seven Ways to Pray. 1982. pap. 2.95 (ISBN 0-8423-4849-2). Tyndale.

Savage, Robert L., jt. auth. see Nimmo, Dan.

Savage, Stephen P. The Theories of Talcott Parsons. LC 80-13828. 1980. 26.00 (ISBN 0-312-79699-4). St Martin.

Savage, Teresa. The Chalkboard in the Kitchen: A Step-by-Step Program to Teach Your Preschooler to Read & Count. (Illus.). 288p. 1983. 15.95 (ISBN 0-89479-101-X). A & W Pubs.

Savage, Thomas. The Power of the Dog. 300p. 1982. pap. 5.95x (ISBN 0-941324-01-X). Van Vactor & Goodheart.

Savage, Tom V., jt. auth. see Armstrong, David G.

Savage, W. Sherman. Blacks in the West. LC 75-44657. (Contributions in Afro-American & African Studies: No. 23). 288p. (Orig.). 1976. lib. bdg. 27.50x (ISBN 0-8371-8775-3, SBW/). Greenwood.

--Blacks in the West. LC 75-44657. (Contributions in Afro-American & African Studies: No. 23). xvi, 230p. 1977. pap. text ed. 6.95 (ISBN 0-313-20161-7, SBW/). Greenwood.

Savage, William W., Jr. Singing Cowboys & All That Jazz: A Short History of Popular Music in Oklahoma. LC 82-17560. (Illus.). 200p. 1983. 14.95 (ISBN 0-8061-1648-X). U of Okla Pr.

Savageau, M. Biochemical Systems Analysis: A Study of Function & Design in Molecular Biology. 1976. 31.50 (ISBN 0-201-06738-2, Adv Bk Prog); pap. 24.50 (ISBN 0-201-06739-0, Adv Bk Prog). A-W.

Savalle, Don, jt. ed. see Jones, George F.

Savannah Junior Auxiliary. Savannah: Proud As A Peacock. Barker, Carol & Patrick, Lynn, eds. 320p. 1982. pap. 9.95 (ISBN 0-939114-45-3). Savannah Jr Aux.

Savary, Louis M., jt. auth. see Anderson.

Savary, Louis M., jt. auth. see Berne, Patricia H.

Savary, Louis M., jt. auth. see Linde, Shirley M.

Savas, E. S. The Organization & Efficiency of Solid Waste Collection. LC 76-43606. 320p. 1977. 18.95x o.p. (ISBN 0-669-01095-2). Lexington Bks.

--Privatizing the Public Sector. (Change in American Politics Ser.). 192p. 1982. 15.00 (ISBN 0-934540-15-2); pap. text ed. 8.95x (ISBN 0-934540-14-4). Chatham Hse Pubs.

Savas, E. S., ed. Alternatives for Delivering Public Services: Toward Improved Performance. LC 77-6335. 1977. lib. bdg. 20.50x o.p. (ISBN 0-89158-306-8). Westview.

Savasini, Jose A. Export Promotion: The Case of Brazil. LC 78-16883. (Praeger Special Studies). 1978. 24.95 o.p. (ISBN 0-03-041616-7). Praeger.

Savastano, G., jt. ed. see Dekker, L.

Save, M. A. & Massonnet, C. C. Plastic Analysis & Design of Plates, Shells & Disks. 1972. 85.00 (ISBN 0-444-10113-6, North-Holland). Elsevier.

Saveland, Robert N., ed. Handbook of Environmental Education with International Case Studies. LC 76-4659. 1976. 29.75 o.p. (ISBN 0-471-75535-4, Pub. by Wiley-Interscience). Wiley.

Savelle, Jerry. Energizing Your Faith. Date not set. pap. price not set (ISBN 0-89274-285-2, HH-285). Harrison Hse.

--Giving Birth to a Miracle. 60p. 1981. pap. 1.95 (ISBN 0-89274-171-6, HH-171). Harrison Hse.

--Giving: The Essence of Living. 87p. (Orig.). 1982. pap. 2.25 (ISBN 0-89274-250-X). Harrison Hse.

--If Satan Can't Steal Your Joy, He Can't Have Your Goods. 160p. 1983. pap. 2.95 (ISBN 0-686-83912-9). Harrison Hse.

--Living in Divine Prosperity. 256p. 1983. pap. 3.95 (ISBN 0-89274-247-X). Harrison Hse.

--Man's Crown of Glory. 96p. (Orig.). 1983. pap. 2.25 (ISBN 0-89274-169-4, HH-169). Harrison Hse.

--Nature of Faith. Date not set. pap. price not set (ISBN 0-89274-284-4, HH-284). Harrison Hse.

--Sharing Jesus Effectively. (Orig.). 1982. pap. 3.95 (ISBN 0-89274-251-8). Harrison Hse.

--Sowing in Famine. 32p. (Orig.). 1982. pap. 1.50 (ISBN 0-686-83911-0). Harrison Hse.

--Spirit of Might. 77p. 1982. pap. 2.25 (ISBN 0-89274-242-9, HH-242). Harrison Hse.

--Victory & Success Are Yours. 41p. (Orig.). 1982. pap. text ed. 1.75 (ISBN 0-89274-236-4, HH-236). Harrison Hse.

Saver, F. D., jt. ed. see Kramer, J. K.

Savers, Millicent E., tr. see Bresciani-Turroni, Constantino.

Savery, C. Meg Play Fair. 1970. pap. 1.50 (ISBN 0-87508-722-1). Chr Lit.

Save-Soderbergh, Torgny, ed. The Scandinavian Joint Expedition to Sudanese Nubia: The Rock Drawings, 2 pts, Vol. 1. (Illus.). 238p. Set. 55.00x (ISBN 0-8419-8800-5). Holmes & Meier.

--The Scandinavian Joint Expedition to Sudanese Nubia, Vol.5: Pharaonic New Kingdom Sites - The Pottery. 190p. 37.75x (ISBN 0-8419-8804-8). Holmes & Meier.

--The Scandinavian Joint Expedition to Sudanese Nubia, Vol. 3: Neolithic & A-Group Sites, 2 pts. 420p. 65.00x set (ISBN 0-686-81195-X). Holmes & Meier.

--The Scandinavian Joint Expedition to Sudanese Nubia, Vol. 8: Late Nubian Textiles. 87p. 25.00x (ISBN 0-8419-8807-2). Holmes & Meier.

--The Scandinavian Joint Expedition to Sudanese Nubia. Vol. 9: Human Remains. 139p. 20.00x (ISBN 0-8419-8808-0). Holmes & Meier.

Saveth, Edward N. American History & the Social Sciences. LC 64-20308. 1964. 18.00 (ISBN 0-02-927750-7). Free Pr.

Savetnick, Harold A. Plastisols & Organosols. 248p. 1983. text ed. write for info. (ISBN 0-89874-614-0). Krieger.

Saviano, Eugene & Winget, Lynn W. Two Thousand & One Spanish & English Idioms: 2001 Modismos Espanoles E Ingleses. rev. ed. LC 75-11955. 1983. pap. text ed. cancelled o.p. (ISBN 0-8120-2090-1). Barron.

Savicki, Victor & Brown, Rosemary S. Working with Troubled Children. LC 80-15953. 408p. 1981. text ed. 29.95 (ISBN 0-87705-087-2). Human Sci. Pr.

Savidan, L. Chromatography. 9.00x o.p. (ISBN 0-685-20565-7). Transatlantic.
Savigny, Friedrich Carl Von see Von Savigny, Friedrich Carl.
Savile, Anthony. The Test of Time: An Essay on Philosophical Aesthetics. 1982. 39.95x (ISBN 0-19-824590-4). Oxford U Pr.
Savilescu, S., ed. Computer Operation of Power Systems. 1976. 64.00 (ISBN 0-444-41431-2). Elsevier.
Saville, Anthony & Kavina, George. The Will of the People: Education in Nevada. 1977. pap. text ed. 11.00 o.p. (ISBN 0-8191-0162-1). U Pr of Amer.
Saville, Diana. Walled Gardens: Their Planting & Design. (Illus.). 168p. 1982. 42.00 (ISBN 0-7134-1494-4, Pub. by Batsford England). David & Charles.
Saville, Florence R. Real Food for Your Baby. LC 72-90402. 1973. 8.95 o.p. (ISBN 0-671-21475-6). S&S.
Saville, John, jt. ed. see Bellamy, Joyce M.
Saville, John, jt. ed. see Milband, Ralph.
Saville, John, jt. ed. see Miliband, Ralph.
Saville-Troike. Ethnography of Communication. (Language in Society Ser.). 260p. 1982. text ed. 27.50 (ISBN 0-8391-1764-7); pap. text ed. 22.95 (ISBN 0-8391-1763-9). Univ Park.
Saville-Troike, Muriel. Foundations for Teaching English As a 2nd Language: Theory & Method for Multicultural Education. 200p. 1976. pap. 11.95 (ISBN 0-13-329946-5). P-H.
--A Guide to Culture in the Classroom. LC 78-61039. 80p. 1978. pap. 6.75 (ISBN 0-89763-000-9). Natl Clearinghse Bilingual Ed.
Savin, Marion B., jt. ed. see Abrahams, Harold J.
Savin, William, jt. auth. see Gautreau, Ronald.
Savini, Tom. Grande Illusions: The Art & Technique of Special Make-up Effects. (Illus.). 136p. 1983. pap. 12.95 (ISBN 0-911137-00-9). Imagine.
Saviolo, Vincentio see Jackson, James L.
Savishinsky, Joel S. The Trail of the Hare. (Library of Anthropology Ser.). (Illus.). 286p. 1974. 30.00x (ISBN 0-677-04140-3). Gordon.
Savitch, Jessica. Anchorwoman. 176p. 1982. 12.95 (ISBN 0-399-12735-6). Putnam Pub Group.
Savitch, Marie. Marie Steiner-Von Sivers: Fellow Worker with Rudolf Steiner. Compton-Burnett, Juliet, tr. from Ger. (Illus.). 239p. 1967. 11.95 (ISBN 0-88010-057-5, Pub. by Steinerbooks). Anthroposophic.
Savitski, V. M., jt. auth. see Bassiouni, M. Cherif.
Savitt, Lynne. Lust in Twenty-Eight Flavors. LC 79-63970. (Illus., Orig.). 1979. pap. 3.00 (ISBN 0-915016-26-5). Second Coming.
--No Apologies. 48p. 1981. 4.00. Cardinal Pr.
Savitt, Sam, jt. auth. see Marlin, Herb.
Savitt, Sam, jt. auth. see Steinkraus, William.
Savitt, Sam, jt. auth. see Wilding, Suzanne.
Savitz, Harriet M. If You Can't Be the Sun, Be a Star. 1982. pap. 1.75 (ISBN 0-451-11755-7, Sig Vista). NAL.
--The Lionhearted. (Signet Young Adult Books). (RL 6). 1977. pap. 1.25 o.p. (ISBN 0-451-07364-9, Y7364, Sig). NAL.
--Run, Don't Walk. 1980. pap. 1.75 (ISBN 0-451-11488-4, AE1488, Sig). NAL.
--Run, Don't Walk. (gr. 7 up). 1979. PLB 8.90 s&l (ISBN 0-531-02897-6). Watts.
--Wait until Tomorrow. (Orig.). 1981. pap. 1.95 (ISBN 0-451-09780-7, J9780, Sig). NAL.
Savitz, Leonard D. Dilemmas in Criminology. 1967. pap. text ed. 13.50 (ISBN 0-07-054975-3, C). McGraw.
Savitz, Leonard D. & Johnston, Norman. Contemporary Criminology. LC 81-15975. 379p. 1982. pap. 12.95 (ISBN 0-471-08336-4). Wiley.
--Crime in Society. LC 78-806. 963p. 1978. pap. text ed. 26.95 (ISBN 0-471-03385-5). Wiley.
Savitz, Leonard D., jt. auth. see Johnston, Norman.
Savitz, Leonard D., jt. auth. see Lombroso-Ferrero, Gina.
Savon, Herve. Johann Adam Mohler: The Father of Modern Theology. LC 66-28321. 134p. pap. 1.50 o.p. (ISBN 0-8091-1961-7). Paulist Pr.
Savory, Roger M. Iran Under the Safavids. LC 78-73817. (Illus.). 300p. 1980. 37.50 (ISBN 0-521-22483-7). Cambridge U Pr.
Savory, Roger M., ed. Introduction to Islamic Civilization. LC 74-25662. 220p. 1976. 44.50 (ISBN 0-521-20777-0); pap. 12.95 (ISBN 0-521-09948-X). Cambridge U Pr.
Savory, T. H., jt. auth. see Sankey, J. P.
Savory, Teo, tr. see Queneau, Raymond.
Savoy, Gene. THe Miracle of the Second Advent: Emerging New Christianity & the Secret Church at Work in the World. 1983. text ed. 39.50 (ISBN 0-936202-04-1). Intl Comm Christ.
Savoy, Louis G. Savoy Heritage-1621 to the Present. 144p. 1983. 8.00 (ISBN 0-682-49955-2). Exposition.
Savvas, Minas, tr. see Ritsos, Yannis.
Sawamura, Kaichi, intro. by. Graphic Arts Japan, 1980-81, Vol. 22. LC 64-43886. 178p. (Orig.). 1981. pap. 35.00x o.p. (ISBN 0-8002-2760-3). Intl Pubns Serv.
--Graphic Arts Japan, 1981-82. 23rd ed. LC 64-43886. (Illus.). 170p. (Orig.). 1982. pap. 37.50x (ISBN 0-8002-3065-5). Intl Pubns Serv.
Sawaragi, Yoshikazu, et al. Statistical Decision Theory in Adaptive Control Systems. (Mathematics in Science & Engineering Ser: Vol. 39). 1967. 43.50 (ISBN 0-12-620350-4). Acad Pr.
Saward, Blanche C., jt. auth. see Caulfeild, S. F.
Saward, Blanche C., jt. auth. see Caulfield, Sophia F.
Saward, Susan. The Golden Age of Marie de' Medici. Harris, Ann S., ed. LC 82-2001. (Studies in Baroque Art History: No. 2). 334p. 1982. 44.95 (ISBN 0-8357-1307-5, Pub. by UMI Res Pr). Univ Microfilms.
Sawatsky, John. For Services Rendered: Leslie James Bennett & the RCMP Security Service. LC 82-45272. (Illus.). 320p. 1983. 22.95 (ISBN 0-385-17660-0). Doubleday.
Sawatzky, Harry L. They Sought a Country: Mennonite Colonization in Mexico. LC 78-92673. 1971. 37.50x (ISBN 0-520-01704-8). U of Cal Pr.
Sawatzky, Jasper J. & Chen, Shu-Jen. Programming in Basic-Plus. LC 80-27869. 273p. 1981. pap. 17.95 (ISBN 0-471-07729-1); sol. man. avail. (ISBN 0-471-86867-1). Wiley.
Sawer, David, jt. auth. see Miller, Ronald E.
Sawers, Larry, jt. ed. see Tabb, William K.
Sawey, Orlan. Bernard De Voto. (United States Authors Ser.). 13.95 (ISBN 0-8057-0200-8, Twayne). G K Hall.
--Charles Siringo. (United States Authors Ser.). 1981. 13.95 (ISBN 0-8057-7312-6, Twayne). G K Hall.
Sawhill, Isabel V., jt. ed. see Palmer, John L.
Sawicki, E., jt. auth. see Mulik, J. D.
Sawicki, Eugene, ed. Handbook of Enviromental Genotoxicology: Dictionary of Environ Gene, Vol. I. (Handbook Ser.). 336p. 1982. 69.50 (ISBN 0-8493-3401-2). CRC Pr.
Sawicki, Eugene, et al, eds. Ion Chromatographic Analysis of Environmental Pollutants, Vol. 1. LC 77-92589. 1978. 47.50 (ISBN 0-250-40211-4). Ann Arbor Science.
Sawicki, Marianne. Faith & Sexism: Guidelines for Religious Educators. 112p. 1979. pap. 3.95 (ISBN 0-8164-0105-5). Seabury.
Sawin, Dwight H. Microprocessors & Microcomputer Systems. 288p. 1977. 25.95x (ISBN 0-669-00564-9). Lexington Bks.
Sawin, Lewis, ed. see Meredith, George & Sutro, Alfred.
Sawin, Nancy C. & Perkins, Esther R. Backroading Through Cecil County, Maryland. (Illus.). 71p. 1977. pap. 11.75 (ISBN 0-686-36654-9). Md Hist.
Sawistowski, H. & Smith, W. Mass Transfer Process Calculations. LC 62-21630. (Chemical Engineering Ser: Vol. 2). (Illus.). 1963. 26.00 o.p. (ISBN 0-471-75554-0, Pub. by Wiley). Krieger.
Sawitz, Mike. Fit As a Fiddle. (gr. 1-8). 1981. 4.95 (ISBN 0-86653-007-X, GA 235). Good Apple.
Sawkins, F. J., et al. Evolving Earth. 2nd ed. 1978. 24.95x (ISBN 0-02-406510-2, 40651). Macmillan.
Sawko, F., ed. Developments in Prestressed Concrete, 2 vols, Vol. 1. (Illus.). 1978. Vol. 1. 49.25x (ISBN 0-85334-790-5, Pub. by Applied Sci England); Vol. 2. 30.75x (ISBN 0-85334-811-1). Elsevier.
Sawko, F., jt. auth. see Cope, R.
Sawmill Clinic, 3rd, Portland, Oregon, Feb.1974. Modern Sawmill Techniques Vol. 3: Proceedings. White, Vernon S., ed. LC 73-88045. (Sawmill Clinic Library: A Forest Industries Bk.). (Illus.). 327p. 1974. 29.50 o.p. (ISBN 0-87930-026-4). Miller Freeman.
Sawmill Clinic, 4th, New Orleans, Nov. 1974. Modern Sawmill Techniques Vol. 4: Proceedings. Lambert, Herbert G., ed. LC 73-88045. (Sawmill Clinic Library: A Forest Industries Bk.). (Illus.). 296p. 1975. 29.50 o.p. (ISBN 0-87930-039-6). Miller Freeman.
Sawrey, James, jt. auth. see Telford, Charles W.
Sawusch, Mark. One Thousand One Things to Do with Your Personal Computer. (Illus.). 336p. (Orig.). 1980. 13.95 (ISBN 0-8306-9963-5); pap. 9.95 (ISBN 0-8306-1160-6, 1160). TAB Bks.
Sawvel, Franklin R., ed. see Jefferson, Thomas.
Sawyer. Epithelial-Mesenchymal Interactions. 270p. 1983. 32.95 (ISBN 0-03-060326-9). Praeger.
Sawyer, Alex. In a Time Meant for Love. LC 80-65678. 1980. 9.95 o.p. (ISBN 0-89754-017-4); pap. 2.95 o.p. (ISBN 0-89754-016-6). Dan River Pr.
Sawyer, Carolyn, ed. see Center for Business & Economic Research.
Sawyer, Clair & McCarty, Perry L. Chemistry for Environmental Engineering. 3rd ed. (Water Resources & Environmental Engineering Ser). (Illus.). 1978. text ed. 34.95 (ISBN 0-07-054971-0, C). McGraw.
Sawyer, David. Vibrations. LC 76-11499. (The Resources of Music Series). (Illus.). 1978. 10.95 (ISBN 0-521-20812-2). Cambridge U Pr.
Sawyer, Donald T. & Roberts, Julian L., Jr. Experimental Electrochemistry for Chemists. LC 74-3235. 435p. 1974. 33.95x (ISBN 0-471-75560-5, Pub. by Wiley-Interscience). Wiley.
Sawyer, Frank. Nymphs & the Trout. (Sportsman's Classics Ser.). 272p. 1973. 5.95 o.p. (ISBN 0-517-50336-0). Crown.
Sawyer, George. Business & Society: Managing Corporate & Social Impact. LC 78-69570. (Illus.). 1979. text ed. 23.95 (ISBN 0-395-26541-X); instr's. manual o.p. (ISBN 0-395-26534-7). HM.
Sawyer, Howard G. Business-to-Business Advertising. LC 78-72289. 1978. 21.95 (ISBN 0-87251-034-4). Crain Bks.
Sawyer, J. A., ed. Modelling the International Transmission Mechanism. (Contributions to Economic Analysis Ser.: Vol. 121). 1979. 72.50 (ISBN 0-444-85223-9, North Holland). Elsevier.
Sawyer, Jack, jt. ed. see Pleck, Joseph H.
Sawyer, Jesse. Studies in American Indian Languages. (California Library Reprint). 1974. 31.50x (ISBN 0-520-02525-3). U of Cal Pr.
Sawyer, John. The Dusty Heroes. (Illus.). 1978. 24.95 o.p. (ISBN 0-915088-16-9). C Hungness.
Sawyer, John F. A Modern Introduction to Biblical Hebrew. (Orig.). 1976. pap. 14.00 (ISBN 0-85362-159-4, Oriel). Routledge & Kegan.
Sawyer, John W., ed. Sawyer's Gas Turbine Engineering Handbook, 3 Vols. Incl. Vol. I. Theory & Design. 42.50 (ISBN 0-937506-05-2); Vol. II. Applications. 42.50 (ISBN 0-937506-06-0). LC 74-140403. 1976. Set. 85.00x (ISBN 0-937506-04-4). Turbo Intl Pubn.
Sawyer, John W. & Hallberg, Kurt, eds. Sawyer's Turbomachinery Maintenance Handbook, 3 vols. LC 80-53539. (Illus.). 1060p. 1981. Set. 127.50x (ISBN 0-937506-03-6). Turbo Intl Pubn.
--Sawyer's Turbomachinery Maintenance Handbook: Gas Turbines - Turbocompressors. (Illus.). 375p. 1980. 42.50x (ISBN 0-937506-01-X). Turbo Intl Pubn.
--Sawyer's Turbomachinery Maintenance Handbook: Steam Turbines - Power Recovery Turbines. (Illus.). 350p. 1981. 42.50x (ISBN 0-937506-00-1). Turbo Intl Pubn.
--Sawyer's Turbomachinery Maintenance Handbook, Vol. III: Support Services & Equipment. (Illus.). 340p. 1981. 42.50x (ISBN 0-937506-02-8). Turbo Intl Pubn.
Sawyer, Malcolm C. Macro-Economics in Question: The Keynesian-Monetarist Orthodoxies & the Kaleckian Alternative. LC 82-3221. 224p. 1982. 25.00 (ISBN 0-87332-218-5); pap. 14.95 (ISBN 0-87332-220-7). M E Sharpe.
--Theories of the Firm. LC 79-14662. 1979. 22.50x (ISBN 0-312-79703-6). St Martin.
Sawyer, Michael E., compiled by. A Bibliographical Index of Five English Mystics: Richard Rolle, Julian of Norwich, The Author of the Cloud of Unknowing, Walter Hilton, Margery Kempe. LC 73-110788. 1978. 10.00 (ISBN 0-931222-09-5). Pitts Theolog.
Sawyer, P. H. From Roman Britain to Norman England. LC 78-17640. 1979. 26.00x (ISBN 0-312-30783-7). St Martin.
Sawyer, Ruth. Journey Cake, Ho! (Illus.). (gr. k-3). 1953. PLB 9.95 (ISBN 0-670-40943-X). Viking Pr.
--Maggie Rose. (Illus.). (gr. 3-6). 1952. PLB 9.89 (ISBN 0-06-025201-4, HarpJ). Har-Row.
--Roller Skates. 1981. pap. 14.95 (ISBN 0-670-60310-4). Viking Pr.
Sawyer, W. W. Engineering Approach to Linear Algebra. LC 70-184143. (Illus.). 350p. 1972. text ed. 32.50x (ISBN 0-521-08476-8). Cambridge U Pr.
--Prelude to Mathematics. (Popular Science Ser.). 224p. 1983. pap. 4.50 (ISBN 0-486-24401-6). Dover.
Sawyers, Phyllis & Henry, Frances L. Song of the Coyote: Freeing the Imagination Through the Arts. (Illus.). 173p. (Orig.). 1980. pap. text ed. 21.95x (ISBN 0-89641-036-6). American Pr.
Sax, Gilbert. Foundations of Educational Research. 2nd ed. 1979. 26.95 (ISBN 0-13-329300-9). P-H.
--Principles of Educational & Psychological Measurement & Evaluation. 2nd ed. 704p. 1980. text ed. 25.95x (ISBN 0-534-00832-1); wkbk 8.95x (ISBN 0-534-00833-X). Wadsworth Pub.
Sax, Joseph L. Mountains Without Handrails: Reflections on the National Parks. 160p. 1980. 12.50x (ISBN 0-472-09324-X); pap. 5.95 (ISBN 0-472-06324-3). U of Mich Pr.
Sax, Richard & Ricketts, David. Cooking Great Meals Every Day: Techniques, Recipes & Variations. 320p. 1982. 15.95 (ISBN 0-394-51601-X). Random.
Saxberg, Borje O., jt. auth. see Knowles, Henry P.
Saxby, Graham. The Focalguide to Slides. (Focalguide Ser.). (Illus.). 1979. pap. 7.95 (ISBN 0-240-51004-6). Focal Pr.
Saxe, Leonard, jt. auth. see Bar-Tal, Daniel.
Saxe, Leonard, ed. Making Evaluations Useful to Congress. LC 81-48578. 1982. 7.95x (ISBN 0-87589-916-1, PE-14). Jossey-Bass.
Saxe, Richard. Educational Administration Today: An Introduction. LC 79-91196. 1980. 20.75 (ISBN 0-8211-1858-7); text ed. 18.60 10 or more copies (ISBN 0-686-65584-2). McCutchan.
--Opening the Schools: Alternative Ways of Learning. LC 78-190056. 1972. 22.75 o.p. (ISBN 0-8211-1851-X); text ed. 20.50x o.p. (ISBN 0-685-24961-1). McCutchan.
--School Community Interaction. LC 74-13595. 288p. 1975. 21.75x (ISBN 0-685-52301-2); text ed. 19.50x (ISBN 0-685-52302-0). McCutchan.
Saxe, Richard W., jt. auth. see Dickson, George E.
Saxena, Brij B., et al. Gonadotropins. LC 73-38948. 830p. 1972. 46.50 o.p. (ISBN 0-471-75570-2, Pub. by Wiley). Krieger.
Saxena, Jitendra, ed. Hazard Assessment of Chemicals, Vol. 2. (Serial Publication). 332p. 1983. price not set (ISBN 0-12-312402-6). Acad Pr.
Saxena, S. C. Namibia: Challenge to the United Nations. 15.00 o.p. (ISBN 0-8364-0108-5). South Asia Bks.
Saxena, S. K. Aesthetical Essays: Studies in Aesthetics; Hindustani Music & Kathak Dance. 1982. 18.00x (ISBN 0-8364-0898-5, Pub. by Chanakya). South Asia Bks.
Saxena, Sateshwari. Educational Planning in India: A Study in Approach & Methodology. LC 79-900462. (Illus.). 202p. 1979. 14.00x (ISBN 0-8002-0394-1). Intl Pubns Serv.
Saxon, Arthur H. Selected Letters of P. T. Barnum. LC 82-12843. (Illus.). 360p. 1983. 19.95 (ISBN 0-231-05412-2). Columbia U Pr.
Saxon, J. & Englander, W. ANS COBOL Programming. 2nd ed. 1978. pap. text ed. 16.95 (ISBN 0-13-037770-8). P-H.
Saxon, James A. & Fritz, Robert E. Beginning Programming with ADA. 240p. 1983. pap. text ed. 16.95 (ISBN 0-686-38833-X). P H.
Saxon, John H. Algebra One & Half: An Incremental Development. 1983. text ed. 15.94 (ISBN 0-939798-03-4). Grassdale.
Saxon, John H., Jr. Algebra: An Incremental Approach, Vol. I. (Illus.). 1980. pap. 19.95 ref. ed. (ISBN 0-13-021600-3). P-H.
--Algebra: An Incremental Approach, Vol. II. (Illus.). 1980. 19.95 (ISBN 0-13-021618-6). P-H.
--Algebra Half: An Incremental Development. 1983. text ed. 13.18 (ISBN 0-939798-05-0); tchr's ed. 13.18 (ISBN 0-939798-06-9). Grassdale.
--Algebra I: An Incremental Development. 462p. 1982. tchr's. ed 14.51 (ISBN 0-939798-02-6). Grassdale.
Saxon, Lyle. Fabulous New Orleans. (Illus.). 1950. 12.50 o.p. (ISBN 0-685-08691-7). Pelican.
Saxov, Svend, jt. ed. see Bott, Martin H.
Saxton, Dolores. Mosby's AssessTest for Evaluation of Basic Professional Nursing Knowledge. (Illus.). 86p. 1982. pap. text ed. 19.95 (ISBN 0-8016-4326-0). Mosby.
Saxton, Dolores F. & Hyland, Patricia A. Planning & Implementing Nursing Intervention: Stress & Adaptation Applied to Patient Care. 2nd ed. LC 78-31818. (Illus.). 1979. pap. 11.95 (ISBN 0-8016-4337-6). Mosby.
Saxton, Dolores F., et al. Programmed Instruction in Arithemetic, Dosages, & Solutions. 5th ed. LC 81-18766. (Illus.). 84p. pap. text ed. 9.95 (ISBN 0-8016-4327-9). Mosby.
Saxton, Dolores F., et al, eds. Mosby's Comprehensive Review of Nursing. 10th ed. LC 80-26510. (Illus.). 690p. 1981. text ed. 16.95 (ISBN 0-8016-3530-6). Mosby.
Saxton, J. Edwin. Monoterpenoid Indole Alkaloids, Part 4. (Chemistry of Heterocyclic Compounds Monographs). 1000p. 1983. 200.00 (ISBN 0-471-89748-5). Ronald Pr.
Saxton, Lloyd. Individual, Marriage & the Family. 4th ed. 672p. 1980. text ed. 21.95x (ISBN 0-534-00799-6); study guide 7.95x (ISBN 0-534-00800-3). Wadsworth Pub.
--The Individual, Marriage, & the Family. 5th ed. 512p. 1982. text ed. 22.95x (ISBN 0-534-01003-2). Wadsworth Pub.
Saxton, Martha. The Fifties. Weiss, Jeffrey, ed. (Illus.). 144p. 1975. pap. 4.95 (ISBN 0-8256-4195-0, Quick Fox). Putnam Pub Group.
--The Twenties. Weiss, Jeffrey, ed. LC 75-32890. (Illus.). 144p. (Orig.). 1976. pap. 5.95 (ISBN 0-8256-4197-7, Quick Fox). Putnam Pub Group.
Saxton, Martha & Williams, Gordon. Love Songs. LC 76-8067. 1976. pap. 5.95 (ISBN 0-8256-4199-3, Quick Fox). Putnam Pub Group.
Saxton, W. O. & Cavendish Laboratory, Electron Microscopy Section. Computer Techniques for Image Processing in Electron Microscopy: Supplement 10 to Advances in Electronics & Electron Physics. 1978. 45.50 (ISBN 0-12-014570-7). Acad Pr.
Say, Allen. The Bicycle Man. (Illus.). (gr. k-3). 1982. PLB 12.45 (ISBN 0-395-32254-5); 11.95. HM.
Say, Jean-Baptiste. Olbie: Ou Essai sur les Moyens de Reformer les Moeurs d'une Nation. (Utopias in the Enlightenment Ser.). 141p. (Fr.). 1974. Repr. of 1800 ed. lib. bdg. 44.00x o.p. (ISBN 0-8287-0763-4, 055). Clearwater Pub.
Sayce, Olive. The Medieval German Lyric, Eleven Fifty-Thirteen Hundred: The Development of Its Themes & Forms in Their European Context. 540p. 1982. 83.00x (ISBN 0-19-815772-X). Oxford U Pr.
Sayce, Roderick U. Primitive Arts & Crafts. (Illus.). 1963. Repr. of 1933 ed. 10.00x (ISBN 0-8196-0124-1). Biblo.
Saye, Albert & Allums, John. Principles of American Government. 9th ed. (Illus.). 368p. 1982. pap. text ed. 15.95 (ISBN 0-13-701110-5). P-H.
Saye, Albert B. American Constitutional Law: Cases & Text. 2nd ed. LC 78-20883. 597p. 1979. text ed. 19.95 (ISBN 0-8299-2028-5). West Pub.
Sayegh, Lily. Arabic Handwriting Workbook. 1982. 4.95x (ISBN 0-917062-03-5); book & cassette 15.00x (ISBN 0-686-86193-0). Intl Bk Ctr.
Sayer, jt. auth. see Latimer.
Sayer, James E. Guide to Confident Public Speaking. LC 82-8080. 150p. 1983. text ed. 16.95x (ISBN 0-88229-734-1); pap. text ed. 8.95x (ISBN 0-88229-808-9). Nelson-Hall.
Sayer, M. S., tr. see Hausen, Helmuth.

Sayer, Shannon. Orchids for Hilary. (YA) 1978. 6.95 (ISBN 0-685-19064-1, Avalon). Bouregy.
--Summer of Pearls. (YA) 1979. 6.95 (ISBN 0-685-95879-5, Avalon). Bouregy.
Sayer, Staurt. Introduction to Macroeconomic Policy. 320p. 1982. text ed. 17.95 (ISBN 0-408-10779-0). Butterworth.
Sayers, B. M., et al. Engineering in Medicine. (Science & Engineering Policy Ser.). (Illus.). 1975. text ed. 11.95x o.p. (ISBN 0-19-858315-X). Oxford U Pr.
Sayers, Dorothy. Lord Peter. 1972. pap. 6.95 o.p. (ISBN 0-380-01694-X, 59683-0). Avon.
Sayers, Dorothy L. Busman's Honeymoon. 1968. pap. 2.95 (ISBN 0-380-01076-3, 62489-3). Avon.
--Clouds of Witness. LC 55-10717. 1956. 14.37i (ISBN 0-06-013770-3, HarpT). Har-Row.
--Five Red Herrings. 1968. pap. 2.95 (ISBN 0-380-01187-5, 62109-6). Avon.
--Five Red Herrings. LC 58-8894. 1958. 14.37i (ISBN 0-06-013775-4, HarpT). Har-Row.
--Further Papers on Dante. LC 79-13588. 1980. Repr. of 1957 ed. lib. bdg. 21.00x (ISBN 0-313-22005-0, SAFP). Greenwood.
--Gaudy Night. 1970. pap. 3.50 (ISBN 0-380-01207-3, 62513). Avon.
--Gaudy Night. LC 60-9117. 1960. 14.37i (ISBN 0-06-013780-0, HarpT). Har-Row.
--Have His Carcase. (Reader's Request Ser.). 1980. lib. bdg. 17.95 (ISBN 0-8161-3043-4, Large Print Bks). G K Hall.
--In the Teeth of the Evidence. pap. 2.95 (ISBN 0-380-01280-4, 62943-7). Avon.
--Lord Peter Views the Body. 1969. pap. 2.50 (ISBN 0-380-00946-3, 62075-8). Avon.
--The Man Born to Be King. 1970. pap. 6.95 o.p. (ISBN 0-8028-1329-1). Eerdmans.
--A Matter of Eternity. Sprague, Rosamond K., ed. 128p. 1973. 2.95 o.p. (ISBN 0-8028-1681-9). Eerdmans.
--The Mind of the Maker. LC 78-19503. 1979. pap. 6.68i (ISBN 0-06-067071-1, RD 295, HarpR). Har-Row.
--Murder Must Advertise. (Reader's Request Ser.). 1980. lib. bdg. 15.95 (ISBN 0-8161-3045-0, Large Print Bks). G K Hall.
--The Nine Tailors. LC 34-6048. (Modern Classic Ser.). (gr. 10 up). 11.95 (ISBN 0-15-165897-8). HarBraceJ.
--Strong Poison. (Reader's Request Ser.). 1980. lib. bdg. 15.95 (ISBN 0-8161-3042-6, Large Print Bks). G K Hall.
--Strong Poison. LC 68-28234. 1958. 13.41i (ISBN 0-06-013795-9, HarpT). Har-Row.
--Two Plays About God & Man: With Plans for Amateur Production. LC 77-70559. 1977. pap. 3.00 (ISBN 0-8164-0907-2). Seabury.
--Unpleasantness at the Bellona Club. 1967. pap. 2.50 (ISBN 0-380-01597-8, 62257-2). Avon.
--Whose Body? 1961. pap. 2.50 (ISBN 0-380-00897-1, 62240-8). Avon.
Sayers, Janet. Biological Politics: Feminist & Anti-Feminist Perspectives. 1982. 23.00x (ISBN 0-422-77870-2, Pub. by Tavistock); pap. 9.95x (ISBN 0-422-77880-X). Methuen Inc.
Sayers, R. S. The Bank of England: 1891-1944. LC 75-46116. 1976. 185.00 set (ISBN 0-521-21475-0); Vol. 1. (ISBN 0-521-21067-4); Vol. 2. (ISBN 0-521-21068-2); Vol. 3 (appendixes) (ISBN 0-521-21066-6). Cambridge U Pr.
Sayers, Richard S. Central Banking after Bagehot. LC 82-18693. 149p. 1982. Repr. of 1957 ed. lib. bdg. 29.75x (ISBN 0-313-23743-3, SACB). Greenwood.
Sayers, Robert. Fathering: It's Not the Same. (Illus.). 95p. 1983. pap. 10.95 (ISBN 0-686-38770-8). Nurtury Fam.
Sayigh, A. A. Solar Energy Application in Buildings. LC 78-67882. 1979. 55.00 (ISBN 0-12-620860-3). Acad Pr.
Sayigh, Rosemary. Palestinians: From Peasants to Revolutionaries. 206p. (Orig.). 1979. 31.00 (ISBN 0-905762-24-X, Pub. by Zed Pr England); pap. 8.50 (ISBN 0-905762-25-8, Pub. by Zed Pr England). Lawrence Hill.
Sayigh, Yusif. The Determinants of Arab Economic Development. LC 77-3846. 1978. 18.95x o.p. (ISBN 0-312-19583-4). St Martin.
--The Economies of the Arab World: Development Since 1945. LC 77-3844. 1978. 70.00x (ISBN 0-312-22690-X). St Martin.
Sayler, Mary H. Bible-Times Activity Book. (Pelican Activity Ser.). pap. 0.89 o.p. (ISBN 0-8010-8172-6). Baker Bk.
--Downhill Flats. LC 81-67373. (gr. 5-8). 1982. pap. 5.95 (ISBN 0-8054-4805-5). Broadman.
--Why Are You Home, Dad? (gr. 1-6). 1983. 4.95 (ISBN 0-8054-4276-6). Broadman.
Sayler, Oliver M. Inside the Moscow Art Theatre. Repr. of 1925 ed. lib. bdg. 19.25x (ISBN 0-8371-4014-5, SAMA). Greenwood.
--Our American Theatre. Repr. of 1923 ed. lib. bdg. 18.75x (ISBN 0-8371-4015-3, SAAT). Greenwood.
Sayles, E. B., et al. The Cochise Cultural Sequence in Southeastern Arizona. (Anthropological Papers: No. 42). 1983. pap. 12.95x (ISBN 0-8165-0806-2). U of Ariz Pr.
Sayles, Leonard & Strauss, G. Human Behavior in Organizations. 1966. ref. ed. 23.00 (ISBN 0-13-444703-4). P-H.
Sayles, Leonard, jt. auth. see Wegner, Robert.
Sayles, Leonard R. Leadership, What Effective Managers Really Do & How They Do It: Effective Behavioral Skills. (Management Ser.). (Illus.). 1979. text ed. 23.95 (ISBN 0-07-055012-3, C); pap. text ed. 12.95 (ISBN 0-07-055011-5). McGraw.
--Managerial Behavior: Administration in Complex Organizations. 2nd ed. LC 78-31454. 312p. 1979. lib. bdg. 16.50 (ISBN 0-88275-854-3). Krieger.
Sayles, Leonard R., jt. auth. see Dowling, William F.
Sayles, Leonard R., jt. auth. see Strauss, George.
Sayles, S., jt. auth. see Hall, C.
Sayles, Stephen P. Clair Engle: The Forging of a Public Servant: A Study of Sacramento Valley Politics, 1933-1944. (ANCRR Occasional Publication: No. 1). 1976. 6.00 (ISBN 0-686-38940-9). Assn NC Records.
Saylor, Dennis. Songs in the Night, S.C. 8.00 (ISBN 0-686-71747-3). Palos Verdes.
Saylor, Henry H. Dictionary of Architecture. LC 52-8260. 221p. 1952. pap. 11.95 (ISBN 0-471-75601-6). Wiley.
Saylor, William L. & Ames, Thomas E. Dosage Calculations in Radiation Therapy. LC 79-18920. (Illus.). 112p. 1979. spiral bdg. 19.50 (ISBN 0-8067-1841-2). Urban & S.
Saypol, Judyth & Wikler, Madeline. My Very Own Haggadah. Rev. ed. (Illus.). 32p. (ps-4). pap. text ed. 2.50 (ISBN 0-930494-23-7). Kar Ben.
Saypol, Judyth & Wikler, Madeline, illus. My Very Own Simchat Torah. (gr. k-6). 1981. pap. 2.95 (ISBN 0-930494-11-3). Kar Ben.
Saypol, Judyth R. & Wikler, Madeline. Come Let Us Welcome Shabbat. (Illus.). (gr. k-6). 1978. pap. 2.95 (ISBN 0-930494-04-0). Kar Ben.
--My Very Own Chanukah Book. LC 77-23682. (Illus.). (gr. k-5). 1977. pap. 2.95 (ISBN 0-930494-03-2). Kar-Ben.
--My Very Own Shavuot Book. (Illus.). 32p. (gr. k-6). 1982. pap. 2.95 (ISBN 0-930494-15-6). Kar Ben.
--My Very Own Yom Kippur Book. (Illus.). (gr. k-6). 1978. pap. 2.95 (ISBN 0-930494-05-9). Kar Ben.
Sayre, Alex. Puget Sound: A Poem. (Shorey Historical Ser.). 34p. Repr. of 1883 ed. pap. 0.95 (ISBN 0-8466-0083-8, SJS83). Shorey.
Sayre, David. Computational Crystalaography. 1982. 34.50x (ISBN 0-19-851954-0). Oxford U Pr.
Sayre, Francis B. To Stand in the Cross. 1978. 3.00 (ISBN 0-8164-0380-5). Seabury.
Sayre, Joan M. Helping the Child to Listen & Talk. (Illus.). 1966. pap. text ed. 0.50x (ISBN 0-8134-0883-0); pap. 8.00 25 copies (ISBN 0-686-82924-7); pap. text ed. 25.00 100 copies (ISBN 0-686-82925-5, 883). Interstate.
Sayre, Kenneth M. Plato's Late Ontology: A Riddle Resolved. LC 82-61382. 370p. 1983. 25.00 (ISBN 0-691-07277-9). Princeton U Pr.
Sayre, Lombard. Celestial Shaggy Dog Joke, No. 2. (Illus.). 51p. (Orig.). 1981. pap. 3.95 o.p. (ISBN 0-89260-194-9). Hwong Pub.
Sayre, Rose, jt. ed. see Villani, Jim.
Sayre, Wallace S. & Kaufman, Herbert. Governing New York City. LC 60-8408. 816p. 1960. 15.00x (ISBN 0-87154-732-5). Russell Sage.
Sayre, Wallace S. & Parris, Judith H. Voting for President: The Electoral College & the American Political System. (Studies in Presidential Selection). 169p. 1970. pap. 6.95 (ISBN 0-8157-7719-1). Brookings.
Sayville, Winthrop, jt. auth. see Leventhal, Lance A.
Sayyed Mohammad Ali Jamalzadeh & Heston, W. L. Isfahan Is Half the World: Memories of a Persian Boyhood. LC 82-61370. (Princeton Library of Asian Translations). (Illus.). 384p. 1983. 37.50 (ISBN 0-691-06563-2). Princeton U Pr.
Sazonov, Nicolas I. La Verite sur l'Empereur Nicholas. (Nineteenth Century Russia Ser.). 319p. (Fr.). 1974. Repr. of 1854 ed. lib. bdg. 84.00x o.p. (ISBN 0-8287-0764-2, R49). Clearwater Pub.
SBalaskas, Arthur & Stirk, JOhn L. Soft Exercise. (Illus.). 160p. 1983. pap. 9.95 (ISBN 0-684-17508-8, ScribT). Scribner.
Sbrocchi, Leonard G., ed. see Ariosto.
Scadding, J G. & Cumming, Gordon. Scientific Foundations of Respiratory Medicine. (Illus.). 746p. 1981. 115.00 o.p. (ISBN 0-7216-7959-5). Saunders.
Scaduto, Anthony. A Terrible Time to Die. LC 78-5223. 1978. 7.95 o.p. (ISBN 0-399-12233-8). Putnam Pub Group.
Scaduto, Tony. Scapegoat: The Lonesome Death of Bruno Richard Hauptmann. LC 76-15205. (Illus.). 1976. 12.50 o.p. (ISBN 0-399-11660-5). Putnam Pub Group.
Scaer, David. Getting into the Story of Concord. 1978. pap. 3.75 (ISBN 0-570-03768-9, 12-2703). Concordia.
Scafe, Marla G., jt. auth. see Brooks, William D.
Scaff, Alvin H. Current Social Theory for Philippine Research. 118p. 1982. pap. 7.50 (ISBN 0-686-37570-X, Pub. by New Day Philippines). Cellar.
Scagell, Robin. How to Be an Astronomer. LC 80-53612. (Whizz Kids Ser.). 8.00 (ISBN 0-382-06460-7). Silver.
Scaglia, Gustina & Prager, Frank D. Mariano Taccola & His Book De Ingeneis. 1972. 15.00 o.p. (ISBN 0-262-16045-5). MIT Pr.
Scaglia, Gustina, jt. auth. see Prager, Frank D.
Scaglione, Aldo, tr. see McCrickard, Eleanor F.
Scagnetti, Jack. Bicycle Motocross. (Illus.). (gr. 4-7). 1976. 9.95 o.p. (ISBN 0-525-26505-8). Dutton.
--The Intimate Life of Rudolph Valentino. LC 74-31270. (Illus.). 160p. 1975. 12.95 o.p. (ISBN 0-8246-0197-1). Jonathan David.
--The Laurel & Hardy Scrapbook. LC 76-6566. (Illus.). 160p. 1976. 12.95 o.p. (ISBN 0-8246-0207-2). Jonathan David.
--The Laurel & Hardy Scrapbook. 1982. pap. 8.95 (ISBN 0-8246-0278-1). Jonathan David.
--The Life & Loves of Gable. LC 75-43842. (Illus.). 160p. 1976. 12.95 o.p. (ISBN 0-8246-0205-6). Jonathan David.
--The Life & Loves of Gable. 1982. pap. 8.95 (ISBN 0-8246-0279-X). Jonathan David.
Scahill, jt. auth. see Black, Perry O.
Scaife, Charles W., jt. auth. see Baum, Stuart J.
Scaife, P. F., illus. New Zealand Birds. 64p. 1982. pap. 2.50 (ISBN 0-686-92714-1, Pub. by Viking Sevenseas New Zealand). Intl Schol Bk Serv.
Scala, Bea & Nicholson, Joan. Katharine Gibbs Business Wordbook. 256p. 1982. 11.95 (ISBN 0-02-911670-8). Free Pr.
Scalapino, Leslie. Considering How Exaggerated Music Is. LC 81-84819. 152p. 1982. pap. 10.50 (ISBN 0-86547-066-9). N Point Pr.
Scalapino, Robert A. Asia & the Road Ahead: Issues for the Major Powers. LC 75-15219. 1975. 26.50x (ISBN 0-520-03066-4); pap. 4.95 (ISBN 0-520-03173-3). U of Cal Pr.
--The Foreign Policy of Modern Japan. LC 75-15219. 1977. 21.50 o.p. (ISBN 0-520-03196-2); pap. 9.95x (ISBN 0-520-03499-6). U of Cal Pr.
Scalapino, Robert A. & Wanandi, Jusuf, eds. Economic, Political & Security Issues in Southeast Asia in the 1980s. (Research Papers & Policy Studies: No. 7). 240p. (Orig.). 1982. pap. 10.00x (ISBN 0-912966-52-1). IEAS.
Scales, Alice M. & Biggs, Shirley A. Reading to Achieve: Strategies for Adult-College Learners. 224p. Date not set. pap. text ed. 8.95 (ISBN 0-675-20034-2). Additional supplements may be obtained from publisher. Merrill.
SCales, John L., ed. see Koll, Elsie.
Scales, Part R., jt. ed. see Aaron, Shirley L.
Scalf, Henry P. The Stepp-Stapp Families of America: A Source Book. (Illus.). 430p. pap. write for info. (ISBN 0-933302-20-7). Pikeville Coll.
Scalia, Joni L. The Cutting Edge. 1978. 10.95 o.p. (ISBN 0-07-055019-0, GB). McGraw.
--The Cutting Edge. 240p. 1983. pap. 2.95 (ISBN 0-425-05598-1). Berkley Pub.
Scalia, S. Eugene, jt. ed. see Marchione, Margherita.
Scaliger, Julius C. De Causis Linguae Latinae. (Linguistics 13th-18th Centuries Ser.). 474p. (Fr.). 1974. Repr. of 1598 ed. lib. bdg. 118.00 o.p. (ISBN 0-8287-0765-0, 71-5012). Clearwater Pub.
Scalingi, Paula. The European Parliament: The Three-Decade Search for a United Europe. LC 79-52323. (Contributions in Political Science: No. 37). 1980. lib. bdg. 25.00x (ISBN 0-313-21493-X, SEP/). Greenwood.
Scally, John, jt. auth. see Kakonis, Thomas E.
Scalzi, John B., jt. auth. see Podolny, Walter, Jr.
Scalzo, Frank & Hughes, Rowland. Elementary Computer, Assisted Statistics. rev. ed. 362p. 1983. Repr. of 1978 ed. text ed. avail. (ISBN 0-89874-618-3). Krieger.
Scammell, Michael. Passion for Truth: The Life of Alexander Solzhenitsyn. 1983. write for info (ISBN 0-393-01644-7). Norton.
Scammell, Michael, tr. see Marchenko, Anatoly.
Scammell, W. M. The International Economy Since Nineteen Forty-Five. LC 79-27416. 1980. 27.50 (ISBN 0-312-42191-5). St Martin.
Scammon, Richard. The Odds: On Virtually Everything. 1980. 12.95 (ISBN 0-399-12483-7). Putnam Pub Group.
Scammon, Richard M. & Wattenberg, Ben J. The Real Majority. 1971. pap. 3.75 o.p. (ISBN 0-698-10308-4, Coward). Putnam Pub Group.
Scamozzi, Ottavio B. Le Fabbriche e i Disegni di Andrea Palladio. (Illus., It.). 1968. 22.50 o.s.i. (ISBN 0-8038-0079-7). Architectural.
Scandalios, John G., ed. Physiological Genetics. (Physiological Ecology Ser.). 1979. 29.50 (ISBN 0-12-620980-4). Acad Pr.
Scandalios, John G., jt. ed. see Rattazzi, Mario C.
Scandizzo, Pasquale L. & Swamy, Gurushri. Benefits & Costs of Food Distribution Policies: The India Case. LC 82-8543. (World Bank Staff Working Papers: No. 509). (Orig.). 1982. pap. 3.00 (ISBN 0-8213-0011-3). World Bank.
Scandizzo, Pasquale L., jt. auth. see Harbert, Lloyd.
Scandizzo, Pasquale L., jt. auth. see Knudsen, Odin K.
Scandura, Alice M., ed. see Scandura, Jeanne M.
Scandura, Jeanne M. Critical Reading: Primers A-D. Scandura, Alice M., ed. (Critical Reading Primer Ser.). (Illus.). (gr. 1-3). 1978. 4.00 ea.; Level 1. 4.00 (ISBN 0-89039-250-1); Level 2. 4.00 (ISBN 0-89039-252-8); Level 3. 4.00 (ISBN 0-89039-254-4); Level 4. 4.00 (ISBN 0-89039-256-0). Ann Arbor Pubs.
Scandura, Joseph M., et al. Problem Solving: A Structural-Process with Instructional Implications. 1977. 31.50 (ISBN 0-12-620650-3). Acad Pr.
Scandure, Alice M., jt. auth. see Lowerre, George F.
Scanduzzo, Pasquale L. & Bruce, Colin. Methodologies for Measuring Agricultural Price Intervention Effects. (Working Paper: No. 394). x, 96p. 1980. 5.00 (ISBN 0-686-36089-3, WP-0394). World Bank.
Scanes, C. G. & Ottinger, M. A. Aspect of Avian Endocrinology: Practical & Theoretical Implications. (Graduate Studies: No. 26). 411p. 1982. 59.95 (ISBN 0-89672-103-5); pap. 29.95 (ISBN 0-89672-102-7). Tex Tech Pr.
Scanlan, B. K. & Keys, B. Practice in Management, a Study Guide: Cases & Readings to Accompany Management & Organizational Behavior. 329p. 1979. pap. text ed. 13.50 (ISBN 0-471-04773-2). Wiley.
Scanlan, Burt & Keys, Bernard. Management & Organizational Behavior. 2nd ed. LC 82-13536. (Management Ser.). 666p. 1983. text ed. 26.95 (ISBN 0-471-86183-9); avail. tchr's ed. (ISBN 0-471-89854-6); avail. study guide. Wiley.
Scanlan, Burt & Keys, J. Bernard. Management & Organizational Behavior. LC 78-15477. (Management Ser.). 1979. text ed. 29.95 (ISBN 0-471-02484-8); tchrs. manual avail. (ISBN 0-471-04774-0); study guide (ISBN 0-471-04773-2). Wiley.
Scanlan, Burt K. Management Eighteen: Results Management Practice. 2nd. ed. LC 81-16473. (Wiley Professional Development Programs: Business Administration Ser.). 333p. 1981. 55.95 (ISBN 0-471-86232-0). Wiley.
Scanlan, James P., tr. see Lavrov, Peter.
Scanlan, Michael. Inner Healing. LC 74-81901. 96p. (Orig.). 1974. pap. 2.95 o.p. (ISBN 0-8091-1846-7). Paulist Pr.
--The Power in Penance. 64p. 1972. pap. 0.95 (ISBN 0-87793-092-9). Ave Maria.
Scanlan, Richard A. & Tannenbaum, Steven R., eds. N-Nitroso Compounds. (ACS Symposium Ser.: No. 174). 1981. write for info. (ISBN 0-8412-0667-8). Am Chemical.
Scanlan, Robert H., jt. auth. see Simiu, Emil.
Scanlan, Tom. Family, Drama, & American Dreams. LC 77-83896. (Contributions in American Studies: No. 35). 1978. lib. bdg. 27.50x (ISBN 0-8371-9827-5, SFW/). Greenwood.
Scanlin, Margery, jt. auth. see Kraus, Richard.
Scanlon, David G. Traditions of African Education. LC 60-14305. (Orig.). 1964. text ed. 8.75 (ISBN 0-8077-2107-7); pap. text ed. 5.00x (ISBN 0-8077-2104-2). Tchrs Coll.
Scanlon, David G., ed. International Education: A Documentary History. LC 64-12575. (Orig.). 1960. text ed. 9.50 (ISBN 0-8077-2098-4); pap. 5.00x (ISBN 0-8077-2095-X). Tchrs Coll.
Scanlon, Henry. You Can Sell Your Photos. LC 80-7854. (Illus.). 256p. 1980. 16.95i o.p. (ISBN 0-06-014049-6, CN845, HarpT); pap. 10.50xi (ISBN 0-06-090845-9, CN845, HarpT). Har-Row.
Scanlon, J. W. A System of Newborn Physical Examination. 112p. 1979. pap. text ed. 9.95 (ISBN 0-8391-1392-7). Univ Park.
Scanlon, James E. Randolph-Macon College: A Southern History, 1825-1967. LC 82-16072. 1983. 15.00x (ISBN 0-8139-0928-7). U Pr of Va.
Scanlon, John W., jt. auth. see Daze, Ann M.
Scanlon, L. Aim Sixty-Five Laboratory Manual. (Electronic Technology Ser.). 179p. 1981. pap. text ed. 10.95 (ISBN 0-471-06488-2). Wiley.
Scanlon, Leo. IBM PC Assembly Language: A Guide for Programmers. (Illus.). 384p. 1983. 27.95 (ISBN 0-89303-534-3); pap. 19.95 (ISBN 0-89303-241-7). R J Brady.
Scanlon, Lynne W., jt. auth. see Ehret, Charles F.
Scanlon, Lynne W., jt. auth. see Mandell, Marshall.
Scanlon, Mark & Grill, Tom. The Art of Photographing Women. (Illus.). 144p. 1981. 19.95 o.p. (ISBN 0-8174-3535-2). Watson-Guptill.
Scanlon, Mark, jt. auth. see Grill, Tom.
Scanlon, Michael. A Portion of My Spirit. LC 79-51723. 1979. 8.95 (ISBN 0-89310-047-1); pap. 4.95 o.p. (ISBN 0-89310-048-X). Carillon Bks.
Scanlon, Pat, jt. auth. see Broccoletti, Peter P.
Scanlon, Patrick H., ed. see Junior League of Jackson, Mississippi.
Scannel, Vernon & Harrison, Gregory. Catch the Light. (Illus.). 48p. (gr. 5-8). 1983. text ed. 9.95 (ISBN 0-19-276050-5, Pub. by Oxford U Pr Childrens). Merrimack Bk Serv.
Scannell, Dale & Tracy, Dick. Testing & Measurement in the Classroom. 1975. pap. text ed. 12.50 (ISBN 0-395-18608-0). HM.
Scannell, Mary J., jt. auth. see Webb, David A.
Scanu, Angelo M. & Landsberger, Frank R., eds. Lipoprotein Structure. (Annals of the New York Academy of Sciences: Vol. 348). 436p. 1980. 78.00x (ISBN 0-89766-082-X). NY Acad Sci.
Scanzoni, J., jt. auth. see Scanzoni, L.
Scanzoni, John. Is Family Possible? Theory & Policy for the 21st Century. (Sage Library of Social Research). 224p. 1983. 22.00 (ISBN 0-8039-1920-4); pap. 10.95 (ISBN 0-8039-1921-2). Sage.
--Sex Roles, Women's Work, & Marital Conflict. LC 78-58981. (Illus.). 192p. 1978. 19.95x (ISBN 0-669-02400-7). Lexington Bks.
--Sexual Bargaining: Power Politics in the American Marriage. 1972. pap. 2.95 o.p. (ISBN 0-13-807453-4, Spec). P-H.
Scanzoni, John, jt. auth. see Scanzoni, Letha D.

Scanzoni, L. & Scanzoni, J. Planning the New Office. (Illus.). 1978. 27.50 (ISBN 0-07-054721-1, P&RB). McGraw.

Scanzoni, Letha & Mollenkott, Virginia R. Is the Homosexual My Neighbor? Another Christian View. LC 77-20445. 176p. 1980. pap. 6.95i (ISBN 0-06-067076-2, RD 337, HarpR). Har-Row.

Scanzoni, Letha D. & Scanzoni, John. Men, Women, & Change. 2nd ed. (Illus.). 576p. 1981. 22.50 (ISBN 0-07-055054-9); instr's. manual 6.95 (ISBN 0-07-055055-7). McGraw.

Scapagnini, Umberto, jt. ed. see MacLeod, Robert.

Scaparro, Jack. Worst Enemies. 352p. 1983. pap. 3.75 (ISBN 0-440-09590-5). Dell.

Scarborough, Chuck & Murray, William. The Myrmidon Project. 320p. 1981. 12.95 (ISBN 0-698-11054-4, Coward). Putnam Pub Group.

Scarborough, Don L., jt. auth. see Reber, Arthur S.

Scarborough, Dorothy. The Wind. (Barker Texas History Center Ser: No. 4). 357p. 1979. 14.95 (ISBN 0-292-79012-0); pap. 0.00 o.p. U of Tex Pr.

Scarborough, Elizabeth. The Unicorn Creed. 352p. 1983. pap. 3.95 (ISBN 0-686-82108-4). Bantam.

Scarborough, Hollis, jt. auth. see Haviland, Jeannette.

Scarborough, John. Facets of Hellenic Life. LC 75-29704. (Illus.). 320p. 1976. pap. text ed. 18.95 (ISBN 0-395-20368-6). HM.

Scarborough, Katherine. Homes of the Cavaliers. (Illus.). 392p. 1969. 7.50 (ISBN 0-686-36819-3). Md Hist.

Scarborough, Lee R. With Christ after the Lost. rev. ed. Head, E. D., ed. 1953. 9.95 (ISBN 0-8054-6203-1). Broadman.

Scarcella, Robin C. & Krashen, Stephen D., eds. Research in Second Language Acquisition: Selected Papers of the Los Angeles Second Language Acquisition Research Forum. (Issues in Second Language Research Ser.). 1981. pap. 18.95 (ISBN 0-88377-143-8). Newbury Hse.

Scarf, Maggie. Body, Mind, Behavior. LC 76-9079. 200p. 1976. 9.95 (ISBN 0-915220-14-8, 23045). New Republic.

Scarfe, Brian L. Cycles, Growth & Inflation. (Illus.). 1977. text ed. 32.50x (ISBN 0-07-055039-5, C). McGraw.

Scarfe, Francis, tr. see Aragon, Louis & Cocteau, Jean.

Scarfe, Gerald. Gerald Scarfe. (Illus., Orig.). 1982. pap. 12.95 (ISBN 0-500-27268-9). Thames Hudson.

Scarfe, Herbert. Cutting & Setting Stones. 1972. 17.50 (ISBN 0-7134-2302-1, Pub. by Batsford England). David & Charles.

Scarff, R. W. & Torloni, H. Histological Typing of Breast Tumours. (World Health Organization: International Histological Classification of Tumours Ser.). (Illus.). 1977. 20.00 (ISBN 0-89189-111-0, 70-1-002-20). Am Soc Clinical.

Scargill, D. I. The Form of Cities. (Illus.). 1979. 26.00x (ISBN 0-312-29935-4). St Martin.

Scariano, Margaret M. Bigfoot & the Timberland Mystery. (Voyager Ser.). 96p. (Orig.). 1982. pap. 4.45 (ISBN 0-8010-8225-0). Baker Bk.

Scarinci, Tom. After the Last Heartbeat. LC 79-55679. 1980. 8.95 o.p. (ISBN 0-915684-55-1). Christian Herald.

Scarisbrick, J. J. Henry VIII. LC 68-10995. (English Monarchs Series). (Illus.). 1968. 34.50x (ISBN 0-520-01129-5); pap. 6.95 (ISBN 0-520-01130-9, CAL195). U of Cal Pr.

Scarlatti. The Operas of Alessandro Scarlatti: Vol. III-Tigrane. Collins, Michael, ed. (Harvard Publications in Music: No. 13). (Illus.). 192p. 1983. text ed. 35.00x. Harvard U Pr.

Scarlett, Bernard. Shipminder: The Story of Her Majesty's Coastguard. 1972. 9.75 o.p. (ISBN 0-7207-0480-4). Transatlantic.

Scarlett, Frank & Townley, Marjorie. Arts Decoratifs 1925: A Personal Recollection of the Paris Exhibition. LC 75-33515. (Illus.). 104p. 1976. 17.95 o.p. (ISBN 0-685-63273-3). St Martin.

Scarlett, James. Scotland's Clans & Tartans. (Illus.). 152p. 1982. 16.00 (ISBN 0-85683-049-6, Pub by Shepheard-Walwyn England). Flatiron Book.

Scarne, John. Scarne on Cards. 1973. pap. 2.95 (ISBN 0-451-11380-2, AE1380, Sig). NAL.

--Scarne's Guide to Modern Poker. 1981. 21.00x o.p. (ISBN 0-686-75468-9, Pub. by Constable Pubs). State Mutual Bk.

Scaroamp, Margaret. The Winchester Connection. (Perspectives II Ser.). (Illus.). 48p. (gr. 7-12). 1982. pap. 2.50 (ISBN 0-87879-314-3). Acad Therapy.

Scarpa, Antonio & Carafoli, Ernesto, eds. Calcium Transport & Cell Function. (Annals of the New York Academy of Sciences Ser.: Vol. 307). 655p. 1978. pap. 70.00x professional (ISBN 0-89072-063-0). NY Acad Sci.

Scarpaci, Vincenza. A Portrait of the Italians in America. (Illus.). 256p. 1982. 30.00 (ISBN 0-684-16992-4, ScribT). Scribner.

Scarpato, Maria & Fattoross, Camille. The Simpleton of Naples & Other Italian Folktales. LC 82-81946. (Illus.). 84p. (gr. 3-8). 1983. 13.95 (ISBN 0-88100-010-8). Capricorn Bks.

Scarpelli, Emile M. & Cosmi, Ermelando V., eds. Reviews in Perinatal Medicine, Vol. 2. LC 77-74616. 405p. 1978. 38.00 (ISBN 0-89004-195-4). Raven.

--Reviews in Perinatal Medicine, Vol. 3. LC 77-74616. 493p. 1979. text ed. 50.00 (ISBN 0-89004-249-7). Raven.

Scarpelli, Emilie & Cosmi, Ermelando, eds. Reviews in Perinatal Medicine, Vol. 4. 544p. 1981. 60.50 (ISBN 0-89004-364-7). Raven.

Scarpitti, Frank, jt. auth. see Stephenson, Richard.

Scarpitti, Frank R., jt. auth. see McGrath, John H.

Scarr, Deryck. Fragments of Empire: A History of the Western Pacific High Commission, 1877-1914. LC 67-28350. (Illus.). 1968. text ed. 16.00x o.p. (ISBN 0-87022-730-0). UH Pr.

Scarr, Deryck, ed. see Giles, William E.

Scarritt, James R., ed. Analyzing Political Change in Africa. (A Westview Replica Edition). 344p. 1980. lib. bdg. 32.00 (ISBN 0-89158-275-4). Westview.

Scarron, Paul. The Whole Comical Works of Monsr. Scarron, Part One. LC 78-170503. (Foundations of the Novel Ser.: Vol. 2). lib. bdg. 50.00 o.s.i. (ISBN 0-8240-0514-7). Garland Pub.

--The Whole Comical Works of Monsr. Scarron, Parts Two & Three. LC 78-170503. (Foundations of the Novel Ser.: Vol. 3). lib. bdg. 50.00 o.s.i. (ISBN 0-8240-0515-5). Garland Pub.

Scarry, Huck. Huck Scarry's Steam Train Journey. LC 79-11532. (Illus.). 1979. 5.95 (ISBN 0-529-05538-4, Philomel); PLB 5.99 (ISBN 0-529-05550-3). Putnam Pub Group.

--Huck Scarry's Steam Train Press-Outs. (Illus.). 32p. (Orig.). (gr. 2-5). 1980. pap. 4.95 (ISBN 0-529-05588-0, Philomel). Putnam Pub Group.

--On the Road: A Panaroma of Early Automobiles. 1981. 8.95 (ISBN 0-399-20818-6, Philomel); lib. bdg. 8.99 (ISBN 0-399-61183-5). Putnam Pub Group.

--On Wheels. LC 79-22940. (Illus.). 32p. (ps-2). 1980. 7.95 (ISBN 0-399-20751-1, Philomel); PLB 7.99 (ISBN 0-399-61161-4). Putnam Pub Group.

Scarry, John, jt. auth. see Kirby, Lee.

Scarry, R. Min Forste Ordbog: English & Danish. (Illus.). 1975. 12.00x (ISBN 8-7009-2642-6, D740). Vanous.

Scarry, Richard. All Day Long. (Golden Look-Look Book Ser). (Illus.). 1976. limp bdg. 1.25 (ISBN 0-307-11825-8, Golden Pr); PLB 6.08 (ISBN 0-307-61825-0). Western Pub.

--All Year Long. (Golden Look-Look Bks.). (Illus.). (ps-1). 1976. PLB 6.08 (ISBN 0-307-61826-9, Golden Pr); pap. 1.25 (ISBN 0-307-11826-6). Western Pub.

--At Work. (Golden Look-Look Ser.). (Illus.). 24p. 1976. limp bdg. 1.25 (ISBN 0-307-11824-X, Golden Pr); PLB 6.08 (ISBN 0-307-61824-2). Western Pub.

--Early Words. LC 75-36466. (Illus.). 14p. (ps-1). 1976. 3.50 (ISBN 0-394-83238-8, BYR). Random.

--In My Town. (Golden Look-Look Bks.). (Illus.). (ps-1). 1976. PLB 6.08 (ISBN 0-307-61828-5, Golden Pr); pap. 1.25 (ISBN 0-307-11828-2). Western Pub.

--On Vacation. (Golden Look-Look Ser.). (Illus.). 1976. PLB 6.08 (ISBN 0-307-61823-4, Golden Pr); pap. 1.25 (ISBN 0-307-11823-1). Western Pub.

--Richard Scarry's Best Christmas Book Ever. LC 80-5172. (Illus.). 48p. (ps-2). 1981. 4.95 (ISBN 0-394-84936-1); PLB 5.99 o.p. (ISBN 0-394-94936-6). Random.

--Richard Scarry's Color Book. LC 75-36465. (Illus.). 14p. (ps-1). 1976. 3.50 (ISBN 0-394-83237-X, BYR). Random.

--Richard Scarry's Find Your ABC's. (Pictureback Bks.). (Illus.). (ps-1). 1973. pap. 1.50 (ISBN 0-394-82683-3). Random.

--Richard Scarry's Great Big Air Book. LC 79-146649. (Illus.). (gr. k-3). 1971. 5.95 (ISBN 0-394-82167-X, BYR); PLB 5.99 (ISBN 0-394-92167-4). Random.

--Richard Scarry's Great Big Mystery Book. (Illus.). (ps-2). 5.95 (ISBN 0-394-82431-8, BYR); PLB 5.99 (ISBN 0-394-92431-2). Random.

--Richard Scarry's Great Big Schoolhouse. (Illus.). (ps-2). 1969. 5.95 (ISBN 0-394-80874-6, BYR); PLB 5.99 (ISBN 0-394-90874-0). Random.

--Richard Scarry's Great Steamboat Mystery. LC 75-6237. (Picturebacks Ser). (Illus.). 32p. (ps-1). 1975. pap. 1.50 (ISBN 0-394-83124-1, BYR). Random.

--Richard Scarry's Lowly Worm Car & Truck Book. LC 82-61012. (Illus.). 16p. (ps-2). 1983. pap. 2.95 (ISBN 0-394-85760-7). Random.

--Richard Scarry's Lowly Worm Word Book. LC 80-53103. (Chunky Bks.). (Illus.). 28p. (ps). 1981. pap. 2.95 board (ISBN 0-394-84728-8). Random.

--Richard Scarry's Please & Thank You Book. LC 73-2441. (Pictureback Library Editions). (ps-2). 1978. PLB 4.99 (ISBN 0-394-92681-1, BYR); 1.50 (ISBN 0-394-82681-7). Random.

Scase, Richard. The State in Western Europe. LC 80-10364. 113p. 1980. 30.00 (ISBN 0-312-75610-0). St Martin.

Scase, Richard, ed. Industrial Society: Class, Cleavage & Control. LC 76-47126. 1977. 22.50x (ISBN 0-312-41545-1). St Martin.

Scattergood, John, ed. see Skelton, John.

Scattergood, V. J., ed. The Works of Sir John Clanvowe. 96p. 1975. 13.50x o.p. (ISBN 0-87471-688-8). Rowman.

Scauenstein, E., et al. Aldehydes in Biological Systems: Their Natural Occurence & Biological Activities. (Advanced Biochemistry Ser.). 205p. 1980. 28.00x (ISBN 0-85086-059-8, Pub. by Pion England). Methuen Inc.

Scavullo, Francesco. Scavullo on Beauty. LC 78-23526. (Illus.). 1979. pap. 15.00 (ISBN 0-394-40728-8, Vin). Random.

--Scavullo Women. LC 81-48326. (Illus.). 192p. 1982. 23.99i (ISBN 0-06-014838-1, HarpT). Har-Row.

Scermino, Daniele. Fun with Land Hermit Crabs. 1978. pap. 2.95 (ISBN 0-915096-08-0). Palmetto Pub.

Scerrato, Umberto. Islam. Nannicini, Giuliana, ed. LC 75-21858. (Monuments of Civilization). (Illus.). 192p. 1976. 25.00 o.p. (ISBN 0-448-02027-0, G&D). Putnam Pub Group.

Schaad, U. B., ed. Paediatrische Infektionskrankheiten III. (Paediatrische Fortbildungskurse fuer die Praxis: Vol. 58). (Illus.). viii, 120p. 1983. pap. 54.00 (ISBN 3-8055-3680-1). S Karger.

Schaaf, Fred. Wonders of the Sky: Observing Rainbows, Comets, Eclipses, the Stars, & Other Phenomena. (Illus.). 224p. (Orig.). 1983. pap. 5.95 (ISBN 0-486-24402-4). Dover.

Schaaf, Richard, tr. see Vallejo, Ceasar.

Schaafsma, Polly. The Rock Art of Utah. Flint, Emily, ed. LC 72-173663. (Peabody Museum Papers: Vol.65). (Illus.). 1976. pap. 18.50 (ISBN 0-87365-186-3). Peabody Harvard.

Schaal, John H. Three Letters from Prison. (Layman's Bible Study Ser.). pap. 2.95 o.p. (ISBN 0-8010-7994-2). Baker Bk.

Schaap, A. P., ed. Singlet Molecular Oxygen. LC 76-3496. (Benchmark Papers in Organic Chemistry Ser.: Vol. 5). 400p. 1976. 58.50 (ISBN 0-12-787415-1). Acad Pr.

Schaap, Dick. Steinbrenner! 336p. 1982. 14.95 (ISBN 0-399-12703-8). Putnam Pub Group.

--Steinbrenner! 320p. 1983. pap. 3.50 (ISBN 0-380-62752-3). Avon.

Schaap, Dick & Beamon, Bob. The Perfect Jump. 1976. pap. 1.75 o.p. (ISBN 0-451-07248-0, E7248, Sig). NAL.

Schaap, Dick, jt. auth. see Breslin, Jimmy.

Schaap, James C. CRC Family Portrait: Sketches of Ordinary Christians in a 125-Year-Old Church. 275p. (Orig.). 1982. pap. 4.35 (ISBN 0-933140-60-6). Bd of Pubns CRC.

Schaap, Walter, tr. see Goffin, Robert.

Schaarschmidt-Richter, Irmtraud & Mori, Osamu. Japanese Gardens. Seligman, Janet, tr. from Ger. LC 79-87439. 1979. 70.00 (ISBN 0-688-03538-8). Morrow.

Schabacker, Joseph & Schroeder, Paul. Accounting Problems & How to Solve Them. (Orig.). 1952. pap. 3.95 (ISBN 0-06-460085-8, CO 85, COS). B&N NY.

Schabacker, R. W. Stock Market Profits. 1967. Repr. of 1934 ed. flexible cover 10.00 (ISBN 0-87034-022-0). Fraser Pub Co.

Schaber, Will, ed. AUFBAU (Reconstruction) LC 72-81086. (Illus.). 416p. (Ger.). 1972. 11.95 o.p. (ISBN 0-87951-001-3). Overlook Pr.

Schach, Paul & Hollander, Lee M., trs. Eyrbyggja Saga. LC 59-11221. (Landmark Edition). (Illus.). 1959. 12.95x o.p. (ISBN 0-8032-0164-8). U of Nebr Pr.

Schach, Paul, tr. see Hallberg, Peter.

Schachar, Ronald A. & Levy, Norman S. Radial Keratotomy. LC 80-84337. (Illus.). 244p. (Orig.). 1980. pap. text ed. 50.00 (ISBN 0-910737-01-0). LAL Pub.

Schachar, Ronald A., et al. Understanding Radial Keratotomy. LC 81-84395. (Illus.). 225p. 1981. text ed. 75.00 (ISBN 0-910737-03-7). LAL Pub.

--Refractive Keratoplasty. 350p. 1982. pap. text ed. 50.00 (ISBN 0-910737-04-5). LAL Pub.

--Refractive Modulation of the Cornea. LC 81-82183. (Illus.). 338p. 1981. pap. text ed. 50.00 (ISBN 0-910737-02-9). LAL Pub.

Schachat, Walter S., ed. see Meltzer, Murray A.

Schacher, Ronald A. & Levy, Norman S. Keratore Fraction. (Illus.). 244p. (Orig.). 1980. pap. text ed. 45.00 (ISBN 0-686-37372-3). A & L Pubns.

Schacher, Ronald A., et al. Kerotorefraction. LC 80-81914. (Illus.). 244p. (Orig.). 1980. pap. text ed. 45.00 (ISBN 0-910737-00-2). LAL Pub.

Schacheter, C., jt. auth. see Salzer, F.

Schachman, Howard K. Ultracentrifugation in Biochemistry. 1959. 50.00 (ISBN 0-12-621050-0). Acad Pr.

Schacht, Jochen, jt. ed. see DeRobertis, Eduardo.

Schacht, Joseph & Bosworth, C. E., eds. The Legacy of Islam. 2nd ed. (Legacy Ser). (Illus.). 1974. text ed. 29.95x (ISBN 0-19-821913-X). Oxford U Pr.

Schacht, Richard. Hegel & After: Studies in Continental Philosophy Between Kant & Sartre. LC 74-4526. 1975. pap. 6.95x (ISBN 0-8229-5254-8). U of Pittsburgh Pr.

--Nietzsche. (Arguments of the Philosophers Ser.). 560p. 1983. 38.95 (ISBN 0-7100-9191-5). Routledge & Kegan.

Schacht, Wilhelm. Rock Gardens. Archibald, Jim, ed. LC 80-54398. (Illus.). 190p. 1983. pap. 9.95 (ISBN 0-87663-588-5). Universe.

Schachter, Bruce J., jt. auth. see Ahuja, Narendra.

Schachter, E. Neil, jt. auth. see Lehnert, Bruce E.

Schachter, Frances F. Everyday Mother Talk to Toddlers: Early Intervention. LC 78-20049. 1979. 18.50 (ISBN 0-12-621360-7). Acad Pr.

Schachter, H. Calculus & Analytic Geometry. 1972. text ed. 26.95 (ISBN 0-07-055056-5, G); ans. 3.00 (ISBN 0-07-055057-3). McGraw.

Schachter, Howard & Kirsner, Joseph B. Crohn's Disease of the Gastrointestinal Tract. LC 80-10339. (Clinical Gastroenterology Monographs). 182p. 1980. 44.50x (ISBN 0-471-48896-8, Pub. by Wiley Medical). Wiley.

Schachter, Jacqueline, jt. auth. see Robinett, Betty W.

Schachter, Paul & Otanes, Fe T. Tagalog Reference Grammar. (California Library Reprint Ser.). 600p. 1983. text ed. 35.00x (ISBN 0-520-04943-8, CLRS 122). U of Cal Pr.

Schachter, Stanley & Rodin, Judith. Obese Humans & Rats. LC 74-7179. 192p. 1974. text ed. 24.95 (ISBN 0-89859-294-1). L Erlbaum Assocs.

Schachter-Shalomi, Zalman & Gropman, Donald. The First Step: A Guide to the New Jewish Spirit. 144p. 1983. pap. 5.95 (ISBN 0-553-01418-8). Bantam.

Schackleton, V. J., jt. auth. see Davies, D. R.

Schacter, Daniel L. Stranger Behind the Engram: Theories of Memory & the Psychology of Science. 288p. 1982. text ed. 24.95 (ISBN 0-89859-245-3). L Erlbaum Assocs.

Schacter, Norm see NFL & Walsh, Bill.

Schad, N., et al. Differential Diagnosis of Congenital Heart Disease. Bar, Hans, ed. LC 64-12879. 450p. 1966. 110.00 o.p. (ISBN 0-8089-0403-5). Grune.

Schad, Tennyson & Shapiro, Ira, eds. American Showcase, Vol.1. (Illus.). 226p. pap. 19.95 o.p. (ISBN 0-931144-01-9). Am Showcase.

--American Showcase, Vol. 2. (Photography, Illustration, & Graphic Design Ser.: Vol. 2). 266p. 1979. 35.00 (ISBN 0-931144-04-3); pap. 22.50 (ISBN 0-931144-03-5). Am Showcase.

Schad, Wolfgang. Man & Mammals: Toward a Biology of Form. new ed. Scherer, Carroll, tr. from Ger. LC 76-52049. Orig. Title: Saugetiere und Mensch: Zur Gestaltbiologie Vom Gesichtspunkt der Dreigliederung. (Illus.). 1978. 14.95 (ISBN 0-914614-10-X). Waldorf Pr.

Schade, Charlene, jt. auth. see Johnson, Leslie.

Schade, George D., tr. see Rulfo, Juan.

Schade, J., jt. auth. see Bernhard, C. G.

Schade, J. & Smith, J., eds. Computers & Brains. (Progress in Brain Research: Vol. 33). 1971. 68.00 (ISBN 0-444-40855-X, North Holland). Elsevier.

Schade, J, jt. ed. see Meyer, J. S.

Schade, J., jt. ed. see Purpura, Dominick.

Schade, J. P. Introduction to Functional Human Anatomy: An Atlas. LC 73-76188. (Illus.). 190p. 1974. text ed. 10.00 (ISBN 0-7216-7945-5). Saunders.

--The Peripheral Nervous System. 2nd ed. 1973. 14.00 (ISBN 0-444-40509-7, North Holland). Elsevier.

Schade, J. P., jt. auth. see Eccles, John C.

Schade, J. P., jt. auth. see Himwich, W. A.

Schade, J. P., jt. auth. see Wiener, Norbert.

Schade, J. P., jt. ed. see Bargmann, W.

Schade, J. P., jt. ed. see Bargmann, Wolfgang.

Schade, J. P., jt. ed. see Singer, Marcus.

Schade, Richard, jt. ed. see Harris, Edward P.

Schade, Richard E., ed. Lessing Yearbook XIII, 1981. 336p. 1982. 27.00 (ISBN 0-8143-1703-0). Wayne St U Pr.

Schade, Werner. Cranach: A Family of Master Painters. (Illus.). 476p. 1980. 50.00 (ISBN 0-399-11831-4). Putnam Pub Group.

Schadler, Reuben, jt. auth. see Seymour, Dale.

Schad-Somers, Suzanne P. Sadomasochism: Etiology & Treatment. LC 81-6460. 300p. 1982. 29.95x (ISBN 0-89885-059-2). Human Sci Pr.

Schadt, Armin L. Counterfeit Reality. 1975. 5.95 o.p. (ISBN 0-8158-0323-0). Chris Mass.

Schaedel, Richard, jt. ed. see Rubin, Vera.

Schaefer. What Is Operations? (Research Bulletin: No. 6). pap. 0.69 (ISBN 0-685-57183-1). Assn Sch Busn.

Schaefer, Arlene B., jt. auth. see Wright, Logan.

Schaefer, Carl. Home Maintenance & Repair. 1977. text ed. 8.52 (ISBN 0-02-827410-5). Glencoe.

Schaefer, Carl J. & Smith, Robert E. Home Mechanics. 1961. text ed. 6.00 o.p. (ISBN 0-02-827400-8). Glencoe.

Schaefer, Charles E. How to Influence Children: A Complete Guide for Becoming a Better Parent. 2nd ed. 320p. 1982. text ed. 14.95 (ISBN 0-442-27492-0). Van Nos Reinhold.

Schaefer, Charles E. & Millman, Howard L. Therapies for Children: A Handbook of Effective Treatments for Problem Behaviors. LC 77-79481. (Social & Behavioral Science Ser). 1977. text ed. 22.95x (ISBN 0-87589-337-6). Jossey-Bass.

Schaefer, Charles E. & O'Connor, Kevin J. Handbook of Play Therapy. (Personality Processes Ser.). 489p. 1983. 34.95 (ISBN 0-471-09462-5, Pub. by Wiley-Interscience). Wiley.

Schaefer, Charles E., et al. Group Therapies for Children & Youth: Principles & Practices of Group Treatment. LC 82-48061. (Social & Behavioral Science Ser.). 1982. text ed. 19.95x (ISBN 0-87589-545-X). Jossey Bass.

Schaefer, F. P., ed. Dye Lasers. LC 73-11593. (Topics in Applied Physics: Vol. 1). (Illus.). xi, 285p. 1974. 25.00 (ISBN 0-387-08470-3). Springer-Verlag.

Schaefer, George. Expectant Father. (Everyday Handbook Ser.). pap. 3.95 (ISBN 0-06-463331-4, EH 331, EH). B&N NY.

Schaefer, Halmuth & Martin, Patrick. Behavioral Therapy. 2nd ed. (Illus.). 352p. 1975. pap. text ed. 14.95 o.p. (ISBN 0-07-055062-X, HP). McGraw.

Schaefer, Hans. Skin Permeability. (Illus.). 360p. 1982. pap. 57.60 (ISBN 0-387-11797-0). Springer-Verlag.

Schaefer, James R. Program Planning for Adult Christian Education. LC 72-88324. 262p. 1972. 7.50 o.p. (ISBN 0-8091-0175-0); pap. 5.50 o.p. (ISBN 0-8091-1755-X). Paulist Pr.

Schaefer, K., ed. Hemofiltration. (Contributions to Nephrology Ser.: Vol. 32). (Illus.). viii, 228p. 1982. pap. 58.75 (ISBN 3-8055-3515-5). S Karger.

Schaefer, R. T. Sociology: Student's Guide with Readings. Date not set. 8.95 (ISBN 0-07-055066-2). McGraw.

Schaefer, Richard. Racial & Ethnic Groups. 1979. text ed. 18.95 (ISBN 0-316-77274-7); tchrs' manual avail. (ISBN 0-316-77275-5). Little.

Schaefer, Richard T. & Lamm, Robert P. Sociology. (Illus.). 608p. 1983. text ed. 21.95x (ISBN 0-07-055065-4, C); student's guide 8.95x (ISBN 0-07-055066-2); instr's manual 15.00 (ISBN 0-07-055067-0); test bank 20.00 (ISBN 0-07-055068-9). McGraw.

Schaefer, Susan D. The Motivation Process. (Orig.). 1977. pap. text ed. 7.95 (ISBN 0-316-77285-2). Little.

Schaefer, V. A., ed. see Brewer, J. E.

Schaefer, William D. James Thomson, (B. V.): Beyond "The City". LC 65-23462. (Perspectives in Criticism: No. 17). 1965. 30.00x (ISBN 0-520-01138-4). U of Cal Pr.

Schaefer, William D., ed. The Speedy Extinction of Evil & Misery: Selected Prose of James Thomson (B. V.) 1967. 36.50x (ISBN 0-520-01139-2). U of Cal Pr.

Schaefer-Simmern, Henry. The Unfolding of Artistic Activity: Its Basis, Processes, & Implications. (Illus.). 1948. 29.50x (ISBN 0-520-01141-4). U of Cal Pr.

Schaefer-Simmern, Henry, tr. see Fiedler, Conrad.

Schaeffer, Dirk L., tr. see Cohen, Rudolf.

Schaeffer, Edith. L' Abri. 1969. pap. 3.95 (ISBN 0-8423-2101-2). Tyndale.

--Christianity Is Jewish. 1975. pap. 6.95 (ISBN 0-8423-0242-5). Tyndale.

--Common Sense Christian Living. 272p. 1983. 14.95 (ISBN 0-8407-5280-6). Nelson.

--Hidden Art. 1971. pap. 6.95 (ISBN 0-8423-1421-0). Tyndale.

Schaeffer, Francis. Basic Bible Studies. 1972. pap. 2.95 (ISBN 0-8423-0103-8). Tyndale.

--He Is There & He Is Not Silent. pap. 4.95 (ISBN 0-8423-1413-X). Tyndale.

--Pollution & the Death of Man. pap. 4.95 (ISBN 0-8423-4840-9). Tyndale.

--True Spirituality. pap. 5.95 (ISBN 0-8423-7351-9). Tyndale.

Schaeffer, Francis A. Art & the Bible. LC 73-75891. 64p. 1973. pap. 2.25 (ISBN 0-87784-443-7). Inter-Varsity.

--The Complete Works of Francis A. Schaeffer: A Christian World View, 5 Vols. 2237p. 1982. Set. slipcase 89.95 (ISBN 0-89107-241-1, Crossway Bks). Good News.

--Genesis in Space & Time. LC 72-78406. 144p. 1972. pap. 4.95 (ISBN 0-87784-636-7). Inter-Varsity.

--No Final Conflict. 48p. 1975. pap. 1.95 o.p. (ISBN 0-87784-417-8). Inter-Varsity.

Schaeffer, Glen N. & Spielman, Patrick E. Basic Mechanical Drawing. 1982. pap. 4.32 (ISBN 0-02-827940-9, 82795). Glencoe.

Schaeffer, Jerry. Churches Don't Grow on Trees. (Home Mission Graded Ser.). 39p. (gr. 8-12). Date not set. pap. 1.50 (ISBN 0-937170-51-8). Home Mission.

Schaeffer, Julius. Die Pilze Mitteleuropas: Vol. 3, Russula-Monographie. (Illus.). 1970. Repr. of 1952 ed. 80.00 (ISBN 3-7682-0689-0). Lubrecht & Cramer.

Schaeffer, Mallor. Young Voices. 1971. 5.95 o.p. (ISBN 0-685-01113-5, 80669). Glencoe.

Schaeffer, Morris, jt. ed. see Hijams, Willy.

Schaeffer, N. M. Reactor Shielding for Nuclear Engineers. LC 73-600001. (AEC Technical Information Center Ser.). 801p. 1973. pap. 28.00 (ISBN 0-87079-004-8, TID-25951); microfiche 4.50 (ISBN 0-87079-339-X, TID-25951). DOE.

Schaeffer, Riley S., jt. auth. see Cordes, Eugene.

Schaeffer, Susan F. Falling. 240p. 1974. pap. 1.50 o.p. (ISBN 0-451-05897-6, W5897, Sig). NAL.

--Granite Lady: Poems. LC 73-21294. 150p. 1974. 6.95 o.p. (ISBN 0-686-67048-5). Macmillan.

--The Madness of a Seduced Woman: A Novel. LC 82-17771. 560p. 1983. 16.95 (ISBN 0-525-24165-5, 1646-490). Dutton.

Schaeffer, Wendell G., jt. auth. see Worcester, Donald E.

Schaeper, Thomas J. The French Council of Commerce, 1700-1715: A Study of Mercantilism after Colbert. 300p. 1983. 30.00 (ISBN 0-8142-0341-8). Ohio St U Pr.

Schaeppi, U. The Neurologic Examination of Beagle Dogs in Toxicity Tests. (Lectures in Toxicology Ser.: No. 18). (Illus.). 1982. 60.00 (ISBN 0-08-029787-0). Pergamon.

Schaerf, Carlo, jt. ed. see Carlton, David.

Schaf, Frank, Jr., jt. auth. see Blackstock, Paul W.

Schafer, Charles & Schafer, Violet. Teacraft. LC 74-14291. (Illus.). 120p. 1975. pap. 5.95 (ISBN 0-394-70636-6, Dist. by Random). Taylor & Ng.

--Wokcraft. LC 73-183774. (Illus.). 1972. pap. 5.95 (ISBN 0-394-70788-5, Dist. by Random). Taylor & Ng.

Schafer, Charles, jt. auth. see Schafer, Violet.

Schafer, Edward. Ancient China. LC 67-30847. (Great Ages of Man). (Illus.). (gr. 6 up). 1967. PLB 11.97 o.p. (ISBN 0-8094-0379-X, Pub. by Time-Life). Silver.

Schafer, Edward H. The Divine Woman: Dragon Ladies & Rain Maidens in T'ang Literature. LC 80-15073. 264p. 1980. pap. 10.00 (ISBN 0-86547-009-X). N Point Pr.

--The Divine Woman: Dragon Ladies & Rain Maidens in T'ang Literature. LC 73-78543. 1973. 12.50x o.s.i. (ISBN 0-520-02465-6). U of Cal Pr.

--The Golden Peaches of Samarkand: A Study of T'ang Exotics. LC 63-8922. 1963. 42.50x (ISBN 0-520-01144-9). U of Cal Pr.

--Pacing the Void: T'ang Approaches to the Stars. LC 76-48362. 1978. 48.50x (ISBN 0-520-03344-2). U of Cal Pr.

--Shore of Pearls: Hainan Island in Early Times. LC 78-94990. (Illus.). 1970. 30.00x (ISBN 0-520-01592-4). U of Cal Pr.

--Tu Wan's Stone Catalogue of Cloudy Forest: A Commentary & Synopsis. LC 60-10361. (Illus.). 1961. 24.50x (ISBN 0-520-01143-0). U of Cal Pr.

--The Vermilion Bird: T'ang Images of the South. LC 67-10463. 1967. 34.50x o.s.i. (ISBN 0-520-01145-7). U of Cal Pr.

Schafer, Eldon L., et al. Practical Financial Management for Dental Practice Administration, 4 vols. Center for Research in Ambulatory Health Care Administration, ed. 1982. slipcase 65.00 (ISBN 0-686-36938-6). Ctr Res Ambulatory.

Schafer, Harald. Chemical Transport Reactions. Frankfort, Hans, tr. 1964. 34.00 (ISBN 0-12-621750-5). Acad Pr.

Schafer, John, jt. auth. see Foth, Henry.

Schafer, Kermit. Blooper Tube. 1979. 10.00 o.p. (ISBN 0-517-53789-3); pap. 5.95 o.p. (ISBN 0-517-53790-7). Crown.

--The Blunderful World of Bloopers. (Illus.). 1976. 5.98 o.p. (ISBN 0-517-52630-1, Bounty Bk.). Crown.

Schafer, P. Process Control Computer Technology. 29.95 (ISBN 0-471-26013-4, Wiley Heyden). Wiley.

Schafer, R. Murray. The Public of the Music Theatre--Louis Riel: A Case Study. 1972. pap. 7.25 (ISBN 0-685-93739-9, 51-26702). Eur-Am Music.

--The Rhinoceros in the Classroom. 1975. pap. 10.00 (ISBN 0-900938-44-7, 50-26922). Eur-Am Music.

Schafer, Richard C. Chiropractic Management of Sports & Recreational Injuries. (Illus.). 580p. 1982. lib. bdg. 44.00 (ISBN 0-683-07581-0). Williams & Wilkins.

Schafer, Richard D. Introduction to Nonassociative Algebras. (Pure & Applied Mathematics: Vol. 22). 1966. 34.50 (ISBN 0-12-622450-1). Acad Pr.

Schafer, Robert & Ladd, Helen F. Discrimination in Mortgage Lending. (MIT-Harvard Joint Center for Urban Studies). 448p. 1981. 45.00x (ISBN 0-262-19192-X). MIT Pr.

Schafer, Rollie, jt. auth. see Oakley, Bruce.

Schafer, Ronald W., jt. auth. see Oppenheim, Alan V.

Schafer, Ronald W., jt. auth. see Rabiner, Lawrence R.

Schafer, Ronald W. & Markel, John D., eds. Speech Analysis. LC 78-65706. 1979. 40.95 (ISBN 0-87942-119-3). Inst Electrical.

Schafer, Roy. The Analytic Attitude. 1983. 20.95 (ISBN 0-465-00267-6). Basic.

--A New Language for Psychoanalysis. LC 75-18185. 432p. 1976. 30.00x o.p. (ISBN 0-300-01894-0); pap. 9.95x o.p. (ISBN 0-300-02761-3, Y-403). Yale U Pr.

Schafer, Stephen. Compensation & Restitution to Victims of Crime. 2nd ed. LC 74-108237. (Criminology, Law Enforcement, & Social Problems Ser.: No. 120). 227p. (Orig.). 1970. 12.00x (ISBN 0-87585-120-7); pap. 6.00x (ISBN 0-87585-901-1). Patterson Smith.

--Introduction to Criminology. 352p. 1976. 19.00 o.p. (ISBN 0-87909-390-0). Reston.

--Readings in Contemporary Criminology. 1976. pap. text ed. 12.95 (ISBN 0-87909-702-7). Reston.

--Victimology: The Victim & His Criminal. 192p. 1977. ref. ed. 16.95 (ISBN 0-87909-874-0). Reston.

Schafer, Stephen & Knudten, Richard D., eds. Criminological Theory: Foundations & Perceptions. LC 76-18488. 288p. 1977. 24.95x (ISBN 0-669-00795-1). Lexington Bks.

Schafer, Violet & Schafer, Charles. Coffee. LC 76-14182. (Illus.). 1976. pap. 5.95 (ISBN 0-394-73253-7, Dist. by Random). Taylor & Ng.

Schafer, Violet, jt. auth. see Schafer, Charles.

Schafer, Walt. Stress, Distress & Growth. LC 78-51073. (Dialogue Bks). (Illus.). 1978. pap. 7.75 o.p. (ISBN 0-931364-00-0); student manual 4.75 o.p. (ISBN 0-931364-01-9). Intl Dialogue Pr.

--Wellness Managing Stress Through Stress Management. LC 82-80484. (Dialogue Bks.). 368p. 1982. pap. 15.75 (ISBN 0-89881-012-4). Intl Dialogue Pr.

Schafer, William J. Confessions & Statements. 104p. 1968. photocopy ed. spiral 10.75x (ISBN 0-398-01655-0). C C Thomas.

Schaff, Harrison H., ed. Three Irish Plays. Incl. Land of Heart's Desire. Yeats, William B; Twisting of the Rope. Hyde, Douglas; Riders to the Sea. Synge, John M. 1962. pap. 3.00 (ISBN 0-8283-1457-8, IPL). Branden.

Schaff, Joanne D. The Language Arts Idea Book: Classroom Activities for Children. LC 75-16597. 1976. 10.95 o.p. (ISBN 0-87620-520-1); pap. text ed. 11.95x (ISBN 0-673-16380-6). Scott F.

Schaff, M. E. & Siebring, B. R. Basic Chemistry. 416p. 1982. pap. text ed. 19.95 (ISBN 0-8403-2802-8). Kendall-Hunt.

--Basic Chemistry: Problems Book. 64p. 1982. saddle stitched 3.95 (ISBN 0-8403-2819-2). Kendall-Hunt.

Schaff, M. E., jt. auth. see Siebring, B. R.

Schaff, Mary E., jt. auth. see Siebring, B. Richard.

Schaff, Philip. The Creeds of Christendom, 3 vols. Incl. The History of Creeds. Vol. 1; The Greek & Latin Creeds with Translations. Vol. 2; The Evangelical Protestant Creeds with Translations. Vol. 3. 1977. Set. 65.00 (ISBN 0-8010-8090-8). Baker Bk.

--The Creeds of Christendom, 3 vols. 1983. price not set (ISBN 0-8010-8232-3). Baker Bk.

Schaffarcick, Jon & Hampson, David. Strategies for Curriculum Development. LC 75-24652. 250p. 1975. 20.75x (ISBN 0-8211-0756-9); text ed. 18.60x (ISBN 0-685-57429-6). McCutchan.

Schaffarzick, Jon & Sykes, Gary. Value Conflicts & Curriculum Issues. LC 79-88125. 1980. 22.00 (ISBN 0-8211-1857-9); text ed. 20.20 in copies of 10 (ISBN 0-685-96794-8). McCutchan.

Schaffer, jt. auth. see Tuazon.

Schaffer, jt. auth. see Tuazon, Redentor M.

Schaffer, Barbara. Hush, Little Baby. (Platt & Munk Peggy Cloth Squeekum Bks.). (Illus.). 10p. (ps). 1982. 3.50 (ISBN 0-448-46829-8, G&D). Putnam Pub Group.

Schaffer, Daniel. Garden Cities for America: The Radburn Experience. 276p. 1982. 29.95 (ISBN 0-87722-258-4). Temple U Pr.

Schaffer, Elyse, jt. auth. see Ross, Diane.

Schaffer, Jeffrey P. Crater Lake National Park & Vicinity. Winnett, Thomas, ed. (Illus.). 160p. (Orig.). 1983. pap. 8.95 (ISBN 0-89997-020-6). Wilderness Pr.

--Yosemite National Park & Vicinity. Winnett, Thomas, ed. (Illus.). 304p. 1983. pap. 12.95 (ISBN 0-89997-028-1). Wilderness Pr.

Schaffer, Jeffrey P., et al. Pacific Crest Trail, Vol. 2: Oregon & Washington. 3rd ed. Winnett, Thomas, ed. LC 72-96122. (Illus.). 328p. (Orig.). 1979. pap. 14.95 (ISBN 0-911824-82-0). Wilderness.

Schaffer, Ronald. The United States in World War I: A Selected Bibliography. Burns, Richard D., ed. LC 78-18456. (War-Peace Bibliography Ser.: No. 7). 224p. 1978. text ed. 24.75 (ISBN 0-87436-274-1). ABC-Clio.

Schaffer, Ulrich. Searching for You. LC 77-20458. 1978. pap. 9.57i (ISBN 0-06-067083-5, RD 259, HarpR). Har-Row.

--Surprised by Light. LC 80-7751. (Illus.). 80p. 1980. 10.53i (ISBN 0-06-067086-X, HarpR); pap. 9.95i (ISBN 0-06-067087-8, RD 335). Har-Row.

Schaffert, Arthur. The Aquanauts. LC 78-125401. (Science Is What & Why Ser). (Illus.). (gr. k-3). 1971. PLB 4.49 o.p. (ISBN 0-698-30015-7, Coward). Putnam Pub Group.

Schaffner, Betty. Designs to Color, 6 bks. (ps-2). 1968. Bk. 1. 2.50 (ISBN 0-8431-0005-2); Bk. 2. 2.50 (ISBN 0-8431-0006-0); Bk. 3. 2.50 (ISBN 0-8431-0007-9); Bk. 4. 2.50 (ISBN 0-8431-0008-7); Bk. 5. 2.50 (ISBN 0-8431-0104-0); Bk. 6. 1.95 (ISBN 0-8431-0218-7). Price Stern.

Schaffner, Fenton, jt. ed. see Popper, Hans.

Schaffner, Nicholas. The Beatles Forever. (Illus.). 1978. pap. 9.95 (ISBN 0-07-055087-5, SP). McGraw.

--The Boys from Liverpool. LC 79-25917. (Illus.). (gr. 6 up). 1980. 11.95 (ISBN 0-416-30661-6). Methuen Inc.

Schaffner, Nicholas, jt. auth. see Shotton, Peter.

Schaffner, Val. Algonquin Cat. (Illus.). 1980. 9.95 o.s.i. (ISBN 0-440-00073-4). Delacorte.

Schafritz, Jay M. Dictionary of Personnel Management & Labor Relations. LC 79-24632. (Orig.). 1980. 29.00 (ISBN 0-935610-09-X). Moore Pub IL.

Schaie, K. Warner & Geiwitz, James. Adult Development & Aging. 1982. text ed. 22.95 (ISBN 0-316-77271-2); tchrs.' manual avail. (ISBN 0-316-77273-9). Little.

Schaifers, K. & Voigt, H. H., eds. Astronomy & Astrophysics: Interstellar Matter, Galaxy, Universe. (Landolt-Boernstein, New Series. Group VI: Vol. 2, Subvol. C). (Illus.). 490p. 1983. 780.00 (ISBN 0-387-10977-3). Springer-Verlag.

Schain, Martin, jt. ed. see Cerny, Philip.

Schain, Martin A. French Communism & Local Power: Urban Politics & Political Change. LC 81-84035. 1983. write for info (ISBN 0-312-30445-5). St Martin.

Schainblatt, Al & Hatry, Harry. Mental Health Services: What Happens To the Client? (Illus.). 119p. (Orig.). 1980. pap. text ed. 5.50 (ISBN 0-87766-275-4). Urban Inst.

Schainblatt, Al & Koss, Margo. Fire Code Inspections & Fire Prevention: What Methods Lead to Success? (Illus.). 122p. (Orig.). pap. text ed. 5.00 (ISBN 0-686-84409-2). Urban Inst.

Schakel, David J. Volleyball. (Illus.). 145p. 1980. pap. text ed. 4.95x (ISBN 0-89641-060-9). American Pr.

Schakel, Peter G., ed. The Longing for a Form: Essay on the Fiction of C. S. Lewis. (Illus.). 256p. 1977. 14.50x (ISBN 0-87338-234-X). Kent St U Pr.

Schalet, Lilian L. Reality. 70p. (Orig.). 1983. pap. 5.00 (ISBN 0-682-49940-4). Exposition.

Schalit, M. Guide to the Literature of the Sugar Industry. 1970. 21.50 (ISBN 0-444-40839-8). Elsevier.

Schall, James V. Distinctiveness of Christianity. LC 81-83566. 298p. (Orig.). 1983. pap. 9.95 (ISBN 0-89870-012-4). Ignatius Pr.

--Liberation Theology. LC 80-82266. 402p. (Orig.). 1982. pap. 10.95 (ISBN 0-89870-006-X). Ignatius Pr.

--The Sixth Paul. LC 77-71026. (Illus., Orig.). 1977. pap. 1.75 o.p. (ISBN 0-8189-1147-6, 147, Pub. by Alba Bks). Alba.

--Welcome, Number 4,000,000,000! LC 77-71021. (Orig.). 1977. pap. 1.75 o.p. (ISBN 0-8189-1145-X, 145, Pub. by Alba Bks). Alba.

Schall, Larry, jt. auth. see Haley, Charles W.

Schall, Lawrence D. & Haley, Charles W. Introduction to Financial Management. 2nd ed. (Finance Ser.). (Illus.). 1980. text ed. 24.95 (ISBN 0-07-055100-6); instr's manual 25.00 (ISBN 0-07-055101-4); study guide 9.95 (ISBN 0-07-055102-2). McGraw.

--Introduction to Financial Management. (Finance Ser.). (Illus.). 1977. text ed. 21.00 (ISBN 0-07-055097-2, C). McGraw.

--Introduction to Financial Management. 3rd ed. (McGraw-Hill Ser. in Finance). (Illus.). 944p. 1983. text ed. 25.95 (ISBN 0-07-055106-5, C); instr's manual 8.95 (ISBN 0-07-055108-1); study guide 9.95 (ISBN 0-07-055107-3). McGraw.

Schall, Lawrence D., jt. auth. see Haley, Charles W.

Schall, Maxine. Limits: A Search for New Values. 352p. 1981. 12.95 (ISBN 0-517-54143-2, C N Potter Bks). Crown.

Schallenberg, Richard H. Bottled Energy: Electrical Engineering & the Evolution of Chemical Energy. LC 80-68493. (Memoirs Ser.: Vol. 148). 1982. 20.00 (ISBN 0-686-82855-0). Am Philos.

Schallenberger, E., jt. auth. see Karg, H.

Schaller, Frank, ed. see World Food Conference, Ames, Iowa June, 1976.

Schaller, Frank W. & Bailey, George W., eds. Agricultural Management & Water Quality. (Illus.). 400p. 1983. text ed. 16.95 (ISBN 0-8138-0082-X). Iowa St U Pr.

Schaller, George B. Golden Shadows, Flying Hooves: With a New Afterword. LC 82-23731. (Illus.). 344p. 1983. pap. 9.95 (ISBN 0-226-73632-6). U of Chicago Pr.

--Mountain Monarchs: Wild Sheep & Goats of the Himalaya. LC 77-1336. (Wildlife Behavior & Ecology Ser.). 1977. lib. bdg. 27.50x (ISBN 0-226-73641-5); pap. 12.50 (ISBN 0-226-73642-3). U of Chicago Pr.

Schaller, George B. & Selsam, Millicent E. The Tiger: Its Life in the Wild. LC 69-14447. 72p. (gr. 5-8). 1969. PLB 8.79 (ISBN 0-06-025280-4, HarpJ). Har-Row.

Schaller, Lyle E. Growing Plans: Strategies to Increase your Church's Membership. 176p. 1983. pap. 6.95 (ISBN 0-687-15962-8). Abingdon.

Schaller, Lyle E. & Tidwell, Charles A. Creative Church Administration. LC 75-15953. 208p. (Orig.). 1975. pap. 4.95 o.p. (ISBN 0-687-09816-5). Abingdon.

Schaller, Michael. The United States & China in the Twentieth Century. (Illus.). 1979. 13.95x (ISBN 0-19-502598-9). Oxford U Pr.

--The United States & China in the Twentieth Century. (Illus.). 1979. pap. text ed. 5.95x (ISBN 0-19-502599-7). Oxford U Pr.

Schaller, W., jt. auth. see Worick, W.

Schaller, Waldemar T. & Vlisidis, Angelina C. Mineralogy & Geochemistry of the Read Magnetite Deposit, Southwestern Stevens County, Washington: & Ludwigite from Read Magnetite Deposit, Stevens County, Washington. (Reprint Ser.: No. 7). 13p. Repr. of 1962 ed. 0.25 (ISBN 0-686-36914-9). Geologic Pubns.

Schallert, William F. & Clark, Carol R. Programming in FORTRAN. LC 78-74039. 1979. pap. text ed. 18.95 (ISBN 0-201-06716-1). A-W.

Schalles, Wade. A Pictorial History of Wrestling. LC 82-81800. (Illus.). 300p. 1983. 29.95 (ISBN 0-88011-074-0). Leisure Pr.

Scham, Alan. Lyautey in Morocco: Protectorate Administration, 1912-1925. LC 74-92680. 1970. 33.00x (ISBN 0-520-01602-5). U of Cal Pr.

Schama, Simon. Two Rothschilds & the Land of Israel. LC 77-20367. (Illus.). 1978. 15.95 o.p. (ISBN 0-394-50137-3). Knopf.

Schambach, Mardel C. & Campbell, Evelyn. The Kings Diet. LC 79-89582. 1979. 5.95 (ISBN 0-89221-068-0). New Leaf.

Schambra, William A., jt. ed. see Goldwin, Robert A.

Schamroth, Leo. Diagnostic Pointers in Electrocardiology, Vol. I. (Illus.). 268p. 1978. text ed. 24.95 o.p. (ISBN 0-913486-87-6). Charles.

--Diagnostic Pointers in Electrocardiology, Vol. 2. LC 79-51385. (Cardiology & Critical Care Ser.). (Illus.). 248p. 1979. text ed. 24.95 o.p. (ISBN 0-89303-004-X). Charles.

Schank, Kenneth, jt. ed. see Arnold, Joseph.

Schank, R. C. Conceptual Information Processing. LC 74-84874. (Fundamental Studies in Computer Science: Vol. 3). 374p. 1975. 64.00 (ISBN 0-444-10773-8, North-Holland). Elsevier.

Schank, Roger & Abelson, Robert. Scripts, Plans, Goals, & Understanding: An Inquiry into Human Knowledge Structures. 256p. 1977. text ed. 14.95 (ISBN 0-89859-138-4). L Erlbaum Assocs.

Schank, Roger C. Dynamic Memory: A Theory of Reminding & Learning in Computers & People. LC 82-1353. 240p. 1983. 29.95 (ISBN 0-521-24858-2); pap. 10.95 (ISBN 0-521-27029-4). Cambridge U Pr.

Schank, Roger C. & Riesbeck, Christopher K. Inside Computer Understanding: Five Programs Plus Miniatures. LC 80-18314. (Artificial Intelligence Ser.). 400p. 1981. text ed. 29.95x (ISBN 0-89859-071-X). L Erlbaum Assocs.

Schanker, H. H., jt. auth. see Ommanney, K. A.

Schanker, Harry H. The Spoken Word. Rothermich, John A., ed. LC 80-24143. (Illus.). 384p. 1981. text ed. 14.60 (ISBN 0-07-055135-9); tchrs. manual 2.44 (ISBN 0-07-055136-7). McGraw.

Schanker, Harry H., jt. auth. see Ommanney, K. A.

Schansberg, David. Homeowner's Guide to Wood Refinishing. (Do-It-Yourself Bks.). (Illus.). 96p. 1982. pap. 3.95 (ISBN 0-686-84011-9). Ideals.

Schantz, Maria E. & Brynner, Joseph F., eds. Reading in American Schools: A Guide to Information Sources. LC 79-23770. (Education Information Guide Ser.: Vol. 5). 1980. 42.00x (ISBN 0-8103-1456-8). Gale.

Schanz, Holly L. Greek Sculptural Groups: Archaic & Classical. LC 78-74971. (Outstanding Dissertations in the Fine Arts Ser.). 190p. 1979. lib. bdg. 20.00 o.s.i. (ISBN 0-8240-3973-4). Garland Pub.

Schanz, John P. Sacraments of Life & Worship. (Orig.). 1966. 4.75 o.p. (ISBN 0-685-07664-4, 80667); pap. 3.95x o.p. (ISBN 0-685-07665-2, 82752). Glencoe.

--A Theology of Community. 1977. pap. text ed. 12.50 (ISBN 0-8191-0177-X). U Pr of Amer.

Schanz, John T., jt. auth. see Frank, Helmut.

Schanzenbach, Douglas T. Vietnam: My Recollections & Reflections. LC 82-80703. 64p. 1983. pap. 4.95 (ISBN 0-86666-088-7). GWP.

Schanzenbach, Gordon, ed. see Ridgley, Marlene.

Schanzer, Ernest. The Problem Plays of Shakespeare: A Study of Julius Caesar, Measure for Measure, Antony & Cleopatra. LC 63-9752. 1963. pap. 1.95 o.p. (ISBN 0-8052-0110-6). Schocken.

Schanzer, Stephan N., jt. auth. see Brown, Herbert P.

Schaper, Robert N. Why Me, God? 2nd ed. LC 73-82763. 160p. 1977. pap. 2.50 o.p. (ISBN 0-8307-0452-3, S273-1-28). Regal.

Schaper, W. Pathophysiology of Myocardial Perfusion. 1980. 141.75 (ISBN 0-444-80048-4). Elsevier.

Schapera, J. Kinship Terminology in Jane Austen's Novels. 1977. 35.00x (ISBN 0-686-98250-9, Pub. by Royal Anthro Ireland). State Mutual Bk.

Schapira, Jay N, et al. Two Dimensional Echocardiography. (Illus.). 368p. 1982. lib. bdg. 38.00 (ISBN 0-683-07521-7). Williams & Wilkins.

Schapiro, Harriette, jt. auth. see Parsons, John A.

Schapiro, Leonard see Hayward, Max.

Schapiro, Melvin & Kuritsky, Joel. The Gastroenterology Assistant: A Laboratory Manual. 2nd ed. LC 81-50268. (Illus.). 150p. 1981. 22.50x (ISBN 0-9605718-3-3). Valley Presbyterian.

Schapiro, Robert, jt. auth. see Feinberg, Gerald.

Schapiro, Ruth G., ed. Tax Shelters. 3rd ed. 500p. 1983. text ed. 65.00 (ISBN 0-686-62638-9, J3-1436). PLI.

Schapp, Dick. Ted. LC 79-91296. (Illus., Orig.). 1980. cancelled (ISBN 0-448-16551-1, G&D). Putnam Pub Group.

Schappacher, W., jt. auth. see Kappel, F.

Schappacher, W., jt. ed. see Kappel, F.

Schaps, Hilda W., jt. auth. see Schutz, Albert L.

Schapsmeier, Edward L. & Schapsmeier, Frederick H. Ezra Taft Benson & the Politics of Agriculture: The Eisenhower Years, 1953-61. LC 74-21896. 374p. 1975. pap. 6.50x (ISBN 0-8134-1697-3, 1697). Interstate.

--Prophet in Politics: Henry A. Wallace & the War Years, 1940-1965. LC 70-114795. (Illus.). 1970. 8.95 o.p. (ISBN 0-8138-1295-X). Iowa St U Pr.

Schapsmeier, Edward L., jt. auth. see Schapsmeier, Frederick H.

Schapsmeier, Frederick H. & Schapsmeier, Edward L. Encyclopedia of American Agricultural History. LC 74-34563. 467p. (Orig.). 1975. lib. bdg. 35.00x (ISBN 0-8371-7958-0, SAA/). Greenwood.

Schapsmeier, Frederick H., jt. auth. see Schapsmeier, Edward L.

Schar, Kenneth V. Eight Lines-Plus, 1490-1981. LC 81-52652. 331p. 1982. lib. bdg. 30.00 (ISBN 0-686-36427-9). Print Shop.

Schara, Ron. Ron Schara's Twin Cities Fishing Guide. LC 81-22555. (Illus.). 120p. 1982. pap. 6.95 (ISBN 0-932272-08-8). Minneapolis Tribune.

Schardt, Emma Von, ed. see Kohler, Carl.

Scharer, Peter & Rinn, L. A., eds. Esthetic Guidelines for Restorative Dentistry. Koehler, Henry M., tr. from Ger. (Illus.). 236p. 1982. text ed. 72.00 (ISBN 0-86715-111-0). Quint Pub Co.

Scharf, Bertram, et al. Experimental Sensory Psychology. 286p. 1975. text ed. 18.95x (ISBN 0-673-05428-4). Scott F.

Scharf, C. Bradley. Politics & Social Change in East Germany: An Evaluation of Socialist Democracy. (Westview Special Studies on the Soviet Union & Eastern Europe). 215p. 1983. lib. bdg. 18.50x; pap. text ed. price not set (ISBN 0-86531-451-9). Westview.

Scharf, Lois. To Work & to Wed: Female Employment, Feminism, & the Great Depression. LC 79-52325. (Contributions in Women's Studies: No. 15). 1980. lib. bdg. 27.50x (ISBN 0-313-21445-X, STW/). Greenwood.

Scharf, Lois & Jensen, Joan M., eds. Decades of Discontent: The Women's Movement 1920-1940. LC 81-4243. (Contributions in Women's Studies: No. 28). 352p. 1983. lib. bdg. 35.00 (ISBN 0-313-22694-6). Greenwood.

Scharf, Peter. Moral Education. LC 78-51097. (Dialogue Bks). (Illus.). 224p. 1978. pap. 7.75 (ISBN 0-931364-02-7); wkbk., 144p. 9.75 (ISBN 0-89881-003-5). Intl Dialogue Pr.

Scharf, Peter, jt. auth. see Binder, Arnold.

Scharf, Robert. Wall Coverings: Paneling, Painting, & Papering. 96p. 1982. pap. 3.95 (ISBN 0-8249-6123-4). Ideals.

Scharf, T. Dictionary of Development Economics. (Eng. & Fr. & Ger.). 1969. 46.50 (ISBN 0-444-40799-5). Elsevier.

Scharf, Thomas J. History of Maryland from the Earliest Period to the Present Day, 3 vols. LC 67-5141. (Illus.). 1967. Repr. of 1879 ed. incl. index 109.00x (ISBN 0-8103-5037-8); index only 27.00 (ISBN 0-8103-5038-6). Gale.

Scharf, W. Particle Accelerators & Their Uses. Lepa, E., tr. from Polish. (Accelerators & Storage Rings Ser.: Vol. 3). 500p. Date not set. 99.50 o.p. (ISBN 3-7186-0034-X). Harwood Academic.

Scharfetter, C. General Psychopathology. Marshall, Helen, tr. from Ger. LC 79-52853. (Illus.). 1980. 54.50 (ISBN 0-521-22812-3); pap. 17.95x (ISBN 0-521-29655-2). Cambridge U Pr.

Scharff, B. Basics of Electric Appliance Servicing. 1976. 19.95 (ISBN 0-07-055141-3, P&RB). McGraw.

--Refrigeration, Air-Conditioning, Range & Oven Servicing. 1976. 22.95 o.p. (ISBN 0-07-055144-8, P&RB). McGraw.

--Small Appliance Servicing Guide: Motor-Driven & Resistance-Heated Appliances. 1976. 19.95 (ISBN 0-07-055142-1, P&RB). McGraw.

Scharff, David E. The Sexual Relationship: An Object Relations View of Sex & the Family. 288p. 1983. 27.50 (ISBN 0-7100-9072-2). Routledge & Kegan.

Scharff, Robert. The Complete Book of Home Remodeling. 1975. 27.50 (ISBN 0-07-055167-7, P&RB). McGraw.

--The Complete Book of Home Workshop Tools. LC 78-14822. (Illus.). 1979. 16.95 o.p. (ISBN 0-07-055042-5, P&RB). McGraw.

--Complete Book of Wood Finishing. 2nd ed. (Illus.). 384p. 1974. 24.95 (ISBN 0-07-055166-9, P&RB). McGraw.

--First Aid for Your Car. 1980. pap. 3.50 (ISBN 0-451-11150-8, AE1150, Sig). NAL.

--Hunter's Game, Gun & Dog Guide. (Quick & Easy Ser). (Orig.). 1967. pap. 1.95 o.p. (ISBN 0-02-081570-0, Collier). Macmillan.

--Ice Hockey Rules in Pictures. LC 73-3667. (Sports Handbooks Ser.). (Illus.). 1973. pap. 2.95 o.p. (ISBN 0-448-01547-1, G&D). Putnam Pub Group.

Scharff, Robert, rev. by see Swezey, Kenneth.

Scharfstein, Ben-Ami. The Philosophers: Life & Thought. 1980. 29.95x (ISBN 0-19-520137-X). Oxford U Pr.

Scharfstein, Ben-Ami, ed. Philosophy East-Philosophy West: A Critical Comparison of Indian, Chinese, Islamic & European Philosophy. 1979. 22.50x (ISBN 0-19-520064-0). Oxford U Pr.

Scharnhorst, Gary. Horatio Alger, Jr. (United States Authors Ser.). 1980. lib. bdg. 11.95 (ISBN 0-8057-7252-9, Twayne). G K Hall.

Scharnhorst, Gerhard J. von see Von Scharnhorst, Gerhard J.

Scharper, Philip J., jt. ed. see Cassidy, Richard J.

Scharzenberger, Georg, jt. ed. see Keeton, George W.

Schatborn, Peter & Van Hasselt, Carlos. Dutch Genre Drawings. LC 72-86013. (Illus.). 162p. (Orig.). 1972. pap. 7.50 (ISBN 0-88397-022-8). Intl Exhibit Foun.

Schatell, Brian. Midge & Fred. LC 82-48540. (Illus.). 32p. (ps-2). 1983. 8.61i (ISBN 0-397-32046-9, JBL-J); PLB 8.89g (ISBN 0-397-32047-7). Har-Row.

Schatt, Roy. James Dean: A Portrait. (Illus.). 144p. (Orig.). 1982. pap. 8.95 (ISBN 0-933328-24-9). Delilah Bks.

Schatt, Stanley. Kurt Vonnegut, Jr. (United States Authors Ser.). 1976. lib. bdg. 12.95 (ISBN 0-8057-7176-X, Twayne). G K Hall.

Schatt, Stanley, jt. ed. see Mandelik, Peter.

Schattenkirchner, M. & Mueller, W., eds. Gold Therapy. (Rheumatology Ser.: Vol. 8). (Illus.). viii, 200p. 1983. 78.00 (ISBN 3-8055-3630-5). S Karger.

Schatter, Richard, ed. see Morgan, Joseph.

Schattle, M., tr. see Brentano, Franz.

Schattle, Margarete, tr. see Wittgenstein, Ludwig.

Schattner, Gertrud & Courtney, Richard, eds. Drama in Therapy, 2 vols. Incl. Drama in Therapy Vol. 1: Children. 392p. 1981. text ed. 19.95x (ISBN 0-89676-013-8); Drama in Therapy Vol. II: Adults. 392p. 1981. text ed. 19.95x (ISBN 0-89676-014-6). LC 80-15680. Drama Bk.

Schattner, Regina. Early Childhood Curriculum for Multiply Handicapped Children. (John Day Bk.). 1971. 10.53xi (ISBN 0-381-97033-7, A20700). T Y Crowell.

Schattschneider, E. E. Party Government. LC 76-56414. 1977. Repr. of 1942 ed. lib. bdg. 21.00x (ISBN 0-8371-9412-1, SCPG). Greenwood.

Schattschneider, Elmer E., et al. Guide to the Study of Public Affairs. LC 73-1406. 135p. 1973. Repr. of 1952 ed. lib. bdg. 18.75x (ISBN 0-8371-6800-7, SCPA). Greenwood.

Schatz, Anne E. & Funk, Berverley M. Transcription Skills for Information Processing, Unit 2. 112p. 1981. pap. text ed. 4.24 (ISBN 0-07-055201-0, G); tchrs. manual & key 4.00 (ISBN 0-07-055212-6); cassettes 120.00 (ISBN 0-07-087832-3). McGraw.

Schatz, Anne E. & Funk, Beverley M. Transcription Skills for Information Processing, Unit 1. 96p. 1981. pap. text ed. 4.24 (ISBN 0-07-055200-2, G); cassettes 120.00 (ISBN 0-07-087831-5). McGraw.

Schatz, Anne E. & Funk, Beverly M. Transcription Skills for Information Processing: Incorporating a Sequence Language Arts Program, Unit 3. (Illus.). 112p. 1981. pap. 4.24 text-wkbk. (ISBN 0-07-055202-9, G); dictation tapes 850.00 (ISBN 0-07-087830-7); tchr's. manual & key 4.00 (ISBN 0-07-055213-4). McGraw.

Schatz, Evalina. Revolutionary Textile Design: Russia in the 1920's & 1930's. 1983. 26.95 (ISBN 0-670-59712-0); pap. 14.95 (ISBN 0-670-59713-9). Viking Pr.

Schatz, G., ed. see Lee, C. P., et al.

Schatz, Howard. Essential Flourescein Angiography: A Compendium of 100 Classic Cases. (Illus.). 1982. text & slides 155.00 (ISBN 0-9608102-1-8). Pacific Med Pr.

Schatz, Howard, et al. Interpretation of Fundus Fluorescein Angiography. new ed. LC 77-19094. (Illus.). 762p. 1977. text ed. 84.50 o.p. (ISBN 0-8016-4343-0). Mosby.

Schatz, Letta. Banji's Magic Wheel. (Picture Bk). (Illus.). 32p. (gr. k-3). 1974. 5.95 o.s.i. (ISBN 0-695-80441-3); PLB 5.97 o.s.i. (ISBN 0-695-40441-5). Follett.

Schatz, Pauline. Manual in Clinical Dietetics. 2nd ed. (Plycon Home Economics Ser.). 142p. 1978. spiral 6.95x. Burgess.

Schatz, Sayre P. Nigerian Capitalism. LC 74-16718. 1978. 40.00x (ISBN 0-520-02859-7). U of Cal Pr.

Schatz, Sayre P., ed. South of the Sahara: Development in African Economies. LC 72-84173. 371p. 1973. 24.95 (ISBN 0-87722-014-X). Temple U Pr.

Schatz, Thomas. Hollywood Genres: Formulas, Filmmaking & the Studio System. (Illus.). 320p. 1981. 29.95 (ISBN 0-87722-222-3). Temple U Pr.

Schatz, Thomas G. Old Hollywood-New Hollywood: Ritual, Art, & Industry. Kirkpatrick, Diane, ed. LC 82-1910. (Studies in Cinema: No. 15). 326p. 1983. 44.95 (ISBN 0-8357-1308-3, Pub. by UMI Res Pr). Univ Microfilms.

Schatzker, J., et al, trs. see Mueller, M. E., et al.

Schatzki, Walter, ed. Old & Rare Children's Books Offered for Sale by Walter Schatzki, Dealer in Rare Books, Prints & Autographs. LC 73-16044. (Illus.). 46p. 1974. Repr. of 1941 ed. 30.00x (ISBN 0-8103-3878-5). Gale.

Schatzman, Leonard & Strauss, Anselm L. Field Research: Strategies for a Natural Society. (Methods of Social Science Ser). 176p. 1973. pap. text ed. 13.95 (ISBN 0-13-314351-1). P-H.

Schatzman, Morton. Soul Murder: Persecution in the Family. 1976. pap. 1.75 o.p. (ISBN 0-451-61499-2, ME1499, Ment). NAL.

--The Story of Ruth: One Women's Haunting Psychiatric Odyssey. 1980. 11.95 (ISBN 0-399-12234-6). Putnam Pub Group.

Schatzman, Morton, ed. see De Saint-Denys, Hervey.

Schaub, J. H. & Dickison, S. K. Engineering & the Humanities. 503p. 1982. text ed. 29.95x (ISBN 0-471-08909-5, Pub. by Wiley-Interscience). Wiley.

Schaudinischky, L. H. Sound, Man, & Building. (Illus.). 1976. 57.50x (ISBN 0-85334-655-0, Pub. by Applied Sci England). Elsevier.

Schauensee, Max De see De Schauensee, Max.

Schauer & Caspari. A Field Guide to the Wild Flowers of Britain & Europe. pap. 18.95 (ISBN 0-686-42739-4, Collins Pub England). Greene.

Schauer, Frederick. Free Speech: A Philosophical Enquiry. LC 82-4170. 250p. 1982. 34.50 (ISBN 0-521-24340-8); pap. 9.95 (ISBN 0-521-28617-4). Cambridge U Pr.

Schauer, R., ed. Sialic Acids: Chemistry, Metabolism, & Function. (Cell Biology Monographs: Vol. 10). (Illus.). 344p. 1983. 68.00 (ISBN 0-387-81707-7). Springer-Verlag.

Schauer, William H. The Politics of Space: A Comparison of the Soviet & American Space Programs. LC 74-84657. 317p. 1976. text ed. 35.00x (ISBN 0-8419-0185-6). Holmes & Meier.

Schaum, Konrad, ed. Deutsche Lyrik. (Orig., Ger.). 1963. pap. 2.95x o.p. (ISBN 0-393-09612-2, NortonC). Norton.

Schaumann, et al. Modern Active Filter Design. LC 81-2368. 426p. 1981. 30.95x (ISBN 0-471-09734-9, Pub. by Wiley-Interscience); pap. 20.00 (ISBN 0-471-09733-0, Pub. by Wiley-Interscience). Wiley.

Schaumberg, Herbert H., jt. auth. see Spencer, Peter S.

Schaumberg-Lever, Gundula, jt. auth. see Lever, Walter F.

Schaumburg, Herbert H., et al. Disorders of Peripheral Nerves. LC 82-22143. (Contemporary Neurology Ser.: No. 24). (Illus.). 240p. 1983. 35.00 (ISBN 0-8036-7732-4). Davis Co.

Schaupp, Dietrich L. A Cross-Cultural Study of a Multinational Company: Attitudinal Responses to Participative Management. LC 78-8453. (Praeger Special Studies). 184p. 1978. 24.95 o.p. (ISBN 0-03-022871-9). Praeger.

Schaupp, Wilhelm. External Walls: Cladding, Thermal Insulation, Dampproofing. 1967. 15.00x o.p. (ISBN 0-685-20580-0). Transatlantic.

Schauss, Alexander. Diet, Crime & Delinquency. 5.95 (ISBN 0-939764-00-8). Cancer Control Soc.

Schaya, Leo. The Universal Meaning of the Kabbalah. 1973. pap. 2.95 (ISBN 0-14-003614-8). Penguin.

Scheader, Catherine. Mary Cassatt. LC 77-7359. (They Found a Way Ser.). (Illus.). 80p. (gr. 4-12). 1978. PLB 10.60 (ISBN 0-516-01852-3). Childrens.

Scheaff, Nicholas. Iveagh House. (Aspects of Ireland Ser.: Vol. 2). (Illus.). 65p. (Orig.). 1978. pap. 5.95 (ISBN 0-906404-02-9, Pub. by Dept Foreign Ireland). Irish Bks Media.

Schebera, Richard L. Christian, Non-Christian Dialogue: The Vision of Robert C. Zaehner. LC 78-64369. 1978. pap. text ed. 9.50 (ISBN 0-8191-0629-1). U Pr of Amer.

Schechner, Richard. The End of Humanism: Writings on Performance. LC 82-62094. 1982. 18.95 (ISBN 0-933826-18-4); pap. 6.95 (ISBN 0-933826-19-2). Performing Arts.

Schechter, Harold & Semeiks, Jonna G. Discoveries: Fifty Stories of the Quest. 608p. (Orig.). 1983. pap. text ed. 10.95t (ISBN 0-672-61563-0); instr's. guide 3.33 (ISBN 0-672-61564-9). Bobbs.

Schechter, Martin. Modern Methods in Partial Differential Equations. 1977. text ed. 42.50x (ISBN 0-07-055193-6, C). McGraw.

Schechter, R. S., jt. ed. see Shah, D. O.

Schechter, Robert S., jt. auth. see Beveridge, S. G.

Schechter, Solomon. Aspects of Rabbinic Theology: Major Concepts of the Talmud. LC 61-14919. 1961. pap. 8.95 (ISBN 0-8052-0015-0). Schocken.

Scheck, Joan. Two Men in the Temple. (Arch Bks: Set 5). (Illus.). (gr. 5). 1968. laminated bdg. 0.89 (ISBN 0-570-06036-2, 59-1149). Concordia.

Scheck, Joann. Man Who Couldn't Wait: Story of Peter. (Arch Bks: Set 8). (Illus., Orig.). (ps-4). 1971. pap. 0.89 (ISBN 0-570-06056-7, 59-1173). Concordia.

--Man Who Took Seven Baths. (Arch Bks, Set 7). (Illus., Orig.). (ps-3). 1970. pap. 0.89 (ISBN 0-570-06048-6, 59-1164). Concordia.

--Three Men Who Walked in Fire. (Arch Bks: Set 4). 1967. laminated bdg. 0.89 (ISBN 0-570-06026-5, 59-1137). Concordia.

Scheckman, Claudia S. The Perfect Chocolate Chip Cookie. LC 80-67918. (Illus.). 44p. (ps-6). Date not set. pap. cancelled (ISBN 0-916634-09-4). Double M Pr.

Schecter, Susan. Women & Male Violence: The Visions & Struggles of the Battered Women's Movement. 300p. 1982. 20.00 (ISBN 0-89608-160-5); pap. 7.50 (ISBN 0-89608-159-1). South End Pr.

Schedel, J. J. The Splendor of Jade: Four Thousand Years of the Art of Chinese Jade Carving. LC 74-9855. 1974. 37.50 o.p. (ISBN 0-525-49505-3). Dutton.

Schedler, Gilbert. Waking Before Dawn. 1978. pap. 2.95 o.p. (ISBN 0-931694-03-5). Wampeter Pr.

Schedler, Norbert O. Philosophy of Religion: Contemporary Perspectives. (Illus.). 512p. 1974. pap. text ed. 12.95x (ISBN 0-02-406720-2). Macmillan.

Scheel, Joegen. Rivulins of the Old World. 19.95 (ISBN 0-87666-137-1, PS660). TFH Pubns.

Scheel, Lyman. Gas Machinery. LC 70-149760. 270p. 1972. 29.95x (ISBN 0-87201-309-X). Gulf Pub.

Scheer, Arnold H. & Juergenson, E. M. Approved Practices in Fruit & Vine Production. 2nd ed. (Illus.). 550p. 1976. 16.50 (ISBN 0-8134-1704-X, 1704); text ed. 12.50x. Interstate.

Scheer, Bradley T. Animal Physiology. LC 63-12289. 409p. 1963. 17.50 (ISBN 0-471-75805-1, Pub. by Wiley). Krieger.

Scheer, George F., ed. see Martin, Joseph P.

Scheer, Julian. Rain Makes Applesauce. (Illus.). 36p. (gr. k-3). 1964. 10.95 (ISBN 0-8234-0091-3). Holiday.

Scheer, Linda & Ramirez, Miguel, eds. Anthology of Mexican Modern Poetry. 170p. Date not set. 20.00 (ISBN 0-931556-06-6); pap. 7.00 (ISBN 0-931556-07-4). Translation Pr. Postponed.

Scheer, Richard K., jt. auth. see Carney, James D.

Scheer, Robert. What Happened? The Story of Election 1980. 1981. 14.45 (ISBN 0-394-41482-9). Random.

--With Enough Shovels: Reagan, Bush, & Nuclear War. 256p. 1982. 14.95 (ISBN 0-394-41482-9). Random.

Scheer, Samuel, jt. auth. see Schultz, Donald.

Scheer, Steven C. Kalman Mikszath. (World Authors Ser.). 1977. lib. bdg. 15.95 (ISBN 0-8057-6299-X, Twayne). G K Hall.

Scheerenberger, R. C. A History of Mental Retardation. LC 82-9489. (Illus.). 336p. 1982. text ed. 23.95 (ISBN 0-933716-27-3). P H Brookes.

Scheer-Schaezler, Brigitte. Saul Bellow. LC 70-178167. (Literature and Life Ser.). 128p. 1972. 11.95 (ISBN 0-8044-2765-8). Ungar.

Scheff, Michael. The Pushbutton Telephone Songbook. (Illus.). 48p. (Orig.). 1972. pap. 1.75 (ISBN 0-8431-0258-6). Price Stern.

Scheff, Peter A., jt. auth. see Wadden, Richard A.

Scheff, Thomas J. Catharsis in Healing, Ritual & Drama. LC 78-57314. 1980. 19.95x (ISBN 0-520-03710-3); pap. 6.50x (ISBN 0-520-04125-9, CAMPUS NO. 249). U of Cal Pr.

--Labeling Madness. 192p. 1975. 8.95 (ISBN 0-13-517367-1, Spec); pap. 3.95 o.p. (ISBN 0-13-517359-0, Spec). P-H.

Scheff, Thomas J., ed. Mental Illness & Social Processes. (Readers in Social Problems Ser). (Orig.). 1967. pap. 13.50 scp o.p. (ISBN 0-06-045762-7, HarpC). Har-Row.

Scheffauer, Herman, tr. see Kaiser, Georg.

Scheffel, Josef V. Ekkehard. abridged ed. Delffs, Sofie, tr. LC 64-20049. 1965. 9.00 (ISBN 0-8044-2767-4); pap. 3.95 (ISBN 0-8044-6802-8). Ungar.

Scheffer, I. The Progressive in English. (Linguistics Ser.: Vol. 15). 397p. 1975. pap. 51.00 (ISBN 0-444-10770-3, North-Holland). Elsevier.

Scheffer, Paul. Seven Years in Soviet Russia. Livingston, Arthur, tr. from Ger. LC 73-853. (Russian Studies: Perspectives on the Revolution Ser.). 357p. 1973. Repr. of 1932 ed. 26.50 (ISBN 0-88355-050-4). Hyperion Conn.

Scheffer, Victor. Natural History of Marine Mammals. LC 76-14820. (Illus.). 170p. (gr. 8 up). 1976. 7.95 o.p. (ISBN 0-686-96884-0, ScribJ); pap. 5.95 (ISBN 0-684-16952-5). Scribner.

Scheffler, H. W. Australian Kin Classification. LC 77-78391. (Studies in Social Anthropology). (Illus.). 1978. 42.50 (ISBN 0-521-21906-X). Cambridge U Pr.

Scheffler, H. W., ed. see Thomson, Donald F.

Scheffler, Hannah N., ed. Resources for Early Childhood: An Annotated Bibliography & Guide for Educators, Librarians, & Parents. LC 81-48421. 400p. 1982. lib. bdg. 38.50 (ISBN 0-8240-9390-9). Garland Pub.

Scheffler, Israel. Conditions of Knowledge: An Introduction to Epistemology & Education. LC 78-54987. (Midway Reprints Ser.). 1983. pap. 3.95 o.s.i. (ISBN 0-226-73668-7, P789, Phoen); price not set (ISBN 0-226-73669-5). U of Chicago Pr.

--Reason & Teaching. LC 72-86641. 214p. lib. bdg. 17.50x (ISBN 0-672-51854-6); pap. text ed. 5.95x (ISBN 0-672-61253-4). Hackett Pub.

Scheffler, Israel, jt. ed. see Rudner, Richard S.

Scheffler, Richard M., ed. Advances in Health Economics & Health Services Research, Vol. 2. 300p. 1981. 45.00 (ISBN 0-89232-100-8). Jai Pr.

--Health Economics & Health Service Research: An Annual Compilation of Research, VBol. I. 1979. lib. bdg. 45.00 (ISBN 0-89232-042-7). Jai Pr.

Scheffler, Samuel. The Rejection of Consequentialism: A Philosophical Investigation of the Considerations Underlying Rival Moral Conceptions. 1982. 12.95x (ISBN 0-19-824657-9). Oxford U Pr.

Scheffman, David T., jt. auth. see Melvin, James R.

Scheflan, Leopold & Jacob, Morris B. The Handbook of Solvents. LC 53-8766. 736p. 1973. Repr. of 1953 ed. 41.50 (ISBN 0-88275-130-1). Krieger.

Scheflen, Albert E. Body Language & the Social Order. (Illus.). 192p. 1972. 12.95 (ISBN 0-13-079590-9, Spec); pap. 5.95 (ISBN 0-13-079582-8, Spec). P-H.

Scheibe, Karl, jt. auth. see Sarbin, Theodore R.

Scheibenpflug, Lotte. Specialties of Austrian Cooking. (Illus.). 113p. 1980. 12.50x (ISBN 3-524-00091-6). Intl Pubns Serv.

Scheiber, Jane L. see O'Toole, James, et al.

Scheiber, Stephen C., jt. ed. see Doyle, Brian B.

Scheick, William J. & Doggett, Joella. Guide to Seventeenth Century American Poetry: A Reference Guide. 1977. lib. bdg. 18.00 (ISBN 0-8161-7983-2, Hall Reference). G K Hall.

Scheid, Francis. Introduction to Computer Science. (Schaum Outline Ser). 1970. pap. 7.95 (ISBN 0-07-055195-2, SP). McGraw.

--Numerical Analysis. (Schaum's Outline Ser). (Orig.). 1968. pap. 8.95 (ISBN 0-07-055197-9, SP). McGraw.

Scheidegger. Physical Aspects of Natural Catastrophes. 300p. 1975. 61.75 (ISBN 0-444-41216-6). Elsevier.

Scheidegger, A. Foundations of Geophysics. 1976. pap. text ed. 36.50 (ISBN 0-444-41389-8). Elsevier.

Scheidel, Thomas M. Persuasive Speaking. 1967. pap. 7.95x (ISBN 0-673-05724-0). Scott F.

--Speech Communication & Human Interaction. 2nd ed. 1976. text ed. 14.50x (ISBN 0-673-15005-4). Scott F.

Scheidel, Thomas M. & Crowell, Laura E. Discussing & Deciding: A Deskbook for Group Leaders & Members. (Illus.). 1979. text ed. 19.95x (ISBN 0-02-406750-4). Macmillan.

Scheidemandel, P. L., jt. auth. see Kanno, C. K.

Scheidemandel, Patricia, et al. Health Insurance for Mental Illness. 89p. 1968. pap. 3.00 o.p. (ISBN 0-685-24845-3, P195-0). Am Psychiatric.

Scheidemandel, Patricia L., jt. auth. see Kanno, Charles.

Scheidemandel, Patricia L., jt. auth. see Kanno, Charles K.

Scheider, William L. Nutrition: Basic Concepts & Applications. (Illus.). 560p. 1983. pap. 19.95x (ISBN 0-07-055230-4); instr's manual 10.00 (ISBN 0-07-055231-2); test bank 11.00 (ISBN 0-07-055232-0). McGraw.

Scheier, Michael & Frankel, Julie. The Whole Mirth Catalog. (Illus.). (gr. 5 up). 2.95 (ISBN 0-531-02494-6); PLB 7.90 s&l (ISBN 0-531-02226-9). Watts.

Scheimann, Eugene, jt. auth. see Mariken, Gene.

Schein, Clarence J. Introduction to Abdominal Surgery: Fifty Clinical Studies. (Illus.). 416p. 1981. pap. text ed. 34.50x (ISBN 0-06-142381-5, Harper Medical). Lippincott.

Schein, Edgar G. Organizational Psychology. 3rd ed. (Foundations of Modern Psychology Ser.). (Illus.). 1980. text ed. 15.95 o.p. (ISBN 0-13-641340-4); pap. text ed. 13.95 (ISBN 0-13-641332-3). P-H.

Schein, Edgar H., jt. auth. see Bailyn, Lotte.

Schein, Jerome & Naiman, Doris. For Parents of Deaf Children. (Illus.). 1978. pap. 7.95 (ISBN 0-913072-31-1). Natl Assn Deaf.

Schein, Jerome D., ed. A Rose for Tomorrow: Biography of Frederick C. Schreiber. (Illus.). 148p. 1981. text ed. 14.95x (ISBN 0-686-32096-4). Natl Assn Deaf.

Schein, Martin, jt. ed. see Goodman, Irving.

Schein, Martin W., ed. Social Hierarchy & Dominance. LC 74-26937. (Benchmark Papers in Animal Behavior, Ser. 3). 401p. 1975. 52.50 (ISBN 0-12-787419-4). Acad Pr.

Schein, P., jt. auth. see Serrou, B.

Schein, Richard D., jt. auth. see Zadoks, Jan C.

Scheinberg, Labe C. & Giesser, Barbara. Neurology Handbook. 2nd ed. 1982. pap. text ed. 11.95 (ISBN 0-87488-604-X). Med Exam.

Scheinberg, Labe C., et al. Neurology Handbook. 1972. spiral bdg. 11.95 o.p. (ISBN 0-87488-604-X). Med Exam.

Scheinberg, Peritz. Modern Practical Neurology. 2nd ed. 360p. 1981. 32.00 (ISBN 0-89004-521-6); pap. 18.00 (ISBN 0-686-69137-7). Raven.

Scheinberg, Peritz, ed. see Princeton Conferences on Cerebrovascular Diseases, 10th.

Scheiner, Albert P. & Abroms, Israel F. The Practical Management of the Developmentally Disabled Child. LC 80-13725. (Illus.). 454p. 1980. text ed. 42.50 (ISBN 0-8016-0061-8). Mosby.

Scheiner, Irwin. Christian Converts & Social Protest in Meiji Japan. LC 74-94981. (Center for Japanese & Korean Studies, UC Berkeley). 1970. 29.50x (ISBN 0-520-01585-1). U of Cal Pr.

Scheinman, Martin F. Evidence & Proof in Arbitration. 48p. 1977. pap. 2.00 (ISBN 0-87546-240-5). ILR Pr.

Scheinmann, F., jt. ed. see Roberts, S. M.

Scheit, Karl H. Nucleotide Analogs: Synthesis & Biological Function. LC 79-25445. 288p. 1980. 50.50 (ISBN 0-471-04854-2, Pub. by Wiley-Interscience). Wiley.

Schell, C., jt. auth. see Kunz, M.

Schell, Catherine, jt. auth. see Kunz, Marilyn.

Schell, D. & LeBoeuf, C. Behavior of Nine Solar Pond Candidate Salts. (Progress in Solar Energy Supplements). 60p. 1983. pap. text ed. 9.00x (ISBN 0-89553-086-4). Am Solar Energy.

Schell, F. Practical Problems in Mathematics--Metric System. LC 78-73133. 1980. pap. text ed. 7.00 (ISBN 0-8273-1418-3); instructor's guide 2.50 (ISBN 0-8273-1419-1). Delmar.

Schell, Frank R. Welding Procedures: Electric Arc. LC 76-14084. (gr. 10-12). 1977. pap. text ed. 7.00 (ISBN 0-8273-1603-8); instr's manual 4.75 (ISBN 0-8273-1697-6). Delmar.

--Welding Procedures: Oxyacetylene. LC 76-4306. 1977. pap. text ed. 7.00 (ISBN 0-8273-1600-3); instr's. guide 4.75 (ISBN 0-8273-1697-6). Delmar.

Schell, Frank R. & Matlock, Bill. Industrial Welding Procedures. LC 77-80481. 1979. text ed. 18.00 (ISBN 0-8273-1696-8); instructor's guide 4.75 (ISBN 0-8273-1697-6). Delmar.

Schell, Frank R. & Matlock, Bill J. Practical Problems in Mathematics for Welders. LC 80-70699. (Practical Problems in Mathematics Ser.). (Illus.). 218p. (Orig.). 1982. pap. text ed. 6.60 (ISBN 0-8273-2076-0); instr.'s guide 3.75 (ISBN 0-8273-2077-9). Delmar.

--Welding Procedures: MIG & TIG. LC 76-62715. 1978. pap. text ed. 11.00 (ISBN 0-8273-1646-1); instr's. manual 4.75 (ISBN 0-8273-1697-6). Delmar.

Schell, Jonathan. The Fate of the Earth. 1982. pap. 2.50 (ISBN 0-380-61325-5, 61325, Discus). Avon.

--The Fate of the Earth. large type ed. LC 82-10299. 405p. 1982. Repr. of 1982 ed. 10.95 (ISBN 0-89621-380-3). Thorndike Pr.

Schell, Josef, jt. ed. see Kahl, Gunter.

Schell, Leo M. Fundamentals of Decoding for Teachers. 2nd ed. 1980. pap. 7.50 (ISBN 0-395-30724-4). HM.

Schell, Lois W., jt. auth. see Schell, Rolfe F.

Schell, Merle. Tasting Good: The International Salt-Free Diet Cookbook. 1982. pap. 7.95 (ISBN 0-452-25364-0, Z5364, Plume). NAL.

Schell, Musher. Pathogenesis & Immunology of Treponemal Infections. (Immunology Ser.). 424p. 1983. 65.00 (ISBN 0-8247-1384-2). Dekker.

Schell, Orville, jt. auth. see Crews, Frederick.

Schell, Peter. How to Succeed at Tennis. (Illus.). 128p. 1982. 12.95 (ISBN 0-8069-4162-6); lib. bdg. 15.69 (ISBN 0-8069-4163-4); pap. 6.95 (ISBN 0-8069-4150-2). Sterling.

Schell, Rolfe F. & Schell, Lois W. Schell's Guide to Eastern Mexico: 1975. rev. ed. LC 73-87598. Orig. Title: Yank in Yucatan. (Illus.). 302p. 1975. 3.95 (ISBN 0-87208-025-0); pap. 2.95 (ISBN 0-87208-024-2). Island Pr.

Schellenberg, James A. The Science of Conflict. (Illus.). 1982. 17.50x (ISBN 0-19-502973-9); pap. text ed. 8.95x (ISBN 0-19-502974-7). Oxford U Pr.

Schellenberg, T. R. Modern Archives: Principles & Techniques. LC 56-58525. (Midway Reprint Ser.). xvi, 248p. 1975. pap. text ed. 11.00x (ISBN 0-226-73684-9). U of Chicago Pr.

--Modern Archives: Principles & Techniques. 248p. 1956. pap. 8.50 member (ISBN 0-686-95767-9, 5002); pap. 9.50 non-member (ISBN 0-686-99606-2). Soc Am Archivists.

Schellenberg, Theodore R. The Management of Archives. 383p. 1965. member 25.00 (ISBN 0-686-95764-4, 5001); non-member 30.00 (ISBN 0-686-99605-4). Soc Am Archivists.

Schellenberger, R. & Boseman, G. MANSYM III: A Dynamic Management Simulator with Decision Support System. (Management Ser.). 94p. 1982. pap. text ed. 12.95 (ISBN 0-471-08581-2); tchrs. manual 6.00 (ISBN 0-471-86815-9). Wiley.

Schellenberger, Robert E. & Boseman, Glenn. Policy Formulation & Strategy Management: Text & Cases. 2nd ed. LC 81-14739. (Management Ser.). 760p. 1982. text ed. 28.95 (ISBN 0-471-08215-5); tchrs'. ed. (ISBN 0-471-86332-7). Wiley.

Scheller, Arnold, jt. ed. see Turner, Roderick.

Scheller, William G. Energy Saving Home Improvements. 1979. pap. 8.95 (ISBN 0-672-21605-1). Sams.

--Randonnees aux Environs de Montreal. Booth, Janine, tr. from English. (AMC Country Walks Bks.). Orig. Title: Country Walks Near Montreal. (Illus.). 200p. (Orig., French.). 1983. pap. 6.95 (ISBN 0-910146-46-2). Appalach Mtn.

--Solar Heating. 1980. pap. 8.95 (ISBN 0-686-82335-4). Sams.

Schellhammer, Hans. International Dimensions of Business Polices & Strategies. Ricks, David A., ed. (International Dimensions of Business Ser.). 200p. 1983. text ed. write for info. Kent Pub Co.

Schellie, Don. Vast Domain of Blood. LC 68-29143. ixx, 268p. 9.95 (ISBN 0-686-74355-5). Westernlore.

Schelling, Friedrich. On University Studies. Guterman, Norbert, ed. Morgan, E. S., tr. LC 65-15086. xxii, 166p. 1966. 12.00x (ISBN 0-8214-0015-0, 82-80166). Ohio U Pr.

Schelling, Friedrich W. Of Human Freedom. Gutmann, James, tr. 180p. 1936. 16.00x (ISBN 0-87548-024-1); pap. 4.95 o.p. (ISBN 0-87548-025-X). Open Court.

Schelling, Thomas C. Arms & Influence. LC 76-41307. 1976. Repr. of 1966 ed. lib. bdg. 21.00x (ISBN 0-8371-8980-2, SCAI). Greenwood.

--Micromotives & Macrobehavior. (Illus.). 1978. 19.95 o.p. (ISBN 0-393-05701-1); pap. 5.95x (ISBN 0-393-09009-4). Norton.

Schellman, James M. Ecumenical Services of Prayer: Consultation on Common Texts. 80p. 1982. pap. 1.95 (ISBN 0-8091-5180-4). Paulist Pr.

Schellman, Pernod. Christo: Complete Editions 1964-1982. 132p. 1982. 32.50 (ISBN 0-8147-3417-0); pap. 17.95 (ISBN 0-8147-3418-9). NYU Pr.

Schelly, William. Harry Langdon. LC 82-6035. (Filmmakers Ser.: No. 3). 249p. 1982. 16.00 (ISBN 0-8108-1567-2). Scarecrow.

Schempp, Walter & Zeller, Karl, eds. Multivariate Approximation Theory Two. (International Series of Numerical Mathematics Ser.: Vol. 61). Date not set. text ed. 34.95 (ISBN 3-7643-1373-0). Birkhauser.

Schenck, Eva, ed. A Sampler of Community Tones Around the Country-World. new ed. LC 77-79357. 1977. pap. 3.00 (ISBN 0-932044-00-X). M O Pub Co.

Schenck, H. V., jt. auth. see Cichy, F. C.

Schenck, Hilbert. Introduction to Ocean Engineering. (Illus.). 384p. 1975. text ed. 33.50 (ISBN 0-07-055240-1, C); solutions manual 7.95 (ISBN 0-07-055241-X). McGraw.

--A Rose for Armageddon. (Orig.). 1982. pap. 2.25 (ISBN 0-671-44311-9, Timescape). PB.

--Theories of Engineering Experimentation. 3rd ed. (Illus.). 1978. text ed. 34.50 (ISBN 0-07-055267-3, C); wkbk. 10.50 (ISBN 0-07-055268-1). McGraw.

Schenck, Linda, tr. see Ekman, Kerstin.

Schenck, Noella L. Winter Park's Old Alabama Hotel. (Illus., Orig.). 1982. pap. 6.95 (ISBN 0-89305-043-1). Anna Pub.

Schendel, Arthur van see Van Schendel, Arthur.

Schendel, Dan E., jt. auth. see Hofer, Charles W.

Schendelen, M. P. van see Herman, V. & Van Schendelen, M. P.

Schenk, Brian, ed. Another Page-General Reading. (Kentucky Educational Television Reading Comprehension Ser.). 176p. (Orig.). 1981. pap. text ed. 6.33 (ISBN 0-8428-9372-5). Cambridge Bk.

--Another Page-Prose Literature. (Kentucky Educational Television Reading Comprehension Ser.). 160p. (Orig.). 1981. pap. text ed. 6.33 (ISBN 0-8428-9364-4). Cambridge Bk.

--The Cambridge Program for the GED Reading Skills Test. (GED Preparation Ser.). 256p. (Orig.). 1981. pap. text ed. 5.87 (ISBN 0-8428-9390-3); Cambridge Exercise Book for the Reading Skills Test 96p. wkbk. 3.33 (ISBN 0-8428-9396-2). Cambridge Bk.

--The Cambridge Program for the GED Science Test. (GED Preparation Ser.). (Illus.). 224p. (Orig.). 1981. pap. 5.87 (ISBN 0-8428-9389-X); Cambridge Exercise Book for the Science Test. wkbk. 3.33 (ISBN 0-8428-9395-4). Cambridge Bk.

Schenk, Brian, ed. see Howett, Jerry.

Schenk, Brian, ed. see Long, Jerry & Tenzer, Jeff.

Schenk, Emmy L., jt. auth. see Schenk, Quentin F.

Schenk, Emmy Lou, jt. auth. see Schenk, Quentin.

Schenk, Joyce. Caves of Darkness. (YA) 1977. 6.95 (ISBN 0-685-73814-0, Avalon). Bouregy.

Schenk, Quentin & Schenk, Emmy Lou. Pulling up Roots: For Parents-How to Let Go - for Young Adults-How to Get Free. LC 78-1873. 1978. 9.95 (ISBN 0-13-740423-9, Spec); pap. 4.95 o.p. (ISBN 0-13-740415-8, Spec). P-H.

Schenk, Quentin F. & Schenk, Emmy L. Welfare, Society & the Helping Professions: An Introduction. 1981. text ed. 13.95x (ISBN 0-02-406800-4). Macmillan.

Schenk De Regniers, Beatrice. Everyone One Is Good for Something. LC 79-12223. (Illus.). (gr. k-4). 1980. 9.95 (ISBN 0-395-28967-X, Clarion). HM.

Schenk de Regniers, Beatrice see Regniers, Beatrice Schenk de.

Schenker, Hillel, ed. After Lebanon: The Israeli-Palestinian Connection. 320p. 1983. 15.95 (ISBN 0-8298-0654-7). Pilgrim NY.

Schenkkan, Robert, ed. see Ibsen, Henrik.

Schenkkan, Robert, tr. see Ibsen, Henrik.

Schepens, Charles L. Retinal Detachment & Allied Diseases. (Illus.). 600p. Date not set. text ed. 198.00 (ISBN 0-7216-7956-0). Saunders. Postponed.

Scheper-Hughes, Nancy. Saints, Scholars, & Schizophrenics: Mental Illness in Rural Ireland. LC 77-71067. 1979. 18.95 (ISBN 0-520-03444-9). U of Cal Pr.

--Saints, Scholars & Schizophrenics: Mental Illness in Rural Ireland. 259p. 1982. 19.95x (ISBN 0-520-03444-9); pap. 9.95 (ISBN 0-520-04786-9). U of Cal Pr.

Scheppach, Raymond C. & Ehrlich, Everett M. Energy-Policy Analysis & Congressional Action. LC 80-8993. (Illus.). 272p. 1981. 27.95x (ISBN 0-669-04490-3). Lexington Bks.

Scheppach, Raymond C., Jr. State Projection of the Gross National Product, 1970, 1980. LC 72-8038. (Multiregional Input-Output Study: Vol. 3). (Illus.). 304p. 1972. 30.95x (ISBN 0-669-84996-0). Lexington Bks.

Scher, Jonathan & Dix, Carol. Will My Baby Be Normal? 352p. 1983. 15.95 (ISBN 0-385-27651-6). Dial.

Scher, S., jt. auth. see Mosesson, G.

Scheraga, Harold A. Protein Structure. (Molecular Biology Ser: Vol. 1). 1961. 41.00 (ISBN 0-12-623850-2). Acad Pr.

Scherer, Carroll, tr. see Schad, Wolfgang.

Scherer, Donald. Personal Values & Environmental Issues. 256p. 1978. pap. 6.95 o.s.i. (ISBN 0-89104-256-3, A & W Visual Library). A & W Pubs.

Scherer, Donald & Attig, Thomas. Ethics & the Environment. (Illus.). 1983. pap. 9.95 (ISBN 0-13-290163-3). P-H.

Scherer, Donald, jt. auth. see Facione, Peter.

Scherer, Donald, et al. Introduction to Philosophy: From Wonder to World View. (Illus.). 1979. text ed. 22.95 (ISBN 0-13-491860-6). P-H.

Scherer, Edmond. Essays on English Literature. Saintsbury, George, tr. 272p. 1982. Repr. of 1891 ed. lib. bdg. 4.00 (ISBN 0-8495-4966-3). Arden Lib.

Scherer, F. M., et al. The Economics of Multi-Plant Operation. LC 74-33697. (Harvard Economic Studies: N0. 145). 448p. 1975. text ed. 22.50x (ISBN 0-674-23340-9). Harvard U Pr.

Scherer, Frederic M. Industrial Market Structure & Economic Performance. 2nd ed. 1980. 26.95 (ISBN 0-395-30726-0). HM.
--The Weapons Acquisition Process: Economic Incentives. LC 64-12400. (Illus.). 1964. 20.00x (ISBN 0-87584-034-5). Harvard Busn.
Scherer, J. L. Handbook on Soviet Military Deficiencies. 128p. 1983. pap. 12.00 (ISBN 0-9607258-1-4). J L Scherer.
Scherer, Jeanne C. Introductory Clinical Pharmacology. 2nd ed. (Illus.). 224p. 1982. pap. text ed. 16.00 (ISBN 0-397-54272-0, Lippincott Nursing); pap. text ed. 8.00 student manual (ISBN 0-397-54374-3). Lippincott.
--Introductory Medical-Surgical Nursing. 3rd ed. (Illus.). 1982. pap. text ed. 25.00 (ISBN 0-397-54280-1, Lippincott Nursing); 12.50. Lippincott.
Scherer, John L., ed. China Facts & Figures Annual. (CHIFFA). 1978. Vol. 1. 34.50 (ISBN 0-87569-029-7). Vol. 2. 35.00. Academic Intl.
--China Facts & Figures Annual, Vol. 4. 1981. 46.50 (ISBN 0-87569-044-0). Academic Intl.
--China Facts & Figures Annual: CHIFFA, Vol. 5. Vol. 5. 47.00 (ISBN 0-87569-049-1). Academic Intl.
Scherer, Klaus R. & Giles, Howard, eds. Social Markers in Speech. LC 79-4080. (Illus.). 1980. 49.50 (ISBN 0-521-22321-0); pap. 15.95 (ISBN 0-521-29590-4). Cambridge U Pr.
Scherer, Klaus R., jt. ed. see Fraser, Colin.
Scherer, Thomas. Phraseologie Im Schulalter. 174p. (Ger.). 1982. write for info. (ISBN 3-261-05015-2). P Lang Pubs.
Scherf, D. & Cohen, J. The Atrioventricular Node & Selected Cardiac Arrhythmias. 480p. 1964. 86.50 o.p. (ISBN 0-8089-0407-8). Grune.
Scherf, W. & Lisieski, W. Amplitude Distribution Spectrometers. (Fundamental Studies in Engineering: Vol. 3). 1980. 106.50 (ISBN 0-444-99777-6). Elsevier.
Scherfig, Hans. Stolen Spring. Brondum, Jack, tr. from Danish. Orig. Title: Det Forsoemte Foraar. 192p. (Orig.). 1983. pap. 6.95 (ISBN 0-940242-00-1). Fjord Pr.
Scherie, Strom. Stuffin' Muffin: Muffin Pan Cooking for Kids. (Illus.). 100p. (Orig.). (ps-9). 1982. pap. 8.95 (ISBN 0-9606964-9-0). Young People's Pr.
Schering, Arnold. Die Niederlandische Orgelmesse Im Zeitalter Des Josquin: Eine Stilkritische Untersuchung. (Bibliotheca Oeganologica: Vol. 16). 1971. Repr. of 1912 ed. wrappers 22.50 o.s.i. (ISBN 90-6027-154-8, Pub. by Frits Knuf Netherlands). Pendragon NY.
Scherman, Katharine. Slave Who Freed Haiti: The Story of Toussaint Louverture. (World Landmark Ser: No. 15). (gr. 7-9). 1964. PLB 5.99 o.p. (ISBN 0-394-90515-6). Random.
Scherman, William. How to Get the Right Job in Publishing. (Illus.). 256p. (Orig.). 1983. pap. 9.95 (ISBN 0-8092-5683-5). Contemp Bks.
Schermer, Irwin E. Automobile Liability Insurance. 2nd ed. LC 81-15532. 1981. looseleaf with annual rev. pages 140.00 (ISBN 0-87632-365-4). Boardman.
Schermerhorn, Gene. Letters to Phil, Memories of a New York Boyhood, 1848-1856. Gill, Brendan, frwd. by. (Illus.). 96p. 1982. 10.95 (ISBN 0-9608788-0-7); Ltd. Ed 35.00 (ISBN 0-9608788-1-5). NY Bound.
Schermerhorn, John R., et al. Managing Organizational Behavior. LC 81-16267. 622p. 1982. text ed. 25.95 (ISBN 0-471-04497-0); tchrs. manual avail. (ISBN 0-471-86233-9). Wiley.
Scherr, Frederick C., jt. auth. see Mathur, Iqbal.
Scherr, G. H., ed. J.I.R. Selected Papers. 2nd ed. 296p. 1981. text ed. 14.95 (ISBN 0-9605852-1-4). JIR.
Scherr, George H. see Hart, Ronald & Massoud, Aly.
Scherrer, Robert A. & Whitehouse, Michael W., eds. Antiinflamatory Agents: Chemistry & Pharmacology, Vols. 1 & 2. 1974. Vol. 1. 67.00 (ISBN 0-12-623901-0); Vol. 2. 67.00 (ISBN 0-12-623902-9); Set. 95.00 (ISBN 0-685-48715-6). Acad Pr.
Schertel, A. Abkuerzungen in der Medizin: Abbreviations in Medicine - Abreviations en Medecine. 3rd ed. 200p. 1983. pap. 12.00 (ISBN 3-8055-3669-0). S Karger.
Schertel, Lothar, et al. Atlas of Xeroradiography. LC 76-14693. (Illus.). 1977. text ed. 15.00 (ISBN 0-7216-7970-6). Saunders.
Schertl, Albrecht. Abbreviations in Medicine. 204p. 1977. pap. 20.00x (ISBN 3-7940-7017-8, Pub. by K G Saur). Gale.
Schertle, Alice. Hob Goblin & the Skeleton. (ps-3). 1982. 8.50 (ISBN 0-688-00279-X); PLB 7.63 (ISBN 0-688-00282-X). Morrow.
--In My Treehouse. LC 82-10016. (Illus.). 32p. (gr. k-3). 1983. 9.50 (ISBN 0-688-01638-3); PLB 9.12 (ISBN 0-688-01639-1). Lothrop.
Schertz, Lyle P., jt. auth. see Baum, Kenneth H.
Schervish, Paul G. The Structural Determinants of Unemployment: Vulnerability & Power in Market Relations. (Quantitative Studies in Social Relations). Date not set. price not set (ISBN 0-12-623950-9). Acad Pr.
Scherzer, Alfred L. & Tscharnuter, Ingrid. Early Diagnosis & Therapy in Cerebral Palsey. 304p. 1982. 35.00 (ISBN 0-8247-1828-3). Dekker.
Schetky, L. McDonald, jt. auth. see LeMay, Iain.
Schettler, F. G., et al, eds. Atherosclerosis VI: Proceedings. (Illus.). 982p. 1983. 44.00 (ISBN 0-387-11450-5). Springer-Verlag.
Schetzen, Martin. The Volterra & Weiner Theories of Nonlinear Systems. LC 79-13421. 531p. 1980. 39.95x (ISBN 0-471-04455-5, Pub. by Wiley-Interscience). Wiley.
Scheub, Harold. African Oral Narratives, Proverbs, Riddles, Poetry & Song: An Annotated Bibliography. (Reference Publications Ser.). 1977. lib. bdg. 45.00 (ISBN 0-8161-8034-2, Hall Reference). G K Hall.
Scheuer, P. Liver Biopsy Interpretation. 3rd ed. 1980. text ed. 70.00 (ISBN 0-02-859180-1, Pub. by Bailliere-Tindall). Saunders.
Scheuer, Paul J., ed. Marine Natural Products: Chemical & Biological Perspectives, Vol. III. LC 77-10960. 1980. 30.00 (ISBN 0-12-624003-5). Acad Pr.
--Marine Natural Products: Chemical & Biological Perspectives, Vol. 2. (Marine Natural Products: Chemical & Biological Perspectives Ser.). 1978. 53.00 (ISBN 0-12-624002-7). Acad Pr.
Scheuer, Steven. TV Annual 1978-1979. (Illus.). 1979. 19.95 o.p. (ISBN 0-02-607070-7); pap. 9.95 o.p. (ISBN 0-02-081830-0). Macmillan.
Scheuer, Steven H. Movies on TV Nineteen Eighty-Two to Nineteen Eighty-Three. 768p. (Orig.). 1982. pap. 3.95 (ISBN 0-553-14806-0). Bantam.
Scheuerman, Richard & Trafzer, Clifford. The Volga Germans: Pioneers in the Pacific Northwest. LC 80-52314. (GEM Books-Historical Ser.). (Illus.). 240p. (Orig.). 1981. 19.95 o.p. (ISBN 0-89301-073-1). U Pr of Idaho.
Scheuerman, Richard V., jt. auth. see Barner, Herbert E.
Scheuermann, Peter, ed. Database Usability & Responsiveness. 1982. 34.00 (ISBN 0-12-624080-9). Acad Pr.
Scheuring, Ann, et al. Agricultural Resources of California Counties. 136p. (Orig.). 1982. pap. text ed. 5.00x (ISBN 0-931876-57-5, 3275). Ag Sci Pubns.
Scheuring, Ann F., ed. A Guidebook to California Agriculture. LC 82-2669. (Illus.). 544p. 1983. 22.50x (ISBN 0-520-04709-5). U of Cal Pr.
Scheuring, Lynn, jt. auth. see Scheuring, Tom.
Scheuring, Tom & Scheuring, Lynn. Two for Joy: Reflections for a Husband & Wife on Their Spirit Led Journey Through Jesus to the Father. LC 76-28274. 1976. pap. 4.95 o.p. (ISBN 0-8091-1985-4). Paulist Pr.
Scheurwater, W. & Van Acht, R. Oude Klavecimbels, Hun Bouw En Restauratie: Old Harpsichords, Their Construction & Restauration. (Haags Gemeentemuseum, 'kijkboekjes' Ser.: Vol. 2). (Dutch & Eng.). 1976. wrappers 15.00 o.s.i. (ISBN 90-6027-337-0, Pub. by Frits Knuf Netherlands). Pendragon NY.
Scheven, Albert. Swahili Proverbs: Nia Zikiwa Moja, Kilicho Mbali Huja. LC 80-8273. 608p. (Orig.). 1981. lib. bdg. 35.25 (ISBN 0-8191-1845-1); pap. text ed. 22.50 (ISBN 0-8191-1846-X). U Pr of Amer.
Scheveningen Conference on Differential Equations, 2nd, the Netherlands, 1975 & Eckhaus, W. New Developments in Differential Equations: Proceedings. (North Holland Mathematics Studies: Vol. 21). 1976. 47.00 (ISBN 0-444-11107-1, North-Holland). Elsevier.
Schevill, James. The American Fantasies: Collected Poems 1945-1980. LC 82-75372. 224p. 1983. lib. bdg. 27.95x (ISBN 0-8040-0393-9); pap. 12.95 (ISBN 0-8040-0394-7). Swallow.
--Breakout: In Search of New Theatrical Environments. LC 82-73047. (Illus.). 411p. 1972. 15.00x (ISBN 0-8040-0574-5); pap. 4.95x o.s.i. (ISBN 0-8040-0640-7). Swallow.
--The Buddhist Car & Other Characters. LC 82-73401. 83p. 1973. 6.00 (ISBN 0-8040-0628-8). Swallow.
--Lovecraft's Follies: A Play. LC 77-150761. 90p. 1971. 5.00 o.p. (ISBN 0-8040-0501-X); pap. 2.95 o.p. (ISBN 0-8040-0502-8). Swallow.
--Stalingrad Elegies. LC 64-16113. 53p. (Orig.). 1964. pap. 2.25 o.p. (ISBN 0-8040-0281-9, 59). Swallow.
--Violence & Glory: Poems, Nineteen-Sixty-Two to Nineteen-Sixty-Eight. LC 76-75733. 148p. 1969. 7.95 o.p. (ISBN 0-8040-0313-0); pap. 6.95 (ISBN 0-8040-0314-9). Swallow.
Schewe, Charles & Smith, Reuben. Marketing: Concepts & Applications. 2nd ed. 736p. 1983. 25.95 (ISBN 0-07-055251-7, C); write for info. instr's manual (ISBN 0-07-055252-5); study guide 8.95 (ISBN 0-07-055253-3); write for info. test book (ISBN 0-07-055254-1). McGraw.
Schewe, Charles D. & Smith, Rueben. Marketing: Concepts & Applications. (Marketing Ser.). (Illus.). 1979. text ed. 22.95 (ISBN 0-07-055272-X); instrs' manual 45.00 (ISBN 0-07-055273-8); study guide 9.50 (ISBN 0-07-055278-9); test bank 25.00 (ISBN 0-07-055280-0). McGraw.
Schexnayder, C. J. Construction Equipment & Techniques for the Eighties. LC 81-71797. 404p. 1982. pap. text ed. 29.50 (ISBN 0-87262-293-2). Am Soc Civil Eng.
Schey, Harry M. Div, Grad, Curl & All That: An Informal Text on Vector Calculus. (Illus.). 150p. 1973. pap. text ed. 6.95x (ISBN 0-393-09367-0). Norton.
Schey, John A. Introduction to Manufacturing Processes. (Illus.). 1977. text ed. 33.50 (ISBN 0-07-055274-6, C); solutions manual 7.95 (ISBN 0-07-055275-4). McGraw.
--Metal Deformation Processes: Friction & Lubrication. (Illus.). 824p. 1980. 110.00 (ISBN 0-08-024658-3); soft cover 95.00 (ISBN 0-08-024657-5); microfiche x 58.00 (ISBN 0-08-024656-7); microfilm xx 35.00 (ISBN 0-08-024655-9). Pergamon.
Schiamberg, Lawrence B. & Smith, Karl U. Human Development. 1982. text ed. 23.95x (ISBN 0-02-406840-3). Macmillan.
Schiaparelli, G. V. Le Opere Publicate per Cura Della Reale Specola Di Brera, Vols. 1-11. (Sources of Science Ser). (It). Repr. of 1930 ed. Set. 440.00 (ISBN 0-384-53780-4). Johnson Repr.
Schiavetti, Nicholas, jt. auth. see Ventry, Ira M.
Schiavone, Guiseppe, ed. East-West Relations: Prospects for the 1980s. LC 81-21433. 315p. 1982. 32.50x (ISBN 0-312-22496-6). St Martin.
Schibilla, Linda, jt. auth. see Christman, Ronald.
Schick, Alice. Serengeti Cats. LC 77-812. (gr. 4 up). 1977. 10.53i (ISBN 0-397-31757-3, JBL-J). Har-Row.
Schick, Allen. Budget Innovation in the States. 223p. 1971. pap. 7.95 (ISBN 0-8157-7731-0). Brookings.
--Congress & Money: Budgeting, Spending & Taxing. LC 80-53322. 600p. 1980. 27.50 (ISBN 0-87766-278-9); pap. 12.95 (ISBN 0-87766-294-0, 31800). Urban Inst.
--Reconciliation & the Congressional Budget Process. 1981. pap. 4.25 (ISBN 0-8447-3471-3). Am Enterprise.
Schick, Allen & Pfister, Adrienne. American Government: Continuity & Change. (Illus.). 629p. (gr. 10-12). 1975. 19.56 (ISBN 0-395-18825-3); instrs' guide & key 7.68 (ISBN 0-395-18816-4); student's wk. guide 6.80 (ISBN 0-395-18824-5). HM.
Schick, Allen, ed. Perspective On Budgeting (Par Classics II) LC 80-81208. 1980. 10.95 (ISBN 0-936678-01-1). Am Soc Pub Admin.
Schick, Barbara A., jt. auth. see Rose, Allen J.
Schick, C. Dennis & Book, Albert C. Fundamentals of Creative Advertising. LC 82-71763. 1983. write for info. (ISBN 0-87251-035-2). Crain Bks.
Schick, George B., jt. auth. see Raygor, Alton L.
Schick, K. Principios of Electricidad. 1970. text ed. 15.95 (ISBN 0-07-091840-6, G). McGraw.
Schick, Kurt. Introduction to Electricity. 1975. 16.05 o.p. (ISBN 0-07-077678-4, G). McGraw.
Schick, Richard P. & Couturier, Jean J. The Public Interest in Government Labor Relations. LC 76-46642. 288p. 1977. prof ref 22.00x (ISBN 0-88410-245-9). Ballinger Pub.
Schick, William & Merz, Charles. Fortran for Engineering. (Illus.). 384p. 1972. text ed. 21.95 (ISBN 0-07-055276-2, C); solutions manual 25.00 (ISBN 0-07-055277-0). McGraw.
Schickedanz, et al. Strategies for Teaching Young Children. (Early Childhood Series). 1977. text ed. 21.95 (ISBN 0-13-851105-5). P-H.
Schickedanz, Judith & York, Mary. Strategies for Teaching Young Children. 2nd ed. (Illus.). 416p. 1983. 22.95 (ISBN 0-13-851139-X). P-H.
Schickedanz, Judith A., et al. Toward Understanding Children. 1982. text ed. 22.95 (ISBN 0-316-77324-7); tchrs' manual avail. (ISBN 0-316-77323-9); student guide 7.95 (ISBN 0-316-77322-0); TB avail. (ISBN 0-316-77319-0). Little.
Schickel, Richard. World of Goya. LC 68-56432. (Library of Art Ser.). (Illus.). (gr. 6 up). 1968. 19.92 (ISBN 0-8094-0276-9, Pub. by Time-Life). Silver.
Schickele, Peter. The Definitive Biography of P. D. Q. Bach. 1976. 12.50 (ISBN 0-394-46536-9); pap. 8.95 (ISBN 0-394-73409-2). Random.
Schickling, Wanda. Chipper Picks a Family. (gr. 4-6). 1952. pap. 1.25 o.p. (ISBN 0-8024-1135-5). Moody.
Schiefelbusch. Language Intervention Strategies. 432p. 1978. text ed. 24.95 (ISBN 0-8391-1238-6). Univ Park.
Schiefelbusch, R. Language Perspectives-Acquisition, Retardation, & Intervention. 686p. 1974. text ed. 24.95 (ISBN 0-8391-0687-4). Univ Park.
--Nonspeech Language & Communication. 544p. 1979. text ed. 27.95 (ISBN 0-8391-1558-X). Univ Park.
Schiefelbusch, Richard L. & Bricker, Dianne D., eds. Early Language: Intervention. 616p. 1981. text ed. 27.95 (ISBN 0-8391-1618-7). Univ Park.
Schiefelbusch, Richard L. & Hollis, John H., eds. Language Intervention from Ape to Child. (Language Intervention Ser.). 552p. 1979. text ed. 32.95 (ISBN 0-8391-1413-3). Univ Park.
Schiefelbush, Richard L. The Bases of Language Intervention. (Illus.). 488p. 1978. text ed. 24.95 (ISBN 0-8391-1197-5). Univ Park.
Schiefer, G. W., jt. auth. see Hanf, C. H.
Schiel, Jacob H. Journey Through the Rocky Mountains & the Humboldt Mountains to the Pacific Ocean. Bonner, Thomas N., ed. (American Exploration & Travel Ser.: No. 27). (Illus.). 1959. 9.95 o.p. (ISBN 0-8061-0422-8). U of Okla Pr.
Schier, Steven E. The Rules & the Game: Democratic National Convention Delegate Selection in Iowa & Wisconsin. LC 79-5495. 1980. text ed. 26.50 (ISBN 0-8191-0891-X); pap. text ed. 16.25 (ISBN 0-8191-0892-8). U Pr of Amer.
Schierbeek, Bert. Shapes of the Voice. (Twayne International Translations Ser: No. 9). 1977. lib. bdg. 10.00 o.p. (ISBN 0-8057-8156-0, Twayne). G K Hall.
Schierlova, M., tr. see Stembera, Z., et al.
Schiesel, Jane. The Otis Redding Story. LC 70-144294. 144p. (gr. 5-7). 1973. 7.95 o.p. (ISBN 0-385-02335-9). Doubleday.
Schiesl, Martin. The Politics of Efficiency: Municipal Administration & Reform in America, 1880-1920. LC 75-17285. 1977. 29.50x (ISBN 0-520-03067-2); pap. 8.50x (ISBN 0-520-04086-4). U of Cal Pr.
Schiff, Barry & Fishman, Hal. The Vatican Target. LC 78-221421. 1979. 8.95 o.p. (ISBN 0-312-83801-8). St Martin.
Schiff, Barry J. The Boeing 707. (Illus.). 180p. 1983. pap. 7.95 (ISBN 0-8168-5653-2). Aero.
Schiff, David. The Music of Elliott Carter. (Illus.). 370p. 1983. lib. bdg. 39.50 (ISBN 0-903873-06-0). Da Capo.
Schiff, Ellen. From Stereotype to Metaphor: The Jew in Contemporary Drama. (SUNY Series in Modern Jewish Literature & Culture). (Illus.). 275p. 1982. 30.50x (ISBN 0-87395-621-4); pap. 9.95x (ISBN 0-87395-622-2). State U NY Pr.
Schiff, Eric, tr. from Ger. Switzerland: An International Banking & Finance Center M. Ikle. LC 72-76544. 156p. 1972. 34.50 (ISBN 0-12-786720-1). Acad Pr.
Schiff, Eric, tr. see Ikle, Max.
Schiff, Irwin A. & Murzin, Howy. How Anyone Can Stop Paying Income Taxes. LC 81-71431. 1982. 11.50 (ISBN 0-930374-03-7, Dist. by S&S). Freedom Bks.
Schiff, Laura, tr. see Mihaly, Ida F.
Schiff, Leon. Diseases of the Liver. 5th ed. (Illus.). 1424p. 1982. text ed. 95.00 (ISBN 0-397-50458-6, Lippincott Medical). Lippincott.
Schiff, Leonard I. Quantum Mechanics. 3rd ed. LC 68-25665. (International Pure & Applied Physics Ser). (Illus.). 1968. text ed. 35.00 (ISBN 0-07-055287-8, C). McGraw.
Schiff, Roselyn L., et al. Communication Strategy: A Guide to Speech Preparation. 1981. pap. text ed. 8.95x (ISBN 0-673-15437-8). Scott F.
Schiff, Stuart D. Whispers Four. LC 82-45337. (Science Fiction Ser.). 192p. 1983. 11.95 (ISBN 0-385-18028-4). Doubleday.
Schiff, Stuart D., ed. Mad Scientists: An Anthology of Fantasy & Horror. LC 79-8943. 312p. 1980. 9.95a o.p. (ISBN 0-385-14906-9); PLB (ISBN 0-385-14907-7). Doubleday.
Schiff, Susan, ed. see Postal, Bernard & Koppman, Lionel.
Schiff, William. Perception: An Applied Approach. LC 79-88717. 1980. text ed. 23.50 (ISBN 0-395-27054-5). HM.
Schiffer, Charles A., jt. ed. see Sohmer, Paul R.
Schiffer, Don & Duroska, Lud. Football Rules in Pictures. rev. ed. LC 72-86663. (Sports Handbooks Ser.). (Illus., Orig.). (gr. 7 up). 1969. pap. 3.95 (ISBN 0-448-01785-7, G&D). Putnam Pub Group.
Schiffer, Herbert F., jt. auth. see Peter, Nancy.
Schiffer, Judith. School Renewal Through Staff Development. LC 80-10594. 1980. pap. 12.95x (ISBN 0-8077-2582-X). Tchrs Coll.
Schiffer, M. B. & Gumerman, G. J., eds. Conservation Archaeology: A Guide for Cultural Resources Management Studies. 1977. 31.50 (ISBN 0-12-624160-0). Acad Pr.
Schiffer, Margaret B. Arts & Crafts of Chester County, Pa. (Illus.). 285p. 1981. 29.95 (ISBN 0-916838-35-8). Schiffer.
--Historical Needlework of Pennsylvania. (Illus.). 160p. 10.00 o.p. (ISBN 0-685-78508-4). Schiffer.
Schiffer, Michael. Lessons of the Road. 1980. 10.95 o.p. (ISBN 0-671-25380-8). S&S.
Schiffer, Michael B., jt. auth. see Rathje, William L.
Schiffer, Michael B., ed. Advances in Archaeological Method & Theory, Vol. 6. Date not set. price not set (ISBN 0-12-003106-X). Acad Pr.
--Advances in Archaeological Method & Theory: Selections for Students, Vols. 1-4. LC 82-13810. (Serial Publication). 712p. 1982. text ed. 19.95 (ISBN 0-12-624180-5). Acad Pr.
Schiffer, Nancy, jt. auth. see Herbert, Peter.
Schiffer, Nancy, compiled by. Matchbox Toys. (Illus.). 204p. (Orig.). 1983. pap. 14.95 (ISBN 0-916838-74-9). Schiffer.
Schifferes, J. J. & Synovitz, R. J. Healthier Living. 4th ed. 558p. 1979. text ed. 29.95 (ISBN 0-471-01944-5). Wiley.
Schifferes, Justus J. & Peterson, Louis J. Healthier Living Highlights. 2nd ed. LC 74-24339. (Illus.). 289p. 1975. text ed. 22.50 (ISBN 0-471-76071-4); tchr's manual avail. (ISBN 0-471-76072-2). Wiley.
Schiffhorst, Gerald J. & Fear, David E. Short English Workbook. 2nd ed. 1981. pap. text ed. 8.95x (ISBN 0-673-15534-X). Scott F.
Schiffhorst, Gerald J., jt. auth. see Fear, David E.
Schiffman, Gilbert B., jt. auth. see Goldberg, Herman K.
Schiffman, Harold F., jt. auth. see Shapiro, Michael C

Schiffman, Leon G. & Kanuk, Leslie L. Consumer Behavior. 2nd ed. 592p. 1982. 25.95 (ISBN 0-13-168880-4). P-H.

Schiffman, Leon G., et al. Consumer Behavior. LC 77-25032. (Illus.). 1978. ref. ed. 24.95x (ISBN 0-13-169201-1). P-H.

Schiffman, Susan, et al. Introduction to Multidimensional Scaling: Theory, Methods & Applications. LC 81-10842. 1981. 29.50 o.p. (ISBN 0-12-624350-6). Acad Pr.

Schiffman, Ted, jt. auth. see Lariviere, Susan.

Schiffman, Yale M. & D-Alessio, Gregory J. Limits to Solar & Biomass Energy Growth. LC 81-48071. 1983. price not set (ISBN 0-669-05253-1). Lexington Bks.

Schiffman, Yale M. & D'Alessio, Gregory J. Solar Energy Systems: An Alternative Perspective. LC 81-48071. 1983. write for info. (ISBN 0-669-05253-1). Lexington Bks.

Schiffrin, Harold Z. Sun Yat-sen & the Origins of the Chinese Revolution. LC 68-26530. (Center for Chinese Studies, UC Berkeley). 1968. 30.00x (ISBN 0-520-01142-2). U of Cal Pr.

Schifftner, Kenneth C. & Hesketh, Howard E. Wet Scrubbers. LC 82-70703. (The Environment & Energy Handbook Ser.). (Illus.). 140p. 1982. 19.95 (ISBN 0-250-40456-7). Ann Arbor Science.

Schild, Erich, et al. Environmental Physics in Construction: Its Application in Architectural Design. 211p. 1982. text ed. 65.00 (ISBN 0-246-11224-7). Renouf.

--Environmental Physics in Construction: Its Applications in Architectural Design. 220p. 1982. 95.00x (ISBN 0-246-11224-7, Pub. by Granada England). State Mutual Bk.

--Structural Failure in Residential Buildings, 3 vols. Incl. Vol. 1. Flat Roofs, Roof Terraces & Balconies. 186p. 34.95x o.p. (ISBN 0-470-26305-9); Vol. 2. External Walls & Openings. 154p. 34.95x (ISBN 0-470-26789-5); Vol. 3. Basement & Adjoining Land Drainage. 154p. 39.95x (ISBN 0-470-26846-8). LC 77-28647. 1978-80. Set. 85.85x o.p. (ISBN 0-470-26898-0). Halsted Pr.

Schilder, Klass. The Trilogy, 3 vols. 1978. Set. 48.00 (ISBN 0-86524-126-0, 9501). Klock & Klock.

Schildknecht, C. E. & Skeist, I., eds. Polymerization Processes. LC 76-17108. (High Polymer Ser.: Vol. 29). 768p. 1977. 65.95x (ISBN 0-471-39381-9, Pub. by Wiley-Interscience). Wiley.

Schildkrout, Enid. People of the Zongo: The Transformation of Ethnic Identities in Ghana. LC 76-47188. (Cambridge Studies in Social Anthropology: No. 20). 1978. 34.50 (ISBN 0-521-21483-1). Cambridge U Pr.

Schildt, John W. Drums Along the Antietam. 1972. 19.95 (ISBN 0-87012-128-6). McClain.

Schill, Gottfried. Catenanes, Rotaxanes & Knots. Boeckmann, J., tr. from Ger. LC 78-127702. (Organic Chemistry Ser.: Vol. 22). 1971. 39.00 (ISBN 0-12-625450-8). Acad Pr.

Schillebeeckx, Edward. God among Us: The Gospel Proclaimed. 278p. 1983. 12.95 (ISBN 0-8245-0575-1). Crossroad NY.

--God is New Each Moment: Conversations with Huub Oosterhuis & Piet Hoogeveen. 160p. (Orig.). 1983. pap. price not set (ISBN 0-8164-2475-6). Seabury.

--Paul the Apostle. (Illus.). 128p. 1983. 14.95 (ISBN 0-8245-0574-3). Crossroad NY.

Schillebeeckx, Edward & Baptist-Metz, Johannes. Martyrdom Today. (Concilium 1983: Vol. 163). 128p. 1983. pap. 6.95 (ISBN 0-8164-2443-8). Seabury.

Schillebeeckx, Edward, ed. The Movement of Theology Since the Council. (Concilium 1983: Vol. 170). 128p. (Orig.). 1983. pap. 6.95 (ISBN 0-8164-2450-0). Seabury.

Schillebeeckx, Edward & Metz, Johannes B., eds. The Right of the Community to a Priest. (Concilium Ser.: Vol. 133). 128p. (Orig.). 1980. pap. 5.95 (ISBN 0-8164-2275-3). Seabury.

Schillebeeckx, Edward, jt. ed. see Kung, Hans.

Schillebeeckz, Edward, jt. ed. see Kung, Hans.

Schiller. Wilhelm Tell. Prudhoe, J., tr. from Ger. (Classics of Drama in English Translation Ser.). 1970. pap. 6.50 (ISBN 0-7190-0426-8). Manchester.

Schiller, A. Arthur. Foreign Law Classification in the Columbia University Law Library. LC 64-66321. 93p. 1964. 12.50 (ISBN 0-379-00254-X). Oceana.

Schiller, Bradley R. Economics of Poverty & Discrimination. 3rd ed. (Illus.). 1980. pap. text ed. 14.95 (ISBN 0-13-232025-8). P-H.

Schiller, Dan. Telematics & Government. 256p. 1982. 24.50 (ISBN 0-89391-106-2); pap. 12.50 (ISBN 0-89391-129-1). Ablex Pub.

Schiller, Donald. CATV Program Origination & Production. Brock, Bill, ed. 1978. 14.95 o.p. (ISBN 0-8306-8865-X, 865). TAB Bks.

Schiller, E. J. & Droste, R. L., eds. Water Supply & Sanitation in Developing Countries. LC 81-86538. (Illus.). 368p. 1982. 29.95 (ISBN 0-250-40490-7). Ann Arbor Science.

Schiller, Ferdinand C. Humanism: Philosophical Essays. Repr. of 1912 ed. lib. bdg. 17.25x (ISBN 0-8371-2837-4, SCHU). Greenwood.

--Studies in Humanism. Repr. of 1912 ed. lib. bdg. 19.75x (ISBN 0-8371-2812-9, SCSH). Greenwood.

Schiller, Francis. A Mobius Strip: Fin-de-Sicle Neuropsychiatry & Paul Mobius. LC 81-40317. (Illus.). 110p. 1981. 16.95x (ISBN 0-520-04467-3). U of Cal Pr.

--Paul Broca, Eighteen Twenty-Four to Eighteen Eighty: Founder of French Anthropoogy, Explorer of the Brain. LC 78-59453. 1979. 37.50x (ISBN 0-520-03744-8). U of Cal Pr.

Schiller, Friedrich. Mary Stuart. Passage, Charles E., tr. & intro. by. Bd. with The Maid of Orleans. LC 60-13991. xxviii, 259p. pap. 4.95 (ISBN 0-8044-6818-4). Ungar.

Schiller, Herbert I. Who Knows: Information in the Age of the Fortune 500. (Communications & Information Science Ser.). 150p. 1981. text ed. 19.50x (ISBN 0-89391-069-4); pap. 11.95. Ablex Pub.

Schiller, Herbert I., jt. ed. see Nordenstreng, Kaarle.

Schiller, J. Friedrich. On the Aesthetic Education of Man, in a Series of Letters. Wilkinson, Elizabeth M. & Willoughby, L. A., eds. 1982. 32.50x o.p. (ISBN 0-19-815359-7); pap. 16.95x (ISBN 0-19-815786-X). Oxford U Pr.

Schiller, Joseph. Physiology & Classification: Historical Relations. 214p. 1980. 36.75x (ISBN 2-224-00588-1). Masson Pub.

Schiller, Justin G., ed. see Ballantyne, Robert.

Schiller, Justin G., ed. see Boreman, Thomas.

Schiller, Justin G., ed. see Charlesworth, Maria L.

Schiller, Justin G., ed. see D'Aulnoy, Marie C.

Schiller, Justin G., ed. see Finley, Martha.

Schiller, Justin G., ed. see Harris, Benjamin.

Schiller, Justin G., ed. see Newbery, F.

Schiller, Justin G., ed. see Wilde, Oscar.

Schiller, Marc, jt. auth. see Moffat, Anne.

Schiller, Patricia. Creative Approach to Sex Education & Counseling: With a New Section on Sex Therapy. 1978. pap. 12.00 o.s.i. (ISBN 0-695-81178-9). Follett.

Schiller, Siegfried, et al. Electron Beam Technology. 416p. 1982. 52.50 o.s.i. (ISBN 0-471-06056-9, Pub. by Wiley-Interscience). Wiley.

Schillereff, Ronald L. Multibank Holding Company Performance. Dufey, Gunter, ed. LC 82-8583. (Research for Business Decisions Ser.: No. 52). 122p. 1982. 34.95 (ISBN 0-8357-1348-2, Pub. by UMI Res Pr). Univ Microfilms.

Schilling, Bernard M. Dryden & the Conservative Myth. 1961. 47.50x (ISBN 0-685-69862-9). Elliots Bks.

Schilling, Donald & Belove, Charles. Electronic Circuits: Discrete & Integrated. 2nd ed. (Electical & Electronic Engineering). (Illus.). 1979. text ed. 34.95 (ISBN 0-07-055294-0, C); manual 24.00solutions (ISBN 0-07-055299-1). McGraw.

Schilling, Donald, jt. auth. see Taub, Herbert.

Schilling, H. D., et al. Coal Gasification-Exisiting Processes & New Developments. 330p. 1983. 40.00x (ISBN 0-8448-1421-0). Crane-Russak Co.

Schilling, J. S. & Shelton, R. N. Physics of Solids Under High Pressure. 1982. 61.75 (ISBN 0-444-86326-5). Elsevier.

Schilling, Jane M., jt. auth. see Chamberlain, Neil W.

Schilling, Michael, jt. ed. see Harms, Wolfgang.

Schilling, R. S., ed. Occupational Health Practice. (Illus.). 1973. 32.95 o.p. (ISBN 0-407-33700-8). Butterworth.

Schilling, Ronald B., jt. auth. see Herskowitz, G. P.

Schilling, S. Paul. The Faith We Sing. LC 82-21749. 240p. 1983. pap. write for info. (ISBN 0-664-24434-3). Westminster.

Schilpp, Paul A., ed. Albert Einstein Autobiographical Notes: A Centennial Edition. LC 78-13925. 1979. 13.50x (ISBN 0-87548-352-6). Open Court.

--Albert Einstein: Philosopher-Scientist. LC 50-5340. (Library of Living Philosophers: Vol. Vii). 799p. 1973. 33.00x (ISBN 0-87548-133-7); pap. 16.00x (ISBN 0-87548-286-4). Open Court.

--The Philosophy of Brand Blanshard. (The Library of Living Philosophers: Vol. XV). 1161p. 1980. 38.00x (ISBN 0-87548-349-6). Open Court.

Schilpp, Paul A., ed. & intro. by. The Philosophy of C. D. Broad. LC 60-12084. (Library of Living Philosophers: Vol. X). 878p. 1959. 33.00x (ISBN 0-87548-128-0). Open Court.

--The Philosophy of C. I. Lewis. LC 67-10007. (Library of Living Philosophers: Vol. Xiii). 727p. 1968. 30.00x (ISBN 0-87548-135-3). Open Court.

Schilpp, Paul A., ed. Philosophy of Ernst Cassirer. LC 72-83947. (Library of Living Philosophers Ser.: Vol. VI). 954p. 1949. 36.00x (ISBN 0-87548-131-0); pap. 18.00x (ISBN 0-87548-146-9). Open Court.

Schilpp, Paul A., ed. & intro. by. The Philosophy of G. E. Moore. LC 68-57206. (Library of Living Philosophers: Vol. Iv). 744p. 1942. 30.00x (ISBN 0-87548-136-1); Vol. 1 $ 2. pap. 8.00x (ISBN 0-87548-280-5); Vol. 2. pap. 8.00x (ISBN 0-87548-281-3). Open Court.

--The Philosophy of George Santayana. LC 75-154024. (Library of Living Philosophers: Vol. II). 715p. 1951. 30.00x (ISBN 0-87548-139-6). Open Court.

Schilpp, Paul A., intro. by. The Philosophy of Jean-Paul Sartre. (Library of Living Philosophers Ser.: Vol. XVI). xiv, 754p. 1981. 27.50x (ISBN 0-87548-354-2). Open Court.

Schilpp, Paul A., ed. The Philosophy of Karl Jaspers. augmented ed. LC 57-14578. (Library of Living Philosophers: Vol. IX). xxvi, 992p. 1981. Repr. of 1957 ed. 33.00x (ISBN 0-87548-361-5). Open Court.

--The Philosophy of Karl Popper, 2 vols. LC 78-186983. (The Library of Living Philosophers: Vol. Xiv). 1357p. 1974. Set. 42.00x (ISBN 0-87548-353-4); Vol. 1. (ISBN 0-87548-141-8); Vol. 2. (ISBN 0-87548-142-6). Open Court.

Schilpp, Paul A., ed. & intro. by. The Philosophy of Rudolf Carnap. LC 62-9577. (Library of Living Philosophers: Vol. XI). xvi, 1104p. 1963. 42.00x (ISBN 0-87548-130-2). Open Court.

--The Philosophy of Sarvepalli Radhakrishnan. (Library of Living Philosophers: Vol. Viii). 813p. 1952. 33.50x (ISBN 0-87548-137-X). Open Court.

Schilpp, Paul A. & Friedman, Maurice, eds. The Philosophy of Martin Buber. LC 65-14535. (The Library of Living Philosophers: Vol. Xii). 831p. 1967. 33.50x (ISBN 0-87548-129-9). Open Court.

Schilt, A. A. Analytical Applications of 1, 10-Phen'-antroline & Related Compounds. 1969. inquire for price o.p. (ISBN 0-08-012877-7). Pergamon.

Schima, M., ed. Advances in Voluntary Sterilization. (International Congress Ser.: No. 284). 1974. 61.50 (ISBN 0-444-15075-7). Elsevier.

Schima, Marilyn & Bolian, Polly. I Know a Nurse. (Community Helper Bks.). (Illus.). (gr. 1-3). 1969. PLB 4.29 o.p. (ISBN 0-399-60287-9). Putnam Pub Group.

Schimberg, Albert P. Tall in Paradise: The Story of Saint Coletta of Corbie. 2.75 o.p. (ISBN 0-8338-0059-0). M Jones.

Schimizzi, Ned V. Mastering the Metric System. (Orig.). 1975. pap. 2.50 (ISBN 0-451-62194-8, ME2194, Ment). NAL.

Schimke, Robert T., ed. Gene Amplification. LC 81-70729. 339p. 1982. text ed. 38.50x (ISBN 0-87969-151-4). Cold Spring Harbor.

Schimke, Robert T. & Katunuma, Nobuhiko, eds. Intracellular Protein Turnover. 1975. 35.00 (ISBN 0-12-625550-4). Acad Pr.

Schimmel, jt. auth. see Lieberman.

Schimmel, Annemarie. Islam in India & Pakistan. (Iconography of Religions Ser.: XXII 9). (Illus.). x, 34p. 1982. pap. write for info. (ISBN 90-04-06479-6). E J Brill.

Schimmel, David, jt. auth. see Fischer, Louis.

Schimmel, Nancy. Just Enough to Make a Story: A Sourcebook for Storytelling. Rev. ed. 1982. pap. 6.00 (ISBN 0-932164-00-5). Sisters Choice.

Schimmelpfeng, Richard H. & Cook, Donald, eds. Use of the Library of Congress Classification. LC 68-27829. 1968. pap. 8.50 (ISBN 0-8389-3082-4). ALA.

Schimmels, Cliff. How to Survive & Thrive in College. 160p. 1983. pap. 5.95 (ISBN 0-8007-5104-3, Power Bks). Revell.

Schimper, A. F. Plant Geography Upon a Physiological Basis. Fisher, W. R., tr. (Illus.). 1960. Repr. of 1903 ed. 80.00 (ISBN 3-7682-0901-6). Lubrecht & Cramer.

Schimpff, Jill W. Open Sesame Picture Dictionary: Featuring Jim Henson's Sesame Street Muppets, Children's Television Workshop. 84p. 1982. pap. text ed. 4.95x (ISBN 0-19-503035-4). Oxford U Pr.

--Oxford Picture Dictionary of American English Workbook. (Illus.). 1981. 3.75x (ISBN 0-19-502819-8). Oxford U Pr.

Schinauer, Betty, jt. auth. see Wilkerson, Gwen.

Schindler, G. E., ed. see Joel, A. E., Jr.

Schindler, Gene & Schindler, Roana. Hawaii Kai Cookbook. (Illus.). 1970. 7.95 (ISBN 0-8208-0225-5). Hearthside.

Schindler, Harold. Orrin Porter Rockwell: Man of God, Son of Thunder. 2nd ed. (University of Utah Publications in the American West: Vol. 15). (Illus.). 1983. 25.00 (ISBN 0-87480-204-0). U of Utah Pr.

Schindler, John. How to Live Three Hundred & Sixty Five Days a Year. 1954. pap. 3.95 o.p. (ISBN 0-13-416792-9, Parker). P-H.

Schindler, Margaret. Living with a Colostomy. (Illus.). 128p. (Orig.). 1983. pap. 6.95 (ISBN 0-7225-0681-3, Pub. by Thorsons Pubs England). Sterling.

Schindler, Maria. Europe: A Cosmic Picture. Fletcher, John, ed. Gorge, Peter, tr. from Ger. (Illus.). 240p. 1975. 18.95 (ISBN 0-88010-041-9, Pub. by New Knowledge Bks England). Anthroposophic.

--Goethe's Theory of Colour. Mery, Eleanor C., tr. from Ger. (Illus.). 210p. 1970. 23.95 (ISBN 0-88010-047-8, Pub. by New Knowledge Bks England). Anthroposophic.

Schindler, Paul E. Aspirin Therapy. LC 77-56688. 1978. 8.95 o.s.i. (ISBN 0-8027-0565-0). Walker & Co.

Schindler, Regine. The Lost Sheep. LC 80-68546. Orig. Title: Das Verlorene Shaf. 32p. (gr. k-3). 1982. Repr. 6.95g (ISBN 0-687-22780-1). Abingdon.

Schindler, Roana, jt. auth. see Schindler, Gene.

Schindler-Rainman, Eva & Lippitt, Ronald. Taking Your Meetings Out of the Doldrums. LC 75-41890. (Illus.). 100p. 1975. 10.50 (ISBN 0-88390-136-6). Univ Assocs.

Schine, Cathleen. Alice in Bed. LC 82-48721. 1983. 12.95 (ISBN 0-394-52982-0). Knopf.

Schinke, Steven P. & Gilchrist, LeWayne D. Teaching Adolescents Life Skills. 1983. pap. text ed. price not set (ISBN 0-8391-1795-7, 18570). Univ Park.

Schinkel, K. F. K. F. Schinkel: Collected Architectural Designs. (Academy Architecture Ser.). (Illus.). 128p. 1983. 29.95 (ISBN 0-312-44952-6); pap. 19.95 (ISBN 0-312-44953-4). St Martin.

Schinnerer, Otto P., ed. see Kaestner, Erich.

Schinzinger, Roland, jt. auth. see Martin, Michael.

Schioler, Gail. The Non-Drinker's Drink Book. (Illus.). 160p. 1981. 12.95 (ISBN 0-920510-16-7, Pub. by Personal Lib); pap. 8.95 (ISBN 0-920510-80-9). Dodd.

Schippers, M. E., jt. auth. see Duvis, Fritz D.

Schirman, Lucille. Lady on the Run. 1982. pap. 2.95 (ISBN 0-451-11831-6, AE1831, Sig). NAL.

Schirmbeck, Egon. Restaurants: Architecture & Ambience. (Illus.). 144p. (Eng. & Ger.). 1983. 35.00 (ISBN 0-8038-5081-6). Architectural.

Schirmer, Henry W., ed. Profile - Architectural Firms - The American Institute of Architects. 1980. 96.00 o.p. (ISBN 0-931392-02-0). Am Inst Arch.

Schiro, George J., jt. auth. see Katsaros, Thomas.

Schirokauer, Conrad. A Brief History of Chinese & Japanese Civilizations. (Illus., Orig.). 1978. pap. text ed. 18.95 (ISBN 0-15-505570-4, HC). HarBraceJ.

--Modern China & Japan: A Brief History. 358p. 1982. pap. text ed. 13.95 (ISBN 0-15-559870-8, HC). HarBraceJ.

Schissel, Marvin. Dentistry & Its Victims. 336p. 1981. 11.95 o.p. (ISBN 0-312-19391-2). St Martin.

Schiwetz, E. M. Six Spanish Missions in Texas: A Portfolio of Paintings by E. M. Schiwetz. 1968. 60.00 o.s.i. (ISBN 0-292-73650-9). U of Tex Pr.

Schjeldahl, Peter. Since Nineteen Sixty-Four: New & Selected Poems. LC 78-15572. 1978. pap. 5.00 (ISBN 0-915342-26-X). SUN.

Schla, jt. auth. see Barish.

Schlaadt, Richard G. & Shannon, Peter T. Drugs of Choice: Current Perspectives on Drug Use. (Illus.). 464p. 1982. pap. 17.95 (ISBN 0-13-220772-9). P-H.

Schlachter, Gail & Thomison, Dennis. Library Science Dissertations, Nineteen Seventy-Three to Nineteen Eighty: An Annotated Bibliography. (Research Studies in Library Science: No. 18). 400p. 1982. 45.00 (ISBN 0-87287-299-8). Libs Unl.

Schlachter, Gail A. Directory of Financial Aids for Women. 2nd ed. LC 82-6778. 344p. 1982. text ed. 26.00 (ISBN 0-87436-340-3); pap. 16.00 (ISBN 0-87436-344-6). ABC-Clio.

Schlachter, Gail M. A Guide to the Reference Literature on Women in the Social Sciences, Humanities, and Sciences. (Clio Reference Guide Ser.). 1982. cancelled (ISBN 0-87436-313-6). ABC Clio.

Schlack, A. L., jt. auth. see Sandor, Bela I.

Schlack, Beverly Ann. Continuing Presences: Virginia Woolf's Use of Literary Allusion. LC 78-68163. 1979. 15.95x (ISBN 0-271-00208-5). Pa St U Pr.

Schlaefke, M. E., et al, eds. Central Neurone Environment & the Control Systems of Breathing & Circulation. (Proceedings in Life Sciences Ser.). 275p. 1982. 35.00 (ISBN 0-387-11671-0). Springer-Verlag.

Schlafly, Phyllis. The End of an Era. 1982. 12.95 (ISBN 0-89526-659-8). Regnery-Gateway.

Schlaifer, R. & Heron, S. D. Development of Aircraft Engines & Fuels. 1970. Repr. of 1950 ed. 54.00 o.p. (ISBN 0-08-018740-4). Pergamon.

Schlaifer, Robert. Analysis of Decisions under Uncertainty. LC 77-5729. (Illus.). 746p. 1978. Repr. of 1969 ed. 31.50 (ISBN 0-88275-560-9). Krieger.

--Computer Programs for Elementary Decision Analysis. LC 75-151633. (Illus.). 1971. 14.00x (ISBN 0-87584-091-4). Harvard Busn.

--Introduction to Statistics for Business Decisions. 1961. text ed. 20.95 o.p. (ISBN 0-07-055308-4, C); solutions manual 4.95 o.p. (ISBN 0-07-055305-X). McGraw.

--Probability & Statistics for Business Decisions. LC 79-23042. 744p. Date not set. Repr. of 1959 ed. lib. bdg. cancelled (ISBN 0-89874-029-0). Krieger.

Schlamm, Rhoda, ed. see Goldblatt, Burt.

Schlanger, S. O. & Cita, M. B., eds. Nature & Origin of Cretaceous Carbonrich Facies. write for info. (ISBN 0-12-624950-4). Acad Pr.

Schlant, Ernestine, tr. see Habermann, Gerhard.

Schlant, Ernestine S. Hermann Broch. (World Authors Ser.). 1978. lib. bdg. 15.95 (ISBN 0-8057-6326-0, Twayne). G K Hall.

Schlatter, Richard, jt. ed. see McCormick, Richard P.

Schlawin, Sheila, jt. auth. see Chew, Charles.

Schlechter, R. Beitraege zur Orchideenkunde von Colombia. (Feddes Repertorium: Beiheft 27). 183p. (Ger.). 1980. Repr. of 1924 ed. lib. bdg. 31.20x (ISBN 3-87429-182-0). Lubrecht & Cramer.

--Beitraege zur Orchideenkunde von Zentralamerika, 2 vols. in one. (Feddes Repertorium: Beiheft 17 & 18). 402p. (Ger.). 1980. Repr. of 1922 ed. lib. bdg. 54.00x (ISBN 3-87429-181-2). Lubrecht & Cramer.

--Orchidaceae Perrierianae: Zur Orchideenkunde der Insel Madagascar. (Feddes Repertorium: Beiheft 33). 391p. (Ger.). 1980. Repr. of 1925 ed. lib. bdg. 46.00x (ISBN 3-87429-183-9). Lubrecht & Cramer.

--Orchideenflora von Rio Grande do Sul. (Feddes Repertorium: Beiheft 35). 108p. (Ger.). 1980. Repr. of 1925 ed. lib. bdg. 23.60x (ISBN 3-87429-185-5). Lubrecht & Cramer.

Schlede, Nancy, ed. see Parsons, James.

Schlegal, John P., et al, eds. Towards a Re-Definition of Development: Essays & Discussion on the Nature of Development in an International Perspective. Birou. LC 76-28753. 1977. text ed. 17.75 (ISBN 0-08-020580-1). Pergamon.

Schlegel, Friedrich. Dialogue on Poetry & Literary Aphorisms. Behler, Ernst & Struc, Roman, trs. LC 67-27115. 1968. 16.95x (ISBN 0-271-73136-2). Pa St U Pr.

--Ueber Die Sprache und Weisheit der Indier: Ein Beitrag Zur Begrundung der Altertumskunde. (Amsterdam Classics in Linguistics Ser.). lvii, 194p. 1977. 32.00 (ISBN 90-272-0872-7, 1). Benjamins North Am.

Schlegel, H & Wulverhorst, A. H. Verster Van. Traite De Fauconnerie. 1600.00 (ISBN 0-384-53920-3); Portfolio 500.00 (ISBN 0-384-53925-4). Johnson Repr.

Schlegel, H. G. Microbial Energy Conversion. LC 76-56894. 1977. pap. text ed. write for info. (ISBN 0-08-021791-5). Pergamon.

Schlegel, John P. The Deceptive Ash: Bilingualism & Canadian Policy in Africa, 1957-1971. LC 78-64827. 1978. pap. text ed. 16.00 (ISBN 0-8191-0637-2). U Pr of Amer.

Schlegel, Karl F., jt. auth. see Wilhelm, Friedrich.

Schlegel, Stuart A. Tiruray Justice: Traditional Tiruray Law & Morality. LC 72-107660. 1970. 28.50x (ISBN 0-520-01686-6). U of Cal Pr.

Schleh, Edward C. Management by Results: The Dynamics of Profitable Management. (Illus.). 1961. 26.50 (ISBN 0-07-055320-3, P&RB). McGraw.

--The Management Tactician: Executive Tactics for Getting Results. (Illus.). 288p. 1974. 19.95 (ISBN 0-07-055293-2, P&RB). McGraw.

Schlehofer, Jo. Joy in Parenting: Parenting Skills with Pre-Schoolers Through Adolescents. pap. 3.95 o.p. (ISBN 0-8091-2125-5). Paulist Pr.

Schlei, Barbara L. & Grossman, Paul. Employment Discrimination Law. 1600p. 1983. 95.00 (ISBN 0-87179-386-5). BNA.

--Employment Discrimination Law: 1979 Supplement. LC 79-881. 488p. 1979. pap. 8.50 o.p. (ISBN 0-87179-296-6); student ed. o.p. 4.00 o.p. (ISBN 0-87179-301-6). BNA.

Schleicher, August. Die Sprachen Europas in Systematischer Uebersicht (Bonn; 1850) Linguistische Untersuchungen. (Amsterdam Classics in Linguistics: 4). 325p. 1983. 32.00 (ISBN 90-272-0875-1). Benjamins North Am.

Schleichkorn, Jay. Coping with Cerebral Palsy: Answers to Questions Parents Often Ask. 1983. pap. text ed. 14.95 (ISBN 0-8391-1768-X, 19186). Univ Park.

Schleien, Stuart, jt. auth. see Wehman, Paul.

Schleier, Curt. You'd Better Not Tell. LC 78-20921. 1979. 7.50 (ISBN 0-664-32646-3). Westminster.

Schleiermacher, Friedrich. On the Glaubenslehre: Two Letters to Dr. Lucke. Massey, James A., ed. Duke, James & Fiorenza, Francis S., trs. from Ger. LC 80-20717. (American Academy of Religion, Texts & Translations Ser.: No. 3). Orig. Title: Sendschreiben Uber Seine Glaubenslehre an Lucke. 1981. 9.95 (ISBN 0-686-86731-9, 01-02-03); pap. 9.95 (ISBN 0-89130-420-7). Scholars Pr CA.

Schleifer, Abdullah. The Fall of Jerusalem. LC 79-178713. (Illus.). 256p. 1972. 7.50 (ISBN 0-85345-204-0, CL2040); pap. 3.45 (ISBN 0-85345-249-0, PB2490). Monthly Rev.

Schlein, Miriam. Metric: The Modern Way to Measure. LC 76-29665. (gr. 3-7). 1977. pap. 1.95 (ISBN 0-15-659310-6, VoyB). HarBraceJ.

--My House. LC 79-165820. (Illus.). (ps-2). 1971. 5.50g o.p. (ISBN 0-8075-5357-3). A Whitman.

Schleker, Peggy J., ed. see Roberts, Duane F.

Schleker, Peggy J., ed. see Weisbrod, Harry, et al.

Schlemm, Betty L. Painting with Light. (Illus.). 1978. 19.95 o.p. (ISBN 0-8230-3881-5). Watson-Guptill.

Schlemmer. Handbook of Advertising Art Production. 2nd ed. 1976. text ed. 17.95 (ISBN 0-13-372524-3); pap. text ed. 12.95 (ISBN 0-13-372516-2). P-H.

Schlemmer, Oskar. Man: Teaching Notes from the Bauhaus. 1971. 10.00 (ISBN 0-262-19095-8). MIT Pr.

Schlenker, B. R. An Introduction to Materials Science: S. I. Edition. LC 73-16682. 364p. 1974. 27.95x o.s.i. (ISBN 0-471-76177-X). Wiley.

Schlenker, Barry R. Impression Management: The Self-Concept, Social Identity, & Interpersonal Relations. LC 80-15047. 250p. 1980. text ed. 18.95 (ISBN 0-8185-0398-X). Brooks-Cole.

Schlepp, Wayne. San-ch'u: Its Technique & Imagery. 160p. 1970. 19.50 (ISBN 0-299-05540-X). U of Wis Pr.

Schlereth, Hewitt. Celestial Navigation by Sun Lines. (The Cruising Navigator Ser.: Vol. 2). (Illus.). 352p. 1983. 25.00 (ISBN 0-915160-53-6). Seven Seas.

--Commonsense Celestial Navigation. 1979. pap. 8.95 (ISBN 0-8092-7219-9). Contemp Bks.

--Latitude & Longitude By the Noon Sight. LC 82-50249. (Crusing Navigatar: Vol. 1). (Illus.). 320p. 1982. 25.00 (ISBN 0-915160-51-X). Seven Seas.

--Sight Reduction Tables for Small Boat Navigation. LC 82-19210. (The Cruising Navigator Ser.: Vol. 00). 196p. 1983. 25.00 (ISBN 0-915160-54-4). Seven Seas.

Schlereth, Thomas. Material Culture Studies in America. LC 82-8812. (Illus.). 1982. cloth 22.95 (ISBN 0-910050-61-9); pap. 15.00x (ISBN 0-910050-67-8). AASLH.

Schlereth, Thomas J. Artifacts & the American Past: Techniques for the Teaching Historian. LC 80-19705. 300p. 1981. text ed. 14.95 (ISBN 0-910050-47-3). AASLH.

--The Cosmopolitan Ideal in Enlightenment Thought. LC 76-22405. 1977. text ed. 15.95x (ISBN 0-268-00720-9). U of Notre Dame Pr.

--The University of Notre Dame: A Portrait of Its History & Campus. LC 74-27890. 1976. text ed. 25.00 o.p. (ISBN 0-268-01906-1); pap. text ed. 9.95x (ISBN 0-268-01905-3). U of Notre Dame Pr.

Schlesinger. Neurophysical Peptide Hormones & Other Biologically Active Peptides. (Developments in Endocrinology Ser.: Vol. 3). 1982. 60.00 (ISBN 0-444-00605-2). Elsevier.

--Quality of Worklife & the Supervisor. 208p. 1982. 26.95 (ISBN 0-03-061598-4). Praeger.

Schlesinger, Alice, illus. Big Book of Mother Goose. (Nursery Treasure Bks.). (Illus.). (gr. k-3). 1.50 o.p. (ISBN 0-448-04200-2, G&D). Putnam Pub Group.

Schlesinger, Arthur M. Learning How to Behave: A Historical Study of American Etiquette Books. LC 68-28296. 95p. 1968. Repr. of 1946 ed. 17.50x (ISBN 0-8154-0201-5). Cooper Sq.

--New Viewpoints in American History. LC 76-49146. 1977. Repr. of 1922 ed. lib. bdg. 19.25x (ISBN 0-8371-9314-1, SCNV). Greenwood.

Schlesinger, Arthur M., Jr., ed. & intro. by. The Dynamics of World Power, 5 vols. Incl. Vol. 1. Western Europe (ISBN 0-07-055322-X); Vol. 2. Eastern Europe & the Soviet Union (ISBN 0-07-055323-8); Vol. 3. Latin America (ISBN 0-07-055324-6); Vol. 4. Far East (ISBN 0-07-055325-4); Vol. 5. United Nations, Middle East, Subsaharan Africa (ISBN 0-07-055326-2). LC 78-150208. 4500p. 1973. Set. 225.00 (ISBN 0-07-079729-3, P&RB). McGraw.

Schlesinger, Arthur M., Sr. Critical Period in American Religion 1875-1900. Wolf, Richard C., ed. LC 67-24338. (Facet Bks.). 1967. pap. 0.50 o.p. (ISBN 0-8006-3044-0, 1-3044). Fortress.

Schlesinger, Elfriede, jt. auth. see DeVore, Wynetta.

Schlesinger, G. Testing Machine Tools: For the Use of Machine Tool Makers, Users Inspectors & Plant Engineers. 8th ed. 1978. text ed. 19.25 (ISBN 0-08-021685-4). Pergamon.

Schlesinger, George N. Metaphysics: Issues & Techniques. LC 82-24408. 288p. 1983. text ed. 28.50x (ISBN 0-389-20380-7); pap. text ed. 16.50x (ISBN 0-389-20381-5). B&N Imports.

Schlesinger, Hilde S. & Meadow, Kathryn P. Sound & Sign: Childhood Deafness & Mental Health. LC 77-174455. 294p. 1973. 18.50x (ISBN 0-520-02136-3). U of Cal Pr.

Schlesinger, I. M. & Namir, L. Sign Language of the Deaf: Psychological Linguistic & Sociological Perspectives. (Perspectives in Neurolinguistics & Psycholinguistics Ser.). 1978. 33.00 (ISBN 0-12-625150-9). Acad Pr.

Schlesinger, Kurt, et al. Psychology: A Dynamic Science. 784p. 1976. text ed. write for info. (ISBN 0-697-06620-7); study guide avail. (ISBN 0-697-06621-5); instrs. manual avail. (ISBN 0-697-06657-6). Wm C Brown.

Schlesinger, Leonard & Eccles, Robert G. Managing Behavior in Organizations: Texts, Cases, Readings Led. (Illus.). 704p. 1983. text ed. 23.95 (ISBN 0-07-055332-7, C); instructor's manual 13.95 (ISBN 0-07-055333-5). McGraw.

Schlesinger, Louis B., jt. auth. see Revitch, Eugene.

Schlesinger, Ludwig. Handbuch der Theorie der Linearen Differentialgleichungen, 2 Vols. (Bibliotheca Mathematica Teubneriana, 30-31). (Ger). Repr. Set. 88.00 (ISBN 0-384-53978-5). Johnson Repr.

Schlesinger, Mark. Reconstructing General Education: An Examination of Assumptions, Practices & Prospects. Woditsch, Gary, ed. LC 77-72184. (CUE Project Occasional Paper Ser.: No. 2). 1977. pap. 3.00 (ISBN 0-89372-002-X). General Stud Res.

Schlesinger, Mark, jt. auth. see Cappuzzello, Paul.

Schlesinger, Milton J., et al, eds. Heat Shock: From Bacteria to Man. LC 82-61222. 440p. 1982. 45.00X (ISBN 0-87969-158-1). Cold Spring Harbor.

Schlesinger, R. Walter, ed. The Togaviruses. 1980. 66.50 (ISBN 0-12-625380-3). Acad Pr.

Schlesinger, Reuben & Wolfson, Marty. Todays Economic Issues. (Illus.). 1974. pap. 5.95 (ISBN 0-916114-04-X). Wolfson.

Schlesinger, Richard B., jt. auth. see Lippmann, Morton.

Schlesinger, Rudolf B., ed. Formation of Contracts: A Study of the Common Core of Legal Systems, 2 Vols. LC 67-25905. (No. 269). 1968. Set. 75.00 (ISBN 0-379-00269-8). Oceana.

Schlesinger, Stephen, jt. auth. see Kinzer, Stephen.

Schlesinger, Tom. Fighting Strategy: Winning Combinations. LC 82-70680. (Illus.). 101p. (Orig.). 1982. pap. 5.95 (ISBN 0-86568-035-3, 306). Unique Pubns.

Schlessinger, Bernard. The Basic Business Library: Core Resources. 240p. 1983. lib. bdg. 32.50 (ISBN 0-89774-038-6). Oryx Pr.

Schleyer, Paul, jt. ed. see Olah, George A.

Schlichmann, M., jt. auth. see Paden, I.

Schlichting, Hermann. Boundary Layer Theory. 7th ed. Kestin, J., tr. from Ger. (Mechanical Engineering Ser.). (Illus.). 1979. 39.95 (ISBN 0-07-055334-3, C). McGraw.

Schlichting, Hermann T. & Truckenbrodt, Erich A. Aerodynamics of the Airplane. (Illus.). 1979. text ed. 79.00 (ISBN 0-07-055341-6). McGraw.

Schlichting, Marvin. Intermediate Algebra. Date not set. text ed. price not set o.s.i. (ISBN 0-442-21214-3). Van Nos Reinhold.

Schlick, Arnolt. Spiegel der Orgelmacher un(D) Organisten. (Bibliotheca Organologica: Vol. 63). 1981. 60.00 o.s.i. (ISBN 90-6027-395-8, Pub. by Frits Knuf Netherlands); wrappers 47.50 o.s.i. (ISBN 90-6027-338-9). Pendragon NY.

Schliemann, Peter U. Strategy of British & German Investors in Brazil. 200p. 1981. text ed. 49.25x (ISBN 0-566-00435-6). Gower Pub Ltd.

Schlier, C., ed. Molecular Beams & Reaction Kinetics. (Italian Physical Society: Course No. 44). 1970. 64.50 (ISBN 0-12-368844-2). Acad Pr.

Schlimbach, Alice, jt. ed. see Kritsch, Erna.

Schlimbach, Georg C. Ueber Die Structur, Erhaltung Stimmung, Prufung der Orgel: Leipzig 1801. (Bibliotheca Organologica: Vol. 8). Repr. of 1966 ed. wrappers 27.50 o.s.i. (ISBN 90-6027-025-8, Pub. by Frits Knuf Netherlands). Pendragon NY.

Schlinger, Evert L., jt. auth. see Cole, Frank R.

Schlink, Basilea. Asi Seremos Diferentes. 224p. Date not set. 2.95 (ISBN 0-88113-004-4). Edit Betania.

--Dear Brothers & Sisters in Christ: Five Letters of Comfort. 1978. pap. 0.75 (ISBN 3-87209-622-2). Evang Sisterhood Mary.

--Encontre la Llave al Corazon De Dios. 304p. Date not set. 2.50 (ISBN 0-88113-070-2). Edit Betania.

--The Grace of Love. 1974. gift edition 0.75 (ISBN 3-87209-662-1). Evang Sisterhood Mary.

--The Holy Land Today. rev. ed. 1975. 5.50 (ISBN 3-87209-610-9). Evang Sisterhood Mary.

--Let Me Stand at Your Side. 1975. 2.75 (ISBN 3-87209-614-1). Evang Sisterhood Mary.

--Mi Oracion. 96p. Date not set. 1.75 (ISBN 0-88113-201-2). Edit Betania.

--O None Can Be Loved Like Jesus. 1974. pap. 1.00 (ISBN 3-87209-651-6). Evang Sisterhood Mary.

--Realidades. 160p. Date not set. 2.25 (ISBN 0-88113-262-4). Edit Betania.

--The Royal Priesthood. 1971. pap. 0.75 (ISBN 3-87209-654-0). Evang Sisterhood Mary.

--Songs & Prayers of Victory. 1978. pap. 1.50 (ISBN 3-87209-652-4). Evang Sisterhood Mary.

--The Weapon of Prayer. 1974. Gift ed. 0.75 (ISBN 3-87209-658-3). Evang Sisterhood Mary.

--What Made Them So Brave? (Illus.). (gr. 3 up). 1978. gift edition 2.25 (ISBN 3-87209-655-9). Evang Sisterhood Mary.

--Why Doesn't God Intervene? Evangelical Sisterhood of Mary, tr. from Ger. 32p. 1982. pap. 0.30 (ISBN 3-87209-629-X). Evang Sisterhood Mary.

--Words for the Servants of God. 1974. pap. 0.60 (ISBN 3-87209-661-3). Evang Sisterhood Mary.

Schlink, Edmund. The Doctrine of Baptism. Bouman, Herbert, tr. from Ger. LC 78-159794. 256p. 1972. pap. 9.50 (ISBN 0-570-03726-3, 12-2628). Concordia.

Schlissel, Lillian, ed. see Irving, Washington.

Schlitt, Dorothy M., et al. Life: A Question of Survival. (Illus., Orig.). (gr. 7-11). 1972. pap. text ed. 9.88x (ISBN 0-913688-03-7); teacher's guide 5.32 (ISBN 0-913688-04-5). Pawnee Pub.

Schlitt, W. J., intro. by. Interfacing Technologies in Solution Mining. LC 82-71423. (Illus.). 370p. (Orig.). 1982. pap. 30.00 (ISBN 0-89520-295-6, 295-6). Soc Mining Eng.

Schlitt, W. J., ed. Leaching & Recovering Copper from As-Mined Materials. LC 79-57347. (Illus.). 124p. 1980. pap. 20.00x (ISBN 0-89520-272-7). Soc Mining Eng.

Schlitt, W. J. & Larson, W. C., eds. Gold & Silver Leaching, Recovery & Economics. LC 81-68558. (Illus.). 148p. 1981. pap. text ed. 20.00x (ISBN 0-89520-289-1). Soc Mining Eng.

Schlitt, W. J. & Shock, D. A., eds. In Situ Uranium Leaching & Ground Water Restoration. LC 79-52217. (Illus.). 137p. 1979. pap. 20.00x (ISBN 0-89520-267-0). Soc Mining Eng.

Schlittler, Emil, ed. Antihypertensive Agents. (Medicinal Chemistry: Vol. 7). 1967. 67.50 (ISBN 0-12-625650-0). Acad Pr.

Schlobin, Roger C. Andre Norton: A Primary & Secondary Bibliography. 1979. lib. bdg. 13.00 (ISBN 0-8161-8044-X, Hall Reference). G K Hall.

--Urania's Daughters: A Checklist of Women Science Fiction Writers, 1692-1982. (Illus., Orig.). 1982. 11.95x (ISBN 0-916732-57-6); pap. 5.95x (ISBN 0-916732-56-8). Starmont Hse.

Schlobin, Roger C., jt. auth. see Tymn, Marshall B.

Schlobin, Roger C., ed. see Beauchamp, Gorman.

Schlobin, Roger C., ed. see Clareson, Thomas D.

Schlobin, Roger C., ed. see Collings, Michael R.

Schlobin, Roger C., ed. see Crossley, Robert.

Schlobin, Roger C., ed. see Diskin, Lahna.

Schlobin, Roger C., ed. see Elliot, Jeffrey M.

Schlobin, Roger C., ed. see Hassler, Donald M.

Schlobin, Roger C., ed. see Joshi, S. T.

Schlobin, Roger C., ed. see Kinnaird, John.

Schlobin, Roger C., ed. see Murphy, Brian.

Schlobin, Roger C., ed. see Pierce, Hazel.

Schlobin, Roger C., ed. see Weedman, Jane B.

Schlobin, Roger C., ed. see Winter, Douglas E.

Schlobin, Roger C., ed. see Wolfe, Gary K.

Schlobin, Roger C., ed. see Yoke, Carl B.

Schloegl, Irmgard, ed. The Wisdom of the Zen Masters. LC 75-42115. (The Wisdom Bks). 96p. 1976. pap. 4.95 o.s.i. (ISBN 0-8112-0609-2). New Directions.

Schloss, Christine S. Travel, Trade, & Temptation: The Dutch Italianate Harbor Scene, 1640-1680. Harris, Ann S., ed. LC 82-1864. (Studies in Baroque Art History: No. 3). 214p. 1982. 39.95 (ISBN 0-8357-1309-1, Pub. by UMI Res Pr). Univ Microfilms.

Schloss, Joseph D., Sr., ed. Handbook of Arrest, Search & Seizure. 90p. (Orig.). 1982. pap. text ed. 6.95 (ISBN 0-942728-02-5). Custom Pub Co.

Schloss, S. Pollenanalytische und Stratigraphische Untersuchungen im Sewensee. Ein Beitrag Zur Spaet- und Postglazealen Vegetations-Geschichte der Suedvogesen. (Dissertationes Botanica 52 Ser.). (Illus., Ger.). 1980. lib. bdg. 20.00x (ISBN 3-7682-1240-8). Lubrecht & Cramer.

Schlossberg, Dan. Baseballaffs. LC 82-10020. (Illus.). 96p. 1982. pap. 3.95 (ISBN 0-8246-0288-9). Jonathan David.

Schlossberg, Edwin & Brockman, John. The Kids' Pocket Calculator Game Book. (Illus.). 1977. 6.95 o.p. (ISBN 0-688-03233-8); pap. 3.95 o.s.i. (ISBN 0-688-08233-5). Morrow.

--The Philosopher's Game: Match Your Wits Against the One Hundred Greatest Thinkers of All Time. LC 76-62793. 1977. 6.98 (ISBN 0-312-60462-9); pap. 6.95 (ISBN 0-312-60463-7). St Martin.

--The Pocket Calculator Game Book. LC 75-26562. (Illus.). 1975. pap. 3.95 o.s.i. (ISBN 0-688-07983-0). Morrow.

--Pocket Calculator Game Book, No. 2. LC 77-7054. (Illus.). 1977. 6.95 (ISBN 0-688-03234-6); pap. 4.95 (ISBN 0-688-08234-3). Morrow.

Schlossberg, Harvey & Freeman, Lucy. Psychologist with a Gun. 1974. 6.95 o.p. (ISBN 0-698-10598-2, Pub. by Coward). Putnam Pub Group.

Schlossberg, Herbert. Idols for Destruction. 320p. 1983. 14.95; pap. 8.95 (ISBN 0-8407-5832-4). Nelson.

Schlossberg, Nancy, et al. Perspectives on Counseling Adults: Issues & Goals. LC 77-16292. (Psychology Ser.). 1978. text ed. 16.95 (ISBN 0-8185-0261-4). Brooks-Cole.

Schlossberg, Stephen I. & Scott, Judy M. Organizing & the Law. 3rd. ed. 1983. 20.00 (ISBN 0-87179-118-8); pap. 15.00 (ISBN 0-87179-119-6). BNA.

Schlosser, Felix. Forms of Christian Life. Wilson, R. A., tr. LC 69-20476. 1969. 4.50 o.p. (ISBN 0-685-07633-4, 80670). Glencoe.

Schlosser, Robert. The Humidity Readings. 16p. 1981. pap. 1.00 o.p. (ISBN 0-686-33137-0). Samisdat.

Schlosstein, Karl-Hans. Die Westfalischen Fabrikengerichtsdeputationen: Vorbilder, Werdegang und Scheitern. 219p. (Ger.). 1982. write for info. (ISBN 3-8204-7111-1). P Lang Pubs.

Schlote, Werner. British Overseas Trade from 1700 to the 1930's. LC 75-40922. 181p. 1976. Repr. of 1952 ed. lib. bdg. 15.75x (ISBN 0-8371-8692-7, SCBO). Greenwood.

Schlotterback, Thomas. Five Thousand Years of Faces. (Illus.). 72p. 1983. pap. 9.95 (ISBN 0-942342-02-X). Bellevue Art.

Schlottmen, Alan M. Environmental Regulation & the Allocation of Coal: A Regional Analysis. LC 76-56841. (Special Studies). 1977. 22.95 o.p. (ISBN 0-275-24090-8). Praeger.

Schluchter, Wolfgang, jt. auth. see Roth, Guenther.

Schluep, J., jt. auth. see Westcott, Alvin.

Schlueter, David A. Military Criminal Justice: Practice & Procedure. 425p. 1982. 35.00 (ISBN 0-87215-417-3). Michie-Bobbs.

Schlueter, June, jt. auth. see Schlueter, Paul.

Schlueter, Paul. Names & American Literature. (International Library of Names). 250p. 1983. text ed. 24.50x (ISBN 0-8290-1284-2). Irvington.

--The Novels of Doris Lessing. LC 72-10281. (Crosscurrents-Modern Critiques Ser.). 155p. 1973. 6.95 o.p. (ISBN 0-8093-0612-3). S Ill U Pr.

--Shirley Ann Grau. (United States Authors Ser.). 1981. lib. bdg. 13.95 (ISBN 0-8057-7316-9, Twayne). G K Hall.

Schlueter, Paul & Schlueter, June. English Novel Twentieth Century Criticism: Vol. II, Twentieth Century Authors. LC 82-75695. xxxiv, 380p. 1982. lib. bdg. 30.00x (ISBN 0-8040-0424-2). Swallow.

Schlumberger, Anne G. The Schlumberger Adventure. LC 82-8830. (Illus.). 135p. 1983. 22.50 (ISBN 0-668-05644-4, 5644). Arco.

Schlumpf, Lester, ed. Barron's Three-Year Sequence for High School Mathematics - Course I. 250p. (gr. 9-12). 1981. pap. text ed. 3.95 (ISBN 0-8120-3183-0). Barron.

Schlumpf, M. & Lichtensteiger, W., eds. Drugs & Hormones in Brain Development. (Monographs in Neural Sciences: Vol. 10). (Illus.). iv, 180p. 1983. 75.50 (ISBN 3-8055-3514-7). S Karger.

Schlunder, E. U., jt. auth. see Afgan, N. H.

Schlunder, E. U, et al, eds. Heat Exchanger Design Handbook, 5 vols. LC 82-9267. (Illus.). 2000p. 1982. Set. looseleaf 600.00 (ISBN 0-89116-125-2). Hemisphere Pub.

Schlundt, Christena L. Tamiris: A Chronicle of Her Dance Career 1929-1955. LC 72-86181. (Illus., Orig.). 1972. pap. 11.00 o.p. (ISBN 0-87104-233-9). NY Pub Lib.

Schlundt, Christena L., ed. Professional Appearances of Ruth St. Denis & Ted Shawn: A Chronology & an Index of Dances, 1906-1932. LC 62-17441. (Illus., Orig.). 1962. pap. 5.50 o.p. (ISBN 0-87104-147-2). NY Pub Lib.

--Professional Appearances of Ted Shawn & His Men Dancers: A Chronology & an Index of Dances, 1933-1940. LC 67-17590. (Illus., Orig.). 1967. pap. 5.00 o.p. (ISBN 0-87104-148-0). NY Pub Lib.

Schluter, Hans, compiled by. Index Libycus: Bibliography of Libya 1957-1969 with Supplementary Material 1915-1956. 1972. 22.50 (ISBN 0-8161-0939-7, Hall Reference). G K Hall.

Schluter, Hans, et al. Index Libycus: Supplement I, 1970-75. 1979. lib. bdg. 25.00 (ISBN 0-8161-8076-8, Hall Reference). G K Hall.

Schluter, Herman. Lincoln, Labor & Slavery. LC 65-17920. 1965. Repr. of 1913 ed. 7.50x (ISBN 0-8462-0570-X). Russell.

Schmalenberg, Claudia, jt. auth. see Kramer, Marlene.

Schmalensee, Richard. The Control of Natural Monopolies. LC 78-6061. 1979. 21.95 (ISBN 0-669-02322-1). Lexington Bks.

Schmalleger, Frank & Gustafson, Robert. The Social Basis of Criminal Justice: Ethical Issues for the 80's. LC 80-6175. 328p. (Orig.). 1981. lib. bdg. 22.25 (ISBN 0-8191-1685-8); pap. text ed. 12.25 (ISBN 0-8191-1686-6). U Pr of Amer.

Schmalstieg, William R. Indo-European Linguistics: A New Synthesis. LC 79-65827. 224p. 1980. text ed. 17.50x (ISBN 0-271-00240-9). Pa St U Pr.

--Introduction to Old Church Slavic. 1976. soft cover 12.95 (ISBN 0-89357-027-3). Slavica.

--Studies in Old Prussian. LC 76-19017. 1977. text ed. 17.95x (ISBN 0-271-01231-5). Pa St U Pr.

Schmalstieg, William R., jt. ed. see Magner, Thomas F.

Schmalz, N., jt. auth. see Pfeilschifter, B.

Schmalzl, F., et al, eds. Disorders of the Monocyte Macrophage System: Pathophysiological & Clinical Aspects. (Hematology & Blood Transfusion Ser.: Vol. 27). (Illus.). 200p. 1982. 45.60 (ISBN 0-387-10980-3). Springer-Verlag.

Schmandt, Henry J. Fundamentals of Government. rev. ed. 1963. 6.50 o.p. (ISBN 0-02-827660-4). Glencoe.

Schmandt, Jugen. Financing & Control of Academic Research. (Working Paper Ser.: No. 6). 1977. 2.50 (ISBN 0-686-10610-5). LBJ Sch Public Affairs.

Schmandt, Jurgen, et al, eds. Nutrition Policy in Transition. LC 79-9628. (Illus.). 320p. 1980. 24.95x (ISBN 0-669-03596-3). Lexington Bks.

Schmandt-Besserat, Denise, ed. Early Technologies. LC 78-59574. (Invited Lectures on the Middle East at the University of Texas at Austin Ser.: Vol. 3). (Illus.). iv, 105p. 1979. 16.00x (ISBN 0-89003-031-6); pap. 12.00x (ISBN 0-89003-032-4). Undena Pubns.

--The Legacy of Sumer. LC 76-18604. (Bibliotheca Mesopotamica: Vol.4). (Illus.). 1976. 18.50x o.p. (ISBN 0-89003-044-8); pap. 12.00x o.p. (ISBN 0-89003-043-X). Undena Pubns.

Schmardt-Besserat, Denise, ed. Immortal Egypt. LC 78-53515. (Invited Lectures on the Middle East at the University of Texas at Austin Ser.: Vol. 2). (Illus.). 62p. 1978. text ed. 16.00x o.p. (ISBN 0-89003-056-1); pap. text ed. 9.50x o.p. (ISBN 0-89003-057-X). Undena Pubns.

Schmeck, Ronald R., jt. ed. see Dillon, Ronna F.

Schmeckebier, Laurence F. Congressional Apportionment. LC 74-4731. (Studies in Administration Ser.: No. 40). 233p. 1976. Repr. of 1941 ed. lib. bdg. 16.25x (ISBN 0-8371-7486-4, SCCA). Greenwood.

--History of the Know Nothing Party in Maryland. 1973. Repr. of 1899 ed. pap. 10.00 (ISBN 0-384-54020-1). Johnson Repr.

Schmeid, Wieland. Tobey. (Modern Painters Ser.). (Illus.). Date not set. pap. 3.95 o.p. (ISBN 0-452-00352-0, FM 352, Mer). NAL.

Schmeidler, Gertrude R. & McConnell, R. A. ESP & Personality Patterns. LC 73-9258. 136p. 1973. Repr. of 1958 ed. lib. bdg. 21.25x (ISBN 0-8371-6992-5, SCES). Greenwood.

Schmeidler, R., jt. auth. see Mintz, Elizabeth.

Schmelcher, T. Low Voltage Switch Gear. 1976. 42.95 (ISBN 0-471-26014-2, Wiley Heyden). Wiley.

Schmeling, Gareth L. Chariton. (World Authors Ser.). 1974. lib. bdg. 15.95 (ISBN 0-8057-2207-6, Twayne). G K Hall.

--Xenophon of Ephesus. (World Authors Ser.). 1980. lib. bdg. 15.95 (ISBN 0-8057-6455-0, Twayne). G K Hall.

Schmeling, Marianne. Flee the Wolf. LC 78-24154. 1978. 9.95 o.p. (ISBN 0-915442-73-6, Unilaw); pap. 5.95 o.s.i. (ISBN 0-915442-67-1). Donning Co.

Schmeltz, L. R. Playing the Stock & Bond Markets with Your Personal Computer. 308p. 1981. 16.95 (ISBN 0-8306-9647-4); pap. 9.95 (ISBN 0-8306-1251-3, 1251). TAB Bks.

Schmelzenbach, Elmer & Parrott, Leslie. Sons of Africa. 217p. 1979. 9.95 (ISBN 0-8341-0601-9). Beacon Hill.

Schmenner, Roger W. Production-Operations Management. 480p. 1980. text ed. 21.95 (ISBN 0-574-19500-9, 13-2500); instr's. guide avail. (ISBN 0-574-19501-7, 13-2501). SRA.

Schmer, Gottfried & Strandjord, Paul E., eds. Current Topics in Coagulation. 1973. 29.50 (ISBN 0-12-626250-0). Acad Pr.

Schmerling, Louis. Organic & Petroleum Chemistry for Nonchemists. 109p. 1981. 29.95x (ISBN 0-87814-173-1). Pennwell Books Division.

Schmertz, Eric J., jt. auth. see Greenman, Russell L.

Schmid, A. Allan. Property, Power & Public Choice: An Inquiry into Law & Economics. LC 78-5930. (Praeger Special Studies). 1978. 28.95 o.p. (ISBN 0-03-042956-0). Praeger.

Schmid, Andrea B. Modern Rhythmic Gymnastics. LC 75-21074. 379p. 1976. pap. text ed. 12.95 o.p. (ISBN 0-87484-280-8). Mayfield Pub.

Schmid, Andrea B. & Drury, Blanche J. Gymnastics for Women. 4th ed. LC 76-56510. 396p. 1977. spiral bdg. 13.95 (ISBN 0-87484-364-2); 19.95 o.p. (ISBN 0-87484-365-0). Mayfield Pub.

Schmid, C. F., jt. auth. see Dornbusch, S. M.

Schmid, Calvin F. Statistical Graphics: Design Principles & Practices. 300p. 1983. 21.95x (ISBN 0-471-87525-2, Pub. by Wiley Interscience). Wiley.

Schmid, Calvin F. & Schmid, Stanton E. Handbook of Graphic Presentation. 2nd ed. LC 78-13689. 308p. 1979. 26.95 (ISBN 0-471-04724-4, Pub. by Wiley-Interscience). Wiley.

Schmid, E. Atlas of Animal Bones. (Eng. & Ger.). 1972. 75.75 (ISBN 0-444-40831-2). Elsevier.

Schmid, E. D., et al, eds. Proceedings of the Sixth International Conference of Raman Spectroscopy. 1978. pap. 114.00 set (ISBN 0-471-26015-0, Wiley Heyden). Wiley.

Schmid, Eleonore. Tonia: The Mouse with the White Stone & What Happened on Her Way to See Uncle Tobias. LC 73-88947. (Illus.). 32p. (gr. 2-5). 1974. 4.95 o.p. (ISBN 0-399-20396-6). Putnam Pub Group.

Schmid, Hermann. Decimal Computation. LC 80-29514. 280p. 1983. Repr. of 1974 ed. lib. bdg. 27.50 (ISBN 0-89874-318-4). Krieger.

Schmid, Herta & Van Kesteren, Aloysius, eds. Semiotics, Theatre & Drama. (Linguistic & Literary Studies in Eastern Europe: 10). 480p. 1983. 54.00 (ISBN 90-272-1513-8). Benjamins North Am.

Schmid, Jean, tr. see Biesantz, Hagen & Klingborg, Arne.

Schmid, Otto & Klay, Ruedi. Green Manuring: Principles & Practice. Brinton, William, Jr., ed. 41p. (Orig.). 1981. pap. 4.00 (ISBN 0-9603554-1-3). W F Brinton.

Schmid, Rex E. & Nagata, Lynn. Contemporary Issues in Special Education. 2nd ed. 304p. 1983. 13.95x (ISBN 0-07-055331-9, C). McGraw.

Schmid, Rex E., et al. Contemporary Issues in Special Education. (Special Education Ser.). (Illus.). 1976. text ed. 14.95 (ISBN 0-07-055330-0, C). McGraw.

Schmid, Roland & Sapunov, Valentin N. Non-Formal Kinetics: In Search of Chemical Reaction Pathways, Vol. 14. Ebel, Hans F., ed. (Monographs in Modern Chemistry Vol. 14). (Illus.). 210p. 1982. 51.60x (ISBN 0-89573-055-3). Verlag Chemie.

Schmid, Stanton E., jt. auth. see Schmid, Calvin F.

Schmid, Vernon L. Media & Methods for Your Church. Zapel, Arthur L., ed. (Illus.). 56p. (Orig.). 1980. pap. 3.95 (ISBN 0-916260-06-2). Meriwether Pub.

Schmid, W. & Nielsen, J. Human Behaviour & Genetics. 1981. 56.25 (ISBN 0-444-80357-2). Elsevier.

Schmidek, Henry H. Pineal Tumors. LC 77-78560. (Masson Cancer Management Ser.: Vol. 3). 152p. 1977. 42.00x (ISBN 0-89352-007-1). Masson Pub.

Schmidek, Henry H. & Sweet, William D., eds. Current Techniques in Operative Neurosurgery. 624p. 1978. 99.50 o.p. (ISBN 0-8089-1026-4). Grune.

Schmidek, Henry H. & Sweet, William H., eds. Operative Neurosurgical Techniques: Indications & Methods, 2 Vols. 1982. write for info. (ISBN 0-8089-1440-5, 793903); Vol. 2. 195.00 (ISBN 0-8089-1439-1, 793902). Grune.

Schmidgall, Gary. Literature As Opera. LC 76-57264. (Illus.). 1977. 25.00x (ISBN 0-19-502213-0). Oxford U Pr.

--Literature As Opera. (Illus.). 1980. pap. 9.95 (ISBN 0-19-502706-X, GB 598, GB). Oxford U Pr.

Schmidgall-Tellings, A. Ed. & Stevens, Alan. Contemporary Indonesian-English Dictionary. LC 80-20994. xvi, 388p. 1981. 28.95x (ISBN 0-8214-0424-5, 82-83152); pap. 14.95x (ISBN 0-8214-0435-0, 82-83160). Ohio U Pr.

Schmidhauser, John R. & Totten, George O., III, eds. The Whaling Issue in U. S.-Japan Relations. 1978. lib. bdg. 30.00 o.p. (ISBN 0-89158-176-6). Westview.

Schmidman, John. Unions in Post-Industrial Society. LC 78-112229. 1979. text ed. 14.95x (ISBN 0-271-00209-3). Pa St U Pr.

Schmid-Schonbein, Feder. English for Mopsy & Me: Pupils' Workbook I. (Illus.). 40p. (ps-2). 1981. pap. 3.95 (ISBN 0-08-027227-4). Pergamon.

--English for Mopsy & Me: Pupils' Workbook II. (Illus.). 40p. (ps-2). 1981. pap. 3.95 (ISBN 0-08-027228-2). Pergamon.

--English for Mopsy & Me: Teacher's Book One. 64p. 1982. pap. 4.50 (ISBN 0-08-027226-6). Pergamon.

Schmidt & Tembrock. Evolution & Determination of Animal & Human Behavior. Date not set. 34.00 (ISBN 0-444-86346-X). Elsevier.

Schmidt, jt. auth. see Andraeson, Tjalve.

Schmidt, A. M. Island of Nose. 1977. 8.95 o.p. (ISBN 0-416-86210-1). Methuen Inc.

Schmidt, A. P., jt. auth. see Hachenberg, H.

Schmidt, A. V. & Jacobs, Nicolas. Medieval English Romances, 2 pts. LC 79-48002. (The London Medieval & Renaissance Ser.). 1980. write for info.; Pt. 1, 210p. 29.50x (ISBN 0-8419-0604-1); Pt. 2, 285p. 32.50x (ISBN 0-8419-0605-X). Holmes & Meier.

Schmidt, Alfred. The Concept of Nature in Marx. 1978. pap. 7.00 o.p. (ISBN 0-8052-7019-1, Pub by NLB). Schocken.

Schmidt, Alois X. & List, H. Material & Energy Balances. 1962. ref. ed. 32.95 (ISBN 0-13-560219-X). P-H.

Schmidt, Alvin J. Oligarchy in Fraternal Organizations: A Study in Organizational Leadership. LC 73-15732. 104p. 1973. 15.00x (ISBN 0-8103-0345-0). Gale.

Schmidt, Arno. Evening Edged in Gold. LC 79-3373. (Helen & Kurt Wolff Bk.). 224p. 1980. 74.95 (ISBN 0-15-129376-7). HarBraceJ.

Schmidt, B. GPSS FORTRAN. LC 80-40968. (Computing Ser.). 523p. 1980. 43.95 (ISBN 0-471-27881-5, Pub. by Wiley-Interscience). Wiley.

Schmidt, Benno C., Jr. Freedom of the Press vs. Public Access. LC 75-19818. (Special Studies). 1976. text ed. 29.95 o.p. (ISBN 0-275-01620-X); pap. text ed. 13.95 o.p. (ISBN 0-275-89430-4). Praeger.

Schmidt, Bill, jt. auth. see Nelson, Bill.

Schmidt, Bob. Great Fishing Close to Chicago. LC 77-91188. 1978. pap. 7.95 o.p. (ISBN 0-8092-7676-3). Contemp Bks.

Schmidt, C. W. Marta. LC 82-80825. 360p. 1982. 10.95 (ISBN 0-89407-059-2). Strawberry Hill.

Schmidt, Charles T., Jr., jt. auth. see Kruger, Daniel H.

Schmidt, Chester M., Jr., jt. auth. see Meyer, Jon K.

Schmidt, Cynthia E. The Story of Colorado, 6 units. Incl. Unit 1. Colorado - Land & Animals (ISBN 0-913688-50-9); Unit 2. Prehistoric People (ISBN 0-913688-51-7); Unit 3. Tribes & Trailblazers (ISBN 0-913688-52-5); Unit 4. Gold Fever (ISBN 0-913688-53-3); Unit 5. Early Statehood (ISBN 0-913688-54-1); Unit 6. Twentieth Century Colorado (ISBN 0-913688-55-X). (Illus.). Set. 385.00 (ISBN 0-913688-56-8); 75.00 ea.; each set contains a tchr's manual, 2 film strips, 2 cassette tapes, 10 spirit duplications masters, 8 learning center cards, 2 color posters. Pawnee Pub.

Schmidt, D. & Seldon, H. L., eds. Adverse Effects of Antiepileptic Drugs. 250p. 1982. text ed. 45.00 (ISBN 0-89004-567-4). Raven.

Schmidt, Daryl D. Hellenistic Greek Grammar & Noam Chomsky: Nominalizing Transformations. LC 81-13544. (Society of Biblical Literature Dissertation Ser.). 1981. pap. 12.00 (ISBN 0-89130-527-0, 06-01-62). Scholars Pr CA.

Schmidt, Donald H., jt. auth. see Pollock, Michael L.

Schmidt, Dorey, ed. see Seale, Jan.

Schmidt, E. H. & Hildebrandt, A., eds. Health Evaluation of Heavy Metals in Infant Formula & Junior Food, Berlin: 1981, Proceedings. (Illus.). 192p. 1983. 16.00 (ISBN 0-387-11823-3). Springer-Verlag.

Schmidt, E. M., jt. ed. see Nielsen, M.

Schmidt, E. T., jt. auth. see Huhn, A. P.

Schmidt, Frank L., jt. ed. see Hamner, W. Clay.

Schmidt, Frank L., jt. auth. see Hunter, John E.

Schmidt, Frank L., jt. auth. see Pearlman, Kenneth.

Schmidt, Frank W. & Willmott, A. John. Thermal Energy Storage & Regeneration. (Illus.). 352p. 1981. 42.50 (ISBN 0-07-055346-7). McGraw.

Schmidt, Franz. Hangman's Diary, Being the Journal of Master Franz Schmidt Public Executioner of Nuremburg, 1573-1617. Keller, Albrecht, ed. LC 79-172586. (Criminology, Law Enforcement, & Social Problems Ser., No. 176). (With essay Criminal Procedure in Germany in Middle Ages by C. V. Calvert). 1973. Repr. of 1928 ed. 15.00x (ISBN 0-87585-176-2). Patterson Smith.

Schmidt, G., jt. ed. see Broy, M.

Schmidt, Gail R. Francis: A Saint We Share, a Discussion Guide for Lutherns & Roman Catholics. LC 82-60848. 1982. pap. 3.95 (ISBN 0-8091-2496-3). Paulist Pr.

Schmidt, Gerald D. & Roberts, Larry S. Foundations of Parasitology. 2nd ed. LC 81-1342. (Illus.). 795p. 1981. pap. text ed. 27.95 (ISBN 0-8016-4344-9). Mosby.

Schmidt, Gerald D., ed. Problems in Systematics of Parasites. (Illus.). 1974. 16.50 o.p. (ISBN 0-8391-0010-8). Univ Park.

Schmidt, Gerard F. Hoer Gut Zu: A Beginning German Audio-Lingual Reader. 1964. text ed. 14.95x (ISBN 0-02-407700-3). Macmillan.

Schmidt, Gunter, jt. ed. see Arentewicz, Gerd.

Schmidt, H. L. & Forste, L. H, eds. Stable Isotopes. (Analytical Chemistry Symposia Ser.: Vol. 11). 1982. 117.00 (ISBN 0-444-42076-2). Elsevier.

Schmidt, H. L. & Forstel, H, eds. Stable Isotopes: Proceedings of the 4th International Conference, Julich, Mar. 23-26, 1981, No. 11. (Analytical Chemistry Symposia Ser.). 758p. 1982. 117.00 (ISBN 0-444-42076-2). Elsevier.

Schmidt, Helmut & Von Stackelberg, Mark. Modern Polarographic Methods. Maddison, R. E., tr. 1963. 23.00 (ISBN 0-12-626950-5). Acad Pr.

Schmidt, Henry, ed. see Buckley, Joseph C.

Schmidt, Henry J., jt. auth. see Blume, Bernhard.

Schmidt, Hubert G. Agriculture in New Jersey: A Three Hundred Year History. (Illus.). 352p. 1973. 27.50 (ISBN 0-8135-0756-1). Rutgers U Pr.

--Rural Hunterdon: An Agricultural History. LC 77-139149. (Illus.). 331p. 1972. Repr. of 1945 ed. lib. bdg. 20.25x (ISBN 0-8371-5765-X, SCRH). Greenwood.

Schmidt, I., et al, eds. Optometry Examination Review Book, Vol. 1. 2nd ed. 1978. pap. 16.50 o.s.i. (ISBN 0-87488-469-1). Med Exam.

Schmidt, J., jt. auth. see Csakany, B.

Schmidt, J. D. Yang Wan-Li. (World Authors Ser.). 1976. lib. bdg. 15.95 (ISBN 0-8057-6255-8, Twayne). G K Hall.

Schmidt, J. E. Practical Nurses' Medical Dictionary: A Cyclopedic Medical Dictionary for Practical Nurses, Vocational Nurses, & Nurses' Aides. 300p. 1968. 11.75x o.p. (ISBN 0-398-01675-5). C C Thomas.

--Structural Units of Medical & Biological Terms: A Convenient Guide, in English, to the Roots, Stems, Prefixes, Suffixes, & Other Combining Forms Which Are the Building Blocks of Medical & Related Scientific Words. 180p. 1969. 11.75x o.p. (ISBN 0-398-01676-3). C C Thomas.

Schmidt, J. H. & Neimark, Paul. Getting Along: How to Be Happy with Yourself & Others. LC 78-14309. (gr. 5-8). 1979. 7.95 (ISBN 0-399-20654-X). Putnam Pub Group.

Schmidt, J. W. & Brodie, M. L., eds. Relational Database Systems: Analysis & Comparison. 618p. 1983. 19.80 (ISBN 0-387-12032-7). Springer-Verlag.

Schmidt, Janet. Demystifying Parole. LC 76-48375. (Illus.). 208p. 1977. 22.95x o.p. (ISBN 0-669-01145-2). Lexington Bks.

Schmidt, Jerry. New Beginnings. LC 77-92734. 1978. pap. 2.95 (ISBN 0-89081-069-9, 0699). Harvest Hse.

Schmidt, Jerry & Brock, Raymond. The Emotions of a Man. LC 82-84070. 192p. (Orig.). 1983. pap. 4.95 (ISBN 0-89081-330-2). Harvest Hse.

Schmidt, Jerry A. Do You Hear What You're Thinking? 1983. pap. 4.50 (ISBN 0-88207-381-8). Victor Bks.

Schmidt, Joel. Larousse Greek & Roman Mythology. LC 80-15046. (Illus.). 320p. 1980. 16.95 o.p. (ISBN 0-07-055342-4). McGraw.

Schmidt, John. Successful Dream Interpretation. LC 81-83112. 135p. (Orig.). 1982. pap. 5.95x (ISBN 0-9608336-1-7). Dreambooks.

Schmidt, Karl A. Easy Ways to Enlarge Your German Vocabulary. LC 73-92020. (Orig.). 1974. 4.50 (ISBN 0-486-23044-9). Dover.

Schmidt, Karl P. & Davis, D. Dwight. Field Book of Snakes of United States & Canada. (Putnam Nature Field Bks.). (Illus.). 1941. 5.95 o.p. (ISBN 0-399-10295-7). Putnam Pub Group.

Schmidt, L. M., jt. auth. see Lee, Leslie W.

Schmidt, Marlin R. & Sprandel, Hazel Z., eds. Helping the Learning Disabled. LC 81-48489. 1982. 7.95x (ISBN 0-87589-920-X, SS-18). Jossey-Bass.

Schmidt, Michael, ed. Ten English Poets: An Anthology. (Poetry Ser.). 1979. pap. 5.95 o.p. (ISBN 0-85635-167-9, Pub. by Carcanet New Pr England). Humanities.

Schmidt, Michael, ed. see Sisson, C. H.

Schmidt, Michael, tr. see Paz, Octavio.

Schmidt, Nancy J. Children's Books on Africa & Their Authors: An Annotated Bibliography. LC 74-23783. (African Bibliography Ser.: Vol. 3). 400p. 1975. text ed. 32.50x (ISBN 0-8419-0166-X, Africana). Holmes & Meier.

Schmidt, O. J., ed. see Brontman, Lazar K.

Schmidt, Paul, ed. Meyerhold at Work. Levin, Ilya & McGee, Vern, trs. 261p. 1981. text ed. 22.50x (ISBN 0-292-75058-7). U of Tex Pr.

Schmidt, Paul, tr. see Rimbaud, Arthur.

Schmidt, Paul J., ed. see Firkin, Barry G., et al.

Schmidt, R. A. Coal in America: Reserves, Production & Use. 1979. 62.25 (ISBN 0-07-055347-5). McGraw.

Schmidt, R. E. & Stroehmann, I., eds. Immunglobulintherapie. (Beitraege zu Infusionstherapie und klinische Ernaehrung: Vol. 11). viii, 160p. 1983. pap. 36.00 (ISBN 3-8055-3660-7). S Karger.

Schmidt, R. F. & Thews, G., eds. Human Physiology. Biederman-Thorson, M. A., tr. from Ger. (Illus.). 750p. 1982. 36.00 (ISBN 0-387-11669-9). Springer-Verlag.

Schmidt, R. R., jt. auth. see Lemmerz, A. H.

Schmidt, Richard A. Motor Control & Learning: A Behavioral Emphasis. LC 81-82449. (Illus.). 700p. 1982. text ed. 29.95x (ISBN 0-931250-21-8). Human Kinetics.

Schmidt, Richard P., jt. ed. see Mayersdorf, Assa.

Schmidt, Robert. Welding Skills & Techniques. 1982. text ed. 20.95 (ISBN 0-8359-8611-X); instrs'. manual avail. (ISBN 0-8359-8612-8). Reston.

Schmidt, Robert P. Autobody Repair & Refinishing. 350p. 1981. text ed. 22.95 (ISBN 0-8359-0247-1); instr's. manual free (ISBN 0-8359-0248-X). Reston.

Schmidt, Roland & Khoury, George H. Pediatric Cardiology: A Tape-Filmstrip Presentation. (Illus.). 83p. 1973. pap. 75.00 incl. cassettes o.p. (ISBN 0-7216-9832-8). Saunders.

Schmidt, Stanley, ed. Analog: Writers' Choice. 288p. 1983. 12.95 (ISBN 0-385-27913-2). Davis Pubns.

--Analog's Golden Anniversary Anthology. 384p. 1980. 10.95 o.s.i. (ISBN 0-8037-0217-5). Davis Pubns.

--War & Peace: Possible Futures from "Analog". 1983. 12.95 (ISBN 0-385-27916-7). Davis Pubns.

Schmidt, Steffen W., et al. Friends, Followers & Factions: A Reader in Political Clientelism. LC 73-93060. 1977. 47.50x (ISBN 0-520-02696-9); pap. 10.95x (ISBN 0-520-03156-3). U of Cal Pr.

Schmidt, Steven. Creating the Technical Report. (Illus.). 160p. 1983. 17.95 (ISBN 0-13-189027-1). P-H.

Schmidt, T. H., jt. ed. see Dembroski, T. M.

Schmidt, Terry D. Managing Your Career Success: Practical Strategies for Engineers, Scientists & Technical Managers. (Career Development Ser.). 216p. 1982. 19.95 (ISBN 0-534-97948-3). Lifetime Learn.

Schmidt, Terry D., jt. auth. see Holtz, Herman R.

Schmidt, Victor E. & Rockcastle, Verne N. Teaching Science with Every Day Things. 2nd ed. (Illus.). 224p. 1982. pap. 14.95 (ISBN 0-07-055355-6). McGraw.

--Teaching Science with Everyday Things. 1968. pap. text ed. 17.95 (ISBN 0-07-055351-3, C). McGraw.

Schmidt, W. German. 660p. 1980. 10.00x o.p. (ISBN 0-569-05867-8, Pub. by Collet's). State Mutual Bk.

Schmidt, Waldemar A. Principles & Techniques of Surgical Pathology. 1982. text ed. 55.00 (ISBN 0-201-07139-8, 07139, Med-Nurse). A-W.

Schmidt, Walter A., jt. auth. see Bellis, Herbert F.

Schmidt, Werner H. The Faith of the Old Testament: A History. Sturdy, John, tr. LC 82-21780. 336p. (Orig.). 1983. price not set (ISBN 0-664-21826-1); pap. price not set (ISBN 0-664-24456-4). Westminster.

Schmidt, Wilhelm. The Culture Historical Method of Ethnology. LC 73-10761. 383p. 1974. Repr. of 1939 ed. lib. bdg. 20.75x (ISBN 0-8371-7036-2, SCET). Greenwood.

Schmidt, Winsor C., et al. Public Guardianship & the Elderly. 300p. 1981. prof ref 25.00x (ISBN 0-88410-596-2). Ballinger Pub.

Schmidt-Neubauer, Joachim. Die Bedeutung des Gluckseligkeitsbegriffes fur die Dramentheorie und -Praxis der Aufklarung und Des Sturm und Drang. 164p. (Ger.). 1982. write for info. (ISBN 3-261-05011-X). P Lang Pubs.

Schmidt-Nielsen, B., ed. Urea & the Kidney. 1970. 55.75 (ISBN 90-219-0127-7, Excerpta Medical). Elsevier.

Schmidt-Nielsen, Knut. Animal Physiology. 2nd ed. LC 78-56822. (Illus.). 1978. 26.95x (ISBN 0-521-22178-1). Cambridge U Pr.

--Animal Physiology. 3rd ed. (Biological Science & Foundations of Modern Biology Ser). 1970. ref. ed. 15.95x (ISBN 0-13-037390-7); pap. 12.95x ref. ed. (ISBN 0-13-037382-6). P-H.

--How Animals Work. LC 77-174262. (Illus.). 100p. 1972. 21.95 (ISBN 0-521-08417-2); pap. 7.95x (ISBN 0-521-09692-8). Cambridge U Pr.

Schmidt-Nielsen, Knut, et al, eds. Comparative Physiology: Water, Ions & Fluid Mechanics. LC 77-7320. (Illus.). 1978. 62.50 (ISBN 0-521-21696-6). Cambridge U Pr.

--Comparative Physiology: Primitive Mammals. LC 77-7320. (Illus.). 1980. 49.50 (ISBN 0-521-22847-6). Cambridge U Pr.

Schmidt-Radefeldt, J. Reading in Portuguese Linguistics. new ed. (North Holland Linguistics Ser.: Vol. 22). 1976. pap. 49.00 (ISBN 0-444-10910-2, North-Holland). Elsevier.

Schmied, Elsie, ed. Maintaining Cost Effectiveness. LC 79-84505. 259p. 1979. pap. 19.95 (ISBN 0-913654-53-1). Aspen Systems.

Schmieg, Glenn, jt. auth. see Dittman, Richard.

Schmincke-Ott, Eva, jt. ed. see Bisswanger, Hans.

Schmit, R. Eugene Boudin, 3 vols. (Illus., Fr.). 1975. Set. text ed. 500.00 o.p. (ISBN 0-685-55902-5). Newbury Bks.

Schmits, Larry J. & Ray, Jack H. The Missouri Archaeologist, Vol. 43. LC 44-14131. (Illus.). 120p. 1982. pap. 6.00 (ISBN 0-943414-05-9). MO Arch Soc.

Schmitt, Bernard. Protein, Calories & Development: Nutritional Variables in the Economics of Developing Nations. (Westview Special Studies in Society, Politics & Economic Development). 1979. lib. bdg. 28.50 o.p. (ISBN 0-89158-185-5). Westview.

Schmitt, Charles. John Case & Aristotelianism in Renaissance England. (McGill-Queen's Studies in the History of Ideas). 368p. 1983. 37.50x (ISBN 0-7735-1005-2). McGill-Queens U Pr.

Schmitt, Charles, ed. History of Universities: Continuity & Change in Early Modern Universities, Vol. 1. 1981. 100.00x o.p. (ISBN 0-86127-051-7, Pub. by Avebury Pub England). State Mutual Bk.

--History of Universities, Vol. 1. 225p. 1981. text ed. 29.00x (ISBN 0-86127-051-7, Pub. by Avebury England). Humanities.

Schmitt, Charles B. Aristotle & the Renaissance. (Martin Classical Lectures: No. XXVII). (Illus.). 208p. 1983. text ed. 18.50x (ISBN 0-674-04525-4). Harvard U Pr.

Schmitt, Conrad J. A Cada Paso: Lengua, Lectura y Cultura, Bk. 1. (Illus.). (gr. 1). 1978. text ed. 10.00 (ISBN 0-07-055489-7, W); tchr's. manual 7.84 (ISBN 0-07-055490-0); wkbk. 4.68 (ISBN 0-07-055491-9); cue cards 82.08 (ISBN 0-07-098489-1). McGraw.

--A Cada Paso: Lengua, Lectura y Cultura, Bk. 2. Saslow, Joan, ed. (Illus.). (gr. 4). 1978. text ed. 10.92 (ISBN 0-07-055492-7, W); tchr's. ed. 11.84 (ISBN 0-07-055493-5); wkbk. 4.68 (ISBN 0-07-055494-3). McGraw.

--A Cada Paso: Lengua, Lectura y Cultura, Bk. 3. Saslow, Conad J., ed. (Illus.). (gr. 3). 1978. text ed. 10.92 (ISBN 0-07-055495-1, W); tchr's. manual 11.84 (ISBN 0-07-055496-X); wkbk. 4.68 (ISBN 0-07-055497-8). McGraw.

--A Cada Paso: Lengua, Lectura y Cultura, Bk. 4. (Illus.). (gr. 2). 1978. text ed. 10.92 (ISBN 0-07-055498-6, W); tchr's. manual 11.84 (ISBN 0-07-055499-4); wkbk. 4.68 (ISBN 0-07-055500-1). McGraw.

--Espanol: Comencemos. 2nd ed. 1974. text ed. 14.48 (ISBN 0-07-055501-X, W); tchr's. ed. 16.28 (ISBN 0-07-055502-8); wkbk. 4.68 (ISBN 0-07-055503-6). McGraw.

--Espanol: Comencemos. (gr. 7-9). 1969. text ed. 11.60 o.p. (ISBN 0-07-055410-2, W); tchr's. ed. o.p. 11.96 o.p. (ISBN 0-07-055411-0); wkbk. 3.60 o.p. (ISBN 0-07-055412-9). McGraw.

--Espanol, Comencemos: Pupil's Edition. 3rd ed. Chimienti, Teresa, ed. LC 80-13033. (Illus.). 280p. (Span.). (gr. 7). 1980. text ed. 14.24 (ISBN 0-07-055573-7, W); tchr's ed. 16.56 (ISBN 0-07-055574-5); wkbk. 4.64 (ISBN 0-07-055575-3); tests 80.60 (ISBN 0-07-055576-1); filmstrips 116.12 (ISBN 0-07-098991-5); test replacements 48.36 (ISBN 0-07-055577-X). McGraw.

--Espanol: Sigamos. (gr. 7-9). 1969. text ed. 16.56 (ISBN 0-07-055420-X, W); tchr's ed. 17.04 (ISBN 0-07-055421-8). McGraw.

--Espanol: Sigamos. 2nd ed. 1974. text ed. 14.48 (ISBN 0-07-055511-7, W); tchr's. ed. 16.28 (ISBN 0-07-055512-5); wkbk. 4.68 (ISBN 0-07-055513-3). McGraw.

--Espanol: Sigamos, Pupil's Edition. 3rd ed. Chimienti, Teresa, ed. LC 80-13032. (Illus.). 282p. (Span.). (gr. 8). 1980. text ed. 14.24 (ISBN 0-07-055578-8, W); tchrs. ed. 16.56 (ISBN 0-07-055579-6); wkbk. 4.64 (ISBN 0-07-055575-3); filmstrips 116.12 (ISBN 0-07-098994-X). McGraw.

--Let's Speak Spanish, 4 bks. Incl. Bk. 1. 1964. o.p. (ISBN 0-07-055371-8); Bk. 2. 1965. 6.60 (ISBN 0-07-055362-9); Bk. 3. 1966. text ed. 9.32 (ISBN 0-07-055364-5); Bk. 4. 1966. text ed. 9.32 (ISBN 0-07-055367-X). (gr. 3-6, W). McGraw.

--Let's Speak Spanish, Bk. 1. 2nd ed. LC 77-8914. (Illus.). 1977. text ed. 11.08 (ISBN 0-07-055481-1, W); tchr's. manual 11.76 (ISBN 0-07-055482-X). McGraw.

--Let's Speak Spanish, Bk. 2. 2nd ed. LC 77-8916. (Illus.). 1977. text ed. 11.08 (ISBN 0-07-055483-8, W); tchr's. manual 11.76 (ISBN 0-07-055484-6). McGraw.

--Let's Speak Spanish, Bk. 4. 2nd ed. LC 77-8915. (Illus.). 1978. text ed. 10.92 (ISBN 0-07-055487-0, W); tchr's. ed. 11.84 (ISBN 0-07-055488-9). McGraw.

--Schaum's Outline of Spanish Grammar. 2nd ed. (Schaum's Outline Ser.). 1980. pap. 4.95 (ISBN 0-07-055431-5). McGraw.

Schmitt, Conrad J., jt. auth. see Okin, Josee.

Schmitt, Conrad J., jt. auth. see Okin, Josee P.

Schmitt, Conrad J., et al. Espanol: A Descubrirlo, Learning Spanish the Modern Way. 3rd ed. 1971. 19.32 (ISBN 0-07-055375-0, W); tchr's. ed. 20.72 (ISBN 0-07-055376-9); wkbk. 5.84 (ISBN 0-07-055377-7). McGraw.

--Espanol: A Descubrirlo. 5th ed. Saslow, Joan, ed. (Illus.). 416p. (Span.). (gr. 9). 1981. text ed. 18.44 (ISBN 0-07-055404-8); tchrs. ed. 19.76 (ISBN 0-07-055405-6); wkbk. 5.32 (ISBN 0-07-055406-4); test pkg. 54.64 (ISBN 0-07-055408-0); tapes 341.88 (ISBN 0-07-098710-6); cassettes 412.92 (ISBN 0-07-098711-4); filmstrips 143.88 (ISBN 0-07-098713-0); complete kit 75.48 (ISBN 0-07-098712-2). McGraw.

Schmitt, Daniel, jt. ed. see Thivolet, Jean.

Schmitt, E. William, Jr., jt. auth. see Hilt, Nancy E.

Schmitt, F. O., ed. Neurosciences: Second Study Program. LC 78-136288. (Illus.). 1088p. (Charts, Photos, Micrographs, Tabs). 1971. ref. ed. 60.00 o.p. (ISBN 0-87470-014-0); prof. ed. 25.00x o.p. (ISBN 0-686-96876-X). Rockefeller.

Schmitt, F. O., et al, eds. Functional Linkage in Biomolecular Systems. LC 74-14479. 366p. 1975. 34.50 (ISBN 0-89004-006-0). Raven.

Schmitt, Francis O. & Worden, Frederic G., eds. The Neurosciences: Fourth Study Program. 1979. 60.00x (ISBN 0-262-19162-8). MIT Pr.

--The Neurosciences: Third Study Program. 1250p. 1974. 55.00x (ISBN 0-262-19112-1). MIT Pr.

Schmitt, Francis O., et al, eds. Molecular Genetic Neuroscience. 725p. 1982. text ed. 74.00 (ISBN 0-89004-744-8). Raven.

--Neurosciences Research Symposium Summaries, Vols. 5-8. Incl. Vol. 5. 1971. 30.00x (ISBN 0-262-19100-8); Vol. 6. 1973. 30.00x (ISBN 0-262-19107-5); Vol. 7. 1975. 30.00x (ISBN 0-262-19117-2); Vol 8. 1977. 35.00x (ISBN 0-262-19141-5). LC 66-22645. MIT Pr.

--The Organization of the Cerebral Cortex. (Illus.). 576p. 1981. text ed. 55.00x (ISBN 0-262-19189-X). MIT Pr.

Schmitt, Francis P. Church Music Transgressed: Reflections on Reform. LC 77-9424. 1977. 3.00 (ISBN 0-8164-0355-4). Seabury.

Schmitt, Karl M., ed. The Roman Catholic Church in Modern Latin America. (A Borzio Book on Latin America). pap. text ed. 4.95x (ISBN 0-685-77216-0, 31352). Phila Bk Co.

Schmitt, Klaus, ed. Delay & Functional Differential Equations & Their Applications. 1972. 64.50 (ISBN 0-12-627250-6). Acad Pr.

Schmitt, Marshall L., jt. auth. see Buban, Peter.

Schmitt, N. M. & Farwell, R. F. Understanding Electronic Control of Automation Systems. LC 81-85603. (Understanding Ser.). (Illus.). 280p. 1983. pap. 6.95 (ISBN 0-89512-052-6). Tex Instr Inc.

Schmitt, Richard. Alienation & Class. 236p. 1983. 18.95 (ISBN 0-87073-497-0); pap. 9.95 (ISBN 0-87073-498-9). Schenkman.

Schmitt, Robert C. Demographic Statistics of Hawaii, 1778-1965. LC 67-50840. (Illus.). 1968. pap. text ed. 6.00x (ISBN 0-87022-740-8). UH Pr.

--Historical Statistics of Hawaii. LC 77-90997. 1978. text ed. 30.00x (ISBN 0-8248-0505-4). UH Pr.

Schmitt, Waldo L., jt. ed. see Llano, George A.

Schmitter, Dean, ed. Mark Twain. LC 74-9583. 160p. 1975. pap. 2.45 o.p. (ISBN 0-07-055394-7, SP). McGraw.

Schmitter, Philippe C., jt. ed. see Lehmbruch, Gerhard.

Schmitthoff, Clive. International Commercial Arbitration, 2 bdrs. & Rel. 2, 4, 6. LC 74-17320. 1975. bdr. 75.00 ea. (ISBN 0-379-00266-3); Rel. 2. 35.00; Rel. 4. 75.00; Rel. 6. 30.00; Set. 225.00. Oceana.

Schmittroth, John, Jr., ed. Abstracting & Indexing Services Directory. 400p. 1982. pap. 96.00x (ISBN 0-8103-1649-8). Gale.

--Encyclopedia of Information Systems & Services. 5th ed. 1100p. 1982. 260.00x (ISBN 0-8103-1138-0). Gale.

Schmittroth, John, Jr. & Kruzas, Anthony T., eds. Encyclopedia of Information Systems & Services. 4th ed. 1500p. 1980. 235.00 o.p. (ISBN 0-8103-0942-4). Gale.

Schmittroth, John, Jr., jt. ed. see Kruzas, Anthony T.

Schmitz, Andrew, et al. Grain Export Cartels. Mitchell, Donald O. & Carter, Colin A., eds. 320p. 1981. prof ref 35.00x (ISBN 0-88410-690-X). Ballinger Pub.

Schmitz, Andrew, jt. ed. see Sarris, Alexander.

Schmitz, Dorothy C. Chris Evert: Women's Tennis Champion. LC 77-70891. (Pros Ser.). (Illus.). (gr. 2). 1977. PLB 7.95 (ISBN 0-913940-64-X). Crestwood Hse.

--Dorothy Hamill: Skate to Victory. LC 77-70888. (Pros Ser.). (Illus.). (gr. 2). 1977. PLB 7.95 (ISBN 0-913940-62-3). Crestwood Hse.

--Evel Knievel: Motorcycle Daredevil. LC 77-70889. (Pros Ser.). (Illus.). (gr. 2). 1977. PLB 7.95 (ISBN 0-913940-61-5). Crestwood Hse.

--The Fabulous Frisbee. Schroeder, Howard, ed. LC 78-7416. (Funseekers Ser.). (Illus.). (gr. 3-4). 1978. PLB 7.95 (ISBN 0-913940-88-7); pap. 3.95 (ISBN 0-89686-009-4). Crestwood Hse.

--Fran Tarkenton: Master of the Gridiron. LC 77-70890. (Pros Ser.). (Illus.). (gr. 2). 1977. PLB 7.95 (ISBN 0-913940-63-1). Crestwood Hse.

--Hang Gliding. Schroeder, Howard, ed. LC 78-6200. (Funseekers Ser.). (Illus.). (gr. 3-4). 1978. PLB 7.95 (ISBN 0-913940-94-1); pap. 3.95 (ISBN 0-89686-015-9). Crestwood Hse.

--Kite Flying. Schroeder, Howard, ed. LC 78-6876. (Funseekers Ser.). (Illus.). (gr. 3-4). 1978. PLB 7.95 (ISBN 0-913940-92-5); pap. 3.95 (ISBN 0-89686-013-2). Crestwood Hse.

--Muhammad Ali: The Greatest. LC 77-70893. (Pros Ser.). (Illus.). (gr. 2). 1977. PLB 7.95 (ISBN 0-913940-60-7). Crestwood Hse.

--O. J. Simpson: The Juice Is Loose. LC 77-70892. (gr. 2). 1977. PLB 7.95 (ISBN 0-913940-65-8). Crestwood Hse.

--Skateboarding. Schroeder, Howard, ed. LC 78-7048. (Funseekers Ser.). (Illus.). (gr. 3-4). 1978. PLB 7.95 (ISBN 0-913940-91-7); pap. 3.95 (ISBN 0-89686-012-4). Crestwood Hse.

Schmitz, E. Robert. The Piano Works of Claude Debussy. (Music Reprint Ser.). 238p. 1983. Repr. of 1950 ed. lib. bdg. 25.00 (ISBN 0-306-76199-8). Da Capo.

Schmitz, Ettore. Confessions of Zeno. DeZoete, Beryl, tr. from It. LC 70-137074. 412p. 1973. Repr. of 1930 ed. lib. bdg. 19.25x (ISBN 0-8371-5537-1, SCCZ). Greenwood.

Schmitz, Helga. Untersuchungen Zur Konservierung der Frucht Koerper des Speisepilzes Pleurotus ostreatus (Jacqu. ex Fr.) Kummer in der Partiellen Autlyse von Pilzzellwaenden. (Bibliothaca Mycologica: No. 77). (Illus.). 85p. (Ger.). 1980. pap. text ed. 12.00x (ISBN 3-7682-1278-5). Lubrecht & Cramer.

Schmitz, J. V. & Brown. Testing of Polymers, 4 vols, Vol. 2. 1966. 33.00 o.s.i. (ISBN 0-87245-561-0). Textile Bk.

--Testing of Polymers, 4 vols, Vol. 3. 1967. 36.50 o.s.i. (ISBN 0-87245-562-9). Textile Bk.

Schmitz, James H. The Universe Against Her. 1981. PLB 13.50 (ISBN 0-8398-2597-8, Gregg). G K Hall.

--The Universe Against Her. 192p. 1982. pap. 2.25 (ISBN 0-441-84576-2, Pub. by Ace Science Fiction). Ace Bks.

Schmitz, Kenneth L. The Gift: Creation. (Aquinas Lecture Ser.). 160p. 1982. 12.95 (ISBN 0-87462-149-6). Marquette.

Schmitz, L. Dora, tr. see Elze, Karl.

Schmitz, Neil. Of Huck & Alice: Humorous Writing in American Literature. (Illus.). 160p. 1982. 25.00x (ISBN 0-8166-1155-6); pap. 10.95x (ISBN 0-8166-1156-4). U of Minn Pr.

Schmitz, Walter J. Learning the Mass. rev. ed. 1966. pap. 2.50 o.p. (ISBN 0-685-07648-2, 80673). Glencoe.

Schmokel, W., jt. auth. see Andrea, Alfred J.

Schmookler, Jacob. Invention & Economic Growth. LC 66-14453. 1966. 17.50x (ISBN 0-674-46400-1). Harvard U Pr.

--Patents, Inventions & Economic Change: Data & Selected Essays. Griliches, Zvi & Hurwicz, Leonid, eds. LC 74-188355. (Illus.). 320p. 1972. 16.00x (ISBN 0-674-65770-5). Harvard U Pr.

Schmottlach, Neil & Clayton, Irene. Physical Education Handbook. 7th ed. 448p. 1983. 17.95 (ISBN 0-13-667535-2); pap. 14.95 (ISBN 0-13-667527-1). P-H.

Schmuck, Patricia A., jt. auth. see Schmuck, Richard A.

Schmuck, Philip, jt. auth. see Eberhart, Perry.

Schmuck, Richard A. & Schmuck, Patricia A. Group Processes in the Classroom. 3rd ed. 234p. 1979. pap. text ed. write for info. o.p. (ISBN 0-697-06091-8). Wm C Brown.

Schmucker, Kurt J. Fuzzy Sets, Natural Language Computation & Risk Analysis. 1983. text ed. price not set (ISBN 0-914894-83-8). Computer Sci.

Schmudde, Theodore H., jt. auth. see Harper, Robert A.

Schmuller, Alan, jt. auth. see Mortensen, Donald.

Schmutterer, H. Pests of Crops in Northeast & Central Africa, with Particular Reference to the Sudan. (Illus.). 296p. 1969. 75.00x (ISBN 3-437-20047-X). Intl Pubns Serv.

Schnabel, Ernst. Anne Frank: A Portrait in Courage. LC 53-12702. 1967. pap. 0.65 (ISBN 0-15-607530-X, Harv). HarBraceJ.

Schnabel, Harry, Jr. Tiebacks. (Illus.). 192p. 1982. 29.50x (ISBN 0-07-055516-8). McGraw.

Schnabel, John F. Sociology: Human Society, Study Guide. 3rd ed. 1981. pap. text ed. 6.95x o.p. (ISBN 0-673-15479-3). Scott F.

Schnabel, Robert B., jt. auth. see Dennis, John E.

Schnabel, Wolfram. Polymer Degradation. 1981. text ed. 32.00x (ISBN 0-02-949640-3, Pub. by Hanser International). Macmillan.

Schnack, Asgar. Aqua. 32p. 1982. pap. 3.50 (ISBN 0-915306-34-4). Curbstone.

Schnacke, Dick. American Folk Toys: How to Make Them. (Handbook Ser). 1974. pap. 7.95 (ISBN 0-14-046209-0). Penguin.

--American Folk Toys, How to Make Them. (Illus.). 160p. 1973. pap. 4.95 (ISBN 0-686-36485-6). Md Hist.

Schnackenberg, Gjertrud. Portraits & Elegies. LC 80-39824. (Poetry Chapbook, Fourth Ser.). 48p. 1981. 8.95 (ISBN 0-87923-368-0). Godine.

Schnaiberg, Allan. The Environment: From Surplus to Scarcity. 1980. text ed. 15.95x o.p. (ISBN 0-19-502610-1); pap. text ed. 13.95x (ISBN 0-19-502611-X). Oxford U Pr.

Schnapper, Antoine. David. (Illus.). 311p. 1982. 75.00 (ISBN 0-933516-59-2). Alpine Fine Arts.

Schnapper, Dominique. Jewish Identities in France: An Analysis of Contmporary French Jewry. Goldhammer, Arthur, tr. LC 82-17495. (Illus.). 224p. 1983. lib. bdg. 25.00x (ISBN 0-226-73910-4). U of Chicago Pr.

Schnare, Sharon, ed. see Draze, Dianne.

Schnebli, H. P., jt. ed. see Bittiger, H.

Schneck, Eleanor M. Reading America. (Illus.). 288p. 1978. pap. text ed. 11.95 (ISBN 0-13-753293-8). P-H.

Schneck, Joshua J. Acid Rain: A Critical Perspective. Johnson, Harriett S., ed. LC 80-54417. (Illus.). 64p. (Orig.). (gr. 7-12). 1981. pap. text ed. 4.95 (ISBN 0-935698-03-5). Tasa Pub Co.

Schneck, N. C., ed. Methods & Principles of Mycarrhizal Research. (Illus.). 256p. 1982. text ed. 24.00 (ISBN 0-89054-046-2). Am Phytopathol.
Schneck, Paul D. Why Do We Have Skeletons? (Creative Questions & Answers Ser.). (Illus.). 32p. (gr. 3-4). 1982. PLB 5.65 (ISBN 0-87191-750-5). Creative Ed.
Schneck, Stephen & Norris, Nigel. Complete Home Medical Guide for Cats. LC 74-31109. (Illus.). 286p. 1975. 8.95 o.p. (ISBN 0-8128-1797-4); pap. 1.95 (ISBN 0-8128-7014-X); pap. 5.95 (ISBN 0-8128-6180-9). Stein & Day.
--The Complete Home Medical Guide for Dogs. LC 74-31110. (Illus.). 286p. 1980. 8.95 o.p. (ISBN 0-8128-1798-2); pap. 5.95 (ISBN 0-8128-6181-7). Stein & Day.
Schnede, Brenda, ed. Chicago Performs: A Guide to Theatre & Dance. LC 77-87358. (Illus.). 93p. (Orig.). 1977. pap. 5.95 o.p. (ISBN 0-8040-0795-0). Swallow.
Schnedier, Meg, ed. see Cahn, Julie.
Schnee, Sandra, jt. auth. see Heffernan, Ildiko.
Schneebaum, Tobias. Keep the River on Your Right. (Illus.). 1969. pap. 9.95 (ISBN 0-394-62438-6, E838, Ever). Grove.
Schneeberger, Kenneth, jt. auth. see Osburn, Donald.
Schneeberger, Pierre-F. Chinese Jades & Other Hardstones. Watson, Katherine, tr. from Fr. (Illus.). 1976. 235.00 (ISBN 0-7100-0455-9). Routledge & Kegan.
Schneede, Uwe M., et al. George Grosz: His Life & Work. Flatauer, Susanne, tr. LC 78-64969. (Illus.). 184p. 1980. 12.50x (ISBN 0-87663-333-5); pap. 8.95 (ISBN 0-87663-990-2). Universe.
Schneeman, Peter. Through the Finger Goggles: Stories. LC 81-69834. (Breakthrough Ser.: No. 37). 112p. pap. 6.95 (ISBN 0-8262-0360-4). U of Mo Pr.
Schneer, C. J., ed. Crystal Form & Structure. (Benchmark Papers in Geology: Vol. 34). 1977. 55.00 (ISBN 0-12-787425-9). Acad Pr.
Schneer, Cecil J., ed. Two Hundred Years of Geology in America: Proceedings of the New Hampshire Bicentennial Conference. LC 78-63149. (Illus.). 401p. 1979. text ed. 30.00x (ISBN 0-87451-160-7). U Pr of New Eng.
Schneer, Jonathan. Ben Tillet: Portrait of Labor Leader. LC 82-13653. (Working Class in European History Ser.). 256p. 1983. 21.95 (ISBN 0-252-01025-6). U of Ill Pr.
Schneerer, W. F. Programmed Graphics. 1967. text ed. 27.95 (ISBN 0-07-055402-1, C); instructor's manual 2.00 (ISBN 0-07-055403-X). McGraw.
Schneeweiss, Adam, jt. auth. see Neufeld, Henry N.
Schneeweiss, R. Dictionary of Cereal Processing & Cereal Chemistry. (Eng. & Fr. & Ger. & Rus.). 1982. 121.50 (ISBN 0-444-42049-5). Elsevier.
Schneewind, Elizabeth H., tr. see Brentano, Franz.
Schneewind, J. B. Sidgwick's Ethics & Victorian Moral Philosophy. 1977. 49.95x (ISBN 0-19-824552-1). Oxford U Pr.
Schneewind, J. B., ed. see Hume, David.
Schneid, Hayyim, ed. Family. 128p. pap. 4.50 (ISBN 0-686-95121-2). ADL.
--Marriage. 128p. pap. 4.50 (ISBN 0-686-95140-9). ADL.
Schneider. Distributed Data Bases. 1982. 44.75 (ISBN 0-444-86474-1). Elsevier.
Schneider, Al. Five Hundred Power Packed Pronouncements. (Anthology of Familiar Quotes Ser.). 88p. (Orig.). 1980. pap. 1.95 (ISBN 0-938784-00-5). Dicul Pub.
--Ouch!! My Ego's Hurting. 48p. 1982. pap. 1.95 (ISBN 0-938784-01-3). Dicul Pub.
Schneider, Allen M. & Tarshis, Barry. An Introduction to Physiological Psychology. 2nd ed. 528p. 1980. text ed. 19.00 (ISBN 0-394-32157-X); wkbk. 7.95 (ISBN 0-394-32149-9). Random.
Schneider, Andre, jt. auth. see Rordorf, Willy.
Schneider, Anne & Schneider, Steven. The Climber's Sourcebook. LC 75-21251. 321p. 1976. pap. 5.95 o.p. (ISBN 0-385-11081-2, Anch). Doubleday.
Schneider, Arnold E., et al. Understanding Business Law. 4th ed. 1967. text ed. 12.20 o.p. (ISBN 0-07-055433-1, G); activity guide 5.00 o.p. (ISBN 0-07-055434-X); tests 1.40 o.p. (ISBN 0-07-055435-8). McGraw.
--Organizational Communications. (Illus.). 448p. 1975. text ed. 24.95 (ISBN 0-07-055465-X, C); instructors' manual 16.95 (ISBN 0-07-055466-8). McGraw.
Schneider, Benjamin. Staffing Organizations. Porter, Lyman W., ed. LC 75-20584. (Scott, Foresman Series in Management & Organizations). (Illus.). 200p. 1976. text ed. 16.50x (ISBN 0-673-16148-X); pap. text ed. 12.50x (ISBN 0-673-16147-1). Scott F.
Schneider, Bernard. Getting & Holding a Job. rev. ed. 1983. pap. 2.95x (ISBN 0-88323-020-8, 120). Richards Pub.
Schneider, Bill. Bicyclist's Guide to Glacier National Park. (Illus.). 48p. 1983. pap. 3.95 (ISBN 0-934318-17-4). Falcon Pr MT.
--The Hiker's Guide to Montana. LC 79-55480. 208p. (Orig.). 1979. pap. text ed. 6.95 o.p. (ISBN 0-934318-01-8). Falcon Pr MT.
--Hiker's Guide to Montana. rev. ed. LC 82-84323. (Illus.). 256p. pap. 7.95 (ISBN 0-934318-08-5). Falcon Pr MT.
--Where the Grizzly Walks. 1982. pap. 8.95 (ISBN 0-87842-153-X). Mountain Pr.
Schneider, Bruno F. Renoir. (Q L P Art Ser). (Illus.). 1958. 7.95 (ISBN 0-517-00498-4). Crown.
Schneider, Carl & Vinovskis, Maris A., eds. The Law & Politics of Abortion. LC 79-3134. 320p. 1980. 18.95x (ISBN 0-669-03386-3). Lexington Bks.
Schneider, Charlotte, jt. ed. see Schneider, Siegfried.
Schneider, Coleman. Embroidery Schiffli Multi Head. LC 78-53521. (Illus.). 1978. 35.00 (ISBN 0-9601662-1-1). C Schneider.
Schneider, David J. Introduction to Social Psychology. LC 75-18160. (Social Psychology Ser.). (Illus.). 656p. 1976. text ed. 23.95 (ISBN 0-201-06728-5); instr's manual 3.50 (ISBN 0-201-06724-2). A-W.
Schneider, David M. History of Public Welfare in New York State: 1609-1866. LC 69-14944. (Criminology, Law Enforcement, & Social Problems Ser.: No. 44). (Illus.). 1969. Repr. of 1938 ed. 18.00x (ISBN 0-87585-044-8). Patterson Smith.
Schneider, David M. & Deutsch, Albert. History of Public Welfare in New York State: 1867-1940. LC 69-14944. (Criminology, Law Enforcement, & Social Problems Ser.: No. 45). (Illus.). 1969. Repr. of 1941 ed. 18.00x (ISBN 0-87585-045-6). Patterson Smith.
Schneider, Dennis M., et al. Linear Algebra: A Concrete Approach. 1982. 22.95x (ISBN 0-02-476810-3). Macmillan.
Schneider, Diana, jt. ed. see Bradshaw, Ralph.
Schneider, Dick, jt. auth. see Jaworski, Leon.
Schneider, Duane, jt. auth. see Franklin, Benjamin.
Schneider, E. V. Industrial Sociology: The Social Relations of Industry & the Community. 2nd ed. (Sociology Ser.). 1969. text ed. 27.00 o.p. (ISBN 0-07-055461-7, C). McGraw.
Schneider, Earl. All About Aquariums. (Illus., Orig.). pap. 6.95 (ISBN 0-87666-768-X, PS601). TFH Pubns.
Schneider, Earl & Vriends, Matthew M. Australian Shell Parakeets. 2nd rev. ed. (Illus.). 1979. 4.95 (ISBN 0-87666-998-4, KW-036). TFH Pubns.
Schneider, Eberhard. The G. D. R. The History, Politics, Economy & Society of East Germany. 1978. 18.95x (ISBN 0-312-31491-4). St Martin.
Schneider, Edward L., ed. The Aging Reproductive System. LC 77-83693. (Aging Ser: Vol. 4). 291p. 1978. 38.00 (ISBN 0-89004-176-8). Raven.
Schneider, Elisabeth. The Dragon in the Gate: Studies in the Poetry of G. M. Hopkins. LC 68-31434. (Perspectives in Criticism: No. 20). 1968. 34.75x (ISBN 0-520-01150-3). U of Cal Pr.
Schneider, Elizabeth W. T. S. Eliot: The Pattern in the Carpet. LC 73-90655. 1975. 26.50x (ISBN 0-520-02648-9). U of Cal Pr.
Schneider, F. Richard. Orthopaedics in Emergency Care. LC 80-12233. (Illus.). 178p. 1980. pap. text ed. 15.00 (ISBN 0-8016-4348-1). Mosby.
Schneider, Frank L. Qualitative Organic Microanalysis. 1964. 64.50 (ISBN 0-12-627750-8). Acad Pr.
Schneider, G. W. Export-Import Financing: A Practical Guide. 1974. 49.95x (ISBN 0-471-06578-1). Ronald Pr.
Schneider, George A., ed. The Freeman Journal: The Infantry in the Sioux Campaign of 1876. LC 76-29573. (Illus.). 1978. 15.00 o.p. (ISBN 0-89141-060-0). Presidio Pr.
Schneider, Gotthard. Die Flechtengattung Psora Sensu Zahlbruckner. (Bibliotheca Lichenologica: 13). (Illus.). 308p. (Ger.). 1980. lib. bdg. 32.00x (ISBN 3-7682-1257-2). Lubrecht & Cramer.
Schneider, H. The Africans: An Ethnological Account. 1981. pap. 14.95 (ISBN 0-13-018648-1). P-H.
--Laser Light. 1978. 8.95 (ISBN 0-07-055451-X). McGraw.
Schneider, H. G. & Schneider, Ruth V., eds. Advances in Epitaxy & Endotaxy: Physical Problems of Epitaxy. LC 72-182289. 251p. 1971. 22.50x o.p. (ISBN 0-8002-0323-2). Intl Pubns Serv.
Schneider, H. J. & Wasserman, A. I., eds. Automated Tools for Information Systems Design: Proceedings IFIP WG Working Conference on Automated Tools for Information Systems Design & Development, 8.1, New Orleans, January 26-28, 1982. 262p. 1982. 36.25 (ISBN 0-444-86338-9). Elsevier.
Schneider, H. J., jt. ed. see Salton, G.
Schneider, Hannes, jt. auth. see Mueller, Rudolf.
Schneider, Harriet, jt. auth. see Tanner, Christine A.
Schneider, Henry & Korth, Russ. Helping People To Solo. LC 82-72562. 72p. pap. text ed. 3.00 (ISBN 0-934396-31-0). Churches Alive.
Schneider, Herman & Schneider, N. Science Fun with a Flashlight. LC 74-9982. (Illus.). 48p. (gr. k-3). 1975. PLB 6.95 o.p. (ISBN 0-07-055455-2, GB). McGraw.
Schneider, Herman & Schneider, Nina. How Scientists Find Out: About Matter, Time, Space, & Energy. (gr. 7 up). 1976. 6.95 (ISBN 0-07-055447-1, GB); PLB 8.95 (ISBN 0-07-055448-X). McGraw.
--Science Fun for You in a Minute or Two: Quick Science Experiments You Can Do. (Illus.). 48p. (gr. 4-6). 1975. PLB 7.95 (ISBN 0-07-055432-3, GB). McGraw.
Schneider, Herman M., jt. auth. see Crestol, Jack.
Schneider, Ingun, tr. see Neuschutz, Karin.
Schneider, J. & Kaffarnick, H. Lipoproteins & Age. 74p. 17.00 (ISBN 0-86577-068-9). Thieme-Stratton.
Schneider, Jane & Schneider, Peter. Culture & Political Economy in Western Sicily. (Studies in Social Discontinuity Series). 1976. 32.50 (ISBN 0-12-627850-4). Acad Pr.
Schneider, Jerome. Using an Offshore Bank for Profit, Privacy & Tax Protection. Benavidez, Max & Vozoff, Kate, eds. (Illus.). 259p. 1982. 15.00 (ISBN 0-933560-03-6). WFI Pub Co.
Schneider, Jerome & Laurins, Alex. How to Start Your Own International Bank. LC 79-64158. pap. cancelled. WFI Pub Co.
Schneider, Jerrold E. Ideological Coalitions in Congress. LC 78-4019. (Contributions in Political Science Ser.: No. 16). (Illus.). 1978. lib. bdg. 29.95x (ISBN 0-313-20410-1, SID/). Greenwood.
Schneider, John. The Contemporary Guitar. LC 81-4797. 250p. (Orig.). Date not set. pap. 22.95 (ISBN 0-520-04048-1). U of Cal Pr. Postponed.
Schneider, John, et al, eds. Survey of Commercially Available Computer-Readable Bibliographic Data Bases. LC 72-97793. cancelled (ISBN 0-87715-102-4). Am Soc Info Sci.
Schneider, Jost & Delaigue, Joelle. La Fugue d'Isabelle. LC 82-9671. (Illus.). 56p. (Fr.). (gr. 7-12). 1982. pap. text ed. 2.35 (ISBN 0-88436-909-9, 40286). EMC.
Schneider, Joyce A. Flora Tristan: Feminist, Socialist & Free Spirit. LC 80-20067. 256p. (gr. 7-9). 1980. 10.75 (ISBN 0-688-22250-1); PLB 10.32 (ISBN 0-688-32250-6). Morrow.
Schneider, L. & Bonjean, C., eds. The Idea of Culture in the Social Sciences. (Illus.). 144p. 1973. 21.95 (ISBN 0-521-20209-4); pap. 5.95x o.p. (ISBN 0-521-09810-6). Cambridge U Pr.
Schneider, Laurence A. Ku Chieh-kang & China's New History: Nationalism & the Quest for Alternative Traditions. LC 73-129608. (Center for Chinese Studies, UC Berkeley). 1971. 36.50x (ISBN 0-520-01804-4). U of Cal Pr.
--A Madman of Ch'u: The Chinese Myth of Loyalty & Dissent. LC 78-54800. 1980. 28.50x (ISBN 0-520-03685-9). U of Cal Pr.
Schneider, Lewis M. The Future of the U. S. Domestic Air Freight Industry: An Analysis of Management Strategies. LC 72-94363. (Illus.). 216p. 1973. 12.50x (ISBN 0-87584-106-6). Harvard Busn.
Schneider, Louis. The Freudian Psychology & Veblen's Social Theory. LC 73-19119. 270p. 1974. Repr. of 1948 ed. lib. bdg. 15.50x (ISBN 0-8371-7308-6, SCFP). Greenwood.
--The Sociological Way of Looking at the World. LC 74-30460. (Illus.). 1975. 19.95 o.p. (ISBN 0-07-055463-3, P&RB). McGraw.
Schneider, M. J., jt. ed. see Fickeisen, D. H.
Schneider, Manfred. Erziehung der Erzieher? 253p. (Ger.). 1982. write for info. (ISBN 3-8204-6997-4). P Lang Pubs.
Schneider, Marcel. Schubert. Poston, Elizabeth, tr. from Fr. LC 75-28926. (Illus.). 191p. 1976. Repr. of 1959 ed. lib. bdg. 18.00x (ISBN 0-8371-8472-X, SCSCH). Greenwood.
Schneider, Mark, jt. ed. see Kraft, Michael.
Schneider, Mark, jt. ed. see Kraft, Michael E.
Schneider, Max F. Beitrage Zu Einer Anleitung Clavichord und Cembalo Zu Spielen. (Keyboard Studies: Vol. 2). (Illus.). xi, 120p. 30.00 o.s.i. (ISBN 90-6027-339-7, Pub. by Frits Knuf Netherlands). Pendragon NY.
Schneider, Meg, ed. see Arneson, D. J.
Schneider, Meg, ed. see Cahn, Julie.
Schneider, Meg, ed. see Dixon, Franklin W.
Schneider, Meg, ed. see Hirsch, Phil.
Schneider, Meg, ed. see Koziakin, Vladimir.
Schneider, Meg, ed. see Kushner, Maureen.
Schneider, Meg, ed. see Milton, Hilary.
Schneider, Meg, ed. see Nash, Bruce.
Schneider, Meg, ed. see Phillips, Louis.
Schneider, Meg, ed. see Rotsler, William.
Schneider, Meg, ed. see Shea, George.
Schneider, Meg, ed. see Sheldon, Ann.
Schneider, Meg, ed. see Tallarico, Tony.
Schneider, Meg, ed. see Taylor, L. B., Jr.
Schneider, Michael G. & Bruell, Steven C. Advanced Programming & Problem Solving with Pascal. LC 81-1344. 506p. 1981. text ed. 26.95 (ISBN 0-471-07876-X). Wiley.
Schneider, Michele, tr. see Kennedy, D. J.
Schneider, N., jt. auth. see Schneider, Herman.
Schneider, Nina, jt. auth. see Schneider, Herman.
Schneider, P. B. & Treves, S. Nuclear Medicine in Clinical Practice. 1978. 114.00 (ISBN 0-444-80052-2, Biomedical Pr). Elsevier.
Schneider, Peter, jt. auth. see Schneider, Jane.
Schneider, Pierre. World of Manet. LC 68-58484. (Library of Art Ser.). (Illus.). (gr. 6 up). 1968. 19.92 (ISBN 0-8094-0277-7, Pub. by Time-Life). Silver.
--World of Watteau. LC 67-20332. (Library of Art Ser.). (Illus.). (gr. 6 up). 1967. 19.92 (ISBN 0-8094-0267-X, Pub. by Time-Life). Silver.
Schneider, R. Guten Tag: A German Language Course for Television. 1974. pap. text ed. 7.95x (ISBN 0-685-47484-4). Schoenhof.
Schneider, R. & Dickey, W. Reinforced Masonry Design. 1980. 44.95 (ISBN 0-13-771733-4). P-H.
Schneider, Raymond K. HVAC Control Systems. LC 80-23588. 358p. 1981. text ed. 27.95 (ISBN 0-471-05180-2); avail. tchr's manual (ISBN 0-471-09274-6). Wiley.
Schneider, Rex. Ain't We Got Fun? (Illus.). 68p. (Orig.). 1982. pap. 3.95 (ISBN 0-9609640-0-2). Blue Mouse.
Schneider, Richard C. The Natural History of the Minocki of the Lakeland Region of Wisconsin. (Illus.). 255p. 1980. 9.95 (ISBN 0-936984-03-1). Schneider Pubs.
Schneider, Richard P., jt. ed. see Sanders, Charles L.
Schneider, Russell J. Frank Robinson: The Making of a Manager. LC 75-43864. (Illus.). 256p. 1976. 8.95 o.p. (ISBN 0-698-10731-4, Coward). Putnam Pub Group.
Schneider, Ruth V., jt. ed. see Schneider, H. G.
Schneider, Siegfried & Schneider, Charlotte, eds. Imagining Success. 330p. Date not set. pap. 14.95 (ISBN 0-9605392-0-4). Gold Key Succ.
Schneider, Steven & Mestrow, L. E. Genesis Strategy. 1977. pap. 4.95 o.s.i. (ISBN 0-440-52792-9, Delta). Dell.
Schneider, Steven, jt. auth. see Schneider, Anne.
Schneider, T., ed. Automatic Air Quality Monitoring Systems: Proceedings of the Conference Held in Bilthorn in 1973. 1974. 21.50 (ISBN 0-444-41202-6). Elsevier.
Schneider, T. & Grant, L., eds. Air Pollution by Nitrogen Oxides: Proceedings of the US-Dutch International Symposium, Maastricht, May 24-28, 1982. (Studies in Environmental Science: No. 21). 1118p. 1982. 159.75 (ISBN 0-444-42127-0). Elsevier.
Schneider, T., et al, eds. Air Pollution Reference Measurement Methods & Systems. (Studies in Environmental Science: Vol. 2). 1979. 47.00 (ISBN 0-444-41764-8). Elsevier.
Schneider, Thomas, ed. see DiFranco, Anthony.
Schneider, Thomas, ed. see Woods, Harold & Woods, Geraldine.
Schneider, Tom. Everybody's a Winner: A Kid's Guide to New Sports & Fitness. (Illus.). (gr. 3 up). 1976. 8.95 (ISBN 0-316-77398-0, Brown Paper School); pap. 6.70i (ISBN 0-316-77399-9). Little.
--The Moveable Nest. (Orig.). 1981. pap. 8.95 o.s.i. (ISBN 0-440-56383-6, Delta). Dell.
Schneider, Tom, ed. see DiFranco, Anthony.
Schneider, Tom, ed. see Filstrup, Chris & Filstrup, Janie.
Schneider, Tom, ed. see Meyer, Kathleen A.
Schneider, Tom, ed. see Smith, Eileen.
Schneider, Tom, ed. see Westman, Paul.
Schneider, Vimala. Infant Massage: A Handbook for Loving Parents. 128p. 1982. pap. 4.95 (ISBN 0-553-01409-9). Bantam.
Schneider, Volker, tr. see Schondorf, Hubert.
Schneider, W. & Sagvall Hein, A. -L., eds. Computational Linguistics in Medicine: Proceedings of the IFIP Working Conference on Computational Linguistics in Medicine. 1978. 42.75 (ISBN 0-444-85040-6, North-Holland). Elsevier.
Schneider, William, jt. auth. see Lipset, Seymour L.
Schneider, William S., Jr., et al. U. S. Strategic-Nuclear Policy & Ballistic Missile Defense: The 1980s & Beyond. LC 79-3296. (Special Reports). 61p. 1980. 6.50 o.p. (ISBN 0-89549-018-8). Inst Foreign Policy Anal.
Schneider-Cuvay, M. Michaela & Rainer, Werner, eds. Salzburg, Pt. 2. (The Symphony 1720-1840 Series B: Vol. 8). lib. bdg. 90.00 (ISBN 0-8240-3818-5). Garland Pub.
Schneiderman, Ben, ed. Data Bases: Improving Usability & Effectiveness. 1978. 36.00 (ISBN 0-12-642150-1). Acad Pr.
Schneiderman, Harry, tr. see Rothgiesser, Ruben.
Schneiderman, Stuart. Jacques Lacan: The Death of an Intellectual Hero. (Illus.). 192p. 1983. 14.95 (ISBN 0-674-47115-6). Harvard U Pr.
Schneiderman, William. Dissent on Trial: The Story of a Political Life. LC 82-17940. 224p. 1983. 17.50x (ISBN 0-930656-25-3); pap. 6.95 (ISBN 0-930656-26-1). MEP Pubns.
Schneiders, Alexander A. Personality Development & Adjustment in Adolescence. 1960. 7.95 o.p. (ISBN 0-02-827760-0). Glencoe.
Schneidman, J. Lee. John F. Kennedy. (World Leaders Ser). 1974. lib. bdg. 11.95 (ISBN 0-8057-3696-4, Twayne). G K Hall.
Schneier, Craig E. & Beatty, Richard W. Personnel Administration Today. 1978. pap. text ed. 16.95 (ISBN 0-201-00503-4). A-W.
Schneier, Craig E., jt. auth. see Beatty, Richard W.
Schneier, Craig E., jt. auth. see Carroll, Stephen J.
Schneierson, Vic, tr. see Ponomarev, Boris N.
Schneir, Miriam, ed. Feminism. 1971. pap. 4.95 (ISBN 0-394-71738-4, Vin). Random.
Schneiter, Paul H. & Nelson, Donald T. The Thirteen Most Common Fund-Raising Mistakes & How to Avoid Them. Kalish, Susan E., ed. LC 82-51251. (Illus.). 95p. (Orig.). 1982. pap. 14.95 (ISBN 0-914756-53-2). Taft Corp.
Schnell, Barry T. The Child Support Survivor's Guide. LC 82-73099. 174p. 1983. pap. price not set. Consumer Aware.

Schnell, George A. & Monmonier, Mark S. The Study of Population: A Geographic Approach. 362p. Date not set. text ed. 24.95 (ISBN 0-675-20046-6). Merrill.

Schnell, Mildred. The Shoemaker's Dream. 28p. 1982. 7.95. Judson.

Schnell, R. L., jt. ed. see Lawson, Robert F.

Schnell, Robert W. Bonko. LC 77-99446. (Illus.). 28p. (ps-3). 5.75 (ISBN 0-87592-008-X). Scroll Pr.

Schnell, William J. How to Witness to a Jehovah's Witness. Orig. Title: Christians, Awake! 160p. 1975. pap. 3.50 (ISBN 0-8010-8048-7). Baker Bk.

Schnelle, Helmut, jt. ed. see Heny, Frank W.

Schnelle, Kenneth E. Case Analysis & Business Problem Solving. 1967. pap. text ed. 16.50 (ISBN 0-07-055470-6, C). McGraw.

Schneller, Eugene S. The Physician's Assistant. LC 76-11974. (Innovation in the Medical Division of Labor). 192p. 1978. 19.95x o.p. (ISBN 0-669-00715-3). Lexington Bks.

Schnepp, A. F. & Schnepp, G. J. To God Through Marriage. rev. ed. (Orig.). 1967. pap. 3.96 o.p. (ISBN 0-02-827860-7). Glencoe.

Schnepp, G. J., jt. auth. see Schnepp, A. F.

Schnessel, S. Michael. Icart. (Illus.). 1976. 25.00 (ISBN 0-517-52498-8, C N Potter Bks). Crown.

--Icart. (Illus.). 192p. 1981. pap. 10.95 (ISBN 0-517-54399-0, C N Potter Bks). Crown.

Schnessel, S. Michael & Karmel, Mel. The Etchings of Louis Icart. LC 82-50430. (Illus.). 192p. 1982. 50.00 (ISBN 0-916838-64-1). Schiffer.

Schnetter, R. Marine Algen der Karibischen Kuest E Von Kolumbien: Chlorophyceae, Vol. II. (Bibliotheca Phycologica Ser.: No. 42). (Illus.). 1978. lib. bdg. 24.00x (ISBN 3-7682-1204-1). Lubrecht & Cramer.

Schnexaydre, Linda & Robins, Kaylyn. Workshops for Jail Library Service: A Planning Manual. 160p. 1981. pap. 17.00 (ISBN 0-8389-3259-2). ALA.

Schniederjans, Marc J., jt. auth. see Kwak, N. K.

Schniedewind, Nancy. Confronting Racism & Sexism: A Practical Handbook for Educators. 1977. 5.00 o.p. (ISBN 0-686-00840-5). Commonground Pr.

Schniedewind, Nancy & Davidson, Ellen. Open Minds to Equality. (Illus.). 272p. 1983. pap. 16.95 (ISBN 0-13-637264-3). P-H.

Schniedman, Rose & Lambert, Susan. Workbook for Being a Nursing Assistant. 3rd ed. 240p. 1981. wkbk. 4.95 (ISBN 0-89303-049-X). R J Brady.

Schnirring, Melissa. The Well-Being Guide to Health Spas in North America. LC 82-45311. 160p. 1982. pap. 6.95 (ISBN 0-689-11195-9). Atheneum.

Schnitger, Carol, jt. auth. see Beatty, Eleanor.

Schnitman, Jorge A. Film Industries in Latin America: Dependency & Development. (Communication & Information Science Ser.). 1983. write for info. (ISBN 0-89391-095-3). Ablex Pub.

Schnitzer. Contemporary Government & Business Relations. 2d ed. text ed. 21.95 (ISBN 0-686-84539-0, BS46); instr's manual avail. HM.

Schnitzer, M. & Khan, S. U., eds. Soil Organic Matter. (Developments in Soil Science: Vol. 8). 1978. 78.75 (ISBN 0-444-41610-2). Elsevier.

Schnitzer, Martin. Contemporary Government & Business Relations. 1978. 23.50 (ISBN 0-395-30727-9). HM.

--Contemporary Government & Business Relations. 2d ed. 608p. text ed. 21.95 (ISBN 0-395-31764-9); write for info. instr's manual (ISBN 0-395-34027-6). HM.

Schnitzer, Martin, jt. auth. see Fox, Harrison W., Jr.

Schnitzer, Robert J. & Grunberg, Emanuel. Drug Resistance of Microorganisms. 1957. 43.00 (ISBN 0-12-628450-4). Acad Pr.

Schnitzer, Robert J., et al, eds. Advances in Pharmacology & Chemotherapy, Vol. 17. 1980. 41.50 (ISBN 0-12-032917-4); lib. ed. 54.00 (ISBN 0-12-032984-0); microfiche ed. 29.50 (ISBN 0-12-032985-9). Acad Pr.

Schnitzlein, H. Norman. Computed Tomography of the Head & Spine: A Photographic Atlas of CT, Gross & Microscopic Anatomy. LC 82-13515. (Illus.). 126p. 1982. text ed. 59.00 (ISBN 0-8067-1771-8). Urban & S.

Schnitzler, Arthur. Anatol. Marcus, Frank, tr. 1982. pap. 7.50 (ISBN 0-413-49880-8). Methuen Inc.

--The Farewell Supper. Brown, Edmund R., ed. (International Pocket Library). pap. 3.00 (ISBN 0-686-77247-4). Branden.

--Liebelei, Leutnant Gustl, Die Letzten Masken. Stern, J. P., ed. 1966. text ed. 8.50x (ISBN 0-521-06201-2). Cambridge U Pr.

--La Ronda. Marcus, Frank, tr. 1982. pap. 5.95 (ISBN 0-413-49530-2). Methuen Inc.

--La Ronde. Barton, John, adapted by. Davies, Sue, tr. from Fr. 1983. pap. 3.95 (ISBN 0-14-048171-0). Penguin.

--The Round Dance (La Ronde) & Other Plays. Osborne, Charles, tr. 222p. 1982. text ed. 14.75x (ISBN 0-85635-398-1, 90198, Pub. by Carcanet New Pr England). Humanities.

--Vienna Nineteen Hundred: Games with Love & Death. 365p. 1974. pap. 3.95 (ISBN 0-14-003759-4). Penguin.

Schnitzler, Arthur see Brown, Edmund R.

Schnitzler, Jean-Henri. Etudes sur l'Empire des Tsars, 2 vols. (Nineteenth Century Russia Ser.). (Fr.). 1974. Repr. of 1847 ed. lib. bdg. 262.00x set o.p. (ISBN 0-8287-0766-9). Clearwater Pub.

Schnurnberger, Lynn E. A World of Dolls That You Can Make. LC 80-8450. (Illus.). 128p. (gr. 3 up). 1982. pap. 9.57i (ISBN 0-06-025231-6, HarpJ); PLB 16.89g (ISBN 0-06-025232-4). Har-Row.

Schnurnberger, Lynn E. & Metropolitan Museum of Art. Kings, Queens, Knights, & Jesters: Making Medieval Costumes. LC 77-25682. (Illus.). (gr. 3 up). 1978. 12.45i (ISBN 0-06-025241-3, HarpJ); PLB 12.89 (ISBN 0-06-025242-1). Har-Row.

Schnurre. Die Tat. (Easy Reader, C). pap. 3.95 (ISBN 0-88436-040-7, 45272). EMC.

Schnurre, Wolfdietrich. Man Sollte Dagegen Sein & Other Stories. Watt, Roderick & Smith, Ursula, eds. 176p. (Orig.). 1982. pap. text ed. 8.50x (ISBN 0-435-38750-2). Heinemann Ed.

Schnurrenger. Principles of Health Maintenance. 272p. 1983. 32.00 (ISBN 0-03-062828-8). Praeger.

Schnytzer, A. The Albanian Economy. (Economics of the World Ser.). (Illus.). 224p. 39.95x (ISBN 0-19-877125-8). Oxford U Pr.

Schnytzer, Adi. Stalinist Economic Strategy in Practice: The Case of Albania. (Economies of the World Ser.). (Illus.). 180p. 1983. 34.95 (ISBN 0-686-84829-2). Oxford U Pr.

Schoberl, F., jt. auth. see Flamm, D.

Schobinger, R. A. Intra-Ossesus Venography. LC 59-14373. 256p. 1960. 59.50 o.p. (ISBN 0-8089-0415-9). Grune.

Schochet, Sidney S., jt. auth. see McCormick, William F.

Schochet, Sydney S., Jr. & McCormick, William F. Neuropathology Case Studies. 2nd ed. 1979. pap. 19.50 (ISBN 0-87488-046-7). Med Exam.

Schochet, Victoria & Silbersack, John, eds. The Berkley Showcase: New Writings in Science Fiction & Fantasy, Vol. 3. 256p. (Orig.). 1981. pap. 2.25 o.p. (ISBN 0-425-04697-4). Berkley Pub.

Schodek, D. Structures. 1980. 27.95 (ISBN 0-13-855304-1). P-H.

Schoder, Judith. Brotherhood of Pirates. LC 79-16061. (Illus.). 96p. (gr. 4-6). 1979. PLB 7.29 o.p. (ISBN 0-671-32965-0). Messner.

Schoder, Judith & Shebar, Sharon. The Bell Witch. (Jem High Interest-Low Reading Level). (Illus.). 64p. (gr. 7-9). 1983. PLB 9.29 (ISBN 0-671-44005-5). Messner.

Schoder, Judy. The Hides-It. (Beginning-to-Read Ser.). 32p. (gr. k-3). 1982. PLB 4.39 (ISBN 0-695-41669-3, Dist. by Caroline Hse); pap. 1.95 (ISBN 0-695-31669-9). Follett.

Schoedinger, Andrew B. Wants, Decisions & Human Action: A Praxeological Investigation. LC 78-62705. 1978. pap. text ed. 10.50 (ISBN 0-8191-0591-0). U Pr of Amer.

Schoeffler, James D. IBM Series 1: Small Computer Concept. 1980. pap. text ed. 12.95 (ISBN 0-574-21330-9, 13-4330). SRA.

Schoelcher, Victor. Des Colonies Francaises; Abolition Immediate De L'esclavage. (Slave Trade in France, 1744-1848, Ser.). 494p. (Fr.). 1974. Repr. of 1842 ed. lib. bdg. 123.00 o.p. (ISBN 0-8287-0768-5, TN133). Clearwater Pub.

--De l'Esclavage des Noirs et de la Legislation Coloniale. (Slave Trade in France Ser., 1744-1848). 160p. (Fr.). 1974. Repr. of 1833 ed. lib. bdg. 48.50x o.p. (ISBN 0-8287-0767-7, TN125). Clearwater Pub.

Schoeloher, Victor. Histoire de l'Esclavage Pendant les deux Dernieres Annees, 2 vols. (Slave Trade in France Ser., 1744-1848). 1053p. (Fr.). 1974. Repr. of 1847 ed. lib. bdg. 260.00x o.p. (ISBN 0-8287-0769-3); Vol. 1. (ISBN 0-685-49223-0, TN 138); Vol. 2. (ISBN 0-685-49224-9, TN 139). Clearwater Pub.

Schoemaker, S. Computer Network & Simulations. 1978. 47.00 (ISBN 0-444-85208-5). Elsevier.

Schoemaker, S., ed. Computer Networks & Simulation II. 326p. 1982. 51.00 (ISBN 0-444-86438-5, North Holland). Elsevier.

Schoeman, Elna. The Namibian Issue: A Select & Annotated Bibliography. 234p. 1982. lib. bdg. 38.00 (ISBN 0-8161-8437-2, Pub. by Hall Reference Bks). G K Hall.

Schoen, A. H., jt. auth. see Compton, D. M.

Schoen, Carol. Anzia Yezierska. (Twayne's United States Authors Ser.). 1982. lib. bdg. 14.95 (ISBN 0-8057-7358-4, Twayne). G K Hall.

Schoen, Carol, et al. The Writing Experience. 2nd ed. 1982. pap. text ed. 10.95 (ISBN 0-316-77415-4); tchrs' manual avail. (ISBN 0-316-77414-6). Little.

Schoen, Cathy, jt. auth. see Davis, Karen.

Schoen, Douglas E. Enoch Powell & the Powellites. LC 77-70333. 1977. 25.00 (ISBN 0-312-25672-8). St Martin.

Schoen, Elin. The Closet Book. (Illus.). 144p. 1982. 22.50 (ISBN 0-517-54285-4, Harmony); pap. 10.95 (ISBN 0-517-54575-6). Crown.

Schoen, Harold L. & Marcucci, Robert. Elementary Algebra Through Problem-Solving. 1981. text ed. 22.50x (ISBN 0-8162-7630-7); study guide & instrs.' manual avail. Holden-Day.

Schoen, Kenneth F., jt. auth. see Ward, David A.

Schoen, Linda, ed. The AMA Book of Skin & Hair Care. 1978. pap. 3.50 (ISBN 0-380-01871-3, 58800-5). Avon.

Schoen, R. & Sudhof, H., eds. Biochemical Findings in the Differential Diagnosis of Internal Diseases. 1963. 22.10 (ISBN 0-444-40511-9). Elsevier.

Schoen, S., jt. auth. see Goodard, T.

Schoen, Sterling H. & Durand, Douglas E. Supervision: The Management of Organizational Resources. (Illus.). 1979. ref. ed. 21.95 (ISBN 0-13-876235-X). P-H.

Schoenbaum, E., jt. auth. see Lomax, P.

Schoenbaum, S. Shakespeare: The Globe & the World. (Illus.). 1979. 35.00x (ISBN 0-19-502645-4); pap. 7.95 (ISBN 0-19-502646-2). Oxford U Pr.

--William Shakespeare: A Compact Documentary Life. LC 76-47436. (Illus.). 1977. 18.95x (ISBN 0-19-502211-4). Oxford U Pr.

--William Shakespeare: A Compact Documentary Life. LC 75-46358. 1978. pap. 7.95 (ISBN 0-19-502433-8, GB 551, GB). Oxford U Pr.

--William Shakespeare: A Documentary Life. (Illus.). 1975. 75.00x (ISBN 0-19-812046-X). Oxford U Pr.

Schoenbaum, Samuel. Shakespeare's Lives. LC 74-118290. 1970. 29.95x (ISBN 0-19-501243-7). Oxford U Pr.

Schoenbaum, Thomas J. Islands, Capes, & Sounds: The North Carolina Coast. LC 81-21557. (Illus.). 352p. 1982. 22.50 (ISBN 0-89587-021-5). Blair.

Schoenberg & Strang, eds. Fundamentals of Music Composition. 8.95 (ISBN 0-686-84403-3). Faber & Faber.

Schoenberg, Arnold. Fundamentals of Musical Composition. Strang, Gerald & Stein, Leonard, eds. 240p. 1982. pap. 8.95 (ISBN 0-571-09276-4). Faber & Faber.

--Preliminary Exercises in Counterpoint. Stein, Leonard, ed. 248p. 1982. pap. 6.95 (ISBN 0-571-09275-6). Faber & Faber.

--Style & Idea: Selected Writings of Arnold Schoenberg. Stein, Leonard, ed. 560p. 1982. Repr. 45.00 (ISBN 0-571-09722-7). Faber & Faber.

Schoenberg, B. Mark, ed. Bereavement Counseling: A Multidisciplinary Handbook. LC 79-7471. 1980. lib. bdg. 29.95x (ISBN 0-313-21434-4, SBR/). Greenwood.

--A Handbook & Guide for College & University Counseling Center. LC 77-87975. 1978. lib. bdg. 29.75x (ISBN 0-313-20050-5, SCH/). Greenwood.

Schoenberg, Bruce S., ed. Neurological Epidemiology: Principles & Clinical Applications. LC 77-72796. (Advances in Neurology Ser.: Vol. 19). 678p. 1978. 70.00 (ISBN 0-89004-212-8). Raven.

Schoenberg, I. J. Cardinal Spline Interpolation. (CBMS-NSF Regional Conference Ser.: No. 12). vi, 125p. 1973. pap. 11.00 (ISBN 0-89871-009-X). Soc Indus-Appl Math.

Schoenberg, Robert J. Art of Being a Boss: Inside Intelligence from Top-Level Business Leaders & Young Executives on the Move. 1978. 13.41i (ISBN 0-397-01291-8). Har-Row.

Schoenblum, Jeffrey. Multistate & Multinational Estate Planning. 1400p. 1982. 125.00 set (ISBN 0-316-77419-7); Vol. 2. (ISBN 0-316-77418-9). Little.

Schoenbrun, David. Soldiers of the Night: The Story of the French Resistance. (Illus.). 1980. 15.95 o.p. (ISBN 0-525-20663-9). Dutton.

--Soldiers of the Night: The Story of the French Resistance. 1981. pap. 9.95 (ISBN 0-452-00612-0, F612, Mer). NAL.

Schoendoerffer, Pierre. The Paths of the Sea. LC 77-18148. 1978. 8.95 o.p. (ISBN 0-698-10903-1, Coward). Putnam Pub Group.

Schoenfeld, David & Natella, Arthur A. The Consumer & His Dollars. new & 3rd ed. LC 74-19030. 365p. 1975. 7.50 (ISBN 0-379-00470-4); wkbk & study guide 2.00 (ISBN 0-379-00808-4); write for info. tchr's answer key (ISBN 0-379-00807-6). Oceana.

Schoenfeld, Dianne B. Games Kids Like. 1974. loose-leaf text 15.95 (ISBN 0-88450-750-5, 2124-B). Communication Skill.

--Games Kids Like & More Games Kids Like: Combination Binder. 1975. loose-leaf 28.00 (ISBN 0-88450-778-5, 2024-B). Communication Skill.

Schoenfeld, Eric, ed. see Beckett, Samuel.

Schoenfeld, Madalynne, jt. ed. see Greene, Ellin.

Schoenfeld, Maxwell P. War Ministry of Winston Churchill. LC 72-153159. (Illus.). 1972. 10.95 (ISBN 0-8138-0260-1). Iowa St U Pr.

Schoenfeld, Norman, jt. auth. see Parker, Frank J.

Schoenfield, Leslie J. Diseases of the Gallbladder & Biliary System. LC 77-5695. (Clinical Gastroenterology Monographs). 1977. 55.50 (ISBN 0-471-76246-6, Pub. by Wiley Medical). Wiley.

Schoenhals, Alvin & Schoenhals, Louise. Vocabulario Mixe de Totontepec. (Vocabularios Indigenas Ser.: No. 14). 353p. 1965. pap. 5.00x (ISBN 0-88312-659-1); microfiche 3.75 (ISBN 0-88312-319-3). Summer Inst Ling.

Schoenhals, Lawrence R. Companion to Hymns of Faith & Life. (Orig.). 1980. pap. 7.95 (ISBN 0-89367-040-5). Light & Life.

Schoenhals, Louise, jt. auth. see Schoenhals, Alvin.

Schoenmaker, Anneke. Praatpaal: Dutch for Beginners. 160p. 1981. 32.00x (ISBN 0-85950-474-3, Pub. by Thornes England). State Mutual Bk.

Schoenstadt, A. L., et al, eds. Information Linkage Between Applied Mathematics & Industry II. LC 80-17975. 1980. 23.00 (ISBN 0-12-628750-3). Acad Pr.

Schoenstein, Ralph. Wasted on the Young. LC 73-11795. 112p. 1974. 4.95 o.p. (ISBN 0-672-51839-2). Bobbs.

Schoeny, Donna H. & Decker, Larry E., eds. Community, Educational & Social Impact Perspectives. LC 82-84309. 232p. (Orig.). Date not set. pap. 5.95 (ISBN 0-911525-00-9). Mid-At Ctr.

Schoep, Arthur, jt. auth. see Goldovsky, Boris.

Schoer, Karl J., compiled by. Christmas Plays From Oberufer. 3rd ed. Harwood, A. C., tr. & intro. by. 64p. 1973. pap. 3.50 (ISBN 0-85440-279-9, Pub. by Steinerbooks). Anthroposophic.

Schoer, Lowell A., jt. auth. see Albers, Henry H.

Schofer, Lawrence. The Formation of a Modern Labor Force: Upper Silesia 1865-1914. LC 73-90658. 1975. 30.00x (ISBN 0-520-02651-9). U of Cal Pr.

Schofer, Peter, et al, eds. Poemes, Pieces, Prose: Introduction a l'analyse De textes litteraires francais. (Illus.). 742p. (Fr.). 1973. pap. text ed. 19.95x (ISBN 0-19-501643-2). Oxford U Pr.

Schoffeniels, E., ed. Biochemical Evolution & the Origin of Life. 1971. 30.75 (ISBN 0-444-10081-4). Elsevier.

Schoffeniels, E. & Neumann, E., eds. Molecular Aspects of Bioelectricity: Proceedings of the Symposium in Honour of 1980 David Nachmansohn, Liege, May 19-20, 1980. (Illus.). 360p. 1980. 72.00 (ISBN 0-08-026371-2). Pergamon.

Schoffer, Herbert & Weis, Erich. Schoffer-Weis German & English Dictionary. 1974. 8.95 o.s.i. (ISBN 0-695-80458-8). Follett.

Schofield. Black & White in School. 272p. 1982. 29.95 (ISBN 0-03-056977-X). Praeger.

Schofield, A. N., ed. see Malushitsky, Yuri N.

Schofield, Bernard. Events in Britain. (Illus.). 256p. 1981. 19.95 o.p. (ISBN 0-7137-1230-9, Pub. by Blandford Pr England). Sterling.

Schofield, Diane. Beginning with Tropicals. pap. 2.95 (ISBN 0-87666-165-7, M523). TFH Pubns.

Schofield, Edmund, ed. Earthcare: Global Protection of Natural Areas; Proceedings of the Fourteenth Biennial Walderness Conference. LC 76-29358. (14th Biennial Wilderness Conference). 1978. lib. bdg. 45.00 o.p. (ISBN 0-89158-034-4). Westview.

Schofield, J. Microcumputer-Based Aids for the Disabled. 1981. pap. text ed. 29.95x (ISBN 0-471-87721-2, Pub. by Wiley Heyden). Wiley.

Schofield, Jack, jt. ed. see Angeloglou, Christopher.

Schofield, K., et al. Heteroaromatic Nitrogen Compounds: The Azoles. LC 74-17504. (Illus.). 500p. 1976. 90.00 (ISBN 0-521-20519-0). Cambridge U Pr.

Schofield, M., pseud. A Minority. LC 76-7604. 1976. Repr. of 1960 ed. lib. bdg. 17.25x (ISBN 0-8371-8877-6, SCAMI). Greenwood.

Schofield, Mary A. Quiet Rebellion: The Fictional Heroines of Eliza Fowler Haywood. LC 81-40664. 148p. (Orig.). 1982. lib. bdg. 19.00 (ISBN 0-8191-2150-9); pap. text ed. 8.25 (ISBN 0-8191-2151-7). U Pr of Amer.

Schofield, Robert E., ed. see Priestley, Joseph.

Schofield, Russell P. Joyous Exploration. LC 82-60316. (Illus.). 104p. (Orig.). 1982. leather ed. 73.95 (ISBN 0-9608720-0-0); pap. 16.95 (ISBN 0-9608720-2-7). Schofield Pub.

Schofield, W. Engineering Surveying. 2nd ed. (Illus.). 1978. pap. 13.95 (ISBN 0-408-00333-2). Butterworth.

Schofield, William H. English Literature, from the Norman Conquest to Chaucer. Repr. of 1906 ed. lib. bdg. 20.00x (ISBN 0-8371-4100-1, SCEL). Greenwood.

Schohl, Wolfgang W. Estimating Shadow Prices for Colombia in an Input-Output Table Framework. (Working Paper: No. 357). 147p. 1979. 5.00 (ISBN 0-686-36085-0, WP-0357). World Bank.

Schoitz & Dahlstrom. Collins Guide to Aquarium Fishes & Plants. 29.95 (ISBN 0-686-42787-4, Collins Pub England). Greene.

Scholars on the Staff of the Pforzheimer Library. Byron on the Continent: A Memorial Exhibition, 1824-1974. LC 74-75534. 88p. (Orig.). 1974. pap. 6.00 o.p. (ISBN 0-87104-248-7, 248). NY Pub Lib.

Scholastic Testing Service. Practice for High School Minimum Educational Competency Tests in Reading & Mathematics. LC 78-78331. (Orig.). pap. 4.95 (ISBN 0-671-47101-5). Monarch Pr.

Scholastic Testing Service Editors. Practice for High School Competency Test in English: Reading & Writing Skills. (Illus.). 160p. 1983. pap. 4.95 (ISBN 0-668-05550-2, 5550). Arco.

--Practice for High School Competency Tests in Mathematics. 160p. 1983. pap. 4.95 (ISBN 0-668-05548-0, 5548). Arco.

Scholberg, Diana E., jt. auth. see Scholberg, Kenneth R.

Scholberg, Henry. Bibliography of Goa & the Portuguese in India. 413p. 1982. text ed. 64.50x (ISBN 0-391-02762-X, Pub. by Promilla & Co India). Humanities.

--Bibliography of Goa & the Portuguese in India. 1982. 55.00x (ISBN 0-8364-0896-9, Pub. by Promilla). South Asia Bks.

Scholberg, Kenneth R. & Scholberg, Diana E. Aqui Mismo. (Illus., Orig.). 1980. pap. text ed. 8.95 (ISBN 0-88377-148-9). Newbury Hse.

Scholberg, Kenneth R., jt. auth. see Rooks, George.

Scholem, Gershom. Kabbalah. 1978. pap. 8.95 (ISBN 0-452-00570-1, F570, Mer). NAL.

--Messianic Idea in Judaism & Other Essays on Jewish Spirituality. 376p. pap. 7.95 (ISBN 0-686-95141-7). ADL.

Scholen, Kenneth & Yung-Ping Chen, eds. Unlocking Home Equity for the Elderly. 320p. 1980. prof ref 32.50x (ISBN 0-88410-595-4). Ballinger Pub.

Scholes, Mary, et al. Handbook of Nursing Procedures. (Illus.). 371p. 1982. pap. text ed. 10.95 (ISBN 0-632-00687-0, B 4361-9). Mosby.

Scholes, Percy A. Oxford Companion to Music. 10th ed. Ward, John O., ed. 1970. 39.95x (ISBN 0-19-311306-6). Oxford U Pr.

Scholes, Robert. Elements of Fiction. 1968. pap. 3.95x (ISBN 0-19-501046-9). Oxford U Pr.

--Elements of Poetry. (Orig.). 1969. pap. text ed. 3.95x (ISBN 0-19-501047-7). Oxford U Pr.

--Structuralism in Literature: An Introduction. LC 73-90578. 250p. 1974. 17.50x (ISBN 0-300-01750-2); pap. 5.95x (ISBN 0-300-01850-9). Yale U Pr.

Scholes, Robert & Kellogg, Robert. Nature of Narrative. 1968. pap. 7.95 (ISBN 0-19-500773-5, GB). Oxford U Pr.

Scholes, Robert & Klaus, Carl H. Elements of Writing. 1972. pap. text ed. 5.95x (ISBN 0-19-501535-5). Oxford U Pr.

Scholes, Robert & Rabkin, Eric. Science Fiction: History-Science-Vision. LC 76-42615. 1977. 18.95x (ISBN 0-19-502173-8). Oxford U Pr.

--Science Fiction: History-Science-Vision. 1977. pap. 6.95 (ISBN 0-19-502174-6, 498, GB). Oxford U Pr.

Scholes, Robert, ed. Some Modern Writers: Essays & Fiction by Conrad, Dinesen, Lawrence, Orwell, Faulkner & Ellison. (Orig.). 1971. pap. 7.95x (ISBN 0-19-501271-2). Oxford U Pr.

Scholes, Robert, et al, eds. Elements of Literature Three: Fiction, Poetry, Drama. 1982. pap. text ed. 12.95x (ISBN 0-19-503071-0); tchr's manual avail. (ISBN 0-19-503190-3). Oxford U Pr.

Scholes, Robert J., jt. ed. see Simon, Thomas W.

Scholes, Roberte, et al, eds. Elements of Literature Five: Fiction, Poetry, Drama, Essay, Film. rev. ed. (Illus.). 1982. pap. text ed. 14.95x (ISBN 0-19-503070-2); tchr's manual avail. (ISBN 0-19-503190-3). Oxford U Pr.

Scholl, Friedrich, jt. auth. see Hummel, Dieter O.

Scholl, H. Dieter. Europe Camping & Caravaning, Nineteen Seventy-Eight to Seventy-Nine. 1978. pap. text ed. 7.00 (ISBN 0-685-52229-6). Campgrounds.

Schollander, Don & Cohen, Joel H. Inside Swimming. LC 74-6908. (Illus.). 96p. 1974. pap. 5.95 o.p. (ISBN 0-8092-8905-9). Contemp Bks.

Schollhammer, Hans & Kuriloff, Arthur. Entrepreneurship & Small Business Management. LC 78-9443. (Management & Administration Ser.). 608p. 1979. text ed. 31.95 (ISBN 0-471-76260-1). Wiley.

Scholnick, Ellin K. New Trends in Conceptual Representation: Challanges to Piaget's Theory? (Jean Piaget Symposium). 320p. 1983. text ed. write for info. (ISBN 0-89859-260-7). L Erlbaum Assocs.

Scholnick, Robert J. Edmund Clarence Stedman. (United States Authors Ser.). 1977. lib. bdg. 13.95 (ISBN 0-8057-7188-3, Twayne). G K Hall.

Scholt, Grayce, jt. ed. see Bingham, Jane.

Scholten, Robert, jt. ed. see De Jong, Kees A.

Scholtz, P. L. Race Relations at the Cape of Good Hope, 1652-1795: A Select Bibliography. 1981. lib. bdg. 30.00 (ISBN 0-8161-8500-X, Hall Reference). G K Hall.

Scholz, Joachim J. Blake & Novalis, Vol. 19. (European University Studies: Series 18, Comparative Literature). 404p. 1978. 64.00 (ISBN 3-261-02576-X). P Lang Pubs.

Scholz, John T., jt. auth. see Rose, Leo E.

Scholz, Nellie. How to Decide: A Workbook for Women. 1978. pap. 7.95 (ISBN 0-380-37309-2, 59394-7). Avon.

Schomer, Karine. Mahadevi Varma & the Chhayavad Age of Modern Hindi Poetry. LC 81-13002. (Illus.). 368p. 1983. text ed. 30.00 (ISBN 0-520-04255-7). U of Cal Pr.

Schomp, Gerald. Alcohol: Its Use, Abuse & Therapy. 5.95 o.p. (ISBN 0-686-92257-3, 8005). Hazelden.

--Overcoming Anxiety: A Christian Guide to Personal Growth. 2.50 o.p. (ISBN 0-686-92388-X, 6584). Hazelden.

Schon, Donald A. The Reflective Practitioner: How Professionals Think in Action. LC 82-70855. 355p. 1983. 19.95 (ISBN 0-465-06874-X). Basic.

Schon, Donald A., jt. auth. see Argyris, Chris.

Schon, Gunter. Simon & Schuster World Coin Catalogue: 1982 - 1983 Twentieth Century. 1982. 19.95 (ISBN 0-671-45606-7); pap. text ed. 13.50 (ISBN 0-671-45612-1). S&S.

Schonberg, Harold C. The Lives of the Great Composers. Rev. ed. (Illus.). 24.95 (ISBN 0-393-01302-2). Norton.

Schonberg, James. The Comparative Trilby Glossary, French-English. 60p. 1983. Repr. of 1895 ed. lib. bdg. 30.00 (ISBN 0-89984-614-9). Century Bookbindery.

Schonberger, Howard B. Transportation to the Seaboard: The Communication Revolution & American Foreign Policy, 1860-1900. LC 75-105979. (Contributions in American History: No. 8). 1971. lib. bdg. 29.95x (ISBN 0-8371-3306-8, SCT/). Greenwood.

Schonberger, Richard J. Japanese Manufacturing Techniques: Nine Hidden Lessons in Simplicity. LC 82-48495. 1982. 14.95 (ISBN 0-02-929100-3). Free Pr.

Schondorf, Hubert. Aspiration Cytology of the Breast. Schneider, Volker, tr. LC 77-24004. (Illus.). 1978. text ed. 16.00 (ISBN 0-7216-8013-5). Saunders.

Schone, Alfred & Hiller, Ferdinand, eds. The Letters of a Leipzig Cantor: Being the Letters of Moritz Hauptmann to Franz Hauser, Ludwig Spohr, & Other Musicians, 2 vols. Coleridge, A. D., tr. LC 75-163789. Date not set. Repr. of 1892 ed. price not set. Vienna Hse.

Schone, H. H., jt. ed. see Winnacker, Ernest L.

Schoner, Bertram & Uhl, Kenneth P. Marketing Research: A Short Course for Professionals. (Wiley Professional Development Programs). 352p. 1976. 39.95 (ISBN 0-471-01701-9). Wiley.

Schoner, Bertran & Uhl, Kenneth P. Marketing Research: Information Systems & Decision Making. 2nd ed. LC 80-11127. 608p. 1980. Repr. of 1975 ed. 28.50 (ISBN 0-89874-184-X). Krieger.

Schonfeld, Josef, jt. auth. see Frank, Samuel B.

Schongut, Emanuel. Catch Kitten. Klimo, Kate, ed. (Kitten Board Bks.). (Illus.). 14p. (ps-k). 1983. 3.95 (ISBN 0-671-46382-9, Little). S&S.

--Hush Kitten. Klimo, Kate, ed. (Kitten Board Bk.). (Illus.). 14p. 1983. 3.95 (ISBN 0-671-46386-1, Little). S&S.

--Look Kitten. Klimo, Kate, ed. (Kitten Board Bks.). (Illus.). 14p. 1983. 3.95 (ISBN 0-671-46388-8, Little). S&S.

--Play Kitten. Klimo, Kate, ed. (Kitten Board Bks.). (Illus.). 14p. 1983. 3.95 (ISBN 0-671-46387-X, Little). S&S.

--Wake Kitten. Klimo, Kate, ed. (Kitten Board Bks.). (Illus.). 14p. 1983. 3.95 (ISBN 0-671-46383-7, Little). S&S.

Schonland, David. Molecular Symmetry. (Illus.). 1965. 14.95 o.p. (ISBN 0-442-07423-9). Van Nos Reinhold.

Schonle, Volker. Johannes, Jesus und die Juden. 288p. (Ger.). 1982. write for info. (ISBN 3-8204-5877-8). P Lang Pubs.

Schonwetter, Norma, ed. see National Council of Jewish Women Greater Detroit Section.

School Library Association of California. Library Skills. rev ed. LC 73-78275. 1973. pap. 5.50 (ISBN 0-8224-4300-7). Pitman Learning.

School of Economic Science, London, Language Dept., tr. see Ficino, Marsilio.

School of Oriental & African Studies, University of London. Library Catalogue of the School of Oriental & African Studies: Third Supplement, 19 vols. 1979. Set. lib. bdg. 1990.00 (ISBN 0-8161-0261-9, Hall Library). G K Hall.

School of Social Work, Columbia University. Dictionary Catalog of the Whitney M. Young, Jr., Memorial Library of Social Work. 1980. lib. bdg. 1275.00 (ISBN 0-8161-0307-0, Hall Library). G K Hall.

Schoolcraft, Henry R. Literary Voyager or Muzzeniegun. Mason, Philip P., ed. LC 74-12581. (Illus.). 193p. 1974. Repr. of 1962 ed. lib. bdg. 15.00x o.p. (ISBN 0-8371-7724-3, SCLV). Greenwood.

Schooler, Carmi, jt. auth. see Kohn, Melvin L.

Schoolfield, George C. Janus Secundus. (World Authors Ser.). 1980. lib. bdg. 15.95 (ISBN 0-8057-6378-3, Twayne). G K Hall.

Schoolfield, George C., tr. Swedo-Finnish Short Stories. LC 74-8724. (International Studies & Translations Ser.). 344p. 1974. lib. bdg. 13.50 o.p. (ISBN 0-8057-3367-1, Twayne). G K Hall.

Schoolfield, Lucille D. Better Speech & Better Reading. 1973. text ed. 7.00 o.p. (ISBN 0-686-09394-1). Expression.

Schools Council & Sixth Form Mathematics Project. Mathematics Applicable: Polynomial Models. 1977. pap. text ed. 8.50x o.p. (ISBN 0-435-51699-X). Heinemann Ed.

--Mathematics Applicable: Vector Models. 1977. pap. text ed. 8.50x o.p. (ISBN 0-435-51700-7). Heinemann Ed.

Schools Council History 13-16 Project. Arab-Israeli Conflict. (Modern World Problems Ser.). (Illus.). 1979. Repr. of 1977 ed. lib. bdg. 12.95 (ISBN 0-912616-68-7); pap. text ed. 5.95 (ISBN 0-912616-67-9). Greenhaven.

--The Rise of Communist China. (Modern World Problems Ser.). (Illus.). 1979. lib. bdg. 12.95 (ISBN 0-912616-70-9); pap. text ed. 5.95 (ISBN 0-912616-69-5). Greenhaven.

Schools Council Sixth Form Mathematics Projects. Mathematics Applicable: Geometry from Coordinates. 1975. pap. text ed. 8.50x o.p. (ISBN 0-435-51697-3). Heinemann Ed.

Schools Council Sixth Form Mathematics Project. Mathematics Applicable: Introductory Probability. 1975. pap. text ed. 6.50x o.p. (ISBN 0-435-51698-1). Heinemann Ed.

--Mathematics Applicable: Logarithmic, Exponential. 1975. pap. text ed. 8.50x o.p. (ISBN 0-435-51703-1). Heinemann Ed.

--Mathematics Applicable: Mathematics Changes Gear. 1975. pap. text ed. 4.00x o.p. (ISBN 0-435-51695-7). Heinemann Ed.

--Mathematics Applicable: Understanding Indices. 1975. pap. text ed. 8.50x o.p. (ISBN 0-435-51696-5). Heinemann Ed.

Schools Councils History 13-16 Project. The Irish Question. (Modern World Problems Ser.). (Illus.). 1979. lib. bdg. 12.95 (ISBN 0-912616-72-5); pap. text ed. 5.95 (ISBN 0-912616-71-7). Greenhaven.

Schoonmaker, Alan. Students' Survival Manual: Or How to Get an Education Despite It All. 1971. pap. 9.50 scp (ISBN 0-06-045791-0, HarpC). Har-Row.

Schoonover, Shirley. Mountain of Winter. 192p. 1980. pap. 2.25 o.p. (ISBN 0-380-76513-6, 76513). Avon.

--A Season of Hard Desires. 240p. 1981. pap. 2.50 o.p. (ISBN 0-380-77149-7, 77149). Avon.

--Winter Dream. 240p. 1980. pap. 2.25 o.p. (ISBN 0-380-75671-4, 75671). Avon.

Schoor, Gene. Bart Starr: A Biography. LC 76-56332. (gr. 4-7). 1977. PLB 7.95 o.p. (ISBN 0-385-11695-0). Doubleday.

--Billy Martin. LC 79-7699. (Illus.). 1980. 11.95 o.p. (ISBN 0-385-15280-9). Doubleday.

--Joe Dimaggio: A Biography. LC 79-7700. (Illus.). (gr. 7-9). 1980. 8.95a (ISBN 0-385-12290-X); PLB (ISBN 0-385-12291-8). Doubleday.

--The Scooter: The Phil Rizzuto Story. (Illus.). 192p. (gr. 5 up). 1982. 11.95 (ISBN 0-684-17635-1, ScribT). Scribner.

Schoore. Sports Illustrated Swimming & Diving. 1973. 5.95i (ISBN 0-397-01002-8); pap. 2.95i (ISBN 0-397-01003-6, LP-084). Har-Row.

Schopenhauer, Arthur. On the Fourfold Root of the Principle of Sufficient Reason. Payne, E. F., ed. LC 76-156072. 302p. 1974. 21.00x (ISBN 0-87548-278-3); pap. 8.50x (ISBN 0-87548-201-5). Open Court.

--The Psychological Theory of Positive Thinking. (An Essential Knowledge Library Book). (Illus.). 119p. 1983. 76.85 (ISBN 0-686-82204-8). Am Inst Psych.

--The Schopenhauer's Interpretation of the History of Philosophy. (The Essential Library of the Great Philosophers). (Illus.). 129p. 1983. 69.85 (ISBN 0-89901-093-8). Found Class Reprints.

--The Schopenhauer's Theory of the Essence of Man & of Life. (The Essential Library of the Great Philosophers). (Illus.). 109p. 1983. 71.45 (ISBN 0-89901-094-6). Found Class Reprints.

--World As Will & Representation, 2 Vols. Payne, E. F., tr. 1966. pap. text ed. 7.95 ea.; Vol. 1. pap. text ed. (ISBN 0-486-21761-2); Vol. 2. pap. text ed. (ISBN 0-486-21762-0). Dover.

--World As Will & Representation, 2 vols. Payne, E. F., tr. Set. 25.00 (ISBN 0-8446-2885-9). Peter Smith.

Schopf, J. William. Cradle of Life. 1983. write for info. (ISBN 0-87735-339-5). Freeman C.

Schopf, J. William, ed. Earth's Earliest Biosphere: Its Origin & Evolution. LC 82-61383. (Illus.). 1000p. 1983. 60.00 (ISBN 0-691-08323-1); pap. 22.50 (ISBN 0-691-02375-1). Princeton U Pr.

Schopf, Susan. Eating Within the Limits: An Oxford Dining Guide. Northcutt, Mary Jean, ed. (Illus.). 40p. (Orig.). 1982. 0.75 (ISBN 0-934172-08-0). Wim Pubns.

Schopflin, George. Censorship & Political Communication. LC 82-42712. 250p. 1982. 27.50x (ISBN 0-312-12728-6). St Martin.

Schopler, E. Individualized Assessment & Treatment for Autistic & Developmentally Disabled Children. Incl. Vol. I. Psycho-Educational Profile. 256p. 1978. pap. text ed. 29.95 (ISBN 0-8391-1279-3); Vol. II. Teaching Strategies for Parents & Professionals. 272p. 1979. pap. text ed. 19.95 (ISBN 0-8391-1521-0). Univ Park.

Schopler, Eric, jt. ed. see Mesibov, Gary.

Schopper, H., ed. Elastic & Charge Exchange Scattering of Elementary Particles: Pion Nucleon Scattering-Methods & Results of Phenomenological Analyses. (Landolt-Boernstein-New Series. Group I: Vol. 9, Subvol. B, Pt. 2). (Illus.). 610p. 1983. 400.00 (ISBN 0-387-11282-0). Springer-Verlag.

Schopper, H., ed. see International School of Nuclear Physics, Sept 23-30, 1974.

Schor, Amy. Line by Line. 256p. 1981. 11.95 o.s.i. (ISBN 0-399-90083-7, Marek). Putnam Pub Group.

Schor, Joel A. Henry Highland Garnet: A Voice of Black Radicalism in the 19th Century. LC 76-8746. (Contributions in American History Ser.: No. 54). (Illus.). 256p. 1977. lib. bdg. 22.50x (ISBN 0-8371-8937-3, SHG/). Greenwood.

Schor, Lynda. True Love & Real Romance. LC 79-13135. 1979. 9.95 (ISBN 0-698-11004-8, Coward). Putnam Pub Group.

Schor, Sandra & Fishman, Judith. The Random House Guide to Basic Writing. 1978. pap. text ed. 13.95 (ISBN 0-394-32608-3). Random.

Schorer, Mark. The Wars of Love. LC 82-61041. 176p. 1982. Repr. of 1954 ed. 16.95 (ISBN 0-933256-34-5). Second Chance.

Schorer, Mark, ed. Story: A Critical Anthology. 2nd ed. 1967. pap. text ed. 13.95 (ISBN 0-13-850263-3). P-H.

Schorer, Mark, ed. see Austen, Jane.

Schorer, Mark, ed. see Lawrence, D. H.

Schorer, Mark F. The State of Mind: Thirty-Two Stories. LC 73-156208. 346p. 1972. Repr. of 1947 ed. lib. bdg. 15.75x (ISBN 0-8371-6158-4, SCSM). Greenwood.

Schories, Pat. Let's Pretend. (Peggy Cloth Bks.). (Illus.). 10p. (ps-1). 1980. pap. 3.50 (ISBN 0-448-40026-X, G&D). Putnam Pub Group.

Schork, M. A., jt. auth. see Remington, R.

Schorr, Mark. Red Diamond: Private Eye. 256p. 1983. 12.95 (ISBN 0-312-66645-4). St Martin.

Schorr, Martyn. Guide to Mechanical Toy Collecting. (Illus.). pap. 10.00 (ISBN 0-940346-02-8). Wallace-Homestead.

Schorr, Michael. Corrosion Manual: Wet-Process Phosphoric Acid, Pt. I. (Reference Manual Ser.: No. R-3). (Illus.). 96p. (Orig.). 1981. pap. 4.00 (ISBN 0-88090-025-3). Intl Fertilizer.

Schorr, Natalie G. En Revue: Le Francais Par le Journalisme. 272p. 1983. pap. 9.95 (ISBN 0-686-82409-1). Heath.

Schorsch, Anita. The Art of the Weaver. LC 77-91925. (Antiques Magazine Library). (Illus.). 1978. 14.50x o.p. (ISBN 0-87663-311-4, Main St); pap. 8.95 (ISBN 0-87663-982-1). Universe.

Schorsch, Louis, jt. auth. see Barnett, Donald F.

Schorske, Carl E. German Social Democracy, Nineteen Five to Nineteen Eighteen: The Development of the Great Schism. (Harvard Historical Studies: No. 65). 384p. 1983. pap. text ed. 4.95x (ISBN 0-674-35125-8). Harvard U Pr.

Schotland, Donald L. Disorders of the Motor Unit. LC 81-13119. 954p. 1982. 75.00 (ISBN 0-471-09507-9, Pub. by Wiley Med). Wiley.

Schots, C., jt. auth. see Adams, A.

Schott, Max. Murphy's Romance. LC 82-22137. 132p. 1983. pap. 5.95 (ISBN 0-88496-197-4). Capra Pr.

Schottelius, Byron A. & Schottelius, Dorothy D. Textbook of Physiology. 18th ed. LC 77-17844. (Illus.). 624p. 1978. text ed. 23.95 (ISBN 0-8016-4356-2). Mosby.

Schottelius, Dorothy D., jt. auth. see Schottelius, Byron A.

Schotter, Andrew. The Economic Theory of Social Institutions. (Illus.). 240p. 1981. 34.50 (ISBN 0-521-23044-6). Cambridge U Pr.

Schotter, Roni. A Matter of Time. 1979. 8.95 o.p. (ISBN 0-399-20804-6, Philomel). Putnam Pub Group.

Schottle, Hugo. Color Photography: The Landscape. (Illus.). 1979. 12.95 o.p. (ISBN 0-8174-2463-6, Amphoto). Watson-Guptill.

--Color Photography: The Portrait. (Illus.). 1979. 12.95 o.p. (ISBN 0-8174-2462-8, Amphoto). Watson-Guptill.

Schou, M. Lithium Treatment of Manic-Depressive Illness. 2nd, rev. ed. (Illus.). x, 70p. 1983. pap. 11.50 (ISBN 3-8055-3678-X). S Karger.

Schoude, Lee E., jt. auth. see Cope, Dwight W.

Schoustra, J. J., jt. auth. see Scott, Ronald F.

Schouten, Alet. Flight into Danger. Berends, Jan & McHargue, Georgess, trs. (Illus.). (gr. 4-7). 1972. PLB 5.69 o.s.i. (ISBN 0-394-92283-2). Random.

Schouten, Jan A. & Van Der Kulk, W. Pfaff's Problem & Its Generalizations. LC 75-77140. 1969. Repr. of 1949 ed. 25.00 (ISBN 0-8284-0221-3). Chelsea Pub.

Schouten, Joop Van see Van Schouten, Joop.

Schoville, Keith N. Biblical Archaeology in Focus. LC 78-62914. 19.95 (ISBN 0-8010-8112-2). Baker Bk.

Schow, Ronald L., et al, eds. Communication Disorders of the Aged. 448p. 1978. pap. 19.95 (ISBN 0-8391-1237-8). Univ Park.

Schoyer, Maxine, jt. auth. see Eckel, Lorelei.

Schrader, Anna. Prophecies of the Ages, Vol. 11. 1.00 o.p. (ISBN 0-89985-102-9). Christ Nations.

--Prophecies of the Ages, Vol. 12. 1.00 o.p. (ISBN 0-89985-103-7). Christ Nations.

--Prophecies of the End-Time, Vol. 4. 1.00 o.p. (ISBN 0-89985-097-9). Christ Nations.

--Prophecies of the End-Time, Vol. 7. 1.00 o.p. (ISBN 0-89985-098-7). Christ Nations.

Schrader, Barry. Introduction to Electro-Acoustic Music. (Illus.). 224p. 1982. 15.95 (ISBN 0-13-481523-8); pap. 12.95 (ISBN 0-13-481515-7). P-H.

Schrader, C., ed. see Comins, Jeremy.

Schrader, Constance. Nine to Five: The Complete Looks, Clothes & Personality Handbook for the Working Woman. (Illus.). 200p. 1981. o. p. 13.95 (ISBN 0-13-622555-1); pap. 6.95 (ISBN 0-13-622563-2). P-H.

Schrader, Diana. A Guide for Using Television in the Classroom. (gr. k-8). 1980. 11.95 (ISBN 0-916456-70-6, GA 161). Good Apple.

Schrader, H. J. Die Pennaten Diatomeen Aus Dem Obereozaen Von Oamaru, Neuseeland. (Illus.). 1969. 16.00 (ISBN 3-7682-5428-3). Lubrecht & Cramer.

Schrader, Lee F. & Goldberg, Ray A. Farmers' Cooperatives & Federal Income Taxes. LC 74-13729. (Concepts in Agribusiness Management). 120p. 1975. prof ref 20.00x (ISBN 0-88410-269-6). Ballinger Pub.

Schrader, Richard J. God's Handiwork: Images of Women in Early Germanic Literature. LC 82-21005. (Contributions in Women's Studies: No. 41). 144p. 1983. lib. bdg. 23.95 (ISBN 0-313-23666-6, SGH/). Greenwood.

Schrader, William B., ed. Measurement, Guidance, & Program Improvement. LC 81-48491. 1982. 7.95x (ISBN 0-87589-927-7, TM-13). Jossey-Bass.

Schrader, William J., et al. Financial Accounting: An Events Approach. 520p. 1981. text ed. 28.95x (ISBN 0-931920-29-9). Dame Pubns.

Schraeger, Sam. Breaking In: A Beginner's Guide to News Writing for Print & Radio. 72p. (Orig.). pap. text ed. 6.95 (ISBN 0-9609268-0-1). H & S Pub Co.
Schraff, A. E. Black Courage. LC 76-87984. (Illus.). (gr. 3 up). 1969. PLB 5.97 (ISBN 0-8255-7801-9). Macrae.
--North Star. 176p. (gr. 7up). 1972. 6.25 (ISBN 0-8255-7810-8). Macrae.
Schraff, Anne. Christians Courageous. (Illus.). (gr. 2-5). 1980. pap. 3.50 (ISBN 0-570-03488-4, 56-1342). Concordia.
--Faith of the Presidents. (Greatness with Faith Ser.). (Illus.). (gr. 5-8). 1978. 4.95 (ISBN 0-570-07877-6, 39-1202); pap. 3.50 (ISBN 0-570-07882-2, 39-1212). Concordia.
Schrag, A., jt. auth. see Slebert, J.
Schrag, Peter. Mind Control. 1979. pap. 5.95 o.s.i. (ISBN 0-440-55870-0, Delta). Dell.
--Test of Loyalty. 1974. 9.95 o.p. (ISBN 0-671-21787-9). S&S.
--Test of Loyalty. LC 74-111. 416p. 1975. pap. 3.95 o.p. (ISBN 0-671-22021-7, Touchstone Bks). S&S.
Schrag, Philip G., jt. auth. see Meltsner, Michael.
Schrage, Linus. Linear Programming Models: Lindo. (Illus.). 288p. (Orig.). 1981. pap. text ed. 20.00 (ISBN 0-89426-031-6); solutions manual 11.25x (ISBN 0-89426-033-2). Scientific Pr.
--User's Manual for LINDO. (Orig.). 1981. pap. text ed. 11.25x (ISBN 0-89426-032-4). Scientific Pr.
Schram, Barbara & Mandell, Betty. Human Services: Strategies of Intervention. 450p. 1983. text ed. 17.95 (ISBN 0-471-87068-4). Wiley.
Schram, Barbara, jt. auth. see Mandell, Betty R.
Schram, Glenn N. Toward a Response to the American Crisis. LC 81-40575. 146p. 1981. lib. bdg. 19.00 (ISBN 0-8191-1957-1); pap. text ed. 8.25 (ISBN 0-8191-1958-X). U Pr of Amer.
Schram, Joseph & Boeschen, John. Children's Rooms & Play Areas. (Do-It-Yourself Bks.). (Illus.). 96p. 1982. pap. 3.95 (ISBN 0-8249-6119-6). Ideals.
Schram, Louis M. Monguors of the Kansu-Tibetan Frontier Part 3: Records of the Monguor Clans, History of the Monguors in Huangchung & the Chronicles of the Lu Family. LC 54-6120. (Transactions Ser.: Vol. 51, Pt. 3). (Illus.). 1961. pap. 1.00 o.p. (ISBN 0-87169-513-8). Am Philos.
Schram, S. T., ed. Authority, Participation & Cultural Change in China. (Contemporary China Institute Publications). (Illus.). 260p. 1973. 54.50 (ISBN 0-521-20296-5); pap. 17.95x (ISBN 0-521-09820-3). Cambridge U Pr.
Schramm, Carl J., ed. Alcoholism & Its Treatment in Industry. 18.95 o.p. (ISBN 0-686-92154-2, 9005). Hazelden.
Schramm, Carl J., et al. Workers Who Drink: Their Treatment in an Industrial Setting. LC 76-58248. 176p. 1978. 21.95x (ISBN 0-669-01342-0). Lexington Bks.
Schramm, Carol, jt. auth. see Highberger, Ruth.
Schramm, David N. & Arnett, W. David, eds. Explosive Nucleosynthesis: Proceedings of the Conference on Explosive Nucleosynthesis Held in Austin, Texas, on April 2-3, 1973. 313p. 1973. 17.95x (ISBN 0-292-72006-8); pap. 9.95x (ISBN 0-292-72007-6). U of Tex Pr.
Schramm, Wilbur, jt. auth. see Rivers, William L.
Schramm, Wilbur, ed. Quality in Instructional Television. 232p. 1973. pap. 5.00 o.p. (ISBN 0-8248-0255-1, Eastwest Ctr). UH Pr.
Schramm, Wilbur & Lerner, Daniel, eds. Communication & Change: The Last Ten Years - & the Next. LC 76-18893. 1976. pap. text ed. 6.95x (ISBN 0-8248-0645-X, Eastwest Ctr). UH Pr.
Schramm, Wilbur, et al. Handbook of Communication. 1973. 52.95 (ISBN 0-395-30728-7). HM.
Schramm, Wilbur L. The Story Workshop. 458p. 1980. Repr. of 1938 ed. lib. bdg. 30.00 (ISBN 0-89984-423-5). Century Bookbindery.
Schran, Peter. Guerrilla Economy: The Development of the Shensi Kansu Ninghsia Border Region, 1937-1945. LC 75-45052. 1976. 44.50x (ISBN 0-87395-344-4). State U NY Pr.
Schrand, H., jt. auth. see Dunlop, I.
Schrand, Heinrich, jt. auth. see Dunlop, Ian.
Schrank, Jeffrey. The Guide to Short Films. LC 78-24701. (gr. 10 up). 1979. pap. text ed. 7.75 (ISBN 0-8104-6035-1). Boynton Cook Pubs.
--Teaching Human Beings: 101 Subversive Activities for the Classroom. LC 73-179154. 288p. (Orig.). 1972. 7.93x (ISBN 0-8070-3176-3); pap. 4.95x (ISBN 0-8070-3177-1, BP425). Beacon Pr.
--Understanding Mass Media. LC 75-20876. (Illus.). 260p. 1976. pap. 10.00 o.p. (ISBN 0-8174-2902-6, Amphoto). Watson-Guptill.
--Understanding Mass Media. (Illus.). 260p. 1981. pap. 11.95 (ISBN 0-8174-6334-8, Amphoto). Watson-Guptill.
Schrank, Robert. American Workers Abroad. 200p. 1979. pap. 6.95 (ISBN 0-262-69078-0). MIT Pr.
--Ten Thousand Working Days. LC 77-14521. 1978. 16.50x (ISBN 0-262-19169-5); pap. 4.95x (ISBN 0-262-69064-0). MIT Pr.
Schrank, Robert, ed. American Workers Abroad. 1979. 15.00 o.p. (ISBN 0-262-19178-4). MIT Pr.
Schreck, James O., jt. auth. see James, M. Lynn.
Schregle, Johannes. Labour Relations & Development in Southern Asia: Problems & Prospects. International Labour Office, ed. vi, 186p. 1982. 22.80 (ISBN 92-2-103026-1); pap. 17.10 limp (ISBN 92-2-103027-X). Intl Labour Office.
Schreiber, Aaron. Jewish Law & Decision-Making: A Study Through Time. 456p. 1980. lib. bdg. 39.95 (ISBN 0-87722-120-0). Temple U Pr.
Schreiber, Arthur F. & Clemmer, Richard B. Economics of Urban Problems. 3rd ed. LC 81-82567. 1982. 23.95 (ISBN 0-395-31742-8); instr's manual 1.00 (ISBN 0-395-31743-6). HM.
Schreiber, Carol T. Changing Places: Men & Women in Transitional Occupations. 1979. 20.00 (ISBN 0-262-19177-6); pap. 6.95 (ISBN 0-262-69075-6). MIT Pr.
Schreiber, Edward, et al. Elastic Constants & Their Measurements. (Illus.). 240p. 1974. 32.50 o.p. (ISBN 0-07-055603-2, P&RB). McGraw.
Schreiber, Flora R. The Shoemaker. 1983. write for info. (ISBN 0-671-22652-5). S&S.
Schreiber, Gerhard. The History of the Former Yen Dynasty. (Perspectives in Asian History: No. 18). 310p. (Repr. of 1949-56 ed.). lib. bdg. 25.00x (ISBN 0-87991-064-X). Porcupine Pr.
Schreiber, Howard G. What Does a Woman Want? 1978. 4.95 o.p. (ISBN 0-533-03231-8). Vantage.
Schreiber, J. & Elliotts, R., eds. In Search of the American Dream. pap. 4.50 o.p. (ISBN 0-452-00421-7, F421, Mer). NAL.
Schreiber, Jan, ed. see Baron, Mary.
Schreiber, Jan, ed. see Gunn, Thom.
Schreiber, Lee & Backpacking Journal Editors. Backpacking. LC 77-8743. 1978. pap. 7.95 (ISBN 0-8128-6187-6). Stein & Day.
Schreiber, Melvyn H., jt. auth. see Cooley, Robert N.
Schreiber, Michael. The Art of Running: From Around the Block to the Perfect Marathon. (Illus.). 208p. (Orig.). 1982. pap. 9.00 (ISBN 0-912528-29-X). John Muir.
Schreiber, Ralph W. Maintenance Behavior & Communication in the Brown Pelican. 78p. 1977. 6.50 (ISBN 0-943610-22-2). Am Ornithologists.
Schreiber, W. G. A Bullet or a Rope. 192p. (YA) 1976. 6.95 (ISBN 0-685-64244-5, Avalon). Bouregy.
--The Mansville Brand. (YA) 1978. 6.95 (ISBN 0-685-84749-7, Avalon). Bouregy.
--Massacre at Fort Caid. (YA) 1977. 6.95 (ISBN 0-685-74265-2, Avalon). Bouregy.
--Revenge at Blue Valley. (YA) 1978. 6.95 (ISBN 0-685-86412-X, Avalon). Bouregy.
Schreibman, Fay, jt. ed. see Adams, William.
Schreibner, Vernon. My Servant Job: A Devotional Guide to the Book of Job. LC 74-14169. 144p. 1974. pap. 0.95 o.p. (ISBN 0-8066-1454-4, 10-4602). Augsburg.
Schreibner, Vernon R. My Redeemer Lives: Messages from the Book of Job for Lent & Easter. LC 74-14170. 80p. 1974. pap. 2.50 o.p. (ISBN 0-8066-1453-6, 10-4600). Augsburg.
Schreier, Carl. Grand Teton Explorers Guide. (Explorers Guides Ser.). (Illus.). 50p. 1982. pap. 3.95 (ISBN 0-943972-01-9). Homestead WY.
--Yellowstone Explores Guide. LC 82-84287. (Explores Guides Ser.). (Illus.). 52p. (Orig.). 1983. pap. 3.95 (ISBN 0-943972-02-7); lib. bdg. 11.95 (ISBN 0-943972-03-5). Homestead NY.
Schreier, James W. Management Ideas: Study Guide & Excercises. (Illus.). 291p. Date not set. pap. text ed. 7.95 (ISBN 0-201-04989-9). A-W.
Schreier, Stefan. Compressible Flow. LC 80-20607. 577p. 1982. 59.95x (ISBN 0-471-05691-X, Pub. by Wiley-Interscience). Wiley.
Schreiner, George E., ed. see Controversies in Nephrology Conference Sponsored by the American Kidney Fund.
Schreiner, George E., et al, eds. Controversies in Nephrology, 1981. (Illus.). 300p. 1982. text ed. write for info. (ISBN 0-89352-177-9). Masson Pub.
Schreiner, Olive. Dream Life & Real Life. LC 77-21347. 1977. lib. bdg. 8.95 (ISBN 0-915864-32-0); pap. 3.95 (ISBN 0-915864-31-2). Academy Chi Ltd.
Schreiner, Richard L., ed. Care of the Newborn. 318p. 1981. text ed. 26.50 (ISBN 0-89004-518-6). Raven.
Schreiner, Richard L. & Kisling, Jeffrey A., eds. Practical Neonatal Respiratory Care. 481p. 1982. text ed. 46.00 (ISBN 0-89004-559-3). Raven.
Schrenk, Martin. Managerial Structures & Practices in Manufacturing Enterprises: A Yugoslav Case Study. (Working Paper: No. 455). iv, 100p. 1981. 5.00 (ISBN 0-686-36177-6, WP-0455). World Bank.
Schrepfer, Susan R. The Fight to Save the Redwoods: A History of Environmental Reform, 1917-1978. LC 81-69828. (Illus.). 352p. 1983. 22.50 (ISBN 0-299-08850-2). U of Wis Pr.
Schreuder, D. M. The Scramble for Southern Africa: 1877-1895. LC 78-58800. (Cambridge Commonwealth Ser.). 1980. 34.50 (ISBN 0-521-20279-5). Cambridge U Pr.
Schreyer, W., ed. High-Pressure Researches in Geoscience: Behavior & Properties of Earth Materials at High Pressure & Temperatures. (Illus.). 545p. 1983. 86.50x (ISBN 3-510-65111-1). Lubrecht & Cramer.
Schriber, Fritz, ed. Antique Auto Body Decoration for the Restorer. LC 82-62673. (Vintage Craft Ser.: No. 6). (Illus.). 1970. pap. 6.00 (ISBN 0-911160-06-X). Post-Era.
Schriber, T. J. Simulation Using GPSS. LC 73-21896. 533p. 1974. 38.95 (ISBN 0-471-76310-1). Wiley.
Schriber, Thomas J. Fundamentals of Flowcharting. LC 79-21692. 1980. Repr. of 1969 ed. 12.00 (ISBN 0-89874-023-1). Krieger.
Schricker, Gale C. A New Species of Man. LC 81-65860. 216p. 1982. 24.50 (ISBN 0-8387-5033-8). Bucknell U Pr.
Schricker, Gerhard, ed. see Bochnovic, John.
Schrickey, Harry G., jt. ed. see Runes, Dagobert.
Schrier, Allan M., ed. Behavioral Primatology: Advances in Research & Theory, Vol. I. 194p. 1977. 14.95 o.s.i. (ISBN 0-470-99268-9). Halsted Pr.
Schrier, Robert W., jt. auth. see Anderson, Robert J.
Schriever, B. A., jt. ed. see Seifert, William W.
Schrini, John E. Guide for Tipping. Date not set. price not set. Tippers Intl.
Schrock, Gladden see Lion, Eugene & Ball, David.
Schrock, Johnny, et al, eds. Wonderful Good Cooking. LC 75-1726. 136p. 1975. pap. 5.95 (ISBN 0-8361-1765-4). Herald Pr.
Schrock, Miriam M. Holistic Assessment of the Healthy Aged. LC 80-10198. 174p. 1980. pap. 14.50 (ISBN 0-471-05597-2, Pub. by Wiley Med). Wiley.
Schrocter, Bob, jt. auth. see Kaufman, Hal.
Schrocter, Bob, jt. auth. see Kaufman, Mal.
Schroder, Eberhard & Lubke, Kraus, eds. The Peptides, 2 vols. Incl. Vol. 1. Methods of Peptide Synthesis. 1965. 76.50 (ISBN 0-12-629801-7); Vol. 2. Synthesis, Occurrence & Action of Biologically Active Polypeptides. 1966. o. p. 81.50 (ISBN 0-12-629802-5). Acad Pr.
Schroder, Jack E. How to Build & Fly Radio Control Gliders. Angle, Burr, ed. (Illus., Orig.). 1980. pap. 4.00 (ISBN 0-89024-549-5). Kalmbach.
Schroder, Johann. Operator Inequalities. LC 79-28754. (Mathematics in Science & Engineering Ser.). 1980. 45.50 (ISBN 0-12-629750-9). Acad Pr.
Schroder, Johannes H. Genetics for Aquarists. (Illus.). 1976. pap. 9.95 (ISBN 0-87666-461-3, PS-656). TFH Pubns.
Schrodinger, Erwin. What Is Life? Bd. with Mind & Matter. pap. 9.95x (ISBN 0-521-09397-X). Cambridge U Pr.
Schrody, Marjorie F. The T. F. H. Book of Kittens. (Illus.). 96p. 6.95 (ISBN 0-686-97808-0, HP-012). TFH Pubns.
Schroedel, John G. Attitudes Toward Persons With Disabilities: A Compendium of Related Literature. LC 78-62049. 182p. 1978. 8.25 (ISBN 0-686-38794-5). Human Res Ctr.
Schroedel, John G. & Jacobsen, Richard J. Employer Attitudes Towards Hiring Persons With Disabilities: A Labor Market Research Model. LC 78-70971. 60p. 1978. 5.75 (ISBN 0-686-42975-3). Human Res Ctr.
Schroeder, A. & Bonnet, L. Evangelios Sinopticos: Tomo I. Cativiela, A., tr. (Comentario Del Nuevo Testamento). 1977. Repr. of 1971 ed. 12.95 (ISBN 0-311-03050-5). Casa Bautista.
Schroeder, Albert. Gold & Silver Coins of Annam. Permar, B. & Novak, J., eds. (Illus.). 1983. Repr. of 1968 ed. softcovered 10.00 (ISBN 0-686-80446-5). S J Durst.
Schroeder, Albert H., jt. auth. see Jenkins, Myra E.
Schroeder, Andre. Endodontics-Science & Practice: A Textbook for Student & Practitioners. (Illus.). 286p. 1981. vinyl bound 64.00 (ISBN 0-931386-36-5). Quint Pub Co.
Schroeder, Carol. A Bibliography of Danish Literature in English Translation, 1950-1980. 197p. 1982. 19.95x (ISBN 87-7429-044-4). Nordic Bks.
Schroeder, Carolyn, tr. see Leray, Jean.
Schroeder, David. Solid Ground: Facts on the Faith for Young Christians. Bubna, Paul, frwd. by. 255p. 1982. pap. 5.95 (ISBN 0-87509-323-X); Leader's guide 3.50 (ISBN 0-87509-326-4). Chr Pubns.
Schroeder, E. H., ed. see Freligh, H. M.
Schroeder, E. H., ed. see Mangham, Evelyn.
Schroeder, Edward D. Water & Wastewater Treatment. (Environmental Engineering & Water Resources Ser.). (Illus.). 1976. text ed. 31.50 (ISBN 0-07-055643-1, C); solutions manual 7.95 (ISBN 0-07-055644-X). McGraw.
Schroeder, Eileen. Going to the Dogs. (Illus.). 128p. 1980. 7.95 o.p. (ISBN 0-517-54025-8). Crown.
Schroeder, Ernst. Algebra der Logik, 5 vols. in 3. 2nd ed. LC 63-11315. 2192p. (Ger.). 1980. Set. 85.00 (ISBN 0-8284-0171-3). Chelsea Pub.
Schroeder, F. H. & De Voogl, H. J., eds. Steroid Receptors, Metabolism & Prostate Cancer. (International Congress Ser.: Vol. 494). 1980. 58.50 (ISBN 0-444-90119-1). Elsevier.
Schroeder, George A. The Man in the White Robe. 1983. 10.95 (ISBN 0-533-05560-1). Vantage.
Schroeder, Gertrude E., jt. ed. see Koropeckyj, I. S.
Schroeder, H. E. Pathobiologie oraler Strukturen. (Illus.). x, 198p. 1983. pap. 23.50 (ISBN 3-8055-3692-5). S Karger.
Schroeder, Henry A. The Trace Elements & Man. LC 72-85731. (Illus.). 192p. 1973. 7.95 (ISBN 0-686-66795-6); pap. 6.95 (ISBN 0-8159-6907-4). Devin.
Schroeder, Howard, ed. see Abels, Harriette S.
Schroeder, Howard, ed. see Ahlstrom, Mark.
Schroeder, Howard, ed. see East, Ben & Nentl, Jerolyn.
Schroeder, Howard, ed. see Fenton, Don & Fenton, Barb.
Schroeder, Howard, ed. see Hahn, James & Hahn, Lynn.
Schroeder, Howard, ed. see Holmgren, Virginia.
Schroeder, Howard, ed. see Hull, Jesse R.
Schroeder, Howard, ed. see Johnson, Martha P.
Schroeder, Howard, ed. see Kinter, Judith.
Schroeder, Howard, ed. see Letchworth, Beverly J.
Schroeder, Howard, ed. see Levinson, Nancy S.
Schroeder, Howard, ed. see McConoughey, Jana.
Schroeder, Howard, ed. see Miner, Jane C.
Schroeder, Howard, ed. see Miner, Jane Claypool.
Schroeder, Howard, ed. see Nentl, Jerolyn.
Schroeder, Howard, ed. see Reece, Collen L.
Schroeder, Howard, ed. see Robison, Nancy.
Schroeder, Howard, ed. see Schmitz, Dorothy C.
Schroeder, Howard, ed. see Sheffer, H. R.
Schroeder, Howard, ed. see Sirof, Harriet.
Schroeder, Howard, ed. see Thorn, Ian.
Schroeder, Howard, ed. see Thorne, Ian.
Schroeder, Howard, ed. see Zeleznak, Shirley.
Schroeder, J. W., ed. High Energy Rate Fabrication. (PVP Ser.: Vol. 70). 1982. 20.00 (H00246). ASME.
Schroeder, John S. & Daily, Elaine K. Techniques in Bedside Hemodynamic Monitoring. LC 75-31957. (Illus.). 212p. 1976. pap. text ed. 9.95 o.p. (ISBN 0-8016-4362-7). Mosby.
Schroeder, John S., jt. auth. see Daily, Elaine K.
Schroeder, Joseph J., ed. Gun Collector's Digest. 2nd ed. 1976. pap. 7.95 o.s.i. (ISBN 0-695-80684-X). Follett.
Schroeder, Joseph J., ed. see Editors of Gun Digest.
Schroeder, L. Bonnety A. Juan y Hechos: Tomo II. Cativiela, A., tr. Repr. of 1977 ed. 12.95 (ISBN 0-311-03051-3). Casa Bautista.
Schroeder, Larry D. & Sjoquist, David L. The Property Tax & Alternative Local Taxes: An Economic Analysis. LC 75-3751. (Special Studies). (Illus.). 128p. 1975. text ed. 23.95 o.p. (ISBN 0-275-07480-3). Praeger.
Schroeder, Leila O. The Legal Environment of Social Work. 288p. 1982. text ed. 21.95 (ISBN 0-13-528356-6). P-H.
Schroeder, Lelah Crabbs, jt. auth. see McCall, William A.
Schroeder, Lynn, jt. auth. see Ostrander, Sheila.
Schroeder, Mayme, jt. auth. see Bajza, Charles C.
Schroeder, Paul, jt. auth. see Schabacker, Joseph.
Schroeder, R. Operations Management. (Management Ser.). (Illus.). 736p. 1981. text ed. 25.95 (ISBN 0-07-055612-1, C); instructor's manual 18.95 (ISBN 0-07-055613-X). McGraw.
Schroeder, Richard. Politics of Drugs. 2nd ed. Congessional Quarterly, ed. LC 79-27927. 204p. 1980. pap. 8.25 (ISBN 0-87187-193-9). Congr Quarterly.
Schroeder, Richard G., jt. auth. see McCullers, Levis D.
Schroeder, Susan. Cuba: A Handbook of Historical Statistics. 550p. 1982. lib. bdg. 85.00 (ISBN 0-8161-8213-2, Hall Reference). G K Hall.
Schroeder, W. Widick, jt. ed. see Cobb, John B., Jr.
Schroeder, Walter W., III, et al, eds. Readings in Urban Dynamics, Vol. 2. LC 73-89545. (Illus.). 1975. 45.00x (ISBN 0-262-19170-9). MIT Pr.
Schroeder, Warren L., ed. Soils in Construction. 2nd ed. LC 79-22775. 315p. 1980. deluxe ed. 25.95 (ISBN 0-471-05648-0); avail. tchr's manual (ISBN 0-471-07785-2). Wiley.
Schroeder, William J. The Dangerous Role of Soviet Russia at the End of the Twentieth Century with Respect to the United States, Europe, Asia, Saudi Arabia, Israel & the Middle East. (Illus.). 171p. 1982. 98.45 (ISBN 0-86722-004-X). Inst Econ Pol.
Schroeppel, Tom. The Bare Bones Camera Course for Film & Video. 2nd rev. ed. LC 82-90651. (Illus.). 89p. (Orig.). 1982. pap. 5.95 (ISBN 0-9603718-1-8). Schroeppel.
Schroeter, Bob. Hocus-Focus, No. 4. 1982. pap. 1.75 (ISBN 0-451-11880-4, AE1880, Sig). NAL.
Schroeter, J. Die Pilze Schlesiens, 2 vols. (Illus.). 1973. Repr. of 1908 ed. Set. 100.00 (ISBN 3-7682-0761-7). Lubrecht & Cramer.
Schrorder, E. H., ed. see Pardington, G. P.
Schrotenboer, P. Man in God's World. 1977. pap. 1.00 o.p. (ISBN 0-88906-200-5). Wedge Pub.
Schroth, Raymond A. The Eagle & Brooklyn: A Community Newspaper, 1841-1955. LC 73-20972. (Contributions in American Studies: No. 13). 304p. 1974. lib. bdg. 25.00x (ISBN 0-8371-7335-3, SBE/). Greenwood.
Schubel, J. R. The Living Chesapeake. 113p. 1981. 19.95 (ISBN 0-686-36773-1). Md Hist.
Schubel, Jerry R. & Marcy, Barton C., Jr., eds. Power Plant Entrainment: A Biological Assessment. 1978. 28.50 (ISBN 0-12-631050-5). Acad Pr.
Schubert, D., jt. auth. see Schubert, I.
Schubert, Dexter R., jt. auth. see Thomas, Violet S.
Schubert, Earl D., ed. Psychological Acoustics. LC 78-23369. (Benchmark Papers in Acoustics Ser.: Vol. 13). 416p. 1979. 52.50 (ISBN 0-87933-338-3). Hutchinson Ross.
Schubert, Franz. Complete Sonatas for Pianoforte Solo. 293p. 1970. pap. 8.50 (ISBN 0-486-22647-6). Dover.

--Complete Song Cycles. Mandyczewski, Euseblus, ed. Drinker, Henry S., tr. LC 74-116821. Orig. Title: Lieder & Gesange. 1970. pap. 6.95 (ISBN 0-486-22649-2). Dover.
Schubert, Gerald, jt. auth. see Turcotte, Donald L.
Schubert, Glendon. Human Jurisprudence: Public Law As Political Science. LC 74-78862. 416p. 1975. text ed. 17.50x (ISBN 0-8248-0294-2). UH Pr.
--Judicial Mind, 1946-1969. 1976. codebk. write for info. (ISBN 0-89138-154-6). ICPSR.
--Judicial Policy Making: The Political Role of the Courts. rev. ed. 1974. pap. 9.95x (ISBN 0-673-07914-7). Scott F.
Schubert, Glendon A. The Public Interest: A Critique of the Theory of a Political Concept. LC 82-15509. x, 244p. 1982. Repr. of 1960 ed. lib. bdg. 29.75x (ISBN 0-313-22364-5, SCPU). Greenwood.
Schubert, Gottfried. Cure & Recognize Aquarium Fish Diseases. (Illus.). 128p. 1974. 7.95 (ISBN 0-87666-773-6, PS-210). TFH Pubns.
Schubert, Herbert G. Complete Sales Conference Desk Handbook. LC 79-25233. 392p. 1981. 34.50 o.p. (ISBN 0-13-162453-9, Parker). P-H.
Schubert, I. & Schubert, D. There's a Crocodile under My Bed. 9.95 (ISBN 0-07-055614-8). McGraw.
Schubert, K. Spontinis Italienische Schule. (Illus.). xii, 224p. 30.00 o.s.i. (ISBN 90-6027-340-0, Pub. by Frits Knuf Netherlands). Pendragon NY.
Schubert, Paul B., ed. Die Methods: Design, Frabrication, Maintainance & Application, Bk. 1. LC 66-19984. (Illus.). 464p. 1966. 20.00 o.p. (ISBN 0-8311-1013-9). Indus Pr.
Schubert, R. & Ryan, L. Fundamentals of Solar Heating. 1981. 29.95 (ISBN 0-13-344457-0). P-H.
Schubert, W. Communications Cables & Transmission Systems. 1976. 41.00 (ISBN 0-471-26016-9, Pub. by Wiley Heyden). Wiley.
Schubert, William H. Curriculum Books: The First Eighty Years. LC 80-8275. 371p. 1980. lib. bdg. 25.25 (ISBN 0-8191-1261-5); pap. text ed. 14.75 (ISBN 0-8191-1262-3). U Pr of Amer.
Schuberth, Christopher J. & Cashatt, Everett D. Fluorspar Mining District, Cave-in-Rock & Shawnee National Forest. (Guidebooklet Ser.: No. 3). 42p. 1979. pap. 2.55x (ISBN 0-89792-076-7). Ill St Museum.
Schuchard, Oliver, photos by. Missouri. Hall, John M. LC 81-86039. (Illus.). 128p. 1982. 29.50 (ISBN 0-912856-76-9). Graphic Arts Ctr.
Schuchert, Richard, tr. see Endo, Shusaku.
Schuchhardt, Walter-Herwig. Greek Art. LC 70-175860. (History of Art Ser.). (Illus.). 192p. 1972. 10.00x o.p. (ISBN 0-87663-169-3). Universe.
Schuck, Peter H. Suing Government: Citizen Remedies for Official Wrongs. LC 82-48907. 320p. 1983. text ed. 25.00x (ISBN 0-300-02957-8). Yale U Pr.
Schuckers, Gordon H., jt. auth. see Daniloff, Raymond G.
Schuckit, Marc A. Psychiatry Specialty Board Review. 2nd ed. Feighner, John P., ed. 1977. spiral bdg. 22.50 (ISBN 0-87488-312-1). Med Exam.
Schuder, D. L., jt. auth. see Wilson, M. C.
Schuder, P., jt. auth. see Glover, B.
Schuder, Pete, jt. auth. see Glover, Bob.
Schudson, Michael. Discovering the News: A Social History of American Newspapers. LC 78-54997. 1978. 14.95x (ISBN 0-465-01669-3). Basic.
Schuell, Hildred. Aphasia Theory & Therapy: Selected Lectures & Papers of Hildred Schuell. 2nd ed. Sies, Luther F., ed. LC 82-20228. (Illus.). 344p. 1983. pap. text ed. 12.25 (ISBN 0-8191-2768-X). U Pr of Amer.
Schueller, Wolfgang. High-Rise Building Structures. LC 76-28734. 274p. 1977. 38.95x (ISBN 0-471-01530-X, Pub. by Wiley-Interscience). Wiley.
Schuessler, Karl F. Measuring Social Life Feelings: Improved Methods for Assessing How People Feel About Society & Their Place in Society. LC 82-48063. (Social & Behavioral Science Ser.). 1982. text ed. 18.95x (ISBN 0-87589-548-4). Jossey Bass.
Schuett, F. Die Peridineen der Plankton-Expedition der Humboldt-Stiftung I: Allgemeiner Teil. (Illus.). 1978. Repr. of 1895 ed. 40.00 (ISBN 3-7682-0806-0). Lubrecht & Cramer.
Schuettinger, Robert. Lord Acton: Historian of Liberty. LC 74-20792. 263p. 1974. 17.00x (ISBN 0-87548-294-5). Open Court.
Schuetz, Harald. Benzodiazepines: A Handbook. (Illus.). 460p. 1982. 88.00 (ISBN 0-387-11270-7). Springer-Verlag.
Schuetz, Robert D., jt. auth. see Hart, Harold.
Schufreider, Gregory. An Introduction to Anslem's Argument. 131p. 1978. 29.95 (ISBN 0-87722-133-2); pap. 10.00 (ISBN 0-87722-129-4). Temple U Pr.
Schug, Mark C. Economic Education Across the Curriculum. LC 82-60803. (Fastback Ser.: No. 183). 50p. 1982. pap. 0.75 (ISBN 0-87367-183-X). Phi Delta Kappa.
Schugart, Gary L., et al. A Survey of Accounting. LC 82-71247. 837p. 1982. text ed. 24.95x (ISBN 0-931920-40-X); study guide 6.95 (ISBN 0-931920-57-4); practice problem o.p. 4.95 (ISBN 0-686-68566-0); working papers o.p. 6.95 (ISBN 0-686-68567-9). Dame Pubns.
Schuh, G. Edward & Tollini, Helio. Costs & Benefits of Agricultural Research: The State of the Arts. (Working Paper: No. 360). iv, 70p. 1979. 5.00 (ISBN 0-686-36065-6, WP-0360). World Bank.
Schuh, J. F. Mathematical Tools for Modern Physics. 456p. 1968. 103.00x (ISBN 0-677-61090-4). Gordon.
Schuh, Russell G. A Dictionary of Ngizim. (U.C. Publications in Linguistics: Vol. 99). 256p. 1981. 12.50x (ISBN 0-520-09636-3). U of Cal Pr.
Schuh, Willi. Richard Strauss: A Chronicle of the Early Years 1864-1898. Whittall, Mary, tr. LC 81-12200. (Illus.). 576p. 1982. 59.50 (ISBN 0-521-24104-9). Cambridge U Pr.
Schuhholz, Annaliese & Diekmann, Jens. Romantik Hotels & Restaurants. (Illus.). 160p. 1981. pap. 4.98 o.p. (ISBN 0-912944-66-8). Berkshire Traveller.
--Romantik Hotels & Restaurants: Multilingual Guide. Rev. ed. (Illus.). 170p. 1983. pap. 5.95 (ISBN 0-912944-73-0). Berkshire Traveller.
Schuijf, A. & Hawkins, A. D., eds. Sound Reception in Fish. LC 76-54648. (Developments in Aquaculture & Fisheries Science: Vol. 5). 1977. 55.50 (ISBN 0-444-41540-8). Elsevier.
Schukert, Michael A., ed. see University Aviation Association.
Schulberg, Budd. Everything That Moves. LC 78-62604. 1980. 12.95 o.p. (ISBN 0-385-00521-0). Doubleday.
--Moving Pictures: Memories of a Hollywood Prince. LC 80-9055. 448p. pap. 11.95 (ISBN 0-8128-6157-4). Stein & Day.
--On the Waterfront: A Screenplay. Bruccoli, Matthew J., ed. LC 80-15734. (Screenplay Library). (Illus.). 166p. 12.50 (ISBN 0-8093-0956-4); pap. 6.95 (ISBN 0-8093-0957-2). S Ill U Pr.
Schulberg, Cecilia. The Music Therapy Sourcebook: A Collection of Activities Categorized & Analyzed. LC 80-12945. 296p. 1981. 24.95 (ISBN 0-89885-007-X). Human Sci Pr.
Schulberg, Herbert C. & Killilea, Marie, eds. The Modern Practice of Community Mental Health: A Volume in Honor of Gerald Caplan. LC 82-48066. (Social & Behavioral Science Ser.). 1982. text ed. 27.95x (ISBN 0-87589-550-6). Jossey Bass.
Schuld, Frank P. The Simple Squeeze in Bridge. LC 74-6305. (Illus.). 1977. 10.95 o.p. (ISBN 0-8069-8662-X); PLB 9.29 o.p. (ISBN 0-8069-8663-8); pap. 5.95 o.p. (ISBN 0-8069-8664-6). Sterling.
Schulder, Diane & Kennedy, Florynce. Abortion Rap. (Orig.). 1971. pap. 3.95 o.p. (ISBN 0-07-055713-6, GB). McGraw.
Schuler, Carol A., jt. auth. see Stein, Sandra K.
Schuler, Charles, ed. see Fowler, Richard J.
Schuler, Charles A. Electronics: Principles & Applications. (Basic Skills in Electricity & Electronics Ser.). (Illus.). 1979. text ed. 21.96 (ISBN 0-07-055572-9, G); activities manual 10.96 (ISBN 0-07-055619-9); teacher's manual 2.00 (ISBN 0-07-055620-2). McGraw.
--Introduction to Television Servicing. Schuler, Charles A., ed. (Basic Skills in Electricity & Electronics Ser.). (Illus.). 1979. pap. text ed. 14.96 (ISBN 0-07-007176-4, G); teacher's manual 2.00 (ISBN 0-07-007178-0); activities manual 8.96 (ISBN 0-07-007177-2). McGraw.
Schuler, Charles A., ed. see Gilmore, Charles M.
Schuler, Charles A., ed. see Palmore, Phyllis & Andre, Nevin.
Schuler, Charles A., ed. see Tokheim, Roger.
Schuler, D., jt. ed. see Freeman, A. J.
Schuler, Edgar A., et al, eds. Readings in Sociology. 5th ed. LC 79-146068. (Illus., Orig.). 1974. pap. text ed. 12.50 scp o.p. (ISBN 0-690-00461-3, HarpC); instr's manual avail. o.p. (ISBN 0-690-00659-4). Har-Row.
Schuler, Jeanne L. City Bred Daughter. 12p. (Orig.). 1982. pap. 1.50 (ISBN 0-910083-08-8). Heritage Trails.
Schuler, K., jt. ed. see Freeman, A. J.
Schuler, Randall S. Effective Personal Management. (Illus.). 600p. 1983. text ed. 19.95 (ISBN 0-314-69676-8); instrs.' manual avail. (ISBN 0-314-71144-9); study guide avail. (ISBN 0-314-71122-8). West Pub.
--Personnel & Human Resource Management. (Management Ser.). (Illus.). 572p. 1981. text ed. 24.50 (ISBN 0-8299-0406-9). West Pub.
Schuler, Randall S. & Dalton, Dan R. Case Problems in Management. 2nd ed. (Management Ser.). (Illus.). 315p. 1983. pap. text ed. 11.95 (ISBN 0-314-69677-6). West Pub.
Schuler, Randall S., jt. auth. see Carroll, Stephen J., Jr.
Schuler, Randall S., et al. Applied Readings in Personnel & Human Resource Management. (Management Ser.). (Illus.). 328p. 1981. pap. text ed. 10.95 (ISBN 0-8299-0408-5). West Pub.
Schuler, Robert. Floating Out of Stone. signed 20.00 (ISBN 0-686-84323-1); 10.00 (ISBN 0-686-84324-X); pap. 4.50 (ISBN 0-686-84325-8). Juniper Pr WI.
Schuler, Ruth W. Beware of the Wolves. 24p. (Orig.). 1982. pap. 2.50 (ISBN 0-910083-07-X). Heritage Trails.
--Born of Buffalo Bone. 24p. (Orig.). 1978. pap. 2.50 (ISBN 0-910083-03-7). Heritage Trails.
Schuler, Ruth W., ed. Dreaming in the Dawn. 50p. (Orig.). 1980. pap. 3.00 (ISBN 0-910083-07-X). Heritage Trails.
Schuler, Stanley. The Homeowner's Directory. 1978. 12.50x o.s.i. (ISBN 0-671-22597-9); pap. 7.95x o.p. (ISBN 0-671-23016-6). S&S.
Schuler, Stanley, ed. Simon & Schuster's Guide to Trees. (Illus.). 1978. 19.95 (ISBN 0-671-24124-9); pap. 9.95 (ISBN 0-671-24125-7). S&S.
Schuler, Stanley, ed. see Moggi, Guido, et al.
Schulian, John. Writers' Fighters & Other Sweet Scientists. 300p. 1983. 12.95 (ISBN 0-8362-6704-4); pap. 7.95 (ISBN 0-8362-6703-6). Andrews & McMeel.
Schulke, Flip, ed. Martin Luther King, Jr. A Documentary...Montgomery to Memphis. (Illus.). 224p. 1976. 19.95 (ISBN 0-393-07487-0); limited ed. o.p. 100.00 (ISBN 0-685-62030-1); pap. 10.95 (ISBN 0-393-07492-7). Norton.
Schull, W. J. & Chakraborty, R., eds. Human Genetics: A Selection of Insights. LC 78-13701. (Benchmark Papers in Genetics: Vol. 10). 359p. 1979. 43.50 (ISBN 0-87933-321-9). Hutchinson Ross.
Schuller, Ahuva, jt. auth. see Strauss, Ruby G.
Schuller, Gunther. Early Jazz: Its Roots & Musical Development. (Illus.). 1968. 22.50x (ISBN 0-19-500097-8). Oxford U Pr.
Schuller, Linda J., jt. auth. see Barrett, Janice R.
Schuller, Robert. The Inside Story. 8.95 (ISBN 0-686-82099-1). Word Pub.
--Power Ideas for a Happy Family. 1982. pap. 1.95 (ISBN 0-515-64094-8). Jove Pubns.
--Voce Pode Ser Quem Deseja. (Port.). 1981. 1.60 (ISBN 0-8297-1104-X). Life Pubs Intl.
Schuller, Robert H. Descubra Como Amarse a Si Mismo. (La Serie Descubra). 48p. Date not set. 1.35 (ISBN 0-88113-066-4). Edit Betania.
--Descubra Como Florecer en Cualquier Ambiente. (La Serie Descubra). 48p. Date not set. 1.35 (ISBN 0-88113-067-2). Edit Betania.
--Descubra Como Sentirse Seguro de Si Mismo. (La Serie Descubra). 48p. Date not set. 1.35 (ISBN 0-88113-068-0). Edit Betania.
--Descubra Como Transformar Su Actividad en Energia. (La Serie Descubra). 48p. Date not set. 1.35 (ISBN 0-88113-069-9). Edit Betania.
--Descubra Cuales Deben Ser Sus Prioridades. (La Serie Descubra). 48p. Date not set. 1.35 (ISBN 0-88113-078-8). Edit Betania.
--Descubra el Poder para Sobreponerse a las Derrotas. (La Serie Descubra). 48p. Date not set. 1.35 (ISBN 0-88113-071-0). Edit Betania.
--Descubra el Valor de Enfrentarse al Futuro. (La Serie Descubra). 48p. Date not set. 1.35 (ISBN 0-88113-072-9). Edit Betania.
--Descubra la Hermosura de la Vida. (La Serie Descubr). 48p. Date not set. 1.35 (ISBN 0-88113-073-7). Edit Betania.
--Descubra la Libertad. (La Serie Descubra). 48p. Date not set. 1.35 (ISBN 0-88113-074-5). Edit Betania.
--Descubra la Salud y la Felicidad. (La Serie Descubra). 48p. Date not set. 1.35 (ISBN 0-88113-075-3). Edit Betania.
--Descubra Los Milagros En Su Vida. (La Serie Descubra). 48p. Date not set. 1.35 (ISBN 0-88113-076-1). Edit Betania.
--Descubra Sus Oportunidades. (La Serie Descubra). 48p. Date not set. 1.35 (ISBN 0-88113-077-X). Edit Betania.
--Living Powerfully One Day at a Time. 400p. 1983. pap. 6.95 (ISBN 0-8007-5113-2, Power Bks). Revell.
--Peace of Mind Through Possibility Thinking. 1978. pap. 2.50 (ISBN 0-515-06585-4). Jove Pubns.
--The Peak to Peek Principle. LC 80-1693. 192p. 1980. 11.95 (ISBN 0-385-17319-9). Doubleday.
--Self-Love. (Orig.). 1982. pap. 2.50 (ISBN 0-515-06491-2). Jove Pubns.
--Self-Love. 1975. pap. 2.95 (ISBN 0-8007-8195-3, Spire Bks). Revell.
--Self Love: The Dynamic Force of Success. 1969. 6.95 o.p. (ISBN 0-8015-6714-9, Hawthorn); pap. 5.25 (ISBN 0-8015-6720-3, 0510-150, Hawthorn). Dutton.
--Tough Times Never Last, But Tough People Do. (Illus.). 224p. 1983. 12.95 (ISBN 0-8407-5287-3). Nelson.
--You Can Become the Person You Want to Be. 224p. 1973. 10.95 o.p. (ISBN 0-8015-9048-5, Hawthorn); pap. 4.95 (ISBN 0-8015-9049-3, 0481-140, Hawthorn). Dutton.
Schullery, Paul. American Bears: Selections from the Writings of Theodore Roosevelt. (Illus.). 1983. 17.50 (ISBN 0-87081-135-5); pap. 6.95 (ISBN 0-87081-136-3). Colo Assoc.
Schullery, Paul, ed. Old Yellowstone Days. LC 78-6732. (Illus.). 1979. 15.00 (ISBN 0-87081-120-7); pap. 5.95 (ISBN 0-87081-121-5). Colo Assoc.
Schulman, Benson R. & Hart, Monte M. English Mechanics. 1978. pap. text ed. 8.95 (ISBN 0-669-00775-7). Heath.
Schulman, Eveline D. Intervention in Human Services: A Guide to Skills & Knowledge. 3rd ed. LC 81-16989. 1982. pap. text ed. 16.95 (ISBN 0-8016-4371-6). Mosby.
Schulman, Gerda L. Family Therapy: Teaching, Learning, Doing. LC 81-40525. 198p. (Orig.). 1982. lib. bdg. 21.25 (ISBN 0-8191-2081-2); pap. text ed. 10.25 (ISBN 0-8191-2082-0). U Pr of Amer.
Schulman, Grace, tr. see Carmi, T.
Schulman, Ivan A., jt. auth. see Chamberlin, Vernon A.
Schulman, Janet. The Great Big Dummy. LC 78-27728. (Greenwillow Read-Alone Bks.). (Illus.). 32p. (gr. 1-3). 1979. PLB 5.95 (ISBN 0-688-84208-9). Greenwillow.
--The Nutcracker. LC 79-11223. (Illus.). (gr. 1-5). 1979. 9.25 (ISBN 0-525-36245-2, 0898-270). Dutton.
Schulman, Janet, ed. see Sesame Street.
Schulman, Jerome L. Coping with Tragedy: Successfully Facing the Problem of a Seriously Ill Child. 1976. 9.95 o.s.i. (ISBN 0-695-80604-1). Follett.
Schulman, Jerome L. & Irwin, Martin. Psychiatric Hospitalization of Children. (Illus.). 406p. 1982. 45.50x (ISBN 0-398-04686-7). C C Thomas.
Schulman, Jerome L., jt. auth. see Buist, Charlotte A.
Schulman, Ken. Connecting. 1979. text ed. 11.95 (ISBN 0-914094-13-0). Symphony.
Schulman, Martin. The Ascendant: Your Karmic Doorway. Date not set. pap. 6.95 (ISBN 0-87728-507-1). Weiser.
--Karmic Astrology: Joy & the Part of Fortune. (Vol. 3). 1982. pap. 4.95 (ISBN 0-686-98128-6). Weiser.
--Karmic Astrology: The Karma of the Now, Vol. 4. 1978. pap. 4.95 (ISBN 0-87728-416-4). Weiser.
--Karmic Astrology: The Moon's Nodes & Reincarnation. (Vol. 1). 1975. 4.95 (ISBN 0-87728-288-9). Weiser.
--Karmic Relationships. Date not set. pap. 6.95 (ISBN 0-87728-508-X). Weiser.
--Student Handbook: A Review Guide, Activities Manual & Reader for "Understanding Psychology" 2nd ed. 1977. 5.50 (ISBN 0-394-32205-3). Random.
--Venus: The Gift of Love. LC 81-90119. (Illus.). 152p. (Orig.). 1981. pap. 7.95 (ISBN 0-940086-00-X). Golden Light.
Schulman, Neil J. The Rainbow Cadenza: A Novel in Logosta Form. 1983. price not set (ISBN 0-671-42003-8). S&S.
Schulman, P. R. Large-Scale Policy Making. 1980. 17.95 (ISBN 0-444-99075-5). Elsevier.
Schulman, Sylvia, jt. auth. see Wong, S. T.
Schulman, Sylvia, jt. auth. see Wong, Ting.
Schulster, D. & Levitzki, A. Cellular Receptors for Hormones & Neurotransmitters. LC 79-41216. 412p. 1980. 83.95x (ISBN 0-471-27682-0, Pub. by Wiley-Interscience). Wiley.
Schult, Martha, jt. auth. see Dickason, Jean.
Schulte. Reporting Public Affairs. 1981. 21.95x (ISBN 0-02-408040-3). Macmillan.
Schulte, Elaine L. Whither the Wind Bloweth. 1982. pap. 2.25 (ISBN 0-380-79384-9, 79384, Flare). Avon.
Schulte, Rainer, ed. Contemporary Writing from the Continents. xviii, 431p. 1982. lib. bdg. 21.95x (ISBN 0-8214-0656-6, 82-84267); pap. 14.95 (ISBN 0-8214-0657-4, 82-84275). Ohio U Pr.
Schultejann, Marie. Ministry of Service: A Manual for Social Involvement. LC 76-16901. 120p. (Orig.). 1976. pap. 1.95 o.p. (ISBN 0-8091-1967-6). Paulist Pr.
Schulte Nordholt, Jan W. The Dutch Republic & American Independence. Rowen, Herbert H., tr. from Dutch. LC 82-2563. (Illus.). xii, 351p. 1982. 29.95x (ISBN 0-8078-1530-6). U of NC Pr.
Schulterbrandt, Joy G. & Raskin, Allen, eds. Depression in Childhood: Diagnosis, Treatment & Conceptual Models. LC 76-47122. 192p. 1977. o. p. 17.00 (ISBN 0-89004-147-4); pap. 16.00 (ISBN 0-685-74515-5). Raven.
Schultes, Richard & Davis, William. The Glass Flowers at Harvard. (Illus.). 128p. 1983. 25.75 (ISBN 0-525-93250-X, 02501-740); pap. 15.95 (ISBN 0-525-47711-X, 01549-460). Dutton.
Schulte Strathaus, Ulrike J. Das Zuercher Kunsthaus-ein Museumsbau Von Moser. (Institut fuer Geschichte und Theorie der Architecture Ser.: Vol. 22). 158p. Date not set. pap. text ed. 18.95 (ISBN 3-7643-1242-4). Birkhauser.
Schultheis, Rob. The Hidden West: Journeys in the American Outback. 1982. 11.50 (ISBN 0-394-50612-X). Random.
--The Hidden West: Journeys in the American Outback. LC 82-73719. 192p. 1983. pap. 9.50 (ISBN 0-86547-087-1). N Point Pr.
Schultheiss, Tom. A Day in the Life. (Illus.). 336p. 1981. pap. 8.95 (ISBN 0-8256-3229-3, Quick Fox). Putnam Pub Group.
--A Day in the Life: The Beatles Day-by-Day 1960-1970. LC 79-91185. (Rock & Roll Reference Ser.: No. 3). 354p. 1980. individuals 11.95 (ISBN 0-87650-120-X); institutions 15.95. Pierian.
Schults, Dorothy, jt. auth. see Sturman, Julie.
Schultz. Biochemistry of the Phagocytic Process. 1970. pap. 8.00 (ISBN 0-444-10267-1). Elsevier.
Schultz, Arlo, tr. see Zankov, L. V., et al.
Schultz, Arlo A., tr. see Vasil eva, E. K.
Schultz, Barbara, jt. ed. see Schultz, Mark.
Schultz, Birl E., jt. auth. see Beard, Charles A.

Schultz, Cathy, ed. Alcoholism: Triad to Recovery. 160p. 1983. 12.95 (ISBN 0-89769-075-3); pap. 6.95 (ISBN 0-89769-047-8). Pine Mntn.

Schultz, Dave & Fischler, Stan. The Hammer: Confessions of a Hockey Enforcer. 224p. 1983. pap. 2.95 (ISBN 0-425-05887-5). Berkley Pub.

Schultz, David A. & Rodgers, Stanley F. Marriage,the Family & Personal Fullfillment. (Illus.). 432p. 1975. text ed. 21.95 o.p. (ISBN 0-13-559377-8). P-H.

Schultz, Dieter. Fluchtpunkte der Negativitat Spiegelungen der Dramatik Samuel Becketts In Der Marxistischen Literaturkritik. 231p. (Ger.). 1982. write for info. (ISBN 3-8204-7113-8). P Lang Pubs.

Schultz, Dodi, jt. auth. see Pomerantz, Virginia.

Schultz, Dodie, jt. auth. see Pomerantz, Virginia E.

Schultz, Don E. & Martin, Dennis. Strategic Advertising Campaigns. LC 79-92171. 1980. 22.95x (ISBN 0-87251-043-3). Crain Bks.

Schultz, Don E., jt. auth. see Robinson, William A.

Schultz, Donald. Principles of Physical Security. 168p. 1978. 15.95 (ISBN 0-87201-748-6). Gulf Pub.

Schultz, Donald & Melsa, J. State Functions & Linear Control Systems. (Electronic Systems Ser.). 1967. text ed. 39.00 (ISBN 0-07-055655-5, C); solutions manual 15.50 (ISBN 0-07-055656-3). McGraw.

Schultz, Donald & Scheer, Samuel. Crime Scene Investigation. LC 76-7559. (Criminal Justice Ser.). (Illus.). 1977. 22.95x (ISBN 0-13-192864-3). P-H.

Schultz, Donald, jt. auth. see Melsa, James L.

Schultz, Donald E. Essentials of Advertising Strategy. LC 80-70203. 131p. 1981. pap. text ed. 10.95 (ISBN 0-87251-045-X). Crain Bks.

Schultz, Donald O. Criminal Investigation Techniques. 229p. 1978. 15.95 (ISBN 0-87201-164-X). Gulf Pub.

--Police Pursuit Driving Handbook. 96p. 1979. pap. 7.95 (ISBN 0-87201-771-0). Gulf Pub.

Schultz, Donald O. & Hunt, Derald D. Traffic Investigation & Enforcement. rev. ed. LC 82-73387. (Illus.). 225p. 1983. text ed. 15.95 (ISBN 0-942728-07-6); pap. text ed. 12.95 (ISBN 0-942728-06-8). Custom Pub Co.

Schultz, Donald O. & Service, J. Gregory. Security Litigations & Related Matters. (Illus.). 152p. 1982. 22.50x (ISBN 0-398-04706-5). C C Thomas.

Schultz, Donald O., ed. Modern Police Administration. 172p. 1979. 14.95 (ISBN 0-87201-720-6). Gulf Pub.

Schultz, Duane. A History of Modern Psychology. 3rd ed. LC 80-616. 1981. 20.00 (ISBN 0-12-633060-3); solutions manual 5.50 (ISBN 0-12-633065-4). Acad Pr.

--Wake Island. (War Bks.). 224p. 1983. pap. 2.50 (ISBN 0-86721-122-9). Jove Pubns.

Schultz, Duane P. Psychology & Industry Today. 3rd ed. 1982. text ed. 24.95x (ISBN 0-02-408020-9). Macmillan.

--Psychology in Use: Applications to Everyday Life. 1978. text ed. 26.95x (ISBN 0-02-408060-8). Macmillan.

Schultz, Edna M. Kathy. 1972. pap. 5.95 (ISBN 0-8024-4525-X). Moody.

Schultz, Edward J., tr. see Lee, Ki-Baik.

Schultz, Edward W. & Huechert, Charles M. Childhood Stress & the School Experience. 160p. 1983. text ed. 19.95 (ISBN 0-89885-132-7); pap. text ed. 12.95 (ISBN 0-89885-151-3). Human Sci Pr.

Schultz, Frederick M. Social-Philosophical Foundations of Education. 2nd ed. 1977. pap. text ed. 10.95 (ISBN 0-8403-0969-4). Kendall-Hunt.

Schultz, George A. Species of Asellotes (Isopoda: Paraselloidea) from Anvers Island, Antarctica: Paper 1 in Antarctic Biology of the Antarctic Seas VI. Pawson, David L., ed. (Antarctic Research Ser.: Vol. 26). 1976. pap. 14.95 (ISBN 0-87590-129-8). Am Geophysical.

Schultz, George J., ed. Foreign Trade Marketplace. LC 76-20342. 1977. 94.00x (ISBN 0-8103-0981-5). Gale.

Schultz, George P., jt. auth. see Myers, Charles A.

Schultz, Gordon, jt. auth. see Jensen, Clayne.

Schultz, Gordon W., jt. auth. see Jensen, Clayne R.

Schultz, Gwen. The Blue Valentine. LC 78-12184. (Illus.). (gr. k-3). 1979. Repr. of 1965 ed. 8.25 (ISBN 0-688-22176-9); lib. bdg. 6.96 o.p. (ISBN 0-688-32176-3). Morrow.

--Icebergs & Their Voyages. LC 75-9958. (Illus.). 96p. (gr. 7-9). 1975. PLB 8.59 (ISBN 0-688-32047-3). Morrow.

--Icebergs & Their Voyages. LC 75-9958. 95p. 1975. 6.00 (ISBN 0-688-32047-3). Reading Gems.

Schultz, H. Milton & Forbidden Knowledge. 1955. pap. 24.00 (ISBN 0-527-80600-5). Kraus Repr.

Schultz, Harry D. Panics & Crashes: How You Can Make Money from Them. rev. ed. 256p. 1980. 12.95 o.p. (ISBN 0-87000-491-3, Arlington Hse). Crown.

Schultz, Harry D., jt. auth. see Sinclair, James E.

Schultz, I. & Sachs, G. Hydrogen Ion Transport in Epithelia. (Developments in Bioenergetics & Biomembranes Ser.: Vol. 4). 1981. 84.75 (ISBN 0-444-80015-8). Elsevier.

Schultz, J. & Gratzner, H. G., eds. The Role of Cyclic Nucleotides in Carsinogenesis. 1973. 42.00 (ISBN 0-12-632750-5). Acad Pr.

Schultz, J. & Whelan, W. J., eds. Genetic Manipulation As It Affects the Cancer Problem. 1977. 28.50 (ISBN 0-12-632755-6). Acad Pr.

Schultz, J., jt. ed. see Cramer, H.

Schultz, James A. The Shape of the Round Table: Structures of Middle High German Arthurian Romance. 240p. 1983. 25.00x (ISBN 0-8020-2466-1). U of Toronto Pr.

Schultz, James E. Mathematics for Elemenatry School Teachers. (Mathematics Ser.). 1977. text ed. 22.95 (ISBN 0-675-08509-8). Additional supplements may be obtained from publisher. Merrill.

--Mathematics for Elementary School Teachers. 2nd ed. 528p. 1982. text ed. 22.95 (ISBN 0-675-09860-2). Additional supplements may be obtained from publisher. Merrill.

Schultz, James W. & Betts, Wilbur. Bear Chief's War Shirt. (Illus.). 240p. 1983. 14.95 (ISBN 0-87842-129-7); pap. 7.95 (ISBN 0-87842-130-0). Mountain Pr.

Schultz, Janet L. Biology & Man Laboratory Guide. 80p. 1981. pap. text ed. 6.95 (ISBN 0-8403-2351-4). Kendall-Hunt.

Schultz, Jerelyn. Contemporary Parenting Choices. 260p. 1983. pap. text ed. 14.95 (ISBN 0-8138-0358-6). Iowa St U Pr.

Schultz, Jerold. Polymer Materials Science. (P-H Int'l Series in the Physical & Chemical Engineering Sciences). (Illus.). 496p. 1973. ref. ed. 35.95 (ISBN 0-13-687038-4). P-H.

Schultz, John. Writing from Start to Finish. LC 82-14595. 408p. 1982. 13.50x (ISBN 0-86709-039-1). Boynton Cook Pubs.

Schultz, John J. Understanding & Using Radio Communications Receivers. LC 72-84080. 192p. 1972. 7.95 o.p. (ISBN 0-8306-2614-X); pap. 3.95 o.p. (ISBN 0-8306-1614-4, 614). TAB Bks.

Schultz, John R. & Cleaves, A. B. Geology in Engineering. LC 55-7317. 592p. 1955. text ed. 35.95 (ISBN 0-471-76461-2). Wiley.

Schultz, Joseph P., jt. auth. see Klausner, Carla L.

Schultz, Julius & Black, Ronald E., eds. Membrane Transformation in Neoplasia. 1974. 34.50 (ISBN 0-12-632760-2). Acad Pr.

Schultz, Ken. Bass Fishing Fundamentals. (Illus.). 272p. 1982. 14.95 (ISBN 0-686-97485-9). Exposition.

Schultz, Lawrence. How to Repair CB Radios. Haas, Mark, ed. (Electro Skills Ser.). (Illus.). 176p. 1980. pap. 10.00 (ISBN 0-07-055638-5, G). McGraw.

Schultz, Leroy G., jt. ed. see Gochros, Harvey L.

Schultz, Lynn H., jt. auth. see Pitcher, Evelyn G.

Schultz, M. J., jt. auth. see Denstman, Harold.

Schultz, Mark & Schultz, Barbara, eds. Bicycles & Bicycling: A Guide to Information Sources. LC 79-22839. (Sports, Games, & Pastimes Information Guide Ser.: Vol. 6). 1979. 42.00x (ISBN 0-8103-1448-7). Gale.

Schultz, Mort J. How to Fix It. 1971. 16.95 (ISBN 0-07-055653-9, P&RB). McGraw.

Schultz, Myron G., intro. by. Current Concepts in Parasitology. (Illus.). 137p. (Orig.). 1979. pap. text ed. 6.00 (ISBN 0-910133-04-2). MA Med Soc.

Schultz, Neil. The Complete Book of Safe Moped Operation & Repair. LC 78-18144. (Illus.). 1980. pap. 5.95 o.p. (ISBN 0-385-13531-9, Dolp). Doubleday.

Schultz, Pearle H. Paul Laurence Dunbar: Black Poet Laureate. LC 73-22071. (Creative People Ser.). (Illus.). 144p. (gr. 4-7). 1974. PLB 7.12 (ISBN 0-8116-4516-9). Garrard.

Schultz, Randall L., ed. Applications of Management Science, Vol. 1. 350p. (Orig.). 1981. lib. bdg. 45.00 (ISBN 0-89232-023-0). Jai Pr.

Schultz, Robert C., ed. see Earthday X Colloquium, University of Denver, April 21-24, 1980.

Schultz, Robert C., tr. see Althaus, Paul.

Schultz, Russel R. Blueprint Reading for the Machine Trades. (Illus.). 304p. 1981. text ed. 17.95 (ISBN 0-13-077727-7). P-H.

Schultz, Sam. One Hundred & One Animal Jokes. LC 81-20955. (Make Me Laugh Bks.). (Illus.). 48p. (gr. k-6). 1982. PLB 5.95g (ISBN 0-8225-0978-4). Lerner Pubns.

--One Hundred & One Family Jokes. LC 81-20861. (Make Me Laugh Bks.). (Illus.). 48p. (gr. k-6). 1982. PLB 5.95g (ISBN 0-8225-0981-4). Lerner Pubns.

--One Hundred & One Knock-Knock Jokes. LC 81-20954. (Make Me Laugh Bks.). (Illus.). 48p. (gr. k-6). 1982. PLB 5.95g (ISBN 0-8225-0976-8). Lerner Pubns.

--One Hundred & One Monster Jokes. LC 81-20953. (Make Me Laugh Bks.). (Illus.). 48p. (gr. k-6). 1982. PLB 5.95g (ISBN 0-8225-0977-6). Lerner Pubns.

--One Hundred & One School Jokes. LC 81-20912. (Make Me Laugh Bks.). (Illus.). 48p. (gr. k-6). 1982. PLB 5.95g (ISBN 0-8225-0979-2). Lerner Pubns.

--One Hundred & One Sports Jokes. LC 81-20913. (Make Me Laugh Bks.). (Illus.). 48p. (gr. k-6). 1982. PLB 5.95g (ISBN 0-8225-0980-6). Lerner Pubns.

Schultz, Samuel. Deuteronomy. (Everyman Bible Commentary Ser). 128p. (Orig.). 1971. pap. 4.50 (ISBN 0-8024-2005-2). Moody.

Schultz, Stanley, ed. Ion Transport by Epithelia. (Society of General Physiologists Ser.: Vol. 36). 288p. 1981. text ed. 35.00 (ISBN 0-89004-610-7). Raven.

Schultz, Stanley G. Principles of Membrane Transport. LC 79-54015. (IUPAB Biophysics Ser.: No. 2). (Illus.). 1980. 29.95 (ISBN 0-521-22992-8); pap. 10.95x (ISBN 0-521-29762-1). Cambridge U Pr.

Schultz, Susan, jt. auth. see Mazel, Judy.

Schultz, Theodore W. Investing in People: The Economics of Population Quality. 187p. 1982. pap. 5.95 (ISBN 0-520-04787-7). U of Cal Pr.

--Transforming Traditional Agriculture. LC 82-20271. xiv, 212p. 1964. pap. 7.95 (ISBN 0-226-74075-7). U of Chicago Pr.

Schultz, Theodore W., ed. Economics of the Family: Marriage, Children, & Human Capital. LC 73-81484. x, 584p. 1975. text ed. 25.00x (ISBN 0-226-74085-4). U of Chicago Pr.

Schultz, Thom, compiled by. Pew Peeves. LC 82-50731. (Illus.). 80p. (Orig.). 1982. pap. 3.95 (ISBN 0-936664-07-X). T Schultz Pubns.

Schultz, V., jt. ed. see Klement, A. W.

Schultz, V., et al. A Bibliography of Quantitative Ecology. 1976. 40.50 (ISBN 0-12-787430-5). Acad Pr.

Schultz, Vincent, compiled by. Ecological Aspects of the Nuclear Age: Selected Readings in Radiation Ecology. LC 72-600120. (AEC Technical Information Center Ser.). 588p. 1972. pap. 22.75 (ISBN 0-87079-183-4, TID-25978); microfiche 4.50 (ISBN 0-87079-184-2, TID-25978). DOE.

Schultze, Charles L. The Distribution of Farm Subsidies: Who Gets the Benefits? 1971. pap. 3.95 (ISBN 0-8157-7753-1). Brookings.

--National Income Analysis. 3rd ed. LC 72-140763. (Foundations of Modern Economics Ser.). (Illus.). 1971. pap. 10.95 ref. ed. (ISBN 0-13-609420-1). P-H.

--The Politics & Economics of Public Spending. 1969. pap. 6.95 (ISBN 0-8157-7751-5). Brookings.

--The Public Use of Private Interest. 1977. 12.95 (ISBN 0-8157-7762-0); pap. 5.95 (ISBN 0-8157-7761-2). Brookings.

Schultze, Charles L., jt. auth. see Kneese, Allen V.

Schultze, Charles L., jt. ed. see Fried, Edward R.

Schultze, Charles L., et al. Setting National Priorities: The 1971 Budget. 1970. 14.95 (ISBN 0-8157-7750-7); pap. 5.95 (ISBN 0-8157-7749-3). Brookings.

Schultze, Donald E. All About Teaching: An Introduction to a Profession. 1977. pap. text ed. 8.25 (ISBN 0-8191-0205-9). U Pr of Amer.

Schultze-Motel, W., ed. Advances in Bryology, 1981, Vol.1. (Illus.). 562p. 1982. lib. bdg. 80.00x (ISBN 3-7682-1296-3). Lubrecht & Cramer.

Schulz, Ann. Local Politics & Nation-States: Case Studies in Politics & Policy. Merkl, Peter H., ed. LC 79-11416. (Studies in International & Comparative Politics: No. 12). 234p. 1979. text ed. 12.75 (ISBN 0-87436-289-X). ABC-Clio.

Schulz, Ann, jt. ed. see Marwah, Onkar.

Schulz, Ann T., ed. International & Regional Politics in the Middle East & North Africa: A Guide to Information Sources. LC 74-11568. (International Relations Information Guide Ser.: Vol. 6). 1977. 42.00x (ISBN 0-8103-1326-X). Gale.

Schulz, Anne M., et al. Studies in the History of Art 1979, Vol. 9. (Illus.). pap. 11.95 (ISBN 0-89468-051-X). Natl Gallery Art.

Schulz, Birger. Der Republikanische Richterbund (1921-1933) 211p. (Ger.). 1982. write for info. (ISBN 3-8204-7122-7). P Lang Pubs.

Schulz, Bruno. Sanatorium under the Sign of the Hourglass. 1979. pap. 4.95 (ISBN 0-14-005272-0). Penguin.

Schulz, Cecilia L. The Bland Diet Cookbook. LC 77-95135. 1978. 8.95 o.p. (ISBN 0-399-11857-8). Putnam Pub Group.

Schulz, Charles. Charlie Brown's All-Stars. (gr. 3 up). 1973. pap. 1.95 (ISBN 0-451-09937-0, AE9937, Sig). NAL.

--It Was a Short Summer, Charlie Brown. pap. 1.25 o.p. (ISBN 0-451-07958-2, Y7958, Sig). NAL.

--It's the Great Pumpkin, Charlie Brown. 1968. pap. 2.50 (ISBN 0-451-11538-4, AE1538, Sig). NAL.

--Snoopy Rockets & Spaceships. 48p. Date not set. pap. cancelled (ISBN 0-8431-0666-2). Price Stern.

--Snoopy Trucks & Trailers. 48p. Date not set. pap. cancelled (ISBN 0-8431-0665-4). Price Stern.

--There's No Time for Love, Charlie Brown. 1976. pap. 1.25 o.p. (ISBN 0-451-06886-6, Y6886, Sig). NAL.

Schulz, Charles M. Charlie Brown Christmas. (gr. 3 up). 1971. pap. 2.50 (ISBN 0-451-12307-7, AE2307, Sig). NAL.

--A Charlie Brown Thanksgiving. (Charlie Brown Ser). (gr. 3 up). 1974. 4.95 (ISBN 0-394-83047-4, BYR); PLB 6.99 (ISBN 0-394-93047-9). Random.

--Charlie Brown's Super Book of Questions & Answers About All Kinds of Animals from Snails to People. LC 75-39340. (Illus.). (gr. 3-6). 1976. 7.95 (ISBN 0-394-83249-3, BYR); PLB 9.99 (ISBN 0-394-93249-8). Random.

--Christmas Is Together Time. LC 80-65226. 1982. Repr. of 1981 ed. 6.95 (ISBN 0-915696-30-4). Determined Prods.

--Happiness Is a Warm Puppy. LC 82-70030. (Illus.). 1982. Repr. 4.95 (ISBN 0-915696-13-4). Determined Prods.

--I Need All the Friends I Can Get. LC 80-65225. (Illus.). 1982. Repr. of 1981 ed. 4.95 (ISBN 0-915696-29-0). Determined Prods.

--It's a Mystery, Charlie Brown. (Charlie Brown Ser.). (Illus.). 48p. (gr. 1 up). 1975. 4.95 (ISBN 0-394-83101-2, BYR); PLB 4.99 o.p. (ISBN 0-394-93101-7). Random.

--It's Chow Time, Snoopy! Selected Cartoons from Dr. Beagle & Mr. Hyde, Vol. I. (Illus.). 128p. 1983. pap. 1.95 (ISBN 0-449-20096-5, Crest). Fawcett.

--Love Is Walking Hand-in-Hand. LC 79-63490. (Illus.). 1982. Repr. of 1979 ed. 4.95 (ISBN 0-915696-14-2). Determined Prods.

--Security Is a Thumb & a Blanket. LC 82-70029. (Illus.). 1982. 6.95 (ISBN 0-686-82897-6). Determined Prods.

--Snoopy on Wheels. LC 82-60878. (Chunky Bks.). (Illus.). 28p. (ps). 1983. 2.95 (ISBN 0-394-85630-9). Random.

--Someday You'll Find Her, Charlie Brown. LC 82-3666. (Charlie Brown TV Specials Ser.). (Illus.). 48p. 1982. PLB 4.99 (ISBN 0-394-95429-7); pap. 4.95 (ISBN 0-394-85429-2). Random.

--You're in Love, Charlie Br own. 1970. pap. 1.75 o.p. (ISBN 0-451-09693-2, E9693, Sig). NAL.

--You're Not Elected Charlie Brown. pap. 1.25 o.p. (ISBN 0-451-07016-X, Y7016, Sig). NAL.

--You're Not Elected, Charlie Brown. (Illus.). (ps up). 1973. 1.95 (ISBN 0-394-83044-X); PLB 3.69 (ISBN 0-394-93044-4). Random.

Schulz, Charles M. & Dutton, June. Great Pumpkin Cookbook. LC 80-65224. 1981. pap. 4.95 (ISBN 0-915696-28-2). Determined Prods.

--Snoopy & the Gang Out West. LC 82-71284. (Illus.). 1982. 6.95 (ISBN 0-915696-55-X). Determined Prods.

Schulz, Charles M. & Kiliper, R. Smith. Charlie Brown, Snoopy & Me & All the Other Peanuts Characters. LC 80-923. (Illus.). 128p. 1980. 9.95a (ISBN 0-385-15805-X); PLB (ISBN 0-385-15806-8). Doubleday.

Schulz, Charles M., jt. auth. see Bayley, Monica.

Schulz, Charles M., jt. auth. see Mendelson, Lee.

Schulz, David A. Human Sexuality. (Illus.). 1979. pap. 18.95 ref. ed. (ISBN 0-13-447557-7). P-H.

Schulz, David A. & Rogers, Stanley F. Marriage, the Family & Personal Fulfillment. 2nd ed. (P-H Ser. in Sociology). (Illus.). 1980. text ed. 22.95 (ISBN 0-13-559385-9). P-H.

Schulz, David A., jt. auth. see Wilson, Robert A.

Schulz, Dora & Griesbach, Heinz. Deutsche Sprachlehre Fuer Auslaender. Incl. Grundstufe in einem Band. 5.80x o.p. (ISBN 0-685-47471-2); pap. text ed. 8.45x (ISBN 0-685-47472-0); glossar deutsch-englisch 3.25x (ISBN 0-685-47473-9); o.p. leseheft 1, by roland hils. (ISBN 0-685-47474-7); schuelerheft.contrastive grammar german-english 5.20x (ISBN 0-685-47475-5); Grundstufe. Ausgabe in zwei Baenden. pap. text ed. 7.80x Grundstufe 1. teil (ISBN 0-685-47476-3); pap. text ed. 8.45x grundstufe 2. teil (ISBN 0-685-47477-1); teaching supplement-phraseological glossary-key 5.20x (ISBN 0-685-47478-X); 2 tonbaender, aufnahme der lesetexte des buches und von uebungen, 9.5 cm/s, tapes 52.00x (ISBN 0-685-47479-8); Mittelstufe; Moderner Deutscher Sprachgebrauch.Ein Lehrgang Fuer Fortgeschrittene. pap. text ed. 12.25x (ISBN 0-685-47480-1); lehrerheft 4.90x (ISBN 0-685-47481-X); schuelerheft mit schluessel zuden uebungen 7.15x (ISBN 0-685-47482-8); 1 tonband, aufnahme von 28 lesetexten des lehrbuchs, 9.5 cm/s, tapes 31.20x **(ISBN 0-685-47483-6). pap. Schoenhof.**

Schulz, E. J. Diesel Mechanics. 2nd ed. 496p. 1983. 24.95x (ISBN 0-07-055639-3, G). McGraw.

Schulz, Eberhard, et al. GDR Foreign Policy. Stahnke, Arthur A., ed. Vale, Michel, tr. from Ger. LC 82-793. Orig. Title: Drei Jahrzehnte Aussenpolitik der DDR. 320p. 1982. 35.00 (ISBN 0-87332-203-7). M E Sharpe.

Schulz, Erich J. Diesel Equipment One: Lubrication, Hydraulics, Brakes, Wheels, Tires. Gilmore, D. E., ed. (Illus.). 56p. 1980. 20.95 (ISBN 0-07-055716-0, G); instructor's guide 4.50 (ISBN 0-07-055718-7); wkbk. 6.95 (ISBN 0-07-055717-9). McGraw.

--Diesel Equipment Two: Design, Electronic Controls, Frames, Suspensions, Steering, Transmissions, Drive Lines, Air Conditioning. Gilmore, D. E., ed. (Illus.). 64p. 1981. 21.95 (ISBN 0-07-055708-X, G); instr's. manual 4.00 (ISBN 0-07-055711-X); wkbk. 6.95 (ISBN 0-07-055709-8). McGraw.

--Diesel Mechanics. (Illus.). 1977. pap. text ed. 24.95 (ISBN 0-07-055664-4, G); wkbk. 11.95 (ISBN 0-07-055665-2); instr's guide 6.95 (ISBN 0-07-055666-0). McGraw.

Schulz, James H. The Economics of Aging. 2nd ed. 208p. 1979. pap. text ed. 9.95x (ISBN 0-534-00772-4). Wadsworth Pub.

Schulz, Martin, ed. Eiliptic Problem Solvers. 1981. 31.50 (ISBN 0-12-632620-7). Acad Pr.

Schulz, Max F. Black Humor Fiction of the Sixties: A Pluralistic Definition of Man & His World. LC 72-85538. xii, 156p. 1973. 12.95x (ISBN 0-8214-0125-4, 82-81271). Ohio U Pr.

--Black Humor Fiction of the Sixties: A Pluralistic Definition of Man & His World. LC 72-85538. 156p. 1980. pap. 5.95x (ISBN 0-8214-0574-8, 82-81289). Ohio U Pr.

--Bruce Jay Friedman. (United States Authors Ser.). 1974. lib. bdg. 13.95 (ISBN 0-8057-0290-3, Twayne). G K Hall.

Schulz, R. & Johnson, A. C. Management of Hospitals. 1975. 24.00 (ISBN 0-07-055651-2, HP). McGraw.

Schulz, Rockwell & Johnson, Alton C. Management of Hospitals. 2nd ed. 352p. 1983. 20.95x (ISBN 0-07-055652-0). McGraw.

Schulz, Wallace W. The Chemistry of Americium. LC 76-25824. (ERDA Critical Review Ser.). 300p. 1976. pap. 15.50 (ISBN 0-87079-040-4, TID-26971); microfiche 4.50 (ISBN 0-87079-163-X, TID-26971). DOE.

Schulz, Wallace W. & Benedict, Glen E. Neptunium-237 Production & Recovery. LC 72-600249. (AEC Critical Review Ser.). 94p. 1972. pap. 10.50 (ISBN 0-87079-001-3, TID-25955); microfiche 4.50 (ISBN 0-87079-465-5). DOE.

Schulz-Bischof, Elsbeth, et al, trs. see Baegert, Jacob.

Schulz-Dubois, E. D., jt. ed. see Arecchi, F. T.

Schulze, B. W., jt. auth. see Rempel, S.

Schulze, Helmut. Anwar-El Sadat: Stony Path to Peace. Madam Sadat, ed. 228p. cancelled 22.95 (ISBN 0-531-09878-8). Watts.

Schulze, Joyce E. The Wang Self-Teaching Program. 125p. 1982. looseleaf bound 295.00 (ISBN 0-935506-06-3); 9 cassette lessons incl. Carnegie Pr.

Schumacher, E. F. A Guide for the Perplexed. 1978. pap. 4.76i (ISBN 0-06-090611-1, CN 611, CN). Har-Row.

--A Guide for the Perplexed. LC 76-54381. 1979. pap. 1.95i o.p. (ISBN 0-06-080463-7, P-463, PL). Har-Row.

--Small Is Beautiful: Economics As If People Mattered. LC 73-12710. 304p. (YA) 1976. 12.45i (ISBN 0-06-013801-7, HarpT); pap. 5.95i (ISBN 0-06-090432-1, CN-432). Har-Row.

--Small Is Beautiful: Economics As If People Mattered. 304p. 1975. pap. 3.50i (ISBN 0-06-080352-5, P 352, PL). Har-Row.

Schumacher, E. F. & Gillingham, Peter N. Good Work. LC 76-5528. 1980. pap. 4.76i (ISBN 0-06-090561-1, CN 561, CN). Har-Row.

Schumacher, Evelyn A. Pray with the Psalmist. (Orig.). 1981. pap. 2.50 (ISBN 0-914544-33-0). Living Flame Pr.

Schumacher, F. Practical Problems in Mathematics for Sheet Metal Technicians. LC 71-74885. 1973. pap. text ed. 7.00 (ISBN 0-8273-0287-8); instructor's guide 2.75 (ISBN 0-8273-0288-6). Delmar.

Schumacher, F. W., jt. auth. see Zinngrabe, C. J.

Schumacher, Gary M., jt. auth. see Moates, Danny R.

Schumacher, H. G., jt. auth. see Hoover, T. W.

Schumacher, John N. Father Jose Burgos, Priest & Nationalist. (Illus.). 1972. wrps. 10.00x (ISBN 0-686-09513-8). Cellar.

--Revolutionary Clergy: The Filipino Clergy & the Nationalist Movement, 1850-1903. 306p. 1982. 36.00x (ISBN 0-686-37013-9, Pub. by Ateneo De Manila U Pr Philippines); pap. 20.00. Cellar.

Schumacher, William A., ed. Roman Replies, Nineteen Eighty-One. 46p. (Orig.). 1981. pap. 3.00x (ISBN 0-943616-09-3). Canon Law Soc.

Schuman, David. Policy Analysis, Education & Everyday Life: An Evaluation of Higher Education. 224p. 1981. pap. text ed. 8.95 (ISBN 0-669-04046-0). Heath.

--A Preface to Politics. 3rd ed. 240p. 1981. pap. text ed. 8.95 (ISBN 0-669-03591-2). Heath.

--A Preface to Politics. 2nd ed. 1977. pap. 8.95x o.p. (ISBN 0-669-00348-4). Heath.

Schuman, Dewey, ed. Headlines: A History of Santa Barbara for the Pages of Its Newspapers, 1855 to 1982. (Illus.). 264p. 1982. 19.95 (ISBN 0-88496-192-3); pap. 11.95 (ISBN 0-88496-191-5). Capra Pr.

Schuman, Howard & Hatchtt, Shirley. Black Racial Attitudes: Trends & Complexities. LC 74-620067. 160p. 1974. 12.00x (ISBN 0-87944-158-5). Inst Soc Res.

Schuman, Howard, jt. auth. see Converse, Jean M.

Schuman, Jo M. Art from Many Hands: Multicultural Art Projects for Home & School. (Illus.). 320p. 1980. 19.95 (ISBN 0-13-047217-4, Spec); pap. 8.95 (ISBN 0-13-047209-3). P-H.

Schuman, Leonard M., jt. ed. see Mortimer, James A.

Schuman, Patricia G. Materials for Occupational Education: An Annotated Source Guide. 2nd ed. (Neal-Schuman Sourcebook Ser.). 1983. 29.95 (ISBN 0-918212-17-0). Neal-Schuman.

Schuman, S. A., jt. ed. see Hibbard, P. G.

Schuman, Samuel. Cyril Tourneur. (English Author Ser.). 1980. lib. bdg. 14.95 (ISBN 0-8057-6690-1, Twayne). G K Hall.

--Vladimir Nabokov: A Reference Guide. 1979. lib. bdg. 26.00 (ISBN 0-8161-8134-9, Hall Reference). G K Hall.

Schuman, Tamara. The Parent Manual: Handbook for a Prepared Childbirth. 3rd ed. (Avery's Childbirth Education Ser.). (Illus.). 128p. 1983. pap. 5.50 (ISBN 0-89529-203-3). Avery Pub.

Schumann. Clinicians Guide to Diagnostic Cytology. 1982. 37.95 (ISBN 0-8151-7582-5). Year Bk Med.

Schumann, Elisabeth. German Song. LC 79-4136. (Illus.). 1980. Repr. of 1948 ed. lib. bdg. 16.00x (ISBN 0-313-20999-5, SCGE). Greenwood.

Schumann, John H. The Pidginization Process: A Model for Second Language Acquisition. LC 77-10920. 1978. pap. text ed. 9.95 o.p. (ISBN 0-88377-096-2). Newbury Hse.

Schumann, John H. & Stenson, Nancy. New Frontiers in Second Language Learning. 1975. pap. 9.95 o.p. (ISBN 0-912066-84-9). Newbury Hse.

Schumann, K. M. & Lauterbach, C. A. Die Flora der Deutschen Schutzgebiete in der Suedsee: With Suppl. 1976. 120.00 (ISBN 3-7682-1078-2). Lubrecht & Cramer.

Schumann, Marguerite. The Living Land: An Outdoor Guide to North Carolina. (Illus.). 178p. Date not set. pap. 4.25 o.p. (ISBN 0-914788-29-9). East Woods.

--Tar Heel Sights: Guide to North Carolina's Heritage. LC 82-49030. (Illus.). 192p. 1983. pap. 8.95 (ISBN 0-914788-64-7). East Woods.

Schumann, Paul L., jt. auth. see Ehrenberg, Ronald G.

Schumann, Robert. Great Works for Piano & Orchestra in Full Score (& Listing) (Music Scores, Music to Play Ser.). 183p. 1982. pap. 7.50 (ISBN 0-486-24340-0). Dover.

--Piano Music of Robert Schumann. Incl. Series I. 274p. pap. 8.95 (ISBN 0-486-21459-1); Series 2. 272p. pap. 7.95 (ISBN 0-486-21461-3). 1972. pap. Dover.

Schumann, Walter. Gemstones of the World. Tennissen, Anthony T., ed. LC 77-79503. (Illus.). 1977. 21.49 (ISBN 0-8069-3088-8); lib. bdg. 16.79 (ISBN 0-8069-3089-6). Sterling.

Schumer, Florence. Abnormal Psychology. 768p. Date not set. 23.95 (ISBN 0-686-82412-1); instr's guide 1.95 (ISBN 0-669-05630-8); 8.95 (ISBN 0-669-05628-6). Heath.

Schumer, William, jt. ed. see Lefer, Allan M.

Schumm, George, jt. auth. see Lemmon, E. J.

Schumm, Stanley A. The Fluvial System. LC 77-9333. 338p. 1977. 39.95 (ISBN 0-471-01901-1, Pub by Wiley-Interscience). Wiley.

Schumm, Stanley A., ed. Drainage Basin Morphology. LC 77-7365. (Benchmark Papers in Geology: Vol. 41). 1977. 48.50 (ISBN 0-12-787438-0). Acad Pr.

--River Morphology. LC 72-78310. (Benchmark Papers in Geology Ser.). 1972. pap. 42.00 (ISBN 0-12-787440-2). Acad Pr.

Schumm, Stanley A. & Mosley, Paul M., eds. Slope Morphology. LC 72-95135. (Benchmark Papers in Geology: Vol. 6). 454p. 1973. text ed. 55.00 (ISBN 0-87933-024-4). Hutchinson Ross.

Schumpeter, Joseph. Tthe Instability of Capitalism. (The Most Meaningful Classics in World Culture Ser.). (Illus.). 101p. 1981. Repr. of 1922 ed. 49.85 (ISBN 0-89266-302-2). Am Classical Coll Pr.

Schumpeter, Joseph A. The Theory of Economic Development. Opie, Redvers, tr. 1961. pap. 8.95x (ISBN 0-19-500461-2). Oxford U Pr.

--The Theory of Economic Development: An Inquiry into Profits, Capital, Credit, Interest & the Business Cycle. Opies, Redvers, tr. (Social Science Classics Ser.). 320p. Date not set. pap. 19.95 (ISBN 0-87855-698-2). Transaction Bks.

Schuncke, George & Krogh, Suzanne. Helping Children Choose. 1983. pap. text ed. 10.95 (ISBN 0-673-16622-8). Scott F.

Schunemann, Georg, ed. see Mozart, Wolfgang A.

Schupp, Orion E., ed. Gas Chromatography. (Technique of Organic Chemistry Ser.: Vol. 13). 437p. Repr. of 1968 ed. text ed. 36.50 (ISBN 0-470-93263-5). Krieger.

Schuppert, Mildred. Digest & Index of the Minutes of General Synod, 1958-1977. pap. 10.95 (ISBN 0-8028-1774-2). Eerdmans.

Schur, Edwin M. The Awareness Trap: Self-Absorption Instead of Social Change. LC 77-1243. 1977. pap. 3.95 (ISBN 0-07-055661-X, SP). McGraw.

--Labeling Deviant Behavior: Its Sociological Implications. (Demearath Ser). 1971. pap. text ed. 12.50 scp o.p. (ISBN 0-06-045812-7, HarpC). Har-Row.

--The Politics of Deviance: Stigma Contests & the Uses of Power. 256p. 1979. text ed. 12.95 (ISBN 0-13-684753-6, Spec); pap. text ed. 5.95 (ISBN 0-13-684746-3). P-H.

Schur, Norman W., ed. English English. 2nd ed. LC 77-20390. 332p. 1980. 42.00x (ISBN 0-8103-1096-1). Gale.

Schur, Peter H., ed. The Clinical Management of Systemic Lupus Erythematosus. Date not set. price not set (ISBN 0-8089-1543-6). Grune.

Schur, Sylvia. The Tappan Creative Cookbook for Microwave Ovens & Ranges. 1977. pap. 6.95 (ISBN 0-452-25312-8, Z5312, Plume). NAL.

--The Tappan Creative Cookbook for Microwave Ovens & Ranges. 1981. pap. 3.50 (ISBN 0-451-12039-6, AE2039, Sig). NAL.

Schure, Edouard. From Sphinx to Christ: An Occult History. LC 70-130818. (Spiritual Science Library). 288p. 1981. Repr. of 1970 ed. 14.00 (ISBN 0-89345-011-1, Steinerbks). Garber Comm.

--From Sphinx to Christ: An Occult History. 2nd ed. LC 82-47754. (Library of Spiritual Wisdom Ser.). (Orig.). 1982. pap. 7.64i (ISBN 0-06-067124-6, HarpR). Har-Row.

Schure, Edward. From Sphinx to Christ: An Occult History. 2nd ed. LC 70-130818. (Steiner Books Spiritual Science Library). 288p. 1981. lib. bdg. 14.00 (ISBN 0-89345-011-1). Garber Comm.

--Great Initiates: Secret History of Religions. LC 61-8623. (Steinerbooks Spiritual Science Library). 528p. 1982. Repr. of 1961 ed. 17.00 (ISBN 0-89345-025-1, Spiritual Sci Lib). Garber Comm.

Schurer, Emil. A History of the Jewish People in the Time of Jesus. Glatzer, Nahum N., ed. LC 61-8195. 1961. pap. 7.95 (ISBN 0-8052-0008-8). Schocken.

--The Literature of the Jewish People in the Time of Jesus. Glatzer, Nahum N., ed. LC 72-80038. 416p. 1972. 7.50 o.p. (ISBN 0-8052-3466-7); pap. 4.50 o.p. (ISBN 0-8052-0363-X). Schocken.

Schurer, Ernst. Georg Kaiser. (World Authors Ser.). lib. bdg. 13.95 (ISBN 0-8057-2480-X, Twayne). G K Hall.

Schurer, John, jt. auth. see Foy, Elizabeth.

Schurer, Marcia L., jt. auth. see Mutkoski, Stephen A.

Schurfranz, Vivian. Roman Hostage. LC 74-83607. (Historical Fiction Ser). 224p. (gr. 4-7). 1975. 6.95 o.s.i. (ISBN 0-695-80514-2); PLB 6.99 o.s.i. (ISBN 0-695-40514-4). Follett.

Schurr, B. Manual of Practical Pipeline Construction. 1982. 17.95 (ISBN 0-87201-696-X). Gulf Pub.

Schurr, Cathleen, jt. auth. see Gager, Nancy.

Schurr, Evelyn L. Movement Experience for Children: A Humanistic Approach to Elementary School Physical Education. 3rd ed. 1980. text ed. 22.95 (ISBN 0-13-604553-7). P-H.

Schurter, Neil, jt. auth. see Ewen, Dale.

Schurz, Carl. Charles Sumner: An Essay. Hogue, Arthur R., ed. LC 73-136083. 152p. 1972. Repr. of 1951 ed. lib. bdg. 15.00 o.p. (ISBN 0-8371-5233-X, SCSU). Greenwood.

Schusky, Ernest & Culbert, T. Patrick. Introducing Culture. 3rd ed. (P-H Anthropology Ser.). (Illus.). 1978. pap. 13.95 ref. (ISBN 0-13-477240-7). P-H.

Schusky, Ernest L. Introduction to Social Science. (Illus.). 512p. 1981. pap. text ed. 20.95 (ISBN 0-13-496703-8). P-H.

Schusky, Ernest L., ed. Political Organization of Native North Americans. LC 79-3715. 1980. text ed. 20.75 (ISBN 0-8191-0909-6); pap. text ed. 12.25 (ISBN 0-8191-0910-X). U Pr of Amer.

Schuss, Zeev. Theory & Applications of Stochastic Differential Equations. LC 80-14767. (Wiley Ser. in Probability & Mathematical Statistics: Applied Probability & Statistics). 321p. 1980. 33.95 (ISBN 0-471-04394-X). Wiley.

Schussler, Theodore. Conflict of Laws. 1981 ed. 200p. 1982. 10.50 (ISBN 0-87526-195-7). Gould.

--Constitutional Law. 328p. (1982 ed.). 1982. pap. text ed. 8.50 (ISBN 0-87526-072-1). Gould.

--Federal Courts, Jurisdiction & Practice. 152p. (Orig.). 1982. pap. 7.50x (ISBN 0-87526-036-5). Gould.

Schuster, Danny, jt. auth. see Jackson, David.

Schuster, E. H. Words Are Important: Primary Level (Tan) Bk. (gr. 4). 1979. pap. 1.80x (ISBN 0-8437-7983-7). Hammond Inc.

--Words Are Important Series. Incl. Level A (Blue) Bk. (gr. 5) (ISBN 0-8437-7985-3); Level B (Red) Bk. (gr. 6) (ISBN 0-8437-7991-8); Level C (Green) Bk. (gr. 7) (ISBN 0-8437-7980-2); Level D (Orange) Bk. (gr. 8) (ISBN 0-8437-7950-0); Level E (Purple) Bk. (gr. 9) (ISBN 0-8437-7955-1); Level F (Brown) Bk. (gr. 10) (ISBN 0-8437-7960-8); Level G (Pink) Bk. (gr. 11) (ISBN 0-8437-7965-9); Level H (Grey) Bk. (gr. 12) (ISBN 0-8437-7970-5). 1979. pap. 1.80x ea. Hammond Inc.

Schuster, E. H., jt. auth. see Guth, Hans P.

Schuster, Edgar H. Sentence Mastery, Bk. C. (Illus.). 160p. (gr. 9). 1981. 5.16 (ISBN 0-07-055623-7, W); tchr's manual 5.16 (ISBN 0-07-055633-4). McGraw.

--Sentence Mastery, Bks. A & B. Weeden, Hester E., ed. (Sentence Mastery Ser.). (Illus.). 160p. (gr. 7). 1980. A. 5.16 (ISBN 0-07-055621-0, W); B. 5.16 (ISBN 0-07-055622-9); tchr's manual A. 5.44 (ISBN 0-07-055631-8); tchr's manual B. 5.44 (ISBN 0-07-055632-6). McGraw.

Schuster, Edgar H., jt. auth. see Guth, Hans P.

Schuster, Fred E. Contemporary Issues in Human Resources Management. (Illus.). 496p. 1980. text ed. 23.95 (ISBN 0-8359-1005-9); instrs'. manual avail. (ISBN 0-8359-1006-7). Reston.

Schuster, George S. Oral Microbiology & Infectious Disease. 2nd ed. (Illus.). 470p. 1982. text ed. 29.95 student ed. (ISBN 0-683-07611-6). Williams & Wilkins.

Schuster, H. Experimentelle Untersuchungen Zur Schwermetallresistenz Von Sumersen Makrophyten. (Dissertationes Botanica 50 Ser.). (Illus., Ger.). 1980. pap. text ed. 16.00x (ISBN 3-7682-1229-7). Lubrecht & Cramer.

Schuster, H. J. Analyse und Bewertung Von Pflanzengesell-Schaften Im Noerdliche Frankenjura - ein Beitrag Zum Problem der Quantifizierung Unter-Schiedlich Anthropogen Beeinflusster Oekosystems. (Dissertationes Botanicae: No. 53). (Illus.). 482p. (Ger.). 1981. pap. text ed. 32.00x (ISBN 3-7682-1264-5). Lubrecht & Cramer.

Schuster, Peter, et al. The Hydrogen Bond: Recent Developments in Theory & Experiments, 3 vols. LC 76-373671. (Illus.). 1976. Set. 259.75 (ISBN 0-444-10805-X, North-Holland). Elsevier.

Schuster, R. M. An Annotated Synopsis of the Genera & Subgenera of Lejeuneacea, 1: Introduction, Annotated Keys to Subfamilies & Genera. 1963. 24.00 (ISBN 3-7682-5409-7). Lubrecht & Cramer.

--Boreal Hepaticae, a Manual of Liverworts of Minnesota & Adjacent Regions. (Bryophytorum Bibliotheca Ser.: No. 11). (Illus.). 1977. lib. bdg. 40.00x (ISBN 3-7682-1150-9). Lubrecht & Cramer.

--Studies in Cephaloziellaceae. (Illus.). 1977. 16.00 (ISBN 3-7682-0823-0). Lubrecht & Cramer.

Schut, Henry J. Ten Years to Live. 7.95 o.p. (ISBN 0-8010-8127-0). Baker Bk.

Schuter, Hans. Index Libycus: A Cumlative Index to Bibliography of Libya, 1915-1975. 1981. 25.00 (ISBN 0-8161-8534-4, Hall Reference). G K Hall.

Schuth, H. Wayne. Mike Nichols. (Filmmakers Ser.). 1978. lib. bdg. 12.95 (ISBN 0-8057-9255-4, Twayne). G K Hall.

Schutte, C. J. The Theory of Molecular Spectroscopy: The Quantum Mechanics & Group Theory of Vibrating & Rotating Molecules, 2 Vols. 1976. Vol. 1. 104.25 (ISBN 0-444-10627-8, North-Holland); Vol. 2. write for info. Elsevier.

Schutte, J. Everything You Always Wanted to Know About Elementary Statistics: But Were Afraid to Ask. (Methods of Social Science Ser.). 1977. 13.95 (ISBN 0-13-293506-6). P-H.

Schutte, William M. Index to Recurrent Elements in James Joyce's "Ulysses". LC 81-18274. 432p. 1982. 20.00x (ISBN 0-8093-1067-8). S Ill U Pr.

Schutte, William M. & Steinberg, Erwin R. Communication in Business & Industry. LC 74-13262. 414p. 1977. Repr. of 1960 ed. 18.50 (ISBN 0-88275-199-9). Krieger.

Schuttenberg, Ernest M. & Poppenhagen, Brent W. Field Experience in Postsecondary Education: A Guidebook for Action. LC 80-8242. 214p. 1980. pap. text ed. 12.75 (ISBN 0-8191-1212-7). U Pr of Amer.

Schutz, Albert J. Nguna Grammar. (Oceanic Linguistics Special Publication: No. 5). (Orig., Nguna & Eng). 1969. pap. text ed. 4.00x (ISBN 0-87022-744-0). UH Pr.

--Nguna Texts: A Collection of Traditional & Modern Narratives from the Central New Hebrides. (Oceanic Linguistics Special Publication: No. 4). (Orig., Nguna & Eng). 1969. pap. text ed. 8.00x (ISBN 0-87022-745-9). UH Pr.

Schutz, Albert J. & Komaitai, Rusiate T. Spoken Fijian. LC 76-157881. 304p. 1971. pap. text ed. 8.00x (ISBN 0-87022-746-7). UH Pr.

Schutz, Albert L. & Schaps, Hilda W. Caucasian Yoga. (Illus.). 140p. 12.95 o.p. (ISBN 0-936596-06-6); pap. 9.95 o.p. (ISBN 0-686-96936-7). Quantal.

Schutz, Alfred. Reflections on the Problem of Relevance. Zaner, Richard M., ed. LC 82-11850. xxiv, 186p. 1982. Repr. of 1970 ed. lib. bdg. 25.00x (ISBN 0-313-22820-5, SCRER). Greenwood.

Schutz, B. Geometrical Methods of Mathematical Physics. LC 80-40211. (Illus.). 300p. 1980. 44.50 (ISBN 0-521-23271-6); pap. 16.95 (ISBN 0-521-29887-3). Cambridge U Pr.

Schutz, J. H. Paul & the Anatomy of Apostolic Authority. LC 74-76573. (Society for New Testament Studies, Monographs: No. 26). 1975. 52.50 (ISBN 0-521-20464-X). Cambridge U Pr.

Schutz, John. Dawning of America: 1492-1789. LC 80-68812. (Orig.). 1981. pap. text ed. 10.95x (ISBN 0-88273-109-2). Forum Pr IL.

Schutz, John A. & Kirkendall, Richard S. The American Republic. LC 77-93846. (Illus.). 1978. text ed. 22.50x (ISBN 0-88273-251-X); Vol. 1, to 1877. pap. text ed. 12.95x (ISBN 0-88273-250-1); Vol. 2, since 1877. pap. text ed. 12.95x (ISBN 0-88273-252-8). Forum Pr IL.

Schutz, John A., ed. see Cherny, Robert W. & Issel, William.

Schutz, John A., ed. see Dasmann, Raymond F.

Schutz, John A., ed. see Hendrick, Irving G.

Schutz, John A., ed. see Hine, Robert V.

Schutz, John A., ed. see Olin, Spencer C., Jr.

Schutz, John A., ed. see Phillips, George H., Jr.

Schutz, John A., ed. see Putnam, Jackson K.

Schutz, John A., ed. see Rolle, Andrew, Jr.

Schutz, John A., ed. see Selvin, David F.

Schutz, Will. Leaders of Schools: FIRO Theory Applied to Administrators. LC 76-41489. 216p. 1977. pap. 8.50 (ISBN 0-88390-053-X). Univ Assocs.

Schutz, William C. The Interpersonal Underworld. LC 66-28683. 1966. pap. 7.95x (ISBN 0-8314-0011-0). Sci & Behavior.

Schutze, Frieda, tr. see Stresau, Hermann.

Schutzer, Daniel, jt. ed. see Hwang, John.

Schutzman, Steve. Smoke the Burning Body Makes. LC 78-2256. (Illus.). 1978. pap. 4.50 (ISBN 0-915572-28-1). Panjandrum.

Schuurman, C. J. Intrance: Fundamental Psychological Problems of the Inner & Outer World. Boer-Hoff, Louise E., tr. from Dutch. LC 78-70618. 1983. pap. 9.95 (ISBN 0-89793-023-1). Hunter Hse.

Schuyler, Arlene A. Wildflowers South Florida Natives: Indentification & Habitat of Indigenous Tropical Flora. Hall, Charlotte & Oppenheimer, Richard, eds. LC 82-90756. (Illus.). 112p. (Orig.). 1982. pap. 5.95 (ISBN 0-910991-00-6). Facts FL.

Schuyler, James. Freely Espousing. LC 79-24866. 92p. (Orig.). 1980. pap. 5.00 (ISBN 0-915342-28-6). SUN.

--Home Book. (Orig.). 1977. pap. 5.00 (ISBN 0-915990-05-9). Z Pr.

--What's for Dinner? 180p. 1978. 10.00 (ISBN 0-87685-382-3); ltd. signed ed. o.p. 15.00 (ISBN 0-87685-383-1); pap. 4.50 (ISBN 0-87685-381-5). Black Sparrow.

Schuyler, James, jt. auth. see Ashbery, John.

Schuyler, James, et al. ZZZZ. Elmslie, Kenward, ed. (Illus.). 96p. (Orig.). 1976. pap. 5.00 (ISBN 0-915990-03-2). Z Pr.

Schuyler, Montgomery. Index Verborum of the Fragments of the "Avesta". LC 2-15630. (Columbia University. Indo-Iranian Ser.: No. 4). Repr. of 1901 ed. 14.50 (ISBN 0-404-50474-4). AMS Pr.

Schvey, Henry I. Oskar Kokoschka: The Painter As Playwright. (Illus.). 160p. 1982. 25.00X (ISBN 0-8143-1702-2). Wayne St U Pr.

Schwab, Adolf J. High-Voltage Measurement Techniques. 1972. 25.00x o.s.i. (ISBN 0-262-19096-6). MIT Pr.

Schwab, Donald P., jt. auth. see Cummings, L. L.

Schwab, F. L., ed. Geosynclines: Concept & Place Within Plate Tectonics. LC 81-6807. (Benchmark Papers in Geology Ser.: Vol. 50). 432p. 1982. 52.00 (ISBN 0-87933-410-X). Hutchinson Ross.

Schwab, G. O., et al. Elementary Soil & Water Engineering. 2nd ed. LC 76-132224. 316p. 1978. 29.95x (ISBN 0-471-76526-0); Arabic Translation 8.80 (ISBN 0-471-04504-7). Wiley.

Schwab, George, ed. Eurocommunism: The Ideological & Political-Theoretical Foundations. (Contributions in Political Science: No. 60). (Illus.). xxvi, 325p. 1981. lib. bdg. 29.95x (ISBN 0-313-22908-2, SEU/). Greenwood.

--United States Foreign Policy at the Crossroads. LC 82-15588. (Contributions in Political Science Ser.: No. 96). 267p. 1982. lib. bdg. 29.95 (ISBN 0-313-23270-9, SFP/). Greenwood.

Schwab, Glenn O. & Frevert, Richard K. Soil & Water Conservation Engineering. 3rd ed. LC 80-27961. 525p. 1981. text ed. 37.95 (ISBN 0-471-03078-3); solutions manual avail. (ISBN 0-471-05018-0). Wiley.

Schwab, John J., jt. ed. see Masserman, J. H.

Schwab, Judith L. Recreation as a Forest Product. (Public Administration Ser.: Bibliography P 1096). 57p. 1982. pap. 8.25 (ISBN 0-88066-286-7). Vance Biblios.

Schwab, Peter, jt. ed. see Pollis, Adamantia.

Schwab, Richard, tr. see D'Alembert, Jean L.

Schwabacker, Eric. Capturing the Profit Potential of the Stock Market New Highs & New Lows. (Research Center for Economic Psychology Library). (Illus.). 138p. 1983. 53.45 (ISBN 0-86654-062-8). Inst Econ Finan.

Schwabe, Moshe & Lifshitz, Baruch. Beth She'arim, Vol. 2: The Greek Inscriptions. (Illus.). 256p. 1975. 30.00x o.p. (ISBN 0-8135-0762-6). Rutgers U Pr.

Schwabe-Braun, Angelika, jt. ed. see Tuexen, R.

Schwaiger, Konrad, jt. auth. see Kirchner, Emil.

Schwait, Allen L., jt. auth. see Garbis, Marvin J.

Schwalb, Ann W., ed. see Champlin, Connie.

Schwalb, Ann W., ed. see Hunt, Tamara & Renfro, Nancy.

Schwalb, Ann W., ed. see Renfro, Nancy.

Schwalb, Marvin N. & Miles, Philip G., eds. Genetics & Morphogenesis in the Basidiomycetes. 1978. 24.00 (ISBN 0-12-632050-0). Acad Pr.

Schwaller de Lubicz, Isha. The Opening of the Light: The Three Principles of Man's Awakening. Resnick, Susan, tr. from Fr. 350p. (Orig.). 1983. pap. 9.95 (ISBN 0-89281-038-6). Inner Tradit.

Schwaller de Lubicz, R. A. The Egyptian Miracle. VandenBroeck, A. & VandenBroeck, G., trs. from Fr. (Illus.). 320p. 1983. 16.95 (ISBN 0-89281-008-4). Inner Tradit.

--Esoterism & Symbol. VandenBroeck, Go & VandenBroeck, Andre, trs. 96p. 1983. pap. 5.95 (ISBN 0-89281-014-9). Inner Tradit.

--Nature Word: Verbe Nature. Lawlor, Deborah, tr. from French. & intro. by. LC 82-81069. (Illus.). 160p. (Orig.). 1982. pap. 6.95 (ISBN 0-940262-00-2). Lindisfarne Pr.

Schwalm, N. Daniel, Jr., ed. The Hessians of Lewis Miller. (Illus.). 30p. 1983. pap. 25.00 (ISBN 0-939016-07-9). Johannes Schwalm Hist.

--Journal of the Johannes Schwalm Historical Association, Vol. 2, No. 2. (Illus.). 62p. (Orig.). 1982. pap. 7.50 (ISBN 0-939016-06-0). Johannes Schwalm Hist.

Schwamm, Ellen. How He Saved Her. LC 82-48885. 1983. 13.95 (ISBN 0-394-52707-0). Knopf.

Schwan, Herman P. Biological Engineering. (Inter-University Electronics Ser). (Illus.). 1969. text ed. 29.50 o.p. (ISBN 0-07-055734-9, C). McGraw.

Schwan, W. Creighton, jt. auth. see Richter, Herbert P.

Schwanauer, Francis. The Flesh of Thought is Pleasure or Pain. LC 82-17674. 136p. (Orig.). 1983. pap. text ed. 8.75 (ISBN 0-8191-2765-5). U Pr of Amer.

--No Many Is Not a One (For the Case Is a Comparison) LC 80-6173. 66p. (Orig.). 1981. pap. text ed. 6.00 o.p. (ISBN 0-8191-1455-3). U Pr of Amer.

--Those Fallacies by Slight of Reason. 1978. pap. text ed. 8.00 (ISBN 0-8191-0619-4). U Pr of Amer.

--To Make Sure is to Cohere. LC 82-17653. 94p. (Orig.). 1983. pap. text ed. 7.50 (ISBN 0-8191-2766-3). U Pr of Amer.

--Truth Is a Neighborhood with Nothing in Between. 127p. 1977. pap. text ed. 8.00 (ISBN 0-8191-0240-7). U Pr of Amer.

--Wahrheit Ist eine Nachbarschaft, Die Nichts Trennt. 196p. (Ger.). 1980. pap. text ed. 10.00 (ISBN 0-8191-0995-9). U Pr of Amer.

Schwandt, P. Risk & Prevention of Arterial Lipidoses. 300p. 1983. 37.50 (ISBN 0-87527-232-0). Green.

Schware, Robert, jt. auth. see Kellogg, William W.

Schwark, Bryan L., jt. auth. see Camp, William L.

Schwarta, M. M. Source Book on Innovative Welding Processes. 1981. 46.00 (ISBN 0-87170-105-7). ASM.

Schwartz. Breast Disease: Diagnosis & Treatment. 1982. 55.00 (ISBN 0-444-00593-5). Elsevier.

Schwartz, A., jt. auth. see Archer, Jerome W.

Schwartz, Alan & Scott, Robert E. Commercial Transactions Principles & Policies. (University Casebook Ser.). 1104p. 1982. text ed. write for info. tchr's manual (ISBN 0-88277-121-3); pap. write for info. Foundation Pr.

--Sales Law & the Contracting Process. LC 82-82575. (University Casebook Ser.). 512p. 1982. text ed. write for info. (ISBN 0-88277-077-2). Foundation Pr.

Schwartz, Alan U., jt. auth. see Ernst, Morris L.

Schwartz, Alvin. Busy Buzzing Bumblebees. LC 81-48639. (I Can Read Bk.). (Illus.). 64p. (gr. k-3). 1982. pap. 2.84i (ISBN 0-06-444036-2, Trophy). Har-Row.

--Busy Buzzing Bumblebees. LC 81-48639. (A Trophy I Can Read Bk.). 64p. (gr. k-3). 1982. pap. 2.84 (ISBN 0-06-444036-2, Trophy). Har-Row.

--Chin Music: Tall Talk & Other Talk. LC 79-2403. (Illus.). (gr. 5 up). 1979. 9.57i (ISBN 0-397-31869-3, JBL-J); PLB 9.89 (ISBN 0-397-31870-7); pap. 3.95 (ISBN 0-397-31871-5). Har-Row.

--Cross Your Fingers, Spit in Your Hat. LC 73-21912. (Illus.). 160p. (gr. 4 up). 1974. 9.57i (ISBN 0-397-31530-9, JBL-J); pap. 2.95 (ISBN 0-397-31531-7). Har-Row.

--Flapdoodle: Pure Nonsense from American Folklore. LC 79-9618. (Illus.). 128p. (gr. 5up). 1980. 9.57 (ISBN 0-397-31919-3, JBL-J); PLB 8.89 o.p. (ISBN 0-397-31920-7); pap. 3.95 (ISBN 0-397-31921-5, JBL-J). Har-Row.

--Kickle Snifters & Other Fearsome Critters. LC 75-29048. (gr. k-4). 1976. 9.57i (ISBN 0-397-31645-3, JBL-J). Har-Row.

--Scary Stories to Tell in the Dark. LC 80-8728. (Illus.). 128p. (gr. 5 up). 1981. 9.57i (ISBN 0-397-31926-6, JBL-J); PLB 9.89g (ISBN 0-397-31927-4); pap. 4.95i (ISBN 0-397-31970-3). Har-Row.

--There Is a Carrot in My Ear & Other Noodle Tales. LC 80-8442. (I Can Read Bk.). (Illus.). 64p. (gr. k-3). 1982. 7.64i (ISBN 0-06-025233-2, HarpJ); PLB 8.89g (ISBN 0-06-025234-0). Har-Row.

--Tomfoolery: Trickery & Foolery with Words. LC 72-12900. 128p. (gr. 10 up). 1973. 9.57i (ISBN 0-397-31466-3, JBL-J); pap. 2.50 (ISBN 0-397-31467-1). Har-Row.

--A Twister of Twists, a Tangler of Tongues. LC 72-1434. (Illus.). 126p. (gr. 6 up). 1972. 9.57i (ISBN 0-397-31387-X, JBL-J); pap. 1.95 (ISBN 0-397-31412-4, LSC-22). Har-Row.

Schwartz, Amy. Bea & Mr. Jones. LC 81-18031. (Illus.). 32p. (ps-2). 1982. 8.95 (ISBN 0-02-781430-0). Bradbury Pr.

--Begin at the Beginning. LC 82-48257. (Illus.). 32p. (ps-3). 1983. 8.61i (ISBN 0-06-025227-8, HarpJ); PLB 8.89g (ISBN 0-06-025228-6). Har-Row.

Schwartz, Anthony M., et al. Surface Active Agents: Vol 1 - Their Chemistry & Technology. LC 74-11051. 592p. 1979. Repr. of 1949 ed. lib. bdg. 30.50 (ISBN 0-88275-684-2). Krieger.

--Surface Active Agents: Vol. 2, Agents & Detergents. exp. ed. LC 74-11051. 888p. 1977. Repr. of 1958 ed. 40.00 o.p. (ISBN 0-88275-157-3). Krieger.

Schwartz, Arthur. Survival Handbook for Children of Aging Parents. 1977. pap. 6.95 (ISBN 0-695-80811-7). Follett.

Schwartz, Arthur P., jt. auth. see Frishman, Austin M.

Schwartz, Audrey J. The Schools & Socialization. (Critical Issues in Education Ser.). 204p. 1975. pap. text ed. 11.50 scp o.p. (ISBN 0-06-045823-2, HarpC). Har-Row.

Schwartz, B. Clinical Venereology. 1966. pap. 9.75 (ISBN 0-08-011601-9). Pergamon.

Schwartz, B., et al. Statutory History of the United States, 3 vols. Incl. Vol. 1. Civil Rights. Schwartz, B. 80.00 o.p. (ISBN 0-07-055681-4); Vol. 2. Labor Relations. Koretz, R. 50.00 o.p. (ISBN 0-07-055682-2); Vol. 3. Income Security. Stevens, R. L. 50.00 o.p. (ISBN 0-07-055683-0). 1970. 135.00 set o.p. (ISBN 0-07-079799-4, P&RB). McGraw.

Schwartz, Barry. Psychology of Learning & Behavior. 2nd ed. 440p. 1983. 19.95x (ISBN 0-393-95276-2). Norton.

--Psychology of Learning & Behavior: Essays on Behavior Theory. 500p. 1982. pap. text ed. 14.95x (ISBN 0-393-95305-X). Norton.

Schwartz, Benjamin. In Search of Wealth & Power: Yen Fu & the West. 320p. 1983. pap. text ed. 7.95x (ISBN 0-674-44652-6, Belknap Pr). Harvard U Pr.

Schwartz, Benjamin, jt. ed. see Rosemont, Henry.

Schwartz, Bernard. Administrative Law: A Casebook. 1977. 22.50 o.p. (ISBN 0-316-77563-0). Little.

--Administrative Law: A Casebook. LC 82-18494. 1982. text ed. 26.50 (ISBN 0-316-77566-5). Little.

--Administrative Law: A Textbook. 1976. 19.95 (ISBN 0-316-77560-6). Little.

--Administrative Law: A Textbook. 1980. pap. 19.00 tchr's manual o.p. (ISBN 0-316-77564-9). Little.

--A Commentary on the Constitution of the United States, 3 pts. in 5 vols. LC 77-79328. 1977. Repr. of 1968 ed. lib. bdg. 27.50x ea. (ISBN 0-8377-1108-8); lib. bdg. 137.50 set price. Rothman.

--The Great Rights of Mankind: A History of the American Bill of Rights. LC 76-42646. 1977. 19.95x (ISBN 0-19-502191-6). Oxford U Pr.

Schwartz, Bernard & Lesher, Stephen. Final Judgement: Inside the Warren Court 1953-69. LC 82-45454. (Illus.). 264p. 1983. 16.95 (ISBN 0-385-18326-7). Doubleday.

Schwartz, Bernard & Wade, H. W. Legal Control of Government: Administrative Law in Britain & the United States. 1972. 49.00x (ISBN 0-19-825315-X). Oxford U Pr.

Schwartz, Bernard, ed. American Law: The Third Century: the Law Bicentennial Volume. LC 76-50507. iv, 454p. 1976. text ed. 22.50x (ISBN 0-8377-0204-6); text ed. 37.50x limited signed, boxed ed. (ISBN 0-8377-0205-4). Rothman.

Schwartz, Betty, ed. see Cahn, Julie.

Schwartz, Bob. Diets Don't Work. rev. ed. LC 82-70262. (Illus.). 204p. (Orig.). Date not set. 14.95 (ISBN 0-942540-01-8); pap. 9.95 (ISBN 0-942540-02-6). Breakthru Pub.

Schwartz, Brian. China off the Beaten Track. (Illus.). 256p. 1983. pap. 10.95 (ISBN 0-312-13304-9). St Martin.

Schwartz, Charles, jt. auth. see Schwartz, Elizabeth.

Schwartz, Charles D. & Schwartz, Ouida D. A Flame of Fire: The Story of Troy Annual Conference. LC 82-70624. (Illus.). 376p. (Orig.). 1982. pap. text ed. 15.00x (ISBN 0-914960-38-5). Academy Bks.

Schwartz, Charles F., ed. see U. S. Office Of Business Economics.

Schwartz, Cipora. How to Run a School Board Campaign & Win. 142p. (Orig.). 1982. pap. 5.95 (ISBN 0-934460-19-1). NCCE.

Schwartz, Daniel. The National Directory of Income Opportunities. LC 77-95320. 1978. 15.00 o.p. (ISBN 0-87863-153-4). Farnswth Pub.

Schwartz, David. Introduction to Management: Principles, Practices, & Processes. 649p. 1980. text ed. 19.95 o.p. (ISBN 0-15-543423-3, HC); Instructor's resource manual avail. o.p. (ISBN 0-15-543424-1); study guide 7.95 o.p. (ISBN 0-15-543425-X). HarBraceJ.

Schwartz, David J. The Magic of Getting What You Want. 224p. 1983. 11.95 (ISBN 0-688-01824-6). Morrow.

--Magic of Thinking Big. 1959. 10.95 o.p. (ISBN 0-13-545178-7). P-H.

--Marketing Today: A Basic Approach. 2nd ed. (Illus.). 1977. text ed. 17.95 o.p. (ISBN 0-15-555086-1, HC); instructor's manual avail. o.p. (ISBN 0-15-555087-X); "Marketing Words & Concepts" 4.95 o.p. (ISBN 0-15-555088-8). HarBraceJ.

--Marketing Today: A Basic Approach. 3rd ed. 630p. 1981. text ed. 22.95 (ISBN 0-15-555089-6); tchr's. manual with tests 2.95 (ISBN 0-15-555090-X); wkbk. 7.95 (ISBN 0-15-555092-6). HarBraceJ.

Schwartz, David J., jt. auth. see Mauser, Ferdinand F.

Schwartz, David M., jt. auth. see Weiner, Neal O.

Schwartz, Delmore. I Am Cherry Alive, the Little Girl Sang. LC 76-58708. (Illus.). (ps-3). 1979. 7.95i o.p. (ISBN 0-06-025243-X, HarpJ); PLB 7.79 (ISBN 0-06-025244-8). Har-Row.

Schwartz, Doris R. Faculty Research Development Grants: A Follow-up Report. (League Exchange Ser.: No. 125). 52p. 1981. 5.95 (ISBN 0-686-38311-7, 14-1835). Natl League Nurse.

Schwartz, Douglas W., et al. Archaeology of the Grand Canyon: Unkar Delta. LC 80-21667. (Grand Canyon Archaeological Ser.: Vol. 2). (Illus.). 405p. (Orig.). 1981. pap. 15.00 (ISBN 0-933452-04-7). Schol Am Res.

--Archaeology of the Grand Canyon: The Walhalla Plateau. LC 81-5730. (Grand Canyon Archaeological Ser.: Vol. 3). (Illus.). 250p. (Orig.). 1981. pap. 12.00 (ISBN 0-933452-06-3). Schol Am Res.

Schwartz, Edmund & Landovitz, Leon. Funk & Wagnall's Crossword Puzzle Word Finder. LC 79-84768. 1979. pap. 6.95 o.p. (ISBN 0-448-15709-8, G&D). Putnam Pub Group.

Schwartz, Edmund I. & Landovitz, Leon F. Funk & Wagnall's Crossword Puzzle Word Finder. 768p. Date not set. pap. price not set (ISBN 0-448-15709-8, G&D). Putnam Pub Group.

Schwartz, Eli, jt. ed. see Aronson, J. Richard.

Schwartz, Elizabeth & Schwartz, Charles. When Flying Animals Are Babies. LC 73-78456. (Illus.). (gr. k-3). 1973. PLB 4.95 (ISBN 0-8234-0229-0). Holiday.

Schwartz, Elroy. Tulsa Gold. (Orig.). 1981. pap. 2.75 o.p. (ISBN 0-451-09566-9, E9566, Sig). NAL.

Schwartz, Elroy, jt. auth. see Woodbury, John.

Schwartz, Estelle R. & Potter, Lillian F. Foundations of Patient Care: Basic Principles for the Health Occupations. (Illus.). 374p. 1981. text ed. 15.75 (ISBN 0-397-54261-5, Lippincott Nursing); pap. text ed. 11.50 (ISBN 0-397-54260-7). Lippincott.

Schwartz, Eugene M. Mail Order: How to Get Your Share of the Hidden Profits That Exist in Your Business. 288p. 1982. 50.00 (ISBN 0-932648-33-9). Boardroom.

Schwartz, Federico. El Corazon Del Comunismo. Moore, Cecil, tr. from English. 1977. pap. 0.60 cancelled (ISBN 0-311-14204-4, Edit Mundo). Casa Bautista.

Schwartz, Florence. Vegetable Cooking of All Nations. (International Cook Book). 1973. 7.95 o.p. (ISBN 0-517-50097-3). Crown.

Schwartz, Gail G. Advanced Industrialization & the Inner Cities. LC 79-3744. (Urban Round Table Ser.). 192p. 1981. 21.95x (ISBN 0-669-03512-2). Lexington Bks.

Schwartz, Gail G. & Choate, Pat. Being Number One: Rebuilding the U. S. Economy. 160p. 1980. 17.95x (ISBN 0-669-04308-7). Lexington Bks.

Schwartz, Gary E., jt. ed. see Davidson, Richard J.

Schwartz, Gordon F. & Markham, Margaret. The Breast Book. (Illus.). 416p. (Orig.). Date not set. pap. cancelled (ISBN 0-448-14347-X, G&D). Putnam Pub Group.

Schwartz, H., ed. Multivariable Technical Control Systems, 4 vols. 1972. Set. 85.00 (ISBN 0-444-10335-X, North-Holland). Elsevier.

Schwartz, Hans-Peter, jt. ed. see Kaiser, Karl.

Schwartz, Helen. The New Jersey House. (Illus.). 238p. 1983. 25.00 (ISBN 0-8135-0965-3); pap. 14.95 (ISBN 0-8135-0990-4). Rutgers U Pr.

Schwartz, Helene. Lawyering. 368p. 1976. 10.00 o.p. (ISBN 0-374-18422-4); pap. 3.95 (ISBN 0-374-51394-5). FS&G.

Schwartz, Howard. Elijah's Violin & Other Jewish Fairy Tales. LC 82-48133. (Illus.). 272p. 1983. 14.95 (ISBN 0-06-015108-0, HarpT). Har-Row.

--Imperial Messages. 1976. pap. 2.50 o.p. (ISBN 0-380-00682-0, 28860, Bard). Avon.

Schwartz, Howard & Jacobs, Jerry. Qualitative Sociology: A Method to the Madness. LC 78-58915. 1979. 19.95 (ISBN 0-02-928170-9); pap. text ed. 10.95 (ISBN 0-02-928160-1). Free Pr.

Schwartz, Jackie. Letting Go of Stress. 352p. (Orig.). 1982. pap. 3.95 (ISBN 0-523-42028-5). Pinnacle Bks.

Schwartz, Jane T. & Schwartz, Lawrence H. Vulnerable Infants: A Psychosocial Dilemma. new ed. (Illus.). 1977. pap. text ed. 17.95 (ISBN 0-07-055764-0, HP). McGraw.

Schwartz, Janet, jt. auth. see Federico, Ronald C.

Schwartz, Jeon-Michael. The Mystery of Easter Island. 1975. pap. 1.95 o.p. (ISBN 0-380-00419-4, 38455). Avon.

Schwartz, Jerome L., jt. ed. see Nolan, Robert L.

Schwartz, Jesse G, ed. A Subtle Anatomy of Capitalism: Selected Readings. LC 76-26192. (Illus.). 1977. pap. 17.95x (ISBN 0-673-16177-3). Scott F.

Schwartz, Joel. Upchuck Summer. (gr. k-6). 1983. pap. 2.25 (ISBN 0-440-49264-5, YB). Dell.

Schwartz, Jonathan. Distant Stations. 320p. 1980. pap. 2.50 o.p. (ISBN 0-380-50583-5, 50583). Avon.

Schwartz, Joseph. Hart Crane: A Reference Guide. 251p. 1983. 36.00 (ISBN 0-8161-8493-3). G K Hall.

Schwartz, Judy I., ed. Teaching the Linguistically Diverse. 138p. 9.00 (ISBN 0-686-95321-5); members 7.50 (ISBN 0-686-99495-7). NCTE.

Schwartz, Jules J. Corporate Policy: A Casebook. (Illus.). 1978. 24.95 (ISBN 0-13-174813-0). P-H.

Schwartz, Julius. Earthwatch: Space-Time Investigations with a Globe. (Illus.). 64p. (gr. 7-9). 1977. PLB 8.95 (ISBN 0-07-055685-7, GB). McGraw.

Schwartz, Laurent. Application des Distributions a l'Etude des Particles Elementaires en Mecanique Quantique. (Cours & Documents de Mathematiques & de Physique Ser.). 148p. (Fr.). 1969. 35.00 (ISBN 0-677-50090-4). Gordon.

--Application of Distributions to the Theory of Elementary Particles in Quantum Mechanics. LC 68-17535. (Documents on Modern Physics Ser.). (Illus.). 144p. 1968. 40.00x (ISBN 0-677-30090-5). Gordon.

--Random Measures on Arbitrary Topological Spaces & Cylindrical Measures. (Tata Institute of Fundamental Research Studies in Mathematics Ser). 1974. text ed. 15.00x o.p. (ISBN 0-19-560516-0). Oxford U Pr.

Schwartz, Lawrence H., jt. auth. see Schwartz, Jane T.

Schwartz, Leni. The Environment of the Pregnant Year: A Guide to Prenatal Bonding for Expectant Parents. 342p. 1980. cancelled o.p. (ISBN 0-399-90090-X, Marek). Putnam Pub Group.

--The World of the Unborn: Nurturing Your Child Before Birth. 1981. 12.95 o.s.i. (ISBN 0-399-90090-X, Marek). Putnam Pub Group.

Schwartz, Leo W., ed. Great Ages & Ideas of the Jewish People. 6.95 (ISBN 0-394-60413-X). Modern Lib.

Schwartz, Leonard, jt. auth. see Schwartz, Roslyn.

Schwartz, Lester & Brechner, Irv. The Career Finder: Pathways to over 1500 Careers. LC 82-90224. 352p. 1983. pap. 8.95 (ISBN 0-345-29772-5). Ballantine.

Schwartz, Lita L. American Education: A Problem-Centered Approach. 3rd ed. LC 78-62182. 1978. pap. text ed. 15.00 (ISBN 0-8191-0508-2). U Pr of Amer.

Schwartz, Lloyd & Estess, Sybil P. Elizabeth Bishop & Her Art. (Under Discussion Ser.). (Illus.). 328p. 1982. 18.50 (ISBN 0-472-09343-6); pap. 8.95 (ISBN 0-472-06343-X). U of Mich Pr.

Schwartz, Louis E. Proof Persuasion & Cross-Examination: A Winning New Approach in the Courtroom. 1973. 74.50 (ISBN 0-13-730820-5). Exec Reports.

Schwartz, Lynne S. The Accounting. (Chapbook Ser.). 32p. 1983. pap. 10.00 (ISBN 0-915778-50-5); deluxe ed. 75.00 deluxe ed. (ISBN 0-915778-49-1); pap. 35.00 signed (ISBN 0-915778-51-3). Penmaen Pr.

--Balancing Acts. LC 80-8366. 224p. 1981. 11.49i (ISBN 0-06-013702-9, HarpT). Har-Row.

--Rough Strife. LC 79-2740. 1980. 11.49i (ISBN 0-06-014024-0, HarpT). Har-Row.

Schwartz, M. Computer-Communications Network Design & Analysis. 1977. 34.95 (ISBN 0-13-165134-X); sol. manual 4.00 (ISBN 0-13-165159-5). P-H.

Schwartz, M. K., jt. ed. see Latner, A. L.

Schwartz, M. M. Metals Joining Manual. (Illus.). 1979. 26.95 (ISBN 0-07-055720-9, P&RB). McGraw.

--Source Book on Brazing & Brazing Technology. 1980. 46.00 (ISBN 0-87170-099-9). ASM.

--Source Book on Electron Beam & Laser Welding. 1981. 46.00 (ISBN 0-87170-104-9). ASM.

Schwartz, Mark, jt. auth. see Kahlenberg, Mary H.

Schwartz, Marla S., jt. auth. see Goss, Dinah B.

Schwartz, Martin F. Stuttering Solved. LC 75-42456. (Illus.). 1976. 9.95i (ISBN 0-397-01134-2). Har-Row.

Schwartz, Marvin. Physiological Psychology. 2nd ed. LC 77-17438. (Century Psychology Ser.). (Illus.). 1978. ref. ed. 24.95 (ISBN 0-13-674895-3). P-H.

Schwartz, Marvin D. American Furniture of the Colonial Period. LC 76-18763. (Illus.). 1976. 4.95 (ISBN 0-87099-149-3). Metro Mus Art.

--Chairs, Tables, Sofas, & Beds. LC 82-47846. (Collector's Guides to American Antiques Ser.). 1982. 13.95 (ISBN 0-394-71269-2). Knopf.

Schwartz, Maurice, ed. The Encyclopedia of Beaches & Coastal Environments. (Encyclopedia of Earth Sciences Ser.: Vol. 15). 1982. cancelled (ISBN 0-12-787449-6). Acad Pr.

Schwartz, Maurice L., ed. Barrier Islands. LC 73-12838. (Benchmark Papers in Geology Ser.). 464p. 1973. text ed. 50.00 o.p. (ISBN 0-12-787447-X). Acad Pr.

--Spits & Bars. LC 72-88983. (Benchmark Papers in Geology Ser). 1973. text ed. 55.00 (ISBN 0-12-787448-8). Acad Pr.

Schwartz, Max. Civil Engineering for the Plant Engineer. 304p. 1983. Repr. of 1972 ed. lib. bdg. write for info. (ISBN 0-89874-050-9). Krieger.

Schwartz, Max, jt. auth. see Besselievre, Edmond.

Schwartz, Mel M. Composite Materials Handbook. (Illus.). 704p. 1983. 34.50 (ISBN 0-07-055743-8, P&RB). McGraw.

--Modern Metal Joining Techniques. LC 71-82976. 1969. 44.95 o.p. (ISBN 0-471-76615-1, Pub. by Wiley-Interscience). Wiley.

Schwartz, Melvin. Information, Transmission, Modulation & Noise. 2nd ed. 1970. text ed. 29.95 (ISBN 0-07-055761-6, C); solutions manual 7.95 (ISBN 0-07-020115-3). McGraw.

--Principles of Electrodynamics. (International Ser. in Pure & Applied Physics). (Illus.). 368p. 1972. text ed. 25.95 o.p. (ISBN 0-07-055675-X, C). McGraw.

Schwartz, Michael. Radical Protest & Social Structure: The Southern Farmer's Alliance & Cotton Tenancy, 1880-1890. (Studies in Social Discontinuity Ser.). 1976. 34.50 (ISBN 0-12-632850-1). Acad Pr.

Schwartz, Michael, ed. The Structure of Power in America: The Corporate Elite As a Ruling Class. 260p. 1983. text ed. 34.00x (ISBN 0-8419-0764-1); pap. text ed. 17.50x (ISBN 0-8419-0765-X). Holmes & Meier.

Schwartz, Mischa. Information Transmission, Modulation & Noise: A Unified Approach. rev. ed. (McGraw-Hill Electrical & Electronic Engineering Ser.). (Illus.). 672p. 1980. text ed. 37.50 (ISBN 0-07-055782-9); solutions manual 15.00 (ISBN 0-07-055783-7). McGraw.

Schwartz, Mischa & Shaw, L. Signal Processing: Discrete Spectral Analysis, Detection & Estimation. text ed. 37.95 (ISBN 0-07-055662-8, C). McGraw.

Schwartz, Mischa, et al. Communication Systems & Techniques. (Inter-University Electronics Ser.). 1966. 57.50 (ISBN 0-07-055754-3, P&RB). McGraw.

Schwartz, Morris S. & Shockley, Emmy L. Nurse & the Mental Patient: A Study of Interpersonal Relations. 284p. 1956. pap. 14.50x (ISBN 0-471-76610-0, Pub. by Wiley-Medical). Wiley.

Schwartz, Mortimer. Environmental Law: A Guide to Information Sources. LC 73-17541. (Man & the Environment Information Guide Series: Vol. 6). 1977. 42.00x (ISBN 0-8103-1339-1). Gale.

Schwartz, Mortimer D., jt. auth. see Rabin, Edward H.

Schwartz, Mortimer D., ed. Conference on Space Science & Space Law: Proceedings. (Illus.). x, 176p. 1964. pap. text ed. 6.75x (ISBN 0-8377-1100-2). Rothman.

Schwartz, Morton. Soviet Perceptions of the United States. LC 76-7767. 1978. 22.50x (ISBN 0-520-03234-9); pap. 4.95 (ISBN 0-520-04094-5, CAL NO. 455). U of Cal Pr.

Schwartz, Murray. Law & the American Future: An American Assembly Book. 1976. 9.95 o.p. (ISBN 0-13-526061-2, Spec); pap. 4.95 o.p. (ISBN 0-13-526053-1, Spec). P-H.

Schwartz, N. L. & Schwartz, S. The Hollywood Writers' Wars. 352p. 1983. pap. 8.95 (ISBN 0-07-055791-8, GB). McGraw.

Schwartz, Narda Lacey. Articles on Women Writers, 1960-1975: A Bibliography. LC 77-9071. 236p. 1977. text ed. 26.50 o.p. (ISBN 0-87436-252-0). ABC-Clio.

Schwartz, Neena B. & Hunzicker-Dunn, Mary, eds. Dynamics of Ovarian Function. 350p. 1981. text ed. 42.50 (ISBN 0-89004-594-1). Raven.

Schwartz, Ouida D., jt. auth. see Schwartz, Charles D.

Schwartz, Pepper, jt. auth. see Laws, Judith L.

Schwartz, Peter, et al. Fabric Forming Systems. LC 82-7967. (Textile Ser.). (Illus.). 175p. 1983. 24.00 (ISBN 0-8155-0908-1). Noyes.

Schwartz, Peter J., et al, eds. Neural Mechanisms in Cardiac Arrhythmias. LC 77-77962. (Perspectives in Cardiovascular Research Ser.: Vol. 2). 460p. 1978. 45.00 (ISBN 0-89004-209-8). Raven.

Schwartz, Richard B. Samuel Johnson & the Problem of Evil. LC 74-27314. 128p. 1975. 22.50 (ISBN 0-299-06790-4). U of Wis Pr.

Schwartz, Richard F., jt. auth. see Spitzer, Harry.

Schwartz, Robert, jt. auth. see Condemi, John J.

Schwartz, Robert A., jt. auth. see Bloch, Ernest.

Schwartz, Robert M., ed. see MassCOSH Legal Committee.

Schwartz, Robert N., ed. see Kevan, Larry.

Schwartz, Ronald. Jose Maria Gironella. (World Authors Ser.). lib. bdg. 15.95 (ISBN 0-8057-2372-2, Twayne). G K Hall.

Schwartz, Ronald D., jt. auth. see Basso, Daivd T.

Schwartz, Ronald D., jt. auth. see Basso, David T.

Schwartz, Ronald O. Common Female Problems & their Surgical Correction: Facts for Men & Women. LC 82-11248. (Illus.). 96p. (Orig.). Date not set. pap. text ed. 2.95 (ISBN 0-9609222-0-2). Med-Ed.

Schwartz, Roslyn & Schwartz, Leonard. Becoming a Couple: Making the Most Out of Every Stage in Your Relationship. 1980. text ed. 10.95 (ISBN 0-13-072173-5, Spec); pap. text ed. 5.95 (ISBN 0-13-072165-4, Spec). P-H.

Schwartz, S., jt. auth. see Schwartz, N. L.

Schwartz, S. I. Principles of Surgery: PreTest Self-Assessment & Review. 2nd ed. 267p. 1983. 32.95 (ISBN 0-07-051927-7). McGraw-Pretest.

Schwartz, Seymour I. Surgical Diseases of the Liver. 1964. 34.00 o.p. (ISBN 0-07-055774-8, HP). McGraw.

Schwartz, Seymour I., et al. Tropical Surgery. 1971. 44.00 o.p. (ISBN 0-07-055670-9, HP). McGraw.

Schwartz, Seymour I., et al, eds. Principles of Surgery: PreTest Self-Assessment & Review with CME Examination. 260p. (Orig.). 1981. 75.00 (ISBN 0-07-079036-1, HP). McGraw.

--Year Book of Surgery, 1982. (Illus.). 550p. 1982. 37.00 (ISBN 0-8151-7622-8). Year Bk Med.

--Year Book of Surgery 1983. (Illus.). 1983. 40.00 (ISBN 0-8151-7692-9). Year Bk Med.

Schwartz, Sheila. The Solid Gold Circle. 448p. 1980. 9.95 o.p. (ISBN 0-517-54163-7). Crown.

Schwartz, Stephan. The Secret Vaults of Time. Markel, Bob, ed. 6.95 o.p. (ISBN 0-448-12717-2, G&D). Putnam Pub Group.

Schwartz, Stephan A. The Alexandria Project. Date not set. 15.95 (ISBN 0-440-00078-5, E Friede). Delacorte.

Schwartz, Stephen E. Trace Atmospheric Constituents: Properties Transformations & Fates. (Advances in Environmental Science & Technology Ser.). 560p. 1983. 60.00 (ISBN 0-471-87640-2, Pub. by Wiley-Interscience). Wiley.

Schwartz, Steven, jt. auth. see Heller, Steven.

Schwartz, Stuart B. Sovereignty & Society in Colonial Brazil: The High Court of Bahia & Its Judges, 1609-1751. LC 76-186112. 1973. 40.00x (ISBN 0-520-02195-9). U of Cal Pr.

Schwartz, Stuart E. Dealing with the Unexpected: Situational Approach for Teachers. 240p. 1982. pap. text ed. 8.95x (ISBN 0-534-01233-7). Wadsworth Pub.

Schwartz, Susan H., jt. auth. see Camden, Thomas M.

Schwartz, Ted. Amphoto Guide to Photographing Models. (Amphoto Guide Ser.). 1979. 10.95 o.p. (ISBN 0-8174-2474-1, Amphoto); pap. 7.95 (ISBN 0-8174-2146-7). Watson-Guptill.

--Business Side of Photography. (Illus.). 1979. 11.95 o.p. (ISBN 0-8174-2518-7, Amphoto). Watson-Guptill.

--Professional Photographer's Handbook. (Illus.). 320p. 1983. 29.50 (ISBN 0-07-055690-3, P&RB). McGraw.

Schwartz, Theodore, ed. Socialization As Cultural Communication. LC 75-17282. 1976. 19.50x (ISBN 0-520-03061-3); pap. 8.50x (ISBN 0-520-03955-6). U of Cal Pr.

Schwartz, Theodore B. Year Book of Endocrinology 1983. 1983. 40.00 (ISBN 0-8151-7725-9). Year Bk Med.

Schwartz, Theodore B. & Ryan, Will G., eds. Year Book of Endocrinology, 1982. (Illus.). 1982. 37.00 (ISBN 0-8151-7594-9). Year Bk Med.

Schwartz, Toby D. Mercy, Lord! My Husband's in the Kitchen & Other Equal Opportunity Conversations with God. LC 80-715. (Illus.). 96p. 1980. 6.95 (ISBN 0-385-17058-0). Doubleday.

Schwartz, Tony. Media: The Second God. LC 81-5312. (Illus.). 1982. 13.50 (ISBN 0-394-50247-7). Random.

Schwartz, Warren C., jt. ed. see Martin, Donald L.

Schwartz, William F. Dreams: Your Personal Genie. Horwege, Richard A., ed. 160p. 1983. pap. 6.95 (ISBN 0-89865-175-1). Donning Co.

Schwartzburg, Leon. The North Indian Peasant Goes to Market. 176p. 1979. text ed. 13.95 (ISBN 0-89684-097-2, Pub. by Motilal Banarsidass India). Orient Bk Dist.

Schwartzman, Sylvan D., jt. auth. see Miller, Milton G.

Schwartz-Nobel, Loretta. Starving in the Shadow of Plenty. 256p. 1981. 12.95 (ISBN 0-399-12522-1). Putnam Pub Group.

Schwarz, Alfred. From Buchner to Beckett: Dramatic Theory & the Modes of Tragic Drama. LC 77-92255. xxiv, 360p. 1978. 20.00x (ISBN 0-8214-0391-5, 82-82840). Ohio U Pr.

Schwarz, Boris. Music & Musical Life in Soviet Russia: Enlarged Edition, 1917-1981. LC 82-48267. 736p. 1983. write for info. (ISBN 0-253-33956-1). Ind U Pr.

Schwarz, Daniel R. Conrad: The Later Fiction, Vol. 2. 192p. 1982. text ed. 24.00x (ISBN 0-333-28308-2, Pub. by Macmillan England). Humanities.

Schwarz, Egon. Joseph von Eichendorff. (World Authors Ser.). lib. bdg. 15.95 (ISBN 0-8057-2296-3, Twayne). G K Hall.

Schwarz, Haller. More Pac-Mania. 96p. (Orig.). 1982. pap. cancelled (ISBN 0-523-41993-7). Pinnacle Bks.

Schwarz, Harold, jt. auth. see Weston, Ralph.

Schwarz, Henry G., ed. see Poppe, Nicholas.

Schwarz, Jack. The Path of Action. LC 77-2247. 1977. pap. 5.95 (ISBN 0-525-47466-8, 0578-170). Dutton.

--Voluntary Controls: Exercises for Creative Meditation & for Activating the Potential of the Chakras. 1978. pap. 6.75 (ISBN 0-525-47494-3). Dutton.

Schwarz, Philip J. Coalition Bargaining. (Key Issues Ser.: No. 5). 44p. 1970. pap. 2.00 (ISBN 0-87546-241-3). ILR Pr.

Schwarz, R. H., jt. auth. see Bolognese, Ronald J.

Schwarz, Rae P. see Peyo.

Schwarz, Ralph & Friedland, B. Linear Systems. (Electronic & Electrical Engineering Ser.). 1965. text ed. 42.00 (ISBN 0-07-055778-0, C). McGraw.

Schwarz, Richard H., jt. auth. see Bolognese, Ronald J.

Schwarz, Richard H., ed. Handbook of Obstetric Emergencies. 2nd ed. 1977. 11.95 o.p. (ISBN 0-87488-634-1). Med Exam.

Schwarz, Richard W. John Harvey Kellogg. LC 75-137. 256p. 1981. pap. 6.95 (ISBN 0-943872-80-4). Andrews Univ Pr.

Schwarz, S. Knowledge & Concepts in Future Studies. LC 76-54238. (Westview Replica Edition Ser.). 1977. lib. bdg. 24.50 o.p. (ISBN 0-89158-123-5). Westview.

Schwarz, S. J., tr. see Brommer, Frank.

Schwarz, Ted. Amphoto Guide to Photographing Buildings & Real Estate. (Illus.). 168p. 1980. 10.95 o.p. (ISBN 0-8174-2508-X, Amphoto); pap. 6.95 o.p. (ISBN 0-8174-2170-X). Watson-Guptill.

--Beginner's Guide to Coin Collecting. LC 78-22353. (Illus.). 1980. pap. 6.95 o.p. (ISBN 0-385-14491-1, Dolp). Doubleday.

--The Hillside Strangler. 1982. pap. 2.75 (ISBN 0-451-11452-3, AE1452, Sig). NAL.

Schwarz, W. M. Intermediate Electromagnetic Theory. LC 74-163568. 454p. 1973. Repr. of 1964 ed. 22.50 (ISBN 0-88275-093-3). Krieger.

Schwarzenbach, G., et al. Complexometric Titrations. 2nd ed. 1969. 21.95x o.p. (ISBN 0-416-19290-4). Methuen Inc.

Schwarzenberger, G., jt. auth. see Keeton, G. W.

Schwarzenberger, Georg. Economic World Order: A Basic Problem of International Economic Law. LC 70-132276. (The Melland Schill Lectures). 159p. 1970. 11.00 (ISBN 0-379-11911-0). Oceana.

Schwarzenberger, Georg & Brown, E. D. A Manual of International Law. 6th ed. lix, 612p. 1976. text ed. 34.00x (ISBN 0-903486-26-1). Rothman.

Schwarzenberger, Georg, jt. ed. see Keeton, George W.

Schwarzenberger, George. International Constitutional Law: International Law As Applied by International Courts & Tribunals, Vol. 3. LC 57-59355. 1976. lib. bdg. 100.00 o.p. (ISBN 0-89158-542-7). Westview.

Schwarzenberger, R. L. Elementary Differential Equations. 1969. pap. 6.95x o.p. (ISBN 0-412-09580-7, Pub. by Chapman & Hall). Methuen Inc.

--N-Dimensional Crystallography. LC 79-19693. (Research Notes in Mathematics Ser.: No. 41). 139p. (Orig.). 1980. pap. text ed. 18.95 (ISBN 0-686-31215-5). Pitman Pub MA.

Schwarzenegger, Arnold & Hall, Douglas K. Arnold: The Education of a Bodybuilder. (Illus.). 320p. 1982. pap. 3.95 (ISBN 0-671-46139-7). PB.

Schwarzenneger, Arnold & Dobbins, Bill. Arnold's Bodybuilding for Men. 1981. 17.50 (ISBN 0-671-25613-0). S&S.

Schwarzer, William W. Managing Antitrust & Other Complex Litigation. 465p. 1982. 35.00 (ISBN 0-686-84229-4). Michie-Bobbs.

Schwarzkopf, A. B., et al, eds. Optimal Control & Differential Equation. 1978. 30.50 (ISBN 0-12-632250-3). Acad Pr.

Schwarzkopf, Friedemann, tr. see Emmichoven, F. W.

Schwarzrock, Shirley & Wrenn, C. Gilbert. Alcohol As a Crutch. (Coping with Ser.). (Illus.). (gr. 7-12). 1971. pap. text ed. 2.25 (ISBN 0-913476-17-X). Am Guidance.

--Can You Talk with Someone Else? (Coping with Ser.). (Illus.). 36p. (gr. 7-12). 1970. pap. text ed. 2.25 (ISBN 0-913476-22-6). Am Guidance.

--Changing Roles of Men & Women. (Coping with Ser.). (Illus.). 31p. (gr. 7-12). 1970. pap. text ed. 2.25 (ISBN 0-913476-29-3). Am Guidance.

--Coping with Cliques. (Coping with Ser.). (Illus.). 31p. (gr. 7-12). 1971. pap. text ed. 2.25 (ISBN 0-913476-30-7). Am Guidance.

--The Coping with Series. (Illus., Orig.). (gr. 7-12). 1970-73. pap. text ed. 34.50 complete ref. set (ISBN 0-913476-10-2); manual 4.50 (ISBN 0-913476-11-0). Am Guidance.

--Crises Youth Face Today. (Coping with Ser.). (Illus.). 64p. (gr. 7-12). 1973. pap. text ed. 2.25 (ISBN 0-913476-28-5). Am Guidance.

--Do I Know the "Me" Others See? (Coping With Ser.). (Illus.). 55p. (gr. 7-12). 1973. pap. text ed. 2.25 (ISBN 0-913476-27-7). Am Guidance.

--Easing the Scene. (Coping with Ser.). (Illus.). (gr. 7-12). 1970. pap. text ed. 2.25 (ISBN 0-913476-23-4). Am Guidance.

--Facts & Fantasies About Alcohol. (Coping with Ser.). (Illus.). (gr. 7-12). 1971. pap. text ed. 2.25 (ISBN 0-913476-13-7). Am Guidance.

--Facts & Fantasies About Drugs. (Coping with Ser.). (Illus.). (gr. 6-9). 1970. pap. text ed. 2.25 (ISBN 0-913476-12-9). Am Guidance.

--Facts & Fantasies About Smoking. (Coping with Ser.). (Illus.). 40p. (gr. 7-12). 1971. pap. text ed. 2.25 (ISBN 0-913476-14-5). Am Guidance.

--Food As a Crutch. (Coping with Ser.). (Illus.). (gr. 7-12). 1971. pap. text ed. 2.25 (ISBN 0-913476-18-8). Am Guidance.

--Grades, What's So Important About Them, Anyway? (Coping with Ser.). (Illus.). 33p. (gr. 7-12). pap. text ed. 2.25 (ISBN 0-913476-34-X). Am Guidance.

--I'd Rather Do It Myself, If You Don't Mind. (Coping with Ser.). (Illus.). 39p. (gr. 7-12). 1970. pap. text ed. 2.25 (ISBN 0-913476-31-5). Am Guidance.

--In Front of the Table & Behind It. (Coping with Ser.). (Illus.). 41p. (gr. 7-12). 1971. pap. text ed. 2.25 (ISBN 0-913476-24-2). Am Guidance.

--Living with Differences. (Coping with Ser.). (gr. 7-12). 1973. pap. text ed. 2.25 (ISBN 0-913476-19-6). Am Guidance.

--Living with Loneliness. (Coping with Ser.). (Illus.). 31p. (gr. 7-12). 1970. pap. text ed. 2.25 (ISBN 0-913476-32-3). Am Guidance.

--The Mind Benders. (Coping with Ser.). (gr. 10 up). 1971. pap. text ed. 2.25 (ISBN 0-913476-16-1). Am Guidance.

--My Life - What Shall I Do with It? (Coping with Ser.). (Illus.). 50p. (gr. 7-12). 1973. pap. text ed. 2.25 (ISBN 0-913476-26-9). Am Guidance.

--Parents Can Be a Problem. (Coping with Ser.). (Illus.). (gr. 7-12). 1970. pap. text ed. 2.25 (ISBN 0-913476-33-1). Am Guidance.

--Some Common Crutches. (Coping with Ser.). (Illus.). 43p. (gr. 7-12). pap. text ed. 2.25 (ISBN 0-913476-15-3). Am Guidance.

--To Like & Be Liked. (Coping with Ser.). (Illus.). 37p. (gr. 7-12). 1970. pap. text ed. 2.25 (ISBN 0-913476-25-0). Am Guidance.

--Understanding the Law of Our Land. (Coping with Ser.). (Illus.). 51p. (gr. 7-12). 1973. pap. text ed. 2.25 (ISBN 0-913476-21-8). Am Guidance.

--You Always Communicate Something. (Coping with Ser.). (Illus.). 58p. (gr. 7-12). 1973. pap. text ed. 2.25 (ISBN 0-913476-20-X). Am Guidance.

Schwarzrock, Shirley P. & Jensen, James R. Effective Dental Assisting. 6th ed. 848p. 1982. text ed. write for info. (ISBN 0-697-05664-3); instrs. manual avail. (ISBN 0-697-05666-X); student workbook wire coil avail. (ISBN 0-697-05665-1). Wm C Brown.

Schwarzweller, Harry K., et al. Mountain Families in Transition: A Case Study of Appalachian Migration. LC 71-138090. 1971. 17.95x (ISBN 0-271-01149-1). Pa St U Pr.

Schwarzwer, R., et al. Advances in Test Anxiety Research, Vol. 1. xii, 176p. 1982. pap. text ed. 19.95 (ISBN 0-89859-256-9). L Erlbaum Assocs.

Schwebke, Phyllis W. How to Tailor. (gr. 9 up). 1965. 6.95 o.p. (ISBN 0-685-07642-3, 80704). Glencoe.

Schwed, Peter, jt. auth. see Lopez, Nancy.

Schwede, Olga. An Early Childhood Activity Program for Handicapped Children. 1977. pap. 7.95 (ISBN 0-914420-59-3). Exceptional Pr Inc.

Schweer, Kathryn D., jt. ed. see Warner, Steven D.

Schwefel, Hans-Paul. Numerical Optimization of Computer Models. 389p. 1981. 36.95 (ISBN 0-471-09988-0, Pub. by Wiley-Interscience). Wiley.

Schweickart, David. Capitalism or Worker Control: An Ethical & Economic Appraisal. 266p. 1980. 29.95 (ISBN 0-03-056724-6). Praeger.

Schweid, Richard. Hot Peppers: Cajuns & Capsicum in New Iberia la. LC 80-23160. 200p. 1980. 11.95 (ISBN 0-914842-50-1); pap. 6.95 (ISBN 0-914842-51-X). Madrona Pubs.

Schweiker, Roioli. Canoe Camping Vermont & New Hampshire Rivers. Baker, Catherine J., ed. LC 76-52884. (Illus.). 1977. pap. 4.95 (ISBN 0-912274-71-9). Backcountry Pubns.

Schweinitz, L. D. Synopsis Fungorum in America Boreali Media Degentium. 1962. Repr. of 1834 ed. 40.00 (ISBN 3-7682-0117-1). Lubrecht & Cramer.

Schweinitz, L. D. Von see Von Schweinitz, L. D.

Schweisguth, Odile. Solid Tumors in Children. LC 82-2008. 517p. 1982. 55.00 (ISBN 0-471-07733-X, Pub. by Wiley Med). Wiley.

Schweiter, John C. The ABC of Doll Collecting. LC 81-8764. (Illus.). 160p. 1983. pap. 8.95 (ISBN 0-8069-7696-9). Sterling.

Schweitzer & Sklar. Probabilistic Metric Spaces. (Probability & Applied Mathematics Ser.: Vol. 5). 1982. 39.00 (ISBN 0-444-00666-4). Elsevier.

Schweitzer, Albert. J. S. Bach, 2 vols. (Illus.). 1962. Set. pap. 12.90 (ISBN 0-8283-1733-X, 64); pap. 6.50 ea. Branden.

--J. S. Bach, 2 vols. Newman, Ernest, tr. (Illus.). (YA) (gr. 7-12). pap. 6.00 ea.; Vol. 1. pap. (ISBN 0-486-21631-4); Vol. 2. pap. (ISBN 0-486-21632-2). Dover.

--J. S. Bach, 2 vols. Newman, Ernest, tr. Set. 23.00 (ISBN 0-8446-0902-1). Peter Smith.

Schweitzer, Burton L. & Aarons, Howell. Word Attack: An Individualized Approach. 1980. text ed. 8.95 (ISBN 0-675-08187-4). Additional supplements may be obtained from publisher. Merrill.

Schweitzer, Darrell. Conan's World & Robert E. Howard. LC 78-14569. (The Milford Ser.: Popular Writers of Today: Vol. 17). 1978. lib. bdg. 9.95x (ISBN 0-89370-123-8); pap. 3.95x (ISBN 0-89370-223-4). Borgo Pr.

--The Dream Quest of H. P. Lovecraft. LC 78-891. (The Milford Ser: Popular Writers of Today: Vol. 12). 1978. lib. bdg. 9.95x (ISBN 0-89370-117-3); pap. 3.95x (ISBN 0-89370-217-X). Borgo Pr.

--Exploring Fantasy Worlds: Essays on Fantastic Literature. LC 81-21657. (I. O. Evans Studies in the Philosophy & Criticism of Literature: Vol. 3). 64p. 1983. lib. bdg. 9.95x (ISBN 0-89370-162-9); pap. 3.95x (ISBN 0-89370-262-5). Borgo Pr.

--Science Fiction Voices: No. 1. LC 79-1396. (The Milford Ser.: Popular Writers of Today: Vol. 23). 1979. lib. bdg. 9.95x (ISBN 0-89370-133-5); pap. 3.95x (ISBN 0-89370-233-1). Borgo Pr.

--Science Fiction Voices, No. 5: Interviews with Science-Fiction Writers. LC 81-21624. (The Milford Series: Popular Writers of Today: Vol. 35). 64p. 1981. lib. bdg. 9.95x (ISBN 0-89370-151-3); pap. text ed. 3.95x (ISBN 0-89370-251-X). Borgo Pr.

--The Shattered Goddess. Stine, Hank, ed. LC 82-5012. (Illus.). 186p. 1983. pap. 5.95 (ISBN 0-89865-197-2, AACR2, Starblaze). Donning Co.

--We Are All Legends. Stine, Hank, ed. LC 81-5041. (Illus., Orig.). 1981. pap. 5.95 (ISBN 0-89865-062-3, Starblaze). Donning Co.

Schweitzer, Gemello, jt. auth. see Gordon, Robert J.

Schweitzer, Gertrude. Stand Before Kings. 336p. 1982. 14.95 (ISBN 0-399-12702-X). Putnam Pub Group.

Schweitzer, Iris. Hilda's Restful Chair. LC 81-67667. (Illus.). 32p. (ps-3). 1982. PLB 9.95 (ISBN 0-689-50230-3, McElderry Bk). Atheneum.

--In a Forest of Flowers. LC 73-87216. (Illus.). 32p. (gr. 4-8). 1974. PLB 5.29 o.p. (ISBN 0-399-60872-9). Putnam Pub Group.

--Tiglis & the Bird-Machine. LC 78-18146. (Reading-on-My-Own Book Ser.). (Illus.). (gr. 1). 1980. PLB 6.95a o.p. (ISBN 0-385-12161-X). Doubleday.

Schweitzer, John C. The ABC's of Doll Collecting. LC 81-8764. (Illus.). 160p. 1981. 14.95 (ISBN 0-8069-5428-0); lib. bdg. 17.79 (ISBN 0-8069-5429-9). Sterling.

Schweitzer, N. M. Ophthalmology. (Jonxis Lectures Ser.: Vol. 8). Date not set. 28.50 (ISBN 0-444-90275-9). Elsevier.

Schweitzer, Philip A. Handbook of Corrosion Resistant Piping. LC 81-19291. 368p. 1984. Repr. of 1969 ed. lib. bdg. write for info. (ISBN 0-89874-457-1). Krieger.

--Handbook of Separation Techniques for Chemical Engineers. (Illus.). 1979. 54.90 (ISBN 0-07-055790-X, P&RB). McGraw.

Schweitzer, Robert, jt. ed. see Havrilesky, Thomas M.

Schweitzer, Sydney C. Winning with Deception & Bluff. LC 78-25798. 1979. 8.95 o.p. (ISBN 0-13-961276-9). P-H.

Schweizer, Eduard. Church As the Body of Christ. LC 64-16282. (Orig.). 1964. pap. 2.95 (ISBN 0-8042-3376-4). John Knox.

--Good News According to Mark. Madvig, Donald, tr. LC 77-93828. 1970. 16.95 (ISBN 0-8042-0250-8). John Knox.

--Good News According to Matthew. Green, David E., tr. LC 74-3717. 1975. 17.95 (ISBN 0-8042-0251-6). John Knox.

--Jesus. LC 76-107322. 1979. pap. 5.95 (ISBN 0-8042-0331-8). John Knox.

Schweizer, Edward. The Letter to the Colossians: A Commentary. Chester, Andrew, tr. LC 81-65657. 352p. (Orig.). 1981. pap. 12.50 (ISBN 0-8066-1893-0, 10-3823). Augsburg.

Schweizer, Niklaus R. Hawaii & the German Speaking Peoples. (Illus.). 232p. (Orig.). pap. 15.00 (ISBN 0-914916-60-2). Topgallant.

Schweizer, Susanna, jt. auth. see Ching-hih Chen.

Schweizer, W. Basel. 1975. bds. 7.50 o.p. (ISBN 0-911268-27-8). Rogers Bk.

Schweke, William, jt. ed. see Friedman, Robert E.

Schweltzer, Frederick. A History of the Jews Since the First Century A. D. 319p. pap. 1.95 (ISBN 0-686-95171-9). ADL.

Schwemm, Robert G. Housing Discrimination Law. 500p. 1983. text ed. 35.00 (ISBN 0-87179-389-X). BNA.

Schwendowius, Barbara & Domling, Wolfgang, eds. Johann Sebastian Bach: Life, Times, Influence. Coombs, John & Salter, Lionel, trs. from Ger. (Illus.). 1978. 45.00 o.s.i. (ISBN 3-7618-0589-6). Eur-Am Music.

Schweninger, Ann. The Hunt for Rabbit's Galosh. LC 74-33659. 32p. (ps-3). 1976. 5.95 o.p. (ISBN 0-385-00130-4); PLB write for info. o.p. (ISBN 0-385-00274-2). Doubleday.

Schwenke, Karl & Schwenke, Sue. Build Your Own Stone House: Using the Easy Slipform Method. LC 75-16831. (Illus.). 156p. 1975. 10.95 o.p. (ISBN 0-88266-071-3); pap. 6.95 o.p. (ISBN 0-88266-069-1). Garden Way Pub.

Schwenke, Sue, jt. auth. see Schwenke, Karl.

Schwenker, Robert F., Jr. & Garn, Paul. Thermal Analysis, 2 Vols. 1969. Vol. 1. 67.00 (ISBN 0-12-633201-0); Vol 2. 67.00 (ISBN 0-12-633202-9); Set. 95.00 (ISBN 0-686-66357-8). Acad Pr.

Schweppe, Fred C. Uncertain Dynamic Systems. (Illus.). 576p. 1973. ref. ed. 35.95 (ISBN 0-13-935593-6). P-H.

Schwer, L. E., ed. Nonlinear Numerical Analysis of Reinforced Concrete. 1982. 30.00 (H00242). ASME.

Schwerdtfeger, Friedrich W. Traditional Housing in African Cities: A Comparative Study of Houses in Zaria, Ibadan & Marrakech. LC 80-41693. 480p. 1982. 59.95x (ISBN 0-471-27953-6, Pub. by Wiley-Interscience). Wiley.

Schwerdtfeger, P. Physical Principles of Micro-Meteorological Measurements. (Developments in Atmospheric Science Ser.: Vol. 6). 1976. 51.00 (ISBN 0-444-41489-4). Elsevier.

Schwerdtfeger, W., ed. Climates of Central & South America. (World Survey of Climatology: Vol. 12). 1976. 121.50 (ISBN 0-444-41271-9). Elsevier.

Schwerer, Fred C., ed. see AIP Conference, 84th, APS-AISI, Lehigh University, 1981.

Schwerin, Horace S. & Newell, Henry H. Persuasion in Marketing: Dynamics of Marketing's Great Untapped Resource. LC 80-23133. (Ronald Series on Marketing Management). 259p. 1981. 29.95 (ISBN 0-471-04554-3, Pub. by Wiley-Interscience). Wiley.

Schwerin, Kurt. A Bibliography of German. (Language Legal Monograph Ser.). 383p. 1977. text ed. 58.00x (ISBN 3-7940-7037-2, Pub. by K G Saur). Gale.

Schwerner, Armand. The Tablets I-XXIV & Sounds of the River Naranjana. 124p. 1983. ltd., signed ed. 15.95 (ISBN 0-930794-59-1); pap. 6.95 (ISBN 0-930794-60-5). Station Hill Pr.

Schwicker, A., jt. auth. see Cagnacci.

Schwiebert, Ernest. Trout Strategies: Observations on Modern Fly Fishing, Including Tested Methods of Matching the Hatch, Fishing the Nymph, Bucktails & Streamers, Wet & Dry Flies; & Techniques for Eastern & Western Lakes, Ponds, Rivers & Streams--Drawn from the Author's Masterwork "Trout". (Illus.). 288p. 1983. pap. 10.95 (ISBN 0-525-48052-8, 01064-310). Dutton.

Schwiebert, Ernest G. Luther & His Times: The Reformation from a New Perspective. (Illus.). (gr. 9 up). 1950. 23.95 (ISBN 0-570-03246-6, 15-1164). Concordia.

Schwieder, Dorothy. Black Diamonds: Life & Work in Iowa's Coal Mining Communities, 1895-1925. (Illus.). 176p. 1983. 13.95 (ISBN 0-8138-0991-6). Iowa St U Pr.

Schwieder, Dorothy, ed. Patterns & Perspectives in Iowa History. 450p. 1973. 9.50x (ISBN 0-8138-1215-1). Iowa St U Pr.

Schwimmer, Eric. The World of the Maori. (Illus.). 1978. pap. 5.25 o.p. (ISBN 0-589-05085-0, Pub. by Reed Books Australia). C E Tuttle.

Schwimmer, Erik. Exchange in the Social Structure of the Orokaiva. LC 73-87566. 280p. 1974. 26.00 (ISBN 0-312-27405-X). St Martin.

Schwimmer, Erik, ed. see Williams, Francis E.

Schwind, J. Von see Von Schwind, J.

Schwinger, Julian. Particles, Sources & Fields, Vol. 1. LC 73-119670. (Physics Ser). 1970. text ed. 30.50 (ISBN 0-201-06782-X, Adv Bk Prog). A-W.

--Particles, Sources, & Fields, Vol. 2. (Physics Ser.). 1973. 30.50 (ISBN 0-201-06783-8, Adv Bk Prog). A-W.

Schwinger, Julian, ed. Selected Papers on Quantum Electrodynamics. LC 58-8524. 1958. lib. bdg. 15.00x (ISBN 0-88307-648-9). Gannon.

Schwirian, Kent P. Comparative Urban Structure: Studies in the Ecology of the Cities. 1973. text ed. 19.95x o.p. (ISBN 0-669-82966-8). Heath.

Schwitzgebel, R. Kirkland, jt. auth. see Schwitzgebel, Robert L.

Schwitzgebel, Robert L. & Schwitzgebel, R. Kirkland. Law & Psychological Practice. LC 79-20112. 416p. 1980. text ed. 21.95 (ISBN 0-471-76694-1). Wiley.

Schwizer, Eduard. Luke: A Challenge to Present Theology. LC 81-85332. 144p. 1982. pap. 9.95 (ISBN 0-8042-0686-4). John Knox.

Schwob, Marcel. The King of the Golden Mask & Other Stories. White, Iain, tr. from French. 224p. 1982. text ed. 14.75x (ISBN 0-85635-403-1, 30268, Pub. by Carcanet New Pr England). Humanities.

Schwoebel, Robert. Shadow of the Crescent: The Renaissance Image of the Turk. (Illus.). 1967. 25.00 (ISBN 0-312-71400-9). St Martin.

Schyler, Randall S., jt. ed. see Sethi, Amarjit.

Sciacchetano, Larry & McCallum, Jack. Sports Illustrated Wrestling. 1979. 5.95 o.p. (ISBN 0-397-01275-6, LP-130); pap. 2.95i (ISBN 0-397-01276-4). Har-Row.

Sciama, Dennis W. Modern Cosmology. LC 73-142961. (Cambridge Science Classics Ser.). (Illus.). 220p. 1982. pap. 12.95 (ISBN 0-521-28721-9). Cambridge U Pr.

--Modern Cosmology. LC 73-142961. (Illus.). 1971. text ed. 21.95x (ISBN 0-521-08069-X). Cambridge U Pr.

Sciarra, D. J., jt. auth. see Milgram, J. I.

Sciarra, Dorothy J. & Dorsey, Anne G. Developing & Administering a Child Care Center. LC 78-69564. (Illus.). 1979. 20.95 (ISBN 0-395-26263-1). HM.

Sciarra, John J., jt. auth. see Demarest, Robert J.

Sciarra, John J. & Stoller, Leonard, eds. The Science & Technology of Aerosol Packaging. 710p. 1974. 79.95x (ISBN 0-471-76693-3, Pub. by Wiley-Interscience). Wiley.

Sciascia, Leonardo. Candido; or, a Dream Dreamed in Sicily. 168p. 1982. pap. text ed. 12.50x (ISBN 0-85635-404-X, Pub. by Carcanet Pr England). Humanities.

Scibak, John W., jt. ed. see Whitman, Thomas L.

Sciberras, Edmond. Multinational Electronic Companies & National Economic Policies. Altman, Edward I. & Walter, Ingo, eds. LC 76-10398. (Contemporary Studies in Economic & Financial Analysis: Vol. 6). 1977. lib. bdg. 36.50 (ISBN 0-89232-016-8). Jai Pr.

Scibor-Rylski, A. J. Road Vehicle Aerodynamics. LC 74-26859. 213p. 1975. 43.95 o.p. (ISBN 0-470-75920-8); pap. 22.95 o.p. (ISBN 0-470-26655-4). Halsted Pr.

Science Action Coalition & Conry, Tom. A Consumer's Guide to Cosmetics. LC 79-7193. (Illus.). 384p. 1980. pap. 5.95 (ISBN 0-385-13503-3, Anch). Doubleday.

Science & Public Policy Papers I. Proceedings, Vol. 368. 235p. 1981. 50.00 (ISBN 0-89766-125-7, Rosenberg Pub); pap. write for info. (ISBN 0-89766-126-5). NY Acad Sci.

Science Council of Japan, ed. see International Seaweed Symposium, 7th, Sappora, Japan, Aug. 1971.

Science Investigator. Popular Scientific Recreations. 9.50x o.p. (ISBN 0-392-12671-0, SpS). Sportshelf.

Science Policy & Biomedical Research Symposium, Paris, 1968. Proceedings. (Science Policy Studies & Documents Ser., No. 16). (Orig.). 1969. pap. 2.50 o.p. (ISBN 92-3-100751-3, UNESCO). Unipub.

Scientific American Editors. Medicine, 2 vols. 2500p. 1982. 2.20 (ISBN 0-686-94061-X). W H Freeman.

Scientific American, Inc. Scientific American Cumulative Index 1948-1978. 1979. 45.00 o.s.i. (ISBN 0-89454-002-5). Sci Am Illus Lib.

Scientific Research (SIR), ed. Drugs Studies in CVD & PVD: Proceedings of the International Symposium, Geneva, May 25-26, 1981. (Illus.). 250p. 1982. 41.00 (ISBN 0-08-027084-0). Pergamon.

Scientific Workshop on Atmospheric Carbon Dioxide, Washington, D.C., 1976. Report. pap. 10.00 (ISBN 0-686-93941-7, W218, WMO). Unipub.

Scientists for Life. The Position of Modern Science on the Beginning of Human Life. 47p. (Orig.). 1975. pap. 1.00 (ISBN 0-937930-02-4). Sun Life.

Sciff, G., ed. Picasso in Perspective. 1975 (ISBN 0-13-675801-0, Spec). pap. 3.95 o.p. (ISBN 0-13-675793-6, Spec). P-H.

Scimecca, Joseph A. Society & Freedom: An Introduction to Humanist Sociology. 250p. 1981. text ed. 16.95x (ISBN 0-312-73806-4); pap. text ed. 8.95x (ISBN 0-312-73807-2). St Martin.

Scioletti, Daniel C. Legal Decisions for CPA's & Business People. 1979. text ed. 18.95 (ISBN 0-8403-1922-3). Kendall-Hunt.

Scioli, Frank & Cook, Thomas, eds. The Methodology of Policy Studies. 1973. pap. 6.00 (ISBN 0-918592-05-4). Policy Studies.

Scioli, Frank P. & Cook, Thomas J. Methodologies for Analyzing Public Policies. LC 75-8152. (Policy Studies Organization Policy Study Ser.). 192p. 1975. 18.95 (ISBN 0-669-00596-7, Dist. by Transaction Bks). Lexington Bks.

Scipien. Comprehensive Pediatric Nursing. 1983. write for info. (ISBN 0-07-055554-0). McGraw.

Scipio. Emergent Africa. rev. ed. 1967. pap. 1.95 o.p. (ISBN 0-671-20155-7, Touchstone Bks). S&S.

Scipio, Alice R., jt. auth. see Jamieson, Graham A.

Scithers, George A., ed. Isaac Asimov's Worlds of Science Fiction. 288p. 1980. 9.95 o.s.i. (ISBN 0-8037-4192-8). Davis Pubns.

Scithers, George H., ed. Isaac Asimov's Adventures of Science Fiction. 1980. 9.95 o.s.i. (ISBN 0-686-85857-3). Davis Pubns.

--Isaac Asimov's Marvels of Science Fiction. 1979. 9.95 o.s.i. (ISBN 0-8037-3773-4). Davis Pubns.

--Isaac Asimov's Masters of Science Fiction. 1978. 8.95 o.s.i. (ISBN 0-8037-3697-5). Davis Pubns.

Scitovsky, Tibor. The Joyless Economy. (Illus.). 1976. 19.95x (ISBN 0-19-501974-1). Oxford U Pr.

Sclafani, R. J., jt. auth. see Dickie, George.

Sclove, Stanley L., jt. auth. see Anderson, T. W.

Scnmelzer, R., jt. auth. see Raygor, A.

Scobel, Don N. Creative Worklife. 244p. 1981. 17.95x (ISBN 0-87201-905-5). Gulf Pub.

Scobie, G. E. Psychology of Religion. LC 74-21832. 189p. 1975. text ed. 19.95 o.p. (ISBN 0-470-76712-X); pap. text ed. 9.95 (ISBN 0-470-26689-9). Halsted Pr.

Scobie, Grant M. Investment in International Agricultural Research: Some Economic Dimensions. (Working Paper: No. 361). iv, 98p. 1979. 5.00 (ISBN 0-686-36067-2, WP-0361). World Bank.

Scobie, James R. Argentina: A City & a Nation. 2nd ed. (Latin American Histories Ser). 1971. 14.95 o.p. (ISBN 0-19-501479-0); pap. text ed. 6.95x (ISBN 0-19-501480-4). Oxford U Pr.

--Buenos Aires: Plaza to Suburb Eighteen Seventy - Nineteen Ten. 1978. text ed. 17.50 o.p. (ISBN 0-19-501821-4); pap. text ed. 7.95x (ISBN 0-19-502437-0). Oxford U Pr.

Scoble, Harry M., jt. ed. see Wiseberg, Laurie S.

Scoby, Joan & McGrath, Lee P. What Is a Friend. 1971. pap. 1.95 o.p. (ISBN 0-671-10539-6, Fireside). S&S.

Scofield, C. I. Rightly Dividing the Word of Truth. 72p. (Orig.). 1974. pap. 2.50 (ISBN 0-310-32662-1, 6364P). Zondervan.

Scofield, W. M. Washington's Historical Markers. (Illus.). 80p. 1967. pap. 1.95 o.p. (ISBN 0-911518-15-0). Touchstone Pr Ore.

Scoggan, Nita. Pillars of the Pentagon. (Illus.). 176p. 1982. pap. 4.95 (ISBN 0-910487-00-6). Royalty Pub.

Scoggin, Margaret, ed. Chucklebait: Funny Stories for Everyone. (Illus.). (gr. 7 up). 1947. PLB 5.69 o.p. (ISBN 0-394-91026-5). Knopf.

Scoggin, Margaret C., ed. More Chucklebait: Funny Stories for Everyone. (Illus.). (gr. 7 up). 1949. PLB 5.69 o.p. (ISBN 0-394-91420-1). Knopf.

Scoggins, Bruce, jt. ed. see Stanley, Philip E.

Scoles. Pediatric Orthopedics in Clinical Practice. 1982. 39.95 (ISBN 0-8151-7583-3). Year Bk Med.

Scoles, Eugene F. & Hay, Peter. Conflict of Laws. LC 82-11120. (Hornbook Ser.). 987p. 1982. text ed. 20.95 (ISBN 0-314-65345-7). West Pub.

Scoles, Eugene F., jt. auth. see Halbach, Edward C.

Scollon, Ron & Scollon, Suzanne. Narrative, Literacy, & Face in Interethnic Communication. (Advances in Discourse Processes: Vol. 7). 188p. 1981. text ed. 18.95 (ISBN 0-89391-076-7); pap. text ed. 14.95 (ISBN 0-89391-086-4). Ablex Pub.

Scollon, Ronald. Conversations with a One Year Old: A Case Study of the Developmental Foundation of Syntax. 1976. text ed. 12.00x (ISBN 0-8248-0479-1). UH Pr.

Scollon, Ronald & Scollon, Suzanne B. Linguistic Convergence: An Ethnography of Speaking at Fort Chipewyan, Alberta. (Language, Thought & Culture Ser.). 1979. 28.50 (ISBN 0-12-633380-7). Acad Pr.

Scollon, Suzanne, jt. auth. see Scollon, Ron.

Scollon, Suzanne B., jt. auth. see Scollon, Ronald.

Sconce, J. S., ed. Chlorine: Its Manufacture, Properties & Uses. LC 62-20781. 912p. 1972. Repr. of 1962 ed. 54.50 (ISBN 0-88275-075-5). Krieger.

Scoones, William B., ed. Four Centuries of English Letters. LC 79-142558. 1971. Repr. of 1893 ed. 40.00x (ISBN 0-8103-3638-3). Gale.

Scopes, Nigel, ed. Pest & Disease Control Handbook. 250p. 1979. 35.00x (ISBN 0-901436-42-9, Pub. by British Crop Protection England). Intl Schol Bk Serv.

Scopes, P. G. Mathematics in Secondary Schools. LC 72-78894. (Illus.). 128p. 1973. pap. text ed. 8.95x (ISBN 0-521-09728-2). Cambridge U Pr.

Scopes, R. K. Protein Purifaction: Principles & Practice. (Springer Advanced Texts in Chemistry). (Illus.). 282p. 1983. 29.95 (ISBN 0-387-90726-2). Springer-Verlag.

Scoppettone, Sandra. Innocent Bystanders. 1982. 13.95 (ISBN 0-453-00422-9, H422). NAL.

--The Late Great Me. LC 75-27416. 1976. 7.95 (ISBN 0-399-11620-6). Putnam Pub Group.
--The Late Great Me. 1.95 o.p. (ISBN 0-686-92244-1, 5021). Hazelden.
--Some Unknown Person. LC 77-2910. 1977. 8.95 (ISBN 0-399-11999-X). Putnam Pub Group.
--Such Nice People. LC 79-22855. 1980. 10.95 (ISBN 0-399-12353-9). Putnam Pub Group.
--Trying Hard to Hear You. LC 74-2611. 272p. (gr. 7-12). 1974. 9.57i (ISBN 0-06-025246-4, HarpJ); PLB 10.89 (ISBN 0-06-025247-2). Har-Row.
Scoppettoone, Sandra, jt. auth. see Fitzhugh, Louise.
Scorer, C. G. & Farrington, G. H. Congenital Deformities of the Testis & Epididymis. 1971. 16.20 o.p. (ISBN 0-407-13891-9). Butterworth.
Scorer, R. S. The Clever Moron. 1977. 15.00 o.p. (ISBN 0-7100-8552-4). Routledge & Kegan.
--Pollution in the Air: Problems, Policies & Priorities. 156p. 1973. 14.95 (ISBN 0-685-30197-4). Routledge & Kegan.
Scorer, R. S. & Wexler, H. A Colour Guide to Clouds. 1964. 16.25 (ISBN 0-08-010375-8); pap. 7.00 (ISBN 0-08-010374-X). Pergamon.
Scorer, Richard. Clouds of the World: A Complete Color Encyclopedia. (Illus.). 176p. 1983. 60.00 (ISBN 0-7153-8442-2). David & Charles.
Scoresby, William. Account of the Arctic Regions, 2 Vols. LC 69-10853. Set. 50.00x o.p. (ISBN 0-678-05626-9). Kelley.
--Journal of a Voyage to the Northern Whale Fishery: 1822. 1981. 45.00x (ISBN 0-686-98244-4, Pub. by Caedmon of Whitby). State Mutual Bk.
--My Father, Eighteen Fifty-one. 1981. 30.00x (ISBN 0-686-98242-8, Pub. by Caedmon of Whitby). State Mutual Bk.
--The Polar Ice & the North Pole. 1981. 30.00x (ISBN 0-686-98241-X, Pub. by Caedmon of Whitby). State Mutual Bk.
Scotland, James, jt. auth. see Rusk, Robert R.
Scotland. Treaties. Treaty of Union of Scotland & England. Pryde, George S., ed. LC 78-24202. 1979. Repr. of 1950 ed. lib. bdg. 17.50x (ISBN 0-313-20829-8, SCTR). Greenwood.
Scott. The Cultural Significance of Accounts. LC 73-84524. 1973. Repr. of 1931 ed. text ed. 13.00 (ISBN 0-914348-08-6). Scholars Bk.
--Underground Homes: An Alternative Lifestyle. 400p. 1981. 18.95 (ISBN 0-8306-9626-1); pap. 10.95 o.p. (ISBN 0-8306-1372-2, 1372). TAB Bks.
--Window on the Wild. 8.95 (ISBN 0-399-20722-8). Putnam Pub Group.
Scott, A., jt. ed. see Ricciardi, L.
Scott, A. A. Engineering Outlines, Vols. 1-2. (gr. 9 up). Vol. 1. 9.50x o.p. (ISBN 0-333-03318-3); Vol. 2. 14.00x o.p. (ISBN 0-685-04850-0). Transatlantic.
Scott, A. C., ed. Traditional Chinese Plays, 3 vols. Incl. Vol. 1. Ssu Lang Visits His Mother; The Butterfly Dream. (Illus.). 180p. 1967. pap. 6.95 (ISBN 0-299-04134-4); Vol. 2. Longing for Worldly Pleasures; Fifteen Strings of Cash. (Illus.). 172p. 1969. 20.00 (ISBN 0-299-05370-9); pap. 6.95 (ISBN 0-299-05374-1); Vol. 3. Picking up the Jade Bracelet; a Girl Setting Out for Trial. LC 66-22854. (Illus.). 112p. 1975. 17.50 (ISBN 0-299-06630-4). pap. U of Wis Pr.
Scott, A. F. Close Readings. 1968. pap. text ed. 5.95x o.p. (ISBN 0-435-18801-1). Heinemann Ed.
--The Plantagenet Age. LC 75-4880. (Everyone a Witness Ser.). (Illus.). 328p. 1976. 9.95i o.p. (ISBN 0-690-01002-8); pap. 4.95 o.p. (ISBN 0-8152-0393-4, A-393). T Y Crowell.
--What Fires Kindle Genius? LC 81-90430. 97p. 8.95 (ISBN 0-533-05188-6). Vantage.
--What Makes a Prose Genius? 1983. 10.95 (ISBN 0-533-05623-3). Vantage.
Scott, A. I., jt. auth. see Devon, T. K.
Scott, A. J. The Urban Land Nexus & the State. 256p. 1980. 24.00x (ISBN 0-85086-079-2, Pub. by Pion England). Methuen Inc.
Scott, Adolphe C. The Classical Theatre of China. LC 77-16447. (Illus.). 1978. Repr. of 1957 ed. lib. bdg. 29.75x (ISBN 0-313-20022-X, SCCT). Greenwood.
Scott, Alexander, ed. see MacDiarmid, Hugh.
Scott, Alexandra. Catch a Star. (Harlequin Romances Ser.). 192p. 1983. pap. 1.75 (ISBN 0-373-02554-8). Harlequin Bks.
Scott, Alexis, ed. The Workbook: California Edition. (Illus.). 700p. 1977. Set. 33.95 (ISBN 0-911113-00-2). Scott & Daughters.
Scott, Alice. How to Raise & Train a Pekingese. (Illus.). pap. 2.95 (ISBN 0-87666-346-3, DS1028). TFH Pubns.
Scott, Allan W. Cooling of Electronic Equipment. LC 73-11154. 283p. 1974. 34.95x (ISBN 0-471-76780-8, Pub. by Wiley-Interscience). Wiley.
Scott, Allen J., jt. auth. see Dear, Michael J.
Scott, Amanda. The Fugitive Heiress. (Orig.). 1981. pap. 1.95 o.p. (ISBN 0-451-09974-5, J9974, Sig). NAL.
Scott, Andrew M., jt. auth. see Scott, Anne F.
Scott, Ann, jt. auth. see First, Ruth.
Scott, Ann, jt. auth. see Hanak, Marcia.
Scott, Ann H. On Mother's Lap. LC 76-39726. (Illus.). 39p. (ps-k). 1972. PLB 10.95 (ISBN 0-07-055897-3); pap. 6.95 o.p. (ISBN 0-07-055896-5). McGraw.
Scott, Anne F. & Scott, Andrew M. One Half the People: The Fight for Woman Suffrage. 1982. 18.95 (ISBN 0-252-01011-6); pap. 5.95 (ISBN 0-252-01005-1). U of Ill Pr.
Scott, Arthur F., ed. Survey of Progress in Chemistry, 8 vols. Incl. Vol. 1. 1963. 46.50 (ISBN 0-12-610501-4); Vol. 2. 1965. 46.50 (ISBN 0-12-610502-2); Vol. 3. 1966. 46.50 (ISBN 0-12-610503-0); Vol. 4. 1968. 46.50 (ISBN 0-12-610504-9); Vol. 5. 1969. 46.50 (ISBN 0-12-610505-7); Vol. 6. 1974. 59.00 (ISBN 0-12-610506-5); Vol. 7. 1976. 42.50 (ISBN 0-12-610507-3); lib. ed 52.50 (ISBN 0-12-610574-X); microfiche 31.50 (ISBN 0-12-610575-8); Vol. 8. 1978. 47.50 (ISBN 0-12-610508-1); lib. ed. 59.50 (ISBN 0-12-610576-6); microfiche 36.50 (ISBN 0-12-610577-4); Vol. 9. 1980. 35.00 (ISBN 0-12-610509-X); lib. ed. 52.00 (ISBN 0-12-610578-2); microfiche 24.50 (ISBN 0-12-610579-0). Acad Pr.
--Survey of Progress in Chemistry, Vol. 10. (Serial Publication). Date not set. price not set (ISBN 0-12-610510-3). Acad Pr.
Scott, Austin. Interim Supplement to Scott on Trusts. LC 67-19987. pap. write for info. o.s.i. (ISBN 0-316-77645-9). Little.
Scott, Austin W. Abridgement of The Law of Trusts. 5th ed. 796p. 1960. 22.00 (ISBN 0-316-77640-8). Little.
--Interim Supplement to Law of Trusts. 1981. pap. 37.50 o.p. (ISBN 0-316-77645-9). Little.
--The Law of Trusts, 6 Vols. 3rd ed. 1982. Set. with 1980 supplement 295.00 (ISBN 0-316-77686-6). Little.
Scott, Austin W. & Scott, Austin W., Jr. Cases on Trusts. 5th ed. 1966. 23.00 o.p. (ISBN 0-316-77652-1). Little.
Scott, Authur F. America Grows. 1981. 10.95 (ISBN 0-533-04906-7). Vantage.
Scott, Bev, ed. see Trotsky, Leon.
Scott, Beverly, ed. see Trotsky, Leon.
Scott, Blackie. It's Fun to Entertain. 200p. 1983. 8.95 (ISBN 0-931948-42-8). Peachtree Pubns.
Scott, Brent-Wood. Love Is the Message. 1969. pap. 1.75 (ISBN 0-910140-20-0). Anthony.
Scott, C. Initiate in the Dark Cycle. pap. 5.95 (ISBN 0-87728-362-1). Weiser.
--Principles of Management Information Systems. 1983. write for info. (ISBN 0-07-056103-6). McGraw.
Scott, C. D. Biotechnology in Energy Production & Conservation: (Biotechnology & Bioengineering Symposia Ser.). 514p. 1979. pap. 45.95x (ISBN 0-471-05745-2, Pub. by Wiley-Interscience). Wiley.
--Second Symposium on Biotechnology in Energy Production & Conservation. 353p. 1980. pap. 55.95 (ISBN 0-471-09015-8, Pub. by Wiley-Interscience). Wiley.
Scott, C. R. Introduction to Soil Mechanics & Foundation. 3rd ed. 1980. 26.75 (ISBN 0-85334-873-1, Pub. by Applied Sci England). Elsevier.
Scott, C. R., ed. Developments in Soil Mechanics, Vol. 1. (Illus.). 1978. text ed. 86.00 (ISBN 0-85334-771-9, Pub. by Applied Sci England). Elsevier.
Scott, Carroll L. Successful Retirement in Florida. rev. ed. (Illus.). Date not set. cancelled (ISBN 0-915764-02-4); pap. price not set (ISBN 0-915764-01-6). SunRise Hse.
Scott, Catherine D., et al, eds. Directory of Aerospace Resources: A Guide to Special Collections in College, University, Historical Societies, & the National, State, & Local Archives of the United States. (Smithsonian Institution Libraries Research Guides). 112p. 1982. pap. 9.95x (ISBN 0-87474-851-8). Smithsonian.
Scott, Charles, ed. On Dreaming: An Encounter with Medard Boss. LC 82-21429. (Scholars Press General Series). 124p. 1982. pap. text ed. 9.95 (ISBN 0-89130-603-X, 00-03-06). Scholars Pr CA.
Scott, Charles E. Boundaries in Mind: A Study of Immediate Awareness Based on Psychotherapy. LC 81-18366. (AAR Studies in Religion). 1982. 10.95 (ISBN 0-89130-554-8, 01-00-27). Scholars Pr CA.
--Boundaries in Mind: A Study of Immediate Awareness Based on Psychotherapy. (American Academy of Religion Studies in Religion Series Co-Published with Scholars Press). 112p. 1982. 12.95 (ISBN 0-8245-0529-8). Crossroad NY.
Scott, Charles R., Jr. & Strickland, Alonzo J., III. Tempomatic IV: A Management Simulation. 2nd ed. LC 79-89182. (Illus.). 1980. pap. text ed. 12.95 (ISBN 0-395-28731-6); instr's. manual 1.00 (ISBN 0-395-28732-4); computer centers manual 1.75 (ISBN 0-395-28733-2); punched card deck avail. (ISBN 0-395-28734-0). HM.
Scott, Charlotte A. Projective Methods in Plane Analytical Geometry. 3rd ed. LC 49-4920. 11.95 (ISBN 0-8284-0146-2). Chelsea Pub.
Scott, Clifford H. Lester Frank Ward. LC 76-16539. (United States Authors Ser.). 1976. lib. bdg. 13.95 (ISBN 0-8057-7175-1, Twayne). G K Hall.
Scott, Cyril. Music: Its Secret Influence Throughout the Ages. LC 79-16380. 208p. 1981. pap. 6.95 (ISBN 0-87728-315-X). Weiser.
Scott, D. F., Jr., et al. Cases in Finance. (Illus.). 1977. pap. 13.95x ref. ed. (ISBN 0-13-115337-4). P-H.
Scott, D. J., jt. auth. see Basawa, I. V.
Scott, Daphne H., jt. auth. see Hoenig, Stuart A.
Scott, David H., ed. see Miller, Madeleine S. & Miller, J. Lane.
Scott, David L. Financing the Growth of Electric Utilities. LC 75-25024. (Illus.). 1976. 26.95 o.p. (ISBN 0-275-56460-6). Praeger.
Scott, David L. & Scott, Kay W. Traveling & Camping in the National Park Areas: Eastern States. LC 78-69951. (Illus.). 200p. 1979. pap. 4.95 (ISBN 0-87106-972-5). Globe Pequot.
Scott, David L., jt. auth. see Ferretti, Val S.
Scott, Desmond. Typhoon Pilot. (Illus.). 196p. 1983. 22.50 (ISBN 0-686-43268-1, Pub. by Secker & Warburg). David & Charles.
Scott, Diana. Bread & Roses. 300p. 1983. pap. 9.95 (ISBN 0-86068-235-8, Virago Pr). Merrimack Bk Serv.
Scott, Donald M. & Wishy, Bernard, eds. America's Families: A Documentary History. LC 79-3402. (Illus.). 688p. 1982. pap. 12.45i (ISBN 0-06-090903-X, CN 903, CN). Har-Row.
Scott, Donald M., ed. see O'Hara, Betsy.
Scott, Doug, tr. see Zimmerli, Walther.
Scott, Douglas. Operation Artemis. LC 79-2077. 1979. 10.95 o.p. (ISBN 0-672-52610-7). Bobbs.
--The Spoils of War. LC 77-14032. 1978. 8.95 o.p. (ISBN 0-698-10868-X, Coward). Putnam Pub Group.
Scott, Dru. How to Put More Time in Your Life. 1981. pap. 2.95 (ISBN 0-451-11958-4, AE1958, Sig). NAL.
Scott, Ed. Honda XL-XR125-200 Singles 1979-1982. Wauson, Sydnie A., ed. (Illus.). 352p. (Orig.). 1982. pap. text ed. 10.95 (ISBN 0-89287-355-8, M318). Clymer Pubns.
Scott, Edna see Lyman, Edna, pseud.
Scott, Edward M. Struggles in an Alcoholic Family. (Illus.). 280p. 1970. photocopy ed. spiral 15.75x (ISBN 0-398-01702-6). C C Thomas.
Scott, Eileen P. Your Visually Impaired Student: A Guide for Teachers. (Illus.). 224p. 1983. pap. text ed. 14.95 (ISBN 0-8391-1703-5, 16241). Univ Park.
Scott, Elaine. Adoption. LC 80-14848. (First Bks.). (Illus.). (gr. 4 up). 1980. 8.90 (ISBN 0-531-02937-9). Watts.
Scott, Eleanor. Fin De Fiesta: A Journey to Yucatan. (Illus.). 1974. pap. 6.95 (ISBN 0-913270-39-3). Sunstone Pr.
Scott, Ernest. Working in Wood: An Illustrated Encyclopedia. (Illus.). 272p. 1980. 25.00 (ISBN 0-399-12550-7). Putnam Pub Group.
Scott, Ernie. Building a Successful Ceramic Studio. (Illus.). 182p. 1980. 10.00 (ISBN 0-686-36025-7); pap. o.p. (ISBN 0-686-37270-0). Scott Pubns MI.
Scott, Eugene. Racquetball: The Cult. LC 77-75883. (Illus.). 1979. pap. 6.95 (ISBN 0-385-13006-6, Dolp). Doubleday.
Scott, Eugene L. The Tennis Experience. LC 79-7519. (Illus.). 1982. cancelled 19.95 (ISBN 0-88332-119-X). Larousse.
Scott, Evelyn. Background in Tennessee. facsimile ed. LC 80-15703. (Tennesseana Editions). 324p. 1980. Repr. of 1937 ed. 12.50 (ISBN 0-87049-297-7). U of Tenn Pr.
Scott, Frank, jt. ed. see Martin, Cliff.
Scott, G. Atmospheric Oxidation & Antioxidants. 1966. 95.75 (ISBN 0-444-40519-4). Elsevier.
Scott, G., ed. Developments in Polymer Stabilization, Vols. 1-6. 1979-82. Vol. 1. 69.75 (ISBN 0-85334-838-3, Pub. by Applied Sci England); Vol. 2. 45.00 (ISBN 0-85334-885-5); Vol. 3. 41.00 (ISBN 0-85334-890-1); Vol. 4. 55.50 (ISBN 0-85334-920-7); Vol. 5. 59.50 (ISBN 0-85334-967-3); Vol. 6. 81.60 (ISBN 0-85334-168-0). Elsevier.
Scott, Gavin. A Flight of Lies. 224p. 1981. 9.95 o.p. (ISBN 0-312-29614-2). St Martin.
Scott, Gay. The European Economic Community. 80p. (Orig.). 1981. pap. text ed. 20.00 (ISBN 0-906011-04-3, Pub by Capital Plan Info). Oryx Pr.
Scott, Geoffrey. Egyptian Boats. LC 80-27676. (A Carolrhoda on My Own Bk). (Illus.). 48p. (gr. k-3). 1981. PLB 6.95g (ISBN 0-87614-138-6). Carolrhoda Bks.
--Labor Day. LC 81-15485. (Carolrhoda on My Own Bks.). (Illus.). 48p. (gr. k-3). 1982. PLB 6.95g (ISBN 0-87614-178-5). Carolrhoda Bks.
Scott, George D. Plant Symbiosis. (Studies in Biology: No. 16). 64p. 1969. pap. text ed. 8.95 (ISBN 0-7131-2237-4). E Arnold.
Scott, George H. Bulbs: How to Select, Grow & Enjoy. 160p. 1982. pap. 7.95 (ISBN 0-89586-146-1). H P Bks.
Scott, George P. & Wahner, Heinz W., eds. Radiation & Cellular Response. (Illus.). 160p. 1983. pap. text ed. 5.95x (ISBN 0-8138-1496-0). Iowa St U Pr.
Scott, George R. The History of Corporal Punishment: A Survey of Flagellation in Its Historical, Anthropological & Sociological Aspects. LC 74-1088. (Illus.). 261p. 1974. Repr. of 1938 ed. 34.00x (ISBN 0-8103-3978-1). Gale.
Scott, Gerald, ed. Developments in Polymer Stabilisation, Vol. 1. (Illus.). 1979. 70.00x (ISBN 0-85334-838-3, Pub. by Applied Sci England). Burgess-Intl Ideas.
--Developments in Polymer Stabilisation, Vol. 2. (Illus.). x, 245p. 1980. 45.00x (ISBN 0-85334-885-5). Burgess Intl Ideas.
Scott, Gini G. Cult & Countercult: A Study of a Spiritual Growth Group & a Witchcraft Order. LC 79-54057. (Contributions in Sociology: No. 38). (Illus.). 1980. lib. bdg. 25.00x (ISBN 0-313-22074-3, SCC/). Greenwood.
Scott, Gwendolyn D. & Carlo, Mona. Learning, Feeling, Doing: Designing Creative Learning Experiences for Elementary Health Education. (Illus.). 1978. ref. ed. 15.95 o.p. (ISBN 0-13-527689-6). P-H.
Scott, H. B. & Pooley, A. C. The Status of Crocodiles in Africa. 1972. pap. 10.00 (ISBN 2-88032-010-0, IUCN43, IUCN). Unipub.
Scott, H. M., jt. auth. see Mckay, Derek.
Scott, Hardiman. Operation Ten. LC 82-47542. (A Cornelia & Michael Bessie Bk.). 224p. 1982. 12.45i (ISBN 0-06-039011-5, HarpT). Har-Row.
Scott, Harriet F., jt. auth. see Scott, William F.
Scott, Harriet F., tr. see Sokolovskiy, V. D.
Scott, Henry J. & Scott, Lenore. Hieroglyphs for Fun. (gr. 3-7). 1974. 7.95 o.p. (ISBN 0-442-27523-4). Van Nos Reinhold.
Scott, Henry W. The Evolution of Law: A Historical Review. 165p. 1982. Repr. of 1908 ed. lib. bdg. 22.50x (ISBN 0-8377-1127-4). Rothman.
Scott, Herschel L., Jr. Dehydrator Gourmet. LC 82-61641. (Western Backpacking Ser.). (Illus.). 65p. (Orig.). 1983. pap. 3.95 (ISBN 0-88083-003-4). Poverty Hill Pr.
--Passport to Prosperity. 60p. 1983. pap. 3.95 (ISBN 0-88083-005-0). Poverty Hill Pr.
Scott, Herschel L., Jr., jt. auth. see Stevens, Douglas L.
Scott, Hilda, jt. ed. see Eichler, Margrit.
Scott, Hildreth. I'm Free. (Uplook Ser.). 31p. 1973. pap. 0.75 o.p. (ISBN 0-8163-0073-9, 09340-1). Pacific Pr Pub Assn.
Scott, J. A. & Clark, Jane E. The Development of Movement Control & Coordination. (Series on Developmental Psychology). 376p. 1982. 48.00x (ISBN 0-471-10048-X, Pub. by Wiley-Interscience). Wiley.
Scott, J. M., jt. auth. see Theobald, Robert.
Scott, J. P., ed. Critical Periods. LC 78-632. (Benchmark Papers in Animal Behavior: Vol. 12). 381p. 1978. 48.50 (ISBN 0-87933-119-4). Hutchinson Ross.
Scott, J. T. Arthritis & Rheumatism: The Facts. (The Facts Ser.). (Illus.). 1980. 12.95x (ISBN 0-19-261168-2). Oxford U Pr.
Scott, Jack, jt. auth. see Lowder, Hughston E.
Scott, Jack D. The Book of the Goat. (Illus.). (gr. 6-8). 1979. 8.95 (ISBN 0-399-20681-7). Putnam Pub Group.
--The Book of the Pig. (Illus.). 64p. (ps up). 1981. 8.95 (ISBN 0-399-20718-X). Putnam Pub Group.
--Moose. (Illus.). 64p. (gr. 5 up). 1981. 9.95 (ISBN 0-399-20721-X). Putnam Pub Group.
--Orphans from the Sea. 64p. 1982. 10.95 (ISBN 0-399-20858-5). Putnam Pub Group.
--The Sea File. 288p. 1981. 10.95 o.p. (ISBN 0-07-056110-9, GB). McGraw.
--The Submarine Bird. LC 79-18297. (Illus.). (gr. 1 up). 1980. 8.95 (ISBN 0-399-20701-5). Putnam Pub Group.
--The Survivors: Enduring Animals of North America. LC 75-10132. (Illus.). 128p. (gr. 5 up). 1975. 7.50 o.p. (ISBN 0-15-283257-2, HJ). HarBraceJ.
Scott, Jack D. & Scott, Maria L. A World of Pasta. LC 77-25251. 1978. 12.95 o.p. (ISBN 0-07-055792-6, GB). McGraw.
Scott, Jack D. & Sweet, Ozzie. Canada Geese. LC 76-871. (Illus.). 64p. (gr. 5 up). 1976. 8.95 o.p. (ISBN 0-399-20492-X). Putnam Pub Group.
--City of Birds & Beasts: Behind the Scenes at the Bronx Zoo. LC 77-13888. (Illus.). (gr. 6 up). 1978. 8.95 (ISBN 0-399-20633-7). Putnam Pub Group.
--The Gulls of Smuttynose Island. LC 77-7870. (Illus.). (gr. 6-8). 1977. 8.95 (ISBN 0-399-20618-3). Putnam Pub Group.
--Island of Wild Horses. LC 78-17380. (Illus.). (gr. 6-8). 1978. 8.95 (ISBN 0-399-20648-5). Putnam Pub Group.
--Little Dogs of the Prairie. LC 76-56217. (Illus.). (gr. 6-8). 1977. 8.95 (ISBN 0-399-20561-6). Putnam Pub Group.
--The Loggerhead Turtle: Survivor from the Sea. new ed. LC 73-83993. (Illus.). 64p. (gr. 4 up). 1974. 8.95 o.p. (ISBN 0-399-20379-6). Putnam Pub Group.
--Return of the Buffalo. LC 76-19019. (Illus.). (gr. 6-8). 1976. 8.95 (ISBN 0-399-20552-7). Putnam Pub Group.
--That Wonderful Pelican. LC 74-21064. (Illus.). 64p. (gr. 6 up). 1975. 8.95 (ISBN 0-399-20449-0). Putnam Pub Group.
Scott, Jack S. A Clutch of Vipers. LC 78-22451. (Harper Novel of Suspense). 1979. 11.49i (ISBN 0-06-014008-9, HarpT). Har-Row.
--The Gospel Lamb. LC 80-7609. 192p. 1980. 11.49i (ISBN 0-06-014029-1, HarpT). Har-Row.
--The Local Lads: A Novel of Suspense. 1983. 12.95 (ISBN 0-525-24159-0, 01258-370). Dutton.
Scott, James. Yearbook Forty-Three, Nineteen Eighty-One, Association of Pacific Coast Geographers. LC 37-13376. (Illus.). 176p. 1982. pap. text ed. 7.00 (ISBN 0-87071-243-8). Oreg St U Pr.

Scott, James B. Djuna Barnes. (U.S. Authors Ser.: No. 262). 1976. lib. bdg. 7.95 o.p. (ISBN 0-8057-7153-0, Twayne). G K Hall.

--Hague Conference of Eighteen Ninety-Nine & Nineteen Seven, 2 vols. LC 79-147589. (Library of War & Peace; Int'l. Organization, Arbitration & Law). Set. lib. bdg. 76.00 o.s.i. (ISBN 0-8240-0350-0); lib. bdg. 38.00 ea. o.s.i. Garland Pub.

Scott, James C. The Moral Economy of the Peasant: Rebellion & Subsistence in Southeast Asia. LC 75-43334. 1976. 20.00x o.p. (ISBN 0-300-01862-2); pap. 5.95x (ISBN 0-300-02190-9). Yale U Pr.

Scott, James G; see Muller, W. Max.

Scott, Jane. To Keep an Island. LC 82-16299. 180p. (gr. 4-7). 1983. 10.95 (ISBN 0-689-50272-9, McElderry Bk). Atheneum.

Scott, Jeremy. The Two Faces of Robert Just. LC 80-14206. Orig. Title: Angels in Your Beer. 286p. 1980. 9.95 o.p. (ISBN 0-688-03621-X). Morrow.

Scott, Joan E. Introduction to Interactive Computer Graphics. LC 81-7621. 255p. 1982. 29.95 (ISBN 0-471-05773-8, Pub. by Wiley-Interscience); pap. 15.50x (ISBN 0-471-86623-7). Wiley.

Scott, John. Basic Computer Logic. LC 80-5074. (The Lexington Books Series in Computer Science). 256p. 1981. 24.95x (ISBN 0-669-03706-0). Lexington Bks.

--Behind the Urals: An American Worker in Russia's City of Steel. LC 72-88916. (Classics in Russian Studies: No. 3). 288p. 1973. pap. 4.95x (ISBN 0-253-10600-1). Ind U Pr.

--Corporations, Classes & Capitalism. LC 80-5097. 219p. 1980. 26.00 (ISBN 0-312-17011-4). St Martin.

Scott, John, tr. see Dolby, William.

Scott, John A. The Ballad of America: The History of the United States in Song & Story. 1983. pap. 12.95 (ISBN 0-8093-1061-9). S Ill U Pr.

--Unity of Homer. LC 65-15246. 1921. 10.00x (ISBN 0-8196-0152-7). Biblo.

Scott, John A., tr. see Olschki, Leonardo.

Scott, John B. Intermediate Algebra. 2nd ed. 332p. 1980. pap. text ed. 14.95x (ISBN 0-89641-033-1). American Pr.

Scott, John I., ed. Getting the Most Out of High School. 2nd rev. ed. LC 67-26419. 165p. (gr. 9 up). 1967. 6.50 (ISBN 0-379-00089-X). Oceana.

Scott, Jonathan. Piranesi. LC 74-81701. (Illus.). 400p. 1975. 29.98 o.p. (ISBN 0-312-61355-5). St Martin.

Scott, Joseph, jt. auth. see Davis, Gary.

Scott, Joseph E. & Dinitz, Simon, eds. Criminal Justice Planning. LC 76-14129. (Praeger Special Studies). 1977. 25.95 o.p. (ISBN 0-03-040896-2). Praeger.

Scott, Joseph W. Woman Know Thyself. LC 76-14588. (Illus.). 1976. 12.50 o.p. (ISBN 0-913590-44-4). Slack Inc.

Scott, Judy M., jt. auth. see Schlossberg, Stephen I.

Scott, Justin. Normandie Triangle. 576p. 1982. pap. 3.95 (ISBN 0-345-30640-6). Ballantine.

--A Pride of Royals. LC 81-71676. 570p. 1983. 15.95 (ISBN 0-87795-382-1). Arbor Hse.

Scott, K. Counterfeiting in Colonial Rhode Island. (Illus.). 1960. softcover 20.00 (ISBN 0-915262-76-2). S J Durst.

Scott, K. J., jt. auth. see Hall, E. G.

Scott, Kay W., jt. auth. see Scott, David L.

Scott, Kenneth, ed. see Needleman, Jacob, et al.

Scott, Kenneth J., ed. see Nye, F. Ivan & Berardo, Felix M.

Scott, Kenneth J., ed. see Tyson, Joseph B.

Scott, Kenneth W. Zane Grey, Born to the West: A Reference Guide. 1979. lib. bdg. 23.00 (ISBN 0-8161-7875-5, Hall Reference). G K Hall.

Scott, L. B. A New Time for Phonics, 6 Bks. 1980. Bks. A-C. text ed. 3.16 ea. Bk. A: Consonants (ISBN 0-07-056111-7). Bk. B: Short Vowels (ISBN 0-07-056112-5). Bk. C: Long Vowels (ISBN 0-07-056113-3). Bks. D-F. text ed. 4.72 ea. Bk. D: Consonant Pairs (ISBN 0-07-056114-1). Bk. E: Patterns (ISBN 0-07-056115-X). Bk. F: Sounds & Syllables (ISBN 0-07-056116-8). tchr's manuals for ea. bk. avail. McGraw.

Scott, L. L., tr. see Serre, J. P.

Scott, Lenore, jt. auth. see Scott, Henry J.

Scott, Lou P. Self Instruction & Review in Nursing. 2nd ed. (Illus.). 1980. pap. text ed. 13.95x ea. Vol. III (ISBN 0-02-408320-8). Vol. IV (ISBN 0-02-408370-4). Macmillan.

Scott, Louise B. Developing Communication Skills: A Guide for the Classroom Teacher. 1971. text ed. 19.72 (ISBN 0-07-055828-0, W). McGraw.

--Developing Phonics Skills: Listening, Reading, & Writing. LC 81-23225. 1982. pap. text ed. 16.95x (ISBN 0-8077-2718-0). Tchrs Coll.

--Reading Skills: A Phonics Approach. 1975. text ed. 2.12 o.p. (ISBN 0-07-055906-6, W). McGraw.

Scott, Louise B. & Garner, Jewell. Mathematical Experiences for Young Children. (Illus.). 1977. text ed. 19.24 (ISBN 0-07-055585-0, W). McGraw.

Scott, Louise B., et al. Learning Time with Language Experiences for Young Children. (Illus.). 1968. text ed. 19.30 o.p. (ISBN 0-07-055800-0, W). McGraw.

Scott, Marcia. Daring Sea Captains. LC 72-3592. (Pull Ahead Bks.). (Illus.). 96p. (gr. 6-11). 1973. PLB 4.95g (ISBN 0-8225-0465-0). Lerner Pubns.

Scott, Margaret K. & Beazley, Mary. Making Pressed Flower Pictures. (Illus.). 120p. 1980. 18.95 o.p. (ISBN 0-7134-1970-9, Pub. by Batsford England). David & Charles.

--Pressed Flowers Through the Seasons. (Illus.). 120p. 1983. 19.95 (ISBN 0-7134-4039-2, Pub. by Batsford England). David & Charles.

Scott, Maria L., jt. auth. see Scott, Jack D.

Scott, Martyn J., jt. auth. see Birley, Arthur W.

Scott, Mary. Kundalini in the Physical World. (Illus.). 240p. (Orig.). 1983. pap. price not set (ISBN 0-7100-9417-5). Routledge & Kegan.

Scott, Mel. American City Planning Since 1890. LC 70-84533. (California Studies in Urbanization & Environmental Design). 1969. 57.50x (ISBN 0-520-01382-4); pap. 14.95x (ISBN 0-520-02051-0, CAL235). U of Cal Pr.

Scott, Michael. Abortion, the Facts. 1980. 11.00x o.p. (ISBN 0-686-75606-1, Pub. by Darton-Longman-Todd England). State Mutual Bk.

Scott, Michael D. & Powers, William G. Interpersonal Communication: A Question of Needs. LC 77-76342. (Illus.). 1978. text ed. 16.95 (ISBN 0-395-25055-2); instr's. manual 1.00 (ISBN 0-395-25056-0). HM.

Scott, Michael W. Rakehell Dynasty: No. 2, China Bride. 512p. 1981. pap. 3.50 (ISBN 0-446-30309-7). Warner Bks.

--Rakehell Dynasty: No. 3, Orient Affair. 512p. (Orig.). 1982. pap. 3.95 (ISBN 0-446-30771-8). Warner Bks.

Scott, Miriam M. & Stratton, Carol. The Art of Sukhothai. (Illus.). 1981. 69.00x (ISBN 0-19-580434-1). Oxford U Pr.

Scott, N. R. Electronic Computer Technology. 1970. text ed. 24.95 o.p. (ISBN 0-07-055814-0, C). McGraw.

Scott, Natalie. Mandy's Favorite Louisiana Recipes. 64p. 1978. pap. 2.50 (ISBN 0-88289-142-1). Pelican.

Scott, Niki. The Balancing Act: A Handbook for Working Mothers. LC 78-10166. 1978. pap. 4.95 o.s.i. (ISBN 0-8362-6404-5). Andrews & McMeel.

Scott, O., et al. Prentice-Hall Textbook of Cosmetology. 1976. 16.95 (ISBN 0-13-695312-3); pap. text ed. 8.95 student's guide (ISBN 0-13-695304-2). P-H.

Scott, P. G. Strategies for Postsecondary Education. LC 75-8372. 161p. 1975. 17.25 o.p. (ISBN 0-470-76860-6). Krieger.

Scott, P. J. Anne Bronte: A New Critical Assessment. LC 82-22793. (Critical Studies). 208p. 1983. text ed. 27.50x (ISBN 0-389-20345-9). B&N Imports.

--E. M. Forster: Our Permanent Contemporary. (Critical Studies). (Illus.). 208p. 1983. text ed. 26.50x (ISBN 0-389-20368-8). B&N Imports.

Scott, Patricia E., jt. ed. see Fivaz, Derek.

Scott, Paul. The Raj Quartet, 4 Vols. LC 76-13249. 1978. Set. boxed set 29.95 (ISBN 0-688-03337-7). Morrow.

Scott, Peter. Australian Agriculture: Resource Development & Spatial Organization. (Geography of World Agriculture Ser.: Vol.9). (Illus.). 150p. 1981. 15.00x (ISBN 963-05-2445-7). Intl Pubns Serv.

--A Coloured Key to the Wildfowl of the World. rev. ed. (Illus.). 95p. 1972. 12.50x (ISBN 0-85493-013-2). Intl Pubns Serv.

--Strategies for Postsecondary Education. LC 75-8372. 161p. 1975. 29.95 o.s.i. (ISBN 0-470-76860-6). Halsted Pr.

Scott, Peter C. Foundations of College Chemistry: Study Guide. alternate ed. (Orig.). 1980. pap. text ed. 8.95 (ISBN 0-8185-0404-8). Brooks-Cole.

--Hein's Foundations of College Chemistry: Study Guide. 4th ed. 1977. study guide 8.95x o.p. (ISBN 0-8221-0197-1). Dickenson.

Scott, Peter D. Beyond Conspiracy. Stetler, Russell, ed. LC 81-51702. (Illus.). 1981. 19.00 o.p. (ISBN 0-87867-087-4); pap. 7.95 o.p. (ISBN 0-87867-088-2). Ramparts.

Scott, Peter W. Axolotls. (Illus.). 96p. 1981. 4.95 (ISBN 0-87666-937-2, KW-132). TFH Pubns.

Scott Publishing Co. Postage Stamp Catalogue & Inventory Checklist, 1983. (Illus.). 288p. (Orig.). 1982. pap. 2.84i (P-BN 5149). B&N NY.

Scott Publishing Company, ed. Scott Nineteen Eighty-One Stamp Catalogue: United States-United Nations-Canada. 1981. pap. 2.95 o.p. (ISBN 0-15-679672-4). HarBraceJ.

Scott, R., ed. Contemporary Liquid Chromotography. LC 74-15553. (Techniques of Chemistry Ser.: Vol. XI). 1976. 38.50x (ISBN 0-471-92900-X, Pub. by Wiley-Interscience). Wiley.

Scott, R. B., ed. Proverbs & Ecclesiastes. LC 65-13988. (Anchor Bible Ser.: No. 18). 1965. 14.00 (ISBN 0-385-02177-1, Anch). Doubleday.

Scott, R. C. & Sondak, N. E. PL-One for Programmers. 1970. pap. 18.95 (ISBN 0-201-07081-2). A-W.

Scott, R. W. Developments in Flow Measurement, Vol. 1. 1982. 74.00 (ISBN 0-85334-976-2, Pub. by Applied Sci England). Elsevier.

Scott, Ray G. How to Build Your Own Underground Home. (Illus.). 1979. 15.95 (ISBN 0-8306-9744-6); pap. 8.95 (ISBN 0-8306-1172-X, 1172). TAB Bks.

Scott, Raymond L. The Hiding God: Jesus in the Old Testament. 192p. 1982. pap. 4.95 (ISBN 0-8010-8221-8). Baker Bk.

Scott, Richard, et al. Auditing: A Systems Approach. (Illus.). 720p. 1982. text ed. 26.95 (ISBN 0-8359-0238-2); instr's manual free (ISBN 0-8359-0239-0); practical case 8.95 (ISBN 0-8359-0240-4); instr's. manual to case free (ISBN 0-8359-0274-9); sampling package free (ISBN 0-8359-0285-4). Reston.

Scott, Richard A., jt. ed. see Tschudy, Robert H.

Scott, Robert & Nigro, Nic. Principles of Economics. 1982. text ed. 25.95x (ISBN 0-02-408360-7). Macmillan.

Scott, Robert E., jt. auth. see Schwartz, Alan.

Scott, Robert F., ed. Shooter's Bible 1982, No. 73. 576p. 1981. pap. 10.95 o.p. (ISBN 0-88317-105-8). Stoeger Pub Co.

Scott, Robert G. Design Fundamentals. (Illus.). 1951. text ed. 16.95 o.p. (ISBN 0-07-055805-1, C). McGraw.

Scott, Robert H. Problems in National Income Analysis & Forecasting. rev. ed. 1972. pap. 8.95x o.p. (ISBN 0-673-07793-4). Scott F.

Scott, Robert H. & Nigro, Nic. Principles of Macroeconomics. 502p. 1982. pap. 18.95 (ISBN 0-02-408380-1). Macmillan.

--Principles of Microeconomics. 516p. 1982. pap. text ed. 18.95 (ISBN 0-02-408370-4). Macmillan.

--Principles of Microeconomics. 516p. 1982. pap. 18.95 (ISBN 0-02-408370-4). Macmillan.

Scott, Robert J. Fiberglass Boat Design & Construction. LC 72-83719. 1973. 12.50 o.p. (ISBN 0-8286-0059-7). De Graff.

Scott, Robert L., jt. auth. see Brockreide, Wayne.

Scott, Robert L. & Brockriede, Wayne, eds. The Rhetoric of Black Power. LC 78-31755. 1979. Repr. of 1969 ed. lib. bdg. 20.75x (ISBN 0-313-20973-1, SCRB). Greenwood.

Scott, Robert S. Voyage of the 'Discovery' (Illus.). 1951. 18.00 (ISBN 0-685-20649-1). Transatlantic.

Scott, Robert W. & West, Ronald R., eds. Structure & Classification of Paleocommunities. LC 76-4587. 352p. 1976. 49.50 (ISBN 0-12-787455-0). Acad Pr.

Scott, Roland B., ed. Advances in the Pathophysiology, Diagnosis & Treatment of Sickle Cell Disease. LC 82-12658. (Progress in Clinical & Biological Research Ser.: Vol. 98). 180p. 1982. 22.00 (ISBN 0-8451-0098-X). A R Liss.

Scott, Ronald B. Cancer: The Facts. 1980. text ed. 12.95x (ISBN 0-19-261149-6). Oxford U Pr.

Scott, Ronald B. & Fraser, James, eds. The Medical Annual 1982-83. (Illus.). 408p. 1982. pap. text ed. 29.50 (ISBN 0-7236-0655-2). Wright-PSG.

Scott, Ronald F. Foundation Analysis. (Civil Engineering & Engineering Mechanics Ser.). (Illus.). 496p. 1981. text ed. 33.95 (ISBN 0-13-329169-3). P-H.

Scott, Ronald F. & Schoustra, J. J. Soil Mechanics & Engineering. 1968. text ed. 23.95 (ISBN 0-07-055798-5, G). McGraw.

Scott, Ronald M., jt. auth. see Anderson, Kim E.

Scott, Rosemary. The Female Consumer. LC 75-31648. 300p. 1976. 39.95 o.p. (ISBN 0-470-76789-8). Halsted Pr.

Scott, Russell, Jr., et al, eds. Current Controversies in Urologic Management. LC 70-173342. (Illus.). 391p. 1972. 20.00 o.p. (ISBN 0-7216-8043-7). Saunders.

Scott, Samantha. Love's Unveiling. (Candlelight Ecstasy Ser.: No. 147). (Orig.). 1983. pap. 1.95 (ISBN 0-440-15022-1). Dell.

Scott, Samuel H., jt. ed. see Soderlund, G. F.

Scott, Sandra. The Hare Lay Trembling. 1981. 8.95 (ISBN 0-533-04662-9). Vantage.

Scott, Sarah. The History of Cornelia, 1750. (The Flowering of the Novel, 1740-1775 Ser: Vol. 29). 1974. lib. bdg. 50.00 o.s.i. (ISBN 0-8240-1128-7). Garland Pub.

Scott, T. Carcinogenic & Chronic Toxic Hazards of Aromatic Amines. 1962. 19.50 (ISBN 0-444-40520-8). Elsevier.

Scott, Thomas, jt. auth. see Henry, Matthew.

Scott, Thomas G., ed. Checklist of North American Plants for Wildlife Biologists. Wasser, Clinton H. LC 79-89208. 58p. (Orig.). 1980. pap. 4.50 (ISBN 0-933564-07-4). Wildlife Soc.

Scott, Tom, jt. auth. see Cousins, Geoffrey.

Scott, Tom, jt. ed. see MacQueen, John.

Scott, Virginia M. The Palace of the Princess. 1978. 7.95 o.p. (ISBN 0-533-03352-7). Vantage.

Scott, W. Bible Handbook, 2 vols. 18.00 (ISBN 0-88172-123-9). Believers Bkshelf.

Scott, W., jt. auth. see Curtis, J.

Scott, W. A. & Werner, R., eds. Molecular Cloning of Recombinant DNA. 1977. 25.00 (ISBN 0-12-634250-4). Acad Pr.

Scott, W. Richard. Organizations: Rational, Natural, & Open Systems. (Ser. in Sociology). (Illus.). 320p. 1981. text ed. 22.95 (ISBN 0-13-641977-1). P-H.

SCott, W. Stephen. Bankruptcy: A Virginia Law Practice System. 417p. 1982. looseleaf with forms 75.00 (ISBN 0-87215-507-2). Michie-Bobbs.

Scott, Walter. The Heart of Midlothian. Lamot, Clare, ed. (World's Classics Ser.). 1983. pap. 10.95 (ISBN 0-19-281583-0). Oxford U Pr.

--Ivanhoe. (RL 7). pap. 2.95 (ISBN 0-451-51684-2, CE1684, Sig Classics). NAL.

--Ivanhoe. (Penguin English Library). pap. 4.95 (ISBN 0-14-043143-8). Penguin.

--Ivanhoe. 1982p. Repr. lib. bdg. 18.95x (ISBN 0-89967-043-1). Harmony Raine.

--Kenilworth. new ed. (Classics Series). (gr. 10 up). 1968. pap. 2.50 (ISBN 0-8049-0193-7, CL-193). Airmont.

--Minstrelsy of the Scottish Border, 4 Vols. Henderson, T. F., ed. LC 67-23924. 1968. Repr. of 1902 ed. Set. 132.00x (ISBN 0-8103-3418-6). Gale.

--Old Mortality. Calder, Angus, ed. 1975. pap. 4.95 (ISBN 0-14-043098-9). Penguin.

--Waverley. 1976. 12.50x (ISBN 0-460-00075-6, Evman); pap. 4.95x (ISBN 0-460-01075-1, Evman). Biblio Dist.

Scott, Walter, tr. see Trismegistus, Hermes.

Scott, Walter A., et al, eds. Mobilization & Reassembly of Genetic Information: Vol. 17 of the Miami Winter Symposia. LC 80-18845. 1980. 40.00 (ISBN 0-12-633360-2). Acad Pr.

Scott, Sir Walter. Monastery. 1969. Repr. of 1906 ed. 9.95x (ISBN 0-460-00136-1, Evman). Biblio Dist.

Scott, Willard. Willard Scott's The Joy of Living. LC 82-4956. 1982. 12.95 (ISBN 0-698-11130-3, Coward). Putnam Pub Group.

Scott, William A. Money & Banking. Bruchey, Stuart, ed. LC 80-1168. (The Rise of Commercial Banking Ser.). 1981. Repr. of 1910 ed. lib. bdg. 35.00x (ISBN 0-405-13678-1). Ayer Co.

Scott, William A. & Wertheimer, Michael. Introduction to Psychological Research. LC 62-15190. 1962. 19.95x o.p. (ISBN 0-471-76857-X). Wiley.

Scott, William A. & Withey, Stephen B. The United States & the United Nations. (National Studies on International Organization - the Carnegie Endowment for International Peace). (Illus.). 314p. 1974. Repr. of 1958 ed. lib. bdg. 20.75x (ISBN 0-8371-7537-2, SCUS). Greenwood.

Scott, William A., ed. Sources of Protestant Theology. 1971. pap. 5.95 o.p. (ISBN 0-02-828010-5). Glencoe.

Scott, William E. Orthoptics & Ocular Examination Techniques. (Illus.). 416p. 1983. lib. bdg. 39.95 (ISBN 0-683-07614-0). Williams & Wilkins.

Scott, William F. The Discovery of the Igorots: Spanish Contacts with the Pagans of Northern Luzon. rev. ed. 1982. wrps. 10.75x (ISBN 0-686-18708-3). Cellar.

Scott, William F. & Scott, Harriet F. The Soviet Control Structure. (Strategy Papers Ser.: No. 39). 150p. 1983. pap. price not set (ISBN 0-8448-1452-0). Crane-Russak Co.

Scott, William H. Cracks in the Parchment Curtain & Other Essays in Philippine History. (Orig.). 1982. pap. 14.00 (ISBN 0-686-37571-8, Pub. by New Day Philippines). Cellar.

Scott, William H., jt. ed. see Filipiniana Book Guild.

Scott, William R. & Cunnison, J. Industries of the Clyde Valley During the War. (Economic & Social History of the World War Ser.). 1924. text ed. 49.50x (ISBN 0-686-83583-2). Elliots Bks.

Scott, William R., jt. auth. see New, Paul F.

Scott, William R. & Gross, Fletcher, eds. Proceedings of the Conference on Finite Groups. 1976. 58.50 (ISBN 0-12-633650-4). Acad Pr.

Scott, William T. The Physics of Electricity & Magnetism. 2nd ed. LC 75-42235. 722p. 1977. Repr. of 1966 ed. 29.50 (ISBN 0-88275-375-4). Krieger.

Scott, William W. A History of Orange County, Virginia. (Illus.). 292p. Repr. of 1907 ed. 16.00x o.p. (ISBN 0-685-65084-7). Va Bk.

Scott-Craig, T. S. K. A Guide to Pronouncing Biblical Names. LC 81-84713. 112p. (Orig.). 1982. pap. 3.50 (ISBN 0-8192-1292-X). Morehouse.

Scott-Fox, L., tr. see Descombes, Vincent.

Scotti, Paul. Seaports: Ships, Piers, & People. LC 80-21655. (Illus.). 64p. (gr. 4-6). 1980. PLB 7.29 o.p. (ISBN 0-671-34032-8). Messner.

Scottish Classics Group. Versiculi: A Companion in Verse. 1976. pap. text ed. 2.95x (ISBN 0-05-002897-9); tchr's notes 1.75x (ISBN 0-05-002898-7). Longman.

Scottish Classics Group, ed. Cicero: Pro Lege Manilia. (Ecce Romani Ser.). (Illus.). 64p. (Lat.). 1980. pap. text ed. 3.50x (ISBN 0-05-003259-3). Longman.

Scottish Tourist Board. Scotland: Bed & Breakfast. (Illus.). 208p. 1982. pap. 4.95 o.p. (ISBN 0-85419-192-5, Pub. by Auto Assn-British Tourist Authority England). Merrimack Bk Serv.

--Scotland: Hotels & Guesthouses. (Illus.). 296p. 1982. pap. 4.95 o.p. (ISBN 0-85419-191-7, Pub. by Auto Assn-British Tourist Authority England). Merrimack Bk Serv.

Scott-James, Anne & Lancaster, Osbert. The Pleasure Garden: An Illustrated History of English Gardening. LC 77-84332. (Illus.). 1978. 7.95 o.s.i. (ISBN 0-87645-109-1). Gambit.

Scott-Kilvert, Ian see Henderson, Philip.

Scott-Moncrieff, C. K., tr. see Stendhal.

Scott-Morgan, John. The Colonel Stephens Railways. LC 77-91737. 1978. 17.95 o.p. (ISBN 0-7153-7544-X). David & Charles.

Scott-Morton, Michael S., jt. auth. see Keen, Peter F.

Scott-Morton, Michael S., jt. auth. see McCosh, Andrew M.

Scott Russell, R. Plant Root Systems: Their Function & Interaction with the Soil. LC 77-6394. 1977. 39.50x (ISBN 0-07-084068-7). McGraw.

Scott-Taggart, John. Italian Maiolica. (Country Life Collector's Guides Ser). 1972. 4.95 o.p. (ISBN 0-600-43184-3). Transatlantic.

Scottus, Sedulius. Sedulius Scottus: On Christian Rulers & the Poems. Doyle, Edward, tr. from Latin. 200p. 1983. 16.00 (ISBN 0-86698-024-5). Medieval & Renaissance NY.

Scoufos, Alice-Lyle. Shakespeare's Typological Satire: A Study of the Falstaff-Oldcastle Problem. LC 77-92256. (Illus.). xvii, 378p. 1979. 24.95x (ISBN 0-8214-0390-7, 82-82832). Ohio U Pr.

Scouten, Arthur, intro. by. Restoration & Eighteenth Century Drama. 160p. 1981. pap. 5.95 o.p. (ISBN 0-312-67787-1). St Martin.

Scouten, Arthur H., jt. auth. see Avery, Emmett L.

Scouten, William H. Affinity Chromatography, Vol. 59. LC 80-20129. (Analytical Chemistry & Applications Monographs). 348p. 1981. 53.95 (ISBN 0-471-02649-2, Pub. by Wiley-Interscience). Wiley.

--Solid Phase Biochemistry: Analytical & Synthetic Aspects. (Chemical Analysis: Monographs on Analytical Chemistry & its Application). 632p. 1983. 75.00x (ISBN 0-471-08585-5, Pub. by Wiley-Interscience). Wiley.

Scovell, E. J. The Space Between. 64p. (Orig.). 1982. 12.50 (ISBN 0-436-44446-1, Pub. by Secker & Warburg). David & Charles.

Scoville, Herbert, Jr. The MX: Prescription for Disaster. (Illus.). 224p. 1981. 16.50x (ISBN 0-262-19199-7); pap. 6.95 (ISBN 0-262-69077-2). MIT Pr.

Scoville, Jon, jt. auth. see Banek, Reinhold.

Scowcroft, Brent, ed. Military Service in the United States. (Illus.). 226p. 1982. 14.95 (ISBN 0-13-583062-1); pap. 7.95 (ISBN 0-13-583054-0). P-H.

Scowcroft, Brent, ed. see Atlantic Council.

Scoy-Mosher, Michael B. Van see Van Scoy-Mosher, Michael B.

Scragg, D. G. A History of English Spelling. 1975. pap. 7.00 (ISBN 0-7190-0639-2). Manchester.

Scragg, D. G., ed. The Battle of Maldon. (Old & Middle English Texts). 128p. Date not set. pap. 5.95 (ISBN 0-7190-0838-7). Manchester.

Scragg, Leah. The Metamorphosis of Gallathea: A Study in Creative Adaptation. LC 81-40846. 150p. (Orig.). 1982. lib. bdg. 19.75 (ISBN 0-8191-2303-X); pap. text ed. 8.25 (ISBN 0-8191-2304-8). U Pr of Amer.

Scranton, Pierce E. Practical Techniques in Venipuncture. (Illus.). 180p. 1977. pap. 5.00 o.p. (ISBN 0-683-07551-9). Williams & Wilkins.

Scranton, Robert. Architecture of the Sanctuary of Apollo Hylates at Kourion. LC 67-27069. (Transactions Ser.: Vol. 57, Pt. 5). (Illus.). 1967. pap. 1.00 o.p. (ISBN 0-87169-575-8). Am Philos.

Scranton, Robert L. Greek Architecture. LC 62-7531. (Great Ages of World Architecture Ser). 1962. 7.95 o.s.i. (ISBN 0-8076-0175-6); pap. 7.95 o.s.i. (ISBN 0-8076-0337-6). Braziller.

Scrase, David. Wilhelm Lehmann: A Critical Biography. LC 81-69880. (Studies in German Literature, Linguistics, & Culture: Vol. 13). (Illus.). 1983. Set. 33.00x (ISBN 0-938100-14-9); Pt. I, 200 Pp. 17.00x (ISBN 0-938100-15-7); Pt. II, 200 Pp. 16.00x (ISBN 0-938100-16-5). Camden Hse.

Scrase, David, tr. see Melchinger, Siegfried.

Screen, J. E. O. Finland. (World Bibliographical Ser.: No. 31). 212p. 1981. text ed. 30.50 (ISBN 0-903450-55-0). ABC-Clio.

Scriabin, Alexander. The Complete Preludes & Etudes for Pianoforte Solo. Igumnov, K. N. & Mil'Shteyn, Y. I., eds. 250p. 1973. pap. 7.50 (ISBN 0-486-22919-X). Dover.

Scriabine, A., ed. New Antihypertensive Drugs: A. N. Richards Symposium. Sweet, C. S. LC 76-20746. (Monographs of the Physiological Society of Philadelphia). 1976. 40.00 o.s.i. (ISBN 0-470-15181-1). Halsted Pr.

Scriabine, Alexander, ed. The Pharmacology of Antihypertensive Drugs. 472p. 1980. text ed. 43.50 (ISBN 0-89004-329-9). Raven.

Scriabine, Alexander, et al, eds. Prostaglandins in Cardiovascular & Renal Function. (Monographs of the Physiology. Soc. of Phila.: Vol. 6). (Illus.). 481p. 1980. text ed. 70.00 (ISBN 0-686-24956-9). Spectrum Pub.

Scribner, Kimball. Your Future in Aviation Careers in the Air. rev. ed. (Careers in Depth Ser.). (Illus.). (gr. 7-12). 1982. PLB 7.97 (ISBN 0-8239-0490-3). Rosen Pr.

Scribner, R. W. For the Sake of Simple Folk: Popular Propaganda for the German Reformation. (Cambridge Studies in Oral & Literate Culture: No. 2). (Illus.). 350p. 1981. 47.50 (ISBN 0-521-24192-8). Cambridge U Pr.

Scribner, Robert L. & Tarter, Brent, eds. Revolutionary Virginia: The Road to Independence, Clash of Arms & the Fourth Convention, 1775-1776, a Documentary Record, Vol. V. LC 72-96023. 471p. 1979. 30.00x (ISBN 0-8139-0806-X). U Pr of Va.

Scribner, Robert L., jt. ed. see Tartar, Brent.

Scribner, S., jt. auth. see Cole, M.

Scrignar, C. B. Stress Strategies. (Karger Biobehavioral Medicine Ser.: Vol. 1). (Illus.). 1983. 28.75 (ISBN 3-8055-3605-4). S Karger.

Scrimgeour, G. J. A Woman of Her Times. LC 81-15722. 408p. 1982. 13.95 (ISBN 0-399-12711-9). Putnam Pub Group.

Scrimgeour, James R. Sean O'Casey. (English Authors Ser.). 1978. 12.95 (ISBN 0-8057-6735-5, Twayne). G K Hall.

Scrimshaw, Nevin S. & Altschul, Aaron M., eds. Amino Acid Fortification of Protein Foods. 1971. 33.00x (ISBN 0-262-19091-5). MIT Pr.

Scrimshaw, Nevin S., jt. ed. see Chen, Lincoln C.

Scripta Technica, tr. see Turov, E. A.

Scripta Technica, tr. see Veselov, M. G.

Scripta Technica Inc., tr. see Postnikov, M. M.

Scripture Union. Every Day: Bible Readings for Each Day of the Year. LC 72-4169. 1972. 3.95 o.p. (ISBN 0-87981-015-7). Holman.

Scriven, Carl & Stevens, James. Food Equipment Facts: A Handbook for the Food Service Industry. LC 81-24977. 429p. 1982. pap. text ed. 15.95 (ISBN 0-471-86819-1). Wiley.

Scriven, F. B. Sports Facilities for Schools in Developing Countries. LC 72-96367. (Educational Studies & Documents). (Illus.). 39p. (Orig.). 1973. pap. 2.50 o.p. (ISBN 92-3-101049-2, U629, UNESCO). Unipub.

Scriven, M. S., jt. auth. see Madaus, G.

Scriven, Michael. Primary Philosophy. 1966. text ed. 25.00 (ISBN 0-07-055860-4, C). McGraw.

--Reasoning. 1977. pap. text ed. 17.50 (ISBN 0-07-055882-5, C). McGraw.

Scrivenor, Patrick. In Praise of Male Chauvinism. 2.95 o.p. (ISBN 0-7153-7488-5). David & Charles.

Scriver, Bob. No More Buffalo. LC 82-15194. (Illus.). 150p. 1982. 35.00 (ISBN 0-913504-75-0). Lowell Pr.

Scrivin, Peter. The Tintookies & Little Fella Bindi. (Illus.). (gr. 1 up). 10.00x (ISBN 0-392-04991-0, ABC). Sportshelf.

Scrivner, Charles L. Empire Express. LC 76-17672. (Worldwar II Naval History). (Illus.). 56p. 1976. pap. 6.50 o.p. (ISBN 0-911852-78-6). Hist Aviation.

Scrivner, Louise. Guide to Oral Interpretation. LC 79-11940. (Orig.). 1980. pap. 11.95 (ISBN 0-672-61476-6). Odyssey Pr.

Scroeder, John S., jt. auth. see Page, Helen C.

Scroggie, W. Graham. Know Your Bible. 608p. 1965. 17.95 (ISBN 0-8007-0169-0). Revell.

--Studies in Philemon. LC 77-79186. 1982. 6.95 (ISBN 0-8254-3718-0); pap. 3.95 (ISBN 0-8254-3739-3). Kregel.

--W. Graham Scroggie Library Series, 6 vols. 1981. pap. 14.50 (ISBN 0-8254-3738-5). Kregel.

--W. Graham Scroggie Library Series, 7 Vols. 1982. pap. 18.00 (ISBN 0-8254-3740-7). Kregel.

Scroggs, James. Letting Love in. LC 77-27268. 1978. 11.95 o.p. (ISBN 0-13-531566-2, Spec); pap. 4.95 (ISBN 0-13-531558-1, Spec). P-H.

Scruton, R. Fortnight's Anger. 224p. 1981. text ed. 15.00x (ISBN 0-85635-376-0, Pub. by Carcanet Pr England). Humanities.

Scruton, Robert. A Dictionary of Political Thought. LC 82-47532. 352p. 1982. write for info. (ISBN 0-06-015044-0, HarpT). Har-Row.

Scruton, Roger. Art & Imagination: A Study in the Philosophy of Mind. 256p. 1982. pap. 8.95 (ISBN 0-686-80814-2). Routledge & Kegan.

Scrutton, D. R. & Gilbertson, M. P. Physiotherapy in Pediatric Practice. (Postgraduate Pediatric Ser.). 1975. 19.95 o.p. (ISBN 0-407-00017-8). Butterworth.

Scrutton, R. A. & Talwani, M. The Ocean Floor: Bruce Heezen Memorial Volume. LC 81-14700. 318p. 1982. 106.00 (ISBN 0-471-10091-9, Pub. by Wiley-Interscience). Wiley.

Scudder, Norma. Elmo. (Illus.). 33p. 1982. pap. 3.50 (ISBN 0-942316-03-7). Pueblo Pub Pr.

Scudder, Vida D. Social Ideals in English Letters. (Belles Lettres in English Ser). Repr. of 1898 ed. 33.00 (ISBN 0-384-54520-3). Johnson Repr.

Scull, Andrew. Museums of Madness: The Social Organization of Insanity in Nineteenth Century England. LC 78-73732. (Illus.). 1979. 22.50 (ISBN 0-312-55355-2). St Martin.

Scullard, H. H. From the Gracchi to Nero: A History of Rome from 133 B.C. to A.D. 68. 5th ed. LC 76-1802. 488p. 1983. 30.00x (ISBN 0-416-56090-3); pap. 14.95x (ISBN 0-416-56100-4). Methuen Inc.

--History of the Roman World: 753-146 BC. 4th ed. xiv, 480p. 1980. 35.00x (ISBN 0-416-71480-3); pap. 14.95x (ISBN 0-416-71490-0). Methuen Inc.

--Roman Britain: Outpost of the Empire. (Illus.). 1979. 17.95 (ISBN 0-500-45019-6). Thames Hudson.

Scullard, H. H., jt. ed. see Hammond, N. G.

Scullard, H. H., ed. see McKay, Alexander G.

Scullard, H. H., ed. see Toynbee, J. M.

Sculley, Dean, ed. Cooper Union School of Architecture: Solitary Travelers, Vols. 1 & 2. (Illus.). 149p. 1983. pap. 35.00 (ISBN 0-8390-0310-2). Allanheld & Schram.

Scullion, Hugh, jt. auth. see Edwards, P. K.

Scullion, John. Isaiah Forty to Sixty-Six, Vol. 12. 1982. 12.95 (ISBN 0-89453-246-4); pap. 7.95 (ISBN 0-686-32765-9). M Glazier.

Scullion, John J., tr. see Westermann, Claus.

Scully, C. & Cawson, R. A. Medical Problems in Dentistry. (Illus.). 528p. 1982. pap. 33.50 (ISBN 0-7236-0607-2). Wright-PSG.

Scully, James. May Day. LC 80-80653. 72p. (Orig.). 1980. pap. 3.00 o.p. (ISBN 0-936484-00-4). Minn Rev Pr.

Scully, James, ed. see Vallejo, Ceasar.

Scully, M. O., jt. ed. see Ter Haar, D.

Scully, V. J., Jr., jt. auth. see Downing, A. F.

Scully, Vincent. Pueblo: Mountain, Village, Dance. LC 73-16935. (Illus.). 398p. 1975. 25.00 o.p. (ISBN 0-670-58209-3). Viking Pr.

Scully, Vincent, ed. see Trager, Philip, et al.

Sculthorpe, C. Duncan. Biology of Aquatic Vascular Plants. (Illus.). 1967. 39.95 o.p. (ISBN 0-312-07945-1). St Martin.

Sculthorpe, William L. Design of High Pressure Steam & High Temperature Water Plants. LC 81-19340. 112p. 1983. Repr. of 1972 ed. lib. bdg. write for info. (ISBN 0-89874-466-0). Krieger.

Scuola, Editrice, Brescia, Italy, tr. see Bettoni, Efrem.

Scupham, Peter. The Hinterland. 1977. pap. 5.95x o.p. (ISBN 0-19-211871-4). Oxford U Pr.

Scura, Dorothy M. Henry James, 1960-1974: A Reference Guide. 1979. lib. bdg. 40.00 (ISBN 0-8161-7850-X, Hall Reference). G K Hall.

Scurlock, John. Retroactive Legislation Affecting Interests in Land. LC 54-62006. (Michigan Legal Studies). xv, 390p. 1982. Repr. of 1953 ed. lib. bdg. 30.00 (ISBN 0-89941-175-4). W S Hein.

Scurlock, R. G. Low Temperature Behaviour of Solids. (Solid-State Physics Ser). 1966. pap. 3.75 o.p. (ISBN 0-7100-4383-X). Routledge & Kegan.

Scuro, Vincent, jt. auth. see Lavine, Sigmund A.

Scurr & Feldman. Scientific Foundations of Anaesthesia. 3rd ed. 1982. 74.50 (ISBN 0-8151-7628-7). Year Bk Med.

Scutchfield, F., jt. auth. see Pieroni, Robert E.

Scutt, Jocelynne A., jt. ed. see Mukherjee, Satyanshu K.

Scwartz, Seymour I., et al. Principles of Surgery. 3rd ed. (Illus.). 1979. 1 vol. ed. 60.00 (ISBN 0-07-055735-7, HP); text ed. 80.00 2 vol. ed. (ISBN 0-07-055736-5). McGraw.

Scyoc, Sydney J. Van see Van Scyoc, Sydney J.

S. D. de Lerin, Olivia, tr. see Sutton, Joan L. & Watson de Barros, Leda.

Sea, Beth. I Am what I Am-Human. (Illus.). 40p. (Orig.). Date not set. pap. 3.50 (ISBN 0-9608796-0-9). B S Beaulieu.

Sea World Press & Alan Sloan, Inc. The Sea World Alphabet Book. LC 79-65202. (Sea World Press Ser.). (Illus.). 32p. (ps-3). 1980. 4.95 (ISBN 0-15-271946-6, 015-65202, HJ). HarBraceJ.

Seabloom, R. W., jt. auth. see Crandall, K. C.

Seabloom, R. W., jt. auth. see Eikum, A. S.

Seaborg, G. T. & Loveland, W. Nuclear Chemistry. (Benchmark Papers in Physical & Chemical Physics: Vol. 5). 1982. cancelled (ISBN 0-12-787454-2). Acad Pr.

Seaborg, G. T., ed. Transuranium Elements: Products of Modern Alchemy. LC 78-7803. (Benchmark Papers in Physical Chemistry & Chemical Physics: Vol. 1). 488p. 1978. 56.00 (ISBN 0-87933-326-X). Hutchinson Ross.

Seaborg, Glenn & Katzin, Leonard I., eds. Production & Separation of U-233: Survey. (National Nuclear Energy Ser.: Division IV, Vol. 17A). 236p. 1951. pap. 20.50 (ISBN 0-87079-384-5, TID-5222); microfilm 4.50 (ISBN 0-87079-342-X, TID-5222). DOE.

Seaborg, Glenn T. & Loeb, Benjamin S. Kennedy, Khrushchev, & the Test Ban. (Illus.). 336p. 1983. pap. 7.95 (ISBN 0-520-04961-6, CAL 629). U of Cal Pr.

Seaborne, A. E., jt. auth. see Borger, Robert.

Seabough, Ed. So You're Going to College. LC 73-91607. 5.95 (ISBN 0-8054-5321-0). Broadman.

Seabrook, Peter. The Complete Vegetable Gardener. (Illus.). 128p. 1983. pap. 7.95 (ISBN 0-89104-059-5, A & W Visual Library). A & W Pubs.

Seabrooke, Brenda. The Best Burglar Alarm. LC 78-7455. (Illus.). (gr. k-3). 1978. 9.75 (ISBN 0-688-22165-3); PLB 9.36 (ISBN 0-688-32165-8). Morrow.

--Home Is Where They Take You in. LC 79-24508. 192p. (gr. 7-9). 1980. 9.75 (ISBN 0-688-22221-8); PLB 9.36 (ISBN 0-688-32221-2). Morrow.

Seabrooke, W., jt. auth. see Miles, C. W.

Seaburg, K. G., et al. The Algae of Southern Victorialand, Antarctica, Taxonomic & Distributional Study. (Illus.). 1980. lib. bdg. 40.00 (ISBN 3-7682-1249-1). Lubrecht & Cramer.

Seabury, David. Art of Selfishness: How to Deal with the Tyrants & Tyrannies in Your life. 1966. 8.95 o.p. (ISBN 0-671-05460-0). S&S.

--How to Live With Yourself. 104p. 1972. pap. 3.95 (ISBN 0-911336-39-7). Sci of Mind.

Seabury, Paul. The Wilhelmstrasse: A Study of German Diplomats Under the Nazi Regime. LC 76-2403. (Illus.). 217p. 1976. Repr. of 1954 ed. lib. bdg. 17.25x (ISBN 0-8371-8790-7, SEWI). Greenwood.

Seabury, Paul, et al, eds. Bureaucrats & Brainpower: Government Regulation of Universities. Weinberger, Caspar & Lyman, Richard. LC 79-51328. 171p. 1979. pap. text ed. 6.95 (ISBN 0-917616-35-9). ICS Pr.

Seabury, William M. The Public & the Motion Picture Industry. LC 75-160247. (Moving Pictures Ser.). xiv, 340p. 1971. Repr. of 1926 ed. lib. bdg. 19.95x (ISBN 0-89198-048-2). Ozer.

Seaby, B. A. Roman Silver Coins: Gordian III to Postumus, Vol. IV. 4th ed. 1982. 22.50 (ISBN 0-686-37931-4). Numismatic Fine Arts.

--Roman Silver Coins: Pertinax, to Balbinus & Pupienus, Vol. III. 4th ed. 1982. 22.50 (ISBN 0-686-37930-6). Numismatic Fine Arts.

Seaby, H. A. Roman Silver Coins: The Republic to Augustus, Vol. 1. 3rd ed. 1978. 16.00. Numismatic Fine Arts.

--Roman Silver Coins: Tiberius to Commodus, Vol. 2. 3rd ed. 1979. 30.00. Numismatic Fine Arts.

--Standard Catalogue of British Coins: Coins of England & the United Kingdom. 18th ed. 1981. write for info. o.p. Numismatic Fine Arts.

Seacole, Mary. Wonderful Adventures of Mrs. Seacole in Many Ways. Alexander, Ziggi & Dewjee, Audrey, eds. 192p. 1983. 13.95 (ISBN 0-905046-22-6); pap. 7.95 (ISBN 0-905046-23-4). Falling Wall.

Seader, J. D., jt. auth. see Henley, Ernest J.

Seaford, Richard. Pompeii. (Illus.). 1979. pap. 9.95 o.p. (ISBN 0-500-27168-2). Thames Hudson.

Seager, R., tr. see Gelzer, Matthias.

Seager, Spencer L. & Slabaugh, Michael R. Introductory Chemistry: General, Organic, Biological. 1979. text ed. 25.50x (ISBN 0-673-15026-7); study guide 9.95x (ISBN 0-673-15215-4). Scott F.

Seager, Spencer L. & Stoker, H. Stephen. Chemistry: A Science for Today. 1973. text ed. 18.95x (ISBN 0-673-07808-6). Scott F.

Seager, Spencer L., jt. auth. see Slabaugh, Michael R.

Seager, Spencer L., jt. auth. see Stoker, H. Stephen.

Seagle, Janet, jt. ed. see Murdoch, Joseph S.

Seagrave. Soldiers of Fortune. LC 81-13599. (Epic of Flight Ser.). PLB 19.96 (ISBN 0-8094-3326-5). Silver.

Seagrave, Sterling. The Bush Pilots. (Epic of Flight Ser.). 1983. lib. bdg. 19.96 (ISBN 0-8094-3309-5, Pub. by Time-Life). Silver.

Seagren, Daniel R. Congratulations Graduate. (Contempo Ser.). pap. 1.25 (ISBN 0-8010-8139-4). Baker Bk.

--Love Carved in Stone: Ten Commandments. 1983. pap. text ed. 2.50 (ISBN 0-8307-0840-5). Regal.

Seagrin, G. N., tr. see Piaget, Jean.

Seagull, Louis M. Southern Republicanism 1940-1972. LC 74-17381. 1974. 10.95x o.s.i. (ISBN 0-470-76875-4); pap. 5.95x o.s.i. (ISBN 0-470-76876-2). Halsted Pr.

Seal, Anil. Emergence of Indian Nationalism. (Political Change in Modern Asia: No. 1). (Illus.). 1968. 42.50 (ISBN 0-521-06274-8); pap. 12.95x (ISBN 0-521-09652-9). Cambridge U Pr.

Seal, Hilary L. Survival Probabilities: The Goal of Risk Theory. LC 78-8599. (Probability & Mathematical Statistics Ser.). 103p. 1978. 44.95 (ISBN 0-471-99683-1, Pub. by Wiley-Interscience). Wiley.

Sealander, Judith. As Minority Becomes Majority: Federal Reaction to the Phenomenon of Women in the Work Force 1920-1963. LC 82-15820. 224p. 1983. lib. bdg. 27.95 (ISBN 0-313-23750-6). Greenwood.

Seale, Arthur C., Jr., jt. auth. see Pansini, Anthony J.

Seale, Barbara. Writing Efficiently: A Step-by-Step Composition Course. (Illus.). 1978. pap. text ed. 10.25 (ISBN 0-13-970160-5). P-H.

Seale, David. Vision & Stagecraft in Sophocles. LC 82-50459. 270p. 1982. lib. bdg. 27.50x (ISBN 0-226-74404-3). U of Chicago Pr.

Seale, J. N. Car Service Data. 3rd ed. 1979. 13.95 o.p. (ISBN 0-600-32016-2). Transatlantic.

Seale, J. N., compiled by. Car Service Data. 2nd ed. (Illus.). 272p. 1976. 10.00 o.p. (ISBN 0-600-31832-X). Transatlantic.

Seale, Jan. Sharing the House. Schmidt, Dorey, ed. (River Sedge Poetry Ser.: No. 3). (Illus.). 50p. (Orig.). 1982. pap. 4.00 (ISBN 0-938884-05-0). RiverSedge Pr.

Seale, M. S. Qur'an & Bible: Studies in Interpretation & Dialogue. 124p. 1978. 23.50x (ISBN 0-85664-818-3, Pub. by Croom Helm Ltd England). Biblio Dist.

Seale, Roland. Practical Designs for Wood Turning. LC 79-65084. (Illus.). 1979. pap. 6.95 (ISBN 0-8069-8874-6). Sterling.

Seale, Sara. The Young Amanda, The Truant Bride & Beggars May Sing. (Harlequin Romances (3-in-1) Ser.). 576p. 1983. pap. 3.95 (ISBN 0-373-20070-6). Harlequin Bks.

Seale, William. Sam Houston's Wife: A Biography of Margaret Lea Houston. LC 77-123341. (Illus.). 1970. 12.50 o.p. (ISBN 0-8061-0926-2). U of Okla Pr.

--A Tasteful Interlude: American Interiors Through the Camera's Eye, 1860 to 1917. LC 80-27341. (Illus.). 288p. 1981. pap. 14.00 (ISBN 0-910050-49-X). AASLH.

Seales, John B. The Travel Game: An Insider's Guide to Getting the Most for Your Travel Dollar. Rand, Elizabeth, ed. 192p. (Orig.). 1983. pap. 6.95 (ISBN 0-914488-28-7). Rand-Tofua.

Sealey, Raphael. A History of the Greek States, 700-338 BC. 1977. 38.50x (ISBN 0-520-03125-3); pap. 10.95x (ISBN 0-520-03177-6, CAMPUS 165). U of Cal Pr.

Sealey, Richard. How to Keep Your VW Rabbit Alive, a Manual of Step by Step Procedures for the Compleat Idiot. LC 79-91278. (Illus.). 432p. (Orig.). 1980. pap. 15.00 (ISBN 0-912528-17-6). John Muir.

Sealfon, Peggy. The Magic of Book of Instant Photography. (Illus.). 256p. 1982. 25.95 (ISBN 0-8436-0137-X); pap. 14.95 (ISBN 0-8436-0138-8). CBI Pub.

Seals, Monroe. History of White County Tennessee. LC 74-13633. 168p. 1975. Repr. of 1935 ed. 17.50 (ISBN 0-87152-186-5). Reprint.

Seals, Thomas L. Proverbs: Wisdom for All Ages. 4.95. Quality Pubns.

Sealts, M. M., Jr. see Emerson, Ralph W.

Sealts, Merton M., Jr. The Early Lives of Melville: Nineteenth-Century Biographical Sketches & Their Authors. LC 74-5906. (Illus.). 296p. 1974. 27.50x (ISBN 0-299-06570-7). U of Wis Pr.

Sealts, Merton M., Jr. see Emerson, Ralph W.

Sealts, Merton M., Jr., ed. see Melville, Herman.

Sealy, Adrienne. And Even a Child Shall Lead Them. 7.50 o.p. (ISBN 0-533-00895-6). Vantage.

Sealy, Lloyd G., jt. auth. see Fink, Joseph.

Seaman, Barrett, jt. auth. see Moritz, Michael.

Seaman, Betty M. What Is Bertha Gray Doing in the Kitchen? 1980. 4.50 o.p. (ISBN 0-533-04456-1). Vantage.

Seaman, David, jt. auth. see Buttimer, Anne.

Seaman, Don, ed. see Boyle, Patrick G.

Seaman, Donald. The Terror Syndicate. LC 76-25011. 1976. 7.95 o.p. (ISBN 0-698-10791-8, Coward). Putnam Pub Group.

--Working Effectively with Task Force Oriented Groups. Pardoen, Alan, ed. (Adult Education Association Professional Development Ser.). (Illus.). 144p. 1981. text ed. 14.95x (ISBN 0-07-000554-0, C). McGraw.

Seaman, Dorothy, jt. auth. see Smith, Paula.

Seaman, Gary. Temple Organization in a Chinese Village. (Asian Folklore & Social Life Monographs: Vol. 101). 173p. 1978. 14.50 (ISBN 0-89986-332-9). Oriental Bk Store.

Seaman, Janet & Depauw, Karen. The New Adapted Physical Education: A Developmental Approach. LC 81-84691. (Illus.). 507p. 1982. text ed. 19.95 (ISBN 0-87484-524-6); instrs'. man avail. Mayfield Pub.

Seaman, L. C. Post-Victorian Britain: 1902-1951. 531p. 1968. 15.95x (ISBN 0-416-69760-7). Methuen Inc.

--Victorian England: Aspects of English & Imperial History 1837-1901. 500p. 1973. pap. 13.95x (ISBN 0-416-77550-0). Methuen Inc.

Seaman, L. C. B, ed. see Packe, Michael.

Seaman, Patricia, jt. auth. see Martinell, Patricia.

Seamands, David A. Healing for Damaged Emotions. 1981. pap. 4.50 (ISBN 0-88207-228-5). Victor Bks.

Seamans, Eldon L. Studies in American Minority Life. 1976. pap. text ed. 8.25 (ISBN 0-8191-0092-7). U Pr of Amer.

Seamark, R. F., jt. ed. see Matthew, C. D.

Seamon, David. A Geography of the Life World: Movement, Rest & Encounter. 1979. 27.50x (ISBN 0-312-32257-7). St Martin.

Seamon, Harold P., intro. by see Genck, Fredric H. & Klingenberg, Allen J.

Seamon, John G. Memory & Cognition: An Introduction. (Illus.). 1980. text ed. 13.95x (ISBN 0-19-502642-X); pap. text ed. 11.95x (ISBN 0-19-502643-8). Oxford U Pr.

Seamon, John G., ed. Human Memory: Contemporary Readings. (Illus.). 1980. text ed. 27.50x (ISBN 0-19-502738-8); pap. text ed. 13.95x (ISBN 0-19-502739-6). Oxford U Pr.

Seanor, Donald, ed. Electrical Properties of Polymers. 1982. 52.00 (ISBN 0-12-633680-6). Acad Pr.

Seaquist, Alfred J., compiled by. Nonwood Plant Fiber Pulping, Progress Report, No. 12. (TAPPI Press Reports Ser.). (Illus.). 88p. 1982. 48.95 (ISBN 0-89852-397-4, 01-01-R097). TAPPI.

Seaquist, Edgar O. How to Diagnose & Repair House Structure Problems. (Illus.). 1980. 17.50 (ISBN 0-07-056013-7). McGraw.

Sear, David. The Emperors of Rome & Byzantium: Chronological & Genealogical Tables for History Students & Coin Collectors. 2nd ed. 12.50x. Numismatic Fine Arts.

--Greek Coins & Their Values, Vol. 1. 1978. 27.50. Numismatic Fine Arts.

--Greek Coins & Their Values, Vol. 2. 1979. 35.00. Numismatic Fine Arts.

--Roman Coins & Their Values. 1981. 25.00. Numismatic Fine Arts.

Searby, Ellen. The Inside Passage Traveler. 6th ed. (Illus.). 144p. 1983. pap. 5.95 (ISBN 0-9605526-3-4). Windham Bay.

--Inside Passage Traveler: Getting Around in Southeastern Alaska. 5th ed. (Illus.). 136p. 1983. pap. 5.95 (ISBN 0-9605526-2-6). Windham Bay.

Search, Gay. Surviving Divorce: A British Handbook for Men. (Illus.). 128p. 1983. 16.50 (ISBN 0-241-10954-X, Pub. by Hamish Hamilton England). David & Charles.

Searcy, Margaret Z. Race of Flitty Hummingbird & Flappy Crane. (Illus.). (gr. 2-4). 1980. 7.50 (ISBN 0-916620-21-2). Portals Pr.

--Wolf Dog of the Woodland Indians. LC 81-19763. (Illus.). 114p. (gr. 4-8). 1982. 9.95 (ISBN 0-8173-0091-0). U of Ala Pr.

Searcy, Ronald L. Diagnostic Biochemistry. 1969. 37.00 o.p. (ISBN 0-07-055892-2, HP). McGraw.

Seare, Nicholas. Rude Tales & Glorious. 1983. 13.95 (ISBN 0-517-54986-7, C N Potter Bks). Crown.

Searfoss, D. Gerald, jt. auth. see Seawell, L. Vann.

Searfoss, Lyndon W. & Moorman, Gary B. Learning to Teach Reading: Instructional Units for Developing Basic Teaching Skills. 1980. pap. text ed. 7.95 (ISBN 0-8403-2123-6). Kendall-Hunt.

Searight, Ellen. Golden Interlude. (Orig.). 1980. pap. 1.25 o.s.i. (ISBN 0-440-13916-3). Dell.

Searight, Mary W. Your Career in Nursing. rev. ed. LC 77-6180. (Messner Career Books). (Illus.). 192p. (gr. 7 up). 1977. PLB 7.79 o.p. (ISBN 0-671-32922-7). Messner.

Searight, Sarah. The British in the Middle East. (Illus.). 290p. 1982. 21.95 (ISBN 0-85692-018-5, Pub. by Salem Hse Ltd). Merrimack Bk Serv.

Searing, Helen. New American Art Museums. Date not set. text ed. 24.95 (ISBN 0-520-04895-4); pap. text ed. write for info. (ISBN 0-520-04896-2). U of Cal Pr. Postponed.

Searing, Susan E. Introduction to Library Research in Women's Studies. (Guides to Library Research). 200p. 1983. lib. bdg. 17.50 (ISBN 0-86531-267-2). Westview.

Searl, C., jt. auth. see Irving, J.

Searl, Stanford J., Jr., ed. see Miller, Perry.

Searle, Anthony G. Comparative Genetics of Coat Colour in Mammals. 1968. 53.50 (ISBN 0-12-633450-1). Acad Pr.

Searle, C. Ronald, jt. auth. see Shaw, Irwin.

Searle, Campbell L., jt. auth. see Gray, Paul E.

Searle, Campbell L., et al. Elementary Circuit Properties of Transistors, Vol. 3. LC 64-8766. (Semiconductor Electronics Education Committee Ser.). 306p. 1964. pap. 17.95 o.s.i. (ISBN 0-471-76937-1); avail. sol. circuits o.s.i. (ISBN 0-471-76942-8). Wiley.

Searle, Chris. We're Building the New School! Diary of a Teacher in Mozambique. (Illus.). 192p. (Orig.). 1981. 9.95 (ISBN 0-905762-87-8, Pub. by Zed Pr England); pap. cancelled (ISBN 0-905762-88-6). Lawrence Hill.

Searle, J. R., ed. Philosophy of Language. (Oxford Readings in Philosophy Ser). (Orig.). 1971. pap. text ed. 8.95x (ISBN 0-19-875015-3). Oxford U Pr.

Searle, John R. Speech Acts. LC 68-24484. 1970. 29.95 (ISBN 0-521-07184-4); pap. 8.95x (ISBN 0-521-09626-X). Cambridge U Pr.

Searle, Judith. Lovelife. 1981. 13.95 o.p. (ISBN 0-453-00409-1). NAL.

--Lovelife. 1982. pap. 2.95 (ISBN 0-451-11822-7, AE1822, Sig). NAL.

Searle, Leroy, jt. auth. see Berger, Paul.

Searle, Mark, ed. Sunday Morning: A Time for Worship. LC 82-15306. 200p. (Orig.). 1982. pap. 5.95 (ISBN 0-8146-1259-8). Liturgical Pr.

Searle, Ronald. The Big Fat Cat Book. 1982. 12.95 (ISBN 0-316-77898-2). Little.

Searle, S. R. Matrix Algebra for the Biological Sciences: Including Applications in Statistics. LC 66-11528. (Quantitative Methods for Biologists & Medical Statistics Ser.). 296p. 1966. 36.95 o.p. (ISBN 0-471-76930-4, Pub. by Wiley-Interscience). Wiley.

Searle, S. R. & Hausman, W. H. Matrix Algebra for Business & Economics. LC 66-11528. 362p. 1970. 36.95x (ISBN 0-471-76941-X, Pub. by Wiley-Interscience). Wiley.

Searles, Baird & Meacham, Beth. A Reader's Guide to Fantasy. 224p. 1982. 15.95x (ISBN 0-87196-772-3). Facts on File.

Searls, Hank. Sounding. LC 81-69190. 369p. 1982. 13.50 (ISBN 0-394-52471-3). Random.

Sears, C., jt. auth. see Stanitski, Conrad L., Jr.

Sears, Curtis & Stanitski, Conrad. Chemistry for Health-Related Sciences: Laboratory Manual. (2nd). (Illus.). 400p. 1983. pap. 13.95 (ISBN 0-686-38830-5). P H.

Sears, Curtis T., jt. auth. see Stanitski, Conrad L.

Sears, D. W. The Nature & Origin of Meteorites. LC 78-10127. (Monographs on Astronomical Subjects). (Illus.). 1979. 19.95x o.p. (ISBN 0-19-520121-3). Oxford U Pr.

Sears, David O. & McConahay, John B. The Politics of Violence: The New Urban Blacks & the Watts Riot. LC 80-6312. 255p. 1982. lib. bdg. 20.00 (ISBN 0-8191-1628-9); pap. text ed. 10.25 (ISBN 0-8191-1629-7). U Pr of Amer.

Sears, Donald A. John Neal. (United States Authors Ser.). 1978. lib. bdg. 13.95 (ISBN 0-8057-7230-8, Twayne). G K Hall.

Sears, Donald A., jt. auth. see Bolinger, Dwight.

Sears, Francis W. & Salinger, Gerhard L. Thermodynamics, the Kinetic Theory of Gases & Statistical Mechanics. 3rd ed. 464p. 1975. text ed. 28.95 (ISBN 0-201-06894-X). A-W.

Sears, Francis W., et al. University Physics. 6th ed. LC 81-17551. (Physics Ser.). (Illus.). 900p. 1981. text ed. 33.95 (ISBN 0-201-07195-9); Part I. text ed. 19.95 (ISBN 0-201-07196-7); Part II. study guide 15.95; sol. guide 6.95. A-W.

--College Physics. 5th ed. LC 79-20729. (Physics Ser.). 1980. text ed. 28.95 (ISBN 0-201-07681-0); sol.guide 5.95. A-W.

Sears, Glenn A., jt. auth. see Clough, Richard H.

Sears, J. Kern & Darby, Joseph R. The Technology of Plasticizers. LC 80-10225. (SPE Monographs). 1166p. 1982. 130.00x (ISBN 0-471-05583-2, Pub. by Wiley-Interscience). Wiley.

Sears, Joel L. Optimization Techniques in FORTRAN. 1979. 10.00 o.p. (ISBN 0-07-091042-1, P&RB). McGraw.

Sears, Louis M. George Washington & the French Revolution. LC 73-8258. 378p. 1973. Repr. of 1960 ed. lib. bdg. 18.75x (ISBN 0-8371-6975-5, SEGW). Greenwood.

Sears, M. & Warren, Bruce, eds. Progress in Oceanography, Vols. 1 & 4-6. LC 63-15353. text ed. write for info. Vol. 1 1964 (ISBN 0-08-010199-2). Vol. 4 1967 (ISBN 0-08-012124-1). Vol. 5 1969. (ISBN 0-08-012631-6). Vol. 6, 1974 (ISBN 0-08-017707-7). Pergamon.

Sears, Mary, compiled by. Oceanographic Index, Woods Hole Oceanographic Institution Author Cumulation, 1971-1974. 1976. lib. bdg. 115.00 (ISBN 0-8161-0029-2, Hall Library). G K Hall.

--Oceanographic Index, Woods Hole Oceanographic Institution, Regional Cumulation, 1971-1974. 1976. lib. bdg. 105.00 (ISBN 0-8161-0943-5, Hall Library). G K Hall.

--Oceanographic Index, Woods Hole Oceanographic Institution, Subject Cumulation 1971-1974, 2 vols. 1976. Set. lib. bdg. 230.00 (ISBN 0-8161-0030-6, Hall Library). G K Hall.

--Oceanographic Index: Author Cumulation, 1946-1970: Woods Hole Oceanographic Institution, Mass, 3 vols. 1972. Set. 285.00 (ISBN 0-8161-0931-1, Hall Library). G K Hall.

--Oceanographic Index: Organismal Cumulation, 1946-1973, Marine Organisms, Chiefly Planktonic: Woods Hole Oceanographic Institution, Mass, 3 vols. 1454p. 1974. Set. lib. bdg. 260.00 (ISBN 0-8161-0933-8, Hall Library). G K Hall.

--Oceanographic Index: Regional Cumulation, 1946-1970: Woods Hole Oceanographic Institution, Mass. 1972. 95.00 (ISBN 0-8161-0117-5, Hall Library). G K Hall.

--Oceanographic Index: Subject Cumulation, 1946-1971: Woods Hole Oceanographic Institution, Mass, 4 vols. 1972. Set. 380.00 (ISBN 0-8161-0932-X, Hall Library). G K Hall.

Sears, Mason. Years of High Purpose: From Trusteeship to Nationhood. LC 80-5161. (Illus.). 205p. 1980. text ed. 18.00 (ISBN 0-8191-1052-3); pap. text ed. 9.50 (ISBN 0-8191-1053-1). U Pr of Amer.

Sears, Pauline S., ed. Intellectual Development. new ed. LC 73-146672. (Readings in Educational Research Ser.). 1971. 30.75 (ISBN 0-471-76975-4); text ed. 28.00 10 or more copies (ISBN 0-686-67150-3). McCutchan.

Sears, Priscilla F. A Pillar of Fire to Follow: American Indian Dramas 1808-1859. LC 81-85523. 149p. 1982. 11.95 (ISBN 0-87972-193-6); pap. 5.95 (ISBN 0-87972-194-4). Bowling Green Univ.

Sears, Robert R. Survey of Objective Studies of Psychoanalytic Concepts. LC 79-4476. 1979. Repr. of 1943 ed. lib. bdg. 19.00x (ISBN 0-313-21249-X, SESO). Greenwood.

Sears, Robert R. & Feldman, S. Shirley, eds. The Seven Ages of Man: A Survey of Human Development. LC 73-12029. 155p. 1973. pap. 5.50x (ISBN 0-913232-06-8). W Kaufmann.

Sears, Ruth M. Nurse Nora's Folly. (YA) 1979. 6.95 (ISBN 0-685-65272-6, Avalon). Bouregy.

Sears, Ruth McCarthy. Dr. Sara's Vigil. (YA) 1978. 6.95 (ISBN 0-685-84746-2, Avalon). Bouregy.

--Ordeal of Love. (YA) 1977. 6.95 (ISBN 0-685-73815-9, Avalon). Bouregy.

--Tiger by the Tail. (YA) 1978. 6.95 (ISBN 0-685-85783-2, Avalon). Bouregy.

Sears, Stephen. Landscape Turned Red: The Battle of Antietam. LC 82-19519. (Illus.). 416p. 1983. 17.95 (ISBN 0-89919-172-X). Ticknor & Fields.

Sears, Wellington, ed. see Kaswell, E. R.

Sears, William B. Creative Parenting. (Illus.). 576p. 1982. 19.95 (ISBN 0-89696-179-6, An Everest House Book). Dodd.

Sears, William H. Fort Center: An Archaeological Site in the Lake Okeechobee Basin. Milanich, Jerald T., ed. LC 82-10898. (Florida State Museum, Ripley P. Bullen Monographs in Anthropology & History: No. 4). (Illus.). xii, 212p. 1982. 21.00 (ISBN 0-8130-0740-2). U Presses Fla.

Seashore, Stanley E. & Lawler, Edward. Assessing Organization Change: A Guide to Methods, Measures & Practices. (Organizational Assessment & Change Ser.). 500p. 1983. price not set (ISBN 0-471-89484-2, Pub. by Wiley-Interscience). Wiley.

Seasoltz, R., ed. Living Bread, Saving Cup: Readings on the Eucharist. LC 81-20813. 350p. 1982. pap. 12.95 (ISBN 0-8146-1257-1). Liturgical Pr.

Seaton, Albert. The Battle for Moscow. (War Bks.). 336p. 1983. pap. 2.75 (ISBN 0-86721-158-X). Jove Pubns.

--The Crimean War: A Russian Chronicle. LC 77-82643. (Illus.). 1978. 20.00 (ISBN 0-312-17206-0). St Martin.

--The Russian Army of the Napoleonic Wars. LC 73-83326. (Men-at-Arms Ser). (Illus.). 40p. 1973. pap. 7.95 o.p. (ISBN 0-88254-167-6). Hippocrene Bks.

--The Soviet Army. LC 73-83324. (Men-at-Arms Ser). (Illus.). 40p. 1973. pap. 7.95 o.p. (ISBN 0-88254-166-8). Hippocrene Bks.

Seaton, Donald C., et al. Physical Education Handbook. 6th ed. (Illus.). 438p. 1974. text ed. 20.95 (ISBN 0-13-667501-8); pap. text ed. 15.95 (ISBN 0-13-667493-3). P-H.

Seaton, Jerome P., tr. see Cheng, Francois.

Seaton, Lionel, tr. see Boger, Jan.

Seaton, S. Lee, jt. ed. see Watson-Gegeo, Karen A.

Seats, Melainie R. Mostly About Love. 1977. pap. 1.50 (ISBN 0-686-18834-9). Windmill Pr.

Seattle Art Museum. Brian Wall. LC 82-60696. (Illus.). 28p. (Orig.). 1982. pap. 6.95x (ISBN 0-932216-09-9). Seattle Art.

Seaver, David-Linn. Moto-Cross Racing. LC 78-38590. (Speed Sports Ser.). (Illus.). (gr. 9 up). 1972. 6.50 o.p. (ISBN 0-397-31294-6). Har-Row.

Seaver, G. Edward Wilson of the Antarctic. 14.50 o.p. (ISBN 0-685-91531-X). Transatlantic.

Seaver, Jeannette. Soups. 214p. 1983. 13.95 (ISBN 0-86579-031-0). Seaver Bks.

Seaver, Richard, ed. see Sade, Marquis De.

Seaver, Richard, tr. see Sade, Marquis De.

Seaward, Eileen, jt. auth. see Ardiff, Martha B.

Seawell, L. Vann. Hospital Financial Accounting Theory & Practice. LC 74-27241. (Illus.). 569p. 1975. text ed. 19.95x (ISBN 0-930228-00-6, 1454); instr's manual 39.90 (ISBN 0-686-77079-X). Healthcare Fin Man Assn.

--Introduction to Hospital Accounting. rev. ed. LC 77-74543. (Illus.). 508p. 1977. text ed. 14.95x (ISBN 0-930228-05-7); Practice Set (1978) 7.00 (ISBN 0-930228-08-1); Solutions Manual (1977) 29.90 (ISBN 0-930228-06-5). Healthcare Fin Man Assn.

Seawell, L. Vann & Searfoss, D. Gerald. Accounting. (College Outlines Ser). pap. text ed. 4.95 o.p. (ISBN 0-671-08040-7). Monarch Pr.

Seay, Albert. Music in the Medieval World. 2nd ed. (Illus.). 202p. 1975. 13.95 (ISBN 0-13-608133-9); pap. text ed. 12.95 (ISBN 0-13-608125-8). P-H.

Seay, Bill M. & Gottfried, Nathan. The Development of Behavior: A Synthesis of Developmental & Comparative Psychology. LC 78-50639. (Illus.). 1978. text ed. 26.50 (ISBN 0-395-24747-0); instr's. manual 1.00 (ISBN 0-395-24746-2). HM.

Seay, Davin R., jt. auth. see Bell, Gary.

Seay, Thomas A. Systematic Eclectric Therapy. 126p. 1979. softcover 9.75 o.p. (ISBN 0-932930-03-4). Pilgrimage Inc.

Sebald, Hans. Adolescence: A Social Psychological Analysis. 2nd ed. 1977. pap. text ed. 21.95 (ISBN 0-13-008599-5). P-H.

Sebaly, Kim, jt. auth. see Poffenberger, Thomas.

Sebatier, Paul A., jt. auth. see Mazmanian, Daniel A.

Sebba, G. Bibliographia Cartesiana: A Critical Guide to the Descartes Literature (1800-1960) 1964. 50.00 (ISBN 0-685-11995-5). Heinman.

Sebba, Helen, tr. see Bastide, Roger.

Sebba, Helen, tr. see Frenz, Horst.

Sebba, Leslie, jt. auth. see Landau, Simha F.

Sebeok, Thomas, ed. see Johnson, Sahnny.

Sebeok, Thomas A., ed. A Perfusion of Signs. LC 76-29318. (Advance in Semiotics Ser.). 224p. 1977. 15.00x o.p. (ISBN 0-253-34352-6). Ind U Pr.

Sebeok, Thomas A. & Rosenthal, Robert, eds. The Clever Hans Phenomenon: Communication with Horses, Whales, Apes, and People. LC 81-2806. 311p. 1981. 62.00x (ISBN 0-89766-113-3). NY Acad Sci.

Seber, G. A. Elementary Statistics. LC 73-16685. 240p. 1974. pap. 18.95 o.p. (ISBN 0-471-77092-2, Pub. by Wiley-Interscience). Wiley.

--Linear Regression Analysis. (Wiley Ser. in Probability & Mathematical Statistics). 465p. 1977. 47.95x (ISBN 0-471-01967-4, Pub by Wiley-Interscience). Wiley.

Seber, George A. Elementary Statistics. 226p. 1981. pap. text ed. cancelled o.p. (ISBN 0-89874-263-3). Krieger.

Sebesta, Robert W. & Kraushaar, James M. Computer Concepts, Structured Programming & Interactive BASIC. LC 82-81084. (Illus.). 240p. 1982. pap. text ed. 14.95x (ISBN 0-938188-04-6). Mitchell Pub.

Sebesta, Sam L. & Iverson, William. Literature for Thursday's Child. LC 74-32421. (Illus.). 1975. text ed. 19.95 (ISBN 0-574-18615-8, 13-6015). SRA.

Sebestyen, Gyula. Lightweight Building Construction. LC 77-21902. 383p. 1978. 64.95 o.s.i. (ISBN 0-470-99166-6). Halsted Pr.

Sebestyen, Tibor. Lake Balaton: A Comprehensive Guide. Halapy, Lilli, tr. from Hungarian. (Illus.). 206p. 1982. 10.00x (ISBN 963-13-1234-8). Intl Pubns Serv.

Sebold, F. D., jt. auth. see Venieris, Y. P.

Sebree, Mac, jt. auth. see Kirkland, John F.

Sebree, Mac, ed. see Keilty, Ed.

Sebrell, Jr. & Haggerty. Food & Nutrition. rev. ed. LC 80-52153. (Life Nature Library). 13.40 (ISBN 0-8094-4063-6). Silver.

Sebrell, W. H., Jr. & Harris, Robert S., eds. Chemistry, Physiology, Pathology, Metdhods. Incl. Vol. 1. 2nd ed. 1967. o.s. 63.00 (ISBN 0-12-633761-6); Vol. 2. 1968. o.s. 60.50 (ISBN 0-12-633762-4); Vol. 3. 1971. 71.50 (ISBN 0-12-633763-2); Vol. 5. 1972. 59.50 (ISBN 0-12-633765-9); Vols. 6-7. Gyorgy, Paul & Pearson, W. N., eds. 1968. Vol. 6. 46.00 (ISBN 0-12-633706-3); Vol. 7. 46.00 (ISBN 0-12-633707-1). Acad Pr.

Sechan, Edmond. The String Bean. LC 81-43242. (Illus.). 64p. 1982. 12.95 (ISBN 0-385-17135-8). Doubleday.

Sechehaye, Marguerite. Autobiography of a Schizophrenic Girl. Rubin-Rabson, Grace, tr. 1970. pap. 1.75 (ISBN 0-451-09775-0, E9775, Sig). NAL.

Sechrist, Elizabeth H. Christmas Everywhere. rev. ed. (Illus.). (gr. 5 up). 1962. 6.75 (ISBN 0-8255-8130-3); PLB 6.71 (ISBN 0-8255-8131-1). Macrae.

--Heigh-Ho for Halloween. (Illus.). (gr. 7-11). 1948. PLB 6.71 (ISBN 0-8255-8139-7). Macrae.

--Once in the First Times. (gr. 3-7). 1969. 6.50 (ISBN 0-8255-8140-0); PLB 5.97 (ISBN 0-8255-8141-9). Macrae.

--Poems for Red Letter Days. (Illus.). (gr. 3-7). 1951. PLB 5.97 (ISBN 0-8255-8155-9). Macrae.

--Red Letter Days. rev. ed. (Illus.). (gr. 3-7). 1965. 6.67 (ISBN 0-8255-8162-1); PLB 6.47 (ISBN 0-8255-8163-X). Macrae.

Sechrist, Elizabeth H. & Woolsey, Janette. It's Time for Brotherhood. rev. ed. LC 72-11098. 256p. (gr. 4 up). 1973. PLB 7.97 (ISBN 0-8255-8191-5). Macrae.

--It's Time for Christmas. (Illus.). (gr. 5 up). 1959. 6.50 (ISBN 0-8255-8222-9); PLB 5.97 (ISBN 0-8255-8223-7). Macrae.

--It's Time for Easter. (Illus.). (gr. 5-9). 1961. 8.50 (ISBN 0-8255-8198-2). Macrae.

--It's Time for Story Hour. (Illus.). (gr. 1-5). 1964. PLB 6.97 (ISBN 0-8255-8211-3). Macrae.

--It's Time for Thanksgiving. (Illus.). (gr. 1-5). 1957. PLB 5.97 (ISBN 0-8255-8215-6). Macrae.

Sechrist, Elizabeth H., ed. One Thousand Poems for Children. rev. ed. (Illus.). (gr. k-8). 1946. 9.75 (ISBN 0-8255-8146-X). Macrae.

--Thirteen Ghostly Yarns. rev. ed. (Illus.). (gr. 3 up). 1963. PLB 7.97 (ISBN 0-8255-8171-0). Macrae.

Sechrist, Elsie. Dreams Your Magic Mirror: With Interpretations of Edgar Cayce. 256p. 1974. pap. 2.95 (ISBN 0-446-30832-3). Warner Bks.

--Meditation: Der Weg Zum Licht. Kronberger, Helge F., tr. from Eng. (Illus.). 53p. (Ger.). 1980. pap. 10.00 o.p. (ISBN 0-87604-131-4). ARE Pr.

Seck, Assane, intro. by. Contemporary Art of Senegal. (Illus.). 54p. 1980. pap. 5.00 (ISBN 0-686-83420-8). Mus Fine Arts Boston.

Secka, Pap-Cheyassin O. Southern Africa: Action for Peaceful Change. (IPA Reports Ser.: No. 2). 31p. 1972. 1.50x (ISBN 0-686-36940-8). Intl Peace.

Seckinger, Donald S. A Problems Approach to Foundations of Education. LC 75-25869. 220p. 1975. pap. text ed. 17.50 (ISBN 0-471-77100-7). Wiley.

Seckler, Bernard. The Programmable Hand Calculator: A Teacher's Tool for Mathematics Classroom Lectures. 207p. (Orig.). 1982. handbk. 10.00 (ISBN 0-686-36869-X). Sigma Pr NY.

Seckler, David. Thorstein Veblen & the Institutionalists: A Study in the Philosophy of Economics. LC 73-91642. 175p. 1975. text ed. 13.50x (ISBN 0-87081-055-3). Colo Assoc.

Second International Congress on Analytical Techniques in Environmental Chemistry. Analytical Techniques in Environmental Chemistry 2: Proceedings of the Second International Congress, Barcelona, Spain, November 1981. Albaiges, J., ed. LC 82-15047. (Series on Environmental Science: Vol. 7). (Illus.). 482p. 1982. 75.00 (ISBN 0-08-028740-9). Pergamon.

Second International Symposium on Nitrite in Meat Products, Zeist, the Netherlands, 7-10 Sept. 1976. Proceedings. Tinbergen, B. J., ed. 1977. pap. 52.00 o.p. (ISBN 90-220-0607-7, Pub. by PUDOC). Unipub.

Secor, Marie & Fahnestock, Jeanne. A Rhetoric for Argument. 416p. 1982. text ed. 13.95 (ISBN 0-394-32416-1). Random.

Secor, Robert. American Literature One (Colonial Period to 1890) (Monarch College Outlines). pap. 4.95 o.p. (ISBN 0-671-08041-5, 08028). Monarch Pr.

Secor, Robert A. & Pickering, John M., eds. Pennsylvania Seventeen Seventy-Six. LC 75-27232. (Illus.). 352p. 1975. 27.50 (ISBN 0-271-01217-X). Pa St U Pr.

Secord, Paul F. & Backman, Carl W. Social Psychology. 2nd ed. (Illus.). 704p. 1973. text ed. 17.95 o.p. (ISBN 0-07-055914-7, C); instructor's manual by K. Blau 3.95 o.p. (ISBN 0-07-005881-4). McGraw.

Secord, Paul F., jt. auth. see Guttentag, Marcia.

Secord, Paul F., et al. Understanding Social Life: An Introduction to Social Psychology. (Illus.). 1976. text ed. 26.95 (ISBN 0-07-055917-1, C); instr's manual 3.95 (ISBN 0-07-055918-X). McGraw.

Secretan, Dominique. Classicism. (Critical Idiom Ser.). 1973. pap. 4.95x (ISBN 0-416-75020-6). Methuen Inc.

Secretariat d'Etat au Plan et au Development Regional, Direction de la Statistique. Annuaire Statistique Du Maroc 1975. 1976. pap. 12.50x o.p. (ISBN 0-8002-2356-X). Intl Pubns Serv.

Secretariat for Futures Studies, Stockholm. Solar Vs. Nuclear: The Solar Nuclear Alternative. 1980. 43.00 (ISBN 0-08-024758-X); pap. 18.00 (ISBN 0-08-024759-8). Pergamon.

Secrist, Sally, jt. auth. see Brindle, John.

Seculoff, James. Holy Hour for a New People. LC 76-27491. (Orig.). 1976. pkg. of 10 8.50 (ISBN 0-87973-645-3). Our Sunday Visitor.

Sedaka, Neil. Laughter in the Rain: My Own Story. (Illus.). 256p. 1982. 14.95 (ISBN 0-399-12744-5). Putnam Pub Group.

Sedano, H. O., et al. Oral Manifestations of Inherited Disorders. 1977. 29.95 (ISBN 0-409-95050-5). Butterworth.

Seddiqui, Fred R. Engineering Functions: Concerns of the Industry. 1983. 20.00 (ISBN 0-533-05497-4). Vantage.

Seddon, John. John Seddon: The Penman's Paradise, 1695. limited ed. (Illus.). 1966. 25.00 o.s.i. (ISBN 0-685-16848-4). Museum Bks.

Seder, John & Burrell, Berkeley G. Getting It Together: Black Businessmen in America. LC 70-142096. 1971. 6.95 o.p. (ISBN 0-15-135275-5). HarBraceJ.

Sederberg, Arelo. Power Players. LC 79-15126. 1980. 11.95 o.p. (ISBN 0-688-03514-0). Morrow.

Sederberg, Peter C. Interpreting Politics: An Introduction to Political Science. LC 77-1657. (Chandler & Sharp Publications in Political Science). 378p. 1977. pap. text ed. 9.95x (ISBN 0-88316-529-5). Chandler & Sharp.

Sederer, Lloyd I. Inpatient Psychiatry: Diagnosis & Treatment. 323p. 1982. 35.00 (ISBN 0-683-07627-2). Williams & Wilkins.

Sedgwick, Adam. Discourse on the Studies of the University. (Victorian Library). 1969. Repr. of 1833 ed. text ed. 15.00x (ISBN 0-7185-5004-8, Leicester). Humanities.

Sedgwick, Alexander. Jansenism in Seventeenth-Century France: Voices from the Wilderness. LC 77-2812. 243p. 1977. 14.95x (ISBN 0-8139-0702-0). U Pr of Va.

--Third French Republic, 1870-1914. LC 68-13384. (Europe Since 1500 Ser. 4). (Orig.). 1969. pap. 6.95x (ISBN 0-88295-763-5). Harlan Davidson.

Sedgwick, Ellery. The Happy Profession. LC 78-152604. (Illus.). 343p. 1972. Repr. of 1946 ed. lib. bdg. 17.75x (ISBN 0-8371-6039-1, SEHP). Greenwood.

Sedgwick, John. Night Vision: Confessions of Gil Lewis, Private Eye. 176p. 1982. 12.95 (ISBN 0-671-43237-0). S&S.

Sedgwick, Peter. Psycho Politics. LC 82-47555. 292p. 1982. 15.34i (ISBN 0-06-015058-0, HarpT); pap. 6.68i (ISBN 0-06-090964-1, CN-964). Har-Row.

Sedgwick, Rae. The White Frame House: A Novel. LC 80-65838. 144p. (gr. 3-6). 1980. 8.95 o.s.i. (ISBN 0-440-09018-0); PLB 8.44 o.s.i. (ISBN 0-440-09019-9). Delacorte.

Sedgwick, Robert P., et al. Cerebral Degenerations in Childhood. 1975. spiral bdg. 12.00 o.p. (ISBN 0-87488-759-3). Med Exam.

Sedgwick, W. B., ed. see Plautus.

Sediacek, B. & Overberger, C. G. Microcalorimetry of Macromolecules. 112p. 1981. pap. 13.95 (ISBN 0-471-86313-0, Pub. by Wiley-Interscience). Wiley.

Sedivec, V. & Flek, J. The Handbook of Analysis of Organic Solvents. Sommernitz, Harry, tr. LC 75-44239. (Ser. in Analytical Chemistry). 1976. 89.95 (ISBN 0-470-15010-6). Halsted Pr.

Sedlacek, B., et al. Polymer Catalysts & Affinants: Polmers in Chromatography. 254p. 1981. pap. 35.95 (ISBN 0-471-09014-X, Pub. by Wiley-Interscience). Wiley.

Sedlacek, Keith, jt. auth. see Culligan, Matthew J.

Sedlak, Michael W., jt. ed. see Walch, Timothy.

Sedlar, Jean W., jt. auth. see McNeill, William H.

Sedlar, Jean W., jt. ed. see McNeill, William H.

Sedley, Dorothy. College Writer's Workbook. 240p. 1981. pap. text ed. 10.95 (ISBN 0-675-08022-3). Additional supplements may be obtained from publisher. Merrill.

Sedley, Dorothy, jt. auth. see Bramer, George R.

Sed-Rajna, Gabrielle, jt. ed. see Narkis, Bezalel.

Sedriks, A. John. Corrosion of Stainless Steels. LC 79-11985. (Corrosion Monographs). 282p. 1979. 41.50x (ISBN 0-471-05011-3, Pub. by Wiley-Interscience). Wiley.

Sedunov, Yu. S. Physics of Drop Formation in the Atmosphere. Greenberg, P., ed. Lederman, D., tr. from Rus. LC 74-8198. 233p. 1974. 36.95 o.s.i. (ISBN 0-470-77111-9). Halsted Pr.

Sedwick, jt. auth. see Gallo.

Sedwick, jt. auth. see Paolozzi.

Sedwick, Angie. Synergy. LC 72-86429. 64p. 1972. 4.00 (ISBN 0-911838-23-6). Windy Row.

Sedwick, Frank. Conversation in Spanish: Points of Departure. 3rd ed. (Orig.). 1981. pap. text ed. write for info. (ISBN 0-442-24467-3). Van Nos Reinhold.

--Spanish for Careers: Conversational Perspectives. (Orig.). 1980. pap. text ed. 8.95 (ISBN 0-442-20562-7). Van Nos Reinhold.

Sedwick, Frank & Azana, Manuel M. Conversaciones con Madrilenos. (Span.). 1974. pap. 5.95 (ISBN 0-442-25081-9). Van Nos Reinhold.

Sedwick, Frank, jt. auth. see Bonnell, Peter.

Sedwick, Frank, jt. auth. see Paolozzi, Gabriel J.

See, Carolyn. Blue Money. 1976. pap. 1.95 o.p. (ISBN 0-671-80581-9). PB.

--Mother, Daughters. 1977. 8.95 o.p. (ISBN 0-698-10837-X, Coward). Putnam Pub Group.

--Rhine Madens. 304p. 1981. 13.95 (ISBN 0-698-11105-2, Coward). Putnam Pub Group.

--Rhine Maidens. 1983. pap. 4.95 (ISBN 0-14-006361-7). Penguin.

See, Henri. Economic Interpretation of History. Knight, Melvin M., tr. LC 67-30863. Repr. of 1929 ed. 15.00x (ISBN 0-678-00354-8). Kelley.

Seebeck, jt. auth. see Hummel.

Seeber, Gerd C. The Abduction. LC 81-47465. 272p. 1983. 16.50 (ISBN 0-03-059404-9). HR&W.

Seebohm, Caroline & Pool, Mary J., eds. The House & Garden's Book of Total Health. LC 78-5048. (Illus.). 1978. 11.95 o.p. (ISBN 0-399-12154-4). Putnam Pub Group.

Seeborg, Irmtraud & Ma, Cynthia. BASIC for the DEC-10. LC 82-13957. 204p. 1982. pap. 8.95x (ISBN 0-910554-37-4). Eng Pr.

Seecharan, Sheila. Conversations with Christ. 1983. 5.95 (ISBN 0-533-05303-X). Vantage.

Seed, Allen H., IV. The Impact of Inflation on Internal Planning & Control. 239p. pap. 17.95 (ISBN 0-86641-010-4, 81131). Natl Assn Accts.

Seed, Geoffrey. James Wilson. LC 78-2034. (KTO Studies in American History). 1978. lib. bdg. 30.00 (ISBN 0-527-81050-9). Kraus Intl.

Seed, Pat. Another Day. 100p. 1983. 16.50 (ISBN 0-434-67862-7, Pub. by Heinemann England); pap. 9.95 (ISBN 0-434-68533-X). David & Charles.

Seed, Philip. The Expansion of Social Work in Britain. (Library of Social Work). 128p. 1973. 12.95x (ISBN 0-7100-7536-7). Routledge & Kegan.

Seed, Suzanne. Saturday's Child. LC 72-12599. (Illus.). (gr. 6-12). 1973. PLB 8.95 (ISBN 0-87955-803-2); pap. 5.95 (ISBN 0-87955-203-4). O'Hara.

Seedor. Body Mechanics & Patient Positioning. pap. text ed. 8.75 (ISBN 0-8077-2524-2, Lippincott Nursing). Lippincott.

--Introduction to Asepsis: A Programmed Unit in Fundamentals of Nursing. 3rd rev. ed. pap. text ed. 8.95 (ISBN 0-8077-2555-2, Lippincott Nursing). Lippincott.

--The Physical Assessment. 2nd ed. pap. text ed. 10.95 (ISBN 0-8077-2642-7, Lippincott Nursing). Lippincott.

Seedor, Marie M. Aids to Nursing Diagnosis: A Programmed Unit in Fundamentals of Nursing. 3rd ed. 378p. (Orig.). 1980. pap. text ed. 9.50x (ISBN 0-8077-2630-3). Tchrs Coll.

--Body Mechanics & Patient Positioning: A Programmed Unit of Study for Nurses. LC 73-85804. 1977. pap. 9.50x (ISBN 0-8077-2524-2). Tchrs Coll.

--Introduction to Asepsis. 3rd ed. LC 79-514. 1979. pap. text ed. 9.50x (ISBN 0-8077-2555-2). Tchrs Coll.

--A Nursing Guide To Oxygen Therapy: A Programed. 3rd ed. (Orig.). 1980. pap. 9.50x o.p. (ISBN 0-8077-2578-1). Tchrs Coll.

--The Physical Assessment: A Programmed Unit of Studies for Nurses. 2nd ed. LC 73-85804. (Illus.). 344p. 1981. pap. text ed. 11.50x (ISBN 0-8077-2642-7). Tchrs Coll.

Seeds, H. Fortran IV for Business & General Applications. LC 74-34058. 422p. 1975. 19.95 (ISBN 0-471-77109-0, Pub. by Wiley-Interscience). Wiley.

Seeds, Harice L. Programming RPG II. LC 79-127669. 1971. pap. 22.95 (ISBN 0-471-77113-9). Wiley.

--Structured FORTRAN 77 for Business & General Applications. LC 81-125. 512p. 1981. text ed. 20.95 (ISBN 0-471-07836-0). Wiley.

Seefeldt, Carol. A Curriculum for Preschools. 2nd ed. (Early Childhood Education Ser.: No. C24). 368p. 1980. text ed. 19.95 (ISBN 0-675-08137-8). Additional supplements may be obtained from publisher. Merrill.

--Social Studies for the Preschool-Primary Child. (Elementary Education Ser.). (Illus.). 1977. pap. text ed. 16.95 (ISBN 0-675-08593-4). Merrill.

--Teaching Young Children. (Illus.). 1980. text ed. 23.95 (ISBN 0-13-896423-8). P-H.

Seeger, A., ed. Vacancies & Interstitials in Metals. 1970. 107.50 (ISBN 0-444-10268-X). Elsevier.

Seeger, C. Ronald. Problems for Exploration Geophysics. LC 78-62263. 1978. pap. text ed. 4.75 (ISBN 0-8191-0573-2). U Pr of Amer.

Seeger, Charles. Studies in Musicology, 1935-1975. LC 76-19668. 1977. 38.50x (ISBN 0-520-02000-6). U of Cal Pr.

Seeger, K. Semiconductor Physics: An Introduction. 2nd ed. (Springer Series in Solid-State Sciences: Vol. 40). (Illus.). 510p. 1982. 39.00 (ISBN 0-387-11421-1). Springer-Verlag.

Seeger, Peggy, jt. auth. see MacColl, Ewan.

Seeger, Raymond J. Galileo Galilei, His Life & Work. (Men of Physics Ser.). 1966. text ed. 17.75 (ISBN 0-08-012025-3); pap. 7.75 (ISBN 0-08-012024-5). Pergamon.

--Josiah Willard Gibbs-American Physicist Par Excellance. (Men of Physics Ser.). 1974. 37.00 (ISBN 0-08-018013-2). Pergamon.

See-Lasley, Kay & Ignoffo, Robert. Manual of Oncology Therapeutics. LC 81-1998. 457p. 1981. pap. text ed. 25.95 (ISBN 0-8016-4448-8). Mosby.

Seeley, Burns K. Meditations on St. John. Coniker, Jerome F. & Francis, Dale, eds. LC 81-65808. (Living Meditation & Prayerbook Ser.). (Illus.). 245p. (Orig.). 1981. pap. text ed. 6.00 (ISBN 0-932406-03-3). AFC.

--Meditations on St. Matthew. Coniker, Jerome F., ed. LC 82-71700. (Living Meditation & Prayerbook ser.). (Illus.). 250p. (Orig.). 1982. pap. text ed. 6.00 (ISBN 0-932406-05-X). AFC.

--Meditations on St. Paul. Coniker, Jerome F., ed. LC 82-72201. (Living Meditation & Prayerbook Ser.). (Illus.). 270p. (Orig.). 1982. pap. text ed. 6.00 (ISBN 0-932406-06-8). AFC.

--Reflections on St. Paul. Coniker, Jerome F., ed. LC 82-72202. (Living Meditation & Prayerbook Ser.). (Illus.). 270p. (Orig.). 1982. pap. text ed. 6.00 (ISBN 0-932406-07-6). AFC.

Seeley, Colleen, jt. auth. see Seeley, Mildred.

Seeley, David. Education Through Partnership: Mediating Structures & Education. 328p. 1981. prof ref 29.50x (ISBN 0-88410-825-2). Ballinger Pub.

Seeley, Mildred & Seeley, Colleen. Doll Collecting for Fun & Profit. LC 82-84016. (Illus.). 144p. 1983. 14.95 (ISBN 0-89586-207-7). H P Bks.

Seelig, Michael Y. The Architecture of Self Help Communities. LC 77-15116. (Illus.). 1978. 25.00 o.p. (ISBN 0-07-099901-5, Architectural Rec Bks). McGraw.

Seelig, Sharon C. The Shadow of Eternity: Belief & Structure in Herbert, Vaughan, & Traherne. LC 80-51018. 200p. 1981. 16.50x (ISBN 0-8131-1444-6). U Pr of Ky.

Seely, Clinton, tr. see Sen, Ramprasad.

Seely, G. R., jt. auth. see Vernon, Leo P.

Seely, Pauline A., ed. ALA Rules for Filing Catalog Cards. 2nd ed. LC 68-21019. 1968. 10.00 (ISBN 0-8389-0002-X); pap. 5.00 abr. ed (ISBN 0-8389-0001-1). ALA.

Seely, Rebecca, jt. auth. see Roberts, Carey.

Seely, Samuel & Poularikas, Alexander. Electrical Engineering: Introduction & Concepts. 650p. 1981. text ed. 26.95 (ISBN 0-916460-31-2). Matrix Pub.

Seelye, E. Data Book for Civil Engineers, 3 vols. Incl. Manual Metal-Arc Welding. 85.50 (ISBN 0-85083-026-5, Pub. by); Vol. 2. Specifications & Costs. 3rd ed. 566p. 1957. 79.95 (ISBN 0-471-77319-0); Vol. 3. Field Practice. 2nd ed. 394p. 1954. 59.95 (ISBN 0-471-77352-2). LC 57-5932 (Pub. by Wiley-Interscience). Wiley.

Seelye, E. E. Data Book for Civil Engineers: Design, Vol. 1. 3rd ed. 670p. 1960. text ed. 85.50x (ISBN 0-471-77286-0, Pub. by Wiley-Interscience). Wiley.

Seelye, John. Prophetic Waters: The River in Early American Life. LC 76-46353. 1977. 22.50x (ISBN 0-19-502047-2). Oxford U Pr.

--True Adventures of Huckleberry Finn. 1971. pap. 3.45 o.p. (ISBN 0-671-20951-5, Touchstone Bks). S&S.

Seeman, Ernest. American Gold. 1979. pap. 2.50 o.s.i. (ISBN 0-380-43679-5, 43679). Avon.

Seeman, Julius M. Personality Integration: Studies & Reflections. 192p. 1983. 19.95x (ISBN 0-89885-084-3). Human Sci Pr.

Seemann, B. Flora Vitiensis. (Historia Naturalis Classica 103 Ser.). 1978. Repr. of 1865 ed. lib. bdg. 160.00x (ISBN 3-7682-1144-4). Lubrecht & Cramer.

Seemann, Caroline, tr. see Hobsley, M.

Seemann, H. E. Physical & Photographic Principles of Medical Radiography. LC 68-18631. (Photographic Science & Technology & Graphic Arts Ser.). 1968. 16.95 o.p. (ISBN 0-471-77387-5, Pub. by Wiley-Interscience). Wiley.

Seers, Dudley, ed. Dependency Theory: A Critical Reassessment. 211p. 1982. 30.00 (ISBN 0-903804-84-0). F Pinter Pubs.

Seers, Dudley & Vaitsos, Constantine, eds. The Second Enlargement of the EEC: The Integration of the Unequal Partners. 312p. 1982. 60.00x (ISBN 0-333-29189-1, Pub. by Macmillan England). State Mutual Bk.

--The Second Enlargement of the EEC: The Integration of Unequal Partners. LC 81-8750. 312p. 1982. 29.95 (ISBN 0-312-70830-0). St Martin.

Seese, William S. & Daub, Guido H. Basic Chemistry. 3rd ed. 608p. 1981. text ed. 24.95 (ISBN 0-13-057653-0). P-H.

--In Preparation for College Chemistry. 2nd ed. (Illus.). 1980. pap. text ed. 16.95 (ISBN 0-13-453670-3). P-H.

Seev, Neumann, jt. auth. see Borovits, Israel.

Seevers, James A. Space. LC 77-18976. (Read About Science Ser.). (Illus.). (gr. k-3). 1978. PLB 13.30 (ISBN 0-8393-0076-X). Raintree Pubs.

Sefton, Catherine. The Emma Dilemma. (Illus.). 96p. (gr. 4-6). 1983. 8.95 (ISBN 0-571-11841-0). Faber & Faber.

--Ghost & Bertie Boggin. 94p. (gr. 2-6). 1982. 5.95 (ISBN 0-571-11524-1). Faber & Faber.

Sefton, Donald, jt. auth. see Brown, Gary D.

Sefton, James E. Andrew Johnson & the Uses of Constitutional Power. (Library of American Biography). 1980. 9.95 (ISBN 0-316-77988-1); pap. 5.95. Little.

Segal. Be My Friend. 1.95 o.p. (ISBN 0-8065-0308-4); pap. 1.10 o.p. (ISBN 0-685-38413-6). Citadel Pr.

Segal, Abraham. One People: A Study in Comparative Judaism. Zlotowitz, Bernard M., ed. 160p. (Orig.). (gr. 7-9). 1983. pap. text ed. 6.95 (ISBN 0-8074-0169-2, 140025). UAHC.

Segal, Abraham, jt. auth. see Essrig, Harry.

Segal, Arthur. City Planning in Ancient Times: Digging up the Past. LC 75-5294. (Lerner Archaeology Ser.: Digging up the Past). (Illus.). (gr. 5 up). 1977. PLB 7.95g (ISBN 0-8225-0836-2). Lerner Pubns.

Segal, Bernard L. & Likoff, William. Auscultation of the Heart. LC 65-14909. (Illus.). 208p. 1965. 45.00 o.p. (ISBN 0-8089-0419-1); record o.p. 20.50 o.p. (ISBN 0-8089-0420-5); tape at 3 3/4 51.00 o.p. (ISBN 0-8089-0421-3); tape at 7 1/2 39.50 o.p. (ISBN 0-8089-0422-1). Grune.
Segal, Brenda L. Aliya. 1979. pap. 1.95 o.p. (ISBN 0-515-04773-2). Jove Pubns.
--If I Forget Thee. 1983. 16.95 (ISBN 0-312-40489-1). St Martin.
--Tenth Measure. 576p. 1980. 13.95 o.p. (ISBN 0-312-79110-0). St Martin.
Segal, Brenda L. & Kanter, Marianne. Aliya: A Love Story. LC 77-9217. 1978. 8.95 o.p. (ISBN 0-312-01865-7). St Martin.
Segal, Charles, ed. see Whitman, Cedric H.
Segal, Charles M. & Stineback, David, eds. Puritans, Indians & Manifest Destiny. LC 77-3858. 1977. 8.95 o.p. (ISBN 0-399-11928-0). Putnam Pub Group.
Segal, Daniel. Polycyclic Groups. LC 82-9476. (Cambridge Tracts in Mathematics Ser.: No. 82). 200p. Date not set. price not set (ISBN 0-521-24146-4). Cambridge U Pr.
Segal, E. Mathematical Cosmology & Extragalactic Astronomy. (Pure & Applied Mathematics Ser.: Vol. 68). 1976. 29.50 (ISBN 0-12-635250-X). Acad Pr.
Segal, Edith. Come with Me: Poems for the Young. pap. 1.25 o.p. (ISBN 0-8065-0179-0). Citadel Pr.
Segal, Erich. Love Story. 1977. pap. 2.50 (ISBN 0-380-01760-1, 62158-4). Avon.
--Man, Woman & Child. (General Ser.). 1980. lib. bdg. 10.95 (ISBN 0-8161-3124-4, Large Print Bks). G K Hall.
--Oliver's Story. LC 75-6359. 160p. (YA) 1977. 13.41i (ISBN 0-06-013852-1, HarpT). Har-Row.
Segal, Erich, tr. Plautus: Three Comedies. 1969. pap. 5.95xi o.p. (ISBN 0-06-131932-5, TB1932, Torch). Har-Row.
Segal, G., ed. New Development in Topology. LC 73-84323. (London Mathematical Society Lecture Notes Ser.: No. 11). 120p. 1973. 15.95 (ISBN 0-521-20354-6). Cambridge U Pr.
Segal, Gary L. Immigrating to Canada: Who is Allowed? What is Required? How to do It? Rev. ed. 1983. pap. price not set (ISBN 0-88908-565-X). Self Counsel Pr.
Segal, Hanna. Melanie Klein. (Modern Masters Ser.). 204p. 1980. 12.95 o.p. (ISBN 0-670-46474-0). Viking Pr.
Segal, Harold & Doyle, Darrell J., eds. Protein Turnover & Lysosome Function. 1978. 60.00 (ISBN 0-12-636150-9). Acad Pr.
Segal, Hillel & Berst, Jesse. How to Manage Your Small Computer: Without Frustration. (Illus.). 1983. text ed. 22.95 (ISBN 0-13-423665-3); pap. text ed. 14.95 (ISBN 0-13-423681-5). P-H.
Segal, J., jt. auth. see Mardesic, S.
Segal, Joyce. The Scariest Witch in Wellington Towers. (Break-of-Day Ser.). (gr. 1-4). 1981. 6.99 (ISBN 0-698-30722-4, Coward). Putnam Pub Group.
Segal, Julius & Yahraes, Herbert. A Child's Journey: Forces That Shape the Lives of Our Young. LC 77-17602. 1978. 16.95 (ISBN 0-07-056039-0, P&RB). McGraw.
--Child's Journey: Forces That Shape the Lives of Our Young. (McGraw-Hill Paperbacks Ser.). 1979. pap. 5.95 (ISBN 0-07-056038-2, SP). McGraw.
Segal, Julius, jt. auth. see Luce, Gay G.
Segal, Margaret, ed. see Yorkey, Richard.
Segal, Marilyn & Adcock, Doon. Feelings. LC 80-83445. (Illus.). 69p. 1981. pap. 8.95 (ISBN 0-89334-062-6). Humanics Ltd.
Segal, Marilyn & Tomasello, Len. Nuts & Bolts: Organization & Management Techniques for an Interest Centered Pre-School Classroom. LC 80-83444. (Illus.). 77p. 1981. pap. 8.95 (ISBN 0-89334-063-4). Humanics Ltd.
Segal, Morley, jt. auth. see Kalvelage, Carl.
Segal, Morley, ed. Foundations of Human Resource Development. 175p. 1983. pap. text ed. 399.00 (ISBN 0-934698-18-X). New Comm Pr.
Segal, Muriel. Virgins: Reluctant, Dubious, & Avowed. 1977. 9.95 o.p. (ISBN 0-02-609070-8, 60907). Macmillan.
Segal, Naomi. The Banal Object: Theme & Thematics in Proust, Rilke, Hofmannsthal & Sartre. 147p. 1981. 49.00x (ISBN 0-85457-099-3, Pub. by Inst Germanic Stud England). State Mutual Bk.
Segal, Patrick. The Man Who Walked in His Head. Stephens, John, tr. from Fr. LC 79-21426. 1980. Repr. 10.95 o.p. (ISBN 0-688-03529-9). Morrow.
Segal, Robert, jt. auth. see Kelley, Susan.
Segal, Ryna A. New York City Department of Cultural Affairs, 1976-1973: A Record of Government's Involvement in the Arts. LC 76-22386. 88p. 1976. pap. 1.75x (ISBN 0-89062-037-7, Pub. by NYC Cultural). Pub Ctr Cult Res.
Segal, S. & Yager, J. Foundations of Biochemical Psychiatry. 1977. 29.95 (ISBN 0-409-95001-7). Butterworth.
Segal, S. L. Nine Introductions in Complex Analysis. (Mathematics Studies Ser.: Vol. 53). 1981. 64.00 (ISBN 0-444-86226-9, North Holland). Elsevier.
Segal, Steven P. & Aviram, Uri. The Mentally Ill in Community-Based Sheltered Care: A Study of Community Care & Social Integration. (Health, Medicine & Society Ser.). 441p. 1978. 38.50 (ISBN 0-471-77400-6, Pub. by Wiley-Interscience). Wiley.
Segal, Zev & Ayalon, Ofra. Getting Along: Games for Couple Compatibility. (Illus.). 128p. (Orig.). 1981. pap. 6.95 (ISBN 0-448-16169-9, G&D). Putnam Pub Group.
Segalen, Martine. Love & Power in the Peasant Family. Matthews, Martine, tr. LC 82-50495. (Illus.). 224p. 1983. 21.00x (ISBN 0-226-74451-5). U of Chicago Pr.
Segalen, Victor. Rene Leys. Underwood, J. A., tr. from Fr. LC 72-13317. 224p. 1974. cancelled 6.95 o.p. (ISBN 0-87955-901-2). O'Hara.
Segall, Ascher, et al. Systematic Course Design for the Health Fields. LC 75-20398. 171p. 1975. 20.95 o.p. (ISBN 0-471-77410-3, Pub. by Wiley Med). Wiley.
Segall, Helen, tr. see Mayakovsky, Vladimir & Brik, Lily.
Segall, Marshall H., jt. ed. see Goldstein, Arnold P.
Segalla, Rosemary A. Departure from Traditional Roles: Mid-LIfe Women Break the Daisy Chains. Nathan, Peter E., ed. LC 82-20089. (Research in Clinical Psychology Ser.: No. 5). 164p. 1982. 34.95 (ISBN 0-8357-1386-5). Univ Microfilms.
Segalman, Ralph. Conflicting Rights: Social Legislation & Policy, the Deviant, the Society, & the Law, Vol. II. 1978. pap. text ed. 12.50 (ISBN 0-8191-0526-0). U Pr of Amer.
--Conflicting Rights: Social Legislation & Policy, Vol. 1. 537p. 1977. pap. text ed. 19.50 (ISBN 0-8191-0193-1). U Pr of Amer.
Segalowitz, S. J. & Gruber, F. A. Language Development & Neurological Theory. 1977. 32.50 (ISBN 0-12-635650-5). Acad Pr.
Segalowitz, S. J., ed. Language Functions & Brain Organization. Date not set. 43.50 (ISBN 0-12-635640-8). Acad Pr.
Segalowitz, Sid J. Two Sides of the Brain: Brain Lateralization Explored. 252p. 1983. 12.95 (ISBN 0-13-935296-1); pap. 6.95 (ISBN 0-13-935304-6). P-H.
Segar, E. C. Popeye the Sailor 1936-1937: A Classic from the Golden Age of the Comics. (Illus.). 1976. pap. 7.95 o.p. (ISBN 0-517-52820-7). Crown.
Segar, William. The Booke of Honor & Armes & Honor Military & Civil, 2 vols. in 1. LC 74-20543. 475p. 1975. Repr. of 1590 ed. 52.00x (ISBN 0-8201-1138-4). Schol Facsimiles.
Segawa, Tomio, et al, eds. Molecular Pharmacology of Neurotransmitter Receptors. (Advances in Biochemical Psychopharmacology Ser.: Vol. 35). 1982. text ed. 31.00 (ISBN 0-89004-736-7). Raven.
Segel, I. H. Enzyme Kinetics: Behavior & Analysis of Rapid Equilibrium & Steady State Enzyme Systems. LC 74-26546. 957p. 1975. 39.95x (ISBN 0-471-77425-1, Pub. by Wiley-Interscience). Wiley.
Segel, Irwin H. Biochemical Calculations: How to Solve Mathematical Problems in General Biochemistry. 2nd ed. LC 75-23140. 441p. 1976. text ed. 15.50 (ISBN 0-471-77421-9). Wiley.
Segel, L. A., jt. auth. see Lin, C. C.
Segel, L. A., ed. Mathematical Models of Molecular & Cellular Biology. LC 79-52854. (Illus.). 767p. Date not set. pap. price not set (ISBN 0-521-27054-5). Cambridge U Pr.
Segel, Lee A. Mathematics Applied to Continuum Machanics. 1977. 32.95x (ISBN 0-02-408700-9, 40870). Macmillan.
Segel, Leon. The Problem Solver's Universal Checklist. 17p. (Orig.). 1983. pap. text ed. 5.00 (ISBN 0-9607160-0-9). Ed Acad.
Seger, Gerhart H. Germany. rev. ed. LC 77-83909. (World Cultures Ser.). (Illus.). 188p. (gr. 6 up). 1978. text ed. 11.20 ea. 1-4 copies o.s.i. (ISBN 0-88296-180-2); text ed. 8.96 ea. 5 or more copies o.s.i.; tchrs'. guide o.s.i. 8.94 o.s.i. (ISBN 0-686-85958-8). Fideler.
Seger, John H. Early Days Among the Cheyenne & Arapahoe Indians. Vestal, Stanley, ed. (CAI Ser.: Vol. 5). (Illus.). 1934. 8.95 o.p. (ISBN 0-8061-0344-2); pap. 5.95 (ISBN 0-8061-1533-5). U of Okla Pr.
Segerberg, Osborn. Living to be a One Hundred: 1,200 Who Did & How They Did It. (Illus.). 416p. 1983. pap. 9.95 (ISBN 0-686-83778-9, ScribT). Scribner.
Segerlind, Larry J. Applied Finite Element Analysis. LC 76-6958. 422p. 1976. text ed. 35.95 (ISBN 0-471-77440-5). Wiley.
Segerstedt, T., ed. Ethics for Science Policy: Proceedings. (Illus.). 1979. 38.00 (ISBN 0-08-024464-5); pap. 14.75 (ISBN 0-08-024463-7). Pergamon.
Segev, Eli, jt. auth. see Ein-Dor, Philip.
Segger, S. W. Version & Themes Models. 1973. pap. text ed. 7.95x (ISBN 0-521-06276-4). Cambridge U Pr.
Segler, Franklin M. Theology of Church & Ministry. LC 60-14146. 1960. bds. 8.95 (ISBN 0-8054-2506-3). Broadman.
Seglow, Peter. Trade Unionism in Television. 1978. text ed. 28.00x (ISBN 0-566-00203-5). Gower Pub Ltd.
Segmuller, Gottfried. Surgical Stabilization of the Skeleton of the Hand. (Illus.). 170p. 1977. pap. 22.50 o.p. (ISBN 0-683-07751-1). Krieger.
Segonzac, Catherine de see De Segonzac, Catherine.
Segovia, Andres & Mendoza, George. Andres Segovia, My Book of the Guitar: Guidance for the Young Beginner. LC 79-10277. (Illus.). 1979. 9.95 (ISBN 0-529-05539-2, Philomel). Putnam Pub Group.
Segraves, Kelly L., jt. auth. see Kofahl, Robert E.
Segraves, R. T. Marital Therapy: A Combined Psychodynamic-Behavioral Approach. (Critical Issues in Psychiatry Ser.). 295p. 1982. 24.50x (ISBN 0-306-40936-4, Plenum Pr). Plenum Pub.
Segre, Dan V. A Crisis of Identity: Israel & Zionism. 1980. 17.95x (ISBN 0-19-215862-7). Oxford U Pr.
Segre, E., et al, eds. Annual Review of Nuclear Science, Vol. 26. LC 53-995. (Illus.). 1976. text ed. 19.50 (ISBN 0-8243-1526-X). Annual Reviews.
Segre, Emilio. Enrico Fermi, Physicist. LC 71-107424. (Illus.). 1970. 12.50x o.s.i. (ISBN 0-226-74472-8). U of Chicago Pr.
Segre, Emilio, et al, eds. Annual Review of Nuclear Science, Vol. 24. LC 53-995. (Illus.). 1974. text ed. 19.50 (ISBN 0-8243-1524-3). Annual Reviews.
--Annual Review of Nuclear Science, Vol. 27. LC 53-995. (Illus.). 1977. text ed. 19.50 (ISBN 0-8243-1527-8). Annual Reviews.
Seguin, Edward. Idiocy & Its Treatment by the Physiological Method. LC 79-12541. Repr. of 1866 ed. 35.00x (ISBN 0-678-00731-4). Kelley.
--Report on Education. LC 76-39942. (History of Psychology Ser.). 1976. Repr. of 1880 ed. 29.00x (ISBN 0-8201-1282-8). Schol Facsimiles.
Segulin, Fran see Zoch, Barbara.
Segundo, Jean L. Grace & the Human Condition. Drury, John, tr. from Span. LC 72-85794. (A Theology for Artisans of a New Humanity Ser: Vol. 2). Orig. Title: Gracia y Condicion Humana. 196p. 1973. 7.95x o.p. (ISBN 0-88344-482-8); pap. 4.95x o.p. (ISBN 0-88344-488-7). Orbis Bks.
Segundo, Juan L. The Hidden Motives of Pastoral Action: Latin American Reflections. Drury, John, tr. from Sp. LC 77-13420. Orig. Title: Accion Pastoral latinoamericana: Sus motivos ocultos. 156p. 1977. 12.95x o.p. (ISBN 0-88344-185-3); pap. 5.95x o.s.i. (ISBN 0-88344-186-1). Orbis Bks.
Segura, Chris. Marshland Brace: Two Louisiana Stories. 256p. 1982. 14.95 (ISBN 0-8071-1040-X). La State U Pr.
Segura, Pancho & Heldman, Gladys. Pancho Segura's Championship Strategy: How to Play Winning Tennis. LC 75-43500. (Illus.). 160p. 1976. 12.95 o.p. (ISBN 0-07-056040-4, GB); pap. 6.95 o.p. (ISBN 0-07-056041-2). McGraw.
Segura, Robert, jt. auth. see Hanson, Marilyn.
Seguras, S. L., jt. ed. see Jamison, P. L.
Seguy, E. A. The Spectacular Color Floral Designs of E.A. Seguy. (Illus.). 48p. (Orig.). 1983. pap. 2.95 (ISBN 0-486-24488-1). Dover.
Segy, Ladislas. Masks of Black Africa. LC 74-15005. (Illus.). 246p. 1975. pap. 8.95 (ISBN 0-486-23181-X). Dover.
Sehlin, Gunhild. Mary's Little Donkey. (Illus.). 1979. 10.95 (ISBN 0-903540-29-0, Pub. by Floris Books). St George Bk Serv.
Sehlinger, Bob & Finley, John. Southern Florida Attractions: A Consumer Guide. (Illus.). 140p. 1982. pap. 3.95 (ISBN 0-89732-017-4). Menasha Ridge.
Sehlinger, Peter J., jt. ed. see Klotter, James C.
Sehmel, George A. see Engelmann, Rudolf J.
Sehnert, Keith & Eisenberg, Howard. How to Be Your Own Doctor (Sometimes) rev. ed. LC 81-47701. 368p. 1981. pap. 7.95 (ISBN 0-448-12027-5, G&D). Putnam Pub Group.
Sehnert, Keith W. The Family Doctor's Health Tips. Grooms, Kathe, ed. LC 81-16858. (Illus.). 180p. 1981. 9.95 o.p. (ISBN 0-915658-45-3); pap. 4.95 o.p. (ISBN 0-915658-39-9). Meadowbrook Pr.
Sehnert, Keith W. & Eisenberg, Howard. How to Be Your Own Doctor - Sometimes. LC 74-18875. (Illus.). 416p. 1981. pap. 7.95 (ISBN 0-448-12027-5, G&D). Putnam Pub Group.
Seibel, H. Dieter. The Dynamics of Achievement: A Radical Perspective. LC 73-13502. (Studies in Sociology Ser). 1974. pap. text ed. 2.50 o.p. (ISBN 0-672-61335-2). Bobbs.
Seibel, Hugo & Guyer, Kenneth E. Barron's How to Prepare for the New Medical College Admission Test (MCAT) LC 80-15470. 1981. pap. text ed. 7.95 (ISBN 0-8120-2190-8). Barron.
Seiber, R. Timothy & Gordon, Andrew J., eds. Children & Their Organizations: Investigations in American Culture. 1981. lib. bdg. 21.95 (ISBN 0-8161-9024-0, Univ Bks). G K Hall.
Seiberling, Grace. Monet's Series. LC 79-57497. (Outstanding Dissertations in the Fine Arts Ser.: No. 5). 470p. 1982. lib. bdg. 50.00 o.s.i. (ISBN 0-8240-3941-6). Garland Pub.
Seibert, Helen K., ed. see Hershey, Ronald A.
Seibert, Johann. Fruchtanatomische Untersuchungen an Lithospermeae (Boraginaceae) (Dissertationes Botanicae 40). (Illus.). 1978. pap. text ed. 20.00x (ISBN 3-7682-1179-7). Lubrecht & Cramer.
Seibert, Joseph C., jt. auth. see Nunlist, Robert A.
Seibert, M. Angelice. Pediatric Assistant's Handbook. (Allied Health Professions Monograph). 1983. write for info. (ISBN 0-87527-287-8). Green.
Seibert, Michael & Bolton, James R., eds. Biomass Production & Photobiological Conversion of Solar Energy. (Biological & Chemical Energy Conversion Ser.: Vol. 2). (Illus.). 1983. lib. bdg. 55.00x (ISBN 0-89553-042-2). Am Solar Energy.
Seibert, Robert F. & Anderson, Roy R. Politics & Change in the Middle East: Sources of Conflict & Accommodation. 352p. 1982. pap. 14.95 (ISBN 0-13-685057-X). P-H.
Seibert, W. H. The Lincoln Library of Essential Information, 2 vols. 42nd ed. LC 24-14708. (Illus.). (gr. 5 up). 1982. Set. 109.95 (ISBN 0-912168-09-9). Frontier Pr Co.
Seibert-Shook, Mavis, jt. auth. see Beveridge-Wavering, Agnes.
Seide, Diane. Careers in Health Services. rev. ed. 160p. (YA) 1982. 10.50 (ISBN 0-525-66768-7, 01019-310). Lodestar Bks.
Seide, Diane, jt. auth. see Traynor, Mark.
Seide, Michael. The Common Wilderness. 600p. 1982. 16.95 (ISBN 0-914590-74-X). Fiction Coll.
Seidel, Andrew D. & Ginsberg, Philip M. Commodities Trading: Analysis & Operations. (Illus.). 448p. 1982. text ed. 39.95 (ISBN 0-13-152678-2). P-H.
Seidel, Frank, jt. auth. see Ellis, William.
Seidel, J. J. Die Orgel und Ihr Bau: Ein Systematisches Handbuch. (Bibliotheca Organologica: Vol. 2). Repr. of 1966 ed. wrappers 22.50 o.s.i. (ISBN 90-6027-001-0, Pub. by Frits Knuf Netherlands). Pendragon NY.
Seidel, Kathleen G. The Same Last Name. (American Romance Ser.). 192p. 1983. pap. 2.25 (ISBN 0-686-38730-9). Harlequin Bks.
Seidel, L. E. Applied Textile Marketing. 1970. 5.95x (ISBN 0-87245-296-4). Textile Bk.
Seidel, Linda, ed. see Durantini, Mary F.
Seidel, Linda, ed. see Smith, David R.
Seidel, Robert J., ed. Computer Literacy: Issues & Directions for 1985. LC 82-1677. 308p. 1982. 23.00 (ISBN 0-12-634960-6). Acad Pr.
Seidel, Robert J., ed. see Conference on Computer Technology in Education for 1985 at Arlie House, Warrenton, Va., Sept. 15-18, 1975.
Seiden, Art. Michael Shows Off Baltimore. (Show Off Ser.). (Illus.). 32p. (gr. 1-5). 1982. 4.95 (ISBN 0-942806-01-8). Outdoor Bks.
Seiden, Art, illus. Look on the Ground. (Illus.). 14p. (ps). 1982. 2.95 (ISBN 0-448-12310-X, G&D). Putnam Pub Group.
--Tick-Tock. (Platt & Munk Peggy Cloth Clock Bks.). (Illus.). 10p. (ps). 1982. 3.50 (ISBN 0-448-46828-X, G&D). Putnam Pub Group.
Seiden, Rudolph. Livestock Health Encyclopedia. 3rd ed. Gough, W. James, ed. LC 68-8793. (Illus.). 1968. text ed. 27.50 (ISBN 0-8261-0003-1). Springer Pub.
Seidenberg, Dana A. Uhuru & the Kenya Indians: The Role of a Minority Community in Kenya-1939-1963-Politics. Date not set. text ed. price not set (ISBN 0-7069-1959-9, Pub. by Vikas India). Advent NY.
Seidenberg, Jacob. Labor Injunction in New York City, 1935-1950. (Cornell Studies in Industrial & Labor Relations: No. 4). 192p. 1953. pap. 3.00 (ISBN 0-87546-001-1). ILR Pr.
Seidenberg, Robert. Marriage in Life & Literature. LC 70-97939. 1970. 5.95 o.p. (ISBN 0-8022-2331-1). Philos Lib.
Seidenberg, Robert & DeCrow, Karen. Women Who Marry Houses: Panic & Protest in Agoraphobia. LC 82-14934. 204p. 1983. 15.95 (ISBN 0-07-016284-0, GB); pap. 7.95 (ISBN 0-07-016283-2). McGraw.
Seidenspinner-Nunez, Dayle. The Allegory of Love: Parodic Perspectivism in the Libro De Buon Amor. (U.C. Publications in Modern Philology: Vol. 112). 1981. pap. 12.00x o.s.i. (ISBN 0-520-09630-4). U of Cal Pr.
Seidensticker, Edward G. Low City, High City: Tokyo from Edo to the Earthquake. LC 82-48867. (Illus.). 320p. 1983. 18.95 (ISBN 0-394-50730-4). Knopf.
Seidensticker, Edward G., tr. see Kawabata, Yasunari.
Seidensticker, Edward G., tr. see Tanizaki, Junichiro.
Seidensticker, Edward T., tr. see Tanizaki, Junichiro.
Seiders, E. J., ed. Pipline Supervisory & Control Systems Workshop. 90p. 1982. 25.00 (I00149). ASME.
Seidl, Frederick & Applebaum, Robert. Delivering In-Home Services to the Aged & Disabled: The Wisconsin Experiment. LC 81-48068. (Illus.). 1983. write for info. (ISBN 0-669-05243-4). Lexington Bks.
Seidle, Helmut A. Medizinische Sprichwortr Im Englischen und Deutschen. 410p. (Ger.). 1981. write for info. (ISBN 3-8204-5985-5). P Lang Pubs.
Seidler, L. J. & Carmichael, D. R. Accountants' Handbook, 2 vols. 6th ed. LC 80-25239. (Professional Acounting & Business Ser.). 2064p. 1981. 85.00 (ISBN 0-471-05505-0, Pub. by Wiley Interscience). Wiley.
Seidler, Lee J. Social Accounting: Theory, Issues & Cases. LC 74-12116. (Management, Accounting & Information Systems Ser). 547p. 1975. 33.95 o.p. (ISBN 0-471-77488-X). Wiley.
Seidler, Lee J. & Carmichael, Douglas R. Accountants' Handbook. 6th ed. LC 80-25239. 2064p. 1981. 85.00x (ISBN 0-471-05505-0). Ronald Pr.

Seidler, Lee J., et al. The Equity Funding Papers: The Anatomy of a Fraud. LC 77-9921. (Accounting & Information Systems Ser.). 578p. 1977. text ed. 37.95 (ISBN 0-471-02273-X). Wiley.

Seidler, Tor. Terpin. (Illus.). 128p. (gr. 6 up). 1982. 8.95 (ISBN 0-374-37413-9). FS&G.

Seidl-Hohenveldern, I. American-Austrian Private International Law. LC 62-20879. (Bilateral Studies in Private International Law: No. 11). 1963. 15.00 (ISBN 0-379-11411-9). Oceana.

Seidman, A., jt. auth. see Kaufman, Milton.

Seidman, Ann. Working Women: A Study of Women in Paid Jobs. LC 77-13074. (Special Studies on Women in Contemporary Society Ser.). 1978. lib. bdg. 20.00 o.p. (ISBN 0-89158-051-4). Westview.

Seidman, Ann, ed. Natural Resources & National Welfare: The Case of Copper. LC 75-60. (Illus.). 476p. 1975. 42.95 o.p. (ISBN 0-275-05450-0). Praeger.

Seidman, Arthur, jt. auth. see Prensky, Sol.

Seidman, Arthur H. Integrated Circuits Applications Handbook. (Electrical & Electronics Technology Handbook). 704p. 1983. text ed. 39.95 (ISBN 0-471-07765-8). Wiley.

Seidman, Arthur H. & Mahrous, Haroun. Handbook of Electric Power Calculations. 608p. 1983. 29.50 (ISBN 0-07-056061-7, P&RB). McGraw.

Seidman, Arthur H. & Waintraub, Jack L. Electronics: Devices, Discrete & Integrated Circuits. (Electronics Technology Ser.). 1977. text ed. 26.95 (ISBN 0-675-08494-6). Additional supplements may be obtained from publisher. Merrill.

Seidman, Arthur H., jt. auth. see Kaufman, Milton.

Seidman, Arthur H., jt. auth. see Loveday, George C.

Seidman, Edward, ed. Handbook of Social Intervention. x ed. 736p. 1983. 49.95 (ISBN 0-8039-1971-9). Sage.

Seidman, Eric, jt. auth. see Denenberg, R. V.

Seidman, Harold. Politics, Position & Power: The Dynamics of Federal Organization. 3rd ed. 1980. text ed. 7.95x (ISBN 0-19-502659-4). Oxford U Pr.

Seidman, Hillel. The Glory of the Jewish Holidays. 2nd ed. LC 68-58504. (Illus.). 1980. 15.95 (ISBN 0-88400-065-6). Shengold.

Seidman, Hugh & Whyatt, Frances, eds. Equal Time. 101p. 1972. pap. 8.00 (ISBN 0-89366-130-9). Ultramarine Pub.

Seidman, Laurence I. Once in the Saddle. 1973. pap. 2.25 (ISBN 0-686-95754-7). Jefferson Natl.

Seidman, Robert. Bucks County Idyll. 1980. pap. 10.95 o.p. (ISBN 0-671-24825-1). S&S.

--One Smart Indian. LC 77-1174. 1977. 9.95 o.p. (ISBN 0-399-11929-9). Putnam Pub Group.

Seidman, Robert, jt. auth. see Chambliss, William.

Seidman, Robert B. The State, Law & Development. LC 78-18769. 1978. 35.00 (ISBN 0-312-75613-5). St Martin.

Seidman, Steve. The Film Career of Billy Wilder. 1977. lib. bdg. 15.00 (ISBN 0-8161-7934-4, Hall Reference). G K Hall.

Seidmann, Gertrud. Reise Nach Salzburg. (Illus.). 1975. pap. 3.95x (ISBN 0-582-36188-5); cassette 10.50x (ISBN 0-582-37521-5). Longman.

Seifer, Nancy. Nobody Speaks for Me. 1977. pap. 4.95 o.p. (ISBN 0-671-23026-3, Touchstone Bks). S&S.

Seifert, Anne. The Intelligent Woman's Diet. LC 82-42532. (Illus.). 269p. (Orig.). 1982. pap. 8.95 (ISBN 0-943584-01-9). Varnes Pubs.

Seifert, Anne & Hoyt, Fred. Hydroponic Home Gardening: Made Easy! (Illus.). 120p. (Orig.). 1983. pap. 4.50 (ISBN 0-943584-00-0). Varnes Pubs.

Seifert, Edward H., jt. ed. see Hefner, Robert L.

Seifert, Elizabeth. Doctor Tuck. 1980. pap. 1.75 o.p. (ISBN 0-451-09205-8, E9205, Sig). NAL.

--The Doctor's Desperate Hour. 1977. pap. 1.50 o.p. (ISBN 0-451-07787-3, W7787, Sig). NAL.

--Doctors on Eden Place. 1979. pap. 1.75 o.p. (ISBN 0-451-08852-2, E8852, Sig). NAL.

--The Doctors Were Brothers. (General Ser.). 1979. lib. bdg. 12.95 (ISBN 0-8161-6705-2, Large Print Bks). G K Hall.

--The Story of Andrea Fields. 208p. 1974. pap. 1.25 o.p. (ISBN 0-451-06535-2, Y6535, Sig). NAL.

--Two Doctors, Two Loves. LC 82-7436. 1982. 10.95 (ISBN 0-396-08101-0). Dodd.

--Two Doctors, Two Loves. (General Ser.). 1983. lib. bdg. 13.50 (ISBN 0-8161-3496-0, Large Print Bks). G K Hall.

--Two Faces of Dr. Collier - The Doctor's Reputation. 1980. pap. 1.95 o.p. (ISBN 0-451-09469-7, J9469, Sig). NAL.

Seifert, George G. Applying Statistical Concepts: A Workbook to Accompany Albert E. Bartz's Basic Statistical Concepts. 2nd ed. 1981. pap. text ed. 7.95x (ISBN 0-8087-4201-9). Burgess.

Seifert, Hans T., ed. see Streaborg, L.

Seifert, Harvey, jt. auth. see Bennett, John C.

Seifert, Herbert & Threlfall, W. Lehrbuch Der Topologie. (Ger). 18.50 (ISBN 0-8284-0031-8). Chelsea Pub.

--Variationsrechnung Im Grossen. LC 77-160837. (Ger.). 9.95 (ISBN 0-8284-0049-0). Chelsea Pub.

Seifert, Kelvin. Educational Psychology. 464p. 1982. pap. text ed. 18.95 (ISBN 0-395-32790-3); write for info. tchr's. manual (ISBN 0-395-32791-1); study guide 6.95 (ISBN 0-395-33183-8). HM.

Seifert, Wilfried, ed. Neurobiology of the Hippocampus. Date not set. price not set (ISBN 0-12-634880-4). Acad Pr.

Seifert, William W. & Schriever, B. A., eds. Air Transportation Nineteen Seventy-Five & Beyond: A Systems Approach. 1968. 25.00x (ISBN 0-262-19042-7). MIT Pr.

Seiffert, Dorothy, jt. auth. see Glenn, Peter.

Seigel, Alan H. Breakin' In...to the Music Business. (Illus.). 272p. (Orig.). 1983. text ed. 14.95 (ISBN 0-89524-171-4, 8609); pap. 8.95 (ISBN 0-89524-156-0, 8604). Cherry Lane.

Seigfried, Charlene H. Chaos & Context: A Study in William James. LC 77-86346. xiii, 137p. 1978. 12.95x (ISBN 0-8214-0378-8, 82-82766). Ohio U Pr.

Seigfried, F. R. & Pueschel, M. Down's Syndrome: Growing & Learning. LC 78-19184. 1978. pap. 6.95 (ISBN 0-8362-2805-7). Andrews & McMeel.

Seiler, F. R. & Geursen, R. G., eds. Seven S-Immunglobulin zur intravenoesen Anwendung. (Beitraege zu Infusionstherapie und klinische Ernaehrung: Vol. 9). (Illus.). viii, 176p. 1982. pap. 36.00 (ISBN 3-8055-3632-1). S Karger.

Seiler, Hans J. Cahuilla Text with an Introduction. (Language Science Monographs: Vol. 6). 1970. pap. text ed. 8.50x o.p. (ISBN 0-87750-148-3). Res Ctr Lang Semiotic.

Seiler, Hansjakob. Possession as an Operational Dimension of Language. (Language Universal Ser.: 2). 140p. 1983. pap. write for info (ISBN 3-87808-980-5). Benjamins North Am.

Seiler, John, ed. Southern Africa Since the Portuguese Coup. (Westview Special Studies on Africa). (Illus.). 272p. 1980. 26.50 (ISBN 0-89158-767-5). Westview.

Seiler, N. & Jung, M. J., eds. Enzyme Activated Irreversable Inhibitors: Proceedings of the Int'l. Symposium Held in Strasbourg, July, 1978. 1978. 77.00 (ISBN 0-444-80080-8, Biomedical Pr). Elsevier.

Seiler, Robert E. & Collins, Frank. Accounting Principles for Management: An Introduction. 3rd ed. Date not set. text ed. 22.95 (ISBN 0-675-08267-6); wkbk. 8.95 (ISBN 0-675-08106-8). Additional supplements may be obtained from publisher. Merrill.

Seilhamer, Frank H. Prophets & Prophecy: Seven Key Messengers. LC 76-62603. 96p. (Orig.). 1977. pap. 0.50 o.p. (ISBN 0-8006-1254-X, 1-1254). Fortress.

Sein, Kenneth & Withey, J. A. The Great Po Sein: A Chronicle of the Burmese Theater. LC 75-46553. 170p. 1976. Repr. of 1966 ed. lib. bdg. 16.25x (ISBN 0-8371-8737-0, SEGP). Greenwood.

Seinfeld, John. Air Pollution: Physical & Chemical Fundamentals. (Illus.). 544p. 1974. text ed. 39.50 (ISBN 0-07-056042-0, C); solution's manual 5.00 (ISBN 0-07-056043-9). McGraw.

Seip, G. G. Electrical Installations Handbook, 2 vols. Set. 137.95 (ISBN 0-471-26018-5, Pub. by Wiley Heyden). Wiley.

Seip, Terry L. The South Returns to Congress: Men, Economic Measures, & Intersectional Relationships, 1868-1879. LC 82-4654. (Illus.). 344p. 1983. 25.00 (ISBN 0-8071-1052-3). La State U Pr.

Seipel, L., jt. ed. see Loogen, F.

Seipp, Conrad, jt. auth. see Ramirez de Arellano, Annette B.

Seippel. Optoelectronics. 1981. text ed. 24.95 (ISBN 0-8359-5255-X). Reston.

Seiss, Joseph. The Great Pyramid: A Miracle in Stone. LC 72-81590. (Illus.). 256p. 1973. pap. 3.50 (ISBN 0-89345-218-1, Steinerbks). Garber Comm.

Seitel, Fraser P. The Practice of Public Relations. (Marketing & Management Ser.). 352p. 1980. text ed. 22.95 (ISBN 0-675-08147-5). Additional supplements may be obtained from publisher. Merrill.

Seitz & Finegold. Silversmithing. LC 82-70657. 500p. 1983. 35.00 (ISBN 0-8019-7232-9). Chilton.

Seitz, Don C. Dreadful Decade: Detailing Some Phases in the History of the United States from Reconstruction to Resumption, 1869-1879. LC 68-28646. (Illus.). 1968. Repr. of 1926 ed. lib. bdg. 18.75x (ISBN 0-8371-0216-2, SEDD). Greenwood.

--The James Gordon Bennetts, Father & Son: Proprietors of the New York Herald. (Illus.). 405p. 1974. Repr. of 1928 ed. 18.50x (ISBN 0-8464-0008-1). Beekman Pubs.

--Under the Black Flag. LC 78-167167. 1971. Repr. of 1925 ed. 37.00x (ISBN 0-8103-3805-X). Gale.

Seitz, Neil & Yeager, Frederick. Financial Institution Management. 450p. 1982. text ed. 23.95 (ISBN 0-8359-2022-4); instr's. manual free (ISBN 0-8359-2023-2). Reston.

Seitz, Neil E. Financial Analysis: A Programmed Approach. 2nd ed. (Illus.). 1979. pap. text ed. 12.95 (ISBN 0-8359-1992-7); instrs'. manual avail. (ISBN 0-8359-1993-5). Reston.

Seitz, Nick. Improve Your Game (& Learn About) the Superstars of Golf. 192p. Date not set. pap. cancelled (ISBN 0-346-12477-8). Cornerstone.

Seitz, Steven T. Bureaucracy Policy & the Public. new ed. LC 77-26656. (Illus.). 216p. 1978. pap. text ed. 4.95 o.p. (ISBN 0-8016-4482-8). Mosby.

Seitz, William C. The Sixties: Art in the Age of Aquarius. LC 78-60217. 1978. 20.00 o.p. (ISBN 0-8076-0906-4); pap. (ISBN 0-8076-0907-2). Braziller.

Seitzinger, Jack M. & Kelley, Thomas M. Police Terminology: Programmed Manual for Criminal Justice Personnel. (Illus.). 152p. 1974. spiral 11.75x (ISBN 0-398-02947-4). C C Thomas.

Seiverd, Charles E. Hematology for Medical Technologists. 5th ed. LC 81-8265. (Illus.). 946p. 1983. text ed. write for info o.p. (ISBN 0-8121-0805-1). Lea & Febiger.

Seixas, Frank A. Currents in Alcoholism: Biochemical, Biological & Clinical Topics. 512p. 1977. Vol. I. 45.50 (ISBN 0-8089-1007-8). Grune.

Seixas, Judith S. Alcohol: What it Is, What it Does. 5.95 o.p. (ISBN 0-686-92239-5, 5002). Hazelden.

Seixas, Vic, Jr. & Cohen, Joel. Prime Time Tennis. (Illus.). 256p. 1982. 12.95 (ScribT). Scribner.

Seiyama, S. & Kozo, T. New Horizons in Catalysis, 2 vols. (Studies in Surface Science & Catalysis: Vol. 7). 1981. Set. 149.00 (ISBN 0-444-99750-4). Elsevier.

Sejna, Jan. We Will Bury You. 206p. 1983. 17.50 (ISBN 0-283-98862-2, Pub by Sidgwick & Jackson). Merrimack Bk Serv.

Sejourne, Laurette. Burning Water: Thought & Religion in Ancient Mexico. LC 76-14205. (Illus.). 1976. pap. 3.95 o.p. (ISBN 0-394-73276-6). Shambhala Pubns.

Sekey, Andrew. Electroacoustic Analysis & Enhancement of Alaryngeal Speech. (Illus.). 368p. 1982. 49.75x (ISBN 0-398-04547-X). C C Thomas.

Sekhar, Uday, jt. auth. see Gulhati, Ravi.

Sekhesa, Tholoana, jt. auth. see Demuth, Katherine.

Seki, Hozen, tr. see Okada, Barbara T.

Sekiguchi, Sueo, jt. ed. see Krause, Lawrence B.

Sekka, Kanzaka. A Flight of Butterflies. (Illus.). 1979. 9.98 (ISBN 0-500-01227-X). Thames Hudson.

Seklemian, M., jt. auth. see Paganetti, J.

Sekora, John & Turner, Darwin, eds. The Art of Slave Narrative: Original Essays in Criticism & Theory. (Essays in Literature Ser.: Bk. 5). 144p. 1982. pap. text ed. 8.00 (ISBN 0-934312-04-4). Western Ill Univ.

Sekowsky, JoAnne. My Father Has A Green Thumb. 32p. 1981. pap. 0.75 (ISBN 0-930756-63-0). Women's Aglow.

Sela. Role of Non-Specific Immunity in the Prevention & Treatment of Cancer. 1980. 102.25 (ISBN 0-444-80156-1). Elsevier.

Sela, M. & Prywes, M., eds. Topics in Basic Immunology. 1969. 43.00 (ISBN 0-12-635550-9). Acad Pr.

Sela, Michael, ed. The Antigens. 1974. Vol. 1. by subscription 45.00 64.00 (ISBN 0-12-635501-0). Acad Pr.

--The Antigens, Vol. 4. 1977. 62.50 (ISBN 0-12-635504-5); subscription 53.50. Acad Pr.

--The Antigens, Vol. 5. 1979. 41.00 (ISBN 0-12-635505-3); by subscription 35.00. Acad Pr.

Selakovich, Daniel. Schools & American Society. 2nd ed. LC 70-173274. 1973. text ed. 15.95x o.p. (ISBN 0-471-00715-3). Wiley.

Selbert, Ingrid. Our Changing World. (Illus.). 12p. 1982. 10.95 (ISBN 0-399-20869-0, Philomel). Putnam Pub Group.

Selbo, M. L. Adhesive Bonding of Wood. LC 77-88958. (Drake Home Craftsman Ser.). (Illus.). 1978. pap. 6.95 (ISBN 0-8069-8104-0). Sterling.

Selbst, Paul L. & Launer, Deborah J. Modern Health Care Forms. 1976. 54.00 (ISBN 0-88262-114-9). Warren.

Selby, Curt. Blood County. (Science Fiction Ser.). 1981. pap. 2.25 o.p. (ISBN 0-87997-622-5, UE1622). DAW Bks.

Selby, D. J. Introduction to the New Testament: The Word Became Flesh. 1971. text ed. 20.95x (ISBN 0-02-408870-6). Macmillan.

Selby, Donald J. Toward the Understanding of St. Paul. 1962. ref. ed. 18.95 (ISBN 0-13-925693-8). P-H.

Selby, Earl & Selby, Miriam. Odyssey: Journey Through Black America. 1971. 7.95 o.p. (ISBN 0-399-10590-5). Putnam Pub Group.

Selby, Edward B., Jr., jt. auth. see Timberlake, Richard H., Jr.

Selby, F. G., ed. see Burke, Edmund.

Selby, Hubert. The Demon. 1977. pap. 1.95 o.p. (ISBN 0-451-07611-7, J7611, Sig). NAL.

Selby, Hubert, Jr. The Room. LC 72-155129. 1971. pap. 1.95 o.s.i. (ISBN 0-394-17816-5, B363, BC). Grove.

Selby, John. Powerpoint. 304p. 1982. pap. 2.95 o.p. (ISBN 0-446-90673-5). Warner Bks.

Selby, M. J. Hillslope Materials & Processes. (Illus.). 1982. 46.00x (ISBN 0-19-874126-X); pap. 24.00x (ISBN 0-19-874127-8). Oxford U Pr.

Selby, Miriam, jt. auth. see Selby, Earl.

Selby, Peter H. Interpreting Graphs & Tables. LC 75-25761. (Self-Teaching Guides Ser.). 1976. pap. text ed. 4.95x o.p. (ISBN 0-471-77559-2). Wiley.

--Quick Algebra Review. (Self Teaching Guide Ser.). 192p. 1983. pap. 8.95 (ISBN 0-471-86471-4). Wiley.

Selby-Lowndes, Joan. Your Book of the English Church. 3.25 o.p. (ISBN 0-685-91532-8). Transatlantic.

Selcher, Wayne A. The Afro-Asian Dimensions of Brazilian Foreign Policy, 1956-1972. LC 73-19968. (Latin American Monographs 2: No. 13). 1974. 11.00 (ISBN 0-8130-0384-9). U Presses Fla.

--Brazil's Multilateral Relations Between First & Third Worlds. LC 77-25273. (A Westview Replica Edition Ser.). 1978. lib. bdg. 26.00 o.p. (ISBN 0-89158-088-3). Westview.

Selcher, Wayne A., ed. Brazil in the International System. (Special Studies on Latin America & the Caribbean). 300p. 1981. lib. bdg. 30.00 o.p. (ISBN 0-89158-907-4). Westview.

Selcraig, James T. The Red Scare in the Midwest, 1945-1955: A State & Local Study. Berkhofer, Robert, ed. LC 82-17545. (Studies in American History & Culture: No. 36). 226p. 1982. 39.95 (ISBN 0-8357-1380-6, Pub. by UMI Res Pr). Univ Microfilms.

Selden, Bernice. The Body-Mind Book: Nine Ways to Awareness. LC 79-17571. (Illus.). 160p. (gr. 8-12). 1979. PLB 7.29 o.p. (ISBN 0-671-32918-9). Messner.

Selden, David. The Teacher Rebellion. 336p. 1983. 14.95 (ISBN 0-88258-099-X). Howard U Pr.

Selden, George. Cricket in Times Square. (Illus.). (gr. 2-7). 1970. pap. 2.25 (ISBN 0-440-41563-2, YB). Dell.

--Cricket in Times Square. LC 60-12640. (Illus.). 192p. (gr. 4 up). 1960. 9.95 (ISBN 0-374-31650-3). FS&G.

--Irma & Jerry. 1982. pap. 2.50 (ISBN 0-380-80978-8, 80978, Camelot). Avon.

--Oscar Lobster's Fair Exchange. (Illus.). (gr. 3-7). 1974. pap. 2.25 (ISBN 0-380-00703-7, 61085X, Camelot). Avon.

Selden, John. Table-Talk. large type ed. Arber, Edward, ed. 1972. Repr. of 1869 ed. 10.00x (ISBN 0-87556-314-7). Saifer.

Selden, Kyoko, jt. ed. see Lippit, Noriko.

Selden, Kyoko, tr. see Reiitsu, Kojima.

Selden, Mark, ed. The People's Republic of China: A Documentary History of Revolutionary Change. 1980. pap. 12.50 (ISBN 0-85345-532-5, PB5325). Monthly Rev.

Selden, Mark, ed. see Reiitsu, Kojima.

Selden, Samuel, Jr. & Rezzuto, Thomas. Essentials of Stage Scenery. LC 70-182307. (Illus.). 1972. 21.95 (ISBN 0-13-289215-4). P-H.

Selden, William, jt. auth. see Nanassy, Louis C.

Seldes, George, ed. Great Quotations. 1966. 15.00 o.p. (ISBN 0-8184-0036-6). Lyle Stuart.

Seldin, Joel. Automation: The Challenge of Men & Machines. rev. ed. (Challenge Bk). (Illus.). (gr. 6-8). 1971. 4.00e o.p. (ISBN 0-698-20008-X, Coward). Putnam Pub Group.

Seldin, Marian, jt. ed. see Silberstein, Suzanne.

Seldin, Maury, ed. The Real Estate Handbook. LC 79-51783. 1980. 45.00 (ISBN 0-87094-184-4). Dow Jones-Irwin.

Seldin, Ruth. Teacher's Guide to Jews & Their Religion. 150p. 5.95 (ISBN 0-686-95154-9); pap. 2.95 (ISBN 0-686-99468-X). ADL.

Seldin, Ruth R., jt. auth. see Routtenberg, Lilly S.

Seldin, Scott. Yes, Boss. LC 82-72103. (Illus.). 128p. 1982. 10.95 (ISBN 0-943778-01-8); pap. 5.95 (ISBN 0-943778-02-6). Blythe-Pennington.

Seldis, Henry J. Helen Lundeberg: A Retrospective Exhibition. (Illus.). 32p. 1971. 5.00x (ISBN 0-686-99825-1). La Jolla Mus Contemp Art.

Seldon, Arthur. Charge. 1977. 12.50 o.p. (ISBN 0-85117-115-X). Transatlantic.

Seldon, Arthur, ed. see Plant, Sir Arnold.

Seldon, George. Chester Cricket's Pigeon Ride. (gr. k-6). 1983. pap. 1.95 (ISBN 0-440-41389-3, YB). Dell.

Seldon, H. L., jt. ed. see Schmidt, D.

Seldon, Philip. How to Buy Wine. LC 79-8504. (Illus.). 224p. (Orig.). 1981. pap. 9.95 (ISBN 0-385-14961-1, Dolp). Doubleday.

Selecky, Paul A. Pulmonary Disease. LC 82-1903. (Internal Medicine Today: A Comprehensive Postgraduate Library). 345p. 1982. 40.00 (ISBN 0-471-09554-0, Pub. by Wiley Med). Wiley.

Selekman, Benjamin M., et al. Problems in Labor Relations. 3rd ed. 1964. text ed. 18.95 o.p. (ISBN 0-07-056083-8, C); key 3.50 o.p. (ISBN 0-07-056084-6). McGraw.

Selender, Michael D. The Anal Period. LC 78-51335. (Illus.). 1978. pap. 3.25 o.s.i. (ISBN 0-931354-00-5). Stone-Crock-Buzzard-Pr.

Seletz, Jeanette. Jone Brent, Neurosurgeon. LC 78-50163. 320p. 1983. 12.50 (ISBN 0-87527-136-7). Green.

Self, Charles. Bathroom Remodeling. (Illus.). 224p. 1980. 14.95 (ISBN 0-8359-0436-9); pap. 7.95 (ISBN 0-8359-0435-0). Reston.

--Do-It-Yourselfer's Guide to Auto Body Repair & Painting. (Illus.). 1978. 10.95 (ISBN 0-8306-7949-9); pap. 6.95 (ISBN 0-8306-6949-3, 949). TAB Bks.

Self, Charles R. Country Living: The Homesteader's Bible. (Illus.). 512p. 1981. 21.95 (ISBN 0-8306-9672-5, 1301); pap. 12.95 (ISBN 0-8306-1301-3, 1301). TAB Bks.

--Wood Heating Handbook. LC 77-1816. (Illus.). 1977. 8.95 o.p. (ISBN 0-8306-7872-7); pap. 5.95 o.p. (ISBN 0-8306-6872-1, 872). TAB Bks.

Self, Charles R., Jr. Underground Plant Life. LC 77-88947. 1978. pap. 4.95 o.p. (ISBN 0-8069-8752-9, 046510). Sterling.

Self, George. Make a New Sound. 1976. pap. 15.50 (ISBN 0-900938-46-3, 50-26909). Eur-Am Music.

Self, Margaret, ed. Now What Can We Do? LC 76-62687. 144p. (ps). 1977. pap. 2.50 o.p. (ISBN 0-8307-0517-1, 56-031-02). Regal.

Self, Margaret C. At the Horse Show. LC 72-92310. (Illus.). 1966. 8.95 o.p. (ISBN 0-668-02747-9). Arco.

--Complete Book of Horses & Ponies. (Illus.). (gr. 6 up). 1963. 8.95 (ISBN 0-07-056109-5, GB). McGraw.

--Horses - Their Selection, Care & Handling. pap. 4.00 (ISBN 0-87980-195-6). Wilshire.

--Young Rider & His First Pony. LC 69-14892. (Illus.). 178p. 1974. pap. 2.95 o.p. (ISBN 0-668-03408-4). Arco.

Self, Margaret M. Effective Year-Round Bible Ministries. LC 80-52962. 144p. 1981. pap. 3.95 o.p. (ISBN 0-8307-0751-4, 5414318). Regal.

--Who Helps Betsy & Brian? 8p. (ps). 1975. pap. 0.49 o.p. (ISBN 0-8307-0383-7, 56-014-01). Regal.

Self, Robert T. Barrett Wendell. LC 75-12735. (United States Authors Ser.). 1975. lib. bdg. 13.95 (ISBN 0-8057-7160-3, Twayne). G K Hall.

Selfe, Lorna, ed. Normal & Anomalous Representationl Drawing Ability in Children. Date not set. price not set (ISBN 0-12-635760-9). Acad Pr.

Selfoh, Nicolaas. Catalogue d'une Tres Belle Bibliotheque de Livres de Musique, Ainsi Qu'une Collection de Toutes Sortes d'Instruments. (Auction Catalogues of Music Ser.: Vol. 1). 1973. wrappers 50.00 o.s.i. (ISBN 90-6027-341-9, Pub. by Frits Knuf Netherlands). Pendragon NY.

Selfridge, Oliver. A Primer for FORTRAN IV: On-Line. 1972. pap. 7.95x o.p. (ISBN 0-262-69035-7). MIT Pr.

Selick, et al, eds. Current Trends in Algebraic Topology. (Canadian Mathematical Ser.: Vol.2). Pt.1. 26.00 (ISBN 0-686-84832-2, CMS2.1); Pt.2. 24.00 (ISBN 0-8218-6002-X, CMS2.2); Set (Vols. 1 & 2) 42.00 (ISBN 0-8218-6003-8). Am Math.

Selig, E. T., jt. ed. see Yong, R. N.

Selig, Robert L. George Gissing. (English Authors Ser.). 192p. 1983. lib. bdg. 15.95 (ISBN 0-8057-6831-9, Twayne). G K Hall.

Seliger, Herbert W. & Long, Michael H., eds. Classroom Oriented Research in Second Language Acquisition. 364p. 1983. pap. text ed. 15.95 (ISBN 0-88377-267-1). Newbury Hse.

Seliger, M. The Marxist Conception of Ideology. LC 76-11092. (International Studies). 1977. 32.50 (ISBN 0-521-21229-4); pap. 12.95x (ISBN 0-521-29625-0). Cambridge U Pr.

Seliger, Martin. Ideology & Politics. LC 75-15430. 1976. 14.95 (ISBN 0-02-928360-4). Free Pr.

Seligman, Dee, compiled by. Doris Lessing: An Annotated Bibliography of Criticism. LC 80-24540. xv, 139p. 1981. lib. bdg. 27.50x (ISBN 0-313-21270-8, SDL/). Greenwood.

Seligman, Gerald. Business Spelling the Easy Way. 144p. 1983. pap. 4.95 (ISBN 0-8120-2523-7). Barron.

Seligman, Gustav L., jt. auth. see Jones, Robert.

Seligman, Janet, tr. see Schaarschmidt-Richter, Irmtraud & Mori, Osamu.

Seligman, Joel. The High Citadel. 1978. 10.95 o.p. (ISBN 0-395-26301-8). HM.

Seligman, Martin E. & Rosenhan, David L. Abnormal Psychology. 1983. write for info (ISBN 0-393-95277-0). Norton.

Seligman, Milton. Group Counseling & Group Psychotherapy with Special Populations. 372p. 1981. text ed. 23.95 (ISBN 0-8391-1691-8). Univ Park.

--A Guide to Understanding & Treating the Family with a Handicapped Child. write for info (ISBN 0-8089-1561-4). Grune.

Seligman, Susan M. Now That I'm a Mother...What Do I Do for Me. 1980. 9.95 o.p. (ISBN 0-8092-7156-7); pap. 5.95 o.p. (ISBN 0-8092-7155-9). Contemp Bks.

Seligman, Thomas K., jt. auth. see Berrin, Kathleen.

Seligmann & Nitzig. Primary Immunodeficiencies. (Inserm Symposia Ser.: Vol. 16). 1980. 96.75 (ISBN 0-444-80296-7). Elsevier.

Seligson, David see Reiner, Miriam, et al.

Seligson, Harry & Bardwell, George. Labor-Management Relations in Colorado. LC 82-71140. 1961. 12.00 (ISBN 0-8040-0178-2, SB). Swallow.

Seligson, Tom. Stalking. 1979. 8.95 o.p. (ISBN 0-89696-037-4, An Everest House Book). Dodd.

Selikoff, Irving & Lee, Douglas H. Asbestos & Disease. LC 77-25735. (Environmental Sciences Ser.). 1978. 54.00 (ISBN 0-12-636050-2). Acad Pr.

Selikoff, Irving J., jt. auth. see Hammond, E. Cuyler.

Selikoff, Irving J. & Hammond, E. Cuyler, eds. Health Hazards of Asbestos Exposure, Vol. 330. LC 79-24999. (Annals of the New York Academy of Sciences). 814p. 1979. 151.00x (ISBN 0-89766-033-1). NY Acad Sci.

Selin, W. E., ed. see Jonson, Ben.

Selincourt, Ernest De see Wordsworth, William.

Selinker, Larry, et al, eds. English for Academic & Technical Purposes: Studies in Honor of Louis Trimble. (Orig.). 1981. pap. 16.95 (ISBN 0-88377-178-0). Newbury Hse.

Selinko, Annemarie see Allen, W. S.

Seljeskog, Edward L., jt. ed. see Chou, Shelley N.

Selkov, E., jt. auth. see Reich, J. G.

Sell & Wright. Haemophilus Influenza: Epidemiology, Immunology & Prevention of Disease. 352p. 1982. 50.00 (ISBN 0-444-00683-4). Elsevier.

Sell, Betty, jt. ed. see Sell, Kenneth D.

Sell, Charles, jt. auth. see Perry, Lloyd.

Sell, G. R., jt. auth. see Naylor, A. W.

Sell, Kenneth D. & Sell, Betty, eds. Divorce in the United States, Canada & Great Britain: A Guide to Information Sources. LC 78-15894. (Social Issues & Social Problems Information Guide Ser.: Vol. 1). 1978. 42.00x (ISBN 0-8103-1396-0). Gale.

Sell, R. G. & Shipley, P., eds. Satisfactions in Work Design: Ergonomics & Other Approaches. 220p. 1979. write for info. (ISBN 0-686-81311-1, Pub. by Taylor & Francis). Intl Pubns Serv.

Sell, R. G. & Shipley, Patricia, eds. Satisfactions in Work Design: Ergonomics & Other Approaches. LC 79-311845. 202p. 1979. 25.00x (ISBN 0-85066-180-3). Intl Pubns Serv.

Sell, Violet, compiled by see American Library Association.

Sella, Amnon. Soviet Political & Military Conduct in the Middle East. 1981. 26.00 (ISBN 0-312-74845-0). St Martin.

Sellar, Walter C. & Yeatman, Robert J. Ten Sixty-Six & All That. 1958. pap. 4.50 (ISBN 0-525-47025-5, 0437-130). Dutton.

Sellars, Wilfrid. Naturalism & Ontology. viii, 182p. (Orig.). 1980. lib. bdg. 24.00 (ISBN 0-917930-36-3); pap. text ed. 7.50x (ISBN 0-917930-16-9). Ridgeview.

--Philosophical Perspectives: History of Philosophy. 1979. lib. bdg. 23.00 (ISBN 0-917930-24-X); pap. text ed. 6.50x (ISBN 0-917930-04-5). Ridgeview.

--Philosophical Perspectives: Metaphysics & Epistemology. 1979. lib. bdg. 23.00 (ISBN 0-917930-25-8); pap. text ed. 6.50x (ISBN 0-917930-05-3). Ridgeview.

--Pure Pragmatics & Possible Worlds: The Early Essays of Wilfrid Sellars. Sicha, Jeffrey, ed. LC 78-65271. (Orig.). 1980. lib. bdg. 24.00 (ISBN 0-917930-26-6); pap. text ed. 9.50x (ISBN 0-917930-06-1). Ridgeview.

--Science & Metaphysics: Variations on Kantian Themes. LC 68-12258. (International Library of Philosophy & Scientific Method). 1968. pap. text ed. 21.00x o.p. (ISBN 0-7100-3501-2). Humanities.

Sellars, Wilfrid & Hospers, John, eds. Readings in Ethical Theory. 2nd ed. 1970. text ed. 27.95 (ISBN 0-13-756007-9). P-H.

Sellars, Wilfrid, jt. ed. see Feigl, Herbert.

Sellars, Wilfrid, jt. ed. see Freeman, Eugene.

Sellassie, Sahle. Firebrands. (Orig.). 9.00 o.s.i. (ISBN 0-89410-103-X); pap. 5.00 o.s.i. (ISBN 0-89410-102-1). Three Continents.

Selleck, Jack. Contrast: A Design Principle. LC 75-21110. (Concepts of Design Ser.). (Illus.). 80p. (gr. 7-12). 1975. 9.95 (ISBN 0-87192-074-3). Davis Mass.

--Line: A Design Element. LC 74-82679. (Concepts of Design Ser). (Illus.). 80p. (gr. 7 up). 1974. 9.95 (ISBN 0-87192-063-8). Davis Mass.

Selleck, R. J. English Primary Education & the Progressives: 1914-1939. (Students Library of Education). 1972. 14.95x (ISBN 0-7100-7208-2). Routledge & Kegan.

Sellen, Betty-Carol, jt. ed. see Berkner, Dimity S.

Sellens, Alvin. The Stanley Plane: A History & Descriptive Inventory. LC 75-9509. (Illus.). 1975. 13.50 (ISBN 0-686-27737-6). Sellens.

--Woodworking Planes: A Descriptive Register of Wooden Planes. LC 78-52687. (Illus.). 1978. 13.50 (ISBN 0-686-15773-7). Sellens.

Seller, Maxine S. To Seek America: A History of Ethnic Life in the United States. LC 77-8248. 1977. lib. bdg. 15.95x (ISBN 0-89198-117-9); pap. text ed. 8.75x (ISBN 0-89198-118-7). Ozer.

Seller, Maxine S., ed. Immigrant Women. 347p. 1980. 27.95 (ISBN 0-87722-190-1); pap. text ed. 10.95 (ISBN 0-87722-191-X). Temple U Pr.

Sellers, C. G. As It Happened: A History of the United States. 1974. text ed. 13.20 (ISBN 0-07-056179-6); tchr's ed. 18.72 (ISBN 0-07-056180-X). McGraw.

Sellers, Charles, et al. A Synopsis of American History: Complete Volume. 5th ed. 1981. 15.95 (ISBN 0-395-30735-X); Vol. 1. pap. 11.95 (ISBN 0-395-30736-8); Vol. 2. pap. 11.95 (ISBN 0-395-30737-6); instr's manual 1.25 (ISBN 0-395-30738-4). HM.

Sellers, Frank. Sharps Firearms. (Illus.). 1978. 34.95 o.s.i. (ISBN 0-695-80912-1). Follett.

Sellers, Gene. Understanding Algebra & Trigonometry. 1979. text ed. 22.95 (ISBN 0-675-08306-0). Additional supplements may be obtained from publisher. Merrill.

Sellers, Gene R. Understanding College Algebra. 1979. text ed. 19.95 (ISBN 0-675-08294-3). Additional supplements may be obtained from publisher. Merrill.

Sellers, I., jt. ed. see Briggs, J. H.

Sellers, James. Warming Fires: The Quest for Community in America. 224p. 1975. 2.00 (ISBN 0-8164-0273-6). Seabury.

Sellers, Jill, ed. see Adams, Carol & Laurikietis, Rae.

Sellers, L. Cooking with Love. LC 77-99864. (Illus.). 1969. 12.00 (ISBN 0-08-006908-8); pap. 4.80 (ISBN 0-08-006907-X). Pergamon.

--The Simple Subs Book. 1968. 23.00 o.s.i. (ISBN 0-08-013042-9); pap. 12.75 (ISBN 0-08-013041-0). Pergamon.

Sellers, Leonard & Rivers, William R. Mass Media Issues: Articles & Commentaries. (Illus.). 432p. 1977. pap. text ed. 16.95 (ISBN 0-13-559500-2). P-H.

Sellers, Michael. Cache on the Rocks. LC 82-45606. (Crime Club Ser.). 192p. 1983. 11.95 (ISBN 0-385-18416-6). Doubleday.

--P.S. I Love You: An Intimate Portrait of Peter Sellers. 264p. 1982. 12.95 (ISBN 0-525-24123-X, 01258-370). Dutton.

Sellers, O. R. & Baramki, D. C. A Roman-Byzantine Burial Cave in Northern Palestine. (American Schools of Oriental Research, Supplementary Ser.: Vols. 15-16). 55p. 1953. pap. text ed. 3.50x (ISBN 0-89757-315-3, Am Sch Orient Res). Eisenbrauns.

Sellers, Ovid R., et al. The Excavations at Beth-Zur, 1957. (American Schools of Oriental Research Ser.). 87p. 1968. text ed. 6.00x (ISBN 0-89757-038-3, Am Sch Orient Res). Eisenbrauns.

Selley, N. J. Experimental Approach to Electrochemistry. LC 77-7914. 211p. 1977. 29.95x o.s.i. (ISBN 0-470-99204-2). Halsted Pr.

Selley, R. C. Introduction to Sedimentology. 2nd ed. 18.50; pap. write for info. (ISBN 0-12-636362-5). Acad Pr.

Selley, Richard C. Ancient Sedimentary Environments. 2nd ed. LC 78-58627. (Illus.). 1978. pap. 12.95x (ISBN 0-8014-9869-4). Cornell U Pr.

--Petroleum Geology for Geophysicists & Engineers. LC 82-81124. (Short Course Handbooks). (Illus.). 96p. 1982. text ed. 22.00 (ISBN 0-934634-49-1); pap. 15.00 (ISBN 0-934634-42-4). Intl Human Res.

Sellick, Douglas, jt. auth. see Addkison, Roy.

Sellin, Don & Birch, Jack. Psychoeducational Development of Gifted & Talented Learners. LC 81-3467. 319p. 1981. text ed. 26.50 (ISBN 0-89443-362-8). Aspen Systems.

Sellin, Thorsten. Culture Conflict & Crime. LC 39-7280. 1938. pap. 4.00 (ISBN 0-527-03277-8). Kraus Repr.

Sellin, Thorsten & Wolfgang, Marvin E. The Measurement of Delinquency. (Criminology, Law Enforcement, & Social Problems Ser.: No. 209). 433p. 1975. Repr. of 1964 ed. 20.00x (ISBN 0-87585-209-2). Patterson Smith.

Sellin, Thorsten & Wolfgang, Marvin E., eds. Delinquency: Selected Studies. LC 78-84961. 161p. 1969. 11.50 (ISBN 0-471-77568-1, Pub. by Wiley). Krieger.

Sellin, Thorsten & Young, Donald, eds. China, the Annals of the American Academy of Political & Social Science. LC 80-8830. (China During the Interregnum 1911-1949, The Economy & Society Ser.). 431p. 1982. lib. bdg. 43.00 (ISBN 0-8240-4685-4). Garland Pub.

Sellin, Thorsten, ed. see Conrad, John P.

Sellin, Thorsten, jt. ed. see Hottel, Althea K.

Sellin, Thorsten, jt. ed. see Peel, Roy V.

Sellin, Thorsten, ed. see Simpson, Smith.

Sellink, J. L. & Miller, R. E. Radiology of the Small Bowel, Modern Enteroclysis Technique & Atlas. 1982. text ed. 98.00 (ISBN 90-247-2460-0, Pub. by Martinus Nijhoff Netherlands). Kluwer Boston.

Sells, A. Lytton, tr. see James Second, King of Great Britain.

Sells, Arthur L. Italian Influence in English Poetry from Chaucer to Southwell. LC 76-136893. 1971. Repr. of 1955 ed. lib. bdg. 19.75x (ISBN 0-8371-5336-0, SEIF). Greenwood.

Sells, Saul B. & Berry, Charles A., eds. Human Factors in Jet & Space Travel: A Medical-Psychological Analysis. (Illus.). 1961. 18.50 o.p. (ISBN 0-8260-8015-4, Pub. by Wiley Medical). Wiley.

Sellwood, A. V., jt. auth. see Mohr, Ulrich.

Selman & Selman-Reimer. Energy Coupling in Photosynthesis. (Developments in Biochemistry Ser.: Vol. 20). 1981. 65.00 (ISBN 0-444-00675-3). Elsevier.

Selman, Brian, et al, eds. Insects. 1979. 19.95 o.p. (ISBN 0-448-15467-6, G&D). Putnam Pub Group.

Selman, Edythea G. & Lindenauer, Nancy. I Am Me. (gr. 1-5). 1979. pap. 1.25 (ISBN 0-448-16587-2, G&D). Putnam Pub Group.

Selman, G. G., jt. auth. see Jurand, A.

Selman, Joseph. Elements of Radiobiology. (Illus.). 312p. 1983. 28.75x (ISBN 0-398-04753-7). C C Thomas.

Selman, Robert L. The Growth of Interpersonal Understanding: Developmental & Clinical Analysis. (Developmental Psychology Ser.). 1980. 28.50 (ISBN 0-12-636450-8). Acad Pr.

Selmanowitz, Victor J. & Pereira, Frederick A. Dermatology Specialty Board Review. 4th ed. 1982. pap. 28.50 (ISBN 0-87488-311-3). Med Exam.

Selman-Reimer, jt. auth. see Selman.

Selmes, Cyril. New Movements in the Study & Teaching of Biology. (Illus.). 363p. 1975. 10.00 o.s.i. (ISBN 0-85117-049-8). Transatlantic.

Selowsky, Marcelo, jt. auth. see Martin, Ricardo.

Selsam, Howard, et al, eds. Dynamics of Social Change: A Reader in Marxist Social Science. LC 77-120820. 1970. 10.00 o.p. (ISBN 0-7178-0242-6); pap. 4.95 (ISBN 0-7178-0264-7). Intl Pub Co.

Selsam, Millicent. Tyrannosaurus Rex. LC 77-25677. (Illus.). (gr. 3-5). 1978. 7.95 o.p. (ISBN 0-06-025423-8, HarpJ); PLB 10.89 (ISBN 0-06-025424-6). Har-Row.

Selsam, Millicent & Dewey, Kenneth. Up, Down & Around: The Force of Gravity. LC 76-23796. (gr. 1-3). 1977. PLB 7.95a o.p. (ISBN 0-385-09865-0). Doubleday.

Selsam, Millicent & Hunt, Joyce. A First Look at Fish. LC 72-81377. (First Look at Ser). 32p. (gr. 2-4). 1972. 4.50 o.s.i. (ISBN 0-8027-6119-4); PLB 8.85 (ISBN 0-8027-6120-8). Walker & Co.

Selsam, Millicent E. The Apple & Other Fruits. (Illus.). 48p. (gr. k-3). 1973. 6.95 o.p. (ISBN 0-688-20089-3); PLB 9.55 (ISBN 0-688-30089-8). Morrow.

--Birth of a Forest. LC 63-17281. (Illus.). (gr. 3-7). 1964. PLB 9.89 o.p. (ISBN 0-06-025276-6, HarpJ). Har-Row.

--Harlequin Moth: Its Life Story. LC 75-17862. (Illus.). 48p. (gr. 2-5). 1975. 9.95 (ISBN 0-688-22049-5); PLB 9.55 (ISBN 0-688-32049-X). Morrow.

--How Animals Tell Time. (Illus.). (gr. 5-9). 1967. PLB 9.55 (ISBN 0-688-31407-4). Morrow.

--Maple Tree. LC 68-25933. (Illus.). (gr. 2-5). 1968. PLB 9.55 (ISBN 0-688-31496-1). Morrow.

--Microbes at Work. (Illus.). (gr. 5-9). 1953. PLB 9.55 (ISBN 0-688-31497-X). Morrow.

--Mimosa, the Sensitive Plant. (Illus.). (gr. 4-6). 1978. 9.75 (ISBN 0-688-22167-X); PLB 9.36 (ISBN 0-688-32167-4). Morrow.

--Peanut. LC 70-81886. (Illus.). (gr. 2-5). 1969. PLB 9.55 (ISBN 0-688-31803-7). Morrow.

--Play with Plants. rev. ed. LC 78-8509. (Illus.). (gr. 4-6). 1978. PLB 9.36 (ISBN 0-688-32166-6). Morrow.

--Popcorn. (Illus.). (gr. 2-5). 1976. 7.25 o.p. (ISBN 0-688-22083-5); PLB 8.59 (ISBN 0-688-32083-X). Morrow.

--See Through the Jungle. LC 57-5018. 48p. (gr. 3-6). 1957. PLB 9.89 o.p. (ISBN 0-06-025366-5, HarpJ). Har-Row.

Selsam, Millicent E. & Hunt, Joyce. A First Look at Spiders. (A First Look at Ser.). (Illus.). 32p. (gr. 1-3). 1983. 7.95 (ISBN 0-8027-6480-0); lib. bdg. 8.85 (ISBN 0-8027-6481-9). Walker & Co.

Selsam, Millicent E. & Morrow, Betty. See Through the Sea. LC 54-8990. 48p. (gr. 3-6). 1955. PLB 9.89 o.p. (ISBN 0-06-025456-4, HarpJ). Har-Row.

Selsam, Millicent E. & Wexler, Jerome. The Amazing Dandelion. (Illus.). (gr. 2-5). 1977. 8.95 (ISBN 0-688-22129-7); PLB 8.59 (ISBN 0-688-32129-1). Morrow.

--Eat the Fruit, Plant the Seed. LC 80-13720. (Illus.). 48p. (gr. k-3). 1980. 9.75 (ISBN 0-688-22236-6); PLB 9.36 (ISBN 0-688-32236-0). Morrow.

Selsam, Millicent E., jt. auth. see Schaller, George B.

Selser, Gregorio. Sandino. Belfrage, Cedric, tr. LC 80-8086. 256p. 1982. 16.00 (ISBN 0-85345-558-9, CL5589); pap. 7.50 (ISBN 0-85345-559-7, PB5597). Monthly Rev.

Seltz, David. Food Service Marketing & Promotion. LC 76-566430. (Illus.). 1977. 21.95 (ISBN 0-86730-211-9). Lebhar Friedman.

--How to Get Started in Your Own Franchise Business. rev. ed. LC 79-27945. 1980. 19.95 (ISBN 0-87863-172-0). Farnswth Pub.

Seltz, David D. Branchising: Proven Techniques for Rapid Company Expansion. LC 79-19549. (Illus.). 288p. 1980. 24.95 (ISBN 0-07-056215-6, P&RB). McGraw.

--Handbook of Effective Sales Prospecting Techniques. LC 81-22919. (Illus.). 256p. Date not set. pap. text ed. 25.00 (ISBN 0-201-07138-X). A-W.

--Industrial Selling: Gateway to the Million Dollar Sale! new ed. (Illus.). 1976. 26.50 (ISBN 0-07-056209-1, P&RB). McGraw.

--A Treasury of Business Opportunities for the Eighties. 3rd ed. 283p. 1983. 19.95 (ISBN 0-686-89906-8). Farnswth Pub.

--Treasury of Business Opportunities...Featuring Over 400 Ways to Make a Fortune Without Leaving Your House. LC 76-47103. 1981. 19.95 (ISBN 0-87863-097-X). Farnswth Pub.

Seltzer, Alvin J. Chaos in the Novel - The Novel in Chaos. LC 73-91347. 384p. 1974. 17.50x o.p. (ISBN 0-8052-3543-4). Schocken.

Seltzer, D., ed. see Shakespeare, William.

Seltzer, David. The Omen. (Illus.). (RL 10). 1976. pap. 2.95 (ISBN 0-451-11989-4, AE1989, Sig). NAL.

Seltzer, Lawrence H., ed. New Horizons in Economic Progress. LC 64-13304. (Leo M. Franklin Memorial Lectures in Human Relations Ser: No. 12). 1964. 5.95x o.p. (ISBN 0-8143-1238-1). Wayne St U Pr.

Seltzer, Leon F. The Vision of Melville & Conrad. LC 78-108735. xxxvi, 132p. 1970. 12.00x (ISBN 0-8214-0065-7, 82-80783). Ohio U Pr.

Seltzer, M. Seligson & Baden, R. Kramer. School-Age Child Care: An Action Manual. 480p. (Orig.). 1982. pap. 12.00 (ISBN 0-86569-112-6). Auburn Hse.

Seltzer, Robert M. Jewish People, Jewish Thought. (Illus.). 1980. text ed. 22.95x (ISBN 0-02-408950-8). Macmillan.

Seltzer, Sandra, et al. Discovering American English: Writing. 1981. pap. text ed. 12.95x (ISBN 0-02-408960-5). Macmillan.

Selucky, Radoslav. Marxism, Socialism, Freedom: Towards a General Theory of Labor-Managed Systems. LC 79-14913. 1979. 26.00 (ISBN 0-312-51855-2). St Martin.

Selvadurai, A. P. Elastic Analysis of Soil-Foundation Interactions. (Developments in Geotechnical Engineering Ser.: Vol. 17). 1979. 102.25 (ISBN 0-444-41663-3). Elsevier.

Selvdurai, A. P. Mechanics of Structural Media, 2 Vols. (Studies in Applied Mechanics: Vol. 5). 1981. Set. 161.75 (ISBN 0-444-41982-9); Pt. A. 79.50 (ISBN 0-444-41979-9); 79.50 (ISBN 0-444-41983-7, PT. B). Elsevier.

Selvig, Dick & Riley, Don. High & Dry. 368p. 1983. pap. 3.50 (ISBN 0-523-41921-X). Pinnacle Bks.

Selvik, Arne, jt. ed. see Summers, Gene F.

Selvin, David F. A History of California's Labor. Hundley, Norris, Jr. & Schutz, John A., eds. LC 81-66062. (Golden State Ser.). (Illus.). 110p. 1981. pap. text ed. 5.95x (ISBN 0-87835-117-5). Boyd & Fraser.

Selvon, Samuel. A Brighter Sun. 215p. 1979. 10.00x o.s.i. (ISBN 0-89410-111-0); pap. 5.00 o.s.i. (ISBN 0-89410-110-2). Three Continents.

--The Lonely Londoners. 126p. (Orig.). 1979. 10.00 o.s.i. (ISBN 0-89410-113-7); pap. 5.00 o.s.i. (ISBN 0-89410-112-9). Three Continents.

--Ways of Sunlight. 188p. (Orig.). 1979. 10.00 o.s.i. (ISBN 0-89410-109-9); pap. 5.00 o.s.i. (ISBN 0-89410-108-0). Three Continents.

Selwood, Neville & Hedges, Alan. Transplantation Antigens: A Study in Serological Data Analysis. LC 78-5708. 1978. 30.25 o.p. (ISBN 0-471-99657-2, Pub. by Wiley-Interscience). Wiley.

Selwood, Pierce W. Adsorption & Collective Paramagnetism. 1962. 40.00 (ISBN 0-12-636550-4). Acad Pr.

Selwyn, Victor & Maury de, Eric, eds. Return to Oasis-War Poems & Recollections from the Middle East, 1940-1946. 288p. 1982. 16.00 (ISBN 0-85683-047-X, Pub by Shepheard-Walwyn England); pap. 8.50 (ISBN 0-85683-051-8). Flatiron Book.

Selye, Hans. The Chemical Prevention of Cardiac Necroses. LC 58-12955. 1958. 14.95 o.p. (ISBN 0-8260-8053-7, Pub. by Wiley Medical). Wiley.

--The Stress of Life. rev. ed. LC 75-12746. 554p. 1976. 12.95 o.p. (ISBN 0-07-056208-3, GB). McGraw.

--The Stress of Life. 2nd ed. (McGraw Hill Paperbacks). 1978. pap. 5.95 (ISBN 0-07-056212-1, SP). McGraw.

--Stress Without Distress. LC 74-1314. (Illus.). 1974. 10.95i (ISBN 0-397-01026-5). Har-Row.

--Stress Without Distress. 1975. pap. 2.95 (ISBN 0-451-12417-0, AE2417, Sig). NAL.

Selye, Hans, ed. Selye's Guide to Stress Research, Vol. 2. 448p. 1982. text ed. write for info. (ISBN 0-442-26264-7). Van Nos Reinhold.

Selz, J. Edvard Munch. (Q.A.P. Art Ser.). (Illus.). pap. 4.95 (ISBN 0-517-51837-6). Crown.

Selz, Jean. Boudin. (Quality-Low-Price Art Ser.). (Illus.). 96p. 1982. 7.95 (ISBN 0-517-54710-4). Crown.

--Edvard Munch. (Q L P Art Ser.). (Illus.). 96p. 1974. 7.95 (ISBN 0-517-51571-7). Crown.

--Foujita. 96p. 1981. 6.95 o.p. (ISBN 0-517-54429-6). Crown.

--Gustave Moreau. (Q. L. P. Ser.). (Illus.). 1979. 7.95 (ISBN 0-517-53449-5). Crown.

--Matisse. (Q L P Art Ser.). (Illus.). 7.95 (ISBN 0-517-03723-8). Crown.

--Odilon Redon. LC 73-147349. (Q L P Art Ser). (Illus.). 1971. 7.95 (ISBN 0-517-50799-4). Crown.

--Turner. (Q L P Art Ser.). (Illus.). 96p. 1975. 7.95 (ISBN 0-517-52361-2). Crown.

--Vlaminck. (Q L P Art Ser.). (Illus.). 7.95 (ISBN 0-517-03726-2, 037262). Crown.

Selz, Peter. Art in Our Times: A Pictorial History 1890-1980. 590p. 1981. pap. text ed. 22.95 (ISBN 0-15-503473-1, HC). HarBraceJ.

--Fletcher Benton-Recent Work. (Illus.). 4p. 1972. 0.50x (ISBN 0-686-99824-3). La Jolla Mus Contemp Art.

--German Expressionist Painting. LC 57-10501. (Illus.). 1957. 49.50x (ISBN 0-520-01161-9); pap. 10.95 (ISBN 0-520-02515-6). U of Cal Pr.

--Sam Francis. LC 74-16096. (Contemporary Artist Ser.). (Illus.). 296p. 1982. 65.00 o.p. (ISBN 0-8109-0265-6). Abrams.

Selz, Peter & Einstein, Susan. Sam Francis. (Illus.). 296p. 1982. 65.00 (ISBN 0-686-82699-X). Abrams.

Selzer, Arthur. The Heart: Its Function in Health & Disease. rev. ed. (Perspectives in Medicine: No. 1). (YA) (gr. 9 up). 1968. 19.50x (ISBN 0-520-01162-7). U of Cal Pr.

--Principles of Clinical Cardiology. LC 74-17762. (Illus.). 735p. 1975. text ed. 25.00 o.p. (ISBN 0-7216-8060-7). Saunders.

Selzer, Joae. When Children Ask About Sex: A Guide for Parents. LC 74-4879. (Illus.). 158p. 1975. Repr. of 1974 ed. 7.25 (ISBN 0-8070-2376-0). Beacon Pr.

Selzer, Richard. Confessions of a Knife. 1979. 8.95 o.p. (ISBN 0-671-24292-X). S&S.

--Confessions of a Knife. 1981. pap. 4.95 o.p. (ISBN 0-671-41385-6, Touchstone Bks). S&S.

--Letters to a Young Doctor. 195p. 1982. 13.95 (ISBN 0-671-25339-5). S&S.

--Mortal Lessons: Notes on the Art of Surgery. 1978. pap. 5.95 (ISBN 0-671-24074-9, Touchstone Bks). S&S.

--Rituals of Surgery. 1980. pap. 3.95 o.s.i. (ISBN 0-671-25340-9, Touchstone Bks). S&S.

Selznick, Irene M. A Private View. 1983. 16.95 (ISBN 0-394-40192-1). Knopf.

Selznick, Philip. T. V. A. & the Grass Roots: A Study in the Sociology of Formal Organization. LC 65-25023. (California Library Reprint Ser.: No. 103). 1980. 24.50x (ISBN 0-520-03979-3). U of Cal Pr.

Semaan, Khalil I., ed. see Makdisi, George.

Semanov, V. I. Lu Hsun & His Predecessors. Alber, Charles A., tr. from Rus. LC 80-50885. Orig. Title: Lu Sin': Ego Predshestvenniki. 1980. 27.50 (ISBN 0-87332-153-7). M E Sharpe.

Semb, George, jt. auth. see Ramp, Eugene.

Sembene, Ousmane. Man is Culture. (Hans Wolff Memorial Lecture Ser.). 24p. (Orig., Eng. & Fr.). 1979. pap. text ed. 2.50 (ISBN 0-941934-14-4). Ind U Afro-Amer Arts.

--Xala. Wake, Clive, tr. from Fr. (Illus.). 120p. 1983. pap. 6.95 (ISBN 0-88208-068-7). Lawrence Hill.

Semchyshen, M. Advanced Materials for Pressure Vessel Service with Hydrogen at High Temperature & Pressures. (MPC-18). 288p. 1982. 50.00 (H00227). ASME.

Semeiks, Jonna G., jt. auth. see Schechter, Harold.

Semel, Ann. Black American Poetry. (Monarch Notes). (Orig.). 1977. pap. 2.25 o.p. (ISBN 0-671-00981-8). Monarch Pr.

Semel, Eleanor M., jt. auth. see Wiig, Elisabeth H.

Semenko, Irina M. Vasily Zhukovsky. (World Authors Ser.). 1976. lib. bdg. 15.95 (ISBN 0-8057-2995-X, Twayne). G K Hall.

Semenkov, O. I., jt. auth. see Ellis, T. M.

Semenov, E. P. The Russian Government & the Massacres. LC 70-97304. (Judaica Ser.). 265p. 1972. Repr. of 1907 ed. lib. bdg. 15.75x (ISBN 0-8371-2632-0, SERG). Greenwood.

Semenza, G. Of Oxygen, Fuels & Living Matter, Vol. 2, Pt. 2. (Evolving Life Sciences: Recollections on Scientific Ideas & Events Ser.). 508p. 1982. text ed. 65.00x (ISBN 0-471-27924-2, Pub. by Wiley-Interscience). Wiley.

Semenza, G., ed. Of Oxygen, Fuels & Living Matter, Pt. 1, Vol. 1. LC 80-41420. (Evolving Life Sciences Ser.: Recollections of Scientific Ideas & Events). 349p. 1982. 73.00x (ISBN 0-471-27923-4, Pub. by Wiley-Interscience). Wiley.

Semeomoff, Boris. Projective Techniques. LC 75-37872. 336p. 1976. 52.95 (ISBN 0-471-01490-7); pap. 26.95 (ISBN 0-471-01684-5, Pub. by Wiley-Interscience). Wiley.

Semere, Mario G. A Guide to Hand Lettering. 2nd ed. (Illus.). 1977. pap. text ed. 11.95 (ISBN 0-8403-1780-8). Kendall-Hunt.

Semin, G. K., et al. Nuclear Quadrupole Resonance in Chemistry. Shelnitz, P., tr. from Rus. 517p. 1975. 89.95x o.s.i. (ISBN 0-470-77580-7). Halsted Pr.

Semin, Gun R. & Manstead, S. R., eds. The Accountability of Conduct. (European Monograph Soc.: No. 33). Date not set. price not set (ISBN 0-12-636650-0). Acad Pr.

Seminar & Study Tour on Electricity Distribution Systems in Urban Areas & Their Integration with Transmission Systems. Proceedings. (Energy Resources Development Ser.: No. 18). pap. 12.00 (ISBN 0-686-93055-X, UN78/2F8, UN). Unipub.

Seminar on Agricultural Credit for Small Farmers in Latin America, Quito, Ecuador, 1974. Report. (Development Documents Ser.: No. 20). 130p. 1975. pap. 11.50 (ISBN 0-686-92819-9, 683, FAO). Unipub.

Seminar on Grant Proposal Development. Successful Grant Proposals: Proceedings. Mackenna, David W., ed. 108p. 1975. pap. 5.00 (ISBN 0-936440-40-6). Inst Urban Studies.

Seminar on Petroleum Legislation. Offshore Operation: Proceedings. (Mineral Resources Development Ser.: No. 40). pap. 5.00 (ISBN 0-686-94654-5, UN73/2F13, UN). Unipub.

Seminar on Population Growth & India's Economic Development. India's Population: Some Problems in Perspective Planning-Proceedings. Agarwala, S. N., ed. LC 74-27391. 1974. Repr. of 1960 ed. lib. bdg. 18.50x (ISBN 0-8371-7905-X, AGIP). Greenwood.

Seminar on the Design & Construction of Ferro-Cement Fishing Vessels, Wellington, N.Z., 1972. Working Papers. (FAO Fisheries Reports: No. 131). 456p. 1973. pap. 26.00 o.p. (ISBN 0-686-93079-7, FAO). Unipub.

Semlak, William D. Conflict Resolving Communication: A Skill Development Approach. 60p. 1982. pap. text ed. 3.50x (ISBN 0-917974-76-X). Waveland Pr.

Semm, K. Atlas of Gynecologic Laparoscopy & Hysteroscopy. Borow, Lawrence S., ed. Rice, Allan L., tr. LC 76-20941. (Illus.). 352p. 1977. text ed. 45.00 o.p. (ISBN 0-7216-8063-1). Saunders.

Semm, K. & Mettler, L., eds. Human Reproduction: Proceedings of World Congress, 3rd, Berlin, Mar. 22-26, 1981. (International Congress Ser.: No. 551). 586p. 1981. 101.50 (ISBN 0-444-90214-7). Elsevier.

Semm, Kurt & Greenblatt, Robert B. Genital Endometriosis in Infertility. 110p. 15.95 (ISBN 0-86577-059-X). Thieme-Stratton.

Semmel, Bernard. Jamaican Blood & Victorian Conscience: The Governor Eyre Controversy. LC 76-7623. 1976. Repr. of 1963 ed. lib. bdg. 15.50x (ISBN 0-8371-8653-6, SEJB). Greenwood.

--Rise of Free Trade Imperialism. LC 71-112473. 1970. 44.50 (ISBN 0-521-07725-7). Cambridge U Pr.

Semmes, Raphael. Crime & Punishment in Early Maryland. LC 77-108227. (Criminology, Law Enforcement, & Social Problems Ser.: No. 110). 1970. Repr. of 1938 ed. 16.00x (ISBN 0-87585-110-X). Patterson Smith.

Semmler, Clement. Douglas Stewart. (World Authors Ser.). 1974. lib. bdg. 15.95 (ISBN 0-8057-2863-5, Twayne). G K Hall.

Semonche, John E. Charting the Future: The Supreme Court Responds to a Changing Society, 1890-1920. LC 77-94745. (Contributions in Legal Studies Ser.: No. 5). 1978. lib. bdg. 29.95x (ISBN 0-313-20314-8, SCF/). Greenwood.

Semonin, Richard W. & Beadle, Robert W., eds. Precipitation Scavenging (1974) Proceedings. LC 76-53788. (ERDA Symposium Ser.). 856p. 1977. pap. 29.50 (ISBN 0-87079-309-8, CONF-741003); microfiche 4.50 (ISBN 0-87079-310-1, CONF-741003). DOE.

Sempangi, F. Kefa. Trapped. LC 79-50394. 192p. 1979. pap. 4.95 o.p. (ISBN 0-8307-0684-4, 5411807). Regal.

Semper, Edward & Coggin, Philip, eds. Hidden Factors in Technological Change. 1976. pap. text ed. 10.00 (ISBN 0-08-021007-4). Pergamon.

Semple, J. G., jt. auth. see Tyrrell, J. A.

Semple, Jean E. Hearing-Impaired Pre-School Child: A Book for Parents. 104p. 1970. photocopy ed. spiral 10.50x (ISBN 0-398-01724-7). C C Thomas.

Semprevivo, Philip C. Systems Analysis. 2nd ed. 416p. 1982. text ed. 18.95 write for info. (ISBN 0-574-21355-4, 13-4355); instr. guide avail. (ISBN 0-574-21356-2, 13-4356); study guide 8.95 (ISBN 0-574-21357-0, 13-4357). SRA.

--Teams in Information Systems Development. LC 80-50608. 144p. (Orig.). 1980. pap. 18.50 (ISBN 0-917072-20-0). Yourdon.

Semprun, Jorge. What a Beautiful Sunday! Sheridan, Alan, tr. from Fr. LC 82-47662. (A Helen & Kurt Wolff Bk.). 444p. 1982. 14.95 (ISBN 0-15-195857-2). HarBraceJ.

Semrad, Alice. Comprehensive Review for Medical Technologists. 2nd ed. LC 78-31823. 222p. 1979. pap. text ed. 14.95 o.p. (ISBN 0-8016-4487-9). Mosby.

Sems, Charles. Trolley Days in Pasadena. (Illus.). 196p. Date not set. 34.95 (ISBN 0-87095-086-X). Golden West.

Sen, Amartya. Employment, Technology & Development. (Economic Development Ser.). 1975. text ed. 29.00x (ISBN 0-19-877052-9); pap. text ed. 7.95x (ISBN 0-19-877053-7). Oxford U Pr.

--Levels of Poverty: Policy & Change. (Working Paper: No. 401). 91p. 1980. 5.00 (ISBN 0-686-36132-6, WP-0401). World Bank.

Sen, Amartya K. Choice of Techniques: An Aspect of the Theory of Planned Economic Development. 3rd ed. LC 68-3220. 1968. 12.50x o.p. (ISBN 0-678-06266-8). Kelley.

--Choice, Welfare & Measurement. 440p. 1983. 37.50x (ISBN 0-262-19214-4). MIT Pr.

Sen, Asok, et al. Perspectives in Social Science: Three Studies on the Agrarian Structure in Bengal, 1850-1947, Vol. 2. 1982. 13.00x (ISBN 0-19-561019-9). Oxford U Pr.

Sen, Bandhudas. The Green Revolution in India: A Perspective. LC 74-11066. 118p. 1974. 15.95x o.s.i. (ISBN 0-470-77590-4). Halsted Pr.

Sen, D. N. Contributions to the Ecology of Halophytes. 1982. 69.50 (ISBN 90-6193-942-9, Pub. by Junk Pubs Netherlands). Kluwer Boston.

Sen, Jyoti P. The Progress of T. S. Eliot As Poet & Critic. 1971. text ed. 5.00x o.p. (ISBN 0-391-01101-4). Humanities.

Sen, K. M. Hinduism. lib. bdg. 10.50x (ISBN 0-88307-248-3). Gannon.

Sen, Mohit. Revolution in India: Path & Problems. 1977. 5.50x o.p. (ISBN 0-88386-951-9, Pub. by Peoples Pub. House). South Asia Bks.

Sen, P. C. Thyristor DC Drives. LC 80-21226. 307p. 1981. 44.95x (ISBN 0-471-06070-4, Pub. by Wiley-Interscience). Wiley.

Sen, P. K. Logic, Induction & Ontology. (Jadavpur Studies in Philosophy: Vol. 2). 241p. 1982. text ed. 16.25x (ISBN 0-391-02491-4). Humanities.

Sen, P. K., jt. auth. see Puri, M. L.

Sen, Pranab Kumar. Sequential Nonparametrics: Invariance Principles & Statistical Inference. LC 81-4432. (Probability & Mathematical Statistics Ser.). 421p. 1981. 42.50x (ISBN 0-471-06013-5, Pub. by Wiley-Interscience). Wiley.

Sen, R. N. & Weil, C., eds. Statistical Mechanics & Field Theory. LC 72-4108. 340p. 1972. 55.95 o.s.i. (ISBN 0-470-77595-5). Halsted Pr.

Sen, Ramprasad. Grace & Mercy in Her Wild Hair. Nathan, Leonard & Seely, Clinton, trs. from Bengali. LC 82-904. 100p. (Orig.). 1982. pap. 7.00 (ISBN 0-87773-761-4). Great Eastern.

Sen, S. K., jt. ed. see Giles, Kenneth L.

Sen, Sudhir. Turning the Tide: A Strategy to Conquer Hunger & Poverty. 1978. 11.00x o.p. (ISBN 0-8364-0260-X). South Asia Bks.

Sena, Jorge de see De Sena, Jorge.

Senatore, John, jt. auth. see Joohnson, Kenneth.

Senay, Edward C. Substance Abuse Disorders in Clinical Practice. (Senay Ser.). 256p. 1983. text ed. 22.50 (ISBN 0-7236-7031-5). Wright PSG.

Sendak, Jack. Second Witch. LC 65-20255. (Illus.). (gr. 2-6). 1965. PLB 9.89 (ISBN 0-06-025476-9, HarpJ). Har-Row.

Sendall, Bernard. Independent Television in Britain: Origin & Foundation 1946-62, Vol. 1. 418p. 1982. text ed. 21.00x (ISBN 0-333-30941-3, Pub. by Macmillan England). Humanities.

Sender. Requiem por un Campesino. (Easy Reader, C). 1972. pap. 3.95 (ISBN 0-88436-055-5, 70273). EMC.

Sender, Ramon J. Mosen Millan. Duncan, R. M., ed. 1964. pap. text ed. 7.95 (ISBN 0-669-32631-3). Heath.

Senderens, Alain. The Three-Star Recipes of Alain Senderens. Hyman, Philip & Hyman, Mary, trs. LC 82-6488. (Illus.). 352p. 1982. 22.50 (ISBN 0-688-00728-7). Morrow.

Sendler, Dave, jt. auth. see Sabin, Lou.

Seneca. Dialogues. Reynolds, Leighton D., ed. (Oxford Classical Texts). 1977. text ed. 19.95x (ISBN 0-19-814659-0). Oxford U Pr.

--Oedipus. Hadas, Moses, tr. LC 55-13616. 1955. pap. 2.95 o.p. (ISBN 0-672-60210-5, LLA44). Bobbs.

--Stoic Philosophy of Seneca: Essays & Letters. Hadas, Moses, ed. 1968. pap. 5.95 (ISBN 0-393-00459-7, Norton Lib). Norton.

Seneca Corporation, jt. auth. see Copeland, William C.

Seneca, Joseph J. & Taussig, Michael K. Environmental Economics. 2nd ed. (Illus.). 1979. ref. ed. 23.95 (ISBN 0-13-283291-7). P-H.

Seneca, L. Thyestes: A Tragedy. Elder, Jane, tr. from Latin. 58p. 1982. pap. text ed. 6.25x (ISBN 0-85635-434-1, 80730, Pub. by Carcanet Pr England). Humanities.

Senelick, Laurence, ed. Russian Satirical Comedy. 1983. 19.95 (ISBN 0-933826-52-4); pap. 7.95 (ISBN 0-933826-53-2). Performing Arts.

Senese, Donald J. Modernizing the Chinese Dragon: The Prospective Impact of Western Aid & Technology on Mainland China. 1980. pap. 10.00 (ISBN 0-686-64115-9). Coun Am Affairs.

Senesh, Lawrence. The Optimum of Knowledge Academy of Independent. Boulding, Kenneth E., ed. (Academy of Independent Scholars Forum Ser.). 1983. lib. bdg. 20.00 (ISBN 0-86531-544-2). Westview.

Seneviratne, H. L. Rituals of the Kandyan State. LC 77-80842. (Cambridge Studies in Social Anthropology: No. 22). (Illus.). 1978. 32.50 (ISBN 0-521-21736-9). Cambridge U Pr.

Seng, You Poh, jt. ed. see Hughes, Helen.

Sengbush, Ray L. Seismic Exploration Methods. LC 82-81559. (Illus.). 289p. 1983. text ed. 38.00 (ISBN 0-934634-21-1). Intl Human Res.

Sengel, Bill, jt. auth. see Takken, Suzzane.

Sengel, Bill, ed. Basic Well Logging. 1982. 20.00 (ISBN 0-89419-183-7). Inst Energy.

Sengel, E. W., jt. ed. see Abell, J. M.

Sengel, P. Morphogenesis of Skin. LC 74-25659. (Developmental & Cell Biology Ser.: No. 2). (Illus.). 300p. 1975. 75.00 (ISBN 0-521-20644-8). Cambridge U Pr.

Senger, Leslie W., jt. auth. see Estes, John E.

Senghor, Leopold S. Ethiopiques. Harris, Jessica, tr. from Fr. LC 75-18602. 130p. cancelled 0.00 (ISBN 0-89388-210-0). Okpaku Communications.

--Negritude & Humanism. Jeanpierre, Wendell A., tr. from Fr. LC 75-508. Date not set. cancelled 0.00 o.p. (ISBN 0-89388-197-X). Okpaku Communications. Postponed.

Senglor, Leopold S. Nocturnes. Reed, John & Wake, Clive, trs. LC 75-162958. 96p. 1971. 6.95 o.p.; pap. 2.95 (ISBN 0-89388-015-9). Okpaku Communications.

Sengstock, Mary. Chaldean Americans Changing Conceptions of Ethnic Identity. 220p. 1982. text ed. 14.95 (ISBN 0-913256-43-9, Dist. by Ozer); pap. text ed. 9.95x (ISBN 0-913256-42-0, Dist. by Ozer). Ctr Migration.

Sengupta, Arjun, ed. Commodities, Finance & Trade: Issues in the North-South Negotiations. LC 79-17881. (Contributions in Economics & Economic History: No. 30). (Illus.). 1980. lib. bdg. 35.00x (ISBN 0-313-21469-7, SEC/). Greenwood.

Sen Gupta, Bhabani. Soviet-Asian Relations in the 1970s & Beyond: An Interperceptional Study. LC 76-24368. 1976. 36.95 o.p. (ISBN 0-275-23740-0). Praeger.

Sengupta, Jati K., jt. auth. see Tintner, Gerhard.

Sengupta, Nirmal. Destitutes & Development. 1979. text ed. 9.50x (ISBN 0-391-01864-7). Humanities.

Sengupta, Padmini. Red Hibiscus: A Novel. 4.50x o.p. (ISBN 0-210-33989-6). Asia.

Sengupta, Subrata & Lee, Samuel S., eds. Waste Heat: Utilization & Management. LC 82-6095. (Illus.). 1200p. 1983. text ed. 125.00 (ISBN 0-89116-256-9). Hemisphere Pub.

Sengupta, Subrata & Wong, Kau-Fui V., eds. Resource Recovery from Solid Wastes: Proceedings of a Conference in Miami Beach, Florida, May 10-12, 1982. LC 82-18145. 600p. 1982. 97.50 (ISBN 0-08-028825-1, A125). Pergamon.

Sengupta, Surajit. Business Law in India. 894p. (Orig.). 1979. pap. text ed. 9.95x o.p. (ISBN 0-19-560658-2). Oxford U Pr.

Senick, Gerard J., ed. Children's Literature Review, Vol. 5. 350p. 1983. 56.00x (ISBN 0-8103-0330-2). Gale.

--Children's Literature Review: Excerpts from Critical Commentaries on Juvenile & Young People's Authors & Their Books, 4 vols. Incl. Vol. 1. 1976 (ISBN 0-8103-0077-X); Vol. 2. 1976 (ISBN 0-8103-0078-8); Vol. 3 (ISBN 0-8103-0079-6); Vol. 4. 1982 (ISBN 0-8103-0080-X). LC 75-34953. (Children's Literature Review Ser.). 56.00x ea. Gale.

Seniff, Dennis P., ed. Libro de Monteria Alfonso XI. (Spanish Ser.: No. 8). 1983. 24.00x (ISBN 0-942260-27-9). Hispanic Seminary.

Senior, Clarence. Land Reform & Democracy. LC 74-8261. (Illus.). 269p. 1974. Repr. of 1958 ed. lib. bdg. 16.25x (ISBN 0-8371-7563-1, SELR). Greenwood.

Senior, Donald & Stuhlmueller, Carroll. The Biblical Foundations for Mission. LC 82-22430. 368p. (Orig.). 1983. 25.00 (ISBN 0-88344-046-6); pap. 14.95 (ISBN 0-88344-047-4). Orbis Bks.

Senior, Michael. The Life & Times of Richard II. Fraser, Antonia, ed. (Kings & Queens of England Ser.). (Illus.). 224p. 1981. text ed. 17.50x (ISBN 0-686-36953-X, Pub. by Weidenfeld & Nicolson England). Biblio Dist.

Senior, Patrick, pseud. Self-Solving: The Key to Making Business a Pleasure. 30p. 1982. bklet 2.00 (ISBN 0-911201-00-9). New Age Bus Bks.

Senior, Robert. The World Travel Market. 266p. 1982. 115.00x (ISBN 0-686-92044-9, Euromonitor). State Mutual Bk.

Seniz, Refah, jt. auth. see Blackburn, Jeanne M.

Senje, Sigurd. Escape! Ramsden, Evelyn, tr. LC 64-12509. (gr. 7 up). 1966. pap. 1.25 (ISBN 0-15-629041-3, VoyB). HarBraceJ.

Senkevitch, Anatole, Jr. Soviet Architecture, 1917-62: A Bibliographic Guide to Source Material. LC 73-75335. 300p. 1974. 15.00 (ISBN 0-8139-0415-3). U Pr of Va.

Senn, Alfred E. The Emergence of Modern Lithuania. LC 74-14028. 272p. 1975. Repr. of 1959 ed. lib. bdg. 18.25x (ISBN 0-8371-7780-4, SEML). Greenwood.

Senn, Frank C. Christian Worship & Its Cultural Setting. LC 82-48587. 160p. 1983. pap. 8.95 (ISBN 0-8006-1700-2, 1-1700). Fortress.

--The Pastor As Worship Leader: A Manual for Corporate Worship. LC 77-72452. 1977. 4.95 o.p. (ISBN 0-8066-1593-1, 10-4871). Augsburg.

Senn, James. Information Systems in Management. 2nd ed. 544p. 1982. text ed. 28.95x (ISBN 0-534-01023-7). Wadsworth Pub.

Senn, James A. Information Systems in Management. 1978. text ed. 27.95x o.p. (ISBN 0-534-00563-2). Wadsworth Pub.

Senn, Steve. The Double Disappearance of Walter Fozbek. new ed. 128p. (gr. 8-12). 1980. 8.95 o.s.i. (ISBN 0-8038-1571-9). Hastings.

--The Double Disappearance of Walter Fozbek. (Illus.). 120p. (gr. 3-5). 1983. pap. 1.95 (ISBN 0-380-62737-X, 380-62737X, Camelot). Avon.

Senna & Siegel. Cases & Comments on Juvenile Law. (Criminal Justice Ser.). 600p. 1976. pap. text ed. 21.50 (ISBN 0-8299-0629-0). West Pub.

Senna, Carl, ed. The Fallacy of I. Q. LC 72-93380. 180p. 1973. 8.95 o.p. (ISBN 0-685-28733-5, 89388-X). Okpaku Communications.

Senna, Joseph J. & Siegel, Larry J. Introduction to Criminal Justice. 2nd ed. (Criminal Justice Ser.). (Illus.). 656p. 1981. text ed. 22.50 (ISBN 0-8299-0409-3). West Pub.

--Juvenile Law: Cases & Comments. (Criminal Justice Ser.). 1976. text ed. 21.50 o.p. (ISBN 0-8299-0629-0). West Pub.

Senna, Joseph J., jt. auth. see Siegel, Larry J.

Sennett, Richard, jt. auth. see Cobb, Jonathan.

Sennett, Richard, ed. Classic Essays on the Culture of Cities. (Orig.). 1969. pap. text ed. 13.95 (ISBN 0-13-135194-X). P-H.

Sennewald, Charles A. Effective Security Management. LC 78-6058. (Illus.). 1978. 18.95 (ISBN 0-913708-30-5). Butterworth.

Sennholz, Hans F., ed. Gold Is Money. LC 74-15161. (Contributions in Economics & Economic History Ser.: No. 12). 1975. lib. bdg. 25.00x (ISBN 0-8371-7804-5, SGM/). Greenwood.

Senter, R. J. Analysis of Data: Introductory Statistics for the Behavioral Sciences. 1969. text ed. 17.95x o.p. (ISBN 0-673-05448-9). Scott F.

Senter, R. J. & Dimond, Richard E. Psychology: The Exploration of Human Behavior. 1976. text ed. 14.50x (ISBN 0-673-07632-6). Scott F.

Senter, Sylvia & Howe, Marguerite. Women at Work: A Psychologist's Secrets to Getting Ahead in Business. Saco, Don, ed. 304p. 1982. 12.95 (ISBN 0-698-11157-5, Coward). Putnam PubGroup.

Senter Fitt, Arnold D. Airports of Mexico & Centro America. 15th ed. (Illus.). 560p. (Orig.). 1982. pap. 24.95 (ISBN 0-937260-00-2). Senterfitt.

Sentlowitz, Michael & Thelen, James. Baseball: A Game of Numbers. (gr. 7-12). 1977. pap. text ed. 9.92 (ISBN 0-201-06798-6, Sch Div); tchr's man. 2.96 (ISBN 0-201-06816-8). A-W.

Sentlowitz, Michael & Trivisone, Margaret. College Algebra. (Math - Remedial & Precalculus Ser.). 576p. 1981. text ed. 19.95 (ISBN 0-201-06626-2); student solution bk. 5.95 (ISBN 0-201-06627-0); calculator suppl. 1.50 (ISBN 0-201-06628-9). A-W.

--College Algebra & Trigonometry. 1981. text ed. 21.95 (ISBN 0-201-06676-9). A-W.

--Dice & Dots. (gr. 4-8). 1979. pap. text ed. 9.15 (ISBN 0-201-06982-2, Sch Div). A-W.

Sentlowitz, Michael, jt. auth. see Brett, William.

Senturia, Stephen D. & Wedlock, Bruce D. Electronic Circuits & Applications. LC 74-7404. 623p. 1975. text ed. 33.95 (ISBN 0-471-77630-0); avail. tchr's manual (ISBN 0-471-77632-7). Wiley.

Senzel, Howard. Cases. LC 82-70132. 276p. 1982. 14.95 (ISBN 0-670-20603-2). Viking Pr.

Seo, Hiroshi. Civil Aircraft of the World. (Illus.). 96p. 1982. 12.95 (ISBN 0-86720-559-8). Sci Bks Intl.

--Military Aircraft of the World. (Illus.). 96p. 1982. 12.95. Sci Bks Intl.

Seo, K. K., jt. auth. see Long, William A.

Seon, Manley. Long Island Discovery. 10.95 o.p. (ISBN 0-911660-19-4). Yankee Peddler.

Sepharial. Manual of Astrology. 4.95 o.p. (ISBN 0-685-22026-5); pap. 12.95 o.p. (ISBN 0-685-22027-3). Wehman.

Seplaki, Les. Antitrust & the Economics of the Market: Text, Readings, Cases. 690p. 1982. pap. text ed. 15.95 (ISBN 0-15-502860-X, HC). HarBraceJ.

--Antitrust & the Economics of the Market Text, Readings, Cases. 640p. (Orig.). 1982. pap. text ed. 15.95 (ISBN 0-686-83984-6). HarBraceJ.

Seppala, John. Is That Troubled Employee Still Troubling You? A Strategy for Supervisors. 1.50 (ISBN 0-89486-138-7). Hazelden.

Seppala, M., jt. ed. see Grudzinskas, J. B.

Septier, A., ed. Focusing of Charged Particles, 2 Vols. 1967. Vol. 1. 63.00 o.s.i. (ISBN 0-12-636901-1); Vol. 2. 60.00 o.s.i. (ISBN 0-12-636902-X); Set. 100.00 o.s.i. (ISBN 0-685-05127-7). Acad Pr.

Septier, A., jt. ed. see Marton, C.

Sequeira, M. S. Motorcycles. LC 78-5963. (Easy-Read Fact Bks). (Illus.). (gr. 2-4). 1978. PLB 8.60 s&l (ISBN 0-531-01373-1). Watts.

Sequin, Jim, jt. auth. see Head, Barry.

Sequoia, Anna. The Official J. A. P. Handbook: The Complete Guide to Jewish American Princesses & Princes. (Illus.). 1982. pap. 5.95 (ISBN 0-452-25359-4, Plume). NAL.

Serafian, Michael. The Pilgrim. 281p. 1964. 4.50 o.p. (ISBN 0-374-23304-7). FS&G.

Serafica, Felicisima C. Social-Cognitive Development in Context. LC 82-2933. 283p. 1982. text ed. 24.50x (ISBN 0-89862-623-4). Guilford Pr.

Serafin, David. Christmas Rising. 192p. 1983. 10.95 (ISBN 0-312-13414-2). St Martin.

Serafin, Donald & Buncke, Harry. Microsurgical Composite Tissue Transplantation. LC 78-12297. (Illus.). 792p. 1979. text ed. 62.50 (ISBN 0-8016-0882-1). Mosby.

Serafin, Joan M. Faulkner's Uses of the Classics. (Studies in Modern Literature: No. 1). 208p. 1983. 34.95 (ISBN 0-8357-1397-0, Pub. by UMI Res Pr). Univ Microfilms.

Serafini, V., ed. Allergology. (International Congress Ser.: No. 211). (Abstracts - 7th Congress). 1970. pap. 19.00 (ISBN 90-219-1180-9, Excerpta Medica). Elsevier.

Serane, Abbe. Neutonianisme De Voltaire. Repr. of 1779 ed. 42.00 o.p. (ISBN 0-8287-0773-1). Clearwater Pub.

Serane, Phillipe. L' Heureux Naufrage. (Utopias in the Enlightenment Ser.). 28p. (Fr.). 1974. Repr. of 1789 ed. 22.50x o.p. (ISBN 0-8287-1379-0, 008). Clearwater Pub.

Seranne, Ann. All About Small Dogs in the Big City. (Illus.). 1975. 8.95 o.p. (ISBN 0-698-10668-7, Coward). Putnam Pub Group.

--The Complete Book of Egg Cookery. 224p. 1983. 14.95 (ISBN 0-02-609620-X). Macmillan.

--The Home Canning & Preserving Book. 1975. pap. 5.95 (ISBN 0-06-463424-8, EH 424, EH). B&N NY.

Seranne, Ann & Miller, Lise M. The Joy of Owning a Shih Tzu. LC 82-11786. (Illus.). 272p. 1982. 17.95 (ISBN 0-87605-334-7). Howell Bk.

Seranne, Ann, ed. America Cooks: The General Federation of Women's Clubs Cookbook. 1967. 16.95 (ISBN 0-399-10020-2). Putnam Pub Group.

Seraphin, B. O. Optical Properties of Solids: New Developments. 1976. 166.00 (ISBN 0-444-11005-4, North-Holland). Elsevier.

Serapiao, Luis B. & El-Khawas, Mohamed A. Mozambique in the Twentieth Century: From Colonialism to Independence. LC 79-64964. 1979. pap. text ed. 13.75 (ISBN 0-8191-0502-3). U Pr of Amer.

Seraydarian, Patricia M. The Church Secretary's Handbook. 159p. 1982. pap. 5.95 (ISBN 0-8423-0281-6). Tyndale.

Serazzi, Guiseppe, jt. auth. see Ferrari, Domenico.

Serban, George. The Tyranny of Magical Thinking: The Child's World of Belief & Adult Neurosis. 256p. 1982. 17.95 (ISBN 0-525-24140-X, 01743-520). Dutton.

Serban, George, ed. Social & Medical Aspects of Drug Abuse. 288p. 1983. text ed. 35.00 (ISBN 0-89335-191-1). SP Med & Sci Bks.

Serban, George, ed. see International Symposium on the Kittay Scientific Foundation, 4th.

Serban, William, jt. ed. see Brady, Darlene.

Serbein, Oscar N., jt. auth. see Green, Mark R.

Sercarz, Eli, ed. Regulatory Genetics of the Immune System. 1977. 47.50 (ISBN 0-12-637160-1). Acad Pr.

Sercarz, Eli, et al, eds. The Immune System: Genes, Receptors, Signals. 1974. 34.00 (ISBN 0-12-637150-4). Acad Pr.

Sercarz, Eli E. & Cunningham, Alastair J., eds. Strategies of Immune Regulation. LC 79-28392. 1980. 44.50 (ISBN 0-12-637140-7). Acad Pr.

Serebriakoff, Victor. A Mensa Puzzle Book. 128p. 1982. 20.00x (ISBN 0-584-11020-0, Pub. by Muller Ltd). State Mutual Bk.

--Puzzles, Problems, & Pastimes for the Superintelligent. 131p. 1983. 9.95 (ISBN 0-13-744664-0); pap. 3.95 (ISBN 0-13-744656-X). P-H.

Serebriakoff, Victor & Langer, Steven. Test Your Child's I.Q. 1982. pap. 1.95 (ISBN 0-451-11461-2, AJ1461, Sig). NAL.

Serebrianskii, N., ed. Zhitie Prepodobnoevfrosina Pskovskogo: Pervonachal'naia Redaktsiia. (Monuments of Early Russian Literature: Vol. 3). 118p. 1982. pap. 8.00 (ISBN 0-933884-21-4). Berkeley Slavic.

Seredy, Kate. The White Stag. (Story Bks. Ser.). (gr. 4-7). 1979. pap. 3.50 (ISBN 0-14-031258-7, Puffin). Penguin.

Sereno, Kenneth & Bodaken, Edward. Trans-per: Understanding Human Communication. 1975. 18.95 (ISBN 0-395-18701-X); teaching strategies guide 1.65 (ISBN 0-395-18783-4). HM.

Sereny, Gitta. Into That Darkness. LC 82-40049. 400p. 1982. pap. 6.95 (ISBN 0-394-71035-5, Vin). Random.

Serfass, Robert C., ed. see American College of Sports Medicine.

Serfass, Ronald E. Porcelain: The Elite of Ceramics. (Illus.). 192p. 1980. 10.95 o.p. (ISBN 0-517-53621-8); pap. 8.95 o.p. (ISBN 0-517-53623-4). Crown.

Serfaty, Simon, ed. see Braga de Macedo, Jorge.

Serfling, R. J., jt. ed. see Proschan, Frank.

Serfling, Robert J. Approximation Theorems of Mathematical Statistics. LC 80-13493. (Wiley Ser. in Probability & Mathematical Statistics). 371p. 1980. 41.95 (ISBN 0-471-02403-1). Wiley.

Serfozo, Mary. Welcome Roberto! Bienvenido, Roberto! (Illus.). (gr. 1-3). 1969. PLB 4.98 (ISBN 0-695-49225-X). Follett.

Sergeant, Howard. Poems from the Medical World. 192p. 1980. 19.95 o.p. (ISBN 0-85200-289-0). Wright-PSG.

Sergeant, Howard, jt. auth. see Porter, Peter.

Sergeant, Howard, ed. The Two Continents Book of Childrens Verse. 1977. Repr. of 1972 ed. 7.95 o.p. (ISBN 0-8467-0238-X, Pub. by Two Continents). Hippocrene Bks.

Sergeant, Philip W. Witches & Warlocks. LC 72-164055. (Illus.). 290p. 1975. Repr. of 1936 ed. 34.00x (ISBN 0-8103-3979-X). Gale.

Sergeant, Philip W., tr. see Znosko-Borovsky, Eugene.

Sergeeva, L. M., jt. auth. see Lipatov, Yu. S.

Sergievsky, Orest. Memoirs of a Dancer: Shadows, Dreams, Memories. LC 79-87806. (Illus.). 276p. 1980. 20.00 (ISBN 0-87127-113-3); pap. 10.95 (ISBN 0-87127-129-X). Dance Horiz.

Sergiovanni, Thomas J., jt. auth. see Carver, Fred D.

Sergrovanni, T., et al. Educational Governance & Administration. 1980. 24.95 (ISBN 0-13-236653-3). P-H.

SERI. A New Prosperity: Building a Sustainable Energy Future the SERI (Solar Conservation Study) LC 81-6089. 450p. (Orig.). 1981. 39.95x (ISBN 0-471-88652-1, Brick Hse Pub.). Wiley.

Serio, M. & Pazzagli, M., eds. Luminescence Assays: Perspectives in Endocrinology & Clinical Chemistry. (Serono Symposia Publications from Raven Press Ser.). 301p. 1982. text ed. 38.50 (ISBN 0-89004-740-5). Raven.

Serio, Mario & Martini, Luciano, eds. Animal Models in Human Reproduction. 499p. 1980. text ed. 49.50 (ISBN 0-89004-522-4). Raven.

Serjeant. Private Flying for Leisure & Business. 16.50x (ISBN 0-392-06630-0, LTB). Sportshelf.

Serjeant, Graham R. The Clinical Features of Sickle Cell Disease. (Clinical Studies Ser.: Vol. 4). 357p. 1975. 110.00 (ISBN 0-444-10592-1, North-Holland). Elsevier.

Serjeant, R. B. Portuguese of the Arabian Coast. (Arab Background Ser.). 1968. 16.00x (ISBN 0-86685-027-9). Intl Bk Ctr.

Serle & Morel. A Field Guide to the Birds of West Africa. 29.95 (ISBN 0-686-42763-7, Collins Pub England). Greene.

Serling, Robert J. The Jet Age. (Epic of Flight Ser.). 1982. lib. bdg. 19.96 (ISBN 0-8094-3301-X, Pub. by Time-Life). Silver.

--The Only Way to Fly: The Story of Western Airlines, America's Senior Air Carrier. (Airlines History Project Ser.). (Illus.). Date not set. price not set (ISBN 0-404-19334-X). AMS Pr.

Serlio, Sebastiano. The Five Books of Architecture. Unabridged ed. (Architecture Ser.). (Illus.). 416p. 1982. pap. 14.95 (ISBN 0-486-24349-4). Dover.

--On Domestic Architecture: The Sixth Book: Different Dwellings from the Meanest Hovel to the Most Ornate Palace. 1978. 95.00x (ISBN 0-262-19174-1). MIT Pr.

Serman, Ilya Z. Konstantin Batyushkov. (World Authors Ser.). 1974. lib. bdg. 15.95 (ISBN 0-8057-2118-5, Twayne). G K Hall.

Serna, Gomez De La see Gomez de la Serna, Ramon.

Sernka, Thomas & Jacobson, Eugene. Gastrointestinal Physiology: The Essentials. 1979. pap. 12.95 o.p. (ISBN 0-683-07720-1). Williams & Wilkins.

Sernka, Thomas J. & Jacobson, Eugene D. Gastrointestinal Physiology: The Essentials. 2nd ed. 184p. 1983. pap. text ed. write for info. (ISBN 0-683-07721-X). Williams & Wilkins.

Seronde, Joseph, jt. ed. see Peyre, Henri.

Seronsy, Cecil. Samuel Daniel. (English Authors Ser.). 13.95 (ISBN 0-8057-1136-8, Twayne). G K Hall.

Seros, Kathleen, adapted by. Sun & Moon: Fairy Tales from Korea. LC 82-82510. (Illus.). 61p. (gr. 4-6). 1982. PLB 14.95 (ISBN 0-930878-25-6). Hollym Intl.

Serota, Gary, jt. auth. see Dumbaugh, Kerry.

Serow, Robert C. Schooling for Social Diversity: An Analysis of Policy & Practice. 1983. pap. text ed. 14.95x (ISBN 0-8077-2729-6). Tchrs Coll.

Serpe, Abbe. Analyses et Critiques Des Oubrages De M. De Voltaire. Repr. of 1789 ed. 71.00 o.p. (ISBN 0-8287-0775-8). Clearwater Pub.

Serpico, Tom. Tom, the Poet & Gadgetmaker. 86p. 1980. 6.00 (ISBN 0-682-49622-7). Exposition.

Serra, M. A., jt. auth. see Camarao, P. C.

Serraillier, Ian. Silver Sword. LC 59-6556. (Illus.). (gr. 7-9). 1959. 10.95 (ISBN 0-87599-104-1). S G Phillips.

Serraillier, Ian see Allen, W. S.

Serrano, Antonio, jt. auth. see Cowman, Charles E.

Serrano, Miguel. The Serpent of Paradise. pap. 7.95 (ISBN 0-7100-7785-8). Routledge & Kegan.

--The Ultimate Flower. MacShane, Frank, tr. LC 69-19629. (Illus., Span.). 1970. 8.95x o.p. (ISBN 0-8052-3351-2). Schocken.

Serrano-Plaja, Arturo. Magic Realism in Cervantes: Don Quixote As Seen Through Tom Sawyer & the Idiot. Rudder, Robert S., tr. LC 71-94991. 232p. 1970. 26.50x (ISBN 0-520-01591-6). U of Cal Pr.

Serran-Pagan, Gines. Estudios Sociales: Preparacion para el Examen de Equivalencia en Espanol de la Escuela Superior. LC 81-15016. 192p. 1982. pap. 5.00 (ISBN 0-668-05373-9, 5373). Arco.

Serratrice, G., ed. Peroneal Atrophy & Related Disorders. Roux, H. LC 78-62593. (Illus.). 376p. 1979. 52.50x (ISBN 0-89352-028-4). Masson Pub.

Serre, J. A Course in Arithmetic. LC 70-190089. (Graduate Texts in Mathematics: Vol. 7). (Illus.). 115p. 1973. pap. 20.00 (ISBN 0-387-90040-3). Springer-Verlag.

Serre, J. P. Linear Representations of Finite Groups. Scott, L. L., tr. from Fr. LC 76-12585. (Graduate Texts in Mathematics: Vol. 42). 170p. (Corrected Second Printing). 1983. 24.00 (ISBN 0-387-90190-6). Springer-Verlag.

Serrell, Beverly. Making Exhibit Labels: A Step-by-Step Guide. (Illus.). 128p. 1983. pap. text ed. 11.95 (ISBN 0-910050-64-3). AASLH.

Serres, F. J. De see De Serres, F. J., et al.

Serrou. Immune Complexes & Plasma Exchanges in Cancer Patients. (Human Cancer Immunology Ser.: Vol. 1). 1981. 82.75 (ISBN 0-444-80237-1). Elsevier.

--Suppressor Cells. (Human Cancer Immunology Ser.: Vol. 2). 1981. 75.50 (ISBN 0-444-80306-8). Elsevier.

Serrou, B. & Schein, P. Nitrosoureas in Cancer Treatment. (Inserm Symposia Ser.: Vol. 19). 1981. 61.00 (ISBN 0-444-80343-2). Elsevier.

Serrou, B. & Rosenfeld, C., eds. Current Concepts in Human Immunology & Cancer Immunomodulation: Proceedings of the International Symposium, Montpellier, France, January 18-20, 1982. (Developments in Immunology Ser.: Vol. 17). 664p. 1982. 84.95 (ISBN 0-444-80426-9, Biomedical Pr). Elsevier.

--Natural Killer Cells. (Human Cancer Immunology Ser.: Vol. 4). 284p. 1982. 96.00 (ISBN 0-444-80414-5). Elsevier.

Serrou, B. & Rosenfeld, S., eds. New Immunomodulating Agents & Biological Response Modifiers. (Human Cancer Immunology Ser.: Vol. 3). 400p. 1982. 106.50 (ISBN 0-444-80401-3, Biomedical Pr). Elsevier.

Serrulaz, Maurice. French Impressionists: A Selection of Drawings of the French 19th Century. Moscowitz, Ira, ed. (Drawings of the Masters Ser.). (Illus.). 1975. pap. 5.95 (ISBN 0-316-58560-2). Little.

Serruys, Henry, ed. Kumiss Ceremonies & Horse Races: Three Mongolian Texts. 124p. 1974. pap. 27.50x (ISBN 0-686-82196-3). Intl Pubns Serv.

Sertel, M. R. Workers & Incentives. (Contributions to Economic Analysis: Vol. 140). 1982. 59.75 (ISBN 0-444-86360-5). Elsevier.

Serti, Luciano, ed. Fra Angelico. (Art Library: Vol. 22). (Illus., Orig.). 1969. pap. 3.50 (ISBN 0-448-00471-2, G&D). Putnam Pub Group.

SerVaas, Cory, et al. The Saturday Evening Post Fiber & Bran Better Health Cookbook. abr. ed. LC 80-67052. (Illus.). 320p. 1977. pap. 6.50 (ISBN 0-89387-048-X, Co-Pub by Sat Eve Post). Curtis Pub Co.

--The Saturday Evening Post Fiber & Bran Better Health Cookbook. LC 77-7804. (Illus.). 320p. 1977. 12.95 (ISBN 0-89387-008-0, Co-Pub by Sat Eve Post). Curtis Pub Co.

Servan-Schreiber, Jean-Jacques. Lieutenant in Algeria. Matthews, Ronald, tr. from Fr. LC 76-30382. 1977. Repr. of 1957 ed. lib. bdg. 17.25x (ISBN 0-8371-9420-2, SELI). Greenwood.

--The World Challenge: OPEC & the New World Order. 1981. 14.95 o.p. (ISBN 0-671-42524-2). S&S.

Serve, M. Paul. A Step-by-Step Approach to Elementary Organic Synthesis. LC 75-10413. 1979. pap. text ed. 14.95 (ISBN 0-250-40098-7). Ann Arbor Science.

Service, Alastair. The Architects of London. (Illus.). 1979. 22.95 o.s.i. (ISBN 0-8038-0017-7). Architectural.

Service, Elman R. The Hunters. 2nd ed. (Foundations of Modern Anthropology Ser.). (Illus.). 1979. pap. 9.95 ref. (ISBN 0-13-448100-3). P-H.

Service, J. Gregory, jt. auth. see Schultz, Donald O.

Service, John S. The Amerasia Papers: Some Problems in the History of US-China Relations. LC 72-635322. (China Research Monographs: No. 7). 218p. 1971. pap. 4.00x (ISBN 0-912966-08-4). IEAS.

Service, M. W. Methods for Sampling Adult Simulidae, with Special Reference to the Simulium Damnosum Complex. 1977. 35.00x (ISBN 0-85135-087-9, Pub. by Centre Overseas Research). State Mutual Bk.

Service, Robert W. Best Tales of the Yukon. 208p. (Orig.). 1983. lib. bdg. 12.90 (ISBN 0-89471-202-0); pap. 4.95 (ISBN 0-89471-201-2). Running Pr.

Service, William. Owl. (Illus.). 1979. pap. 2.95 o.p. (ISBN 0-14-005267-4). Penguin.

Servieres. Memoires Pour Servir a L'histoire De M. De Voltaire. Repr. of 1785 ed. 539.00 o.p. (ISBN 0-8287-0776-6). Clearwater Pub.

Servies, James & Rea, Robert R., eds. The Log of H. M. S. Mentor, Seventeen Eighty to Seventeen Eighty-One: A New Account of the British Navy at Pensacola. LC 80-28006. (Illus.). xiv, 206p. 1982. 11.75 (ISBN 0-8130-0704-6). U Presses Fla.

Serviss, Garrett P. Columbus of Space. LC 73-13265. (Classics of Science Fiction Ser.). (Illus.). 331p. 1973. 12.50 (ISBN 0-88355-119-5); pap. 3.95 (ISBN 0-88355-148-9). Hyperion Conn.

Servodidio, Mirella & Welles, Marcia L., eds. From Fiction to Metafiction: Essays in Honor of Carmen Martin Gaite. LC 82-61181. 200p. (Orig.). 1983. pap. 25.00 (ISBN 0-89295-023-4). Society Sp & Sp-Am.

Serwadda, W. Moses. Songs & Stories from Uganda. Pantaleoni, Hewitt, ed. LC 72-7556. (Illus.). (gr. 2 up). 1974. 9.57i (ISBN 0-690-75240-7, TYC-J); PLB 9.89 (ISBN 0-690-75241-5). Har-Row.

Serwer, Jacquelyn D., jt. auth. see Calingaert, Efrem F.

Sesame Street. Bathtime on Sesame Street. Schulman, Janet, ed. LC 82-80571. (Little Pops). (Illus.). 12p. (ps-3). 1983. pap. 2.50 (ISBN 0-394-85449-7). Random.

--Big Bird's Farm. LC 81-50537. (Board Bks.). (Illus.). 14p. (ps). 1981. bds. 3.50 (ISBN 0-394-84812-8). Random.

--Ernie & Bert Can...Can You. LC 81-83696. (Chunky Bks.). (Illus.). 28p. (ps). 1982. 2.95 (ISBN 0-394-85150-1). Random.

--Ernie & Bert's Delivery Service. LC 82-61011. (Illus.). 16p. (ps-2). 1983. pap. 2.95 (ISBN 0-394-85761-5). Random.

--Grover's Monster Album. LC 80-50179. (Board Books). (Illus.). 14p. (ps). 1980. 3.50 (ISBN 0-394-84577-3). Random.

--Grover's New Kitten. LC 81-50538. (Board Bks.). (Illus.). 14p. (ps). 1981. bds. 3.50 (ISBN 0-394-84872-1). Random.

--The King on a Swing. (Sesame Street Pop-up Ser: No. 6). (Illus.). (ps-2). 1972. 3.50 o.p. (ISBN 0-394-82461-X, BYR). Random.

--Sweet Dreams on Sesame Street. Schulman, Janet, ed. LC 82-80572. (Little Pops Ser.). (Illus.). 12p. (ps-3). 1983. pap. 2.50 (ISBN 0-394-85448-9). Random.

--In & Out, Up & Down. LC 81-83697. (Chunky Books Ser.). (Illus.). 28p. (ps). 1982. bds. 2.95 (ISBN 0-394-85151-X). Random.

Seshadri, R. K. A Swadeshi Bank from South India: A History of the Indian Bank 1907-1982. (Illus.). 249p. 1982. text ed. 22.50x (ISBN 0-86131-341-0, Pub. by Orient Longman Ltd India). Apt Bks.

Seshadri, S. R. Fundamentals of Transmission Lines & Electromagnetic Fields. LC 77-128908. (Engineering Science Ser). 1971. text ed. 31.95 (ISBN 0-201-06722-6). A-W.

Seshamani, Geeta, ed. see Wilde, Oscar.

Sesiano, J. Diophantus' Arithmetica: Books IV to VI in the Arabic Translation of Qusta ibn Luqa. (Sources in the History of Mathematics & Physical Sciences Ser.: Vol. 3). (Illus.). 502p. 1983. 72.00 (ISBN 0-387-90690-8). Springer-Verlag.

Seskin, Jane. More Than Mere Survival: Conversations with Women Over Sixty-Five. LC 79-3549. 1980. 8.95 o.p. (ISBN 0-88225-288-7). Newsweek.

Sesma, Candido. El Espanol Multilinque. 200p. (Span.). 1982. pap. 7.50 (ISBN 0-686-97293-7). Orbis Pubns.

--Multilingual E.S.L. Textbook in 17 Languages. 150p. 6.95 (ISBN 0-933146-00-0). Orbis Pubns.

Sessions, K. W. & Fischer, W. Understanding Oscilloscopes & Display Waveforms. 327p. 1978. 35.95 (ISBN 0-471-02625-5). Wiley.

Sessions, Keith. Fixin up Your Van on a Budget. (Illus.). 1977. 13.95 (ISBN 0-8306-7982-0); pap. 8.95x (ISBN 0-8306-6982-5, 982). TAB Bks.

Sessions, Ken, ed. Master Handbook of One Thousand & One Practical Electronic Circuits. LC 75-31458. 602p. 1975. 15.95 o.p. (ISBN 0-8306-5800-9); pap. 14.95 (ISBN 0-8306-4800-3, 800). TAB Bks.

Sessions, Kendall W. The Homeowner's Handbook of Plumbing & Repair. LC 77-2133. 1978. text ed. 23.95x o.p. (ISBN 0-471-02550-X). Wiley.

Sessions, Kendall Webster. Discrete-Transistor Circuit Sourcemaster. LC 78-6774. 411p. 1978. text ed. 54.50 o.p. (ISBN 0-471-02626-3). Wiley.

Sessions, Kendell W. IC Schematic Sourcemaster. LC 77-13404. 557p. 1978. text ed. 49.95 (ISBN 0-471-02623-9). Wiley.

Sessions, Kenneth W. Amateur FM Conversion & Construction Projects. LC 74-79584. (Illus.). 256p. 1974. 8.95 (ISBN 0-8306-4722-8); pap. 5.95 o.p. (ISBN 0-8306-3722-2, 722). TAB Bks.

Sessions, Roger. Questions About Music. 1971. pap. 4.95 (ISBN 0-393-00571-2). Norton.

Sessions, Thelma A. Country Folk Ain't So Bad. 72p. 1983. 5.50 (ISBN 0-682-49956-0). Exposition.

Sessoms, H. Douglas, et al. Leisure Services: The Organized Recreation & Parks System. rev. 5th ed. (Illus.). 416p. 1975. text ed. 20.95 (ISBN 0-13-530105-X). P-H.

Sestay, Catherine J. Needlework: A Selected Bibliography with Special Reference to Embroidery & Needlepoint. LC 82-5806. 162p. 1982. 12.00 (ISBN 0-8108-1554-0). Scarecrow.

Sesto, Steven L. Del see Del Sesto, Steven L.

Setai, Bethuel. The Political Economy of South Africa: The Making of Poverty. 1977. pap. text ed. 10.75 (ISBN 0-8191-0171-0). U Pr of Amer.

Setchell, W. A. & Gardener, N. L. The Marine Algae of the Pacific Coast of North America: 1919-29, 3parts in 1. (Bibl. Phyco.). 1967. 72.00 (ISBN 3-7682-0454-5). Lubrecht & Cramer.

Setchell, W. A. & Gardner, N. L. Algae of Northwestern America. (Illus.). 1968. pap. 48.00 (ISBN 0-686-31750-5). Lubrecht & Cramer.

Setek, William M. Fundamentals of Mathematics. 2nd ed. 621p. 1979. text ed. 22.95 (ISBN 0-02-477690-4). Macmillan.

Setek, William M., Jr. Algebra: A Fundamental Approach. LC 81-8363. 718p. 1983. Repr. of 1977 ed. lib. bdg. write for info. o.p. (ISBN 0-89874-376-1). Krieger.

--Fundamentals of Mathematics. 3rd ed. 640p. 1983. text ed. 22.95 (ISBN 0-02-477960-1). Macmillan.

Seters, John Van see Van Seters, John.

Seth, H. K. A Monograph of the Genus Chaetomium. (Illus.). 1971. 40.00 (ISBN 3-7682-5437-2). Lubrecht & Cramer.

Seth, Marie. Dream of the Dead: (Pacesetters) LC 77-75946. (Illus.). (gr. 4 up). 1978. 8.65 (ISBN 0-516-02154-0). Childrens.

Seth, Ronald. Secret Servants: A History of Japanese Espionage. LC 75-393. 278p. 1975. Repr. of 1957 ed. lib. bdg. 21.00x (ISBN 0-8371-8021-X, SESS). Greenwood.

--True Book About the Secret Service. (Illus.). (gr. 7 up). 8.75x o.p. (ISBN 0-392-05199-0, LTB). Sportshelf.

Seth, S. Up Against the Corporate Wall: Modern Corporations & Social Issues of the 80's. 4th ed. 1982. pap. 14.95 o.p. (ISBN 0-13-938308-5); 19.95 o.p. (ISBN 0-13-938316-6). P-H.

Sethares, George C., jt. auth. see Bent, Robert J.

Sethi, A. S. & Pummer, Reinhard, eds. Comparative Religion. LC 79-905771. 200p. 1979. 12.50x (ISBN 0-7069-0810-4). Intl Pubns Serv.

Sethi, Amarjit & Schyler, Randall S., eds. Handbook of Stress Coping Strategies & Techniques. 1983. write for info. Prof. Ref. (ISBN 0-88410-745-0). Ballinger Pub.

Sethi, G. S. & Kakkar, K. C. Workshop Calculations. 150p. Date not set. 6.95x (ISBN 0-07-451903-4). McGraw.

Sethi, S. Prakash. The Unstable Ground: Corporate Social Policy in a Dynamic Society. LC 73-18300. (Management, Accounting, & Information Systems Ser.). 557p. 1974. 24.95 o.s.i. (ISBN 0-471-77685-8). Wiley.

Sethi, S. Prakash & Swanson, Carl L. Private Enterprise & Public Purpose. LC 80-26590. (Management Ser.). 461p. 1981. pap. text ed. 18.95 (ISBN 0-471-07697-X). Wiley.

Sethna, Minocher J., ed. Contributions to Synthetic Jurisprudence. LC 62-11118. 273p. 1962. 10.00 (ISBN 0-379-00113-6). Oceana.

Seth-Smith, David. Small Parrots: Parrakeets. (Illus.). 1979. 14.95 (ISBN 0-87666-978-X, H-1017). TFH Pubns.

Setliff, Gail. Meg & Nan: A Rebus Reader. 16p. 1982. 6.95 (ISBN 0-943124-00-X, Pub. by Third Century Pr). Educ Prog Dev.

Setliff, Gail & Gilliam, Brenda. Bob & Pat: A Rebus Reader. 16p. 1982. 6.95 (ISBN 0-943124-01-8, Pub. by Third Century Pr). Educ Prog Dev.

Seto, William W. Acoustics. (Schaum Outline Ser). 1971. pap. 7.95 (ISBN 0-07-056328-4, SP). McGraw.

--Mechanical Vibrations. (Orig.). 1964. pap. 7.95 (ISBN 0-07-056327-6, SP). McGraw.

Seton, Cynthia P. A Fine Romance. 1977. pap. 1.75 o.p. (ISBN 0-451-07455-6, E7455, Sig). NAL.

--A Fine Romance. 192p. 1976. 7.95 (ISBN 0-393-08742-5); pap. 3.95 (ISBN 0-393-30032-3). Norton.

Seton, Ernest T. Two Little Savages. (Illus.). 9.50 (ISBN 0-8446-2909-X). Peter Smith.

--Two Little Savages. 552p. 1982. Repr. of 1903 ed. lib. bdg. 45.00 (ISBN 0-89984-443-X). Century Bookbindery.

--Wild Animals I Have Known. Kottmeyer, William A., et al, eds. 1970. pap. 5.76 (ISBN 0-07-009288-5, W). McGraw.

Seton, Julia M. Trail & Campfire Stories. 3.35 (ISBN 0-686-96391-1, SL3529). BSA.

Seton-Watson, Christopher. Italy from Liberalism to Fascism, 1870-1925. (Illus.). 1967. 65.00x (ISBN 0-416-18940-7). Methuen Inc.

Seton-Watson, Hugh. Nations & States: An Enquiry into the Origins of Nations & the Politics of Nationalism. 563p. soft 16.00 (ISBN 0-89158-227-4). Westview.

Seton-Williams, Veronica, jt. auth. see Stocks, Peter.

Setright, L. J. Motorcycling Facts & Feats. 258p. 1980. 19.95 (ISBN 0-85112-200-0, Pub. by Guinness Superlatives England). Sterling.

Settari, A., jt. auth. see Aziz, K.

Sette, D., ed. Dispersion & Absorption of Sound by Molecular Processes. (Italian Physical Society Ser.: Course No. 27). (Illus.). 1964. 63.00 (ISBN 0-12-368827-2). Acad Pr.

Sette, D., ed. see Enrico Fermi Course 63, Vareno, Italy 1974.

Settel, Irving, jt. ed. see Kleppner, Otto.

Setterdahl, Lilly, compiled by. Swedish-American Newspapers: A Guide to the Microfilms Held by Swenson Swedish Immigration Research Center. LC 81-68299. (Augustana College Library Ser.: No. 35). 1981. 3.00x o.p. (ISBN 0-910182-41-8). Augustana.

Setterington, R. E., jt. ed. see Randeraat, J. Van.

Settgast, Edward E. & Anderson, Gerald F. Basic Spanish: Essentials for Mastery. 3rd ed. 359p. 1982. text ed. 18.95 scp (ISBN 0-06-045908-5, HarpC); instr's. manual avail. (ISBN 0-06-366062-8); scp cassette tapes 219.00 (ISBN 0-06-047444-0); wkbk. scp 8.95 (ISBN 0-06-045922-0). Har-Row.

Setti, Ginancarlo, jt. auth. see Brecher, Kenneth.

Setti, Umm. Daily Life in Ancient & Modern Egypt. Fairservis, Walter A., Jr., ed. (Illus.). 336p. 1983. write for info o.p. (ISBN 0-8014-1501-2). Cornell U Pr.

Settin, Joan. Gerontologic Human Resources: The Role of the Paraprofessional. LC 81-6315. 192p. 1983. 24.95x (ISBN 0-89885-042-8). Human Sci Pr.

Settle, Allen K., jt. auth. see Lutrin, Carl E.

Settle, Elizabeth A. & Settle, Thomas A. Ishmael Reed: A Primary & Secondary Bibliography. 155p. 1982. lib. bdg. 25.00 (ISBN 0-8161-8514-X, Hall Reference). G K Hall.

Settle, Mary L. The Killing Ground. 1982. 14.95 (ISBN 0-374-18107-1); slip-cased ltd. ed. 75.00 (ISBN 0-374-18109-8). FS&G.

Settle, Mary Lee. Blood Tie. 1977. 10.95 o.s.i. (ISBN 0-395-25401-9). HM.

--The Scapegoat. large print ed. LC 81-5636. 534p. 1981. Repr. of 1980 ed. 12.95x o.p. (ISBN 0-89621-285-8). Thorndike Pr.

Settle, Russell F., jt. auth. see Anderson, Lee G.

Settle, Thomas A., jt. auth. see Settle, Elizabeth A.

Settler, H., jt. auth. see Newton, S.

Settles, William F. Communist Life Revisited. 3rd ed. 186p. 1982. pap. 3.95 (ISBN 0-686-36920-3). Settles Bks.

Setton, C., et al. Dictionnaire Hachette de la Langue Francaise. 1813p. (Fr.). 1980. 65.00 (ISBN 0-686-97331-3, M-9373). French & Eur.

Setton, Kenneth M., jt. ed. see Hazard, Harry W.

Seturaman, V. S., jt. auth. see Ramaswami, S.

Sety, Omm & El Zeini, Hanny. Abydos: Holy City of Ancient Egypt. Wallace, Arthur, ed. LC 81-81128. (Illus.). 284p. 1983. 29.95 (ISBN 0-937892-07-6). LL Co.

Setzekorn, William D. Formerly British Honduras: A Profile of the New Nation of Belize. rev. ed. LC 81-80917. (Illus.). x, 299p. 1981. pap. 8.95x (ISBN 0-8214-0568-3, 82-83608). Ohio U Pr.

Seuling, Barbara. You Can't Eat Peanuts in Church & Other Little-Known Laws. LC 74-19384. 64p. (gr. 4-7). 1975. 6.95 (ISBN 0-385-01393-0). Doubleday.

Seume, Richard. Nehemiah: God's Builder. 1978. pap. 3.95 o.p. (ISBN 0-8024-5868-8). Moody.

Seunig, Waldemar. Horsemanship. rev. ed. LC 56-5594. (Illus.). 1961. 17.95 (ISBN 0-385-01015-X). Doubleday.

Seurat, Georges. The Drawings of George Seurat. Appelbaum, Stanley, tr. from Fr. LC 73-131438. (Illus.). 1971. pap. 6.00 (ISBN 0-486-22786-3). Dover.

Seuren, Pieter A., ed. Semantic Syntax. (Oxford Readings in Philosophy Ser.). (Illus.). 1974. pap. text ed. 8.95x (ISBN 0-19-875028-5). Oxford U Pr.

Seuss, Dr. Bartholomew & the Oobleck. (Illus.). (gr. k-3). 1949. 4.95 (ISBN 0-394-80075-3, BYR); PLB 5.99 (ISBN 0-394-90075-8); pap. 2.95 (ISBN 0-394-84539-0). Random.

--Horton Hears a Who. (Illus.). (gr. k-3). 1954. 6.95 (ISBN 0-394-80078-8, BYR); PLB 5.99 (ISBN 0-394-90078-2). Random.

--I Had Trouble in Getting to Solla Sollew. (Illus.). (ps-3). 1965. 5.95 (ISBN 0-394-80092-3, BYR); PLB 6.99 (ISBN 0-394-90092-8). Random.

--If I Ran the Circus. (Illus.). (gr. k-3). 1956. 5.95 (ISBN 0-394-80080-X, BYR); PLB 5.99 (ISBN 0-394-90080-4). Random.

--Scrambled Eggs Super. (Illus.). (gr. k-3). 1953. 2.95 (ISBN 0-394-84544-7, BYR); PLB 5.99 (ISBN 0-394-90085-5). Random.

Sevareid, Eric. Small Sounds in the Night: A Collection of Capsule Commentaries on the American Scene. LC 76-56347. 1977. Repr. of 1956 ed. lib. bdg. 19.25x (ISBN 0-8371-9421-0, SESM). Greenwood.

Sevareid, Eric & Case, John. Enterprise. 224p. 1983. 12.95 (ISBN 0-07-056336-5). McGraw.

Sevastopoulos, Julie. Keys to Spelling, Vol. 2. 64p. (Orig.). (gr. 5-10). Date not set. pap. text ed. price not set (ISBN 0-88499-542-9). Inst Mod Lang. Postponed.

Sevcik, J. Detectors in Gas Chromatography. (Journal of Chromatography Library: Vol. 4). 1976. 40.50 (ISBN 0-444-99857-8). Elsevier.

Seve, Lucien. Man in the Marxist Theory & the Psychology of Personality. (Marxist Theory & Contemporary Capitalism Ser.). 508p. 1980. text ed. 42.00x (ISBN 0-391-00743-2); pap. text ed. 17.00x (ISBN 0-391-01913-9). Humanities.

Sevela, Efraim. The Standard Bearer. Arthur, Donald & Lourie, Richard, trs. from Russian. 1983. 14.95 (ISBN 0-89651-701-2); pap. 8.95 (ISBN 0-89651-703-9). Icarus.

Seventh Asian Regional Conference, Teheran, 1971. Agenda for Asia: The Social Perplexities of the Second Development Decade. 48p. 1971. write for info. (ISBN 92-2-100103-2). Intl Labour Office.

Seventh International Heat Transfer Conference, Munich, 1982. Heat Transfer Nineteen Eighty Two: Proceedings, 6 Vols. Grigull, U. & Hahne, E., eds. LC 82-9369. 3260p. 1982. text ed. 395.00 set (ISBN 0-89116-299-2). Hemisphere Pub.

Seventh Technical Conference of the BPMA in Conjunction with BHRA. Pumps-the Developing Needs. Stephens, H. S. & Hanson, J. A., eds. (Illus.). 250p. 1981. pap. 62.50x (ISBN 0-906085-52-7). BHRA Fluid.

Seventy First Infantry Division, U.S. Army. The Seventy-First Came to Gunskirchen Lager. 2nd ed. Blumenthal, David R., intro. by. (Witness to the Holocaust Ser.: No. 1). (Illus.). 28p. 1983. pap. 1.50 (ISBN 0-89937-036-5). Witness Holocaust.

Seventy-Three Magazine Editors. The Giant Handbook of Computer Projects. (Illus.). 1979. 16.95 (ISBN 0-8306-9724-1); pap. 12.95 (ISBN 0-8306-1169-X, 1169). TAB Bks.

--The Power Supply Handbook. (Illus.). 1979. 16.95 (ISBN 0-8306-9806-X); pap. 10.95 (ISBN 0-8306-8806-4, 806). TAB Bks.

Sever, John L. & Madden, David, eds. Polyomaviruses & Human Neurological Disease. LC 82-22945. (Progress in Clinical & Biological Research Ser.: Vol. 105). 376p. 1983. 66.00 (ISBN 0-8451-0105-6). A R Liss.

Severance, Gordon, ed. see Hoeber, Ralph, et al.

Severance, Jane. When Megan Went Away. LC 79-90437. 32p. (gr. k-2). 1979. pap. 2.75 (ISBN 0-914996-22-3). Lollipop Power.

Severance, Tom, jt. auth. see Erb, Gary E.

Severens, Kenneth. Southern Architecture: An Architectural & Cultural History of the South from the Colonization of America to the 20th Century. LC 80-24727. 208p. 1981. 19.75 o.p. (ISBN 0-525-20692-2, 01917-580). Dutton.

Se Vere Stacpoole, H see Swan, D. K.

Severi, Francesco. Vorlesungen Uber Algebraische Geometrie. (Bibliotheca Mathematica Teubneriana Ser: No. 32). (Ger). Repr. of 1921 ed. 45.00 (ISBN 0-384-54945-4). Johnson Repr.

Severin, C. S., jt. ed. see Bell, Rebecca S.

Severin, Frank T. Discovering Man in Psychology. 2nd ed. Orig. Title: Humanistic Viewpoints in Psychology. (Illus.). 420p. 1973. pap. text ed. 13.00 o.p. (ISBN 0-07-056340-3, C). McGraw.

Severin, Tim. The Brendan Voyage. LC 78-867. (Illus.). 1978. 12.95 o.p. (ISBN 0-07-056335-7, GB). McGraw.

--The Sinbad Voyage. (Illus.). 256p. 1983. 17.95 (ISBN 0-399-12757-7). Putnam Pub Group.

Severn, Bill. Bill Severn's Big Book of Magic. (Illus.). (gr. 7 up). 1980. pap. 4.95 o.p. (ISBN 0-679-20534-9). McKay.

--Bill Severn's Impromptu Magic. (Illus.). 192p. 1982. 12.95 (ISBN 0-684-17606-8, ScribT). Scribner.

Severns, William H. & Fellows, Julian R. Air Conditioning & Refrigeration. LC 58-7908. 563p. 1958. text ed. 35.95x o.p. (ISBN 0-471-77781-1). Wiley.

Severs, J. Burke. Literary Relationships of Chaucer's Clerkes Tale. (Yale Studies in English Ser.: No. 96). 1972. Repr. of 1942 ed. 18.50 o.p. (ISBN 0-208-01138-2, Archon). Shoe String.

Severs, Vesta N. Lucinda. (Midwestern Memories Ser.). (Illus.). (gr. 5-9). 4.95 (ISBN 0-570-07805-9, 39-1000); pap. 3.50 (ISBN 0-570-07800-8, 39-1010). Concordia.

Severson, R., ed. see Avens, Roberts.

Severy, Lawrence J., et al. A Contemporary Introduction to Social Psychology. (Illus.). 1976. text ed. 23.95 (ISBN 0-07-056330-6, C); instructor's manual 2.95 (ISBN 0-07-056331-4). McGraw.

Sewall, Marcia. The Cobbler's Song. (A Unicorn Bk.). (Illus.). 32p. (gr. 1-4). 1982. 8.95 (ISBN 0-525-44005-4, 0869-260). Dutton.

Seward, Desmond. Monks & Wine. (Illus.). 1979. 14.95 o.p. (ISBN 0-517-53914-4). Crown.

Seward, Georgene H. Psychotherapy & Culture Conflict - In Community Mental Health. 2nd ed. 220p. 1972. 13.50 o.p. (ISBN 0-8260-8045-6). Wiley.

Seward, Georgene H., jt. auth. see Seward, John P.

Seward, John P. & Seward, Georgene H. Sex Differences: Mental & Tempermental. LC 79-48004. 240p. 1980. 24.95x (ISBN 0-669-03629-3). Lexington Bks.

Sewell, Anna. Black Beauty. (Childrens Illustrated Classics Ser). (Illus.). 237p. 1977. Repr. of 1950 ed. 10.50x (ISBN 0-460-05012-5, Pub. by J. M. Dent England). Biblio Dist.

--Black Beauty. (Nancy Drew's Favorite Classics). (Illus.). (gr. 6-9). 1978. 2.95 (ISBN 0-448-14940-0, G&D). Putnam Pub Group.

--Black Beauty. (Illus.). (gr. 4-6). illus. jr. lib. o.p. 5.95 (ISBN 0-448-05807-3, G&D); lib. bdg. 2.95 companion lib. ed. o.p. (ISBN 0-448-05457-4); deluxe ed. 8.95 (ISBN 0-448-06007-8); pap. 4.95 (ISBN 0-448-11007-5). Putnam Pub Group.

--Black Beauty. (gr. 1-6). 1982. pap. 2.25 (ISBN 0-14-035006-3, Puffin). Penguin.

--Black Beauty. LC 78-3823. (Raintree's Illustrated Classics). (Illus.). (gr. 5-8). 1978. PLB 13.30 (ISBN 0-8393-6209-9). Raintree Pubs.

--Black Beauty. Vance, Eleanor G., ed. (Illus.). (gr. k-3). 1949. 5.95 (ISBN 0-394-80637-9, BYR); PLB 5.99 (ISBN 0-394-90637-3). Random.

--Black Beauty. (gr. 3 up). 1979. pap. 1.50 (ISBN 0-307-21604-7, Golden Pr). Western Pub.

--Black Beauty. Barish, Wendy, ed. (Illus.). 240p. 1982. 14.95 (ISBN 0-671-43789-5). Wanderer Bks.

--Black Beauty & the Runaway Horse. Richardson, I. M., ed. LC 82-7029. (Adventures of Black Beauty Ser.). (Illus.). 32p. (gr. 2-5). 1982. PLB 8.79 (ISBN 0-89375-812-4); pap. 2.50 (ISBN 0-89375-813-2). Troll Assocs.

--Black Beauty Finds a Home. Richardson, I. M., ed. LC 82-7024. (Adventures of Black Beauty Ser.). (Illus.). 32p. (gr. 2-5). 1982. PLB 8.79 (ISBN 0-89375-816-7); pap. 2.50 (ISBN 0-89375-817-5). Troll Assocs.

--Black Beauty Grows Up. Richardson, I. M., ed. LC 82-7075. (Adventures of Black Beauty Ser.). (Illus.). 32p. (gr. 2-5). 1982. PLB 8.79 (ISBN 0-89375-810-8); pap. 2.50 (ISBN 0-89375-811-6). Troll Assocs.

--The Courage of Black Beauty. Richardson, I. M., ed. LC 82-7090. (Adventures of Black Beauty Ser.). (Illus.). 32p. (gr. 2-5). 1982. PLB 8.79 (ISBN 0-89375-814-0); pap. 2.50 (ISBN 0-89375-815-9). Troll Assocs.

Sewell, Anna see Swan, D. K.

Sewell, Brocard, jt. ed. see Woolf, Cecil.

Sewell, Elizabeth. Acquist. LC 82-83593. 116p. 1983. 9.95 (ISBN 0-89386-006-9); pap. 6.95 (ISBN 0-89386-007-7). Acorn NC.

Sewell, Elizabeth M. Margaret Percival, 1847. Bd. with The Experience of Life; or, Aunt Sarah, 1852. (Victorian Fiction Ser). 1975. lib. bdg. 66.00 o.s.i. (ISBN 0-8240-1550-9). Garland Pub.

Sewell, Geof. Reshaping Remedial Education. 140p. 1982. text ed. 26.00x (ISBN 0-7099-2348-1, Pub. by Croom Helm Ltd England). Biblio Dist.

Sewell, John W. The United States & World Development: Agenda 1977. LC 76-30725. (Special Studies). 1977. pap. 8.95 (ISBN 0-275-65000-6). Praeger.

Sewell, M. J., jt. ed. see Hopkins, H. G.

Sewell, P. A., jt. auth. see Hamilton, R. J.

Sewell, Richard H. Ballots for Freedom: Antislavery Politics in the United States 1837-1860. LC 75-25464. 1976. 22.50x (ISBN 0-19-501997-0). Oxford U Pr.

Sewell, W. Derrick & Coppock, J. T. Public Participation in Planning. LC 76-56800. 217p. 1977. 44.95 (ISBN 0-471-99474-X, Pub. by Wiley-Interscience). Wiley.

Sewell, W. H., Jr. Work & Revolution in France. LC 80-12103. (Illus.). 336p. 1980. 39.50 (ISBN 0-521-23442-5); pap. 9.95 (ISBN 0-521-29951-9). Cambridge U Pr.

Sewell, W. R., jt. auth. see O'Riordan, Timothy.

Sewell, Walter E. Degree of Approximation by Polynomials in the Complex Domain. (Annals of Mathemartic Studies: No. 9). 1942. pap. 20.00 (ISBN 0-527-02725-1). Kraus Repr.

Sewell, William H. & Hauser, Robert M. Education, Occupation, & Earnings: Achievement in the Early Career. 1975. 29.50 (ISBN 0-12-637850-9). Acad Pr.

Sewell, William H. & Hauser, Robert M, eds. Schooling & Achievement in American Society. (Studies in Population Ser.). 1976. 42.50 (ISBN 0-12-637860-6). Acad Pr.

Sewoster, Edward. Eight Place Tables of Arc Lengths. text ed. 15.00 o.p. (ISBN 0-8284-0240-X). Chelsea Pub.

Sewter, E. R., tr. The Alexiad of Anna Comnena. (Classic Ser.). 1979. pap. 6.75 (ISBN 0-14-044215-4). Penguin.

Sewter, E. R., tr. see Psellus, Michael.

Sexias, Frank A. Work in Progress on Alcoholism, Vol. 273. Eggleston, Suzie, ed. (Annals of the New York Academy of Sciences). 664p. 1976. 43.00x (ISBN 0-89072-052-5). NY Acad Sci.

Sexton, Ann, jt. auth. see Kumin, Maxine.

Sexton, Anne. The Awful Rowing Toward God. LC 74-23618. 96p. 1975. o.s. 8.95 (ISBN 0-395-20365-1); pap. 5.50 (ISBN 0-395-20366-X). HM.

--The Book of Folly. LC 72-3839. 1972. 5.95 (ISBN 0-395-14014-5). pap. 3.95 (ISBN 0-395-14075-7). HM.

--The Death Notebooks. LC 73-17311. 1974. 8.95 o.s.i. (ISBN 0-395-18281-6); pap. 3.45 o.s.i. (ISBN 0-395-18462-2). HM.

Sexton, Anne, jt. auth. see Kumin, Maxine.

Sexton, Donald L. & Van Auken, Philip M. Experiences in Entrepreneurship & Small Business Management. (Illus.). 240p. 1982. pap. text ed. 16.95 (ISBN 0-13-294884-2). P-H.

Sexton, Donald L., jt. auth. see Jenkins, Michael D.

Sexton, Donald L., et al. Encyclopedia of Entrepreneurship. (Illus.). 512p. 1982. text ed. 29.95 (ISBN 0-13-275826-1). P-H.

Sexton, J. E., jt. auth. see Rosenberg, R. Robert.

Sexton, Patricia C. American School: A Sociological Analysis. (Orig.). 1967. pap. 9.95 ref. ed. o.p. (ISBN 0-13-029504-3). P-H.

Sexton-Jones, Sondra. Outside, Looking in. LC 72-185926. 64p. 1972. 4.00 (ISBN 0-911838-17-1). Windy Row.

Seybert, Michael, ed. Fleet Reports & Records Encyclopedia (21m) 300p. 1982. 3-ring binder 45.00 (ISBN 0-934674-43-4, 81-86198). J J Keller.

--National Backhaul Guide: Trip Leasing, Source Directory, Exempt Commodities. LC 76-18485. (4g). 1982. looseleaf 95.00 (ISBN 0-934674-02-7). J J Keller.

Seybert, Michael, ed. see Keller, J. J., & Assocs., Inc.

Seybert, Michael, ed. see Keller, John J.

Seybert, Michael, et al, eds. see Keller, John J.

Seybold, D. & Gessler, U., eds. Acute Renal Failure. (Illus.). viii, 268p. 1982. pap. 24.75 (ISBN 3-8055-3579-1). S Karger.

Seybolt, Peter J., ed. The Rustication of Urban Youth in China: A Social Experiment. LC 76-17395. 1977. 27.50 (ISBN 0-87332-082-4). M E Sharpe.

Seybolt, Peter J & Chiang, Gregory K., eds. Language Reform in China: Documents & Commentary. LC 76-4302. 1979. 30.00 (ISBN 0-87332-081-6). M E Sharpe.

Seyersted, Brita L., ed. see Pound, Ezra & Ford, Ford Madox.

Seyfer, Eudora, jt. auth. see Bell, Lorna.

Seyferth, D. & King, R. Organometallic Chemistry Reviews: Annual Surveys 1977 - Silicon-Germanium-Tin-Lead. (Journal of Organometallic Chemistry: Vol. 8). 1979. 117.00 (ISBN 0-444-41789-3). Elsevier.

Seyferth, D., ed. Organometallic Chemistry Reviews: Annual Surveys 1975 - Silicon-Tin-Lead. (Journal of Organometallic Chemistry Library: Vol. 4). 1977. 95.75 (ISBN 0-444-41591-2). Elsevier.

Seyferth, D. & Davies, A. G., eds. Organometallic Chemistry Reviews. (Journal of Organometallic Chemistry Library: Vol. 9). 1980. 106.50 (ISBN 0-444-41840-7). Elsevier.

Seyferth, D. & King, R., eds. Annual Surveys of Organometallic Chemistry, Vols. 1-3. 1965-68. 38.50 ea. Vol. 1, 1964 (ISBN 0-444-40527-5). Vol. 2, 1965 (ISBN 0-444-40528-3). Vol. 3, 1966 (ISBN 0-444-40529-1). Elsevier.

--Organometallic Chemistry Reviews: Annual Surveys, 1976: Silicon, Germanium, Tin & Lead. (Junior Organometallic Library Ser.: Vol. 6). 1978. 106.50 (ISBN 0-444-41698-6). Elsevier.

Seyferth, D. & King, R. B., eds. Organometallic Chemistry Reviews Annual Surveys: Silicon, Germanium, Tin & Lead. (Journal of Organometallic Chemistry Library: Vol. 10). 1980. 117.00 (ISBN 0-444-41876-8). Elsevier.

--Organometallic Chemistry Reviews Annual Surveys: Silicon, Tin & Lead. (Journal of Organometallic Chemistry Library: Vol. 11). 1981. 117.00 (ISBN 0-444-41985-3). Elsevier.

Seyferth, D., et al, eds. Organometallic Chemistry Reviews. (Journal of Organometallic Chemistry Library: Vol. 5). 1977. 95.75 (ISBN 0-444-41633-1). Elsevier.

Seyferth, D, et al, eds. Organometallic Chemistry Reviews. (Journal of Organometallic Chemistry Library: Vol. 3). 1977. 95.75 (ISBN 0-444-41538-6). Elsevier.

Seyferth, D., et al, eds. Organometallic Chemistry Reviews. (Journal of Organometallic Chemistry Library: Vol. 7). 1979. 106.50 (ISBN 0-444-41788-5). Elsevier.

--Organometallic Chemistry Reviews: Organosilicon Reviews. (Journal of Organometallic Chemistry Library: Vol. 2). 1976. 95.75 (ISBN 0-444-41488-6). Elsevier.

--Organometallic Chemistry Reviews: Proceedings. (Journal of Organometallic Chemistry Library: Vol. 12). 1982. 117.00 (ISBN 0-444-42025-8). Elsevier.

Seyler, Dorothy, jt. auth. see Boltz, Carol.

Seyler, Dorothy U. & Sipple, M. Noel. Thinking for Writing. LC 77-22730. 1978. pap. text ed. 12.95 (ISBN 0-574-22035-6, 13-5035); instr's guide avail. (ISBN 0-574-22036-4, 13-5036). SRA.

Seyling, Barbara & Glasgow, Winnette. Fun with Crafts. (Elephant Bks). (gr. 1-6). 1977. pap. 1.25 (ISBN 0-448-14450-6, G&D). Putnam Pub Group.

Seymor, John. The Gardeners Delight. 1979. 5.95 o.p. (ISBN 0-517-53805-9). Crown.

Seymour, A. B. Host Index of the Fungi of North America. (Bibl. Myco. Ser.: No.2). 1967. pap. 40.00 (ISBN 3-7682-0461-8). Lubrecht & Cramer.

Seymour, A. C; see Brooke, Charlotte.

Seymour, Charles. Woodrow Wilson & the World War. 1921. text ed. 8.50x (ISBN 0-686-83860-2). Elliots Bks.

Seymour, Charles, Jr., ed. & intro. by. Michelangelo: The Sistine Chapel Ceiling. (Critical Studies in Art History). (Illus.). 243p. 1972. pap. 7.95x (ISBN 0-393-09889-3). Norton.

Seymour, Claire. Precipice: Learning to Live with Alzheimer's Disease. 10.00 (ISBN 0-686-84433-5). Vantage.

Seymour, D. see Bassett, T.

Seymour, D. G. Divided Loyalties. 324p. 1982. 25.00 (ISBN 0-686-43275-4). Pr of Morningside.

Seymour, Dale & Gidley, Richard. Eureka. 1970. pap. 9.50 wkbk. (ISBN 0-88488-048-6). Creative Pubns.

Seymour, Dale & Greenes, Carole. Activities with Geoblocks. 1975. pap. 5.00 wkbk. cancelled (ISBN 0-88488-049-4). Creative Pubns.

Seymour, Dale & Schadler, Reuben. Creative Constructions. rev. ed. (Illus.). 62p. (gr. 5-12). 1970. wkbk. 6.50 (ISBN 0-88488-007-9). Creative Pubns.

Seymour, Dale & Silvey, Linda. Line Designs. rev. ed. (Illus.). (gr. 5-12). 1970. wkbk. 6.50 (ISBN 0-88488-008-7). Creative Pubns.

Seymour, Dale, et al. Number Sentence Games. rev. ed. 1973. pap. 4.25 wkbk. cancelled (ISBN 0-88488-024-9). Creative Pubns.

--Aftermath Ser. rev. ed. (Illus.). 122p. 1970. Bks. 1-4. wkbks. 7.95 ea. Bk. 1 (ISBN 0-88488-033-8). Bk. 2 (ISBN 0-88488-034-6). Bk. 3 (ISBN 0-88488-035-4). Bk. 4 (ISBN 0-88488-036-2). Creative Pubns.

Seymour, Edward L., ed. Wise Garden Encyclopedia. 1970. 14.95 o.p. (ISBN 0-448-01997-3, G&D). Putnam Pub Group.

Seymour, Gerald. Archangel. 352p. 1982. 14.95 (ISBN 0-525-24129-9, 01451-440). Dutton.

--The Glory Boys. 1976. 1.95 (ISBN 0-449-23392-8). Random.

Seymour, Harold J. Campanas para Obtencion de Fondus. 194p. 1964. 9.50 (ISBN 0-686-82669-8). CASE.

Seymour, Ian. OPEC: An Instrument of Change. 256p. 1981. 26.00x (ISBN 0-312-58605-1). St Martin.

Seymour, Jack L. From Sunday School to Church School: Continuities in Protestant Church Education in the United States, 1860-1929. LC 82-15977. 188p. 1982. lib. bdg. 22.00 (ISBN 0-8191-2726-4); pap. text ed. 10.00 (ISBN 0-8191-2727-2). U Pr of Amer.

Seymour, Jane. Dressing Thin. 1979. pap. text ed. 8.95 o.p. (ISBN 0-914094-11-4). Symphony.

Seymour, John. The Lore of the Land. LC 82-16887. (Illus.). 160p. 1983. 14.95 (ISBN 0-8052-3836-0). Schocken.

Seymour, M. C., ed. Selections from Hoccleve. (Illus.). 1982. 23.50x (ISBN 0-19-871083-6); pap. 11.95x (ISBN 0-19-871084-4). Oxford U Pr.

Seymour, Miranda. Count Manfred. 1977. 8.95 o.p. (ISBN 0-698-10796-9, Coward). Putnam Pub Group.

--Daughter of Shadows. LC 77-22844. 1977. 8.95 o.p. (ISBN 0-698-10784-5, Coward). Putnam Pub Group.

--The Goddess. LC 78-24536. 1979. 10.95 o.p. (ISBN 0-698-10972-4, Coward). Putnam Pub Group.

Seymour, P. H. Human Visual Cognition. 1979. 26.00x (ISBN 0-312-39966-9). St Martin.

Seymour, Peter. Busy Bears. (Surprise Bks.). (Illus.). 22p. 1982. 4.95 (ISBN 0-8431-0640-9). Price Stern.

--Frontier Town. LC 82-80754. (Illus.). (gr. 1-4). 1982. 7.50 (ISBN 0-03-062077-5). HR&W.

--The Fuzzy What-Was-He. (Surprise Bks.). (Illus.). 22p. (ps-2). 1982. 4.95 (ISBN 0-8431-0639-5). Price Stern.

--Pendragon Castle. Moseley, Keith, designed by. LC 82-80753. (Illus.). (gr. 1-4). 1982. 7.50 (ISBN 0-03-062076-7). HR&W.

Seymour, Peter, compiled by. Moments Bright & Shining: Three Hundred & Sixty-Five Thoughts to Enjoy Day by Day. (Illus.). 1979. boxed 5.50 (ISBN 0-8378-1706-4). Gibson.

Seymour, R. A Monograph of the Genus Saprolegnia. (Illus.). 1970. 16.00 (ISBN 3-7682-0657-2). Lubrecht & Cramer.

Seymour, R. B. Plastics vs. Corrosives. (Society of Plastics Engineers Monographs). 285p. 1982. text ed. 47.50x (ISBN 0-471-08182-5, Pub. by Wiley-Interscience). Wiley.

Seymour, Raymond B. Additives for Plastics, 2 vols. Incl. Vol. 1. State of the Art. 31.00 (ISBN 0-12-637501-1); Vol. 2. New Developments. 18.50 (ISBN 0-12-637502-X). 1978. Acad Pr.

--Introduction to Polymer Chemistry. LC 77-19164. 448p. 1978. Repr. of 1971 ed. lib. bdg. 23.50 (ISBN 0-88275-650-8). Krieger.

--Modern Plastics Technology. (Illus.). 256p. 1975. 19.95 (ISBN 0-87909-500-8). Reston.

Seymour, Smith F. Bibliography in the Bookshop. 192p. 1972. 18.00 (ISBN 0-233-95971-8, 05817-8, Pub. by Gower Pub Co England). Lexington Bks.

--An English Library: A Bookman's Guide. 384p. 1963. 12.50 (ISBN 0-233-95810-X, 05816-5, Pub. by Gower Pub Co England). Lexington Bks.

Seymour, Thomas D. Introduction to the Language & Verse of Homer. (College Classical Ser.). iv, 104p. 1981. lib. bdg. 20.00 (ISBN 0-686-95464-5); pap. text ed. 12.50 (ISBN 0-89241-117-1). Caratzas Bros.

--Life in the Homeric Age. LC 63-12451. (Illus.). 1907. 12.00x (ISBN 0-8196-0125-X). Biblo.

Seymour, William. Battles in Britain Ten Sixty-Six to Seventeen Forty-Six, 2 vols. in one. (Illus.). 1979. 19.95 o.s.i. (ISBN 0-88254-493-4). Hippocrene Bks.

--Battles in Britian & Their Political Background, 1642-1746, Vol. 2. LC 75-34555. (Illus.). 1976. 14.95 o.p. (ISBN 0-88254-379-2). Hippocrene Bks.

Seymour-Smith, Martin. The New Astrologer. (Illus.). 320p. 1983. 17.75 (ISBN 0-02-609740-0); pap. 8.95 (ISBN 0-02-081940-4). Macmillan.

--Robert Graves: His Life & Work. (Illus.). 624p. 1983. 22.50 (ISBN 0-03-022171-4). HR&W.

--Who's Who in Twentieth-Century Literature. (McGraw-Hill Paperbacks). 1977. pap. 4.95 o.p. (ISBN 0-07-056350-0, SP). McGraw.

Seymour-Smith, Martin, jt. auth. see Reeves, James.

Seymour-Smith, Martin, ed. The English Sermon Fifteen Hundred Fifty to Sixteen Hundred Fifty, Vol. 1. 491p. 1976. text ed. 22.25x (ISBN 0-85635-093-1, Pub. by Carcanet New Pr England). Humanities.

Seymour-Ure, Colin. The American President: Power & Communication. LC 82-5772. 1982. 22.50x (ISBN 0-312-02786-9). St Martin.

Seyppel, Joachim. T. S. Eliot. LC 75-143187. (Literature and Life Ser.). 1971. 11.95 (ISBN 0-8044-2818-2). Ungar.

Seznec, Jean, ed. Diderot: Salons, Vol. III, Seventeen Sixty-Seven. 2nd ed. (Illus.). 1982. 110.00 (ISBN 0-19-817372-5). Oxford U Pr.

Sfikas, George. Wild Flowers of Greece. (Illus.). 125p. (Orig.). 1981. pap. 10.00x (ISBN 0-8002-2951-7). Intl Pubns Serv.

Sgall, Peter, ed. Contributions to Functional Syntax & Semantics. (Linguistic & Literary Studies in Eastern Europe: 16). 300p. 1983. 36.00 (ISBN 9-027215-20-0). Benjamins North Am.

Sgontz, Larry G., jt. auth. see Pogue, Thomas F.

Sgro, Joseph A., ed. Virginia Tech Symposium on Applied Behavioral Science, Vol. I. LC 80-8614. 320p. 1981. 31.95x (ISBN 0-669-04332-X). Lexington Bks.

Sgroi, Peter. Blue Jeans & Black Robes: Teenagers & the Supreme Court. LC 79-115. 192p. (gr. 7 up). 1979. PLB 7.79 o.p. (ISBN 0-671-32884-0). Messner.

Shaanan, Alexander. Dear God, is Justice Still With You? (Illus.). 144p. 1983. 8.95 (ISBN 0-89962-306-9). Todd & Honeywell.

Shaban, M. A. The Abbasid Revolution. 1979. 37.50 (ISBN 0-521-07849-0); pap. 12.95 (ISBN 0-521-29534-3). Cambridge U Pr.

--Islamic History A. D. Six Hundred to Seven Fifty: New Interpretation I. LC 79-145604. 1971. 42.50 (ISBN 0-521-08137-8); pap. 13.95 (ISBN 0-521-29131-3). Cambridge U Pr.

--Islamic History: A.D. 750 to 1055, (A.H. 132 to 448) New Interpretation II. LC 75-39390. (Illus.). 190p. 1976. 42.50 (ISBN 0-521-21198-0); pap. 13.95 (ISBN 0-521-29453-3). Cambridge U Pr.

Shabtai, Sabi H. Five Minutes to Midnight. 1980. 9.95 o.s.i. (ISBN 0-440-02569-9). Delacorte.

Shachter-Haham, Mayer, ed. Compound of Hebrew. 776p. 1982. text ed. 15.00 (ISBN 0-686-38112-2). K Sefer.

Shachtman, Tom. The Day America Crashed. LC 78-12963. 1979. 10.95 (ISBN 0-399-11613-3). Putnam Pub Group.

--Edith & Woodrow. 288p. 1981. 12.95 (ISBN 0-399-12446-2). Putnam Pub Group.

Shack, William A. The Central Ethiopians: Amhara, Tigrina & Related People. LC 75-320468. (Ethnographic Survey of Africa Ser.). (Illus.). 1974. pap. 17.50x (ISBN 0-85302-040-X). Intl Pubns Serv.

Shack, William A. & Skinner, Elliott P., eds. Strangers in African Society. LC 77-73501. (Campus Ser.: No. 220). 1979. 37.50x (ISBN 0-520-03458-9); pap. 8.95x (ISBN 0-520-03812-6). U of Cal Pr.

Shackel, B., ed. Man-Computer Interaction: Human Factors of Computers & People. (NATO Advanced Study Institute Ser.: Applied Sciences, No. 44). 550p. Date not set. 60.00x (ISBN 90-286-0910-5). Sijthoff & Noordhoff. Postponed.

Shackelford, Jean A., ed. Urban & Regional Economics: A Guide to Information Sources. LC 74-11556. (Economics Information Guide Ser.: Vol. 14). 190p. 1980. 42.00x (ISBN 0-8103-1303-0). Gale.

Shackelford, Richard T. & Zuidema, George D. Surgery of the Alimentary Tract, Vol. 2. (Illus.). 634p. 1981. text ed. 65.00 (ISBN 0-7216-8084-4). Saunders.

Shackelton, Alberta D. Practical Nurse Nutrition Education. 3rd ed. LC 77-176216. (Illus.). 1972. pap. 6.50 o.p. (ISBN 0-7216-8112-3). Saunders.

Shackle, George L. An Economic Querist. LC 72-96679. 120p. 1973. 19.95 (ISBN 0-521-20188-8). Cambridge U Pr.

--Economics for Pleasure. 2nd ed. 1968. 44.50 (ISBN 0-521-06282-9); pap. 15.95x (ISBN 0-521-09507-7, 170). Cambridge U Pr.

--Epistemics & Economics: A Critique of Economic Doctrine. LC 72-76091. (Illus.). 400p. 1973. 59.50 (ISBN 0-521-08626-4). Cambridge U Pr.

--Nature of Economic Thought. 1966. 49.50 (ISBN 0-521-06278-0). Cambridge U Pr.

--Scheme of Economic Theory. 1965. 42.50 (ISBN 0-521-06280-2). Cambridge U Pr.

--Years of High Theory. 1967. 47.50 (ISBN 0-521-06279-9). Cambridge U Pr.

Shackle, P. Siraiki Language of Central Pakistan. 1977. 22.50x o.p. (ISBN 0-88386-306-5). South Asia Bks.

Shackleford, Richard T. & Zuidema, George D. Surgery of the Alimentary Tract: Colon & Anorectal Tract, Vol. 3. 2nd ed. (Illus.). 705p. 1982. 70.00 (ISBN 0-7216-8085-2). Saunders.

Shackleford, Ruby P. Ascend the Hill & Other Poems. 64p. 1974. 4.00 (ISBN 0-911838-38-4). Windy Row.

Shackleton, Basil. The Grape Cure. 1978. pap. 5.95 (ISBN 0-7225-0202-8). Newcastle Pub.

Shackleton, Elizabeth, jt. auth. see Shackleton, Robert.

Shackleton, J. R. & Locksley, G. Twelve Contemporary Economists. 263p. 1981. 27.95 o.p. (ISBN 0-470-27168-X). Halsted Pr.

Shackleton, J. R. & Locksley, Gareth. Twelve Contemporary Economists. LC 81-2403. 263p. 1982. pap. 17.95x (ISBN 0-470-27367-4). Halsted Pr.

Shackleton, M., ed. see Gide, Andre.

Shackleton, Robert & Shackleton, Elizabeth. Quest of the Colonial. LC 72-99075. (Illus.). 1970. Repr. of 1907 ed. 37.00x (ISBN 0-8103-3574-3). Gale.

Shackleton, Robert, pref. by. Computers & Early Books. vii, 131p. 1975. 12.00x o.p. (ISBN 0-7201-0444-0, Pub. by Mansell England). Wilson.

Shackley, M. L. Rocks & Man. LC 76-52809. (Illus.). 1977. 16.95 o.p. (ISBN 0-312-68799-0). St Martin.

Shackley, Myra. Rocks & Man. (Illus.). 160p. 1982. pap. text ed. 9.95x (ISBN 0-04-913019-6). Allen Unwin.

--Still Living. (Illus.). 1983. 16.95 (ISBN 0-500-01298-9). Thames Hudson.

Shackley, T. The Third Option. 1981. 12.00 (ISBN 0-07-056382-9). McGraw.

Shacter, Helen S., jt. auth. see Jenkins, Gladys G.

Shactman, Tom. The Phony War: Nineteen Thirty-Nine to Nineteen Forty. LC 81-47971. 304p. 1982. 16.30i (ISBN 0-06-038036-5, HarpT). Har-Row.

Shad, A. R. A.B.C. Islamic Reader. 2.00 (ISBN 0-686-97874-9). Kazi Pubns.

Shadbolt, Maurice, jt. auth. see Brake, Brian.

Shadburne, William, jt. auth. see Ascher, Scott.

Shade, William G. & Friedman, Jean E., eds. Our American Sisters: Women in American Life & Thought. 3rd ed. 448p. 1982. pap. text ed. 12.95 (ISBN 0-669-04755-4). Heath.

Shader, R. I., jt. auth. see DiMascio, A.

Shadid, Mohammed K. The United States & the Palestinians. 240p. 1981. 26.00x (ISBN 0-312-83315-6). St Martin.

Shadily, Hassan, jt. auth. see Echols, John M.

Shadman, Alonzo J. Who Is Your Doctor & Why? LC 80-82320. 1980. 3.95x (ISBN 0-87983-227-4, Pub. by Keats). Formur Intl.

Shadwell, Thomas. The Virtuoso. Nicolson, Marjorie H. & Rodes, David S., eds. LC 65-19466. (Regents Restoration Drama Ser). xxvi, 153p. 1966. 13.95x o.p. (ISBN 0-8032-0368-3); pap. 3.95x o.p. (ISBN 0-8032-5368-0, BB 254, Bison). U of Nebr Pr.

Shadwell, Thomas, jt. auth. see Dryden, John.

Shady, Raymond C. & Shand, G. B., eds. Play-Texts in Old Spelling. LC 81-69123. 1982. 24.50 (ISBN 0-404-62276-3). AMS Pr.

Shaeffer, Claire B. The Complete Book of Sewing Shortcuts. LC 81-50981. (Illus.). 256p. 1981. 19.95 (ISBN 0-8069-5433-7); lib. bdg. 23.59. Sterling.

--The Complete Book of Sewing Shortcuts. LC 81-8818. 256p. 1983. pap. 12.95 (ISBN 0-8069-7564-4). Sterling.

Shaevel, M. Leonard, jt. auth. see Paul, Richard S.

Shaevitz, Marjorie, jt. auth. see Lenz, Marjorie.

Shafarevich, I. R. Basic Algebraic Geometry. LC 77-6425. (Springer Study Edition). 1977. pap. 28.00 (ISBN 0-387-08264-6). Springer-Verlag.

Shafarevich, Igor. The Socialist Phenomenon. Tjalsma, William, tr. from Rus. LC 79-1684. 1980. 17.26i (ISBN 0-06-014017-8, HarpT). Har-Row.

Shafer. Urban Growth & Economics. 1977. 16.95 (ISBN 0-87909-853-8). Reston.

Shafer, Donald M. Manual on Retina Detachment. (Handbook in Ophthalmology Ser.). 1984. price not set (ISBN 0-683-07688-4). Williams & Wilkins.

Shafer, Kathleen N., et al. Medical-Surgical Nursing. 6th ed. LC 74-20829. 1032p. 1975. text ed. 21.95 o.p. (ISBN 0-8016-4516-6). Mosby.

Shafer, Michael. The Language of the Horse. LC 74-24802. (Illus.). 1975. 15.95 (ISBN 0-668-03762-8). Arco.

Shafer, Neil, ed. see Pick, Albert.

Shafer, Richard A & Coghill, Mary A. Personnel Research Abstracts. LC 73-1670. (ILR Bibliography Ser.: No. 10). 60p. 1973. pap. 3.00 (ISBN 0-87546-050-X); pap. 6.00 special hard bdg. (ISBN 0-87546-281-2). ILR Pr.

Shafer, Robert. Paul Elmermoore & American Criticism. 1935. text ed. 19.50x (ISBN 0-686-83688-X). Elliots Bks.

--Progress & Science. 1922. text ed. 37.50x (ISBN 0-686-83714-2). Elliots Bks.

Shafer, Robert E. & Staab, Claire. Language Functions & School Success. 1983. text ed. 8.95x (ISBN 0-673-15834-9). Scott F.

Shafer, Robert J. History of Latin America. 1978. text ed. 20.95 (ISBN 0-669-01283-1). Heath.

Shafer, Ronald G., jt. auth. see Carlson, Margaret B.

Shafer, Ronald G., jt. auth. see Sumichrast, Michael.

Shafer, Thomas. Real Estate & Economics. (Illus.). 320p. 1976. 18.95 (ISBN 0-87909-715-9). Reston.

Shaffer, Arthur. The Politics of History: Writing the History of the American Revolution, 1783-1815. LC 75-7865. 227p. 1975. 19.95 (ISBN 0-913750-09-3). Precedent Pub.

Shaffer, Carol, jt. auth. see Cooley, Marcia.

Shaffer, Carolyn & Fielder, Erica. Nature & the City: An Explorer's Guide for Kids & Grownups. (Illus.). 112p. (Orig.). Date not set. pap. 6.95 (ISBN 0-938530-12-7, 12-7). Lexikos.

Shaffer, David & Dunn, Judy. The First Year of Life: Psychological & Medical Implications of Early Experience. LC 78-11237. (Studies in Psychiatry). 221p. 1980. 49.95 (ISBN 0-471-99734-X, Pub. by Wiley-Interscience). Wiley.

Shaffer, David R. Social & Personality Development. LC 78-12032. (Psychology Ser.). (Illus.). 1979. text ed. 22.95 (ISBN 0-8185-0289-4). Brooks-Cole.

Shaffer, E. S. Comparative Criticism: A Yearbook, Vol. 4. (Illus.). 320p. 1982. 49.50 (ISBN 0-521-24578-8). Cambridge U Pr.

--Kubla Khan & the Fall of Jerusalem. LC 74-79141. 320p. 1975. 57.50 (ISBN 0-521-20478-X). Cambridge U Pr.

--Kubla Khan & the Fall of Jerusalem. LC 79-8492. 362p. 1980. pap. 15.95 (ISBN 0-521-29807-5). Cambridge U Pr.

Shaffer, E. S., ed. Comparative Criticism: A Yearbook, Vol. 1. 1980. 37.50 (ISBN 0-521-22296-6). Cambridge U Pr.

Shaffer, Ed. The United States & the Control of World Oil. LC 82-42720. 256p. 1983. 27.50x (ISBN 0-312-83314-8). St Martin.

Shaffer, Frederick. Mola Design Coloring Book: Forty-Five Authentic Indian Motifs from Panama. (Illus.). 48p. (gr. 3 up). Date not set. pap. 2.75 (ISBN 0-486-24289-7). Dover.

Shaffer, Gail. Women's Fight for Liberation. (Topics of Our Times Ser.: No. 11). 32p. lib. bdg. 2.95 incl. catalog cards (ISBN 0-87157-812-3); pap. 1.95 vinyl laminated covers (ISBN 0-87157-312-1). SamHar Pr.

Shaffer, H. & Greenwald, H. Independent Retailing: A Money Making Manual. (Illus.). 400p. 1976. 18.95 (ISBN 0-13-456780-3); pap. 14.50 (ISBN 0-686-96834-4). P-H.

Shaffer, Harry G. Free Periodicals from Socialist Countries: An Annotated Bibliography. 1977. 0.60 o.p. (ISBN 0-89977-018-5). Am Inst Marxist.

Shaffer, Harry G., ed. Soviet Agriculture: An Assessment of Its Contributions to Economic Development. LC 77-7512. (Praeger Special Studies). 1977. 26.95 (ISBN 0-03-021976-0). Praeger.

Shaffer, James H. Explorations in Psychological Experimentation. LC 79-65010. 1979. pap. text ed. 9.50 (ISBN 0-8191-0778-6). U Pr of Amer.

Shaffer, Janet. Peter Fracisco-Virginia Giant. LC 76-25334. 1976. 8.95 (ISBN 0-87716-068-6, Pub. by Moore Pub Co). F Apple.

Shaffer, Jerome A. Philosophy of Mind. LC 68-24352. (Foundations of Philosophy Ser.). (Orig.). 1968. pap. 10.95 ref. ed. (ISBN 0-13-663724-8). P-H.

Shaffer, John B. Humanistic Psychology. LC 77-15044. (Foundations of Modern Psychology Ser.). (Illus.). 1978. ref. ed. 17.95 (ISBN 0-13-447698-0); pap. text ed. 13.95 (ISBN 0-13-447680-8). P-H.

Shaffer, John B. & Galinsky, M. David. Models of Group Therapy & Sensitivity Training. (Personal, Clinical & Social Psychology Ser). 228p. 1974. 23.95 (ISBN 0-13-586081-4). P-H.

Shaffer, John W. Family & Farm: Agrarian Change & Household Organization in the Loire Valley, 1500-1900. LC 81-9335. (European Social History Ser.). 268p. 1982. 39.00x (ISBN 0-87395-562-5); pap. 12.95x (ISBN 0-87395-563-3). State U NY Pr.

Shaffer, Katherine A., jt. auth. see Unger, June D.

Shaffer, Kenneth, jt. auth. see Snyder, Graydon.

Shaffer, Louis R., et al. Critical-Path Method. (Illus.). 1965. 24.50 o.p. (ISBN 0-07-056371-3, P&RB). McGraw.

Shaffer, Lynda. Mao & the Workers: The Hunan Labor Movement, 1920-23. LC 82-5923. 300p. 1982. 30.00 (ISBN 0-87332-204-5). M E Sharpe.

Shaffer, Martin. Life after Stress. (Illus.). 288p. 1983. pap. 8.95 (ISBN 0-8092-5622-3). Contemp Bks.

Shaffer, Peter. Equus. 1977. pap. 2.50 (ISBN 0-380-00357-0, 51797, Bard). Avon.

Shaffer, R. D., jt. auth. see Nanney, J. L.

Shaffer, Robert H., jt. auth. see Hammond, Edward H.

Shaffer, W. D. & Wheelwright, Richard, eds. Creating Original Programming for Cable TV. 175p. 1983. 29.95 (ISBN 0-86729-043-9). Knowledge Indus.

Shaffer, William R. Party and Ideology in the United States Congress. LC 80-8277. 372p. 1980. lib. bdg. 23.50 (ISBN 0-8191-1232-1); pap. text ed. 13.75 (ISBN 0-8191-1233-X). U Pr of Amer.

Shafii, Mohammad & Shafii, Sharon L., eds. Pathways of Human Development: Treatment of Emotional Disorders in Infancy, Childhood & Adolescence. LC 82-80780. (Orig.). 1982. pap. text ed. 24.95 (ISBN 0-686-81689-7). Thieme-Stratton.

Shafii, Sharon L., jt. ed. see Shafii, Mohammad.

Shafiroff, Ira L. The Taxpayers' Survival Guide: All You Want to Know About IRS Tax Audits. 133p. 1981. 11.00 (ISBN 0-938648-10-1). T-C Pubns CA.

Shafiroff, Martin D. & Shook, Robert L. Successful Telephone Selling in the 80's. 176p. 1983. pap. 4.76i (ISBN 0-06-463569-4, EH 569). B&N NY.

Shafran, Avi. Jewthink: A Guide to Real Judaism for the Thinking Individual. 1977. pap. 3.95 o.p. (ISBN 0-87203-064-4). Hermon.

Shafrir, E., ed. Contemporary Topics in the Study of Diabetes & Metabolic Endocrinology. (Based upon a symposium). 1976. 46.00 (ISBN 0-12-638060-0). Acad Pr.

--Impact of Insulin on Metabolic Pathways. 1972. 49.50 (ISBN 0-12-638050-3). Acad Pr.

Shafritz. Personnel Management in Government. 2nd rev. ed. (Public Administration & Public Policy Ser.: Vol. 10). 448p. 1981. 21.75 (ISBN 0-8247-1454-7). Dekker.

Shafritz, Jay M. & Hyde, Albert C., eds. Classics of Public Administration. LC 78-6950. (Classics Ser.). (Orig.). 1978. pap. 12.50x (ISBN 0-935610-00-6). Moore Pub IL.

Shafritz, Jay M. & Whitbeck, Philip H., eds. Classics of Organization Theory. (Classics Ser.). (Orig.). 1978. pap. 10.00x (ISBN 0-935610-02-2). Moore Pub IL.

Shafritz, Jay M., jt. ed. see Hyde, Albert C.

Shafritz, Jay M., jt. ed. see Neugarten, Dail A.

Shaftel, Fannie R., jt. auth. see Shaftel, George.

Shaftel, George & Shaftel, Fannie R. Role Playing in the Curriculum. 2nd ed. 464p. 1982. 23.95 (ISBN 0-13-782482-3). P-H.

Shaftel, Oscar. An Understanding of the Buddha. LC 72-80041. 256p. 1974. 10.00x o.p. (ISBN 0-8052-3544-2). Schocken.

Shagan, Steve. The Formula. 352p. 1982. pap. 2.75 (ISBN 0-553-13801-4). Bantam.

Shagass, Charles, et al, eds. Psychopathology & Brain Dysfunction. LC 76-55487. (American Psychopathological Association Ser). 399p. 1977. 31.00 (ISBN 0-89004-120-2). Raven.

Shah, A. M. The Household Dimension of the Family in India. LC 71-126757. 1974. 36.50x (ISBN 0-520-01790-0). U of Cal Pr.

Shah, Ahmed. The Bijak or the Complete Works of Kabir. 1981. Repr. 16.50 (ISBN 0-89684-256-8, Pub. by Asian Pubn India). Orient Bk Dist.

Shah, D. O. & Schechter, R. S., eds. Improved Oil Recovery by Surfactant & Polymer Flooding. 1977. 42.00 (ISBN 0-12-641750-4). Acad Pr.

Shah, Giri Raj. Indian Heritage. 187p. 1982. text ed. 12.00x (ISBN 0-391-02806-5, Pub. by Abhinav India). Humanities.

Shah, Giriraj. Kingdom of Gods: Uttarakhand. LC 75-908038. 1975. 7.00 o.p. (ISBN 0-88386-724-9). South Asia Bks.

Shah, Idries. The Exploits of the Incomparable Mulla Nasrudin. 1972. pap. 4.25 (ISBN 0-525-47339-4). Dutton.

--Learning How to Learn: Psychology & Spirituality in the Sufi Way. LC 80-8892. 304p. 1981. pap. 7.95i (ISBN 0-06-067255-2, CN4015, HarpR). Har-Row.

--A Perfumed Scorpion. 1982. pap. 5.72i (ISBN 0-06-067254-4, CN-4036). Har-Row.

--Pleasantries of Mulla Nasrudin. 1971. pap. 6.75 (ISBN 0-525-47306-8, 0655-200). Dutton.

--Tales of the Dervishes. 1970. pap. 5.50 (ISBN 0-525-47262-2, 0534-160). Dutton.

--Thinkers of the East. 1972. pap. 3.50 (ISBN 0-14-003410-2). Penguin.

--Way of the Sufi. 1970. pap. 5.95 (ISBN 0-525-47261-4, 0578-170). Dutton.

--Wisdom of the Idiots. 1971. pap. 4.50 (ISBN 0-525-47307-6, 0437-130). Dutton.

--World Tales. LC 79-1734. (Illus.). 1979. 19.95 o.p. (ISBN 0-15-199434-X). HarBraceJ.

Shah, J. J., ed. Form, Structure & Function in Plants, Pt. 2. (Current Trends in Life Sciences Ser.: Vol. 8). (Illus.). 150p. 20.00x (ISBN 0-88065-240-3, Pub. by Messers Today & Tommorrow Printers & Publishers). Scholarly Pubns.

Shah, Kirit N. Learn Hindi: Hindi Sikhiye. Parikh, Bharat, ed. LC 82-99946. (Illus.). 192p. (Orig.). 1983. pap. text ed. 9.95 (ISBN 0-9609614-1-0). K N Shah.

Shah, N. S. Water Supply Engineering. 1972. 4.50x o.p. (ISBN 0-210-31171-1). Asia.

Shah, Narayan K., jt. auth. see Worth, Robert M.

Shah, Pravin. Cost Control & Information Systems: A Complete Guide to Effective Design & Implementation. (Illus.). 608p. 1981. 27.50 (ISBN 0-07-056369-1, P&RB). McGraw.

Shah, Ramesh & London, A. L. Laminar Flow Forced Convection in Ducts: Supplement 1 to Advances in Heat Transfer. (Supplement I to Advances in Heat Transfer). 1978. 68.50 (ISBN 0-12-020051-1). Acad Pr.

Shah, Ramesh K., jt. ed. see Kakac, Sadik.

Shah, Y. T. Gas Liquid Solid Reactor Design. 1979. text ed. 68.50 (ISBN 0-07-056370-5, C). McGraw.

Shaha, Rishikesh. Nepali Politics: Retrospect & Prospect. 2nd ed. 1978. 14.95x o.p. (ISBN 0-19-560890-9). Oxford U Pr.

Shahan, Lynn. Living Alone & Liking It. LC 80-53332. 1981. 10.95 (ISBN 0-936906-02-2). Stratford Pr.

Shahan, Robert W. & Mohanty, J. N. Thinking About Being: Aspects of Heidegger's Thought. LC 81-40297. 208p. Date not set. 17.50X (ISBN 0-8061-1780-X). U of Okla Pr.

Shahana, V. A., ed. Focus on Forster's "A Passage to India". Indian Essays in Criticism. 137p. 1975. text ed. 9.00x (ISBN 0-391-01071-9). Humanities.

Shahane, V. A. Leaves of Grass Notes. 80p. (Orig.). 1972. pap. text ed. 2.50 (ISBN 0-8220-0723-1). Cliffs.

Shahane, V. A., ed. Indian Poetry in English: A Critical Assessment. 1981. 14.00x o.p. (ISBN 0-8364-0685-0, Orient Longman). South Asia Bks.

Shahane, V. R., ed. Focus on Forster's "A Passage to India". Indian Essays in Criticism. LC 76-900437. 1976. 9.50x o.p. (ISBN 0-88386-748-6). South Asia Bks.

Shahane, Vasant A. Ruth Prawer Jhabvala. enl. ed. (Indian Writers Ser.: Vol. 11). 1983. 12.00 (ISBN 0-89253-074-X). Ind-US Inc.

Shahastra. From My Heart. (Magical Rainbow Ser.). (Illus.). 32p. (ps-7). 1982. coloring book 2.95 (ISBN 0-911281-02-9). Magical Rainbow.

--Invisible Worlds. (Magical Rainbow Ser.). (Illus.). 52p. 1982. 2.95 (ISBN 0-911281-03-7). Magical Rainbow.

--Magical Rainbow Man. (Magical Rainbow Ser.). (Illus.). 64p. (ps-7). 1982. pap. 8.95 (ISBN 0-911281-00-2). Magical Rainbow.

--Missing Magical Energy. (Magical Rainbow Ser.). (Illus.). 64p. (ps-7). 1982. pap. 8.95 (ISBN 0-686-38241-2). Magical Rainbow.

Shaheen, Esber I. Arabic: English with a Petroleum Accent. 176p. 1978. 29.95x (ISBN 0-87814-043-3). Pennwell Book Division.

--Basic Practice of Chemical Engineering. 1975. text ed. 35.95 (ISBN 0-395-17645-X); solutions manual o.p. 4.35 (ISBN 0-395-18791-5). HM.

Shaher, Reda M. Complete Transposition of the Great Arteries. 1973. 72.50 (ISBN 0-12-638150-X). Acad Pr.

Shahid, Irfan. Omar Khayyam, the Philosopher-Poet of Medieval Islam. LC 82-12023. 32p. 1982. lib. bdg. 5.95 (ISBN 0-87840-022-2). Georgetown U Pr.

Shahid Javed Burki. Pakistan Under Bhutto. LC 78-31358. 1979. 26.00x (ISBN 0-312-59471-2). St Martin.

Shahn, Ben. The Alphabet of Creation: An Ancient Legend from the Zohar. LC 54-11739. (Illus.). 1965. pap. 3.95 (ISBN 0-8052-0359-1). Schocken.

Shaifer, Edward F., jt. auth. see Lifson, Melvin W.

Shain, Henry, jt. auth. see Milberg, Aaron S.

Shain, M. & Longley, D. A Dictionary of Information Technology. 1982. 75.00x (ISBN 0-686-42940-0, Pub. by Macmillan England). State Mutual Bk.

Shain, Martin & Groeneveld, Judith. Employee Assistance Programs: Philosophy, Theory, & Practice. LC 78-20375. 256p. 1980. 25.95x (ISBN 0-669-02737-5). Lexington Bks.

Shain, Martin, et al. Influence, Choice & Drugs: Toward a Systematic Approach to the Prevention of Substance Abuse. LC 77-5230. 160p. 1977. 17.95x o.p. (ISBN 0-669-01597-0). Lexington Bks.

Shain, Merle. Some Men Are More Perfect Than Others. 1979. 9.57i (ISBN 0-397-01360-4). Har-Row.

--When Lovers Are Friends. 1978. 9.57i (ISBN 0-397-01265-9). Har-Row.

Shain, Michael, jt. auth. see Longley, Dennis.

Shainberg, Diane. Healing in Psychotherapy: The Process of Holistic Change. 170p. 1983. 37.50 (ISBN 0-677-06100-5). Gordon.

Sha'ked, Ami. Human Sexuality & Rehabilitation Medicine: Sequel Functioning Following Equal Card Injury. 288p. 1981. 25.00 (ISBN 0-683-07749-X). Williams & Wilkins.

Shaked, Gerson, jt. ed. see Lelchuk, Alan.

Shaked, Haim, jt. ed. see Legum, Colin.

Shaked, Shaul, tr. Wisdom of the Sasanian Sages: Denkard Book Six. (Bibliotheca Persica: Persian Heritage Ser.: No. 36). 1979. lib. bdg. 50.00 (ISBN 0-89158-376-9). Westview.

--Wisdom of the Sasanian Sages: Denkard Book VI. LC 79-2957. (Persian Heritage Ser.). 400p. 1983. 50.00x (ISBN 0-89158-376-9). Caravan Bks.

Shakely, Lauren, ed. see Husband, Timothy & Gilmore-House, Gloria.

Shakepeare & Donne. Shakespeare's "Sonnets". Bd. with The Love Poems of John Donne. 128p. 160p. 1982. Deluxe boxed set. 17.95 (ISBN 0-312-74500-1). St Martin.

Shaker, Peggy, ed. see Hendricks, Evan.

Shakespear, William. Four Great Tragedies: Hamlet, Othello, King Lear & Macbeth. 1982. pap. 4.50 (ISBN 0-451-51638-9, CE1638, Sig Classics). NAL.

Shakespeare, William. All's Well That Ends Well. Quiller-Couch, Arthur, et al, eds. (New Shakespeare Ser). 23.95 (ISBN 0-521-07525-4); pap. 4.95x (ISBN 0-521-09468-2). Cambridge U Pr.

--All's Well That Ends Well. pap. 1.95 (ISBN 0-451-51657-5, CJ1657, Sig Classics). NAL.

--All's Well That Ends Well. rev. ed. Harbage, Alfred, ed. (Shakespeare Ser.). 1965. pap. 2.95 (ISBN 0-14-071430-8). Penguin.

--Anthony & Cleopatra. Quiller-Couch, Arthur, et al, eds. (New Shakespeare Ser). 23.95 o.p. (ISBN 0-521-07526-2); pap. 4.95x (ISBN 0-521-09469-0). Cambridge U Pr.

--Antony & Cleopatra. Ridley, M. R., ed. (Arden Shakespeare Ser.). 278p. 1954. 30.00x (ISBN 0-416-47290-7); pap. 5.95 (ISBN 0-416-47630-9). Methuen Inc.

--Antony & Cleopatra. Everett, B., ed. pap. 2.25 (ISBN 0-451-51772-5, CE1772, Sig Classics). NAL.

--Antony & Cleopatra. rev. ed. Kittredge, George L. & Ribner, Irving, eds. 1966. pap. 4.50x o.p. (ISBN 0-471-00508-8). Wiley.

--As You Like It. Quiller-Couch, Arthur, et al, eds. (New Shakespeare Ser). 1968. 23.95 o.p. (ISBN 0-521-07527-0); pap. 4.95x (ISBN 0-521-09470-4). Cambridge U Pr.

--As You Like It. 2nd ed. Latham, Agnes, ed. LC 75-2896. (Arden Shakespeare Ser.). 224p. 1975. 30.00x (ISBN 0-416-17830-8); pap. 5.95 (ISBN 0-416-17840-5). Methuen Inc.

--As You Like It. Gilman, Albert, ed. pap. 1.95 (ISBN 0-451-51667-2, CJ1667, Sig Classics). NAL.

--Comedy of Errors. rev. ed. Quiller-Couch, Arthur, et al, eds. (New Shakespeare Ser). 1968. 24.95 (ISBN 0-521-07528-9); pap. 4.95x (ISBN 0-521-09471-2). Cambridge U Pr.

--Comedy of Errors. Levin, Harry, ed. pap. 2.25 (ISBN 0-451-51742-3, CE1742, Sig Classics). NAL.

--Comedy of Errors. rev. ed. Kittredge, George L. & Ribner, Irving, eds. 1966. pap. 3.95x o.p. (ISBN 0-471-00530-4). Wiley.

--Complete Works. Craig, W. J., ed. (Oxford Standard Authors Ser). (Illus.). 1943. 15.95 (ISBN 0-19-254174-9). Oxford U Pr.

--Coriolanus. Quiller-Couch, Arthur, et al, eds. (New Shakespeare Ser). 1969. 24.95 (ISBN 0-521-07529-7); pap. 4.95x (ISBN 0-521-09472-0). Cambridge U Pr.

--Coriolanus. Brockbank, Phillip, ed. LC 76-9167. (Arden Shakespeare Ser.). 300p. 1976. 30.00x (ISBN 0-416-17870-7); pap. 5.95 (ISBN 0-416-17880-4). Methuen Inc.

--Coriolanus. Brower, Reuben, ed. pap. 2.25 (ISBN 0-451-51576-5, CJ1576, Sig Classics). NAL.

--Coriolanus. 1967. pap. text ed. 3.50x o.p. (ISBN 0-471-00538-X). Wiley.

--Cymbeline. Quiller-Couch, Arthur, et al, eds. (New Shakespeare Ser). 1968. 24.95 (ISBN 0-521-07530-0); pap. 4.95x (ISBN 0-521-09473-9). Cambridge U Pr.

--Four Great Comedies. 1982. pap. 4.50 (ISBN 0-451-51693-1, CE1693, Sig Classics). NAL.

--Hamlet. Quiller-Couch, Arthur, et al, eds. (New Shakespeare Ser). 24.95 (ISBN 0-521-07531-9); pap. 4.95x (ISBN 0-521-09474-7). Cambridge U Pr.

--Hamlet, 2 Vols. new variorum ed. Furness, Horace H., ed. pap. 5.50 ea. o.p.; Vol. 1. pap. (ISBN 0-486-21004-9); Vol. 2. pap. (ISBN 0-486-21005-7). Dover.

--Hamlet. Harrison, George B., ed. LC 62-21849. 1963. pap. 1.85 o.p. (ISBN 0-15-638410-8, Harv). HarBraceJ.

--Hamlet. Mack, Maynard & Boynton, Robert W., eds. LC 82-14753. (Shakespeare Ser). (Illus.). 192p. (gr. 10-12). 1981. pap. text ed. 2.25x (ISBN 0-86709-019-7). Boynton Cook Pubs.

--Hamlet. Barnet, Sylvan, ed. pap. 1.95 (ISBN 0-451-51763-6, CJ1763, Sig Classics). NAL.

--Hamlet. Wright, Louis B. & LaMar, Virginia, eds. (Folger Lib. Ser). (Illus.). 352p. (gr. 12 up). 1958. pap. text ed. 2.95 (ISBN 0-671-44721-1). WSP.

--Hamlet. Jenkins, Harold, ed. (Arden Shakespeare Ser.). 1982. 30.00x (ISBN 0-416-17910-X); pap. 8.95 (ISBN 0-416-17920-7). Methuen Inc.

--Henry Eighth. Quiller-Couch, Arthur, et al, eds. (New Shakespeare Ser.). 1969. 23.95 o.p. (ISBN 0-521-07538-6); pap. 4.95 (ISBN 0-521-09481-X). Cambridge U Pr.

--Henry Fifth. Quiller-Couch, Arthur, et al, eds. (New Shakespeare Ser.). 24.95 (ISBN 0-521-07534-3); pap. 4.95x (ISBN 0-521-09477-1). Cambridge U Pr.

--Henry Fifth. Brown, John R., ed. pap. 1.95 (ISBN 0-451-51575-7, CJ1575, Sig Classics). NAL.

--Henry Fifth. Wright, Louis B. & LaMar, Virginia A., eds. (Folger Lib.). 304p. (gr. 11-12). pap. text ed. 2.95 (ISBN 0-671-41519-0). WSP.

--Henry Fourth, Pt. 1. Quiller-Couch, Arthur, et al, eds. (New Shakespeare Ser.). 24.95 (ISBN 0-521-07532-7); pap. 4.95x (ISBN 0-521-09475-5). Cambridge U Pr.

--Henry Fourth, Pt. 1. Mack, Maynard, ed. pap. 1.95 (ISBN 0-451-51535-8, CJ1535, Sig Classics). NAL.

--Henry Fourth, Pt. 1. rev. ed. Sanderson, James L., ed. (Critical Editions Ser.). (Annotated). (gr. 9-12). 1969. text ed. 5.00 (ISBN 0-393-04234-0); pap. text ed. 6.95x (ISBN 0-393-09554-1, 9554, NortonC). Norton.

--Henry Fourth, Pt. 2. Quiller-Couch, Arthur, et al, eds. (New Shakespeare Ser.). 24.95 (ISBN 0-521-07533-5); pap. 4.95x (ISBN 0-521-09476-3). Cambridge U Pr.

--Henry Fourth, Pt. 2. Holland, Norman N., ed. pap. 2.50 (ISBN 0-451-51722-9, CE1722, Sig Classics). NAL.

--Henry Sixth, Pt. 1. Quiller-Couch, Arthur, et al, eds. (New Shakespeare Ser). 1968. 24.95 (ISBN 0-521-07535-1); pap. 4.95x (ISBN 0-521-09478-X). Cambridge U Pr.

--Henry Sixth, Pt. 1. Ryan, Lawrence V., ed. pap. 3.50 (ISBN 0-451-51705-9, CE1705, Sig Classics). NAL.

--Henry Sixth, Pt. 2. Quiller-Couch, Arthur, et al, eds. (New Shakespeare Ser). 1968. 24.95 (ISBN 0-521-07536-X); pap. 4.95x (ISBN 0-521-09479-8). Cambridge U Pr.

--Henry Sixth, Pt. 3. Quiller-Couch, Arthur, et al, eds. (New Shakespeare Ser). 1968. 24.95 (ISBN 0-521-07537-8); pap. 4.95x (ISBN 0-521-09480-1). Cambridge U Pr.

--Henry V. 1967. pap. text ed. 3.95x o.p. (ISBN 0-471-00519-3). Wiley.

--Julius Caesar. Quiller-Couch, Arthur, et al, eds. (New Shakespeare Ser). 1968. 24.95 (ISBN 0-521-07539-4); pap. 4.95x (ISBN 0-521-09482-8). Cambridge U Pr.

--Julius Caesar. Mack, Maynard & Boynton, Robert W., eds. LC 82-14755. (Shakespeare Ser). (Illus.). 160p. (gr. 10-12). 1981. pap. text ed. 2.25x (ISBN 0-86709-023-5). Boynton Cook Pubs.

--Julius Caesar. Barnet, Sylvan, ed. pap. 1.95 (ISBN 0-451-51785-7, CJ1785, Sig Classics). NAL.

--Julius Caesar. Kittredge, George L. & Ribner, Irving, eds. 1966. pap. 6.95x (ISBN 0-673-15700-8). Scott F.

--Julius Caesar. Wright, Louis B. & LaMar, Virginia, eds. 240p. pap. 2.25 (ISBN 0-671-45914-7). WSP.

--King Henry Eighth. Foakes, R. A., ed. (Arden Shakespeare Ser.). 1957. 30.00x (ISBN 0-416-47230-3); pap. 5.95 (ISBN 0-416-10450-9). Methuen Inc.

--King Henry Fourth, Pt. 1. rev. 6th ed. Humphreys, Arthur R., ed. (Arden Shakespeare Ser.). 1960. Repr. of 1960 ed. 30.00x (ISBN 0-416-47420-9); pap. 5.95 (ISBN 0-416-47660-0). Methuen Inc.

--King Henry Fourth, Pt. 2. Humphresy, A. R., ed. (Arden Shakespeare Ser.). 242p. 1966. 30.00x (ISBN 0-416-47430-6); pap. 5.95 (ISBN 0-416-49640-7). Methuen Inc.

--King Henry Sixth, Pt. 1. 3rd rev. ed. Cairncross, Andrew S., ed. (Arden Shakespeare Ser.). 1962. 30.00x (ISBN 0-416-47200-1); pap. 7.95x (ISBN 0-416-27840-X). Methuen Inc.

--King Henry Sixth, Pt. 3. 3rd rev. ed. Cairncross, Andrew S., ed. (Arden Shakespeare Ser.). 1965. 30.00x (ISBN 0-416-47220-6); pap. 7.95 (ISBN 0-416-27910-4). Methuen Inc.

--King John. Quiller-Couch, Arthur, et al, eds. (New Shakespeare Ser). 1969. 23.95 o.p. (ISBN 0-521-07540-8); pap. 4.95x (ISBN 0-521-09483-6). Cambridge U Pr.

--King John. Matchett, William M., ed. pap. 1.95 (ISBN 0-451-51399-1, CJ1399, Sig Classics). NAL.

--King Lear. Quiller-Couch, Arthur, et al, eds. (New Shakespeare Ser). 1968. 23.95 o.p. (ISBN 0-521-07541-6); pap. 4.95x (ISBN 0-521-09484-4). Cambridge U Pr.

--King Lear. Muir, Kenneth, ed. (Arden Shakespeare Ser.). 1972. 30.00x (ISBN 0-416-76110-0); pap. 5.95 (ISBN 0-416-10170-4). Methuen Inc.

--King Lear. Fraser, Russell, ed. pap. 2.25 (ISBN 0-451-51768-7, CE1768, Sig Classics). NAL.

--King Lear. Kittredge, George L. & Ribner, Irving, eds. 1967. pap. 6.95x (ISBN 0-673-15709-1). Scott F.

--King Richard the Third. Hammond, Antony, ed. (Arden Shakespeare Ser.). 1982. 30.00x (ISBN 0-416-17970-3); pap. 6.95 (ISBN 0-416-17980-0). Methuen Inc.

--Love Poems & Sonnets of William Shakespeare. LC 57-11411. 1957. 8.95 (ISBN 0-385-01733-2). Doubleday.

--Love's Labor's Lost. pap. 2.50 (ISBN 0-451-51773-3, CE1773, Sig Classics). NAL.

--Love's Labour's Lost. Quiller-Couch, Arthur, et al, eds. (New Shakespeare Ser). (Illus.). 1969. 24.95 (ISBN 0-521-07542-4); pap. 4.95x (ISBN 0-521-09485-2). Cambridge U Pr.

--Macbeth. Quiller-Couch, Arthur, et al, eds. (New Shakespeare Ser.). 23.95 o.p. (ISBN 0-521-07543-2); pap. 4.95x (ISBN 0-521-09486-0). Cambridge U Pr.

--Macbeth. Harrison, George B., ed. LC 62-21851. 1963. pap. 1.45 o.p. (ISBN 0-15-654998-0, Harv). HarBraceJ.

--Macbeth. Mack, Maynard & Boynton, Robert W., eds. LC 82-14754. (Shakespeare Ser.). (gr. 10-12). 1981. pap. text ed. 2.25x (ISBN 0-86709-021-9). Boynton Cook Pubs.

--Macbeth. 9th ed. Muir, Kenneth, ed. (Arden Shakespeare Ser.). 1956. 30.00x (ISBN 0-416-47320-2); pap. 5.95 (ISBN 0-416-10160-7). Methuen Inc.

--Measure for Measure. Quiller-Couch, Arthur, et al, eds. (New Shakespeare Ser.). 1969. 23.95 o.p. (ISBN 0-521-07544-0); pap. 4.95x (ISBN 0-521-09487-9). Cambridge U Pr.

--Measure for Measure. rev. ed. Kittredge, George L. & Ribner, Irving, eds. 1967. pap. 3.95x o.p. (ISBN 0-471-00536-3). Wiley.

--Merchant of Venice. Quiller-Couch, Arthur, et al, eds. (New Shakespeare Ser). 24.95 (ISBN 0-521-07545-9); pap. 4.95x (ISBN 0-521-09488-7). Cambridge U Pr.

--Merchant of Venice. 1974. pap. 2.25 (ISBN 0-451-51598-6, CE1598, Sig Classics). NAL.

--Merry Wives of Windsor. Quiller-Couch, Arthur, et al, eds. (New Shakespeare Ser). 1969. 24.95 (ISBN 0-521-07546-7); pap. 4.95x (ISBN 0-521-09489-5). Cambridge U Pr.

--Merry Wives of Windsor. Oliver, H. J., ed. (Arden Shakespeare Ser.). 1971. 30.00x (ISBN 0-416-47690-2); pap. 6.95 (ISBN 0-416-17780-8). Methuen Inc.

--Merry Wives of Windsor. rev. ed. Kittredge, George L. & Ribner, Irving, eds. LC 69-15381. 1969. pap. 3.95x o.p. (ISBN 0-471-00533-9). Wiley.

--A Midsummer Night's Dream. Shrimpton, Nick, ed. (Plays in Performance). (Illus.). 176p. 1983. text ed. 19.50x (ISBN 0-389-20178-2). B&N Imports.

--Midsummer Night's Dream. Quiller-Couch, Arthur, et al, eds. (New Shakespeare Ser). 24.95 (ISBN 0-521-07547-5); pap. 4.95x (ISBN 0-521-09490-9). Cambridge U Pr.

--Midsummer Night's Dream. Cleman, Wolfgang, ed. pap. 1.95 (ISBN 0-451-51619-2, CJ1619, Sig Classics). NAL.

--Much Ado About Nothing. Quiller-Couch, Arthur, et al, eds. (New Shakespeare Ser). 1969. 24.95 (ISBN 0-521-07548-3); pap. 4.95x (ISBN 0-521-09491-7). Cambridge U Pr.

--Much Ado About Nothing. new variorum ed. Furness, Horace H., ed. pap. 4.00 o.p. (ISBN 0-486-21187-8). Dover.

--Much Ado About Nothing. rev. ed. Kittredge, George L. & Ribner, Irving, eds. 1967. pap. 4.50x o.p. (ISBN 0-471-00524-X). Wiley.

--Othello. Quiller-Couch, Arthur, et al, eds. (New Shakespeare Ser). 1969. 23.95 o.p. (ISBN 0-521-07549-1); pap. 4.95x (ISBN 0-521-09492-5). Cambridge U Pr.

--Othello. rev. 7th ed. Ridley, M. R., ed. (Arden Shakespeare Ser.). 1965. 30.00x (ISBN 0-416-47440-3); pap. 5.95 (ISBN 0-416-47650-3). Methuen Inc.

--Othello. Kernan, Alvin, ed. pap. 2.95 (ISBN 0-451-51740-7, CE1740, Sig Classics). NAL.

--Pericles. Quiller-Couch, Arthur, et al, eds. (New Shakespeare Ser). 1969. 24.95 (ISBN 0-521-07550-5); pap. 4.95x (ISBN 0-521-09494-1). Cambridge U Pr.

--Pericles. 3rd ed. Hoeniger, F. D., ed. (Arden Shakespeare Ser.). 1963. 30.00x (ISBN 0-416-47570-1); pap. 6.95 (ISBN 0-416-27850-7). Methuen Inc.

--Poems. Quiller-Couch, Arthur, et al, eds. (New Shakespeare Ser). 1969. 23.95 o.p. (ISBN 0-521-07551-3); pap. 4.95x (ISBN 0-521-09493-3). Cambridge U Pr.

--Poems. 3rd ed. Prince, F. T., ed. (Arden Shakespeare Ser.). 1969. Repr. of 1960 ed. 30.00x (ISBN 0-416-47610-4); pap. 6.95 (ISBN 0-416-27870-1). Methuen Inc.

--Richard Second. Quiller-Couch, Arthur, et al, eds. (New Shakespeare Ser). 24.95 (ISBN 0-521-07552-1); pap. 4.95x (ISBN 0-521-09495-X). Cambridge U Pr.

--Richard Third. Quiller-Couch, Arthur, et al, eds. LC 68-133495. (New Shakespeare Ser). 1968. 23.95 o.p. (ISBN 0-521-07553-X); pap. 4.95x (ISBN 0-521-09496-8). Cambridge U Pr.

--Richard Third. Eccles, Mark, ed. pap. 2.50 (ISBN 0-451-51728-8, CE1728, Sig Classics). NAL.

--The Riverside Shakespeare. Evans, G. Blakemore, et al, eds. 1728p. 1974. text ed. 24.95 (ISBN 0-395-04402-2). HM.

--The Riverside Shakespeare. Evans, Cruynne, ed. 1974. 22.95 (ISBN 0-686-97265-1). HM.

--Romeo & Juliet. Quiller-Couch, Arthur, et al, eds. (New Shakespeare Ser). 1969. 24.95 (ISBN 0-521-07554-8); pap. 4.95x (ISBN 0-521-09497-6). Cambridge U Pr.

--Romeo & Juliet. 1980. 30.00x (ISBN 0-416-17850-2); pap. 4.95 (ISBN 0-416-17860-X). Methuen Inc.

--Romeo & Juliet. Bryant, Joseph, ed. pap. 1.95 (ISBN 0-451-51635-4, CJ1635, Sig Classics, L1040). NAL.

--Romeo & Juliet. LC 82-48874. (Illus.). 136p. Date not set. 8.95 (ISBN 0-394-53027-6). Knopf. Postponed.

--Shakespeare Simplified. Davidson, Diane, ed. Incl. Vol. 1. Macbeth. LC 79-65834 (ISBN 0-934048-03-7). pap. (ISBN 0-934048-02-9); Vol. 2. Julius Caesar. LC 79-65835 (ISBN 0-934048-05-3). pap. (ISBN 0-934048-04-5); Vol. 3. Romeo & Juliet. LC 79-65836 (ISBN 0-934048-07-X). pap. (ISBN 0-934048-06-1); Vol. 4. Merchant of Venice. LC 79-65837 (ISBN 0-934048-09-6). pap. (ISBN 0-934048-08-8); Vol. 5. Midsummer Night's Dream. LC 79-65838 (ISBN 0-934048-11-8). pap. (ISBN 0-934048-10-X); Vol. 6. Hamlet. LC 79-65884 (ISBN 0-934048-13-4). pap. (ISBN 0-934048-12-6). 1983. casebound ea. 7.95 (ISBN 0-686-37767-2); pap. 3.95 ea. (ISBN 0-686-37768-0). Swan Books.

--Shakespeare's Plays in Quarto: A Facsimilie Edition of Copies Primarily from the Henry E. Huntington Library. Allen, Michael J. & Muir, Kenneth, eds. LC 81-40322. 936p. 1982. 125.00x (ISBN 0-520-04077-5). U of Cal Pr.

--Sonnets. Quiller-Couch, Arthur, et al, eds. (New Shakespeare Ser). 1969. 23.95 o.p. (ISBN 0-521-07555-6); pap. 4.95x (ISBN 0-521-09498-4). Cambridge U Pr.

--Sonnets. Rollins, Hyder E., ed. LC 51-6753. (Crofts Classics Ser.). 1950. pap. text ed. 0.85x o.p. (ISBN 0-88295-082-7). Harlan Davidson.

--Sonnets. Bush, Douglas & Harbage, Alfred, eds. (Shakespeare Ser.). (YA) (gr. 9 up). 1963. pap. 2.95 (ISBN 0-14-071423-5, Pelican). Penguin.

--The Sonnets of William Shakespeare: The Royal Shakespeare Theatre Edition. 170p. 1982. 16.00 (ISBN 0-85683-013-5, Pub by Shepheard-Walwyn England). Flatiron Book.

--Taming of the Shrew. Quiller-Couch, Arthur, et al, eds. (New Shakespeare Ser). 24.95 (ISBN 0-521-07556-4); pap. 4.95x (ISBN 0-521-09499-2). Cambridge U Pr.

--Taming of the Shrew. Heilman, Robert, ed. pap. 2.25 (ISBN 0-451-51637-0, CE1637, Sig Classics). NAL.

--Taming of the Shrew. Wright, Louis B. & LaMar, Virginia A., eds. (Folger Library). (Illus.). 272p. (gr. 11 up). 1963. pap. text ed. 2.50 (ISBN 0-671-45751-9). WSP.

--Taming of the Shrew. Morris, Brian, ed. 1982. 30.00x (ISBN 0-416-47580-9); pap. 6.95 (ISBN 0-416-17800-6). Methuen Inc.

--Tempest. Quiller-Couch, Arthur, et al, eds. (New Shakespeare Ser). 1969. 23.95 o.p. (ISBN 0-521-07557-2); pap. 4.95x (ISBN 0-521-09500-X). Cambridge U Pr.

--Tempest. 6th ed. Kermode, Frank, ed. (Arden Shakespeare Ser.). 1962. Repr. of 1958 ed. 30.00x (ISBN 0-416-47360-1); pap. 5.95 (ISBN 0-416-10190-9). Methuen Inc.

--Tempest. Langbaum, Robert, ed. pap. 1.95 (ISBN 0-451-51562-5, CJ1562, Sig Classics). NAL.

--The Tempest. Wright, Louis B. & La Mar, Virginia A., eds. (Folger Library Ser.). 216p. pap. 1.95 (ISBN 0-686-37066-X). WSP.

--Timon of Athens. Quiller-Couch, Arthur, et al, eds. (New Shakespeare Ser). 23.95 o.p. (ISBN 0-521-07558-0); pap. 4.95x (ISBN 0-521-09501-8). Cambridge U Pr.

--Timon of Athens. Date not set. pap. 2.50 (ISBN 0-451-51640-0, CE1640, Sig Classics). NAL.

--Timon of Athens. rev. ed. Hinman, Charlton, ed. (Shakespeare Ser.). 1982. pap. 2.95 (ISBN 0-14-071429-4, Pelican). Penguin.

--Titus Andronicus. Quiller-Couch, Arthur, et al, eds. LC 68-133497. (New Shakespeare Ser). 1968. 24.95 (ISBN 0-521-07559-9); pap. 4.95x (ISBN 0-521-09502-6). Cambridge U Pr.

--Titus Andronicus, Pericles & Two Noble Kinsman. pap. 3.95 (ISBN 0-451-51639-7, CE1639, Sig Classics). NAL.

--Troilus & Cressida. Quiller-Couch, Arthur, et al, eds. (New Shakespeare Ser). 1969. 23.95 (ISBN 0-521-07560-2); pap. 4.95x (ISBN 0-521-09503-4). Cambridge U Pr.

--Troilus & Cressida. Seltzer, D., ed. 1974. pap. 2.25 (ISBN 0-451-51697-4, CE1697, Sig Classics). NAL.

--Troilus & Cressida. Palmer, Kenneth, ed. (Arden Shakespeare Ser.). 1982. 30.00x (ISBN 0-416-47680-5); pap. 6.95 (ISBN 0-416-17790-5). Methuen Inc.

--Twelfth Night. Quiller-Couch, Arthur, et al, eds. (New Shakespeare Ser). 1968. 23.95 o.p. (ISBN 0-521-07561-0); pap. 4.95x (ISBN 0-521-09504-2). Cambridge U Pr.

--Twelfth Night. Lothian, J. M. & Craik, T. W., eds. (Arden Shakespeare Ser.). 1975. 30.00x (ISBN 0-416-17950-9); pap. 4.95 (ISBN 0-416-17960-6). Methuen Inc.

--Twelfth Night. pap. 2.25 (ISBN 0-451-51774-1, CE1774, Sig Classics). NAL.

--Twelfth Night. Wright, Louis B. & La Mar, Virginia A., eds. (Folger Library Ser.). 256p. pap. 2.50 (ISBN 0-671-45752-7). WSP.

--Two Gentlemen of Verona. Quiller-Couch, Arthur, et al, eds. (New Shakespeare Ser). 1969. 23.95 o.p. (ISBN 0-521-07562-9); pap. 4.95x (ISBN 0-521-09505-0). Cambridge U Pr.

--Two Gentlemen of Verona. Date not set. pap. 2.50 (ISBN 0-451-51649-4, CE1649, Sig Classics). NAL.
--Two Gentlemen of Verona. Wright, Louis B. & La Mar, Virginia A., eds. (Folger Library). 224p. (gr. 10 up). 1983. pap. 1.95 (ISBN 0-671-49113-X). WSP.
--When Daisies Pied, & Violets Blue. (Illus.). 32p. (gr. 1-3). 1974. 5.95 o.p. (ISBN 0-698-20286-4, Coward). Putnam Pub Group.
--Winter's Tale. Quiller-Couch, Arthur, et al, eds. (New Shakespeare Ser). 1968. 23.95 o.p. (ISBN 0-521-07563-7); pap. 4.95x (ISBN 0-521-09506-9). Cambridge U Pr.
--Winter's Tale. Kermode, Frank, ed. 1974. pap. 2.50 (ISBN 0-451-51700-8, CE1700, Sig Classics). NAL.
Shakespeare, William see Allen, W. S.
Shakespeare, William see Swan, D. K.
Shakespeare, William, ed. see Muir, Kenneth.
Shakespeare, William, jt. ed. see Oliver, H. J.
Shakhashiri, Bassam Z., et al. Chemical Demonstrations: A Handbook for Teachers of Chemistry, Vol. 1. LC 81-70016. (Illus.). 256p. 1983. 25.00 (ISBN 0-299-08890-1). U of Wis Pr.
Shakhnazarov, G. Futurology Fiasco. 230p. 1982. 6.50 (ISBN 0-8285-2275-8, Pub. by Progress Pubs USSR). Imported Pubns.
Shakibi, Jami G. & Liebson, Philip R., eds. Cardiology Review. 3nd. ed. 1981. pap. 25.00 (ISBN 0-87488-337-7). Med Exam.
Shakir, M. H., tr. Holy Qur'an. 660p. (Eng. & Arabic.). 1982. 15.00 (ISBN 0-940368-17-X); pap. 7.96 (ISBN 0-940368-16-1). Tahrike Tarsile Quran.
Shakman, Robert A. Poison-Proof Your Body. 192p. 1980. 12.95 o.p. (ISBN 0-87000-478-6, Arlington Hse). Crown.
Shakow, David. Adaptation in Schizophrenia: The Theory of Segmental Set. LC 79-14979. (Personality Processes Ser.). 245p. 1979. 32.95 (ISBN 0-471-05756-8, Pub. by Wiley-Interscience). Wiley.
Shaku, Soyen. Zen for Americans: Including the Sutra of Forty-Two Chapters. Suzuki, D. T., tr. 226p. 1974. lib. bdg. 15.50x (ISBN 0-87548-279-1); pap. 6.00x (ISBN 0-87548-273-2). Open Court.
Shale, Richard. Academy Awards: An Ungar Reference Index. 2nd ed. (Ungar Film Library Ser.). (Illus.). 650p. 1983. 28.50 (ISBN 0-8044-2813-1); pap. 14.50 (ISBN 0-8044-6861-3). Ungar.
Shales, Tom. On the Air! 1982. 14.95 (ISBN 0-671-44203-1). Summit Bks.
Shaliapin, Fedor I. Man & Mask: Forty Years in the Life of a Singer. Megroz, Phyllis, tr. from Fr. LC 70-109841. (Illus.). xxvi, 358p. Repr. of 1932 ed. lib. bdg. 19.00x (ISBN 0-8371-4332-2, SHMM). Greenwood.
Shalit, Nathan. Cup & Saucer Chemistry. (Elephant Bks). 96p. (gr. 3-6). 1974. pap. 2.95 o.s.i. (ISBN 0-448-11690-1, G&D). Putnam Pub Group.
Shallcross, Doris & Sisk, Dorothy. The Growing Person: How to Encourage Healthy Emotional Development in Children. (Illus.). 179p. 1982. 13.95 (ISBN 0-13-367847-4); pap. 5.95 (ISBN 0-13-367839-3). P-H.
Shalom, Stephen R. The Human Costs of Chinese Communism: Propaganda Versus Reality. (Occasional Paper Arizona State Univ., Center for Asian Studies Ser.: No. 15). 200p. 1983. pap. 4.00 (ISBN 0-939252-11-2). ASU Ctr Asian.
--Socialist Visions. 350p. 1982. 20.00 (ISBN 0-89608-170-2); pap. 7.50 (ISBN 0-89608-169-9). South End Pr.
Shama, Avraham, ed. see Farhar-Pilgrim, Barbara & Unseld, Charles T.
Shamai, Ruth, tr. see Muir, John.
Shaman, Harvey. The View Camera: Operations & Techniques. LC 75-42770. (Illus.). 128p. 1977. pap. 9.95 (ISBN 0-8174-0598-4, Amphoto). Watson-Guptill.
Shaman, Margaret & Wilson, Derek. The Illustrated Book of World History. (Illus.). 1978. 14.95 o.p. (ISBN 0-8467-0532-X, Pub. by Two Continents). Hippocrene Bks.
Shaman, Sanford S. The Contemporary American Potter: Recent Vessels. LC 80-50438. (Illus.). 24p. (Orig.). 1980. pap. text ed. 3.00 o.p. (ISBN 0-932660-03-7). U of NI Dept Art.
Shambaugh, George & Shea, John J. Proceedings of the Shambaugh Fifth International Workshop on Middle Ear Microsurgery and Fluctant Hearing Loss. LC 77-79552. 1977. 35.00 o.p. (ISBN 0-87397-125-6). Strode.
Shamberger, Raymond J. Biochemistry of Selenium. (Biochemistry of the Elements Ser.: Vol. 2). 346p. 1983. 42.50x (ISBN 0-306-41090-7, Plenum Pr). Plenum Pub.
Shamburger, Page, jt. auth. see Christy, Joe.
Shame, George H. & Egolf, Donald B. Operant Conditioning & the Management of Stuttering: A Book for Clinicians. 250p. 1976. 19.95 o.p. (ISBN 0-13-637322-4). P-H.
Shames, jt. auth. see Botvinick.
Shames, George H. & Florance, Cheri L. Stutter-Free Speech: A Goal for Therapy. (Special Education Ser.). 184p. (Orig.). 1980. pap. text ed. 15.95 (ISBN 0-675-08178-5). Merrill.
Shames, George H. & Wiig, Elisabeth H. Human Communication Disorders: An Introduction. 544p. 1982. pap. text ed. 24.95 (ISBN 0-675-09837-8). Additional supplements may be obtained from publisher. Merrill.
Shames, I. Engineering Mechanics, 2 vols. 3rd ed. 1980. Vol. 1, Statics. 25.95 (ISBN 0-13-279141-2); Vol. 2, Dynamics. 25.95 (ISBN 0-13-279158-7); combined ed. 36.95 (ISBN 0-13-279166-8). P-H.
Shames, I. H. Mechanics of Fluids. 2nd ed. 768p. 1982. 31.95x (ISBN 0-07-056385-3); solutions manual 15.00 (ISBN 0-07-056386-1). McGraw.
Shames, Irving H. Introduction to Solid Mechanics. (Illus.). 688p. 1975. ref. ed. 31.95 (ISBN 0-13-497503-0). P-H.
--Mechanics of Deformable Solids. LC 79-17373. 544p. 1979. Repr. of 1964 ed. lib. bdg. 26.50 (ISBN 0-89874-013-4). Krieger.
--Mechanics of Fluids. 1962. text ed. 32.50 (ISBN 0-07-056390-X, C); solutions manual 25.00 (ISBN 0-07-056391-8). McGraw.
Shamir, Ruth. All Our Vows. LC 82-61795. 1983. 11.95 (ISBN 0-88400-090-7). Shengold.
Shamma, jt. auth. see Byrkit.
Shampo, M. A., jt. auth. see Kyle, R. A.
Shamuyarira, Nathan. Crisis in Rhodesia. 1965. 9.95 o.p. (ISBN 0-685-20570-3). Transatlantic.
--Liberation Movements in Southern Africa. (Hans Wolff Memorial Lecture Ser.). 38p. (Orig.). 1978. pap. text ed. 3.00 (ISBN 0-941934-21-7). Ind U Afro-Amer Arts..
Shan, Han. The White Crane Has No Mourners. Hardesty, Jim & Tobias, Art, trs. Bd. with Honking Geese. Basho & Etsujin. Terasaki, Etsuko & Jorgensen, Rich, trs.. 1978. pap. 3.00 (ISBN 0-686-37611-0). Stone Pr Calif.
Shanahan, Louise, jt. auth. see Rue, James.
Shanahan, Louise, jt. auth. see Rue, James J.
Shanahan, William F. Arco's Guide to Apprenticeship Programs. (Arco Occupational Guides Ser.). 216p. 1983. lib. bdg. 12.95 (ISBN 0-668-05454-9); pap. 6.95 (ISBN 0-668-05461-1). Arco.
--College: Yes or No? The High School Student's Career Decision-Making Handbook. LC 82-6775. 256p. (gr. 9 up). 1983. lib. bdg. 12.95 (ISBN 0-668-05589-8); pap. 7.95 (ISBN 0-668-05590-1). Arco.
--Resumes for Engineers: A Resume Preparation & Job-Getting Guide. 128p. 1983. lib. bdg. 11.95 (ISBN 0-668-05664-9); pap. 6.95 (ISBN 0-668-05668-1). Arco.
--Your Career in Engineering. LC 80-24731. (Arco's Career Guidance Ser.). (Illus.). 176p. 1981. lib. bdg. 7.95 (ISBN 0-668-05195-7); pap. 4.50 (ISBN 0-668-05201-5). Arco.
Shand, Errol B. Glass Engineering Handbook. 2nd ed. 1958. 45.00 o.p. (ISBN 0-07-056395-0, P&RB). McGraw.
Shand, G. B., jt. ed. see Shady, Raymond C.
Shandler, Michael & Shandler, Nina. The Complete Guide to Raising Your Child & Cookbook for Raising Your Child as a Vegetarian. 384p. 1982. pap. 3.50 (ISBN 0-345-30685-6). Ballantine.
Shandler, Michael, jt. auth. see Shandler, Nina.
Shandler, Nina & Shandler, Michael. Yoga for Pregnancy & Birth: A Guide for Expectant Parents. LC 78-21099. (Illus.). 1979. text ed. 11.95x o.p. (ISBN 0-8052-3704-6); pap. 5.95 (ISBN 0-8052-0612-4). Schocken.
Shandler, Nina, jt. auth. see Shandler, Michael.
Shandong Medical College. Anatomical Atlas of Chinese Acupuncture Points. (Illus.). 265p. 1982. 50.00 (ISBN 0-8351-0954-2). China Bks.
Shane, Alex M. The Life & Work of Evgenij Zamjatin. LC 68-19643. 1968. 38.50x (ISBN 0-520-01164-3). U of Cal Pr.
Shane, Don G., jt. auth. see Van Osdol, William R.
Shane, Donea L. Returning to School: A Guide for Nurses. 320p. 1983. text ed. 18.95 (ISBN 0-13-779165-8); pap. 14.95 (ISBN 0-13-779157-7). P-H.
Shane, Harold, jt. auth. see Shane, Ruth.
Shane, Ruth & Shane, Harold. The New Baby. LC 79-10844. (Illus.). (ps-k). 1979. PLB 9.15 (ISBN 0-307-60822-0, Golden Pr); pap. 2.95 (ISBN 0-307-10822-8). Western Pub.
Shane, Simon. What I'd Tell You If You'd Listen. 1978. 4.95 o.p. (ISBN 0-533-03699-2). Vantage.
Shaner, Dorcas D. Short Dramas for the Church. 224p. 1980. pap. 11.95 (ISBN -08170-0883-7). Judson.
Shaner, Richard C., jt. ed. see Murphy, George E., Jr.
Shaner, W. W. & Phillip, Perry P. Farming Systems Research & Development: Guidelines for Developing Countries. (WVSS in Agriculture Science & Policy Ser.). (Illus.). 1982. lib. bdg. 25.00 (ISBN 0-86531-389-X); pap. 10.95 (ISBN 0-86531-425-X). Westview.
Shaner, W. W. & Philipp, P. F., eds. Readings in Farming Systems Research & Development. (Special Studies in Agriculture-Aquaculture Science & Policy). 166p. 1982. lib. bdg. 19.00 (ISBN 0-86531-502-7). Westview.
Shanes, Ethel. National Survey of the Aged 1975. LC 82-80683. 1982. write for info. (ISBN 0-89138-938-5). ICPSR.
Shanet, Howard. Learn to Read Music. (Illus.). 184p. (Orig.). 1964. pap. 5.95 (ISBN 0-571-05849-3). Faber & Faber.
Shange, Ntozake. Sassafrass. (Illus.). 40p. 1976. pap. 1.95 o.p. (ISBN 0-915288-14-1). Shameless Hussy.
--Three Pieces. 1982. pap. 5.95 (ISBN 0-14-048170-2). Penguin.
Shanghai College of Traditional Medicine. Acupuncture: A Comprehensive Text. O'Conner, John & Bensky, Dan, eds. O'Connor, John & Bensky, Dan, trs. from Chinese. LC 81-65416. (Illus.). 741p. 1981. 55.00 (ISBN 0-939616-00-9). Eastland.
Shanin, Teodor & Alavi, Hamza, eds. Introduction to the Sociology of " Developing Societies". 1982. 25.00 (ISBN 0-85345-595-3, CL5953); pap. 12.50 (ISBN 0-85345-596-1, PB5961). Monthly Rev.
Shanina, N., compiled by. Victor Vasnetsov. 1980. 14.95 (ISBN 0-89893-073-1). CDP.
Shank, et al. Guide to Modern Meals. 3rd ed. O'Neill, Martha, ed. (Illus.). 640p. (gr. 10-12). 1980. 19.80 (ISBN 0-07-056416-7, W); tchr's. resource guide 7.92 (ISBN 0-07-047514-8). McGraw.
Shank, Adele, tr. see Arrabal, Fernando.
Shank, Alan. Presidential Policy Leadership: Kennedy & Social Welfare. LC 80-8278. 309p. 1980. lib. bdg. 21.50 (ISBN 0-8191-1265-8); pap. text ed. 12.50 (ISBN 0-8191-1266-6). U Pr of Amer.
Shank, Alan, jt. ed. see Levin, Melvin R.
Shank, Carolyn. A Child's Way to Water Play. LC 82-82119. (Illus.). 176p. (Orig.). 1983. pap. 6.95 (ISBN 0-88011-053-8). Leisure Pr.
Shank, Dorothy E., et al. Guide to Modern Meals. 2nd ed. (American Home & Family Ser). (gr. 10-12). 1970. text ed. 22.32 (ISBN 0-07-056404-3, W). McGraw.
Shank, John, jt. auth. see Dearden, John.
Shank, John K. Contemporary Managerial Accounting: A Casebook. (Illus.). 352p. 1981. 15.95 (ISBN 0-13-170357-9). P-H.
Shank, Stanley, ed. Test Your Bible Power: A Good Book Quiz. (Epiphany Bks.). 1983. pap. 1.95 (ISBN 0-345-30663-5). Ballantine.
Shank, Theodore. American Alternative Theater. LC 81-84701. (Grove Press Modern Dramatists Ser.). (Illus.). 224p. (Orig.). 1982. pap. 12.50 (ISBN 0-394-17963-3, E-798, Ever). Grove.
Shank, W. H. Indian Trails to Superhighways. 1975. 3.00 (ISBN 0-933788-39-8). Am Canal & Transport.
--Vanderbilt's Folly: History of Pennsylvania Turnpike. 6th ed. 1979. 3.00 (ISBN 0-933788-41-X). Am Canal & Transport.
Shank, W. H. & Mayo. Towpaths to Tugboats,1982: A History of American Canal Engineering. 1982. 6.00 (ISBN 0-933788-40-1). Am Canal & Transport.
Shankar, Kripa. Concealed Tenancy & Its Implications for Economic Growth: A Case Study of Eastern Uttar Pradesh. 144p. 1980. text ed. 10.00x (ISBN 0-391-02137-0). Humanities.
Shankara. Brahma-Sutra Bhasya of Sankaracarya. Gambhirananda, Swami, tr. (Sanskrit & Eng). 16.95 (ISBN 0-87481-066-3). Vedanta Pr.
--Vakyavritti & Atmajnanopadeshavidhi. (Sanskrit & Eng). pap. 1.75 (ISBN 0-87481-424-3). Vedanta Pr.
Shankaranarayanan, S. Sri Chakra. 1979. 12.00 (ISBN 0-941524-11-6). Lotus Light.
Shankaranarayanan, S. Glory of the Divine Mother: Devi Mahatmyam. 330p. (Eng. & Sanskrit.). 1983. 12.95 (ISBN 0-941524-08-6). Lotus Light.
Shanken, Marvin R. The Impact American Beer Market Review & Forecast: 1982 Edition. 3rd ed. (Illus.). 55p. 1982. pap. 150.00 (ISBN 0-918076-19-6). M Shanken Comm.
--The Impact American Distilled Spirits Market Review & Forecast: 1982 Edition. 7th ed. (Illus.). 64p. 1982. pap. 150.00 (ISBN 0-918076-18-8). M Shanken Comm.
--The Impact American Wine Market Review & Forecast: 1982 Edition. 8th ed. (Illus.). 72p. 1982. pap. 150.00 (ISBN 0-918076-17-X). M Shanken Comm.
Shankland, Craig, et al. The Golfer's Stroke-Saving Handbook. (Illus.). 1979. pap. 2.95 (ISBN 0-451-11586-4, AE1586, Sig). NAL.
Shankland, Virginia, ed. Animal Heroes. 8.00 (ISBN 0-392-10046-0, SpS). Sportshelf.
Shankle, George E. American Nicknames. 2nd ed. 524p. 1955. 18.00 (ISBN 0-8242-0004-7). Wilson.
Shanklin, Eugenia, jt. ed. see Berleant-Schiller, Riva.
Shankman, Arnold, jt. auth. see Wright, Marion A.
Shankman, Arnold, jt. ed. see Chepesiuk, Ronald.
Shankman, Steven. Pope's Iliad: Homer in the Age of Passion. LC 82-61384. 176p. 1983. 19.50x (ISBN 0-691-06566-7). Princeton U Pr.
Shanks, Daniel. Solved & Unsolved Problems in Number Theory. 2nd ed. LC 77-13019. 1978. text ed. 12.95 (ISBN 0-8284-0297-3). Chelsea Pub.
Shanks, Lewis. Baudelaire: Flesh & Spirit. LC 74-34363. (Studies in French Literature, No. 45). 1974. lib. bdg. 38.95x (ISBN 0-8383-2058-9). Haskell.
Shanks, M., et al. Pre-Calculus Mathematics. 3rd ed. (gr. 10-12). 1976. text ed. 20.40 (ISBN 0-201-00768-1, Sch Div). A-W.
Shanks, Merrill, et al. Pre-Calculus Mathematics. 4th ed. (gr. 11-12). 1981. text ed. 20.88 (ISBN 0-201-07684-5, Sch Div); tchr's ed. 9.72 (ISBN 0-201-07685-3); solution manual 17.12 (ISBN 0-201-07686-1). A-W.
Shanks, Michael. Planning & Politics: The British Experience 1960-76. (Political & Economic Planning Ser.). 1977. text ed. 22.50x (ISBN 0-04-330283-1); pap. text ed. 8.95x (ISBN 0-04-330284-X). Allen Unwin.
Shanks, R. G. Cardio Vascular Systems. (British Journal of Clinical Pharmacology Ser., Vol. I--Methods in Clinical Pharmacology). 106p. 1980. text ed. 39.50 o.p. (ISBN 0-8391-1486-9). Univ Park.
Shanks, Robert. I Can Make It Without You. 1979. 9.95 o.p. (ISBN 0-399-12345-8). Putnam Pub Group.
Shanmugam, K. Sam. Digital & Analog Communication Systems. LC 78-26191. 600p. 1979. text ed. 35.95 (ISBN 0-471-03090-2); tchr's manual avail. (ISBN 0-471-07832-8). Wiley.
--Digital & Analog Communication Systems. 600p. 1979. 32.95 (ISBN 0-686-98113-8). Telecom Lib.
Shannon, Alice R. Decorative Treasures from Papier-Mache. 1970. 6.95 (ISBN 0-8208-0334-0). Hearthside.
Shannon, Barbara, jt. auth. see Long, Patricia J.
Shannon, Claude E. & Weaver, Warren. The Mathematical Theory of Communication. LC 49-11922. 1949. 10.00 o.p. (ISBN 0-252-72548-4); pap. 4.95 (ISBN 0-686-96903-0). U of Ill Pr.
Shannon, David. Consumer Rights in Oregon. 99p. 1978. 3.50 (ISBN 0-88908-807-1). Self Counsel Pr.
Shannon, David A. Between the Wars: America, Nineteen Nineteen to Nineteen Forty-One. 2nd ed. LC 78-69558. (Illus.). 1979. pap. text ed. 11.50 (ISBN 0-395-26535-5). HM.
--Southern Business: The Decades Ahead. (ITT Key Issues Lecture Ser.). 123p. 1981. pap. text ed. 6.50 (ISBN 0-672-97877-6). Bobbs.
Shannon, Dell. Appearances of Death. LC 77-5709. 1977. 7.95 o.p. (ISBN 0-688-03238-9). Morrow.
--Exploit of Death. 228p. 1983. 11.95 (ISBN 0-688-02018-6). Morrow.
--Felony at Random. LC 78-27317. 1979. 8.95 o.p. (ISBN 0-688-03474-8). Morrow.
--Felony File. 1980. 9.95 (ISBN 0-688-03593-0). Morrow.
--Murder Most Strange. large type ed. LC 82-10340. 354p. 1982. 10.95 (ISBN 0-89621-377-3). Thorndike Pr.
Shannon, Doris. Beyond the Shining Mountains. LC 78-21358. 1979. 10.95 o.p. (ISBN 0-312-07782-3). St Martin.
Shannon, Doug. Off the Record: Everything Related to Playing Recorded Dance Music in the Entertainment Business. Kutnick, Richard W., ed. LC 79-92926. 403p. 1982. pap. 19.95 (ISBN 0-9603826-1-5). Pacesetter Pub. Hse., OH.
Shannon, Elizabeth. Up in the Dark. LC 82-73037. (Illus.). 384p. 1983. 14.95 (ISBN 0-689-11364-1). Atheneum.
Shannon, Foster. Green Leaf Bible Series, Vol. II. Rew, Lois J., ed. (Orig.). 1983. pap. 2.50 (ISBN 0-938462-11-3). Green Leaf CA.
Shannon, Foster H. The Green Leaf Bible Series, Vol. I. Rew, Lois J., ed. 1982. Set. pap. write for info. (ISBN 0-938462-05-9); Vol. I. pap. 12.50 (ISBN 0-938462-06-7); 2.50 (ISBN 0-938462-09-1). Green Leaf CA.
Shannon, Fred A. Appraisal of Walter Prescott Webb's "The Giant Plains.". LC 78-12508. (Critiques of Research in the Social Sciences: No. III). 1979. Repr. of 1940 ed. lib. bdg. 19.75x (ISBN 0-313-21211-2, SHWP). Greenwood.
--The Farmer's Last Frontier: Agriculture, 1860-1897. LC 76-48797. (The Economic History of the United States Ser.). 1977. pap. 10.95 (ISBN 0-87332-099-9). M E Sharpe.
--The Organization & Administration of the Union Army 1861-1865, 2 vols. Set. 20.00 (ISBN 0-8446-1402-5). Peter Smith.
Shannon, George. Dance Away. (Illus.). (ps-3). 1982. 9.50 (ISBN 0-688-00838-0); PLB 8.59 (ISBN 0-688-00839-9). Greenwillow.
Shannon, Harper. Riches in Romans. LC 70-95323. (Orig.). 1969. pap. 2.25 (ISBN 0-8054-1318-9). Broadman.
Shannon, Jasper B. Toward a New Politics in the South. 1949. 9.50x (ISBN 0-87049-006-0). U of Tenn Pr.
Shannon, Jasper B., ed. Study of Comparative Government, an Appraisal of Contemporary Trends: Essays Written in Honor of Frederic Austin Ogg. LC 68-54435. (Illus.). 1968. Repr. of 1949 ed. lib. bdg. 18.50x (ISBN 0-8371-0219-7, SHCG). Greenwood.
Shannon, Jeanene P. Don't Give Up on Tatting Yet, Bk. I. LC 79-52545. (Illus.). 1979. pap. 12.95 (ISBN 0-931716-01-2). Bradford Pub.
--Don't Give up on Tatting Yet, Bk. II. LC 79-52545. (Illus.). 126p. 1979. pap. 10.00 o.s.i. (ISBN 0-931716-02-0). Bradford Pub.
Shannon, John. Each Soul Is Where It Wishes to Be. 1973. pap. 3.00 (ISBN 0-87924-023-7). Membrane Pr.
Shannon, John K. W: Tungsten. 1976. pap. 3.00 (ISBN 0-87924-037-7). Membrane Pr.
Shannon, John K., ed. see Trollope, Anthony.
Shannon, Lytle. Golden Stallion. (YA) 1972. 6.95 (ISBN 0-685-02720-1, Avalon). Bouregy.
Shannon, Magdaline W., tr. see Price-Mars, Jean.

Shannon, Michael O. Modern Ireland: A Bibliography for Research, Planning & Development. 760p. 1982. 65.00 (ISBN 0-85365-914-1, Pub. by Lib Assn England). Oryx Pr.

Shannon, Monica. Dobrey. (Orig.). 1981. pap. 12.95 (ISBN 0-670-27513-1). Viking Pr.

Shannon, P., jt. auth. see Naylor, D.

Shannon, Patrick, jt. auth. see Groebner, David.

Shannon, Peter T., jt. auth. see Schlaadt, Richard G.

Shannon, R. E. Engineering Management. 400p. 1980. 32.95 (ISBN 0-471-03408-8). Wiley.

Shannon, Robert C. The New Testament Church. (Orig.). 1964. pap. 2.95 (ISBN 0-87239-335-6, 3052). Standard Pub.

Shannon, Robert E. Systems Simulation: The Art & Science. (Illus.). 368p. 1975. ref. ed. 24.95 (ISBN 0-13-881839-8). P-H.

Shannon, Robert H. Handbook of Coal-Based Electric Power Generation: The Technology, Utilization, Application & Economics of Coal for Generating Electric Power. LC 82-7916. (Illus.). 372p. 1983. 45.00 (ISBN 0-8155-0907-3). Noyes.

Shannon, Roger H., ed. Hospital Information Systems. LC 79-15608. 405p. 1979. 51.00 (ISBN 0-444-85341-3, North Holland). Elsevier.

Shannon, Salley R. Bedtime Without Tears. (Illus.). 1983. 11.95 (ISBN 0-915556-07-3). Great Ocean.

Shannon, Thomas A. What Are They Saying About Peace & War? (WATSA Ser.). 128p. 1983. pap. 3.95 (ISBN 0-8091-2499-8). Paulist Pr.

Shannon, Thomas A. & DiGiacomo, James. An Introduction to Bioethics. LC 79-66585. 160p. 1979. pap. 4.95 (ISBN 0-8091-2224-3). Paulist Pr.

Shannon, Thomas R., jt. auth. see Daley, Nelda K.

Shannon-Thornberry, Milo. The Alternate Celebrations Catalogue. LC 82-3638. (Illus.). 192p. 1982. pap. 8.95 (ISBN 0-8298-0601-6). Pilgrim NY.

Shanson, D. C. Microbiology in Clinical Practice. (Illus.). 600p. 1982. 32.50 (ISBN 0-7236-0636-6). Wright-PSG.

Shanteau, Doreen, ed. Audiovisuals About Birth & Family Life, 1970-1980. 128p. 1981. saddle stitched 5.00 (ISBN 0-934024-05-7). ICEA.

Shao, Stephen. Statistics for Business & Economics. 2nd ed. 1973. 9.95 (ISBN 0-675-08898-4). Additional supplements may be obtained from publisher. Merrill.

Shao, Stephen P. Essentials of Business Statistics. (Business Ser.). 1977. text ed. 19.95 (ISBN 0-675-08507-1). Additional supplements may be obtained from publisher. Merrill.

Shao Shankang, jt. auth. see Cai Longyun.

Shapcott, Thomas, ed. Consolidation: The Second Poets Anthology. 265p. 1983. text ed. 18.00 (ISBN 0-7022-1677-1); pap. 9.50 (ISBN 0-7022-1676-3). U of Queensland Pr.

Shapira, Abraham, ed. The Seventh Day: Soldiers Talk about the Six-Day War. 276p. 6.95 o.p. (ISBN 0-686-95163-8); pap. 2.65 o.p. (ISBN 0-686-99470-1). ADL.

Shapira, Morris, ed. see James, Henry.

Shapiro. Assault on Tarawa. 6.95 o.p. (ISBN 0-679-20679-5). McKay.

--Clinical Application of Blood Gases. 3rd ed. 1982. 27.50 (ISBN 0-8151-7632-5). Year Bk Med.

--D-Day-Omaha Beach. 1981. 6.95 o.p. (ISBN 0-679-20575-6). McKay.

Shapiro, A. H. The Dynamics & Thermodynamics of Compressible Fluid Flow, Vol. 1. 647p. 1953. 36.95 (ISBN 0-471-06691-5). Wiley.

Shapiro, Andrew O., jt. auth. see Striker, John M.

Shapiro, Arnold. Kenny's Crazy Kite. (Surprise Bk). (Illus.). (ps-4). 1978. 4.95 (ISBN 0-8431-0445-7). Price Stern.

Shapiro, Arnold, jt. auth. see Kolman, Bernard.

Shapiro, Arnold, jt. ed. see Kolman, Bernard.

Shapiro, Arthur K., et al, eds. Gilles de la Tourette Syndrome. LC 74-21986. 447p. 1978. 36.00 (ISBN 0-89004-057-5). Raven.

Shapiro, Ascher H. The Dynamics & Thermodynamics of Compressible Fluid Flow, 2 Vols. (Illus.). 647p. 1953-54. Vol. 1. 32.95 o.p. (ISBN 0-471-06845-4); Vol. 2. 29.95 o.p. (ISBN 0-8260-8075-8). Wiley.

--The Dynamics & Thermodynamics of Compressible Fluid Flow, Vol. 2. LC 82-17967. 550p. 1983. Repr. of 1954 ed. lib. bdg. price not set (ISBN 0-89874-566-7). Krieger.

Shapiro, Barbara J. John Wilkins, 1614-1672: An Intellectual Biography. LC 73-84042. 1969. 37.50x (ISBN 0-520-01396-4). U of Cal Pr.

--Probability & Certainty in Seventeenth Century England: A Study of the Relationships Between Natural Science, Religion, History, Law, Literature. LC 82-61385. 368p. 1983. 35.00x (ISBN 0-691-05379-0). Princeton U Pr.

Shapiro, Barry & Boericke, Arthur. Handmade Homes: The Natural Way to Build Houses. LC 80-22607. (Illus.). 1981. 17.95 o.s.i. (ISBN 0-440-03340-3). Delacorte.

Shapiro, Barry, jt. auth. see Shapiro, Evelyn.

Shapiro, Barry A. Clinical Application of Blood Gases. 2nd ed. (Illus.). 1977. 21.50 o.p. (ISBN 0-8151-7638-4). Year Bk Med.

Shapiro, Benson P. Sales Program Management. 1976. text ed. 24.95 (ISBN 0-07-056413-2, C); instructor's manual 20.95 (ISBN 0-07-056414-0). McGraw.

Shapiro, Dan, jt. auth. see Parsler, Ron.

Shapiro, Daniel Z. Thinking Divorce-Consider the Shocking Personal & Financial Reality. 125p. (Orig.). 1983. pap. price not set (ISBN 0-930256-11-5). Almar.

Shapiro, David. Neurotic Styles. 1965. 12.95x o.s.i. (ISBN 0-465-04958-3); pap. 5.95x (ISBN 0-465-09502-X, TB5003). Basic.

--To an Idea: A Book of Poems. LC 82-22288. 96p. 11.95 (ISBN 0-87951-176-1); deluxe ed. 40.00 (ISBN 0-87951-181-8). Overlook Pr.

Shapiro, David, et al, eds. Behavior Disorders & Stress: Causes, Prevention, & Treatment. 700p. Date not set. 20.00 o.p. (ISBN 0-88437-005-4). Psych Dimensions.

Shapiro, David L., ed. see Harlan, John M.

Shapiro, Deane H., Jr. & Walsh, Roger N., eds. The Art & Science of Meditation, Vol. II, a Reader. 600p. 1983. write for info (ISBN 0-202-25136-5). Aldine Pub.

Shapiro, Deborah. Parents & Protectors: A Study in Child Abuse & Neglect. 1979. pap. text ed. 6.50 (ISBN 0-87868-139-6, G-19). Child Welfare.

Shapiro, Deborah, jt. auth. see Grow, Lucille J.

Shapiro, Diane R. Foundations for Sociology. 1977. pap. 15.95 (ISBN 0-395-30742-2); instr's manual 1.00 (ISBN 0-395-30743-0). HM.

Shapiro, E. Donald, jt. auth. see Curran, William.

Shapiro, E. Donald, jt. auth. see Curran, William J.

Shapiro, Edna. Windwagon Smith. LC 69-12924. (American Folktales Ser.). (Illus.). (gr. 2-5). 1969. PLB 6.69 (ISBN 0-8116-4016-7). Garrard.

Shapiro, Eileen C. & Lowenstein, Leah M., eds. Becoming a Physician: Development of Values & Attitudes in Medicine. Boston University School of Medicine. LC 79-10958. 314p. 1979. prof ref 28.00x (ISBN 0-88410-527-X). Ballinger Pub.

Shapiro, Eugene. The Condo & Co-op Book: A Game Plan for Winning the Condo-Co-op Conversion Battle. 186p. 1983. 14.95 (ISBN 0-13-167171-5); pap. 6.95 (ISBN 0-13-167163-4). P-H.

Shapiro, Evelyn & Shapiro, Barry. The Women Say, the Men Say: Women's Lib & Mens Consciousness. 1979. pap. 8.95 o.s.i. (ISBN 0-440-59831-1, Delta). Dell.

Shapiro, Fred C. Radwaste: A Reporter's Investigation of Nuclear Waste Disposal. LC 81-40238. 288p. 1981. 14.50 (ISBN 0-394-51159-X). Random.

Shapiro, Gary, jt. auth. see Williams, J. Mark.

Shapiro, Gilbert. Physics Without Math: A Descriptive Introduction. (Illus.). 1979. text ed. 21.95 (ISBN 0-13-674317-X). P-H.

Shapiro, H. L., jt. auth. see Alo, R. A.

Shapiro, Harold N. Introduction to the Theory of Numbers. (Pure & Applied Mathematics Ser.). 480p. 1983. 39.95 (ISBN 0-471-86737-3, Pub. by Wiley-Interscience). Wiley.

Shapiro, Harold T. & Fulton, George A. A Regional Econometric Forecasting System: Major Economic Areas of Michigan. 1983. 35.00 (ISBN 0-472-10035-1). U of Mich Pr.

Shapiro, Harvey L. Introduction to Assembly Language Programming on the PDP-10 & PDP-11. (Illus.). 441p. 1982. pap. text ed. 19.95 (ISBN 0-88284-171-8); instructor' manual avail. Alfred Pub.

Shapiro, Howard I. The Birth Control Book. 1982. pap. 3.50 (ISBN 0-380-40139-8, 569868). Avon.

--Cranes & Derricks. (Illus.). 1979. 32.50 (ISBN 0-07-056420-5, P&RB). McGraw.

--The Pregnancy Book for Today's Woman: An Obstetrician Answers all Your Questions About Pregnancy & Childbirth & Some You May Not Have Considered. LC 80-7916. (Illus.). 448p. 1983. 17.26i (ISBN 0-06-181766-X, HarpT). Har-Row.

Shapiro, Ira, jt. ed. see Schad, Tennyson.

Shapiro, Irwin. Dan McCann & His Fast Sooner Hound. LC 74-28287. (American Folktales Ser). (Illus.). 48p. (gr. 2-5). 1975. PLB 6.69 (ISBN 0-8116-4043-4). Garrard.

--Darwin & the Enchanted Isles. LC 77-7544. (Science Discovery Bks.). (Illus.). (gr. 3-6). 1977. PLB 5.99 o.p. (ISBN 0-698-30679-1, Coward). Putnam Pub Group.

--The Gift of Magic Sleep: Early Experiments in Anesthesia. (Science Discovery Bks). (Illus.). (gr. 2-6). reinforced bdg. 5.99 (ISBN 0-698-30694-5, Coward). Putnam Pub Group.

--Gretchen & the White Steed. LC 72-1471. (Venture Ser). (Illus.). 64p. (gr. 2). 1972. PLB 6.89 (ISBN 0-8116-6962-9). Garrard.

--The Hungry Ghost Mystery. LC 78-5841. (Mystery Ser.). (Illus.). (gr. 2-6). 1978. PLB 6.89 (ISBN 0-8116-6403-1). Garrard.

--Joe Magarac & His U. S. A. Citizen Papers. LC 78-66070. (Illus.). 1979. pap. 2.50 (ISBN 0-8229-5305-6). U of Pittsburgh Pr.

--Paul Bunyan Tricks a Dragon. LC 74-19059. (American Folktales Ser). (Illus.). 48p. (gr. 2-5). 1975. PLB 6.69 (ISBN 0-8116-4042-6). Garrard.

--Willie's Whizmobile. LC 72-10559. (Venture Ser). (Illus.). 40p. (gr. 1). 1973. PLB 6.69 (ISBN 0-8116-6726-X). Garrard.

Shapiro, Jacqueline R. & Swaybill, Marion L. Sexibody Diet & Exercise Program. 1982. text ed. 10.95 (ISBN 0-914094-19-X). Symphony.

Shapiro, James A., ed. Mobile Genetic Elements. LC 82-11624. Date not set. 65.00 (ISBN 0-12-638680-3). Acad Pr.

Shapiro, James E. Meditations from the Breakdown Lane: Running Across America. 1982. 12.50 (ISBN 0-394-51438-6). Random.

Shapiro, Jane P. & Potichnyj, Peter J., eds. Change & Adaptation in Soviet & East European Politics. LC 76-8415. (Special Studies). (Illus.). 275p. 1976. 31.95 o.p. (ISBN 0-275-56190-9). Praeger.

Shapiro, Jane P., jt. ed. see Potichnyj, Peter J.

Shapiro, Jed, jt. auth. see Malocsay, Zoltan.

Shapiro, Jeremy F. Mathematical Programming: Structures & Algorithms. LC 79-4478. 388p. 1979. 37.50x (ISBN 0-471-77886-9, Pub by Wiley-Interscience). Wiley.

Shapiro, Jerome H. & Hipona, Florencio A. Radiology. 2nd ed. (Medical Examination Review Book: Vol. 17). 1972. spiral bdg. 19.00 (ISBN 0-87488-117-X). Med Exam.

Shapiro, Jerrold L. Methods of Group Psychotherapy & Encounter: A Tradition of Innovation. LC 77-83390. 1978. text ed. 16.95 (ISBN 0-87581-229-5). Peacock Pubs.

Shapiro, Judith, jt. auth. see Heng, Liang.

Shapiro, Kenneth, ed. Pediatric Head Trauma. LC 82-84516. (Illus.). 1983. price not set monograph (ISBN 0-87993-191-4). Futura Pub.

Shapiro, Leonard R. The Petro-Dollar Circuit, Bk. 1. Rev. ed. 98p. (Orig.). 1982. pap. 7.00 (ISBN 0-686-36032-X). Shapiro.

Shapiro, Lillian, ed. Fiction for Youth: A Recommended Guide to Books. LC 80-22480. 252p. 1981. 21.95 (ISBN 0-918212-34-0). Neal-Schuman.

Shapiro, Lillian L. Teaching Yourself in Libraries. 180p. 1978. 7.00 ea. (ISBN 0-8242-0628-2); 25 or more copies 5.00 ea. Wilson.

Shapiro, Louis. Clinical Trials. (Statistics, Textbook & Monographs). 280p. 1983. price not set (ISBN 0-8247-1741-4). Dekker.

Shapiro, Louis W. Introduction to Abstract Algebra. (International Ser. in Pure & Applied Mathematics). (Illus.). 448p. 1975. text ed. 17.95 o.p. (ISBN 0-07-056415-9, C). McGraw.

Shapiro, M. Asymmetry. (North Holland Linguistic Ser.: Vol. 26). 1976. pap. 30.00 (ISBN 0-7204-0415-0, North-Holland). Elsevier.

Shapiro, Martin & Tresolini, Rocco J. American Constitutional Law. 5th ed. 1979. 26.95x (ISBN 0-02-409570-2). Macmillan.

--American Contitutional Law. 6th ed. 816p. 1983. text ed. 24.95 (ISBN 0-02-409580-X). Macmillan.

Shapiro, Mary J. The Dover New York Walking Guide: From the Battery to Wall Street. (New York Walking Guide Ser.). (Illus.). 64p. 1982. pap. 1.50 (ISBN 0-486-24225-0). Dover.

--The Dover New York Walking Guide: From Wall Street to Chambers Street. (New York Walking Guide Ser.). (Illus.). 64p. 1982. pap. 1.50 (ISBN 0-486-24226-9). Dover.

--A Picture History of the Brooklyn Bridge. (New York City Ser.). (Illus.). 96p. (Orig.). 1983. pap. 5.95 (ISBN 0-486-24403-2). Dover.

Shapiro, Michael C. & Schiffman, Harold F. Language & Society in South Asia. 306p. 1983. 25.00x (ISBN 90-70176-55-6). Foris Pubns.

Shapiro, Michael H. & Morse, Stephen. Biological & Behavioral Technology & the Law. 396p. 1982. 34.50 (ISBN 0-03-056974-5). Praeger.

Shapiro, Milton. Ranger Battalion: American Rangers in World War Two. LC 79-9548. (Illus.). 192p. (gr. 7 up). 1979. PLB 8.29 o.p. (ISBN 0-671-32928-6). Messner.

Shapiro, Milton J. The Screaming Eagles: The 101st Airborne Division in World War II. LC 76-15568. 192p. (gr. 7 up). 1976. PLB 7.29 o.p. (ISBN 0-671-32808-5). Messner.

Shapiro, Murray, et al. Barron's How to Prepare for the American College Testing Program (ACT) rev. ed. LC 79-20856. (gr. 11-12). 1982. pap. text ed. 6.95 (ISBN 0-8120-0636-4). Barron.

--Basic Tips on the American College Testing Program (ACT) 150p. (gr. 11-12). 1983. pap. text ed. 2.95 (ISBN 0-8120-2415-X). Barron.

Shapiro, Nat, ed. Popular Music: An Annotated Index of Popular Songs. (Popular Music Ser.). (350 pages per vol.). 40.00x ea. Vol. 1, 1950-1959 (ISBN 0-8103-0839-8). Vol. 2, 1940-1949 (ISBN 0-8103-0840-1). Vol. 3, 1960-1964 (ISBN 0-8103-0841-X). Vol. 4, 1930-1939 (ISBN 0-8103-0842-8). Vol. 5, 1920-1929 (ISBN 0-8103-0843-6). Vol. 6, 1965-1969 (ISBN 0-8103-0844-4). Vol. 7, 1970-74 (ISBN 0-8103-0845-2). Gale.

Shapiro, Norman, tr. & pref. by. Fables from Old French: Aesop's Beasts & Bumpkins. 1982. 19.95 (ISBN 0-8195-5074-4). Wesleyan U Pr.

Shapiro, Norman R., ed. & tr. see Feydeau, Georges.

Shapiro, Pamela, jt. auth. see Anderson, Barbara.

Shapiro, Patricia. Caring for the Mentally Ill. (Impact Bks). (Illus.). 96p. (gr. 7 up). 1982. PLB 8.90 (ISBN 0-531-04399-1). Watts.

Shapiro, Raymond, ed. Lonely in Baltimore: Personal Columns. (Illus., Orig.). 1983. pap. 4.95 (ISBN 0-394-71465-2, Vin). Random.

Shapiro, Ronald M., et al. Securities Regulation Forms - Compliance-Practice, 3 vols. LC 75-17451. 1975. 210.00 (ISBN 0-87632-194-5). Boardman.

Shapiro, Roy D., jt. auth. see Dyer, James S.

Shapiro, S. S., jt. auth. see Hahn, Gerald J.

Shapiro, Stanley. Simon's Soul. LC 77-6119. 1977. 7.95 o.p. (ISBN 0-399-11858-6). Putnam Pub Group.

Shapiro, Stanley S., ed. see New York Academy of Sciences, March 10-12, 1980.

Shapiro, Stephen R., jt. auth. see DeVries, Pieter A.

Shapiro, Stuart. Lisp: An Interactive Approach. 1983. text ed. p.n.s. (ISBN 0-914894-44-7). Computer Sci.

Shapiro, Stuart C. Techniques of Artificial Intelligence. 1978. pap. 9.95 (ISBN 0-442-80501-2). Van Nos Reinhold.

Shapiro, Stuart L. & Teukolsky, Saul A. Black Holes, White Dwarfs, & Neutron Stars: The Physics of Compact Objects. 650p. 1983. 39.95 (ISBN 0-471-87317-9, Pub. by Wiley-Interscience). Wiley.

Shapiro, Sue A. Contemporary Theories of Schizophrenia: Review & Synthesis. LC 79-27499. 290p. 1981. 19.95 (ISBN 0-07-056423-X). McGraw.

Shapiro, Warren. Social Organization in Aboriginal Australia. LC 78-32074. 1979. 22.50x (ISBN 0-312-73316-X). St Martin.

Shapiro, William E., ed. New Book of Knowledge, 21 Vols. LC 81-82202. (Illus.). 1982. write for info. (ISBN 0-7172-0513-4). Grolier Ed Corp.

Shapiro-Bertolini, Ethel. When the Storm Broke. 6.95 o.s.i. (ISBN 0-8283-1307-5). Branden.

Shapley, Fern R. Catalog of the Italian Paintings, 2 vols. LC 79-4410. pap. 10.00 set (ISBN 0-89468-053-6). Vol. 1 (ISBN 0-89468-054-4). Vol. 2 (ISBN 0-89468-055-2). Natl Gallery Art.

Shapley, Harlow. Inner Metagalaxy. 1957. text ed. 39.50x (ISBN 0-686-83589-1). Elliots Bks.

Sharabati, Doreen. Saudi Arabian Seashells. 1982. 50.00x (ISBN 0-9507641-0-8, Pub. by Cave Pubns England). State Mutual Bk.

Sharaf, Myron. Fury on Earth: A Biography of Wilhelm Reich. LC 82-5707. (Illus.). 560p. 1983. 24.95 (ISBN 0-312-31370-5). St Martin.

Sharan, Mahesh Kumar. Studies in Sanskrit Inscriptions of Ancient Cambodia. (Illus.). 372p. 1974. 17.50x o.p. (ISBN 0-88386-293-X). South Asia Bks.

Sharbrough, David. American Premium Guide to Olde Cameras. (Illus.). 192p. (Orig.). 1982. pap. 9.95 (ISBN 0-89689-037-6). Bks Americana.

Sharda, Bam D. Status Attainment in Rural India. 1977. 8.00x o.p. (ISBN 0-88386-144-5). South Asia Bks.

Share, Allen J. Cities in the Commonwealth: Two Centuries of Urban Life in Kentucky. LC 81-51015. (Kentucky Bicentennial Bookshelf Ser.). 160p. 1982. 6.95 (ISBN 0-8131-0252-9). U Pr of Ky.

Share Working Conference on Data Base Management Systems, 2nd, Canada, 1977. The ANSI-SPARC DBMS Model: Proceedings. Jardine, D. A., ed. 1977. 59.75 (ISBN 0-7204-0719-2, North-Holland). Elsevier.

Sharfman, I. Harold. Jews of Jackson, California. LC 76-79574. (Illus.). 1969. 11.50 o.p. (ISBN 0-87062-054-1). A H Clark.

Sharfstein, Steven, jt. auth. see Foley, Henry A.

Shargel, Harry D., jt. auth. see Lowe, E. Nobles.

Shariati, Ali. Man & Islam. Marjani, Fatollah, tr. from Farsi. 150p. (Orig.). 1982. pap. 4.95 (ISBN 0-941722-00-7, Pub. by Handami Found Iran). Book Dist Ctr.

Sharick, Gilbert. Grounding & Bonding, Vol. XIII. 1981. 18.00 (ISBN 0-686-98069-7). Telecom Lib.

Sharif, Omar. Omar Sharif's Life in Bridge. Reese, Terence, tr. from French. 144p. 1983. pap. 6.95 (ISBN 0-571-13098-4). Faber & Faber.

Sharif, Zeenat. Muslim Womans Home Companion. Quinlan, Hamid, ed. LC 82-70459. (Illus.). 180p. 1983. text ed. 6.50 (ISBN 0-89259-042-4); pap. 4.50 (ISBN 0-686-42956-7). Am Trust Pubns.

Sharitz, Rebecca R., jt. ed. see Gibbons, J. Whitfield.

Sharkansky, I. The Maligned States: Policy Accomplishments, Problems & Opportunities. 2nd ed. 1977. 15.95 (ISBN 0-07-056434-5). McGraw.

Sharkansky, Ira & Van Meter, Donald. Policy & Politics in American Governments. (Illus.). 360p. 1975. pap. text ed. 18.95 (ISBN 0-07-056428-0, C); instructors' manual 2.95 (ISBN 0-07-056429-9). McGraw.

Sharkey, Brian J. Coaches' Guide to Sport Physiology. 1983. pap. text ed. price not set (ISBN 0-931250-38-2). Human Kinetics.

Sharkey, Paul W., ed. Philosophy, Religion & Psychotherapy: Essays in the Philosophical Foundations of Psychotherapy. LC 81-40828. 242p. (Orig.). 1982. lib. bdg. 23.00 (ISBN 0-8191-2331-5); pap. text ed. 10.75 (ISBN 0-8191-2332-3). U Pr of Amer.

Sharkey, Thomas. Sanctity Is a Broken Television Set on a Rainy Day. LC 76-122719. 1970. 3.95 o.p. (ISBN 0-8199-0411-2). Franciscan Herald.

Sharkey, William W. The Theory of Natural Monopoly. LC 82-1136. (Illus.). 1982. 32.50 (ISBN 0-521-24394-7); pap. 9.95 (ISBN 0-521-27194-0). Cambridge U Pr.

Sharlin, Harold & Sharlin, Tiby. Lord Kelvin: The Dynamic Victorian. LC 78-50771. (Illus.). 1979. 22.50 (ISBN 0-271-00203-4). Pa St U Pr.

Sharlin, Harold I., ed. Business & Its Environment: Essays for Thomas C. Cochran. LC 82-6143. (Contributions in American Studies: No. 63). (Illus.). 264p. 1983. lib. bdg. 35.00 (ISBN 0-313-21438-7, SHB/). Greenwood.
Sharlin, Tiby, jt. auth. see Sharlin, Harold.
Sharlot, M. Michael, jt. auth. see Dix, George E.
Sharma & Sharma. Chromosome Techniques. 3rd ed. LC 79-41279. 1980. 149.00 (ISBN 0-408-70942-1). Butterworth.
Sharma, Archana. The Chromosomes. 286p. 1976. 50.00x (ISBN 0-686-84450-5, Pub. by Oxford & I B H India). State Mutual Bk.
Sharma, B., jt. auth. see Reddy, G. Ram.
Sharma, B. N. Social & Cultural History of Northern India c. 1000-1200 A.D. 1972. text ed. 15.00x (ISBN 0-391-00300-3). Humanities.
Sharma, C. H. & Leland, David. A Manual of Homoeopathy & Natural Medicine: Principles of an Age-Old Practice of Alternative Medicine with Step-by-Step Remedies. 1976. pap. 3.50 o.p. (ISBN 0-525-47432-3). Dutton.
Sharma, D. S., jt. auth. see Sharma, K. K.
Sharma, Govind N. Munshi Prem Chand. (World Author Ser.). 1978. 15.95 (ISBN 0-8057-6329-5, Twayne). G K Hall.
Sharma, H. S. The Physiography of the Lower Chambal Valley & Its Agricultural Development. 1979. text ed. 15.75x (ISBN 0-391-01927-9). Humanities.
--Ravine Erosion in India. (Illus.). 100p. 1980. text ed. 11.75x (ISBN 0-391-02142-7). Humanities.
Sharma, Hari P., jt. ed. see Gough, Kathleen.
Sharma, I. C., tr. see Bhatt, R. Kaladhar.
Sharma, J. N. The International Fiction of Henry James. 1980. text ed. 13.00x (ISBN 0-333-90300-5). Humanities.
Sharma, Jagdish S. Encyclopedia India, 2 Vols. 2nd & rev. ed. 1407p. 1981. Set. 195.00 (ISBN 0-940500-78-7, Pub by S Chand India). Asia Bk Corp.
Sharma, Joseph see Zweig, Gunter.
Sharma, K. D. Fundamentals of Machine Design. 1971. 15.00x (ISBN 0-210-27015-2). Asia.
Sharma, K. K. Joyce Cary His Theme & Technique. 208p. 1976. text ed. 8.75x (ISBN 0-391-02550-3). Humanities.
--Perspectives on Raja Rao. (Indo-English Writers Ser.: No. 2). 237p. 1980. text ed. 13.00x (ISBN 0-391-02520-1). Humanities.
Sharma, K. K. & Sharma, D. S. Introduction to Practical Chemistry. 240p. 1982. 50.00x (ISBN 0-686-83156-X, Pub. by Garlandfold England); pap. 40.00x (ISBN 0-686-83157-8). State Mutual Bk.
--An Introduction to Practical Chemistry. 500p. 1982. text ed. 35.00x (ISBN 0-7069-1767-7, Pub. By Vikas India). Advent NY.
Sharma, K. K., ed. Indo-English Literature: A Collection of Critical Essays on Indian Creative Writers in English. 273p. 1977. text ed. 13.00x (ISBN 0-391-02534-1). Humanities.
Sharma, Krishan. The Konds of Orissa. 1979. text ed. 10.50x (ISBN 0-391-01816-7). Humanities.
Sharma, L. S. Coleridge: His Contribution to English Criticism. 224p. 1982. text ed. 14.00x (ISBN 0-391-02459-0). Humanities.
Sharma, M. M., jt. auth. see Doraiswamy, L. K.
Sharma, Miriam. The Politics of Inequality: Competition & Control in an Indian Village. LC 78-5526. (Asian Studies at Hawaii: No. 22). 1978. pap. text ed. 10.50x (ISBN 0-8248-0569-0). UH Pr.
Sharma, N. K., jt. auth. see Dandekar, M. M.
Sharma, N. N. Kalpa Chintamani of Damodara Bhatta. 160p. 1979. 16.95 o.p. (ISBN 0-89684-093-X, Pub. by Eastern Bk India). Orient Bk Dist.
Sharma, R. K., ed. Economics of Soviet Assistance to India. 167p. 1981. 14.95 (ISBN 0-940500-73-6, Pub by Allied Pubs India). Asia Bk Corp.
Sharma, R. N. Political Science in India. 1979. 28.50x o.p. (ISBN 0-8364-0328-2). South Asia Bks.
--Spatial Approach for District Planning: A Case Study of Karnal District. 138p. 1981. text ed. 14.25x (ISBN 0-391-02272-5, Pub. by Concept India). Humanities.
Sharma, R. N., jt. auth. see Singh, Mohinder.
Sharma, R. N., ed. Indian Librarianship. 1982. 20.00x (ISBN 0-8364-0890-X, Pub. by Kalyani). South Asia Bks.
Sharma, R. R. A Marxist Model of Social Change. 256p. 1980. text ed. 15.25x (ISBN 0-391-01766-7). Humanities.
Sharma, R. S. Anita Desai. (Indian Writers Ser.: Vol. 18). 1981. 12.00 (ISBN 0-86578-071-4). Ind-US Inc.
Sharma, Rama & Gopal. The History of Vijayanagar Empire. 1980. Vols. 1 & 2. 74.95 (ISBN 0-940500-93-0); Vol. 1 Beginnings & Expansion, 247p. Vol. 2 Decline & Disappearance, 611p. Asia Bk Corp.
Sharma, Rameshwar K. & Criss, Wayne E., eds. Endocrine Control in Neoplasia. LC 77-72623. (Progress in Cancer Research & Therapy Ser.: Vol. 9). 391p. 1978. 45.00 (ISBN 0-89004-244-6). Raven.
Sharma, Ravindra N., ed. Indian Librarianship: Perspectives & Prospects. 333p. 1981. 22.95x (ISBN 0-940500-01-9); lib. bdg. 22.95x (ISBN 0-686-92290-5); text ed. 22.95x (ISBN 0-686-98499-4). Asia Bk Corp.
Sharma, S. C., jt. ed. see Coleman, P. G.
Sharma, S. R., tr. see Hillebrandt, Alfred.
Sharma, Savitri. Women Students in India. 1979. text ed. 13.00x (ISBN 0-391-01831-0). Humanities.
Sharma, Sue, jt. auth. see Gargan, William.
Sharma, V. K., jt. ed. see Agarwal, V. P.
Sharman, D. F., tr. see Youdim, M. B. & Lovenberg, W.
Sharman, Lyon. Sun Yat-sen, His Life & Its Meaning: A Critical Biography. LC 68-17141. 1934. text ed. 20.00x (ISBN 0-8047-0609-3); pap. 4.95 o. p. (ISBN 0-8047-0610-7). Stanford U Pr.
Sharman, Nick. Judgement Day. 1982. pap. 2.95 (ISBN 0-451-11450-7, AE1450, Sig). NAL.
--The Scourge. (Orig.). 1980. pap. 2.25 o.p. (ISBN 0-451-09114-0, E9114, Sig). NAL.
--The Surrogate. (Orig.). 1980. pap. 2.75 o.p. (ISBN 0-451-09957-5, E9957, Sig). NAL.
Sharmat, Marjorie. Gila Monsters Meet You At. 1983. pap. 3.50 (ISBN 0-14-050430-3, Puffin). Penguin.
--I Saw Him First. LC 82-14839. 128p. (YA) (gr. 7 up). 1983. 12.95 (ISBN 0-440-03975-4). Delacorte.
--Mooch the Messy Meets Prudence the Neat. LC 77-29049. (Break-of-Day Bk.). (Illus.). (gr. 1-3). 1979. PLB 6.99 (ISBN 0-698-30703-8, Coward). Putman Pub.
Sharmat, Marjorie W. Best Valentine in the World. LC 81-13345. (Illus.). 32p. (gr. k-3). 1982. 9.95 (ISBN 0-8234-0440-4). Holiday.
--A Big Fat Enormous Lie. LC 77-15645. (Illus.). (ps-2). 1978. 10.25 (ISBN 0-525-26510-4, 0995-300). Dutton.
--Burton & Dudley. LC 75-1091. (Illus.). 48p. (gr. k-3). 1975. PLB 6.95 (ISBN 0-8234-0260-6). Holiday.
--Edgemont. (Illus.). 32p. (gr. 3-5). 1980. pap. 2.95 (ISBN 0-698-20523-5, Coward). Putnam Pub Group.
--Edgemont. LC 76-113. (Illus.). (gr. k-2). 1976. 6.95 o.p. (ISBN 0-698-20375-5, Coward). Putnam Pub Group.
--Frizzy the Fearful. LC 82-12093. (Illus.). 32p. (ps-3). reinforced binding 8.95 (ISBN 0-8234-0475-7). Holiday.
--Grumley the Grouch. LC 79-28290. (Illus.). 32p. (ps-3). 1980. PLB 8.95 (ISBN 0-8234-0410-2). Holiday.
--I Saw Him First. (Young Love Romance Ser.). (YA) (gr. 7-12). 1983. pap. 1.95 (ISBN 0-440-94009-5, LFL). Dell.
--I Want Mama. LC 74-3584. (Illus.). 32p. (gr. k-3). 1974. PLB 9.89 o.p. (ISBN 0-06-025554-4, HarpJ). Har-Row.
--I'm Not Oscar's Friend Anymore. (gr. k-2). 1975. 9.95 (ISBN 0-525-32537-9, 0966-290). Dutton.
--I'm Terrific. LC 76-9094. (Illus.). 32p. (ps-3). 1977. PLB 8.95 (ISBN 0-8234-0282-7). Holiday.
--Morris Brookside, a Dog. LC 73-76797. (Illus.). 48p. (gr. k-3). 1973. PLB 6.95 (ISBN 0-8234-0225-8). Holiday.
--Mysteriously Yours, Maggie Marmelstein. LC 81-48656. (Illus.). 160p. (gr. 3-6). 1982. 8.61i (ISBN 0-06-025516-1, HarpJ); PLB 8.89g (ISBN 0-06-025517-X). Har-Row.
--Nate the Great. (Break-of-Day Bk.). (Illus.). 64p. (gr. 1-3). 1972. PLB 6.99 (ISBN 0-698-30444-6, Coward). Putman Pub.
--Nate the Great & the Lost List. (Break-of-Day Bk.). (Illus.). (gr. k-2). 1975. PLB 6.99 (ISBN 0-698-30593-0, Coward). Putnam Pub Group.
--Nate the Great & The Missing Key. (Illus.). 48p. (gr. 7-10). 1981. PLB 6.99 (ISBN 0-698-30726-7, Coward). Putman Pub.
--Nate the Great & the Missing Key. 48p. (gr. 1-4). 1982. pap. 1.75 (ISBN 0-440-46191-X, YB). Dell.
--Nate the Great & The Phony Clue. (Break-of-Day Bk.). (Illus.). 48p. (gr. k-3). 1977. PLB 6.99 (ISBN 0-698-30650-3, Coward). Putnam Pub.
--Nate the Great & The Snowy Trail. (Break of Day Ser.). (Illus.). 48p. (gr. 6-9). 1982. pap. 6.99 (ISBN 0-698-30738-0, Coward). Putnam Pub.
--Nate the Great & The Sticky Case. LC 77-17011. (Break of Day Bk.). (Illus.). (gr. 1-3). 1978. PLB 6.99 (ISBN 0-698-30697-X, Coward). Putman Pub.
--Nate the Great Goes Undercover. (Break-of-Day Bk.). (Illus.). 48p. (gr. 1-3). 1974. PLB 6.99 (ISBN 0-698-30547-7, Coward). Putman Pub.
--Rex. LC 67-14075. (Illus.). (gr. k-3). 1967. PLB 8.89 (ISBN 0-06-025544-7, HarpJ). Har-Row.
--Rollo & Juliet Forever. LC 80-628. 32p. (gr. 2-3). 1981. 9.95a (ISBN 0-385-15784-3); PLB (ISBN 0-385-15785-1). Doubleday.
--The Trolls of Twelfth Street. LC 78-31788. (Break-of-Day Bk.). (Illus.). (gr. k-3). 1979. PLB 6.99 (ISBN 0-698-30716-X, Coward). Putman Pub.
--Walter the Wolf. LC 74-26659. (Illus.). 32p. (gr. k-3). 1975. PLB 8.95 (ISBN 0-8234-0253-3). Holiday.
Sharmat, Mitchell. Reddy Rattler & Easy Eagle. LC 78-20924. (Reading-on-My-Own Bk.). (Illus.). (gr. 1). 1979. PLB 6.95a o.p. (ISBN 0-385-14216-1). Doubleday.
--The Seven Sloppy Days of Phineas Pig. LC 81-6954. (Illus.). 48p. (gr. 4-8). 11.95 (ISBN 0-15-272936-4, HJ). HarBraceJ.
Sharnoff, J. G. The Prevention of Venous Thrombosis & Pulmonary Embolism. 1980. lib. bdg. 29.95 (ISBN 0-8161-2223-7, Hall Medical). G K Hall.
Sharoff, Victor. The Heart of the Wood. (Break-of-Day Bk.). (Illus.). (gr. k-3). 1971. PLB 4.69 o.p. (ISBN 0-698-30187-0, Coward). Putnam Pub Group.
Sharon, Arieh. Planning Jerusalem: The Master Plan for the Old City of Jerusalem & Its Environs. LC 73-8521. (Illus.). 208p. 1974. 37.50 (ISBN 0-07-056450-7, P&RB). McGraw.
Sharon, Elizabeth, tr. see Tobin, William J.
Sharon, Nathan. Complex Carbohydrates: Their Chemistry, Biosynthesis, & Function, a Set of Lecture Notes. (Illus.). 1975. 24.50 (ISBN 0-201-07324-2, Adv Bk Prog); pap. 22.50 (ISBN 0-201-07323-4). A-W.
Sharouni, Yusuf. Blood Feud. LC 82-50881. 130p. 1983. 12.00X (ISBN 0-89410-358-X); pap. 5.00X (ISBN 0-89410-350-4). Three Continents.
Sharow, Nancy, jt. auth. see Levine, Susan P.
Sharp, jt. auth. see Roberts.
Sharp, A. M., jt. auth. see Lipman, Matthew.
Sharp, Alan A. Hemostasis & Thrombosis. new ed. (BIMR Hematology Ser.: vol. 1). 1983. text ed. price not set (ISBN 0-407-02335-6). Butterworth.
Sharp, Amy. Victorian Poets. 207p. 1982. Repr. of 1891 ed. lib. bdg. 35.00 (ISBN 0-89987-792-3). Darby Bks.
Sharp, Andrew, jt. auth. see Rogers, Frank.
Sharp, Ann M., jt. auth. see Lipman, Matthew.
Sharp, Ann M., jt. ed. see Lipman, Matthew.
Sharp, Ansel M. & Olson, Kent W. Public Finance: The Economics of Government Revenues & Expenditures. (Illus.). 1978. text ed. 20.95 (ISBN 0-8299-0172-8). West Pub.
Sharp, Archibald. Bicycles & Tricycles: An Elementary Treatise on Their Design & Construction. 1977. pap. 9.95 (ISBN 0-262-69066-7). MIT Pr.
--Bicycles & Tricycles; Elementary Treatise on Their Design & Construction: 1896. (Illus.). 536p. Date not set. pap. 35.00 (ISBN 0-87556-579-4). Saifer.
Sharp, B. B. Water Hammer: Problems & Solutions. 152p. 1981. text ed. 26.50 (ISBN 0-7131-3427-5). E Arnold.
Sharp, B. L., jt. ed. see Dawson, J. B.
Sharp, Buchanan. In Contempt of All Authority: Rural Artisans & Riot in the West of England. LC 78-54801. 1980. 27.50x (ISBN 0-520-03681-6). U of Cal Pr.
Sharp, Cecil J. The Idiom of the People: English Traditional Verse. Reeves, James, ed. LC 76-2536. 244p. 1976. Repr. of 1965 ed. lib. bdg. 17.50x (ISBN 0-8371-8769-9, SHIP). Greenwood.
Sharp, Cecil J., jt. ed. see Karpeles, Maud.
Sharp, D. H., jt. ed. see Wightman, A. S.
Sharp, Evelyn. Thinking Is Child's Play. 1970. pap. 1.95 o.p. (ISBN 0-380-01580-3, 41103, Discus). Avon.
Sharp, Flo, jt. auth. see Derig, Betty.
Sharp, Gary D. & Dizon, Andrew E., eds. Physiological Ecology of the Tunas. LC 78-26514. 1979. 46.50 (ISBN 0-12-639180-7). Acad Pr.
Sharp, H. M., jt. auth. see Kinzey, Bertram Y., Jr.
Sharp, Hal. Sportsman's Digest of Fishing. 1953. pap. 3.95 o.p. (ISBN 0-06-463247-4, EH 247, EH). B&N NY.
Sharp, J. A. Introduction to Animal Tissue Culture. (Studies in Biology: No. 82). 64p. 1977. pap. text ed. 8.95 (ISBN 0-7131-2645-0). E Arnold.
Sharp, J. C. Casting Pit Practice. (Illus.). 1969. 9.50x o.p. (ISBN 0-685-20564-9). Transatlantic.
Sharp, J. J. Hydraulic Modelling: Theory & Practice. 1981. text ed. 53.95 (ISBN 0-408-00482-7, Newnes-Butterworth). Butterworth.
Sharp, J. R. & Mann, M., eds. A Select List of Newsletters in the Field of Librarianship & Information Science. 63p. 1981. pap. 40.00x (ISBN 0-905984-72-2, Pub. by Brit Lib England). State Mutual Bk.
Sharp, John R. Information Retrieval: Notes for Students. 96p. 1970. 8.50 (ISBN 0-233-96166-6, 05818-1, Pub. by Gower Pub Co England). Lexington Bks.
--Some Fundamentals of Information Retrieval. 224p. 1965. 14.00 (ISBN 0-233-95712-X, 05820-3, Pub. by Gower Pub Co England). Lexington Bks.
Sharp, M. A. No Sour Grapes. 134p. (Orig.). 1981. pap. write for info. Grape Pr.
Sharp, Margery. Bernard into Battle. (gr. k-6). 1983. pap. 1.75 (ISBN 0-440-40306-5, YB). Dell.
--Bernard the Brave. (gr. k-6). 1983. pap. 1.95 (ISBN 0-440-40305-7, YB). Dell.
--Miss Bianca in the Orient. 1978. pap. 2.25 (ISBN 0-440-45716-5, YB). Dell.
--Miss Bianca in the Salt Mines. 1978. pap. 2.25 (ISBN 0-440-45717-3, YB). Dell.
--Rescuers. 160p. 1974. pap. 1.50 (ISBN 0-440-47378-0, YB). Dell.
Sharp, Marilyn. Masterstroke. 338p. 1981. 12.95 o.p. (ISBN 0-399-90106-X, Marek). Putnam Pub Group.
--Sunflower. LC 78-24428. 1979. 9.95 (ISBN 0-399-90035-7, Marek). Putnam Pub Group.
Sharp, Martin. The History of De-Havillands. 1982. 70.00x (ISBN 0-906393-20-5, Pub. by Airlife England). State Mutual Bk.
Sharp, Mary. Point & Pillow Lace: A Short Account of Various Kinds, Ancient & Modern, & How to Recognize Them. LC 72-141752. (Tower Bks). (Illus.). 1971. Repr. of 1905 ed. 34.00x (ISBN 0-8103-3912-9). Gale.
Sharp, R. Farquharson, ed. Dictionary of English Authors: Biographical & Bibliographical. LC 75-35577. 1978. Repr. of 1904 ed. 45.00x (ISBN 0-8103-4281-2). Gale.
Sharp, R. Farquharson, tr. see Bjornson, Bjornstjerne.
Sharp, R. Farquharson, tr. see Ibsen, Henrik.
Sharp, R. Y., ed. Commutative Algebra: Durham, 1981. LC 82-12781. (London Mathematical Society Lecture Note Ser.: No. 72). 200p. Date not set. pap. 24.95 (ISBN 0-521-27125-8). Cambridge U Pr.
Sharp, Rachel & Green, Anthony. Education & Social Control. 1975. 21.95x (ISBN 0-7100-8160-X); pap. 10.00 (ISBN 0-7100-8161-8). Routledge & Kegan.
Sharp, Richard. Diplomacy. (Illus.). 1978. 15.95x o.p. (ISBN 0-8464-0336-6). Beekman Pubs.
Sharp, Robert L. Big Outfit: Ranching on the Baca Float. LC 74-75821. 1974. pap. 4.95 o.p. (ISBN 0-8165-0410-5). U of Ariz Pr.
Sharp, Vicki F. Statistics for the Social Sciences. 1979. text ed. 18.95 (ISBN 0-316-78324-2); tchrs' manual avail. (ISBN 0-316-78325-0). Little.
Sharp, William R. & Evans, David A. Crop Species, Vol. 2. LC 82-73774. (Handbook of Plant Cell Culture). 550p. 1982. 49.50 (ISBN 0-02-949230-0). Free Pr.
Sharpe, A. G. & Emeleus, H. J., eds. Advances in Inorganic Chemistry & Radiochemistry, Vol. 26. (Serial Publication). Date not set. price not set (ISBN 0-12-023626-5); price not set lib. ed. (ISBN 0-12-023692-3); price not set microfiche (ISBN 0-12-023693-1). Acad Pr.
Sharpe, A. G., jt. ed. see Emeleus, H. J.
Sharpe, Caroline, illus. Sindbad the Sailor. (Illus.). 32p. 1974. 5.50 (ISBN 0-85953-030-2, Pub. by Child's Play England). Playspaces.
Sharpe, Charles K. Historical Account of the Belief in Witchcraft in Scotland. LC 74-8196. 1974. Repr. of 1884 ed. 42.00x (ISBN 0-8103-3590-5). Gale.
Sharpe, Deborah T. The Psychology of Color & Design. (Quality Paperback: No. 313). 170p. 1975. pap. 4.95 (ISBN 0-8226-0313-6). Littlefield.
Sharpe, Eric J., jt. ed. see Hinnells, John R.
Sharpe, Glyn, ed. see Smith, Harold & Keiffer, Mildred.
Sharpe, Grant W. Interpreting the Environment. 2nd ed. LC 81-10391. 694p. 1982. text ed. 27.95 (ISBN 0-471-09007-7). Wiley.
Sharpe, Grant W., ed. Interpreting the Environment. LC 76-4564. 505p. 1976. 24.95 o.p. (ISBN 0-471-77896-6). Wiley.
Sharpe, Grant W., et al. Introduction to Forestry. 4th ed. (Forest Resources Ser.). 1976. text ed. 28.50 (ISBN 0-07-056480-9, C). McGraw.
Sharpe, John C. & Marx, Fredrick. Management of Medical Emergencies. 2nd ed. (Illus.). 1969. 27.00 o.p. (ISBN 0-07-056484-1, HP). McGraw.
Sharpe, Jon. Dakota Wild. (The Trailsman Ser.: No. 6). (Orig.). 1981. pap. 2.50 (ISBN 0-451-11988-6, AE1988, Sig). NAL.
--Mountain Man Kill. (The Trailsman Ser.: No. 3). (Orig.). 1980. pap. 2.50 (ISBN 0-451-12100-7, AE2100, Sig). NAL.
--The River Raiders. (The Trailsman Ser.: No. 5). (Orig.). 1981. pap. 2.25 o.p. (ISBN 0-451-11199-0, AE1199, Sig). NAL.
--Six-Gun Drive. (Trailsman Ser.: No. 8). (Orig.). 1981. pap. 2.50 (ISBN 0-451-12172-4, AE2172, Sig). NAL.
--The Sundown Searchers. (The Trailsman Ser.: No. 4). (Orig.). 1980. pap. 2.50 (ISBN 0-451-12200-3, AE2200, Sig). NAL.
--The Trailsman, No. 10: Slave Hunter. Date not set. pap. 2.25 (ISBN 0-451-11465-5, AE1465, Sig). NAL.
--The Trailsman, No. 12: Condor Pass. 176p. Date not set. pap. 2.50 (ISBN 0-451-11837-5, AE1837, Sig). NAL.
--Trailsman, No. 3: Blood Chase. 1982. pap. 2.50 (ISBN 0-451-11927-4, AE1927, Sig). NAL.
--The Trailsman, No. 8: Six Gun Drive. Date not set. pap. 2.50 (ISBN 0-451-12172-4, AE2172, Sig). NAL.
--Wolf Country. (The Trailsman Ser.: No. 7). (Orig.). 1981. pap. 2.25 (ISBN 0-451-09905-2, E9905, Sig). NAL.
Sharpe, Lesley. Schiller & the Historical Character: Presentation & Interpretation in the Historiographical Works & in the Historical Dramas. (Modern Languages & Literature Monographs). 220p. 1982. 29.50x (ISBN 0-19-815537-9). Oxford U Pr.
Sharpe, Melvin A., jt. auth. see Black, Sam.
Sharpe, Mitchell R., jt. auth. see Ordway, Frederick I.
Sharpe, Myron E. John Kenneth Galbraith & the Lower Economics. 2nd ed. LC 74-21267. 1974. 12.50 (ISBN 0-87332-040-9). M E Sharpe.
Sharpe, Pamela. French-English ESL Card Guide. 12p. (gr. 9-12). Date not set. 2.95 (ISBN 0-8120-5479-2). Barron.
--Spanish-English ESL Card Guide. 12p. (gr. 9-12). Date not set. 2.95 (ISBN 0-8120-5480-6). Barron.
Sharpe, Pamela J. How to Prepare for the Michigan Test Battery. (Barron's Educational Ser.). 160p. 1982. pap. 7.95 (ISBN 0-8120-2419-2). Barron.
Sharpe, R. A., jt. auth. see Currie, B.

Sharpe, Robert B. Irony in the Drama: An Essay on Impersonation, Shock & Catharsis. LC 74-8121. 222p. 1975. Repr. of 1959 ed. lib. bdg. 16.25x (ISBN 0-8371-7552-6, SHID). Greenwood.

Sharpe, Robert F. The Planned Giving Idea Book. 1981. 22.00 (ISBN 0-686-31966-4). Public Serv Materials.

Sharpe, Robert J. The Law of Habeas Corpus. 1976. 42.50x (ISBN 0-19-825332-X). Oxford U Pr.

Sharpe, Sara. Gardener George Goes to Town. LC 82-47577. (Illus.). 40p. (gr. k-3). 1982. 8.61i (ISBN 0-06-025619-2, HarpJ); PLB 9.89g (ISBN 0-06-025620-6). Har-Row.

Sharpe, W. Investments. 2nd ed. 1981. 25.95 (ISBN 0-13-504613-0). P-H.

Sharpe, W. F. Portfolio Theory & Capital Markets. (Foundations of American Government & Political Science). 1970. 31.95 (ISBN 0-07-056487-6, C). McGraw.

Sharpe, William F. & Cootner, Cathryn M., eds. Financial Economics: Essays in Honor of Paul Cootner. (Illus.). 272p. 1982. 29.95 (ISBN 0-13-315291-X). P-H.

Sharper, C. R., jt. auth. see Prus, Robert C.

Sharpes, Donald K., jt. auth. see English, Fenwick W.

Sharples, Stephen P., jt. auth. see Morrison, Leonard A.

Sharpless, John W. Mossman's A Problem Oriented Approach to Stroke Rehabilitation. 1982. 39.75 (ISBN 0-686-95716-4); pap. 32.50 (ISBN 0-686-99586-4). Sis Kenny Inst.

--Mossman's Problem-Oriented Approach to Stroke Rehabilitation. 2nd ed. (Illus.). 456p. 1982. 39.75x (ISBN 0-398-04443-0); pap. 32.50x (ISBN 0-398-04570-4). C C Thomas.

Sharpless, Richard E. Gaitan of Colombia: A Political Biography. LC 77-74552. (Pitt Latin American Ser.). 1977. 14.95 (ISBN 0-8229-3354-3). U of Pittsburgh Pr.

Sharpley, J. Miles & Kaplan, Arthur M., eds. Proceedings of the Third International Biodegradation Symposium. (Illus.). xiv, 1138p. 1976. 199.00 (ISBN 0-85334-679-8, Pub. by Applied Sci England). Elsevier.

Sharrad, L., jt. auth. see Botham, Mary.

Sharrock, E. M., jt. auth. see Sharrock, J. T. R.

Sharrock, J. T. R. & Sharrock, E. M. Rare Birds in Britain & Ireland. (Illus.). 1976. 21.00 o.p. (ISBN 0-85661-014-3, Pub by T & A D Poyser). Buteo.

Sharrock, Roger, ed. & intro. by see Bunyan, John.

Sharry, John J. Complete Denture Prosthodontics. rev. ed. (Illus.). 384p. 1974. text ed. 37.50 o.p. (ISBN 0-07-056496-5, HP). McGraw.

Sharsmith, Helen K. Spring Wildflowers of the San Francisco Bay Region. (California Natural History Guides: No. 11). (Illus.). 1965. 14.95x (ISBN 0-520-03098-2); pap. 5.95 (ISBN 0-520-01168-6). U of Cal Pr.

Shartse, O., tr. see Virta, Nikolai E.

Shartse, Olga, ed. see Poliakova, Liudmila V.

Shashua, Leon & Goldschmidt, Yaaqov. Tools for Financial Management: Emphasis on Inflation. LC 82-47951. 448p. 1983. 36.95x (ISBN 0-669-05720-7). Lexington Bks.

Shastri, H. P., tr. The Ramayana of Valmiki, 3 vols. 3rd ed. 1976. Set. pap. 65.00 (ISBN 0-85424-016-0); Vol. 1. Vol. 2. (ISBN 0-85424-000-4); Vol. 3. (ISBN 0-85424-017-9). Orient Bk Dist.

Shatsky, S. Teacher's Experience. 342p. 1981. 8.00 (ISBN 0-8285-2158-1, Pub. by Progress Pubs USSR). Imported Pubns.

Shattock, E. H. A Manual of Self-Healing. 96p. 1983. pap. 5.95 (ISBN 0-89281-040-8). Destiny Bks.

Shattuck, Clifford. The Nubble: Cape Neddick Lightstation, York, Maine. LC 79-53507. (Illus.). 1979. pap. 4.95 (ISBN 0-87027-195-4). Cumberland Pr.

Shattuck, Louise F. In Stiches Over Bitches: And Now Your Vet Wants a Rolls-Royce! LC 82-23276. (Illus.). 160p. 1983. 10.95 (ISBN 0-87605-549-8). Howell Bk.

Shattuck, Roger, tr. see Daumal, Rene.

Shatz, Marshall S. Soviet Dissent in Historical Perspective. LC 80-13318. 240p. 1981. 24.95 (ISBN 0-521-23172-8). Cambridge U Pr.

Shatzkin, Mike, jt. auth. see Funt, Peter.

Shatzmiller, Maya. L'Historiographie Merinde: Ibn Khaldun et ses Contemporains. (Illus.). xii, 163p. 1982. write for info. (ISBN 90-04-06759-0). E J Brill.

Shaners, Margaret. Dark Knight. 192p. (YA) 1976. 6.95 (ISBN 0-685-61052-7, Avalon). Bouregy.

Shaughnessy, Edward J. Bail & Preventive Detention in New York. (Illus.). 260p. (Orig.). 1982. lib. bdg. 24.00 (ISBN 0-8191-2574-1); pap. text ed. 11.75 (ISBN 0-8191-2575-X). U Pr of Amer.

Shaughnessy, Edward J. & Trebbi, Diana. A Standard for Miller: A Community Response to Pornography. LC 80-5648. (Illus.). 256p. 1980. lib. bdg. 21.25 (ISBN 0-8191-1280-1); pap. text ed. 11.50 (ISBN 0-8191-1281-X). U Pr of Amer.

Shaughnessy, John J., jt. auth. see Underwood, Benton.

Shaughnessy, Mina P. Errors & Expectations: A Guide for the Teacher of Basic Writing. 1977. text ed. 16.95x (ISBN 0-19-502157-6); pap. 8.95x (ISBN 0-19-502507-5). Oxford U Pr.

Shaull, Richard, jt. auth. see Gutierrez, Gustavo.

Shaum, John H., Jr. & Flayhart, William J., III. Majesty at Sea: The Four-Stackers. (Illus.). 1981. 29.95 (ISBN 0-393-01527-0). Norton.

Shave, W. North Atlantic Neighbors: Britain, Canada, U.S.A. (The Life & Livelihood Geographies Ser.: Bk. 1). (Illus.). 8.95 o.p. (ISBN 0-7195-0829-0). Transatlantic.

Shaver, Chester L. see Wordsworth, William & Wordsworth, Dorothy.

Shaver, James P. & Larkins, A. Guy. Analysis & Public Issues: Decision-Making in a Democracy. 232p. (gr. 9-12). 1973. pap. text ed. 12.40 (ISBN 0-395-13466-8); tchr's. guide & ans. key. pap. 20.20 (ISBN 0-395-13467-6). HM.

Shaver, James P. & Strong, William. Facing Value Decisions: Rationale-Building for Teachers. LC 81-18235. 1982. text ed. pap. text ed. 14.95x (ISBN 0-8077-2681-8). Tchrs Coll.

Shaver, Jesse M. Ferns of Eastern Central States. Orig. Title: Ferns of Tennessee. (Illus.). 1970. pap. 4.00 o.p. (ISBN 0-486-22541-0). Dover.

Shaver, Kelley G. Principles of Social Psychology. 2nd ed. 1981. text ed. 20.95 (ISBN 0-316-78329-3); tchr's ed. avail. (ISBN 0-316-78330-7). Little.

Shaver, Phillip R., jt. auth. see Robinson, John P.

Shavin, Norman & Galphin, Bruce. Atlanta: Triumph of a People. (Illus.). 456p. 1982. 29.95 (ISBN 0-910719-00-4). Capricorn Corp.

Shavitt, Isaiah, jt. ed. see Lykos, Peter.

Shaviv, G., ed. see International Conference, 7th, Tel Aviv, June 23-28, 1974.

Shaw & Kellam. Brain Science for Psychiatry. 1982. text ed. pns (ISBN 0-407-00236-7); pap. text ed. 69.95 (ISBN 0-407-00237-5). Butterworth.

Shaw & Kirkwood. Your World. (Illus.). 10.50x (ISBN 0-392-02030-0, ABC). Sportshelf.

Shaw, Alan, jt. auth. see Pohl, Ira.

Shaw, Alan C. Logical Design of Operating Systems. (Illus.). 304p. 1974. 28.95 (ISBN 0-13-540112-7). P-H.

Shaw, Arnold. A Dictionary of American Pop-Rock. 475p. 1982. pap. 12.95 (ISBN 0-686-83163-2). Macmillan.

--A Dictionary of American Pop-Rock. LC 82-50382. 440p. 1983. 19.95 (ISBN 0-02-872350-3); pap. 12.95. Schirmer Bks.

--Sinatra: The Entertainer. Allan, Ted, ed. (Illus.). 160p. 1980. 19.95 (ISBN 0-933328-43-5). Delilah Bks.

Shaw, B. L. Inorganic Hydrides. 1967. 21.00 o.s.i. (ISBN 0-08-012110-1); pap. 9.75 (ISBN 0-08-012109-8). Pergamon.

Shaw, Bernard. Collected Plays with Their Prefaces: Definitive Edition in Seven Volumes. 1975. 20.00 ea.; Vol. 1. (ISBN 0-396-07125-2); Vol. 2. (ISBN 0-396-07126-0); Vol. 3. (ISBN 0-396-07127-9); Vol. 4. (ISBN 0-396-07128-7). Vol. 5 (ISBN 0-396-07129-5). Vol. 6 (ISBN 0-396-07130-9). Vol. 7 (ISBN 0-396-07131-7). Dodd.

--Four Plays by Bernard Shaw. Incl. Candida. 1953; Caesar & Cleopatra; Pygmalion; Heartbreak House. 1962. 3.95 o.s.i. (ISBN 0-394-60019-3, M19). Modern Lib.

--Saint Joan. Bd. with Major Barbara; Androcles & the Lion. LC 56-5413. 6.95 (ISBN 0-394-60480-6). Modern Lib.

Shaw, Bernard & Douglas, Alfred. Bernard Shaw & Alfred Douglas: A Correspondence. Hyde, Mary, ed. LC 82-5567. (Illus.). 280p. 1982. 25.00 (ISBN 0-89919-128-2). Ticknor & Fields.

Shaw, Bob. Pitching. (Illus.) 1981. pap. 7.95 (ISBN 0-8092-5913-3). Contemp Bks.

Shaw, Bradley & Gonzalez-Del Valle, Luis. Luis Romero. (World Authors Ser.). 1979. lib. bdg. 11.95 (ISBN 0-8057-6361-9, Twayne). G K Hall.

Shaw, Bruce. My Country of the Pelican Dreaming: The Life of an Australian Aborigine of the Gadjerong, Grant Ngabidji, 1904-1977. (AIAS New Ser.). 202p. 1981. pap. text ed. 11.25x (ISBN 0-391-02218-0, Pub. by Australian Inst Australia). Humanities.

Shaw, Bryce R. Personalized Computational Skills Program. LC 79-90570. 544p. 1980. Set. pap. text ed. 19.95 (ISBN 0-395-29032-5); Mod. A. pap. text ed. 7.50 (ISBN 0-395-29033-3); Mod. B. pap. text ed. 7.50 (ISBN 0-395-29034-1); Mod. C. pap. text ed. 7.50 (ISBN 0-395-29035-X); pap. 1.25 inst. manual (ISBN 0-395-29036-8). HM.

Shaw, Bynum. Days of Power, Nights of Fear. 288p. 1980. 10.95 o.p. (ISBN 0-312-18483-2). St Martin.

--Divided We Stand: The Baptists in American Life. LC 73-86777. 250p. 1974. 12.95 (ISBN 0-87716-044-9, Pub. by Moore Pub Co). F Apple.

Shaw, Bynum & Folk, Edgar E. W. W. Holden: A Political Biography. (Illus.). 288p. 1982. 24.95 (ISBN 0-89587-025-8). Blair.

Shaw, Catherine M. Richard Brome. (English Author Ser.). (gr. 10-12). 1980. lib. bdg. 14.95 (ISBN 0-8057-6783-5, Twayne). G K Hall.

Shaw, Charles R., ed. see Annual Symposium on Fundamental Cancer Research, No. 31.

Shaw, Chris, jt. auth. see Abraham, Ralph.

Shaw, Clifford R. Natural History of a Delinquent Career. LC 68-56042. (Illus.). 1968. Repr. of 1931 ed. lib. bdg. 18.50x (ISBN 0-8371-0654-0, SHDC). Greenwood.

Shaw, D. The Dissuaders: Three Explanations of Religion. (Student Christian Movement Press Ser.). (Orig.). 1978. pap. 4.95x (ISBN 0-19-520339-9). Oxford U Pr.

Shaw, D. J. Introduction to Colloid & Surface Chemistry. 2nd ed. 248p. 1970. 12.95 o.p. (ISBN 0-408-70021-1). Butterworth.

Shaw, D. L., ed. Eduardo Mallea: Todo verdor perecera. 1968. 8.30 o.p. (ISBN 0-08-012868-8); pap. 5.75 o.p. (ISBN 0-08-012867-X). Pergamon.

Shaw, D. T. Recent Developments in Aerosol Science. 327p. 1978. 59.95 (ISBN 0-471-02950-5, Pub. by Wiley-Interscience). Wiley.

Shaw, Daniel, ed. Kinship Studies in Papua, New Guinea. 246p. 1974. 5.00x (ISBN 0-7263-0245-7); microfiche 3.00 (ISBN 0-88312-396-7). Summer Inst Ling.

Shaw, David, jt. auth. see Cartlidge, Niall.

Shaw, David T. Fundamentals of Aerosol Science. LC 77-19331. 372p. 1978. 60.00 (ISBN 0-471-02949-1, Pub. by Wiley-Interscience). Wiley.

Shaw, Denis. Pakistani Twins. (Twins Ser). (gr. 6-9). 1965. 7.50 (ISBN 0-8023-1094-X). Dufour.

Shaw, Diana & Berry, Caroline F. Options: The Female Teen's Guide to Coping with the Problems of Today's World. LC 80-2871. 168p. 1983. pap. 4.95 (ISBN 0-385-17057-2, Anch). Doubleday.

Shaw, E. M. History of the Currency of South Africa. (Illus.). 1983. Repr. of 1956 ed. pap. 10.00 (ISBN 0-942666-07-0). S J Durst.

Shaw, E. N. Europe's Nuclear Power Experiment: History of the OECD Dragon Project. (Illus.). 300p. 1982. 25.00 (ISBN 0-08-029324-7). Pergamon.

Shaw, Edward P. Problems & Policies of Malesherbes As Directeur De la Librarie in France, 1750-1763. LC 66-63787. 1966. 24.50x (ISBN 0-87395-018-6). State U NY Pr.

Shaw, Edward S. Financial Deepening in Economic Development. (Economic Development Ser.). 1973. text ed. 15.95x (ISBN 0-19-501633-5); pap. text ed. 7.95x (ISBN 0-19-501632-7). Oxford U Pr.

Shaw, Edward S., jt. auth. see Gurley, John G.

Shaw, Edwin, jt. auth. see Goldsmith, M.

Shaw, Evelyn. Fish Out of School. LC 77-105477. (Science I Can Read Books). (Illus.). (ps-3). 1970. 7.64i (ISBN 0-06-025563-3, HarpJ); PLB 8.89 o.p. (ISBN 0-06-025564-1). Har-Row.

--Octopus. LC 74-135779. (Science I Can Read Books). (Illus.). (gr. k-3). 1971. PLB 8.89 o.p. (ISBN 0-06-025559-5, HarpJ). Har-Row.

--Sea Otters. LC 79-2017. (Nature I Can Read Bks.). (Illus.). 64p. (gr. k-3). 1980. 7.64i (ISBN 0-06-025613-3, HarpJ); PLB 8.89 (ISBN 0-06-025614-1). Har-Row.

--The Snoopy Doghouse Cookbook. LC 78-68776. (Illus.). 1979. pap. 4.95 (ISBN 0-915696-12-6). Determined Prods.

Shaw, Frank R., jt. auth. see Eckert, John E.

Shaw, G., jt. auth. see Brooks, J.

Shaw, G. B. The Intelligent Woman's Guide to Socialism, Capitalism, Sovietism, & Fascism. (Pelican Classic Ser.). 1982. pap. 4.95 (ISBN 0-14-020001-0). Penguin.

Shaw, G. B. & Lerner, Alan J. Pygmalion. Bd. with My Fair Lady. pap. 2.50 (ISBN 0-451-51760-1, CE1760, Sig Classics). NAL.

Shaw, G. K., jt. auth. see Peacock, Alan.

Shaw, George B. Back to Methuselah. rev. ed. 1947. 6.95x (ISBN 0-19-500181-8). Oxford U Pr.

--Bernard Shaw's Plays: Major Barbara, Heartbreak House, Saint Joan, Too True to Be Good. Smith, Warren S., ed. (Critical Editions Ser). 1970-71. pap. text ed. 8.95x (ISBN 0-393-09942-3). Norton.

--Caesar & Cleopatra: A History. Forter, Elizabeth T., ed. LC 65-14791. (Crofts Classics Ser.). 1965. pap. text ed. 3.75x (ISBN 0-88295-086-X). Harlan Davidson.

--Candida & How She Lied to Her Husband. Smith, J. Percy, intro. by. LC 79-56703. (Bernard Shaw Early Texts: Play Manuscripts in Facsimile). 1981. lib. bdg. 45.00 o.s.i. (ISBN 0-8240-4579-3). Garland Pub.

--The Devil's Disciple. Whitman, Robert F., ed. LC 79-56706. (Bernard Shaw Early Texts: Play Manuscripts in Facsimile). 1981. lib. bdg. 45.00 o.s.i. (ISBN 0-8240-4581-5). Garland Pub.

--Major Barbara. Forter, Elizabeth T., ed. LC 77-145842. (Crofts Classics Ser.). 1971. text ed. 10.00x (ISBN 0-88295-087-8); pap. text ed. 3.75x (ISBN 0-88295-088-6). Harlan Davidson.

--The Man of Destiny & Caesar & Cleopatra. Wisenthal, J. L., ed. LC 79-56707. (Bernard Shaw Early Texts: Play Manuscripts in Facsimile). 1981. lib. bdg. 70.00 o.s.i. (ISBN 0-8240-4582-3). Garland Pub.

--Mrs. Warren's Profession. Peters, Margot, ed. LC 79-56701. (Bernard Shaw Early Texts: Play Manuscripts in Facsimile). 1981. lib. bdg. 50.00 o.s.i. (ISBN 0-8240-4577-7). Garland Pub.

--On Going to Church. Brown, Edmund R., ed. (International Pocket Library). pap. 3.00 (ISBN 0-686-77248-2). Branden.

--On Going to Church. 24p. pap. 1.25 (ISBN-0-934676-13-5). Greenlf Bks.

--The Portable Bernard Shaw. Weintraub, Stanley, ed. (Viking Portable Library Ser: P90). 1977. pap. 6.95 (ISBN 0-14-015090-0). Penguin.

--Pygmalion. Shefter, Harry, ed. (Enriched Classics Edition Ser.). 176p. 1983. pap. 2.25 (ISBN 0-671-43298-2). WSP.

--Widowers' Houses. Bringle, Jerald, ed. LC 79-56699. (Bernard Shaw Early Texts: Play Manuscripts in Facsimile). 1981. lib. bdg. 50.00 o.s.i. (ISBN 0-8240-4575-0). Garland Pub.

Shaw, George B; see Brown, Edmund R.

Shaw, George B; see Laurel Editions Editors.

Shaw, George Bernard. Plays. pap. 3.95 (ISBN 0-451-51786-5, CE1786, Sig Classics). NAL.

Shaw, George R. Knots: Useful & Ornamental. 3rd ed. (Illus.). 1972. pap. 6.95 (ISBN 0-02-082030-5, Collier). Macmillan.

Shaw, Grace, jt. auth. see Lemond, Alan.

Shaw, Grace, ed. see Harrison, Harry.

Shaw, Grace, ed. see Howard, Robert E.

Shaw, Grace, ed. see Hutchinson, Warner.

Shaw, Grace, ed. see Roth, June.

Shaw, Graham. The Cost of Authority: Manipulation & Freedom in the New Testament. LC 82-48545. 320p. 1983. pap. 16.95 (ISBN 0-8006-1707-X). Fortress.

Shaw, Graham W. & Quraishi, Salim, eds. The Bibliography of South Asian Periodicals: A Union List of Periodicals in South Asian Languages. LC 82-16454. 148p. 1983. text ed. 26.50x (ISBN 0-389-20338-6). B&N Imports.

Shaw, H. Fly-Tying: Materials-Tools-Techniques. 2nd ed. LC 79-18416. 310p. 1979. 18.50 (ISBN 0-471-05516-6, Pub. by Wiley-Interscience). Wiley.

Shaw, H. Curtis. Temptation & Release. 1978. 6.95 o.p. (ISBN 0-533-03383-7). Vantage.

Shaw, Harlan. American Men's Wear, Eighteen Sixty-One to Nineteen Eighty-Two. LC 82-81871. (Illus.). 327p. (Orig.). 1982. pap. 21.50 (ISBN 0-88127-008-3). Oracle Pr LA.

Shaw, Harry. Concise Dictionary of Literary Terms. (McGraw-Hill Paperbacks). Orig. Title: Dictionary of Literary Terms. 224p. 1976. pap. 4.95 (ISBN 0-07-056483-3, SP). McGraw.

--Dictionary of Literary Terms. LC 72-179884. 418p. 1972. 29.95 (ISBN 0-07-056490-6, P&RB). McGraw.

--Dictionary of Problem Words & Expressions. 1975. 19.95 (ISBN 0-07-056489-2, P&RB). McGraw.

--The Harper Handbook of College Composition. 5th ed. 609p. 1981. text ed. 14.50 scp (ISBN 0-06-045976-X, HarpC); scp wkbk. 9.95 (ISBN 0-06-045982-4); ans. key avail. (ISBN 0-06-366036-9); diagnostic tests avail. (ISBN 0-06-366037-7). Har-Row.

--McGraw Hill Handbook of English. 3rd ed. 1969. text ed. 11.20 o.p. (ISBN 0-07-056492-2, W); pap. text ed. 8.20 o.p. (ISBN 0-07-056493-0); tchr's. key 2.56 o.p. (ISBN 0-07-056494-9). McGraw.

--McGraw-Hill Handbook of English. 4th ed. (Illus.). (gr. 9-12). 1977. pap. text ed. 11.20 (ISBN 0-07-056506-6, W); tchr's. manual 5.28 (ISBN 0-07-056507-4). McGraw.

--Punctuate It Right! (Orig.). 1963. pap. 3.50 (ISBN 0-06-463255-5, EH 255, EH). B&N NY.

--Twenty Steps to Better Writing. (Quality Paperback: No. 289). 146p. (Orig.). 1978. pap. 3.95 (ISBN 0-8226-0289-X). Littlefield.

Shaw, Harry B. Gwendolyn Brooks. (United States Authors Ser.). 1980. lib. bdg. 10.95 (ISBN 0-8057-7287-1, Twayne). G K Hall.

Shaw, Henry. The Encyclopedia of Ornament. (Illus.). 1974. 12.50 o.p. (ISBN 0-312-24920-9); pap. 5.50 o.p. (ISBN 0-312-24955-1). St Martin.

Shaw, Irwin. Bread upon the Waters. 1981. 14.95 o.s.i. (ISBN 0-440-00884-0); ltd. signed ed. 50.00 o.s.i. (ISBN 0-440-00908-1). Delacorte.

--Bread Upon the Waters. 1982. pap. 3.95 (ISBN 0-440-10845-4). Dell.

--Evening in Byzantium. 352p. 1974. pap. 3.95 (ISBN 0-440-13150-2). Dell.

--Rich Man, Poor Man. 1970. 12.50 o.s.i. (ISBN 0-440-07423-1). Delacorte.

--Rich Man, Poor Man. 1976. pap. 4.25 (ISBN 0-440-17424-4). Dell.

--Short Stories: Five Decades. 1983. pap. 6.95 (ISBN 0-686-82566-7, LE). Dell.

--Short Stories of Five Decades. 1978. 16.95 o.s.i. (ISBN 0-440-04147-3). Delacorte.

--The Top of the Hill. 1979. 12.95 o.s.i. (ISBN 0-440-08976-X). Delacorte.

--Top of the Hill. 1980. pap. 3.95 (ISBN 0-440-19026-6). Dell.

--The Troubled Air. 1978. pap. 2.75 (ISBN 0-440-18608-0). Dell.

--The Young Lions. Date not set. 7.95 (ISBN 0-394-60809-7). Modern Lib.

Shaw, Irwin & Searle, C. Ronald. Paris Paris. 1978. pap. 3.95 o.s.i. (ISBN 0-440-56850-1, Delta). Dell.

Shaw, J. T. Pushkin's Rhymes: A Dictionary. LC 73-15263. 718p. 1974. 50.00 (ISBN 0-299-06480-8). U of Wis Pr.

Shaw, J. Thomas, tr. see Puskin, Alexander.

Shaw, Jackie. Freehanding with Jackie. (Illus.). 48p. (Orig.). 1980. pap. 6.50 (ISBN 0-941284-12-3). Deco Design Studio.

--Painting in the Pantry with Jackie. (Illus.). 32p. (Orig.). 1982. pap. 5.50 (ISBN 0-941284-15-8). Deco Design Studio.

--Pigments of your Imagination, Vol. 1 - 3. (Orig.). 1978. Vol. 1. pap. 5.95 (ISBN 0-941284-06-9); Vol. 2. pap. 5.95 (ISBN 0-941284-07-7); Vol. 3. pap. 8.95 (ISBN 0-941284-08-5). Deco Design Studio.

--Rock 'N Tole. (Orig.). 1980. pap. 8.50 (ISBN 0-941284-10-7). Deco Design Studio.

--There's a Rainbow in my Paintbox. (Orig.). 1977. pap. 5.95 (ISBN 0-941284-05-0). Deco Design Studio.
--Tole Technique & Decorative Arts, 4 Vols. (Orig.). 1974. Vol. 1. pap. 3.95 (ISBN 0-941284-01-8); Vol. 2. pap. 3.95 (ISBN 0-941284-02-6); Vol. 3. pap. 3.95 (ISBN 0-941284-03-4); Vol. 4. pap. 3.95 (ISBN 0-941284-04-2). Deco Design Studio.
--You Can Do-Things By Yourself. 72p. (gr. 1-4). 1977. pap. 4.00 (ISBN 0-941284-00-X). Deco Design Studio.
Shaw, James H, ed. Sweeteners & Dental Caries: Proceedings. LC 78-52278. 404p. 1978. 15.00 (ISBN 0-917000-05-6). IRL Pr.
Shaw, Janet, jt. auth. see Shaw, John R.
Shaw, Jean. The Better Half of Life: Meditations from Ecclesiastes. 192p. 1983. pap. 5.95 (ISBN 0-310-43551-X). Zondervan.
Shaw, Jean W. TV: Friend or Foe? 1983. pap. cancelled (ISBN 0-8054-5652-X). Broadman.
Shaw, Joan. The Uncle & Other Stories. Jaffray, Angela, ed. LC 82-70936. 101p. 1983. pap. 6.00 (ISBN 0-932274-31-5); signed 15.00 (ISBN 0-932274-32-3). Cadmus Eds.
Shaw, John. The Self in Social Work. (Library of Social Work). 1974. 14.95x (ISBN 0-7100-7920-6); pap. 6.95 (ISBN 0-7100-7921-4). Routledge & Kegan.
Shaw, John A., jt. auth. see Leet, Don R.
Shaw, John M., ed. Childhood in Poetry: A Catalogue, with Biographical & Critical Annotations, of the Books of English & American Poets Comprising the Shaw Childhood in Poetry Collection in the Library of the Florida State University, 5 Vols. LC 67-28092. (Illus.). 1967. 245.00x (ISBN 0-8103-0475-9). Gale.
--Childhood in Poetry: First Supplement, 3 Vols. LC 67-28092. (Illus.). 1972. Set. 170.00x (ISBN 0-8103-0476-7). Gale.
--Childhood in Poetry: Second Supplement - a Catalogue, with Biographical & Critical Annotations, of the Books of English & American Poets Comprising the Shaw Childhood in Poetry Collection in the Library of the Fla. St. U, 2 vols. LC 67-28092. 1500p. 1976. Set. 170.00x (ISBN 0-8103-0477-5); Vol. 1. 42.50 o.p. (ISBN 0-8103-0479-1); Vol. 2. index 75.00 (ISBN 0-686-67256-9). Gale.
--Childhood in Poetry: Third Supplement. LC 67-28092. (Childhood in Poetry Ser.). (Illus.). 96.00x (ISBN 0-8103-0480-5). Gale.
Shaw, John R. & Shaw, Janet. The New Horizon Ladder Dictionary of the English Language for Young Readers. rev. ed. (Illus.). 686p. 1973. pap. 2.50 (ISBN 0-451-11332-2, AE1332, Sig). NAL.
Shaw, Joseph M. Pulpit Under the Sky: A Life of Hans Nielson Hauge. LC 78-12391. 1979. Repr. of 1955 ed. lib. bdg. 20.50x (ISBN 0-313-21123-X, SHPU). Greenwood.
Shaw, K. Ceramic Glazes. 1971. 24.95 (ISBN 0-444-20107-6). Elsevier.
Shaw, L., jt. auth. see Schwartz, Mischa.
Shaw, Leo. Battle of the Bulge. (Illus.). 80p. (Orig.). 1980. pap. 8.00x (ISBN 0-686-27285-4). Servicios Intles.
--Battle of the Bulge. 2nd ed. (Illus.). 80p. 1982. pap. 8.00 (ISBN 0-686-34569-X). Servicios Intles.
--Blazing Lecterns. (Illus.). 130p. (Orig.). 1983. pap. 8.00 (ISBN 0-943236-06-1). Servicios Intles.
--Dolly. (Illus.). 132p. 1982. pap. 8.00 (ISBN 0-686-34570-3). Servicios Intles.
--Female Charioteers (Women Drivers) 130p. (Orig.). 1983. pap. text ed. 8.00 (ISBN 0-943236-07-X). Servicios Intles.
--Kalifunkens. (Illus.). 130p. (Orig.). 1983. pap. text ed. 8.00 (ISBN 0-943236-05-3). Servicios Intles.
--Retirement Reverly. pap. 8.00 (ISBN 0-686-34571-1). Servicios Intles.
--Unsafe to Read at Any Speed. (Illus.). 85p. (Orig.). 1980. pap. 8.00x (ISBN 0-686-27286-2). Servicios Intles.
Shaw, Lois B., ed. Unplanned Careers: The Working Lives of Middle-Aged Women. LC 82-47925. 160p. 1982. 19.95x (ISBN 0-669-05701-0). Lexington Bks.
Shaw, Loretta. The Human Machine. LC 82-73479. 140p. (Orig.). 1982. pap. 6.95 (ISBN 0-931494-33-8). Brunswick Pub.
Shaw, Luci. The Sighting. LC 81-9342. (The Wheaton Literary Ser.). (Illus.). 96p. 1981. pap. 4.95 (ISBN 0-87788-768-3). Shaw Pubs.
Shaw, Luci, ed. see Boom, Corrie ten.
Shaw, M. Group Dynamics: The Psychology of Small Group Behavior. 1975. text ed. 23.95 o.p. (ISBN 0-07-056501-5, C). McGraw.
Shaw, M. & Costanzo, P. R. Theories in Social Psychology. 1970. text ed. 31.00 (ISBN 0-07-056495-7, C). McGraw.
Shaw, M. E. & Costanzo, P. R. Theories of Social Psychology. 2nd ed. 1982. 30.00 (ISBN 0-07-056512-0). McGraw.
Shaw, M. E. & Wright, J. M. Scales for the Measurement of Attitudes. (Psychology Ser.). 1967. text ed. 55.00 (ISBN 0-07-056498-1, C). McGraw.
Shaw, M. P., et al. The Gunn-Hilsum Effect. LC 76-45995. 1979. 31.00 (ISBN 0-12-638350-2). Acad Pr.
Shaw, Maie-Jose. Basic Skills Reading Workbook: Grade 7. (Basic Skills Workbooks). 32p. (gr. 7). 1982. tchrs' ed. 0.99 (ISBN 0-8209-0369-8, W-H). ESP.
Shaw, Malcolm, et al. Using AACR2: A Diagrammatic Approach. 224p. 1981. text ed. 27.50x (ISBN 0-912700-88-2). Oryx Pr.
Shaw, Margery W., jt. ed. see Doudera, A. Edward.
Shaw, Marie. Basic Skills Spelling Tests Workbook. (Basic Skills Workbooks). 32p. (gr. 5-6). 1983. 0.99 (ISBN 0-8209-0567-4, STW-2). ESP.
--Basic Skills Spelling Tests Workbook. (Basic Skills Workbooks). 32p. (gr. 3-4). 1983. 0.99 (ISBN 0-8209-0566-6, STW-1). ESP.
--Spelling Tests: Grade 3. Incl. Grade 4. wkbk. 5.00 (ISBN 0-8209-0169-5, ST-4); Grade 5. wkbk. 5.00 (ISBN 0-8209-0170-9, ST-5); Grade 6. wkbk. 5.00 (ISBN 0-8209-0171-7, ST-6). (Spelling Ser.). 24p. 1979. wkbk. 5.00 (ISBN 0-8209-0168-7, ST-3). ESP.
Shaw, Marie-Jose. Basic Skills English Workbook: Grade 10. (Basic Skills Workbooks). 32p. 1982. wkbk. 0.99 (ISBN 0-8209-0359-0, EW-K). ESP.
--Basic Skills English Workbook: Grade 11. (Basic Skills Workbooks). 32p. 1982. wkbk. 0.99 (EW-L). ESP.
--Basic Skills English Workbook: Grade 12. (Basic Skills Workbooks). 32p. 1982. wkbk. 0.99 (ISBN 0-8209-0361-2, EW-M). ESP.
--Basic Skills English Workbook: Grade 2. (Basic Skills Workbooks). 32p. 1982. tchrs' ed. 0.99 (ISBN 0-8209-0351-5, EW-C). ESP.
--Basic Skills English Workbook: Grade 3. (Basic Skills Worbooks). wkbk. 0.99 (ISBN 0-8209-0352-3, EW-D). ESP.
--Basic Skills English Workbook: Grade 4. (Basic Skills Workbooks). 32p. 1982. wkbk. 0.99 (ISBN 0-686-38394-X). ESP.
--Basic Skills English Workbook: Grade 5. (Basic Skills Workbooks). 32p. 1982. wkbk. 0.99 (ISBN 0-8209-0354-X, EW-F). ESP.
--Basic Skills English Workbook: Grade 6. (Basic Skills Workbook). 32p. 1982. wkbk. 0.99 (ISBN 0-8209-0355-8, EW-G). ESP.
--Basic Skills English Workbook: Grade 7. (Basic Skills Workbooks). 32p. 1982. wkbk. 0.99 (ISBN 0-8209-0356-6, EW-H). ESP.
--Basic Skills English Workbook: Grade 8. (Basic Skills Workbooks). 32p. 1982. wkbk. 0.99 (ISBN 0-8209-0357-4, EW-I). ESP.
--Basic Skills English Workbook: Grade 9. (Basic Skills Workbooks). 32p. 1982. wkbk. 0.99 (ISBN 0-8209-0358-2, EW-J). ESP.
--Basic Skills Reading Workbook: Grade 2. (Basic Skills Workbooks). 32p. (gr. 2). 1982. tchrs' ed. 0.99 (ISBN 0-8209-0364-7, RW-C). ESP.
--Basic Skills Reading Workbook: Grade 4. (Basic Skills Workbooks). 32p. (gr. 4). 1982. tchrs' ed. 0.99 (ISBN 0-8209-0366-3, RW-E). ESP.
--Basic Skills Reading Workbook: Grade 5. (Basic Skills Workbooks). 32p. (gr. 5). 1982. tchrs' ed. 0.99 (ISBN 0-8209-0367-1, W-F). ESP.
--Basic Skills Reading Workbook: Grade 6. (Basic Skills Workbooks). 32p. (gr. 6). 1982. wkbk. 0.99 (ISBN 0-8209-0368-X, RW-G). ESP.
--Basic Skills Reading Workbooks: Grade 3. (Basic Skills Workbooks). 32p. (gr. 3). 1982. wkbk. 0.99 (ISBN 0-8209-0365-5, RW-D). ESP.
--Basic Skills Spelling Workbook: Grade 3. (Basic Skills Workbooks). 32p. (gr. 3). 1982. wkbk. 0.99 (ISBN 0-8209-0373-6, SPW-D). ESP.
--Basic Skills Spelling Workbook: Grade 4. (Basic Skills Workbooks). 32p. (gr. 4). 1982. wkbk. 0.99 (ISBN 0-8209-0374-4, SPW-E). ESP.
--Basic Skills Spelling Workbook: Grade 5. (Basic Skills Workbooks). 32p. (gr. 5). 1982. wkbk. 0.99 (ISBN 0-8209-0375-2, SPW-F). ESP.
--Basic Skills Spelling Workbook: Grade 6. (Basic Skills Workbooks). 32p. (gr. 6). 1982. wkbk. 0.99 (ISBN 0-8209-0376-0, SPW-G). ESP.
--Basic Skills Vocabulary Workbook: Grade 2. (Basic Skills Workbooks). 32p. (gr. 2). 1982. wkbk. 0.99 (ISBN 0-8209-0378-7, VW-C). ESP.
--Basic Skills Vocabulary Workbook: Grade 3. (Basic Skills Workbooks). 32p. (gr. 3). 1982. wkbk. 0.99 (ISBN 0-8209-0379-5, VW-D). ESP.
--Basic Skills Vocabulary Workbook: Grade 4. (Basic Skills Workbooks). 32p. (gr. 4). 1982. wkbk. 0.99 (ISBN 0-8209-0380-9, VW-E). ESP.
--Basic Skills Vocabulary Workbook: Grade 5. (Basic Skills Workbooks). 32p. (gr. 5). 1982. wkbk. 0.99 (ISBN 0-8209-0381-7, VW-F). ESP.
--Basic Skills Vocabulary Workbook: Grade 6. (Basic Skills Workbooks). 32p. (gr. 6). 1982. wkbk. 0.99 (ISBN 0-8209-0382-5, VW-G). ESP.
--Combining Forms: Grade 5. (English Sound Filmstrip Kits Ser.). (gr. 5). 1980. tchrs ed. 24.00 (ISBN 0-8209-0512-7, FCW5E-19). ESP.
--Combining Forms: Grade 6. (English Sound Filmstrip Kits Ser.). (gr. 6). 1980. tchrs ed. 24.00 (ISBN 0-8209-0532-1, FCW6E-19). ESP.
--Commands. (English Sound Filmstrip Kits Ser.). (gr. 3). 1979. tchrs ed. 24.00 (ISBN 0-8209-0466-X, FCW3E-13). ESP.
--Compounding Sentence Parts. (English Sound Filmstrip Kits Ser.). (gr. 5). 1980. tchrs ed. 24.00 (ISBN 0-8209-0508-9, FCW5E-15). ESP.
--Conjunctions & Interjections. (English Sound Filmstrip Kits Ser.). (gr. 6). 1980. tchrs ed. 24.00 (ISBN 0-8209-0520-8, FCW6E-7). ESP.
--Conjunctions & Prepositions. (English Sound Filmstrip Kits Ser.). (gr. 5). 1980. tchrs ed. 24.00 (ISBN 0-8209-0501-1, FCW5E-8). ESP.
--The Dewey Decimal Classification. (Sound Filmstrip Kits Ser.). (gr. 4-8). 1981. tchrs ed. 24.00 (ISBN 0-8209-0447-3, FCW-24). ESP.
--The Dictionary. (Sound Filmstrip Kits Ser.). (gr. 3-6). 1981. tchrs ed. 24.00 (ISBN 0-8209-0441-4, FCW-18). ESP.
--Did-Done, Ran-Run, & Saw-Seen. (English Sound Filmstrip Kits Ser.). (gr. 3). 1980. tchrs ed. 24.00 (ISBN 0-8209-0471-6, FCW3E-18). ESP.
--Direct & Indirect Objects. (English Sound Filmstrip Kits Ser.). (gr. 5). 1980. tchrs ed. 24.00 (ISBN 0-8209-0505-4, FCW5E-12). ESP.
--Direct Objects. (English Sound Filmstrips Kits Ser.). (gr. 4). 1979. tchrs ed. 24.00 (ISBN 0-8209-0483-X, FCW4E-10). ESP.
--The Encyclopedia. (Sound Filmstrip Kits Ser.). (gr. 3-6). 1981. tchrs ed. 24.00 (ISBN 0-8209-0442-2, FCW-19). ESP.
--Energy & Man. (Sound Filmstrip Kits Ser.). (gr. 3-6). 1981. 24.00 (ISBN 0-8209-0435-X, FCW-12). ESP.
--First Aid. (Sound Filmstrip Kits Ser.). (gr. 3-6). 1981. tchrs ed. 24.00 (ISBN 0-8209-0434-1, FCW-11). ESP.
--Following Directions. (Sound Filmstrip Kits Ser.). (gr. 2-4). 1981. tchrs ed. 24.00 (ISBN 0-8209-0449-X, FCW-26). ESP.
--Four Kinds of Sentences: Grade 4. (English Sound Filmstrip Kits Ser.). (gr. 4). 1979. tchrs ed. 24.00 (ISBN 0-8209-0486-4, FCW4E-13). ESP.
--Four Kinds of Sentences: Grade 5. (English Sound Filmstrip Kits Ser.). (gr. 5). 1980. tchrs ed. 24.00 (ISBN 0-8209-0509-7, FCW5E-16). ESP.
--Four Sentence Patterns. (English Sound Filmstrip Kits Ser.). (gr. 6). 1980. tchrs ed. 24.00 (ISBN 0-8209-0528-3, FCW6E-15). ESP.
--Four Sentence Types. (English Sound Filmstrip Kits Ser.). (gr. 6). 1980. tchrs ed. 24.00 (ISBN 0-8209-0529-1, FCW6E-16). ESP.
--How to Make Comparisons. (English Sound Filmstrip Kits Ser.). (gr. 6). 1980. tchrs ed. 24.00 (ISBN 0-8209-0519-4, FCW6E-6). ESP.
--Indirect Objects. (English Sound Filmstrip Kits Ser.). (gr. 4). 1979. tchrs ed. 24.00 (ISBN 0-8209-0484-8, FCW4E-11). ESP.
--Jumbo English Yearbook: Grade 10. (Jumbo English Ser.). (gr. 10). 1979. wkbk. 14.00 (ISBN 0-8209-0008-7, JEY-8). ESP.
--Jumbo English Yearbook: Grade 11. (Jumbo English Ser.). (gr. 11). 1982. wkbk. 14.00 (ISBN 0-8209-0009-5, JEY-9). ESP.
--Jumbo English Yearbook: Grade 12. (Jumbo English Ser.). (gr. 12). 1982. wkbk. 14.00 (ISBN 0-8209-0010-9, JEY-10). ESP.
--Jumbo English Yearbook: Grade 2. (Jumbo English Ser.). 96p. (gr. 2). 1980. wkbk. 14.00 (ISBN 0-8209-0000-1, JEY-0). ESP.
--Jumbo English Yearbook: Grade 3. (Jumbo English Ser.). 96p. (gr. 3). 1977. wkbk. 14.00 (ISBN 0-8209-0001-X, JEY-1). ESP.
--Jumbo English Yearbook: Grade 4. (Jumbo English Ser.). (gr. 4). 1977. wkbk. 14.00 (ISBN 0-8209-0002-8, JEY-2). ESP.
--Jumbo English Yearbook: Grade 5. (Jumbo English Ser.). (gr. 5). 1977. wkbk. 14.00 (ISBN 0-8209-0003-6, JEY-3). ESP.
--Jumbo English Yearbook: Grade 6. (Jumbo English Ser.). (gr. 6). 1977. wkbk. 14.00 (ISBN 0-8209-0004-4, JEY-4). ESP.
--Jumbo English Yearbook: Grade 7. (Jumbo English Ser.). (gr. 7). 1982. wkbk. 14.00 (ISBN 0-8209-0005-2, JEY-5). ESP.
--Jumbo English Yearbook: Grade 8. (Jumbo English Ser.). (gr. 8). 1979. wkbk. 14.00 (ISBN 0-8209-0006-0, JEY-6). ESP.
--Jumbo English Yearbook: Grade 9. (Jumbo English Ser.). (gr. 9). 1979. wkbk. 14.00 (ISBN 0-8209-0007-9, JEY-7). ESP.
--Jumbo Reading Yearbook: Grade 2. (Jumbo Reading Ser.). 96p. (gr. 2). 1978. 14.00 (ISBN 0-8209-0013-3, JRY 2). ESP.
--Jumbo Reading Yearbook: Grade 3. (Jumbo Reading Ser.). 96p. (gr. 3). 1978. 14.00 (ISBN 0-8209-0014-1, JRY 3). ESP.
--Jumbo Reading Yearbook: Grade 4. (Jumbo Reading Ser.). 96p. (gr. 4). 1978. 14.00 (ISBN 0-8209-0015-X, JRY 4). ESP.
--Jumbo Reading Yearbook: Grade 5. (Jumbo Reading Ser.). 96p. (gr. 5). 1978. 14.00 (ISBN 0-8209-0016-8, JRY 5). ESP.
--Jumbo Reading Yearbook: Grade 6. (Jumbo Reading Ser.). 96p. (gr. 6). 1978. 14.00 (ISBN 0-8209-0017-6, JRY 6). ESP.
--Jumbo Reading Yearbook: Grade 7. (Jumbo Reading Ser.). 96p. (gr. 7-12). 1980. 14.00 (ISBN 0-8209-0018-4, JRY 7). ESP.
--Jumbo Spelling Yearbook: Grade 3. (Jumbo Spelling Ser.). 96p. (gr. 3). 1979. 14.00 (ISBN 0-8209-0020-6, JSPY 3). ESP.
--Jumbo Spelling Yearbook: Grade 4. (Jumbo Spelling Ser.). 96p. (gr. 4). 1979. 14.00 (ISBN 0-8209-0021-4, JSPY 4). ESP.
--Jumbo Spelling Yearbook: Grade 5. (Jumbo Spelling Ser.). 96p. (gr. 5). 1980. 14.00 (ISBN 0-686-38407-5, JSPY 5). ESP.
--Jumbo Spelling Yearbook: Grade 6. (Jumbo Spelling Ser.). 96p. (gr. 6). 1980. 14.00 (ISBN 0-8209-0023-0, JSPY 6). ESP.
--Jumbo Vocabulary Development Yearbook: Grade 3. (Jumbo Vocabulary Ser.). 96p. (gr. 3). 1980. 14.00 (ISBN 0-8209-0052-4, JVDY 3). ESP.
--Jumbo Vocabulary Development Yearbook: Grade 4. (Jumbo Vocabulary Ser.). 96p. (gr. 4). 1980. 14.00 (ISBN 0-8209-0053-2, JVDY 4). ESP.
--Jumbo Vocabulary Development Yearbook: Grade 5. (Jumbo Vocabulary Ser.). 96p. (gr. 5). 1981. 14.00 (ISBN 0-8209-0054-0, JVDY 5). ESP.
--Mr. Fish Talks About Subjects. (English Sound Filmstrip Kits Ser.). 1p. (gr. 4). 1980. 24.00 (ISBN 0-8209-0482-1, FCW4E-9). ESP.
--Mr. Tense. (English Sound Filmstrip Kits Ser.). 1p. (gr. 4). 1980. 24.00 (ISBN 0-8209-0480-5, FCW4E-7). ESP.
--Pronouns. (English Sound Filmstrip Kits Ser.). 1p. (gr. 6). 1980. 24.00 (ISBN 0-8209-0515-1, FCW6E-2). ESP.
--Written Problems in Math: Grade 3. (Math Ser.). 24p. 1982. wkbk. 5.00 (ISBN 0-8209-0123-7, A-33). ESP.
Shaw, Martin & Coleman, Henry. National Anthems of the World. 5th, rev. & enl. ed. Cartledge, T. M. & Reed, W. L., eds. 511p. 1983. 19.95 (ISBN 0-7137-0888-3, Pub. by Blandford Pr England). Sterling.
Shaw, Martin, ed. see Dearmer, Percy.
Shaw, Marvin. Group Dynamics. 3rd ed. (Illus.). 560p. 1980. 26.50 (ISBN 0-07-056504-X). McGraw.
Shaw, Michael, tr. see Jauss, Hans R.
Shaw, Michael T., ed. Chronic Granulocytic Leukaemia. 264p. 1982. 36.95 (ISBN 0-03-060053-7). Praeger.
Shaw, Milton C., jt. ed. see Mueller, William M.
Shaw, Pat, jt. ed. see Karples, Maud.
Shaw, Patrick W. Literature: A College Anthology. LC 76-19905. (Illus.). 1977. text ed. 18.50 (ISBN 0-395-24841-8); instr's. manual 2.35 (ISBN 0-395-24842-6). HM.
Shaw, R. Paul. Mobilising Human Resources in the Arab World. (Arab World Ser.). 288p. 1983. price not set (ISBN 0-7103-0040-9, Kegan Paul). Routledge & Kegan.
Shaw, Richard. The Hard Way Home. (YA) (gr. 7-12). 1983. pap. 2.25 (ISBN 0-440-93865-1, LFL). Dell.
--Lamprey's Legacy. 256p. 1983. pap. 2.75 (ISBN 0-380-61721-8). Avon.
--Tree for Rent. LC 72-165821. (Illus.). (gr. k-2). 1971. 5.25g o.p. (ISBN 0-8075-8082-1). A Whitman.
Shaw, Rita G. Sons & Lovers Notes. (Orig.). 1965. pap. 2.75 (ISBN 0-8220-1210-3). Cliffs.
Shaw, Robert, tr. see Kuhne, Karl.
Shaw, Robert B., jt. auth. see Gould, Frank W.
Shaw, Robert B., ed. see Vaughan, Henry.
Shaw, Robert J., ed. see Library Buildings Institute And Alta Workshop - Detroit - 1965.
Shaw, Robin. The Climber's Bible: A Complete Basic Guide to Rock & Ice Climbing & an Introduction to Mountaineering. LC 78-20097. (Outdoor Bible Ser.). (Illus.). 144p. 1983. pap. 5.95 (ISBN 0-385-14075-4). Doubleday.
Shaw, Ronald. Wave Energy: A Design Challenge. (Ellis Horwood Series in Energy & Fuel Science). 202p. 1982. 49.95x (ISBN 0-470-27539-1). Halsted Pr.
Shaw, Ronald E. Andrew Jackson, Seventeen Sixty-Seven to Eighteen Forty-Five: Chronology, Documents, Bibliographical Aids. LC 71-83748. (Presidential Chronology Ser.: No. 13). 123p. 1969. 8.00 (ISBN 0-379-12063-1). Oceana.
Shaw, Russell. Choosing Well. LC 82-40375. 96p. 1982. pap. text ed. 2.95 (ISBN 0-268-00737-3). U Of Notre Dame Pr.
Shaw, Russell, jt. auth. see Grisez, Germain.
Shaw, Ruth W. J. M. Synge's Guide to Aran Islands. 1983. pap. 5.95 (ISBN 0-8159-6835-3). Devin.
Shaw, S. J. History of the Ottoman Empire & Modern Turkey. LC 76-9179. (Illus.). 1977. Set. 95.00 (ISBN 0-521-08772-4); Vol. 1. 49.50 (ISBN 0-521-21280-4); Vol. 2. 69.50 (ISBN 0-521-21449-1); Set. pap. 35.00 (ISBN 0-521-08759-7); Vol. 1. pap. 19.95 (ISBN 0-521-29163-1); Vol. 2. pap. 22.95 (ISBN 0-521-29166-6). Cambridge U Pr.
Shaw, Samuel. Ernest Hemingway. LC 78-134827. (Literature and Life Ser.). 11.95 (ISBN 0-8044-2823-9). Ungar.
--Ernest Hemingway. LC 78-134827. (Literature & Life). 144p. 1982. pap. 5.95 (ISBN 0-8044-6859-1). Ungar.
Shaw, Sandy, jt. auth. see Pearson, Durk.
Shaw, Sheilah. Kaleidometrics: The Art of Making Beautiful Patterns from Circles. 40p. 1982. pap. 3.95 (ISBN 0-13-514505-8). P-H.
Shaw, Stella, jt. auth. see Lees, Dennis.
Shaw, Stephen M. Surfboard: How to Build Surfboards & How to Surf. Brown, Aileen, ed. (Illus.). 1981. Transmedia.
Shaw, Stephen M. & Brown, Aileen, eds. Surfboard: How to Build Surfboard & Sailboards, How to Surf. (Illus.). 1983. 10.00 (ISBN 0-912750-04-9). Transmedia.
Shaw, Susan, jt. auth. see Axelrod, Herbert.
Shaw, T., jt. auth. see Roberts, P.

Shaw, T. L. An Environmental Appraisal of Tidal Power Stations with Particular Reference to the Severn Barrage. (Water Resources Engineering Ser.). 220p. 1980. pap. text ed. 27.50 (ISBN 0-686-31208-2). Pitman Pub MA.

Shaw, T. L., ed. Mechanics of Wave-Induced Forces on Cylinders. new ed. (Illus.). 1979. cancelled o.p. (ISBN 0-8224-8433-1). Pitman Pub MA.

--Mechanics of Wave-Induced Forces on Cylinders. (Water Resources Engineering Ser.). 752p. 1979. text ed. 59.95 (ISBN 0-273-08433-X). Pitman Pub MA.

Shaw, Terry, jt. auth. see Meyer, John S.

Shaw, Thomas. Roughshod. 208p. (Orig.). 1982. pap. 2.25 (ISBN 0-449-14503-4, GM). Fawcett.

Shaw, Thurstan. Igbo-Ukwu, 2 vols. (Illus.). 888p. 1970. 68.00 set o.p. (ISBN 0-686-31721-1). Vol. 1 (ISBN 0-571-09123-7). Vol. 2 (ISBN 0-571-09124-5). Faber & Faber.

Shaw, Timothy M. Dependence & Underdevelopment: The Development & Foreign Policies of Zambia. LC 76-620013. (Papers in International Studies: Africa: No. 28). (Illus.). 1976. pap. 5.00 o.p. (ISBN 0-89680-061-X, Ohio U Ctr Intl). Ohio U Pr.

Shaw, Timothy M., jt. auth. see Anglin, Douglas G.

Shaw, William. Legal Norms in a Confucian State. (Korea Research Monographs: No. 5). 280p. 1981. 10.00x (ISBN 0-912966-32-7). IEAS.

Shaw, William, jt. ed. see Arthur, John.

Shaw, William H. Presenting Entertainment Arts: Stage, Film, Television. 192p. 1980. pap. text ed. 10.95 (ISBN 0-8403-2226-7). Kendall-Hunt.

Shaw, William T. Computer Control of BATCH Processes. McMenamin, James F., ed. LC 82-82986. (Illus.). 400p. 1982. 49.50 (ISBN 0-9609256-0-0). EMC Controls.

Shawchuck, Norman, jt. auth. see Lindgren, Alvin J.

Shawchuck, Norman, jt. auth. see Perry, Lloyd M.

Shawcross, John T., ed. The Complete Poetry of John Donne. LC 67-15386. pap. 8.95 (ISBN 0-385-05256-1, Anch). Doubleday.

--Complete Poetry of John Milton. LC 72-150934. 1971. pap. 8.95 (ISBN 0-385-02351-0, Anch). Doubleday.

Shawcross, Mike. San Cristobal de las Casas (Chiapas) City & Area Guide. 3rd ed. (Illus.). 75p. 1980. pap. 5.95 (ISBN 0-933982-16-X). Bradt Ent.

Shawe, Daniel R., ed. Guidebook on Fossil Fuels & Metals, Eastern Utah & Western-Southwestern Central Colorado. (Professional Contributions Ser.: No. 9). (Illus.). 150p. 1978. pap. 8.50 (ISBN 0-918062-04-7). Colo Sch Mines.

Shawker, Thomas H., jt. auth. see Brascho, Donn J.

Shawn, Bernard. Foundations of Citizenship, 2 bks. 1971 ed. Bk. 1. fabrikoid 6.95x (ISBN 0-88323-015-1, 115); Bk. 2. fabrikoid 6.95x (ISBN 0-88323-016-X, 116); combo fabrikoid 9.95x (ISBN 0-88323-017-8, 117); tchr's guide (ISBN 0-88323-018-6, 118). Richards Pub.

Shawn, Ted. Dance We Must. LC 74-28011. (Studies in Music, No. 42). 1974. lib. bdg. 22.95x o.p. (ISBN 0-8383-2032-5). Haskell.

Shawn, Wallace & Gregory, Andre. My Dinner with Andre. LC 81-47639. (Illus.). 240p. (Orig.). 1981. pap. 6.95 (ISBN 0-394-17948-X, E763, Ever). Grove.

Shay, Arthur. What Happens in a Skyscraper. LC 72-183834. (What It's Like Ser.). (Illus.). 32p. (gr. 2-4). 1972. 5.95 o.p. (ISBN 0-8092-8611-4); PLB avail o.p. (ISBN 0-685-23701-X). Contemp Bks.

Shay, Arthur & Leve, Chuck. Winning Raquetball. LC 75-32992. (Winning Ser). 176p. 1976. 8.95 (ISBN 0-8092-8086-8); pap. 7.95 (ISBN 0-8092-8062-0). Contemp Bks.

Shay, Arthur, jt. auth. see Fancher, Terry.

Shay, Arthur, jt. auth. see Groppel, Jack L.

Shay, Arthur, jt. auth. see Sauser, Jean.

Shay, Frank. Judge Lynch: His First Hundred Years. LC 70-75359. 1969. Repr. of 1938 ed. 10.00x (ISBN 0-8196-0231-0). Biblo.

--Judge Lynch: His First Hundred Years. Bd. with Lynching & Racial Exploitation. Raper, Arthur F. LC 69-14945. (Criminology, Law Enforcement, & Social Problems Ser., No. 55). (With introductory essay). 1969. Repr. of 1938 ed. 11.00x (ISBN 0-87585-055-3). Patterson Smith.

Shay, Jerry W., ed. Techniques in Somatic Cell Genetics. (Illus.). 568p. 1982. 49.50x (ISBN 0-306-41040-0, Plenum Pr). Plenum Pub.

Shay, Jerry W., jt. ed. see Dowben, Robert M.

Shay, Mary L. The Ottoman Empire from Seventeen Twenty to Seventeen Thirty-Four: As Revealed in Despatches from the Venetian Baili. LC 75-18363. (Illinois Studies in the Social Sciences: Vol. XXVII, No. 3). 1978. Repr. of 1944 ed. lib. bdg. 18.25x (ISBN 0-8371-8319-7, SHOTE). Greenwood.

Shay, Sunny & Barbaresi, Sara M. How to Raise & Train an Afghan. (Orig.). pap. 2.95 (ISBN 0-87666-232-7, DS1001). TFH Pubns.

Shayon, Robert L. Television: The Dream & the Reality. 1960. pap. 1.95 o.p. (ISBN 0-87462-416-9). Marquette.

Shea, Carole A., jt. auth. see Clark, Carolyn.

Shea, Edward, jt. auth. see Bender, Jay.

Shea, George. Alligators. LC 76-58509. (Four (Not So) Awful Creatures Ser.). (Illus.). (gr. 2-6). 1977. PLB 6.95 (ISBN 0-88436-310-4); pap. 3.95 (ISBN 0-88436-311-2). EMC.

--Bats. LC 77-23287. (Four (Not So) Awful Creatures Ser.). (Illus.). (gr. 2-6). 1977. PLB 6.95 (ISBN 0-88436-304-X); pap. 3.95 (ISBN 0-88436-305-8). EMC.

--Bears. LC 80-20367. (Creatures Wild & Free Ser.). (gr. 1-6). 1981. 6.95 (ISBN 0-88436-772-X). EMC.

--Big Cats. LC 80-22377. (Creatures Wild & Free). (gr. 1-6). 1981. text ed. 6.95 (ISBN 0-88436-774-6). EMC.

--Dolphins. LC 80-18259. (Creatures Wild & Free Ser.). (gr. 1-6). 1981. 6.95 (ISBN 0-88436-770-3). EMC.

--Snakes. LC 80-21294. (Creatures Wild & Free Ser.). (gr. 1-6). 1981. 6.95 (ISBN 0-88436-776-2). EMC.

--Spiders. LC 77-338. (Four (Not So) Awful Creatures Ser.). (Illus.). (gr. 2-6). 1977. PLB 6.95 (ISBN 0-88436-306-6); pap. 3.95 (ISBN 0-88436-307-4). EMC.

--Whales. LC 80-18413. (Creatures Wild & Free Ser.). (gr. 1-6). 1981. 6.95 (ISBN 0-88436-768-1). EMC.

--What to Do When You Are Bored. Schneider, Meg, ed. (Illus.). 64p. (Orig.). (gr. 8-12). 1983. pap. 3.95 (ISBN 0-671-44426-3). Wanderer Bks. Postponed.

--Wolves. LC 77-556. (Four (Not So) Awful Creatures Ser.). (Illus.). (gr. 2-6). 1977. PLB 6.95 (ISBN 0-88436-308-2); pap. 3.95 (ISBN 0-88436-309-0). EMC.

Shea, Gordon F. Creative Negotiating: Productive Tools & Techniques for Solving Problems, Resolving Conflicts & Settling Differences. 1983. 17.95 (ISBN 0-8436-0885-4). CBI Pub.

Shea, John. Stories of Faith. 1980. pap. 7.95 (ISBN 0-88347-112-4). Thomas More.

Shea, John J. & Akens, David S. Hearing Help. (Illus.). 112p. 1979. 7.95 (ISBN 0-87397-128-0). Strode.

Shea, John J., jt. auth. see Shambaugh, George.

Shea, Margaret, ed. see Chase, Virginia.

Shea, Michael. Nifft the Lean. 304p. 1982. pap. 2.95 (ISBN 0-686-82129-7). DAW Bks.

Shea, Robert. Last of the Zinja. (Shike Ser.: Bk. 2). 460p. (Orig.). 1981. pap. 3.50 (ISBN 0-515-07145-5). Jove Pubns.

--Last of the Zinja. (Shike Ser.). 488p. 1982. 14.95 (ISBN 0-399-12729-1). Putnam Pub Group.

--Shike: Book 1: Time of the Dragons. 1981. pap. 3.50. Jove Pubns.

--Time of the Dragons. (Shike Ser.). 488p. 1982. 14.95 (ISBN 0-399-12728-3). Putnam Pub Group.

--Time of the Dragons Shike, Bk. I. 464p. (Orig.). 1981. pap. 3.50 (ISBN 0-515-07119-6). Jove Pubns.

Shea, T. E. Transmission Networks & Wave Filters. 512p. 1929. 24.50 (ISBN 0-442-07535-9, Pub. by Van Nos Reinhold). Krieger.

Shea, Victoria, jt. auth. see Mount, Marianne.

Shea, William R. Nature Mathematized. 1983. 56.50 (ISBN 90-277-1402-9, Pub. by Reidel Holland). Kluwer Boston.

Shead, Richard. Music in the Nineteen Twenties. LC 77-82644. 1977. 20.00x (ISBN 0-312-55482-6). St Martin.

Sheahan, Desmond & Johnson, Robert, eds. Modern Crystal & Mechanical Filters. LC 76-57822. 1977. 37.95 (ISBN 0-87942-095-2). Inst Electrical.

Sheahan, Richard. Coal Conversion Decisionmaking: Industry Notebook. 250p. 1982. Wkbk. 48.00 (ISBN 0-86587-101-9). Gov Insts.

Sheally, John H., II. Morgans in the Colonies & Across the Pond. LC 78-54664. (Illus.). 143p. 1978. write for info. JCP Corp VA.

Sheals, J. G., jt. auth. see Lincoln, R. J.

Shealy, C. N. & Shealy, Mary C. To Parent or Not? LC 80-21104. (Orig.). 1980. text ed. 11.95 o.p. (ISBN 0-89865-065-8); pap. 6.95 o.p. (ISBN 0-89865-039-9). Donning Co.

Shealy, Mary C., jt. auth. see Shealy, C. N.

Shean, Glenn. Schizophrenia: An Introduction to Research & Theory. 1978. text ed. 13.95 (ISBN 0-316-78352-8); pap. text ed. 9.95 (ISBN 0-316-78353-6). Little.

Shean, Glenn D. Dimensions in Abnormal Psychology. 2nd ed. 1976. pap. 15.95 (ISBN 0-395-30837-2). HM.

Sheard, James L. & Stalley, Rodney E. Opening Doors to the Job Market. LC 82-72642. 176p. 1983. pap. 8.95 (ISBN 0-8066-1948-1, 10-4811). Augsburg.

Shearer, Alistair, jt. auth. see Russell, Peter.

Shearer, I. A., ed. see O'Connell, D. P.

Shearer, John. Billy Jo Jive & the Case of the Midnight Voices. LC 81-15281. 48p. (gr. k-3). 1982. 8.95 o.s.i. (ISBN 0-440-00752-6); PLB 8.89 o.s.i. (ISBN 0-440-00758-5). Delacorte.

--Billy Jo Jive & the Walkie-Talkie Caper: A Mystery. LC 80-17780. (Illus.). 48p. (gr. k-3). 1981. 7.95 o.s.i. (ISBN 0-440-00791-7); PLB 7.45 o.s.i. (ISBN 0-440-00792-5). Delacorte.

--Billy Jo Jive, Super Private Eye: The Case of the Missing Ten Speed Bike. LC 75-43563. (Illus.). (gr. 1-4). 1976. 5.95 o.s.i. (ISBN 0-440-00533-7); PLB 5.47 o.s.i. (ISBN 0-440-00534-5). Delacorte.

--Billy Jo Jive: The Case of the Missing Pigeons. LC 78-50409. (Illus.). (gr. 1-4). 1978. 5.95 o.s.i. (ISBN 0-440-00567-1); PLB 5.47 o.s.i. (ISBN 0-440-00568-X). Delacorte.

--Billy Jo Jive: The Case of the Sneaker Snatcher. LC 76-47242. (Illus.). (gr. 1-3). 1977. 6.95 o.s.i. (ISBN 0-440-00546-9); PLB 6.46 o.s.i. (ISBN 0-440-00548-5). Delacorte.

--Billy Jo Jive: The Case of the Sneaker Snatcher. (gr. 1-3). 1979. pap. 1.75 (ISBN 0-440-40569-6, YB). Dell.

Shearer, William M. Research Procedures in Speech-Language-Hearing. (Illus.). 272p. 1981. lib. bdg. 22.00 (ISBN 0-683-07724-4). Williams & Wilkins.

Shearman, Hugh. Approach to the Occult. 2.25 o.p. (ISBN 0-8356-7026-0). Theos Pub Hse.

Shears, Carl L. Niggers & Po' White Trash. LC 79-167825. 72p. 2.95 (ISBN 0-912444-15-0). Gaus.

Shears, Judith, jt. auth. see Hotchkiss, Bill.

Sheats, John E., jt. ed. see Carraher, Charles E., Jr.

Sheatz, Guy C. Missie, Equus Sapiens. LC 81-81613. 1983. 7.95 (ISBN 0-87212-159-3). Libra.

Shebar, Sharon, jt. auth. see Schoder, Judith.

Shebar, Sharon S. The Mysterious World of Honeybees. LC 79-11828. (Illus.). 64p. (gr. 4-6). 1979. PLB 6.97 o.p. (ISBN 0-671-32985-5). Messner.

--Whaling for Glory. LC 78-18247. (Illus.). 96p. (gr. 4-6). 1978. PLB 7.29 o.p. (ISBN 0-671-32917-0). Messner.

Shechner, Mark. Joyce in Nighttown: A Psychoanalytic Inquiry into Ulysses. 1974. 22.50x (ISBN 0-520-02398-6). U of Cal Pr.

Shechtman, Stephen & Singer, Wenda G. Real Men Enjoy their Kids. 176p. (Orig.). 1983. pap. 6.95 (ISBN 0-687-35598-2). Abingdon.

Sheckley, Robert. Futuropolis. LC 78-56317. (Illus.). 120p. 1978. 14.95 o.s.i. (ISBN 0-89104-124-9, A & W Visual Library); pap. 7.95 o.s.i. (ISBN 0-89104-123-0). A & W Pubs.

--The Robot Who Looks Like Me. 192p. 1982. pap. 2.50 (ISBN 0-553-13031-5). Bantam.

Sheckleye, Robert. The Tenth Victim. (Science Fiction Ser.). 1978. lib. bdg. 9.95 o.p. (ISBN 0-8398-2440-8, Gregg). G K Hall.

Shecter, Ben. Molly Patch & Her Animal Friends. LC 75-6304. (Illus.). 64p. (ps-3). 1975. PLB 8.89 o.p. (ISBN 0-06-025589-7, HarpJ). Har-Row.

--The River Witches. LC 75-25397. (Illus.). 192p. (gr. 5 up). 1979. 7.95i o.p. (ISBN 0-06-025607-9, HarpJ); PLB 7.89 o.p. (ISBN 0-06-025608-7). Har-Row.

--A Summer Secret. LC 76-41512. (Illus.). (gr. k-3). 1977. 4.95i o.p. (ISBN 0-06-025597-8, HarpJ); PLB 4.79 (ISBN 0-06-025598-6). Har-Row.

--The Toughest & Meanest Kid on the Block. (Illus.). 32p. (ps-3). 1973. PLB 4.69 o.p. (ISBN 0-399-60797-8). Putnam Pub Group.

--The Whistling Whirligig. LC 74-5493. (Illus.). 154p. (gr. 5 up). 1974. 8.89i o.p. (ISBN 0-06-025584-6, HarpJ). Har-Row.

Shedd, C. W. You Are Somebody Special. 2nd ed. 1982. 10.95 (ISBN 0-07-056511-2). McGraw.

Shedd, Charles W. Grandparents: Then God Created Grandparents & It Was Very Good. LC 75-42892. (Illus.). 144p. 1976. 9.95 (ISBN 0-385-11067-7, Galilee); pap. 7.95 (ISBN 0-385-13115-1, Galilee). Doubleday.

Shedd, Charlie. Devotions for Dieters. 1983. 8.95 (ISBN 0-8499-0330-0). Word Bks.

--The Stork is Dead. 1982. pap. 2.50 (ISBN 0-8499-4167-9). Word Pub.

Shedd, Charlie & Shedd, Martha. Grandparents Family Book: A Keepsake for Our Grandchild. LC 78-20098. (Illus.). 128p. 1982. 10.95 (ISBN 0-385-13469-X). Doubleday.

Shedd, Charlie, ed. You Are Somebody Special. 1978. 7.95 o.p. (ISBN 0-07-056509-0, GB). McGraw.

Shedd, Charlie W. Grandparents. (Inspirational Bks). 1977. lib. bdg. 9.95 o.p. (ISBN 0-8161-6519-X, Large Print Bks). G K Hall.

--Grandparents: Then God Created Grandparents & It Was Very Good. LC 77-80913. (Illus.). 1978. pap. 7.95 (Galilee). Doubleday.

--Letters to Philip. (Orig.). pap. 2.50 (ISBN 0-515-06495-5). Jove Pubns.

--The Pastoral Ministry of Church Officers. LC 65-11504. 1965. pap. 4.25 (ISBN 0-8042-1788-2). John Knox.

--Stork Is Dead. 1976. pap. 1.50 o.s.i. (ISBN 0-89129-134-2). Jove Pubns.

--Talk to Me. 1976. pap. 1.50 o.s.i. (ISBN 0-89129-112-1). Jove Pubns.

--Talk to Me. rev. ed. LC 82-45455. 120p. 1983. pap. 5.95 (ISBN 0-385-18328-3, Galilee). Doubleday.

Shedd, Donald P. & Weinberg, Bernd. Surgical & Prosthetic Approaches to Speech Rehabilitation. 1980. lib. bdg. 35.50 (ISBN 0-8161-2186-9, Hall Medical). G K Hall.

Shedd, Joe. White Workers & Black Trainees: An Outline of Some of the Issues Raised by Special Training Programs for the Disadvantaged. (Key Issues Ser.: No. 13). 40p. 1973. pap. 2.00 (ISBN 0-87546-243-X). ILR Pr.

Shedd, Martha, jt. auth. see Shedd, Charlie.

Shedd, Robert, jt. ed. see Block, Haskell.

Shedd, W. G. The Doctrine of Endless Punishment. 1980. 8.25 (ISBN 0-86524-019-1, 9803). Klock & Klock.

--Theological Essays. 1981. lib. bdg. 26.00 (ISBN 0-86524-079-5, 8602). Klock & Klock.

Shedd, William G. Dogmatic Theology, 4 vols. 1979. Repr. of 1889 ed. Set. 52.50 o.p. (ISBN 0-86524-033-7); text ed. 44.95 o.p. (ISBN 0-686-25157-1). Klock & Klock.

--History of Christian Doctrine, 2 vols. 1978. 31.50 (ISBN 0-86524-124-4, 8701). Klock & Klock.

Shedd, William G. T. Critical & Doctrinal Commentary on Romans. 1978. 17.00 o.p. (ISBN 0-86524-955-5). Klock & Klock.

Shedden, John. Ski Teaching. 2nd, rev. ed. (Illus.). 137p. 1980. 20.00x o.p. (ISBN 0-584-10477-4). Intl Pubns Serv.

Shedenhelm, W. R. The Young Rockhound's Handbook. LC 77-12632. (Illus.). (gr. 6 up). 1978. 7.95 (ISBN 0-399-20624-8). Putnam Pub Group.

Shedlock, J. S., tr. Richard Wagner's Letters to His Dresden Friends. LC 72-163800. 512p. Date not set. Repr. of 1890 ed. price not set. Vienna Hse.

Shedlock, J. S., tr. see Beethoven, Ludwig Van.

Shedlovsky, Theodore, ed. Electrochemistry in Biology & Medicine. LC 55-8561. 369p. 1955. 18.00 (ISBN 0-471-78177-0, Pub. by Wiley). Krieger.

Sheed, F. J. Our Hearts Are Restless: The Prayer of St. Augustine. 1976. pap. 2.50 (ISBN 0-8164-2127-7). Seabury.

Sheed, Frank, tr. see Augustine, Saint.

Sheed, Wilfred. Clare Booth Luce. large type ed. LC 82-5871. 378p. 1982. Repr. of 1982 ed. 11.95 (ISBN 0-89621-366-8). Thorndike Pr.

Sheed, Wilfrid. The Blacking Factory. Bd. with Pennsylvania Gothic. 246p. 1968. 5.95 o.p. (ISBN 0-374-11428-5). FS&G.

--Transatlantic Blues. 1979. pap. 2.25 o.p. (ISBN 0-380-42259-X, 42259). Avon.

Sheehan, Angela. The Duck. LC 78-63093. (First Look at Nature Bks). (Illus.). (gr. 2-4). 1979. 2.50 (ISBN 0-531-09098-1, Warwick Pr); PLB 7.90 s&l (ISBN 0-531-09074-4). Watts.

Sheehan, Angela, ed. Discovering Nature. LC 77-6206. (Illus.). (gr. 3-12). 1977. PLB 21.30 (ISBN 0-8393-0025-5). Raintree Pubs.

Sheehan, Bernard. Savagism & Civility. LC 79-18189. 1980. 37.50 (ISBN 0-521-22927-8); pap. 8.95 (ISBN 0-521-29723-0). Cambridge U Pr.

Sheehan, Bernard S., ed. Information Technology: Advances & Applications. LC 81-48575. 1982. 7.95x (ISBN 0-87589-905-6, IR-35). Jossey-Bass.

Sheehan, Carol. Pipes That Won't Smoke; Coal That Won't Burn: Haida Sculpture in Argillite. (Illus.). 214p. 1982. pap. 19.95 (ISBN 0-686-84107-7, 28739-4). U of Chicago Pr.

Sheehan, Denza C. & Hrapchak, Barbara B. Theory & Practice of Histotechnology. 2nd ed. LC 80-11807. 462p. 1980. text ed. 37.95 (ISBN 0-8016-4573-5). Mosby.

Sheehan, Donald & Syrett, Harold C., eds. Essays in American Historiography. LC 72-9833. (Illus.). 320p. 1973. Repr. of 1960 ed. lib. bdg. 17.00x (ISBN 0-8371-6268-8, SMAH). Greenwood.

Sheehan, George. Dr. Sheehan on Fitness. (Illus.). 1983. price not set (ISBN 0-671-45478-1). S&S.

--Running & Being: The Total Experience. 1983. pap. 3.95 (ISBN 0-446-97090-5). Warner Bks.

Sheehan, H. L. & Davis, J. C. Post-Partum Hypopituitarism. (Illus.). 600p. 1982. 69.75x (ISBN 0-398-04523-2). C C Thomas.

Sheehan, Larry, ed. see Smith, Stan, et al.

Sheehan, Margaret A. & Robinson, Michael J. Over the Wire & on TV: CBS & UPI in Campaign '80. 1982. 16.95 (ISBN 0-87154-722-8). Basic.

Sheehan, P. W. & Perry, C. W. Methodologies of Hypnosis: A Critical Appraisal of Contemporary Paradigms of Hypnosis. LC 76-3543. 329p. 1976. 18.00x o.p. (ISBN 0-470-15028-9). Halsted Pr.

Sheehan, Peter W., ed. The Function & Nature of Imagery. 1972. 55.50 (ISBN 0-12-638950-0). Acad Pr.

Sheehan, Susan. Is there No Place on Earth for Me? Coles, Robert M., frwd. by. LC 82-40424. 352p. 1983. pap. 4.95 (ISBN 0-394-71378-8, Vin). Random.

Sheehan, Valerie H., ed. Unmasking: Ten Women in Metamorphosis. LC 82-73393. 286p. 1973. 12.95 (ISBN 0-8040-0626-1). Swallow.

Sheehy, Emma D. Fives & Sixes Go to School. Repr. of 1954 ed. lib. bdg. 19.75x (ISBN 0-8371-2572-3, SHFS). Greenwood.

Sheehy, Eugene P. Guide to Reference Books. 9th ed. 1976. text ed. 40.00 (ISBN 0-8389-0205-7). ALA.

Sheehy, Eugene P. & Lohf, Kenneth A. Index to the Little Review, 1914-1929. 1961. pap. 5.00 o.p. (ISBN 0-87104-096-4). NY Pub Lib.

Sheehy, Eugene P., ed. Guide to Reference Books: 2nd Supplement. 9th ed. 252p. 1982. pap. text ed. 15.00 (ISBN 0-8389-0361-4). ALA.

Sheehy, Gail. Pathfinders. 1982. pap. 4.50 (ISBN 0-686-83415-1). Bantam.

Sheeler, P. Centrifugation in Biology & Medical Science. 269p. 1981. 39.50 (ISBN 0-471-05234-5, Pub. by Wiley-Interscience). Wiley.

Sheeler, P. & Bianchi, D. E. Cell Biology: Structure, Biochemistry & Function. 578p. 1980. text ed. 29.95 (ISBN 0-471-78220-3). Wiley.

Sheeler, Phillip. Cell Biology: Structure, Biochemistry & Function. 2nd ed. Bianchi, Donald E., ed. (Illus.). 700p. 1983. text ed. 29.95 (ISBN 0-471-09308-4). Wiley.

Sheeler, W. D. & Bayley, S. C. Foundations for Reading & Writing: Workbooks 3 & 4. Evans, A. R., ed. (Welcome to English Ser.). (Illus.). 1978. 3.45 ea. Bk. 3 (ISBN 0-89285-035-3). Bk. 4 (ISBN 0-89285-036-1). English Lang.

Sheeler, W. D. & Markley, R. W. Words, Words, Words, Bk 2. (Words, Words, Words). 128p. (gr. 9-12). 1982. pap. text ed. 6.95 (ISBN 0-88345-424-6). Regents Pub.

Sheeler, W. D., et al. Foundations for Reading & Writing: Workbooks 1 & 2. Evans, A. R., ed. (Welcome to English Ser.). (Illus.). 1977. No. 1. wkbk 3.45 ea. (ISBN 0-89285-033-7). No. 2 (ISBN 0-89285-034-5). Bk. 1. cassettes 12.00 (ISBN 0-89285-044-2); Bk. 2. (ISBN 0-89285-045-0); Bk. 3. (ISBN 0-89285-046-9); Bk. 4. (ISBN 0-89285-047-7). English Lang.

Sheeler, Willard D. Elementary Course in English, 2 bks. 1971. pap. text ed. 4.75 ea.; student text 1 avail. (ISBN 0-87789-046-3); student text 2 avail. (ISBN 0-87789-049-8). Cassettes 1. cassettes 175.00 (ISBN 0-87789-110-9); Cassettes 2. cassettes 175.00 (ISBN 0-87789-111-7); tchrs' manual 1 & 2 2.95 (ISBN 0-87789-002-1). Eng Language.

--Extra Drills & Practices. 1978. 5.25 (ISBN 0-89285-039-6). English Lang.

--Grammar & Drillbook. 1978. 5.50 (ISBN 0-89285-037-X). English Lang.

Sheeler, Willard D., jt. auth. see Dale, Jean N.

Sheeler, Williard D., jt. auth. see Dale, Jean N.

Sheen, Fulton J. On Being Human. LC 81-43373. 400p. 1983. pap. text ed. 5.95 (ISBN 0-385-18469-7, Im). Doubleday.

--The Way of the Cross: Pocket-Size, Giant Print Edition. rev. ed. (Illus.). 64p. 1982. Repr. of 1932 ed. pap. 2.95 (ISBN 0-87973-659-3, 659); roncote 2.95 (ISBN 0-87973-660-7, 660). Our Sunday Visitor.

--The World's First Love. 240p. 1976. 4.50 (ISBN 0-385-11559-8, Im). Doubleday.

--The World's Great Love: The Prayer of the Rosary. (Illus.). 1978. pap. 2.00 (ISBN 0-8164-2182-X). Seabury.

Sheen, Jack H. Aesthetic Rhinoplasty. LC 78-27554. (Illus.). 608p. 1978. text ed. 115.00 (ISBN 0-8016-4575-1). Mosby.

Sheenan, J. A Guide to Sources of Information on Australian Business. (Guides to Australian Information Sources Ser.). 120p. 1983. pap. 10.50 (ISBN 0-08-029831-1). Pergamon.

Sheerin, John, ed. see Vatican Council Two.

Sheet Music Magazine & Keyboard Classics Magazine, ed. The Do-it Yourself Handbook for Keyboard Playing. Date not set. price not set (ISBN 0-943748-00-3). Shacor Inc.

Sheets, Herman E. & Boatwright, Victor T., eds. Hydronautics. 1970. 68.00 (ISBN 0-12-639150-5). Acad Pr.

Sheets, Leslie P., jt. auth. see Humphries, James T.

Sheets, Payson D. & Grayson, Donald K., eds. Volcanic Activity & Human Ecology. LC 79-51701. 1979. 57.50 (ISBN 0-12-639120-3). Acad Pr.

Sheets, Robin, jt. auth. see Helsinger, Elizabeth.

Shefer, Daniel, jt. auth. see Guldmann, Jean-Michel.

Sheff, Alexander L. Bookkeeping Made Easy. (Orig.). 1971. pap. 4.09i (ISBN 0-06-463235-0, EH 235, EH). B&N NY.

Sheff, David. The Playboy Interviews with John Lennon & Yoko Ono. Golson, G. Barry, ed. 256p. 1982. pap. 3.50 (ISBN 0-425-05989-8). Berkley Pub.

Sheff, Donald, et al. The World's First Quiz Almanac. 544p. (Orig.). 1983. pap. 9.95 (ISBN 0-89104-295-4, A & W Visual Library). A & W Pubs.

Sheffer, H. R. Airplanes. Schroeder, Howard, ed. LC 81-19524. (Movin' on Ser.). (Illus.). 48p. (Orig.). (gr. 4-8). 1982. PLB 7.95 (ISBN 0-89686-195-3); pap. 3.95 (ISBN 0-89686-205-4). Crestwood Hse.

--Cycles. Schroeder, Howard, ed. (Movin' On Ser.). (Illus.). 48p. (Orig.). (gr. 5-6). 1983. lib. bdg. 7.95 (ISBN 0-89686-199-6); pap. text ed. 3.95 o.p. (ISBN 0-89686-209-7). Crestwood Hse.

--Great Cars. Schroeder, Howard, ed. (Movin' On Ser.). (Illus.). 48p. (Orig.). (gr. 5-6). 1983. lib. bdg. 7.95 (ISBN 0-89686-192-9); pap. text ed. 3.95 o.p. (ISBN 0-89686-202-X). Crestwood Hse.

--Paddlewheelers. Schroeder, Howard, ed. LC 81-19456. (Movin' on Ser.). (Illus.). 48p. (Orig.). (gr. 4-8). 1982. PLB 7.95 (ISBN 0-89686-194-5); pap. 3.95 (ISBN 0-89686-204-6). Crestwood Hse.

--Race Cars. Schroeder, Howard, ed. (Movin' On Ser.). (Illus.). 48p. (gr. 3-10). 1982. PLB 7.95 (ISBN 0-89686-200-3); pap. 3.95 (ISBN 0-89686-210-0). Crestwood Hse.

--R.V.'s. Schroeder, Howard, ed. (Movin' On Ser.). (Illus.). 48p. (Orig.). (gr. 5-6). 1983. lib. bdg. 7.95 (ISBN 0-89686-198-8); pap. text ed. 3.95 o.p. (ISBN 0-89686-208-9). Crestwood Hse.

--Tractors. Schroeder, Howard, ed. (Movin' On Ser.). (Illus.). 48p. (Orig.). (gr. 5-6). 1983. lib. bdg. 7.95 (ISBN 0-89686-196-1); pap. text ed. 3.95 o.p. (ISBN 0-89686-206-2). Crestwood Hse.

--Trains. Schroeder, Howard, ed. LC 81-19452. (Movin' on Ser.). (Illus.). 48p. (Orig.). (gr. 4-8). 1982. PLB 7.95 (ISBN 0-89686-193-7); pap. 3.25 (ISBN 0-89686-203-8). Crestwood Hse.

--Trucks. Schroeder, Howard, ed. (Movin' On Ser.). (Illus.). 48p. (Orig.). (gr. 5-6). 1983. lib. bdg. 7.95 (ISBN 0-89686-197-X); pap. text ed. 3.95 o.p. (ISBN 0-89686-207-0). Crestwood Hse.

--Vans. Schroeder, Howard, ed. (Movin' On Ser.). (Illus.). 48p. (Orig.). (gr. 3-10). 1982. PLB 7.95 (ISBN 0-89686-201-1); pap. 3.95 (ISBN 0-89686-211-9). Crestwood Hse.

Sheffield, Edward, et al. Systems of Higher Education: Canada. rev. ed. 1982. pap. 8.00 o.p. (ISBN 0-89192-204-0). Interbk Inc.

Sheffield, J. B. & Hilfer, S. R., eds. Cellular Communication During Ocular Development. (Cell & Developmental Biology of the Eye Ser.). (Illus.). 196p. 1983. 32.50 (ISBN 0-387-90773-4). Springer-Verlag.

Sheffield, James R. Education in Kenya: An Historical Study. LC 72-88639. (Illus.). 126p. 1973. pap. text ed. 5.95x (ISBN 0-8077-2419-X). Tchrs Coll.

Sheffield, John. Plasma Scattering of Electromagnetic Radiation. 1975. 63.00 (ISBN 0-12-638750-8). Acad Pr.

Sheffield, Lyn. Total Fitness for Women. 1980. pap. text ed. 6.95x o.p. (ISBN 0-673-16207-9). Scott F.

Sheffield, Riley, Jr. Floating Drilling: Equipment & Its Use. (Practical Drilling Technology Ser.: Vol. 2). 258p. 1980. 24.95x (ISBN 0-87201-289-1). Gulf Pub.

Shefler, Oscar. I'd Rather Be in Philadelphia. 304p. (Orig.). 1981. pap. 2.75 o.p. (ISBN 0-523-41152-9). Pinnacle Bks.

Shefner, Jeremy M., jt. auth. see Levine, Michael W.

Shefrin, Steven M. Rational Expectations. LC 82-19747. (Cambridge Surveys of Economic Literature Ser.). 215p. Date not set. 29.95 (ISBN 0-521-24310-6); pap. 8.95 (ISBN 0-521-28595-X). Cambridge U Pr.

Shefter, ed. see Stevenson, Robert L.

Shefter, Harry, ed. see Buck, Pearl S.

Shefter, Harry, ed. see Goldsmith, Oliver.

Shefter, Harry, ed. see Shaw, George B.

Shehadi, Fadlou. Metaphysics in Islamic Philosophy. LC 81-18069. 1983. 35.00x (ISBN 0-88206-049-X). Caravan Bks.

Shehan, Lawrence. A Blessing of Years: The Memoirs of Lawrence Cardinal Shehan. 1983. price not set. U of Notre Dame Pr.

Sheidley, William E. Barnabe Googe. (English Authors Ser.). 1981. lib. bdg. 13.95 (ISBN 0-8057-6798-3, Twayne). G K Hall.

Sheidley, William E. see Butler, Francelia, et al.

Sheikh, Ahmed. International Law & National Behavior: A Behavioral Interpretation of Contemporary International Law & Politics. LC 73-19922. 352p. 1974. pap. text ed. 18.95 (ISBN 0-471-78230-0). Wiley.

Sheikh, Anees A. Imagery: Current Theory, Research, & Application. (Personality Processes Ser.). 450p. 1983. 39.95 (ISBN 0-471-09225-8, Pub. by Wiley-Interscience). Wiley.

Sheilds, Nwanganga. Women in the Urban Labor Markets of Africa: The Case of Tanzania. (Working Paper: No. 380). 136p. 1980. 5.00 (ISBN 0-686-36152-0, WP-0380). World Bank.

Sheils, W. J. & Baker, Derek, eds. The Church & Healing. (Studies in Church History: Vol. 19). 400p. 1983. text ed. 36.00x (ISBN 0-631-13117-5, Pub by Basil Blackwell England). Biblio Dist.

Shein, Harvey M., jt. ed. see Ingle, David J.

Shein, Keith. An Intimate Distance. LC 81-50229. 48p. 1982. pap. 6.00 (ISBN 0-917588-06-1). Trike.

Sheinkin, David, et al. Food, Mind & Mood. 304p. 1980. pap. 3.95 (ISBN 0-446-30737-8). Warner Bks.

Sheinkopf, David I. Gelatin & Jewish Law. 1982. pap. 7.95 (ISBN 0-8197-0488-1). Bloch.

Sheinwold, Alfred. Duplicate Bridge. LC 75-156814. 1971. lib. bdg. 10.50x (ISBN 0-88307-572-5). Gannon.

--First Book of Bridge. 1962. pap. 3.50 (ISBN 0-06-463242-3, EH 242, EH). B&N NY.

Sheinwold, Alfred, jt. auth. see Kaplan, Edgar.

Shejbal, J. Controlled Atmosphere Storage of Grains. (Developments in Agricultural Engineering Ser.: Vol. 1). 1981. 83.00 (ISBN 0-444-41939-X). Elsevier.

Shekelle, R. B., jt. ed. see Lauer, R. M.

Shekhar, K. C. & Nair, R. R. Elements of Commerce. 225p. 1982. text ed. 20.00x (ISBN 0-7069-2020-1, Pub. by Vikas India). Advent NY.

Shekleton, Maureen E., jt. auth. see Groer, Maureen W.

Shelah, S. Classification Theory & the Number of Non Isomorphic Models. (Studies in Logic & the Foundations of Mathematics: Vol. 92). 1978. 85.00 (ISBN 0-7204-0757-5, North-Holland). Elsevier.

--Proper Forcing. (Lecture Notes in Mathematics: Vol. 940). 496p. 1983. pap. 25.00 (ISBN 0-387-11593-5). Springer-Verlag.

Shelbourne, Cecily. Stage of Love. LC 77-9005. 1978. 8.95 o.p. (ISBN 0-399-12078-5). Putnam Pub Group.

Shelby, David S. Anterior Restoration, Fixed Bridgework, & Esthetics. (Illus.). 416p. 1976. 38.75x o.p. (ISBN 0-398-03322-6). C C Thomas.

Shelby, Donald J. Bold Expectations of the Gospel. 96p. (Orig.). 1983. pap. 3.95 (ISBN 0-8358-0454-2). Upper Room.

--Meeting the Messiah. LC 79-57363. 96p. (Orig.). 1980. pap. 3.50x (ISBN 0-8358-0398-8). Upper Room.

Shelby, Graham. The Cannaways. 1983. pap. 3.50 (ISBN 0-8217-1124-5). Zebra.

Sheldahl, Terry K. Beta Alpha Psi, from Alpha to Omega: Pursuing a Vision of Professional Education for Accountants, 1919-1945. LC 82-48386. (Accountancy in Transition Ser.). 800p. 1982. lib. bdg. 60.00 (ISBN 0-8240-5301-X). Garland Pub.

Sheldon, Alan, et al, eds. Systems & Medical Care. 1970. 19.00x (ISBN 0-262-19077-X). MIT Pr.

Sheldon, Ann. Linda Craig: Secret of the Old Sleigh. Schneider, Meg, ed. (Linda Craig Ser.). 192p. (gr. 3-7). 1983. pap. 3.50 (ISBN 0-671-46459-0). Wanderer Bks.

--Linda Craig: The Clue on the Desert Trail. (Linda Craig Ser.: No. 3). 192p. (gr. 3-7). 1981. 8.95 (ISBN 0-671-42651-6); pap. 2.95 (ISBN 0-671-42652-4). Wanderer Bks.

--Linda Craig: The Ghost Town Treasure. (Linda Craig Ser.: No. 6). 192p. (gr. 3-7). 1982. 8.95 (ISBN 0-671-44527-8); pap. 2.95 (ISBN 0-671-44526-X). Wanderer Bks.

--Linda Craig: The Haunted Valley. Barish, Wendy, ed. (Linda Craig Ser.: No. 7). 192p. (gr. 3-7). 1982. cancelled (ISBN 0-671-45551-6); pap. 2.95 (ISBN 0-671-45550-8). Wanderer Bks.

--Linda Craig: The Mystery in Mexico. rev. ed. (Linda Craig Ser.: No. 5). 192p. (Orig.). (gr. 3-7). 1981. 8.95 (ISBN 0-671-42706-7); pap. 2.95 (ISBN 0-671-42703-2). Wanderer Bks.

--Linda Craig: The Mystery of Horseshoe Canyon. (Linda Craig Ser.: No. 4). 192p. (gr. 3-7). 1981. 8.95 (ISBN 0-671-42653-2); pap. 2.95 (ISBN 0-671-42654-0). Wanderer Bks.

--Linda Craig: The Palomino Mystery. (The Linda Craig Ser.: No. 1). (gr. 3-7). 1981. 8.95 (ISBN 0-671-42649-4); pap. 2.95 (ISBN 0-671-42650-8). Wanderer Bks.

--Linda Craig: The Secret of Rancho Del Sol. (Linda Craig Ser.: No. 2). 192p. (gr. 3-7). 1981. 8.95 (ISBN 0-671-42647-8); pap. 2.95 (ISBN 0-671-42648-6). Wanderer Bks.

Sheldon, Brian. Behavior Modification. 1982. 26.00x (ISBN 0-422-77060-4, Pub. by Tavistock, England); pap. 11.95x (ISBN 0-422-77070-1). Methuen Inc.

Sheldon, Charles. In His Steps. (Family Library). 1973. pap. 1.25 o.p. (ISBN 0-89129-178-4). Jove Pubns.

--In His Steps. pap. 4.95 (ISBN 0-8007-5011-X, Power Bks); pap. 2.95 (ISBN 0-8007-8022-1, Spire Bks). Revell.

Sheldon, Charles H. & Weaver, Frank P. Politicians, Judges, & the People: A Study in Citizens' Participation. LC 79-7472. (Contributions in Political Science: No. 36). 1980. lib. bdg. 25.00x (ISBN 0-313-21492-1, SPJ/). Greenwood.

Sheldon, Charles H., jt. auth. see Baker, Donald G.

Sheldon, Charles M. En Sus Pasos. Reuben, Ruth, tr. from Eng. Orig. Title: In His Steps. 92p. (Span.). 1981. pap. 1.75 (ISBN 0-311-37011-X). Casa Bautista.

--In His Steps. 6.95 (ISBN 0-8054-7302-5). Broadman.

--In His Steps. Rev. ed. 256p. 1982. 5.95 (ISBN 0-448-01662-1, G&D). Putnam Pub Group.

Sheldon, Charls M. Bible Stories. LC 74-4817. (Illus.). 1978. pap. 4.95 (ISBN 0-448-14612-6, G&D). Putnam Pub Group.

Sheldon, Dyan. Victim of Love. 228p. 1983. 14.75 (ISBN 0-670-74586-3). Viking Pr.

Sheldon, Eleanor B. & Moore, Wilbert E., eds. Indicators of Social Change: Concepts & Measurements. LC 68-54407. 822p. 1968. 17.95x (ISBN 0-87154-771-6). Russell Sage.

Sheldon, Eric, jt. auth. see Marmier, Pierre.

Sheldon, George. History of Deerfield, Massachusetts, 2 vols. LC 79-189321. (Illus.). 1972. Repr. of 1895 ed. Set. 75.00x (ISBN 0-912274-14-X). NH Pub Co.

Sheldon Landwehr & Associates. Who's Who in America's Restaurants: New York & Eastern States Limited, 1983 Ed. Landwehr, Sheldon, ed. (Illus.). 220p. 1983. 129.50 (ISBN 0-910297-00-2). Whos Who Rest.

Sheldon, Margaret & Lockwood, Barbara. All About Poodles. (The All About Ser.). (Illus.). 150p. 1983. 12.95 (ISBN 0-7207-1440-0, Pub. by Michael Joseph). Merrimack Bk Serv.

Sheldon, Mary. Perhaps I'll Dream of Darkness. LC 81-40217. 224p. 1981. 11.50 (ISBN 0-394-51175-1). Random.

Sheldon, R. P. Composite Polymeric Materials. (Applied Science Publications). 228p. 1982. 39.00 (ISBN 0-85334-129-X, Pub. by Applied Sci England). Elsevier.

Sheldon, Richard, tr. see Shklovsky, Viktor.

Sheldon, Sidney. Masters of the Game. LC 82-60920. 448p. 1982. 15.95 (ISBN 0-688-01365-1). Morrow.

--The Naked Face. 1975. pap. 3.50 (ISBN 0-440-15921-0). Dell.

--The Other Side of Midnight. 1977. pap. 3.95 (ISBN 0-440-16067-7). Dell.

--Rage of Angels. 504p. 1983. pap. 3.95 o.p. (ISBN 0-446-36214-X). Warner Bks.

Sheldon, Stephen. Pediatric Differential Diagnosis: A Problem-Oriented Approach. 159p. 1979. softcover 9.95 (ISBN 0-89004-351-5). Raven.

Sheldon, Stephen H. Manual of Practical Pediatrics. 302p. 1981. pap. 12.95 (ISBN 0-89004-632-8). Raven.

Sheldon, William H. Penny Whimsy. LC 76-19190. (Illus.). 1976. Repr. 35.00x (ISBN 0-88000-136-4). Quarterman.

Sheldon-Wildgen, Jan, jt. auth. see VanBiervliet, Alan.

Sheldrake, P. Accountability in Higher Education. LC 79-83555. 1979. text ed. 22.50x (ISBN 0-86861-121-2). Allen Unwin.

Sheldrake, Rupert. A New Science of Life: The Hypothesis of Formative Causation. 256p. 1981. 60.00x o.p. (ISBN 0-85634-115-0, Pub. by Muller Ltd). State Mutual Bk.

Shelef, G. & Soeder, C. J. Algae Biomass: Productions & Use. 1981. 151.50 (ISBN 0-444-80242-8). Elsevier.

Sheleff, Leon. Generations Apart: Adult Hostility to Youth. 352p. 1981. 19.95 (ISBN 0-07-056540-6, P&RB). McGraw.

Sheleff, Leon S. The Bystander: Behavior, Law & Ethics. LC 77-18577. 240p. 1978. 21.95x (ISBN 0-669-02110-5). Lexington Bks.

Sheley, Joseph F. Understanding Crime. 1979. pap. text ed. 14.95x (ISBN 0-534-00695-7). Wadsworth Pub.

Shelgren, Margaret, jt. auth. see Lauderdale, Beverly.

Sheline, Glenn E., et al. Pituitary Adenomas. (Oncologic Multidisciplinary Decisions in Onology Ser.). (Illus.). 248p. 1981. pap. 100.00 (ISBN 0-08-027463-3). Pergamon.

Shell, Ella Jo. Recipes From Our Front Porch. (Illus.). 152p. 1982. pap. 10.00 (ISBN 0-939114-65-8). Wimmer Bks.

Shell, Kurt L. Transformation of Austrian Socialism. LC 61-8738. 1961. 39.50x (ISBN 0-87395-005-4). State U NY Pr.

Shell, Marc. Money, Language & Thought: Literary & Philosophic Economies from the Medieval to the Modern Era. (Illus.). 219p. 1982. 22.50 (ISBN 0-520-04379-0). U of Cal Pr.

Shell, Merle. Tasting Good: The International Salt-Free Diet Cookbook. LC 80-2729. 1981. 14.95 (ISBN 0-672-52623-9). Bobbs.

Shell, R. L. & Jeffries, N. P. Engineering Fundamentals. new ed. LC 74-32613. 150p. 1975. 10.50x o.p. (ISBN 0-87263-032-3). SME.

Sheller, Roscoe. Me & the Model T. (Illus.). 1982. pap. 7.95 (ISBN 0-686-84255-3). Binford.

Shelley, jt. ed. see Medawar.

Shelley, Bruce. What Is the Church? 132p. 1983. pap. cancelled o.p. (ISBN 0-88207-105-X). Penguin.

--What is the Church? God's People. 132p. 1983. pap. 4.50 (ISBN 0-88207-105-X). Victor Bks.

Shelley, Donald A. The Fraktur Writings or Illuminated Manuscripts of the Pennsylvania Germans. (Pennsylvania German Folklore Society Ser.: Vol. 23). 1958. 50.00 (ISBN 0-911122-21-4). Penn German Soc.

Shelley, J. Pocket Guide to... Programming. 64p. 1982. spiral bdg. 6.95 (ISBN 0-201-07736-1). A-W.

Shelley, Joseph F. Engineering Mechanics: Statics & Dynamics, 2 vols. (Illus.). 1980. Set. text ed. 36.95 (ISBN 0-07-056555-4). Statics Vol. text ed. 26.95 (ISBN 0-07-056551-1); Dynamics Vol. text ed. 26.95 (ISBN 0-07-056553-8); Statics Vol. solutions manual 25.00 (ISBN 0-07-056552-X); Dynamics Vol. solutions manual 30.50 (ISBN 0-07-056554-6). McGraw.

Shelley, Mary. The Annotated Frankenstein. (Illus.). 1977. 14.95 o.p. (ISBN 0-517-53071-6, C N Potter Bks). Crown.

--Frankenstein. (Bantam Classics Ser.). 240p. (Orig.). (gr. 9-12). 1981. pap. text ed. 1.50 (ISBN 0-553-21044-0). Bantam.

--Frankenstein. 1979. pap. 2.95x (ISBN 0-460-01616-4, Evman). Biblio Dist.

--Frankenstein. 1964. pap. 1.95 (ISBN 0-440-32717-2, LE). Dell.

--Frankenstein. (gr. 3 up). 1978. pap. 1.50 (ISBN 0-307-21632-2, Golden Pr); Golden Pr. PLB 6.08 (ISBN 0-307-61632-0). Western Pub.

--Robert Andrew Parker's Illustrated Frankenstein. 1976. pap. 5.95 o.p. (ISBN 0-517-51697-7, C N Potter Bks). Crown.

Shelley, Mary see Swan, D. K.

Shelley, Mary W. Tales & Stories. (Science Fiction Ser). 416p. 1975. Repr. of 1891 ed. lib. bdg. 18.00 o.p. (ISBN 0-8398-2311-8, Gregg). G K Hall.

Shelley, Percy B. Cenci: A Tragedy in Five Acts. LC 79-93255. 1970. Repr. of 1886 ed. 8.00x (ISBN 0-87753-035-1). Phaeton.

--The Complete Poetical Works of Percy Bysshe Shelley: 1814-1817, Vol. 2. (Oxford English Texts Ser.). 1974. 59.00x (ISBN 0-19-812707-3). Oxford U Pr.

--Hellas: A Lyrical Drama. Wise, Thomas J., ed. LC 72-93256. 1970. Repr. of 1886 ed. 8.00x (ISBN 0-87753-036-X). Phaeton.

--The Poetical Works of Shelley. rev. ed. Ford, Newell F., intro. by. LC 74-11133. (Cambridge Editions Ser.). 704p. 1975. 16.95 (ISBN 0-395-18461-4). HM.

--Shelley's Critical Prose. McElderry, B. R., Jr., ed. LC 66-19856. (Regents Critics Ser.). xxiv, 183p. 1967. 14.50x o.p. (ISBN 0-8032-0461-2); pap. 2.95x o.p. (ISBN 0-8032-5462-8, BB 407, Bison). U of Nebr Pr.

Shellhaas, Glen W., ed. see Parnell, Richard B.

Shelly, Gary B. & Cashman, Thomas J. Introduction to BASIC Programming. 1982. pap. text ed. 14.95x (ISBN 0-88236-118-X). Anaheim Pub Co.

Shelly, Judith A. Caring in Crisis: Bible Studies for Helping People. LC 78-13878. 1979. pap. 3.95 (ISBN 0-87784-563-8). Inter-Varsity.

Shelly, Judith A., jt. auth. see Fish, Sharon.

Shelly, Marshall, jt. auth. see Heck, Glenn.
Shelnitz, P., tr. see Brainina, K. Z.
Shelnitz, P., tr. see Semin, G. K., et al.
Shelsby, Earl, ed. NRA Gunsmithing Guide: Updated. rev. ed. (Illus.). 336p. (Orig.). 1980. pap. text ed. 11.95 (ISBN 0-935998-47-0). Natl Rifle Assn.
Shelsby, Earl & Gilford, James, eds. Basic Hunter's Guide. rev. ed. (Illus.). 280p. (Orig.). 1982. pap. text ed. 14.95 (ISBN 0-935998-46-2). Natl Rifle Assn.
Shelsby, Earl, ed. see Mitchell, Jack D.
Shelston, Alan. Biography. (The Critical Idiom Ser.). 1977. text ed. 9.95x (ISBN 0-416-83680-1); 4.95x (ISBN 0-416-83690-9). Methuen Inc.
Shelton, Alphonse, jt. auth. see Sanderson, Gretchen.
Shelton, Austin J. Igbo-Igala Borderland: Religion & Social Control in Indigenous African Colonialism. LC 70-141493. 1971. 39.50x (ISBN 0-87395-082-8). State U NY Pr.
Shelton, Brenda K. Reformers in Search of Yesterday: Buffalo in the 1890's. LC 76-22699. 1976. 34.50x (ISBN 0-87395-352-5). State U NY Pr.
Shelton, Carrie & Shelton, Donald. The Christian Children's Cookbook. 80p. (gr. k-5). 1982. cancelled (ISBN 0-9607468-2-X). GloryPatri.
Shelton, Donald, jt. auth. see Shelton, Carrie.
Shelton, G. A., ed. Electrical Conduction & Behavior in "Simple" Invertebrates. (Illus.). 1982. 98.00x (ISBN 0-19-857171-2). Oxford U Pr.
Shelton, Gilbart. Best of the Rip Off Press, Vol. 2: The Fabulous Furry Freak Brothers. (Best of the Rip Off Press Ser.). (Illus.). 96p. (Orig.). 1974. pap. 5.95 (ISBN 0-89620-076-0). Rip Off.
Shelton, Gilbert. More Adventures of Fat Freddy's Cat. (Illus.). 96p. (Orig.). 1981. pap. 4.95 (ISBN 0-89620-057-4). Rip Off.
--Wonder Wart-Hog & the Nurds of November. (Illus.). 216p. (Orig.). Date not set. pap. 6.95 (ISBN 0-89620-083-3). Rip Off.
Shelton, Gilbert & Richards, Ted. Give Me Liberty. (Illus.). 48p. (Orig.). 1976. pap. 3.50 (ISBN 0-89620-085-X). Rip Off.
Shelton, Gilbert & Sheridan, Dave. The Adventures of Fat Freddy's Cat. rev. ed. (Illus.). 160p. (Orig.). 1982. pap. 5.95 (ISBN 0-89620-058-2). Rip Off.
Shelton, Gilbert, ed. see Williams, Robert.
Shelton, Herbert M. Hygienic Care of Children. 430p. pap. 6.95 (ISBN 0-686-97975-3). Natural Hygiene.
Shelton, Ingrid. The Lollipop Dragon & the Writing Contes. Gambill, Henrietta, ed. (Tiny Tumtum Tales Ser.). (Illus.). 80p. (Orig.). (gr. k-4). 1983. pap. 0.98 (ISBN 0-87239-698-3, 2914). Standard Pub.
--The Lollipop Dragon Finds the Missing Teddy Bear. Gambill, Henrietta, ed. (Tiny Tumtum Tales Ser.). (Illus.). 80p. (Orig.). (gr. k-4). 1983. pap. 0.98 (ISBN 0-87239-697-5, 2913). Standard Pub.
--The Lollipop Dragon Helps the Flower Lady. Gambill, Henrietta, ed. (Tiny Tumtum Tales Ser.). (Illus.). 80p. (Orig.). (gr. k-4). 1983. pap. 0.98 (ISBN 0-87239-696-7, 2912). Standard Pub.
--The Lollipop DRagon Plans a Potluck Picnic. Gambill, Henriette, ed. (Tiny Tumtum Tales Ser.). (Illus.). 80p. (Orig.). (gr. k-4). 1983. pap. 0.98 (ISBN 0-87239-695-9, 2911). Standard Pub.
--The Lord's Prayer. (Arch Bks.). 1982. pap. 0.89 (ISBN 0-570-06161-X, 59-1308). Concordia.
Shelton, Jack & Juhasz, Jack R. How to Enjoy One to Ten Perfect Days in San Francisco. rev. 3rd ed. Swedin, Diane, ed. LC 82-61645. (Illus.). 192p. 1983. pap. 3.95 (ISBN 0-918742-02-1). Shelton.
Shelton, Jaki. Dead on Arrival. 2nd ed. 100p. (Orig.). Date not set. pap. 5.00 (ISBN 0-932112-08-0). Carolina Wren. Postponed.
Shelton, John C., jt. auth. see Monson, Richard S.
Shelton, Kodikara. Foreign Policy of Sri Lanka. 1982. 18.50x (ISBN 0-8364-0905-1, Pub. by Heritage India). South Asia Bks.
Shelton, Margaret R., et al. First Aid for Your Dog. Foyle, Christina, ed. 1972. 3.95 (ISBN 0-685-55804-5). Palmetto Pub.
Shelton, Oscar D. Canadian Dominion. 1919. text ed. 8.50x (ISBN 0-686-83498-4). Elliots Bks.
Shelton, R. L., jt. ed. see Hartley, John E.
Shelton, R. N., jt. auth. see Schilling, J. S.
Shelton, Ralph L., jt. auth. see Skinner, Paul H.
Shelton, Regina M. To Lose a War: Memories of a Young German Girl. 1982. 19.95 (ISBN 0-8093-1074-0). S Ill U Pr.
Shelton, Richard. Selected Poems, Nineteen Sixty-Nine to Nineteen Eighty-One. LC 82-2680. (Pitt Poetry Ser.). 233p. (YA) 1982. 14.95 (ISBN 0-8229-3470-1); pap. 6.95 (ISBN 0-8229-5343-9). U of Pittsburgh Pr.
Shelton, Ronald L., jt. auth. see Myers, Wayne L.
Shelton, W. G. Dean Tucker & Eighteenth Century Economic & Political Thought. LC 79-29742. 1980. 26.00 (ISBN 0-312-18538-3). St Martin.
Shely, Patricia. Los Animales Del Arca. Cranberry, Nola, tr. from Eng. (Libros Para Colorear). (Illus.). 16p. (Span.). 1982. pap. 1.20 (ISBN 0-311-38561-3). Casa Bautista.
--El Nino Jesus. Cranberry, Nola, tr. (Libros Para Colorear). (Illus.). 16p. (Span.). 1982. pap. 1.20 (ISBN 0-311-38563-X). Casa Bautista.
--Pre-School Pocketbook of Crafts. LC 74-28722. (Illus.). 96p. (ps-1). 1975. pap. 2.25 (ISBN 0-87239-045-4, 2135). Standard Pub.
Shem, Samuel. The House of God. LC 78-18368. 1978. 9.95 (ISBN 0-399-90023-3, Marek). Putnam Pub Group.
Shemberg, Kenneth M., jt. auth. see Doherty, Michael E.
Shemel, Sidney & Krasilovsky, M. William. This Business of Music. 4th ed. 1979. 18.50 (ISBN 0-8230-7753-5, Billboard Bks). Watson-Guptill.
Shemel, Sidney & Krislovsky, M. William. More About This Business of Music. rev ed. Zhito, Lee, ed. 204p. (Orig.). 1982. Repr. 12.95 (ISBN 0-8230-7567-2, Billboard Bks). Watson-Guptill.
Shen, Hsieh W. Modeling of Rivers. LC 79-3913. 1000p. 1979. 61.95x (ISBN 0-471-05474-7, Pub. by Wiley-Interscience). Wiley.
Shen, James. Is the U. S. True to its Friends? A View from the Former Ambassador of Free China. 300p. 1983. 14.95 (ISBN 0-686-82487-3). Acropolis.
Shen, Liang & Kong, J. A. Applied Electromagnetism. (Electrical Engineering Ser.). 584p. 1983. text ed. 33.95 (ISBN 0-534-01358-9). Brooks-Cole.
Shen, Peter & Wilson, Joyce. Make Your Face Your Fortune. (Illus.). 160p. 1982. pap. 8.95 (ISBN 0-89696-181-8, An Everest House Book). Dodd.
--Peter Shen's Face Fortunes. (Illus.). 276p. 1982. 14.95 (ISBN 0-399-12669-4, Perige); pap. 6.95 (ISBN 0-399-50585-7). Putnam Pub Group.
--Peter Shen's Make-up for Success. LC 79-28306. (Illus.). 192p. 1980. 14.95 (ISBN 0-89696-075-7, An Everest House Book). Dodd.
Shenberg, Yitzhak. Under the Fig Tree: Palestinian Stories. 1951. 1.50 o.p. (ISBN 0-8052-3274-5). Schocken.
Shendge, Malati J. The Civilized Demons: The Harappans in the Rgveda. (Illus.). 1977. 30.00x o.p. (ISBN 0-8364-0077-1). South Asia Bks.
Shenfeld, Gary. Famous Firsts in Space. (Famous Firsts Ser.). (Illus.). (gr. 5 up). 1972. PLB 4.49 o.p. (ISBN 0-399-60160-0). Putnam Pub Group.
Shenfield, Margaret, tr. see Eimert, Herbert & Stockhausen, Karlheinz.
Shenitzer, Abe, tr. see Yaglom, I. M.
Shenk, Carol. Measurements in Cooking. 1983. pap. 2.95x (ISBN 0-88323-065-8, 162); tchr's ed. 1.00 (ISBN 0-88323-066-6, 163). Richards Pub.
Shenk, Michel, tr. see Trocme, Andre.
Shenk, Norman A. Calculus & Analytic Geometry. 2nd ed. (Illus.). 1979. 35.50x (ISBN 0-673-16059-9). Scott F.
Shenk, Wilbert R. Exploring Church Growth. 336p. 1983. pap. 12.95 (ISBN 0-8028-1962-1). Eerdmans.
--Henry Venn: Missionary Statesman. LC 82-18779. 192p. (Orig.). 1983. pap. 9.95 (ISBN 0-88344-181-0). Orbis Bks.
Shenkel, William M. Modern Real Estate Appraisal. (Illus.). 1978. text ed. 25.95 (ISBN 0-07-056548-1, C); instructor's manual 4.95 (ISBN 0-07-056549-X). McGraw.
--Modern Real Estate Management. (Illus.). 1979. text ed. 25.95x (ISBN 0-07-056546-5); instructor's manual 9.00 (ISBN 0-07-056547-3). McGraw.
Shennan, Stephen, jt. ed. see Renfrew, Colin.
Shennum, David. English-Egyptian Index of Faulkner's Concise Dictionary of Middle Egyptian. LC 77-15699. (Aids & Research Tools in Ancient Near Eastern Studies: Vol. I). 178p. 1979. pap. 8.00 o.p. (ISBN 0-89003-054-5). Undena Pubns.
Shenov, G. V., jt. auth. see Srivastava, U. K.
Shenoy, G. K. & Wagner, F. E., eds. Mossbauer Isomer Shifts. 1978. 138.50 (ISBN 0-7204-0314-6, North-Holland). Elsevier.
Shenson, Howard L. Consulting Handbook. 5th ed. 213p. 1982. pap. 39.00 (ISBN 0-910549-00-1). H L Shenson.
--How to Create & Market Successful Seminars. 1981. 27.00 (ISBN 0-686-30968-5, An Everest House Book). Dodd.
Shenstone, William. Poetical Works. LC 68-54436. (Illus.). 1968. Repr. of 1854 ed. lib. bdg. 15.75x (ISBN 0-8371-0655-9, SHWS). Greenwood.
Shenstone, William, ed. Miscellany, Seventeen Fifty-Nine to Seventeen Sixty-Three. LC 78-16381. 1978. Repr. of 1952 ed. lib. bdg. 18.50x (ISBN 0-313-20591-4, SHMI). Greenwood.
Shenton, Stan. Triumph Speed Tuning. 2nd ed. Arman, Mike, ed. (Illus.). 64p. 1982. pap. 8.00 (ISBN 0-933078-09-9). M Arman.
Shepard. Antitrust & American Business Abroad. 2nd ed. 1981. 120.00 (ISBN 0-07-002435-9). McGraw.
--California Construction Law Manual. 2nd ed. 1977. 42.00 (ISBN 0-07-000223-1). McGraw.
--Civil Rights & Civil Liberties Litigation: A Guide to S1983. 1979. 50.00 (ISBN 0-07-045856-1). McGraw.
--Creditor's Rights in Bankruptcy. 1980. 70.00 (ISBN 0-07-044060-3); annual suppl. 25.00 (ISBN 0-07-044064-6). McGraw.
--Environmental Protection: The Legal Framework. 1981. 60.00 (ISBN 0-07-057883-4). McGraw.
--Estate Planning for Farmers & Ranchers. 1980. 65.00 (ISBN 0-07-033500-1). McGraw.
--Fritz. 1980. 7.95 (ISBN 0-531-07313-0, Pub. by Second Change Pr); 15.95 (ISBN 0-686-83006-7). Watts.
--Guide to International Law. 1983. 75.00 (ISBN 0-07-067513-9). McGraw.
--Hearsay Handbook. (incl. 1980 suppl.). 1975. 50.00 (ISBN 0-07-005270-0). McGraw.
--Inter-Vivos Trusts. 1975. 37.50 (ISBN 0-07-011554-0). McGraw.
--International Corporation Taxation. 1980. 70.00 (ISBN 0-07-050537-3). McGraw.
--International Estate Planning. 1981. 80.00 (ISBN 0-07-046430-8). McGraw.
--International Individual Taxation, 2 vols. 1981. 75.00 (ISBN 0-07-050544-6). McGraw.
--Mental Capacity. 1977. 50.00 (ISBN 0-07-000756-X); annual pocket suppl. 1979 15.00 (ISBN 0-07-000761-6). McGraw.
--Solar Law. (incl. 1981 suppl.). 1978. 55.00 (ISBN 0-07-035400-6); annual pocket part suppl. 16.00 (ISBN 0-07-035404-9). McGraw.
--Statistical Proof of Discrimination. 1980. 50.00 (ISBN 0-07-003470-2). McGraw.
Shepard, Dennis D. The Intraocular Lens Manual. 4th, rev. ed. (Illus.). 498p. 1982. pap. text ed. 45.00 (ISBN 0-686-97269-4). D D Shepard.
Shepard, Greg. Bigger, Stronger, Faster. new ed. (Illus.). 1977. pap. 5.95 (ISBN 0-89036-102-9). Hawkes Pub Inc.
Shepard, J. M. & Stewart. Sociology & Social Problems: A Conceptual Approach. (Illus.). 336p. 1976. pap. text ed. 14.95 (ISBN 0-13-821652-5). P-H.
Shepard, J. W. see Gospel Advocate.
Shepard, John, jt. auth. see Painter, Desmond.
Shepard, John W. Christ of the Gospels. rev. ed. 1946. 10.95 (ISBN 0-8028-1779-3). Eerdmans.
Shepard, Jon M. Automation & Alienation: A Study of Office & Factory Workers. 1st U. S. ed. 1971. 17.50x (ISBN 0-262-19075-3). MIT Pr.
--Organizational Issues in Industrial Society: A Book of Readings. (General Sociology Ser.). 496p. 1972. ref. ed. 16.95 o.p. (ISBN 0-13-641001-4). P-H.
--Sociology. (Illus.). 533p. 1980. text ed. 21.95 (ISBN 0-8299-0412-3). West Pub.
Shepard, Jon M. & Voss, Harwin L. Social Problems. (Illus.). 1978. pap. text ed. 15.95x (ISBN 0-02-409670-9). Macmillan.
Shepard, Judith. More Food of My Friends: Their Favorite Recipes. LC 82-84010. 176p. (Orig.). 1983. pap. 8.95 (ISBN 0-932966-29-2). Permanent Pr.
Shepard, Leslie. Encyclopedia of Occultism & Parapsychology: A Compendium of Information on the Occult Sciences, Magic, Demonology, Superstitions, Spiritism, Mysticism, Metaphysics, Psychical Science & Parapsychology. 2nd ed. (Illus.). 400p. Date not set. 125.00x (ISBN 0-8103-0196-2). Gale.
--History of Street Literature: The Story of Broadside Ballads, Chapbooks, Proclamations, News-Sheets, Etc. LC 72-12953. (Illus.). 240p. 1973. 30.00x (ISBN 0-8103-2006-1). Gale.
--John Pitts, Ballad Printer of Seven Dials, London, 1765-1844. (Illus.). 1969. 24.00x (ISBN 0-8103-2007-X). Gale.
Shepard, Leslie, ed. Encyclopedia of Occultism & Parapsychology: A Compendium of Information on the Occult Sciences, Magic, Demonology, Superstition, Spiritism, Mysticism, Metaphysics, Psychical Science & Parapsychology, 2 vols. LC 77-92. (Illus., Supplemented by Occultism update). 1978. Set. 120.00x (ISBN 0-8103-0185-7); pap. 75.00x occultism update: a periodical supplement (4 issues subscription) (ISBN 0-685-79636-1). Gale.
Shepard, Leslie A. Encyclopedia of Occultism & Parapsychology: Vols. 1 & 2. 1980. pap. 19.90 o.p. boxed set (ISBN 0-380-50112-0, 50112); Vol. 1. pap. 9.95 o.s.i. (ISBN 0-380-48835-3, 48835); Vol. 2. pap. 9.95 o.s.i. (ISBN 0-380-48975-9, 48975). Avon.
Shepard, Marion L., et al. Introduction to Energy Technology. LC 75-36284. 1976-80. 23.95 (ISBN 0-250-40123-1); 10.95 o.p. softcover (ISBN 0-250-40239-4). Ann Arbor Science.
Shepard, Odell, jt. ed. see Manchester, Frederick A.
Shepard, Paul & McKinley, Daniel, eds. Subversive Science: Essays Toward an Ecology of Man. LC 69-15029. (Illus., Orig.). 1969. pap. text ed. 15.50 (ISBN 0-395-05399-4). HM.
Shepard, Priscilla, ed. What Is a Mother? 1977. pap. 5.50 boxed (ISBN 0-8378-5010-X). Gibson.
Shepard, Ray. Autobiography of Malcolm X: Notes. 69p. (Orig.). 1973. pap. text ed. 2.50 (ISBN 0-8220-0802-5). Cliffs.
Shepard, Ricahrd F. & Levi, Vicki G. Live & Be Well: A Celebration of Yiddish Culture in America from the First Immigrants to the Second World War. (Illus.). 192p. Date not set. price not set (ISBN 0-345-30752-6); pap. 9.95 (ISBN 0-345-29435-1). Ballantine.
Shepard, Roger N., et al, eds. Multidimensional Scaling: Theory & Applications in the Behavioral Sciences. Incl. Volume 1: Theory. 250p. 29.00 (ISBN 0-12-785781-8); Volume 2: Applications. 320p. 34.00 (ISBN 0-12-785782-6). LC 74-187260. 1972. Set. 50.00 (ISBN 0-685-25831-9). Acad Pr.
Shepard, Sam. Angel City; Curse of the Starving Class: & Other Plays. 246p. 1982. pap. 7.95 cancelled (ISBN 0-8264-0218-6). Continuum.
--Buried Child. 160p. 1982. pap. 6.95 cancelled (ISBN 0-8264-0220-8). Continuum.
--Chicago & Other Plays. 172p. 1982. pap. 6.95 cancelled (ISBN 0-8264-0222-4). Continuum.
--Four Two-Act Plays. 226p. 1982. pap. 7.95 cancelled (ISBN 0-8264-0221-6). Continuum.
--Hawk Moon: A Book of Short Stories, Poems & Monologues. LC 80-85347. 93p. 1981. 12.95 (ISBN 0-933826-22-2); pap. 4.95 (ISBN 0-933826-23-0); ltd. signed 25.00 (ISBN 0-686-86591-X). Performing Arts.
--Motel Chronicles. 144p. (Orig.). 1983. 14.95 (ISBN 0-87286-144-9); pap. 5.95 (ISBN 0-87286-143-0). City Lights.
--The Unseen Hand: And Other Plays. 234p. 1982. pap. 6.95 cancelled (ISBN 0-8264-0219-4). Continuum.
Shepard, Sanford. Lost Lexicon: Secret Meanings in the Vocabulary of Spanish Literature During the Inquisition. LC 82-70140. (Hispanic Studies Collection). 143p. (Orig.). 1982. pap. 19.95 (ISBN 0-89729-309-6). Ediciones.
Shepard, T. H., et al, eds. see Gaudeloupe Confernce by L'Institut de la Vie, et al.
Shepard, William C. The Prosecutor's Reach: Legal Issues & the New Religions. 200p. 1983. 12.95 (ISBN 0-8245-0582-4). Crossroad NY.
Sheperd, A. P., tr. see Steiner, Rudolf.
Shephard, Priscilla, compiled by. The Hymn of St. Francis. 1978. 3.95 (ISBN 0-8378-2011-1). Gibson.
Shephard, R. J. Human Physiological Work Capacity. LC 77-80847. (International Biological Programme Ser.: No. 15). (Illus.). 1978. 70.00 (ISBN 0-521-21781-4). Cambridge U Pr.
Shephard, Roy J. The Risks of Passive Smoking. (Illus.). 196p. 1982. text ed. 27.95x (ISBN 0-19-520393-3). Oxford U Pr.
Shephard, Susan, ed. The Books That Have Been Shaping American Foreign Policy. 130p. 1983. 9.95 (ISBN 0-8180-2303-1). Horizon.
Shepherd. College Study Skills. 1983. pap. text ed. 10.95 (ISBN 0-686-84577-3, RD02); instr's. manual avail. (RD03). HM.
--College Vocabulary Skills. 2d ed. 1983. pap. text ed. 11.95 (ISBN 0-686-84578-1, RD05); instr's. manual avail. (RD06). HM.
Shepherd, D. M., jt. ed. see McKay, Alexander G.
Shepherd, David. Comprehensive High School Reading Methods. 3rd ed. 416p. 1982. text ed. 19.95 (ISBN 0-675-09881-5). Merrill.
Shepherd, Dorothy. Homoeopathy for the First Aider. 1982. pap. 3.95 (ISBN 0-85032-091-7, Pub. by C. W. Daniels). Formur Intl.
--More Magic of the Minimum Dose. 1974. 10.95 (ISBN 0-85032-056-9, Pub. by C. W. Daniels). Formur Intl.
Shepherd, Eric & Watson, J. P. Personal Meanings: The First Guy's Hospital Symposium on the Individual Frame of Reference. LC 82-1986. 202p. 1982. 54.95 (ISBN 0-471-10220-2, Pub. by Wiley-Interscience). Wiley.
Shepherd, F. A. Advance Engineering Surveying. 288p. 1982. pap. text ed. 24.95 (ISBN 0-7131-3416-X). E Arnold.
--Engineering Surveying. 2nd ed. 304p. 1983. pap. text ed. write for info. (ISBN 0-7131-3478-X). E Arnold.
--Engineering Surveying Problems & Solutions. 384p. 1977. pap. text ed. 19.95 (ISBN 0-7131-3370-8). E Arnold.
Shepherd, Geoff, jt. ed. see Spence, Sue.
Shepherd, Geoffrey, ed. Ancrene Wisse, Pts. 6 & 7. (Old & Middle English Texts). 116p. 1972. pap. 10.95x o.p. (ISBN 0-06-496228-8). B&N Imports.
Shepherd, Geoffrey, et al. Marketing Farm Products: Economic Analysis. 6th ed. (Illus.). 1976. text ed. 19.95x o.p. (ISBN 0-8138-1080-9). Iowa St U Pr.
Shepherd, Geoffrey S. Agricultural Price Analysis. 5th rev. ed. (Illus.). 1963. 9.50x (ISBN 0-8138-0070-6). Iowa St U Pr.
Shepherd, George W., Jr. Anti-Apartheid: Transnational Conflict & Western Policy in the Liberation of South Africa. LC 77-71868. (Studies in Human Rights: No. 3). 1977. lib. bdg. 27.50x (ISBN 0-8371-9537-3, SHA/). Greenwood.
Shepherd, Gordon M. Neurobiology. 1982. 35.00x (ISBN 0-19-503054-0); pap. 21.95x (ISBN 0-19-503055-9). Oxford U Pr.
--The Synaptic Organization of the Brain. 2nd ed. LC 79-899. (Illus.). 1979. text ed. 24.95x (ISBN 0-19-502548-2); pap. text ed. 14.95x (ISBN 0-19-502549-0). Oxford U Pr.
Shepherd, J. & Morton, A. H. Higher Electrical Engineering. (Pitman Paperback Ser.). (Illus.). 877p. pap. text ed. 35.00x (ISBN 0-273-40063-0, LTB). Sportshelf.
Shepherd, J. Barrie. Diary of Daily Prayer. LC 74-14176. 136p. (Orig.). 1975. pap. 4.50 (ISBN 0-8066-1459-5, 10-1900). Augsburg.
--Encounters: Poetic Meditations on the Old Testament. LC 82-22422. 176p. (Orig.). 1983. pap. 8.95 (ISBN 0-8298-0637-7). Pilgrim NY.
Shepherd, J. F. & Walton, G. Shipping, Maritime Trade & the Economic Development of Colonial America. LC 76-176256. (Illus.). 350p. 1972. 32.50 (ISBN 0-521-08409-1). Cambridge U Pr.
Shepherd, J. F., jt. auth. see Walton, G. M.
Shepherd, J. T. & Vanhoutte, P. M., eds. The Human Cardiovascular System: Facts & Concepts. 363p. 1979. 30.00 (ISBN 0-89004-367-1); softcover 15.95 (ISBN 0-686-52359-8). Raven.
Shepherd, J. W. Church, Falling Away & Restoration. 8.95 (ISBN 0-89225-065-8); pap. 5.95 (ISBN 0-89225-191-3). Gospel Advocate.
--Handbook on Baptism. 10.95 (ISBN 0-89225-097-6). Gospel Advocate.

Shepherd, J. W. & Ellis, H. D. Identification Evidence: A Psychological Evaluation. 164p. 1982. 23.50 (ISBN 0-08-028441-8). Pergamon.

Shepherd, J. W. see Gospel Advocate.

Shepherd, J. W see Gospel Advocate.

Shepherd, Jack, jt. auth. see Glover, Bob.

Shepherd, James F. College Study Skills. LC 78-69533. (Illus.). 1978. pap. text ed. 10.50 (ISBN 0-395-26261-5); instr's. manual 0.50 (ISBN 0-395-26260-7). HM.

--College Vocabulary Skills. LC 78-69548. (Illus.). 1978. pap. text ed. 10.95 (ISBN 0-395-26851-6); instr's. manual 0.50 (ISBN 0-395-26852-4). HM.

--The Houghton Mifflin Study Skills Handbook. (Illus.). 368p. 1982. pap. text ed. 10.50 (ISBN 0-395-31709-6). HM.

--Reading Skills for College Study. LC 79-89520. (Illus.). 1980. pap. text ed. 11.95 (ISBN 0-395-28503-8); instr's. manual 1.00 (ISBN 0-395-28504-6). HM.

--RSVP: The Houghton Mifflin Reading, Study, & Vocabulary Program. LC 80-82698. (Illus.). 352p. 1981. pap. text ed. 10.95 (ISBN 0-395-29342-1); instr's manual 0.75 (ISBN 0-395-29343-X). HM.

Shepherd, James L., tr. see Gaillardet, Frederic.

Shepherd, James M. From Lot to Chimney Top. LC 81-83926. (Illus.). 273p. 1982. pap. 12.5005619816x (ISBN 0-9607308-0-X). Stuart Pubs VA.

Shepherd, Jean. A Fistful of Fig Newtons. LC 80-2872. (Illus.). 288p. 1981. 15.95 (ISBN 0-385-17503-5). Doubleday.

--In God We Trust: All Others Pay Cash. pap. 5.95 (ISBN 0-385-02174-7, Dolp). Doubleday.

--Wanda Hickey's Night of Golden Memories & Other Disasters. LC 72-161317. (Illus.). 1976. pap. 7.95 (ISBN 0-385-11632-2, Dolp). Doubleday.

Shepherd, John. Tin Pan Alley. (Routledge Popular Music Ser.). 128p. 1982. 12.95 (ISBN 0-7100-0904-6). Routledge & Kegan.

Shepherd, John A. Management of the Acute Abdomen. (Illus.). 1982. 42.50x (ISBN 0-19-261322-7). Oxford U Pr.

Shepherd, John T. & Vanhoutte, Paul M. Veins & Their Control. LC 75-15353. (Illus.). 269p. 1975. text ed. 12.00 (ISBN 0-7216-8220-0). Saunders.

Shepherd, Leslie. Encyclopedia of Occultism: Supplement to 1st Edition. 1982. 74.00x (ISBN 0-8103-0198-9). Gale.

Shepherd, Margaret. Capitals for Calligraphy: A Sourcebook of Decorated Letters. (Illus.). 128p. 1981. pap. 9.95 (ISBN 0-02-029960-5, Collier). Macmillan.

--Learning Calligraphy: A Book of Lettering, Design & History. 1978. pap. 9.95 (ISBN 0-02-015550-6, Collier). Macmillan.

Shepherd, Massey H. Oxford American Prayer Book Commentary. 1950. 24.95x (ISBN 0-19-501202-X). Oxford U Pr.

Shepherd, Michael, ed. Psychiatrists on Psychiatry. LC 81-21750. (Illus.). 200p. 1983. 29.50 (ISBN 0-521-24480-3); pap. 13.95 (ISBN 0-521-28863-0). Cambridge U Pr.

Shepherd, Michael & Zangwill, O. L., eds. General Psychopathology. LC 81-21575. (Handbook of Psychiatry Ser.: Vol. 1). (Illus.). 500p. 1983. 49.50 (ISBN 0-521-23649-5); pap. 19.95 (ISBN 0-521-28137-7). Cambridge U Pr.

Shepherd, Ray. This Business of Writing. 1980. pap. text ed. 10.95 (ISBN 0-574-20035-5, 13-3035); instr's. guide avail. (ISBN 0-574-20036-3, 13-3036). SRA.

Shepherd, Rebecca A., ed. Peterson's Annual Guide to Independent Secondary Schools 1983. 924p. 1983. pap. 10.95 (ISBN 0-87866-212-X). Petersons Guides.

Shepherd, Richard. Bibliography of Carlyle. LC 70-116801. (Reference Ser., No. 44). 1970. Repr. of 1881 ed. lib. bdg. 43.95x (ISBN 0-8383-1043-5). Haskell.

--Bibliography of Tennyson. LC 73-116802. (Studies in Tennyson, No. 27). 1970. Repr. of 1896 ed. lib. bdg. 27.95x (ISBN 0-8383-1044-3). Haskell.

Shepherd, Robert, Jr. John Milton: Paradise Lost a Prose Rendition. (Illus.). 160p. (Orig.). 1983. 17.95 (ISBN 0-8164-0534-4); pap. 8.95 (ISBN 0-8164-2415-2). Seabury.

Shepherd, Roberta B., jt. auth. see Carr, Janet H.

Shepherd, Stella. Like a Mantle, the Sea. LC 73-85450. (Illus.). 184p. 1971. 9.50x (ISBN 0-8214-0133-5, 82-81362). Ohio U Pr.

Shepherd, W. & Zand, P. Energy Flow & Power Factor in Nonsinusoidal Circuits. LC 78-51684. (Illus.). 1979. 64.50 (ISBN 0-521-21990-6). Cambridge U Pr.

Shepherd, W. G., tr. see Horace.

Shepherd, W. R. Guide to the Materials for the History of the United States in Spanish Archives. 1907. pap. 13.00 (ISBN 0-527-00701-3). Kraus Repr.

Shepherd, Walter. Flint: Its Origin, Properties & Uses. (Illus.). 1972. 18.50x o.s.i. (ISBN 0-571-09926-2). Transatlantic.

--Let's Look at Trees. (Illus.). (gr. 4 up). 9.50x o.p. (ISBN 0-392-03761-0, LTB). Sportshelf.

Shepherd, William G. The Economics of Industrial Organization. LC 78-6285. 1979. 24.95 (ISBN 0-13-231464-9). P-H.

Shepherd, William R. Hispanic Nations of a New World. 1921. text ed. 8.50x (ISBN 0-686-83565-4). Elliots Bks.

--Shepherd's Historical Atlas. 9th rev. ed. (Illus.). (gr. 7 up). 1980. 28.50x (ISBN 0-389-20155-3). B&N Imports.

Shepley, John, tr. see Courthion, Pierre.

Shepp, Bryan E. see Tighe, Thomas J.

Shepp, Lawrence A., ed. see Symposian Applied Mathematics.

Sheppard, A., jt. ed. see Toebes, G. H.

Sheppard, Ann, ed. see Little, Geraldine.

Sheppard, Anne. BivaD (David) For Parents of Learning Disabled Children. 24p. (Orig.). 1983. pap. 1.25 (ISBN 0-8298-0650-4). Pilgrim NY.

Sheppard, Bruce D. & Sheppard, Carroll A. The Complete Guide to Women's Health. LC 82-14802. (Illus.). 421p. 1982. 19.95 (ISBN 0-936166-07-X). Mariner Pub.

Sheppard, C. Stewart, ed. Working in the Twenty-First Century. Carroll, Donald C. LC 79-24775. 235p. 1980. 26.95 (ISBN 0-471-07755-0, Pub. by Wiley-Interscience). Wiley.

Sheppard, Carroll A., jt. auth. see Sheppard, Bruce D.

Sheppard, Charles. Natural History of the Coral Reef. (Illus.). 160p. 1983. 16.95 (ISBN 0-7137-1268-6, Pub. by Blandford Pr England). Sterling.

Sheppard, Donna C., ed. see Colonial Williamsburg Foundation Staff.

Sheppard, Donna C., ed. see Turgeon, Charlotte.

Sheppard, E. J. Ancient Athens. Reeves, Marjorie, ed. (Then & There Ser.). (Illus.). 110p. (gr. 7-12). 1967. pap. text ed. 3.10 (ISBN 0-582-20406-2). Longman.

--Ancient Egypt. Reeves, Marjorie, ed. (Then & There Ser.). (Illus.). 80p. (gr. 7-12). 1960. pap. text ed. 3.10 (ISBN 0-582-20361-9). Longman.

Sheppard, Eugenia & Blackwell, Earl. Skyrocket. LC 79-8012. 1980. 12.95 (ISBN 0-385-15695-2). Doubleday.

Sheppard, Francis. London, Eighteen Eight to Eighteen Seventy: The Infernal Wen. LC 71-142067. (History of London Series). (Illus.). 1971. 42.50x (ISBN 0-520-01847-8). U of Cal Pr.

Sheppard, Georgie M., jt. auth. see Liebers, Arthur.

Sheppard, Jill. The Redlegs of Barbados. LC 76-56886. (Caribbean Monographs). 1977. lib. bdg. 30.00 (ISBN 0-527-82230-2). Kraus Intl.

Sheppard, John R. & Anderson, V. Elving, eds. Membranes & Genetic Disease. LC 82-12672. (Progress in Clinical & Biological Research Ser.: Vol. 97). 422p. 1982. 68.00 (ISBN 0-8451-0097-1). A R Liss.

Sheppard, Joseph J. Human Color Perception. 1968. text ed. 23.95 (ISBN 0-444-00030-5, North Holland). Elsevier.

Sheppard, K. The Treatment of Cats by Homoeopathy. 1979. pap. 3.95x (ISBN 0-85032-120-4, Pub. by C. W. Daniels). Formur Intl.

--The Treatment of Dogs by Homoeopathy. 1981. pap. 3.95x (ISBN 0-85032-079-8, Pub. by C. W. Daniels). Formur Intl.

Sheppard, Leslie & Axelrod, R. Herbert. Paganini. (Illus.). 704p. 1979. 25.00 (ISBN 0-87666-618-7, Z-28). Paganiniana Pubns.

Sheppard, Mary. All Angels Cry. LC 77-88211. 1977. 9.95 (ISBN 0-87716-085-6, Pub. by Moore Pub Co). F Apple.

Sheppard, Mubin. Taman Budiman: Memoirs of an Unorthodox Civil Servant. 278p. (Orig.). 1979. pap. text ed. 11.95x (ISBN 0-686-98151-0). Heinemann Ed.

Sheppard, P. A. see Landsberg, H. E.

Sheppard, P. M., ed. Practical Genetics. LC 73-9709. 337p. 1973. text ed. 55.95x o.s.i. (ISBN 0-470-78360-5). Halsted Pr.

Sheppard, Stephen. The Four Hundred. LC 79-12362. 1979. 11.95 o.p. (ISBN 0-671-40071-1). Summit Bks.

--Monte Carlo. 416p. 1983. 15.95 (ISBN 0-671-44789-0). Summit Bks.

Sheppard, Valerie & Premazon, Judith. Carnival of Language Fun. (gr. 4-8). 1982. 5.95 (ISBN 0-86653-085-1, GA 431). Good Apple.

Sheppard, Vincent F., jt. auth. see Reed, Gretchen M.

Sheppard, Walter L., Jr. Ancestry & Descendants of Thomas Stickney Evans & Sarah Ann Fifield, His Wife. (Illus.). 214p. 1940. 15.00 (ISBN 0-9607610-0-4); pap. 10.00 (ISBN 0-9607610-3-9). W L Sheppard.

--Ancestry of Edward Carleton & Ellen Newton His Wife. (Illus.). 860p. 1978. text ed. write for info. (ISBN 0-9607610-2-0). W L Sheppard.

--A Handbook of Chemically Resistant Masonry. (Illus.). 260p. 1977. 40.00 (ISBN 0-9607610-1-2). W L Sheppard.

Sheppard, William A. Organic Syntheses. LC 21-17747. (Organic Syntheses Ser.: Vol. 58). 240p. 1978. 21.50 (ISBN 0-471-04739-2, Pub. by Wiley-Interscience). Wiley.

Sheppard, William C. & Willoughby, Robert H. Child Behavior. 1975. 24.50 (ISBN 0-395-30838-0); Personalized Student Guide. pap. 11.50 (ISBN 0-395-30839-9). HM.

Sheppard, William F; see Klein, Felix.

Sheppard-Landis, Sara. Just Your Size: A Guide to Fashion, Health & Beauty for the Woman Size 14 & up. (Illus.). 192p. 1982. 14.95 (ISBN 0-698-11154-0, Coward). Putnam Pub Group.

Shepperd, G. A. A History of War & Weapons, 1660-1918. (Illus.). 224p. 1972. 12.45i (ISBN 0-690-39367-9). T Y Crowell.

Shepperd, Gladys B. The Montgomery Saga: From Slavery to Black Power. 1983. 10.00 (ISBN 0-533-05553-9). Vantage.

Shepperd, M. J., jt. auth. see Minski, L.

Shepperson, George A & Edwards, Owen D., eds. Scotland, Europe & the American Revolution. LC 76-48756. 1977. 20.00x (ISBN 0-312-70402-X). St Martin.

Shepperson, Wilbur S. Samuel Roberts: A Welsh Colonizer in Civil War Tennessee. LC 60-12777. (Illus.). 1961. 13.50x (ISBN 0-87049-032-X). U of Tenn Pr.

Shepro, David & Fulton, George P. Microcirculation As Related to Shock. 1968. 51.00 (ISBN 0-12-639650-7). Acad Pr.

Sheps, Cecil G., jt. auth. see Lewis, Irving J.

Sheps, Cecil G., jt. ed. see Burrell, Craig D.

Sher, Barbara. Wishcraft: How to Get What You Really Want. 1983. pap. price not set (ISBN 0-449-90083-5, Columbine). Fawcett.

Sher, George, ed. see Mill, John S.

Sher, Jonathan P., ed. Rural Education in Urbanized Nations: Issues & Innovations. (Special Studies in Education). 425p. 1981. lib. bdg. 30.00 (ISBN 0-89158-964-3). Westview.

Sher, Jonathon P. Education in Rural America: A Reassessment of Conventional Wisdom. LC 76-57184. 1977. lib. bdg. 29.00 (ISBN 0-89158-201-0); softcover 12.95 (ISBN 0-89158-203-7). Westview.

Sherard, James L., et al. Earth & Earth-Rock Dams: Engineering Problems of Design & Construction. LC 63-14068. 725p. 1963. 66.50 (ISBN 0-471-78547-4, Pub. by Wiley-Interscience). Wiley.

Sherarts, I. Karon, ed. see Mittlefehldt, Pamela.

Sheraton, Mimi. From My Mother's Kitchen: Recipes & Reminiscences. LC 75-6360. (Illus.). 1979. 14.37i (ISBN 0-06-013846-7, HarpT). Har-Row.

--German Cookbook. 1965. 19.95 (ISBN 0-394-40138-7). Random.

Sheratt, A. F., ed. Integrated Environment in Building Design. (Illus.). x, 281p. 1974. 51.25 (ISBN 0-85334-609-7, Pub. by Applied Sci England). Elsevier.

Sherbiny, Nalem A. & Sirageldin, Ismail, eds. Manpower Planning in the Oil Countries. (Research in Human Capital & Development: Supplement No. 1). 350p. 1981. 42.50 (ISBN 0-89232-129-6). Jai Pr.

Sherbo, Arthur, ed. see Johnson, Samuel.

Sherbon, Elizabeth. On the Count of One: Modern Dance Methods. 3rd ed. (Illus.). 284p. 1982. spiral bdg. 12.95 (ISBN 0-87484-541-6). Mayfield Pub.

Sherborn, C. D. Index Animalium Sive Index Nominum Quae ab A.D. MDCCLVIII Generibus et Speciebus Animalium Inposita Sunt: Sectio Secunda, (1801-1850), Pts. 1-33. 1922. text ed. 437.50x (ISBN 0-565-00801-3, Pub. by Brit Mus Nat Hist). Sabbot-Natural Hist Bks.

Sherbowitz-Wetzor, O. P., tr. see Cross, Samuel H.

Sherburne, Zoa. Almost April. (gr. 7 up). 1956. PLB 9.12 (ISBN 0-688-31013-3). Morrow.

--Girl in the Mirror. (gr. 7 up). 1966. 9.50 (ISBN 0-688-21344-8). Morrow.

--The Girl Who Knew Tomorrow. (gr. 7 up). 1970. PLB 9.12 (ISBN 0-688-31347-7). Morrow.

--Too Bad About the Haines Girl. (gr. 9-12). 1967. PLB 9.12 (ISBN 0-688-31646-8); pap. 2.95 (ISBN 0-688-26646-0). Morrow.

--Why Have the Birds Stopped Singing? 192p. (gr. 7 up). 1974. PLB 8.59 (ISBN 0-688-30111-8). Morrow.

Shercliff, J. A. Vector Fields. LC 76-8153. (Illus.). 1977. 64.50 (ISBN 0-521-21306-1); pap. 16.95x (ISBN 0-521-29092-9). Cambridge U Pr.

Sherer, Michael L. Good News for Children: Object Lessons on Epistle Texts. LC 81-65655. (Series B). 128p. (Orig.). 1981. pap. 4.50 (ISBN 0-8066-1891-4, 10-2809). Augsburg.

Shereshefsky, Pauline M. & Yarrow, Leon J. Psychological Aspects of a First Pregnancy & Early Postnatal Adaptation. LC 73-87877. 391p. 1973. 22.50 (ISBN 0-911216-65-0). Raven.

Shereshevsky, Esra. Rashi: The Man & His World. 288p. 1982. 17.50 (ISBN 0-87203-101-2). Hermon.

Sherf, A. F., jt. auth. see Chupp, C.

Sheridan, Alan. Michel Foucault: The Will to Truth. 1980. 25.00x (ISBN 0-422-77350-6, Pub. by Tavistock England); pap. 9.95 (ISBN 0-422-76570-8). Methuen Inc.

Sheridan, Alan, tr. see Ladurie, Emmanuel L.

Sheridan, Alan, tr. see Semprun, Jorge.

Sheridan, Dave, jt. auth. see Shelton, Gilbert.

Sheridan, David & Rifkin, Erik. The Management of Scarcity. 1983. 26.00x (ISBN 0-88410-866-X). Ballinger Pub.

Sheridan, Frances see Boswell, James.

Sheridan, Frank J. Italian, Slavic & Hungarian Unskilled Immigrant Laborers in the United States. LC 70-145492. (The American Immigration Library). 84p. 1971. Repr. of 1907 ed. lib. bdg. 8.95x (ISBN 0-89198-025-3). Ozer.

Sheridan, James F. Mystery Delight: An Unnatural Philosophy. 1980. pap. text ed. 9.50 (ISBN 0-8191-1089-2). U Pr of Amer.

--Psyche: Lectures on Psychology & Philosophy. LC 79-66579. 1979. pap. text ed. 9.75 (ISBN 0-8191-0843-X). U Pr of Amer.

Sheridan, James F., Jr. Once More from the Middle: A Philosophical Anthropology. LC 72-85543. ix, 157p. 1973. 10.00x (ISBN 0-8214-0108-4, 82-81115). Ohio U Pr.

Sheridan, Jane. My Lady Hoyden. 1982. pap. 2.95 (ISBN 0-451-11511-2, AE1511, Sig). NAL.

Sheridan, John V. Tourist in His Footsteps. LC 79-53024. (Presence Ser., Vol. 1). (Orig.). 1979. pap. 2.95 (ISBN 0-89003-034-0). Undena Pubns.

Sheridan, Kimberly. Felis-Hade. (Aura Felis-Hade: No. 1). 331p. (gr. 5). 1983. 9.95 (ISBN 0-9609262-5-9). Felis-Hadiken.

Sheridan, M. D. From Birth to Five Years: Children's Developmental Processes. (General Ser). (Illus.). 72p. 1975. pap. text ed. 7.00x (ISBN 0-85633-074-4, NFER). Humanities.

Sheridan, Michael. The Fifth Season. LC 78-7507. 52p. 1978. 8.50 (ISBN 0-8214-0405-9, 82-82972); pap. 4.95 (ISBN 0-8214-0407-5, 82-82980). Ohio U Pr.

Sheridan, Richard B. The Rivals. Downer, Alan S., ed. LC 52-13686. (Crofts Classics Ser.). 1953. pap. text ed. 3.25x (ISBN 0-88295-091-6). Harlan Davidson.

Sheridan, Richard B; see Morrell, Janet M.

Sheridan, T. Mindful Militants. LC 74-17503. 352p. 1976. 39.50 (ISBN 0-521-20680-4). Cambridge U Pr.

Sheridan, T. J. Seven Chinese Stories. (Oxford Progressive English Readers Ser.). (Illus.). 1975. pap. 3.50x (ISBN 0-19-638230-0). Oxford U Pr.

Sheridan, Thomas B. & Ferrell, William R. Man-Machine Systems: Information, Control, & Decision Models of Human Performance. LC 73-19777. (Illus.). 707p. 1974. 27.50x o.p. (ISBN 0-262-19118-0). MIT Pr.

Sherif, Carolyn W. & Sherif, Muzafer. Reference Groups: Exploration into Conformity & Deviation of Adolescents. LC 64-10594. 384p. 1972. 5.25 (ISBN 0-89526-954-6). Regnery-Gateway.

Sherif, Mohamed A. Ghazali's Theory of Virtue. LC 71-38000. 200p. 1975. 34.50x (ISBN 0-87395-206-5). State U NY Pr.

Sherif, Muzafer, jt. auth. see Sherif, Carolyn W.

Sheriff, R. E. & Geldart, L. P. Exploration Seismology: History, Theory, & Data Acquisition, Vol. I. LC 81-18176. (Illus.). 300p. Date not set. price not set (ISBN 0-521-24373-4). Cambridge U Pr.

Sheriff, Robert E. A First Course in Geophysical Exploration & Interpretation. LC 78-70766. (Illus.). 313p. 1979. text ed. 32.00 (ISBN 0-934634-02-5). Intl Human Res.

--Seismic Stratigraphy. LC 80-83974. (Illus.). 224p. 1980. text ed. 29.00 (ISBN 0-934634-08-4); pap. 22.00 (ISBN 0-934634-51-3). Intl Human Res.

Sherill, John. Mi Amiga, la Biblia. 160p. Date not set. 2.50 (ISBN 0-88113-305-1). Edit Betania.

Sherington, Geoffrey. Australia's Immigrants. (Australian Experience Ser.). 216p. 1981. text ed. 22.50x (ISBN 0-86861-010-0); pap. text ed. 9.95x (ISBN 0-86861-018-6). Allen Unwin.

--English Education, Social Change & War: 1911-1920. 176p. 1982. text ed. 19.00x (ISBN 0-7190-0840-9, Pub. by Manchester England). Humanities.

Sherk, William. Five Hundred Years of New Words. LC 82-45307. (Illus.). 200p. 1983. pap. 9.95 (ISBN 0-385-17902-2). Doubleday.

Sherley-Price, Leo, tr. see Thomas a Kempis, Saint.

Sherlock, A. J. & Roebuck, E. M. Calculus: Pure & Applied. 544p. 1982. pap. text ed. 16.95 (ISBN 0-7131-3446-1). E Arnold.

Sherlock, Connie. Bible Families. Beegle, Shirley, ed. (Think 'N Check Quizzes Ser.). (Illus.). 16p. (Orig.). (gr. 4-8). 1983. pap. 1.50 (ISBN 0-87239-688-6, 2792). Standard Pub.

--Life of Jesus. Beegle, Shirley, ed. (Think 'N Check Quizzes Ser.). (Illus.). 16p. (Orig.). (gr. 4-8). 1983. pap. 1.50 (ISBN 0-87239-689-4, 2793). Standard Pub.

Sherlock, John & Westheimer, David. The Amindra Gamble. 350p. 1982. 13.95 (ISBN 0-698-11100-1, Coward). Putnam Pub Group.

--The Amindra Gamble. 1983. pap. price not set. Zebra.

Sherlock, Paul, jt. ed. see Jerzy, George B.

Sherlock, Philip M. West Indian Folk Tales. (Oxford Myths & Legends Ser.). (Illus.). (gr. 6-12). 1978. Repr. of 1966 ed. 12.95 (ISBN 0-19-274116-0). Oxford U Pr.

Sherlock, Sheila. Disease of the Liver & Biliary System. 6th ed. (Illus.). 552p. 1981. text ed. 57.50 (ISBN 0-632-00766-4, B-4588-3). Mosby.

Sherlock, Thomas. The Tryal of the Witnesses of the Resurrection of Jesus, 1973 & the Use & Extent of Prophecy, 1728. Wellek, Rene, ed. LC 75-25131. (British Philosophers & Theologians of the 17th & 18th Centuries Ser.). 1978. lib. bdg. 42.00 o.s.i. (ISBN 0-8240-1761-7). Garland Pub.

Sherma, J., jt. auth. see Touchstone, J. C.

Sherma, Joseph see Zweig, Gunter.

Sherma, Joseph, jt. ed. see Zweig, Gunter.

Sherman, Alan & Sherman, Sharon J. The Elements of Life: Approach to Chemistry for the Health Sciences. (Illus.). 1980. text ed. 26.95 (ISBN 0-13-266130-6); lab. man. 12.95 (ISBN 0-13-266148-9). P-H.

Sherman, Alan, et al. Basic Concepts of Chemistry. 2nd ed. LC 79-88447. (Illus.). 1980. text ed. 23.95 (ISBN 0-395-28153-9); instr's. manual 1.10 (ISBN 0-395-28154-7); study guide 8.95 (ISBN 0-395-28702-2); lab experiments 12.95 (ISBN 0-395-28155-5). HM.

Sherman, Barrie, jt. auth. see Jenkins, Clive.

Sherman, Bill, ed. see Kvasnicker, Ted, et al.

Sherman, Charles D. Clinical Concepts in Cancer Management. (Illus.). 1976. pap. text ed. 19.95 o.p. (ISBN 0-07-056580-5, HP). McGraw.

Sherman, Dan. The Prince of Berlin. 1983. 15.95 (ISBN 0-87795-480-1). Arbor Hse.

Sherman, Florence J. How to Raise & Train a West Highland White Terrier. (Orig.). pap. 2.95 (ISBN 0-87666-408-7, DS1133). TFH Pubns.

Sherman, Franklin, ed. see Milford, T. R.

Sherman, Franklin, ed. see Temple, William.

Sherman, Franklin, ed. see Van Oyen, Hendrik.

Sherman, Franklin, tr. see Tillich, Paul.

Sherman, Frederick C. Combat Command. 400p. 1982. pap. 2.95 (ISBN 0-553-22917-6). Bantam.

Sherman, Fredrick T., jt. auth. see Libow, Leslie S.

Sherman, Geraldine. Animals with Pouches: The Marsupials. LC 77-27592. (Illus.). 40p. (gr. 1-4). 1978. PLB 7.95 (ISBN 0-8234-0324-6). Holiday.

--Caverns: A World of Mystery & Beauty. LC 80-15865. (Illus.). 64p. (gr. 4-6). 1980. PLB 7.29 o.p. (ISBN 0-671-33081-0). Messner.

Sherman, H. J. Sociology: Traditional & Radical Perspectives. 1982. pap. text ed. 15.50 (ISBN 0-06-318190-8, Pub. by Har-Row Ltd England). Har-Row.

Sherman, H. J., jt. auth. see Edginton, J. K.

Sherman, Harold. You Live After Death. 1949. 8.95 (ISBN 0-910140-16-2). Anthony.

--Your Mysterious Powers of E.S.P. pap. 1.95 (ISBN 0-451-09315-1, J9315, Sig). NAL.

Sherman, Herbert L., Jr., et al, eds. see Labor Law Group.

Sherman, Howard. Stagflation: An Introduction to Traditional & Radical Macroeconomic. 2nd ed. 320p. 1983. pap. text ed. 10.95 scp (ISBN 0-06-046108-X, HarpC). Har-Row.

Sherman, Howard J., jt. auth. see Hunt, E. K.

Sherman, Irwin W. & Sherman, Vilia G. Biology: A Human Approach. 3rd ed. (Illus.). 748p. 1983. 25.00x (ISBN 0-19-503176-8); tchrs.' companion free (ISBN 0-19-503296-9). Oxford U Pr.

--The Invertebrates: Function & Form: A Laboratory Guide. 2nd ed. (Illus.). 352p. 1976. pap. text ed. 13.95x (ISBN 0-02-409840-X). Macmillan.

Sherman, J. A. & Denmark, F. L. The Psychology of Women: Future Directions in Research. LC 78-31824. 800p. 1979. 59.95 (ISBN 0-88437-009-7). Psych Dimensions.

Sherman, Jacques L., Jr. & Fields, Sylvia K., eds. Guide to Patient Evaluation. 4th ed. LC 78-50128. 1982. 28.50 (ISBN 0-87488-883-2); pap. 17.95 (ISBN 0-87488-985-5). Med Exam.

Sherman, James R. Escape to the Gunflint. (Illus.). 175p. (Orig.). 1982. pap. 3.95 (ISBN 0-935538-03-8). Pathway Bks.

--Stop Procrastinating--Do It! LC 80-82893. (Orig.). 1981. pap. 2.25 (ISBN 0-935538-01-1). Pathway Bks.

Sherman, Joan. Jack London: A Reference Guide. (Reference Publications Ser.). 1977. lib. bdg. 22.00 o.p. (ISBN 0-8161-7849-6, Hall Reference). G K Hall.

Sherman, Joel D. & Kutner, Mark A., eds. New Dimensions of the Federal-State Partnership in Education. 168p. (Orig.). 1983. pap. write for info. (ISBN 0-937846-98-8). Inst Educ Lead.

Sherman, Johanna. The Sacred Rose Tarot. 56p. 1982. pap. 12.00 (ISBN 0-88079-012-1). US Games Syst.

Sherman, John C., jt. ed. see Chapman, John D.

Sherman, Jory. The Bamboo Demons. (Chill Ser.: No. 3). 1979. pap. 1.75 o.p. (ISBN 0-523-40222-8). Pinnacle Bks.

--Chill, No. 2. 1978. pap. 1.75 o.p. (ISBN 0-523-40221-X). Pinnacle Bks.

--Gunn, No. 1: Dawn of Revenge. 224p. (Orig.). 1980. pap. 1.95 (ISBN 0-89083-594-2). Zebra.

--Gunn, No. 1: Dawn of Revenge. (Orig.). pap. 2.25 (ISBN 0-89083-590-X). Zebra.

--Gunn, No. 10: Hard Bullets. (Orig.). 1981. pap. 2.25 (ISBN 0-89083-896-8). Zebra.

--Gunn, No. 11: Trial by Sixgun. (Orig.). 1982. pap. 2.25 (ISBN 0-89083-918-2). Zebra.

--Gunn, No. 12: The Widowmaker. 1982. pap. 2.25 (ISBN 0-89083-987-5). Zebra.

--Gunn, No. 13: Arizona Hardcase. (Orig.). 1982. pap. 2.25 (ISBN 0-8217-1039-7). Zebra.

--Gunn, No. 14: The Buff Runners. 1982. pap. 2.25 (ISBN 0-8217-1093-1). Zebra.

--Gunn, No. 15: Drygulched. 1983. pap. 2.25 (ISBN 0-8217-1142-3). Zebra.

--Gunn, No. 2: Mexican Showdown. 224p. (Orig.). 1980. pap. 1.95 (ISBN 0-89083-628-0). Zebra.

--Gunn, No. 3: Death's-Head Trail. 240p. (Orig.). 1980. pap. 1.95 (ISBN 0-89083-648-5). Zebra.

--Gunn, No. 4: Blood Justice. 256p. (Orig.). 1980. pap. 1.95 (ISBN 0-89083-670-1). Zebra.

--Gunn, No. 5: Winter Hell. 256p. (Orig.). 1981. pap. 1.95 (ISBN 0-89083-708-2). Zebra.

--Gunn, No. 6: Duel in Purgatory. 1981. pap. 1.95 (ISBN 0-89083-739-2). Zebra.

--Gunn, No. 7: Law of the Rope. (Orig.). 1981. pap. 2.25 (ISBN 0-89083-766-X). Zebra.

--Gunn, No. 8: Apache Arrows. 1981. pap. 2.25 (ISBN 0-89083-791-0). Zebra.

--Gunn, No. 9: Boothill Bounty. (Orig.). 1981. pap. 2.25 (ISBN 0-686-79736-1). Zebra.

--House of Scorpions. (Chill Ser.: No. 6). 192p. 1980. pap. 1.95 o.p. (ISBN 0-523-40699-1). Pinnacle Bks.

--The Phoenix Man. (Chill Ser.: No. 5). 192p. (Orig.). 1980. pap. 1.75 o.p. (ISBN 0-523-40698-3). Pinnacle Bks.

--Satan's Seed, No. 1. 1978. pap. 1.50 o.p. (ISBN 0-523-40220-1). Pinnacle Bks.

--Shadows. (Chill Ser.: No. 7). 192p. (Orig.). 1980. pap. 1.95 o.p. (ISBN 0-523-41058-1). Pinnacle Bks.

Sherman, Julia A. & Beck, Evelyn T., eds. The Prism of Sex: Essays in the Sociology of Knowledge. LC 79-3969. 320p. 1979. 19.50 (ISBN 0-299-08010-2). U of Wis Pr.

Sherman, Kenneth. Data Communication Systems: A User's Guide. (Illus.). 368p. 1980. 23.95 (ISBN 0-8359-1227-2). Reston.

--Data Communications: A User's Guide. 348p. 1981. 21.95 (ISBN 0-686-98096-4). Telecom Lib.

Sherman, Lawrence W. Scandal & Reform: Controlling Police Corruption. LC 77-79236. 1978. 28.50x (ISBN 0-520-03523-2). U of Cal Pr.

Sherman, Lawrence W. & Lambert, Richard D., eds. Police & Violence. LC 80-68055. (The Annals of the American Academy of Political & Social Science Ser.: No. 452). 1980. 7.50 o.p. (ISBN 0-87761-256-0); pap. text ed. 7.95 (ISBN 0-87761-257-9). Am Acad Pol Soc Sci.

Sherman, Lila. Art Museums of America: A Guide to Collections in the United States & Canada. LC 81-11062. (Illus.). 1981. pap. 6.95 (ISBN 0-688-00744-9). Quill NY.

Sherman, Margaret. Sweet Puddings & Desserts. (International Wine & Food Society Ser.). (Illus.). 4.50 o.p. (ISBN 0-7153-5177-X). David & Charles.

Sherman, Margaret E. Where to Stay U. S. A. from Fifty Cents to Fifteen Dollars a Night. Cohen, Marjorie A., ed. 1980. 5.95 (ISBN 0-671-25496-0). S&S.

Sherman, Michael & Hawkins, Gordon. Imprisonment in America: Choosing the Future. LC 81-10453. xii, 146p. 1981. pap. 5.95 (ISBN 0-226-75280-1). U of Chicago Pr.

Sherman, Michael I., ed. Concepts in Mammalian Embryogenesis. LC 77-4144. (Cell Monograph). 1977. 30.00x (ISBN 0-262-19158-X). MIT Pr.

Sherman, Michael I., ed. see Symposium Held at the Roche Institute of Molecular Biology, Nutley, New Jersey, May, 1975.

Sherman, Murray H., ed. Psychoanalysis & Old Vienna: Freud, Reik, Schnitzler, Kraus. LC 76-89968. (Special Issue of Psychoanalytic Review Ser.). 192p. 1978. 12.95 (ISBN 0-87705-333-2). Human Sci Pr.

Sherman, N., jt. auth. see Kieffer.

Sherman, Natalie, jt. auth. see Cappucino, James C.

Sherman, Paul D. Color Vision in the Nineteenth Century: The Young-Helmholtz-Maxwell Theory. 233p. 1981. 49.50 (ISBN 0-9960022-6-X, Pub. by A Hilger England). Heyden.

Sherman, Richard. Eritrea: The Unfinished Revolution. 222p. 1982. 19.95 (ISBN 0-03-055921-9); pap. 6.00 (ISBN 0-03-062803-2). Praeger.

Sherman, Richard B. The Republican Party & Black America: From McKinley to Hoover, 1896-1933. LC 72-96714. 274p. 1973. 13.95x (ISBN 0-8139-0467-6). U Pr of Va.

Sherman, Robert, jt. auth. see Borge, Victor.

Sherman, Robert M. & Sherman, Ruth W. Vital Records of Yarmouth, Mass. to 1850, 2 vols. LC 79-189435. 1975. Set. 20.00x o.p. (ISBN 0-930272-00-5). RI Mayflower.

Sherman, Robert W. & Knight, Morris H. Aural Comprehension in Music, 2 vols. (Illus.). 672p. (Orig.). 1972. wkbk. 22.50 ea. (C). Vol. 1 (ISBN 0-07-056569-4). Vol. 2 (ISBN 0-07-056570-8). instructor's manual 3.95 (ISBN 0-07-056573-2); test manual 3.95 (ISBN 0-07-056574-0). McGraw.

Sherman, Roger. The Shermans: A Sketch of Family History & a Genealogical Record, 1570-1890 with Some Account of Families Intermarried. 1946. pap. 29.50x (ISBN 0-685-89781-8). Elliots Bks.

Sherman, Ruth W., jt. auth. see Sherman, Robert M.

Sherman, Ruth W., jt. auth. see Wakefield, Robert S.

Sherman, Ruth W., ed. see Wakefield, Robert S.

Sherman, Sharon J., jt. auth. see Sherman, Alan.

Sherman, Steve. Cheese Sweets & Savories. 176p. 1983. pap. 8.95 (ISBN 0-8289-0498-7). Greene.

Sherman, Stuart C. The Voice of the Whaleman: With an Account of the Nicholson Whaling Collection. LC 65-18564. (Illus.). 219p. 1965. 15.00x (ISBN 0-8139-0945-7, Pub. by Providence Public Library). U Pr of Va.

Sherman, Stuart P. Shaping Men & Women: Essay on Literature & Life. Zeitlin, Jacob, ed. LC 69-10153. 1969. Repr. of 1928 ed. lib. bdg. 18.00x (ISBN 0-8371-0221-9, SHEL). Greenwood.

Sherman, T. D. O & M in Local Government. 1969. 24.00 o.p. (ISBN 0-08-013317-7); pap. 10.75 o.p. (ISBN 0-08-013309-6). Pergamon.

Sherman, Theodore A. & Johnson, Simon. Modern Technical Writing. 3rd ed. (Illus.). 480p. 1975. 18.95 (ISBN 0-13-598763-6). P-H.

Sherman, Thomas M. & Wildman, Terry M. Proven Strategies for Successful Test Taking. 160p. 1982. pap. text ed. 7.50 (ISBN 0-675-09843-2). Merrill.

Sherman, Vilia G., jt. auth. see Sherman, Irwin W.

Sherman, William L., jt. auth. see Meyer, Michael C.

Shern, Roald J, jt. ed. see Bibby, Basil G.

Sheroner, Charles M., ed. see Rousseau, Jean J.

Sherouse, Deborah L. Professional's Handbook on Geriatric Alcoholism. (Illus.). 288p. 1983. text ed. price not set (ISBN 0-398-04828-2). C C Thomas.

Sherover, Charles M. Heidegger, Kant & Time. LC 74-135011. 344p. 1971. 15.00x o.p. (ISBN 0-253-32720-2). Ind U Pr.

Sherover, Charles M., ed. The Development of the Democratic Idea. 1974. pap. 2.50 o.s.i. (ISBN 0-451-61303-1, ME1303, Ment). NAL.

Sherr, Paul. Short Story & the Oral Tradition. LC 70-101314. 1970. pap. text ed. 8.95x (ISBN 0-87835-002-0). Boyd & Fraser.

Sherr, Sol. Video & Electronic Displays: A User's Guide. LC 81-21915. 352p. 1982. 29.50x (ISBN 0-471-09037-9, Pub. by Wiley-Interscience). Wiley.

Sherr, Solomon, ed. Fundamentals of Display System Design. LC 78-96045. 1970. 46.00 o.p. (ISBN 0-471-78570-9, Pub. by Wiley-Interscience). Wiley.

Sherrard, Philip. Byzantium. LC 66-28334. (Great Ages of Man Ser). (Illus.). (gr. 6 up). 1966. PLB 11.97 o.p. (ISBN 0-8094-0372-2, Pub. by Time-Life). Silver.

--The Wound of Greece: Studies in Neo-Hellenism. LC 78-27758. 1979. 15.95x (ISBN 0-312-89300-0). St Martin.

Sherrard, Philip, tr. see Christopoulos, George A.

Sherrard, Philip, tr. see Christopoulos, George A. & Bastias, John C.

Sherrard, Philip, jt. tr. see Palmer, G. E.

Sherrat, A. F. Air Conditioning System Design for Buildings. 256p. 1983. 30.00 (ISBN 0-07-084591-3). McGraw.

Sherratt, A. F. Air Conditioning Design for Buildings. Date not set. price not set (ISBN 0-444-20041-X). Elsevier.

Sherratt, A. F., ed. Energy Conservation & Energy Management in Buildings. (Illus.). 1976. text ed. 57.50x (ISBN 0-85334-684-4, Pub. by Applied Sci England). Elsevier.

--Integrated Environment in Building Design. LC 74-22250. 281p. 1975. 54.95x o.s.i. (ISBN 0-470-78575-6). Halsted Pr.

Sherratt, A. F., jt. ed. see Croome, D. J.

Sherrer, jt. auth. see Nadel.

Sherrer, Jr., jt. auth. see Nadel.

Sherrill, Anne H., jt. auth. see Kushner, Howard I.

Sherrill, Chris & Aiello, Roger. Key West, the Last Resort. (Illus.). 171p. Date not set. pap. 6.95 (ISBN 0-686-84261-8). Banyan Bks.

Sherrill, John, jt. auth. see Blair, Charles.

Sherrill, John L. My Friend the Bible. 1978. 5.95 (ISBN 0-912376-37-6). Chosen Bks Pub.

Sherrington, Charles S. Man on His Nature. 1951. 45.00 (ISBN 0-521-06436-8); pap. 13.95x (ISBN 0-521-09203-5). Cambridge U Pr.

Sherrington, P. J. & Oliver, R. Granulation: Monographs in Powder Science & Technology. 1980. 42.95 (ISBN 0-471-26019-3, Pub. by Wiley Heyden). Wiley.

Sherrod, H. Floyd, ed. Environment Law Review: Annual. Incl. 1970 (ISBN 0-87632-042-6); 1971 (ISBN 0-87632-048-5); 1972 (ISBN 0-87632-082-5); 1973 (ISBN 0-87632-090-6); 1974 (ISBN 0-87632-115-5). 42.50 ea. o.p. Boardman.

Sherrod, John, ed. Information Systems & Networks: Eleventh Annual Symposium. LC 74-11941. 200p. 1975. lib. bdg. 25.00x (ISBN 0-8371-7717-0, ISN/). Greenwood.

Sherrod, Philip L. Thirty-One Mentatalia. (Orig.). 1980. pap. 5.00 (ISBN 0-934536-03-1). Merging Media.

Sherrod, Rod. The Aftermath: Asia. (World War II Ser.). 1983. lib. bdg. 19.92 (ISBN 0-8094-3436-9, Pub. by Time-Life). Silver.

Sherry, Norman, ed. see Conrad, Joseph.

Sherry, Pearl A., jt. auth. see Vidaver, Doris.

Sherry, Richard. A Treatise of Schemes & Tropes. LC 61-5030. 1977. Repr. of 1550 ed. 31.00x (ISBN 0-8201-1258-5). Schol Facsimiles.

Sherry, Ruth, ed. see O'Connor, Frank & Hunt, Hugh.

Sherster, Joyce. OJT File Clerk Resource Materials. 2nd ed. (Gregg Office Job Training Program). (Illus.). 104p. (gr. 11-12). soft-cover 5.60 (ISBN 0-07-056640-2, G). McGraw.

Sherster, Joyce A. OJT File Clerk Training Manual. 2nd ed. (Gregg Office Job Training Program Ser.). (Illus.). 80p. (gr. 11-12). 1981. pap. 4.16x (ISBN 0-07-056641-0). McGraw.

Shertenlieb, Bill & Sanders, Phronie. Focus on Competition: A Tennis Manual. rev. ed. (Illus.). 1980. pap. 4.50 (ISBN 0-9606066-0-2). Tennis Manual.

Shertzer, B., jt. auth. see Belman, H. S.

Shertzer, Bruce. Career Planning: Freedom to Choose. 2nd ed. LC 80-81846. (Illus.). 416p. 1981. pap. text ed. 10.95 (ISBN 0-395-29738-9); 1.00 (ISBN 0-395-29739-7). HM.

Shertzer, Bruce & Linden, James D. Fundamentals of Individual Appraisal: Assessment Techniques for Counselors. LC 78-69542. (Illus.). 1979. text ed. 24.50 (ISBN 0-395-26536-3); instr's. manual 1.00 (ISBN 0-395-26537-1). HM.

Shertzer, Bruce & Stone, Shelley C. Fundamentals of Guidance. 4th ed. LC 80-81917. (Illus.). 576p. 1981. text ed. 22.95 (ISBN 0-395-29712-5); instr's. manual 1.10 (ISBN 0-395-29713-3). HM.

Shertzer, Bruce, jt. auth. see Peters, Herman J.

Shertzer, Bruce, jt. auth. see Stone, Shelley C.

Shertzer, Bruce E. & Stone, Shelley C. Fundamentals of Counseling. 3rd ed. LC 79-88448. (Illus.). 1980. text ed. 22.95 (ISBN 0-395-28580-1); instr's. manual 1.10 (ISBN 0-395-28579-8). HM.

Sherwani, H. K. Cultural Trends in Medieval India: Architecture, Painting, Literature, Language. 4.50x o.p. (ISBN 0-210-98143-1). Asia.

--Studies in Muslim Political Thought & Administration. 6.50 (ISBN 0-686-18544-7). Kazi Pubns.

Sherwen, Laurie N. & Weingarten, Carol-Grace. Analysis & Application of Nursing Research: Parent-Neonate Issues Studies. LC 82-20201. 300p. 1983. pap. text ed. 13.95 (ISBN 0-534-01292-2). Brooks-Cole.

Sherwen, Laurie N., jt. auth. see Smith, Dorothy W.

Sherwin, Byron. Abraham Joshua Heschel. LC 78-71051. (Makers of Contemporary Theology Ser.). 1979. pap. 1.99 (ISBN 0-8042-0466-7). John Knox.

Sherwin, Dee, jt. auth. see Hayek, Ann.

Sherwin, E. & Weston, G. J. Chemistry of the Non-Metallic Elements. 1966. 15.00 o.p. (ISBN 0-08-011296-X); pap. 7.00 o.p. (ISBN 0-08-011295-1). Pergamon.

Sherwin, Keith. Engineering Design for Performance. (Ellis Horwood Series in Civil & Mechanical Engineering). 162p. 1982. 49.95X (ISBN 0-470-27534-0). Halsted Pr.

Sherwin, Martin J. A World Destroyed: The Atomic Bomb & the Grand Alliance. 1977. pap. 4.95 (ISBN 0-394-72148-9, Vin). Random.

Sherwin, Mary, jt. auth. see Patton, Marion.

Sherwin, Sally. Seven Steps to Rock-Bottom Food Costs: A Guide to Kitchen Economy. LC 76-12637. (Illus.). 192p. 1976. 6.95 o.p. (ISBN 0-688-03069-6); pap. 3.95 o.p. (ISBN 0-688-08069-3). Morrow.

Sherwin-White, A. N., et al, eds. see Pliny.

Sherwood, Arthur W. Understanding the Chesapeake. (Illus.). 114p. 1980. pap. 5.00 (ISBN 0-686-36776-6). Md Hist.

Sherwood, Charles S., jt. auth. see Davis, Grant M.

Sherwood, Dennis H. Crystals, X-Rays, & Proteins. LC 73-7098. 702p. 1976. 55.95 o.s.i. (ISBN 0-470-78590-X). Halsted Pr.

Sherwood, George, jt. auth. see Sherwood, Ruth.

Sherwood, Hugh C. How Corporate & Municipal Debt Is Rated: An Inside Look at Standard & Poor's Rating System. LC 76-12099. 1976. 29.95 o.p. (ISBN 0-471-78585-7, Pub by Wiley-Interscience). Wiley.

--How to Invest in Bonds. LC 74-81543. 176p. 1976. pap. 5.95 (ISBN 0-07-056685-2, SP). McGraw.

--How to Invest in Bonds. 192p. 1983. 13.95 (ISBN 0-8027-0732-7). Walker & Co.

Sherwood, J. N. Diffusion Process, Vol. 1. 410p. 1971. 92.00x (ISBN 0-677-14820-8). Gordon.

Sherwood, J. N., ed. see Thomas Graham Memorial Symposium.

Sherwood, James. James Sherwood's Discriminating Guide to London. pap. 4.95 o.p. (ISBN 0-448-14057-8, G&D). Putnam Pub Group.

Sherwood, John J., et al. Management Development Strategies. 34p. 1983. 35.00 (ISBN 0-08-029510-X). Pergamon.

Sherwood, John N. The Plastically Crystalline State: Orientationally-Disordered Crystals. LC 78-16086. 383p. 1979. 81.95 (ISBN 0-471-99715-3, Pub. by Wiley-Interscience). Wiley.

Sherwood, Martha. How to Build a Comfortable Campsite: A Beginner's Guide. LC 78-24726. (Illus.). 1979. 12.50 o.p. (ISBN 0-89196-050-3, Domus Bks); pap. 6.95 o.p. (ISBN 0-89196-024-4). Quality Bks IL.

Sherwood, Mary. The History of the Fairchild Family. LC 75-32157. (Classics of Children's Literature, 1621-1932: Vol. 22). 1976. Repr. of 1818 ed. lib. bdg. 38.00 o.s.i. (ISBN 0-8240-2271-8). Garland Pub.

Sherwood, Michael. Logic of Explanation in Psychoanalysis. 1969. 39.00 (ISBN 0-12-639450-4). Acad Pr.

Sherwood, Nancy & Timiras, Paola. A Stereotaxic Atlas of the Developing Rat Brain. LC 70-103674. (Illus., Fr. & Ger.). 1970. 68.50x (ISBN 0-520-01656-4). U of Cal Pr.

Sherwood, Peter B., jt. ed. see Johnson, Willard E.

Sherwood, Philip, jt. auth. see Stevens, Robert.

Sherwood, Robert D., jt. auth. see Goldberg, Kenneth P.

Sherwood, Roger, jt. auth. see Polyzoides, Stefanos.

Sherwood, Ruth & Sherwood, George. Homes, Today & Tomorrow. rev. ed. (gr. 9-12). 1976. text ed. 15.92 o.p. (ISBN 0-87002-173-7); trans. master 15.96 (ISBN 0-87002-357-8); student guide 6.60 (ISBN 0-87002-346-2); tchrs.' guide 7.28 (ISBN 0-87002-347-0). Bennett IL.

Sherwood, Sylvia, et al. An Alternative to Institutionalization: The Highland Heights Experiment. (Cushing Hospital Series on Aging & Terminal Care). 352p. 1981. prof ref 29.00x (ISBN 0-88410-720-5). Ballinger Pub.

--The Hidden Patient. (Cushing Hospital Ser. on Aging & Terminal Care). 1983. prof ref 24.50x (ISBN 0-88410-722-1). Ballinger Pub.

Sherwood, T., et al. Roads to Radiology: An Imaging Guide to Medicine & Surgery. (Illus.). 96p. 1983. pap. 16.00 (ISBN 0-387-11801-2). Springer-Verlag.

Sherwood, T. K., et al. Mass Transfer. 1975. 39.50 (ISBN 0-07-056692-5, C). McGraw.

Sherwood, Valerie. Bold Breathless Love. 576p. (Orig.). 1981. pap. 3.95 (ISBN 0-446-30702-5). Warner Bks.

--Her Shining Splendor. 576p. (Orig.). 1980. pap. 3.95 (ISBN 0-446-30536-7). Warner Bks.

--Rash, Reckless Love. 576p. (Orig.). 1981. pap. 3.50 (ISBN 0-446-90915-7). Warner Bks.

--Rich Radiant Love. 576p. 1983. pap. 3.95 (ISBN 0-446-30555-3). Warner Bks.

--These Golden Pleasures. 512p. (Orig.). 1977. pap. 3.95 (ISBN 0-446-30761-0). Warner Bks.

--This Loving Torment. 528p. (Orig.). 1977. pap. 3.95 (ISBN 0-446-30724-6). Warner Bks.

--This Towering Passion. 512p. (Orig.). 1978. pap. 3.95 (ISBN 0-446-30770-X). Warner Bks.

Sherwood, William & Cohen, Alan, eds. Transfusion Therapy in Infancy & Childhood: The Fetus, Infant & Child. LC 80-80304. (Masson Monographs in Pediatrics - Pediatric Hematology Oncology: Vol. 1). (Illus.). 232p. 1980. text ed. 40.00x (ISBN 0-89352-074-8). Masson Pub.

Sherzer, J. An Areal-Typological Study of American Indian Languages North of Mexico. (North-Holland Linguistics Ser.: Vol. 20). 1976. 39.00 (ISBN 0-444-11046-1, North-Holland); pap. 25.75 (ISBN 0-444-10911-0). Elsevier.

Sherzer, Joel. Kuna Ways of Speaking: An Ethnographic Perspective. (Texas Linguistic Ser.). 288p. 1983. 22.50 (ISBN 0-292-74305-X). U of Tex Pr.

Shesgreen, Sean. William Hogarth's Four Times of the Day & the Points du Jour Tradition. LC 82-71597. (Illus.). 144p. 1982. 22.50x (ISBN 0-8014-1504-7). Cornell U Pr.

Shestack, Alan, jt. auth. see Baier, Lesley K.

Shestack, Robert. Handbook of Physical Therapy. 3rd ed. LC 66-30317. 1977. text ed. 20.95 (ISBN 0-8261-0173-9); pap. text ed. 12.95 (ISBN 0-8261-0174-7). Springer Pub.

Shestov, Lev. All Things Are Possible & Penultimate Words & Other Essays. LC 76-8303. xiii, 239p. 1977. 13.50x (ISBN 0-8214-0237-4, 82-82394). Ohio U Pr.

--Dostoevsky, Tolstoy & Nietzsche. Martin, Bernard & Roberts, Spencer E., trs. LC 74-78504. xxx, 322p. 1969. 16.00x (ISBN 0-8214-0053-3, 82-80596). Ohio U Pr.

--In Job's Balances: On the Sources of the Eternal Truths. Coventry, Camilla & Macartney, C. A., trs. from Ger. LC 73-92902. l, 379p. (Eng.). 1975. 18.00x (ISBN 0-8214-0143-2, 82-81461). Ohio U Pr.

--Potestas Clavium. Martin, Bernard, tr. LC 67-24282. 1968. 20.00x (ISBN 0-8214-0040-1, 82-80448). Ohio U Pr.

--Speculation & Revelation. Martin, Bernard, tr. from Rus. LC 81-38425. Orig. Title: Umozrenie I Otkrovenie. x, 312p. 1982. lib. bdg. 32.95x (ISBN 0-8214-0422-9, 82-83145). Ohio U Pr.

Sheth, Jagdish N., ed. Research in Marketing, Vol. 2. 357p. 1979. 40.00 (ISBN 0-89232-059-1). Jai Pr.

--Research in Marketing, Vol. 3. (Orig.). 1979. lib. bdg. 40.00 (ISBN 0-89232-060-5). Jai Pr.

--Research in Marketing, Vol. 4. 300p. 1981. 40.00 (ISBN 0-89232-169-5). Jai Pr.

--Research in Marketing, Vol. 5. 325p. 1981. 42.50 (ISBN 0-89232-211-X). Jai Pr.

--Research in Marketing: An Annual Compilation of Research, Vol. 1. (Annual Ser.). (Orig.). 1978. lib. bdg. 40.00 (ISBN 0-89232-041-9). Jai Pr.

Sheth, N. J., jt. auth. see Lipson, Charles.

Shetler, Joanne. Notes on Balangao Grammar. (Languages Data, Asian-Pacific Ser.: No. 9). 254p. 1976. pap. 5.25x (ISBN 0-88312-209-X); microfiche 3.00x (ISBN 0-88312-309-6). Summer Inst Ling.

Shetler, St. G. Variation & Evolution of the Nearctic Harebells (Campanula Subsect-Heterophylla) (Phanerogamarum Monagraphiae: No. XI). (Illus.). 516p. 1982. lib. bdg. 80.00x (ISBN 3-7682-1241-6). Lubrecht & Cramer.

--Variation & Evolution of the Neartic Harebells: Campanula Subsect. Heterophylla. (Phanerogamarum Monographiae: No. XI). (Illus.). 1980. lib. bdg. 60.00x (ISBN 3-7682-1241-6). Lubrecht & Cramer.

Shetreet, S. Judges on Trial. 1976. 59.75x (ISBN 0-444-10958-7, North-Holland). Elsevier.

Shetter, W. Z., jt. auth. see Bird, R. B.

Shetty, C. M., jt. auth. see Bazaraa, Mokhtar S.

Shetty, Y. Krishna, jt. auth. see Prasad, S. Benjamin.

Shevchenko, Viktor V. Continuous Transitions in Open Waveguides. Beckmann, Petr, tr. from Rus. LC 72-145593. (Electromagnetics Ser.: Vol. 5). (Illus.). 1971. 25.00x (ISBN 0-911762-08-6). Golem.

Shevell, Richard S. Fundamentals of Flight. (Illus.). 464p. 1983. 28.95 (ISBN 0-13-339093-4). P-H.

Shevin, Aliza, tr. see Aleichem, Sholom.

Shevin, Jann, jt. auth. see Hutcheson, John D., Jr.

Shevky, Eshref & Williams, Marilyn. The Social Areas of Los Angeles: Analysis & Typology. LC 72-138180. (Illus.). 172p. 1972. Repr. of 1949 ed. lib. bdg. 18.50x (ISBN 0-8371-5637-8, SHLA). Greenwood.

Shevtsov, V. S. State & Nations in the U. S. S. R. 208p. 1982. 6.45 (ISBN 0-8285-2419-X, Pub. by Progress Pubs). Imported Pubns.

Shewan, M. J., jt. ed. see Skinner, F. A.

Shewan, Rodney, ed. see Ashbee, C. R.

Shewan, Rodney, ed. see Cobden-Sanderson, T. J.

Shewan, Rodney, ed. see Crane, Walter.

Shewan, Rodney, ed. see Cust, M. M.

Shewan, Rodney, ed. see Dresser, Christopher.

Shewan, Rodney, ed. see Godwin, E. W.

Shewan, Rodney, ed. see Rational Dress Association.

Shewan, Rodney, ed. see Sylvia's Home Help Series.

Shewan, Rodney, ed. see Wilde, Oscar.

Shewell-Cooper, W. E. Basic Book of Greenhouse Growing. (Illus.). 1978. 15.00 o.p. (ISBN 0-214-20499-5). Transatlantic.

--Plants, Flowers & Herbs of the Bible. LC 76-58772. (Illus.). 180p. 1977. 7.95 o.p. (ISBN 0-87983-166-9); pap. 3.95 o.p. (ISBN 0-87983-147-2). Keats.

Shewmake, Georgia M. Balcony of Evil. 192p. (YA) 1976. 6.95 (ISBN 0-685-62023-9, Avalon). Bouregy.

--The Curse of the Rebellars. 192p. (YA) 1975. 6.95 (ISBN 0-685-52654-2, Avalon). Bouregy.

--Ghosts of Yesterday. 1983. 6.95 (ISBN 0-686-84192-1, Avalon). Bouregy.

--Lake of Shadows. (YA) 1980. 6.95 (ISBN 0-686-73931-0, Avalon). Bouregy.

--Love's Strange Mysteries. 1982. pap. 6.95 (ISBN 0-686-84710-5, Avalon). Bouregy.

--Ridge of Fear. (YA) 1979. 6.95 (ISBN 0-685-93878-6, Avalon). Bouregy.

--The Shadow of Dolores. (YA) 1978. 6.95 (ISBN 0-685-86413-8, Avalon). Bouregy.

--Thicket of Terror. (YA) 1981. 6.95 (ISBN 0-686-73956-6, Avalon). Bouregy.

Shewmon, Paul G. Diffusion in Solids. (Materials Science & Engineering Ser.). 1963. text ed. 33.00 (ISBN 0-07-056695-X, C). McGraw.

--Transformations in Metals. (Materials Science & Engineering Ser.). 1969. text ed. 38.00 (ISBN 0-07-056694-1, C). McGraw.

Shew-Pincar. Writing Skills. Raygor, Alton L., ed. (Basic Skills Ser.). (Illus.). 1980. pap. 13.95x (ISBN 0-07-056690-9). McGraw.

Shewring, Walter, tr. see Homer.

Shibata, Katsue, tr. see Soseki, Natsume.

Shibel, Elaine & Moser, Kenneth M. Respiratory Emergencies. LC 77-8139. (Illus.). 290p. 1977. pap. text ed. 24.50 o.p. (ISBN 0-8016-4583-2). Mosby.

Shibuya, Yusaburo, tr. see Takeda, Taijun.

Shichor, David, jt. auth. see Decker, David L.

Shichor, Y. The Middle East in China's Foreign Policy: 1949-1977. LC 78-58801. (International Studies). (Illus.). 1979. 37.50 (ISBN 0-521-22214-1). Cambridge U Pr.

Shidle, Norman G. Art of Successful Communication: Business & Personal Achievement Through Written Communication. 1965. 17.00 o.p. (ISBN 0-07-056798-0, P&RB). McGraw.

Shieh, Francis. A Glimpse of Chinese Language: Peking's Language Reforms & the Teaching of Chinese in the U.S. pap. 8.50 (ISBN 0-686-09053-5, AD612722); microfiche 4.50 (ISBN 0-686-09054-3). Natl Tech Info.

Shieh, Francis, jt. auth. see Elliot, Jeffrey M.

Shiel. The Shetland Sheepdog. 1977. pap. 2.50 (ISBN 0-7028-1005-3). Palmetto Pub.

Shiel, M. P. The Purple Cloud. (Science Fiction Ser.). 1977. Repr. of 1901 ed. lib. bdg. 20.00 o.p. (ISBN 0-8398-2381-9, Gregg). G K Hall.

--The Rajah's Sapphire. (The Nautilus Ser.). (Illus.). 163p. 1981. pap. 6.00 (ISBN 0-686-92118-6). Highflyer Pr.

Shield, R., jt. ed. see Carlson, D.

Shields, jt. auth. see O'Reilly, P H.

Shields, Art. My Shaping-Up Years: The Early Life of Labor's Great Reporter. LC 82-21176. (Illus.). 240p. (Orig.). 1983. 14.00 (ISBN 0-7178-0597-2); pap. 4.95 (ISBN 0-7178-0571-9). Intl Pub Co.

Shields, C. Boilers. 1961. 62.50 (ISBN 0-07-056801-4, P&RB). McGraw.

Shields, Carrington, jt. auth. see Oppenheim, S. Chesterfield.

Shields, Geoffrey B., ed. Debt Financing & Capital Formation in Health Care Institutions. LC 82-11407. 334p. 1982. 32.50 (ISBN 0-89443-662-7). Aspen Systems.

Shields, Gerald, jt. auth. see Robotham, John.

Shields, J. B. The Gifted Child. (Exploring Education Ser.). 1968. pap. text ed. 5.00x o.p. (ISBN 0-901225-42-8, NFER). Humanities.

Shields, Jack W. The Trophic Function of Lymphoid Elements. (Illus.). 456p. 1972. photocopy ed. spiral 44.75x (ISBN 0-398-02412-X). C C Thomas.

Shields, James J. & Greer, Colin, eds. Foundations of Education: Dissenting Views. LC 73-16438. 202p. 1974. pap. text ed. 18.95 (ISBN 0-471-78635-7). Wiley.

Shields, Jerry A. The Diagnosis & Management of Intraocular Tumors. (Illus.). 703p. 1983. text ed. 89.50 (ISBN 0-8016-4585-9). Mosby.

Shields, Jerry A., jt. auth. see Tasman, William.

Shields, Kenneth, Jr. Indo-European Noun Inflection: A Developmental History. LC 82-467. 120p. 1982. 13.75x (ISBN 0-271-00311-1). Pa St U Pr.

Shields, M. Bruce. A Study Guide for Glaucoma. (Illus.). 560p. 1982. lib. bdg. 60.00 (ISBN 0-683-07691-4). Williams & Wilkins.

Shields, Mary R. The Construction & Use of Teacher-Made Tests. 2nd ed. 116p. 1965. 4.95 (ISBN 0-686-38287-0, 14-136). Natl League Nurse.

Shields, Paul C. Elementary Linear Algebra. 3rd rev. ed. (Illus.). 1980. text ed. 22.95x (ISBN 0-87901-121-1). Worth.

Shields, Steven L. Divergent Paths of the Restoration: A History of the Latter Day Saint Movement. LC 81-86304. (Illus.). 288p. 1982. 12.95 (ISBN 0-942284-00-3). Restoration Re.

Shields, Thomas W., ed. General Thoracic Surgery. 2nd ed. LC 82-17942. (Illus.). 1072p. 1983. text ed. 118.00 (ISBN 0-8121-0782-9). Lea & Febiger.

Shields, William M. Philopatry, Inbreeding & the Evolution of Sex. 250p. 1982. 49.00x (ISBN 0-87395-617-6); pap. 16.95x (ISBN 0-87395-618-4). State U NY Pr.

Shiels, Frederick L. America, Okinawa, & Japan: Case Studies for Foreign Policy Theory. LC 79-5496. 1980. text ed. 21.75 (ISBN 0-8191-0893-6); pap. text ed. 12.50 (ISBN 0-8191-0894-4). U Pr of Amer.

--Tokyo & Washington: Dilemmas of a Mature Alliance. LC 79-3339. 1980. 22.95x (ISBN 0-669-03378-2). Lexington Bks.

Shiels, William E. Gonzalo De Tapia, 1561-1594: Founder of the First Permanent Jesuit Mission in North America. LC 74-12835. (U.S. Catholic Historical Society Monograph: No. XIV). 1978. Repr. of 1934 ed. lib. bdg. 20.50x (ISBN 0-8371-7758-8, SHGT). Greenwood.

Shier, L. A., ed. see Kammerer, W.

Shiers, D, jt. ed. see Krudy, E. S.

Shiers, George. Electronic Drafting. 1962. ref. ed. 24.95 (ISBN 0-13-250563-0). P-H.

--Electronic Drafting Techniques & Exercises. (Illus.). 1963. pap. text ed. 14.95 (ISBN 0-13-250605-X). P-H.

Shiffer, M. M. & Bowden, Leon. The Role of Mathematics in Science. (New Mathematical Library: No. 30). 150p. 1983. pap. write for info. (ISBN 0-88385-630-1). Math Assn.

Shifflett, Crandall A. Patronage & Poverty in the Tobacco South: Louisa County, Virginia, 1860-1900. LC 82-6996. (Illus.). 144p. 1982. text ed. 12.00x (ISBN 0-87049-359-0). U of Tenn Pr.

Shiflett, John M. & Brown, George I. Confluent Education: Attitudinal & Behavioral Consequences of Confluent Teacher Training. LC 78-60626. (Illus.). 1978. pap. 5.00 (ISBN 0-930626-02-8). Psych & Consul Assocs.

Shiflett, Orvin L. The Origins of American Academic Librarianship. (Libraries & Information Science Ser.). 250p. 1981. text ed. 27.50x (ISBN 0-89391-082-1). Ablex Pub.

Shifrin, Avraham. U. S. S. R. Labor Camps. 1982. 3.95. Diane Bks.

--U. S. S. R. Prison Camps. 506p. (Orig.). pap. 3.95 o.p. (ISBN 0-88264-159-X). Diane Bks.

Shifrin, Avrahan. The First Guidebook to the USSR. 1981. pap. 7.95x (ISBN 0-88264-157-3). Diane Bks.

Shifrine, Moshe, ed. The Canine as a Biomedical Research Model: Immunological, Hematological & Oncological Aspects. LC 80-24174. (DOE Technical Information Center Ser.). 435p. 1980. pap. 19.00 (ISBN 0-87079-122-2, DOE/TIC-10191); microfiche 4.50 (ISBN 0-87079-457-4, DOE/TIC-10191). DOE.

Shigley, F. D. Randy Raindrop Takes a Trip. (Nature & Science Bk.). (Illus.). (gr. k-6). PLB 5.95 o.p. (ISBN 0-513-00397-5). Denison.

Shigley, Joseph E. Applied Mechanics of Materials. (Illus.). 1975. text ed. 34.00 (ISBN 0-07-056845-6); solutions manual 6.00 (ISBN 0-07-056846-4). McGraw.

--Dynamic Analysis of Machines. (Mechanical Engineering Ser.). 1961. text ed. 37.50 (ISBN 0-07-056858-8, C); solutions manual 18.00 (ISBN 0-07-056859-6). McGraw.

--Kinematic Analysis of Mechanisms. 2nd ed. LC 68-9559. (Mechanical Engineering Ser). (Illus.). 1969. text ed. 34.95 (ISBN 0-07-056868-5, C); instructor's manual 25.00 (ISBN 0-07-056874-X). McGraw.

--Mechanical Engineering Design. 3rd ed. (Mechanical Engineering Ser.). (Illus.). 1976. text ed. 33.50 (ISBN 0-07-056881-2); solutions manual 22.00 (ISBN 0-07-056882-0). McGraw.

--Mechanical Engineering Design. 2nd ed. LC 74-167497. (Mechanical Engineering Ser.). (Illus.). 768p. 1972. text ed. 19.50 o.p. (ISBN 0-07-056869-3, C). McGraw.

Shigley, Joseph E. & Mitchell, Larry D. Mechanical Engineering Design. 4th ed. (In Mechanical Engineering Ser.). (Illus.). 778p. 1983. text ed. 34.95 (ISBN 0-07-056888-X, C); Supplementary materials avail. solutions manual 10.00 (ISBN 0-07-056889-8). McGraw.

Shigley, Joseph E. & Uiker, John J. Theory of Machines & Mechanisms. (Mechanical Engineering Ser.). (Illus.). 576p. 1980. text ed. 36.95x (ISBN 0-07-056884-7); solutions manual 17.50 (ISBN 0-07-056885-5). McGraw.

Shih, Chung-Wen. Injustice to Tou O Yuan: A Study & Translation. LC 74-155585. (Princeton-Cambridge Studies in Chinese Linguistics, No. 4). 480p. 1973. 49.50 o.p. (ISBN 0-521-08228-5); pap. 22.95x (ISBN 0-521-09739-8). Cambridge U Pr.

Shih Nai-An. Water Margin, 2 vols. Jackson, J. H., tr. LC 67-31568. 1968. 16.50x (ISBN 0-8188-0208-1). Paragon.

Shih, Vivian E. Laboratory Techniques for the Detection of Hereditary Metabolic Disorders. LC 82-8920. 134p. 1982. Repr. of 1973 ed. lib. bdg. 34.95 (ISBN 0-89874-492-X). Krieger.

Shihata, Ibrahim F. The Other Face of OPEC. LC 82-15301. (Energy Resources & Policies of the Middle East & North Africa Ser.). (Illus.). 320p. (Orig.). 1982. pap. 12.95x (ISBN 0-582-78336-4). Longman.

Shih-Chen, Li. Chinese Medicinal Herbs. 1973. pap. 7.95 (ISBN 0-914558-00-5). Georgetown Pr.

Shih-Tsai Chen, Samuel. Basic Documents of International Organization. rev. ed. 1979. pap. text ed. 10.95 (ISBN 0-8403-1947-9, 40194701). Kendall-Hunt.

--The Theory & Practice of International Organization. rev. ed. 1979. text ed. 15.95 (ISBN 0-8403-1946-0, 40194601). Kendall-Hunt.

Shilling, A. G. & Sokoloff, Kiril. Is Inflation Ending? Are You Ready? LC 82-23962. (Illus.). 320p. 1983. 17.95 (ISBN 0-07-056879-0, P&RB). McGraw.

Shilling, Alison W., jt. auth. see Holm, John A.

Shilling, Dana. Be Your Own Boss: A Step-by-Step Guide to Financial Independence Through Your Own Small Business. 490p. 1983. 14.95 (ISBN 0-688-01572-7). Morrow.

--Fighting Back: A Consumer's Guide for Getting Satisfaction, Including Plaintext Form Letters to Rip Out When You're Ripped Off. LC 82-3497. 256p. (Orig.). 1982. pap. 8.00 (ISBN 0-688-01316-3). Quill NY.

--Making Wise Decisions: Plaintext Forms for Analyzing Your Options in Financial, Legal, Health, & Consumer Markets. 256p. (Orig.). 1982. pap. 8.00 (ISBN 0-688-01941-2). Quill NY.

Shilling, Diana. Fighting Back: A Consumer's Guide for Getting Satisfaction. 1982. 8.00 (ISBN 0-688-01316-3). Morrow.

Shilling, John. Thailand: Income Growth & Poverty Alleviation. viii, 56p. 1980. 10.00 (ISBN 0-686-36121-0, RC-8011). World Bank.

Shilling, John, jt. auth. see Lim, E. R.

Shilling, N. A. Doing Business in Saudi Arabia & the Arab Gulf States. LC 75-37251. (Doing Business in the Middle East Ser.). 185.00 (ISBN 0-916400-01-8); supplement o.p. 65.00 (ISBN 0-685-83461-1); 40.00 o.p. (ISBN 0-686-96749-6); 55.00 o.p. (ISBN 0-686-96750-X). Inter-Crescent.

Shillingburg, Herbert T., Jr. & Kessler, James C. Restoration of the Endodontically Treated Tooth. (Illus.). 374p. 1982. text ed. 68.00 (ISBN 0-86715-108-0). Quint Pub Co.

Shillingford, J. P. Coronary Heart Disease: The Facts. (The Facts Ser.). (Illus.). 1981. text ed. 12.95x (ISBN 0-19-261262-X). Oxford U Pr.

Shillingford, John & Stringer, Michael. Pocket Guide to Common Wild Flowers. (Illus.). 100p. 7.95 (ISBN 0-7028-8040-X, Pub. by Salem Hse Ltd.). Merrimack Bk Serv.

Shillito, John, Jr. & Matson, Donald D. An Atlas of Pediatric Neurosurgical Operations. (Illus.). 497p. 1982. 175.00 (ISBN 0-7216-8242-1). Saunders.

Shiloh, Allen. Modern Book for All Ages. 50p. 1982. pap. 4.95. Adams Pr.

Shilov, Georgi E. Linear Algebra. Silverman, Richard, tr. from Rus. LC 77-75267. 1977. pap. text ed. 6.95 (ISBN 0-486-63518-X). Dover.

--Mathematical Analysis, 2 vols. Incl. Vol. 1. Elementary Real & Complex Analysis. 1973 (ISBN 0-262-19109-1); Vol. 2. Elementary Functional Analysis. 1974 (ISBN 0-262-19122-9). 1974. 25.00x ea. MIT Pr.

Shilov, V. N., jt. auth. see Dukhin, S. S.

Shilova, I., jt. auth. see Dulmatovskaya, G.

Shils, Edward. Tradition. LC 80-21643. viii, 334p. 1981. pap. 10.95 (ISBN 0-226-75326-3). U of Chicago Pr.

Shils, Edward, ed. Criteria for Scientific Development: Public Policy & National Goals. 1968. 17.50x (ISBN 0-262-19043-5); pap. 4.95 (ISBN 0-262-69020-9). MIT Pr.

Shils, Edward, jt. ed. see Daalder, Hans.

Shilton, Neale. A Million Miles Ago. (Illus.). 140p. 1982. 19.95 (ISBN 0-85429-313-2). Haynes Pubns.

Shilton, Peter, jt. auth. see Tomas, Jason.

Shilts, Randy. The Mayor of Castro Street: The Life & Times of Harvey Milk. (Illus.). 388p. 1983. pap. 9.95 (ISBN 0-312-52331-9). St Martin.

Shim, Jae K., jt. auth. see Siegel, Joel G.

Shimamoto, et al, eds. see International Symposium, 2nd, Tokyo, 1972.

Shiman, Alexander, jt. auth. see Shimanovskaya, K.

Shiman, D. A., et al. Teachers on Individualization: The Way We Do It. 1974. 11.95 (ISBN 0-07-056895-2, P&RB). McGraw.

Shimanovskaya, K. & Shiman, Alexander. Radiation Injury of Bone: Bone Injuries Following Radiation Therapy of Tumors. Haigh, Basil, tr. (Illus.). 300p. 1983. 40.00 (ISBN 0-08-028821-9). Pergamon.

Shimek, William. Patterns: What Are They? LC 68-56710. (Math Concept Bks). (gr. 3-6). 1969. PLB 3.95g (ISBN 0-8225-0581-9). Lerner Pubns.

Shimek, William J. The Celsius Thermometer. LC 74-11898. (The Early Metric Ser.). (Illus.). 32p. (gr. 2-5). 1975. PLB 4.95g (ISBN 0-8225-0589-4). Lerner Pubns.

--The Gram. LC 74-11897. (The Early Metric Ser.). (Illus.). 32p. (gr. 2-5). 1975. PLB 4.95g (ISBN 0-8225-0588-6). Lerner Pubns.

--The Liter. LC 74-11895. (The Early Metric Ser.). (Illus.). 32p. (gr. 2-5). 1975. PLB 4.95g (ISBN 0-8225-0587-8). Lerner Pubns.

--The Meter. LC 74-11894. (The Early Metric Ser.). (Illus.). 32p. (gr. 2-5). 1975. PLB 4.95g (ISBN 0-8225-0586-X). Lerner Pubns.

Shimer. Drawing Chicken. (The Grosset Art Instruction Ser.: No. 9). (Illus.). 48p. Date not set. pap. price not set (ISBN 0-448-00518-2, G&D). Putnam Pub Group.

--Drawing Children. (Grosset Art Introduction Ser.: Vol. 9). pap. 2.95 (ISBN 0-448-00518-2, G&D). Putnam Pub Group.

Shimer, Dorothy B. Bhabani Bhattacharya. (World Authors Ser.). 1975. lib. bdg. 15.95 (ISBN 0-8057-2151-7, Twayne). G K Hall.

--Rice Bowl Women. 1982. pap. 3.95 (ISBN 0-451-62082-8, ME2082, Ment). NAL.

Shimer, Harvey W. & Shrock, Robert R. Index Fossils of North America. (Illus.). 1944. 60.00x (ISBN 0-262-19001-X). MIT Pr.

Shimi, I. N., jt. ed. see Tsokos, C. P.

Shimidzu, T., et al. Reactivities. LC 61-642. (Advances in Polymer Science: Vol. 23). (Illus.). 1977. 35.00 o.p. (ISBN 0-387-07943-2). Springer-Verlag.

Shimin, Symeon. A Special Birthday. (Illus.). (ps-4). 1976. 5.95 (ISBN 0-07-056901-0, GB); PLB 7.95 (ISBN 0-07-056902-9). McGraw.

Shimizu, Akinao & Aoki, Katsutada. Application of Invariant Imbedding to Reactor Physics. (Nuclear Science & Technology Ser). 1972. 39.50 (ISBN 0-12-640150-0). Acad Pr.

Shimizu, Kay. Weight Control with Asian Foods. (Illus.). 92p. 1975. pap. 3.95 o.p. (ISBN 0-87040-355-9). Japan Pubns.

Shimoda, S., jt. auth. see Sudo, T.

Shimoni, S. Legends of Queen Esther. (Biblical Ser.). (Illus.). (gr. 1-5). 1975. 5.00 o.p. (ISBN 0-914080-15-6). Shulsinger Sales.

--Legends of Ruth. (Biblical Ser.). (Illus.). (gr. 1-5). 1975. 5.00 o.p. (ISBN 0-914080-10-5). Shulsinger Sales.

Shimony, Abner, ed. see Carnap, Rudolf.

Shimshoni, Daniel. Israeli Democracy. 1982. text ed. 34.95 (ISBN 0-02-928620-4). Free Pr.

Shin, Y. W. & Moody, F. J., eds. Fluid Transients & Fluid-Structure Interaction. (PVP Ser.: Vol. 64). 381p. 1982. 60.00 (H00221). ASME.

Shin Ch'Eng-Chih. Urban Commune Experiments in Communist China. LC 74-3621. 167p. 1974. Repr. of 1962 ed. lib. bdg. 17.25x (ISBN 0-8371-7451-1, SHUC). Greenwood.

Shine, H. Aromatic Rearrangements. 1967. 49.00 (ISBN 0-444-40534-8). Elsevier.

Shine, Ted, jt. ed. see Hatch, James V.

Shinebourne, Elliot A. & Anderson, Robert H. Current Paediatric Cardiology. (Illus.). 1980. text ed. 32.50x (ISBN 0-19-261141-0). Oxford U Pr.

Shinefield, Henry R., jt. auth. see Aly, Raza.

Shiner, Margot. Ultrastructure of the Small Intestinal Mucosa: Normal & Disease-Related Appearances. (Illus.). 175p. 1982. 70.00 (ISBN 0-387-11732-6). Springer-Verlag.

Shing, M. T., jt. auth. see Hu, T. C.

Shingarev, A. I. The Shingarev Diary: How It Was, Nov. 1917-Jan. 1918. Ashbee, F. & Tidmarsh, I., trs. from Russ. 1978. 11.50x (ISBN 0-931554-06-3); pap. 6.00 (ISBN 0-931554-07-1). Strathcona.

Shingleton, John. Career Decision Making. (Illus.). 1982. pap. text ed. 9.95 (ISBN 0-07-056904-5, C). McGraw.

Shin Jo Joo Hwang. Korean Clause Structure. (Publications in Linguistics & Related Fields Ser: No. 50). 1976. pap. 4.00x (ISBN 0-88312-060-7); microfiche 1.50x (ISBN 0-686-67551-7). Summer Inst Ling.

Shinkokai, Kokusai B., compiled by. Current Contents of Academic Journals in Japan, 1971. 246p. 1973. 10.00x (ISBN 0-86008-057-9, Pub. by Japan Sci Soc). Intl Schol Bk Serv.

--Current Contents of Academic Journals in Japan, 1970. 208p. 1971. 10.00x (ISBN 0-86008-056-0, Pub. by Japan Sci Soc). Intl Schol Bk Serv.

Shinn, Bev & Shinn, Duane. Free & Low Cost Things for New Mothers. 1978. pap. 3.95 o.p. (ISBN 0-912732-47-4). Duane Shinn.

Shinn, Duane. Piano Breakthrough: How to Revolutionize Your Playing Through Chords & Broken Chords. 1978. pap. 25.00 o.p. (ISBN 0-912732-44-X). Duane Shinn.

Shinn, Duane, jt. auth. see Shinn, Bev.

Shinn, F. Game of Life & How to Play It. text ed. 3.95 o.s.i. Wehman.

--Secret Door to Success. 3.95x o.s.i. (ISBN 0-685-70721-0). Wehman.

--Your Word Is Your Wand. 3.95x. Wehman.

Shinn, Florence S. Your Word Is Your Wand. 1978. pap. 2.50 (ISBN 0-87516-259-2). De Vorss.

Shinn, G. Introduction of Professional Selling. 1982. 16.25x (ISBN 0-07-056906-1); cancelled tchrs'. manual 4.00 (ISBN 0-07-056907-X). McGraw.

Shinn, George. The Miracle of Motivation. 246p. 1983. 9.95 (ISBN 0-8423-4353-9); pap. 6.95 (ISBN 0-8423-4354-7). Tyndale.

Shinn, Glen C. & Weston, Curtis. Working in Agricultural Mechanics. Amberson, Max L., ed. (Illus.). 1978. pap. text ed. 10.96 (ISBN 0-07-000843-4, G); activity guide & project plan bk. 6.96 (ISBN 0-07-000844-2); tchrs. manual & key 4.95 (ISBN 0-07-000845-0); transparency masters 9.96 (ISBN 0-07-000846-9); boxed set 110.00 (ISBN 0-07-079314-X). McGraw.

Shinn, Roger L. Forced Options: Social Decisions for the 21st Century. LC 82-47755. (Religious Perspective Ser.). 256p. 1982. 19.18i (ISBN 0-06-067282-X, HarpR). Har-Row.

Shinn, Roger L., ed. Faith & Science in an Unjust World, Vol. 1: Plenary Presentations. LC 80-81141. 408p. 1980. pap. 12.95 o.p. (ISBN 0-8006-1390-2, 1-1390). Fortress.

Shinn, W. E. Flat Knitting. (Knitting Technology Ser). 22.00x (ISBN 0-87245-303-0). Textile Bk.

Shinners, Stanley M. A Guide to Systems Engineering & Management. LC 76-7289. (Illus.). 1976. 25.95x (ISBN 0-669-00680-7). Lexington Bks.

Shinozuka, M., jt. ed. see Moan, T.

Shins, Susan. Food by Phone: Manhattan's Best Meals & Munchies Delivered to Your Door. 256p. 1983. pap. 8.95 (ISBN 0-517-54923-9). Crown.

Shinskey, F. G. Conservation: Individual Efforts for Preserving Resources. 1978. 29.50 (ISBN 0-12-641650-8). Acad Pr.

--PH & P Ion: Control in Process & Waste Streams. LC 73-7853. (Environmental Science & Technology Ser.). 259p. 1973. 43.50 (ISBN 0-471-78640-3, Pub. by Wiley-Interscience). Wiley.

--Process Control Systems. 2nd ed. 1979. 34.75 (ISBN 0-07-056891-X). McGraw.

Shinskey, F. Greg. Distillation Control: For Productivity & Energy Conservation. 1976. 30.95 (ISBN 0-07-056893-6, P&RB). McGraw.

Shio, Mitsuru, jt. auth. see Kono, Shigemi.

Shiokawa, ed. New Horizons in Rheumatoid Arthritis. (International Congress Ser.: Vol. 535). 1981. 75.75 (ISBN 0-444-90185-X). Elsevier.

Shiota, H. Y., et al, eds. Herpes Virus: Clinical, Pharmacological, & Basic Aspects; Proceedings of the International Symposium, Tokushima City, Japan, July 27-30, 1981. (International Congress Ser.: No. 571). 486p. 1982. 97.75 (ISBN 0-444-90248-1, EXcerpta Medica). Elsevier.

Shipka, Thomas A., jt. auth. see Minton, Arthur J.

Shiplett, Gary R. Worship & Hymnody. (Illus.). 122p. (Orig.). 1980. pap. text ed. 8.95 (ISBN 0-916260-08-9). Meriwether Pub.

Shiplett, June. Reap the Bitter Winds. 1979. pap. 2.95 (ISBN 0-451-11690-9, AE1690, Sig). NAL.

Shiplett, June L. The Wild Storm of Heaven. (Orig.). 1980. pap. 2.95 (ISBN 0-451-11247-4, AE1247, Sig). NAL.

Shipley, Arthur H. Gray Shadow. 6.95 o.p. (ISBN 0-914330-19-5); pap. 3.45 o.p. (ISBN 0-914330-20-9). Pioneer Pub Co.

Shipley, Joseph T. In Praise of English: The Growth & Use of Language. 1982. 8.95 (ISBN 0-8129-6325-3). Times Bks.

Shipley, Kenneth G. & Banis, Carolyn S. Teaching Morphology Developmentally: Methods & Materials for Teaching Bound Morphology. 1981. 70.00 (ISBN 0-88450-728-9, 3137-B). Communication Skill.

Shipley, P., jt. ed. see Sell, R. G.

Shipley, Patricia, jt. ed. see Sell, R. G.

Shipley, R. Bruce. Introduction to Matrices & Power Systems. LC 76-16482. 274p. 1976. 39.95x (ISBN 0-471-78642-X, Pub. by Wiley-Interscience). Wiley.

Shipley, Vivian. Jack Tales. LC 82-82421. 64p. 1982. pap. 5.00 (ISBN 0-912678-49-6). Greenfld Rev Pr.

Shipman, Bret. Old California: The Missions, Ranchos, & Romantic Adobes. (Old California Ser.: No. 2). (Illus.). 1983. 4.95 (ISBN 0-913290-17-3). Camaro Pub.

Shipman, Carl. Motorcycle Tuning for Performance. LC 73-82437. (Illus.). 1973. pap. 7.95 (ISBN 0-912656-33-6). H P Bks.

Shipman, Chris. Exercise: The New Language of Love. LC 82-83946. (Illus.). 176p. (Orig.). 1983. pap. 7.95 (ISBN 0-88011-113-5). Leisure Pr.

Shipman, David. The Story of the Cinema: From Beginnings to "Gone with the Wind", Vol. 1. (Illus.). 1982. 30.50 o.p. (ISBN 0-8090-8874-6). Hill & Wang.

Shipman, Gordon. Handbook for Family Analysis. LC 82-47579. 400p. 1982. 27.95x (ISBN 0-669-05548-4); pap. 17.95 (ISBN 0-669-05549-2). Lexington Bks.

Shipman, Harry L. Black Holes, Quasars, & the Universe. 2nd ed. (Illus.). 1980. pap. 12.50 (ISBN 0-395-28499-6). HM.

--The Restless Universe: An Introduction to Astronomy. LC 77-78584. (Illus.). 1978. text ed. 26.95 (ISBN 0-395-25392-6); instr's. manual 0.50 (ISBN 0-395-25393-4). HM.

Shipman, James T. & Adams, Jerry L. An Introduction to Physical Science. 4th ed. 736p. 24.95 (ISBN 0-669-05391-0); instr's. guide 1.95 (ISBN 0-669-05394-5); lab. guide 10.95 (ISBN 0-669-05393-7). Heath.

Shipman, James T., et al. An Introduction to Physical Science. 3rd ed. 1979. text ed. 24.95x (ISBN 0-669-01720-5); instr's manual 1.95 (ISBN 0-669-01723-X); lab. manual 10.95 (ISBN 0-669-01722-1); student guide 8.95 (ISBN 0-669-01721-3). Heath.

Shipman, M. D., et al. Inside a Curriculum Project. LC 74-12560. 190p. 1974. pap. 9.95x (ISBN 0-416-78050-4). Methuen Inc.

Shipman, Natalie. Follow Your Heart. (YA) 1971. 6.95 (ISBN 0-685-03336-8, Avalon). Bouregy.

Shipman, S. S., jt. auth. see Bogen, J. I.

Shipman, Thomas. Carolina. LC 80-17666. 1980. Repr. of 1683 ed. 34.00x (ISBN 0-8201-1355-7). Schol Facsimiles.

Shipmen, Marten, ed. Organisation & Impact of Social Research: Six Original Case Studies in Education & Behavioural Sciences. 1976. 14.95x (ISBN 0-7100-8320-3). Routledge & Kegan.

Shipp, Audrey, ed. see Koch, Hugh.

Shipp, Bill. Murder at Broad River Bridge: The Slaying of Lemuel Penn by Members of the Ku Klux Klan. LC 81-10624. 91p. 1982. 8.95 (ISBN 0-931948-20-7). Peachtree Pubs.

Shipp, G. P. Studies in the Language of Homer. 2nd ed. LC 76-149439. (Cambridge Classical Studies). 1972. 44.50 (ISBN 0-521-07706-0). Cambridge U Pr.

Shipp, James F. Russian-English Dictionary of Abbreviations & Initialisms. 637p. (Orig.). 1982. flexi 60.00x (ISBN 0-917564-12-X). Translation Research.

--Russian-English Glossary of Scientific Surnames & Eponyms. 1978. pap. 15.00 (ISBN 0-932386-00-8). Wychwood Pr.

--Russian-English Index to Scientific Apparatus Nomenclature. 2nd ed. 1983. pap. text ed. 14.00x (ISBN 0-917564-15-4). Transaction Research.

Shipp, Ralph D., Jr. Practical Selling. LC 79-88039. 1980. text ed. 20.95 (ISBN 0-395-28181-4); instr's. manual 1.90 (ISBN 0-395-28182-2); dialogue tape 1.65 (ISBN 0-395-29303-0). HM.

--Retail Merchandising: Principles & Applications. LC 75-31040. (Illus.). 352p. 1976. text ed. 22.95 (ISBN 0-395-20271-X); instr's. manual o.p. 1.90 (ISBN 0-395-20270-1). HM.

Shippen, J. M. & Turner, J. C. Basic Farm Machinery. 2nd ed. LC 73-7618. 392p. 1973. text ed. 15.50 o.p. (ISBN 0-08-017652-6). Pergamon.

Shippen, J. W. Gold Is Where You Find It. 1982. 10.95 (ISBN 0-533-05219-X). Vantage.

Shippey, T. A. Old English Verse. 1972. text ed. 14.50x o.p. (ISBN 0-09-111030-0, Hutchinson U Lib); pap. text ed. 7.50x o.p. (ISBN 0-09-111031-9). Humanities.

Shipsides, Frank & Eason, Helena. Bristol: Profile of a City. 87p. 1982. 30.00x (ISBN 0-905459-21-0, Pub. by Redcliffe England). State Mutual Bk.

Shipton, Clifford K. Index to the Proceedings of the American Antiquarian Society, 1812 to 1961. LC 78-52372. vii, 603p. 1978. 45.00x (ISBN 0-912296-12-7, Dist. by U Pr of Va). Am Antiquarian.

Shirai, Shohei. Pearls. (Illus.). 168p. (Eng, Fr, Japanese & Span.). 1981. 47.50x (ISBN 0-8002-2870-7). Intl Pubns Serv.

Shiraki, H., jt. ed. see Roizin, L.

Shircore, Ina E. Treasure Hunting. LC 80-52199. (Whizz Kids Ser.). 8.00 (ISBN 0-382-06459-3). Silver.

Shire, Ellen. The Mystery at Number Seven, Rue Petite. LC 77-79854. (ps-3). 1978. 3.95 (ISBN 0-394-83664-2, BYR); PLB 4.99 (ISBN 0-394-93664-7). Random.

Shire, T. Hebrew Magic Amulets. (Illus.). 224p. 1982. pap. text ed. 9.95x (ISBN 0-87441-340-0). Behrman.

Shirer, William L. Ghandi: A Memoir. 1982. pap. 3.95 (ISBN 0-671-46147-8). WSP.

Shires, D. B., ed. see World Conference on Medical Informatics, 2nd.

Shires, David B. & Hennen, Brian. Family Medicine: A Guidebook for Practitioners of the Art. (Illus.). 1980. pap. text ed. 19.95 (ISBN 0-07-056920-7). McGraw.

Shires, G. Thomas, ed. Care of the Trauma Patient. 2nd ed. (Illus.). 1979. text ed. 48.00 (ISBN 0-07-056916-9, HP). McGraw.

Shires, G. Tomas, et al. Shock. LC 73-85076. (Major Problems in Clinical Surgery Ser.: Vol. 13). (Illus.). 175p. 1973. text ed. 14.00 o.p. (ISBN 0-7216-8250-2). Saunders.

Shirk, Evelyn U. Adventurous Idealism: Philosophy of Alfred Lloyd. 1968. Repr. of 1952 ed. lib. bdg. 16.00x (ISBN 0-8371-0223-5, SHAI). Greenwood.

Shirk, George H. Oklahoma Place Names. 2nd ed. LC 73-7424. 248p. 1974. 12.95 (ISBN 0-8061-1140-2). U of Okla Pr.

Shirkey, Harry C. Pediatric Therapy. 6th ed. LC 80-14601. (Illus.). 1321p. 1980. text ed. 67.50 (ISBN 0-8016-4596-4). Mosby.

Shirkov, D. V., jt. auth. see Bogoliubov, N. N.

Shirl-E. Princess Love. 1982. 5.75 (ISBN 0-8062-1884-3). Carlton.

Shirley. A User's Guide to Diagnostic Ultrasound. 352p. 1978. text ed. 19.95 o.p. (ISBN 0-8391-1307-2). Univ Park.

Shirley, D. A., jt. ed. see Matthias, E.

Shirley, Frances A., ed. see Webster, John.

Shirley, Glenn. Belle Starr & Her Times: The Literature, the Facts, & the Legends. LC 81-14683. (Illus.). 334p. (YA) 1982. 19.95 (ISBN 0-8061-1713-3). U of Okla Pr.

--Shotgun for Hire: The Story of Deacon Jim Miller, Killer of Pat Garrett. (Illus.). 1970. 4.95 (ISBN 0-8061-1646-3). U of Okla Pr.

--West of Hell's Fringe: Crime, Criminals, & the Federal Peace Officer in Oklahoma Territory, 1889-1907. LC 77-9112. (Illus.). 1978. 19.95 (ISBN 0-8061-1444-4). U of Okla Pr.

Shirley, Grace. Shirley's Twentieth Century Lovers' Guide. 160p. (Orig.). 1981. pap. 2.25 o.p. (ISBN 0-523-40868-4). Pinnacle Bks.

Shirley, Hardy L. Forestry & Its Career Opportunities. 3rd ed. (Forest Resources Ser). (Illus.). 544p. 1973. text ed. 28.95 (ISBN 0-07-056978-9, C). McGraw.

Shirley, Hunter B. Inside the Human Control System. LC 81-81614. 1983. 8.95 (ISBN 0-87212-153-4). Libra.

Shirley, M. Margaret. The First Two Years; A Study of Twenty-Five Babies, Vol. I: Postural & Locomotor Development. LC 76-142316. (U of Minnesota Institute of Child Welfare, Monnograph: No. VI). (Illus.). 1973. Repr. of 1931 ed. lib. bdg. 15.00 (ISBN 0-8371-5905-9, CWSG). Greenwood.

Shirley, R. C. & Peters, M. H. Strategy & Policy Formation: A Multifunctional Orientation. 2nd ed. 286p. 1981. pap. 17.95 (ISBN 0-471-06510-2). Wiley.

Shirley, Robert C., et al. The Study of Strategy & Policy Formation: A Multifunctional Orientation. LC 75-25814. 232p. 1976. text ed. 10.95x o.p. (ISBN 0-471-78643-8). Wiley.

Shirley, V. S., jt. auth. see Lederer, C. Michael.

Shirly, Hunter B. Mapping the Mind. (Illus.). 376p. 1983. text ed. 27.95 (ISBN 0-911012-19-2). Nelson-Hall.

Shirokogoroff, Sergei M. Anthropology of Northern China. (Orig.). 1966. Repr. of 1923 ed. text ed. 17.50x (ISBN 90-6234-039-3). Humanities.

Shirokov, Y. M. & Yudin, N. P. Nuclear Physics, 2 vols. 749p. 1982. Set. 16.95 (ISBN 0-8285-2451-3, Pub. by Mir Pubs USSR). Imported Pubns.

Shirreffs, Gordon. The Lone Rifle-Barranca. 1978. pap. 1.75 o.p. (ISBN 0-451-08052-1, E8052, Sig). NAL.

Shirreffs, Janet H. Community Health: Contemporary Perspectives. (Illus.). 416p. 1982. 24.95 (ISBN 0-13-153494-7). P-H.

Shirts, Morris. Warm Up for Little League Baseball. LC 70-151708. (Illus.). 176p. (gr. 2 up). 1976. 8.95 (ISBN 0-8069-4044-1); PLB 10.99 (ISBN 0-8069-4045-X). Sterling.

Shirts, Morris A. Warm up for Little League Baseball. rev. ed. (Illus.). (gr. 3-5). 1977. pap. 2.25 (ISBN 0-671-42422-X). Archway.

Shirts, Morris A. & Myers, Kent E. Call It Right! Umpiring in the Little League. LC 76-51169. (Illus.). 1977. 7.95 o.p. (ISBN 0-8069-4108-1); lib. bdg. 7.49 o.p. (ISBN 0-8069-4109-X). Sterling.

Shirwood, William. William of Sherwood's Introduction to Logic. Kretzmann, Norman, tr. LC 75-3998. 187p. 1976. Repr. of 1966 ed. lib. bdg. 15.50x (ISBN 0-8371-7412-0, SHSI). Greenwood.

Shisha, Oved, ed. Inequalities: Proceedings, 3 vols. Vol. 1, 1967. 36.00 (ISBN 0-12-640350-3); Vol. 2, 1970. 72.00 (ISBN 0-12-640302-3); Vol. 3, 1972. 62.50 (ISBN 0-12-640303-1). Acad Pr.

Shishkoff, Serge, tr. see Dostoevsky, Fyodor.

Shisko, Robert, jt. auth. see Raffel, Jeffrey A.

Shisler, William, jt. auth. see Eisner, Vivien.

Shissler, Barbara. New Testament in Art. LC 70-84411. (Fine Art Books). (Illus.). (gr. 5-11). 1970. PLB 4.95g (ISBN 0-8225-0169-4). Lerner Pubns.

--Sports & Games in Art. LC 65-29038. (Fine Art Bks.). (Illus.). (gr. 5-11). 1966. PLB 4.95g (ISBN 0-8225-0161-9). Lerner Pubns.

--Worker in Art. LC 72-84409. (Fine Art Ser). (Illus.). (gr. 5-11). 1970. PLB 4.95g (ISBN 0-8225-0167-8). Lerner Pubns.

Shiva Das Floating Eagle Feather. Kiss of God. 100p. 1979. pap. 3.50 (ISBN 0-686-95426-2). Ananda Marga.

Shivanandan, Mary. Nasser, Modern Leader of Egypt. new ed. Rahmas, D. Steve, ed. LC 73-87627. (Outstanding Personalities Ser.: No. 64). 32p. (Orig.). (gr. 7-12). 1973. lib. bdg. 2.95 incl. catalog cards (ISBN 0-87157-564-7); pap. 1.95 vinyl laminated covers (ISBN 0-87157-064-5). SamHar Pr.

Shiv Brat Lal. Light on Ananda Yoga. Morrow, Steve, tr. LC 82-61990. 160p. 1982. pap. 10.00 (ISBN 0-89142-041-X). Sant Bani Ash.

Shive, John N. & Weber, Robert L. Similarities in Physics. 277p. 1982. 27.95 (ISBN 0-471-89795-7, Pub. by Wiley-Interscience). Wiley.

Shively, Ann. Pedigrees. LC 80-7888. 408p. 1980. 14.37i (ISBN 0-690-02002-3). Har-Row.

--Whirlwind. 1982. 13.94i (ISBN 0-06-014995-7, HarpT). Har-Row.

Shively, W. Phillips. The Craft of Political Research. 2nd ed. (Contemporary Comparative Politics Ser.). (Illus.). 1980. pap. text ed. 11.95 (ISBN 0-13-188748-3). P-H.

Shivers, Alfred S. Jessamyn West. (United States Authors Ser.). lib. bdg. 10.95 (ISBN 0-8057-0784-0, Twayne). G K Hall.

--Maxwell Anderson. (United States Authors Ser.). 1976. lib. bdg. 12.95 (ISBN 0-8057-7179-4, Twayne). G K Hall.

Shivers, Jay S. & Calder, Clarence R. Recreational Crafts. (Health, Physical Education, Recreation Ser.). (Illus.). 448p. 1974. 31.50 (ISBN 0-07-056980-0, C). McGraw.

Shivers, Louise. Here to Get My Baby Out of Jail. LC 82-18536. 165p. 1983. 11.95 (ISBN 0-394-52388-1). Random.

Shklar. Oral Oncology: Diagnosis, Therapy, Management & Rehabilitation of the Oral Cancer Patient. 1983. 59.50t (ISBN 0-8151-7672-4). Year Bk Med.

Shklar, G. & McCarthy, P. Oral Manifestations of Systemic Disease. 1976. 29.95 (ISBN 0-409-95002-5). Butterworth.

Shklar, Judith N. Freedom & Independence. LC 75-26273. (Cambridge Studies in the History & Theory of Politics). 200p. 1976. 22.95x (ISBN 0-521-21025-9). Cambridge U Pr.

Shklovsky, Viktor. Sentimental Journey: Memoirs, 1917-1922. Sheldon, Richard, tr. LC 71-87022. 304p. 1972. 14.50x o.p. (ISBN 0-8014-0536-X). Cornell U Pr.

Shlaim, A. & Yannopoulos, G. N. The EEC & Eastern Europe. LC 78-51675. 1979. 49.50 (ISBN 0-521-22072-6). Cambridge U Pr.

Shlaim, A. & Yannopoulos, G., eds. The EEC & the Mediterranean Countries. LC 75-3858. (Illus.). 356p. 1976. 57.50 (ISBN 0-521-20817-3). Cambridge U Pr.

Shlaim, Avi. The United States & the Berlin Blockade, Nineteen Forty-Eight to Nineteen Forty-Nine: A Study in Crisis Decision-Making. LC 81-19363. (International Crisis Behavior Ser.: Vol. 2). 440p. 1983. 38.00x (ISBN 0-520-04385-5). U of Cal Pr.

Shlaim, Avi, ed. International Organizations in World Politics Yearbook, 1975. 1976. 27.50 (ISBN 0-89158-608-3). Westview.

Shloming, Robert, jt. auth. see Carnevale, Thomas.

Shneiderman, Ben, ed. Database Management Systems. LC 76-41070. (Information Technology Ser.: Vol. I). (Illus.). 137p. 1976. pap. 17.25 (ISBN 0-88283-014-7). AFIPS Pr.

Shneiderman, Ben, jt. ed. see Badre, Albert.

Shneiderman, Ben, ed. see Hiltz, S. R.

Shneidman, Edwin S. Suicide Thoughts & Reflections, 1960-1980. LC 81-81844. (Special Issues of SLTB Ser.: Vol. 11). 172p. 1981. 19.95 (ISBN 0-89885-090-8). Human Sci Pr.

--Voices of Death. LC 79-2636. 1980. 14.49i (ISBN 0-06-014023-2, HarpT). Har-Row.

--Voices of Death. 224p. 1982. pap. 2.95 (ISBN 0-553-13997-5). Bantam.

Shneidman, Edwin S., ed. Death: Current Perspectives. 2nd ed. LC 80-81360. 557p. 1980. pap. text ed. 14.95 (ISBN 0-87484-508-4). Mayfield Pub.

Shnitzler, Arthur. The Bachelor's Death. (Arabic.). pap. 8.95x o.p. (ISBN 0-686-63549-3). Intl Bk Ctr.

Shnol, S. E. Physico-Chemical Factors of Biological Evolution. (Soviet Scientific Reviews, Biology Reviews Supplement Ser.: Vol. 1). 296p. 1981. 85.00 (ISBN 3-7186-0044-7). Harwood Academic.

Shoben, Edward J., Jr., jt. ed. see Milton, Ohmer.

Shoben, J. Edward, Jr. Lionel Trilling. LC 81-40472. (Literature and Life Ser.). 280p. 1982. 14.50 (ISBN 0-8044-2815-8). Ungar.

Shoch, J. Design & Performance of Local Computer Networks. Date not set. price not set (ISBN 0-07-056984-3). McGraw.

Shock, D. A., jt. ed. see Schlitt, W. J.

Shock, Julian. Extraterrestrial. (Orig.). 1982. pap. 2.95 (ISBN 0-686-97466-2). Zebra.

Shockley, A. A., jt. ed. see Josey, E. J.

Shockley, Ann A. Loving Her. 1978. pap. 1.75 o.p. (ISBN 0-380-38935-5, 38935). Avon.

--Loving Her. LC 73-13227. 192p. 1974. 6.95 o.p. (ISBN 0-672-51835-X). Bobbs.

Shockley, Emmy L., jt. auth. see Schwartz, Morris S.

Shockley, Martin S. The Richmond Stage, 1784-1812. LC 76-16866. 451p. 1977. 20.00x (ISBN 0-8139-0686-5). U Pr of Va.

Shocpol, Theda, jt. ed. see Burawoy, Michael.

Shoden, Rebecca & Griffin, Sue. Fundamentals of Clinical Nutrition. (Illus.). 1980. pap. text ed. 11.95 (ISBN 0-07-056991-6). McGraw.

Shoebridge, D. J., jt. auth. see Giggins, L. W.

Shoecraft, Paul. Arithmetic Primer. (gr. 4 up). 1979. pap. text ed. 13.95 (ISBN 0-201-07321-8, Sch Div); tchrs'. materials 5.95 (ISBN 0-201-07143-6, Sch Div). A-W.

Shoehmelian, O. Three Apples from Heaven: Armenian Folk Tales. Avakian, Arra & Bond, Harold, eds. Shoehmelian, O., tr. from Armenian. (Illus.). 150p. (Orig.). 1982. pap. 6.95 (ISBN 0-933706-23-5). Ararat Pr.

Shoehmelian, O., tr. see Shoehmelian, O.

Shoemaker, David, et al. Experiments in Physical Chemistry. 4th ed. (Illus.). 736p. 1980. text ed. 29.00 (ISBN 0-07-057005-1, C). McGraw.

Shoemaker, Donald P. Abortion, the Bible & the Christian. 1976. 4.50 (ISBN 0-910728-15-1); pap. 1.25 (ISBN 0-910728-08-9). Hayes

Shoemaker, Helen S. Secret of Effective Prayer. 1976. pap. 1.75 o.s.i. (ISBN 0-89129-211-X). Jove Pubns.

Shoemaker, Hurst H. Science-Hobby Book of Fishing. rev. ed. LC 68-28033. (Science-Hobby Books). (Illus.). (gr. 5-9). 1968. PLB 4.95g (ISBN 0-8225-0555-X). Lerner Pubns.

Shoemaker, Hurst H., jt. auth. see Zim, Herbert S.

Shoemaker, Ken, ed. see Kunz, Kevin & Kunz, Barbara.

Shoemaker, Lynn. Coming Home. 67p. 1973. 4.95 (ISBN 0-87886-037-1); pap. 2.45 (ISBN 0-87886-038-X). Ithaca Hse.

--Curses & Blessings. LC 77-19321. 63p. 1978. 3.50 (ISBN 0-87886-092-4). Ithaca Hse.

Shoemaker, Norma J., jt. ed. see Adler, Diane.

Shoemaker, Robert S., jt. auth. see McGuiston, Frank W., Jr.

Shoemaker, Robert S., jt. auth. see McQuiston, Frank W., Jr.

Shoemaker, Sydney, jt. ed. see Ginet, Carl.

Shoemaker, William H. The Multiple Stage in Spain During the Fifteenth & Sixteenth Centuries. LC 78-137076. 150p. 1973. Repr. of 1935 ed. lib. bdg. 18.75x (ISBN 0-8371-5539-8, SHMS). Greenwood.

Shoemark, Pete. Yamaha XS 1100 Fours. 190p. 1982. pap. 9.50 (ISBN 0-85696-483-2). Haynes Pubns.

Shoenberg, David. Superconductivity. 2nd ed. (Cambridge Monographs on Physics). (Illus.). 1960-1965. pap. 7.95 (ISBN 0-521-09254-X). Cambridge U Pr.

Shoenberg, Isaac J. Mathematical Time Exposures. 200p. 1983. write for info. (ISBN 0-88385-438-4). Math Assn.

Shoenberg, Z., tr. see Turgenev, Ivan S.

Shoenberg, Z., tr. see Lermontov, M. Y.

Shoenberg, Zlata, tr. see Tolstoi, L. N.

Shoesmith. Excavations on & Close to the Defences: Hereford City Excavations, Vol. 2. (CBA Research Report: No. 46). 120p. 1982. pap. text ed. 31.50x (ISBN 0-906780-16-0, 41410, Pub. by Coun Brit Archaeology England). Humanities.

Shoesmith, R. Excavations at Castle Green, Hereford. (CBA Research Reports Ser.: No. 36). 70p. 1980. pap. text ed. 24.00x (ISBN 0-906780-05-5, Pub. by Coun Brit Archaeology). Humanities.

Shofner, Vaughn D. Varietal Verses. LC 78-63416. 1979. 4.95 o.p. (ISBN 0-533-03979-7). Vantage.

Shogan, Robert. None of the Above: Why Presidents Fail & What Can Be Done about It. 15.95 (ISBN 0-453-00426-1, H426). NAL.

Shoham, Giora S. & Rahav, Giora. The Mark of Cain: The Stigma Theory of Crime & Social Deviance. LC 82-3173. 240p. 1982. 27.50x (ISBN 0-312-51446-8). St Martin.

Shoham, S. G., ed. Israel Studies in Criminology: The Many Faces of Crime & Deviance, Vol. 6. 270p. 1983. 27.50x (ISBN 0-911378-41-3). Sheridan.

Shoham, S. G. & Grahame, A., eds. Alientation & Anomie Revisited. 280p. 1982. pap. text ed. 23.50x (ISBN 0-391-02817-0, Pub. by Ramot Pub Co Israel). Humanities.

Shoham, S. Giora, ed. Alienation & Anomie Revisited. Grahame, Anthony. 280p. (Orig.). 1982. pap. text ed. 23.50x (ISBN 0-911378-44-8). Sheridan.

Shoham, Sigiora, jt. ed. see Mednick, Sarnoff A.

Shokeid, Moshe & Deshen, Schlomo. Distant Relations: Ethnicity & Politics Among Arabs & North African Jews in Israel. (Isreali Studies). 256p. 1982. 27.95 (ISBN 0-03-059856-7). Praeger.

Shokeid, Moshe & Deshen, Shlomo. Distant Relations: Ethnicity & Politics Among Arabs & North African Jews in Israel. 192p. 1982. 25.95x (ISBN 0-686-86217-1). J F Bergin.

Shokmori, T., jt. auth. see Kohsaka, M.

Sholevar, G. P. The Handbook of Marriage & Marital Therapy. 600p. 1981. text ed. 40.00 (ISBN 0-89335-120-2). Spectrum Pub.

Sholinsky, Jane. In the Saddle. Horseback Riding for Girls & Boys. LC 76-52388. (Illus.). 80p. (gr. 3-6). 1977. PLB 6.97 o.p. (ISBN 0-671-32825-5). Messner.

--Peanut Parade. LC 78-25852. (Illus.). 80p. (gr. 3-5). 1979. PLB 7.29 o.p. (ISBN 0-671-32944-8). Messner.

Sholokhov, Mikhail. And Quiet Flows the Don. Stevens, H. C., tr. 1965. pap. 6.95 (ISBN 0-394-70330-8, Vin). Random.

Shomaker, Diana, jt. auth. see Furukawa, Chiyoko.

Shomaker, Gordon. The Arrow of the Years. 1976. 5.00 o.p. (ISBN 0-8233-0242-3). Golden Quill.

Shoman, S. Giora. The Violence of Silence: The Impossibility of Dialogue. 300p. 1982. 27.00 (ISBN 0-905927-06-0). Transaction Bks.

Shon, David N., ed. Graft Copolymerization of Lignocellulosic Fibers. (ACS Symposium Ser.: No. 187). 1982. write for info. (ISBN 0-8412-0721-6). Am Chemical.

Shondell, Donald S. & McManama, Jerre. Volleyball. (Sports Ser). (Illus.). 1971. pap. 6.95 ref. ed. (ISBN 0-13-943761-4). P-H.

Shonfield, Andrew. Modern Capitalism: The Changing Balance of Public & Private Power. 1969. pap. 8.95 (ISBN 0-19-500298-9, GB). Oxford U Pr.

--The Use of Public Power. Shonfield, Zuzanna, ed. 140p. 1983. 19.95 (ISBN 0-19-215357-9). Oxford U Pr.

Shonfield, Andrew, jt. ed. see Kindleberger, Charles.

Shonfield, Zuzanna, ed. see Shonfield, Andrew.

Shonick, William. Elements of Planning for Area-Wide Personal Health Services. LC 76-6445. (Issues & Problems in Health Care Ser.). (Illus.). 227p. 1976. pap. text ed. 8.50 o.p. (ISBN 0-8016-4592-1). Mosby.

Shont, Esther M. Internal Bank Auditing. LC 82-2851. 249p. 1982. 24.95x (ISBN 0-471-08918-4, Pub. by Wiley-Interscience). Wiley.

Shontz, F. C. Perceptual & Cognitive Aspects of Body Experience. 1969. 48.00 (ISBN 0-12-640650-2). Acad Pr.

Shook, Frederick & Lattimore, Dan. The Broadcast News Process. 2nd ed. (Illus.). 1983. pap. text ed. 14.95x (ISBN 0-89582-084-6). Morton Pub.

Shook, Georg. Painting Watercolors from Photographs. (Illus.). 144p. 1983. 22.50 (ISBN 0-8230-3873-4). Watson-Guptill.

Shook, Robert L. The Book of Why. (Illus.). 160p. 1983. 9.95 (ISBN 0-8437-3335-7). Hammond Inc.

--The Chief Executive Officers: Men Who Run Big Business in America. LC 81-47238. (Illus.). 224p. 1981. 12.98 (ISBN 0-06-014897-7, HarpT). Har-Row.

--The Entrepreneurs. LC 79-2735. (Illus.). 192p. 1981. pap. 3.95i (ISBN 0-06-464043-4, BN 4043); 9.95 (ISBN 0-06-014025-9). Har-Row.

--The Real Estate People: Top Salespersons, Brokers, & Realtors Share the Secrets of Their Success. LC 80-7599. (Illus.). 208p. 1981. pap. 5.05i (ISBN 0-06-464047-7, BN 4047, BN). B&N NY.

--The Real Estate People: Top Salespersons, Brokers, & Realtors Share the Secrets of Their Success. LC 80-7599. (Illus.). 192p. 1980. 11.49i (ISBN 0-06-014038-0, HarpT). Har-Row.

--Ten Greatest Salespersons. pap. 2.64i (ISBN 0-06-465104-5, BN). B&N NY.

--Ten Greatest Salespersons. 208p. 1980. pap. 2.25i (ISBN 0-06-465104-5, PBN 5104); 11.49i (ISBN 0-06-014012-7). Har-Row.

--Why Didn't I Think of That! 208p. 1982. 11.95 (ISBN 0-453-00419-9, H419). NAL.

Shook, Robert L., jt. auth. see Shafiroff, Martin D.

Shooltz, Danna, ed. see Reggio, Kathryn & Davidson, Josephine.

Shooman, M. L. Software Engineering: Reliability, Development & Management. 1982. text ed. 34.95 (ISBN 0-07-057021-3); instr's manual avail. McGraw.

Shooman, Martin L. Probabilistic Reliability: An Engineering Approach. (Electrical & Electronic Engineering Series). 1968. text ed. 45.00 (ISBN 0-07-057015-9, C). McGraw.

Shope, Robert K. The Analysis of Knowing. LC 82-15099. 377p. 1983. 25.00x (ISBN 0-691-07275-2); pap. 8.95x (ISBN 0-691-02025-6). Princeton U Pr.

Shopen, Timothy. Languages & Their Speakers. 1979. text ed. 15.95 (ISBN 0-316-78728-0). Little.

Shopsin, Baron, ed. Manic Illness. LC 78-66347. 252p. 1979. text ed. 23.00 (ISBN 0-89004-211-X). Raven.

Shopsin, Baron, jt. ed. see Greenhill, Lawrence.

Shor, Elizabeth N. Fossils & Flies: The Life of a Compleat Scientist, Samuel Wendell Williston 1851-1918. LC 77-145503. (Illus.). 1971. 14.95x o.p. (ISBN 0-8061-0949-1). U of Okla Pr.

Shore, Ann. The Faraway Land. (Candlelight Romance Ser.: No. 697). (Orig.). 1982. pap. 1.75 o.s.i. (ISBN 0-440-12487-5). Dell.

--The Searching Heart. (Orig.). 1980. pap. 1.50 o.s.i. (ISBN 0-440-17731-6). Dell.

Shore, anne. The Searching Heart. (Nightingale Series Paperbacks). 1983. pap. 7.95 (ISBN 0-8161-3472-3, Large Print Bks). G K Hall.

--Valley of the Butterflies. (Candlelight Romance Ser.: No. 668). (Orig.). 1981. pap. 1.50 o.s.i. (ISBN 0-440-19195-5). Dell.

--Whispers of the Heart. 1978. pap. 1.25 o.s.i. (ISBN 0-440-14541-4). Dell.

Shore, B. W. & Menzel, D. H. Principles of Atomic Spectra. LC 67-27275. (Wiley Series in Pure & Applied Spectroscopy). 1968. 37.95 o.p. (ISBN 0-471-78835-X, Pub. by Wiley-Interscience). Wiley.

Shore, Barry. Introduction to Quantitative Methods for Business Decisions: Text & Cases. (Illus.). 1978. text ed. 25.95 (ISBN 0-07-057050-7, C); instructor's manual 6.95 (ISBN 0-07-057051-5). McGraw.

--Operations Management. (Management Ser.). (Illus.). 544p. 1973. text ed. 29.95 (ISBN 0-07-057045-0, C); instructor's manual 10.95 (ISBN 0-07-057046-9). McGraw.

Shore, Bernard, ed. Biological Implications of the Nuclear Age: Proceedings. Hatch, Frederick. LC 74-603800. (AEC Symposium Ser.). 334p. 1969. pap. 16.25 (ISBN 0-87079-150-8, CONF-690303); microfiche 4.50 (ISBN 0-87079-151-6, CONF-690303). DOE.

Shore, Bradd. Sala'ilua: A Samoan Mystery. (Illus.). 338p. 1982. 28.00x (ISBN 0-231-05383-5); pap. 14.00x (ISBN 0-231-05382-7). Columbia U Pr.

Shore, Bruce H. New Electronics. LC 78-81612. 1970. 27.50 o.p. (ISBN 0-07-057042-6, P&RB). McGraw.

Shore, David A., jt. ed. see Conte, Jon R.

Shore, Elliot, et al, eds. The Alternative Papers: Selections from the Alternative Press, 1979-1980. LC 82-3250. (Illus.). 521p. 1982. 34.95 (ISBN 0-87722-243-6); pap. 14.95 (ISBN 0-87722-244-4). Temple U Pr.

Shore, Michael. Act Now. 183p. (Orig.). 1982. pap. 6.95 (ISBN 0-910243-00-X). M Shore Assocs.

Shore, R. W., jt. auth. see Holt, C. A.

Shore, Sidney, jt. auth. see Smith, Frank E.

Shore, Susan, illus. Strawberry Shortcake's Year-Round Coloring Book. (Illus.). 80p. (ps-2). 1983. pap. 1.95 (ISBN 0-394-85626-0). Random.

Shore, W. Shakespeare's Self. LC 72-179265. (Studies in Shakespeare, No. 24). 1971. Repr. of 1920 ed. lib. bdg. 49.95x (ISBN 0-8383-1366-3). Haskell.

Shorell, Irma & Davis, Julie. A Lifetime of Skin Beauty: The Irma Shorell Program. 1982. 14.95 (ISBN 0-671-42274-X). S&S.

Shores, Christopher F. Second Tactical Air Force: November 1943 to the End of World War II. (Illus.). 298p. 1970. 14.95x o.p. (ISBN 0-8464-0828-7). Beekman Pubs.

Shores, Christopher F. & Ward, Richard. North American Mustang Mk. 1-4. LC 73-88967. (Arco-Aircam Aviation Ser., No. 3). (Illus., Orig.). 1968. lib. bdg. 5.00 o. p. (ISBN 0-668-02098-9); pap. 2.95 o.p. (ISBN 0-668-02097-0). Arco.

Shores, Edward. George Roy Hill. (Filmmakers Ser.). 208p. 1983. lib. bdg. 19.95 (ISBN 0-8057-9290-2, Twayne). G K Hall.

Shorey, H. H. & McKelvey, John J., Jr. Chemical Control of Insect Behavior: Theory & Application. LC 76-46573. (Environmental Science & Technology Ser.). 414p. 1977. 38.95x (ISBN 0-471-78840-6, Pub. by Wiley-Interscience). Wiley.

Shorney, George H, Jr., jt. auth. see Hustad, Donald P.

Shorr, Joseph E. Psycho-Imagination Therapy. LC 72-180903. 1972. 17.50 o.p. (ISBN 0-685-40256-8); pap. 12.75 o.p. (ISBN 0-913258-00-8). Thieme-Stratton.

--Psychotherapy Through Imagery. 2nd ed. (Illus.). 216p. 1983. write for info. (ISBN 0-86577-083-2). Thieme-Stratton.

Shorris, Earl. Under the Fifth Sun. 1980. 14.95 o.s.i. (ISBN 0-440-09388-0). Delacorte.

Shors, jt. auth. see Hood.

Short, Andrew & Kinnibugh, William. Lightweight Concrete. 3rd ed. (Illus.). 1978. text ed. 76.00 (ISBN 0-85334-734-4, Pub. by Applied Sci England). Elsevier.

Short, Byron, et al. Pressure Enthalpy Charts. 1970. 9.95x (ISBN 0-87201-105-4). Gulf Pub.

Short, Frederick, jt. auth. see Eden, Douglas.

Short, I., ed. see Benedeit.

Short, J. A. Fishing & Casing Repair. 365p. 1982. 55.00x (ISBN 0-87814-191-X). Pennwell Books Division.

Short, J. R. Urban Data Sources. LC 79-42888. (Sources & Methods in Geography Ser.). 1980. pap. text ed. 9.95 (ISBN 0-408-10640-9). Butterworth.

Short, James F., Jr., ed. Law & Order: Modern Criminals. rev. 2nd. ed. LC 72-87662. 312p. 1970. o. p. 9.95 (ISBN 0-87855-049-6); pap. text ed. 4.95 (ISBN 0-87855-542-0). Transaction Bks.

Short, James F., Jr., jt. ed. see Wolfgang, Marvin E.

Short, James R. & Tate, Thad W., eds. The Journal of Major George Washington. facsimile ed. LC 59-9062. (Eyewitness to History Ser.). (Illus., Orig.). 1959. 3.95 (ISBN 0-910412-57-X). Williamsburg.

Short, John. Public Expenditure & Taxation in the UK Regions. 160p. 1981. text ed. 38.50x (ISBN 0-566-00403-8). Gower Pub Ltd.

Short, John & Nicholas, David. Money Flows in the Regions of the United Kingdom. 232p. 1981. text ed. 47.50x (ISBN 0-566-00421-6). Gower Pub Ltd.

Short, John & Williams, Ederyn. The Social Psychology of Telecommunications. 195p. 1976. 37.50 (ISBN 0-686-98124-3). Telecom Lib.

Short, John, et al. The Social Psychology of Telecommunications. LC 75-44335. 195p. 1976. 41.95 (ISBN 0-471-01581-4, Pub. by Wiley-Interscience). Wiley.

Short, John R. Introduction to Political Geography. 200p. 1982. 29.95 (ISBN 0-7100-0964-X); pap. 13.50 (ISBN 0-7100-0965-8). Routledge & Kegan.

Short, K. Microprocessors & Programmed Logic. 1980. 32.95 (ISBN 0-13-581173-2). P-H.

Short, K. R. Film & Propaganda in World War II. LC 82-23838. 300p. 1983. text ed. 23.95x (ISBN 0-87049-386-8). U of Tenn Pr.

Short, Lester L., jt. auth. see Mayr, Ernst.

Short, Luke. King Colt. (General Ser.). 1980. lib. bdg. 11.95 (ISBN 0-8161-3110-4, Large Print Bks). G K Hall.

--Last Hunt. 128p. 1982. pap. 1.95 (ISBN 0-553-20677-X). Bantam.

--Luke Short's Best of the West. 1983. 14.95 (ISBN 0-87795-471-2). Arbor Hse.

Short, Max H. & Felton, Elizabeth N. The United States Book: Facts & Legends About the Fifty States. LC 75-7008. (Illus.). 112p. (gr. 3-9). 1975. PLB 5.95g (ISBN 0-8225-0298-4). Lerner Pubns.

Short, Michael. Your Book of Music. LC 82-9377. (Your Book Of...Ser.). (Illus.). 96p. (gr. 3-6). 1983. 8.95 (ISBN 0-571-18031-0). Faber & Faber.

Short, Philip. Banda. 358p. 1974. 22.50x (ISBN 0-7100-7631-2). Routledge & Kegan.

--The Dragon & the Bear: Inside China & Russia Today. LC 82-12427. (Illus.). 504p. 1983. 19.95 (ISBN 0-688-01524-7). Morrow.

Short, R. V., jt. ed. see Austin, C. R.

Short, Robert. The Gospel from Outer Space. 1983. pap. 5.95 (ISBN 0-686-43269-X, HarpR). Har-Row.

Short, Walter & Solar Energy Research Int. Economic Assessment of Conservation & Solar Technologies: Method & Data. (Progress in Solar Energy Ser.: Suppl.). 150p. 1983. pap. 13.50 (ISBN 0-89553-131-3). Am Solar Energy.

Shortall, Leonard. Sam's First Fish. (Illus.). (ps-3). 1962. PLB 9.12 (ISBN 0-688-31658-1). Morrow.

Shortell, Stephen M. & Brown, Montague, eds. Organizational Research in Hospitals. LC 76-46140. 112p. (Orig.). 1976. pap. 10.00 (ISBN 0-914818-02-3). Blue Cross Shield.

Shorter, Aylward. East African Societies. (Library of Man). 1974. 14.95x (ISBN 0-7100-7957-5); pap. 6.95 (ISBN 0-7100-7958-3). Routledge & Kegan.

Shorter, Clement K. Charlotte Bronte & Her Circle. LC 78-78241. 1969. Repr. of 1896 ed. 42.00x (ISBN 0-8103-3138-1). Gale.

--Charlotte Bronte & Her Circle. Repr. of 1896 ed. lib. bdg. 21.00x (ISBN 0-8371-2811-0, SHCB). Greenwood.

Shorter, E. & Tilly, C. Strikes in France, 1930-1968. LC 73-80475. (Illus.). 400p. 1974. 54.50 (ISBN 0-521-20293-0). Cambridge U Pr.

Shorter, John. Correlation Analysis of Organic Reactivity: With Particular Reference to Multiple Regression. LC 82-7655. 235p. 1982. 41.95 (ISBN 0-471-10479-5, Pub. by Wiley-Interscience). Wiley.

Shortley, George H., jt. auth. see Condon, Edward U.

Shortliffe. Computer Based Medical Consultations: Mycin. 1976. 28.50 (ISBN 0-444-00179-4). Elsevier.

Shortridge, Lillie M. & Lee, Juanita E. Introduction to Nursing Practice. new ed. (Illus.). 1980. text ed. 26.50 (ISBN 0-07-057056-6, HP); introductory skills 15.95 (ISBN 0-07-057057-4). McGraw.

Shortt, Joseph & Wilson, Thomas C. Problem Solving & the Computer: A Structured Concept with PL 1 (PLC) 2nd ed. 1979. pap. text ed. 18.95 (ISBN 0-201-06916-4). A-W.

Shortt, Samuel E. Psychiatric Illness in Physicians. (Illus.). 344p. 1982. 34.75x (ISBN 0-398-04638-7). C C Thomas.

Shoshkes, Lila. Space Planning. LC 76-41305. (Illus.). 1977. 25.95 o.p. (ISBN 0-07-057060-4, Architectural Rec Bks). McGraw.

Shostak, Arthur B. Blue Collar Stress. LC 79-16531. (A-W Occupational Stress Ser.). 1979. pap. text ed. 7.00 (ISBN 0-201-07688-8). A-W.

Shostak, Jerome. Barron's How to Prepare for the College Board Achievement Tests - English. 4th ed. 224p. (gr. 11-12). 1981. pap. text ed. 5.95 (ISBN 0-8120-2282-3). Barron.

Shostak, Stanley. Hydra: A Photomicrographic Book. LC 77-9875. (Illus.). (gr. 6-8). 1978. PLB 5.99 (ISBN 0-698-30671-6, Coward). Putnam Pub Group.

Shosteck, Robert. Weekender's Guide to the Four Seasons: Sports & Recreation, Scenic, Historic & Cultural Places & Activities Within 200 Miles of Washington, Baltimore & Richmond. 7th ed. Grayson, Cary T., Jr. & Lukowski, Susan, eds. LC 71-58813. 504p. (Orig.). 1982. pap. 7.95 (ISBN 0-87107-043-X). Potomac.

Shostrum, Everett L., jt. auth. see Brammer, Lawrence M.

Shotland, R. Lance. University Communication Networks: The Small World Method. LC 76-6079. 179p. 1976. pap. 11.50 (ISBN 0-471-78855-4, Pub. by Wiley). Krieger.

Shotton, Peter & Schaffner, Nicholas. John Lennon in My Life. LC 82-42853. (Illus.). 224p. 1983. 22.50 (ISBN 0-8128-2916-6); deluxe signed edition 200.00 (ISBN 0-8128-2915-8); pap. 14.95 (ISBN 0-8128-6185-X). Stein & Day.

Shotwell, Louisa R. Roosevelt Grady. LC 63-14778. (Illus.). 152p. (gr. 4-6). 1963. 7.99 o.s.i. (ISBN 0-529-03781-5, Philomel). Putnam Pub Group.

Shoukri, Ghali. Egypt: Portrait of a President: Sadat's Road to Jerusalem. 465p. 1982. 30.00 (ISBN 0-86232-062-3, Pub. by Zed Pr England); pap. 14.50 (ISBN 0-86232-072-0, Pub. by Zed Pr England). Lawrence Hill.

Shouksmith, George. Assessment Through Interviewing. 1978. text ed. 8.55 o.p. (ISBN 0-08-012826-2); pap. text ed. 4.40 o.p. (ISBN 0-08-012825-4). Pergamon.

Shoumatoff, Alex. The Capital of Hope. 240p. 1980. 11.95 (ISBN 0-698-11048-X, Coward). Putnam Pub Group.

--Russian Blood: A Family Chronicle. (Illus.). 320p. 1982. 17.95 (ISBN 0-698-11139-7, Coward). Putnam Pub Group.

--Westchester: Portrait of a County. (Illus.). 1979. 9.95 o.p. (ISBN 0-698-10925-2, Coward). Putnam Pub Group.

Shoup, Barbara. Night Watch. LC 82-47543. 224p. 1982. 12.45i (ISBN 0-06-039012-3, HarpT). Har-Row.

Shoup, Carl S. The Value-Added Tax. LC 76-381204. (Center of Planning & Economic Research, Athens, Lecture Ser: No. 27). 43p. 1973. pap. 8.50x (ISBN 0-8002-2214-8). Intl Pubns Serv.

Shoup, Cynthia A. Laboratory Exercises in Respiratory Therapy. 2nd ed. (Illus.). 266p. 1983. pap. text ed. 15.95 (ISBN 0-8016-4594-8). Mosby.

Shoup, T. Practical Guide to Computer Methods for Engineers. 1979. 26.95 (ISBN 0-13-690651-6). P-H.

Shoup, T. E., jt. auth. see Fletcher, L. S.

Shourd, Melvin L., jt. auth. see Winter, H. Frank.

Shourds, Harry & Hillman, Anthony. Carving Shorebirds: With Full-Size Patterns. (Illus.). 72p. 1982. pap. 4.95 (ISBN 0-486-24287-0). Dover.

Shouse, Dennis, et al. Handbook for Volunteers in Substance Abuse Agencies. 32p. 1983. pap. 9.95x pkg. of 4 (ISBN 0-918452-40-6). Learning Pubns.

Shouse, Margaret N., jt. ed. see Sterman, M. B.

Shoushen, Jin. Beijing Legends. Yang, Gladys, tr. (Illus.). 141p. (Orig.). 1982. pap. 2.95 (ISBN 0-8351-1042-7). China Bks.

Shout, Howard F. Start Supervising. rev. ed. LC 77-10068. 154p. 1977. pap. 10.00 (ISBN 0-87179-263-X). BNA.

Shouten, J., jt. auth. see Reinders Folmer, A. N.

Shover, John L., jt. auth. see Rogin, Michael P.

Shover, Michele. Chico's Little Chapman Mansion: The House & Its People. (ANCRR Research Paper: No. 7). 1981. 6.00 (ISBN 0-686-38941-7). Assn NC Records.

Shovers, Aaron H. Visions of Peace. LC 81-86206. 352p. 1983. pap. 9.95 (ISBN 0-86666-078-X). GWP.

Showalter, Carol. Three D: The Story of the New Christian Group Diet Program that is Sweeping the Country. 4.95 (ISBN 0-941478-05-X). Paraclete Pr.

Showalter, English, Jr. Exiles & Strangers: A Reading of Camus' "Exile & the Kingdom". 200p. 1983. price not set (ISBN 0-8142-0353-1). Ohio St U Pr.

Showalter, Lester. Boy - Girl Friendships. 70p. 1982. pap. 2.00 (ISBN 0-686-35751-5). Rod & Staff.

Showalter, R. E. Hilbert Space Methods for Partial Differential Equations. (Monographs & Studies: No. 1). 196p. 1977. pap. text ed. 21.95 (ISBN 0-273-08440-2). Pitman Pub MA.

Showalter, Rachel. Home Fires at the Foot of the Rockies. 248p. 1973. 6.45 (ISBN 0-686-05599-3). Rod & Staff.

Show-Chih Rai Chu. Chinese Grammer & English Grammer: A Comparative Study. 417p. 1982. 12.95 (ISBN 0-686-37710-9); pap. 10.95 (ISBN 0-686-37711-7). Inst Sino Amer.

Showell, Ellen H. Cecilia & the Blue Mountain Boy. LC 82-10098. (Illus.). 96p. (gr. 4 up). 1983. 9.00 (ISBN 0-688-01514-X). Lothrop.

Showell, J. P. The German Navy in World War Two: An Illustrated Reference Guide to the Kriegsmarine, 1920-1945. LC 75-84933. (Illus.). 1979. 22.95 (ISBN 0-87021-933-2). Naval Inst Pr.

--U-Boats Under the Swastika. LC 73-93152. 10.00 o.p. (ISBN 0-668-03457-2); pap. 4.95 o.p. (ISBN 0-668-04290-7). Arco.

Showerman, Grant, tr. see Salustri, Carlo A.

Showers, Kay S., jt. auth. see Showers, Paul.

Showers, Mary Jane, jt. auth. see King, Barry G.

Showers, Norman. Bowling. 3rd ed. 1980. 7.95x (ISBN 0-673-16183-8). Scott F.

Showers, Paul. Baby Starts to Grow. LC 69-11827. (A Let's-Read-&-Find-Out Science Bk). (Illus.). (gr. k-3). 1969. PLB 10.89 (ISBN 0-690-11320-X, TYC-J); (ISBN 0-685-20467-7). Har-Row.

--A Baby Starts to Grow. LC 69-11827. (Crocodile Paperbacks Ser.). (Illus.). 33p. (gr. k-3). 1972. pap. 3.95 (ISBN 0-690-11325-0, TYC-J). Har-Row.

--Columbus Day. LC 65-16186. (Holiday Ser.). (Illus.). (gr. k-3). 1965. 10.89 (ISBN 0-690-19982-1, TYC-J). Har-Row.

--Drop of Blood. LC 67-23672. (A Let's-Read-&-Find-Out Science Bk). (Illus.). (gr. k-3). 1967. PLB 10.89 (ISBN 0-690-24526-2, TYC-J); Har-Row.

--Find Out by Touching. LC 60-13242. (A Let's-Read-&-Find-Out Science Bk). (Illus.). (gr. k-3). 1961. PLB 10.89 (ISBN 0-690-29782-3, TYC-J). Har-Row.

--Follow Your Nose. LC 63-15097. (A Let's-Read-&-Find-Out Science Bk). (Illus.). (gr. k-3). 1963. PLB 10.89 (ISBN 0-690-31273-3, TYC-J); Har-Row.

--Hear Your Heart. LC 68-11067. (A Let's Read & Find Out Science Bk.). (Illus.). (gr. k-3). 1968. bds. 6.95 o.p. (ISBN 0-690-37378-3, TYC-J); PLB 10.89 (ISBN 0-690-37379-1). Har-Row.

--How Many Teeth. LC 62-11004. (A Let's-Read-&-Find-Out Science Bk). (Illus.). (gr. k-3). 1962. PLB 10.89 (ISBN 0-690-40716-5, TYC-J). Har-Row.

--How You Talk. LC 66-15766. (A Let's-Read-&-Find-Out Science Bk). (Illus.). (ps-3). 1967. 10.89 (ISBN 0-690-42136-2, TYC-J). Har-Row.

--How You Talk. LC 66-15766. (Crocodile Paperbacks Ser.). (Illus.). 40p. (gr. k-3). 1975. pap. 2.95 (ISBN 0-690-00637-3, TYC-J). Har-Row.

--In the Night. LC 61-6138. (A Let's-Read-&-Find-Out Science Bk). (Illus.). (gr. k-3). 1961. PLB 10.89 (ISBN 0-690-44621-7, TYC-J). Har-Row.

--Indian Festivals. LC 70-78266. (Holiday Ser.). (Illus.). (gr. k-3). 1969. 6.95 o.p. (ISBN 0-690-43697-1, TYC-J); PLB 8.89 o.p. (ISBN 0-690-43698-X). Har-Row.

--Listening Walk. LC 61-10495. (A Let's-Read & Find-Out Science Bk). (Illus.). (gr. k-3). 1961. 10.89 (ISBN 0-690-49663-X, TYC-J). Har-Row.

--Look at Your Eyes. LC 62-12821. (A Let's-Read-&-Find-Out Science Bk). (Illus.). (gr. k-3). 1962. bds. 6.95 o.p. (ISBN 0-690-50727-5, TYC-J); PLB 10.89 (ISBN 0-690-50728-3). Har-Row.

--Me & My Family Tree. LC 77-26595. (A Let's-Read-&-Find-Out Science Bk.). (Illus.). (gr. k-3). 1978. 8.95 o.p. (ISBN 0-690-03886-0, TYC-J); PLB 10.89 (ISBN 0-690-03887-9). Har-Row.

--No Measles, No Mumps for Me. LC 79-7106. (Let's-Read-&-Find-Out Science Book). (Illus.). 40p. (gr. k-3). 1980. 10.53i (ISBN 0-690-04017-2, TYC-J); PLB 10.89 (ISBN 0-690-04018-0). Har-Row.

--Sleep Is for Everyone. LC 72-83785. (A Let's Read-&-Find-Out Science Bk). (Illus.). (ps-3). 1974. 10.89 (ISBN 0-690-01118-0, TYC-J). Har-Row.

--Use Your Brain. LC 79-157646. (A Let's-Read-&-Find-Out Science Bk). (Illus.). (gr. k-3). 1971. 10.53i (ISBN 0-690-85410-2, TYC-J); PLB 7.95 o.p. (ISBN 0-690-85411-0); pap. 2.95 crocodile paperback ser. (ISBN 0-690-00204-1). Har-Row.

--What Happens to a Hamburger. LC 70-106578. (A Let's Read & Find Out Science Bks.). (Illus.). (gr. k-3). 1970. bds. 7.95 o.p. (ISBN 0-690-87540-1, TYC-J); PLB 10.89 (ISBN 0-690-87541-X). Har-Row.

--Where Does the Garbage Go? LC 73-14881. (A Let's-Read-&-Find-Out Science Bks.). (Illus.). (ps-3). 1974. 7.95 o.p. (ISBN 0-690-00392-7, TYC-J); PLB 10.89 (ISBN 0-690-00402-8). Har-Row.

--Your Skin & Mine. LC 65-16185. (A Let's-Read-&-Find-Out Science Bk). (Illus.). (gr. k-3). 1965. PLB 10.89 (ISBN 0-690-91127-0, TYC-J); pap. 3.95 crocodile paperback ser. (ISBN 0-690-00205-X). Har-Row.

Showers, Paul & Showers, Kay S. Before You Were a Baby. LC 68-13588. (A Let's-Read-&-Find-Out Science Bk). (Illus.). (gr. k-3). 1968. PLB 10.89 (ISBN 0-690-12882-7, TYC-J). Har-Row.

Showers, Ralph. Reach for a Rainbow. 1983. 8.95 (ISBN 0-8499-0342-4). Word Bks.

Showers, Renald E. What on Earth Is God Doing? Satan's Conflict with God. 48p. 1983. pap. 3.50 study guide (ISBN 0-87213-785-6). Loizeaux.

Showers, Victor. World Facts & Figures. LC 78-14041. 757p. 1979. 28.95x (ISBN 0-471-04941-7, Pub. by Wiley-Interscience). Wiley.

--The World in Figures. LC 73-9. 585p. 1973. 19.95 o.p. (ISBN 0-471-78859-7, Pub. by Wiley-Interscience). Wiley.

Showler, Brian & Sinfield, Adrian, eds. The Workless State: Studies in Unemployment. 288p. 1981. 19.95x (ISBN 0-85520-327-7, Pub. by Martin Robertson England). Biblio Dist.

Showman, Richard K., et al, eds. The Papers of General Nathanael Greene, Vol. 1: December, 1766 to December 1776. LC 76-20441. xxxix, 606p. 1976. 22.00x o.p. (ISBN 0-8078-1285-4). U of NC Pr.

Showman, Richard K., et al, eds. see Greene, Nathanael.

Shows, Hal. A Breath for Nothing. pap. 3.00 o.s.i. (ISBN 0-686-81810-5). Anhinga Pr.

Shpigler, B., jt. auth. see Beraha, E.

Shpilberg, David. Statistical Decomposition of Industrial Fire Loss. LC 80-52616. (Huebner Foundation Monograph Ser.). 104p. (Orig.). 1982. pap. 14.95 (ISBN 0-918930-11-1). Huebner Foun Insur.

Shrader, Elizabeth H. & Hand, Katherine. Meditations on Ancient Wisdom. 1977. pap. 1.75 (ISBN 0-685-82000-9). Creative Pr.

Shrader, R. L. Amateur Radio: Theory & Practice. 352p. 1982. 16.95x (ISBN 0-07-057146-5). McGraw.

Shrader, Robert L. Electrical Fundamentals for Technicians. 2nd ed. (Illus.). 1977. text ed. 23.95 (ISBN 0-07-057141-4, G). McGraw.

--Electronic Communication. 4th rev. ed. LC 79-13336. (Illus.). 1980. text ed. 26.95x (ISBN 0-07-057150-3). McGraw.

--Electronic Communication. 3rd ed. (Illus.). 720p. 1975. text ed. 24.10 (ISBN 0-07-057138-4, G). McGraw.

--Electronic Fundamentals for Technicians. 1972. text ed. 23.95 (ISBN 0-07-057142-2, G). McGraw.

Shrader, Robert L. & Boyce, Jefferson C. Practice Tests for Radiotelephone Licenses. (Illus.). 1977. pap. text ed. 11.50 (ISBN 0-07-057130-9, G). McGraw.

Shrader, Stephen. Leaving by the Closet Door. 82p. 1970. 2.95 (ISBN 0-87886-001-0). Ithaca Hse.

Shrader-Frechette, K. Environmental Ethics. 1981. 12.95 (ISBN 0-910286-77-9); pap. 9.95 (ISBN 0-910286-75-2). Boxwood.

Shrago, Jackie, jt. auth. see Jewett, Jim.

Shreck, Peter. First Letters. (Macmillan Learning Window Book Ser.). (Illus.). 48p. (ps-k). 1982. 7.95 (ISBN 0-02-782590-6). Macmillan.

Shreffler, Philip A. The H. P. Lovecraft Companion. LC 76-52605. (Illus.). 1977. lib. bdg. 25.00x (ISBN 0-8371-9482-2, SHP/). Greenwood.

Shreir, L. L. Corrosion, Vol. I & II. 2nd ed. 1976. 229.95 (ISBN 0-408-00267-0). Butterworth.

Shreve, F., et al. Plant Life of Maryland. 1969. pap. 32.00 (ISBN 3-7682-0626-2). Lubrecht & Cramer.

Shreve, G. M. & Arewa, E. O. Genesis of Structures in African Narrative: Dahomean Narratives, Vol. 2. (Studies in African Semiotics Ser.). 1982. 35.00 (ISBN 0-914970-01-1). Conch Mag.

Shreve, L. G. The Phoenix with Oily Feathers. LC 80-80510. 275p. 1980. 10.95 (ISBN 0-87716-116-X, Pub. by Moore Pub Co). F Apple.

--Tench Tilghman: The Life & Times of Washington's Aide-de-Camp. LC 82-60330. (Illus.). 288p. 1982. 15.95 (ISBN 0-87033-293-7). Cornell Maritime.

Shreve, R. Norris & Brink, Joseph. Chemical Process Industries. 4th ed. (Illus.). 1977. 34.75 (ISBN 0-07-057145-7, P&RB). McGraw.

Shreve, Steven E., jt. auth. see Bertsekas, Dimitri P.

Shreve, Susan. Family Secrets: Five Very Important Stories. (Illus.). 60p. (gr. 2-6). 1983. pap. 1.75 (ISBN 0-440-42856-4, YB). Dell.

Shrewsbury, Marvin M., jt. auth. see Chin, Edwin, Jr.

Shriberg, Lawrence D. & Kent, Raymond D. Clinical Phonetics. LC 81-15988. (Wiley Communications Ser.). 481p. 1982. 21.95 (ISBN 0-471-08654-1); tapes avail. (ISBN 0-471-08655-X). Wiley.

Shriberg, Lawrence D. & Kwiatkowski, Joan. Natural Process Analysis (NPA) A Procedure for Phonological Analysis of Continuous Speech Analysis. LC 80-51707. (Wiley Ser. on Communication Disorders). 175p. 1980. pap. 16.50 (ISBN 0-471-07893-X). Wiley.

Shrier, Clarence. God of Health. 2.50 (ISBN 0-87509-088-5); pap. 1.50 (ISBN 0-87509-089-3). Chr Pubns.

Shrier, Nettie Vander see Vander Shrier, Nettie.

Shrii Prabhat Rainjain Sarkar. Human Society, Vol. I. 185p. 1970. pap. 2.00 (ISBN 0-686-36520-8). Ananda Marga.

--Problem of the Day. 64p. 1968. pap. 1.00 (ISBN 0-686-95454-8). Ananda Marga.

Shrimpton, Nick, ed. see Shakespeare, William.

Shriner, Charles A. Wit, Wisdom & Foibles of the Great. LC 68-30617. 1969. Repr. of 1918 ed. 40.00x (ISBN 0-8103-3297-3). Gale.

Shriner, D. S., et al, eds. Atmospheric Sulfur Deposition: Environmental Impact & Health Effects. LC 80-68667. 586p. 1980. 39.95 (ISBN 0-250-40380-3). Ann Arbor Science.

Shriner, R. H., jt. auth. see Shriner, R. L.

Shriner, R. L. & Shriner, R. H. Organic Syntheses Collective Volumes Cumulative Indices for Collective Volumes 1-5. (Organic Synthesis Collective Volumes). 432p. 1975. 34.95x (ISBN 0-471-78885-6, Pub. by Wiley-Interscience). Wiley.

Shriner, Ralph, et al. The Systematic Identification of Organic Compounds: A Laboratory Manual. 6th ed. LC 79-13365. 604p. 1980. 29.95 (ISBN 0-471-78874-0). Wiley.

Shrivastava, B. K. & Casstevens, Thomas B., eds. American Government & Politics. 1980. text ed. 21.00x (ISBN 0-391-01798-5). Humanities.

Shrivastava, O. S. Demography. 500p. 1983. text ed. 37.50x (ISBN 0-7069-1109-1, Pub. by Vikas India). Advent NY.

Shriver, Donald W., Jr. Rich Man, Poor Man. LC 71-37003. (Christian Ethics for Modern Man Ser.). (Illus.). 112p. (Orig.). 1972. pap. 1.95 o.p. (ISBN 0-8042-9092-X). John Knox.

Shriver, Donald W., Jr., jt. auth. see Pasquariello, Ronald D.

Shriver, Duward F. Inorganic Syntheses, Vol. 19. LC 39-23015. (Inorganic Synthesis Ser.). 327p. 1979. 38.50x (ISBN 0-471-04542-X, Pub. by Wiley-Interscience). Wiley.

Shriver, William P. Immigrant Forces: Factors in the New Democracy. LC 74-145493. (The American Immigration Library). 312p. 1971. Repr. of 1913 ed. lib. bdg. 18.95x (ISBN 0-89198-026-1). Ozer.

Shrock, Robert. Geology at MIT Eighteen Sixty-five to Nineteen Sixty-five: A History of the First Hundred Years of Geology at Massachusetts Institute of Technology. Vol. I: The Faculty & Supporting Staff. LC 77-71235. (Illus.). 1977. 30.00x (ISBN 0-262-19161-X). MIT Pr.

Shrock, Robert R. Geology at MIT Eighteen Sixty-five to Nineteen Sixty-five: A History of the First Hundred Years of Geology at Massachusetts Institute of Technology Vol. II: Departmental Operations & Products. (Illus.). 1176p. 1982. 60.00x (ISBN 0-262-19211-X). MIT Pr.

Shrock, Robert R. & Twenhofel, William H. Principles of Invertebrate Paleontology. 2nd ed. (International Ser. in the Earth & Planetary Sciences: Geography Ser.). 1953. text ed. 44.95 (ISBN 0-07-057165-1, C). McGraw.

Shrock, Robert R., jt. auth. see Shimer, Harvey W.

Shrodes, Carolina, et al. Conscious Reader. 2nd ed. 992p. 1978. 12.95x (ISBN 0-02-410320-9, 41032). Macmillan.

Shrodes, Caroline, et al. Reading for Rhetoric: Applications to Writing. 4th ed. 1979. pap. 11.95x (ISBN 0-02-410240-7); instr's. manual avail. Macmillan.

Shrope, Wayne A. Speaking & Listening: A Contemporary Approach. 2nd ed. 305p. 1979. pap. text ed. 11.95 (ISBN 0-15-583182-8, HC); instructor's manual avail. (ISBN 0-15-583183-6). HarBraceJ.

Shropshire, Rebecca, tr. see Watts, Alan.

Shrott, Gail, jt. auth. see Cassedy, David.

Shrout, Beatrice L. How To: Programs & Skits. LC 82-60776. 240p. (Orig.). 1982. 8.50 (ISBN 0-9609070-0-9). B L Shrout.

Shroyer, Edgar H. Signs of the Times. LC 82-81441. (Illus.). xii, 436p. 1982. pap. text ed. 14.95 (ISBN 0-913580-76-7). Gallaudet Coll.

Shroyer, Frederick B. & Gardemal, Louis G. Types of Drama: A Critical & Historical Introduction. 1970. pap. 10.95x (ISBN 0-673-05667-8). Scott F.

Shrubb, Lee, jt. ed. see Coleman, Peter.
Shry, Carroll L., Jr., jt. auth. see Reiley, H. Edward.
Shryock, Clifford. How to Raise & Train a Chow Chow. (Orig.). pap. 2.95 (ISBN 0-87666-268-8, DS1070). TFH Pubns.
Shryock, R. H. The Development of Modern Medicine: An Interpretation of the Social & Scientific Factors Involved. LC 79-5401. 1980. 22.50 (ISBN 0-299-07530-3); pap. 9.95 (ISBN 0-299-07534-6). U of Wis Pr.
Shtern, V. Y. The Gas-Phase Oxidation of Hydrocarbons. Mullins, B. P., ed. 1964. inquire for price o.p. (ISBN 0-08-010202-6). Pergamon.
Shtipelman, Boris A. Design & Manufacture of Hypoid Gears. LC 78-8591. 432p. 1978. 67.50x (ISBN 0-471-03648-X, Pub. by Wiley-Interscience). Wiley.
Shuangshoti, Samruay, jt. auth. see Netsky, Martin G.
Shub, Elizabeth, tr. see Nikly, Michelle.
Shuba, M. F., jt. ed. see Bulbring, E.
Shubert, Bruno O., jt. auth. see Larson, Harold J.
Shubik, Martin. Game Theory in the Social Sciences. 1982. 35.00 (ISBN 0-686-36255-1). MIT Pr.
Shubik, Martin, ed. Game Theory & Related Approaches to Social Behavior. LC 74-26575. 402p. 1975. Repr. of 1964 ed. 22.00 (ISBN 0-88275-229-4). Krieger.
Shubnikov, A. V. & Belov, N. V. Colored Symmetry. 1964. inquire for price (ISBN 0-08-010505-X); pap. 24.00 (ISBN 0-08-013790-3). Pergamon.
Shuch, Milton L. Women in Management: Environment & Role. (ITT Key Issues Lecture Ser.). 93p. 1981. pap. text ed. 6.50 (ISBN 0-672-97919-5). Bobbs.
Shuchman, Philip. Cohen & Cohen's Readings in Jurisprudence & Legal Philosophy. 2nd ed. 1099p. 1979. text ed. 26.00 (ISBN 0-316-78877-5). Little.
Shuckburgh, E. S., ed. De Senectute. 1983. 11.50 (ISBN 0-89241-348-4). Caratzas Bros.
Shuckburgh, Evelyn S., tr. see Polybius.
Shuckrow, Alan J., et al. Hazardous Waste Leachate Management Manual. LC 82-7924. (Pollution Technology Rev. 92). (Illus.). 379p. 1983. 36.00 (ISBN 0-8155-0910-3). Noyes.
Shucksmith, Mark. No Homes for Locals? 154p. 1981. text ed. 39.00x (ISBN 0-566-00465-8). Gower Pub Ltd.
Shue, Henry, jt. ed. see Brown, Peter G.
Shue, Vivienne. Peasant China in Transition: The Dynamics of Development Toward Socialism 1949 to 1956. LC 80-13109. 500p. 1980. 29.75x (ISBN 0-520-03734-0). U of Cal Pr.
Shuely, Ahmed A. Ahlam's Quest. 1977. 5.95 o.p. (ISBN 0-533-02598-2). Vantage.
Shuey, R. T. Semi-Conducting Ore Minerals. (Developments in Economic Geology Ser: Vol. 4). 415p. 1975. 59.75 (ISBN 0-444-41357-X). Elsevier.
Shuey, William C., ed. The Amylograph Handbook. 2nd rev. ed. LC 82-82980. (Illus.). 440p. 1981. 12.00 (ISBN 0-913250-15-5). Am Assn Cereal Chem.
Shufelt, Gwen, ed. The Agenda in Action: Yearbook, 1983. LC 82-22367. (Illus.). 256p. 1983. 14.50 (ISBN 0-87353-201-5). NCTM.
Shufunotomo Editors. The Essentials of Bonsai. (Illus.). 108p. 1982. 9.95. Timber.
Shugar, G. J. Chemical Technicians' Ready Reference Handbook. 1973. 32.50 o.p. (ISBN 0-07-057175-9, P&RB). McGraw.
Shugar, Gershon, et al. Chemical Technicians' Ready Reference Handbook. 2nd ed. (Illus.). 864p. 1981. 44.50 (ISBN 0-07-057176-7, P&RB). McGraw.
Shugart, Cecil G., jt. auth. see Rains, Karen J.
Shugart, Cooksey & Engle, Tom. Complete Guide to American Pocket Watches. 3rd ed. (Illus.). 320p. 1983. pap. 9.95 (ISBN 0-517-54916-6). Overstreet.
--The Complete Guide to American Pocket Watches 1983: Pocket Watches from 1809-1950. 1983. pap. 9.95 (ISBN 0-517-54916-6, Harmony). Crown.
Shugart, H. H. & O'Neill, R. V., eds. Systems Ecology. LC 79-970. (Benchmark Papers in Ecology: Vol. 9). 368p. 1979. 43.00 (ISBN 0-87933-347-2). Hutchinson Ross.
Shugart, H. H., Jr., ed. Time Series & Ecological Processes: Proceedings. LC 78-5410. (SIAM-SIMS Conference Ser.: Vol. 5). (Illus.). xxi, 303p. (Orig.). 1978. pap. text ed. 24.00 (ISBN 0-89871-032-4). Soc Indus-Appl Math.
Shugrue, Michael, ed. see Burnet, Sir Thomas & Duckett, George.
Shugrue, Michael F., ed. Foundations of the Novel Series: Representative Early Eighteenth-Century Fiction, 71 vols. lib. bdg. 50.00 ea. o.p. Garland Pub.
Shugrue, Michael F., ed. see Boswell, James.
Shugrue, Michael F., ed. see Fielding, Sarah.
Shugrue, Michael F., ed. see Lennox, Charlotte.
Shugrue, Michael F., ed. see McCarthy, Charlotte.
Shugrue, Michael F., ed. see Richardson, Samuel.
Shugrve, Michael, ed. see Walker, Charles.
Shukla, A. C. & Misra, S. P. Essentials of Paleobotany. 2nd ed. (Illus.). 1982. text ed. 20.00 (ISBN 0-7069-1450-3, Pub. by Vikas India). Advent NY.
Shukla, Ashok C. & Misra, Shital P. Essentials of Paleobotany. 1975. 15.00x o.p. (ISBN 0-7069-0381-1, Pub. by Vikas India). Advent NY.
Shukla, K. S. Adolescent Thieves. 1979. text ed. 15.75x (ISBN 0-391-01925-2). Humanities.
Shukla, P. Physics of Disordered Solids. 200p. 1982. text ed. 16.00x (ISBN 0-391-02755-7, Pub. by Concept India). Humanities.
Shukri, Muhammed F. The Khedive Ismail & Slavery in the Sudan 1863-1879. (Illus.). Repr. of 1930 ed. 35.00x (ISBN 0-87991-056-9). Porcupine Pr.
Shula, Dorothy, et al. Souper Bowl of Recipes. 1980. 15.00 (ISBN 0-89002-164-3); pap. 9.95 (ISBN 0-89002-163-5). Northwoods Pr.
Shulan, Michael. The Truth About Monsters. LC 80-13490. (Monsters & Mysteries Ser.). (gr. 4-10). 1980. pap. 2.25 (ISBN 0-88436-761-4). EMC.
Shulberg, Lucille. Historic India. LC 68-22440. (Great Ages of Man Ser.). (gr. 6 up). 1968. PLB 11.97 o.p. (ISBN 0-8094-0381-1, Pub. by Time-Life). Silver.
Shuldener, Henry L. & Fullman, James B. Water & Piping Problems: A Troubleshooter's Guide for Large & Small Buildings. LC 80-28287. 207p. 1981. 27.95 (ISBN 0-471-08082-9, Pub. by Wiley-Interscience). Wiley.
Shuldiner, Paul W., jt. auth. see Oi, Walter Y.
Shuldner, Herbert. The Popular Science Book of Gadgets: Ingenious Devices for the Home. Michaelman, Herbert, ed. 1980. 19.95 (ISBN 0-517-54280-3, Michelman Books); pap. 10.95 (ISBN 0-517-54443-1, Michelman Books). Crown.
Shuler, Charles, ed. Residential Wiring. (Basic Skills in Electricity & Electronics Ser.). Date not set. text ed. price not set (ISBN 0-07-053354-7); price not set tchr's. manual (ISBN 0-07-053356-3); price not set activity manual (ISBN 0-07-053355-5). McGraw.
Shuler, Ellis W. Rocks & Rivers of America. (Illus.). 1945. 15.00 o.p. (ISBN 0-8260-8165-7, Pub. by Wiley-Interscience). Wiley.
Shuler, J. L. Give Your Guilt Away. LC 72-79605. 1972. pap. 0.95 o.p. (ISBN 0-8163-0134-4, 07150-6). Pacific Pr Pub Assn.
Shuler, John L. Making Jesus Real. LC 79-83591. (Stories That Win Ser.). 1979. pap. 0.95 o.p. (ISBN 0-8163-0324-X, 13051-8). Pacific Pr Pub Assn.
Shuler, K. E., ed. Advances in Chemical Physics: Stochastic Processes in Chemical Physics, Vol. 15. LC 58-9935. 391p. 1969. 24.00 (ISBN 0-471-78967-4). Krieger.
Shuler, Philip L. A Genre for the Gospels: The Biographical Character of Matthew. LC 81-71384. 144p. 1982. 14.95 (ISBN 0-8006-0677-9). Fortress.
Shulevitz, Uri. Writing with Pictures: A Visual Approach to Creating Children's Books. (Illus.). 256p. 1983. 24.95 (ISBN 0-8230-5940-5). Watson-Guptill.
Shull, F. A., et al. Organizational Decision Making. 1970. 18.95 o.p. (ISBN 0-07-057182-1, C). McGraw.
Shull, Henry, jt. auth. see Krause, Peter.
Shulman, Abraham. The Story of Hotel Polski. 256p. 12.95 (ISBN 0-686-95088-7); pap. 5.95 (ISBN 0-686-99461-2). ADL.
Shulman, Alix K. Memoirs of an Ex-Prom Queen. 1972. 11.95 o.p. (ISBN 0-394-47156-3). Knopf.
Shulman, Arnold. Optical Data Processing. LC 70-82970. (Pure & Applied Optics Ser). 1970. 57.50 o.p. (ISBN 0-471-78980-1, Pub. by Wiley-Interscience). Wiley.
Shulman, Bernard H. Essays in Schizophrenia. 2nd ed. LC 82-72136. 191p. 1983. pap. 14.50x (ISBN 0-918560-29-2). A Adler Inst.
Shulman, Bernard H. & Forgus, Ronald. Personality: A Cognitive View. 1979. text ed. 25.95 (ISBN 0-13-657882-9). P-H.
Shulman, Frank J. Doctoral Dissertations on South Asia, 1966-1970: An Annotated Bibliography Covering North America, Europe, & Australia. LC 78-186256. (Michigan Papers on South & Southeast Asia: No. 4). 228p. 1971. pap. 6.75x o.p. (ISBN 0-89148-004-8). Ctr S&SE Asian.
Shulman, Frank J., jt. auth. see Ward, Robert E.
Shulman, Frank J., compiled by. Doctoral Dissertations on Japan & on Korea, 1969-1979: An Annotated Bibliography of Studies in Western Languages. LC 82-13563. 489p. 1982. 35.00 (ISBN 0-295-95895-2); pap. 14.95 (ISBN 0-295-95961-4). U of Wash Pr.
Shulman, Lawrence. The Skills of Helping Individuals & Groups. LC 78-71816. 1979. text ed. 18.50 (ISBN 0-87581-243-0). Peacock Pubs.
--Skills of Supervision & Staff Management. LC 81-83338. 384p. 1982. text ed. 17.95 (ISBN 0-87581-278-3). Peacock Pubs.
Shulman, R. G., ed. Biological Applications of Magnetic Resonance. LC 79-16020. 1979. 40.00 (ISBN 0-12-640750-9). Acad Pr.
Shulov, A. The Development of Eggs of the Red Locust, Nomandacris Septemfasciata (Serville) & the African Migratory Locust, Locusta Migratoria Migratoria Migratorioides (R&F), & Its Interruption under Particular Conditions of Humidity. 1970. 35.00x (ISBN 0-85135-001-1, Pub. by Centre Overseas Research). State Mutual Bk.
Shulov, A. & Pener, M. P. Studies on the Development of Eggs of the Desert Locust (Schistocerca Gregaria Forskal) & Its Interruption under Particular Conditions of Humidity. 1963. 35.00x (ISBN 0-85135-035-6, Pub. by Centre Overseas Research). State Mutual Bk.
Shulte, Albert P. & Choate, Stuart A. What Are My Chances, Book A. Thompson, Virginia, ed. (Illus.). (gr. 4-6). 1977. pap. 7.95 (ISBN 0-88488-082-6). Creative Pubns.
--What Are My Chances, Book B. Thompson, Virginia, ed. (Illus.). (gr. 7-9). 1977. pap. 7.95 (ISBN 0-88488-083-4). Creative Pubns.
Shultz, Ellen, ed. see Crosby, Sumner M., et al.
Shultz, Ellen, ed. see Curators at the Musei Vaticani & the Metropolitan Museum of Art.
Shultz, George & Weber, Arnold R. Strategies for the Displaced Worker. LC 76-7418. 1976. Repr. of 1966 ed. lib. bdg. 17.00x (ISBN 0-8371-8855-5, WEDW). Greenwood.
Shultz, George P. & Dam, Kenneth W. Economic Policy Beyond the Headlines. (Illus.). 1978. 8.95 o.p. (ISBN 0-393-05674-0); pap. 3.25x o.s.i. (ISBN 0-393-09059-0). Norton.
Shultz, T. J., tr. see Cremer, L. & Muller, H.
Shulvass, Moses A. The History of the Middle Ages, 2 Vols. Incl. Vol. 1. The Antiquity (ISBN 0-89526-660-1); Vol. 2. The Early Middle Ages (ISBN 0-89526-842-6). LC 81-85564. 19.95 ea. Regnery-Gateway.
Shumacher, Harold V. Atlanta Restaurant Guide. LC 82-10134. 272p. (Orig.). 1982. pap. 4.95 (ISBN 0-88289-248-7). Pelican.
Shumacher, William A. Roman Replies, Nineteen Eighty-Two. 42p. (Orig.). 1982. pap. 3.00x (ISBN 0-943616-13-1). Canon Law Soc.
Shumaker, Terence M., jt. auth. see Madsen, David A.
Shumaker, Terrence M. Process Piping Blueprint Reading. (Illus.). 176p. 1982. 13.95 (ISBN 0-13-723502-X). P-H.
Shumaker, Virginia O. The Alaska Pipeline. LC 79-13696. (Illus.). 64p. (gr. 3-5). 1979. PLB 7.29 o.p. (ISBN 0-671-32975-8). Messner.
Shumaker, Wayne. The Occult Sciences in the Renaissance: A Study in Intellectual Patterns. LC 70-153552. (Illus.). 1972. 38.50x (ISBN 0-520-02021-9); pap. 6.95 (ISBN 0-520-03840-1). U of Cal Pr.
Shumaker, Wayne & Heilbron, J. L. John Dee on Astronomy: Propaedeumata Aphoristica (1558 & 1568) LC 76-50254. 1978. 34.50x (ISBN 0-520-03376-0). U of Cal Pr.
Shuman, Bernard, jt. auth. see Gross, Barbara.
Shuman, D. R., jt. auth. see Andreoli, Anthony L.
Shuman, John T. English for Vocational & Technical Schools. 2nd ed. (Illus.). (gr. 9-12). 1954. 20.95x (ISBN 0-673-15724-5). Scott F.
Shuman, R. Baird. Robert E. Sherwood. (United States Authors Ser.). lib. bdg. 13.95 (ISBN 0-8057-0660-7, Twayne). G K Hall.
Shuman, R. Baird, ed. Creative Approaches to the Teaching of English: Secondary. LC 73-85766. 288p. 1974. pap. text ed. 7.95 (ISBN 0-87581-159-0). Peacock Pubs.
--Education in the 80s: English. 167p. 9.95 (ISBN 0-686-95337-1); members 8.95 (ISBN 0-686-99498-1). NCTE.
--Galaxy of Black Writing. LC 70-99294. 1970. 11.95 (ISBN 0-87716-018-X, Pub. by Moore Pub Co); pap. 5.95 (ISBN 0-686-66328-4). F Apple.
--Nine Black Poets. LC 68-57162. 1968. 10.95 (ISBN 0-87716-001-5, Pub. by Moore Pub Co). F Apple.
Shuman, Robert M., jt. auth. see Leech, Richard W.
Shumrick, Donald A., jt. ed. see Paparella, Michael.
Shumrick, Donald A., jt. ed. see Paparella, Michael M.
Shumsky, Abraham & Shumsky, Adaia. Ahavat Chesed - Love Mercy: Reader. (Mah Tov Hebrew Teaching Ser.: Bk. 2). (Illus.). (gr. 4 up). 1970. text ed. 5.50 (ISBN 0-8074-0175-7, 405304); tchrs'. guide 3.50 (ISBN 0-8074-0176-5, 205305); wkbk. 4.25 (ISBN 0-8074-0177-3, 405303). UAHC.
--Asot Mishpat. (Mah Tov Hebrew Teaching Ser.: Bk. 1). (Illus.). (gr. 4-8). 1969. text ed. 5.50 (ISBN 0-8074-0178-1, 405301); tchrs'. guide 3.50 (ISBN 0-8074-0179-X, 205302); wkbk. 4.25 (ISBN 0-8074-0180-3, 405300). UAHC.
--Hatznea Lechet: Walk Humbly. Spiro, Jack D., ed. (Mah Tov Hebrew Teaching Ser.: Bk. 3). (Illus.). (gr. 4). 1971. text ed. 5.00 (ISBN 0-8074-0181-1, 405307); tchrs'. guide 3.50 (ISBN 0-8074-0182-X, 205308); wkbk. 4.25 (ISBN 0-8074-0183-8, 405306). UAHC.
--Olam Gadol, 2 bks. Incl. Alef: a Big World. (Preprimer). text ed. 5.50 o.p. (ISBN 0-8074-0184-6, 405250); Bet. (Primer). 1973. text ed. 5.50 o.p. (ISBN 0-8074-0185-4, 405252); wkbk. with record 4.25 o.p. (ISBN 0-8074-0186-2, 405253). (Mah Tov Hebrew Program Ser.). (gr. 1-2). tchrs'. guide 5.00 o.p. (ISBN 0-8074-0187-0, 205254). UAHC.
Shumsky, Adaia, jt. auth. see Shumsky, Abraham.
Shumsky, Neil L. & Crimmins, Timothy, eds. Urban America: A Historical Bibliography. LC 82-24292. (Clio Bibliography Ser.: No. 11). 422p. 1982. lib. bdg. 55.00 (ISBN 0-87436-038-2). ABC-Clio.
Shumway, Eric B. Intensive Course in Tongan. (PALI Language Texts: Polynesia). 1971. pap. text ed. 15.00x (ISBN 0-87022-757-2). UH Pr.
Shun-Ichi Ohnishi, jt. ed. see Sato, Ryo.
Shunk, F. A. Constitution of Binary Alloys: 2nd Supplement. 1969. 59.00 o.p. (ISBN 0-07-057315-8, P&RB). McGraw.
Shupe, Anson & Stacey, William A. Born Again Politics & the Moral Majority: What Social Surveys Really Show. LC 82-8078. (Studies in American Religion: Vol. 5). 128p. 1982. 29.95x (ISBN 0-88946-919-9); Softcover 14.95x (ISBN 0-88946-920-2). E Mellen.
Shupe, Anson, jt. auth. see Bromley, David.
Shupp, Robert P., jt. auth. see Bragger, Jeanette D.
Shur, Irene G. & Littell, Franklin H. Reflection on the Holocaust. Lambert, Richard D., ed. LC 80-66618. (The Annals of the American Academy of Political & Social Science: No. 450). 272p. 1980. 5.50x o.s.i. (ISBN 0-87761-252-8); pap. text ed. 7.95 (ISBN 0-87761-253-6). Am Acad Pol Soc Sci.
Shura, Mary F. Eleanor. LC 82-19795. (Illus.). 128p. (gr. 4 up). 1983. PLB 8.95 (ISBN 0-396-08116-9). Dodd.
Shurcliff, William. Air-to-Air Heat Exchangers for Houses: How to Bring Air Into Your Home & Expel Polluted Air, While Recovering Valuable Heat. 224p. 1982. 21.95 (ISBN 0-471-88652-1, Pub. by Brick Hse Pub.). Wiley.
--Super Solar Houses: Saunder's Low-Cost, One Hundred Percent Solar Designs. (Illus.). 196p. 1983. 16.95 (ISBN 0-931790-48-4); pap. 11.95 (ISBN 0-931790-47-6). Brick Hse Pub.
--Superinsulated Houses. 1982. pap. 7.95 (ISBN 0-931790-25-5). Brick Hse Pub.
Shurcliff, William A. Air to Air Heat Exchanges for Houses. 224p. 1982. pap. 12.95 (ISBN 0-931790-40-9). Brick Hse Pub.
--Superinsulated Houses & Double-Envelope Houses: A Survey of Principles & Practice. (Illus.). 228p. 1981. 24.95 (ISBN 0-471-88647-5, Pub. by Brick Hse Pub.). Wiley.
--Thermal Shutters & Shades: Over One-Hundred Schemes for Reducing Heat-Loss Through Windows. LC 80-11574. 272p. 1980. 26.95 (ISBN 0-471-88648-3, Pub. by Brick Hse Pub.). Wiley.
Shurden, Kay W. & Dinwiddie, Dottie, eds. Women on Pilgrimage. LC 81-70975. 1982. pap. 4.95 (ISBN 0-8054-5428-4). Broadman.
Shure, Myrna B. & Spivack, George. Problem-Solving Techniques in Childrearing. LC 77-93677. (Social & Behavioral Science Ser.). (Illus.). 1978. text ed. 19.95x (ISBN 0-87589-366-X). Jossey-Bass.
Shurin, Aaron. The Graces. (Writing Ser.: No. 43). 80p. (Orig.). 1983. pap. 5.95 (ISBN 0-87704-060-5). Four Seasons Foun.
Shurkin, Joel. The Invisible Fire: Story of Mankind's Triumph Over the Ancient Scourge of Smallpox. LC 79-13415. 1979. 12.95 (ISBN 0-399-12286-9). Putnam Pub Group.
Shurkin, Joel N. Jupiter: The Star That Failed. LC 78-10885. 1979. 8.95 (ISBN 0-664-32642-0). Westminster.
Shurley, Jay T., ed. Relating Environment to Mental Health & Illness: The Ecopsychiatric Base. (Task Force Reports: 16). 58p. 1979. pap. 5.00 o.p. (ISBN 0-685-95864-7, P147-0). Am Psychiatric.
Shurter, Robert L. Effective Letters in Business. 2nd ed. 1954. text ed. 9.50 o.p. (ISBN 0-07-057339-5, C); pap. 5.95 (ISBN 0-07-057340-9). McGraw.
--Handy Grammar Reference. 1959. pap. 3.95 (ISBN 0-07-057345-X). McGraw.
--Written Communication in Business. 3rd ed. 1971. text ed. 15.95 o.p. (ISBN 0-07-057325-5, C); instructor's manual 4.95 o.p. (ISBN 0-07-057326-3). McGraw.
Shurter, Robert L., et al. Business Research & Report Writing. 1965. pap. 4.95 (ISBN 0-07-057329-8, SP). McGraw.
Shurtleff, M. C. Compendium of Corn Diseases. 2nd ed. LC 80-67517. (Compendium Ser.: No. 1). (Illus.). 124p. 1980. 12.00 (ISBN 0-89054-021-7). Am Phytopathol Soc.
Shurtleff, William & Aoyagi, Akiko. The Book of Kudzu. LC 77-74891. 104p. 1977. pap. 4.95 (ISBN 0-933332-11-4). Soyfoods Center.
--The Book of Miso. 768p. 1981. pap. 3.50 (ISBN 0-345-29107-7). Ballantine.
--The Book of Miso. LC 76-19599. (Soyfoods Ser.). (Illus.). 256p. 1976. pap. 8.95 (ISBN 0-933332-10-6). Soyfoods Center.
--The Book of Miso. rev. ed. (Illus.). 256p. 14.95 (ISBN 0-89815-098-1); pap. 9.95 (ISBN 0-89815-097-3). Ten Speed Pr.
--The Book of Tempeh: Professional Edition. LC 78-20185. (Illus.). 248p. Repr. of 1979 ed. 16.95 (ISBN 0-933332-05-X). Soyfoods Center.
--The Book of Tofu. LC 74-31629. (Soyfoods Ser.). (Illus.). 336p. 1975. pap. 9.95 (ISBN 0-933332-09-2). Soyfoods Center.
--The Book of Tofu. rev. ed. (Illus.). 336p. 16.95 (ISBN 0-89815-096-5); pap. 11.95 (ISBN 0-89815-095-7). Ten Speed Pr.
--Miso Production: The Book of Miso, Vol. II. rev. ed. LC 76-19599. (Illus.). 80p. 1979. pap. 9.95 (ISBN 0-933332-00-9). Soyfoods Center.
--Miso Production: The Book of Miso, Vol. II. rev. ed. LC 76-19599. (Soyfood Production Ser.: No. 1). (Illus.). 80p. 1979. pap. 9.95 (ISBN 0-933332-00-9). Soyfoods Center.
--Soyfoods Industry Directory & Databook. (Soyfoods Production Ser.: No. 4). (Illus.). 56p. (Orig.). 1982. pap. text ed. 75.00 (ISBN 0-933332-06-8). Soyfoods Center.

--Soyfoods Labels, Posters & Other Graphics. (Soyfoods Production Ser.: No. 6). 185p. (Orig.). 1982. pap. 35.00 spiral bdg. (ISBN 0-933332-08-4). Soyfoods Center.

--Tempeh Production: The Book of Tempeh, Vol. II. LC 79-89281. (Soyfood Production Ser.: No. 3). (Illus.). 256p. 1980. 22.95 (ISBN 0-933332-04-1); pap. 19.95 (ISBN 0-933332-02-5). Soyfoods Center.

--Tofu & Soymilk Production: The Book of Tofu, Vol. II. LC 74-31629. (Soyfood Production Ser.: No. 2). (Illus.). 336p. 1979. 24.95 o.s.i. (ISBN 0-933332-03-3); pap. 24.95 (ISBN 0-933332-01-7). Soyfoods Center.

--Using Tofu, Tempeh & Other Soyfoods in Restaurants, Delis & Cafeterias. (Soyfoods Production Ser.: No. 5). 135p. (Orig.). 1982. pap. text ed. 32.95 spiral bound (ISBN 0-933332-07-6). Soyfoods Center.

Shuster, Albert H., jt. auth. see Ploghoft, Milton E.

Shuster, Bud. Believing in America. 288p. 1983. 13.95 (ISBN 0-688-01834-3). Morrow.

Shuster, Sam. Dermatology in Internal Medicine. 1979. pap. 18.95x (ISBN 0-19-261142-9). Oxford U Pr.

Shusterich, Kurt M. Resource Management & the Oceans: The Political Economy of Deep Seabed Mining. (A Westview Replicia Edition Ser.). (Illus.). 280p. 1982. softcover 22.50 (ISBN 0-86531-901-4). Westview.

Shusterman, David. C. P. Snow. LC 74-23949. (English Authors Ser.: No. 179). 1975. lib. bdg. 12.95 (ISBN 0-8057-1510-X, Twayne). G K Hall.

Shute, C. D. The McCollough Effect. LC 78-15609. (Illus.). 1979. 34.95 (ISBN 0-521-22395-4). Cambridge U Pr.

Shute, Nevil. In the Wet. 1982. 14.95 (ISBN 0-434-69913-6, Pub. by Heinemann). David & Charles.

--Marazan. 1982. 14.95 (ISBN 0-434-69901-2, Pub. by Heinemann). David & Charles.

--An Old Captivity. 1982. 13.95 (ISBN 0-434-69906-3, Pub. by Heinemann). David & Charles.

--Pied Piper. 1982. 13.95 (ISBN 0-434-69908-X, Pub. by Heinemann). David & Charles.

--Requiem for a Wren. 1982. 13.95 (ISBN 0-434-69916-0, Pub. by Heinemann). David & Charles.

--Round the Bend. 1977. Repr. of 1951 ed. lib. bdg. 16.95x (ISBN 0-89244-053-8). Queens Hse.

--Ruined City. 1982. 13.95 (ISBN 0-434-69904-7, Pub. by Heinemann). David & Charles.

--Trustee from the Toolroom. 311p. 1976. Repr. of 1960 ed. lib. bdg. 17.95x (ISBN 0-89244-016-3). Queens Hse.

--What Happened to the Corbetts. 1982. 13.95 (ISBN 0-434-69905-5, Pub. by Heinemann). David & Charles.

Shute, Stephanie. Variety Show, to Go! Zapel, Arthur L., ed. LC 82-82077. (Illus.). 90p. (Orig.). 1982. pap. text ed. 5.50 (ISBN 0-916260-18-6). Meriwether Pub.

Shute, Wilfrid. Vitamin E: Ailing & Healthy Hearts. pap. 2.75x (ISBN 0-686-29960-4). Cancer Control Soc.

Shute, Wilfrid E. Dr. Wilfrid E. Shute's Complete, Updated Vitamin E Book. LC 75-7808. 228p. 1975. pap. 2.95 (ISBN 0-87983-151-0). Keats.

--The Health Preserver. LC 77-14086. 1977. 8.95 o.p. (ISBN 0-87857-189-2). Rodale Pr Inc.

Shutler, Richard, Jr., ed. Early Man in the New World. (Illus.). 200p. 1983. 29.95 (ISBN 0-8039-1958-1); pap. 14.95 (ISBN 0-8039-1959-X). Sage.

Shutt, R. P., ed. Bubble & Spark Chambers: Principles & Use, 2 vols. (Pure & Applied Physics Ser.: Vol. 27). 1967. Vol. 1. 67.00 (ISBN 0-12-641001-1); Vol. 2. 67.00 (ISBN 0-12-641002-X); Set. 94.00 (ISBN 0-685-23204-2). Acad Pr.

Shuttle, Penelope. The Orchard Upstairs. 1980. pap. 11.95 (ISBN 0-19-211938-9). Oxford U Pr.

Shuttle, Penelope & Redgrove, Peter. Wise Wound: Eve's Curse & Everywoman. LC 78-6402. 1978. 9.95 o.p. (ISBN 0-399-90024-1, Marek). Putnam Pub Group.

Shuttlesworth, Dorothy E. The Story of Monkeys, Great Apes, & Small Apes. LC 76-150872. 112p. (gr. 3-7). 1972. 6.95 (ISBN 0-385-06055-6); PLB o.p. (ISBN 0-385-04724-X). Doubleday.

Shuttlesworth, Dorothy E. & Shuttlesworth, Gregory J. Farms for Today & Tomorrow: The Wonders of Food Production. LC 78-22356. (Illus.). 1979. PLB 7.95a o.p. (ISBN 0-385-14539-X). Doubleday.

Shuttlesworth, Gregory J., jt. auth. see Shuttlesworth, Dorothy E.

Shuttleworth, Charles, jt. auth. see Comber, Leon.

Shuttleworth, Riley & Verma, Kiran. Mechanical & Electrical Systems for Construction. (Construction Ser.). (Illus.). 736p. 1984. text ed. 32.95x (ISBN 0-07-057215-1, C). McGraw.

Shutz, John A., ed. see Lapp, Rudolph M.

Shuval, Hillel I. Environmental Quality & Exology, Vol. II. 400p. 1983. pap. text ed. 44.00 (ISBN 0-86689-020-3). Balaban Intl Sci Serv.

Shuval, Hillel I., ed. Water Quality Management Under Conditions of Scarcity: Israel As a Case Study. LC 79-8848. (Water Pollution Ser.). 1980. 40.00 (ISBN 0-12-641280-4). Acad Pr.

Shuval, Judith T. Newcomers & Colleagues: Soviet Immigrant Physicians in Israel. LC 82-72536. 250p. 1983. 16.95 (ISBN 0-88105-002-4). Cap & Gown.

Shuy, Roger. Discovering American Dialects. 1967. pap. 3.00 (ISBN 0-8141-1206-4); pap. 2.20 members (ISBN 0-686-86403-4). NCTE.

Shvidkovsky, Oleg A., jt. auth. see Burian, Jiri.

Shvyrkov, V. V. S. Legend in Applied Probability & Statistics. Rev. ed. LC 81-85204. (Illus.). 224p. 1982. 13.80 o.s.i. (ISBN 0-942004-00-0, 1A). G Throwkoff.

--S. Legend in Statistical Science. LC 81-86400. (Illus.). 257p. (Orig.). 1982. wkbk. o.s.i. 18.20 (ISBN 0-942004-01-9). G Throwkoff.

--Statistic: Art or Science? LC 82-61951. (Illus.). 105p. (Orig.). 1982. text ed. 11.60 (ISBN 0-942004-05-1). G Throwkoff.

--Statistical Science in Economic Forecasting. (Illus.). 212p. (Orig.). 1983. pap. 18.30 wkbk. (ISBN 0-942004-04-3). G Throwkoff.

--Statistical Science in Economics, Vol. I. LC 82-50717. 206p. 1982. wkbk. 17.30 (ISBN 0-942004-02-7). G Throwkoff.

--Statistical Science in Economics, Vol. II. LC 82-50717. (Illus.). 224p. (Orig.). 1982. wkbk. 19.20 (ISBN 0-942004-03-5). G Throwkoff.

--Statistical Science in Economics. (Volume II). (Illus.). 207p. (Orig.). 1983. wkbk. 19.10 (0686387597). G Throwkoff.

Shwartz, Susan, ed. Hecate's Cauldron. 256p. 1982. pap. 2.95 (ISBN 0-87997-705-1, UE1705). DAW Bks.

Shy, John. The American Revolution. 1983. write for info (ISBN 0-393-95278-9). Norton.

Shyer, Marlene F. Adorable Sunday. 192p. (gr. 6-8). 1983. 11.95 (ISBN 0-684-17848-6). Scribner.

--Never Trust a Handsome Man. LC 78-11220. 1979. 8.95 o.p. (ISBN 0-698-10963-5, Coward). Putnam Pub Group.

Shyne, Ann W., jt. auth. see Russo, Eva M.

Shyne, Ann W., ed. Child Welfare Perspectives. 1979. 7.95 (ISBN 0-87868-133-7, CW-32). Child Welfare.

Shyne, Kevin. The Man Who Dropped from the Sky. Rosoff, Iris, ed. (Illus.). 64p. 1982. lib. bdg. 9.29 (ISBN 0-671-44164-7). Messner.

Sia, Mary L. Mary Sia's Chinese Cookbook. 3rd ed. (Illus.). 1964. pap. 4.95 (ISBN 0-8248-0402-3). UH Pr.

Siafaca, Ekaterini. Medical Technology & Government Research: Key Trends in Medical Devices, Instrumentation & Diagnostics Research. (F & S Press Bk.). 200p. 1983. prof ref 34.95x (ISBN 0-686-97887-0). Ballinger Pub.

Siafaca, Katie & F & S Press Book. Investor Owned Hospitals & Their Role in the Changing U. S. Health Care System. 224p. 1981. prof ref. 32.95x (ISBN 0-86621-000-8). Ballinger Pub.

SIAM Institute for Mathematics & Society Conference, Alta, Utah, July 5-9, 1976. Environmental Health: Quantitative Methods. Proceedings. Whittemore, Alice, ed. LC 77-70937. (SIAM-SIMS Conference Ser.: Vol. 4). (Illus.). vii, 259p. (Orig.). 1977. pap. text ed. 25.50 (ISBN 0-89871-030-8). Soc Indus-Appl Math.

Sibbald, William J. Synopsis of Critical Care. (Illus.). 274p. 1983. lib. bdg. price not set (ISBN 0-683-07710-4). Williams & Wilkins.

Sibbes, Richard. Works of Robert Sibbes, Vol. 1. 1979. 14.95 (ISBN 0-85151-169-4). Banner of Truth.

Sibbett, Ed. Easy-to-Make Stained Glass Lampshades. (Illus., Orig.). 1980. pap. 4.50 (ISBN 0-486-23997-7). Dover.

Sibbett, Ed, Jr. Art Nouveau Stained Glass Coloring Book. (Illus.). 1982. pap. 2.50 (ISBN 0-486-23399-5). Dover.

--Art Nouveau Stained Glass Pattern Book. LC 77-87497. (Pictorial Archives Ser.). (Illus.). 1978. pap. 3.00 (ISBN 0-486-23577-7). Dover.

--Celtic Design Coloring Book. 48p. 1979. pap. 2.00 (ISBN 0-486-23796-6). Dover.

--Christmas Cut & Use Stencils. 64p. 1978. pap. 3.25 (ISBN 0-486-23636-6). Dover.

Sibbett, Ed., Jr. Easy-to Make Articulated Wooden Toys: Patterns & Instructions for 18 Playthings That Move. (General Crafts Ser.). (Illus.). 48p. 1983. pap. 2.50 (ISBN 0-486-24411-3). Dover.

Sibbett, Ed, Jr. Easy-to-Make Stained Glass Panels: With Full-Size Templates for 32 Projects. (Illus.). 64p. (Orig.). 1983. pap. 3.95 (ISBN 0-486-24448-2). Dover.

--Fantastic Super Stickers: One-Hundred-Fifty Colorful Pressure-Sensitive Stickers. (Illus.). 16p. (Orig.). 1983. pap. 2.95 (ISBN 0-486-24471-7). Dover.

--Floral Cut & Use Stencils: 54 Full-Size Stencils Printed on Durable Stencil Paper. LC 78-67294. (Cut & Use Stencil Ser.). (Illus.). 1979. pap. 3.50 (ISBN 0-486-23742-7). Dover.

--Floral Stained Glass Pattern Book. (Illus.). 64p. 1982. pap. 3.50 (ISBN 0-486-24259-5). Dover.

--Gift Labels for Holidays & Special Occasions. (Illus.). pap. 2.50 (ISBN 0-486-24190-4). Dover.

--Historic Styles Stained Glass Pattern Book. (Illus.). 64p. (Orig.). 1981. pap. 3.50 (ISBN 0-486-24176-9). Dover.

--Iron-On T-Shirt Transfers for Hand Coloring. (Illus., Orig.). 1976. pap. 1.95 (ISBN 0-486-23395-2). Dover.

Sibbett, Ed., Jr. Peasant Designs for Artists & Craftsmen. LC 76-58079. (Dover Needlepoint Ser.). (Illus.). 1977. pap. 4.00 (ISBN 0-486-23478-9). Dover.

Sibbett, Ed, Jr. Ready-to-Use Christmas Designs. (Clip Art Ser.). (Illus.). 1979. pap. 2.95 (ISBN 0-486-23900-4). Dover.

--Stained Glass Pattern Book: 88 Designs for Workable Projects. 8.50 (ISBN 0-8446-5522-8). Peter Smith.

--Turn of the Century Posters Coloring Book. 48p. 1978. pap. 2.00 (ISBN 0-486-23705-2). Dover.

Sibbett, Ed, Jr., ed. Ready-to-Use Illustrations for Holidays & Special Occasions. (Illus.). 64p. (Orig.). 1983. pap. 2.95 (ISBN 0-486-24440-7). Dover.

Sibeko, David. South Africa's Secret Trial: The PAC Bethal 18 Case. (International Ser.). 1979. pap. 1.50 (ISBN 0-930720-63-6). Liberator Pr.

Siberell, Anne. Whale in the Sky. LC 82-2483. (A Unicorn Bks.). (Illus.). 32p. (ps-3). 1982. 10.95 (ISBN 0-525-44021-6, 01063-320). Dutton.

Sibert, Jody, ed. The Incredible Shrinking Woman. 160p. (Orig.). 1981. pap. 2.50 o.s.i. (ISBN 0-515-05753-3). Jove Pubns.

Sibinga, C. Th. & Das, P. C. Blood Transfusion & Problems of Bleeding. 1982. text ed. 39.50 (ISBN 90-247-3058-9, Pub. by Martinus Nijhoff Netherlands). Kluwer Boston.

Sibley, Agnes. Charles Williams. (English Author Ser.). 1982. lib. bdg. 14.95 (ISBN 0-8057-6811-4, Twayne). G K Hall.

--May Sarton. (U. S. Authors Ser.: No. 213). lib. bdg. 10.95 o.p. (ISBN 0-8057-0656-9, Twayne). G K Hall.

Sibley, Celestine. Children, My Children. LC 80-8231. 210p. 1981. 11.49i (ISBN 0-06-014872-1, HarpT). Har-Row.

Sibley, Charles G. & American Ornithologists' Union, eds. Proceedings: International Ornithological Congress, 13th, 2 vols. 1250p. 1963. 10.00 (ISBN 0-943610-00-1). Am Ornithologists.

Sibley, Elbridge. Recruitment, Selection & Training of Social Scientists. LC 48-9155. (Social Science Research Council Bulletin: No. 58). 1948. pap. 6.00 (ISBN 0-527-03286-7). Kraus Repr.

--Support for Independent Scholarship & Research. LC 51-5070. (Social Science Research Council Bulletin). 1951. pap. 4.00 (ISBN 0-527-03310-3). Kraus Repr.

Sibley, Frederic M. An Iambic Odyssey. 1982. 5.75 (ISBN 0-8062-1865-7). Carlton.

Sibley, Hi. One Hundred & Two Bird Houses, Feeders You Can Make. (Illus.). 1980. pap. 5.40 (ISBN 0-87006-304-9). Goodheart.

--Wood Projects, Bk. 1. LC 71-111283. (Illus.). 1970. pap. 5.40 (ISBN 0-87006-110-0). Goodheart.

Sibley, Jack R. & Gunter, Pete A., eds. Process Philosophy: Basic Writings. LC 78-57668. 1978. pap. text ed. 17.75 (ISBN 0-8191-0531-7). U Pr of Amer.

Sibley, Marilyn M. Lone Stars & State Gazettes: Texas Newspapers Before the Civil War. LC 82-45898. (Illus.). 408p. 1983. 21.50 (ISBN 0-89096-149-2). Tex A&M Univ Pr.

Sibley, Susan. Woodsmoke. 1979. pap. 1.95 o.p. (ISBN 0-380-45435-1, 45435). Avon.

Sibmacher, Johan, illus. Baroque Charted Designs for Needlework. LC 75-2820. Orig. Title: Kreuzstich-Muster, 36 Tafeln. (Illus.). 48p. 1975. pap. 1.95 (ISBN 0-486-23186-0). Dover.

Sibson, jt. auth. see Falla.

Sibson, R. B., jt. auth. see Falla, R. A.

Sibyll, Claus, jt. auth. see Von Lang, Jochen.

Sica, Joseph F. God So Loved the World. LC 81-40441. 120p. (Orig.). 1981. lib. bdg. 17.75 (ISBN 0-8191-1677-7); pap. text ed. 8.00 (ISBN 0-8191-1678-5). U Pr of Amer.

Sicard, Gerald L. & Weinberger, Philip R. Sociology for Our Times. 1977. pap. 7.95x o.p. (ISBN 0-673-07989-9). Scott F.

Siccardi, Mirtha. Luz Que No Se Apaga. (Span.). pap. 3.95 (ISBN 0-8024-5195-0). Moody.

Sices, David, jt. auth. see Denoeu, Francois.

Sicha, Jeffrey, ed. see Sellars, Wilfrid.

Sichel, Betty A. Value Education for an Age of Crisis. LC 81-40642. 204p. (Orig.). 1982. lib. bdg. 22.25 (ISBN 0-8191-2361-7); pap. text ed. 10.75 (ISBN 0-8191-2362-5). U Pr of Amer.

Sichel, Joyce L. Program Evaluation Guidelines: A Research Handbook for Agency Personnel. LC 81-4148. 108p. 1982. 19.95x (ISBN 0-89885-030-4). Human Sci Pr.

Sichel, Marion. History of Children's Costume. (Costume Reference Ser.). (Illus.). 72p. 1983. 10.95 (ISBN 0-8238-0259-0). Plays.

Sichel, Werner. Public Utility Rate Making in an Energy Conscious Environment. 1979. lib. bdg. 25.00 (ISBN 0-89158-180-4). Westview.

Sichel, Werner & Eckstein, Peter. Basic Economic Concepts: Microeconomics. 2nd ed. 1977. pap. 12.50 (ISBN 0-395-30745-7); instr's manual 0.75 (ISBN 0-395-30747-3). HM.

Sichel, Werner, jt. ed. see Gies, Thomas G.

Sicher, Harry & DuBrul, E. Lloyd. Oral Anatomy. 6th ed. LC 74-20890. 554p. 1975. text ed. 24.50 o.p. (ISBN 0-8016-4604-9). Mosby.

Sicignano, Robert & Prichard, Doris. Special Issues Index: Specialized Contents of Business, Industrial, & Consumer Journals. LC 82-11725. 315p. 1982. lib. bdg. 35.00 (ISBN 0-313-23278-4, SII/). Greenwood.

Sicilia, Dominic. Instant Photo - Instant Art. 1977. pap. 5.95 o.s.i. (ISBN 0-8431-0423-6). Price Stern.

Sick, H., jt. auth. see Korite, J. C.

Sickels, Robert J. The Presidency: An Introduction. 1980. pap. text ed. 14.95 (ISBN 0-13-697433-3). P-H.

Sickinghe, Jhr. W., jt. ed. see Kaempfer, H. M.

Sickle, Larry van see Van Sickle, Larry.

Sickle, Sylvia Van see Van Sickle, Sylvia.

Sickles, Margaret, jt. auth. see Walsh, Mary A.

Sickman, John, jt. auth. see Birnbaum, Mark.

Sidar, Alexander G., Jr. & Potter, David A. No-Need Merit Awards: A Survey of Their Use at Four-Year Public & Private Colleges & Universities. 1978. pap. 4.00 o.p. (ISBN 0-87447-064-1, 218383). College Bd.

Sidar, Alexander, III. The Dorset Disaster. 1980. 10.95 o.p. (ISBN 0-448-15713-6, G&D). Putnam Pub Group.

Siddall, G. & Zemel, J., eds. Application Thin Films, 2 Vols. 1972. 109.75 (ISBN 0-444-41095-3). Elsevier.

Siddiqi, Amir H. Caliphate & Kingship in Mediaeval Persia. LC 77-10621. (Studies in Islamic History: No. 14). 112p. Repr. of 1937 ed. lib. bdg. 15.00x (ISBN 0-87991-463-7). Porcupine Pr.

Siddique, Kankab. Islamic Revolution: The Iranian Experiment. Naeem, Nadrat, ed. (Illus.). 100p. (Orig.). pap. 3.50 (ISBN 0-942978-03-X). Am Soc Ed & Rel.

Siddique, Kaukab. Islam-the Wave of the Future. LC 82-83624. 75p. (Orig.). 1983. pap. 2.00 (ISBN 0-942978-04-8). Am Soc Ed & Rel.

Siddiqui, A. H. Arabic for Beginners. pap. 8.95 (ISBN 0-686-63894-8). Kazi Pubns.

--The Cracy & the Islamic State. 2.50 (ISBN 0-686-83892-0). Kazi Pubns.

--Islam & Remaking of Humanity. 13.95 (ISBN 0-686-83885-8); pap. 9.95 (ISBN 0-686-83886-6). Kazi Pubns.

--Main Springs of Western Civilization. 6.50 (ISBN 0-686-18567-6). Kazi Pubns.

--Philosophical Interpretation of History. 9.95 (ISBN 0-686-83884-X). Kazi Pubns.

--Prayers of the Prophet with Arabic Text. pap. 2.00 (ISBN 0-686-18345-2). Kazi Pubns.

--Sahih Muslim, 4 vols. 60.00 (ISBN 0-686-18341-X). Kazi Pubns.

--Selections from Quran & Hadith. pap. 18.50 ea. (ISBN 0-686-63914-6). Kazi Pubns.

--What Islam Gave to Humanity? pap. 2.00 (ISBN 0-686-63918-9). Kazi Pubns.

Siddiqui, M. A. A. Principle of Islam. pap. 0.75 o.p. (ISBN 0-686-18486-6). Kazi Pubns.

Siddiqui, M. I. Economic Security in Islam. 1981. 14.95 (ISBN 0-686-97853-6). Kazi Pubns.

--Excellent Qualities of Holy Quran. 2.50 (ISBN 0-686-83882-3). Kazi Pubns.

--Martyrdom of Husain. 3.95 (ISBN 0-686-83883-1). Kazi Pubns.

--Penal Law of Islam. 1980. 12.00 (ISBN 0-686-64662-2). Kazi Pubns.

--Qualities of Holy Quran. 1981. 2.50 (ISBN 0-686-97854-4). Kazi Pubns.

--Rights of Allah & Human Rights. 1981. 12.95 (ISBN 0-686-97876-5). Kazi Pubns.

--Rights of Allah (God) & Human Rights. 12.50 (ISBN 0-686-83894-7). Kazi Pubns.

--Theocracy & the Islamic State. 12.95 (ISBN 0-686-97875-7). Kazi Pubns.

--What Agitates the Mind of the East. 1981. 1.25 (ISBN 0-686-97862-5). Kazi Pubns.

--Why Islam Forbids Gambling & Alcohol. 12.50 (ISBN 0-686-83890-4). Kazi Pubns.

--Why Islam Forbids Intoxicants & Gambling. 1981. 12.50 (ISBN 0-686-97852-8). Kazi Pubns.

Siddiqui, M. M. Women in Islam. pap. 4.75 (ISBN 0-686-18462-9). Kazi Pubns.

Siddiqui, M. S. Blessed Women of Islam. 12.50 (ISBN 0-686-83898-X). Kazi Pubns.

Siddiqui, Moulana M. Elementary Teachings of Islam. LC 82-72579. 88p. (Orig.). 1982. pap. 1.50 o.p. (ISBN 0-686-92010-4). Contemp Bks.

Siddiqui, Muhammad A. Elementary Teachings of Islam. Date not set. price not set (ISBN 0-89259-022-X). Am Trust Pubns.

Siddiqui, S. A. Public Finance in Islam. 5.75 (ISBN 0-686-18375-4). Kazi Pubns.

Siddiqui, Zeba. Kareem & Fatimah. Quinlan, Hamid, ed. LC 82-70452. 50p. 1982. pap. 3.50 (ISBN 0-89259-032-7). Am Trust Pubns.

Siddons, Arthur W., et al. New Calculus. 1950. Pt. 1. text ed. 6.95x (ISBN 0-521-06465-1). Cambridge U Pr.

Sidebotham, R. Introduction to the Theory & Context of Accounting. 2nd ed. 1970. pap. 11.00 o.p. (ISBN 0-08-015620-7). Pergamon.

Sidel, Ruth. Families of Fengsheng: Urban Life in China. 1974. 9.95 o.p. (ISBN 0-14-061616-0, PB16); pap. 3.95 (ISBN 0-14-003948-1, 3948). Penguin.

--Women & Child Care in China. rev. ed. (Illus.). 1973. pap. 5.95 (ISBN 0-14-003718-7). Penguin.

Sidel, Ruth & Sidel, Victor W. The Health of China. LC 81-68353. 272p. 1983. pap. 7.64 (ISBN 0-8070-2161-X, BP651). Beacon Pr.

Sidel, Victor W., jt. auth. see Sidel, Ruth.

Sider, Ronald J. & Taylor, Richard K. Nuclear Holocaust & Christian Hope. (Illus.). 492p. (Orig.). 1982. pap. 6.95 (ISBN 0-87784-386-4). Inter-Varsity.

--Nuclear Holocaust & Christian Hope: A Book for Christian Peacemakers. 360p. 1983. pap. 6.95 (ISBN 0-8091-2512-9). Paulist Pr.

Sider, Ronald J., ed. Evangelicals & Development: Toward a Theology of Social Change. LC 82-6970. (Contemporary Issues in Social Ethics Ser.). 1982. pap. 6.95 (ISBN 0-664-24445-9). Westminster.

--Lifestyle in the Eighties: An Evangelical Commitment to Simple Lifestyle. LC 82-7067. (Contemporary Issues in Social Ethics Ser.). 1982. pap. 10.95 (ISBN 0-664-24437-8). Westminster.

Sider, Ronald J. & Brubaker, Darrel J., eds. Preaching on Peace. LC 82-10958. 96p. 1982. pap. 3.95. Fortress.

Sides, C. M., ed. Transactions of the American Association of Cost Engineers, 1979. (Illus.). 28p. 1979. pap. 30.00 (ISBN 0-930284-03-8). Am Assn Cost Engineers.

Sides, Dorothy. Decorative Art of the Southwest Indians. 1961. pap. 2.25 (ISBN 0-686-95773-3). Jefferson Natl.

Sidgwick, A. Sidgwick's Greek Prose Composition. 150p. 1983. pap. text ed. 10.95x (ISBN 0-7156-1675-7, Pub. by Duckworth England). Biblio Dist.

Sidgwick, A., ed. see Aeschylus.

Sidgwick, J. B. Amateur Astronomer's Handbook. 4th, rev. ed. LC 80-20596. (Illus.). 568p. 1980. text ed. 24.95x (ISBN 0-89490-049-8); pap. 7.95 (ISBN 0-89490-076-5). Enslow Pubs.

Sidgwick, Jean, tr. see Del Vasto, Lanza.

Sidhanta, Mirmal K. The Heroic Age of India: A Comparative Study. LC 75-928104. 1975. Repr. of 1929 ed. 12.75x o.p. (ISBN 0-8364-0409-2). South Asia Bks.

Sidley, Nathan T., jt. auth. see Ammer, Christine.

Sidney, Margaret. Five Little Peppers & How They Grew. (Illus.). (gr. 4-6). illus. jr. lib. o.p. 5.95 (ISBN 0-448-05808-1, G&D); companion lib. & ed. 2.95 (ISBN 0-448-05459-0); deluxe ed. 8.95 (ISBN 0-448-06008-6); pap. 4.95 (ISBN 0-448-11008-3). Putnam Pub Group.

--Five Little Peppers & How They Grew. (Grow-up Books Ser.). (Illus.). (gr. 4-6). 1.95 o.p. (ISBN 0-448-02239-7, G&D). Putnam Pub Group.

Sidney, Philip. Complete Prose Works, 4 vols. Feuillerat, A., ed. Incl. Vol. 1. The Countesse of Pembroke's Arcadia. 69.50 (ISBN 0-521-06468-6); Vol. 2. The Last Part of Countesse of Pembroke's Arcadia & the Lady of May. 47.50 (ISBN 0-521-06469-4); Vol. 3. The Defence of Poesie, Political Discourses, Correspondence, Translations. 59.50 (ISBN 0-521-06470-8); Vol. 4. The Older Arcadia. 59.50 (ISBN 0-521-06471-6). 190.00 set (ISBN 0-521-08770-8). Cambridge U Pr.

--The Countesse of Pembroke's Arcadia. LC 82-10288. 1983. 35.00x (ISBN 0-8201-1382-4). Schol Facsimiles.

--Miscellaneous Prose of Sir Philip Sidney. Van Dorsten, Jan & Duncan-Jones, Katherine, eds. (Oxford English Texts Ser.). 1973. 29.00x o.p. (ISBN 0-19-811880-5). Oxford U Pr.

Sidney, Philip, tr. see Mornay, Philippe de.

Sidowski, Joseph B. Experimental Methods & Instrumentation in Psychology. (Psychology Ser.). 1966. text ed. 38.00 (ISBN 0-07-057347-6, C). McGraw.

Sidran, Ben. Black Talk. (Quality Paperbacks Ser.). 244p. 1983. pap. 7.95 (ISBN 0-306-80184-1). Da Capo.

Sidwell, Duncan. Expedition Two Thousand Sixty-One. LC 73-145608. (Illus.). 1971. text ed. 3.50x (ISBN 0-521-08087-8). Cambridge U Pr.

Sidwell, E. H., jt. auth. see Jennings, R.

Sidwell, Ron. West Midland Gardens. 252p. 1981. text ed. 18.00x (ISBN 0-904387-71-2, 61110, Pub. by Sutton England). Humanities.

Sieben, J. Kenneth. Composition Five: Basic Skills for Writing. Anthony, Lillian S., ed. 1982. pap. text ed. 13.50x (ISBN 0-673-15539-0). Scott F.

Siebenheller, Norma. P. D. James. LC 81-40473. (Recognitions Series.). 162p. 1981. 11.95 (ISBN 0-8044-2817-4); pap. 5.95 (ISBN 0-8044-6862-1). Ungar.

Siebenmann, R. E., jt. auth. see Williams, E. D.

Siebenschuh, William R. Fictional Techniques & Factual Works. LC 82-8373. 200p. 1983. text ed. 18.00x (ISBN 0-8203-0636-3). U of Ga Pr.

--Form & Purpose in Boswell's Biographical Works. LC 74-171621. 1972. 23.50x (ISBN 0-520-02246-7). U of Cal Pr.

Siebenschuh, William R., jt. auth. see Mundhenk, Robert T.

Sieber, Harry. The Picaresque. (The Critical Idiom Ser.). 1977. 9.95x (ISBN 0-416-82710-1); pap. 4.95x o.p. (ISBN 0-416-82720-9). Methuen Inc.

Siebert, C. A. & Doane, D. V. The Hardenability of Steels. 1977. 44.00 o.p. (ISBN 0-87170-047-6). ASM.

Siebert, E. D. Foundations of Chemistry. 1982. text ed. 26.50 (ISBN 0-07-057285-2, C); study guide 8.95 (ISBN 0-07-057286-0); instr's manual 10.00 (ISBN 0-07-057287-9). Mcgraw.

Siebert, Fredrick S. Freedom of the Press in England, Fourteen Seventy-Six to Seventeen Seventy-Six: The Rise & Decline of Government Controls. LC 52-5892. 1965. pap. 8.95 o.p. (ISBN 0-252-72431-3). U of Ill Pr.

--The Rights & Privileges of the Press. LC 70-100243. xvii, 429p. Repr. of 1934 ed. lib. bdg. 19.75x (ISBN 0-8371-4021-8, SIRP). Greenwood.

Siebert, H. & Eichberger, J. Trade & Environment: A Theoretical Enquiry. (Studies in Environmental Science Ser.: Vol. 6). 1980. 59.75 (ISBN 0-444-41875-X). Elsevier.

Siebert, Horst. Economics of the Environment. LC 80-7442. 1981. 26.95x (ISBN 0-669-03693-5). Lexington Bks.

Siebert, Horst, et al. The Political Economy of Environmental Protection. Altman, Edward I., ed. LC 78-13843. (Contemporary Studies in Economic & Financial Analysis Ser.). 1979. lib. bdg. 36.00 (ISBN 0-89232-116-4). Jai Pr.

Siebert, Rudolf J. From Critical Theory of Society to Theology of Communicative Praxis. LC 79-65296. 1979. pap. text ed. 10.50 (ISBN 0-8191-0783-2). U Pr of Amer.

--Hegel's Concept of Marriage & Family: The Origin of Subjective Freedom. LC 78-78401. 1979. pap. text ed. 8.25 (ISBN 0-8191-0710-7). U Pr of Amer.

--Hegel's Philosophy of History: Theological, Humanistic & Scientific Elements. LC 78-66279. 1979. pap. text ed. 9.75 (ISBN 0-8191-0689-5). U Pr of Amer.

--Horkheimer's Critical Sociology of Religion: The Relative & the Transcendent. LC 78-66280. 1979. pap. text ed. 8.25 (ISBN 0-8191-0688-7). U Pr of Amer.

Siebert, W. S., jt. auth. see Addison, John.

Siebold. Attitudes & Behavior. 256p. 1983. 22.95 (ISBN 0-03-060293-9). Praeger.

Siebold, Philipp F. Von see Von Siebold, Philipp F.

Siebrand, J. C., jt. auth. see Lenderink, R. S.

Siebring, B. R. & Schaff, M. E. Chemistry: A Basic Approach. 1971. text ed. 22.00 (ISBN 0-07-057349-2, C); instr's manual 1.95 (ISBN 0-07-057354-9); wkbk. 12.95 (ISBN 0-07-057352-2). McGraw.

Siebring, B. R., jt. auth. see Schaff, M. E.

Siebring, B. Richard & Schaff, Mary E. General Chemistry. 864p. 1980. text ed. 29.95x (ISBN 0-534-00802-X); lab manual 14.95x (ISBN 0-534-00838-0); study guide 9.95x (ISBN 0-534-00839-9); solns. manual 9.95x (ISBN 0-534-00859-3). Wadsworth Pub.

Siedel, Frank. The Ohio Story. 288p. 1973. pap. 3.95 o.s.i. (ISBN 0-913428-08-6). Landfall Pr.

Siedel, George J. & Willing, Jean S. Michigan Guide to Real Estate Licensing Examinations for Salespersons & Brokers. LC 81-16394. 160p. 1982. pap. text ed. 12.95 (ISBN 0-471-87760-3). Wiley.

Siedentop, Daryl. Developing Teaching Skills in Physical Education. 2nd ed. LC 82-60884. 295p. 1982. pap. text ed. 10.95 (ISBN 0-87484-550-5). Mayfield Pub.

Siedentop, Larry, jt. ed. see Miller, David.

Siedentopf, Heinrich, jt. auth. see Caiden, Gerald E.

Siedhoff, Thomas, jt. auth. see Ruecker, Norbert.

Siefert, Susan S. The Dilemma of the Talented Heroine: A Study in Nineteenth Century Fiction. 1978. 14.95 (ISBN 0-88831-018-8). Eden Pr.

Siefkin, David. The City at the End of the Rainbow: San Francisco & Its Grand Hotels. LC 75-45100. (Illus.). 265p. 1976. 9.95 o.p. (ISBN 0-399-11742-3). Putnam Pub Group.

Sieg, Theodore Le see Le Sieg, Theodore.

Siegal, Alex, ed. see Fishbein, Harold.

Siegal, Aranka. Upon the Head of the Goat. 1983. pap. 2.25 (ISBN 0-686-43018-2). NAL.

Siegal, B. S. & Gillespie, A. R. Remote Sensing in Geology. 702p. 1980. text ed. 51.95 (ISBN 0-471-79052-4). Wiley.

Siegal, Harvey A. Outposts of the Forgotten: Socially Terminal People in Slum Hotels & Single Room Occupancy Tenements. LC 76-1777. 220p. 1978. 12.95 (ISBN 0-87855-141-7). Transaction Bks.

Siegal, Marcia B. Watching the Dance Go by. (Houghton Mifflin Paperbacks Ser.). 1977. pap. 7.95 o.s.i. (ISBN 0-395-25833-2). HM.

Siegal, Mordecai. The Good Cat Book: How to Live & with & Take Loving Care of Your Cat. 1981. 14.95 o.s.i. (ISBN 0-671-24640-2). S&S.

Siegal, Mordecai & Margolis, Matthew. Good Dog, Bad Dog. (Illus.). 1974. pap. 2.95 (ISBN 0-451-12370-0, AE2370, Sig). NAL.

Siegal, Sanford. Dr. Siegal's No-Hunger Diet. 320p. 1983. 14.75 (ISBN 0-02-610660-4). Macmillan.

Siegan, Bernard. Planning Without Prices. 160p. 1977. 16.95x o.p. (ISBN 0-669-00247-X). Lexington Bks.

Siegan, Bernard H. Economic Liberties & the Constitution. LC 80-15756. viii, 384p. 1980. pap. 9.95 (ISBN 0-226-75664-5). U of Chicago Pr.

--Land Use Without Zoning. LC 72-4936. (Illus.). 304p. 1972. 16.95x (ISBN 0-669-82040-7). Lexington Bks.

Siegan, Bernard H., ed. Government, Regulation & the Economy. LC 78-14150. 160p. 1980. 19.95x (ISBN 0-669-02664-6). Lexington Bks.

--Regulation, Economics, & the Law. LC 77-11398. 144p. 1979. 18.95x (ISBN 0-669-02091-5). Lexington Bks.

Siegbahn, K. Alpha, Beta & Gamma Ray Spectroscopy, 2 Vols. 1965. 170.25 (ISBN 0-7204-0083-X, North Holland). Set. Elsevier.

Siegel, jt. auth. see Senna.

Siegel, A. Politics & the Media in Canada. 192p. Date not set. 10.95 o.p. (ISBN 0-07-077866-3). McGraw.

Siegel, A. & Fawcett, B. Transformation el Utilisation des Legumineuses Alimentaires (Application Particuliere aux Pays en Development) 63p. 1978. pap. 6.00 o.p. (ISBN 0-88936-123-1, IDRC-TS1F, IDRC). Unipub.

Siegel, Abraham J. & Lipsky, David B., eds. Unfinished Business: An Agenda for Labor, Management, & the Public. 1978. 12.50x (ISBN 0-262-19175-X). MIT Pr.

Siegel, Adrienne. Philadelphia: A Chronological & Documentary History. LC 74-23205. (American Cities Chronology Ser.). 154p. 1975. 8.50 (ISBN 0-379-00621-9). Oceana.

Siegel, Beatrice. Indians of the Woodland Before & After the Pilgrims. LC 74-186176. (Illus.). 96p. (gr. 3-7). 1972. PLB 5.85 (ISBN 0-8027-6108-9). Walker & Co.

--Lillian Wald of Henry Street. LC 82-20359. (Illus.). 224p. (gr. 7 up). 1983. 12.95 (ISBN 0-02-782630-9). Macmillan.

--A New Look at the Pilgrims: Why They Came to America. LC 76-57060. (Illus.). (gr. 3-7). 1977. 5.95 o.p. (ISBN 0-8027-6291-3); PLB 5.85 (ISBN 0-8027-6292-1). Walker & Co.

Siegel, Benjamin, jt. ed. see Rose, Noel R.

Siegel, Benjamin M., ed. Modern Developments in Electron Microscopy. 1964. 55.00 (ISBN 0-12-641450-5). Acad Pr.

Siegel, Bernard J. Slavery During the Third Dynasty of Ur. LC 48-8755. 1947. pap. 8.00 (ISBN 0-527-00565-7). Kraus Repr.

Siegel, Bernard J., et al, eds. Annual Review of Anthropology, Vol. 11. LC 72-82136. (Illus.). 1982. text ed. 22.00 (ISBN 0-8243-1911-7). Annual Reviews.

Siegel, Bertram M. Reviewing Basic EMT Skills: A Guide for Self-Evaluation. 1981. 12.95 (ISBN 0-940432-00-5, Pub. by Emergency Training); 15 or more copies 10.95 (ISBN 0-686-96964-2). Educ Direction.

Siegel, Boaz. Proving Your Arbitration Case. LC 61-13660. 48p. 1961. pap. 3.50 (ISBN 0-87179-087-4). BNA.

Siegel, Brian. How to Succeed in Law School. rev. ed. LC 75-17848. 96p. 1983. pap. text ed. 4.95 (ISBN 0-8120-2365-X). Barron.

Siegel, C. L. Topics in Complex Function Theory, 3 vols. Incl. Vol. 1. Elliptical Functions & Uniformization Theory. 186p. 1969. 34.95x (ISBN 0-471-79070-2); Vol. 2. Automorphic Functions & Abelian Integrals. 193p. 1972. 39.95x (ISBN 0-471-79080-X); Vol. 3. Abelian Functions & Modular Functions of Several Variables. Tretkoff, M. & Gottschling, E., trs. 244p. 1973. 44.95x (ISBN 0-471-79090-7). LC 69-19931. (Pure & Applied Mathematics Ser., Pub. by Wiley-Interscience). Wiley.

Siegel, Carole & Fischer, Susan K. Psychiatric Records in Mental Health Care. LC 80-23099. (Illus.). 352p. (Orig.). 1981. pap. 29.95 (ISBN 0-87630-241-X). Brunner Mazel.

Siegel, David D. Handbook on New York Practice, Nineteen Eighty Two Pocket Part. (Hornbook Ser.). 119p. 1982. pap. text ed. 7.95 (ISBN 0-314-66866-7). West Pub.

Siegel, Dorothy S. Winners: Eight Special Young People. LC 77-27985. 192p. (gr. 7 up). 1978. PLB 7.79 o.p. (ISBN 0-671-32861-1). Messner.

Siegel, Eli. The Aesthetic Method in Self-Conflict: Accompanied by Psychiatry, Economics, Aesthetics. 2nd ed. LC 79-55196. 91p. 1976. pap. text ed. 2.50 o.s.i. (ISBN 0-910492-29-8). Definition.

--Definitions & Comment: Being a Description of the World. Reiss, Ellen, intro. by. 320p. Date not set. 15.95 (ISBN 0-910492-31-X); pap. 8.95 (ISBN 0-910492-32-8). Definition.

--Hot Afternoons Have Been in Montana: Poems. LC 57-10740. (Orig.). 1958. 5.00 o.p. (ISBN 0-910492-05-0); pap. 2.50 (ISBN 0-910492-20-4). Definition.

Siegel, Eli, et al. Goodbye Profit System: Update. Baird, Martha, ed. LC 82-72727. 200p. (Orig.). 1982. pap. 4.95 (ISBN 0-910492-33-6). Definition.

Siegel, Ernest & Gold, Ruth. Educating the Learning Disabled. 1982. text ed. 22.95x (ISBN 0-02-410400-0). Macmillan.

Siegel, Esther, jt. auth. see Parker, David L.

Siegel, Frederic R. Applied Geochemistry. LC 74-13486. 353p. 1974. 35.95 (ISBN 0-471-79095-8, Pub. by Wiley-Interscience). Wiley.

Siegel, Gary L. & Loman, L. Anthony. Missouri at Ground Zero: What Nuclear War Would Do to One State. (Illus.). 165p. (Orig.). 1982. pap. 8.95 (ISBN 0-686-37613-7). IAR Press.

Siegel, Gilbert B. Breaking with Orthodoxy in Public Administration. LC 80-5081. 706p. 1980. text ed. 28.25 o.p. (ISBN 0-8191-1042-6). U Pr of Amer.

--The Vicissitudes of Governmental Reform in Brazil: A Study of the DASP. LC 78-62264. 1978. pap. text ed. 9.50 o.p. (ISBN 0-8191-0572-4). U Pr of Amer.

Siegel, Harry. Business Guide for Interior Designers: A Practical Checklist for Analyzing the Various Conditions of a Design Project & the Related Clauses for a Letter of Agreement. 1976. pap. 5.95 (ISBN 0-8230-7460-9, Whitney Lib). Watson-Guptill.

Siegel, Irving. Productivity Measurement: An Evolving Art, Vol. 16. (Studies in Productivity-Highlights of the Literature). (Orig.). 1982. pap. 35.00 (ISBN 0-08-029497-9). Pergamon.

Siegel, Irwin M., jt. auth. see Carr, Ronald E.

Siegel, J. H. Schaum's Outline of Managerial Accounting. (Schaum Outline Ser.). 320p. 1983. 7.95x (ISBN 0-07-057305-0, GB). McGraw.

Siegel, James E. Comeuppance. 96p. 1983. 13.95 (ISBN 0-8022-2413-X). Philos Lib.

Siegel, James T. The Rope of God. LC 69-15942. (Library Reprint: Vol. 96). 1978. 29.50x (ISBN 0-520-03714-6). U of Cal Pr.

Siegel, Joel G. How to Analyze Businesses, Financial Statements & the Quality of Earnings. LC 82-9125. 284p. 1982. 29.95 (ISBN 0-13-396135-4, Busn). P-H.

Siegel, Joel G. & Shim, Jae K. Schaum's Outline of Financial Accounting. (Schaum's Outline Ser.). 272p. 1983. pap. 7.95 (ISBN 0-07-057304-2). McGraw.

Siegel, Larry J. Criminology. 650p. 1983. text ed. write for info. (ISBN 0-314-69678-4). West Pub.

Siegel, Larry J. & Senna, Joseph J. Juvenile Delinquency: Theory, Practice & Law. (Criminal Justice Ser.). (Illus.). 554p. 1981. text ed. 22.95 (ISBN 0-8299-0414-X). West Pub.

Siegel, Larry J., jt. auth. see Senna, Joseph J.

Siegel, Lee. Fires of Love-Waters of Peace. LC 82-21767. 1983. text ed. 12.50 (ISBN 0-8248-0828-2). UH Pr.

Siegel, Linda S., ed. Alternatives to Piaget: Critical Essays on the Theory. 1977. 19.50 (ISBN 0-12-641950-7). Acad Pr.

Siegel, Mark A & Jacobs, Nancy R., eds. Arms Sales: A Reflection of Foreign Policy? 80p. 1982. pap. 11.95 (ISBN 0-936474-26-2). Instruct Aides TX.

Siegel, Mark A. & Jacobs, Nancy R., eds. Consumer Regulation Needed Protection or Too Much Bureaucracy. Rev. ed. (Instructional Aides Ser.). 80p. 1982. pap. text ed. 11.95 (ISBN 0-936474-23-8). Instruct Aides TX.

--Crime: A Serious American Problem. rev. ed. (Instructional Aides Ser.). 88p. 1982. pap. 11.95 (ISBN 0-936474-24-6). Instruct Aides TX.

--Minorities: A Changing Role in American Society. rev. ed. (Instructional Aides Ser.). 88p. 1982. pap. text ed. 11.95 (ISBN 0-936474-25-4). Instruct Aides TX.

Siegel, Mary-Ellen, jt. auth. see Greenberger, Monroe E.

Siegel, Morris. Mackenzie Collection: A Study of West African Carved Gambling Chips. LC 41-25906. 1940. pap. 10.00 (ISBN 0-527-00554-1). Kraus Repr.

Siegel, Patricia J. Alfred de Musset: A Reference Guide. 1982. lib. bdg. 48.00 (ISBN 0-8161-8233-7, Hall Reference). G K Hall.

Siegel, Paul S., jt. auth. see Miller, Howard L.

Siegel, R. & Howell, J. R. Thermal Radiation Heat Transfer. 1971. text ed. 26.50 o.p. (ISBN 0-07-057318-2, C); solution manual 5.00 o.p. (ISBN 0-07-057319-0). McGraw.

Siegel, R. K. & West, L. J., eds. Hallucinations: Behavior, Experience, & Theory. LC 75-12670. 322p. 1975. 60.00x (ISBN 0-471-79096-6, Pub. by Wiley Medical). Wiley.

Siegel, Richard & Owen, David. Fantastic Planets. LC 78-64553. (Illus.). 1979. 17.95 (ISBN 0-89169-535-4); pap. 9.95 (ISBN 0-89169-534-6). Reed Bks.

Siegel, Richard & Suares, J. C. Alien Creatures. LC 77-94830. (Illus.). 1978. 14.95 (ISBN 0-89169-521-4); pap. 6.95 (ISBN 0-89169-501-X). Reed Bks.

Siegel, Robert. The Kingdom of Wundle. 48p. (gr. 1-6). 1982. 8.95 (ISBN 0-89107-261-6, Crossway Bks). Good News.

--Whalesong. 144p. 1983. pap. 3.95 (ISBN 0-425-05874-3). Berkley Pub.

Siegel, Robert & Howell, John R. Thermal Radiation Heat Transfer. 2nd ed. LC 79-17242. (Thermal & Fluids Engineering Hemisphere Ser.). (Illus.). 928p. 1980. text ed. 38.50 (ISBN 0-07-057316-6, C); solutions manual 18.50 (ISBN 0-07-057317-4). McGraw.

Siegel, Robert, jt. auth. see Butterfield, John H.

Siegel, Sidney. Nonparametric Statistics for the Behavioral Sciences. (Psychology Ser.). 1956. text ed. 37.50 (ISBN 0-07-057348-4, C). McGraw.

Siegel, Sidney & Fouraker, Lawrence E. Bargaining & Group Decision Making: Experiments in Bilateral Monopoly. LC 77-14561. 1977. Repr. of 1960 ed. lib. bdg. 18.00x (ISBN 0-8371-9837-2, SIBG). Greenwood.

Siegel, Stanley E. A History of Texas to Eighteen Sixty-Five. 262p. 1981. pap. text ed. 8.95x (ISBN 0-89641-062-5). American Pr.

Siegel, William L. Franchising. (Small Business Ser.). 160p. 1983. pap. 7.95 (ISBN 0-471-09965-1). Wiley.

Siegele, H. H. Cabinets & Built-Ins. LC 80-52589. (Illus.). 104p. 1980. pap. 6.95 (ISBN 0-8069-8188-1). Sterling.

--Roof Framing. rev. ed. LC 74-25285. (Illus.). 176p. 1980. pap. 7.95 (ISBN 0-8069-8626-3). Sterling.

--The Steel Square. LC 79-63089. (Illus.). 1979. pap. 6.95 (ISBN 0-8069-8854-1). Sterling.

Siegel-Gorelick, Bryna. The Working Parents' Guide to Child Care. 1983. 15.45i (ISBN 0-316-79004-4); pap. 8.70i (ISBN 0-316-79003-6). Little.

Siegelman, Ellen Y. Personal Risk: Mastering Change in Love & Work. 240p. 1983. pap. text ed. 12.95 scp (ISBN 0-06-046136-5, HarpC). Har-Row.

Siegelman, Irwin, ed. see Williams, George A. & Barnes, Richard.

Siegfried. Complete Memoirs of George Sherston. 656p. 1937. 23.95 (ISBN 0-571-06146-X); pap. 13.95 (ISBN 0-571-09913-0). Faber & Faber.

Siegfried, Joan C., jt. auth. see Prokopoff, Stephen S.

Siegfried, Robert & Dott, Robert H., Jr., eds. Humphry Davy on Geology: The 1805 Lectures for the General Audience. LC 79-5022. 192p. 1980. 22.50 (ISBN 0-299-08030-7). U of Wis Pr.

Siegfried, W. Typing Medical Forms. 1969. 9.80 (ISBN 0-07-057342-5, G). McGraw.

Sieghart, Paul. The International Law of Human Rights. 600p. 1983. 74.00 (ISBN 0-19-876096-5). Oxford U Pr.

Siegle, Arthur. Basic Plane Surveying. LC 77-87883. 1979. pap. text ed. 12.00 (ISBN 0-8273-1698-4); instructor's guide 3.75 (ISBN 0-8273-1699-2). Delmar.

Siegler, Arthur B., Jr., jt. ed. see Baker, James R.

Siegler, Miriam & Osmond, Humphrey. Models of Madness, Models of Medicine. 1976. pap. 5.95xi o.p. (ISBN 0-06-131953-8, TB 1953, Torch). Har-Row.

Siegler, Robert S. Children's Thinking: What Develops? 384p. 1978. text ed. 19.95 (ISBN 0-89859-161-9). L Erlbaum Assocs.

Siegler, Rodie, jt. auth. see Pressman, Robert M.

Siegler, Susan. Needlework Patterns from the Metropolitan Museum of Art. LC 76-10097. (Illus.). 1976. 19.95 (ISBN 0-8212-0639-7, 599700). NYGS.

--Needlework Patterns from the Metropolitan Museum of Art. LC 76-10097. (Illus.). 1978. pap. 14.95 (ISBN 0-8212-0736-9, 599719). NYGS.

Siegman, A. E. Introduction to Lasers & Masers. 1971. text ed. 44.50 (ISBN 0-07-057362-X, C). McGraw.

Siegman, Anthony E. Lasers. LC 81-51269. (Illus.). 575p. 1983. 30.00x (ISBN 0-935702-12-1). Univ Sci Bks.

Siegmeister, Elie. Invitation to Music. LC 61-15658. (Illus.). (gr. 8-12). 1961. PLB 6.27 o.p. (ISBN 0-8178-3182-7). Harvey.

Siegmeister, Elie & Downes, Olin. A Treasury of American Song. 3rd ed. Siegmeister, Elie, ed. 412p. 1983. pap. 11.95 (ISBN 0-89524-152-8, 8607). Cherry Lane.

Siegmeister, Elie, ed. see Siegmeister, Elie & Downes, Olin.

Siegrist, Rachel. Spelling by Sound & Structure: Grade Four. 1979. write for info. (ISBN 0-686-25261-6); tchrs' ed. avail. (ISBN 0-686-25262-4). Rod & Staff.

Siekert, Robert & Whisnant, J. P., eds. Cerebral Vascular Diseases: 6th Conference. (Illus.). 288p. 1969. 10.75 o.p. (ISBN 0-8089-0507-4). Grune.

Siekmann, J. & Wrightson, G., eds. The Automation of Reasoning I: Classical Papers on Computational Logic 1957-1966. (Symbolic Computation Ser.). 516p. 1983. 35.00 (ISBN 0-387-12043-2). Springer-Verlag.

--The Automation of Reasoning II: Classical Papers on Computational Logic 1967-1970. (Symbolic Computation Ser.). 640p. 1983. 39.00 (ISBN 0-387-12044-0). Springer-Verlag.

Siemankowski, Francis T., jt. auth. see Cazeau, Charles J.

Siemaszko, Frederick. Computing in Clinical Laboratories. LC 77-94061. 1978. 31.95 o.p. (ISBN 0-471-04321-4, Pub. by Wiley Medical). Wiley.

Siemens. Basic Electricity. 1979. 11.95 (ISBN 0-471-26022-3, Pub. by Wiley Heyden). Wiley.

--Quantities, Formulae, Definitions. 1979. 4.95 (ISBN 0-471-26120-3, Wiley Heyden). Wiley.

--Telephone Traffic Theory: Tables & Charts, Pt. 1. 1979. 44.95 (ISBN 0-471-26021-5, Wiley Heyden). Wiley.

Siemens, Sydney & Brandzel, Rose. Sexuality: Nursing Assessment & Intervention. (Illus.). 448p. 1982. pap. text ed. 14.75 (ISBN 0-397-54326-3, Lippincott Nursing). Lippincott.

Siemens Team of Authors. Electrical Engineering Handbook. 1976. 57.95 (ISBN 0-471-26020-7, Pub. by Wiley Heyden). Wiley.

Siemens Teams of Authors. Optoelectronics: Liquid-Crystal Display. (Siemens Team of Authors Ser.). 1981. text ed. 57.00x (ISBN 0-471-26125-4, Pub. by Wiley Heyden). Wiley.

--Optoelects Components. (Siemens Team of Authors Ser.). 1981. text ed. 45.95 (ISBN 0-471-26132-7, Pub. by Wiley Heyden). Wiley.

--Software Engineering. (Siemens Team of Authors Ser.). 1980. text ed. 16.95x (ISBN 0-471-26123-8, Pub. by Wiley Heyden). Wiley.

--Video Workstation Ergonomics. (Siemens Teams of Authors Ser.). 1981. text ed. 14.95x (ISBN 0-471-26126-2, Pub. by Wiley Heyden). Wiley.

Siemon, Charles L. & Larsen, Wendy U. Vested Rights: Balancing Public & Private Development Expectations. LC 82-50897. 106p. (Orig.). 1982. pap. text ed. 42.00 (ISBN 0-87420-612-X, VO1). Urban Land.

Sien, Chia Lin, jt. ed. see MacAndrews, Colin.

Siena, James V., ed. Antitrust & Local Government. LC 82-16825. 224p. 1982. text ed. 32.95 (ISBN 0-932020-16-X); pap. text ed. 19.95 (ISBN 0-932020-17-8). Seven Locks Pr.

Sienkewicz, Thomas J. Classical Gods & Heroes in the National Gallery of Art. LC 82-23818. (Illus.). 50p. (Orig.). 1983. pap. text ed. 8.75 (ISBN 0-8191-2967-4). U Pr of Amer.

Sienkiewicz, Henryk. Quo Vadis? Hogarth, C. J., tr. 1980. Repr. of 1941 ed. 9.95x (ISBN 0-460-00970-2, Evman). Biblio Dist.

Sienko, M. J. & Plane, R. A. Chemistry: Principles & Applications. 1979. text ed. 27.50 (ISBN 0-07-057321-2); instructor's manual 15.00 (ISBN 0-07-057322-0); student & instructor solution suppl. 13.50 (ISBN 0-07-057327-1); study guide 11.50 (ISBN 0-07-057323-9). McGraw.

Sienko, Michael J. Chemistry Problems. 2nd ed. LC 70-151306. (Chemistry Ser). 1972. pap. text ed. 12.95 (ISBN 0-8053-8808-7). Benjamin-Cummings.

Sienko, Michell J. Freshman Chemistry Problems & How to Solve Them, 2 pts. Incl. Pt. 1. Stoichiometry & Structure. pap. 9.95 (ISBN 0-8053-8801-X); Pt. 2. Equilibrium. pap. 7.50 (ISBN 0-8053-8805-2). 1964. Benjamin-Cummings.

Sienko, Michell J. & Plane, Robert A. Chemistry. 4th ed. (gr. 11up). 1971. text ed. 20.95 (ISBN 0-07-057334-4, C); study guide 11.95 (ISBN 0-07-054318-6). McGraw.

--Chemistry. 5th ed. 1976. text ed. 27.50 (ISBN 0-07-057335-2, C); instructors' manual 15.00 (ISBN 0-07-057344-1); study guide 11.95 (ISBN 0-07-054319-4). McGraw.

--Experimental Chemistry. 5th ed. 1976. text ed. 16.50 (ISBN 0-07-057331-X, C); instructor's manual 15.00 (ISBN 0-07-057346-8). McGraw.

Siepmann, R., jt. auth. see Zycha, H.

Sierpinski, W. Two Hundred & Fifty Problems in Elementary Number Theory. 1970. 21.50 (ISBN 0-444-00071-2). Elsevier.

Sierra, Gregorio Martinez see Martinez Sierra, Gregorio.

Sierra-Franco, Miriam. Therapeutic Communication in Nursing. 1977. pap. text ed. 14.95 (ISBN 0-07-057280-1, HP). McGraw.

Siers, James. Fiji in Colour. (Illus.). 124p. 1982. cancelled (ISBN 0-908582-52-8, Pub by Salem Hse Ltd.). Merrimack Bk Serv.

Sies, Luther F., ed. see Schuell, Hildred.

Siesjo, B. K. Brain Energy Metabolism. 607p. 1978. 107.95 (ISBN 0-471-99515-0). Wiley.

Siesler, H. W. & Holland-Moritz, K. Infared & Raman Spectroscopy of Polymers. (Practical Spectroscopy Ser.: Vol. 4). (Illus.). 400p. 1980. 55.00 (ISBN 0-8247-6935-X). Dekker.

Siever, Norman L. Intermediate Algebra: A Clear Approach. 1981. text ed. 21.95x (ISBN 0-673-16236-2). Scott F.

Sieverding, C. H., jt. auth. see Moore, M. J.

Sievers, Harry J. William McKinley, 1843-1901: Chronology, Documents, Bibliographical Aids. LC 72-116065. (Presidential Chronology Ser.). 83p. 1970. text ed. 8.00 (ISBN 0-379-12074-7). Oceana.

Sievers, Robert E. Nuclear Magnetic Resonance Shift Reagents. 1973. 30.50 (ISBN 0-12-643050-0). Acad Pr.

Sievers, Sharon L. Flowers in Salt: The Beginnings of Feminist Consciousness in Modern Japan. LC 82-60104. (Illus.). 256p. 1983. 22.50x (ISBN 0-8047-1165-8). Stanford U Pr.

Sievert, Heidi, compiled by. The Big Book for Little Dancers. (Coppenrath Ser.). (Illus.). 58p. 1983. 17.95 o.p. (ISBN 0-914676-85-7, Star & Eleph Bks). Green Tiger Pr.

Sievert, Norman W. Career Education & Industrial Education. 1975. pap. 2.60 o.p. (ISBN 0-395-20048-2). HM.

Sieverts, Steven. Health Planning Issues & Public Law 93-641. LC 77-1306. 120p. 1977. pap. 14.50 o.p. (ISBN 0-87258-201-9, 076135). Am Hospital.

Siewert, Carol H., et al. Basic Textiles: A Learning Package. 228p. 1973. 15.50 (ISBN 0-395-14220-2). HM.

Siewiorek, D., et al. Computer Structures: Principles & Examples. (Computer Science Ser.). 1982. 38.95 (ISBN 0-07-057302-6); wkbk. 13.95x (ISBN 0-07-057303-4). McGraw.

Siewiorek, Daniel, jt. auth. see Stone, Harold.

Siewiorek, Daniel P. & Barbacci, Mario. The Design & Analysis of Instruction Set Processors. Vastyan, James E., ed. 320p. 1982. 13.95x (ISBN 0-07-057303-4). McGraw.

Sifakis, Carl. A Catalogue of Crime. (Orig.). 1979. pap. 1.95 o.p. (ISBN 0-451-08821-2, J8821, Sig). NAL.

Siffert, Robert. How Your Child's Body Grows. LC 78-74040. (Illus.). 1980. 8.95 (ISBN 0-448-15491-9, G&D). Putnam Pub Group.

Siffert, Robert S., jt. ed. see Katz, Jacob F.

Siffin, William J. The Thai Bureaucracy. LC 75-29033. 291p. 1976. Repr. of 1966 ed. lib. bdg. 18.50x (ISBN 0-8371-7429-5, SITB). Greenwood.

Sifford, Darrell. Father & Son. LC 82-11063. 270p. 1982. 9.95 (ISBN 0-664-27004-2, Pub. by Bridgebooks). Westminster.

Sigafoos, Robert A. Corporate Real Estate Development: The Pursuit of America's Leading Corporations for Profit in Housing & Land Use. LC 76-3874. (Special Ser. in Real Estate & Urban Land Economics). (Illus.). 224p. 1976. 23.95x (ISBN 0-669-00644-0). Lexington Bks.

Sigafoos, Robert A. & Oslin, Ronald. Tennessee Guide to Real Estate Licensing Examinations for Salespersons & Brokers. LC 81-11540. 120p. 1982. pap. text ed. 10.95 (ISBN 0-471-87759-X). Wiley.

Sigafoos, Robert A., et al. Real Estate Review's Tennessee Guide to Real Estate Licensing Examination. LC 81-11540. 1981. pap. text ed. 7.95 o.p. (ISBN 0-88262-646-9). Warren.

Sigal, Leon V. Reporters & Officials: The Organization & Politics of Newsmaking. 1973. pap. text ed. 8.95 (ISBN 0-669-89276-9). Heath.

--Reporters & Officials: The Organization & Politics of Newsmaking. LC 72-7014. (Illus.). 240p. 1973. 19.95 (ISBN 0-669-85035-7). Lexington Bks.

Sigall, Michael W. & Ottensoser, Milton D. The American Political Reality. 1972. pap. text ed. 3.50x (ISBN 0-685-55638-7, 31334). Phila Bk Co.

Sigaud, Louis A. Belle Boyd, Confederate Spy. 1945. 3.00 o.p. (ISBN 0-685-09008-6). Dietz.

Sigband, Norman B. Communication for Management & Business. 3rd ed. 1982. text ed. 25.50x (ISBN 0-673-15579-X). Scott F.

Sigband, Norman B. & Bateman, David N. Communicating in Business. 1981. text ed. 23.95x (ISBN 0-673-15175-1); study guide 8.95x (ISBN 0-673-15429-7). Scott F.

Sigband, Norman B., et al. Successful Business English. 1983. pap. text ed. 14.95x (ISBN 0-673-15589-7). Scott F.

Sigel. Metal Ions in Biological Systems, Vol. 15. 520p. 1983. 75.00 (ISBN 0-8247-1750-3). Dekker.

Sigel, Efrem, ed. Videotext: The Coming Revolution in Home-Office Information Retrieval. LC 79-18935. (Communications Library). 1979. text ed. 27.95x (ISBN 0-914236-41-5). Knowledge Indus.

Sigel, Efrem, et al. The Future of Videotext: Worldwide Prospects for Home-Office Electronic Information Services. LC 82-14836. (Communications Library). 197p. 1983. text ed. 34.95 (ISBN 0-86729-025-0). Knowledge Indus.

--Books, Libraries & Electronics: Essays on the Future of Written Communication. LC 82-15229. (Communications Library). 139p. 1982. text ed. 24.95 (ISBN 0-86729-024-2). Knowledge Indus.

--Video Discs: The Technology, the Applications & the Future. LC 80-23112. (Video Bookshelf Ser.). (Illus.). 183p. 1980. text ed. 29.95x (ISBN 0-914236-56-3). Knowledge Indus.

--Video Discs: The Technology, the Applications & the Future. 1980. pap. 16.95 (ISBN 0-442-27784-9). Knowledge Indus.

Sigel, I. E., et al, eds. New Directions in Piagetian Theory & Practice. LC 81-61600. 320p. 1981. text ed. 24.95 (ISBN 0-89859-072-8). L Erlbaum Assocs.

Sigel, Michael, jt. ed. see Cohen, Nicholas.

Sigelman, Daniel W. Your Money or Your Health: A Senior Citizen's Guide to Avoiding High Charging Medicare Doctors. 134p. 1982. 4.00 (ISBN 0-686-96304-0). Pub Citizen Health.

Sigerist, Henry A. A History of Medicine, 2 vols. Incl. Vol. 1. Primitive & Archaic Medicine. 1951. 29.95x (ISBN 0-19-500102-8); Vol. 2. Early Greek, Hindu & Persian Medicine. 1961. 27.50x (ISBN 0-19-500103-6). Oxford U Pr.

Sigerist, Henry E. Medicine & Human Welfare. 1941. text ed. 29.50x (ISBN 0-686-83623-5). Elliots Bks.

Sigerius De Cortraco. Summa Modorum Significandi: Sophismata. (Studies in the History of Linguistics Ser.). 1977. 21.00 (ISBN 90-272-0955-3, 14). Benjamins North Am.

Sigford, Ann. Eight Words for Thirsty. LC 79-13892. (Story of Environmental Action Ser.). (Illus.). (gr. 7 up). 1979. PLB 9.95 (ISBN 0-87518-183-X). Dillon.

Sigg, E., jt. ed. see Garattini, S.

Siggia, Sidney & Hanna, J. Gordon. Quantitative Organic Analysis via Functional Groups. 4th ed. LC 78-5940. 883p. 1979. 81.00 (ISBN 0-471-03273-5, Pub. by Wiley-Interscience). Wiley.

Sigham & Van Dihn, eds. From Bandung to Colombo: Conference of the Non-Aligned Countries. LC 76-11432. 1975. pap. 7.95 (ISBN 0-89388-221-6). Okpaku Communications.

Sightler, Verna W. Reach for the Stars. (YA) 6.95 (ISBN 0-685-07456-0, Avalon). Bouregy.

Sigillito, V. G. Explicit A Priori Inequalities with Applications to Boundary Value Problems. (Research Notes in Mathematics: No. 13). (Orig.). 1977. pap. text ed. 15.50 (ISBN 0-273-01022-0). Pitman Pub MA.

Sigler, Jay A. Understanding Criminal Law. 1981. text ed. 17.95 (ISBN 0-316-79054-0); teachers manual avail. (ISBN 0-316-79055-9). Little.

Sigler, P. B., ed. The Molecular Basis of Mutant Hemoglobin Dysfunction. (The University of Chicago Sickle Cell Center Hemoglobin Symposia: Vol. 1). 1981. 65.00 (ISBN 0-444-00631-1). Elsevier.

Sigman, David S. & Brazier, Mary, eds. The Evolution of Protein Structure & Function: A Symposium in Honor of Prof. Emil L. Smith. LC 80-18140. (UCLA Forum in Medical Science Ser.: Vol. 21). 1980. 28.50 (ISBN 0-12-643150-7). Acad Pr.

Sigmund, Paul, jt. ed. see Aspe, Pedro.

Sigmund, Paul E. Multinationals in Latin America: The Politics of Nationalization. 448p. 1980. 27.50 (ISBN 0-299-08260-1); pap. 9.95 (ISBN 0-299-08264-4). U of Wis Pr.

--Natural Law in Political Thought. LC 81-40937. 224p. 1982. lib. bdg. 22.25 (ISBN 0-8191-2099-5); pap. text ed. 11.00 (ISBN 0-8191-2100-2). U Pr of Amer.

Signitzer, Benno. Regulation of Direct Broadcasting from Satellites: The UN Involvement. LC 76-14372. (Special Studies). (Illus.). 175p. 1976. text ed. 27.95 o.p. (ISBN 0-275-56800-8). Praeger.

Signor, John. Rails in the Shadow of Mt. Shasta: One Hundred Years of Railroading Along Southern Pacific's Shasta Division. LC 81-20194. (Illus.). 176p. 1982. 25.00 (ISBN 0-8310-7141-9). Howell North.

Signy, F. C. History of the Queen's Park Rangers. 15.00x (ISBN 0-392-07910-0, SpS). Sportshelf.

Sigrist, Rene M. Les Sattukku dans l'Esumesa durant la periode d'Isin et Larsa. LC 79-65002. (Bibliotheca Mesopotamica Ser.: Vol. 11). 166p. (Fr.). 1983. write for info (ISBN 0-89003-047-2); pap. write for info (ISBN 0-89003-048-0). Undena Pubns.

Sigur, Gastonz & Kim, Young C. Japanese & U. S. Policy in Asia. 208p. 1982. 22.95 (ISBN 0-03-061849-5). Praeger.

Sigwart. Bridge over the River. new ed. Wetzel, Joseph, tr. from Ger. 110p. 1974. pap. 2.95 (ISBN 0-910142-59-9). Anthroposophic.

Sigworth, Oliver. Four Styles of a Decade, 1740-1750. LC 60-15544. (Illus.). 1960. pap. 3.00 o.p. (ISBN 0-87104-078-6). NY Pub Lib.

Sigworth, Oliver F. William Collins. (English Authors Ser.). 14.95 (ISBN 0-8057-1108-2, Twayne). G K Hall.

Sih, G. & Czoboly, E. Absorbed Specific Energy & or Strain Energy Density Criterion. 1982. lib. bdg. 65.00 (ISBN 90-247-2598-4, Pub. by Martinus Nijhoff Netherlands). Kluwer Boston.

Sih, G. C. & Francois, D., eds. Progress in Fracture Mechanics: Fracture Mechanics Research & Technological Activities of Nations Around the World. (International Series on Strength & Fracture of Materials). (Illus.). 96p. 1983. 19.95 (ISBN 0-08-028691-7). Pergamon.

Sihler, William W., ed. Classics in Commercial Bank Lending. LC 81-83354. 556p. 1981. pap. 24.00 members (ISBN 0-936742-03-8); pap. 28.00 non-members (ISBN 0-686-86675-4). Robt Morris Assocs.

Sik, Chai Sin & Hun, Hyon Jong. Cultural Policy in the Democratic People's Republic of Korea. (Studies & Documents on Cultural Policies Ser.). (Illus.). 40p. 1980. pap. 5.00 (ISBN 92-3-101645-8, U991, UNESCO). Unipub.

Sik, Ota. The Communist Power System. 192p. 1981. 23.95 (ISBN 0-03-044106-4). Praeger.

--The Third Way: Marxist-Leninist Theory & Modern Industrial Society. Sling, Marian, tr. from Ger. LC 76-8032. 512p. 1976. 37.50 (ISBN 0-87332-084-0). M E Sharpe.

Sikat, Dorian. To Where Streets Are Made of Gold: The Story of A Filipino Immigrant. 1982. 7.50 (ISBN 0-682-49405-4). Exposition.

Sikes, Bette, ed. see Maru, Olavi.

Siklossy, Laurent. Let's Talk Lisp. ref. ed. 456p. 1976. 21.95 (ISBN 0-13-532762-8). P-H.

Sikonowiz, Walter. The Complete Book of Word Processing & Business Graphics. 250p. 1983. 21.95 (ISBN 0-13-158667-X); pap. 14.95 (ISBN 0-13-158659-9). P-H.

--Guide to the IBM Personal Computer. (Illus.). 352p. 1983. pap. text ed. 19.95 (ISBN 0-07-057484-7, P&RB). McGraw.

Sikora, Mieczyslaw S. Talisman. Topham, J., ed. 28p. Date not set. pap. 3.95 (ISBN 0-933486-27-8); pap. text ed. 3.95 (ISBN 0-933486-41-3). Am Poetry Pr.

Sikora, R. I. & Barry, Brian, eds. Obligations to Future Generations. LC 78-5495. (Philosophical Monographs: Second Annual Ser.). 272p. 1978. 14.95 (ISBN 0-87722-122-4); pap. 12.95 (ISBN 0-87722-128-6). Temple U Pr.

Sikorowa, Ludwika, et al, eds. Salivary Gland Tumors. LC 80-14975. 200p. 1983. 9.50 (ISBN 0-08-025557-4). Pergamon.

Sikorsky, R. Drive it Forever: Your Key to Long Automobile Life. 144p. 1983. 12.95 (ISBN 0-07-057294-1, GB). McGraw.

Sikov, M. R. see Mahlum, D. D.

Sikov, Melvin R. & Mahlum, D. Dennis, eds. Radiation Biology of the Fetal & Juvenile Mammal: Proceedings. LC 74-603748. (AEC Symposium Ser.). 1026p. 1969. pap. 33.75 (ISBN 0-87079-318-7, CONF-690501); microfiche 4.50 (ISBN 0-87079-319-5, CONF-690501). DOE.

Siks, Geraldine B. Drama with Children. (Illus.). 1977. text ed. 16.50 scp o.p. (ISBN 0-06-046151-9, HarpC). Har-Row.

--Drama With Children. 2nd ed. 368p. 1983. text ed. 16.95 scp (ISBN 0-06-046152-7, HarpC). Har-Row.

Sikula, Andrew F. Management & Administration. LC 72-95954. 1973. text ed. 15.95x o.p. (ISBN 0-675-09000-8). Merrill.

--Personnel Administration & Human Resources Management. LC 75-8691. (Management & Administration Ser.). 456p. 1976. 29.95 (ISBN 0-471-79140-7). Wiley.

--Personnel Management: A Short Course for Professionals. (Wiley Professional Development Programs). 340p. 1977. Set. 39.95 (ISBN 0-471-01931-3). Wiley.

Silador, Sidney, jt. auth. see Kay, Norman.

Silber, Bettina & Stern, Thomas, eds. The Oil Glut: How Deep & How Long. LC 82-71507. (Americans for Energy Independence Energy Policy Ser.). 43p. (Orig.). 1982. pap. 6.00 (ISBN 0-934458-04-9). Americans Energy Ind.

Silber, Earl N. & Katz, Louis N. Heart Disease. (Illus.). 1975. text ed. 70.00x (ISBN 0-02-410450-7). Macmillan.

Silber, Kathleen & Speedlin, Phylis. Dear Birthmother. Myers, Gail E., ed. 214p. (Orig.). 1983. 16.00 (ISBN 0-931722-20-9); pap. 7.95 (ISBN 0-931722-19-5). Corona Pub.

Silber, Kenneth, ed. see Association for Educational Communications & Technology. Task Force on Definition & Terminology.

Silber, Mark. Rural Maine. LC 72-75136. (Illus.). 60p. (Orig.). 1972. 12.50 (ISBN 0-87923-057-6); pap. 5.95 (ISBN 0-87923-056-8). Godine.

Silber, Norman I. Test & Protest: Social Criticism at Consumers Union. 220p. 1983. text ed. 34.50x (ISBN 0-8419-0749-8). Holmes & Meier.

Silber, William L., jt. auth. see Ritter, Lawrence.

Silber, William L., jt. auth. see Ritter, Lawrence S.

Silberbauer, George B. Hunter & Habitat in the Central Kalahari Desert. LC 80-16768. (Illus.). 288p. 1981. 42.50 (ISBN 0-521-23578-2); pap. 14.95 (ISBN 0-521-28135-0). Cambridge U Pr.

Silberberg, Eugene. The Structure of Economics: A Math Analysis. 1978. text ed. 28.95 (ISBN 0-07-057453-7, C); instructor's manual 20.95 (ISBN 0-07-057454-5). McGraw.

Silberberg, H. The German Standard Contracts Act. 124p. 1979. 75.00 (ISBN 0-7121-5485-X, Pub. by Macdonald & Evans). State Mutual Bk.

Silberfein, Marilyn. Constraints on the Expansion of Commercial Agriculture: Iringa District, Tanzania. LC 73-620257. (Papers in International Studies: Africa: No. 21). (Illus.). 1974. pap. 4.50x (ISBN 0-89680-054-7, Ohio U Ctr Intl). Ohio U Pr.

Silberg, Richard. Translucent Gears. 64p. 1982. pap. 4.95 (ISBN 0-938190-06-7). North Atlantic.

Silberkleit, Tom & Biederman, Jerry. The Do-It-Yourself Best Seller. LC 81-43418. (Illus.). 160p. 1982. pap. 8.95 (ISBN 0-385-17919-7, Dolp). Doubleday.

Silberman, Bernard S. Japan & Korea: A Critical Bibliography. LC 82-11841. 120p. 1982. Repr. of 1962 ed. lib. bdg. 25.00x (ISBN 0-313-23594-5, SIJK). Greenwood.

Silberman, Charles E. Crisis in the Classroom: The Remaking in American Education. 1970. 3.95 (ISBN 0-394-71353-2). Random.

Silberman, Leonard & Rothaus, Barbara. Rehabilitation: The California System. 160p. 1980. pap. text ed. 18.95x (ISBN 0-686-97703-3). L Silberman.

Silberman, Mary, jt. auth. see Young, Hy.

Silbermann, Eileen Z. The Savage Sacrament: A Theology of Marriage after American Feminism. 128p. (Orig.). 1983. pap. 6.95 (ISBN 0-89622-165-2). Twenty-Third.

Silbermann, M. & Slavkin, H., eds. Current Advances in Skeletogenesis: Development, Biomineralization, Mediators & Metabolic Bone Diseases (Selected Proceedings of the Fifth International Workshop on Calcified Tissues, Kiryat-Anavim, March 1982) (International Congress Ser.: No. 589). 594p. 1982. 127.75 (ISBN 0-444-90274-0). Elsevier.

Silbersack, John, jt. ed. see Schochet, Victoria.

Silberstang, Edwin. Abandoned. LC 80-1071. 312p. 1981. 10.95 o.p. (ISBN 0-385-15978-1). Doubleday.

--Play Chess Tonight. (Gambler's Book Shelf). (Illus.). 64p. (Orig.). 1976. pap. 2.95 o.p. (ISBN 0-911996-68-0). Gamblers.

--The Winner's Guide to Casino Gambling. 1981. pap. 7.11 (ISBN 0-452-25385-3, Z5385, Plume). NAL.

Silberstein, Jack S., jt. auth. see Prior, John A.

Silberstein, Michael J., jt. auth. see Brodeur, Armand E.

Silberstein, Suzanne & Seldin, Marian, eds. Sense & Style: The Craft of the Essay. 1962. text ed. 4.50 (ISBN 0-685-19703-4). Phila Bk Co.

Silberstein-Storfer, Muriel & Jones, Mablen. Doing Art Together: The Remarkable Parent-Child Workshop of the Metropolitan Museum of Art. (Illus.). 1982. 16.95 (ISBN 0-671-24109-5). S&S.

Silberston, A., jt. auth. see Boehm, K. H.

Silberston, Z. A., jt. auth. see Taylor, C. T.

Silbert, Jerry, jt. auth. see Carnine, Douglas.

Silbert, Jerry, et al. Direct Instruction Mathematics. (Illus., Orig.). 1981. pap. text ed. 23.95 (ISBN 0-675-08047-9). Merrill.

Silbert, Layle. Making a Baby in Union Park, Chicago. 68p. 1982. pap. 4.00 (ISBN 0-917402-19-7). Downtown Poets.

Silberton, A., jt. auth. see Cockerill, A.

Silbey, Joel H., ed. National Development & Sectional Crisis, 1815-1860. (Orig.). 1970. pap. text ed. 3.95 (ISBN 0-685-19748-4). Phila Bk Co.

Silbiger, Alexander. Italian Manuscript Sources of 17th Century Keyboard Music. Buelow, George, ed. LC 79-25558. (Studies in Musicology: No. 18). 244p. 1980. 39.95 (ISBN 0-8357-1075-0, Pub. by UMI Res Pr). Univ Microfilms.

Silen, William, ed. see Cope, Zachary.

Silet, Charles P. Henry Blake Fuller & Hamlin Garland: A Reference Guide. 1977. lib. bdg. 17.00 (ISBN 0-8161-7988-3, Hall Reference). G K Hall.

Silfen, Martin E. Counseling Clients in the Entertainment Industry, 1981: A Course Handbook. 645p. 1981. 30.00 (ISBN 0-686-96109-9, G4-3685). PLI.

--Counseling Clients in the Entertainment Industry 1982 Course Handbook. Rev. ed. (Patents, Copywrights, Trademarks, & Literary Property Ser. 1981-82). 1465p. 1982. pap. text ed. 30.00 (ISBN 0-686-97764-5, G6-3703). PLI.

Silgalis, Eugene, jt. auth. see Taber, Margaret R.

Siliconix, Inc. Designing with Field Effect Transistors. (Illus.). 352p. 1981. 26.90 (ISBN 0-07-057449-9). McGraw.

Silitch, Clarissa, ed. Old Farmers Almanac Colonial Cookbook. Rev. ed. LC 82-50962. (Illus.). 64p. 1982. pap. 5.95 (ISBN 0-89909-008-7). Yankee Bks.

--The Old Farmer's Almanac Heritage Cookbook. LC 82-70482. (Illus.). 64p. (Orig.). 1982. pap. 4.95 (ISBN 0-911658-39-4). Yankee Bks.

Silitch, Clarissa M., ed. Danger, Disaster, & Horrid Deeds. LC 74-83983. (Illus.). 288p. 1979. 12.95 (ISBN 0-911658-62-9); pap. 10.95 (ISBN 0-686-86922-2). Yankee Bks.

--The Old Farmers Almanac Colonial Cookbook. LC 75-41662. (Illus.). 64p. (Orig.). pap. 4.95 o.p. (ISBN 0-911658-70-X). Yankee Bks.

Silk, Alvin J., jt. auth. see Davis, Harry L.

Silk, D. B. Clinical Nutrition in Hospital Practice. 250p. 1983. pap. text ed. 24.00 (ISBN 0-632-86286-6, B4610-3). Mosby.

Silk, Gerald & De Limce, Alison. The Wadsworth Atheneum. LC 81-85340. (Museums Discovered Ser.: Vol.6). (Illus.). 208p. 1982. 25.00 (ISBN 0-9605574-3-1); pap. 18.00 (ISBN 0-9605574-6-6). Shorewood Fine Art.

Silk, John. Statistical Concepts in Geography. (Illus.). 1979. text ed. 25.00x (ISBN 0-04-910065-3); pap. text ed. 11.95x (ISBN 0-04-910066-1). Allen Unwin.

Silk, Leonard. Economics in Plain English: Everything You Need to Know About Economics, in Language You Can Understand. 1978. 8.95 o.p. (ISBN 0-671-22604-5). S&S.

--The Economists. 1978. pap. 3.95 (ISBN 0-380-01835-7, 61309-3, Discus). Avon.

Silk, Leonard & Silk, Mark. The American Establishment. LC 80-50533. 351p. 1980. 15.50 (ISBN 0-465-00134-3). Basic.

Silk, Leonard S. Contemporary Economics. 2nd ed. (Illus.). 544p. 1975. 14.95 o.p. (ISBN 0-07-057441-3, C); instructor's manual 4.95 o.p. (ISBN 0-07-034227-X). McGraw.

Silk, M. S. Interaction in Poetic Imagery. LC 73-90813. 304p. 1974. 44.50 (ISBN 0-521-20417-8). Cambridge U Pr.

Silk, Mark, jt. auth. see Silk, Leonard.

Silke. Kinsale. 224p. 1982. 49.00x (ISBN 0-85323-090-0, Pub. by Liverpool Univ England). State Mutual Bk.

Silkin, Jon, ed. Living Voices. (Pocket Poet Ser.). 1961. pap. 1.25 (ISBN 0-8023-9051-X). Dufour.

Silko, Leslie M. Ceremony. (RL 6). 1978. pap. 3.50 (ISBN 0-451-12028-0, AE2028, Sig). NAL.

Sill, Gertrude G. Handbook of Symbols in Christian Art. (Illus.). 1975. pap. 8.95 (ISBN 0-02-000850-3, Collier). Macmillan.

Sill, Sterling W. The Laws of Success. LC 75-18818. 219p. 1975. 7.95 (ISBN 0-87747-556-3). Deseret Bk.

--Thy Kingdom Come. LC 75-37275. 239p. 1975. 6.95 o.p. (ISBN 0-87747-602-0). Deseret Bk.

Sill, Webster H., Jr. The Plant Protection Discipline. LC 78-59171. 1978. text ed. 25.00x o.p. (ISBN 0-470-26443-8). Allanheld.

--The Plant Protection Discipline: Problems & Possible Developmental Strategies. LC 78-59171. 190p. 1979. 39.95x o.s.i. (ISBN 0-470-26443-8). Halsted Pr.

Sillanpaa, Frans E. The Maid Silja. new ed. Matson, Alexander, tr. from Finnish. LC 33-32586. 316p. 1974. 14.95 (ISBN 0-910220-66-2). Berg.

Silliman, Ron. Crow. 32p. 1971. 1.95 o.p. (ISBN 0-87886-004-5). Ithaca Hse.

Silliphant, Leigh. The No Nonsense Guide to Becoming a Self-Employed Manufacturer's Representative. 58p. (Orig.). 1982. lib. bdg. 8.21 o.p. (ISBN 0-686-82433-4, 0-9609148); pap. 10.95 o.p. (ISBN 0-686-82434-2). L & S Pr.

Silliphant, Sterling. Steel Tiger. 320p. (Orig.). 1983. pap. 3.50 (ISBN 0-345-30428-4). Ballantine.

Sillitoe, Alan. Her Victory. 590p. 1982. 16.95 (ISBN 0-531-09884-2). Watts.

--Loneliness of the Long-Distance Runner. 1960. 10.95 (ISBN 0-394-43389-0). Knopf.

--Loneliness of the Long-Distance Runner. 1971. pap. 1.95 (ISBN 0-451-11436-1, AJ1436, Sig). NAL.

--Saturday Night & Sunday Morning. 192p. 1973. pap. 2.50 (ISBN 0-451-12162-7, AE2162, Sig). NAL.

Sillitoe, Paul. Give & Take: Exchange in Wola Society. LC 79-5084. 1979. 34.00x (ISBN 0-312-32735-8). St Martin.

--Roots of the Earth: Crops in the Highlands of Papua New Guinea. 320p. 1983. 35.00 (ISBN 0-686-82458-X). Manchester.

Sillman, S. The Analysis of on Site Use & Sell Back in Residental Photovoltaic Systems. (Progress in Solar Energy Supplements Ser.). 70p. 1983. pap. text ed. 9.00x (ISBN 0-89553-064-3). Am Solar Energy.

Sills, David L., jt. ed. see Moss, Thomas H.

Sills, David L., et al, eds. Accident at Three Mile Island: The Human Dimensions. 200p. (Orig.). Jan., 1981. lib. bdg. 20.00x (ISBN 0-86531-165-X); Jan., 1981. pap. 12.00 (ISBN 0-86531-187-0). Westview.

Silman, James B. Espanol: Lo Essential Para el Bilingue. 157p. 1977. pap. text ed. 12.25 (ISBN 0-8191-0149-4). U Pr of Amer.

Silman, James B., jt. auth. see Quintanilla, Guadalupe C.

Silone, Ignazio. Bread & Wine. rev. ed. Fergusson, Harvey, Jr., tr. (Orig.). pap. 2.75 (ISBN 0-451-51624-9, CE1624, Sig Classics). NAL.

--Fontamara. Mosbacher, Eric, tr. 1981. pap. 2.95 (ISBN 0-451-51525-0, CE1525, Sig Classics). NAL.

--Vino E Pane. (Easy Readers, Ser. B). 96p. (Ital.). 1976. pap. 3.95 (ISBN 0-88436-269-8, 55253). EMC.

Silton, Lawrence C. Taking Cash Out of the Closely-Held Corporation. LC 79-25961. 330p. 1980. 59.50 (ISBN 0-87624-534-3). Inst Busn Plan.

Siltzbach, Louis E., ed. Seventh International Conference on Sarcoidosis & Other Granulomatous Disorders, Vol. 278. (Annals of the New York Academy of Sciences). 1976. 55.00x (ISBN 0-89072-057-6). NY Acad Sci.

Silva, Clarence De see De Silva, Clarence W. & Wormley, David N.

Silva, Clarence W. de see De Silva, Clarence W.

Silva, da see Wilson, Barbara & Da Silva.

Silva, Jose, tr. see Cook, Jerry.

Silva, Jose D., tr. see Nee, T. S.

Silva, Julian. The Gunnysack Castle. 285p. 1983. 15.95 (ISBN 0-8214-0743-0, 82-85124); pap. 6.95 (ISBN 0-8214-0744-9, 82-85132). Ohio U Pr.

Silva, K. M. De see De Silva, K. M.

Silva, Rita. Fatidic Numbers, Destiny & You. LC 80-17284. 1983. 14.95 (ISBN 0-87949-178-7). Ashley Bks.

Silva, Tony & Kotlar, Barbara. Breeding Lovebirds. (Illus.). 96p. 1981. 4.95 (ISBN 0-87666-831-7, KW-125). TFH Pubns.

--Conures. (Illus.). 96p. 1980. 4.95 (ISBN 0-87666-893-7, KW-121). TFH Pubns.

--Discus. (Illus.). 98p. 1980. 4.95 (ISBN 0-87666-535-0, KW-097). TFH Pubns.

Silva, Zenia S. Da see Da Silva, Zenia S.

Silva-Michelena, Jose A., jt. auth. see Bonilla, Frank.

Silvaroli, Nicholas J. & Kear, Dennis J. A Classroom Guide to Reading Assessment & Instruction. 176p. 1982. text ed. 12.95 (ISBN 0-8403-2633-5). Kendall-Hunt.

Silvaroli, Nicholas J., et al. Oral Language Evaluation. 1977. pap. text ed. 6.95 (ISBN 0-88436-470-4). EMC.

Silvelra, T. The McGraw-Hill Guide for Preparing Students for the New High School Equivalency Examination (GED) 1979. 3.30 (ISBN 0-07-057447-2). McGraw.

Silvennoinen, P. Nuclear Fuel Cycle Optimization: Methods & Modelling Techniques. (Illus.). 138p. 1982. 25.00 (ISBN 0-08-027310-6). Pergamon.

Silver, A. David. The Entrepreneurial Life: How to Go for It & Get It. 288p. 1983. 22.95 (ISBN 0-471-87382-9). Ronald Pr.

--The Radical New Road to Wealth. rev. ed. 1983. pap. 15.00 (ISBN 0-914306-77-4). Intl Wealth.

Silver, Abba H. Where Judaism Differed. 1956. 5.95 o.s.i. (ISBN 0-02-610690-6); pap. 2.95 o.p. (ISBN 0-02-089360-4). Macmillan.

Silver, Alain. The Samurai Film. LC 82-22288. (Illus.). 242p. 1983. 17.95 (ISBN 0-87951-175-3). Overlook Pr.

Silver, Alain & Ward, Elizabeth. The Film Director's Team: A Practical Guide to Organizing & Managing Film Production. LC 82-18181. (Illus.). 224p. 1983. 12.95 (ISBN 0-668-05466-2). Arco.

--Film Noir: An Encyclopedic Reference to the American Style. LC 76-47092. (Illus.). 400p. 1980. 30.00 (ISBN 0-87951-055-2). Overlook Pr.

--Robert Aldrich: A Guide to References & Resources. 1979. lib. bdg. 17.50 (ISBN 0-8161-7993-X, Hall Reference). G K Hall.

Silver, Ann, ed. The Biology of Cholinesterases. LC 74-79240. (Frontiers of Biology Ser.: Vol. 36). 250p. 1975. 166.00 (ISBN 0-444-10652-9, North-Holland). Elsevier.

Silver, Brian D., jt. ed. see McCagg, William O.

Silver, Burr A. Exploration Geology. 1982. 43.00 (ISBN 0-89419-253-1). Inst Energy.

--Subsurface Exploration Stratigraphy. 1982. 45.00 (ISBN 0-89419-254-X). Inst Energy.

--Technique of Using Geologic Data. 1982. 32.00 (ISBN 0-89931-040-0). Inst Energy.

Silver, Carole. The Romance of William Morris. LC 82-2278. xviii, 233p. 1983. text ed. 20.95x (ISBN 0-8214-0651-5, 82-84200); pap. 12.95 (ISBN 0-8214-0706-6, 82-84739). Ohio U Pr.

Silver, Catherine, ed. see Le Play, Frederic.

Silver, Daniel J. Images of Moses. LC 82-70854. 1982. 16.95 (ISBN 0-465-03201-X). Basic.

Silver, Daniel J. & Martin, Bernard. History of Judaism, 2 vols. Incl. Vol. 1. From Abraham to Maimonides. 20.00x o.s.i. (ISBN 0-465-03006-8); pap. 9.95 (ISBN 0-465-03004-1); Vol. 2. Europe & the New World. 20.00x (ISBN 0-465-03007-6); pap. 10.95 (ISBN 0-465-03005-X). LC 73-90131. 1974. Set. 40.00 (ISBN 0-465-03008-4). Basic.

Silver, Edward A., jt. auth. see Peterson, Rein.

Silver, George see Jackson, James L.

Silver, Gerald. Graphic Layout & Design. LC 80-65062. (Graphic Arts Ser.). 312p. 1981. pap. text ed. 12.60 (ISBN 0-8273-1374-8); instr.'s guide 2.50 (ISBN 0-8273-1375-6). Delmar.

Silver, Gerald A. Introduction to Business. (Illus.). 1978. text ed. 23.95 (ISBN 0-07-057495-2, C); study guide 9.95 (ISBN 0-07-057497-9); transparency masters 20.95 (ISBN 0-07-057499-5); instructor's manual 20.95 (ISBN 0-07-057496-0). McGraw.

--Introduction to Management. (Illus.). 530p. 1981. text ed. 22.95 (ISBN 0-8299-0415-8). West Pub.

--Small Computer Systems for Business. (Illus.). 1978. text ed. 18.95 (ISBN 0-07-057463-4, C); solutions manual 7.95 (ISBN 0-07-057464-2). McGraw.

Silver, Gerald A. & Silver, J. Introduction to Programming: Programming Logic & Flowcharting. 1975. text ed. 12.50 (ISBN 0-07-057445-6, G); instructor's manual 4.50 (ISBN 0-07-057446-4). McGraw.

Silver, Gerald A. & Silver, Joan B. Data Processing for Business. 3rd ed. 622p. 1981. text ed. 22.95 (ISBN 0-15-516814-2, HC); instructor's manual avail. 1.95; study guide 7.95 (ISBN 0-15-516815-0); transparency master program avail 5.95 (ISBN 0-15-516817-7); test bklt. avail. 1.50 (ISBN 0-15-516819-3). HarBraceJ.

--Introduction to Systems Analysis. (Illus.). 1976. 22.95x o.p. (ISBN 0-13-498683-0). P-H.

Silver, Gerald A. & Silver, Myrna. Weekend Fathers. LC 81-51695. 1981. 13.95 (ISBN 0-936906-06-5). Stratford Pr.

Silver, Harold, jt. auth. see Lawson, John.

Silver, Harold, jt. auth. see Ryder, Judith.

Silver, Harold, jt. auth. see Silver, Pamela.

Silver, Harold, ed. Concept of Popular Education. 1977. 38.00x o.p. (ISBN 0-416-70740-8). Methuen Inc.

--Equal Opportunity in Education. 1979. pap. 13.00x (ISBN 0-416-78540-9). Methuen Inc.

--Robert Owen on Education. LC 69-10432. (Cambridge Texts & Studies in Education). 1969. 32.50 (ISBN 0-521-07353-7). Cambridge U Pr.

Silver, Helene, jt. auth. see Zell, Hans.

Silver, Herbert, ed. Blood, Blood Components & Derivatives in Transfusion Therapy. 226p. 1980. 25.00 (ISBN 0-914404-55-5). Am Assn Blood.

--Probability of Inclusion in Paternity Testing. 106p. 1982. 17.00 (ISBN 0-914404-77-6); non-members 19.00 (ISBN 0-686-83043-1). Am Assn Blood.

Silver, Howard & Nydahl, John. Introduction to Engineering Thermodynamics. LC 76-3601. (Illus.). 500p. 1977. text ed. 26.95 (ISBN 0-8299-0053-5); solutions manual avail. (ISBN 0-8299-0573-1). West Pub.

Silver, Howard A. Elementary Algebra. (Illus.). 352p. 1982. 19.95 (ISBN 0-13-252817-7). P-H.

--Mathematics: Contemporary Topics & Applications. (Illus.). 1979. text ed. 22.95 (ISBN 0-13-563304-4). P-H.

Silver, Isidore. Law & Economics. LC 71-84422. (Real World of Economics Ser). (Illus.). (gr. 5-11). 1970. PLB 4.95g (ISBN 0-8225-0619-X). Lerner Pubns.

Silver, J., jt. auth. see Silver, Gerald A.

Silver, James W., ed. see Wilson, LeGrand J.

Silver, Jeffery H. & Topolski, Diane F. The Clay Babies & Other Puget Sound Stories. 32p. (Orig.). (gr. 5 up). 1982. pap. 4.00 (ISBN 0-910867-00-3). Silver Seal Bks.

Silver, Joan B., jt. auth. see Silver, Gerald A.

Silver, Maury, jt. auth. see Sabini, Jon.

Silver, Milton, jt. auth. see Garrett, Leonard J.

Silver, Morris. Prophets & Markets. 1982. lib. bdg. 35.00 (ISBN 0-89838-112-6). Kluwer-Nijhoff.

Silver, Murray, jt. auth. see Lewis, Myra.

Silver, Myrna, jt. auth. see Silver, Gerald A.

Silver, Nathan. Lost New York. LC 66-11220. (Illus.). 1971. pap. 7.95 o.p. (ISBN 0-8052-0328-1). Schocken.

Silver, P. H., jt. auth. see Green, J. H.

Silver, Pamela & Silver, Harold. The Education of the Poor: The History of a National School 1824-1974. (Routledge Library in the History of Education). 208p. 1974. 24.50x (ISBN 0-7100-7804-8). Routledge & Kegan.

Silver, Paula. Educational Administration: Theoretical Perspectives on Practice & Research. 416p. 1983. text ed. 17.50 scp (ISBN 0-06-046161-6, HarpC). Har-Row.

Silver, Philip, tr. see Ferrater Mora, Jose.

Silver, Rae, ed. Parental Behavior in Birds. (Benchmark Papers in Animal Behavior: Vol. 11). 1978. 44.50 (ISBN 0-12-787457-7). Acad Pr.

Silver, Rawley. Developing Cognitive & Creative Skills Through Art. 286p. 1978. pap. text ed. 19.95 (ISBN 0-8391-1248-3). Univ Park.

Silver, Richard. Reaching Out to the Alcoholic & the Family. 1.50 (ISBN 0-89486-042-9, 1408B). Hazelden.

--The Wonder of It All. LC 81-86426. 64p. 1983. pap. 5.95 (ISBN 0-686-42890-0). GWP.

Silver, Robert S. & Watt, James. Introduction to Thermodynamics. LC 79-138380. (Illus.). 1971. 22.50 (ISBN 0-521-08064-9). Cambridge U Pr.

Silver, Samuel M., jt. auth. see Braverman, Libbie L.

Silver, Samuel M., jt. auth. see Freedman, Melvin H.

Silver, Theodore & Sacks, Howard R. Your Key to Success in Law School. 128p. 1982. pap. 7.95 o.p. (ISBN 0-671-09256-1). Messner.

Silverberg, Barry, jt. auth. see Ferri, Robert.

Silverberg, James, jt. ed. see Barlow, George W.

Silverberg, Katherine D., ed. see Thibodaux Service League Members.

Silverberg, Mervin. Advanced Textbook of Pediatric Gastroenterology. (Advanced Textbook Ser.). 1982. pap. text ed. 32.50 (ISBN 0-87488-657-0). Med Exam.

Silverberg, Robert. The Best of Robert Silverberg, 2 vols. (Science Fiction Ser.). 1978. Vol. 1. lib. bdg. 13.00 (ISBN 0-8398-2445-9, Gregg); Vol. 2. lib. bdg. 15.00 (ISBN 0-8398-2439-4). G K Hall.

--Capricorn Games. Freas, Polly & Freas, Kelly, eds. LC 78-15284. (Illus.). 1979. pap. 4.95 o.p. (ISBN 0-915442-62-0, Starblaze). Donning Co.

--Earth's Other Shadow. pap. 0.95 o.p. (ISBN 0-451-05538-1, Q5538, Sig). NAL.

--John Muir: Prophet Among the Glaciers. (Lives to Remember Ser.). 224p. (gr. 6 up). 1972. PLB 4.97 o.p. (ISBN 0-399-60714-5). Putnam Pub Group.

--Lord of Darkness. 1983. 15.95 (ISBN 0-87795-443-7). Arbor Hse.

--Lord Valentine's Castle. LC 79-2658. 1980. 14.37i (ISBN 0-06-014026-7, HarpT). Har-Row.

--Majipoor Chronicles. 1983. pap. 3.50 (ISBN 0-686-43062-X). Bantam.

--The Man in the Maze. 192p. 1978. pap. 2.50 o.p. (ISBN 0-380-00198-5, 62794-9). Avon.

--A Robert Silverberg Omnibus: Downward to Earth, the Man in the Maze, & Nightwings. LC 80-8232. 540p. 1981. 16.30i (ISBN 0-06-014047-X, HarpT). Har-Row.

--The Seed of Earth. 192p. 1982. pap. 2.25 (ISBN 0-441-75876-2, Pub. by Ace Science Fiction). Ace Bks.

--Those Who Watch. pap. 2.25 (ISBN 0-451-12022-1, AE2022, Sig). NAL.

--To Open the Sky. 1977. Repr. of 1967 ed. lib. bdg. 11.00 o.p. (ISBN 0-8398-2382-7, Gregg). G K Hall.

--World of a Thousand Colors. 1983. 6.95 (ISBN 0-87795-493-3, Pub. by Priam). Arbor Hse.

--World's Fair Nineteen Ninety-Two. 256p. 1982. pap. 2.50 (ISBN 0-441-90923-X, Pub. by Ace Science Fiction). Ace Bks.

Silverberg, Robert & Garrett, Randall. The Dawning Light. LC 81-4905. (Illus., Orig.). 1981. pap. 5.95 (ISBN 0-89865-034-8, Starblaze). Donning Co.

--The Shrouded Planet. LC 80-22472. 1980. pap. 5.95 (ISBN 0-89865-033-X). Donning Co.

Silverberg, Robert, ed. The Mirror of Infinity. 288p. 1973. pap. 1.95i o.p. (ISBN 0-06-080306-1, P306, PL). Har-Row.

--Mutants: Eleven Stories of Science Fiction. LC 74-10278. (Nelson's Science Fiction Ser.). 224p. 1974. 7.95 o.p. (ISBN 0-525-66412-2). Lodestar Bks.

Silverberg, Robert & Greenberg, Martin H., eds. The Arbor House Treasury of Science Fiction Masterpieces. 1983. 16.95 (ISBN 0-87795-445-3). Arbor Hse.

Silverberg, Robert, ed. see Gotlieb, Phyllis, et al.

Silverberg, Steven G. Principles & Practice of Surgical Pathology, 2 vols. 2048p. 1982. 140.00x (ISBN 0-471-05221-3, Pub. by Wiley Med.). Wiley.

--Principles & Practices of Surgical Pathology, 2 vols. 2048p. 1982. Set. 140.00 (ISBN 0-471-05221-3, Pub. by Wiley Med). Wiley.

--Surgical Pathology of the Uterus. LC 77-8569. (Surgical Pathology Ser.). 130p. 1977. 41.95x (ISBN 0-471-01476-1, Pub. by Wiley Medical). Wiley.

Silverberg, Steven G. & Major, Francis J. Estrogens & Cancer. LC 78-17275. 1978. 37.95 o.p. (ISBN 0-471-04172-6, Pub. by Wiley Medical). Wiley.

Silverbird, Kira, ed. see Mogollon Conference, March 27-28,1980, Las Cruces, New Mexico.

Silvergleid, Arthur, ed. Clinical Hematology for Blood Bankers. 181p. 1979. 25.00 (ISBN 0-914404-47-4). Am Assn Blood.

Silvergleid, Arthur, jt. ed. see Umlas, Joel.

Silvergleid, Arthur J., jt. ed. see Keating, Louise J.

Silverman, Al. Sports Titans of the Twentieth Century. (Putnam Sports Shelf). (Illus.). (gr. 5 up). 1968. PLB 4.97 o.p. (ISBN 0-399-60602-5). Putnam Pub Group.

Silverman, Alan S. Handbook of Chinese for Mathematicians. (Current Chinese Language Project: No. 17). 1976. pap. 3.50x (ISBN 0-912966-17-3). IEAS.

Silverman, Arnold & Roy, Claude C. Pediatric Clinical Gastroenterology. 3rd ed. (Illus.). 978p. 1983. text ed. 66.00 (ISBN 0-8016-4623-5). Mosby.

Silverman, Burt. Breaking the Rules of Watercolor. (Illus.). 144p. 1983. 22.50 (ISBN 0-8230-0523-2). Watson-Guptill.

Silverman, D. P. Interrogative Construction with jn & Jn-jw in Old & Middle Egyptian. LC 79-63266. (Bibliotheca Aegyptia Ser.: Vol. 1). 150p. 1979. text ed. 20.50x (ISBN 0-89003-061-8); pap. 15.50x (ISBN 0-89003-060-X). Undena Pubns.

Silverman, David. Reading Castaneda: A Prologue to the Social Sciences. 1975. 16.00 (ISBN 0-7100-8145-6); pap. 7.95 (ISBN 0-7100-8146-4). Routledge & Kegan.

--Theory of Organizations. LC 72-150812. 1971. text ed. 12.95x (ISBN 0-465-08438-9). Basic.

Silverman, Dee. How to Turn Your Kitchen Talents Into Extra Cash. 101p. 1980. pap. text ed. write for info. (ISBN 0-938908-00-6). Opportunity Knocks.

Silverman, F. Communication for the Speechless. 1980. 22.95 (ISBN 0-13-153361-4). P-H.

Silverman, Frank H. Research Design in Speech Pathology & Audiology: Asking & Answering Questions. (Illus.). 1977. text ed. 27.95 (ISBN 0-13-774117-0). P-H.

Silverman, Franklin H. Legal Aspects of Speech-Language Pathology & Audiology. (Illus.). 240p. 1983. 20.95 (ISBN 0-13-528109-1). P-H.

Silverman, Goldie, jt. auth. see Williams, Jacqueline B.

Silverman, Harold L. & Simon, Gilbert I. The Pill Book. 432p. (Orig.). 1982. pap. 3.95 (ISBN 0-553-22527-8). Bantam.

Silverman, Harold M., et al. The Pill Book. 2nd ed. LC 82-90322. 620p. 1982. 19.95 (ISBN 0-553-05013-3); pap. 9.95 (ISBN 0-553-01377-7). Bantam.

Silverman, Herb. Complex Variables. 1975. text ed. 26.50 o.p. (ISBN 0-395-18582-3). HM.

Silverman, Hillel, jt. auth. see Silverman, Morris.

Silverman, Hugh, jt. ed. see Sallis, John.

Silverman, Jerry. Beginning the Five String Banjo. 1974. pap. 3.95 o.s.i. (ISBN 0-02-082070-4, Collier). Macmillan.

--Folk Guitar - Folk Song. LC 77-71706. (Illus.). 1977. 35.00x o.p. (ISBN 0-8128-2264-1); pap. 9.95 (ISBN 0-8128-2255-2). Stein & Day.

--How to Play Better Guitar. LC 79-180109. pap. 7.95 (ISBN 0-385-00579-2). Doubleday.

--Yiddish Song Book. LC 81-40331. (Illus.). 176p. 1982. 17.95 (ISBN 0-8128-2829-1); pap. 9.95 (ISBN 0-8128-6130-2). Stein & Day.

Silverman, Jonathan. For the World to See: The Life of Margaret Bourke-White. (Illus.). 224p. 1983. 46.95 (ISBN 0-686-82650-7). Viking Pr.

Silverman, Julian. Health Care & Consciousness: Think of Yourself Now & Then. 1982. text ed. 16.95x (ISBN 0-686-83109-8). Irvington.

Silverman, Kaja. The Subject of Semiotics. 250p. 1983. 20.00 (ISBN 0-19-503177-6). Oxford U Pr.

Silverman, Manuel S., jt. auth. see Kroll, Larry J.

Silverman, Maxwell & Bowman, Ned A. Contemporary Theatre Architecture: An Illustrated Survey & a Checklist of Publications, 1946-1964. LC 65-12942. (Illus.). 1965. 12.50 o.p. (ISBN 0-87104-055-7). NY Pub Lib.

Silverman, Maxwell, ed. see Frueh, Alfred J.

Silverman, Melvin. Project Management: A Short Course for Professionals. LC 75-39751. 328p. 1976. Set. text ed. 55.95x (ISBN 0-471-79163-6, Pub. by Wiley-Professional Development Programs). Wiley.

Silverman, Meyer M. Occlusion in Prosthodontics & in the Natural Dentition. (Illus.). 1962. 16.50x (ISBN 0-9600244-1-7). Mutual.

Silverman, Milton. The Drugging of the Americas: How Multinational Drug Companies Say One Thing About Their Products to Physicians in the United States, & Another Thing to Physicians in Latin America. LC 75-27935. 1976. 19.95x (ISBN 0-520-03122-9). U of Cal Pr.

Silverman, Milton & Lee, Philip R. Pills, Profits, & Politics. 1974. 23.75x (ISBN 0-520-02616-0); pap. 4.95 o.s.i. (ISBN 0-520-03050-8). U of Cal Pr.

--Prescription for Death: The Drugging of the Third World. LC 82-1896. 208p. 1982. 16.95 o.s.i. (ISBN 0-520-04721-4). U of Cal Pr.

Silverman, Morris. Memorial Service at the Cemetery. pap. 0.95 (ISBN 0-685-64878-8). Prayer Bk.

--Prayers of Consolation. 1972. 5.95x (ISBN 0-87677-062-6); pap. 4.95x (ISBN 0-87677-063-4). Prayer BK.

--Torah Readings for the Three Festivals. 4.95x (ISBN 0-685-40682-2). Prayer Bk.

Silverman, Morris & Arzt, Max. Selihot Service. rev. ed. pap. 1.95x (ISBN 0-685-40684-9). Prayer Bk.

Silverman, Morris & Hillel. Tishah B'av Service. pap. 1.95x (ISBN 0-685-40683-0). Prayer Bk.

Silverman, Morris & Neusner, Jacob. Complete Purim Service. pap. 2.95 (ISBN 0-685-40685-7). Prayer Bk.

Silverman, Morris & Silverman, Hillel. Prayer Book for Summer Camps. (gr. 3-12). 5.95x (ISBN 0-685-23438-X); pap. 4.95x (ISBN 0-685-23439-8). Prayer Bk.

Silverman, Morris & United Synagogue. High Holiday Prayer Book. 10.95 (ISBN 0-87677-051-0); simulated leather 12.95 (ISBN 0-87677-012-X). Prayer Bk.

--Weekday Prayer Book. 5.95 (ISBN 0-685-40680-6); large ed. o.p. 17.50 (ISBN 0-685-40681-4). Prayer Bk.

Silverman, Morris, jt. auth. see Greenberg, Sidney.

Silverman, Morris, ed. Passover Haggadah. pap. 4.95 (ISBN 0-686-02386-2). Hartmore.

--Passover Haggadah. rev. ed. (Illus.). 1975. 4.95 o.p. (ISBN 0-87677-025-1); pap. 3.95 (ISBN 0-87677-029-4). Prayer Bk.

Silverman, Paul. Animal Behavior in the Laboratory. LC 77-8842. (Illus.). 1978. text ed. 35.00x (ISBN 0-87663-727-6, Pica Pr). Universe.

Silverman, Phyllis R. Helping Women Cope with Grief. (Sage Human Services Guides Ser.: Vol. 25). 111p. 1981. pap. 6.50 (ISBN 0-8039-1735-X). Sage.

Silverman, R. Essentials of Psychology. 1979. pap. 19.95 (ISBN 0-13-286658-7); study guide & wkbk. 8.95 (ISBN 0-13-286666-8). P-H.

Silverman, R., tr. see Gelfand, Izrail M. & Fomin, S. V.

Silverman, Richard, tr. see Shilov, Georgi E.

Silverman, Richard A., tr. see Markushevich, A. I.

Silverman, Rita H. Sufferance Is the Badge of All Our Tribe: A Study of Shylock in the Merchant of Venice. LC 81-40041. 56p. (Orig.). 1981. pap. text ed. 5.25 (ISBN 0-8191-1664-5). U Pr of Amer.

Silverman, Robert J. Getting Published in Education Journals. 118p. 1982. 17.50x (ISBN 0-398-04622-0). C C Thomas.

Silverman, S. Richard, jt. auth. see Calvert, Donald R.

Silverman, S. Richard, tr. Stuttering: Integrating Theory & Practice. LC 82-13818. 215p. 1982. 22.50 (ISBN 0-89443-665-1). Aspen Systems.

Silverman, Sondra. Black Revolt & Democratic Politics. (Problems in Political Science Ser). 1970. pap. text ed. 2.95 o.p. (ISBN 0-669-52357-7). Heath.

Silverman, Stephen. Public Spectacles. 1981. 11.50 o.p. (ISBN 0-525-18605-0, 01117-330). Dutton.

Silverman, William A. The Violin Hunter. (Illus.). 256p. 1981. Repr. of 1957 ed. 17.95 (ISBN 0-87666-577-6, Z-47). Paganiniana Pubns.

Silverman, William B. Rabbinic Wisdom & Jewish Values. rev. ed. Orig. Title: Rabbinic Stories for Christian Ministers & Teachers. 1971. pap. 5.00 o.p. (ISBN 0-8074-0190-0, 383210). UAHC.

Silvern, Leonard C. Basic Analysis. LC 65-22295. (Prog. Bk.). 1965. text ed. write for info o.p.; Set. text ed. 100.00 o.p. (ISBN 0-685-09256-9); color film, educational kit, magnetic tape, picture viewer incl. o.p. Ed & Training.

--Systems Engineering of Education: The Evolution of Systems Thinking in Education, No. 1. 3rd ed. LC 73-150823. (Illus.). vi, 128p. 1975. 20.00 (ISBN 0-87657-107-0). Ed & Training.

--Systems Engineering of Education Twenty: Systems Engineering Applied to Training. (Illus.). 1983. 25.00 (ISBN 0-87657-127-5). Ed & Training.

Silvers, J. B., et al, eds. Health Care Financial Management in the 1980's: Time of Transition. (Illus.). 275p. (Orig.). 1983. pap. text ed. price not set (ISBN 0-914904-86-8). Health Admin Pr.

Silvers, John B. & Prahalad, C. K. Financial Management of Health Institutions. 339p. 1974. 17.95 (ISBN 0-686-68576-8, 14910). Healthcare Fin Man Assn.

Silvers, Ronald J., jt. auth. see Darroch, Vivian.

Silverson, Sarah & Smith, Jan. Speak Easy. 1982. with 3-4inch Umatic Videocassettes 395.00x (ISBN 0-88432-113-4); with Betamax Videocassette 380.00x (ISBN 0-88432-114-2); with VHS videocassette 380.00x (ISBN 0-88432-115-0); manual 4.95x (ISBN 0-88432-085-5). J Norton Pubs.

Silverstein, Albert, ed. Human Communication: Theoretical Explorations. LC 74-14880. 264p. 1974. 14.95x o.s.i. (ISBN 0-470-79172-1). Halsted Pr.

Silverstein, Alvin. Human Anatomy & Physiology. LC 79-13053. 887p. 1980. text ed. 33.95 (ISBN 0-471-79166-0). experiments avail. (ISBN 0-471-79164-4) (ISBN 0-471-07781-X). Wiley.

Silverstein, Alvin & Silverstein, Virginia B. Allergies. LC 77-1284. (gr. 4 up). 1977. 9.57 (ISBN 0-397-31758-1, HarpJ); pap. 2.95 (ISBN 0-397-31759-X). Har-Row.

Silverstein, Alvin & Silverstein, Virginia. Code of Life. LC 77-175558. (Illus.). (gr. 5-9). 1972. 6.95 o.p. (ISBN 0-689-30038-7). Atheneum.

Silverstein, Alvin & Silverstein, Virginia B. Diabetes: The Sugar Disease. LC 78-11631. 1979. 8.61i (ISBN 0-397-31844-8). Har-Row.

Silverstein, Alvin & Silverstein, Virginia. Heartbeats: Your Body, Your Heart. LC 82-48465. (Illus.). 48p. (gr. 3-5). 1983. 9.57i (ISBN 0-397-32037-X, JBL-J); PLB 9.89g (ISBN 0-397-32038-8). Har-Row.

Silverstein, Alvin & Silverstein, Virginia B. Runaway Sugar: About Diabetes. LC 80-8727. (Illus.). 48p. (gr. 3-5). 1981. 9.89i (ISBN 0-397-31928-2, JBL-J); PLB 8.89g (ISBN 0-397-31929-0). Har-Row.

Silverstein, Alvin & Silverstein, Virginia. Sleep & Dreams. LC 73-13825. (Illus.). 160p. (gr. 7 up). 1974. 9.89 (ISBN 0-397-31325-X, HarpJ). Har-Row.

Silverstein, Alvin & Silverstein, Virginia B. The Story of Your Ear. 64p. (gr. 5-9). 1981. lib. bdg. 6.99 (ISBN 0-698-30704-6, Coward). Putnam Pub Group.

Silverstein, Alvin, et al. Aging. LC 79-11890. (Illus.). (gr. 5 up). 1979. PLB 7.90 s&l (ISBN 0-531-02863-1). Watts.

Silverstein, Arthur M. & O'Connor, G. Richard. Immunology & Immunopathology of the Eye. LC 79-84781. 416p. 1979. 66.00x (ISBN 0-89352-042-X). Masson Pub.

Silverstein, Charles. Man to Man: Gay Couples in America. Landis, James, ed. LC 81-15734. 384p. 1982. pap. 7.50 (ISBN 0-688-00803-8). Quill NY.

Silverstein, Harry, jt. auth. see Rosenberg, Bernard.

Silverstein, Harvey. Superships & Nation-States: The Transnational Politics of the Intergovernmental Maritime Consultative Organization. LC 77-27662. (Illus.). 1978. lib. bdg. 27.50 o.p. (ISBN 0-89158-058-1). Westview.

Silverstein, Josef, ed. The Future of Burma in Perspective: A Symposium. LC 76-620184. (Papers in International Studies: Southeast Asia: No. 35). (Illus.). 1974. pap. 7.00 o.p. (ISBN 0-89680-021-0, Ohio U Ctr Intl). Ohio U Pr.

Silverstein, Martin E., et al, eds. Acupuncture & Moxibustion: A Handbook for the Barefoot Doctors of China. LC 74-26919. 1975. 7.00x o.p. (ISBN 0-8052-3585-X); pap. 3.95 (ISBN 0-8052-0476-8). Schocken.

Silverstein, Michael, ed. see Whitney, William D.

Silverstein, Norman, jt. auth. see Huss, Roy.

Silverstein, Pam & Srb, Jozetta H. Flexitime: Where, When, & How? LC 79-88670. (Key Issues Ser.: No. 24). 60p. 1979. pap. 3.50 (ISBN 0-87546-074-7). ILR Pr.

Silverstein, Robert M. & Bassler, G. Clayton. Spectrometric Indentification of Organic Compounds. 4th ed. Morrill, Terence C., ed. LC 80-20548. 442p. 1981. text ed. 28.95 (ISBN 0-471-02990-4). Wiley.

Silverstein, Ruth, et al. Spanish Now! 4th ed. Quinones, Nathan, ed. (Illus.). 480p. (gr. 7-12). 1977. text ed. 14.95 (ISBN 0-8120-5202-1); pap. text ed. 8.95 (ISBN 0-8120-0928-2). Barron.

Silverstein, Samuel. The Child Is Superior to the Man: Children's Experiences with God in the Public School Classroom. (Illus.). 1980. 6.50 o.p. (ISBN 0-682-49541-7). Exposition.

Silverstein, Shel. Giving Tree. LC 64-11840. (Illus.). (ps-3). 1964. 7.95 (ISBN 0-06-025665-6, HarpJ); PLB 8.89 (ISBN 0-06-025666-4). Har-Row.

--A Light in the Attic. LC 80-8453. (Illus.). 176p. 1981. 12.45 (ISBN 0-06-025673-7, HarpJ); PLB 12.89g (ISBN 0-06-025674-5). Har-Row.

--The Missing Piece. LC 75-37408. (Illus.). 112p. (gr. 7 up). 1976. 8.95 (ISBN 0-06-025671-0, HarpJ); PLB 9.89 (ISBN 0-06-025672-9). Har-Row.

--The Missing Piece Meets the Big O. LC 80-8721. (Illus.). 112p. (gr. 3 up). 1981. 8.95 (ISBN 0-06-025657-5, HarpJ); PLB 8.79g (ISBN 0-06-025658-3). Har-Row.

--Where the Sidewalk Ends: Poems & Drawings. LC 73-105486. (Illus.). 176p. (gr. k-3). 1974. 12.45 (ISBN 0-06-025667-2, HarpJ); PLB 12.89 (ISBN 0-06-025668-0). Har-Row.

--Who Wants a Cheap Rhinoceros? LC 82-23945. (Illus.). 56p. (ps-3). 1983. 8.95 (ISBN 0-02-782690-2). Macmillan.

Silverstein, Theodore, ed. see Auerbach, Erich.

Silverstein, Virginia, jt. auth. see Silverstein, Alvin.

Silverstein, Virginia B., jt. auth. see Silverstein, Alvin.

Silverstone, jt. auth. see Simon.

Silverstone, Lou & Rickard, Jack. Politically Mad. (Illus.). 1982. pap. 1.95 (ISBN 0-446-30479-4). Warner Bks.

Silverstone, Sidney. A Player's Guide to Casino Games. LC 80-84947. (Illus.). 155p. (Orig.). 1981. pap. 7.95 (ISBN 0-448-12249-9, G&D). Putnam Pub Group.

Silverstone, Trevor. Obesity: Its Pathogenesis & Management. LC 75-18338. (Illus.). 250p. 1975. 20.00 o.p. (ISBN 0-88416-038-6). Wright-PSG.

Silverstone, Trevor & Turner, Paul. Drug Treatment in Psychiatry. rev. ed. (Social & Psychological Aspects of Medical Practice Ser.). 1978. 22.00 o.p. (ISBN 0-7100-8933-3); pap. 9.75 o.p. (ISBN 0-7100-8934-1). Routledge & Kegan.

Silvert, Frieda, jt. auth. see Krueger, Marlis.

Silvert, K. H. & Reissman, L. Education, Class & Nation. (Studies on Education: Vol. 7). 1976. 19.95 (ISBN 0-444-99018-6). Elsevier.

Silverton, R. E., jt. auth. see Baker, F. J.

Silvester, John R. Introduction to Algebraic K-Theory. 250p. 1981. 29.95x (ISBN 0-412-22700-2, Pub by Chapman & Hall England); pap. 15.95x (ISBN 0-412-23740-7). Methuen Inc.

Silvester, P., jt. ed. see Chari, M. V.

Silvester, R. Coastal Engineering, Vol. 1: Generation, Propagation & Influence of Waves. LC 72-97435. (Developments in Geotechnical Engineering: Vol. 4A). 450p. 1974. 61.75 (ISBN 0-444-41101-1). Elsevier.

--Coastal Engineering, Vol. 2: Sedimentation, Estuaries, Tides, Effluents, Modelling. LC 72-97435. (Developments in Geotechnical Engineering: Vol. 4B). 232p. 1974. 61.75 (ISBN 0-444-41102-X). Elsevier.

Silvester, Richard, intro. by. Coastal & Ocean Engineering: Offshore Structures. (Australian Conference: No. 5). 471p. (Orig.). 1981. pap. text ed. 37.50x (ISBN 0-85825-159-0, Pub. by Inst Engineering Australia). Renouf.

Silvestone, T. & Whelan, H., eds. Obesity: A Bibliography, 1964-1973. 263p. 25.00 (ISBN 0-904147-01-0). IRL Pr.

Silvestri, L., ed. Biology of Oncogenic Viruses. (Proceedings). 1971. 17.30 (ISBN 0-444-10079-2). Elsevier.

Silvestro, Clement M. Organizing a Local Historical Society. 2nd ed. 1968. pap. 3.50 (ISBN 0-910050-03-1). AASLH.

Silvet, J. Estonian-English Dictionary. 2nd ed. 508p. 1980. 55.00x (ISBN 0-686-82326-5, Pub. by Collets). State Mutual Bk.

Silvette, H., jt. auth. see Larson, P. S.

Silvey, Kitty, ed. see Atwood, Evangeline.

Silvey, Kitty, ed. see Elliott, Gerald.

Silvey, Kitty, ed. see Guinther, John.

Silvey, Kitty, ed. see MacArthur, William J.

Silvey, Linda. Geo-Ring Polyhedra. 1972. pap. text ed. 5.75 (ISBN 0-88488-045-1). Creative Pubns.

--Money Matters. 1973. pap. 4.95 wkbk. cancelled (ISBN 0-88488-037-0). Creative Pubns.

--Polyhedra Dice Games for Grades 5 to 10. (Illus.). (gr. 5-10). 1978. 7.25 (ISBN 0-88488-103-2). Creative Pubns.

Silvey, Linda & Taylor, Loretta. Paper & Scissors Polygins. (gr. 4-12). 1976. wkbk. 6.35 (ISBN 0-88488-057-5). Creative Pubns.

Silvey, Linda, jt. auth. see Pasternack, Marian.

Silvey, Linda, jt. auth. see Seymour, Dale.

Silvey, S. D. Optimal Design. 1981. 17.95x (ISBN 0-412-22910-2). Methuen Inc.

--Statistical Inference. (Monographs on Statistics & Applied Probability). 1975. 14.95x (ISBN 0-412-13820-4, Pub. by Chapman & Hall). Methuen Inc.

Silvia, M. T. & Robinson, E. A. Deconvolution of Geophysical Time Series in the Exploration of Oil & Natural Gas. (Developments in Petroleum Science Ser.: Vol. 10). 1979. 55.50 (ISBN 0-444-41679-X). Elsevier.

Silvia, Manual T., jt. auth. see Robinson, Enders A.

Silvian, Leonore. Understanding Diabetes. (Illus., Orig.). 1977. pap. 2.95 o.p. (ISBN 0-671-18330-3). Monarch Pr.

Silvius, G. Harold & Bohn, Ralph C. Planning & Organizing Instruction. rev. ed. Orig. Title: Organizing Course Materials for Industrial Education. 1976. text ed. 19.35 (ISBN 0-87345-720-X). McKnight.

Silvius, George H. & Curry, Estell H. Managing Multiple Activities in Industrial Education. new ed. 1971. text ed. 19.35 (ISBN 0-87345-456-1). McKnight.

Sim, Duncan. Change in the City Centre. 124p. 1982. text ed. 29.50x (ISBN 0-566-00405-4). Gower Pub Ltd.

Sim, Edith. Membrane Biochemistry. (Outline Studies in Biology). 1982. pap. 6.50x (ISBN 0-412-23810-1, Pub. by Chapman & Hall). Methuen Inc.

Sim, F. Robert Browning: The Poet & the Man. LC 72-3196. (Studies in Browning, No. 4). 1972. Repr. of 1923 ed. lib. bdg. 49.95x (ISBN 0-8383-1538-0). Haskell.

Sim, Fan Kok. Women in Southeast Asia: A Bibliography. 1982. lib. bdg. 55.00 (ISBN 0-8161-8407-0, Hall Reference). G K Hall.

Sim, Joseph M. Minor Tooth Movement in Children. 2nd ed. LC 77-24370. (Illus.). 494p. 1977. 49.50 o.p. (ISBN 0-8016-4616-2). Mosby.

Sim, Kevin. Women at War: Five Heroines Who Defied the Nazis & Survived. LC 82-8092. 1982. 12.95 (ISBN 0-688-01324-4). Morrow.

Sim, M. E., jt. auth. see Eccles, M. J.

Sim, T. R. Bryophyta of South Africa. 1973. 70.40 (ISBN 3-87429-053-0). Lubrecht & Cramer.

Simak, Clifford. Destiny Doll. 1982. pap. 2.50 (ISBN 0-87997-772-8, UE1772). DAW Bks.

Simak, Clifford D. All Flesh Is Grass. 1978. pap. 1.75 o.s.i. (ISBN 0-380-39933-4, 39933). Avon.

--Shakespeare's Planet. 224p. 1982. pap. 2.75 (ISBN 0-686-81744-3, Del Rey). Ballantine.

--Special Deliverance. 224p. (Orig.). 1982. pap. 2.75 (ISBN 0-345-29140-9, Del Rey). Ballantine.

--Time & Again. 256p. 1983. pap. 2.50 (ISBN 0-441-81003-9, Pub. by Ace Science Fiction). Ace Bks.

--The Trouble with Tycho. pap. 2.50 (ISBN 0-441-82443-9, Pub. by Ace Science Fiction). Ace Bks.

Simart, G., jt. auth. see Picard, Emile.

Simatupang, T. B. Report from Banaran: The Story of the Experiences of a Soldier During the War of Independence. Anderson, Benedict & Graves, Elizabeth, trs. 186p. 1972. pap. 6.50 (ISBN 0-87763-005-4). Cornell Mod Indo.

Simbulam, Roland G. Her Fall Is Her Triumph. 1978. 5.95 o.p. (ISBN 0-533-03594-5). Vantage.

Simcoe, Frank. The Official Guide to Outdoor Skating. LC 79-67000. (Illus.). 96p. 1980. 5.98 o.p. (ISBN 0-89196-061-9, Domus Bks). Quality Bks IL.

Sime, James. Life of Johann Wolfgang Goethe. LC 77-160782. 1971. Repr. of 1888 ed. 12.00 o.p. (ISBN 0-8046-1614-0). Kennikat.

Sime, Max S. & Coombs, Michael J., eds. Designing for Human-Computer Communication. write for info. (ISBN 0-12-643820-X). Acad Pr.

Simenon. Les Enigmes. (Easy Reader, B). pap. 3.95 (ISBN 0-88436-058-X, 40269). EMC.

--Maigret et le Clochard. (Easy Reader, B). pap. 3.95 (ISBN 0-88436-047-4, 40270). EMC.

Simenon, Georges. Aunt Jeanne. Sainsbury, Geoffrey, tr. 160p. 13.95 (ISBN 0-15-109792-5). HarBraceJ.

--The Iron Staircase. LC 80-25624. 1981. pap. 2.95 (ISBN 0-15-645484-X, Harv). HarbraceJ.

--The Long Exile. Ellenbogen, Eileen, tr. LC 81-48019. (A Helen & Kurt Wolff Bk.). 372p. 1982. 15.95 (ISBN 0-15-152997-3). HarBraceJ.

--Maigret Afraid. Duff, Margaret, tr. 192p. 13.95 (ISBN 0-15-155560-5). HarBraceJ.

--Maigret & the Hotel Majestic. Hillier, Caroline, tr. LC 77-84398. 176p. 1982. pap. 3.95 (ISBN 0-15-655133-0, Harv). HarBraceJ.

--Maigret & the Nahour Case. LC 82-47661. (A Helen & Kurt Wolff Bk.). 168p. 1982. 10.95 (ISBN 0-15-155559-1). HarBraceJ.

--Maigret & the Spinster. Ellenbogen, Eileen, tr. LC 76-27416. (A Helen & Kurt Wolff Bk). 1977. Repr. 6.95 o.p. (ISBN 0-15-155550-8). HarBraceJ.

--Maigret & the Spinster. LC 76-27416. 1982. pap. 3.95 (ISBN 0-15-655129-2, Harv). HarBraceJ.

--Maigret et le Fantome. (Easy Readers, B). (Illus.). 1976. pap. text ed. 3.95 (ISBN 0-88436-287-6). EMC.

--Maigret in Exile. Ellenbogen, Eileen, tr. LC 78-13771. (A Helen & Kurt Wolff Bk.). 1979. 7.95 (ISBN 0-15-155147-2, Harv); pap. 3.95 (ISBN 0-15-655136-5). HarBraceJ.

--Maigret Mystified. Orig. Title: Shadow in the Courtyard. 1964. pap. 1.95 o.p. (ISBN 0-14-002024-1). Penguin.

--A Maigret Trio: Maigret's Failure, Maigret in Society, & Maigret & the Lazy Burglar. Woodard, Daphne & Eglesfield, Robert, trs. 288p. pap. 6.95 (ISBN 0-15-655137-3, Harv). HarBraceJ.

--Pipe de Maigret. Goodall, Geoffrey, ed. 70p. (Fr.). 1969. 4.95 (ISBN 0-312-46235-2). St Martin.

--The Venice Train. Hamilton, Alastair, tr. 156p. pap. 3.95 (ISBN 0-15-693523-6, Harv). HarBraceJ.

Simeone, Frederick A., jt. ed. see Rothman, Richard H.

Simeone, Joseph F. Complete Spanish-English Reference Guide. 1983. 11.95 (ISBN 0-533-05530-X). Vantage.

Simer, Peter & Sullivan, John. The National Outdoor Leadership School's Official Wilderness Guide. (Illus.). 1983. price not set (ISBN 0-671-24996-7); pap. price not set (ISBN 0-671-24997-5). S&S.

Simha, Robert, jt. ed. see Goldstein, Martin.

Simic, Andrei. The Peasant Urbanites: A Study of Rural-Urban Mobility in Serbia. (Studies in Anthropology). 150p. 1972. 30.50 (ISBN 0-12-785790-7). Acad Pr.

Simic, Charles. Weather Forecast For Utopia & Vicinity. 56p. (Orig.). 1983. 11.95 (ISBN 0-930794-82-6); pap. 5.95 (ISBN 0-930794-83-4). Station Hill Pr.

Simic, Z. English-Serbocroatian Dictionary. 446p. (Eng. & Serbocroatian.). 1979. pap. text ed. 14.95 (ISBN 0-686-97375-5, M-9634). French & Eur.

--Yugoslavian Dictionary: English-Serbocroatian. 446p. 1977. pap. text ed. 6.50x (ISBN 0-89918-784-6). Vanous.

Simini, Joseph Peter. Accounting Made Simple. LC 66-12174. pap. 4.95 (ISBN 0-385-02032-5, Made). Doubleday.

Siminoff, Jonathan. The Timex Personal Computer Made Simple. 1982. pap. 3.50 (ISBN 0-451-12138-4, AE2138, Sig). NAL.

Simionescu, C. I., jt. auth. see Vogl, O.

Simitses, George J. An Introduction to the Elastic Stability of Structures. (Illus.). 288p. 1976. 31.95 (ISBN 0-13-481200-X). P-H.

Simiu, Emil & Scanlan, Robert H. Wind Effects on Structures: An Introduction to Wind Engineering. LC 77-21192. 458p. 1978. 41.95 (ISBN 0-471-02175-X, Pub. by Wiley-Interscience). Wiley.

Simkin, James S. Mini-Lectures in Gestalt Therapy. Levitsky, Abraham & Snyder, Mary A., eds. 1974. pap. 3.95 (ISBN 0-915104-01-6). Wordpress.

Simkin, Mark G., jt. auth. see Moscove, Stephen A.

Simkin, Peter A. Heart & Rheumatic Disease, Vol. 2. new ed. (BIMR Rheumatology Ser.). 320p. 1983. text ed. price not set (ISBN 0-407-02353-4). Butterworth.

Simkin, Tom & Fiske, Richard. Krakatau: The Volcanic Eruption & its Effects - A Centennial Retrospective. (Illus.). 400p. 1983. text ed. 15.00 (ISBN 0-87474-842-9). Smithsonian.

Simkin, Tom, et al. Volcanoes of the World: A Regional Gazetteer & Chronology of Volcanism During the Last 10,000 Years. LC 81-6594. 240p. 1981. 24.95 (ISBN 0-87933-408-8). Hutchinson Ross.

Simkin, William E. Mediation & the Dynamics of Collective Bargaining. LC 73-161510. 424p. 1971. 20.00 (ISBN 0-87179-127-7); pap. 10.50 (ISBN 0-87179-115-3). BNA.

Simkins, Francis B. & Roland, Charles P. A History of the South. 4th ed. 744p. 1972. text ed. 24.00 (ISBN 0-394-31646-0, RanC). Random.

Simkins, M. A., jt. auth. see International Symposium on Medicinal Chemistry, Brighton, U. K., 6th, Sept. 4-7, 1978.

Simkins, Paul D. & Wernstedt, Frederick L. Philippine Migration: The Settlement of the Digos-Padada Valley, Davao Province. LC 73-154010. (Monograph Ser.: No. 16). (Illus.). 147p. 1970. 8.25x (ISBN 0-686-30902-2). Yale U SE Asia.

Simko, J. Czechoslovakian Dictionary: English-Sloviak Dictionary. 1971. text ed. 15.00x o.p. (ISBN 0-89918-260-7, C260). Vanous.

Simler, Norman J. The Impact of Unionism on Wage-Income Ratios in the Manufacturing Sector of the Economy. LC 82-21141. (University of Minnesota Studies in Economics & Business: No. 22). iii, 71p. 1983. Repr. of 1961 ed. lib. bdg. 22.50x (ISBN 0-313-23700-X, SIIM). Greenwood.

Simma, Bruno, jt. auth. see Ruster, Bernd.

Simma, Maria. My Personal Experiences with the Poor Souls. Helena, M., tr. from Ger. 1978. 7.95 o.p. (ISBN 0-8199-0744-8). Franciscan Herald.

Simmang, Clifford M., jt. auth. see Faires, Virgil M.

Simmel, E. C., jt. ed. see Fuller, J. L.

Simmel, Edward C. & Hahn, Martin E., eds. Aggressive Behavior: Genetic & Neural Approaches. 1983. text ed. write for info. (ISBN 0-89859-253-4). L Erlbaum Assocs.

Simmel, Edward G., ed. Early Experiences & Early Behavior: Implications for Social Development. LC 79-21421. 1979. 19.50 (ISBN 0-12-644080-8). Acad Pr.

Simmel, Georg. Philosophy of Money. Bottomore, Tom & Frisby, David, trs. from Fr. 1978. 40.00x (ISBN 0-7100-8874-4); pap. 10.95 (ISBN 0-7100-9205-9). Routledge & Kegan.

Simmen, Edward, ed. Chicano: From Caricature to Self-Portrait. 1971. pap. 3.50 (ISBN 0-451-62132-8, ME2132, Ment). NAL.

--Pain & Promise: The Chicano Today. 1972. pap. 1.50 o.p. (ISBN 0-451-61507-7, MW1507, Ment). NAL.

Simmerman, Jim. Home. 104p. 1983. 13.00 (ISBN 0-937872-10-5); pap. 6.00 (ISBN 0-937872-11-3). Dragon Gate.

Simmerman, Nancy, jt. auth. see Nienheuser, Helen.

Simmers, Louise M. Diversified Health Occupations. LC 82-73084. (Illus.). 480p. (Orig.). 1983. text ed. 20.00 (ISBN 0-8273-2288-7); write for info. set wkbk. (ISBN 0-8273-2289-5); write for info. instr's guide (ISBN 0-8273-2290-9). Delmar.

Simmie, Lois. They Shouldn't Make you Promise That. 1982. pap. 2.50 (ISBN 0-451-11866-9, AE1866, Sig). NAL.

Simmonds, D., jt. auth. see Reynolds, L.

Simmonds, Harvey. John Quinn: An Exhibition to Mark the Gift of the John Quinn Memorial Collection. (Illus.). 1968. pap. 2.00 o.p. (ISBN 0-87104-224-X). NY Pub Lib.

Simmonds, Harvey, jt. auth. see Szladits, Lola L.

Simmonds, Harvey, ed. Choreography by George Balanchine. LC 82-83072. 75.00 (ISBN 0-87130-050-8). Eakins.

Simmonds, James D., ed. Milton Studies, Vol. 16. LC 69-12335. (Illus.). vi, 199p. 1983. 17.95x (ISBN 0-8229-3465-5). U of Pittsburgh Pr.

Simmonds, James D., jt. ed. see Marilla, Esmond L.

Simmonds, K. Multinational Corporations Law, 2 bdrs. LC 78-277044. 1979. Set. loose-leaf 225.00 (ISBN 0-379-20373-1). Oceana.

Simmonds, K. R., ed. Cases on Law of the Sea, 7 vols. LC 76-27559. 1977. 42.50 ea. (ISBN 0-379-00885-8). Oceana.

Simmonds, N. W. Bananas. 2nd ed. LC 82-116. (Tropical Agriculture Ser.). (Illus.). 568p. 1982. pap. text ed. 29.95x (ISBN 0-582-46355-6). Longman.

Simmonds, W. H., jt. ed. see Linstone, Harold A.

Simmons, A. & Diaz, Briquets S. Evolution Sociale et Migration Interne en Afrique. 55p. 1978. pap. 3.50 o.p. (ISBN 0-88936-160-6, IDRC-TS11F, IDRC). Unipub.

Simmons, Adelma G. The Illustrated Herbal Handbook. 120p. 1972. pap. 5.25 o.p. (ISBN 0-8015-3960-9, Hawthorn). Dutton.

--A Merry Christmas Herbal. LC 68-56414. (Illus.). 160p. 1968. pap. 7.95 (ISBN 0-688-07080-9). Morrow.

Simmons, Alan F. Potted Orchards: Growing Fruit in Small Spaces. (Illus.). 192p. 1975. 4.95 o.p. (ISBN 0-7153-6666-1). David & Charles.

Simmons, Allison, jt. ed. see Davis, Douglas.

Simmons, Bob & Simmons, Coleen. Crepes & Omelets. Walsh, Jackie, ed. LC 76-8426. (Illus., Orig.). 1976. pap. 5.95 (ISBN 0-911954-73-2). Nitty Gritty.

Simmons, Charles. Wrinkles. 1982. pap. 2.95 (ISBN 0-686-82396-6). Bantam.

Simmons, Charles M. Your Subconscious Power. pap. 5.00 (ISBN 0-87980-178-6). Wilshire.

Simmons, Charles W. & Morris, Harry W. Afro-American History. LC 71-184567. 344p. 1972. pap. text ed. 8.95x (ISBN 0-675-09131-4). Merrill.

Simmons, Coleen, jt. auth. see Simmons, Bob.

Simmons, Colin, jt. ed. see Ingham, Barbara.

Simmons, D. H. Current Pulmonology, Vol. 3. LC 79-643614. 441p. 1981. 55.00 (ISBN 0-471-09505-2, Pub. by Wiley Med). Wiley.

Simmons, D. R. The Great New Zealand Myth. 1978. 24.75 o.p. (ISBN 0-589-00949-4, Pub. by Reed Books Australia). C E Tuttle.

Simmons, Daniel E. Current Pulmonology, Vol. 2. (Current Pulmonology Ser.). (Illus.). 384p. 1980. text ed. 55.00x (ISBN 0-471-09496-X, Pub. by Wiley Med). Wiley.

Simmons, Daniel H. Current Pulmonology, Vol. 4. (Current Pulmonology Ser.). 239p. 1982. 60.00 (ISBN 0-471-09558-3, Pub. by Wiley Med). Wiley.

Simmons, Daniel H., ed. Current Pulmonology, Vol. 1. (Current Pulmonology Ser.). (Illus.). 278p. 1979. 55.00 (ISBN 0-471-09495-1, Pub. by Wiley Med). Wiley.

Simmons, David J. & Kukin, Arthur S., eds. Skeletal Research: An Experimental Approach. 1979. 65.00 (ISBN 0-12-644150-2). Acad Pr.

Simmons, Diane. Joanna, the Crowing Hen of Bethel. 1979. pap. 2.25 (ISBN 0-570-07976-4, 39-1116). Concordia.

Simmons, E. D. Scientific Art of Logic. 1st ed. 1961. 4.80 o.p. (ISBN 0-02-829000-3). Glencoe.

Simmons, Edith, tr. see Berthold, Margot.

Simmons, Emmy B., jt. auth. see Norman, David W.

Simmons, Ernest J., ed. & intro. by see Tolstoy, Leo.

Simmons, Gene & Wang, Herbert. Single Crystal Elastic Constants & Calculated Aggregate Properties. 1971. 22.50x (ISBN 0-262-19092-3). MIT Pr.

Simmons, George F. Differential Equations with Applications & Historical Notes. (Pure & Applied Mathematics Ser.). (Illus.). 480p. 1972. text ed. 29.00 (ISBN 0-07-057375-1, C). McGraw.

--Introduction to Topology & Modern Analysis. (International Series in Pure & Applied Mathematics). 1963. text ed. 30.00 o.p. (ISBN 0-07-057389-1, C). McGraw.

--Introduction to Topology & Modern Analysis. 388p. 1982. Repr. of 1963 ed. lib. bdg. 23.50 (ISBN 0-89874-551-9). Krieger.

Simmons, Gustavus J., ed. Secure Communications & Asymetric Crypto-Systems. (Selected Symposium Ser. 69). 225p. 1982. lib. bdg. 30.00 (ISBN 0-86531-338-5). Westview.

Simmons, Harold E. California Mental Health: The Struggle for Turf. 1978. pap. 10.00 (ISBN 0-87312-008-6). Gen Welfare Pubns.

--California Welfare Reform: Recycling the 1601 Elizabethan Poor Law. 1975. pap. 10.00 (ISBN 0-87312-006-X). Gen Welfare Pubns.

--A Microcosm of Events: Inside California State Bureaucracy. 1978. pap. 5.00 (ISBN 0-87312-009-4). Gen Welfare Pubns.

--Psychogenic Theory of Disease: A New Approach to Cancer Research. 1966. pap. 10.00 o.p. (ISBN 0-87312-000-0). Gen Welfare Pubns.

--Work Relief to Rehabilitation. (Orig.). 1969. pap. 12.00 (ISBN 0-87312-002-7). Gen Welfare Pubns.

--Your Psyche, the Cigarette & the Pill: The Psychogenic Theory of Disease. 1969. pap. 10.00 o.p. (ISBN 0-87312-003-5). Gen Welfare Pubns.

Simmons, Ian. The Ecology of Natural Resources. LC 74-4812. 432p. 1974. pap. text ed. 22.95x o.p. (ISBN 0-470-79194-2). Halsted Pr.

Simmons, J. H. & Uhlmann, D. K., eds. Advances in Ceramics: Vol. 4: Nucleation & Crystallization in Glasses. 1982. non-members 45.00 (ISBN 0-916094-50-2); student members 30.00 (ISBN 0-686-83185-3); members 35.00 (ISBN 0-686-83186-1). Am Ceramic.

Simmons, J. L. Shakespeare's Pagan World: The Roman Tragedies. LC 73-80126. 1973. 14.95x (ISBN 0-8139-0488-9). U Pr of Va.

Simmons, Jack. The Railway in England & Wales, 1830-1914. Incl. Vol. 2. Town & Country. text ed. price not set (ISBN 0-391-01168-5); Vol. 3. Mind & Eve. text ed. price not set (ISBN 0-391-01169-3); Vol. 4. The Community. text ed. price not set (ISBN 0-391-01170-7). (Illus.). Date not set. text ed. price not set (ISBN 0-685-51832-9, Leicester). Humanities.

Simmons, James. Creative Business Financing: How to Make Your Best Deal When Negotiating Equipment, Leases & Business Loans. (Illus.). 310p. 1983. 23.95 (ISBN 0-13-189159-6); pap. 12.95 (ISBN 0-13-189142-1). P-H.

Simmons, James C., jt. auth. see Rudisill, Marie.

Simmons, Janet A. The Nurse-Client Relationship in Mental Health Nursing: Workbook Guides to Understanding & Management. LC 75-40639. 240p. 1978. pap. 9.95 o.p. (ISBN 0-7216-8286-3). Saunders.

Simmons, Joe. The Warrior: Brief Studies in the Sources of Spiritual Mastery, Sport, & Military Power. LC 81-40925. 196p. (Orig.). 1982. lib. bdg. 22.00 (ISBN 0-8191-2293-9); pap. text ed. 10.00 (ISBN 0-8191-2294-7). U Pr of Amer.

Simmons, John. The Life of Plants. LC 77-88438. (Easy Reading Edition of Introduction to Nature Ser.). (Illus.). 1978. PLB 12.68 (ISBN 0-382-06128-4). Silver.

Simmons, John & Mares, William J. Working Together. LC 82-47826. (Illus.). 320p. 1983. 15.00 (ISBN 0-394-51343-6). Knopf.

Simmons, John, ed. Cocoa Production: Economic & Botanical Perspectives. LC 75-19821. (Special Studies). 1976. 52.95 o.p. (ISBN 0-275-56030-9). Praeger.

Simmons, M. Leigh. Career Guide to the Animal Health Field. 1980. pap. 6.95 o.p. (ISBN 0-932036-01-5). Petersons Guides.

Simmons, Marc. The Little Lion of the Southwest: A Life of Manuel Antonio Chaves. Cisneros, Jose, tr. LC 73-1500. 263p. 1974. 12.95 o.p. (ISBN 0-8040-0632-6, SB). Swallow.

--Turquoise & Six-Guns: The Story of Cerrillos, New Mexico. new rev. ed. (Illus.). 1975. pap. 3.95 (ISBN 0-913270-33-4). Sunstone Pr.

Simmons, Mary Ann, jt. ed. see Knight, Allen W.

Simmons, Merle E., ed. Folklore Bibliography for 1976. (Indiana University Folklore Institute Monograph Ser.: Vol. 33). 240p. 1981. text ed. 17.50x (ISBN 0-89727-023-1). Inst Study Hum.

Simmons, Paul D. Birth & Death: Bioethical Decision-Making. LC 82-20160. (Biblical Perspectives on Current Issues). 276p. 1983. pap. price not set (ISBN 0-664-24463-7). Westminster.

Simmons, Paul D. & Crawford, Kenneth. Mi Desarrollo Sexual. Sabanes De Plou, Dafne, tr. from Eng. (El Sexo En la Vida Cristiana). 96p. (Span.). (gr. 10-12). 1980. Repr. of 1979 ed. pap. 2.50 (ISBN 0-311-46257-X, Edit Mundo). Casa Bautista.

Simmons, R. C. & Thomas, P. D. G., eds. Great Britain-Parliament-Proceedings & Debates of the British Parliaments, Respecting North America, 1754 to 1783. LC 81-20814. 1982. Vol. 1. lib. bdg. 75.00 (ISBN 0-527-35723-5); Vol. 2. lib. bdg. 90.00. Kraus Intl.

Simmons, Richard. Richard Simmons' Never-Say-Diet Cook Book. (Illus.). 1980. 14.95 (ISBN 0-446-51209-5); pap. 7.95 (ISBN 0-446-97041-7). Warner Bks.

Simmons, Richard A., jt. auth. see Lasker, Michael.

Simmons, Richard E. Managing Behavioral Processes: Applications of Theory & Research. Mackenzie, Kenneth D., ed. LC 77-86007. (Organizational Behavior Ser.). (Illus.). 1978. pap. text ed. 13.95x (ISBN 0-88295-454-7). Harlan Davidson.

Simmons, Roberta G., ed. Research in Community & Mental Health: An Annual Compilation of Research, Vol. 1. 1979. lib. bdg. 42.50 (ISBN 0-89232-063-X). Jai Pr.

--Research in Community & Mental Health, Vol. 2. 400p. 1981. 42.50 (ISBN 0-89232-152-0). Jai Pr.

Simmons, Roberta G., et al. Gift of Life: The Social & Psychological Impact of Organ Transplantation. LC 77-2749. (Health, Medicine & Society Ser.). 526p. 1977. 45.00 (ISBN 0-471-79197-0, Pub by Wiley-Interscience). Wiley.

Simmons, Roger, tr. see Kutac, Edward A. & Caran, S. Christopher.

Simmons, Seymour & Winer, Marc S. Drawing: The Creative Process. (Illus.). 1977. 22.95 (ISBN 0-13-219378-7, Spec); pap. 10.95 (ISBN 0-13-219360-4, Spec). P-H.

Simmons, Steven J. The Fairness Doctrine & the Media. LC 77-85740. 1978. 19.95x (ISBN 0-520-03585-2). U of Cal Pr.

Simmons, Vickie & Williams, Irene. Attending: Steps Up to Language for the Learning Impaired. Rev. ed. 64p. 1982. 7.95 (ISBN 0-88450-755-6, 4015-B). Communication Skill.

--Pre-Math: The Success Training Program of Increasingly Complex Number Skills. (Steps up to Number Skills for the Learning Impaired Ser.). 96p. 1982. pap. text ed. 10.95 (ISBN 0-88450-820-X, 2068-B). Communication Skill.

Simmons, William S. Kasimir Malevich's Black Square & the Gensis of Suprematism 1907-1915. LC 79-57496. (Outstanding Dissertations in the Fine Arts Ser.). 334p. 1982. lib. bdg. 35.00 o.s.i. (ISBN 0-8240-3942-4). Garland Pub.

Simms & Lindberg. The Nurse Person: Developing Perspectives for Contemporary Nursing. text ed. 17.95 (ISBN 0-06-046216-7, Lippincott Nursing). Lippincott.

Simms, Eric. A Natural History of Britain & Ireland. (Illus.). 258p. 1979. 15.75x o.p. (ISBN 0-460-04372-2, Pub. by J. M. Dent England). Biblio Dist.

Simms, G. O. The Book of Kells: A Selection of Pages Reproduced with a Description & Notes. 1976. Repr. of 1961 ed. pap. text ed. 4.25x (ISBN 0-391-00608-8, Dolmen Pr). Humanities.

Simms, J. A. & Simms, T. H. From Three to Thirteen: Socialization & Achievement in School. (Longman Sociology of Education Ser.). 1969. text ed. 5.00x o. p. (ISBN 0-582-32436-X); pap. text ed. 3.00x (ISBN 0-582-32437-8). Humanities.

Simms, J. G. see Kelly, P. H.

Simms, John D., jt. auth. see Logue, H. E.

Simms, John G. The Williamite Confiscation in Ireland, 1690-1703. LC 76-44839. (Studies in Irish History: Vol. 7). (Illus.). 1977. Repr. of 1956 ed. lib. bdg. 17.75x (ISBN 0-8371-9306-0, SIWI). Greenwood.

Simms, Richard L. & Contreras, Gloria, eds. Racism & Sexism: Responding to the Challenge. LC 79-92018. (Bulletin Ser.: No. 61). 96p. (Orig.). 1980. pap. 7.25 (ISBN 0-87986-025-1). Coun Soc Studies.

Simms, T. H., jt. auth. see Simms, J. A.

Simms, William G., ed. The Charleston Book: A Miscellany in Prose & Verse. (The South Caroliniana Ser.: No. 8). 432p. 1983. Repr. of 1845 ed. 25.00 (ISBN 0-87152-378-7). Reprint.

Simnad, M. T. & Zumwatt, L. R., eds. Materials & Fuels for High-Temperature Nuclear Applications. 1964. 25.00x (ISBN 0-262-19012-5). MIT Pr.

Simoes, Antonio, Jr., ed. The Bilingual Child: Research & Analysis of Existing Educational Themes. 1976. 28.50 (ISBN 0-12-644050-6). Acad Pr.

Simon. Necronomicon. 288p. 1979. pap. 3.50 (ISBN 0-380-75192-5, 82008-0). Avon.

--A Time for Action. 1980. 10.00 (ISBN 0-07-057493-6). McGraw.

--Watercolor. (Grosset Art Introduction Ser.: Vol. 42). pap. 2.95 (ISBN 0-448-00551-4, G&D). Putnam Pub Group.

Simon & Hamilton. X-Ray Anatomy. (Illus.). 1978. 64.95 o.p. (ISBN 0-407-00096-8). Butterworth.

Simon & Silverstone. Cancer of the Uterus. 1983. cancelled (ISBN 0-89352-016-0). Masson Pub.

Simon, Albert & Thompson, William B. Advances in Plasma Physics, 5 vols. Incl. Vol. 1. 1968. 25.50 o.p. (ISBN 0-470-79199-3); Vol. 2. 1969. 21.00 o.p. (ISBN 0-471-79195-4); Vol. 3. 1969. o.p. (ISBN 0-471-79203-9); Vol. 4. 1971. 31.95 o.p. (ISBN 0-471-79204-7); Vol. 5. 1974. 31.95 o.p. (ISBN 0-471-79196-2). LC 67-29541 (Pub. by Wiley-Interscience). Wiley.

Simon, Alexander & Epstein, Leon J., eds. Aging in Modern Society. 1968. pap. 7.50 o.p. (ISBN 0-685-24866-6, P023-0). Am Psychiatric.

Simon, Alfred E., jt. auth. see Kimball, Robert E.

Simon, Andre L. A Concise Encyclopedia of Gastronomy. LC 81-47413. 832p. 1981. pap. 11.95 (ISBN 0-87951-180-X). Overlook Pr.

Simon, Andrea, tr. see Musil, Robert.

Simon, Andrew L. Basic Hydraulics. LC 80-15341. 226p. 1981. text ed. 24.95 (ISBN 0-471-07965-0); tchr's manual (ISBN 0-471-08944-3). Wiley.

--Practical Hydraulics. 2nd ed. LC 79-27270. 403p. 1981. text ed. 24.95 (ISBN 0-471-05381-3); tchrs. ed. avail. (ISBN 0-471-07783-6). Wiley.

Simon, Andrew L. & Ross, David A. Principles of Statics & Strength of Materials. 475p. 1983. text ed. write for info. (ISBN 0-697-08604-6); instr's. manual avail. (ISBN 0-697-08605-4). Wm C Brown.

Simon, Anita, jt. auth. see Bramnick, Lea.

Simon, Anne, et al. Coast Alert: Scientists Speak Out. Jackson, Tom & Reische, Diana, eds. LC 81-68549. (Illus.). 204p. (Orig.). 1981. pap. 7.95 (ISBN 0-931790-44-1). Brick Hse Pub.

Simon, Arthur B. Calculus with Analytic Geometry. 1982. text ed. 35.50x (ISBN 0-673-16044-0). Scott F.

Simon, B. X. The California Directory of Healing Arts, Holistic & Homeopathic Practitioners. (Orig.). 1982. pap. write for info. o.s.i. (ISBN 0-935618-01-5). Rossi Pubns.

Simon, Barry. Trace Ideals & Their Applications. LC 78-20867. (London Mathematical Society Lecture Notes Ser.: No. 35). 1979. pap. 18.95x (ISBN 0-521-22286-9). Cambridge U Pr.

Simon, Brian, jt. auth. see Rubinstein, David.

Simon, Brian, ed. Education in the Eighties in Britain: A Central Issue. Taylor, William. 256p. 1981. 45.00 o.p. (ISBN 0-7134-3679-4, Pub. by Batsford England); pap. 14.95 (ISBN 0-7134-3680-8). David & Charles.

Simon, Brian & Bradley, Ian, eds. The Victorian Public School: Studies in the Development of an Educational Institution; a Symposium. (Illus.). 215p. 1975. text ed. 21.50x o.p. (ISBN 0-7171-0740-X). Humanities.

Simon, C. P., tr. see Martinet, Jean.

Simon, Charlann S. Communicative Competence: A Functional-Pragmatic Approach to Language Therapy. 149p. 1979. pap. text ed. 12.95 (ISBN 0-88450-704-1, 3103-B). Communication Skill.

Simon, Charles E., jt. auth. see Kennedy, Tom.

Simon, Claude. The World About Us. Weissbort, Daniel, tr. from Fr. 120p. 1983. 13.95 (ISBN 0-86538-033-3); pap. 6.95 (ISBN 0-86538-034-1). Ontario Rev NJ.

Simon, Eckehard. Neidhart von Reuental. LC 75-2067. (World Authors Ser.: Germany: No. 364). 1975. lib. bdg. 15.95 o.p. (ISBN 0-8057-6215-9, Twayne). G K Hall.

Simon, Ericka. The Ancient Theatre. 1982. 14.95x (ISBN 0-416-32520-3); pap. 5.95x (ISBN 0-416-32530-0). Methuen Inc.

Simon, Erika. Festivals of Attica: An Archaeological Commentary. 160p. 1983. text ed. 21.50 (ISBN 0-299-09180-5). U of Wis Pr.

Simon, Erika, jt. auth. see Hampe, Roland.

Simon, Ethelyn & Stahl, Nanette. The First Hebrew Primer for Adults. 2nd ed. 320p. (Orig.). 1983. pap. text ed. 14.95 (ISBN 0-939144-05-0). EKS Pub Co.

--The First Hebrew Primer for Adults. 2nd ed. 320p. 1983. lib. bdg. 34.95 (ISBN 0-939144-06-9). EKS Pub Co.

Simon, G. Principles of Bone X-Ray Diagnosis. 3rd ed. 1973. 49.95 o.p. (ISBN 0-407-36319-X). Butterworth.

--Principles of Chest X-Ray Diagnosis. 4th ed. 1978. 64.95 o.p. (ISBN 0-407-36323-8). Butterworth.

--X-Ray Diagnosis for Clinical Students. 3rd ed. 1975. 37.50 o.p. (ISBN 0-407-00004-6). Butterworth.

Simon, George T. The Big Bands. 4th ed. (Illus.). 600p. 1981. 20.00 (ISBN 0-02-872420-8); pap. 11.95 (ISBN 0-02-872430-5). Schirmer Bks.

--The Big Bands Songbook. LC 75-14419. (Illus.). 384p. 1981. pap. 11.06i (ISBN 0-06-464049-3, BN 4049, BN). B&N NY.

Simon, Gerald A., jt. ed. see Glover, John D.

Simon, Gerhard. Church, State & Opposition in U. S. S. R. LC 73-87754. 1974. 32.50x (ISBN 0-520-02612-8). U of Cal Pr.

Simon, Gilbert L., jt. auth. see Silverman, Harold L.

Simon, H. A., jt. auth. see Ijiri, Y.

Simon, H. A., jt. ed. see Bugliarello, George.

Simon, Hansjorg & Bloomfield, Dennis A. Cardioactive Drugs: A Pharmacological Basis for Practice. LC 82-13593. 187p. 1982. pap. 18.00 (ISBN 0-8067-1851-X). Urban & S.

Simon, Henry W. New Victor Book of the Opera. 1968. 21.75 (ISBN 0-671-20054-2). S&S.

Simon, Herbert, jt. ed. see Meynell, Francis.

Simon, Herbert A. Models of Bounded Rationality, 2 vols. Incl. Vol. 1. Economic Analysis & Public Policy. 392p. 30.00x (ISBN 0-262-19205-5); Vol. 2. Behavioral Economics & Business Organization. 496p. 30.00x (ISBN 0-262-19206-3). 1982. MIT Pr.

--Reason in Human Affairs. LC 82-62448. 128p. 1983. 10.00x (ISBN 0-8047-1179-8). Stanford U Pr.

--Sciences of the Artificial. 2nd ed. 192p. 1981. text ed. 16.50x (ISBN 0-262-19193-8); pap. 5.95 (ISBN 0-262-69073-X). MIT Pr.

Simon, Herbert A., jt. auth. see March, James G.

Simon, Herbert A., et al. Centralization vs. Decentralization in Organizing the Controller's Department. LC 77-90343. 1978. Repr. of 1954 ed. text ed. 13.00 (ISBN 0-914348-24-8). Scholars Bk.

Simon, Herbert A., et al, eds. Founders Symposium 1979, the Institute for Social Research: Honoring George Katona. LC 80-23866. 80p. 1980. pap. 6.50x (ISBN 0-87944-259-X). Inst Soc Res.

Simon, Hilda. Frogs & Toads of the World. LC 75-14095. (Illus.). 128p. (gr. 4-6). 1975. 10.53i (ISBN 0-397-31634-8, HarpJ). Har-Row.

--Milkweed Butterflies: Monarchs, Models, & Mimics. LC 68-56601. (Illus.). (gr. 4 up). 1968. 10.95 (ISBN 0-8149-0389-4). Vanguard.

Simon, J. Malcolm & Reeves, John A. Soccer Games Book. LC 82-81817. (Illus.). 160p. (Orig.). 1982. pap. 6.95 (ISBN 0-88011-064-3). Leisure Pr.

Simon, Jacques, jt. auth. see Rouard, Marguerite.

Simon, James & Chadwick. Herbs: An Indexed Bibliography of Last Decade, 1971-1980. (The Scientific Literature on Selected Temperate Herb, Aromatic, & Medicine Plants Ser.). 1983. 49.50 (ISBN 0-208-01990-1, Archon Bks). Shoe String.

Simon, James F. Independent Journey: The Life of William O. Douglas. LC 79-2637. (Illus.). 464p. 1980. 18.22i (ISBN 0-06-014042-9, HarpT). Har-Row.

Simon, Jo-Ann. Hold Fast to Love. 288p. 1982. pap. 3.95 (ISBN 0-380-80945-1, 81778-0). Avon.

Simon, Joan. Education & Society in Tudor England. LC 79-50915. 1979. 49.50 (ISBN 0-521-22854-9); pap. 15.95x (ISBN 0-521-29679-X). Cambridge U Pr.

--The Social Origins of English Education. (Students Library of Education). 1971. 7.50 o.p. (ISBN 0-7100-6945-6). Routledge & Kegan.

Simon, John. European Films in Review. 1982. 17.95 o.p. (ISBN 0-517-54903-4, C N Potter). Crown.

--Paradigms Lost: Literacy & Its Decline. (Illus.). 224p. 1980. 12.95 o.p. (ISBN 0-517-54034-7, C N Potter Bks). Crown.

--Reverse Angle. 1982. pap. 11.95 (ISBN 0-517-54697-3, C N Potter Bks). Crown.

--Reverse Angle: American Film 1970-1980. 384p. 1981. 17.95 (ISBN 0-517-54471-7, C N Potter Bks). Crown.

--Something to Declare: Twelve Years of Films from Abroad. LC 82-16534. 422p. 1983. 19.95 (ISBN 0-686-42946-X, C N Potter). Crown.

Simon, John, frwd. by see Young, Dennis R.

Simon, John B. To Become Somebody. 1982. 12.95 o.p. (ISBN 0-395-32052-6). HM.

Simon, John M. Abingdon Clergy Tax Record Book, 1983. 80p. (Orig.). 1983. pap. 5.95 (ISBN 0-687-00386-5). Abingdon.

Simon, John Y., ed. Personal Memoirs of Julia Dent Grant (Mrs. Ulysses S. Grant) 1975. 12.50 o.p. (ISBN 0-399-11386-X). Putnam Pub Group.

Simon, John Y., ed. see Grant, Ulysses S.

Simon, Julian, ed. Research in Population Economics, Vol. 3. 300p. 1981. 47.50 (ISBN 0-89232-207-1). Jai Pr.

--Research in Population Economics, Vol. 4. 325p. 1981. 49.50 (ISBN 0-89232-242-X). Jai Pr.

Simon, Julian L. Basic Research Methods in Social Science. 2nd ed. 1978. pap. text ed. 23.00x (ISBN 0-394-32049-2). Random.

--How to Start & Operate a Mail Order Business. 3rd. ed. LC 80-13807. (Illus.). 544p. 1980. 24.95 (ISBN 0-07-057417-0, P&RB). McGraw.

Simon, Julian L., ed. Research in Population Economics, Vol. 1. (Orig.). 1978. lib. bdg. 45.00 (ISBN 0-89232-018-4). Jai Pr.

--Research in Population Economics, Vol. 2. (Orig.). 1980. lib. bdg. 45.00 (ISBN 0-89232-125-3). Jai Pr.

Simon, Kate. Mexico: Places & Pleasures. rev ed. LC 78-3317. (Illus.). 1979. 16.30i (ISBN 0-690-01653-0, Tyc-T); pap. 7.95xi (ISBN 0-690-01778-2). T y Crowell.

Simon, Kathrin, tr. see Wolfflin, Heinrich.

Simon, Kia & Bosserman, Lorelei. And Everybody Is a Children. new ed. (Children's Poetry Ser.). (Illus.). 32p. 1974. pap. 0.50 o.p. (ISBN 0-915288-09-5). Shameless Hussy.

Simon, L. M., jt. ed. see Price, P. F.

Simon, Laurence R. El Salvador Land Reform: Nineteen Eighty to Nineteen Eighty-One. Stephens, James C., Jr., ed. (Impact Audit Ser.: No. 2). 55p. (Orig.). 1981. pap. 5.00 (ISBN 0-910281-01-7). Oxfam Am.

Simon, Leslie. High Desire. 80p. 1983. pap. 4.95 (ISBN 0-914728-41-5). Wingbow Pr.

Simon, Linda. Thornton Wilder-His World. LC 78-73193. (Illus.). 1979. 10.95 o.p. (ISBN 0-385-12840-1). Doubleday.

Simon, Louis. Shaw on Education. LC 73-16953. 290p. 1974. Repr. of 1958 ed. lib. bdg. 17.00x (ISBN 0-8371-7245-4, SISH). Greenwood.

Simon, Louise A., jt. ed. see Norman, Hope J.

Simon, M. K., jt. auth. see Lindsey, W. C.

Simon, Mark K., jt. ed. see Lindsey, William C.

Simon, Martin P., jt. auth. see Jahsmann, Allan H.

Simon, Marvin K., jt. auth. see Lindsey, William C.

Simon, Maurice D., jt. auth. see Kanet, Roger E.

Simon, Michael A. Understanding Human Action: Social Explanation of the Vision of Social Science. LC 88-5280. (Systematic Philosophy Ser.). 170p. 1981. 34.50x (ISBN 0-87395-498-X); pap. 10.95x (ISBN 0-87395-499-8). State U NY Pr.

Simon, Michael S. Construction Contracts & Claims. 1979. 27.50 (ISBN 0-07-057433-2, P&RB). McGraw.

Simon, Myron. The Georgian Poetic. (Library Reprint: Vol. 89). 1978. 21.00x (ISBN 0-520-03618-2); pap. 5.95x o.p. (ISBN 0-520-09495-6). U of Cal Pr.

Simon, Nathan, ed. The Psychological Aspects of Intensive Care Nursing. 295p. 1980. text ed. 16.95 o.p. (ISBN 0-87619-663-6). R J Brady.

Simon, Neil. The Collected Plays of Neil Simon, Vol. 2. 1980. pap. 7.95 (ISBN 0-380-51904-6, 51904-6). Avon.

--Fools. 1982. 10.50 (ISBN 0-394-52390-3). Random.

Simon, Noel, jt. auth. see Duplaix, Nicole.

Simon, Norma. I Wish I Had My Father. Tucker, Kathleen, ed. (Concept Bks.). (Illus.). 32p. (gr. 1-4). 1983. PLB 7.50 (ISBN 0-8075-3522-2). A Whitman.

Simon, Peter, jt. auth. see Davis, Stephen.

Simon, Peter, illus. On the Vineyard. LC 79-7878. (Illus.). 192p. 1980. 24.95 (ISBN 0-385-17176-5, Anchor Pr). Doubleday.

Simon, R. L., jt. auth. see Bowie, Norman E.

Simon, Raymond. Publicity & Public Relations Worktext. 5th ed. LC 82-9305. (Grid Series in Advertising & Journalism). 272p. 1982. 14.95 (ISBN 0-88244-253-8). Grid Pub.

Simon, Reeva S. The Modern Middle East: A Guide to Research Tools in the Social Sciences. LC 77-27319. (Westview Special Studies on the Middle East Ser.). 1978. lib. bdg. 29.00 o.p. (ISBN 0-89158-059-X); pap. 12.00 o.p. (ISBN 0-89158-158-8). Westview.

Simon, Rita J. Continuity & Change. LC 77-15090. (ASA Rose Monograph Ser.: No. 6). (Illus.). 1978. 24.95 (ISBN 0-521-21938-8); pap. 8.95x (ISBN 0-521-29318-9). Cambridge U Pr.

--The Jury: Its Role in American Society. LC 77-17682. 176p. 1980. 21.95x (ISBN 0-669-02086-9). Lexington Bks.

--Women & Crime. LC 74-25067. 144p. 1975. 17.95 (ISBN 0-669-97428-5). Lexington Bks.

Simon, Rita J. & Altstein, Howard. Transracial Adoption. LC 76-44817. 197p. 1977. 29.95 (ISBN 0-471-79208-X, Pub. by Wiley-Interscience). Wiley.

--Transracial Adoption: A Follow-Up. LC 80-8770. 160p. 1981. 21.95x (ISBN 0-669-04357-5). Lexington Bks.

Simon, Rita J., jt. auth. see Adler, Freda.

Simon, Rita J., ed. Research in Law & Sociology: An Annual Compilation of Research, Vol. 1. 1978. lib. bdg. 40.00 (ISBN 0-89232-024-9). Jai Pr.

Simon, Rita J. & Spitzer, Steven, eds. Research in Law, Deviance & Social Control, Vol. 4. 325p. (Orig.). 1981. 40.00 (ISBN 0-89232-241-1). Jai Pr.

Simon, Robert & Brenner, Barry E. Procedures & Techniques in Emergency Medicine. (Illus.). 415p. 1982. lib. bdg. 44.00 (ISBN 0-683-07715-5). Williams & Wilkins.

Simon, Robert, jt. ed. see Bloch, Donald.

Simon, Roger. Gramsci's Political Thought: An Introduction. 160p. 1982. text ed. 17.00x (ISBN 0-85315-523-2, Pub. by Lawrence & Wishart Ltd England). Humanities.

Simon, Roger L. Peking Duck. 1979. 9.95 o.p. (ISBN 0-671-22880-3). S&S.

Simon, S., tr. see Djoszegi, V. & Hoppal, M.

Simon, Sam & Waz, Joe. Reverse the Charges: How to Save Money on Your Phone Bill. 3rd ed. 1982. pap. 4.95 (ISBN 0-943444-00-4). NCCB.

Simon, Seymour. About the Food You Eat. LC 79-14395. (Let's-Try-It-Out Ser.). (Illus.). (gr. 1-3). 1979. 8.95 (ISBN 0-07-057457-X). McGraw.

--About Your Heart. LC 73-8019. (Illus.). 48p. (ps-4). 1974. PLB 7.95 o.p. (ISBN 0-07-057440-5, GB). McGraw.

--Body Sense-Body Nonsense. LC 81-47104. (Illus.). 48p. (gr. 3-5). 1981. 9.13i (ISBN 0-397-31943-6, JBL-J); PLB 9.89g (ISBN 0-397-31944-4). Har-Row.
--Creatures from Lost Worlds. LC 78-25875. (Eerie Ser.). (Illus.). (gr. 2-4). 1979. 9.57i (ISBN 0-397-31834-0, HarpJ); PLB 9.89 (ISBN 0-397-31852-9). Har-Row.
--Discovering What Garter Snakes Do. (Illus.). 48p. (gr. 3-7). 1975. PLB 6.95 o.p. (ISBN 0-07-057439-1, GB). McGraw.
--Discovering What Gerbils Do. (Illus.). (gr. 2-6). 1971. PLB 7.95 (ISBN 0-07-057434-0, GB). McGraw.
--Discovering What Puppies Do. (Illus.). 48p. (gr. 4-6). 1977. PLB 6.95 o.p. (ISBN 0-07-057424-3, GB). McGraw.
--Einstein Anderson Lights Up the Sky. LC 82-2689. (Einstein Anderson Mystery-Science Ser.: No. 6). (Illus.). 80p. (gr. 3-7). 1982. 9.95 (ISBN 0-670-29066-1). Viking Pr.
--Ghosts. LC 75-37520. (gr. 1-3). 1976. 9.57i (ISBN 0-397-31664-X, HarpJ); pap. 2.95 (ISBN 0-397-31665-8). Har-Row.
--How to Be a Space Scientist in Your Own Home. LC 81-47759. (Illus.). (gr. 5 up). 1982. 9.57i (ISBN 0-397-31990-8, JBL-J); PLB 8.89g (ISBN 0-397-31991-6); pap. 4.75i (ISBN 0-397-31996-7). Har-Row.
--Life & Death. (Illus.). (gr. 4-6). 1976. PLB 7.95 (ISBN 0-07-057456-1, GB). McGraw.
--Mad Scientists, Weird Doctors, & Time Travelers in Movies, TV, & Books. (Eerie Ser.). (Illus.). (gr. 2-4). 1981. PLB 7.89 (ISBN 0-686-71676-0, HarpJ). Har-Row.
--Silly Animal Jokes & Riddles. 64p. (gr. 1-3). 7.95 o.p. (ISBN 0-07-057397-2). McGraw.
--Weather & Climate. (Science Library: No. 7). (gr. 4-6). 1969. PLB 4.99 (ISBN 0-394-90804-X); pap. 1.50 (ISBN 0-394-80805-3). Random.
Simon, Shirley. Best Friend. (gr. 4-6). 1969. pap. 1.95 (ISBN 0-686-85641-4). Archway.
Simon, Sidney B. Vulture, a Modern Allegory on the Art of Putting Oneself Down. 2.25 (ISBN 0-686-92252-2, 5019). Hazelden.
Simon, Sidney B. & Olds, Sally W. Helping Your Child Learn Right from Wrong: A Guide to Values Clarification. (McGraw-Hill Paperbacks Ser.). 1977. pap. 4.95 (ISBN 0-07-057459-6, SP). McGraw.
Simon, Sidney B., jt. auth. see Read, Donald C.
Simon, Sidney B., et al. Composition for Personal Growth: Values Clarification Through Writing. 192p. (Orig.). 1973. pap. 6.95 o.s.i. (ISBN 0-89104-228-8, A & W Visual Library). A & W Pubs.
Simon, Sidney B., jt. auth. see Howley, Robert C.
Simon, Thomas W. & Scholes, Robert J., eds. Language, Mind, & Brain. (Illus.). 288p. 1982. text ed. 29.95 (ISBN 0-89859-153-8). L Erlbaum Assocs.
Simon, William. Mathematical Techniques for Biology & Medicine. rev. ed. LC 77-24347. (Illus.). 1977. pap. text ed. 9.95x o.p. (ISBN 0-262-69057-8). MIT Pr.
Simon, William, jt. ed. see Gagnon, John H.
Simon, William E. Time for Action. 1980. 10.00 o.p. (ISBN 0-07-057493-6). Readers Digest Pr.
--A Time for Truth. LC 77-25465. 1978. 12.50 o.p. (ISBN 0-07-057378-6). Readers Digest Pr.
Simon, Yves. Nature & Functions of Authority. (Aquinas Lecture). 1940. 7.95 (ISBN 0-87462-104-6). Marquette.
Simond, Ada D. Let's Pretend: Mae Dee & Her Family Ten Years Later. LC 78-62431. (National History Ser.). (Illus.). (gr. 5 up). 1982. 8.95 (ISBN 0-89482-012-5); softcover 5.95 (ISBN 0-89482-013-3). Stevenson Pr.
Simonds, A. P. Karl Mannheim's Sociology of Knowledge. 1978. text ed. 28.95x (ISBN 0-19-827238-3). Oxford U Pr.
Simonds, Calvin. The Weather-Wise Gardener. Halpin, Anne, ed. LC 1-63000001. (Illus.). 300p. 1983. 16.95 (ISBN 0-87857-428-X). Rodale Pr Inc.
Simonds, H. R. & Church, J. M. A Concise Guide to Plastics. 2nd ed. LC 74-32300. 404p. 1975. Repr. of 1963 ed. 22.50 (ISBN 0-88275-269-3). Krieger.
Simonds, J. O. Landscape Architecture. 1961. 39.95 (ISBN 0-07-057391-3, P&RB). McGraw.
Simonds, John O. Earthscape. (Illus.). 352p. 1978. 44.95 (ISBN 0-07-057395-6, P&RB). McGraw.
--Landscape Architecture. (Illus.). 384p. 1983. text ed. 34.95 (ISBN 0-07-057448-0, PRB). McGraw.
Simonds, Nina, tr. see Huang Su Huei.
Simonds, Raymond L. Handbook of Trailer Camping. 4.95 (ISBN 0-910872-16-3). Lee Pubns.
Simonds, Roger T. Beginning Philosophical Logic. 1977. pap. text ed. 10.00 (ISBN 0-8191-0262-8). U Pr of Amer.
Simone, C. B. Cancer & Nutrition: A Ten-Point Plan to Reduce Your Chances of Getting Cancer. 260p. 1983. 15.95 (ISBN 0-07-057466-9, GB). McGraw.
Simone, Diane de see Durden-Smith, Jo & De Simone, Diane.
Simone, Franco. French Renaissance: Medieval Tradition & Italian Influence in Shaping the Renaissance in France. Hall, H. Gaston, ed. LC 70-88170. (Illus.). 1970. 17.95 o.p. (ISBN 0-312-30520-6). St Martin.
Simoneau, Karin, jt. ed. see Wilbert, Johannes.
Simonett, David S., jt. ed. see Lintz, Joseph, Jr.
Simonetti, L., jt. auth. see Banti, Alberto.
Simonian, Charles. Basic Foil Fencing. (Orig.). 1982. pap. text ed. 6.50 (ISBN 0-8403-2726-9, 40272601). Kendall-Hunt.
--Fundamentals of Sports Biomechanics. (Illus.). 224p. 1981. text ed. 17.95 (ISBN 0-13-344499-6). P-H.
Simons & Menzies. Short Course in Foundation Engineering. 1977. 24.95 (ISBN 0-408-00295-6). Butterworth.
Simons, Barbara B. Volcanoes: Mountains of Fire. LC 76-15550. (Science Information Ser.). (Illus.). (gr. 4). 1976. PLB 12.50 o.p. (ISBN 0-8172-0350-8). Raintree Pubs.
Simons, C. J., jt. auth. see Ritchie, Robert L.
Simons, David G., jt. auth. see Travell, Janet G.
Simons, David J., jt. ed. see Kunin, Arthur S.
Simons, Elwyn L. Paleocene Pantodonta. LC 60-13623. (Transactions Ser.: Vol. 50, Pt. 6). (Illus.). 1960. pap. 1.00 o.p. (ISBN 0-87169-506-5). Am Philos.
Simons, Eric N. Dictionary of Ferrous Metals. (Illus.). 1971. 14.00 o.p. (ISBN 0-584-10059-0). Transatlantic.
Simons, Frans. Man kann wieder Christ sein: Eine Abrechnung mit der Theologie und der "kritischen" Bibelwissenschaft. 231p. 1978. write for info. (ISBN 3-261-03011-9). P Lang Pubs.
Simons, G. L. The Illustrated Book of Sexual Records. (Illus.). 192p. (Orig.). 1983. pap. 7.95 (ISBN 0-933328-63-X). Delilah Bks.
Simons, Gene M. Early Childhood Musical Development: A Bibliography of Research Abstracts, 1960-1975. 136p. 1978. 3.00 (ISBN 0-686-37913-6). Music Ed.
Simons, Geoffrey L. Privacy in the Computer Age. 147p. (Orig.). 1982. pap. 22.50x (ISBN 0-85012-348-8). Intl Pubns Serv.
Simons, George F. How Big Is a Person? LC 82-61423. 72p. 1983. 3.95 (ISBN 0-8091-0336-2). Paulist Pr.
--Keeping Your Personal Journal. LC 77-99299. 156p. 1978. pap. 5.95 (ISBN 0-8091-2092-5). Paulist Pr.
Simons, Gerald. Barbarian Europe. LC 68-54209. (Great Ages of Man). (Illus.). (gr. 6 up). 1968. PLB 11.97 o.p. (ISBN 0-8094-0380-3, Pub. by Time-Life). Silver.
Simons, H. Choral Conducting: A Leadership, Teaching Approach. LC 82-70397. 85p. (Orig.). 1983. pap. text ed. write for info (ISBN 0-916656-18-7). Mark Foster Mus.
Simons, Herbert W. Persuasion: Understanding, Practice & Analysis. LC 75-9015. (Speech Communication Ser.). (Illus.). 400p. 1976. text ed. 18.95 (ISBN 0-201-07082-0). A-W.
Simons, J. H., ed. Fluorine Chemistry, 5 vols. 1950-64. Vol. 1. 77.00 (ISBN 0-12-643901-X); Vol. 2. 77.00 (ISBN 0-12-643902-8); Vol. 3. 77.00 (ISBN 0-12-643903-6); Vol. 4. 89.00 (ISBN 0-12-643904-4); Vol. 5. 67.00 (ISBN 0-12-643905-2). Acad Pr.
Simons, John D. Friedrich Schiller. (World Authors Ser.). 15.95 (ISBN 0-8057-6445-3, Twayne). G K Hall.
Simons, Joseph H. Structure of Science. LC 60-13640. 1960. 4.75 o.p. (ISBN 0-685-78048-1). Philos Lib.
Simons, Leon A. Lipids. 96p. 1980. pap. text ed. 17.95 (ISBN 0-8391-1496-6). Univ Park.
Simons, Les. Gila! (Orig.). 1981. pap. 1.95 o.p. (ISBN 0-451-11073-0, AE1073, Sig). NAL.
Simons, M. Laird, ed. see Duyckinck, Evert A. & Duyckinck, George L.
Simons, Mary. Color Me Princess. (Illus.). 1982. pap. 2.95 (ISBN 0-440-51634-X, Dell Trade Pbks). Dell.
Simons, R. H., jt. auth. see Bean, A. R.
Simons, Richard C. & Pardes, Herbert. Understanding Human Behavior in Health & Illness. 2nd ed. (Illus.). 734p. 1981. 29.95 (ISBN 0-686-77743-3, 7740-6). Williams & Wilkins.
Simons, S. Vector Analysis for Mathematicians, Scientists & Engineers. 2nd ed. 1970. 16.25 o.p. (ISBN 0-08-006988-6); pap. 9.25 (ISBN 0-08-006895-2). Pergamon.
Simons, Thomas G. Blessings for God's People: A Book of Blessings for All Occasions. LC 82-62045. 112p. (Orig.). 1983. pap. 5.95 (ISBN 0-87793-264-6). Ave Maria.
Simons, Walter. Evolution of International Public Law in Europe Since Grotius. 1931. text ed. 29.50x (ISBN 0-686-83542-5). Elliots Bks.
Simonsen, Clifford & Gordon, Marshall. Juvenile Justice in America. 2nd ed. 1982. text ed. 23.95x (ISBN 0-02-475770-5). Macmillan.
Simonsen, Paul. Hyacinthe. LC 82-82726. 352p. 1983. 11.95 (ISBN 0-86666-113-1). GWP.
--The Roues. LC 81-81950. 252p. 1983. 11.95 (ISBN 0-86666-045-3). GWP.
Simonsen, R., ed. Bacillaria: International Journal for Diatom Research, Vol. 2. (Illus.). lib. bdg. 32.00x (ISBN 0-686-25191-1). Lubrecht & Cramer.
--Fifth Symposium on Recent & Fossil Diatoms, Antwerp, 1978: Proceedings. (Illus.). 1979. lib. bdg. 80.00 (ISBN 3-7682-5464-X). Lubrecht & Cramer.
--Fourth Symposium on Recent & Fossil Marine Diatoms, Oslo 1976: Proceedings. (Beiheft zur Nova Hedwigia Ser.: No. 54). (Illus.). 1977. lib. bdg. 80.00x (ISBN 3-7682-5454-2). Lubrecht & Cramer.
--Symposium on Recent & Fossil Marine Diatoms, 3rd, Oslo, 1976: Proceedings. (Illus.). 1977. text ed. 80.00x (ISBN 3-7682-5453-4). Lubrecht & Cramer.
Simonsen, R., ed. see Recent & Fossil Marine Diatoms, 3rd Symposium, 1975.
Simonsen, R., ed. see Symposium on Recent & Fossil Marine Diatoms, First, 1972.
Simonsen, R., ed. see Symposium on Recent & Fossil Marine Diatoms, Second, 1974.
Simonsen, Richard & Thompson, Van. Etched Cast Restorations: Clinical & Laboratory Techniques. (Illus.). 180p. 1982. text ed. 46.00 (ISBN 0-86715-120-X). Quint Pub Co.
Simonsen, Sharon. God Never Slept. (Daybreak Ser.). 78p. Date not set. pap. 3.95 (ISBN 0-8163-0472-6). Pacific Pr Pub Assn.
Simonsohn, Shlomo. A History of the Jews in the Duchy of Mantua. (Illus.). 902p. 1977. text ed. 22.00 (ISBN 0-686-42970-2). K Sefer.
Simonson, G. R., ed. The History of the American Aircraft Industry. 1968. 22.50x (ISBN 0-262-19045-1). MIT Pr.
Simonson, Harold P. Zona Gale. (United States Authors Ser.). 13.95 (ISBN 0-8057-0308-X, Twayne). G K Hall.
Simonson, L. A. A Curriculum Model for Individuals with Severe Learning & Behavior Disorders. 320p. 1979. pap. text ed. 12.95 (ISBN 0-8391-1322-6). Univ Park.
Simonson, Leroy. Private Pilot Study Guide: Textbook & Exams. 3rd, rev. ed. LC 76-120103. (Illus.). 368p. 1978. pap. 15.00 o.p. (ISBN 0-911720-01-4). Aviation.
Simonson, Walter, jt. auth. see Claremont, Chris.
Simonton, Wesley & McClaskey, Marilyn J. AACR 2 & the Catalog: Theory-Structure-Changes. LC 81-11757. 78p. 1981. pap. 9.50 (ISBN 0-87287-267-X). Libs Unl.
Simony, Maggie, ed. Traveler's Reading Guides: The Rest of the World, Vol. 3. (Traveler's Reading Guides Ser.). 275p. (Orig.). 1983. pap. 12.95 (ISBN 0-9602050-4-7). Freelance Pubns.
Simony, Maggy. Traveler's Reading Guides Update: January-June, 1983. (Background Books, Novels, Travel Literature & Articles). 150p. (Orig.). 1983. price not set (ISBN 0-9602050-6-3). Freelance Pubns.
Simony, Maggy, ed. Traveler's Reading Guides: Background Books, Novels, Travel Literature & Articles, (Rest of the World, Vol. 3. (Orig.). 1983. pap. 12.95 (ISBN 0-9602050-4-7). Freelance Pubn.
Simony, Maggy, et al, eds. Traveler's Reading Guides: Background Books, Novels, Travel Literature & Articles, Vol. 2 (North America) (Orig.). 1982. pap. 12.95 (ISBN 0-9602050-3-9). Freelance Pubns.
--Traveler's Reading Guides: Background Books, Novels, Travel Literature & Articles, Vol. 1 (Europe) LC 80-65324. 285p. 1981. pap. 12.95 (ISBN 0-9602050-1-2). Freelance Pubns.
Simonyi, K. Foundations of Electrical Engineering. 1964. inquire for price (ISBN 0-08-010204-2); pap. 28.00 (ISBN 0-08-019001-4). Pergamon.
Simos, Bertha G. A Time to Grieve: Loss a Universal Human Experience. LC 75-27964. 1979. 15.95 (ISBN 0-87304-141-0); pap. 10.95 (ISBN 0-87304-153-4). Family Serv.
Simpkin, Diana. The Complete Pregnancy Exercise Program. LC 82-36712. (Medical Library). 176p. 1982. pap. 5.95 (ISBN 0-452-25343-8, 4622-7). Mosby.
Simpkin, Mike. Trapped Within Welfare: Surviving Social Work. (Social Points Ser.). 1979. pap. text ed. 20.00x o. p. (ISBN 0-333-23024-8); pap. text ed. 7.75x (ISBN 0-333-23177-5). Humanities.
Simpkins, C. O. Coltrane: A Biography. LC 75-7459. (Illus.). 287p. 1977. pap. 7.95 (ISBN 0-915542-83-8). Herndon Hse.
Simpkins, Mark A. What Every Woman Should Know About Child Support, Getting It! 1983. 14.95 (ISBN 0-87949-226-0). Ashley Bks.
Simplan Systems, Inc. Corporate Planning & Modeling with Simplan. 2nd ed. 598p. Date not set. pap. text ed. 25.00 (ISBN 0-201-07830-9). A-W.
Simpson, A. B. Danger Lines in the Deeper Life. 133p. 1966. pap. 2.50 (ISBN 0-87509-007-9). Chr Pubns.
--Days of Heaven & Earth. 371p. 1945. pap. 6.95 (ISBN 0-87509-312-4). Chr Pubns.
--El Evangelifo Cuadruple: Fourfold Gospel, Spanish. Bucher, Dorothy, tr. from Eng. 96p. 1981. pap. 2.00 (ISBN 0-87509-268-3). Chr Pubns.
--Holy Spirit, 2 Vols. 15.95 ea.; Vol. 1. 11.00 ea. (ISBN 0-87509-015-X). Vol. 2 (ISBN 0-87509-016-8). pap. 4.50 ea. Vol. 1 (ISBN 0-87509-018-4). Vol. 2 (ISBN 0-87509-019-2). Chr Pubns.
--In the School of Faith. 1974. pap. 2.25 o.p. (ISBN 0-87509-022-2). Chr Pubns.
--Is Life Worth Living? 30p. pap. 1.00 (ISBN 0-87509-045-1). Chr Pubns.
--Life of Prayer. 122p. 1975. pap. 2.50 (ISBN 0-87509-164-4). Chr Pubns.
--The Love Life of Our Lord. pap. 2.95 (ISBN 0-87509-028-1). Chr Pubns.
--Practical Christianity. 1975. Repr. 1.75 (ISBN 0-87509-032-X). Chr Pubns.
--Santificados por Completo-Wholly Sanctified. 136p. (Eng.). 1981. 2.50 (ISBN 0-87509-307-8). Chr Pubns.
--Spirit Filled Church in Action. 112p. 1975. 2.50 (ISBN 0-87509-037-0). Chr Pubns.
--Walking in Love. 1975. Repr. 2.95 (ISBN 0-87509-040-0). Chr Pubns.
--Wholly Sanctified: Legacy Edition. Rev. ed. King, L. L., intro. by. 136p. 1982. pap. 5.95 (ISBN 0-87509-306-X). Chr Pubns.
Simpson, Alan, ed. The Office of the Future, No. 1: Planning for the Office of the Future. 140p. 1981. pap. text ed. 23.50x (ISBN 0-566-03404-2). Gower Pub Ltd.
--The Office of the Future, No. 2: Planning for the Electronic Mail. 133p. 1982. pap. text ed. 23.50x (ISBN 0-566-03406-9). Gower Pub Ltd.
--The Office of the Future, No. 3: Planning for Word Processing. 150p. 1982. pap. text ed. 23.50x (ISBN 0-566-03414-X). Gower Pub Ltd.
--Planning for Telecommunications. (The Office of the Future Ser.). 158p. (Orig.). 1982. pap. text ed. 23.50x (ISBN 0-566-03415-8). Gower Pub Ltd.
Simpson, Alan & Simpson, Mary, eds. I Too Am Here. LC 76-11093. (Illus.). 1977. 27.95 (ISBN 0-521-21304-5). Cambridge U Pr.
Simpson, Albert B. But God. rev. ed. pap. 1.75 (ISBN 0-87509-000-1). Chr Pubns.
--Christ in the Tabernacle. pap. 2.95 (ISBN 0-87509-003-6). Chr Pubns.
--The Christ Life. LC 80-69301. 96p. pap. 2.50 (ISBN 0-87509-291-8). Chr Pubns.
--Christ of the Forty Days. pap. 1.25 o.p. (ISBN 0-87509-004-4). Chr Pubns.
--Cross of Christ. pap. 2.95 (ISBN 0-87509-006-0). Chr Pubns.
--Days of Heaven Upon Earth. pap. 4.25 (ISBN 0-87509-008-7). Chr Pubns.
--Four-Fold Gospel. pap. 2.95 (ISBN 0-87509-011-7). Chr Pubns.
--Gospel of Healing. 1915. pap. 4.50 (ISBN 0-87509-012-5). Chr Pubns.
--In Heavenly Places. pap. 3.25 (ISBN 0-87509-021-4). Chr Pubns.
--Land of Promise. 1969. pap. 2.95 (ISBN 0-87509-024-9). Chr Pubns.
--Larger Christian Life. 2.50 (ISBN 0-87509-025-7); pap. 2.95 mass market (ISBN 0-87509-026-5). Chr Pubns.
--Lord for the Body. pap. 2.95 (ISBN 0-87509-027-3). Chr Pubns.
--Names of Jesus. pap. 3.75 (ISBN 0-87509-030-3). Chr Pubns.
--Present Truths or the Supernatural. 1967. pap. 1.25 (ISBN 0-87509-033-8). Chr Pubns.
--Songs of the Spirit. pap. 2.50 (ISBN 0-87509-036-2). Chr Pubns.
--Walking in the Spirit. pap. 2.95 (ISBN 0-87509-041-9). Chr Pubns.
--When the Comforter Came. pap. 2.95 (ISBN 0-87509-042-7). Chr Pubns.
Simpson, Amos, et al. Death of an Old World: 1914-1945. LC 78-67276. 1979. pap. text ed. 2.95x (ISBN 0-88273-326-5). Forum Pr IL.
Simpson, Amos E., et al. Genesis of a New World: Nineteen Forty-five to Present. LC 78-67276. 1979. pap. text ed. 2.95x (ISBN 0-88273-327-3). Forum Pr IL.
Simpson, B. B., ed. Mesquite: Its Biology in Two Desert Scrub Ecosystems. (US-IBP Synthesis Ser.: Vol. 4). 1977. 40.50 (ISBN 0-12-787460-7). Acad Pr.
Simpson, C. Adventures of Huckleberry Finn: Twentieth Century Interpretations. 1968. 9.95 (ISBN 0-13-013995-5, Spec). P-H.
Simpson, C. F. Practical High Performance Liquid Chromatography. 1976. 57.00 (ISBN 0-471-26025-8, Wiley Heyden). Wiley.
--Techniques of Liquid Chromatography. 400p. 1982. 54.95x (ISBN 0-471-26220-X, Pub. by Wiley Heyden). Wiley.
Simpson, Charles M. Inside the Green Berets: The First Thirty Years a History of the U.S. Army Special Forces. (Illus.). 272p. 1983. 15.95 (ISBN 0-89141-163-1). Presidio Pr.
Simpson, D. H. Commercialisation of the Regional Press: The Development of Monopoly, Profit & Control. 224p. 1981. text ed. 37.25x (ISBN 0-566-00441-0). Gower Pub Ltd.
--First Supplement to the Subject Catalogue of the Royal Commonwealth Society. 1977. lib. bdg. 240.00 (ISBN 0-8161-0075-6, Hall Library). G K Hall.
Simpson, David. General Equilibrium Analysis: An Introduction with Applications. LC 74-31814. 164p. 1975. text ed. 22.95x o.p. (ISBN 0-470-79209-4). Halsted Pr.
Simpson, David W. & Richards, Paul A., eds. Earthquake Prediction. 1981. 38.00 (ISBN 0-87590-403-3). Am Geophysical.
Simpson, Dick. Who Rules: An Introduction to the Study of Politics. LC 82-72528. 162p. (Orig.). 1971. pap. text ed. 5.00x (ISBN 0-8040-0511-7). Swallow.
--Winning Elections: A Handbook in Participatory Politics. rev. & enl. ed. LC 82-75133. (Illus.). x, 237p. 1982. 19.95 (ISBN 0-8040-0365-3); text ed. 9.95 (ISBN 0-8040-0366-1). Swallow.

Simpson, Dick & Beam, George. Strategies for Change: How to Make the American Political Dream Work. LC 82-73856. 258p. 1976. 12.00 (ISBN 0-8040-0696-2). Swallow.

Simpson, Donald H., ed. Biography Catalogue of the Library of the Royal Commonwealth Society. 511p. 1961. 60.00x (ISBN 0-686-80389-2). Gale.

--The Manuscript Catalogue of the Royal Commonwealth Society. 144p. 1976. 15.00x o.p. (ISBN 0-7201-0448-3, Pub. by Mansell England). Wilson.

Simpson, Dorothy. A Puppet for a Corpse: A Luke Thanet Mystery. 192p. 12.95 (ISBN 0-686-83661-8, ScribT). Scribner.

Simpson, Eileen. The Maze. LC 74-23536. 1975. 7.95 o.p. (ISBN 0-671-21960-X). S&S.

--Poets in their Youth: A Memoir. LC 81-48295. 256p. 1982. 15.50 (ISBN 0-394-52317-2). Random.

--Poets in their Youth: A Memoir. LC 82-40429. (Illus.). 288p. 1983. pap. 5.95 (ISBN 0-394-71382-6, Vin). Random.

Simpson, Elizabeth & Gray, Mary A. Humanistic Education: An Interpretation. LC 76-15280. (Ford Foundation Ser.). 352p. 1976. prof ref 11.00x (ISBN 0-88410-168-1). Ballinger Pub.

Simpson, Elizabeth, ed. see Rourke, Margaret V. & Gentry, Christine A.

Simpson, Ethel C., ed. Simpkinsville & Vicinity: The Arkansas Stories of Ruth McEnery Stuart. 208p. 1983. 19.00 (ISBN 0-938626-12-4); pap. 8.95 (ISBN 0-938626-16-7). U of Ark Pr.

Simpson, Evelyn M., ed. & intro. by see Donne, John.

Simpson, F. P., ed. see Catullus.

Simpson, Frank, tr. see Lem, Stanislaw.

Simpson, George & Burger, Neal. Severed Ties. (Orig.). 1983. pap. 3.50 (ISBN 0-440-17705-7). Dell.

Simpson, George E. & Burger, Neal R. Fair Warning. 1980. 10.95 o.s.i. (ISBN 0-440-02474-9). Delacorte.

Simpson, George G. Attending Marvels: A Patagonian Journal. LC 82-13438. (Phoenix Ser.). 296p. 1982. pap. 9.50 (ISBN 0-226-75935-0). U of Chicago Pr.

--Major Features of Evolution. 1967. pap. 2.95 o.p. (ISBN 0-671-23103-0, Touchstone Bks). S&S.

--This View of Life: The World of an Evolutionist. LC 64-14636. 1966. pap. 2.15 (ISBN 0-15-690070-X, Harv). HarBraceJ.

Simpson, George G., ed. Book of Darwin. 300p. 1983. pap. price not set (ISBN 0-671-43126-9). WSP.

Simpson, Hassell A. Rumer Godden. (English Authors Ser.: No. 151). 1973. lib. bdg. 10.95 o.p. (ISBN 0-8057-1219-4, Twayne). G K Hall.

Simpson, Hilary. D. H. Lawrence & Feminism. 174p. 1982. text ed. write for info (ISBN 0-87580-090-4). N Ill U Pr.

Simpson, I. M. Fieldwork in Geology. (Introducing Geology Ser.). (Illus.). 1977. pap. text ed. 6.95x (ISBN 0-04-550025-8). Allen Unwin.

Simpson, I. S. Basic Statistics for Librarians. 2nd ed. 128p. 1983. 19.50 (ISBN 0-85157-352-5, Pub. by Bingley England). Shoe String.

Simpson, Ida. From Student to Nurse. LC 78-31933. (American Sociological Association Rose Monographs). 1979. 24.95 (ISBN 0-521-22683-X); pap. 8.95x (ISBN 0-521-29616-1). Cambridge U Pr.

Simpson, Ida Harper & Simpson, Richard L., eds. Research in the Sociology of Work, Vol. 1. 500p. 1981. 47.50 (ISBN 0-89232-124-5). Jai Pr.

Simpson, J. A., ed. The Concise Oxford Dictionary of Proverbs. 272p. 1983. 16.95 (ISBN 0-19-866131-2). Oxford U Pr.

Simpson, J. Ernest, et al. An Outline of Organic Chemistry. 3rd ed. (Illus.). 448p. 1975. pap. text ed. 18.95 (ISBN 0-07-057436-7, C). McGraw.

Simpson, J. L., ed. Disorders of Sexual Differentiation: Etiology & Clinical Delineation. 1977. 68.50 (ISBN 0-12-644450-1). Acad Pr.

Simpson, Jack B. Hay...But Not in the Barn. 138p. (Orig.). 1982. pap. 3.95 (ISBN 0-686-84394-0). J B Simpson.

Simpson, Jacqueline, ed. Icelandic Folktales & Legends. LC 71-172391. (Cal Ser.: No. 412). 224p. 1972. pap. 4.95 (ISBN 0-520-03835-5). U of Cal Pr.

Simpson, James W. The Editor's Study: A Comprehensive Edition of W. D. Howell's Column. LC 81-50049. 464p. 1983. 38.50X (ISBN 0-87875-213-7). Whitston Pub.

Simpson, James Y. Nature: Cosmic, Human & Divine. 1929. text ed. 29.50x (ISBN 0-686-83632-4). Elliots Bks.

Simpson, Jan. Citizens' Energy Directory. 2nd, rev. ed. (Illus.). 185p. 1980. pap. 6.00 (ISBN 0-89988-055-X). Citizens Energy.

Simpson, Jan, jt. auth. see Bossong, Ken.

Simpson, Janice. Andrew Young: A Matter of Choice. LC 77-29229. (Headliners I). (gr. 3-5). 1978. 6.95 (ISBN 0-88436-472-0); pap. 3.50 o.p. (ISBN 0-88436-473-9). EMC.

--Kate Jackson: Special Kind of Angel. LC 78-18850. (Headliners II). (gr. 3-5). 1978. text ed. 6.95 (ISBN 0-88436-430-5). EMC.

--Ray Kroc: Big Mac Man. LC 78-18752. (Headliners II). (gr. 3-5). 1978. text ed. 6.95 (ISBN 0-88436-434-8). EMC.

--Sylvester Stallone: Going the Distance. LC 78-18845. (Headliners II). (gr. 3-5). 1978. text ed. 6.95 (ISBN 0-88436-436-4). EMC.

Simpson, Jeffrey. Discipline of Power: The Conservative Interlude & the Liberal Restoration. 392p. 1980. 17.95 (ISBN 0-920510-24-8, An Everest House Book). Dodd.

--Officers & Gentlemen: Historic West Point in Photographs. LC 82-16820. (Illus.). 223p. 1982. 24.95 (ISBN 0-912882-53-0). Sleepy Hollow.

Simpson, Keith. The Old Contemptibles. (Illus.). 176p. 1982. 16.95 (ISBN 0-04-940062-2). Allen Unwin.

Simpson, Kieran, ed. Canadian Who's Who, 1982. 17th ed. 1100p. 1982. 85.00x (ISBN 0-8020-4604-5). U of Toronto Pr.

Simpson, Kieth. Police: The Investigation of Violence. 240p. 1978. 39.00x (ISBN 0-7121-1689-3, Pub. by Macdonald & Evans). State Mutual Bk.

Simpson, L. L., ed. Drug Treatment of Mental Disorders. LC 74-14480. 336p. 1976. 24.00 (ISBN 0-89004-007-9). Raven.

Simpson, Lesley B. The Encomienda in New Spain: The Beginning of Spanish Mexico. (California Library Reprint Ser.). (Illus.). 279p. 1982. 18.50x (ISBN 0-520-04629-3, CLRS 115); pap. 6.95 (ISBN 0-520-04630-7). U of Cal Pr.

--Many Mexicos, Silver Anniversary Edition. (YA) (gr. 9 up). 1966. 27.50x (ISBN 0-520-01179-1); pap. 8.65 (ISBN 0-520-01180-5, CAL29). U of Cal Pr.

Simpson, Lesley B., ed. & frwd. by see Chevalier, Francois.

Simpson, Lesley B., tr. see Iglesia, Ramon.

Simpson, Lesley B., tr. see Ricard, Robert.

Simpson, Louis. At the End of the Open Road. LC 63-17792. (Poetry Program). 72p. 1982. pap. 6.95 (ISBN 0-8195-1020-3). Wesleyan U Pr.

--A Company of Poets. LC 80-24888. (Poets on Poetry Ser.). 368p. 1981. pap. 7.95 (ISBN 0-472-06326-X). U of Mich Pr.

--A Dream of Governors. LC 59-12480. (Poetry Program: No. 3). 88p. pap. 6.95 (ISBN 0-8195-1003-3). Wesleyan U Pr.

--An Introduction to Poetry. 2nd ed. 480p. 1972. pap. text ed. 10.95 (ISBN 0-312-43155-4). St Martin.

Simpson, M. A. Medical Education: A Critical Approach. 214p. 1972. 18.95 o.p. (ISBN 0-407-26495-7). Butterworth.

Simpson, Mark S. The Officer in Nineteenth-Century Russian Literature. LC 81-40633. 142p. 1982. lib. bdg. 19.00 (ISBN 0-8191-1888-5); pap. text ed. 8.25 (ISBN 0-8191-1889-3). U Pr of Amer.

Simpson, Mary, jt. ed. see Simpson, Alan.

Simpson, Michael. The Facts of Death. (Illus.). 1979. 11.95 (ISBN 0-13-299636-7, Spec); pap. 5.95 (ISBN 0-13-299628-6). P-H.

Simpson, Norman T. Bed & Breakfast, American Style. rev. ed. LC 81-65526. (Illus.). 350p. 1983. pap. 8.95 (ISBN 0-912944-77-3). Berkshire Traveller.

--Country Inns & Back Roads: Britain & Ireland. LC 79-57146. (Illus., Orig.). 1980. pap. 6.95 (ISBN 0-912944-58-7). Berkshire Traveller.

--Country Inns & Back Roads: Continental Europe. 3rd ed. LC 78-51115. 380p. (Orig.). 1983. pap. 8.95 (ISBN 0-912944-76-5). Berkshire Traveller.

--Country Inns & Back Roads: European Edition II. LC 78-51115. (Illus.). 1978. pap. 6.95 o.p. (ISBN 0-912944-48-X). Berkshire Traveller.

--Country Inns & Back Roads, North America. 17th ed. LC 70-615664. (Illus.). 476p. (Orig.). 1982. pap. 7.95 o.p. (ISBN 0-912944-70-6). Berkshire Traveller.

--Country Inns & Back Roads: North America. 18th ed. LC 70-615664. (Illus.). 486p. (Orig.). 1983. pap. 8.95 (ISBN 0-912944-75-7). Berkshire Traveller.

Simpson, Norman T., ed. Country Inns & Back Roads Cookbook. LC 79-52080. 176p. (Orig.). 1980. pap. 7.95 (ISBN 0-912944-56-0). Berkshire Traveller.

Simpson, P. G., jt. auth. see Davies, E. J.

Simpson, Patricia, jt. auth. see Darnell, Frank.

Simpson, Peggy. Hospitality: In the Spirit of Love. 1980. pap. 4.60 (ISBN 0-89137-416-7). Quality Pubns.

Simpson, R. H. & Dickinson, O. P. A Gasetteer of Aegean Civilization in the Bronze Age. (Studies in Mediterranean Archaeology: No. LII). (Orig.). 1979. pap. text ed. 60.00x (ISBN 91-85058-81-5). Humanities.

Simpson, Richard L., jt. ed. see Simpson, Ida Harper.

Simpson, Robert J., jt. auth. see Power, Henry M.

Simpson, Roger. The Trial of Ned Kelly. (Australian Theatre Workshop Ser.). 1977. pap. text ed. 4.50x o.p. (ISBN 0-85859-153-7, 00530). Heinemann Ed.

Simpson, Ronald D. & Anderson, Norman D. Science, Students, & Schools: A Guide for the Middle & Secondary Teacher. LC 80-23124. 358p. 1981. text ed. 23.95 (ISBN 0-471-02477-5). Wiley.

Simpson, Rosemary. The Seven Hills of Paradise. LC 79-8439. 1980. 13.95 o.p. (ISBN 0-385-15775-4). Doubleday.

Simpson, S. R. Land Law & Registration. LC 74-16994. 700p. 1976. 97.50 (ISBN 0-521-20628-6); pap. 24.95 o.p. (ISBN 0-521-29419-3). Cambridge U Pr.

Simpson, Smith. Resources & Needs of American Diplomacy. Sellin, Thorsten, ed. LC 68-57759. (Annals: Vol. 380). 1968. 15.00 (ISBN 0-87761-111-4); pap. 6.00 (ISBN 0-87761-110-6, 380). Am Acad Pol Soc Sci.

Simpson, Stephen G., jt. auth. see Hamilton, Leicester F.

Simpson, T., et al. Mathematics of Finance. 4th ed. 1969. ref. ed. 24.95 (ISBN 0-13-565036-4). P-H.

Simpson, Thomas D. Money, Banking & Economic Analysis. 2nd ed. (Illus.). 480p. 1981. 23.95 (ISBN 0-13-600205-6). P-H.

Simpson, W., jt. auth. see Smith, W. S.

Simpson, W. D., et al. Ninety-Nine Hundred Family Systems Design Book. new ed. LC 78-58005. (Microprocessor Ser.). (Illus.). 1064p. 1978. pap. 19.50 o.p. (ISBN 0-89512-026-7, LCC4400). Tex Instr Inc.

Simpson, W. Douglas. The Highlands of Scotland. (Hale Topographical Ser.). (Illus.). 1979. pap. 4.50 o.p. (ISBN 0-7091-5887-4). Hippocrene Bks.

Simpson, W. G., jt. auth. see Pinner, S. H.

Simpson, William. The Jonah Legend: A Suggestion of Interpretation. LC 72-177422. (Illus.). vi, 182p. 1971. Repr. of 1899 ed. 30.00x (ISBN 0-8103-3820-3). Gale.

--Poem Panarama. 1983. 5.95 (ISBN 0-533-05352-8). Vantage.

Simpson, William K. Heka-Nefer & the Dynastic Material from Toshka & Arminna. (Pubns of the Penn-Yale Expedition to Egypt: No. 1). (Illus.). 1963. 11.00x (ISBN 0-686-17767-3). Univ Mus of U PA.

Simring, Steven S., jt. auth. see Weber, Eric.

Sims, Chester T. & Hagel, William C., eds. The Superalloys. LC 72-5904. (Science & Technology of Materials Ser.). 614p. 1972. 64.95x (ISBN 0-471-79207-1, Pub. by Wiley-Interscience). Wiley.

SIMS Conference on Epidemiology, Alta, UT, July 8-12, 1974. Epidemiology: Proceedings. Ludwig, D. & Cooke, K. L., eds. LC 75-22944. (SIAM-SIMS Conference Ser.: No. 2). ix, 164p. 1975. pap. 20.50 (ISBN 0-89871-031-6). Soc Indus-Appl Math.

Sims, Donald, jt. auth. see Steinheimer, Richard.

Sims, Donald G. & Whitehead, Robert L. Deafness & Communication: Assessment & Training. (Illus.). 416p. 1982. lib. bdg. 37.00 (ISBN 0-683-07755-4). Williams & Wilkins.

Sims, Dori, jt. auth. see Sims, Dorothy.

Sims, Dorothea F. Diabetes: Reach for Health & Freedom. LC 80-16065. (Illus.). 130p. 1980. pap. 6.95 (ISBN 0-8016-4657-X). Mosby.

Sims, Dorothy. Highchair Gourmet. (Illus.). 1980. 12.95 (ISBN 0-8256-3192-0, Quick Fox). Putnam Pub Group.

Sims, Dorothy & Malone, Barbara. The Food Processor-Microwave Oven Cookbook. (Illus.). 1980. 12.95 (ISBN 0-8256-3189-0, Quick Fox). Putnam Pub Group.

Sims, Dorothy & Sims, Dori. The Low Calorie Food Processor Cookbook. (Illus.). 192p. 1980. 14.95 (ISBN 0-8256-3185-8, Quick Fox). Putnam Pub Group.

Sims, Dorothy D. Chinese Recipes for the Food Processor. LC 77-88748. 1978. 12.95 (ISBN 0-8256-3191-2, Quick Fox). Putnam Pub Group.

--The Food Processor Cookbook. 1978. 4.95 (ISBN 0-8256-3142-4, Quick Fox). Putnam Pub Group.

--Recipes for the Food Processor. LC 77-88749. 1978. 12.95 (ISBN 0-8256-3190-4, Quick Fox). Putnam Pub Group.

Sims, Harold W. Ecology Selected Readings. 2nd ed. 1977. pap. text ed. 11.95 (ISBN 0-8403-2169-4). Kendall-Hunt.

Sims, Janet L., jt. auth. see Davis, Lenwood G.

Sims, Janet L., compiled by. The Progress of Afro-American Women: A Selected Bibliography & Resource Guide. LC 79-8948. 400p. 1980. lib. bdg. 35.00x (ISBN 0-313-22083-2, SAF/). Greenwood.

Sims, Janet L., jt. ed. see Davis, Lenwood G.

Sims, Jean & Connelly, Michael. Time & Space: A Basic Reader. (Illus.). 176p. 1982. pap. text ed. 10.95 (ISBN 0-13-922005-4). P-H.

Sims, John A. Edward John Carnell: Defender of the Faith. LC 78-57980. 1978. pap. text ed. 9.75 (ISBN 0-8191-0658-5). U Pr of Amer.

Sims, John H. & Baumann, Duane D., eds. Human Behavior & the Environment Interactions Between Man & His Physical World. LC 73-89450. (Maaroufa Press Geography Ser.). (Illus.). 354p. 1974. pap. text ed. 5.95x (ISBN 0-88425-002-4). Maaroufa Pr.

Sims, Naomi. All About Hair Care for the Black Woman. LC 81-43267. (Illus.). 224p. 1982. 12.95 (ISBN 0-385-14819-4). Doubleday.

Sims, Odette P. Spelling: Patterns of Sound. 128p. 1974. pap. 12.95 wktxt. (ISBN 0-07-057500-2, W); instructor's manual 15.00 (ISBN 0-07-057517-7); tapes 349.95 (ISBN 0-07-079492-8). McGraw.

Sims, P. K. & Morey, G. B., eds. Geology of Minnesota. LC 73-62334. 1972. pap. 9.05 (ISBN 0-934938-00-8). Minn Geol Survey.

Sims, Patsy. The Klan. LC 77-2335. (Illus.). 384p. 1982. pap. 10.95 (ISBN 0-8128-6096-9). Stein & Day.

Sims, Phillip L., jt. ed. see Vallentine, John F.

Sims, Reginald W. & Price, James H., eds. Evolution, Time & Space. Date not set. price not set (ISBN 0-12-644550-8). Acad Pr.

Sims, Robert L. The Evolution of Myth in Garcia Marquez from La Hojarasca to Cien Anos de Soledad. LC 81-69541. (Hispanic Studies Collection). (Illus.). 153p. (Orig.). 1982. pap. 19.95 (ISBN 0-686-82200-5). Ediciones.

Sims, Rudine. Shadow & Substance. 112p. 1982. pap. text ed. 9.00 (ISBN 0-8389-3278-9). ALA.

--Shadow & Substance: Afro-American Experience in Contemporary Children's Fiction. LC 82-6518. (Orig.). 1982. pap. 6.00 (ISBN 0-8141-4376-8); members 5.50 (ISBN 0-686-87114-6). NCTE.

Sims, William E. Black Studies: Pitfalls & Potential. LC 77-18563. 1978. pap. text ed. 8.25 (ISBN 0-8191-0316-0). U Pr of Amer.

Sims, William E. & Bass de Martinez, Bernice B. Perspectives in Multicultural Education. LC 81-40171. (Illus.). 230p. (Orig.). 1981. lib. bdg. 19.75 (ISBN 0-8191-1687-4); pap. text ed. 10.25 (ISBN 0-8191-1688-2). U Pr of Amer.

Simson, Eve. The Corona Affair. (A Mark Malone Dossier Mystery Ser.). (Illus.). 165p. 1983. pap. 15.95 (ISBN 0-89651-101-4). Icarus.

Simson, F. H., tr. see Hegel, Georg W.

Simson, H. J. British Rule in Palestine & the Arab Rebellion of 1936 - 1937. 1977. Repr. of 1938 ed. 24.95 o.p. (ISBN 0-89712-018-3). Documentary Pubns.

Simson, Howard. The Social Orgins of Afrikaner Fascism & Its Apartheid Policy. (Uppsala Studies in Economic History: No. 21). 234p. 1981. pap. text ed. 23.25x o.p. (ISBN 91-554-1070-7, Pub. by Almqvist & Wiksell Sweden). Humanities.

Simsova, Sylva. A Primer of Comparative Librarianship. 96p. 1982. 14.50 (ISBN 0-85157-341-X, Pub. by Bingley England). Shoe String.

Simtek Inc. International Business Games Directory. (Orig.). 1981. pap. 5.95 (ISBN 0-933836-15-5). Simtek.

Simul International, tr. see Moritani, Masanori.

Sina, Ibn. The Life of Ibn Sina: A Critical Edition & Annotated Translation. Gohlman, William E., tr. from Arabic. & ed. LC 73-6793. 1974. 39.50x (ISBN 0-87395-226-X). State U NY Pr.

Sinacore, A. S., jt. auth. see Sinacore, John S.

Sinacore, Angela, jt. auth. see Sinacore, John.

Sinacore, John & Sinacore, Angela. Health: A Quality of Life. 3rd ed. 514p. 1982. text ed. 21.95 (ISBN 0-02-410820-0). Macmillan.

Sinacore, John S. & Sinacore, A. S. Introductory Health: A Vital Issue. 1975. pap. 9.95 o.p. (ISBN 0-02-410690-9). Macmillan.

Sinaer, George, jt. auth. see Campbell, Frank.

Sinai, Ya G. Mathematical Problems in the Theory of Phase Transitions. 164p. 1982. 27.00 (ISBN 0-08-026469-7, C111, D125). Pergamon.

Sinanoglu, Oktay, ed. Modern Quantum Chemistry, 3 Vols. (Istanbul Lectures). 1965. Vol. 1. 52.50 (ISBN 0-12-645001-3); Vol. 2. 52.50 (ISBN 0-12-645002-1); Vol. 3. 52.50 (ISBN 0-12-645003-X); Set. 112.50 (ISBN 0-685-05137-4). Acad Pr.

Sinanoglu, Paula A. & Maluccio, Anthony N., eds. Parents of Children in Placement: Perspectives & Programs. 1981. 15.95 (ISBN 0-87868-205-8, F-58); pap. 10.95 (ISBN 0-87868-181-7). Child Welfare.

Sinanoglu, Paula A., jt. ed. see Maluccio, Anthony N.

Sinaoglu, Paula A., jt. auth. see Maluccio, Anthony N.

Sincebaugh, Els, jt. auth. see Ericksenn, Lief.

Sinclair. Beginner's Guide to Audio. 1977. pap. 9.95 (ISBN 0-408-00274-3). Focal Pr.

--Beginner's Guide to Tape Recording. (Illus.). 1978. pap. 9.95 (ISBN 0-408-00330-8). Focal Pr.

--Master Stereo Cassette Recording. (Illus.). 1976. pap. 9.95 (ISBN 0-408-00238-7). Focal Pr.

Sinclair, jt. auth. see Hellyer.

Sinclair, A. M. Automatic Continuity of Linear Operators. LC 74-31804. (London Mathematical Society Lecture Note Ser.: No. 21). 120p. 1976. 14.95x (ISBN 0-521-20830-0). Cambridge U Pr.

Sinclair, C. A., jt. auth. see Birks, J. S.

Sinclair, Caroline B. Movement of the Young Child: Ages Two to Six. LC 72-96100. 1973. pap. text ed. 10.95 o.p. (ISBN 0-675-08975-1). Merrill.

Sinclair, D. J., jt. auth. see Jones, E.

Sinclair, David. Human Growth After Birth. 3rd ed. 1978. pap. text ed. 18.95x (ISBN 0-19-263329-5). Oxford U Pr.

--Mechanisms of Cutaneous Sensation. 2nd ed. (Illus.). 1981. pap. text ed. 38.50x (ISBN 0-19-261174-7). Oxford U Pr.

Sinclair, David C. Basic Medical Education. 212p. 1972. text ed. 13.50x o.p. (ISBN 0-19-264913-2). Oxford U Pr.

Sinclair, Dorothy. Administration of the Small Public Library. 2nd ed. LC 79-12338. 1979. 15.00 (ISBN 0-8389-0291-X). ALA.

Sinclair, George. Satan's Invisible World Discovered. LC 68-17017. 1969. Repr. of 1685 ed. 36.00x (ISBN 0-8201-1068-X). Schol Facsimiles.

Sinclair, Heather. Follow the Heart. Bd. with For the Love of a Stranger. 1978. pap. 2.50 (ISBN 0-451-11594-5, AE1594, Sig). NAL.

Sinclair, Ian R. Introducing Amateur Electronics. 96p. 1980. 12.00x o.p. (ISBN 0-85242-394-2, Pub. by K Dickson). State Mutual Bk.

--Introducing Electronics Systems. 112p. 1980. 10.00x o.p. (ISBN 0-85242-395-0, Pub. by K Dickson). State Mutual Bk.

--Introducing Microprocessors. 128p. 1981. 25.00x o.p. (ISBN 0-907266-01-0, Pub. by Dickson England). State Mutual Bk.

Sinclair, Ian R. & McCarty, Nan. Inside Your Computer. (Illus.). 1983. write for info. (ISBN 0-88006-058-1). Green.

Sinclair, J. & Coulthard, R. M. Towards an Analysis of Discourse: The English Used by Teachers & Pupils. (Illus.). 168p. 1975. pap. text ed. 8.50x o.p. (ISBN 0-19-436011-3). Oxford U Pr.

Sinclair, J. B. Compendium of Soybean Diseases. 2nd, rev. ed. LC 81-70509. (Compendium Ser.: No. 2). (Illus.). 120p. 1982. 12.00 (ISBN 0-89054-043-8). Am Phytopathol Soc.

Sinclair, James. The Outside Man: Jack Hades of Papua. 17.50x (ISBN 0-392-16221-0, ABC). Sportshelf.

Sinclair, James E. & Parker, Robert. Strategic Metals: America's Achilles Heel. (Illus.). 256p. 1982. 14.95 o.p. (ISBN 0-87000-530-8, Arlington Hse). Crown.

--Strategic Metals, War Crisis & Investment Opportunities. 1982. 17.50 (ISBN 0-517-54826-7, Arlington Hse). Crown.

Sinclair, James E. & Schultz, Harry D. How You Can Profit from Gold. 1980. 14.95 o.p. (ISBN 0-87000-473-5, Arlington Hse). Crown.

Sinclair, James P. How to Write Successful Corporate Appeals: With Full Examples. 19.75 (ISBN 0-686-37105-4). Public Serv Materials.

Sinclair, John. Bangkok by Night. (Asia by Night Ser.). (Illus.). 64p. (Orig.). 1981. pap. 4.95 (ISBN 962-7031-10-0, Pub. by CFW Pubns Hong Kong). C E Tuttle.

--Quarrying, Opencast & Alluvial Mining. (Illus.). 1969. 51.25 (ISBN 0-444-20040-1, Pub. by Applied Sci England). Elsevier.

Sinclair, John D, tr. see Dante Alighieri.

Sinclair, John L. Cowboy Riding Country. (Illus.). 1982. 19.95 (ISBN 0-8263-0645-4). U of NM Pr.

--New Mexico: The Shining Land. 224p. 1983. Repr. of 1980 ed. 10.95 (ISBN 0-8263-0654-3). U of NM Pr.

Sinclair, Keith. Towards Independence. (Studies in 20th Century History Ser.). 1976. pap. text ed. 4.50x o.p. (ISBN 0-86863-537-5, 00546). Heinemann Ed.

Sinclair, Keith V., compiled by. French Devotional Texts of the Middle Ages: A Bibliographic Manuscript Guide. LC 79-7587. 1979. lib. bdg. 45.00x (ISBN 0-313-20649-X, SFT/). Greenwood.

Sinclair, Keith V., ed. French Devotional Texts of the Middle Ages: A Bibliographic Manuscript Guide, First Supplement. LC 82-11773. 246p. 1982. lib. bdg. 65.00 (ISBN 0-313-23664-X, SIF/). Greenwood.

Sinclair, Kent, Jr. Federal Rules of Evidence at a Glance - Trial Objections at a Glance. 1978. A 3 Page Chart. 10.00 (ISBN 0-685-65699-3, H1-2943). PLI.

Sinclair, Lytton. Diana's Debut. 256p. (Orig.). 1983. pap. 2.75 (ISBN 0-446-30321-6). Warner Bks.

--Diana's Desire. 256p. 1983. pap. 2.75 (ISBN 0-446-30509-X). Warner Bks.

Sinclair, M. A., jt. ed. see Clare, J. N.

Sinclair, Marjorie. Nahi'ena 'ena: Sacred Daughter of Hawaii. LC 76-27896. 1976. 10.95 (ISBN 0-8248-0367-1). UH Pr.

Sinclair, Marjorie, ed. The Path of the Ocean: Traditional Poetry of Polynesia. LC 82-8611. 239p. 1982. 17.95 (ISBN 0-8248-0804-5). UH Pr.

Sinclair, Marti, et al. Darker the Night. 1982. pap. 4.95cancelled (ISBN 0-89191-110-3). Cook.

Sinclair, May. Mary Olivier: A Life. LC 74-169850. 380p. 1972. Repr. of 1919 ed. lib. bdg. 18.50x (ISBN 0-8371-6244-0, SIMA). Greenwood.

Sinclair, Olivia. Ecstasy's Torment. 1982. pap. 3.50 (ISBN 0-8217-1089-3). Zebra.

Sinclair, R. S. Numerical Problems in Colour Physics. 1982. 27.00 (ISBN 0-686-81691-9, Pub. by Soc Dyers & Colour). State Mutual Bk.

Sinclair, Robert & Thompson, Bryan. Metropolitan Detroit: An Anatomy of Social Change. LC 76-48300. (Contemporary Metropolitan Analysis Project Ser.). 1977. pap. 8.95x prof ref (ISBN 0-88410-469-9). Ballinger Pub.

Sinclair, Stuart. The Third World Economic Handbook. (Illus.). 224p. 1982. text ed. 55.00x (ISBN 0-903706-85-7). Irvington.

--The Third World Economic Handbook. 224p. 1982. 137.00x (ISBN 0-686-83129-2, Pub. by Euromonitor). State Mutual Bk.

Sinclair, Stuart W. Urbanization & Labor Markets in Developing Countries. LC 77-25913. 1978. 18.95x (ISBN 0-312-83492-6). St Martin.

Sinclair, Stuart W., jt. auth. see Hallwood, C. Paul.

Sinclair, Tracy. Paradise Island. 192p. (Orig.). 1980. pap. 1.50 (ISBN 0-671-57039-0, Pub. by Silhouette Bks). S&S.

Sinclair, Upton. The Coal War. Graham, John, ed. & intro. by. LC 75-40885. 335p. 1976. text ed. 17.50x (ISBN 0-87081-067-7). Colo Assoc.

--The Jungle. (Bantam Classics Ser). 368p. (gr. 9-12). 1981. pap. text ed. 1.95 (ISBN 0-553-21056-4). Bantam.

Sinclair, William A. Socialism & the Individual: Notes on Joining the Labour Party. LC 77-18930. 1978. Repr. of 1955 ed. lib. bdg. 17.50x (ISBN 0-313-20199-4, SISO). Greenwood.

Sinclair, William A., jt. auth. see Arnheim, Daniel D.

Sinclair, William A., jt. auth. see Pestolesi, Robert A.

Sinden, Frank W. see Feiveson, Harold A., et al.

Sinden, J. A. & Worrell, Albert C. Unpriced Values: Decisions Without Market Prices. LC 78-24183. 511p. 1979. 44.95 (ISBN 0-471-02742-1, Pub. by Wiley-Interscience). Wiley.

Sinderman, C. J. Principal Diseases of Marine Fish & Shellfish. 1970. 59.00 (ISBN 0-12-645850-2). Acad Pr.

Sindermann, Carl J. Winning the Games Scientists Play. (Illus.). 300p. 1982. 15.95x (ISBN 0-306-41075-3, Plenum Pr). Plenum Pub.

Sindermann, Carl J., ed. Disease Diagnosis & Control in North American Marine Aquaculture. (Developments in Aquaculture & Fisheries Science Ser.: Vol. 6). 1977. 59.75 (ISBN 0-444-00237-5). Elsevier.

Sindler, Allan P. American Politics & Public Policy: Seven Case Studies. LC 82-12524. 272p. 1982. pap. 8.95 (ISBN 0-87187-237-4). Congr Quarterly.

--Unchosen Presidents: The Vice-President & Other Frustrations of Presidential Succession. LC 75-46041. (A Quantum Book). 1976. 17.95x (ISBN 0-520-03185-7); pap. 2.95 (ISBN 0-520-03493-7). U of Cal Pr.

Sine, Robert D., et al. Basic Rehabilitation Techniques: A Self-Instructional Guide. 2nd. ed. LC 80-25506. 268p. 1981. text ed. 22.95 (ISBN 0-89443-342-3). Aspen Systems.

Sinek, Jeremy. Supercars. LC 79-10851. (Illus.). 128p. 1979. 14.95 o.p. (ISBN 0-89196-041-4, Domus Bks). Quality Bks IL.

Sinema, William & McGovern, Thomas. Digital, Analog & Data Communications. 1982. text ed. 29.95 (ISBN 0-8359-1301-5); solutions manual free (ISBN 0-8359-1302-3). Reston.

Sines, jt. auth. see Bicknell.

Sinex, F. Marott, ed. see Kroc Foundation Conference, Oct. 12-16, 1981.

Siney, Marion C. The Allied Blockade of Germany: 1914-1916. LC 73-15208. x, 339p. 1974. Repr. of 1957 ed. lib. bdg. 18.75x (ISBN 0-8371-7161-X, SIAB). Greenwood.

Sinfield, A. Dramatic Monologue. (Critical Idiom Ser.). 96p. 1977. 9.95x (ISBN 0-416-70540-5); pap. 4.95x (ISBN 0-416-70630-4). Methuen Inc.

Sinfield, Adrian, jt. ed. see Showler, Brian.

Sinfield, Alan. Literature in Protestant England 1560-1660. LC 82-18408. 168p. 1983. text ed. 23.50x (ISBN 0-389-20341-6). B&N Imports.

Sing, Charles F., jt. auth. see Brewer, George J.

Sing, K. S., jt. auth. see Rouquerol, J.

Sing, Phia. Traditional Recipes of Laos. (Illus.). 320p. 1981. 20.00x (ISBN 0-907325-02-5, Pub. by Prospect England); pap. 15.00. U Pr of Va.

Sing, Shirley, ed. see Nelson, Meryl & Thoman, Frances.

Sing, Shirley, ed. see Thoman, Frances & Nelson, Meryl.

Singarimbun, Masri. Kinship, Descent & Alliance Among the Karo Batak. LC 73-93061. 1975. 34.50x (ISBN 0-520-02692-6). U of Cal Pr.

Singell, Larry D., ed. The Collected Papers of Kenneth E. Boulding, Vol. 4. 1982. 20.00x (ISBN 0-87081-139-8). Colo Assoc.

Singell, Larry D., ed. see Boulding, Kenneth E.

Singer & Ondarza. Molecular Basis of Drug Action. (Developments in Biochemistry Ser.: Vol. 19). 1981. 61.00 (ISBN 0-444-00632-X). Elsevier.

Singer & Statsky. Alternatives to Institutionalization. 1974. softcover 7.00 o.p. (ISBN 0-672-82001-3, Bobbs-Merrill Law). Michie-Bobbs.

--The Criminal Process: Sentencing & Criminal Commitment. 1974. softcover 13.00 o.p. (ISBN 0-672-82003-X, Bobbs-Merrill Law). Michie-Bobbs.

--The Therapeutic State. 1974. softcover 7.00 o.p. (ISBN 0-672-82002-1, Bobbs-Merrill Law). Michie-Bobbs.

Singer, A. Guardians of the North-West Frontier: The Pathans. (Peoples of the Wild Ser.). 1982. 15.96 (ISBN 0-7054-0702-0, Pub. by Time-Life). Silver.

Singer, Albert, jt. auth. see Lees, David H.

Singer, Albert, jt. ed. see Jordan, Joseph A.

Singer, Andrew, jt. auth. see Ledgard, Henry.

Singer, Armand E. Paul Bourget. (World Authors Ser.). 1976. lib. bdg. 15.95 (ISBN 0-8057-6235-3, Twayne). G K Hall.

Singer, Arthur. Wild Animals from Alligator to Zebra. (A Pictureback Bk). (ps-1). 1973. pap. 1.50 (ISBN 0-394-82701-5, BYR). Random.

Singer, Barnett. Village Notables in Nineteenth Century France: Priests, Mayors, Schoolmasters. LC 82-3195. (European Social History Ser.). 208p. 1982. 34.50x (ISBN 0-87395-629-X); pap. 10.95x (ISBN 0-87395-630-3). State U NY Pr.

Singer, Barry, jt. auth. see Abell, George.

Singer, Barry, jt. auth. see Weil, Susanne.

Singer, Bernard M. Mathematics for Industrial Careers. 1973. 13.80 o.p. (ISBN 0-07-057475-8, W); ans. key 2.00 o.p. (ISBN 0-07-057476-6). McGraw.

--Programming in BASIC, with Applications. 1973. text ed. 19.75 (ISBN 0-07-057480-4, G); instructor's manual 4.50 (ISBN 0-07-057481-2). McGraw.

Singer, Bertrand B. Basic Mathematics for Electricity & Electronics. 4th ed. (Illus.). 1978. text ed. 21.95 (ISBN 0-07-057472-3, G); instructor's manual 4.00 (ISBN 0-07-057473-1). McGraw.

--Mathematics at Work: Algebra. (Illus.). (gr. 9-12). 1977. pap. text ed. 18.95x (ISBN 0-07-057491-X, G); ans. key 1.95x (ISBN 0-07-057492-8); instructor's manual 8.95x (ISBN 0-07-057486-3). McGraw.

--Mathematics at Work: Decimals. (gr. 9-12). 1977. pap. text ed. 18.95 (ISBN 0-07-057489-8, G); answer key 1.95 (ISBN 0-07-057490-1). McGraw.

--Mathematics at Work: Fractions. (Illus.). (gr. 9-12). 1977. pap. 15.95 (ISBN 0-07-057487-1, G); instr's manual 8.95 (ISBN 0-07-057486-3); answer key 1.95 (ISBN 0-07-057488-X). McGraw.

Singer, Burns. Burns Singer: Selected Poems. Cluysenaar, Anne, ed. (Poetry Ser.). 1979. 7.95 o.p. (ISBN 0-85635-177-6, Pub. by Carcanet New Pr England). Humanities.

Singer, C. Gregg, jt. auth. see Evans, G. Russell.

Singer, Daniel. The Road to Gdansk: Poland & the U.S.S.R. LC 80-39914. 256p. 1982. 15.00 (ISBN 0-85345-567-8, CL5678); pap. 6.50 (ISBN 0-85345-568-6, PB5686). Monthly Rev.

Singer, David, jt. ed. see Farb, Milton H.

Singer, David, jt. ed. see Himmelfarb, Milton.

Singer, Erwin. Key Concepts in Psychotherapy. LC 78-110104. 1970. 16.95x (ISBN 0-465-03708-9); pap. 10.95x (ISBN 0-465-03709-7). Basic.

Singer, F. Industrial Ceramics. Singer, S., ed. 1963. 85.00x (ISBN 0-412-06610-6, Pub by Chapman & Hall England). Methuen Inc.

Singer, Ferdinand L. Mecanica Para Ingenieros, Tomo Primero: Estatica. 1976. text ed. 13.50x o.p. (ISBN 0-06-316997-5, IntlDept). Har-Row.

Singer, Ferdinand L. & Pytel, Andrew. Strength of Materials. 3rd ed. (Illus.). 1980. text ed. 31.50 scp (ISBN 0-06-046229-9, HarpC); solutions manual avail. (ISBN 0-06-366232-9); scp problem suppl. 1.95 (ISBN 0-06-046234-5). Har-Row.

Singer, Ferndinand. Mechanica Para Ingenieros: Dinamica. 3rd ed. (Span.). 1982. pap. text ed. write for info. (ISBN 0-06-317001-9, Pub. by HarLA Mexico). Har-Row.

Singer, Fred, jt. auth. see Mundlak, Yair.

Singer, Godfrey F. Epistolary Novel: Its Origin, Development, Decline & Residuary Influence. LC 63-9508. 1963. Repr. of 1933 ed. 10.00x o.p. (ISBN 0-8462-0396-0). Russell.

Singer, Greta L., et al. Child Welfare Problems: Prevention, Early Identification, & Intervention. LC 82-20263. 180p. (Orig.). 1983. lib. bdg. 19.75 (ISBN 0-8191-2874-0); pap. text ed. 9.50 (ISBN 0-8191-2875-9). U Pr of Amer.

Singer, H. W. Standardized Accountancy in Germany with A New Appendix. LC 82-48372. (Accountancy in Transition Ser.). 94p. 1982. lib. bdg. 18.00 (ISBN 0-8240-5329-X). Garland Pub.

--The Strategy of International Development: Essays in the Economics of Backwardness. Cairncross, Alec & Puri, Mohinder, eds. LC 74-21810. 256p. 1975. 27.50 (ISBN 0-87332-068-9). M E Sharpe.

Singer, Hans. Technologies for Basic Needs. 2nd ed. x, 161p. 1982. 8.55 (ISBN 92-2-103068-7); pap. 11.40 (ISBN 92-2-103069-5). Intl Labour Office.

Singer, Harry & Donlan, Dan. Reading & Learning from Text. 543p. 1980. text ed. 18.95 (ISBN 0-316-79274-8). Little.

Singer, Helen, tr. see Gratry, A.

Singer, I. J. Family Carnovsky. Singer, Joseph, tr. LC 68-8089. 1969. 10.00 o.s.i. (ISBN 0-8149-0202-2). Vanguard.

--Of a World That Is No More. LC 73-134665. 1970. 10.00 o.s.i. (ISBN 0-8149-0683-4). Vanguard.

Singer, Irving. The Goals of Human Sexuality. LC 72-6598. 1974. pap. 2.95 (ISBN 0-8052-0444-X). Schocken.

Singer, Isaac B. A Crown of Feathers. 342p. 1973. 12.95 (ISBN 0-374-51624-3); pap. 7.95 (ISBN 0-374-51367-8). FS&G.

--A Day of Pleasure: Stories of a Boy Growing up in Warsaw. LC 70-95461. (Illus.). 160p. (gr. 7 up). 1969. 8.95 o.p. (ISBN 0-374-31749-6); pap. 5.95 (ISBN 0-374-51367-8). FS&G.

--The Golem. (Illus.). 86p. (gr. 3 up). 1982. 10.95 (ISBN 0-374-32741-6); slipcased 40.00 (ISBN 0-374-32742-4). FS&G.

--Hasidim. LC 72-84288. (Illus.). 160p. 1973. 10.00 o.p. (ISBN 0-517-50047-7). Crown.

--In My Father's Court. 307p. 1966. 10.95 o.p. (ISBN 0-374-17560-8); pap. 5.95 (ISBN 0-374-50592-6). FS&G.

--An Isaac Bashevis Singer Reader. 586p. 1971. 17.95 (ISBN 0-374-17747-3); pap. 12.50 (ISBN 0-374-64030-0). FS&G.

--The Power of Light. 80p. 1982. pap. 2.25 (ISBN 0-380-60103-6, 60103, Camelot). Avon.

Singer, Ivan. The Theory of Best Approximation & Functional Analysis: Proceedings. (CBMS Regional Conference Ser.: Vol. 13). vii, 95p. (Orig.). 1974. pap. text ed. 12.00 (ISBN 0-89871-010-3). Soc Indus-Appl Math.

Singer, J. David & Small, Melvin. Wages of War, Eighteen Sixteen to Eighteen Sixty-Five: A Statistical Handbook. LC 75-39120. 384p. 1972. 24.95 o.p. (ISBN 0-471-79300-0). Wiley.

--Wages of War, 1816-1865. 1974. codebk. write for info. (ISBN 0-89138-068-X). ICPSR.

Singer, J. David, jt. auth. see LaBarr, Dorothy F.

Singer, J. E., jt. ed. see Baum, A.

Singer, Jeanne. Selected Songs. LC 82-71820. (Living Composers' Ser.: No. 3). 1982. pap. 12.50 (ISBN 0-934218-26-9). Dragons Teeth.

Singer, Jerome E., jt. ed. see Baum, Andrew.

Singer, Jerome L. Imagery & Daydream Methods in Psychotherapy & Behavior Modification. 1974. 37.50 (ISBN 0-12-646665-3). Acad Pr.

Singer, Jerome L., ed. Control of Aggression & Violence. (Personality & Psychopathology Ser: Vol. 10). 1971. 30.00 (ISBN 0-12-646650-5). Acad Pr.

Singer, Joe. How to Paint Figures in Pastel. (Illus.). 168p. 1976. 19.95 o.p. (ISBN 0-8230-2460-1). Watson-Guptill.

Singer, Joe, jt. auth. see Adams, Norman.

Singer, Joe, ed. see Greene, Daniel E.

Singer, Joseph, tr. see Singer, I. J.

Singer, Julia. We All Come from Someplace: Children of Puerto Rico. LC 75-46577. (Illus.). 96p. (gr. 4-6). 1976. 6.95 o.p. (ISBN 0-689-30531-1). Atheneum.

Singer, June F. Star Dreams. 448p. 1983. 14.95 (ISBN 0-87131-396-0). M Evans.

Singer, K. The Prognosis of Narcotic Addiction. 1975. 9.95 o.p. (ISBN 0-407-00021-6). Butterworth.

Singer, Larry M. The Data Processing Manager's Survival Manual: A Guide for Managing People & Resources. 226p. 1982. 24.95x (ISBN 0-471-86476-5). Ronald Pr.

Singer, Lester. Sociology: A Student's Introduction. LC 79-48092. 347p. 1980. pap. text ed. 11.50 o.p. (ISBN 0-8191-1011-6). U Pr of Amer.

Singer, Linda R. Standards Relating to Dispositions. LC 76-14412. (IJA-ABA Junvenile Justice Standards Project Ser.). 156p. 1980. prof ref 20.00x (ISBN 0-88410-229-7); pap. 10.00x prof ref (ISBN 0-88410-816-3). Ballinger Pub.

Singer, Linda R., jt. auth. see Goldfarb, Ronald L.

Singer, M. Introduction to the DEC System Ten Assembler Language Programming. LC 78-8586. 147p. 1978. 17.50 (ISBN 0-471-03458-4). Wiley.

Singer, M., ed. see Meigs, Walter B. & Meigs, Robert F.

Singer, M. H., ed. Competent Reader, Disabled Reader: Research & Application. (Illus.). 192p. 1982. text ed. 19.95x (ISBN 0-89859-196-1). L Erlbaum Assocs.

Singer, Marcus & Schade, J. P., eds. Degeneration Patterns in the Nervous System. (Progress in Brain Research: Vol. 14). 1965. 68.00 (ISBN 0-444-40542-9). Elsevier.

Singer, Marilyn. The Course of True Love Never Did Run Smooth. LC 82-48630. 256p. (YA) (gr. 7 up). 1983. 10.10i (ISBN 0-06-025753-9, HarpJ); PLB 10.89g (ISBN 0-06-025754-7). Har-Row.

--Tarantulas on the Brain. LC 81-48659. (Illus.). 192p. (gr. 4-7). 1982. 9.13i (ISBN 0-06-025745-8, HarpJ); PLB 9.89g (ISBN 0-06-025750-4). Har-Row.

Singer, Michael. PDP-11 Assembler Language Programming & Machine Organization. 178p. 1980. text ed. 17.95 (ISBN 0-471-04905-0). Wiley.

Singer, Michael & Flying Armadillo Staff, eds. Directors: A Complete Guide. 300p. 1982. pap. text ed. 30.00 (ISBN 0-943728-00-2). Lone Eagle Prods.

Singer, Milton, tr. see Gratry, A.

Singer, Neil M. Public Microeconomics: An Introduction to Government Finance. 2nd ed. (Ser. in Economics). 1976. 18.95 (ISBN 0-316-79277-2). Little.

Singer, Pamela M., jt. auth. see Pike, Jody P.

Singer, Penny. The Underground Economy: Earnings That Go Undeclared on Income Tax Forms. (Vital Issues, Vol. XXX 1980-81: No. 8). 0.60 (ISBN 0-686-81603-X). Ctr Info Am.

Singer, Peter. Practical Ethics. LC 79-52328. 1980. 34.95 (ISBN 0-521-22920-0); pap. 8.95 (ISBN 0-521-29720-6). Cambridge U Pr.

Singer, Peter, jt. auth. see Walters, William.

Singer, Philip. Road to Megiddo. LC 77-94858. 1978. softcover 7.00 o.p. (ISBN 0-89430-025-3). Morgan-Pacific.

Singer, Philip, ed. see Johnson, O.

Singer, R. Boletinae of Florida with Notes on Extralimital Species: 4 Parts in One Vol. (Bibliotheca Mycologica Ser.: No. 58). (Illus.). 1977. lib. bdg. 24.00x (ISBN 3-7682-1145-2). Lubrecht & Cramer.

--The Genera Marasmiellus, Crepidotus & Simocybe in the Neotropics. 1973. 80.00 (ISBN 3-7682-5444-5). Lubrecht & Cramer.

--A Monograph of Favolaschia. 1974. 24.00 (ISBN 3-7682-5450-X). Lubrecht & Cramer.

Singer, Richard B. & Levinson, Louis, eds. Medical Risks: Patterns of Mortality & Survival. LC 74-31609. 768p. 1976. 39.95x (ISBN 0-669-98228-8). Lexington Bks.

Singer, Richard G. Just Deserts: Sentencing Based on Equality & Desert. LC 79-915. 240p. 1979. prof ref 22.50x (ISBN 0-88410-799-X). Ballinger Pub.

Singer, Robert. Coaching, Athletics & Psychology. (Education Ser). (Illus.). 464p. 1971. text ed. 26.95 (ISBN 0-07-057465-0, C). McGraw.

Singer, Robert N. The Learning of Motor Skills. 1982. text ed. 20.95x (ISBN 0-02-410790-5). Macmillan.

--Motor Learning & Human Performance: An Application to Motor & Movement Behaviors. 3rd ed. (Illus.). 1980. text ed. 22.95x (ISBN 0-02-410780-8). Macmillan.

Singer, Robert N. & Dick, Walter. Teaching Physical Education: A Systems Approach. 2nd ed. LC 79-88450. (Illus.). 1980. text ed. 20.95 o.p. (ISBN 0-395-28359-0); instr's. manual 0.80 o.p. (ISBN 0-395-28360-4). HM.

Singer, Rolf. Boletes & Related Groups in South America. (Illus.). pap. 6.40 (ISBN 3-7682-0212-7). Lubrecht & Cramer.

--Hydropus (Basidiomycetes-Tricholomataceae-Myceneae) (Flora Neotropica Ser.: No. 32). (Illus.). 1982. pap. 25.00 (ISBN 0-89327-242-6). NY Botanical.

--Mycoflora Australis. 1969. pap. 64.00 (ISBN 3-7682-5429-1). Lubrecht & Cramer.

--Die Pilze Mitteleuropas: Vol. 5, Die Roehrlinge- Pt. 1, Die Boletaceae (Ohne Boletoideae) (Illus.). 1965. 48.00 (ISBN 3-7682-0526-6). Lubrecht & Cramer.

--Die Pilze Mitteleuropas: Vol. 5, Die Roehrlinge- Pt. 2, Die Boletoiceae una Strobilomycetaceae. (Illus.). 1967. 72.00 (ISBN 3-7682-0529-0). Lubrecht & Cramer.

Singer, Ronald & Wymer, John. The Middle Stone Age at Klasies River Mouth in South Africa. LC 81-16081. (Illus.). 1982. lib. bdg. 30.00x (ISBN 0-226-76103-7). U of Chicago Pr.

Singer, S., ed. see Singer, F.

Singer, S. Fred, ed. Torques & Attitude Sensing in Earth Satellites. (Applied Mathematics & Mechanics Ser.: Vol. 7). 1964. 43.50 (ISBN 0-12-646850-8). Acad Pr.

Singer, Sally. Giver of Song. 608p. (Orig.). 1982. pap. 3.50 (ISBN 0-446-90682-4). Warner Bks.

Singer, Stuart R. & Weiss, Stanley. Foreign Investment in the United States 1981: A Course Handbook. 754p. 1981. pap. 25.00 o.p. (ISBN 0-686-96147-1, B4-6579). PLI.

Singer, T. P. Biological Oxidations. LC 66-22060. 722p. 1968. 28.50 (ISBN 0-470-79275-2, Pub. by Wiley). Krieger.

Singer, T. P., ed. Flavins & Flavoproteins. 1976. 200.00 (ISBN 0-444-41458-4). Elsevier.

Singer, Thomas P., et al, eds. Monoamine Oxidase: Structure, Function & Altered Functions. LC 79-24107. 1980. 43.50 (ISBN 0-12-646880-X). Acad Pr.

Singer, Wenda G., jt. auth. see Shechtman, Stephen.

Singh, Ajit. Takeovers: Their Relevance to the Stock Market & the Theory of the Firm. (Department of Applied Economics Monographs: No. 19). 1972. 34.50 (ISBN 0-521-08245-5). Cambridge U Pr.

Singh, Alam. Soil Engineering in Theory & Practice: Fundamentals & General Principles, Vol. 1. 2nd ed. 1983. lib. bdg. 25.00x (ISBN 0-210-22552-1). Asia.

--Soil Engineering in Theory & Practice, Vol. 2. 2nd ed. 1982. 45.00 (ISBN 0-86590-024-8). Apt Bks.

Singh, Amritjit. The Novels of the Harlem Renaissance: Twelve Black Writers, 1923-1933. LC 75-27170. 224p. 1976. 16.95x (ISBN 0-271-01208-0). Pa St U Pr.

Singh, Amritjit, jt. ed. see Ray, David.

Singh, Armitjit, et al, eds. Indian Literature: A Guide to Information Sources. LC 74-11532. (American Literature, English Literature & World Literatures in English Information Guide Ser.: Vol. 36). 450p. 1981. 42.00x (ISBN 0-8103-1238-7). Gale.

Singh, B. N. Use of Calcium Antagonists in Cardiology: Proceedings of the 1st International Symposium on Tiapamil, Lausanne, April 1981. (Journal, Cardiology,: Vol. 69, Supplement 1, 1982). (Illus.). vi, 242p. 1982. pap. 45.00 (ISBN 3-8055-3588-0). S Karger.

Singh, B. P. & Raychaudhuri, S. P., eds. Currnet Trends in Plant Virology: Proceedings of Group Discussions on Plant Virology, National Botanical Research Institute, Lucknow. xvi, 224p. 1982. 19.00 (ISBN 0-686-97972-9, Pub. by Messers Today & Tomorrow Printers & Publishers). Scholarly Pubns.

Singh, Baljit & Misra, Shridhar. Study of Land Reforms in Uttar Pradesh. (Illus.). 1965. 12.00x (ISBN 0-8248-0020-6, Eastwest Ctr). UH Pr.

Singh, Bhaghat, jt. auth. see Naps, Thomas.

Singh, Bhupinder & Bhandari, J. R., eds. The Tribal World & Its Transformation. 1980. text ed. 15.75x (ISBN 0-391-01933-3). Humanities.

Singh, Chandramani. Centres of Pahari Paintings. 174p. 1981. text ed. 62.00x (ISBN 0-391-02412-4, Pub. by Abhinav India). Humanities.

Singh, Darshan. Spiritual Awakening. LC 81-50726. (Illus.). 338p. (Orig.). 1982. pap. 5.50 (ISBN 0-918224-11-X). Sawan Kirpal Pubns.

Singh, Dharamjit. Indian Cookery. (Handbook Ser.). 1970. pap. 3.95 (ISBN 0-14-046141-8). Penguin.

Singh, G., ed. see Leavis, F. R.

Singh, Gurdit. The Visions of James Thomson ("B.V.") An Exploration. (English Language & Literature Ser.: No. 6). 185p. 1980. text ed. 12.00x (ISBN 0-391-02522-8). Humanities.

Singh, I. B., jt. auth. see Reineck, H. E.

Singh, Indera P. & Tiwari, S. C., eds. Man & His Environment. (International Conference of Anthropological & Ethnological Sciences Ser.: No. 10). 299p. 1980. text ed. 19.00x (ISBN 0-391-02140-0). Humanities.

Singh, Inderbir. A Textbook of Human Neuronatomy. 360p. 1982. 60.00x (ISBN 0-686-94065-2, Pub. by Garlandfold England); pap. 50.00x (ISBN 0-7069-1193-8). State Mutual Bk.

Singh, Inderjit. Small Farmers & the Landless in South Asia. (Working Paper: No. 320). xii, 194p. 1979. 5.00 (ISBN 0-686-36077-X, WP-0320). World Bank.

Singh, Indra J. Indian Prison. 1979. text ed. 15.75 (ISBN 0-391-01849-3). Humanities.

Singh, Indu. Telematics in the Year Two Thousand. Voigt, Melvin J., ed. (Communication & Information Science Ser.). 224p. 1983. text ed. 24.95 (ISBN 0-89391-137-2). Ablex Pub.

Singh, J. P. Urban Land Use Planning in Hill Areas: A Case Study of Shillong. 192p. 1980. text ed. 19.00x (ISBN 0-391-02122-2). Humanities.

Singh, Jag J. & Deepak, Adarsh, eds. Environmental & Climatic Impact of Coal Utilization. LC 79-28681. 1980. 42.50 (ISBN 0-12-646360-3). Acad Pr.

Singh, Jagjit. Great Ideas & Theories of Modern Cosmology. 1966. pap. text ed. 6.75 (ISBN 0-486-20925-3). Dover.

--Great Ideas in Information Theory, Language & Cybernetics. (Orig.). 1966. pap. text ed. 5.50 (ISBN 0-486-21694-2). Dover.

Singh, K. S. Economies of the Tribes & Their Transformation. 400p. 1982. text ed. 41.00x (ISBN 0-391-02786-7, 40956, Pub. by Concept India). Humanities.

Singh, K. S., ed. Tribal Movements in India, Vol. 1. 1982. 25.00X (ISBN 0-8364-0901-9, Pub. by Manohar India). South Asia Bks.

Singh, Kala S., jt. auth. see Singh, Sadanand.

Singh, Khushwant. A Bride for the Sahib & Other Stories. 168p. 1967. pap. 2.50 (ISBN 0-88253-087-9). Ind-US Inc.

--Gurus, Godmen & Good People. LC 75-905201. 1975. 9.00x o.p. (ISBN 0-8364-0487-4, Orient Longman). South Asia Bks.

Singh, Kirpal. Spirituality: What It Is. 3rd ed. LC 81-52000. (Illus.). 112p. 1982. Repr. of 1959 ed. pap. 3.50 (ISBN 0-918224-16-0). Sawan Kirpal Pubns.

Singh, Lalita P. Power Politics & Southeast Asia. 1979. text ed. 13.00x (ISBN 0-391-00985-0). Humanities.

Singh, M. G. Dynamical Heirarchical Control. rev. ed. 1980. 55.50 (ISBN 0-444-85488-6). Elsevier.

Singh, M. G., ed. Handbook of Large Scale Systems Engineering Applications. Titl, A. 561p. 1979. 117.00 (ISBN 0-444-85283-2, North Holland). Elsevier.

Singh, Manju S. The Spice Box: A Vegetarian Indian Cookbook. LC 81-2061. (Illus.). 224p. 1981. 15.95 (ISBN 0-89594-052-3); pap. 6.95 (ISBN 0-89594-053-1). Crossing Pr.

Singh, Mohinder & Sharma, R. N. A Cummulative Index to Public Administration: Journal of the Royal Institute of Public Administration, Vols. 1-55, 1928-1977, 1979. text ed. 18.25x (ISBN 0-391-01871-X). Humanities.

Singh, P. Financing of University Education. 236p. 1982. text ed. 17.25x (ISBN 0-391-02727-1, Pub. by Concept India). Humanities.

Singh, R. Electoral Politics in Manipur. 1981. text ed. 16.50x (ISBN 0-391-02271-7, Pub. by Concept India). Humanities.

Singh, R. John. French Diplomacy in the Caribbean & the American Revolution. 1977. 10.00 o.p. (ISBN 0-682-48891-7, University). Exposition.

Singh, R. R., ed. Social Work Perspectives on Poverty. 1980. text ed. 13.00x (ISBN 0-391-01832-9). Humanities.

Singh, R. S. Indian Novel in English: A Critical Study. 1977. text ed. 11.25x o.p. (ISBN 0-391-01079-4). Humanities.

--Plant Diseases. 564p. 1978. 62.00x (ISBN 0-686-84464-5, Pub. by Oxford & I B H India). State Mutual Bk.

Singh, Rajendra. Jaishankar Prasad. (World Authors Ser.). 1982. lib. bdg. 18.95 (ISBN 0-8057-6474-7, Twayne). G K Hall.

Singh, Roderick P. Anatomy of Hearing & Speech. (Illus.). 1980. text ed. 16.95x (ISBN 0-19-502665-9); pap. text ed. 9.95x (ISBN 0-19-502666-7). Oxford U Pr.

Singh, S. Diagnostic Procedures in Hearing, Speech & Langauge. 672p. 1978. text ed. 29.95 (ISBN 0-8391-1217-3). Univ Park.

--Distinctive Features: Theory & Validation. (Illus.). 280p. 1976. text ed. 22.95 (ISBN 0-8391-0754-4). Univ Park.

Singh, S. K. Development Economics: Theory & Findings. LC 72-1966. (Illus.). 320p. 1975. 25.95x o.p. (ISBN 0-669-83626-5). Lexington Bks.

Singh, S. P. & Burry, J. H., eds. Nonlinear Analysis & Applications. (Lecture Notes in Pure & Applied Mathematics: Vol. 80). (Illus.). 488p. 49.75 (ISBN 0-8247-1790-2). Dekker.

Singh, S. P., jt. ed. see Agarwala, Amar N.

Singh, S. R., et al, eds. Pests of Grain Legumes: Ecology & Control. 1979. 42.50 o.s.i. (ISBN 0-12-646350-6). Acad Pr.

Singh, Sadanand. Phonetics: Principles & Practices. (Illus.). 1976. 12.95 o.p. (ISBN 0-8391-0822-2). Univ Park.

Singh, Sadanand & Singh, Kala S. Phonetics: Principles & Practices. 2nd ed. (Illus.). 288p. 1983. pap. 14.95 (ISBN 0-8391-1701-9, 16411). Univ Park.

Singh, Sadanand, ed. Measurement Proceedures in Speech, Hearing & Language. (Illus.). 480p. 1976. text ed. 27.95 (ISBN 0-8391-0753-6). Univ Park.

Singh, Sukhwant. India's Wars Since Independence, Vol. III. 400p. 1982. text ed. 18.95x (ISBN 0-686-73083-6, Pub. by Vikas India). Advent NY.

Singh, Tarlok. Poverty & Social Change: With a Reappraisal. 2nd ed. LC 74-33899. 352p. 1975. Repr. of 1969 ed. lib. bdg. 20.75x (ISBN 0-8371-8000-7, SIPO). Greenwood.

--Towards an Integrated Society. 1969. lib. bdg. 29.95x (ISBN 0-8371-2338-0, SIT/). Greenwood.

Singh, V. B. Social & Economic Change in India. 1967. 7.50x o.p. (ISBN 0-8188-1138-2). Paragon.

Singh, Y., jt. auth. see Unnithan, T. K.

Singhal, Radhey L. & Thomas, John A., eds. Lead Toxicity. LC 79-16784. (Illus.). 524p. 1980. text ed. 42.50 (ISBN 0-8067-1801-3). Urban & S.

Singlemann, Jay & Longhurst, Jean. Business Programming Logic: A Structured Approach. 2nd ed. (Illus.). 288p. 1982. text ed. 16.95 (ISBN 0-13-107623-X). P-H.

Singler, Charles H., jt. auth. see Hughes, C. David.

Singletary, Ernest E., et al. Law Briefs on Litigation & the Rights of Exceptional Children, Youth, & Adults. 1977. pap. text ed. 17.75 o.p. (ISBN 0-8191-0188-5). U Pr of Amer.

Singletary, Milly. The Best One Hundred Ninety-Nine & a Half Restaurants of Hawaii. 34p. 1977. pap. 2.50 o.p. (ISBN 0-9601256-1-2). Singletary.

--Hawaiian Quilting Made Easy. (Illus.). 48p. pap. 5.00 (ISBN 0-9601256-8-X). Sunset Pubns.

--Hilo Hattie: A Legend in our Time. (Illus.). 191p. ltd. ed. 10.95 (ISBN 0-9601256-5-5); pap. 5.95 (ISBN 0-9601256-6-3). Sunset Pubns.

--Three Days in Downtown Honolulu. (Illus.). 48p. (Orig.). 1982. pap. 4.95 (ISBN 0-941244-02-4). Sunset Pubns.

Singletary, W. E. & Overbeek, Ross A. ANS COBOL: A Pragmatic Approach. (Illus.). 288p. 1975. text ed. 21.95 (ISBN 0-07-057469-3, C). McGraw.

Singletary, Wilson E., jt. auth. see Overbeek, Ross A.

Singleton, Charles S., tr. see Dante Alighieri.

Singleton, Esther. The Shakespeare Garden: With Numerous Illustrations from Photographs & Reproductions of Old Wood Cuts. LC 74-8203. 1974. Repr. of 1922 ed. 40.00x (ISBN 0-8103-4048-8). Gale.

Singleton, Fred, ed. Environmental Misuse in the Soviet Union. LC 75-19823. (Special Studies). (Illus.). 140p. 1976. text ed. 28.95 o.p. (ISBN 0-275-56210-7). Praeger.

Singleton, Laurel R., ed. Data Book of Social Studies Materials & Resources, Vol. 8. (Data Book Ser.). 192p. 1983. pap. 10.00 (ISBN 0-89994-279-2). Soc Sci Ed.

--Tips for Social Studies Teachers: Activities from ERIC. 192p. 1983. pap. 10.95 (ISBN 0-89994-280-6). Soc Sci Ed.

Singleton, Mack, tr. see Ruiz, Juan.

Singleton, Mary C. & LeVeau, Barney. The Hip Joint. 1975. pap. 2.00 cancelled (ISBN 0-912452-13-7). Am Phys Therapy Assn.

Singleton, Mary C., jt. auth. see Montgomery, Royce L.

Singleton, Paul & Sainsbury, Diana. Dictionary of Microbiology. LC 78-4532. 481p. 1978. 71.95 (ISBN 0-471-99658-0, Pub. by Wiley-Interscience). Wiley.

--Introduction to Bacteria: For Students in the Biological Sciences. 166p. 1981. 27.95x (ISBN 0-471-10034-X, Pub. by Wiley-Interscience); pap. 12.95x (ISBN 0-471-10035-8, Pub. by Wiley-Interscience). Wiley.

Singleton, Ralph S. & Vietor, Joan E. Budget It Right. 300p. 1983. text ed. 42.50 (ISBN 0-943728-04-5); pap. text ed. 30.00 (ISBN 0-943728-02-9). Lone Eagle Prods.

--Schedule It Right! (Illus.). 300p. 1983. text ed. 42.50 (ISBN 0-943728-03-7); pap. text ed. 30.00 (ISBN 0-943728-01-0). Lone Eagle Prods.

Singleton, W. T. Management Skills. (Study of Real Skills Ser. III). 320p. 1981. text ed. 34.95 (ISBN 0-8391-1683-7). Univ Park.

Singleton, W. T. & Debney, L. M., eds. Occupational Disability. (Illus.). 307p. 1982. 36.80 (ISBN 0-942068-02-5). Bogden & Son.

Singleton, W. T. & Fox, J. C., eds. Measurement of Man at Work. 268p. 1973. write for info. (ISBN 0-85066-041-6, Pub. by Taylor & Francis). Intl Pubns Serv.

Singleton, W. T. & Spurgeon, P., eds. Measurement of Human Resources. LC 74-14848. 370p. 1975. 32.50x (ISBN 0-85066-068-8). Intl Pubns Serv.

Sinha, A. K., ed. Perspectives in Yoga. 1976. 7.50x o.p. (ISBN 0-88386-815-6). South Asia Bks.

Sinha, B. C. Tree Worship in Ancient India. (Illus.). 1979. 18.50x o.p. (ISBN 0-8364-0366-5). South Asia Bks.

Sinha, C. P. Eugene O'Neill's Tragic Vision. 1981. text ed. 18.50x (ISBN 0-391-02203-2). Humanities.

Sinha, D. P. Culture Change in an Inter-Tribal Market. 7.50x o.p. (ISBN 0-210-27031-4). Asia.

Sinha, H. S. Communism & Gita: A Philosophico-Ethical Study. 1979. text ed. 16.25x (ISBN 0-391-01869-8). Humanities.

Sinha, Jai B. The Nurturant Task Leader: A Model of the Effective Executive. 1980. text ed. 11.75x (ISBN 0-391-01823-X). Humanities.

Sinha, M. M. The Impact of Urbanization on Land Use in the Rural-Urban Fringe: A Case Study of Patna. 258p. 1980. text ed. 19.00x (ISBN 0-391-02141-9). Humanities.

Sinha, V. N. John Donne: A Study of His Dramatic Imagination. 1978. pap. 9.00x (ISBN 0-210-40621-6). Asia.

Sinha, V. N., jt. ed. see Mandal, R. B.

Sinibaldi, Thomas. Tap Dancing Step by Step. LC 81-50990. (Illus.). 96p. (gr. 7 up). 1981. 12.95 o.p. (ISBN 0-8069-4656-3); lib. bdg. 11.69 (ISBN 0-8069-4657-1); pap. 6.95 (ISBN 0-8069-7556-3). Sterling.

Sinick, Daniel. Occupational Information & Guidance. (Guidance Monograph). 1970. pap. 2.40 o.p. (ISBN 0-395-09938-2). HM.

Sinicropi, Anthony V., jt. auth. see Hill, Marvin, Jr.

Sinitsyna, I. V., tr. see Pugachev.

Sink, Jack M., jt. auth. see Gannaway, Thomas W.

Sink, L. & Godden, J., eds. Conflicts in Childhood Cancer. 1976. 32.25 (ISBN 0-444-99839-X). Elsevier.

Sinkey, Joseph F., Jr. Commercial Bank Financial Management. 704p. 1983. text ed. 26.95 (ISBN 0-02-410590-2). Macmillan.

--Problem & Failed Institutions in the Commercial Banking Industry. Altman, Edward I. & Walter, Ingo, eds. LC 76-5760. (Contemporary Studies in Economic & Financial Analysis: Vol. 4). 1979. lib. bdg. 36.50 (ISBN 0-89232-005-2). Jai Pr.

Sinkin, Richard N. The Mexican Reform, 1855-1876: A Study in Liberal Nation-Building. LC 78-620053. (Latin American Monograph: No. 49). 273p. 1979. 18.95x o.p. (ISBN 0-292-75044-7); pap. text ed. 8.95x (ISBN 0-292-75045-5). U of Tex Pr.

Sinkler, Lorraine, ed. see Goldsmith, Joel S.

Sinkov, Abraham. Elementary Cryptanalysis: A Mathematical Approach. LC 72-89953. (New Mathematical Library: No. 22). 1980. pap. 8.75 (ISBN 0-88385-622-0). Math Assn.

Sinks, Thomas A. & Hess, John E., eds. Knowledge for What? LC 73-79438. 1969. pap. 2.50x (ISBN 0-8134-1102-5, 1102). Interstate.

Sinn, Gerald R. Cash Operations Management: Profit from Within. 1981. 19.00 (ISBN 0-89433-116-7). Petrocelli.

Sinn, H. W. Economic Decisions Under Uncertainty. (Studies in Mathematical & Managerial Economics: Vol. 32). 350p. 1982. 68.00 (ISBN 0-444-86387-7, North Holland). Elsevier.

Sinnecker, Herbert. General Epidemiology. Walker, N., tr. from Ger. LC 74-4655. 228p. 1977. 41.25 o.p. (ISBN 0-471-79318-3, Pub. by Wiley-Interscience). Wiley.

Sinnema, John R. Hendrik van Veldeke. (World Authors Ser.). lib. bdg. 15.95 (ISBN 0-8057-2936-4, Twayne). G K Hall.

Sinnes, A. Cort. Easy Maintenance Gardening. Burke, Ken, ed. LC 82-82160. (Illus.). 96p. 1982. pap. 5.95 (ISBN 0-89721-004-2). Ortho.

--Shade Gardening. Burke, Ken, ed. LC 82-82159. (Illus.). 96p. (Orig.). 1982. pap. 5.95 (ISBN 0-89721-005-0). Ortho.

--Spas & Hot Tubs: How to Plan, Install & Enjoy. 160p. 1982. pap. 7.95 (ISBN 0-89586-161-5). H P Bks.

Sinnett, A. P. Occult World. 9th ed. 1969. 10.75 (ISBN 0-8356-5019-7). Theos Pub Hse.

Sinnhuber, Karl A. Germany. 2nd ed. (Geography & Growth Ser.). 1970. 12.50x o.p. (ISBN 0-7195-1286-7). Intl Pubns Serv.

Sinnigen, William G. & Boak, Arthur E. A History of Rome to A.D. 565. 6th ed. 1977. 25.95x (ISBN 0-02-410800-6). Macmillan.

Sinnott, Edmund G. Problem of Organic Form. 1963. 29.50x (ISBN 0-685-69864-5). Elliots Bks.

Sinnott, Edmund W. The Bridge of Life. 1972. pap. 3.45 o.p. (ISBN 0-671-21329-6, Touchstone Bks). S&S.

--Plant Morphogenesis. LC 79-4660. 560p. 1979. Repr. of 1960 ed. lib. bdg. 29.50 (ISBN 0-88275-922-1). Krieger.

Sinnott, Loraine T., jt. auth. see Cline, Hugh F.

Sinnott, Roger, jt. ed. see Hirschfeld, Alan.

Sinnott, Roger W., jt. auth. see Hirshfeld, Alan.

Sinor, Denis. History of Hungary. LC 76-26674. 1976. Repr. of 1959 ed. lib. bdg. 21.00x (ISBN 0-8371-9024-X, SIHH). Greenwood.

Sinor, John. Eleven Albatrosses in My Bluebird Tree. Barone, Steve, ed. LC 76-2305. (Illus.). 1976. 8.95 (ISBN 0-89325-001-5). Joyce Pr.

--Finsterhall Goes Over the Wall. new ed. 1978. 5.95 (ISBN 0-89325-011-2). Joyce Pr.

--Finsterhall of San Pasqual. LC 76-20961. (Illus.). (gr. 4-9). 1976. 5.95 (ISBN 0-89325-002-3). Joyce Pr.

--Ghosts of Cabrillo Lighthouse. LC 77-72577. (Illus.). (gr. 4 up). 1977. 5.95 (ISBN 0-89325-004-X). Joyce Pr.

--Ladies in My Life. LC 79-87472. 1979. 9.95 (ISBN 0-89325-015-5). Joyce Pr.

Sinotte, Stephen R. The Fabulous Keokuk Geodes, Vol. I. (Illus.). 7.95 (ISBN 0-686-51555-2, 99023). Wallace-Homestead.

Sintes, J. Diccionario Humoristico. Orig. Title: Span. 900p. 41.95 (ISBN 0-686-57940-0, S-37666). French & Eur.

Sin The & Hiang The. The Big Guys Fall the Hardest. LC 82-72608. (Illus.). 208p. (Orig.). 1982. pap. 9.95 (ISBN 0-89708-099-8). And Bks.

Sinyavsky, Andrei, jt. auth. see Tertz, Abram.

Sinz & Rosenzweig. Psychophysiology, 1980. Date not set. 95.75 (ISBN 0-444-80370-X). Elsevier.

Siotani, Minoru & Hayakawa, T. Modern Multivariate Statistical Analysis & Its Applications: A Graduate Course & Handbook. LC 82-72549. (The American Sciences Press Series in Mathematical & Management Sciences: Vol. 9). 1983. text ed. price not set (ISBN 0-935950-06-0). Am Sciences Pr.

Sioussat, Annie L. Old Manors in the Colony of Maryland, 2 pts. (Illus.). 64p. Date not set. 15.00 (ISBN 0-686-36503-8). Md Hist.

Sipe, H. Craig & Farmer, Walter A. A Summary of Research in Science Education 1980. 208p. 1982. 25.00x (ISBN 0-471-87028-5, Pub. by Wiley Interscience). Wiley.

Siporin, Max. Introduction to Social Work Practice. (Illus.). 416p. 1975. text ed. 22.95x (ISBN 0-02-410850-2). Macmillan.

Siposs, Allan J. Exporting: Practical Handbook for Entrepreneurs & Managers. rev. ed. (Illus.). 103p. (Orig.). 1981. pap. 25.00x looseleaf (ISBN 0-935402-01-2); lib. bdg. 26.00x (ISBN 0-935402-06-3). Intl Comm Serv.

--How to Win the Import Game: Practical Tips & Ideas on Importing. (Illus.). 110p. 1980. pap. 25.00x o.p. (ISBN 0-935402-00-4); lib. bdg. 26.00x o.p. (ISBN 0-686-86197-3). Intl Comm Serv.

--Importing: Practical Tips & Ideas for Entrepreneurs & Managers. rev. ed. (Illus.). 109p. 1981. looseleaf 25.00x (ISBN 0-935402-04-7); lib. bdg. 26.00x (ISBN 0-935402-05-5). Intl Comm Serv.

Sipowicz, A. Edwin, tr. see Graham, Billy.

Sipowicz, Edwin, tr. see Coleman, William L.

Sipowicz, Eswin, tr. see Wirt, Sherwood E.

Sipper, Ralph, ed. see Macdonald, Ross.

Sippl, C., jt. auth. see Sippl, R.

Sippl, Charles J. & Dahl, Fred. Video Computers: How to Select, Mix, & Operate Personal Computers & Home Video Equipment. (Illus.). 256p. 1981. 15.95 (ISBN 0-13-941856-3, Spec); pap. 7.95 (ISBN 0-13-941849-0). P-H.

Sippl, R. & Sippl, C. Personal & Home Electronic Buyers Guide. 1979. 16.95 o.p. (ISBN 0-13-657403-3, Spec); pap. 7.95 o.p. (ISBN 0-13-657395-9, Spec). P-H.

Sipple, Horace & McNutt, Kristen W., eds. Sugars in Nutrition. 1974. 75.50 (ISBN 0-12-646750-1). Acad Pr.

Sipple, M. Noel, jt. auth. see Seyler, Dorothy U.

SIPRI. Strategic Disarmament: Verification & National Security. LC 77-85318. 174p. 1978. 19.50x (ISBN 0-8448-1227-7). Crane-Russak Co.

Sir Thomas Beecham Society. Sir Thomas Beecham Discography. LC 78-2261. 1978. Repr. of 1975 ed. lib. bdg. 17.00x (ISBN 0-313-20367-9, STBD). Greenwood.

Siracusa, Joseph & Laurenti, Josephcompiled by. Literary Relations Between Spain & Italy: A Bibliographic Survey of Comparative Literature (Relaciones Literarias Entre Espana e Italia Ensayo de una Bibliografia de Literature comparada) 1972. lib. bdg. 25.00 (ISBN 0-8161-1010-7, Hall Reference). G K Hall.

Siracusa, Joseph M. New Left Diplomatic Histories & Historians: The American Revisionists. LC 73-75575. (National University Publications). 1973. 14.00 o.p. (ISBN 0-8046-9037-5). Kennikat.

Siracusa, Joseph M. & Smith, Daniel M. The Testing of America: Nineteen Fourteen to Nineteen Forty-Five. rev. ed. 1979. pap. text ed. 10.95x (ISBN 0-88273-101-7). Forum Pr IL.

Sirageldin, Ismail, ed. Research in Human Capital & Development: An Annual Compilation of Research, Vol. 1. 1979. lib. bdg. 42.50 (ISBN 0-89232-019-2). Jai Pr.

--Research in Human Capital & Development, Vol. 2. 325p. 1981. 42.50 (ISBN 0-89232-098-2). Jai Pr.

Sirageldin, Ismail, jt. ed. see Sherbiny, Nalem A.

Sirageldin, Ismail Abdel-Hamid. Non-Market Components of National Income. LC 78-627964. 127p. 1969. pap. 5.00 (ISBN 0-87944-056-2). Inst Soc. Res.

Sirages, H. Elsevier's Football Dictionary. (Eng. & Ger.). 1980. 40.50 (ISBN 0-444-41890-3). Elsevier.

Siragusa, Chris R. Introduction to Programming BASIC. 2nd ed. 340p. 1983. pap. text ed. write for info. (ISBN 0-87150-386-7, 8020). Prindle.

Sircar, D. C. Some Epigraphical Records of the Medieval Period from Eastern India. 1979. 22.00x o.p. (ISBN 0-8364-0349-5). South Asia Bks.

Sircus, Wilfred & Smith, Adam N. Scientific Foundations of Gastroenterology. LC 80-5260. (Illus.). 650p. 1980. 45.00 (ISBN 0-7216-8319-3). Saunders.

Siregar, Susan R. Adat, Islam & Christianity in a Batak Homeland. LC 81-11073. (Papers in International Studies: Southeast Asia Ser.: No. 57). 108p. pap. text ed. 10.00x (ISBN 0-89680-110-1, Ohio U Ctr Intl). Ohio U Pr.

Siren, Osvald. The Chinese on the Art of Painting. LC 63-20263. (Illus.). 1963. pap. 7.50 (ISBN 0-8052-0057-6). Schocken.

Sirianni, Carmen, jt. ed. see Cronin, James E.

Sirico, Louis J., jt. auth. see Waz, Joseph.

Sirico, Louis J., Jr. How to Talk Back to the Telephone Company. 210p. 1979. pap. 10.00 (ISBN 0-686-36551-8). Ctr Responsive Law.

Siringo, Charles. A Texas Cowboy. LC 80-18961. (Classics of the Old West Ser.). PLB 17.28 (ISBN 0-8094-3567-5). Silver.

Siris, Peter. The Peking Mandate. 312p. 1983. 14.95 (ISBN 0-399-12752-6). Putnam Pub Group.

Sirka, Ann. The Nationality Question in Austrian Education: The Case of Ukranians in Galicia, 1867-1914. (European University Studies; Series 3, History & Allied Studies: Vol. 124). 230p. 1980. write for info. (ISBN 3-8204-6618-5). P Lang Pubs.

Sirka, Josef. The Development of Ukrainian Literature in Czechoslovakia 1945-1975: Slavonic Languages & Literatures, Vol. 11. (European University Studies: Ser. 16). 210p. 1978. pap. write for info. (ISBN 3-261-02479-8). P Lang Pubs.

Sirken, Irving A. Education Programs & Projects: Analytical Techniques, Case Studies, & Exercises. rev. ed. ix, 287p. 1979. pap. 6.00 (ISBN 0-686-36036-2). World Bank.

Sirkin, Esther, jt. auth. see Baranov, Alvin B.

Sirkis, Susan B. Fashions Eighteen Fifty-Three to Eighteen Fifty-Eight, Vol. 18. (The Wish Bklets). (Illus.). 44p. 1976. pap. 5.50x (ISBN 0-913786-18-7). Wish Bklets.

--Fashions Eighteen Forty to Eighteen Forty-Five, Vol. 17. (The Wise Bklets). (Illus.). 36p. 1976. pap. 5.50x (ISBN 0-913786-17-9). Wish Bklets.

--Fashions Eighteen Ninety-five to Nineteen Ninety-Six, Vol. 19. (The Wish Bklets). 44p. 1977. pap. 5.50x (ISBN 0-913786-19-5). Wish Bklets.

--Fashions Eighteen Sixty-One to Eighteen Sixty-Five, Vol. 1. (The Wish Bklets). (Illus.). 40p. 1965. pap. 5.50x (ISBN 0-913786-01-2). Wish Bklets.

--Fashions Eighteen Thirty-One to Eighteen Thirty-Five, Vol. 2. (The Wish Bklets). 40p. 1966. pap. 5.50x (ISBN 0-913786-02-0). Wish Bklets.

--Fashions Eighteen Twenty to Eighteen Twenty-Five, Vol. 16. (The Wish Bklets). 40p. 1975. pap. 5.50x (ISBN 0-913786-16-0). Wish Bklets.

--Fashions in Tirm, Vol. 24. (The Wish Bklets). (Illus.). 32p. 1983. pap. 5.50x (ISBN 0-913786-24-1). Wish Bklets.

--Fashions Nineteen Hundred, Vol. 6. (The Wish Bklets). (Illus.). 44p. 1970. pap. 5.50x (ISBN 0-913786-06-3). Wish Bklets.

Sirlin, J. L. Biology of RNA. 1972. 60.00 (ISBN 0-12-646950-4). Acad Pr.

Sirluck, Ernest see Milton, John.

Sirmans, C. F. Research in Real Estate, Vol. 1. 350p. 1981. 49.50 (ISBN 0-89232-217-9). Jai Pr.

Sirmans, C. F. & Kau, James B. Tax Planning for Real Estate Investors: How to Take Advantage of Real Estate Tax Shelters. 2nd ed. (Illus.). 260p. 1982. 18.95 (ISBN 0-13-885285-5, Spec); pap. 9.95 (ISBN 0-13-885277-4). P-H.

Sirnis, A., tr. see Liebknecht, Karl.

Sirof, Harriet. Save the Dam! Schroeder, Howard, ed. LC 81-3198. (Roundup Ser.). (Illus.). 48p. (gr. 3 up). 1981. PLB 7.95 (ISBN 0-89686-156-2); pap. 3.95 (ISBN 0-89686-164-3). Crestwood Hse.

Sirohi, R. S. Mechanical Measurements. LC 80-27233. 210p. 1981. 16.95x o.s.i. (ISBN 0-470-27107-8). Halsted Pr.

Sirois. Immunopharmacology. (Research Monographs in Immunology: Vol. 4). Date not set. 98.00 (ISBN 0-444-80416-1). Elsevier.

Siroky, Mike & Bertucci, Bob. Orange Lightnin': Inside University of Tennessee Football. LC 82-81804. (Illus.). 192p. 1982. 12.95 (ISBN 0-88011-082-1). Leisure Pr.

Siropolis, Nicholas C. Small Business Management. 2nd ed. LC 81-82561. 1982. 22.95 (ISBN 0-395-31732-0); instr's manual 3.00 (ISBN 0-395-31733-9); avail. test bank 1.50 (ISBN 0-395-31770-3). HM.

Sirota, A. G. Polyolefins: Modifications of Structure & Properties. 120p. 1969. 31.95 o.p. (ISBN 0-470-79330-9). Halsted Pr.

Sirota, Adair. Preparing for Childbirth: A Couple's Manual. (Illus.). 192p. (Orig.). 1983. pap. 7.95 (ISBN 0-8092-5625-8). Contemp Bks.

Sirota, David. Essentials of Real Estate. (Illus.). 304p. 1980. ref. ed. 19.95 (ISBN 0-8359-1776-2). Reston.

Siry, Joseph V. Marshes of the Ocean Shore: Development of an Ecological Ethic. LC 82-45899. (Environmental History Ser.: No. 6). 264p. 1983. 22.50x (ISBN 0-89096-150-6). Tex A&M Univ Pr.

Sisam, Kenneth, ed. Fourteenth Century Prose & Verse. (Smith, D. N., Ser). 1921. pap. 14.95x (ISBN 0-19-871093-3). Oxford U Pr.

Sisco, John I., jt. auth. see Koehler, Jerry W.

Sisemore, J. T. Practiquemos la Visitacion. Gonzalez, Ananias, ed. Grijalva, Josue, tr. Orig. Title: The Ministry of Visitation. 1981. Repr. of 1979 ed. 2.50 (ISBN 0-311-11034-7). Casa Bautista.

Sisemore, John T. Church Growth Through the Sunday School. (Orig.). 1983. pap. 5.95 (ISBN 0-8054-6237-6). Broadman.

Sisemore, John T., ed. The Ministry of Religious Education. LC 78-50388. 1978. 8.95 (ISBN 0-8054-3220-5). Broadman.

Sisic, Natasa. Vilem Mathesius Als Bohemist. 240p. (Ger.). 1982. write for info. (ISBN 3-8204-5826-3). P Lang Pubs.

Sisk, Dorothy, jt. auth. see Shallcross, Doris.

Siskin, Bernard R., jt. auth. see Johnson, Rodney D.

Siskind, Aaron. Bucks County Photographs of Early Architecture. (Illus.). 112p. 1974. 12.95 (ISBN 0-910302-02-2). Bucks Co Hist.

Siskind, Charles S. Direct-Current Machinery. 1952. text ed. 23.50 o.p. (ISBN 0-07-057740-4, C). McGraw.

--Electrical Control Systems in Industry. 1963. text ed. 23.95 (ISBN 0-07-057746-3, G). McGraw.

--Electrical Machines: Direct & Alternating Currents. 2nd ed. 1959. text ed. 24.95 (ISBN 0-07-057728-5, G). McGraw.

Siskind, Janet. To Hunt in the Morning. LC 73-82674. (Illus.). 1975. pap. 6.95x (ISBN 0-19-501891-5). Oxford U Pr.

Sisler, Harry H. Electronic Structure, Properties & the Periodic Law. 2nd ed. (Orig.). 1973. pap. text ed. 3.95x (ISBN 0-442-27653-2). Van Nos Reinhold.

Sisler, Harry H., et al. Chemistry: A Systematic Approach. (Illus.). 1980. text ed. 23.95x (ISBN 0-19-502630-6); pap. text ed. 8.95x study guide (ISBN 0-19-502719-1); text ed. 3.95 instructor's manual (ISBN 0-19-502718-3). Oxford U Pr.

Sislowitz, Marcel J. Look! How Your Eyes See. LC 76-56180. (Science Is What & Why Bk.). (Illus.). 48p. (gr. k-3). 1977. PLB 6.99 (ISBN 0-698-30654-6, Coward). Putnam Pub Group.

Sismondi, Simonde de. De l'Interet de la France a l'Egard de la Traite des Negres. (Slave Trade in France Ser., 1744-1848). 35p. 1974. Repr. of 1814 ed. lib. bdg. 20.50x o.p. (ISBN 0-8287-0778-2, TN145). Clearwater Pub.

Sissam, Leighton E., jt. auth. see Pitts, Donald R.

Sissom, Leighton E. & Pitts, Donald R. Elements of Transport Phenomena. LC 75-161670. 1972. text ed. 38.00 o.p. (ISBN 0-07-057749-8, C). McGraw.

Sisson, A. F. Sisson's Synonyms: An Unabridged Synonym & Related-Terms Locator. LC 74-77314. 1970. 22.50 (ISBN 0-13-810630-4, Parker). P-H.

--Sisson's Word & Expression Locater. 1977. pap. 2.50 o.p. (ISBN 0-685-79537-3, 40-073-X). Pinnacle Bks.

--Sisson's Word & Expression Locater. 371p. 1966. 17.95 (ISBN 0-13-810671-1, Busn). P-H.

--Unabridged Crossword Puzzle Dictionary. 1963. 8.95 (ISBN 0-385-02843-1); thumb-indexed edition 10.95 (ISBN 0-385-01350-7). Doubleday.

Sisson, C. H. Anchises. (Poetry Ser.). 1979. 5.95 o.p. (ISBN 0-85635-178-4, Pub. by Carcanet New Pr England). Humanities.

--Anchises-Poems. 55p. 1976. text ed. 6.25x (ISBN 0-85635-178-4, Pub. by Carcanet New Pr England). Humanities.

--Anglican Essays. 208p. 1983. text ed. 14.75x (ISBN 0-85635-456-2, Pub. by Carcanet New Pr England). Humanities.

--The Avoidance of Literature: Collected Essays. Schmidt, Michael, ed. 581p. 1978. text ed. 22.25x (ISBN 0-85635-229-2, Pub. by Carcanet New Pr England). Humanities.

--Christopher Homm: A Novel. (Prose Ser.). 1980. 7.95 o.p. (ISBN 0-85635-103-2, Pub. by Carcanet New Pr England). Humanities.

--Edward Fitzgerald: A Life. 192p. 1983. pap. text ed. 8.50x (ISBN 0-85635-465-1, Pub. by Carcanet New Pr England). Humanities.

--English Poetry Nineteen Hundred to Nineteen Fifty: An Assessment. 274p. 1981. Repr. of 1971 ed. text ed. 21.00x (ISBN 0-85635-393-0, 90202, Pub. by Carcanet New Pr England). Humanities.

--Exactions. 96p. (Orig.). 1981. pap. 7.95 o.p. (ISBN 0-85635-332-9, Pub. by Carcanet New Pr England). Humanities.

--In the Trojan Ditch: Collected Poems & Selected Translations. (Poetey Ser.). 1979. 10.50 o.p. (ISBN 0-85635-074-5, Pub. by Carcanet New Pr England). Humanities.

--Selected Poems. (Literary Ser.). 104p. 1982. 17.50x (ISBN 0-933806-15-9). Black Swan CT.

Sisson, C. H., ed. The English Sermon Sixteen Hundred Fifty to Seventeen Hundred Fifty, Vol. 2. 358p. 1976. text ed. 22.25x (ISBN 0-85635-094-X, Pub. by Carcanet New Pr England). Humanities.

--The Poetic Art: A Translation of Horace's "Ars Poetica". (Translation Ser.). 55p. 1975. pap. 6.25x (ISBN 0-85635-114-8, Pub. by Carcanet New Pr England, Pub. by Carcanet New Pr England). Humanities.

Sisson, C. H., ed. & tr. from Fr. The Song of Roland: A Verse Translation. 192p. 1983. text ed. 14.75x (ISBN 0-85635-421-X, Pub. by Carcanet New Pr England). Humanities.

Sisson, C. H., ed. see Mairet, Philip.

Sisson, C. H., ed. see Swift, Jonathan.

Sisson, C. H., tr. see Du Bellay, Joachim.

Sisson, C. H., tr. see Lucretius.

Sisson, C. J. The Boar's Head Theatre: An Inn-Yard Theatre of the Elizabethan Age. (Illus.). 1972. 16.95x (ISBN 0-7100-7252-X). Routledge & Kegan.

Sisson, Edward B. Reports of the Coxcatlan Project. Incl. First Annual Report. 1973. 4.00 (ISBN 0-939312-13-1); Second Annual Report. 1974. 3.00 o.p. (ISBN 0-686-86586-3); 3.00 (ISBN 0-939312-14-X). Peabody Found.

Sisson, James E. & Martens, Robert W. Jack London First Editions. LC 78-63374. (Illus.). 1978. 29.50 (ISBN 0-932458-00-9). Star Rover.

Sisson, Mark & Hosler, Ray. Runner's World Triathlon Training Book. 140p. 1983. pap. 6.95 (ISBN 0-89037-262-4). Anderson World.

Sisson, Richard. Answering Christianity's Most Puzzling Questions, Vol. I. LC 82-12467. 1982. pap. 7.95 (ISBN 0-8024-5149-7). Moody.

--Answering Christianity's Most Puzzling Questions, Vol. 2. 240p. (Orig.). 1983. pap. 7.95 (ISBN 0-8024-5148-9). Moody.

--Training for Evangelism: Leader's Guide. 8.95 (ISBN 0-8024-8793-9). Moody.

Sisson, Roger L., jt. auth. see Emshoff, James R.

Sisson, Rosemary A. Will in Love. (gr. 7 up). 1977. 10.95 (ISBN 0-688-22107-6); lib. bdg. 10.51 (ISBN 0-688-32107-0). Morrow.

Sissors, Jack & Goodrich, William. Media Planning Workbook. 240p. 1983. pap. text ed. write for info. (ISBN 0-87251-080-8, CB063). Crain Bks.

Sissors, Jack Z. & Surmanek, Jim. Advertising Media Planning. 2nd ed. LC 82-70975. 448p. 1982. 22.95 (ISBN 0-87251-057-3). Crain Bks.

Sit, Amy. The Rib. LC 76-22278. 1976. pap. 3.95 (ISBN 0-89221-026-5). New Leaf.

Sitaram, K. S. & Cogdell, Roy T. Foundations of Intercultural Communication. new ed. 1976. text ed. 14.95x (ISBN 0-675-08626-4). Merrill.

Sitchin, Zecharia. Stairway to Heaven. 336p. 1983. pap. 3.50 (ISBN 0-380-63339-6). Avon.

--The Twelfth Planet. 1978. pap. 3.95 (ISBN 0-380-39362-X, 62588-1). Avon.

Sitenko, A. G. Electromagnetic Fluctuations in Plasma. 1967. 48.50 (ISBN 0-12-647050-2). Acad Pr.

Sites, Frederick, ed. MacRae's Florida state Industrial Directory, 1982. 1982. pap. 75.00 (ISBN 0-686-35981-X). MacRaes Blue Bk.

Sites, W. Kilmer & Blossom, Barbara C. Ethics in Perspective & Practice. new rev ed. LC 72-10273. 128p. 1972. pap. 5.00 incl. tchr's manual (ISBN 0-379-00023-7); write for info. tchr's manual (ISBN 0-379-00824-6). Oceana.

Sithole, Ndabaningi. African Nationalism. 2nd ed. LC 68-133467. (Illus.). 1968. 14.95x o.p. (ISBN 0-19-215631-4); pap. 4.95x (ISBN 0-19-501053-1). Oxford U Pr.

--The Polygamist. LC 79-169156. 160p. 1972. 6.95 o.p. (ISBN 0-89388-036-1). Okpaku Communications.

Sitkoff, Harvard. A New Deal for Blacks: The Emergence of Civil Rights As a National Issue: the Depression Decade. LC 78-2633. 1978. 19.95x (ISBN 0-19-502418-4). Oxford U Pr.

--A New Deal for Blacks: The Emergence of Civil Rights As a National Issue; the Depression Decade. 1981. pap. 8.95 (ISBN 0-19-502893-7, GB 627). Oxford U Pr.

Sitkoff, Harvard, jt. ed. see Chafe, William H.

Sitney, P. Adams. Visionary Film: The American Avant-Garde 1943-1978. 2nd ed. (Illus.). 1979. 25.00x (ISBN 0-19-502485-0). Oxford U Pr.

--Visionary Film: The American Avant-Garde 1943-1978. 2nd ed. (Illus.). 1979. pap. 9.95 (ISBN 0-19-502486-9, GB565, GB). Oxford U Pr.

Sitomer, Harry & Sitomer, Mindel. Zero Is Not Nothing. LC 77-11562. (A Young Math Book). (gr. 1-3). 1978. PLB 10.89 (ISBN 0-690-03829-1, TYC-J). Har-Row.

Sitomer, Harry, jt. auth. see Sitomer, Mindel.

Sitomer, Mindel & Sitomer, Harry. Circles. LC 71-113856. (Young Math Ser.). (Illus.). (gr. 1-4). 1971. 6.95 o.p. (ISBN 0-690-19430-7, TYC-J); PLB 10.89 (ISBN 0-690-19431-5). Har-Row.

--How Did Numbers Begin? LC 75-11756. (Young Math Ser.). (Illus.). 40p. (gr. k-3). 1976. 10.89 (ISBN 0-690-00794-9, TYC-J). Har-Row.

Sitomer, Mindel, jt. auth. see Sitomer, Harry.

Sitte, K. see Fluegge, E.

Sitter, John. Literary Loneliness. LC 82-5105. 240p. 1982. 19.50x (ISBN 0-8014-1499-7). Cornell U Pr.

Sitter, Lamoraal U. De see De Sitter, Lamoraal U.

Sittig, M. Toxic Metals-Pollution Control & Worker Protection. LC 76-24142. (Pollution Technology Review: No. 30). (Illus.). 1977. 39.00 o.p. (ISBN 0-8155-0636-8). Noyes.

Sittig, Marshall. Aromatic Hydrocarbons: Manufacture & Technology. LC 75-32114. (Chemical Technology Review Ser.: No. 56). (Illus.). 357p. 1976. 39.00 o.p. (ISBN 0-8155-0600-7). Noyes.

Sittig, Marshall, jt. ed. see Davidson, Robert L.

Sittig, Roland, jt. ed. see Roggwiller, P.

Sittler, Joseph. Ecology of Faith. LC 61-10278. 112p. 1970. pap. 0.50 o.p. (ISBN 0-8006-1882-3, 1-1882). Fortress.

Sitwell, Edith. I Live Under a Black Sun: A Novel. LC 70-171419. 326p. 1938. Repr. lib. bdg. 17.00x (ISBN 0-8371-6260-2, SIBS). Greenwood.

--A Poet's Notebook. LC 71-152605. xviii, 276p. Repr. of 1950 ed. lib. bdg. 20.50x (ISBN 0-8371-6040-5, SIPN). Greenwood.

Sitwell, Osbert. Discursions on Travel, Art & Life. 1925. lib. bdg. 16.25x (ISBN 0-8371-4336-5, SIDI). Greenwood.

--Great Morning. LC 79-156212. 360p. 1972. Repr. of 1951 ed. lib. bdg. 19.25x (ISBN 0-8371-6162-2, SIGM). Greenwood.

--Laughter in the Next Room. LC 79-152607. 400p. 1972. Repr. of 1948 ed. lib. bdg. 20.50x (ISBN 0-8371-6042-1, SILA). Greenwood.

--Nobel Essences: A Book of Characters. LC 72-152608. 356p. 1973. Repr. of 1950 ed. lib. bdg. 19.25x (ISBN 0-8371-6043-X, SINE). Greenwood.

Siu, Bobby. Women of China: Imperialism & Women's Resistance, 1900-1949. 210p. 1982. text ed. 23.00 (ISBN 0-905762-58-4, Pub. by Zed Pr); pap. text ed. 9.95 (ISBN 0-905762-63-0). Lawrence Hill.
Siu, Helen & Stern, Zelda, eds. Mao's Harvest: Voices from China's New Generation. LC 82-14300. (Illus.). 384p. 1983. 17.95 (ISBN 0-19-503274-8). Oxford U Pr.
Siu, R. G. The Master Manager. LC 80-13390. 341p. 1980. 22.50 (ISBN 0-471-07961-8). Wiley.
Siu, Ralph G. The Craft of Power. LC 78-23393. 255p. 1979. 20.50 (ISBN 0-471-04628-0, Pub. by Wiley-Interscience). Wiley.
--Tao of Science: An Essay on Western Knowledge & Eastern Wisdom. (Illus.). 1958. pap. 5.95 (ISBN 0-262-69004-7). MIT Pr.
--Transcending the Power Game: The Way to Executive Serenity. LC 79-25299. 249p. 1980. 20.50 (ISBN 0-471-06001-1, Pub. by Wiley-Interscience). Wiley.
Siu, Ralph Gun Hoy see Gun Hoy Siu, Ralph.
Siudzinski, Paul. Sumi-E: A Meditation in Ink. LC 77-87475. (Illus.). 1978. pap. 6.95 o.p. (ISBN 0-8069-8698-0). Sterling.
Sivachev, Nikolai V. & Yakovlev, Nikolai N. Russia & the United States. Titelbaum, Olga A., tr. LC 78-10554. (U. S. in the World: Foreign World Perspectives Ser). 1979. 12.95x (ISBN 0-226-76149-5); pap. 8.00x (ISBN 0-226-76150-9, P902, Phoen). U of Chicago Pr.
Sivaji Rao, K. H., jt. auth. see Philip, A. T.
Sivakumar, Chitra. Education, Social Inequality & Social Change in Karnataka. (Studies in Sociology & Social Anthropology). 160p. 1982. text ed. 12.00x (ISBN 0-391-02797-2, Pub. by Hindustan India). Humanities.
Sivan, Audrey J. Can You Help This Puppy Find His Family? An Educational Aid for Learning Verb Tenses in Hebrew. (gr. 3up). 1983. pap. write for info. (ISBN 0-86628-044-8). Ridgefield Pub.
Sivan, Emmanuel. Communisme et Nationalisme En Algerie, 1920-1962. (Travaux et Recherches Ser.: No. 41). (Fr.). 1977. lib. bdg. 30.50x o.p. (ISBN 2-7246-0349-4, Pub. by Presses De la Fondation Nationale Des Sciences Politiques); pap. text ed. 23.00x o.p. (ISBN 2-7246-0342-7). Clearwater Pub.
Sivan, Raphael, jt. auth. see Kwakernaak, Huibert.
Sivan, Reuban, jt. ed. see Levenston, Edward A.
Sivan, Reuven & Levenston, Edward A. The New Bantam-Megiddo Hebrew & English Dictionary. LC 77-75289. 1977. 24.95 (ISBN 0-8052-3666-X). Schocken.
Sivananda, Swami. Practice of Karma Yoga. 1974. 5.50 (ISBN 0-8426-0675-0); pap. 3.50 o.s.i. (ISBN 0-686-67764-1). Orient Bk Dist.
Sivanesan, A. The Bitunicate Ascomycetes & their Anamorphs. (Illus.). 500p. 1983. lib. bdg. 56.00X (ISBN 3-7682-1329-3). Lubrecht & Cramer.
--Taxonomy & Pathology of Venturia Species. (Bibliotheca Mycologica Ser.: No. 59). 1977. lib. bdg. 16.00x (ISBN 3-7682-1167-3). Lubrecht & Cramer.
Sivasankara, Pillai T. Chemmeen: A Novel. Menon, Narayana & Rau, Santha R., trs. LC 78-12828. 1979. Repr. of 1978 ed. lib. bdg. 20.00x (ISBN 0-313-21213-9, SICH). Greenwood.
Sivazlian, B. D. & Stanfel, Larry E. Optimization Techniques in Operations Research. (Industrial Engineering Ser). (Illus.). 448p. 1974. ref. ed. 31.95 (ISBN 0-13-638163-4). P-H.
Sive, Mary R. Media Selection Handbook. 230p. 1982. lib. bdg. 22.50 (ISBN 0-87287-350-1). Libs Unl.
--Selecting Instructional Media: A Guide to Audiovisual & Other Instructional Media Lists. LC 77-27278. 1978. lib. bdg. 18.50 (ISBN 0-87287-181-9). Libs Unl.
--Selecting Instructional Media: A Guide to Audiovisual & Other Instructional Media Lists. 300p. 1983. 22.50 (ISBN 0-87287-342-0). Libs Unl.
Siven, C. H. A Study in the Theory of Inflation & Unemployment. LC 78-24271. (Studies in Monetary Economics: Vol. 4). 1979. 51.00 (ISBN 0-444-85252-2, North Holland). Elsevier.
Siver, Edward W. An Executive Guide to Commercial Property & Casualty Insurance. LC 81-66512. 1981. 34.95 (ISBN 0-87251-049-2). Crain Bks.
Siverd, Bonnie. Count Your Change: A Woman's Guide to Sudden Financial Change. 1983. 6.95 (ISBN 0-87795-460-7, Pub. by Priam). Arbor Hse.
Sivers, Marie Steiner Von see Steiner, Rudolf & Steiner-von Sivers, Marie.
SI Version, ed. see Meriam, J. L.
Siverson, J. W. Europe Nineteen Thirty-Seven. 1982. 5.75 (ISBN 0-8062-1953-X). Carlton.
Siviter, R. E. A Handbook of Railway Photography. (Illus.). 128p. 1983. 24.95 (ISBN 0-7153-8265-9). David & Charles.
Sixth Form Mathematics Project, jt. auth. see Schools Council.
Sixth International Liquid Crystals Conference, Kyoto, Japan, June 30-July 4, 1980. Molecular Crystals & Liquid Crystals Special Topics: Proceedings, 5 vols. Dienes, G. J. & Labes, M. M., eds. 1981. 605.00x (ISBN 0-677-40295-3). Gordon.
Sixth NASW Professional Symposium, 1979, jt. ed. see Dea, Kay.
Siy, L., jt. auth. see Bennett, A. E.
Siyar al-Muluk. The Book of Government or Rules for Kings: The Siyar Al-Muluk or Siyasat-nama of Nizam Al-Mulk. rev. ed. Darke, Hubert, tr. from Persian. (Persian Heritage Ser.). 288p. 1978. 25.00 (ISBN 0-7100-8619-9). Routledge & Kegan.
Sizemore, Barbara A. The Ruptured Diamond: The Politics of the Decentralization of the District of Columbia Public Schools. LC 80-5698. (Illus.). 569p. (Orig.). 1981. lib. bdg. 29.75 (ISBN 0-8191-1617-3); pap. text ed. 18.75 (ISBN 0-8191-1618-1). U Pr of Amer.
Sizemore, Michael, et al. Energy Planning for Buildings. (Illus.). 1979. 44.00x (ISBN 0-913962-08-2). Am Inst Arch.
Sizer, Richard, jt. auth. see Kelman, Alistair.
Sizer, Sandra S. Gospel Hymns & Social Religion: The Rhetoric of Nineteenth-Century Revivalism. Davis, Allen F., ed. LC 78-10165. (American Civilization Ser.). 222p. 1979. lib. bdg. 24.95 (ISBN 0-87722-142-1). Temple U Pr.
Sizer, Theodore R. Age of the Academies. LC 64-24230. (Orig.). 1964. text ed. 10.50 (ISBN 0-8077-2164-6); pap. text ed. 5.50x (ISBN 0-8077-2161-1). Tchrs Coll.
Sizer, Theodore R., ed. Religion & Public Education. LC 80-6223. 384p. 1982. lib. bdg. 25.50 (ISBN 0-8191-2000-6); pap. text ed. 14.25 (ISBN 0-8191-2001-4). U Pr of Amer.
Sizoo, Nugent, et al. Guidelines to Student Activity Fund Accounting. rev. ed. (Bulletin 17). 1977. 5.00 (ISBN 0-910170-01-0). Assn Sch Busn.
Sjo, J. Economics for Agriculturalists. 232p. 1976. 23.95 (ISBN 0-471-87003-X). Wiley.
Sjoberg, Leif, tr. see Lundkvist, Artur.
Sjoden, Per-Olow & Bates, Sandra, eds. Trends in Behavior Therapy. 1979. 35.00 (ISBN 0-12-647450-8). Acad Pr.
Sjodin, R. A. Ion Transport in Skeletal Muscle. (Transport in the Life Sciences Ser.). 157p. 1982. text ed. 35.00x (ISBN 0-471-05265-5, Pub. by Wiley-Interscience). Wiley.
Sjolund, B. H., ed. Brain Stem Control of Spinal Mechanisms: Proceedings of the First Eric K. Fernstrom Symposium, Lund, Sweden, 10-13 November, 1981. Bjorklund, A. (Ferrnstrom Foundation Ser.: Vol. I). 519p. 1982. 110.50 (ISBN 0-444-80429-3). Elsevier.
Sjoman, Vilgot. Diary with Ingmar Bergman. 243p. 1978. 9.95 o.p. (ISBN 0-89720-015-2, L136); pap. 5.50 o.p. (ISBN 0-89720-016-0). Karoma.
Sjoquist, David L., jt. auth. see Schroeder, Larry D.
Sjoqvist, Folke & Tottie, Malcolm, eds. Abuse of Central Stimulants. LC 72-116704. (Illus.). 536p. 1969. 15.00 (ISBN 0-911216-28-6). Raven.
Sjostrand, Fritiof S. Electron Microscopy of Cells & Tissues. Vol. 1, 1967. 58.00, by subscription 43.50 o.p. (ISBN 0-12-647550-4). Acad Pr.
Sjostrom, Ingrid. Quadratura: Studies in Italian Ceiling Painting. (Stockholm Studies in the History of Art: No. 30). (Illus.). 1978. pap. text ed. 22.00x o.p. (ISBN 91-22-00176-X). Humanities.
Sjovaag, E. ABC in Rosemaling. 6th ed. 1982. pap. 8.00x (ISBN 8-2531-9190-1, N519). Vanous.
Sjowall, Maj & Wahloo, Per. The Man on the Balcony. 1976. pap. 2.95 (ISBN 0-394-71777-5, Vin). Random.
--The Man Who Went up in Smoke. 1976. pap. 2.95 (ISBN 0-394-71778-3, Vin). Random.
Skadden, D. H., jt. auth. see Gaffney, D. J.
Skaer, R. J., jt. auth. see Grimstone, A. V.
Skaff, L. B., jt. auth. see Hansen, B. E.
Skagen-Munshi, Kiki, jt. auth. see Kaushall, Phillip.
Skaggs, David C. Roots of Maryland Democracy, 1753-1776. LC 72-833. (Contributions in American History: No. 30). (Illus.). 253p. 1973. lib. bdg. 29.95x (ISBN 0-8371-6402-8, SMD/). Greenwood.
Skaggs, Merrill M. Autobiography of Benjamin Franklin Notes. 1969. pap. 2.75 (ISBN 0-8220-0216-7). Cliffs.
Skaggs, Merrill M., jt. auth. see Barber, Virginia.
Skaife, Sydney H. African Insect Life. 2nd, Rev. ed. LC 80-477821. (Illus.). 352p. 1979. 32.50x (ISBN 0-86977-087-X). Intl Pubns Serv.
Skains, Margo F. Change Your Mind. (Orig.). (YA) 1983. pap. write for info. (ISBN 0-911197-01-X). Miracle Pub Co.
--The Rainbow Train. (Miracle Books Collection for Children). 70p. (Orig.). 1983. pap. text ed. 7.00 (ISBN 0-911197-00-1). Miracle Pub Co.
Skal, David J. & Finnegan, Michael, eds. Theatre Profiles Four. (Illus.). 288p. (Orig.). 1980. pap. 12.95 (ISBN 0-930452-07-0). Theatre Comm.
Skalak, R. & Nerem, R. M., eds. Biomechanics Symposium-AMD-Vol. 10, 1975. (No. 100090). 152p. 1975. pap. text ed. 16.00 o.p. (ISBN 0-685-61215-5). ASME.
Skalimierski, B. & Bogdan. Mechanics & Strength of Materials. LC 78-10900. (Studies in Applied Mechanics Ser.: Vol. 1). 432p. 1979. 68.00 (ISBN 0-444-99793-8). Elsevier.
Skalka, Patricia, ed. see Gibson, Karon W., et al.
Skalley, Michael R. A Medal for Marigold: Seattle's Marine Medic. (Illus.). 160p. (Orig.). 1983. pap. 8.95 (ISBN 0-87564-226-8). Superior Pub.
Skamene, Emil, ed. Genetic Control of Natural Resistance to Infection & Malignancy. (Perspectives in Immunology Ser.). 1980. 38.00 (ISBN 0-12-647680-2). Acad Pr.
Skandalakis, John E. & Gray, Stephen W. Anatomical Complications in General Surgery. (Illus.). 576p. 1982. text ed. 55.00x (ISBN 0-07-057785-4). McGraw.
Skandalakis, John E., jt. auth. see Gray, Stephen W.
Skander, G. A. Supernova: The Exploding Star. 1979. 7.50 o.p. (ISBN 0-533-03600-3). Vantage.
Skard, Sigmund. The U. S. in Norwegian History. LC 76-5263. (Contributions in American Studies: No. 26). (Orig.). 1976. lib. bdg. 25.00x (ISBN 0-8371-8909-8, SKU/). Greenwood.
Skarda, Patricia L. & Jaffe, Nora C., eds. The Evil Image: Two Centuries of Gothic Short Fiction & Poetry. 1981. pap. 8.95 (ISBN 0-452-00549-3, F549, Mer). NAL.
Skardinsky, S. Trudel's Siege. (Illus.). (gr. 4-6). 1976. 5.95 o.p. (ISBN 0-07-057791-9, GB). McGraw.
Skarin, Annalee. Celestial Song of Creation. 1962p. pap. 4.95 (ISBN 0-87516-090-5). De Vorss.
--Man Triumphant. 1966p. pap. 4.95 (ISBN 0-87516-091-3). De Vorss.
--Secrets of Eternity. 1960. pap. 4.95 o.p. (ISBN 0-87516-092-1). De Vorss.
--Temple of God. pap. 4.95 o.p. (ISBN 0-87516-093-X). De Vorss.
--To God the Glory. pap. 4.95 o.p. (ISBN 0-87516-094-8). De Vorss.
Skarmeta, Antonio. Chileno! Carpentier, Hortense, tr. from Span. LC 79-17540. 96p. (gr. 7-9). 1979. 8.75 (ISBN 0-688-22213-7); PLB 8.40 (ISBN 0-688-32213-1). Morrow.
--La Insurreccion. 240p. (Span.). 1982. pap. 8.00 (ISBN 0-910061-05-X). Ediciones Norte.
Skarsgard. International Workshop on Pion & Heavy Ion Radiotherapy. 1982. 80.00 (ISBN 0-444-00765-2). Elsevier.
Skates, Craig B., jt. auth. see Brinegar, Bonnie C.
Skates, John R. Mississippi. (States & the Nation Ser.). 1979. 14.95 (ISBN 0-393-05678-3). Norton.
Skeat, W. W., ed. see Langland, William.
Skeat, Walter W., ed. see Chaucer, Geoffrey.
Sked, Alan & Cook, Chris, eds. Crisis & Controversy: Essays in Honor of A. J. P. Taylor. LC 75-42863. 192p. 1976. 22.50 (ISBN 0-312-17290-7). St Martin.
Skeda, et al. Statistical Climatology. (Developments in Atmosphere Science Ser.: Vol. 13). 1980. 66.00 (ISBN 0-444-41923-3). Elsevier.
Skee, Stanley, jt. auth. see Chaney, Charles.
Skeel, Roland T. Manual of Cancer Chemotherapy. (Spiral Manual Ser.). 279p. 1982. spiralbound 13.95 (ISBN 0-316-79572-0). Little.
Skeem, Jeanette L., ed. see Skeem, Kenneth A.
Skeem, Kenneth A. In the Beginning... Skeem, Jeanette L., ed. LC 81-68054. (Illus.). 256p. 1981. 14.00 (ISBN 0-9606782-0-4). Behemoth Pub.
Skeen, C. Edward, ed. Description of Louisiana by Thomas Jefferys: From His "Natural & Civil History of the French Dominions in North & South America". (Mississippi Valley Collection Bulletin, No. 6). (Illus.). 50p. 1973. pap. 5.95x facsimile ed. o.p. (ISBN 0-87870-082-X). Memphis St Univ.
Skeens, Gary. Poems & Roses: A Lady. 70p. 1978. pap. 4.25 (ISBN 0-9601808-1-8). Quality Ohio.
Skeens, Gary S. The Dancer. (Illus.). 64p. 1979. pap. 3.50 (ISBN 0-9601808-2-6). Quality Ohio.
Skees, William D. Before You Invest in a Small Business Computer. (Management Ser.). 344p. 1982. 27.50 (ISBN 0-534-97937-8). Lifetime Learn.
--Computer Software for Data Communications. LC 80-24266. 192p. 1982. 19.95 (ISBN 0-534-97979-3). Lifetime Learn.
Skeet, Muriel. Emergency Procedures & First Aid for Nurses. (Illus.). 296p. 1981. pap. text ed. 15.50 (ISBN 0-632-00594-7, B 4663-4). Mosby.
Skehan, Everett M. A Bullet for Georgie. 1979. 9.95 o.p. (ISBN 0-395-26294-1). HM.
Skehan, James W., jt. ed. see Carovillano, Robert L.
Skeist, I., jt. ed. see Schildknecht, C. E.
Skelcher, Derek. Word Processing Equipment Survey. 222p. (Orig.). 1980. pap. 137.50 o.p. (ISBN 0-903796-56-2, Pub. by Online Conferences England). Renouf.
Skelland, A. H. Diffusional Mass Transfer. LC 73-12976. 510p. 1974. 64.95 (ISBN 0-471-79374-4, Pub. by Wiley-Interscience). Wiley.
Skellern, Claire & Rogers, Paul. Classic Botany. 208p. 1977. 19.00x (ISBN 0-7121-0255-8, Pub. by Macdonald & Evans). State Mutual Bk.
Skelley, Esther. Medications & Mathematics for the Nurse. 5th ed. (Practical Nursing Ser.). (Illus.). 280p. 1982. pap. text ed. 12.00 (ISBN 0-8273-1923-1); instr's. guide 2.75 (ISBN 0-8273-1950-9). Delmar.
Skelley, Esther G., jt. auth. see Ferris, Elvira.
Skelly, James R., jt. auth. see Zim, Herbert S.
Skelly, James R., jt. ed. see Zim, Herbert S.
Skelly, Timothy. Shoot the Robot, Then Shoot Mom. (Illus.). 112p. (Orig.). 1983. pap. 4.95 (ISBN 0-8092-5541-3). Contemp Bks.
Skelsy, Alice F., jt. auth. see Crockett, James U.
Skelton, Geoffrey, tr. see Frisch, Max.
Skelton, John. Ballade of the Scottysshe Kynge. LC 67-23927. 1969. Repr. of 1882 ed. 30.00x (ISBN 0-8103-3461-5). Gale.
--John Skelton: The Complete English Poems. Scattergood, John, ed. LC 82-16075. (Yale English Poets Ser.). 560p. 1983. text ed. 30.00 (ISBN 0-300-02970-5); pap. text ed. 9.95x (ISBN 0-300-02971-3). Yale U Pr.
--Selected Poems. Hammond, Gerald, ed. (Fyfield Ser.). 142p. 1980. pap. 5.25x (ISBN 0-85635-308-6, Pub. by Carcanet New Pr England). Humanities.
Skelton, Mary L. & Rao, G. Gopal. South Indian Cookery. 115p. 1975. pap. 2.75 (ISBN 0-89253-030-8). Ind-US Inc.
Skelton, Mary L., ed. see Desikachar, T. K.
Skelton, Mollie. You & Your Poodle. 7.95 (ISBN 0-87666-362-5, PS641). TFH Pubns.
Skelton, Peter & Huxtable, Nils. British Steam Revival. (Illus.). 96p. 1983. 14.95 (ISBN 0-86720-640-3). Sci Bks Intl.
Skelton, R. A. & Harvey, P. D. Local Maps & Plans from Medieval England. (Illus.). 344p. 1982. 25.00x (ISBN 0-19-822363-3). Oxford U Pr.
Skelton, Robert, intro. by. The Indian Heritage: Court Life & Art under the Mughal Emperors. (Illus.). 176p. 1982. text ed. 25.00x (ISBN 0-87663-410-2, Herbert Pr). Universe.
Skelton, Robin. J. M. Synge. 1983. pap. 3.95 (ISBN 0-8387-7687-6). Devin.
Skelton, Robin, ed. see Synge, John M.
Skelton, Robin see Synge, John M.
Skemer, Don C. & Morris, Robert C. Guide to the Manuscript Collections of the New Jersey Historical Society, Vol. 15. 245p. 1979. 20.00 (ISBN 0-911020-00-4). NJ Hist Soc.
Skemp, A. Robert Browning. LC 73-21961. (Studies in Browning, No. 4). 1974. lib. bdg. 47.95x (ISBN 0-8383-1813-4). Haskell.
Skemp, Richard R. Intelligence, Learning & Action: A New Model for Theory & Practice in Education. 324p. 1979. 59.95 (ISBN 0-471-99747-1, Pub. by Wiley-Interscience); pap. text ed. 22.00x (ISBN 0-471-27575-1). Wiley.
Skene, William F. The Four Ancient Books of Wales, 2 vols. LC 78-72644. (Celtic Language & Literature: Goidelic & Brythonic). (Illus.). 1136p. Repr. of 1868 ed. Set. 95.00 (ISBN 0-404-17584-8). AMS Pr.
Skene Melvin, Ann, jt. auth. see Skene Melvin, David.
Skene Melvin, David & Skene Melvin, Ann. Crime, Detective, Espionage, Mystery, & Thriller Fiction & Film: A Comprehensive Bibliography of Critical Writing Through 1979. LC 80-1194. xx, 367p. 1980. lib. bdg. 35.00x (ISBN 0-313-22062-X, MCD/). Greenwood.
Skeoch. Life in New France. (Focus on Canadian History). 1981. 8.40 (ISBN 0-531-02181-5). Watts.
Skeoch, Alan. The United Empire Loyalists & the American Revolution. (Focus on Canadian History Ser.). (Illus.). 96p. (gr. 6 up). 1983. PLB 8.40 (ISBN 0-531-04595-1). Watts.
Skeri, J., jt. auth. see Komac.
Skerman, V. B. & McGowan, Vicki, eds. Approved Lists of Bacterial Names. 200p. 1980. 10.00 (ISBN 0-686-95354-1). Am Soc Microbio.
Sketchley, Rose E. English Book-Illustration of To-Day: Appreciations of the Work of Living English Illustrators with Lists of Their Books. LC 78-179655. (Illus.). xxx, 175p. 1974. Repr. of 1903 ed. 42.00x (ISBN 0-8103-4052-6). Gale.
Ski Magazine Editors. Skier's Handbook. (Illus.). 1965. 14.37i (ISBN 0-06-111710-2, HarpT). Har-Row.
Skidelsky, Robert, ed. The End of the Keynesian Era: Essays on the Disintegration of the Keynesian Political Economy. LC 77-8878. 1978. text ed. 21.00x o.p. (ISBN 0-8419-0329-8); pap. text ed. 8.00x (ISBN 0-8419-0340-9). Holmes & Meier.
Skidmore, Felicity, ed. Social Security Financing. 312p. 1981. 32.50x (ISBN 0-262-19196-2). MIT Pr.
Skidmore, Rex A. & Thackeray, Milton G. Introduction to Social Work. 3rd ed. (Illus.). 448p. 1982. text ed. 23.95 (ISBN 0-13-497040-3). P-H.
Skidmore, Rex A., jt. auth. see Thackery, Milton G.
Skidmore, W. L. Sociology's Models of Man. 216p. 1975. 37.00x (ISBN 0-677-04780-0). Gordon.
Skidmore, William L. Theoretical Thinking in Sociology. 2nd ed. LC 78-74540. (Illus.). 1979. 27.50 o.p. (ISBN 0-521-22663-5); pap. 10.95x (ISBN 0-521-29606-4). Cambridge U Pr.
Skilken, Patricia. Never Apologize, Always Explain. (Illus.). 216p. 1982. 11.95 (ISBN 0-89696-176-1, An Everest House Book). Dodd.
Skill, Thomas, jt. auth. see Cassata, Mary.
Skillen, Charles R. Combat Shotgun Training. (Illus.). 224p. 1982. 26.75x (ISBN 0-398-04672-7). C C Thomas.
Skillen, James, ed. see Hatfield, Mark, et al.
Skillen, James, jt. auth. see McCarthy, Rockne.
Skillen, James W. Christians Organizing for Political Service: A Study Guide Based on the Work of the Association for Public Justice. LC 80-66190. 113p. (Orig.). 1982. pap. 3.95 (ISBN 0-936456-01-9). Assn Public Justice.
Skillin, M. & Gay, R. Words into Type. 3rd ed. 1974. 22.95 (ISBN 0-13-964262-5). P-H.
Skilling, H. H. Fundamentals of Electric Waves. 2nd ed. LC 74-8930. 256p. 1974. Repr. of 1948 ed. 12.75 (ISBN 0-88275-180-8). Krieger.

Skilling, Hugh. Electric Networks. LC 73-14870. 480p. 1974. text ed. 36.95 (ISBN 0-471-79420-1); sol. manual avail. (ISBN 0-471-79422-8). Wiley.

Skilling, Hugh Hildreth. Teaching - Engineering, Science, Mathematics. abr. ed. LC 76-47476. 128p. 1977. pap. text ed. 5.50 (ISBN 0-88275-461-0). Krieger.

Skillings, R. D. Alternative Lives. (Ithaca House Fiction Ser.). 149p. 1974. 4.95 o.p. (ISBN 0-87886-032-0). Ithaca Hse.

--In a Murderous Time. 180p. 1982. signed ltd. ed. 17.95 (ISBN 0-918222-35-4); pap. 5.95 (ISBN 0-918222-34-6). Apple Wood.

Skillman, Penny. The San Francisco Fatty Arbuckle-Past & Virginia Present. 72p. (Orig.). 1979. pap. 2.95 (ISBN 0-9603974-0-X). Winona Catawba.

Skillman, William. Radar Calculations Using the TI-59 Programmable Calculator. (Illus.). 350p. 1983. 40.00 (ISBN 0-89006-112-2). Artech Hse.

Skilton, Charles. Old London Postcard Album. 146p. 1982. 35.00x (ISBN 0-686-81688-9, Pub. by C Skilton Scotland). State Mutual Bk.

Skilton, M. Deutsche Texte und Wortschatzuebungen. LC 76-93127. 4.60 o.p. (ISBN 0-08-006462-0); pap. 4.60 o.p. (ISBN 0-08-006461-2); tchr's. ed. 4.40 o.p. (ISBN 0-08-015811-0). Pergamon.

Skimin, E. & McMurtrie, P. Gregg Shorthand Structured Learning Method. (Diamond Jubilee Ser.). 1971. text ed. 18.30 (ISBN 0-07-057895-8, G); instructor's handbk. 6.45 (ISBN 0-07-057896-6). McGraw.

Skimin, Robert. Soldier for Hire, No. 1: Zulu Blood. 1981. pap. 2.50 (ISBN 0-89083-777-5). Zebra.

--Soldier for Hire, No. 2: Trojan in Iran. (Orig.). 1981. pap. 2.50 (ISBN 0-89083-793-7). Zebra.

--Soldier for Hire, No. 3: U. N. Sabotage. (Orig.). 1981. pap. 2.50 (ISBN 0-89083-894-1). Zebra.

--Soldier for Hire, No. 4: Bloodletting! (Orig.). 1982. pap. 2.50 (ISBN 0-89083-939-5). Zebra.

--Soldier for Hire, No. 5: Libyan Warlord. 1982. pap. 2.50 (ISBN 0-89083-988-3). Zebra.

Skinner, A., jt. auth. see Campbell, R. H.

Skinner, A. S., jt. auth. see Campbell, R. H.

Skinner, Andrew, jt. auth. see Taylor, George.

Skinner, B. Behavior of Organisms: Experimental Analysis. 1966. 27.95 (ISBN 0-13-073213-3). P-H.

Skinner, B. F. Contingencies of Reinforcement: A Theoretical Analysis. 1969. pap. 18.95 (ISBN 0-13-171728-6). P-H.

--Notebooks. Epstein, Robert, ed. 386p. 1982. pap. 9.95 (ISBN 0-13-624098-4); 15.95 (ISBN 0-13-624106-9). P-H.

--Skinner for the Classroom: Selected Papers. Epstein, Robert, ed. LC 82-80868. (Illus.). 304p. (Orig.). 1982. Set 1-9. pap. text ed. 11.95 (ISBN 0-87822-261-8, 2618); pap. text ed. 10.75 each (ISBN 0-686-83021-0). Res Press.

--Technology of Teaching. (Orig.). 1968. pap. text ed. 12.95 (ISBN 0-13-902163-9). P-H.

--Walden Two Revisited. 1976. 9.95 (ISBN 0-02-411520-7); pap. 2.95 (ISBN 0-02-411510-X). Macmillan.

Skinner, B. F., jt. auth. see Holland, James.

Skinner, B. F., jt. auth. see Dennis, Wayne.

Skinner, Brian J. & Turekian, Karl K. Man & the Ocean. (Foundations of Earth Science Ser.). (Illus.). 160p. 1973. pap. 11.95 (ISBN 0-13-550970-X). P-H.

Skinner, Brian J., jt. auth. see Dietrich, Richard V.

Skinner, Brian J., jt. auth. see Flint, Richard F.

Skinner, Charles M. American Myths & Legends, 2 vols. LC 78-175743. (Illus.). 697p. 1975. Repr. of 1903 ed. Set. 66.00x (ISBN 0-8103-4036-4). Gale.

--Myths & Legends of Our New Possessions & Protectorate. LC 73-140399. 1971. Repr. of 1900 ed. 37.00x (ISBN 0-8103-3634-0). Gale.

--Myths & Legends of Our Own Land, 2 Vols. LC 79-76999. 1969. Repr. of 1896 ed. Set. 40.00x (ISBN 0-8103-3851-3). Gale.

Skinner, Constance L. Adventures of Oregon. 1920. text ed. 8.50x (ISBN 0-686-83454-2). Elliots Bks.

--Pioneers of the Old Southwest. 1919. text ed. 8.50x (ISBN 0-686-83700-2). Elliots Bks.

Skinner, D. B., jt. ed. see Zuidema, G. D.

Skinner, D. B. see Zuidema, G. D. & Skinner, D. B.

Skinner, Dana R. Our Changing Theatre. 327p. 1982. Repr. of 1931 ed. lib. bdg. 35.00 (ISBN 0-8495-4967-1). Arden Lib.

Skinner, David R. Drilling, Well Completion, Reservoir Engineering, Vol. 1. (Introduction to Petroleum Productions Ser.). 200p. 1981. 21.95x (ISBN 0-87201-767-2). Gulf Pub.

Skinner, Donald G. & De Kernion, Jean B. Genitourinary Cancer. LC 77-84690. 1978. text ed. 45.00 (ISBN 0-7216-8340-1). Saunders.

Skinner, E. M. The Modern Organ. (Bibliotheca Organologica: Vol. 62). Repr. of 1974 ed. wrappers 15.00 o.s.i. (ISBN 90-6027-342-7, Pub. by Frits Knuf Netherlands). Pendragon NY.

Skinner, Elliot P., jt. ed. see Robinson, Pearl T.

Skinner, Elliott P., jt. ed. see Shack, William A.

Skinner, F. A. & Shewan, M. J., eds. Aquatic Microbiology. (Society of Applied Bacteriology Symposia: No. 6). 1978. 57.50 (ISBN 0-12-648030-3). Acad Pr.

Skinner, Gordon B. Introduction to Chemical Kinetics. 1974. 30.00 (ISBN 0-12-647850-3). Acad Pr.

Skinner, Gordon S., jt. auth. see Herman, E. Edward.

Skinner, Hubert M. The Story of the Letters & Figures. LC 71-175744. (Illus.). 1971. Repr. of 1905 ed. 34.00x (ISBN 0-8103-3035-0). Gale.

Skinner, Mark F. & Sperber, Geoffrey H., eds. Atlas of Radiographs of Early Man. LC 82-13989. 346p. 1982. 70.00 (ISBN 0-8451-0218-4). A R Liss.

Skinner, Michael. USAFE: A Primer for Modern Air Combat in Europe. (Illus.). 144p. (Orig.). 1983. pap. 9.95 (ISBN 0-89141-151-8). Presidio Pr.

Skinner, Nancy, jt. auth. see Hall, Eleanor.

Skinner, Orten C. Basic Microbiology. LC 74-78590. (Allied Health Ser). 1975. pap. 9.50 o.p. (ISBN 0-672-61390-5). Bobbs.

Skinner, Otis. Footlights & Spotlights. LC 76-164474. (Illus.). 366p. 1972. Repr. of 1924 ed. lib. bdg. 19.75x (ISBN 0-8371-6216-5, SKSF). Greenwood.

Skinner, Patricia. Marketing Community Health Services. (League Exchange Ser.: No. 121). 42p. 1978. 3.95 (ISBN 0-686-38161-0, 21-1757). Natl League Nurse.

Skinner, Paul, jt. auth. see Hodgson, William R.

Skinner, Paul H. & Shelton, Ralph L. Speech, Language & Hearing: Normal Processes & Disorders. LC 77-73956. (Speech Pathology & Audiology Ser.). 1978. text ed. 20.95 (ISBN 0-201-07461-3); instr's man. price not set (ISBN 0-201-07462-1). A-W.

Skinner, Q. The Foundations of Modern Political Thought: The Renaissance, 2 vols. LC 78-51676. 1978. Vol. 1. 44.50 (ISBN 0-521-22023-8); Vol. 1 pap. 12.95x (ISBN 0-521-29337-5); Vol. 2. 44.50 (ISBN 0-521-22284-2); Vol. 2. pap. 12.95x (ISBN 0-521-29435-5). Cambridge U Pr.

Skinner, Stephen. The Oracle of Geomancy. 400p. pap. 1.95 o.p. (ISBN 0-686-33185-0). Inner Tradit.

Skinner, Stephen, ed. The Magical Diaries of Aleister Crowley, 1923-25. 1981. 8.95 (ISBN 0-87728-514-4). Weiser.

Skinner, Stephen, ed. see Crowley, Aleister.

Skinner, Thomas. How Black Is the Gospel? 1976. pap. 1.25 o.s.i. (ISBN 0-89129-185-7). Jove Pubns.

Skinner, Tom. How Black Is the Gospel? (Trumpet Bks). 1976. pap. 1.25 o.p. (ISBN 0-87981-061-0). Holman.

--How Black Is the Gospel. Montgomery, John W., ed. LC 75-124544. (Evangelical Prospectives Ser). 1970. pap. 2.25 o.p. (ISBN 0-87981-061-0, A Trumpet Book, LP39). Holman.

Skinner, Wickham. Manufacturing in the Corporate Strategy. LC 78-602. (Manufacturing Management Ser.). 327p. 1978. 36.95x (ISBN 0-471-01612-8, Pub. by Wiley-Interscience). Wiley.

Skinulis, Richard, jt. auth. see Mann, Dale.

Skipp, V. Crisis & Development. LC 77-71426. (Illus.). 1978. 22.95 (ISBN 0-521-21660-5). Cambridge U Pr.

Skipper, G. C. Battle of Stalingrad. LC 80-27474. (World at War Ser.). (Illus.). 48p. (gr. 3-8). 1981. PLB 8.65 (ISBN 0-516-04789-2); pap. 2.95 (ISBN 0-516-44789-0). Childrens.

--Battle of the Atlantic. LC 81-6186. (World at War Ser.). (Illus.). 48p. (gr. 3-8). 1981. PLB 8.65 (ISBN 0-516-04793-0); pap. 2.95 (ISBN 0-516-44793-9). Childrens.

--Death of Hitler. LC 80-17180. (World at War Ser.). (Illus.). 48p. (gr. 3-8). 1980. PLB 8.65 (ISBN 0-516-04783-3); pap. 2.95 (ISBN 0-516-44783-1). Childrens.

--MacArthur & the Philippines. LC 81-38520. (World At War Ser.). (Illus.). 48p. (gr. 3-8). 1982. PLB 8.65 (ISBN 0-516-04794-9); pap. 2.95 (ISBN 0-686-97307-0). Childrens.

Skipwith, Peyton. Great Bird Illustrators & Their Art, 1730-1930. LC 78-71382. (Illus.). 176p. 1979. 25.00 o.s.i. (ISBN 0-89479-044-7). A & W Pubs.

Skirrow, G., jt. ed. see Riley, S. P.

Skitok, J. & Marshall, R. Electromagnetic Concepts & Applications. 1981. 34.95 (ISBN 0-13-248963-5). P-H.

Skitt, Jack. Waste Disposal Management & Practice. LC 79-14109. 216p. 1979. 69.95x o.p. (ISBN 0-470-26747-X). Halsted Pr.

Skjei, Eric, jt. auth. see Smith, Craig.

Skjei, Eric W., jt. auth. see Smith, Craig W.

Skjonsberg, Else. A Special Caste? Tamil Women of Sri Lanka. 160p. 1983. pap. 9.95 (ISBN 0-86232-071-2, Pub. by Zed Pr England). Lawrence Hill.

Sklansky, David. Getting the Best of It. 224p. (Orig.). 1982. pap. 9.95 (ISBN 0-89650-721-1). Gamblers.

Sklansky, David & Dionne, Roger. Winning Power. (Illus.). 192p. 1983. 15.95 (ISBN 0-13-961060-X); pap. 7.95 (ISBN 0-13-961052-9). P-H.

Sklansky, J. & Bisconte, J. C., eds. Biomedical Images & Computers: St. Pierre de Chartreuse, France 1980, Proceedings. (Lecture Notes in Medical Informatics: Vol. 17). 332p. 1982. pap. 21.00 (ISBN 0-387-11579-X). Springer-Verlag.

Sklansky, Jack, ed. Pattern Recognition: Introduction & Foundation. LC 73-12568. (Benchmark Papers in Electrical Engineering & Computer Science: Vol. 4). 421p. 1973. text ed. 54.00 o.p. (ISBN 0-87933-045-7). Hutchinson Ross.

Sklansky, Morris A., jt. auth. see Rabichow, Helen G.

Sklar, jt. auth. see Schweitzer.

Sklar, Kathryn F., ed. Three Novels: Harriet Beecher Stowe. LC 81-18629. 1448p. 1982. 27.50 (ISBN 0-940450-01-1). Literary Classics.

Sklar, Kathryn K. Catharine Beecher: A Study in American Domesticity. 376p. 1976. pap. 6.95 (ISBN 0-393-00812-6, N812, Norton Lib). Norton.

Sklar, Morty, intro. by. Cross-Fertilization: The Human Spirit As Place. LC 81-215660. (Contemporary Anthology Ser.: No. 3). (Illus.). 64p. 1980. pap. 2.50 (ISBN 0-930370-10-4). Spirit That Moves.

Sklar, Morty, ed. A Spirit That Moves Us Reader: Seventh Anniversary Anthology. LC 82-10685. (The Contemporary Anthology Ser.: No. 4). (Illus.). 208p. 1982. 12.00 (ISBN 0-930370-13-9); pap. 6.00 (ISBN 0-930370-14-7); signed A-Z 25.00 (ISBN 0-930370-12-0). Spirit That Moves.

Sklar, Richard L. Corporate Power in an African State: The Political Impact of Multinational Mining Companies in Zambia. LC 74-81440. 1975. 38.50x (ISBN 0-520-02814-7). U of Cal Pr.

Sklar, Robert. Movie-Made America: A Cultural History of American Movies. 1976. pap. 8.95 (ISBN 0-394-72120-9, Vin). Random.

Sklare, Marshall. Conservative Judaism: An American Religious Movement. new ed. LC 76-183618. 320p. 1972. pap. 4.95 o.p. (ISBN 0-8052-0345-1). Schocken.

Sklare, Marshall, ed. American Jews. 352p. 1983. pap. text ed. 9.95x (ISBN 0-87441-348-6). Behrman.

--Jewish Community in America. LC 74-8678. (Library of Jewish Studies). (Illus.). 416p. 1974. text ed. 15.95x o.p. (ISBN 0-87441-204-8). Behrman.

--Understanding American Jewry. LC 81-14795. 400p. 1982. text ed. 21.95 (ISBN 0-87855-454-8). Transaction Bks.

Sklarew, jt. auth. see Steckman.

Skloot, Robert, ed. The Theatre of the Holocaust: Four Plays. 352p. 1982. text ed. 25.00 (ISBN 0-299-09070-1); pap. 10.95 (ISBN 0-299-09074-4). U of Wis Pr.

Skobel, Sammy. Semka. 1982. 12.95 (ISBN 0-686-33353-5). Caroline Hse.

Skocpol, Theda. States & Social Revolutions. LC 78-14314. 1979. 39.50 (ISBN 0-521-22439-X); pap. 10.95 (ISBN 0-521-29499-1). Cambridge U Pr.

Skofronick, James G., jt. auth. see Cameron, John R.

Skogan, Wesley G., ed. Sample Surveys of the Victims of Crime. LC 76-24831. 256p. 1976. prof ref 25.00x (ISBN 0-88410-221-1). Ballinger Pub.

Skoglund, Elizabeth. Coping. LC 79-65538. 128p. 1980. pap. 3.95 o.p. (ISBN 0-8307-0727-1, 5413109). Regal.

Skoglund, John E. The Baptists. 1967. pap. 1.25 (ISBN 0-8170-0386-X). Judson.

Skold, Betty W. Lord, I Have a Question: Story Devotions for Girls. LC 79-50079. (gr. 3-6). 1979. pap. 3.50 (ISBN 0-8066-1718-7, 10-4096). Augsburg.

Skoldberg, Phyllis. The Strings: A Comparative View, Vol. I. 1982. pap. text ed. 19.95 (ISBN 0-89917-316-0). TIS Inc.

--Strings: A Comparative View, Vol. II. 1983. pap. text ed. 19.95 (ISBN 0-89917-367-5, Frangipana Press). TIS Pr.

Skolem, Thoralf. Diophantische Gleichungen. LC 51-6891. (Ger). 10.95 (ISBN 0-8284-0075-X). Chelsea Pub.

Skoler, Martin E., ed. Health Care Labor Manual, 3 vols. LC 74-24672. (Updated bimonthly). 1974. Set. loose-leaf metal binding 350.00 (ISBN 0-912862-11-4). Aspen Systems.

Skolimowski, H., tr. see Ajdukiewicz, K.

Skolka, J. V., ed. Compilation of Input-Output Tables, Gouvieux, France, 1981: Proceedings. (Lecture Notes in Economics & Mathematical Sciences Ser.: Vol. 203). 307p. 1983. pap. 21.00 (ISBN 0-387-11553-6). Springer-Verlag.

Skolka, Jiri, ed. see International Conference Sixth Vienna, 1974.

Skolnick, Arlene. The Intimate Environment: Exploring Marriage & Family. 2nd ed. 1978. 18.95 (ISBN 0-316-79700-6); Instr's. manual by Dale Harrentsian (ISBN 0-316-79701-4). Little.

Skolnick, Jerome. Politics of Protest. 1969. 6.95 o.p. (ISBN 0-671-20381-9). S&S.

--Politics of Protest: A Task Force Report Submitted to the National Commission on the Cause & Prevention of Violence Under the Direction of Jerome H. Skolnick. 1969. pap. 2.95 o.p. (ISBN 0-671-20416-5, Touchstone Bks). S&S.

Skolnick, Jerome & Currie, Elliott. Crisis in American Institutions. 5th ed. 1982. pap. text ed. 12.95 (ISBN 0-316-79696-4); tchrs'. manual avail. (ISBN 0-316-79695-6). Little.

Skolnick, Jerome H. Justice Without Trial: Law Enforcement in Democratic Society. 2nd ed. LC 74-34145. 320p. 1975. pap. text ed. 11.50 (ISBN 0-471-79542-9). Wiley.

Skolnick, Jerome H., jt. auth. see Kaplan, John.

Skolnick, Jerome H. & Currie, Elliott, eds. Crisis in American Institutions. 4th ed. 1979. pap. 10.95 o.p. (ISBN 0-316-79697-2); teacher's manual free o.p. (ISBN 0-316-79698-0). Little.

Skolnick, Joan, et al. How To Encourage Girls in Math & Science: Strategies for Parents & Educators. (Illus.). 192p. 1982. 15.95 (ISBN 0-13-405670-1, Spec); pap. 7.95 (ISBN 0-13-405662-0). P-H.

Skolnik, Herman. The Literature Matrix of Chemistry. LC 81-22002. 297p. 1982. 33.95x (ISBN 0-471-79545-3, Pub. by Wiley-Interscience). Wiley.

Skolnik, Louise. Public Assistance & Your Client: A Handbook. 1981. loose-leaf 12.00 o.p. (ISBN 0-88461-008-X); with binder 15.00 o.p. (ISBN 0-536-03925-9). Adelphi Univ.

Skolnik, Merrill I. Introduction to Radar Systems. 2nd ed. (Electrical Engineering Ser.). (Illus.). 1980. text ed. 39.95x (ISBN 0-07-057909-1). McGraw.

--Radar Handbook. 1970. 75.90 o.p. (ISBN 0-07-057908-3, P&RB). McGraw.

Skolnik, Peter L., et al. Fads: America's Crazes, Fevers & Fancies from the 1890s to the 1970s. LC 77-886. (Illus.). 1978. 9.95 (ISBN 0-690-01215-2, TYC-T); pap. 5.95 o.p. (ISBN 0-690-01216-0, TYC-T). T Y Crowell.

Skolsky, Mindy W. Carnival & Kopeck & More About Hannah. LC 77-25643. (Illus.). (gr. 2-5). 1979. 7.95i (ISBN 0-06-025686-9, HarpJ); PLB 9.89 (ISBN 0-06-025692-3). Har-Row.

--Hannah & the Best Father on Route 9W. LC 80-8940. (Illus.). 128p. (gr. 3-6). 1982. 11.06i (ISBN 0-06-025743-1, HarpJ); PLB 11.89g (ISBN 0-06-025744-X). Har-Row.

Skoog, Tord. Plastic Surgery. LC 74-11691. (Illus.). 500p. 1975. text ed. 150.00 o.p. (ISBN 0-7216-8355-X). Saunders.

Skopec, Eric W. Business & Professional Speaking. (Illus.). 288p. 1983. pap. 16.95 (ISBN 0-13-107532-2). P-H.

Skorova, A. E., jt. auth. see Lukevics, E.

Skorpen, Liesel M. Elizabeth. LC 76-105490. 32p. (ps-3). 1970. 6.95i o.p. (ISBN 0-06-025708-3, HarpJ); PLB 7.89 (ISBN 0-06-025709-1). Har-Row.

--Plenty for Three. (Illus.). (gr. k-3). 1971. PLB 4.39 o.p. (ISBN 0-698-30284-2, Coward). Putnam Pub Group.

--We Were Tired of Living in a House. (Illus.). (gr. k-2). 1969. PLB 4.99 o.p. (ISBN 0-698-30394-6, Coward). Putnam Pub Group.

Skorupski, John. Symbol & Theory: A Philosophical Study of Theories of Religion in Social Anthropology. LC 76-3037. 280p. Date not set. pap. 10.95 (ISBN 0-521-27252-1). Cambridge U Pr.

Skorupski, T., jt. auth. see Snellgrove, D. L.

Skousen, K. Fred, et al. Principles of Accounting. 1981. text ed. 25.95x (ISBN 0-87901-137-8); study guide 8.95 (ISBN 0-87901-147-5); practice set, transaction analysis 6.95x (ISBN 0-87901-150-5); practice set, financial statement analysis 6.95x (ISBN 0-87901-151-3); practice set, master budget 4.95x (ISBN 0-87901-152-1); working papers, vol. 1 8.50x (ISBN 0-87901-148-3); working papers, vol. 2 8.50x (ISBN 0-87901-149-1). Worth.

--Financial Accounting. 1981. text ed. 23.95x (ISBN 0-87901-156-4); study guide 8.95x (ISBN 0-87901-157-2); practice set, transaction analysis 6.95x (ISBN 0-87901-150-5); practice set, financial statement analysis 6.95 (ISBN 0-87901-151-3); working papers 8.50 (ISBN 0-87901-158-0). Worth.

Skousen, Mark. Mark Skousen's Guide to Financial Privacy. 1983. write for info (ISBN 0-671-47060-4). S&S.

--The One Hundred Percent Gold Standard. 1977. 12.00 (ISBN 0-8191-0328-4). U Pr of Amer.

--Playing the Price Controls Game. (Illus.). 1977. 10.95 o.p. (ISBN 0-87000-374-7, Arlington Hse). Crown.

--Tax Free. 191p. 1983. 12.95 (ISBN 0-671-46061-7). S&S.

Skousen, W. Cleon. Fantastic Victory. LC 67-30390. 1967. 5.95 o.p. (ISBN 0-685-48243-X). Bookcraft Inc.

--The First Two Thousand Years. 1953. 7.95 (ISBN 0-685-48240-5). Bookcraft Inc.

--The Five Thousand Year Leap: Twenty-Eight Ideas That Changed the World. (Illus.). xx, 337p. (Orig.). 13.95 (ISBN 0-88080-003-8); pap. 9.95 (ISBN 0-88080-004-6). Freemen Inst.

--Prophecy & Modern Times. 150p. pap. 2.95 o.p. (ISBN 0-87747-680-2). Deseret Bk.

--So You Want to Raise a Boy? LC 61-9555. 1962. 12.95 (ISBN 0-385-02408-8). Doubleday.

--The Third Thousand Years. 1964. 12.95 (ISBN 0-685-48241-3). Bookcraft Inc.

Skousgaard, Stephen. Language & the Existence of Freedom: A Study in Paul Ricoeur's Philosophy of Will. LC 79-63257. 1979. pap. text ed. 8.25 (ISBN 0-8191-0725-5). U Pr of Amer.

Skousgaard, Stephen, ed. Phenomenology & the Understanding of Human Destiny. LC 81-40793. (Current Continental Research Ser.: No. 1). 398p. (Orig.). 1982. lib. bdg. 25.50 (ISBN 0-8191-2085-5); pap. text ed. 14.50 (ISBN 0-8191-2086-3). U Pr of Amer.

Skouson, Sandra & Anderson, Peggy. Taming the Video Monster: How Your Family Can Control TV Watching & Video Games. 168p. 1983. pap. 9.95 (ISBN 0-525-93290-9, 0966-290). Dutton.

Skowronski, Deborah. The Non-Reader's Telephone Directory. LC 82-61510. (Illus.). 36p. 1982. pap. text ed. 5.95 (ISBN 0-9609618-0-1). Sunburst.

Skowronski, Sharon, jt. ed. see McHale, Vincent.

Skowrup, Drew, jt. auth. see Verner, Bill.

Skrabanek, D. W., ed. Freelance Opportunities in Texas Publishing. 1982. pap. 5.00 (ISBN 0-934646-10-4). S & S Pr TX.

Skrabanek, P. & Powell, D. Substance P, Vol. 1. 1978. 21.60 (ISBN 0-88831-019-6). Eden Pr.

Skrabanek, Petr & Powell, David. Substance P, Vol. 2. Horrobin, D. F., ed. LC 80-646426. (Annual Research Reviews Ser.). 175p. 1980. 26.00 (ISBN 0-88831-073-0). Eden Pr.

Skrebtsov, G. P., tr. see Glebov, I. A. & Komarsky, E. G.

Skrine, Peter N., jt. auth. see Furst, Lillian R.

Skripkin, Yu. K. Skin & Venereal Diseases. 556p. 1981. 14.00 (ISBN 0-8285-2174-3, Pub. by Mir Pubs USSR). Imported Pubns.

Skrjabin, K. I., et al. Essentials of Nematodology: Vol. 13, Oxyurata of Animals & Man. 486p. 1976. 99.95x o.p. (ISBN 0-470-98978-5). Halsted Pr.

Skrjabina, Elena. Siege & Survival. 1979. pap. 1.95 o.p. (ISBN 0-523-40479-4). Pinnacle Bks.

Skrotzki, Bernhardt G. Basic Thermodynamics: Elements of Energy Systems. 1963. text ed. 24.95 (ISBN 0-07-057945-8, G). McGraw.

Skrotzki, Bernhardt G. & Vopat, W. A. Power Station Engineering & Economy. 2nd ed. 1960. text ed. 37.50 (ISBN 0-07-057940-7, C). McGraw.

Skrovan, Daniel J., ed. see American Society for Training & Development Inc.

Skrupskelis, Ignas K. William James: A Reference Guide. 1977. lib. bdg. 21.00 (ISBN 0-8161-7805-4, Hall Reference). G K Hall.

Skrynnikov, R. G. Boris Godunov. Graham, Hugh F., ed. (Russian Ser.: No. 35). 1978. 16.50 (ISBN 0-87569-046-7). Academic Intl.

--Ivan the Terrible. Graham, Hugh F., ed. (Russian Ser.: No. 32). 1981. 16.50 (ISBN 0-87569-039-4). Academic Intl.

Skucas, J., jt. auth. see Miller, R. E.

Skudlarek, William, ed. The Continuing Quest for God: Monastic Spirituality in Tradition & Transition. LC 81-23614. x, 302p. (Orig.). 1982. pap. 8.95 (ISBN 0-8146-1235-0). Liturgical Pr.

Skujins, J., jt. ed. see West, N. E.

Skulachev, V. P., ed. Soviet Scientific Reviews: Biology Reviews, Vol. 1, Section D. 486p. 1980. lib. bdg. 97.00 (ISBN 3-7186-0020-X). Harwood Academic.

--Soviet Scientific Reviews: Biology Reviews, Vol. 2, Section D. 400p. 1981. 85.00 (ISBN 3-7186-0058-7). Harwood Academic.

--Soviet Scientific Reviews: Biology Review, Vol. 3, Section D. 452p. 1982. write for info. (ISBN 3-7186-0111-7). Harwood Academic.

Skulicz, Matthew. Right on, Shane! (gr. 7-11). 1972. 5.95 o.p. (ISBN 0-399-20198-X). Putnam Pub Group.

Skully, Michael T., ed. Financial Institutions & Markets in the Far East: A Study of China, Hong Kong, Japan, South Korea & Taiwan. LC 82-5652. 240p. 1982. 27.50x (ISBN 0-312-28961-8). St Martin.

Skulsky, S. Legends of Bar Kochba. (Jewish History Ser.). (Illus.). (gr. 5-10). 1975. 5.00 o.p. (ISBN 0-914080-20-2). Shulsinger Sales.

--Legends of King David. (Biblical Ser.). (Illus.). (gr. 5-10). 1975. 6.00 o.p. (ISBN 0-914080-16-4). Shulsinger Sales.

--Legends of King Solomon. (Biblical Ser.). (Illus.). (gr. 5-10). 1975. 6.00 o.p. (ISBN 0-914080-17-2). Shulsinger Sales.

--Legends of Rabbi Akiva. (Jewish History Ser.). (Illus.). (gr. 5-10). 1975. 6.00 o.p. (ISBN 0-914080-18-0). Shulsinger Sales.

Skultans, Vieda. English Madness: Ideas on Insanity Fifteen Eighty to Eighteen Ninety. (Illus.). 1979. 22.50x (ISBN 0-7100-0329-3). Routledge & Kegan.

Skupien, Janet, jt. auth. see Davis, Martha.

Skurka, Norma. Alternate Interiors. (Illus.). 1979. 15.95 o.p. (ISBN 0-399-12288-5). Putnam Pub Group.

Skurnick, Blanch J. The Heath Basic Writer. 448p. 1982. pap. text ed. 11.95 (ISBN 0-669-05172-1). Heath.

Skurnik, W. A., ed. Sub-Saharan Africa: A Guide to Information Sources. LC 73-17513. (International Relations Information Guide Ser.: Vol. 3). 1977. 42.00x (ISBN 0-8103-1391-X). Gale.

Skurski, Roger. New Directions in Economic Justice. 304p. 1983. text ed. 20.95x (ISBN 0-268-01460-4); pap. text ed. 10.95x (ISBN 0-268-01461-2). U of Notre Dame Pr.

--Soviet Marketing & Economic Development. LC 82-792. 256p. 1983. 27.50x (ISBN 0-312-74842-6). St Martin.

Skurzynski, Gloria. The Tempering. 192p. (gr. 6 up). 1983. 11.50 (ISBN 0-89919-152-5, Clarion). HM.

Skuse, Allen. Government Intervention & Industrial Policy. 2nd ed. (Studies in the British Economy Ser.). 1972. pap. text ed. 6.50x o.p. (ISBN 0-435-84556-X). Heinemann Ed.

Skutch, Alexander F. Birds of Tropical America. (Corrie Herring Hooks Ser.: No. 5). (Illus.). 316p. 1983. 29.95 (ISBN 0-292-74634-2). U of Tex Pr.

--Life Histories of Central American Highland Birds. (Illus.). 213p. 1967. 8.00 (ISBN 0-686-35794-9). Nuttall Ornithological.

--New Studies of Tropical American Birds. (Illus.). 281p. 1981. 29.50 (ISBN 0-686-35809-0). Nuttall Ornithological.

--Studies of Tropical American Birds. (Illus.). 228p. 1972. 12.00 (ISBN 0-686-35798-1). Nuttall Ornithological.

Skutnabb-Kangas, Tove. Language in the Process of Cultural Assimilation & Structural Incorporation of Linguistic Minorities. 32p. 1979. pap. 4.50 (ISBN 0-89763-005-X). Natl Clearinghse Bilingual Ed.

Skvirsky, David, tr. see Ponomarev, Boris N.

Skvorecky, Josef. Contemporary Czech Cinematography: Jiri Menzel & the History of the "Closely Watched Trains". (East European Monographs: No. 118). 144p. 1982. 17.50x (ISBN 0-88033-011-2). East Eur Quarterly.

Skwirzynski, J. F. Theoretical Methods for Determining the Interaction of Electromagnetic Waves with Structures. 1981. 99.00 (ISBN 0-686-36958-0, Pub. by Martinus Nijhoff Netherlands). Kluwer Boston.

Sky, Alison & Stone, Michelle. Unbuilt America: Forgotten Architecture in the United States from Thomas Jefferson to the Space Age. (Illus.). 308p. 1983. Repr. of 1976 ed. 24.95 (ISBN 0-89659-341-X). Abbeville Pr.

Skydell, Ruth H., jt. auth. see Belkin, Gary S.

Slaatte, Howard A. Discovering Your Real Self: Sermons of Existential Relevance. LC 80-8289. 156p. 1980. lib. bdg. 18.00 (ISBN 0-8191-1177-5); pap. text ed. 8.25 (ISBN 0-8191-1178-3). U Pr of Amer.

--The Dogma of Immaculate Perception: A Critique of Positivistic Thought. LC 79-66858. 1979. pap. text ed. 8.25 (ISBN 0-8191-0849-9). U Pr of Amer.

--Modern Science & the Human Condition. LC 81-40185. 230p. 1981. pap. text ed. 10.25 (ISBN 0-8191-1586-X); lib. bdg. 19.75 (ISBN 0-8191-1676-9). U Pr of Amer.

--The Pertinence of the Paradox: A Study of the Dialectics of Reason-In-Existence. LC 81-43797. 286p. 1982. pap. text ed. 11.50 (ISBN 0-8191-2245-9). U Pr of Amer.

--The Seven Ecumenical Councils. LC 80-5755. 55p. 1980. pap. text ed. 6.00 (ISBN 0-8191-1204-6). U Pr of Amer.

--Time & Its End: A Comparative Existential Interpretation of Time & Eschatology. LC 80-7814. 298p. 1980. lib. bdg. 21.25 (ISBN 0-8191-1069-8); pap. text ed. 11.50 (ISBN 0-8191-1070-1). U Pr of Amer.

Slaatten, Evelyn. The Good, the Bad & the Rest of Us. LC 80-15595. 160p. (gr. 4-6). 1980. 9.75 (ISBN 0-688-22251-X); PLB 9.36 (ISBN 0-688-32251-4). Morrow.

Slabaugh, Michael R. & Seager, Spencer L. Laboratory Experiments in Introductory Chemistry: General, Organic, Biological. 1979. pap. text ed. 8.95x (ISBN 0-673-15216-2). Scott F.

Slabaugh, Michael R., jt. auth. see Seager, Spencer L.

Slabaugh, Michael R., jt. auth. see Stoker, H. Stephen.

Slabbert, F. Van Zyl see Van Zyl Slabbert, F. & Welsh, David.

Slaby, Andrew E., jt. auth. see Giannini, A. James.

Slaby, Andrew E., jt. auth. see Goldberg, Richard J.

Slaby, Andrew E., jt. auth. see Lieb, Julian.

Slaby, Andrew E., et al. Handbook of Psychiatric Emergencies. 2nd. ed. 1980. 26.95 (ISBN 0-87488-655-4); pap. 17.95 (ISBN 0-87488-645-7). Med Exam.

Slaby, R. J. & Grossman, R., eds. Spanish & German Dictionary, 2 vols. Incl. Vol. 1. Spanish-German. 17.00 (ISBN 0-8044-0581-6); Vol. 2. German-Spanish. 28.00 (ISBN 0-8044-0582-4). 2172p. Set. 45.00 (ISBN 0-8044-0580-8). Ungar.

Slaby, S. M. Fundamentals of Three-Dimensional Geometry. 2nd ed. 416p. 1976. 32.95x (ISBN 0-471-79621-2); wkbk. 16.50x (ISBN 0-471-79622-0); avail. suppl. materials (ISBN 0-471-02478-3); avail. suppl. materials (ISBN 0-471-01914-3); avail. suppl. materials (ISBN 0-471-01913-5). Wiley.

Slaby, Steve M. Engineering Descriptive Geometry. (Orig.). 1969. pap. 5.72i (ISBN 0-06-460101-3, CO 101, COS). B&N NY.

Slack & Mueller. A Propos! Communication et Culture: Un Debut. 1985. text ed. 22.95 (ISBN 0-686-84591-9, FR34); write for info. supplementary materials. HM.

Slack, Adrian. Carnivorous Plants. (Illus.). 240p. 1980. 25.00 (ISBN 0-262-19186-5). MIT Pr.

Slack, Anne & Mueller, Marlies. A Propos! Communication et Culture: Un Debut. LC 82-82509. 1983. 23.95 (ISBN 0-395-32728-8); write for info. supplementary materials. HM.

Slack, Anne, et al. French for Communication, One. LC 77-87429. (Illus., Gr. 9). 1978. text ed. 15.28 (ISBN 0-395-20159-4); complete program avail. write for info. 0.00. HM.

Slack, Claudia. The Moon in Eclipse. (Orig.). 1978. pap. 1.50 o.p. (ISBN 0-451-08132-3, W8132, Sig). NAL.

--Outrageous Fortune. 1978. pap. 1.50 o.p. (ISBN 0-451-07894-2, W7894, Sig). NAL.

--Web of Enchantment. Bd. with Outrageous Fortune. 1980. pap. 1.95 (ISBN 0-451-09357-7, J9357, Sig). NAL.

Slack, Claudia see Cooper, Lynna.

Slack, Jennifer D. Communication Technologies & Society: Conceptions of Causality & the Politics of Technical Intervention. (Communication & Information Science Ser.). 176p. 1983. 19.95 (ISBN 0-89391-124-0). Ablex Pub.

Slack, Paul A. Death & Disease in Pre-Industrial Europe. (Pre-Industrial Europe Ser.: No. 3). Date not set. text ed. price not set (ISBN 0-391-01042-5). Humanities.

Slack, Robert C. & Cottrell, Beekman W. Writing: A Preparation for College Composition. 2nd ed. 1978. pap. text ed. 13.95x (ISBN 0-02-478250-5). Macmillan.

Slack, Robert C., ed. see Hardy, Thomas.

Slack, Steven J. & DeKornfeld, Thomas J. Anesthesiology: Continuing Education Review. 2nd ed. 1983. pap. text ed. price not set (ISBN 0-87488-353-9). Med Exam.

Slack, Walter H. The Surplus Species: Need Man Prevail? LC 81-40833. 172p. (Orig.). 1982. lib. bdg. 22.00 (ISBN 0-8191-2231-9); pap. text ed. 10.00 (ISBN 0-8191-2232-7). U Pr of Amer.

Sladden, John C. Boniface of Devon: Apostle of Germany. 254p. 1980. text ed. 18.75 (ISBN 0-85364-275-3). Attic Pr.

Slade, Carole, jt. auth. see Cummins, Martha H.

Slade, David H., ed. Meteorology & Atomic Energy: 1968. LC 68-60097. (AEC Technical Information Center Ser.). 445p. 1968. pap. 6.00 (ISBN 0-87079-274-1, TID-24190); microfiche 4.50 (ISBN 0-87079-275-X, TID-24190). DOE.

Slade, Herbert. Exploration into Contemplative Prayer. 228p. 1975. pap. 4.95 o.p. (ISBN 0-8091-1904-8). Paulist Pr.

Slade, Jack. Bandido. (Lassiter Ser.: No. 2). 192p. 1982. pap. 2.25 o.p. (ISBN 0-505-51845-7). Tower Bks.

--Bandido. (Lassiter Ser.: No. 2). 192p. 1983. pap. 2.25 (ISBN 0-8439-2005-X, Leisure Bks). Dorchester Pub Co.

--Lassiter. (Lassiter Ser.: No. 1). 192p. 1982. pap. 2.25 o.p. (ISBN 0-505-51833-3). Tower Bks.

--The Man from Cheyenne. (Lassiter Ser.: No. 4). 192p. 1982. pap. write for info o.p. (ISBN 0-505-51860-0). Tower Bks.

--Renegade. (Sundance Ser.: No. 12). 192p. 1982. pap. 2.25 o.s.i. (ISBN 0-8439-1146-8, Leisure Bks). Dorchester Pub Co.

Slade, K. A. Steel Boat Construction. (Questions & Answers Ser.). (Illus.). 115p. (Orig.). 1979. pap. 7.50 o.s.i. (ISBN 0-686-64487-5). Transatlantic.

Slade, R. C., jt. auth. see Gerloch, M.

Slade, Richard. Geometrical Patterns. (Illus.). (gr. 4 up). 1970. 5.95 o.p. (ISBN 0-571-08793-0). Transatlantic.

--Take an Egg Box: How to Make Some Interesting Models. (gr. 4-7). 6.75 o.p. (ISBN 0-571-06359-4). Transatlantic.

Slade, Ruth. King Leopold's Congo. LC 73-21103. (Illus.). 230p. 1974. Repr. of 1962 ed. lib. bdg. 15.75x (ISBN 0-8371-5953-9, SLLC). Greenwood.

Sladek, John. Invisible Green. 186p. 1983. pap. 2.95 (ISBN 0-8027-3020-5). Walker & Co.

Sladen, Douglas. Queer Things About Japan, to Which Is Added a Life of the Emperor of Japan. 4th ed. LC 68-26607. (Illus.). 1968. Repr. of 1913 ed. 37.00x (ISBN 0-8103-3500-X). Gale.

Sladen, F. & Bang, B., eds. Biology of Populations. 1969. 25.00 (ISBN 0-444-00063-1). Elsevier.

Sladkovsky, M. I., ed. Leninism & Modern China's Problems. 253p. 1972. pap. 3.45 (ISBN 0-686-98351-3, Pub. by Progress Pubs USSR). Imported Pubns.

Slaff, Betrand. What Happens in Therapy. (gr. 7 up). 1982. pap. 6.00 (ISBN 0-688-01459-3); PLB 8.63 (ISBN 0-688-01458-5). Morrow.

Slafter, Edmund see Ryder, Hillyer.

Slaga, Thomas J., ed. Modifiers of Chemical Carcinogenesis. LC 77-504. (Carcinogenesis: a Comprehensive Survey Ser.: Vol. 5). 285p. 1979. text ed. 36.00 (ISBN 0-89004-232-2). Raven.

Slaga, Thomas J., et al, eds. Mechanisms of Tumor Promotion & Cocarcinogenesis. LC 77-17752. (Carcinogenesis: a Comprehensive Survey: Vol. 2). 605p. 1978. 58.00 (ISBN 0-89004-208-X). Raven.

Slagle, J. Artificial Intelligence, the Heuristic Programming Approach. 1970. text ed. 31.95 o.p. (ISBN 0-07-058005-7, C). McGraw.

Slagle, Uhlan & Anttila, Raimo. Dynamic Fields & the Structure of Language. (Current Issues in Linguistic Theory: 6). 250p. 1983. 26.00 (ISBN 90-272-3510-4). Benjamins North Am.

Slama, Chester C., ed. Manual of Photogrammetry. 4th ed. LC 80-21514. (Illus.). 1980. (44.95 member) 59.95 (ISBN 0-937294-01-2). ASP.

Slamecka, V. & Borka, H., eds. Planning & Organisation of National Research Programs in Information Science. (Illus.). 83p. 1982. pap. 60.00 (ISBN 0-08-026472-7). Pergamon.

Slane, Alton. Major Supreme Court Decisions in American Government. LC 81-40049. 232p. 1982. lib. bdg. 21.75 (ISBN 0-8191-1870-2); pap. text ed. 10.75 (ISBN 0-8191-1871-0). U Pr of Amer.

Slate, William G. Disorders of the Female Urethra & Urinary Incontinence. 2nd ed. (Illus.). 296p. 1982. lib. bdg. 34.00 (ISBN 0-683-07746-5). Williams & Wilkins.

Slater. Sex Hormones & Behavior. (Studies in Biology: No. 103). 1979. 5.95 o.p. (ISBN 0-8391-0253-4). Univ Park.

Slater & Smith. Basic Plumbing. LC 77-85751. 1979. pap. text ed. 9.80 (ISBN 0-8273-1204-0); instructor's guide 3.25 (ISBN 0-8273-1205-9). Delmar.

Slater, Abby. In Search of Margaret Fuller: A Biography. LC 77-86335. (gr. 7 up). 1978. 7.50 o.s.i. (ISBN 0-440-03944-4). Delacorte.

Slater, Ann P. Shakespeare The Director. LC 82-6704. 256p. 1982. text ed. 23.50x (ISBN 0-389-20304-1). B&N Imports.

Slater, Barbara & Slater, Ron. Tracking Down Trivia. (gr. 5-12). 1982. 4.95 (ISBN 0-86653-078-9, GA 423). Good Apple.

Slater, Barbara R. & Thomas, John M. Psychodiagnostic Evaluation of Children: A Casebook Approach. 1983. pap. text ed. price not set (ISBN 0-8077-2734-2). Tchrs Coll.

Slater, D. W. A Collection of Thoughts into Words. 1983. 5.95 (ISBN 0-533-05452-4). Vantage.

Slater, Frank, ed. Cost Reduction for Special Libraries and Information Centers. LC 73-81388. 1973. 12.50 (ISBN 0-87715-104-0). Am Soc Info Sci.

Slater, Harry. Advanced Plumbing. LC 79-89242. (Construction Ser.). 1980. pap. text ed. 9.80 (ISBN 0-8273-1111-7); instructor's guide 3.25 (ISBN 0-8273-1112-5). Delmar.

Slater, Herbert J., ed. see Burton, John H.

Slater, Herman, ed. A Book of Pagan Rituals, Vols. 1 & 2. 1978. pap. 8.95 (ISBN 0-87728-348-6). Weiser.

Slater, J. Man the Artist. 1970. 3.35 (ISBN 0-08-006899-5). Pergamon.

--Practical Accounting Procedures. 1979. 18.95 (ISBN 0-13-688101-7); pap. 10.95 study guide & wkg. papers (ISBN 0-13-688119-X); pap. 9.95 practice set (ISBN 0-13-688135-1). P-H.

Slater, Jim. The Boy Who Saved Earth. 128p. (YA) (gr. 7 up). 1983. pap. 1.75 (LFL). Dell.

Slater, John C. The Calculation of Molecular Orbitals. LC 78-323. 104p. 1979. 41.50x (ISBN 0-471-03181-X, Pub. by Wiley-Interscience). Wiley.

--Quantum Theory of Matter. 2nd ed. LC 77-3479. (International Ser. in Pure & Applied Physics). (Illus.). 1977. Repr. of 1968 ed. lib. bdg. 39.50 (ISBN 0-88275-553-6). Krieger.

--Quantum Theory of Molecules & Solids, Vol. 1, 3 & 4. Incl. Vol. 1. Electronic Structure of Molecules. 1963. o.p. (ISBN 0-07-058035-9); Vol. 3. Insulators, Semiconductors & Solids. 1969. o.p. (ISBN 0-07-058037-5); Vol. 4. The Self-Consistent Field for Molecules & Solids. 39.50 (ISBN 0-07-058038-3, C). C). McGraw.

--Solid State & Molecular Theory: A Scientific Biography. LC 74-22367. 357p. 1975. text ed. 36.95x (ISBN 0-471-79681-6, Pub. by Wiley-Interscience). Wiley.

Slater, John H. Illustrated Sporting Books. LC 71-75800. 1969. Repr. of 1899 ed. 30.00x (ISBN 0-8103-3889-0). Gale.

Slater, John M. El Morro, Inscription Rock, New Mexico. (Illus.). 157p. 1961. 60.00 o.p. (ISBN 0-87093-305-1). Dawsons.

Slater, L. J. Gem, a General Econometric Matrix Program. LC 76-16920. (Applied Economics, Occasional Papers Ser.: No. 46). (Illus.). 1976. pap. 13.95x (ISBN 0-521-29114-3). Cambridge U Pr.

Slater, L. J., jt. auth. see Pesaran, M. H.

Slater, Lucy J. More Fortran Programs for Economists. (Department of Applied Economics, Occasional Papers: No. 3). (Illus.). 150p. 1972. 17.95x (ISBN 0-521-09722-3). Cambridge U Pr.

Slater, Michael. Dickens & Women. LC 82-62351. (Illus.). 512p. 1983. 28.50x (ISBN 0-8047-1180-1). Stanford U Pr.

Slater, Michael, ed. see Dickens, Charles.

Slater, Montagu. Maria Marten or the Murder in the Red Barn. 1971. pap. text ed. 3.00x o.p. (ISBN 0-435-23810-8). Heinemann Ed.

Slater, P. The Measurements of Intrapersonal Space by Grid Technique: Dimensions of Intrapersonal Space, Vol. 2. 270p. 1977. 52.95 (ISBN 0-471-99450-2). Wiley.

Slater, P., ed. The Measurement of Intrapersonal Space by Grid Techniques: Explorations of Intrapersonal Space, Vol. 1. LC 76-8908. 258p. 1976. 54.95x (ISBN 0-471-01360-9, Pub. by Wiley-Interscience). Wiley.

Slater, Philip. The Pursuit of Loneliness: American Culture at the Breaking Point. rev. ed. LC 75-36045. 256p. 1976. 9.13 (ISBN 0-8070-4158-0); pap. 3.79 (ISBN 0-8070-4159-9, BP535). Beacon Pr.

--Wealth Addiction. 224p. 1983. pap. 5.95 (ISBN 0-525-47704-7, 0577-180). Dutton.

Slater, Philip N. Remote Sensing: Optics & Optical Systems. (Illus.). 450p. 1980. text ed. 38.50 (ISBN 0-201-07250-5). A-W.

Slater, R. A. Engineering Plasticity: Theory & Its Application to Metal Forming, Processes. LC 73-10606. 1977. text ed. 59.95 o.s.i. (ISBN 0-470-79647-2). Halsted Pr.

Slater, Ray. Texas Night Riders. 176p. 1982. pap. 1.95 o.s.i. (ISBN 0-8439-1063-1, Leisure Bks). Nordon Pubns.

Slater, Robert. Israel's Aid to Developing Nations. 104p. pap. 1.95 (ISBN 0-686-95161-0). ADL.

Slater, Ron, jt. auth. see Slater, Barbara.

Slater, S. D. The Strategy of Cash: A Liquidity Approach to Maximizing the Company's Profits. LC 74-9811. (Systems & Controls for Financial Management Ser.). 392p. 1974. 37.95x (ISBN 0-471-79640-9, Pub. by Wiley-Interscience). Wiley.

Slater, Sarah W., jt. auth. see Brauns, Robert.

Slatkes, Leonard. Rembrandt. LC 79-57583. (Abbeville Library of Art Ser.: No. 7). (Illus.). 112p. 1980. pap. 4.95 o.p. (ISBN 0-89659-134-4). Abbeville Pr.

Slatkes, Leonard J. Vermeer & His Contemporaries. Greenberg, Mark D., ed. (Illus.). 200p. 1981. text ed. 25.00 o.p. (ISBN 0-89659-195-6); pap. text ed. 14.95 o.p. (ISBN 0-89659-156-5). Abbeville Pr.

Slatkin, Montgomery, jt. ed. see Futuyma, Douglas J.

Slatkin, Wendy. Aristide Maillol in the 1890s. Foster, Stephen, ed. LC 82-4799. (Studies in Fine Arts: The Avant-Garde: No. 30). 178p. 1982. 39.95 (ISBN 0-8357-1333-4, Pub. by UMI Res Pr). Univ Microfilms.

Slatoff, Walter J. Quest for Failure: A Study of William Faulkner. LC 72-4084. 275p. 1972. Repr. of 1960 ed. lib. bdg. 17.75x (ISBN 0-8371-6432-X, SLQF). Greenwood.

Slatt, Bernard J., jt. auth. see Stein, Harold A.

Slatte, Howard A. The Paradox of Existentialist Theology: The Dialectics of a Faith-Subsumed Reason-in-Existence. LC 81-43508. 272p. 1982. lib. bdg. 23.00 (ISBN 0-8191-2187-8); pap. text ed. 11.50 (ISBN 0-8191-2188-6). U Pr of Amer.

Slattery, David. Washington Redskins: A Pictorial History. LC 77-15328. (Illus.). 168p. 1977. 14.95 (ISBN 0-686-84393-2). JCP Corp VA.

Slattery, Matthew T. Felipe Angeles & the Mexican Revolution. LC 82-91102. (Illus.). 214p. (Orig.). 1982. write for info (ISBN 0-932970-35-4); pap. write for info (ISBN 0-932970-34-6). Greenbriar Bks.

Slatyer, R. D. Plant-Water Relations. (Experimental Botany Ser.: Vol. 2). 1967. 56.00 o.p. (ISBN 0-12-648650-6). Acad Pr.

Slatzer, Robert F. The Life & Curious Death of Marilyn Monroe. (Illus.). 1977. pap. 2.25 o.p. (ISBN 0-523-40090-X). Pinnacle Bks.

Slaughter, Carolyn. The Heart of the River. 288p. 1983. 11.95 (ISBN 0-312-36600-0). St Martin.

Slaughter, Frank G. Doctors at Risk. LC 81-43921. 264p. 1983. 14.95 (ISBN 0-385-17876-X). Doubleday.

--Doctor's Daughters. large type ed. LC 82-3362. 446p. 1982. Repr. of 1981 ed. 13.95 (ISBN 0-89621-355-2). Thorndike Pr.

Slaughter, J. C., jt. auth. see Duffus, C. M.

Slaughter, Mary. Universal Languages & Scientific Taxonomy in the Seventeenth Century. LC 81-20147. 304p. 1982. 47.50 (ISBN 0-521-24477-3). Cambridge U Pr.

Slaughter, S. L., jt. auth. see Hyatt, Christopher S.

Slaus, Ivo, jt. ed. see Paic, Guy.

Slauson, David O. Mechanisms of Disease: A Textbook of Comparative General Pathology. 390p. 1982. 36.00 (ISBN 0-683-07742-2). Williams & Wilkins.

Slauson, Nedra, jt. ed. see Thompson, John W.

Slaven, A. & Aldcroft, D., eds. Business, Banking & Urban History: Essays in Honour of S. G. Checkland. 235p. 1982. text ed. 31.50x (ISBN 0-85976-083-9, 40292, Pub. by Donald Scotland). Humanities.

Slaven, Anthony. Development of the West of Scotland. (Regional History of the British Isles Ser.). 1975. 23.95x (ISBN 0-7100-8097-2). Routledge & Kegan.

Slavens, Thomas P., jt. auth. see Kleinbauer, W. E.

Slavens, Thomas P., jt. ed. see Wilson, John F.

Slavick, William H. DuBose Heyward. (United States Authors Ser.). 1981. lib. bdg. 13.95 (ISBN 0-8057-7342-8, Twayne). G K Hall.

Slavin, Arthur J. The Way of the West, 5 vols. 1973-1975. Vols. A & 1-3. pap. text ed. 16.95x ea. o.p; Vol. A. 20.95 (ISBN 0-471-00907-5); Vol. B. pap. text ed. 19.95 (ISBN 0-471-00908-3); Vol. 1. o.p. (ISBN 0-471-00788-9); Vol. 2. 18.95 (ISBN 0-471-00789-7); Vol. 3. 20.50 (ISBN 0-471-00891-5). Wiley.

Slavin, Morris. Atomic Absorption Spectroscopy, Vol. 25. 2nd ed. LC 78-16257. (Chemical Analysis: Series of Monographs on Analytical Chemistry & Its Applications: Vol. 25). 1978. 36.00 (ISBN 0-471-79652-2, Pub. by Wiley-Interscience). Wiley.

Slavin, Robert E. Cooperative Learning. LC 82-16188. (Research on Teaching Ser.). 208p. 1983. text ed. 22.50x (ISBN 0-582-28355-8). Longman.

Slavin, Sarah, ed. The Equal Rights Amendment: The Policy & Process of Ratification of the 27th Amendment to the U. S. Constitution. LC 82-9340. (Women & Politics Ser.: Vol. 2, Nos. 1 & 2). 163p. 1982. pap. text ed. 15.00 (ISBN 0-917724-86-0, B86). Haworth Pr.

Slavin, Simon, ed. Applying Computers in Social Service & Mental Health Agencies. LC 81-20102. (Administration in Social Work Ser.: Vol. 5, Nos. 3 & 4). 200p. 1982. text ed. 30.00 (ISBN 0-86656-102-1, B102). Haworth Pr.

--Social Administration: The Management of the Social Services. LC 77-88090. 650p. 1978. 32.95 (ISBN 0-917724-01-1, B1); pap. 15.00 (ISBN 0-917724-02-X, B2). Haworth Pr.

Slavin, Simon, jt. ed. see Perlmutter, Felice D.

Slavitt, Dave. King of Hearts. 1977. pap. 1.95 o.p. (ISBN 0-515-04401-6). Jove Pubns.

Slavitt, David. Cold Comfort. LC 79-24475. 1980. 10.95 o.p. (ISBN 0-416-00621-3). Methuen Inc.

--Ringer. Rosenman, Jane, ed. LC 82-5103. 256p. 1982. 13.95 (ISBN 0-525-24139-6, 01354-410). Dutton.

Slavitt, David R. Big Nose: Poems. LC 82-21643. 1983. text ed. 13.95 (ISBN 0-8071-1072-8); pap. 5.95 (ISBN 0-8071-1073-6). La State U Pr.

Slavkin, H., jt. ed. see Silbermann, M.

Slavkin, Harold C., ed. The Comparative Molecular Biology of Extracellular Matrices. 1972. 47.50 (ISBN 0-12-648340-X). Acad Pr.

Slavkin, Harold C. & Bavetta, Lucien A., eds. Developmental Aspects of Oral Biology. 1972. 68.00 (ISBN 0-12-648350-7). Acad Pr.

Slavkin, Harold C. & Greulich, Richard C., eds. Extracellular Matrix Influences on Gene Expression. 1975. 66.00 (ISBN 0-12-648360-4). Acad Pr.

Slavov, Atanas. Ms. Lampedusa Has Vanished. LC 82-62316. 6.00 (ISBN 0-911050-53-1). Occidental.

Slawski, Carl J. Social Psychological Theories: A Comparative Handbook. 1981. pap. text ed. 9.95x o.p. (ISBN 0-673-15333-9). Scott F.

Slawsky, Norman L., jt. auth. see Weeks, J. Devereux.

Slawson, Chester B., jt. auth. see Kraus, Edward H.

Slawson, John. Unequal Americans: Practices & Politics of Intergroup Relations. LC 78-67909. (Contributions in Political Science: No. 24). 1979. lib. bdg. 25.00x (ISBN 0-313-21118-3, SUA/). Greenwood.

Sleator, William. The Green Futures of Tycho. LC 80-23020. (gr. 5-9). 1981. 10.25 (ISBN 0-525-31007-X, 0996-290). Dutton.

--House of Stairs. (gr. 7 up). 1975. pap. 1.50 o.p. (ISBN 0-380-00507-7, 43786). Avon.

--House of Stairs. LC 73-17417. 176p. (gr. 5-8). 1974. 12.95 (ISBN 0-525-32335-X, 0128-370). Dutton.

--Into the Dream. LC 78-11825. (Illus.). (gr. 4-7). 1979. 9.95 (ISBN 0-525-32583-2, 0966-290). Dutton.

Sleator, William, jt. auth. see Redd, William H.

Slebert, J. & Schrag, A. Office Update: Returning Worker: A Gregg Text Kit. 1982. 20.00 (ISBN 0-07-057291-7); tchr's manual & key 3.50 (ISBN 0-07-057292-5). McGraw.

Sledge, Linda. All Dad's Hats. (Home Mission Graded Ser.). 24p. (gr. 1-3). Date not set. pap. 2.00 (ISBN 0-937170-24-0). Home Mission.

Sledge, Linda C. Shivering Babe, Victorious Lord: The Nativity in Poetry & Art. 1981. 24.95 (ISBN 0-8028-3553-8). Eerdmans.

Sleeman, Brian D. Multiparameter Spectral Theory in Hilbert Space. (Research Notes in Mathematics Ser.: No. 22). 118p. (Orig.). pap. text ed. 17.50 (ISBN 0-273-08414-3). Pitman Pub MA.

Sleeman, Phillip, jt. ed. see McBeath, Ron.

Sleeman, Phillip J., et al. Designing Learning Programs & Environments for Students with Special Learning Needs. (Illus.). 304p. 1983. pap. text ed. 24.75x (ISBN 0-398-04770-7). C C Thomas.

Sleeper, Ann, compiled by. The Concise Metric Conversion Tables. (Illus.). 1980. pap. 2.25 o.p. (ISBN 0-385-14044-4, Dolp). Doubleday.

Sleeper, Harold R. Building Planning & Design Standards for Architects, Engineers, Designers, Consultants, Building Committees, Draftsman & Students. 331p. 1955. 45.95 (ISBN 0-471-79761-8, Pub. by Wiley-Interscience). Wiley.

Sleet, R. J., jt. auth. see Fraser, M. J.

Sleeth, Ronald E. Look Who's Talking: A Guide for Lay Speakers in the Church. LC 77-1171. 1982. pap. 4.95 (ISBN 0-687-22630-9). Abingdon.

--Persuasive Preaching. LC 55-8527. viii, 96p. 1981. pap. 4.95 (ISBN 0-943872-81-2). Andrews Univ Pr.

Sleffel, Linda. The Law & the Dangerous Criminal: Statutory Attempts at Definition & Control. LC 77-287. (Dangerous Offender Project Ser.). 208p. 1977. 19.95x (ISBN 0-669-01481-8). Lexington Bks.

Sleigh. Biology of Protozoa. 1973. 25.50 (ISBN 0-444-19553-X). Elsevier.

Sleigh & Freis. BIMR Cardiology: Vol. 1: Hypertension. 1982. 49.95 (ISBN 0-407-02266-X). Butterworth.

Sleigh, Julian. Thirteen to Nineteen: Growing Free. 1982. pap. 2.50 (ISBN 0-903540-58-4, Pub. by Floris Books). St George Bk Serv.

Sleigh, Michael A. The Biology of Protozoa. 324p. 1973. pap. text ed. 18.50 (ISBN 0-686-43104-9). E Arnold.

Sleight, Jack & Hull, Raymond. The Home Book of Smoke Cooking, Meat, Fish & Game. 1975. pap. 1.50 o.s.i. (ISBN 0-515-03638-2). Jove Pubns.

Sleight, Peter & Freis, Edward. Hypertension: Cardiology, Vol. I. (BIMR Ser.). 320p. 1982. text ed. 39.95 (ISBN 0-686-37992-6). Butterworth.

Sleight, Peter, ed. Arterial Baroreceptors & Hypertension. (Illus.). 1981. text ed. 75.00x (ISBN 0-19-261259-X). Oxford U Pr.

Sleightholme, Des. Better Boat Handling. (Illus.). 192p. 1983. 15.00 (ISBN 0-915160-30-7). Seven Seas.

--The Trouble with Cruising. (Illus.). 113p. 11.95cancelled (ISBN 0-914814-40-0). Sail Bks.

Sleisenger, Marvin H. & Fordtran, John S. Gastrointestinal Disease: Pathophysiology, Diagnosis, Management. 2nd ed. LC 77-2104. (Illus.). 1978. text ed. 80.00 o.p. (ISBN 0-7216-8362-2). Saunders.

Slemmer, Robert E. An Atlas of Gross Neuropathology. 326p. 1983. 48.50 (ISBN 0-87527-239-8). Green.

Slemmons, J. W. Microwelding. 2.50 o.p. (ISBN 0-685-65959-3). Am Welding.

Slemon, G. R. & Straughen, A. Electric Machines. LC 79-16369. (Illus.). text ed. 33.95 (ISBN 0-201-07730-2); solutions manual 3.00 (ISBN 0-201-07731-0). A-W.

Slepian, David, ed. Key Papers in the Development of Information Theory. LC 73-77997. (Illus.). 1974. 30.95 (ISBN 0-87942-027-8). Inst Electrical.

Slesin, Suzanne. The New York Times Home Book of Modern Design: Styles, Problems & Solutions. (Illus.). 280p. 1982. 35.00 (ISBN 0-8129-1027-3). Times Bks.

Slesin, Suzanne, jt. auth. see Kron, Joan.

Slesin, Suzanne, et al. French Style. (Illus.). 288p. 1982. 35.00 (ISBN 0-517-54580-2, C N Potter Bks). Crown.

Slesinger, Doris P. Mothercraft & Infant Health: A Sociodemographic & Sociocultural Approach. LC 81-47181. (Illus.). 224p. 1981. 23.95x (ISBN 0-669-04562-4). Lexington Bks.

Slesnick, William E., jt. auth. see Crowell, Richard H.

Slessarev, Helga. Eduard Morike. (World Authors Ser.). 15.95 (ISBN 0-8057-2634-9, Twayne). G K Hall.

Slesser, Malcolm. The Dictionary of Energy. LC 82-10252. 1983. 29.95 (ISBN 0-8052-3816-6). Schocken.

--Energy in the Economy. LC 78-4234. 1978. 26.00x (ISBN 0-312-25141-6). St Martin.

Slesser, Malcolm & Lewis, Chris. Biological Energy Resources. LC 79-10255. (Energy Ser.). 250p. 1979. 23.50x (ISBN 0-419-11340-1, Pub. by E & FN Spon England); pap. text ed. 15.95x 1982 (ISBN 0-419-12570-1). Methuen Inc.

Slichter, Sumner. The American Economy: Its Problems & Prospects. LC 78-12055. 1979. Repr. of 1948 ed. lib. bdg. 18.75x (ISBN 0-313-21083-7, SLAE). Greenwood.

Slichter, Sumner H., et al. The Impact of Collective Bargaining on Management. 1960. 24.95 (ISBN 0-8157-7984-4). Brookings.

Slide, Anthony, ed. Selected Film Criticism: 1896-1911. LC 82-10623. 134p. 1982. 11.00 (ISBN 0-8108-1575-3). Scarecrow.

--Selected Film Criticism, 1931-1940. LC 82-10642. 292p. 1982. 16.00 (ISBN 0-8108-1570-2). Scarecrow.

--Selected Film Criticism, 1941-1950. LC 81-23344. 280p. 1983. 17.50 (ISBN 0-8108-1593-1). Scarecrow.

Slider, H. C. Practical Petroleum Reservoir Engineering Methods. LC 74-33712. 600p. 1976. 55.95x (ISBN 0-87814-061-1). Pennwell Pub.

S.L.I.G. Buyers Guide. Starting, Lighting, Ignition & Generating Systems. 8th ed. 1983. 8.00 (ISBN 0-685-78814-8). IBMA Pubns.

Sligar, Steve, jt. ed. see Ornston, L. Nicholas.

Slik, Sheila T., jt. auth. see Taynton, Mark.

Slik, Shelia, jt. auth. see Taynton, Mark.

Slikkerveer, L., jt. auth. see Buschkens, W.

Sling, Marian, tr. see Sik, Ota.

Slingerland, Aart, jt. auth. see Wilmot, Philip D.

Slingerland, H. Dixon. The Testaments of the Twelve Patriarchs: A Critical History of Research. LC 75-34233. (Society of Biblical Literature. Monograph). 1977. 13.50 (ISBN 0-89130-062-7, 060021); pap. 9.95 (ISBN 0-686-96882-4). Scholars Pr Ca.

Slinn, W. G., jt. ed. see Engelmann, R. J.

Sliosberg, A. Elsevier's Dictionary of Pharmaceutical Science & Techniques, 2 vols. Incl. Vol. 1: Pharmaceutical Technology. 1968. 132.00 (ISBN 0-444-40544-5); Vol. 2: Materia Medica. 1980. 123.50 (ISBN 0-444-41664-1). Set. 255.50 (ISBN 0-686-85925-1). Elsevier.

--Elsevier's Medical Dictionary. rev. 2nd ed. LC 72-97436. 1452p. (Eng. & Fr. & Ital. & Span. & Ger.). 1975. 181.00 (ISBN 0-444-41103-8). Elsevier.

Slipp, Freude N. Joy of the Limerick Sex Manual: Sex for Sophisticates. 1979. 6.95 o.p. (ISBN 0-934622-01-9). Agora Pr.

Slipp, Samuel. Curative Factors in Dynamic Psychotherapy. (Illus.). 448p. 1981. 23.95 (ISBN 0-07-058190-8). McGraw.

Slive, Seymour. Jacob Van Ruisdael. LC 81-65933. (Illus.). 270p. 1981. 45.00 (ISBN 0-89659-226-X). Abbeville Pr.

Sliwa, Curtis & Alliance of Guardian Angels, Inc. Street-Smart: The Guardian Angel Guide to Safe Living. LC 82-16238. (Illus.). 192p. 1982. pap. 5.95 (ISBN 0-686-82142-4). A-W.

Sloan, Alan D., jt. auth. see Berger, Marc A.

Sloan, Allan. Three Plus One Equals Billions: The Bendix-Martin Marietta War. (Illus.). 1983. 16.50 (ISBN 0-87795-504-2). Arbor Hse.

Sloan, Allan K. Citizen Participation in Transportation Planning: The Boston Experience. LC 74-13977. 200p. 1974. text ed. 17.50 prof ref (ISBN 0-88410-413-3). Ballinger Pub.

Sloan, Anne B., jt. auth. see Pacela, Allan F.

Sloan, Bernard. The Best Friend You'll Ever Have. 224p. 1980. 9.95 o.p. (ISBN 0-517-54003-7). Crown.

Sloan, Blanche C. & Swinburne, Bruce R. Campus Art Museums & Galleries: A Profile. LC 80-23418. 64p. (Orig.). 1981. pap. 9.95x (ISBN 0-8093-1005-8). S Ill U Pr.

Sloan Commission on Government & Higher Education. Program for Renewed Partnership: A Report. 1980. prof ref 22.50x (ISBN 0-88410-193-2). Ballinger Pub.

Sloan, Douglas. Education & Values. LC 79-19832. 1980. pap. text ed. 10.95x (ISBN 0-8077-2574-9). Tchrs Coll.

--Scottish Enlightenment & the American College Ideal. LC 75-132938. 1971. text ed. 14.50x (ISBN 0-8077-2168-9). Tchrs Coll.

Sloan, Earl S. Treatise on the Horse. (Illus.). 1983. Repr. of 1897 ed. softcover 5.00 (ISBN 0-686-64453-0). S J Durst.

Sloan, Ethel. A Kangaroo in the Kitchen: And Other Adventures of an American Family Down Under. LC 77-15437. 1978. 7.95 o.p. (ISBN 0-672-52378-7). Bobbs.

Sloan, Frank A. & Bentkover, Judith D. Access to Ambulatory Care & the U. S. Economy. LC 78-19537. 193p. 1979. 19.95x o.p. (ISBN 0-669-02510-0). Lexington Bks.

Sloan, Frank A. & Steinwald, Bruce. Hospital Labor Markets: Analysis of Wages & Work Force Composition. LC 79-5324. (Illus.). 208p. 1980. 24.95x (ISBN 0-669-03385-5). Lexington Bks.

--Insurance, Regulation, & Hospital Costs. LC 79-3752. (Illus.). 288p. 1980. 28.95x (ISBN 0-669-03472-X). Lexington Bks.

Sloan, Glenna. The Child As Critic: Teaching Literature in the Elementary School. LC 75-23360. 1975. pap. text ed. 6.95x (ISBN 0-8077-2482-3). Tchrs Coll.

Sloan, Harold S. & Zurcher, Arnold J. Dictionary of Economics. LC 70-118099. pap. text ed. 5.95 (ISBN 0-06-463266-0, EH 266, EH). B&N NY.

Sloan, I. Alcohol & Drug Abuse & the Law. LC 80-36962. (Legal Almanac Ser.: No. 27). 117p. 1980. 5.95 (ISBN 0-379-11137-3). Oceana.

Sloan, Irving J. American Landmark Legislation: Primary Materials, 10 vols. LC 75-42876. 1975. 50.00 ea. (ISBN 0-379-10125-4); Set. 500.00. Oceana.

--The Blacks in America 1492-1977: A Chronology & Fact Book. 4th rev. ed. LC 76-5910. (Ethnic Chronology Ser.: No. 2). 169p. 1977. lib. bdg. 8.50x (ISBN 0-379-00524-7). Oceana.

--Environment & the Law. 2nd ed. LC 79-156377. (Legal Almanac Ser: No. 65). 120p. 1979. 5.95 (ISBN 0-379-11114-4). Oceana.

--The Jews in America 1621-1977: A Chronology & Fact Book. 2nd ed. LC 77-26768. (No. 3). 1978. lib. bdg. 8.50 (ISBN 0-379-00530-1). Oceana.

Sloan, Irving J., ed. Child Abuse: Governing Law & Legislation. 128p. 1982. lib. bdg. 5.95 (ISBN 0-379-11142-X). Oceana.

--Protection of Abused Victims: State Laws & Decisions. 1982. 35.00 (ISBN 0-379-10237-4). Oceana.

Sloan, Irving J., ed. see Callahan, Parnell J. & Nussbaum, Louis M.

Sloan, Irving J., ed. see Zarr, Melvyn.

Sloan, Jacob, ed. & tr. see Ringelblum, Emmanuel.

Sloan, Jane. Robert Bresson: A Guide to References & Resources. 1983. 35.00 (ISBN 0-8161-8502-6, Hall Reference). G K Hall.

Sloan, John. New York Etchings: Nineteen Five to Nineteen Forty-Nine. 1978. pap. 5.00 (ISBN 0-486-23651-X). Dover.

Sloan, L. L. & Ragaway, Martin, eds. World's Worst Show Me Jokes. (Humor Special Ser). (Illus.). 1978. pap. 1.50 o.s.i. (ISBN 0-8431-0476-7). Price Stern.

Sloan, M. E. Computer Hardware & Organization. 2nd ed. 500p. 1983. text ed. write for info. (ISBN 0-574-21425-9, 13-4425); write for info. instr's. guide (ISBN 0-574-21426-7). SRA.

Sloan, Marjorie, jt. auth. see Holmquist, Emily.

Sloan, Martha E. Introduction to Minicomputers & Microcomputers. LC 78-74693. 1980. text ed. 28.95 (ISBN 0-201-07279-3). A-W.

Sloan, Mohammad I. Khowar English Dictionary. LC 81-90111. 151p. 1981. 8.95 (ISBN 0-686-36937-8). M Ismail Sloan Pubs.

Sloan, Robert C. A Nice Place to Live. 1982. pap. 2.95 (ISBN 0-553-22507-3). Bantam.

Sloan, Samuel. Sloan's Victorian Buildings: Illustrations & Floor Plans for 60 Residences & Other Structures, 2 vols. in 1. (Illus.). 400p. 1981. pap. 13.95 (ISBN 0-486-24009-6). Dover.

Sloan, Thomas O. & Waddington, Raymond B., eds. The Rhetoric of Renaissance Poetry. LC 73-80824. 1974. 28.50x (ISBN 0-520-02501-6). U of Cal Pr.

Sloan, Thomas O., jt. ed. see Maclay, Joanna M.

Sloan, Tod. Tod Sloan. Luckman, A. Dick, ed. 310p. 1982. Repr. of 1915 ed. lib. bdg. 45.00 (ISBN 0-8495-4965-5). Arden Lib.

Sloane, Arthur. Personnel: The Managing of Human Resources. (Illus.). 608p. 1983. 24.95 (ISBN 0-13-658278-8). P-H.

Sloane, Beverly L., jt. auth. see Sloane, Robert M.

Sloane, David E. The Literary Humor of the Urban Northeast, 1830 to 1890. LC 82-12688. (Illus.). 319p. 1983. text ed. 22.50X (ISBN 0-8071-1055-8). La State U Pr.

Sloane, Eric. Diary of an Early American Boy. (Illus.). 128p. 1983. 14.95 (ISBN 0-8038-1583-2). Hastings.

--Eric Sloane's Weather Book. (Illus.). 1977. pap. 6.25 (ISBN 0-8015-2365-6, 0607-180, Hawthron). Dutton.

--Folklore of American Weather. 1976. pap. 5.95 (ISBN 0-8015-2719-8, 0578-170, Hawthorn). Dutton.

--The Legacy. LC 78-22455. (Funk & W Bk.). (Illus.). 1979. 9.95i (ISBN 0-308-10351-3). T Y Crowell.

--A Museum of Early American Tools. (Illus.). 128p. (Orig.). 1983. 14.95 (ISBN 0-8038-4746-7). Hastings.

--A Reverence for Wood. (Illus.). 128p. 1983. 14.95 (ISBN 0-8038-6367-5). Hastings.

--School Days, 2 vols. Incl. ABC of Early Americana. 64p; The Little Red Schoolhouse. 64p. LC 73-80015. (Illus.). 1973. boxed set 12.95 o.p. (ISBN 0-385-07423-9). Doubleday.

--School Days: Early Americana-Little Red School House, 2 Vols. (Illus.). 112p. (Orig.). 1983. boxed set 12.95 (ISBN 0-8038-6781-6). Hastings.

--Sloan's Almanac & Weather Forecaster. 1977. pap. 5.95 (ISBN 0-8015-6877-3, 0578-170, Hawthorn). Dutton.

Sloane, Ethel. Biology of Women. LC 79-15256. 544p. 1980. 24.00x (ISBN 0-471-02165-2, Pub. by Wiley-Medical). Wiley.

Sloane, Eugene A. The Complete Book of Locks, Keys, Burglar & Smoke Alarms & Other Security Devices. 1979. pap. 2.95 o.p. (ISBN 0-451-08713-5, E8713, Sig). NAL.

Sloane, Howard N., Jr. & MacAulay, Barbara D., eds. Operant Procedures in Remedial Speech & Language Training. LC 81-43724. (Illus.). 458p. 1982. pap. text ed. 14.25 (ISBN 0-8191-2216-5). U Pr of Amer.

Sloane, Irving. Classic Guitar Construction. (Illus.). 1966. 14.00 (ISBN 0-525-08200-X, 01359-410). Dutton.

Sloane, Irving, jt. auth. see Pollack, Richard.

Sloane, Martin. The Supermarket Shopper's Guide to Coupons & Refunds, 1980. 224p. (Orig.). Date not set. pap. 2.95 (ISBN 0-686-65664-4). Bantam.

Sloane, N. J. A Short Course on Error Correcting Codes. (CISM (International Centre for Mechanical Sciences) Ser.: Vol. 188). (Illus.). 76p. 1982. pap. 11.20 (ISBN 0-387-81303-9). Springer-Verlag.

Sloane, N. J., jt. auth. see MacWilliams, F. J.

Sloane, Peter, jt. auth. see Chiplin, Brian.

Sloane, Richard & Wallace, Marie. Private Law Library: Nineteen Eighties & Beyond. LC 79-87893. (Patents, Copyrights, Trademarks, & Literary Property Course Handbook Ser.: 1978-1979). 1979. pap. text ed. 20.00 o.p. (ISBN 0-686-59557-2, G4-3653). PLI.

Sloane, Robert M. & Sloane, Beverly L. A Guide to Health Facilities: Personnel and Management. 2nd ed. LC 76-39863. (Illus.). 210p. 1977. pap. 13.95 o.p. (ISBN 0-8016-4653-7). Mosby.

Sloane, Roscoe C. & Montz, John M. Elements of Topographic Drawing. 2nd ed. (Illus.). 1963. text ed. 19.00 o.p. (ISBN 0-07-058210-6, C). McGraw.

Sloane, Sheila B. The Medical Word Book: A Spelling & Vocabulary Guide to Medical Transcription. LC 72-86455. (Illus.). 923p. 1973. pap. 16.95 o.p. (ISBN 0-7216-8364-9). Saunders.

Sloans, N. J. A Handbook of Integer Sequences. 1973. 27.50 (ISBN 0-12-648550-X). Acad Pr.

Sloat, Barbara F., jt. auth. see Elliott, Alfred M.

Sloat, Clarence, et al. Introduction to Phonology. LC 77-23100. (Illus.). 1978. ref. 16.95 (ISBN 0-13-492207-7). P-H.

Slobin, Dan I. Psycholinguistics. 2nd ed. 1979. pap. text ed. 12.50x (ISBN 0-673-15140-9). Scott F.

Slobodchikoff, C. N., ed. Concepts of Species. LC 76-17090. (Benchman Papers in Systematic & Evolutionary Biology: Vol. 3). 1976. 49.50 (ISBN 0-12-787468-2). Acad Pr.

Slobodkin, Louis. Space Ship Returns to the Apple Tree. LC 58-11080. (Illus.). 128p. (gr. 3-5). 1972. pap. 2.95 (ISBN 0-02-045010-9, Collier). Macmillan.

Slochower, Joyce A. Excessive Eating: The Role of Emotions & Environment. (Center for Policy for Research Monographs: Vol. 3). 128p. 1982. 18.95x (ISBN 0-89885-097-5). Human Sci Pr.

Slockbower, Jean & Blumenfield, Thomas, eds. Collection & Handling of Laboratory Specimens: A Practical Guide. (Illus.). 250p. 1983. pap. text ed. 10.95 (ISBN 0-397-50520-5, Lippincott Medical). Lippincott.

Slocombe, Lorna. Sailing Basics. (Sports Basics Ser.). (Illus.). 48p. (gr. 3-7). 1982. 8.95 (ISBN 0-13-786053-6). P-H.

Slocum. In Place of Transition Metals in Organic Synthesis, Vol. 295. 1977. 12.00 (ISBN 0-89072-041-X). NY Acad Sci.

Slocum, Alfred A., ed. see Council on Legal Education Opportunity.

Slocum, D. W. & Hughes, O. R., eds. Transition Metal Mediated Organic Syntheses. LC 79-24735. (N.Y. Academy of Sciences Annals: Vol. 333). 301p. 1980. 57.00x (ISBN 0-89766-039-0). NY Acad Sci.

Slocum, John, jt. auth. see Hellriegel, Don.

Slocum, John J. A Bibliography of James Joyce: Eighteen Eighty-Two to Nineteen Forty-One. LC 70-138182. 195p. 1972. Repr. of 1953 ed. lib. bdg. 18.50x (ISBN 0-8371-5639-4, SLJJ). Greenwood.

Slocum, John W., Jr., jt. auth. see Hellriegel, Don.

Slocum, Jonah. Celestial Navigation with a Pocket Calculator. 2nd ed. (Illus.). 130p. 1982. pap. text ed. 14.95 (ISBN 0-917410-06-8). Basic Sci Pr.

Slocum, Keith, jt. auth. see McCauley, Rosemarie.

Slocum, Marianna, jt. auth. see Gerdel, Florence.

Slocum, Robert B., ed. Biographical Dictionaries & Related Works: An International Bibliography. LC 67-27789. 1967. 68.00x (ISBN 0-8103-0972-6); supplement no. 1 68.00x (ISBN 0-8103-0973-4); supplement no. 2 68.00x (ISBN 0-8103-0974-2). Gale.

Slocum, Victor. Capt. Joshua Slocum: The Life & Voyages of America's Best Known Sailor. LC 80-28585. (Illus.). 384p. 1983. Repr. of 1950 ed. 17.50 (ISBN 0-911378-04-9). Sheridan.

Sloma, Richard. No-Nonsense Government. LC 82-42727. 248p. 1983. 16.95 (ISBN 0-8128-2901-8). Stein & Day.

Sloman, A. Terence Phormio. (Bolchazy-Carducci Textbook). (Illus.). 176p. 1981. pap. text ed. 7.50x (ISBN 0-86516-003-1). Bolchazy-Carducci.

Sloman, Anne, jt. ed. see Butler, David E.

Sloman, Larry. Reefer Madness: A of Marijuana in America. (Illus.). 360p. 1983. pap. 8.95 (ISBN 0-394-62446-7, Ever). Grove.

--Thin Ice: A Season in Hell with the New York Rangers. 1983. pap. 3.95 (ISBN 0-440-18571-8). Dell.

Slomson, A. B., jt. auth. see Bell, J. L.

Slone, Verna M. What My Heart Wants to Tell. (General Ser.). 1979. lib. bdg. 10.95 (ISBN 0-8161-3007-8, Large Print Bks). G K Hall.

--What My Heart Wants to Tell. LC 78-31688. (Illus.). 1979. 8.95 (ISBN 0-915220-47-4). New Republic.

Slonim, Elsie. Mousie Longtail: The Mouse Who Rose to Fame. 1979. 6.95 o.p. (ISBN 0-533-03622-4). Vantage.

Slonim, Jacob, jt. auth. see Fisher, P. S.

Slonim, Marc. Epic of Russian Literature: From Its Origins Through Tolstoy. 1964. pap. 6.95 o.p. (ISBN 0-19-500713-1, GB). Oxford U Pr.

--Soviet Russian Literature: Writers and Problems, 1917-1977. 2nd ed. LC 76-426661. 1977. 22.50x (ISBN 0-19-502151-7). Oxford U Pr.

--Soviet Russian Literature: Writers & Problems, 1917-1977. 2nd ed. 1977. pap. 9.95 (ISBN 0-19-502152-5, GB184, GB). Oxford U Pr.

Slonim, N. Balfour. Respiratory Physiology. 4th ed. LC 81-11055. (Illus.). 301p. 1981. pap. text ed. 19.95 (ISBN 0-8016-4668-5). Mosby.

Slonneger, J. C. Dynagraph Analysis of Sucker Rod Pumping. 216p. 1961. 24.95x (ISBN 0-87201-216-6). Gulf Pub.

Sloop, Joseph. Television Servicing with Basic Electronics. Date not set. pap. 14.50 Instrs' Guide (ISBN 0-672-21885-2); Student's Manual 10.00 (ISBN 0-672-21880-1). Sams.

Slosberg, Paul S. Neurology. 7th ed. (Medical Examination Review Book Ser.: Vol. 8). 1981. pap. 11.95 (ISBN 0-87488-108-0). Med Exam.

Sloshberg, Willard. Contemporary Society. (Illus.). 1978. pap. text ed. 14.95 (ISBN 0-8299-0140-X); wkbk. avail. (ISBN 0-8299-0574-X). West Pub.

Sloshberg, Willard & Nessmith, William C. Contemporary American Society: An Introduction to Social Science. (Illus.). 600p. 1983. pap. text ed. 13.95 (ISBN 0-314-69671-7). West Pub.

Slosson, Edwin E. American Spirit in Education. 1921. text ed. 8.50x (ISBN 0-686-83467-4). Elliots Bks.

Slosson, Edwin E., tr. see Bergson, Henri.

Slosson, Preston. A Pictorial History of the American People. LC 82-80280. (Illus.). 320p. Date not set. price not set (ISBN 0-528-81548-2). Rand.

Slote, Al. The Devil Rides with Me, Six Fantastic Stories. LC 79-23092. (gr. 4-9). 1980. 8.95 (ISBN 0-416-30141-X). Methuen Inc.

Slote, Alfred. The Biggest Victory. (gr. 3-7). 1977. pap. 1.95 o.p. (ISBN 0-380-00907-2, 52787, Camelot). Avon.

--C.O.L.A.R. LC 80-8723. (Illus.). 160p. (gr. 2-5). 1981. 9.57i (ISBN 0-686-75355-0, JBL-J); PLB 9.89 (ISBN 0-397-31937-1). Har-Row.

--Coraje, Campeon! Ortiz, Victoria, ed. Costantini, Humberto & Brof, Janet, trs. LC 78-20548. (gr. 4-7). 1979. 9.57i (ISBN 0-397-31849-9, HarpJ). Har-Row.

--The Hotshot. (Triumph Books). (Illus.). (gr. 4 up). 1977. PLB 8.90 s&l (ISBN 0-531-00330-2). Watts.

--Jake. 155p. (gr. 5-6). 9.57i (ISBN 0-397-31414-0, HarpJ); pap. 2.50 (ISBN 0-397-31327-6). Har-Row.

--My Father, the Coach. (gr. 3-7). 1977. pap. 1.75 o.p. (ISBN 0-380-01724-5, 54080, Camelot). Avon.

--My Trip to Alpha 1. LC 78-6463. (Illus.). (gr. 3-5). 1978. 9.57i (ISBN 0-397-31810-3, HarpJ). Har-Row.

--Omega Station. LC 82-48461. (Illus.). 160p. (gr. 2-5). 1983. 9.57i (ISBN 0-397-32036-1, JBL-J); PLB 9.89g. Har-Row.

--Rabbit Ears. LC 81-47760. 128p. (gr. 4-7). 1982. 9.57i (ISBN 0-397-31988-6, JBL-J); PLB 8.89g (ISBN 0-397-31989-4). Har-Row.

--Rabbit Ears. LC 81-47760. (A Trophy Bk.). 128p. (gr. 4-7). 1983. pap. 2.84i (ISBN 0-06-440134-0, Trophy). Har-Row.

--Termination: The Closing at Baker Plant. LC 69-13100. 360p. 1969. 12.00x (ISBN 0-87944-219-0). Inst Soc Res.

--Tony & Me. LC 74-5182. 160p. (gr. 4-6). 1974. 8.95i (ISBN 0-397-31507-4, HarpJ). Har-Row.

Slote, Michael A. Reason & Scepticism. (Muirhead Library of Philosophy). 1970. text ed. 17.50x (ISBN 0-391-00026-8). Humanities.

Slotkin, Richard, jt. ed. see Folsom, James K.

Slotnick, Daniel L. & Slotnick, Joan L. Computers: Their Structure, Use, & Influence. (Illus.). 1979. ref. 19.95 (ISBN 0-13-165068-8). P-H.

Slotnick, Joan L., jt. auth. see Slotnick, Daniel L.

Slottman, William B., jt. ed. see Janos, Andrew C.

Slover, Elizabeth, jt. auth. see Harris, Ollie K.

Slowe, Richard. Innocents in Africa. 1980. 25.00x o.p. (ISBN 0-902628-79-8, Pub. by RAC). State Mutual Bk.

Sloyan, Gerard S. Jesus on Trial: The Development of the Passion Narratives & Their Historical & Ecumenical Implications. 156p. pap. 3.75 (ISBN 0-686-95173-5). ADL.

Sloyan, Gerard S., jt. ed. see Swidler, Leonard.

Sloyan, Virginia, ed. Liturgy Committee Handbook. 1971. pap. 5.75 o.p. (ISBN 0-918208-00-9). Liturgical Conf.

--Signs, Songs & Stories. (Illus.). 160p. 1982. pap. 8.50 (ISBN 0-8146-1285-7). Liturgical Pr.

Sluglett, Peter, compiled by. Theses on Islam, Middle East, & Northwest Africa, 1880-1978. 200p. 1982. 28.00 (ISBN 0-7201-1651-1, Pub. by Mansell England). Wilson.

Slurzberg, Morris & Osterheld, William. Essentials of Communication Electronics. 3rd ed. (Illus.). 784p. 1973. text ed. 24.95 (ISBN 0-07-058309-9, G); ans 1.50 (ISBN 0-07-058310-2). McGraw.

--Essentials of Electricity-Electronics. 3rd ed. 1965. text ed. 17.95 o.p. (ISBN 0-07-058260-2, G); answers 1.50 o.p. (ISBN 0-07-058261-0). McGraw.

SLUSA, ed. see Hanriot, Hugo.

Slusher, Harold S. Critique of Radiometric Dating. LC 73-79063. (ICR Technical Monograph: No. 2). (Illus.). 46p. 1973. pap. 5.95 (ISBN 0-89051-011-3). CLP Pubs.

Slusky, Thea D. The Skier's Year-Round Exercise Guide: Safe, Effective Techniques for Men & Women. 1978. 11.95 (ISBN 0-8128-2512-8); pap. 11.95 (ISBN 0-8128-6003-9). Stein & Day.

Slusser, George E. The Bradbury Chronicles. LC 77-774. (The Milford Series: Popular Writers of Today Vol. 4). 1977. lib. bdg. 9.95x (ISBN 0-89370-107-6); pap. 3.95x (ISBN 0-89370-207-2). Borgo Pr.

--The Classic Years of Robert A. Heinlein. LC 77-24626. (The Milford Ser.: Popular Writers of Today Ser.: Vol. 11). 1977. lib. bdg. 9.95x (ISBN 0-89370-116-5); pap. 3.95x (ISBN 0-89370-216-1). Borgo Pr.

--The Delany Intersection: Samuel R. Delany Considered As a Writer of Semi-Precious Words. LC 77-24580. (The Milford Ser.: Popular Writers of Today: Vol. 10). 1977. lib. bdg. 9.95x (ISBN 0-89370-114-9); pap. 3.95x (ISBN 0-89370-214-5). Borgo Pr.

--Frank Herbert: Prophet of Dune. LC 78-1310. (The Milford Ser: Popular Writers of Today: Vol. 14). Date not set. lib. bdg. 9.95x (ISBN 0-89370-119-X); pap. 3.95x (ISBN 0-89370-219-6). Borgo Pr. Postponed.

--Harlan Ellison: Unrepentant Harlequin. LC 77-768. (Milford Ser.: Popular Writers of Today: Vol. 6). 1977. lib. bdg. 9.95x (ISBN 0-89370-109-2); pap. 3.95x (ISBN 0-89370-209-9). Borgo Pr.

--I. Asimov: The Foundations of His Science Fiction. LC 78-1042. (Milford Ser.: Popular Writers of Today: Vol. 15). Date not set. lib. bdg. 9.95x (ISBN 0-89370-122-X); pap. 3.95x (ISBN 0-89370-222-6). Borgo Pr. Postponed.

--Robert A. Heinlein: Stranger in His Own Land. 2nd rev. ed. LC 77-5657. (The Milford Ser: Popular Writers of Today Vol. 1). 1977. lib. bdg. 9.95x (ISBN 0-89370-110-6); pap. 3.95x (ISBN 0-89370-210-2). Borgo Pr.

--The Space Odysseys of Arthur C. Clarke. LC 77-24438. (The Milford Ser: Popular Writers of Today: Vol. 8). 1978. lib. bdg. 9.95x (ISBN 0-89370-112-2); pap. 3.95x (ISBN 0-89370-212-9). Borgo Pr.

Slusser, George E., et al, eds. Bridges to Science Fiction. LC 80-16622. (Alternatives Ser.). 176p. 1980. 12.95 (ISBN 0-8093-0961-0). S Ill U Pr.

--Coordinates: Placing Science Fiction & Fantasy. (Alternatives Ser.). 264p. 1983. price not set (ISBN 0-8093-1105-4). S Ill U Pr.

Slusser, Robert M., jt. ed. see Wolin, Simon.

Slutzkin, D., ed. see Emanuel, N. M. & Knorre, D. G.

Slutzkin, D., ed. see Kiselev, A. V. & Lygin, V. I.

Slutzkin, D., ed. see Lipatov, Yu. S & Sergeeva, L. M.

Slutzkin, D., tr. see Tugarinov, A. I.

Sluyser, M., jt. ed. see Hilgers, J.

Sluzar, Sophia, jt. ed. see Bialers, Seweryn.

Sly, Michael R. Pediatric Allergy. 2nd ed. (Medical Outline Ser.). 1980. pap. 25.00 (ISBN 0-87488-624-4). Med Exam.

Sly, Peter G. Sediment-Freshwater Interaction. 1982. text ed. 125.00 (ISBN 90-6193-760-4, Pub. by Junk Pubs Netherlands). Kluwer Boston.

Slyke, Helen Van see Van Slyke, Helen.

Slyke, Helen van see Van Slyke, Helen.

Slyke, Helen Van see Van Slyke, Helen.

Slyke, Helen Van see Van Slyke, Helen & Ashton, Sharon.

Slyke, Helen Van see Van Slyke, Helen & Elward, James.

Slyke, L. L. van see Van Slyke, L. L. & Price, W. V.

Smagula, Howard J. Currents: Contemporary Directions in the Visual Arts. 384p. 1983. text ed. 16.95 (ISBN 0-13-195743-0). P-H.

Smail, R. C. Crusading Warfare, 1097-1193: A Contribution to Medieval Military History. LC 67-26956. (Cambridge Studies in Medieval Life & Thought Ser: No. 3). 1967. 42.50 (ISBN 0-521-21315-0); pap. 13.95 (ISBN 0-521-09730-4). Cambridge U Pr.

Smail, William M., ed. Quintilian on Education. LC 66-13554. 1966. text ed. 9.50 (ISBN 0-8077-2173-5); pap. text ed. 4.50x (ISBN 0-8077-2170-0). Tchrs Coll.

Smaldon, G. British Coastal Shrimps & Prawns. (Synposes of the British Fauna Ser.). 1979. 12.00 o.s.i. (ISBN 0-12-649250-6). Acad Pr.

Smaldone, J. P. Warfare in the Sokoto Caliphate. LC 75-27795. (African Studies Ser.: No. 19). (Illus.). 1977. 44.50 (ISBN 0-521-21069-0). Cambridge U Pr.

Small, Arnold M. Elements of Hearing Science: A Programmed Text. LC 77-20110. (Communications Disorders Ser.). 1978. 17.95 (ISBN 0-471-01732-9). Wiley.

Small, Bertrice. Beloved. 560p. (Orig.). 1983. pap. 6.95 (ISBN 0-345-29356-8). Ballantine.

--The Kadin. 1978. pap. 3.50 (ISBN 0-380-01699-0, 80002). Avon.

--Love Wild & Fair. 1978. pap. 3.95 (ISBN 0-380-40030-8, 82867-7). Avon.

--Skye O'Malley. 480p. 1981. pap. 2.95 (ISBN 0-345-28680-4). Ballantine.

Small Business Tax Equity Conference. Proceedings. 1983. write for info. Am Inst CPA.

Small, Christopher. Music, Society, Education. LC 77-81648. (Illus.). 1977. 15.50 (ISBN 0-02-872440-2). Schirmer Bks.

Small Computers in Business Seminar, London. Small Computers in Business. 37p. 1981. pap. 28.60x (ISBN 0-686-97777-7). Renouf.

Small, David & Small, Sandy, eds. The Creative Atari. LC 82-71997. (Illus.). 250p. 1983. pap. 15.95 (ISBN 0-916688-34-8). Creative Comp.

Small, Dwight H. After You've Said I Do. 1976. pap. 1.75 (ISBN 0-515-09678-4). Jove Pubns.

--Marriage As Equal Partnership. 1980. pap. 3.95 (ISBN 0-8010-8177-7). Baker Bk.

Small, Emmett, ed. see De Purucker, G.

Small, Emmett, ed. see Wright, L. L.

Small, Emmett, ed. see Wright, Leoline L., et al.

Small, Harold A., ed. see Davis, William H.

Small, Herbert. The Library of Congress: Its Architecture & Decoration. Reed, Henry H., ed. (Classical America in Art & Architecture Ser.). (Illus.). 1983. 19.95 (ISBN 0-393-01587-4); pap. 6.50 (ISBN 0-393-30038-2). Norton.

Small, HyDee. The Complete Bed Building Book. (Illus.). 1979. 12.95 o.p. (ISBN 0-8306-9822-1); pap. 7.95 o.p. (ISBN 0-8306-1124-X, 1124). TAB Bks.

Small, Jacquelyn. Transformers: The Therapists of the Future. 2nd ed. (Illus.). 325p. 1983. pap. 9.95 (ISBN 0-939344-01-7). Eupsychian.

Small, John & Clark, Michael. Slopes & Weathering. LC 81-18025. (Cambridge Topics in Geography Second Ser.). 112p. 1982. 12.95 (ISBN 0-521-23340-2); pap. 6.95 (ISBN 0-521-29926-8). Cambridge U Pr.

Small, John, ed. see Monkhouse, F. J.

Small, Kenneth A. Geographically Differentiated Taxes & the Location of Firms. 27p. 1982. pap. 5.00 (ISBN 0-938882-03-1, Dist. by Transaction Bks). PURRC.

Small, Laurence, jt. auth. see Hyatt, Herman R.

Small, Leonard. The Minimal Brain Dysfunctions: Diagnosis & Treatment. 320p. 1982. text ed. 22.95 (ISBN 0-02-929300-6). Free Pr.

Small, Lucile J. Not by Prescription. 64p. pap. 2.95 (ISBN 0-686-82633-7). Review & Herald.

Small, Melvin, jt. auth. see Singer, J. David.

Small, Miriam R. Oliver Wendell Holmes. (U. S. Authors Ser.: No. 29). 1962. lib. bdg. 10.95 o.p. (ISBN 0-8057-0380-2, Twayne). G K Hall.

Small, Robert Van Dyke. Crystals of Indoctrination. 80p. 1982. 6.00 (ISBN 0-682-49906-4). Exposition.

Small, Ruth. Fatsy Patsy. (Illus.). 64p. 1983. 6.95 (ISBN 0-89962-329-8). Todd & Honeywell.

Small, Ruth & Sundick, Sherry. Potpourri. new ed. (Illus.). 48p. 1978. pap. 2.00 (ISBN 0-932044-07-7). M O Pub Co.

Small, Sandy, jt. ed. see Small, David.

Small, Verna, ed. see Hoffman, Emanuel.

Small, W. Emmett & Todd, Helen, eds. Theosophical Manuals. Incl. Vol. 1. What Is Theosophy? pap. 2.25 (ISBN 0-913004-18-9); Vol. 2. Reincarnation. pap. 3.25 (ISBN 0-8356-0453-5); Vol. 3. Karma. pap. 2.00 (ISBN 0-913004-16-2); Vol. 5. After Death What? pap. 2.50 (ISBN 0-913004-15-4, 913004-15); Vol. 8. Cycles. pap. 2.50 (ISBN 0-913004-19-7); Theosophy & Christianity. pap. 2.00 (ISBN 0-913004-17-0). (Twelve in Ser.). 1975. pap. 24.00 set. Point Loma Pub.

Small, W. Emmett, ed. see Benjamin, Elsie.

Small, W. Emmett, ed. see De Purucker, G.

Small, W. Emmett, ed. see De Purucker, G. & Tingley, Katherine.

Small, W. Emmett, ed. see De Zirkoff, Boris.

Small, W. Emmett, ed. see Edge, Henry T.

Small, W. Emmett, ed. see Greenwalt, Emmett A.

Small, W. Emmett, ed. see Ross, Lydia.

Small, W. Emmett, ed. see Ryan, Charles J.

Small, W. Emmett, ed. see Tingley, Katherine.

Small, W. Emmett, ed. see Van Pelt, G.

Small, W. Emmett, ed. see Van Pelt, Gertrude W.

Small, W. Emmett, ed. see Wright, Leoline L.

Smalley, Barbara. George Eliot & Flaubert: Pioneers of the Modern Novel. LC 73-85446. ix, 240p. 1974. 13.50x (ISBN 0-8214-0136-X, 82-81396). Ohio U Pr.

Smalley, Barbara, ed. see Lewes, George H.

Smalley, Harold E. Hospital Management Engineering: A Guide to the Improvement of Hospital Management Systems. (Illus.). 480p. 1982. 29.95 (ISBN 0-13-394775-0). P-H.

Smalley, I. J., ed. Loess: Lithology & Genesis. LC 75-30690. (Benchmark Papers in Geology: Vol. 26). 448p. 1975. 56.00 (ISBN 0-12-787472-0). Acad Pr.

Smalley, James. Funding Sources for Fire Departments. LC 82-62452. 75p. 1982. pap. text ed. 15.00 (ISBN 0-87765-246-5, FSP-60). Natl Fire Prot.

Smalley, S. S., jt. auth. see Lindars, B.

Smalley, W. A., jt. auth. see De Waard, J.

Smalley, Webster, ed. see Hughes, Langston.

Smalley, William A., ed. Readings in Missionary Anthropology II. 2nd rev. enl. ed. LC 78-6009. (Applied Cultural Anthropology Ser.). 1978. pap. text ed. 12.95x o.p. (ISBN 0-87808-731-1). William Carey.

Smallman, R. E., jt. auth. see Loretto, M. H.

Smallpiece, Basil. Of Comets & Queens. 300p. 1981. 35.00x (ISBN 0-906393-10-8, Pub. by Airlife England). State Mutual Bk.

Smallwood, Charles, et al. The Cable Car Book. LC 80-65238. (Illus.). 160p. 1980. 25.00 o.p. (ISBN 0-89087-280-5). Celestial Arts.

Smallwood, FRank. The Other Candidates: Third Parties in Presidential Elections. LC 82-40478. (Illus.). 312p. 1983. 20.00; pap. 10.95 (ISBN 0-87451-257-3). U Pr of New Eng.

Smallwood, James M., jt. auth. see Bell, Samuel E.

Smallwood, James M., ed. see Rogers, Will.

Smallwood, W. L. Life Science. 1972. 19.64 (ISBN 0-07-058415-X); tchr's. ed. 24.00 (ISBN 0-07-058416-8); work study guide, pupil's ed. 5.32 (ISBN 0-07-058418-4); work study guide, tchr's ed. 6.84 (ISBN 0-07-058419-2); tests 48.20 (ISBN 0-07-058417-6). McGraw.

Smallwood, William. Challenges to Science: General Science for Tomorrow's World, Pupil's Edition. (Illus.). 1980. text ed. 18.96 (ISBN 0-07-058431-1, W); tchr's. ed. 23.20 (ISBN 0-07-058432-X); wkbk. 6.36 (ISBN 0-07-059350-7); tests 46.64 (ISBN 0-07-058433-8). McGraw.

Smallwood, William L. Life Science. 2nd ed. (Challenges to Science Ser.). (Illus.). 1978. text ed. 18.96 (ISBN 0-07-058420-6, W); tchr's. ed. 23.20 (ISBN 0-07-058421-4); wk. study guide 6.36 (ISBN 0-07-068310-7); tests 46.64 (ISBN 0-07-058422-2). McGraw.

Smal-Stocki, Roman. Shevchenko Meets America. LC 64-20248. pap. 6.95 (ISBN 0-87462-310-3). Marquette.

Smal-Stocki, Roman & Sokolnicki, Alfred J., eds. Russian & Communist Imperialism in Action, 2 vols. (Marquette Slavic Ser.). Vol. 1. pap. 12.95 (ISBN 0-87462-306-5); Vol. 2. pap. 13.95 (ISBN 0-87462-307-3). Marquette.

Smardon, Richard C., ed. The Future of Wetlands: Assessing Visual-Cultural Values. LC 78-72316. (Illus.). 240p. 1983. text ed. 34.50x (ISBN 0-86598-020-9). Allanheld.

Smaridge, Norah. The Mysteries in the Commune. LC 82-45389. (High Interest, Low Vocabulary Ser.). (Illus.). 160p. (gr. 4). 1982. PLB 10.95 (ISBN 0-396-08076-6). Dodd.

--The Mystery at Greystone Hall. LC 79-52045. (High Interest-Low Vocabulary Ser.). (Illus.). (gr. 6-9). 1979. 7.95 (ISBN 0-396-07733-1). Dodd.

--What's on Your Plate? LC 81-17684. 32p. (gr. k-3). 1982. 7.50 (ISBN 0-687-44911-1). Abingdon.

Smarr, Janet L., tr. from Ital. Italian Renaissance Tales. (Illus.). 375p. 1983. pap. 13.95 (ISBN 0-933760-03-5). Solaris Pr.

Smarr, Larry. Sources of Gravitational Radiation. LC 79-50177. (Illus.). 1979. 32.50 (ISBN 0-521-22778-X). Cambridge U Pr.

Smart, Alastair. The Assisi Problem & the Art of Giotto. LC 81-81724. (Illus.). 310p. 1983. Repr. of 1971 ed. lib. bdg. 85.00 (ISBN 0-87817-283-1). Hacker.

Smart, Albert. Planning Guide for the Beginning Retailer. LC 79-25510. 1979. 6.95 (ISBN 0-86730-540-1). Lebhar Friedman.

Smart, Barry see Littlejohn, Gary, et al.

Smart, Bath C. & Crofton, H. T. Dialect of the English Gypsies. 2nd ed. LC 68-22050. 1968. Repr. of 1875 ed. 34.00x (ISBN 0-8103-3292-2). Gale.

Smart, Borlase. Seascape Painting Step-By-Step. LC 70-82748. (Illus.). 144p. 1969. 15.00 o.p. (ISBN 0-8230-4740-7); pap. 9.95 o.p. (ISBN 0-8230-4741-5). Watson-Guptill.

Smart, Christopher. Selected Poems. Rev. ed. Walsh, Marcus, ed. (Fyfield Ser.). 118p. (Orig.). 1979. pap. 5.25x (ISBN 0-85635-307-8, Pub. by New Pr England). Humanities.

Smart, D. R. Fixed Point Theorems. (Cambridge Tracts in Mathematics: No. 66). (Illus.). 100p. 1980. pap. 14.95x (ISBN 0-521-29833-4). Cambridge U Pr.

Smart, H. R. Philosophy & Its History. LC 62-9573. vi, 170p. 1962. pap. 5.00x (ISBN 0-87548-050-0). Open Court.

Smart, James D. The Cultural Subversion of the Biblical Faith: Life in the 20th Century Under the Sign of the Cross. LC 77-22063. 1977. pap. 5.95 (ISBN 0-664-24148-4). Westminster.

--The Past, Present, & Future of Biblical Theology. LC 79-16943. 1979. softcover 8.95 (ISBN 0-664-24284-7). Westminster.

--The Strange Silence of the Bible in the Church: A Study in Hermeneutics. LC 72-118323. 1970. 6.00 (ISBN 0-664-20894-0); pap. 4.95 (ISBN 0-664-24894-2). Westminster.

--The Teaching Ministry of the Church: An Examination of Basic Principles of Christian Education. LC 54-10569. 1971. pap. 5.95 (ISBN 0-664-24910-8). Westminster.

Smart, James D., jt. ed. see Olin, John C.

Smart, James G., ed. A Radical View: Agate Dispatches of Whitelaw Reid, 1861-1865, 2 vols. LC 75-20227. (Illus.). 1976. 22.95xset o.p. (ISBN 0-87870-030-7). Vol. 1 (ISBN 0-87870-031-5). Vol. 2 (ISBN 0-87870-032-3). Memphis St Univ.

Smart, James R. Modern Geometries. 2nd ed. Wisner, Robert J., ed. LC 77-15784. (Contemporary Undergraduate Mathematics). (Illus.). 1978. text ed. 23.95 (ISBN 0-8185-0265-7); inst. manual upon adoption of text free (ISBN 0-685-86623-8). Brooks-Cole.

Smart, John J. Philosophy & Scientific Realism. 1963. text ed. 8.50x (ISBN 0-7100-3617-5). Humanities.

Smart, K. F., ed. Malnutrition & Endemic Diseases: Their Effects on Education in the Developing Countries. (Educational Research & Practice Ser., No. 3). (Illus.). 135p. (Orig.). 1972. pap. 7.50 o.p. (ISBN 0-685-38711-9, U364, UNESCO). Unipub.

Smart, Lana. Recruiting Qualified Disabled Workers: An Employer's Directory to Placement Services in the Greater New York Area. LC 79-92836. 160p. 1980. 5.59 (ISBN 0-686-38817-8). Human Res Ctr.

Smart, Lana, jt. auth. see McCarthy, Henry.

Smart, Lana, compiled by. Recruting Qualified Disabled Workers: An Employer's Directory to Placement Services in the Greater New York Area. LC 79-92836. 160p. 1980. 5.95 (ISBN 0-686-38815-1). Human Res Ctr.

Smart, Laura S & Smart, Mollie S. Families: Developing Realtionships. 2nd ed. (Illus.). 1980. text ed. 22.95x (ISBN 0-02-411930-X). Macmillan.

Smart, Margaret A. Focus on Pre-Algebra. (Illus.). 48p. (Orig.). (gr. 6-9). 1983. pap. text ed. 4.94 (ISBN 0-918932-81-5). Activity Resources.

Smart, Mollie S. & Smart, Russell C. Development & Relationships, 4 vols. 2nd ed. Incl. Vol. 1. Infants. 370p. 11.95x (ISBN 0-02-411970-9); Vol. 2. Pre-School Children. 356p. 11.95x (ISBN 0-02-412040-5); Vol. 3. School-Age Children. 340p. 11.95x (ISBN 0-02-411990-3); Vol. 4. Adolescents. 310p. 11.95 (ISBN 0-02-412120-7). (Illus.). 1978. 11.95 ea. Macmillan.

Smart, Mollie S., jt. auth. see Smart, Laura S.

Smart, Mollie S., et al. Children-Development & Relationships. 4th ed. 1982. text ed. 23.95 (ISBN 0-02-411910-5). Macmillan.

Smart, Ninian. The Concept of Worship. 1972. 12.95 o.p. (ISBN 0-312-16030-5). St Martin.

--A Dialogue of Religions. LC 79-8730. (The Library of Philosophy & Theology). 142p. 1981. Repr. of 1960 ed. lib. bdg. 19.25x (ISBN 0-313-22187-1, SMDR). Greenwood.

--Doctrine & Argument in Indian Philosophy. 1964. text ed. 13.50x o.p. (ISBN 0-391-00696-7). Humanities.

--The Philosophy of Religion. 1979. 15.95x (ISBN 0-19-520138-8); pap. 6.95 (ISBN 0-19-520139-6). Oxford U Pr.

--Secular Education & the Logic of Religion: Heslington Lectures, University of York, 1966. 1969. text ed. 5.00x o.p. (ISBN 0-571-08284-X). Humanities.

--Worldviews: Crosscultural Explorations in Human Beliefs. (Illus.). 224p. 1983. 12.95 (ISBN 0-686-83823-8, ScribT). Scribner.

Smart, Ninian & Hecht, Richard, eds. Sacred Texts of the World: A Universal Anthology. 1982. 27.50 (ISBN 0-8245-0483-6). Crossroad NY.

Smart, Paul. The Illustrated Encyclopedia of the Butterfly World. (Illus.). 275p. 1981. 14.98 o.p. (ISBN 0-89196-106-2, Bk Value Intl). Quality Bks IL.

Smart, Reginald G. The New Drinkers: Teenage Use & Abuse of Alcohol. 5.95 o.p. (ISBN 0-686-92230-1, 4287). Hazelden.

Smart, Russell C., jt. auth. see Smart, Mollie S.

Smart, T., jt. auth. see Hodgetts, R.

Smart, Terry L., jt. auth. see Kownslar, Allan O.

Smart, W. M. Textbook on Spherical Astronomy. 6th ed. LC 76-50643. (Illus.). 1977. 57.50 (ISBN 0-521-21516-1); pap. 21.95x (ISBN 0-521-29180-1). Cambridge U Pr.

Smart, Walter K. English Review Grammar. 4th ed. 1940. pap. 11.95 (ISBN 0-13-282897-9). P-H.

Smart, William. Eight Modern Essayists. 3rd ed. 382p. 1980. pap. text ed. 9.95x (ISBN 0-312-23976-9); instr's. manual avail. (ISBN 0-312-23977-7). St Martin.

Smeathers, Bryan K. Prepare for & Survive a Nuclear Attack! LC 82-73105. (Illus.). 120p. (Orig.). 1983. pap. write for info. (ISBN 0-910629-00-5). Audubon Pub Co.

Smeaton, R. W. Motor Application & Maintenance Handbook. 1969. 51.25 (ISBN 0-07-058438-9, P&RB). McGraw.

--Switchgear & Control Handbook. 1976. 51.25 (ISBN 0-07-058439-7, P&RB). McGraw.

Smedes, Lewis. Sexologia para Cristianos. Sanchez, Jorge, tr. from Eng. 288p. 1982. pap. 4.95 (ISBN 0-89922-175-0). Edit Caribe.

Smedes, Lewis B. How Can It Be All Right When Everything Is All Wrong. LC 82-47756. 128p. (Orig.). 1982. pap. 5.72i (ISBN 0-06-067409-1, HarpR). Har-Row.

--Mere Morality: What God Expects from Ordinary People. 336p. 1983. 14.95 (ISBN 0-8028-3571-6). Eerdmans.

--Union with Christ: A Biblical View of the New Life in Jesus Christ. rev. ed. Orig. Title: All Things Made New. 208p. 1983. pap. 4.95 (ISBN 0-8028-1963-X). Eerdmans.

Smedley, Agnes. Daughter of Earth: A Novel. 420p. 1973. 10.00 (ISBN 0-912670-87-8); pap. 5.50 (ISBN 0-686-85951-0). Feminist Pr.

Smedley, Dan. Programming the PL-I Way. (Illus.). 294p. 1982. 15.95 (ISBN 0-8306-0092-2); pap. 9.95 (ISBN 0-8306-1414-1, 1414). TAB Bks.

Smeed, Victor E. Power Model Boats. (Illus.). 128p. 7.25x o.p. (ISBN 0-85344-065-4). Intl Pubns Serv.

Smeets, J. R. La Bible de Mace de la Charite Vol. V: Cantiques des Catntiques, Maccabees. (Leidse Romanistische Reeks: Vol. 10). (Illus.). vii, 303p. 1982. pap. write for info. (ISBN 90-04-06776-0). E J Brill.

Smellie & Adams. Biochemistry of Nucleic Acids. 9th ed. 420p. 41.00x (ISBN 0-412-22680-4, Pub. by Chapman & Hall England); pap. 19.95x (ISBN 0-412-22690-1). Methuen Inc.

Smelser, George K., ed. Structure of the Eye. 1961. 64.00 (ISBN 0-12-648950-5). Acad Pr.

Smelser, Marshal L. Democratic Republic, 1801-1815. Commager, Henry S. & Morris, Richard S., eds. LC 68-28218. (New American Nation Series). (Illus.). 1968. 21.10i (ISBN 0-06-013927-7, HarpT). Har-Row.

Smelser, Marshall. Democratic Republic, Eighteen Hundred One to Eighteen Fifteen. Commager, Henry S. & Morris, Richard B., eds. (New American Nations Ser). 1968. pap. 8.95xi (ISBN 0-06-131406-4, TB1406, Torch). Har-Row.

Smelser, Neil J. Comparative Methods in the Social Science. LC 75-42020. (Illus.). 272p. 1976. pap. text ed. 16.95x (ISBN 0-13-154138-2). P-H.

--Sociology. (Ser. in Sociology). (Illus.). 640p. 1981. text ed. 22.95 (ISBN 0-13-820829-8). P-H.

--The Sociology of Economic Life. 2nd ed. (Illus.). text ed. 11.95 op (ISBN 0-13-821579-0); pap. text ed. 9.95 (ISBN 0-13-821561-8). P-H.

Smelser, Neil J. & Content, Robin. The Changing Academic Market: General Trends & a Berkeley Case Study. 1980. 24.95x (ISBN 0-520-03753-7). U of Cal Pr.

Smelser, Neil J. & Almond, Gabriel, eds. Public Higher Education in California. 1974. 38.50x (ISBN 0-520-02510-5). U of Cal Pr.

Smelser, Neil J., ed. see Handel, Judith.

Smereczynska, Anastasia, compiled by. How to Make Christmas Tree Ornaments. Jarymowycz, Mary, tr. from Ukranian. (Illus.). 80p. (Orig.). 1982. 6.00 (ISBN 0-686-38965-4). UNWLA.

Smernoff, Richard A. Andre Chenier. (World Author Ser.). 1977. lib. bdg. 15.95 (ISBN 0-8057-6258-2, Twayne). G K Hall.

Smetana, Andrew O., jt. auth. see Smetana, Frederick O.

Smetana, Frederick O. & Smetana, Andrew O. FORTRAN Codes for Classical Methods in Linear Dynamics. 408p. 1982. 12.95x (ISBN 0-07-058440-0). McGraw.

Smethurst, Richard J. A Social Basic for Prewar Japanese Militarism: The Army & the Rural Community. (Center for Japanese & Korean Studies). 1974. 38.50x (ISBN 0-520-02552-0). U of Cal Pr.

Smethurst, Wood. Teaching Young Children to Read at Home. 1975. 14.95 (ISBN 0-07-058443-5, P&RB). McGraw.

Smeyak, G. Paul. Broadcast News Writing. 2nd ed. LC 82-9293. (Grid Series in Advertising & Journalism). 216p. 1983. pap. text ed. 11.95 (ISBN 0-88244-255-4). Grid Pub.

Smeyak, Paul. Broadcast News Writing. 2nd ed. LC 82-9293. (Grid Series in Advertising & Journalism). 300p. 1983. pap. text ed. 11.95 (ISBN 0-686-42906-0). Grid Pub.

Smialowski, Arthur, jt. auth. see Currie, Donald J.

Smiddy, F. G. Tutorials in Surgery, No. 3. 288p. 1982. text ed. 22.95 (ISBN 0-272-79661-1). Pitman Pub MA.

Smidt, J., ed. see Joint ISMAR-AMPERE International Conference on Magnetic Resonance.

Smidt, Rita, tr. see Petonnet, Colette.

Smidt, Seymour, jt. auth. see Bierman, Harold, Jr.

Smil, Vaclav & Nachman, Paul. Energy Analysis & Agriculture: An Application to U. S. Corn Production. (Special Studies in Agricultural Science & Policy). 175p. 1982. lib. bdg. 25.00 (ISBN 0-86531-167-6). Westview.

Smilansky, M. Priorities in Education: Preschool; Evidence & Conclusions. (Working Paper: No. 323). ii, 72p. 1979. 5.00 (ISBN 0-686-36041-9, WP-0323). World Bank.

Smiles, Samuel. Josiah Wedgewood. LC 71-141603. 1971. Repr. of 1894 ed. 37.00x (ISBN 0-8103-3617-0). Gale.

--Lives of the Engineers: Selections from Samuel Smiles. Hughes, Thomas P., ed. 1966. 15.00 (ISBN 0-262-08026-5). MIT Pr.

Smiley, Albert K. Competitive Bidding Under Uncertainty: The Case of Offshore Oil. LC 79-856. 136p. 1979. prof ref 22.50x (ISBN 0-88410-671-3). Ballinger Pub.

Smiley, Emma. Search for Certainty. 1972. pap. 2.50 (ISBN 0-87516-159-6). De Vorss.

Smiley, Jane. At Paradise Gate. 1981. 12.95 o.s.i. (ISBN 0-671-42598-6). S&S.

Smiley, Nixon. Crowder Tales. (Illus.). 169p. Date not set. 5.95 (ISBN 0-686-84216-2). Banyan Bks.

Smiley, R. W., ed. Compendium of Turfgrass Diseases. LC 82-73593. (Ninth in Compendium Ser.). (Illus.). 100p. 1983. pap. 12.00 member (ISBN 0-89054-049-7); pap. 15.00 nonmember (ISBN 0-686-82687-6). Am Phytopathological Soc.

Smiley, Sam. Playwriting: The Structure of Action. LC 78-125077. (Theatre & Drama Ser). 1971. pap. 14.95 ref. ed. (ISBN 0-13-684530-4). P-H.

Smiley, Virginia. Liza Hunt, Pediatric Nurse. 192p. (YA) 1976. 6.95 (ISBN 0-685-64248-8, Avalon). Bouregy.

--Nurse Karen's Summer of Fear. (YA) 1979. 6.95 (ISBN 0-685-90725-2, Avalon). Bouregy.

--Return to Love. (Silver Bell). 192p. 1982. pap. 1.95 o.s.i. (ISBN 0-8439-1156-5, Leisure Bks). Nordon Pubns.

--Sugar Bush Nurse. (YA) 1981. 6.95 (ISBN 0-686-73948-5, Avalon). Bouregy.

Smiley, Virginia K. Love Rides the Rapids. (YA) 1980. 6.95 (ISBN 0-686-59787-7, Avalon). Bouregy.

Smillie, Benjamin G., ed. Political Theology in the Canadian Context. (SR Supplements: No. 11). xxii, 272p. 1982. pap. text ed. 7.50x (ISBN 0-919812-16-3, Pub. by Wilfrid Laurier U Pr). Humanities.

Smirfitt, J. A. Introduction to Weft Knitting. 1975. 18.00x (ISBN 0-87245-567-X). Textile Bk.

Smirnitsky, A. I. Russian English Dictionary. rev. ed. 1973. 24.75 (ISBN 0-525-19520-3, 02403-720). Dutton.

Smirnov, B. M. Negative Ions. 1982. 58.50 (ISBN 0-07-058447-8). McGraw.

--Physics of Weakly Ionized Gas. 428p. 1981. 12.00 (ISBN 0-8285-2197-2, Pub. by Mir Pubs USSR). Imported Pubns.

Smirnov, L. N. Legislative Acts of the U. S. S. R., 1977-1979. 381p. 1981. 8.00 (ISBN 0-8285-2235-9, Pub by Progress Pubs USSR). Imported Pubns.

Smirnov, V. I. see Alexandrov, Eugene.

Smirnov, V. N., jt. ed. see Chazov, E. I.

Smirnov, Vladimir I. & Lebedev, N. A. Functions of a Complex Variable. LC 68-20049. 1968. 22.50x (ISBN 0-262-19046-X). MIT Pr.

Smirnova, M. A. The Hausa Language: A Descriptive Grammar, Vol. 4. (Languages of Asia & Africa Ser.). 100p. (Orig.). 1982. pap. 13.95 (ISBN 0-7100-9076-5). Routledge & Kegan.

Smisek, M. & Cerny, S. Active Carbon. 1970. 41.75 (ISBN 0-444-40773-1). Elsevier.

Smissen, Betty van Der see Van der Smissen, Betty.

Smit, J. Magnetic Properties of Materials. (Inter-University Electronics Ser.). 1971. 33.00 o.p. (ISBN 0-07-058445-1, C). McGraw.

Smit, J. W., jt. ed. see Smit, P.

Smit, P. & Smit, J. W., eds. The Dutch in America 1609-1970: A Chronology & Factbook. LC 72-8684. (Ethnic Chronology Ser.: No. 5). 1160p. 1972. 8.50 (ISBN 0-379-00504-2). Oceana.

--The Netherlands: A Chronology & Fact Book. LC 73-5599. (World Chronology Ser.). 152p. 1973. lib. bdg. 8.50 (ISBN 0-379-16301-2). Oceana.

Smith. Advances in Nuclear Quadrupole Resonance, Vol. 4. 1980. 114.00 (ISBN 0-471-26030-4, Pub. by Wiley Heyden). Wiley.

--Basic Hydraulics. 1982. text ed. 19.95 (ISBN 0-408-01112-2). Butterworth.

--A Biographical Index of America Artists. Date not set. 30.00 (ISBN 0-686-43139-1). Apollo.

--Chemotaxonomy of Plants. 1976. 26.00 (ISBN 0-444-19454-1); pap. 12.00 (ISBN 0-444-19455-X). Elsevier.
--Fundamentals of Oral Interpretation. Applbaum, Ronald & Hart, Roderick, eds. LC 77-12697. (MODCOM - Modules in Speech Communication Ser.). 1978. pap. text ed. 2.75 (ISBN 0-574-22532-3, 13-5532). SRA.
--Fungal Differentiations. (Mycology Ser.). 600p. 1983. price not set (ISBN 0-8247-1734-1). Dekker.
--Ground Ladder Operations. LC 77-19332. 1977. pap. 10.95 o.p. (ISBN 0-87618-884-6). R J Brady.
--Illustrated History of Pro Football Sports. 8.95 o.p. (ISBN 0-448-14416-6, G&D). Putnam Pub Group.
--Mallett's Index of Artists, 2 Vols. Date not set. 50.00 (ISBN 0-686-43138-3). Apollo.
--Orientations to Speech Criticism. Applbaum, Ronald & Hart, Roderick, eds. (MODCOM Modules in Speech Communication Ser.). 1976. pap. text ed. 2.75 (ISBN 0-574-22526-9; 13-5526). SRA.
--Spiritual Living. 1978. pap. 2.50 (ISBN 0-8423-6410-2). Tyndale.
Smith & Bass. Communication for Health Care Team. 1982. pap. text ed. 12.95 (ISBN 0-06-318210-6, Pub. by Har-Row Ltd England). Har-Row.
Smith & Prout. Bladder Cancer: BIMR Urology. 1983. text ed. price not set (ISBN 0-407-02358-5). Butterworth.
Smith & Weiss. Circulation, Neurobiology & Behavior. 1982. 59.00 (ISBN 0-444-00759-8). Elsevier.
Smith, jt. auth. see Cheng.
Smith, jt. auth. see McDonald.
Smith, jt. auth. see Perry.
Smith, jt. auth. see Slater.
Smith, ed. see Ballantyne, J.
Smith, ed. see Dudley, H.
Smith, et al. PCP: Problems & Prevention. 1982. pap. text ed. 15.95 (ISBN 0-8403-2809-5). Kendall-Hunt.
Smith, A. D. International Industrial Productivity: A Comparison of Britian, America & Germany. LC 82-4348. (National Institute of Economic & Social Research Occasional Papers 34). (Illus.). 200p. 1982. 24.95 (ISBN 0-521-24901-5). Cambridge U Pr.
Smith, A. E. Express Yourself, Vols. 1-4. (gr. 7-12). 1.95 ea. o.p. Transatlantic.
Smith, A. G. & Briden, J. C. Mesozoic & Cenozoic Paleocontinental Maps. LC 76-114025. (Cambridge Earth Science Ser.). (Illus.). 1977. 8.95x (ISBN 0-521-29117-8). Cambridge U Pr.
Smith, A. G., et al. Phanerozoic Paleocontinental World Maps. LC 79-42669. (Cambridge Earth Science Ser.). 96p. 1981. 34.50 (ISBN 0-521-23257-0); pap. 14.95 (ISBN 0-521-23258-9). Cambridge U Pr.
Smith, A. H. North American Species of Mycena. (Bibl. Myco.: Vol. 31). 1971. Repr. of 1947 ed. 48.00 (ISBN 3-7682-0699-8). Lubrecht & Cramer.
Smith, A. Hassell. County & Court: Government & Politics in Norfolk 1558-1603. 1974. 39.95x o.p. (ISBN 0-19-822407-9). Oxford U Pr.
Smith, A. I. Advances in Creep Design. 1971. 49.25 (ISBN 0-444-20119-X). Elsevier.
Smith, A. J. Literary Love: The Role of Passion in English Poems & Plays of the 17th Century. 192p. 1983. text ed. price not set (ISBN 0-7131-6388-7). E Arnold.
--The Moss Flora of Britain & Ireland. LC 77-71428. (Illus.). 1978. 85.00 (ISBN 0-521-21648-6). Cambridge U Pr.
Smith, A. J. Ward. Pressure Losses in Ducted Flows. 1971. 16.50 o.p. (ISBN 0-408-70153-6). Butterworth.
Smith, A. L. Analytical Infrared Spectroscopy: Fundamentals, Techniques, & Analytical Problem Solving, Vol. 54. 322p. 1979. 44.00 (ISBN 0-471-04378-8, Pub. by Wiley-Interscience). Wiley.
--Handbook of the British Lichens. 1964. Repr. of 1921 ed. 5.00 (ISBN 3-7682-0215-1). Lubrecht & Cramer.
Smith, A. L., ed. Analysis of Silicones. LC 74-13522. (Chemical Analysis Ser: Vol. 41). 407p. 1975. 52.00 o.s.i. (ISBN 0-471-80010-4, Pub. by Wiley-Interscience). Wiley.
Smith, A. M., jt. auth. see Cebeci, Tuncer.
Smith, A. M., tr. see Foucault, Michel.
Smith, A. R. Models of Manpower Systems. 1971. 26.95 (ISBN 0-444-19634-X). Elsevier.
Smith, A. R., ed. Corporate Manpower Planning. 187p. 1980. text ed. 27.00x (ISBN 0-566-02167-6). Gower Pub Ltd.
Smith, A. Robert & Giles, James V. An American Rape: A True Account of the Giles-Johnson Case. LC 75-17823. (Illus.). 300p. 1975. 10.00 (ISBN 0-915220-05-9); pap. 4.95 (ISBN 0-915220-32-6, 522967). New Republic.
Smith, A. Sheridan, tr. see Foucault, Michel.
Smith, A. W. Captain Departed. 1935. text ed. 24.50 (ISBN 0-686-83500-X). Elliots Bks.
Smith, A. W. & Stearn, W. T. A Gardener's Dictionary of Plant Names: A Handbook on the Origin & Meaning of Some Plant Names. LC 72-79502. 391p. 1972. 11.95 o.p. (ISBN 0-312-31710-7). St Martin.
Smith, Adam. Adam Smith Today: An Inquiry in to the Causes of the Wealth of Nations. Jenkins, Arthur H., ed. LC 68-8231. 1969. Repr. of 1948 ed. 17.50 o.p. (ISBN 0-8046-0238-7). Kennikat.
--Essai sur la Primiere Formation des Langues et sur la Difference du Genie. (Linguistics 13th-18th Centuries Ser.). 258p. (Fr.). 1974. Repr. of 1809 ed. lib. bdg. 70.00x o.p. (ISBN 0-8287-0779-0, 5050). Clearwater Pub.
--Essays on Philosophical Subjects. LC 82-7121. 392p. 1982. pap. 5.50X (ISBN 0-86597-023-8). Liberty Fund.
--An Inquiry into the Nature & Causes of the Wealth of Nations, 2 vols. in one. Cannan, Edwin, ed. LC 76-21934. 1977. pap. 10.95 (ISBN 0-226-76374-9, P707, Phoen). U of Chicago Pr.
--An Inquiry into the Nature & Causes of The Wealth of Nations: Glasgow Edition, 2 Vols. LC 81-15578. 1982. Set. pap. 11.00 ea. (ISBN 0-86597-008-4). Vol. I, 620p (ISBN 0-86597-006-8). Vol. II, 544p (ISBN 0-86597-007-6). Liberty Fund.
--Lectures on Historic & Belles Lettres. Bryce, J. C., ed. (The Glasgow Edition of the Works & Correspondence of Adam Smith). 416p. 1982. 48.00x (ISBN 0-19-828186-2). Oxford U Pr.
--The Wealth of Nations, 2 vols. in 1. 1977. Repr. of 1910 ed. 14.95x (ISBN 0-460-00412-3, Evman). Biblio Dist.
--Wealth of Nations. 1982. 3.95 o.p. (ISBN 0-14-043208-6). Penguin.
--The Wealth of Nations. Cannan, Edwin, ed. & intro. by. 9.95 (ISBN 0-394-60409-1). Modern Lib.
--Wealth of Nations. LC 37-3720. 1976. 24.95 (ISBN 0-910220-79-4). Berg.
--Wealth of Nations: Selections. Stigler, George J., ed. LC 57-12307. (Crofts Classics Ser.). 1957. pap. text ed. 3.25x (ISBN 0-88295-093-2). Harlan Davidson.
Smith, Adam N., jt. auth. see Sircus, Wilfred.
Smith, Adeline, jt. auth. see Meredith, Howard.
Smith, Adrian. APL: A Design Handbook for Commercial Systems. (Wiley Ser. in Information Processing). 352p. 1982. 24.95x (ISBN 0-471-10092-7, Pub. by Wiley-Interscience). Wiley.
Smith, Adrian, tr. see De Finetti, Bruno.
Smith, Al J. Managing Hazardous Substances Accidents. (Illus.). 224p. 1981. 21.95 (ISBN 0-07-058467-2). McGraw.
Smith, Alan, ed. Country Life International Dictionary of Clocks. LC 78-65713. (Illus.). 1979. 45.00 (ISBN 0-399-12338-5). Putnam Pub Group.
Smith, Alan B., ed. Neutron Standards & Flux Normalization: Proceedings. LC 77-611328. (AEC Symposium Ser.). 525p. 1971. pap. 21.25 (ISBN 0-87079-294-6, CONF-701022); microfiche 4.50 (ISBN 0-87079-295-4, CONF-701022). DOE.
Smith, Alan E. Protein Biosynthesis. (Outline Studies in Biology Ser.). 1976. pap. 6.50x (ISBN 0-412-13460-8, Pub. by Chapman & Hall). Methuen Inc.
Smith, Alan G., ed. The Reign of James VI & I. LC 73-79379. (Problems in Focus Ser.). 275p. 1973. 25.00 (ISBN 0-312-67025-7). St Martin.
Smith, Alan R. Taxonomy of Thelypteris Subgenus Steiropteris (Including Glaphyropteris) (U. C. Publications in Botany Ser.: Vol. 76). 1980. pap. 10.50x (ISBN 0-520-09602-9). U of Cal Pr.
Smith, Alasdair. A Mathematical Introduction to Economics. LC 82-11560. (Illus.). 270p. 1982. text ed. 29.95x (ISBN 0-389-20325-4). B&N Imports.
Smith, Albert. Mont Blanc. 88p. 1983. Repr. of 1852 ed. lib. bdg. 45.00 (ISBN 0-89984-613-0). Century Bookbindery.
Smith, Albert A., Jr. The Coupling of External Electromagnetic Fields to Transmission Lines. LC 76-49504. 132p. 1977. 29.95 (ISBN 0-471-01995-X, Pub. by Wiley-Interscience). Wiley.
Smith, Albert G., Jr. The American House Styles of Architecture Coloring Book. (Illus.). 48p. (Orig.). (gr. 3 up). 1983. pap. 2.25 (ISBN 0-486-24472-5). Dover.
--Cut & Assemble Main Street: Nine Easy-to-Make Full-Color Buildings in H-C Scale. (Illus.). 48p. (Orig.). (gr. 4 up). 1983. pap. 4.95 (ISBN 0-486-24473-3). Dover.
Smith, Alberta, jt. auth. see Holmes, Ernest.
Smith, Alexander. Memoirs of the Life & Times of the Famous Jonathan Wilde. LC 76-170567. (Foundations of the Novel Ser.: Vol. 48). lib. bdg. 50.00 o.s.i. (ISBN 0-8240-0560-0). Garland Pub.
Smith, Alexander B. & Berlin, Louis. Introduction to Probation & Parole. 2nd ed. (Criminal Justice Ser.). (Illus.). 1979. text ed. 18.50 (ISBN 0-8299-0235-X); instrs.' manual avail. (ISBN 0-8299-0601-0). West Pub.
--Treating the Criminal Offender. 2nd ed. 368p. 1981. text ed. 19.95 (ISBN 0-13-930735-4). P-H.
Smith, Alexander M., jt. auth. see Carty, Tony.
Smith, Alice G. Sharing Literature with Children & Youth through School & Public Libraries. 250p. 1982. 28.50 (ISBN 0-87287-341-2). Libs Unl.
Smith, Alice L. Microbiology & Pathology. 12th ed. LC 79-27338. (Illus.). 844p. 1980. text ed. 24.95 (ISBN 0-8016-4673-1). Mosby.
--Principles of Microbiology. 9th ed. LC 80-26593. (Illus.). 724p. 1981. text ed. 24.95 (ISBN 0-8016-4682-0). Mosby.
Smith, Allan B. Nine Hundred Open Salts. (Illus.). 1982. 16.00 (ISBN 0-940554-09-9). Country Hse.
Smith, Allan B. & Smith, Helen B. Eight Hundred Forty Individual Open Salts Illustrated: The Seventh Book. (Illus.). 1980. pap. 12.00 (ISBN 0-940554-00-3). Country Hse.
Smith, Alpheus & Cooper, John N. Elements of Physics. 9th ed. (Illus.). 1979. text ed. 28.50x (ISBN 0-07-058634-9); instructor's manual 15.00 (ISBN 0-07-058638-1); study guide 11.50 (ISBN 0-07-058639-X). McGraw.
Smith, Andrew J., tr. see Vasil eva, E. K.
Smith, Ann. The Tummy Trimmer Primer. LC 78-74043. (Illus., Orig.). 1979. pap. 4.94 o.p. (ISBN 0-448-16293-8, G&D). Putnam Pub Group.
Smith, Ann, jt. auth. see Taebel, Del.
Smith, Anne, ed. Obesity: A Bibliography 1974-1979. 340p. 1980. 55.00 (ISBN 0-904147-17-7). IRL Pr.
Smith, Anne W. Blue Denim Blues. LC 82-1744. 144p. (gr. 4-8). 1982. 9.95 (ISBN 0-689-30942-2). Atheneum.
Smith, Anthony. Goodbye Gutenberg: The Newspaper Revolution of the 1980's. LC 79-24263. (Illus.). 1980. 19.95x (ISBN 0-19-502709-4). Oxford U Pr.
--Goodbye Gutenberg: The Newspaper Revolution of the 1980's. (Illus.). 1981. pap. 7.95 (ISBN 0-19-503006-0, GB 660, GB). Oxford U Pr.
--Television & Political Life: Studies of Six European Countries. LC 78-24334. 1979. 26.00x (ISBN 0-312-79073-2). St Martin.
Smith, Anthony, ed. Newspapers & Democracy. 320p. 1980. text ed. 27.50x (ISBN 0-262-19184-9). MIT Pr.
Smith, Anthony D. The Ethnic Revival. (Themes in the Social Sciences Ser.). 224p. 1981. 29.95 (ISBN 0-521-23267-8); pap. 9.95 (ISBN 0-521-29885-7). Cambridge U Pr.
--Nationalist Movements. LC 77-75680. 1977. 16.95x o.p. (ISBN 0-312-56012-5). St Martin.
--State & Nation in the Third World: The Western State & African Nationalism. LC 82-10672. 180p. 1983. 25.00x (ISBN 0-312-75605-4). St Martin.
--Theories of Nationalism. 2nd ed. 392p. 1983. text ed. 36.00x (ISBN 0-8419-0846-X); pap. text ed. 16.00x (ISBN 0-8419-0845-1). Holmes & Meier.
Smith, Anthony D., ed. Labour Market & Inflation. LC 68-10752. (International Institute for Labour Studies Ser.). (Illus.). 1968. 19.95 o.p. (ISBN 0-312-46305-7). St Martin.
--Wage Policy Issues in Economic Development. LC 69-13690. (International Institute for Labour Studies). 1969. 32.50 (ISBN 0-312-85330-0). St Martin.
Smith, Arthur B., Jr. & Craver, Charles B. Employment Discrimination Law, Cases & Materials. 2nd ed. (Contemporary Legal Education Ser). 1982. text ed. 28.50 (ISBN 0-87215-407-6, Bobbs-Merrill Law); 1980 suppl. 6.00 (ISBN 0-87215-409-2). Michie-Bobbs.
Smith, Arthur H. Village Life in China: A Study in Sociology. Repr. of 1899 ed. lib. bdg. 16.25x (ISBN 0-8371-1167-6, SMVL). Greenwood.
Smith, Arthur J., ed. Oxford Book of Canadian Verse. 1960. pap. 9.95x (ISBN 0-19-540106-9). Oxford U Pr.
Smith, Arthur J., jt. auth. see Moriei, Peter.
Smith, Arthur L., jt. auth. see Rich, Andrea.
Smith, Arthur L., Jr., jt. auth. see Jacobsen, Hans-Adolf.
Smith, Augustus H. Economics for Our Times. 4th ed. (gr. 9-12). 1966. text ed. 7.68 o.p. (ISBN 0-07-058509-1, W). McGraw.
Smith, B. Babington, ed. Training in Small Groups: A Study of Five Methods. rev. ed. Farrell, B. A. 114p. 1979. 25.00 (ISBN 0-08-023689-8). Pergamon.
Smith, B. H. Bridged Aromatic Compounds. (Organic Chemistry: Vol. 2). 1965. 67.50 (ISBN 0-12-650350-8). Acad Pr.
Smith, B. J., jt. auth. see Pain, R. H.
Smith, B. L., ed. see Bureau of Social Science Research.
Smith, B. Othanel, jt. auth. see Orlosky, Donald E.
Smith, Bailey E. Real Revival Preaching. LC 81-86667. 1982. 7.95 (ISBN 0-8054-6235-X). Broadman.
Smith, Barbara, jt. auth. see Gagnon, John H.
Smith, Barbara, ed. Home Girls: A Black Feminist Anthology. 384p. (Orig.). 1983. pap. 10.95 (ISBN 0-930436-16-4). Persephone.
Smith, Barbara A., ed. see Halliburton, John H., Jr.
Smith, Barbara H. On the Margins of Discourse: The Relation of Literature to Language. LC 78-18274. xviii, 226p. 1978. pap. 7.50 (ISBN 0-226-76453-2). U of Chicago Pr.
Smith, Barbara K., jt. auth. see Smith, Jerome F.
Smith, Barbara L. Techniques of Professional Pursuits. 1979. pap. text ed. 6.75 o.p. (ISBN 0-8191-0714-X). U Pr of Amer.
Smith, Barbara L., et al. Political Research Methods: Foundations & Techniques. (Illus.). 352p. 1976. pap. text ed. 21.95 (ISBN 0-395-20363-5). HM.
Smith, Bardwell, ed. Essays on Gupta Culture. 1983. 34.00x (ISBN 0-8364-0871-3); text ed. 20.00x (ISBN 0-686-42974-5). South Asia Bks.
Smith, Bardwell, ed. see Sato, Giei & Nishimura, Eshin.
Smith, Bardwell L., jt. ed. see Elison, George.
Smith, Barry D. & Vetter, Harold J. Theoretical Approaches to Personality. (Illus.). 416p. 1982. 23.95 (ISBN 0-13-913491-3). P-H.
Smith, Barry D., jt. auth. see Cummins, J. David.
Smith, Beatrice S. Proudest Horse on the Prairie. LC 74-128804. (Real Life Bks). (gr. 4-9). 1971. PLB 3.95g (ISBN 0-8225-0702-1). Lerner Pubns.
--The Road to Galveston. LC 72-7657. (Adult & Young Adult Bks). (Illus.). (gr. 5-12). 1973. PLB 5.95g (ISBN 0-8225-0755-2). Lerner Pubns.
Smith, Bede. The Lancashire Watch Company, Prescott, Lancashire, England 1889-1910. 1973. 10.50 (ISBN 0-913602-08-6). K Roberts.
Smith, Bernard. Australian Painting, Seventeen-Eighty Eight to Nineteen-Seventy. (Illus.). 1971. 48.00x o.p. (ISBN 0-19-550270-1). Oxford U Pr.
--Ion Implantation Range Data for Silicon & Geranium Device Technologies. 1977. write for info (ISBN 0-471-05517-4). Res Stud Pr.
Smith, Bernard, ed. Concerning Contemporary Art: The Power Lectures 1968-1973. (Illus.). 1975. pap. 8.50x o.p. (ISBN 0-19-920062-9). Oxford U Pr.
Smith, Bert K. Looking Forward: New Options for Your Later Years. LC 82-70573. 224p. 1982. 12.45 (ISBN 0-8070-4146-7). Beacon Pr.
Smith, Bertha. How the Spirit Filled My Life. LC 73-87068. 6.95 (ISBN 0-8054-5540-X). Broadman.
Smith, Bessie G., jt. auth. see Brian, George C.
Smith, Betty. Joy in the Morning. LC 62-14560. 1963. lib. bdg. 11.87i (ISBN 0-06-013931-5, HarpT). Har-Row.
--A Tree Grows in Brooklyn. 1968. pap. 2.95i (ISBN 0-06-080126-3, P126, PL). Har-Row.
Smith, Betty & Block, Ira. Textiles in Perspective. (Illus.). 512p. 1982. text ed. 23.95 (ISBN 0-13-912808-5). P-H.
Smith, Billy A., jt. ed. see Bonneau, B. Lee.
Smith, Bobbi. Rapture's Rage. 1983. pap. 3.50 (ISBN 0-8217-1121-0). Zebra.
Smith, Bonnie S. If You Love Me, Call Me Dorrie. (Pennypincher Bks.). (gr. 3-6). 1982. pap. 1.75 (ISBN 0-89191-710-1). Cook.
Smith, Bradley & Stevens, Gus. The Emergency Book: You Can Save a Life. (Illus.). 1979. 8.95 o.p. (ISBN 0-671-24115-X). S&S.
Smith, Bradley F. Heinrich Himmler: A Nazi in the Making, 1900-1926. LC 79-137403. (Publications Ser.: No. 93). (Illus.). 1971. 10.95x o.p. (ISBN 0-8179-1931-7). Hoover Inst Pr.
--The Shacow Warriors: O.S.S. & the Origins of the C.I.A. 400p. 1983. 14.95 (ISBN 0-465-07756-0). Basic.
Smith, Brenda. Bridging the Gap: College Reading. 1981. pap. text ed. 10.95x (ISBN 0-673-15364-9). Scott F.
Smith, Brenda D. Breaking Through: Beginning College Reading. 1983. pap. text ed. 10.95x (ISBN 0-673-15543-9). Scott F.
Smith, Brian C. & Stanyer, Jeffrey. Administering Britain. (Studies in Public Administrative Institutions Ser.). 288p. 1980. pap. 9.95x o.p. (ISBN 0-85520-374-9, Pub. by Martin Robertson England). Biblio Dist.
Smith, Brian J., jt. auth. see Lewis, Theodore G.
Smith, Brian R. The Country Consultant. 310p. 1982. 18.95 (ISBN 0-916654-23-0). Consultants NE.
--How to Prosper in Your Own Business. (Illus.). 1983. pap. 11.95 (ISBN 0-86616-025-6). Greene.
--The Small Computer in Small Business. 1983. pap. 9.95 (ISBN 0-86616-024-8). Greene.
Smith, Brian R. & Austin, Daniel J. Word Processing: A Guide for Small Business. 146p. 1983. pap. 9.95 (ISBN 0-86616-021-3). Lewis.
Smith, Bruce. The Common Wages. 80p. 1983. 13.50 (ISBN 0-935296-42-5); pap. 7.95. Sheep Meadow.
--State Police, Organization & Administration. LC 69-14946. (Criminology, Law Enforcement, & Social Problems Ser.: No. 64). 1969. Repr. of 1925 ed. 12.50x (ISBN 0-87585-064-2). Patterson Smith.
--The World According to Warbucks: Capitalist Quotations from the Richest Man in the World. (Illus.). 96p. 1982. 6.95 (ISBN 0-8329-0266-7). New Century.
Smith, Bruce D., ed. Mississippian Settlement Patterns. (Studies in Archaeology Ser.). 1978. 48.00 (ISBN 0-12-650640-X). Acad Pr.
Smith, Bryan C. Community Health: An Epidemiological Approach. (Illus.). 1979. text ed. 21.95x (ISBN 0-02-412570-9). Macmillan.
Smith, Buford D. Design of Equilibrium Stage Processes. (Chemical Engineering Ser.). 1963. text ed. 42.00 (ISBN 0-07-058637-3, P&RB). McGraw.
Smith, Byron C. & Bosniak, Stephen L., eds. Advances in Ophthalmic Plastic & Reconstructive Surgery. (Illus.). 278p. 1983. 60.00 (ISBN 0-08-029656-4). Pergamon.
Smith, C. B., jt. ed. see Fazzolare, Rocco.
Smith, C. Colin, ed. Spanish Ballads. 1964. 8.75 (ISBN 0-08-010914-4); pap. 6.95 (ISBN 0-08-010913-6). Pergamon.
Smith, C. E. Applied Mechanics-Dynamics. 2nd ed. 518p. 1982. text ed. 27.95x (ISBN 0-471-02966-1). Wiley.
Smith, C. Henry, jt. ed. see Bender, Harold S.
Smith, C. M., ed. see Bureau of Social Science Research.
Smith, C. R., jt. ed. see Grood, E. S.
Smith, C. R., jt. ed. see Mates, R. E.
Smith, C. Ray. Supermannerism: New Attitudes in Post-Modern Architecture. LC 76-44664. 1977. pap. 9.95 o.p. (ISBN 0-525-47424-2). Dutton.
Smith, C. Ray, ed. Theatre Crafts Book of Makeup, Masks & Wigs. Theatre Craft Editors. LC 72-94992. (Illus.). 1974. pap. 6.95 o.p. (ISBN 0-87857-058-6). Rodale Pr Inc.

Smith, C. V. Meteorology & Grain Storage. (Technical Note Ser.: No. 101). (Illus., Orig.). 1970. pap. 10.00 (ISBN 0-685-22323-X, W71, WMO). Unipub.

Smith, C. V., ed. Meteorological Observations in Animal Experiments. (Technical Note Ser.). (Orig.). 1970. pap. 6.00 (ISBN 0-685-04918-3, W78, WMO). Unipub.

Smith, Campbell, tr. see Kant, Immanuel.

Smith, Carlton G. Serial Dissections of the Human Brain. LC 81-2540. (Illus.). 100p. 1981. text ed. 17.00 (ISBN 0-8067-1811-0). Urban & S.

Smith, Carol. Auditory Discrimination Practice Exercises. 1981. pap. text ed. 3.95x (ISBN 0-8134-2168-3, 2168). Interstate.

--Cancer: Nursing Assessment & Care: A Self-Learning Text. (Illus.). 1980. pap. text ed. 12.95 (ISBN 0-07-059106-7). McGraw.

--How Products Are Made. (Science Ser.). 24p. (gr. 5-8). 1979. wkbk. 5.00 (ISBN 0-8209-0151-2, S-13). ESP.

Smith, Carol, jt. auth. see Danhof, Kenneth.

Smith, Carol E. Better Meetings: A Handbook for Trainers of Policy Councils & Other Decision-Making Groups. LC 75-4255. 102p. 1975. 9.95 (ISBN 0-89334-009-X, 105). Humanics Ltd.

Smith, Carole. Danger at the Golden Dragon. Fay, Ann, ed. (High-Low Mysteries Ser.). (Illus.). 128p. (gr. 3-8). 1983. PLB 7.50 (ISBN 0-8075-1449-7). A Whitman.

Smith, Carole R. Social Work with the Dying & Bereaved. Campling, Jo, ed. (Practical Social Work Ser.). 160p. 1982. 40.00x (ISBN 0-333-30894-8, Pub. by Macmillan England). State Mutual Bk.

Smith, Carole S. The End. 1978. pap. 1.75 o.p. (ISBN 0-380-01978-7, 38919). Avon.

Smith, Catherine R., tr. see Sokolov, Yury M.

Smith, Cathy. Food One Hundred One: A Student Guide to Quick & Easy Cooking. (Illus.). 155p. 1982. 7.95 (ISBN 0-914718-75-4). Pacific Search.

Smith, Cecil. Worlds of Music. LC 73-7312. 328p. 1973. Repr. of 1952 ed. lib. bdg. 17.00x (ISBN 0-8371-6925-9, SMWM). Greenwood.

Smith, Cecil L., jt. auth. see Murrill, Paul W.

Smith, Cedric M. Alcoholism-Treatment. Horrobin, David F., ed. (Alcohol Research Review Ser.: Vol. III). 1981. 26.95x (ISBN 0-87705-956-X). Human Sci Pr.

Smith, Charles A. Promoting the Social Development of Young Children. LC 81-83085. 261p. 1981. pap. 9.95 (ISBN 0-87484-528-9); instr's guide avail. Mayfield Pub.

Smith, Charles E. Applied Mechanics-More Dynamics. LC 75-44021. 1976. text ed. 23.95x o.p. (ISBN 0-471-79996-3). Wiley.

--Applied Mechanics: Statics. 2nd ed. LC 81-4232. 316p. 1982. text ed. 25.95 (ISBN 0-471-02965-3). Wiley.

--Commitment: The Cement of Love. LC 82-71915. (Orig.). 1983. pap. 4.50 (ISBN 0-8054-5651-1). Broadman.

Smith, Charles H., jt. auth. see Bergendorff, Fred.

Smith, Charles J. Synonyms Discriminated. Smith, Percy H., ed. LC 78-126007. 1970. Repr. of 1903 ed. 42.00x (ISBN 0-8103-3010-5). Gale.

Smith, Charles L. Fight That Ticket in Washington. 73p. 1977. 1.95 (ISBN 0-88908-701-6). Self Counsel Pr.

Smith, Charles M. Reverend Randollph & the Avenging Angel. LC 77-6617. 1977. 7.95 (ISBN 0-399-11859-4). Putnam Pub Group.

--Reverend Randolph & the Fall from Grace, Inc. LC 78-19097. 1978. 8.95 (ISBN 0-399-12289-3). Putnam Pub Group.

--Reverend Randolph & the Holy Terror. 192p. 1980. 10.95 (ISBN 0-399-12461-6). Putnam Pub Group.

--Reverend Randolph & the Unholy Bible. 224p. 1983. 12.95 (ISBN 0-399-12796-8). Putnam.

Smith, Charles O. Introduction to Reliability in Design. LC 82-14854. 284p. 1982. Repr. of 1976 ed. lib. bdg. 18.50 (ISBN 0-89874-553-5). Krieger.

--Products Liability: Are You Vulnerable? (Illus.). 368p. 1981. text ed. 30.00 (ISBN 0-13-725036-3). P-H.

--Science of Engineering Materials. 2nd ed. (Illus.). 1977. text ed. 29.95 (ISBN 0-13-794990-1). P-H.

Smith, Charles P., ed. Achievement-Related Motives in Children. LC 75-81045. 264p. 1969. 10.50x (ISBN 0-87154-811-9). Russell Sage.

Smith, Charles R. Mechanics of Secondary Oil Recovery. LC 74-32220. 512p. 1975. Repr. of 1966 ed. 30.50 (ISBN 0-88275-270-7). Krieger.

Smith, Charles W. The Mind of the Market. LC 82-48235. 224p. 1983. pap. 5.72i (ISBN 0-06-090993-5, CN 993, CN). Har-Row.

Smith, Charlotte. Desmond: A Novel, 3 vols. Luria, Gina, ed. LC 73-22133. (The Feminist Controversy in England, 1788-1810 Ser.). 1974. lib. bdg. 50.00 ea. o.s.i. (ISBN 0-8240-0879-0). Garland Pub.

Smith, Chris & Hoath, David C. Law & the Underprivileged. 280p. 1975. 21.95x (ISBN 0-7100-8259-2). Routledge & Kegan.

Smith, Christine, jt. auth. see Isard, Walter.

Smith, Christopher & Smith, I. C. Microcomputers in Education. (Computers & Their Applications Ser.). 212p. 1982. 49.95 o.s.i. (ISBN 0-470-27319-4). Halsted Pr.

Smith, Christopher J. & Hanham, Robert Q. Alcohol Abuse: Geographical Perspectives. Knight, C. Gregory, ed. LC 82-25529. (Resource Publications in Geography Ser.). 85p. (Orig.). 1983. pap. 5.00 (ISBN 0-89291-166-2). Assn Am Geographers.

Smith, Chuck. Bible Prophecy for Today. 80p. (Orig.). 1982. pap. 1.50 (ISBN 0-936728-32-9). Word For Today.

--Charisma vs. Charismania. LC 82-2241. 176p. (Orig.). 1983. pap. 3.95 (ISBN 0-89081-353-1). Harvest Hse.

--The Gospel of John. LC 78-64556. (Illus.). 1980. cancelled (ISBN 0-89169-531-1); pap. cancelled (ISBN 0-89169-530-3). Reed Bks.

Smith, Clifford N. Federal Land Series, Vol. 3. LC 72-328. 382p. 1980. 45.00 (ISBN 0-8389-0278-2). ALA.

--Federal Land Series, Vol. 4, Pt. 1. 406p. 1982. text ed. 35.00 (ISBN 0-8389-0364-9). ALA.

Smith, Clifford N., compiled by. British Colonial Land Grants in North Carolina. (British-American Genealogical Research Monograph: No. 3). 80p. 1981. pap. cancelled (ISBN 0-915162-27-X). Westland Pubns.

Smith, Clifford Neal. Eighteenth-Century Emigrants from Kreis Simmern (Hunsrueck), Rheinland-Pfalz, Germany, to Central Europe, Pfalzdorf am Niederrhein, & North America. (German-American Genealogical Research Monograph: No. 15). 25p. (Orig.). 1982. pap. 10.00 (ISBN 0-915162-15-6). Westland Pubns.

Smith, Clifford T., jt. ed. see Blakemore, Harold.

Smith, Clive. The Performing World of the Actor. LC 81-50297. (The Performing World Ser.). PLB 15.20 (ISBN 0-382-06589-1). Silver.

Smith, Clive R., compiled by. Flying at Hendon: A Pictorial Record on Art Paper. (Illus.). 31p. (Orig.). 1975. pap. 2.50 o.p. (ISBN 0-7100-8294-0). Routledge & Kegan.

Smith, Clyde, photos by. Pennsylvania. LC 78-51218. (Belding Imprint Ser.). (Illus.). 192p. (Text by Cronan Minton). 1978. 32.50 (ISBN 0-912856-40-8). Graphic Arts Ctr.

Smith, Colin. Contemporary French Philosophy: A Study in Norms & Values. LC 75-8489. 1976. Repr. of 1964 ed. lib. bdg. 19.25x (ISBN 0-8371-8156-9, SMFP). Greenwood.

--The Cut-Out. 1981. pap. 10.95 (ISBN 0-670-25192-5). Viking Pr.

Smith, Colin, tr. see Merleau-Ponty, M.

Smith, Colin, tr. see Merleau-Ponty, Maurice.

Smith, Colin L. The Embassy of Sir William White of Constantinople 1886-1891. LC 78-1011. (Oxford Historical Series, British Ser.). 1979. Repr. of 1957 ed. lib. bdg. 17.75x (ISBN 0-313-21155-8, SMES). Greenwood.

Smith College. The Sophia Smith Collection. The Author, Subject & Manuscript Catalogs of the Sophia Smith Collection (Women's History Archive, 7 vols. 1975. Set. lib. bdg. 630.00 (ISBN 0-8161-0001-2, Hall Library). G K Hall.

Smith, Cornelius C., Jr. Don't Settle for Second: Life & Times of Cornelius C. Smith. LC 76-52040. (Illus.). 1977. 14.95 o.p. (ISBN 0-89141-007-4). Presidio Pr.

Smith, Courtney. Commodity Spreads: Techniques & Methods for Spreading Financial Futures, Grains, Meats, & Other Commodities. LC 82-10924. 211p. 1982. 34.95x (ISBN 0-471-09178-2). Ronald Pr.

Smith, Courtney, jt. auth. see Grushcow, Jack.

Smith, Craig & Skjei, Eric. Getting Grants. LC 78-20187. 1980. 14.37i (ISBN 0-06-014013-5, HarpT). Har-Row.

Smith, Craig, jt. auth. see Bolling, Landrum R.

Smith, Craig R., jt. auth. see Robertson, David H.

Smith, Craig W. & Skjei, Eric W. Getting Grants. 14.00 (ISBN 0-686-38890-9). Public Serv Materials.

Smith, Curt. Long Time Gone: The Years of Turmoil Remembered. (Illus.). 264p. 1982. 15.95 (ISBN 0-89651-425-0). Icarus.

Smith, Cynthia J., jt. auth. see Frazer, Joan M.

Smith, Cyril. Adolescence. 1968. text ed. 6.00x (ISBN 0-582-48775-7); pap. text ed. 2.50x o.p. (ISBN 0-582-48776-5). Humanities.

Smith, Cyril E. The University of Toulouse in the Middle Ages. 1959. 29.95 (ISBN 0-87462-402-9). Marquette.

Smith, Cyril S. A Search for Structure: Selected Essays on Science, Art & History. (Illus.). 410p. 1981. 32.50x (ISBN 0-262-19191-1). MIT Pr.

Smith, Cyril S., ed. Sources for the History of the Science of Steel, 1532-1786. (Society for the History of Technology Ser.: No. 4). 1968. 25.00x (ISBN 0-262-19041-9). MIT Pr.

Smith, Cyril S., ed. see Rozdzienski, Walenty.

Smith, D. Rhodesia, the Problem. 1969. Repr. 15.50 o.p. (ISBN 0-08-007094-9). Pergamon.

Smith, D. Howard. The Wisdom of the Taoists. LC 80-15629. (Wisdom Ser.). 96p. 1980. 5.25 (ISBN 0-8112-0777-3, NDP509). New Directions.

Smith, D. I. & Stopp, P. The River Basin. LC 77-85688. (Topics in Geography Ser.). (Illus.). 1979. 18.50 (ISBN 0-521-21900-0); pap. 8.95x (ISBN 0-521-29307-3). Cambridge U Pr.

Smith, D. K., jt. auth. see Borg, I. Y.

Smith, D. N. A Forgotten Sector: The Training of Ancillary Staff in Hospitals. 1969. text ed. 24.00 (ISBN 0-08-013379-7); write for info. (ISBN 0-08-013378-9); write for info. Pergamon.

Smith, D. N., ed. see Swift, Jonathan.

Smith, Dale. Forage Management in the North. 4th ed. 272p. 1981. perfect bdg. 11.95 (ISBN 0-8403-2377-8, 40237704). Kendall-Hunt.

Smith, Dale R., ed. see Tucker, Bettie C.

Smith, Daniel M. Aftermath of War: Bainbridge Colby & Wilsonian Diplomacy. LC 77-115881. (Memoirs Ser.: Vol. 80). 1970. pap. 2.50 o.p. (ISBN 0-87169-080-2). Am Philos.

--Great Departure: The United States in World War 1, 1914-1920. LC 65-19813. (America in Crisis Ser.). 1965. pap. text ed. 11.95 (ISBN 0-471-80006-6). Wiley.

Smith, Daniel M., jt. auth. see Siracusa, Joseph M.

Smith, Darrell. Integrative Counseling & Psychotherapy. 1975. pap. 2.60 o.p. (ISBN 0-395-20033-4). HM.

Smith, Datus C, Jr. The Land & People of Indonesia. Rev. ed. LC 82-48964. (Portraits of the Nations Ser.). (Illus.). 160p. (gr. 4 up). 1983. 10.53i (ISBN 0-397-32048-5, JBL J); PLB 10.89g (ISBN 0-397-32049-3). Har-Row.

Smith, Dave. Blue Spruce. (Illus.). 24p. 1980. 15.00 o.p. (ISBN 0-918092-17-5); pap. 3.50 o.p. (ISBN 0-918092-19-1); signed paper 8.00 o.p. (ISBN 0-918092-18-3). Tamarack Edns.

--The Fisherman's Whore. LC 73-85445. 74p. 1974. 7.50 (ISBN 0-8214-0137-8, 82-81404). Ohio U Pr.

Smith, Dave J. The Giver of Morning: On the Poetry of Dave Smith. Weigl, Bruce, ed. LC 81-86003. (Thunder City Press Profile Ser.). (Illus.). 104p. 1982. cancelled 9.95 (ISBN 0-918644-26-7); pap. 5.95 (ISBN 0-686-96900-6). Thunder City.

Smith, David & Neal, Peters. Peter Allen: Between the Moon & New York City. (Illus.). 160p. (Orig.). 1983. pap. 9.95 (ISBN 0-933328-57-5). Delilah Bks.

Smith, David, jt. auth. see Peters, Neal.

Smith, David, ed. A People & a Proletariat. cloth. 19.95 (ISBN 0-86104-321-9); pap. 9.95 (ISBN 0-686-96855-7). Pluto Pr.

Smith, David, tr. see Ruyslinck, Ward.

Smith, David A. Interface: Calculus & the Computer. LC 75-25016. (Illus.). 288p. 1975. pap. text ed. 13.95 (ISBN 0-395-21875-6); instr's. manual 2.45 (ISBN 0-395-21876-4). HM.

--Subsidized Housing as a Tax Shelter. LC 82-60131. 288p. 1982. 35.00 (ISBN 0-943570-00-X). R A Stanger.

Smith, David B. & Kaluzny, Arnold D. The White Labyrinth: Understanding the Organization of Health Care. LC 75-7012. 250p. 1975. 25.00x (ISBN 0-8211-1854-4); text ed. 22.95x (ISBN 0-685-53678-5). McCutchan.

Smith, David C. The Master of Evil. 352p. (Orig.). 1983. pap. 2.95 (ISBN 0-523-41738-1). Pinnacle Bks.

--Oron, No. 4: The Valley of Ogrum. (Orig.). 1982. pap. 2.25 (ISBN 0-686-83074-1). Zebra.

--The Sorcerer's Shadow. 1982. pap. 2.50 (ISBN 0-686-97453-0). Zebra.

Smith, David C. & Tierney, Richard L. Red Sonja, No. 4: Endithor's Daughter. 1982. pap. 2.50 (ISBN 0-441-71159-6, Pub. by Ace Science Fiction). Ace Bks.

--Red Sonja, No. 6: Star of Doom. 1983. pap. 2.50 (ISBN 0-441-71162-6, Pub. by Ace Science Fiction). Ace Bks.

Smith, David E. History of Mathematics, 2 vols. Incl. Vol. 1. General Survey of the History of Elementary Mathematics. Repr. of 1923 ed. 8.00 (ISBN 0-486-20429-4); Vol. 2. Special Topics of Elementary Mathematics. Repr. of 1925 ed (ISBN 0-486-20430-8). pap. text ed. 10.00 ea. Dover.

--Number Stories of Long Ago. LC 70-167181. (Illus.). 150p. (gr. 1 up). 1973. Repr. of 1951 ed. 34.00x (ISBN 0-8103-3273-6). Gale.

--Prairie Liberalism: The Liberal Party in Saskatchewan, 1905-1971. LC 74-78676. 1975. 30.00x (ISBN 0-8020-5313-0); pap. 9.50 (ISBN 0-8020-6290-3). U of Toronto Pr.

--Quantitative Business Analysis. LC 82-7833. 670p. 1982. Repr. lib. bdg. 39.50 (ISBN 0-89874-504-7). Krieger.

Smith, David E. & De Morgan, Augustus. Rara Arithmetica & Arithmetical Books, 2 vols. in 1. 4th ed. LC 74-113148. (Illus., Eng.). 1970. text ed. 35.00 (ISBN 0-8284-0192-6). Chelsea Pub.

Smith, David E. & Luce, John. Love Needs Care. LC 77-121434. (Illus.). 1971. 8.95 o.p. (ISBN 0-316-80143-7). Little.

Smith, David E., ed. A Multicultural View of Drug Abuse: Proceedings of the National Drug Abuse Conference, 1977. 1978. 39.95 (ISBN 0-8161-2127-3, Hall Medical). G K Hall.

Smith, David E., ed. see De Morgan, Augustus.

Smith, David E., tr. see Descartes, Rene.

Smith, David Eugene & Mikami, Yoshio. History of Japanese Mathematics. 280p. 1914. 18.00x (ISBN 0-87548-170-1). Open Court.

Smith, David H., jt. auth. see Katz, Alfred H.

Smith, David H. & Til, John Van, eds. International Perspectives on Voluntary Action Research. LC 82-20090. 430p. (Orig.). 1983. lib. bdg. 36.50 (ISBN 0-8191-2862-7); pap. text ed. 21.50 (ISBN 0-8191-2863-5). U Pr of Amer.

Smith, David K. Network Optimisation Practice: A Computational Guide. (Ellis Horwood Series in Mathematics Its Applications). 237p. 1982. 59.95X (ISBN 0-470-27347-X). Halsted Pr.

Smith, David M. Human Geography: A Welfare Approach. LC 77-70203. 1977. 22.50 (ISBN 0-312-39946-4). St Martin.

--Industrial Location: An Economic Geographical Analysis. 2nd ed. LC 80-19231. 450p. 1981. text ed. 32.95 (ISBN 0-471-06078-X). Wiley.

--Living Under Apartheid. (London Research Series in Geography: No. 2). 296p. 1983. text ed. 35.00x (ISBN 0-04-309110-5). Allen Unwin.

--Practice of Silviculture. 7th ed. LC 62-16244. 1962. 30.95 (ISBN 0-471-80017-1). Wiley.

Smith, David N. & Wells, Louis T., Jr. Negotiating Third World Mineral Agreements, Promises As Prologue. LC 75-29274. 288p. 1976. prof ref 27.50x (ISBN 0-88410-041-3). Ballinger Pub.

Smith, David N., ed. see Johnson, Samuel.

Smith, David R. Masks of Wedlock: Seventeenth-Century Dutch Marriage Portraiture. Seidel, Linda, ed. LC 82-8618. (Studies in Fine Arts: Iconography: No. 8). 304p. 1982. 39.95 (ISBN 0-8357-1353-9, Pub. by UMI Res Pr). Univ Microfilms.

Smith, David S. Insect Cells, Their Structure & Function. text ed. 17.65 o.p. (ISBN 0-934454-51-5). Lubrecht & Cramer.

Smith, David W. The Friendless American Male. LC 82-21518. 1983. pap. 4.95 (ISBN 0-8307-0863-4, 5417309). Regal.

--Helvetius: A Study in Persecution. LC 82-15841. (Illus.). viii, 250p. 1982. lib. bdg. 35.00x (ISBN 0-313-23744-1, SMHL). Greenwood.

--Mothering Your Unborn Baby. LC 78-64724. (Illus.). 1979. pap. text ed. 6.95 (ISBN 0-7216-8416-5). Saunders.

--Recognizable Patterns of Human Deformation: Identification & Management of Mechanical Effects on Morphogenesis. (Illus.). 240p. 1981. text ed. 22.50 (ISBN 0-7216-8401-7). Saunders.

--Recognizable Patterns of Human Malformation: Genetic, Embryologic & Clinical Aspects, Vol. 7. 2nd ed. LC 75-21150. (Illus.). 528p. 1976. text ed. 32.50 o.p. (ISBN 0-7216-8376-2). Saunders.

Smith, David W., ed. Introduction to Clinical Pediatrics. 2nd ed. LC 76-50157. (Illus.). 1977. pap. text ed. 15.95 (ISBN 0-7216-8396-7). Saunders.

Smith, David W. & Bierman, Edwin L., eds. The Biologic Ages of Man: From Conception Through Old Age. LC 73-81837. (Illus.). 211p. 1973. text ed. 8.00 o.p. (ISBN 0-7216-8423-8). Saunders.

Smith, Debbi K. Secrets from a Stargazer's Notebook. 512p. 1982. pap. 3.50 (ISBN 0-553-22587-1). Bantam.

Smith, DeBoyd L. A Guide to Marine Coastal Plankton & Marine Invertebrate Larvae. LC 76-62564. (Illus.). 1978. pap. text ed. 9.95 (ISBN 0-8403-1672-0). Kendall-Hunt.

Smith, Delbert D. Space Stations: International Law & Policy. (Illus.). 1979. lib. bdg. 32.00 (ISBN 0-89158-654-7). Westview.

Smith, Denis M. Mussolini. LC 81-48127. (Illus.). 448p. 1982. 20.00 (ISBN 0-394-50694-4). Knopf.

Smith, Dennis. The Aran Islands: A Personal Journey. LC 77-25609. (Illus.). 160p. 1980. 17.95 o.p. (ISBN 0-385-13591-2). Doubleday.

--Barrington Moore Jr. A Critical Appraisal. 224p. (Orig.). 1983. lib. bdg. 17.50 (ISBN 0-87332-241-X); pap. text ed. 8.95 (ISBN 0-87332-242-8). M E Sharpe.

--Dennis Smith's Fire Safety Book: Everything You Need to Know to Save Your Life. 1983. pap. 2.95 (ISBN 0-686-43213-4). Bantam.

--The Final Fire. 1976. pap. 1.95 o.p. (ISBN 0-451-07141-7, J7141, Sig). NAL.

--Glitter & Ash. 1981. pap. 2.95 o.p. (ISBN 0-451-09761-0, E9761, Sig). NAL.

--The Little Fire Engine: That Saved the City. Kraus, Robert, ed. (Illus.). 32p. (gr. k-3). Date not set. bds. 6.95 (ISBN 0-671-45564-8). Windmill Bks.

Smith, Denzell S., ed. see May, Thomas.

Smith, DeVerne R. Palauan Social Structure. 345p. Date not set. 35.00 (ISBN 0-8135-0953-X). Rutgers U Pr.

Smith, Dick, jt. auth. see Amann, Dick.

Smith, Divine & Smith, Van. The Simply Divine Paperdoll Book. (Illus.). 32p. 1983. pap. 7.95 (ISBN 0-312-72593-0). St Martin.

Smith, Donald. How to Be Moderately Successful. 200p. (Orig.). 1982. pap. 7.95 (ISBN 0-89182-061-2). Charles River Bks.

Smith, Donald A. & Mukerjee, Gitanjali, eds. Assuring Quality Ambulatory Health Care: The Martin Luther King, Jr. Health Center. (Westview Special Studies in Health Care Ser.). 1978. lib. bdg. 30.00 o.p. (ISBN 0-89158-409-9). Westview.

Smith, Donald E., jt. auth. see Smith, Judith M.

Smith, Donald F. & Horrobin, D. F. Lithium & Animal Behavior. LC 81-13321. (Lithium Research Review Ser.: Vol. II). 134p. 1982. 16.95 (ISBN 0-89885-075-4). Human Sci Pr.

Smith, Donald M. & Mitchell, John. Aquametry, Vol. 5, Pt. 2. 2nd ed. (Chemical Analysis Monographs). 852p. 1983. 110.00 (ISBN 0-471-02265-9, Pub. by Wiley-Interscience). Wiley.

Smith, Donald M., jt. auth. see Mitchell, John, Jr.

Smith, Donald R. Variational Methods in Optimization. (Illus.). 464p. 1974. 28.95 (ISBN 0-13-940627-1). P-H.

Smith, Donald R., ed. see State Bar of Texas Council of the Family Law Section.

Smith, Doris. The Travels of J. B. Rabbit. LC 82-80876. Orig. Title: Les Vacances de Jeremy. (Illus.). 48p. (gr. k-2). 1982. 5.95 (ISBN 0-448-16585-6, G&D). Putnam Pub Group.
Smith, Doris, illus. The Tortoise & the Hare. LC 78-12525. (A Goodnight Bk.). (Illus.). (ps-1). 1979. 1.75 o.p. (ISBN 0-394-84102-6). Knopf.
Smith, Doris B. The First Hard Times. 144p. 1983. 10.95 (ISBN 0-670-31571-0). Viking Pr.
--Kelly's Creek. LC 75-6761. (Illus.). 80p. (gr. 3-7). 1975. 12.45i (ISBN 0-690-00731-0, TYC-J). Har-Row.
Smith, Dorothy. In Our Own Interest: A Handbook for the Citizen Lobbyist in State Legislatures. LC 78-10625. 144p. 1979. pap. 5.95 (ISBN 0-914842-33-1). Madrona Pubs.
Smith, Dorothy E., jt. auth. see McGinnis, Dorothy J.
Smith, Dorothy H. The Tall Book of Christmas. LC 54-9002. (Tall Bks). (Illus.). 96p. (gr. k-3). 1980. 5.95i (ISBN 0-06-025700-8, HarpJ); PLB 7.89 (ISBN 0-06-025701-6). Har-Row.
Smith, Dorothy V. This Was Staten Island. (Illus.). 1968. pap. 7.95 (ISBN 0-686-20335-6). Staten Island.
Smith, Dorothy V., jt. auth. see Dubois, Theodora.
Smith, Dorothy W. & Sherwen, Laurie N. Mothers & Their Adopted Children: The Bonding Process. LC 82-62153. 166p. (Orig.). 1983. pap. text ed. 10.95 (ISBN 0-913292-39-7). Tiresias Pr.
Smith, Douglas, et al. A Transition in Advanced Mathematics. LC 82-20737. 200p. 1983. text ed. 21.95 (ISBN 0-534-01249-3). Brooks-Cole.
Smith, Douglas K. Classroom Teacher & the Special Child. (Special Education Ser.). (Illus.). 224p. 1980. pap. text ed. 15.00 (ISBN 0-89568-187-0). Spec Learn Corp.
Smith, Douglass & Gibbons, John T. Real Estate Education Company: Real Estate Exam Manual. 200p. 1980. pap. 11.95 o.s.i. (ISBN 0-695-81408-7). Follett.
Smith, Duane A. Song of the Hammer & Drill: The Colorado San Juans, 1860-1914. Raese, Jon W. & Goldberg, J. H., eds. (Illus.). 194p. 1982. 28.95 (ISBN 0-918062-49-7). Colo Sch Mines.
--A Taste of the West: Essays in Honor of Robert G. Athearn. Smith, Duane A., ed. 1983. write for info. (ISBN 0-87108-641-7). Pruett.
Smith, Dwight L., ed. Afro-American History: A Bibliography. new ed. LC 73-87155. (Clio Bibliography Ser.: No. 2). 856p. 1974. text ed. 55.00 o.p. (ISBN 0-87436-123-0). ABC-Clio.
--Afro-American History: A Bibliography, Vol. 2. (Clio Bibliography Ser.: No. 8). 394p. 1981. 98.50 (ISBN 0-87436-314-4). ABC-Clio.
--The American & Canadian West: A Bibliography. (Clio Bibliography Ser.: No. 6). 558p. 1979. text ed. 69.00 (ISBN 0-87436-272-5). ABC-Clio.
--The History of Canada: An Annotated Bibliography. (Clio Bibliography Ser.: No. 10). 336p. 1983. lib. bdg. 55.00 (ISBN 0-87436-047-1). ABC-Clio.
--Indians of the United States & Canada: A Bibliography. LC 73-87156. (Clio Bibliography Ser.: No. 3). 453p. 1974. 48.00 o.p. (ISBN 0-87436-124-9). ABC-Clio.
Smith, E. A. A Comprehensive Approach to Rehabilitation of the Cancer Patient. 1976. text ed. 7.95 o.p. (ISBN 0-07-058492-3, HP). McGraw.
--Psychosocial Aspects of Cancer Patient Care. 1976. text ed. 7.95 o.p. (ISBN 0-07-058493-1, HP). McGraw.
Smith, E. Boyd. The Farm Book. 1982. PLB 12.95 (ISBN 0-395-32951-5); 12.45. HM.
Smith, E. Brian. Basic Chemical Thermodynamics. 2nd ed. (Oxford Chemistry Ser.). (Illus.). 1977. 13.95x o.p. (ISBN 0-19-855507-5); pap. 7.95x o.p. (ISBN 0-19-855508-3). Oxford U Pr.
--Basic Chemical Thermodynamics. 3rd ed. (Illus.). 160p. 1982. 19.50x (ISBN 0-19-855521-0); pap. 8.95x (ISBN 0-19-855522-9). Oxford U Pr.
Smith, E. Brooks & Meredith, Robert. Pilgrim Courage. (Illus.). (gr. 5 up). 1962. 9.95 (ISBN 0-316-80045-7). Little.
Smith, E. D. Battle for Burma. 1979. 25.00 o.p. (ISBN 0-7134-0737-9, Pub. by Batsford England). David & Charles.
--Britain's Brigade of Gurkhas. (Illus.). 291p. 1983. 22.50 (ISBN 0-436-47510-3, Pub. by Secker & Warburg). David & Charles.
Smith, E. D., jt. auth. see Nyman, R. Carter.
Smith, E. E. First Lensman. 1973. pap. 1.75 o.s.i. (ISBN 0-515-05332-5). Jove Pubns.
--Galactic Patrol. 1973. pap. 1.75 o.s.i. (ISBN 0-515-05288-4, V3084). Jove Pubns.
--Masters of Space. (The Family D'Alembert Ser.). (Orig.). 1979. pap. 1.75 o.s.i. (ISBN 0-515-04335-4). Jove Pubns.
--Masters of the Vortex. (The Lensman Ser.). pap. 1.75 o.s.i. (ISBN 0-515-05328-7). Jove Pubns.
Smith, E. E. & Goldin, Stephen. Appointment at Bloodstar. (The Family d'Alembert Ser.: No. 5). 192p. 1983. pap. 2.25 (ISBN 0-425-05821-2). Berkley Pub.
--The Clockwork Traitor. (The Family d'Alembert Ser.). 160p. 1982. pap. 2.25 (ISBN 0-425-05661-9). Berkley Pub.
--Eclipsing Binaries. (The Family d'Alembert Ser.: No. 8). 192p. (Orig.). 1983. pap. 2.50 (ISBN 0-425-05848-4). Berkley Pub.
--Getaway World. (The Family d'Alembert Ser.: No. 4). 192p. (Orig.). pap. 1.75 o.p. (ISBN 0-515-04809-7). Jove Pubns.
Smith, E. E. & Ribbons, D. W., eds. Molecular Approaches to Immunology. (Miami Winter Symposia Ser.). 1975. 37.50 (ISBN 0-12-651050-4). Acad Pr.
Smith, E. N., jt. auth. see Melvin, B. L.
Smith, E. Newbold. American Naval Broadsides: Seventeen Forty-Five to Eighteen Fifteen. (Illus.). 221p. 1974. 35.00 o.p. (ISBN 0-517-51761-2, C N Potter Bks). Crown.
Smith, E. Peshine. Manual of Political Economy. LC 66-17864. Repr. of 1853 ed. 19.50x (ISBN 0-678-00127-8). Kelley.
Smith, Ed. Blacks Students in Interracial Schools: A Guide for Students, Teachers, & Parents. 134p. 6.95 o.p. (ISBN 0-686-97219-8). Garrett Pk.
Smith, Ed., jt. auth. see Cannon, Joan B.
Smith, Edith K. How to Raise & Train a Great Pyrenees. (Orig.). pap. 2.50 o.p. (ISBN 0-87666-311-0, DS1084). TFH Pubns.
Smith, Edward C. & Zurcher, Arnold J. Dictionary of American Politics. 2nd ed. LC 67-28530. (Orig., Maps). 1968. pap. 5.72i (ISBN 0-06-463261-X, EH 261, EH). B&N NY.
Smith, Edward E. Children of the Lens. 1970. pap. 1.75 o.s.i. (ISBN 0-515-05326-0, V3251). Jove Pubns.
--Skylark Three. Del Rey, Lester, ed. LC 75-429. (Library of Science Fiction). 1975. lib. bdg. 17.50 o.s.i. (ISBN 0-8240-1433-2). Garland Pub.
--Subspace Explorers. LC 64-25828. 1965. 15.00x (ISBN 0-940724-15-4). Canaveral.
--Triplanetary. (The Lensman Ser.). 1970. pap. 1.75 o.s.i. (ISBN 0-515-05331-7). Jove Pubns.
Smith, Edward H. & Pimentel, David, eds. Pest Control Strategies. 1978. 30.50 (ISBN 0-12-650450-4). Acad Pr.
Smith, Edward R. Practical Guide for Private Investigators. 144p. 1982. pap. 8.95 (ISBN 0-87364-255-4). Paladin Ent.
Smith, Edward S. Unified Calculus. 507p. 1947. text ed. 14.50 (ISBN 0-471-80487-8, Pub. by Wiley). Krieger.
Smith, Edwin. All the Photo-Tricks. 4th ed. (Illus.). 280p. 1973. 24.95 (ISBN 0-240-50837-8). Focal Pr.
--Literacy Education for Adolescents & Adults: A Teacher's Resource Book. LC 74-101315. 1970. text ed. 13.95x (ISBN 0-87835-001-2). Boyd & Fraser.
Smith, Edwin, jt. auth. see Boas, Ralph P.
Smith, Edwin R., jt. auth. see Carmichael, Robert D.
Smith, Egerton. Principles of English Metre. Repr. of 1923 ed. lib. bdg. 16.25x (ISBN 0-8371-4340-3, SMEM). Greenwood.
Smith, Eileen. Mexico: Giant of the South. Schneider, Tom, ed. (Discovering our Heritage Ser.). (Illus.). 144p. (gr. 5 up). 1983. PLB 9.95 (ISBN 0-87518-242-9). Dillon Pr.
Smith, Elaine, jt. auth. see Smith, Eugene.
Smith, Elaine C. Love's Brightest Hour. (Candlelight Romance Ser.: No. 688). (Orig.). 1981. pap. 1.75 o.s.i. (ISBN 0-440-18530-0). Dell.
Smith, Elbert B. Magnificent Missourian: The Life of Thomas Hart Benton. LC 73-7459. 351p. 1973. Repr. of 1958 ed. lib. bdg. 18.75x (ISBN 0-8371-6933-X, SMMM). Greenwood.
Smith, Eleanor, jt. auth. see DiLeo, Michael.
Smith, Elihu H., ed. American Poems. LC 66-60007. 352p. 1979. 40.00x (ISBN 0-8201-1042-6). Schol Facsimiles.
Smith, Elinor. Aviatrix. (Illus.). 288p. 1981. 13.95 (ISBN 0-15-110372-0). HarBraceJ.
--Aviatrix. large type ed. LC 82-5849. 466p. 1982. Repr. of 1981 ed. 12.95 (ISBN 0-89621-368-4). Thorndike Pr.
Smith, Elise C., ed. Toward Internationalism: Readings in Cross-Cultural Communication. LC 78-17153. 1979. pap. text ed. 11.95 (ISBN 0-88377-123-3). Newbury Hse.
Smith, Elizabeth, ed. see Larsen, Norma S.
Smith, Elizabeth H., jt. ed. see Blocker, H. Gene.
Smith, Elliott. Contemporary Vocabulary. LC 78-65215. 1979. pap. text ed. 9.95x (ISBN 0-312-16847-0); inst. manual avail. (ISBN 0-312-16848-9). St Martin.
Smith, Elliott L. & Smith, Wanda V. Access to Literature. 600p. 1981. pap. 11.95x (ISBN 0-312-00213-0); instr. manual avail. (ISBN 0-312-00214-9). St Martin.
Smith, Elna N., jt. auth. see Melvin, Bruce L.
Smith, Elsdon C. The Book of Smith. LC 79-10098. (Illus.). 1979. pap. 4.95 (ISBN 0-399-50393-5, Perige). Putnam Pub Group.
--The New Dictionary of Family Names. LC 72-79693. 512p. 1973. 19.18i (ISBN 0-06-013933-1, HarpT). Har-Row.
--Personal Names: A Bibliography. LC 66-31855. 1965. Repr. of 1952 ed. 30.00x (ISBN 0-8103-3134-9). Gale.
--Story of Our Names. LC 71-109181. 1970. Repr. of 1950 ed. 29.00x (ISBN 0-8103-3858-0). Gale.
Smith, Elton E. Charles Reade. (English Authors Ser.: No. 186). 14.95 (ISBN 0-8057-6660-X, Twayne). G K Hall.
--Louis MacNeice. (English Authors Ser.: No. 99). lib. bdg. 10.95 o.p. (ISBN 0-8057-1364-6, Twayne). G K Hall.
Smith, Elwood. The See & Hear & Smell & Taste & Touch Book. LC 72-13890. (Illus.). (ps-3). 1973. 5.95 (ISBN 0-87955-105-4); PLB 4.98 (ISBN 0-87955-705-2). O'Hara.
Smith, Emil L. & Hill, Robert L. Principles of Biochemistry. 7th ed. Incl. General Aspects. 960p. text ed. 36.00x (ISBN 0-07-069762-0); Mammalian Biochemistry. 672p. text ed. 42.00x (ISBN 0-07-069763-9). (Illus.). 1983 (HP). McGraw.
Smith, Emily A., jt. auth. see Peck, Elisabeth S.
Smith, Eph. Riding to Win. (Illus.). 12.50x (ISBN 0-392-04411-0, SpS). Sportshelf.
Smith, Eric. Collecting Stamps. 15.50x (ISBN 0-392-09205-0, SpS). Sportshelf.
--How to Repair Clocks. (Illus.). 1979. 10.95 (ISBN 0-8306-9723-3); pap. 5.95 (ISBN 0-8306-1168-1, 1168). TAB Bks.
Smith, Eric, tr. see Eimert, Herbert & Stockhausen, Karlheinz.
Smith, Erik. Mozart Serenades, Divertimenti, & Dances. LC 81-71300. (BBC Music Guides Ser.). (Orig.). 1983. pap. 4.95 (ISBN 0-686-43217-7). U of Wash Pr.
Smith, Estellie, jt. auth. see Press, Irwin.
Smith, Esther M. Mrs. Humphry Ward. (English Author Ser.). 1980. lib. bdg. 14.95 (ISBN 0-8057-6766-5, Twayne). G K Hall.
Smith, Euclid O. Social Plays in Primates. 1978. 30.50 (ISBN 0-12-652750-4). Acad Pr.
Smith, Eugene & Smith, Elaine. Mind Matter Motion: Prescription Running. LC 82-99857. (Illus.). 240p. (Orig.). 1982. pap. 11.95 (ISBN 0-9608910-0-5). Neihardt-Smith.
Smith, Eunice, jt. auth. see Moura, Bernard.
Smith, Eunice C. & Savacool, John K. Voix du Siecle. 276p. (Orig.). pap. text ed. 9.95 (ISBN 0-15-595006-1). HarBraceJ.
Smith, Eunice C. & Savacool, John K., eds. Voix Du Siecle. 276p. (Fr.). 1980. pap. text ed. 9.95 o.p. (ISBN 0-15-595006-1, HC). HarBraceJ.
Smith, Evelyn R. Name Index to Arad Thomas' 1871: Pioneer History of Orleans County, New York. 32p. 1982. lib. bdg. 12.00x (ISBN 0-932334-55-5); pap. text ed. 8.00x (ISBN 0-932334-56-3). Heart of the Lakes.
Smith, Everett L. & Stoedefalke, Karl. Aging & Exercise. LC 80-20596. 1983. pap. 8.95 (ISBN 0-89490-040-4). Enslow Pubs.
Smith, Everett L., ed. see American College of Sports Medicine.
Smith, F. B. Florence Nightingale: Reputation & Power. LC 81-21332. 1982. 25.00 (ISBN 0-312-29649-5). St Martin.
Smith, F. B., jt. auth. see Kamenkay, Eugene.
Smith, F. G. Pulsars. LC 75-44569. (Cambridge Monographs on Physics). (Illus.). 1977. 44.50 (ISBN 0-521-21241-3). Cambridge U Pr.
Smith, F. Graham & Thomson, J. H. Optics. LC 71-146547. (Manchester Physics Ser). 350p. 1971. 19.95 (ISBN 0-471-80360-X, Pub. by Wiley-Interscience). Wiley.
Smith, F. J. Experiencing Musical Sound. 256p. 1979. 21.00x (ISBN 0-677-04430-5). Gordon.
Smith, F. Seymour, jt. auth. see Bell, F. T.
Smith, Francis B. Radical Artisan: William James Linton 1812-1897. LC 73-1933. (Illus.). 254p. 1973. 17.50x o.p. (ISBN 0-87471-180-0). Rowman.
Smith, Frank. History of English Elementary Education, 1760-1902. Repr. of 1931 ed. 25.00x (ISBN 0-678-08046-1). Kelley.
--Reading Without Nonsense. LC 79-11078. 1979. pap. text ed. 7.95x (ISBN 0-8077-2567-6). Tchrs Coll.
--Walt Disney's Tron Electronic Mixed up Mazes. Barish, Wendy, ed. (Illus.). 64p. (gr. 3-7). 1982. pap. 1.95 (ISBN 0-671-44541-3). Wanderer Bks.
--Walt Disney's Tron Electronic Puzzle World. Barish, Wendy, ed. (Illus.). 64p. (gr. 3-7). 1982. pap. 1.95 (ISBN 0-671-44540-5). Wanderer Bks.
Smith, Frank & Miller, George, eds. Genesis of Language: A Psycholinguistic Approach. 1966. pap. 4.95x (ISBN 0-262-69022-5). MIT Pr.
Smith, Frank C. Mr. Merlin's Mazes. (Illus.). 64p. (Orig.). (gr. 3-7). 1981. pap. 2.50 o.p. (ISBN 0-671-44478-6). Wanderer Bks.
Smith, Frank C. & Chang, Richard C. The Practice of Ion Chromatography. 200p. 1983. 35.00 (ISBN 0-471-05517-4, Pub. by Wiley-Interscience). Wiley.
Smith, Frank E. & Shore, Sidney. It Doesn't Pay to Work too Hard. 200p. (Orig.). 1979. pap. 9.00 (ISBN 0-9602288-0-2). Smith F E.
Smith, Frank J. & Hester, Randolph T., Jr. Community Goal Setting. LC 81-7090. 152p. 1982. 29.50 (ISBN 0-87933-405-3). Hutchinson Ross.
Smith, Frank J., jt. auth. see Dunham, Randall.
Smith, Frank K. Private Pilot's Survival Manual. (Modern Aviation Ser.). (Illus.). 1979. 9.95 o.p. (ISBN 0-8306-9766-7); pap. 5.95 o.p. (ISBN 0-8306-2261-6, 2261). TAB Bks.
--Weekend Wings: The Complete Adventures of the Original Weekend Pilot. 1982. 13.95 (ISBN 0-394-52527-2). Random.
Smith, Fred H. The Neanderthal Remains from Krapina: A Descriptive & Comparative Study. 1976. pap. 11.95x (ISBN 0-87049-226-8). U of Tenn Pr.
Smith, Frederick M. Surgery of the Elbow. 2nd ed. LC 75-183457. (Illus.). 360p. 1972. 14.00 o.p. (ISBN 0-7216-8382-7). Saunders.
Smith, G., jt. auth. see Lees, R.
Smith, G. B., jt. auth. see Tozer, A. W.
Smith, G. B., ed. see Tozer, A. W.
Smith, G. Barnett & Martin, Dorothy. John Knox: Apostle of the Scottish Reformation. LC 82-12608. 128p. 1982. pap. 3.95 (ISBN 0-8024-4354-0). Moody.
Smith, G. C., ed. The Boole-DeMorgan Correspondence, 1842-1864. (Logic Guides Ser.). (Illus.). 162p. 1982. 44.00x (ISBN 0-19-853183-4). Oxford U Pr.
Smith, G. C., et al. Laboratory Manual for Meat Science. 2nd ed. (Illus.). 316p. 1982. pap. text ed. 13.95x (ISBN 0-89641-112-5). American Pr.
Smith, G. Dallas. Outline of Bible Study. pap. 2.95 (ISBN 0-89225-192-1); pap. 2.95 o.p. (ISBN 0-686-96726-7). Gospel Advocate.
Smith, G. Hubert. Omaha Indians. Horr, David A., ed. (American Indian Ethnohistory Ser. - Plains Indians). 1974. lib. bdg. 42.00 o.s.i. (ISBN 0-8240-0739-5). Garland Pub.
Smith, G. L. & Davis, P. E. Medical Terminology. 4th ed. LC 80-17970. 325p. 1981. pap. 16.50 (ISBN 0-471-05827-0, Pub. by Wiley Med); material 1.95 supplementary (ISBN 0-471-09071-9). Wiley.
Smith, G. M. Phytoplankton of the Inland Lakes of Wisconsin, 2 vols. in one. 1977. Repr. of 1924 ed. 48.00 (ISBN 3-7682-1134-7). Lubrecht & Cramer.
Smith, G. N. Elements of Soil Mechanics. 5th ed. 440p. 1982. 49.00x (ISBN 0-246-11334-0, Pub. by Granada England). State Mutual Bk.
--Elements of Soil Mechanics for Civil & Mining Engineers. 342p. 1968. 65.00x (ISBN 0-677-61280-X). Gordon.
--Elements of Soil Mechanics for Civil & Mining Engineers. 493p. 1982. pap. text ed. 21.75x (ISBN 0-246-11765-6, Pub. by Granada England). Renouf.
--Introduction to Matrix & Finite Elements in Civil Engineering. (Illus.). 1971. text ed. 20.50 (ISBN 0-85334-502-3, Pub. by Applied Sci England). Elsevier.
Smith, G. R. & Dorr, E. Display & Promotion. (Occupational Manuals & Projects in Marketing Ser.). 1970. text ed. 6.96 (ISBN 0-07-058605-5, G). McGraw.
Smith, Gaddis. American Diplomacy During the Second World War: 1941-1945. LC 64-8713. 194p. 1965. 11.95 (ISBN 0-471-80177-1). Wiley.
--Foreign Policy in Perilous Times: Who's in Charge? (Vital Issues, Vol. XXIX: No. 8). 0.50 (ISBN 0-686-81613-7). Ctr Info Am.
Smith, Gary. Money & Banking: Financial Markets & Institutions. (Illus.). 1981. text ed. 22.95 (ISBN 0-201-07696-9); instr's manual 2.50 (ISBN 0-201-07697-7). A-W.
Smith, Gaylord. The Briton Manufacturing Company: A Microcomputer Simulation. user's guide scp 8.00 (ISBN 0-06-046314-7, HarpC); complete package scp 225.00 (ISBN 0-06-046313-9). Har-Row.
Smith, Gene. Where Are My Legions. LC 79-28277. 320p. 1980. 12.95 o.p. (ISBN 0-688-03645-7). Morrow.
Smith, Genevie L. Spelling by Principles. 1966. text ed. 9.95 (ISBN 0-13-834242-3). P-H.
Smith, Genevieve. Genevieve Smith's Deluxe Handbook for the Executive Secretary. 267p. 1979. 17.50 (ISBN 0-686-84017-8, Busn). P-H.
Smith, Genevieve & Davis, Phyllis E. Medical Terminology: A Programmed Text. 3rd ed. LC 75-30952. 1976. 11.95 o.p. (ISBN 0-471-80200-X, Pub. by Wiley Medical). Wiley.
Smith, Genevieve L. & Davis, Phyllis E. Quick Medical Terminology. LC 72-4193. (Wiley Self-Teaching Guides Ser). 248p. 1972. 8.95x (ISBN 0-471-80198-4); cassettes 8.95 (ISBN 0-471-80201-8). Wiley.
Smith, Genny, ed. see Bateman, Paul, et al.
Smith, Genny, ed. see Lane, Paul H. & Rossman, Antonio.
Smith, Genny, ed. see Reed, Adele.
Smith, Genny, ed. see Rinehart, C. Dean & Smith, Ward C.
Smith, Genny S., ed. see Rinehart, Dean, et al.
Smith, Geoffrey Nowell- see Nowell-Smith, Geoffrey.
Smith, Geoffrey R. & Toynbee, Margaret. Leaders of the Civil Wars, Sixteen Forty-Two to Sixteen Forty-Eight. 1980. 30.00x o.p. (ISBN 0-900093-56-0, Pub. by Roundwood). State Mutual Bk.
Smith, George. The Coronation of Elizabeth Wydeville. 90p. 1975. Repr. of 1935 ed. text ed. 10.50x (ISBN 0-904586-00-6, Pub. by Alan Sutton England). Humanities.
--Storage Batteries: Including Operation, Charging, Maintenance & Repair. 3rd, rev. ed. (Illus.). 248p. (gr. 9 up). 1980. text ed. 39.95x o.s.i. (ISBN 0-273-08416-X, LTB). Sportshelf.
Smith, George A. Encyclopedia of Cockatiels. (Illus.). 1978. 14.95 (ISBN 0-87666-958-5, PS-743). TFH Pubns.
--Lovebirds & Related Parrots. (Illus.). 1979. pap. 14.95 (ISBN 0-87666-974-7, PS-774). TFH Pubns.
Smith, George C., ed. see Livermore Arms Control Conference.
Smith, George H. Motivation Research in Advertising & Marketing. LC 70-100175. (Illus.). 1971. Repr. of 1954 ed. lib. bdg. 21.00x (ISBN 0-8371-4023-4, SMMO). Greenwood.

Smith, George I. The Ghosts of Kampala: The Rise & Fall of Idi Amin. 208p. 1980. 10.95 o.p. (ISBN 0-312-32662-9). St Martin.

Smith, George M. Hebron Church Register 1750-1825, Madison, Virginia, 2 vols. 1981. pap. 12.00 set (ISBN 0-917968-08-5). Shenandoah Hist.

Smith, George O. Scientists' Nightmares: The Baffling, the Fake, & the Unsolvable. (Illus.). 160p. (gr. 7-11). 1972. PLB 5.29 o.p. (ISBN 0-399-60715-3). Putnam Pub Group.

--Worlds of George O. 352p. 1982. pap. 3.50 (ISBN 0-553-22532-4). Bantam.

Smith, George P. & Gallo, Barbara G. Virginia Forms, Vol. II. 368p. 1982. 65.00 (ISBN 0-87215-527-7). Michie-Bobbs.

Smith, George P., ed. Wills & Administration for Virginia & West Virginia, 3 vols. 2nd ed. 1960. with 1975 cum. suppl. 100.00 (ISBN 0-87215-114-X); 1975 cum. suppl. only 20.00 (ISBN 0-87215-296-0). Michie-Bobbs.

Smith, George P., II, ed. Challenges to the Brave New World, 2. LC 81-68023. (New Studies on Law & Society). (Orig.). 1982. Vol. 1. PLB 32.00x (ISBN 0-86733-015-5); Vol. 2. PLB 28.50x (ISBN 0-686-91870-3); Vol. 1 o.p. pap. text ed. 19.75x (ISBN 0-686-98370-X); Vol. 2. pap. text ed. 18.50x o. p (ISBN 0-686-98371-8). Assoc Faculty Pr.

Smith, George W., jt. auth. see Judah, Charles.

Smith, Gerald, jt. auth. see Belstock, Alan.

Smith, Gerald, ed. Tragedy in the Church. 1978. pap. 2.50 (ISBN 0-87509-215-2). Chr Pubns.

Smith, Gerald B., jt. ed. see Mathews, Shailer.

Smith, Gerald B., ed. see Tozer, A. W.

Smith, Geraldine, ed. Phase Diagrams for Ceramists, Vol. 4, 1981. (Illus.). 80.00 (ISBN 0-916094-40-5); members 60.00 (ISBN 0-686-85613-9); students 40.00 (ISBN 0-686-91505-4). Am Ceramic.

Smith, Gerard. The Philosophy of Being. 1964. 12.95 (ISBN 0-87462-530-0). Marquette.

--Truth That Frees. (Aquinas Lecture). 1956. 7.95 (ISBN 0-87462-121-6). Marquette.

Smith, Gerard V., ed. Catalysis in Organic Synthesis, 1977. 1978. 29.50 (ISBN 0-12-650550-0). Acad Pr.

Smith, Gerry, tr. see Galich, Alexander.

Smith, Gilbert. Juan Pablo Forner. (World Authors Ser.). 1976. lib. bdg. 15.95 (ISBN 0-8057-6170-5, Twayne). G K Hall.

Smith, Gilbert M. Crypotogamic Botany, 2 vols. 2nd ed. Incl. Vol. 1. Algae & Fungi. text ed. 28.00 o.p. (ISBN 0-07-058839-2); Vol. 2. Bryophytes & Pteridophytes. text ed. o.p. (ISBN 0-07-058849-X). (Botanical Sciences Ser.). 1955 (C). McGraw.

Smith, Glenn H. Langer of North Dakota. Freidel, Frank, ed. LC 78-62502. (Modern American History Ser.: Vol. 16). 1979. lib. bdg. 25.00 o.s.i. (ISBN 0-8240-3639-5). Garland Pub.

Smith, Godfrey. Caviare. 1976. 8.95 o.p. (ISBN 0-698-10800-0, Coward). Putnam PubGroup.

Smith, Gordon. Democracy in Western Germany: Parties & Politics in the Federal Republic. 2nd ed. 180p. (Orig.). 1983. pap. text ed. 8.50x (ISBN 0-686-82618-3). Holmes & Meier.

--Politics in Western Europe. LC 73-75192. 398p. 1973. text ed. 19.50x o.p. (ISBN 0-8419-0137-6); pap. text ed. 9.75x o.p. (ISBN 0-8419-0143-0). Holmes & Meier.

--Politics in Western Europe. 3rd ed. LC 80-81211. 344p. 1980. 27.50x (ISBN 0-8419-0627-0); pap. 12.50x (ISBN 0-8419-0628-9). Holmes & Meier.

Smith, Graham E. The Latvian Nation. (Studies in Russian & East European History). (Illus.). 1983. price not set (ISBN 0-389-20025-5). B&N Imports. Postponed.

Smith, Grahame. Dickens, Money & Society. 1968. 34.50x (ISBN 0-520-01190-2). U of Cal Pr.

Smith, Gregory W. & Naifeh, Steven. What Every Client Needs to Know about Using a Lawyer. 256p. 1982. 13.95 (ISBN 0-399-12761-5). Putnam Pub Group.

Smith, Grey. Better Grades in Ten Minutes. rev. ed. 49p. 1983. pap. text ed. 4.95 (ISBN 0-686-84030-5). WordShop Pubns.

Smith, Gudmund, jt. ed. see Froehlich, Werner.

Smith, Guillaume. Nouveau Voyage de Guinee, Description des Coutumes, Manieres, Terrain, Climat, etc. Habillements, Batiments, Education, Arts Manuels, Agriculture, Commerce, Emplois, Langages, Rangs de Distinction, Habitations, Divertissements, 2 vols. (Bibliotheque Africaine Ser.). 580p. (Fr.). 1974. Repr. of 1751 ed. lib. bdg. 155.00x o.p. (ISBN 0-8287-0780-4, 72-2159). Clearwater Pub.

Smith, Gus, jt. auth. see Hickey, Des.

Smith, Guy. Bats Out of Hell. 1979. pap. 1.75 o.p. (ISBN 0-451-08925-1, E8925, Sig). NAL.

Smith, Guy E. English Literature: After Neo-Classicism. (Quality Paperback: No. 59). (Orig.). 1967. pap. 1.95 o.p. (ISBN 0-8226-0059-5). Littlefield.

Smith, Guy N. Killer Crabs. 1979. pap. 1.75 o.p. (ISBN 0-451-08954-5, E8954, Sig). NAL.

Smith, Guy N., ed. Sleeping Beauty. LC 79-89578. (Disney Classics Ser.). (Illus.). (gr. k-4). 1980. pap. 0.95 (ISBN 0-448-16108-7, G&D). Putnam Pub Group.

Smith, Guy V. Master Guide to Real Estate Valuation. 1973. 79.50 (ISBN 0-13-559922-9). Exec Reports.

--Portable Home Valuation Guide. 1982. 59.50 (ISBN 0-13-686428-7). Exec Reports.

Smith, H. The Last Words. pap. 3.75 (ISBN 0-88172-124-7). Believers Bkshelf.

--An Outline of the Book of Nehemiah. pap. 3.50 (ISBN 0-88172-125-5). Believers Bkshelf.

--Strategies of Social Research. 2nd ed. 1980. 22.95 (ISBN 0-13-851154-3). P-H.

--You Can Survive. 1982. 9.95 (ISBN 0-07-058960-7). McGraw.

Smith, H., jt. auth. see Draper, N. R.

Smith, H., jt. auth. see Draper, Norman.

Smith, H., ed. The Molecular Biology of Plant Cells. (Botanical Monographs: Vol. 14). 1978. 48.50x (ISBN 0-520-03465-1). U of Cal Pr.

Smith, H. Allen. Larks in the Popcorn. LC 74-15560. (Illus.). 256p. 1974. Repr. of 1948 ed. lib. bdg. 17.00x (ISBN 0-8371-7791-X, SMLP). Greenwood.

Smith, H. G., ed. Thermal Neutron Scattering Applied to Chemical & Solid State Physics. pap. 5.00 (ISBN 0-686-60374-5). Polycrystal Bk Serv.

Smith, H. R., et al. Management: Making Organizations Perform. (Illus.). 1980. text ed. 23.95x (ISBN 0-02-412500-8). Macmillan.

Smith, H. T. & Green, T. Human Interaction with Computers. LC 79-42930. 1980. 33.50 (ISBN 0-12-652850-0); pap. 15.50 o.s. (ISBN 0-12-652852-7). Acad Pr.

Smith, H. W. On Paper. 2nd ed. 1978. pap. 10.95x o.p. (ISBN 0-534-00561-6). Wadsworth Pub.

Smith, H. Wendell. Elements of the Essay. 1979. pap. text ed. 9.95x o.p. (ISBN 0-534-00701-5). Wadsworth Pub.

Smith, Hanna W. El Secreto de una Vida Feliz. 224p. Date not set. 2.95 (ISBN 0-88113-270-5). Edit Betania.

Smith, Harlan M. Elementary Monetary Theory. (Orig.). 1968. pap. text ed. 3.95x (ISBN 0-685-19722-0). Phila Bk Co.

Smith, Harold & Baker, William. The Administrative Manager. LC 78-6085. 1978. text ed. 19.95 (ISBN 0-574-20030-4, 13-3030); instr's guide avail. (ISBN 0-574-20031-2, 13-3031); study guide 7.95 (ISBN 0-574-20032-0, 13-3032). SRA.

Smith, Harold & Keiffer, Mildred. Pathways in Mathematics: Level II. 3rd ed. Sharpe, Glyn, ed. (Illus.). (gr. 8). 1980. pap. text ed. 7.26x (ISBN 0-913688-37-1); tchr's guide 6.00 (ISBN 0-686-96846-8). Pawnee Pub.

Smith, Harold, jt. auth. see Keiffer, Mildred.

Smith, Harold I. Pastoral Care for Single Parents. 158p. 1982. pap. 3.95 (ISBN 0-8341-0782-1). Beacon Hill.

--Single Life in a Double Bed: How to Cope with Life After Divorce. LC 79-65543. 1979. pap. 2.50 (ISBN 0-89081-360-4). Harvest Hse.

Smith, Harold W. Approximate Analysis of Randomly Excited Non-Linear Controls. (Press Research Monographs: No. 34). 1966. 15.00x (ISBN 0-262-19027-3). MIT Pr.

Smith, Harriet L. American Indian Foods & Vegetables. (A Western Americana Book). (Illus., Orig.). 1982. pap. 3.00x (ISBN 0-913626-23-6). S S S Pub Co.

Smith, Harriet L., et al. Academic Sketches. (Illus.). 104p. (Orig.). 1973. pap. 4.00 (ISBN 0-913626-03-1). S S S Pub Co.

--Spring Sketches. (Humor Ser.). (Illus.). 50p. (Orig.). 1973. pap. 3.00x (ISBN 0-913626-01-5). S S S Pub Co.

--Oregon Vignettes Series One: Joel Palmer & Other Diarist of the Oregon Trail. (Illus.). 104p. (Orig.). pap. cancelled o.p. (ISBN 0-913626-06-6). S S S Pub Co.

--Oregon Vignettes Series Three: Pioneer Jills of All Trades. (Illus.). 104p. (Orig.). pap. cancelled o.p. (ISBN 0-913626-16-3). S S S Pub Co.

--Oregon Vignettes Series Two: Pioneer Jack of All Trade. (Illus.). 104p. (Orig.). pap. cancelled o.p. (ISBN 0-913626-14-7). S S S Pub Co.

Smith, Harris P. & Wilkes, Lambert H. Farm Machinery & Equipment. 6th ed. (Illus.): 1976. text ed. 39.50 (ISBN 0-07-058957-7, C). McGraw.

Smith, Harry. Biography of a Bee. (Illus.). (gr. 5-7). 1970. PLB 4.49 o.p. (ISBN 0-399-60057-4). Putnam Pub Group.

--Me, the People. LC 79-63451. 116p. 1979. 6.50 (ISBN 0-912292-61-X). The Smith.

--Phytochrome & Photomorphogenesis. (Illus.). 242p. 1975. text ed. 24.00 o.p. (ISBN 0-07-084038-5, C). McGraw.

Smith, Harry, jt. auth. see Cruchon, Steve.

Smith, Harry, ed. see Greenberg, Alvin, et al.

Smith, Harry, et al. The Word & Beyond. LC 81-51491. 400p. 1981. 12.95 (ISBN 0-912292-70-9); pap. 5.95 (ISBN 0-912292-67-9). The Smith.

Smith, Harry, Jr., jt. auth. see Kuebler, Roy R., Jr.

Smith, Harry W. The Art of Making Furniture in Miniature. (Illus.). 288p. 1983. 32.50 (ISBN 0-525-93249-6, 03155-950); pap. 21.95 (ISBN 0-525-47713-6, 02131-640). Dutton.

--Michael & the Mary Day. (Illus.). 1979. 9.95 (ISBN 0-89272-077-8); pap. 6.95 (ISBN 0-89272-046-8). Down East.

--Windjammers of the Maine Coast. (Illus.). 128p. 1983. 12.95t (ISBN 0-89272-120-0); pap. 7.95 (ISBN 0-89272-135-9). Down East.

Smith, Helen B., jt. auth. see Smith, Allan B.

Smith, Helen D., jt. auth. see Hopkins, Helen L.

Smith, Helen D., jt. ed. see Hopkins, Helen L.

Smith, Helen K. Presumptuous Dreamers: A Sociological History of the Life & Times of Abigail Scott Duniway, 1872-1886, Vol. 2. LC 74-79460. (Western Americana Bk.). (Orig.). 1983. 20.00t (ISBN 0-913626-26-0); pap. 15.00t (ISBN 0-913626-27-9). S S S Pub Co.

Smith, Helena H., jt. auth. see Alderson, Nannie T.

Smith, Helene, jt. auth. see Swetnam, George.

Smith, Henry. Amazing Air. LC 82-80991. (Science Club Ser.). (Illus.). 48p. (gr. 3-6). 1983. PLB 8.16 (ISBN 0-688-00973-5); pap. 5.25 (ISBN 0-688-00977-8). Lothrop.

Smith, Henry C. Sensitivity Training: The Scientific Understanding of Individuals. 1973. text ed. 21.95 (ISBN 0-07-058481-8, C). McGraw.

Smith, Henry C. & Wakeley, John H. Psychology of Industrial Behavior. 3rd ed. 400p. 1972. text ed. 32.50 (ISBN 0-07-058900-3, C); instructor's manual 2.95 (ISBN 0-07-058901-1). McGraw.

Smith, Henry J. Collected Mathematical Papers, 2 Vols. LC 65-11859. 75.00 (ISBN 0-8284-0187-X). Chelsea Pub.

--Report on the Theory of Numbers. LC 64-8080. 1966. 15.95 (ISBN 0-8284-0186-1). Chelsea Pub.

Smith, Henry L. Airways Abroad: The Story of American World Air Routes. (Airlines History Project Ser.). Date not set. price not set (ISBN 0-404-19336-6). AMS Pr.

--Airways: The History of Commercial Aviation in the United States. (Airlines History Project Ser.). (Illus.). Date not set. price not set (ISBN 0-404-19335-8). AMS Pr.

Smith, Henry N. Democracy & the Novel: Popular Resistance to Classic American Writers. (A Galaxy Book: No. 633). 1978. pap. 6.95 (ISBN 0-19-502896-1). Oxford U Pr.

Smith, Henry P. Glossary of Terms & Phrases. LC 79-175746. x, 521p. 1972. Repr. of 1889 ed. 45.00x (ISBN 0-8103-3816-5). Gale.

Smith, Herbert. Dreams of Natural Places: A New England Schooner Odyssey. LC 80-69529. (Illus.). 104p. 1981. 18.95 (ISBN 0-89272-107-3, PIC470). Down East.

Smith, Herbert F. John Muir. (United States Authors Ser.). 13.95 (ISBN 0-8057-0536-8, Twayne). G K Hall.

--Living for Resurrection. pap. 1.95 o.p. (ISBN 0-685-61278-3). Alba.

--The Popular American Novel, 1865-1920. (United States Author Ser.). 1980. lib. bdg. 11.95 (ISBN 0-8057-7310-X, Twayne). G K Hall.

Smith, Herbert F., ed. Bracebridge Hall: Washington Irving. (Critical Editions Program). 1977. lib. bdg. 25.00 (ISBN 0-8057-8506-X, Twayne). G K Hall.

Smith, Herbert H. The Citizen's Guide to Planning. 2nd ed. LC 78-72486. (Illus.). 198p. 1979. pap. 8.95 (ISBN 0-918286-14-X). Planners Pr.

--Citizen's Guide to Zoning. LC 82-62237. (Illus.). 256p. 1983. pap. write for info (ISBN 0-918286-28-X). Planners Pr.

Smith, Herschel. Aircraft Piston Engines: From the Manly Baltzer to the Continental Tiara. (Aviation Ser.). (Illus.). 264p. 1981. 21.95 (ISBN 0-07-058472-9, P&RB). McGraw.

Smith, Hervey G. Marlinspike Sailor. rev. ed. LC 77-143856. (Illus.). 1969. 12.50 (ISBN 0-8286-0044-9). De Graff.

--The Small-Boat Sailor's Bible. rev ed. LC 73-82247. (Outdoor Bible Ser.). 144p. 1974. pap. 3.95 (ISBN 0-385-05527-7). Doubleday.

Smith, Hobart M. Amphibians of North America. (Golden Field Guide Ser.). (Illus.). 1978. 9.95 (ISBN 0-307-47008-3, Golden Pr); PLB 13.08 (ISBN 0-307-63662-3); pap. 6.95 (ISBN 0-307-13662-0). Western Pub.

--Snakes As Pets. (Illus.). 1958. 14.95 (ISBN 0-87666-908-9, AP925). TFH Pubns.

Smith, Hobart M., jt. auth. see Zim, Herbert S.

Smith, Homer. Organizing for Better Meetings. 1976. pap. 21.00 plastic spiral binding (ISBN 0-686-98291-6). Sales & Mktg.

Smith, Homer W. Kidney: Structure & Functions in Health & Disease. (Illus.). 1951. 45.00x (ISBN 0-19-501140-6). Oxford U Pr.

Smith, Howard E. Sensual Explorer: Stimulating Your Pleasure Senses. LC 77-9068. 1977. 8.95 o.p. (ISBN 0-399-12079-3). Putnam Pub Group.

Smith, Howard E., Jr. Killer Weather: Stories of Great Disasters. LC 81-22114. 256p. 1982. 12.95 (ISBN 0-396-08055-3). Dodd.

--Play with the Sun. (gr. 2-4). 1975. PLB 6.95 o.p. (ISBN 0-07-059105-9, GB). McGraw.

Smith, Howard, Jr. The Animal Olympics. LC 78-60302. (Illus.). 1979. 7.95a o.p. (ISBN 0-385-14354-0). Doubleday.

Smith, Howard M. Principles of Holography. 2nd ed. LC 75-5631. 279p. 1975. 32.50 (ISBN 0-471-80341-3, Pub. by Wiley-Interscience). Wiley.

Smith, Howard Van see Van Dusen, C. Raymond & Van Smith, Howard.

Smith, Huston. Forgotten Truth: The Primordial Tradition. LC 74-15850. (Illus.). 192p. 1976. 8.95i o.p. (ISBN 0-06-013902-1, HarpT). Har-Row.

--Religions of Man. pap. 5.95i (ISBN 0-06-090043-1, CN43, CN). Har-Row.

Smith, Hyman. Preventing Alcohol Consumption. 1983. 30.00 (ISBN 0-533-05043-X). Vantage.

Smith, I., jt. auth. see Hellerman, Herbert.

Smith, I. C. Microcomputers in Education. LC 81-20176. (Computers & Their Applications Ser.). 212p. 1982. 34.95 (ISBN 0-470-27362-3). Halsted Pr.

Smith, I. C., jt. auth. see Smith, Christopher.

Smith, I. M. Programming the Finite Element Method with Application to Geomechanics. 351p. 1982. 47.50x (ISBN 0-471-28003-8, Pub. by Wiley-Interscience); pap. 21.95x (ISBN 0-471-10098-6, Pub. Bu Wiley-Interscience). Wiley.

Smith, Iain C. The Search. 192p. 1983. 16.95 (ISBN 0-575-03297-9, Pub. by Gollancz England). David & Charles.

Smith, Ian Mayo. Planning a Performance Improvement Project: A Practical Guide. 3rd rev. ed. LC 80-8175. (Guideline Ser.). 61p. (Orig.). 1981. pap. write for info. (ISBN 0-931816-26-2); wkbk. avail.; 5.45x (ISBN 0-686-86268-6). Kumarian Pr.

Smith, Ian W. Kinetics & Dynamics of Elementary Gas Reactions. LC 79-40533. (Illus.). 1980. 39.95 (ISBN 0-408-70790-9). Butterworth.

Smith, Irene. Diary of a Small Business. 192p. 1982. 14.95 (ISBN 0-686-83056-3, ScribT). Scribner.

Smith, Irving D., ed. Doane's Farm Management Guide. 14th ed. LC 79-56892. (Illus.). 1980. pap. cancelled (ISBN 0-932250-09-2). Doane-Western.

Smith, Ivan C. & Carson, Bonnie. Indium. LC 77-88486. (Trace Metals in the Environment Ser.: Vol. 5). 1978. 39.50 o.p. (ISBN 0-250-40232-7). Ann Arbor Science.

Smith, Ivan C. & Carson, Bonnie L. Silver, Vol. 2. LC 77-88486. (Trace Metals in the Environment Ser.). 1977. 39.50 o.p. (ISBN 0-250-40215-7). Ann Arbor Science.

--Thallium, Vol. 1. LC 77-88486. (Trace Metals in the Environment Ser.). 1977. 39.50 o.p. (ISBN 0-250-40214-9). Ann Arbor Science.

--Zirconium, Vol. 3. LC 77-88486. (Trace Metals in the Environment Ser.). 1978. 39.50 o.p. (ISBN 0-250-40216-5). Ann Arbor Science.

Smith, Ivan C. & Carson, Bonnie L., eds. Cobalt, Vol. 6. LC 77-88486. (Trace Metals in the Environment Ser.). 1981. 59.95 (ISBN 0-250-40362-5). Ann Arbor Science.

Smith, Ivan C., et al. Palladium-Osmium, Vol. 4. LC 77-88486. (Trace Metals in the Environment Ser.). 1978. 39.50 o.p. (ISBN 0-250-40217-3). Ann Arbor Science.

Smith, J. Instant Medical Advisor. (Career Institute Instant Reference Library). 1970. 3.95 o.p. (ISBN 0-531-02011-8). Watts.

--Shakespearian & Other Essays. LC 73-83110. 368p. 1974. 39.50 (ISBN 0-521-20373-2). Cambridge U Pr.

Smith, J., jt. auth. see Lynch, B.

Smith, J., jt. ed. see Schade, J.

Smith, J. A., ed. Advances in Nuclear Quadrupole Resonance. Vol. 3. 1978 ed. 114.00 (ISBN 0-471-26029-0, Pub. by Wiley Heyden); Vol. 2. 1975 ed. 114.00 (ISBN 0-471-26028-2); Vol. 1. 1974 ed. 114.00 (ISBN 0-471-26027-4). Wiley.

Smith, J. C. Study of Wordsworth. LC 68-26218. 1969. Repr. of 1944 ed. 7.50 o.p. (ISBN 0-8046-0427-4). Kennikat.

Smith, J. E. Industrial Mycology. Berry, D. R., ed. (Filamentous Fungi Ser.: Vol. 1). 352p. 1975. text ed. write for info (ISBN 0-7131-2467-9). E Arnold.

--Integrated Injection Logic. 421p. 1980. 38.95x (ISBN 0-471-08675-4, Pub. by Wiley-Interscience); pap. 24.95x (ISBN 0-471-08676-2). Wiley.

Smith, J. E. & Berry, D. B. Biosynthesis & Metabolism. (Filamentous Fungi Ser.: Vol. 2). (Illus.). 654p. 1976. text ed. 64.50 (ISBN 0-7131-2537-3). E Arnold.

--Developmental Mycology. (Filamentous Fungi Ser.: Vol. 3). 480p. 1978. text ed. 74.50 (ISBN 0-7131-2642-6). E Arnold.

Smith, J. E. & Berry, D. R. Fungal Technology. (Filamentous Fungi Ser.: Vol. 4). 320p. 1983. text ed. 74.50 (ISBN 0-7131-2857-7). E Arnold.

Smith, J. E., ed. Integrated Injection Logic. LC 80-18841. 1980. 38.95 (ISBN 0-87942-137-1). Inst Electrical.

Smith, J. F., et al. Thorium: Preparation & Properties. 382p. 1975. text ed. 12.50x (ISBN 0-8138-1635-1). Iowa St U Pr.

Smith, J. G., jt. ed. see Roosevelt, Anna C.

Smith, J. H. Digital Logic: Basic Theory & Practice. 1972. 12.75 o.p. (ISBN 0-408-00060-0). Transatlantic.

Smith, J. Lawton. Neuro-Ophthalmology Update. LC 77-78562. (Illus.). 412p. 1977. 66.75x (ISBN 0-89352-005-5). Masson Pub.

Smith, J. Lawton, ed. Neuro-Ophthalmology Focus, 1980. LC 79-87484. (Illus.). 472p. 1979. text ed. 66.75x (ISBN 0-89352-071-3). Masson Pub.

--Neuro-Ophthalmology Focus 1982. LC 81-15581. (Illus.). 340p. 1981. 66.75x (ISBN 0-89352-157-4). Masson Pub.

Smith, J. Lawton, ed. see Neuro-Opthamology Symposia of the University of Miami & the Bascom Palmer Eye Institute.

Smith, J. M. Advanced Analysis with the Sharp 5100 Scientific Calculator. LC 79-22505. 132p. 1979. 8.95 o.p. (ISBN 0-471-07753-4, Pub. by Wiley-Interscience). Wiley.

--A History of Australian Vegetation. 216p. 1981. 18.50 (ISBN 0-07-072953-0). McGraw.

--Mathematical Modeling & Digital Simulation for Engineers & Scientists. LC 76-52419. 332p. 1977. 34.95 (ISBN 0-471-80344-8, Pub. by Wiley-Interscience). Wiley.
Smith, J. M. & VanNess, H. C. Introduction to Chemical Engineering Thermodynamics. 3rd ed. (Illus.). 672p. 1975. text ed. 36.95 (ISBN 0-07-058701-9, C); solutions manual 25.00 (ISBN 0-07-058702-7). McGraw.
Smith, J. Maynard. The Evolution of Sex. LC 77-85689. (Illus.). 1978. 37.50 (ISBN 0-521-21887-X); pap. 11.95x (ISBN 0-521-29302-2). Cambridge U Pr.
--Mathematical Ideas in Biology. LC 68-25088. (Illus.). 1968. 22.50 (ISBN 0-521-07335-9); pap. 9.95 (ISBN 0-521-09550-6). Cambridge U Pr.
Smith, J. Percy, intro. by see Shaw, George B.
Smith, J. Russell. Tree Crops. 1978. pap. 5.95i o.p. (ISBN 0-06-090610-3, CN 610, CN). Har-Row.
Smith, J. V. Geometrical & Structural Crystallography. (Smith-Wylie Intermediate Geology Ser.). 450p. 1982. text ed. 29.95 (ISBN 0-471-86168-5). Wiley.
Smith, J. Warren, jt. auth. see Francis, Nelle.
Smith, Jack L. & Keith, Robert M. Accounting for Financial Statement Presentation. 1979. text ed. 24.95 (ISBN 0-07-058890-2); instructor's manual 14.00 (ISBN 0-07-058891-0). McGraw.
--Accounting Principles. 1152p. 1983. 25.00 (ISBN 0-07-059060-5, C); study guide, 320p 9.95x (ISBN 0-07-059062-1). Supplementary materials avail. McGraw.
Smith, James. History of Chenango County, New York, 1784-1880. Orig. Title: History of Chenago & Madison Counties. (Illus.). 499p. 1979. Repr. of 1880 ed. 25.00x o.p. (ISBN 0-931308-01-1). Molly Yes.
Smith, James, ed. see Leffler, John F.
Smith, James A. Classroom Organization for the Language Arts. LC 76-9555. 1977. pap. text ed. 5.50 (ISBN 0-87581-195-7). Peacock Pubs.
--Dress 'Em Out. (Illus.). 256p. 1983. pap. 11.95 (ISBN 0-88317-107-4). Stoeger Pub Co.
Smith, James C., ed. see Paul, Aileen, Jr.
Smith, James C., ed. see Woods, Betty.
Smith, James C., Jr., jt. auth. see Martinez, Eluid L.
Smith, James C., Jr., ed. see Byrnes, Patricia & Krenz, Nancy.
Smith, James C., Jr., ed. see Chapman, Al.
Smith, James C., Jr., ed. see Foust, Juana.
Smith, James C., Jr., ed. see Hodge, Gene M.
Smith, James C., Jr., ed. see McGreevy, Susan B.
Smith, James C., Jr., ed. see Romero, Mary A. & Romero, Carlos.
Smith, James C., Jr., ed. see Stedman, Myrtle.
Smith, James C., Jr., ed. see Young, Ezra.
Smith, James D. Gears & Their Vibration: A Basic Approach to Understanding Gear Noise. (Mechanical Engineering Ser.: Vol. 17). (Illus.). 192p. 1983. 29.50 (ISBN 0-8247-1797-X). Dekker.
Smith, James E. Divided We Fall. LC 79-67439. 96p. (Orig.). 1980. pap. 1.95 (ISBN 0-87239-381-X, 40086). Standard Pub.
--Ezekiel. (Bible Study Textbook Ser.). 1979. 14.30 o.s.i. (ISBN 0-89900-024-X). College Pr Pub.
Smith, James E., ed. Torrey Canyon-Pollution & Marine Life. (Illus.). 1968. 45.00 (ISBN 0-521-07144-5). Cambridge U Pr.
Smith, James R. Hard-Core: A Study of the Unemployables in Contemporary American Society. 100p. (Orig.). 1970. pap. text ed. 6.95x (ISBN 0-686-94119-5). Irvington.
Smith, James W., jt. ed. see Grabb, William X.
Smith, Jan, jt. auth. see Silverson, Sarah.
Smith, Jane F. & Kvasnicka, Robert M., eds. Indian-White Relations: A Persistent Paradox. LC 75-22316. 1981. pap. 6.95 (ISBN 0-88258-094-9). Howard U Pr.
Smith, Jane I. An Historical & Semantic Study of the Term "Islam" As Seen in a Sequence of Qur'an Commentaries. LC 75-22485. (Harvard Dissertations in Religion). 1975. 9.00 (ISBN 0-89130-020-1, 03-00-01). Scholars Pr Ca.
Smith, Jane I. & Haddad, Yvonne Y. Islamic Understanding of Death & Resurrection. LC 80-21303. 270p. 1981. 39.50x (ISBN 0-87395-506-4); pap. 14.95x (ISBN 0-87395-507-2). State U NY Pr.
Smith, Jane S. & Carlson, Betty. A Gift of Music: Great Composers & Their Influence. 243p. 1979. 9.95 (ISBN 0-89107-159-8). Crossway Bks.
Smith, Janet, ed. see Twain, Mark.
Smith, Janis. Pediatric Critical Care Nursing. (Series in Critical Care Nursing). (Illus.). 500p. (Orig.). 1982. pap. text ed. 14.95. Wiley.
Smith, Jared. Song of the Blood. 1983. 4.00 (ISBN 0-912292-67-9). Horizon.
Smith, Jean. Tapu Removal in Maori Religion. 1974. text ed. 12.00x (ISBN 0-8248-0591-7). UH Pr.
Smith, Jean R., jt. auth. see McGill, Shirley L.
Smith, Jeffrey A. American Presidential Elections: Trust & the Rational Voter. 224p. 1980. 25.95 (ISBN 0-03-056143-4). Praeger.
Smith, Jennifer see Bates, Martin & Dudley-Evans, Tony.
Smith, Jerald R. BUSOP. rev. ed. (Business Adventures Ser.). 1978. pap. 4.95 (ISBN 0-933836-04-X). Simtek.
Smith, Jerome & Miroff, Franklin I. You're Our Child: A Social-Psychological Approach to Adoption. LC 80-5957. 110p. (Orig.). 1981. lib. bdg. 18.00 (ISBN 0-8191-1416-2); pap. text ed. 8.25 (ISBN 0-8191-1417-0). U Pr of Amer.
Smith, Jerome F. & Smith, Barbara K. Silver Profits in the Eighties. 1982. 16.95 (ISBN 0-916728-56-0). Bks in Focus.
Smith, Jerry C. & Urban, William L., trs. The Livonian Rhymed Chronicle. LC 77-78928. (Uralic & Altaic: No. 128). 1977. pap. text ed. 10.00x o.p. (ISBN 0-87750-213-7). Res Ctr Lang Semiotic.
Smith, Jerry J., jt. auth. see Moyle, Peter B.
Smith, Jerry L. The Searcher---How to Satisfy a Searching Soul. new ed. (Illus., Orig.). 1979. pap. 1.95 (ISBN 0-9602136-0-0). J L Smith.
--The Secret of a Powerful & Victorious Life. new ed. (Illus., Orig.). 1979. pap. 3.95 (ISBN 0-9602136-1-9). J L Smith.
Smith, Jessie C. Black Academic Libraries & Research Collections: An Historical Survey. LC 77-71857. (Contributions in Afro-American & African Studies: No. 34). 1977. lib. bdg. 29.95x (ISBN 0-8371-9546-2, SBA/). Greenwood.
Smith, Jim. Frog Band & Durrington Dormouse. (The Frog Band Ser.). (Illus.). 32p. (gr. 1-3). 1980. pap. 3.95g o.p. (ISBN 0-316-80159-3). Little.
Smith, Jo R., jt. auth. see Black, Ann N.
Smith, Joan. Babe. (General Ser.). 1980. lib. bdg. 13.95 (ISBN 0-8161-3112-0, Large Print Bks). G K Hall.
--The Gift of Umtal. (Julia MacRae Ser.). 144p. (gr. 5 up). 1983. 8.95 (ISBN 0-531-04580-3, MacRae). Watts.
--Imprudent Lady. (General Ser.). 1979. lib. bdg. 13.95 (ISBN 0-8161-6746-X, Large Print Bks). G K Hall.
--Imprudent Lady. LC 77-90132. 1978. 8.95 o.s.i. (ISBN 0-8027-0589-8). Walker & Co.
--Prelude to Love. 192p. (Orig.). 1983. pap. 2.25 (ISBN 0-449-20092-2, Crest). Fawcett.
--Social Issues & the Social Order: The Contradictions of Capitalism. (Orig.). 1981. pap. text ed. 13.95 (ISBN 0-316-79907-6). Little.
--Talk of the Town. (General Ser.). 1979. lib. bdg. 12.50 (ISBN 0-8161-3004-3, Large Print Bks). G K Hall.
Smith, Joanmarie, jt. auth. see Durka, Gloria.
Smith, Joanna. Farm Your Garden. (Illus.). 1977. 14.95x o.p. (ISBN 0-8464-0405-2). Beekman Pubs.
Smith, Jody B. The Image of Guadalupe: Myth or Miracle? LC 80-2066. (Illus.). 192p. 1983. 14.95 (ISBN 0-385-15971-4). Doubleday.
Smith, Joe, jt. auth. see Ray, Graham H.
Smith, John. Captain John Smith's History of Virginia. Hawke, David F., ed. LC 74-12083. (American History Landmarks Ser.). 1970. 6.50 o.p. (ISBN 0-672-60881-2). Bobbs.
--Select Discourses. Wellek, Rene, ed. LC 75-11252. (British Philosophers & Theologians of the 17th & 18th Centuries Ser.). 1978. Repr. of 1660 ed. lib. bdg. 42.00 o.s.i. (ISBN 0-8240-1803-6). Garland Pub.
--Select Discourses. Patrides, C. A., ed. LC 79-15690. 1979. Repr. of 1660 ed. 65.00x (ISBN 0-8201-1335-2). Schol Facsimiles.
Smith, John, ed. Modern Love Poems. (Pocket Poet Ser.). 1966. pap. 1.25 (ISBN 0-8023-9050-1). Dufour.
Smith, John C. From Colonialism to World Community: The Church's Pilgrimage. LC 82-12138. 1982. pap. 8.95 (ISBN 0-664-24452-1). Westminster.
Smith, John D., compiled by. Black Slavery in the Americas: An Interdisciplinary Bibliography, 1865-1980, 2 vols. LC 82-11737. 1982. Set. lib. bdg. 95.00 (ISBN 0-313-23118-4, SMB/). Greenwood.
Smith, John E. Biotechnology. (Studies in Biology: No. 136). 64p. 1981. pap. text ed. 8.95 (ISBN 0-7131-2835-6). E Arnold.
--Experience & God. 1968. 11.95x (ISBN 0-19-501207-0). Oxford U Pr.
--Experience & God. LC 68-18566. 1974. pap. 5.95 (ISBN 0-19-501847-8, GB424, Gb). Oxford U Pr.
--Religion & Empiricism. (Aquinas Lecture Ser.). 1967. 7.95 (ISBN 0-87462-132-1). Marquette.
--The Spirit of American Philosophy. (SUNY Series in Philosophy). 272p. 1982. 29.50x (ISBN 0-87395-650-8); pap. 7.95x (ISBN 0-87395-651-6). State U NY Pr.
Smith, John E. & Berry, David, eds. Filamentous Fungi. Incl. Vol. 1. Industrial Mycology. LC 75-2101. 340p. 69.95 o.p. (ISBN 0-470-80187-5); Vol. 2. Biosynthesis & Metabolism. LC 75-41613. 89.95 o.p. (ISBN 0-470-15005-X); Vol. 3. Developmental Mycology. LC 75-2101. 69.95 o.p. (ISBN 0-470-99352-9). (Filamentous Fungi Ser.: Vols. 1-3). 1975-78. Halsted Pr.
Smith, John H. The University Teaching of Social Sciences: Industrial Sociology. 1961. pap. 2.75 o.p. (ISBN 92-3-100461-1, UNESCO). Unipub.
Smith, John H., et al see Dryden, John.
Smith, John I. Modern Operational Circuit Design. LC 79-165950. (Illus.). 1971. 33.95 o.p. (ISBN 0-471-80194-1, Pub. by Wiley-Interscience). Wiley.
Smith, John M. Evolution & the Theory of Games. 200p. 1982. 34.50 (ISBN 0-521-24673-3); pap. 11.95 (ISBN 0-521-28884-3). Cambridge U Pr.
Smith, Jon M. Financial Analysis & Business Decisions on the Pocket Calculator. LC 75-39752. (Systems & Controls for Financial Management Ser.). 317p. 1976. 29.95 (ISBN 0-471-80184-4, Pub. by Wiley-Interscience). Wiley.
--Scientific Analysis on the Pocket Calculator. 2nd ed. LC 77-6662. 445p. 1977. 25.50 (ISBN 0-471-03071-6, Pub. by Wiley-Interscience). Wiley.
Smith, Jonathan Z. Imagining Religion: From Babylon to Jonestown. LC 82-2734. (Studies in the History of Judaism). 1982. 15.00 (ISBN 0-226-76358-7). U of Chicago Pr.
Smith, Josefa J., et al, eds. Cortina-Grosset Basic German Dictionary. LC 73-18523. 384p. 1975. pap. 3.50 (ISBN 0-686-96722-4, G&D). Putnam Pub Group.
Smith, Joseph. Doctrine & Covenants of the Church of Jesus Christ of Latter-Day Saints: Containing the Revelations Given to Joseph Smith, Jun, the Prophet, for the Building up of the Kingdom of God in the Last Days. Pratt, Orson, ed. LC 69-14082. 1971. Repr. of 1880 ed. lib. bdg. 29.75x (ISBN 0-8371-4101-X, SMCC). Greenwood.
Smith, Joseph B. The Plot to Steal Florida: James Madison's Phony War. 1983. 15.95 (ISBN 0-87795-477-1). Arbor Hse.
--Portrait of a Cold Warrior. LC 76-13567. 1976. 10.95 o.p. (ISBN 0-399-11788-1). Putnam Pub Group.
Smith, Joseph C. The Day the Music Died. LC 80-8914. 416p. 1982. pap. cancelled (ISBN 0-394-62422-X, E827, Ever). Grove.
Smith, Joseph F. Gospel Doctrine. 553p. 1975. 10.95 (ISBN 0-87747-101-0); pap. 2.50 (ISBN 0-87747-663-2). Deseret Bk.
--Pediatric Neuropathology. (Illus.). 288p. 1973. pap. 29.00 (ISBN 0-07-058490-7, HP). McGraw.
--The Way to Perfection. 365p. 1972. 6.95 o.p. (ISBN 0-87747-300-5). Deseret Bk.
Smith, Joseph M. Chemical Engineering Kinetics. 3rd ed. (Chemical Engineering Ser.). (Illus.). 704p. 1980. text ed. 35.95 (ISBN 0-07-058710-8, C); solution manual 8.95 (ISBN 0-07-058711-6). McGraw.
Smith, Josie, tr. see Hill, Tomas.
Smith, Josie De. Senor: No Me Dejes Rodar. (Illus.). 96p. 1981. pap. 2.50 (ISBN 0-311-40042-6). Casa Bautista.
Smith, Josie de see De Smith, Josie.
Smith, Joyce M. Art History: A Study Guide. Masters, Janet F., tr. (Illus.). 256p. 1982. pap. text ed. 9.95 (ISBN 0-13-047324-3). P-H.
--Coping with Life & Its Problems. 1976. pap. 2.50 (ISBN 0-8423-0434-7). Tyndale.
--Fulfillment: Bible Studies for Women. 1975. pap. 2.50 (ISBN 0-8423-0980-2). Tyndale.
--Learning to Talk with God. 1976. pap. 2.50 (ISBN 0-8423-2140-3). Tyndale.
--A Rejoicing Heart. 1979. pap. 2.50 (ISBN 0-8423-5418-2). Tyndale.
--Understanding Your Emotions. 1977. pap. 2.50 (ISBN 0-8423-7770-0). Tyndale.
--A Woman's Priorities. 1976. pap. 2.50 (ISBN 0-8423-8380-8). Tyndale.
Smith, Joyce Marie. The Significance of Jesus. 1976. pap. 2.50 (ISBN 0-8423-5887-0). Tyndale.
Smith, Judith M. Designing Instructional Tasks: A Primer. (Michigan Learning Modules Ser.: No. 6). 1979. write for info. (ISBN 0-914004-09-3). Ulrich.
--A Technology of Reading & Writing Vol. 4: Designing Instructional Tasks. (Educational Psychology Ser.). 1979. 15.00 (ISBN 0-12-651704-5). Acad Pr.
Smith, Judith M. & Smith, Donald E. Child Management: A Program for Parents & Teachers. LC 76-22829. 1976. pap. text ed. 6.95 (ISBN 0-87822-125-5); discussion guide 2.95 (ISBN 0-87822-126-3). Res Press.
Smith, Judy G. Celebrating Special Days in the Church School Year. Zapel, Arthur L., ed. LC 81-83441. (Illus.). 125p. (Orig.). 1981. pap. text ed. 8.95 (ISBN 0-916260-14-3). Meriwether Pub.
Smith, Julian. Nevil Shute. (English Authors Ser.). 1976. lib. bdg. 12.95 (ISBN 0-8057-6664-2, Twayne). G K Hall.
Smith, Julian C., jt. auth. see McCabe, Warren.
Smith, Julian P., jt. auth. see Delgado, Gregorio.
Smith, Juliet. Airport. LC 80-52521. (Starters Ser.). PLB 8.00 (ISBN 0-382-06488-7). Silver.
Smith, K., jt. auth. see Ryles, A. P.
Smith, K. A., jt. ed. see Nukols, M. L.
Smith, K. G. Insects & Other Arthropods of Medical Importance. LC 74-594820. 561p. 1973. 64.95 (ISBN 0-471-99684-X, Pub. by Wiley-Interscience). Wiley.
Smith, K. G., jt. auth. see Cogan, B. H.
Smith, K. M. Plant Viruses. 6th ed. 1977. 12.95x o.p. (ISBN 0-412-14710-6, Pub. by Chapman & Hall); pap. 12.50x (ISBN 0-412-14740-8). Methuen Inc.
Smith, K. M. & Ritchie, D. A. Introduction to Virology. 250p. 1980. 33.00x (ISBN 0-412-21960-3, Pub by Chapman & Hall England); pap. 15.95x (ISBN 0-412-21970-0). Methuen Inc.
Smith, K. T. Primer of Modern Analysis. 2nd ed. (Undergraduate Texts in Mathematics Ser.). 482p. 1983. 28.00 (ISBN 0-387-90797-1). Springer-Verlag.
Smith, K. W. Hamsters & Gerbils. (Illus.). 93p. 1977. pap. 3.95 (ISBN 0-7028-1082-7). Avian Pubns.
Smith, Karl J. Arithmetic for College Students. LC 80-21125. 400p. 1981. text ed. 19.95 (ISBN 0-8185-0422-6). Brooks-Cole.
--Basic Mathematics for College Students. LC 80-20492. 400p. (Orig.). 1981. pap. text ed. 20.95 (ISBN 0-8185-0419-6). Brooks-Cole.
--Essentials of Trigonometry. LC 82-12994. (Mathematics Ser.). 280p. 1983. text ed. 21.95 (ISBN 0-534-01224-8). Brooks-Cole.
--Finite Mathematics: A Discrete Approach. 1975. text ed. 18.95x (ISBN 0-673-07921-X). Scott F.
--The Nature of Modern Mathematics. 3rd ed. LC 79-20064. 1980. text ed. 22.95 (ISBN 0-8185-0352-1). Brooks-Cole.
--Precalculus Mathematics: A Functional Approach. 2nd ed. LC 82-20719. 512p. 1983. text ed. 22.95 (ISBN 0-534-01223-X). Brooks-Cole.
--Trigonometry for College Students. 2nd ed. LC 79-9122. 1980. text ed. 20.95 (ISBN 0-8185-0340-8). Brooks-Cole.
Smith, Karl J. & Boyle, Patrick J. Beginning Algebra for College Students. 2nd ed. LC 80-12572. 1980. text ed. 20.95 (ISBN 0-8185-0365-3). Brooks-Cole.
--College Algebra. 2nd ed. LC 81-10233. (Mathematics Ser.). 420p. 1982. text ed. 21.95 (ISBN 0-8185-0489-7). Brooks-Cole.
Smith, Karl U., jt. auth. see Schiamberg, Lawrence B.
Smith, Katherine V. Chickens, Cookies, & Cozzin George. 144p. (Orig.). 1983. pap. text ed. 6.95 (ISBN 0-687-06485-6). Abingdon.
Smith, Kathleen, jt. auth. see Ulett, George A.
Smith, Kathy. A Rainy Day Guide to Portland. (Orig.). 1983. pap. 6.95 (ISBN 0-87701-288-1). Chronicle Bks.
Smith, Kay N. Catching Fire. 272p. 1982. 12.95 (ISBN 0-698-11134-6, Coward). Putnam Pub Group.
--Mindspell. 288p. 1983. 12.95 (ISBN 0-688-01928-5). Morrow.
--The Watcher. LC 79-2366. 1980. 10.95 (ISBN 0-698-11006-4, Coward). Putnam Pub Group.
Smith, Keith V. Guide to Working Capital Management. (Illus.). 1979. 19.95 (ISBN 0-07-058546-6, P&RB); pap. 14.95 (ISBN 0-07-058545-8). McGraw.
--The Management of Working Capital: Readings. LC 74-2811. 400p. 1974. pap. text ed. 12.95 o.s.i. (ISBN 0-8299-0018-7). West Pub.
--Readings on the Management of Working Capital. 2nd ed. (Illus.). 1980. pap. 15.95 (ISBN 0-8299-0296-1). West Pub.
Smith, Ken. Southern Home Landscaping. (Illus.). 192p. (Orig.). 1982. pap. 7.95 (ISBN 0-89586-063-5). H P Bks.
--Work, Distances: Poems. LC 82-73187. 98p. 1972. 7.95 (ISBN 0-8040-0588-5); pap. 5.00 o.p. (ISBN 0-8040-0589-3). Swallow.
Smith, Ken D. A Phonological Reconstruction of Proto-North-Bahnaric. (Language Data, Asian-Pacific Ser.: No. 2). v, 109p. 1972. pap. 3.00x (ISBN 0-88312-202-2); microfiche 2.25x (ISBN 0-88312-302-9). Summer Inst Ling.
Smith, Kenn. Flower of Gold. 304p. (Orig.). 1982. pap. 3.25 o.p. (ISBN 0-505-51836-8). Tower Bks.
Smith, Kenneth G. Learning to Be a Man. LC 78-120413. (Orig.). 1970. pap. 3.95 (ISBN 0-87784-692-8). Inter-Varsity.
Smith, Kenneth H. American Economic History. LC 75-84415. (Real World of Economics Ser.). (Illus.). (gr. 5-11). 1970. PLB 4.95g (ISBN 0-8225-0612-2). Lerner Pubns.
--International Trade. LC 70-84419. (Real World of Economics Ser). (Illus.). (gr. 5-11). 1970. PLB 4.95g (ISBN 0-8225-0616-5). Lerner Pubns.
--Money & Banking. LC 72-84417. (Real World of Economics Ser). Orig. Title: Banking. (Illus.). (gr. 5-11). 1970. PLB 4.95g (ISBN 0-8225-0614-9). Lerner Pubns.
--Taxes. LC 79-84416. (Real World of Economics Ser). Orig. Title: Taxation. (Illus.). (gr. 5-11). 1970. PLB 4.95g (ISBN 0-8225-0613-0). Lerner Pubns.
Smith, Kenneth M., et al, eds. Advances in Virus Research. Incl. Vol. 1. 1953. 51.50 (ISBN 0-12-039801-X); Vol. 2. 1954. 51.50 (ISBN 0-12-039802-8); Vol. 3. 1955. 51.50 (ISBN 0-12-039803-6); Vol. 4. 1957. 51.50 (ISBN 0-12-039804-4); Vol. 5. 1958. 51.50 (ISBN 0-12-039805-2); Vol. 6. 1962. 51.50 (ISBN 0-12-039806-0); Vol. 7. 1963. 51.50 (ISBN 0-12-039807-9); Vol. 8. 1961. 51.50 (ISBN 0-12-039808-7); Vol. 9. 1962. 51.50 (ISBN 0-12-039809-5); Vol. 10. 1967. 51.50 (ISBN 0-12-039810-9); Vol. 11. 1965. 51.50 (ISBN 0-12-039811-7); Vol. 12. 1969. 51.50 (ISBN 0-12-039812-5); Vol. 13. 1968. 51.50 (ISBN 0-12-039813-3); Vol. 14. 1968. 51.50 (ISBN 0-12-039814-1); Vol. 15. 1969. 59.50 (ISBN 0-12-039815-X); Vol. 16. 1970. 59.50 (ISBN 0-12-039816-8); Vol. 17. 1972. 51.50 (ISBN 0-12-039817-6); Vol. 21. 1977. 50.50 (ISBN 0-12-039821-4); Vol. 22. 1978. 49.50 (ISBN 0-12-039822-2); Vol. 23. 1979. 51.50 (ISBN 0-12-039823-0); Vol. 24. 1979. 47.50 (ISBN 0-12-039824-9). Acad Pr.
Smith, Kenwyn K. Groups in Conflict: Prisons & Disguise. 272p. 1982. pap. text ed. 10.95 (ISBN 0-8403-2752-8). Kendall-Hunt.
Smith, Kerry V., ed. Advances in Applied Micro-Economics, Vol. 1. 300p. 1981. 40.00 (ISBN 0-89232-171-7). Jai Pr.

Smith, L. A., jt. auth. see Storr, G. M.

Smith, L. Neil. The Nagasaki Vector. 256p. (Orig.). 1983. pap. 2.75 (ISBN 0-345-30382-2, Del Rey). Ballantine.

Smith, L. P. Methods in Agricultural Meteorology. LC 74-21868. (Developments in Atmospheric Science Ser: Vol. 3). 210p. 1975. 57.75 (ISBN 0-444-41286-7). Elsevier.

Smith, Lacey B. Elizabeth Tudor: Biography of a Queen. (Library of World Biography). 1975. 8.95 (ISBN 0-316-80152-6); pap. 5.95 (ISBN 0-316-80153-4). Little.

--A History of England, Vol. I: The Making of England 55 B. C. to 1399. 4th ed. Hollister, C. W., ed. 320p. 1983. pap. text ed. 10.95 (ISBN 0-669-04377-X). Heath.

Smith, Lacey B., ed. A History of England Vol. II: This Realm of England 1399 to 1688. 4th ed. 336p. 1983. pap. text ed. 10.95 (ISBN 0-669-04378-8). Heath.

Smith, Lacey B., ed. see Arnstein, Walter L.

Smith, Lacey B., ed. see Willcox, William B. & Arnstein, Walter L.

Smith, Larry. Lawrence Ferlinghetti: Poet-at-Large. LC 82-10835. 144p. 1983. 22.50 (ISBN 0-8093-1101-1); pap. 9.95 (ISBN 0-8093-1102-X). S Ill U Pr.

Smith, Larry E. English for Cross-Cultural Communication. LC 79-11303. 1979. 35.00x (ISBN 0-312-25423-7). St Martin.

Smith, Larry L. Crisis Intervention Theory & Practice: A Source Book. 1976. pap. text ed. 11.25 (ISBN 0-8191-0077-3). U Pr of Amer.

Smith, Larry R. Kenneth Patchen. (United States Authors Ser.). 1978. lib. bdg. 13.95 (ISBN 0-8057-7195-6, Twayne). G K Hall.

Smith, Laura, jt. ed. see Lehmkuhl, Donald.

Smith, Laura A. Music of the Waters. LC 69-16479. 1969. Repr. of 1888 ed. 37.00x (ISBN 0-8103-3552-2). Gale.

Smith, Lawrence & Harris, Victor. Japanese Decorative Arts. 128p. 1982. 40.00x (ISBN 0-7141-1421-9, Pub. by Brit Mus Pubns England). State Mutual Bk.

Smith, Lawrence B., jt. auth. see Officer, Lawrence H.

Smith, Lee. Black Mountain Breakdown. 230p. 1981. 10.95 (ISBN 0-399-12531-0). Putnam Pub Group.

--Cakewalk. 256p. 1981. 12.95 (ISBN 0-399-12666-X). Putnam Pub Group.

--Oral History. LC 82-18081. 288p. 1983. 14.95 (ISBN 0-399-12794-1). Putnam.

Smith, Leial R. English for Careers Business Professionals & Technical. 2nd ed. 410p. 1981. pap. text ed. 19.95 (ISBN 0-471-09353-X); tchrs.' ed. 10.00 (ISBN 0-471-08991-5); personal learning guide 7.95 (ISBN 0-471-09191-X). Wiley.

Smith, Len Y. & Roberson, G. Gale. Smith & Roberson's Business Law: U.C.C. 5th ed. 264p. 1982. text ed. 25.95 (ISBN 0-314-63286-7). West Pub.

Smith, Len Young & Gale, Roberson G. Smith & Roberson's Essentials of Business Law. (Illus.). 1008p. 1982. text ed. 23.95 (ISBN 0-314-69680-6); tchrs.' manual avail. (ISBN 0-314-71127-9); study guide avail. (ISBN 0-314-71145-7); transparency masters avail. (ISBN 0-314-71128-7). West Pub.

Smith, Lendon. The Children's Doctor. LC 72-77666. 1977. 4.95 (ISBN 0-13-131904-3, Reward). P-H.

--Feed Your Kids Right. 1980. pap. 6.95 (ISBN 0-440-52704-X, Dell Trade Pbks). Dell.

--Feed Your Kids Right: Dr. Smith's Program for Your Child's Total Health. 1979. 10.95 (ISBN 0-07-058496-6, GB). McGraw.

Smith, Lendon H. The Encyclopedia of Baby & Child Care. LC 70-180226. (Illus.). 548p. 1972. 12.95 o.p. (ISBN 0-13-275198-4). P-H.

--The Encyclopedia of Baby & Child Care. 1980. pap. 9.95 (ISBN 0-446-37502-0). Warner Bks.

--The Encyclopedia of Baby Child Care. rev. ed. 1981. 13.95 (ISBN 0-13-275503-3). P-H.

Smith, Leona W. The Forgotten Art of Flower Cookery. LC 73-4124. (Illus.). 192p. 1973. 11.49i (ISBN 0-06-013934-X, HarpT). Har-Row.

Smith, Lillian E. Strange Fruit. LC 44-40028. 12.95 (ISBN 0-15-185769-5). HarBraceJ.

Smith, Linda C. New Information Technologies-New Opportunities: Proceedings of the Clinic on Library Applications of Data Processing, 1981. LC 82-10947. 119p. 1982. 11.00 (ISBN 0-87845-066-1). U of Ill Lib Info Sci.

Smith, Linda H., jt. auth. see Renzulli, Joseph S.

Smith, Linda H., ed. see Ciabotti, Patricia.

Smith, Linda H., ed. see Dow, Clista.

Smith, Linda H., ed. see Dutton, Nancy C.

Smith, Linda H., ed. see Johnson, Judith M.

Smith, Linda H., ed. see Krause, Claire S.

Smith, Linda H., ed. see Mathews, F. Neil.

Smith, Linda H., ed. see Page, Beverly.

Smith, Lindsay, ed. see Mitchell, Meredith.

Smith, Lloyd. Hangin' Round the Ohio Bar: Poems for Bar People. 1983. 6.95 (ISBN 0-533-05489-3). Vantage.

Smith, Lloyd H., Jr. & Wyngaarden, James B., eds. Review of General Internal Medicine: A Self-Assessment Manual. LC 79-3922. (Illus.). 330p. 1980. pap. text ed. 16.95 o.p. (ISBN 0-7216-8419-X). Saunders.

Smith, Logan P. Words & Idioms. LC 77-148923. 1971. Repr. of 1925 ed. 40.00x (ISBN 0-8103-3651-0). Gale.

Smith, Lotsee P., jt. auth. see Hale, Robert G.

Smith, Louis M. & Keith, Pat M. Anatomy of Educational Innovation: An Organizational Analysis of an Elementary School. LC 70-150613. 420p. 1971. 22.50 (ISBN 0-471-80179-8). Krieger.

Smith, Louis M. & Hudgins, Bryce B., eds. Educational Psychology. 1964. 9.50x (ISBN 0-685-84262-2). Phila Bk Co.

Smith, Lowell. Average American. LC 82-84427. (Illus.). 112p. (Orig.). 1983. pap. 8.00 (ISBN 0-937088-03-X). Illum Pr.

Smith, Lucinda. Movie Palaces. 1980. 17.95 o.p. (ISBN 0-517-53857-1, C N Potter Bks). Crown.

Smith, Luther E., Jr. Howard Thurman: The Mystic As Prophet. LC 80-5961. 208p. (Orig.). 1982. lib. bdg. 21.25 (ISBN 0-8191-1986-5); pap. text ed. 10.25 (ISBN 0-8191-1987-3). U Pr of Amer.

Smith, Lynn, jt. auth. see Tuttle, Marcia.

Smith, Lynn S. A Practical Approach to Serials Cataloging, Vol. 2. Stueart, Robert W., ed. LC 76-5645. (Foundations in Library & Information Science). 1978. lib. bdg. 40.00 (ISBN 0-89232-007-9). Jai Pr.

Smith, Lynwood S. Introduction to Fish Physiology. (Illus.). 256p. 1982. 29.95 (ISBN 0-87666-542-3, PS-785). TFH Pubns.

Smith, M. Monograph of the Sea Snakes. (Illus.). 1964. Repr. of 1926 ed. 16.00 (ISBN 3-7682-0260-7). Lubrecht & Cramer.

Smith, M. A., jt. ed. see Haworth, J. T.

Smith, M. Brewster. Humanizing Social Psychology. LC 73-21076. (Social & Behavioral Science Ser.). 358p. 1974. 22.95x (ISBN 0-87589-229-9). Jossey-Bass.

Smith, M. Easterby, et al. Auditing Managment Development. 180p. 1980. text ed. 32.50x (ISBN 0-566-02131-5). Gower Pub Ltd.

Smith, M. Estellie. Those Who Live from the Sea: A Study in Maritime Anthropology. (AES Ser.). (Illus.). 1977. text ed. 23.95 (ISBN 0-8299-0139-6). West Pub.

Smith, M. Hamblin. The Psychology of the Criminal. (Historical Foundations of Forensic Psychiatry & Psychology Ser.). viii, 182p. 1983. Repr. of 1922 ed. lib. bdg. 22.50 (ISBN 0-306-76176-9). Da Capo.

Smith, M. J., jt. ed. see Gavriel, Salvendy.

Smith, M. W., et al. Bibliography of Electrophoretic Studies of Biochemical Variation in Natural Vertebrate Populations. 105p. 1982. 19.95 (ISBN 0-89672-106-X); pap. 8.00 (ISBN 0-89672-105-1); looseleaf 5.00 (ISBN 0-89672-104-3). Tex Tech Pr.

Smith, M. Z., jt. auth. see Lewis, T. G.

Smith, Malcolm. Life Beyond Life. 1978. 1.25 (ISBN 0-88270-317-X). Bridge Pub.

Smith, Manual J. When I Say No, I Feel Guilty. 3.50 o.p. (ISBN 0-686-92415-0, 6655). Hazelden.

Smith, Margaret. The Way of the Mystics: The Early Christian Mystics & the Rise of the Sufis. 1979. 16.95x o.p. (ISBN 0-19-520039-X). Oxford U Pr.

Smith, Margaret, jt. ed. see Jack, Ian.

Smith, Margaret, ed. see Lacayo, Carmela G.

Smith, Margaret B. The First Forty Years of Washington Society. LC 65-19563. (American Classics Ser.). 1975. 19.00 (ISBN 0-8044-1865-9). Ungar.

Smith, Margaret G., jt. auth. see Kissane, John M.

Smith, Marilyn, jt. auth. see Titus, Harold.

Smith, Marilyn Z. Standard COBOL: A Problem-Solving Approach. 308p. 1974. pap. text ed. 18.50 (ISBN 0-395-17091-5). HM.

Smith, Marilyn Z., jt. auth. see Cooper, Laura G.

Smith, Marion. A Mother Bear's Troubled Trip, on the Way North. LC 67-28219. (Illus.). 1976. pap. 2.95 (ISBN 0-87027-093-1). Cumberland Pr.

Smith, Marion B. Dualities in Shakespeare. LC 66-5056. 1966. 22.50x o.p. (ISBN 0-8020-5171-5). U of Toronto Pr.

Smith, Marion J. Pokey & Timothy of Stonehouse Farm. LC 73-80612. 72p. (gr. 4-6). 1973. pap. 2.95 (ISBN 0-87027-129-6). Cumberland Pr.

Smith, Marion R. Fremont see Fremont-Smith, Marion R.

Smith, Marjorie & Goodman, Julie. Child & Family: Concepts of Nursing Practice. (Illus.). 1184p. 1982. 32.95x (ISBN 0-07-048720-0); instr's manual 8.95 (ISBN 0-07-048721-9). McGraw.

Smith, Marjorie, jt. auth. see Williams, Joyce W.

Smith, Mark. Doctor Blues. 484p. 1983. 15.95 (ISBN 0-688-01553-0). Morrow.

--The Moon Lamp. 1977. pap. 1.75 o.p. (ISBN 0-380-00992-7, 32698). Avon.

Smith, Mark S. Chronic Disorders in Adolescence. 1982. text ed. 35.00 (ISBN 0-7236-7031-5). Wright-PSG.

Smith, Marsella, jt. auth. see Mummah, Hazel.

Smith, Martha L. Catalog Shopping. (Illus.). 1979. pap. 2.75x (ISBN 0-88323-147-6). Richards Pub.

Smith, Martin, ed. Benson of Cowley. 1980. 22.50x (ISBN 0-19-213112-5). Oxford U Pr.

Smith, Martin C. Canto for a Gypsy. 176p. 1983. pap. 2.50 (ISBN 0-345-30615-5). Ballantine.

--Nightwing: A Novel. 1977. 10.95 o.p. (ISBN 0-393-08783-2). Norton.

Smith, Martin L., ed. Benson of Cowley. 153p. 1983. pap. 8.00 (ISBN 0-936384-12-3). Cowley Pubns.

Smith, Marvin B. Handbook of Ocular Pharmacology. 2nd ed. LC 77-94882. (Illus.). 256p. 1978. spiral bd. 20.00 (ISBN 0-88416-246-X). Wright-PSG.

Smith, Mary A. Gustav Stickley: The Craftsman. (A New York State Study Ser.). (Illus.). 200p. 1983. text ed. 22.00x (ISBN 0-686-84444-0). Syracuse U Pr.

Smith, Mary C. All the Gods Are Dying Gods. 191p. 1983. Repr. of 1977 ed. 7.95 (ISBN 0-9609286-0-X). St Peters Pr.

Smith, Max J. Daddy Cries Too. Monroe, Charles P., ed. (Illus.). 1977. pap. 3.95 (ISBN 0-916674-04-5). Blue Max Pr.

--Hi, Lady & Other Random Thoughts. Monroe, Charles P., ed. 104p. (Orig.). 1973. pap. 3.95 (ISBN 0-916674-00-2). Blue Max Pr.

--I'll Say Goodby Tomorrow. Monroe, Charles P., ed. 108p. (Orig.). 1976. 5.95 (ISBN 0-916674-03-7). Blue Max Pr.

--Pieces of Love. Monroe, Charles P., ed. 82p. 1973. pap. 3.95 (ISBN 0-916674-01-0). Blue Max Pr.

--Touch Me to Sleep. Monroe, Charles P., ed. 104p. (Orig.). 1974. pap. 3.95 (ISBN 0-916674-02-9). Blue Max Pr.

Smith, Maxwell A. Prosper Merimee. (World Authors Ser.). lib. bdg. 15.95 (ISBN 0-8057-2612-8, Twayne). G K Hall.

Smith, Merriman. A President's Odyssey. LC 74-28759. 272p. 1975. Repr. of 1961 ed. lib. bdg. 18.25x (ISBN 0-8371-7921-1, SMPR). Greenwood.

Smith, Michael. Secrets. 238p. 1981. 10.95 o.p. (ISBN 0-312-70913-7). St Martin.

Smith, Michael, ed. The Duchess of Duke Street Entertains. LC 77-24315. (Illus.). 1977. 8.95 o.p. (ISBN 0-698-10850-7, Coward). Putnam Pub Group.

--National Media Conference Report, 1980. 1980. pap. text ed. 49.95 o.p. (ISBN 0-935224-02-5). Larimi Comm.

--TV News, 1980-1981. 1980. 70.00 o.p. (ISBN 0-935224-03-3). Larimi Comm.

Smith, Michael, et al. Preparing for Confirmation: Student Text. (Illus.). 64p. (Orig.). 1974. pap. 1.50 (ISBN 0-87793-066-X). Ave Maria.

Smith, Michael A. Landscapes, Nineteen Seventy-Five to Nineteen Seventy-Nine, 2 vols. (Illus.). 1981. Set. 325.00 (ISBN 0-9605646-0-8). Vol. 1, 116pgs (ISBN 0-9605646-1-6). Vol. II, 52pgs (ISBN 0-9605646-2-4). Lodima.

Smith, Michael L. Ionian Vision: Greece in Asia Minor, 1919-1922. LC 73-80083. 350p. 1973. 22.50 o.p. (ISBN 0-312-43540-1). St Martin.

Smith, Michael M., ed. Radio Contacts Nineteen Eighty-Two. 1982. pap. text ed. 126.00 o.p. (ISBN 0-935224-11-4). Larimi Comm.

--Television Contracts, Nineteen Eighty-Two. 1982. pap. text ed. 116.00 o.p. (ISBN 0-935224-10-6). Larimi Comm.

--TV News, 1980-82. 1981. pap. text ed. 90.00 o.p. (ISBN 0-935224-05-X). Larimi Comm.

Smith, Michael R. Law & the North Carolina Teacher. LC 74-21897. xvi, 196p. 1975. pap. text ed. 5.65x (ISBN 0-8134-1696-5, 1696). Interstate.

Smith, Mickey & Brown, Thomas. Handbook of Institutional Pharmacy Practice. (Illus.). 718p. 1979. 31.00 o.p. (ISBN 0-683-07884-4). Williams & Wilkins.

Smith, Mickey C. & Knapp, David A. Pharmacy, Drugs & Medical Care. 3rd ed. (Illus.). 352p. 1981. soft cover 19.95 (ISBN 0-686-77763-8, 7761-9). Williams & Wilkins.

Smith, Mickey C., ed. Principles of Pharmaceutical Marketing. 3rd ed. LC 82-6624. (Illus.). 529p. 1983. text ed. write for info. (ISBN 0-8121-0858-2). Lea & Febiger.

Smith, Mike, jt. auth. see Acheson, Dean.

Smith, Mike, jt. auth. see Achison, Dean.

Smith, Milton. Money Today, More Tomorrow. (Orig.). 1981. text ed. 15.95 (ISBN 0-316-79902-5); pap. text ed. 9.95 (ISBN 0-316-79903-3). Little.

Smith, Mimi. This Is a Test. LC 82-51221. (Artists' Bk.). 48p. (Orig.). 1983. pap. 8.50 (ISBN 0-89822-031-9). Visual Studies.

Smith, Mina. Arranging Flowers. 13.50x o.p. (ISBN 0-392-07373-0, LTB). Sportshelf.

Smith, Minor J. Abused. 1983. 7.95 (ISBN 0-533-05633-0). Vantage.

Smith, Mont. What the Bible Says about the Covenant. LC 81-65516. (What the Bible Says Ser.). 400p. 1981. 13.50 (ISBN 0-89900-083-5). College Pr Pub.

Smith, Moody D., jt. auth. see Spivey, Robert A.

Smith, Munroe. The Development of European Law. LC 79-1621. 1980. Repr. of 1928 ed. 24.50 (ISBN 0-88355-925-0). Hyperion Conn.

Smith, Myron J., Jr. Air War Bibliography, 1939-1945: English Language Sources, Vol. 5, Pt. 7. (Aerial Support Ser.). 162p. 1982. 21.50 (ISBN 0-686-96376-8). MA-AH Pub.

--American Navy, Seventeen Eighty-nine to Eighteen Sixty: A Bibliography. LC 73-18464. (American Naval Bibliography Ser.: Vol. 2). 1974. 20.00 (ISBN 0-8108-0659-2). Scarecrow.

--Cloak & Dagger Fiction: An Annotated Guide to Spy Thrillers. 2d ed. LC 82-6655. 431p. 1982. text ed. 34.50 (ISBN 0-87436-328-4). ABC-Clio.

--Keystone Battlewagon, U.S.S. Pennsylvania (BB-38) (Illus.). 48p. 1983. 4.95 (ISBN 0-933126-27-1). Pictorial Hist.

--The Secret Wars: A Guide to Sources in English: Vol. 1, Intelligence, Propaganda & Psychological Warfare, Resistance Movements & Secret Operations, 1939-1945. Burns, Richard D., ed. LC 79-25784. (War-Peace Bibliography Ser.: No. 12). 250p. 1980. 32.95 (ISBN 0-87436-271-7). ABC-Clio.

--The Secret Wars: A Guide to Sources in English: Vol. 2, Intelligence, Propaganda & Psychological Warfare, Covert Operations, 1945-1980. Burns, Richard D., ed. LC 79-25784. (War-Peace Bibliography Ser.: No. 13). 389p. 1981. 32.95 (ISBN 0-87436-303-9). ABC-Clio.

--The Secret Wars: A Guide to Sources in English: Vol. 3, International Terrorism, 1968-1980. Burns, Richard D., ed. LC 79-25784. (War-Peace Bibliography Ser.: No. 14). 237p. 1980. 32.95 (ISBN 0-87436-304-7). ABC-Clio.

--The Soviet Air & Strategic Rocket Forces, 1939-1980: A Guide to Sources in English. Burns, Richard D., ed. LC 80-22514. (War-Peace Bibliography Ser.: No. 10). 321p. 1981. 26.25 (ISBN 0-87436-306-3). ABC-Clio.

--The Soviet Army, Nineteen Thirty-Nine to Nineteen Eighty: A Guide to Sources in English. Burns, Richard D., ed. LC 82-4107. (War-Peace Bibliography Ser.: No. 11). 720p. 1982. 26.25 (ISBN 0-87436-307-1). ABC-Clio.

--The Soviet Navy, Nineteen Forty-One to Nineteen Seventy-Eight: A Guide to Sources in English. Burns, Richard D., ed. LC 79-26542. (War-Peace Bibliography Ser.: No. 9). 211p. 1980. text ed. 26.25 (ISBN 0-87436-265-2). ABC-Clio.

--The U. S. Gunboat Carondolet, 1861-1865. 1982. 25.00 (ISBN 0-686-96381-4). MA-AH Pub.

--World War Two at Sea: A Bibliography of Sources in English, 3 vols. Incl. Vol. 1. The European Theater. 16.50 (ISBN 0-8108-0884-6); Vol. 2. The Pacific Theater. 19.50 (ISBN 0-8108-0969-9); Vol. 3. 26.00 (ISBN 0-8108-0970-2). Pt. 1: Gen. Works, Naval Hardware, & The All Hands Chronology (1941-1945) Pt. 2: Home Fronts & Special Studies. LC 75-34098. 1976. Set. 3 vol. set 47.50,. Scarecrow.

Smith, N., jt. auth. see Robinson, H.

Smith, N. D., tr. see Bockle, Franz.

Smith, N. Ty, jt. auth. see Saidman, Lawrence J.

Smith, N. V. The Acquisition of Phonology. LC 72-95409. 228p. 1973. 37.50 (ISBN 0-521-20154-3). Cambridge U Pr.

Smith, Nana B. The World Is Wide & Memories of My Life. 1979. 5.95 o.p. (ISBN 0-533-03192-3). Vantage.

Smith, Nancy, jt. auth. see Coyne, Marla.

Smith, Nancy C. The Falling-Apart Winter. LC 82-70071. 128p. (gr. 4-7). 1982. 9.95 (ISBN 0-8027-6461-4); PLB 10.85 (ISBN 0-8027-6464-9). Walker & Co.

Smith, Nancy R. Experience & Art: Teaching Children to Paint. (Illus.). 1983. pap. text ed. 11.95x (ISBN 0-8077-2700-8). Tchrs Coll.

Smith, Nelson C. James Hogg. (English Authors Ser.). 1980. lib. bdg. 12.95 (ISBN 0-8057-6803-3, Twayne). G K Hall.

Smith, Nicholas D., jt. ed. see Miller, Fred D.

Smith, Nila B., et al. Best of Literature. Incl. Voyages in Reading. (gr. 7). text ed. 6.00 o.p. (ISBN 0-672-70565-6); tchrs' ed 6.00 o.p. (ISBN 0-685-23133-X); Challenges in Reading. (gr. 8). text ed. 6.40 o.p. (ISBN 0-672-70569-9); tchrs' ed 6.40 o.p. (ISBN 0-685-23134-8); Riches in Reading. (gr. 9). text ed. 6.76 o.p. (ISBN 0-672-70562-1). (Reading Literature Ser.). (gr. 7-9). 1969. tchrs' manuals o.p. 1.40 o.p. (ISBN 0-686-76920-1). Bobbs.

--Best of Children's Literature. Incl. Sunny & Gay. (gr. 1). text ed. 3.12 o.p. (ISBN 0-672-70530-3); Fun All Around. (gr. 3). text ed. 3.56 o.p. (ISBN 0-672-70538-9); Shining Hours. (gr. 4). text ed. 3.76 o.p. (ISBN 0-672-70542-7); Time for Adventure. (gr. 5). text ed. 4.04 o.p. (ISBN 0-672-70546-X); Beyond the Horizon. (gr. 6). text ed. 4.16 o.p. (ISBN 0-672-70550-8). (gr. 1-6). 1968. tchrs' manuals o.p. 1.40 o.p. (ISBN 0-686-76921-X). Bobbs.

Smith, Norman. If It Shines, Clangs & Bends, Its Metal. LC 79-227. (Science Is What & Why Ser.). (Illus.). (gr. 2-4). 1980. PLB 6.99 (ISBN 0-698-30717-8, Coward). Putnam Pub Group.

--Moonhopping: Through Our Solar System. (Science Is What & Why Ser.). (Illus.). (gr. k-3). 1977. PLB 5.99 o.p. (ISBN 0-698-30643-0, Coward). Putnam Pub Group.

--Space: What's Out There. (What Lives There Ser.). (Illus.). 32p. (gr. 2-6). 1976. PLB 5.99 (ISBN 0-698-30585-X, Coward). Putnam Pub Group.

--Sunpower. (Science Is What & Why Ser.). (Illus.). (gr. k-2). 1976. PLB 6.99 (ISBN 0-698-30626-0, Coward). Putnam Pub Group.

--Wind Power. (Science Is What & Why Ser.). (gr. 3-7). 1981. 6.99 (ISBN 0-698-30732-1, Coward). Putnam Pub Group.

Smith, Norman F. Inside Story of Metal. LC 77-10768. (Illus.). 192p. (gr. 7 up). 1977. PLB 7.79 o.p. (ISBN 0-671-32860-3). Messner.

Smith, Norman K. Credibility of Divine Existence. Porteous, A. J., et al, eds. 1967. 26.00 (ISBN 0-312-17185-4). St Martin.

Smith, Norman K., ed. see Kant, Immanuel.

Smith, Norman L. The Return of Billy the Kid. LC 77-7541. (Illus.). 1977. 8.95 o.p. (ISBN 0-698-10834-5, Coward). Putnam Pub Group.

Smith, Norman O. Elementary Statistical Thermodynamics: A Problems Approach. 225p. 1982. 25.00x (ISBN 0-306-41205-5, Plenum Pr); pap. 14.95x (ISBN 0-306-41216-0). Plenum Pub.

Smith, Norval, jt. ed. see Van der Hulst, Harry.

Smith, Oscar E., Jr. Yankee Diplomacy: U. S. Intervention in Argentina. LC 79-25196. (Arnold Foundation Studies: Vol. III, New Ser.). 196p. 1980. Repr. of 1953 ed. lib. bdg. 19.00x (ISBN 0-313-22124-3, SMYD). Greenwood.

Smith, Owen T., jt. auth. see Arnold, Alvin L.

Smith, P. The Chemotaxonomy of Plants. (Contemporary Biology Ser). 324p. 1978. text ed. 26.00 o.p. (ISBN 0-7131-2544-6); pap. 16.95 (ISBN 0-444-19455-X). Univ Park.

Smith, P. & Morrison, W. I. Simulating the Urban Economy. (Monographs in Spatial & Environmental Analysis). 152p. 1975. 15.50x (ISBN 0-85086-046-6, Pub. by Pion England). Methuen Inc.

Smith, P., jt. auth. see Diamond, W. I.

Smith, P., ed. The Historian & Film. LC 75-19577. 235p. 1976. 27.95 (ISBN 0-521-20992-7). Cambridge U Pr.

Smith, P., tr. see Palm, Goran.

Smith, P. Christopher, tr. see Gadamer, Hans-Georg.

Smith, P. E., ed. Applying Research to Hydraulic Engineering. LC 82-72777. 752p. 1982. pap. text ed. 53.00 (ISBN 0-87262-316-5). Am Soc Civil Eng.

Smith, P. R. & Julian, W. G. Building Services. (Illus.). 1976. 55.50x (ISBN 0-85334-657-7, Pub. by Applied Science). Elsevier.

Smith, P. R., ed. see Computer Assisted Learning Symposium, 1981.

Smith, Page. Trial by Fire: The Civil War & Reconstruction, Vol. 5, pt. 1. LC 81-18573. (A People's History of the United States Ser.). 1056p. 1982. 29.95 (ISBN 0-07-058571-7). McGraw.

Smith, Page & Daniel, Charles. The Chicken Book. LC 81-83967. 400p. 1982. pap. 12.00 (ISBN 0-86547-067-7). N Point Pr.

Smith, Page, ed. A Letter from My Father: The Strange Intimate Correspondence of W. Ward Smith to His Son Page Smith. LC 81-15890. (Illus.). 472p. 1982. pap. 8.50 (ISBN 0-688-00798-8). Quill NY.

Smith, Pat, jt. auth. see Fulton, Eleanor.

Smith, Patricia. Effanbee Dolls. 248p. Date not set. 19.95 (ISBN 0-89145-202-8). Collector Bks.

Smith, Patricia, jt. auth. see Barrow, Georgia.

Smith, Patricia A., jt. auth. see Barrow, Georgia M.

Smith, Patrick. A Year at the Met. LC 82-47829. Date not set. 15.00 (ISBN 0-394-51783-0). Knopf. Postponed.

Smith, Patti. Babel. (Illus.). 1978. 4.95 (ISBN 0-399-12000-9); pap. 4.95 (ISBN 0-399-12102-1). Putnam Pub Group.

Smith, Paul. Aerobic Rope Skipping. (Illus.). 1981. 6.95 (ISBN 0-914296-04-3); kit with lP record & book 15.95 (ISBN 0-685-64474-X) (ISBN 0-685-64475-8). Activity Rec.

--Key to the Ulysses of James Joyce. LC 68-54175. (Studies in Fiction, No. 34). 1969. Repr. of 1934 ed. lib. bdg. 22.95x (ISBN 0-8383-0625-X). Haskell.

--Pound Revised. 204p. 1983. text ed. 29.25x (ISBN 0-7099-2346-5, Pub. by Croom Helm Ltd England). Biblio Dist.

Smith, Paul, jt. auth. see Ayllon, Candido.

Smith, Paul A. Electing a President: Information & Control. Pomper, Gerald M., ed. 256p. 1982. 28.95 (ISBN 0-03-059664-5). Praeger.

Smith, Paul F. Money & Financial Intermediation: The Theory & Structure of Financial Systems. LC 77-21636. (Illus.). 1978. 23.95 (ISBN 0-13-600288-9). P-H.

Smith, Paul F., ed. Underwater Photography: Scientific & Engineering Applications. (Illus.). 1983. text ed. write for info. Sci Bks Intl.

Smith, Paul H. & Gawalt, Gerard W., eds. Letters of Delegates to Congress, Seventeen Seventy-Four to Seventeen Eighty-Nine, 8 Vols. Incl. Vol. I. August Seventeen Seventy-Four to August Seventeen Seventy-Five. LC 76-2592. (Illus.). xxxvii, 751p. 1976. 18.00 (ISBN 0-8444-0191-9); Vol. 2. September to December Seventeen Seventy-Five. LC 76-2592. (Illus.). xxvii, 735p. 1978. 15.00 (ISBN 0-8444-0230-3); Vol. 3. January First to May Fifteenth, Nineteen Seventy-Six. LC 76-2592. (Illus.). xxix, 735p. 1978. 18.00 (ISBN 0-8444-0259-1); May Sixteenth to August Fifteenth, Seventeen Seventy-Six. LC 76-2592. (Illus.). xxviii, 739p. 1979. 18.00 (ISBN 0-8444-0260-5); Vol. 5. August Sixteenth to December Thirty-First, Seventeen Seventy-Six. LC 76-2592. (Illus.). xxx, 767p. 1979. 19.00 (ISBN 0-8444-0276-1); Vol. 6. January First to April Thirtyith, Nineteen Eighty-One. LC 76-2592. (Illus.). xxviii, 760p. 1981. 19.00 (ISBN 0-8444-0310-5); Vol. 7. May First to September Eighteenth, Seventeen Seventy-Seven. LC 76-2592. (Illus.). xxvi, **749p. 1981. 15.00 (ISBN 0-8444-0350-4); Vol. 8. September Nineteenth, Seventeen Seventy-Seven to January Thirty First, Seventeen Seventy-Eight. LC 76-2592. (Illus.). xxxii, 745p. 1981. 17.00 (ISBN 0-8444-0356-3). Set. write for info. (ISBN 0-8444-0177-3). Lib Congress.**

Smith, Paul J. Key to the Ulysses of James Joyce. pap. 3.00 o.s.i. (ISBN 0-87286-058-2). City Lights.

Smith, Paula & Seaman, Dorothy. Not Chopped Herring! The Kosher Way to Cook Gourmet. 288p. (Orig.). 1983. pap. 10.75 (ISBN 0-933374-01-1). Jetsand Pr.

Smith, Pauline C. Brush Fire! LC 78-14768. (A Hiway Bk.). 1979. pap. 8.95 (ISBN 0-664-32639-0). Westminster.

Smith, Peggy. Proofreading Manual & Reference Guide. (Illus.). 426p. 1981. incl. wkbk. 35.50x (ISBN 0-935012-02-8); wkbk sep. 11.00 (ISBN 0-935012-03-6). Edit Experts.

Smith, Peggy B. & Mumford, David M. Adolescent Pregnancy: Perspectives for the Health Professional. 1980. lib. bdg. 19.95 (ISBN 0-8161-2121-4, Hall Medical). G K Hall.

Smith, Penelope. Animal Talk: A Guide to Communicating with & Understanding Animals. (Illus.). 76p. 1982. pap. 5.00 (ISBN 0-936552-02-6). Pegasus Pubns.

--Body Operator's Manuals, No. 2-4. rev. ed. (Illus.). 48p. 1981. Set. pap. 5.95 (ISBN 0-936552-01-8). Pegasus Pubns.

Smith, Pennie see Eel Pie, pseud.

Smith, Percy H., ed. see Smith, Charles J.

Smith, Peter. Dive Bomber! 1982. 15.95 (ISBN 0-87021-930-8). Naval Inst Pr.

Smith, Peter & Summerfield, Geoffrey, eds. Matthew Arnold & the Education of the New Order. LC 69-10433. (Cambridge Texts & Studies in Education: No. 3). 1969. 25.95 (ISBN 0-521-07341-3). Cambridge U Pr.

Smith, Peter H. Upgrading Lecture-Rooms. (Illus.). 1979. 43.00x (ISBN 0-85334-849-9, Pub. by Applied Sci England). Elsevier.

Smith, Peter M. On the Hymm to Zeus in Aeschylus' Agamemnon. LC 80-11327. (American Classical Studies: No. 5). 12.00x (ISBN 0-89130-387-1, 40-04-05); pap. 9.00 (ISBN 0-89130-388-X). Scholars Pr CA.

Smith, Philip C., ed. Seafaring in Colonial Massachusetts. LC 80-51256. (Illus.). xvii, 240p. 1980. 25.00x (ISBN 0-8139-0897-3, Colonial Soc MA). U Pr of Va.

Smith, Philip L. Sources of Progressive Thought in American Education. LC 80-8290. 217p. 1980. lib. bdg. 18.75 (ISBN 0-8191-1300-X); pap. text ed. 10.25 (ISBN 0-8191-1301-8). U Pr of Amer.

Smith, Philip R., jt. auth. see Thrush, John C.

Smith, Phillip H. Electronic Applications of the Smith Chart. LC 82-14829. 250p. 1983. Repr. of 1969 ed. lib. bdg. price not set (ISBN 0-89874-552-7). Krieger.

Smith, R. & James, G. V. Analytical Sciences Monographs: The Sampling of Bulk Materials. 200p. 1982. 90.00x (ISBN 0-85186-810-X, Pub. by Royal Soc Chem England). State Mutual Bk.

Smith, R., jt. auth. see Aaronovitch, S.

Smith, R. A. Semiconductors. 2nd ed. LC 77-82515. 1978. 96.50 (ISBN 0-521-21824-1); pap. 29.50 (ISBN 0-521-29314-6). Cambridge U Pr.

Smith, R. B. Setting up Shop: The Do's & Dont's of Starting a Small Business. 256p. 1982. 21.95 (ISBN 0-07-058531-8). McGraw.

Smith, R. C. Materials of Construction. 3rd ed. (Illus.). 1979. text ed. 25.95 (ISBN 0-07-058497-4, G); answer key 1.50 (ISBN 0-07-058498-2). McGraw.

--Principles & Practices of Heavy Construction. 2nd ed. (Illus.). 448p. 1976. 26.95 (ISBN 0-13-701995-5). P-H.

Smith, R. E. Peasant Farming in Muscovy. LC 75-23843. (Illus.). 1977. 44.50 (ISBN 0-521-20912-9). Cambridge U Pr.

Smith, R. E., jt. ed. see Butt, C. R.

Smith, R. J. Electronics Circuits & Devices, Vol. 1. 2nd ed. 494p. 1980. 33.95 (ISBN 0-471-05344-9). Wiley.

Smith, R. L. The Excretory Function of Bile: The Elimination of Drugs & Toxic Substances in Bile. 1973. 40.00x (ISBN 0-412-11140-3, Pub. by Chapman & Hall). Methuen Inc.

Smith, R. M., jt. ed. see Hetzel, B. S.

Smith, R. P. Consumer Demand for Cars in the U. S. A. LC 74-31802. (Department of Applied Economics, Occasional Papers Ser.: No. 44). (Illus.). 200p. 1975. 27.95 (ISBN 0-521-20770-3); pap. 14.95x (ISBN 0-521-09947-1). Cambridge U Pr.

Smith, R. Philip. The La Costa Diet & Exercise Book. (Illus.). 1977. 14.95 (ISBN 0-448-12978-7, G&D); pap. 8.95 (ISBN 0-448-16529-5). Putnam Pub Group.

Smith, R. S. Warfare & Diplomacy in Pre-Colonial West Africa. 240p. 1976. 10.95x o.p. (ISBN 0-416-55060-6); pap. 5.95x o.p. (ISBN 0-416-55070-3). Methuen Inc.

Smith, R. T. Beasts Did Leap. 28p. 1982. 15.00 (ISBN 0-918092-29-9); pap. 5.00 (ISBN 0-918092-30-2). Tamarack Edns.

--Good Water. (Tamarack Awards Ser.). (Orig.). 1979. signed ed. 6.50 (ISBN 0-918092-13-2); pap. 3.50 (ISBN 0-686-51189-1). Tamarack Edns.

--Rural Route. 96p. 1981. cancelled (ISBN 0-918092-23-X); pap. 6.00 (ISBN 0-918092-25-6); signed ed., paper ed. 10.00 (ISBN 0-918092-24-8). Tamarack Edns.

Smith, R. T., jt. auth. see Frederick, M. T.

Smith, R. W. Chinese Boxing. 8.95x (ISBN 0-685-63749-2). Wehman.

Smith, Ralph & Butler, Blaine. Engineering as a Career. 4th rev. ed. (Illus.). 448p. 1983. pap. text ed. 18.95 (ISBN 0-07-058788-4, C); write for info. instr's manual (ISBN 0-07-058789-2). McGraw.

Smith, Ralph, ed. Breeding the Colorful Little Grass Parakeet. (Illus.). 1979. 4.95 (ISBN 0-87666-982-8, KW-006). TFH Pubns.

Smith, Ralph C. A Biographical Index of American Artists. LC 79-167186. 1976. Repr. of 1930 ed. 34.00x (ISBN 0-8103-4251-0). Gale.

Smith, Ralph I., ed. see Light.

Smith, Ralph J. Circuits, Devices, & Systems: A First Course in Electrical Engineering. 3rd ed. LC 75-29290. 1976. text ed. 33.95 (ISBN 0-471-80171-2); instructor's manual avail. (ISBN 0-471-01556-3). Wiley.

--Engineering As a Career. 3rd ed. LC 69-17192. 1969. pap. text ed. 16.95 (ISBN 0-07-058786-8, C); instructors' manual 7.95 (ISBN 0-07-058787-6). McGraw.

Smith, Ralph L., jt. ed. see Jesuale, Nancy J.

Smith, Ralph Lee, jt. ed. see Jesuale, Nancy J.

Smith, Randy B. Setting Up Shop. 288p. 1983. pap. 6.95 (ISBN 0-446-37533-0). Warner Bks.

Smith, Raymond J. Charles Churchill. (English Authors Ser.). 1977. lib. bdg. 14.95 (ISBN 0-8057-6669-3, Twayne). G K Hall.

Smith, Raymond J. & Oates, Joyce Carol, eds. Ontario Review, No. 15. 120p. (Orig.). 1981. 3.95 (ISBN 0-686-86540-5). Ontario Rev NJ.

--Ontario Review, Number 16. 116p. (Orig.). 1982. pap. 3.95 o.p. (ISBN 0-686-32782-9). Ontario Rev NJ.

Smith, Rebecca. The Telephone Connection. 1981. pap. 1.50 (ISBN 0-686-37154-2). Eldridge Pub.

Smith, Rebecca M. Klemer's Marriage & Family Relationships. 2nd ed. 424p. 1975. text ed. 22.95 scp (ISBN 0-06-046311-2, HarpC); instructor's manual avail. (ISBN 0-06-366303-1). Har-Row.

Smith, Reginald H. Justice & the Poor: A Study of Present Day Denial of Justice to the Poor. 3rd ed. (Criminology, Law Enforcement, & Social Problems Ser.: No. 139). (With introductory essay added). 1972. Repr. of 1924 ed. 10.00x (ISBN 0-87585-139-8). Patterson Smith.

Smith, Reid. Majestic Middle Tennessee. new ed. (Illus.). 143p. 1975. 9.95 (ISBN 0-88289-121-9). Pelican.

Smith, Reuben, jt. auth. see Schewe, Charles.

Smith, Richard. Mercenaries & Mandarins: Ever Victorious Army in Nineteenth Century China. LC 78-6394. (Studies in American History). 1978. lib. bdg. 30.00 (ISBN 0-527-83950-7). Kraus Intl.

Smith, Richard, jt. auth. see Kreps, Karen.

Smith, Richard A., ed. Manpower & Primary Health Care: Guidelines for Improving - Expanding Health Service Coverage in Developing Countries. LC 78-17554. 1978. 10.00x (ISBN 0-8248-0607-7). UH Pr.

--Thinking, Knowing, Living: An Introduction to Philosophy. LC 78-52290. 1978. pap. text ed. 8.50 o.p. (ISBN 0-8191-0492-2). U Pr of Amer.

Smith, Richard C., jt. ed. see Webster, Richard C.

Smith, Richard E. Richard Aldington. (English Authors Ser.). 1977. lib. bdg. 14.95 (ISBN 0-8057-6691-X, Twayne). G K Hall.

Smith, Richard H. A Concise Coptic-English Lexicon. 96p. 1983. 10.95 (ISBN 0-8028-3581-3). Eerdmans.

--Spymaster's Odyssey: The Secret Service of Allen Dulles. (Illus.). 1979. write for info. o.p. (ISBN 0-698-10703-9, Coward). Putnam Pub Group.

Smith, Richard J., jt. auth. see Otto, Wayne.

Smith, Richard J., et al. The School Reading Program: A Handbook for Teachers, Supervisors, & Specialists. LC 77-77993. (Illus.). 1978. text ed. 23.50 (ISBN 0-395-25452-3). HM.

Smith, Richard K. First Across! The U. S. Navy's Transatlantic Flight of 1919. LC 72-85396. 279p. 1973. 11.00 o.p. (ISBN 0-87021-184-6). Naval Inst Pr.

Smith, Richard L., jt. auth. see Thacker, Ronald J.

Smith, Richard T. Analysis of Electrical Machines. LC 81-4541. (Illus.). 240p. 1982. 36.00 (ISBN 0-08-027174-X). Pergamon.

Smith, Richard T. & Landy, Maurice, eds. Immune Surveillance. LC 73-138439. (Perspectives in Immunology Ser). 1971. 49.50 (ISBN 0-12-652250-2). Acad Pr.

--Immunobiology of the Tumor-Host Relationship: Proceedings. (Perspectives in Immunology Ser.). 1975. 49.50 (ISBN 0-12-652260-X). Acad Pr.

Smith, Richard W., jt. auth. see Giannotti, John B.

Smith, Rob. General Principles Breast & Extracranial Endocrines: Operative Surgery. 4th ed. 1982. text ed. 130.00 (ISBN 0-407-00650-8). Butterworth.

Smith, Robb. Amphoto Guide to Filters. (Illus.). 1979. 10.95 o.p. (ISBN 0-8174-2458-X, Amphoto); pap. 7.95 (ISBN 0-8174-2132-7). Watson-Guptill.

--Mamiya Professional Systems Handbook. (Illus.). 224p. 1974. 17.50 o.p. (ISBN 0-8174-0557-7, Amphoto). Watson-Guptill.

--The Tiffen Practical Filter Manual. (Illus.). 96p. 1975. pap. 5.95 o.p. (ISBN 0-8174-0180-6, Amphoto). Watson-Guptill.

Smith, Robert. Applied General Mathematics. LC 79-51586. (General Mathematics Ser.). (Illus.). 349p. 1982. text ed. 18.20 (ISBN 0-8273-1674-7); instr's. guide 4.75 (ISBN 0-8273-1675-5); test booklet 4.75 (ISBN 0-8273-2075-2). Delmar.

--Hiking Oahu. 2nd ed. Winnett, Thomas, ed. LC 80-53464. (Trail Guide Ser.). (Illus.). 128p. (Orig.). 1980. pap. 5.95 (ISBN 0-89997-006-0). Wilderness.

--Illustrated History of Baseball. LC 72-77101. 288p. 1973. Repr. 3.95 (ISBN 0-448-02081-5, G&D). Putnam Pub Group.

--Introduction to Mental Retardation. 1971. 26.50 (ISBN 0-07-058903-8, C). McGraw.

--MacArthur in Korea: The Naked Emperor. 1982. 15.95 (ISBN 0-671-24062-5). S&S.

Smith, Robert & John, Tommy. The Sally & Tommy John Story: Our Life in Baseball. (Illus.). 288p. 1983. 13.95 (ISBN 0-02-559260-2). Macmillan.

Smith, Robert, jt. auth. see Draeger, Donn F.

Smith, Robert, jt. auth. see Neisworth, John.

Smith, Robert & Winnett, Thomas, eds. Hiking Hawaii: The Big Island. 2nd ed. LC 79-93248. (Trail Guide Ser.). (Illus.). 116p. (Orig.). 1980. pap. 5.95 (ISBN 0-89997-000-1). Wilderness.

Smith, Robert A. Science of Life: With Affirmations of Jesus Christ. 1970. 2.25 o.s.i. (ISBN 0-912128-07-0). Pubns Living.

--Science of Life: With Affirmations of Jesus Christ. 1970. 2.95 o.s.i. (ISBN 0-912128-07-0). Pubns Living.

--Seeking & Finding. 1974. 1.75 o.s.i. (ISBN 0-912128-08-9). Pubns Living.

Smith, Robert B., ed. An Introduction to Social Research. LC 82-11529. (Handbook of Social Science Methods Ser.: Vol. 1). 444p. 1983. text ed. 37.50x (ISBN 0-88410-890-2). Ballinger Pub.

Smith, Robert B. & Manning, Peter K., eds. Qualitative Methods. (Handbook of Social Science Methods Ser.: Vol. 2). 360p. 1982. text ed. 30.00x (ISBN 0-88410-909-7). Ballinger Pub.

Smith, Robert C. How to Survive a Nuclear Disaster. 1983. pap. 3.95 (ISBN 0-8217-1131-8). Zebra.

Smith, Robert C., jt. ed. see Howard, John R.

Smith, Robert D. Vocational-Technical Mathematics. LC 81-70966. (Illus.). 576p. (Orig.). 1983. pap. text ed. 19.80 (ISBN 0-8273-1882-0); instr's guide 7.25 (ISBN 0-8273-1883-9). Delmar.

Smith, Robert D., jt. auth. see Burack, Elmer H.

Smith, Robert E. A Ceramic Sequence from the Pyramid of the Sun at Teotihuacan, Mexico. (Peabody Museum Papers: Vol. 75). (Illus.). 300p. (Orig.). 1983. pap. text ed. 40.00x (ISBN 0-87365-201-0). Peabody Harvard.

--Forging & Welding. rev. ed. (Illus.). (gr. 7 up). 1956. text ed. 17.28 (ISBN 0-87345-120-1). McKnight.

--Patternmaking & Founding. (gr. 9 up). 1959. pap. 6.36 (ISBN 0-87345-020-5). McKnight.

--Privacy: How to Protect What's Left of It. LC 78-55857. 1980. pap. 4.95 o.p. (ISBN 0-385-14270-6, Anch). Doubleday.

--Workrights: How to Draw the Line Without Losing Your Job. 236p. 1983. 14.95 (ISBN 0-525-24179-5, 01451-440); pap. 8.95 (ISBN 0-525-48047-1, 0801-240). Dutton.

Smith, Robert E. & Johnson, Dora E. Fortran Autotester. 176p. (Prog. Bk.). 1962. pap. 13.00 o.p. (ISBN 0-471-80337-5, Pub. by Wiley-Interscience). Wiley.

Smith, Robert E., jt. auth. see Schaefer, Carl J.

Smith, Robert F., ed. The United States & the Latin American Sphere of Influence, 2 vols. Incl. Vol. 1. The Era of Caribbean Intervention, 1898-1930 (ISBN 0-89874-153-X); Vol. 2. The Era of Good Neighbors, Cold Warriors & Hairshirts, 1930-1982 (ISBN 0-89874-154-8). 1983. pap. text ed. 5.50 (ISBN 0-686-86266-X). Krieger.

Smith, Robert F., Jr. Organic Gardening in the West: Raising Vegetables in a Short, Dry Growing Season. (Illus.). 1976. pap. 4.95 (ISBN 0-913270-60-1). Sunstone Pr.

Smith, Robert J. Crime Against the Elderly: Implications for Policy-Makers & Practitioners. 61p. 1979. pap. text ed. 5.00 (ISBN 0-910473-07-2). Intl Fed Ageing.

Smith, Robert J. & Wiswell, Ella L. The Women of Suye Mura. LC 82-2708. (Illus.). 320p. 1983. lib. bdg. 20.00x (ISBN 0-226-76344-7); pap. 7.50 (ISBN 0-226-76345-5). U of Chicago Pr.

Smith, Robert J., jt. auth. see Cornell, John B.

Smith, Robert J., ed. The Psychopath in Society. (Personality & Psychopathology Ser.). 1978. 18.00 (ISBN 0-12-652550-1). Acad Pr.

Smith, Robert K. Chocolate Fever. 1978. pap. 1.95 (ISBN 0-440-41369-9, YB). Dell.

--Jane's House. LC 82-2277. 352p. 1982. 13.95 (ISBN 0-688-01255-8). Morrow.

--Jelly Belly: A Novel. LC 80-23898. (Illus.). 160p. (gr. 4-8). 1981. 9.95 o.s.i. (ISBN 0-440-04186-4); PLB 9.89 o.s.i. (ISBN 0-440-04190-2). Delacorte.

--Sadie Shapiro, Matchmaker. (General Ser.). 1980. lib. bdg. 10.95 (ISBN 0-8161-3108-2, Large Print Bks). G K Hall.

--Sadie Shapiro, Matchmaker. 1980. 7.95 o.p. (ISBN 0-671-24014-5). S&S.

Smith, Robert L. Ecology & Field Biology. 3rd ed. 800p. 1980. 28.50scp (ISBN 0-06-046329-5, HarpC). Har-Row.

--Electrical Wiring: Industrial. 4th ed. LC 81-71831. (Illus.). 160p. 1982. pap. text ed. 12.80 (ISBN 0-8273-1947-9); instr's guide 2.10 (ISBN 0-8273-1948-7). Delmar.

--Refractions. LC 79-53012. (Living Poets' Library: Vol. 21). 1979. pap. 3.50 (ISBN 0-934218-11-0). Dragons Teeth.

Smith, Robert M. Anesthesia for Infants & Children. 4th ed. LC 79-18284. (Illus.). 698p. 1979. text ed. 67.50 (ISBN 0-8016-4699-5). Mosby.

--Clinical Teaching. 2nd ed. (Illus.). 448p. 1974. text ed. 26.50 (ISBN 0-07-058906-2, C); instr's manual 16.00 (ISBN 0-07-058907-0). McGraw.

Smith, Robert M. & Neisworth, John. The Exceptional Child. 2nd ed. (McGraw-Hill Ser. in Special Education). (Illus.). 1983. text ed. 22.95 (ISBN 0-07-058976-3, C); write for info instr's manual (ISBN 0-07-058977-1); write for info study guide (ISBN 0-07-058978-X). McGraw.

Smith, Robert M. & Neisworth, John T. The Exceptional Child: A Functional Approach. (Illus.). 384p. 1975. text ed. 25.50 (ISBN 0-07-058975-5, C); instructor's manual by Greer 11.00 (ISBN 0-07-024377-8). McGraw.

Smith, Robert M., jt. auth. see Neisworth, John T.

Smith, Robert M., et al. Evaluating Educational Environments. 1978. pap. text ed. 12.95 (ISBN 0-675-08388-5). Additional supplements may be obtained from publisher. Merrill.

Smith, Robert O., jt. auth. see Rouse, Robert S.

Smith, Robert R., et al, eds. Vascular Malformations & Fistulas of the Brain. (Seminars in Neurological Surgery). 267p. 1982. text ed. 35.00 (ISBN 0-89004-683-2). Raven.

Smith, Robert S. Kingdoms of the Yoruba. 2nd ed. (Studies in African History). (Illus.). 1976. 19.95x (ISBN 0-416-84710-2); pap. 12.95x (ISBN 0-416-84720-X). Methuen Inc.

Smith, Robert S. & Kensicki, Peter R. Principles of Insurance Protection. LC 80-84218. 752p. 1981. pap. text ed. 17.00 (ISBN 0-89462-006-1). IIA.

Smith, Robert S., jt. auth. see Ehrenberg, Ronald.

Smith, Robert S., et al. Principles of Insurance Production. 1980. write for info. o.p. (PRO 81). IIA.

Smith, Robert W. Shaolin Temple Boxing Secrets. 7.95x o.p. (ISBN 0-685-22107-5). Wehman.

Smith, Roberta H. In Vitro: Propagation of Kalanchoe. (Avery's Plant Tissue Culture Ser.). (Illus.). 16p. (Orig.). 1982. pap. text ed. 2.95 (ISBN 0-89529-163-0). Avery Pub.

Smith, Robin, jt. auth. see Georgacarakos, George N.

Smith, Robin, jt. auth. see Willey, Keith.

Smith, Robin, tr. see Mann, Klaus.

Smith, Robin L. Passage to Glory. 400p. Date not set. pap. 3.50 (ISBN 0-441-65219-0). Ace Bks.

Smith, Roch C. Gaston Bachelard. (World Authors Ser.). 1982. lib. bdg. 16.95 (ISBN 0-8057-6511-5, Twayne). G K Hall.

Smith, Rodney see London, P. S.

Smith, Rodney, jt. ed. see Ballantyne, J.

Smith, Rodney, ed. see Symon, Lindsay.

Smith, Roge T. Gothic Architecture in England with an Illustrated Glossary of Technical Terms. (Illus.). 164p. 1983. 91.85 (ISBN 0-86650-059-6). Gloucester Art.

Smith, Roger. Brittle Bone Syndrome. (Illus.). 224p. 1983. text ed. 69.95 (ISBN 0-407-00211-1). Butterworth.

--Greta the Green Cow. (Umbrella Books). (Illus.). 30p. (ps). 1983. bds. 5.95 (ISBN 0-19-278200-2, Pub by Oxford U Pr Childrens). Merrimack Bk Serv.

--Hiking Maui: The Valley Isle. 2nd ed. Winnett, Thomas, ed. LC 79-93159. (Trail Guide Ser.). (Illus.). 144p. (Orig.). 1980. pap. 5.95 (ISBN 0-911824-99-5). Wilderness.

--The Penguin Book of Orienteering. 1983. pap. 4.95 (ISBN 0-14-046438-7). Penguin.

Smith, Roger & Apley, Alan. Biochemical Disorders of the Skeleton. (Postgraduate Orthopedic Ser.). (Illus.). 1979. text ed. 59.95 (ISBN 0-407-00122-0). Butterworth.

Smith, Roger C., et al. Smith's Guide to the Literature of the Life Sciences. 9th ed. LC 79-55580. 1980. pap. 13.95x (ISBN 0-8087-3576-4). Burgess.

Smith, Roger H. Paperback Parnassus: The Birth, the Development, the Pending Crises of the Modern American Paperbound Book. 100p. 1976. 18.00 o.p. (ISBN 0-89158-007-7). Westview.

Smith, Roger T., ed. see Rosengarten, A.

Smith, Ronald. Principles & Practices of Light Construction. 3rd ed. (Illus.). 1980. text ed. 26.95 (ISBN 0-13-701979-3). P-H.

Smith, Ronald C. Materials of Construction. 2nd ed. (Illus.). 448p. 1972. text ed. 23.05 o.p. (ISBN 0-07-058477-X, G). McGraw.

Smith, Ronald D. December King. LC 82-70368. (gr. 5-9). 1983. pap. 3.95 (ISBN 0-8054-4516-1). Broadman.

Smith, Ronald E. & Nozik, Robert M. Uveitis: A Clinical Approach to Diagnosis & Management. (Illus.). 232p. 1983. lib. bdg. 49.95 (ISBN 0-683-07768-6). Williams & Wilkins.

Smith, Ronald E., et al. Psychology: The Frontiers of Behavior. 2nd ed. 717p. 1982. text ed. 24.50 scp (ISBN 0-06-045729-5, HarpC); scp study guide 8.95 (ISBN 0-06-044886-5); instr's manual avail. (0-06-365850-X); test bank avail. (ISBN 0-06-364925-X); test bank II avail. (ISBN 0-06-364926-8). Har-Row.

Smith, Ronald L. Let Peas Be With You: Food Poems. LC 82-72607. (Illus.). 106p. (Orig.). 1982. pap. 4.95 (ISBN 0-89708-108-0). And Bks.

Smith, Ronald W. & Preston, Frederick W. Sociology: An Introduction. 2nd ed. LC 80-51057. 673p. 1982. text ed. 18.95 (ISBN 0-312-73992-3); instr's. manual & test item file avail.; study guide 6.95 (ISBN 0-312-73995-8). St Martin.

Smith, Rosemary, jt. auth. see Hackett, Brian.

Smith, Roswell C. English Grammar on the Productive System. (American Linguistics Ser.). 1983. Repr. of 1864 ed. 30.00x (ISBN 0-8201-1377-8). Schol Facsimiles.

Smith, Ruby G. People's Colleges: A History of the New York State Extension Service in Cornell University & the State, 1876-1948. (Illus.). 614p. 1949. 27.50x (ISBN 0-8014-0396-0). Cornell U Pr.

Smith, Rueben, jt. auth. see Schewe, Charles D.

Smith, Russell E. Electricity for Refrigeration, Heating, & Air Conditioning. 2nd ed. 1983. text ed. 24.95 (ISBN 0-534-01316-3, Pub. by Breton Pubs). Wadsworth Pubs.

Smith, Ruth E. Miniature Lamps II. LC 82-50618. (Illus.). 249p. 1982. 28.50 (ISBN 0-916838-65-X). Schiffer.

Smith, Ruth E. & Feltner, Helen A. Price Guide to Miniature Lamps Book I & II. 48p. 1982. pap. 10.00 (ISBN 0-916838-72-2). Schiffer.

Smith, Ruth S. Cataloging Made Easy: How to Organize Your Congregation's Library. (Illus.). 263p. 1978. pap. 4.95 o.p. (ISBN 0-686-95421-1). CSLA.

--Getting the Books Off the Shelves: Making the Most of Your Congregation's Library. (Illus.). 117p. 1975. pap. 4.95 o.p. (ISBN 0-686-95423-8). CSLA.

--Getting the Books Off the Shelves: Making the Most of Your Congregation's Library. 126p. (Orig.). 1975. pap. 4.95 (ISBN 0-8164-1236-7). Seabury.

Smith, Ruth S., jt. auth. see Werner, Emmy E.

Smith, S., jt. auth. see Keedy, M.

Smith, S. E. & Rawlins, M. D. Variability in Human Drug Response. 1976. 19.95 (ISBN 0-407-43301-5). Butterworth.

Smith, S. E., jt. ed. see Harley, J. L.

Smith, Sally. Parachuting & Skydiving. (Illus.). 1978. 14.50 o.p. (ISBN 0-7207-1063-4). Transatlantic.

Smith, Sally L. No Easy Answers: Teaching the Learning Disabled Child. 1979. text ed. 14.95 (ISBN 0-316-79904-1); pap. text ed. 9.95 (ISBN 0-316-79906-8). Little.

Smith, Sally T. House on Stone Quarry. (YA) 1980. 6.95 (ISBN 0-686-73937-X, Avalon). Bouregy.

--Incident at Caprock. 1981. pap. 6.95 (ISBN 0-686-84681-8, Avalon). Bouregy.

--Return to Terror. 1982. 6.95 (ISBN 0-686-84183-2, Avalon). Bouregy.

--The Secret of Harpen's Landing. (YA) 1978. 6.95 (ISBN 0-685-86414-6, Avalon). Bouregy.

Smith, Sally Tyree. The Visitors at Merville House. (YA) 1979. 6.95 (ISBN 0-685-93881-6, Avalon). Bouregy.

Smith, Sam B. & Owsley, Harriet C., eds. The Papers of Andrew Jackson: 1770-1803, Vol. 1. LC 79-15078. (Illus.). 656p. 1980. 27.50x (ISBN 0-87049-219-5). U of Tenn Pr.

Smith, Samuel. Ideas of the Great Psychologists. LC 82-48135. 224p. 1983. pap. 6.68 (ISBN 0-06-463561-9, EH 561, EH). Har-Row.

--Ideas of the Great Psychologists. LC 82-48135. 304p. 1983. 14.34i (ISBN 0-06-015087-4, HarpT). Har-Row.

Smith, Sanderson M. Mastering Multiple-Choice Mathematics Tests: Algebra, Geometry, Trigonometry. LC 81-20675. (Illus.). 224p. (Orig.). 1982. pap. 6.95 (ISBN 0-668-05409-3). Arco.

Smith, Sandra, tr. see Stehle, Hansjakob.

Smith, Sara L., jt. auth. see Lynch, Jane S.

Smith, Sara R. Manchurian Crisis Nineteen Thirty One to Nineteen Thirty Two: A Tragedy in International Relations. Repr. of 1948 ed. lib. bdg. 16.00x (ISBN 0-8371-3344-0, SMMC). Greenwood.

Smith, Sarah. Jessica's First Prayer, Repr. Of 1867 Ed. Wolff, Robert L., ed. Bd. with Little Meg's Children; Alone in London. Repr. of 1869 ed; Pilgrim Street. Repr. of 1872 ed. (Victorian Fiction Ser.). 1975. lib. bdg. 60.00 o.s.i. (ISBN 0-8240-1569-X). Garland Pub.

Smith, Sarah W., tr. see Colette.

Smith, Scottie F. An Alabama Journal 1977. LC 76-40827. 1976. 5.95 o.p. (ISBN 0-87397-109-4). Strode.

Smith, Selwyn. The Maltreatment of Children: A Comprehensive Guide to the Battered Baby Syndrome. 464p. 1978. text ed. 19.95 (ISBN 0-8391-1220-3). Univ Park.

Smith, Sharon. Basic Skills Travel & Transportation Workbook. (Basic Skills Workbooks). 32p. (gr. 4-7). 1983. 0.99 (ISBN 0-8209-0561-5, SW-9). ESP.

--Craftsmen of Colonial America. (Social Studies). 24p. (gr. 5-8). 1977. wkbk. 5.00 (ISBN 0-8209-0258-6, SS-25). ESP.

--Electricity. (Science Ser.). 24p. (gr. 5-9). 1977. wkbk. 5.00 (ISBN 0-8209-0157-1, S-19). ESP.

--Money Management. (Math Ser.). 24p. (gr. 7 up). 1982. wkbk. 5.00 (ISBN 0-8209-0121-0, A-31). ESP.

--Travel & Transportation. (Social Studies Ser.). 24p. (gr. 5-9). 1976. wkbk. 5.00 (ISBN 0-8209-0247-0, SS-14). ESP.

--Yankee Magazine's Travel Guide to New England: Summer-Fall 1983. (Illus.). 200p. 1983. pap. 2.50 (ISBN 0-89909-004-4). Yankee Bks.

Smith, Shea & Walsh, John E., Jr. Strategies in Business. LC 77-25091. (Systems & Controls for Financial Management Ser). 1978. 33.95 o.p. (ISBN 0-471-80002-3). Ronald Pr.

Smith, Sherry A., jt. auth. see Rogers, Mary B.

Smith, Sidonie. Where I'm Bound. LC 73-20973. 194p. 1974. lib. bdg. 25.00x (ISBN 0-8371-7337-X, SPS/). Greenwood.

Smith, Stan, et al. Modern Tennis Doubles. Sheehan, Larry, ed. LC 75-13514. (Illus.). 1977. o. p 9.95 (ISBN 0-689-10687-4); pap. 4.95 (ISBN 0-689-70556-5). Atheneum.

Smith, Stanley B., ed. see Lucretius.

Smith, Stephen L. Recreation Geography. (Themes in Resource Management Ser.). (Illus.). 240p. 1982. pap. text ed. write for info. (ISBN 0-582-30050-9). Longman.

Smith, Steve. Fly the Biggest Piece Back. LC 78-13586. (Illus.). 278p. 1979. limited ed. 49.50 (ISBN 0-87842-118-1); 15.95 (ISBN 0-87842-108-4). Mountain Pr.

Smith, Steve L., jt. auth. see Taylor, Fred I.

Smith, Steven P. The Long Riders. 192p. 1980. pap. 2.25 o.p. (ISBN 0-380-76174-2, 76174). Avon.

--Walking Wounded. 1979. 9.95 (ISBN 0-399-12320-2). Putnam Pub Group.

Smith, Stevie. Me Again: Uncollected Writings of Stevie Smith. LC 82-40430. (Illus.). 400p. 1983. pap. 6.95 (ISBN 0-394-71362-1, Vin). Random.

--Stevie Smith: A Selection. Lee, Hermione, ed. 224p. 1983. 18.95 (ISBN 0-571-13029-1); pap. 6.95 (ISBN 0-571-13030-5). Faber & Faber.

Smith, Susan. Made in America. LC 71-145708. 1971. Repr. of 1929 ed. 30.00x (ISBN 0-8103-3396-1). Gale.

Smith, Susan, jt. auth. see Thwaite, Jean.

Smith, Susan H. How, When & Where in Atlanta. Nicholson, Diana M., ed. (Marmac Guidebook Ser.). 288p. (Orig.). 1981. pap. 8.95 (ISBN 0-939944-00-6). Marmac Pub.

--Marmac Guide to Atlanta. 2nd ed. Nicholson, Diana M., ed. (Marmac Guide Ser.). (Illus.). 296p. 1983. pap. 6.95 (ISBN 0-939944-27-8). Marmac Pub.

Smith, Susan S. Complete Poems & Collected Letters of Adelaide Crapsey. LC 76-25509. (Illus.). 1977. 34.50x (ISBN 0-87395-342-8). State U NY Pr.

Smith, Susan T. Communication & Other Social Behavior in Parus Carolinensis. (Illus.). 125p. 1972. 7.75 (ISBN 0-686-35799-X). Nuttall Ornithological.

Smith, Suzanne, jt. auth. see Olmstead, Barney.

Smith, Suzy. Enigma of Out of Body Travel. pap. 1.25 o.p. (ISBN 0-451-06967-6, Y6967, Sig). NAL.

Smith, Sydney G. Collected Poems. (The Scottish Library Ser). 269p. 1975. text ed. 22.25x o.p. (ISBN 0-7145-3511-7). Humanities.

Smith, Syndey B. Sherca. (Short Play Ser.). pap. 1.95x (ISBN 0-912262-57-5). Proscenium.

Smith, T. C. Trojan Peace: Some Deterrence Propositions Tested, Vol. 19, Bk. 2. (Monograph Series in World Affairs). (Orig.). 1982. pap. 5.00 (ISBN 0-87940-069-2). U of Denver Intl.

Smith, T. J., jt. ed. see Steinhart, J. S.

Smith, T. Lynn. The Sociology of Agricultural Development. (Monographs & Theory Studies in Sociology & Anthropology in Honor of N. Anderson). 101p. 1974. text ed. 22.25x (ISBN 90-04-03540-0). Humanities.

Smith, Terrence L. The Money War. LC 78-55022. 1978. 9.95 o.p. (ISBN 0-689-10900-8). Atheneum.

Smith, Thelma, ed. see Lowell, James R.

Smith, Thelma M. & Miner, Ward L. Transatlantic Migration: The Contemporary American Novel in France. LC 68-29749. (Illus.). 1968. Repr. of 1955 ed. lib. bdg. 15.75x (ISBN 0-8371-0232-4, SMCA). Greenwood.

Smith, Theodore A. Dynamic Business Strategy: The Art of Planning for Success. (Illus.). 1977. 21.00 (ISBN 0-07-059090-7, P&RB). McGraw.

Smith, Thomas. De Republica Anglorum. Dewar, Mary, ed. LC 81-21634. (Cambridge Studies in the History & Theory of Politics). 192p. 1982. 39.50 (ISBN 0-521-24109-X). Cambridge U Pr.

--Euclid: His Life & His System. (The Essential Library of the Great Philosophers). (Illus.). 113p. 1983. Repr. of 1902 ed. 67.85 (ISBN 0-89901-092-X). Found Class Reprints.

Smith, Thomas E. Industrial Energy Management for Cost Reduction. LC 79-89733. (Illus.). 1979. 39.95 (ISBN 0-250-40340-4). Ann Arbor Science.

Smith, Thomas F. The Powerticians: Politics & Social Life in Jersey City. (Illus.). 256p. 1982. 15.00 (ISBN 0-8184-0328-4). Lyle Stuart.

Smith, Thomas V. & White, Leonard D. Chicago, an Experiment in Social Science Research. LC 68-57639. 1968. Repr. of 1929 ed. lib. bdg. 15.75x (ISBN 0-8371-0661-3, SMCH). Greenwood.

Smith, Thomas V., ed. Philosophers Speak for Themselves: From Aristotle to Plotinus. 2nd ed. LC 56-4949. 1956. pap. 7.50 (ISBN 0-226-76479-6, P9, Phoen). U of Chicago Pr.

Smith, Tim D., jt. auth. see Fowler, Charles W.

Smith, Timothy. Revivalism & Social Reform: American Protestantism on the Eve of the Civil War. LC 80-8114. 272p. 1980. pap. text ed. 5.95x (ISBN 0-8018-2477-X). Johns Hopkins.

Smith, Timothy J. Combustion Noise Control. (Illus.). 180p. pap. text ed. 45.00 (ISBN 0-89671-042-4). Southeast Acoustics.

Smith, Toby. Dateline New Mexico. 2nd ed. (Illus.). 252p. 1982. 14.95 (ISBN 0-8263-0628-4). U of NM Pr.

--Pieces of the Promise. (Illus.). 90p. (Orig.). 1982. pap. 7.95 (ISBN 0-9608762-0-0). T Smith.

Smith, Tom. Singing the Middle Ages. 64p. 1982. 11.95 (ISBN 0-914378-87-2); pap. 5.95 (ISBN 0-914378-88-0). Countryman.

Smith, Tony. The End of the European Empire. (Problems in European Civilization Ser.). 240p. 1975. pap. text ed. 5.95 (ISBN 0-669-93195-0). Heath.

--Gymnastics: A Mechanical Understanding. (Illus.). 192p. 1983. text ed. 15.00 (ISBN 0-8419-0829-X). Holmes & Meier.

Smith, Tracy E., jt. auth. see Lee, Ellen W.

Smith, Uriah. Daniel & the Revelation. 768p. 1944. pap. 3.50 o.p. (ISBN 0-8163-0028-3, 04079-0). Pacific Pr Pub Assn.

Smith, Ursula, jt. auth. see Peavy, Linda.

Smith, Ursula, ed. see Schnurre, Wolfdietrich.

Smith, V. Jackson. Programming for Radio & Television. LC 80-5635. 141p. 1980. pap. text ed. 7.75 o.p. (ISBN 0-8191-1250-X). U Pr of Amer.

--Programming for Radio & Television. rev. ed. LC 82-21887. (Illus.). 180p. 1983. lib. bdg. 18.75 (ISBN 0-8191-2887-2); pap. text ed. 8.25 (ISBN 0-8191-2888-0). U Pr of Amer.

Smith, V. Kerry. Economic Consequences of Air Pollution. LC 76-25901. 136p. 1976. prof ref 25.00x (ISBN 0-88410-026-X). Ballinger Pub.

Smith, V. Kerry, jt. auth. see Cicchetti, Charles J.

Smith, Van, jt. auth. see Smith, Divine.

Smith, Vearl R., jt. ed. see Larson, Bruce L.

Smith, Verity. Ramon de Valle-Inclan. (World Authors Ser.). lib. bdg. 15.95 (ISBN 0-8057-2924-0, Twayne). G K Hall.

Smith, Vernon, jt. ed. see Keen, John.

Smith, Vernon L., ed. Research in Experimental Economics, Vol. 1. (Orig.). 1979. lib. bdg. 45.00 (ISBN 0-89232-030-3). Jai Pr.

Smith, Veronica B., ed. International Directory of Exhibiting Artists 1982. 1982. Vol. 1: Painters, Printmakers, & Draughtsmen 485 pgs. text ed. 44.75 (ISBN 0-903450-61-5); Vol. 2: Sculptors, Photographers, Performance Artists, & Others 306 pgs. text ed. 28.75 (ISBN 0-903450-62-3). ABC-Clio.

Smith, Vincent. The Oxford History of India. 4th ed. Spear, Percival, ed. (Illus.). 1981. pap. 10.95x (ISBN 0-19-561297-3). Oxford U Pr.

Smith, Vincent E. Science & Philosophy. (Illus.). 1965. 5.50 o.p. (ISBN 0-02-829100-X). Glencoe.

--Science of Nature: An Introduction. rev. ed. Orig. Title: General Science of Nature. 1966. pap. 4.95x o.p. (ISBN 0-02-829120-4). Glencoe.

Smith, Vincent E., tr. Saint Thomas & the Object of Geometry. (Aquinas Lecture). 1953. 7.95 (ISBN 0-87462-118-6). Marquette.

Smith, Vincent G., tr. see Alba, Victor.

Smith, Virginia. Lion Rugs from Fars. 1982. 12.95 (ISBN 0-89754-030-1); pap. 8.95 (ISBN 0-89754-027-1). Dan River Pr.

Smith, Virginia W. The Single Parent: Revised, Updated & Expanded. 192p. 1983. pap. 5.95 (ISBN 0-8007-5105-1, Power Bks). Revell.

Smith, Vivian. Vance & Nettie Palmer. (World Authors Ser.). 1974. lib. bdg. 15.95 (ISBN 0-8057-2667-5, Twayne). G K Hall.

Smith, W. Elementary Complex Variables. LC 43-87526. 352p. 1974. text ed. 17.95x (ISBN 0-675-08870-4). Merrill.

Smith, W., jt. auth. see Sawistowski, H.

Smith, W. Allen. Elementary Numerical Analysis. 1979. text ed. 25.95 scp (ISBN 0-06-046312-0, HarpC). Har-Row.

Smith, W. D. Under the Influence: A History of Nitrous Oxide & Oxygen Anaesthesia. 208p. 1982. 40.00 (ISBN 0-333-31681-9, Pub. by Macmillan England). State Mutual Bk.

Smith, W. F. Structure & Properties of Engineering Alloys. 1980. 36.50 (ISBN 0-07-058560-1). McGraw.

Smith, W. H. Basic Manual of Military Small Arms. (Illus.). 216p. 1979. Repr. of 1943 ed. 22.95 (ISBN 0-8117-0409-2). Stackpole.

Smith, W. H., ed. see Deffand, Madame du.

Smith, W. J. Communication & Relationships in the Genus Tyrannus. (Illus.). 250p. 1966. 8.00 (ISBN 0-686-35792-2). Nuttall Ornithological.

--Modern Optical Engineering. 1966. 47.50 (ISBN 0-07-058690-X, P&RB). McGraw.

Smith, W. L., jt. auth. see Cox, D. R.

Smith, W. L., et al, eds. Neurological Evaluation of the Psychogenic Patient. 160p. 1982. text ed. 15.00 (ISBN 0-686-73345-2). SP Med & Sci Bks.

Smith, W. Lynn & Kling, Arthur, eds. Issues in Brain Behavior Control. LC 76-4949. 1976. 12.50x o.s.i. (ISBN 0-470-15038-6). Halsted Pr.

Smith, W. R. & Missen, R. W. Chemical Reaction Equilibrium Analysis: Theory & Algorithms. 352p. 1982. 42.95 (ISBN 0-471-09347-5, Pub. by Wiley-Interscience). Wiley.

Smith, W. Ramsay, ed. Energy from Forest Biomass. LC 82-20745. (Symposium). Date not set. 27.50 (ISBN 0-686-42980-X). Acad Pr.

Smith, W. S. & Simpson, W. Art & Architect of Ancient Egypt. (Pelican History of Art Ser.: No. 14). 1981. pap. 35.00 (ISBN 0-670-13378-7). Viking Pr.

Smith, W. S., jt. auth. see Hebden, Norman.

Smith, W. Stevenson. The Art & Architecture of Ancient Egypt. rev ed. (Pelican History of Art Ser). (Illus.). 360p. 1981. pap. 16.95x (ISBN 0-14-056114-5, Pelican). Penguin.

Smith, W. W., et al. The Genus Primula, 22 pts. in one vol. (Plant Monograph Reprints: No. 11). 1977. lib. bdg. 80.00 (ISBN 3-7682-1118-5). Lubrecht & Cramer.

Smith, Wallace F. Housing: The Social & Economic Elements. LC 71-86372. (California Studies in Urbanization & Environmental Design). (Illus.). 1970. 28.50x (ISBN 0-520-01561-4). U of Cal Pr.

--Urban Development: The Process & the Problems. LC 74-79772. 320p. 1975. 30.00x (ISBN 0-520-02780-9); pap. 8.95x (ISBN 0-520-03956-4). U of Cal Pr.

Smith, Wanda V., jt. auth. see Smith, Elliott L.

Smith, Ward C., jt. auth. see Rinehart, C. Dean.

Smith, Warren H. Originals Abroad. 1952. text ed. 29.50x (ISBN 0-686-83662-6). Elliots Bks.

Smith, Warren H., ed. see Walpole, Horace.

Smith, Warren S. Bishop of Everywhere: Bernard Shaw & the Life Force. LC 81-17700. 196p. 1982. 17.95x (ISBN 0-271-00306-5). Pa St U Pr.

Smith, Warren S., ed. see Shaw, George B.

Smith, Watson. The Story of the Museum of Northern Arizona. 1969. pap. 0.75 (ISBN 0-89734-045-0). Mus Northern Ariz.

Smith, Wendell & Rohrman, N. Human Learning. text ed. 18.95 (ISBN 0-07-058695-0, C); pap. text ed. 13.95 (ISBN 0-07-058694-2). McGraw.

Smith, Wendy. Rubik's Revenge. Kraus, Robert, ed. (Illus.). 128p. 1982. pap. 3.95 o.s.i. (ISBN 0-671-45749-7). Windmill Bks.

Smith, Wheaton, Jr. A Life to Live. 96p. 1983. 8.95 (ISBN 0-89962-324-7). Todd & Honeywell.

Smith, Wilbur. The Diamond Hunters. 1974. pap. 1.25 o.p. (ISBN 0-451-05977-8, Y5977, Sig). NAL.

--Flight of the Falcon. 576p. 1983. pap. 3.95 (ISBN 0-449-20271-2, Crest). Fawcett.

--Hungry As the Sea. 1981. pap. 3.95 (ISBN 0-451-12218-6, E9599, Sig). NAL.

--Men of Men. LC 82-45566. 528p. 1983. 17.95 (ISBN 0-385-17834-4). Doubleday.

--Shout at the Devil. LC 77-87166. 1978. Repr. of 1968 ed. lib. bdg. 12.50x o.p. (ISBN 0-8376-0421-4). Bentley.

--A Sparrow Falls. LC 78-218. 1978. 10.95 o.p. (ISBN 0-385-13603-X). Doubleday.

--The Sunbird. LC 72-94173. 480p. 1973. 10.95 (ISBN 0-385-00710-8). Doubleday.

Smith, Wilbur M. The Biblical Doctrine of Heaven. 1980. text ed. 7.95 o.p. (ISBN 0-8024-0705-6). Moody.

Smith, Wilfred & Wise, M. J. A Historical Introduction to the Economic Geography of Great Britain. (Advanced Economic Geography Ser.). 1968. lib. bdg. 20.00 o.p. (ISBN 0-7135-1509-0). Westview.

Smith, Wilfred C. Towards a World Theology: Faith & the Comparative History of Religion. LC 80-50826. 1981. 20.00 (ISBN 0-664-21380-4). Westminster.

Smith, William. New Smith's Bible Dictionary. rev. ed. Lemmons, Reuel G., et al, eds. LC 66-20927. 1966. 9.95 (ISBN 0-385-04869-6); thumb-indexed 10.95 (ISBN 0-385-04872-6). Doubleday.

--The Particular Description of England in 1588. (Illus.). 124p. 1982. text ed. 76.00x (ISBN 0-86299-015-7, Pub. by Sutton England). Humanities.

--Smaller Classical Dictionary. Blakeney, E. H. & Warrington, John, eds. 1958. pap. 4.95 o.p. (ISBN 0-525-47012-3). Dutton.

--Smith's Bible Dictionary. rev. ed. 9.95 (ISBN 0-87981-033-5); thumb-indexed 10.95 (ISBN 0-87981-035-1). Holman.

--Smith's Bible Dictionary. (Family Library). (YA) (gr. 7-12). 1967. pap. 4.95 (ISBN 0-515-06701-6). Jove Pubns.

--Smith's Bible Dictionary. Peloubet, F. N. & Peloubet, M. A., eds. 1979. 8.95 (ISBN 0-8407-5170-2); pap. 5.95 (ISBN 0-8407-5700-X). Nelson.

--Smith's Bible Dictionary. 800p. pap. 4.95 (ISBN 0-8007-8039-6, Spire Bks). Revell.

Smith, William, tr. see Fichte, Johann G.

Smith, William A. Giovanni Gentile on the Existence of God. Matczak, S. A., ed. & intro. by. LC 70-111087. (Philosophical Questions Ser.: No. 7). 1970. 18.00 (ISBN 0-912116-04-8). Learned Pubns.

Smith, William A., Jr. & Wechsler, Ben L. Planning Guide for Information System Evaluation Studies. 1973. pap. text ed. 12.00 (ISBN 0-89806-016-8, 98); pap. text ed. 6.00 members. Inst Indus Eng.

Smith, William C. Reactions to Delinquency. LC 78-70859. 1978. pap. text ed. 8.25 (ISBN 0-8191-0649-6). U Pr of Amer.

Smith, William D., et al, eds. Reflections on Black Psychology. LC 79-63256. 1979. pap. text ed. 17.00 (ISBN 0-8191-0722-0). U Pr of Amer.

Smith, William F. Noticiario: Primer Nivel. (Orig.). 1981. pap. text ed. 8.95 (ISBN 0-88377-161-6). Newbury Hse.

Smith, William H. Tree Pathology. 1970. text ed. 22.50 (ISBN 0-12-652650-8). Acad Pr.

Smith, William J. Laughing Time: Nonsense Poems. LC 80-65839. (Illus.). 96p. 1980. 9.95 o.s.i. (ISBN 0-440-05534-2). Delacorte.

--The Traveler's Tree: New & Selected Poems. (Illus.). 200p. 1980. deluxe ed. 90.00 signed ltd ed. o.p. (ISBN 0-89255-048-1); 13.95 o.p. (ISBN 0-89255-049-X). Persea Bks.

Smith, William J. see Brasil, Emanuel.

Smith, William J., tr. see Chukovsky, Kornei.

Smith, William Jay, tr. see Lundkvist, Artur.

Smith, William O. Food Services. Lynch, Richard, ed. (Career Competencies in Marketing Ser.). (Illus.). (gr. 11-12). 1979. pap. text ed. 7.32 (ISBN 0-07-058541-5); tchr's. manual & key 4.50 (ISBN 0-07-058542-3). McGraw.

Smith, William R. The Prophets of Israel. (Social Science Classics Ser.). 446p. 1983. cancelled (ISBN 0-87855-318-5); text ed. 19.95 cancelled (ISBN 0-686-68059-6); pap. cancelled (ISBN 0-87855-700-8); pap. text ed. 7.95 cancelled (ISBN 0-686-68060-X). Transaction Bks.

--Rhetoric of American Politics: A Study of Documents. 1969. lib. bdg. 29.95x (ISBN 0-8371-1495-0). Greenwood.

Smith, Willie. Stories from the Microwave. 24p. 1983. pap. text ed. 2.00 (ISBN 0-686-38441-5). Skydog OR.

Smith, Willie Mae. One Step at a Time. 1979. 4.95 o.p. (ISBN 0-533-04046-9). Vantage.

Smith, Wm. Flint & Medley, Frank. Noticiario: Segundo Nivel. (Noticiario Ser.). 184p. 1982. pap. text ed. 8.95 (ISBN 0-88377-219-1). Newbury Hse.

Smith, Wm. Flint & Nieman, Linda. Noticiario: Tercer Nivel. (Noticiario Ser.). 176p. 1982. pap. text ed. 8.95 (ISBN 0-88377-277-9). Newbury Hse.

Smith, Woodruff D. European Imperialism in the Nineteenth & Twentieth Centuries. LC 82-7859. 296p. 1982. text ed. 20.95x (ISBN 0-88229-706-6); pap. text ed. 10.95x (ISBN 0-88229-812-7). Nelson-Hall.

Smithberger, Andrew T., ed. Essays: British & American. Repr. of 1953 ed. lib. bdg. 20.25x (ISBN 0-8371-2328-3, SMEB). Greenwood.

Smithe, P. C. Medical Typewriting. 2nd ed. 288p. 1983. text ed. 9.80 (ISBN 0-07-058925-9, G). McGraw.

Smithells, C. J., ed. Metals Reference Book. 5th ed. 1976. 160.00 o.p. (ISBN 0-408-70627-9). Butterworth.

Smithers, G. V., jt. ed. see Bennett, J. A.

Smith-Glendenning, Ruby. All about Scales, Step by Step. 1983. 7.95 (ISBN 0-533-05472-9). Vantage.

Smith-Gordon, Lionel. Rural Reconstruction in Ireland. 1919. 49.50x (ISBN 0-685-69866-1). Elliots Bks.

Smith-Perkins, Staunton E. Satan in the Pulpit. (Illus.). 104p. (Orig.). 1982. pap. 4.95 (ISBN 0-943982-00-6). SES Development.

Smithsi, T. Basic Mathematical Skills. 1974. pap. 16.95 (ISBN 0-13-063420-4). P-H.

Smithson, Alison & Smithson, Peter. A. & P. Smithson. Dunster, David, ed. LC 79-92593. (Architectural Monograph). (Illus.). 112p. (Orig.). 1983. pap. 19.95 (ISBN 0-8478-0294-9). Rizzoli Intl.

--Ordinariness & Light. (Illus.). 1970. 14.50x o.p. (ISBN 0-262-19082-6). MIT Pr.

--Without Rhetoric: An Architectural Aesthetic 1955-1972. 1974. 12.50x (ISBN 0-262-19119-9). MIT Pr.

Smithson, M. & Amato, P. R. Dimensions of Helping Behaviour. (The International Series in Experimental Social Psychology). 165p. 1983. 22.50 (ISBN 0-08-027412-9). Pergamon.

Smithson, Peter, jt. auth. see Smithson, Alison.

Smithsonian Institute. A Zoo for All Seasons: The Smithsonian Animal World. (Illus.). 1979. 16.95 (ISBN 0-89577-003-2). Norton.

Smithsonian Institution, Washington, D.C. National Museum of Natural History. Catalog to Manuscripts at the National Anthropological Archives, 4 vols. 1975. Set. lib. bdg. 380.00 (ISBN 0-8161-1194-4, Hall Library). G K Hall.

Smithsonian Institution, Washington D.C. Descriptive Catalog of Painting & Sculpture in the National Museum of American Art. 1983. lib. bdg. 125.00 (ISBN 0-8161-0408-5, Hall Library). G K Hall.

Smithsonian Institution, Washington, D. C. Dictionary Catalog of the Library of the Freer Gallery of Art, 6 Vols. 1967. Set. lib. bdg. 530.00 (ISBN 0-8161-0799-8, Hall Library). G K Hall.

--Index to Grass Species, 3 Vols. Chase, Agnes & Niles, Cornelia D., eds. 1963. Set. 285.00 (ISBN 0-8161-0445-X, Hall Library). G K Hall.

Smithwick, Noah. The Evolution of a State or Recollections of Old Texas Days. (Barker Texas History Center Ser.: No. 5). (Illus.). 248p. 1983. 19.95 (ISBN 0-292-72043-2); pap. 8.95 (ISBN 0-292-72045-9). U of Tex Pr.

Smithy-Willis, Debra & Willis, Jerry. How to Use Supercalc. 200p. 1982. pap. 19.95 (ISBN 0-88056-095-9). Dilithium Pr.

Smitley, Robert L. Popular Financial Delusions. 1963. Repr. of 1933 ed. flexible cover 10.00 (ISBN 0-87034-004-2). Fraser Pub Co.

Smits Van Waesberghe, J. Dia-Pason: Ausgewahlte Aufsatze Von Joseph Smits Van Waesberghe. 200p. 1976. 32.50 o.s.i. (ISBN 90-6027-345-1, Pub. by Frits Knuf Netherlands). Pendragon NY.

--Expositiones in Micrologum Guidonis Arentini. 175p. 1957. 30.00 o.s.i. (ISBN 90-6027-343-5, Pub. by Frits Knuf Netherlands). Pendragon NY.

--Organicae Voces: Festschrift Joseph Smits Van Waesberghe Angeboten Anlasslich Seienes 60. 180p. 1963. 30.00 o.s.i. (ISBN 90-6027-344-3, Pub. by Frits Knuf Netherlands). Pendragon NY.

Smitty, William H. Three Hundred Sermon Outlines From the New Testament. LC 81-86666. (Orig.). 1983. pap. 4.50 (ISBN 0-8054-2246-3). Broadman.

Smitty, William H., ed. Three-Hundred Sermon Outlines from the Old Testament. LC 81-67996. 1982. pap. 3.95 (ISBN 0-8054-2242-0). Broadman.

Smock, Ann, tr. see Blanchot, Maurice.

Smock, Audrey C., jt. auth. see Smock, David R.

Smock, David R. & Smock, Audrey C. The Politics of Pluralism: A Comparative Study of Lebanon and Ghana. LC 75-8278. 356p. 1975. 19.95 (ISBN 0-444-99008-9). Elsevier.

Smock, Raymond & Daniel, Pete. A Talent for Detail: The Photographs of Frances B. Johnson from 1899 to 1910. Date not set. 15.00 o.p. (ISBN 0-517-51642-X, Harmony). Crown.

Smoeyenbos, Milton & Almeder, Robert, eds. Business Ethics: Corporate Values & Society. 400p. 1983. pap. 12.95 (ISBN 0-87975-207-6). Prometheus Bks.

Smoke, Jim. Every Single Day. 256p. 1983. 6.95 (ISBN 0-8007-5120-5, Power Bks). Revell.

--Growing Through Divorce. LC 76-21980. 1979. pap. 2.50 o.p. (ISBN 0-89081-151-2). Harvest Hse.

Smokler, Howard E., jt. auth. see Kyburg, Henry E.

Smola, B. K. & Mason, M. A. Basic Medical-Surgical Nursing Workbook. 2nd ed. 1978. pap. 9.95x (ISBN 0-02-412960-7, 41296). Macmillan.

Smolarski, Dennis C. Eucharistia: A Study of the Eucharistic Prayer. LC 82-60850. 1982. pap. 7.95 (ISBN 0-8091-2474-2). Paulist Pr.

Smolderen, J. J., jt. auth. see Wirz, H. J.

Smoldyrev, A. Ye. Pipeline Transport: Principles of Design. Cooley, W. C., ed. Peaboby, A. L., tr. from Rus. (Illus.). 345p. 1982. 60.00x (ISBN 0-918990-09-2). Terraspace.

Smole, William J. The Yanoama Indians: A Cultural Geography. (Texas Pan American Ser.). (Illus.). 286p. 1976. 20.00x o.p. (ISBN 0-292-71019-4). U of Tex Pr.

Smolen, Maxine. Wheelchair Recipes from the Collection of Momma Wheels. Hammond, Debbie, ed. LC 80-11153. 1983. pap. 9.95 (ISBN 0-87949-171-X). Ashley Bks.

Smolin, Pauline & Clayton, Philip T. Words: Form & Function. 1980. pap. text ed. 8.95 (ISBN 0-669-02573-9). Heath.

Smolinski, Leon, intro. by. Leonid V. Kantorovich: Essays in Optimal Planning. LC 75-46110. 1976. 30.00 (ISBN 0-87332-076-X). M E Sharpe.

Smolira, M. Analysis of Structures by the Force-Displacement Method. 1980. 61.50 (ISBN 0-85334-814-6, Pub. by applied Sci England). Elsevier.

--Analysis of Tall Buildings by the Force Displacement Method. LC 74-19011. 299p. 1975. 59.95x o.s.i. (ISBN 0-470-80620-6). Halsted Pr.

Smolitskii, jt. auth. see Mikhlin.

Smolka, Richard G., jt. auth. see Gosnell, Harold F.

Smoller, J. Shock Waves & Reaction-Diffusion Equations. (Grundlehren der Mathematischen Wissenschaften: Vol. 258). (Illus.). 581p. 1983. 39.00 (ISBN 0-387-90752-1). Springer-Verlag.

Smollett, tr. see Voltaire, Francois M. De.

Smollett, Tobias. Humphrey Clinker. pap. 2.95 (ISBN 0-451-51557-9, CE1557, Sig Classics). NAL.

--Humphry Clinker. Ross, Angus, ed. (English Library Ser.). 1967. pap. 3.95 (ISBN 0-14-043021-0). Penguin.

--Tobias Smollett: Travels Through France & Italy. facsimile ed. Felsenstein, Frank, ed. 59.00x (ISBN 0-19-812611-5). Oxford U Pr.

Smollett, Tobias, tr. see Voltaire.

Smollett, Tobias G. The Expedition of Humphrey Clinker. Thorson, James, ed. (Norton Critical Edition Ser.). 1983. write for info (ISBN 0-393-01592-0); pap. write for info (ISBN 0-393-95283-5). Norton.

--Expedition of Humphry Clinker (NCE) Thorson, James L., ed. (Norton Critical Edition Ser.). 1983. text ed. write for info (ISBN 0-393-95283-5). Norton.

--Roderick Random. 1982. pap. 5.95x (ISBN 0-460-01790-X, Evman). Biblio Dist.

Smollin, Michael J. Learning Colors with Strawberry Shortcake. LC 79-66564. (Shape Bks.). (Illus.). 24p. (ps). 1980. 2.95 (ISBN 0-394-84388-6, BYR). Random.

Smollon, Jim, ed. see Steinmetz, Bob.

Smooha, Sammy. Israel: Pluralism & Conflict. LC 74-76390. 1978. 39.75x (ISBN 0-520-02722-1). U of Cal Pr.

Smookler, Helene V. Economic Integration in New Communities: An Evaluation of Factors Affecting Policies & Implementation. LC 76-18298. (New Communities Research Ser.). 264p. 1976. prof ref 17.50x (ISBN 0-88410-457-5). Ballinger Pub.

Smoot, Dan. The Invisible Government. 3rd ed. 240p. 1977. pap. 4.95 (ISBN 0-88279-125-7). Western Islands.

Smoot, Shields, jt. auth. see Brenner, Shauna C.

Smoots, Vernon A., jt. auth. see Fletcher, Gordon A.

Smorsten, Kenneth. A Preface to Action: An Introduction to American Politics. 2nd ed. 1980. pap. text ed. 15.50x (ISBN 0-673-16062-9). Scott F.

Smorto, Mairo P. & Basmajian, John V. Clinical Electroneurography: An Introduction to Nerve Conduction Tests. 2nd ed. 312p. 1979. 29.95 (ISBN 0-683-07812-7). Williams & Wilkins.

Smothermon, Ron. Transforming, No. 1. LC 81-14356. 200p. (Orig.). 1982. pap. 7.95 (ISBN 0-932654-04-5). Context Pubns.

--Winning Through Enlightenment. 2nd ed. 226p. 1982. pap. 7.95 (ISBN 0-932654-01-0). Context Pubns.

Smout, T. C., jt. ed. see Flinn, M. W.

Smoyak, Shirley, ed. The Psychiatric Nurse As a Family Therapist. LC 75-5813. 251p. 1975. 18.95 (ISBN 0-471-80770-2, Pub. by Wiley Medical). Wiley.

Smoyak, Shirley A. & Rouslin, Sheila, eds. A Collection of Classics in Psychiatric Nursing Literature. LC 82-61592. 1982. 30.00 (ISBN 0-913590-96-7). Slack Inc.

Smucker, Barbara. Runaway to Freedom: A Story of the Underground Railway. LC 77-11834. (Illus.). 1978. 10.53i o.p. (ISBN 0-06-025724-5, HarpJ); PLB 7.89 o.p. (ISBN 0-06-025725-3). Har-Row.

Smulkstys, Julius. Karl Marx. (World Authors Ser.: Germany: No. 296). 1974. lib. bdg. 10.95 o.p. (ISBN 0-8057-2595-4, Twayne). G K Hall.

Smullen, Clinton W., jt. auth. see Detmar, Richard C.

Smullyan, R. M. First-Order Logic. LC 68-13495. (Ergebnisse der Mathematik und Ihrer Grenzgebiete: Vol. 43). 1968. Repr. 23.00 o.p. (ISBN 0-387-04099-4). Springer-Verlag.

Smullyan, Raymond. Alice in Puzzle-Land: A Carrolian Tale for Children Under Eighty. LC 82-2215. (Illus.). 200p. 1982. 12.50 (ISBN 0-688-00748-1). Morrow.

--The Chess Mysteries of the Arabian Knights. LC 81-47482. 1981. 13.50 (ISBN 0-394-51467-X); pap. 6.95 (ISBN 0-394-74869-7). Knopf.

--Five Thousand B.C. & Other Philosophical Fantasies. 224p. 1983. 13.95 (ISBN 0-312-29516-2). St Martin.

--The Lady or the Tiger? & Other Logic Puzzles. LC 81-48098. 224p. 1982. 13.95 (ISBN 0-394-51466-1). Knopf.

--This Book Needs No Title: A Budget of Living Paradoxes. LC 79-27862. (Illus.). 1980. 9.95 (ISBN 0-13-919035-X); pap. 4.95 (ISBN 0-13-919027-9). P-H.

Smullyan, Raymond M. The Tao Is Silent. LC 76-62939. (Orig.). 1977. 7.95i (ISBN 0-06-067469-5, RD 206, HarpR). Har-Row.

Smurthwaite & Udall. Starting Work. 14.50x (ISBN 0-392-13268-0, SpS). Sportshelf.

Smutek, Ray, ed. Off the Walls: An Anthology of Mountaineering Cartoons. (Illus.). 176p. (Orig.). 1982. pap. cancelled o.p. (ISBN 0-89886-062-8). Mountaineers.

Smuts, J. C. Selections from the Smuts Papers, 4 vols. Hancock, William K. & Van Der Poel, Jean, eds. Vol. 1, 1886-1902. 94.50 (ISBN 0-521-05190-8); Vol. 2, From 1902-1910. 94.50 (ISBN 0-521-05191-6); Vol. 3, From 1910-1918. 94.50 (ISBN 0-521-05192-4); Vol. 4, From 1918-1919. 94.50 (ISBN 0-521-05193-2); Vol. 5. from 1945-1950 94.00 (ISBN 0-521-08604-3); Vol. 5, From 1919-1943. 94.50 (ISBN 0-521-08602-7); Vol. 6, From 1934-1945. 94.00 (ISBN 0-521-08603-5). Cambridge U Pr.

Smuts, Robert W. Women & Work in America. LC 72-139843. 1971. pap. 4.95 (ISBN 0-8052-0298-6). Schocken.

Smykla, John. Community Based Corrections. 1981. text ed. 23.95x (ISBN 0-02-477790-0). Macmillan.

Smyrl, Frank H. Poley Morgan, Son of a Texas Scalawag. (Illus.). 65p. 1982. 10.95 (ISBN 0-910779-00-7). Book Texas.

Smyser, Carol. Nature's Design: A Practical Guide to Natural Landscaping. Rodale Press & Hylton, Bill, eds. (Illus.). 432p. 1982. 22.95 (ISBN 0-87857-343-7, 01-618-0). Rodale Pr Inc.

Smyser, W. R. The Independent Vietnamese: Vietnamese Communism Between Russia & China, 1956 to 1969. (Southeast Asia Ser., Ohio University Center for International Studies). 143p. (Orig.). 1980. pap. 12.75 (ISBN 0-89680-105-5, 80-18308, Ohio U Ctr Intl). Ohio U Pr.

Smyslov, V. V. Selected Games. LC 81-23466. (Russian Chess Ser.). 250p. 1983. 19.95 (ISBN 0-08-026912-5). Pergamon.

Smyth, Albert H. Philadelphia Magazines & Their Contributors 1741-1850. LC 77-140401. 1970. Repr. of 1892 ed. 42.00x (ISBN 0-8103-3596-4). Gale.

Smyth, Alfred P. Celtic Leinster: Towards an Historical Geography of Early Irish Civilization. (Illus.). 200p. 1983. 50.00x (ISBN 0-7165-0097-3, Pub. by Irish Academic Pr Ireland). Biblio Dist.

Smyth, Charles H. Cranmer & the Reformation Under Edward Sixth. Repr. of 1926 ed. lib. bdg. 15.75x (ISBN 0-8371-4025-0, SMCR). Greenwood.

Smyth, Donna E. Quilt. 144p. 1982. pap. 5.95 (ISBN 0-88961-073-8). Crossing Pr.

Smyth, G. D. Diagnostic ENT. (Illus.). 1978. text ed. 14.95x (ISBN 0-19-261133-X). Oxford U Pr.

Smyth, Herbert W. Aeschylean Tragedy. LC 67-19531. 1969. Repr. of 1924 ed. 8.00x (ISBN 0-8196-0235-3). Biblo.

Smyth, Herbert W., ed. Greek Melic Poets. LC 63-10769. 1899. 8.00x (ISBN 0-8196-0120-9). Biblo.

Smyth, J. D. Introduction to Animal Parasitology. 2nd ed. LC 76-26911. 466p. 1962. pap. 21.50 o.p. (ISBN 0-470-98921-1, Pub. by Wiley). Krieger.

Smyth, John. Rebellious Ranie. 16.50x (ISBN 0-392-04358-0, LTB). Sportshelf.

Smyth, Norman. Story of Church Unity: The Lambeth Conference of Anglican Bishops & the Congregational-Episcopal Approaches. 1923. text ed. 29.50x (ISBN 0-686-83788-6). Elliots Bks.

Smyth, Norman & Walker, Williston. Approaches Toward Church Unity. 1919. text ed. 24.50x (ISBN 0-686-37862-8). Elliots Bks.

Smyth, Piazzi. Our Inheritance in the Great Pyramids. LC 77-5284. (Illus.). 672p. 1980. Repr. of 1877 ed. 20.00x (ISBN 0-89345-029-4, Biograf Pubns). Garber Comm.

Smyth, Robert. Broken Arrows. 36p. saddle 4.00 (ISBN 0-938756-05-2). Yellow Moon.

Smyth, Thomas. Wandering Thoughts Still Come. 80p. 1983. 6.50 (ISBN 0-682-49943-9). Exposition.

Smyth, W. F. Electroanalysis in Hygiene, Environmental, Clinical & Pharmaceutical Chemistry. (Analytical Chemistry Symposia Ser.: Vol. 2). 1980. 68.00 (ISBN 0-444-41850-4). Elsevier.

Smythe, Dallas W. Dependency Road: Communications, Capitalism, Consciousness & Canada. 300p. 1981. text ed. 29.50 (ISBN 0-89391-067-8); pap. 15.95 (ISBN 0-89391-088-0). Ablex Pub.

Smythe, Daniel. Strange Element. 1966. 4.00 o.p. (ISBN 0-8233-0101-X). Golden Quill.

Smythe, R. H. Cat Psychology. (Illus.). 1978. 7.95 (ISBN 0-87666-854-6, PS-748). TFH Pubns.

--Vision in the Animal World. LC 75-13590. (Illus.). 175p. 1975. 26.00 (ISBN 0-312-84980-X). St Martin.

Smythe, Reginald H. How to Raise & Train a Shih Tzu. (Orig.). pap. 2.95 (ISBN 0-87666-388-9, DS1117). TFH Pubns.

--Mind of the Horse. LC 65-22225. 1965. 9.95 (ISBN 0-8289-0042-6). Greene.

Smythe, Ted C., jt. auth. see Emery, Michael.

Smythe, Ted C., jt. auth. see Emery, Michael C.

Smythe, William R. Static & Dynamic Electricity. 3rd ed. (International Series in Pure & Applied Physics). (Orig.). 1968. text ed. 49.95 (ISBN 0-07-059420-1, C). McGraw.

Smythies, J. R. Brain Mechanisms & Behaviour. 1970. 24.00 (ISBN 0-12-653240-0). Acad Pr.

Smythies, John & Bradley, Ronald, eds. International Review of Neurobiology, Vol. 23. 446p. 1982. 52.00 (ISBN 0-12-366823-9). Acad Pr.

Smythies, John R., jt. ed. see Pfeiffer, Carl C.

Snaith, Norman H. The Distinctive Ideas of the Old Testament. LC 64-24013. 1964. pap. 3.45 o.p. (ISBN 0-8052-0090-8). Schocken.

Snaith, Philip. Clinical Neurosis. 1981. pap. text ed. 18.95x (ISBN 0-19-261251-4). Oxford U Pr.

Snapp, Allen & Anderson, John. Studies in Uto-Aztecan Grammar Vol. 3: Uto-Azetican Grammatical Sketches, 4 vols. LC 82-86. (Publications in Linguistics: No. 56). 393p. 1982. pap. text ed. 14.00 Set (ISBN 0-88312-086-0, 51800); Five microfiche. 4.50. Summer Inst Ling.

Snatzke. ORD & CD in Organic Chemistry. (Chemical Analysis Ser.). 1981. 85.95 (ISBN 0-85501-000-2). Wiley.

Snatzke, G., ed. Optical Rotatory Dispersion & Circular Dichroism in Organic Chemistry. 1976. 85.95 (ISBN 0-471-26031-2, Wiley Heyden). Wiley.

Snead, Rodman E. Coastal Landforms & Surface Features: A Photographic Atlas & Glossary. LC 81-2949. 272p. 1982. 40.00 (ISBN 0-87933-052-X). Hutchinson Ross.

Sneath, E. Hershey, ed. Evolution of Ethics. 1927. 49.50x (ISBN 0-685-69867-X). Elliots Bks.

Sneck, William J. Charismatic Spiritual Gifts: A Phenomenological Analysis. LC 80-8291. 312p. (Orig.). 1981. lib. bdg. 23.75 (ISBN 0-8191-1765-X); pap. text ed. 12.75 (ISBN 0-8191-1766-8). U Pr of Amer.

Sneddon, I. N., ed. Encyclopedic Dictionary of Mathematics for Engineers. LC 73-6800. 1976. write for info. (ISBN 0-08-021149-6). Pergamon.

Sneed, Marcy C., et al. Human Life: Our Legacy & Our Challenge. new ed. LC 75-22323. (Illus.). 1976. pap. text ed. 7.56 (ISBN 0-07-059440-6, W). McGraw.

Sneeden, R. P. Organochromium Compounds. (Organometalic Chemistry Ser.). 1975. 65.00 (ISBN 0-12-653850-6). Acad Pr.

Sneider, Lea, jt. auth. see Levy, Dana.

Snelbecker, Glenn E. Learning Theory: Instructional Theory & Psychoeducational Design. (Illus.). 544p. 1974. text ed. 23.95 o.p. (ISBN 0-07-059450-3, C). McGraw.

Snelgrove, Dudley, jt. auth. see Egerton, Judy.

Snell, B., ed. Translating & the Computer. 1979. 38.50 (ISBN 0-444-85302-2, North Holland). Elsevier.

Snell, Betty E. Machiguenga: Fonologia y Vocabulario Breve. (Documentos Del Trabajo (Peru): No. 5). 34p. 1975. pap. 2.00x (ISBN 0-685-51605-9); microfiche 1.50 (ISBN 0-88312-327-4). Summer Inst Ling.

Snell, Bruno. The Discovery of the Mind in Early Greek Philosophy & Literature. (Illus.). 128p. 1982. pap. 6.00 (ISBN 0-486-24264-1). Dover.

--Scenes from Greek Drama. (Sather Classical Lectures: No. 34). 1964. 30.00x (ISBN 0-520-01191-0). U of Cal Pr.

Snell, Daniel C. A Workbook of Cuneiform Signs. (Aids & Research Tools in Ancient Near Eastern Studies Ser.: Vol. 3). 140p. 1979. pap. text ed. 13.00x (ISBN 0-89003-058-8). Undena Pubns.

Snell, E. E., et al, eds. Annual Review of Biochemistry, Vol. 51. LC 32-25093. (Illus.). 1982. text ed. 23.00 (ISBN 0-8243-0851-4). Annual Reviews.

--Annual Review of Biochemistry, Vol. 52. LC 32-25093. (Illus.). 1175p. 1983. 29.00 (ISBN 0-8243-0852-2). Annual Reviews.

--Chemical & Biological Aspects of Pyridoxal Catalysis. 1964. 48.00 (ISBN 0-08-010423-1). Pergamon.

Snell, Esmond E., et al, eds. Annual Review of Biochemistry, Vol. 50. LC 32-25093. (Illus.). 1981. text ed. 21.00 (ISBN 0-8243-0850-6). Annual Reviews.

Snell, F. D. Photometric & Flourometric Methods of Analysis: Nonmetals, 2 Pt. Set. 818p. 1981. 95.00 (ISBN 0-471-81023-1, Pub. by Wiley-Interscience). Wiley.

Snell, F. D., et al. Encyclopedia of Industrial Chemical Analysis, 20 vols. (Vol. 1 avail. only with set). 1975. Set. 400.00 o.s.i. (ISBN 0-471-81006-1). Krieger.

Snell, Forster D. Photometric & Fluorometric Methods of Analysis: Metals, 2 pts. LC 77-25039. 2192p. 1978. Set. 315.00 (ISBN 0-471-81014-2, Pub. by Wiley-Interscience). Wiley.

Snell, J. B. One Man's Railway: J. E. P. Howey & the Romney, Hythe & Dymchurch Railway. (Illus.). 96p. (Orig.). 1983. 17.50 (ISBN 0-7153-8325-6). David & Charles.

Snell, J. Laurie, jt. auth. see Kemeny, John.

Snell, John L. Nazi Revolution: Hitler's Dictatorship & the German Nation. 2nd ed. Mitchell, Allan, rev. by. (Problems in European Civilization Ser). 1973. pap. text ed. 5.95 (ISBN 0-669-81752-X). Heath.

Snell, John L., jt. auth. see Perkins, Dexter.

Snell, Joseph, ed. see Triplett, Frank.

Snell, Keith, ed. Developmental Toxicology. 350p. 1982. 47.50 (ISBN 0-03-060408-7). Praeger.

Snell, Martha E. Systematic Instruction of the Moderately & Severely Handicapped. 2nd ed. 550p. (pb). 1983. pap. 23.95 (ISBN 0-675-20035-0). Merrill.

Snell, Martha E., jt. auth. see Mercer, Cecil D.

Snell, Martha E., ed. Systematic Instructional of the Moderately & Severely Handicapped. (Special Education Ser.). 1978. text ed. 24.95 (ISBN 0-675-08390-7). Merrill.

Snell, Robert. Theophile Gautier: A Romantic Critic of the Visual Arts. (Illus.). 1981. 34.50x (ISBN 0-19-815768-1). Oxford U Pr.

Snell, W. H. & Dick, E. A. The Boleti of Northeastern North America. (Illus.). 1970. 100.00 (ISBN 3-7682-0681-5). Lubrecht & Cramer.

Snell, Wilma S. How to Build an Heirloom Miniature House from a Kit. Stern, Marcia & Hayden, Bob, eds. (Illus., Orig.). 1985. pap. price not set (ISBN 0-89024-062-0). Kalmbach.

Snellgrove, D. L. & Skorupski, T. The Cultural Heritage of Ladakh, - Two: Zangskar & the Cave Temples of Ladakh. 166p. 1981. text ed. 48.00x (ISBN 0-85668-148-2, Pub. by Aris & Phillips England). Humanities.

Snellgrove, L. E. The Early Modern Age. (Longman Secondary Histories Ser.). (Illus.). 256p. (Orig.). (gr. 7-12). 1980. pap. text ed. 9.50 (ISBN 0-582-20511-5). Longman.

--The Modern World Since Eighteen Seventy. 2nd ed. (Longman Secondary Histories Ser.). (Illus.). 352p. (Orig.). (gr. 9-12). 1981. pap. text ed. 11.75 (ISBN 0-582-22299-0). Longman.

Snellgrove, L. E., jt. auth. see Cootes, R. J.

Snelling, John. Painter & Decorator's Book of Facts. (Illus.). 150p. 1973. 12.50x (ISBN 0-291-39316-0). Scholium Intl.

Snelling, Lauraine. Tragedy on the Toutle. (Voyager Ser.). 96p. (Orig.). 1982. pap. 3.95 (ISBN 0-8010-8226-9). Baker Bk.

Sneve, Virginia D. High Elk's Treasure. LC 72-75600. (Illus.). (gr. 4-6). 1972. PLB 8.95 (ISBN 0-8234-0212-6). Holiday.

Sneyers, R. Sur L'analyse Statistique des Series D'observations. (Note Technique: No. 143). 192p. 1976. pap. 45.00 (ISBN 92-63-20415-2, W181, WMO). Unipub.

Snider, Arthur D., jt. auth. see Soff, Edward B.

Snider, Delbert A. International Monetary Relations. (Orig.). 1966. pap. text ed. 3.50 (ISBN 0-685-19737-9). Phila Bk Co.

Snider, Frederick, tr. see Polisensky, Josef.

Snider, Gordon, jt. auth. see Berland, Theodore.

Snider, Ray S., jt. auth. see Fox, Clement A.

Snider, Sandra, jt. auth. see McAdam, Pat.

Sniderman, Florence M., jt. auth. see Breed, Paul F.

Sniderman, Paul M. Personality & Democratic Politics. 1975. 30.00x (ISBN 0-520-02324-2). U of Cal Pr.

--A Question of Loyalty. 200p. 1982. 18.95x (ISBN 0-520-04196-8); pap. 6.95 (ISBN 0-520-04413-4, CAL 524). U of Cal Pr.

Snieszko, S. F., ed. see Anderson, Douglas P.

Snieszko, Stanislas F., ed. see Neish, Gordon A. & Hughes, Gilbert C.

Sniezko, S., et al. Diseases of Fishes, Book 2: Bacteria. (Illus.). 19.95 (ISBN 0-87666-038-3, PS202). TFH Pubns.

Snipes, Katherine. Robert Graves. LC 78-20943. (Literature and Life Ser.). 1979. 14.50 (ISBN 0-8044-2825-5). Ungar.

Snitow, Ann & Stansell, Christine, eds. Powers of Desire: The Politics of Sexuality. LC 82-48037. (Monthly Review Series on Women, Politics, & Revolutionary Change). (Illus.). 448p. 1982. 25.00 (ISBN 0-85345-609-7, CL6097); pap. 12.50 (ISBN 0-85345-610-0, PB6100). Monthly Rev.

Snively, W. D., Jr., jt. auth. see Metheny, Norma.

Snizek, William E., et al, eds. Contemporary Issues in Theory & Research: A Metasociological Perspective. LC 78-4024. (Contributions in Sociology Ser.: No. 33). (Illus.). 1979. lib. bdg. 35.00x (ISBN 0-313-20409-8, FCI/). Greenwood.

Snodderly, Daniel R. Ithaca & It's Past: The History & Architecture of the Downtown. LC 82-70370. (Illus.). 100p. (Orig.). 1982. pap. 6.50 (ISBN 0-942690-00-1). DeWitt Hist.

Snodgrass, Coral, jt. auth. see Mathur, Iqbal.

Snodgrass, Joan G. The Numbers Game: Statistics in Psychology. 1977. 19.95x (ISBN 0-19-502301-3). Oxford U Pr.

Snodgrass, Robert E. Principles of Insect Morphology. (Zoological Sciences Ser.). 1935. 55.00 (ISBN 0-07-059510-0, C). McGraw.

Snodgrass, W. D. After Experience: Poems & Translations. LC 67-22508. 92p. 1968. 8.00 (ISBN 0-06-013947-1). Ultramarine Pub.

--Six Minnesinger Songs. (Burning Deck Poetry Ser.). (Illus.). 40p. (Orig.). 1983. signed ed. 25.00x (ISBN 0-930901-04-5); pap. 5.00 (ISBN 0-930901-05-3). Burning Deck.

Snodk, J. R., et al. A Cross-Section of Nevada-Style Thrust in Northeast Washington. (Reports of Investigations: No. 25). (Illus.). 1981. 0.50 (ISBN 0-686-38466-0). Geologic Pubns.

Snodrass, Jon, jt. auth. see Jack-Roller.

Snoeyink, Vernon L. & Jenkins, David. Water Chemistry. (SPE Monographs). 1980. 34.95xz (ISBN 0-471-05196-9); 16.95 (ISBN 0-471-06272-3). Wiley.

Snook, Barbara. Needlework Stitches. (Illus.). 1963. 3.50 o.p. (ISBN 0-517-02516-7); pap. 1.95 o.p. (ISBN 0-517-50079-5). Crown.

Snook, Donald I. Hospitals: What They Are & How They Work. LC 80-26956. 275p. 1981. text ed. 24.50 (ISBN 0-89443-339-3). Aspen Systems.

Snook, I. A., ed. & intro. by. Concepts of Indoctrination: Philosophical Essays. (International Library of the Philosophy of Education). 224p. 1972. 22.00x (ISBN 0-7100-7279-1). Routledge & Kegan.

Snooks, Margaret, jt. auth. see Steglich, W. G.

Snopek, Albert M. Fundamentals of Special Radiographic Procedures. (Illus.). 352p. 1975. text ed. 27.50 (ISBN 0-07-059515-1, C). McGraw.

Snorre, Sturleson. Edda. Deuxieme Partie: Tractatus Philogicus et Addimenta ex Lodicibus Manuscripts. (Linguistics 13th-18th Centuries Ser.). 260p. (Fr.). 1974. Repr. of 1852 ed. lib. bdg. 71.00x o.p. (ISBN 0-8287-0781-2, 71-5003). Clearwater Pub.

Snorri Sturleson. Heimskringla: History of the Kings of Norway. Hollander, Lee M., tr. (Illus.). 880p. 1964. 40.00x o.p. (ISBN 0-292-73262-7). U of Tex Pr.

Snouffer, Nancy K. & Thistlethwaite, Linda L. College Reading Power. 2nd ed. 1979. pap. text ed. 12.95 (ISBN 0-8403-2092-2). Kendall-Hunt.

Snover, Stephen & Spikell, Mark. Programming the TI-55 Slide Rule Calculator. 117p. 1982. 15.95 (ISBN 0-13-729921-4); pap. 7.95 (ISBN 0-13-729913-3). P-H.

Snow, Anthony & Hopewell, Graham. Planning Your Bathroom. LC 77-78532. (Design Centre Books). (Illus.). 1977. pap. 4.95 o.p. (ISBN 0-85072-026-5, 030078, Quick Fox). Putnam Pub Group.

Snow, C. P. Death Under Sail. LC 75-46000. (Crime Fiction Ser). 1976. Repr. of 1932 ed. lib. bdg. 17.50 o.s.i. (ISBN 0-8240-2393-5). Garland Pub.

--The Masters. 384p. 1982. pap. 6.95 (ISBN 0-684-71897-9, ScribT). Scribner.

Snow, Catherine & Ferguson, C. Talking to Children. LC 76-11094. 1977. 44.50 (ISBN 0-521-21318-5); pap. 15.95 (ISBN 0-521-29513-0). Cambridge U Pr.

Snow, Catherine, jt. ed. see Waterson, Natalie.

Snow, Charles C., jt. auth. see Miles, Raymond E.

Snow, Charles P. Two Cultures: And a Second Look. LC 64-1425. 1969. 18.95 (ISBN 0-521-06520-8); pap. 5.50 (ISBN 0-521-09576-X). Cambridge U Pr.

Snow, Charles W. Electrical Drafting & Design. (Illus.). 416p. 1976. 22.95 (ISBN 0-13-247379-8). P-H.

Snow, D. W., ed. Atlas of Speciation in African Non-Passerine Birds. (Illus.). 1978. 124.00x (ISBN 0-565-00787-4, Pub. by Brit Mus Nat Hist). Sabbot-Natural Hist Bks.

Snow, Donald M. Introduction to World Politics: A Conceptual & Developmental Perspective. LC 80-5851. 230p. 1981. lib. bdg. 20.50 (ISBN 0-8191-1398-0); pap. text ed. 10.25 (ISBN 0-8191-1399-9). U Pr of Amer.

--The Nuclear Future: Toward a Strategy of Uncertainty. LC 82-7110. 224p. 1983. text ed. 25.00 (ISBN 0-8173-0117-8); pap. text ed. 12.95 (ISBN 0-8173-0118-6). U of Ala Pr.

Snow, Dorothea J. By Love Bewitched. (YA) 1981. 6.95 (ISBN 0-686-73945-0, Avalon). Bouregy.

--Gardens of Love. 1982. 6.95 (ISBN 0-686-84169-7, Avalon). Bouregy.

--Love's Dream Remembered. (YA) 1979. 6.95 (ISBN 0-685-90722-8, Avalon). Bouregy.

--Love's Wondrous Ways. 1981. pap. 6.95 (ISBN 0-686-84699-0, Avalon). Bouregy.

Snow, Dudley. The Progress of Public Health in Western Australia. 185p. 1982. 27.00 (ISBN 0-7244-8478-7, Pub. by U of W Austral Pr); pap. 16.25 (ISBN 0-686-83112-8). Intl Schol Bk Serv.

Snow, Edith. Hold Your Hands to the Earth. 12.00 o.p. (ISBN 0-912950-25-0); pap. 7.00 o.p. (ISBN 0-912950-26-9). Blue Oak.

--Selected Poems. 1978. 10.00 o.s.i. (ISBN 0-912950-51-X); pap. 4.50 o.s.i. (ISBN 0-912950-52-8). Blue Oak.

--The Water Mill. 88p. 1971. pap. 4.00 o.p. (ISBN 0-912950-09-9). Blue Oak.

Snow, Edward R. The Romance of Casco Bay. LC 75-29352. (Illus.). 1975. 7.95 o.p. (ISBN 0-396-07214-3). Dodd.

--Supernatural Mysteries & Other Tales: New England to the Bermuda Triangle. LC 74-25671. (Illus.). 288p. 1974. 7.95 o.p. (ISBN 0-396-07028-0). Dodd.

--Tales of Terror & Tragedy. LC 79-21872. (Illus.). 1979. 8.95 o.p. (ISBN 0-396-07775-7). Dodd.

Snow, George, jt. auth. see Farren, Mick.

Snow, Horace. Dear Charlie. Rev. ed. (Illus.). 1983. softcover 3.95 (ISBN 0-914330-22-5). Pioneer Pub Co.

Snow, John. Secrets of Ponds & Lakes. Jack, Susan, ed. (Secrets of Ser.). (Illus.). 96p. (Orig.). 1982. pap. 5.95 (ISBN 0-930096-30-4). G Gannett.

Snow, John C. Manual of Anesthesia. 1977. spiral bound 15.95 o.p. (ISBN 0-316-80220-4). Little.

--Manual of Anesthesia. (Spiral Manual Ser.). 1982. spiralbound 15.95 (ISBN 0-316-80222-0). Little.

Snow, John W., jt. ed. see Macavoy, Paul W.

Snow, Keith R. Insects & Disease. LC 73-15433. 208p. 1974. 11.50 (ISBN 0-470-81017-3, Pub. by Wiley). Krieger.

Snow, Laurence H., jt. auth. see Madow, Leo.

Snow, Lois W. Edgar Snow's China. LC 82-49084. (Illus.). 304p. 1983. pap. 11.95 (ISBN 0-394-71500-4, Vin). Random.

Snow, Phillip. Stranger & Brother: A Portrait of C. P. Snow. (Illus.). 256p. 1983. 14.95 (ISBN 0-684-17801-X, ScribT). Scribner.

Snow, Richard. The Funny Place. Ashbery, John, ed. LC 74-6145. 72p. 1975. 6.95 (ISBN 0-87955-502-5); pap. 2.95 (ISBN 0-87955-505-X). O'Hara.

Snow, Suzanne, jt. auth. see Douillard, Jeanne.

Snow, Theodore P., Jr. The Dynamic Universe: An Introduction to Astronomy. 500p. 1983. text ed. 19.95 (ISBN 0-314-69681-4); instrs.' manual avail. (ISBN 0-314-71129-5); study guide avail. (ISBN 0-314-71130-9). West Pub.

Snowden, Derek, jt. auth. see Jackson, Betty.

Snowden, Frank M., Jr. Before Color Prejudice: The Ancient View of Blacks. (Illus.). 224p. 1983. text ed. 17.50x (ISBN 0-674-06380-5). Harvard U Pr.

Snowden, Lonnie, ed. Reaching the Underserved: Mental Health Needs of Neglected Populations. (Sage Annual Review of Community Mental Health: Vol. 3). (Illus.). 1982. pap. 25.00 (ISBN 0-8039-1856-9); pap. 12.50 (ISBN 0-8039-1857-7). Sage.

Snowden, M. Management of Engineering Projects. 1977. 26.95 (ISBN 0-408-00273-5). Butterworth.

Snowden, R. & Mitchell, G. D. The Artificial Family: A Consideration of Artificial Insemination by Donor. 138p. 1981. text ed. 14.95 (ISBN 0-04-176001-8). Allen Unwin.

Snowdon, J. C. Vibration & Shock in Damped Mechanical Systems. 486p. 1968. 49.95x (ISBN 0-471-81000-2, Pub. by Wiley-Interscience). Wiley.

Snowdon, Lynda, compiled by. Baa, Baa, Black Sheep & Other Rhymes. (First Nursery Rhyme Bks.). (Illus.). 12p. (ps-1). 1981. 1.95 o.p. (ISBN 0-517-54532-2). Crown.

--Doctor Foster & Other Rhymes. (First Nursery Rhyme Bks.). (Illus.). 12p. (ps-1). 1981. 1.95 o.p. (ISBN 0-517-54533-0). Crown.

--Hey Diddle Diddle & Other Rhymes. (First Nursery Rhyme Bks.). (Illus.). 12p. (ps-1). 1981. 1.95 o.p. (ISBN 0-517-54530-6). Crown.

--Jack & Jill & Other Rhymes. (First Nursery Rhyme Bks.). (Illus.). 12p. (ps-1). 1981. 1.95 o.p. (ISBN 0-517-54534-9). Crown.

--Tom, Tom, the Piper's Son & Other Rhymes. (First Nursery Rhyme Bks.). (Illus.). 12p. (ps-1). 1981. 1.95 o.p. (ISBN 0-517-54531-4). Crown.

Snowman, Daniel. Britain & America: An Interpretation of Their Cultures, 1945-1975. LC 76-48858. (Orig.). 1977. pap. text ed. 6.50x o.p. (ISBN 0-06-131922-8, TB1922, Torch). Har-Row.

Snowran, Jack, jt. auth. see Biehler, Robert F.

Snow-Smith, Joanne. The Salvator Mundi of Leonardo da Vinci. LC 82-21190. (Illus.). 96p. (Orig.). 1982. pap. 24.00 (ISBN 0-686-83066-0) (ISBN 0-935558-11-X). Henry Art.

Snustad, D. Peter, jt. auth. see Gardner, Eldon J.

Snyder, Al. Lightplane Construction & Repair. 1968. 7.95 (ISBN 0-8306-9992-9); pap. 3.95 o.p. (ISBN 0-8306-2220-9, 2220). TAB Bks.

Snyder, Anne. Counter Play. (Orig.). 1981. pap. 2.25 (ISBN 0-451-11898-7, AE1898, Sig). NAL.

--First Step. (RL 7). 1976. pap. 1.75 (ISBN 0-451-11757-3, AE1757, Sig). NAL.

--First Step. 1.50 o.p. (ISBN 0-686-92243-3, 5009). Hazelden.

--Goodbye Paper Doll. (Orig.). 1980. pap. 1.95 (ISBN 0-451-09826-9, E9826, Sig). NAL.

--My Name Is Davy-I'm an Alcoholic. (RL 5). 1978. pap. 1.95 (ISBN 0-451-12336-0, AJ2336, Sig). NAL.

--My Name Is Davy, I'm an Alcoholic. 1.50 o.p. (ISBN 0-686-92248-4, 5016). Hazelden.

Snyder, Anne & Pelletier, Louis. Nobody's Brother. 1982. pap. 2.25 (ISBN 0-451-11756-5, AE1756, Sig). NAL.

--Two Point Zero. 1982. pap. 1.75 (ISBN 0-451-11476-0, AE1476, Vista). NAL.

Snyder, Arnold. Blackbelt in Blackjack. 120p. 1982. pap. 12.95 (ISBN 0-910575-02-9). R G Enterprises.

Snyder, Bernadette. Graham Crackers, Galoshes & God. 96p. 1982. pap. 2.95 (ISBN 0-89243-164-4). Liguori Pubns.

Snyder, Bernadette M. & Terry, Hazelmai M. Decorations for Forty-Four Parish Celebrations: Enhancing Worship Experiences Tastefully & Simply. (Illus., Orig.). 1982. pap. 9.95 (ISBN 0-89622-167-9). Twenty-Third.

Snyder, Bernhart R. Fundamentals of Individual Retirement Plans. 1980. 8.95 o.p. (ISBN 0-87863-206-9). Farnswth Pub.

Snyder, Bernhart R., rev. by see Keir, Jack & Lundy, Carl P.

Snyder, Carol. The Great Condominium Rebellion. LC 81-65491. (Illus.). 128p. (gr. 3-7). 1981. 9.95 o.s.i. (ISBN 0-440-03062-5); PLB 9.89 o.s.i. (ISBN 0-440-03063-3). Delacorte.

--Ike & Mama & the Block Wedding. LC 78-11702. (Illus.). (gr. 2-6). 1979. 7.95 (ISBN 0-698-20461-1, Coward). Putnam Pub Group.

--Ike & Mama & the Once-a-Year Suit. LC 77-21429. (Illus.). (gr. 3-6). 1978. 7.95 (ISBN 0-698-20436-0, Coward). Putnam Pub Group.

--Ike & Mama & the Once-in-a-Lifetime Movie. (Mike & Mama Ser.). (Illus.). 96p. 1981. 7.95 (ISBN 0-698-20501-4, Coward). Putnam Pub Group.

Snyder, Carole. The Great Condominium Rebellion. (gr. k-6). 1983. pap. 2.25 (ISBN 0-440-43123-9, YB). Dell.

Snyder, Charles R., jt. ed. see Pittman, David J.

Snyder, David P., ed. The Family in Post-Industrial America: Some Fundamental Perceptions for Public Policy Development. (AAAS Selected Symposium: No. 32). 1979. lib. bdg. 16.00 (ISBN 0-89158-482-X). Westview.

Snyder, Don, ed. see Woods, Sylvia.

Snyder, Donald L. Random Point Processes. LC 75-11556. 485p. 1975. 49.50 (ISBN 0-471-81021-5, Pub. by Wiley-Interscience). Wiley.

Snyder, Eldon E. & Spreitzer, Elmer M. Social Aspects of Sport. 2nd ed. (Illus.). 368p. 1983. pap. 18.95 (ISBN 0-13-815639-5). P-H.

Snyder, Ernest E. Man & the Physical Universe. LC 75-30446. (Physical Science Ser.). 373p. 1976. text ed. 21.95 o.p. (ISBN 0-675-08631-0). Additional supplements may be obtained from publisher. Merrill.

--Physical Science for Today. LC 72-96694. 1973. pap. text ed. 8.95x o.p. (ISBN 0-675-08964-6). Merrill.

Snyder, F. G., ed. Symposium on Mineral Resources of the Southeastern United States. 1950. 16.50x (ISBN 0-87049-007-9). U of Tenn Pr.

Snyder, Fred L., ed. Ether Lipids: Chemistry & Biology. 1972. 65.00 (ISBN 0-12-654150-7). Acad Pr.

Snyder, Gary. The Old Ways: Six Essays. 1977. pap. 3.00 (ISBN 0-87286-091-4). City Lights.

--The Real Work: Interviews & Talks. McLean, Scott, ed. LC 79-27319. 224p. 1980. 10.95 (ISBN 0-8112-0760-9); pap. 5.50 (ISBN 0-8112-0761-7, NDP499). New Directions.

--Regarding Wave. LC 72-122107. 1970. 6.00 (ISBN 0-8112-0386-7); pap. 5.25 (ISBN 0-8112-0196-1, NDP306). New Directions.

--Riprap & Cold Mountain Poems. rev. ed. LC 66-3169. (Writing Ser.: No. 7). (Illus.). 1965. pap. 3.50 o.p. (ISBN 0-87704-002-8). Four Seasons Foun.

--Riprap & Cold Mountain Poems. LC 66-3169. (Illus.). 72p. 1965. pap. 3.95 (ISBN 0-912516-47-X). Grey Fox.

--Turtle Island. LC 74-8542. (Illus.). 128p. 1974. pap. 3.95 (ISBN 0-8112-0546-0, NDP381). New Directions.

Snyder, Gerald S. Human Rights. (gr. 4 up). 1980. PLB 8.90 (ISBN 0-531-04103-4). Watts.

--Is There a Loch Ness Monster? The Search for a Legend. LC 77-22700. (Illus.). 192p. (gr. 7 up). 1977. PLB 7.79 o.p. (ISBN 0-671-32853-0). Messner.

--The Royal Oak Disaster. LC 78-19095. (Illus.). 1978. Repr. 10.95 o.p. (ISBN 0-89141-063-5). Presidio Pr.

Snyder, Glenn H. Deterrence & Defense: Toward a Theory of National Security. LC 75-18405. (Illus.). 294p. 1975. Repr. of 1961 ed. lib. bdg. 39.75x (ISBN 0-8371-8333-2, SNDD). Greenwood.

Snyder, Graydon & Shaffer, Kenneth. Texts in Transit. (Orig.). 1976. pap. 2.95 (ISBN 0-685-61334-8). Brethren.

Snyder, Howard A. The Community of the King. LC 77-6030. (Illus.). 1977. pap. 5.95 (ISBN 0-87784-752-5). Inter-Varsity.

--Liberating the Church: The Ecology of Church & Kingdom. 280p. (Orig.). 1982. pap. 6.95 (ISBN 0-87784-385-6); cloth 12.95 (ISBN 0-87784-894-7). Inter-Varsity.

--The Problem of Wineskins: Church Renewal in Technological Age. LC 74-31842. (Illus.). 216p. 1975. pap. text ed. 4.95 (ISBN 0-87784-769-X); study guide o.p. 0.95 (ISBN 0-87784-460-7). Inter-Varsity.

Snyder, J. Richard. William S. Culbertson: In Search of a Rendezvous. LC 79-6025. 156p. 1980. text ed. 17.75 (ISBN 0-8191-0972-X); pap. text ed. 9.50 (ISBN 0-8191-0973-8). U Pr of Amer.

Snyder, J. W. Alexander the Great. (World Leaders Ser.). 12.50 (ISBN 0-8057-3004-4, Twayne). G K Hall.

Snyder, James C. Fiscal Management & Planning in Local Government. LC 76-43218. 336p. 1977. 19.95x o.p. (ISBN 0-669-01055-3). Lexington Bks.

Snyder, James C., jt. auth. see Catanese, Anthony J.

Snyder, James C., et al, eds. Introduction to Architecture. (Illus.). 1979. text ed. 32.50 (ISBN 0-07-059547-X, C). McGraw.

Snyder, John & Larsen, Arthur. Administration & Supervision in Laboratory Medicine. (Illus.). 560p. 1982. text ed. 35.00 (ISBN 0-06-142415-3, Harper Medical). Lippincott.

Snyder, John, jt. auth. see Conner, Floyd.

Snyder, Julian. The Way of the Hunter Warrior: How to Make a Killing in Any Market. LC 82-61459. 190p. 1982. 12.95 (ISBN 0-943940-00-1). Dutton.

Snyder, Karl E. & Rall, Eilene M. Structures in Composition. 1970. pap. 9.95x (ISBN 0-673-05884-0). Scott F.

Snyder, L. R. & Kirkland, J. J. Introduction to Modern Liquid Chromatography. 2nd ed. LC 79-4537. 863p. 1979. 43.95x (ISBN 0-471-03822-9, Pub. by Wiley-Interscience). Wiley.

Snyder, Leon C. Flowers for Northern Gardens. (Illus.). 464p. 1983. 25.00 (ISBN 0-8166-1229-3). U of Minn Pr.

Snyder, Llewellyn R. Computational Arithmetic. LC 67-26174. 1968. text ed. 19.95 (ISBN 0-07-059552-6, C). tchrs' manual & key 3.00 (ISBN 0-07-059550-X). McGraw.

Snyder, Llewellyn R. & Jackson, William F. Essential Business Mathematics. 7th ed. (Illus.). 1979. text ed. 21.95 (ISBN 0-07-059567-4, C); wkbk. 10.95 (ISBN 0-07-059568-2); instructor's manual 29.95 (ISBN 0-07-059569-0). McGraw.

Snyder, Louis. First Book of World War Two. LC 81-5021. (First Bks). (Illus.). (gr. 7 up). 1958. PLB 6.45 o.p. (ISBN 0-531-00676-X); pap. 1.25 o.p. (ISBN 0-531-02319-2). Watts.

Snyder, Louis L. The First Book of the Soviet Union. rev. ed. LC 78-4842. (First Bks.). (Illus.). 96p. (gr. 7 up). 1978. PLB 7.90 (ISBN 0-531-02230-7). Watts.

--Louis L. Snyder's Historical Guide to World War II. LC 81-13433. 750p. 1982. 39.95 (ISBN 0-313-23216-4). Greenwood.

--War: A Concise History, 1939-1945. 1966. 17.50 o.s.i. (ISBN 0-671-79652-6). S&S.

--World War I. (First Bks.). (Illus.). 96p. (gr. 4up). 1981. lib. bdg. 8.90 o.p. (ISBN 0-531-04332-0). Watts.

--World War II. (First Bks.). (Illus.). 96p. (gr. 4 up). 1981. lib. bdg. 8.90 (ISBN 0-531-04333-9). Watts.

Snyder, Louis L., ed. Historic Documents of World War I. LC 76-13149. 1977. Repr. of 1958 ed. lib. bdg. 17.75x (ISBN 0-8371-9398-2, SNHD). Greenwood.

Snyder, Mariah. A Guide to Neurological & Neurosurgical Nursing. 768p. 1983. 25.95 (ISBN 0-471-09835-3, Pub. by Wiley Med). Wiley.

Snyder, Mary A., ed. see Simkin, James S.

Snyder, Neil, jt. auth. see Glueck, William.

Snyder, Noel F. & Wiley, James W. Sexual Size Dimorphism in Hawks & Owls of North America. 95p. 1976. 7.00 (ISBN 0-943610-20-6). Am Ornithologists.

Snyder, R. D., jt. auth. see Byars, E. F.

Snyder, Rachel, ed. see National Passive Solar Conference, 5th, Amherst, 1980.

Snyder, Richard C., jt. auth. see Byrne, Kathleen D.

Snyder, Robert. Anais Nin Observed: From a Film Portrait of a Woman As Artist. LC 82-73922. (Illus.). 116p. 1976. pap. 9.95 (ISBN 0-8040-0708-X). Swallow.

Snyder, Robert L. Biology of Population Growth. LC 75-32937. (Biology & Environment Ser.). 250p. 1976. text ed. 18.95 o.p. (ISBN 0-312-08015-8). St Martin.

Snyder, Solomon H. Biological Aspects of Mental Disorder. 1980. 16.95x (ISBN 0-19-502715-9). Oxford U Pr.

--Biological Aspects of Mental Disorder. (Illus.). 1981. pap. 7.95x (ISBN 0-19-502888-0). Oxford U Pr.

Snyder, Solomon H. & Matthysse, Steven. Opiate Receptor Mechanisms: Neurochemical & Neurophysiological Processes in Opiate Drug Action & Addiction. LC 75-7828. 172p. 1975. text ed. 20.00x (ISBN 0-262-19132-6). MIT Pr.

Snyder, Stephen. Pier Paolo Pasolini. (Filmmakers Ser.). 1980. lib. bdg. 13.95 (ISBN 0-8057-9271-6, Twayne). G K Hall.

Snyder, Thomas F. Archeology Search Book. O'Neill, Martha, ed. (Search Ser.). (Illus.). 32p. (gr. 4-12). 1982. 32.46 (ISBN 0-07-059467-8, W). McGraw.

Snyder, Thomas F. & O'Neill, Martha. Community Searchbook. (Search Ser.). (Illus.). 32p. (gr. 4-12). 1982. reorders 32.46 (ISBN 0-07-059463-5). McGraw.

Snyder, Thomas F. F. Energy Search Apple Set. O'Neill, Martha, ed. (Search Ser.). (Illus.). 35p. 1982.. 180.00 (ISBN 0-07-079002-7, W). McGraw.

Snyder, Thomas L. & Domer, Larry R. Personalized Guide to Practice Evaluation. Felmeister, Charles J., ed. (Dental Practice Management Ser.). 216p. 1982. pap. text ed. 12.95 (ISBN 0-8016-4715-0). Mosby.

Snyder, Thomas L., ed. see Bosmajian, C. Perry & Bosmajian, Linda S.

Snyder, Thomas L., ed. see Domer, Larry R. & Bauer, Jeffrey C.

Snyder, Thomas L., ed. see Felmeister, Charles J. & Tulman, Michael M.

Snyder, Thomas L., ed. see Haver, Jurgen F.

Snyder, Virgil, et al. Selected Topics in Algebraic Geometry, 2 Vols in 1. 2nd ed. LC 78-113149. 1970. text ed. 17.50 (ISBN 0-8284-0189-6). Chelsea Pub.

Snyder, William P., jt. auth. see Hambrick, Ralph S., Jr.

Snyder, William U. Thomas Wolfe: Ulysses & Narcissus. LC 78-141381. xxiv, 234p. 1971. 12.95x (ISBN 0-8214-0087-8, 82-80919). Ohio U Pr.

Snyder, Zilpha K. And All Between. LC 75-29315. (Illus.). 224p. (gr. 5-8). 1976. 8.95 (ISBN 0-689-30514-1). Atheneum.

--The Birds of Summer. LC 82-13756. 204p. (gr. 7 up). 1983. 10.95 (ISBN 0-689-30967-8). Atheneum.

--Come on, Patsy. LC 81-10814. (Illus.). 32p. (ps-2). 1982. PLB 9.95 (ISBN 0-689-30892-2). Atheneum.

--The Famous Stanley Kidnapping Case. LC 79-12308. (gr. 4-7). 1979. 10.95 (ISBN 0-689-30728-4). Atheneum.

Snypp, Wilbur. The Buckeyes: A Story of Ohio State Football. Rev. & enl. ed. LC 74-77737. (College Sports Ser.). Orig. Title: Ohio State Football. 1974. 10.95 o.p. (ISBN 0-87397-031-4). Strode.

Soare, M. Application of Finite Difference Equations to Shell Analysis. 1968. inquire for price___00 (ISBN 0-08-010214-X). Pergamon.

Soaring Bear. Dental Self Help: New edition of Natural Dental Wellness. 2nd ed. 160p. 1983. pap. 6.95 (ISBN 0-9607518-1-5). Dental Info.

--Natural Dental Wellness. (Illus.). 90p. (Orig.). 1980. pap. 5.95 (ISBN 0-9607518-0-7). Dental-Info.

Sobel, B. Z. Hebrew Christianity: The Thirteenth Tribe. LC 74-3351. 428p. 1974. 11.50 (ISBN 0-471-81025-8). Krieger.

Sobel, David S., ed. Ways of Health: Holistic Approaches to Ancient & Contemporary Medicine. LC 78-14081. 1979. pap. 8.95 (ISBN 0-15-694992-X, Harv). HarBraceJ.

Sobel, Harry, ed. Behavior Therapy in Terminal Care: A Humanistic Approach. (Cushing Hospital Ser. on Aging & Terminal Care). 336p. 1981. prof ref 29.00x (ISBN 0-88410-716-7). Ballinger Pub.

Sobel, Lester A., ed. U. S. Military Dilemma. 200p. 1981. cancelled (ISBN 0-87196-202-0, Checkmark). Facts on File.

Sobel, M. J., jt. auth. see Heyman, D. P.

Sobel, Max & Maletsky, Evan. Teaching Mathematics: A Source Book for Aids, Activities, & Strategies. (Illus.). 288p. 1975. pap. text ed. 18.95 (ISBN 0-13-894121-1). P-H.

Sobel, Max A. & Banks, J. Houston. Algebra: Its Elements & Structure, Bk. 1. 3rd rev. ed. (gr. 9). 1976. text ed. 16.64 (ISBN 0-07-059581-X, W); tchr's ed. 18.08 (ISBN 0-07-059582-8); test 3.68 (ISBN 0-07-059583-6); solutions manual 9.84 (ISBN 0-07-059584-4). McGraw.

--Algebra: Its Elements & Structure, Bk. 2. 3rd, rev. ed. 624p. (gr. 11). 1977. text ed. 17.28 (ISBN 0-07-059585-2, W). McGraw.

Sobel, Max A. & Lerner, Norbert. Algebra & Trigonometry: A Pre-Calculus Approach. 2nd ed. (Illus.). 608p. 1983. text ed. 24.95 (ISBN 0-13-021634-8). P-H.

--Algebra & Trigonometry: A Precalculus Approach. (Illus.). 1979. ref. ed. 24.95 (ISBN 0-13-021709-3). P-H.

--College Algebra. (Illus.). 576p. 1983. text ed. 21.95 (ISBN 0-13-141796-7). P-H.

Sobel, Max A., jt. auth. see Merserve, Bruce E.

Sobel, Max A., jt. auth. see Meserve, Bruce E.

Sobel, Mechal. Trabelin' On: The Slave Journey to an Afro-Baptist Faith. LC 77-84775. (Contributions in Afro-American & African Studies: No. 36). 1978. lib. bdg. 35.00x (ISBN 0-8371-9887-9, STO/). Greenwood.

Sobel, Nathan, ed. see Haffner, Sylvia.

Sobel, Nathan R. Eye-Witness Identification. 2nd ed. LC 81-170436. 1981. 45.00 (ISBN 0-87632-367-0) (ISBN 0-685-99205-5). Boardman.

Sobel, Robert. The Age of Giant Corporations: A Microeconomic History of American Business, 1914-1970. LC 72-835. (Contributions in Economics & Economic History). 1974. lib. bdg. 29.95x (ISBN 0-8371-6404-4, SAB/); pap. text ed. 5.95x (ISBN 0-8371-7339-6, SAB/). Greenwood.

Sobel, Robert, ed. Biographical Directory of the United States Executive Branch, 1774-1977. 2nd ed. LC 77-84. 1977. lib. bdg. 45.00x (ISBN 0-8371-9527-6, SBU/). Greenwood.

Sobel, Rochelle S. Mi Ani? (Who Am I?) (Illus.). 40p. (Hebrew & Eng.). (gr. 1-4). 1982. 3.95 (ISBN 0-686-83445-3). Kar Ben.

Sobel, Ruth. Gogol's Forgotten Book: Selected Passages & Its Contemporary Readers. LC 80-8292. 1981. lib. bdg. 20.75 (ISBN 0-8191-1630-0); pap. text ed. 11.00 (ISBN 0-8191-1631-9). U Pr of Amer.

Sobell, Linda C., ed. Evaluating Alcohol & Drug Abuse Treatment Effectiveness. 1980. 24.00 (ISBN 0-08-022997-2). Pergamon.

Sober, Elliott. Simplicity. (Clarendon Library of Logic & Philosophy). (Illus.). 1975. 27.50x (ISBN 0-19-824407-X). Oxford U Pr.

Soberman, Richard M. Transport Technology for Developing Regions: A Study of Road Transportation in Venezuela. 1967. 20.00x (ISBN 0-262-19032-X). MIT Pr.

Sobey, Edwin J. & Burns, Gary. Runner's World: Aerobic Weight Training Book. 181p. 1982. pap. 9.95 (ISBN 0-89037-241-1). Anderson World.

Sobey, Francine, ed. Changing Roles in Social Work Practice. LC 77-70327. 305p. 1977. 17.50 (ISBN 0-87722-092-1); pap. 10.95 (ISBN 0-87722-096-4). Temple U Pr.

Sobie, Keith, et al. The Video Wizard Handbook. (Illus.). 196p. 1982. pap. 6.95 (ISBN 0-686-35866-X). Video Wizard.

Sobieski, jt. auth. see Anderson.

Sobieszek, Barbara, jt. auth. see Webster, Murray, Jr.

Sobieszek, Robert & Appel, Odette. Spirit of Fact: The Daguerreotypes of Southworth & Hawes, 1843-1862. LC 75-43054. (International Museum of Photography Series: Vol. 1). (Illus.). 192p. 1976. 40.00 (ISBN 0-87923-179-3). Godine.

Sobin, Anthony. The Sunday Naturalist. LC 82-6316. xii, 75p. 1982. text ed. 14.95x (ISBN 0-8214-0636-1, 82-84093); pap. 7.95 (ISBN 0-8214-0637-X, 82-84101). Ohio U Pr.

Sobin, Julian M. The China Trade: A Practical Guide to Buying, Selling, & Marketing in the People's Republic of China. 320p. 1980. 25.00 o.p. (ISBN 0-471-07999-5, Pub. by Wiley-Interscience). Wiley.

Sobin, L. H., jt. auth. see Zimmerman, L. E.

Soble, Ron. Smart Money in Hard Times: A Guide to Inflationproof Investments. Orig. Title: Smart Money. 1975. pap. 1.75 o.p. (ISBN 0-451-06447-X, E6447, Sig). NAL.

Soble, Ronald L. Whatever Became of Free Enterprise? (Orig.). 1977. pap. 1.75 o.p. (ISBN 0-451-07542-0, E7542, Sig). NAL.

Sobol, Donald J. Encyclopedia Brown's Book of Wacky Crimes. (Illus.). 128p. (gr. 3-5). 1982. 8.95 (ISBN 0-525-66786-5, 0869-260). Lodestar Bks.

--Encyclopedia Brown's Record Book of Weird & Wonderful Facts. LC 78-72857. (Illus.). (gr. 3 up). 1979. 4.95 o.p. (ISBN 0-440-02329-7); PLB 9.89 (ISBN 0-440-02330-0). Delacorte.

--Encyclopedia Brown's Record Book of Weird & Wonderful Facts. (Illus.). (gr. 3-7). 1981. pap. 1.75 (ISBN 0-440-42361-9, YB). Dell.
--Encyclopedia Brown's Second Record Book of Weird & Wonderful Facts. (Illus.). (gr. 3-7). 1982. pap. 1.95 (ISBN 0-440-42421-6, YB). Dell.
Sobol, Harriet. The Interns. (Illus.). (gr. 6 up). 1981. 8.95 (ISBN 0-698-20518-9, Coward). Putnam Pub Group.
Sobol, Harriet L. Clowns. (gr. 6-9). 1982. 9.95 (ISBN 0-698-20558-8, Coward). Pub. by Coward.
--Grandpa: A Young Man Grown Old. (Illus.). (YA) 1980. 8.95 (ISBN 0-698-20508-1, Coward). Putnam Pub Group.
Sobol, Max A. & Lerner, Norbert. Algebra for College Students: An Intermediate Approach. 2nd ed. 1980. text ed. 22.95 (ISBN 0-13-021584-8). P-H.
Sobolev, N. V. Deep-Seated Inclusions in Kimberlites & the Problems of the Upper Mantle Composition. Brown, David A., tr. from Rus. LC 76-62627. (Eng.). 1977. 28.00 (ISBN 0-87590-202-2). Am Geophysical.
Sobolev, V. S., et al, eds. Metamorphic Complexes of Asia. (Illus.). 350p. 1982. 60.01 (ISBN 0-08-022854-2). Pergamon.
Sobolev, V. V. Light Scattering in Planetary Atmospheres. Irvine, W. M., tr. 1975. text ed. 49.00 (ISBN 0-08-017934-7). Pergamon.
Sobotka, Harry & Stewart, C. P., eds. Advances in Clinical Chemistry. Incl. Vol. 1. 1958. 59.00 (ISBN 0-12-010301-X); Vol. 2. 1959. 59.00 (ISBN 0-12-010302-8); Vol. 3. 1960. 59.00 (ISBN 0-12-010303-6); Vol. 4. 1961. 59.00 (ISBN 0-12-010304-4); Vol. 5. 1963. 59.00 (ISBN 0-12-010305-2); Vol. 6. 1963. 59.00 (ISBN 0-12-010306-0); Vol. 7. 1964. 59.00 (ISBN 0-12-010307-9); Vol. 8. 1966. 59.00 (ISBN 0-12-010308-7); Vol. 9. 1967. 59.00 (ISBN 0-12-010309-5); Vol. 10. Bodansky, Oscar & Stewart, C. P., eds. 1967. 59.00 (ISBN 0-12-010310-9); Vol. 11. 1969. 59.00 (ISBN 0-12-010311-7); Vol. 12. 1969. 59.00 (ISBN 0-12-010312-5); Vol. 13. 1970. 62.50 (ISBN 0-12-010313-3); Vol. 14. Bodansky, Oscar & Latner, A. L., eds. 1971. 62.50 (ISBN 0-12-010314-1); Vol. 15. 1972. 60.00 (ISBN 0-12-010315-X). Acad Pr.
Sobotta, Johannes. Atlas of Human Anatomy. Figge, Frank H. & Hild, Walter J., eds. Incl. Vol. 1. Regions, Bones, Ligaments & Muscles. 290p. text ed. 39.50 (ISBN 0-8067-1719-X); Vol. 2. Visceral Anatomy (Cardiovascular, Lymphatic, Digestive, Respiratory & Urogenital Systems) 255p. text ed. 39.50 (ISBN 0-8067-1729-7); Vol. 3. Central Nervous System, Autonomic Nervous System, Sense Organs & Skin, Peripheral Nerves & Vessels. 366p. text ed. 45.00 (ISBN 0-686-83002-4). (Illus.). 1978. Repr. of 1974 ed. complete set 112.00 (ISBN 0-686-77287-3). Urban & S.
Soboul, Albert. A Short History of the French Revolution, 1789-1799. Symcox, Geoffrey, tr. 1977. 23.75x (ISBN 0-520-02855-4); pap. 5.95x (ISBN 0-520-03419-8). U of Cal Pr.
Soboul, Albert, ed. see Babeuf, Francois-Noel.
Sobran, Joseph. The Conservative Manifesto: The Philosophy, the Passion, the Promise. LC 81-68540. 304p. 1983. 12.95 (ISBN 0-88015-001-7). Empire Bks.
Sobrero, A. & Harvey, R., eds. Advances in Planned Parenthood, Vols 3-7. (International Congress Ser.: Nos. 156, 177, 207, 224 & 246). 1968-72. Vol. 3. pap. 13.75 (ISBN 90-219-0099-8, Excerpta Medica); Vol. 4. pap. 20.00 (ISBN 90-219-0114-5); Vol. 5. pap. 27.50 (ISBN 90-219-0138-2); Vol. 6. pap. 22.25 (ISBN 90-219-0171-4); Vol. 7. pap. 25.50 (ISBN 90-219-0193-5). Elsevier.
Sobrero, Acquiles, ed. see Stone, Hannah & Stone, Abraham.
Sobue, Itsurd. Spinocerebellar Degenerations. 294p. 1980. text ed. 64.50 o.p. (ISBN 0-8391-4123-8). Univ Park.
Sobul, DeAnne. Bill of Rights, a Handbook. 1968. pap. text ed. 4.40 o.p. (ISBN 0-02-640700-0, 64070). Glencoe.
Sochen, June. Consecrate Every Day: The Public Lives of Jewish American Women, Eighteen Eighty to Nineteen Eighty. LC 80-29169. (Modern Jewish History Ser.). 180p. 1981. 34.50x (ISBN 0-87395-526-9); pap. 10.95x (ISBN 0-87395-527-7). State U NY Pr.
Social Science Education Consortium, Inc. Family Development. (Adoption Builds Families Ser.: Unit I). (Illus.). 1980. multimedia teaching kit 24.95 (ISBN 0-89994-256-3); storybook 0.75 (ISBN 0-686-86748-3). Soc Sci Ed.
Social Science Research Council, et al. Farm Management Research, Nineteen Forty-Nineteen Forty One. LC 44-4129. 1943. pap. 4.00 (ISBN 0-527-03281-6). Kraus Repr.
Social Science Research Council - Committee on Historiography. Theory & Practice in Historical Study. LC 46-3597. 1946. pap. 5.00 (ISBN 0-527-03283-2). Kraus Repr.
Social Science Research Council Conference on Social Experiments. Experimental Testing of Public Policy: Proceedings, 1974. Boruch, Robert F. & Riecken, Henry W., eds. LC 75-30613. 180p. 1976. lib. bdg. 22.00 o.p. (ISBN 0-89158-004-2). Westview.
Social Security Administration. Survey of Low Income Aged & Disabled, 1973-1975. LC 79-67535. 1979. codebk. write for info. o.p. (ISBN 0-89138-965-2). ICPSR.
Social Systems, Inc., jt. auth. see Mayo, R. Britton.
Societe de Chimie Physique, International Meeting, 29th, Orsay, Oct. 1976. Electrical Phenomena at the Biological Membrane Level: Proceedings. Roux, E., ed. 1977. 106.50 (ISBN 0-444-41572-6). Elsevier.
Society for Historians of American Foreign Relations, jt. auth. see Burns, Richard D.
Society for Hospital Planning of the American Hospital Association. Compendium of Resources for Strategic Planning in Hospitals. LC 80-28585. 132p. (Orig.). 1981. pap. 15.00 (ISBN 0-87258-326-0, AHA-127188). Am Hospital.
Society for Hospital Social Work Directors of the American Hospital Association. Cost Accountability for Hospital Social Work. LC 80-12334. 48p. (Orig.). 1980. pap. 12.50 (ISBN 0-87258-278-7, AHA-187123). Am Hospital.
--Documentation by Social Workers in Medical Records. 1978. pap. 7.50 (ISBN 0-87258-256-6, AHA-187115). Am Hospital.
--Quality & Quantity Assurance for Social Workers in Health Care: A Training Manual. LC 80-26488. (Illus.). 96p. (Orig.). 1980. manual 27.50 (ISBN 0-87258-325-2, AHA-187128). Am Hospital.
--Reporting System for Hospital Social Work. LC 78-5696. 32p. 1978. pap. 11.25 (ISBN 0-87258-237-X, AHA-187118). Am Hospital.
--Social Work Staff Development for Health Care. LC 76-41793. 36p. 1976. pap. 8.75 (ISBN 0-87258-322-8, AHA-187105). Am Hospital.
Society for International Development. International Development, 1965. LC 64-8541. 1966. 12.50 (ISBN 0-379-12000-3). Oceana.
--International Development 1968: Accomplishments & Apprehensions. LC 64-8541. (Society for International Development Ser.: No. 5). 1969. 17.50 (ISBN 0-379-12005-4). Oceana.
Society for Nutrition Education Resource Center. Vegetarians & Vegetarian Diets. rev. ed. (Nutrition Education Resource Ser.: No. 8). 10p. 1982. pap. 4.00 (ISBN 0-910869-14-6). Soc Nutrition Ed.
Society for Nutrition Education. A Brief Guide to Becoming a Nutrition Advocate. 19p. (Orig.). 1982. pap. 3.75 (ISBN 0-910869-15-4). Soc Nutrition Ed.
--Fitness & Nutrition. (Nutrition Education Source Ser.). (Orig.). 1981. pap. 4.00 (ISBN 0-910869-11-1). Soc Nutrition Ed.
Society for Psychical Research London, England. Catalogue of the Library of the Society for Psychical Research, London, England. 1976. lib. bdg. 70.00 (ISBN 0-8161-0008-X, Hall Library). G K Hall.
Society for Technical Communciation, ed. International Technical Communication Conference, 29th. (Illus.). 532p. (Orig.). 1982. pap. text ed. 45.00x (ISBN 0-914548-38-7); microfiche 30.00. Soc Tech Comm.
Society for the Study of Development & Growth - Symposium. Cytodifferentiation & Macromolecular Synthesis: Proceedings. Locke, M., ed. 1963. 42.50 (ISBN 0-12-454156-9). Acad Pr.
Society For The Study Of Developmental Biology - 27th Symposium. Emergence of Order in Developing Systems: Proceedings. Locke, N., ed. 1969. 46.50 (ISBN 0-12-612960-6); pap. 37.00 (ISBN 0-12-612966-5). Acad Pr.
Society For The Study Of Developmental Biology - 24th Symposium. Reproduction: Molecular, Subcellular & Cellular. Locke, M., ed. 1966. 52.50 (ISBN 0-12-454174-7). Acad Pr.
Society for the Study of Experimental Biology - 28th Symposium, 1969. Communication in Development. Lang, Anton, ed. (Journal of Developmental Biology: Suppl. 3). 1970. 45.00 (ISBN 0-12-612968-1); pap. 32.50 (ISBN 0-12-612969-X). Acad Pr.
Society of Brothers, ed. Children in Community: A Photographic Essay. rev. ed. LC 74-4383. (Illus.). 180p. 1975. 14.95 (ISBN 0-87486-015-6). Plough.
Society Of Brothers, ed. see Blumhardt, Christoph.
Society Of Brothers, ed. see Swinger, Marlys.
Society of Education Officers. Management in the Education Service: Challenge & Response. (Open University Set Bk.). 128p. 1975. pap. 5.25 o.p. (ISBN 0-7100-8292-4). Routledge & Kegan.
Society of Experimental Stress Analysis. Manual of Engineering Stress Analysis. 3rd ed. 1982. 15.95 (ISBN 0-686-83114-4). P-H.
Society Of Friends Of Eastern Art, ed. Index of Japanese Painters. LC 58-9985. 1958. 7.95 (ISBN 0-8048-0262-9). C E Tuttle.
Society of Industrial Realtors & Economics & Research Division of the National Association of Realtors. S. I. R. Industrial Real Estate Market Survey. 17.50 (ISBN 0-686-37026-0). Soc Industrial Realtors.
Society of Manufacturing Engineers. BASIC Programming Solutions for Manufacturing. 300p. 1982. 43.00 (ISBN 0-13-066332-8). P-H.
Society of Manufacturing Engineers & Fabricating Manufacturers Association, eds. FABTECH International Conference Proceedings. LC 81-52608. (Illus.). 529p. 1981. pap. 35.00 o.p. (ISBN 0-87263-072-2). SME.
Society Of Manufacturing Engineers. Surface Preparation & Finishes for Metals. Murphy, J. A., ed. 1971. 42.50 (ISBN 0-07-059557-7, P&RB). McGraw.
--Tool & Manufacturing Engineers Handbook. 3rd ed. Dallas, D. B., ed. (Illus.). 1976. 82.50 (ISBN 0-07-059558-5, P&RB). McGraw.
Society of Mining Engineers of AIME, 1973. Hydrometallurgy: Proceedings. LC 72-88874. 30.00x (ISBN 0-89520-017-1). Soc Mining Eng.
Society of Naval Architects & Marine Engineers. Furnace Performance Criteria for Gas, Oil & Coal Fired Boilers. (Ships Machinery Bulletin). 16p. 1981. member 7.00 (ISBN 0-686-95823-3, 3-32); non-member 10.50 (ISBN 0-686-99626-7). Soc Naval Arch.
--Guide for the Disposal of Shipboard Wastes. (Ship Machinery Bulletin). 60p. 1982. member 11.00 (ISBN 0-686-95837-3, 3-33); non-member 16.50 (ISBN 0-686-99634-8). Soc Naval Arch.
Society of Naval Architecture & Marine Engineers. The Status of Commercial Seakeeping Research. (Hydrodynamic Bulletins). 70p. 1982. member 19.00 (ISBN 0-686-95801-2, 1-39); non-member 28.50 (ISBN 0-686-99617-8). Soc Naval Arch.
Society of Patient Representatives of the American Hospital Association. Essentials of Patient Representative Programs in Hospitals. LC 78-26889. 40p. 1978. pap. 11.25 (ISBN 0-87258-255-8, AHA-157142). Am Hospital.
--The Patient Representative's Participation in Risk Management. 40p. (Orig.). 1980. pap. 10.00 (ISBN 0-87258-315-5, AHA-157152). Am Hospital.
Society of Photographic Scientists & Engineers. SPSE Handbook of Photographic Science & Engineering. LC 72-10168. (Wiley Ser. on Photographic Science & Technology & the Graphic Arts). 1416p. 1973. 82.50x (ISBN 0-471-81880-1, Pub. by Wiley-Interscience). Wiley.
Soclof, S. I., jt. auth. see Iles, P. A.
Socolich, Sally. Bargain Hunting in the Bay Area. 4th & rev. ed. pap. 5.95 (ISBN 0-914728-32-6). Wingbow Pr.
Socolow, Robert H. see Feiveson, Harold A., et al.
Socolow, Robert H., ed. Saving Energy in the Home: Princeton's Experiments at Twin Rivers. LC 78-2598. 368p. 1978. prof ref 25.00x (ISBN 0-88410-080-4). Ballinger Pub.
Socolow, Susan M. Merchants of Buenos Aires, Seventeen Seventy-Eight to Eighteen Hundred & Ten. LC 77-85216. (Cambridge Latin American Studies: No. 30). (Illus.). 1979. 39.50 (ISBN 0-521-21812-8). Cambridge U Pr.
Socrates, G. Infrared Characteristic Group Frequencies. LC 79-1406. 153p. 1980. 79.95 (ISBN 0-471-27592-1, Pub. by Wiley-Interscience). Wiley.
--Thermodynamics & Statistical Mechanics. 374p. 1971. 14.95 o.p. (ISBN 0-408-70179-X). Butterworth.
Soda, ed. Drug Induced Sufferings: Medical, Pharmaceutical & Legal Aspects. (International Congress Ser.: Vol. 513). 1980. 105.75 (ISBN 0-444-90140-X). Elsevier.
Sodaro & Wolchik. Foreign & Domestic Policy in Eastern Europe in the 1980's: Trends & Prospects. LC 82-3265. 192p. 1983. 25.00x (ISBN 0-312-29843-9). St Martin.
Soddy, Frederick. The Story of Atomic Energy. 1949. 35.00 o.p. (ISBN 0-911268-29-4). Rogers Bk.
Sodee, D. Bruce & Early, Paul J. Technology & Interpretation of Nuclear Medicine Procedures. 2nd ed. LC 75-15607. (Illus.). 520p. 1975. text ed. 31.95 o.p. (ISBN 0-8016-4732-0). Mosby.
Sodek, George, jt. auth. see Pell, Arthur.
Sodeman, William, ed. Self-Assessment of Current Knowledge in Internal Medicine. 6th ed. 1982. pap. text ed. 26.00 (ISBN 0-87488-257-5). Med Exam.
Sodeman, William A., Jr. & Saladin, Thomas A. Gastroenterology Specialty Board Review. 2nd ed. 1981. pap. 28.50 (ISBN 0-87488-316-4). Med Exam.
Soden, John V., jt. auth. see McLean, Ephraim R.
Soderberg. Drawing Boats & Ships. (Pitman Art Ser.: Vol. 7). pap. 1.95 o.p. (ISBN 0-448-00516-6, G&D). Putnam Pub Group.
Soderberg, George A. Finishing Technology. rev. ed. (gr. 10-12). 1969. text ed. 21.28 (ISBN 0-87345-016-7). McKnight.
Soderberg, P. M. All About Lovebirds. new ed. Orig. Title: Foreign Birds for Cage & Aviary; Lovebirds, Cardinals & Buntings. (Illus.). 1977. pap. 5.95 (ISBN 0-87666-957-7, PS-742). TFH Pubns.
Soderberg, Percy M. Cat Diseases. (Orig.). pap. 2.95 (ISBN 0-87666-171-1, AP4800). TFH Pubns.
Soderholm, Marjorie E. Understanding the Pupil, 3 pts. Incl. Pt. 1. The Pre-School Child. pap. 2.50 o.p. (ISBN 0-8010-7906-3); Pt. 2. The Primary & Junior Child. pap. 2.50 (ISBN 0-8010-7953-5); Pt. 3. The Adolescent. pap. 2.50 (ISBN 0-8010-7922-5). pap. Baker Bk.
Soderlind, Arthur. Colonial Connecticut. LC 76-3588. (Colonial History Ser.). (Illus.). 176p. (gr. 5 up). 1976. 7.95 o.p. (ISBN 0-525-67136-6). Lodestar Bks.
Soderlund, G. F. & Scott, Samuel H., eds. Examples of Gregorian Chant & Other Sacred Music of the 16th Century. LC 70-129090. (Orig.). 1971. 20.95 (ISBN 0-13-293753-0). P-H.
Soderlund, Gustave F. Direct Approach to Counterpoint in Sixteenth Century Style. 1947. 16.95 (ISBN 0-13-214569-3). P-H.
Soderlund, Jean R. & Dunn, Richard S., eds. William Penn & the Founding of Pennsylvania, 1680-1684: A Documentary History. (Illus.). 380p. 1982. 20.00x (ISBN 0-8122-7862-3); pap. 8.95x (ISBN 0-8122-1131-6). U of Pa Pr.
Soderman, Joanne, ed. see Morningside Associates.
Soderquist, Larry D. Securities Regulation: 1983 Supplement. (University Casebook Ser.). 612p. 1982. pap. text ed. write for info. (ISBN 0-88277-072-1). Foundation Pr.
Soderstrom, Mary. Maybe Tomorrow I'll Have a Good Time. LC 80-25357. (Illus.). 32p. (gr. 4-8). 1981. 9.95 (ISBN 0-89885-012-6). Human Sci Pr.
Soderstrom, Neil. Chainsaw Savvy: A Complete Guide. (Illus.). 144p. (Orig.). 1983. pap. 9.95 (ISBN 0-87100-187-X, 2187). Morgan.
--Heating Your Home with Wood. LC 77-26480. (Popular Science Skill Bks.). 1978. pap. 3.95i o.p. (ISBN 0-06-090649-9, CN 649, CN). Har-Row.
Soderstrom, Nils. Fine-Needle Aspiration Biopsy: Used As a Direct Adjunct in Clinical Diagnostic Work. (Illus.). 159p. 1965. 59.50 (ISBN 0-8089-0608-9). Grune.
Soebadio, H. & Sarvaas, C. Dynamics of Indonesian History. 1978. 81.00 (ISBN 0-444-85023-6, North-Holland). Elsevier.
Soeder, C. J., jt. auth. see Shelef, G.
Soeder, C. J., ed. Microalgae for Food & Feed; a Status Analysis: Proceedings. Binsack, R. (Ergebnisse der Limnologie: Vol. II). (Illus.). 300p. 1978. pap. text ed. 65.00x (ISBN 3-510-47009-5). Intl Pubns Serv.
Soedharno, R. & Bergau, Nancy. Using Consultants for Materials Development. (Technical Note Ser.: No. 19). (Illus.). 20p. (Orig.). 1982. pap. 1.00 (ISBN 0-932288-65-0). Ctr Intl Ed U of MA.
Soehner, E. Die Gattung Hymenogaster Vitt. 1962. pap. 16.00 (ISBN 3-7682-5402-X). Lubrecht & Cramer.
Soelle, Dorothee. The Arms Race Kills Even Without War. LC 82-48543. 128p. 1983. pap. 6.95 (ISBN 0-8006-1701-0). Fortress.
Soemardjan, Selo. Imbalances in Development: The Indonesian Experience. LC 72-619654. (Papers in International Studies: Southeast Asia: No. 25). 1972. pap. 3.50x (ISBN 0-89680-013-X, Ohio U Ctr Intl). Ohio U Pr.
Soergel, Dagobert. Indexing Languages & Thesauri: Construction & Maintenance. LC 73-20301. (Information Sciences Ser.). 632p. 1974. 56.95 (ISBN 0-471-81047-9, Pub. by Wiley-Interscience). Wiley.
Soest, Peter J. Van see Van Soest, Peter J.
Sofaer, Abraham D. War, Foreign Affairs & Constitutional Power, Vol. 1: The Origins. LC 76-15392. 1976. prof ref 20.00x (ISBN 0-88410-222-X). Ballinger Pub.
Sofer, Barbara. Holiday Adventures of Achbar. (Illus.). (gr. 2-6). 1983. pap. 4.95 (ISBN 0-930494-22-9). Kar Ben.
Sofer, Cyril. Men in Mid-Career: A Study of British Managers & Technical Specialists. (Studies in Sociology: No. 4). 1970. 32.50 (ISBN 0-521-07788-5); pap. 16.95x (ISBN 0-521-09606-5). Cambridge U Pr.
Sofer, Eugene. From Pale to Pampa: The Jewish Immigrant Experience in Buenos Aires. 1982. text ed. 29.50x (ISBN 0-8419-0428-6). Holmes & Meier.
Sofer, Nat. How You Can Build a Fortune Investing in Land. (Illus.). 224p. 1983. 15.95 (ISBN 0-13-444026-9); pap. 7.95 (ISBN 0-13-444018-8). P-H.
Soff, Edward B. & Snider, Arthur D. Fundamentals of Complex Analysis for Mathematics, Science & Engineering. (Illus.). 1976. 29.95 (ISBN 0-13-332148-7). P-H.
Soffer, Reba N. Ethics & Society in England: The Revolution in the Social Sciences, 1870-1914. 1978. 33.00x (ISBN 0-520-03521-6). U of Cal Pr.
Soffer, Richard L. Biochemical Regulation of Blood Pressure. LC 80-39522. 456p. 1981. 62.50 (ISBN 0-471-05600-6, Pub. by Wiley-Interscience). Wiley.
Sofowora, Abayomi. Medicinal Plants & Traditional Medicine in Africa. 192p. 1983. 31.95 (ISBN 0-471-10367-5, Pub. by Wiley Interscience). Wiley.
Softly, Barbara. Lemon-Yellow Elephant Called Trunk. LC 71-115818. (Illus.). 48p. (gr. k-2). PLB 5.29 o.p. (ISBN 0-8178-4772-3). Harvey.
Soggin, J. Alberto. Introduction to the Old Testament. Rev. ed. Bowden, John, tr. LC 81-3422. (Old Testament Library). 544p. 1982. 27.50 (ISBN 0-664-21385-5). Westminster.
--Joshua: A Commentary. Wilson, R. A., tr. LC 72-76954. (Old Testament Library). 1972. 11.95 (ISBN 0-664-20938-6). Westminster.
Soghoian, Richard J. The Ethics of G. E. Moore & David Hume: The Treatise As a Response to Moore's Refutation of Ethical Naturalism. LC 79-88306. 1979. pap. text ed. 8.25 (ISBN 0-8191-0774-3). U Pr of Amer.
Sohal. Age Pigments. 1981. 103.50 (ISBN 0-444-80277-0). Elsevier.
Sohl, Damian G., jt. auth. see Rehg, Kenneth L.
Sohl, Robert & Carr, Audrey. Games Zen Masters Play: The Writings of R. H. Blyth. 1976. pap. 2.25 (ISBN 0-451-62105-0, ME2105, Ment). NAL.

Sohl, Robert & Carr, Audrey, eds. Gospel According to Zen: Beyond the Death of God. (Orig.). 1970. pap. 2.95 (ISBN 0-451-62184-0, ME2184, Ment). NAL.

Sohmer, Bernard, jt. auth. see Gondin, William R.

Sohmer, Paul R. & Schiffer, Charles A., eds. Blood Storage & Preservation. 62p. 1982. 11.00 (ISBN 0-914404-73-3); non-members 13.00 (ISBN 0-686-83047-4). Am Assn Blood.

Sohn, David A., ed. see Poe, Edgar Allan.

Sohn, Ho-Min. Woleaian Reference Grammar. (PALI Language Texts: Micronesia). 336p. (Orig.). 1975. pap. text ed. 14.00x (ISBN 0-8248-0356-6). UH Pr.

Sohn, Ho-Min & Tawerilmang, Anthony F. Woleaian-English Dictionary. (Pali Language Texts: Micronesia). 328p. 1976. pap. text ed. 12.00x (ISBN 0-8248-0415-5). UH Pr.

Sohner, Charles P. California Government & Politics Today. 3rd ed. 1980. pap. text ed. 4.50x (ISBN 0-673-15242-1). Scott F.

--The People's Power: American Government & Politics Today. 1973. pap. 14.50x (ISBN 0-673-07646-6). Scott F.

Sohner, Charles P. & Martin, Helen P. American Government & Politics Today. 3rd. ed. 1980. pap. text ed. 15.50x (ISBN 0-673-15241-3); study guide 5.50x (ISBN 0-673-15243-X). Scott F.

Soifer, David, ed. Biology of Cytoplasmic Microtubules. (Annals of the New York Academy of Sciences Ser.: Vol. 253). 848p. 1975. 99.50x (ISBN 0-89072-007-X). NY Acad Sci.

Soisson. Egypt. 224p. 1982. 5.98 o.p. (ISBN 0-517-28279-8). Crown.

Soisson, Harold E. Instrumentation in Industry. LC 74-23222. 563p. 1975. 44.95x (ISBN 0-471-81049-5, Pub. by Wiley-Interscience). Wiley.

Sokal, Michael M., ed. An Education in Psychology: James McKeen Cattell's Journal & Letters from Germany & England 1880-1888. 508p. 1981. text ed. 32.50x (ISBN 0-262-19185-7). MIT Pr.

Sokeland, jt. auth. see Alken.

Sokol, David M. American Architecture & Art: A Guide to Information Sources. LC 73-17563. (American Studies Information Guide Ser.: Vol. 2). 480p. 1976. 42.00x (ISBN 0-8103-1255-7). Gale.

Sokol, David M., ed. American Decorative Arts & Old World Influences: A Guide to Information Sources. (Art & Architecture Information Guide Ser.: Vol. 14). 256p. 1980. 42.00x (ISBN 0-8103-1465-7). Gale.

Sokol, Gerald H. & Maickel, Roger P. Radiation Drug Interactions in the Treatment of Cancer. 235p. 1980. text ed. 44.50 (ISBN 0-471-04697-3, Pub. by Wiley Med). Wiley.

Sokol, Hilda W., ed. see International Symposium on the Brattleboro Rat, Sept. 4-7, 1981.

Sokol, Ronald P. Justice After Darwin. LC 75-9170. 141p. 1975. 12.50 (ISBN 0-87215-167-0). Michie-Bobbs.

--Language & Litigation. 1967. 12.50 (ISBN 0-87215-053-4). Michie-Bobbs.

--Puzzle of Equality. 1967. 12.50 (ISBN 0-87215-055-0). Michie-Bobbs.

Sokol, Saul. Your Insurance Adviser. LC 76-12063. (Illus.). 256p. (Orig.). 1977. pap. text ed. 3.50 (ISBN 0-06-463405-1, EH 405, EH). B&N NY.

Sokolinsky, Martin, tr. see Paris, Alain.

Sokolnicki, Alfred J., jt. ed. see Smal-Stocki, Roman.

Sokolnikoff, I. S. Mathematical Theory of Elasticity. LC 82-14844. 488p. 1982. Repr. of 1956 ed. lib. bdg. 29.50 (ISBN 0-89874-555-1). Krieger.

Sokolnikoff, Ivan S. Tensor Analysis. 2nd ed. LC 64-13223. (Applied Mathematical Ser.). 1964. 38.50 (ISBN 0-471-81052-5). Wiley.

Sokolnikoff, Ivan S. & Redheffer, R. M. Mathematics of Physics & Modern Engineering. 2nd ed. 1966. text ed. 39.50 (ISBN 0-07-059625-5, C). McGraw.

Sokoloff, Alexander see Demerec, M.

Sokoloff, Alice H. Cosima Wagner: Extraordinary Daughter of Franz Liszt. LC 72-11253. (Illus.). 1969. 7.50 o.p. (ISBN 0-396-05893-0). Dodd.

Sokoloff, Georges & Lemoine, Francoise. China & the USSR: Limits to Trade with the West. 70p. 1982. pap. text ed. 6.50x (ISBN 0-86598-104-3). Allanheld.

Sokoloff, Kiril. The Paine Webber Handbook to Stock & Bond Analysis. new ed. (Illus.). 1979. 39.95 (ISBN 0-07-059576-3). McGraw.

--The Thinking Investor's Guide to the Stock Market. (Illus.). 1978. 22.50 (ISBN 0-07-059615-8, P&RB). McGraw.

Sokoloff, Kiril, jt. auth. see Shilling, A. G.

Sokoloff, L. The Joints & Synovial Fluid, Vol. 1. Sokoloff, Leon, ed. 1978. 56.50 (ISBN 0-12-655101-4); 42.00 set (ISBN 0-685-80835-1). Acad Pr.

Sokoloff, Leon, ed. see Sokoloff, L.

Sokolov, E. N., et al. Neuronal Mechanisms of the Orienting Reflexes. 322p. 1975. 19.95 o.s.i. (ISBN 0-470-92562-0, SI25). Halsted Pr.

Sokolov, Raymond. Fading Feast: A Compendium of Disappearing American Regional Foods. (Illus.). 288p. 1983. pap. 6.95 (ISBN 0-525-48030-7, 0674-210, Obelisk). Dutton.

--Native Intelligence: A Novel. 240p. 1983. pap. 5.95 (ISBN 0-525-48029-3, 0577-180, Obelisk). Dutton.

--The Saucier's Apprentice: A Modern Guide to Classic French Sauces for the Home. 1976. 13.50 (ISBN 0-394-48920-9). Knopf.

--The Wayward Reporter: The Life of A. J. Liebling. LC 79-3403. (Illus.). 1980. 16.95i o.p. (ISBN 0-06-014061-5, HarpT). Har-Row.

Sokolov, Sasha. Shkola Dlya Durakov. 1976. 10.00 (ISBN 0-88233-189-2); pap. 5.00 (ISBN 0-88233-188-4). Ardis Pubs.

Sokolov, V., jt. auth. see Gligoric, S.

Sokolov, Yury M. Russian Folklore. Smith, Catherine R., tr. LC 79-134444. (Illus.). 1971. Repr. of 1966 ed. 50.00x (ISBN 0-8103-5020-3). Gale.

Sokolovskill. Statics of Granular Media. 1965. pap. inquire for price o.p. (ISBN 0-08-013624-9). Pergamon.

Sokolovskiy, V. D. Soviet Military Strategy. 3rd ed. Scott, Harriet F., tr. from Rus. LC 73-94042. (Illus.). 560p. 1975. 39.50x o.s.i. (ISBN 0-8448-0311-1); pap. 29.50x (ISBN 0-8448-1382-6). Crane-Russak Co.

Sokolow, Asa D. Political Theory of Arthur J. Penty. 1940. pap. text ed. 22.50x (ISBN 0-686-83707-X). Elliots Bks.

Sokolyszyn, Aleksander & Wertsman, Vladimir, eds. Ukrainians in Canada & the United States: A Guide to Information Sources. (Ethnic Studies Information Guide Ser.: Vol. 7). 375p. 1981. 42.00x (ISBN 0-8103-1494-0). Gale.

Sokya, Lester F. & Redmond, Geoffrey P., eds. Drug Metabolism in the Immature Human. 302p. 1981. text ed. 32.00 (ISBN 0-89004-600-X). Raven.

Sola, Pool Ithiel de see De Sola Pool, Ithiel.

Sola, Ralph De see De Sola, Ralph.

Sola Pinto, Vivian De see De Sola Pinto, Vivian.

Sola Pool, Ithiel de see De Sola Pool, Ithiel.

Solar Age Magazine, ed. The Solar Age Resource Book: A Complete Guidebook for the Consumer to Harnessing the Power of Solar Energy, in Depth & up-to-Date. LC 78-74580. (Illus.). 1979. pap. 7.95 (ISBN 0-89696-050-1). SolarVision.

Solar Age Magazine Editors, ed. Solar Age Catalog: A Guide to Solar Energy Knowledge & Materials. LC 77-79117. (Illus.). 1977. pap. 4.50 (ISBN 0-918984-00-9). SolarVision.

Solar, Edmundo Del see Del Solar, Edmundo.

Solar Energy Research Institute. Annual Review of Solar Energy (Nineteen Seventy-Eight) 166p. 1981. pap. 19.95x (ISBN 0-930978-77-3, V029). Solar Energy Info.

--Fermentation Guide for Common Grains: A Step-by-Step Procedure for Small-Scale Ethanol Fuel Production. 1982. pap. 9.95 o.p. (ISBN 0-89934-157-8). Solar Energy Info.

--A New Prosperity: Building a Sustainable Energy Future (Solar Conservation Study) LC 81-6089. 1981. 19.95x (ISBN 0-931790-53-0). Brick Hse Pub.

--Performance Criteria for Photovoltaic Energy Systems: Performance Criteria. 228p. 1981. pap. 29.50x (ISBN 0-89934-150-0, P0-43). Solar Energy Info.

Solar Energy Research Institute, jt. auth. see Masterson, Keith.

Solar Energy Research Int., jt. auth. see Short, Walter.

Solberg, Carl. The Humphrey Story: A Comprehensive, Independent Biography of Hubert H. Humphrey. 1983. write for info (ISBN 0-393-01645-5). Norton.

Solberg, Harry L., et al. Thermal Engineering. LC 60-11730. 1960. text ed. 32.95 (ISBN 0-471-81147-5). Wiley.

Solberg, Winton U., ed. The Federal Convention & the Formation of the Union of the American States. LC 58-9959. (YA) (gr. 9 up). 1958. pap. 12.95 o.p. (ISBN 0-672-60024-2, AHS19). Bobbs.

Solbrig, Otto T., ed. Demography & Evolution in Plant Populations. (Botanical Monographs Ser.: Vol. 15). 1980. monograph 40.00x (ISBN 0-520-03931-9). U of Cal Pr.

Soldan, Kurt, ed. see Mozart, Wolfgang A.

Soldano, B. A. Mass, Measurement & Motion Sequel Two: A New Look at Maxwell's Equations & the Permittivity of Free Space. Brantley, William H., ed. (Illus.). 50p. (Orig.). 1982. pap. 7.00x (ISBN 0-943410-00-2). Grenridge Pub.

Soldo, Beth J., jt. auth. see Struyk, Raymond J.

Sole, Carlos, jt. auth. see Sole, Yolanda.

Sole, S. De see De Sole, S.

Sole, Yolanda & Sole, Carlos. Modern Spanish Syntax. 1976. text ed. 21.95 (ISBN 0-669-00193-7). Heath.

Solecki, Rose L. An Early Village Site at Zawi Chemi Shanidar. LC 80-54671. (Bibliotheca Mesopotamica: Vol. 13). (Illus.). xi, 102p. 1981. 21.50x (ISBN 0-89003-067-7); pap. 16.50x (ISBN 0-89003-068-5). Undena Pubns.

Soled, Alex J. Federal Income of Estates & Beneficiaries. LC 82-73532. 915p. (Orig.). 1982. compression binder 79.00 (ISBN 0-940024-01-2). Chancery Pubs.

Soleillant, Claude. Activities & Projects: India in Color. LC 77-79499. (Activities & Projects Ser.). (Illus.). (gr. 2 up). 1977. 10.95 (ISBN 0-8069-4550-8); PLB 13.29 (ISBN 0-8069-4551-6). Sterling.

--Japan: Activities & Projects in Color. LC 79-91394. (Illus.). 96p. (gr. 2-12). 1980. 10.95 (ISBN 0-8069-4556-7); PLB 13.29 (ISBN 0-8069-4557-5). Sterling.

--Mexico: Activities & Projects in Color. LC 77-81955. (Activities & Projects Ser.). (Illus.). 96p. (English.). (gr. 3 up). 1978. 10.95 (ISBN 0-8069-4552-4); PLB 13.29 (ISBN 0-8069-4553-2). Sterling.

Soleillant, Claude, jt. auth. see Farnay, Josie.

Sole-Levis, Amadey. Spanish Pastoral Novel. (World Authors Ser.). 13.95 (ISBN 0-8057-6417-8, Twayne). G K Hall.

Solem, Alan. The Shell Makers: Introducing Mollusks. LC 73-20315. 304p. 1974. 17.95 o.p. (ISBN 0-471-81210-2, Pub. by Wiley-Interscience). Wiley.

Solensten, John. Good Thunder: Associated Writing Programs Novel Ser. 172p. 1983. 10.95 (ISBN 0-87395-712-1). State U NY Pr.

--The Heron Dancer. LC 81-83878. (Minnesota Voices Project Ser.: No. 3). (Illus.). 155p. 1981. pap. 5.00 (ISBN 0-89823-026-8). New Rivers Pr.

Solheim, Bjarte G., jt. ed. see Ferrone, Soldano.

Solheim, Wilhelm G., ed. Anthropology at the Eighth Pacific Science Congress. (Social Science & Linguistics Institute Special Publications). (Illus.). 285p. 1968. pap. 6.00x o.p. (ISBN 0-8248-0243-8). UH Pr.

Solian, Alexandru. Theory of Modules. LC 76-47588. 1977. 55.50 o.p. (ISBN 0-471-99462-6, Pub. by Wiley-Interscience). Wiley.

Solinger, Dorothy J. Regional Government & Political Integration in Southwest China, 1949-1954: A Case Study. LC 75-22662. 1977. 40.00x (ISBN 0-520-03104-0). U of Cal Pr.

Solinus, C. Julius. The Excellent & Pleasant Work Collectanea Rerum Memorabilium of Caius Julius Solinus. LC 55-10771. Repr. of 1587 ed. 29.00x (ISBN 0-686-63879-4). Schol Facsimiles.

Solis, Raul F., I. Upper Tertiary & Quaternary Depositional Systems, Central Coastal Plain, Texas: Regional Geology of the Coastal Aquifer & Potential Liquid-Waste Repositories. (Report of Investigations Ser.: No. 108). (Illus.). 89p. 1982. 3.00 (ISBN 0-686-36992-0). U of Tex Econ Geology.

Sollacher, Hans. Stoppregeln. xv, 621p. (Ger.). 1982. write for info. P Lang Pubs.

Sollberger, A. Biological Reactors Caused by Electrical Currents & X-Rays. 1965. 66.00 (ISBN 0-444-40549-6). Elsevier.

Sollenberger, Harold M. Management Control of Information Systems Development. 204p. 17.95 (ISBN 0-86641-047-3, 7150). Natl Assn Accts.

Sollenberger, N. J., jt. auth. see Preston, Howard K.

Sollov, Jacques. Reborn Again in the Kingdom. LC 81-71382. (The Temple of Love Ser.). (Illus.). 128p. (Orig.). 1982. pap. 9.95 (ISBN 0-941804-04-6). White Eagle Pub.

Solly, Henry. Working Men's Social Clubs & Educational Institutes. LC 79-56943. (The English Working Class Ser.). 1980. lib. bdg. 22.00 o.s.i. (ISBN 0-8240-0124-9). Garland Pub.

Solman, Paul & Friedman, Thomas. Life & Death on the Corporate Battlefield. 1983. 13.95 (ISBN 0-671-25564-9). S&S.

Solmon, Lewis C. Macroeconomics. 3rd ed. LC 79-25516. 480p. 1980. pap. text ed. 16.95 (ISBN 0-201-07217-3); student guide avail. (ISBN 0-201-07220-3). A-W.

--Microeconomics. 3rd ed. LC 79-25515. 528p. 1980. pap. text ed. 16.95 (ISBN 0-201-07218-1); student guide avail. (ISBN 0-201-07221-1). A-W.

Solmon, Lewis C. & Gordon, Joanne J. The Characteristics & Needs of Adults in Postsecondary Education. 176p. 1981. 22.95x (ISBN 0-669-04361-3). Lexington Bks.

Solmon, Lewis C. & Taubman, Paul J., eds. Does College Matter: Some Evidence on the Impact of Higher Education. 1973. 17.50 o.s.i. (ISBN 0-12-655050-6). Acad Pr.

Solmon, Lewis C., et al. College As a Training Ground for Jobs. LC 77-2939. (Special Studies). 1977. text ed. 26.95 o.p. (ISBN 0-275-24450-4). Praeger.

--Underemployed Ph.D.'s. LC 80-8951. 368p. 1981. 34.95x (ISBN 0-669-04482-2). Lexington Bks.

Solnick, Bruce B. West Indies & Central America. (Orig.). 1970. pap. text ed. 3.95 (ISBN 0-685-04148-4). Phila Bk Co.

Solnit, Albert, jt. auth. see Jones, Warren W.

Solo, Dan X. Art Deco Display Alphabets: 100 Complete Fonts. (Pictural Archive Ser.). (Illus.). 104p. (Orig.). 1982. pap. 4.00 (ISBN 0-486-24372-9). Dover.

--Art Nouveau Display Alphabets: One Hundred Complete Fonts. LC 76-18408. (Pictorial Archives Ser.). (Illus.). (Orig.). 1976. pap. 4.00 (ISBN 0-486-23386-3). Dover.

--Art Nouveau Typographic Ornaments. (Pictorial Archives Ser.). (Illus.). 100p. (Orig.). 1982. pap. 4.00 (ISBN 0-486-24366-4). Dover.

Solo, Len. Alternative, Innovative & Traditional Schools: Some Personal Views. LC 80-7950. 232p. 1980. lib. bdg. 20.25 (ISBN 0-8191-1087-6); pap. text ed. 10.00 o.p. (ISBN 0-8191-1088-4). U Pr of Amer.

Soloff, A., et al. Torataynu. (Sacred Hebrew Ser.). (Illus.). 168p. (gr. 2-8). 1981. pap. text ed. 4.95 (ISBN 0-86628-026-X). Ridgefield Pub.

Soloff, Mordecai, et al. Jewish Life. (Sacred Hebrew Ser.). (Illus.). 112p. (Orig.). 1980. pap. 3.95 (ISBN 0-86628-000-6). Ridgefield Pub.

Sologub, Feodor. The White Dog. Goldberg, Isaac, ed. Cournos, John, tr. (International Pocket Library). pap. 2.00 o.s.i. (ISBN 0-686-77249-0). Branden.

Sologub, Fyodor. The Petty Demon. Cioran, Sam, tr. from Rus. 400p. 1983. 25.00 (ISBN 0-88233-807-2); pap. 5.95 (ISBN 0-88233-808-0). Ardis Pubs.

Sologub, Fyodor see Goldberg, Isaac.

Soloman, Eldra P. & Davis, P. William. Understanding Human Anatomy & Physiology. (Illus.). 1978. text ed. 29.95 (ISBN 0-07-059645-X, C); instructor's manual 10.95 (ISBN 0-07-059646-8); lab manual 14.95 (ISBN 0-07-059649-2); study guide 11.95 (ISBN 0-07-059647-6). McGraw.

Soloman, Martin B., jt. auth. see Kennedy, Michael.

Solomon. Arise, My Love. LC 75-4077. (Illus.). 56p. (From King James Version - Song of Songs). 1975. 15.95 o.p. (ISBN 0-570-03253-9, 15-2161); pap. 6.95 o.p. (ISBN 0-570-03712-3, 12-2614). Concordia.

Solomon, Arthur, et al. Interpersonal Communication: A Cross-Disciplinary Approach. 120p. 1970. 12.75x o.p. (ISBN 0-398-01810-3). C C Thomas.

Solomon, Arthur P. Housing the Urban Poor: A Critical Analysis of Federal Housing Policy. (Joint Center for Urban Studies). 300p. 1974. 20.00x (ISBN 0-262-19120-2); pap. 4.95x (ISBN 0-262-69058-6). MIT Pr.

Solomon, Arthur P., ed. The Prospective City: Economic, Population, Energy, & Environmental Developments Shaping Our Cities & Suburbs. (MIT-Harvard Joint Center for Urban Studies). 1980. text ed. 32.50x (ISBN 0-262-19182-2); pap. 9.95x (ISBN 0-262-69071-3). MIT Pr.

Solomon, Barbara. Experience of American Women: Thirty Stories. 1978. pap. 3.95 (ISBN 0-451-62115-8, ME2115, Ment). NAL.

Solomon, Barbara, ed. The Awakening & Selected Stories of Kate Chopin. (Orig.). 1976. pap. 2.95 (ISBN 0-451-51749-0, CE1749, Sig Classics). NAL.

Solomon, Barbara P. Short Flights. 348p. 1983. 18.75 (ISBN 0-670-33053-1). Viking Pr.

Solomon, Bernard, jt. auth. see Howe, Leland W.

Solomon, Brad. Jake & Katie. 304p. 1980. pap. 2.50 o.p. (ISBN 0-380-52969-6, 52969). Avon.

Solomon, Bruce, jt. auth. see Olsen, Michael.

Solomon, C. The Complete Curry Cookbook. 13.95 (ISBN 0-07-059639-5). McGraw.

Solomon, C. R. Hacia la Felicidad: Como Vivir una Vida Victoriosa y Practicar la Terapia Espiritual. Repr. of 1979 ed. 3.25 (ISBN 0-311-42060-5). Casa Bautista.

Solomon, Charles. Handbook to Happiness. 1975. pap. 4.95 (ISBN 0-8423-1280-3). Tyndale.

Solomon, Charles R. The Rejection Syndrome. 144p. 1982. pap. 4.95 (ISBN 0-8423-5417-4). Tyndale.

Solomon, Charmaine. Chinese Diet Cookbook. LC 79-19679. (Illus.). 1980. pap. 9.95 o.p. (ISBN 0-07-059637-9). McGraw.

Solomon, D. H. & Hawthorne, D. G. Chemistry of Pigments & Fillers. 392p. 1983. 50.00 (ISBN 0-471-81223-4, Pub. by Wiley-Interscience). Wiley.

Solomon, Diane S. Teaching Riding: Step-by-Step Schooling for Horse & Rider. LC 81-40281. (Illus.). 321p. 1982. 17.95 (ISBN 0-8061-1580-7). U of Okla Pr.

Solomon, E. P., jt. auth. see Davis, P. W.

Solomon, Evelyn. The Big Flood. Sparks, Judith, ed. (A Happy Day Book). (Illus.). 24p. (gr. k-2). 1980. 1.29 (ISBN 0-87239-407-7, 3639). Standard Pub.

Solomon, Ezra & Pringle, John J. An Introduction to Financial Management. 2nd ed. 1980. text ed. 25.50x (ISBN 0-673-16172-2); o.p. inst. manual by john j. pringle (ISBN 0-8302-4753-X); study guide by john a. holloran & howard p. lanser 10.95x (ISBN 0-673-16173-0). Scott F.

Solomon, Gail E. & Kutt, Henn, eds. Epilepsy: A Clinical Textbook. (Contemporary Neurology Ser.: No. 25). (Illus.). 350p. 1983. cancelled (ISBN 0-8036-7972-6). Davis Co.

Solomon, Harry M. Sir Richard Blackmore. (English Authors Ser.). 1980. lib. bdg. 14.95 (ISBN 0-8057-6782-7, Twayne). G K Hall.

Solomon, Herbert. Geometric Probability. (CBMS-NSF Regional Conference Ser.: Vol. 28). (Illus.). vi, 174p. (Orig.). 1978. pap. text ed. 19.00 (ISBN 0-89871-025-1). Soc Indus-Appl Math.

Solomon, J. B., ed. Developmental & Comparative Immunology I: First Congress of Developmental & Comparative Immunology, 27 July-1 August 1980, Aberdeen. (Illus.). 580p. 1981. 110.00 (ISBN 0-08-025922-7). Pergamon.

Solomon, J. B. & Horton, J. D., eds. Developmental Immunobiology: Proceedings of the Symposia on Developmental Immunobiology, Aberdeen, U.K., Sept. 1977. 1978. 95.75 (ISBN 0-444-80034-4, Biomedical Pr). Elsevier.

Solomon, Karey, jt. auth. see Fritchman, June.

Solomon, Kenneth & Levy, Norman B., eds. Men in Transition: Theory & Therapy. 500p. 1982. 39.50x (ISBN 0-306-40976-3, Plenum Pr). Plenum Pub.

Solomon, Lanny M., et al. Accounting Principles. 1152p. 1983. scp 26.95 (ISBN 0-06-046348-1, HarpC); Vol. I. instr's. solutions manual avail. (ISBN 0-06-366392-9); test bank (Walther) avail. (ISBN 0-06-366393-7); transparencies avail. (ISBN 0-06-366394-5); study guide 8.50 (ISBN 0-06-046881-5); Vol. I. scp work papers 8.50 (ISBN 0-06-046354-6); Vol. II. scp work papers 8.50 (ISBN 0-06-046356-2); Vol. I. scp practice set 5.95 (ISBN 0-06-046353-8); Vol. II. practice set avail. (ISBN 0-06-046355-4). Har-Row.

Solomon, Larry, ed. Complete Book of Modern Fly Fishing. (Illus.). 288p. 1979. pap. 8.95 (ISBN 0-695-81312-9). DBI.

--The Complete Book of Modern Fly Fishing. (Illus.). 288p. 1979. pap. 7.95 o.s.i. (ISBN 0-695-81312-9). Follett.

Solomon, Lawrence & Spector, Leo. Chemistry Achievement Test. 2d ed. LC 76-47486. 1978. pap. 3.95 o.p. (ISBN 0-668-04101-3). Arco.

Solomon, Lewis C. Economics. LC 79-25514. 832p. 1980. text ed. 23.95 (ISBN 0-201-07635-7); avail. student guide 8.95 (ISBN 0-201-07637-3); tchr's manual 3.00 (ISBN 0-201-07636-5); test items 10.95 (ISBN 0-201-07638-1); transparency 12.95 (ISBN 0-201-07639-X). A-W.

Solomon, Lewis D. & Stevenson, Russell, Jr. Corporations Law & Policies. LC 82-11128. (American Casebook Ser.). 1161p. 1982. text ed. 24.95 (ISBN 0-314-65583-2); tchrs' manual avail. (ISBN 0-314-71638-6). West Pub.

Solomon, Linda L., jt. auth. see Solomon, Richard.

Solomon, Martin B., jt. auth. see Kennedy, Michael.

Solomon, Miriam L., ed. see Art Directors Club of New York.

Solomon, Morton B., et al. Main Hurdman & Cranston Guide to Preparing Financial Reports, 1981. LC 81-2454. 290p. 1981. 80.00x (ISBN 0-471-09104-9, Pub. by Wiley-Interscience). Wiley.

Solomon, Nathan A., ed. Nuclear Medicine. 2nd. ed. (Medical Examination Review Bk. Ser.: Vol. 25). 1977. spiral bdg. 23.00 (ISBN 0-87488-133-1). Med Exam.

Solomon, Neil. Dr. Solomon's High Health Diet & Exercise Plan: How to Make Cholesterol Work for You. 1980. 9.95 (ISBN 0-399-12450-0). Putnam Pub Group.

--Stop Smoking, Lose Weight. 320p. 1981. 10.95 (ISBN 0-399-12600-7). Putnam Pub Group.

Solomon, Neil & Harrison, Evalee. Doctor Solomon's Proven Master Plan for Total Body Fitness & Maintenance. LC 75-43745. (Illus.). 1976. 7.95 (ISBN 0-399-11591-9). Putnam Pub Group.

Solomon, Richard & Solomon, Linda L. Residential Home Management: A Handbook for Managers of Community-Living Facilities. LC 81-6554. 144p. 1982. 19.95x (ISBN 0-89885-037-1). Human Sci Pr.

Solomon, Richard H. Mao's Revolution & the Chinese Political Culture. (Center for Chinese Studies, Univ. of Michigan). 1971. 40.00x (ISBN 0-520-01806-0); pap. 5.95 (ISBN 0-520-02250-5, CAL246). U of Cal Pr.

Solomon, Robert. From Rationalism to Existentialism: The Existentialist & Their Nineteenth Century Backgrounds, 1972. 1978. pap. text ed. 9.95x (ISBN 0-391-00850-1). Humanities.

--The International Monetary System: 1945-1976: an Insiders View. LC 76-10094. 1977. 17.50i o.p. (ISBN 0-06-013898-X, HarpT). Har-Row.

Solomon, Robert C. The Big Questions: A Short Introduction to Philosophy. 352p. (Orig.). 1982. pap. text ed. 10.95 (ISBN 0-15-505410-4, HC). HarBraceJ.

--Existentialism. 1974. pap. text ed. 7.00 (ISBN 0-394-31704-1). Random.

--Existentialism. 1974. pap. 5.95 (ISBN 0-686-38912-3, Mod LibC). Modern Lib.

--History & Human Nature: A Philosophical Review of European History & Culture, 1750-1850. LC 79-1846. (Illus.). 1979. 18.95 o.p. (ISBN 0-15-140547-6). HarBraceJ.

--Introducing Philosophy: Problems & Perspectives. 2nd ed. 560p. 1981. pap. text ed. 13.95 (ISBN 0-15-541559-X, HC). HarBraceJ.

--Introducing the German Idealists. (Philosophical Dialogue Ser.). 80p. 1981. lib. bdg. 9.50 (ISBN 0-915145-02-2); pap. text ed. 2.95 (ISBN 0-915145-03-0). Hackett Pub.

--The Passions. LC 74-33691. 1977. pap. 3.95 o.p. (ISBN 0-385-12220-9, Anch). Doubleday.

--The Passions. xxv, 448p. 1983. text ed. 22.95x (ISBN 0-268-01551-1); pap. text ed. 9.95x (ISBN 0-268-01552-X). U of Notre Dame Pr.

Solomon, Robert C., ed. Phenomenology & Existentialism. LC 79-66420. 1979. pap. text ed. 11.00 (ISBN 0-8191-0826-X). U Pr of Amer.

Solomon, Ruth F. The Eagle & the Dove. 512p. 1980. pap. 2.75 o.s.i. (ISBN 0-515-05248-5). Jove Pubns.

Solomon, Sheila, jt. auth. see Cassin, Barbara.

Solomon, Shirl. Knowing Your Child Through His Handwriting & Drawing. (Illus.). 1978. 8.95 o.p. (ISBN 0-517-53287-5). Crown.

Solomon, Stanley J. Beyond Formula: American Film Genres. (Illus., Orig.). 1976. pap. text ed. 14.95 (ISBN 0-15-505400-7, HC). HarBraceJ.

Solomon, Susan G. The Soviet Agrarian Debate: A Controversy in Social Science, 1923-1929. LC 77-21555. 309p. 1978. 32.00 (ISBN 0-89158-339-4). Westview.

Solomon, Susan G., jt. ed. see Lubrano, Linda L.

Solomons, T. W. Fundamentals of Organic Chemistry. LC 81-16021. 865p. 1982. text ed. 27.95 (ISBN 0-471-02980-7); 13.95 (ISBN 0-471-86182-0). Wiley.

Solomons, T. W. Graham. Organic Chemistry. 2nd ed. 1980. text ed. 34.50 (ISBN 0-471-04213-7); sol. manual 13.95 (ISBN 0-471-05770-3); 50.00 tests (ISBN 0-471-05137-3). Wiley.

Solotaroff, Lynn, tr. see Luria, A. R.

Solotaroff, Lynn, tr. see Tolstoy, Leo.

Solotaroff, Ted, ed. Many Windows: 23 Stories from American Review. 1982. pap. 7.64i (ISBN 0-06-090923-4, CN-923, HarpT). Har-Row.

Solotorovsky, Morris, jt. ed. see Lynn, Melvyn.

Soloukhin, Vladimir. Sentenced & Other Stories. Martin, D. W., tr. from Rus. 200p. Date not set. 20.00 (ISBN 0-88233-802-1); pap. 6.50 (ISBN 0-88233-803-X). Ardis Pubs.

Solov'Ev, Vladimir S. A Solovyov Anthology. Frank, S. L., ed. Duddington, Natalie, tr. LC 74-7614. 256p. 1974. Repr. of 1950 ed. lib. bdg. 17.50x (ISBN 0-8371-7592-5, SOSA). Greenwood.

Soloveytchik, George. Switzerland in Perspective. LC 82-11781. 306p. 1982. Repr. of 1954 ed. lib. bdg. 39.75x (ISBN 0-686-83187-X). Greenwood.

Soloviev, Vladimir. The Antichrist. 1982. pap. 5.50 (ISBN 0-86315-501-4). St George Bk Serv.

Solovyev, Vladimir. God, Man & the Church. Attwater, Donald, tr. from Rus. 192p. 1975. 10.95 (ISBN 0-227-67690-4). Attic Pr.

Solovyov, A. A., ed. Against Trotskyism. 406p. 1972. 4.10 (ISBN 0-8285-0391-5, Pub. by Progress Pubs USSR). Imported Pubns.

Solow, Daniel. How to Read & Do Proofs: An Introduction to Mathematical Thought Process. 172p. 1982. text ed. 9.95 (ISBN 0-471-86645-8). Wiley.

Solow, Robert & Brown, E. Carey, eds. Paul Samuelson & Modern Economic Theory. 350p. 1983. 27.00 (ISBN 0-07-059667-0, C). McGraw.

Solow, Robert M. Growth Theory: An Exposition. (Illus.). 1970. 6.95x (ISBN 0-19-501295-X). Oxford U Pr.

Solso, Robert L, ed. Information Processing & Cognition: The Loyola Symposium. LC 75-14324. 438p. 1975. 19.95x o.s.i. (ISBN 0-470-81230-3). Halsted Pr.

Solt, David L., jt. auth. see Naiman, Robert J.

Solt, J., jt. ed. see Striker, G.

Solt, Marilyn L., jt. auth. see Peterson, Linda K.

Solter, Davor, ed. see Symposium Held at the Roche Institute of Molecular Biology, Nutley, New Jersey, May, 1975.

Soltera, Maria. Lady's Ride Across Spanish Honduras. Stone, Doris, ed. LC 64-66325. (Latin American Gateway Ser.). (Illus.). 1964. Repr. of 1884 ed. 12.50 (ISBN 0-8130-0215-X). U Presses Fla.

Soltis, A. Pawn Structure Chess. 1976. 10.95 o.p. (ISBN 0-679-13050-0); pap. 5.95 o.p. (ISBN 0-679-14475-7). McKay.

Soltis, Jonas F., jt. ed. see Chazan, Barry I.

Soltow, Martha J. & Gravelle, Susan. Worker Benefits: Industrial Welfare in America 1900-1935. LC 82-25494. 242p. 1983. 16.50 (ISBN 0-8108-1614-8). Scarecrow.

Soltz, Vicki, jt. auth. see Dreikurs, Rudolf.

Soltzberg, Len, et al. BASIC & Chemistry. 1975. pap. text ed. 13.50 (ISBN 0-395-21720-2). HM.

Solum, Nora O., tr. see Rolvaag, O. E.

Solvay American Corporation, tr. see Lefevre, M. J.

Solvay Conference on Physics. Symmetry Properties of Nuclei. 372p. 1974. 94.00 (ISBN 0-677-14450-4). Gordon.

Solvit, Marie-Janine. Magnificent Macrame: 50 Projects You Can Create. LC 78-66295. (Illus.). 1979. 19.95 (ISBN 0-8069-5390-X); lib. bdg. 17.59 o.p. (ISBN 0-8069-5391-8). Sterling.

Solymar, Istvan, ed. Collections of the Hungarian National Gallery. Bodoczky, Caroline & Bodoczky, Istvan, trs. 1980. 15.95 (ISBN 0-89893-159-2). CDP.

Solymar, L. A Review of the Principles of Electrical & Electronic Engineering. Incl. Vol. 1. Principles of Heavy Current Engineering. LC 73-15220. 115p. 1974. pap. 9.95x (ISBN 0-412-11660-X); Vol. 2. From Circuits to Computers. LC 73-15221. 184p. 1974. pap. 9.95x (ISBN 0-412-11670-7); Vol. III. Modern Physical Electronics. LC 73-15223. 213p. 1975. pap. 11.95x (ISBN 0-412-11680-4); Vol. 4. Microwaves, Communications & Radar. LC 73-15224. 190p. 1975. pap. 11.95x (ISBN 0-412-11690-1). pap. (Pub. by Chapman & Hall England). Methuen Inc.

--Superconductive Tunnelling & Applications. 1972. 37.00x o.p. (ISBN 0-412-10210-2, Pub. by Chapman & Hall). Methuen Inc.

Solymosi, F. Structure & Stability of Salts of Halogen Oxyacids in the Solid Phase. LC 75-19287. 1977. 77.25 o.p. (ISBN 0-471-81275-7, Pub. by Wiley-Interscience). Wiley.

Solzhenitsyn, Aleksandr. Detente: Prospects for Democracy & Dictatorship. 2nd ed. 134p. 1980. text ed. 7.95 o. p. (ISBN 0-87855-352-5); pap. text ed. 8.95 (ISBN 0-87855-750-4). Transaction Bks.

Solzhenitsyn, Aleksandr I. East & West: The Nobel Lecture on Literature, a World Split Apart, Letter to the Soviet Leaders, & a BBC Interview with Aleksandr I. Solzhenitsyn. LC 79-5222. 1980. pap. 1.95i o.p. (ISBN 0-06-080508-0, P 508, PL). Har-Row.

--Gulag Archipelago, 3 vols. 1979. Boxed Set. pap. 7.50i o.p. (ISBN 0-06-080503-X, P 503, PL). Har-Row.

--The Gulag Archipelago, One, Pts. 1 & 2. Whitney, Thomas P., tr. from Rus. LC 73-22756. (Illus.). 1974. 20.14i (ISBN 0-06-013914-5, HarpT). Har-Row.

--The Gulag Archipelago, Three, Pts. 5, 6, & 7. Willetts, Harry, tr. from Rus. LC 73-22756. (Illus.). 1978. 20.14i (ISBN 0-06-013912-9, HarpT). Har-Row.

--The Gulag Archipelago, Two, Pts. 3 & 4. Whitney, Thomas P., tr. from Rus. LC 73-22756. (Illus.). 1975. 20.14i (ISBN 0-06-013911-0, HarpT). Har-Row.

--The Oak & the Calf: A Memoir. Willetts, Harry, tr. from Rus. LC 79-1685. 1980. 17.26i (ISBN 0-06-014014-3, HarpT). Har-Row.

--A World Split Apart. LC 78-19593. (Rus. & Eng.). 1979. 9.57i (ISBN 0-06-014007-0, HarpT). Har-Row.

Solzhenitsyn, Alexander. August Nineteen Fourteen. 736p. 1974. pap. 2.50 (ISBN 0-553-02997-5). Bantam.

--Nobel Lecture. bi-lingual ed. Reeve, F. D., tr. from Rus. 80p. 1973. 4.00 o.p. (ISBN 0-374-22300-9); pap. 1.50 (ISBN 0-374-51063-6). FS&G.

--Prisoners. Rapp, Helen & Thomas, Nancy, trs. from Rus. 1983. 12.50 (ISBN 0-374-23739-5). FS&G.

--Victory Celebrations. Rapp, Helen & Thomas, Nancy, trs. from Rus. 1983. 10.50 (ISBN 0-374-28356-7). FS&G.

Solzman, E. Twentieth Century Music: An Introduction. 2nd ed. 1974. pap. 13.95 (ISBN 0-13-935007-1). P-H.

Som, Ranjan K. Recall Lapse in Demographic Enquiries. 280p. 1973. lib. bdg. 18.95x (ISBN 0-210-98167-9). Asia.

Soma, H., ed. Morphological & Functional Aspects of Placental Dysfunction. (Contributions to Gynecology & Obstetrics: Vol. 9). (Illus.). viii, 180p. 1982. pap. 76.75 (ISBN 3-8055-3510-4). S Karger.

Soma, John T. The Computer Industry: An Economic-Legal Analysis of Its Technology & Growth. LC 76-2989. (Illus.). 240p. 1976. 22.95x o.p. (ISBN 0-669-00643-2). Lexington Bks.

Somasundaran, P., ed. Fine Particles Processing, 2 vols. LC 79-57344. (Illus.). 1865p. 1980. text ed. 50.00x (ISBN 0-89520-275-1). Soc Mining Eng.

Somasundaran, P. & Arbiter, N., eds. Beneficiation of Mineral Fines. LC 79-91945. (Illus.). 406p. (Orig.). 1979. pap. text ed. 24.00x (ISBN 0-89520-259-X). Soc Mining Eng.

Somba, J. N. Alipanda Upepo Na Kuvuna. (Swahili Literature). (Orig., Swahili.). 1978. pap. text ed. 2.95x o.p. (ISBN 0-686-74438-1, 00606). Heinemann Ed.

Sombart, Werner. New Social Philosophy. Geiser, Karl F., ed. LC 69-14085. 1969. Repr. of 1937 ed. lib. bdg. 17.00x (ISBN 0-8371-1042-4, SONP). Greenwood.

Somer, John & Klinkowitz, Jerome. Writing Under Fire. 1978. pap. 4.95 o.s.i. (ISBN 0-440-59345-X, Delta). Dell.

Somer, John, jt. ed. see Hoy, James F.

Somer, John, ed. see Vonnegut, Kurt.

Somerfield, Benita, ed. see Howett, Jerry.

Somers, Anne, ed. Promoting Health: Consumer Education & National Policy. LC 76-21444. 240p. 1977. 22.95 (ISBN 0-912862-25-4). Aspen Systems.

Somers, Anne R. & Somers, Herman M. Health & Health Care: Policies in Perspective. LC 77-76921. 528p. 1978. 42.50 (ISBN 0-912862-45-9); pap. text ed. 24.50 (ISBN 0-912862-49-1). Aspen Systems.

Somers, David J. Learning Functional Words & Phrases for Everyday Living. Bk. 1, 1977. pap. 2.75x (ISBN 0-88323-135-2, 223); Bk. 2, 1980. pap. 2.75x (ISBN 0-88323-159-X, 249). Richards Pub.

Somers, Gerald G., ed. see National Academy of Arbitrators-22nd Annual Meeting.

Somers, Gerald G., ed. see National Academy of Arbitrators-23nd Annual Meeting.

Somers, Gerald G., ed. see National Academy of Arbitrators-24th Annual Meeting.

Somers, Gerald G., ed. see National Academy of Arbitrators-25th Annual Meeting.

Somers, Gerald G., ed. see National Academy of Arbitrators-26th Meeting.

Somers, Gerald G., ed. see National Academy of Arbitrators-27th Annual Meeting.

Somers, Gerald G., ed. see National Academy of Arbitrators-28th Annual Meeting.

Somers, Gerald G., ed. see National Academy of Arbitrators-29th Annual Meeting.

Somers, Gerald G., ed. see National Academy of Arbitrators-30th Annual Meeting.

Somers, Herman M., jt. auth. see Somers, Anne R.

Somers, Jane. The Diary of a Good Neighbor. 1983. 12.95 (ISBN 0-394-52970-7). Knopf.

Somers, R., jt. ed. see Epstein, S.

Somers, R., ed. see Stout, R. D. & Doty, W. D.

Somerset, Anthony, jt. auth. see Marris, Peter.

Somerset, Douglas P. The Destructive Conception of God in Kant's "Philosophy of Man". (Illus.). 129p. 1982. 63.45 (ISBN 0-89266-355-3). Am Classical Coll Pr.

Somerset House Editorial Staff. Index to the Archives of George Allen & Co., 1893-1915. (The Archives of British Publishers on Microfilm). 126p. (Orig.). 1974. pap. 45.00x (ISBN 0-914146-11-4). Somerset Hse.

--Index to the Archives of Swan Sonnenschein & Co., 1878-1911. (The Archives of British Publishers on Microfilm). 132p. (Orig.). 1975. pap. 45.00x (ISBN 0-914146-12-2). Somerset Hse.

--Index to the Authors & Titles of Kegan Paul, Trench, Trubner & Henry S. King 1858-1912. (Archives of British Publishers on Microfilm). 130p. (Orig.). 1974. pap. 45.00x (ISBN 0-914146-13-0). Somerset Hse.

Somervell, D. C., ed. see Toynbee, Arnold J.

Somervell, David. A Companion to Palgrave's Golden Treasury. 147p. 1983. Repr. of 1917 ed. lib. bdg. 25.00 (ISBN 0-89984-611-4). Century Bookbindery.

Somervell, David C. English Thought in the Nineteenth Century. LC 77-21468. 1977. Repr. of 1962 ed. lib. bdg. 20.50x (ISBN 0-8371-9793-7, SOET). Greenwood.

Somerville, Christopher. Walking Old Railways. LC 78-74078. 1979. 17.50 (ISBN 0-7153-7681-0). David & Charles.

Somerville, John. The Peace Revolution: Ethos & Social Process. LC 74-5993. (Contributions in Philosophy: No. 7). 1975. lib. bdg. 25.00x (ISBN 0-8371-7532-1, SPR/). Greenwood.

--Philosophy of Marxism: An Exposition. 1967. pap. text ed. 3.95x (ISBN 0-394-30658-9). Phila Bk Co.

--Soviet Philosophy, a Study of Theory & Practice. LC 68-19296. (Illus.). 1968. Repr. of 1946 ed. lib. bdg. 16.00x (ISBN 0-8371-0234-0, SOSP). Greenwood.

Somerville, John & Parsons, Howard L. Dialogues on the Philosophy of Marxism: Proceedings of the Society for the Philosophical Study of Dialectical Materialism. LC 77-149963. (Contributions in Philosophy Ser.: No. 6). 1974. lib. bdg. 35.00x (ISBN 0-8371-6062-6, PAD/). Greenwood.

Somerville, Robert. Pope Alexander III & the Council of Tours (1163) A Study of Ecclesiastical Politics & Institutions in the Twelfth Century. (UCLA Center for Medieval & Renaissance Studies: Vol. 12). 1978. 21.50x (ISBN 0-520-03184-9). U of Cal Pr.

Somerville, Rose M. Introduction to Family Life & Sex Education. (Family & Consumer Sciences Ser). 432p. 1972. ref. ed. o.p. 18.95 (ISBN 0-13-483149-7); pap. text ed. 14.95 op (ISBN 0-13-483131-4). P-H.

Somerville, Rose M., ed. Intimate Relationships: Marriage, Family & Lifestyles Through Literature. (Family & Consumer Science Ser.). (Illus.). 480p. 1975. ref. ed. o.p. 16.95 (ISBN 0-13-476861-2); pap. 15.95 (ISBN 0-13-476879-5). P-H.

Somjee, A. H. Democratic Processes in a Developing Society. LC 79-4035. 1979. 22.50 (ISBN 0-312-19373-4). St Martin.

--Political Capacity in Developing Societies. 1982. 20.00x (ISBN 0-312-62145-0). St Martin.

Somjen, George G. Neurophysiology: The Essentials. 400p. 1983. text ed. price not set (ISBN 0-683-07856-9). Williams & Wilkins.

Somma, Antonio. Ballo in Maschera. Dent, E. J., ed. 1952. 3.00 o.p. (ISBN 0-19-313313-X). Oxford U Pr.

Sommar, H. G. A Brief Guide to Sources of Fiber & Textile Information. 15.00 o.p. (ISBN 0-87245-606-4). Textile Bk.

Sommer, Alfred. Epidemiology & Statistics for the Ophthalmologist. (Illus.). 1980. pap. text ed. 14.95x (ISBN 0-19-502656-X). Oxford U Pr.

Sommer, Armand & Kedzie, Daniel P. Your Future in Insurance. LC 70-114117. (Career Guidance Ser). 1971. pap. 4.50 (ISBN 0-668-02249-3). Arco.

Sommer, Barbara B. Puberty & Adolescence. (Illus.). 1978. text ed. 9.95x o.p. (ISBN 0-19-502376-5); pap. text ed. 6.95x (ISBN 0-19-502377-3). Oxford U Pr.

Sommer, Barbara B., jt. auth. see Sommer, Robert.

Sommer, Bobbe L. Never Ask a Cactus for a Helping Hand! Today is my Time. 80p. 1982. pap. text ed. 3.50 (ISBN 0-8403-2710-2). Kendall-Hunt.

Sommer, Carl. Schools in Crisis: Training for Success or Failure? (Orig.). 1983. write for info. Cahill Pub Co.

Sommer, Carol, jt. ed. see Wilgus, D. K.

Sommer, Elyse. Career Opportunities in Crafts: The First Complete Guide for Success as a Crafts Professional. 1977. 10.95 (ISBN 0-517-52873-8); pap. 6.95 (ISBN 0-517-52874-6). Crown.

--Rock & Stone Craft. (Arts & Crafts Ser.). (Illus.). 96p. 1973. 5.95 o.p. (ISBN 0-517-50353-0). Crown.

--Textile Collector's Guide. (Illus.). 1978. pap. 5.95 o.p. (ISBN 0-671-18093-2). Monarch Pr.

Sommer, Elyse & Sommer, Mike. Creating with Driftwood & Weathered Wood. (Arts & Crafts Ser.). (Illus.). 96p. 1974. 5.95 o.p. (ISBN 0-517-51572-5). Crown.

--Wearable Crafts. 1976. o. p. 10.95 o.p. (ISBN 0-517-52395-7); pap. 5.95 o.p. (ISBN 0-517-52518-6). Crown.

Sommer, Mike, jt. auth. see Sommer, Elyse.

Sommer, Peter, jt. auth. see Spigai, Frances.

Sommer, Robert. The End of Imprisonment. LC 75-38097. 1976. 15.95x (ISBN 0-19-502045-6). Oxford U Pr.

--The End of Imprisonment. (Reconstruction of Society Ser.). 1976. pap. text ed. 5.95x (ISBN 0-19-502046-4). Oxford U Pr.

--The Minds Eye. 1978. pap. 4.50 o.s.i. (ISBN 0-440-55610-4, Delta). Dell.

Sommer, Robert & Sommer, Barbara B. A Practical Guide to Behavioral Research. (Illus.). 272p. 1980. text ed. 15.95x o.p. (ISBN 0-19-502691-8); pap. text ed. 11.95x (ISBN 0-19-502692-6). Oxford U Pr.

Sommer, Scott. Last Resort. 1982. 12.50 (ISBN 0-394-52290-7). Random.

Sommerfeld, Arnold. Atombau und Spektrallinien, 2 Vols. 1951. Set. 95.00 o.p. (ISBN 0-8044-4886-8); Vol. 1. 35.00 o.p. (ISBN 0-8044-4887-6); Vol. 2. 40.00 o.p. (ISBN 0-8044-4888-4). Ungar.

--Lectures on Theoretical Physics. Incl. Vol. 1. Mechanics. 1952. text ed. 24.00 (ISBN 0-12-654668-1); pap. 15.25 (ISBN 0-12-654670-3); Vol. 2. Mechanics of Deformable Bodies. 1950. text ed. 24.00 (ISBN 0-12-654650-9); pap. text ed. 15.25 (ISBN 0-12-654652-5); Vol. 3. Electrodynamics. 1952. text ed. 24.00 (ISBN 0-12-654662-2); pap. 15.25 (ISBN 0-12-654664-9); Vol. 4. Optics. 1954. text ed. 24.00 (ISBN 0-12-654674-6); pap. 15.25 (ISBN 0-12-654676-2); Vol. 5. Thermodynamics & Statistical Mechanics. 1956. text ed. 24.00 (ISBN 0-12-654680-0); pap. 15.25 (ISBN 0-12-654682-7); Vol. 6. Partial Differential Equations in Physics. 1949. 24.00 (ISBN 0-12-654656-8); pap. text ed. 15.25 (ISBN 0-12-654658-4). pap. Acad Pr.

Sommerfeld, Ray M. & Anderson, Hershel M. An Introduction to Taxation Advanced Topics. 583p. 1982. text ed. 28.95 (ISBN 0-15-546321-7, HC). HarBraceJ.

Sommerfeld, Ray M., et al. An Introduction to Taxation: Advanced Topics. (Illus.). 592p. 1980. text ed. 28.95 (ISBN 0-15-546315-2, HC); solutions manual avail. (ISBN 0-15-546316-0). HarBraceJ.

--Introduction to Taxation 1983 Edition. 1983. text ed. 24.95 (ISBN 0-15-546319-5, HC); instructors' manual avail. (ISBN 0-15-546308-X); packet of tax forms avail. (ISBN 0-685-83244-9); study guide avail. (ISBN 0-15-546320-9). HarBraceJ.

Sommerfeldt, John R., ed. ABBA: Guides to Wholeness & Holiness East & West. (Cistercian Studies: No. 38). 1982. 22.95 (ISBN 0-87907-838-3). Cistercian Pubns.

Sommerfield, Sylvie F. Kristen's Passion. 1983. pap. 3.75 (ISBN 0-8217-1169-5). Zebra.

--Savage Rapture. 1982. pap. 3.50 (ISBN 0-8217-1085-0). Zebra.

Sommerhoff, Gerd. Logic of the Living Brain. LC 73-8198. 413p. 1974. 51.95 (ISBN 0-471-81305-2, Pub. by Wiley-Interscience). Wiley.

Sommerman, Susan, ed. see Waltz, Julie.

Sommernitz, Harry, tr. see Sedivec, V. & Flek, J.

Sommers, Beverly. City Life, City Love. (Harlequin American Romance (Canada) Ser.). 256p. 1983. pap. 2.25 (ISBN 0-373-16011-9). Harlequin Bks.

Sommers, Nancy, ed. see Kane, Thomas S.

Sommers, P. D., jt. ed. see Lerner, D. E.

Sommers, Richard J. & Vandiver, Frank E. Richmond Redeemed: The Seige at Petersburg. LC 79-7844. (Illus.). 696p. 1981. 22.50 o.p. (ISBN 0-385-15626-X). Doubleday.

Sommers, Ronald K. Articulation Disorders. 240p. 1983. 20.95 (ISBN 0-13-049080-6). P-H.

Sommers, Sheldon C., jt. auth. see Parsons, Langdon.

Sommers, Sheldon C., jt. auth. see Rotterdam, Heidrun Z.

Sommers, Sheldon C., jt. ed. see Barber, Hugh R. K.

Sommers, Susan. Beauty after Forty: How to put Time on your Side. (Illus.). 288p. 1983. 19.95 (ISBN 0-385-27229-4). Dial.

Sommerville, Duncan Y. Bibliography of Non-Euclidean Geometry. 2nd ed. LC 72-113150. 1960. text ed. 22.50 (ISBN 0-8284-0175-6). Chelsea Pub.

Sommerville, Paul. Dictionary of Geotechnics. 1983. text ed. 49.95 (ISBN 0-408-00437-1). Butterworth.

Somogyi, Ede see Feher, Matyas & Erdy, Miklos.

Somogyi, J. C. World-Wide Problems of Nutrition Research & Nutrition Education. (Bibliotheca Nutritio et Dieta: No. 32). (Illus.). xvi, 76p. 1983. pap. 45.00 (ISBN 3-8055-3586-4). S Karger.

Somogyi, J. C., ed. Nutrition in Early Childhood & Its Effects in Later Life. (Bibliotheca Nutritio et Dieta: No. 31). (Illus.). viii, 144p. 1982. pap. 63.50 (ISBN 3-8055-3527-9). S Karger.

Somogyi, J. C. & Fidanza, F., eds. Nutritional Problems of the Elderly. (Bibliotecha Nutritio et Dieta Ser.: No. 33). (Illus.). viii, 190p. 1983. pap. 78.00 (ISBN 3-8055-3700-X). S Karger.

Somorjai, G. A. The Structure & Chemistry of Solid Surfaces. LC 71-90401. 1576p. 1969. 62.00 (ISBN 0-471-81320-6, Pub. by Wiley). Krieger.

Somorjai, G. A., jt. ed. see Templeton, David H.

Sondak, N. E., jt. auth. see Scott, R. C.

Sonde, B. S. Introduction to System Design Using Integrated Circuits. LC 80-26988. 261p. 1981. 34.95x (ISBN 0-470-27110-8). Halsted Pr.

Sonde, Susan. Inland Is Parenthetical. LC 79-9105. pap. 3.75 (ISBN 0-931848-28-8). Dryad Pr.

Sonder, Otto W., jt. auth. see Harvey, William H.

Sonderman, Judith & Zwitman, Daniel. More Programmed Articulation Skills: Carryover Stories. (Illus.). 1979. pap. text ed. 16.50 (ISBN 0-88450-705-X, 3107-B). Communication Skill.

Sondermann, Fred, et al. The Theory & Practice of International Relationships. 5th ed. (Illus.). 1979. pap. text ed. 14.95 (ISBN 0-13-914507-9). P-H.

Sondheim, Alan, ed. Individuals: Post-Movement Art. 1977. pap. 7.95 o.p. (ISBN 0-525-47428-5). Dutton.

Sondheim, Stephen & Hugh, Wheeler. Sweeney Todd, the Demon Barber of Fleet Street. LC 79-18468. (Illus.). 1979. 7.95 (ISBN 0-396-07776-5). Dodd.

Sondheim, Stephen, jt. auth. see Goldman, James.

Sondheim, Stephen, et al. Pacific Overtures. LC 76-55020. 1977. 6.95 o.p. (ISBN 0-396-07414-6). Dodd.

Sondheimer, Ernst & Rogerson, Alan. Numbers & Infinity: An Historical Account of Mathematical Concepts. LC 81-7660. 150p. 1981. 17.95 (ISBN 0-521-24091-3); pap. 7.95 (ISBN 0-521-28433-3). Cambridge U Pr.

Sondheimer, Janet, tr. see Bloch, Marc.

Soneblum, Sidney. The Energy Connections: Between Energy & the Economy. LC 78-15374. 288p. 1978. prof ref 25.00x (ISBN 0-88410-076-6). Ballinger Pub.

Sonenblum, Sidney, et al. How Cities Provide Services: An Evaluation of Alternative Delivery Structures. LC 77-2313. 296p. 1977. prof ref 22.50x (ISBN 0-88410-439-7). Ballinger Pub.

Sonfist, Alan. Art in the Land: A Critical Anthology. (Illus.). 240p. Date not set. pap. 10.75 (ISBN 0-525-47702-0, 01044-310). Dutton.

Song, Cathy. Picture Bride. LC 82-48910. (Younger Poets Ser.: No. 78). 80p. 1983. text ed. 10.95x (ISBN 0-300-02959-4); pap. text ed. 4.95x (ISBN 0-300-02969-1). Yale U Pr.

Songes, Chevalier de la Marmotte. Au Palais De Morphee. (Fr.). 1977. Repr. of 1745 ed. lib. bdg. 20.50x o.p. (ISBN 0-8287-0783-9). Clearwater Pub.

Songying, Lin. Hatching a Cuckoo Bird. (Illus.). 24p. (Orig.). (ps). 1982. pap. 1.00 (ISBN 0-8351-1023-0). China Bks.

Soni, Atmaram H. Mechanism Synthesis & Analysis. LC 81-11723. 512p. 1981. Repr. of 1974 ed. 25.00 (ISBN 0-89874-380-X). Krieger.

--Mechanism Synthesis & Analysis. (Illus.). 550p. 1974. text ed. 19.95 o.p. (ISBN 0-07-059640-9, C); test manual avail. o.p. (ISBN 0-07-059641-7). McGraw.

Sonka, A. Skillful Reading: A Text & Workbook for Students of English as a Second Language. 1981. pap. 11.95 (ISBN 0-13-812404-3). P-H.

Sonka, S. T. Computers in Farming: Selection & Use. 356p. 1983. 19.95 (ISBN 0-07-059653-0). McGraw.

Sonkin, Daniel J. & Durphy, Michael. Learning to Live Without Violence: A Handbook for Men. 140p. 1982. pap. 10.00 (ISBN 0-912078-72-3). Volcano Pr.

Sonne, Conway B. Saints on the Seas: A Maritime History of Mormon Migration, 1830-1890. (Publications in the American West: Vol. 17). (Illus.). 240p. 1983. 20.00 (ISBN 0-87480-221-0). U of Utah Pr.

Sonneborn, Ruth A. Question & Answer Book of Everyday Science. (Illus.). (gr. k-3). 1961. 4.95 o.p. (ISBN 0-394-80781-2, BYR); PLB 4.99 o.p. (ISBN 0-394-90781-7). Random.

--Question & Answer Book of Space. (Illus.). (gr. k-3). 1965. 5.95 (ISBN 0-394-84053-4, BYR); PLB 6.99 (ISBN 0-394-94053-9). Random.

Sonnedecker, Glenn. Kremers & Urdang's History of Pharmacy. 4th ed. LC 75-40104. (Illus.). 1976. text ed. 30.00 o.p. (ISBN 0-397-52074-3, Lippincott Medical). Lippincott.

Sonnedecker, Glenn, ed. Early Years of Federal Food & Drug Control. (New Ser.: No. 7). (Orig.). 1982. pap. 4.90 (ISBN 0-931292-11-5). Am Inst Hist Pharm.

Sonnenberg, G. J. Radar & Electronic Navigation. 5th ed. LC 77-30476. 1978. 49.95 (ISBN 0-408-00272-7). Butterworth.

Sonnenblick, Carol, jt. auth. see Friedman, Judith.

Sonnenburg, David & Birnbaum, Michael. Understanding Pacemakers. (Illus.). 192p. 1982. pap. 12.95 (ISBN 0-686-83697-9, ScribT). Scribner.

Sonnenfeld, Albert. Crossroads: Essays on the Catholic Novelists. 15.00. French Lit.

Sonnenfeld, Peter, ed. Tethys: The Ancestral Mediterranean. LC 80-13974. (Benchmark Papers in Geology Ser.: Vol. 53). 352p. 1981. 40.00 (ISBN 0-87933-355-3). Hutchinson Ross.

Sonnenfield, Marion, ed. The World of Yesterday's Humanist Today: Proceedings of the 1981 Stefan Zweig Symposium. 384p. 1983. 50.00x (ISBN 0-87395-599-4). State U NY Pr.

Sonnenschein, William S. Best Books, 6 Vols. 3rd. ed. LC 68-58760. 1969. Repr. of 1935 ed. Set. 310.00x (ISBN 0-8103-3362-7). Gale.

Sonnett, Sherry. Smoking. (First Bks.). (Illus.). (gr. 4-6). 1977. PLB 8.90 (ISBN 0-531-01299-9). Watts.

Sonnevi, Goran. The Economy Spinning Faster & Faster. Bly, Robert, intro. by. LC 82-16719. 45p. 1982. signed ltd ed 20.00 (ISBN 0-915342-40-5); pap. 5.00 (ISBN 0-915342-39-1). SUN.

Sonnichsen, C. L. The Mescalero Apaches. LC 58-11610. (Civilization of the American Indian Ser.: Vol. 51). (Illus.). 300p. 1973. pap. 9.95 (ISBN 0-8061-1615-3). U of Okla Pr.

--Outlaw: Bill Mitchell, Alias Baldy Russell: His Life & Times. LC 65-25798. 1965. 9.95 o.p. (ISBN 0-8040-0238-X, SB). Swallow.

--Roy Bean: Law West of the Pecos. (Illus.). 5.95 o.s.i. (ISBN 0-8159-6715-2). Devin.

Sonnino, Lee A. A Handbook to Sixteenth Centruy Rhetoric. 278p. 1968. 22.75 (ISBN 0-7100-2935-7). Routledge & Kegan.

Sonnino, Paul, tr. see Frederick Of Prussia.

Sonnleitner, A. T. Cave Children. Bell, Anthea, tr. from Ger. LC 70-120785. (Illus.). (gr. 8 up). 1971. 10.95 (ISBN 0-87599-169-6). S G Phillips.

Sonntag, Linda. Butterflies. (The Leprechaun Library). (Illus.). 64p. 1980. 3.95 (ISBN 0-399-12546-9). Putnam Pub Group.

--Eggs. (The Leprechaun Library). 64p. 1980. 3.95 (ISBN 0-399-12543-4). Putnam Pub Group.

--Frogs. (The Leprechaun Library). (Illus.). 64p. 1981. 4.95 (ISBN 0-399-12611-2). Putnam Pub Group.

Sonntag, R. E. & Van Wylen, G. J. Fundamentals of Statistical Thermodynamcis. LC 65-27654. 1966. text ed. 40.95 (ISBN 0-471-81360-5). Wiley.

Sonntag, Richard E. & Van Wylen, Gordon J. Introduction to Thermodynamics: Classical & Statistical. 2nd ed. 832p. 1982. text ed. 34.95 (ISBN 0-471-03134-8). Wiley.

Sonntag, Richard E., jt. auth. see Van Wylen, Gordon J.

Sonntag, Stanley, jt. auth. see Emmons, Shirlee.

Sonntag, Wendy W. A Working Approach to Chemistry. 1979. pap. text ed. 15.95 (ISBN 0-8403-2048-5). Kendall-Hunt.

Sonquist, John A., et al. Searching for Structure. rev. ed. LC 73-620236. 236p. 1974. 15.00x (ISBN 0-87944-110-0); pap. 10.00x (ISBN 0-87944-109-7). Inst Soc Res.

Sons, Ray. Andrea Jaeger: Pro in Ponytails. LC 81-6097. (Sports Stars Ser.). (Illus.). 48p. (gr. 2-8). 1981. PLB 7.95 (ISBN 0-516-04314-5); pap. 2.50 (ISBN 0-516-44314-3). Childrens.

Sonstegard, Lois, ed. Women's Health: Ambulatory Care, Vol. 1. 368p. 1982. 24.50 (ISBN 0-8089-1501-0). Grune.

--Women's Health: Childbearing, Vol. 2. Date not set. price not set (ISBN 0-8089-1508-8). Grune.

Sontag, Frederick & Bryant, M. Darrol, eds. God: The Contemporary Discussion. LC 82-70771. (Conference Ser.: No. 12). vi, 419p. (Orig.). 1982. pap. text ed. 12.95 (ISBN 0-932894-12-7). Unif Theol Seminary.

Sontag, Susan. Against Interpretation. 146p. 1966. 14.50 (ISBN 0-374-97514-0). FS&G.

--The Benefactor. 1978. pap. 4.95 o.s.i. (ISBN 0-440-50632-8, Delta). Dell.

--A Susan Sontag Reader. 420p. 1982. 17.95 (ISBN 0-374-27215-8); slip-cased ltd. ed. 60.00 (ISBN 0-374-27216-6). FS&G.

Sontag, Susan, ed. Death Kit. 1978. pap. 4.95 o.s.i. (ISBN 0-440-52171-8, Delta). Dell.

Sontag, Susan, intro. by see Barthes, Roland.

Sontagg, Karlheinz. Inhalte und Strukturen Industrieller Berufsausbildung. iv, 240p. (Ger.). 1982. write for info. (ISBN 3-8204-7223-1). P Lang Pubs.

Sontheimer, Kurt & Bleek, Wilhelm. The Government & Politics of East Germany. LC 75-43485. 205p. 1976. 18.95 (ISBN 0-312-34125-3). St Martin.

Sood, A., jt. auth. see Dhir, K. K.

Sood, Mohan K. Modern Igneous Petrology. LC 81-8220. 244p. 1981. 29.95x (ISBN 0-471-08915-X, Pub. by Wiley-Interscience). Wiley.

Soong, T. T. Probabilistic Modeling & Analysis in Science & Engineering. LC 81-19686. 384p. 1981. text ed. 32.95 (ISBN 0-471-08061-6); solutions manual avail. (ISBN 0-471-08575-8); tchr's manual avail. (ISBN 0-471-08983-4). Wiley.

--Random Differential Equations in Science & Engineering. (Mathematics in Science & Engineering Ser.). 1973. 54.00 (ISBN 0-12-654850-1). Acad Pr.

Soon Man Rhim. Women of Asia: Yesterday & Today. Fowler, Ruth, ed. 140p. (Orig.). 1982. pap. 6.95 (ISBN 0-377-00134-1). Friend Pr.

Soons, Alan. Alonso De Castillo Solorzano. (World Author Ser.). 1978. 15.95 (ISBN 0-8057-6294-9, Twayne). G K Hall.

--Juan de Mariana. (World Authors Ser.). 1982. lib. bdg. 17.95 (ISBN 0-8057-6497-6, Twayne). G K Hall.

Soonsawad, Thong-In, tr. Thai Poets. 1968. pap. 1.50x o.p. (ISBN 0-8188-0210-3). Paragon.

Sooter, Wilburn L. Eye: A Light Receiver. LC 81-68313. 1981. pap. 3.95 (ISBN 0-89051-076-8); tchr's guide 2.95x (ISBN 0-686-33036-6). CLP Pubs.

Soothill, Eric & Soothill, Richard. Wading Birds of the World. (Illus.). 334p. 1983. 29.95 (ISBN 0-7137-0913-8, Pub. by Blandford Pr England). Sterling.

Soothill, Richard, jt. auth. see Soothill, Eric.

Soothill, William E., ed. see Confucius.

Sootin, Laura. Let's Go to a Bank. (Let's Go Ser.). (Illus.). (gr. 2-5). 1957. PLB 4.29 o.p. (ISBN 0-399-60352-2). Putnam Pub Group.

--Let's Go to a Newspaper. (Let's Go Ser.). (Illus.). (gr. 2-5). 1956. PLB 4.29 o.p. (ISBN 0-399-60387-5). Putnam Pub Group.

--Let's Go to a Police Station. (Let's Go Ser.). (Illus.). (gr. 2-4). 1957. PLB 4.29 o.p. (ISBN 0-399-60392-1). Putnam Pub Group.

Soper, Davison E. Classical Field Theory. LC 75-37659. 259p. 1976. text ed. 44.95x o.s.i. (ISBN 0-471-81368-0, Pub. by Wiley-Interscience). Wiley.

Soper, Robert T., jt. auth. see Liechty, Richard D.

Sopher, Charles & Baird, Jack. Soils & Soil Management. 2nd ed. 1981. text ed. 18.95 (ISBN 0-8359-7031-0); instr's. manual free (ISBN 0-8359-7032-9). Reston.

Sophian, J. Pregnancy Nephropathy, 2 vols. (Illus.). 1972. Set. 65.00 o.p. (ISBN 0-407-36200-2). Butterworth.

Sophocles. Oedipus Rex. Dawe, R. D., ed. LC 81-21626. (Cambridge Greek & Latin Classics Ser.). 256p. 1982. 37.50 (ISBN 0-521-24543-5); pap. 12.95 (ISBN 0-521-28777-4). Cambridge U Pr.

--Oedipus The King. Bagg, Robert, tr. from Greek. LC 81-19735. 96p. 1982. lib. bdg. 10.00x (ISBN 0-87023-361-0); pap. text ed. 5.00x (ISBN 0-87023-362-9). U of Mass Pr.

--Philoctetes. Webster, ed. 1970. pap. 11.95 (ISBN 0-521-09890-4). Cambridge U Pr.

--Sophocles Two. Greene, David & Lattimore, Richmond, eds. Incl. Ajax. Moore, John; The Women of Trachis. Jameson, Michael; Electra. Grene, David; Philoctetes. Grene, David. LC 54-10731. (Complete Greek Tragedies Ser: No. 4). 70p. 1957. pap. 5.50 (ISBN 0-226-30786-7, P314, Phoen). U of Chicago Pr.

--Three Tragedies: Antigone, Oedipus the King, & Electra. Kitto, H. D., tr. from Gr. 1962. pap. text ed. 4.95 (ISBN 0-19-500374-8). Oxford U Pr.

--Trachiniae. Easterling, P. E., ed. LC 81-21680. (Cambridge Greek & Latin Classics). 256p. 1982. 37.50 (ISBN 0-521-20087-3); pap. 12.95 (ISBN 0-521-28776-6). Cambridge U Pr.

Sophocles see Hadas, Moses.

Sophocles, jt. auth. see Aeschylus.

Sopka, Katherine R., jt. auth. see Holton, Gerald.

Sopp, LaVerne. Personal Name Index to the Eighteen Fifty-Six City Directories of Iowa. (Genealogy & Local History Ser.: Vol. 13). 400p. 1980. 42.00x (ISBN 0-8103-1486-X). Gale.

Sopper, William E. & Kardos, Louis T., eds. Recycling Treated Municipal Wastewater & Sludge Through Forest & Cropland. LC 73-2382. (Illus.). 479p. 1973. 20.00x (ISBN 0-271-01159-9). Pa St U Pr.

Sorabji, Richard. Necessity, Cause & Blame: Perspectives on Aristotle's Theory. LC 79-2449. (Orig.). 1983. 42.50x (ISBN 0-8014-1162-9); pap. 12.95x (ISBN 0-8014-9244-0). Cornell U Pr.

Sorani, Robert P. Circuit Training. (Physical Education Activities Ser.). 80p. 1966. pap. text ed. write for info. (ISBN 0-697-07006-9); tchrs.' manual avail. (ISBN 0-697-07215-0). Wm C Brown.

Soranna, Morag, jt. auth. see Miller, Duncan.

Soranna, Morag, jt. ed. see Miller, Duncan.

SorBello, Marisa. Woman in Reformation Europe. LC 81-1190. (Woman in History Ser.: Vol. 19). (Illus.). 210p. (Orig.). 1983. (ISBN 0-86663-053-8); pap. (ISBN 0-86663-054-6). Ide Hse.

Sorbom, Dag, jt. auth. see Joreskog, Karl G.

Sorcar, Prafulla C. Rapid Lighting Design & Cost Estimating. LC 79-4690. (Illus.). 1979. 39.50 (ISBN 0-07-059651-4). McGraw.

Sorce, Rose L. Complete Italian Cookbook. 1955. 3.95 (ISBN 0-448-01364-9, G&D). Putnam Pub Group.

Sorcher, Melvin, jt. auth. see Goldstein, Arnold P.

Sorcher, Melvin, jt. auth. see Hakel, Milton D.

Sordat, B., ed. International Workshop on Immune-Deficient Animals in Experimental Research, 4th, Chexbres, October 1982. (Journal: Experimental Cell Biology: Vol. 50, No. 6). 60p. 1983. pap. 22.75 (ISBN 3-8055-3647-X). S Karger.

Sordillo, Donald A. The Programmer's ANSI COBOL Reference Manual. (Illus.). 1978. ref. 32.00 (ISBN 0-13-729491-3). P-H.

Soreff, S. M. Management of the Psychiatric Emergency. 290p. 1981. pap. 16.50 (ISBN 0-471-06012-7, Pub. by Wiley Med). Wiley.

Sorel, Albert. The Eastern Question in the Eighteenth Century: The Partition of Poland & the Treaty of Kainardji. LC 68-9661. 1969. Repr. of 1898 ed. 24.00x (ISBN 0-86527-048-1). Fertig.

Sorel, George. Social Foundation of Contemporary Economy. Stanley, John L., ed. 270p. 1983. Repr. 39.95 (ISBN 0-87855-482-3). Transaction Bks.

Sorel, Georges. From Georges Sorel: Essays in Socialism & Philosophy. Stanley, John L., ed. Stanley, Charlotte & Stanley, John L., trs. 1974. pap. 9.95x (ISBN 0-19-501716-1). Oxford U Pr.

--The Illusions of Progress. Stanley, John & Stanley, Charlotte, trs. LC 69-16511. 1969. 29.50x (ISBN 0-520-01531-2); pap. 3.25 (ISBN 0-520-02256-4, CAL251). U of Cal Pr.

Sorelle, Rupert P., et al. Mecanografia: Metodo Racional. 2nd ed. 1962. text ed. 11.00 (ISBN 0-07-059650-6, G). McGraw.

Soren, David, jt. ed. see Biers, Jane C.

Sorensen, Andrew A. Alcoholic Priests: A Sociological Study. 1977. 2.00 (ISBN 0-8164-0317-1). Seabury.

Sorensen, Grethe. Needlepoint Designs from Oriental Rugs. (Illus.). 112p. 1983. pap. 12.95 (ISBN 0-686-83779-7, ScribT). Scribner.

Sorensen, H. The Alkaline Rocks. LC 75-11556. 622p. 1974. 136.95 (ISBN 0-471-81383-4, Pub. by Wiley-Interscience). Wiley.

Sorensen, Harry A. Energy Conversion Systems. 750p. 1983. text ed. 30.95 (ISBN 0-471-08872-2); price not set solutions manual (ISBN 0-471-87156-7). Wiley.

Sorensen, J. M. & Arlt, W. Liquid-Liquid Equilibrium Data Collection: Ternary & Quaternary Systems, Vol. V, Pt. 3. Behrens, D. & Eckermann, R., eds. (Dechema Chemistry Data Ser.). 605p. 1981. lib. bdg. 120.00x (ISBN 0-686-73456-4, Pub. by Dechema Germany). Scholium Intl.

--Liquid-Liquid Equilibrium Data Collection: Ternary Systems, Vol. V, Pt. 2. Behrens, D. & Eckermann, R., eds. (Dechema Chemistry Data Ser.). 1981. lib. bdg. 122.00x (ISBN 3-921-56718-1, Pub. by Dechema Germany). Scholium Intl.

Sorensen, K. E., jt. auth. see Davis, Calvin V.

Sorensen, Karen C. & Luckmann, Joan. Basic Nursing: A Psychophysiologic Approach. LC 77-84691. (Illus.). 1979. text ed. 37.50 (ISBN 0-7216-8498-X). Saunders.

Sorensen, Karen C., jt. auth. see Luckmann, Joan.

Sorensen, L. O. A Guide To the Seaweed of South Padre Island, Texas. 123p. 1979. pap. text ed. 8.95 (ISBN 0-89787-101-4). Gorsuch Scarisbrick.

Sorensen, Otto M., tr. see Petersen, Nis.

Sorensen, Robert. Shadow of the Past. Uhlich, Richard, ed. (Bluejeans Paperback Ser.). (Illus., Orig.). (gr. 7-12). 1978. pap. text ed. 1.25 o.p. (ISBN 0-8374-0042-2). Xerox Ed Pubns.

Sorensen, Robert M. Basic Coastal Engineering. LC 77-29256. (Ocean Engineering Ser.). 227p. 1978. 35.95 (ISBN 0-471-81370-2, Pub. by Wiley-Interscience). Wiley.

Sorensen, Theodore. Kennedy. LC 65-14660. 1965. 17.50i (ISBN 0-06-013950-1, HarpT). Har-Row.

--Watchmen in the Night: Presidential Accountability After Watergate. LC 75-1273. 1975. 15.00x (ISBN 0-262-19133-4); pap. 5.95 (ISBN 0-262-69055-1). MIT Pr.

Sorensen, Virginia. Miracles on Maple Hill. LC 56-8358. (Illus.). (gr. 4-6). 1956. 7.95 (ISBN 0-15-254558-1, HJ). HarBraceJ.

--Miracles on Maple Hill. LC 56-8358. (Illus.). (gr. 4-7). 1972. pap. 4.95 (ISBN 0-15-660440-X, VoyB). HarBraceJ.

--Plain Girl. LC 55-8681. (Illus.). (gr. 4-6). 1965. pap. 2.95 (ISBN 0-15-672020-5, VoyB). HarBraceJ.

Sorenson, Al. Hands Up! The History of a Crime. (Early West Ser.). (Illus.). 160p. 1982. Repr. of 1877 ed. 24.95 (ISBN 0-932702-19-8). Creative Texas.

Sorenson, Anton M., Jr. Animal Reproduction: Principles & Practice. Zappa, C. Robert, ed. (Agriculture Sciences Ser.). (Illus.). 1979. text ed. 33.50 (ISBN 0-07-059670-0). McGraw.

Sorenson, C. D. & Wets, R. J. Nondifferential & Variational Techniques in Optimization. (Mathematical Programming Studies: Vol. 17). 1982. 25.75 (ISBN 0-444-86392-3). Elsevier.

Sorenson, D. & Wets, R. J. Algorithms & Theory in Filtering & Control. (Mathematical Programming Studies: Vol. 18). 1982. 25.75 (ISBN 0-444-86399-0). Elsevier.

Sorenson, Darrell. The Art of Preserving Human Resources. 6.95 o.p. (ISBN 0-686-92158-5, 9010). Hazelden.

Sorenson, Don L., ed. see Christian, Esther.

Sorenson, Don L., ed. see Morrison, Kenneth & Havens, Robert I.

Sorenson, Herbert. Psychology in Education. 4th ed. 1964. text ed. 11.50 o.p. (ISBN 0-07-059685-9, C); teacher's manual o.p. (ISBN 0-07-059686-7). McGraw.

Sorenson, Herbert, et al. Psychology for Living. 3rd ed. 1971. text ed. 14.00 o.p. (ISBN 0-07-059733-2, W); tchr's manual 1.44 o.p. (ISBN 0-07-059734-0); tests 3.72 o.p. (ISBN 0-07-059735-9). McGraw.

Sorenson, J. A., jt. auth. see DeBlanc, H. J.

Sorenson, J. M. & Arlt, W. Liquid-Liquid Equilibrium Data Collection: Binary Systems, Vol. V, Pt. 1. Behrens, Dieter & Eckermann, Reiner, eds. (Dechema Chemistry Data Ser.). (Illus.). 622p. 1980. text ed. 120.00x (ISBN 3-921-56717-3, Pub by Dechema Germany). Scholium Intl.

Sorenson, Jacki & Bruns, Bill. Jacki Sorenson's Aerobic Lifestyles. 1983. 15.95 (ISBN 0-671-45616-4, Poseidon). PB.

Sorenson, James, jt. ed. see Esser, Peter.

Sorenson, James A., ed. Physics in Nuclear Medicine: The Slide Set. 1982. slide set 295.00 (ISBN 0-8089-1530-4). Grune.

Sorenson, James E., jt. auth. see Newman, Frederick L.

Sorenson, Lorin. The Classy Ford V8. (Illus.). 240p. 1982. 35.00 (ISBN 0-686-82139-4, F705). Motorbooks Intl.

Sorenson, Marge, jt. auth. see Hannawell, Peggy.

Sorenson, P. G., jt. auth. see Tremblay, J. P.

Sorenson, Robert J. Design for Accessibility. LC 78-11801. (Illus.). 1979. 28.95 (ISBN 0-07-059680-8, P&RB). McGraw.

Sorenson, Stephen. Growing up Isn't Easy, Lord: Story Devotions for Boys. LC 79-50080. (gr. 3-6). 1979. pap. 3.50 (ISBN 0-8066-1713-6, 10-2904). Augsburg.

Sorescu, Marin. This Hour. Hamburger, Michael, tr. from Romanian. 28p. (Eng.). 1982. pap. 2.50 (ISBN 0-937406-22-8); limited ed. 12.50 (ISBN 0-937406-23-6). Logbridge-Rhodes.

Sorge, Bart W., jt. auth. see Weston, J. Fred.

Sorge, G. A. Die Geheim Gehaltene Kunst Von Mensuration Von Orgel-Pfeiffen: The Secretly Kept Art of the Scaling of Organ Pipes. (Bibliotheca Organologica: Vol. 33). 1979. 57.50 o.s.i. (ISBN 0-686-30869-7, Pub by Frits Knuf Netherlands); wrappers 45.00 o.s.i. (ISBN 90-6027-346-X). Pendragon NY.

Sorger, James, jt. auth. see Dawley, Gloria.

Sorger, T. J. Buying a Computer Micro-Mini or Main Frame. (Illus.). pap. 12.95 (ISBN 0-9604072-1-9). Sorger Assocs.

--Managements Guide to Software Development. (Illus., Orig.). pap. 12.95 (ISBN 0-9604072-2-7). Sorger Assocs.

Sorin, Gerald. The New York Abolitionists: A Case Study of Political Radicalism. LC 73-105981. 172p. 1970. lib. bdg. 25.00x (ISBN 0-8371-3308-4, SNY/). Greenwood.

Sorin, Martin D. Data Entry Without Keypunching: Improved Preparation for Social-Data Analysis. LC 78-24637. 288p. 1982. 28.95x (ISBN 0-669-02803-7). Lexington Bks.

Sorine, Stephanie. The French Riviera Body Book. (Illus.). 128p. 1983. 12.95 (ISBN 0-312-30527-3). St Martin.

Sork, David & Boyd, Don. Master Catechist Guide for the Catechist Formation Book. LC 82-60853. 1982. pap. 3.95 (ISBN 0-8091-2471-8). Paulist Pr.

Sorkin. Education, Unemployment & Economic Growth. LC 73-11656. 208p. 1974. 18.95 (ISBN 0-669-85498-0). Lexington Bks.

Sorkin, Alan. The Economics of the Postal System: Alternatives & Reform. LC 78-19228. 224p. 1980. 24.95x (ISBN 0-669-02460-0). Lexington Bks.

--Health Economics: An Introduction. LC 73-11656. (Illus.). 224p. 1975. 18.95x (ISBN 0-669-93393-7). Lexington Bks.

--Health Manpower: An Economic Perspective. LC 75-17335. 192p. 1977. 19.95x (ISBN 0-669-00086-8). Lexington Bks.

Sorkin, Alan L. Economic Aspects of Natural Hazards. LC 79-48027. (Illus.). 192p. 1981. 24.95x (ISBN 0-669-03639-0). Lexington Bks.

--The Urban American Indian. LC 76-54459. (Illus.). 176p. 1978. 19.95x (ISBN 0-669-01296-3). Lexington Bks.

Sorkin, Ernst, jt. ed. see Normann, Sigurd J.

Sorkin, Robert D., jt. auth. see Kantowitz, Barry H.

Sorley, Imogene, jt. auth. see Carr, Jo.

Sorley, Lewis. Arms Transfers Under Nixon: A Policy Analysis. Davis, Vincent, ed. LC 82-15970. (Essays for the Third Century: America & a Changing World Ser.). 248p. 1983. 22.00 (ISBN 0-8131-0404-1). U Pr of Ky.

Sorlien, Robert P., ed. see Manningham, John.

Sorlier, Charles, ed. Chagall by Chagall. (Illus.). 1980. 65.00 o.p. (ISBN 0-8109-0758-5). Abrams.

Sorm, Frantisek & Dolejs, Ladislaw. Guaianolides & Germacranolides. LC 66-16515. 1966. write for info. Holden-Day.

Sormo, Maitland C. De see De Sormo, Maitland C.

Sormus, L., jt. auth. see Bicudo, C.

Sorochan, Walter D. Personal Health Appraisal. LC 75-31788. 302p. 1980. Repr. of 1976 ed. pap. 11.50 (ISBN 0-471-81384-2). Krieger.

--Promoting Your Health. LC 80-24347. 577p. 1981. pap. text ed. 18.95 (ISBN 0-471-04681-7). Wiley.

Sorochan, Walter D. & Bender, Stephen J. Teaching Elementary Health Science. 2nd ed. LC 78-62551. (Health Education Ser.). (Illus.). 1979. text ed. 20.95 (ISBN 0-201-07492-3). A-W.

--Teaching Secondary Health Science. LC 78-1760. 1978. text ed. 32.95 (ISBN 0-471-81387-7). Wiley.

Soroka, Marguerite C., jt. ed. see Baker, John B.

Sorokin, Pitirim. Social & Cultural Dynamics. LC 80-23730. (Social Science Classics Ser.). 720p. Date not set. cancelled (ISBN 0-87855-363-0); pap. 19.95 (ISBN 0-87855-787-3). Transaction Bks.

Sorosky, Marlene. Cookery for Entertaining. LC 78-71788. (Illus.). 1979. pap. 7.95 (ISBN 0-89586-019-8). H P Bks.

--Marlene Sorosky's Year-Round Holiday Cookbook. LC 82-47533. (Illus.). 320p. 1982. 19.18i (ISBN 0-06-015045-9, HarpT). Har-Row.

Sorrell, Mark. The Peculiar People. (Illus.). 168p. 1979. text ed. 15.00 (ISBN 0-85364-263-X). Attic Pr.

Sorrell, Martin. Francis Ponge. (World Authors Ser.). 1981. 14.95 (ISBN 0-8057-6419-4, Twayne). G K Hall.

Sorrels, Rosalie, ed. What, Woman, & Who, Myself, I Am. LC 74-21892. 1978. pap. 5.25 (ISBN 0-8256-9905-3, Quick Fox). Putnam Pub Group.

Sorrels, William W. Memphis' Greatest Debate: A Question of Water. LC 74-130973. 1970. 7.50x o.p. (ISBN 0-87870-005-6). Memphis St Univ.

Sorrenson, Keith. Integration or Identity? (Studies in 10th Century Hisory). (Orig.). 1977. pap. text ed. 4.50x o.p. (ISBN 0-86863-542-1, 00547). Heinemann Ed.

Sorrenson, M. P. Europe & Southern Africa. (A History Monograph). 1978. pap. text ed. 4.50x o.p. (ISBN 0-686-71774-0, 00543). Heinemann Ed.

Sorrentino, Anthony. The Delinquent & His Neighbors. 250p. 1977. pap. text ed. 11.00 (ISBN 0-8191-0069-2). U Pr of Amer.

--How to Organize the Neighborhood for Delinquency Prevention. LC 79-1279. 224p. 1979. 26.95 (ISBN 0-87705-391-X); pap. 14.95 o.p. (ISBN 0-87705-413-4). Human Sci Pr.

Sorrentino, Frank M. American Government: Power & Politics in America. LC 82-21748. (Illus.). 452p. (Orig.). 1983. pap. text ed. 16.75 (ISBN 0-8191-2946-1). U Pr of Amer.

Sorrentino, Gilbert. Blue Pastoral. LC 82-73720. 320p. 1983. 18.00 (ISBN 0-86547-095-2). N Point Pr.

--Crystal Vision. LC 81-2628. 320p. 1981. 17.50 (ISBN 0-86547-041-3). N Point Pr.

--Crystal Vision. 1982. pap. 6.95 (ISBN 0-14-006320-X). Penguin.

--The Orangery. LC 77-13099. (University of Texas Poetry Ser.: No. 3). 94p. 1978. 7.95 (ISBN 0-292-76008-6); pap. 0.00 o. p. U of Tex Pr.

Sors, Andrew I. & Coleman, David, eds. Pollution Research Index: A Guide to World Research in Environmental Pollution. 2nd ed. 555p. 220.00x (ISBN 0-686-75642-8, Pub. by Longman). Gale.

Sors, L. Fatigue Design of Machine Components. 224p. 1971. text ed. inquire for price (ISBN 0-08-016138-3); write for info. xerox copyflo avail. Pergamon.

Sorsa, Marja & Vainio, Harri, eds. Mutagens in Our Enviroment. LC 82-20320. (Progress in Clinical & Biological Research Ser.: V0l. 109). 502p. 1982. 50.00 (ISBN 0-8451-0109-9). A R Liss.

Sorsa, Marja, jt. ed. see Hemminki, Kari.

Sorsabal, jt. auth. see Burns.

Sorsby, A. Diseases of the Fundus Oculi. 1976. 79.95 (ISBN 0-407-00023-2). Butterworth.

Sorsby, A. & Miller, S., eds. Modern Trends in Ophthalmology, Vol. 5. (Illus.). 256p. 1973. 29.95 o.p. (ISBN 0-407-30603-X). Butterworth.

Sorum, C. Harvey, jt. auth. see Boikess, Robert S.

Sorum, Henry & Lagowski, Joseph J. Introduction to Semimicro Qualitative Analysis. 5th ed. LC 76-51795. (Illus.). 320p. 1977. pap. text ed. 14.95 (ISBN 0-13-496059-9). P-H.

Sosa, Ernest, ed. Causation & Conditionals. (Oxford Readings in Philosophy Ser). (Illus.). 1975. pap. text ed. 8.95x (ISBN 0-19-875030-7). Oxford U Pr.

Soseki, Natsuem. Mon. 1982. 8.95 (ISBN 0-686-91896-7, Coward). Putnam Pub Group.

Soseki, Natsume. And Then. Field, Norma M., tr. from Japanese. (The Perigee Japanese Library). 1982. pap. 6.95 (ISBN 0-399-50611-X, Perige). Putnam Pub Group.

--I Am a Cat. Shibata, Katsue & Kai, Motonari, trs. from japanese. LC 81-17271. (UNESCO Collection of Representative Works, Japanese Ser.). 431p. 1982. 15.95 (ISBN 0-698-11144-3, Coward); pap. 8.95 (ISBN 0-686-83013-X). Putnam Pub Group.

--Kokoro. McClellan, Edwin, tr. 256p. 1957. pap. 4.95 (ISBN 0-89526-951-1). Regnery-Gateway.

--Light & Darkness. Viglielmo, V. H., tr. from Japanese. (The Perigee Japanese Library). 397p. 1982. pap. 7.95 (ISBN 0-399-50610-1, Perige). Putnam Pub Group.

--Mon. Mathy, Francis, tr. from Japanese. (The Perigee Japanese Library). 217p. 1982. pap. 5.95 (ISBN 0-399-50608-X, Perige). Putnam Pub Group.

--Mon: ("The Gate") Mathy, Francis, tr. 217p. 12.95 (ISBN 0-698-11145-1, Coward). Putnam Pub Group.

--Sanshiro. Rubin, Jay, tr. from Japanese. (The Perigee Japanese Library). 248p. 1982. pap. 5.95 (ISBN 0-399-50613-6, Perige). Putnam Pub Group.

--The Three-Cornered World. Turney, Alan, tr. from Japanese. (The Perigee Japanese Library). 184p. 1982. pap. 4.95 (ISBN 0-399-50607-1, Perige). Putnam Pub Group.

--The Wayfarer. Yu, Beongcheon, tr. from Japanese. (The Perigee Japanese Library). 324p. 1982. pap. 6.95 (ISBN 0-399-50612-8, Perige). Putnam Pub Group.

Sosin, J. M. English America & the Revolution of 1688: Royal Administration & the Structure of Provincial Government. LC 81-16084. x, 321p. 1982. 25.00x (ISBN 0-8032-4131-3). U of Nebr Pr.

Sosin, Mark & Dance, Bill. Practical Black Bass Fishing. LC 73-41507. (Sportsmen's Classics Ser.). (Illus.). 192p. 1974. 8.95 o.p. (ISBN 0-517-51497-4); pap. 5.95 o.p. (ISBN 0-517-52137-7). Crown.

--Practical Black Bass Fishing. (Illus.). 224p. pap. 5.95 o.p. (ISBN 0-88317-064-7). Stoeger Pub Co.

Sosin, Mark & Kreh, Lefty. Fishing the Flats. (Illus.). 160p. 1983. 14.95 (ISBN 0-8329-0278-0); pap. 8.95 (ISBN 0-8329-0280-2). Winchester Pr.

Sosin, Mark, jt. auth. see Kreh, Lefty.

Sosin, Mark, ed. Angler's Bible No. 2, 1977 Ed. 1977. pap. 7.95 o.s.i. (ISBN 0-695-80722-6). Follett.

Soskis, David A., jt. ed. see Eichelman, Burr.

Sosnowski, Kiryl. The Tragedy of Children under Nazi Rule. LC 81-19506. 380p. (Pol.). 1983. Repr. of 1962 ed. 20.00x (ISBN 0-86527-342-1). Fertig.

Sossi, Ron, et al. West Coast Plays Seven: The Chicago Conspiracy Trial, Camp Shepard, Exploring the Geography of Character, from the Coyote Cycle. (Illus.). 1980. pap. 6.00 (ISBN 0-934782-06-7). West Coast Plays.

Sostek, Anita, jt. ed. see Field, Tiffany.

Soth, Lauren. Farm Trouble. LC 75-27658. 221p. 1976. Repr. of 1957 ed. lib. bdg. 15.50x (ISBN 0-8371-8445-2, SOFT). Greenwood.

Sotheby, William. Oberon: A Poem from the German of Wieland. Reiman, Donald H., ed. LC 75-31258. (Romantic Context Ser.: Poetry 1789-1830). 1978. Repr. of 1798 ed. lib. bdg. 47.00 o.s.i. (ISBN 0-8240-2205-X). Garland Pub.

Sotkin, Marc. Official Rock 'n' Roll Trivia Quiz Book, No. 2. (Illus., Orig.). 1978. pap. 1.75 o.p. (ISBN 0-451-08299-0, E8299, Sig). NAL.

Soto, Benigno, et al. Radiographic Anatomy of the Coronary Arteries: An Atlas. LC 74-33209. 320p. 1976. monograph 35.00 (ISBN 0-87993-066-7). Futura Pub.

Soto, Kanzan. The Japanese Sword. Earle, Joe, tr. LC 82-48779. (Japanese Arts Library). (Illus.). 220p. 1983. 91.95 (ISBN 0-87011-562-6). Kodansha.

Soto, Osvaldo N. Repaso De Gramatica. 2nd ed. 360p. 1974. pap. text ed. 14.95 (ISBN 0-15-576617-1, HC); wkbk. o.p. 5.95 (ISBN 0-15-576618-X); student wkbk. 6.95 (ISBN 0-15-576622-8); tapes. set 1 165.00 (ISBN 0-15-576619-8); tapes. set 2 50.00 (ISBN 0-15-576623-6). HarBraceJ.

Soto, Roberto J. & Sartorio, Giorgio, eds. New Concepts in Thyroid Disease. LC 82-24926. (Progress in Clinical & Biological Research Ser.: Vol. 116). 250p. 1983. 26.00 (ISBN 0-8451-0116-1). A R Liss.

Sotomayor, Antonio. Balloons: The First Two Hundred Years. (Illus.). (gr. 4-9). 1972. PLB 5.49 o.p. (ISBN 0-399-60753-6). Putnam Pub Group.

Soto-Ruiz, Luis, ed. see Gorostiza, C.

Souaid, Robert, et al. Adoption: A Guide for Those Who Want to Adopt. 25p. (Orig.). 1982. pap. 1.00 (ISBN 0-686-37425-8). Coun NY Law.

Soubrier, J. P. & Vedrinne, J., eds. Depression & Suicide: Medical, Psychological & Socio-Cultural Aspects, Proceedings of the XI Congress of the International Association for Suicide Prevention, Paris, July 5-9, 1981. (Illus.). 912p. 1983. 100.00 (ISBN 0-08-027080-8); pap. 60.00 (ISBN 0-08-027081-6). Pergamon.

Soucek, Branko. Microprocessors & Microcomputers. LC 75-33123. 607p. 1976. 39.95x (ISBN 0-471-81391-5, Pub. by Wiley-Interscience). Wiley.

--Minicomputers in Data Processing & Simulation. LC 77-37436. 467p. 1972. 39.95x (ISBN 0-471-81390-7, Pub. by Wiley-Interscience). Wiley.

Soucek, Branko & Carlson, Albert D. Computers in Neurobiology & Behavior. LC 75-25677. 368p. 1976. 32.50 o.p. (ISBN 0-471-81389-3, Pub. by Wiley-Interscience). Wiley.

Soucek, Priscilla, jt. auth. see Goffen, Rona.

Soucheray, Joe. Sooch! LC 81-11322. (Illus.). 270p. 1984. 8.95 (ISBN 0-932272-07-X). Minneapolis Tribune.

--Walter Payton. (Sports Superstars Ser.). (Illus.). (gr. 3-9). 1979. PLB 6.95 o.p. (ISBN 0-89813-002-6); pap. 3.25 (ISBN 0-89812-160-4). Creative Ed.

Souchotte, E. Marine Auxiliary Machinery. 6th ed. 512p. 1983. text ed. 49.95 (ISBN 0-408-01123-8). Butterworth.

Soucie, Gary. Hook, Line, & Sinker: The Complete Angler's Guide to Terminal Tackle. LC 81-20251. (Illus.). 480p. 1983. 22.50 (ISBN 0-03-048261-5). HR&W.

Souders, Mott. Engineer's Companion. LC 65-26851. 426p. 1966. 29.95x (ISBN 0-471-81395-8, Pub. by Wiley-Interscience). Wiley.

Souders, Mott, jt. auth. see Eshbach, Ovid W.

Soule, Gardner. The Maybe Monsters. (Illus.). (gr. 5 up). 1963. PLB 5.69 o.p. (ISBN 0-399-60457-X). Putnam Pub Group.

--The Mystery Monsters. (Illus.). (gr. 5 up). 1965. PLB 5.79 o.p. (ISBN 0-399-60483-9). Putnam Pub Group.

--Mystery Monsters of the Deep. LC 80-24617. (gr. 5 up). 1979. PLB 9.90 (ISBN 0-531-04258-8). Watts.

--New Discoveries in Oceanography. (Illus.). 128p. (gr. 6 up). 1974. PLB 4.99 o.p. (ISBN 0-399-60877-X). Putnam Pub Group.

--Remarkable Creatures of the Seas. LC 74-33148. (Illus.). 96p. (gr. 5 up). 1975. 5.95 o.p. (ISBN 0-399-20414-8). Putnam Pub Group.

--Strange Things Animals Do: How Scientists Probe Their Secrets. (Illus.). (gr. 5 up). 1970. PLB 4.98 o.p. (ISBN 0-399-60614-9). Putnam Pub Group.

--The Trail of the Abominable Snowman. (Illus.). (gr. 7 up). 1966. PLB 5.49 o.p. (ISBN 0-399-60642-4). Putnam Pub Group.

--UFO & IFO: A Factual Report on Flying Saucers. (Illus.). (gr. 5-9). 1967. PLB 5.49 o.p. (ISBN 0-399-60647-5). Putnam Pub Group.

Soule, George. Prosperity Decade from War to Depression: 1917-1929. LC 76-48796. (The Economic History of the United States Ser.). 1977. pap. 9.95 (ISBN 0-87332-098-0). M E Sharpe.

Soule, John W., jt. auth. see Abcarian, Gilbert.

Soule, M. E., jt. auth. see Frankel, O. H.

Soule, Sandra, jt. ed. see Beckham, Barry.

Soule, Sandra, ed. see Cohen, Marjorie A.

Soulez. Reflexions sur l'Etude Sociologique des Centres Semi-Urbains de la Cote d'Ivoire. (Black Africa Ser.). 11p. (Fr.). 1974. Repr. of 1967 ed. 20.50 o.p. (ISBN 0-8287-1410-X, 71-2056). Clearwater Pub.
Soulik, Tobias, jt. auth. see Carroll, Vern.
Soulsby, E. J., ed. Pathophysiology of Parasitic Infections. 1976. 27.50 (ISBN 0-12-655365-3). Acad Pr.
Soulsby, J., jt. auth. see Marsh, S. B.
Soulsby, John. Sale of Goods. 96p. 1980. 25.00x (ISBN 0-906501-18-0, Pub. by Keenan England). State Mutual Bk.
Soulsby, E. J., ed. Parasitic Zoonoses: Clinical & Experimental Studies. 1974. 44.00 (ISBN 0-12-655360-2). Acad Pr.
Soumaoro, Bourama & Bird, Charles S. Seyidu Kamara Ka Donkiliw. (Occasional Papers in Mande Studies). 101p. (Orig.). 1976. pap. text ed. 5.00 (ISBN 0-941934-18-7). Ind U Afro-Amer Arts.
Soupault, Philippe. Last Nights of Paris. Williams, William C., tr. from Fr. 250p. 17.95 (ISBN 0-916190-18-8); pap. 8.95 (ISBN 0-916190-19-6). Full Court NY.
Soupault, Re, tr. Breton Folktales. 215p. 1974. 12.95 o.p. (ISBN 0-7135-1890-1). Transatlantic.
Souper. About to Teach: An Introduction to Method in Teaching. 1976. 18.95x (ISBN 0-7100-8311-4); pap. 9.95 (ISBN 0-7100-8315-7). Routledge & Kegan.
Sourd, Leonard Le see Marshall, Catherine & Le Sourd, Leonard.
Sourek, Otakar. The Orchestral Works of Antonin Dvorak. Samsour, Roberta F., tr. LC 77-109851. (Illus.). 351p. Repr. of 1958 ed. lib. bdg. 17.75x (ISBN 0-8371-4342-X, SOOW). Greenwood.
Sourirajan, S. Reverse Osmosis. 1970. 67.50 (ISBN 0-12-655650-4). Acad Pr.
Sours, John A., jt. auth. see Goodman, Jerome D.
Sours, Keith J. SCSS Short Guide: An Introduction to the SCSS Conversational System. 144p. 1981. pap. text ed. 8.95 (ISBN 0-07-046539-8, C). McGraw.
Souryal, Sam. Police Administration & Management. (Criminal Justice Ser.). 1977. text ed. 21.50 (ISBN 0-8299-0141-8); instrs.' manual avail. (ISBN 0-8299-0371-2). West Pub.
Souryal, Sam S. Police Organization & Administration. (Criminal Justice Ser.). 150p. 1981. pap. text ed. 9.95 (ISBN 0-15-570701-9, HC). HarBraceJ.
Sousa, John P. The Fifth String. (Illus.). 144p. 1981. Repr. 9.95 (ISBN 0-87666-623-3, Z-35). Paganiniana Pubns.
Sousa, Maria De see De Sousa, Maria.
Sousa, Ronald W. The Rediscoverers: Major Writers in the Portuguese Literature of National Regeneration. LC 80-21453. (Illus.). 208p. 1981. 18.50x (ISBN 0-271-00300-6). Pa St U Pr.
Sousanis, Marti E. The Art of Filo Cookbook. Virbila, Sherry, ed. (Illus.). 160p. (Orig.). 1983. pap. 7.95 (ISBN 0-943186-05-6). Aris Bks.
Souter, John. Personal Bible Study Notebook I. 1975. pap. 4.95 (ISBN 0-8423-4817-4). Tyndale.
--What's the Good Word? The All New Super Incredible Bible Study Book for Junior Highs. 64p. 1983. pap. 2.50 (ISBN 0-310-45891-9). Zondervan.
Souter, John & Souter, Susan. Youth Bible Study Notebook. 1977. pap. 4.95 (ISBN 0-8423-8790-0). Tyndale.
Souter, John C. Date. 1981. pap. 3.95 (ISBN 0-8423-0636-6). Tyndale.
--Grow! 1979. pap. 2.50 (ISBN 0-8423-1231-5). Tyndale.
--Personal Prayer Notebook. 1976. pap. 4.95 (ISBN 0-8423-4819-0). Tyndale.
Souter, John C. & O'Brosky, James. Getting to Know God: A Family Hour Funbook. LC 78-56877. (Illus., Orig.). 1978. pap. 3.95 (ISBN 0-89081-357-4, 1466). Harvest Hse.
Souter, Liedekens. Ghemaect Ter Eeren Gods, Op Alle Dye Psalmen Van David: Tot Stichtinghe, En Een Gheestelijcke Vermakinghe Van Alle Christe Mensche. (Facs. of Dutch Songbooks: Vol. 2). 1982. Set. 50.00 o.s.i. (ISBN 0-686-30870-0, Pub. by Frits Knuf Netherlands). Vol. 1 (ISBN 90-6027-348-6). Vol. 2 Intro., Notes, Commentary & Bibliography (ISBN 90-6027-349-4). Pendragon NY.
Souter, Susan, jt. auth. see Souter, John.
Souter, Susan J. How to Be a Confident Woman: A Bible Study Guide for Women. LC 78-51904. 1978. pap. 2.95 (ISBN 0-89081-124-5, 1245). Harvest Hse.
South Africa Dept. of Statistics. South African Statistics, 1980. 7th ed. (Illus.). 625p. (Orig.). 1980. pap. 35.00x o.p. (ISBN 0-621-06028-3). Intl Pubns Serv.
South Oaks Foundation Conference, April 8-9 1976. Women in Industry: Medical, Emotional & Career Problems. Yolles, Stanley, ed. LC 77-4285. 1977. 34.50x (ISBN 0-87395-804-7). State U NY Pr.
South, R. Biogeography & Ecology of the Island of Newfoundland. 1983. 120.00 (ISBN 90-6193-101-0, Pub. by Junk Pubs Netherlands). Kluwer Boston.
South, Raymond. Royal Castle, Rebel Town. 1981. 39.50x o.p. (ISBN 0-86023-131-3, Pub. by Barracuda England). State Mutual Bk.
South, Stanley. Method & Theory in Historical Archeology. (Studies in Archeology Ser.). 1977. 27.50 (ISBN 0-12-655750-0). Acad Pr.
South, Stanley, ed. Research Strategies in Historical Archaeology. (Studies in Archaeology). 1977. 29.50 (ISBN 0-12-655760-8). Acad Pr.
Southall, Aidan, ed. Urban Anthropology: Cross-Cultural Studies of Urbanization. (Illus.). 1973. pap. text ed. 8.95x o.p. (ISBN 0-19-501691-2). Oxford U Pr.
Southall, Ivan. Journey into Mystery, Story of Explorers Burke & Wills. 13.50x (ISBN 0-392-08006-0, ABC). Sportshelf.
Southam, B. C., ed. Critical Essays on Jane Austen. 1968. 14.00x o.p. (ISBN 0-7100-6243-5); pap. 6.95 (ISBN 0-7100-6904-9). Routledge & Kegan.
Southam, Brian, ed. Jane Austen's "Sir Charles Grandison". (Illus.). 1981. 21.95x (ISBN 0-19-812637-9). Oxford U Pr.
Southam, Chester & Friedman, Herman, eds. International Conference on Immunotherapy of Cancer, Vol. 277. (Annals of the New York Academy of Sciences). 741p. 1976. 53.00x (ISBN 0-89072-056-8). NY Acad Sci.
Southam, Chester, jt. ed. see Friedman, Herman.
Southampton Conf. on Short-Run Econometric Models of UK Economy. Econometric Study of the UK: Proceedings. Hilton, Kenneth & Heathfield, David, eds. LC 73-101418. 1970. lib. bdg. 35.00x (ISBN 0-678-07004-0). Kelley.
Southard, Doris. North American Game Birds & Mammals. (Illus.). 224p. 1983. pap. 10.95 (ISBN 0-686-83781-9, ScribT). Scribner.
Southard, Edna C. Decorative Arts of the Russian Royalty. LC 82-61597. (Illus.). 32p. 1982. pap. 3.00 (ISBN 0-940784-04-1). Miami Univ Art.
Southard, Edna C., jt. auth. see Cook, Sterling.
Southard, Edna C., jt. auth. see Sanabria, Sergio.
Southard, Samuel. Pastoral Evangelism. LC 80-82196. 192p. 1981. pap. 4.49 (ISBN 0-8042-2037-9). John Knox.
Southball, Raymond, ed. Pope: An Essay on Criticism, the Rape of the Lock & Epistles to Several Persons (Moral Essays) 352p. 1973. 29.00x (ISBN 0-7121-0147-0, Pub. by Macdonald & Evans). State Mutual Bk.
Souther, J. W. Technical Report Writing. 2nd ed. 1977. 19.95 (ISBN 0-471-81412-1). Wiley.
Southerington, F. R., ed. see Hardy, Thomas.
Southerland, Ellease. Let the Lion Eat Straw. 1980. pap. 2.25 (ISBN 0-451-11687-9, AE1687, Sig). NAL.
Southerland-Holmes, Nancy. Creative Christmas. (Illus.). 18p. 1981. pap. 5.00 (ISBN 0-943574-09-9). That Patchwork.
--Muslin Mummies & Daddies. (Illus.). 10p. 1980. pap. 4.00 (ISBN 0-943574-01-3). That Patchwork.
--Soft Structures. (Illus.). 10p. 1980. pap. 4.00 (ISBN 0-943574-02-1). That Patchwork.
--This Little Pig... (Illus.). 42p. 1982. pap. 6.00 (ISBN 0-943574-10-2). That Patchwork.
Southern California Research Council. The Air of Southern California: How Clean & at What Price? (Report Ser.: No. 22). 1975. pap. 4.00 o.p. (ISBN 0-686-15200-X). Econ Res Ctr.
--Dignity or Despair: The Economics of Aging in Southern California, Rpt. No. 21. 1973. pap. 4.00 o.p. (ISBN 0-686-15201-8). Econ Res Ctr.
Southern, Carol, ed. see Penney, Alexandra.
Southern, Carol, ed. see Rosenfeld, Lulla.
Southern, Eileen. Music of Black Americans. 2nd ed. 600p. 1983. text ed. write for info. (ISBN 0-393-95270-3). Norton.
Southern Living Magazine Food Editors. Southern Living: Nineteen Eighty-Two Annual Recipes. (Illus.). 352p. 1983. 14.95 (ISBN 0-8487-0537-8). Oxmoor Hse.
Southern Oregon Chapter-AIA. Architectural Guidebook to Lane Country. (Illus.). 156p. (Orig.). 1983. pap. price not set (ISBN 0-87595-085-X, Western Imprints). Oreg Hist Soc.
Southern, R., tr. see Gongora, M.
Southern, R. W., ed. Essays in Medieval History. 1968. 20.00 (ISBN 0-312-26250-7). St Martin.
Southern, Richard W. Making of the Middle Ages. (Illus.). 1953. 20.00x o.p. (ISBN 0-300-00967-4); pap. 5.95x 1961 (ISBN 0-300-00230-0, Y46). Yale U Pr.
--St. Anselm & His Biographer. 62.50 (ISBN 0-521-06532-1). Cambridge U Pr.
Southern, Terry. Blue Movie. 1971. pap. 1.50 o.p. (ISBN 0-451-06173-X, W6173, Sig). NAL.
Southgate, D. A., jt. auth. see Paul, A. A.
Southmayd, William, jt. auth. see Hoffman, Marshall.
Southwart, Elizabeth. Bronte Moors & Villages from Thorton to Haworth. 190p. 1982. Repr. of 1923 ed. lib. bdg. 65.00 (ISBN 0-89984-609-2). Century Bookbindery.
Southwell, Sheila. Painting China & Porcelain. (Illus.). 104p. 1983. pap. 7.50 (ISBN 0-7137-1341-0, Pub. by Blandford Pr England). Sterling.
Southwell-Sander, Peter. Verdi, His Life & Times. expanded ed. (Illus.). 192p. Repr. of 1978 ed. 12.95 (ISBN 0-87666-639-X, Z-38). Paganiniana Pubns.
Southwest Asian Ceramic Society: West Malaysia Chapter. Nonya Ware & Kitchen Ch'ing: Ceremonial & Domestic Pottery of the 19th-20th Centuries Commonly Found in Malaysia. (Illus.). 136p. 39.00x (ISBN 0-19-582516-0). Oxford U Pr.
Southwest Center for Urban Research. Principles for Local Environmental Management. LC 77-28081. 1978. prof ref 19.50x (ISBN 0-88410-077-4). Ballinger Pub.
Southwick, Albert P. Quizzism & Its Key. LC 68-22051. 1970. Repr. of 1884 ed. 30.00x (ISBN 0-8103-3094-6). Gale.
--Wisps of Wit & Wisdom, or Knowledge in a Nutshell. LC 68-30582. 1968. Repr. of 1892 ed. 30.00x (ISBN 0-8103-3095-4). Gale.
Southwick, Charles E., jt. auth. see Vermeersch, LaVonne F.
Southwick, Lawrence, compiled by. Yankee Verse by Nathan Marshall Southwick (1872-1963) The Wit & Wisdom of a New England Philosopher. 1979. 10.00 o.p. (ISBN 0-682-49205-1). Exposition.
Southwick, Marcia. Build with Adobe. 3rd rev. & enl. ed. LC 82-73443. (Illus.). 230p. 1974. pap. 7.95 (ISBN 0-8040-0634-2). Swallow.
Southwood, Art, jt. auth. see Poticha, Joseph S.
Southwood, James, jt. auth. see Saunders, Frank.
Southwood, T. R. Ecological Methods: With Particular Reference to the Study of Insect Population. 2nd ed. 1978. 29.00x (ISBN 0-412-15760-8, Pub. by Chapman & Hall). Methuen Inc.
Southworth, Herbert R. Guernica! Guernica! A Study of Journalism, Diplomacy, Propaganda, & History. LC 74-82850. 1977. 37.50x (ISBN 0-520-02830-9). U of Cal Pr.
Southworth, Michael, jt. auth. see Southworth, Susan.
Southworth, R. & De Leeuw, S. Digital Computation & Numerical Methods. 1965. text ed. 34.95 (ISBN 0-07-059799-5, C); solutions manual 25.00 (ISBN 0-07-059801-0). McGraw.
Southworth, Susan & Southworth, Michael. Maps: A Visual Survey & Design Guide. 224p. 1982. 39.95 (ISBN 0-8212-1503-5). NYGS.
Soutter, John C. Survive! (Orig.). (gr. 9-12). 1983. pap. 3.95 (ISBN 0-8423-6694-6). Tyndale.
Soutter-Perrot, Andrienne. Air. (First Book of Nature Ser.). (Illus.). 28p. (gr. k-5). 1983. 2.95 (ISBN 0-8120-5487-3). Barron.
--Earth. (First Book of Nature Ser.). (Illus.). 28p. (gr. k-5). 1983. 2.95 (ISBN 0-8120-5486-5). Barron.
--The Earthworm. (First Book of Nature Ser.). (Illus.). 28p. (gr. k-5). 1983. 2.95 (ISBN 0-8120-5488-1). Barron.
--The Egg. (First Book of Nature Ser.). (Illus.). 28p. (gr. k-5). Date not set. cancelled (ISBN 0-8120-5490-3). Barron.
--The Toad. (First Book of Nature Ser.). 28p. (gr. k-5). Date not set. cancelled (ISBN 0-8120-5492-X). Barron.
--Water. (First Book of Nature Ser.). (Illus.). 28p. (gr. k-5). 1983. 2.95 (ISBN 0-8120-5485-7). Barron.
Souvarine, Boris, ed. Bulletin Communiste, 6 vols. (The Communist International: 1919-1939). (Fr.). 1978. lib. bdg. 400.00x set o.p. (ISBN 0-8287-1337-5); lib. bdg. 70.00x ea. o.p. Clearwater Pub.
Souweine, Judith, et al. Mainstreaming: Ideas for Teaching Young Children. LC 81-83869. 98p. 1981. pap. text ed. 5.00 (ISBN 0-912674-77-6, 114). Natl Assn Child Ed.
Souza, Anthony De see Vogeler, Ingolf & De Souza, Anthony.
Souza, Chris de see De Souza, Chris.
Souza, Raymond D. Lino Novas Calvo. (World Author Ser.). 1981. lib. bdg. 14.95 (ISBN 0-8057-6440-2, Twayne). G K Hall.
Sova, Margaret, jt. auth. see Kreitner, Robert.
Sovani, N. V. Urbanization & Urban India. 7.50x o.p. (ISBN 0-210-22695-1). Asia.
Sovold, Pamela, et al. Market Notebook. LC 80-16856. 230p. 1980. pap. 7.95 (ISBN 0-914842-44-7). Madrona Pubs.
Sovran, Gino, ed. see Symposium, Michigan, 1965.
Sowa, Cora A. Traditional Themes & the Homeric Hymns. 250p. 1982. 39.00x (ISBN 0-86516-018-X). Bolchazy-Carducci.
Sowa, John F. Conceptual Structures: Information Processing in Mind & Machine. LC 82-20720. (Systems Programming Ser.). 300p. 1983. text ed. 20.95 (ISBN 0-201-14472-7). A-W.
Sowande, Bode. Farewell to Babylon. 179p. (Orig.). 1979. 10.00 o.s.i. (ISBN 0-89410-107-2); pap. 5.00 o.s.i. (ISBN 0-89410-106-4). Three Continents.
Soward, A. M. Stellar & Planetary Magnetism. (The Fluid Mechanics of Astrophysics & Geophysics Ser.: Vol. 2). 1982. write for info. (ISBN 0-677-16430-0). Gordon.
Soward, Frederic H. & McInnis, Edgar. Canada & the United Nations. LC 74-6712. (National Studies on International Organization Ser). 285p. 1975. Repr. of 1957 ed. lib. bdg. 18.75x (ISBN 0-8371-7546-1, SOCU). Greenwood.
Sowards, J. Kelley. Desiderius Erasmus. (World Authors Ser.). 1975. lib. bdg. 13.95 (ISBN 0-8057-2302-1, Twayne). G K Hall.
Sowby, F. D., ed. Limits for Inhalation of Radon Daughters by Workers: ICRP Publication No. 32. ICRP. 32p. 1981. pap. 10.00 (ISBN 0-08-028864-2). Pergamon.
--Limits for Intakes of Radionuclides by Workers: ICRP Publication No. 30, Part 3. (Annals of the ICRP Ser.: Vol. 5, Nos. 2-3). 128p. 1982. pap. 25.00 (ISBN 0-08-026834-X). Pergamon.
--Limits for Intakes of Radionuclides by Workers, 7 vols. ICRD. (ICRP Publications: No. 30). 2500p. 1982. 370.00 (ISBN 0-08-028863-4). Pergamon.
Sowby, F. D. & International Commission on Radiological Protection, eds. General Principles of Monitoring for Radiation Protection of Workers: ICRP Publication, No. 35. 40p. 1982. pap. 15.00 (ISBN 0-08-029816-8). Pergamon.
--Protection Against Ionizing Radiation in the Teaching of Science: ICRP Publication, No. 36. 14p. 1982. pap. 10.00 (ISBN 0-08-029818-4). Pergamon.
Sowby, F. D. & International Commission on Radiology Protection, eds. Protection of the Patient in Diagnostic Radiology: ICRP Publication, No. 34. 88p. 1982. pap. 25.00 (ISBN 0-08-029797-8). Pergamon.
Sowden, J. K. The German Question, 1945-1973. LC 75-21518. 400p. 1975. 29.95 o.p. (ISBN 0-312-32620-3). St Martin.
Sowder, Barbara J. & Burt, Marvin R. Children of Heroin Addicts: An Assessment of Health, Learning, Behavioral, & Adjustment Problems. 176p. 1980. 22.95 (ISBN 0-03-057033-6). Praeger.
Sowell, Ellis. The Evolution of the Theories & Techniques of Standard Costs. LC 73-2027. 548p. 1973. 17.60 o.p. (ISBN 0-8173-8901-6). U of Ala Pr.
Sowell, Evelyn & Casey, Rita. Research Methods in Education. 416p. 1982. text ed. 23.95x (ISBN 0-534-01025-3). Wadsworth Pub.
Sowell, Judith B. & May, Ruth G. Yes, Johnny Can Read. 192p. 1982. pap. text ed. 10.36 (ISBN 0-8403-2874-5). Kendall-Hunt.
Sowell, Thomas. Ethnic America: A History. 353p. 1983. pap. 9.50 (ISBN 0-465-02075-5). Basic.
--Markets & Minorities. LC 81-66107. 160p. 1981. 12.98 (ISBN 0-465-04398-4); pap. 6.00x (ISBN 0-465-04399-2). Basic.
Sowell, Thomas, et al, eds. The Fairmont Papers: Black Alternatives Conference, December, 1980. LC 81-80735. 174p. (Orig.). 1981. pap. text ed. 5.95 (ISBN 0-917616-42-1). ICS Pr.
Sowers, George F. Introductory Soil Mechanics & Foundations: Geotechnic Engineering. 4th ed. (Illus.). 1979. text ed. 33.95x (ISBN 0-02-413870-3). Macmillan.
Sowers, J. R., ed. Hypothalmic Hormones. LC 79-19856. (Benchmark Papers in Human Physiology Ser.: Vol. 14). 368p. 1980. 46.00 (ISBN 0-87933-358-8). Hutchinson Ross.
Sowers, Robert. The Language of Stained Glass. (Illus.). 220p. 1981. 24.95 (ISBN 0-917304-61-6). Timber.
Soyer, Raphael. Diary of an Artist. LC 77-4798. (Illus.). 1977. 15.95 (ISBN 0-915220-29-6); deluxe ed. 200.00 (ISBN 0-915220-33-4). New Republic.
Soyinka, W. Myth, Literature & the African World. LC 75-38184. 180p. 1976. 27.50 (ISBN 0-521-21190-5); pap. 9.95 (ISBN 0-521-29394-4). Cambridge U Pr.
Soyinka, Wole. Ake: The Years of Childhood. 230p. 1982. 14.95 (ISBN 0-394-52807-7). Random.
--Camwood on the Leaves & Before the Blackout: Plays. LC 73-92792. Date not set. 5.95 (ISBN 0-89388-150-3); pap. 2.95 (ISBN 0-686-70398-7). Okpaku Communications.
--Collected Plays, Vol. 1. new ed. 1973. pap. 7.95 (ISBN 0-19-281136-3, 392, GB). Oxford U Pr.
Soyka, Fred. The Ion Effect. 2.95x (ISBN 0-553-14388-3). Cancer Control Soc.
Soyster, Allen L., jt. auth. see Murphy, Frederic H.
Sozan, Michael. The History of Hungarian Ethnography. 437p. 1978. pap. text ed. 15.75 (ISBN 0-8191-0361-6). U Pr of Amer.
Sozen, Mete A., ed. Significant Developments in Engineering Practice & Research. LC 81-69911. (SP-72). 425p. (Orig.). 1981. pap. 76.95 (ISBN 0-686-95236-7). ACI.
Sozuki, Taki. East Asian Cooking. (Illus.). 1983. cancelled (ISBN 0-8120-5401-6). Barron.
Space, Mark, et al. English Comprehensive. (Arco's Regents Review Ser.). 288p. (Orig.). 1983. pap. 3.95 o.p. (ISBN 0-668-05698-3, 5698). Arco.
Space Science Board. Biology & the Exploration of Mars. 1966. 8.75 (ISBN 0-309-01296-1). Natl Acad Pr.
Spache, George D. & Berg, Paul C. Art of Efficient Reading. 3rd ed. (Orig.). (YA) (gr. 9-12). 1978. pap. text ed. 13.95x (ISBN 0-02-413990-4, 41399). Macmillan.
Spackman, W. M. An Armful of Warm Girl. LC 81-19669. 144p. 1981. pap. 5.95 (ISBN 0-941324-00-1). Van Vactor & Goodheart.
--A Difference of Design. LC 82-48873. 1983. 10.95 (ISBN 0-394-53130-2). Knopf.
--A Presence with Secrets. 160p. 1982. pap. 4.95 (ISBN 0-525-48022-6, 0481-140, Obelisk). Dutton.
Spacks, Patricia M. The Adolescent Idea: Myths of Youth & the Adult Imagination. 352p. 1981. 17.00 (ISBN 0-465-00057-6). Basic.
--The Female Imagination. 1976. pap. 3.95 (ISBN 0-380-00599-9, 62901, Discus). Avon.
Spada, James. Spada Report: The Newest Survey of Gay Male Sexuality. 1979. pap. 2.50 o.p. (ISBN 0-451-08660-0, E8660, Sig). NAL.
Spadaccini, Victor M. & Whiting, Karen L. Minnesota Pocket Data Book 1983-1984. 300p. (Orig.). 1983. pap. 24.95 (ISBN 0-911493-00-X). Blue Sky.
Spadone, Frank G. Major Variety & Oddity Guide of U. S. Coins. 8th ed. LC 80-84159. (Collector Ser.). (Illus.). 128p. 1981. pap. 4.95 o.p. (ISBN 0-87637-162-4, 162-04). Hse of Collectibles.

Spadoni, H., jt. ed. see Ferrari, D.
Spady, Richard H., jt. auth. see Friedlaender, Ann F.
Spaet, Theodore, ed. Progress in Hemostasis & Thrombosis, Vol. 6. X ed. write for info. (ISBN 0-8089-1493-6). Grune.
Spaet, Theodore H., ed. Progress in Hemostasis & Thrombosis, Vol. 2. LC 72-2917. (Illus.). 384p. 1974. 63.50 o.p. (ISBN 0-8089-0816-2). Grune.
Spaeth. Collecting Art. (Pitman Art Ser.: Vol. 59). pap. 1.95 o.p. (ISBN 0-448-00568-9, G&D). Putnam Pub Group.
Spaeth, Marcia J., jt. ed. see Zeigler, Earle F.
Spaeth, Sigmund G. The Common Sense of Music. LC 74-163550. (Illus.). 375p. 1972. Repr. of 1924 ed. lib. bdg. 18.50x (ISBN 0-8371-6210-6, SPSM). Greenwood.
--Great Symphonies: How to Recognize & Remember Them. rev. ed. LC 77-138184. (Illus.). 308p. 1972. Repr. of 1952 ed. lib. bdg. 29.75x (ISBN 0-8371-5641-6, SPGS). Greenwood.
Spaeth, Steven E., jt. ed. see Loomis, Kristin S.
Spaethling, Robert & Weber, Eugene, eds. Literature One: Supplementary Readings with Exercises. (Ger). 1972. pap. text ed. 7.95x (ISBN 0-19-501550-9); tapes set 29.95 (ISBN 0-19-501703-X). Oxford U Pr.
Spaggiari, Albert. Fric-Frac: The Great Riviers Train Robbery. 1979. 8.95 o.p. (ISBN 0-395-27764-7). HM.
Spahr, Ronald C. The Impressive & Convincing Case for a Personal God. (The Science of Man Library Book). (Illus.). 139p. 1982. 51.45 (ISBN 0-686-83075-X). Am Classical Coll Pr.
Spain, Peter. Blood Scenario. 1980. 11.95 (ISBN 0-698-11029-3, Coward). Putnam Pub Group.
Spain, Stanley. Rajac: A Story. (Illus.). 192p. 1982. 13.95 (ISBN 0-02-612580-3). Macmillan.
Spalding, Dudley B., ed. GENMIX: A General Computer Program for Two-Dimensional Parabolic Flow. LC 77-7978. 1977. text ed. write for info. (ISBN 0-08-021708-7). Pergamon.
Spalding, Henry D. Irish Laffs. (Illus.). 96p. 1982. pap. 3.95 (ISBN 0-8246-0289-7). Jonathan David.
--Jewish Laffs. LC 82-9990. (Illus.). 96p. 1982. pap. 3.95 (ISBN 0-8246-0290-0). Jonathan David.
Spalding, J. M., jt. auth. see Johnson, R. H.
Spalek, John M. Guide to the Archival Materials of the German-Speaking Emigration to the United States After 1933: Verzeichnis der Quellen und Materialien der Deutschspragen Emigration in den U. S. A. Seit 1933. LC 78-10847. 1133p. 1978. 27.50x (ISBN 0-8139-0749-7). U Pr of Va.
Spalinger, Anthony J. Aspects of the Military Documents of the Ancient Egyptians. LC 81-14680. (Near Eastern Researches Ser.: No. 9). 352p. 1983. text ed. 30.00x (ISBN 0-300-02381-2). Yale U Pr.
Spalinger, Donald E., jt. ed. see Yoakum, James D.
Spallanzani, Lazaro. Opere, 5 vols. (It). Repr. of 1826 ed. Set. 245.00 (ISBN 0-384-56850-5). Johnson Repr.
Spanbauer, Larry, jt. auth. see Hancock, Virgil.
Spangenberg, Bradford, ed. British Attitude Towards the Employment of Indians in Civil Service. 2nd ed. 1977. 15.00x o.p. (ISBN 0-88386-140-2). South Asia Bks.
Spangle, Francis & Rusmore, Jean. South Bay Trails: Outdoor Adventures in Santa Clara Valley. Winnett, Thomas, ed. (Illus.). 224p. 1983. pap. 8.95 (ISBN 0-89997-022-2). Wilderness Pr.
Spangler, Charles W. Organic Chemistry: A Brief Contemporary Perspective. (Illus.). 1980. text ed. 25.95 (ISBN 0-13-640318-2); pap. 8.95 (ISBN 0-13-640342-5). P-H.
Spangler, David, ed. Cooperation with Spirit: Further Conversations with John. 32p. 1982. pap. 3.00 (ISBN 0-936878-07-X). Lorian Pr.
Spangler, E. R., jt. auth. see Mueller, G. E.
Spangler, Earl. Presidential Tenure & Constitutional Limitation. 190p. 1977. pap. text ed. 9.50 (ISBN 0-8191-0158-3). U Pr of Amer.
Spangler, John, jt. auth. see Williams, Dudley.
Spangler, Mary & Werner, Rita. The Structured Essay: A Formula for Writing. 288p. 1982. pap. text ed. 19.95 (ISBN 0-8403-2701-3). Kendall-Hunt.
Spangler, Mary M. Principles of Education: A Study of Aristotelian Thomism Contrasted with Other Philosophies. LC 82-24757. 306p. (Orig.). lib. bdg. 23.50 (ISBN 0-8191-3015-X); pap. text ed. 12.50 (ISBN 0-8191-3016-8). U Pr of Amer.
Spangler, Richard J., ed. see International Computer Programs, Inc.
Spangler, Richard J., ed. see International Computer Programs Inc.
Spangler, Richard J., ed. see International Computers Programs Inc.
Spanier, Graham B., jt. auth. see Bowman, Henry A.
Spanier, Graham B., jt. auth. see Lerner, Richard M.
Spaniol, Otto. Computer Arithmetic: Logic & Design. LC 80-41867. (Computing Ser.). 280p. 1981. 44.95 (ISBN 0-471-27926-9, Pub. by Wiley-Interscience). Wiley.
Spann, Edward K. The New Metropolis: New York City, 1840-1857. (Illus.). 546p. 1983. pap. 12.50 (ISBN 0-231-05085-2). Columbia U Pr.
Spann, Gloria C. Lillian Carter: A Portrait. Date not set. cancelled (ISBN 0-698-10995-3, Coward). Putnam Pub Group.
Spann, Meno. Franz Kafka. LC 75-26548. (World Authors Ser.: No. 381). 1976. lib. bdg. 12.95 o.p. (ISBN 0-8057-6182-9, Twayne). G K Hall.
Spann, Meno & Goedsche, Curt R. Deutsche Denker und Forscher. (Orig., Ger.). (gr. 10-12). 1967. pap. text ed. 11.95 (ISBN 0-13-204008-5). P-H.
Spann, Meno, jt. auth. see Goedsche, C. R.
Spann, Sylvia, jt. auth. see Culp, Mary B.
Spannaus, N., ed. see Kalimtgis, Konstandinos, et al.
Spannbauer, Paul. Laboratory Excercises in Human Physiology. 166p. 1983. pap. text ed. 12.95 scp (ISBN 0-06-046372-4, HarpC); instr's. manual avail. (ISBN 0-06-366350-3). Har-Row.
Spano, Pier F., et al, eds. Sulpiride & Other Benzamides. 326p. 1979. text ed. 30.00 (ISBN 0-89004-502-X). Raven.
Spano, Rick. The Rank & File Movement in Social Work. LC 81-40161. 290p. (Orig.). 1982. lib. bdg. 22.50 (ISBN 0-8191-2539-3); pap. text ed. 11.50 (ISBN 0-8191-2540-7). U Pr of Amer.
Spanoghe & Feenstra. Honderdvijftig jaar Rechtsleven in Belgie en Nederland, 1830-1980: Praeadviezen Uitgebracht Vooreen Colloquium Georganiseerd door de Juridische Faculteiten van de Universiteiten van Gent en Leiden. Gent, 1980. (Leidse Juridische Reeks Ser.: Vol. 15). (Illus.). xvii, 534p. 1981. pap. write for info. E J Brill.
Spanswick, R. M. & Lucas, W. J. Plant Membrane Transport. (Developments in Plant Biology Ser.: Vol. 4). 1980. 92.00 (ISBN 0-444-80082-4). Elsevier.
Spar, J. Willy, a Story of Water. LC 68-56819. (Illus.). (gr. 2-3). 1968. PLB 6.75x (ISBN 0-87783-051-7); pap. 2.95 deluxe edx (ISBN 0-87783-117-3); cassette 5.95x (ISBN 0-87783-233-1). Oddo.
Spar, James E., jt. auth. see Colby, Kenneth M.
Sparafucile, Tony, ed. see Hammett, Dashiell & Raymond, Alex.
Sparano, Vin. Complete Outdoors Encyclopedia. LC 72-90934. 1980. 18.22i (ISBN 0-06-014033-X, HarpT). Har-Row.
Sparano, Vin T., ed. The American Fisherman's Fresh & Salt Water Guide. (Illus.). 1978. pap. 5.95 o.s.i. (ISBN 0-695-80930-X). Follett.
Sparberg, Marshall, jt. auth. see Goodman, Michael J.
Sparck Jones, Karen & Kay, Martin. Linguistic & Information Science. (Library & Information Science Ser.). 244p. 1974. 31.50 (ISBN 0-12-656250-4). Acad Pr.
Spargo, Benjamin H., et al. Renal Biopsy Pathology with Diagnostic & Therapeutic Implications. 469p. 1979. 60.00 (ISBN 0-471-03119-4, Pub. by Wiley-Interscience). Wiley.
Spargo, Edward. The Now Student: Reading & Study Skills. rev ed. (Illus.). (gr. 12 up). 1977. pap. text ed. 7.20x (ISBN 0-89061-120-3, 71); instructor's guide free (ISBN 0-89061-121-1, 712). Jamestown Pubs.
--Skills Drills, Book 1. (Skills Drills Ser.). 100p. 1983. price not set spirit masters (ISBN 0-89061-321-4); price not set reproducibles (ISBN 0-89061-324-9). Jamestown Pubs.
--Skills Drills, Book 2. (Skills Drills Ser.). 100p. 1983. price not set spirit masters (ISBN 0-89061-322-2); price not set reproducibles (ISBN 0-89061-350-8). Jamestown Pubs.
--Skills Drills, Book 3. (Skills Drills Ser.). 100p. 1983. price not set spirit masters (ISBN 0-89061-323-0); price not set reproducibles (ISBN 0-89061-351-6). Jamestown Pubs.
Spargo, Edward & Harris, Raymond. Reading the Content Fields: English. (Content Skills Ser. - Middle Level). (Illus.). 96p. (Orig.). (gr. 6-8). 1978. pap. text ed. 3.20x (ISBN 0-89061-125-4, 551M). Jamestown Pubs.
--Reading the Content Fields: Mathematics. (Content Skills Ser - Advanced Level). (Illus.). 96p. (gr. 9-12). 1978. pap. text ed. 3.20x (ISBN 0-89061-139-4, 553A). Jamestown Pubs.
--Reading the Content Fields: Mathematics. (Content Skills Ser. - Middle Level). (Illus.). 96p. (gr. 6-8). 1978. pap. text ed. 3.20x (ISBN 0-89061-129-7, 553M). Jamestown Pubs.
--Reading the Content Fields: Practical Arts. (Content Skills Ser. - Advanced Level). (Illus.). 96p. (gr. 9-12). 1978. pap. text ed. 3.20x (ISBN 0-89061-143-2, 555A). Jamestown Pubs.
--Reading the Content Fields: Practical Arts. (Contents Skills Ser. - Middle Level). (Illus.). 96p. (gr. 6-8). 1978. pap. text ed. 3.20x (ISBN 0-89061-133-5, 555M). Jamestown Pubs.
--Reading the Content Fields: Science. (Content Skills Ser. - Advanced Level). (Illus.). 96p. (gr. 9-12). 1978. pap. text ed. 3.20x (ISBN 0-89061-141-6, 554A). Jamestown Pubs.
--Reading the Content Fields: Science. (Content Skills Ser. - Middle Level). (Illus.). 96p. (gr. 6-8). 1978. pap. text ed. 3.20x (ISBN 0-89061-131-9, 554M). Jamestown Pubs.
--Reading the Content Fields: Social Studies. (Content Skills Ser. - Middle Level). (Illus.). 96p. (Orig.). (gr. 6-8). 1978. pap. text ed. 3.20x (ISBN 0-89061-127-0, 552M). Jamestown Pubs.
--Reading the Content Fields: Social Studies. (Content Skills Ser. - Advanced Level). (Illus.). 96p. (Orig.). (gr. 9-12). 1978. pap. text ed. 3.20x (ISBN 0-89061-137-8, 552A). Jamestown Pubs.
Spargo, Edward, ed. Selections from the Black (Brown Book) 2nd ed. (The College Reading Skills Ser). (Illus.). 176p. (gr. 12 up). 1974. pap. text ed. 6.00x (ISBN 0-89061-001-0, 702). Jamestown Pubs.
--Selections from the Black (Olive Book) 2nd ed. (The College Reading Skills Ser). (Illus.). 176p. (gr. 12 up). 1974. pap. text ed. 6.00x (ISBN 0-89061-000-2, 701). Jamestown Pubs.
--Selections from the Black (Purple Book) 2nd ed. (The College Reading Skills Ser). (Illus.). 176p. (gr. 12 up). 1974. pap. text ed. 6.00x (ISBN 0-89061-002-9, 703). Jamestown Pubs.
--Topics for the Restless (Brown Book) (The College Reading Skills Ser). (Illus.). 176p. (gr. 9-11). 1974. pap. text ed. 6.00x (ISBN 0-89061-007-X, 742). Jamestown Pubs.
--Topics for the Restless (Olive Book) (The College Reading Skills Ser). (Illus.). 176p. (gr. 6-8). 1974. pap. text ed. 6.00 (ISBN 0-89061-006-1, 741). Jamestown Pubs.
--Topics for the Restless (Purple Book) (The College Reading Skills Ser). (Illus.). 176p. (gr. 12 up). 1974. pap. text ed. 6.00x (ISBN 0-89061-008-8, 743). Jamestown Pubs.
Spargo, Edward, ed. see Giroux, James A.
Spargo, Edward, ed. see Giroux, James A. & Twining, James E.
Spargo, Edward, ed. see Giroux, James A. & Williston, Glenn R.
Spargo, Edward, et al. Timed Readings. (Illus., Orig.). (gr. 4-5). 1979. Bk. 1, 120p. pap. text ed. 4.00 (ISBN 0-89061-198-X, 801); Bk. 2, 120p. pap. text ed. 4.00 (ISBN 0-89061-199-8, 802). Jamestown Pubs.
Spargo, Edward, et al, eds. Voices from the Bottom (Brown Book) (The College Reading Skills Ser). (Illus.). 176p. (gr. 9-11). 1972. pap. text ed. 6.00x (ISBN 0-89061-004-5, 722). Jamestown Pubs.
--Voices from the Bottom (Olive Book) (The College Reading Skills Ser). (Illus.). 176p. (gr. 6-8). 1972. pap. text ed. 6.00x (ISBN 0-89061-003-7, 721). Jamestown Pubs.
--Voices from the Bottom (Purple Book) (The College Reading Skills Ser). (Illus.). 176p. (gr. 12 up). 1972. pap. text ed. 6.00x (ISBN 0-89061-005-3, 723). Jamestown Pubs.
--Timed Readings. Incl. Book Three (ISBN 0-89061-031-2, 803); Book Four (ISBN 0-89061-032-0, 804); Book Five (ISBN 0-89061-033-9, 805); Book Six (ISBN 0-89061-034-7, 806); Book Seven (ISBN 0-89061-035-5, 807); Book Eight (ISBN 0-89061-036-3, 808); Book Nine (ISBN 0-89061-037-1, 809); Book Ten (ISBN 0-89061-038-X, 810). (Illus.). 120p. 1975. pap. text ed. 4.00x ea.; Set. (ISBN 0-89061-099-1). Jamestown Pubs.
Spariosu, Mihai. Literature, Mimesis & Play. (Kodikas Supplement Ser.: No. 15). 200p. (Orig.). 1982. pap. 16.50 (ISBN 3-87808-943-0). Benjamins North Am.
Spark, Muriel. The Ballad of Peckham Rye. 208p. 1982. pap. 4.95 (ISBN 0-399-50650-0, Perige). Putnam Pub Group.
--The Girls of Slender Means. 192p. 1982. pap. 4.95 (ISBN 0-399-50659-4, Perige). Putnam Pub Group.
--Loitering with Intent. 1981. 12.95 o.p. (ISBN 0-698-11047-1, Pub. by Coward). Putnam Pub Group.
--Loitering with Intent. 224p. 1982. pap. 4.95 (ISBN 0-399-50663-2, Perige). Putnam Pub Group.
--Memento Mori. 224p. 1982. pap. 4.95 (ISBN 0-399-50665-9, Perige). Putnam Pub Group.
--Not to Disturb. 1977. pap. 3.95 (ISBN 0-14-003774-8). Penguin.
--The Takeover. 1978. pap. 3.95 (ISBN 0-14-004596-1). Penguin.
--Territorial Rights. LC 78-24146. 1979. 9.95 (ISBN 0-698-10929-5, Coward). Putnam Pub Group.
Spark, Muriel & Standford, Derek. Emily Bronte: Her Life & Work. 272p. 1982. pap. 9.95 (ISBN 0-7206-0194-0, Pub. by Peter Owen). Merrimack Bk Serv.
Sparke, Archibald, ed. see Corns, Albert R.
Sparkes, Brian, jt. ed. see Kurtz, Donna.
Sparkes, Ivan. The Windsor Chair: An Illustrated History of a Classic English Chair. (Illus.). 1975. 17.50 o.s.i. (ISBN 0-902875-62-0). Transatlantic.
Sparkes, Ivan G., ed. A Dictionary of Collective Nouns & Group Terms. LC 75-4117. 213p. 1975. 42.00x (ISBN 0-8103-2016-9, Pub. by White Lion Publishers). Gale.
Sparkes, J. J. Transistor Switching & Sequential Circuits. 1969. 24.00 o.s.i. (ISBN 0-08-012982-X); pap. 10.75 o.p. (ISBN 0-08-012981-1). Pergamon.
Sparkes, J. R. & Pass, C. L. Monopoly. 2nd ed. (Studies in the British Economy Ser.). (Orig.). 1980. pap. text ed. 10.00x o.p. (ISBN 0-435-84582-9). Heinemann Ed.
--Trade & Growth. (Studies in the British Economy). 1977. pap. text ed. 5.50x o.p. (ISBN 0-435-84555-1). Heinemann Ed.
Sparkes, Roy. A Handbook of Art Techniques. (Illus.). 120p. 1981. 14.95 (ISBN 0-7134-3386-8, Pub. by Batsford England). David & Charles.
Sparkia, Roy. The Dirty Rotten Truth. 1973. pap. 1.25 o.p. (ISBN 0-451-07721-0, Y7721, Sig). NAL.
--Swap. pap. 1.25 o.p. (ISBN 0-451-07719-9, Y7719, Sig). NAL.
Sparkman, Brandon & Carmichael, Ann. Blueprint for a Brighter Child. LC 72-10307. (Illus.). 184p. 1975. pap. 2.95 o.p. (ISBN 0-07-059891-6, SP). McGraw.
Sparks, B. W. & West, R. G. The Ice Age in Britain. (Methuen Library Reprint Ser.). (Illus.). 320p. 1982. 45.00x (ISBN 0-416-32160-7, 3583). Methuen Inc.
Sparks, Esther. Ernst Damitz: 1805-1883. LC 76-56874. (Illus.). 56p. (Orig.). 1976. pap. 3.75 (ISBN 0-86559-021-4). Art Inst Chi.
Sparks, Fred W. Survey of Basic Mathematics. 3rd ed. 1971. text ed. 13.50 o.p. (ISBN 0-07-059900-9, C); instructor's manual 2.95 o.p. (ISBN 0-07-059901-7). McGraw.
Sparks, Fred W. & Rees, Charles S. A Survey of Basic Mathematics. 4th ed. (Illus.). 1979. pap. text ed. 23.95 (ISBN 0-07-059902-5, C); answer manual 15.00 (ISBN 0-07-059903-3). McGraw.
Sparks, Fred W., jt. auth. see Rees, Paul K.
Sparks, J. E. & Johnson, Carl E. Read Right: Comprehension Power. 1971. pap. text ed. 11.95x (ISBN 0-02-478390-0, 47839). Macmillan.
Sparks, Jack, ed. The Apostolic Fathers: New Translations of Early Christian Writings. LC 78-14870. 1978. pap. 7.95 (ISBN 0-8407-5661-5). Nelson.
Sparks, James C., Jr., jt. auth. see McFarland, Kenton.
Sparks, Jared, ed. see Franklin, Benjamin.
Sparks, John. The Discovery of Animal Behavior. 1982. 24.95 (ISBN 0-316-80492-4). Little.
Sparks, Judith, ed. Christmas Programs for the Church, No. 14. 64p. (Orig.). 1981. pap. 2.75 o.p. (ISBN 0-87239-437-9, 8614). Standard Pub.
Sparks, Judith, ed. see Bachman, Mary.
Sparks, Judith, ed. see Balika, Susan S.
Sparks, Judith, ed. see Bennett, Marian.
Sparks, Judith, ed. see Crandall, Ruth.
Sparks, Judith, ed. see Eberle, Sarah.
Sparks, Judith, ed. see Gambill, Henrietta.
Sparks, Judith, ed. see Grubb, Reba.
Sparks, Judith, ed. see Humble, Linda.
Sparks, Judith, ed. see Johnson, Irene L.
Sparks, Judith, ed. see Mueller, Virginia.
Sparks, Judith, ed. see Odor, Ruth.
Sparks, Judith, ed. see O'Rourke, Robert.
Sparks, Judith, ed. see Patterson, Yvonne.
Sparks, Judith, ed. see Solomon, Evelyn.
Sparks, Judith A., ed. see Jessie, Karen.
Sparks, Judith A., ed. see Staton, Knofel.
Sparks, Judith Ann, ed. see Maschke, Ruby.
Sparks, Judy, ed. Christmas Programs for the Church. (No. 16). 64p. 1983. pap. 2.95 (ISBN 0-87239-614-2). Standard Pub.
--Standard Christmas Program Book, No. 44. 48p. 1983. pap. 1.95 (ISBN 0-87239-621-5). Standard Pub.
Sparks, Judy, ed. see Odor, Ruth.
Sparks, Kimberly & Vail, Van Horn. German in Review. 1967. text ed. 16.95 (ISBN 0-15-529590-X, HC); tapes 75.00 (ISBN 0-15-529591-8, HC). HarBraceJ.
Sparks, Kimberly, jt. auth. see Vail, Van Horn.
Sparks, Lee, ed. Youth Group Travel Directory, 1983. LC 81-64228. 150p. 1982. 7.95 (ISBN 0-936664-09-6). T Schultz Pubns.
Sparks, Richard, jt. auth. see Elstein, Max.
Sparks, Richard F., et al. Surveying Victims: A Study of the Measurement of Criminal Victimization, Perceptions of Crime & Attitudes to Criminal Justice. LC 76-52393. 276p. 1978. 59.95 (ISBN 0-471-99494-4, Pub. by Wiley-Interscience). Wiley.
Sparling, S. R. Botany: A Laboratory Manual. 1966. 13.95x (ISBN 0-02-414240-9). Macmillan.
Sparnon, Norman. Creative Japanese Flower Arrangement. Stuart, Isla, ed. (Illus.). 133p. 1982. 15.00 (ISBN 0-8048-1404-X, Pub. by Shufunomoto Co Ltd Japan). C E Tuttle.
Sparr, Theanna, illus. Christian Mother Goose: Color-Me Rhymes, No. 2. (Color-Me Ser.). (Illus.). 64p. (gr. k-4). 1981. pap. 1.75 (ISBN 0-933724-04-7). Decker Pr Inc.
Sparrow, Arnold H., jt. ed. see Bensen, David W.
Sparrow, C. The Lorenz Equations: Bifurcations, Chaos, & Strange Attractors. (Applied Mathematical Sciences Ser.: Vol. 41). (Illus.). 288p. 1983. 19.80 (ISBN 0-387-90775-0). Springer-Verlag.
Sparrow, E. M. & Cess, R. D. Radiation Heat Transfer: Augmented Edition. LC 77-24158. (McGraw-Hill Series in Thermal & Fluids Engineering). (Illus.). 1978. text ed. 38.00 (ISBN 0-07-059910-6, Hemisphere Pub. Corp.). McGraw.
Sparrow, F. K., Jr., jt. auth. see Johnson, T. W., Jr.
Sparrow, Gerald. Great Defamers. (Crime in Fact Ser.). 1971. 16.50x (ISBN 0-392-00956-0, LTB). Sportshelf.
Sparrow, Gregory S. Lucid Dreaming: Dawning of the Clear Light. 76p. 1982. pap. 3.95 (ISBN 0-87604-086-5). ARE Pr.
Sparrow, John. Independent Essays. LC 76-49841. 1977. Repr. of 1963 ed. lib. bdg. 15.50x (ISBN 0-8371-9361-3, SPIE). Greenwood.
Sparrow, John, jt. auth. see England, Martha W.
Sparrow, John, jt. ed. see Gere, J. A.
Sparrow, W. Keats & Cunningham, Donald H. The Practical Craft: Readings for Business & Technical Writers. LC 77-93967. (Illus.). 1978. pap. text ed. 13.95 (ISBN 0-395-25590-2); instr's. manual o.p. 0.25 (ISBN 0-395-25591-0). HM.

Sparrow, W. Keats & Pickett, Nell Ann, eds. Technical & Business Communication in Two-Year Programs. (Orig.). 1983. pap. write for info. (ISBN 0-8141-5298-8). NCTE.

Spate, O. H. The Pacific Since Magellan, Vol. II: Monopolists & Freebooters. (Illus.). xxiii, 426p. 1983. 59.50x (ISBN 0-686-43209-6). U of Minn Pr.

Spatola, Anthony L. Mastering Medical Language. (Illus.). 464p. 1981. pap. text ed. 18.95 (ISBN 0-13-560151-7). P-H.

Spatt, Leslie & Koegler, Horst. Stuttgart Ballet. 1978. 14.95 o.p. (ISBN 0-903102-42-0). Dance Horiz.

Spatt, Leslie E., illus. Antoinette Sibley. Clarke, Mary. (Illus.). 128p. (gr. 6-12). 1981. 28.50 (ISBN 0-903102-64-1). Princeton Bk Co.

Spatz, Chris & Johnston, James O. Basic Statistics: Tales of Distributions. 2nd ed. 1980. text ed. 20.95 (ISBN 0-8185-0384-X). Brooks-Cole.

Spatz, Laura, ed. see U. S. Bureau of Labor Statistics.

Spatz, Lois. Aeschylus. (World Authors Ser.). 1982. lib. bdg. 15.95 (ISBN 0-8057-6522-0, Twayne). G K Hall.

Spatz, Lois S. Aristophanes. (World Authors Ser.). 1978. lib. bdg. 12.95 (ISBN 0-8057-6323-6, Twayne). G K Hall.

Spaulding. Syntax of the Spanish Verbs. 156p. 1982. 30.00x (ISBN 0-85323-143-5, Pub. by Liverpool Univ England). State Mutual Bk.

Spaulding, C. E. A Veterinary Guide for Animal Owners: Cattle, Goats, Sheep, Horses, Pigs, Poultry, Rabbits, Dogs, Cats. LC 76-10641. (Illus.). 1976. 16.95 (ISBN 0-87857-118-3). Rodale Pr Inc.

Spaulding, C. E. & Spaulding, Jackie. The Complete Care of Orphaned or Abandoned Baby Animals. (Illus.). 1979. 12.95 (ISBN 0-87857-266-X); pap. 8.95 (ISBN 0-87857-265-1). Rodale Pr Inc.

Spaulding, Edith R. Experimental Study of Psychopathic Delinquent Women. LC 69-14947. (Criminology, Law Enforcement, & Social Problems Ser.: No. 60). (Illus.). 1969. Repr. of 1923 ed. 17.00x (ISBN 0-87585-060-X). Patterson Smith.

--An Experimental Study of Psychopathic Delinquent Women. (Historical Foundations of Forensic Psychiatry & Psychology Ser.). (Illus.). xviii, 368p. 1983. Repr. of 1923 ed. lib. bdg. 45.00 (ISBN 0-306-76185-8). Da Capo.

Spaulding, Elbridge G. Resource of War: The Credit of the Government Made Immediately Available-History of the Legal Tender Paper Money Issued During the Great Rebellion Being a Loan Without Interest & a National Currency. LC 69-19681. (Money Markets Ser). 1971. Repr. of 1869 ed. lib. bdg. 16.75x (ISBN 0-8371-0662-1, SPRW). Greenwood.

Spaulding, J. L., jt. ed. see O'Fahey, R. S.

Spaulding, Jackie. The Family Horse. (Illus.). 1982. write for info. (ISBN 0-88930-050-X, Pub. by Cloudburst Canada); pap. 9.95 (ISBN 0-88930-049-6). Madrona Pubs.

Spaulding, Jackie, jt. auth. see Spaulding, C. E.

Spaulding, M. L., jt. auth. see Gordon, R.

Speads, Carola H. Breathing: The ABC's. LC 77-11537. (Illus.). 1978. 12.45i (ISBN 0-06-013996-X, HarpT). Har-Row.

Spear, Arthur, ed. The Journals of Hezekiah Prince, Jr., 1822-1828. 1965. 6.50 o.p. (ISBN 0-915592-06-1). Maine Hist.

Spear, George E., jt. ed. see Mocker, Donald W.

Spear, Jeffrey L. Dreams of an English Eden: Ruskin & His Tradition in Social Criticism. 224p. 1983. text ed. 25.00x (ISBN 0-231-05536-6); pap. 12.50 (ISBN 0-231-05537-4). Columbia U Pr.

Spear, Judy, ed. see Department of American Decorative Arts & Sculpture & Fairbanks, Jonathan L.

Spear, Judy, ed. see Poulet, Anne.

Spear, Mary E. Practical Charting Techniques. 1969. 32.95 (ISBN 0-07-060010-4, P&RB). McGraw.

Spear, Norman, jt. ed. see Isaccson, Robert L.

Spear, Percival, ed. see Smith, Vincent.

Spear, Richard E. Caravaggio & His Followers. rev. ed. (Icon Editions Ser.). (Illus.). 256p. 1975. pap. 6.95xi o.p. (ISBN 0-06-430034-X, IN34, HarpT). Har-Row.

--Renaissance & Baroque Paintings from the Sciarra & Fiano Collections. LC 72-1141. (Illus.). 112p. 1973. 24.50x (ISBN 0-271-01156-4). Pa St U Pr.

Spear, Thomas. Traditions of Origin & Their Interpretation: The Mijikenda of Kenya. (African Series, Ohio University Papers in International Studies: No. 42). (Illus., Orig.). 1981. pap. text ed. 13.50x (ISBN 0-89680-109-8, Ohio U Ctr Intl). Ohio U Pr.

Spear, Thomas J. Mijikenda Historical Traditons. 180p. 1982. pap. 13.50 (ISBN 0-89680-109-8, Ohio U Ctr Intl). Ohio U Pr.

Spear, Victor I. Sports Illustrated Racquetball. 1979. 9.95i (ISBN 0-397-01306-X); pap. 5.95i (ISBN 0-397-01307-8, LP-134). Har-Row.

Speare, Alden, et al. Residential Mobility, Migration & Metropolitan Change. LC 74-23550. 1975. prof ref 17.50x (ISBN 0-88410-406-0). Ballinger Pub.

Speare, Elizabeth. The Witch of Blackbird Pond. 256p. (gr. 5-8). 1972. pap. 2.50 (ISBN 0-440-49569-5, YB). Dell.

Speare, Elizabeth G. The Sign of the Beaver. 144p. (gr. 5 up). 1983. 8.95 (ISBN 0-395-33890-5). HM.

Spearing, A. C. Gawain-Poet. LC 72-112476. 1971. 44.50 (ISBN 0-521-07851-2); pap. 12.50 (ISBN 0-521-29119-4). Cambridge U Pr.

Spearl, Alexander. Living with a Car. 14.50x (ISBN 0-392-05915-0, SpS). Sportshelf.

Spearman, R. I. The Integument: A Textbook of Skin Biology. LC 72-88612. (Biological Structure & Function Ser.: No. 3). (Illus.). 200p. 1973. 49.50 (ISBN 0-521-20048-2). Cambridge U Pr.

Spearritt, Peter & Walker, David, eds. Australian Popular Culture. 1979. text ed. 25.00x (ISBN 0-86861-145-X); pap. text ed. 9.95x (ISBN 0-86861-153-0). Allen Unwin.

Spears, Betty & Swanson, Richard A. History of Sport & Physical Activity in the United States. 2nd ed. 416p. 1983. text ed. write for info. (ISBN 0-697-07212-6). Wm C Brown.

Spears, Harold. High School for Today. Repr. of 1950 ed. lib. bdg. 16.25x (ISBN 0-8371-2531-6, SPHS). Greenwood.

Spears, Richard A. Slang & Euphemism: Abridged Edition. 1982. pap. 4.50 (ISBN 0-451-11889-8, AE1889, Sig). NAL.

Spears, Stanley. Mysteries of Eternal Life. 3rd ed. 1970. pap. 2.95 o.p. (ISBN 0-87516-095-6). De Vorss.

Speas, Jan C. My Love, My Enemy. 1978. pap. 1.95 o.p. (ISBN 0-380-01869-1, 369540). Avon.

Speca, Bob, Jr. & Sugar, Bert. The Great Falling Domino Book. (Illus., Orig.). 1979. pap. 4.95 o.p. (ISBN 0-446-97046-8). Warner Bks.

Spechler, Dina R. Domestic Influences on Soviet Foreign Policy. LC 78-61396. 1978. pap. text ed. 7.25 (ISBN 0-8191-0596-1). U Pr of Amer.

Specht, E. K. Foundation of Wittgenstein's Late Philosophy. 218p. 1969. 14.50 (ISBN 0-7190-0312-1). Manchester.

Specht, Harry, jt. auth. see Gilbert, Neil.

Specht, Harry, ed. see Jaffe, Eliezer F.

Specht, Harry, jt. ed. see Kramer, Ralph M.

Specht, Irene, jt. auth. see Huffman, Robert.

Specht, R. L., ed. Heathlands & Related Shrublands, 2 Vols. (Ecosystems of the World Ser.: Vol. 9A-B). 1980-81. Set. 144.75 (ISBN 0-444-41810-5); Vol. 1: Descriptive Studies. 78.75 (ISBN 0-444-41701-X); Vol. 2: Analytical Studies. 78.75 (ISBN 0-444-41809-1). Elsevier.

Specht, Richard. Giacomo Puccini, the Man, His Life, His Work. Phillips, Catherine A., tr. 1933. lib. bdg. 17.75x (ISBN 0-8371-4030-7, SPPU). Greenwood.

Specht, Riva & Craig, Grace. Human Development: A Social Work Perspective. (Illus.). 384p. 1982. text ed. 23.95 (ISBN 0-13-444778-6). P-H.

Specht, Sally & Rawlings, Sandra. Creating with Card Weaving. (Arts & Crafts Ser.). 96p. 1973. 4.95 o.p. (ISBN 0-517-50348-4); pap. 2.95 o.p. (ISBN 0-517-50379-4). Crown.

Specht, Walter, jt. auth. see Kubo, Sakae.

Special Committee of the Section of Labor Relations Law, ABA, ed. The Developing Labor Law: The Board, the Courts, & the National Labor Relations Act, 1978 Supplement. 298p. 1979. 7.50 o.p. (ISBN 0-87179-312-1). BNA.

Special Learning Corp. Identification & Evaluation of Exceptional Children. (Special Education Ser.). (Illus.). 224p. (Orig.). 1980. pap. text ed. 15.00 (ISBN 0-89568-113-7). Spec Learn Corp.

--Readings in the Severely & Profoundly Handicapped Education. (Special Education Ser). (Illus.). 1978. 15.00 (ISBN 0-89568-079-3). Spec Learn Corp.

Special Learning Corporation. Readings in Law & the Exceptional Child: Due Process. (Special Education Ser.). (Illus., Orig.). 1980. pap. text ed. 15.00 (ISBN 0-89568-192-7). Spec Learn Corp.

--Readings in Mainstreaming. rev. ed. (Special Education Ser.). (Illus.). 224p. 1981. pap. text ed. 15.00 (ISBN 0-89568-293-1). Spec Learn Corp.

Special Learning Corporation, ed. Readings in Child Abuse. (Special Education Ser.). (Illus., Orig.). 1979. pap. text ed. 15.00 (ISBN 0-89568-103-X). Spec Learn Corp.

--Readings in Mainstreaming. rev. ed. (Special Education Ser.). 1978. pap. text ed. 15.00 (ISBN 0-89568-011-4). Spec Learn Corp.

Specialist Symposium on Geophysical Fluid Dynamics, European Geophysical Society, Fourth Meeting, Munich September, 1977. Proceedings. Davies, P. A. & Roberts, P. H., eds. 156p. 1978. 26.00 (ISBN 0-677-40115-9). Gordon.

Speck, F. G., et al. Rappahannock Taking Devices: Traps, Hunting & Fishing. (Joint Publications: No. 1). (Illus.). 28p. 1946. 1.00x (ISBN 0-686-17764-9). Univ Mus of U PA.

Speck, Frank G. Creek Indians of Taskigi Town. LC 8-10851. (AAA Memoirs Ser.: No. 8). 1907. pap. 8.00 (ISBN 0-527-00507-X). Kraus Repr.

--Functions of Wampum among the Eastern Algonkian. LC 19-12781. (AAA Memoirs Ser.: No. 25). 1919. pap. 12.00 (ISBN 0-527-00524-X). Kraus Repr.

--Iroquois. 2nd ed. LC 46-2147. (Bulletin Ser.: No. 23). (Illus.). 95p. (Orig.). 1955. pap. 4.50x (ISBN 0-87737-007-9). Cranbrook.

--Penobscot Shamanism. LC 20-13167. (AAA Memoirs Ser.: No. 25). 1919. pap. 8.00 (ISBN 0-527-00527-4). Kraus Repr.

Speck, Henry E., Jr. Old Testament Survey, Part 1, 2 Pts. (Living Word Paperback Ser.). (Orig.). 1963. pap. 2.95; Pt. 1. (ISBN 0-8344-0038-3); Pt. 2. pap. o.p. (ISBN 0-8344-0039-1). Sweet.

Speck, Von S. & Riggle, H. M. Biblische Lehren. 343p. 1982. pap. 4.00 (ISBN 0-686-36267-5). Faith Pub Hse.

Speck, W. A. The Butcher: The Duke of Cumberland & the Suppression of the Forty-Five. (Illus.). 240p. 1981. text ed. 25.00x (ISBN 0-631-10501-8, Pub. by Basil Blackwell England). Biblio Dist.

--Society & Literature in England 1700-1760. 220p. 1982. 40.00x (ISBN 0-7171-0977-1, Pub. by Macmillan England). State Mutual Bk.

Speck, W. H. Tory & Whig: The Struggle in the Constituencies, 1701-1715. LC 73-97057. 200p. 1970. 22.50 (ISBN 0-312-80955-7). St Martin.

Speckhart, Frank H. & Green, Walter L. A Guide to Using CSMP: The Continuous System Modeling Program - a Program for Simulating Physical Systems. 1976. 23.95 (ISBN 0-13-371377-6); solutions manual 4.50 (ISBN 0-13-371351-2). P-H.

Speckmann, E. J. & Elger, C. E., eds. Epilepsy & Motor System. (Illus.). 359p. pap. text ed. 27.50 (ISBN 0-8067-1821-8). Urban & S.

Specter, Gerald & Claiborn, William, eds. Crisis Intervention. LC 73-4360. (Continuing Series in Community-Clinical Psychology: Vol. 2). 210p. 1973. text ed. 22.95 (ISBN 0-87705-118-6); pap. 12.95 (ISBN 0-87705-124-0). Human Sci Pr.

Spector, jt. auth. see Rawson.

Spector, Gerald A., jt. auth. see Zax, Melvin.

Spector, Leo, jt. auth. see Solomon, Lawrence.

Spector, Marshall. Concepts of Reduction in Physical Science. LC 78-5441. (Philosophical Monographs: Second Annual Ser.). 126p. 1978. 24.95 (ISBN 0-87722-131-6); pap. 14.95 (ISBN 0-87722-127-8). Temple U Pr.

Spector, Robert D. Arthur Murphy. (English Authors Ser.). 1979. lib. bdg. 14.95 (ISBN 0-8057-6751-7, Twayne). G K Hall.

--Par Lagerkvist. (World Authors Ser.: Sweden: No. 267). 1973. lib. bdg. 13.95 o.p. (ISBN 0-8057-2509-1, Twayne). G K Hall.

--Tobias George Smollett. (English Authors Ser.: No. 75). 12.50 o.p. (ISBN 0-8057-1508-8, Twayne). G K Hall.

--Tobias Smollett: A Reference Guide. 1980. lib. bdg. 30.00 (ISBN 0-8161-7960-3, Hall Reference). G K Hall.

Spector, Robert D., ed. see Hawthorne, Nathaniel.

Spector, Robert D., ed. see Twain, Mark.

Spector, Sherman D. A History of the Balkan People. 10.95 o.s.i. (ISBN 0-685-60129-3, Pub by Twayne). Cyrco Pr.

Spectorsky, A. C., jt. auth. see Iselin, Fred.

Spectre, Peter, jt. auth. see Lang, Steven.

Spectre, Peter, jt. auth. see Putz, George.

Speculator Morum. Bibliotheca Arcana: Brief Notices of Books that have been Secretly Printed, Prohibited by Law, Seized, Anathematized, Burnt or Bowdlerized. 189p. 1982. 60.00x (ISBN 0-284-79523-2, Pub. by C Skilton Scotland). State Mutual Bk.

Spedding, C. R. An Introduction to Agricultural Systems. 1979. 20.50 (ISBN 0-85334-823-5, Pub. by Applied Sci England). Elsevier.

Spedding, E. H. & Danne, A. H., eds. Rare Earths. LC 61-15413. 654p. 1971. Repr. of 1961 ed. 28.50 (ISBN 0-88275-052-6). Krieger.

Speed, Eric. Dead Heat at Le Mans. (Wynn & Lonny Racing Bks.: Vol. 5). (gr. 3-6). 1977. 2.95 o.p. (ISBN 0-448-12807-1, G&D); lib. bdg. 3.39 o.p. (ISBN 0-448-13409-8). Putnam Pub Group.

--Gold Cup Rookies. LC 75-17388. (Wynn & Lonnie Racing Books Ser.: Vol. 4). 196p. (gr. 3-6). 1976. 2.95 o.p. (ISBN 0-448-12166-2, G&D); lib. bdg. 3.99 o.p. (ISBN 0-448-13329-6). Putnam Pub Group.

--GT Challenge. LC 75-17390. (Wynn & Lonnie Racing Books Ser.: Vol. 3). 196p. (gr. 3-6). 1976. 2.95 o.p. (ISBN 0-448-12167-0, G&D); lib. bdg. 3.99 o.p. (ISBN 0-448-13330-X). Putnam Pub Group.

--The Mexicali One Thousand. LC 74-1898. (Wynn & Lonny Racing Books Ser.: Vol. 1). (Illus.). 182p. (gr. 3-6). 1975. 2.95 o.s.i. (ISBN 0-448-11790-8, G&D); PLB 3.39 o.s.i. (ISBN 0-448-13220-6). Putnam Pub Group.

--Midnight Rally. LC 77-89962. (Wynn & Lonny Ser.: Vol. 6). (gr. 3-6). 1978. 2.95 (ISBN 0-448-14558-8, G&D). Putnam Pub Group.

--Road Race of Champions. LC 74-1899. (Wynn & Lonny Racing Books Ser.: Vol. 2). 196p. (gr. 3-6). 1975. 2.95 o.s.i. (ISBN 0-448-11791-6, G&D). Putnam Pub Group.

Speed, F. Maurice, ed. Film Review, Nineteen Seventy-Seven to Seventy-Eight. (Illus.). 1978. 15.00 o.p. (ISBN 0-491-02211-5). Transatlantic.

Speed, Harold. The Practice & Science of Drawing. (Illus.). 304p. 1972. pap. 5.50 (ISBN 0-486-22870-3). Dover.

Speed, P. F. The Potato Famine & the Irish Emigrants. Reeves, Marjorie, ed. (Then & There Ser.). (Illus.). 96p. (Orig.). (gr. 7-12). 1976. pap. text ed. 3.10 (ISBN 0-582-21721-0). Longman.

Speedlin, Phylis, jt. auth. see Silber, Kathleen.

Speedling, Edward J. Heart Attack. 1982. 19.95x (ISBN 0-422-77790-0, Pub. by Tavistock); pap. 8.95 (ISBN 0-422-77800-1). Methuen Inc.

Speedwriting Institute. Typing for Beginners. 1976. pap. 3.80 (ISBN 0-671-18138-6). Monarch Pr.

Speegle, Roger & Giesecke, William B. Business World. (Illus.). 192p. (Orig.). 1983. pap. text ed. 7.95x (ISBN 0-19-503230-6). Oxford U Pr.

Speek, P. A; see Bernard, William S.

Speelman, Arlene. Examination Review for Practical Nurses. 3rd rev. ed. LC 76-14540. 384p. 1976. pap. text ed. 7.95 o.p. (ISBN 0-399-40052-4). Putnam Pub Group.

Speer, Albert. Inside the Third Reich. (Illus.). 624p. 1981. pap. 8.95 (ISBN 0-02-037500-X); prepack(10) 89.50. Macmillan.

Speer, Dana C., jt. auth. see Dwight, John A.

Speer, Frederic. Food Allergy. 2nd ed. 1983. text ed. write for info. (ISBN 0-7236-7016-1). Wright-PSG.

Speer, Robert E. Five Minutes a Day. LC 43-16427. 1977. softcover 3.95 (ISBN 0-664-24139-5). Westminster.

Speeth, Kathleen, jt. auth. see Goleman, Daniel.

Spehlmann, R. EEG Primer. 1981. 70.75 (ISBN 0-444-80260-6); pap. 26.95 (ISBN 0-444-80299-1). Elsevier.

Speicher, Klaus. Singing Canaries. (Illus.). 96p. 1981. 4.95 (ISBN 0-87666-875-9, KW-047). TFH Pubns.

Speidel, Hans. Invasion Nineteen Forty-Four: Rommel & the Normandy Campaign. LC 79-147223. (Illus.). 1971. Repr. of 1950 ed. lib. bdg. 20.75x (ISBN 0-8371-5988-1, SPIN). Greenwood.

Speier, Hans. Force & Folly: Essays on Foreign Affairs & the History of Ideas. 1968. pap. 2.95x o.p. (ISBN 0-262-69025-X). MIT Pr.

--Social Order & the Risks of War: Papers in Political Sociology. 1969. pap. 3.95x o.p. (ISBN 0-262-69016-0). MIT Pr.

Speijer, J. S. Sanskrit Syntax. 412p. 1981. Repr. 15.00 (ISBN 0-89581-205-3). Lancaster-Miller.

Speir, Jerry. Raymond Chandler. LC 80-5347. (Recognitions Ser.). 180p. 1981. 11.95 (ISBN 0-8044-2826-3); pap. 5.95 (ISBN 0-8044-6872-9). Ungar.

--Ross MacDonald. LC 78-4297. (Recognitions Ser.). 1978. 11.95 (ISBN 0-8044-2824-7); pap. 5.95 (ISBN 0-8044-6871-0). Ungar.

Speirs, Gill, jt. auth. see Koenig, Marion.

Speirs, Ronald. Brecht's Early Plays. 224p. 1982. text ed. 35.00x (ISBN 0-391-02554-6). Humanities.

Speis, Werner. Loplop: The Artist in the Third Person. Gabriel, J. W., tr. from Ger. (Illus.). 200p. 1983. 50.00 (ISBN 0-8076-1065-8). Braziller.

Speiser, jt. ed. see Breimer.

Speiser, A. Die Theorie der Gruppen Von Endlicher Ordnung. (MA Ser.: No. 22). 272p. (Ger.). 1980. 36.30x (ISBN 3-7643-1151-7). Birkhauser.

Speiser, D., ed. Daniel Bernoulli: Werke Band 2: Mathematische Schriften. 403p. 1982. text ed. 60.00x (ISBN 3-7643-1084-7). Birkhauser.

Speiser, Ephraim A. United States & the Near East. rev. ed. LC 73-100244. (Illus.). 1971. Repr. of 1950 ed. lib. bdg. 16.25x (ISBN 0-8371-4031-5, SPUS). Greenwood.

Speiser, Stuart M. Superstock. 284p. 1982. 14.95 (ISBN 0-89696-165-6, An Everest House Book). Dodd.

Speiser, Werner. China. (Art of the World Library Ser.). 6.95 o.p. (ISBN 0-517-50833-8). Crown.

Speisman, Joseph C., jt. auth. see White, Kathleen M.

Speissl, B., et al. TNM-Atlas: Illustrated Guide to the Classification of Malignant Tumors. (UICC International Union Against Cancer Ser.). (Illus.). 240p. 1982. pap. 14.00 (ISBN 0-387-11429-7). Springer-Verlag.

Spekman, Robert E. & Wilson, David T., eds. Issues in Industrial Marketing: A View to the Future Proceedings. LC 81-8054. (Illus.). 99p. (Orig.). 1982. pap. text ed. 10.00 (ISBN 0-87757-154-6). Am Mktg.

Spell, Lota M. Research Materials for the Study of Latin-America at the University of Texas. Repr. of 1954 ed. lib. bdg. 15.75x (ISBN 0-8371-5033-7, TLSR). Greenwood.

Speller, D. C. Anti Fungal Chemotherapy. LC 79-40524. 446p. 1980. 119.95 (ISBN 0-471-27620-0, Pub. by Wiley-Interscience). Wiley.

Speller, Jon P., ed. Cyclopedia of American Genealogy, 2 Vols. Vol. 1. 1978 50.00 (ISBN 0-8315-0159-6); Vol. 2. 1980 50.00 (ISBN 0-8315-0160-X). Speller.

Spellerberg, Ian F. Biology of Reptiles. 1982. 39.95x (ISBN 0-412-00161-6, Pub. by Chapman & Hall England); pap. 21.00x (ISBN 0-412-00171-3, Pub. by Chapman & Hall England). Methuen Inc.

Spelllerberg, Ian F. Ecological Evaluation for Conservation. (Studies in Biology: No. 133). 64p. 1981. pap. text ed. 8.95 (ISBN 0-7131-2823-2). E Arnold.

Spellman, A. B. Black Music: Four Lives. LC 66-10410. 1971. pap. 3.95 o.p. (ISBN 0-8052-0281-1). Schocken.

Spellman, Cathy C. Notes to My Daughters. 320p. 1981. 10.95 o.p. (ISBN 0-517-54331-1). Crown.

--So Many Partings. 640p. 1983. 16.95 (ISBN 0-440-07812-1). Delacorte.

Spellman, Shirley, jt. auth. see Davis, Judy.

Spence. Basic Human Anatomy. 1982. 28.95 (ISBN 0-8053-6994-5); instr's guide avail. (ISBN 0-8053-6996-1). Benjamin-Cummings.

--Basic Industrial Drafting. 1979. pap. text ed. 12.68 (ISBN 0-87002-297-0); 7.96 (ISBN 0-87002-142-7). Bennett IL.
--Drafting Technology & Practice. rev ed. (gr. 9-12). 1980. text ed. 24.60 (ISBN 0-87002-303-9); worksheets 13.28 (ISBN 0-87002-355-1). Bennett IL.
--Graphic Reproductions. 1980. text ed. 23.84 (ISBN 0-87002-285-7); student guide 3.80 (ISBN 0-87002-319-5). Bennett IL.

Spence & Atkins. Technical Drafting. (gr. 9-12). 1980. text ed. 22.00 (ISBN 0-87002-305-5); Inst. Resource Guide 80 10.00 (ISBN 0-87002-314-4). Bennett IL.

Spence, A. Michael, jt. auth. see Hayes, Samuel L., III.

Spence, Alexander & Mason, Elliott. Human Anatomy & Physiology. LC 78-57266. (Illus.). 1979. text ed. 26.95 (ISBN 0-8053-6990-2); instr's resource package 150.00 (ISBN 0-8053-6991-0); transparencies 150.00 (ISBN 0-8053-6992-9). Benjamin-Cummings.

Spence, Gerry L. & Polk, Anthony. Gerry Spence: Gunning for Justice. LC 81-43926. 480p. 1982. 17.95 (ISBN 0-385-17703-8). Doubleday.

Spence, Inez. Coping with Loneliness. 2.45 o.p. (ISBN 0-686-92313-8, 6369). Hazelden.

Spence, J. C. Experimental High-Resolution Electron Microscopy. (Monographs on the Physics & Chemistry of Materials). (Illus.). 1981. 79.00x (ISBN 0-19-851365-8). Oxford U Pr.

Spence, J. D., jt. auth. see Teer, F.

Spence, J. T. see Spence, Kenneth W., et al.

Spence, J. Wayne. COBOL for the 80's. (Illus.). 608p. 1982. pap. 18.95 (ISBN 0-314-63290-5). West Pub.

Spence, Jack. Search for Justice: Neighborhood Courts in Allende's Chile. 1979. lib. bdg. 24.75 (ISBN 0-89158-279-7). Westview.

Spence, Janet T. see Spence, Kenneth W., et al.

Spence, Janet T., et al. Elementary Statistics. 3rd ed. (Illus.). 288p. 1976. ref. ed. 19.95 (ISBN 0-13-260109-5, Busn); wkbk. 8.95 (ISBN 0-13-260091-9). P-H.

Spence, Jim & Brown, Gar. Motorcycle Racing in America: A Definitive Look at the Sport. LC 74-6144. (Illus.). 144p. 1977. pap. 5.95 (ISBN 0-87955-418-5). O'Hara.

Spence, Kenneth W., et al, eds. The Psychology of Learning & Motivation: Advances in Research & Theory, 14 vols. Incl. Vol. 1. Spence, Kenneth W. & Spence, Janet T., eds. 1967. 43.00 (ISBN 0-12-543301-8); Vol. 2. 1968. 49.50 (ISBN 0-12-543302-6); Vol. 3. Bower, G. H. & Spence, J. T., eds. 1970. 49.50 (ISBN 0-12-543303-4); Vol. 4. Bower, G. H., ed. 1970. 49.50 (ISBN 0-12-543304-2); Vol. 5. 1972. 49.50 (ISBN 0-12-543305-0); Vol. 6. 1972. 49.50 (ISBN-0-12-543306-9); Vol. 7. 1973. 49.50 (ISBN 0-12-543307-7); Vol. 8. 1974. 52.50 (ISBN 0-12-543308-5); Vol. 9. 1975. 49.50 (ISBN 0-12-543309-3); Vol. 10. 1976. 43.00 (ISBN 0-12-543310-7); Vol. 12. Spence, Kenneth W., ed. 1977. 38.50 (ISBN 0-12-543312-3); Vol. 13. 1979. 43.50 (ISBN 0-12-543311-5); Vol. 14. 1980. 41.50 (ISBN 0-12-543314-X). Acad Pr.

Spence, Lawrence E. Finite Mathematics. 544p. 1981. text ed. 22.50 scp (ISBN 0-06-046369-4, HarpC); scp sol. manual 8.95 (ISBN 0-06-041842-7); instr's. manual avail. (ISBN 0-06-366385-6). Har-Row.

Spence, Lewis. Atlantis Discovered. 1973. Repr. of 1924 ed. 34.00x (ISBN 0-685-70656-7). Gale.
--Myths & Legends of Babylonia & Assyria. LC 77-167199. (Illus.). 414p. 1975. Repr. of 1916 ed. 47.00x (ISBN 0-8103-4089-5). Gale.
--Occult Sciences in Atlantis. LC 70-16446. 1970. pap. 6.95 (ISBN 0-87728-136-X). Weiser.

Spence, Martha I., jt. auth. see Vinsant, Marielle.

Spence, Michelle. Rebekka Moon. (Orig.). 1983. pap. 3.25 (ISBN 0-440-17099-0). Dell.

Spence, R. & Brayton, R. Sensitivity & Optimization. (Computer Aided Design of Electrical Circuits Ser.: Vol. 2). 1977. 61.75 (ISBN 0-444-41929-2). Elsevier.

Spence, R. J. Small-Scale Production of Cementitious Materials. (Illus.). 49p. (Orig.). 1981. pap. 4.25x (ISBN 0-903031-74-4, Pub. by Intermediate Tech England). Intermediate Tech.

Spence, Robert. Linear Active Networks. LC 73-88242. 1970. 32.95 o.p. (ISBN 0-471-81525-X, Pub. by Wiley-Interscience). Wiley.

Spence, Sue & Shepherd, Geoff, eds. Developments in Social Skills Training. Date not set. price not set (ISBN 0-12-656620-8). Acad Pr.

Spence, William P. Architecture: Design-Engineering-Drawing. rev. ed. (gr. 9-12). 1979. text ed. 21.97 (ISBN 0-87345-099-X); quizzes & problems 6.00 (ISBN 0-87345-098-1); ans. key avail. (ISBN 0-685-14523-9). McKnight.

Spencer. Playing the Guitar. (Beginner's Guides Ser.). (gr. 4-9). 1980. 6.95 (ISBN 0-686-36438-4, Usborne-Hayes); PLB 8.95 (ISBN 0-88110-038-2). EDC.

Spencer, jt. auth. see Green, H.

Spencer, et al, eds. AIA Building Construction Legal Citator, 1981, 2 vols. 1982. Set. loose leaf 120.00x (ISBN 0-913962-44-9). Am Inst Arch.

Spencer, A. J. Death in Ancient Egypt. 1983. pap. 5.95 (ISBN 0-14-022294-4, Pelican). Penguin.

Spencer, Albert, et al. Materials of Construction. 1982. text ed. 22.95 (ISBN 0-8359-4291-0); solutions manual o.p. avail. (ISBN 0-8359-4292-9). Reston.

Spencer, Anne. On the Edge of the Organization: The Role of the Outside Director. 120p. 1983. 24.95 (ISBN 0-471-90018-4, Pub. by Wiley-Interscience). Wiley.

Spencer, Anne M. In Praise of Heroes: Contemporary African Commemorative Cloth. Sweeney, Mary S. & Bartle, Wilmot T., eds. LC 82-14299. (Illus.). 44p. (Orig.). pap. 4.95 (ISBN 0-932828-09-4). Newark Mus.

Spencer, Arthur. Gotland. (Islands Ser.). 1974. 12.95 o.p. (ISBN 0-7153-6373-5). David & Charles.

Spencer, Baldwin & Gillen, F. J. Native Tribes of Central Australia. (Illus.). 1969. Repr. of 1899 ed. text ed. 32.25x o.p. (ISBN 90-6234-041-5). Humanities.

Spencer, Charles. Blue Collar: An Internal Examination of the Workplace. LC 76-50937. 1977. pap. 6.95 (ISBN 0-918206-01-4). Lakeside Chart.
--Erte. (Illus.). 1970. pap. 12.95 (ISBN 0-517-54391-5, C N Potter Bks). Crown.
--Erte. (Illus.). 192p. 1970. 25.00 o.p. (ISBN 0-517-54564-0, C N Potter Bks). Crown.

Spencer, Chas. L. Knots, Splices, & Fancy Work. 1981. 25.00x (ISBN 0-85174-157-6, Pub. by Brown, Son & Ferguson). State Mutual Bk.

Spencer, Christopher. Davenant's MacBeth From the Yale Manuscript. 1961. text ed. 39.50x (ISBN 0-686-83523-9). Elliots Bks.
--Drug Abuse in East Asia. 1981. 29.95x (ISBN 0-19-580476-7). Oxford U Pr.
--Nahum Tate. (English Authors Ser.). lib. bdg. 14.95 (ISBN 0-8057-1536-3, Twayne). G K Hall.

Spencer, Cornelia. The Yangtze: China's River Highway. (Rivers of the World Ser.). (Illus.). (gr. 4-7). 1963. PLB 3.98 (ISBN 0-8116-6357-4). Garrard.

Spencer, D. A. Focal Dictionary of Photographic Technologies. (Illus.). 1973. 39.95 (ISBN 0-240-50747-9). Focal Pr.

Spencer, D. A., et al. Color Photography in Practice. rev. 6th ed. LC 76-133457. (Illus.). 408p. 1975. 35.95 (ISBN 0-240-50902-1); pap. 19.95 (ISBN 0-240-50928-5). Focal Pr.

Spencer, David, et al. Contexts for Composition. 5th ed. 1979. pap. text ed. 13.95 (ISBN 0-13-171512-7). P-H.

Spencer, Domina E., jt. auth. see Moon, Parry.

Spencer, Donald. Computer Dictionary for Everyone. 1981. pap. 5.95 (ISBN 0-686-96885-9, ScribT). Scribner.

Spencer, Donald A. Computer Literacy Test Questions. 1983. 6.95x (ISBN 0-89218-074-9). Camelot Pub.
--Hymn & Scripture Selection Guide. LC 76-48529. 1977. text ed. 9.85 (ISBN 0-8170-0705-9). Judson.

Spencer, Donald D. BASIC Programming. LC 82-17689. 1983. 14.95 (ISBN 0-89218-062-5). Camelot Pub.
--BASIC Quiz Book. 1983. 5.95x (ISBN 0-89218-076-5). Camelot Pub.
--BASIC Workbook for Microcomputers. 1983. 7.95x (ISBN 0-89218-040-4). Camelot Pub.
--Computer Awareness Book. 2nd ed. 1982. pap. 2.90 (ISBN 0-89218-051-X). Camelot Pub.
--Computer Dictionary. 2nd ed. LC 78-31738. 1979. 11.95 o.p. (ISBN 0-89218-037-4); pap. 6.95 (ISBN 0-89218-038-2). Camelot Pub.
--Computer Poster Book. 1982. 14.95x (ISBN 0-89218-067-6). Camelot Pub.
--Computer Science Mathematics. (Mathematics Ser.). 320p. 1976. text ed. 20.95 (ISBN 0-675-08650-7). Merrill.
--Computers in Number Theory. (Illus.). 1982. pap. 13.95 (ISBN 0-914894-27-7). Computer Sci.
--Data Processing: An Introduction. (Business C11 Ser.). 1978. pap. text ed. 16.95 (ISBN 0-675-08416-4). Additional supplements may be obtained from publisher. Merrill.
--Data Processing: An Introduction with BASIC. 2nd ed. 576p. 1982. pap. text ed. 19.95 (ISBN 0-675-09854-8); guide 6.95 study (ISBN 0-675-09803-3). Additional Supplements May Be Obtained From Publisher. Merrill.
--Famous People of Computing: A Book of Posters. 1982. 12.95x (ISBN 0-89218-068-4). Camelot Pub.
--Fortran Programming. 2nd ed. 1980. pap. 8.95 (ISBN 0-89218-042-0); tchr's manual 3.95x (ISBN 0-686-80432-5); wkbk. o.p. 4.95x (ISBN 0-686-80433-3). Camelot Pub.
--Guide to BASIC Programming. 2nd ed. 1975. text ed. 18.95 (ISBN 0-201-07106-1). A-W.
--Illustrated Computer Dictionary for Young People. LC 81-21795. (Illus.). 1982. 8.95x (ISBN 0-89218-052-8). Camelot Pub.
--An Introduction to Computers: Developing Computer Literacy. 1983. 18.95 (ISBN 0-675-20030-X). Additional supplements may be obtained from publisher. Merrill.
--Introduction to Information Processing. 3rd ed. 650p. 1981. text ed. 23.95 (ISBN 0-675-08073-8); basic supplement 2.95 (ISBN 0-675-09917-X); additional suppl. mat. avail. Merrill.
--Introduction to Information Processing. 2nd ed. (Business Ser.). 1977. text ed. 17.95 o.s.i. (ISBN 0-675-08520-9); Student Guide 6.95 (ISBN 0-675-08519-5). Merrill.
--Microcomputer Coloring Book. 1982. 2.90. Camelot Pub.
--Problem Solving with FORTRAN. LC 76-26040. (Illus.). 1977. pap. text ed. 15.95 (ISBN 0-13-720094-3). P-H.
--Some People Just Won't Believe a Computer. 1978. pap. 1.50x (ISBN 0-89218-032-3). Camelot Pub.
--Understanding Computers. (gr. 9-12). 1982. 13.95x (ISBN 0-89218-057-9); instr's. guide 12.95x (ISBN 0-89218-059-5); student wkbk. 5.95x (ISBN 0-89218-058-7). Camelot Pub.
--Visual Masters for BASIC Programming. 2d ed. 1982. 9.95x (ISBN 0-89218-049-8). Camelot Pub.
--Visual Masters for Teaching About Computers. 2d ed. 1982. 9.95x (ISBN 0-89218-050-1). Camelot Pub.
--Visual Masters for Teaching FORTRAN Programming. 1978. 9.95x (ISBN 0-89218-035-8). Camelot Pub.
--What Computers Can Do. 2nd ed. LC 81-21664. 1982. 12.95x (ISBN 0-89218-043-9). Camelot Pub.

Spencer, E., ed. Hand Atlas of the Urinary Sediment. 2nd ed. 68p. 1977. text ed. 19.95 (ISBN 0-8391-0989-X). Univ Park.

Spencer, Edgar. Dynamics of the Earth: An Introduction to Physical Geology. 1972. text ed. 25.50 scp (ISBN 0-690-24844-X, HarpC). Har-Row.

Spencer, Edgar W. Introduction to the Structure of the Earth. 2nd ed. 1977. text ed. 35.00 (ISBN 0-07-060197-6, C). McGraw.
--Physical Geology. (Biology Ser.). (Illus.). 656p. 1983. text ed. 26.95 (ISBN 0-201-06423-5); Laboratory Manual avail.; Instrs's Manual avail.; Study Guide avail. A-W.

Spencer, Elizabeth. Ship Island & Other Stories. 1968. 5.95 o.p. (ISBN 0-07-060182-8, GB). McGraw.
--The Snare. LC 72-3846. 384p. 1972. 8.95 o.p. (ISBN 0-07-060178-X, GB). McGraw.

Spencer, Everett R., Jr. A Society of Physicians. LC 81-81396. 410p. 1981. 26.00 (ISBN 0-9608238-0-8). MA Med Soc.

Spencer, F. Introduction to Human & Molecular Biology. 235p. 1970. 9.95 o.p. (ISBN 0-407-55900-0). Butterworth.

Spencer, Frances A. Bible Facts in Crossword Puzzles. (Quiz & Puzzle Bks.). 1979. pap. 2.95 (ISBN 0-8010-7972-1). Baker Bk.

Spencer, Frank, ed. A History of American Physical Anthropology: 1930-1980. 1982. 44.50 (ISBN 0-12-656660-7). Acad Pr.

Spencer, Frank C., jt. ed. see Sabiston, David C.

Spencer, Hanna. Heinrich Heine. (World Authors Ser.: No. 669). 1982. lib. bdg. 13.95 (ISBN 0-8057-6516-6, Twayne). G K Hall.

Spencer, Hazelton, et al. British Literature, 2 vols. 3rd ed. 1974. text ed. 19.95 ea.; Vol. 1. text ed. (ISBN 0-669-84129-3); Vol. 2. text ed. (ISBN 0-669-84137-4). Heath.

Spencer, Henry C., et al. Technical Drawing Problems: Series Two. 4th ed. (Illus.). 1980. pap. text ed. 14.95x (ISBN 0-02-414330-8). Macmillan.
--Technical Drawing Problems: Series Three. 3rd ed. (Illus.). 1980. pap. text ed. 14.95x (ISBN 0-02-414360-X). Macmillan.

Spencer, Herbert. Pathology of the Lung, 2 vols. LC 76-56633. 1977. Vol. 2. text ed. 22.50 (ISBN 0-7216-8515-3). Saunders.
--Pioneers of Modern Typography. (Illus.). 160p. 1983. pap. 15.00 (ISBN 0-262-69081-0). MIT Pr.

Spencer, J. E. Shifting Cultivation in Southeastern Asia. (California Library Reprint Ser.). 1978. 30.00x (ISBN 0-520-03517-8). U of Cal Pr.

Spencer, J. E. & Thomas, W. L. Introducing Cultural Geography. 2nd ed. LC 77-20230. 1978. text ed. 27.95 (ISBN 0-471-81631-0); avail. tchr's manual (ISBN 0-471-03422-3). Wiley.

Spencer, J. R. Titian. (Color Slide Program of the Great Masters). 1968. 17.95 (ISBN 0-07-060146-1, P&RB). McGraw.

Spencer, Jack, jt. auth. see Chartock, Roselle.

Spencer, John D. & Pippenger, Dale E. The Voltage Regulator Handbook for Design Engineers. LC 77-87869. 1977. pap. 5.65 (ISBN 0-89512-101-8, LCC4350). Tex Instr Inc.

Spencer, John R., tr. see Alberti, Leone B.

Spencer, Kevin, jt. ed. see Price, Christopher P.

Spencer, L. J. A Key to Precious Stones. (Illus.). 237p. 1971. 9.95 (ISBN 0-87523-054-7). Emerson.

Spencer, L. J., tr. see Bauer, Max.

Spencer, LaVyrle. Forsaking All Others, No. 76. 1982. pap. 1.75 o.p. (ISBN 0-515-06687-7). Jove Pubns.
--Hummingbird. 416p. 1983. pap. 3.50 (ISBN 0-515-07108-0). Jove Pubns.
--A Promise to Cherish. (Second Chance at Love Ser.: No. 100). 1983. pap. 1.75 (ISBN 0-515-06864-0). Jove Pubns.

Spencer, Louise. Cake Decorating Ideas & Designs. LC 80-54334. (Illus.). 1981. 13.95 (ISBN 0-8069-0214-0); lib. bdg. 16.79 (ISBN 0-8069-0215-9); pap. 7.95 (ISBN 0-8069-7502-4). Sterling.
--Decorating Cakes & Party Foods. (Illus.). 1969. 8.95 (ISBN 0-8208-0219-0). Hearthside.

Spencer, M. C. Charles Fourier. (World Authors Ser.). 15.95 (ISBN 0-8057-6420-8, Twayne). G K Hall.

Spencer, Margaret R., jt. auth. see Hall, Vivian S.

Spencer, May & Tait, Katherine M. Introduction to Nursing. 5th ed. (Illus.). 544p. 1982. pap. text ed. 15.95 (ISBN 0-632-00705-2, B 4635-9). Mosby.

Spencer, Metta & Inkeles, Alex. Foundations of Modern Sociology. 3rd ed. (Prentice Hall Foundations of Modern Sociology Ser.). (Illus.). 672p. 1982. text ed. 22.95 (ISBN 0-13-330290-3). P-H.

Spencer, Michael. Michael Bufor. (World Authors Ser.: No. 275). 10.95 o.p. (ISBN 0-686-75275-9, Twayne). G K Hall.

Spencer, Michael, tr. see Butor, Michel.

Spencer, Milton H. Contemporary Economics. 4th rev. ed. 1980. text ed. 25.95x (ISBN 0-87901-113-0); study guide 9.95 (ISBN 0-87901-109-2). Worth.
--Contemporary Macroeconomics. 4th ed. (Illus.). text ed. 16.95x (ISBN 0-87901-114-9); study guide 7.95 (ISBN 0-87901-110-6). Worth.
--Contemporary Microeconomics. 4th ed. 1980. text ed. 16.95x (ISBN 0-87901-115-7); study guide 7.95 (ISBN 0-87901-111-4). Worth.

Spencer, Natalie, compiled by. References for Debtor's or Bill Payor's; Data Notes. 75p. Date not set. 12.95 (ISBN 0-686-37648-X). Data Notes Pub.

Spencer, Peter S. & Schaumberg, Herbert H. Experimental & Clinical Neurotoxicology. (Illus.). 956p. 1980. lib. bdg. 125.00 (ISBN 0-683-07854-2). Williams & Wilkins.

Spencer, Phillis. Vacation Timesharing. 160p. (Orig.). 1982. pap. cancelled (ISBN 0-920510-71-X, Pub. by Personal Lib). Dodd.

Spencer, Ray, jt. auth. see Laubich, Arnold.

Spencer, Richard A. The Fire of Truth. LC 82-71218. (Orig.). 1982. pap. 5.95 (ISBN 0-8054-2248-X). Broadman.

Spencer, Richard H. Planning Implementation & Control in Product Test Assurance. (Illus.). 240p. 1983. text ed. 27.50 (ISBN 0-13-679506-4). P-H.

Spencer, Richard P. Nuclear Medicine-Focus on Clinical Diagnosis. 2nd ed. 1980. pap. 23.00 (ISBN 0-87488-825-5). Med Exam.

Spencer, Robert E., jt. auth. see Campbell, Hugh G.

Spencer, Roberta T. & Nichols, Lynn W. Clinical Pharmacology & Nursing Management. (Illus.). 1056p. 1983. text ed. 29.50 (ISBN 0-397-54304-2, Lippincott Medical). Lippincott.

Spencer, Samuel R., Jr. Booker T. Washington & the Negro's Place in American Life. (The Library of American Biography). 212p. 1965. pap. 5.95 (ISBN 0-316-80621-8). Little.

Spencer, Sharon. Collage of Dreams: The Writings of Anais Nin. LC 82-74201. 188p. 1977. 12.95x (ISBN 0-8040-0760-8). Swallow.
--Space, Time & Structure in the Modern Novel. LC 82-72387. 251p. 1971. pap. 6.95x (ISBN 0-8040-0334-3). Swallow.

Spencer, Sharon, tr. see Chedid, Andree.

Spencer, Sidney. Mysticism in World Religion. 9.50 (ISBN 0-8446-0927-7). Peter Smith.

Spencer, Stanley. The Man: Correspondence & Reminiscences. Rothenstein, John, ed. LC 79-63683. (Illus.). 156p. 1979. 18.95x (ISBN 0-8214-0431-8, 82-83202). Ohio U Pr.

Spencer, Sue. Bitten in the Outback. 1978. 6.95 o.p. (ISBN 0-533-03782-4). Vantage.

Spencer, T. J. & Wells, S. E. Book of Masques. 1967. 69.50 (ISBN 0-521-05455-9). Cambridge U Pr.

Spencer, W. Wylie. Our Knowledge of Other Minds. 1930. text ed. 29.50x (ISBN 0-686-83671-5). Elliots Bks.

Spencer, Warren F. The Confederate Navy in Europe. LC 81-23283. 288p. 1983. text ed. 19.95 (ISBN 0-8173-0115-1). U of Ala Pr.

Spencer, William. Art of Bassoon Playing. rev. ed. Muellet, Frederick A., ed. (Illus.). 1969. pap. text ed. 8.50 (ISBN 0-87487-073-9). Summy.
--The Islamic States in Conflict. (Impact Ser.). 96p. (gr. 7 up). 1983. PLB 8.90 (ISBN 0-531-04544-7). Watts.

Spencer, Zane, jt. auth. see Leech, Jay.

Spender, Dale. Women of Ideas & What Men Have Done to Them: From Aphra Behn to Adrenne Rich. 576p. 1983. 23.95 (ISBN 0-7100-9353-5). Routledge & Kegan.

Spender, Humphrey. Worktown People: Photographs from Northern England, 1937-1938. Mulford, Jeremy, ed. (Illus.). 128p. 1982. 14.95 (ISBN 0-905046-20-X). Falling Wall.

Spender, John A. Short History of Our Times. LC 72-110865. (Illus.). 1971. Repr. of 1934 ed. lib. bdg. 15.75x (ISBN 0-8371-4538-4, SPSH). Greenwood.

Spender, S. Life & the Poet. LC 74-7171. (Studies in Poetry, No. 38). 1974. lib. bdg. 39.95x (ISBN 0-8383-1924-6). Haskell.
--Poetry Since Nineteen Thirty Nine. LC 74-7038. (Studies in Poetry, No. 38). 1974. lib. bdg. 39.95x (ISBN 0-8383-1930-0). Haskell.

Spender, Stephen. Henry Moore: Sculptures in Landscape. (Illus.). 1979. 25.00 o.p. (ISBN 0-517-53676-5, C N Potter Bks). Crown.
--Learning Laughter. (Illus.). Repr. of 1953 ed. lib. bdg. 16.00x (ISBN 0-8371-1958-8, SPLL). Greenwood.
--The Magic Flute. (Opera Stories for Young People Ser.). (Illus.). (gr. 3 up). 1966. PLB 4.89 o.p. (ISBN 0-399-60436-7). Putnam Pub Group.
--Selected Poems. 80p. 1965. pap. 4.95 (ISBN 0-571-06358-6). Faber & Faber.

--Selected Poems. 1964. pap. 8.95 (ISBN 0-394-40445-9). Random.

--T. S. Eliot. (Modern Masters Ser.). 1976. pap. 3.95 (ISBN 0-14-004321-7). Penguin.

--The Thirties & After: Poetry, Politics, People, 1930s-1970s. LC 78-23721. 1979. pap. 10.00 (ISBN 0-394-50173-X, Vin). Random.

Spender, Stephen & Hockney, David. China Diary. 1983. 28.50 (ISBN 0-686-42992-3). Abrams.

Spender, Stephen, jt. auth. see Hogarth, Paul.

Spender, Stephen, ed. Great Writings of Goethe. 1978. pap. 4.95 (ISBN 0-452-00524-8, F524, Mer). NAL.

Spener, Philip J. Pia Desideria. Tappert, Theodore G., ed. & tr. LC 64-12995. 1964. pap. 4.75 (ISBN 0-8006-1953-6, 1-1953). Fortress.

Spengemann, William C. The Forms of Autobiography: Episodes in the History of a Literary Genre. LC 79-22575. 1980. 22.50x (ISBN 0-300-02473-8); pap. 7.95x (ISBN 0-300-02886-5, Y-436). Yale U Pr.

Spengler, Dan M. Low Back Pain: Assessment & Management. 176p. 1982. 24.00 (ISBN 0-8089-1468-5, 794238). Grune.

Spengler, Joseph J. France Faces Depopulation. LC 69-10158. (Illus.). 1968. Repr. of 1938 ed. lib. bdg. 18.50x (ISBN 0-8371-0235-9, SPFD). Greenwood.

--Origins of Economic Thought & Justice. LC 79-27026. (Political & Social Economy Ser.). 192p. 1980. 16.95x (ISBN 0-8093-0947-5). S Ill U Pr.

Spengler, Oswald. The Decline of the West. Werner, Helmut, ed. 7.95 (ISBN 0-394-60488-1). Modern Lib.

Spenner, Helmut. I Am a Little Cat. (Little Animal Stories Ser.). (Illus.). 24p. 1983. 5.95 (ISBN 0-8120-5513-6). Barron.

Spenner, Kenneth I. & Otto, Luther B. Career Lines & Careers: Entry into Careers Sales, Vol. III. LC 82-47855. (Entry into Careers Ser.). (Illus.). 256p. 1982. 24.95x (ISBN 0-669-03645-5). Lexington Bks.

Spens, Janet. Spenser's Faerie Queene: An Interpretation. LC 66-27149. 1967. Repr. of 1934 ed. 10.00x (ISBN 0-8462-1796-1). Russell.

Spenser, Dwight. Word Games in English. 1981. 15.00x o.p. (ISBN 0-686-75663-0, Pub. by European Schoolbks England). State Mutual Bk.

Spenser, Edmund. Faerie Queen. Roche, Thomas P. & O'Donnell, C. Patrick, Jr., eds. (Poetry Ser.). 1979. pap. 12.95 o.p. (ISBN 0-14-042207-2). Penguin.

--Faerie Queen (A Selection) 1976. 12.95x (ISBN 0-460-01443-9, Evman); pap. 3.95x (ISBN 0-460-01443-9, Evman). Biblio Dist.

--The Faerie Queene, Book 1. Jussawala, M. C., ed. (Annotated OL Texts). viii, 279p. 1982. pap. text ed. 7.95x (ISBN 0-86131-185-X, Pub. by Orient Longman Ltd India). Apt Bks.

--Shepherd's Calendar & Other Poems. 1978. Repr. of 1932 ed. 9.95x (ISBN 0-460-00879-X, Evman). Biblio Dist.

Spenser, Edmund & Davies, John. Ireland under Elizabeth & James the First. Morley, Henry, ed. 445p. 1982. Repr. of 1890 ed. lib. bdg. 50.00 (ISBN 0-89987-647-1). Darby Bks.

Spenser, Jay P. Bellanca C. F. The Emergence of the Cabin Monoplane in the United States. LC 81-607557. (Famous Aircraft of the National Air & Space Museum Ser.: Vol. 6). (Illus.). 96p. 1982. pap. 7.95 (ISBN 0-87474-881-X). Smithsonian.

Sper, Felix. From Native Roots. (Illus.). 6.00 o.p. (ISBN 0-910294-03-8). Brown Bk.

Sperandeo, Andy. Introduction of Model Railroad Wiring. Hayden, Bob, ed. (Illus., Orig.). 1984. pap. price not set (ISBN 0-89024-060-4). Kalmbach.

Speranskii, M. N., ed. Iz Starinnoi Novgorodskoi Literatury XIV Veka. (Monuments of Early Russian Literature: Vol. 4). 140p. (Russian.). 1982. pap. 9.00 (ISBN 0-933884-24-9). Berkeley Slavic.

Speraw, Linda. How to Buy Your First Home. 192p. 1983. 14.95 (ISBN 0-87196-609-3). Facts on File.

Sperber, D. Rethinking Symbolism. Morton, A. L., tr. from Fr. LC 75-18433. (Studies in Social Anthropology: No. 11). 164p. 1975. 21.95 (ISBN 0-521-20834-3); pap. 8.95 (ISBN 0-521-09967-6). Cambridge U Pr.

Sperber, Geoffrey H., jt. ed. see Skinner, Mark F.

Sperber, Milo. Zarabanda. 1972. pap. text ed. 4.95 (ISBN 0-912022-32-9). EMC.

Sperber, Murray, ed. Arthur Koestler: A Collection of Critical Essays. 1977. 12.95 (ISBN 0-13-049213-2, Spec). P-H.

Sperber, Nathaniel N. & Lerbinger, Otto. Manager's Public Relations Handbook. LC 81-22896. 256p. 1982. text ed. 25.00 (ISBN 0-201-14199-X). A-W.

Sperber, Paula & Pezzano, Chuck. Inside Bowling for Women. LC 77-75852. (Inside Ser.). (Illus.). 1977. 7.95 o.p. (ISBN 0-8092-7995-9); pap. 5.95 o.p. (ISBN 0-8092-7980-0). Contemp Bks.

Sperber, Philip. Fail-Safe Business Negotiating: Strategies & Tactics for Success. (Illus.). 302p. 1982. 19.95 (ISBN 0-13-299586-7); pap. 10.95 (ISBN 0-13-299578-6). P-H.

--Intellectual Property Management - Law - Business - Strategy. LC 74-21479. 1974. with 1980 rev. pages 75.00 (ISBN 0-87632-150-3). Boardman.

Speriglio, Milo A. Marilyn Monroe: Murder Cover-Up. LC 82-51319. (Illus.). 276p. (Orig.). 1983. pap. 7.95 (ISBN 0-930990-77-3). Seville Pub.

Sperisen, Francis J. Art of the Lapidary. rev. ed. 1961. 9.95 o.p. (ISBN 0-685-07609-1, 80712). Glencoe.

Sperline, Meredith E. Ordinary Differential Equations: Solutions & Applications. LC 80-6101. 584p. 1981. pap. text ed. 18.75 (ISBN 0-8191-1358-1). U Pr of Amer.

Sperling, A. P. Arithmetic Made Simple. pap. 4.95 (ISBN 0-385-00983-6, Made). Doubleday.

Sperling, Abraham & Stuart, Monroe. Mathematics Made Simple. rev. ed. LC 80-2627. (Made Simple Bk.). (Illus.). 192p. 1982. pap. 4.95 (ISBN 0-385-17481-0). Doubleday.

Sperling, D., jt. ed. see Kanafani, A.

Sperling, Dan. A Spectator's Guide to Baseball. 96p. (Orig.). 1983. pap. 2.50 (ISBN 0-380-82628-3). Avon.

Sperling, Susan K. Poplollies & Bellibones. (Illus.). 1979. pap. 3.95 (ISBN 0-14-005190-2). Penguin.

--Poplollies & Bellibones: A Celebration of Lost Words. (Illus.). 1977. 7.95 (ISBN 0-517-53079-1, C N Potter Bks). Crown.

Sperlinger, David. Animals in Research: New Perspectives in Animal Experimentation. 373p. 1981. 49.95 (ISBN 0-471-27843-2, Pub. by Wiley-Interscience). Wiley.

Spero, Joan E. The Politics of International Economic Relations. 2nd ed. 350p. 1981. text ed. 16.95x (ISBN 0-312-62704-1); pap. text ed. 9.95x (ISBN 0-312-62705-X). St Martin.

Spero, Robert. The Duping of the American: Dishonesty & Deception in Presidential Television Advertising. 1980. 14.37i (ISBN 0-690-01884-3). Har-Row.

Speroff, Leon, et al. Clinical Gynecological Endocrinology & Infertilty. 450p. 1983. lib. bdg. price not set (ISBN 0-683-07895-X). Williams & Wilkins.

--Clinical Gynecological Endocrinology & Infertility. 2nd ed. (Illus.). 444p. 1978. 38.00 o.p. (ISBN 0-683-07894-1). Williams & Wilkins.

Speroni, Charles & Kany, Charles K. Spoken Italian for Students & Travelers. 2nd ed. 1978. pap. text ed. 7.95 (ISBN 0-669-00577-0). Heath.

Sperounis, Frederick P. The Limits of Progressive School Reform in the Nineteen Seventies: A Case Study. LC 80-5063. 286p. 1980. pap. text ed. 11.25 (ISBN 0-8191-1031-0). U Pr of Amer.

Sperry, Armstrong. All About the Jungle. (Allabout Ser: No. 29). (Illus.). (gr. 5-9). 1959. PLB 5.39 o.p. (ISBN 0-394-90229-7, BYR). Random.

Sperry, Kip. Index to Genealogical Periodical Literature, 1960-1977. LC 79-9407. (Gale Genealogy & Local History Ser.: Vol. 9). 1979. 42.00x (ISBN 0-8103-1403-7). Gale.

Sperry, Kip, ed. Survey of American Genealogical Periodicals & Periodical Indexes. LC 78-55033. (Genealogy & Local History Ser.: Vol. 3). 1978. 42.00x (ISBN 0-8103-1401-0). Gale.

Sperry, Len. Learning Performance & Individual Differences: Essays & Readings. 1972. pap. 7.95x (ISBN 0-673-07799-3). Scott F.

Sperry, Ralph A. Status Quotient: The Carrier. 1981. pap. 2.50 o.p. (ISBN 0-380-78766-0, 78766). Avon.

Spetgang, Tilly & Wells, Malcolm. The Children's Solar Energy Book: Even Grown-Ups Can Understand. LC 81-85022. (Illus.). 160p. (gr. 4 up). 1982. 12.95 (ISBN 0-8069-3118-3); PLB 15.69 (ISBN 0-8069-3119-1); pap. 7.95 (ISBN 0-8069-7584-9). Sterling.

Speth, John D. Bison Kills & Bone Counts: Decision Making by Ancient Hunters. LC 82-21976. (Prehistoric Archaeology & Ecology Ser.). (Illus.). 272p. 1983. pap. 9.00 (ISBN 0-226-76949-6). U of Chicago Pr.

Speth, Linda & Hirsch, Alison D. Women, Family, & Community in Colonial America: Two Perspectives. LC 82-23326. (Women & History Ser.: No. 4). 85p. 1983. text ed. 20.00 (ISBN 0-86656-191-9). Haworth Pr.

Spevack, J. M. Teaching Sucks. 130p. pap. 2.95 (ISBN 0-9604448-2-3). Spevack.

--Thought Disorder. 188p. pap. 2.00 (ISBN 0-9604448-1-5). Spevack.

Speyer, A. James. Idea & Image in Recent Art. LC 74-76720. (Illus.). 50p. (Orig.). 1974. pap. 2.50x (ISBN 0-86559-015-X). Art Inst Chi.

Speyer, A. James & Rorimer, Anne. Seventy-fourth American Exhibition. (Illus.). 64p. Date not set. pap. 8.95 (ISBN 0-86559-050-8). Art Inst Chi.

Spicehandler, Daniel. The Serpent & the Eagle. 300p. 1983. 14.95 (ISBN 0-937444-05-7); pap. 9.95 (ISBN 0-937444-06-5). Caislan Pr.

Spicer, A. Advances in Preconcentration & Dehydration of Food. 1974. 67.75 (ISBN 0-85334-599-6). Elsevier.

Spicer, Arnold, ed. Bread: Social, Nutritional, & Agricultural Aspects of Wheaten Bread. (Illus.). 1975. 57.50x (ISBN 0-85334-637-2, Pub. by Applied Sci England). Elsevier.

Spicer, Dorothy. Desert Adventure. (YA) 1968. 6.95 (ISBN 0-685-07428-5, Avalon). Bouregy.

--Humming Top. LC 68-31176. (gr. 7-11). 1968. 10.95 (ISBN 0-87599-147-5). S G Phillips.

Spicer, Dorothy G. Book of Festivals. LC 75-92667. 1969. Repr. of 1937 ed. 42.00x (ISBN 0-8103-3143-8). Gale.

--Folk Festivals & the Foreign Community. LC 70-167201. 1976. Repr. of 1923 ed. 34.00x (ISBN 0-8103-4301-0). Gale.

--Forty Six Days of Christmas. (Illus.). (gr. 3-6). 1960. PLB 4.99 o.p. (ISBN 0-698-30091-2, Coward). Putnam Pub Group.

--The Owl's Nest: Folk Tales from Friesland. (Illus.). (gr. 3-7). 1968. PLB 4.99 o.p. (ISBN 0-698-30277-X, Coward). Putnam Pub Group.

--Thirteen Dragons. (Illus.). 128p. (gr. 3-6). 1974. PLB 5.86 o.p. (ISBN 0-698-30506-X, Coward). Putnam Pub Group.

--Thirteen Ghosts. (Illus.). (gr. 3-6). 1965. PLB 5.29 o.p. (ISBN 0-698-30357-1, Coward). Putnam Pub Group.

--Thirteen Giants. (Illus.). (gr. 3-6). 1966. PLB 4.99 o.p. (ISBN 0-698-30358-X, Coward). Putnam Pub Group.

--Thirteen Jolly Saints. (Illus.). (gr. 3-5). 1970. PLB 4.99 o.p. (ISBN 0-698-30360-1, Coward). Putnam Pub Group.

--Thirteen Monsters. (Illus.). (gr. 3-6). 1964. PLB 4.99 o.p. (ISBN 0-698-30361-X, Coward). Putnam Pub Group.

--Thirteen Rascals. (Illus.). 1972. PLB 4.99 o.p. (ISBN 0-698-30362-8, Coward). Putnam Pub Group.

--Thirteen Witches, Two Wizards, the Devil & a Pack of Goblins. (Illus.). (gr. 3-6). 1970. PLB 4.99 o.p. (ISBN 0-698-30363-6, Coward). Putnam Pub Group.

--Yearbook of English Festivals. LC 74-162632. (Illus.). 298p. 1954. Repr. lib. bdg. 18.75x (ISBN 0-8371-6132-0, SPEF). Greenwood.

Spicer, Edward H. The American Indians. (Dimensions of Ethnicity Ser.). 176p. 1982. pap. text ed. 5.95x (ISBN 0-674-02476-1). Harvard U Pr.

Spicer, Edward H., ed. Human Problems in Technological Change. LC 52-11862. 302p. 1952. 9.50x (ISBN 0-87154-824-0). Russell Sage.

Spicer, Jerry & Barnett, Peggy. Hospital-Based Chemical Dependency Treatment: A Model for Outcome Evaluation. 3.50 (ISBN 0-89486-078-X, 1935B). Hazelden.

--The Outcomes of Employer Referrals to Treatment. 3.50 (ISBN 0-686-92445-2, 1943B). Hazelden.

Spicer, Jerry & McKenna, Thomas. Apples & Oranges: A Comparison of Inpatient & Outpatient Programs. 2.50 (ISBN 0-89486-125-5, 1928B). Hazelden.

Spicer, Jerry, jt. auth. see Laundergan, J. Clark.

Spicer, Keith. Winging It: A Guide to Making Speeches Fly Without Notes. LC 80-8644. 264p. 1982. 13.95 (ISBN 0-385-15764-9). Doubleday.

Spiegal, Murray R. Applied Differential Equations. 3rd ed. 1980. text ed. 27.95 (ISBN 0-13-040097-1). P-H.

Spiegel, Allen, et al, eds. Medical Technology, Health Care & the Consumer. LC 79-25559. 352p. 1981. 34.95x (ISBN 0-87705-498-3). Human Sci Pr.

Spiegel, Allen D. & Hyman, Herbert Harvey. Basic Health Planning Methods. LC 78-10780. 508p. 1979. 52.50 (ISBN 0-89443-077-7). Aspen Systems.

Spiegel, E. A. Guided Brain Operations. (Illus.). x, 246p. 1982. 88.75 (ISBN 3-8055-3451-5). S Karger.

Spiegel, Henry W. The Growth of Economic Thought. rev. ed. 880p. 1983. text ed. 37.50 (ISBN 0-8223-0550-X); pap. text ed. 22.50 (ISBN 0-8223-0551-8). Duke.

Spiegel, Herbert J. & Gruber, Arnold. From Weather Vanes to Satellites: An Introduction to Meteorology. LC 82-8349. 241p. 1983. text ed. 16.95 (ISBN 0-471-86401-3). Wiley.

Spiegel, Leonard & Limbrunner, George F. Reinforced Concrete Design. (Illus.). 1980. text ed. 20.95 (ISBN 0-13-771659-1). P-H.

Spiegel, Marianne A. United States Policy Options in Southern Africa: The Next Five Years. (Seven Springs Studies). 49p. 1982. pap. 3.00 (ISBN 0-943006-07-4). Seven Springs.

Spiegel, Murray R. Advanced Calculus. (Orig.). 1963. pap. 8.95 (ISBN 0-07-060229-8, SP). McGraw.

--Advanced Mathematics for Engineers & Scientists. (Schaum Outline Ser). 1970. pap. 8.95 (ISBN 0-07-060216-6, SP). McGraw.

--Calculus of Finite Differences & Differential Equations. (Schaum's Outline Ser). pap. 7.95 (ISBN 0-07-060218-2, SP). McGraw.

--College Algebra. (Orig.). 1956. pap. 6.95 (ISBN 0-07-060226-3, SP). McGraw.

--Complex Variables. (Orig.). 1964. pap. 7.95 (ISBN 0-07-060230-1, SP). McGraw.

--Fourier Analysis. 1974. pap. text ed. 7.95 (ISBN 0-07-060219-0, SP). McGraw.

--Laplace Transforms. (Orig.). 1965. pap. 8.95 (ISBN 0-07-060231-X, SP). McGraw.

--Mathematical Handbook of Formulas & Tables. (Schaum's Outline Ser.). 1968. pap. text ed. 7.95 (ISBN 0-07-060224-7, SP). McGraw.

--Probability & Statistics. 304p. (Orig.). 1975. pap. text ed. 7.95 (ISBN 0-07-060220-4, SP). McGraw.

--Real Variables. 1969. pap. 7.95 (ISBN 0-07-060221-2, SP). McGraw.

--Statistics. 1961. pap. text ed. 7.95 (ISBN 0-07-060227-1, SP). McGraw.

--Theoretical Mechanics. (Schaum's Outline Ser). 1967. pap. 8.95 (ISBN 0-07-060232-8, SP). McGraw.

Spiegel, Shalom. The Last Trial: On the Legend & Lore of the Command to Abraham to Offer Isaac As a Sacrifice - the Akedah. LC 79-12664. (The Jewish Legacy Ser.). 1979. pap. 7.95x (ISBN 0-87441-290-0). Behrman.

Spiegel, Stephen L. & Becker, Carol, eds. At Issue: Politics in the World Arena. 3rd ed. LC 80-52377. 534p. 1981. pap. text ed. 9.95x (ISBN 0-312-05882-9). St Martin.

Spiegel, Steven L. Dominance & Diversity: The International Hierarchy. LC 80-8295. 317p. 1980. lib. bdg. 21.50 (ISBN 0-8191-1331-X); pap. text ed. 11.00 (ISBN 0-8191-1332-8). U Pr of Amer.

Spiegel, Timothy M. Practical Rheumatology. 384p. 1983. 35.00 (ISBN 0-471-09567-2, Pub. by Wiley Med). Wiley.

Spiegelberg, H. & Ave-Lallemant, E. Pfander-Studien. 1982. 69.50 (ISBN 90-247-2490-2, Pub. By Martinus Nijhoff Netherlands). Kluwer Boston.

Spiegelberg, Stanley, jt. tr. see Pearson, Nancy.

Spiegelman. The Knight: The Theory & Method of Jung's Active Imagination Techique. (Illus.). 1982. pap. 6.95 (ISBN 0-941404-23-4). Falcon Pr Az.

Spiegelman, J. Marvin. The Tree. 2nd ed. 464p. 1982. pap. 12.95 (ISBN 0-941404-04-8). Falcon Pr Az.

Spiegelstein. Behavior Models & the Analysis of Drug Action. (Proceedings). 1982. 127.75 (ISBN 0-444-42125-4). Elsevier.

Spielberg, Danielson, jt. auth. see Spielberg, Maier.

Spielberg, Maier & Spielberg, Danielson. Tenant Resource & Advocacy Center. 57p. Date not set. pap. 5.00 (ISBN 0-686-36543-7). Ctr Responsive Law.

Spielberg, Peter, ed. James Joyce's Manuscripts & Letters at the University of Buffalo. LC 62-19657. (Illus.). 1962. 32.50x (ISBN 0-87395-009-7). State U NY Pr.

Spielberger, C. D., jt. auth. see Gaudry, Eric.

Spielberger, C. D., ed. Current Topics in Clinical & Community Psychology. Vol. 1. 43.50 (ISBN 0-12-153501-0); Vol. 2. 43.50 (ISBN 0-12-153502-9); Vol. 3. 43.50 (ISBN 0-12-153503-7). Acad Pr.

Spielberger, C. D., et al. Stress & Anxiety, Vol. 8. 1981. 34.95 (ISBN 0-07-060239-5). McGraw.

Spielberger, Charles, jt. ed. see O'Neil, Harold F., Jr.

Spielberger, Charles D. & Diaz-Guerrero, Rogelio, eds. Cross-Cultural Anxiety, Vol. 2. LC 76-28389. (Clinical & Community Psychology Ser.). (Illus.). 350p. 1982. text ed. 34.50 (ISBN 0-89116-242-9). Hemisphere Pub.

Spielberger, Charles D. & Vagg, Peter R., eds. The Assessment & Treatment of Test Anxiety. (Clinical & Community Psychology Ser.). 352p. Date not set. text ed. 35.00 (ISBN 0-89116-212-7). Hemisphere Pub. Postponed.

Spielberger, Charles D., jt. ed. see Butcher, James N.

Spielberger, Walter J. Gepard. (Illus.). 255p. (Ger.). 1982. 39.95x (ISBN 0-933852-30-4). Nautical & Aviation.

Spieler, Carolyn, ed. Women in Medicine-1976. LC 77-82299. (Illus.). 1977. pap. 4.00 o.p. (ISBN 0-914362-21-6). J Macy Foun.

Spielman, John see Chang, Raymond.

Spielman, Patrick. Alphabets & Designs For Wood Signs. (Illus.). 132p. 1983. 13.95 (ISBN 0-8069-5482-5); pap. 6.95 (ISBN 0-8069-7702-7). Sterling.

--Make Your Own Sports Gear. 1970. 7.95 o.p. (ISBN 0-685-07653-9, 80721). Glencoe.

--Making Wood Decoys. LC 82-50556. (Illus.). 160p. 1982. 16.95 (ISBN 0-8069-5476-0); lib. bdg. 19.99 (ISBN 0-8069-5477-9); pap. 8.95 (ISBN 0-8069-7660-8). Sterling.

--Making Wood Signs. LC 80-54342. (Illus.). 144p. 1981. 13.95 (ISBN 0-8069-5434-5); lib. bdg. 9.89 o.p. (ISBN 0-8069-5435-3); pap. 6.95 (ISBN 0-8069-8984-X). Sterling.

--Working Green Wood with Peg. LC 79-91406. (Illus.). 160p. 1980. lib. bdg. 13.29 (ISBN 0-8069-5417-5). pap. 8.95 (ISBN 0-8069-8924-6). Sterling.

Spielman, Patrick E., jt. auth. see Schaeffer, Glen N.

Spielmann, Karl F. Analyzing Soviet Strategic Arms Decisions. LC 78-6007. 184p. 1978. 20.00 o.p. (ISBN 0-89158-162-6). Westview.

Spielmann, M. H. History of Punch. LC 69-16069. 1969. Repr. of 1895 ed. 47.00x (ISBN 0-8103-3553-0). Gale.

Spier, Peter. Crash! Bang! Boom. LC 70-157625. (Illus.). (ps-1). 1972. 9.95a (ISBN 0-385-06780-1); PLB (ISBN 0-385-02496-7). Doubleday.

--The Erie Canal. LC 70-102055. (Illus.). 36p. (ps up). 1970. 8.95 (ISBN 0-385-06777-1); PLB 7.90 (ISBN 0-385-05452-1); pap. 1.95 o.p. (ISBN 0-385-05234-0). Doubleday.

--Fast-Slow High-Low: A Book of Opposites. LC 72-76207. (Illus.). 48p. (gr. k-3). 1972. 9.95a (ISBN 0-385-06781-X); PLB (ISBN 0-385-02876-8). Doubleday.

--Gobble, Growl, Grunt. LC 79-144300. (Illus.). (ps-1). 1971. 10.95a (ISBN 0-385-06779-8); PLB (ISBN 0-385-00681-0). Doubleday.

--People. (Illus.). 48p. (gr. 1-3). 1980. 10.95 (ISBN 0-385-13181-X); PLB (ISBN 0-385-13182-8). Doubleday.

--Tin Lizzie. LC 74-1510. 48p. (gr. 3-5). 1975. 8.95a (ISBN 0-385-09470-1); PLB (ISBN 0-385-07069-1); pap. 2.50 (ISBN 0-385-13342-1). Doubleday.

--The Toy Store. LC 80-1847. (Balloon Bks.). (Illus.). 14p. (ps-k). 1981. 3.95 (ISBN 0-385-15729-0). Doubleday.
Spiering, Frank. Prince Jack. LC 77-16950. 8.95 o.p. (ISBN 0-385-12537-2). Doubleday.
Spiers, A. L. Basic Paediatrics for Nurses. (Illus.). 1973. text ed. 11.00x o.p. (ISBN 0-685-83070-5); pap. text ed. 5.00x o.p. (ISBN 0-685-83071-3). State Mutual Bk.
Spiers, M. Victoria Park, Manchester. 1976. 21.00 (ISBN 0-7190-1333-X). Manchester.
Spiertz, J. H. & Kramer, T., eds. Crop Physiology & Cereal Breeding: Proceedings of a Eucarpia Workshop held in Wageningen, 13-16 November 1978. 193p. 1979. pap. 33.00 (ISBN 0-686-93150-5, 0705-7, Pudoc). Unipub.
Spies, Joseph R. Wild Ponies of Chincoteague. (Illus.). 130p. 1977. 8.95 (ISBN 0-686-36724-3). Md Hist.
Spies, Richard R. The Effect of Rising Costs on College Choice: A Study of the Application Decisions of High-Ability Students. LC 78-51251. (Illus.). 1978. pap. 7.00 o.p. (ISBN 0-87447-038-2, 223412). College Bd.
Spiess, Eliot B. Genes in Populations. LC 77-3990. 1977. text ed. 35.95 (ISBN 0-471-81612-4); solutions manual 7.95 (ISBN 0-471-03720-6). Wiley.
Spiess, Gerry & Bree, Marlin. Alone Against the Atlantic. (Illus.). 256p. 1981. 12.95 (ISBN 0-89893-506-7). CDP.
--Alone Against the Atlantic. (Illus.). 208p. 1983. pap. 2.95 (ISBN 0-425-05844-1). Berkley Pub.
Spiess, Gesine. Zum Rollenspieleinsatz In der Grundschule. 338p. (Ger.). 1982. write for info. (ISBN 3-8204-5831-X). P Lang Pubs.
Spiess, H. W., jt. auth. see Steigel, A.
Spiessens, G. Leven En Werken Van De Antwerpse Luitcomponist Emanuel Adriaenssen, 2 vols. (Illus.). xiv, 479p. 1974. Set. 180.00 o.s.i. (ISBN 90-6027-350-8, Pub. by Frits Knuf Netherlands). Pendragon NY.
Spieth, Philip T., jt. auth. see Fristrom, James W.
Spigai, Frances & Sommer, Peter. A Guide to Electronic Publishing: Opportunities in Online & Viewdata Services. LC 81-20787. (Publishing Technology & Management Reports). 163p. 1982. pap. text ed. 95.00 (ISBN 0-914236-87-3). Knowledge Indus.
Spigai, Frances, jt. auth. see Dicaro, Deborah.
Spigai, Frances, et al, eds. see ASIS Mid-Year Meeting, 4th.
Spigai, Frances G. Invisible Medium: State of the Art of Microform & a Guide to the Literature. 1973. 6.50 (ISBN 0-685-33433-3). Am Soc Info Sci.
Spigelman, James, jt. auth. see Pringle, Peter.
Spike, Paul. Last Rites. 1982. pap. 3.50 (ISBN 0-451-11612-7, AE1612, Sig). NAL.
--The Night Letter. 1979. pap. 2.50 o.p. (ISBN 0-451-08947-2, E8947, Sig). NAL.
--The Night Letter. LC 78-18379. 1979. 9.95 (ISBN 0-399-12213-3). Putnam Pub Group.
Spikell, Mark, jt. auth. see Snover, Stephen.
Spiker, C. C., jt. ed. see Lipsitt, L. P.
Spiker, Charles G see Reese, Hayne.
Spiker, Louise C. No Instant Grapes in God's Vineyard. 112p. 1982. pap. 5.95 (ISBN 0-686-82282-X). Judson.
Spikes, W. Franklin, ed. The University & the Inner City. LC 79-3285. (A Redefinition of Relationships). 208p. 1980. 23.95x (ISBN 0-669-03444-4). Lexington Bks.
Spilerman, Seymour, jt. ed. see Land, Kenneth C.
Spilke, Francine S. What About Me? (The Divorced Family Ser.). (Illus.). 80p. (gr. 3-9). 1979. 6.95 o.p. (ISBN 0-517-53784-2, Michelman Bks). Crown.
Spilken, Aron. Escape! The Story the Newspapers Couldn't Print. 1983. 14.95 (ISBN 0-453-00433-4). NAL.
Spilker, J., Jr. Digital Communication by Satellite. 1976. 44.95 (ISBN 0-13-214155-8). P-H.
Spilker, James J., Jr., ed. Digital Communications by Satellite. 670p. 1977. 41.00 (ISBN 0-686-98091-3). Telecom Lib.
Spillane, J. A., jt. auth. see Spillane, J. D.
Spillane, J. D. & Spillane, J. A. An Atlas of Clinical Neurology. 3rd ed. (Illus.). 1982. text ed. 39.50x (ISBN 0-19-261286-7). Oxford U Pr.
Spillane, John D. Atlas of Clinical Neurology. 2nd ed. (Illus.). 1975. text ed. 39.50x o.p. (ISBN 0-19-264172-7). Oxford U Pr.
--The Doctrine of the Nerves: Chapters in the History of Neurology. (Illus.). 1981. text ed. 55.00x (ISBN 0-19-261135-6). Oxford U Pr.
Spillane, John D., ed. Tropical Neurology. (Illus.). 1973. text ed. 39.00x (ISBN 0-19-264154-9). Oxford U Pr.
Spillane, Mickey. Big Kill. 1952. pap. 1.95 (ISBN 0-451-11441-8, AJ1441, Sig). NAL.
--Bloody Sunrise. pap. 2.25 (ISBN 0-451-12050-7, AE2050, Sig). NAL.
--Body Lovers. 1967. pap. 1.95 (ISBN 0-451-09698-3, J9698, Sig). NAL.
--Day of the Guns. pap. 1.95 (ISBN 0-451-09653-3, J9653, Sig). NAL.
--Death Dealers. 1971. pap. 1.95 (ISBN 0-451-09650-9, J9650, Sig). NAL.
--Deep. pap. 1.95 (ISBN 0-451-11402-7, AJ1402, Sig). NAL.
--Delta Factor. 1968. pap. 2.50 (ISBN 0-451-12208-9, AE2208, Sig). NAL.
--Erection Set. pap. 2.95 (ISBN 0-451-11808-1, AE1808, Sig). NAL.
--Girl Hunters. pap. 1.95 (ISBN 0-451-09558-8, AE9558, Sig). NAL.
--The Girl Hunters. Bd. with Survival...Zero. 352p. 1980. pap. 2.50 o.p. (ISBN 0-451-09352-6, E9352, Sig). NAL.
--I, the Jury. 1972. pap. 2.95 (ISBN 0-451-11396-9, AE1396, Sig). NAL.
--Killer Mine. 1968. pap. 1.95 (ISBN 0-451-11797-2, AJ1797, Sig). NAL.
--Kiss Me, Deadly. pap. 2.50 (ISBN 0-451-12134-1, Q6492, Sig). NAL.
--The Last Cop Out. 192p. 1973. pap. 2.50 (ISBN 0-451-11905-3, AE1905, Sig). NAL.
--The Long Wait. 184p. 1972. pap. 2.50 (ISBN 0-451-12190-2, AE2190, Sig). NAL.
--Me, Hood. (Orig.). 1969. pap. 1.95 (ISBN 0-451-11679-8, AJ1679, Sig). NAL.
--One Lonely Night. pap. 2.50 (ISBN 0-451-12165-1, AE2165, Sig). NAL.
--One Lonely Night - The Twisted Thing. 1980. pap. 2.50 o.p. (ISBN 0-451-09465-4, E9465, Sig). NAL.
--The Snake. pap. 2.50 (ISBN 0-451-12209-7, AE2209, Sig). NAL.
--Survival-Zero. 1971. pap. 2.50 (ISBN 0-451-12105-8, AE2105, Sig). NAL.
--Tomorrow I Die. LC 82-60903. 260p. 1983. 13.95 (ISBN 0-89296-061-2); write for info. limited ed. (ISBN 0-89296-062-0). Mysterious Pr.
--Twisted Thing. 1971. pap. 2.50 (ISBN 0-451-12207-0, AE2207, Sig). NAL.
--Vengeance Is Mine. pap. 1.95 (ISBN 0-451-11734-4, AJ1734, Sig). NAL.
Spiller, Brian, ed. see Cowper, William.
Spiller, Robert, ed. see Adams, Henry.
Spiller, Robert E. Milestones in American Literary History. LC 76-47170. (Contributions in American Studies Ser.: No. 27). 1977. lib. bdg. 25.00x (ISBN 0-8371-9403-2, SMI/). Greenwood.
Spiller, Robert E., ed. see Emerson, Ralph Waldo.
Spillman, jt. auth. see Davis.
Spillman, Betty E., tr. see Jacob, Francois.
Spillman, James R. Omega Cometh: How to Live in the Last Days. 160p. 1980. 7.95 o.p. (ISBN 0-8007-1071-1). Revell.
Spillman, Jane S. Glass Tableware, Bowls, & Vases. LC 82-47849. (Collector's Guides to American Antiques Ser.). (Illus.). 1982. write for info. (ISBN 0-394-71272-2). Knopf.
Spillman, Nancy Z. Consumers: A Personal Planning Reader. LC 75-28369. (Illus.). 350p. 1975. pap. text ed. 12.50 (ISBN 0-8299-0065-9). West Pub.
Spillman, Ronald. Good Basic Photography. pap. 5.00x o.p. (ISBN 0-392-14212-0, SpS). Sportshelf.
Spillmann, Lothar & Wooten, Bill, eds. Sensory Experience, Adaptation & Perception: Festschrift for Ivo Kohler. 800p. 1982. text ed. 49.95 (ISBN 0-89859-218-6). L Erlbaum Assocs.
Spillner, Bernd. Error Analysis: A Comprehensive Bibliography. (Library & Information Sources in Linguistics: 12). 250p. 1983. 26.00 (ISBN 90-27237-31-X). Benjamins North Am.
Spina, D. A., jt. auth. see Dixon, Franklin W.
Spina, Tony. On Assignment: Projects in Photo-Journalism. (Illus.). 192p. 1982. 24.95 (ISBN 0-8174-5275-3, Amphoto). Watson-Guptill.
Spinar, Z. V. Life Before Man. LC 72-1866. (Illus.). 228p. (gr. 7 up). 1972. 12.50 o.p. (ISBN 0-07-060240-9, GB). McGraw.
Spinard, Norman. The Mind Game. (Orig.). pap. 2.50 o.s.i. (ISBN 0-515-04847-X). Jove Pubns.
Spinden, Herbert J. Ancient Civilizations of Mexico & Central America. 3rd rev. ed. LC 67-29554. (Illus.). 1968. Repr. of 1928 ed. 10.00x (ISBN 0-8196-0215-9). Biblo.
--Nez Perce Indians. LC 8-34805. 1908. pap. 13.00 (ISBN 0-527-00508-8). Kraus Repr.
--Songs of the Tewa. (Illus.). 1976. 12.95 (ISBN 0-913270-55-5). Sunstone Pr.
Spindle, Richard. They Never Stopped Teaching. 96p. 1982. pap. 2.50 (ISBN 0-8341-0735-X). Beacon Hill.
Spindler, George D., ed. The Making of Psychological Anthropology. LC 76-24597. 1978. 50.00x o.s.i. (ISBN 0-520-03320-5); pap. 12.75x (ISBN 0-520-03957-2). U of Cal Pr.
Spinell, Donald, ed. see Educational Research Council of America.
Spinelli, Jackaline. Who Is My Neighbor? (Color Us Wonderful Ser.). (ps). 1971. pap. 0.35 o.p. (ISBN 0-8091-6521-X). Paulist Pr.
Spinelli, Jerry. Space Station Seventh Grade. LC 82-47915. 192p. (gr. 7 up). 1982. 11.95 (ISBN 0-316-80709-5). Little.
Spingarn, Lawrence P. The Belvedere. (Illus.). 16p. 1982. pap. 15.00x (ISBN 0-930126-11-4). Typographeum.
--Moral Tales. LC 82-6216. (Illus.). 70p. 1983. pap. 4.75 (ISBN 0-912288-19-1). Perivale Pr.
Spink, John S. French Free-Thought from Gassendi to Voltaire. Repr. of 1960 ed. lib. bdg. 17.00x (ISBN 0-8371-0663-X, SPFF). Greenwood.
Spink, Kathryn, tr. see Bang, Kirsten.
Spink, R. Hans Christian Andersen: The Man & His Work. (Illus.). 64p. 1975. pap. 6.00x (ISBN 8-7142-7882-0, D-742). Vanous.
Spink, Reginald. Hans Christian Andersen & His World. LC 72-77072. (Pictorial Biography Ser.). (Illus.). 128p. 1972. 6.95 o.p. (ISBN 0-399-11070-4). Putnam Pub Group.
Spinks, J. W. & Woods, R. J., eds. An Introduction to Radiation Chemistry. 2nd ed. LC 75-46589. 504p. 1976. 43.50x (ISBN 0-471-81670-1, Pub. by Wiley-Interscience). Wiley.
Spinner, Manuel. Elements of Project Management: Plan, Schedule, & Control. (Illus.). 240p. 1981. text ed. 24.00 (ISBN 0-13-269852-8). P-H.
Spinner, Stephanie. How it All Began. 1982. 4.95 o.p. (ISBN 0-672-52730-8). Bobbs.
--How Raggedy Ann Began. (Illus.). (gr. 3-6). 1983. 4.95 (ISBN 0-686-95253-7). Bobbs.
Spinner, Stephanie, ed. see Farley, Walter.
Spinner, T. J., Jr. George Joachim Goschen: The Transformation of a Victorian Liberal. (Conference on British Studies Biographical Ser.). 268p. 1973. 39.50 (ISBN 0-521-20210-8). Cambridge U Pr.
Spinoza, Baruch. Letters to Friend & Foe. LC 66-22242. 1967. pap. 2.75 o.p. (ISBN 0-8022-1620-X). Philos Lib.
Spinoza, Benedictus de see De Spinoza, Benedictus.
Spinrad. Speaker's Lifetime Library. 1979. 29.50 (ISBN 0-13-824557-6, Parker). P-H.
Spinrad, Bernard I. Use of Computers in Analysis of Experimental Data & the Control of Nuclear Facilities: Proceedings. LC 67-60057. (AEC Symposium Ser.). 306p. 1967. pap. 15.75 (ISBN 0-87079-214-8, CONF-660527); microfiche 4.50 (ISBN 0-87079-215-6, CONF-660527). DOE.
Spinrad, Norman. Bug Jack Barron. (Science Fiction Ser.). 1981. lib. bdg. cancelled o.s.i. (ISBN 0-8398-2617-6, Gregg). G K Hall.
--The Iron Dream. 1977. Repr. of 1972 ed. lib. bdg. 13.00 o.p. (ISBN 0-8398-2361-4, Gregg). G K Hall.
--Modern Science Fiction. 560p. 1976. Repr. of 1974 ed. lib. bdg. 25.00 (ISBN 0-8398-2339-8, Gregg). G K Hall.
--Songs from the Stars. 1980. 11.95 o.p. (ISBN 0-671-25326-3). S&S.
--Staying Alive: A Writer's Guide. Stine, Hank, ed. LC 82-14736. 162p. 1983. pap. 5.95 (ISBN 0-89865-259-6). Donning Co.
--The Void Captain's Tale. 1983. 15.50 (ISBN 0-671-43483-7, Timescape). PB.
Spiotta, Loren. Macaws. (Illus.). 1979. 4.95 (ISBN 0-87666-975-5, KW-003). TFH Pubns.
Spira, Harold R. Canine Terminology. (Illus.). 147p. 1983. 29.95 (ISBN 0-06-312047-X, Dist. by Har-Row). Howell Bk.
Spira, Robert. Craps: Pressing Your Luck. 32p. (Orig.). 1982. pap. 2.00 (ISBN 0-911455-01-9). Quartz Pr.
Spira, Ruth R. Naturally Chinese. 1978. pap. 8.95 o.p. (ISBN 0-87857-219-8). Rodale Pr Inc.
--Naturally Chinese: Healthful Cooking from China. LC 73-20862. (Illus.). 384p. 1974. 12.95 o.p. (ISBN 0-87857-080-2). Rodale Pr Inc.
Spirer, H. F., jt. auth. see Spirer, L. Z.
Spirer, Herbert F., jt. auth. see Spirer, Louise Z.
Spirer, L. Z. & Spirer, H. F. German Shorthaired Pointer. 1970. 12.95 (ISBN 0-87666-303-X, PS635). TFH Pubns.
Spirer, Louise. This Is the Miniature Schnauzer. 12.95 (ISBN 0-87666-339-0, PS627). TFH Pubns.
Spirer, Louise Z. & Miller, E. This Is the Doberman Pinscher. 1963. 12.95 (ISBN 0-87666-283-1, PS622). TFH Pubns.
Spirer, Louise Z. & Spirer, Herbert F. This Is the Pomeranian. (Illus.). 1965. 12.95 (ISBN 0-87666-354-4, PS634). TFH Pubns.
Spirit, Diana, jt. auth. see Ettlinger, John R.
Spiritual Counterfeits Project Staff. Spiritual Warfare. Orig. Title: Exorcism. 32p. 1977. pap. 0.50 o.p. (ISBN 0-87784-161-6). Inter-Varsity.
Spirko, Christina. Your Future in Radiologic Technology. LC 66-14028. (Careers in Depth Ser). (gr. 7 up). PLB 7.97 o.p. (ISBN 0-8239-0076-2). Rosen Pr.
Spirn, Steven & Benfer, David W. Issues in Health Care Management. LC 82-8842. 498p. 1983. 32.50 (ISBN 0-89443-826-3). Aspen Systems.
Spiro. Clinical Gastroenterology. 3rd ed. 1983. 85.00 (ISBN 0-02-415250-1). Macmillan.
Spiro, George W. & Houghteling, James L., Jr. The Dynamics of Law. 2nd ed. 229p. 1981. pap. text ed. 9.95 (ISBN 0-15-518513-6, HC). HarBraceJ.
Spiro, Herbert T. Finance for the Nonfinancial Manager, Student Edition. LC 76-56371. 281p. 1978. 22.50 (ISBN 0-471-04803-8, Pub. by Wiley-Interscience). Wiley.
--Financial Planning for the Independent Professional. LC 78-18179. 235p. 1978. 37.95 (ISBN 0-471-03111-9, Pub. by Wiley-Interscience). Wiley.
Spiro, Howard M. Clinical Gastroenterology. 2nd ed. (Illus.). 1977. text ed. 72.00x (ISBN 0-02-415260-9). Macmillan.
Spiro, Jack D., ed. see Shumsky, Abraham & Shumsky, Adaia.
Spiro, Melford E. Kibbutz: Venture in Utopia. rev. ed. LC 70-132260. (Studies in the Libertarian & Utopian Tradition). 1963. pap. 4.95 o.p. (ISBN 0-8052-0063-0). Schocken.
--Kinship & Marriage in Burma: A Cultural & Psychodynamic Analysis. 1977. 34.50x (ISBN 0-520-03220-9). U of Cal Pr.
--Oedipus in the Trobriands. LC 82-7032. (Chicago Original Paperbacks Ser.). 224p. 1983. lib. bdg. 26.00x (ISBN 0-226-76988-7); pap. text ed. 12.95x (ISBN 0-226-76989-5). U of Chicago Pr.
Spiro, Shimon E. & Yuchtman-Yaar, Ephraim, eds. Evaluating the Welfare State: Social & Political Perspectives. LC 82-22596. Date not set. price not set. Acad Pr.
Spiro, Thomas G. Copper Proteins. LC 81-7465. (Metal Ions in Biology Ser.). 363p. 1981. 61.50 (ISBN 0-471-04400-8, Pub. by Wiley-Interscience). Wiley.
--Iron-Sulfur Proteins. (Metal Ions in Biology Ser.). 434p. 1982. 80.00x (ISBN 0-471-07738-0, Pub. by Wiley-Interscience). Wiley.
Spiro, Thomas G. & Stigliani, William. Environmental Issues in Chemical Perspective. 1980. 23.50x (ISBN 0-87395-427-0). State U NY Pr.
Spiro, Thomas G., ed. Metal Ion Activation of Dioxygen. LC 79-13808. (Metal Ions in Biology Ser.: Vol. 2). 247p. 1980. 50.50 (ISBN 0-471-04398-2, Pub. by Wiley-Interscience). Wiley.
--Nucleic Acid-Metal Ion Interactions. LC 79-13808 (Metals Ions in Biology Ser.: Vol. 1). 256p. 1980. 43.95 (ISBN 0-471-04399-0, Pub. by Wiley-Interscience). Wiley.
Spirt, Diana L. Library-Media Manual. 192p. 1979. 7.00 (ISBN 0-8242-0615-0). Wilson.
Spirt, Diana L., jt. auth. see Gillespie, John T.
Spiselman, Anne, jt. auth. see Kelson, Allen H.
Spitell, John A., et al, eds. Clinical Medicine, 12 vols. 1983. looseleaf 600.00 (ISBN 0-686-97944-3, Harper Medical); revision pages 75.00 (ISBN 0-686-97945-1). Lippincott.
Spitler, Sue & Hauser, Nao. The Popcorn Lover's Book. (Illus.). 96p. (Orig.). 1983. pap. 3.95 (ISBN 0-8092-5542-1). Contemp Bks.
Spitta, Edmund. Photo-Micrography 1899. (Illus.). 163p. pap. 35.00 (ISBN 0-87556-580-8). Saifer.
Spitta, Philip. Johann Sebastian Bach, 2 vols. 17.50 ea. Vol. 1 (ISBN 0-486-22278-0). Vol. 2 (ISBN 0-486-22279-9). Dover.
Spitta, Philip, ed. see Frederick The Great.
Spittell, John A., Jr., ed. Clinical Medicine, 12 vols. (Annual Revision Service). loose leaf 600.00 o.p. (ISBN 0-686-97855-2, Harper Medical); revision pages 70.00 o.p. (ISBN 0-686-97856-0). Lippincott.
--Clinical Vascular Disease. LC 82-12974. (Cardiovascular Clinics Ser.: Vol. 13, No. 2). (Illus.). 384p. 1983. 45.00 (ISBN 0-8036-8087-2). Davis Co.
Spitz, A. Edward & Flaschner, Alan B. Retailing. 1980. text ed. 19.95 (ISBN 0-316-80710-9); tchr's ed. avail. (ISBN 0-316-80711-7). Little.
Spitz, Bruce. Medicaid Nursing Home Reimbursment in New York. (Illus.). 65p. (Orig.). 1981. pap. text ed. 7.00 (ISBN 0-87766-289-4). Urban Inst.
Spitz, Bruce & Weeks, Jane. Medicaid Nursing Home Reimbursement in Minnesota. LC 80-54798. (Illus.). 64p. (Orig.). 1981. pap. text ed. 6.00. Urban Inst.
--Medicaid Nursing Home Reimbursment in Illinois. LC 80-54797. (Illus.). 55p. (Orig.). 1981. pap. text ed. 6.00 (ISBN 0-87766-287-8). Urban Inst.
Spitz, Edna H., jt. ed. see Herrmann, Elizabeth R.
Spitz, Lewis W., ed. Reformation: Basic Interpretations. 2nd ed. (Problems in European Civilization Ser.). 1972. pap. text ed. 5.95 (ISBN 0-669-81620-5). Heath.
Spitz, Lewis W., Jr. The Northern Renaissance. LC 70-178767. (Sources of Civilization in the West Ser). 1972. 5.95t (ISBN 0-13-623801-7, Spec); pap. 2.45 (ISBN 0-13-623793-2, Spec). P-H.
Spitzbart, Abraham. Analytic Geometry. 1969. text ed. 19.95x (ISBN 0-673-05389-X). Scott F.
--Calculus with Analytic Geometry. 1975. text ed. 24.50x (ISBN 0-673-07907-4). Scott F.
Spitzberg, Irving R., Jr., ed. Exchange of Expertise: The Counterpart System in the New International Order. (Westview Replica Edition). 1978. lib. bdg. 20.25 o.p. (ISBN 0-89158-280-0). Westview.
Spitze, Glenna, jt. ed. see Huber, Joan.
Spitzer, Adrian, ed. The Kidney During Development: Morphology & Function. LC 81-15567. (Illus.). 320p. 1982. 70.25x (ISBN 0-89352-160-4). Masson Pub.
Spitzer, Dan. Wanderlust: Overland Through Asia & Africa. LC 78-27894. (Illus.). 1979. 10.95 o.p. (ISBN 0-399-90036-5, Marek). Putnam Pub Group.
Spitzer, Harry & Schwartz, Richard F. Inside Retail Sales Promotion & Advertising. 434p. 1982. text ed. 20.95 scp (ISBN 0-06-046383-X, HarpC). Har-Row.
Spitzer, Leo. The Creoles of Sierra Leone: Responses to Colonialism, 1870-1945. LC 74-5908. (Illus.). 272p. 1974. 27.50x (ISBN 0-299-06590-1). U of Wis Pr.
--Essays on English & American Literature. Hatcher, Anna, ed. 307p. 1983. Repr. of 1968 ed. 15.00 (ISBN 0-87752-227-8). Gordian.
Spitzer, Leo & Brody, Jules. Approaches Textuelles des "Memoires" de Saint-Simon. (Etudes Litteraires Francaise: No. 9). 107p. (Orig., Fr.). 1980. pap. 10.50 (ISBN 3-87808-888-4). Benjamins North Am.
Spitzer, Lyman, Jr. Diffuse Matter in Space. (Tracts on Physics & Astronomy, Vol. 28). 1968. 27.00 o.p. (ISBN 0-470-81710-0, Pub. by Wiley-Interscience). Wiley.

--Physical Processes in the Interstellar Medium. LC 77-14273. 315p. 1978. 31.95 (ISBN 0-471-02232-2, Pub. by Wiley-Interscience). Wiley.

Spitzer, Robert J. The Presidency & Public Policy: The Four Arenas of Presidential Power. LC 81-19802. (Illus.). 224p. 1983. text ed. 18.75 (ISBN 0-8173-0109-7). U of Ala Pr.

Spitzer, Robert L. Psychopathology: A Case Book. (Illus.). 320p. 1983. pap. text ed. 12.95 (ISBN 0-07-060350-2, C). McGraw.

Spitzer, Robert L. & Klein, Donald F., eds. Critical Issues in Psychiatric Diagnosis. LC 77-72812. (American Psychopathological Association Ser.). 355p. 1978. 34.50 (ISBN 0-89004-213-6). Raven.

Spitzer, Robert S., ed. Tidings of Comfort & Joy: An Anthology of Change. LC 75-7997. 1975. pap. 5.95 (ISBN 0-685-50622-3). Sci & Behavior.

Spitzer, S. P. & Denzin, N. K. Mental Patient: Studies in the Sociology of Deviance. 1968. pap. text ed. 17.95 (ISBN 0-07-060332-4, C). McGraw.

Spitzer, Steven, ed. Research in Law & Sociology, Vol. 2. 1979. lib. bdg. 40.00 (ISBN 0-89232-111-3). Jai Pr.

--Research in Law & Sociology, Vol. 3. 368p. 1980. 40.00 (ISBN 0-89232-186-5). Jai Pr.

Spitzer, Steven, jt. ed. see Simon, Rita J.

Spitzing, G. Focalguide to Effects & Tricks. (Focalguide Ser.). (Illus.). 192p. 1974. pap. 7.95 (ISBN 0-240-50761-4). Focal Pr.

--Focalguide to Enlarging. (Focalguide Ser.). (Illus.). 1973. pap. 7.95 (ISBN 0-240-50760-6). Focal Pr.

Spitzing, Gunter. La Ampliacion: Una Guia Para Aficionados. Estadella, Victor, tr. from Eng. (Focalguide Ser.). 196p. (Span.). 1977. pap. 8.95 o.p. (ISBN 0-240-51094-1, Pub. by Ediciones Spain). Focal Pr.

--Focalguide to Portraits. (Focalguide Ser.). (Illus.). 1974. pap. 7.95 (ISBN 0-240-50758-4). Focal Pr.

Spitznas, M., ed. Current Research in Ophthalmic Electron Microscopy: Transactions of the 5th Annual Meeting of the European Club for Opthalmic Fine Structure in Zuerich, March 25 & 26, 1977. (Illus.). 1978. pap. 28.40 (ISBN 0-387-08508-4). Springer-Verlag.

Spivack, George, jt. auth. see Shure, Myrna B.

Spivack, Jane F., ed. Careers in Information. LC 82-7188. (Professional Librarian Ser.). 250p. 1982. text ed. 34.50 (ISBN 0-914236-70-9); pap. text ed. 27.50 (ISBN 0-914236-83-0). Knowledge Indus.

Spivack, Mayer. Institutional Settings: An Environmental Design Approach. Tamer, Joanna, ed. 208p. 1983. 24.95 (ISBN 0-89885-105-X). Human Sci Pr.

Spivak, John L. Georgia Nigger. LC 69-14948. (Criminology, Law Enforcement, & Social Problems Ser.: No. 32). (Illus.). 1969. Repr. of 1932 ed. 10.00x (ISBN 0-87585-032-4). Patterson Smith.

Spivak, Michael. Calculus on Manifolds: A Modern Approach to Classical Theorems of Advanced Calculus. (Orig.). 1965. pap. 14.95 (ISBN 0-8053-9021-9). Benjamin-Cummings.

Spivey, Donald. Schooling for the New Slavery: Black Industrial Education, 1868-1915. LC 77-87974. (Contributions in Afro-American & African Studies: No. 38). 1978. lib. bdg. 25.00x (ISBN 0-313-20051-3, SSN/). Greenwood.

Spivey, Morma G., jt. auth. see Barbour, Pamela G.

Spivey, Robert A. & Smith, Moody D. Anatomy of the New Testament: A Guide to Its Structure & Meaning. 3rd ed. 544p. 1982. text ed. 22.95 (ISBN 0-02-415300-1). Macmillan.

Spivey, W. Allen. Economic Policies in France, 1976-81: The Barre Program in a West European Perspective. (Michigan International Business Studies: No. 18). (Illus.). 90p. (Orig.). 1982. pap. 6.00 (ISBN 0-87712-223-7). U Mich Busn Div Res.

Spizzichins, F., jt. auth. see Koch, G.

Spizzirri, Linda, ed. see Spizzirri Publishing Co. Staff.

Spizzirri, Peter M. History of the American Truck. (Illus.). 32p. (gr. 3-8). 1979. pap. 1.00 o.p. (ISBN 0-86545-018-8). Spizzirri.

Spizzirri Publishing Co. Staff. Animal Alphabet: An Educational Coloring Book. Spizzirri, Linda, ed. (Illus.). 32p. (gr. 1-8). 1982. pap. 1.25 (ISBN 0-86545-042-0). Spizzirri.

--Cats of the Wild: An Educational Coloring Book. Spizzirri, Linda, ed. (Illus.). 32p. (gr. 1-8). 1982. pap. 1.25 (ISBN 0-86545-045-5). Spizzirri.

--Counting & Coloring Dinosaurs: An Educational Coloring Book. Spizzirri, Linda, ed. (Illus.). 32p. (gr. 1-8). 1982. pap. 1.25 (ISBN 0-86545-044-7). Spizzirri.

--Endangered Species: An Educational Coloring Book. Spizzirri, Linda, ed. (Illus.). 32p. (gr. 1-8). 1982. pap. 1.25 (ISBN 0-86545-041-2). Spizzirri.

--Kachina Dolls: An Educational Coloring Book. Spizzirri, Linda, ed. (Illus.). 32p. (gr. 1-8). 1982. pap. 1.25 (ISBN 0-86545-046-3). Spizzirri.

--Northeast Indians: An Educational Coloring Book. Spizzirri, Linda, ed. (Illus.). 32p. (gr. 1-8). 1982. pap. 1.25 (ISBN 0-86545-040-4). Spizzirri.

--Northwest Indians: An Educational Coloring Book. Spizzirri, Linda, ed. (Illus.). 32p. (gr. 1-8). 1982. pap. 1.25 (ISBN 0-86545-047-1). Spizzirri.

--Picture Dictionary: An Educational Coloring Book. Spizzirri, Linda, ed. (Illus.). 32p. (gr. 1-8). 1982. pap. 1.25 (ISBN 0-86545-049-8). Spizzirri.

--Planets: An Educational Coloring Book. Spizzirri, Linda, ed. (Illus.). 32p. (gr. 1-8). 1982. pap. 1.95 (ISBN 0-86545-043-9). Spizzirri.

--State Birds: An Educational Coloring Book. Spizzirri, Linda, ed. (Illus.). 32p. (gr. 1-8). 1982. pap. 1.25 (ISBN 0-86545-050-1). Spizzirri.

--Trucks: An Educational Coloring Book. Spizzirri, Linda, ed. (Illus.). 32p. (gr. 1-8). 1982. pap. 1.25 (ISBN 0-86545-051-X). Spizzirri.

--Whales: An Educational Coloring Book. Spizzirri, Linda, ed. (Illus.). 32p. (gr. 1-8). 1982. pap. 1.25 (ISBN 0-86545-039-0). Spizzirri.

Spjut, Harlin, jt. ed. see Ackerman, Lauren.

Splaver, Bernard R. Successful Catering. 2nd ed. 352p. 1982. text ed. 24.95 (ISBN 0-8436-2219-9). CBI Pub.

Splaver, Sarah. Paraprofessions: Careers of the Future & the Present. LC 72-1417. (Career Bks.). 192p. (gr. 9 up). 1972. PLB 7.29 o.p. (ISBN 0-671-32546-9). Messner.

--Your Career - If You're Not Going to College. rev. ed. LC 72-161518. (Career Bks). 224p. (gr. 9 up). 1971. PLB 7.29 o.p. (ISBN 0-671-32461-6). Messner.

--Your Handicap: Don't Let It Handicap You. rev. ed. LC 67-10635. 224p. (gr. 7 up). 1974. PLB 7.29 o.p. (ISBN 0-671-32654-6). Messner.

--Your Personality & Your Career. LC 77-22787. (Messner Career Books). 192p. (gr. 7 up). 1977. PLB 7.79 o.p. (ISBN 0-671-32862-X). Messner.

Spock, Benjamin. Baby & Child Care. new rev. ed. 1976. 15.95 (ISBN 0-8015-0481-3, 01549-460, Hawthorn). Dutton.

Spock, Marjorie. In Celebration of the Human Heart. 1982. pap. 5.95 (ISBN 0-916786-65-X). St George Bk Serv.

Spodek, Bernard. Teaching in the Early Years. 2nd ed. (Early Childhood Ser.). (Illus.). 1978. ref. ed. 23.95 (ISBN 0-13-892562-3). P-H.

Spodek, Bernard, ed. Handbook of Research in Early Childhood Education. LC 81-71152. (Illus.). 640p. 1982. text ed. 49.95 (ISBN 0-02-930570-5). Free Pr.

Spodek, Bernard & Walberg, Herbert J., eds. Early Childhood Education: Issues & Insights. LC 76-62804. 1977. 18.50 (ISBN 0-8211-1856-0); text ed. 16.95x 10 or more copies (ISBN 0-685-74999-1). McCutchan.

Spodek, Bernard, jt. ed. see Saracho, Olivia N.

Spoel, S. Van der see Van der Spoel, S. & Pierrot-Bults, A. C.

Spoerl, Heinrich. Der Gasmann. (Easy Readers B Ser.). 64p. (Ger.). 1976. pap. text ed. 3.95 (ISBN 0-88436-275-2, 45265). EMC.

Spoerri, Daniel. Mythology & Meatballs: A Greek Island Diary-Cookbook. Williams, Emmett, tr. from Fr. LC 82-16355. 238p. 1982. 14.95 (ISBN 0-943186-01-3); pap. 8.95 o.p (ISBN 0-943186-02-1). Aris Bks.

Spofford, Ainsworth R. The Founding of Washington City. 62p. 1883. 5.50 (ISBN 0-686-36845-2). Md Hist.

Spohn, Eric E., et al. Operative Dentistry Procedures for Dental Auxiliaries. LC 81-907. (Illus.). 298p. 1981. pap. text ed. 18.95 (ISBN 0-8016-2580-7). Mosby.

Spolsky, Bernard. Educational Linguistics. LC 78-2904. 1978. pap. 10.95 o.p. (ISBN 0-88377-094-6). Newbury Hse.

Spolsky, Bernard & Cooper, Robert L., eds. Case Studies in Bilingual Education. 1978. pap. text ed. 17.95 (ISBN 0-88377-092-X). Newbury Hse.

--Frontiers of Bilingual Education. LC 76-56747. 1977. pap. 14.95 o.p. (ISBN 0-88377-066-0). Newbury Hse.

Spolton, L. The Upper Secondary School. 1967. write for info. o.p. (ISBN 0-08-012497-6) (ISBN 0-08-012496-8). Pergamon.

Spong, John S. Into the Whirlwind: The Future of the Church. 192p. 1983. price not set (ISBN 0-8164-0539-5). Seabury.

--This Hebrew Lord. 1976. pap. 4.95 (ISBN 0-8164-2133-1). Seabury.

Sponsel, Johann U. Orgelhistorie: Nurnberg 1771. (Bibliotheca Organologica Ser.: Vol. 18). Date not set. Repr. of 1968 ed. wrappers 20.00 o.s.i. (ISBN 90-6027-049-5, Pub. by Frits Knuf Netherlands). Pendragon NY.

Spooner, jt. auth. see Coggin.

Spooner, J. D. Ocular Anatomy. (Illus.). 1972. pap. 32.50 (ISBN 0-407-93412-X). Butterworth.

Spooner, Maggie. Sunpower Experiments. LC 79-65077. (Illus.). (gr. 5 up). 1979. 9.95 (ISBN 0-8069-3110-8); PLB 12.49 (ISBN 0-8069-3111-6). Sterling.

Sporer, Siegfried L. Reducing Disparity in Judicial Sentencing: A Social-Psychological Approach. (European University Studies-Ser. 6, Psychology: Vol. 97). 114p. 1982. write for info. (ISBN 3-8204-7208-8). P Lang Pubs.

Spores, Ronald. Mixtec Kings & Their People. (Civilization of the American Indian Ser.: No. 85). (Illus.). 1967. 17.50 (ISBN 0-8061-0726-X). U of Okla Pr.

Sporne, K. R. The Morphology of Angiosperms. LC 74-29412. 200p. 1975. 17.95 o.p. (ISBN 0-312-54845-1). St Martin.

Sporre, Dennis. Perceiving the Arts: An Introduction to the Humanities. (Illus.). 256p. 1981. text ed. 12.95 (ISBN 0-13-657031-3). P-H.

Sports Illustrated Editors. Sports Illustrated Baseball. rev. ed. LC 77-37610. (Illus.). (YA) 1972. 5.95i (ISBN 0-397-00857-0); pap. 2.95i (ISBN 0-397-00831-7, LP-60). Har-Row.

--Sports Illustrated Basketball. LC 76-168552. (Illus.). (gr. 7-9). 1971. 5.95 o.p. (ISBN 0-397-00881-3); pap. 2.95 o.p. (ISBN 0-397-00882-1, LP54). Har-Row.

--Sports Illustrated Dog Training. LC 72-3179. (Illus.). (YA) 1972. 5.95i (ISBN 0-397-00906-2); pap. 2.95 o.p. (ISBN 0-397-00907-0, LP-66). Har-Row.

--Sports Illustrated Horseback Riding. LC 74-161580. (Illus.). (gr. 7-9). 1971. 5.95 o.p. (ISBN 0-397-00736-1); pap. 2.95 o.p. (ISBN 0-397-00735-3, LP55). Har-Row.

--Sports Illustrated Ice Hockey. LC 78-156366. (Illus.). (gr. 7-9). 1971. 5.95i o.p. (ISBN 0-397-00835-X); pap. 2.95 o.p. (ISBN 0-397-00836-8). Har-Row.

--Sports Illustrated Squash. rev. ed. LC 70-161579. (Illus.). 1971. 4.95 o.s.i. (ISBN 0-397-00837-6); pap. 2.95i (ISBN 0-397-00838-4, LP58). Har-Row.

Sports Illustrated Editors & Dunaway, James O. Sports Illustrated Book of Track & Field: Running Events. rev. ed. LC 76-8268. (Illus.). (gr. 7-9). 1971. 5.95i (ISBN 0-397-01172-5); pap. 2.95 (ISBN 0-397-01171-7, LP-064). Har-Row.

Sports Illustrated Editors & Jerome, John. Sports Illustrated Skiing. rev. ed. LC 71-146685. 1971. 5.95 o.p. (ISBN 0-397-00840-6); pap. 2.95i (ISBN 0-397-00839-2, LP57). Har-Row.

Sports Illustrated Editors, jt. auth. see Hidy, Vernon S.

Sports Illustrated Editors, jt. auth. see Robison, Bonnie.

Sports Illustrated Editors, jt. auth. see Talbert, Bill.

Sports Illustrated Editors, jt. auth. see Wilkinson, Bud.

Sports Products, Inc. Staff. Beat the Spread: The Pro Football Bettor's Companion. LC 82-82191. (Illus.). 160p. 1982. pap. 8.00 (ISBN 0-688-01261-2). Quill NY.

Sports Products Inc. Staff. Beat the Spread: The 1982 Pro Football Bettor's Companion. 1982. pap. 8.00 (ISBN 0-688-01261-2); ten copy prepack 80.00 (ISBN 0-688-01609-X). Morrow.

Spoto, Donald. The Dark Side of Genius: The Life of Alfred Hitchcock. 576p. 1983. 21.50i (ISBN 0-316-80723-0). Little.

--Stanley Kramer: Film Maker. LC 78-18834. (Illus.). 1978. 12.95 (ISBN 0-399-12214-1); pap. 6.95 (ISBN 0-399-12249-4). Putnam Pub Group.

Spotte, S. Fish & Invertebrate Culture: Water Management in Closed Systems. 2nd ed. 179p. 1979. 21.50x (ISBN 0-471-02306-X, Pub. by Wiley-Interscience). Wiley.

Spotte, Stephen. Marine Aquarium Keeping: The Science, Animals & Art. LC 73-4425. (Illus.). 171p. 1973. 17.95 (ISBN 0-471-81759-7, Pub. by Wiley-Interscience). Wiley.

--Seawater Aquariums: The Captive Environment. LC 79-11038. 413p. 1979. 34.95 (ISBN 0-471-05665-0, Pub. by Wiley-Interscience). Wiley.

Spottiswood, David J. & Kelly, Errol G. Introduction to Mineral Processing. 544p. 1982. 65.95 o.s.i. (ISBN 0-471-03379-0, Pub. by Wiley-Interscience). Wiley.

Spottiswoode, Raymond. The Focal Encyclopedia of Film & Television: Techniques. (Illus.). 1969. 57.95 (ISBN 0-240-50654-5). Focal Pr.

Spotts, M. F. Design of Machine Elements. 5th ed. (Illus.). 1978. ref. ed. 35.95 (ISBN 0-13-200576-X). P-H.

Sprachman, Paul, tr. see Al-Ahmad, Jalal.

Sprachman, Susan, jt. auth. see Stevenson, Jane.

Spradley, James P. & McCurdy, David W. The Cultural Experience: Ethnography in Complex Society. (Illus.). 246p. 1972. pap. text ed. 11.95 (ISBN 0-574-18575-5, 13-1575). SRA.

Spradley, James P. & McCurdy, David. Anthropology: A Cultural Perspective. 2nd ed. LC 74-23259. 672p. 1980. text ed. 20.50 (ISBN 0-471-04601-9); avail. tchr's manual (ISBN 0-471-06231-6). Wiley.

Spradling, Mary M., ed. In Black & White, 2 Vols. 3rd ed. 1980. Set. 92.00x (ISBN 0-8103-0438-4). Gale.

Sprafkin, Joyce, et al, eds. RX Television: Enhancing the Preventive Impact of TV. LC 82-15778. (Prevention in Human Services Ser.: Vol. 2, Nos. 1-2). 176p. 1983. text ed. 20.00 (ISBN 0-86656-168-4, B168). Haworth Pr.

Sprafkin, Robert, ed. see Claiborn, William L., et al.

Spragens, Thomas S., Jr. Understanding Political Theory: An Introduction. LC 75-33578. 150p. 1976. 17.95 (ISBN 0-312-83160-9); pap. text ed. 9.95 (ISBN 0-312-83195-1). St Martin.

Spragens, William C. The Presidency & the Mass Media in the Age of Television. LC 78-51149. 1978. pap. text ed. 12.25 (ISBN 0-8191-0476-0). U Pr of Amer.

Spragens, William C. & Terwoord, Carole A. From Spokesman to Press Secretary: White House Media Operations. LC 80-8296. 276p. 1980. lib. bdg. 21.25 (ISBN 0-8191-1246-1); pap. text ed. 11.25 (ISBN 0-8191-1247-X). U Pr of Amer.

Spragens, William T. Options & Oversight: Programs, Planning, Process, Performance. 1979. pap. 5.50x (ISBN 0-89917-007-2). TIS Inc.

Spragg, Roger G., jt. auth. see Moser, Kenneth M.

Spragg, S. P. The Physical Behavior of Macromolecules with Biological Functions. LC 80-40280. (Biophysics & Biochemistry Monographs). 202p. 1980. 43.95 (ISBN 0-471-27784-3, Pub. by Wiley-Interscience). Wiley.

Spraggett, Allen. Arthur Ford: The Man Who Talked with the Dead. 1974. pap. 1.50 o.p. (ISBN 0-451-05804-6, W5804, Sig). NAL.

--The Case for Immortality. 1975. pap. 1.50 o.p. (ISBN 0-451-06373-2, W6373, Sig). NAL.

--Ross Peterson: A New Edgar Cayce. 1978. pap. 1.95 o.s.i. (ISBN 0-515-04579-9). Jove Pubns.

Sprague, Arthur, tr. see Miliutin, Nikolai A.

Sprague, Charles E. The Philosophy of Accounts. LC 72-81869. 1972. Repr. of 1919 ed. text ed. 13.00 (ISBN 0-914348-09-4). Scholars Bk.

Sprague, Claire, ed. Virginia Woolf: A Collection of Critical Essays. LC 73-133057. (Twentieth Century Views Ser). 1971. 12.95t (ISBN 0-13-962837-1, Spec). P-H.

Sprague, Gretchen. White in the Moon. LC 68-16877. (gr. 8 up). 1968. 5.95 o.p. (ISBN 0-396-05699-7). Dodd.

Sprague, Gretchen A. Question of Harmony. LC 65-13511. (gr. 7 up). 1965. 4.50 o.p. (ISBN 0-396-05111-1). Dodd.

Sprague, Howard B. Turf Management Handbook. 3rd ed. LC 74-19656. 1982. 17.25 (ISBN 0-8134-2187-X); text ed. 12.95x. Interstate.

Sprague, Howard B., ed. Grasslands of the United States: Their Economic & Ecological Importance. (Illus.). 375p. 1974. text ed. 9.50x (ISBN 0-8138-0745-X). Iowa St U Pr.

Sprague, James & Epstein, Alan, eds. Progress in Psychobiology & Physiological Psychology, Vol. 8. LC 66-29640. 1979. 50.00 (ISBN 0-12-542108-7); lib. ed. 58.00 (ISBN 0-12-542178-8); microfiche 42.00 (ISBN 0-12-542179-6). Acad Pr.

Sprague, James M. & Epstein, Alan N., eds. Progress in Psychobiology & Physiological Psychology, Vol. 9. 1980. 43.00 (ISBN 0-12-542109-5); lib. ed. 55.50 (ISBN 0-12-542180-X); microfiche 30.50 (ISBN 0-12-542181-8). Acad Pr.

Sprague, Janet, jt. auth. see Austin-Lett, Genelle.

Sprague, Ken & Reynolds, Bill. The Gold's Gym Book of Bodybuilding. (Illus.). 288p. (Orig.). 1983. 17.95 (ISBN 0-8092-5694-0); pap. 10.95 (ISBN 0-8092-5693-2). Contemp Bks.

Sprague, Marshall. Newport in the Rockies: The Life & Good Times of Colorado Spring. rev. ed. LC 82-75570. (Illus.). 382p. 1981. 15.95 (ISBN 0-8040-0412-9); pap. 9.95 (ISBN 0-8040-0413-7). Swallow.

Sprague, R. H., Jr., jt. ed. see Fick, G.

Sprague, Richard W., ed. see White, Marjorie L.

Sprague, Robert L., ed. Advances in Law & Child Development, Vol. 1. 300p. 1981. 40.00 (ISBN 0-89232-094-X). Jai Pr.

Sprague, Rosamond K., ed. see Sayers, Dorothy L.

Sprague, Stuart & Perkins, Elizabeth. Frankfort: A Pictorial History. LC 80-23571. (Illus.). 1980. pap. 12.95 (ISBN 0-89865-003-8); ltd. ed. 24.95 (ISBN 0-89865-001-1). Donning Co.

Sprague De Camp, L. The Queen of Zamba. LC 77-82627. 1977. pap. 1.50 o.s.i. (ISBN 0-89559-006-9). Davis Pubns.

Sprandel, Hazel Z., jt. ed. see Schmidt, Marlin R.

Sprandel, U. & Stark, F. Kompendium der Inneren Medizin. viii, 300p. 1983. pap. 23.50 (ISBN 3-8055-3562-7). S Karger.

Spratley, Richard D., jt. auth. see Pimentel, George C.

Spratt, John S. The Road to Spindletop: Economic Change in Texas, 1875-1901. (Texas History Paperbacks Ser: No. 5). 367p. 1970. pap. 7.95x o.p. (ISBN 0-292-70030-X). U of Tex Pr.

Spratt, John S., Jr., et al. Exenterative Surgery of the Pelvis. LC 72-90729. (Major Problems in Clinical Surgery Ser.: No. 12). (Illus.). 177p. 1973. text ed. 9.95 o.p. (ISBN 0-7216-8523-4). Saunders.

Spratt, Philip. Beyond Communism. 1982. Repr. of 1947 ed. 8.50 (ISBN 0-8364-0882-9, Pub. by Ajanta). South Asia Bks.

Sprawls, Perry, Jr. The Physics & Instrumentation of Nuclear Medicine. 198p. 1981. text ed. 24.95 (ISBN 0-8391-0544-4). Univ Park.

Spray, Pauline. Rx for Happiness. 1978. 2.50 o.p. (ISBN 0-8341-0545-4). Beacon Hill.

Spray, Russell E. Amazing Grace Sermon Outlines. (Pocket Pulpit Library). 96p. (Orig.). 1982. pap. 2.95 (ISBN 0-8010-8222-6). Baker Bk.

--Simple Outlines on the Christian Faith. (Dollar Sermon Library). 1977. pap. 1.95 (ISBN 0-8010-8120-3). Baker Bk.

Spreadbury, P. J., jt. auth. see Ahmed, H.

Sprecher, C. Ronald. Essentials of Investments. LC 77-74380. (Illus.). 1979. text ed. 25.95 (ISBN 0-395-25454-X); instr's. manual 1.00 (ISBN 0-395-25455-8). HM.

Sprecher, R. Ronald. Introduction to Investment Management. 1975. text ed. 26.95 (ISBN 0-395-18706-0); instr's. manual 1.65 (ISBN 0-395-18784-2). HM.

Spreckelmeyer, Kent F., jt. auth. see Marans, Robert W.

Spreckley, Val. Keeping a Cow. LC 78-74083. 1979. 11.95 o.p. (ISBN 0-7153-7655-1). David & Charles.

Spreiregen, Paul D., ed. see Peets, Elbert.

Spreitzer, Elmer M., jt. auth. see Snyder, Eldon E.

Sprengel, Christian K. Das Entdeckte Geheimnis der Natur Im Bau & der Befruchtung der Blumen. 1973. Repr. of 1793 ed. 40.00 (ISBN 3-7682-0828-1). Lubrecht & Cramer.
Sprenkle, Robert & Ledet, David. Art of Oboe Playing. (Illus.). 1961. pap. text ed. 10.95 (ISBN 0-87487-040-2). Summy.
Sprent, Janet. The Biology of Nitrogen Fixing Organisms. (Illus.). 1979. text ed. 39.95 (ISBN 0-07-084087-3). McGraw.
Spretnak, Charlene. Politics of Women's Spirituality: Essays on the Rise of Spiritualist Power Within the Feminist Movement. LC 80-2876. 624p. 1981. 22.50 (ISBN 0-385-17770-4, Anch); pap. 12.95 (ISBN 0-385-17241-9). Doubleday.
Sprieregen, P. Design Competitions. 1979. 36.50 (ISBN 0-07-060381-2). McGraw.
Spriestersbach, D. C. Research Administration in Academic Institutions. 1975. 0.75 o.p. (ISBN 0-8268-1378-X). ACE.
Sprigge, Cecil. Development of Modern Italy. 1943. text ed. 18.50x (ISBN 0-686-83525-5). Elliots Bks.
Sprigge, Sylvia, tr. see Croce, Benedetto.
Sprigge, Sylvia, tr. see Treves, Giuliana A.
Sprigge, T. L., ed. see Bentham, Jeremy.
Spriggle, H. Kenwood, compiled by. Ninety-Nine Advertising Layout Designs. (Illus.). 1980. write for info. o.p. H Spriggle.
Spriggle, Judith A., ed. An Apple a Day, in a Different Way: 365 Wholesome & Tasty Recipes. 1980. spiral bdg. 5.95 o.p. (ISBN 0-938686-02-X). H Spriggle.
Spriggle, Kenwood. Basic Advertising Layout Designs. wire-o bdg. 50.00 o.p. (ISBN 0-938686-05-4). H Spriggle.
Spriggle, Kenwood, ed. Consumer's Nineteen Seventy-Eight Guide to Wholesale Prescription Drug Prices. LC 77-92884. (First annual suppl. 1980). 1978. spiral bdg. 8.95x o.p. (ISBN 0-938686-00-3). H Spriggle.
Spriggs, Marshall T., ed. see Harak, Charles.
Spriggs, Marshall T., ed. see Rodgers, Allan G.
Spriggs, Marshall T., ed. see Winsor, Ernest.
Sprinchorn, Evert, ed. see Wagner, Richard.
Spring, Harry M. Boiler Operator's Guide. 1940. 29.50 (ISBN 0-07-060510-6, P&RB). McGraw.
Spring, Ira & Manning, Harvey. One Hundred & Two Hikes in the Alpine Lakes, South Cascades & Olympics. 2nd ed. LC 79-166974. (Illus.). 232p. (Orig.). 1978. pap. 7.95 o.p. (ISBN 0-916890-24-4). Mountaineers.
Springarn, Natalie D., ed. see Conference on Confidentiality of Health Records, Key Biscayne, Fla., Nov. 6-9, 1974.
Springer, Edward, ed. The Penthouse Letters. 1983. pap. 3.95 (ISBN 0-446-30681-9). Warner Bks.
Springer, George. Introduction to Riemann Surfaces. 2nd ed. LC 80-67978. (Illus.). viii, 309p. 1981. text ed. 14.95 (ISBN 0-8284-0313-9). Chelsea Pub.
Springer, Haskell S. Washington Irving: A Reference Guide. 1976. lib. bdg. 25.00 (ISBN 0-8161-1101-4, Hall Reference). G K Hall.
Springer, Haskell S., ed. see Irving, Washington.
Springer, Imogene, ed. Recommended English Language Arts Curriculum Guides, K-2. 23p. 1981. 1.40 (ISBN 0-686-95303-7); members 1.00 (ISBN 0-686-99490-6). NCTE.
Springer, J. Frederick, jt. auth. see Musolf, Lloyd D.
Springer, Jeanne A. Fitness for You: A Head-to-Toe Stretching Strengthening & Body-Toning Exercise Program for Women. LC 82-90713. (Illus.). 68p. (Orig.). 1982. pap. 3.95 (ISBN 0-9609394-0-7). Kelane Pub.
Springer, John. Fondas: Films & Careers of Henry, Jane & Peter Fonda. 1970. 10.00 (ISBN 0-8065-0014-X); pap. 6.95 o.p. (ISBN 0-8065-0383-1). Citadel Pr.
--Forgotten Films to Remember. 256p. 1982. 8.95 (ISBN 0-8065-0797-7). Citadel Pr.
Springer, Marlene. Edith Wharton & Kate Chopin: A Reference Guide. 1976. lib. bdg. 30.00 (ISBN 0-8161-1099-9, Hall Reference). G K Hall.
--Hardy's Use of Allusion. LC 82-21977. 22.50x (ISBN 0-7006-0231-3). Univ Pr KS.
Springer, Melvin D. The Algebra of Random Variables. LC 78-9315. (Wiley Ser. in Probability & Mathematical Statistics: Applied Section). 470p. 1979. 49.95 (ISBN 0-471-01406-0, Pub. by Wiley-Interscience). Wiley.
Springer, Rebecca R. My Dream of Heaven. 160p. 1979. 6.95 o.p. (ISBN 0-8007-0989-6). Revell.
Springer, Robert. The Digest Book of Skin & Scuba Diving. (Sports & Leisure Library). (Illus.). 1979. pap. 2.95 o.s.i. (ISBN 0-695-81286-6). Follett.
Springer, Robert, jt. ed. see Lewis, Jack.
Springer, Victor G. Pacific plate Biogeography, with Special Reference to Shorefishes. LC 82-600146. (Contributions to Zoology Ser.: No. 367). (Illus.). 182p. 1982. pap. text ed. 7.95x (ISBN 0-87474-883-6). Smithsonian.
Springer, William. Cinderella? 1979. pap. 1.50 (ISBN 0-686-38384-2). Eldridge Pub.
--Snow White & the Little Men. 1979. pap. 1.50 (ISBN 0-686-38381-8). Eldridge Pub.
Springfield Museum of Fine Arts. John Sloan: The Glouster Years. LC 80-82281. (Illus.). 1980. 8.00 (ISBN 0-686-30581-7). Springfield Lib & Mus.
Springford, Michael, ed. Electrons at the Fermi Surface. LC 79-50509. (Illus.). 496p. 1980. 89.50 (ISBN 0-521-22337-7). Cambridge U Pr.
Springham, D. G., jt. auth. see Moses, V.
Springstubb, Tricia. The Blueberry Troll. LC 81-3872. (Carolrhoda on My Own Bks.). (Illus.). 48p. (gr. k-3). 1981. PLB 6.95g (ISBN 0-87614-167-X, AACR2). Carolrhoda Bks.
--The Magic Guinea Pig. LC 81-22285. (Illus.). 32p. (gr. k-3). 1982. 9.50 (ISBN 0-688-01151-9); lib. bdg. 8.59 (ISBN 0-688-01152-7). Morrow.
--My Minnie Is a Jewel. LC 80-66712. (Carolrhoda on My Own Bks.). (Illus.). 48p. (gr. k-3). 1980. PLB 6.95g (ISBN 0-87614-131-9). Carolrhoda Bks.
Sprinkel, Beryl W. & Genetski, Robert J. Winning with Money. 245p. 1982. pap. 6.95 (ISBN 0-87094-355-3). Dow Jones-Irwin.
Sprinkle, Patricia. Hunger: Understanding the Crisis Through Games, Dramas & Songs. 5.95 (ISBN 0-686-95934-5). Alternatives.
Sprinkle, Patricia H. Hunger: Understanding the Crisis Through Games, Dramas, & Songs. LC 78-52451. 112p. (Orig.). 1980. pap. 6.95 (ISBN 0-8042-1312-7). John Knox.
Sprinthall, Normal, jt. auth. see Sprinthall, Richard.
Sprinthall, Norman A. & Collins, W. Andrews. Adolescent Psychology: A Developmental View. (Illus.). 608p. Date not set. text ed. price not set (ISBN 0-201-16301-2). A-W.
Sprinthall, Richard & Sprinthall, Normal. Educational Psychology: A Developmental Approach. 3rd ed. LC 80-15223. (Illus.). 624p. 1981. pap. text ed. 18.95 (ISBN 0-201-06872-9); instr's. manual avail. (ISBN 0-201-06873-7); solutions manual avail. (ISBN 0-201-06876-1). A-W.
Sprintzen, David A. The Drama of Thought: An Inquiry into the Place of Philosophy in Human Experience. LC 78-64821. 1978. pap. text ed. 9.75 (ISBN 0-8191-0640-2). U Pr of Amer.
Sproat, John G. The Best Men: Liberal Reformers in the Gilded Age With a New Preface. LC 82-10948. (Phoenix Ser.). 376p. 1983. pap. 9.95 (ISBN 0-226-76990-9). U of Chicago Pr.
Sprogle, Howard O. The Philadelphia Police: Past & Present. LC 70-172570. (Criminology, Law Enforcement, & Social Problems Ser.: No. 151). (Illus.). Date not set. Repr. of 1887 ed. lib. bdg. price not set (ISBN 0-87585-151-7). Patterson Smith.
Spronck, Lambert H. The Financial Executive's Handbook for Managing Multinational Corporations. 1980. 42.95x (ISBN 0-471-05277-9). Ronald Pr.
--Managing Coordinated External & Internal Audits. LC 82-16150. 254p. 1983. 34.95x (ISBN 0-471-86140-5). Ronald Pr.
Spronk, N., jt. ed. see Addink, A. D.
Sprose, Judith, jt. auth. see Hamric, Ann B.
Sproston, E., jt. ed. see Garattini, S.
Sprott, Julien C. Introduction to Modern Electronics. LC 80-25366. 349p. 1981. text ed. 25.95 (ISBN 0-471-05840-8); 10.50 (ISBN 0-471-86375-0). Wiley.
Sprott, S. E. English Debate on Suicide. LC 61-11287. 176p. 1973. 16.00x (ISBN 0-87548-013-6); pap. 4.95 o.p (ISBN 0-87548-014-4). Open Court.
Sproul, R. C. Basic Training: Plain Talk on the Key Truths of the Faith. 176p. (Orig.). 1982. pap. 5.95 (ISBN 0-310-44921-9). Zondervan.
--Discovering the Intimate Marriage. LC 72-23494. 160p. 1981. pap. 2.95 o.p. (ISBN 0-87123-118-2, 200118). Bethany Hse.
--In Search of Dignity. LC 82-18576. (In Search Of Ser.). 1983. 10.95 (ISBN 0-8307-0869-3, 5110407). Regal.
--Stronger Than Steel: The Wayne Alderson Story. LC 80-7746. 244p. 1980. 11.95i (ISBN 0-06-067502-0, HarpR). Har-Row.
Sproule, J. Michael. Argument: Language & Its Influence. new ed. (Illus.). 1980. text ed. 23.50x (ISBN 0-07-060520-3). McGraw.
--Communication Today. 1981. pap. text ed. 13.50x (ISBN 0-673-15168-9); study guide 6.95x (ISBN 0-673-15469-6). Scott F.
Sproull, R. L. & Phillips, W. A. Modern Physics. 3rd ed. LC 79-26680. 682p. 1980. text ed. 33.95 (ISBN 0-471-81840-2). Wiley.
Sproull, Robert, jt. auth. see Newman, William.
Sproull, Robert F., jt. auth. see Newman, William M.
Sprouse, Jean. The Secret of the Satin Doll. (YA) 1978. 6.95 (ISBN 0-685-87349-8, Avalon). Bouregy.
Sprouse, Mary L. How to Survive a Tax Audit: What to Do Before & After You Hear from the IRS. LC 80-1127. (Illus.). 288p. 1981. 11.95 o.p. (ISBN 0-385-17260-5). Doubleday.
Sprout, Harold & Sprout, Margaret. The Context of Environmental Politics: Unfinished Business for America's Third Century. LC 77-84066. (Essays for the Third Century Ser.). (Illus.). 224p. 1978. 12.00x (ISBN 0-8131-0400-9). U Pr of Ky.
Sprout, Harold H. & Sprout, Margaret. The Ecological Perspective on Human Affairs, with Special Reference to International Politics. LC 78-27759. 1979. Repr. of 1965 ed. lib. bdg. 20.75x (ISBN 0-313-20914-6, SPEP). Greenwood.
--Toward a New Order of Sea Power: American Naval Policy & the World Scene, 1918-1922. Repr. of 1946 ed. lib. bdg. 17.50x (ISBN 0-8371-1168-4, SPAN). Greenwood.
Sprout, Margaret, jt. auth. see Sprout, Harold.
Sprout, Margaret, jt. auth. see Sprout, Harold H.
Sprowls, James T. Discretion & Lawlessness: Compliance in the Juvenile Court. LC 79-6735. 144p. 1980. 16.95x (ISBN 0-669-03540-8). Lexington Bks.
Sprowls, R. Clay. Management Data Bases. LC 76-6100. 382p. 1976. text ed. 31.95x o.p. (ISBN 0-471-81865-8, Pub. by Wiley Hamilton); TM Bases 5.50x (ISBN 0-471-02547-X). Wiley.
Spruch, Grace M. & Spruch, Larry. Twenty-One Astounding Science Quizzes. (Illus.). 160p. 1982. pap. 4.76i (ISBN 0-06-463550-3, EH550). B&N NY.
Spruch, Larry, jt. auth. see Spruch, Grace M.
Sprudz, Adolf, ed. see Holborn, Hajo.
Sprudzs, Adolf. Benelux Abbreviations & Symbols: Law & Related Subjects. LC 74-140620. 129p. 1971. lib. bdg. 20.00 (ISBN 0-379-00120-9). Oceana.
--Italian Abbreviations & Symbols: Law & Related Subjects. LC 70-95307. 124p. 1969. 20.00 (ISBN 0-379-00451-8). Oceana.
Sprudzs, Adolf, jt. ed. see Kavass, Igor I.
Sprung, Charles L. The Pulmonary Artery Catheter: Methodology & Clinical Applications. 1983. pap. 16.95 (ISBN 0-8391-1808-2, 15520). Univ Park.
Sprung, Mervyn, ed. The Question of Being: East-West Perspectives. 1978. text ed. 15.95x (ISBN 0-271-01242-0). Pa St U Pr.
Sprunt, Alexander, Jr. & Dick, John H. Carolina Low Country Impressions. (Illus.). 1964. 14.95 (ISBN 0-8159-5201-5). Devin.
Sprunt, James, et al. From Bondage to Freedom. (Orig.). 1968. pap. 4.95 o.p. (ISBN 0-8042-9020-2); tchrs' guide pap. 3.00 o.p. (ISBN 0-686-76880-9). John Knox.
SPSS Inc. Analysis of U. S. Census Data. 144p. 1983. 16.95x (ISBN 0-07-060523-8, C). McGraw.
--SPSS-X Analysis of SMF Data. 144p. 1983. 16.95x (ISBN 0-07-060522-X, C). McGraw.
--SPSS-X Basics. 160p. 1983. 12.95x (ISBN 0-07-060524-6, C). McGraw.
SPSS, Inc. SPSS-X Data Management. 256p. 1983. 16.95x (ISBN 0-07-046547-9). McGraw.
--SPSS-X User's Guide. 800p. 1983. 21.95x (ISBN 0-07-046550-9, C). McGraw.
Spude, Robert L. & Paher, Stanley W. Central Arizona Ghost Towns. (Illus.). 1978. 7.50 (ISBN 0-913814-19-9); pap. 3.50 (ISBN 0-913814-20-2). Nevada Pubns.
Spufford, Margaret. Contrasting Communities: English Villagers in the Sixteenth & Seventeenth Centuries. LC 73-83105. (Illus.). 1974. 49.50 (ISBN 0-521-20323-6). Cambridge U Pr.
--Contrasting Communities: English Villagers in the Sixteenth & Seventeenth Centuries. LC 73-83105. (Illus.). 1980. pap. 16.95 (ISBN 0-521-29748-6). Cambridge U Pr.
Spulber, D. F., jt. auth. see Mirman, L. J.
Spunt, Georges. A Place in Time. 384p. 1980. pap. 2.50 o.p. (ISBN 0-523-40668-1). Pinnacle Bks.
Spurga, Ronald C. A Practical Guide to the Commodities Markets. 204p. 1983. 19.95 (ISBN 0-13-690644-3); pap. 9.95 (ISBN 0-13-690636-2). P-H.
Spurgeon, C. Gleanings among the Sheaves. 1974. pap. 2.50 o.p. (ISBN 0-87509-085-0). Chr Pubns.
Spurgeon, C. H. Barbed Arrows. 237p. pap. 2.95 o.p. (ISBN 0-87509-049-4). Chr Pubns.
--Infant Salvation. 1981. pap. 0.50 (ISBN 0-686-37176-3). Pilgrim Pubns.
Spurgeon, Carlos M. Discursos a Mis Estudiantes. 1981. pap. 5.75 (ISBN 0-311-42006-0). Casa Bautista.
Spurgeon, Caroline. Shakespeare's Imagery. 1952. 57.50 (ISBN 0-521-06538-0); pap. 11.95 (ISBN 0-521-09258-2). Cambridge U Pr.
Spurgeon, Caroline F. Five Hundred Years of Chaucer Criticism & Allusion, 1357-1900, 3 Vols. LC 60-5339. (Illus.). 1960. Repr. of 1925 ed. Set. 45.00x o.p. (ISBN 0-8462-0279-4). Russell.
Spurgeon, Charles H. All of Grace. (Summit Books). 1976. pap. 2.95 (ISBN 0-8010-8095-9). Baker Bk.
--All of Grace. pap. 2.95 (ISBN 0-8024-0001-9). Moody.
--Charles Haddon Spurgeon: Autobiography, Vol. 1 The Early Years, 1834-1860. 1976. 16.95 (ISBN 0-85151-076-0). Banner of Truth.
--Charles Haddon Spurgeon: Autobiography, Vol. 2 The Full Harvest, 1861-1892. 1975. 16.95 (ISBN 0-85151-182-1). Banner of Truth.
--Commenting & Commentaries. (C. H. Spurgeon Library). 1981. pap. 3.95 (ISBN 0-8010-8194-7). Baker Bk.
--Daily Help. 1959. 3.95 (ISBN 0-448-01637-0, G&D). Putnam Pub Group.
--Faith's Checkbook. pap. 3.95 (ISBN 0-8024-0014-0, 35-14). Moody.
--John Ploughman's Talks. (Summit Bks.). 1976. pap. 3.50 (ISBN 0-8010-8094-0). Baker Bk.
--Psalms. Fuller, David O., ed. LC 76-12085. Orig. Title: Treasury of David. 1976. 11.95 (ISBN 0-8254-3714-8). Kregel.
--Seven Wonders of Grace. (Summit Bks). 1978. 2.95 o.p. (ISBN 0-8010-8131-9). Baker Bk.
--Solamente por Gracia. 128p. 1982. pap. 2.95 (ISBN 0-8024-8116-7). Moody.
--The Soulwinner. (Orig.). 1963. pap. 4.95 (ISBN 0-8028-8081-9). Eerdmans.
--Spurgeon on Inerrancy. LC 81-68636. 176p. 1982. pap. cancelled (ISBN 0-86693-002-7). Christian Herald.
--Spurgeon's Devotional Bible. 1974. Repr. 18.95 (ISBN 0-8010-8043-6). Baker Bk.
--Spurgeon's Sermons, 10 vols. (Charles H. Spurgeon Library). 1983. pap. 99.95 (ISBN 0-8010-8231-5). Baker Bk.
--Twelve Christmas Sermons. (Charles H. Spurgeon Library). 148p. 1976. pap. 3.95 (ISBN 0-8010-8081-9). Baker Bk.
Spurgeon, Charles H. C. H. Spurgeon's Sermons on Christ's Names & Titles. Cook, Charles T., ed. 1965. Repr. of 1961 ed. 7.95 (ISBN 0-87921-033-8). Attic Pr.
Spurgeon, P., jt. ed. see Singleton, W. T.
Spurgeon, Sandra L., jt. auth. see Porter, John W.
Spurling, T. H., jt. auth. see Mason, E. A.
Spurlock, John H. He Sings for Us: A Sociolinguistic Analysis of the Appalachian Subculture & of Jesse Stuart As a Major American Author. LC 80-8297. (Illus.). 190p. 1980. lib. bdg. 18.75 (ISBN 0-8191-1271-2); pap. text ed. 9.50 (ISBN 0-8191-1272-0). U Pr of Amer.
Spurr, R. T., jt. auth. see Newcomb, T. P.
Spurr, Russell. A Glorious Way to Die: The Kamikaze Mission of the Battleship Yamato, April 1945. LC 81-9663. (Illus.). 368p. 1981. 14.95 (ISBN 0-937858-00-5); pap. 8.95 (ISBN 0-937858-17-X). Newmarket.
Spurr, Stephen H. & Barnes, Burton V. Forest Ecology. 3rd ed. LC 79-10007. 1980. text ed. 31.95 (ISBN 0-471-04732-5). Wiley.
Spurs, Jackson see Foreman, Dave & Koehler, Bart.
Spurzheim, Johann C. Observations on the Deranged Manifestations of the Mind, or Insanity. LC 78-81359. (Hist. of Psych. Ser.). (Illus.). 1970. Repr. of 1833 ed. 32.00x (ISBN 0-8201-1078-7). Schol Facsimiles.
Spuy, H. van der see Van Der Spuy, H. I.
Spyers Duran, Peter, ed. see Florida Atlantic University Conference.
Spyers-Duran, Peter, ed. see International Seminar on Approval & Gathering Plans in Large & Medium Size Academic Libraries, 3rd.
Spyker, John H. Little Lives. 1980. pap. 2.25 o.p. (ISBN 0-380-48322-X, 48322). Avon.
Spyker, John Howland. Little Lives. 1978. 10.00 o.p. (ISBN 0-448-15164-2, G&D). Putnam Pub Group.
Spykman, E. C. Edie on the Warpath. LC 66-14797. (gr. 5-9). 1970. pap. 2.95 (ISBN 0-15-627650-X, VoyB). HarBraceJ.
--Terrible, Horrible Edie. LC 60-8412. 1966. pap. 2.95 (ISBN 0-15-688650-2, VoyB). HarBraceJ.
--The Wild Angel. 1981. PLB 9.95 (ISBN 0-8398-2624-9, Gregg). G K Hall.
Spykman, Elizabeth C. Edie on the Warpath. LC 66-14797. 191p. (gr. 4-6). 1970. pap. 2.95 (ISBN 0-15-225045-X, HJ). HarBraceJ.
--Lemon & a Star. LC 55-7614. (gr. 5-9). 1955. 5.95 o.p. (ISBN 0-15-244713-X, HJ). HarBraceJ.
Spykman, Gordon. Christian Faith in Focus. (Orig.). 1967. pap. 3.50 o.p. (ISBN 0-8010-7907-1). Baker Bk.
Spyri, J. Heidi. (Deluxe Illustrated Classics Ser.). 1977. 4.50 (ISBN 0-307-12211-5, Golden Pr). Western Pub.
--Heidi's Children. (Deluxe Illustrated Classics Ser.). 1977. 4.50 (ISBN 0-307-12221-2, Golden Pr). Western Pub.
Spyri, Johanna. Heidi. (Nancy Drew's Favorite Classics). (Illus.). (gr. 6-9). 1978. 2.95 (ISBN 0-448-14941-9, G&D). Putnam Pub Group.
--Heidi. (Illus.). (gr. 4-6). il. jr. lib. 5.95 (ISBN 0-448-05812-X, G&D); Companion Lib. Ed. 2.95 (ISBN 0-448-05463-9); deluxe ed. 8.95 (ISBN 0-448-06012-4). Putnam Pub Group.
--Heidi. LC 78-5489. (Raintree's Illustrated Classics). (Illus.). (gr. 5-8). 1978. PLB 13.30 (ISBN 0-8172-1131-4). Raintree Pubs.
--Heidi. Barish, Wendy, ed. (Illus.). 336p. 1982. 14.95 (ISBN 0-671-43790-9). Wanderer Bks.
--Heidi. 1983. pap. 2.25 (ISBN 0-14-035002-0, Puffin). Penguin.
Squadrito, Kathleen. John Locke. (English Authors Ser.). 1979. 12.95 (ISBN 0-8057-6772-X, Twayne). G K Hall.
Squadrito, Kathleen M. Locke's Theory of Sensitive Knowledge. LC 78-62265. 1978. pap. text ed. 10.00 (ISBN 0-8191-0571-6). U Pr of Amer.
Squibb, George D. Precedence in England & Wales. 158p. 1981. 34.50x (ISBN 0-19-825389-3). Oxford U Pr.
Squier, Charles L. Sir John Suckling. (English Authors Ser.). 1978. 14.95 (ISBN 0-8057-6721-5, Twayne). G K Hall.
Squier, Elizabeth. Guide to Recommended Country Inns of New England. 8th ed. 304p. 1983. pap. 7.95 (ISBN 0-87106-976-8). Globe Pequot.
Squiers, Granville. Secret Hiding-Places the Origins, Histories & Descriptions of English Secret Hiding-Places Used by Priests, Cavaliers, Jacobites & Smugglers. LC 70-157499. (Tower Bks). (Illus.). 1971. Repr. of 1934 ed. 37.00x (ISBN 0-8103-3920-X). Gale.
Squire, Aelred. Summer in the Seed. LC 79-52126. 256p. 1980. pap. 7.95 o.p. (ISBN 0-8091-2237-5). Paulist Pr.

Squire, David. Window-Boxes, Pots & Tubs: A Growing Guide. (Illus.). 168p. 1983. 22.50 (ISBN 0-7153-8385-X). David & Charles.
Squire, Elizabeth D. New Fortune in Your Hand. rev. & enl. ed. LC 60-7508. (Illus.). 1968. 9.95 (ISBN 0-8303-0061-9). Fleet.
Squire, Enid. Introducing Systems Design. LC 78-18651. 1979. pap. text ed. 19.95 (ISBN 0-201-07421-4). A-W.
Squire, Jason E. The Movie Business Book. (Illus.). 448p. 1983. 24.95 (ISBN 0-13-604603-7); pap. 13.95 (ISBN 0-13-604595-2). P-H.
Squire, Jessie & Clayton, Bruce D. Basic Pharmacology for Nurses. 7th ed. LC 80-26574. 296p. 1981. pap. text ed. 16.50 (ISBN 0-8016-4743-6). Mosby.
Squire, Lucy, et al. Exercises in Diagnostic Radiology, Vol. 4: The Total Patient. 2nd ed. (Illus.). 118p. 1981. pap. 13.95 (ISBN 0-7216-8542-0). Saunders.
Squire, Lucy F., jt. auth. see Gosink, Barbara B.
Squire, Lucy F., jt. auth. see Langston, Charles S.
Squire, Lucy F., et al. Exercises in Diagnostic Radiology. Incl. Vol. 1. The Chest. Colaice, William M. & Strutynsky, Natalie S. 1970. pap. 7.95 o.p. (ISBN 0-7216-8525-0); Vol. 2. The Abdomen. Colaice, William M. & Strutynsky, Natalie S. 1971. pap. 7.95 o.p. (ISBN 0-7216-8526-9); Vol. 3. Bone. Colaice, William M. & Strutynsky, Natalie S. 1972. pap. 8.95 o.p. (ISBN 0-7216-8527-7); Vol. 4. The Total Patient. Dreyfuss, Jack R. & Langston, Charles S. 1972. pap. 7.95 o.p. (ISBN 0-7216-8528-5); Vol. 5. Pediatrics. Heller, Richard M. 1973. pap. 8.95 o.p. (ISBN 0-7216-4630-1); Vol. 6. Nuclear Radiology. James, A. Everette. 1973. pap. 7.95 o.p. (ISBN 0-7216-5103-8); Vol. 7. The Emergency Patient. Langston, Charles S. pap. 8.50 o.p. (ISBN 0-685-36219-1). LC 74-113034. (Illus.). pap. Saunders.
--Exercises in Diagnostic Radiology, Vol. 3: Bone. 2nd ed. (Illus.). 85p. 1981. pap. text ed. 11.95 (ISBN 0-7216-8541-2). Saunders.
--Exercises in Diagnostic Radiology, Volume 1: The Chest. 2nd ed. (Illus.). 86p. 1981. pap. 11.95 (ISBN 0-7216-8539-0). Saunders.
--Exercises in Diagnostic Radiology, Volume 2: The Abodomen. 2nd ed. (Illus.). 88p. 1981. pap. 11.95 (ISBN 0-7216-8540-4). Saunders.
Squire, Morris B., jt. auth. see Mathein, J. Daniel.
Squire, Norman. Contract Bridge: How to Become a Champion. (Illus.). 122p. 1975. 7.50 o.p. (ISBN 0-86002-006-1). Transatlantic.
--A Guide to Bridge Conventions. 2nd ed. 100p. 1979. pap. 4.95 (ISBN 0-7156-1426-6). US Games Syst.
Squire, P. S. Third Department: The Political Police in the Russia of Nicholas First. LC 69-10198. (Illus.). 1968. 37.50 (ISBN 0-521-07148-8). Cambridge U Pr.
Squire, Robin. Portrait of Barbara. LC 76-28061. 1978. 8.95 o.p. (ISBN 0-312-63175-8). St Martin.
Squire, Russel & Mountney, Virginia R. Class Piano for Adult Beginners. 2nd ed. LC 70-115130. (Illus.). 1971. pap. text ed. 15.95 (ISBN 0-13-135160-5). P-H.
Squires, D. Practical Physics. 2nd ed. 1977. text ed. 10.95 o.p. (ISBN 0-07-084073-3, C). McGraw.
Squires, Dick. The Other Racquet Sports. (Illus.). 1978. 14.95 o.p. (ISBN 0-07-060532-7, GB). McGraw.
Squires, G. L. Introduction to the Theory of Thermal Neutron Scattering. LC 77-85682. (Illus.). 1978. 59.50 (ISBN 0-521-21884-5). Cambridge U Pr.
Squires, Michael. The Pastoral Novel: Studies in George Eliot, Thomas Hardy, & D. H.Lawrence. LC 74-75793. 1975. 13.95x (ISBN 0-8139-0530-3). U Pr of Va.
Squires, Norman. Squeeze Play Simplified. 184p. 1979. pap. 5.95 (ISBN 0-7156-1348-0). US Games Syst.
Squires, Radcliffe. Gardens of the World. LC 80-21750. x, 60p. 1981. 0.00 o.p. (ISBN 0-8071-0754-9); pap. 4.95 (ISBN 0-8071-0755-7). La State U Pr.
--Journeys. LC 82-84117. 70p. (Orig.). Date not set. pap. 3.95 (ISBN 0-941692-02-7); Ltd. Signed ed. 10.00, (ISBN 0-941692-03-5). Elysian Pr.
Squires, Terence L. Your Book of Electronics. (gr. 7 up). 4.50 o.p. (ISBN 0-571-05792-6). Transatlantic.
Squires, William T. The Metal Craftsman Handbook. 1981. 8.95 o.p. (ISBN 0-89606-050-0). Green Hill.
SRA. Stenospeed for the Legal Secretary. 353p. 1981. pap. text ed. 24.95 (ISBN 0-574-20880-1, 13-3880). SRA.
--Stenospeed for the Medical Secretary. 418p. 1981. pap. text ed. 24.95 (ISBN 0-574-20885-2, 13-3885). SRA.
SRA Data Processing & Curriculum Group. Case Study in Business System Design. (Illus.). 1970. pap. text ed. 7.95 (ISBN 0-574-16094-9, 13-0782); instr's guide avail. (ISBN 0-574-16095-7, 13-0783). SRA.
Sraffa, P. Production of Commodities by Means of Commodities. (Illus.). 99p. 1975. pap. 12.95 (ISBN 0-521-09969-2). Cambridge U Pr.
Sraffa, P., ed. see Ricardo, David.
Srb, Adrian M., jt. auth. see Wallace, Bruce.
Srb, Jozetta H. Communicating with Employees About Pension & Welfare Benefits. (Key Issues Ser.: No. 8). 44p. 1971. pap. 2.00 (ISBN 0-87546-244-8). ILR Pr.
--Portable Pensions. (Key Issues Ser.: No. 4). 1969. pap. 2.00 (ISBN 0-87546-245-6). ILR Pr.
Srb, Jozetta H., jt. auth. see Silverstein, Pam.
Sreedhar. The Gulf. 1982. text ed. 19.25x (ISBN 0-391-02798-0, Pub. by UBS India). Humanities.
Sreenivasan, Kasthuri. Climbing the Coconut Tree: A Partial Autobiography. (Illus.). 1980. 13.95x o.p. (ISBN 0-19-561242-6). Oxford U Pr.
Srere, Paul A. & Estabrook, Ronald W., eds. Microenvironments & Metabolic Compartmentation. 1978. 41.00 (ISBN 0-12-660550-5). Acad Pr.
Sri Alurobindo. Hymns to the Mystic Fire. 1973. 15.00 o.p. (ISBN 0-89071-220-4). Matagiri.
Sri Aurobindo. The Secret of the Veda. 1971. 15.50 o.p. (ISBN 0-89071-219-0). Matagiri.
Srigley, Michael, tr. see Lindroth, Stan, et al.
Srinath, M. D. & Rajasekaran, P. K. An Introduction to Statistical Signal Processing with Applications. LC 78-15417. 499p. 1979. 39.50x (ISBN 0-471-04404-0, Pub. by Wiley-Interscience). Wiley.
Srinivas, M. N. Social Change in Modern India. (Rabindranath Tagore Memorial Lectures). (gr. 9-12). 1966. 22.50x o.p. (ISBN 0-520-01203-8); pap. 6.95x (ISBN 0-520-01421-9, CAMPUS21). U of Cal Pr.
Srinivasadasa. Yatindramatadipika. Adidevananda, Swami, tr. (Sanskrit & Eng.). 2.75 o.p. (ISBN 0-87481-428-6). Vedanta Pr.
Srinivasan, A. V., ed. Structural Dynamic Aspects of Bladed-Disk Assemblies. 1976. pap. text ed. 14.00 o.p. (ISBN 0-685-75518-5, H00098). ASME.
Srinivasan, Dobli, ed. Ocular Therapeutics. LC 80-80728. (Illus.). 248p. 1980. 48.75x (ISBN 0-89352-084-5). Masson Pub.
Srinivasan, P. R., et al, eds. The Origins of Modern Biochemistry: A Retrospect on Proteins. (Annals of the New York Academy of Sciences: Vol. 325). 373p. (Orig.). 1979. pap. 67.00x (ISBN 0-89766-018-8). NY Acad Sci.
Srinivasan, R. Mechanical Vibration Analysis. 480p. Date not set. 12.95x (ISBN 0-07-451932-8). McGraw.
Srinivasan, R., ed. Conformation in Biology: Past, Present & Future. Sarma, R. H. (Illus.). 500p. 1982. text ed. 89.00 (ISBN 0-940030-05-5). Adenine Pr.
Srinivasan, S. K. & Mehata, K. M. Stochastic Processes. LC 77-20511. 1978. text ed. 18.95 o.p. (ISBN 0-07-096612-5, C); pap. text ed. 8.95 o.p. (ISBN 0-07-011548-6). McGraw.
Srinivasan, V. Applied Thermodynamics for Engineers. (Illus.). 400p. Date not set. text ed. cancelled (ISBN 0-7069-1177-6, Pub. by Vikas India). Advent NY.
Srinivasau, Nirmala. Identity Crisis of Muslims: Profiles of Lucknow Youth. 140p. 1981. text ed. 13.00x (ISBN 0-391-02279-2, Pub. by Concept India). Humanities.
Srinivisan, Mangalam, ed. Technology Assessment & Development. 288p. 1982. 29.95 (ISBN 0-03-059543-6). Praeger.
Sri Ram Sharma. The Religious Policy of the Mughal Emperors. 3rd ed. 258p. 1973. lib. bdg. 10.95x (ISBN 0-210-33935-7). Asia.
Srivastava & Carter. Introduction to Applied Multivariate Statistics. Date not set. 34.50 (ISBN 0-444-00621-4). Elsevier.
Srivastava, Dharma. The Province of Agra. 1979. text ed. 19.50x (ISBN 0-391-01814-0). Humanities.
Srivastava, H. M. & Buschman, R. G. Convolution Integral Equations with Special Function Kernals. LC 76-52979. 1977. 16.95x o.s.i. (ISBN 0-470-99050-3). Halsted Pr.
Srivastava, J. Combinatorial Mathematics Optical Designs & Their Applications. (Annals of Discreet Mathematics Ser.: Vol. 6). 1980. 72.50 (ISBN 0-444-86048-7). Elsevier.
Srivastava, J. N., ed. see International Symposium on Statistical Design & Linear Models, March 19-23, 1973.
Srivastava, J. N., et al. A Survey of Combinatorial Theory. LC 72-88578. 470p. 1973. 51.00 (ISBN 0-444-10425-9, North-Holland). Elsevier.
Srivastava, Jane J. Averages. LC 75-5927. (Young Math Ser.). (Illus.). 40p. (gr. 1-5). 1975. 9.57i o.p. (ISBN 0-690-00742-6, TYC-J); PLB 10.89 (ISBN 0-690-00743-4). Har-Row.
--Computers. LC 70-171009. (Young Math Ser.). (Illus.). (gr. 1-4). 1972. 9.57i o.p. (ISBN 0-690-20850-2, TYC-J); PLB 10.89 (ISBN 0-690-20851-0). Har-Row.
--Number Families. LC 78-19511. (Illus.). (gr. 2-5). 1979. PLB 10.89 (ISBN 0-690-03924-7, TYC-J). Har-Row.
--Spaces, Shapes, & Sizes. LC 78-22516. (Illus.). 48p. (gr. 1-3). 1980. 10.53i (ISBN 0-690-03961-1, TYC-J); PLB 10.89 (ISBN 0-690-03962-X). Har-Row.
--Statistics. LC 72-7559. (Young Math Ser.). (Illus.). (gr. 1-5). 1973. PLB 10.89 (ISBN 0-690-77300-5, TYC-J). Har-Row.
Srivastava, Meera. Constitutional Crisis in the States in India. 220p. 1980. text ed. 13.50x (ISBN 0-391-02135-4). Humanities.
Srivastava, U. K. & Shenov, G. V. Quantitative Techniques for Managerial Decision Making: Concepts, Illustrations, & Problems. LC 82-21242. 968p. 1983. 29.95 (ISBN 0-470-27375-5). Wiley.
Srivastava, V., ed. Cultural Contours of India. 419p. 1981. text ed. 120.00x (ISBN 0-391-02358-6). Humanities.
Sroda, George. Life Story of TV Star & Celebrity Herman the Worm. (Illus.). 189p. 1979. 3.95 (ISBN 0-9604486-1-6); pap. 3.95 (ISBN 0-9604486-2-4). G Sroda.
--No Angle Left Unturned: Facts About Nightcrawlers. (Illus.). 111p. (gr. 10 up). 1975. pap. 4.95 (ISBN 0-9604486-0-8). G Sroda.
Sroge, Maxwell H. The Best in Catalog-1983. 180p. 1983. 29.95 (ISBN 0-942674-03-0). Sroge M.
--Catalog Marketer Supplier's Guide, 1982. 116p. 1982. perfect bound 29.95 (ISBN 0-942674-02-2). Sroge M.
Sroog, C. E., jt. auth. see Berry, G. C.
Ssu-Ma, Ch'Ien. Statesman, Patriot & General in Ancient China. Bodde, D., tr. 1940. pap. 10.00 (ISBN 0-527-02691-3). Kraus Repr.
Ssu Shu. Chinese Classical Work Commonly Called the Four Books. 1828. Collie, David, ed. LC 75-122487. 1970. Repr. of 1828 ed. 41.00x (ISBN 0-8201-1079-5). Schol Facsimiles.
Staab, Claire, jt. auth. see Shafer, Robert E.
Staab, Wayne J. The Hearing Aid Book. (Illus.). 1978. 12.95 o.p. (ISBN 0-8306-8987-7); pap. 8.95 o.p. (ISBN 0-8306-7987-1, 987). TAB Bks.
Staal, Frits. Exploring Mysticism: A Methodological. LC 74-76391. 1975. 36.50x (ISBN 0-520-02726-4); pap. 4.95 (ISBN 0-520-03119-9, CAL 313). U of Cal Pr.
Staal, J. F. A Reader on the Sanskrit Grammarians. 1972. 47.50x (ISBN 0-262-19078-8). MIT Pr.
Staar. Yearbook on International Affairs. 1982. 39.95 (ISBN 0-686-96536-1). Hoover Inst Pr.
Staar, Richard F., ed. see De Weydenthal, Jan B.
Stabb, Martin S. Jorge Luis Borges. (World Authors Ser.). lib. bdg. 12.95 (ISBN 0-8057-2168-1, Twayne). G K Hall.
Stableford, Brian. Journey to the Center. 176p. 1982. pap. 2.50 (ISBN 0-87997-756-6, UE1756). DAW Bks.
Stableford, Brian M. The City of the Sun. (Science Fiction Ser). (Orig.). 1978. pap. 1.50 o.p. (ISBN 0-87997-377-3, UW1377). DAW Bks.
--A Clash of Symbols: The Triumph of James Blish. LC 79-13067. (The Milford Ser.: Popular Writers of Today: Vol. 24). 1979. lib. bdg. 9.95x (ISBN 0-89370-134-3); pap. 3.95x (ISBN 0-89370-234-X). Borgo Pr.
--Critical Threshold. (Science Fiction Ser.). 1977. pap. 1.25 o.p. (ISBN 0-87997-282-3, UY1282). DAW Bks.
--Masters of Science-Fiction, No. 1: Essays on Science-Fiction Authors. LC 80-24116. (Milford Series: Popular Writers of Today: Vol. 32). 64p. (Orig.). 1981. lib. bdg. 9.95x (ISBN 0-89370-147-5); pap. text ed. 3.95x (ISBN 0-89370-247-1). Borgo Pr.
--The Mysteries of Modern Science. 1978. 16.95 (ISBN 0-7100-8697-0). Routledge & Kegan.
--The Sociology of Science Fiction. LC 81-21607. (I. O. Evans Studies in the Philosophy & Criticism of Literature: Vol. 4). 192p. 1983. lib. bdg. 12.95x (ISBN 0-89370-165-3); pap. 5.95x (ISBN 0-89370-265-X). Borgo Pr.
Stableford, T. The Literary Appreciation of Russian Writers. LC 81-6192. 1982. text ed. 29.95 (ISBN 0-521-23498-0); pap. text ed. 11.95 (ISBN 0-521-28003-6). Cambridge U Pr.
Stablefore, Brian. The Gates of Eden. 176p. 1983. pap. 2.35 (ISBN 0-686-84669-9). DAW Bks.
Stabler, C. Norman. How to Read the Financial News. 10th ed. 239p. 1972. pap. 4.95 (ISBN 0-06-463327-6, EH 327, EH). B&N NY.
Stabley, Don. System 360 Assembler Language. LC 67-30037. 129p. 1967. pap. 19.95x (ISBN 0-471-81950-6, Pub. by Wiley-Interscience). Wiley.
Stabley, Don H. Assembler Language for Application Programming. (Illus.). 700p. 1982. 35.00 (ISBN 0-89433-176-0). Petrocelli.
Stace, B. C., jt. ed. see Miller, R. G.
Stace, Christopher, tr. see Plautus.
Stace, Walter T. Destiny of Western Man. Repr. of 1942 ed. lib. bdg. 16.25x (ISBN 0-8371-3375-0, STDM). Greenwood.
--Theory of Knowledge & Existence. Repr. of 1932 ed. lib. bdg. 20.50x (ISBN 0-8371-4343-8, STTK). Greenwood.
Stacey, Barrie. Political Socialization in Western Society: An Analysis from a Life-Span Perspective. LC 77-27905. 1978. 25.00x (ISBN 0-312-62513-8). St Martin.
Stacey, David. Interpreting the Bible. 120p. 1977. pap. 2.00 (ISBN 0-8164-1228-6). Seabury.
Stacey, F. D. & Banerjee, S. K. Physical Principles of Rock Magnetism. LC 72-87965. (Developments in Solid Earth Geophysics Ser.: Vol. 5). 224p. 1974. 53.25 (ISBN 0-444-41084-8). Elsevier.
Stacey, Frank D. Physics of the Earth. 2nd ed. LC 76-41891. 414p. 1977. text ed. 31.50 (ISBN 0-471-81956-5). Wiley.
Stacey, Gillian, jt. auth. see Atmore, Anthony.
Stacey, J. The Common People of the Old Testament. 1975. pap. 4.30 (ISBN 0-08-018101-5). Pergamon.
Stacey, Judith. Patriarchy & Socialist Revolution in China. LC 82-8482. 330p. 1983. text ed. 28.50x (ISBN 0-520-04825-3). U of Cal Pr.
Stacey, M. Methods of Social Research. 1969. 14.75 (ISBN 0-08-013355-X); pap. 7.50 (ISBN 0-08-013354-1). Pergamon.
Stacey, Margaret & Price, Marion. Women, Power & Politics. 208p. 1981. 25.00x (ISBN 0-422-76140-0, Pub. by Tavistock England); pap. 9.95 (ISBN 0-422-76150-8). Methuen Inc.
Stacey, W. David. Groundwork of Biblical Studies. LC 82-70961. 448p. 1982. pap. 12.50 (ISBN 0-8066-1936-8, 10-2893). Augsburg.
Stacey, W. H., Jr. Space-Time Nuclear Reactor Kinetics. (Nuclear Science & Technology Ser: Vol. 5). 1969. 40.50 (ISBN 0-12-662050-4). Acad Pr.
Stacey, W. M. Fusion Plasma Analysis. 376p. 1981. 41.95 (ISBN 0-471-08095-0, Pub. by Wiley-Interscience). Wiley.
Stacey, Weston M., Jr. Modal Approximations: Theory & an Application to Fast-Reactor Physics. (Press Research Monographs: No. 41). 1967. 17.50x (ISBN 0-262-19038-9). MIT Pr.
--Variational Methods in Nuclear Reactor Physics. (Nuclear Science & Technology Ser.). 1974. 40.50 (ISBN 0-12-662060-1). Acad Pr.
Stacey, William A., jt. auth. see Shupe, Anson.
Stachowicz, Jim. Diver's Guide to Florida & the Florida Keys. LC 76-12928. (Illus.). 64p. (Orig.). 1983. pap. 4.50 (ISBN 0-89317-007-0). Windward Pub.
Stachura, Peter. The German Youth Movement. LC 80-14527. 1981. 26.00 (ISBN 0-312-32624-6). St Martin.
Stachura, Peter D. Gregor Strasser & the Rise of Nazism. 208p. 1983. text ed. 19.50x (ISBN 0-04-943027-0). Allen Unwin.
--Nazi Youth in the Weimar Republic. LC 74-14196. (Studies in International & Comparative Politics: No. 5). 301p. 1975. text ed. 21.50 o.p. (ISBN 0-87436-198-2); pap. text ed. 11.75 o.p. (ISBN 0-87436-199-0). ABC-Clio.
Stachura, Peter D., ed. The Nazi Machdtergreifung. 208p. 1983. text ed. 19.50x (ISBN 0-04-943026-2). Allen Unwin.
Stack, Barbara. Handbook of Mining & Tunnelling Machinery. LC 80-4159. 742p. 1982. 91.00x o.p. (ISBN 0-471-27937-4, Pub. by Wiley-Interscience). Wiley.
Stack, Carol B., jt. ed. see Hall, Robert L.
Stack, Edward M. Reading French in the Arts & Sciences. 3rd ed. 265p. 1979. pap. text ed. 12.50 o.p. (ISBN 0-395-27505-9). HM.
Stack, Frank, jt. ed. see Bussabarger, Robert F.
Stack, Herbert & Elkow, J. D. Education for Safe Living. 4th ed. (Illus.). 1966. text ed. 18.95 (ISBN 0-13-239194-5). P-H.
Stack, Jack M., ed. The Special Infant: An Interdisciplinary Approach to the Optimal Development of Infants. LC 81-4478. 351p. 1982. 34.95x (ISBN 0-89885-028-2). Human Sci Pr.
Stack, John F., Jr. International Conflict in an American City: Boston's Irish, Italians & Jews, 1935-1944. LC 78-73798. (Contributions in Political Science: No. 26). 1979. lib. bdg. 25.00x (ISBN 0-313-20887-5, SCA/). Greenwood.
Stack, Norman. U. S. Coins of Value. (Orig.). 1981. pap. 2.50 o.s.i. (ISBN 0-440-18759-1). Dell.
Stack, Oswald, ed. Pasolini on Pasolini. LC 79-97238. (Cinema One Ser: No. 11). (Illus.). 176p. 1970. 6.50x o.p. (ISBN 0-253-16130-4); pap. 4.95x o.p. (ISBN 0-253-16131-2). Ind U Pr.
Stackel, Paul. Die Theorie der Parallellinien Von Euklid Bis Auf Gauss. (Bibliotheca Mathematica Teubneriana Ser: No. 41). (Ger.). Repr. of 1895 ed. 39.00 (ISBN 0-384-57410-6). Johnson Repr.
Stackelberg, Mark Von see Schmidt, Helmut & Von Stackelberg, Mark.
Stackpole, Edouard A. & Summerfield, Melvin B. Nantucket Doorways: Thresholds to the Past. (Illus.). 1974. 8.95 o.p. (ISBN 0-8038-5038-7). Hastings.
Stackpole, Everett S. History of Durham, Maine, Sixteen Eighty-Four to Eighteen Ninety-Nine. LC 79-57068. (Illus.). 1979. Repr. of 1899 ed. 35.00x o.p. (ISBN 0-89725-011-7). NH Pub Co.
Stack-Staikidis, William, jt. auth. see LaLonde, William S.
Stacy, Pat & Linet, Beverly. Duke: A Love Story, An Intimate Memoir of John Wayne's Last Years. LC 82-73031. 224p. 1983. 14.95 (ISBN 0-689-11366-8). Atheneum.
Stacy, Ralph W. & Waxman, Bruce. Computers in Biomedical Research, 4 vols. 1965-1964. Vol. 1. 67.00 (ISBN 0-12-662301-5); Vol. 2. 61.001 (ISBN 0-12-662302-3); Vol. 3. 61.00 (ISBN 0-12-662303-1); Vol. 4. 1974. 57.00 (ISBN 0-12-662304-X). Acad Pr.
Staczer, John J., jt. auth. see Roy, Joaquin.
Staddor, J., jt. ed. see Honig, Werner K.
Stadelmann, Rudolph. The Social & Political History of the German 1848 Revolution. Chastain, James G., tr. from Ger. LC 74-27711. Orig. Title: Soziale und Politis Che Geschichet der Revolution Von 1848. xvi, 218p. 1975. 15.00x (ISBN 0-8214-0177-7, 82-81743). Ohio U Pr.
Staden, Von Heinrich see Giamatti, A. Bartlett.
Staden, Wendelgard von. Darkness Over the Valley. Peters, Mollie C., tr. from Ger. LC 80-15579. Orig. Title: Nacht Uber dem Tal. 176p. 1981. 9.95 (ISBN 0-89919-009-X). Ticknor & Fields.
Staden, Wendelgard von see Von Staden, Wendelgard.

Stadiem, William. A Class by Themselves: The Untold Story of the Great Southern Families. (Illus.). 288p. 1980. 12.95 o.p. (ISBN 0-517-53735-4). Crown.
Stadiem, William, jt. auth. see Pepitone, Lena.
Stadlander, Jane. Pomegranate. 48p. 1983. pap. 5.95 (ISBN 0-86666-084-4). GWP.
Stadler, E. M., jt. auth. see Gourevitch, D.
Stadler, Glen M. Courthouse. LC 81-86351. 300p. 1983. pap. 8.95 (ISBN 0-86666-066-6). GWP.
Stadler, John. Animal Cafe. LC 80-15072. (Illus.). 32p. (gr. k-2). 1980. 9.95 (ISBN 0-02-786600-9). Bradbury Pr.
--Gorman & the Treasure Chest. (Illus.). 32p. (ps-2). 1983. 10.95. Bradbury Pr.
--Hector, the Accordion-Nosed Dog. LC 81-7713. (Illus.). 32p. (ps-2). 1983. 10.95 (ISBN 0-02-786680-7). Bradbury Pr.
--Rodney & Lucinda's Amazing Race. LC 80-39848. (Illus.). 32p. (ps-2). 1981. 9.95 (ISBN 0-02-786670-X). Bradbury Pr.
Stadler, Quandra P., ed. Out of Our Lives: A Collection of Contemporary Black Fiction. LC 74-7092. 324p. 1975. 10.95 (ISBN 0-88258-027-2). Howard U Pr.
Stadler, Wolfram, tr. see Hagedoern, Peter.
Stadt, R. & Adams, J. M. Retirement: Planning Tomorrow Today. LC 82-14799. 192p. 1982. 7.95 (ISBN 0-07-000404-8, G). McGraw.
Stadt, R. W. Personal & Family Finance. 256p. 1983. 7.95 (ISBN 0-07-000403-X, G). McGraw.
Stadtler, Bea. The Holocaust: A History of Courage & Resistance. 210p. Repr. 5.50 (ISBN 0-686-95067-4). ADL.
Stadtman, E., jt. ed. see Horecker, Bernard.
Stadtman, Earl R., jt. ed. see Hoercker, Bernard L.
Staebler, Warren. Ralph Waldo Emerson. (World Leaders Ser). 1973. lib. bdg. 11.95 (ISBN 0-8057-3674-3, Twayne). G K Hall.
Staeheli, Alice M. Costuming the Christmas Play. (Illus., Orig.). 1980. pap. text ed. 5.95 (ISBN 0-916260-09-7). Meriwether Pub.
Staeheli, Jean & Robinson, Jo. Unplug the Christmas Machine: How to Really Participate in the Joys of Christmas. LC 82-12465. 1982. 14.50 (ISBN 0-688-01319-8). Morrow.
Stael, De see De Stael.
Staff & Editors of the New York Post, jt. auth. see Blumenfeld, Ralph.
Staff, Hammond, ed. Glove Compartment Road Atlas 1983. Rev. ed. (Illus.). 48p. 1983. pap. 1.95 (ISBN 0-8437-2634-2). Hammond Inc.
Staff of CHHA-CHS, NLN. Publicity for Your Community Health Agency. rev. ed. 37p. 1978. 3.95 (ISBN 0-686-38166-1, 21-1748). Natl League Nurse.
Staff of Public Management Institute. How to Build a Big Endowment. 590p. 75.00 (ISBN 0-686-38885-2). Public Serv Materials.
Staff of the Family Handyman Magazine. Early American Furniture-Making Handbook. (Illus.). 162p. pap. 9.95 (ISBN 0-686-83795-9, ScribT). Scribner.
Staffieri, Anthony, jt. auth. see Post, Elizabeth.
Staffieri, Anthony, jt. auth. see Post, Emily.
Stafford, jt. auth. see Hughes.
Stafford, D. A. Anaerobic Digestion. 1980. 94.50 (ISBN 0-85334-904-5, Pub. by Applied Sci England). Elsevier.
Stafford, D. C., jt. auth. see Corner, D. C.
Stafford, David. Britain & European Resistance, Nineteen Forty to Nineteen Forty-Five: A Survey of the Special Operations Executive, with Documents. LC 79-19224. 1980. 27.50 (ISBN 0-8020-2361-4); pap. 12.50 (ISBN 0-8020-6522-8). U of Toronto Pr.
Stafford, Don G., jt. auth. see Renner, John W.
Stafford, George T., jt. auth. see Florio, A. E.
Stafford, Harold C. The Unknown & Extraordinary Medicinal Properties of Wines & Alcholic Beverages. (An Intimate Life of Man Library Bk.). (Illus.). 118p. 1982. 51.45 (ISBN 0-89266-374-X). Am Classical Coll Pr.
Stafford, Harry C. Culture & Cosmology: Essays on the Birth of World View. LC 80-5642. 371p. 1981. lib. bdg. 24.00 (ISBN 0-8191-1371-9); pap. text ed. 13.75 (ISBN 0-8191-1372-7). U Pr of Amer.
Stafford, Irving, jt. auth. see Leventhal, Lance A.
Stafford, J., jt. auth. see DeNeufville, R.
Stafford, Jean. Boston Adventure. LC 44-40176. 1967. pap. 0.95 (ISBN 0-15-613611-2, Harv). HarBraceJ.
--The Mountain Lion. 244p. 1983. pap. 5.95 (ISBN 0-525-48031-5, 0577-180, Obelisk). Dutton.
Stafford, Kim R. The Granary. LC 81-69799. 1982. 12.95 (ISBN 0-915604-64-7); pap. 4.95 (ISBN 0-915604-65-5). Carnegie-Mellon.
Stafford, L. W. Business Mathematics. 400p. 1981. 25.00x (ISBN 0-7121-0282-5, Pub. by Macdonald & Evans). State Mutual Bk.
Stafford, L. W., jt. auth. see Harper, W. M.
Stafford, Linda. Mind Invaders. (YA) (gr. 9-12). 1982. pap. 0.95. Victor Bks.
Stafford, Marilyn. The Inside Secrets to a Modeling Career! Terschluse, Marilyn, ed. LC 82-60444. (Illus.). 75p. (Orig.). (gr. 12 up). 1982. pap. 7.95 (ISBN 0-910025-00-2). MidCoast Pubns.
Stafford, Marvin W. Exfoliative Cytology of the Female Genital Tract. 32p. 1972. 42.50, incl. filmstrip o.p. (ISBN 0-7216-9817-4); tape suppl. 9.50 o.p. (ISBN 0-7216-9830-1). Saunders.
Stafford, Pauline. Queens, Concubines, & Dowagers: The King's Wife in the Early Middle Ages. LC 82-13368. (Illus.). 264p. 1983. text ed. 22.50 (ISBN 0-8203-0639-8). U of Ga Pr.
Stafford, Peter. Psychedelics Encyclopedia. (Illus.). 400p. 1982. pap. 12.95 (ISBN 0-87477-231-1). J P Tarcher.
Stafford, R. H. Digital Television: Bandwidth Reduction & Communication Aspects. LC 80-17542. 387p. 1980. 39.50 (ISBN 0-471-07857-3, Pub. by Wiley-Interscience). Wiley.
Stafford, William. A Glass Face in the Rain. LC 82-47534. 96p. 1982. 12.45i (ISBN 0-06-015046-7, CN983, CN); pap. 6.68i (ISBN 0-06-090983-8). Har-Row.
--Roving Across Fields: A Conversation with William Stafford. Tammaro, Thom, ed. & intro. by. 48p. (Orig.). 1983. pap. 6.95 (ISBN 0-935306-15-3). Barnwood Pr.
--Stories That Could Be True: New & Collected Poems. LC 77-3775. 1977. 13.41i (ISBN 0-06-013988-9, HarpT); pap. 6.97 (ISBN 0-06-090918-8, CN-0918). Har-Row.
--Unmuzzling Ox Anthology, No. 14. Andre, Michael, et al, eds. Olson & Bukowski. (Illus.). 1980. pap. 4.95 (ISBN 0-686-28477-1). Unmuzzled Ox.
--Writing the Australian Crawl. Hall, Donald, ed. LC 77-5711. (Poets on Poetry Ser.). pap. 7.95 (ISBN 0-472-87300-8). U of Mich Pr.
Stafford, William & Bell, Marvin. Segues. 64p. 1983. 10.95 (ISBN 0-87923-410-5). Godine.
Stafford-Clark, David. What Freud Really Said. LC 66-24900. (What They Really Said Ser.). 1971. 7.50x (ISBN 0-8052-3283-4); pap. 5.50 (ISBN 0-8052-0290-0). Schocken.
Stafford-Dietsch, Jeremy. Polyphemus. 1983. 14.95 (ISBN 0-533-05387-0). Vantage.
Stafl, A., jt. auth. see Kolstad, P.
Stafl, Milos. Electrodynamics of Electrical Machines. Toombs, G. A., ed. 1969. 11.25x o.p. (ISBN 0-592-02518-7). Transatlantic.
Stafleu & Cowan, R. S. Taxonomic Literature: LH-O, Vol. 3. 1982. 135.00 (ISBN 90-313-0444-1, Pub. by Junk Pubs Netherlands). Kluwer Boston.
Stafleu, F. A. Introduction to Jussieu's Genera Plantarum. 8.00 (ISBN 3-7682-0000-0). Lubrecht & Cramer.
Stafleu, F. A., jt. auth. see La Billardiere, J. De.
Stage, John L. & Lacy, Dan. The Birth of America. new ed. Orig. Title: Colonial America. (Illus.). 256p. 1975. 9.95 (ISBN 0-448-11545-X, G&D). Putnam Pub Group.
Stager, Lawrence E., et al, eds. American Expedition to Idalion, Cyprus, First Preliminary Report: Seasons of 1971 & 1972. (American Schools of Oriental Research, Supplement Ser.: Vol. 18). 178p. (Orig.). 1974. pap. text ed. 3.50x (ISBN 0-89757-318-8, Am Sch Orient Res). Eisenbrauns.
Stagg, Albert L. The Almadas & the Alamos. LC 77-74317. 1978. 11.50x o.s.i. (ISBN 0-8165-0609-4); pap. 7.50 (ISBN 0-8165-0474-1). U of Ariz Pr.
Stagg, Frank. Book of Acts. 1955. 12.95 (ISBN 0-8054-1311-1). Broadman.
--Polarities of Man's Existence in Biblical Perspective. LC 73-8812. 1973. 8.95 (ISBN 0-664-20976-9). Westminster.
--Teologia Del Nuevo Testamento. Canclini, Arnoldo, tr. 346p. 1976. pap. 9.95 (ISBN 0-311-09077-X). Casa Bautista.
Stagg, Glenn W. & El-Abiad, Ahmed H. Computer Methods in Power System Analysis. (Electronic Systems Ser.). 1968. text ed. 26.50 o.p. (ISBN 0-07-060658-7, C). McGraw.
--Computer Methods in Power Systems Analysis. LC 82-95. 438p. 1983. Repr. of 1968 ed. cancelled (ISBN 0-89874-394-X). Krieger.
Stagg, K. G. & Zienkiewicz, O. C. Rock Mechanics in Engineering Practice. LC 68-9674. 442p. 1968. 47.95 (ISBN 0-471-81965-4, Pub. by Wiley-Interscience). Wiley.
Stagg, Mildred. Animal & Pet Photography Simplified. (Illus.). 96p. 1975. pap. 4.95 o.p. (ISBN 0-8174-0181-4, Amphoto); Spanish Ed. pap. 6.95 o.p. (ISBN 0-686-67116-3). Watson-Guptill.
Staggs, Kenneth W., ed. see Cooper, James F., et al.
Stagner, Ross & Rosen, Hjalmar. Psychology of Union-Management Relations. LC 67-25148. (Behavioral Science in Industry Ser). (Orig.). 1966. pap. text ed. 7.95 (ISBN 0-8185-0315-7). Brooks-Cole.
Stahel, H. R. Atlantis Illustrated. (Illus.). 144p. 1982. 7.95 (ISBN 0-448-16061-7, G&D). Putnam Pub Group.
Staheli, Julie. Kachinas: A Color & Cut-out Collection. (Illus.). 32p. (gr. 4-10). 1983. pap. 3.95 (ISBN 0-912300-44-2). Troubador Pr.
Stahl, Barbara J. Vertebrate History: Problems in Evolution. (Population Biology Ser). (Illus.). 544p. 1973. text ed. 20.95 o.p. (ISBN 0-07-060698-6, C). McGraw.
Stahl, Dulcelina A., jt. auth. see Baldonado, Ardelina A.
Stahl, E., ed. Thin-Layer Chromatography: A Laboratory Handbook. 2nd. ed. Ashworth, M. R., tr. LC 69-14538. (Illus.). 1969. 83.00 o.p. (ISBN 0-387-04736-0). Springer-Verlag.
Stahl, Elizabeth L., jt. auth. see Madell, Robert.
Stahl, Franklin W. Mechanics of Inheritance. 2nd ed. Suskind, Sigmund & Hartman, Philip, eds. LC 69-19870. (Foundations of Modern Genetics Ser). 1969. pap. 10.95 ref. ed. o.p. (ISBN 0-13-571042-1). P-H.
Stahl, G. Allan, ed. Polymer Science Overview. (ACS Symposium Ser.: No. 175). 1981. write for info. (ISBN 0-8412-0668-6). Am Chemical.
Stahl, Glenn O. Public Personnel Administration. 8th ed. 608p. 1983. text ed. 24.95scp (ISBN 0-06-046404-6, HarpC). Har-Row.
Stahl, Henri. Traditional Romanian Village Communities. Chirot, D. & Chirot, H. C., trs. LC 79-52855. (Studies in Modern Capitalism). (Illus.). 1980. 44.50 (ISBN 0-521-22957-X). Cambridge U Pr.
Stahl, Hilda. Elizabeth Gail & the Dangerous Double. (gr. 4-7). 1980. pap. 2.50 (ISBN 0-8423-0723-0). Tyndale.
--Elizabeth Gail & the Handsome Stranger. 128p. 1983. pap. 2.95 (ISBN 0-686-82692-2, 75-0707-9). Tyndale.
--Elizabeth Gail & the Music Camp Romance. 128p. (gr. 3-7). 1983. pap. 2.95 (ISBN 0-8423-0708-7). Tyndale.
--Elizabeth Gail & the Mystery at the Johnson Farm. 1978. pap. text ed. 2.50 (ISBN 0-8423-0720-6). Tyndale.
--Elizabeth Gail & the Strange Birthday Party. (gr. 4-6). 1980. 2.95 (ISBN 0-8423-0724-9). Tyndale.
--Elizabeth Gail & the Teddy Bear Mystery. 1979. pap. 2.50 (ISBN 0-8423-0722-2). Tyndale.
--Elizabeth Gail & the Terrifying News. (gr. 4-8). 1980. 2.95 (ISBN 0-8423-0725-7). Tyndale.
--Teddy Jo & the Strangers in the Pink House. (gr. 4-7). 1983. pap. 2.95 (ISBN 0-8423-6946-5). Tyndale.
--Tina's Reluctant Friend. (gr. 4-7). 1981. pap. 2.95 (ISBN 0-8423-7216-4). Tyndale.
Stahl, Jaspar J. History of Old Broadbay & Waldoboro, 2 vols. LC 56-5858. 1975. Set. 35.00 (ISBN 0-87027-169-5). Cumberland Pr.
Stahl, Nanette, jt. auth. see Simon, Ethelyn.
Stahl, O. Glenn. Public Personnel Administration. 7th ed. 592p. 1976. text ed. 21.50 scp o.p. (ISBN 0-06-046387-2, HarpC). Har-Row.
Stahl, P. W., ed. KG Two Hundred. (Illus.). 224p. 1981. 19.95 (ISBN 0-86720-564-4). Sci Bks IntL.
Stahl, Sidney M. & Hennes, James D. Reading & Understanding Applied Statistics: A Self-Learning Approach. 2nd ed. LC 79-29760. (Illus.). 1980. pap. text ed. 14.95 (ISBN 0-8016-4754-1). Mosby.
Stahl, Wilda. Teddy Jo & the Stolen Ring. 128p. 1982. pap. 2.95 (ISBN 0-8423-6945-7). Tyndale.
Stahlberg, H., tr. see Hoffmann, M., et al.
Stahle, J. Vestibular Function on Earth & in Space. 1970. 59.00 (ISBN 0-08-015592-8). Pergamon.
Stahlkopf, K. E., jt. auth. see Steele, L. E.
Stahl-Mazor, Emma. Tears & Laughters in My Poetry. 183p. 1981. 7.50 (ISBN 0-682-49708-8). Exposition.
Stahmann, Mark, ed. see International Symposium On Poly-A-Amino Acids - 1st - University Of Wisconsin - 1961.
Stahmann, Robert F. & Hiebert, William. Premarital Counseling: Education for Marriage. LC 78-19727. 192p. 1980. 22.95x (ISBN 0-669-02726-X). Lexington Bks.
Stahmann, Robert F. & Hiebert, William J., eds. Klemer's Counseling in Marital & Sexual Problems: A Clinical Handbook. 2nd ed. 1977. pap. 19.95 o.p. (ISBN 0-683-07911-5). Williams & Wilkins.
Stahnke, A. A., jt. auth. see Ellsworth, J. W.
Stahnke, Arthur A., ed. see Schulz, Eberhard, et al.
Staicar, Tom. Fritz Leiber. LC 82-40260. (Recognitions). 200p. (YA) 1983. 11.95 (ISBN 0-8044-2836-0); pap. 6.95 (ISBN 0-8044-6875-3). Ungar.
Staimle, Fritz, jt. auth. see Von Cube, Hans L.
Stainback, Berry, jt. auth. see Weaver, Earl.
Stainback, William C., et al. Establishing a Token Economy in the Classroom. LC 72-93476. 1973. pap. text ed. 8.95x (ISBN 0-675-09032-6). Merrill.
Stainer, C., jt. auth. see Stainer, J. F.
Stainer, J. F. & Stainer, C. Dufay & His Contemporaries: Fifty Compositions (Ranging from About A.D. Fourteen Hundred to Fourteen Hundred & Forty. 1966. Repr. of 1898 ed. 50.00 o.s.i. (ISBN 90-6027-003-7, Pub. by Frits Knuf Netherlands). Pendragon NY.
Staines, Graham L., jt. auth. see Quinn, Robert P.
Stainforth, J., jt. ed. see McGarry, M. G.
Stainsby, G., jt. auth. see Dickinson, E.
Stair, Joan, jt. ed. see Elliott, Norman F.
Stair, Lila B. Careers in Business. LC 82-73634. 170p. 1983. Repr. of 1980 ed. 12.95 (ISBN 0-87094-398-7). Dow Jones-Irwin.
Stair, Ralph M., Jr. Learning to Live with Computers: Advice for Managers. LC 82-73408. 190p. 1983. 19.95 (ISBN 0-87094-383-9). Dow Jones-Irwin.
Stair, William K., ed. Student, Teacher, & Engineer: Selected Speeches & Articles of Nathan W. Dougherty. LC 76-186707. 1972. 14.50x (ISBN 0-87049-138-5). U of Tenn Pr.
Stakenas, Robert G. & Kaufman, Roger. Technology in Education: Its Human Potential. LC 81-82473. (Fastback Ser.: No. 163). 50p. 1981. pap. 0.75 (ISBN 0-87367-162-7). Phi Delta Kappa.
Stakes, Mary E. & Chandler, R. Michael. Health Care Cost Containment. 62p. (Orig.). 1980. pap. 5.00 o.p. (ISBN 0-89854-061-5). U of GA Inst Govt.
Stakgold, Ivar. Green's Functions & Boundary Value Problems. LC 78-27259. (Pure & Applied Mathematics: Texts, Monographs & Tracts). 638p. 1979. 46.95 (ISBN 0-471-81967-0, Pub. by Wiley-Interscience). Wiley.
Stalberg, Roberta & Nesi, Ruth. China's Crafts: The Story of How They're Made & What They Mean. 1980. 15.95 (ISBN 0-8351-0755-8); pap. 10.95 (ISBN 0-8351-0740-X). China Bks.
Staley, Frederick A. Outdoor Education for the Whole Child. (Illus.). 1979. pap. text ed. 9.95 (ISBN 0-8403-1993-2). Kendall-Hunt.
Staley, H. B., jt. auth. see David, D. J.
Staley, Lucy. New Trends in Table Setting... & Period Designs, Too. (Illus.). 1968. 7.95 (ISBN 0-8208-0056-2). Hearthside.
Staley, T. F. Twentieth-Century Women Novelists. 1982. 70.00x (ISBN 0-686-42935-4, Pub. by Macmillan England). State Mutual Bk.
Staley, Thomas F. Dorothy Richardson. (English Authors Ser.: No. 187). 1976. lib. bdg. 12.50 o.p. (ISBN 0-8057-6662-6, Twayne). G K Hall.
Staley, Thomas F., ed. James Joyce Today: Essays on the Major Works. LC 79-17222. 1979. Repr. of 1966 ed. lib. bdg. 17.75x (ISBN 0-313-21292-9, STJJ). Greenwood.
Staley, Thomas F. & Benstock, Bernard, eds. Approaches to Joyce's Portrait: Ten Essays. LC 76-6670. 1976. 14.95 (ISBN 0-8229-3331-4). U of Pittsburgh Pr.
Stalin, Iosif. Selected Writings. Repr. of 1942 ed. lib. bdg. 20.75x (ISBN 0-8371-4482-5, STWR). Greenwood.
Stalker, David M., tr. see Westermann, Claus.
Stalker, G. M., jt. auth. see Burns, Tom.
Stalker, James. Vida de Jesucristo. 177p. (Span.). 1973. pap. write for info. o.s.i. Edit Caribe.
Stalker, James M. Life of Jesus Christ. 160p. 8.95 (ISBN 0-8007-0177-1). Revell.
--Life of St. Paul. 160p. 8.95 (ISBN 0-8007-0178-X). Revell.
Stalland, Mary K., jt. auth. see Brin, Ruth F.
Stallard, John J., et al. The Electronic Office: A Guide for Managers. LC 82-72866. 180p. 1982. 19.95 (ISBN 0-87094-256-5). Dow Jones-Irwin.
Stallard, Patricia Y. Glittering Misery: Dependents of the Indian Fighting Army. LC 77-94535. (Illus.). 1978. 12.95 o.p. (ISBN 0-88342-054-6). Old Army.
--Glittering Misery: Dependents of the Indian Fighting Army. LC 77-94525. (Illus.). 1978. 10.95 o.p. (ISBN 0-88342-054-6); pap. 4.95 o. p. o.p. (ISBN 0-88342-239-5). Presidio Pr.
--Glittering Misery: Dependents of the Indian Fighting Army. LC 77-94535. (Illus.). 1983. pap. 6.95 (ISBN 0-88342-239-5). Old Army.
Stallard, Richard E., jt. auth. see Caldwell, Robert C.
Stalley, Richard, jt. auth. see Leighton, Neil.
Stalley, Rodney E., jt. auth. see Sheard, James L.
Stallings, Constance, jt. ed. see Mitchell, John G.
Stallings, Frank, jt. auth. see Derfler, Frank, Jr.
Stallings, James D. & Morris, Terry. A New You: How Plastic Surgery Can Change Your Life. 1980. pap. 2.50 o.p. (ISBN 0-451-09023-3, E9023, Sig). NAL.
Stallings, James O. & Powell, Marcia. The Look of Success. LC 82-71744. (Illus.). 224p. 1982. 14.95 (ISBN 0-8119-0456-3). Fell.
Stallings, John W., jt. auth. see Nelson, D. Lloyd.
Stallknecht, Newton P. & Brumbaugh, Robert S. The Compass of Philosophy. LC 74-6121. 258p. 1974. Repr. of 1954 ed. lib. bdg. 17.00x (ISBN 0-8371-7494-5, STTH). Greenwood.
Stallman, Birdie. Learning About Witches. LC 81-10011. (The Learning About Ser.). (Illus.). 48p. (gr. 2-6). 1981. PLB 9.25 (ISBN 0-516-06536-X); pap. 3.95 (ISBN 0-516-46536-8). Childrens.
Stallman, R. W. The Houses That James Built and Other Literary Studies. LC 77-371844. 256p. 1977. 14.00x (ISBN 0-8214-0362-1, 82-82525); pap. 5.50x (ISBN 0-8214-0363-X, 82-82543). Ohio U Pr.
--The Stephen Crane Reader. 604p. 1972. pap. 9.95x (ISBN 0-673-05680-5). Scott F.
Stallman, R. W., ed. The Art of Joseph Conrad: A Critical Symposium. LC 81-82620. xxxii, 354p. 1982. text ed. 22.95x (ISBN 0-8214-0583-7, 82-83707); pap. text ed. 11.95x (ISBN 0-8214-0584-5, 82-83715). Ohio U Pr.
Stallman, Robert. The Beast. (The Book of the Beast: Vol. 3). (Orig.). 1982. pap. 2.50 (ISBN 0-671-41383-X, Timescape). PB.
Stallman, Robert W. Critiques & Essays in Criticism, Nineteen Twenty to Nineteen Forty-Eight: Representing the Achievement of Modern British & American Critics. 1949. text ed. 27.50x (ISBN 0-673-15725-3). Scott F.

Stallman, Robert W., ed. The Critic's Notebook. LC 76-48931. 1977. Repr. of 1950 ed. lib. bdg. 20.00x (ISBN 0-8371-9324-9, STCN). Greenwood.
Stallone, Carol N., ed. The Faces & Phases of Women: An Educational Kit. (Illus.). 76p. (gr. 4-9). 1983. pap. text ed. 5.00 (ISBN 0-9610622-0-7); kit incl. 31 posters 30.00 (ISBN 0-686-38901-8). Natl Wmns Hall Fame.
Stallworth, E. A., jt. auth. see Kharbanda, O. P.
Stallworthy, E. A., jt. auth. see Kharbanda, O. P.
Stallworthy, John, jt. auth. see Howkins, John.
Stallworthy, Jon. A Familiar Tree. (Illus.). 1978. 9.95x (ISBN 0-19-520050-0). Oxford U Pr.
--Root & Branch. 1969. pap. 5.95x (ISBN 0-19-519995-2). Oxford U Pr.
--Wilfred Owen. 1975. 25.00x (ISBN 0-19-211719-X). Oxford U Pr.
Stallybrass, Oliver, ed. see Forster, E. M.
Stalybrass, Oliver, ed. see Forster, E. M.
Stam, David, jt. ed. see Yachnin, Rissa.
Stam, David H. Wordsworthian Criticism 1964-1973: An Annotated Bibliography. LC 72-81870. 120p. 1974. 15.00 (ISBN 0-87104-237-1). NY Pub Lib.
Stamatoyannopoulos, G. & Nienhuis, A., eds. Cellular & Molecular Regulation of Hemoglobin Switching. 856p. 1979. 89.50 (ISBN 0-686-63983-9). Grune.
Stamaty, Mark Alan. MacDoodle Street. 96p. 1981. pap. 6.95 o.p. (ISBN 0-312-92519-0). St Martin.
Stambler, Irwin. Automobiles of the Future. (Illus.). (gr. 8 up). 1966. PLB 5.29 o.p. (ISBN 0-399-60036-1). Putnam Pub Group.
--Bill Walton: Super Center. LC 75-35931. (Putnam Sports Shelf Biography Ser.). 128p. (gr. 5 up). 1976. PLB 6.29 o.p. (ISBN 0-399-60980-6). Putnam Pub Group.
--Catfish Hunter: The Three-Million Dollar Arm. LC 76-10367. (Putnam Sports Shelf). (gr. 5 up). 1976. PLB 6.29 o.p. (ISBN 0-399-61023-5). Putnam Pub Group.
--Dream Machines: Vans & Pickups. (Illus.). 128p. (YA) (gr. 7-12). 1980. 8.95 (ISBN 0-399-20692-2). Putnam Pub Group.
--Encyclopedia of Pop, Rock & Soul. LC 65-20817. (Illus.). 1975. 19.95 o.p. (ISBN 0-312-24990-X). St Martin.
--Great Moments in Stock Car Racing. LC 74-124174. (Putnam Sports Shelf). (Illus.). (gr. 5 up). 1971. PLB 5.29 o.p. (ISBN 0-399-60213-5). Putnam Pub Group.
--Here Come the Funny Cars. LC 75-30596. (Illus.). 128p. (gr. 5-8). 1976. PLB 6.99 (ISBN 0-399-60977-6). Putnam Pub Group.
--Minibikes & Small Cycles. (Illus.). (gr. 6-8). 1977. PLB 6.99 o.p. (ISBN 0-399-61055-3). Putnam Pub Group.
--New Automobiles of the Future. LC 77-24426. (Illus.). (gr. 6 up). 1978. 7.95 o.p. (ISBN 0-399-20623-X). Putnam Pub Group.
--Ocean Liners of the Air. (Illus.). (gr. 6-10). 1969. PLB 4.89 o.p. (ISBN 0-399-60495-2). Putnam Pub Group.
--Racing the Sprint Cars. LC 78-24402. (Illus.). (gr. 5 up). 1979. 7.95 o.p. (ISBN 0-399-20666-3). Putnam Pub Group.
--The Supercars & the Men Who Race Them. LC 74-16630. (Illus.). 160p. (gr. 6 up). 1975. 6.95 o.p. (ISBN 0-399-20437-7). Putnam Pub Group.
--Top Fuelers: Drag Racing Royalty. LC 77-13328. (Illus.). (gr. 5 up). 1978. PLB 5.99 o.p. (ISBN 0-399-61116-9). Putnam Pub Group.
--Unusual Automobiles of Today & Tomorrow. (Illus.). (gr. 5-10). 1972. PLB 4.99 (ISBN 0-399-60719-6). Putnam Pub Group.
Stambler, Irwin & Landon, Grelun. Encyclopedia of Folk, Country & Western. (Illus.). 1200p. 1982. 50.00 (ISBN 0-312-24818-0). St Martin.
Stamford, Sarah. The Magnificent Duchess. 1980. pap. 1.50 o.s.i. (ISBN 0-440-15371-9). Dell.
--The Marshal's Lady. 1981. 13.50 o.p. (ISBN 0-525-15320-9, 01311-390). Dutton.
Stamler, Suzanne. Three Wise Birds. (Jataka Tales for Children Ser.). (Illus.). (gr. 1-6). 1976. 5.95 o.p. (ISBN 0-913546-29-1); pap. 4.95 o.p. (ISBN 0-913546-68-2). Dharma Pub.
Stamm, A. J. Wood & Cellulose Science. (Illus.). 549p. 1964. 42.50 o.s.i. (ISBN 0-471-06843-8, Pub. by Wiley-Interscience). Wiley.
Stamm, Charles F., jt. auth. see Howell, James M.
Stamm, Douglas R. Under Water: The Northern Lakes. (Illus.). 128p. 1977. pap. 9.95 (ISBN 0-299-07264-9). U of Wis Pr.
Stamm, Laura & Fishler, Stan. Power Skating: A Pro Coach's Secrets. LC 82-60068. (Illus.). 192p. 1982. 13.95 (ISBN 0-8069-4164-2); lib. bdg. 16.79 (ISBN 0-8069-4165-0); pap. 8.95 (ISBN 0-8069-7672-1). Sterling.
Stamm, Martha & Stanforth, Deidre. Buying & Renovating a House in the City: A Practical Guide. 1972. pap. 6.95 o.p. (ISBN 0-394-70759-1). Knopf.
Stamm, Millie. Meditation Moments for Women. 1967. pap. 6.95 (ISBN 0-310-32981-7). Zondervan.
Stamm, Rudolf. The Shaping Powers at Work, Fifteen Essays on Poetic Transmutation. LC 68-75100. 320p. 1967. 32.50x (ISBN 3-533-01771-0). Intl Pubns Serv.
Stamos. Iphigenia: The Greek Legends. 1982. 15.00 (ISBN 0-686-98035-2). Byzantine Pr.
Stamov, Stefan. The Architectural Heritage of Bulgaria. (Illus.). 1972. 20.00 o.p. (ISBN 0-685-86584-3, 56911634). State Mutual Bk.
Stamov, Stefan & Angreova, R. The Architectural Heritage of Bulgaria. Caneva-Decevska, N., ed. (Import Ser). (Illus.). 227p. 1974. lib. bdg. 45.00 (ISBN 0-306-70675-X). Da Capo.
Stamp, Cordelia. Mary Linskill. 29.00x (ISBN 0-686-98236-3, Pub. by Caedmon of Whitby). State Mutual Bk.
Stamp, Cordelia, jt. auth. see Stamp, Tom.
Stamp, E. International Auditing Standards. 1979. 28.95 (ISBN 0-13-470948-9). P-H.
Stamp, L. Dudley. Asia: A Regional & Economic Geography. 12th ed. 1967. 49.95x (ISBN 0-416-30400-1). Methuen Inc.
Stamp, L. Dudley & Beaver, S. H. The British Isles. 6th ed. LC 70-17425. (Geographies for Advanced Studies). 1972. 35.00 o.p. (ISBN 0-312-10325-5). St Martin.
Stamp, Tom & Stamp, Cordelia. James Cook, Maritime Scientist. 1981. 25.00x (ISBN 0-686-98237-1, Pub. by Caedmon of Whitby). State Mutual Bk.
--William Scoresby, Arctic Scientist. 1981. 30.00x (ISBN 0-686-98238-X, Pub. by Caedmon of Whitby). State Mutual Bk.
Stampfle, Felice, jt. auth. see Bean, Jacob.
Stampfli, J. G., jt. auth. see Lowengrub, M.
Stampp, Kenneth M. Era of Reconstruction 1865-1877. (YA) 1965. 12.95 (ISBN 0-394-42355-0). Knopf.
--The Imperiled Union: Essays of the Background of the Civil War. 1981. pap. 7.95 (ISBN 0-19-502991-7, GB 654, GB). Oxford U Pr.
--The Imperiled Union: Essays on the American Civil War. 1980. 17.50x (ISBN 0-19-502681-0). Oxford U Pr.
--Peculiar Institution. 1956. 15.50 (ISBN 0-394-44015-3). Knopf.
Stamps, Jeffrey, jt. auth. see Lipnack, Jessica.
Stamps, L. G. An Elegy Written for Atlanta's Children. (Illus.). 24p. (Orig.). 1982. pap. 3.00 (ISBN 0-911087-00-1). Bargara Pr.
Stamps, Paula L. Ambulatory Care Systems, Vol. 3: Evaluation of Outpatient Facilities. LC 76-55865. (Illus.). 272p. 1978. 23.95x (ISBN 0-669-01325-0). Lexington Bks.
Stan, Susan. Careers in an Art Museum. LC 82-18654. (Early Career Bks.). (Illus.). 36p. (gr. 2-5). 1983. PLB 5.95g (ISBN 0-8225-0337-9). Lerner Pubns.
Stanaford, Penny. Create-A-Cookbook: Guide to Easy Meal Planning. (Illus.). 68p. 1980. 11.95 (ISBN 0-9604850-0-7); shrink wrapped 8.95 (ISBN 0-686-96857-3). Postscript.
Stanard, Mary N. Colonial Virginia: Its People & Customs. LC 78-99055. (Social History Reference Ser.). (Illus.). 1970. Repr. of 1917 ed. 42.00x (ISBN 0-8103-0161-X). Gale.
Stanasila, Octavian, jt. auth. see Banica, Constantin.
Stanat, Donald F. & McAllister, David F. Discrete Mathematics in Computer Science. (Illus.). 1977. 27.95 (ISBN 0-13-216150-8). P-H.
Stanaway, John. Cobra in the Sky: Thirty-Ninth Fighter Squadron. (Illus.). 1982. pap. 6.50 (ISBN 0-911852-92-1). Hist Aviation.
Stanbury. Managing Public Enterprises. 320p. 1982. 29.95 (ISBN 0-03-061977-7). Praeger.
Stanbury, John B. Endemic Goiter & Endemic Cretinism: Iodine Nutrition in Health. LC 79-22459. 606p. 1980. 57.95 o.p. (ISBN 0-471-05819-X, Pub. by Wiley Medical). Wiley.
Stanbury, John B., jt. auth. see DeGroot, Leslie J.
Stanbury, W. T. & Thompson, Fred. Regulatory Reform in Canada. 139p. (Orig.). 1982. pap. text ed. 7.95x (ISBN 0-920380-71-9, Pub. by Inst Res Pub Canada). Renouf.
Stanchfield, Jo M. Patterns, Level 3, Bk. B. LC 77-83336. (Vistas Ser.). (Illus., Gr. 9). 1978. pap. text ed. 7.32 (ISBN 0-395-25230-X). HM.
Stanchfield, Jo M., et al. Horizons, Level 1, Bk. A. LC 77-83336. (Vistas Ser.). (Illus., Gr. 7). 1978. pap. text ed. 7.32 (ISBN 0-395-25225-3). HM.
--Networks, Level 3, Bk. A. LC 77-83336. (Vistas Ser.). (Illus., Gr. 9). 1978. pap. text ed. 7.32 (ISBN 0-395-25229-6). HM.
--Paces, Level 2, Bk. B. LC 77-83336. (Vistas Ser.). (Illus., Gr. 8). 1978. pap. text ed. 7.32 (ISBN 0-395-25228-8). HM.
--Summits, Level 1, Bk. B. LC 77-83336. (Vistas Ser.). (Illus., Gr. 7). 1978. pap. text ed. 7.32 (ISBN 0-395-25226-1). HM.
--Tempos, Level 2, Bk. A. LC 77-83336. (Vistas Ser.). (Illus., Gr. 8). 1978. pap. text ed. 7.32 (ISBN 0-395-25227-X). HM.
Stancl, Donald L. & Stancl, Mildred L. Applications of College Mathematics: Management, Life, & Social Sciences. 736p. Date not set. 26.95 (ISBN 0-669-03860-1); instr's guide 1.95 (ISBN 0-669-03861-X); price not set computer supplement (ISBN 0-669-03881-4). Heath.
Stancl, Mildred L., jt. auth. see Stancl, Donald L.
Standard Educational Corporation. New Standard Encyclopedia, 17 vols. Downey, Douglas W., ed. LC 82-3301. (gr. 9-12). 1983. Set. 559.50 (ISBN 0-87392-182-7). Standard Ed.
Standard's & Poor's. Options Handbook. 1982. 29.95 (ISBN 0-07-051884-X). McGraw.
--OTC Handbook. 1982. 39.50 (ISBN 0-07-051885-8). McGraw.
--Stockmarket Encyclopedia of the Fortune. 1982. 27.50 (ISBN 0-07-051886-6). McGraw.
Standford, Derek, jt. auth. see Spark, Muriel.
Standifer, Billie J. Cain: The Neolithic Link. 1982. 8.75 (ISBN 0-8062-1937-8). Carlton.
Standifer, James A., jt. ed. see Hicks, Charles E.
Standing Conference on Library Materials on Africa. Periodicals from Africa: A Bibliography & Union List of Periodicals Published in Africa. Travis, Carole, ed. 1977. lib. bdg. 65.00 (ISBN 0-8161-7946-8, Hall Reference). G K Hall.
Standing, Dorothy. Using Crochet Motifs. (Illus.). 92p. 1975. 5.95 o.p. (ISBN 0-263-05366-0). Transatlantic.
Standing, E. M. Maria Montessori. pap. 3.95 (ISBN 0-451-62108-5, ME2108, Ment). NAL.
Standing, Guy. Conceptualising Territorial Mobility in Low-Income Countries. International Labour Office, ed. 50p. (Orig.). 1982. pap. 5.70 (ISBN 92-2-102929-8). Intl Labour Office.
Standing, Guy, jt. ed. see Peek, Peter.
Standing, Sue. Amphibious Water. 44p. 2.95. Zephyr Pr.
--Amphibious Weather. 52p. 1981. signed ed. 5.00 (ISBN 0-939010-02-X); pap. 2.95. Zephyr Pr.
Standing Bear, Luther. My People the Sioux. Brininstool, E. A., ed. LC 74-77394. xx, 288p. 1975. 19.95x (ISBN 0-8032-0874-X); pap. 5.50 (ISBN 0-8032-5793-7, BB 578, Bison). U of Nebr Pr.
Standish, Marjorie. Cooking Down East. 1979. 8.95 o.p. (ISBN 0-930096-00-2). G Gannett.
Standish, Thomas A. A Data Definition Facility for Programming Languages. LC 79-7307. (Outstanding Dissertations in the Computer Sciences). 1980. lib. bdg. 30.00 o.s.i. (ISBN 0-8240-4422-3). Garland Pub.
--Data Structure Techniques. LC 78-67454. 1979. text ed. 26.95 (ISBN 0-201-07256-4). A-W.
Standley, Arline R. Auguste Comte. (World Authors Ser.). lib. bdg. 14.95 (ISBN 0-8057-6467-4, Twayne). G K Hall.
Standley, Fred L. Stopford Brooke. (English Authors Ser.). lib. bdg. 13.95 (ISBN 0-8057-1060-4, Twayne). G K Hall.
Standley, Fred L. & Standley, Nancy V. James Baldwin: A Reference Guide. 1979. lib. bdg. 35.00 (ISBN 0-8161-7844-5, Hall Reference). G K Hall.
Standley, K. J. Oxide Magnetic Materials. 2nd ed. (Monographs on the Physics & Chemistry of Materials). (Illus.). 1972. 55.00x o.p. (ISBN 0-19-851327-5). Oxford U Pr.
Standley, Nancy V., jt. auth. see Standley, Fred L.
Standley, P. C. Flora of the Glacier National Park, Montana. (Illus.). 1969. pap. 16.00 (ISBN 3-7682-0627-0). Lubrecht & Cramer.
--Flora of the Panama Canal Zone. 1968. pap. 24.00 (ISBN 3-7682-0578-9). Lubrecht & Cramer.
--Trees & Shrubs of Mexico. (Contrib. U. S. Nat'l Herb. Ser.: No. 23, 1-5). 1722p. 1982. Repr. lib. bdg. 100.00 (ISBN 3-7682-1288-2). Lubrecht & Cramer.
Standley, P. C., jt. auth. see Wooton, E. O.
Stands In Timber, John & Liberty, Margot. Cheyenne Memories. LC 67-24515. (Illus.). xvi, 348p. 1972. pap. 7.95 (ISBN 0-8032-5751-1, BB 544, Bison). U of Nebr Pr.
Stanek, Jaroslav, et al. Monosaccharides. Mayer, Karel, tr. 1964. 99.50 (ISBN 0-12-663750-4). Acad Pr.
--Oligosaccharides. Mayer, Karel, tr. 1965. 66.50 (ISBN 0-12-663756-3). Acad Pr.
Stanek, Lou W. Megan's Beat. LC 82-45511. 224p. 1983. 10.95 (ISBN 0-8037-5201-6, 01063-320). Dial Bks Young.
Stanek, V. J. Pictorial Encyclopedia of the Animal Kingdom. (Illus.). 1962. 10.00 o.p. (ISBN 0-517-02963-4). Crown.
Stanerson, Lavon. Creative Stitchery. LC 76-13060. (Early Craft Books). (Illus.). (gr. k-5). 1976. PLB 3.95g (ISBN 0-8225-0885-0). Lerner Pubns.
Stanescu, Nichita. Ask the Circle to Forgive You: Selected Poems, 1964-1979. Irwin, Mark & Carpinisan, Mariana, trs. LC 82-84247. (Contemporary European Poetry Ser.). 84p. (Romanian.). 1983. lib. bdg. 10.00 (ISBN 0-910321-06-X); pap. 5.95 (ISBN 0-910321-05-1). Globe Pr.
Stanfel, Larry E., jt. auth. see Sivazlian, B. D.
Stanfield, J. P., jt. ed. see Jelliffe, D. B.
Stanford, A. L., Jr. Foundations of Biophysics. 1975. text ed. 24.50 (ISBN 0-12-663350-9). Acad Pr.
Stanford, Ann, jt. auth. see Crowell, Pattie.
Stanford Arms Control Group. International Arms Control: Issues & Agreements. Barton, John H. & Weiler, Lawrence D., eds. LC 76-14270. 456p. 1976. 12.95x (ISBN 0-8047-0921-1). Stanford U Pr.
Stanford Central America Action Network, ed. Revolution in Central America. 525p. 1982. lib. bdg. 30.00 (ISBN 0-86531-540-X); pap. text ed. 13.95 (ISBN 0-86531-541-8). Westview.
Stanford, Charles V. Studies & Memories. 224p. 1983. pap. 6.25 (ISBN 0-88072-009-3). Tanager Bks.
Stanford, Dennis, jt. auth. see Frison, George.
Stanford, Derek, ed. Three Poets of the Rhymers Club: Lionel Johnson, John Davidson & Ernest Dowson. 1974. 8.50x (ISBN 0-85635-089-3, Pub. by Carcanet New Pr England); pap. 5.25x (ISBN 0-85635-090-7, Pub. by Carcanet New England). Humanities.
Stanford, Donald, ed. see Bridges, Robert.
Stanford, Donald E., ed. The Selected Letters of Robert Bridges, 2 vols. LC 80-54789. (Illus.). 960p. 1983. Set. 65.00 (ISBN 0-686-86801-3); Vol. 1. (ISBN 0-87413-177-4); Vol. 2. (ISBN 0-87413-204-5). U Delaware Pr.
Stanford, E. P. & Lockery, Shirley, eds. Trends & Status of Minority Aging, Vol. 8. (Proceedings of the Institute on Minority Aging). 150p. (Orig.). 1982. pap. 10.00 (ISBN 0-916304-57-4). Campanile.
Stanford, Edwin G., et al, eds. Progress in Applied Materials Research. 1963-65. Vol. 4, 246p. 60.00x (ISBN 0-677-00920-8); Vol. 5, 238p. 60.00x (ISBN 0-677-00930-5); Vol. 6, 310p. 70.00x (ISBN 0-677-00940-2). Gordon.
Stanford, G. McGraw-Hill Vocabulary, Bk. 6. 2nd ed. 1981. 5.28 (ISBN 0-07-060776-1). McGraw.
Stanford, Gene. Developing Effective Classroom Groups: A Practical Guide for Teachers. 256p. 1977. 10.95 o.s.i. (ISBN 0-89104-230-X, A & W Visual Library); pap. 6.95 (ISBN 0-89104-188-5, A & W Visual Library). A & W Pubs.
--McGraw-Hill Vocabulary, Bk. 1. 2nd ed. Weeden, Hester E., ed. (Illus.). 128p. (gr. 7-12). 1981. pap. text ed. 5.28 (ISBN 0-07-060771-0). McGraw.
--McGraw Hill Vocabulary, Bk. 1. (gr. 7-12). 1971. text ed. 5.48 (ISBN 0-07-060757-5, W). McGraw.
--McGraw-Hill Vocabulary, Bk. 2. 2nd ed. (Illus.). 128p. 1981. pap. text ed. 5.28 (ISBN 0-07-060772-9). McGraw.
--McGraw-Hill Vocabulary, Bk. 3. 2nd ed. (Illus.). 128p. 1981. pap. text ed. 5.28 (ISBN 0-07-060773-7). McGraw.
--McGraw-Hill Vocabulary, Bk. 4. 2nd ed. (Illus.). 128p. (gr. 10). 1981. pap. text ed. 4.76 (ISBN 0-07-060760-5, W). McGraw.
Stanford, J. K. Complex Gun. 17.56x (ISBN 0-392-00519-0, SpS). Sportshelf.
--Last Chukker. 6.50 (ISBN 0-8159-6102-2). Devin.
Stanford, Jay G., jt. auth. see Tees, David W.
Stanford, Mary Lee. Touched by Fire. (Orig.). 1980. pap. 1.25 o.s.i. (ISBN 0-440-17461-9). Dell.
Stanford, Mel. New Enterprise Management. (Illus.). 400p. 1982. text ed. 20.95 (ISBN 0-8359-4886-2); instr's. manual free (ISBN 0-8359-4887-0). Reston.
Stanford, Melvin J. Management Policy. (Illus.). 1979. ref. ed. 24.95 (ISBN 0-13-548974-1). P-H.
Stanford, Miles J. The Ground of Growth. 1976. pap. 2.95 (ISBN 0-310-33011-4). Zondervan.
Stanford, Quentin, ed. The World's Population: Problems of Growth. 1972. pap. 15.95x o.p. (ISBN 0-19-540193-X). Oxford U Pr.
Stanford, Quentin H. & Moran, Warren. Geography: A Study of Its Physical Elements. (Illus.). 1978. text ed. 12.95x o.p. (ISBN 0-19-540282-0). Oxford U Pr.
Stanford, Sandra. Long Winters Night. 192p. 1981. pap. 1.50 (ISBN 0-671-57058-7, Pub. by Silhouette Bks). S&S.
Stanford, Sondra. Golden Tide. 192p. (Orig.). 1980. pap. 1.50 (ISBN 0-671-57006-4, Pub. by Silhouette Bks). S&S.
--No Trespassing. 192p. (Orig.). 1980. pap. 1.50 (ISBN 0-671-57046-3, Pub. by Silhouette Bks). S&S.
--Shadow of Love. 192p. (Orig.). 1980. pap. 1.50 (ISBN 0-671-57025-0, Pub. by Silhouette Bks). S&S.
Stanford, Sondrs. Storm's End. 192p. (Orig.). 1980. pap. 1.50 (ISBN 0-671-57035-8, Pub. by Silhouette Bks). S&S.
Stanford University, Hoover Institution on War, Revolution & Peace. Catalog of the Arabic Collection. 1969. 95.00 (ISBN 0-8161-0170-1, Hall Library). G K Hall.
--Catalog of the Chinese Collection, 13 Vols. 1969. Set. 1180.00 (ISBN 0-8161-0168-X, Hall Library). G K Hall.
--Catalog of the Chinese Collection First Supplement, 2 vols. 1972. Set. lib. bdg. 280.00 (ISBN 0-8161-1046-8, Hall Library). G K Hall.
Stanford University, Hoover Institution on War, Revolution, & Peace. The Catalog of the Chinese Collection: Second Supplement, 2 vols. 1977. Set. lib. bdg. 260.00 (ISBN 0-8161-0039-X, Hall Library). G K Hall.
Stanford University, Hoover Institution on War, Revolution & Peace. Catalog of the Japanese Collection, 7 Vols. 1969. Set. 665.00 (ISBN 0-8161-0169-8, Hall Library). G K Hall.
--Catalog of the Japanese Collection, First Supplement. 581p. 1972. lib. bdg. 120.00 (ISBN 0-8161-1051-4, Hall Library). G K Hall.
Stanford University, Hoover Institution on War, Revolution, & Peace. Catalog of the Japanese Collection: Second Supplement. 1977. lib. bdg. 130.00 (ISBN 0-8161-0040-3, Hall Library). G K Hall.
Stanford University, Hoover Institution on War, Revolution & Peace. Catalog of the Turkish & Persian Collections. 1969. 95.00 (ISBN 0-8161-0171-X, Hall Library). G K Hall.

Stanford University, Hoover Institution on War, Peace & Revolution. Catalog of the Western Language Collections, 63 Vols. 1969. Set. 5985.00 (ISBN 0-8161-0859-5, Hall Library). G K Hall.

Stanford University, Hoover Institution on War, Revolution & Peace. Catalog of the Western Language Collections, First Supplement, 5 vols. 2627p. 1972. Set. lib. bdg. 700.00 (ISBN 0-8161-1019-0, Hall Library). G K Hall.

--The Catalog of the Western Language Collections: Second Supplement, 6 vols. 1977. Set. lib. bdg. 840.00 (ISBN 0-8161-0037-3, Hall Library). G K Hall.

--Catalogs of the Western Language Serials & Newspaper Collection, 3 Vols. 1969. 285.00 (ISBN 0-8161-0167-1, Hall Library). G K Hall.

Stanford, W. B. The Sound of Greek: Studies in the Greek Theory & Practice of Euphony. (Sather Classical Lectures: No. 38). (YA) (gr. 9 up). 1967. 33.00x (ISBN 0-520-01204-6). U of Cal Pr.

Stanford, W. B. & McDowell, R. B. Mahaffy: A Biography of an Anglo-Irishman. 1971. 12.95 o.p. (ISBN 0-7100-6880-8). Routledge & Kegan.

Stanford, W. J. McGraw-Hill Vocabulary, Bk. 5. 2nd ed. (McGraw-Hill Vocabulary Ser.). 1982. 5.28 (ISBN 0-07-060775-3). McGraw.

Stanford, William B. Ulysses Theme. 1968. pap. 9.95 (ISBN 0-472-06143-7, 143, AA). U of Mich Pr.

Stanforth, Deidre, jt. auth. see Stamm, Martha.

Stanforth, Deirdre. Creole! 1972. 4.95 (ISBN 0-88289-360-2). Pelican.

Stang, Alan. The Highest Virtue. LC 74-14602. (Illus.). 500p. 1974. 14.95 (ISBN 0-88279-230-X). Western Islands.

--It's Very Simple: True Story of Civil Rights. LC 65-23268. (Illus.). 1965. 5.00 (ISBN 0-88279-207-5); pap. 0.75 pocketsize o.p. (ISBN 0-88279-007-2). Western Islands.

Stang, David. Introduction to Social Psychology. LC 80-19469. 570p. 1981. text ed. 21.95 (ISBN 0-8185-0427-7). Brooks-Cole.

Stang, David J., jt. auth. see Fretz, Bruce R.

Stang, JoAnne. Shadows on the Sceptered Isle. 224p. 1980. 8.95 o.p. (ISBN 0-517-53958-6). Crown.

Stang, Peter J., et al. Vinyl Cations. LC 79-21330. 1979. 73.00 (ISBN 0-12-663780-6). Acad Pr.

Stang, Sondra J. Ford Madox Ford. LC 77-41. (Literature and Life Ser.). 1977. 11.95 (ISBN 0-8044-2832-8). Ungar.

Stange, G. Robert, jt. auth. see Houghton, Walter E.

Stange, L. A., jt. auth. see Grigarick, A. A.

Stangel, John J. Fertility & Conception: An Essential Guide for Childless Couples. 1980. pap. 5.95 (ISBN 0-452-25316-0, Z5316, Plume). NAL.

Stanger, Frank B. Gifts of the Spirit. 1974. pap. 1.00 (ISBN 0-87509-084-2). Chr Pubns.

Stanger, Margaret A. That Quail, Robert. LC 66-19990. (Illus.). (gr. 4-9). 1966. 8.95i (ISBN 0-397-00451-6). Har-Row.

Stangland, E. C. Norwegian Jokes. (Mitzi's Office Jokes Ser.). (Illus., Orig.). 1979. pap. 1.75 (ISBN 0-9602692-0-7). Norse Pr.

--UFF DA Jokes. (Mitzi's Office Jokes Ser.). (Orig.). 1979. pap. 2.00 (ISBN 0-9602692-4-X). Norse Pr.

--Yankee Jokes. 1982. 2.00 (ISBN 0-9602692-7-4). Norse Pr.

Stangland, Red. Grandson of Norwegian Jokes. 1982. pap. 2.00 (ISBN 0-9602692-9-0). Norse Pr.

Stangler, Sharon, et al. Screening Growth & Development of Preschool Children: A Guide for Test Selection. (Illus.). 1980. text ed. 19.50 (ISBN 0-07-060780-X). McGraw.

Stangos, Niko & Richardson, Tony, eds. Concepts of Modern Art. LC 73-9334. (Icon Editions). (Illus.). 256p. 1974. pap. 9.95xi o.p. (ISBN 0-06-430104-4, IN-41, HarpT). Har-Row.

Stangos, Nikos & Richardson, eds. Concepts of Modern Art. 2nd ed. LC 80-8704. (Icon Editions Ser.). (Illus.). 392p. 1981. 20.00i (ISBN 0-06-438535-3, HarpT); pap. 9.95xi (ISBN 0-06-430104-4, IN104, HarpT). Har-Row.

Stangos, Nikos, ed. see Hockney, David.

Staniar, William, ed. Plant Engineering Handbook. 2nd ed. 1959. 89.50 (ISBN 0-07-060824-5, P&RB). McGraw.

--Prime Movers. 3rd ed. 1966. 9.95 o.p. (ISBN 0-07-060825-3, P&RB). McGraw.

Stanicek, Frank, jt. auth. see Kornhaber, Bruce.

Stanier, Roger, et al. Introduction to the Microbial World. (Illus.). 1979. ref. ed. 25.95 (ISBN 0-13-488049-8); lab. manual 10.95 (ISBN 0-13-488031-5). P-H.

Staniland, Martin. The Lions of Dagbon. LC 74-16989. (African Studies: No. 16). (Illus.). 300p. 1975. 37.50 (ISBN 0-521-20682-0). Cambridge U Pr.

Stanish, Bob. Connecting Rainbows. (gr. 3-12). 1982. 7.95 (ISBN 0-86653-081-9, GA 426). Good Apple.

--Hippogriff Feathers. (gr. 3-12). 1981. 7.95 (ISBN 0-86653-009-6, GA 237). Good Apple.

--The Unconventional Invention Book. (gr. 3-12). 1981. 8.95 (ISBN 0-86653-035-5, GA 263). Good Apple.

Stanislav, J. F. Mathematical Modeling of Transport Phenomena Processes. LC 81-69257. 254p. 1982. text ed. 39.95 (ISBN 0-250-40489-3). Ann Arbor Science.

Stanislawczyk, Irene E. & Yavemer, Symond. Creativity in the Language Classroom. LC 76-2625. 1976. pap. text ed. 6.95 o.p. (ISBN 0-88377-047-4). Newbury Hse.

Stanislawczyk, Irene E., jt. ed. see Gomez-Gil, Orlando.

Stanislawski, Dan. Anatomy of Eleven Towns in Michoacan. (Illus.). Repr. of 1950 ed. lib. bdg. 19.00x (ISBN 0-8371-1029-7, TLSM). Greenwood.

--Individuality of Portugal: A Study in Historical-Political Geography. (Illus.). Repr. of 1959 ed. lib. bdg. 17.75x (ISBN 0-8371-2120-5, STP). Greenwood.

Stanislawski, J. The Great English-Polish Dictionary. 1405p. (Eng. & Pol.). 1979. leatherette 75.00 (ISBN 0-686-97431-X, M-9329). French & Eur.

Stanislawski, Jan. A Practical English-Polish Dictionary. LC 77-578742. 913p. (Polish.). 1981. 17.50x (ISBN 83-214-0245-3). Intl Pubns Serv.

--A Practical Polish-English Dictionary. LC 77-578742. 1036p. (Polish.). 1981. 17.50x (ISBN 83-214-0124-4). Intl Pubns Serv.

Stanislawski, Michael. Tsar Nicholas I & the Jews: The Transformation of Jewish Society in Russia, 1825-1855. (Illus.). 320p. 1983. 17.95 (ISBN 0-8276-0216-2). Jewish Pubn.

Stanislowski, J. Polish Great Dictionary, Vol. 2: Polish-English, 2 vols. 4th ed. 1978. text ed. 42.00x (ISBN 0-89918-521-5, P-521). Vanous.

Staniszkis, Jadwiga. Poland's Self-Limiting Revolution. Gross, Jan T., ed. LC 80-61387. 328p. 1983. 19.50x (ISBN 0-691-09403-9). Princeton U Pr.

Stanitski, Conrad, jt. auth. see Sears, Curtis.

Stanitski, Conrad L. & Sears, Curtis T. Chemistry for Health-Related Sciences: Concepts & Correlations. 1976. 26.95 (ISBN 0-13-129429-6); lab. manual 12.95 (ISBN 0-13-129437-7); student guide 6.95 (ISBN 0-13-129403-2). P-H.

Stanitski, Conrad L., Jr. & Sears, C. Aspects of Chemistry for Health-Related Sciences: Concepts & Correlations. 1979. 26.95 (ISBN 0-13-049262-0); study guide 7.95 (ISBN 0-13-049254-X). P-H.

Stankard, Martin F., Jr. Successful Management of Large Clerical Operations: A Guide to Improving Service Transaction Systems. LC 80-11991. (Illus.). 288p. 1980. 21.95 (ISBN 0-07-060831-8, P&RB). McGraw.

Stanke, Don E., jt. auth. see Parish, James R.

Stankiewicz, W. J. Approaches to Democracy: Philosophy of Government at the Close of the Twentieth Century. 1980. 26.00x (ISBN 0-312-04668-5). St Martin.

--Aspects of Political Theory: Classical Concepts in an Age of Relativism. 175p. 1976. 14.95 (ISBN 0-02-977630-9). Transaction Bks.

--Politics & Religion in Seventeenth-Century France. LC 76-2075. 269p. 1976. Repr. of 1960 ed. lib. bdg. 20.00x (ISBN 0-8371-8770-2, STPR). Greenwood.

Stankiewicz, W. J., ed. The Tradition of Polish Ideals: Essays in History & Literature. 288p. 1981. 27.50x (ISBN 0-901149-18-7, Pub. by Orbis Bks England). State Mutual Bk.

Stankovic, John A. Structured Systems & Their Performance Improvement through Vertical Migration. Stone, Harold S., ed. LC 82-2772. (Computer Science Ser.: Systems Programming: No. 1). 152p. 1982. 39.95 (ISBN 0-8357-1325-3, UMI Res Pr). Univ Microfilms.

Stankovsky, Jan, jt. auth. see Levcik, Friedrich.

Stanley, jt. auth. see Dalton.

Stanley, Arthur P. Epistles of Paul to the Corinthians. 1981. 20.95 (ISBN 0-86524-051-5, 7105). Klock & Klock.

Stanley, Bill, ed. see Thorburn, Craig.

Stanley, Brian H. Experiments in Electric Circuits. 256p. 1982. text ed. 11.95 (ISBN 0-675-09805-X). Additional supplements may be obtained from publisher. Merrill.

Stanley, C. Maxwell. The Consulting Engineer. 2nd ed. LC 81-11593. 303p. 1982. 29.95x (ISBN 0-471-08920-6, Pub. by Wiley-Interscience). Wiley.

--Managing Global Problems: A Guide to Survival. 286p. (Orig.). 1979. text ed. 12.50 (ISBN 0-9603112-1-1); pap. text ed. 7.95 (ISBN 0-9603112-2-X). Stanley Found.

Stanley, Charles J. Boxers. 1982. lib. bdg. 75.00 (ISBN 0-686-81932-2). Porter.

Stanley, Charlotte, tr. see Sorel, Georges.

Stanley, D. J. & Kelling, G., eds. Sedimentation in Submarine Canyons, Fans & Trenches. LC 77-19163. 395p. 1978. 60.50 (ISBN 0-87933-313-8). Hutchinson Ross.

Stanley, David. South Pacific Handbook. 2nd ed. Dalton, Bill, ed. LC 81-80992. (Illus.). 450p. 1982. pap. 12.95 o.p. (ISBN 0-9603322-3-5, Pub. by Moon Pubns). C E Tuttle.

--South Pacific Handbook. 2nd ed. 574p. Date not set. price not set (ISBN 0-9603322-3-5). Moon Pubns CA.

Stanley, David M. Boasting in the Lord. LC 73-84361. 204p. 1973. pap. 3.95 o.p. (ISBN 0-8091-1793-2). Paulist Pr.

Stanley, David T. Managing Local Government Under Union Pressure. (Studies of Unionism in Government). 1972. pap. 7.95 (ISBN 0-8157-8101-6). Brookings.

--Prisoners among Us: The Problem of Parole. 1976. 18.95 (ISBN 0-8157-8106-7); pap. 7.95 (ISBN 0-8157-8105-9). Brookings.

Stanley, Del & Black, John. Practical Accounting. 3rd ed. 1980. pap. text ed. 17.95x o.p. (ISBN 0-673-16133-1). Scott F.

Stanley, Delmar S., jt. auth. see Black, John G.

Stanley, Gary S. The Garimus File. (Illus., Orig.). 1983. pap. 7.95 (ISBN 0-86605-107-4). Heres Life.

Stanley, George F. Canada Invaded: Seventeen Seventy-Five to Seventy-Six. LC 73-88116. (Canadian War Museum Historical Publications Ser.: No. 8). (Illus.). 172p. 1973. 10.95 o.p. (ISBN 0-88866-537-7); pap. 5.95 o.p. (ISBN 0-88866-578-4). Samuel Stevens.

Stanley Gibbons. British Commonwealth. (Stanley Gibbons Stamp Catalogue Ser.: Part 1). 1983. 35.00 (ISBN 0-85259-346-5). StanGib Ltd.

Stanley Gibbons Ltd., ed. Stamps of the World. (Illus.). 1983. Pt. 1,A-J. 24.00 (ISBN 0-85259-018-0); Pt. 2,K-Z. 24.00 (ISBN 0-85259-019-9). StanGib Ltd.

Stanley Gibbons Ltd, ed. Stanley Gibbons British Commonwealth. (Illus.). 35.00 (ISBN 0-85259-017-2). StanGib Ltd.

Stanley, H. Eugene. Introduction to Phase Transitions & Critical Phenomena. (International Series of Monographs on Physics). (Illus.). 1971. text ed. 19.95x (ISBN 0-19-501458-8). Oxford U Pr.

Stanley, Hugh P. The Challenge of Fatherhood. LC 82-73132. 96p. (Orig.). 1982. pap. 2.45 (ISBN 0-87029-185-8, 20279-6). Abbey.

Stanley, J., jt. auth. see Blumberg, A. A.

Stanley, James C., ed. Biologic & Synthetic Prostheses. 681p. 1982. 79.50 (ISBN 0-8089-1491-X). Grune.

Stanley, John, jt. auth. see Baldwin, Ian.

Stanley, John, tr. see Sorel, Georges.

Stanley, John L. The Sociology of Virtue: The Political & Social Theories of George Sorel. LC 81-40318. 320p. 1981. 33.00x (ISBN 0-520-03790-1). U of Cal Pr.

Stanley, John L., ed. see Sorel, George.

Stanley, John L., ed. see Sorel, Georges.

Stanley, John L., tr. see Sorel, Georges.

Stanley, Julian C., jt. auth. see Glass, Gene V.

Stanley, Julian C., jt. auth. see Hopkins, Kenneth D.

Stanley, Keith K., jt. auth. see Houslay, Miles D.

Stanley, Kenneth E., jt. auth. see Mike, Valerie.

Stanley, Linda C. The Foreign Critical Reputation of F. Scott Fitzgerald: An Analysis & Annotated Bibliography. LC 79-7474. 1980. lib. bdg. 35.00x (ISBN 0-313-21444-1, STF/). Greenwood.

Stanley, Liz & Wise, Sue. Breaking Out: Feminist Consciousness & Feminist Research. 192p. (Orig.). 1983. pap. price not set (ISBN 0-7100-9315-2). Routledge & Kegan.

Stanley, Lowell C., jt. auth. see Larson, Martin A.

Stanley, Marland L. Two-Phase Flow Measurements: Principles, Designs & Applications. (Technical Report of an International Colloquim on Two-Phase Flow Instrumentation Ser.). 568p. 1982. pap. text ed. 44.95x (ISBN 0-87664-699-2). Instru Soc.

Stanley, Melissa & Andrykovitch, George. Living: An Interpretive Approach to Biology. 204p. Date not set. price not set Instrs' Manual (ISBN 0-201-07174-6); Study Guide 8.95 (ISBN 0-201-07175-4). A-W.

--A Living Approach to Biology. (Biology Ser.). (Illus.). 640p. 1981. text ed. 24.95x (ISBN 0-201-07173-8); write for info. lab manual (ISBN 0-201-07176-2). A-W.

Stanley, Michael. The Swiss Conspiracy. 1976. pap. 1.95 o.p. (ISBN 0-380-00492-5, 34082). Avon.

Stanley, Michael & Rotrosen, John, eds. The Benzamides: Pharmacology, Neurobiology, & Clinical Aspects. 224p. 1982. text ed. 31.00 (ISBN 0-89004-639-5). Raven.

Stanley, Montes. Creating & Knitting Your Own Designs For A Perfect Fit. LC 82-47549. (Illus.). 176p. 1982. 17.26i (ISBN 0-06-015054-8, HarpT). Har-Row.

Stanley, P. Fracture Mechanics in Engineering Practice. 1982. 94.50 (ISBN 0-85334-723-9, Pub. by Applied Sci England). Elsevier.

Stanley, P., ed. Computing Developments in Experimental & Numerical Stress Analysis. (Illus.). x, 239p. 1976. 35.00 (ISBN 0-85334-680-1, Pub. by Applied Sci England). Elsevier.

--Non-Linear Problems in Stress Analysis. (Illus.). 1978. 102.50 (ISBN 0-85334-780-8, Pub. by Applied Sci England). Elsevier.

Stanley., P., jt. ed. see Richards, T. H.

Stanley, Philip & Miller, John H. Pediatric Angiography. (Illus.). 419p. 1982. 75.00 (ISBN 0-683-07898-4). Williams & Wilkins.

Stanley, Philip E. & Scoggins, Bruce, eds. Liquid Scintillation Counting: Recent Developments. 1974. 45.00 (ISBN 0-12-663850-0). Acad Pr.

Stanley, R. Promotion: Advertising, Publicity, Personal Selling, Sales Promotion. (Illus.). 1977. text ed. 21.95 o.p. (ISBN 0-13-730770-5). P-H.

Stanley, Richard & Neame, Alan. Exploration Diaries of H. M. Stanley. LC 62-11208. (Illus.). 1962. 10.00 o.p. (ISBN 0-8149-0212-X). Vanguard.

Stanley, Steven M. The New Evolutionary Timetable: Fossils, Genes & the Origin of Species. LC 81-66101. (Illus.). 288p. 1981. 16.75 (ISBN 0-465-05013-1). Basic.

Stanley, Thomas. A History of Philosophy, 3 vols. Wellek, Rene, ed. LC 75-11254. (British Philosophers & Theologians of the 17th & 18th Centuries Ser.). 1978. Repr. of 1687 ed. lib. bdg. 42.00 o.s.i. (ISBN 0-8240-1804-4). Garland Pub.

Stanley, Timothy W. & Danielian, Ronald L. U. S. Foreign Economic Strategy for the 1980s. (Replica Edition Ser.). 210p. 1981. 18.50 (ISBN 0-86531-911-1). Westview.

Stanley, Timothy W., jt. auth. see International Economic Studies Institute.

Stanley, W. M., jt. ed. see Burnet, F. M.

Stanley, William D. Digital Signal Processing. (Illus.). 336p. 1975. 24.95 (ISBN 0-87909-199-1). Reston.

Stanley, William T., compiled by. Broadway in the West End: An Index of Reviews of the American Theatre in London, 1950-1975. LC 77-89108. 1978. lib. bdg. 29.95x (ISBN 0-8371-9852-6, STB/). Greenwood.

Stanley-Wood, N. & Allen, T. Particle Size Analysis. 1982. text ed. 74.95x (ISBN 0-471-26221-8, Pub. by Wiley-Interscience). Wiley.

Stanlis, J. P., ed. see Burke, Edmund.

Stannard, David E. The Puritan Way of Death: A Study in Religion, Culture & Social Change. LC 76-42647. (Illus.). 1977. 17.95x (ISBN 0-19-502226-2). Oxford U Pr.

--The Puritan Way of Death: A Study in Religion, Culture, & Social Change. LC 76-42647. (Illus.). 1974. pap. 5.95 (ISBN 0-19-502521-0, GB573, GB). Oxford U Pr.

Stannard-Friel, Don. Harassment Therapy: A Case Study of Psychiatric Violence. 1981. lib. bdg. 16.95 (ISBN 0-8161-9030-5, Univ Bks). G K Hall.

Stanner, W. E. The South Seas in Transition: A Study of Post-War Rehabilitation & Reconstruction in Three British Pacific Dependencies. LC 82-15534. xiv, 448p. 1982. Repr. of 1953 ed. lib. bdg. 39.75x (ISBN 0-313-23661-5, STSOS). Greenwood.

Stano, Michael, jt. auth. see Reinsch, Lamar.

Stanovich, Betty J. Hedgehog Adventures. LC 82-12665. (Illus.). 48p. (gr. 1-3). 1983. 8.00 (ISBN 0-688-01664-2); PLB 7.63 (ISBN 0-688-01669-3). Lothrop.

Stans, Maurice. The Terrors of Justice. LC 78-57417. 1978. 12.95 (ISBN 0-89696-020-X, An Everest House Book). Dodd.

Stansbie, Ken. How to Save Fifty Percent or More on Gas & Car Repairs. 96p. 1983. pap. 4.95 (ISBN 0-86666-035-6). GWP.

Stansby, M. E., jt. ed. see Barlow, S. M.

Stansell, Christine, jt. ed. see Snitow, Ann.

Stansell, Gary, tr. see Wolff, Hans W.

Stansfield. Serology & Immunology. 1981. 24.95x (ISBN 0-02-415740-6). Macmillan.

Stansfield, Charles, jt. auth. see Zimolzak, Chester.

Stansfield, Charles A., jt. auth. see Zimolzak, Chester E.

Stansfield, Charles A., Jr. New Jersey: A Geography. 240p. 1983. lib. bdg. 35.00x (ISBN 0-89158-957-0); pap. text ed. 20.00x (ISBN 0-86531-491-8). Westview.

Stansfield, Malcolm, jt. auth. see Giles, Tony.

Stansfield, Richard H. Advertising Manager's Handbook. 1982. 57.50 (ISBN 0-85013-128-6). Dartnell Corp.

Stansfield, William D. Genetics. (Schaum Outline Ser.). 1969. pap. 6.95 (ISBN 0-07-060842-3, SP). McGraw.

--The Science of Evolution. 1977. 24.95x (ISBN 0-02-415750-3). Macmillan.

Stanski, Donald R. & Watkins, David W. Drug Disposition in Anesthesia. (The Scientific Basis of Clinical Anesthesia Ser.). 1982. 24.50 (ISBN 0-8089-1498-7, 794308). Grune.

Stansky, Peter, ed. see Ashbee, C. R.

Stansky, Peter, ed. see Cobden-Sanderson, T. J.

Stansky, Peter, ed. see Crane, Walter.

Stansky, Peter, ed. see Cust, M. M.

Stansky, Peter, ed. see Dresser, Christopher.

Stansky, Peter, ed. see Godwin, E. W.

Stansky, Peter, ed. see Rational Dress Association.

Stansky, Peter, ed. see Sylvia's Home Help Series.

Stansky, Peter, ed. see Wilde, Oscar.

Stant, Margaret. The Young Child: His Activities & Materials. (Illus.). 160p. 1972. pap. text ed. 15.95 (ISBN 0-13-977157-3). P-H.

Stanton & Ali. The Experienced Hand: A Student Manual for Making the Most of an Internship. LC 81-24199. 1982. pap. 5.95 (ISBN 0-910328-33-1). Carroll Pr.

Stanton, Ann M. When Mothers Go to Jail. LC 79-3522. 224p. 1980. 24.95 (ISBN 0-669-03461-4). Lexington Bks.

Stanton, E. N., jt. auth. see Idleman, H. K.

Stanton, Edgar, ed. Promise of USA. LC 75-39971. (Illus.). 248p. 1975. pap. text ed. 4.95 o.p. (ISBN 0-89260-000-4). Hwong Pub.

--Violence: U.S.A. LC 75-39970. (Illus.). 480p. 1976. pap. text ed. 5.95 o.p. (ISBN 0-89260-004-7). Hwong Pub.

Stanton, Edward, ed. see Da Gama, Jose B.

Stanton, Elinor. Surprise Ending, No. 68. 1982. pap. 1.75 (ISBN 0-515-06679-6). Jove Pubns.

Stanton, Elizabeth C. Eighty Years & More: Reminiscences, 1815-1897. LC 75-162284. (Studies in the Life of Women). (Illus.). 1971. pap. 7.95 (ISBN 0-8052-0324-9). Schocken.

Stanton, G. N. Jesus of Nazareth in New Testament Preaching. LC 73-92782. (Society of New Testament Studies: No. 27). 228p. 1975. 37.50 (ISBN 0-521-20465-8). Cambridge U Pr.

Stanton, H. U. Teaching of the Qur'An, with an Account of Its Growth & Subject Index. LC 74-90040. 1969. Repr. 12.00x (ISBN 0-8196-0253-1). Biblo.

Stanton, Harry E. Helping Students Learn: The Improvement of Higher Education. LC 78-70519. 1978. pap. text ed. 8.00 (ISBN 0-8191-0644-5). U Pr of Amer.

Stanton, Jeffrey & Dickey, John, eds. The Addison-Wesley Book of Apple Computer Software 1983. (Microbooks Ser. Popular). 402p. 1982. pap. text ed. 19.95 (ISBN 0-201-10285-4). A-W.

Stanton, Marjorie & Carlson, Sylvia. The Changing Role of the Professional Nurse: Implications for Nursing Education. (Faculty-Curriculum Development Ser.: Pt. V). 49p. 1975. 4.25 (ISBN 0-686-38269-2, 15-1574). Natl League Nurse.

Stanton, Marjorie, jt. auth. see Torres, Gertrude.

Stanton, Matin. Outside the Dream: Lacan & French Styles of Psychoanalysis. 108p. 1983. pap. 9.95 (ISBN 0-7100-9273-3). Routledge & Kegan.

Stanton, Michael N., ed. English Literary Journals, 1900 to 1950: A Guide to Information Sources. LC 74-32509. (American Literature, English Literature & World Literatures in English Information Ser.: Vol. 32). 200p. 1982. 42.00x (ISBN 0-8103-1359-6). Gale.

Stanton, R. L. Ore Petrology. (International Series in the Earth & Planetary Sciences). (Illus.). 736p. 1971. text ed. 45.00 (ISBN 0-07-060843-1, C). McGraw.

Stanton, Robert B. Colorado River Controversies. Chalfant, James M. & Stone, Julius F., eds. LC 82-60295. (Illus.). 310p. 1982. pap. 12.95 (ISBN 0-916370-09-7). Westwater.

Stanton, Robert J. Gore Vidal: A Primary & Secondary Bibliography. 1980. lib. bdg. 27.00 (ISBN 0-8161-8109-8, Hall Reference). G K Hall.

--Truman Capote: A Reference Guide. 1980. lib. bdg. 21.50 (ISBN 0-8161-8108-X, Hall Reference). G K Hall.

Stanton, Thomas E., ed. see Perry, Elliot.

Stanton, William A. Pulse Technology. LC 64-17153. 225p. 1964. text ed. 11.50 (ISBN 0-471-82080-6, Pub. by Wiley). Krieger.

Stanton, William J. Fundamentals of Marketing. 6th ed. (Illus.). 704p. 1981. text ed. 24.95 (ISBN 0-07-060891-1, C); instrs. manual 20.95 (ISBN 0-07-060892-X); study guide 9.95 (ISBN 0-07-060893-8); test file 20.95 (ISBN 0-07-060894-6); transparency masters 20.95 (ISBN 0-07-060895-4). McGraw.

Stanton, William R. Leopard's Spots: Scientific Attitudes Toward Race in America, 1815-1859. LC 59-11625. (Midway Reprints Ser.). 1982. 6.50x o.s.i. (ISBN 0-226-77122-9); pap. 8.00x (ISBN 0-226-77124-5, P218, Phoen). U of Chicago Pr.

Stanton-Hicks, Michael & Boas, Robert, eds. Chronic Low Back Pain. 247p. 1982. text ed. 27.50 (ISBN 0-89004-598-4). Raven.

Stanway, Andrew. Alternative Medicine: A Guide to Natural Therapies. 1982. pap. 5.95 (ISBN 0-14-022369-X, Pelican). Penguin.

Stanwood, Brooks. The Seventh Child. 1982. 12.95 (ISBN 0-671-43637-6, Linden). S&S.

--The Seventh Child. 1983. pap. 3.50 (ISBN 0-440-19122-X). Dell.

Stanwood, Donald A. The Memory of Eva Ryker. LC 77-23897. (Fic). 1978. 8.95 o.p. (ISBN 0-698-10876-0, Coward). Putnam Pub Group.

Stanworth, P. & Giddens, A., eds. Elites & Power in British Society. LC 73-92788. (Studies in Sociology: No. 8). (Illus.). 280p. 1974. 34.50 (ISBN 0-521-20441-0); pap. 10.95x (ISBN 0-521-09853-X). Cambridge U Pr.

Stanyer, Jeffrey, jt. auth. see Smith, Brian C.

Stapf, O. & Wordsell, W. C. Index Londinensis, 6 vols. & 2 suppl. 1979. Repr. of 1929 ed. 1008.00 (ISBN 3-87429-151-0). Lubrecht & Cramer.

Stapledon, Olaf. Last Men in London. (Science Fiction Ser.). 336p. 1976. Repr. of 1932 ed. lib. bdg. 15.00 o.p. (ISBN 0-8398-2340-1, Gregg). G K Hall.

--Nebula Maker & Four Encounters. LC 82-17684. (Illus.). 288p. 1983. 12.95 (ISBN 0-686-84666-4); pap. 6.95 (ISBN 0-686-84667-2). Dodd.

--To the End of Time. (Science Fiction Ser). 808p. 1975. Repr. of 1953 ed. lib. bdg. 35.00 o.p. (ISBN 0-8398-2312-6, Gregg). G K Hall.

Staples, Caroline M. The Yarn Animal Book. 1976. 9.95 o.p. (ISBN 0-671-22336-4). S&S.

Staples, Frederick. Auditing Manual. 181p. 1980. pap. 9.50 (ISBN 0-686-70151-8). Counting Hse.

--The Inventories. LC 74-20116. 104p. 1975. 6.45 (ISBN 0-915026-19-8). Counting Hse.

Staples, Michael, jt. auth. see Chin, David.

Staples, Michael P. Tibetan Kung-Fu: The Way of the Monk. LC 80-106130. (Illus.). 80p. 1976. pap. 3.75 (ISBN 0-86568-004-3). Unique Pubns.

Staples, R. Introduction to Black Sociology. 1975. 18.95 (ISBN 0-07-060840-7, C). McGraw.

Staples, R. C. & Toenniessen, G. H. Plant Disease Control: Resistance & Susceptibility. 312p. 1981. 35.50x (ISBN 0-471-08196-5, Pub. by Wiley-Interscience). Wiley.

Staples, Richard C., jt. auth. see Mussell, Harry.

Staples, Russell L., jt. auth. see Oosterwal, Gottfried.

Staples, William R. The Documentary History of the Destruction of the Gaspee. Deasy, Richard M., ed. (Rhode Island Revolutionary Heritage Ser.: Vol. IV). 250p. 1983. write for info (ISBN 0-917012-05-4). RI Pubns Soc.

Stapleton, Edmund, tr. see Percheron, Maurice.

Stapleton, John F. Essentials of Clinical Cardiology. LC 82-18223. (Illus.). 490p. 1983. pap. text ed. 19.95 (ISBN 0-8036-8097-X). Davis Co.

Stapleton, John F., jt. auth. see Sussex, Margie.

Stapleton, Richard. Capital Market Equilibrium & Corporate Financial Decisions. Altman, Edward I. & Walter, Ingo, eds. LC 76-52021. (Contemporary Studies in Economic & Financial Analysis Ser.). 1980. lib. bdg. 34.00 (ISBN 0-89232-054-0). Jai Pr.

Stapleton, Richard C. Managing Creatively: Action Learning in Action. 1976. pap. text ed. 10.75 (ISBN 0-8191-0035-8). U Pr of Amer.

Stapleton, Thomas & Katz, Julian. The Prevention of Psychiatric Disorders in Children. (International Lectures in Preventive Medicine). 244p. 1983. 16.00 (ISBN 0-87527-234-7). Green.

Stapleton, W. Vaughan & Teitelbaum, Lee E. In Defense of Youth: A Study of the Role of Counsel in American Juvenile Courts. LC 72-83837. 244p. 1972. 11.95x (ISBN 0-87154-833-X). Russell Sage.

Stapp, Melinda M., jt. ed. see Caskey, Jefferson D.

Stapp, W. B., jt. ed. see Swan, James A.

Stapp, William B. & Liston, Mary D., eds. Environmental Education: A Guide to Information Sources. LC 73-17542. (Man & the Environment Information Guide Ser.: Vol. 1). 350p. 1975. 42.00x (ISBN 0-8103-1337-5). Gale.

Staquet, M., jt. ed. see Klastersky, J.

Staquet, M., jt. ed. see Tagnon, H. J.

Staquet, Maurice J., ed. Cancer Therapy: Prognostic Factors & Criteria of Response. LC 74-14481. (European Organization for Research on Treatment of Cancer Ser.). 405p. 1975. 34.50 (ISBN 0-89004-008-7). Raven.

--Randomized Trials in Cancer: A Critical Review by Sites. LC 77-17753. (European Organization for Research on Treatment of Cancer Monograph: Vol. 4). 445p. 1978. 49.50 (ISBN 0-89004-264-0). Raven.

Staquet, Maurice J., jt. ed. see Klastersky, Jean.

Staquet, Maurice J., jt. ed. see Tagnon, Henri J.

Star, Cima. Understanding Headaches. (Illus.). 1977. pap. 2.95 o.p. (ISBN 0-671-18088-6). Monarch Pr.

Star, Robin R. We Can, Vol. 1. 88p. (gr. 4 up). 1980. PLB 3.95 (ISBN 0-88200-135-3, C2670). Alexander Graham.

--We Can, Vol. 2. 98p. (gr. 4 up). 1980. PLB 3.95 (ISBN 0-88200-136-1, C2786). Alexander Graham.

Star, Steven H., jt. auth. see Corey, E. Raymond.

Star Wars. The Empire Strikes Back: A Pop-up Book. LC 79-92275. (Pop-up Book: No. 41). (Illus.). 16p. (ps-3). 1980. pap. 5.95 (ISBN 0-394-84413-0). Random.

Starbird, William & Oriti, Ronald. Introduction to Astronomy. 1977. text ed. 23.95x (ISBN 0-02-478560-1). Macmillan.

Starbuck, Alexander. The History of Nantucket: County, Island & Town. LC 69-13507. (Illus.). 1969. 32.50 (ISBN 0-8048-0250-5). C E Tuttle.

Starbuck, Carol, jt. auth. see Livingston, Elizabeth.

Starbuck, Gene H. Models of Human Sexuality & Social Control. LC 81-40136. 107p. 1981. lib. bdg. 17.70 (ISBN 0-8191-1651-3); pap. text ed. 8.00 (ISBN 0-8191-1652-1). U Pr of Amer.

Starbuck, George. The Argot Merchant Disaster Poems: New & Selected. 1982. 12.95 (ISBN 0-316-81084-3); pap. 8.95 (ISBN 0-316-81081-9). Little.

Starchild, Adam. Tax Havens for Corporations. 186p. 1979. 19.95 (ISBN 0-87201-818-0). Gulf Pub.

--Tax Havens: What They Are & What They Can Do for the Shrewd Investor. (Dollar-Growth Library). 1979. 12.95 o.p. (ISBN 0-87000-454-9, Arlington Hse). Crown.

Starck, Marcia. Astrology: Key to Holistic Health. Robertson, Arlene, ed. 220p. (Orig.). 1982. pap. 9.95 (ISBN 0-930706-11-0). Seek-It Pubns.

Starck, Walter A. & Brundza, Paul. Art of Underwater Photography. (Illus.). 1966. 8.95 o.p. (ISBN 0-8174-0516-X, Amphoto). Watson-Guptill.

Starcke, Walter. This Double Thread. 160p. 1969. 11.95 (ISBN 0-227-67738-2). Attic Pr.

Stare, Frederick J. & McWilliams, Margaret. Living Nutrition. 3rd ed. LC 80-20470. 580p. 1981. text ed. 27.50 (ISBN 0-471-04940-9). Wiley.

Stare, Fredrick J. & McWilliams, Margaret. Nutrition for Good Health. 224p. 13.95 (ISBN 0-89313-064-8). G F Stickley.

Stare, Fredrick J., jt. auth. see Whelan, Elizabeth M.

Starfield, A. M., jt. auth. see Crouch., S. L.

Stargel, Gloria C. The Healing. (Orig.). 1982. pap. 2.50 (ISBN 0-8423-1425-3). Tyndale.

Starhawk. Dreaming the Dark: Magic, Sex, & Politics. LC 81-70485. 256p. 1982. 13.94 (ISBN 0-8070-1000-6); pap. 6.97 (ISBN 0-8070-1001-4, BP633). Beacon Pr.

Starika, W. A. & Richardson, E. L., eds. The T.F.H. Book of Parrots: With a Special Illustrated Section on Surgical Sexing William C. Satterfield. (Illus.). 80p. 1982. 6.95 (ISBN 0-87666-806-6, HP-015). TFH Pubns.

Stark, tr. see Chekhov, Anton.

Stark, Alice M., ed. see Akhilananda, Swami.

Stark, Barbara L. & Voorhies, Barbara, eds. Prehistoric Coastal Adaptations: The Economy & Ecology of Maritime Middle America. (Studies in Archaeology Ser.). 1978. 32.50 (ISBN 0-12-663250-2). Acad Pr.

Stark, Brian J. Special Situation Investing: Hedging, Arbitrage & Liquidation. LC 82-73635. 250p. 1983. 27.50 (ISBN 0-87094-384-7). Dow Jones-Irwin.

Stark, Bruce P; see Weaver, Glenn.

Stark, Claude. God of All. 1982. 12.00 (ISBN 0-89007-000-8); pap. 6.00 (ISBN 0-89007-102-0). Branden.

Stark, Claude A. God of All: Sri Ramakrishna's Approach to Religious Plurality. LC 74-76001. (God Ser.). (Illus.). 236p. 1974. No. 101. 12.00 (ISBN 0-89007-000-8); No. 102. pap. 6.00 (ISBN 0-89007-102-0). C Stark.

Stark, Claude A., ed. see Akhilananda, Swami.

Stark, F., jt. auth. see Sprandel, U.

Stark, Frederick. Phrase Dictionaries for the American Tourist, 6 bks. Incl. German for the American Tourist. pap. (ISBN 0-8326-2409-8, 6570); Spanish for the English-Speaking Tourist. pap. (ISBN 0-8326-2410-1, 6571); French for the English-Speaking Tourist. pap. (ISBN 0-8326-2411-X, 6572); Italian for the English-Speaking Tourist. pap. (ISBN 0-8326-2412-8, 6573); Greek for the English-Speaking Tourist. pap. (ISBN 0-8326-2413-6, 6574); Russian for the English-Speaking Tourist. pap. (ISBN 0-8326-2414-4, 6575). 128p. (Orig.). 1981. pap. 2.50 ea. Delair.

Stark, Freya. Alexander's Path. 1975. 28.50 (ISBN 0-7195-1332-4). Transatlantic.

--The Southern Gates of Arabia: A Journey to the Hadhramaut. 1972. 28.50 (ISBN 0-7195-2425-3). Transatlantic.

--The Valleys of the Assassins. rev. ed. (Illus.). 1972. 28.50 (ISBN 0-7195-2429-6). Transatlantic.

Stark, Gary D. & Lackner, Bede K., eds. Essays on Culture & Society in Modern Germany. LC 82-40315. (Walter Prescott Webb Memorial Lectures Ser.: No. 15). 216p. 1982. 19.50x (ISBN 0-89096-137-9). Tex A&M Univ Pr.

Stark, Gary D., jt. ed. see Moch, Leslie P.

Stark, George R., ed. Biochemical Aspects of Reactions on Solid Supports. 1971. 43.00 (ISBN 0-12-663950-7). Acad Pr.

Stark, Harry A., ed. Automotive Yearbook. 1981. 60.00x (ISBN 0-686-35934-8). Wards Comm.

--Ward's Automotive Yearbook. LC 40-33639. 1982. 75.00 (ISBN 0-686-35855-4). Wards Comm.

--Ward's Nineteen Eighty-Three Automotive Yearbook. 45th ed. LC 40-33639. (Illus.). 400p. 1983. 85.00 (ISBN 0-910589-00-3). Wards Comm.

Stark, J. P. Solid State Diffusion. LC 80-11750. 252p. 1983. Repr. of 1976 ed. lib. bdg. write for info. (ISBN 0-89874-145-9). Krieger.

Stark, James H. Loyalists of Massachusetts & the Other Side of the American Revolution. LC 68-58022. (Illus.). Repr. of 1910 ed. lib. bdg. 35.00x (ISBN 0-678-00791-8). Kelley.

Stark, Joan S., et al. The Many Faces of Educational Consumerism. LC 77-8722. 240p. 1977. 21.95x o.p. (ISBN 0-669-01631-4). Lexington Bks.

Stark, John O. Pynchon's Fictions: Thomas Pynchon & the Literature of Information. LC 79-28466. x, 183p. 1980. 15.95x (ISBN 0-8214-0419-9, 82-83129). Ohio U Pr.

Stark, Leland A., ed. How to Live & Die with California Probate. pap. 9.95 (ISBN 0-87201-095-3). Gulf Pub.

Stark, Lewis M. Whitney Cookery Collection. rev. ed. 1959. pap. 3.00 o.p. (ISBN 0-87104-216-9). NY Pub Lib.

Stark, M., jt. auth. see Mostowski, J.

Stark, Myra, jt. ed. see Dean, Nancy.

Stark, Myra, jt. ed. see Murray, Janet H.

Stark, Paul & Kramer, Alex. Total Conditioning for Football: The Pitt Panther Way. 2nd ed. LC 82-81449. (Illus.). 152p. (Orig.). 1982. pap. 5.95 (ISBN 0-88011-075-9). Leisure Pr.

Stark, R., ed. Language Behaviour in Infancy & Early Childhood. 1981. 39.50 (ISBN 0-444-00627-3). Elsevier.

Stark, R. M. & Nichols, R. L. Civil Engineering System, Mathematical Foundation for Design. text ed. 36.50 (ISBN 0-07-060857-1, C); solutions manual 6.95 (ISBN 0-07-060859-8). McGraw.

Stark, Raymond. The Book of Aphrodisiacs. LC 80-6206. 212p. 1982. pap. 7.95 (ISBN 0-8128-6164-7). Stein & Day.

Stark, Richard. The Hunter. 1981. lib. bdg. 10.95 (ISBN 0-8398-2706-7, Gregg). G K Hall.

--The Man With the Getaway Face. 1981. lib. bdg. 10.95 (ISBN 0-8398-2707-5, Gregg). G K Hall.

--The Mourner. 1981. lib. bdg. 10.95 (ISBN 0-8398-2708-3, Gregg). G K Hall.

--The Outfit. 1981. lib. bdg. 10.95 (ISBN 0-8398-2710-5, Gregg). G K Hall.

--The Score. 1981. lib. bdg. 10.95 (ISBN 0-8398-2711-3, Gregg). G K Hall.

--The Seventh. 1981. lib. bdg. 10.95 (ISBN 0-8398-2737-7, Gregg). G K Hall.

--Stark Mysteries, 6 bks. 1981. Set. lib. bdg. 60.00 (ISBN 0-8398-2732-6, Gregg). G K Hall.

Stark, Richard, ed. How to Be Rich & Grow Richer. (Illus.). 120p. 1974. 39.15 o.p. (ISBN 0-913314-41-2). Am Classical Coll Pr.

Stark, Rodney & Foster, Bruce D. Wayward Shepards: Prejudice & the Protestant Clergy. 130p. pap. 6.95 (ISBN 0-686-95186-7). ADL.

Stark, Rodney & Glock, Charles Y. American Piety: The Nature of Religious Commitment. (Patterns of Religious Commitment: No. 1). 1968. 28.50x (ISBN 0-520-01210-0); pap. 2.65 (ISBN 0-520-01756-0, CAL197). U of Cal Pr.

Stark, Rodney, jt. auth. see Glock, Charles Y.

Stark, S. Returning to Work: A Planning Book. LC 82-14892. 208p. 1983. 7.95x (ISBN 0-07-060887-3). McGraw.

Stark, Sandra L., jt. auth. see Gainer, Harold N.

Stark, Stephen L. Conducting Community Surveys. (How to Ser.). 1976. pap. text ed. 1.50 o.s.i. (ISBN 0-87812-134-X). Pendell Pub.

Stark, Thomas. Distribution of Personal Income in the United Kingdom, 1949-1963. LC 72-160099. (Illus.). 1972. 37.50 (ISBN 0-521-08258-7). Cambridge U Pr.

Stark, Werner. Safeguards of the Social Bond: Ethos & Religion, Vol. IV. 250p. 1983. cloth 15.00 (ISBN 0-8232-1080-4); pap. 7.50 (ISBN 0-8232-1081-2). Fordham.

Starke, Frederick A., jt. auth. see Gray, Jerry L.

Starke, P. H. Abstract Automata. 1972. 36.25 (ISBN 0-444-10349-X, North-Holland); pap. 23.50 (ISBN 0-444-10354-6, North Holland). Elsevier.

Starker, Leopold A. The Desert. rev. ed. LC 80-52124. (Life Nature Library). PLB 13.40 (ISBN 0-8094-3851-8). Silver.

Starkey, J. Denbigh & Ross, Rockford. Fundamental Programming. 256p. 1982. pap. text ed. write for info. (ISBN 0-314-71810-9). West Pub.

--Fundamental Programming: FORTRAN. 352p. 1982. pap. text ed. write for info. (ISBN 0-314-71812-5). West Pub.

--Fundamental Programming: Pascal. 352p. 1982. pap. text ed. write for info. (ISBN 0-314-71811-7). West Pub.

Starkey, Otis P., et al. The Anglo-American Realm. 2nd ed. (Geography Ser.). (Illus.). 384p. 1975. text ed. 26.95 (ISBN 0-07-060872-5, C). McGraw.

Starkey, Roberta, jt. auth. see Divine, James.

Starkey, Ronald. An Introduction to Organic Chemistry: Study Guide & Solutions Manual. 1978. 13.50x (ISBN 0-8162-8391-5). Holden-Day.

Starkie, D., ed. Pricing & Cost Recovery in Long Distance Transport. 1982. lib. bdg. 39.50 (ISBN 90-247-2683-2, Pub. by Martinus Nijhoff). Kluwer Boston.

Starkie, Enid. Baudelaire. 1958. 12.50 o.p. (ISBN 0-8112-0387-5). New Directions.

Starkie, Walter. Raggle Taggle. (Illus.). 20.00 (ISBN 0-7195-1338-3). Transatlantic.

--Scholars & Gypsies: An Autobiography. (Illus.). 1963. 31.75x (ISBN 0-520-01205-4). U of Cal Pr.

Starkie, Walter, tr. see De Cervantes, Miguel.

Starkman, Mirian K., ed. see Swift, Jonathan.

Starkopf, Adam. There is Always Time to Die. 256p. 10.95 (ISBN 0-686-95091-7); pap. 5.95 (ISBN 0-686-99462-0). ADL.

Starks, Arthur E. Combined Concordances to the Scriptures. 1978. 29.95 (ISBN 0-8309-0255-4). Herald Hse.

Starks, Charles. Free Radical Telomerization. 1974. 55.00 (ISBN 0-12-663650-8). Acad Pr.

Starks, Christopher. Possession. (Orig.). 1983. pap. price not set (ISBN 0-449-12547-5, GM). Fawcett.

Starling, Grover. The Changing Environment of Business. LC 79-26814. 1980. text ed. 21.95x (ISBN 0-87872-251-3); instr's manual avail. Kent Pub Co.

Starling, Kenneth E. Fluid Thermodynamic Properties for Light Petroleum Systems. 270p. 1973. 34.95x (ISBN 0-87201-293-X). Gulf Pub.

Starling, Marion W. The Slave Narrative: Its Place in American History. 1981. lib. bdg. 28.50 (ISBN 0-8161-8459-3, Univ Bks). G K Hall.

Starling, Thomas. The Garlic Kid. LC 77-91896. 227p. 1978. pap. 5.95 autographed (ISBN 0-914864-01-7); pap. 3.95 not autographed. Spindrift.

Starmer, T., jt. ed. see Barker, J. S.

Starmore, Alice. Scandinavian Knitwear: Thirty Original Designs from Traditional Patterns. 128p. 1982. 39.00x (ISBN 0-686-82320-6, Pub. by Bell & Hyman England). State Mutual Bk.

Starn, Randolph, jt. auth. see Partridge, Loren.

Starnes, Kathleen M. Peter Abelard: His Place in History. LC 80-8298. 161p. 1981. lib. bdg. 19.75 (ISBN 0-8191-1510-X); pap. text ed. 9.50 (ISBN 0-8191-1511-8). U Pr of Amer.

Starobinski, Jean. Seventeen Eighty-Nine: The Emblems of Reason. Bray, Barbara, tr. LC 81-13135. Orig. Title: Mille Sept Cent Quatre-Vingt Dix-Neuf, les Emblemes De la Raison. (Illus.). 298p. (Fr.). 1982. 24.95x (ISBN 0-8139-0915-5). U Pr of Va.

Staron, Stanislaw, jt. ed. see Hilberg, Raul.

Starosciak, Jane. Entropy & the Speed of Light. 1982. pap. 7.50 (ISBN 0-686-38085-1). K Starosciak.

Starosciak, Jane, jt. ed. see Starosciak, Kenneth.

Starosciak, Kenneth & Starosciak, Jane, eds. Frank Lloyd Wright: A Bibliography Issued on the Occasion of the Destruction of the F. W. Little House. ltd. ed. 10.00 (ISBN 0-686-05288-9). K Starosciak.

Starosciak, Kenneth, ed. & intro. by see Melville, Herman.

Starr, Anne. Come Kiss a Stranger. 1982. pap. write for info. o.p. (ISBN 0-451-11360-8, AE1360, Sig). NAL.
--Hold Back Tomorrow. (Orig.). 1981. pap. 1.95 o.p. (ISBN 0-451-11033-1, AJ1033, Sig). NAL.
--A Time for Loving. (Adventures in Love Ser.: No. 27). 1982. pap. 1.75 (ISBN 0-451-11706-9, AE1706, Sig). NAL.
Starr, B. D. & Weiner, M. B. The Starr-Weiner Report on Sex & Sexuality in the Mature Years. 312p. 1982. pap. 5.95 (ISBN 0-07-060878-4). McGraw.
Starr, Bernard. The Psychology of School Adjustment: Readings. 1970. pap. text ed. 6.35 (ISBN 0-685-55639-5, 30250). Phila Bk Co.
Starr, Bernard D. & Goldstein, Harris A. Human Development & Behavior: Psychology in Nursing. LC 73-92205. 1975. text ed. 17.50 (ISBN 0-8261-1550-0). Springer Pub.
Starr, Bill. Border Angel. 1979. 5.95 o.p. (ISBN 0-533-03670-4). Vantage.
Starr, Cecie & Taggart, Ralph. Biology: The Unity & Diversity of Life. 2nd ed. 608p. 1981. text ed. 25.95x (ISBN 0-534-00930-1); wkbk. 8.95x (ISBN 0-534-00977-8). Wadsworth Pub.
Starr, Chauncey & Ritterbush, Philip C., eds. Science, Technology & the Human Prospect. (Pergamon Policy Studies). Date not set. 66.00 (ISBN 0-08-024650-8); leather bdg. 350.00 (ISBN 0-685-97190-2) (ISBN 0-08-024652-4). Pergamon. Postponed.
Starr, Chester G. Ancient Romans. (Illus.). 1971. 17.95x (ISBN 0-19-501455-3); pap. 9.95x (ISBN 0-19-501454-5). Oxford U Pr.
--Early Man: Prehistory & the Civilizations of the Ancient Near East. (Illus.). 1973. 17.95x (ISBN 0-19-501641-6); pap. 9.95x (ISBN 0-19-501640-8). Oxford U Pr.
--The Economic & Social Growth of Early Greece: 800--500 B.C. (Illus.). 1977. 19.95x (ISBN 0-19-502223-8). Oxford U Pr.
--The Economic & Social Growth of Early Greece, 800-500 B. C. (Illus.). 1977. pap. text ed. 6.95x (ISBN 0-19-502224-6). Oxford U Pr.
--A History of the Ancient World. 2nd ed. 1974. text ed. 29.95 o.p. (ISBN 0-19-501814-1); text ed. 14.95x o.p. (ISBN 0-19-501815-X). Oxford U Pr.
--A History of the Ancient World. 3rd ed. LC 81-22408. (Illus.). 768p. 1983. 29.95 (ISBN 0-19-503143-1); text ed. 19.95x (ISBN 0-19-503144-X). Oxford U Pr.
--The Roman Empire, Twenty-Seven B.C. Four Hundred Seventy-Six A.D. A Study in Survival. LC 81-22310. (Illus.). 224p. 1983. 17.95 (ISBN 0-19-503129-6); pap. 6.95x (ISBN 0-19-503130-X). Oxford U Pr.
Starr, Douglas P. How to Handle Speechwriting Assignments. LC 78-10843. 1978. pap. 3.95 (ISBN 0-87576-007-4). Pilot Bks.
Starr, Frederick. Headliners & Softliners: More Heat Than Light? "Themes & Sub-Themes in the Salt II Debate". LC 79-67157. (Papers on International Issues: No. 2). 1979. pap. 2.00 (ISBN 0-935082-01-8). Southern Ctr Intl Stud.
Starr, G. Australian Political Parties. LC 78-324684. 1978. pap. text ed. 12.95x o.p. (ISBN 0-85859-178-2, 00513). Heinemann Ed.
Starr, Hampton. Contemporary Illusions People Live by. (Essential Knowledge Library). 1979. 47.45 (ISBN 0-89266-170-4). Am Classical Coll Pr.
Starr, Herbert W. Elegy Written in a Country Churchyard - Thomas Gray. 1968. pap. text ed. 3.50x (ISBN 0-675-09563-8). Merrill.
Starr, Irving S., jt. auth. see Clark, Leonard H.
Starr, Ivan. Rituals of the Diviner. LC 80-53522. (Bibliotheca Mesopotamica Ser.: Vol. 12). 150p. 1983. write for info (ISBN 0-89003-063-4); pap. write for info (ISBN 0-89003-064-2). Undena Pubns.
Starr, John. Dark Side of the Dream. LC 81-21832. 576p. (Orig.). 1982. 15.95 (ISBN 0-446-51239-7). Warner Bks.
--The Dark Side of the Dream. 624p. 1983. pap. 3.95 (ISBN 0-446-30808-0). Warner Bks.
Starr, John B. & Dyer, Nancy A. Post-Liberation Works of Mao Zedong: A Bibliography & Index. LC 67-65707. (China Research Monographs: Special). 1976. pap. 7.50x (ISBN 0-912966-16-5). IEAS.
Starr, Joyce, jt. ed. see Novik, Nimrod.
Starr, Kevin. Americans & the California Dream. (Illus.). 1973. 19.95x (ISBN 0-19-501644-0). Oxford U Pr.
--California! LC 80-51092. (Illus.). 296p. (gr. 4-9). 1980. text ed. 16.00x (ISBN 0-87905-100-0). Peregrine Smith.
Starr, Kevin, ed. see Norris, Frank.
Starr, Louis M., jt. ed. see Mason, Elizabeth B.
Starr, M. K., jt. auth. see Bowen, E. K.
Starr, Martha H. & Hill, Elizabeth W., eds. The Jane Austen Calendar: Diary 1984. (Illus.). 132p. pap. 9.95 (ISBN 0-15-645968-X, Harv). HarBraceJ.
Starr, Martin K. Operations Management. LC 77-22692. (Illus.). 1978. ref. 26.95 (ISBN 0-13-637603-7). P-H.
Starr, Martin K. & Stein, Irving. The Practice of Management Science. (Illus.). 208p. 1976. 15.95 (ISBN 0-13-693630-X). P-H.
Starr, Martin K., jt. auth. see Dannebring, David D.
Starr, Martin K., jt. auth. see Miller, David W.
Starr, Paul. The Social Transformation of American Medicine. 1983. 24.95 (ISBN 0-465-07934-2). Basic.
Starr, Philip C. Economics: Principles in Action. 3rd ed. 1978. pap. 18.95x (ISBN 0-534-00911-5); wkbk. 8.95x (ISBN 0-534-00912-3). Wadsworth Pub.
Starr, R. H., ed. Child Abuse Prediction: Policy Implications. LC 82-1786. 256p. 1982. prof ref 24.50x (ISBN 0-88410-378-1). Ballinger Pub.
Starr, Richard. Woodworking with Kids. LC 82-60026. (Illus.). 216p. 1982. 18.95 (ISBN 0-918804-14-0, Dist. by Van Nostrand Reinhold). Taunton.
Starr, S. Frederick. Red & Hot: The Fate of Jazz in the Soviet Union. (Illus.). 300p. 1983. 16.95 (ISBN 0-19-503163-6). Oxford U Pr.
Starr, Victor P. Physics of Negative Viscosity Phenomena. LC 68-22768. (International Earth & Planetary Sciences Ser). (Illus.). 1968. text ed. 11.50 o.p. (ISBN 0-07-060875-X, C). McGraw.
Starr, Walter A., Jr. Starr's Guide to the John Muir Trail & the High Sierra Region. 12th rev. ed. Robinson, Douglas, ed. LC 67-25840. (Totebook Ser.). (Illus.). 224p. 1974. pap. 7.95 (ISBN 0-87156-172-7); map 1.95 (ISBN 0-87156-173-5). Sierra.
Starr, William. Electrical Wiring & Design: A Practical Approach. (Electronic Technology Ser.). 432p. 1983. text ed. 21.95 (ISBN 0-471-05131-4); write for info. tchr's. ed. (ISBN 0-471-89527-X). Wiley.
Starr, William J. & Devine, George F., eds. Music Scores Omnibus, Vol. 1. 2nd ed. 430p. 1974. pap. text ed. 22.95 (ISBN 0-13-608349-8). P-H.
Starre, H. van Der see International Symposium on Olfaction & Taste, 7th, the Netherlands 1980.
Starrett, Vincent. The Private Life of Sherlock Holmes. rev. ed. LC 81-82191. (Illus.). 150p. Date not set. write for info. (ISBN 0-934468-08-7). Gaslight. Postponed.
Starry, Donn A. Armored Combat in Vietnam. LC 80-69325. 1981. 15.00 (ISBN 0-672-52673-5). Bobbs.
Start, C., jt. auth. see Newsholme, E. A.
Start, L. E., jt. auth. see Haddon, A. C.
Startsev, V. G. Primate Models of Human Neurogenic Disorders. Bowden, D. M., tr. LC 76-21626. 1976. 19.95x o.p. (ISBN 0-470-15193-5). Halsted Pr.
Startt, James D. Journalism's Unofficial Ambassador: A Biography of Edward Price Bell 1869-1943. LC 79-17071. (Illus.). xiii, 260p. 1980. 17.95x (ISBN 0-8214-0415-6, 82-83061). Ohio U Pr.
Startup, Richard. The University Teacher & His World. 1979. text ed. 33.25x (ISBN 0-566-00295-7). Gower Pub Ltd.
Startup, Richard & Whittaker, Elwyn T. Introducing Social Statistics. (Studies in Sociology). 1982. text ed. 28.50x (ISBN 0-04-310012-0); pap. text ed. 12.50x (ISBN 0-04-310013-9). Allen Unwin.
Starworth, I. J. Build Your Own World. 36p. 1982. 14.95 (ISBN 0-399-50652-7, Perige). Putnam Pub Group.
Starzhinskii, V. M., jt. auth. see Yakubovich, V. A.
Stasack, Edward, jt. auth. see Cox, Halley J.
Stasch, Stanley F. Systems Analysis for Marketing Planning & Control. 552p. 1971. pap. 14.50x (ISBN 0-673-07724-1). Scott F.
Stasheff, Edward, et al. The Television Program: Its Direction & Production. 5th ed. 256p. 1976. 12.95 (ISBN 0-8090-9181-X); pap. 7.95 o.p. (ISBN 0-8090-1378-9). Hill & Wang.
Stashower, Gloria, compiled by. To a Delightful Daughter. 1979. pap. 4.95 boxed o.p. (ISBN 0-8378-5029-0). Gibson.
Stasi, Lawrence Di see Di Stasi, Lawrence.
Stasi, Linda. Simply Beautiful: Quick Tips & Pro Tricks for Looking Great in No Time Flat. (Illus.). 128p. 1983. pap. 4.95 (ISBN 0-312-72591-4); pap. 49.50 ppk of 10 (ISBN 0-312-72592-2). St Martin.
Stasiowski, Frank & Burstein, David. Project Management for the Design Professional. (Illus.). 160p. 1982. 24.95 (ISBN 0-8230-7434-X, Whitney Lib). Watson-Guptill.
Stasny, Charles & Tyrnauer, Gabrielle. Who Rules the Joint? A Study of the Changing Political Culture of Maximum-Security Prisons in America. LC 78-14157. 256p. 1982. 26.95x (ISBN 0-669-02661-1). Lexington Bks.
Stason, Edwin B. & Estep, Samuel D. Atoms & the Law, 2 bks. (Michigan Legal Publications Ser.). xxvii, 1512p. 1982. Repr. of 1959 ed. lib. bdg. 55.00 (ISBN 0-89941-176-2). W. S. Hein.
Stasov, V. Russian Peasant Design Motifs for Needleworkers & Craftsmen. (Pictorial Archives Ser.). (Illus.). 32p. (Orig.). 1976. pap. 2.00 (ISBN 0-486-23235-2). Dover.
Stassinopoulos, Arianna. Maria Callas: The Woman Behind the Legend. 1981. 16.95 o.s.i. (ISBN 0-671-25583-5). S&S.
Stastny, F. Glucocorticoids & Brain Development. (Monographs in Neural Sciences: Vol. 9). (Illus.). viii, 200p. 1983. 54.00 (ISBN 3-8055-3626-7). S Karger.
Stasz, Clarice. The American Nightmare: Why Inequality Persists. LC 80-6191. 233p. 1983. pap. 7.95 (ISBN 0-8052-0709-0). Schocken.
Staszak, E. R. Vacuum-Formed Model Aircraft Construction. Angle, Burr, ed. (Illus., Orig.). 1983. pap. price not set (ISBN 0-89024-047-7). Kalmbach.
Staszewski, Jerzy. Epidemiology of Cancer of Selected Sites. LC 74-1096. 300p. 1975. prof ref 25.00 o.p. (ISBN 0-88410-114-2). Ballinger Pub.
Staszkow, Ronald. Developmental Mathematics: Basic Arithmetic with a Brief Introduction to Algebra. 448p. 1982. pap. text ed. 16.50 (ISBN 0-8403-2822-2). Kendall-Hunt.
Stat, Bob & Stat, Susan. Complete Chocolate Chip Cookie Book. (Illus.). 128p. 1982. pap. 4.95 (ISBN 0-440-01273-2, Banbury). Dell.
Stat, Susan, jt. auth. see Stat, Bob.
State Bar of Texas Council of the Family Law Section. Texas Family Practice Manual. Rasor, Reba G. & Smith, Donald R., eds. LC 76-6773. 928p. 1976. includes supplement s 75.00 (ISBN 0-938160-15-X, 6338). State Bar TX.
State Bar of Texas Legal Forms Committee, ed. Legal Form Manual for Real Estate Transactions. rev. ed. 231p. 1976. includes supplement 55.00 (ISBN 0-938160-11-7, 2434). State Bar TX.
State Bar of Texas Pattern Jury Charges Committee. Texas Pattern Jury Charges: Vol. 1. LC 78-13954. 290p. 1969. includes supplement 50.00 (ISBN 0-938160-00-1, 6307). State Bar TX.
--Texas Pattern Jury Charges: 1973 Cumulative Supplement, Vol. 1. LC 78-13954. 91p. 1973. pap. 6.50 (ISBN 0-938160-01-X, 6316). State Bar TX.
State Bar of Texas Professional Efficiency & Economic Research Committee. Texas Probate System: Dependent Administration & Procedures in Lieu of Administration. Chrisman, P. Oswin & Brill, James E., eds. 429p. 1974. One System. 60.00 o.p. (ISBN 0-938160-13-3, 6319); Two Systems. 100.00 o.p. (ISBN 0-938160-13-3). State Bar TX.
State Bar of Texas Real Estate, Probate & Trust Law Sec. Texas Estate Administration. Saunders, Charles A., ed. 1054p. 1975. includes supplement 60.00 (ISBN 0-938160-06-0, 6313). State Bar TX.
State Industrial Directories Corp. Indiana State Industrial Directory, 1981. Date not set. pap. price not set o.s.i. (ISBN 0-89910-046-5). State Indus Dir.
--Kentucky State Industrial Directory, Nineteen Eighty-One. Date not set. pap. price not set o.s.i. (ISBN 0-89910-042-2). State Indus Dir.
--Louisiana State Industrial Directory, Nineteen Eighty-One. Date not set. pap. price not set o.s.i. (ISBN 0-89910-047-3). State Indus Dir.
--Michigan State Industrial Directory, Nineteen Eighty-One. Date not set. pap. price not set o.s.i. (ISBN 0-89910-048-1). State Indus Dir.
--Mississippi State Industrial Directory, Nineteen Eighty-One. Date not set. pap. price not set o.s.i. (ISBN 0-89910-050-3). State Indus Dir.
--Vermont State Industrial Directory, Nineteen Eighty-One. Date not set. pap. price not set o.s.i. (ISBN 0-89910-043-0). State Indus Dir.
--Virginia State Industrial Directory, Nineteen Eighty-One. Date not set. pap. price not set o.s.i. (ISBN 0-89910-044-9). State Indus Dir.
State Library, Pretoria, ed. South African National Bibliography, 1979. 747p. 1979. 66.50x o.p. (ISBN 0-8002-2755-7). Intl Pubns Serv.
--South African National Bibliography, 1981. LC 50-57958. 822p. 1981. 66.50x (ISBN 0-7989-0070-9). Intl Pubns Serv.
State of California, Office of Appropriate Technology. Commonsense Wind Energy. 128p. (Orig.). 1983. pap. 8.95 (ISBN 0-931790-38-7). Brick Hse Pub.
Stateham, B. R. Banners of the Sa'yen. (Science Fiction Ser.). 1981. pap. 2.25 o.p. (ISBN 0-87997-636-5, UE1636). DAW Bks.
Staten, H. Jacqueline. The Power of Meditation & Prayer. 1982. 7.95 (ISBN 0-533-04948-2). Vantage.
Statera, Gianni. Death of a Utopia: the Development & Decline of Student Movements in Europe. 1975. 19.95x (ISBN 0-19-501795-1). Oxford U Pr.
States, Bert O. The Shape of Paradox: An Essay on Waiting for Godot. (Quantum Bk.). 1978. 17.50x (ISBN 0-520-03549-6); pap. 2.65 (ISBN 0-520-03572-0). U of Cal Pr.
Statham, Frances P. Phoenix Rising. 1983. pap. 5.95 (ISBN 0-449-90010-X, Columbine). Fawcett.
Statham, Jane, jt. ed. see ReQua, Eloise.
Stationery Office (Great Britain) Annual Catalogues of British Official & Parliamentary Publications 1910 to 1919. 2042p. 1975. Repr. lib. bdg. 85.00x (ISBN 0-914146-20-3). Somerset Hse.
--Annual Catalogues of British Official & Parliamentary Publications 1894 to 1909. 3076p. 1975. Repr. lib. bdg. 120.00x (ISBN 0-914146-19-X). Somerset Hse.
Statisches Zentralamt. Statistisches Handbuch fur Die Republik Osterreich, 1982. 33rd ed. (Illus.). 662p. (Orig., Ger.). pap. 57.50 (ISBN 0-8002-3048-5). Intl Pubns Serv.
Statistisches Zentralamt, Austria, ed. Statistisches Handbuch fur die Republik Osterreich, 1981. 32nd ed. (Illus.). 668p. (Ger.). pap. 57.50x (ISBN 0-8002-3067-1). Intl Pubns Serv.
Statius. Silvae. Phillimore, J. S., ed. (Oxford Classical Texts). 1905. 13.95x o.p. (ISBN 0-19-814631-0). Oxford U Pr.
Statler, Oliver. Japanese Inn: A Reconstruction of the Past. LC 82-4955. (Illus.). 381p. 1982. pap. 8.95 (ISBN 0-8248-0818-5). UH Pr.
--Japanese Pilgrimage. (Illus.). 288p. 1983. 17.95 (ISBN 0-688-01890-4). Morrow.
Staton, Knofel. Check Your Homelife. Sparks, Judith A., ed. 176p. (Orig.). 1983. pap. 4.95 (ISBN 0-87239-649-5, 39973). Standard Pub.
--Check Your Life in Christ. Root, Orrin, ed. 160p. (Orig.). 1983. pap. 2.95 (ISBN 0-87239-666-5, 41018). Standard Pub.
--Check Your Morality. Underwood, Jon, ed. 194p. (Orig.). 1983. pap. 3.95 (ISBN 0-87239-630-4, 39971). Standard Pub.
--The Servant's Call. LC 75-7462. (New Life Ser.). (Illus.). 96p. 1976. pap. 1.95 (ISBN 0-87239-051-9, 40024). Standard Pub.
--Spiritual Gifts for Christians Today. 118p. (Orig.). 1973. pap. 2.95 (ISBN 0-89900-134-3). College Pr Pub.
--Thirteen Lessons on I, II, III John. LC 80-69722. (Bible Student Study Guide Ser.). 149p. 1980. pap. 2.95 (ISBN 0-89900-169-6). College Pr Pub.
--What to Do Till Jesus Comes. LC 81-14594. 112p. 1983. pap. 2.25 (ISBN 0-87239-481-6, 41016). Standard Pub.
Staton, Natalie M. Come Back Tomorrow. 1977. 4.50 o.p. (ISBN 0-533-02770-5). Vantage.
Staton, Thomas F. How to Study. 1959. pap. text ed. 2.25 (ISBN 0-913476-07-2). Am Guidance.
Staton, Wesley M., jt. auth. see Cornacchia, Harold J.
Statsky, jt. auth. see Singer.
Statsky, William P. Domestic Relations: Law & Skills. LC 78-7303. (Paralegal Ser.). 537p. 1978. text ed. 22.95 (ISBN 0-8299-2007-2). West Pub.
--Legal Research, Writing & Analysis. 2nd ed. (Illus.). 200p. 1982. pap. text ed. 11.95 (ISBN 0-314-65180-2). West Pub.
Statt, David. Dictionary of Psychology. 1982. pap. 4.76i (ISBN 0-06-463553-8, EH-553). Har-Row.
Staub, George E. & Kent, Leona M. The Paraprofessional in the Treatment of Alcoholism: A New Profession. 184p. 1979. 11.00x (ISBN 0-398-02860-5). C C Thomas.
Staubesand, Jochen, jt. ed. see Ferner, Helmut.
Staubus, George J. A Theory of Accounting to Investors. LC 61-7516. 1971. Repr. of 1961 ed. text ed. 13.00 (ISBN 0-914348-10-8). Scholars Bk.
St Aubyn, F. C. Charles Peguy. (World Authors Ser.). 1977. lib. bdg. 15.95 (ISBN 0-8057-6304-X, Twayne). G K Hall.
Staudacher, Joseph H., jt. auth. see Hellman, Hugo E.
Stauder, Jack. Majangir: Ecology & Society of a Southwest Ethiopian People. (Cambridge Studies in Social Anthropology: No. 5). (Illus.). 1971. 24.95 (ISBN 0-521-08094-0). Cambridge U Pr.
Staudohar, Paul D., jt. auth. see Yoder, Dale.
Staudt, F. J., jt. ed. see Van Loon, J. H.
Staudt, Kathleen & Jacquette, Jane, eds. Women in Developing Countries: A Policy Focus. (Women & Politics, Vol. 2, No. 4). 150p. 1983. text ed. 19.95 (ISBN 0-86656-226-5, B226). Haworth Pr.
Staudt, Thomas A. & Taylor, Donald. Managerial Introduction to Marketing. 3rd ed. (Illus.). 576p. 1976. 24.95x o.p. (ISBN 0-13-550186-5). P-H.
Staufenberger, Richard A., ed. see Police Foundation.
Stauffer, Donald, ed. see Coleridge, Samuel T.
Stauffer, Donald A. English Biography Before Seventeen Hundred. 392p. Repr. of 1930 ed. lib. bdg. 25.00x (ISBN 0-87991-065-8). Porcupine Pr.
Stauffer, Francis H. Queer, the Quaint, the Quizzical. LC 68-22052. 1968. Repr. of 1882 ed. 30.00x (ISBN 0-8103-3096-2). Gale.
Stauffer, Helen W. Mari Sandoz: Story Catcher of the Plains. LC 81-22014. (Illus.). xiv, 322p. 1982. 22.50 (ISBN 0-8032-4121-6); pap. 10.95 (ISBN 0-8032-9134-5, BB822, Bison). U of Nebr Pr.
Stauffer, Jay R., Jr., jt. ed. see Hocutt, Charles H.
Stauffer, Richard E. Stauffer-Stouffer-Stover & Related Families. LC 77-78908. 1977. 14.95 o.p. (ISBN 0-9606604-0-2). R E Stauffer.
Stauffer, Robert B. The Development of an Interest Group: The Philippine Medical Association. 1966. 4.00x (ISBN 0-8248-0436-8). UH Pr.
Stauffer, Russell G. The Language-Experience Approach to the Teaching of Reading. 2nd ed. (Illus.). 1980. pap. text ed. 16.50 scp (ISBN 0-06-046409-7, HarpC). Har-Row.
Stauffer, Russell G., et al. Diagnosis, Correction, & Prevention of Reading Disabilities. 1978. text ed. 17.95 scp (ISBN 0-06-046418-6, HarpC). Har-Row.
Stauffer, Thomas M. Assessing Sponsored Research Programs. 1977. 5.50 o.p. (ISBN 0-8268-1207-4). ACE.
Stauffer, Thomas M., ed. Competition & Cooperation in American Higher Education. 1981. 10.50 o.p. (ISBN 0-8268-1450-6). ACE.
Stauth, Cameron. New Approach to Cancer. 1982. 6.95x (ISBN 0-942686-01-2). Cancer Control Soc.
Stave, Bruce M. The New Deal & the Last Hurrah: Pittsburgh Machine Politics. LC 78-93863. 1970. 14.95 o.p. (ISBN 0-8229-3200-8). U of Pittsburgh Pr.
Stave, Bruce M. & Stave, Sondra A. Urban Bosses, Machines, & Progressive Reformers. 2nd. ed. 178p. (Orig.). Date not set. pap. 5.95 o.p. (ISBN 0-89874-119-X). Krieger.
Stave, Sondra A., jt. auth. see Stave, Bruce M.
Staveley, A. L. Memories of Gurdjieff. 1978. 7.95 (ISBN 0-89756-025-6). Two Rivers.
--Themes. xvi, 100p. 1982. 20.00x o.p. (ISBN 0-89756-010-8). Two Rivers.

Stavely, A. L. Where is Beradino? 96p. 1982. 8.95 (ISBN 0-89756-011-6). Two Rivers.

Staver, Allen E., jt. auth. see From, Lester D.

Stavisky, Aron Y. Shakespeare & the Victorians: Roots of Modern Criticism. LC 68-31374. (Illus.). 1969. 9.95x o.p. (ISBN 0-8061-0822-3). U of Okla Pr.

Stavitsky, Gail. Henry Koerner: From Vienna to Pittsburgh. (Illus.). 85p. (Orig.). 1983. pap. 12.95 (ISBN 0-88039-005-0). Mus Art Carnegie.

Stavrakas, Nick & Allen, Keith, eds. Studies in Topology. 1975. 60.00 (ISBN 0-12-663450-5). Acad Pr.

Stavrianos, Leften. Man's Past & Present: A Global History. 2nd ed. LC 74-28215. (Illus.). 576p. 1975. pap. text ed. 19.95 (ISBN 0-13-552091-6). P-H.

--The World Since Fifteen Hundred. 4th ed. (Illus.). 528p. 1982. 16.95 (ISBN 0-13-968164-7). P-H.

Stavropoulos, C. Partakers of Divine Nature. 1976. pap. 3.95 (ISBN 0-937032-09-3). Light&Life Pub Co MN.

Stavrou, Nikolaos A. Edvard Kardelj: The Historical Roots of Non-Alignment. LC 80-5251. 95p. 1980. pap. text ed. 6.75 (ISBN 0-8191-1066-3). U Pr of Amer.

Stavroulakis, P., ed. Interference Analysis of Communication Systems. LC 80-18464. 1980. 38.95 (ISBN 0-87942-135-5). Inst Electrical.

Stavroulakis, Peter. Interference Analysis of Communication Systems. LC 80-18464. 424p. 1980. 38.95x (ISBN 0-471-08674-6, Pub. by Wiley-Interscience); pap. 24.95x (ISBN 0-471-08673-8, Pub. by Wiley-Interscience). Wiley.

Staw, Barry. Psychological Foundations of Organizational Behavior. 2nd ed. 1983. pap. text ed. 15.95x (ISBN 0-673-16005-X). Scott F.

Staw, Barry & Cummings, L. L., eds. Research in Organizational Behavior, Vol. 4. 425p. 1981. 45.00 (ISBN 0-89232-147-4). Jai Pr.

Staw, Barry, jt. ed. see Cummings, L. L.

Staw, Barry H., ed. Research in Organizational Behavior, Vol. 1. 1979. lib. bdg. 42.50 (ISBN 0-89232-045-1). Jai Pr.

Staw, Barry M. & Salancik, Gerald R. New Directions in Organizational Behavior. LC 82-9953. 314p. 1982. Repr. of 1977 ed. 18.50 (ISBN 0-89874-528-4). Krieger.

Staw, Barry M., ed. Psychological Foundations of Organizational Behavior. LC 76-62995. 1977. pap. text ed. 15.50x (ISBN 0-673-16134-X). Scott F.

Staw, Barry M. & Cummings, Larry L., eds. Research in Organizational Behavior, Vol. 2. (Orig.). 1980. lib. bdg. 42.50 (ISBN 0-89232-099-0). Jai Pr.

Stead, Betty A. Women in Management. (Illus.). 1978. 18.95 (ISBN 0-13-961730-2); pap. text ed. 14.95 (ISBN 0-13-961722-1). P-H.

Stead, Dom J., tr. see St. Maximus the Confessor.

Stead, Evelyn S. & Warren, Gloria K. Low-Fat Cookery. new, rev. ed. 1977. pap. 6.95 (ISBN 0-07-060903-9, SP). McGraw.

Stead, Philip J., ed. Pioneers in Policing. LC 75-14556. (Ser. in Criminology, Law Enforcement & Social Problems: No. 213). (Illus.). 1978. 20.00x (ISBN 0-87585-213-0); pap. 9.00x (ISBN 0-87585-803-1). Patterson Smith.

Steadman, David W. Abraham van Diepenbeeck: Seventeenth-Century Flemish Painter. Harris, Ann S., ed. LC 82-8423. (Studies in Baroque Art History: No. 5). 204p. 1982. 39.95 (ISBN 0-8357-1352-0, Pub. by UMI Res Pr). Univ Microfilms.

Steadman, John. Nature into Myth: Medieval & Renaissance Moral Symbols. (Studies in Language & Literature Ser.: No. 1). 1979. text ed. 20.00x o.p. (ISBN 0-391-00752-1). Duquesne.

Steadman, John M. Disembodied Laughter: Troilus & the Apotheosis Tradition. 1972. 28.50x (ISBN 0-520-02047-2). U of Cal Pr.

Steadman, Mimi. One Hundred Inns in Maine. 2nd ed. 224p. 1982. pap. 8.95 (ISBN 0-89272-155-3, 431). Down East.

Steadman, P. Energy, Environment & Building. LC 74-21715. (Cambridge Urban & Architectural Studies: No. 3). (Illus.). 294p. 1975. 39.50 (ISBN 0-521-20694-4); pap. 13.95 (ISBN 0-521-09926-9). Cambridge U Pr.

--The Evolution of Designs. LC 78-18255. (Cambridge Urban & Architectural Studies: No. 5). 37.50 (ISBN 0-521-22302-4). Cambridge U Pr.

Steadman, Philip, jt. auth. see March, Lionel.

Steadman, Ralph. The Jelly Book. LC 73-99918. (Illus.). 32p. (ps-3). 5.75 (ISBN 0-87592-027-6). Scroll Pr.

Steady, Filomina C. Women in Africa. 256p. 1983. pap. 8.95 (ISBN 0-87073-221-8). Schenkman.

Steakley, Douglas. Holloware Techniques. (Illus.). 1979. 15.00 o.p. (ISBN 0-8230-2322-2). Watson-Guptill.

Steane, J. B. Tennyson. LC 75-78854. (Literary Critiques Ser.). (Illus., Orig.). 1969. lib. bdg. 4.95 o.p. (ISBN 0-668-01946-8). Arco.

Steane, J. B., ed. see Jonson, Ben.

Stearn, Colin W., et al. Geological Evolution of North America. 3rd ed. LC 78-8124. 566p. 1979. text ed. 30.95 (ISBN 0-471-07252-4). Wiley.

Stearn, Jess. Power of Alpha Thinking. 1977. pap. 2.50 (ISBN 0-451-11316-0, AE1316, Sig). NAL.

--The Search for a Soul: Taylor Caldwell's Psychic Lives. LC 72-84945. 336p. 1973. 7.95 o.p. (ISBN 0-385-02563-7). Doubleday.

Stearn, Jess & Geller, Larry. The Truth About Elvis. 288p. (Orig.). 1980. pap. 2.50 o.s.i. (ISBN 0-515-05154-3). Jove Pubns.

Stearn, Jess & Thompson, Alec. How to Cure Your Own Aching Back. Friedman, Robert, ed. (Illus.). 208p. (Orig.). 1983. pap. 6.95 (ISBN 0-89865-178-6). Donning Co.

Stearn, Jess, jt. auth. see Caldwell, Taylor.

Stearn, Jesse. Adventures into the Psychic. 1971. pap. 1.50 o.p. (ISBN 0-451-07822-5, W7822, Sig). NAL.

Stearn, Kelly. Consequences. 322p. 1980. 11.95 o.p. (ISBN 0-312-16269-3). St Martin.

Stearn, W. T. The Natural History Museum at South Kensington: A History of the British Museum (Natural History) 1753-1980. (Illus.). 350p. 1981. 37.50x (ISBN 0-434-73600-7). Sabbot-Natural Hist Bks.

Stearn, W. T., jt. auth. see Smith, A. W.

Stearn, William T., ed. Humbolt, Bonpland, Kunth & Tropical American Botany. 1968. pap. 16.00 (ISBN 3-7682-0539-8). Lubrecht & Cramer.

Stearns, Betty & Degen, Clara, eds. Careers in Music. rev. ed. LC 76-150516. (Illus.). 1980. pap. text ed. 2.00 (ISBN 0-918196-00-0). American Music.

Stearns, Bill. From Rock Bottom to Mountaintop. 1979. pap. 3.95 (ISBN 0-88207-580-2). Victor Bks.

--If the World Fits, You're the Wrong Size. 1981. pap. 3.50 (ISBN 0-88207-588-8). Victor Bks.

Stearns, Harold T. Geology of the State of Hawaii. 2nd ed. (Illus.). 1983. 18.95 (ISBN 0-87015-234-3). Pacific Bks.

Stearns, Jean. The Federalist Without Tears. 178p. 1977. pap. text ed. 6.25 (ISBN 0-8191-0106-0). U Pr of Amer.

Stearns, John, jt. auth. see Hinman, Steve.

Stearns, Louis W. Sea Urchin Development: Cellular & Molecular Aspects. LC 73-18054. 352p. 1974. text ed. 51.00 (ISBN 0-12-787488-7). Acad Pr.

Stearns, M. W. Neoplasms of the Colon, Rectum, & Anus. (Memorial Sloane Kettering Cancer Center Ser.). 206p. 1980. 40.00 (ISBN 0-471-05924-2, Pub. by Wiley Med). Wiley.

Stearns, Marshall W. Story of Jazz. 1956. 19.95x (ISBN 0-19-500115-X). Oxford U Pr.

--Story of Jazz. (Illus.). 1970. pap. 9.95 (ISBN 0-19-501269-0, GB). Oxford U Pr.

Stearns, Peter N. European Society in Upheaval: Social History Since 1750. 2nd ed. 416p. 1975. pap. text ed. 13.95x (ISBN 0-02-416210-8). Macmillan.

--Lives of Labor: Work in a Maturing Industrial Society. LC 74-28298. 1975. text ed. 39.50x (ISBN 0-8419-0192-9). Holmes & Meier.

--Old Age in Preindustrial Society. LC 81-6874. 250p. 1983. 27.50x (ISBN 0-8419-0645-9). Holmes & Meier.

Stearns, Robert, jt. auth. see Klein, Michael R.

Stearns, Robert, et al. Constructions. (Illus.). 1982. cancelled (ISBN 0-917562-18-6). Contemp Arts.

--Dynamix. (Illus.). 55p. 1982. 10.00 (ISBN 0-917562-20-8). Contemp Arts.

Stebbens, Theodore E., Jr., jt. auth. see Gerdts, William H.

Stebbing, Peter, tr. from Ger. see Koch, Elisabeth & Wagner, Gerard.

Stebbing, Rita, tr. see Steiner, Rudolf.

Stebbings, R. F. & Dunning, F. B., eds. Rydberg States of Atoms & Molecules. LC 82-1181. (Illus.). 500p. Date not set. price not set (ISBN 0-521-24823-X). Cambridge U Pr.

Stebbins, G. Ledyard. Processes of Organic Evolution. 3rd ed. (Illus.). 1977. pap. text ed. 14.95 (ISBN 0-13-723452-X). P-H.

Stebbins, Madeline, tr. see Couer de Jesus d' Elbee, Jean du.

Stebbins, Natalie & Barbaresi, Sara M. How to Raise & Train a Doberman Pinscher. (Illus.). pap. 2.95 (ISBN 0-87666-282-3, DS1013). TFH Pubns.

Stebbins, Richard P. & Amoia, Alba, eds. The World This Year 1972: Supplement to the Political Handbook & Atlas of the World 1970. 1972. 9.95 o.p. (ISBN 0-671-21288-5). S&S.

Stebbins, Robert A. Commitment to Deviance: The Nonprofessional Criminal in the Community. LC 75-95504. (Contributions in Sociology Ser.: No. 5). 1971. lib. bdg. 25.00x (ISBN 0-8371-2339-9, STD/); pap. 4.95 (ISBN 0-8371-8927-6). Greenwood.

Stebbins, Robert C. Amphibians of Western North America. 1951. 45.00x o.s.i. (ISBN 0-520-01212-7). U of Cal Pr.

--Reptiles & Amphibians of the San Francisco Bay Region. (California Natural History Guides: No. 3). (Illus.). 1959. 14.95x o.p. (ISBN 0-520-03100-8). U of Cal Pr.

Stebbins, Robert L. & Walheim, Lance. Western Fruit, Berries & Nuts: How to Select, Grow & Enjoy. (Illus.). 192p. (Orig.). pap. 7.95 (ISBN 0-89586-078-3). H P Bks.

Stebbins, Robert L., jt. auth. see MacCaskey, Michael.

Steben, Ralph E. & Bell, Sam. Track & Field: An Administrative Approach to the Science of Coaching. LC 77-2001. 1978. text ed. 28.95 (ISBN 0-471-02546-1). Wiley.

Stechow, Wolfgang. Breugel. (Library of Great Painters). (Illus.). 158p. 40.00 o.p. (ISBN 0-8109-0045-9). Abrams.

Steck, Allen, jt. auth. see Roper, Steve.

Steck, Allen & Roper, Steve, eds. Ascent 1980: The Mountaineering Experience in Word & Image. LC 80-13855. (Illus.). 272p. (Orig.). 1980. pap. 14.95 (ISBN 0-87156-240-5). Sierra.

Steckel, Clyde J. Theology & Ethics of Behavior Modification. LC 79-62910. 1979. pap. text ed. 9.75 (ISBN 0-8191-0718-2). U Pr of Amer.

Steckel, R. & Kagan, Robert A., eds. Recent Advances in Cancer Diagnosis. 1982. 34.50 o.p. (ISBN 0-8089-1451-0). Grune.

Steckel, Richard J. & Kagan, A. Robert. Diagnosis & Staging of Cancer: A Radiologic Approach. LC 76-4250. (Illus.). 400p. 1976. text ed. 26.50 o.p. (ISBN 0-7216-8579-X). Saunders.

Steckel, Robert C. Profitable Telephone Sales Operations. 143p. 1976. 15.00 (ISBN 0-686-98054-9). Telecom Lib.

Stecken, Fritz. Training the Horse & Rider. LC 72-2706. (Illus.). 1976. 9.95 (ISBN 0-668-03786-5). Arco.

Stecker, Elinor. How to Create & Use High Contrast Images, Vol. 13. 160p. 1982. pap. 9.95 (ISBN 0-89586-143-7). H P Bks.

Steckler, Doug, jt. auth. see Oberman, Margaret.

Steckman & Sklarew. Amusettes. (Illus.). (gr. 7-9). 1973. pap. text ed. 3.95 (ISBN 0-88345-185-9, 18082). Regents Pub.

Steckmesser, Kent L. Western Outlaws: The "Good Badman" in Fact, Film & Folklore. 170p. Date not set. 17.95 (ISBN 0-941690-07-5); pap. 10.95 (ISBN 0-941690-08-3). Regina Bks.

--Westward Movement: A Short History. LC 68-55275. (Illus.). 1969. text ed. 28.95 (ISBN 0-07-060915-2, C). McGraw.

Steckmest, F. W. Corporate Performance: The Key to Public Trust. LC 81-8347. 1982. 18.95 (ISBN 0-07-009306-7). McGraw.

Stedman, Edmund C., ed. see Poe, Edgar Allan.

Stedman, John C., jt. auth. see Neumeyer, Fredrik.

Stedman, Jon, jt. auth. see Foster, Lewis.

Stedman, Judith, jt. ed. see Jerse, Dorothy W.

Stedman, Myrtle. Adobe Architecture. Smith, James C., Jr., ed. LC 73-77322. (Illus.). 1978. pap. 4.25 (ISBN 0-913270-12-1). Sunstone Pr.

--Adobe Fireplaces. rev. ed. Smith, James C., Jr., ed. LC 77-78520. (Illus., Orig.). 1977. pap. 2.50 (ISBN 0-913270-32-6). Sunstone Pr.

Stedman, Preston. The Symphony. (Illus.). 1979. ref. ed. 20.95 (ISBN 0-13-880062-6). P-H.

Stedman, Ray C. Authentic Christianity. (Orig.). pap. 1.75 o.s.i. (ISBN 0-89129-249-7). Jove Pubns.

--Folk Psalms of Faith. LC 72-90405. 1973. pap. 2.95 o.p. (ISBN 0-8307-0450-7, S264-1-29). Regal.

Stedman, William. A Guide to Public Speaking. 2nd ed. (Illus.). 208p. 1981. pap. text ed. 13.95 (ISBN 0-13-370619-2). P-H.

Stedman-Jones, Gareth, jt. ed. see Samuel, Raphael.

Stedwell, Paki. Vaulting: Gymnastics on Horseback. LC 79-11556. (Illus.). 128p. (gr. 7 up). 1980. PLB 7.79 o.p. (ISBN 0-671-34023-9). Messner.

Stee, Ethard W. van see Van Stee, Ethard W.

Steed, S. Paul, jt. auth. see Van Orden, Naola.

Steedman, Ian. Marx After Sraffa. 1978. 17.50 o.p. (ISBN 0-902308-49-1, Pub by Verso); pap. 6.95 (ISBN 0-8052-7112-0). Schocken.

Steedman, Ian, ed. Fundamental Issues in Trade Theory. 1979. 30.00x (ISBN 0-312-31035-8). St Martin.

Steedman, James C., jt. auth. see Reynolds, Charles E.

Steeds, W., jt. auth. see Newton, K.

Steefel, Lawrence D., Jr. The Position of Duchamp's Glass in the Development of His Art. LC 76-23647. (Outstanding Dissertations in the Fine Arts Ser.). 1977. lib. bdg. 63.00x o.s.i. (ISBN 0-8240-2730-2). Garland Pub.

Steegmuller, Francis, ed. Your Isadora: The Love Story of Isadora Duncan & Gordon Craig. LC 74-5178. (Illus.). 1974. 15.00 (ISBN 0-87104-256-8). NY Pub Lib.

Steegmuller, Francis, ed. & tr. see Flaubert, Gustave.

Steegmuller, Francis, tr. see Flaubert, Gustave.

Steel, Catherine M. & Hochman, Janice M. Assertion Skill Training: A Group Procedure for High School Women. 63p. Date not set. 3.75 (ISBN 0-686-36418-X, 72053); nonmembers 4.50 (ISBN 0-686-37312-X). Am Personnel.

Steel, Danielle. Love: Poems by Danielle Steel. (Orig.). 1981. pap. 2.75 (ISBN 0-440-15377-8). Dell.

--Loving. (Orig.). 1981. pap. 3.75 (ISBN 0-440-14657-7). Dell.

--Now & Forever. 432p. 1982. pap. 3.75 (ISBN 0-440-11743-7). Dell.

--Now & Forever. (General Ser.). 1982. lib. bdg. 16.95 (ISBN 0-8161-3330-1, Large Print Bks). G K Hall.

--Passion's Promise. 1981. pap. 3.75 (ISBN 0-440-12926-5). Dell.

--A Perfect Stranger. (Orig.). 1982. pap. 3.75 (ISBN 0-440-17221-7). Dell.

--The Promise. 1983. pap. 3.50 (ISBN 0-440-17079-6). Dell.

--Remembrance. 1983. pap. 3.95 (ISBN 0-440-17370-1). Dell.

--The Ring. 1980. 11.95 o.s.i. (ISBN 0-440-07622-6). Delacorte.

--The Ring. 1981. pap. 3.75 (ISBN 0-440-17386-8). Dell.

--Season of Passion. 1981. pap. 3.75 (ISBN 0-440-17704-9). Dell.

--Summer's End. 1981. pap. 3.75 (ISBN 0-440-18405-3). Dell.

--Summer's End. (Reader's Request Ser.). 1981. lib. bdg. 15.95 (Large Print Bks). G K Hall.

--Thurston House. (Orig.). 1983. pap. price not set (ISBN 0-440-58655-0, Dell Trade Pbks). Dell.

Steel, David. Preaching Through the Year. LC 80-82191. 168p. 1980. pap. 3.49 (ISBN 0-8042-1801-3). John Knox.

Steel, Donald. Golf Facts & Feats. (Illus.). 256p. 1982. pap. 12.95 (ISBN 0-85112-257-4, Pub. by Guinness Superlatives England); 19.95 (ISBN 0-85112-242-6). Sterling.

Steel, E. W. & McGhee, Terence. Water Supply & Sewerage. 5th ed. (Illus.). 1979. text ed. 36.50 (ISBN 0-07-060929-2, C); soultions manual 13.00 (ISBN 0-07-060930-6). McGraw.

Steel, E. W., jt. auth. see Ehlers, Victor M.

Steel, Flora Annie. Tattercoats. LC 76-9947. (Illus.). 32p. (gr. k-3). 1976. 10.95 (ISBN 0-02-786900-8). Bradbury Pr.

Steel, G. Gordon. Growth Kinetics of Tumours. (Illus.). 1978. text ed. 59.00x (ISBN 0-19-857388-X). Oxford U Pr.

Steel, John E., jt. auth. see Calvert, Robert, Jr.

Steel, Robert G. & Torrie, James H. Principles & Procedures of Statistics: With Special Reference to the Biological Sciences. 1960. text ed. 19.95 o.p. (ISBN 0-07-060925-X, C); ans. bk. 3.50 o.p. (ISBN 0-07-060923-3). McGraw.

Steel, Rodney & Harvey, Anthony. The Encyclopedia of Pre-Historic Life. (Illus.). 1979. 24.95 o.p. (ISBN 0-07-060920-9). McGraw.

Steel, Ronald. Pax Americana. rev. ed. 1977. pap. 4.95 (ISBN 0-14-004664-X). Penguin.

Steel, William H. Interferometry. (Cambridge Monographs on Physics). 1967. 37.50 (ISBN 0-521-06547-X). Cambridge U Pr.

Steele, Colin, ed. Independent Mexico: A Collection of Mexican Pamphlets in the Bodleian Library, Oxford. new ed. Costeloe, Michael. 128p. 1974. 8.00 o.p. (ISBN 0-7201-0383-5, Pub. by Mansell England). Wilson.

Steele, Danielle. Once in a Lifetime. (General Ser.). 1983. lib. bdg. 14.95 (ISBN 0-8161-3407-3, Large Print Bks). G K Hall.

Steele, Frederic L. At Timberline: A Nature Guide to the Mountains of the Northeast. (Illus.). 356p. 1983. pap. 10.95 (ISBN 0-910146-39-X). Appalach Mtn.

Steele, Gerald L. Exploring the World of Plastics. LC 75-42964. (gr. 8-12). 1977. text ed. 19.96 (ISBN 0-87345-411-1). McKnight.

--Fiber Glass. (Illus.). (gr. 11-12). 1962. text ed. 14.64 (ISBN 0-87345-174-0). McKnight.

Steele, Glen, jt. ed. see Eiseman, Ben.

Steele, Henry B., jt. auth. see Griffin, James M.

Steele, J. H., ed. Marine Food Chains: Proceedings of a Symposium Held at the University of Aarhus, Denmark, from 23rd to 26th July 1968. (Illus.). 1973. Repr. of 1970 ed. lib. bdg. 54.00x (ISBN 3-87429-047-6). Lubrecht & Cramer.

Steele, James H., jt. auth. see Myers, J. Arthur.

Steele, James H., jt. ed. see Arambulo, Primo.

Steele, James W. Frontier Army Sketches. LC 73-99567. 1969. pap. 7.95 (ISBN 0-8263-0233-5). U of NM Pr.

Steele, Jessica. Distrust Her Shadow. (Harlequin Romances Ser.). 192p. 1983. pap. 1.75 (ISBN 0-373-02555-6). Harlequin Bks.

--Intimate Enemies. (Harlequin Presents Ser.). 192p. 1983. pap. 1.95 (ISBN 0-373-10605-X). Harlequin Bks.

--Price to Be Met. (Harlequin Presents). 192p. 1983. pap. text ed. 1.95 (ISBN 0-373-10596-7). Harlequin Bks.

Steele, Joan. Captain Mayne Reid. (English Authors Ser). 1978. lib. bdg. 14.95 (ISBN 0-8057-6700-2, Twayne). G K Hall.

Steele, L. E. Assuring Structural Integrity of Steel Reactor Pressure Vessels. 1980. 41.00 (ISBN 0-85334-906-1, Pub. by Applied Sci England). Elsevier.

Steele, L. E. & Stahlkopf, K. E. Structural Integrity of Light Water Reactor Components. (Illus.). 405p. 1982. 82.00 (ISBN 0-85334-157-5, Pub. by Applied Sci England). Elsevier.

Steele, Lowell. Innovation in Big Business. LC 75-14971. 320p. 1975. 26.95 (ISBN 0-444-00170-0, North Holland). Elsevier.

Steele, Mary Q. The Living Year: An Almanac for My Survivors. 1982. 6.50 (ISBN 0-688-00992-1). Morrow.

Steele, Mary Q. see Gage, Wilson, pseud.

Steele, Max. Seasonal Jobs on Land & Sea. LC 78-3171. 1979. pap. 4.50i o.p. (ISBN 0-06-090628-6, CN628, CN). Har-Row.

Steele, Michael R. Knute Rockne: A Bio-Bibliography. LC 82-6107. (Popular Culture Bio-Bibliographies Ser.). (Illus.). 352p. 1983. lib. bdg. 35.00 (ISBN 0-313-22239-8, SNR/). Greenwood.

Steele, Nathan. The Sharecroppers. 1978. 4.95 o.p. (ISBN 0-533-03468-X). Vantage.

Steele, Pauline F., ed. Dimensions of Dental Hygiene. 3rd ed. LC 82-15281. (Illus.). 549p. 1982. text ed. 28.50 (ISBN 0-8121-0846-9). Lea & Febiger.

Steele, Phillip. Going to the Zoo. LC 80-52529. (Starters Ser.). PLB 8.00 (ISBN 0-382-06476-3). Silver.
--The Last of the Cherokee Warriors. 2nd ed. (Illus.). (gr. 6-12). 1978. pap. 3.95 (ISBN 0-88289-203-7); 6.95 (ISBN 0-911116-99-0). Pelican.
Steele, Phillip W. Ozark Tales & Superstitions. LC 82-22425. (Illus.). 100p. 1983. pap. 4.95 (ISBN 0-88289-404-8). Pelican.
Steele, Richard. The Plays of Richard Steele. Kenny, Shirley S., ed. 1971. 59.00x (ISBN 0-19-812414-7). Oxford U Pr.
Steele, Robert C. Modern Topographic Drawing. (Illus.). 208p. 1980. text ed. 16.95x (ISBN 0-87201-870-9). Gulf Pub.
Steele, Robert G. With Pen or Sword. 1978. 11.95 o.p. (ISBN 0-533-03778-6). Vantage.
Steele, Robert S. Freud & Jung: Conflicts of Interpretation. 300p. 1982. 32.50 (ISBN 0-7100-9067-6). Routledge & Kegan.
Steele, Susan, et al. An Encyclopedia of AUX: A Study in Cross-Linguistic Equivalence. (Linguistic Inquiry Monographs). 380p. 1981. 32.50x (ISBN 0-262-19197-0); pap. 15.00x (ISBN 0-262-69074-8). MIT Pr.
Steele, Thomas J. Holy Week in Tome: A New Mexico Passion Play. (Illus., Bilingual, spanish-english). 1976. pap. 8.95 (ISBN 0-913270-63-6). Sunstone Pr.
--Santos & Saints: The Religious Folk Art of Hispanic New Mexico. Rev. ed. LC 74-75452. (Illus.). 228p. 1982. pap. 9.95 (ISBN 0-941270-12-2). Ancient City Pr.
Steele, Wilbur D. Full Cargo: More Stories. LC 75-36514. 1976. Repr. of 1957 ed. lib. bdg. 21.50x o.p. (ISBN 0-8371-8636-6, STFC). Greenwood.
Steele, William O. The Buffalo Knife. LC 52-6460. (Illus.). (gr. 4-6). 1968. pap. 2.75 (ISBN 0-15-614750-5, VoyB). HarBraceJ.
--Flaming Arrows. LC 57-6791. (Illus.). (gr. 4-8). 1972. pap. 1.15 (ISBN 0-15-631550-5, VoyB). HarBraceJ.
--The Lone Hunt. LC 75-29489. (Illus.). 176p. (gr. 4-6). 1976. pap. 1.75 (ISBN 0-15-652983-1, VoyB). HarBraceJ.
--The Perilous Road. LC 58-6820. (Illus.). (gr. 3-7). 1965. pap. 3.95 (ISBN 0-15-671696-8, VoyB). HarBraceJ.
--The War Party. LC 78-52815. (A Let Me Read Bk). (Illus.). (gr. k-4). pap. 1.95 (ISBN 0-15-694697-1, VoyB). HarBraceJ.
Steelman, David C., ed. see National Center for State Courts.
Steelman, Robert. Border Riders. 224p. (Orig.). Date not set. pap. cancelled o.p. (ISBN 0-505-51812-0). Tower Bks.
Steelman, Robert, ed. Catalog of the Lititz Congregation Collection. LC 80-27511. xi, 488p. 1981. 40.00 o.p. (ISBN 0-8078-1477-6). U of NC Pr.
Steelman, Robert J. Man They Hanged. LC 80-1038. (Double D Western Ser.). 192p. 1980. 10.95 o.p. (ISBN 0-385-15829-7). Doubleday.
--Surgeon to the Sioux. LC 78-22799. (Double D Western Ser.). 1979. 9.95 o.p. (ISBN 0-385-14430-X). Doubleday.
Steely, Judy, jt. auth. see Davidson, Tom.
Steeman, Nielson E. Marine Photosynthesis. LC 74-29691. (Oceanography Ser: Vol. 13). 141p. 1975. 51.00 (ISBN 0-444-41320-0). Elsevier.
Steen. Dictionary of Biology. 1983. pap. text ed. 15.50 (ISBN 0-06-318241-6, Pub. by Har-Row Ltd England). Har-Row.
Steen, Edwin B. Abbreviations in Medicine. 4th ed. 1978. pap. 12.95 (ISBN 0-02-859430-4, Pub. by Bailliere-Tindall). Saunders.
--Dictionary of Biology. LC 70-156104. 15.00x o.p. (ISBN 0-06-480827-0, EH 321, EH); pap. 5.95 (ISBN 0-06-463321-7). B&N NY.
--Dictionary of Biology. 630p. 1971. text ed. 15.00x (ISBN 0-686-83546-8). B&N Imports.
Steen, Edwin B. & Ashley Montagu. Anatomy & Physiology, 2 vols. Incl. Cells, Tissues, Integument, Skeletal, Muscular & Digestive Systems, Blood, Lymph, Circulatory System (ISBN 0-06-460098-X, 98); Urinary, Respiratory & Nervous Systems, Sensations & Sense Organs, Endocrine & Reproductive Systems (ISBN 0-06-460099-8, CO 99). 1959. 4.95 ea. (COS). Har-Row.
Steen, Edwin B. & Price, James H. Human Sex & Sexuality: With a Dictionary of Sexual Terms. LC 76-21654. (Illus.). 338p. 1977. 29.50 (ISBN 0-471-82101-2). Wiley.
Steen, Frederick H. & Ballou, D. H. Analytic Geometry. 3rd ed. 1963. text ed. 21.95 (ISBN 0-471-00570-3). Wiley.
Steen, Marguerite. Stallion. LC 33-7951. 1971. 6.50x (ISBN 0-7182-0699-1). Intl Pubns Serv.
Steen, S. W. Mathematical Logic with Special Reference to the Natural Numbers. 1971. 87.50 (ISBN 0-521-08053-3). Cambridge U Pr.
Steenberghen, Fernand Van see Van Steenberghen, Fernand.
Steenbrink, P. A. Optimization of Transport Networks. LC 73-2793. 325p. 1974. 54.95 (ISBN 0-471-82098-9, Pub. by Wiley-Interscience). Wiley.
Steene, B. August Strindberg: An Introduction to His Major Works. rev. ed. Orig. Title: The Greatest Fire- A Study of August Strindberg. 1982. Repr. of 1973 ed. text ed. 28.75x (ISBN 0-391-02715-8, Pub. by Almqvist & Wiksell Sweden). Humanities.
Steene, Birgitta. Ingmar Bergman. LC 74-80081. (Griffin Authors Ser). 158p. 1975. pap. 4.95 o.p. (ISBN 0-312-41790-X). St Martin.
Steene, Roger C. Butterfly & Angelfishes of the World: Australia, Vol. 1. LC 78-17351. 144p. 1977. 30.50 o.p. (ISBN 0-471-04737-6, Pub. by Wiley-Interscience). Wiley.
Steenrod, N. E., jt. auth. see Chinn, W. G.
Steensma, Robert C. Dr. John Arbuthnot. (English Authors Ser.). 1979. lib. bdg. 14.95 (ISBN 0-8057-6749-5, Twayne). G K Hall.
--Sir William Temple. (English Authors Ser.). lib. bdg. 14.95 (ISBN 0-8057-1540-1, Twayne). G K Hall.
Steenwyk, Elizabeth van see Van Steenwyk, Elizabeth.
Steenwyk, Elizabeth Van see Van Steenwyk, Elizabeth.
Steenwyk, Elizbeth Van see Van Steenwyk, Elizabeth.
Steer, Charles & Kelly, John. How to Ace the SAT. 288p. 1981. pap. 8.95 (ISBN 0-671-25300-X, Fireside). S&S.
Steer, Francis W. A Catalogue of Sussex Estate & Tithe Award Maps, Vol. 1. 240p. 1962. 40.00x (ISBN 0-686-82392-3). State Mutual Bk.
--A History of the Worshipful Company of Scrivners of London, Vol. 1. (Illus.). 92p. 1973. 35.00x o.p. (ISBN 0-8476-1379-8). Rowman.
--The Mitford Archives, Vol. 1. 83p. 1961. 29.00x (ISBN 0-900801-23-9). State Mutual Bk.
--The Mitford Archives, Vol. 2. 67p. 1970. 39.00x (ISBN 0-900801-02-6). State Mutual Bk.
Steer, Francis W., ed. The Lavington Estate Archives. 128p. 1964. 30.00x (ISBN 0-900801-12-3). State Mutual Bk.
Steer, John L. & Dudley, Cliff. Vietnam, Curse or Blessing. (Illus.). 192p. (Orig.). 1982. pap. 2.95 (ISBN 0-89221-091-5). New Leaf.
Steer, Roger. George Muller: Delighted in God! rev. ed. LC 81-52600. 351p. 1981. pap. 3.95 (ISBN 0-87788-304-1). Shaw Pubs.
Steere, Daniel C. I Am, I Can. 1976. pap. write for info o.s.i. Jove Pubns.
Steere, David A. Bodily Expressions in Psychotherapy. (Illus.). 352p. 1983. 25.00 (ISBN 0-87630-322-X). Brunner-Mazel.
Steere, Douglas. Together in Solitude. 160p. 1983. 12.95 (ISBN 0-8245-0531-X). Crossroad NY.
Steere, Douglas, tr. see Kierkegaard, Soren.
Steere, William C. The Mosses of Arctic Alaska. (Bryophytorum Bibliotheca: No. 14). (Illus.). 1978. lib. bdg. 60.00 (ISBN 3-7682-1181-9). Lubrecht & Cramer.
Steerl, Francis W. Scriveners' Company Common Papers, 1357-1628. 1968. 50.00x (ISBN 0-686-96616-3, Pub by London Rec Soc England). State Mutual Bk.
Steers, James A. Coast of England & Wales in Pictures. 1960. 26.95 o.p. (ISBN 0-521-06549-6); pap. 14.95 (ISBN 0-521-29274-3). Cambridge U Pr.
Steers, R. & Porter, L. Motivation & Work Behavior. 3rd ed. 720p. (Orig.). 1983. text ed. 24.95x (ISBN 0-07-060942-X, C). McGraw.
Steers, Richard, jt. auth. see Mowday, Richard.
Steers, Richard M. Introduction to Organizational Behavior. 1981. text ed. 24.50x (ISBN 0-673-15598-6). Scott F.
Steers, Richard M. & Porter, Lyman W. Motivation & Work Behavior. (Illus.). 608p. 1975. text ed. 12.95 o.p. (ISBN 0-07-060940-3, C). McGraw.
--Motivation & Work Behavior. 2nd ed. (Management Ser.). (Illus.). 1979. text ed. 23.50 (ISBN 0-07-060941-1, C). McGraw.
Steeves, Edna L. & Backscheider, P. R., eds. The Plays of Mary Pix & Catherine Trotter, 2 Vols. LC 78-66620. (Eighteenth Century English Drama Ser.). Set. lib. bdg. 50.00 (ISBN 0-8240-3606-9). Garland Pub.
Steeves, Edna L., ed. see Pope, Alexander.
Steeves, Frank L. & English, Fenwick W. Secondary Curriculum for a Changing World. 1978. text ed. 18.95 (ISBN 0-675-08424-5). Additional supplements may be obtained from publisher. Merrill.
Stefanelli, John M. Selection & Procurement for the Hospitality Industry. LC 80-20604. (Wiley Service Management Ser.). 502p. 1981. text ed. 26.95 (ISBN 0-471-04538-1); avail. supplementary materials (ISBN 0-471-05953-6). Wiley.
Stefani, P., et al, eds. International College of Surgeouns, Biennial World Congress: Abstracts, Eigheenth Congress. 1972. pap. 19.50 (ISBN 90-219-1201-5, Excerpta Medica). Elsevier.
Stefanics, Charlotte, jt. auth. see Niklas, Gerald R.
Stefanik, Alfred. Copy Cat Sam: Developing Ties with a Special Child. LC 81-20212. 32p. 1982. 9.95 (ISBN 0-89885-058-4). Human Sci Pr.
Stefanile, Felix. In That Far Country: Sonnets. (Sparrow Poetry Pamphlets Ser.: No. 43). 32p. 1982. pap. 2.00x (ISBN 0-935552-14-6). Sparrow Pr.
Stefanis, et al, eds. Hashish: Studies of Long-Term Use. LC 76-19848. 195p. 1977. 17.00 (ISBN 0-89004-138-5). Raven.
Stefanis, C. N. Recent Advances In Depression. 152p. 1983. 18.00 (ISBN 0-08-027954-6). Pergamon.
Stefano, Frank, Jr., jt. auth. see Coysh, A. W.
Stefano, Johanna S. de see DeStefano, Johanna S.
Stefanovich, Hoechst, ed. Stroke: Animal Models: Proceedings of an International Symposium held at Wiesbaden, Germany, 16 November 1981. (Illus.). 200p. 1982. 50.00 (ISBN 0-08-029799-4). Pergamon.
Stefansson, Evelyn & Yahn, Linda C. Here is Alaska. 4th ed. (Illus.). 192p. (gr. 5 up). 1983. 12.95 (ISBN 0-684-17865-6). Scribner.
Stefansson, Vilhjalmur. Adventures in Error. LC 71-121210. 1970. Repr. of 1936 ed. 30.00x (ISBN 0-8103-3838-6). Gale.
--Iceland: The First American Republic. LC 70-138131. 1971. Repr. of 1939 ed. lib. bdg. 17.75x (ISBN 0-8371-5167-8, STIF). Greenwood.
--Northwest to Fortune. LC 73-20881. (Illus.). 356p. 1974. Repr. of 1958 ed. lib. bdg. 19.00x (ISBN 0-8371-5729-3, STNF). Greenwood.
Steffan. Silk Screen. (Pitman Art Ser.: Vol. 47). pap. 1.95 o.p. (ISBN 0-448-00556-5, G&D). Putnam Pub Group.
Steffan, T. G., et al, eds. see Byron, George G.
Steffanides, George F. The Scientist's Thesaurus. 4th ed. 156p. 1978. pap. 3.00 (ISBN 0-9600114-0-4, TX-7-128). Steffanides.
Steffek, Edwin, ed. The Complete Book of Houseplants & Indoor Gardening. (Illus.). 1976. 16.95 o.p. (ISBN 0-517-52614-X). Crown.
Steffel, Edwin, ed. Home Growing. LC 77-256. (Illus.). 1977. 22.50 (ISBN 0-312-38836-5). St Martin.
Steffel, Margaret J., jt. auth. see Alexander, John J.
Steffel, Victor L., jt. auth. see Henderson, Davis.
Steffen, C. & Ludwig, H., eds. Clinical Immunology & Allergology. (Developments in Immmunology: Vol. 14). 1981. 67.00 (ISBN 0-444-80312-2). Elsevier.
Steffen, John J. & Karoly, Paul, eds. Autism & Severe Psychopathology: Advances in Child Behavioral Analysis Therapy, Vol. II. LC 82-47799. 352p. 1982. 31.95x (ISBN 0-669-05639-1). Lexington Bks.
Steffen, John J., jt. ed. see Karoly, Paul.
Steffens, Henry J., jt. auth. see Williams, L. Pearce.
Steffens, Joseph L. The Struggle for Self-Government. (American Studies). Repr. of 1906 ed. 26.00 (ISBN 0-384-57770-9). Johnson Repr.
Steffens, Lincoln. The Autobiography of Lincoln Steffens, 2 Vols. LC 67-7897. (Illus.). 1968. Vol. 1. pap. 5.95 (ISBN 0-15-609395-2, Harv); Vol. 2. pap. 7.95 (ISBN 0-15-609396-0). HarBraceJ.
Steffensen, Arnold J. & Johnson, L. M. Algebra & Trigonometry. 1981. pap. text ed. 20.95x (ISBN 0-673-15371-1). Scott F.
--Intermediate Algebra. 1981. pap. text ed. 18.95x (ISBN 0-673-15369-X). Scott F.
Steffensen, Arnold R. & Johnson, L. M. Trigonometry with Analytic Geometry. 1983. pap. text ed. 17.95x (ISBN 0-673-15633-8). Scott F.
Steffensen, Arnold R. & Johnson, L. Murphy. College Algebra. 1981. pap. text ed. 19.95x (ISBN 0-673-15370-3). Scott F.
--Fundamentals of Arithmetic. 1981. pap. text ed. 18.95x (ISBN 0-673-15481-5). Scott F.
Steffensen, James L., Jr., ed. Great Scenes from the World Theater, Vol. 1. 1965. pap. 3.95 (ISBN 0-380-00793-2, 62927-5, Bard). Avon.
Stefferud, Alfred. The Wonders of Seeds. LC 56-6921. (Illus.). (gr. 5-9). 1966. pap. 0.45 (ISBN 0-15-698350-8, VoyB). HarBraceJ.
Stefflre, Buford & Grant, W. Harold. Theories of Counseling. 2nd ed. (Guidance Counseling & Student Personnel in Education Ser). 352p. 1972. text ed. 15.95 o.p. (ISBN 0-07-060971-3, C). McGraw.
Stefflre, Buford & Matheny, Kenneth. Function of Counseling Theory. (Guidance Monograph). 1968. pap. 2.40 o.p. (ISBN 0-395-09914-5). HM.
Stefflre, Buford, jt. auth. see Burks, Herbert M., Jr.
Steffns, Bradley. The Outcropping. (Living Poets' Library Ser.). 1983. pap. 3.50 (ISBN 0-686-84155-7). Dragons Teeth.
Steffy, Wilbert, jt. auth. see Gray, Steven.
Stegeman, Wilson. Medical Terms Simplified. LC 75-12977. (Illus.). 305p. 1975. pap. text ed. 13.95 (ISBN 0-8299-0062-4). West Pub.
Stegena, Lajos, jt. ed. see Rybach, Ladislaus.
Stegenga, James A. & Axline, Andrew W. The Global Community: A Brief Introduction to International Relations. 2nd ed. 190p. 1981. pap. text ed. 10.50 scp (ISBN 0-06-040404-3, HarpC). Har-Row.
Steger, Jane. Leaves from a Secret Journal. 1978. pap. 3.50 o.s.i. (ISBN 0-932970-05-2). Prinit Pr.
Steger, Wilber A., jt. auth. see House, Peter A.
Steggert, Frank X. Community Action Groups & City Governments. LC 75-5912. 128p. 1975. prof ref 16.50x (ISBN 0-88410-415-X). Ballinger Pub.
Steglich, W. G. & Snooks, Margaret. American Social Problems: An Institutional View. 1980. text ed. 19.95x o.p. (ISBN 0-673-16292-3). Scott F.
Stegman & Tromovitch. Basis of Dermatologic Surgery. (Illus.). 192p. 1981. 29.50 (ISBN 0-8151-8168-X). Year Bk Med.
Stegman, Michael. Housing Investment in the Inner City: The Dynamics of Decline: a Study of Baltimore Maryland, 1968-1970. 320p. 1972. 18.00x o.p. (ISBN 0-262-19103-2). MIT Pr.
Stegman, Michael A. & Sumka, Howard J. Nonmetropolitan Housing Problems & Policies. LC 76-17023. 1976. 19.00 (ISBN 0-88410-581-4). Ballinger Pub.
Stegmann, Boris C. Relationships of the Superorders Alectoromorphae & Charadriomorphae (Aves) A Comparative Study of the Avian Hand. (Illus.). 119p. 1978. 10.00 (ISBN 0-686-35806-6). Nuttall Ornithological.
Stegmann, Robert, jt. auth. see Miller, David.
Stegmueller, W., et al, eds. Philosophy of Economics, Munich, Federal Republic of Germany, 1981: Proceedings. (Studies in Contemporary Economics: Vol. 2). (Illus.). 306p. 1983. pap. 21.00 (ISBN 0-387-11927-2). Springer-Verlag.
Stegner, Mary, jt. ed. see Stegner, Wallace.
Stegner, Page. Sports Car Menopause. 1977. 8.95 o.p. (ISBN 0-316-81224-2, Atlantic-Little, Brown). Little.
Stegner, Wallace. Sound of Mountain Water. 1980. pap. 6.95 o.p. (ISBN 0-525-47631-8). Dutton.
Stegner, Wallace & Stegner, Mary, eds. Great American Short Stories. pap. 3.95 (ISBN 0-440-33060-2, LE). Dell.
Stegun, Irene A., jt. ed. see Abramowitz, Milton.
Stehle, Audrey P. & Ingram, Marilyn, eds. The Southern Heritage Cakes Cookbook. LC 82-62141. (The Southern Heritage Cookbook Library). (Illus.). 144p. 1983. 9.57i (ISBN 0-8487-0601-3). Oxmoor Hse.
--The Southern Heritage Company's Coming Cookbook. LC 82-62140. (The Southern Heritage Cookbook Library). (Illus.). 144p. 1983. 9.57i (ISBN 0-8487-0603-X). Oxmoor Hse.
--The Southern Heritage Poultry Cookbook. LC 82-62142. (The Southern Heritage Cookbook Library). (Illus.). 144p. 1983. 9.57i (ISBN 0-8487-0604-8). Oxmoor Hse.
Stehle, Claudia. Individualitat und Romanform. 186p. (Ger.). 1982. write for info. (ISBN 3-8204-5727-5). P Lang Pubs.
Stehle, Hansjakob. Eastern Politics of the Vatican, 1917-1979. Smith, Sandra, tr. from Ger. LC 80-15236. Orig. Title: Die Ostpolitik Des Vatikans, 1917-1975. (Illus.). 1981. 28.95x (ISBN 0-8214-0367-2, 82-82592); pap. 14.95 (ISBN 0-8214-0564-0, 82-82600). Ohio U Pr.
Stehle, Philip, jt. auth. see Corben, H. C.
Stehli, Francis G., jt. ed. see Nairn, Alan E.
Stehling. Common Problems in Pediatric Anesthesia. 1982. 35.00 (ISBN 0-8151-8181-7). Year Bk Med.
Stehling, Kurt R. Computers & You. 256p. 1973. pap. 2.50 (ISBN 0-451-62080-1, ME2080, Ment). NAL.
Stehsel, Donald L. Cats of California. (Illus.). 126p. (Orig.). 1967. pap. 6.95 (ISBN 0-686-37035-X). Stehsel.
--Crows of California. 110p. (Orig.). 1947. pap. text ed. 7.95 (ISBN 0-686-37033-3). Stehsel.
--Hunting the California Black Bear. LC 65-19814. (Illus.). 194p. 1965. pap. 7.00 (ISBN 0-686-37776-1). Stehsel.
Steich, Marianne, ed. see McAlister, marcia.
Steichen, Edward. Family of Man. 1967. deluxe ed. 15.00 o.p. (ISBN 0-671-24381-0). S&S.
Steichen, Edward, ed. Family of Man. (Photos). pap. 6.95 (ISBN 0-451-79999-2, G9999, Sig). NAL.
Steichen, James B., jt. auth. see Strickland, James W.
Steichen, Jean J., tr. see Amiel-Tison, Claudine & Grenier, Albert.
Steidel, R. F. An Introduction to Mechanical Vibrations. 2nd rev. ed. 400p. 1980. 35.95 (ISBN 0-471-04883-2). Wiley.
Steidl, G. Basics of Assembly Life. pap. 2.75 (ISBN 0-88172-126-3). Believers Bkshelf.
Steidl, G. S. By Faith. 48p. pap. 2.25 (ISBN 0-88172-127-1). Believers Bkshelf.
Steidl, Rose E. & Bratton, Esther C. Work in the Home. LC 67-29007. 419p. 1968. 27.95 o.s.i. (ISBN 0-471-82085-7). Wiley.
Steig, William. C D B. LC 80-12376. (Illus.). 44p. (gr. 1 up). pap. 2.95 (ISBN 0-671-96030-X). Windmill Bks.
--Doctor De Soto. (Illus.). 32p. (ps up). 1982. 10.95 (ISBN 0-374-31803-4). FS&G.
--Drawings. 192p. 1979. 19.95 (ISBN 0-374-29031-8). FS&G.
Steigel, A. & Spiess, H. W. Dynamic NMR Spectroscopy. rev. ed. (NMR - Basic Principles & Progress: Vol. 15). (Illus.). 1982. 61.30 (ISBN 0-387-08784-2). Springer-Verlag.
Steiger, Brad. Astral Projection. 1982. pap. 9.95 (ISBN 0-914918-36-2). Para Res.
--ETs & Poltergeists: Their True Story. Stine, Hank, ed. LC 82-14671. (Illus.). 152p. (Orig.). 1983. pap. 5.95 (ISBN 0-89865-272-3). Donning Co.
--The Hypnotist. 1979. pap. 2.50 o.s.i. (ISBN 0-440-13771-3). Dell.
--Kahuna Magic. 1981. pap. 5.95 (ISBN 0-914918-34-6). Para Res.
--Monsters Among Us. 1982. pap. 9.95 (ISBN 0-914918-38-9). Para Res.
--The Seed. 192p. 1983. pap. 2.75 (ISBN 0-425-05845-X). Berkley Pub.
--Worlds Before Our Own. LC 78-18232. 1978. 8.95 (ISBN 0-399-12215-X, Pub. by Berkley). Putnam Pub Group.
Steiger, Brad, ed. see Gittner, Louis.

Steigleder. Pocket Atlas of Dermatology. (Flexi-Bk.). 1983. write for info. (ISBN 0-86577-092-1). Thieme-Stratton.

Steigleman, Walter A. Newspaperman & the Law. LC 74-141419. 1971. Repr. of 1950 ed. lib. bdg. 20.25x (ISBN 0-8371-3059-X, STNE). Greenwood.

Steiglitz, Kenneth. An Introduction to Discrete Systems. LC 73-6820. 318p. 1974. text ed. 31.95 (ISBN 0-471-82097-0); 8.00 (ISBN 0-471-82103-9). Wiley.

Steiglitz, Kenneth & Papadimitriou, Christos. Combinatorial Optimization: Algorithm & Complexity. (Illus.). 512p. 1982. 35.00 (ISBN 0-13-152462-3). P-H.

Steigman, Gary, ed. see Zel'Dovich, Ya. B. & Novikov, I. D.

Steil, Lyman K. & Barker, Larry L. Effective Listening: Key to Your Success. LC 82-11512. (Illus.). Date not set. pap. text ed. 7.95 (ISBN 0-201-16425-6). A-W.

Steil, Lyman K. & DeMare, George. Listening-It Can Change Your Life: A Handbook for Scientists & Engineers. 170p. 1983. 18.95x (ISBN 0-471-86165-0). Ronald Pr.

Steila, Donal. Geography of Soils: Formation, Distribution & Management. (Illus.). 256p. 1976. 12.95 (ISBN 0-13-351734-9). P-H.

Steila, Donald, et al. Earth & Man: a Systematic Geography. LC 80-19689. 448p. 1981. text ed. 27.95 (ISBN 0-471-04221-8); avail. tchr's manual (ISBN 0-471-09079-4). Wiley.

Steiman, Harvey, jt. auth. see Hom, Ken.

Steimann, I. & Nissen, M. Danish Modern for Udlaendinge. 1974. pap. text ed. 18.50x o.p. (ISBN 8-7008-1281-1, D-728). Vanous.

Stein. Great Cars. 9.95 o.p. (ISBN 0-448-01118-2, G&D). Putnam Pub Group.

--Towards New Towns for America. 264p. 1982. 32.00x (ISBN 0-85323-163-X, Pub. by Liverpool Univ England). State Mutual Bk.

Stein, Aaron M. The Bombing Run. LC 82-45548. (Crime Club Ser.). 192p. 1983. 11.95 (ISBN 0-385-18381-X). Doubleday.

Stein, Allen F. Cornelius Mathews. (United States Authors Ser.). 1974. lib. bdg. 13.95 (ISBN 0-8057-0478-7, Twayne). G K Hall.

Stein, Allen F. & Walters, Thomas N. The Southern Experience in Short Fiction. 1971. pap. 9.95x (ISBN 0-673-07605-9). Scott F.

Stein, Arnold. The Art of Presence: The Poet & Paradise Lost. 1976. 25.00x (ISBN 0-520-03167-9). U of Cal Pr.

Stein, Arthur, jt. auth. see Weisbord, Robert G.

Stein, Aurel. Serindia, 5 Vols. (Illus.). 1980. Set. 350.00x (ISBN 0-8002-2452-3). Intl Pubns Serv.

Stein, Ben. The Manhattan Gambit. LC 81-43637. 336p. 1983. 15.95 (ISBN 0-385-17225-7). Doubleday.

Stein, Ben & Stein, Herbert. Moneypower: How to Profit from Inflation. LC 79-2235. 1980. 12.45i (ISBN 0-06-014073-9, HarpT). Har-Row.

Stein, Benjamin, jt. auth. see McGuinness, William J.

Stein, Burton, ed. Essays on South India. (Asian Studies at Hawaii Ser.: No. 15). 288p. (Orig.). 1975. pap. text ed. 9.50x (ISBN 0-8248-0350-7). UH Pr.

Stein, Charles. Horse Sacrifice. 80p. 1980. 20.00 (ISBN 0-930794-31-1); pap. 4.45 (ISBN 0-930794-30-3). Station Hill Pr.

--Parts & Other Parts. (Illus.). 96p. (Orig.). 1982. 5.50 (ISBN 0-930794-66-4); ltd. signed ed. 20.00 (ISBN 0-930794-79-6). Station Hill Pr.

Stein, Charles, ed. Critical Materials Problems in Energy Production. 1976. 56.50 (ISBN 0-12-665050-0). Acad Pr.

Stein, Charles F., Jr. A History of Calvert County, Maryland. (Illus.). 484p. 1976. 20.00 (ISBN 0-686-36506-2). Md Hist.

--Origin & History of Howard County, Maryland. (Illus.). 383p. 1972. 19.50 (ISBN 0-686-36696-4). Md Hist.

Stein, Charlotte M. The Stained Glass Window. Date not set. cancelled. Double M Pr.

Stein, Clarence S. Toward New Towns for America. (Illus.). 1966. pap. 8.95x (ISBN 0-262-69009-8). MIT Pr.

Stein, Donald, jt. auth. see Finger, Stanley.

Stein, Donald G., et al, eds. Plasticity & Recovery of Function in the Central Nervous System. 1974. 46.50 (ISBN 0-12-664350-4). Acad Pr.

Stein, Edward V. Guilt: Theory & Therapy. 1968. 6.00 o.s.i. (ISBN 0-7100-0009-X). Westminster.

Stein, Elizabeth P. David Garrick, Dramatist. (MLA Revolving Fund Ser.: No. 7). 1938. pap. 32.00 (ISBN 0-527-86100-6). Kraus Repr.

Stein, Emanuel, jt. auth. see Fox, William.

Stein, Eric, jt. auth. see Sandalow, Terrance.

Stein, Frances P. & Udell, Rochelle. Hot Tips: One Thousand Real Life Fashion & Beauty Tricks. (Illus.). 224p. 12.95 (ISBN 0-399-12580-9). Putnam Pub Group.

Stein, Franklin. Anatomy of Research in Allied Health. 272p. 1983. pap. text ed. 12.50x (ISBN 0-87073-007-X). Schenkman.

Stein, Gary see Prescott, David M.

Stein, Gary S., ed. see Symposium, University of Florida, Gainsville, March, 1975.

Stein, Gertrude. The Autobiography of Alice B. Toklas. LC 79-92497. Date not set. 6.95 (ISBN 0-394-60487-3). Modern Lib.

--How Writing Is Written: Previously Uncollected Writings of Gertrude Stein, Vol. 2. Haas, Robert B., ed. 165p. (Orig.). 1977. 14.00 o.p. (ISBN 0-87685-200-2); pap. 5.00 o.p. (ISBN 0-87685-199-5). Black Sparrow.

--Narration. LC 77-24699. 1973. lib. bdg. 8.50 (ISBN 0-8414-7932-1). Folcroft.

--The Yale Gertrude Stein. LC 80-5398. 480p. 1980. text ed. 35.00x (ISBN 0-300-02574-2); pap. 8.95 (ISBN 0-300-02609-9). Yale U Pr.

Stein, Harold A. & Slatt, Bernard J. Ophthalmic Assistant: Fundamentals & Clinical Practice. 3rd ed. LC 75-43808. (Illus.). 594p. 1976. text ed. 30.50 o.p. (ISBN 0-8016-4772-X). Mosby.

Stein, Harold A., et al. Manual of Opthalmic Terminology: LC 81-14136. (Illus.). 269p. 1982. pap. text ed. 18.95 (ISBN 0-8016-4769-X). Mosby.

Stein, Harry. Salem: A Pictorial History. LC 80-27805. (Illus.). 205p. 1981. pap. 12.95 o.p. (ISBN 0-89865-125-5). Donning Co.

Stein, Harry H., jt. ed. see Harrison, John M.

Stein, Herbert. Conservative Economics. 1983. 15.50 (ISBN 0-671-44127-2). S&S.

Stein, Herbert, jt. auth. see Stein, Ben.

Stein, Herman D., ed. Organization & the Human Services: Cross-Disciplinary Reflections. 264p. 1981. 29.95 (ISBN 0-87722-209-6). Temple U Pr.

Stein, Irving, jt. auth. see Starr, Martin K.

Stein, J. F. Introduction to Neurophysiology. (Illus.). 386p. 1982. pap. text ed. write info. (ISBN 0-632-00582-3, B4871-9). Mosby.

Stein, J. L. Monetarism. (Studies in Monetary Economics: Vol. 1). 1976. 55.50 (ISBN 0-444-11001-1, North-Holland). Elsevier.

Stein, J. Stewart. Construction Glossary: An Encyclopedic Reference & Manual. LC 79-19824. (Practical Construction Guides). 1013p. 1980. 77.95x (ISBN 0-471-04947-6, Pub. by Wiley-Interscience). Wiley.

--Construction Regulations: A Glossary of Zoning Ordinances & Building Codes. 750p. 1983. 75.00 (ISBN 0-471-89776-0, Pub. by Wiley Interscience). Wiley.

Stein, Jack M. Richard Wagner & the Synthesis of the Arts. LC 73-1840. (Illus.). 229p. 1973. Repr. of 1960 ed. lib. bdg. 19.00x (ISBN 0-8371-6806-6, STRX). Greenwood.

Stein, Janet, ed. Handbook of Phycological Methods. (Illus.). 512p. 1973. 52.50 (ISBN 0-521-20049-0); pap. 18.95 (ISBN 0-521-29747-8). Cambridge U Pr.

Stein, Janet see Prescott, David M.

Stein, Jay H., ed. Internal Medicine. 1983. single vol. 65.00 (ISBN 0-316-81231-5); 2 vols. 80.00 (ISBN 0-316-81232-3) (ISBN 0-316-81233-1). Little.

Stein, Jean & Pimpton, George, eds. Edie: An American Biography. 1983. pap. 3.95 (ISBN 0-440-13303-3). Dell.

Stein, Jean & Plimpton, George, eds. Edie: An American Biography. LC 81-48118. 1982. 16.95 (ISBN 0-394-48819-9). Knopf.

Stein, Joe & Clark, Diane. Don Coryell Win with Honor. LC 76-28011. (Illus.). 1976. 8.95 (ISBN 0-89325-003-1). Joyce Pr.

Stein, Jonathan B. The Soviet Block, Energy & Western Security. LC 82-49253. 1983. price not set (ISBN 0-669-06441-6). Lexington Bks.

Stein, Judith, jt. auth. see Holcombe, Marya.

Stein, Keith. Art of Clarinet Playing. (Illus.). 1958. pap. text ed. 9.50 (ISBN 0-87487-023-2). Summy.

Stein, Kevin, jt. auth. see Marsh, Dave.

Stein, Leon. Anthology of Musical Forms. 1962. pap. text ed. 13.95 (ISBN 0-87487-044-5). Summy.

--Structure & Style. rev. enlarged ed. LC 78-15541. (Illus.). xx, 297p. (Orig.). (gr. 9 up). 1979. pap. text ed. 14.95 (ISBN 0-87487-164-6). Summy.

Stein, Leonard, ed. see Schoenberg, Arnold.

Stein, Mari. So You're Going to Have Puppies. 108p. 1973. 3.50 o.p. (ISBN 0-913590-13-4). Slack Inc.

Stein, Mark. Good & Bad Feelings. LC 75-28353. (Illus.). 96p. (gr. 3-7). 1976. 6.25 o.p. (ISBN 0-688-22061-4); PLB 8.16 (ISBN 0-688-32061-9). Morrow.

--The Groves of Academe. Bd. with The Plumber's Apprentice. pap. 2.95 (ISBN 0-686-81620-X). Dramatists Play.

Stein, Marvin, jt. auth. see West, Louis J.

Stein, Max. Love Story of a Jewish Cat. (Illus.). 1979. pap. 3.95 o.p. (ISBN 0-8467-0582-6, Pub. by Two Continents). Hippocrene Bks.

Stein, Murray, ed. Jungian Analysis. 1982. 19.95 (ISBN 0-87548-350-X). Open Court.

Stein, Murray, tr. see Guggenbuhl-Craig, A.

Stein, Murray, tr. see Kerenyi, Karl.

Stein, Norman, jt. auth. see Goldstein, Arnold P.

Stein, Peter. Single. 1976. pap. text ed. 2.95x o.p. (ISBN 0-13-810564-2, Spec). P-H.

Stein, Peter, et al. The Marital Game: Understanding Marital Decision Making. 2nd ed. 1977. pap. text ed. 7.95x o.p. (ISBN 0-394-31136-1). Random.

Stein, Peter J., ed. Single Life: Unmarried Adults in Social Context. 350p. 1981. text ed. 16.95x (ISBN 0-312-72596-5); pap. text ed. 9.95x (ISBN 0-312-72597-3). St Martin.

Stein, Philip & Rowe, Bruce M. Introduction to Physical Anthropology. 2nd ed. 1978. pap. text ed. 19.95 (ISBN 0-07-061116-5, C); instructor's manual 3.95 (ISBN 0-07-061118-1); wkbk. 12.95 (ISBN 0-07-061119-X). McGraw.

Stein, Philip G., jt. auth. see Abrams, Marshall D.

Stein, Philip L. & Rowe, Bruce M. Physical Anthropology. 3rd ed. 512p. 1982. 19.95x (ISBN 0-07-061151-3). McGraw.

Stein, R. Incest & Human Love. LC 73-82641. 1973. 8.95 o.p. (ISBN 0-89388-090-6). Okpaku Communications.

Stein, R., jt. auth. see Stone, A.

Stein, R. Conrad. Dunkirk, World at War. LC 82-4595. (Illus.). (gr. 3-8). 1982. PLB 8.65g (ISBN 0-516-04795-7); pap. 2.95 (ISBN 0-516-44795-5). Childrens.

--Fall of Singapore, World at War. LC 82-9416. (Illus.). (gr. 3-8). 1982. PLB 8.65g (ISBN 0-516-04796-5); pap. 2.95 (ISBN 0-516-44796-3). Childrens.

--Hiroshima, World at War. LC 82-4538. (Illus.). (gr. 3-8). 1982. PLB 8.65g (ISBN 0-516-04797-3); pap. 2.95 (ISBN 0-516-44797-1). Childrens.

--Me & Dirty Arnie. LC 81-84216. 132p. (YA) (gr. 8-12). 1982. 9.95 (ISBN 0-15-253141-6, HJ). HarBraceJ.

--Resistance Movements, World at War. LC 82-9399. (Illus.). (gr. 3-8). 1982. PLB 8.65g (ISBN 0-516-04798-1); pap. 2.95 (ISBN 0-516-44798-X). Childrens.

--The Story of the Barbary Pirates. LC 82-4436. (Cornerstones of Freedom Ser.). (Illus.). (gr. 3-6). 1982. PLB 7.95g (ISBN 0-516-04632-2); pap. 2.50 (ISBN 0-516-44632-0). Childrens.

--The Story of the Clipper Ships. LC 81-1299. (Cornerstones of Freedom Ser.). (Illus.). 32p. (gr. 3-6). 1981. PLB 7.95 (ISBN 0-516-04612-8); pap. 2.50 (ISBN 0-516-44612-6). Childrens.

--The Story of the Flight at Kitty Hawk. LC 81-1634. (Cornerstones of Freedom Ser.). (Illus.). 32p. (gr. 3-6). 1981. PLB 7.95 (ISBN 0-516-04614-4); pap. 2.50 (ISBN 0-516-44614-2). Childrens.

--The Story of the Gold at Sutter's Mill. LC 81-6088. (Cornerstones of Freedom Ser.). (Illus.). 32p. (gr. 3-6). 1981. PLB 7.95 (ISBN 0-516-04617-9); pap. 2.50 (ISBN 0-516-44617-7). Childrens.

--The Story of the Nineteenth Amendment. LC 82-4419. (Cornerstones of Freedom Ser.). (Illus.). (gr. 3-6). 1982. PLB 7.95g (ISBN 0-516-04639-X); pap. 2.50 (ISBN 0-516-44639-8). Childrens.

--The Story of the Panama Canal. LC 82-4565. (Cornerstones of Freedom Ser.). (Illus.). (gr. 3-6). 1982. PLB 7.95g (ISBN 0-516-04640-3); pap. 2.50 (ISBN 0-516-44640-1). Childrens.

--The Story of the Pony Express. LC 81-4558. (Cornerstones of Freedom Ser.). (Illus.). 32p. (gr. 3-6). 1981. PLB 7.95 (ISBN 0-516-04631-4); pap. 2.50 (ISBN 0-516-44631-2). Childrens.

--The Story of the Underground Railroad. LC 82-3801. (Cornerstones of Freedom Ser.). (Illus.). 32p. (gr. 3-6). 1981. PLB 7.95 (ISBN 0-516-04643-8); pap. 2.50 (ISBN 0-516-44643-6). Childrens.

Stein, R. J. see Ordway, Frederick I., 3rd.

Stein, Ralph. The Greatest Cars. 1979. 35.00 o.s.i. (ISBN 0-671-25195-3). S&S.

Stein, Rita, et al, eds. Major Modern Dramatists: British, American, German & Scandinavian Dramatists, Vol. 1. LC 78-4310. (Library of Literary Criticism). 550p. 1983. 45.00 (ISBN 0-8044-3267-8). Ungar.

Stein, Robert. The French Slave Trade in the Eighteenth Century: An Old Regime Business. LC 79-3970. 270p. 1979. 22.50 (ISBN 0-299-07910-4). U of Wis Pr.

Stein, Robert E. & Johnson, Brian. Banking on the Biosphere? Environmental Procedures & Practices of Nine Multilateral Development Agencies. 224p. 1979. 25.95x (ISBN 0-669-02734-0). Lexington Bks.

Stein, Robert G. Mathematics: An Exploratory Approach. (Illus.). 352p. 1975. text ed. 20.95 (ISBN 0-07-060993-4, C). McGraw.

Stein, S. K. Calculus & Analytical Geometry. 3rd ed. (Illus.). 1248p. 1982. 33.50x (ISBN 0-07-061153-X); instructor's manual 10.00 (ISBN 0-07-061154-8); solutions manual 12.95 (ISBN 0-07-061155-6). McGraw.

Stein, Sandra K. & Schuler, Carol A. Love Numbers: A Numerological Guide to Compatibility. (Illus.). 384p. 1981. 11.95 (ISBN 0-399-12518-3). Putnam Pub Group.

Stein, Sara. Piece of Red Paper. LC 73-92068. (I Am, I Can, I Will Ser.). 44p. 1979. pap. 3.95 (ISBN 0-8331-0038-6). Hubbard Sci.

Stein, Sara, jt. auth. see Children's TV Workshop.

Stein, Sara B. How to Raise a Puppy: A Child's Book of Pet Care. LC 76-8137. (Illus.). (ps-5). 1976. PLB 5.99 (ISBN 0-394-93223-4, BYR); pap. 3.95 (ISBN 0-394-83223-X). Random.

--The New Parents' Guide to Early Learning. 176p. 1976. pap. 3.95 o.p. (ISBN 0-452-25122-2, Z5122, Plume). NAL.

Stein, Sherman & Crabill, Calvin. Elementary Algebra: A Guided Inquiry. LC 78-17913. 96p. (Orig.). 1972. text ed. 21.95 (ISBN 0-395-12669-X); instr's. ed. 21.95 (ISBN 0-395-12670-3); solution key 2.30 (ISBN 0-395-13756-X). HM.

Stein, Sherman K. Calculus & Analytic Geometry. 3rd ed. (Illus.). 1977. text ed. 27.95 (ISBN 0-07-061008-8, C); solutions manual 25.00 (ISBN 0-07-061110-6). McGraw.

--Calculus: in the First Three Dimensions. 1967. text ed. 24.00 (ISBN 0-07-061000-2, C). McGraw.

Stein, Shifra. Day Trips: Gas-Saving Getaways Less Than Two Hours from Greater Kansas City. (Illus.). 96p. 1980. pap. 4.50 (ISBN 0-9609752-0-9). S Stein Prods.

--Day Trips: Minneapolis. 1982. pap. 5.72i (ISBN 0-06-090948-X, CN-948). Har-Row.

--Day Trips: St. Louis. 1982. pap. 5.72i (ISBN 0-06-090902-1, CN-902). Har-Row.

--Discover Kansas City: A Guide to Unique Shops, Services & Businesses. (Illus.). 1981. pap. 7.95 (ISBN 0-9609752-1-7). S Stein Prods.

--I Love You. 1982. 5.50 (ISBN 0-8378-1711-0). Gibson.

--Pocket Guide to Kansas City, Vol. I. (Illus.). 160p. (Orig.). 1983. pap. 3.98 (ISBN 0-9609752-2-5). S Stein Prods.

--You're A Great Friend! 1982. 5.50 (ISBN 0-8378-1712-9). Gibson.

Stein, Shifra, compiled by. Dear Dad. 1977. 5.50 (ISBN 0-8378-1736-6). Gibson.

Stein, Sol. The Childkeeper. LC 75-15823. 211p. 1975. 7.95 o.p. (ISBN 0-15-117233-1). HarBraceJ.

Stein, Stanley J., jt. ed. see Cortes Conde, Roberto.

Stein, Stephen D., jt. auth. see Moloff, Ronald L.

Stein, Steve. Populism in Peru: The Emergence of the Masses & the Politics of Social Control. LC 79-5415. (Illus.). 320p. 1980. 22.50 (ISBN 0-299-07990-2). U of Wis Pr.

Stein, Theodore J. Social Work Practice in Child Welfare. (Illus.). 288p. 1981. text ed. 21.95 (ISBN 0-13-819524-2). P-H.

Stein, Toby. Getting Thin & Staying Thin. LC 82-48514. 250p. 1983. 14.95 (ISBN 0-8128-2896-8). Stein & Day.

Stein, Walter. Criticism As Dialogue. LC 69-12929. 1969. 42.50 (ISBN 0-521-07439-8). Cambridge U Pr.

Stein, Walter J. California & the Dust Bowl Migration. LC 70-175611. (Contributions in American History: No. 21). 1973. lib. bdg. 29.95x (ISBN 0-8371-6267-X, STC/); pap. text ed. 6.95 (ISBN 0-8371-7229-2, STC/). Greenwood.

--Man & His Place in History. 1980. pap. 4.25x (ISBN 0-906492-35-1, Pub. by Kolisko Archives). St George Bk Serv.

Stein, William B., ed. Two Brahman Sources of Emerson & Thoreau, 1822-1832. LC 67-10340. 1967. 38.00x (ISBN 0-8201-1043-4). Schol Facsimiles.

Stein, Zena, et al. Famine & Human Development: The Dutch Hunger Winter 1944-1945. (Illus.). 1974. text ed. 18.95x (ISBN 0-19-501811-7). Oxford U Pr.

Steinbach, Robert C. Programming Exercises for Problem Oriented Languages. LC 78-85768. (Illus., Orig.). 1969. pap. text ed. 2.95x o.p. (ISBN 0-02-478770-1, 47877). Glencoe.

Steinbach, Robert C. & Bellairs, Donald W. Trigonometry: Its Development & Use. 1971. text ed. 11.95x o.p. (ISBN 0-02-478650-0, 47865); tchrs' bklt. free o.p. (ISBN 0-685-03676-6). Glencoe.

Steinbeck, John. The Acts of King Arthur & His Noble Knights. 464p. 1980. pap. 2.95 (ISBN 0-686-96671-6, Del Rey). Ballantine.

--East of Eden. 1981. pap. 3.95 (ISBN 0-14-004997-5). Penguin.

--East of Eden. T. V. ed. 1979. pap. 3.95 (ISBN 0-14-005829-X). Penguin.

--The Log from the Sea of Cortez. 1977. pap. 4.95 (ISBN 0-14-004261-X). Penguin.

--Moon Is Down. 1982. pap. 3.95 (ISBN 0-14-006222-X). Penguin.

--Of Mice & Men. 1938. 5.95 (ISBN 0-394-60472-5). Modern Lib.

--Once There Was a War. 1977. pap. 3.95 (ISBN 0-14-004291-1). Penguin.

--Short Reign of Pippin IV. 1977. pap. 3.95 (ISBN 0-14-004290-3). Penguin.

--To a God Unknown. 1976. pap. 3.95 (ISBN 0-14-004233-4). Penguin.

Steinbeck, John & Ricketts, Edward F. Sea of Cortez: A Leisurely Journal of Travel & Research. (Illus.). 640p. Repr. of 1941 ed. 30.00 (ISBN 0-911858-08-3). Appel.

Steinberg, Ada. Words & Music in the Novels of Andrey Bely. LC 81-21718. (Cambridge Studies in Russian Literature). 320p. 1982. 57.50 (ISBN 0-521-23731-9). Cambridge U Pr.

Steinberg, Alfred. The Kennedy Brothers. (Lives to Remember Ser.). (gr. 7-11). 1969. PLB 5.49 o.p. (ISBN 0-399-60335-2). Putnam Pub Group.

--Woodrow Wilson. (Lives to Remember Ser.). (gr. 5-9). 1961. PLB 4.97 o.p. (ISBN 0-399-60683-1). Putnam Pub Group.

Steinberg, Arnold. The Political Campaign Handbook: Media, Scheduling, & Advance. LC 75-43130. 288p. 1976. 24.95x (ISBN 0-669-00481-2). Lexington Bks.

--Political Campaign Management: A Systems Approach. LC 75-36014. 320p. 1976. 25.95 (ISBN 0-669-00374-3). Lexington Bks.

Steinberg, Arthur G., et al. Progress in Medical Genetics, Vol. 1. LC 75-21151. (Illus.). 300p. 1976. text ed. 22.00 o.p. (ISBN 0-7216-8586-2). Saunders.

Steinberg, Arthur G., et al, eds. Progress in Medical Genetics, Vol. 2. Childs, Barton. LC 75-21151. 1977. text ed. 27.50 o.p. (ISBN 0-7216-8588-9). Saunders.

Steinberg, Bernard D. Principles of Aperture & Array System Design: Including Random & Adaptive Arrays. LC 75-30847. 356p. 1976. 43.50x (ISBN 0-471-82102-0, Pub. by Wiley-Interscience). Wiley.

Steinberg, C. M. & Lefkovits, I., eds. The Immune System, Vol. 1: Festschrift in Honor of Niels Kaj Jerne, on the Occasion of His 70th Birthday. (Illus.). xx, 440p. 1981. 148.50 (ISBN 3-8055-3407-8). S Karger.

Steinberg, Charles S., ed. Mass Media & Communication. 2nd rev. & enl. ed. (Studies in Public Communication). 650p. 1972. 14.00 o.p. (ISBN 0-8038-4664-9); pap. text ed. 8.50x o.s.i. (ISBN 0-8038-4663-0). Hastings.

Steinberg, D. D. & Jakobovits, L. A. Semantics: An Interdisciplinary Reader in Philosophy, Linguistics & Psychology. LC 78-123675. (Illus.). 1971. 62.50 (ISBN 0-521-07822-9); pap. 16.95 (ISBN 0-521-20499-2). Cambridge U Pr.

Steinberg, Dave S. Cooling Techniques for Electronic Equipment. LC 80-14141. 370p. 1980. 34.95 (ISBN 0-471-04403-2, Pub. by Wiley Interscience). Wiley.

--Vibration Analysis for Electronic Equipment. LC 72-13763. 467p. 1973. 48.95x (ISBN 0-471-82100-4, Pub. by Wiley-Interscience). Wiley.

Steinberg, David. Computational Matrix Algebra. (Illus.). 320p. 1974. text ed. 29.00 (ISBN 0-07-061110-6, C). McGraw.

Steinberg, David J. The Philippines: A Singular & a Plural Place. (Illus.). 135p. 1982. lib. bdg. 18.50 (ISBN 0-89158-990-2). Westview.

Steinberg, David M., tr. see Masson, Francois.

Steinberg, Derek. The Clinical Psychiatry of Adolescence: An Approach to Diagnosis, Treatment, & the Organisation of Work. (Studies in Child Psychiatry). 350p. 1983. price not set (ISBN 0-471-10314-4, Pub. by Wiley Interscience). Wiley.

Steinberg, Donna. I Lost It All in Montreal. 272p. 1983. pap. 2.95 (ISBN 0-380-81836-1, 81836-1). Avon.

Steinberg, E. P. Practice for Navy Placement Tests. 2nd ed. LC 82-4069. 272p. 1982. pap. 8.00 (ISBN 0-668-05354-2, 5354). Arco.

Steinberg, Eleanor B. & Yager, Joseph A. New Means of Financing International Needs. LC 77-21275. 1978. 18.95 (ISBN 0-8157-8116-4); pap. 7.95 (ISBN 0-8157-8115-6). Brookings.

Steinberg, Eleanor B., jt. auth. see Yager, Joseph A.

Steinberg, Eric, ed. see Hume, David.

Steinberg, Erwin R., jt. auth. see Markman, Alan M.

Steinberg, Erwin R., jt. auth. see Schutte, William M.

Steinberg, Eve P. How to Get a Clerical Job in Government. LC 82-16263. 224p. 1983. pap. 8.00 (ISBN 0-686-82499-7, 5647). Arco.

--Post Office Clerk-Carrier. 14th ed. LC 82-1666. 160p. 1982. pap. 6.95 (ISBN 0-668-05388-7, 5388). Arco.

Steinberg, G. M., ed. Immunology of the Eye I: Immunogenetics & Transplantation Immunity: Immunogenetics & Transplantation Immunity. 300p. 1980. pap. 25.00 (ISBN 0-904147-25-8). IRL Pr.

Steinberg, H. Organoboron Chemistry, Vol. 1, Boron-Oxygen & Boron-Sulfur Compounds. LC 62-20337. 950p. 1964. 82.50x (ISBN 0-470-82093-4, Pub. by Wiley-Interscience). Wiley.

Steinberg, Ira. Behaviorism & Schooling. 1980. 25.00 (ISBN 0-312-07253-8). St Martin.

Steinberg, J. Why Switzerland? LC 75-36024. (Illus.). 224p. 1976. 27.95 (ISBN 0-521-21139-5). Cambridge U Pr.

--Why Switzerland? LC 75-36024. (Illus.). 225p. 1981. pap. 9.95 (ISBN 0-521-28144-X). Cambridge U Pr.

Steinberg, Jean, tr. see Doerner, Klaus.

Steinberg, Jean, tr. see Hankel, Wilhelm.

Steinberg, Jules. Locke, Rousseau, & the Idea of Consent: An Inquiry into the Liberal-Democratic Theory of Political Obligation. LC 77-91094. (Contributions in Political Science: No. 6). 1978. lib. bdg. 25.00x (ISBN 0-313-20052-1, SLR/). Greenwood.

Steinberg, Leo. Other Criteria: Confrontations with Twentieth-Century Art. LC 72-77502. (Illus.). 436p. 1975. pap. 18.95 (ISBN 0-19-501846-X, GB438, GB). Oxford U Pr.

Steinberg, Lois. Voices Round the River. Walkup, Kathleen, ed. (Illus.). 25.00 (ISBN 0-686-23234-8); pap. 5.00 (ISBN 0-686-23235-6). Five Trees.

Steinberg, M. W., ed. see Klein, A. M.

Steinberg, Magery A. Handwriting. (Mickey's Practice Workbooks Ser.). (Illus.). (gr. 3-5). 1979. pap. 1.25 (ISBN 0-448-16128-1, G&D). Putnam Pub Group.

Steinberg, Marc I. Corporate Internal Affairs: A Corporate & Securities Law Perspective. LC 82-16619. 296p. 1983. lib. bdg. 35.00 (ISBN 0-89930-039-1, SCS/, Quorum). Greenwood.

Steinberg, Margery. The Christopher Reeve Scrapbook. 160p. (Orig.). (gr. 5 up). 1981. pap. 1.95 (ISBN 0-448-17223-2, G&D). Putnam Pub Group.

Steinberg, Margery A. Advanced Reading Comprehension. (Disney Practice Workbook Ser.). (Illus.). (gr. 3-5). 1979. pap. 1.25 (ISBN 0-448-16129-X, G&D). Putnam Pub Group.

--Beginning to Read. (Mickey's Practice Workbooks). (Illus.). (gr. k-3). 1979. pap. 1.25 (ISBN 0-448-16126-5, G&D). Putnam Pub Group.

--Dictionary & Word Skills. (Mickey's Practice Workbooks). (Illus.). (gr. 3-5). 1979. pap. 1.25 (ISBN 0-448-16127-3, G&D). Putnam Pub Group.

--Mickey's Practice Workbook: Division & Fractions, No. 12. (Mickey's Practice Workbook Ser.). (Illus.). (gr. 3-5). 1980. pap. 1.25 (ISBN 0-448-16131-1, G&D). Putnam Pub Group.

--Mickey's Practice Workbook: Math Puzzles & Games, No. 11. (Mickey's Practice Workbook Ser.). (Illus.). (gr. 3-5). 1980. pap. 1.25 (ISBN 0-448-16130-3, G&D). Putnam Pub Group.

Steinberg, Mark, jt. auth. see Miller, Gerald R.

Steinberg, Miho T. Answer Key to Robert Krohn's English Sentence Structure. 142p. 1977. pap. text ed. 3.95x (ISBN 0-472-08801-7). U of Mich Pr.

Steinberg, Morris. The Designer of a Good Life in a Changing World. 1978. 8.95 o.p. (ISBN 0-533-03507-4). Vantage.

Steinberg, Peter. Play Bridge in Four Hours. LC 77-94853. (Illus.). 1978. 12.95 o.p. (ISBN 0-448-14673-8, G&D). Putnam Pub Group.

--Playbridge in Four Hours. LC 77-94853. (Illus.). 256p. 1981. pap. 7.95 (ISBN 0-448-14687-8, G&D). Putnam Pub Group.

Steinberg, Peter, jt. auth. see Vargoshe, Richard.

Steinberg, Phil. Aquariums. LC 74-11889. (Early Craft Bks.). (Illus.). 32p. (gr. 1-4). 1975. PLB 3.95g (ISBN 0-8225-0870-2). Lerner Pubns.

--Photography. LC 74-11892. (Early Craft Bks). (Illus.). 32p. (gr. 1-4). 1975. PLB 3.95g (ISBN 0-8225-0869-9). Lerner Pubns.

--You & Your Pet: Aquarium Pets. LC 78-54359. (You & Your Pet Bks). (Illus.). (gr. 4 up). 1978. PLB 5.95g (ISBN 0-8225-1255-6). Lerner Pubns.

--You & Your Pet: Birds. LC 78-54352. (You & Your Pet Bks). (Illus.). (gr. 4 up). 1978. PLB 5.95g (ISBN 0-8225-1251-3). Lerner Pubns.

--You & Your Pet: Cats. LC 78-54353. (You & Your Pet Bks). (Illus.). (gr. 4 up). 1978. PLB 5.95g (ISBN 0-8225-1252-1). Lerner Pubns.

--You & Your Pet: Dogs. LC 78-54354. (You & Your Pet Bks). (Illus.). (gr. 4 up). 1978. PLB 5.95g (ISBN 0-8225-1253-X). Lerner Pubns.

--You & Your Pet: Horses. LC 78-54355. (You & Your Pet Bks). (Illus.). (gr. 4 up). PLB 5.95g (ISBN 0-8225-1257-2). Lerner Pubns.

--You & Your Pet: Rodents & Rabbits. LC 78-54365. (You & Your Pet Bks). (Illus.). (gr. 4 up). 1978. PLB 5.95g (ISBN 0-8225-1256-4). Lerner Pubns.

--You & Your Pet: Terrarium Pets. LC 78-54360. (You & Your Pet Bks). (Illus.). (gr. 4 up). 1978. PLB 5.95g (ISBN 0-8225-1254-8). Lerner Pubns.

Steinberg, Rafael. Cooking of Japan. LC 75-84632. (Foods of the World Ser.). (Illus.). (gr. 6 up). 1969. PLB 17.28 (ISBN 0-8094-0067-7, Pub. by Time-Life). Silver.

--Island Fighting. LC 78-52847. (World War II Ser.). (Illus.). 1978. lib. bdg. 19.92 (ISBN 0-8094-2487-8). Silver.

--Pacific & Southeast Asian Cooking. LC 70-114231. (Foods of the World Ser.). (Illus.). (gr. 6 up). 1970. PLB 17.28 (ISBN 0-8094-0072-3, Pub. by Time-Life). Silver.

--Return to the Philippines. LC 78-21648. (World War II Ser.). (Illus.). 1979. lib. bdg. 19.92 (ISBN 0-8094-2515-7). Silver.

Steinberg, Raphael. Man & the Organization. LC 74-23044. (Human Behavior Ser.). (Illus.). 176p. (gr. 5 up). 1975. PLB 13.28 o.p. (ISBN 0-8094-1913-0). Silver.

Steinberg, Raymond M. & Carter, Genevieve W. Case Management & the Elderly: A Handbook for Planning & Administering Programs. 224p. 1982. 25.95 (ISBN 0-669-06089-5). Lexington Bks.

Steinberg, Richard M. & Danker, Harold. Erisa: An Accounting & Management Guide. 2nd ed. 392p. 1983. 49.95x (ISBN 0-471-09798-5). Ronald Pr.

Steinberg, Ronald. Fra Girolamo Savonarola, Florentine Art & Renaissance Historiography. LC 76-8304. (Illus.). 151p. 1977. 12.00x (ISBN 0-8214-0202-1, 82-82097). Ohio U Pr.

Steinberg, S. A Fairy Tale. 1980. 8.95 o.s.i. (ISBN 0-440-00011-4). Delacorte.

Steinberg, S. H. Historical Tables Fifty-Eight BC to AD Nineteen Seventy-Eight. 10th ed. LC 79-16881. 1979. 26.00x (ISBN 0-312-38676-1). St Martin.

Steinberg, S. H., ed. Dictionary of British History. 2nd ed. LC 79-140431. 1971. 17.95 o.p. (ISBN 0-312-20020-X). St Martin.

Steinberg, Saul. The Passport. (Illus.). 1979. 17.95 o.p. (ISBN 0-394-50528-X). Random.

Steinberg, Theodore L. Mendele Mocher Seforim. (World Authors Ser.). 1977. lib. bdg. 15.95 (ISBN 0-8057-6308-2, Twayne). G K Hall.

Steinberg, W. Hasselblad Guide. (Illus.). 1968. pap. 2.95 o.p. (ISBN 0-8174-0174-1, Amphoto). Watson-Guptill.

--Minolta Twin-Lens Reflex Guide. 1968. 2.95 o.p. (ISBN 0-8174-0167-9, Amphoto). Watson-Guptill.

Steinberger, Anna & Steinberger, Emil, eds. Testicular Development: Structure & Function. 556p. 1979. text ed. 61.50 (ISBN 0-89004-397-3). Raven.

Steinberger, Emil, jt. ed. see Steinberger, Anna.

Steinbergh, Judith & McKim, Elizabeth. Beyond Words: Writing Poems with Children. 136p. 1983. pap. 9.95 (ISBN 0-931694-13-2). Wampeter Pr.

Steinbicker, Earl. DayTrips from London by Rail, Bus or Car. (Illus.). 256p. (Orig.). 1983. pap. 8.95 (ISBN 0-8038-1581-6). Hastings.

Steinbock, B. Killing & Letting Die. 239p. 1980. pap. 12.95 (ISBN 0-13-515361-1). P-H.

Steinbrecher, Edwin. Inner Guide Meditation. 200p. 1983. pap. 9.95 (ISBN 0-85030-300-1). Newcastle Pub.

Steinbring, Jack, jt. ed. see Hamer, John.

Steinbruckner, Bruno F. Ludwig Thoma. (World Authors Ser.). 1978. lib. bdg. 14.95 (ISBN 0-8057-6335-X, Twayne). G K Hall.

Steinbruner, John, jt. auth. see Jacoby, Henry D.

Steinbrunner, Chris & Penzler, Otto. Encyclopedia of Mystery & Detection. 1976. 24.50 o.p. (ISBN 0-07-061121-1, P&RB). McGraw.

Steincrohn, Peter J. Low Blood Sugar. 1973. pap. 2.25 (ISBN 0-451-12192-9, AE2192, Sig). NAL.

Steindler, Geraldine. Game Cookbook. 1965. pap. 5.95 o.s.i. (ISBN 0-695-87906-5). Follett.

--Game Cookbook. (Illus.). 240p. pap. 8.95 (ISBN 0-88317-000-0). Stoeger Pub Co.

Steindler, Gerry. Game Cookbook. Rev. ed. Cruson, Charlene S., ed. 256p. 1983. pap. 10.95 (ISBN 0-88317-111-2). Stoeger Pub Co.

Steindler, R. A. Reloader's Guide. 3rd ed. 1975. pap. 6.95 deluxe ed o.s.i. (ISBN 0-695-80551-7). Follett.

--The Rifle Guide. (Illus.). 1978. pap. 8.95 o.s.i. (ISBN 0-695-81128-2). Follett.

Steindler, R. A., ed. & illus. Shooting the Muzzleloaders. new ed. LC 74-29423. (Sports Library). (Illus.). 1975. 11.95 o.s.i. (ISBN 0-89149-032-9); pap. 6.95 o.s.i. (ISBN 0-89149-062-0). Jolex.

Steindler, Robert A. Home Gunsmithing Digest. 1978. pap. 7.95 o.s.i. (ISBN 0-695-81212-2). Follett.

Steindl-Rast, David. A Listening Heart: The Art of Contemplative Living. 96p. 1983. 7.95 (ISBN 0-8245-0576-X). Crossroad NY.

Steinem, Gloria. Picking Up the Pieces: A Chronicle of Our Times. 288p. Date not set. 14.95 (ISBN 0-03-063236-6). HR&W.

Steiner, Barbara. Biography of a Bengal Tiger. LC 78-24470. (Nature Biography Ser.). (Illus.). (gr. 3-6). 1979. PLB 6.99 (ISBN 0-399-61138-X). Putnam Pub Group.

--Biography of a Desert Bighorn. LC 74-16629. (Nature Biography Ser.). (Illus.). (gr. 3-5). 1975. PLB 5.49 o.p. (ISBN 0-399-60923-7). Putnam Pub Group.

--Biography of a Kangaroo Rat. LC 76-5450. (Nature Biography Ser). (Illus.). (gr. 3-5). 1977. PLB 4.97 o.p. (ISBN 0-399-61017-0). Putnam Pub Group.

--Biography of a Killer Whale. LC 77-20982. (Nature Biography Ser.). (Illus.). (gr. 3-5). 1978. PLB 6.99 (ISBN 0-399-61087-1). Putnam Pub Group.

--Biography of a Wolf. (Nature Biography Ser.). (Illus.). 64p. (gr. 3-5). 1973. PLB 6.59 o.p. (ISBN 0-399-60781-1). Putnam Pub Group.

--Stanleigh's Wrong Side Out Day. LC 82-9711. (Illus.). (gr. k-4). 1982. PLB 9.25g (ISBN 0-516-03619-X). Childrens.

Steiner, Barry R. Pay Less Tax Legally: 1983. (Orig.). 1982. pap. 4.95 (ISBN 0-451-82071-1, Sig). NAL.

Steiner, Barry R. & Kennedy, David W. Perfectly Legal: Three Hundred Foolproof Methods for Paying Less Taxes, 1983 Edition. 230p. 1983. 14.95 (ISBN 0-471-89588-1, Pub. by Wiley-Interscience); pap. 7.95 (ISBN 0-471-87020-X). Wiley.

--Perfectly Legal: Two Hundred & Seventy-Five Foolproof Methods for Paying Less Taxes. LC 81-10348. 201p. 1981. 14.95 o.p. (ISBN 0-471-08420-4, Pub. by Wiley-Interscience). Wiley.

Steiner, Bernard C. Reverend Thomas Bray: His Life & Selected Works Relating to Maryland. 252p. 1901. 9.50 (ISBN 0-686-36853-3). Md Hist.

Steiner, Bruce E. Samuel Seabury, Seventeen Twenty-Nine to Seventeen Ninety-Six: A Study in the High Church Tradition. LC 78-181686. (Illus.). xiii, 508p. 1971. 20.00x (ISBN 0-8214-0098-3, 82-81032). Ohio U Pr.

Steiner, Bruce E; see Weaver, Glenn.

Steiner, Christian & Jacobson, Robert M. Opera People. LC 82-7113. (Illus.). 128p. 1982. 30.00 (ISBN 0-86565-027-6). Vendome.

Steiner, Dale R., ed. Historical Journals: A Handbook for Writers & Reviewers. LC 80-26215. 213p. 1981. 28.50 (ISBN 0-87436-312-8); pap. text ed. 13.85 (ISBN 0-87436-337-3). ABC-Clio.

Steiner, Elizabeth. Logical & Conceptual Analytic Techniques for Educational Researchers. LC 77-18575. 1978. pap. text ed. 6.25 (ISBN 0-8191-0406-X). U Pr of Amer.

Steiner, Elizabeth, et al. Education & American Culture. (Illus.). 1980. pap. text ed. 12.95x (ISBN 0-02-416770-3). Macmillan.

Steiner, Erich. Determination & Interpretation of Molecular Wave Functions. LC 75-78120. (Monographs in Physical Chemistry: No. 3). 250p. 1976. 49.50 (ISBN 0-521-21037-2). Cambridge U Pr.

Steiner, Eugen. The Slovak Dilemma. (International Studies). (Illus.). 242p. 1973. 32.50 (ISBN 0-521-20050-4). Cambridge U Pr.

Steiner, Frederick. The Politics of New Town Planning: The Newfields, Ohio, Story. LC 80-12783. (Illus.). xiv, 266p. 1981. 17.95x (ISBN 0-8214-0414-8, 82-83053). Ohio U Pr.

Steiner, George. After Babel: Aspects of Language & Translation. LC 74-29207. 1975. 27.50 o.p. (ISBN 0-19-212196-0); pap. 10.95 (ISBN 0-19-502048-0, GB). Oxford U Pr.

--Anno Domini: Three Stories. LC 80-15345. 205p. 1980. Repr. of 1964 ed. 3.95 (ISBN 0-87951-113-3). Overlook Pr.

--The Death of Tragedy. LC 79-21658. 1980. pap. 6.95 (ISBN 0-19-502702-7, GB 599, GB). Oxford U Pr.

--In Bluebeard's Castle: Some Notes Toward the Redefinition of Culture. LC 70-158141. 1971. pap. 6.95 (ISBN 0-300-01710-3). Yale U Pr.

--The New CEO. LC 82-48599. (Studies of the Modern Corporation-Graduate School of Business-Columbia Univ). 160p. 1983. write for info. (ISBN 0-02-931250-7). Free Pr.

--On Difficulty & Other Essays. 1978. pap. 7.95 (ISBN 0-19-520222-8, G-B613). Oxford U Pr.

--The Portage to San Cristobel of A.H. 1982. 13.50 (ISBN 0-671-44572-3). S&S.

Steiner, George A. & Steiner, John F. Business, Government & Society: A Managerial Perspective. 3rd ed. 625p. 1980. text ed. 24.95 (ISBN 0-394-32445-5). Random.

Steiner, George A., et al. Management Policy & Strategy: Cases & Readings. 2nd ed. 1982. 26.95 (ISBN 0-02-416800-9); text ed. 14.95x (ISBN 0-02-416790-8). Macmillan.

Steiner, Gilbert Y. The Children's Cause. 1976. 22.95 (ISBN 0-8157-8120-2); pap. 8.95 (ISBN 0-8157-8119-9). Brookings.

--The Futility of Family Policy. 250p. 1981. 18.95 (ISBN 0-8157-8124-5); pap. 7.95 (ISBN 0-8157-8123-7). Brookings.

--The State of Welfare. 1971. 22.95 (ISBN 0-8157-8122-9); pap. 8.95 (ISBN 0-8157-8121-0). Brookings.

Steiner, Gilbert Y., ed. The Abortion Dispute & the American System. LC 82-45978. 100p. 1983. pap. 6.95 (ISBN 0-8157-8125-3). Brookings.

Steiner, H. M. Public & Private Investments: Socioeconomic Analysis. 414p. 1980. 39.95 (ISBN 0-471-01625-X, Pub. by Wiley-Interscience). Wiley.

Steiner, Henry J. & Vagts, Detlev F. Case & Documentary Supplement for Use with Transnational Legal Problems, Materials & Text. 2nd ed. (University Casebook Ser.). 273p. 1982. pap. text ed. write for info. (ISBN 0-88277-092-6). Foundation Pr.

Steiner, Henry M. Conflict in Urban Transportation: The People Against the Planners. LC 78-2070. (Illus.). 144p. 1978. 18.95x (ISBN 0-669-02268-3). Lexington Bks.

Steiner, J. E. & Ganchrow, J. R., eds. The Determination of Behavior by Chemical Stimuli: Proceedings of the Fifth European Chemoreception Research Organization Mini-Symposium, Israel, 1981. 287p. 1982. pap. 24.00 (ISBN 0-904147-33-9). IRL Pr.

Steiner, Jacob. Gesammelte Werke, 2 Vols. 2nd ed. LC 76-113151. (Ger). 1971. text ed. 59.50 set (ISBN 0-8284-0233-7). Chelsea Pub.

Steiner, Jean-Francis. Treblinka. 1979. pap. 2.95 (ISBN 0-451-62028-3, ME2028, Ment). NAL.

Steiner, Jesse F. & Brown, Roy M. North Carolina Chain Gang, a Study of County Convict Road Work. LC 69-14949. (Criminology, Law Enforcement, & Social Problems Ser.: No. 39). (Illus.). 1969. Repr. of 1927 ed. 8.50x (ISBN 0-87585-039-1). Patterson Smith.

Steiner, John F., jt. auth. see Steiner, George A.

Steiner, Jorg, jt. auth. see Muller, Jorg.

Steiner, Marie Von Sivers see Steiner, Rudolf & Steiner Von Sivers, Marie.

Steiner, P., et al, eds. The Structure of the Literary Process: Studies Dedicated to the Memory of Felix Vodicka. (Linguistic & Literary Studies in Eastern Europe: No. 8). 450p. 1982. 60.00 (ISBN 90-272-1512-X). Benjamins North Am.

Steiner, Robert, et al. Chemistry of Living Systems. 1981. text ed. write for info. (ISBN 0-442-20052-8). Van Nos Reinhold.

Steiner, Rudlof. The Concepts of Original Sin & Grace. Osmond, D. S., tr. from Ger. 32p. 1973. pap. 1.95 (ISBN 0-85440-275-6, Pub. by Steinerbooks). Anthroposophic.

Steiner, Rudolf. And The Temple Becomes Man. Osmond, D. S., tr. from Ger. 31p. 1979. pap. 2.50 (ISBN 0-85440-337-X, Pub. by Steinerbooks). Anthroposophic.

--The Being of Man & His Future Evolution. Wehrle, Pauline, tr. from Ger. 148p. 1981. 18.00 (ISBN 0-85440-402-3, Pub. by Steinerbooks); pap. 11.95 (ISBN 0-85440-405-8). Anthroposophic.

--The Boundaries of Natural Science. Amrine, Frederick, tr. from Ger. 190p. 1983. 14.00 (ISBN 0-88010-018-4). Anthroposophic.

--The Calendar of the Soul. Pusch, Ruth & Pusch, Hans, trs. from Ger. 62p. 1982. 7.95 (ISBN 0-88010-009-5). Anthroposophic.

--The Change in the Path to Supersensible Knowledge. 22p. 1982. pap. 2.75 (ISBN 0-919924-18-2, Pub. by Steiner Book Centre Canada). Anthroposophic.

--Christianity & Occult Mysteries of Antiquity. 2nd ed. Allen, Paul M., ed. Frommer, E. A., et al, trs. from Ger. LC 61-18165. (The Major Writings of Rudolf Steiner in English Translation Ser.: The Centennial Edition). 256p. 1981. 13.00 (ISBN 0-89345-021-9); pap. 7.50 (ISBN 0-89345-201-7). Garber Comm.
--Christianity As a Mystical Fact & the Occult Mysteries of Antiquity. LC 61-18165. 256p. 1979. 13.00 (ISBN 0-89345-021-9, Spiritual Sci Lib). Garber Comm.
--The Constitution of the School of Spiritual Science. 2nd ed. Adams, George & Rudel, Joan, trs. from Ger. 78p. 1980. pap. 5.00 (ISBN 0-88010-039-7, Pub. by Anthroposophical Society London). Anthroposophic.
--Cosmic Memory: Atlantis & Lemuria. LC 59-13706. 256p. 1981. Repr. of 1959 ed. 13.00 o.p. (ISBN 0-8334-0731-7). Garber Comm.
--Cosmic Memory: Atlantis & Lemuria. 5th ed. LC 59-13706. (Steiner Books Spiritual Science Library). 256p. 1981. lib. bdg. 13.00 (ISBN 0-89345-022-7). Garber Comm.
--Curative Education. 2nd ed. Adams, Mary, tr. (Illus.). 240p. 1981. pap. 13.00 (ISBN 0-85440-244-6). Anthroposophic.
--The Dead Are with Us. Osmond, D. S., tr. from Ger. 32p. 1973. pap. 2.50 (ISBN 0-85440-274-8, Pub. by Steinerbooks). Anthroposophic.
--The Easter Festival in Relation to the Mysteries. Adams, George, tr. 79p. 1968. pap. 5.95 (ISBN 0-85440-194-6). Anthroposophic.
--The Education of the Child. 4th impr. of 2nd ed. Adams, George & Adams, Mary, trs. from Ger. 48p. 1981. pap. 3.00 (ISBN 0-85440-030-3, Pub. by Steinerbooks). Anthroposophic.
--The Effects of Spiritual Development. 3rd ed. Parker, A. H., tr. from Ger. (Illus.). 157p. 1978. 15.00 (ISBN 0-85440-319-1, Pub. by Steinerbooks); pap. 9.95 (ISBN 0-85440-320-5). Anthroposophic.
--Esoteric Development. 190p. 1982. 14.00 (ISBN 0-88010-013-3); pap. 8.95 (ISBN 0-88010-012-5). Anthroposophic.
--The Etherisation of the Blood: The Entry of the Etheric Christ into the Evolution of the Earth. 4th ed. Freeman, Arnold & Osmond, D. S., trs. from Ger. 42p. 1980. pap. 2.95 (ISBN 0-85440-248-9, Pub. by Steinerbooks). Anthroposophic.
--Eurythmy As Visible Music. rev. ed. Compton-Burnett, V. & Compton-Burnett, J., trs. from Ger. (Illus.). 1977. 14.50 (ISBN 0-85440-309-4). Anthroposophic.
--The Evolution of Consciousness. Watkin, V. E. & Davy, C., trs. from Ger. 199p. 1979. pap. 7.95 (ISBN 0-85440-351-5, Pub. by Steinerbooks). Anthroposophic.
--The Festival & Their Meaning. 399p. 1981. 21.00 (ISBN 0-85440-370-1, Pub. by Steinerbooks); pap. 15.00 (ISBN 0-85440-380-9). Anthroposophic.
--The Foundation Stone. 72p. 1979. pap. 5.50 (ISBN 0-85440-346-9, Pub. by Steinerbooks). Anthroposophic.
--Four Mystery Dramas. Pusch, Ruth & Pusch, Hans, trs. from Ger. (Illus.). 565p. 1973. pap. 16.50 (ISBN 0-919924-08-5, Pub. by Steiner Book Centre Canada). Anthroposophic.
--From Jesus to Christ. 185p. 1973. 16.95 o.p. (ISBN 0-85440-277-2). Anthroposophic.
--From Symptom to Reality in Modern History. 245p. 1976. 16.95 (ISBN 0-85440-298-5). Anthroposophic.
--The Gospel of St. John & its Relation to the Other Gospels. rev. ed. Easton, Stewart, ed. Lockwood, Samuel & Lockwood, Loni, trs. from Ger. 298p. 1982. 14.00 (ISBN 0-88010-015-X); pap. 8.95 (ISBN 0-88010-014-1). Anthroposophic.
--Gospel of St. Luke. 1964. 13.95 (ISBN 0-85440-042-7); pap. 8.95 (ISBN 0-85440-299-3). Anthroposophic.
--The Holy Grail: From the Works of Rudolf Steiner. Roboz, Steven, ed. 40p. 1979. pap. 2.95 (ISBN 0-88010-049-4, Pub. by Steiner Book Centre Canada). Anthroposophic.
--The Human Soul & the Universe. (q). Orig. Title: Cosmic & Human Metamorphoses. 24p. 1982. pap. 2.95 (ISBN 0-919924-17-4, Pub. by Steiner Book Centre Canada). Anthroposophic.
--Initiation & Its Results. 134p. 7.00 (ISBN 0-686-38222-6). Sun Bks.
--The Inner Aspect of the Social Question. Davy, Charles, tr. from Ger. 72p. 1974. pap. 3.95 (ISBN 0-85440-050-8, Pub. by Steinerbooks). Anthroposophic.
--Introduction to Spiritual Science. Garber, Bernard J., ed. & intro. by. LC 82-82478. (Steinerbooks Spiritual Science Library). 248p. 1982. 13.00 (ISBN 0-89345-038-3). Garber Comm.
--Jesus & Christ. Bledsoe, John, tr. from Ger. 23p. 1976. pap. 1.50 (ISBN 0-88010-042-7). Anthroposophic.
--Karmic Relationships, 8 vols. Incl. Vol. 1. 14.50; Vol. 2. 14.50 (ISBN 0-685-36128-4); Vol. 3. 12.95 (ISBN 0-685-36129-2); Vol. 4. o.p. (ISBN 0-685-36130-6); Vol. 5. o.p. (ISBN 0-685-36131-4); Vol. 6. 9.75 (ISBN 0-685-36132-2); Vol. 7. 9.95 (ISBN 0-685-36133-0); Vol. 8. 9.95 (ISBN 0-685-36134-9). Anthroposophic.
--Karmic Relationships: Esoteric Studies, Vol. I. Adams, George, tr. from Ger. 205p. 1981. 14.50 (ISBN 0-85440-260-8, Pub. by Steinerbooks). Anthroposophic.
--Karmic Relationships: Esoteric Studies, Vol. 7. Osmond, D. S., tr. from Ger. 140p. 1973. 9.95 (ISBN 0-85440-276-4, Pub. by Steinerbooks). Anthroposophic.
--Karmic Relationships: Esoteric Studies, Vol. 8. Osmond, D. S., tr. from Ger. Orig. Title: Cosmic Christianity & the Impulse of Michael. 102p. 1975. 9.95 (ISBN 0-85440-018-4, Pub. by Steinerbooks). Anthroposophic.
--Karmic Relationships: Esoteric Studies (The Karmic Relationships of the Anthroposophics Movement, Vol. 3. 3rd ed. Adams, George, tr. 179p. 1977. 12.95 (ISBN 0-85440-313-2, Pub. by Steinerbooks). Anthroposophic.
--Karmic Relationships: Esteric Studies, Vol. 2. Adams, George & Cotterell, M., trs. from Ger. Davy, C. & Osmond, D. S. 1974. 14.50 (ISBN 0-85440-281-0, Pub. by Steinerbooks). Anthroposophic.
--Knowledge of the Higher Worlds & Its Attainment. Metaxa, George & Monges, Henry B., trs. from Ger. LC 79-101595. 224p. 1983. 14.00 (ISBN 0-88010-045-1); pap. 6.95 (ISBN 0-88010-046-X). Anthroposophic.
--Knowledge of the Higher Worlds: How Is It Achieved? 6th ed. Davy, Charles & Osmond, D. S., trs. from Ger. 222p. 1976. pap. 5.50 (ISBN 0-85440-221-7, Pub. by Steinerbooks). Anthroposophic.
--A Lecture on Eurythmy. 2nd ed. 37p. 1977. pap. 3.00 o.p. (ISBN 0-85440-189-X). Anthroposophic.
--Links Between the Living & the Dead: Transformation of Earthly Forces into Clairvoyance. Osmond, D. S. & Davy, C., trs. 64p. 1973. pap. 3.00 (ISBN 0-85440-273-X, Pub. by Steinerbooks). Anthroposophic.
--Man as a Being of Sense & Perception. Lenn, Dorothy, tr. from Ger. 53p. 1981. pap. 6.00 (ISBN 0-919924-11-5, Pub. by Steiner Book Centre Canada). Anthroposophic.
--Man as a Picture of the Living Spirit. Adams, George, tr. from Ger. 31p. (Orig.). 1972. pap. 1.95 (ISBN 0-85440-253-5, Pub. by Steinerbooks). Anthroposophic.
--Man as Symphony of the Creative Word. 3rd ed. Compton-Burnett, Judith, tr. from Ger. 223p. 1978. pap. 10.95 (ISBN 0-85440-324-8, Pub. by Steinerbooks). Anthroposophic.
--Man-Hieroglyph of the Universe. Adams, George & Adams, Mary, trs. from Ger. 221p. 1972. 16.00 (Pub. by Steinerbooks). Anthroposophic.
--Manifestations of Karma. 261p. 1976. pap. 6.95 (ISBN 0-85440-305-1). Anthroposophic.
--Mission of the Individual Folk Souls in Relation to Teutonic Mythology. Parker, A. H., tr. from Ger. 1970. 11.95 o.p. (ISBN 0-85440-229-2). Anthroposophic.
--A Modern Art of Education. 3rd ed. Darrell, Jesse, tr. from Ger. 233p. 1981. 16.95 (ISBN 0-85440-261-6, Pub. by Steinerbooks); pap. 11.95 (ISBN 0-85440-262-4). Anthroposophic.
--Mysticism at the Dawn of the Modern Age. 2nd ed. Allen, Paul M., ed. Zimmer, Karl E., tr. from Ger. LC 60-15703. (The Major Writings of Rudolf Steiner in English Translation Ser.: The Centennial Edition). 256p. 1981. 13.00 (ISBN 0-89345-026-X, Steinerbks); pap. 7.50 (ISBN 0-89345-206-8). Garber Comm.
--Occult Readings & Occult Hearing. Osmond, D. S., tr. from Ger. 79p. 1975. pap. 5.50 (ISBN 0-85440-286-1). Anthroposophic.
--Occult Science: An Outline. Adams, George & Adams, Mary, trs. from Ger. 352p. 1969. 14.50 (ISBN 0-85440-207-1, Pub. by Steinerbooks). Anthroposophic.
--The Occult Significance of the Blood. 3rd ed. Barfield, Owen, tr. from Ger. 32p. 1978. pap. 1.95 (ISBN 0-85440-186-5, Pub. by Steinerbooks). Anthroposophic.
--Philosophy of Spiritual Activity. 2nd ed. LC 80-65627. (Steinerbks Spiritual Science Library). 304p. 1980. lib. bdg. 14.00 (ISBN 0-89345-030-8). Garber Comm.
--The Reappearance of Christ in the Etheric. rev. ed. 190p. (Orig.). 1983. 14.00 (ISBN 0-88010-017-6); pap. 8.95 (ISBN 0-88010-016-8). Anthroposophic.
--The Redemption of Thinking: A Study in the Philosophy of Thomas Aquinas. Sheperd, A. P. & Nicoll, Mildred R., trs. from Ger. Orig. Title: Die Philosophie des Thomas von Aquino. 191p. 1983. pap. text ed. 8.95 (ISBN 0-88010-044-3). Anthroposophic.
--Road to Self Knowledge. 1975. 10.95 (ISBN 0-85440-290-X); pap. 6.95 (ISBN 0-85440-291-8). Anthroposophic.
--Rudolf Steiner: An Autobiography. LC 72-95242. (Illus.). 560p. 1978. 20.00x (ISBN 0-89345-031-6, Spiritual Sci Lib); pap. 14.00 (ISBN 0-89345-210-6). Garber Comm.
--Rudolf Steiner: An Autobiography. 2nd ed. LC 72-95242. (Steinerbks Spiritual Science Library). (Illus.). 560p. 1980. lib. bdg. 20.00 (ISBN 0-89345-031-6). Garber Comm.
--Rudolf Steiner: An Autobiography. Allen, Paul M., ed. Stebbing, Rita, tr. LC 72-95242. Orig. Title: Mein Lebensgang. (Illus.). 541p. 1977. pap. 13.95 (ISBN 0-8334-3501-9, Pub. by Steinerbooks NY). Anthroposophic.
--Self-Consciousness: The Spiritual Human Being. Garber, Bernard J., ed. LC 82-82477. (Steinerbooks Spiritual Science Library). 320p. 1982. 14.00 (ISBN 0-89345-020-0). Garber Comm.
--Spiritual Research: Methods & Results. rev. ed. Tapp, Michael, tr. from Ger. LC 81-51763. 288p. 1981. 14.00 (ISBN 0-89345-010-3, Spiritual Sci Lib). Garber Comm.
--Study of Man. 191p. 1981. 11.95 (ISBN 0-85440-104-0); pap. 8.50 (ISBN 0-85440-292-6). Anthroposophic.
--Threefold Social Order. rev. ed. Heckel, Frederick C., ed. LC 66-29676. Orig. Title: Threefold Commonwealth. 82p. (Orig.). 1966. pap. 5.00 (ISBN 0-910142-40-8). Anthroposophic.
--The True Nature of the Second Coming. 81p. 1980. pap. 3.50 (ISBN 0-85440-246-2). Anthroposophic.
--Truth & Knowledge: Introduction to "Philosophy of Spiritual Activity". 2nd ed. Allen, Paul M., ed. Stebbing, Rita, tr. from Ger. LC 62-22389. (The Major Writings of Rudolf Steiner in English Translation Ser.: The Centennial Edition). 112p. 1981. Repr. of 1963 ed. 10.00 (ISBN 0-89345-008-1, Steinerbks). Garber Comm.
--World History in the Light of Anthroposophy. new ed. Adams, George & Adams, Mary, trs. from Ger. 159p. 1977. pap. 9.00 (ISBN 0-85440-316-7). Anthroposophic.
Steiner, Rudolf & Steiner Von Sivers, Marie. Creative Speech: The Nature of Speech Formation. Budgett, Winifred & Hummel, Nancy, trs. from Ger. 240p. 1978. 16.95 (ISBN 0-85440-322-1, Pub. by Steinerbooks). Anthroposophic.
Steiner, Rudolf & Steiner-von Sivers, Marie. Poetry & the Art of Speech. Wedgwood, Julia & Welburn, Andrew, trs. from Ger. 323p. (Orig.). 1981. pap. 14.00 (ISBN 0-85440-407-4, Pub. by Steinerbooks). Anthroposophic.
Steiner, Rudolf, jt. auth. see Roboz, Steven.
Steiner, Rudolf, jt. auth. see Von Goethe, J. W.
Steiner, Rudolf, jt. auth. see Von Goethe, Johann W.
Steiner, Rudolf, et al. Education As an Art. Allen, Paul M., ed. Tapp, Michael & Tapp, Elizabeth, trs. from Ger. LC 73-130816. (Spiritual Science Library). 128p. (Orig.). 1981. 10.00 (ISBN 0-89345-024-3, Steinerbks); pap. 5.00 (ISBN 0-89345-202-5). Garber Comm.
Steiner, Rudolph. Spiritual-Scientific Basis of Goethe's Work. 1982. pap. 2.50 (ISBN 0-916786-66-8). St George Bk Serv.
Steiner, Shari. The Female Factor. LC 81-85717. 330p. 1983. pap. text ed. 19.95 (ISBN 0-933662-47-5). Intercult Pr.
--The Female Factor: A Study of Women in Five Western European Societies. LC 75-45111. 1977. 8.95 o.p. (ISBN 0-399-11582-X). Putnam Pub Group.
Steiner, Stan. Fusang: The Chinese Who Built America. LC 78-2172. 1979. 14.37i (ISBN 0-06-014087-9, HarpT). Har-Row.
--New Indians. 1969. pap. 2.65 o.s.i. (ISBN 0-440-56306-2, Delta). Dell.
--New Indians. LC 67-22509. (Illus.). 1968. 14.37i (ISBN 0-06-014082-8, HarpT). Har-Row.
Steiner, W. A. Classification Scheme & List of Subject Headings for the Squire Law Library of the University of Cambridge. LC 73-19917. 159p. 1974. lib. bdg. 20.00 (ISBN 0-379-20060-0). Oceana.
Steiner, Walter & Tabachnick, WAlter, eds. Recent Development in the Genetics of Insect Disease Vectors. (Illus.). 665p. text ed. 26.00 (ISBN 0-87563-224-6). Stipes.
Steiner, Wendy. The Colors of Rhetoric: Problems in the Relation Between Modern Literature & Painting. LC 81-19753. 1982. text ed. 25.00x (ISBN 0-226-77227-6). U of Chicago Pr.
Steiner, Zara S. Foreign Office & Foreign Policy Eighteen Ninety-Eight to Nineteen Fourteen. LC 70-85739. (Illus.). 1970. 44.50 (ISBN 0-521-07654-4). Cambridge U Pr.
Steinert, Marlis G. Hitler's War & the Germans: Public Mood and Attitude During the Second World War. De Witt, Thomas E., tr. from Ger. LC 76-25618. 387p. 1977. 21.95x (ISBN 0-8214-0186-6, 82-81875); pap. 11.95x (ISBN 0-8214-0402-4, 82-81883). Ohio U Pr.
Steiner Von Sivers, Marie, jt. auth. see Steiner, Rudolf.
Steiner-von Sivers, Marie, jt. auth. see Steiner, Rudolf.
Steiner Von Sivers, Marie see Steiner, Rudolf & Steiner-von Sivers, Marie.
Steinfeld, George J. Taret: An Integrative Approach to Individual & Family Therapy. 107p. 1980. softcover 8.95 (ISBN 0-932930-24-7). Pilgrimage Inc.
Steinfeld, Jeffrey. Molecules & Radiation: An Introduction to Modern Molecular Spectroscopy. 1978. pap. text ed. 14.50x (ISBN 0-262-69059-4). MIT Pr.
Steinfeld, Jeffrey I., ed. Electronic Transition Lasers. LC 76-4504. 300p. 1976. text ed. 22.50x (ISBN 0-262-19146-6). MIT Pr.
Steinfels, Peter. The Neo-Conservatives. 1979. 11.95 o.p. (ISBN 0-671-22665-7). S&S.
Steinfield, M. Cracks in the Melting Pot. 2nd ed. 1973. pap. 11.95x (ISBN 0-02-478670-5, 47867). Macmillan.
Steingart, Irving. Cognition as Pathological Play in Borderline-Narcissistic Personalities. 256p. 1983. text ed. 25.00 (ISBN 0-89335-179-2). SP Med & Sci Bks.
Steingass, David. American Handbook. LC 73-5370. (Pitt Poetry Ser.). 1973. 9.95 (ISBN 0-8229-3270-9); pap. 4.50 (ISBN 0-8229-5239-4). U of Pittsburgh Pr.
Steingass, F. A Comprehensive Persian-English Dictionary: Including the Arabic Words & Phrases to Be Met Within Persian Literature. 1977. text ed. 37.50x o.p. (ISBN 0-391-01967-8). Humanities.
--A Comprehensive Persian-English Dictionary: Including the Arabic Words & Phrases to Be Met with in Persian Literature. 1977. 65.00 o.p. (ISBN 0-7100-2152-6). Routledge & Kegan.
Steingold, Fred. Legal Master Guide for Small Business. 242p. 1983. 21.95 (ISBN 0-13-528422-8); pap. 9.95 (ISBN 0-13-528414-7). P-H.
Steingold, Fred S. The Practical Guide to Michigan Law. LC 82-10965. (Illus.). 184p. 1983. pap. 8.95 (ISBN 0-472-06341-3). U of Mich Pr.
Steinhacker, Charles. Superior: Portrait of a Living Lake. Karlen, Arno, compiled by. LC 74-123962. (Illus.). 1970. 40.00i (ISBN 0-06-014086-0, HarpT). Har-Row.
Steinhart, J. S. & Smith, T. J., eds. The Earth Beneath the Continents. LC 66-62581. (Geophysical Monograph Ser.: Vol. 10). 1966. 21.00 (ISBN 0-87590-010-0). Am Geophysical.
Steinhauer, Harry. Kulturlesebuch Fur Anfanger. 2nd ed. (Orig., Ger.). pap. text ed. 10.95 (ISBN 0-02-416850-5). Macmillan.
Steinhauer, Harry, ed. Twelve German Novellas. Steinhauser, Harry, tr. from Ger. 648p. 1977. 30.00x (ISBN 0-520-03504-6); pap. 11.95 (ISBN 0-520-03002-8, CAL 608). U of Cal Pr.
Steinhauer, Raleigh F. Fundamentals of Business Policy. 1978. pap. text ed. 8.00 (ISBN 0-8191-0370-5). U Pr of Amer.
Steinhaus, H. Mathematical Snapshots. 3rd, rev., & enl. ed. (Illus.). 320p. 1983. pap. 7.95 (ISBN 0-19-503267-5, GB 726, GB). Oxford U Pr.
Steinhaus, Hugo. Mathematical Snapshots. 3rd ed. (Illus.). 1969. 17.95x (ISBN 0-19-500117-6). Oxford U Pr.
Steinhauser, Harry, tr. see Steinhauer, Harry.
Steinheimer, Richard & Sims, Donald. Growing up with Trains: A Southern California Album. Bradley, Bill, ed. (Special Ser.: No. 83). 1982. 16.95 (ISBN 0-916374-53-X). Interurban.
Steinhilber, R. M. & Ulett, G. A., eds. Psychiatric Research in Public Service. 166p. 1962. pap. 3.00 o.p. (ISBN 0-685-24862-3, P015-0). Am Psychiatric.
Steinhoff, Carl R., jt. auth. see Owens, Robert G.
Steinhoff, D. Small Business Management Fundamentals. 3rd ed. (Management Ser.). 1982. 23.95x (ISBN 0-07-061146-7); instr's manual 18.95 (ISBN 0-07-061147-5). McGraw.
Steinhoff, Dan. Small Business Management Fundamentals. 2nd ed. (Illus.). 1977. text ed. 23.95 (ISBN 0-07-061142-4, C); instructors manual 22.50 (ISBN 0-07-061144-0). McGraw.
--The World of Business. (Illus.). 1979. text ed. 23.95 (ISBN 0-07-061134-3, C); tchrs. guide 18.95 (ISBN 0-07-061135-1); study guide 9.95 (ISBN 0-07-061136-X); test file 15.95 (ISBN 0-07-061129-7). McGraw.
Steinhoff, Patricia G. & Diamond, Milton. Abortion Politics: The Hawaii Experience. LC 77-3655. 1977. text ed. 10.00x (ISBN 0-8248-0550-X); pap. 4.95 (ISBN 0-8248-0498-8). UH Pr.
Steinhoff, Richard. Arithmetic. (Illus.). 1977. pap. text ed. 21.00 (ISBN 0-07-061127-0, C); instructor's manual 15.00 (ISBN 0-07-061128-9). McGraw.
--Basic Mathematics. 224p. 1972. 19.95 (ISBN 0-07-061123-8, G); instructor's manual 3.00 (ISBN 0-07-061124-6). McGraw.
Steinike, Otto A. Blueprint Reading, Checking & Testing, 2 Pts. 3rd ed. (Illus.). (gr. 9-10). 1956. Pt. 1. pap. text ed. 5.00 (ISBN 0-87345-080-9); Pt. 2. text ed. 5.00 (ISBN 0-87345-082-5). McKnight.
Steinilber-Oberlin, Emile. The Buddhist Sects of Japan, Their History, Philosophical Doctrines & Sanctuaries. Loge, Marc, tr. LC 78-109854. (Illus.). 303p. Repr. of 1938 ed. lib. bdg. 18.00x (ISBN 0-8371-4349-7, STBS). Greenwood.
Steininger, G. Russell & Van de Velde, Paul. Three Dollars a Year, Being the Story of San Pablo Cuatro Venados, a Typical Zapotecan Indian Village that Hangs on a Slope of the Sierras in Southwestern Mexico: Being the Story of San Pablo Cuatro Venados, a Typical Zapotecan Indian Village that Hangs on a Slope of the Sierras in Southwestern Mexico. LC 71-165660. Repr. of 1935 ed. 12.00 (ISBN 0-87917-016-6). Ethridge.
Steinitz, Carl & Rogers, Peter. Systems Analysis Model of Urbanization & Change: An Experiment in Interdisciplinary Education. 1970. 18.50x (ISBN 0-262-19074-5). MIT Pr.
Steinitz, Ernst. Algebraische Theorie der Koerper. LC 51-10623. 1976. text ed. 14.95 (ISBN 0-8284-0077-6). Chelsea Pub.
Steinitz, H., jt. ed. see Leffkowitz, M.

Steinitz, Kate T. Kurt Schwitters: A Portrait from Life. 1968. 32.50x o.p. (ISBN 0-520-01219-4). U of Cal Pr.
Steinke, Anne. Woman in Flight. (Finding Mr. Right Ser.). Date not set. pap. price not set. Avon.
Steinke, Frank F. Greater Works Shall Ye Do. 101p. (Orig.). 1980. pap. 2.25 (ISBN 0-686-73996-5). Impact Bks Mo.
Steinke, Peter L. Preaching the Theology of the Cross: Sermons & Worship Ideas for Lent & Easter. LC 82-72638. 128p. (Orig.). 1983. pap. 5.95 (ISBN 0-8066-1944-9, 10-5144). Augsburg.
Steinke, Rudolf, jt. ed. see Vale, Michel.
Steinkraus, Warren, ed. see Brightman, Edgar S.
Steinkraus, Warren E. Philosophy of Art. 1974. pap. 5.95x o.p. (ISBN 0-02-829230-8, 82923). Glencoe.
Steinkraus, Warren E., ed. New Studies in Berkeley's Philosophy. LC 81-40866. 218p. 1982. lib. bdg. 23.25 (ISBN 0-8191-2006-5); pap. text ed. 11.25 (ISBN 0-8191-2007-3). U Pr of Amer.
Steinkraus, Warren E., jt. ed. see Beck, Robert N.
Steinkraus, William & Savitt, Sam. Great Horses of the U. S. Equestrian Team. LC 76-53434. (Illus.). (gr. 5 up). 1977. 6.95 o.p. (ISBN 0-396-07432-4). Dodd.
Steinkraus, William, ed. The U. S. Equestrian Team Book of Riding. 1976. 14.95 o.p. (ISBN 0-671-22371-2). S&S.
Steinkuehler, Pearl, jt. auth. see Nordtvedt, Matilda.
Steinkueler, Pearl, jt. auth. see Nordvedt, Matilda.
Steinlage, Ralph. College Algebra & Trigonometry. 1981. text ed. 24.50x (ISBN 0-673-16231-1). Scott F.
Steinman, G. D., jt. auth. see Kenyon, D.
Steinman, Laura, ed. see Levin, Paul.
Steinman, Lisa M. Lost Poems. 51p. 1976. 3.50 (ISBN 0-87886-073-8). Ithaca Hse.
Steinman, Michael. Energy & Environmental Issues: The Making & Implementation of Public Policy Issues. LC 78-13871. 224p. 1979. 23.95x (ISBN 0-669-02699-9). Lexington Bks.
Steinmetz, Andrew. Gaming Table: Its Votaries & Victims, in All Times & Countries, Especially in England & in France, 2 Vols. LC 69-16247. (Criminology, Law Enforcement, & Social Problems Ser.: No. 96). 1969. Repr. of 1870 ed. Set. 40.00x (ISBN 0-87585-096-0). Patterson Smith.
Steinmetz, Bob. In the Land of Funshine. Smollon, Jim, ed. Orig. Title: Jayhawking Florida Traveler. (Illus.). 72p. 1972. pap. 1.00 o.p. (ISBN 0-686-11502-3). Star Pub Fla.
Steinmetz, Charles P. Lectures on Electrical Engineering, 3 vols. Alger, Philip L., ed. Incl. Vol. 1. Elements of Electrical Engineering (ISBN 0-8446-0325-2); Vol. 2. Electric Waves & Impulses (ISBN 0-8446-0326-0); Vol. 3. Transient Electrical Phenomena (ISBN 0-8446-0327-9). 30.00 set (ISBN 0-8446-0324-4). Peter Smith.
Steinmetz, D., jt. auth. see Sandberg, K.
Steinmetz, George H. Freemasonry: Its Hidden Meaning. 1982. Repr. of 1976 ed. 9.50 (ISBN 0-686-43322-X). Macoy Pub.
--The Lost Word: Its Hidden Meaning. 1976. Repr. 9.50 (ISBN 0-88053-052-9). Macoy Pub.
--The Royal Arch: Its Hidden Meaning. 1979. Repr. of 1946 ed. text ed. 9.50 (ISBN 0-685-88808-8, M-302). Macoy Pub.
Steinmetz, Lawrence L. Nice Guys Finish Last. 1983. 12.95 (ISBN 0-8159-6316-5). Devin.
Steinmetz, S. J. Pipe, Bible & Peyote Among the Oglala Lakota. (Stockholm Studies in Comparative Religion: No. 19). 188p. 1981. pap. text ed. 20.00x o.p. (ISBN 91-22-00452-1, Pub. by Almqvist & Wilsell Swed En). Humanities.
Steinmeyer, Henry G. Staten Island, 1524-1898. (Illus.). 1973. Repr. of 1950 ed. 7.95 (ISBN 0-686-20334-8). Staten Island.
Steinmiller, Oswald M. The Approaching Seven Major Political Revolutions Which Will Transform Radically the World. (Illus.). 137p. 1983. 77.85 (ISBN 0-86722-030-9). Inst Econ Pol.
Steinour, Marcus. Dudley Smithwright & the Phantom Voice. LC 82-71048. (Dudley Smithwright Ser.). (Illus.). 96p. (gr. 3-5). 1982. 12.95x (ISBN 0-943864-09-7); pap. 3.95x (ISBN 0-943864-04-6). Davenport.
Steinsaltz, Adin. Beggars & Prayers: Adin Steinsaltz Retells the Tales of Rabbi Nahman of Bratslav. LC 78-54502. 1980. 11.50 (ISBN 0-465-00579-9). Basic.
--The Essential Talmud. Galai, Chaya, tr. from Hebrew. LC 75-36384. 200p. 1976. 15.00 (ISBN 0-465-02060-7). Basic.
--The Thirteen-Petalled Rose. LC 79-3077. 181p. 1980. 15.00 (ISBN 0-465-08560-1). Basic.
Steinwald, Bruce, jt. auth. see Sloan, Frank A.
Steinwede, Dietrich. Reformation: A Picture Story of Martin Luther. Cooperrider, Edward A., tr. from German. LC 82-49055. (Illus.). 56p. 1983. pap. 6.95 (ISBN 0-8006-1710-X, 1-1710). Fortress.
Steinwedel, Louis W. & Newport, Herbert J. The Duesenberg. (Norton Automobile Ser.). (Illus.). 1982. 15.95 (ISBN 0-393-01589-0). Norton.
Steir, Charles. Blue Jolts: True Stories from the Cuckoo's Nest. LC 77-21412. 1978. 8.95 (ISBN 0-915220-30-X, 22969). New Republic.
Steiss, Alan W. Local Government Finance: Capital Facilities Planning & Debt Administration in Local Government. 320p. 1975. 23.95x (ISBN 0-669-00126-0). Lexington Bks.
Steiss, Alan W. & Daneke, Gregory A. Performance Administration. LC 79-48028. 288p. 1980. 24.95x (ISBN 0-669-03637-4). Lexington Bks.
Stekl, William, jt. auth. see Hill, Evan.
Steklov Institute of Mathematics, Academy of Sciences, U S S R, Vol. 136, jt. auth. see Vladimirov, V. S.
Steklov Institute of Mathematics & Kuz'mina, G. V. Moduli of Families of Curves & Quadratic Differentials. LC 82-8902. (Proceedings of the Steklov Institute of Mathematics). 76.00 (ISBN 0-8218-3040-6, STEKLO-1982-1). Am Math.
Steklov Institute of Mathematics & Karacuba, A. A. Multiple Trignometric Sums. LC 82-18403. (Proceedings of the Steklov Institute of Mathematics Ser.: Vol.1982 No. 2). 42.00 (ISBN 0-8218-3067-8, STEKLO/151). Am Math.
Stele, France, compiled by. Slovene Impressionists. Jereb, Elza & Mackinnon, Alasdair, trs. (Illus.). 196p. 1980. 35.00 (ISBN 0-89893-107-X). CDP.
Stella, A. M. Giovanni Alexander. 80p. 1982. pap. 3.50 (ISBN 0-9602044-2-3). Deinotation Seven.
Stella, Alexander A. Giovanni. 1982. 3.50 (ISBN 0-9602044-2-3). A Stella.
Stellar, Eliot, jt. auth. see Dethier, Vincent G.
Stellern, John. Diagnostic Prescriptive Teaching. 1982. 24.95 (ISBN 0-914420-56-9). Exceptional Pr Inc.
Stellern, John & Vasa, Stanley F. Introduction to Diagnostic-Prescriptive Teaching & Programming. 176p. 1976. 18.95 (ISBN 0-686-84869-1). Exceptional Pr Inc.
Stellfeld, J. A. Bibliographie Des Editions Musicales Platiniennes. (Acad. Royale, Mem. Ser.: Vol. 3). (Illus.). 248p. wrappers 35.00 o.s.i. (ISBN 90-6027-353-2, Pub. by Frits Knuf Netherlands). Pendragon NY.
Stellmacher, H. Bob. Cases in Real Estate Practice. (Illus.). 1980. pap. text ed. 13.95x (ISBN 0-02-417040-2). Macmillan.
Stellman, Jeanne M., jt. auth. see Daum, Susan M.
Stellwag, Carion F. Austrian Textiles. (Illus.). 22.50x (ISBN 0-87245-320-0). Textile Bk.
Stelmach, G. A. & Requin, J. Tutorials in Motor Behavior. (Advances in Psychology Ser.: Vol. 1). 1980. 70.25 (ISBN 0-444-85466-5). Elsevier.
Steltenkamp, Michael. The Sacred Vision: Native American Religion & Its Practice Today. LC 82-60594. 1983. pap. 5.95 (ISBN 0-8091-2481-5). Paulist Pr.
Steltzer, Ulli. Health in the Highlands: The Chimaltenango Development Program of Guatemala. LC 82-48872. (Illus.). 128p. 1983. 30.00 (ISBN 0-295-95994-0); pap. 0.00 (ISBN 0-295-96024-8). U of Wash Pr.
--Inuit: The North in Transition. LC 82-50685. (Illus.). 224p. 1983. 29.95 (ISBN 0-295-95951-7). U of Wash Pr.
Stelzel, Christian. Magic Cards. 52p. 1982. pap. 3.95 (ISBN 0-88079-025-3). US Games Syst.
Stelzer, Dick. The Star Treatment. LC 77-76868. 1977. 7.95 o.p. (ISBN 0-672-52290-X). Bobbs.
Stelzer, Ulli. Health in the Guatemalan Highlands. (Illus.). 128p. 1983. 30.00 (ISBN 0-295-95994-0); pap. 9.95 (ISBN 0-295-96024-8). U of Wash Pr.
Stem, Thad, Jr. Entries from Oxford. LC 78-171456. 333p. 1971. 9.95 (ISBN 0-87716-033-3, Pub. by Moore Pub Co). F Apple.
--Ransacking Words & Customs. LC 77-88204. 1977. 10.95 (ISBN 0-87716-086-4, Pub. by Moore Pub Co). F Apple.
--Thad Stem's Ark. LC 79-89864. (Illus.). 1979. 9.95 (ISBN 0-87716-107-0, Pub. by Moore Pub Co). F Apple.
--Thad Stem's First Reader. LC 76-1456. 1976. 9.95 (ISBN 0-87716-061-9, Pub. by Moore Pub Co). F Apple.
Stem, Thad, Jr., jt. auth. see Butler, Alan.
Stember, Charles H. Sexual Racism. 1978. pap. 3.95i o.p. (ISBN 0-06-090598-0, CN 598, CN). Har-Row.
Stembera, Z., et al, eds. High Risk Pregnancy & Child. Schierlova, M., tr. from Czech. (Illus.). 308p. 1976. 27.50 o.p. (ISBN 90-247-1924-0, Pub. by Nijhoff). Wright-PSG.
Stemmler, Theo, ed. English Texts, 15 vols. Incl. Vol. 1. Medieval English Love-Lyrics. 132p. 1970. pap. text ed. 7.50x (ISBN 3-484-44000-7); Vol. 2. English Satirical Poetry from Joseph Hall to Percy B. Shelley. 156p. 1970. pap. text ed. 7.50x (ISBN 3-484-44001-5); Vol. 3. Elizabethan Sonnet Sequences. 179p. 1970. pap. text ed. 7.50x (ISBN 3-484-44002-3); Vol. 4. Augustan Poetry. 158p. 1970. pap. text ed. 7.50x (ISBN 3-484-44003-1); Vol. 5. Linguistics in Great Britain II (Contemporary Linguistics) 164p. 1970. pap. text ed. 5.00x (ISBN 3-484-44004-X); Vol. 6. Medieval English Saints' Legends. 144p. 1970. pap. text ed. 7.50x (ISBN 3-484-44005-8); Vol. 7. English Theories of the Novel II (18 th Century) 158p. 1970. pap. text ed. 7.50 (ISBN 3-484-44006-6); Vol. 8. English Character-Writing. 136p. 1971. pap. text ed. 7.50x (ISBN 3-484-44007-4); Vol. 9. English Theories of the Novel III(19th Century) 150p. 1972. pap. text ed. 5.00x (ISBN 3-484-44012-0); Vol. 12. Mock-Heroic Poetry. 157p. 1971. **pap. text ed. 5.00x (ISBN 3-484-44008-2); Vol. 13. English Dramatic Theories IV (20th Century) 160p. 1972. pap. text ed. 5.00x (ISBN 3-484-44011-2); Vol. 14. Linguistics in Great Britain I (History of Linguistics) 155p. 1971. pap. text ed. 5.00x (ISBN 3-484-44009-0); Vol. 15. British Radicals & Reformers, 1789-1832. 134p. 1971. pap. text ed. 5.00x (ISBN 3-484-44010-4). pap. Intl Pubns Serv.**
Stempel, Guido H., III & Westley, Bruce H. Research Methods in Mass Communication. (Illus.). 550p. 1981. text ed. 26.95 (ISBN 0-13-774240-1). P-H.
Stempell, Dieter. A Programmed Introduction to the Theory of Probability. Baurley, George L., tr. (Illus.). 168p. 1973. pap. 5.50 (ISBN 0-8285-5141-3). Pub. by Verlag die Wirtschaft.
Stemple, David. High Ride Gobbler: The Story of the American Wild Turkey. LC 78-24200. (Illus.). 1979. 8.95 (ISBN 0-529-05524-4, Philomel). Putnam Pub Group.
Stenberg, Odin K. A Church Without Walls. LC 76-7702. 1976. pap. 3.50 (ISBN 0-87123-056-9, 200056). Bethany Hse.
Stendahl. Best Restaurants New York. LC 78-9420. (Best Restaurant Ser.). (Illus.). pap. 3.95 o.p. (ISBN 0-89286-137-1). One Hund One Prods.
--Charter House of Parma. Date not set. pap. 3.95 (ISBN 0-451-51731-8, CE1731, Sig Classics). NAL.
--The Full Flavor Cookbook. LC 82-184519. (Illus.). 160p. 1983. pap. 6.95 (ISBN 0-89709-043-8). Liberty Pub.
Stendahl, Brita K. Soren Kierkegaard. (World Authors Ser.). 1976. lib. bdg. 13.95 (ISBN 0-8057-6234-5, Twayne). G K Hall.
Stendhal. Charterhouse of Parma. Scott-Moncrieff, C. K., tr. (Orig.). pap. 3.95 (ISBN 0-451-51731-8, C1731, Sig Classics). NAL.
Stendhal, pseud. Lucien Leuwen, 2 vols. Varese, Louise, tr. Incl. Vol. 1. Green Huntsman. pap. o.p. (ISBN 0-685-23192-5, NDP107); Vol. 2. Telegraph. LC 50-3663. 5.00 (ISBN 0-8112-0388-3); pap. 1.75 o.p. (ISBN 0-8112-0199-6, NDP108). Set. pap. New Directions.
Stendhal. Lucien Leuwen, 2 vols. Edwards, H. L., tr. LC 82-73493. 645p. Repr. of 1951 ed. lib. bdg. 45.00x (ISBN 0-88116-011-3). Brenner Bks.
--Red & the Black. Parks, Lloyd C., tr. (Orig.). 1970. pap. 3.95 (ISBN 0-451-51793-8, CE1793, Sig Classics). NAL.
Stendhal, Henri. Memoirs of Egotism. Josephson, Matthew & Josephson, Hannah, trs. from Fr. 1975. pap. 2.95 o.p. (ISBN 0-07-061145-9, SP). McGraw.
Stendhal, Henry B. The Life of Henri Brulard. Phillips, Catherine A., tr. from Fr. 361p. 1982. Repr. of 1925 ed. lib. bdg. 40.00 (ISBN 0-89984-091-4). Century Bookbindery.
Steneck, N. H., ed. Risk-Benefit Analysis: The Microwave Case. LC 82-50313. (Illus.). 1982. 15.00 (ISBN 0-911302-44-1). San Francisco Pr.
Stenesh, J. Dictionary of Biochemistry. LC 75-23037. 344p. 1975. 42.50 (ISBN 0-471-82105-5, Pub. by Wiley-Interscience). Wiley.
Stenger, V. A., jt. auth. see Kolthoff, I. M.
Stenger, William, jt. auth. see Weinstein, Alexander.
Stenhagen, E., et al, eds. Registry of Mass Spectral Data, 4 vols. LC 74-910. 3358p. 1974. Set. 575.00 (ISBN 0-471-82115-2, Pub. by Wiley-Interscience). Wiley.
Stenhouse, Lawrence & Gajendra, Verna K. Teaching About Race Relations: Problems & Effects. (Routledge Education Books). 260p. 1982. 26.00 (ISBN 0-7100-9036-6). Routledge & Kegan.
Stenius, E. Critical Essays. (Acta Philosophica Fennica Ser.: Vol. 25). Date not set. pap. 25.75 (ISBN 0-444-10360-0). Elsevier.
Stenning, Eiliah M. Cavalier King Charles Spaniels. Foyle, Christina, ed. (Foyle's Handbks). (Illus.). 1973. 3.95 (ISBN 0-685-55793-6). Palmetto Pub.
Stensbol, Ottar. Model Flying Handbook. LC 75-14507. (Illus.). 1979. pap. 5.95 (ISBN 0-8069-8848-7). Sterling.
Stensland, Anna L. Literature by & about the American Indian: An Annotated Bibliography. LC 79-18073. 382p. 1979. pap. 9.25 (ISBN 0-8141-2984-6); pap. 6.60 members (ISBN 0-686-86437-9). NCTE.
Stensland, Vivian, ed. Daily Light from the New American Standard Bible. 416p. 1975. 8.95 (ISBN 0-8024-1740-X); pap. 4.95 o.p. (ISBN 0-8024-1741-8). Moody.
Stenson, Nancy, jt. auth. see Schumann, John H.
Stensrud, Rockwell, jt. auth. see Kirschenbaum, Howard.
Stenton, Adrian, jt. auth. see DeJoia, Alex.
Stenton, Doris M. The English Woman in History. LC 77-75291. (Studies in the Life of Women). 1977. lib. bdg. 20.00x o.p. (ISBN 0-8052-3669-4). Schocken.
Stenzel, A. M. Approaching the CPA Examination: A Personal Guide to Examination Preparation. 1981. pap. 9.95 (ISBN 0-471-08699-1). Wiley.
Stenzel, George, jt. auth. see Pearce, J. Kenneth.
Stenzel, Larry G. Lillie Seline's Confession. 96p. (Orig.). 1982. pap. 5.75 (ISBN 0-910021-02-3). Samuel P Co.
--Tales to Tell. 128p. (Orig.). 1979. pap. 4.50 (ISBN 0-910021-00-7). Samuel P Co.
Stepan, Nancy. The Idea of Race in Science: Great Britain 1800-1960. 1982. lib. bdg. 27.50 (ISBN 0-208-01972-3). Shoe String.
Stepanchev, Stephen. Mad Bomber. 100p. (Orig.). 1972. pap. 4.00 o.p. (ISBN 0-87685-122-7). Black Sparrow.
Stepanek, Vladimir, jt. auth. see Eckschlager, Karel.
Stepanoff, A. J. Centrifugal & Axial Flow Pumps: Theory, Design & Application. 2nd ed. LC 57-10815. 462p. 1957. 47.95x (ISBN 0-471-82137-3, Pub. by Wiley-Interscience). Wiley.
Stepanoff, Alexely. Gravity Flow & Transportation of Solids in Suspension. LC 72-91156. (Materials Handling & Packaging Ser). 1969. text ed. 12.50 (ISBN 0-471-82202-7, Pub. by Wiley). Krieger.
Stepanoff, Alexey J. Pumps & Blowers. LC 75-11894. 324p. 1978. Repr. of 1965 ed. 19.50 (ISBN 0-88275-306-1). Krieger.
Stepanoff, N. C. & Flier, Michael S. Say It in Russian. (Say It In Ser.). 256p. (gr. 6 up). pap. 2.95 (ISBN 0-486-20810-9). Dover.
Stepanov, B. I. & Gribkovskii, V. P. Theory of Luminescence. 505p. 1969. 98.00x (ISBN 0-677-61530-2). Gordon.
Stepanov, Nikolai L. Ivan Krylov. (World Authors Ser.). lib. bdg. 15.95 (ISBN 0-8057-2504-0, Twayne). G K Hall.
Stepat-Devan, Dorothy, et al. Introduction to Home Furnishings. 3rd ed. (Illus.). 1980. text ed. 22.95x (ISBN 0-02-417090-9). Macmillan.
Stepek, J. & Daoust, H. Additives for Plastics. (Polymers: Properties & Applications Ser.: Vol. 5). (Illus.). 256p. 1983. 69.00 (ISBN 0-387-90753-X). Springer-Verlag.
Stepelevich, L., ed. The Young Hegelians: An Anthology. LC 82-9480. (Texts in German Philosophy). 350p. Date not set. 49.50 (ISBN 0-521-24539-7); pap. 15.95 (ISBN 0-521-28772-3). Cambridge U Pr.
Stepelevich, Lawrence S., ed. & intro. by. The Capitalist Reader. LC 77-6261. 1977. 9.95 o.p. (ISBN 0-87000-379-8, Arlington Hse). Crown.
Stephan, Ruth, jt. ed. see Arguedas, Jose M.
Stephani, Hans. General Relativity: An Introduction to the Theory of the Gravitational Field. Stewart, John, ed. LC 81-10115. (Illus.). 300p. 1982. 49.50 (ISBN 0-521-24008-5). Cambridge U Pr.
Stephanides, Theodore, tr. see Palamas, Kostes.
Stephanits, V. The German Shepherd Dog in Word & Picture. 1925. 65.00 o.p. (ISBN 0-686-19925-1). Quest Edns.
Stephanopoulos, G. Synthesizing Networks of Heat Exchangers. Gyftopoulos, Elias P. & Cohen, Karen C., eds. (Industrial Energy-Conservation Manuals: No. 4). (Illus.). 128p. 1982. 3-ring binder pages 17.50x (ISBN 0-262-19203-9). MIT Pr.
Stephansson, O., ed. Application of Rock Mechanics to Cut & Fill Mining. 376p. (Orig.). 1981. pap. text ed. 132.25x (ISBN 0-900488-60-3). IMM North Am.
Stephen, A. C. & Edmonds, S. J. The Phyla Sipuncula & Echiura. 1972. 77.50x (ISBN 0-565-00717-3, Pub. by Brit Mus Nat Hist England). Sabbot-Natural Hist Bks.
Stephen, B., jt. auth. see Garst, T. E.
Stephen, Barbara B. Creating with Tissue Paper. (Arts & Crafts Ser.). (Illus.). 264p. 1973. 8.95 o.p. (ISBN 0-517-50579-7); pap. 6.95 o.p. (ISBN 0-517-50580-0). Crown.
Stephen, C. R., et al. Elements of Pediatric Anesthesia. 2nd ed. (Illus.). 216p. 1970. 17.75x o.p. (ISBN 0-398-01855-3). C C Thomas.
Stephen, David, ed. Cats. (Animal World Ser). (Illus.). 108p. 1974. 7.95 o.p. (ISBN 0-399-11240-5). Putnam Pub Group.
--Dolphins, Seals & Other Sea Mammals. (Animal World Ser). (Illus.). 88p. 1973. 6.95 o.p. (ISBN 0-399-11153-0). Putnam Pub Group.
Stephen, David, ed. see Hanzak, Jan & Veselovsky, Zdenek.
Stephen, J. M., jt. auth. see Waterlow, J. C.
Stephen, Leslie. English Utilitarians, 3 Vols. LC 67-29517. Repr. of 1900 ed. 67.50x o.p. (ISBN 0-678-00353-X). Kelley.
Stephen, Robert M. Developing an Understanding of World Problems. LC 69-15389. (No. 362). 154p. 1969. text ed. 7.00 incl. tchr's manual (ISBN 0-379-00362-7). Oceana.

Stephen, W. J. An Analysis of Primary Medical Care. LC 77-83999. (Illus.). 1979. 42.50 (ISBN 0-521-21860-8). Cambridge U Pr.

Stephen Chen Chi Aun. God's Plan for Salvation. 1978. 7.50 o.p. (ISBN 0-533-03754-9). Vantage.

Stephens, A. Rainer Maria Rilke's Gedichte an Die Nacht: An Essay in Interpretation. LC 72-178284. (Anglica Germanica Ser.: No. 2). 288p. 1972. 47.50 (ISBN 0-521-08388-5). Cambridge U Pr.

Stephens, Alan. In Plain Air: Poems 1958-1980. LC 82-75257. xii, 203p. 1982. text ed. 22.95x (ISBN 0-8040-0379-3); pap. 10.95 (ISBN 0-8040-0380-7). Swallow.

--Sum. LC 82-72015. (New Poetry Ser.: No. 19). 47p. 1958. 4.95 (ISBN 0-8040-0285-1). Swallow.

--Tree Meditation & Others. LC 82-72098. 53p. 1971. 6.95 (ISBN 0-8040-0296-7); pap. 4.50 (ISBN 0-8040-0622-9). Swallow.

--White River Poems: Conversations, Pronouncements, Testimony, Recollections & Mediations on the Subject of the White River Massacre, Sept. 29, 1879. LC 82-74268. 115p. 1975. 9.50 (ISBN 0-8040-0774-8). Swallow.

Stephens, Alan, ed. see Googe, Barnabe.

Stephens, Bruce M. God's Last Metaphor: The Doctrine of the Trinity in New England Theology. LC 80-11421. (American Academy of Religion Studies in Religion). pap. 11.95 (ISBN 0-89130-386-3, 01-00-24). Scholars Pr CA.

Stephens, Charles, jt. auth. see Suares, Jean-Clande.

Stephens, Christopher. The Lion Paperback: A Checklist. 32p. 1980. pap. 3.50 (ISBN 0-89366-124-4). Ultramarine Pub.

Stephens, Cleo M. Island Adventure. (YA) 6.95 (ISBN 0-685-07438-2, Avalon). Bouregy.

--The Mexican Mantilla. (YA) 1979. 6.95 (ISBN 0-685-90723-6, Avalon). Bouregy.

Stephens, Donald. Bliss Carman. (World Authors Ser.). 1966. lib. bdg. 15.95 (ISBN 0-8057-2200-9, Twayne). G K Hall.

Stephens, E. C., jt. auth. see Dunn, J. D.

Stephens, Edna B. John Gould Fletcher. (United States Author Ser.). 13.95 (ISBN 0-8057-0264-4, Twayne). G K Hall.

Stephens, Gwen J. Pathophysiology for Health Practitioners. (Illus.). 1980. text ed. 27.95x (ISBN 0-02-417120-4). Macmillan.

Stephens, H. A. Poisonous Plants of the Central United States. LC 79-28161. (Illus.). 224p. 1980. 16.00x o.p. (ISBN 0-7006-0202-X); pap. 9.95 (ISBN 0-7006-0204-6). Univ Pr KS.

Stephens, H. S., ed. see Seventh Technical Conference of the BPMA in Conjunction with BHRA.

Stephens, Harold. The Complete Guide to Singapore. (The Complete Asian Guide Ser.). (Illus.). 112p. (Orig.). 1981. pap. 6.95 (ISBN 962-7031-05-4, Pub. by CFW Pubns Hong Kong). C E Tuttle.

--Singapore by Night. (Asia by Night Ser.). (Illus.). 64p. (Orig.). 1981. pap. 4.95 (ISBN 962-7031-09-7, Pub. by CFW Pubns Hong Kong). C E Tuttle.

Stephens, Irving E. & Barnes, Dorothy L. A Bibliography of Noise for 1977-1981. LC 72-87107. (Bibliography of Noise Ser.). 177p. 1983. 22.50x (ISBN 0-686-83742-8). Whitston Pub.

Stephens, J. N. The Fall of the Florentine Republic 1512-1530. (Oxford-Warburg Studies). 300p. 1983. 39.50 (ISBN 0-19-822599-7). Oxford U Pr.

Stephens, James. The Insurrection in Dublin. 1979. text ed. 12.50x o. p. (ISBN 0-391-00942-7); pap. text ed. 6.00x (ISBN 0-391-00943-5). Humanities.

Stephens, James C. Managing Complexity: Work, Technology, Resources, & Human Relations. rev. ed. LC 77-124381. 1977. 26.50 (ISBN 0-912338-13-X); microfiche 9.50 (ISBN 0-912338-14-8). Lomond.

Stephens, James C., Jr., ed. see Simon, Laurence R.

Stephens, John. Incidents of Travel in Central America, Chiapas & Yucatan, 2 Vols. (Illus.). 1969. Vol. 1. pap. 6.50 ea. (ISBN 0-486-22404-X); Vol. 2. pap. (ISBN 0-486-22405-8). Dover.

Stephens, John, tr. see Segal, Patrick.

Stephens, John C., ed. The Guardian. LC 79-57559. 832p. 1982. 55.00x (ISBN 0-8131-1422-5). U Pr of Ky.

Stephens, John F. Spirit Filled Family, No. 11. 48p. (Orig.). 1980. pap. 1.95 (ISBN 0-89841-008-8). Zoe Pubns.

Stephens, John L. Incidents of Travel in Egypt, Arabia Petraea & the Holy Land. (Illus.). 1970. 24.95 o.p. (ISBN 0-8061-0886-X). U of Okla Pr.

Stephens, Ken. Waterskiing. (Illus.). 96p. 1975. 7.95 (ISBN 0-07-077762-4, GB). McGraw.

Stephens, Kent. Matches, Flames & Rails: The Diamond Match Co. in the High Sierra. rev. 2nd ed. 1980. 17.95 o.p. Trans-Anglo.

Stephens, M., jt. ed. see Roderick, G.

Stephens, Meic, ed. The Arts in Wales, Nineteen Fifty to Nineteen Seventy-Five. (Illus.). 342p. 1980. pap. 11.95 (ISBN 0-905171-43-8, Pub. by Welsh Art Wales). Intl Schol Bk Serv.

--Welsh Dylan. 54p. 1980. pap. 3.50 o.p. (ISBN 0-905171-50-0, Pub. by Welsh Art Wales). Intl Schol Bk Serv.

Stephens, R. Theory & Practice of Weed Control. 1982. 45.00x (ISBN 0-333-21294-0, Pub. by Macmillan England). State Mutual Bk.

Stephens, R. C. Mechanics of Machines. 304p. 1982. pap. write for info (ISBN 0-7131-3471-2). E Arnold.

Stephens, R. E., jt. ed. see Inoue, S.

Stephens, R. I., jt. auth. see Fuchs, H. O.

Stephens, R. W., ed. Acoustics, 1974. 18.95x o.p. (ISBN 0-412-12550-1). Methuen Inc.

--Sound: In Eight Languages. LC 74-16209. (International Dictionaries of Science & Technology Ser). 853p. 1974. 69.95 o.s.i. (ISBN 0-470-82200-7). Halsted Pr.

Stephens, Robert. Worktext in Intermediate Algebra. (Illus.). 1977. pap. text ed. 14.50 (ISBN 0-8299-0105-1). West Pub.

Stephens, Sharon. The Black Earl. (Tapestry Romance Ser.). 1982. pap. 2.50 (ISBN 0-686-83759-2). PB.

Stephens, Thomas M. Directive Teaching of Children with Learning & Behavioral Handicaps. 2nd ed. 272p. 1976. pap. 13.95 (ISBN 0-675-08590-X). Merrill.

Stephens, Thomas M. & Hartman, A. Carol. Teaching Children Basic Skills: A Circiculum Handbook. 512p. 1983. pap. text ed. 17.95 (ISBN 0-675-20013-X). Merrill.

Stephens, Thomas M., jt. auth. see Wolf, Joan S.

Stephens, Thomas M., et al. Teaching Mainstreamed Students. 380p. 1982. text ed. 13.95 (ISBN 0-471-02479-1); tchrs' ed. avail. (ISBN 0-471-86479-X). Wiley.

--Teaching Children Basic Skills: A Curriculum Handbook for Directive Teaching. (Special Education Ser.). 1978. pap. text ed. 21.95 (ISBN 0-675-08399-0). Merrill.

Stephens, Thomas W. The United Nations Disaster Relief Office: The Politics & Administration of International Relief Assistance. LC 78-60792. 1978. pap. text ed. 13.25 o.p. (ISBN 0-8191-0414-0). U Pr of Amer.

Stephens, Trent D. Atlas of Human Embryology. (Illus.). 1980. pap. text ed. 12.95x (ISBN 0-02-417150-6). Macmillan.

Stephens, W. B. Sources for English Local History. (The Sources of History Ser.). 336p. 1981. 54.50 (ISBN 0-521-23763-7); pap. 18.95 (ISBN 0-521-28213-6). Cambridge U Pr.

--Teaching Local History. 1977. 16.50 (ISBN 0-7190-0660-0). Manchester.

Stephens, William H. Where Jesus Walked. LC 80-67422. 1981. soft cover 13.95 (ISBN 0-8054-1138-0). Broadman.

Stephens, William N. The Family in Cross-Cultural Perspective. LC 81-40919. 476p. 1982. pap. text ed. 16.50 (ISBN 0-8191-2263-7). U Pr of Amer.

Stephensen, P. R., jt. auth. see Bisset, James.

Stephensen, P. R., jt. auth. see Regardie, Israel.

Stephenson. Beginners Guide to BASIC Programming. 1982. text ed. 9.95. Butterworth.

Stephenson, Ashley. The Garden Planner. (Illus.). 258p. 1983. 25.00 (ISBN 0-312-31688-7); pap. 12.95 (ISBN 0-312-31689-5). St Martin.

Stephenson, Brian. Steam Locomotives. LC 80-50429. (Fact Finders Ser.). PLB 8.00 (ISBN 0-382-06386-4). Silver.

Stephenson, D. Pipeline Design for Water Engineers. 2nd ed. (Developments in Water Science: Vol. 15). 1981. 49.00 (ISBN 0-444-41991-8). Elsevier.

--Rockfill in Hydraulic Engineering, Vol. 27. LC 79-16588. (Developments in Geotechnical Engineering Ser.). 216p. 1979. 47.00 (ISBN 0-444-41828-8). Elsevier.

--Stormwater Hydrology & Drainage. (Developments in Water Science: Vol. 14). 1981. 53.25 (ISBN 0-444-41998-5). Elsevier.

Stephenson, Dianna. Bookshops of London. 120p. (Orig.). 1981. pap. 8.95 (ISBN 0-933982-30-5, Lascelles). Bradt Ent.

Stephenson, Edward P., ed. The Sailboat Owner's Equipment Catalogue. (Illus.). 256p. 1982. 24.95 (ISBN 0-312-69673-6); pap. 13.95 (ISBN 0-312-69674-4). St Martin.

Stephenson, F. W., jt. auth. see Bowron, P.

Stephenson, G. M. & Davis, J. H., eds. Progress in Applied Social Psychology, Vol. 1. LC 80-41694. (Progress in Applied Social Psychology Ser.). 400p. 1981. 46.95 (ISBN 0-471-27954-4, Pub. by Wiley-Interscience). Wiley.

Stephenson, G. R., jt. auth. see McEwen, F. L.

Stephenson, Geoffrey M. & Brotherton, Christopher J. Industrial Relations: A Social Psychological Approach. LC 78-18452. 412p. 1979. 62.95 (ISBN 0-471-99701-3, Pub. by Wiley-Interscience). Wiley.

Stephenson, George E. Small Gasoline Engines. LC 76-51117. 1978. pap. text ed. 8.80 (ISBN 0-8273-1026-9); instructor's guide 3.25 (ISBN 0-8273-1027-7). Delmar.

Stephenson, Gilbert T. & Wiggins, Norman A. Estates & Trusts. 5th ed. (Risk & Insurance Ser.). 480p. 1973. text ed. 24.95 (ISBN 0-13-289546-3). P-H.

Stephenson, H. Handbook of Public Relations: The Standard Guide to Public Affairs & Communications. 2nd ed. 1971. 67.50 o.p. (ISBN 0-07-061183-1, P&RB). McGraw.

--Handbook of Public Relations: The Standard Guide to Public Affairs & Communications. 2nd ed. 1982. (ISBN 0-07-061183-1). McGraw.

Stephenson, Harry, jt. auth. see Duffey, Rick.

Stephenson, Holly. The Space Monster. LC 80-52520. (Starters Ser.). PLB 8.00 (ISBN 0-382-06501-8). Silver.

Stephenson, J. The Oligochaeta. (Illus.). 1930. 80.00 (ISBN 3-7682-0750-1). Lubrecht & Cramer.

Stephenson, J. & Callander, R. A. Engineering Design. LC 73-5277. 705p. 1974. 54.95 (ISBN 0-471-82210-8, Pub. by Wiley-Interscience). Wiley.

Stephenson, J., jt. auth. see Ord-Smith, R. J.

Stephenson, Nathaniel W. Abraham Lincoln & the Union. 1918. text ed. 8.50x (ISBN 0-686-83453-4). Elliots Bks.

--Day of the Confederacy. 1919. text ed. 8.50x (ISBN 0-686-83524-7). Elliots Bks.

--Texas & the Mexican War. 1919. text ed. 8.50x (ISBN 0-686-83810-6). Elliots Bks.

Stephenson, Peter, jt. ed. see GJW Government Relations.

Stephenson, Richard & Scarpitti, Frank. Group Interaction As Therapy. LC 72-810. (Contributions in Sociology Ser.: No. 13). 228p. 1974. lib. bdg. 27.50x (ISBN 0-8371-6399-4, SCG/). Greenwood.

Stephenson, Richard M. Living with Tomorrow: A Factual Look at America's Resources. LC 81-10467. 280p. 1981. 24.50 (ISBN 0-471-09457-9, Pub. by Wiley-Interscience). Wiley.

Stephenson, Richard M. & Iaccarino, Joseph. The Complete Book of Ballroom Dancing. LC 78-22648. (Illus.). 1980. 15.95 (ISBN 0-385-14553-5). Doubleday.

Stephenson, Richard W., compiled by see United States Library of Congress Map Division.

Stephenson, William K. Concepts in Biochemistry. 2nd ed. LC 77-16205. 152p. 1978. pap. text ed. 11.95 (ISBN 0-471-02002-8). Wiley.

--Concepts in Cell Biology. LC 77-16205. 221p. 1978. text ed. 16.50 (ISBN 0-471-03390-1). Wiley.

--Concepts in Neurophysiology. LC 79-19675. 175p. 1980. pap. text ed. 15.50 (ISBN 0-471-05585-9). Wiley.

Stepin, L. D. Quantum Radio Frequency Physics. 1965. 17.50x o.s.i. (ISBN 0-262-19016-8). MIT Pr.

Stepney, Rod, jt. auth. see Ashton, Heather.

Steponaitis, Vincas. Ceramics, Chronology & Community Patterns: An Archaeological Study at Moundville. LC 81-17672. (Studies in Archaeology). 1982. 46.00 (ISBN 0-12-666280-0). Acad Pr.

Steptoe, John. Jeffrey Bear Cleans up His Act. LC 82-12732. (Illus.). 32p. (gr. k-3). 1983. 9.50 (ISBN 0-688-01640-5); PLB 9.12 (ISBN 0-688-01642-1). Lothrop.

Steranko, J. The Steranko History of the Comics, 2 vols, Vol 1-2. (Illus.). 1971. Vol. 1. pap. 4.00 o.p. (ISBN 0-517-50758-7); Vol. 2. pap. 6.00 o.p. (ISBN 0-517-50188-0). Crown.

Sterba, Gunther & Mills, Dick. The Aquarium Encyclopedia: Freshwater & Saltwater Fish & Plants. (Illus.). 608p. 1983. 35.00 (ISBN 0-262-19207-1). MIT Pr.

Sterba, Richard F. Reminiscences of a Viennese Psychoanalyst. (Illus.). 190p. 1982. 17.50 (ISBN 0-8143-1716-2). Wayne St U Pr.

Sterbacek, Z., et al. Calculation of Properties Using Corresponding State Methods. LC 79-10102. (Chemical Engineering Monographs: Vol. 5). 300p. 1979. 57.50 (ISBN 0-444-99807-1). Elsevier.

Sterbenz, Carol E. The Gnomes Book of Christmas Crafts. (Illus.). 162p. 1980. 19.95 o.p. (ISBN 0-686-62718-0, 0967-7). Abrams.

Sterbenz, Carol E. & Johnson, Nancy. The Decorated Tree: Recreating Traditional Christmas Ornaments. LC 82-1774. (Illus.). 168p. 1982. 22.50 (ISBN 0-8109-0805-0). Abrams.

Sterchele, Christina L., illus. Twelve Days of Christmas. (Illus.). (ps-6). 1981. 3.50 (ISBN 0-686-38114-9). Moonlight FL.

Sterling, Bryan. The Best of Will Rogers. 1979. 13.95 (ISBN 0-517-53927-6). Crown.

Sterling, Charles. Still Life Painting. 1981. 27.50i (ISBN 0-06-438530-2, IN-96); pap. 14.95xi (ISBN 0-06-430096-X). Har-Row.

Sterling, Charles & Salinger, Margaretta. A Catalogue of French Paintings: Nineteenth & Twentieth Centuries. LC 41-7098. (Illus.). 1966. 7.50 o.s.i. (ISBN 0-87099-061-6); pap. 4.95 o.s.i. (ISBN 0-87099-062-4). Metro Mus Art.

Sterling, Dorothy. The Outer Lands: A Natural History Guide to Cape Cod, Martha's Vineyard, Nantucket, Block Island, & Long Island. (Illus.). 1978. 11.95 (ISBN 0-393-06438-7); pap. 6.95 (ISBN 0-393-06441-7). Norton.

Sterling, E. M. Trips & Trails, Two: Olympics, South Cascades, & Mt. Rainier. 3rd ed. (Trips & Trails Ser.). (Illus.). 228p. 1983. pap. 7.95 (ISBN 0-89886-069-5). Mountaineers.

--Trips & Trails, 2. 2nd ed. LC 67-26501. (Illus.). 224p. 1978. pap. 7.95 o.p. (ISBN 0-916890-13-9). Mountaineers.

Sterling Editors. Dominican Republic - in Pictures. LC 74-31701. (Visual Geography Ser.). (Illus.). 64p. (gr. 5 up). 1975. PLB 4.99 o.p. (ISBN 0-8069-1197-2); pap. 2.95 (ISBN 0-8069-1196-4). Sterling.

--Horse Identifier. LC 80-50439. (Illus.). 128p. 1980. 12.95 (ISBN 0-8069-3742-4); lib. bdg. 8.29 o.p. (ISBN 0-8069-3743-2). Sterling.

Sterling Editors, ed. East Germany: In Pictures. LC 77-79502. (Visual Geography Ser.). (Illus.). (gr. 4 up). 1977. PLB 6.69 (ISBN 0-8069-1217-0); pap. 2.95 (ISBN 0-8069-1216-2). Sterling.

--The Middle East-The Arab States-In Pictures. (Illus.). (gr. 5 up). 1978. 19.95 (ISBN 0-8069-0156-X); PLB 23.59 (ISBN 0-8069-0157-8). Sterling.

Sterling, Julie, jt. auth. see Lampman, Linda.

Sterling, Louise J., ed. see Gamble, David P.

Sterling, M. J. Power-System Control. (IEE Control Engineering Ser.: No. 6). (Illus.). 250p. 1978. 42.25 (ISBN 0-906048-01-X). Inst Elect Eng.

Sterling Publishing Company Editors. Alaska in Pictures. LC 58-13382. (Visual Geography Ser). (Orig.). (gr. 6 up). 1966. PLB 6.69 (ISBN 0-8069-1001-1); pap. 2.95 (ISBN 0-8069-1000-3). Sterling.

--Brazil in Pictures. LC 67-16015. (Visual Geography Ser.). (gr. 6 up). PLB 4.99 o.p. (ISBN 0-8069-1081-X); pap. 2.95 (ISBN 0-8069-1080-1). Sterling.

--Canada in Pictures. LC 66-16200. (Visual Geography Ser.). (Illus.). (gr. 6 up). 1966. PLB 6.69 (ISBN 0-8069-1067-4); pap. 2.95 (ISBN 0-8069-1066-6). Sterling.

--Denmark in Pictures. LC 61-10396. (Visual Geography Ser). (gr. 5 up). PLB 6.69 (ISBN 0-8069-1003-8); pap. 2.95 (ISBN 0-8069-1002-X). Sterling.

Sterling Publishing Company Editors, ed. Ecuador in Pictures. LC 69-19495. (Visual Geography Ser). (Illus., Orig.). (gr. 7 up). 1969. PLB 4.59 o.p. (ISBN 0-8069-1113-1); pap. 2.50 o.p. (ISBN 0-8069-1112-3). Sterling.

Sterling Publishing Company Editors. Egypt in Pictures. rev. ed. LC 72-81051. (Visual Geography Ser.). (Illus.). 64p. (gr. 6 up). 1978. PLB 4.99 o.p. (ISBN 0-8069-1157-3); pap. 2.95 o.p. (ISBN 0-8069-1156-5). Sterling.

--England in Pictures. LC 65-15825. (Visual Geography Ser.). (Illus., Orig.). (gr. 6 up). PLB 4.99 o.p. (ISBN 0-8069-1055-0); pap. 2.95_o.p. (ISBN 0-8069-1054-2). Sterling.

--Family Book of Crafts. LC 72-95199. (Illus.). 576p. (gr. 6 up). 1973. 20.00 o.p. (ISBN 0-8069-5250-4); PLB 17.59 o.p. (ISBN 0-8069-5251-2). Sterling.

--France in Pictures. LC 65-24384. (Visual Geography Ser). (Illus., Orig.). (gr. 5 up). 1965. PLB 4.99 o.p. (ISBN 0-8069-1057-7); pap. 2.95 (ISBN 0-8069-1056-9). Sterling.

--Greece in Pictures. rev. ed. LC 62-12596. (Visual Geography Ser). (Illus., Orig.). (gr. 6 up). PLB 6.69 (ISBN 0-8069-1023-2); pap. 2.95 (ISBN 0-8069-1022-4). Sterling.

--Holland in Pictures. LC 62-18637. (Visual Geography Ser). (Illus., Orig.). (gr. 6 up). 1962. PLB 4.99 o.p. (ISBN 0-8069-1033-X); pap. 2.95 (ISBN 0-8069-1032-1). Sterling.

--India in Pictures. rev. ed. LC 68-6396. (Visual Geography Ser). (Illus.). (gr. 5 up). 1968. PLB 4.99 o.p. (ISBN 0-8069-1009-7); pap. 2.95 o.p. (ISBN 0-8069-1008-9). Sterling.

--Italy in Pictures. LC 66-16199. (Visual Geography Ser). (Illus., Orig.). (gr. 4-12). 1966. PLB 4.99 o.p. (ISBN 0-8069-1071-2); pap. 2.95 o.p. (ISBN 0-8069-1070-4). Sterling.

--Jamaica in Pictures. LC 67-16016. (Visual Geography Ser.). (Illus.). (gr. 4-12). 1967. PLB 4.99 o.p. (ISBN 0-8069-1085-2); pap. 2.95_o.p. (ISBN 0-8069-1084-4). Sterling.

--Japan in Pictures. rev. ed. LC 60-14338. (Visual Geography Ser.). (Orig.). (gr. 6 up). 1978. PLB 6.69 (ISBN 0-8069-1011-9); pap. 2.95 (ISBN 0-8069-1010-0). Sterling.

--Lebanon in Pictures. rev. ed. LC 73-90809. (Visual Geography Ser). (Illus., Orig.). (gr. 7 up). 1978. PLB 4.99 o.p. (ISBN 0-8069-1123-9); pap. 2.95 (ISBN 0-8069-1122-0). Sterling.

--New Zealand in Pictures. LC 64-24690. (Visual Geography Ser.). (Orig.). (gr. 6 up). PLB 6.69 (ISBN 0-8069-1047-X); pap. 2.95 (ISBN 0-8069-1046-1). Sterling.

--Norway in Pictures. LC 67-16017. (Visual Geography Ser). (Orig.). (gr. 6 up). PLB 6.69 (ISBN 0-8069-1089-5); pap. 2.95 (ISBN 0-8069-1088-7). Sterling.

--Panama & the Canal Zone in Pictures. LC 69-19499. (Visual Geography Ser). (Illus., Orig.). (gr. 7 up). 1969. PLB 6.69 (ISBN 0-8069-1121-2). Sterling.

--Puerto Rico in Pictures. LC 61-10399. (Visual Geography Ser). (gr. 6 up). PLB 6.69 (ISBN 0-8069-1015-1); pap. 2.95 (ISBN 0-8069-1014-3). Sterling.

--Saudi Arabia in Pictures. rev. ed. LC 72-95213. (Visual Geography Ser.). (Illus.). 64p. (Orig.). (gr. 6 up). 1978. PLB 4.99 o.p. (ISBN 0-8069-1169-7). Sterling.

--Spain in Pictures. LC 62-18639. (Visual Geography Ser). (Illus., Orig.). (gr. 6 up). 1962. PLB 6.69 (ISBN 0-8069-1029-1); pap. 2.95 (ISBN 0-8069-1028-3). Sterling.

--Switzerland in Pictures. LC 60-14340. (Visual Geography Ser.). (Orig.). (gr. 6 up). PLB 6.69 (ISBN 0-8069-1017-8); pap. 2.95 (ISBN 0-8069-1016-X). Sterling.

--Thailand in Pictures. rev. ed. LC 63-11593. (Visual Geography Ser.). (Illus., Orig.). (gr. 6 up). 1978. PLB 4.99 o.p. (ISBN 0-8069-1037-2); pap. 2.95 (ISBN 0-8069-1036-4). Sterling.

Sterling, Robert J. Wings. 1979. pap. 2.75 o.p. (ISBN 0-451-08811-5, E8811, Sig). NAL.

Sterling, Robert R., ed. Asset Valuation & Income Determination: A Consideration of the Alternatives. LC 73-160580. 1971. text ed. 13.00 (ISBN 0-914348-11-6). Scholars Bk.

--Research Methodology in Accounting. LC 72-77235. 1972. text ed. 13.00 (ISBN 0-914348-13-2). Scholars Bk.

Sterling, Robert R. & Lemke, Kenneth W., eds. Maintenance of Capital: Financial vs Physical. LC 82-16847. 323p. 1982. 15.00 (ISBN 0-914348-32-9). Scholars Bk.

Sterling Swift Publishing Co. Co-Op East Law Outlines: Wills and Estates. (Co Op East Law Outlines Ser.). (Orig.). 1976. 6.95 o.p. (ISBN 0-88408-086-2). Sterling Swift.

--Swift's Nineteen-Eighty-Two-Eighty-Three Educational Software Directory: Apple II Edition. 358p. 1983. pap. 14.95 (ISBN 0-88408-150-8). Sterling Swift.

Sterman, Donna, jt. auth. see Dunne, Robert L.

Sterman, M. B. & Shouse, Margaret N., eds. Sleep & Epilepsy: Symposium. LC 82-11657. 1982. 39.00 (ISBN 0-12-666360-2). Acad Pr.

Stermer, Bill. Motorcycle Touring. LC 82-82675. 160p. 1982. pap. 7.95 (ISBN 0-89586-170-4). H P Bks.

Stermole, Franklin J. Economic Evaluation & Investment Decision Methods. 4th ed. 1982. text ed. 28.00x (ISBN 0-9603282-4-6); solutions manual 7.00 (ISBN 0-9603282-5-4). Invest Eval.

Stern. Intensive Care in the Newborn, Vol. III. 332p. 1981. 68.75x (ISBN 0-89352-114-0). Masson Pub.

Stern, Alfred. Search for Meaning: Philosophical Vistas. LC 75-134888. 1971. 15.00x o.p. (ISBN 0-87870-006-4). Memphis St Univ.

Stern, Arlene L., ed. Law Librarian's Professional Desk Reference & Diary, 1983. v, 569p. 1982. text ed. 20.00x (ISBN 0-8377-1128-2). Rothman.

Stern, Arthur. Air Pollution, Vol. 5. 3rd ed. 1977. 59.50 (ISBN 0-12-666605-9). Acad Pr.

Stern, Arthur C., et al. Fundamentals of Air Pollution. 1973. text ed. 27.00 (ISBN 0-12-666560-5). Acad Pr.

Stern, B. T., ed. Information & Innovation: Proceedings of a Seminar of ICSU-AB on the Role of Information in the Innovative Process, Amsterdam, The Netherlands, 1982. (Contemporary Topics in Information Transfer Ser.: Vol. 1). 192p. 1982. 38.50 (ISBN 0-444-86496-2, North Holland). Elsevier.

Stern, Bert & Golbitz, Pat. The Last Sitting. LC 82-6350. (Illus.). 192p. 1982. 25.00 (ISBN 0-688-01173-X). Morrow.

Stern, Cecily. A Different Kind of Gold. LC 80-8452. (Illus.). 128p. (gr. 5 up). 1981. pap. 1.88i (ISBN 0-06-440126-X, Trophy). Har-Row.

Stern, Chaim, ed. Gates of Prayer. pulpit ed. 1975. 20.00 o.p. english ed. (ISBN 0-916694-46-1); Hebrew 20.00 (ISBN 0-916694-03-8). Central Conf.

--Gates of Prayer. 1978. gifted edition 12.50 (ISBN 0-916694-69-0). Central Conf.

Stern, Daniel. An Urban Affair. 1980. 12.95 o.p. (ISBN 0-671-41226-4). S&S.

Stern, David, jt. auth. see Bibbero, Robert J.

Stern, David M. How to Make a Fortune Collecting Art & Antiques. (Illus.). 121p. 1980. deluxe ed. 27.85 o.p. (ISBN 0-930582-68-3). Glencoe.

Stern, Don. Backgammon. 1977. PLB 8.90 (ISBN 0-531-01298-0). Watts.

Stern, Edward L. Prescription Drugs & Their Side Effects. rev. ed. 160p. 1981. pap. 5.95 (ISBN 0-448-14734-3, G&D). Putnam Pub Group.

--Prescription Drugs & Their Side Effects. rev. ed. 128p. Date not set. pap. price not set (ISBN 0-448-12025-9, G&D). Putnam Pub Group.

Stern, Edward L., ed. Direct Marketing Market Place 1983. 4th ed. LC 79-649244. 480p. 1983. pap. 48.00 (ISBN 0-934464-04-9). Hilary Hse Pub.

Stern, Ellen. The Best of New York "Best Bets". LC 77-78528. (Illus.). 1977. pap. 3.95 (ISBN 0-8256-3074-6, 030074, Quick Fox). Putnam Pub Group.

Stern, Ellen & Michaels, Jonathan. The Good Heart Diet Cookbook. 256p. 1983. pap. 6.95 (ISBN 0-446-37547-0). Warner Bks.

Stern, Ephraim. The Material Culture of the Land of the Bible in the Persian Period 538-331 B.C. (Illus.). 304p. 1982. pap. text ed. 65.00x (ISBN 0-85668-137-7, 40917, Pub. by Aris & Phillips England). Humanities.

Stern, Frances M. & Zemke, Ron. Stressless Selling: A Guide for Men & Women in Sales. (Illus.). 310p. 1981. 16.95 (ISBN 0-13-852749-0, Spec); pap. 7.95 (ISBN 0-13-852731-8). P-H.

Stern, Fritz R. The Politics of Cultural Despair: A Study in the Rise of the Germanic Ideology. (California Library Reprint Ser.). 1974. 34.50x (ISBN 0-520-02643-8); pap. 7.95x (ISBN 0-520-02626-8). U of Cal Pr.

Stern, Gary H., jt. auth. see DeRosa, Paul.

Stern, Gerald. Lucky Life. LC 77-8541. (New Poetry Ser.). 1977. pap. 6.95 (ISBN 0-395-25809-X). HM.

Stern, Gerald M. The Buffalo Creek Disaster: The Story of the Survivors' Unprecedented Lawsuit. 1976. 4.95 (ISBN 0-394-72343-0). Random.

Stern, Guy. War, Weimar, & Literature: The Story of the Neue Merkur, 1914-1925. LC 71-136960. (Illus.). 1971. 18.95x (ISBN 0-271-01147-5). Pa St U Pr.

Stern, H. I. Transport Scheduling & Routing: An Introduction to Quantitative Methods. Date not set. price not set (ISBN 0-07-061196-3). McGraw.

Stern, Henry R. & Novak, Richie Y. A Handbook of English-German Idioms & Useful Expressions. (Orig.). 1973. pap. text ed. 11.95 (ISBN 0-15-530865-3, HC). HarBraceJ.

Stern, J. P. Re-Interpretations: Seven Studies in Nineteenth Century German Literature. 370p. Date not set. 49.50 (ISBN 0-521-23983-4); pap. 17.95 (ISBN 0-521-28366-3). Cambridge U Pr.

--A Study of Nietzsche. LC 78-54328. (Major European Authors Ser.). 1979. 34.50 (ISBN 0-521-22126-9). Cambridge U Pr.

--A Study of Nietzsche. LC 78-54328. (Major European Authors Ser.). 1982. pap. 12.95 (ISBN 0-521-28380-9). Cambridge U Pr.

Stern, J. P., ed. see Schnitzler, Arthur.

Stern, James, tr. see Kafka, Franz.

Stern, James L. & Dennis, Barbara D., eds. Decisional Thinking of Arbitrators & Judges: National Academy of Arbitrators, 33rd Annual Meeting. 320p. 1981. text ed. 27.50 (ISBN 0-87179-346-6). BNA.

Stern, James L. & Grodin, Joseph R., eds. Public-Sector Bargaining. LC 78-25655. 336p. 1979. 17.50 (ISBN 0-87179-291-5). BNA.

Stern, James L., ed. see National Academy of Arbitrators-32nd Annual Meeting.

Stern, Jane & Stern, Michael. Goodfood: The Adventurous Eaters Guide to Restaurants Serving America's Best Regional Specialties. LC 82-48729. 1983. 17.95 (ISBN 0-394-52448-9); pap. 8.95 (ISBN 0-394-71392-3). Knopf.

--Horror Holiday: Secrets of Vacation Survival. 144p. 1981. pap. 5.95 o.p. (ISBN 0-525-47655-5). Dutton.

--Roadfood. rev. ed. (Illus.). 1980. pap. 7.95 o.p. (ISBN 0-394-73873-X). Random.

Stern, Joel, tr. see Lem, Stanislaw.

Stern, Jonathan P. Soviet Natural Gas Development to Nineteen Ninety: The Implications for the CMEA & the West. LC 79-2705. 208p. 1980. 24.95x (ISBN 0-669-03233-6). Lexington Bks.

Stern, Joseph J. & Lewis, Jeffrey D. Employment Patterns & Income Growth. (Working Paper: No. 419). 70p. 1980. 5.00 (ISBN 0-686-36049-4, WP-0419). World Bank.

Stern, Joseph J., jt. auth. see Roemer, Michael.

Stern, Jossi, jt. ed. see Foster, David.

Stern, Kingsley R. Introductory Plant Biology. 2nd ed. 575p. 1982. pap. text ed. write for info. (ISBN 0-697-04713-X); instrs.' manual avail. (ISBN 0-697-04716-4); lab manual avail. (ISBN 0-697-04572-2); transparencies avail. (ISBN 0-697-04784-9). Wm C Brown.

Stern, Kurt, jt. auth. see Davidsohn, Israel.

Stern, Leo. Drug Use in Pregnancy. 300p. 1983. text ed. write for info. (ISBN 0-86792-011-4, Pub by Adis Pr Australia). Wright-PSG.

Stern, Leo, jt. auth. see Denhoff, Eric.

Stern, Leo, et al. Intensive Care in the Newborn. LC 76-22262. 296p. 1977. 43.50x (ISBN 0-89352-000-4). Masson Pub.

--Intensive Care of the Newborn II. LC 78-63400. (Illus.). 418p. 1979. 52.50x (ISBN 0-89352-022-5). Masson Pub.

Stern, Madeleine B., ed. Publishers for Mass Entertainment in the Nineteenth Century. 1980. lib. bdg. 28.00 (ISBN 0-8161-8471-2, Hall Reference). G K Hall.

Stern, Marcia, ed. see Beals, Judy.

Stern, Marcia, ed. see Snell, Wilma S.

Stern, Marilyn & Powell, Sherry, eds. Telephone Services Directory. 1982. pap. 64.00x (ISBN 0-8103-1542-4). Gale.

Stern, Mark E. Marketing Planning: A Systems Approach. 1966. pap. 12.95 (ISBN 0-07-061211-0, C). McGraw.

Stern, Melvin E. Ocean Circulation Physics. (International Geophysics Ser.). 1975. 42.50 (ISBN 0-12-666750-0). Acad Pr.

Stern, Menahem, ed. Greek & Latin Authors on Jews & Judaism: From Herodotus to Plutarch, Vol. 1. 576p. 1981. Repr. text ed. 43.75x (ISBN 965-208-035-7, Pub. by Brill Holland). Humanities.

Stern, Michael. Douglas Sirk. (Filmmakers Ser.). 1979. lib. bdg. 12.95 (ISBN 0-8057-9269-4, Twayne). G K Hall.

--National Computer Services Register, 1983: Small Computers, North American Edition. 350p. 1983. pap. 39.95 (ISBN 0-911345-00-0). Datanet Pub.

--World Travel Digest 1983. 850p. 1982. pap. 29.95 (ISBN 0-943816-04-1). Spex Intl.

Stern, Michael, jt. auth. see Stern, Jane.

Stern, Michael, compiled by. National Computer Services Register Winter 1983. 300p. 1982. pap. 15.95 (ISBN 0-943816-03-3). Spex Intl.

Stern, Milton, ed. see Melville, Herman.

Stern, Milton R. Critical Essays on Herman Melville's "Typee". (Critical Essays on American Literature Ser.). 1982. lib. bdg. 32.00 (ISBN 0-8161-8445-3). G K Hall.

Stern, Milton R. & Gross, Seymour L, eds. American Literature Survey. Incl. Vol. 1. Colonial & Federal to 1800. 672p. pap. text ed. o.p. (ISBN 0-14-015085-4); Vol. 2. The American Romantics 1800-1860. Brooks, Van W., pref. by. 720p. pap. text ed. o.p. (ISBN 0-14-015086-2); Vol. 3. Nation & Region 1860-1900. Jones, Howard M., pref. by. 736p. pap. text ed. o.p. (ISBN 0-14-015087-0); Vol. 4. The Twentieth Century. Cowley, Malcolm, pref. by. 736p. pap. text ed. 6.95 (ISBN 0-14-015088-9). LC 74-3690. (Viking Portable Library). 1977. pap. Penguin.

Stern, N., jt. auth. see Stern, R. A.

Stern, Nancy & Stern, Robert A. Structured Cobol Programming. 3rd ed. LC 79-18434. 571p. 1980. pap. 25.95 (ISBN 0-471-04913-1). Wiley.

Stern, Nancy, jt. auth. see Stern, Robert A.

Stern, Nancy, et al. Three Seventy Three Sixty Assembler Language Programming. LC 78-10504. 516p. 1979. pap. text ed. 26.95 (ISBN 0-471-03429-0); write for info. tchrs. manual (ISBN 0-471-05393-7). Wiley.

Stern, Naomi M., jt. auth. see Degenshein, Joan.

Stern, Norman B. Baja California, Jewish Refuge & Homeland. LC 72-94422. (Baja California Travels Ser.: No. 32). 1973. 18.00 (ISBN 0-87093-232-2). Dawsons.

Stern, Paul C. Evaluating Social Science Research. (Illus.). 1979. pap. text ed. 9.95x (ISBN 0-19-502480-X). Oxford U Pr.

Stern, Paul F. In Praise of Madness. 1973. pap. 2.25 o.s.i. (ISBN 0-440-54180-8, Delta). Dell.

Stern, Paula. Water's Edge: Domestic Politics & the Making of American Foreign Policy. LC 78-55331. (Contributions in Political Science: No. 15). 1979. lib. bdg. 29.95x (ISBN 0-313-20520-5, SWE/). Greenwood.

Stern, Peter. Floyd, A Cat's Story. LC 81-48657. (Illus.). 32p. (gr. k-3). 1982. 8.61i (ISBN 0-06-025772-5, HarpJ); PLB 8.89g (ISBN 0-06-025779-2). Har-Row.

Stern, Philip. Rape of the Taxpayer. 1974. pap. 1.95 o.p. (ISBN 0-394-71959-X, Vin). Random.

Stern, Philip V. Edgar Allan Poe: Visitor from the Night of Time. LC 72-83786. 176p. (gr. 7-12). 1973. 9.57i o.p. (ISBN 0-690-25554-3, TYC-J). Har-Row.

--Henry David Thoreau: Writer & Rebel. LC 74-139108. (gr. 7-9). 1972. 10.53i (ISBN 0-690-37715-0, TYC-J). Har-Row.

Stern, Philip V., ed. see Thoreau, Henry D.

Stern, Phillip. The Portable Poe. (Orig.). 1983. 18.75 (ISBN 0-670-56178-9). Viking Pr.

Stern, Phillip V. Secret Missions of the Civil War. LC 74-9399. (Illus.). 320p. 1975. Repr. of 1959 ed. lib. bdg. 18.25x (ISBN 0-8371-7657-3, STSM). Greenwood.

Stern, Phillip V., ed. see Poe, Edgar A.

Stern, R. A. & Stern, N. Concepts of Information Processing with Basic. 216p. 1982. pap. text ed. 13.95 (ISBN 0-471-87617-8). Wiley.

Stern, Renee, jt. auth. see Bates, Myrtle.

Stern, Richard. The Chaleaur Network. (Illus.). 1981. pap. 7.95 (ISBN 0-531-07334-3, Pub. by Second Chance Pr); 15.95 (ISBN 0-686-83008-3). Watts.

--Natural Shocks. LC 77-22952. 1978. 8.95 o.p. (ISBN 0-698-10865-5, Coward). Putnam Pub Group.

--Packages. 186p. 1980. 10.95 (ISBN 0-698-11041-2, Pub. by Coward). Putnam Pub Group.

Stern, Rob. SB2C Helldiver in Action. (Aircraft in Action Ser.). (Illus.). 50p. 1982. saddlestitch 4.95 (ISBN 0-89747-128-8, 1054). Squad Sig Pubns.

Stern, Robert. They Were Number One. LC 82-83920. (Illus.). 400p. 1983. 19.95 (ISBN 0-88011-122-4). Leisure Pr.

Stern, Robert, ed. The Anglo-American Suburb Seventeen Ninety to the Present. (Architectural Design Profiles Ser.). (Illus.). 80p. 1980. pap. cancelled o.p. (ISBN 0-8478-5318-7). Rizzoli Intl.

Stern, Robert A. George Howe: Toward a Modern American Architecture. LC 73-86918. (Illus.). 456p. 1975. 34.50x o.p. (ISBN 0-300-01642-5). Yale U Pr.

--New Directions in American Architecture. rev. ed. LC 70-81278. (New Directions in Architecture Ser). 1978. 9.95 o.s.i. (ISBN 0-8076-0523-9); pap. 7.95 o.s.i. (ISBN 0-8076-0527-1). Braziller.

Stern, Robert A. & Stern, Nancy. An Introduction to Computers & Information Processing. LC 81-11428. 637p. 1982. text ed. 24.95 (ISBN 0-471-08723-8); tchrs.' ed 23.00 (ISBN 0-471-09941-4); 22.50 tests (ISBN 0-471-86212-6); study guide 9.95 (ISBN 0-471-09231-2). Wiley.

Stern, Robert A., jt. auth. see Stern, Nancy.

Stern, Robert J., jt. auth. see Morgan, William.

Stern, Robert L. Appellate Practice in the United States. 568p. 1981. text ed. 38.50 (ISBN 0-87179-352-0). BNA.

Stern, Robert L. & Gressman, Eugene. Supreme Court Practice. 5th ed. 1306p. 1978. 47.50 (ISBN 0-87179-213-3). BNA.

Stern, Robert M. & Davis, Christopher M., eds. Gastric Motility: A Selectively Annotated Bibliography. LC 82-12173. 208p. 1982. 19.50 (ISBN 0-87933-430-4). Hutchinson Ross.

Stern, Robert M., et al. Psychophysiological Recording. (Illus.). 1980. text ed. 22.50x (ISBN 0-19-502695-0); pap. text ed. 12.95x (ISBN 0-19-502696-9). Oxford U Pr.

Stern, Robert N. & Comstock, Philip. Employee Stock Ownership Plans (ESOPs) Benefits for Whom? LC 78-620017. (Key Issues Ser.: No. 23). 64p. 1978. pap. 3.00 (ISBN 0-87546-068-2). ILR Pr.

Stern, Roger. Spider-Man: The Secret Story of Marvel's World Famous Wall Crawler. LC 81-10022. (Secret Stories of the Sensational Super Heroes). (Illus.). 64p. (gr. 3 up). 1981. PLB 9.25 (ISBN 0-516-02414-0). Childrens.

Stern, S. M., ed. & tr. see Goldziher, Ignac.

Stern, Sheldon M. The Black Response to Enslavement: Reinterpretations of the Behavior & Personality of American Slaves. 1976. pap. text ed. 9.25 o.p. (ISBN 0-8191-0004-8). U Pr of Amer.

Stern, Simon. Mrs. Vinegar. (Illus.). (ps-2). 1979. 7.95x (ISBN 0-13-604488-3). P-H.

Stern, Stanley. Understanding Accounting. LC 82-18434. 160p. 1983. lib. bdg. 10.95 (ISBN 0-668-05726-2). Arco.

Stern, Stephen. The Sephardic Jewish Community of Los Angeles: A Study in Folklore & Ethnic Identity. Dorson, Richard M., ed. LC 80-734. (Folklore of the World Ser.). 1980. lib. bdg. 35.00x (ISBN 0-405-13324-3). Ayer Co.

Stern, Stephen, jt. auth. see Georges, Robert A.

Stern, Susan, jt. auth. see Hamburger, Robert.

Stern, Thomas, jt. ed. see Silber, Bettina.

Stern, Virginia F. Gabriel Harvey: A Study of His Life, Marginalia & Library. (Illus.). 1979. text ed. 52.00x (ISBN 0-19-812091-5). Oxford U Pr.

Stern, Walter. The New Investor's Guide to Making Money in Real Estate. new ed. LC 74-5626. (Illus.). 160p. (Orig.). 1976. pap. 5.95 o.p. (ISBN 0-448-11832-7, G&D). Putnam Pub Group.

--Stern's Handbook of Package Design Research. LC 80-39935. 576p. 1981. 44.95x (ISBN 0-471-05901-3, Pub. by Wiley-Interscience). Wiley.

Stern, Walter H., ed. Vitrectomy Techniques for the Anterior Segment Surgeon: A Practical Approach. (Current Opthamology Monographs). write for info. Grune.

Stern, Zelda, jt. ed. see Siu, Helen.

Sternbach, Mary. Countries with No Names. 32p. (Orig.). 1982. pap. 3.00 (ISBN 0-941062-08-2); pap. 30.00 ltd. ed. (ISBN 0-941062-09-0). Guignol Bks.

Sternbach, Richard A. Pain Patients: Traits & Treatments. 1974. 22.00 (ISBN 0-12-667235-0). Acad Pr.

Sternbach, Richard A., ed. The Psychology of Pain. LC 77-84554. 282p. 1978. 23.00 (ISBN 0-89004-278-0). Raven.

Sternback-Scott, Sisa, ed. see Mindell, Arnold.

Sternback-Scott, Sisa, ed. see Mitchell, Meredith.

Sternberg. Composition. (The Grosset Art Instruction Ser.: No. 1). (Illus.). 48p. Date not set. pap. 2.95 (ISBN 0-448-00510-7, G&D). Putnam Pub Group.

--Realistic - Abstract Art. (Pitman Art Ser.: Vol. 29). pap. 1.95 o.p. (ISBN 0-448-00538-7, G&D). Putnam Pub Group.

--Woodcut. (Grosset Art Introduction Ser.: Vol. 40). (Illus.). 48p. Date not set. pap. 2.95 (ISBN 0-448-00549-2, G&D). Putnam Pub Group.

Sternberg, Cecilia. Masquerade. 1981. pap. 2.75 o.p. (ISBN 0-451-09603-7, E9603, Sig). NAL.

Sternberg, Charles D. BASIC Computer Programs for Business. Date not set. Vol. 1. 10.95 (ISBN 0-686-92665-X, 5162); Vol. 2. 13.95 (ISBN 0-686-98558-3, 5178). Hayden.

Sternberg, Dick. Fishing with Live Bait. 160p. 1983. 16.95 (ISBN 0-307-46635-3, Golden Pr). Western Pr.

Sternberg, James & Sternberg, Thomas. Great Skin at any Age: How to Keep Your Skin Looking Young without Plastic Surgery. 160p. 1983. 12.95 (ISBN 0-312-34674-3). St Martin.

Sternberg, Les & Adams, Gary. Educating Severely & Profoundly Handicapped Students. LC 82-4102. 366p. 1982. 28.50 (ISBN 0-89443-695-3). Aspen Systems.

Sternberg, Richard, jt. auth. see Anikouchine, William.

Sternberg, Robert. How to Prepare for the Miller Analogies Test. 3rd ed. 192p. 1981. pap. 4.95 (ISBN 0-8120-2325-0). Barron.

--Writing the Psychology Paper. LC 77-9250. 1977. pap. text ed. 4.95 (ISBN 0-8120-0772-7). Barron.

Sternberg, Robert J. Barron's How to Prepare for the Miller Analogies Test (MAT) 3rd ed. LC 81-10762. 1981. pap. text ed. 4.95 (ISBN 0-8120-2325-0). Barron.

Sternberg, Robert J., ed. Handbook of Human Intelligence. LC 82-1160. (Illus.). 832p. 1982. 65.00 (ISBN 0-521-22870-0); pap. 24.95 (ISBN 0-521-29687-0). Cambridge U Pr.

Sternberg, Robert J. & Detterman, Douglas K., eds. Human Intelligence: Perspectives on Its Theory & Measurement. LC 79-17994. 1979. 17.95 (ISBN 0-89391-030-9); 26.50 (ISBN 0-686-85498-5). Ablex Pub.

Sternberg, Robert J., jt. ed. see Detterman, Douglas K.

Sternberg, Shlomo. Lectures on Differential Geometry. 2nd ed. LC 81-71141. xvii, 438p. 1982. text ed. 25.00 (ISBN 0-8284-0316-3, 316). Chelsea Pub.

Sternberg, Thomas, jt. auth. see Sternberg, James.

Sternberg, Thomas H. & Newcomer, Victor D., eds. Evaluation of Therapeutic Agents & Cosmetics. (Illus.). 1964. 26.00 o.p. (ISBN 0-07-061241-2, HP). McGraw.

Sternberger, Ludwig A. Immunocytochemistry. 2nd ed. LC 78-13263. (Basic & Clinical Immunology Ser.). 354p. 1979. 55.00x (ISBN 0-471-03386-3, Pub. by Wiley Medical). Wiley.

Sternburg, Janet, ed. The Writer on Her Work. 228p. 1981. pap. 5.95 (ISBN 0-393-00071-0). Norton.

Sterne, George & Von Hoelscher, Russ. How to Start Making Money in a Business of Your Own. 420p. 1981. 14.95 (ISBN 0-940398-05-2). Profit Ideas.

Sterne, Laurence. A Sentimental Journey Through France & Italy by Mr. Yorick. rev. ed. Stout, Gardner D., Jr., ed. (Illus.). 1967. 39.00x (ISBN 0-520-01228-3). U of Cal Pr.

--The Sermons of Mr. Yorick. David, Marjorie, ed. (Fyfield Ser.). 1979. 7.95 o.p. (ISBN 0-85635-056-7, Pub. by Carcanet New Pr England); pap. 3.95 o.p. (ISBN 0-85635-057-5). Humanities.

--Tristram Shandy. pap. 3.95 (ISBN 0-451-51778-4, CE1778, Sig Classics). NAL.

Sterne, Lawrence. The Life & Opinions of Tristram Shandy, Gentleman. Ross, Ian C., ed. (The World's Classics Ser.). 640p. 1983. pap. 5.95 (ISBN 0-19-281566-0, GB). Oxford U Pr.

Sterne, M. & Batty, I. Pathogenic Clostridia. 1975. 24.95 o.p. (ISBN 0-407-35350-X). Butterworth.

Sterner. Gaudi: The Architecture in Barcelona, Antoni. (Pocket Art Ser.). 1983. pap. 3.50 (ISBN 0-8120-2293-9). Barron.

Sterner, Gabriele. Antoni Gaudi: Architecture in Barcelona. (Pocket Art Ser.). (Illus.). 1983. pap. 3.50 (ISBN 0-8120-2293-9). Barron.

Sternfeld, Frederick see Abraham, Gerald, et al.

Sternheim, M. M., jt. auth. see Kane, J. W.

Sternheim, Morton M., jt. auth. see Kane, Joseph W.

Sternlicht, M., jt. auth. see Bioler, I.

Sternlicht, Sanford. C. S. Forester. (English Authors Ser.). 1981. lib. bdg. 11.95 (ISBN 0-8057-6810-6, Twayne). G K Hall.

--John Masefield. (English Authors Ser.). 1977. lib. bdg. 12.95 (ISBN 0-8057-6678-2, Twayne). G K Hall.

Sternlieb, George & Hughes, James W., eds. America's Housing: Prospects & Problems. LC 80-10700. 480p. 1980. pap. text ed. 15.00 (ISBN 0-88285-063-6). Ctr Urban Pol Res.

Sternlieb, George, jt. ed. see Burchell, Robert W.

Sterns, Indrikis. The Greater Medieval Historians: An Interpretation & a Bibliography. LC 80-5850. 260p. 1980. lib. bdg. 21.25 (ISBN 0-8191-1327-1); pap. text ed. 11.50 (ISBN 0-8191-1328-X). U Pr of Amer.

Sterns, Indrikis, ed. The Greater Medieval Historians: A Reader. LC 82-15919. 472p. (Orig.). 1983. lib. bdg. 30.50 (ISBN 0-8191-2752-3); pap. text ed. 17.25 (ISBN 0-8191-2753-1). U Pr of Amer.

Sterns, Peter N., ed. The Other Side of Western Civilization - Readings in Everyday Life: The Sixteenth Century to the Present, Vol. 2. 370p. 1979. pap. text ed. 11.95 (ISBN 0-15-567649-0, HC). HarBraceJ.

Sternthal, Brian & Craig, C. Samuel. Consumer Behavior: An Information Processing Perspective. (Illus.). 384p. 1982. text ed. 26.95 (ISBN 0-13-169284-4). P-H.

Sterrett, Grace & Aboud, Antone. Right to Strike in Public Employment. 2nd, rev. ed. LC 82-15859. (Key Issues Ser.: No. 15). 1982. pap. 5.00 (ISBN 0-87546-096-8). ILR Pr.

Sterzl, J. & Riha, I., eds. Developmental Aspects of Antibody Formation & Structure: Proceedings, Vols. 1 & 2. 1971. Vol. 1. 67.50 (ISBN 0-12-667901-0); Vol. 2. 67.50 (ISBN 0-12-667902-9). Acad Pr.

Stetler, Cheryl B., et al, eds. see Massachusetts General Hospital.

Stetler, Russell, ed. see Giap, Vo Nguyen.

Stetler, Russell, ed. see Scott, Peter D.

Stetler, Susan T., jt. ed. see Young, Margaret W.

Stetson, Daniel E. Alumni Invitational Exhibition. Boatright, Kevin, ed. (Illus.). 16p. (Orig.). 1982. pap. text ed. 2.50 (ISBN 0-932660-05-3). U of NI Dept Art.

--University of Northern Iowa Department of Art Annual Faculty Exhibition. Boatright, Kevin, ed. LC 82-50565. 16p. (Orig.). 1982. pap. text ed. 2.00 (ISBN 0-932660-05-3). U of NI Dept Art.

Stetson, Fred, ed. see Cook, Jeffrey.

Stetson, Fred, ed. see Graves, Will.

Stetten, Mary. Let's Play Science. LC 78-24698. (Illus.). (ps-3). 1979. pap. 4.95i (ISBN 0-06-090711-8, CN-711, CN). Har-Row.

Stettler, Howard F. Auditing Principles: A System-Based Approach. 5th ed. (Illus.). 704p. 1982. text ed. 27.95 (ISBN 0-13-051722-4). P-H.

Stettler, Howard F. & Newton, Sherwood W. Practice Case for Auditing. 4th ed. 1977. pap. text ed. 13.95 (ISBN 0-13-694521-X). P-H.

Stettner, Allison G. & Cowan, Anita P. Health Aspects of Family Planning: A Guide to Resources in the United States. LC 81-1651. 247p. 1982. 29.95x (ISBN 0-89885-005-3). Human Sci Pr.

Stettner, N. Productivity, Bargaining & Industrial Change. 1969. 17.75 o.p. (ISBN 0-08-006756-5); pap. 7.75 o.p. (ISBN 0-08-006757-3). Pergamon.

Steuart, Justin. Wayne Wheeler, Dry Boss. LC 75-100207. (Illus.). 304p. Repr. of 1928 ed. lib. bdg. 15.50x (ISBN 0-8371-4033-1, STWW). Greenwood.

Steuber, U. International Banking: The Foreign Activities of the Banks of Principal Industrial Countries (1976) rev. ed. Pringle, R. & Pringle, R., trs. from Ger. Repr. of 1974 ed. 47.50 (ISBN 90-286-0375-1). Heinman.

Steuding, Bob. Gary Snyder. (United States Authors Ser.). 1976. lib. bdg. 13.95 (ISBN 0-8057-7174-3, Twayne). G K Hall.

Steuernagel, Gertrude A. Political Philosophy As Therapy: Marcuse Reconsidered. LC 77-94747. (Contributions in Political Science: No. 11). 1979. lib. bdg. 25.00x (ISBN 0-313-20315-6, SPP/). Greenwood.

Stevans, C. M., jt. ed. see Daniels, Cora L.

Steven, Hugh. Good Broth to Warm our Bones. 192p. 1982. pap. 5.95 (ISBN 0-89107-272-1, Crossway Bks). Good News.

--The Man with the Noisy Heart. LC 78-21038. 1979. 7.95 (ISBN 0-8024-5171-3). Moody.

--Never Touch a Tiger. LC 80-18225. 180p. 1980. pap. 4.95 o.s.i. (ISBN 0-8407-5737-9). Nelson.

STeven, Robert K., jt. auth. see Stevens, Revalee R.

Steven, Stewart. The Poles. (Illus.). 320p. 1982. 15.95 (ISBN 0-02-614460-3). Macmillan.

Stevens & Warshofsky, Fred. Sound & Hearing. rev ed. LC 80-52113. (Life Science Library). PLB 13.40 (ISBN 0-8094-4059-8). Silver.

Stevens, A. L., jt. auth. see Gentner, D.

Stevens, Alan, jt. auth. see Schmidgall-Tellings, A. Ed.

Stevens, Albert C. Cyclopaedia of Fraternities. 2nd rev. ed. LC 66-20332. 1966. Repr. of 1907 ed. 37.00x (ISBN 0-8103-3084-9). Gale.

Stevens, Ann, tr. see Eca de Queiroz.

Stevens, Austin N., ed. Yankees Under Steam. LC 71-141043. 12.50 o.p. (ISBN 0-911658-59-9); pap. 7.95 o.p. (ISBN 0-911658-78-5, 3044). Yankee Bks.

Stevens, Barbara, jt. auth. see Rezler, Agnes.

Stevens, Barbara J. First-Line Patient Care Management. 2nd ed. LC 82-13907. 195p. 1982. 22.50 (ISBN 0-89443-845-X). Aspen Systems.

--The Nurse As Executive. 2nd ed. LC 79-90379. (Nursing Dimensions Administrative Ser.). 365p. 1980. Repr. text ed. 25.00 (ISBN 0-913654-62-0); pap. text ed. 21.95 (ISBN 0-89443-800-X). Aspen Systems.

Stevens, Barbara J. & Kelley, Jean A. Cognitive Dissonance: An Examination of CBHDP Stated Beliefs & Their Effect on Education Programs. 49p. 1981. 4.95 (ISBN 0-686-38244-7, 15-1851). Natl League Nurse.

Stevens, Barbara J., ed. Educating the Nurse Manager: Case Studies & Group Work. LC 81-83096. 196p. 1982. 22.50 (ISBN 0-89443-698-8). Aspen Systems.

Stevens, Blaine. The Outlanders. (Orig.). 1979. pap. 2.50 (ISBN 0-515-04861-5). Jove Pubns.

Stevens, Bryna. Ben Franklin's Glass Harmonica. LC 82-9715. (Carolrhoda On My Own Bks). (Illus.). 48p. (gr. 1-4). 1983. PLB 6.95g (ISBN 0-87614-202-1). Carolrhoda Bks.

Stevens, Byron, jt. auth. see Hecht, Arthur.

Stevens, C. A. Your Key to the Cockpit. (Illus.). 1980. pap. 3.00 o.p. (ISBN 0-911721-85-1, Pub. by Inflight). Aviation.

Stevens, C. F. Neurophysiology: A Primer. 182p. 1966. 21.50 (ISBN 0-471-82436-4). Wiley.

Stevens, Carla. Pig & the Blue Flag. LC 76-58384. (Illus.). 48p. (gr. k-3). 1976. 6.95 (ISBN 0-395-28825-8, Clarion). HM.

Stevens, Charles F. & Tsien, Richard W., eds. Ion Permeation Through Membrane Channels, Vol. 3. LC 76-19934. 168p. 1979. text ed. 17.50 (ISBN 0-89004-224-1). Raven.

Stevens, Cheryl J., jt. auth. see Monette, Louis G.

Stevens, Cheryl J., jt. auth. see Wynne, Frances H.

Stevens, Cheryl J., ed. A Medley of English Recipes. (Illus.). 99p. (Orig.). 1982. pap. write for info. (ISBN 0-88127-009-1). Oracle Pr LA.

--Three Plays by Louisiana Playwrights. LC 82-80740. (Illus.). 180p. (Orig.). 1982. pap. 15.00 (ISBN 0-88127-006-7). Oracle Pr LA.

--Two Plays by Louisiana Playwrights. 100p. (Orig.). 1983. pap. write for info (ISBN 0-88127-013-X). Oracle Pr LA.

Stevens, Cheryl J., ed. see Bhacca, Rosaria D.

Stevens, Chris. Fastest Machines. LC 80-10227. (Machine World Ser.). (Illus.). 32p. (gr. 2-4). 1980. PLB 13.85 (ISBN 0-8172-1337-6). Raintree Pubs.

Stevens, Christopher. Food Aid in the Developing World. 1979. 30.00 (ISBN 0-312-29763-7). St Martin.

Stevens, Clifford. The Life of Christ. 196p. (Orig.). 1983. pap. 5.95 (ISBN 0-87973-617-8, 617). Our Sunday Visitor.

--Portraits of Faith. LC 74-21891. 176p. 1975. pap. 2.50 o.p. (ISBN 0-87973-764-6). Our Sunday Visitor.

Stevens, Crystal & Ferneti, Casper. Washing Your Hands. (Project MORE Daily Living Skills Ser.). 32p. 1979. Repr. of 1975 ed. pap. text ed. 5.95 (ISBN 0-8331-1241-4). Hubbard Sci.

Stevens, David. English Renaissance Theatre: A Reference Guide. 1982. lib. bdg. 42.00 (ISBN 0-8161-8361-9, Hall Reference). G K Hall.

--Sunset & Morning Star. 1977. 7.50 o.p. (ISBN 0-200-72448-7). Transatlantic.

Stevens, David H., ed. Ten Talents in the American Theatre. LC 76-20514. 299p. 1976. Repr. of 1957 ed. lib. bdg. 21.00x (ISBN 0-8371-8996-9, STTA). Greenwood.

Stevens, Denis. Letters of Claudio Monteverdi. LC 80-66219. 432p. 1980. 49.50 (ISBN 0-521-23591-X). Cambridge U Pr.

Stevens, Denis, ed. History of Song. rev. ed. (Illus.). 1970. pap. 9.95 (ISBN 0-393-00536-4, Norton Lib). Norton.

Stevens, Dennis W. A History of Song. LC 82-11781. 491p. 1982. Repr. of 1960 ed. lib. bdg. 39.75x (ISBN 0-313-22933-3, STHS). Greenwood.

Stevens, Don E. Man's Search for Certainty. LC 80-15743. 288p. 1980. 9.95 o.p. (ISBN 0-396-07860-5). Dodd.

Stevens, Douglas L. & Scott, Herschel L., Jr. The Grand Canyon & Havasu. LC 82-82171. (Western Backpacking Ser.). (Illus.). 60p. (Orig.). 1982. pap. 4.50 (ISBN 0-88083-002-6). Poverty Hill Pr.

Stevens, Eden V. Buffalo Bill. (See & Read Biography Ser). (Illus.). 64p. (gr. 2-5). 1976. PLB 4.79 o.p. (ISBN 0-399-60983-0). Putnam Pub Group.

Stevens, Edward. Business Ethics. LC 79-91409. 248p. (Orig.). 1979. pap. 8.95 (ISBN 0-8091-2244-8). Paulist Pr.

--An Introduction to Oriental Mysticism. LC 73-87030. 192p. 1973. pap. 2.95 o.p. (ISBN 0-8091-1798-3). Paulist Pr.

--Oriental Mysticism. pap. 2.95 o.p. (ISBN 0-8091-1798-3). Paulist Pr.

Stevens, Elisabeth. Elisabeth Stevens Guide to Baltimore's Inner Harbor. (Illus.). 64p. 1981. pap. 3.50 (ISBN 0-916144-86-0). Stemmer Hse.

--Fire & Water: Short Stories. LC 82-203. (Illus.). 100p. 1983. pap. 5.25 (ISBN 0-912288-20-5). Perivale Pr.

Stevens, Ella. Sex Education: Contraception. (Michigan Learning Module Ser.). 1979. write for info. (ISBN 0-914004-37-9). Ulrich.

--Sex Education: Gonorrhea. (Michigan Learning Module Ser.). 1979. write for info. (ISBN 0-914004-38-7). Ulrich.

Stevens, Evelyn P. Protest & Response in Mexico. 280p. 1974. 30.00x (ISBN 0-262-19128-8). MIT Pr.

Stevens, Franklin. Dance As Life: A Season with American Ballet Theatre. LC 74-15855. (Illus.). 256p. (YA) 1976. 12.45i (ISBN 0-06-014103-4, HarpT). Har-Row.

Stevens, G. T., Jr. Economic & Financial Analysis of Capital Investments. LC 78-27857. 386p. 1979. text ed. 39.95 (ISBN 0-471-04851-8); solutions manual 10.00 (ISBN 0-471-05001-6). Wiley.

Stevens, George. Three Years in the Sixth Corps. (Collector's Library of the Civil War). 1983. 26.60 (ISBN 0-8094-4266-3). Silver.

Stevens, George, jt. auth. see Hardinge, George.

Stevens, George E., jt. auth. see Stevens, Laura J.

Stevens, Gergiana G., ed. The United States & the Middle East. LC 64-14027. 1963. 4.00 (ISBN 0-936904-05-4); pap. 1.95 (ISBN 0-936904-30-5). Am Assembly.

Stevens, Glenn H. Arithmetic on Modular Curves. (Progress in Mathematics Ser.: 20). 1982. text ed. 15.00 (ISBN 3-7643-3088-0). Birkhauser.

Stevens, Gloria. The Metaphorical Eye: Special Effects in Photography. LC 75-39834. (Illus.). 160p. 1976. 15.95 o.p. (ISBN 0-8174-0599-2, Amphoto). Watson-Guptill.

Stevens, Gus, jt. auth. see Smith, Bradley.

Stevens, Gwendolyn & Gardner, Sheldon. The Women of Psychology, 2 vols. 300p. 1982. Set. text ed. 15.25 (ISBN 0-87073-443-1); Set. pap. text ed. 8.95 (ISBN 0-87073-446-6). Schenkman.

Stevens, Gwendolyn, jt. auth. see Gardner, Sheldon.

Stevens, H. C., tr. see Sholokhov, Mikhail.

Stevens, Henry. Recollections of James Lenox & the Formation of His Library. rev. ed. Paltsits, Victor H., ed. 1951. 6.00 o.p. (ISBN 0-87104-155-3). NY Pub Lib.

Stevens, I. N. & Yardley, D. C. The Protection of Liberty. (Mainstream Ser.). 200p. 1982. text ed. 18.50x (ISBN 0-631-12944-8, Pub. by Basil Blackwell England). Biblio Dist.

Stevens, Irving L. Fishbones: Hoboing in the 1930's. LC 82-90088. (Illus.). 136p. (Orig.). 1982. pap. 7.95 (ISBN 0-9609208-0-3). Moosehead Prods.

Stevens, J. E., ed. Music & Poetry in the Early Tudor Court. LC 77-90180. (Cambridge Studies in Music). (Illus.). 1979. 84.50 (ISBN 0-521-22030-0); pap. 19.95 (ISBN 0-521-29417-7). Cambridge U Pr.

Stevens, Jack G., et al, eds. Persistent Viruses. (ICN-UCLA Symposia on Molecular & Cellular Biology, 1978 Ser.: Vol. 11). 1978. 47.50 (ISBN 0-12-668350-6). Acad Pr.

Stevens, James, jt. auth. see Scriven, Carl.

Stevens, Jane, jt. auth. see Perkins, James.

Stevens, Janet, adapted by. & illu see Andersen, Hans Christian.

Stevens, Janice. Take Back the Moment. 1983. pap. 1.75 (ISBN 0-686-43402-1, Sig Vista). NAL.

Stevens, John. Aikido: The Way of Harmony. LC 82-42680. (Illus.). 256p. (Orig.). 1983. pap. 14.95 (ISBN 0-394-71426-1). Shambhala Pubns.

Stevens, John, tr. see Bede The Venerable.

Stevens, John D. Shaping the First Amendment: The Development of Free Expression. (CommText Ser.: Vol. 11). 160p. 1982. 15.00 (ISBN 0-8039-1876-3); pap. 7.95 (ISBN 0-8039-1877-1). Sage.

Stevens, John G. R., jt. auth. see Gunn, Donald L.

Stevens, Karl K. Statics & Strength of Materials. (Illus.). 1979. ref. ed. 31.95 (ISBN 0-13-844688-1). P-H.

Stevens, Kathleen. Molly, McCullough, & Tom the Rogue. LC 82-45584. (Illus.). 32p. (gr. 2-6). 1983. 10.53i (ISBN 0-690-04295-7, TYC-J); PLB 10.89g (ISBN 0-690-04296-5). Har-Row.

Stevens, Kathleen R. Power & Influence: A Source Book for Nurses. LC 82-13397. 304p. 1983. pap. 12.95x (ISBN 0-471-08870-6, Pub. by Wiley Med). Wiley.

Stevens, Kim. The Bee Gees: A Photo-Bio. 1979. pap. 1.95 o.s.i. (ISBN 0-515-05158-6). Jove Pubns.

Stevens, L. A., jt. auth. see Nichols, R.

Stevens, L. Robert. Charles Darwin. (English Authors Ser.). 1978. 12.95 (ISBN 0-8057-6718-5, Twayne). G K Hall.

Stevens, Laura J. & Stevens, George E. How to Feed Your Hyperactive Child. LC 76-23799. 1977. 8.95 (ISBN 0-385-12465-1). Doubleday.

Stevens, Laura J. & Stoner, Rosemary B. How to Improve Your Child's Behavior Through Diet. LC 78-22649. (Illus.). 1979. 9.95 o.p. (ISBN 0-385-14820-8). Doubleday.

Stevens, Laurence. Guide to Travel Agency Security. (The Travel Agency Management Practical Guide Ser.). 36p. 1982. pap. text ed. 5.00x (ISBN 0-916032-15-9). Merton Hse.

Stevens, Leonard A. The Death Penalty: The Case of Life vs. Death in the United States, the 8th Amendment. LC 78-5880. (Great Constitutional Issues Ser.: The 8th Amendment). (gr. 6 up). 1978. PLB 8.99 (ISBN 0-698-30701-1, Coward). Putnam Pub Group.

--Equal! The Case of Integration vs Jim Crow, the Fourteenth Amendment. LC 75-25646. (Great Constitutional Issues Ser.). 228p. (gr. 7 up). 1975. PLB 6.99 (ISBN 0-698-30597-3, Coward). Putnam Pub Group.

--Trespass: The People's Privacy vs Power of the Police, the 4th Amendment. (Great Constitutional Issues Ser.). 160p. (gr. 6-8). 1977. PLB 8.99 (ISBN 0-698-30663-5, Coward). Putnam Pub Group.

Stevens, Lucile V. Of Dreams & Danger. 1981. pap. 6.95 (ISBN 0-686-84674-5, Avalon). Bouregy.

--Phantom Rubies. (YA) 1979. 6.95 (ISBN 0-685-65274-2, Avalon). Bouregy.

--Red Tower. (YA) 6.95 (ISBN 0-685-07457-9, Avalon). Bouregy.

Stevens, Lynsey. Man of Vengeance. (Harlequin Presents Ser.). 192p. 1983. pap. 1.95 (ISBN 0-373-10606-8). Harlequin Bks.

Stevens, Malcolm P. Polymer Chemistry: An Introduction. 1975. text ed. 28.50 (ISBN 0-201-07312-9, Adv Bk Prog); pap. text ed. 24.95 (ISBN 0-201-07313-7, Adv Bk Prog). A-W.

Stevens, Marion K. Geriatric Nursing for Practical Nurses. 2nd ed. LC 74-9441. (Illus.). 244p. 1975. pap. text ed. 11.95x (ISBN 0-7216-8594-3). Saunders.

--The Practical Nurse in Supervisory Roles. LC 73-80982. (Illus.). 160p. 1973. text ed. 7.50x o.p. (ISBN 0-7216-8591-9). Saunders.

Stevens, Mark. How to Borrow A Million Dollars. 224p. 1983. 13.95 (ISBN 0-02-614480-8). Macmillan.

--Like No Other Store in the World: The Inside Story of Bloomingdale's. LC 78-22465. (Illus.). 1979. 10.95i o.p. (ISBN 0-690-01814-2). T Y Crowell.

Stevens, Mary O. & McNulty, Thomas F. World of Variation. LC 79-129359. 1978. 10.00x o.p. (ISBN 0-262-19176-8); pap. 4.95x (ISBN 0-262-69062-4). MIT Pr.

Stevens, Matthew & Phillips, Robert I. Comprehensive Review for the Radiologic Technologist. 3rd ed. LC 76-7476. (Illus.). 243p. 1977. 14.95 o.p. (ISBN 0-8016-4789-4). Mosby.

Stevens, Michael, jt. auth. see Hoy, Michael.

Stevens, Nora B., jt. ed. see Stevens, Norman.

Stevens, Norman & Stevens, Nora B., eds. Author's Guide to Journals in Library & Information Science. LC 80-20964. (Author's Guide to Journals Ser.). 192p. 1982. 19.95 (ISBN 0-917724-13-5, B13). Haworth Pr.

Stevens, Norman D. Communication Throughout Libraries. LC 82-10502. (Scarecrow Library Administration Ser.: No. 6). 195p. 1983. 14.50 (ISBN 0-686-84523-4). Scarecrow.

Stevens, Olive. Children Talking Politics: Political Learning in Childhood. (Issues & Ideas in Education Ser.). 206p. 1982. text ed. 24.95x (ISBN 0-85520-489-3, Pub. by Martin Robertson England). Biblio Dist.

Stevens, Paul, jt. ed. see Granatstein, J. L.

Stevens, Peter, ed. Modern English Canadian Poetry: A Guide to Information Sources. LC 73-16994. (American Literature, English Literature, & World Literatures in English Information Guide Ser.: Vol. 15). 1978. 42.00x (ISBN 0-8103-1244-1). Gale.

Stevens, Peter S. A Handbook of Regular Patterns: An Introduction to Symmetry in Two Dimensions. (Illus.). 384p. 1981. 40.00 (ISBN 0-262-19188-1). MIT Pr.

Stevens, R. L. see Schwartz, B., et al.

Stevens, R. T. A Woman of Texas. LC 79-7212. 1980. 11.95 o.p. (ISBN 0-385-15325-2). Doubleday.

Stevens, Revalee R. & STeven, Robert K. The Protestant Cemetery of Rome. LC 81-84484. (North American Records in Italy). (Illus.). 110p. (Orig.). 1982. pap. 10.00 (ISBN 0-88127-003-2). Oracle Pr LA.

Stevens, Richard G., jt. ed. see Frisch, Morton J.

Stevens, Richard P. Weizmann & Smuts: A Study in Zionist-South African Cooperation. (No. 43). 1976. English. 6.00 o.p. (ISBN 0-686-15605-6); French. pap. 4.00 (ISBN 0-686-15606-4). Inst Palestine.

Stevens, Robert. Law School: Legal Education in America from the 1850s to the 1980s. LC 82-11148. (Studies in Legal History Ser.). xvi, 334p. 1983. 19.95x (ISBN 0-8078-1537-3). U of NC Pr.

Stevens, Robert & Sherwood, Philip. How to Prepare a Feasibility Study: A Step-by-Step Guide Including Three Model Studies. (Illus.). 232p. 1982. 17.95 (ISBN 0-13-429258-8); pap. 8.95 (ISBN 0-13-429241-3). P-H.

Stevens, Robert D., et al, eds. Rural Development in Bangladesh & Pakistan. LC 75-17807. 336p. 1976. text ed. 17.50x (ISBN 0-8248-0332-9, Eastwest Ctr). UH Pr.

Stevens, Robert V. Organic Syntheses, Vol. 61. (Organic Synthesis Ser.). 180p. 1983. 24.50 (ISBN 0-471-87038-2, Pub. by Wiley-Interscience). Wiley.

Stevens, Robert W., ed. Community Self-Help Housing Manual: Partnership in Action. (Illus.). 72p. (Orig.). 1982. pap. 4.75x (ISBN 0-942850-00-9). Intermediate Tech.

Stevens, Roger T. Operational Test & Evaluation: A Systems Engineering Process. LC 78-21932. 275p. 1979. 32.50x (ISBN 0-471-04725-2, Pub. by Wiley-Interscience). Wiley.

Stevens, Rolland E. & Walton, Joan M. Reference Work in the Public Library. 300p. 1982. 28.50 (ISBN 0-87287-332-3). Libs Unl.

Stevens, Ron & Godnic, Joy. How to Make Love to Yourself. Date not set. pap. 3.00 (ISBN 0-686-84098-4). Wilshire.

Stevens, Rosemary, et al. Alien Doctors: Foreign Medical Graduates in American Hospitals. LC 77-12934. (Health, Medicine & Society Ser.). 365p. 1978. 29.95 o.p. (ISBN 0-471-82455-0, Pub. by Wiley-Interscience). Wiley.

Stevens, S. S. Psychophysics: Introduction to Its Perceptual, Neutral & Social Prospects. LC 74-13473. 329p. 1975. 39.50x (ISBN 0-471-82437-2, Pub. by Wiley-Interscience). Wiley.

Stevens, W. A. Virology & Flowering Plants. (Tertiary Level Biology Ser.). 1982. 39.95x (ISBN 0-412-00061-X, Pub. by Chapman & Hall); pap. 19.95x (ISBN 0-412-00071-7). Methuen Inc.

Stevens, W. C. The Book of Daniel. 190p. 1915. pap. 2.95 (ISBN 0-87509-061-3). Chr Pubns.

--Revelation, the Crown Jewel of Biblical Prophecy. pap. 5.95 o.p. (ISBN 0-87509-126-1). Chr Pubns.

Stevens, W. C. & Turner, N. Woodbending Handbook. LC 77-94902. (Illus.). 1979. pap. 9.50 (ISBN 0-918036-06-2). Woodcraft Supply.

Stevens, Wallace. Collected Poems. LC 82-40031. 560p. 1982. pap. 8.95 (ISBN 0-394-71180-7). Random.

--The Necessary Angel. 1965. pap. 3.95 (ISBN 0-394-70278-6, Vin). Random.

Stevens, Warren F. Management & Leadership in Nursing. (Illus.). 1978. text ed. 21.50 (ISBN 0-07-061260-9, HP). McGraw.

Stevens, Wayne P. Using Structured Design: How to Make Programs Simple, Changeable, Flexible & Reusable. LC 80-23481. 213p. 1981. 29.95 (ISBN 0-471-08198-1, Pub. by Wiley-Interscience). Wiley.

Stevens, Wendelle & Herrmann, William J. UFO...Contact from Reticulum. (UFO Factbooks). (Illus.). 398p. 1981. lib. bdg. 16.95 (ISBN 0-686-84864-0). UFO Photo.

Stevens, Wendelle C. UFO Contact from the Pleiades. (UFO Factbooks). (Illus.). 542p. 1982. lib. bdg. 17.95 (ISBN 0-9608558-2-3). UFO Photo.

Stevens, Wendelle C. & Dong, Paul. UFOs Over Modern China. (UFO Factbks.). (Illus.). 452p. 1983. lib. bdg. 17.95 (ISBN 0-9608558-3-1). UFO Photo.

Stevens, Wendelle C., jt. auth. see Denaerde, Stefan.

Stevens, Wendelle C., jt. auth. see Sanchez-Ocejo, Virgilio.

Stevens, William O. Footsteps to Freedom. (gr. 9 up). 1954. 5.95 o.p. (ISBN 0-396-03635-X). Dodd.

Stevens, William R. Deadly Intentions. LC 82-7290. 288p. 1982. 14.95 (ISBN 0-312-92127-6). Congdon & Weed.

Stevens-Long, Judith. Adult Life: Developmental Processes. LC 78-71610. (Illus.). 549p. 1979. text ed. 19.95 (ISBN 0-87484-449-5); instructors manual avail. Mayfield Pub.

Stevenson. Treasure Island. (Illus.). (gr. 1-9). Date not set. price not set (ISBN 0-448-06025-6, G&D). Putnam Pub Group.

Stevenson, Anne. Coil of Serpents. 1977. 7.95 o.p. (ISBN 0-399-11930-2). Putnam Pub Group.

--Mask of Treason. LC 79-14275. 1979. 10.95 (ISBN 0-399-12370-9). Putnam Pub Group.

--Minute by Glass Minute. 64p. 1983. pap. 12.95 (ISBN 0-19-211947-8). Oxford U Pr.

--A Relative Stranger. 1970. 5.95 o.p. (ISBN 0-399-10684-7). Putnam Pub Group.

Stevenson, Arthur J. The New York-Newark Air Freight System. LC 82-160111. (Research Papers: Nos. 199-200). (Illus.). 440p. 1982. pap. 16.00x (ISBN 0-89065-106-X). U Chicago Dept Geog.

Stevenson, Augusta. Abraham Lincoln: The Great Emancipator. (Childhood of Famous Americans Ser.). (gr. 3-8). 1983. pap. 3.95 (ISBN 0-686-95264-2). Bobbs.

--Clara Barton: Founder of the American Red Cross. (Childhood of Famous Americans Ser.). (gr. 3-8). 1983. pap. 3.95 (ISBN 0-686-95254-5). Bobbs.

--Daniel Boone. new ed. (Childhood of Famous Americans Ser.). (Illus.). 204p. (Orig.). (gr. 2 up). 1983. pap. 3.95 (ISBN 0-672-52752-9). Bobbs.

--Israel Putnam: Fearless Boy. LC 59-12853. (Childhood of Famous Americans Ser.). (Illus.). (gr. 3-7). 1959. 3.95 o.p. (ISBN 0-672-50081-7). Bobbs.

--John Fitch: Steamboat Boy. LC 66-18417. (Childhood of Famous Americans Ser.). (Illus.). (gr. 3-7). 1966. 3.95 o.p. (ISBN 0-672-50101-5). Bobbs.

Stevenson, Catherine B. Victorian Women Travel Writers in Africa. (English Authors Ser.). 184p. 1982. lib. bdg. 17.95 (ISBN 0-8057-6835-1, Twayne). G K Hall.

Stevenson, Charles L. see Dewey, John.

Stevenson, Colin. A Quick March to Literacy: A Study of Reading & Writing Disability in the British Army. 1983. price not set (ISBN 0-8077-2737-7). Tchrs Coll.

Stevenson, D. French War Aims Against Germany, Nineteen Fourteen to Nineteen Nineteen. (Illus.). 320p. 1982. 49.00x (ISBN 0-19-822574-1). Oxford U Pr.

Stevenson, D. E. Miss Buncle Married. 323p. 1981. Repr. lib. bdg. 16.95 (ISBN 0-89966-167-X). Buccaneer Bks.

--Miss Buncle's Book. 335p. 1981. Repr. lib. bdg. 16.95 (ISBN 0-89966-168-8). Buccaneer Bks.

Stevenson, David. The Scottish Revolution: Sixteen Thirty-Seven to Sixteen Forty-Four. LC 74-76015. 416p. 1974. 19.95 o.p. (ISBN 0-312-70525-5). St Martin.

Stevenson, David L., jt. ed. see Gold, Herbert.

Stevenson, Dinah, ed. see Mooser, Stephen.

Stevenson, Don & Blyth, Hugh F. The Wonderlamp. (Illus.). 48p. 1983. text ed. 12.95 casebound (ISBN 0-933770-19-7). Kalimat.

Stevenson, Drew. Ballad of Penelope Lou... & Me. LC 78-5105. (Children's Stories Ser.). (Illus.). (gr. 3-5). 1978. 8.95 (ISBN 0-89594-004-3); pap. 2.95 (ISBN 0-89594-003-5). Crossing Pr.

Stevenson, Dwight E. & Diehl, Charles F. Reaching People from the Pulpit a Guide to Effective Sermon Delivery. (Notable Books on Preaching). 1978. pap. 4.50 (ISBN 0-8010-8133-5). Baker Bk.

Stevenson, E. J. Extractive Metallurgy: Recent Advances. LC 77-77021. (Chemical Technology Review Ser.: No. 93). (Illus.). 1977. 39.00 o.p. (ISBN 0-8155-0668-6). Noyes.

Stevenson, Edward. High Tech Bicycle. LC 81-48157. (Illus.). 192p. 1982. 24.04i (ISBN 0-06-014876-4, HarpT). Har-Row.

Stevenson, Edward P. The Avenging Spirit. (Twilight Ser.: No. 10). (YA) (gr. 7-12). 1983. pap. 1.95 (ISBN 0-440-90001-8, LFL). Dell.

Stevenson, Edwina, jt. auth. see Stevenson, James.

Stevenson, F. J. Humus Chemistry: Genesis, Composition Reactions. LC 81-12933. 443p. 1982. 37.50x (ISBN 0-471-09299-1, Pub. by Wiley-Interscience). Wiley.

Stevenson, Florence. Dark Encounter. 1977. pap. 1.50 o.p. (ISBN 0-451-07504-8, W7504, Sig). NAL.

--Dark Odyssey. (Orig.). 1974. pap. 0.95 o.p. (ISBN 0-451-06223-X, Q6223, Sig). NAL.

Stevenson, G. Biology of Fungi. 1970. 12.00 (ISBN 0-444-19674-9). Elsevier.

Stevenson, George A. Graphic Arts Encyclopedia. 2nd ed. (Illus.). 1979. 34.95 (ISBN 0-07-061288-9). McGraw.

Stevenson, George B. Keyguide to Key West & the Florida Keys. (Illus.). 64p. Date not set. pap. 3.50 (ISBN 0-686-84251-0). Banyan Bks.

Stevenson, H. F., compiled by. Light Upon the Word. 1980. pap. 6.95 o.p. (ISBN 0-8007-5046-2, Power Bks). Revell.

Stevenson, Harold W., et al, eds. Early Behavior: Comparative & Developmental Approach. LC 75-5858. 316p. 1975. Repr. of 1967 ed. text ed. 18.50 (ISBN 0-88275-307-X). Krieger.

Stevenson, Ian. Cases of the Reincarnation Type: Vol. IV-Twelve Cases in Thailand & Burma. LC 74-28263. 1983. price not set (ISBN 0-8139-0960-0). U Pr of Va.

--Cases of the Reincarnation Type, Vol. 3: Twelve Cases in Lebanon & Turkey. LC 74-28263. 384p. 1980. 25.00x (ISBN 0-8139-0816-7). U Pr of Va.

Stevenson, J. An Account of Fungus Exiccati Containing Material from the Americas. 1971. 80.00 (ISBN 3-7682-5436-4). Lubrecht & Cramer.

Stevenson, J., jt. ed. see Quinault, R.

Stevenson, James. The Bruckner Octagon. (Illus.). 112p. 1983. 15.75 (ISBN 0-670-19264-3). Viking Pr.

--Could Be Worse! (Picture Puffins Ser). (Illus.). 1979. pap. 3.50 (ISBN 0-14-050285-8, Puffin). Penguin.

--The Great Big Especially Beautiful Easter Egg. LC 82-11731. (Illus.). 32p. (gr. k-3). 1983. 10.00 (ISBN 0-688-01789-4); PLB 9.55 (ISBN 0-688-01791-6). Greenwillow.

--Let's Boogie! LC 78-17558. (Illus.). 1978. 8.95 o.p. (ISBN 0-396-07633-5). Dodd.

--Oliver, Clarence, & Violet. (Illus.). (gr. 3-5). 1982. 9.50 (ISBN 0-688-80275-3); PLB 8.59 (ISBN 0-688-84275-5). Greenwillow.

--We Can't Sleep. 1982. 9.50 (ISBN 0-688-01213-2); PLB 8.59 (ISBN 0-688-01214-0). Morrow.

Stevenson, James & Stevenson, Edwina. Help, Yelled Maxwell. LC 77-21247. (Illus.). 89p. (gr. 3-5). 1978. 9.75 (ISBN 0-688-80133-1); PLB 9.36 (ISBN 0-688-84133-3). Greenwillow.

Stevenson, Jane & Sprachman, Susan. Reading the Social Sciences in English. (English As a Second Language Bk.). 1981. pap. text ed. 5.50x (ISBN 0-582-74809-7). Longman.

Stevenson, John. Writing Commercial Fiction. 128p. 1983. 12.95 (ISBN 0-13-971689-0, Reward); pap. 6.95 (ISBN 0-13-971671-8). P-H.

Stevenson, John, jt. auth. see Cook, Chris.

Stevenson, June & Jones, Catherine. Yearbook of Social Policy in Britain 1982. 260p. 1983. price not set (ISBN 0-7100-9537-6). Routledge & Kegan.

Stevenson, June, jt. ed. see Jones, Catherine.

Stevenson, K. J., et al. Air Pollution in Homes III: Measurements of Carbon Monoxide & Nitrogen Oxides in Two Living Rooms, 1979. 1981. 39.00x (ISBN 0-686-97012-8, Pub. by W Spring England). State Mutual Bk.

Stevenson, Kenneth & Habermas, Gary B. Verdict on the Shroud: Evidence for the Death & Resurrection of Jesus Christ. (Illus.). 220p. 1981. pap. 6.95 (ISBN 0-89283-174-X). Servant.

Stevenson, Leslie. The Metaphysics of Experience. 1982. 16.50x (ISBN 0-19-824655-2). Oxford U Pr.

--Seven Theories of Human Nature. 1974. text ed. 11.95x (ISBN 0-19-875033-1); pap. text ed. 5.95x (ISBN 0-19-875034-X). Oxford U Pr.

Stevenson, Lionel see Baker, Ernest A.

Stevenson, Merritt R., et al. A Marine Atlas of the Pacific Coastal Waters of South America. LC 79-85448. (Illus.). 1970. 110.00x (ISBN 0-520-01616-5). U of Cal Pr.

Stevenson, Olive, jt. auth. see Hallett, Christine.

Stevenson, Peter. Braithwaite's Original Brass Band. LC 80-18065. (Illus.). 32p. (gr. 1-4). 1981. 8.95 o.p. (ISBN 0-7232-6193-8). Warne.

Stevenson, R. H., tr. see Rustaveli, Shota.

Stevenson, Richard. Death Trick. 190p. 1983. pap. 5.95 (ISBN 0-932870-27-9). Alyson Pubns.

--Fundamentals of Finance. (McGraw-Hill Ser. in Finance). (Illus.). 1979. text ed. 23.95x (ISBN 0-07-061275-7); study guide 8.95x (ISBN 0-07-061277-3); instrs.' manual 18.95x (ISBN 0-07-061276-5). McGraw.

Stevenson, Richard A. & Jennings, Edward H. Fundamentals of Investments. 2nd ed. (Illus.). 608p. 1980. text ed. 23.95 (ISBN 0-8299-0299-6). West Pub.

Stevenson, Richard A. & Phillips, Susan M. Investment Environment, Analysis & Alternatives: A Book of Readings. (Illus.). 1977. pap. text ed. 14.95 (ISBN 0-8299-0117-5). West Pub.

Stevenson, Robert. Music in Aztec & Inca Territory. (California Library Reprint Ser.: No. 64). 1977. Repr. of 1968 ed. 55.00x (ISBN 0-520-03169-5). U of Cal Pr.

--Spanish Music in the Age of Columbus. LC 78-20496. (Encore Music Editions Ser.). 1981. Repr. of 1960 ed. 44.75 (ISBN 0-88355-872-6). Hyperion Conn.

Stevenson, Robert A. The Complete Book of Salt-Water Aquariums: How to Equip & Maintain Your Marine Aquarium & Understand Its Ecology. (Funk & W Bk.). 224p. 1974. 11.49i (ISBN 0-308-10090-5). T Y Crowell.

Stevenson, Robert K. The Golden Era of Preventive Medicine. LC 82-99906. 120p. (Orig.). 1982. pap. 8.95 (ISBN 0-9606252-2-4). Stevenson Intl.

Stevenson, Robert L. A Child's Garden of Verses. (Illus.). 86p. (ps-3). Date not set. price not set (ISBN 0-448-40510-5, G&D). Putnam Pub Group.

--Child's Garden of Verses. (Illus.). (gr. k-3). 1957. 4.95 (ISBN 0-448-02878-6, G&D). Putnam Pub Group.

--A Child's Garden of Verses. LC 76-24179. (Picturebacks Ser.). (Illus.). (ps-2). 1978. PLB 4.99 (ISBN 0-394-93739-2, BYR); pap. 1.50 (ISBN 0-394-83739-8). Random.

--Child's Garden of Verses Coloring Book. pap. 2.25 (ISBN 0-486-23481-9). Dover.

--Dr. Jekyll & Mr. Hyde. (Bantam Classics Ser.). 128p. (Orig.). (gr. 7-12). 1981. pap. text ed. 1.95 (ISBN 0-553-21045-9). Bantam.

--In the South Seas. (Pacific Classics Ser.: No. 3). 1971. pap. 4.95 (ISBN 0-87022-933-8). UH Pr.

--An Inland Voyage Travels with a Donkey in the Cevennes, & the Silverado Squatters. 1978. Repr. of 1925 ed. 8.95x (ISBN 0-460-00766-1, Evman). Biblio Dist.

--Island Night's Entertainments. LC 74-31328. (Pacific Classics Ser.: No. 6). 288p. 1975. pap. 3.95 (ISBN 0-8248-0286-1). UH Pr.

--Kidnapped. (Illus.). (gr. 4-6). companion lib. ed. 2.95 (ISBN 0-448-05474-4, G&D); il. jr. lib. 5.95 (ISBN 0-448-05815-4); deluxe ed. 8.95 (ISBN 0-448-06015-9). Putnam Pub Group.

--Kidnapped. (RL 6). 1959. pap. 1.50 (ISBN 0-451-51754-7, CW1754, Sig Classics). NAL.

--Kidnapped. Bd. with Treasure Island. 1981. pap. 2.75 (ISBN 0-451-51545-5, CE1545, Sig Classics). NAL.

--Kidnapped. (gr. 7 up). 1975. pap. 2.25 (ISBN 0-14-030034-1, Puffin). Penguin.

--Strange Case of Doctor Jekyll & Mister Hyde & Other Stories. (Illus.). 1961. 8.00 o.p. (ISBN 0-399-20040-1). Putnam Pub Group.

--Travels in Hawaii. Day, A. Grove, ed. & intro. by. LC 72-91621. (Illus.). 250p. 1973. 10.50 (ISBN 0-8248-0257-8). UH Pr.

--Treasure Island. (Bantam Classics Ser.). (Illus.). 208p. (gr. 7-12). 1981. pap. text ed. 1.75 (ISBN 0-553-21046-7). Bantam.

--Treasure Island. (Hardy Boys' Favorite Classics). (Illus.). (gr. 6-9). 1978. 2.95 (ISBN 0-448-14920-6, G&D). Putnam Pub Group.

--Treasure Island. (Illus.). (gr. 4-6). 1947. 5.95 o.p. (ISBN 0-448-05825-1, G&D). Companion Library 2.95 o.p. (ISBN 0-448-06025-6); il. jr. lib. 5.95 o.p. (ISBN 0-686-60791-0). Putnam Pub Group.

--Treasure Island. (RL 6). pap. 1.50 (ISBN 0-451-51729-6, CW1729, Sig Classics). NAL.

--Treasure Island. LC 78-3553. (Raintree's Illustrated Classics). (Illus.). (gr. 5-8). 1978. PLB 13.30 (ISBN 0-8172-1136-5). Raintree Pubs.

--Treasure Island. Shefter, ed. 304p. pap. 2.95 (ISBN 0-671-48932-1). WSP.

Stevenson, Robert L. & Osbourne, Lloyd. The Wrecker. (Illus.). 448p. 1982. pap. 6.95 (ISBN 0-486-24367-2). Dover.

Stevenson, Robert L see Allen, W. S.

Stevenson, Robert L see Eyre, A. G.

Stevenson, Robert L see Swan, D. K.

Stevenson, Robert Louis. The Body Snatcher. Harris, Raymond, ed. (The Jamestown Classics Ser.). (Illus.). 48p. (Orig.). 1982. pap. text ed. 2.00x (ISBN 0-89061-281-1, 459); tchr's ed 3.00x (ISBN 0-89061-257-9, 461). Jamestown Pubs.

--The Bottle Imp. Harris, Raymond, ed. (The Jamestown Classics Ser.). (Illus.). 48p. (Orig.). 1982. pap. text ed. 2.00x (ISBN 0-89061-259-5, 463); tchr's ed 3.00x (ISBN 0-89061-260-9, 465). Jamestown Pubs.

--Doctor Jekyll & Mister Hyde. (Classics Ser). (gr. 8 up). 1964. pap. 1.25 (ISBN 0-8049-0042-6, CL-42). Airmont.

--Dr. Jekyll & Mr. Hyde. (gr. 3 up). Date not set. price not set (ISBN 0-448-41110-5, G&D). Putnam Pub Group.

--Kidnapped. (Bantam Classics Ser.). 240p. 1982. pap. 1.50 (ISBN 0-553-21067-X). Bantam.

--Kidnapped: Being Memoirs of the Adventures of David Balfour in the Year 1751. (Illus.). 304p. 1982. 75.00 (ISBN 0-684-17794-3, ScribT); pap. 17.95 (ISBN 0-684-17634-3). Scribner.

--Markheim. Harris, Raymond, ed. (Jamestown Classics Ser.). (Illus.). 48p. 1982. pap. text ed. 2.00x (ISBN 0-89061-250-1, 455); tchr's ed 3.00x (ISBN 0-89061-251-X, 457). Jamestown Pubs.

--The Strange Case of Dr. Jekyll & Mr. Hyde. Harris, Raymond, ed. (The Jamestown Classics). (Illus.). 48p. 1982. pap. text ed. 2.00x (ISBN 0-89061-253-6, 451); tchr's ed. 3.00x (ISBN 0-89061-254-4, 453). Jamestown Pubs.

--Treasure Island. (Childrens Illustrated Classics Ser.). 281p. 1975. Repr. of 1948 ed. text ed. 11.00x o.p. (ISBN 0-460-05001-X, Pub. by J. M. Dent England). Biblio Dist.

Stevenson, Russell, Jr., jt. auth. see Solomon, Lewis D.

Stevenson, S. W. A Dictionary of Roman Coins. 1964. 32.00 o.p. (ISBN 0-686-35935-6). Numismatic Fine Arts.

Stevenson, Taloria, ed. see Roberts, Jean & Ahuja, Elizabeth M.

Stevenson, Violet. Flowercraft. (Illus.). 188p. 1978. 12.95 o.s.i. (ISBN 0-89479-083-8). A & W Pubs.

--Gardening Without Gardens. (Illus.). 157p. 1976. 7.50 o.p. (ISBN 0-86002-088-6). Transatlantic.

Stevenson, W. D. Elements of Power System Analysis. 3rd ed. 1975. text ed. 33.95 (ISBN 0-07-061285-4, C); solutions manual 7.95 (ISBN 0-07-061286-2). McGraw.

Stevenson, William. A Man Called Intrepid: The Secret War. Moore, John, tr. LC 75-30730. (Illus.). 486p. 1976. 15.95 (ISBN 0-15-156795-6). HarBraceJ.

Stevenson, William D., Jr. Elements of Power System Analysis. 4th ed. (Electrical Power & Energy Ser.). 416p. 1982. text ed. 36.50x (ISBN 0-07-061278-1); solutions manual 5.00 (ISBN 0-07-061279-X). McGraw.

Stevenson-Hinde, Joan & Parkes, Colin M., eds. The Place of Attachment in Human Behavior. 1982. 20.00 (ISBN 0-465-05771-3). Basic.

Stever, Donald W., Jr. Seabrook & the Nuclear Regulatory Commission: The Licensing of a Nuclear Power Plant. LC 79-56160. (Illus.). 264p. 1980. 18.50x (ISBN 0-87451-181-X). U Pr of New En.

Steves, Ann & Perkins, Deborah A., eds. Clinical Evaluation Methods Guide. 72p. 1982. 18.00 (ISBN 0-932004-11-3). Soc Nuclear Med.

Stevic, Richart R., jt. auth. see Hansen, James C.

Stevick, Earl. Memory, Meaning & Method. LC 76-2032. 1976. 13.95 (ISBN 0-88377-053-9). Newbury Hse.

Stevick, Earl W. Teaching Languages: A Way & Ways. (Orig.). 1980. pap. text ed. 13.95 (ISBN 0-88377-147-0). Newbury Hse.

Stevick, Philip. Chapter in Fiction: Theories of Narrative Division. LC 75-125079. 1970. 14.95x (ISBN 0-8156-0070-4). Syracuse U Pr.

Stevick, Philip, ed. Theory of the Novel. LC 67-25335. 1967. pap. text ed. 13.95 (ISBN 0-02-931490-9). Free Pr.

Steward, D. J., ed. Some Aspects of Paediatric Anaesthesia. (Monographs in Anaesthesiology: Vol. 10). 370p. 1982. 95.00 (ISBN 0-444-80327-0). Elsevier.

Steward, Dick. Money, Marines & Mission: Recent U. S.-Latin American Policy. LC 80-8303. 290p. 1980. pap. text ed. 11.50 (ISBN 0-8191-1244-5). U Pr of Amer.

Steward, F. C., ed. Plant Physiology: A Treatise, 6 vols. Incl. Vol. 1A. Cellular Organization & Respiration. 1960. 47.00 (ISBN 0-12-668601-7); Vol. 1B. Photosynthesis & Chemosynthesis. 1960. 46.50 (ISBN 0-12-668641-6); Vol. 2. Plants in Relation to Water & Solutes. 1959. 75.00 (ISBN 0-12-668602-5); Vol. 3. Inorganic Nutrition of Plants. 1963. 76.00 (ISBN 0-12-668603-3); Vol. 4A. Metabolism: Organic Nutrition & Nitrogen Metabolism. 1965. 72.00 (ISBN 0-12-668604-1); Vol. 4B. Metabolism: Intermediary Metabolism & Pathology. 1966. 67.50 (ISBN 0-12-668644-0); Vol. 5A. Analysis of Growth: Behavior of Plants & Their Organs. 1969. 67.50 (ISBN 0-12-668605-X); Vol. 5B. Analysis of Growth: The Responses of Cells & Tissues in Culture. 1969. 54.00 (ISBN 0-12-668645-9); Vol. 6A. Physiology of Development: Plants & Their Reproduction. 1972. 67.50 (ISBN 0-12-668606-8); Vol. 6B. Physiology of Development: the Hormones. 1972. 55.50 (ISBN 0-12-668646-7); Vol. 6C. From Seeds to Sexuality. 1972. 54.00 (ISBN 0-12-668656-4). **Set. 897.80 (ISBN 0-685-23211-5). Acad Pr.**

Steward, F. C. & Bidwell, R. G., eds. Plant Physiology: A Treatise: Energy & Carbon Metabolism, Vol. 7. Date not set. 67.50 (ISBN 0-12-668607-6). Acad Pr.

Steward, F. G., et al. Growth, Form & Composition of Potato Plants as Affected by Environment. (Botany Supplement Ser.: No. 2). 1982. 12.00 o.s.i. (ISBN 0-12-670380-9). Acad Pr.

Steward, J. K., jt. auth. see Marsden, H. B.

Steward, Joyce S. Contemporary College Reader. 2nd ed. 1981. pap. 10.95x (ISBN 0-673-15404-1). Scott F.

--Themes for Writers: A College Reader. 1982. pap. text ed. 9.95x (ISBN 0-673-15575-7). Scott F.

Steward, Joyce S. & Croft, Mary K. The Writing Laboratory. 1982. pap. text ed. 12.50x (ISBN 0-673-15612-5). Scott F.

Steward, Julian H. Area Research: Theory & Practice. LC 50-14624. 1950. pap. 5.00 (ISBN 0-527-03290-5). Kraus Repr.

Steward, Julian H., ed. Contemporary Change in Traditional Societies, 3 vols. Incl. Vol. 1. African Tribes. (Illus.). 519p. (Includes Introduction). o.p. (ISBN 0-252-74508-6); Vol. 2. Asian Rural Societies. (Illus.). 350p. 25.00 (ISBN 0-252-74510-8); Vol. 3. Mexican & Peruvian Communities. (Illus.). 294p. 25.00 (ISBN 0-252-74511-6); pap. 7.95 (ISBN 0-252-00714-X). LC 66-25557. 1967. U of Ill Pr.

--Handbook of South American Indians, 7 vols. Incl. Vol. 1. The Marginal Tribes. 624p. 35.00x (ISBN 0-8154-0212-0); Vol. 2. The Andean Civilizations. 35.00x o.p. (ISBN 0-8154-0213-9); Vol. 3. The Tropical Forest Tribes. 986p. 35.00x (ISBN 0-8154-0214-7); Vol. 4. The Circum-Caribbean Tribes. 609p. 35.00x (ISBN 0-8154-0215-5); Vol. 5. The Comparative Anthropology of South American Indians. 818p. 35.00x (ISBN 0-8154-0216-3); Vol. 6. Physical Anthropology, Linguistics & Cultural Geography of South American Indians. 715p. 35.00x (ISBN 0-8154-0217-1); Vol. 7. The Index. 11.00x o.p. (ISBN 0-8154-0218-X). LC 63-17285. (Illus.). Repr. of 1957 ed. Cooper Sq.

Steward, M. W. Immunochemistry. (Outline Studies in Biology). 1974. pap. 5.95x o.p. (ISBN 0-412-12450-5, Pub. by Chapman & Hall). Methuen Inc.

Steward, M. W., jt. auth. see Glynn, L. E.

Steward, M. W., jt. ed. see Glynn, L. E.

Steward, Samuel see Andros, Phil, pseud.

Stewart. How to Travel Book for Young People. 1981. 9.95 o.p. (ISBN 0-679-51206-3); pap. 5.95 o.p. (ISBN 0-679-51207-1). McKay.

Stewart & Garson. Organizational Behavior & Public Management. 312p. 1983. price not set. Dekker.

Stewart, jt. auth. see Podel.

Stewart, jt. auth. see Shepard, J. M.

Stewart, et al. Keys to English Mastery, 6 Levels. (gr. 7-12). pap. 3.39 ea.; tchr's eds. 3.96 ea.; dupl. masters 21.12 ea. Bowmar-Noble.

Stewart, A. C. Dark Dove. LC 74-14814. 192p. (gr. 6-9). 1974. 10.95 (ISBN 0-87599-203-X). S G Phillips.

--Elizabeth's Tower. LC 72-4063. 220p. (gr. 6-9). 1972. 10.95 (ISBN 0-87599-193-9). S G Phillips.

--Ossian House. LC 76-9645. (gr. 6 up). 1976. PLB 10.95 (ISBN 0-87599-219-6). S G Phillips.

Stewart, A. T. The Pagoda War: Lord Dufferin & the Fall of the Kingdom of Ava, 1885-86. (Illus.). 223p. 1973. 12.00 o.p. (ISBN 0-571-08722-1). Transatlantic.

Stewart, Adrian. Hurricane: The War Exploits of the Fighter Air-Craft. 1982. 60.00x (ISBN 0-686-82343-5, Pub. by W Kimber). State Mutual Bk.

Stewart, Andrew, jt. auth. see Stewart, Valerie.

Stewart, Angus, ed. Contemporary Britain. 220p. (Orig.). 1983. pap. price not set (ISBN 0-7100-9406-X). Routledge & Kegan.

Stewart, Ann. Housing Action in an Industrial Suburb. (Law, State & Society). 1981. 29.50 (ISBN 0-12-669250-5). Acad Pr.

Stewart, Arlene & Van Raalte, Joan. No Bad Babies: An Owner's Manual. (Illus.). 96p. (Orig.). 1983. pap. 3.95 (ISBN 0-688-02129-8). Quill NY.

Stewart, Aubrey, tr. see Fabri, Felix.

Stewart, Avy. The Travelers. (Orig.). 1982. pap. 2.00 (ISBN 0-937172-36-7). JLJ Pubs.

Stewart, Bhob, jt. ed. see Barlow, Ron.

Stewart, Bobbie, ed. see Christ Episcopal Church.

Stewart, Bruce. Science of Social Issues. 1971. 10.00 o.p. (ISBN 0-8108-0410-7). Scarecrow.

Stewart, Bruce H. Operative Urology: Lower Urinary Tract, Pelvic Structures & Male Reproductive System. 2nd ed. (Illus.). 432p. 1982. lib. bdg. 58.00 (ISBN 0-683-07896-8). Williams & Wilkins.

Stewart, C. M., jt. auth. see Allport, J. A.

Stewart, C. P. & Stolman, A., eds. Toxicology: Mechanisms & Analytical Methods, 2 vols. 1960-61. Vol. 1. 77.00 (ISBN 0-12-669701-9); Vol. 2. 88.00 (ISBN 0-12-669702-7). Acad Pr.

Stewart, C. P., jt. ed. see Sobotka, Harry.

Stewart, C. P. see Sobotka, Harry & Stewart, C. P.

Stewart, C. S. Journal of a Residence in the Sandwich Islands, 1823-1825. LC 71-135064. (Sandwich Islands Publications). (Illus.). 1971. Repr. of 1830 ed. 7.50 (ISBN 0-87022-772-6). UH Pr.

Stewart, Charles E., ed. see Koch, William J.

Stewart, Charles E., ed. see Philippakis, Andreas S. & Kazmier, Leonard J.

Stewart, Charles E., ed. see Rice, John R.

Stewart, Charles E., ed. see Tremblay, Jean-Paul & Bunt, Richard B.

Stewart, Charles T. Air Pollution, Human Health, & Public Policy. LC 78-13818. 160p. 1979. 18.95x (ISBN 0-669-02670-0). Lexington Bks.

Stewart, Charles W. Minister As Marriage Counselor. rev. ed. LC 61-5559. 1970. 8.95 o.p. (ISBN 0-687-26957-1). Abingdon.

Stewart, D. Exploring the Philosophy of Religion. (Illus.). 1980. pap. text ed. 16.95 (ISBN 0-13-297366-9). P-H.

Stewart, D. J., jt. auth. see Paritsis, N. C.

Stewart, D. L. The Man in the Blue Flannel Pajamas. LC 77-18093. (Illus.). 1977. pap. 5.95 o.s.i. (ISBN 0-89645-003-1). Media Ventures.

Stewart, Daniel R., ed. Design & Operation of Caving & Sublevel Stoping Mines. LC 81-68554. (Illus.). 843p. 1981. 66.00x (ISBN 0-89520-287-5). Soc Mining Eng.

Stewart, David & Blocker, H. Gene. Fundamentals of Philosophy. 1982. text ed. 22.95x (ISBN 0-02-417270-7). Macmillan.

Stewart, David & Stewart, Lee. Getting the Childbirth Options You Want... in Less Than Nine Months. LC 81-85423. 300p. (Orig.). 1983. pap. text ed. 9.95 (ISBN 0-934426-03-1). Napsac Reprods.

Stewart, David, ed. see Ricoeur, Paul.

Stewart, David H., jt. auth. see Eckhardt, Caroline D.

Stewart, Desmond. Early Islam. LC 67-27863. (Great Ages of Man Ser.). (gr. 6 up). 1967. PLB 11.97 o.p. (ISBN 0-8094-0377-3, Pub. by Time-Life). Silver.

--Pyramids & Sphinx. LC 76-154725. (Wonders of Man Ser.). (Illus.). 1971. 16.95 (ISBN 0-88225-006-X). Newsweek.

--The Pyramids & Sphinx. Gardner, Joseph L., ed. LC 76-154725. (Illus.). 1979. pap. 8.95 o.p. (ISBN 0-88225-271-2). Newsweek.

Stewart, Dick. Universal Fly Tying Guide. (Illus.). 48p. pap. 7.95 (ISBN 0-936644-00-1). Greene.

Stewart, Don, jt. auth. see McDowell, Josh.

Stewart, Donald A., ed. Children with Sex Chromosome Aneuploidy: Follow-up Studies. LC 82-21657. (Birth Defects: Original Article Ser.: Vol. 18, No. 4). 251p. 1982. write for info. A R Liss.

Stewart, Donald C. Setts of the Scottish Tartans. (Illus.). 154p. 1982. 15.00 (ISBN 0-686-37795-8, Pub by Sheperd-Walwyn England). Flatiron Book.

Stewart, Edward. Ballerina. 1979. 13.95 o.p. (ISBN 0-385-13401-0). Doubleday.

--For Richer for Poorer. LC 81-43112. 528p. 1981. 14.95 (ISBN 0-385-11492-3). Doubleday.

--For Richer, for Poorer. 496p. 1983. pap. 3.50 (ISBN 0-425-05397-0). Berkley Pub.

Stewart, Edward C. American Cultural Patterns: A Cross-Cultural Perspective. LC 70-26361. 101p. 1972. pap. text ed. 6.50 (ISBN 0-933662-01-7). Intercult Pr.

Stewart, Edward T., et al. An Atlas of Endoscopic Retrograde Cholangiopancreatography. LC 77-11169. (Illus.). 366p. 1977. text ed. 53.50 o.p. (ISBN 0-8016-4803-3). Mosby.

Stewart, Elbert. Social Problems in Modern America. 3rd ed. Provenzano, Marian D., ed. (Illus.). 432p. 1983. pap. text ed. 18.00x (ISBN 0-07-061427-X, C); write for info. instr's manual (ISBN 0-07-061428-8). McGraw.

--Sociology: The Human Science. 2nd, rev. ed. 608p. 1981. text ed. 23.95 (ISBN 0-07-061280-3, C); instr's. manual 13.00 (ISBN 0-07-061281-1); test bank 19.95 (ISBN 0-07-061289-7). McGraw.

Stewart, Elbert W. Evolving Life Styles: An Introduction to Cultural Anthropology. (Illus.). 480p. 1973. text ed. 18.50 o.p. (ISBN 0-07-061349-4, C); pap. text ed. 16.50 o.p. (ISBN 0-07-061334-6); instructors' manual 2.95 o.p. (ISBN 0-07-061395-8). McGraw.

--The Human Bond: Introduction to Social Psychology. LC 77-9002. 518p. 1978. pap. text ed. 25.50 (ISBN 0-471-82479-8); tchrs. manual 6.00 (ISBN 0-471-82481-X). Wiley.

--The Troubled Land: Social Problems in Modern America. 2nd ed. 1975. text ed. 15.95 (ISBN 0-07-061417-2); pap. text ed. 17.50 (ISBN 0-07-061418-0); instructor's manual 7.95 (ISBN 0-07-061419-9). McGraw.

Stewart, Elbert W. & Glynn, James A. Introduction to Sociology. 3rd ed. (Illus.). 1979. pap. text ed. 18.95 (ISBN 0-07-061371-0); instructors manual 15.00 (ISBN 0-07-061372-9). McGraw.

--Introduction to Sociology. 2nd ed. LC 74-7357. (Sociology Ser.). (Illus.). 384p. 1974. pap. text ed. 10.50 o.p. (ISBN 0-07-061321-4, C); instructors' manual 4.95 o.p. (ISBN 0-07-061329-X). McGraw.

Stewart, Elinore P. Letters of a Woman Homesteader. (Illus.). 304p. 1982. pap. 6.50 (ISBN 0-395-32137-9). HM.

--Letters of a Woman Homesteader. 1982. 5.95 o.p. (ISBN 0-395-32137-9). HM.

Stewart, Eva M., jt. auth. see Riddick, Walter E.

Stewart, Frances. International Technology Transfer: Issues & Policy Options. (Working Paper: No. 344). xii, 116p. 1979. 5.00 (ISBN 0-686-36131-8, WP-0344). World Bank.

--Work, Income & Inequality. LC 81-24065. 304p. 1982. 32.50x (ISBN 0-312-88943-7). St Martin.

Stewart, Frank & Unterecker, John, eds. Poetry Hawaii: A Contemporary Anthology. LC 79-63338. (Illus., Orig.). 1979. pap. 4.95 (ISBN 0-8248-0642-5). UH Pr.

Stewart, Frank H. Fundamentals of Age-Group Systems. (Studies in Anthropology Ser.). 1977. 48.00 (ISBN 0-12-670150-4). Acad Pr.

Stewart, Frank M. A Half-Century of Municipal Reform. LC 74-168967. 289p. 1972. Repr. of 1950 ed. lib. bdg. 17.00x (ISBN 0-8371-6240-8, STHC). Greenwood.

--Introduction to Linear Algebra. 304p. 1963. 14.00 (ISBN 0-442-07989-3, Pub. by Van Nos Reinhold). Krieger.

Stewart, Fred M. Century. 1982. pap. 3.95 (ISBN 0-451-11407-8, AE1407, Sig). NAL.

--Ellis Island. Golbitz, Pat, ed. LC 82-14301. 384p. 1983. 15.95 (ISBN 0-688-01622-7). Morrow.

--Six Weeks. 1982. pap. 2.95 (ISBN 0-553-22981-8). Bantam.

Stewart, G. B. A New Mythos: The Novel of the Artist As Heroine, 1877-1977. LC 78-74840. 1979. 17.95 (ISBN 0-88831-030-7). Eden Pr.

Stewart, G. F. & Abbott, J. C. Marketing Eggs & Poultry. (FAO Animal Production & Health Series, No. 5; FAO Marketing Guides: No. 4). 194p. 1961. pap. 13.25 (ISBN 0-686-92985-3, F270, FAO). Unipub.

Stewart, G. W. Introduction to Matrix Computations. (Computer Science & Applied Mathematics Ser.). 1973. 27.01 (ISBN 0-12-670350-7). Acad Pr.

Stewart, G. W., jt. ed. see Duff, I. S.

Stewart, George F. & Amerine, Maynard A. Introduction to Food Science & Technology. 2nd ed. (Food Science & Technology Ser.). 1982. 21.00. Acad Pr.

Stewart, George F., jt. ed. see Rockland, Louis B.

Stewart, George R. American Given Names: Their Origin & History in the Context of the English Language. 1979. 18.95 (ISBN 0-19-502465-6). Oxford U Pr.

--American Place-Names: A Concise & Selective Dictionary for the Continental United States of America. LC 72-83018. 1970. 25.00 (ISBN 0-19-500121-4). Oxford U Pr.

--California Trail: An Epic with Many Heroes. (American Trails Library Ser). 1962. 11.95 o.p. (ISBN 0-07-061312-5, GB). McGraw.

--Names on the Land: A Historical Account of Placenaming in the United States. 4th ed. LC 82-6578. 560p. 1982. pap. 10.00 (ISBN 0-938530-02-X, 02-X). Lexikos.

--Storm. LC 82-16098. xiv, 349p. 1983. pap. 8.95 (ISBN 0-8032-9135-3, BB826, Bison). U of Nebr Pr.

--U. S. Forty: Cross Section of the United States of America. (Illus.). 311p. 1973. Repr. of 1953 ed. lib. bdg. 37.50x (ISBN 0-8371-6655-1, STUS). Greenwood.

Stewart, Grace. A New Mythos: The Novel of the Artist As Heroine 1877 - 1977. 2nd ed. 208p. 1981. pap. 8.95 (ISBN 0-920792-11-1). Eden Pr.

Stewart, H. C., jt. auth. see Hughes, W. H.

Stewart, H. L., jt. auth. see Kifer, R. S.

Stewart, Harry L. & Storer, John M. Fluid Power. 3rd ed. LC 79-9123. 1980. 23.50 (ISBN 0-672-97224-7); instructor's manual 3.33 (ISBN 0-672-97226-3); student manual 10.95 (ISBN 0-672-97225-5); transparency masters 42.50 (ISBN 0-672-97228-X). Bobbs.

Stewart, I. Lie Algebra Generated by Finite-Dimensional Ideals. (Research Notes in Mathematics Ser.: No. 2). 154p. 1975. text ed. 18.95 (ISBN 0-273-00142-6). Pitman Pub MA.

Stewart, I. & Tall, D. O. Complex Analysis. LC 82-4351. (Illus.). 250p. Date not set. price not set (ISBN 0-521-24513-3); pap. price not set (ISBN 0-521-28763-4). Cambridge U Pr.

Stewart, I. N. & Tall, D. O. Algebraic Number Theory. LC 78-31625. 200p. 1979. pap. 16.95x (ISBN 0-412-16000-5, Pub. by Chapman & Hall). Methuen Inc.

Stewart, Ian & Jones, Robin. Timex Sinclair One-Thousand: Programs, Games, & Graphics. 100p. 1982. pap. 10.95 (ISBN 3-7643-3080-5). Birkhauser.

Stewart, Ian & Tall, David. The Foundations of Mathematics. (Illus.). 1977. 26.00x o.p. (ISBN 0-19-853164-8); pap. 13.50x (ISBN 0-19-853165-6). Oxford U Pr.

Stewart, Ian see Bates, Martin & Dudley-Evans, Tony.

Stewart, Isobel. A Time in September. (Aston Hall Romances Ser.). 192p. (Orig.). 1981. pap. 1.50 o.p. (ISBN 0-523-41125-1). Pinnacle Bks.

Stewart, J. Of No Fixed Abode. 232p. 1975. 19.50 (ISBN 0-7190-0560-4). Manchester.

Stewart, J., jt. auth. see Pahre, P.

Stewart, J. I. Joseph Conrad. LC 68-15412. 1968. 6.00 o.p. (ISBN 0-396-05711-X). Dodd.

--Thomas Hardy: A Critical Biography. LC 78-159830. 1971. 6.95 o.p. (ISBN 0-396-06338-1). Dodd.

Stewart, J. I. M. A Use of Riches. (Phoenix Fiction Ser.). 246p. 1957. pap. 6.95 (ISBN 0-226-77403-1). U of Chicago Pr.

--A Villa in France. 1983. 15.00x (ISBN 0-393-01646-3). Norton.

Stewart, J. R., jt. auth. see Archer, F. C.

Stewart, J. R., jt. auth. see Huffman, Harry.

Stewart, James A. The Partners: Inside Americ's Most Powerful Law Firms. 384p. 1983. 16.95 (ISBN 0-671-42023-2). S&S.

Stewart, James R., et al. An Atlas of Vascular Rings & Related Malformations of the Aortic Arch System. (Illus.). 184p. 1964. photocopy ed. spiral 19.75x (ISBN 0-398-01861-8). C C Thomas.

Stewart, James S. Faith to Proclaim. (James S. Stewart Library). 2.95 o.p. (ISBN 0-8010-7977-2). Baker Bk.

--The Life & Teaching of Jesus Christ. 1982. pap. 2.95 (ISBN 0-687-21744-X, Festival). Abingdon.

--Man in Christ. (James S. Stewart Library). 1975. pap. 6.95 (ISBN 0-8010-8045-2). Baker Bk.

Stewart, James W. & Zitlow, David R. The Law & the Citizen - Student in Wisconsin: A Handbook for Secondary Students. (Illus.). 225p. 1981. pap. text ed. 6.95 o.s.i. (ISBN 0-314-63146-1). West Pub.

Stewart, Jean, tr. see Majault, Joseph.

Stewart, Jean, tr. see Mosse, Claude.

Stewart, Jeannie C. Ancient & Cherished Treasures of Scotland. (Illus.). 1982. 6.75 (ISBN 0-8062-1774-X). Carlton.

Stewart, Jeffery C., ed. Essays from the Harlem Renaissance: The Critical Temper of Alain Locke. LC 80-9046. 435p. 1982. lib. bdg. 52.00 (ISBN 0-8240-9318-6). Garland Pub.

Stewart, Jeffrey R., jt. auth. see Huffman, Harry.

Stewart, Jeffrey R., et al. Progressive Filing. 9th ed. Pezzuti, Ella, ed. LC 79-26178. (Illus.). 160p. (gr. 9-12). 1980. text ed. 11.16 (ISBN 0-07-061445-8, G); practice set 9.32 (ISBN 0-07-061446-6). McGraw.

Stewart, Jeffrey R., Jr. & Blockhus, Wanda A. Office Procedures. LC 79-9095. (Illus.). 1980. text ed. 15.04 (ISBN 0-07-061440-7); General Office Projects 6.60 (ISBN 0-07-061441-5); Administrative Projects 6.60 (ISBN 0-07-061442-3); tchrs. manual & key 6.80 (ISBN 0-07-061443-1). McGraw.

Stewart, Jeffrey R., Jr. & Kahn, Gilbert. Gregg Quick Filing Practice. 2nd ed. (Illus.). 1979. pap. text ed. 7.32 (ISBN 0-07-061430-X, G); tchr's manual & visual key 7.05 (ISBN 0-07-061431-8). McGraw.

Stewart, Jeffrey R., Jr., et al. Filing Systems & Records Management. 3rd ed. LC 80-21605. (Illus.). 240p. 1981. text ed. 12.70 (ISBN 0-07-061471-7, G); instr's. manual & key 8.25 (ISBN 0-07-061473-3); practice materials 8.75 (ISBN 0-07-061472-5). McGraw.

Stewart, Jo. Andrea. 1982. pap. 2.50 (ISBN 0-451-11654-2, AE1654, Sig Vista). NAL.

Stewart, Joan Hinde. Colette. (World Authors Ser.). 198p. 1983. lib. bdg. 13.95 (ISBN 0-8057-6527-1, Twayne). G K Hall.

Stewart, John. Local Government: The Conditions of Local Choice. (Institute of Local Government Studies). 216p. 1983. text ed. 28.50x (ISBN 0-04-352102-9); pap. text ed. 12.95x (ISBN 0-04-352103-7). Allen Unwin.

Stewart, John & D'Angelo, Gary. Together-Communicating Interpersonally. 2nd ed. LC 79-26426. (Speech Communication Ser.). (Illus.). 1980. pap. 14.95 (ISBN 0-201-07506-7). A-W.

Stewart, John, jt. auth. see Parker, Alan.

Stewart, John, ed. see Jones, Bessie.

Stewart, John, ed. see Stephani, Hans.

Stewart, John Allan. Dangerous Hideaway Assignment. 1983. pap. 2.95 (ISBN 0-8423-5872-2). Tyndale.

Stewart, John B. The Moral & Political Philosophy of David Hume. 422p. 1973. Repr. of 1963 ed. lib. bdg. 35.00x (ISBN 0-8371-6488-5, STDH). Greenwood.

Stewart, John D. Study of Major Religious Beliefs in America. (Living Word Paperback Ser.). (Orig.). 1962. pap. 2.95 cancelled (ISBN 0-8344-0040-5). Sweet.

Stewart, John I. Eight Modern Writers. (Oxford History of English Literature Ser.). 1963. 39.50x (ISBN 0-19-812207-1); pap. 5.95x (ISBN 0-19-881300-7, OPB300). Oxford U Pr.

Stewart, Joseph T. Dynamic Stock Option Trading. LC 80-25957. 193p. 1981. 37.95 (ISBN 0-471-08670-3). Ronald Pr.

Stewart, Joyce L., jt. auth. see Campbell, Mary C.

Stewart, K. K. God Made Me Special. Mahany, Patricia, ed. (Happy Day Bks.). (Illus.). 24p. (ps-2). 1983. 1.29 (ISBN 0-87239-635-5, 3555). Standard Pub.

Stewart, Katie. Short Cut Cookbook. (Illus.). 128p. 1981. 7.95 o.p. (ISBN 0-600-31991-1, 8183). Larousse.

Stewart, Kenneth L., et al. Clinical Removable Partial Prosthodontics. LC 81-22399. (Illus.). 715p. 1983. text ed. 59.50 (ISBN 0-8016-4813-0). Mosby.

Stewart, Kenneth N. News Is What We Make It: A Running Story of the Working Press. Repr. of 1943 ed. lib. bdg. 16.25x (ISBN 0-8371-3378-5, STNM). Greenwood.

Stewart, Lane, jt. auth. see Paine, Shep.

Stewart, Lee, jt. auth. see Stewart, David.

Stewart, Leon. Too Late. pap. 5.95 (ISBN 0-911866-66-3). Advocate.

Stewart, Linda. Panic on Page One. 1979. 8.95 o.s.i. (ISBN 0-440-07120-8). Delacorte.

Stewart, Lois. The Ancestors & Descendants of James Montaney (1799-1857) of Oppenheim, Fulton County, N.Y. LC 82-82521. (Illus.). 448p. 1982. 25.00 (ISBN 0-9609512-0-2). L Stewart.

Stewart, Lucy P. Bride of Torquay. (Candlelight Ser.). 1980. pap. 1.50 o.s.i. (ISBN 0-440-11000-9). Dell.

Stewart, M. M. & Zimmer, K. College English & Communication. 4th ed. 1982. 19.35 (ISBN 0-07-072846-1). McGraw.

--College English & Communication: Berkeley Edition. 4th ed. 1982. 19.35 o.p. (ISBN 0-07-072851-8); communications problems 8.95 o.p. (ISBN 0-07-072852-6); cancelled instructor's guide & key o.p. McGraw.

--Communication Problems Correlated with College English & Communication. 4th ed. 1982. 10.00x (ISBN 0-07-072847-X); instr's. guide & key 9.90 (ISBN 0-07-072848-8). McGraw.

Stewart, M. M., et al. Basic Graphic Arts. 624p. 1983. 15.96 (ISBN 0-07-061420-2, G). McGraw.

Stewart, Maco. Sex, Money & God. 1982. cancelled 14.95 (ISBN 0-87949-228-7). Ashley Bks.

Stewart, Margaret M. Amphibians of Malawi. LC 67-63247. (Illus.). 1967. 24.50x (ISBN 0-87395-027-5). State U NY Pr.

Stewart, Marie M., et al. Business English & Communication. 4th ed. (Illus.). 560p. 1971. 14.64 (ISBN 0-07-061323-0, G); tchr's manual & key 10.64 (ISBN 0-07-061326-5); student projects & activities 6.12 (ISBN 0-07-061324-9); tests 2.08 (ISBN 0-07-061325-7). McGraw.

--College English & Communication. 3rd ed. (Illus.). 544p. 1975. text ed. 20.95 (ISBN 0-07-061401-6); instructor's manual & key o.p. 8.10 (ISBN 0-07-061404-0); wkbk. 9.85 (ISBN 0-07-061402-4). McGraw.

Stewart, Marjabella Y. The Teen Girls Guide to Social Success. 1982. pap. 2.50 (ISBN 0-451-11886-3, Sig Vista). NAL.

Stewart, Marjabelle & Faux, Marian. Executive Etiquette. LC 79-16524. 1979. 12.95 (ISBN 0-312-27427-0). St Martin.

Stewart, Marjorie S. & Stivers, Wendellyn. Teaching Aids & Strategies: Home Economics. LC 72-80153. 1973. pap. text ed. 3.95x (ISBN 0-8134-1489-X, 1489). Interstate.

Stewart, Mark A. & Gath, Ann. Psychlogical Disorders of Children. LC 77-10316. 180p. 1978. pap. 7.50 (ISBN 0-686-74098-X). Krieger.

Stewart, Mark A. & Olds, Sally W. Raising a Hyperactive Child. LC 72-79696. (Illus.). 312p. 1973. 14.37i (ISBN 0-06-014121-2, HarpT). Har-Row.

Stewart, Martha & Hawes, Elizabeth. Entertaining. (Illus.). 308p. 1982. 35.00 (ISBN 0-517-54419-9, Pub. by Potter). Crown.

Stewart, Mary. Ludo & the Star Horse. LC 74-26662. (Illus.). 192p. (gr. 3-7). 1975. 9.50 (ISBN 0-688-22017-7); PLB 9.12 (ISBN 0-688-32017-1). Morrow.

Stewart, Mary see Eyre, A. G.

Stewart, Mary J. El Intrepido Francisco: Vida y Ministerio de un Editor Evangelico. pap. (ISBN 0-311-01069-5). Casa Bautista.

Stewart, Michael. He to Hecuba. 80p. (Orig.). 1968. pap. 3.95 (ISBN 0-910482-15-2). Drama Bk.

--Politics & Economic Policy in the UK Since 1964: The Jekyll & Hyde Years. 1978. pap. 14.00 (ISBN 0-08-022469-5). Pergamon.

Stewart, N. The Effective Woman Manager: Seven Vital Skills Toward Upward Mobility. 219p. 1978. 16.95 (ISBN 0-471-04148-3, Pub. by Wiley-Interscience). Wiley.

Stewart, N., et al. Systematic Counseling. LC 77-24374. (Illus.). 1978. 25.95 (ISBN 0-13-880252-1). P-H.

Stewart, P. R. & Letham, D. S., eds. The Ribonucleic Acids. LC 73-76335. (Illus.). xv, 268p. 1973. 27.00 (ISBN 0-387-90281-3). Springer-Verlag.

Stewart, Pat. The U. S. Fitness Book. 1979. 9.95 o.p. (ISBN 0-671-24678-X). S&S.

Stewart, Pat, jt. auth. see Potter, Beatrix.

Stewart, Paul. Sports Illustrated Judo. LC 75-15827. (Sports Illustrated Ser). (Illus.). 1976. 5.95i (ISBN 0-397-01096-6); pap. 2.95i (ISBN 0-397-01104-0, LP-097). Har-Row.

Stewart, Philip D. Political Power in the Soviet Union: A Study of Decision-Making in Stalingrad. LC 68-17706. 1968. pap. 5.95 (ISBN 0-672-60764-6). Bobbs.

Stewart, Philippa, jt. auth. see Davies, Penelope.

Stewart, R. D. Cost Estimating. 448p. 1981. 32.95 (ISBN 0-471-08175-2, Pub. by Wiley-Interscience). Wiley.

Stewart, R. N. Boys' Book of Boats. 1981. 15.00x o.p. (ISBN 0-904558-94-0, Pub. by Saiga Pub). State Mutual Bk.

Stewart, Ramona. The Nightmare Candidate. 288p. 1980. 9.95 o.s.i. (ISBN 0-440-06135-0). Delacorte.

--Seasons of the Heart. LC 77-15066. 1978. 8.95 o.p. (ISBN 0-399-12135-8). Putnam Pub Group.

Stewart, Richard, jt. auth. see Breyer, Stephen.

Stewart, Richard B. & Krier, James E. Environmental Law & Policy. 2nd ed. (Contemporary Legal Education Ser.). 1978. 26.00 (ISBN 0-672-82859-6, Bobbs-Merrill Law);, 1982 supplement 7.00 (ISBN 0-87215-547-1). Michie-Bobbs.

Stewart, Rob. The Volunteer Firefighters' Management Book. LC 81-18183. 1982. 10.95 (ISBN 0-672-52719-7). Bobbs.

Stewart, Robert. Labrador. (The World's Wild Places Ser.). (Illus.). 1977. lib. bdg. 15.96 (ISBN 0-686-51020-8). Silver.

--Leadership for Agricultural Industry. Amberson, Max L., ed. (Career Preparation for Agricultural-Agribusiness). (Illus.). (gr. 9-10). 1978. pap. text ed. 7.96 (ISBN 0-07-000847-7, G); activity guide 4.96 (ISBN 0-07-000848-5); tchrs. manual & key 3.50 (ISBN 0-07-000849-3); transparency masters 7.96 (ISBN 0-07-000850-7); boxed set 110.00 (ISBN 0-07-079315-8). McGraw.

Stewart, Robert, ed. see Johnson, Dorothy M.

Stewart, Rosemarie. The Best Days of Your Life. 1977. pap. 1.95 o.s.i. (ISBN 0-515-03660-9). Jove Pubns.

Stewart, Rosemary. How Computers Affect Management. 256p. 1972. 20.00x (ISBN 0-262-19105-9). MIT Pr.

Stewart, S. M., ed. see Pejovic, Brian.

Stewart, Sally A., ed. see Kornberg, Patti.

Stewart, Sandra, ed. see Junior League of Sarasota FL, Inc.

Stewart, Seumas. Book Collecting: A Beginner's Guide. 1974. 21.50 (ISBN 0-7153-7754-X). David & Charles.

Stewart, Susan, jt. auth. see Anderson, Carol.

Stewart, T. H., ed. see Pejovic, Brian.

Stewart, Tamara & Rosenbaum, Judith, eds. Judicial Discipline & Disability Digest: 1979 Supplement. LC 81-65601. 350p. 1982. 95.00 (ISBN 0-938870-25-4); lib. bdg. 50.00 (ISBN 0-686-36542-9). Am Judicature.

Stewart, Tamara A., jt. ed. see Brooks, Terrance V.

Stewart, Tony, ed. Cool Cats: Twenty-Five Years of Rock 'n' Roll Style. LC 81-71008. (Illus.). 160p. (Orig.). 1982. pap. 9.95 (ISBN 0-933328-23-0). Delilah Bks.

Stewart, V. Mary, jt. auth. see Kidder, Louise H.

Stewart, Valerie & Stewart, Andrew. Managing the Poor Performer. 1982p. 1982. text ed. 28.50x (ISBN 0-566-02248-6). Gower Pub Ltd.

Stewart, W. A. & McCann, W. P. Educational Innovators: Seventeen-Fifty to Eighteen-Hundred, 2 Vols. (Illus.). 1968. 26.00 ea. Vol. 1 (ISBN 0-312-23765-0). Vol. 2 (ISBN 0-312-23800-2). St Martin.

Stewart, W. A., jt. auth. see Mannheim, Karl.

Stewart, W. D., ed. Algal Physiology & Biochemistry. (Botanical Monographs). 1975. 52.50x o.s.i. (ISBN 0-520-02410-9). U of Cal Pr.

--Nitrogen Fixation by Free-Living Micro-Organisms. LC 75-2731. (International Biological Programme Ser.: Vol. 6). (Illus.). 448p. 1976. 77.50 (ISBN 0-521-20708-8). Cambridge U Pr.

Stewart, Warren E., et al, eds. Dynamics & Modeling of Reactive Systems. LC 80-19714. (Mathematics Research Center Ser.). 1980. 20.00 (ISBN 0-12-669550-4). Acad Pr.

Stewart, William. J. Keir Hardie, a Biography. Repr. of 1921 ed. lib. bdg. 15.75x (ISBN 0-8371-3746-2, STKH). Greenwood.

Stewart, William J. Transforming Traditional Unit Teaching. 87p. 1982. pap. text ed. 3.95x (ISBN 0-89641-107-9). American Pr.

--Unit Teaching: Perspectives & Prospects. LC 82-60785. 125p. (Orig.). 1983. pap. 12.95 (ISBN 0-686-81659-5). R & E Res Assoc.

Stewart, William R. Philanthropic Work of Josephine Shaw Lowell, Containing a Biographical Sketch of Her Life Together with a Selection of Her Public Papers & Private Letters. LC 71-172576. (Criminology, Law Enforcement, & Social Problems Ser.: No. 163). (Illus.). 1974. Repr. of 1911 ed. 20.00x (ISBN 0-87585-163-0). Patterson Smith.

Stewart-Gordon, Faith & Hazelton, Nika. The Russian Tea Room Cookbook. (Illus.). 1981. 14.95 (ISBN 0-399-90128-0, Marek). Putnam Pub Group.

Stewart-Green, Miriam. Women Composers: A Checklist of Works for the Solo Voice. 1980. lib. bdg. 45.00 (ISBN 0-8161-8498-4, Hall Reference). G K Hall.

Stewig, John W. Children & Literature. 1980. 23.50 (ISBN 0-395-30748-1). HM.

--Informal Drama in the Elementary Language Arts Program. (Orig.). 1983. pap. text ed. write for info. Tchrs Coll.

Steyaert, Thomas A. Biology: A Contemporary View. (Illus.). 512p. 1975. text ed. 27.50 (ISBN 0-07-061346-X, C). McGraw.

Steyermark, Julian A. Flora of Missouri. (Illus.). 1963. 39.95x (ISBN 0-8138-0655-0). Iowa St U Pr.

Steyn, Peter. Birds of Prey of Southern Africa. (Illus.). 309p. 1983. 42.00 (ISBN 0-88072-025-5). Tanager Bks.

Steyskal, G. C., et al. Taxonomy of North American Flies of the Genus Limnia (Diptera: Sciomyzidae) (Publications in Entomology Ser.: No. 83). 1978. pap. 14.50x (ISBN 0-520-09577-4). U of Cal Pr.

Stiasny, G., tr. see Wilhelm, Friedrich & Schlegel, Karl F.

Stibble, Hugo L., ed. Cartographic Materials. LC 82-11519. 268p. 1982. text ed. 40.00 (ISBN 0-8389-0363-0). ALA.

Stibbs, Alan. How to Understand Your Bible. Wenham, David & Wenham, Clare, eds. LC 77-72351. Orig. Title: Understanding God's Word. 1978. pap. 1.95 (ISBN 0-87788-365-3). Shaw Pubs.

Stibbs, Alan M. So Great Salvation: The Meaning & Message of the Letter to the Hebrews. 118p. 1970. pap. 4.95 (ISBN 0-85364-102-1). Attic Pr.

Stibic. Tools of the Mind. 1982. 35.00 (ISBN 0-444-86444-X). Elsevier.

Sticca, Sandro. Latin Passion Play: Its Origins & Development. LC 69-11318. (Illus.). 1970. 29.50x (ISBN 0-87395-045-3). State U NY Pr.

Stichman, Barton F., jt. auth. see Rivkin, Robert S.

Stickel, D. L. The Brain Death Criterion of Human Death. (Illus.). 73p. 1982. 19.00 o.s.i. (ISBN 0-08-025814-X). Pergamon.

Stickel, E. Gary, ed. New Uses of Systems Theory in Archaeology. LC 82-13811. (Ballen Press Anthropological Papers: No. 24). (Illus.). 104p. (Orig.). 1982. pap. 9.95 (ISBN 0-87919-096-5). Ballena Pr.

Stickelberger, E. Calvin. Gelser, David, tr. 1977. Repr. of 1959 ed. 12.95 (ISBN 0-227-67424-3). Attic Pr.

Stickle, Warren E., jt. ed. see Brownell, Blaine A.

Stickler, Gunnar B., jt. auth. see Mellinger, James F.

Stickley, Gustav. Craftsman Homes: Architecture & Furnishings of the American Arts & Crafts Movement. LC 78-73519. (Illus.). 1979. pap. 6.50 (ISBN 0-486-23791-5). Dover.

Stickney, Carol, jt. auth. see Bristow, Opal.

Stickney, John. Self-Made: Braving an Independent Career in a Corporate Age. 1980. 10.95 (ISBN 0-399-11931-0). Putnam Pub Group.

Stickney, Matthew. A Genealogical Memoir of the Descendants of Wiliam & Mary Fowler of Ipswich, Massachusetts, Ten Generations 1590-1882. 247p. 18.00 (ISBN 0-88389-003-8). Essex Inst.

Stickney, Robert R. Principles of Warmwater Aquaculture. LC 78-25642. 375p. 1979. 33.95x (ISBN 0-471-03388-X, Pub. by Wiley-Interscience). Wiley.

Stidger, Howe C. & Ruth, W. Inflation Management: One Hundred Practical Techniques for Business & Industry. LC 80-11271. 448p. 1980. Repr. of 1976 ed. lib. bdg. 21.50 (ISBN 0-89874-132-7). Krieger.

Stidger, Howe C. & Stidger, Ruth W. Inflation Management: One Hundred Practical Techniques for Business & Industry. LC 76-8927. 400p. 1976. 19.95 o.p. (ISBN 0-471-82485-2, Pub. by Wiley-Interscience). Wiley.

Stidger, Ruth W., jt. auth. see Stidger, Howe C.

Stidworthy, John. Snakes of the World. rev. ed. LC 74-7546. (Illus.). 160p. 1975. 1.95 (ISBN 0-448-11856-4, G&D). Putnam Pub Group.

Stieber, Jack. Public Employee Unionism: Structure, Growth, Policy. LC 73-1591. (Studies of Unionism in Government). 256p. 1973. 16.95 (ISBN 0-8157-8160-1); pap. 7.95 (ISBN 0-8157-8159-8). Brookings.

Stieber, Jack, jt. ed. see Banks, Robert F.

Stiefel, E. L. Introduction to Numerical Mathematics. Rheinboldt, W. C., tr. 1963. text ed. 22.00 (ISBN 0-12-671150-X); problem bklt. free (ISBN 0-685-05133-1). Acad Pr.

Stieg, Margaret F. Laud's Lavoratory. LC 80-70185. 416p. 1982. 45.00 (ISBN 0-8387-5019-2). Bucknell U Pr.

Stieglitz, Maria. Career Education For Physically Disabled Students: Career Awareness Curriculum. LC 80-83986. (Illus.). 100p. (gr. k-8). 1981. 9.75 (ISBN 0-686-38797-X). Human Res Ctr.

--Career Education For Physically Disabled Students: Self-Concept Curriculum. LC 80-82643. (Illus.). 96p. (gr. k-3). 1981. 9.75 (ISBN 0-686-38800-3). Human Res Ctr.

Stieglitz, Maria & Cohen, James S. Career Education For Physically Disabled Students: Speaker's Bureau. LC 79-93340. (Illus.). 62p. 1980. 6.50 (ISBN 0-686-38801-1). Human Res Ctr.

Stieglitz, Maria N. & Cohen, James S. Career Education For Physically Disabled Students: A Bibliography. LC 79-89057. 152p. 1980. 11.25 (ISBN 0-686-42978-8). Human Res Ctr.

Stieglitz, Maria N., jt. auth. see Cohen, James S.

Stiehl, Ulrich. Dictionary of Book Publishing. 538p. (Eng. & Ger.). 1977. text ed. 55.00x (ISBN 3-7940-4147-X, Pub. by K G Saur). Gale.

Stiehm, E. Richard & Fulginiti, Vincent A. Immunologic Disorders in Infants & Children. LC 72-90730. (Illus.). 637p. 1973. pap. text ed. 27.75x o.p. (ISBN 0-7216-8602-8). Saunders.

Stiehm, J., ed. Women's & Men's Wars. 90p. 1983. 17.00 (ISBN 0-08-027949-X). Pergamon.

Stieneger, Leonard. George Wilheim Steller, the Pioneer of Alaskan Natural History. 548p. 1982. Repr. of 1936 ed. 110.00x (ISBN 0-576-29124-2, Gregg Intl). State Mutual Bk.

Stienhauer, Paul D. & Rae-Grant, Quentin, eds. Psychological Problems of the Child in the Family: A Textbook. 1983. text ed. 29.95x (ISBN 0-465-06676-3). Basic.

Stier, Rudolf E. Words of the Apostles. 1982. lib. bdg. 18.75 (ISBN 0-86524-087-6, 4403). Klock & Klock.

--Words of the Risen Christ. 1982. lib. bdg. 8.25 (ISBN 0-86524-088-4, 9512). Klock & Klock.

Stierlin, Helm. Separating Parents & Adolescents. LC 81-12860. 230p. 1982. 25.00 (ISBN 0-87668-477-0). Aronson.

Stierlin, Henri. The Art of the Aztecs. LC 82-50424. (Illus.). 208p. 1982. 50.00 (ISBN 0-8478-0441-0). Rizzoli Intl.

--Encyclopedia of World Architecture. 416p. 1982. pap. 16.95 (ISBN 0-442-27957-4). Van Nos Reinhold.

Stifel, Laurence D., et al, eds. Social Sciences & Public Policy in the Developing World. LC 81-47748. 384p. 1982. 23.95x (ISBN 0-669-04824-0). Lexington Bks.

Stifle, J. M., jt. auth. see Haskins, Jim.

Stifter, Adalbert. Bergkristall: (Rock Crystal) Foster, J. R., tr. from Ger. (Harrap Bilingual Ser.). 114p. 1950. 5.00 (ISBN 0-911268-55-3). Rogers Bk.

Stigger, Judith A. Coping with Infertility. LC 82-72649. 112p. (Orig.). 1983. pap. 4.95 (ISBN 0-8066-1956-2, 10-1692). Augsburg.

Stigler, George. The Organization of Industry. LC 82-20013. viii, 328p. 1968. pap. 10.95 (ISBN 0-226-77432-5). U of Chicago Pr.

Stigler, George J. The Economist as Preacher, & Other Essays. LC 82-4807. (Illus.). 272p. 1983. lib. bdg. 20.00 (ISBN 0-226-77430-9). U of Chicago Pr.

--Essays in the History of Economics. LC 65-14426. 1965. 20.00x (ISBN 0-226-77426-0). U of Chicago Pr.

--Essays in the History of Economics. LC 65-14426. (Phoenix Ser.). viii, 392p. Date not set. pap. 9.95 (ISBN 0-226-77427-9). U of Chicago Pr.

--Theory of Price. 3rd ed. 1966. text ed. 20.95x (ISBN 0-02-417380-0). Macmillan.

Stigler, George J., ed. see Smith, Adam.

Stigliani, William, jt. auth. see Spiro, Thomas G.

Stiglitz, Bruce M., jt. auth. see Kopple, Robert C.

Stiglitz, Joseph, jt. auth. see Atkinson, Anthony.

Stiglitz, Joseph E. & Uzawa, Hirofumi, eds. Readings in the Modern Theory of Economic Growth. 1969. 25.00x (ISBN 0-262-19055-9); pap. 12.50x (ISBN 0-262-69018-7). MIT Pr.

Stigum, Marcia & Branch, Rene O., Jr. Managing Bank Assets & Liabilities. LC 82-71069. 280p. 1982. 32.50 (ISBN 0-87094-297-2). Dow Jones-Irwin.

Stiles, Beryl S. Cajun Odyssey: From Nova Scotia to Louisiana... with Love. (Illus.). 200p. 1982. pap. 8.99 (ISBN 0-686-37651-X). Thomson-Shore.

Stiles, Bill. How to Be a Champion Wholesale Salesman. 1982. text ed. 19.95 (ISBN 0-8359-2916-7). Reston.

Stiles, David. The Tree House Book. 80p. 1983. pap. 3.95 (ISBN 0-380-43133-5, 43133). Avon.

Stiles, F. Gary & Wolf, Larry L. Ecology & Evolution of Lek Mating Behavior in the Long-tailed Hermit Hummingbird. 78p. 1979. 8.50 (ISBN 0-943610-27-3). Am Ornithologists.

Stiles, Harold, jt. auth. see Nichols, Talmage.

Stiles, Henry R. Bundling: Its Origin, Progress & Decline in America. LC 78-167211. 146p. Repr. of 1934 ed. 34.00x (ISBN 0-8103-3204-3). Gale.

--The History of Ancient Wethersfield Connecticut, Vol. 1. LC 74-83524. 995p. 1974. Repr. of 1904 ed. 75.00x o.p. (ISBN 0-912274-45-X). NH Pub Co.

--History of Ancient Wethersfield Connecticut, Vol. 2. LC 74-83524. (Illus.). 946p. 1975. Repr. of 1904 ed. 75.00x (ISBN 0-912274-50-6). NH Pub Co.

--History of Ancient Windsor Conn, 2 vols. LC 75-27475. (Illus.). 1976. Repr. of 1892 ed. 100.00x set (ISBN 0-912274-79-4); Vol. 1. (ISBN 0-912274-55-7); Vol. 2. (ISBN 0-912274-56-5). NH Pub Co.

Stiles, Karl A. Handbook of Histology. 5th ed. (Illus.). 1968. 21.95 (ISBN 0-07-061426-1, HP). McGraw.

Stiles, Karl A., jt. auth. see Boolootian, Richard A.

Stiles, Karl A., jt. auth. see Burns, Robert D.

Stiles, W. An Introduction to the Principles of Plant Physiology. 3rd ed. 633p. 1969. 40.95x (ISBN 0-416-41850-3). Methuen Inc.

Stiles, W. S., jt. auth. see Wyszecki, Gunter.

Stiling, Marjorie. Famous Brand Names, Emblems & Trademarks. LC 80-69353. (Illus.). 64p. 1981. 8.95 (ISBN 0-7153-8098-2). David & Charles.

Still, Athole. Swimming. 12.95x o.p. (ISBN 0-392-00035-0, SpS). Sportshelf.

Still, James. Early Recollections & Life of Dr. James Still, 1812-1885. (Illus.). 288p. 1973. Repr. 22.50x o.p. (ISBN 0-8135-0769-3). Rutgers U Pr.

--Jack & the Wonder Beans. new ed. LC 77-7982. (Illus.). (gr. k-3). 1977. 7.95 (ISBN 0-399-20498-9). Putnam Pub Group.

--Sporty Creek: A Novel About an Appalachian Boyhood. LC 76-47538. (Illus.). (gr. 6-8). 1977. 5.95 o.p. (ISBN 0-399-20577-2). Putnam Pub Group.

--Way Down Yonder on Troublesome Creek: Appalachian Riddles & Rusties. (Illus.). 64p. (gr. 3 up). 1974. PLB 4.49 o.p. (ISBN 0-399-60850-8). Putnam Pub Group.

--The Wolfpen Rusties: Appalachian Riddles & Gee-Haw Whimmy-Diddles. (Illus.). (gr. 4 up). 1975. 5.95 o.p. (ISBN 0-399-20460-1). Putnam Pub Group.

Still, Jean. Food Selection & Preparation. 1981. text ed. 21.95x (ISBN 0-02-417510-2). Macmillan.

Still, R. R., et al. Sales Management: Decisions, Strategies & Cases. 4th ed. (Illus.). 656p. 1981. text ed. 24.95 (ISBN 0-13-788059-6). P-H.

Still, Richard R. & Cundiff, Edward W. Essentials of Marketing. 2nd ed. LC 79-170644. 1972. ref. ed. 14.95 (ISBN 0-13-286468-1). P-H.

Still, Richard R., jt. auth. see Cundiff, Edward W.

Stille, Charles J. Major-General Anthony Wayne & the Pennsylvania Line of the Continental Army. LC 68-26268. (Keystone State Historical Publications Ser). 1968. Repr. of 1893 ed. 15.00 (ISBN 0-8046-0446-0). Kennikat.

Stille, G., jt. ed. see Hoffmeister, F.

Stiller, Brian. A Generation under Siege. 156p. 1983. pap. 4.95 (ISBN 0-88207-100-9). Victor Bks.

Stiller, Nikki. Eve's Orphans: Mothers & Daughters in Medieval English Literature. LC 79-8954. (Contributions in Women's Studies: No. 16). (Illus.). xii, 152p. 1980. lib. bdg. 25.00x (ISBN 0-313-22067-0, SEO/). Greenwood.

Stilley, Frank. Here Is Your Career: Airline Pilot. LC 78-9087. (Here Is Your Career Ser.). (Illus.). (gr. 6-8). 1978. 7.95 o.p. (ISBN 0-399-20643-4). Putnam Pub Group.

--Here Is Your Career: Veterinarian. LC 76-17924. (Illus.). 1976. PLB 5.89 o.p. (ISBN 0-399-61025-1). Putnam Pub Group.

--One Hundred Thousand Dollar Rat & Other Animal Heroes for Human Health. LC 74-21076. (Illus.). (gr. 5 up). 1975. 6.95 o.p. (ISBN 0-399-20441-5). Putnam Pub Group.

--The Search: Our Quest for Intelligent Life in Outer Space. LC 76-54149. (Illus.). (gr. 6-8). 1977. 7.95 o.p. (ISBN 0-399-20587-X). Putnam Pub Group.

Stillinger, Jack, ed. see Keats, John.

Stillings, Frank S., tr. see Gasparini, Francesco.

Stillman, Beatrice, ed. & tr. see Dostoyevsky, Anna.

Stillman, Damie. The Decorative Work of Robert Adam. 20.00 o.p. (ISBN 0-85458-160-X). Transatlantic.

Stillman, David M. & Gordon, Ronni L. Comunicando: A First Course in Spanish. 1979. text ed. 21.95 (ISBN 0-669-01359-5); instrs'. manual 1.95 (ISBN 0-669-02404-X); wkbk.-lab. manual 8.95 (ISBN 0-669-01708-6); reel tapeset 45.00 (ISBN 0-669-01711-6); cassette tapeset 35.00 (ISBN 0-669-01710-8); demonstration tape avail.; transcript avail. (ISBN 0-669-01709-4). Heath.

Stillman, David M., jt. auth. see Gordon, Ronni L.

Stillman, Deanne, jt. auth. see Weiner, Rex.

Stillman, Frances & Whitfield, Jane S. Poet's Manual & Rhyming Dictionary. LC 65-11650. 1965. 12.45i (ISBN 0-690-64572-4). T Y Crowell.

Stillman, Frances, ed. see Whitfield, Jane S.

Stillman, Irwin & Baker, Sinclair. The Doctor's Quick Weight Loss Diet. 1978. pap. 3.25 (ISBN 0-440-12045-4). Dell.

Stillman, Irwin M. & Baker, Samm S. The Doctor's Quick Inches-off Diet. 1983. pap. 3.50 (ISBN 0-440-12043-8). Dell.

Stillman, Linda K. Alfred Jarry. (World Authors ser.). 184p. 1983. lib. bdg. 16.95 (ISBN 0-8057-6528-X, Twayne). G K Hall.

--La Theatralite dans l'Oeuvre d'Alfred Jarry. (Fr.). 16.00 (ISBN 0-917786-12-2). French Lit.

Stillman, Myra, jt. auth. see Tannenbaum, Beulah.

Stillman, Norman A. The Jews of Arab Lands: A History & Source Book. 416p. 14.95 (ISBN 0-686-95136-0); pap. 9.95 (ISBN 0-686-99467-1). ADL.

Stillman, Peter. Improving Your Camera Handling. Rahmas, D. Steve, ed. (Handicraft Ser.: No. 9). (Illus.). 32p. (Orig.). 1973. lib. bdg. 2.45 incl. catalog cards o.p. (ISBN 0-87157-909-X); pap. 1.25 vinyl laminated covers o.p. (ISBN 0-87157-409-8). SamHar Pr.

--Stained Glass for the Amateur. new ed. Rahmas, D. Steve, ed. (Handicraft Ser.: No. 8). (Illus.). 32p. (Orig.). 1973. lib. bdg. 2.45 incl. catalog cards o.p. (ISBN 0-87157-908-1); pap. 1.25 vinyl laminated covers o.p. (ISBN 0-87157-408-X). SamHar Pr.

Stillman, Richard & Mosher, Frederick C., eds. Professions in Government. LC 79-93072. 102p. 1981. pap. 9.95 (ISBN 0-87855-863-2). Transaction Bk.

Stillman, Richard J. The Rise of the City Manager: A Public Professional in Local Government. LC 74-80742. 170p. 1979. pap. 7.50 o.p. (ISBN 0-8263-0508-3). U of NM Pr.

--Small Business Management: How to Start & Stay in Business. 1982. 18.95 (ISBN 0-316-81608-6); pap. 10.95 (ISBN 0-316-81609-4). Little.

--Your Personal Financial Planner. (Illus.). 176p. 1981. 15.95 (ISBN 0-13-980516-8, Spec); pap. 7.95 (ISBN 0-13-980508-7). P-H.

Stillman, Richard J., II. Public Administration: Concepts & Cases. 2nd ed. LC 79-89817. (Illus.). 1980. text ed. 13.50 (ISBN 0-395-28634-4). HM.

Stillman, Richard J., II, ed. Basic Documents of American Public Administration: Since World War II. 320p. 1983. text ed. 34.50 (ISBN 0-8419-0769-2); pap. text ed. 15.50 (ISBN 0-8419-0770-6). Holmes & Meier.

Stillman, W. J. Construction Practices for Project Managers & Superintendents. (Illus.). 1978. text ed. 21.95 (ISBN 0-87909-164-9). Reston.

Stillwell, G. Keith. Therapeutic Electricity & Ultraviolet Radiation. 3rd ed. (Illus.). 361p. 1983. lib. bdg. price not set (ISBN 0-683-07979-4). Williams & Wilkins.

Stillwell, Hallie, jt. auth. see Madison, Virginia.

Stillwell, James & Stockard, Jerry. Fitness Exercises for Elementary School Children: A Guide for Teachers & Parents. LC 82-83926. (Illus.). 176p. (Orig.). 1983. pap. 7.95 (ISBN 0-88011-093-7). Leisure Pr.

Stillwell, Lyda, jt. auth. see Heinig, Ruth.

Stillwell, Paul, ed. Naval Review Nineteen Eighty-Two. LC 62-21028. (Illus.). 272p. 1982. 12.00x (ISBN 0-87021-500-0). Naval Inst Pr.

Stillwell, William E., ed. The Revolution in Counseling: A Second Look. 1980. members 2.00 (ISBN 0-686-36373-6); non-members 2.75 (ISBN 0-686-37294-8). Am Personnel.

Stilman, Galina, et al. Introductory Russian Grammar. 2nd ed. LC 75-179421. (Illus.). 538p. (Rus.). 1972. text ed. 22.50x (ISBN 0-471-00738-2) (ISBN 0-471-00740-4). wkbk. 8.95x (ISBN 0-471-00906-7) (ISBN 0-685-99773-1). tapes 3.00 (ISBN 0-471-00741-2). Wiley.

Stilman, Leon. Collected Essays. 250p. Date not set. 22.00 (ISBN 0-88233-794-7). Ardis Pubs.

Stilson, Charles B. Polaris & the Immortals. (YA) 6.95 (ISBN 0-685-07455-2, Avalon). Bouregy.

Stilson, Max. Who? What? Where? Bible Quizzes. (Quiz & Puzzle Bks.). 96p. 1980. pap. 2.95 (ISBN 0-8010-8012-6). Baker Bk.

Stilwell, Frank J. Economic Crisis, Cities & Regions: An Analysis of Current Urban & Regional Problems in Australia. 192p. 1980. 21.00 (ISBN 0-08-024810-1); pap. 13.50 (ISBN 0-08-024809-8). Pergamon.

Stimer, Lyn. Beware the Greeks. 256p. (Orig.). 1981. pap. 2.50 o.p. (ISBN 0-523-41115-4). Pinnacle Bks.

Stimmann, M. W. Pesticide Application & Safety Training. 1977. pap. text ed. 8.00x (ISBN 0-931876-17-6, 4070). Ag Sci Pubns.

Stimmel, Barry. Cardiovascular Effects of Mood-Altering Drugs. LC 77-91582. 304p. 1979. text ed. 30.00 (ISBN 0-89004-287-X). Raven.

Stimmel, Barry, ed. Current Controversies in Alcoholism. (Advances in Alcohol & Substance Abuse, Vol 2, No. 3). 128p. 1983. text ed. 19.95 (ISBN 0-86656-225-7, B225). Haworth Pr.

--The Effects of Maternal Alcohol & Drug Abuse on the Newborn. LC 82-9393. (Advances in Alcohol & Substance Abuse Ser.: Vol. 1, Nos. 3 & 4). 168p. 1982. text ed. 32.00 (ISBN 0-917724-92-5, B92). Haworth Pr.

--Evaluation of Drug Treatment Programs. LC 82-21194. (Advances in Alcohol & Substance Abuse Ser.: Vol. 2, No 1). 108p. 1983. text ed. 14.95 (ISBN 0-86656-194-3, B194). Haworth Pr.

--Opiate Receptors, Neurotransmitters, & Drug Dependence: Basic Science-Clinical Correlates. LC 81-7011. (Advances in Alcohol & Substance Abuse Ser.: Vol 1, No. 1). 129p. 1981. text ed. 25.00 (ISBN 0-86656-103-X, B103). Haworth Pr.

Stimpson, Catherine & Person, Ethel S., eds. Women-Sex & Sexuality. 384p. 1981. pap. 7.95 (ISBN 0-226-77476-7); pap. 5.95 (ISBN 0-226-77477-5, P 914, Phoen). U of Chicago Pr.

Stimpson, George W. Nuggets of Knowledge. LC 75-109182. 1970. Repr. of 1928 ed. 40.00x (ISBN 0-8103-3860-2). Gale.

--Popular Questions Answered. LC 74-109601. 1970. Repr. of 1930 ed. 45.00x (ISBN 0-8103-3859-9). Gale.

Stimpson, Kate. Class Notes. 256p. 1980. pap. 2.25 o.p. (ISBN 0-380-50203-8, 50203). Avon.

Stimson, Allen. Photometry & Radiometry for Engineers. LC 74-11253. 446p. 1974. 39.95x (ISBN 0-471-82531-X, Pub. by Wiley-Interscience). Wiley.

Stimson, Ardyth, jt. auth. see Stimson, John.

Stimson, Dorothy. Scientists & Amateurs, a History of the Royal Society. Repr. of 1948 ed. lib. bdg. 15.75x (ISBN 0-8371-0238-3, STHR). Greenwood.

Stimson, Gerry V. & Oppenheimer, Edna. Heroin Addiction. 1982. 32.00x (ISBN 0-422-77890-7, Pub. by Tavistock). Methuen Inc.

Stimson, Hugh M. T'ang Poetic Vocabulary. 8.50 (ISBN 0-686-16504-7). Far Eastern Pubns.

Stimson, Hugh M. & Po-Fei Huang, Parker. Spoken Standard Chinese, Vol. 1. 9.95 (ISBN 0-686-15202-6). Far Eastern Pubns.

--Spoken Standard Chinese, Vol. 2. 1976. 9.95 (ISBN 0-686-15386-3). Far Eastern Pubns.

Stimson, John & Stimson, Ardyth. Sociology: Contemporary Readings. LC 82-82203. 450p. 1983. pap. text ed. 10.00 (ISBN 0-87581-286-4). Peacock Pubs.

Stinchcombe, Arthur L. Theoretical Methods in Social History. (Studies in Social Discontinuity). 1978. 11.50 (ISBN 0-12-672250-1). Acad Pr.

Stinchcombe, Arthur L., ed. Economic Sociology: Monograph. LC 82-13717. (Studies in Social Discontinuity). Date not set. 29.50 (ISBN 0-12-671380-4); pap. price not set (ISBN 0-12-671382-0). Acad Pr.

Stinchcombe, Arthur W. Creating Efficient Industrial Management. 1974. 27.50 (ISBN 0-12-785805-9). Acad Pr.

Stinchcombe, William. The XYZ Affair. LC 80-544. (Contributions in American History: No. 89). (Illus.). 167p. 1980. lib. bdg. 25.00x (ISBN 0-313-22234-7, SXY/). Greenwood.

Stine, Bob. The Great Superman Movie Book. (gr. 3-7). Date not set. pap. 1.95 (ISBN 0-686-97342-9). Schol Bk Serv.

Stine, G. Harry. Handbook of Model Rocketry. 5th ed. LC 82-8913. (Illus.). 352p. 1983. lib. bdg. 16.95 (ISBN 0-668-05358-5); pap. 11.95 (ISBN 0-668-05360-7). Arco.

--The Hopeful Future. 256p. 1983. 15.95 (ISBN 0-02-094140-4). Macmillan.

--Shuttle into Space: A Ride in America's Space Transportation System. (Illus.). (gr. 5). 1978. PLB 8.97 o.s.i. (ISBN 0-695-40920-4); pap. 4.95 o.s.i. (ISBN 0-695-30920-X). Follett.

--The Third Industrial Revolution. LC 75-21783. (Illus.). (YA) 1975. 7.95 o.p. (ISBN 0-399-11552-8). Putnam Pub Group.

Stine, Gerald J. Laboratory Experiments in Genetics. (Illus.). 256p. 1973. pap. text ed. 12.95x (ISBN 0-02-417520-X). Macmillan.

Stine, Hank, ed. see Ackerman, Forrest J.

Stine, Hank, ed. see Aspin, Robert.

Stine, Hank, ed. see Bradley, Marion Z.

Stine, Hank, ed. see Clifton, Mark.

Stine, Hank, ed. see Cole, Adrian.

Stine, Hank, ed. see De Camp, L. Sprague.

Stine, Hank, ed. see Gluckman, Janet.

Stine, Hank, ed. see Lafferty, R. A.

Stine, Hank, ed. see McCarty, James A. & Elkins, Don.

Stine, Hank, ed. see Miller, Ron & Durant, Frederick C.

Stine, Hank, ed. see Myers, John.

Stine, Hank, ed. see Schweitzer, Darrell.

Stine, Hank, ed. see Spinrad, Norman.

Stine, Hank, ed. see Steiger, Brad.

Stine, Hank, ed. see Sucharitkul, Somtow.

Stine, Hank, ed. see Trimble, Bjo.

Stine, Hank, ed. see White, Ted.

Stine, Laura, jt. ed. see Corrie, Sandra.

Stine, Peter. Sense of God: Meditations for Thinking Christians. 128p. 1980. 4.95 o.p. (ISBN 0-8010-8183-1). Baker Bk.

Stine, Whitney. The Oklahomans. 448p. 1980. pap. 2.95 (ISBN 0-523-41886-8). Pinnacle Bks.

--The Second Generation. 1981. pap. 2.95 o.p. (ISBN 0-523-41488-9). Pinnacle Bks.

Stine, Whitney & Davis, Bette. Mother Goddam. 1975. pap. 2.50 o.p. (ISBN 0-425-04444-0, Medallion). Berkley Pub.

Stine, Whitney & Davis, Betty. Mother Goddam. (Illus.). 432p. 1982. pap. 2.95 (ISBN 0-425-05394-6). Berkley Pub.

Stineback, David, jt. ed. see Segal, Charles M.

Stinger, Charles L. Humanism & the Church Fathers: Ambrogio Traversari (1386-1439) & the Revival of Patristic Theology in the Early Italian Renaissance. LC 76-21699. 1977. 49.50x (ISBN 0-87395-304-5). State U NY Pr.

Stingley, James. Mother, Mother. 224p. 1981. 11.95 (ISBN 0-312-92543-3). Congdon & Weed.

Stini, William A., jt. auth. see Greenwood, Davydd J.

Stinnet, Nick, et al, eds. Family Strengths 4: Positive Support Systems. 612p. 1982. pap. 14.50x (ISBN 0-8032-9133-7). U of Nebr Pr.

Stinnett, Nick & Walters, James. Relationships in Marriage & Family. 1977. 20.95 (ISBN 0-02-417530-7). Macmillan.

Stinnett, Roger, jt. auth. see Kirkman, Kay.

Stinnett, T. M. & Henson, Kenneth T. America's Public Schools in Transition: Future Trends & Issues. LC 82-740. 1982. text ed. 24.95x (ISBN 0-8077-2684-2). Tchrs Coll.

Stinnett, T. M., jt. auth. see Haberman, Martin.

Stinson, John E., jt. auth. see Johnson, Thomas W.

Stinson, John E., jt. ed. see Hersey, Paul.

Stinson, Peggy & Robert. The Long Dying of Baby Andrew. (Atlantic Monthly Press Book Ser.). 384p. 1983. 16.50 (ISBN 0-316-81635-3). Little.

Stinson, Robert. Lincoln Steffens. LC 79-4831. (Literature and Life Ser.). 1980. 11.95 (ISBN 0-8044-2829-8). Ungar.

Stinton. Anatomy of the Aeroplane. 1966. 12.50 (ISBN 0-444-19815-6). Elsevier.

Stinton, John E., jt. auth. see Pritchett, S. Travis.

Stiny, George & Gips, James. Algorithmic Aesthetics: Computer Models for Criticism & Design in the Arts. 1979. 28.50x (ISBN 0-520-03467-8). U of Cal Pr.

Stipa, S. & Cavallaro, A., eds. Peripheral Arterial Diseases: Medical & Surgical Problems. (Serono Symposia Ser.: No. 44). 1982. 67.50 (ISBN 0-12-671460-6). Acad Pr.

Stipe, Gordon J. The Development of Physical Theories. LC 77-13632. 494p. (Orig.). 1978. Repr. of 1979 ed. lib. bdg. 27.00 (ISBN 0-88275-623-0). Krieger.

Stire, Tom G., ed. Process Control Computer Systems: Guide for Managers. LC 82-70705. (Illus.). 296p. 1982. 29.95 (ISBN 0-686-82280-3). Ann Arbor Science.

Stirewalt, Edward N., jt. auth. see Maycock, Paul D.

Stirk, JOhn L., jt. auth. see SBalaskas, Arthur.

Stirling, C. J. & Patai. The Chemistry of Sulphoniom Group, Part 2. LC 80-40122. (Chemistry of Functional Group Ser.). 462p. 1981. o. p 112.95x (ISBN 0-471-27770-3, Pub. by Wiley-Interscience); Set. 211.00x (ISBN 0-471-27655-3). Wiley.

--The Chemistry of the Sulphonium Group, 2 pts. LC 80-40122. (Chemistry of Functional Groups). 1981. Pt. 1. 385p. 98.95x, (ISBN 0-471-27769-X, Pub. by Wiley-Interscience); Pt. 2. 462p. 112.95x, (ISBN 0-471-27770-3). Wiley.

Stirling, C. J. M., ed. Organic Sulpher Chemistry. 352p. 1975. 34.50 o.p. (ISBN 0-408-70711-9). Butterworth.

Stirling, Eruera. Eruera: The Teachings of a Maori Elder. Salmond, Anne, ed. (Illus.). 1981. 45.00x (ISBN 0-19-558069-9). Oxford U Pr.

Stirling, James & Maxwell, Robert. James Stirling. (Academy Architecture Ser.). (Illus.). 96p. 1983. pap. 14.95 (ISBN 0-312-43987-3). St Martin.

Stirling, Monica. The Fine & the Wicked: The Life & Times of Ouida. 223p. 1982. Repr. of 1958 ed. lib. bdg. 30.00 (ISBN 0-89760-850-X). Telegraph Bks.

Stirling, Nora. Who Wrote the Modern Classics. (John Day Bk.). (Illus.). 1970. 10.53i (ISBN 0-381-98184-3, A88500). T Y Crowell.

--You Would If You Loved Me. LC 70-88697. (gr. 6 up). 1969. 5.95 (ISBN 0-87131-111-9). M Evans.

Stirling, Patrick J. Australian & Californian Gold Discoveries & Their Probable Consequences. Repr. of 1853 ed. lib. bdg. 21.00x (ISBN 0-8371-0670-2, STGD). Greenwood.

Stirling, William, tr. From Machault to Malherbe Thirteenth to Seventeeth Century. 230p. 1982. Repr. of 1947 ed. lib. bdg. 45.00 (ISBN 0-89760-017-7). Telegraph Bks.

Stirner, Max. The Ego & His Own: The Case of the Individual Against Authority. Martin, James J., ed. Byington, Steven T., tr. from Ger. LC 82-50474. 400p. 1982. pap. 6.95 (ISBN 0-686-35964-X). West World Pr.

Stirrup Associates Inc. My Jesus Pocketbook of Li'l Critters. Phillips, Cheryl M., ed. LC 82-63139. (Illus.). 32p. (Orig.). 1983. pap. text ed. 0.49 (ISBN 0-937420-05-0). Stirrup Assoc.

--My Jesus Pocketbook of Manners. Phillips, Cheryl M., ed. LC 82-63141. (Illus.). 32p. 1983. pap. 0.49 (ISBN 0-937420-06-9). Stirrup Assoc.

Stirrup Associates, Inc. My Jesus Pocketbook of Scripture Pictures. LC 82-80351. (Illus.). 32p. (Orig.). (ps). 1982. pap. 0.49 (ISBN 0-937420-02-6). Stirrup Assoc.

--My Jesus Pocketbook of the 23rd Psalm. Phillips, Cheryl M., ed. LC 82-63140. (Illus.). 32p. (Orig.). 1983. pap. text ed. 0.49 (ISBN 0-937420-04-2). Stirrup Assoc.

Stirzaker, David, jt. auth. see Grimmett, Geoffrey.

Stitch, M. L., ed. Laser Handbook, III. 846p. 1979. 157.50 (ISBN 0-444-85271-9, North Holland). Elsevier.

Stitch, Stephen P., jt. auth. see Jackson, David A.

Stites, Daniel P., et al, eds. Basic & Clinical Immunology. 4th ed. LC 80-82159. (Illus.). 775p. 1982. lexotone cover 22.00 (ISBN 0-87041-223-X). Lange.

Stites, Frances N. John Marshall: Defender of the Constitution. (Library of American Biography). (Orig.). 1981. 11.95 (ISBN 0-316-81669-8); pap. text ed. 5.95 (ISBN 0-316-81667-1). Little.

Stitt, Abby. The Sexually Healthy Woman. LC 77-78345. 1979. pap. 4.95 o.p. (ISBN 0-448-14366-6, G&D). Putnam Pub Group.

Stitt, F. A. Systems Graphics: Breakthroughs in Drawing Production & Project Management for Architects, Designers & Engineers. 224p. 1983. 34.95 (ISBN 0-07-061551-9, P&RB). McGraw.

Stitt, Fred A. Systems Drafting. (Illus.). 1980. 23.95 (ISBN 0-07-061550-0). McGraw.

Stitt, Irene. Japanese Ceramics of the Last Hundred Years. (Illus.). 256p. 1974. 9.95 o.p. (ISBN 0-517-51664-0). Crown.

Stivers, Dick. Amazon Slaughter. (Able Team Ser.). 192p. 1983. pap. 1.95 (ISBN 0-373-61204-4, Pub. by Worldwide). Harlequin Bks.

--Texas Showdown. (Able Team Ser.). 192p. 1982. pap. 1.95 (ISBN 0-373-61203-6, Pub. by Worldwide). Harlequin Bks.

Stivers, Wendellyn, jt. auth. see Stewart, Marjorie S.

Stivers, William. Supremacy & Oil: Iraq, Turkey, & the Anglo-American World Order, 1918-1930. LC 82-5092. 248p. 1983. 19.95x (ISBN 0-8014-1496-2). Cornell U Pr.

Stiverson, Georgy A., jt. auth. see Papenfuse, Edward C.

St John, Patricia. Secret of the Fourth Candle. LC 81-22400. 128p. 1981. pap. 2.95 (ISBN 0-8024-7681-3). Moody.

ST. Johns, A. R. No Good-byes: My Search Into Life Beyond Death. 1981. 10.95 (ISBN 0-07-054450-6). McGraw.

St Joseph, J. K., jt. auth. see Norman, E. R.

Stobart, Tom. Herbs, Spices & Flavorings. LC 81-18886. (Illus.). 320p. 1982. 14.95 (ISBN 0-87951-148-6). Overlook Pr.

Stobaugh, Robert, jt. auth. see Ghadar, Fariborz.

Stobaugh, Robert B., et al. Nine Investments Abroad & Their Impact at Home: Case Studies on Multinational Enterprises & the U.S. Economy. LC 74-20368. 250p. 1976. 14.00x (ISBN 0-87584-113-9). Harvard Busn.

Stobaugh, Robert B., Jr. Petrochemical Manufacturing & Marketing Guide, 2 vols. Incl. Vol. 1. Aromatics & Derivatives. 1967. (ISBN 0-87201-665-X); Vol. 2. Olefins, Diolefins & Acetylene. 1968. (ISBN 0-87201-666-8). 12.95x ea. o.p. Gulf Pub.

Stobbs, Joanna & Stobbs, William. One Sun, Two Eyes, & a Million Stars. (Illus.). 32p. (ps). 1983. bds. 7.95 (ISBN 0-19-279747-6, Pub by Oxford U Pr Childrens). Merrimack Bk Serv.

Stobbs, William. Round & Round the Garden. (Illus.). 32p. (ps). 1983. bds. 7.50 (ISBN 0-370-30497-7, Pub. by The Bodley Head). Merrimack Bk Serv.

--Story of the Three Bears. (Illus.). (gr. k-3). 1965. PLB 6.95 o.p. (ISBN 0-07-061576-4, GB). McGraw.

--There's a Hole in My Bucket. (Umbrella Books). (Illus.). 30p. (ps). 1983. bds. 5.95 (ISBN 0-19-279755-7, Pub by Oxford U Pr Childrens). Merrimack Bk Serv.

Stobbs, William, jt. auth. see Stobbs, Joanna.

Stobie, Margaret R. Frederick Philip Grove. (World Author Ser.). lib. bdg. 15.95 (ISBN 0-8057-2408-7, Twayne). G K Hall.

Stobla, K. Marie, tr. see Bach, Johann S.

Stock, Augustine. Call to Discipleship: A Literary Study of Mark's Gospel. 1982. pap. 7.95 (ISBN 0-89453-273-1). M Glazier.

Stock, Brian. Myth & Science in the Twelfth Century: A Study of Bernard Silvester. LC 72-38385. (Illus.). 320p. 1972. 27.50x o.p. (ISBN 0-691-05201-8). Princeton U Pr.

Stock, Claudette & McClure, Judith S. The Household Curriculum: A Workbook for Teaching Your Young Child to Think. LC 82-48805. (Illus.). 160p. (Orig.). 1983. pap. 6.68i (ISBN 0-06-091019-4, CN 1019, CN). Har-Row.

Stock, D. E., ed. Measurements in Polyphase Flows. 1978. 20.00 o.p. (ISBN 0-685-66803-7, H00121). ASME.

Stock, Eugene. Practical Truths from the Pastoral Epistles. 352p. 1983. Repr. 12.95 (ISBN 0-8254-3746-6). Kregel.

Stock Exchange, London, ed. Stock Exchange Official Year-Book (U.K.), 1981-82. 107 ed. LC 34-16479. 1982. 180.00x (ISBN 0-333-31019-5). Intl Pubns Serv.

Stock, J. P. & Williams, D. O., eds. Diagnosis & Treatment of Cardiac Arrythmias. 3rd ed. (Illus.). 1974. 39.95 (ISBN 0-407-14752-7). Butterworth.

Stock, James R. Energy-Ecology Impacts on Distribution. 1978. 20.95x (ISBN 0-905440-53-6, Pub. by MCB Pubns). State Mutual Bk.

Stock, John T. Amperometric Titrations. 742p. 1975. Repr. of 1965 ed. 41.50 (ISBN 0-88275-268-5). Krieger.

Stock, Leo F., ed. see Great Britain. Parliament.

Stock, M. J. Obesity & Leanness: Basic Aspects. 110p. 1982. 14.95x (ISBN 0-471-89857-0, Pub. by Wiley-Interscience). Wiley.

Stock, Noel. The Life of Ezra Pound: An Expanded Edition. LC 81-86250. 512p. 1982. pap. 15.00 (ISBN 0-86547-075-8). N Point Pr.

Stock, Noel, ed. Ezra Pound Perspectives: Essays in Honor of His Eightieth Birthday. LC 75-40995. 1977. Repr. of 1965 ed. lib. bdg. 19.00x (ISBN 0-8371-8712-5, STEP). Greenwood.

Stock, Patricia, ed. Forum: Essays on Theory & Practice in the Teaching of Writing. 384p. (Orig.). 1983. pap. text ed. 10.50x (ISBN 0-86709-089-8). Boynton Cook Pubs.

Stock, Phyllis. Better Than Rubies: A History of Women's Education. LC 77-21318. 1978. 10.95 o.p. (ISBN 0-399-12081-5). Putnam Pub Group.

--Better Than Rubies: A History of Women's Education. 252p. 1979. pap. 4.95 o.s.i. (ISBN 0-399-50381-1, Perige). Putnam Pub Group.

Stock, R. & Rice, C. B. Chromatographic Methods. 3rd ed. 1974. pap. 15.95x (ISBN 0-412-20810-5, Pub. by Chapman & Hall). Methuen Inc.

Stock, Steve. Disconnections. 1978. pap. 1.00 (ISBN 0-9601624-0-2). Negative Pr.

Stock, Susan. Early Morning Through the Door. Detro, Gene, ed. (Kestrel Ser.: No. 5). 24p. 1983. pap. 3.00 (ISBN 0-914974-37-8). Holmgangers.

Stock, Susan, jt. auth. see Partridge, Bonnie.

Stock, Ursula. Die Bedeutung der Sakramente in Luthers Sermonen von 1519. (Studies in the History of Christian Thought Ser.: Vol. 27). viii, 383p. 1982. write for info. (ISBN 90-04-06536-9). E J Brill.

Stockard, Jean & Johnson, Miriam M. Sex Roles, Sex Inequality, & Sex Role Development. (Illus.). 1980. pap. text ed. 18.95 (ISBN 0-13-807560-3). P-H.

Stockard, Jerry, jt. auth. see Stillwell, James.

Stockbridge, Henry. The Archives of Maryland Illustrating the Spirit of the Times of the Early Colonists. 87p. 1886. 6.50 (ISBN 0-686-36848-7). Md Hist.

Stockdale, Connie R., jt. auth. see Neeson, Jean D.

Stockdale, James B. & Hatfield, Mark O. The Ethics of Citizenship. (The Andrew R. Cecil Lectures on Moral Values in a Free Society Ser.: Vol. II). 167p. 1981. 9.95x (ISBN 0-292-72038-6). U of Tex Pr.

Stockdale, L. A. Servomechanisms. pap. 28.50x (ISBN 0-273-40490-3, SpS). Sportshelf.

Stockel, Martin W. Auto Mechanics Fundamentals. LC 81-20007. (Illus.). 608p. 1982. text ed. 16.80 (ISBN 0-87006-336-7); wkbk. 4.96 (ISBN 0-87006-337-5). Goodheart.

--Auto Service & Repair. LC 77-25054. (Illus.). 864p. 1978. text ed. 17.28 (ISBN 0-87006-248-4). Goodheart.

Stockham, John J. Particle Size Analysis. Fochtman, Edward G., ed. LC 77-78323. 1977. 39.95 (ISBN 0-250-40189-4). Ann Arbor Science.

Stockham, K. A. The Government & Control of Libraries. 112p. 1975. 12.50 (ISBN 0-233-96718-4, 05822-X, Pub. by Gower Pub Co England). Lexington Bks.

Stockham, K. A., ed. British County Libraries Nineteen Nineteen to Nineteen Seventy-Five. 128p. 1969. 15.00 (ISBN 0-233-96111-9, 05821-1, Pub. by Gower Pub Co England). Lexington Bks.

Stockhammer, Morris, ed. Plato Dictionary. LC 63-11488. 1963. 7.50 o.p. (ISBN 0-8022-1651-X). Philos Lib.

Stockhausen, Karlheinz, jt. ed. see Eimert, Herbert.

Stockholm, Alan J. A Biomechanics Manual for Coaches & Physical Educators. (Illus.). 125p. 1983. pap. 7.50 (ISBN 0-935496-03-3). AC Pubns.

Stockholm International Peace Research Institute (SIPRI) The Arms Trade Registers. LC 75-868. 186p. 1975. text ed. 20.00x (ISBN 0-262-19138-5). MIT Pr.

--Incendiary Weapons. 175p. 1975. text ed. 25.00x (ISBN 0-262-19139-3). MIT Pr.

--Nuclear Proliferation Problems. LC 74-8307. 312p. 1975. text ed. 23.00x o.p. (ISBN 0-262-10015-0). MIT Pr.

Stockholm International Peace Research Institute. Problem of Chemical & Biological Warfare: A Study of the Historical, Technical, Military, Legal & Political Aspects of CBW, & Possible Disarmament Measures, Vol. 2, CB Weapons Today. 1973. text ed. 11.75x o.p. (ISBN 0-391-00201-5). Humanities.

--Problem of Chemical & Biological Warfare: A Study of the Historical, Technical, Military, Legal & Political Aspects of CBW, & Possible Disarmament Measures, Vol. 3, C B W & International Law. 1973. text ed. 23.00x (ISBN 0-391-00202-3). Humanities.

--S I P R I Yearbook of World Armaments & Disarmaments 1968-69. 1970. text ed. 19.00x (ISBN 0-391-00012-8); pap. text ed. 15.00x (ISBN 0-391-00085-3). Humanities.

--S I P R I Yearbook of World Armaments & Disarmaments, 1969-70, No. 2, (Illus.). 1971. text ed. 19.25x (ISBN 91-85114-08-1); pap. text ed. 17.50x (ISBN 0-391-00085-3). Humanities.

Stockholm International Peace Research Institute (SIPRI) Safeguards Against Nuclear Proliferation. LC 75-867. 140p. 1975. text ed. 18.00x o.p. (ISBN 0-262-19137-7). MIT Pr.

Stockholm International Peace Research Institute. Southern Africa: The Escalation of a Conflict. LC 76-4518. (Special Studies). 400p. 1976. text ed. 38.95 o.p. (ISBN 0-275-56840-7). Praeger.

Stockholm International Peace Research Institute (SIPRI) Tactical & Strategic Antisubmarine Warfare. LC 74-17775. 135p. 1974. 13.00x o.p. (ISBN 0-262-20031-7). MIT Pr.

Stockholm International Peace Research Institute. World Armaments & Disarmament: SIPRI Yearbook, 1974. 1974. 35.00x (ISBN 0-262-19129-6). MIT Pr.

Stockholm International Peace Research Institute (SIPRI) World Armaments & Disarmament: SIPRI Yearbook 1975. LC 75-13547. 520p. 1975. 35.00x (ISBN 0-262-19140-7). MIT Pr.

Stockholm International Peace Research Institute. World Armaments & Disarmament: SIPRI Yearbook 1976. LC 76-15848. 1976. 35.00x (ISBN 0-262-19149-0). MIT Pr.

--World Armaments & Disarmament: SIPRI Yearbook 1977. 1977. 42.50x (ISBN 0-262-19160-1). MIT Pr.

Stockkigt, J. R., et al, eds. Thyroid Research III: Eighth International Thyroid Congress 3-5 February 1980, Sydney, Australia. 800p. 1980. 140.00 (ISBN 0-08-026361-5). Pergamon.

Stockley, Ivan H. Drug Interaction. (Illus.). 512p. 1981. pap. text ed. 34.00 (ISBN 0-632-00843-1, B 4658-8). Mosby.

--Drug Interactions & Their Mechanisms. 84p. 1980. 5.00 (ISBN 0-85369-119-3, Pub. by Pharmaceutical). Rittenhouse.

Stockley, Tom. Great Wine Values. 150p. (Orig.). 1982. pap. 4.95 (ISBN 0-89716-107-6). Peanut Butter.

Stockmair, W., jt. tr. see Kinkeldey, H.

Stockman, Harry E. Saga of the Amplifying Crystal Nineteen Ten to Nineteen Forty-Eight: Predecessor to the Transistor. Date not set. pap. price not set (ISBN 0-918332-09-5). Sercolab.

Stocks, Broan, jt. auth. see Arnold, Eddie.

Stocks, Eleanor. Educational Methods & Materials. 1977. pap. text ed. 7.50 o.p. (ISBN 0-8191-0174-5). U Pr of Amer.

Stocks, J., jt. auth. see Down, C. G.

Stocks, Peter & Seton-Williams, Veronica. Egypt. (Blue Guides Ser.). 768p. 1983. 28.95 (ISBN 0-393-01557-2); pap. 15.95 (ISBN 0-393-30009-9). Norton.

Stockton, Doris S. Essential Algebra. 1973. pap. 15.50x (ISBN 0-673-07833-7). Scott F.

--Essential Algebra & Trigonometry. LC 77-76337. (Illus.). 1978. text ed. 24.95 (ISBN 0-395-25413-2); instr's. manual 1.00 (ISBN 0-395-25414-0). HM.

--Essential Algebra with Functions. 1973. pap. 15.50x (ISBN 0-673-07862-0). Scott F.

--Essential College Algebra. LC 78-69526. (Illus.). 1979. text ed. 21.95 (ISBN 0-395-26544-4); instr's. manual 1.00 (ISBN 0-395-26538-X). HM.

--Essential Mathematics. 1972. pap. 15.50x (ISBN 0-673-07825-6). Scott F.

--Essential Precalculus. LC 77-75647. (Illus.). 1978. text ed. 24.95 (ISBN 0-395-25417-5); instr's. manual 1.85 (ISBN 0-395-25418-3). HM.

--Essential Trigonometry. LC 78-69543. (Illus.). 1979. text ed. 21.95 (ISBN 0-395-26539-8); instr's. manual 1.00 (ISBN 0-395-26545-2). HM.

Stockton, Elizabeth. Data Entry Drillbook. 1983. spiral 10.00x (ISBN 0-89262-004-8). Career Pub.

--Twenty-Twenty Career Planning: How to Get a Job & Keep It. McFadden, S. Michele, et al, eds. 33p. 1982. 1.25 ea. (ISBN 0-89262-056-0); pak of 30 37.50. Career Pub.

Stockton, Frank. Castaway's. McCallum, Geo, ed. pap. 2.95 o.p. (ISBN 0-89285-150-3). Eng Language.

Stockton, Frank R. The Science Fiction of Frank R. Stockton: An Anthology 1874-1900. 352p. 1976. lib. bdg. 15.00 (ISBN 0-8398-2344-4, Gregg). G K Hall.

Stockton, Ronald R. & Wayman, Frank W. A Time of Turmoil: Values & Voting in the 1970's. 216p. 1983. 18.95. Wayne St U Pr.

--A Time of Turmoil: Values & Voting in the 1970's. 216p. 1983. 18.95 (ISBN 0-87013-232-6). Mich St U Pr.

Stockton, William. Altered Destinies. 1980. pap. 2.50 o.p. (ISBN 0-451-09460-3, E9460, Sig). NAL.

Stockum, Hilda Van see Broger, Achim.

Stockums, Wilhelm. The Priesthood. 242p. 1938. pap. 6.00 (ISBN 0-686-81629-3). TAN Bks Pubs.

Stockwell, jt. auth. see Barber, Hugh O.

Stockwell, Charles. Eng Workbook. 1983. pap. text ed. write for info. (ISBN 0-8391-1743-4, 17566). Univ Park.

Stockwell, Charles W., jt. auth. see Barber, Hugh O.

Stockwell, J. How to Be a Fix-It Genius Using Seven Simple Tools. 1975. 12.95 (ISBN 0-07-061587-X, P&RB). McGraw.

Stockwell, John. Red Sunset. 1982. pap. 3.50 (ISBN 0-451-11912-6, AE1912, Sig). NAL.

Stockwell, John, jt. auth. see Holtje, Herbert.

Stockwell, John & Holtje, Herbert, eds. The Photographer's Business Handbook. (Illus.). 320p. 1981. 16.95 (ISBN 0-07-061585-3, P&RB). McGraw.

Stockwell, R. A. Biology of Cartilage Cells. LC 78-67433. (Biological Structure & Function Ser.: No. 7). (Illus.). 1979. 75.00 (ISBN 0-521-22410-1). Cambridge U Pr.

Stockwell, Richard E. The Stockwell Guide for Technical & Vocational Writing. 2nd ed. LC 81-3675. (Engineering Technology Ser.). 354p. 1981. pap. text ed. 16.95 (ISBN 0-201-07154-1); avail. study wkbk. 8.95 (ISBN 0-201-07155-X). A-W.

Stockwell, Robert P. Foundations of Syntactic Theory. LC 76-8021. (Foundations of Modern Linguistics Ser.). 1977. 14.95 o.p. (ISBN 0-13-329987-2); pap. text ed. 12.95 (ISBN 0-13-329979-1); wkbk. 7.95 (ISBN 0-13-965202-7). P-H.

Stockwin, J. A. Japan: Divided Politics in a Growth Economy. (Comparative Modern Government Ser.). 320p. 1982. pap. text ed. 6.95x (ISBN 0-393-95235-5). Norton.

Stoddard, Alan. Back-Relief from Pain. LC 78-24488. (Positive Health Guides Ser.). (Illus.). 1979. 8.95 o.p. (ISBN 0-668-04677-5, 4677-5); pap. 4.95 (ISBN 0-668-04684-8, 4684-8). Arco.

Stoddard, Charles H. Essentials of Forestry Practice. 3rd ed. LC 78-6652. 387p. 1978. text ed. 23.95 (ISBN 0-471-07262-1). Wiley.

--Looking Forward: Planning a Workable Future. 320p. 1982. 15.95 (ISBN 0-02-614780-7). Macmillan.

Stoddard, Edward. The First Book of Magic. (Illus.). 1980. pap. 2.25 (ISBN 0-380-49221-0, 63750-2, Camelot). Avon.

--The First Book of Magic. LC 76-47643. (First Bks.). (Illus.). 72p. (gr. 4-6). 1977. PLB 7.90 (ISBN 0-531-00575-5). Watts.

Stoddard, Ellwyn R. Mexican Americans. LC 81-40781. 288p. 1981. pap. text ed. 9.25 (ISBN 0-8191-1806-0). U Pr of Amer.

Stoddard, Ellwyn R., et al, eds. Borderlands Sourcebook: A Guide to the Literature on Northern Mexico & the American Southwest. LC 82-40331. (Illus.). 500p. 1983. 48.50x (ISBN 0-8061-1718-4). U of Okla Pr.

Stoddard, Karen M. Saints & Shrews: Women & Aging in American Popular Film. LC 82-15821. (Contributions in Women's Studies: No. 39). 192p. 1983. lib. bdg. 27.95 (ISBN 0-313-23391-8, STS/). Greenwood.

Stoddard, Richard, ed. Stage Scenery, Machinery & Lighting: A Guide to Information Sources. LC 76-13574. (Performing Arts Information Guide Ser.: Vol. 2). 1977. 42.00x (ISBN 0-8103-1374-X). Gale.

--Theatre & Cinema Architecture: A Guide to Information Sources. LC 78-14820. (Performing Arts Information Guide Ser.: Vol. 5). 1978. 42.00x (ISBN 0-8103-1426-6). Gale.

Stoddard, Whitney S. The West Portals of St. Denis & Chartres. 1983. pap. write for info (ISBN 0-393-30043-9). Norton.

Stoddart, D. M., ed. Ecology of Small Mammals. 386p. 1979. 42.00x (ISBN 0-412-14790-4, Pub. by Chapman & Hall England). Methuen Inc.

Stoddart, L. A., et al. Range Management. 3rd ed. (Illus.). 480p. 1975. text ed. 33.50 (ISBN 0-07-061596-9). McGraw.

Stoddart, Michael D. Mammalian Orders & Pheromones. (Studies in Biology: No. 73). 64p. 1976. pap. text ed. 8.95 (ISBN 0-7131-2591-8). E Arnold.

Stodola, Jiri. Encyclopedia of Water Plants. text ed. 12.95 (ISBN 0-87666-169-X, H929). TFH Pubns.

Stodolsky, Susan, et al. Challenging the Myths: The Schools, the Blacks, & the Poor. (Reprint Ser.: No. 5). 5.95 (ISBN 0-916690-03-2). Harvard Educ Rev.

Stoeber, Edward A. Tax & Fringe Benefit Planning for Professional Corporations. 4th ed. LC 78-78161. 1979. pap. 13.75 o.p. (ISBN 0-87218-400-5). Natl Underwriter.

Stoecker, W. F. Design of Thermal Systems. 2nd ed. (Illus.). 1980. 32.00 (ISBN 0-07-061618-3). McGraw.

--Refrigeration & Air Conditioning. (Mechanical Engineer's License Examination Library). 1958. text ed. 37.50 (ISBN 0-07-061615-9). McGraw.

Stoecker, W. F. & Jones, J. W. Refrigeration & Air Conditioning. 2nd ed. 464p. 1982. 33.50x (ISBN 0-07-061619-1). McGraw.

Stoeckl, Agnes De see De Stoeckl, Agnes.

Stoeckley, T. R. The Trippensee Transparent Simplified Celestial Globe. 17p. 1968. pap. text ed. 5.30 (ISBN 0-686-37060-0). Trippensee Pub.

Stoedefalke, Karl, jt. auth. see Smith, Everett L.

Stoel, Thomas B., Jr. & Miller, Alan S. Fluorocarbon Regulation: An International Comparison. LC 79-3178. (Illus.). 320p. 1980. 27.95x o.p. (ISBN 0-669-03393-6). Lexington Bks.

Stoerker, Fredrick C., jt. auth. see Thomas, Norman C.

Stoess, H. A., Jr. Pneumatic Conveying. LC 79-105393. 218p. 1970. 44.95 (ISBN 0-471-82680-4, Pub. by Wiley-Interscience). Wiley.

Stoessinger, John G. Nations in Darkness: China, Russia, & America. 3rd ed. 263p. 1981. pap. text ed. 8.00 (ISBN 0-394-32657-1). Random.

--Why Nations Go to War. 2nd ed. LC 77-86304. 1978. text ed. 15.95x o.p. (ISBN 0-312-87851-6); pap. text ed. 5.95x o.p. (ISBN 0-312-87852-4). St Martin.

Stoesz, Samuel J. Church & Membership Awareness. pap. 2.95 (ISBN 0-87509-066-4); leaders guide 1.25 (ISBN 0-87509-067-2). Chr Pubns.

--Church & Missions Alive. 1975. pap. 2.95 (ISBN 0-87509-068-0); leaders guide 1.25 (ISBN 0-87509-069-9). Chr Pubns.

Stoesz, Samuel S. Life Is for Growth. 1977. pap. 2.75 (ISBN 0-87509-102-4); leaders guide 1.50 (ISBN 0-87509-169-5). Chr Pubns.

Stoever, William A. Renegotiations in International Business Transactions: The Process of Dispute-Resolution Between Multinational Investors & Host Societies. LC 79-4727. 400p. 1981. 29.95x (ISBN 0-669-03057-0). Lexington Bks.

Stoeving, Paul. Violin: Its Famous Makers & Players. (Illus.). Repr. of 1928 ed. lib. bdg. 15.75x (ISBN 0-8371-4346-2, STVI). Greenwood.

Stoff, Jesse A., jt. auth. see Pellegrino, Charles R.

Stoffel, Lester, jt. auth. see Gregory, Ruth.

Stoffels, Robert E. Management in Action, Vol. XII. 1981. 7.50 (ISBN 0-686-98068-9). Telecom Lib.

Stohr, Walter & Taylor, D. R. Development from Above or Below? The Dialects of Regional Planning in Developing Countries. 448p. 1981. 54.95 (ISBN 0-471-27823-8, Pub. by Wiley-Interscience). Wiley.

Stoiaken, Larry, jt. auth. see Marier, Donald.

Stoiber, Richard E. & Morse, Sterns A. Microscopic Identification of Crystals. LC 79-11715. 286p. 1979. Repr. of 1972 ed. lib. bdg. 16.50 o.p. (ISBN 0-88275-975-2). Krieger.

Stokell, Marjorie. A Visitor's Guide to L. A. Harper, Susan, ed. LC 80-67475. (Illus.). 224p. (Orig.). Date not set. pap. 6.95 (ISBN 0-89395-061-0). Cal Living Bks. Postponed.

Stokely, Jim & Johnson, Jeff, eds. An Encyclopedia of East Tennessee. LC 81-68545. (Illus.). 550p. 1981. 21.95 (ISBN 0-9606832-0-8). Children's Mus.

Stoken, Dick. What They Are, What They Mean, How to Profit by Them. (Illus.). 1978. 28.95 (ISBN 0-07-061632-9, P&RB). McGraw.

Stoker, Bram. The Annotated Dracula. (Illus.). 1975. 14.95 (ISBN 0-517-52017-6, C N Potter Bks). Crown.

--Dracula. (Bantam Classics Ser.). 432p. (Orig.). (gr. 9-12). 1981. pap. text ed. 1.75 (ISBN 0-553-21047-5). Bantam.

--Dracula. 1965. pap. 2.50 (ISBN 0-440-92148-1, LE). Dell.

--Dracula. 1959. 7.95 (ISBN 0-385-00383-8). Doubleday.

--Dracula. 1932. 6.95 (ISBN 0-394-60447-4). Modern Lib.

--Dracula. (RL 10). pap. 2.50 (ISBN 0-451-51670-2, CE1670, Sig Classics). NAL.

--Dracula. (Illus.). 1979. write for info (ISBN 0-515-05347-3). Jove Pubns.

--Personal Reminiscences of Henry Irving, 2 Vols. Repr. of 1906 ed. Set. lib. bdg. 32.25x o.p. (ISBN 0-8371-2845-5, STHI). Greenwood.

Stoker, Bram see Swan, D. K.

Stoker, H. Stephen & Seager, Spencer L. Environmental Chemistry: Air & Water Pollution. 2nd ed. 1976. pap. 9.95x (ISBN 0-673-07978-3). Scott F.

Stoker, H. Stephen & Slabaugh, Michael R. General, Organic & Biochemistry: A Brief Introduction. 1981. text ed. 24.50x (ISBN 0-673-15091-7); study guide 7.95x (ISBN 0-673-15501-3). Scott F.

Stoker, H. Stephen, jt. auth. see Seager, Spencer L.

Stoker, H. Stephen, et al. Energy: From Source to Use. 1975. pap. 9.95x (ISBN 0-673-07947-3). Scott F.

Stoker, Howard W. Automated Data Processing in Testing. (Guidance Monograph). 1968. pap. 2.40 o.p. (ISBN 0-395-09931-5). HM.

Stoker, J. J. Nonlinear Elasticity. (Notes on Mathematics & Its Applications Ser). (Illus.). 142p. (Orig.). 1968. 32.00x (ISBN 0-677-00660-8); pap. 9.50 o.p. (ISBN 0-677-00665-9). Gordon.

--Nonlinear Vibrations in Mechanical & Electrical Systems Pure & Aplied Mechanics, Vol. 2. 294p. 1950. 44.95 (ISBN 0-470-82830-7). Wiley.

Stoker, James. Differential Geometry. (Pure & Applied Mathematics Ser.). 404p. 1969. 42.50x (ISBN 0-471-82825-4, Pub. by Wiley-Interscience). Wiley.

Stoker, James J. Water Waves. LC 56-8228. (Pure & Applied Mathematics Ser.). (Illus.). 595p. 1957. 55.00x (ISBN 0-470-82863-3, Pub. by Wiley-Interscience). Wiley.

Stoker, John. The Illustrated Frankenstein. LC 80-52336. (Illus., Orig.). 1980. pap. 6.95 o.p. (ISBN 0-8069-8916-5). Sterling.

Stokes, Adrian. Concise Encyclopedia of Information Technology. 272p. 1983. 17.95 (ISBN 0-13-167205-3); pap. 9.95 (ISBN 0-13-167213-4). P-H.

--A Game That Must Be Lost. (Essays, Prose, & Scottish Literature). 1979. 12.95 o.p. (ISBN 0-85635-069-9, Pub. by Carcanet New Pr England). Humanities.

--A Game that Must Be Lost. 160p. 1973. text ed. 14.75x (ISBN 0-85635-069-9, Pub. by Carcanet New Pr England). Humanities.

--The Quattrocento: A Different Conception of the Italian Renaissance. LC 68-28902. (Illus.). 1969. 8.50x (ISBN 0-8052-3215-X); pap. 3.95 (ISBN 0-8052-0194-7). Schocken.

Stokes, Adrian V. Concise Encyclopedia of Computer Terminology. 289p. 1980. text ed. 37.50x (ISBN 0-905897-32-3). Gower Pub Ltd.

Stokes, Allen W., ed. Territory. LC 73-18327. (Benchmark Papers in Animal Behavior Ser.). 416p. 1974. 49.50 (ISBN 0-12-787490-9). Acad Pr.

Stokes, Antony, jt. auth. see Fennell, John.

Stokes, Bill. You Can Catch Fish. LC 76-12478. (Games & Activities Ser.). 48p. (gr. k-3). 1976. 12.85 o.p. (ISBN 0-8172-0627-2). Raintree Pubs.

Stokes, Charles J. Economics for Managers. (Illus.). 1978. text ed. 25.95 (ISBN 0-07-061663-9); instructor's manual 20.95 (ISBN 0-07-061664-7). McGraw.

Stokes, Curtis. The Evolution of Trotsky's Theory of Revolution. LC 81-40930. 206p. (Orig.). 1982. lib. bdg. 23.25 (ISBN 0-8191-2235-1); pap. text ed. 10.25 (ISBN 0-8191-2236-X). U Pr of Amer.

Stokes, Donald, jt. auth. see Butler, David.

Stokes, Donald W. A Guide to Bird Behavior, Vol. I. (Stokes Nature Guide Ser.). (Illus.). 416p. 1983. pap. 8.70i (ISBN 0-316-81725-2). Little.

--A Guide to Observing Insect Lives. (Stokes Nature Guides). 1983. 15.00i (ISBN 0-316-81724-4). Little.

Stokes, E. T. The Peasant & the Raj. LC 77-77731. (Cambridge South Asian Studies: No. 23). 1978. 42.50 (ISBN 0-521-21684-2). Cambridge U Pr.

--The Peasant & the Raj: Studies in Agrarian Society & Peasant Rebellion in Colonial India. LC 77-77731. (Cambridge South Asian Studies: No. 23). 304p. 1980. pap. 14.95x (ISBN 0-521-29770-2). Cambridge U Pr.

Stokes, Geoffrey. The Village Voice Anthology, Nineteen Fifty-Six to Nineteen Eighty: Twenty-Five Years of Writing from the Village Voice. LC 83-438. (Illus.). 1982. 15.50 (ISBN 0-688-01105-5); pap. 7.50 (ISBN 0-688-01222-1). Quill NY.

Stokes, Gordon. Beginner's Guide to Woodturning. (Illus.). 124p. 1975. 18.00 o.p. (ISBN 0-7207-0637-8). Transatlantic.

--Modern Wood Turning. LC 76-16365. (Illus.). 1979. pap. 6.95 (ISBN 0-8069-8518-6). Sterling.

--Toy Making in Wood. (Pelham Craft Ser.). (Illus.). 1978. 16.50 o.s.i. (ISBN 0-7207-0999-7). Transatlantic.

--Woodturning for Pleasure. (Illus.). 128p. 1980. 13.95 (ISBN 0-13-962563-1, Spec); pap. 4.95 (ISBN 0-13-962555-0). P-H.

Stokes, Gweneth & Reeves, Marjorie. Marco Polo & Cathay. (Then & There Ser.). (Illus.). 90p. (Orig.). (gr. 7-12). 1971. pap. text ed. 3.10 (ISBN 0-582-20465-8). Longman.

Stokes, Gwenneth, jt. auth. see Stokes, John.

Stokes, Henry S. The Life & Death of Yukio Mishima. 368p. 1975. pap. 3.45 o.s.i. (ISBN 0-440-55033-5, Delta). Dell.

Stokes, I. N. & Haskell, Daniel C. American Historical Prints: Early Views of American Cities, Etc., from the Phelps Stokes & Other Collections. LC 77-180284. (Illus.). 235p. 1974. Repr. of 1933 ed. 45.00x (ISBN 0-8103-3950-1). Gale.

Stokes, Jack. Monster Madness Outrageous Jokes About Weird Folks. LC 80-2068. (Illus.). 64p. (gr. 6). 1981. 8.95a o.p. (ISBN 0-385-15690-1); PLB 8.95a (ISBN 0-385-15691-X). Doubleday.

Stokes, John. Seventy Years of Radio Tubes & Valves. LC 82-15899. (Illus.). 256p. Date not set. 21.95 (ISBN 0-911572-27-9). Vestal.

Stokes, John & Stokes, Gwenneth. Europe & the Modern World. (Illus.). 372p. (Orig.). (gr. 10-12). 1973. pap. text ed. 11.95 (ISBN 0-582-31337-6). Longman.

Stokes, John, ed. see Allen, Grant.

Stokes, John, ed. see Brookfield, Charles & Glover, J. M.

Stokes, John, ed. see Dowson, Ernest & Moore, Arthur.

Stokes, John, ed. see Hichens, Robert S.

Stokes, John, ed. see Lee, Vernon.

Stokes, John, ed. see Moore, George.

Stokes, John, ed. see O'Shaughnessy, Arthur.

Stokes, John, ed. see O'Sullivan, Vincent.

Stokes, John, et al. Barbarians in Peking. (Then & There Ser.). (Illus.). 96p. (Orig.). (gr. 7-12). 1979. pap. text ed. 3.10 (ISBN 0-582-22124-2). Longman.

Stokes, John W. How to Manage a Restaurant: Or Institutional Food Service. 4th ed. 416p. 1982. text ed. write for info. (ISBN 0-697-08315-2). Wm C Brown.

Stokes, Lillian G., jt. auth. see Billings, Diane M.

Stokes, M. Conquering Government Regulation: A Business Guide. 288p. 1982. 27.50 (ISBN 0-07-061640-X). McGraw.

Stokes, McNeill. Construction Law in Contractors' Language. 1977. 32.50 (ISBN 0-07-061635-3, P&RB). McGraw.

--Labor Law in Contractors' Language. 1979. 32.50 (ISBN 0-07-061650-7, P&RB). McGraw.

Stokes, Richard, ed. Gefunden: An Anthology of German Literature. 192p. (Orig.). 1981. pap. text ed. 7.50x (ISBN 0-435-38860-6). Heinemann Ed.

Stokes, Susan, jt. auth. see Littlejohn, Patricia.

Stokes, Vernon L. Manufacturing Materials. (Electronics Technology Ser.). 1977. text ed. 23.95 (ISBN 0-675-08493-8). Additional supplements may be obtained from publisher. Merrill.

Stokes, W. Lee. The Creation Scriptures: Witness for God in the Age of Science. LC 78-71714. 1979. pap. 5.95 o.p. (ISBN 0-88290-106-0). Horizon Utah.

Stokes, William L. Essentials of Earth History. 4th ed. (Illus.). 640p. 1982. text ed. 28.95 (ISBN 0-13-285890-8). P-H.

--Essentials of Earth History: An Introduction to Historical Geology. 3rd ed. (Illus.). 512p. 1973. ref. ed. 25.95 o.p. (ISBN 0-13-285932-7). P-H.

Stokes, William L., et al. Introduction to Geology: Physical & Historical. 2nd ed. LC 77-21570. 1978. text ed. 28.95 (ISBN 0-13-484352-5). P-H.

Stokes, William N., Jr. Oil Mill on the Texas Plains: A Study in Agricultural Cooperation. LC 78-6372. (Illus.). 248p. 1979. 10.00 o.p. (ISBN 0-89096-059-3). Tex A&M Univ Pr.

Stokes, William S. Honduras: An Area Study in Government. LC 70-140651. (Illus.). 351p. 1974. Repr. of 1950 ed. lib. bdg. 19.75x (ISBN 0-8371-5813-3, STHO). Greenwood.

Stokes, William T. Gems of Geometry. rev. ed. (Illus.). 1978. pap. text ed. 6.95 (ISBN 0-914534-02-5). Stokes.

--Notable Numbers. rev. ed. (Illus.). 1974. pap. text ed. 6.95 (ISBN 0-914534-01-7). Stokes.

Stokes, William T. & Laycock, Mary. Math Activity Worksheet Masters. 1971. pap. text ed. 6.95 (ISBN 0-88488-012-5). Creative Pubns.

Stokes, Zoe. Zoe's Cats. (Illus.). 1982. 12.95 (ISBN 0-500-01273-3). Thames Hudson.

Stokesburg, Leon. Gaining Speed. 1983. pap. 3.00 (ISBN 0-686-84799-7). Anhinga Pr.

Stokesbury, James L. A Short History of World War I. LC 80-22207. (Illus.). 352p. 1981. pap. 7.95 (ISBN 0-688-00129-7). Quill NY.

Stokke, Allan H., jt. auth. see Ferguson, Robert W.

Stokke, Olav, ed. Reporting Africa. LC 76-163923. 250p. 1971. text ed. 25.00x (ISBN 0-8419-0090-6, Africana). Holmes & Meier.

Stokland, Torill & Vajrathon, Mallica, eds. Creative Women in Changing Societies: A Quest for Alternatives. LC 82-16017. 192p. 1982. lib. bdg. 22.50 (ISBN 0-941320-06-5). Transnatl Pubs.

Stoklitsky, L., tr. see Kotov, A. & Yudovich, M.

Stokoe, John, jt. auth. see Bruce, John C.

Stokoe, William C. see Wescott, Roger W.

Stol, P. T. A Contribution to Theory & Practice of Non-Linear Parameter Optimization. (Agricultural Research Reports Ser.: No. 835). (Illus.). 160p. 1975. pap. 38.00 o.p. (ISBN 90-220-0562-3, Pub. by PUDOC). Unipub.

Stolberg, D., jt. ed. see Johnson, P.

Stoler, Mark A. The Politics of the Second Front: American Military Planning & Diplomacy in Coalition Warfare, 1941-1943. LC 76-47171. (Contributions in Military History Ser.: No 12). 1977. lib. bdg. 27.50x (ISBN 0-8371-9438-5, SPF/). Greenwood.

Stoleru. Economic Equilibrium & Growth, Vol. 1. LC 74-25895. 300p. 1975. 28.00 (ISBN 0-444-10766-5, North-Holland); pap. 19.50 (ISBN 0-444-10866-1). Elsevier.

Stolk, Anthonie, jt. auth. see De Joode, Ton.

Stoll. Hormonal Management of Endocrine-Related Cancer. 260p. 1982. text ed. 49.95 (ISBN 0-85324-148-1). Univ Park.

Stoll, B. A., ed. Mind & Cancer Prognosis. LC 79-40643. 203p. 1980. 41.95 (ISBN 0-471-27644-8, Pub. by Wiley-Interscience). Wiley.

Stoll, Basil A. Prolonged Arrest of Cancer. (New Horizons in Oncology Ser.). 448p. 1982. 59.00 (ISBN 0-471-10221-0, Pub. by Wiley Med). Wiley.

Stoll, Basil A., ed. Endocrine Therapy in Malignant Disease. LC 78-188731. (Illus.). 400p. 1972. 23.00 o.p. (ISBN 0-7216-8615-X). Saunders.

Stoll, Clarice S. Female & Male: Socialization, Social Roles & Social Structure. 2nd ed. 250p. 1978. pap. text ed. write for info. o.p. (ISBN 0-697-07554-0). Wm C Brown.

Stoll, Elmo & Stoll, Mark. The Pioneer Catalogue of Country Living. (Illus.). 112p. 1980. pap. 8.95 (ISBN 0-920510-13-2, Pub. by Personal Lib). Dodd.

Stoll, Mark, jt. auth. see Stoll, Elmo.

Stoll, Sharon K. Roller Skating: Fundamentals & Techniques. LC 82-83932. (Illus.). 144p. (Orig.). 1983. pap. 6.95 (ISBN 0-88011-101-1). Leisure Pr.

Stollberg, Robert & Hill, Faith F. Physics: Fundamental & Frontiers. rev. ed. 1975. text ed. 20.97 (ISBN 0-395-18243-3); write for info. laboratory suppl. (ISBN 0-395-18242-5); progress tests 54.42 (ISBN 0-395-18240-9). HM.

Stolle, C. & Bearden, G. Auditing of Computer-Generated Accounts: A Simulation. 1971. text ed. 10.50 o.p. (ISBN 0-07-061668-X); instructor's manual 5.50 o.p. (ISBN 0-07-061669-8). McGraw.

Stoller, Alan, jt. auth. see Krupinski, Jerzy.

Stoller, Leonard, jt. ed. see Sciarra, John J.

Stoller, Robert J. Perversion. 1976. pap. 3.45 o.s.i. (ISBN 0-440-56907-9, Delta). Dell.

--Sexual Excitement: Dynamics of Exotic Life. 1980. pap. 4.95 o.p. (ISBN 0-671-41394-5, Touchstone). S&S.

--Splitting. 1974. pap. 3.45 o.s.i. (ISBN 0-440-58312-8, Delta). Dell.

Stollerman, Gene H. Advances in Internal Medicine, Vol. 28. 1982. 47.95 (ISBN 0-8151-8298-8). Year Bk Med.

Stolman, A., ed. Progress in Chemical Toxicology. LC 63-22331. 1963-1969. Vols. 1-4. 61.00 ea. Vol. 1 (ISBN 0-12-536501-2). Vol. 2 (ISBN 0-12-536502-0). Vol. 3 (ISBN 0-12-536503-9). Vol. 4 (ISBN 0-12-536504-7). Vol. 5 1974. 69.00 (ISBN 0-12-536505-5); Vol. 6 Date Not Set. price not set (ISBN 0-12-536506-3). Acad Pr.

Stolman, A., jt. ed. see Stewart, C. P.

Stoloff, Carolyn. A Spool of Blue: New & Selected Poems. LC 82-6006. (Poets Now Ser.: No. 5). 194p. 1983. 13.50 (ISBN 0-8108-1563-X). Scarecrow.

--Swiftly Now. LC 81-11150. 52p. 1982. lib. bdg. 13.95x (ISBN 0-8214-0646-9, 82-84150); pap. 6.95 (ISBN 0-8214-0647-7, 80-84168). Ohio U Pr.

Stolojian, Sanda. Duiliu Zamfirescu. (World Authors Ser.). 1980. lib. bdg. 15.95 (ISBN 0-8057-6393-7, Twayne). G K Hall.

Stolovitch, Harold D., jt. auth. see Thiagarajan, Sivasailam.

Stolow, Nathan. Conservation Standards for Works of Art in Transit & on Exhibition. (Museums & Monuments Ser.: No. 17). (Illus.). 129p. 1979. pap. 16.50 (ISBN 92-3-101628-8, U973, UNESCO). Unipub.

Stolpe, Hjalmar. Amazon Indian Designs from Brazilian & Guianan Wood Carvings. LC 73-92501. (Pictorial Archives Ser.). 64p. 1974. 2.50 o.p. (ISBN 0-486-23040-6). Dover.

Stolper, Gustav. This Age of Fable, the Political & Economic World We Live In. LC 68-57641. (Illus.). 1968. Repr. of 1942 ed. lib. bdg. 18.50x (ISBN 0-8371-0671-0, STAF). Greenwood.

Stolper, Wolfgang, ed. see Congress of the International Institute of Public Finance Tokyo, 37th, 1981.

Stoltz, Berdine & Saloom, Pamela. Why, What & How of Interest Development Centers. 1978. pap. text ed. 5.95 (ISBN 0-936386-02-9). Creative Learning.

Stolz, Benjamin A., jt. ed. see Matejka, Ladislav.

Stolz, Lois H., et al. Father Relations of War-Born Children: The Effect of Postwar Adjustment of Fathers on the Behavior & Personality of First Children Born While Fathers Were at War. LC 69-10160. 1969. Repr. of 1954 ed. lib. bdg. 20.50x (ISBN 0-8371-0672-9, STWC). Greenwood.

Stolz, Mary. Cat in the Mirror. LC 75-6307. 256p. (gr. 5 up). 1975. 8.95i o.p. (ISBN 0-06-025832-2, HarpJ); PLB 10.89 (ISBN 0-06-025833-0). Har-Row.

--Cat Walk. LC 82-47576. (Illus.). 128p. (gr. 3-7). 1983. 8.61i (ISBN 0-06-025974-4, HarpJ); PLB 8.89g (ISBN 0-06-025975-2). Har-Row.

--Lands End. LC 73-7139. 176p. (gr. 7 up). 1973. 10.53i (ISBN 0-06-025916-7, HarpJ); PLB 9.89 o.p. (ISBN 0-06-025917-5). Har-Row.

--Pray Love, Remember. LC 54-10048. (gr. 8 up). 1954. PLB 10.89 o.p. (ISBN 0-06-025981-7, HarpJ). Har-Row.

Stolz, P., jt. ed. see Drew, L. R.

Stolzenberg, Mark. Clown: For Circus & Stage. LC 80-54337. (Illus.). 1981. 13.95 (ISBN 0-8069-7034-0); lib. bdg. 16.79 (ISBN 0-8069-7035-9). Sterling.

--Exploring Mime. LC 79-65068. (Illus.). 1979. 13.95 (ISBN 0-8069-7028-6); lib. bdg. 16.79 (ISBN 0-8069-7029-4). Sterling.

Stommel, Elizabeth, jt. auth. see Stommel, Henry.

Stommel, Henry & Stommel, Elizabeth. Volcano Weather. 1983. 15.00 (ISBN 0-915160-71-4). Seven Seas.

Stommmel, Henry. The Gulf Stream: A Physical & Dynamical Description. (California Library Reprint Ser). 1977. Repr. of 1964 ed. 31.50x (ISBN 0-520-03307-8). U of Cal Pr.

Stonar, J. O., Jr., jt. auth. see Bashkin, S.

Stonberg, Selma F. From Start to Finish. (Illus., Orig.). 1970. pap. text ed. 12.50 o.p. (ISBN 0-395-05438-9). HM.

Stone, jt. auth. see Byrns.

Stone, jt. auth. see Warren.

Stone, A. & Stein, R. Biology Project Puzzlers. (gr. 8-12). 1973. 4.95 o.p. (ISBN 0-13-076877-4). P-H.

Stone, A., Jr., ed. Ambassadors: Twentieth Century Interpretations. 1969. 9.95 (ISBN 0-13-023937-2, Spec); pap. 1.25 o.p. (ISBN 0-13-023929-1, Spec). P-H.

Stone, A. R. & Platt, H. M., eds. Concepts in Nematode Systematics. (Systematics Symposium Special Ser.: Vol. 22). write for info. (ISBN 0-12-672680-9). Acad Pr.

Stone, Abraham, jt. auth. see Stone, Hannah.

Stone, Alan. The Political Economy of Public Policy. (Sage Yearbooks in Politics & Public Policy: Vol. 10). 256p. 1982. 25.00 (ISBN 0-8039-1795-3); pap. 12.50 (ISBN 0-8039-1796-1). Sage.

--Regulation & its Alternatives. LC 81-22118. 304p. 1982. pap. 8.50 (ISBN 0-87187-215-3). Congr Quarterly.

Stone, Alan, jt. auth. see Stone, Sue.

Stone, Alan, jt. ed. see Calloway, Barbara.

Stone, Alan, et al, eds. A Catalog of the Diptera of America North of Mexico. 2nd printing ed. 1700p. 1983. Repr. of 1965 ed. text ed. 37.50x (ISBN 0-87474-890-9). Smithsonian.

Stone, Albert, ed. The American Autobiography: A Collection of Critical Essays. 184p. 1981. 12.95 (ISBN 0-13-024638-7); pap. 5.95 (ISBN 0-13-024620-4). P-H.

Stone, Alex P., jt. ed. see Carasso, Alfred.

Stone, Alfred R. & Deluca, Stuart M. Investigating Crimes: An Introduction. LC 79-88446. (Illus.). 1980. text ed. 24.95 (ISBN 0-395-28525-9); instr's. manual 1.10 (ISBN 0-395-28526-7). HM.

Stone, Andy. Song of the Kingdom. LC 78-22424. (Illus.). 240p. 1979. 8.95 o.p. (ISBN 0-385-15035-0). Doubleday.

Stone, Ann. Antique Furniture: Baroque, Rococo, Neoclassical. (Illus.). 240p. 1982. 16.98 (ISBN 0-89673-140-5). Bookthrift.

Stone, Anna. Sculpture: New Ideas & Techniques. (Illus.). 1977. 16.50 o.s.i. (ISBN 0-7135-1943-6). Transatlantic.

Stone, Archie A. Careers in Agribusiness & Industry. 3rd ed. LC 76-106341. (Illus.). (gr. 9-12). 15.35 (ISBN 0-8134-2073-3); text ed. 11.50x. Interstate.

Stone, Archie A. & Gulvin, Harold E. Machines for Power Farming. 3rd ed. LC 76-42244. 533p. 1977. text ed. 34.50 (ISBN 0-471-82556-5). Wiley.

Stone, Arlene. Through a Coal Cellar Darkly. 1979. pap. 3.00 (ISBN 0-686-65849-3). Juniper Pr WI.

Stone, B. C. The Genus Pelea A. Gray: Rutaceae: Evodiiae. (Taxonomic Monograph). 1969. pap. 40.00 (ISBN 3-7682-0635-1). Lubrecht & Cramer.

Stone, Bailey S. The Parlement of Paris 1774-1789. LC 79-27732. x, 227p. 1981. 21.00x (ISBN 0-8078-1442-3). U of NC Pr.

Stone, Bob. Successful Direct Marketing Methods. 2nd, rev. ed. LC 78-74973. (Illus.). 1979. 27.95 (ISBN 0-87251-040-9). Crain Bks.

Stone, Bruce, jt. auth. see Kaufman, Roger.

Stone, C., et al. Urban Policy & Politics in a Bureaucratic Age. pap. 14.95 (ISBN 0-13-939538-5). P-H.

Stone, Carl & Brown, Aggrey, eds. Essays on Power & Change in Jamaica. 207p. (Orig.). 1977. pap. 8.95 (ISBN 0-87855-683-4). Transaction Bks.

Stone, Carl, jt. ed. see Henry, Paget.

Stone, Christopher D. Should Trees Have Standing? Toward Legal Rights for Natural Objects. 1975. pap. 1.50 o.p. (ISBN 0-380-00400-3, 255693, Discus). Avon.

--Should Trees Have Standing? Toward Legal Rights for Natural Objects. LC 73-19535. 121p. 1974. 8.95 o.p. (ISBN 0-913232-09-2); pap. 5.50 (ISBN 0-913232-08-4). W Kaufmann.

Stone, Clarence R. Eye & Ear Fun, 3 bks. 1946. 3.76 ea. Bk. 1 (ISBN 0-07-061701-5). Bk. 2 (ISBN 0-07-061702-3). Bk. 4 (ISBN 0-07-061703-1). McGraw.

Stone, Daniel J. Pulmonary Medicine Case Studies. 1982. pap. text ed. 16.50 (ISBN 0-87488-051-3). Med Exam.

Stone, David. How to Sell New Homes & Condominiums. LC 75-15546. 1977. 32.95 (ISBN 0-07-061735-X). McGraw.

--Leopard Jasmine. 1981. 12.95 o.p. (ISBN 0-89754-028-X); pap. 8.95 o.p. (ISBN 0-89754-027-1). Dan River Pr.

Stone, David A. The Exponential Map at an Isolated Singular Point. LC 81-19100. (Memoirs: 256). 1982. 10.00 (ISBN 0-8218-2256-X). Am Math.

Stone, Donald. France in the Sixteenth Century. LC 75-46622. 180p. 1976. Repr. of 1969 ed. lib. bdg. 18.00x (ISBN 0-8371-8734-6, STFS). Greenwood.

Stone, Doris. Pre-Columbian Man Finds Central America. Flint, Emily, ed. LC 72-801668. (Peabody Museum Press). (Illus.). 1972. 25.00x (ISBN 0-87365-803-5); pap. 15.00 (ISBN 0-87365-776-4). Peabody Harvard.

Stone, Doris, ed. see Soltera, Maria.

Stone, Elaine, jt. auth. see Troxell, Mary D.

Stone, Elberta H. I'm Glad I'm Me. (Illus.). (gr. k-2). 1971. PLB 5.29 o.p. (ISBN 0-399-60298-4). Putnam Pub Group.

Stone, Elizabeth. Continuing Library Education As Viewed in Relation to Other Continuing Professional Education Movements. LC 74-21737. 1974. 25.00 (ISBN 0-87715-108-3). Am Soc Info Sci.

Stone, Elizabeth W., ed. American Library Development: 1600 - 1899. 367p. 1977. 50.00 (ISBN 0-8242-0418-2). Wilson.

--New Directions in Staff Development. LC 72-171618. 70p. 1971. 3.00 o.p. (ISBN 0-8389-3130-8). ALA.

Stone, Elizabeth W., et al. Continuing Library & Information Science Education: Final Report to the National Commission on Libraries & Information Science. LC 74-21738. 478p. 1974. lexhide 10.00 (ISBN 0-87715-109-1). Am Soc Info Sci.

Stone, Elna. How to Choose Your Work. 1969. pap. text ed. 3.00 o.p. (ISBN 0-02-829260-X). Glencoe.

--How to Get a Job. 1969. pap. text ed. 3.00 o.p. (ISBN 0-02-829240-5). Glencoe.

--The Visions of Esmaree. LC 75-26201. 320p. 1976. 8.95 o.p. (ISBN 0-312-85050-6). St Martin.

Stone, Else, tr. see Peinkofer, Karl & Tannigel, Fritz.

Stone, Eugene. Research Methods in Organizational Behavior. 5th ed. LC 77-18755. (Scott, Foresman Series in Management & Organizations). 1978. 16.50x (ISBN 0-673-16140-4); pap. 12.50x (ISBN 0-673-16139-0). Scott F.

Stone, F. G. & West, Robert. Advances in Organometallic Chemistry, Vol. 19. 1980. 48.00 (ISBN 0-12-031119-4); lib. bdg. 62.50 (ISBN 0-12-031183-6); microfiche 34.00 (ISBN 0-12-031184-4). Acad Pr.

Stone, F. G., jt. auth. see Abel, E. W.

Stone, F. G. & West, Robert, eds. Advances in Organometallic Chemistry. Incl. Vol. 1. 1964. 62.00 (ISBN 0-12-031101-1); Vol. 2. 1965. 62.00 (ISBN 0-12-031102-X); Vol. 3. 1966. 62.00 (ISBN 0-12-031103-8); Vol. 4. 1966. 62.00 (ISBN 0-12-031104-6); Vol. 5. 1967. 62.00 (ISBN 0-12-031105-4); Vol. 6. 1968. 62.00 (ISBN 0-12-031106-2); Vol. 7. 1969. 62.00 (ISBN 0-12-031107-0); Vol. 8. 1970. 62.00 (ISBN 0-12-031108-9); Vol. 9. 1971. 68.50 (ISBN 0-12-031109-7); Vol. 10. 1972. 68.50 (ISBN 0-12-031110-0); Vol. 11. 1973. 62.00 (ISBN 0-12-031111-9); Vol. 12. 1974. 68.50 (ISBN 0-12-031112-7); Vol. 13. 1975. 77.00 (ISBN 0-12-031113-5); lib ed. 99.00 (ISBN 0-12-031171-2); microfiche 56.50 (ISBN 0-12-031172-0); Vol. 14. 1976. 67.00 (ISBN 0-12-031114-3); lib ed. 86.00 (ISBN 0-12-031173-9); microfiche 49.00 (ISBN 0-12-031174-7); Vol. 15. 1977. 60.00 (ISBN 0-12-031115-1); lib ed. 76.00 (ISBN 0-12-031175-5); microfiche 45.00 (ISBN 0-12-031176-3); Vol. 16. 1977. 62.00 (ISBN 0-12-031116-X); lib ed. 79.50 (ISBN 0-12-031177-1); **microfiche 45.00 (ISBN 0-12-031178-X); Vol. 17. 1979. 64.50 (ISBN 0-12-031117-8); lib ed. 82.00 (ISBN 0-12-031179-8); microfiche 47.00 (ISBN 0-12-031180-1). Acad Pr.**

--Advances in Organometallic Chemistry, Vol. 18. LC 64-16030. 1980. 46.00 (ISBN 0-12-031118-6); lib ed. 61.00 (ISBN 0-12-031181-X); microfiche 33.00 (ISBN 0-12-031182-8). Acad Pr.

--Advances in Organometallic Chemistry, Vol. 20. (Serial Publication). 384p. 1982. 56.00 (ISBN 0-12-031120-8); lib. ed. 73.00 (ISBN 0-12-031185-2); microfiche 39.50 (ISBN 0-12-031186-0). Acad Pr.

--Advances in Organometallic Chemistry, Vol. 21. 310p. 1982. 52.00 (ISBN 0-12-031121-6). Acad Pr.

Stone, F. G., jt. ed. see Wilkinson, Geoffrey.

Stone, Fred H. Psychiatry & the Pediatrician. Apley, John, ed. (Postgraduate Pediatrics Ser). 1976. 15.95 o.p. (ISBN 0-407-00074-7). Butterworth.

Stone, Frederick B., jt. auth. see McMaster, John.

Stone, G. W., Jr., ed. see Garrick, David.

Stone, George C., et al. Health Psychology-A Handbook: Theories, Applications, & Challenges of a Psychological Approach to the Health Care System. LC 79-83580. (Social & Behavioral Science Ser.). 1979. 35.00 (ISBN 0-87589-411-9). Jossey-Bass.

Stone, George K. More Science Projects You Can Do. (gr. 5 up). 1970. PLB 5.95 o.p. (ISBN 0-13-600924-7). P-H.

--More Science Projects You Can Do. (Illus.). (gr. 5 up). 1981. pap. 2.95 (ISBN 0-13-600916-6). P-H.

Stone, Gerald W., jt. auth. see Byrns, Ralph T.

Stone, Gerald W., Jr., jt. auth. see Byrns, Ralph T.

Stone, Gillian. Land of the Golden Mountains. 384p. (Orig.). 1980. pap. 2.50 o.p. (ISBN 0-451-09344-5, E9344, Sig). NAL.

Stone, Gregory & Lowenstein, Douglas, eds. Lowenstein: Acts of Courage & Belief. 333p. 29.95 (ISBN 0-15-154742-4); pap. 9.95. HarBraceJ.

--Lowenstein: Acts of Courage & Belief. 416p. pap. 9.95 (ISBN 0-15-654302-8, Harv). HarBraceJ.

Stone, Gregory P. & Farberman, Harvey A. Social Psychology Through Symbolic Interaction. 2nd ed. LC 80-23770. 544p. 1981. pap. text ed. 18.95 (ISBN 0-471-03029-5). Wiley.

Stone, H. S. Microcomputer Interfacing. LC 81-17619. 480p. 1982. text ed. 32.95 (ISBN 0-201-07403-6). A-W.

Stone, Hannah & Stone, Abraham. Marriage Manual. rev. & enl. ed. Aitken, Gloria S. & Sobrero, Acquiles, eds. (Illus.). 1968. 8.95 o.p. (ISBN 0-671-45101-4). S&S.

Stone, Harold. Introduction to Computer Organization & Data Structures. (Computer Science Ser.). 1971. text ed. 40.00 (ISBN 0-07-061726-0). McGraw.

Stone, Harold & Siewiorek, Daniel. Introduction to Computer Organization & Data Structure P D P. 11th ed. (Illus.). 352p. 1975. text ed. 33.95 (ISBN 0-07-061720-1). McGraw.

Stone, Harold, ed. see Betteridge, Terry.

Stone, Harold, ed. see Carter, Lynn R.

Stone, Harold, ed. see Dion, Bernard A.

Stone, Harold, ed. see Epstein, Robert S.

Stone, Harold, ed. see Gehringer, Edward F.

Stone, Harold, ed. see Gustavson, Frances G.

Stone, Harold, ed. see Johnson, Scott D.

Stone, Harold, ed. see Karp, Richard A.

Stone, Harold, ed. see Kemmerer, Richard A.

Stone, Harold, ed. see Kwong, Yat-Sang.

Stone, Harold, ed. see Lau, Edwin J.

Stone, Harold, ed. see Merkle, Ralph C.

Stone, Harold, ed. see Reid, Loretta G.

Stone, Harold S. Discrete Mathematical Structures & Their Applications. LC 72-96797. 401p. 1973. text ed. 24.95 (ISBN 0-574-17982-8, 13-0982). SRA.

Stone, Harold S., ed. see Cattell, R. G.

Stone, Harold S., ed. see Stankovic, John A.

Stone, Helen D. & Hunzeker, Jeanne M. Creating a Foster Parent-Agency Handbook. LC 74-81975. 1974. pap. 4.30 (ISBN 0-87868-123-X, F-53). Child Welfare.

--Education for Foster Family Care: Models & Methods for Social Workers & Foster Parents. LC 74-25269. 1974. pap. 7.95 o.p. (ISBN 0-87868-112-4). Child Welfare.

Stone, Howard. Short Bike Rides in Greater Boston & Central Massachusetts. LC 81-86604. (Illus.). 592p. 1982. pap. 8.95 (ISBN 0-87106-965-2). Globe Pequot.

Stone, Howard W. The Caring Church: A Guide for Lay Pastoral Care. LC 82-48415. 144p. (Orig.). 1983. pap. 5.72 (ISBN 0-06-067695-7, HarpR). Har-Row.

--Crisis Counseling. 3.25 o.p. (ISBN 0-686-92184-4, 4235). Hazelden.

Stone, Idella P. Thirty Classic Mexican Menus in Spanish & English. pap. 6.95 o.p. (ISBN 0-517-53768-0, Pub. by Ward Ritchie). Crown.

Stone, Irving. Adversary in the House. LC 47-31015. 1947. 13.95 (ISBN 0-385-04003-2). Doubleday.

--Adversary in the House. 1972. pap. 3.50 (ISBN 0-451-11165-6, AE1165, Sig). NAL.

--Agony & the Ecstasy. pap. 3.95 (ISBN 0-451-11010-2, AE1010, Sig). NAL.

--Clarence Darrow for the Defense. LC 41-20757. 1949. 14.95 (ISBN 0-385-04073-3). Doubleday.

--Clarence Darrow for the Defense. 1971. pap. 3.95 (ISBN 0-451-11166-4, AE1166, Sig). NAL.

--The Greek Treasure. 1976. pap. 3.50 (ISBN 0-451-11684-4, AE1684, Sig). NAL.

--The Greek Treasure: A Biographical Novel of Henry & Sophia Schliemann. LC 74-33740. 480p. 1975. 14.95 (ISBN 0-385-07309-7); Limited edition 40.00 (ISBN 0-385-11170-3). Doubleday.

--Jack London: Sailor on Horseback. 1978. 12.95 (ISBN 0-385-14084-3). Doubleday.

--Love Is Eternal. LC 54-9678. 13.95 (ISBN 0-385-02040-6). Doubleday.

--Love Is Eternal. 512p. (RL 7). 1972. pap. 2.95 (ISBN 0-451-09594-4, F9594, Sig). NAL.

--Lust for Life. 1954. 13.95 (ISBN 0-385-04270-1). Doubleday.

--The Origin. 1981. pap. 8.95 (ISBN 0-452-25284-9, Z5284, Plume). NAL.

--The Origin. 1982. pap. 4.95 (ISBN 0-451-11761-1, AE1761, Sig). NAL.

--The Passionate Journey. 12.95 (ISBN 0-385-17198-6). Doubleday.

--The Passionate Journey. 288p. 1972. pap. 1.25 o.p. (ISBN 0-451-06858-0, E6858, Sig). NAL.

--Passions of the Mind. 816p. 1972. pap. 4.50 (ISBN 0-451-11580-5, AE1580, Sig). NAL.

--President's Lady. 1968. pap. 2.50 (ISBN 0-451-09595-2, AE9595, Sig). NAL.

--They Also Ran. (RL 9). 1968. pap. 2.25 o.p. (ISBN 0-451-07110-7, E7110, Sig). NAL.

Stone, Irving, ed. Dear Theo: The Autobiography of Vincent Van Gogh. LC 46-4152. (Illus.). 14.95 (ISBN 0-385-17197-8). Doubleday.

Stone, Irving, ed. see Van Gogh, Vincent.

Stone, Irwin. The Healing Factor: Vitamin C Against Disease. LC 72-77105. (Illus.). 1972. pap. 3.95 (ISBN 0-448-11693-6, G&D). Putnam Pub Group.

Stone, James. The Church of God of Prophecy: History & Polity. 1977. 11.95 (ISBN 0-934942-02-1). White Wing Pub.

--How To Live In the Fullness of Spirit. 61p. 1982. pap. 1.95 (ISBN 0-934942-33-1). White Wing Pub.

Stone, James W. Van see Van Stone, James W.

Stone, Janet & Bachner, Jane. Speaking up. LC 77-7134. (Illus.). 1977. 9.95 o.p. (ISBN 0-07-061673-6, GB). McGraw.

--Speaking up. 1978. pap. 4.95 o.p. (ISBN 0-07-061674-4, SP). McGraw.

Stone, Janet & Musset, Anthony. Contact Lens Design Tables. 1981. text ed. 25.95 (ISBN 0-407-00219-7). Butterworth.

Stone, John, et al, eds. see Tocqueville, Alexis.

Stone, John F. Plant Modification for More Efficient Water Use. (Developments in Agricultural & Managed Forest Ecology Ser.: Vol. 1). 330p. 1975. Repr. 53.25 (ISBN 0-444-41273-5). Elsevier.

Stone, Jon. Would You Like to Play Hide & Seek in This Book with Lovable, Furry Old Grover? LC 76-8120. (Picturebacks Ser.). (Illus.). (ps-1). 1976. pap. 1.50 (ISBN 0-394-83292-2). Random.

Stone, Julita M. How to Volunteer in Social Service Agencies. (Illus.). 90p. 1982. 14.50x (ISBN 0-398-04719-7). C C Thomas.

Stone, Julius. Aggression & World Order. LC 76-4567. 226p. 1976. Repr. of 1958 ed. lib. bdg. 17.50x (ISBN 0-8371-8806-7, STWO). Greenwood.

Stone, Julius F., ed. see Stanton, Robert B.

Stone, Justin F. The Metaphysics of Wall Street. 175p. 1983. 10.00 (ISBN 0-89540-134-7, SB-134). Sun Pub.

--The Metaphysics of Wallstreet. 152p. 10.00 (ISBN 0-686-38227-7). Sun Bks.

Stone, K., jt. auth. see Kirschner, E.

Stone, K., jt. auth. see Kirshner, C.

Stone, Kate. Brokenburn: The Journal of Kate Stone, 1861-1868. Anderson, John Q., ed. LC 55-7363. (Library of Southern Civilization). 424p. 1972. 25.00x o.p. (ISBN 0-8071-0231-8). La State U Pr.

Stone, Kurt, tr. see Peinkofer, Karl & Tannigel, Fritz.

Stone, L. Joseph & Church, Joseph. Childhood & Adolescence: A Psychology of the Growing Person. 4th ed. LC 78-10730. 1979. text ed. 21.00x (ISBN 0-394-32086-7); study guide 7.00 (ISBN 0-394-32170-7). Random.

Stone, Lawrence. Crisis of the Aristocracy, Fifteen Fifty-Eight to Sixteen Forty-One. abr. ed. (Illus.). 1967. pap. 8.95 (ISBN 0-19-500274-1, GB). Oxford U Pr.

--Family, Sex & Marriage in England, Fifteen Hundred to Eighteen Hundred. abr. ed. LC 79-2028. (Illus.). 1980. pap. 8.95xi (ISBN 0-06-131979-1, TB1979, Torch). Har-Row.

Stone, Lawrence, jt. auth. see Bittker, Boris.

Stone, Lawrence M., jt. auth. see Bittker, Boris.

Stone, Leslie F. Out of the Void. (YA) 6.95 (ISBN 0-685-07452-8, Avalon). Bouregy.

Stone, Linda, jt. auth. see Baratta, Ron.

Stone, Lloyd A., jt. auth. see Bradley, Fred O.

Stone, Lori J., ed. see Stowers, Sharon L.

Stone, Marie. The Covent Garden Cookbook. (Illus.). 256p. 1980. pap. 8.95 (ISBN 0-8052-8021-9, Pub. by Allison & Busby England). Schocken.

Stone, Martha. At the Sign of Midnight: The Concheros Dance Cult of Mexico. LC 73-76303. (Illus.). 262p. 1975. text ed. 16.50x o.s.i. (ISBN 0-8165-0337-0); pap. text ed. 2.00 (ISBN 0-8165-0507-1). U of Ariz Pr.

Stone, Merlin. Marketing & Economics. LC 79-22206. 1980. 26.00 (ISBN 0-312-51527-8). St Martin.

Stone, Merlin & Women Against Racism. Three Thousand Years of Racism. 32p. 1983. pap. 3.00x (ISBN 0-9603352-2-6). New Sibylline.

Stone, Michael. The Armenian Inscriptions from the Sinai. (Armenian Texts & Studies: No. 6). (Illus.). 275p. 1983. text ed. 28.50x (ISBN 0-674-04626-9). Harvard U Pr.

--Signs of the Judgement, Onomastica Sacra & the Generations from Adam. LC 80-28371. (University of Pennsylvania Armenian Texts & Studies). 1981. text ed. 16.50 (ISBN 0-89130-460-6, 21-02-03); pap. 12.00 (ISBN 0-89130-461-4). Scholars Pr CA.

Stone, Michael E., jt. auth. see Nickelsburg, George W.

Stone, Michael H. The Borderline Syndrome: Constitution, Personality & Adaptation. (Illus.). 1980. 31.50 (ISBN 0-07-061685-X, P&RB). McGraw.

Stone, Michael H. & Forest, David. Treating Schizophrenic Patients: A Critical Analytical Approach. Albert, Harry D., ed. (Illus.). 352p. 24.95 (ISBN 0-07-001917-7, P&RB). McGraw.

Stone, Michelle, jt. auth. see Sky, Alison.

Stone, N. J. Fat Chance. 1980. available only in lots of 10 69.50 (ISBN 0-8151-8417-4). Year Bk Med.

Stone, Nancy & Grey, Robert W., eds. White Trash: An Anthology of Contemporary Southern Poets. 2nd ed. 135p. 1983. pap. 7.95 (ISBN 0-917990-06-4). New South Co.

Stone, Nancy W., ed. see Walker, Nancy P.

Stone, Olive M. Family Law. xxxv, 277p. 1977. text ed. 25.00x o.p. (ISBN 0-333-19629-5). Rothman.

Stone, P., jt. ed. see Kelly, E.

Stone, P. A. Building Design Evaluation. 3rd ed. 1980. 28.00x (ISBN 0-419-11720-2, Pub. by E & FN Spon England). Methuen Inc.

--Building Economy: Design, Production & Organisation. 3rd ed. 250p. 1982. 45.00 (ISBN 0-08-028677-1); 17.00 (ISBN 0-08-028678-X). Pergamon.

--Structure, Size & Costs of Urban Settlements. LC 73-80480. (National Institute of Economic & Social Research Economic & Social Studies: No. 28). (Illus.). 300p. 1973. 44.50 (ISBN 0-521-20309-0). Cambridge U Pr.

--Urban Development in Britain: Measurement of Consumer's Expenditure in the United Kingdom, 1920-38. Vol. 1. 47.50 (ISBN 0-521-06932-7); Vol. 2. 59.50 (ISBN 0-521-06558-5). Cambridge U Pr.

Stone, Peter & Edwards, Sherman. Seventeen Seventy-Six: A Musical Play. (Illus.). 1976. pap. 3.95 (ISBN 0-14-048139-7). Penguin.

Stone, Phil, jt. auth. see Rosetti, Rick.

Stone, R. H. & Tripp, D. W. Chemistry. (Secondary Science Ser). (Illus.). (gr. 6-11). 1978. pap. text ed. 8.95 (ISBN 0-7100-8755-1). Routledge & Kegan.

Stone, Richard & Peterson, William, eds. Econometric Contributions to Public Policy. 1979. 39.95x (ISBN 0-312-22631-4). St Martin.

Stone, Robert. Dog Soldiers. LC 74-11441. 384p. 1974. 11.95 o.s.i. (ISBN 0-395-18481-9). HM.

--A Flag for Sunrise. 448p. 1982. pap. 3.95 (ISBN 0-345-30650-3). Ballantine.

Stone, Robert, jt. auth. see Goldstein, Norman.

Stone, Robert B. The Magic of Psychotronic Power. 1978. 14.95 o.p. (ISBN 0-13-545301-1, Parker). P-H.

--The Power of Miracle Metaphysics. 1976. 14.95 o.p. (ISBN 0-13-686683-2, Parker). P-H.

Stone, Robert B., jt. auth. see Petrie, Sidney.

Stone, Robert H. Two Years in Limbo. (Illus.). 85p. 1981. text ed. 7.50 (ISBN 0-9609192-1-X). R H Stone.

--Wild Garlic Islands: A Genealogical Account of the Ramsey Family. LC 82-90342. (Illus.). 191p. (Orig.). 1982. 22.50 (ISBN 0-9609192-0-1). R H Stone.

Stone, Rochelle. Boleslaw Lesmian: The Poet & His Poetry. LC 73-84382. 1976. 35.75x (ISBN 0-520-02549-0). U of Cal Pr.

Stone, Ronald H. Paul Tillich's Radical Social Thought. LC 79-87740. 180p. 1980. pap. 3.99 (ISBN 0-8042-0679-1). John Knox.

--Realism & Hope. 1977. pap. text ed. 10.25 (ISBN 0-8191-0128-1). U Pr of Amer.

--Reinhold Niebuhr: Prophet to Politicians. 270p. 1981. lib. bdg. 21.50 (ISBN 0-8191-1540-1); pap. text ed. 11.00 (ISBN 0-8191-1541-X). U Pr of Amer.

Stone, Rosetta. Because a Little Bug Went Ka-Choo! LC 75-1605. (Illus.). 48p. (gr. k-3). 1975. 4.95 (ISBN 0-394-83130- ... PLB 5.99 (ISBN 0-394-93130-0). Beginner.

Stone, Ruth M. Let the Inside Be Sweet: The Interpretation of Music Event Among the Kpelle of Liberia. LC 81-48628. 208p. 1982. 20.00 (ISBN 0-253-33345-8). Ind U Pr.

Stone, Sandra, et al, eds. Management for Nurses: A Multidisciplinary Approach. LC 75-15561. 280p. 1976. pap. 9.95 o.p. (ISBN 0-8016-4812-2). Mosby.

Stone, Shelley C. & Shertzer, Bruce. Careers in Counseling & Guidance. LC 72-185792. 160p. (Orig.). 1972. pap. text ed. 12.50 (ISBN 0-395-13494-3). HM.

Stone, Shelley C., jt. auth. see Shertzer, Bruce.

Stone, Shelley C., jt. auth. see Shertzer, Bruce E.

Stone, Sue & Stone, Alan. Abnormal Personality Through Literature. (Orig.). 1966. pap. text ed. 13.95 (ISBN 0-13-000786-2). P-H.

Stone, Susanah H. The Oakland Paramount. (Art Ser.). (Illus.). 96p. 1983. 11.95 (ISBN 0-89581-607-5). Lancaster-Miller.

Stone, W. & Packer, N. H. The Short Story: An Introduction. 2nd ed. 640p. 1983. pap. text ed. 9.95x (ISBN 0-07-061693-0, C). McGraw.

Stone, W., et al. The Short Story: An Introduction. 1976. text ed. 13.95 o.p. (ISBN 0-07-061689-2); instructor's manual 15.00 o.p. (ISBN 0-07-061690-6). McGraw.

Stone, Wilfred & Bell, J. G. Prose Style: A Handbook for Writers. 4th ed. (Illus.). 368p. 1983. pap. 13.95x (ISBN 0-07-061734-1). McGraw.

Stone, Wilfred & Hoopes, Robert, eds. Form & Thought in Prose. 4th ed. 1977. text ed. 17.95x (ISBN 0-673-15726-1). Scott F.

Stone, William E., ed. see Walker, Nancy P.

Stone, William F. The Psychology of Politics. LC 73-17647. (Illus.). 1974. 17.00 (ISBN 0-02-931690-1); pap. text ed. 8.95 (ISBN 0-02-931680-4). Free Pr.

Stone, William J. & Rabin, Pauline L., eds. Chronic End-Stage Renal Diseases. Date not set. price not set (ISBN 0-12-672280-3). Acad Pr.

Stone, William S. Idylls of the South Seas. LC 73-128083. 1971. 8.95 (ISBN 0-87022-775-0). UH Pr.

Stone, William T. & Blanchard, Fessenden S. A Cruising Guide to the Chesapeake. LC 73-6038. (Illus.). 1978. 15.00 o.p. (ISBN 0-396-07638-6). Dodd.

Stone, William T. & Blanchard, Fessenden. A Cruising Guide to the Chesapeake. Rev. ed. (Illus.). 1983. 19.95 (ISBN 0-396-08165-7). Dodd.

Stone, William T., jt. auth. see Hart, Jerrems C.

Stone, William W. Balzac, James & the Realistic Novel. LC 82-61388. 224p. 1983. 19.50x (ISBN 0-691-06567-5). Princeton U Pr.

Stoneham, R., jt. auth. see Rees, M.

Stonehill, Arthur, jt. auth. see Eiteman, David K.

Stonehill, Arthur I., jt. auth. see Eiteman, David K.

Stonehill, Edward, jt. auth. see Crisp, Arthur H.

Stonehouse, Bernard. Britain from the Air. LC 82-1507. (Illus.). 160p. 1982. 30.00 (ISBN 0-517-54715-5). Crown.

--Penguins. LC 79-13661. (New Biology Ser.). (gr. 4 up). 1980. 8.95 (ISBN 0-07-061740-6). McGraw.

Stonehouse, Bernard, jt. auth. see Rey, Louis.

Stonehouse, Frederick. The Wreck of the Edmund Fitzgerald. 4th ed. LC 77-93064. (Illus.). 1977. 4.95 o.p. (ISBN 0-685-87719-1). Avery Color.

Stonehouse, John. Death of an Idealist. 245p. 1976. 9.50 o.p. (ISBN 0-491-01615-8). Transatlantic.

Stoneking, Charles E., jt. auth. see Marris, Andrew W.

Stoneman, C. F. & Marsden, J. F. Enzymes & Equillibria. (Scholarship Series in Biology). 1974. text ed. 9.95x o.p. (ISBN 0-435-61840-7). Heinemann Ed.

Stoneman, Elvyn A., jt. auth. see Pearcy, G. Etzel.

Stoneman, P. Technological Diffusion & the Computer Revolution. LC 75-12136. (Department of Applied Economics Monograph: No. 25). (Illus.). 1976. 42.50 (ISBN 0-521-20945-5). Cambridge U Pr.

Stoneman, Richard, ed. see Prorr, Manfred & Limbrunner, Alfred.

Stoneman, Richard, tr. see Pforr, Manfred & Limbrunner, Alfred.

Stoner, Carol, ed. see Hatcher, Richard, et al.

Stoner, Carol, ed. see Sussman, Vic.

Stoner, D. L., et al. Engineering a Safe Hospital Environment. 288p. 1981. 35.00 (ISBN 0-471-04494-6, Pub. by Wiley-Interscience). Wiley.

Stoner, Elisabeth. Watermark. 1983. pap. 2.95 (ISBN 0-939736-37-3). Wings ME.

Stoner, G. O., ed. see Laird, Donald A., et al.

Stoner, J. O., Jr., jt. auth. see Bashkin, S.

Stoner, James A. Management. (Illus.). 1978. text ed. 23.95 (ISBN 0-13-549303-X); study guide & wkbk 8.95 (ISBN 0-13-549329-3). P-H.

--Management. 2nd ed. 704p. 1982. text ed. 25.00 (ISBN 0-13-549667-5); study guide & wkbk. 10.95 (ISBN 0-13-549683-7). P-H.

Stoner, Rosemary B., jt. auth. see Stevens, Laura J.

Stoneridge, M. A. A Horse of Your Own. rev. ed. LC 78-22369. (Illus.). 560p. 1980. 19.95 (ISBN 0-385-14617-5). Doubleday.

--Practical Horseman's Book of Horsekeeping. LC 82-45150. (Illus.). 352p. 1983. 24.95 (ISBN 0-385-17788-7). Doubleday.

Stonerod, David. Puzzles in Space. (Illus.). 1982. pap. text ed. 6.50 (ISBN 0-914534-03-3). Stokes.

Stones, E. Psychopedagogy: Psychological Theory & the Practice of Teaching. 490p. 1979. 24.95x (ISBN 0-416-71330-0); pap. 13.95x (ISBN 0-416-71340-8). Methuen Inc.

--Readings in Educational Psychology: Learning & Teaching. 1970. pap. 11.50x (ISBN 0-416-13750-4). Methuen Inc.

Stones, Edgar & Morris, Sidney. Teaching Practice. 1979. pap. 11.95x (ISBN 0-416-61140-0). Methuen Inc.

Stones, P. B. Viral Vaccines. 1981. write for info. (ISBN 0-471-28015-1, Pub. by Wiley-Interscience). Wiley.

Stonesifer, Roy P., Jr., et al. The American Fabric: Weaving the Past into the Present. 1976. pap. text ed. 3.95x (ISBN 0-88273-242-0). Forum Pr IL.

Stong, Phil. Honk the Moose. LC 35-27382. (Illus.). (gr. 4-6). 1935. PLB 6.95 o.p. (ISBN 0-396-07358-1). Dodd.

Stonorov see Le Corbusier.

Stoodley, K. D., et al. Applied Statistical Techniques. (Ellis Horwood Ser. in Mathematics & Its Applications). 300p. 1980. 74.95x (ISBN 0-470-26951-0). Halsted Pr.

Stoodt, jt. auth. see Roe.

Stoodt, Barbara D. Reading Instruction. 1981. 20.95 (ISBN 0-395-30749-X); instr's manual 1.25 (ISBN 0-395-30750-3). HM.

Stoodt, Barbara D., jt. auth. see Roe, Betty D.

Stookey, R. Yemen. LC 77-454. (Westview Special Studies on the Middle East). 1978. lib. bdg. 30.00 o.p. (ISBN 0-89158-300-9). Westview.

Stookey, Robert W. America & the Arab States: An Uneasy Encounter. LC 75-25874. (America & the World Ser). 298p. 1975. pap. text ed. 15.50 (ISBN 0-471-82976-5). Wiley.

Stopford, J. M. & Channon, D. F. Cases in Strategic Management. 1082p. 1980. 75.95 (ISBN 0-471-27705-3, Pub. by Wiley-Interscience); pap. 32.95 (ISBN 0-686-92660-9). Wiley.

Stopford, John M. & Dunning, John H., eds. World Directory of Multinational Enterprises, 3 Vols. 2nd ed. 1700p. 1982. Set. 365.00x (ISBN 0-8103-0521-6, Pub. by Macmillan England). Gale.

Stopher, Peter R. & Mayburg, Arnim H. Urban Transportation Modeling & Planning. LC 74-21876. 368p. 1975. 26.95x (ISBN 0-669-96941-9). Lexington Bks.

Stopher, Peter R. & Meyberg, Arnim. Transportation Systems Evaluation. 208p. 1976. 20.95x (ISBN 0-669-96958-3). Lexington Bks.

Stopher, Peter R. & Meyburg, Arnim H. Urban Transportation Modeling & Planning. 345p. 1975. pap. 5.00 (ISBN 0-686-94042-3, Trans). Northwestern U Pr.

Stopher, Peter R. & Meyburg, Arnum. Survey Sampling & Multivariate Methods for Social Scientists & Engineers. LC 74-25056. 416p. 1979. 27.95x (ISBN 0-669-96966-4). Lexington Bks.

Stopher, Peter R. & Mevburg, Arnim H., eds. Behavioral Travel-Demand Models. LC 76-14666. 368p. 1976. 28.95x o.p. (ISBN 0-669-00734-X). Lexington Bks.

Stopher, Peter R., et al, eds. New Horizons in Travel-Behavior Research. LC 78-24830. 784p. 1981. 41.95x (ISBN 0-669-02850-9). Lexington Bks.

Stopp, P., jt. auth. see Smith, D. I.

Stoppard, Miriam. Dr. Miriam Stoppard's Book of Baby Care. LC 77-76668. (Illus.). 1977. 10.95 o.p. (ISBN 0-689-10810-9). Atheneum.

Stoppard, Miriam, ed. The Good Looks Book. LC 80-5367. (Illus.). 256p. 1980. 25.00 o.p. (ISBN 0-670-34547-4, Studio). Viking Pr.

Stopple, Libby. A Box of Peppermints. Dromgoole, Dick, ed. LC 75-20957. (Illus.). 96p. (gr. 2-10). 1975. 7.50 (ISBN 0-913632-08-2); pap. 4.50 (ISBN 0-913632-07-4). Am Univ Artforms.

Storandt, Martha, jt. auth. see Botwinick, Jack.

Storch, J. Patient's Rights: Ethical & Legal Issues in Health Case & Nursing. 288p. Date not set. 10.95 (ISBN 0-07-548477-3). McGraw.

Storch, Marcia L. & Carchmichael, Carrie. How to Relieve Cramps & Other Menstrual Problems. LC 81-40508. (Illus.). 128p. 1982. pap. 3.95 (ISBN 0-89480-191-0). Workman Pub.

Storch, O. Industrial Separators for Gas Cleaning. LC 78-10916. (Chemical Engineering Monographs: Vol. 6). 388p. 1979. 61.75 (ISBN 0-444-99808-X). Elsevier.

Storch, Robert D., ed. Popular Culture & Custom in Nineteenth-Century England. LC 82-3302. 232p. 1982. 27.50x (ISBN 0-312-63033-6). St Martin.

Storen, Helen F. Disadvantaged Early Adolescent. 1968. pap. text ed. 4.95 o.p. (ISBN 0-07-061750-3). McGraw.

Storer, J. Don. Simple History of the Steam Engine. (Illus.). 1969. text ed. 12.50x o.p. (ISBN 0-212-98356-3). Humanities.

Storer, John M., jt. auth. see Stewart, Harry L.

Storer, Norman, ed. see Merton, Robert K.

Storer, Tracy I. & Usinger, Robert L. Sierra Nevada Natural History: An Illustrated Handbook. (Illus.). 1963. pap. 7.95 (ISBN 0-520-01227-5). U of Cal Pr.

Storer, Tracy I., et al. General Zoology. 6th ed. 1979. text ed. 28.95 (ISBN 0-07-061780-5); instructor's manual 14.95 (ISBN 0-07-061781-3). McGraw.

Storette, Ronald F. Einreise Und Arbeitserlaubnis in U. S. A. 2nd ed. German American Chamber of Commerce, ed. Theurer, Martin, tr. 155p. (Ger.). 1982. pap. 18.00 (ISBN 0-86640-006-0). German Am Cham.

Storey, Arthur. The Measurement of Classroom Learning: Teacher Directed Assessment. LC 72-130584. (Illus.). 1970. pap. text ed. 6.95 o.p. (ISBN 0-574-17392-7, 13-0392); test set 1.20 o.p. (ISBN 0-574-17393-5, 13-0393). SRA.

Storey, Dale A., jt. auth. see Phillips, Bonnie D.

Storey, David. The Changing Room. Incl. Home; The Contractor. 1975. pap. 2.95 o.p. (ISBN 0-380-00301-5, 48116, Bard). Avon.

--A Prodigal Child. 320p. 1983. 14.95 (ISBN 0-525-24160-4, 01451-440). Dutton.

--Saville. 1978. pap. 2.25 o.p. (ISBN 0-380-01889-6, 37168). Avon.

--This Sporting Life. 1975. pap. 2.95 (ISBN 0-380-00254-X, 58024-1). Avon.

Storey, Edward J. Secrets of Kicking the Football. LC 71-135257. (Putnam Sports Shelf Ser.). (Illus.). (gr. 5 up). 1971. PLB 4.97 o.p. (ISBN 0-399-60572-X). Putnam Pub Group.

Storey, Isabelle, jt. ed. see Howland, Llewellyn.

Storey, James R. & Hendricks, Gary. Retirement Income Issues in an Aging Society. 60p. 1980. pap. text ed. 4.00 (ISBN 0-87766-267-3). Urban Inst.

Storey, Joan & Reece, Daphne E. United States of America West: A Travel Guide to Hawaii, the Pacific States & the Southwest. (Illus.). 1982. pap. 9.95 (ISBN 0-908086-09-1). Hippocrene Bks.

Storey, John. Managerial Prerogative & the Question of Control. (Direct Edition Ser.). 180p. (Orig.). 1983. pap. 18.50 (ISBN 0-7100-9203-2). Routledge & Kegan.

Storey, Joyce. The Thames & Hudson Manual of Dyes & Fabrics. (Illus.). 1978. 17.95 (ISBN 0-500-67016-1). Thames Hudson.

Storey, Margaret. A Quarrel of Witches. (Illus.). (ps-5). 1970. 7.95 o.p. (ISBN 0-571-09416-3). Faber & Faber.

Storey, Mark. The Poetry of John Clare: A Critical Introduction. LC 74-75012. 1974. 18.95 o.p. (ISBN 0-312-61915-4). St Martin.

Storey, Moorfield. Reform of Legal Procedure. 1911. 22.50x o.p. (ISBN 0-685-69871-8). Elliots Bks.

Storey, Reed K. The Search for Accounting Principles. LC 77-81833. 1977. Repr. of 1964 ed. text ed. 13.00 (ISBN 0-914348-20-5). Scholars Bk.

Storey, S. H., jt. auth. see Van Zeggeren, F.

Storey, Wayne, jt. auth. see Klibbe, Lawrence.

Storfer, Paul. Videotext: The Message in the Medium. 240p. 1983. 21.95 (ISBN 0-13-941922-5); pap. 14.95 (ISBN 0-13-941914-4). P-H.

Storing, Herbert J., ed. What Country Have I? Political Writings by Black Americans. LC 77-106206. 1970. pap. 10.95 (ISBN 0-312-86520-1, W21001). St Martin.

Stork, Charles W., tr. see Von Heidenstam, Verner.

Stork, David G., jt. auth. see Berg, Richard E.

Stork, F. C., jt. ed. see Hartmann, R. R.

Storm, Gerrit, ed. see Furst, Bruno.

Storm, Hyemeyohsts. Song of Heyoehkah. 320p. 1983. pap. 12.95 (ISBN 0-345-30731-3). Ballantine.

Storm, Margaret & Ginnett, Elsie. Home Maid Spanish Cookbook. (Illus.). 1977. pap. 3.95 o.p. (ISBN 0-517-53462-2). Crown.

Storm, Theodor. Viola Tricolor. 2.75 o.p. (ISBN 0-592-04223-5). Transatlantic.

Storm, William B., jt. auth. see Jun, Jong S.

Storm, William B., et al. Administrative Alternatives in Development Assistance. LC 73-9774. 128p. 1973. text ed. 17.50 prof ref (ISBN 0-88410-004-9). Ballinger Pub.

Storms, Earl R. Math Made Easy. 1972. 2.75x (ISBN 0-88323-110-7, 198). Richards Pub.

Storms, Edmund K. Refractory Carbides. 1967. 54.00 (ISBN 0-12-672850-X). Acad Pr.

Storms, Laura. The Bird Book. LC 82-15189. (Early Nature Picture Bks.). (Illus.). 32p. (gr. k-3). 1982. lib. bdg. 4.95g (ISBN 0-8225-1116-9). Lerner Pubns.

--Careers with an Orchestra. LC 82-17284. (Early Career Bks.). (Illus.). 36p. (gr. 2-5). 1983. PLB 5.95g (ISBN 0-8225-0344-1). Lerner Pubns.

--The Owl Book. (Early Nature Picture Bks.). (Illus.). 32p. (gr. k-3). 1983. PLB 4.95g (ISBN 0-8225-1117-7). Lerner Pubns.

Storms, Laura, jt. auth. see Thomas, Art.

Storr, Anthony. The Art of Psychotherapy. 204p. 1980. 15.95 (ISBN 0-416-60211-8); pap. 7.95 (ISBN 0-416-60321-1). Methuen Inc.

Storr, Anthony, jt. auth. see Lane, Donald.

Storr, Anthony, ed. The Essential Jung. LC 82-61441. 375p. Date not set. 35.00x (ISBN 0-691-08615-X); pap. 9.95 (ISBN 0-691-02455-3). Princeton U Pr.

Storr, Catherine. Rufus. LC 69-17744. (Illus.). (gr. 4-8). 1969. 6.95 (ISBN 0-87645-010-9). Gambit.

--The Story of the Terrible Scar. (Illus.). 70p. (gr. 2-5). 1978. 6.95 (ISBN 0-571-10996-9). Faber & Faber.

Storr, Catherine, retold by. Adam & Eve. LC 82-23060. (People of the Bible Ser.). (Illus.). 32p. (gr. 1-2). 1983. PLB 11.55 (ISBN 0-8172-1981-1). Raintree Pubs.

Storr, Catherine, ed. The Birth of Jesus. (People of the Bible Ser.). (Illus.). 32p. (gr. 1-2). 1982. PLB 9.95 (ISBN 0-8172-1977-3). Raintree Pubs.

Storr, Catherine & Bennett, Russell, eds. Jonah & the Whale. LC 82-23023. (People of the Bible Ser.). (Illus.). 32p. (gr. 1-2). 1983. PLB 11.55 (ISBN 0-8172-1984-6). Raintree Pubs.

--Miracles By the Sea. LC 82-23022. (People of the Bible Ser.). (Illus.). 32p. (gr. 1-2). 1983. PLB 11.55 (ISBN 0-8172-1983-8). Raintree Pubs.

--The Prodigal Son. LC 82-23011. (People of the Bible Ser.). (Illus.). 32p. (gr. 1-2). 1983. PLB 11.55 (ISBN 0-8172-1982-X). Raintree Pubs.

Storr, G. M. & Smith, L. A. Lizards of Western Astralia: Skinks, Vol. 1. (Illus.). xii, 200p. 1982. pap. 23.00 (ISBN 0-85564-195-9, Pub. by U of W Austral Pr). Intl Schol Bk Serv.

Storr, R. C., jt. auth. see Gilchrist, T. L.

Storrer, Carol M. & Hesterman, Vicki. Walking Home. LC 82-72636. 160p. (Orig.). 1983. pap. 6.95 (ISBN 0-8066-1942-2, 10-6922). Augsburg.

Storrer, William A. The Architecture of Frank Lloyd Wright: A Complete Catalog. 2nd ed. LC 78-1306. 1978. 17.50 (ISBN 0-262-19171-7); pap. 9.95 (ISBN 0-262-69080-2). MIT Pr.

Storry, Richard. Japan & the Decline of the West in Asia. LC 78-31872. (The Making of the Twentieth Century Ser.). 1979. 22.50x (ISBN 0-312-44050-2). St Martin.

Storry, Richard & Forman, Werner. The Way of the Samurai. LC 77-14634. (Illus.). 1978. 14.95 o.p. (ISBN 0-399-12013-0). Putnam Pub Group.

Storsz. Understanding My Church. Date not set. text ed. write for info (ISBN 0-87509-325-6); price not set leader's guide. Chr Pubns.

Stortz, Diane. My Thank You Book. Rev. ed. Miller, Marjorie, ed. (Illus.). 28p. (Orig.). (ps-3). Date not set. PLB 4.95 (ISBN 0-87239-558-8, 2883). Standard Pub. Postponed.

Stortz, Margaret R. Start Living Every Day of Your Life: How to Use the Science of Mind. 96p. 1981. pap. 2.95 (ISBN 0-911336-87-7). Sci of Mind.

Story, Cullen I K. Greek to Me: An Easy Way to Learn New Testament Greek Through Memory Visualization. LC 79-1769. (Illus.). 1979. pap. text ed. 10.53xi (ISBN 0-06-067705-8, RD 307, HarpR). Har-Row.

Story, Donna K. & Rosdahl, Caroline B. Principles & Practices of Nursing Care. 1976. text ed. 21.95 (ISBN 0-07-061770-8); instructor's manual & key 5.00 (ISBN 0-07-061772-4); activities & projects 9.95 (ISBN 0-07-061771-6). McGraw.

Story, G. M., jt. ed. see Halpert, Herbert.

Story, Ronald. The Space Gods Revealed: A Close Look at the Theories of Erich Von Daniken. LC 75-30347. (Illus.). 192p. (YA) 1976. 13.41i (ISBN 0-06-014141-7, HarpT). Har-Row.

Story, Ronald D. Sightings: UFOs & the Limits of Science. LC 81-15773. (Illus.). 224p. 1982. pap. 7.50 (ISBN 0-688-00802-X). Quill NY.

Story, William L. Cemeteries Are for Dying. LC 82-45078. (Crime Club Ser.). 192p. 1982. 10.95 (ISBN 0-385-18190-6). Doubleday.

Storzer, jt. auth. see Gerber.

Storzer, Gerald, jt. auth. see Gerber, Barbara.

Storzer, Gerald H., jt. auth. see Gerber, Barbara L.

Stoskopf, Neal C. Understanding Crop Production. 420p. 1981. text ed. 20.95 (ISBN 0-8359-8027-8). Reston.

Stoss, John. Machines Always Existed. 1983. 8.95 (ISBN 0-916620-57-3). Portals Pr.

Stossel, John. Shopping Smart: The Only Consumer Guide You'll Ever Need. 256p. 1980. 9.95 (ISBN 0-399-12511-6). Putnam Pub Group.

Stotesbury, Sidney D., jt. auth. see Lin Yen Tung.

Stothers, J. B. Carbon-Thirteen NMR Spectra. (Organic Chemistry Ser: Vol. 24). 1972. 69.00 (ISBN 0-12-672950-6). Acad Pr.

Stotler, R. E. The Genus Frullania Subgenus Frullania in Latin America. 1970. 16.00 (ISBN 3-7682-0679-3). Lubrecht & Cramer.

Stott, D. H. Saving Children from Delinquency. 1954. 4.75 o.p. (ISBN 0-8022-1658-7). Philos Lib.

Stott, Denis. Helping the Maladjusted Child: A Guide for Parents & Teachers. 141p. 1982. 11.95 (ISBN 0-13-387068-5); pap. 5.95 (ISBN 0-13-387050-2). P-H.

Stott, Denis H. The Hard-to-Teach Child: A Diagnostic-Remedial Approach. LC 77-25005. 200p. 1977. pap. 17.95 (ISBN 0-8391-1175-4). Univ Park.

Stott, Doug, tr. see Van Der Geest, Bans.

Stott, F. D., et al, eds. ISAM-GENT 1981. 672p. 1982. 65.00 (ISBN 0-12-672360-5). Acad Pr.

Stott, Geraldine & Cook, Bridget. One Hundred Traditional Bobbin Lace Patterns. LC 82-82932. (Illus.). 144p. (Orig.). 1983. pap. 12.95 (ISBN 0-88332-290-0, 8250). Larousse.

Stott, J. R., jt. auth. see Munton, R.

Stott, John. One People. Rev. ed. 128p. 1982. pap. 4.95 (ISBN 0-8007-5099-3, PowerBks). Revell.

Stott, John R. Balanced Christianity. (Orig.). 1975. pap. 1.50 o.p. (ISBN 0-87784-418-6). Inter-Varsity.

--Christian Counter-Culture. LC 77-27687. (Bible Speaks Today Ser.). 1978. pap. 5.95 (ISBN 0-87784-660-X). Inter-Varsity.

--Christian Mission in the Modern World. LC 75-21455. 128p. (Orig.). 1976. pap. 4.95 (ISBN 0-87784-485-2). Inter-Varsity.

--God's Book for God's People. 96p. 1982. pap. 2.95 (ISBN 0-87784-396-1). Inter-Varsity.

--Guard the Gospel. LC 73-75890. (Bible Speaks Today Ser.). 144p. 1973. text ed. 4.25 (ISBN 0-87784-481-X). Inter-Varsity.

--What Christ Thinks of the Church. 1972. pap. 3.95 (ISBN 0-8028-1451-4). Eerdmans.

Stott, William. Documentary Expression & Thirties America. LC 73-82676. (Illus.). 441p. 1976. pap. 8.95 (ISBN 0-19-502099-5, 474, GB). Oxford U Pr.

Stotz, jt. ed. see Florkin, M.

Stotz, E. H., jt. auth. see Florkin, M.

Stotz, E. H., jt. ed. see Florkin, M.

Stoudt, John J. Pennsylvania German Folk Art. (Pennsylvania German Folklore Society Ser.: Vol. 28). 1966. 20.00 o.p. (ISBN 0-686-79894-5). Penn German Soc.

Stough, Ada B. Life Is a Weaver. 1979. pap. 4.95 o.p. (ISBN 0-910286-59-0). Boxwood.

Stough, Charlotte L. Greek Skepticism: A Study in Epistemology. LC 76-82464. 1969. 28.50x (ISBN 0-520-01604-1). U of Cal Pr.

Stough, Furman C. & Holmes, Urban T., 3rd, eds. Realities & Visions: Contributions to the Church's Mission Today. 1976. pap. 1.50 (ISBN 0-8164-2130-7). Seabury.

Stough, Richard H. Dial-A-Prayer. (Orig.). 1983. pap. 1.50 (ISBN 0-937172-44-8). JLJ Pubs.

Stoughton, C. R., ed. Issues in Curriculum Theory. LC 80-5880. 206p. 1981. lib. bdg. 20.25 (ISBN 0-8191-1522-3); pap. text ed. 10.00 (ISBN 0-8191-1523-1). U Pr of Amer.

Stourzh, Gerald, et al. Readings in American Democracy. 2nd ed. 1966. pap. 7.95x (ISBN 0-19-501071-X). Oxford U Pr.

Stout, Ann M., jt. auth. see Stout, James H.

Stout, David F. & Kaufman, Milton. Handbook of Microcircuit Design & Application. (Illus.). 1979. 41.25 (ISBN 0-07-061796-1, P&RB). McGraw.

Stout, G. E., ed. Isotope Techniques in the Hydrologic Cycle. LC 67-60054. (Geophysical Monograph Ser.: Vol. 11). 1967. 10.00 o.p. (ISBN 0-87590-011-9). Am Geophysical.

Stout, Gardner D., Jr., ed. see Sterne, Laurence.

Stout, Gary & Vitt, Joseph E. Public Incentives & Financial Techniques for Codevelopment. LC 82-50705. (Development Component Ser.). (Illus.). 26p. 1982. pap. 10.00 (ISBN 0-87420-610-3, D23). Urban Land.

Stout, George L., jt. auth. see Gettens, Rutherford J.

Stout, James H. & Stout, Ann M. Backpacking with Small Children. LC 74-23854. (Funk & W Bk.). (Illus.). 224p. 1975. 10.53i (ISBN 0-308-10182-0). T Y Crowell.

Stout, Janis P. Sodoms in Eden: The City in American Fiction Before 1860. LC 75-35356. (Contributions in American Studies: No. 19). 192p. 1976. lib. bdg. 25.00x (ISBN 0-8371-8585-8, SSE/). Greenwood.

Stout, Joseph A. The Liberators: Filibustering Expeditions into Mexico, & the Last Gasp of Manifest Destiny. LC 72-83539. (Illus.). 10.50 (ISBN 0-87026-029-4). Westernlore.

Stout, Joseph A., ed. see Rogers, Will, Jr.

Stout, Joseph A., Jr., jt. ed. see Faulk, Odie B.

Stout, Joseph A., Jr., ed. see Rogers, Will.

Stout, Marilyn, jt. auth. see Kunin, Madeleine.

Stout, Melville B. Basic Electrical Measurements. 2nd ed. (Illus.). 1960. ref. ed. 26.95 (ISBN 0-13-059808-9); answers 0.25 (ISBN 0-13-059790-2). P-H.

Stout, Neil R. The Royal Navy in America 1760-1775: A Study of Enforcement of British Colonial Policy in the Era of the American Revolution. LC 73-7771. 350p. 1973. 12.50 o.p. (ISBN 0-87021-553-1). Naval Inst Pr.

Stout, R. D. & Doty, W. D. Weldability of Steels. 3rd ed. Epstein, S. & Somers, R., eds. 430p. 1978. 20.00 (ISBN 0-686-95608-7). Am Welding.

Stout, R. W. Hormones & Atherosclerosis. (Illus.). 300p. 1982. text ed. 55.00 (ISBN 0-686-37160-7, Pub. by MTP Pr England). Kluwer Boston.

Stout, Rex. Black Orchids. 1976. pap. 1.75 o.s.i. (ISBN 0-515-05085-7). Jove Pubns.

--Double for Death. 1979. pap. 1.75 o.s.i. (ISBN 0-515-05277-9). Jove Pubns.

--The Mountain Cat Murders. 176p. 1982. pap. 2.50 (ISBN 0-553-20826-8). Bantam.

--The Nero Wolfe Cookbook. 224p. 1981. pap. 4.95 (ISBN 0-14-005754-4). Penguin.

--Not Quite Dead Enough. (Adventures of Nero Wolfe). pap. 1.75 o.s.i. (ISBN 0-515-05119-5). Jove Pubns.

--Not Quite Dead Enough. 160p. 1982. pap. 2.50 (ISBN 0-553-22589-8). Bantam.

--Over My Dead Body. 1979. pap. 1.75 o.s.i. (ISBN 0-515-04865-8, 04865-8). Jove Pubns.

--The President Vanishes. 272p. 1982. pap. 2.50 (ISBN 0-553-22665-7). Bantam.

--The Red Box. pap. 1.75 o.s.i. (ISBN 0-515-05117-9). Jove Pubns.

--Red Threads. 192p. 1982. pap. 2.50 (ISBN 0-553-22530-8). Bantam.

--Some Buried Caeser. 1979. pap. 1.75 o.s.i. (ISBN 0-515-05118-7). Jove Pubns.

--The Sound of Murder. 1979. pap. 1.75 o.s.i. (ISBN 0-515-05281-7). Jove Pubns.

--Too Many Cooks. LC 75-46002. (Crime Fiction Ser). 1976. Repr. of 1938 ed. lib. bdg. 17.50 o.s.i. (ISBN 0-8240-2394-3). Garland Pub.

--Too Many Cooks. 1976. pap. 1.75 o.s.i. (ISBN 0-515-04866-6). Jove Pubns.

--Where There's a Will: Nero Wolfe. 1941. pap. 1.50 o.p. (ISBN 0-380-01620-6, 39529). Avon.

Stout, Robert J. Camping Out. (Illus.). 1976. pap. 1.00 o.p. (ISBN 0-686-20757-2). Samisdat.

Stout, Robert T. Children's Favorite Story of Santa Claus. (Illus.). 32p. (ps-6). 1982. 5.95 (ISBN 0-911049-08-8); pap. 3.95 (ISBN 0-911049-04-5). Yuletide Intl.

--The Noorps are Coming. (Illus.). 32p. (ps-6). 1982. pap. 3.95 (ISBN 0-911049-05-3). Yuletide Intl.

--The Original Story of Santa Claus. (Illus.). 56p. (ps-8). 1981. 6.95 (ISBN 0-911049-00-2). Yuletide Intl.

--The Secret of Halloween. (Illus.). 24p. (Orig.). (ps-6). 1982. pap. 3.50 (ISBN 0-911049-02-9). Yuletide Intl.

Stout, Ruth & Clemence, Richard. The Ruth Stout No-Work Garden Book. LC 70-152102. (Illus.). 1971. 9.95 (ISBN 0-87857-000-4). Rodale Pr Inc.

Stout, Sandra. Depression Glass in Color. No. 1. plastic bdg. 7.95 (ISBN 0-87069-022-1); No. 2. plastic bdg. 7.95 (ISBN 0-87069-023-X). Wallace-Homestead.

Stout, Sandra M. Depression Glass Book Three in Colors. (Illus.). 7.95 (ISBN 0-87069-181-3); price guide 1.50 (ISBN 0-87069-355-7). Wallace-Homestead.

Stout, Steve. The Starved Rock Murders. (Illus.). 210p. 1982. pap. 6.95 (ISBN 0-686-43142-1). Utica Hse.

Stout, William F. Almost Sure Convergence. 1974. 55.50 (ISBN 0-12-672750-3). Acad Pr.

Stoutenburg, Adrien. American Tall Tales. (Puffin Story Ser.). (Illus.). (gr. 3-7). 1969. pap. 2.95 (ISBN 0-14-030928-4, Puffin). Penguin.

Stoutt, G. The First Month of Life. 1977. pap. 7.95 o.p. (ISBN 0-87489-067-5). Med Economics.

Stoutt, Glenn R., Jr. The First Month of Life. 2nd ed. 175p. 1983. pap. 9.95 (ISBN 0-87489-312-7). Med Economics.

Stovall, Floyd. The Foreground of 'Leaves of Grass' LC 73-87861. 320p. 1974. 20.00 (ISBN 0-8139-0523-0). U Pr of Va.

Stovall, Sidney T., et al. Composition: Skills & Models. 2nd ed. LC 77-77681. (Illus.). 1978. pap. text ed. 14.50 (ISBN 0-395-25749-2); instr's. manual 0.50 (ISBN 0-395-25750-6). HM.

Stove, David. Popper & After: Four Modern Irrationalists. 192p. 1982. 17.50 (ISBN 0-08-026792-0); pap. 9.50 (ISBN 0-08-026791-2). Pergamon.

Stover, A., jt. auth. see Cushman, R. F.

Stover, Alan, ed. Standardized Accounting for Architects. LC 78-70446. (Illus.). 1978. pap. 22.00 o.p. (ISBN 0-913961-06-X). Am Inst Arch.

Stover, Allan C. You & the Metric System. LC 74-2593. (Illus.). 96p. (gr. 5 up). 1974. 4.50 o.p. (ISBN 0-396-06965-7). Dodd.

Stover, Doug. Encyclopedia of Amazing but True Facts. 1982. pap. 3.50 (ISBN 0-451-11559-7, AE1559, Sig). NAL.

Stover, William J. Military Politics in Finland: The Development of Governmental Control Over the Armed Forces. LC 81-40343. 220p. (Orig.). 1982. lib. bdg. 21.25 (ISBN 0-8191-2009-X); pap. text ed. 10.25 (ISBN 0-8191-2010-3). U Pr of Amer.

Stow, Randolph. The Girl Green As Elderflower. 156p. 1980. 9.95 o.p. (ISBN 0-670-34091-X). Viking Pr.

--Tourmaline: A Novel. LC 82-50910. 1983. 10.95 (ISBN 0-8008-7797-7). Taplinger.

Stoward, P. J. & Polak, J. M., eds. Histochemistry: The Widening Horizons, of its Applications in the Biomedical Sciences. LC 81-14704. 293p. 1982. 62.95x (ISBN 0-471-10010-2, Pub. by Wiley-Interscience). Wiley.

Stowe, Charles E. Life of Harriet Beecher Stowe. LC 67-23881. 1967. Repr. of 1889 ed. 34.00x (ISBN 0-8103-3046-6). Gale.

Stowe, Elaine, jt. auth. see Ransom, Grayce A.

Stowe, Harriet B. Uncle Sam's Emancipation, & Other Sketches. LC 76-92442. 1853. 9.00 (ISBN 0-403-00147-1). Scholarly.

--Uncle Tom's Cabin. (Bantam Classics Ser.). 480p. (gr. 7-12). 1981. pap. text ed. 2.25 (ISBN 0-553-21055-6). Bantam.

--Uncle Tom's Cabin. (Illus.). (gr. 6-9). 1929. PLB 5.69 o.p. (ISBN 0-698-30384-9, Coward). Putnam Pub Group.

Stowe, Harriet Beecher. Uncle Tom's Cabin. (RL 7). pap. 2.25 (ISBN 0-451-51755-5, CE1755, Sig Classics). NAL.

Stowe, Keith S. Ocean Science. LC 78-11962. 610p. 1979. pap. text ed. 27.50 (ISBN 0-471-04261-7); tchrs' manual avail. (ISBN 0-471-08084-5). Wiley.

Stowe, Richard S. Alexandre Dumas, pere. (World Authors Ser.). 1976. lib. bdg. 12.95 (ISBN 0-8057-6230-2, Twayne). G K Hall.

Stowe, W. McFerrin. If I were a Pastor. 112p. (Orig.). 1983. pap. 5.95 (ISBN 0-687-18655-2). Abingdon.

Stowe, William W., jt. ed. see Most, Glenn W.

Stowell, Gordon. Abraham. Lerin, S. D. de, tr. from English. (Libros Pescaditos Sobre Perssonajes Biblicos). (Illus.). 24p. 1981. pap. 0.50 (ISBN 0-311-38511-7, Edit Mundo). Casa Bautista.

--Ana. Lerin, S. D. De, tr. from English. (Little Fish Book Ser.). Orig. Title: Hannah. (Illus.). 24p. 1981. pap. 0.50 (ISBN 0-311-38512-5, Edit Mundo). Casa Bautista.

--Dorcas. Lerin, S. D. de, tr. from English. (Libros Pescaditos Sobre Personajes Biblicos). (Illus.). 24p. 1978. pap. 0.50 (ISBN 0-311-38517-6, Edit Mundo). Casa Bautista.

--Jonas. Lerin, S. D. de, tr. from English. (Libros Pescaditos Sobre Personajes Biblicos). Orig. Title: Jonah: The Little Fish Book Ser. (Illus.). 24p. 1978. pap. 0.50 (ISBN 0-311-38514-1, Edit Mundo). Casa Bautista.

--Juan el Bautista. Lerin, S. D. de, tr. from English. (Libros Pescaditos Sobre Personajes Biblicos). Orig. Title: John the Baptist: The Little Fish Book Ser. (Illus.). 24p. 1981. pap. 0.50 (ISBN 0-311-38515-X, Edit Mundo). Casa Bautista.

--Pablo. Lerin, S. D. de, tr. from English. (Libros Pescaditos Sobre Personajes Biblicos). Orig. Title: Paul: The Little Fish Book Ser. (Illus.). 24p. 1981. pap. 0.50 (ISBN 0-311-38518-4, Edit Mundo). Casa Bautista.

--Pedro. Lerin, S. D. de, tr. from English. (Libros Pescaditos Sobre Personajes Biblicos). Orig. Title: Peter: The Little Fish Book Ser. (Illus.). 24p. 1981. pap. 0.50 (ISBN 0-311-38516-8, Edit Mundo). Casa Bautista.

--Rut. Lerin, S. D. de, tr. from English. (Libros Pescaditos Sobre Personajes Biblicos). Orig. Title: Ruth - the Little Fish Book Series. (Illus.). 24p. 1981. pap. 0.50 (ISBN 0-311-38513-3, Edit Mundo). Casa Bautista.

Stowell, Gordon, illus. Jesus & the Fisherman. (Little Fish Books). (Illus.). 14p. 1982. pap. 0.59 (ISBN 0-8307-0831-6, 5608150). Regal.

--Jesus Feeds the People. (Little Fish Books). (Illus.). 14p. 1982. pap. 0.59 (ISBN 0-8307-0832-4, 5608167). Regal.

--Jesus Heals. (Little Fish Books). (Illus.). 14p. 1982. pap. 0.59 (ISBN 0-8307-0828-6, 5608122). Regal.

--Jesus Lives. (Little Fish Books). (Illus.). 14p. 1982. pap. 0.59 (ISBN 0-8307-0834-0, 5608181). Regal.

--Jesus Loves. (Little Fish Books). 14p. 1982. pap. 0.59 (ISBN 0-8307-0830-8, 5608145). Regal.

--Jesus Teaches. (Little Fish Books). (Illus.). 14p. 1982. pap. 0.59 (ISBN 0-8307-0829-4, 5608138). Regal.

--Jesus Tells Some Stories. (Little Fish Books). (Illus.). 14p. 1982. pap. 0.59 (ISBN 0-8307-0833-2, 5608176). Regal.

Stowell, John, ed. see Rhodius, Hans & Darling, John.

Stowell, John C. Carbanions in Organic Synthesis. LC 79-373. 247p. 1979. 30.95x (ISBN 0-471-02953-X, Pub. by Wiley-Interscience). Wiley.

Stower, W. J. The Colour Patterns of Hoppers of the Desert Locust (Schistocerca Gregaria Forskal) 1959. 35.00x (ISBN 0-85135-036-4, Pub. by Centre Overseas Research). State Mutual Bk.

Stower, W. J. & Popov, G. B. Oviposition Behavior & Egg Mortality of the Desert Locust (Schistocerca Gregaria Forskal) on the Coast of Eritrea. 1958. 35.00x (ISBN 0-85135-037-2, Pub. by Centre Overseas Research). State Mutual Bk.

Stowers, Carlton. The Unsinkable Titanic Thompson. 1982. 12.95 (ISBN 0-89015-340-X); pap. 9.95 (ISBN 0-89015-352-3). Eakin Pubns.

Stowers, Carlton & Evans, Wilbur. Champions: University of Texas Track & Field. LC 77-79833. (College Sports Ser.). 1978. 9.95 (ISBN 0-87397-130-2). Strode.

Stowers, Sharon L. Institutional Food Service & Nutritional Care. Stone, Lori J., ed. (Illus.). 151p. 1983. pap. 78.00x (ISBN 0-9609720-0-5). Educ Plan Serv.

Stoy, Joseph E. Denotational Semantics: The Scott-Strachey Approach to Programming Language Theory. 1977. 27.50x (ISBN 0-262-19147-4); pap. 12.50x (ISBN 0-262-69076-4). MIT Pr.

Stoyan, D. & Daley, D. J. Comparison Methods for Queues & Other Stochastic Models. 1982. text ed. write for info. (ISBN 0-471-10122-2, Pub. by Wiley-Interscience). Wiley.

Stoyevsky, Doug. The Paranoids Guide to Them. 96p. 1982. 5.95 (ISBN 0-02-040690-8). Macmillan.

Stoyle, J., jt. auth. see Iglewicz, B.

Straaten, Zac Van see Van Straaten, Zac.

Straaten, Zak Van see Van Straaten, Zak.

Straatveit, Tyyne & Corl, Carolyn K. Easy Art Lessons. (gr. k-6). 1971. 12.95 o.p. (ISBN 0-13-222372-4, Parker). P-H.

Straayer, John. American State & Local Government. 3rd ed. 384p. 1983. text ed. 14.95 (ISBN 0-675-20068-7). Merrill.

Straayer, John A. American State & Local Government. 2nd ed. (Political Science Ser.). 1977. pap. 12.95 (ISBN 0-675-08489-X). Merrill.

Straayer, John A. & Muessig, Raymond H. The Study & Teaching of Political Science. 2nd ed. (Social Science Seminar, Secondary Education Ser.: No. C28). 112p. 1980. pap. text ed. 7.95 (ISBN 0-675-08191-2). Merrill.

Strachan, A. M., jt. auth. see Winter, D. G.

Strachan, Harry W. Family & Other Business Groups in Economic Development: The Case of Nicaragua. LC 75-25025. (Special Studies). (Illus.). 144p. 1976. 24.95 o.p. (ISBN 0-275-56050-3). Praeger.

Strachan, J. George. Alcoholism: Treatable Illness. 12.95 (ISBN 0-89486-149-2, 1066A). Hazelden.

--Recovery from Alcoholism. 5.95 o.p. (ISBN 0-686-92207-7, 7129). Hazelden.

Strachan-Davidson, J. R. Appian Civil Wars, Bk. 1. 158p. Date not set. Repr. of 1902 ed. 7.00x (ISBN 0-86516-021-X). Bolchazy-Carducci.

Stracher, Alfred, ed. Muscle & Non-Muscle Motility, Vol. 1. LC 82-11567. (Molecular Biology Ser.). Date not set. price not set (ISBN 0-12-673001-6); price not set Vol. 2 (ISBN 0-12-673002-4). Acad Pr.

Strachey, Alix, tr. see Freud, Sigmund.

Strachey, Barbara. Remarkable Relations: The Story of the Pearsall Smith Women. LC 82-8429. (Illus.). 370p. 1982. 15.95 (ISBN 0-87663-396-3). Universe.

Strachey, C., jt. auth. see Milne, R.

Strachey, Giles L. Portraits in Miniature & Other Essays by Lytton Strachey. LC 77-10347. 1977. Repr. of 1931 ed. lib. bdg. 19.00x (ISBN 0-8371-9823-2, STPM). Greenwood.

Strachey, James, ed. see Freud, Sigmund.

Strachey, James, ed. & tr. see Freud, Sigmund.

Strachey, James, tr. see Freud, Sigmund.

Strachey, Lytton. Eminent Victorians. 1969. pap. 4.50 (ISBN 0-15-628697-1, Harv). HarBraceJ.

--The Shorter Strachey: Selected Essays of Lytton Strachey. Holroyd, Michael & Levy, Paul, eds. (Illus.). 1980. 19.95x (ISBN 0-19-212211-8). Oxford U Pr.

Strachey, Ray. The Cause: A Short History of the Women's Movement in Great Britain. (Illus.). 432p. 1983. pap. 8.95 (ISBN 0-86068-042-8, Virago Pr). Merrimack Bk Serv.

Strachey, Richard. A Strachey Boy. Strachey, Simonette, ed. 153p. 1981. 14.95 (ISBN 0-7206-0571-7, Pub. by Owen England). State Mutual Bk.

Strachey, Simonette, ed. see Strachey, Richard.

Strachey, William. Lawes Divine, Morall & Martiall, Etc: For the Colony in Virginea Britannia. Flaherty, David H., ed. LC 78-76185. (Jamestown Documents Ser). 160p. (Orig.). 1969. pap. 2.95 (ISBN 0-8139-0271-1). U Pr of Va.

Strachey, William & Jourdain, Sylvester. A Voyage to Virginia in 1609: Two Narratives, Strachey's "True Reportory" & Jourdain's "Discovery of the Bermudas". Wright, Louis B., ed. LC 64-19202. (Jamestown Documents Ser). 1964. pap. 2.95 (ISBN 0-8139-0230-4). U Pr of Va.

Strackbein, Dorothy B., jt. auth. see Strackbein, Ray.

Strackbein, Ray & Strackbein, Dorothy B. Computers & Data Processing Simplified & Self-Taught. LC 82-11664. (Simplified & Self-Taught Ser.). (Illus.). 128p. 1983. lib. bdg. 9.95 (ISBN 0-668-05553-7); pap. 4.95 (ISBN 0-668-05549-9). Arco.

Stracke, E. H. The Man Who Sold Out. (Inflation Fighters Ser.). 176p. (Orig.). 1982. pap. cancelled o.s.i. (ISBN 0-8439-0964-1, Leisure Bks). Nordon Pubns.

Strader, June. The Tide's Rise. LC 73-86776. 1973. 8.95 (ISBN 0-87716-049-X, Pub. by Moore Pub Co). F Apple.

Stradford, H. Todd. Orthopaedics. 4th ed. (Medical Examination Review Book: Vol. 13). 1976. spiral bdg. 23.00 (ISBN 0-87488-113-7). Med Exam.

Stradley, William E. Administrator's Guide to an Individualized Performance Results Curriculum. 1973. 14.95x o.p. (ISBN 0-87628-146-3). Ctr Appl Res.

Stradling, R. A. Europe & the Decline of Spain. (Early Modern Europe Today Ser.). (Illus.). 224p. 1981. text ed. 22.50x (ISBN 0-04-940061-4). Allen Unwin.

Straetz, Ralph, et al, eds. Critical Issues in Health Policy. (A Policy Studies Organization Bk.). 208p. 1981. 27.95x (ISBN 0-669-04504-7). Lexington Bks.

--Critical Perspectives & Issues in Health Policy. (Orig.). 1980. pap. 6.00 (ISBN 0-918592-42-9). Policy Studies.

Straffon, Ralph A., jt. auth. see Novick, Andrew C.

Strahan, Bradley R., ed. see Couch, Larry.

Strahan, Bradley R., ed. see Kramer, Aaron.

Strahl, John W., jt. auth. see Bauer, Dennis E.

Strahler, Arthur N. Physical Geology. 612p. 1981. text ed. 28.50 scp (ISBN 0-06-046462-3, HarpC); instr's. manual avail. (ISBN 0-06-366461-5). Har-Row.

--Principles of Physical Geology. (Illus.). 1977. text ed. 25.50 scp o.p. (ISBN 0-06-046457-7, HarpC); instructor's manual avail. o.p. (ISBN 0-06-366459-3). Har-Row.

Straight, Michael. After Long Silence. (Illus.). 1983. 17.50 (ISBN 0-393-01729-X). Norton.

Strain, John P., ed. Modern Philosophies of Education: A Book of Readings. 1970. text ed. 10.95x o.p. (ISBN 0-394-30837-9, RanC). Random.

Strain, Maurine. My Travel Log. (gr. 3-6). 1982. 4.95 (ISBN 0-86653-062-2, GA 411). Good Apple.

Strain, Philip S. Social Development of Exceptional Children. LC 82-11364. 196p. 1982. 19.95 (ISBN 0-89443-806-9). Aspen Systems.

Strain, Phillip S., et al. Teaching Exceptional Children: Assessing & Modifying Social Behavior. (Educational Psychology Ser.). 1976. 19.00 (ISBN 0-12-673450-X). Acad Pr.

Strain, Virginia S. A Place of Your Own. (Independent Living Ser.). (Illus.). 1978. pap. text ed. 7.96 (ISBN 0-07-061972-7, G); wkbk. 3.96 (ISBN 0-07-061973-5); tchr's manual 4.00 (ISBN 0-07-061974-3). McGraw.

Strait, E. N., jt. auth. see Kim, S. K.

Strait, Newton A., ed. Alphabetical List of Battles, 1754-1900. 1968. Repr. of 1905 ed. 30.00x (ISBN 0-8103-3339-2). Gale.

Strait, Raymond. Star Babies. 1980. 10.95 o.p. (ISBN 0-312-75575-9). St Martin.

Strait, Raymond & Robinson, Terry. Lanza: His Tragic Life. LC 80-17281. 208p. 1980. 10.00 o.p. (ISBN 0-13-523407-7). P-H.

Strait, Raymond, jt. auth. see Clooney, Rosemary.

Strait, Raymond, jt. auth. see Costello, Chris.

Straiton, E. C. The Horse Owner's Vet Book. rev. & updated ed. 1979. 13.41i (ISBN 0-397-01344-2). Har-Row.

Straka, Gerald M., ed. Revolution of Sixteen Eighty-Eight & the Birth of the English Political Nation: Whig Triumph or Palace Revolution. 2nd ed. (Problems in European Civilization Ser.). 1973. pap. text ed. 5.95 (ISBN 0-669-82032-6). Heath.

Straker, Phillip. Night Lust. 1982. pap. 2.95 (ISBN 0-8217-1090-7). Zebra.

Strakosch, G. R. Vertical Transportaion: Elevators & Escalators. 365p. 1967. 41.00x (ISBN 0-471-83167-0, Pub. by Wiley-Interscience). Wiley.

Stralen, D. Van & Cole, Robert. Boiling Phenomena, 2 vols. LC 78-10484. (Series in Thermal & Fluids Engineering). (Illus.). 1979. Vol. 1. text ed. 45.00 (ISBN 0-07-067611-9, C); Vol. 2. text ed. 45.00 (ISBN 0-07-067612-7); Set. text ed. 97.50 (ISBN 0-07-079189-9). McGraw.

Stramm, G. W. Veterinarian Guide. 6.95 (ISBN 0-87666-402-8, AP927). TFH Pubns.

Strand, Fleur L. Physiology: A Regulatory Approach. 2nd ed. 672p. 1983. text ed. 24.95 (ISBN 0-02-417680-X). Macmillan.

Strand, Julie & Boggs, Juanita. Sing a Song of Halloween: With Communication, Arts & Nutrition Activities. (Illus.). 133p. 1982. pap. text ed. 10.95 (ISBN 0-910817-00-6). Collaborative Learn.

Strand, Kenneth A. Catholic German Bibles of the Reformation Era: The Versions of Emser, Dietenberger, Eck, & Others. (Illus.). 1982. 25.00 (ISBN 0-89039-300-1). Ann Arbor FL.

Strand, Mark, ed. Contemporary American Poet. 1971. pap. 3.50 (ISBN 0-451-62098-4, ME2098, Ment). NAL.

--Contemporary American Poets: American Poetry Since 1940. (Illus.). 1969. pap. 6.95 (ISBN 0-452-00592-2, F592, Mer). NAL.

Strand, Paul, photos by. Paul Strand. (Aperture History of Photography Ser.: Vol. 16). (Illus.). 96p. Date not set. cancelled 8.95 (ISBN 0-89381-077-0). Aperture.

Strandberg, Carl H. Aerial Discovery Manual. LC 67-19945. 249p. 1967. pap. 37.95x (ISBN 0-471-83170-0, Pub. by Wiley-Interscience). Wiley.

Strandh, Sigvard. A History of the Machine. LC 77-82279. (Illus.). 240p. 1979. 35.00 o.s.i. (ISBN 0-89479-025-0). A & W Pubs.

Strandjord, Paul E., jt. ed. see Schmer, Gottfried.

Strandness, D. E. & Sumner, David S. Hemodynamics for Surgeons. LC 75-20004. (Modern Surgical Monographs). (Illus.). 662p. 1975. 89.50 o.p. (ISBN 0-8089-0889-8). Grune.

Strang, jt. ed. see Schoenberg.

Strang, Barbara M., ed. A History of English. (University Paperback Ser.). 453p. 1970. 38.00x (ISBN 0-416-16820-5); pap. 15.95x (ISBN 0-416-80660-0). Methuen Inc.

Strang, Gerald, ed. see Schoenberg, Arnold.

Strang, Jeanne, jt. auth. see Fawcett, Hilary.

Strang, Ruth, et al. Improvement of Reading. 4th ed. (Curriculum & Methods in Education Ser.). 1967. text ed. 26.00 (ISBN 0-07-061995-6, C). McGraw.

Strang, W. Gilbert. Linear Algebra & Its Applications. 2nd ed. LC 79-53993. 1980. 27.00 (ISBN 0-12-673660-X). Acad Pr.

Strang, William A. Wisconsin's Economy in Nineteen Ninety: Our History, Our Present, Our Future. (Wisconsin Economy Studies: No. 19). (Orig.). 1982. pap. 12.50 (ISBN 0-86603-014-X). Bureau Res U Wis.

Strange, Allen. Electronic Music: Systems, Techniques & Controls. 2nd ed. 300p. 1982. pap. text ed. write for info. (ISBN 0-697-03602-2). Wm C Brown.

Strange, Edward F. Hiroshige's Woodblock Prints: A Guide. (Fine Art, History of Art Ser.). (Illus.). 336p. 1983. pap. 8.95 (ISBN 0-486-24412-1). Dover.

Strange, Florence. Rock-A-Bye Whale. LC 77-83196. (Illus.). (gr. k-4). 1977. 9.95 (ISBN 0-931644-00-3). Manzanita Pr.

Strange, Jerry, jt. auth. see Rice, Bernard.

Strange, Jerry D. & Rice, Bernard J. Analytical Geometry & Calculus: With Technical Applications. 462p. 1970. text ed. 27.95 (ISBN 0-471-83190-5). Wiley.

Strange, Jerry D., jt. auth. see Rice, B. J.

Strange, Jerry D., jt. auth. see Rice, Bernard J.

Strange, Michael, jt. auth. see Allington, Richard.

Strange, Richard Le see Le Strange, Richard.

Strange, Winifred, jt. ed. see Kavanagh, James F.

Stranger, Joyce. Joyce Stranger's Book of Hanak's Animals. (Illus.). 104p. 1976. 9.00x o.p. (ISBN 0-460-06624-2, Pub. by J. M. Dent England). Biblio Dist.

--Kym. LC 77-22613. (Illus.). 1977. 7.95 o.p. (ISBN 0-698-10854-X, Coward). Putnam Pub Group.

Stranges, Frank E. Nazi UFO Secrets & Bases Exposed. 34p. 1982. pap. 2.95 (ISBN 0-686-37108-9). Intl Evang.

--Saucerama. 5th ed. (Illus.). 4.50 (ISBN 0-686-20563-4). Intl Evang.

Strangio, Christopher E. Digital Electronics: Fundamental Concepts & Applications. (Illus.). 1980. text ed. 29.95 (ISBN 0-13-212100-X). P-H.

Strank, R. H. Management Principles & Practice. (Studies in Cybernetics: Vol. 3). 150p. 1982. write for info. Gordon.

Stranks, D. R., et al. Chemistry: A Structural View. LC 74-31783. 500p. 1975. 41.50 (ISBN 0-521-20707-X); pap. 24.95 (ISBN 0-521-09928-5). Cambridge U Pr.

Stransky, Thomas F., jt. auth. see Henry, Patrick.

Stransky, Thomas F., jt. ed. see Anderson, Gerald H.

Stransky, Thomas F., ed. see Vatican Council Two.

Strapac, Joseph A. Western Pacific's Diesel Years. LC 80-68133. (An Overland Railbook Ser.). (Illus.). 208p. 1980. pap. 18.50 (ISBN 0-916160-08-4). G R Cockle.

Strasberg, Lee, ed. Famous American Plays of the Nineteen Fifties. Incl. Camino Real. Williams, Tennessee; Autumn Garden. Hellman, Lillian; Tea & Sympathy. Anderson, Robert; Zoo Story. Albee, Edward; Hatful of Rain. Gazzo, Michael. (American Drama Ser). pap. 3.50 (ISBN 0-440-32491-2, LE). Dell.

Strasberg, Susan. Bittersweet. 1980. 10.95 (ISBN 0-399-12447-0). Putnam Pub Group.

Strassberg, Richard E. The World of K'ung Shang-Jen: A Man of Letters in Early Ch'ing China. 520p. 1983. text ed. 25.00x (ISBN 0-231-05530-7). Columbia U Pr.

Strassels, Paul. Money in Your Pocket: How to Cut Your Taxes to the Legal Limit. LC 82-45274. 168p. 1982. pap. 6.95 (ISBN 0-385-18236-8, Dolp). Doubleday.

Strassels, Paul N. Money in Your Pocket: Using the New Reagan Tax Laws. 176p. 1981. 9.95 (ISBN 0-89893-508-3). CDP.

Strasser, Alex. The Work of the Science Film Maker. (Library of Film & Television Practice). (Illus.). 328p. 1972. 22.95 o.s.i. (ISBN 0-240-50742-8). Focal Pr.

Strasser, Daniel. The Finances of Europe. LC 77-24408. (Praeger Special Studies). 1977. 36.95 o.p. (ISBN 0-03-022386-5). Praeger.

Strasser, Federico. Metal Stamping Plant Productivity Handbook. (Illus.). 300p. 1983. 29.95 (ISBN 0-8311-1147-X). Indus Pr.

Strasser, Marland K., jt. auth. see Aaron, James E.

Strasser, Maryland K. & Aaron, James. Fundamentals of Safety Education. 3rd ed. 498p. 1981. text ed. 22.95 (ISBN 0-02-417960-4). Macmillan.

Strasser, Todd. Angel Dust Blues. LC 78-31735. 1979. 9.95 (ISBN 0-698-20485-9, Coward). Putnam Pub Group.

--Friends till the End: A Novel. LC 80-68738. 192p. (YA) (gr. 8-12). 1981. 9.95 o.s.i. (ISBN 0-440-02750-0). Delacorte.

--Rock 'n' Roll Nights. (YA) (gr. 7-12). 1983. pap. 2.50 (ISBN 0-440-97318-X, LFL). Dell.

--Workin' for Peanuts. LC 82-14070. 192p. 1983. 12.95 (ISBN 0-440-09401-1). Delacorte.

Strate, James W., jt. auth. see Christiansen, Larry K.

Strate, Jeffrey T. Post-Military Coup Strategy in Uganda: Amin's Early Attempts to Consolidate Political Support in Africa. LC 73-620094. (Papers in International Studies: Africa: No. 18). (Illus.). 1973. pap. 4.50 (ISBN 0-89680-051-2, Ohio U Ctr Intl). Ohio U Pr.

Stratemeyer, Florence, et al. Developing a Curriculum for Modern Living. 2nd ed. LC 57-11371. 1957. text ed. 15.95x (ISBN 0-8077-2221-9). Tchrs Coll.

Stratemeyer Syndicate. Nancy Drew & the Hardy Boys Meet Dracula. Duenewald, Doris, ed. LC 78-52863. (Elephant Books Ser.). (Illus.). (gr. 3-6). 1978. 3.95 o.s.i. (ISBN 0-448-16196-6, G&D). Putnam Pub Group.

Straten, Charles A. Ver see Ver Straten, Charles A.

Stratford, Alan. Airports & the Environment. LC 74-82530. 1975. 19.95 o.p. (ISBN 0-312-01540-2). St Martin.

Stratford, H. Alan. Air Transport Economics in the Supersonic Era. 2nd, new ed. LC 72-84866. 1973. 22.50 o.p. (ISBN 0-312-01610-7). St Martin.

Stratford, Philip. Olive: A Dog - un Chien. (Mini Books for Mini Hands Ser.). (Illus., Fr & Eng., Eng., Fr.). (gr. k-3). 1979. 1.95 (ISBN 0-912766-27-1); pap. 0.79 (ISBN 0-686-86799-8). Tundra Bks.

Strathcarren. Motoring for Pleasure. 14.50x (ISBN 0-392-01637-0, SpS). Sportshelf.

Strathern, Andrew. Rope of Moka. 27.50 o.p. (ISBN 0-521-07987-X); pap. 12.95 (ISBN 0-521-09957-9). Cambridge U Pr.

Strathern, Andrew, ed. Inequalities in New Guinea Highlands Societies. LC 82-4203. (Cambridge Papers in Social Anthropology: No. 11). (Illus.). 224p. 1983. 37.50 (ISBN 0-521-24489-7). Cambridge U Pr.

Strathern, Jeffery N., et al, eds. The Molecular Biology of the Yeast Saccharomyces: Metabolism & Gene Expression. LC 81-68203. (Cold Spring Harbor Monograph: Vol. 11B). 400p. 1982. 75.00x (ISBN 0-87969-149-2). Cold Spring Harbor.

Strathern, Marilyn. Kinship at the Core: An Anthropology of Elmdon, a Village in North-West Essex. LC 80-40550. (Illus.). 336p. 1981. 44.50 (ISBN 0-521-23360-7). Cambridge U Pr.

Strathern, Marilyn, jt. ed. see MacCormack, Carol.

Stratman, Carl J. Bibliography of English Printed Tragedy, Fifteen Sixty-Five to Nineteen Hundred. LC 66-19720. 836p. 1966. 17.50x o.p. (ISBN 0-8093-0230-6). S Ill U Pr.

--Britain's Theatrical Periodicals, 1720-1967: A Bibliography. 2nd rev. ed. LC 72-134260. Orig. Title: British Dramatic Periodicals, 1720-1960. 160p. 1972. 20.00 (ISBN 0-87104-034-4). NY Pub Lib.

--Dramatic Play Lists: 1591-1963. 1966. pap. 5.00 o.p. (ISBN 0-87104-065-4). NY Pub Lib.

Stratman, Chrysostomos H. & Makrakis, Apostolos. The Roman Rite in Orthodoxy, Part I: Additional Testimonies, Pt. II. 62p. 1957. pap. 1.00x (ISBN 0-938366-38-6). Orthodox Chr.

Stratman, Gary D. Pastoral Preaching: Timeless Truth for Changing Needs. 112p. (Orig.). 1983. pap. 6.95 (ISBN 0-687-30139-4). Abingdon.

Stratmann, William C. & Ullman, Ralph. Evaluating Hospital-Based Ambulatory Care: A Case Study. LC 77-11403. 192p. 1980. 26.95x (ISBN 0-669-02096-6). Lexington Bks.

Straton, George D. Theistic Faith for Our Time: An Introduction to the Process Philosophies of Royce & Whitehead. LC 78-65429. 1978. pap. text ed. 12.75 (ISBN 0-8191-0661-5). U Pr of Amer.

Stratonovich, R. L. Topics in the Theory of Random Noise, 2 vols. (Mathematics & Its Applications Ser.). 1963-67. Set. 113.00 (ISBN 0-677-00800-7); Vol. 1, 306p. 65.00x (ISBN 0-677-00780-9); Vol. 2, 344p. 68.00x (ISBN 0-677-00790-6). Gordon.

Stratton, Alan. The Peddlers. 450p. 1982. 13.95 (ISBN 0-531-09875-3). Watts.

Stratton, Andrew. Energy & Feedstocks in the Chemical Industry. 320p. 1981. 89.95 (ISBN 0-470-27396-8). Halsted Pr.

Stratton, Carol, jt. auth. see Scott, Miriam M.

Stratton, Clarence. Handbook of English. LC 74-19222. 1975. Repr. of 1940 ed. 45.00x (ISBN 0-8103-4112-3). Gale.

Stratton, Craig. The Bio-Imagery Method of Breast Enlargement & Waist Reduction. 251p. 1982. 12.95 (ISBN 0-943154-00-6). Ad-Images Pub.

Stratton, Donald B. Neurophysiology. 368p. Date not set. text ed. 24.95 (ISBN 0-07-062151-9). McGraw.

Stratton, Joanna. Pioneer Women. 1982. pap. 8.50 (ISBN 0-671-44748-3, Touchstone Bks). S&S.

Stratton, John, jt. auth. see Montgomery, Michael.

Stratton, John R., jt. auth. see Leger, Robert G.

Stratton, Julius A. Electromagnetic Theory. (International Series in Pure & Applied Physics). (Illus.). 1941. text ed. 44.00 (ISBN 0-07-062150-0, C). McGraw.

Stratton, Peter. Psychobiology of the Human Newborn. LC 81-14756. (Developmental Psychology Ser.). 456p. 1982. 54.95 (ISBN 0-471-10093-5, Pub. by Wiley-Interscience). Wiley.

Stratton, Porter A. Territorial Press of New Mexico, 1834-1912. LC 78-78556. 1969. 15.00x o.p. (ISBN 0-8263-0141-X). U of NM Pr.

Stratton, R. B. Captivity of the Oatman Girls. LC 81-18247. (Classics of the Old West Ser.). lib. bdg. 17.28 (ISBN 0-8094-3991-3). Silver.

Stratton, Rebecca. La Magie D'Une Voix. (Collection Harlequin). 192p. 1983. pap. 1.95 (ISBN 0-373-49320-7). Harlequin Bks.

--The Man From Nowhere. (Harlequin Romances Ser.). 192p. 1983. pap. 1.75 (ISBN 0-373-02543-2). Harlequin Bks.

Stratton, Richard, jt. auth. see Vaughan, Linda K.

Stratton, Richard F. Beginning with Snakes. (Illus.). 96p. 4.95 (ISBN 0-87666-934-8). TFH Pubns.

--The Book of the American Pit Bull Terrier. (Illus.). 352p. 29.95 (ISBN 0-87666-734-5, H-1024). TFH Pubns.

--This Is the American Pit Bull Terrier. (Illus.). 1976. 14.95 (ISBN 0-87666-660-8, PS-613). TFH Pubns.

Stratton, Robert, jt. auth. see Rost, Michael.

Stratton, Robert K., jt. auth. see Rost, Michael A.

Stratton, Stephen S., jt. auth. see Brown, James D.

Stratton-Porter, Gene. Girl of the Limberlost. 4.95 o.p. (ISBN 0-448-01243-X, G&D). Putnam Pub Group.

Straub, Calvin C. The Man-Made Environment. 248p. 1982. pap. text ed. 14.95 (ISBN 0-8403-2903-2). Kendall-Hunt.

Straub, Joseph T. & Kossen, Stan. Introduction to Business. 672p. 1983. text ed. 22.95x (ISBN 0-534-01353-8). Kent Pub Co.

Straub, P. A., jt. auth. see Heilbronner, E.

Straub, Peter. Floating Dragon. 1983. 15.95 (ISBN 0-399-12772-0). Putnam Pub Group.

--Floating Dragon. 578p. 1982. deluxe ed. 50.00 signed (ISBN 0-934438-68-4). Underwood-Miller.

--The General's Wife. (Illus.). 128p. 1983. 25.00 (ISBN 0-937986-54-2). D M Grant.

--Ghost Story. LC 78-27120. 1979. 10.95 (ISBN 0-698-10959-7, Pub. by Coward). Putnam.

--If You Could See Me Now. LC 76-57730. 320p. 1977. 8.95 (ISBN 0-698-10817-5, Coward). Putnam Pub Group.

--Shadowland. 400p. 1980. 12.95 (ISBN 0-698-11045-5, Coward). Putnam Pub Group.

Straub, W., ed. Developments in Opthalmology, Vol. 6: Diagnostic Techniques & Clinical Questions. (Illus.). viii, 140p. 1982. 69.00 (ISBN 3-8055-3431-0). S Karger.

--Turning Points in Cararact Formation, Syndromes & Retinoblastoma. (Developments in Ophthalmology: Vol. 7). (Illus.). viii, 100p. 1982. 56.50 (ISBN 3-8055-3564-3). S Karger.

Straub, William F. The Lifetime Sports-Oriented Physical Education Program. (Illus.). 208p. 1976. ref. ed. 15.95x (ISBN 0-13-536599-6). P-H.

Strauch, Ralph E. The Reality Illusion. LC 82-42705. (Illus.). 230p. (Orig.). 1983. pap. 6.95 (ISBN 0-8356-0571-X, Quest). Theos Pub Hse.

Straughan, B. Instability Non-Existence & the Weighted Energy Method in Fluid Dynamics & Related Theories. (Research Notes in Mathematics Ser.: No. 74). 120p. 1982. pap. text ed. 18.95 (ISBN 0-273-08564-6). Pitman Pub MA.

Straughan, B. P. & Walker, S., eds. Spectroscopy, 3 vols. 2nd ed. Vol. 1. pap. 19.95x (ISBN 0-412-13350-4, Pub by Chapman & Hall England); Vol. 2. pap. 19.95x (ISBN 0-412-13370-9); Vol. 3. pap. 19.95x (ISBN 0-412-13390-3). Methuen Inc.

Straughan, Roger. Can We Teach Children to Be Good? Introductory Studies in the Philosophy of Education. 128p. 1982. text ed. 19.50x (ISBN 0-04-370120-5); pap. text ed. 7.50x (ISBN 0-04-370121-3). Allen Unwin.

Straughen, A., jt. auth. see Slemon, G. R.

Straughen, Alan, jt. auth. see Dewan, Shashi.

Straumanis, Alfreds. Baltic Drama: A Handbook & Bibliography. LC 81-50710. 720p. 1981. 36.50 (ISBN 0-917974-63-8). Waveland Pr.

Straumanis, Alfreds, ed. The Golden Steed: Seven Baltic Plays. LC 78-59271. (Ethnic Heritage Ser.). (Illus.). 1979. 16.50 o.p. (ISBN 0-917974-17-4). Waveland Pr.

Straus, Erwin. Man, Time & World: The Anthropological Psychology of Erwin Straus. Moss, Donald, tr. from Ger. 185p. 1982. text ed. 15.50x (ISBN 0-8207-0159-9, 90007). Duquesne.

Straus, Erwin, ed. see Conference on Phenomenology Pure & Applied, 5th, Lexington, 1972.

Straus, Erwin W. On Obsession: A Clinical & Methodological Study. Repr. of 1948 ed. 14.00 (ISBN 0-384-58630-9). Johnson Repr.

Straus, Marc. Lung Cancer: Clinical Diagnosis & Treatment. Date not set. price not set (ISBN 0-8089-1487-1). Grune.

Straus, Murray, et al. Behind Closed Doors: Violence in the American Family. LC 80-2990. (Illus.). 312p. 1981. pap. 5.95 (ISBN 0-385-14260-9, Anch). Doubleday.

Straus, Ralph. Unspeakable Curll: Being Some Account of Edmund Curll, Bookseller. LC 77-117504. (English Book Trade). (Illus.). Repr. of 1927 ed. 22.50x o.p. (ISBN 0-678-00649-0). Kelley.

Straus, Robert. Medical Care For Seamen. 1950. text ed. 39.50x (ISBN 0-686-83622-7). Elliots Bks.

Strausbaugh, P. D. & Core, Earl L. Flora of West Virginia. LC 78-1146. (Illus.). 1079p. 1979. 25.00 (ISBN 0-89092-010-9). Seneca Bks.

Strausfeld, C., tr. see Bassler, U.

Strauss. Where Did the Justice Go? 1969. 6.95 (ISBN 0-87645-003-6). Gambit.

Strauss & Kaufman. Handbook for Chemical Technicians. new ed. LC 76-10459. (Handbook Ser.). (Illus.). 1976. 32.50 (ISBN 0-07-062164-0, P&RB). McGraw.

Strauss, Albrecht, ed. see Johnson, Samuel.

Strauss, Anselm, et al. Psychiatric Ideologies & Institutions. LC 80-20225. 418p. 1981. cancelled 39.95 (ISBN 0-87855-361-4); pap. 14.95 (ISBN 0-87855-785-7). Transaction Bks.

Strauss, Anselm L. Chronic Illness & the Quality of Life. LC 75-2458. 160p. 1975. pap. text ed. 13.50 (ISBN 0-8016-4837-8). Mosby.

Strauss, Anselm L., jt. auth. see Schatzman, Leonard.

Strauss, David. Menace in the West: The Rise of French Anti-Americanism in Modern Times. LC 77-94748. (Contributions in American Studies: No. 40). 1978. lib. bdg. 29.95x (ISBN 0-313-20316-4, SMW/). Greenwood.

Strauss, Eric. Irish Nationalism & British Democracy. LC 75-8727. 307p. 1975. Repr. of 1951 ed. lib. bdg. 18.25x (ISBN 0-8371-8046-5, STINA). Greenwood.

Strauss, Eric S. & Karpel, Mark A. Family Evaluation. 1983. 26.95 (ISBN 0-89876-038-0). Gardner Pr.

Strauss, Erwin S. The Case Against a Liberatarian Political Party. 1980. pap. 2.25 (ISBN 0-686-29514-5). Loompanics.

Strauss, G., jt. auth. see Sayles, Leonard.

Strauss, Gail, jt. auth. see Relis, Nurie.

Strauss, Gary, jt. auth. see Barber, Cyril.

Strauss, Gary, ed. see Barber, Cyril.

Strauss, Gary H., jt. auth. see Barber, Cyril J.

Strauss, George & Sayles, Leonard R. Personnel: The Human Problem of Management. 4th ed. 1980. text ed. 23.95 (ISBN 0-13-657809-8). P-H.

Strauss, H. William & Pitt, Bertram. Cardiovascular Nuclear Medicine. 2nd ed. LC 79-18410. (Illus.). 430p. 1979. text ed. 67.50 (ISBN 0-8016-2409-6). Mosby.

Strauss, Herbert A. Archival Resources. (Jewish Immigrants of the Nazi Period in the USA: Vol. 1). 1979. 55.00x (ISBN 0-89664-027-2, Pub. by K G Saur). Gale.

Strauss, James D. Job Shattering of Silence. LC 77-155412. (The Bible Study Textbook Ser.). (Illus.). 1976. 14.30 o.s.i. (ISBN 0-89900-015-0). College Pr Pub.

Strauss, Jennifer, jt. auth. see Bragg, Gordon M.

Strauss, Joyce. How Does It Feel...? LC 80-29673. (Illus.). 96p. 1981. pap. 9.95x (ISBN 0-89885-048-7). Human Sci Pr.

--Imagine That...! LC 82-1089. 1983. 9.95 (ISBN 0-89885-128-9). Human Sci Pr.

Strauss, L. Wave Generation & Shaping. 2nd ed. (Electrical & Electronic Engineering Ser.). 1970. text ed. 42.50 (ISBN 0-07-062161-6, C). McGraw.

Strauss, Lawrence. Electronic Marketing: Emerging TV & Computer Channels for Interactive Home Shopping. 160p. 1983. 34.95 (ISBN 0-86729-023-4). Knowledge Indus.

--Home Video & Broadcasting: The Fight for Position, 1981-86. 1981. spiral 795.00 (ISBN 0-686-42877-3). Knowledge Indus.

Strauss, Lehman. John, Epistles of. LC 62-17542. 1962. pap. 3.25 (ISBN 0-87213-821-6). Loizeaux.

--Sense & Nonsense about Prayer. 1976. pap. 4.95 (ISBN 0-8024-7702-X). Moody.
--We Live Forever. 1947. pap. 2.50 (ISBN 0-87213-830-5). Loizeaux.
Strauss, Leo. Liberalism, Ancient & Modern. LC 68-54139. 1968. 15.00x o.s.i. (ISBN 0-465-03928-6). Basic.
--Spinoza's Critique of Religion. LC 65-10948. 1962. 14.00x o.p. (ISBN 0-8052-3246-X). Schocken.
--What Is Political Philosophy? LC 73-1408. 315p. 1973. Repr. of 1959 ed. lib. bdg. 25.00x (ISBN 0-8371-6802-3, STPP). Greenwood.
Strauss, Lucille J., et al. Scientific & Technical Libraries: Their Organization & Administration. 2nd ed. LC 71-173679. 450p. 1972. 39.95 (ISBN 0-471-83312-6, Pub. by Wiley-Interscience). Wiley.
Strauss, P. S., jt. auth. see Fiore, M. V.
Strauss, Raymond, jt. auth. see Minnick, John.
Strauss, Richard. Gane la Batalla de Su Mente. Carrodeguas, Andy & Marosi, Esteban, eds. Taracido, Frank, tr. from Eng. Orig. Title: Win the Battle for Your Mind. 167p. (Span.). 1982. pap. 2.00 (ISBN 0-8297-1262-3). Life Pubs Intl.
--The Metropolitan Opera Classics Library: Der Rosenkavalier. 16.95 (ISBN 0-316-56834-1); 75.00 (ISBN 0-316-56837-6). Little.
--Der Rosenkavalier. (The Metropolitan Opera Classics Library). cancelled (ISBN 0-686-97611-8, Pub. by Reader's Digest) (ISBN 0-686-97612-6). Little.
Strauss, Richard & Von Hofmannsthal, Hugo. The Correspondence Between Richard Strauss & Hugo Von Hofmannsthal. Hammelmann, Hanns & Osers, Ewald, trs. LC 80-40072. 576p. 1981. 67.50 (ISBN 0-521-23476-X); pap. 19.95 (ISBN 0-521-29911-X). Cambridge U Pr.
Strauss, Richard L. Hijos Confiados y Como Crecen. 192p. Date not set. 2.50 (ISBN 0-88113-308-6). Edit Betania.
--Marriage Is for Love. pap. 3.95 (ISBN 0-8423-4181-1). Tyndale.
--Win the Battle for Your Mind. 132p. 1980. pap. 4.50 (ISBN 0-89693-003-3). Victor Bks.
Strauss, Ruby G. & Schuller, Ahuva. I Can Read Hebrew. (Illus.). 64p. (gr. 1-2). 1982. 2.50x (ISBN 0-87441-358-3). Behrman.
Strauss, Sheryl, ed. Security Problems in a Modern Society. (Illus.). 314p. 1980. text ed. 10.95 (ISBN 0-409-95079-3). Butterworth.
Strauss, Steven. Your Prescription & You. 3rd ed. LC 77-26544. 1978. 2.95 o.p. (ISBN 0-686-01087-6). IMS Pr.
--Your Prescription & You. 4th ed. 1980. pap. 2.95 o.p. (ISBN 0-933916-01-9). IMS Pr.
Strauss, Steven, ed. Your Prescription & You. 5th ed. 1982. pap. 3.50 (ISBN 0-933916-07-8). IMS Pr.
Strauss, Sylvia. Traitors to the Masculine Cause: The Men's Campaigns for Women's Rights. LC 81-20299. (Contributions in Women's Studies: No. 35). (Illus.). 370p. 1982. lib. bdg. 35.00 (ISBN 0-313-22238-X, STM/). Greenwood.
Strauss, Walter L. The Complete Drawings of Albrecht Durer: A Complete Catalogue Raisonne, 6 vols. LC 73-80442. (Illus.). Set. 540.00 (ISBN 0-913870-00-5). Abaris Bks.
Strauss, Walter L., ed. Intaglio Prints of Albrecht Durer: Engravings, Etchings, & Drypoints. LC 75-1121. viii, 352p. 1975. lib. bdg. 40.00 (ISBN 0-87920-001-4). Kennedy Gall.
Strauss, Walter L., ed. see Durer, Albrecht.
Strauss, Walter L., tr. see Strieder, P.
Strauss, Werner. Air Pollution Control, 3 pts. LC 69-18013. (Environmental Science & Technology Ser). 1971-72. Pt. I, 457. 40.00 o.p. (ISBN 0-471-83320-7); Pt. 2, 300. o.p 35.95 (ISBN 0-471-83319-3); Pt. 3. 70.00 (ISBN 0-471-83323-1, Pub by Wiley-Interscience). Wiley.
Strausz, Otto P. & Lown, Elizabeth M., eds. Oil Sand & Oil Shale Chemistry. LC 78-19168. (Illus.). 396p. 1978. pap. 37.80x (ISBN 0-89573-102-9). Verlag Chemie.
Stravinskas, Peter M. Catholic Education: A New Dawn? LC 77-71022. (Orig.). 1977. pap. 1.75 o.p. (ISBN 0-8189-1143-3, 143, Pub. by Alba Bks). Alba.
Stravinsky, Igor & Craft, Robert. Dialogues. (Illus.). 152p. pap. 6.95 (ISBN 0-520-04650-1, CAL 548). U of Cal Pr.
Straw, Dorothy, jt. ed. see Kelley, Louise H.
Straw, Stanley B., jt. ed. see Froese, Victor.
Straw Dog, jt. auth. see Heinz, Cecilia.
Strawn, John, jt. auth. see Ramsay, Jack.
Strawser, Robert H., jt. auth. see Francia, Arthur J.
Strawson, John. El Alamein: Desert Victory. 1983. 22.50x (ISBN 0-460-04422-2, Pub. by J. M. Dent England). Biblio Dist.
Strawson, P. F. The Bounds of Sense: An Essay on Kant's Critique of Pure Reason. 296p. 1966. 24.00x (ISBN 0-416-29100-7); pap. 11.50x (ISBN 0-416-83560-0). Methuen Inc.
--Individuals: An Essay in Descriptive Metaphysics. 1964. pap. 11.95x (ISBN 0-416-68310-X). Methuen Inc.
--Logico-Linguistic Papers. 1974. pap. 12.95x (ISBN 0-416-70300-3). Methuen Inc.
Strawson, P. F., ed. Philosophical Logic. (Oxford Readings in Philosophy Ser). (Orig.). 1967. pap. 8.95x (ISBN 0-19-500375-6). Oxford U Pr.
Strayer, Joseph R. Western Europe in the Middle Ages: A Short History. 3rd ed. 1982. pap. text ed. 13.50x (ISBN 0-673-16052-1). Scott F.
Strayer, Joseph R. & Gatzke, Hans W. The Mainstream of Civilization: Two-Vol. Edition. 3rd ed. Incl. Vol. 1. To 1715. 499p. pap. text ed. (ISBN 0-15-551564-0); Vol. 2. Since 1660. 392p. pap. text ed. (ISBN 0-15-551565-9). 1979. pap. text ed. 16.95 ea. (HC); test manual avail. (ISBN 0-15-551563-2). HarBraceJ.
Strayer, Joseph R. & Munro, Dana C. The Middle Ages, Three Ninety-Five to Fifteen Hundred. 5th ed. 1970. text ed. 20.95x (ISBN 0-673-16252-4). Scott F.
Strayer, Joseph R., ed. Dictionary of the Middle Ages, Vol. 1. LC 82-5904. 1982. lib. bdg. 70.00 (ISBN 0-684-16760-3). Scribner.
Streaborg, L. Twelve Melodious Studies for Piano, Op. 63. Seifert, Hans T., ed. (Carl Fischer Music Library: No. 363). 25p. Date not set. pap. 3.25 (ISBN 0-8258-0113-3, L363). Fischer Inc NY.
Streater, R. A. & Greenman, D., eds. Jane's Merchant Ships, 1982-1983. (Jane's Yearbooks). (Illus.). 1000p. 1982. 140.00 (ISBN 0-86720-589-X). Sci Bks Intl.
Streater, Thomas. Bibliography of Texas, Seventeen Ninety-Five to Eighteen Forty-Five. rev. 2nd ed. Hanna, Archibald, ed. 584p. 1983. 225.00 (ISBN 0-89235-060-1). Res Pubns Conn.
Streatfeild, Noel. Ballet Shoes. (gr. 4-6). 1979. pap. 2.75 (ISBN 0-440-41508-X, YB). Dell.
--Circus Shoes. 1981. lib. bdg. 14.95 (ISBN 0-8398-2625-7, Gregg). G K Hall.
--Dancing Shoes. (gr. k-6). 1980. pap. 2.75 (ISBN 0-440-42289-2, YB). Dell.
Streatfield, Noel. Skating Shoes. (Orig.). (gr. 5 up). 1982. pap. 2.75 (ISBN 0-440-47731-X, YB). Dell.
--Theater Shoes. (gr. k-6). 1983. pap. 2.95 (ISBN 0-440-48791-9, YB). Dell.
Strebeck, Mary. Single But Not Alone. (Illus.). 80p. (Orig.). 1982. pap. 4.95 (ISBN 0-939298-16-3, 163). J M Prods.
Strecker, Matthias. Rock Art of East Mexico & Central America: An Annotated Bibliography. (Monograph: X). (Orig.). 1979. pap. 7.00 (ISBN 0-917956-07-9). UCLA Arch.
--Rock Art of East Mexico & Central America: An Annotated Bibliography. 2nd ed. (Monograph X). 86p. pap. 7.00 (ISBN 0-917956-36-2). UCLA Arch.
Streel, M., et al, eds. Advances in Paleozoic Botany. 1972. Repr. 27.75 (ISBN 0-444-41080-5). Elsevier.
Streep, Norbert, jt. auth. see St. Maur, Suzan.
Street, jt. auth. see Kaye.
Street, Alfred B. Woods & Waters: Or, the Saranacs & Racket. LC 75-45369. (Illus.). 1976. Repr. of 1860 ed. 14.50 o.p. (ISBN 0-916346-18-8). Harbor Hill Bks.
Street, Alicia. The Land & People of England. LC 68-10769. (Portraits of the Nations Ser.). (Illus.). (gr. 7-9). 1969. 9.57i o.p. (ISBN 0-397-31373-X, HarpJ). Har-Row.
Street, David, ed. Innovation in Mass Education. 342p. 1969. text ed. 16.00 (ISBN 0-471-83325-8, Pub. by Wiley). Krieger.
Street, David, et al. Handbook of Contemporary Urban Life: An Examination of Urbanization, Social Organization & Metropolitan Politics. LC 78-1155. (Social & Behavioral Science Ser.). (Illus.). 1978. text ed. 38.95x (ISBN 0-87589-372-4). Jossey-Bass.
Street, Donald M., Jr. Street's Cruising Guide to the Eastern Caribbean: Venezuela, Vol. IV. (Illus.). 1981. 25.95 (ISBN 0-393-03260-4). Norton.
Street, Douglas, ed. Children's Novels & the Movies. (Ungar Film Library). (Illus.). 350p. 14.95 (ISBN 0-8044-2840-9); pap. 6.95 (ISBN 0-8044-6883-4). Ungar.
Street, Emma, ed. see Mery, Fernand.
Street, H. E. & Cockburn, W. Plant Metabolism. 2nd ed. LC 76-174629. 332p. 1972. 27.00 (ISBN 0-08-016752-7); pap. 13.25 o.p. (ISBN 0-08-016753-5). Pergamon.
Street, Howard A. A Treatise on the Doctrine of Ultra Vires. LC 81-83532. lxxxviii, 591p. 1981. Repr. of 1930 ed. lib. bdg. 65.00x (ISBN 0-912004-18-5). W W Gaunt.
Street, James H. Look Away, a Dixie Notebook. LC 75-142924. (Illus.). Repr. of 1936 ed. 17.75x (ISBN 0-8371-5950-4, Pub. by Negro U Pr). Greenwood.
Street, James H. & James, Dilmus D., eds. Technological Progress in Latin America: The Prospects for Overcoming Dependency. (Special Studies on Latin America & the Caribbean). 1979. lib. bdg. 28.50 (ISBN 0-89158-255-X). Westview.
Street, John M., jt. ed. see Fuchs, Roland J.
Street, Robert L., jt. auth. see Vennard, John K.
Street, Thomas A. The Foundation of Legal Liability: A Presentation of the Theory & Development of the Common Law, 3 vols. Helmholz, R. H. & Reams, Bernard D., Jr., eds. LC 79-56293. (Historical Writings in Law & Jurisprudence Ser.: No. 5 Bks. 5-7). 1980. Repr. of 1906 ed. Vol. 1, xxix, 500 Pgs. lib. bdg. 30.00 (ISBN 0-89941-044-8); Vol. 2, xviii, 580 Pgs. lib. bdg. 30.00 (ISBN 0-89941-054-5); Vol. 3, xi, 572 Pgs. lib. bdg. 30.00 (ISBN 0-89941-055-3). W S Hein.
Streeten, David H., jt. ed. see Elias, Merrill F.
Streeter, Edwin W. Great Diamonds of the World. Hatton, Joseph & Keane, A. H., eds. LC 76-78238. 1971. Repr. of 1882 ed. 37.00x (ISBN 0-8103-3624-3). Gale.
Streeter, James. Home Is Over the Mountains: The Journey of Five Black Children. LC 70-181763. (Regional American Stories). (Illus.). 64p. (gr. 3-6). 1972. PLB 6.69 (ISBN 0-8116-4256-9). Garrard.
Streeter, Sebastian F. Papers Relating to the Early History of Maryland. 315p. 1876. 15.00 (ISBN 0-686-36840-1). Md Hist.
Streeter, Victor L. Fluid Dynamics. (Aeronautical Science Ser.). 1948. text ed. 33.50 (ISBN 0-07-062179-9, C). McGraw.
--Handbook of Fluid Dynamics. 1961. 71.50 o.p. (ISBN 0-07-062178-0, P&RB). McGraw.
Streeter, Victor L. & Wylie, E. Benjamin. Fluid Mechanics. 7th ed. (Illus.). 1979. text ed. 33.95 (ISBN 0-07-062232-9, C); solutions manual 20.00 (ISBN 0-07-062233-7). McGraw.
Streeter, Victor L., jt. auth. see Wylie, E. Benjamin.
Streetman, B. Solid State Electronic Devices. 2nd ed. 1980. 30.95 (ISBN 0-13-822171-5). P-H.
Street-Porter, Janet. Scandal! (Orig.). 1983. pap. price not set (ISBN 0-440-58260-1). Dell.
Street-Porter, Tim. Interiors. (Illus.). 96p. 1981. pap. 9.95 (ISBN 0-8256-3217-X, Quick Fox). Putnam Pub Group.
Streib, Dan. Counter Force. 192p. (Orig.). 1983. pap. 2.50 (ISBN 0-449-12387-1, GM). Fawcett.
--Hawk: The Power Barons. (The Hawk Ser.: No. 3). (Orig.). pap. 1.95 o.s.i. (ISBN 0-515-05236-1). Jove Pubns.
--The Trident Hijacking. (Counterforce Ser.: No. 2). 208p. (Orig.). 1983. pap. 2.50 (ISBN 0-449-12388-X, GM). Fawcett.
Streich, Marianne, ed. see Maryland Chapter Arthritis Foundation.
Streicher, M. Reshaping Physical Education. 1970. 20.00 (ISBN 0-7190-0412-8). Manchester.
Streiff, Virginia. Classroom Language Assessment. Hayes, Curtis & Kessler, Carolyn, eds. (The Teacher Idea Ser.). 96p. (Orig.). 1983. pap. text ed. 7.95 (ISBN 0-88499-625-5). Inst Mod Lang.
Streifford, David M., ed. Selected Issues in Political Economy. 1977. pap. text ed. 8.00 (ISBN 0-8191-0047-1). U Pr of Amer.
Streika, Joseph P., ed. Literary Theory & Criticism: Essays in Honor of Rene Wellek at the Occasion of His 80th Birthday. 1983. 95.00 (ISBN 0-686-37581-5); pre-pub. 80.00 (ISBN 0-686-37582-3). P Lang Pubs.
Streiker, Lowell D. Cults: The Continuing Threat. 144p. 1983. pap. 2.95 (ISBN 0-687-10069-0). Abingdon.
Streit, Fred. Mainstreaming: Five In-Service Training Sessions. 55p. 1982. pap. 19.95 (ISBN 0-940756-01-3). Essence Pubns.
Streit, Fred, ed. Research Review Nineteen Sixty-Six to Nineteen Eighty: Adolescent Problems. 71p. 1980. pap. 15.00 (ISBN 0-940756-00-5). Essence Pubns.
Streit, Jacob. And There Was Light. Piening, Ekkehard, tr. from Ger. (Illus.). 112p. (gr. 3-4). 1976. pap. 11.00 (ISBN 0-88010-034-6, Pub. by Verlag Walter Keller Switzerland). Anthroposophic.
Streit, Jocob. Animal Stories. Piening, Jacob, tr. from Ger. 36p. (gr. 3-5). 1974. pap. 5.95 (ISBN 0-88010-035-4, Pub. by Verlag Walter Keller Switzerland). Anthroposophic.
Streit, Lois B., jt. auth. see Pall, Michael L.
Streitmatter & Fiore. Microprocessors: Theory & Application. (Illus.). 1979. text ed. 20.95 o.p. (ISBN 0-8359-4371-2); students manual avail. o.p. (ISBN 0-8359-4372-0). Reston.
Streitmatter, Gene. Microprocessor Software: Programming Concepts & Techniques. (Illus.). 400p. 1981. text ed. 20.95 (ISBN 0-8359-4375-5); instructer's manual avail. (ISBN 0-8359-4376-3). Reston.
Streitmatter, Gene & Fiori, Vito. Microprocessor: Theory & Application. 2nd ed. 1980. text ed. 22.95 (ISBN 0-8359-4378-X); solutions manual avail. (ISBN 0-8359-4379-8). Reston.
Streitmatter, Gene & Goldstein, Larry J. Pet CBM: An Introduction to Programming & Applications. (Illus.). 320p. 1983. text ed. 19.95 (ISBN 0-89303-205-0); pap. 14.95 (ISBN 0-89303-204-2). R J Brady.
Streitwiesser & Heathcock. Introduction to Organic Chemistry. 2nd ed. 1981. 32.50 (ISBN 0-02-418050-5). Macmillan.
Strejc, Vladimir. State Space Theory of Discrete Linear Control. LC 79-991. 426p. 1981. 41.00x (ISBN 0-471-27594-8, Pub. by Wiley-Interscience). Wiley.
Strelich, Thomas, Sr. & Strelich, Virginia. The New Basics. (gr. 3-6). 1982. pap. text ed. write for info. (Sch Div). A-W.
Strelich, Virginia, jt. auth. see Strelich, Thomas, Sr.
Strelka, Joseph P., ed. Literary Criticism & Philosophy. LC 82-10137. (Yearbook of Comparative Criticism Ser.: Vol. X). 288p. 1983. text ed. 17.95x (ISBN 0-271-00324-3). Pa St U Pr.
--Patterns of Literary Style. LC 76-123870. (Yearbook of Comparative Criticism, Vol. 3). (Illus.). 1970. 17.95x (ISBN 0-271-00124-0). Pa St U Pr.
--The Personality of the Critic. LC 73-6880. (Yearbook of Comparative Criticism Ser., Vol. 6). 220p. 1973. 17.95x (ISBN 0-271-01120-3). Pa St U Pr.
--Perspectives in Literary Symbolism. LC 67-27116. (Yearbook of Comparative Criticism, Vol. 1). (Illus.). 1968. 17.95x (ISBN 0-271-73137-0). Pa St U Pr.
--Problems of Literary Evaluation. LC 68-56136. (Yearbook of Comparative Criticism, Vol. 2). 1969. 17.95x (ISBN 0-271-00085-6). Pa St U Pr.
Strelka, Joseph P., ed. see Elstun, Esther N.
Strelkova, G. V., tr. see Lazarev, Viktor N.
Strelzoff, Samuel. Technology & Manufacture of Ammonia. LC 80-29078. 283p. 1981. 73.00 (ISBN 0-471-02722-7, Pub. by Wiley-Interscience Ser.). Wiley.
Stremlau, John J. The Foreign Policy priorities of Third World States. (WVSS in International Relations Ser.). 180p. (Orig.). 1982. lib. bdg. 15.00 (ISBN 0-86531-374-1); pap. 8.00 (ISBN 0-86531-383-0). Westview.
Stremlers, Ferrel G. Introduction to Communication Systems. 2nd ed. (Engineering-Electrical Engineering Ser.). (Illus.). 640p. 1982. text ed. 32.95 (ISBN 0-201-07251-3); sol. manual avail. (ISBN 0-201-07252-1). A-W.
Stremnel, Stephen H., jt. auth. see West, William R.
Stremski, Richard. The Shaping of British Policy During the Nationalist Revolution in China. LC 80-110682. Orig. Title: Soochow University Political Science Series. 179p. 1980. text ed. 20.00x (ISBN 0-931712-02-5). Alpine Guild.
Streng, Alice. Syntax, Speech & Hearing: Applied Linguistics for Teachers of Children with Language & Hearing Disabilities. LC 72-1072. 288p. 1972. 32.50 o.p. (ISBN 0-8089-0756-5). Grune.
Streng, Frederick J., et al. Ways of Being Religious: Readings for a New Approach to Religion. (Illus.). 608p. 1973. 23.95 (ISBN 0-13-946277-5). P-H.
Streng, William P. Estate Planning: Principles, Techniques, & Materials for Planning Estates. 35.00 (ISBN 0-686-36922-X). Tax Mgmt.
--International Business Transactions Tax & Legal Handbook. (Illus.). 1977. 39.95 o.p. (ISBN 0-13-467662-9, Busn). P-H.
Strens, R. G., ed. The Physics & Chemistry of Minerals & Rocks. LC 75-6930. 697p. 1975. 149.95 (ISBN 0-471-83368-1, Pub by Wiley-Interscience). Wiley.
Stresau, Hermann. Thornton Wilder. Schutze, Frieda, tr. LC 71-149478. (Literature & Life Ser.). 1971. 11.95 (ISBN 0-8044-2844-1); pap. 4.95 (ISBN 0-8044-6884-2). Ungar.
Streshinsky, Shirley. Hers the Kingdom. 372p. 1982. 14.95 (ISBN 0-399-12576-0). Putnam Pub Group.
--Hers the Kingdom. 608p. 1983. pap. 3.75 (ISBN 0-425-06147-7). Berkley Pub.
Strete, Craig. Dreams That Burn in the Night. LC 81-43660. 192p. 1982. 10.95 (ISBN 0-385-17188-9). Doubleday.
--If All Else Fails... LC 79-7117. (Doubleday D Science Fiction Ser.). 192p. 1980. 10.95 o.p. (ISBN 0-385-15237-X). Doubleday.
Stretton, H. Capitalism, Socialism & the Environment. (Illus.). 368p. 1976. 42.50 (ISBN 0-521-21057-7); pap. 11.95x (ISBN 0-521-29025-2). Cambridge U Pr.
Stretton, R. J., jt. auth. see Dart, R. K.
Streuvels, Stijn. The Long Road. Krispyn, Egbert, ed. LC 75-44092. (International Studies & Translations Program). 1976. lib. bdg. 9.95 (ISBN 0-8057-8155-2, Twayne). G K Hall.
Streuver, Stuart. Koster: Americans in Search of Their Prehistoric Past. 1979. pap. 2.95 (ISBN 0-686-95793-8). Jefferson Natl.
Strevell, et al. Educational Programs for School Business Officials. (Research Bulletin: No. 15). pap. 1.00 o.p. (ISBN 0-685-57175-0). Assn Sch Busn.
--Preconstruction Planning for Educational Facilities. (Research Bulletin: No. 13). pap. 1.00 o.p. (ISBN 0-685-57177-7). Assn Sch Busn.
Stribling, Mary L. Art from Found Materials: Discarded & Natural: Techniques, Design Inspiration. (Illus.). 1970. pap. 5.95 o.p. (ISBN 0-517-54307-9). Crown.
Stribling, Mary Lou. Crafts from North American Indian Arts. (Arts & Crafts Ser.). (Illus.). 308p. 1975. 12.95 o.p. (ISBN 0-517-51612-8); pap. 6.95 (ISBN 0-517-51613-6). Crown.
Strich, Christian, ed. Fellini's Films: The Four Hundred Most Memorable Stills from Frederico Fellini's Fifteen & a Half Films. LC 77-2509. (Illus.). 1977. 45.00 o.p. (ISBN 0-399-12014-9). Putnam Pub Group.
Strich, Fritz. Goethe & World Literature. Sym, C. A., tr. from Ger. LC 71-138188. 1971. Repr. of 1949 ed. lib. bdg. 19.75x (ISBN 0-8371-5645-9, STGO). Greenwood.
Strichart, Stephen S., jt. ed. see Gottlieb, Jay.
Stricherz, Gregory. English Made Casual. 210p. 1980. pap. text ed. 6.50x (ISBN 0-19-581880-6). Oxford U Pr.
Strick, Anne. Injustice for All. LC 76-41405. 1977. 8.95 (ISBN 0-399-11860-8). Putnam Pub Group.
Strickberger, Monroe W. Genetics. 2nd ed. (Illus.). 880p. 1976. text ed. 26.95x (ISBN 0-02-418090-4). Macmillan.
Stricker, George, jt. ed. see Goldman, George D.

Stricker, William F. Keeping Christmas: An Edwardian-Age Memoir. (Illus.). 128p. 1981. 15.00 (ISBN 0-916144-60-7). Stemmer Hse.

Strickland. Immunoparasitology. 304p. 1982. 39.95 (ISBN 0-03-061499-6). Praeger.

Strickland, A. G. How to Get Action: Key to Successful Management. 1976. 14.95 o.p. (ISBN 0-13-407239-1, Parker). P-H.

Strickland, Albert L., jt. auth. see DeSpelder, Lynne A.

Strickland, Allyn, jt. auth. see Weiss, Leonard.

Strickland, Allyn D. Government Regulation & Business. 1981. 23.95 (ISBN 0-395-30751-1). HM.

Strickland, Alonzo J., III, jt. auth. see Scott, Charles R., Jr.

Strickland, Bernard F. & Wilkinson, Charles F., eds. Felix S. Cohen's Handbook of Federal Indian Law. 950p. 1982. 80.00 (ISBN 0-87215-413-0). Michie-Bobbs.

Strickland, C. E. & Burgess, C., eds. Health, Growth, & Heredity: G. Stanley Hall on Natural Education. LC 65-19291. (Orig.). 1965. text ed. 10.50 (ISBN 0-8077-2227-8); pap. text ed. 5.50x (ISBN 0-8077-2224-3). Tchrs Coll.

Strickland, Charles R. Recent Acquisition of Myles Standish Signature. (Pilgrim Society Notes Ser.: No. 5). 1955. 1.00 (ISBN 0-686-30049-1). Pilgrim Hall.

Strickland, Geoffrey. Stendhal: The Education of a Novelist. 276p. 1974. 47.50 (ISBN 0-521-20385-6); pap. 12.95x (ISBN 0-521-09837-8). Cambridge U Pr.

--Structuralism or Criticism? Thought on How We Read. 200p. 1981. 44.50 (ISBN 0-521-23184-1). Cambridge U Pr.

Strickland, James W. & Steichen, James B. Difficult Problems in Hand Surgery. LC 82-2230. (Illus.). 434p. 1982. text ed. 49.50 (ISBN 0-8016-4851-3). Mosby.

Strickland, Joshua. Aliens on Earth. LC 77-71532. (Illus.). (gr. 5-9). 1977. 4.95 o.p. (ISBN 0-448-12898-5, G&D); PLB 5.99 o.p. (ISBN 0-448-13416-0). Putnam Pub Group.

Strickland, R. Mack, jt. auth. see Brown, Arlen D.

Strickland, Rennard. Fire & the Spirits: Cherokee Law from Clan to Court. LC 74-15903. (Civilization of the American Indian Ser.: Vol. 133). (Illus.). 350p. 1975. 16.95 o.p. (ISBN 0-8061-1227-1). U of Okla Pr.

Strickland, Rennard, jt. auth. see Morgan, Anne H.

Strickland, Rennard, jt. auth. see Wade, Edwin L.

Strickland, Richard M. The Fertile Fjord: Plankton in Puget Sound. (A Puget Sound Bk.). (Illus.). 160p. (Orig.). 1983. pap. 8.95 (ISBN 0-295-95979-7, Pub. by Wash Sea Grant). U of Wash Pr.

Strickland, Ruth G. Language Arts in the Elementary School. 3rd ed. 1969. text ed. 16.95 o.p. (ISBN 0-669-20222-3). Heath.

Strickland, Stephen P., jt. auth. see Cater, Douglass.

Strickland, Stephen P., ed. Sponsored Research in American Universities & Colleges. 1968. 7.00 o.p. (ISBN 0-8268-1380-1). ACE.

Strickland, Walter G. Dictionary of Irish Artists, 2 vols. (Illus.). 1358p. 1969. Repr. of 1913 ed. 90.00x set (ISBN 0-7165-0602-5, Pub. by Irish Academic Pr Ireland). Biblio Dist.

Strickland, William D. & Wilder, Aldridge D., Jr. Clinical Chairside Assisting. 3rd ed. (Dental Assisting Manuals: No. 8). ix, 225p. 1980. pap. 10.00x o.p. (ISBN 0-8078-1382-6). U of NC Pr.

--Clinical Sciences. 3rd ed. (Dental Assisting Manuals: No. 7). ix, 170p. 1980. pap. 10.00 o.p. (ISBN 0-8078-1381-8). U of NC Pr.

Strickland, Winifred G. Expert Obedience Training for Dogs. 2nd rev. ed. LC 76-1875. (Illus.). 1976. 15.95 (ISBN 0-02-615020-4). Macmillan.

--Obedience Class Instruction for Dogs: The Trainer's Manual. rev. ed. 1978. 15.95 (ISBN 0-02-615010-7). Macmillan.

Strickler, George M., Jr., jt. auth. see Friedman, Joel Wm.

Strickler, Nancy E., ed. Marketing Life & Health Insurance. LC 81-83848. (FLMI Insurance Education Program Ser.). 471p. 1981. text ed. 25.00 (ISBN 0-915322-47-1). LOMA.

Strid, Arne. Wild Flowers of Mount Olympus. 1981. 125.00x (ISBN 0-686-97063-2, Pub. by Goulandris Greece). State Mutual Bk.

Striebel, Bonnie & Forgan, Ruth A. The Art Corner. 1979. pap. text ed. 11.95x (ISBN 0-673-16342-3). Scott F.

Striebel, C. Optimal Control of Discrete Time Stochastic Systems. (Lecture Notes in Economics & Mathematical Systems Ser.: Vol. 110). 208p. 1975. pap. 14.00 o.p. (ISBN 0-387-07181-4). Springer-Verlag.

Strieder, P. Albrecht Durer, Drawings, Prints, Paintings. Gordon, Nancy M. & Strauss, Walter L., trs. LC 79-50679. (Illus.). 1982. 85.00 (ISBN 0-89835-057-3). Abaris Bks.

Striefel, Sebastian. Teaching a Child to Imitate. (Managing Behavior Ser.: Part 7). 1974. 4.25 o.p. (ISBN 0-89079-007-8). H & H Ent.

Striffler, David F., jt. auth. see Young, Wesley O.

Striffler, Nancy & Willig, Sharon. The Communication Screen: A Preschool Speech-Language Screening Tool. 27p. 1981. pap. text ed. 10.00 (ISBN 0-88450-735-1, 2083-B). Communication Skill.

Strigel, W. Business Cycle Analysis: Papers Presented at the Fourteenth CIRET Conference Proceedings - Lisbon 1979. 446p. 1980. text ed. 50.50x (ISBN 0-566-00368-6). Gower Pub Ltd.

Strik, J. J. & Koeman, J. H., eds. Chemical Porphyria in Man: Porphyrinogenic Action of Halogenated Aromatics in Experimental Animals. LC 79-19486. 236p. 1979. 52.50 (ISBN 0-444-80159-6, North Holland). Elsevier.

Strike, Kenneth. Liberty & Learning. LC 82-5723. 192p. 1982. 20.00x (ISBN 0-312-48353-8). St Martin.

Striker, Fran. The Lone Ranger. 1980. lib. bdg. 9.95 (ISBN 0-8398-2676-1, Gregg). G K Hall.

--The Lone Ranger. (Lone Ranger Ser.: No. 1). 192p. 1978. pap. 1.50 o.p. (ISBN 0-523-40379-8). Pinnacle Bks.

--The Lone Ranger & the Gold Robbery. (Lone Ranger Ser.: No. 3). 1978. pap. 1.75 o.p. (ISBN 0-523-40876-5, Dist. by Independent News Co.). Pinnacle Bks.

--The Lone Ranger & the Mystery Ranch. (The Lone Ranger Ser.: No. 2). 192p. 1978. pap. 1.50 o.p. (ISBN 0-523-40380-1). Pinnacle Bks.

--The Lone Ranger at the Haunted Gulch. (The Lone Ranger Ser.: No. 6). 1979. pap. 1.50 o.p. (ISBN 0-523-40490-5). Pinnacle Bks.

--The Lone Ranger Traps the Smugglers. (Lone Ranger Ser.: No. 7). 1979. pap. 1.75 o.p. (ISBN 0-523-40491-3). Pinnacle Bks.

Striker, G. & Solt, J., eds. Measurement for Progress in Science & Technology: Acta Imeko, 1979, 3 vols. 1980. Set. 223.50 (ISBN 0-444-85477-0). Elsevier.

Striker, Gary E., et al. Use & Interpretation of Renal Biopsy. LC 76-45967. (Major Problems in Pathology: Vol. 8). (Illus.). 1978. text ed. 29.50 o.p. (ISBN 0-7216-8620-6). Saunders.

Striker, John M. & Shapiro, Andrew O. How You Can Sue Without Hiring a Lawyer: A Guide to Winning in Small Claims Court. 1981. 12.95 o.p. (ISBN 0-671-25366-2). S&S.

Striker, Randy. Everglades Assault. (Macmorgan Ser.: No. 6). (Orig.). 1982. pap. 1.95 (AJ1344, Sig). NAL.

--Grand Cayman Slam. (Dusky MacMorgan Ser.: No. 7). 1982. pap. 2.25 (ISBN 0-451-11512-0, AE1512, Sig). NAL.

Striker, Susan. Build a Better Mousetrap. (Illus.). 64p. 1983. pap. 4.95 (ISBN 0-03-057876-0). HR&W.

Strinati, Dominic. Capitalism, the State & Industrial Relations. 236p. 1983. 32.00x (ISBN 0-85664-996-1, Pub. by Croom Helm Ltd England). Biblio Dist.

Strindberg, August. A Dream Play & Four Chamber Plays. Johnson, Walter, tr. 288p. 1975. pap. 6.95 (ISBN 0-393-00791-X, Norton Lib). Norton.

--The Father. Anderson, Valborg, ed. & tr. Bd. with A Dream Play. LC 64-20118. (Crofts Classics Ser.). 1964. pap. text ed. 3.50x (ISBN 0-88295-096-7). Harlan Davidson.

--Married. 254p. 1982. Repr. of 1917 ed. lib. bdg. 20.00 (ISBN 0-89987-793-1). Darby Bks.

--Miss Julie. 1965. pap. 1.75 o.p. (ISBN 0-380-01416-5, 77412, Bard). Avon.

--The Natives of Hemso. Paulson, Arvid, tr. from Swedish. 1973. pap. 2.95 o.s.i. (ISBN 0-87140-284-X). Liveright.

--Open Letters to the Intimate Theater. Johnson, Walter, tr. from Swedish. LC 66-19559. (Illus.). 352p. 1966. 13.50 (ISBN 0-295-74055-8); pap. 2.95 (ISBN 0-295-97874-0, WP28). U of Wash Pr.

--Plays from the Cynical Life. Johnson, Walter, tr. from Swedish. Incl. Debit & Credit; Facing Death; The First Warning; Mother Love; Pariah; Playing with Fire; Simoon. LC 82-13581. (Illus.). 144p. 1983. 22.50 (ISBN 0-295-95980-0). U of Wash Pr.

--Pre-Inferno Plays: The Father, Lady Julie, Creditors, the Stronger, the Bond. Johnson, Walter, tr. & intros by. 1976. pap. 6.95 (ISBN 0-393-00834-7, Norton Lib). Norton.

--Strindberg: Five Plays. Carlson, Harry G., tr. LC 82-15882. 272p. 1983. 20.00 (ISBN 0-520-04697-8); pap. 8.95 (ISBN 0-520-04698-6, CAL 630). U of Cal Pr.

--Three Plays. Incl. Miss Julie; The Outlaw; The Stronger. pap. 2.50 (ISBN 0-8283-1458-6, IPL). Branden.

Strindberg, August & Ibsen, Henrik. Ghost Sonata & When We Dead Awaken. Torp, Thaddeus L., ed. LC 76-4623. (Crofts Classics Ser.). 1977. pap. text ed. 3.75 (ISBN 0-88295-112-2). Harlan Davidson.

Strindberg, August see Dent, Anthony.

Strindberg, August see Moon, Samuel.

Striner, Max. Ego & Its Own. Byington, Steven, tr. from Ger. (Illus.). 366p. 1982. pap. 7.95 (ISBN 0-946061-00-9). Left Bank.

Stringer, Arthur J. Red Wine of Youth: A Life of Rupert Brooke. LC 72-6211. 287p. 1972. Repr. of 1948 ed. lib. bdg. 16.00x (ISBN 0-8371-6456-7, STRW). Greenwood.

Stringer, Bruce. Earlihee the Turtle. (Illus.). pap. 4.95 (ISBN 0-932298-06-0). Copple Hse.

Stringer, James & Clarida, Glen. To Follow Satan's Leading. (Illus.). 128p. 1983. 9.95 (ISBN 0-89962-299-2). Todd & Honeywell.

Stringer, Lorene A. Sense of Self: A Guide to How We Mature. LC 76-157735. 1972. 14.95 (ISBN 0-87722-008-5). Temple U Pr.

Stringer, Michael & Henwood, Kay. Baron Battleaxe & the Magic Carpet. (Illus.). 32p. 1976. 9.00x o.p. (ISBN 0-460-06753-2, Pub. by J. M. Dent England). Biblio Dist.

Stringer, Michael, jt. auth. see Shillingford, John.

Stringer, P. Confronting Social Issues: Applications of Social Psychology, Vol. 2. 1982. 28.00 (ISBN 0-12-673802-5). Acad Pr.

Stringfellow, George. October Night's Feast. LC 81-90721. 50p. 1982. 6.95 (ISBN 0-533-05292-0). Vantage.

Stringfield, V. T., jt. ed. see Herak, M.

Stringham, E. J., jt. auth. see Murphy, Howard A.

Stripling, Scott R. The Picture Theory of Meaning: An Interpretation of Wittgenstein's Tractatus Logico-Philosophicus. LC 78-62176. 1978. pap. text ed. 8.25 (ISBN 0-8191-0109-5). U Pr of Amer.

Stritzke, Barbara. Marieluise Fleisser: Pionere In Ingolstadt. 111p. (Ger.). 1982. write for info. (ISBN 3-8204-5975-8). P Lang Pubs.

Strizower, Schifra. The Bene Israel of Bombay: A Study of a Jewish Community. LC 76-148841. (Pavilion Social Anthropology Ser.). 1971. 8.00x o.p. (ISBN 0-8052-3405-5). Schocken.

Strnad, Wayne, jt. auth. see Gonis, Antonios.

Strobel, H. Computer Controlled Transportation. (Wiley ITASA International Ser. on Applied Systems Analysis). 672p. 1982. 59.95 o.s.i. (ISBN 0-471-10036-6, Pub. by Wiley-Interscience). Wiley.

Strobel, Lee P. Reckless Homicide: Ford's Pinto Trial. LC 80-123374. (Illus.). 220p. 1980. 8.95 (ISBN 0-89708-022-X). And Bks.

Strober, M., jt. auth. see Gordon, F.

Strober, Warren, et al, eds. Recent Advances in Mucosal Immunity. 530p. 1982. text ed. 80.00 (ISBN 0-89004-642-5). Raven.

Strode Publishers. Rivers of Alabama. Klein, E. L., ed. (Illus.). 211p. (gr. 7 up). 1968. 6.95 (ISBN 0-87397-003-9). Strode.

Stroebel, Charles F. QR: The Quieting Reflex. 224p. 1982. 12.95 (ISBN 0-399-12657-0). Putnam Pub Group.

--QR: The Quieting Reflex. 208p. 1983. pap. 2.95 (ISBN 0-425-05867-0). Berkley Pub.

Stroebel, L., et al. Visual Concepts for Photographers. (Illus.). 352p. 1980. 27.95 (ISBN 0-240-51025-9). Focal Pr.

Stroebel, Leslie. View Camera Technique. 4th ed. (Illus.). 1980. 24.95 (ISBN 0-240-51086-0). Focal Pr.

Stroehlein, John R. & Romsdahl, Marvin M., eds. Gastrointestinal Cancer. (M. D. Anderson Clinical Conferences on Cancer Ser.: No. 25). (Illus.). 492p. 1981. text ed. 49.50 (ISBN 0-89004-612-3). Raven.

Stroehmann, I., jt. ed. see Schmidt, R. E.

Stroer, Rosemary, jt. auth. see Ott, John.

Stroethoff, Pieter. Photography for the Scale Modeller. LC 78-55052. (Illus.). 1978. 8.95 o.p. (ISBN 0-8069-8558-5); PLB 7.49 o.p. (ISBN 0-8069-8559-3). Sterling.

Strogonov, B. P., et al. Structure & Function of Plant Cells in Saline Habitats. Gollak, B., ed. Mercado, A., tr. from Rus. LC 73-13609. (Illus.). 284p. 1973. 55.95 o.s.i. (ISBN 0-470-83406-4). Halsted Pr.

Stroh, Thomas F. Managing the Sales Function. (Marketing Ser.). (Illus.). 1977. text ed. 23.95 (ISBN 0-07-062219-1, C); instructor's manual 18.95 (ISBN 0-07-062220-5). McGraw.

Stroheim, Erich Von see Von Stroheim, Erich.

Strohm, Sally. Word Signals. (English Ser.). 24p. (gr. 4-7). 1979. wkbk. 5.00 (ISBN 0-8209-0185-7, E-13). ESP.

Strohmeyer, G., jt. auth. see Hornbostel, H.

Strojan, C. & Lawrence, K. Environmental & Aesthetic Assessment of Small Wind Energy Systems. (Progress in Solar Energy Supplements Ser.). 60p. 1982. pap. text ed. 9.00x (ISBN 0-89553-080-5). Am Solar Energy.

Stroke, George W. Introduction to Coherent Optics & Halography. 2nd ed. (Illus.). 1969. 36.00 (ISBN 0-12-673956-0). Acad Pr.

Stroll, Avrum, jt. auth. see Popkin, Richard H.

Strom, Arlene. Cooking on Wheels. LC 73-112688. (Illus.). 1970. pap. 3.95 (ISBN 0-87027-128-8). Cumberland Pr.

Strom, Fredric A., ed. Zoning & Planning Law Handbook, 1982. 1982. 32.50 (ISBN 0-87632-209-7). Boardman.

Strom, J., jt. auth. see Graef, Judy.

Strom, Margot S. & Parsons, William S. Facing History & Ourselves: Holocaust & Human Behavior. (Illus.). 400p. (gr. 9-12). 1982. pap. text ed. 15.00 (ISBN 0-9607970-1-7). Intentional Ed.

Strom, Robert D. & Bernard, Harold W. Educational Psychology. LC 81-12199. (Psychology Ser.). 720p. 1982. pap. 20.95 (ISBN 0-8185-0453-6). Brooks-Cole.

Stroman, Duane F. The Awakening Minorities: The Physically Handicapped. LC 82-40235. (Illus.). 268p. 1983. lib. bdg. 23.50 (ISBN 0-8191-2694-2); pap. text ed. 11.50 (ISBN 0-8191-2695-0). U Pr of Amer.

Stroman, James, ed. Prize Recipes from Great Restaurants: The Southern States & the Tropics. LC 78-27415. (Prize Recipes Ser.). 128p. 1983. pap. 8.95 (ISBN 0-88289-293-2). Pelican.

Stroman, James H. Secretary's Manual. (Orig.). 1968. pap. 1.95 (ISBN 0-451-11318-7, AJ1318, Sig). NAL.

Stromberg, Ann, ed. Philanthropic Foundations in Latin America. LC 68-54409. 223p. 1968. 9.95x (ISBN 0-87154-837-2). Russell Sage.

Stromberg, Ann H. & Harkess, Shirley, eds. Women Working: Theories & Facts in Perspective. LC 77-89921. 433p. 1978. pap. 12.95 (ISBN 0-87484-301-4). Mayfield Pub.

Stromberg, Karl, jt. auth. see Dressler, Robert E.

Stromberg, Melvin W., jt. auth. see Hebel, Rudolph.

Stromberg, Roland N. European Intellectual History Since Seventeen Eighty-Nine. 2nd ed. LC 74-23541. 384p. 1975. pap. text ed. 16.95x o.p. (ISBN 0-13-292003-4). P-H.

--An Intellectual History of Modern Europe. 2nd ed. LC 74-22388. 595p. 1975. text ed. 24.95 (ISBN 0-13-469106-7). P-H.

Stromberg, Roland N., jt. auth. see Conkin, Paul K.

Stromberg, Marilyn F. & Stromberg, Paul. Primary Care Assessment & Management Skills for Nurses: A Self-Assessment Manual. LC 79-14379. 1979. pap. 17.75x (ISBN 0-397-54233-X, Lippincott Nursing). Lippincott.

Stromberg, Paul, jt. auth. see Stromberg, Marilyn F.

Stromsten, Amy. Recovery: Stories of Alcoholism & Survival. xii, 143p. 1982. 20.00. Rutgers Ctr Alcohol.

Stronck, David, ed. Sex in the Classroom: Readings for Teachers. (Orig.). 1982. pap. 8.00 (ISBN 0-87355-024-2). Natl Sci Tchrs.

Strong, Bethany. Favorite Son. Date not set. price not set. Parable Pr.

--First Love. pap. 1.95 o.p. (ISBN 0-515-04504-7). Jove Pubns.

Strong, Bryan & DeVault, Christine. The Marriage & Family Experience. 2nd ed. (Illus.). 600p. 1983. text ed. 20.95 (ISBN 0-314-69682-2). West Pub.

Strong, Bryan & Reynolds, Rebecca. Understanding Our Sexuality. (Illus.). 598p. 1982. pap. text ed. 17.50 (ISBN 0-314-63294-8). West Pub.

Strong, Bryan, et al. Human Sexuality: Essentials. (Illus.). 1978. pap. text ed. 13.95 (ISBN 0-8299-0154-X); test manual avail. (ISBN 0-8299-0576-6). West Pub.

Strong, Donald S. Organized Anti-Semitism in America: The Rise of Group Prejudice During the Decade 1930-1940. LC 78-26198. 1979. Repr. of 1941 ed. lib. bdg. 18.50x (ISBN 0-313-20883-2, STOA). Greenwood.

Strong, F. Bryan, et al. The Marriage & the Family Experience: A Text with Readings. (Illus.). 1979. pap. text ed. 20.95 (ISBN 0-8299-0278-3); instrs.' manual avail. (ISBN 0-8299-0577-4). West Pub.

Strong, James. Strong's Exhaustive Concordance. 17.95 (ISBN 0-8010-8228-5); pap. 13.95 (ISBN 0-8010-8108-4). Baker Bk.

--Strong's Exhaustive Concordance. LC 78-73138. 1978. pap. 15.95 (ISBN 0-8054-1134-8). Broadman.

Strong, Jo Ann & Egoville, Barbara B. Considerations in Clinical Evaluation: Instructors, Students, Legal Issues, Data. 55p. 1979. 4.95 (ISBN 0-686-38286-2, 16-1764). Natl League Nurse.

Strong, Julia H. A Flock of Blackbirds. write for info. (ISBN 0-89015-122-9). Eakin Pubns.

Strong, Kendrick. All the Master's Men. LC 78-56973. 1978. 7.95 o.p. (ISBN 0-915684-38-1). Christian Herald.

Strong, M. Industrial, Labor & Community Relations. LC 68-59238. 144p. 1974. pap. 7.80 (ISBN 0-8273-0371-8); instructor's guide 3.75 (ISBN 0-8273-0372-6). Delmar.

Strong, Margaret K. Public Welfare Administration in Canada. LC 69-16248. (Criminology, Law Enforcement, & Social Problems Ser.: No. 94). 1969. Repr. of 1930 ed. 14.00x (ISBN 0-87585-094-4). Patterson Smith.

Strong, Michael. The Wolves Came Down the Mountain. (Walker Mystery Ser.). 1979. 7.95 o.s.i. (ISBN 0-8027-5414-7). Walker & Co.

Strong, Michael, jt. auth. see Cathcart, Ruth.

Strong, Patience. The Best Is Yet to Be. pap. 5.50x (ISBN 0-392-09026-0, SpS). Sportshelf.

--Passing Clouds. pap. 5.50x (ISBN 0-392-09012-0, SpS). Sportshelf.

--The Patience Strong Gift Book. 10.00x (ISBN 0-392-08331-0, SpS). Sportshelf.

--The Tapestry of Time. 10.00x (ISBN 0-392-08345-0, SpS). Sportshelf.

Strong, Roy & Oman, Julia T. The English Year. LC 82-804. (Illus.). 224p. 1982. 25.00 (ISBN 0-89919-122-3). Ticknor & Fields.

Strong, Rupert. Come When You Can. LC 82-18970. 86p. (Orig.). 1982. 10.00 (ISBN 0-905888-08-1); pap. 7.00 (ISBN 0-905888-07-3). Dufour.

Strong, Sidney J. Landlord-Tenant Rights for Washington. 3rd ed. 86p. 1982. 4.50 (ISBN 0-88908-718-0). Self Counsel Pr.

Strong, Stanley R. & Claiborn, Charles D. Change Through Interaction: Social Psychological Processes of Counseling & Psychotherapy. LC 81-14631. (Personality Process Ser.). 259p. 1982. 27.95 (ISBN 0-471-05902-1, Pub. by Wiley-Interscience). Wiley.

Strong, Susan, jt. auth. see Toland, Drexel.

Strong, Tracy B. Friedrich Nietzche & the Politics of Transfiguration. LC 74-81442. 380p. 1976. 35.50x (ISBN 0-520-02810-4). U of Cal Pr.

Strong, William, jt. auth. see Shaver, James P.
Strongin, H. Science on a Shoestring. 1976. Tchr's Resource. pap. text ed. 12.00 (ISBN 0-201-07329-3, Sch Div). A-W.
Strongin, Harriet, jt. auth. see Morgenstein, Melvin.
Strongman, Harry, jt. auth. see Crosher, Judith.
Strongman, Harry, jt. auth. see Forman, Joan.
Strongman, Harry, jt. auth. see Gibson, Michael.
Strongman, K. T. The Psychology of Emotion. 2nd. ed. LC 77-26618. 303p. 1978. text ed. 46.95 (ISBN 0-471-99624-6); pap. 19.95 (ISBN 0-471-99625-4, Pub. by Wiley-Interscience). Wiley.
Strony, Madeline S., et al. Refresher Course in Gregg Shorthand. (Diamond Jubilee Ser.). 1970. text ed. 14.00 (ISBN 0-07-062205-1, G). McGraw.
--Refresher Course in Gregg Shorthand Simplified. 1962. 11.95 (ISBN 0-07-062248-5, G). McGraw.
--Secretary at Work. 3rd ed. 1966. text ed. 14.65 (ISBN 0-07-062245-0, G); instructor's manual 5.05 (ISBN 0-07-062250-7). McGraw.
Strooker, J. R. Introduction to Categories, Homological Algebra & Sheaf Cohomology. LC 77-80849. 1978. 49.95 (ISBN 0-521-21699-0). Cambridge U Pr.
Strose, Susanne. Candle-Making. Kuttner, Paul, tr. LC 68-8759. (Little Craft Book Ser). (Illus.). (gr. 5-10). 1968. 6.95 (ISBN 0-8069-5100-1); PLB 6.69 o.p. (ISBN 0-8069-5101-X). Sterling.
Stross, Brian. Variation & Natural Selection As Factors in Linguistic & Cultural Change. (PDR Press Publication in Linguistic Change: No. 2). 1977. pap. text ed. 2.00x o.p. (ISBN 90-316-0062-8). Humanities.
Strother, Edward S. & Huckleberry, Alan W. Effective Speaker. LC 68-7238. (Illus.). 1968. text ed. 19.95 (ISBN 0-395-05441-9). HM.
Strother, Elsie W. Follow Through to Love. (YA) 1977. 6.95 (ISBN 0-685-73816-7, Avalon). Bouregy.
--A Kiss to Remember. (YA) 1980. 6.95 (ISBN 0-686-73932-9, Avalon). Bouregy.
--That Special Kiss. 1982. pap. 6.95 (ISBN 0-686-84744-X, Avalon). Bouregy.
--A Time for Deceit. 1981. pap. 6.95 (ISBN 0-686-84697-4, Avalon). Bouregy.
Strother, G. K. & Weber, Robert L. Physics with Applications in Life Sciences. (Illus.). 1977. text ed. 28.95 (ISBN 0-395-21718-0); instr's. manual 1.00 (ISBN 0-395-21719-9). HM.
Strothmann, F. W., jt. auth. see Lohnes, Walter F.
Strothmann, F. W., ed. see Augustine, Saint.
Stroud, Joanne, ed. see Layard, et al.
Stroud, John. Annals of British & Commonwealth Air Transport, 1919-1960. (Airlines History Project Ser.). Date not set. price not set (ISBN 0-404-19337-4). AMS Pr.
--Famous Airports of the World. 11.75x o.p. (ISBN 0-392-08152-0, SpS). Sportshelf.
Stroud, K. A. Laplace Transforms: Programmes & Problems. LC 73-6317. 273p. 1973. pap. text ed. 16.95x o.p. (ISBN 0-470-83415-3). Halsted Pr.
Stroud, Matthew D., tr. see De la Barca, Pedro C.
Stroud, Oxford S. Writing Prose That Makes a Difference, & the Grammar Minimum. LC 79-84651. 1979. pap. text ed. 6.25 (ISBN 0-8191-0740-9). U Pr of Amer.
Stroud, Parry. Stephen Vincent Benet. (United States Authors Ser.). 1962. lib. bdg. 11.95 (ISBN 0-8057-0052-8, Twayne). G K Hall.
Stroud, R. Diseases of Canaries. 12.95 (ISBN 0-87666-436-2, PS640). TFH Pubns.
Stroud, Robert. Stroud Bird Disease. 14.95 (ISBN 0-87666-435-4, AP926). TFH Pubns.
Stroud, Ronald. The Axones & Kyrbeis of Drakon & Solon. LC 77-20329. (Publications in Classical Studies: Vol. 19). 1979. 12.50x (ISBN 0-520-09590-1). U of Cal Pr.
Stroud, T. Services for Children & Their Families. 1973. 34.00 o.s.i. (ISBN 0-08-016604-0); pap. 17.00 (ISBN 0-08-016605-9). Pergamon.
Stroumillo, Elisabeth De see De Stroumillo, Elisabeth.
Stroumillo, Elizabeth De see De Stroumillo, Elizabeth.
Stroup, Donna F., jt. auth. see Larsen, Richard J.
Stroup, George W. Jesus Christ for Today, Vol. 7. LC 82-13494. (Library of Living Faith). 120p. 1982. pap. 5.95 (ISBN 0-664-24450-5). Westminster.
Stroup, Herbert W., Jr. & Wood, Norma S. Sexuality & the Counseling Pastor. LC 73-88344. 136p. 1974. 5.95 o.p. (ISBN 0-8006-0264-1, 1-264). Fortress.
Stroup, Marjory & Treacy, Margaret. Blood Group Antigens & Antibodies. (Illus.). 255p. (Orig.). 1982. pap. text ed. 35.00 (ISBN 0-910771-00-6). Ortho Diag.
Stroup, Richard & Baden, John. Natural Resources: Bureaucratic Myths & Environmental Management. (Pacific Institute for Public Policy Research Ser.). 264p. 1983. price not set professional reference (ISBN 0-88410-380-3). Ballinger Pub.
Stroup, Thomas B. Works of Nathaniel Lee, 2 vols. Cooke, Arthur L., ed. LC 54-14766. 1954. Set. 30.00 o.p. (ISBN 0-8108-0236-8). Scarecrow.
Strouse, James C. The Mass Media, Public Opinion & Public Policy Analysis. (Political Science Ser). 320p. 1975. text ed. 13.95 (ISBN 0-675-08701-5). Merrill.
Strouse, James C., et al, eds. Making Government Work: Essays in Honor of Conley H. Dillon. LC 80-8308. 478p. 1981. lib. bdg. 26.00 (ISBN 0-8191-1306-9); pap. text ed. 17.00 (ISBN 0-8191-1307-7). U Pr of Amer.
Strout, Cushing. The Pragmatic Revolt in American History: Carl Becker & Charles Beard. LC 79-26417. (The Wallace Notestein Essays: No. 3). 1980. Repr. of 1958 ed. lib. bdg. 19.00x (ISBN 0-313-22203-7, STPG). Greenwood.
Stroynowski, Julius, jt. auth. see Lewytzkyi, Borys.
Strozzi, Barbara. Arie. (Women Composers Ser.). 1983. Repr. of 1970 ed. lib. bdg. write for info (ISBN 0-306-76195-5). Da Capo.
Strub. Energy from Biomass: Proceedings - 2nd EC Conf. (Proceedings - 2nd EC Conf.). Date not set. 106.60 (ISBN 0-85334-196-6, Pub. by Applied Sci England). Elsevier.
Strub, Richard L., jt. auth. see Weisberg, Leon A.
Struble, George W. Assembler Language Programming: The IBM System 360. 2nd ed. 496p. 1975. text ed. 26.95 (ISBN 0-201-07322-6). A-W.
Struble, Raimond A. Nonlinear Differential Equations. LC 79-23165. 1983. Repr. of 1962 ed. lib. bdg. write for info. (ISBN 0-89874-056-8). Krieger.
Struc, Roman, tr. see Schlegel, Friedrich.
Struening, Elmer L. & Guttentag, Marcia, eds. Handbook of Evaluation Research, 2 vols. LC 74-15764. 1975. 30.00 ea. Vol. 1 (ISBN 0-8039-0428-2). Vol. 2 (ISBN 0-8039-0429-0). Set. 55.00x (ISBN 0-686-82964-6). Sage.
Strugatsky, Arkady & Strugatsky, Boris. Roadside Picnic. 1982. pap. 2.25 (ISBN 0-671-45842-6, Timescape). PB.
--Space Apprentice. (Best of Soviet Science Fiction Ser.). 141p. 1981. 11.95 o.p. (ISBN 0-02-615220-7). Macmillan.
Strugatsky, Boris, jt. auth. see Strugatsky, Arkady.
Struglia, Erasmus J., ed. Standards & Specifications Information Sources. LC 65-24659. (Management Information Guide Ser.: No. 6). 1965. 42.00x (ISBN 0-8103-0806-1). Gale.
Struhl, Paula R., jt. auth. see Jaggar, Alison.
Struik, D. J., ed. Source Book in Mathematics: Twelve Hundred to Eighteen Hundred. LC 68-21980. (Source Books in the History of the Sciences Ser). (Illus.). 1969. 22.50x o.p. (ISBN 0-674-82355-9). Harvard U Pr.
Struik, Dirk J., ed. Birth of the Communist Manifesto, Student's Edition. LC 77-148513. (Illus., Incl. the text of The Communist Manifesto by Marx & Engels). 1971. 7.50 o.p. (ISBN 0-7178-0288-4); pap. 3.25 (ISBN 0-7178-0320-1). Intl Pub Co.
Struik, John H., jt. auth. see Fisher, John W.
Struik, L. C. Physical Aging in Amorphous Polymers & Other Materials. 1978. 57.50 (ISBN 0-444-41655-2). Elsevier.
Struin, Leo. The Liver & Anaesthesia. LC 72-97914. (Major Problem in Anaesthesia: Vol. 3). (Illus.). 1976. text ed. 12.00 (ISBN 0-7216-8625-7). Saunders.
Struk, Danylo S., ed. Four Ukranian Poets. Bohachevska-Chomiak, Martha, tr. 1977. cancelled o.p. (ISBN 0-685-79417-2). Cataract Pr.
Strum, Carol Van see Van Strum, Carol.
Strum, Fabienne X. Pautex & His Contemporaries: The Collection of the Museum of Clocks, Watches & Enamels in Geneva. limited ed. (Illus.). 272p. (Eng. & Japanese.). 1982. 265.95 (ISBN 0-8048-1405-8, Pub. by Shufunotomo Co Ltd Japan). C E Tuttle.
Strum, Phillippa. Presidential Power & American Democracy. 2nd ed. LC 79-946. 1979. pap. text ed. 10.95x (ISBN 0-673-16275-3). Scott F.
Strum, Robert D. & Ward, John R. Laplace Transform Solution of Differential Equations. (Orig., Prog. Bk.). 1968. pap. 21.00 ref. ed. (ISBN 0-13-522805-0). P-H.
Strum, Williamson B. Gastroenterology Assistant's Handbook. Gardner, Alvin F., ed. (Allied Professions Monograph Ser.). 224p. 1983. 28.50 (ISBN 0-87527-292-4). Green.
Strumingher, Laura S. What Were Little Girls & Boys Made Of? Primary Education in Rural France, 1830-1880. LC 82-3342. (European Social History Ser.). 192p. 1982. 30.50x (ISBN 0-87395-627-3); pap. 9.95x (ISBN 0-87395-628-1). State U NY Pr.
--Women & the Making of the Working Class: Lyon 1830-1870. LC 78-74841. 1979. 14.95 (ISBN 0-88831-027-7). Eden Pr.
Strumpel, Burkhard, ed. Economic Means for Human Needs; Social Indicators of Well-Being & Discontent. LC 75-620105. 303p. 1976. 20.00x (ISBN 0-87944-193-3). Inst Soc Res.
Strumpel, Burkhard, et al. Surveys of Consumers, 1972-73: Contributions to Behavioral Economics. LC 72-619718. 238p. 1975. pap. 7.00x (ISBN 0-87944-170-4). Inst Soc Res.
Strung, Norman. Deer Hunting. (Illus.). 240p. 1982. pap. 9.95 (ISBN 0-87842-143-2). Mountain Pr.
Strunk, Oliver, ed. Source Readings in Music History, 5 vols. Incl. Vol. 1. Antiquity & the Middle Ages. pap. 4.95x (ISBN 0-393-09680-7); Vol. 2. The Renaissance Era. pap. 4.95x (ISBN 0-393-09681-5); Vol. 3. Baroque Era. pap. 4.95x (ISBN 0-393-09682-3); Vol. 4. Classic Era. pap. 5.95x (ISBN 0-393-09683-1); Vol. 5. Romantic Era. pap. 4.95x (ISBN 0-393-09684-X). 1950. Repr. one vol. ed 24.95x (ISBN 0-393-09742-0, NortonC). Norton.
Strunk, Orlo, Jr. Privacy: Experience, Understanding, Expression. LC 82-16029. 78p. 1983. lib. bdg. 18.00 (ISBN 0-8191-2687-X); pap. text ed. 7.00 (ISBN 0-8191-2688-8). U Pr of Amer.
Strunk, William, Jr. & White, e. B. Elements of Style: With Index. 3rd ed. 92p. 1979. pap. text ed. 2.95 (ISBN 0-02-418200-1); 7.95. Macmillan.
Strupp, H. Psychotherapy & the Modification of Abnormal Behavior. 1970. pap. text ed. 7.95 (ISBN 0-07-062231-0, C). McGraw.
Struppa, Daniele C. The Fundamental Principle for Sysytems of Convolution Equations. LC 82-20614. (Memoirs of the American Mathematical Society Ser.: No. 273). 10.00 (ISBN 0-8218-2273-X, MEMO/273). Am Math.
Strurtridge, Gill, jt. ed. see Geddes, Marion.
Struther, Jan. Mrs. Miniver. LC 40-27553. 1966. pap. 0.50 (ISBN 0-15-663138-5, Harv). HarBraceJ.
Struthers, James. No Fault of Their Own: Unemployment & the Canadian Welfare State, 1914-1941. (State & Economic Life Ser.). 264p. 1983. 31.00 (ISBN 0-8020-2480-7); pap. 12.50 (ISBN 0-8020-6502-3). U of Toronto Pr.
Struthers, John. Dinosaur Cars. LC 77-6202. (Superwheels & Thrill Sports Bks.). (Illus.). (gr. 3-9). 1977. PLB 7.95g (ISBN 0-8225-0416-2). Lerner Pubns.
Struthers, Sally, et al. Sally Struthers' Natural Beauty Book. LC 78-20101. (Illus.). 1979. 6.95 o.p. (ISBN 0-385-14350-8). Doubleday.
Strutt, Joseph. Sports & Pastimes of the People of England: Including Rural & Domestic Recreations. LC 67-23901. (Social History Reference Ser.). (Illus.). 1968. Repr. of 1903 ed. 34.00x (ISBN 0-8103-3260-4). Gale.
Strutt, Max J. Lame, Mathieu Funktionen. LC 66-23757. (Ger). 9.95 (ISBN 0-8284-0203-5). Chelsea Pub.
Strutte, Wilson. Tchaikovsky: His Life & Times. expanded ed. (Life & Times Ser.). (Illus.). 208p. 1981. Repr. of 1979 ed. 12.95 (ISBN 0-87666-641-1, Z-40). Paganiniana Pubns.
Strutynski, Udo, ed. see Dumezil, Georges.
Strutynsky, Natalie S. see Squire, Lucy F., et al.
Strutz, Henry. Dictionary of Five Hundred & One German Verbs: Fully Conjugated in All Tenses. LC 72-92945. 1972. pap. text ed. 5.95 o.p. (ISBN 0-8120-0434-5). Barron.
Strutz, Henry B. Two Hundred & One German Verbs Fully Conjugated in All the Tenses. LC 63-16872. (Orig.). 1964. pap. text ed. 2.95 o.p. (ISBN 0-8120-0210-5). Barron.
Struve, Gleb, jt. ed. see Riasanovsky, Nicholas V.
Struwe, G., jt. auth. see Perris, C.
Struyk, Raymond J. Saving the Housing Assistance Plan: Improving Incentives to Local Governments. 36p. 1980. pap. text ed. 3.50 (ISBN 0-87766-270-3). Urban Inst.
Struyk, Raymond J. & Soldo, Beth J. Improving the Elderly's Housing: A Key to Preserving the Nation's Housing Stock & Neighborhoods. LC 79-3008. 352p. 1982. prof ref 27.50x (ISBN 0-88410-495-8). Ballinger Pub.
Struyk, Raymond J., jt. auth. see Ozanne, Larry.
Struyk, Raymond J., jt. auth. see Rasmussen, David W.
Strydesky, Rebecca, jt. auth. see Moffett, Carol G.
Stryk, Lucien. Awakening. LC 82-72361. 65p. 1973. 7.95 (ISBN 0-8040-0332-7). Swallow.
--Awakening. LC 82-72379. 65p. 1975. pap. 4.95 (ISBN 0-8040-0333-5). Swallow.
--Cherries. LC 82-74411. 1983. pap. 3.00 (ISBN 0-9604740-3-X). Ampersand RI.
--Encounter with Zen: Writings on Poetry & Zen. LC 82-75497. x, 259p. 1982. 26.95x (ISBN 0-8040-0405-6); pap. 10.95 (ISBN 0-8040-0406-4). Swallow.
--Selected Poems. LC 82-74094. 137p. 1976. 10.95 (ISBN 0-8040-0740-3); pap. 5.95 (ISBN 0-8040-0741-1). Swallow.
Stryk, Lucien & Ikemoto, Takashi, eds. The Penguin Book of Zen Poetry. LC 82-74300. 159p. 1978. 10.95 (ISBN 0-8040-0792-6). Swallow.
Stryk, Lucien & Ikemoto, Takashi, trs. from Japanese. Zen: Poems, Prayers, Sermons, Anecdotes, Interviews. LC 82-75232. 210p. 1982. 18.95x (ISBN 0-8040-0377-7); pap. 8.95 (ISBN 0-8040-0378-5). Swallow.
Stryker, John A. & Clement, John A. Therapeutic Radiology Continuing Education Review. 2nd ed. 1981. pap. 23.50 o.p. (ISBN 0-87488-346-6). Med Exam.
Stryker, Ruth, jt. auth. see Gordon, George K.
Stryker, William N. The Stryker Family in America: A Genealogy of the Stryker & Striker Families. LC 78-75351. (Illus.). 500p. 1979. lib. bdg. 48.00 (ISBN 0-9602936-1-2). W N Stryker.
Stryker-Rodda, Harriet. How to Climb Your Family Tree: Genealogy for Beginners. LC 77-24667. (YA) 1977. 5.95 o.s.i. (ISBN 0-397-01159-8); pap. 3.95i (ISBN 0-397-01243-8, LP-121). Har-Row.
Stuart & Murdock. Gymnastics. 8.90 (ISBN 0-531-00446-5). Watts.
Stuart, A. J. Pleistocene Vertebrates in the British Isles. (Illus.). 288p. 1982. 38.00x (ISBN 0-582-30069-X). Longman.
Stuart, Alan, jt. auth. see Kendall, Maurice.
Stuart, Allan, jt. auth. see Kendall, Maurice.
Stuart, Ann. The Demon Count. (Orig.). 1980. pap. 1.25 o.s.i. (ISBN 0-440-11906-5). Dell.
Stuart, Anne. The Demon Count's Daughter. (Orig.). 1980. pap. 1.25 o.s.i. (ISBN 0-440-11907-3). Dell.
--Demonwood. 1979. pap. 1.25 o.s.i. (ISBN 0-440-11774-7). Dell.
--Lord Satan's Bride. (Orig.). 1981. pap. 1.50 o.s.i. (ISBN 0-440-14787-5). Dell.
Stuart, Bruce. State Regulation of Health Service Utilization: Lessons from Michigan. 94p. 1979. pap. text ed. 5.50 (ISBN 0-87766-256-8). Urban Inst.
Stuart, Casey. Passion's Dream. 1982. pap. 3.50 (ISBN 0-8217-1086-9). Zebra.
Stuart, Dabney. Rockbridge Poems. 20p. (Orig.). 1981. pap. 8.00 o.s.i. (ISBN 0-931182-03-4). Iron Mtn Pr.
Stuart, David. Calligraphy: From A to Z. (Illus.). 128p. 1983. 14.95 (ISBN 0-87396-088-2). Stravon.
Stuart, Donald D. Small Claims Court Guide for Washington. 144p. 1979. 4.50 (ISBN 0-88908-712-1). Self Counsel Pr.
Stuart, Dorothy M. Boy Through the Ages. LC 77-89291. (Illus.). 1970. Repr. of 1926 ed. 30.00x (ISBN 0-8103-3578-6). Gale.
--The Girl Through the Ages. LC 70-89292. (Illus.). 264p. 1969. Repr. of 1933 ed. 30.00x (ISBN 0-8103-3581-6). Gale.
Stuart, Douglas T. & Tow, William T., eds. China, the Soviet Union & the West: Strategic & Political Dimensions for the Nineteen Eighties. (Special Studies in International Relations). 320p. (Orig.). 1981. lib. bdg. 30.00 (ISBN 0-86531-091-2); pap. 13.95 (ISBN 0-86531-168-4). Westview.
Stuart, Duane R. Epochs of Greek & Roman Biography. LC 67-19532. 1928. 15.00x (ISBN 0-8196-0193-4). Biblo.
Stuart, Frederic. Watfor Watfiv FORTRAN Programming. LC 78-162424. 239p. 1971. pap. 22.95 (ISBN 0-471-83471-8). Wiley.
Stuart, Frederick. Fortran Programming. rev. ed. LC 68-30922. 371p. 1970. 32.50 (ISBN 0-471-83466-1). Wiley.
Stuart, G. E. Your Career in Archaeology. 1976. pap. 1.50 (ISBN 0-686-36579-8). Am Anthro Assn.
Stuart, Gail W. & Sundeen, Sandra J. Principles & Practice of Psychiatric Nursing. 2nd ed. (Illus.). 1052p. 1983. text ed. 27.95 (ISBN 0-8016-4885-8). Mosby.
Stuart, Isla, ed. see Sparnon, Norman.
Stuart, Jack, ed. Realities of the Truman Presidency. (Controversial Issues in U. S. History Ser.). 160p. 1975. pap. 2.95 o.p. (ISBN 0-671-18734-1). Monarch Pr.
Stuart, Jerome. Those Crazy Wonderful Years: When We Ran Warner Brothers. (Illus.). 256p. 1983. 14.95 (ISBN 0-686-82522-5). Lyle Stuart.
Stuart, Jesse. The Kingdom Within: A Spiritual Autobiography. (Illus.). 1979. 8.95 (ISBN 0-07-062224-8, GB). McGraw.
Stuart, Jessica. Daughters of Moonsong. 384p. 1981. pap. 2.95 o.p. (ISBN 0-523-41168-5). Pinnacle Bks.
Stuart, Lyle. Ultimate Book of Baccarat. (Illus.). 224p. 15.00 (ISBN 0-8184-0339-X). Lyle Stuart.
Stuart, Malcolm. Van Nostrand Reinhold Color Dictionary of Herbs & Herbalism. 160p. 1982. pap. 12.95 (ISBN 0-442-28338-5). Van Nos Reinhold.
Stuart, Malcolm, ed. The Encyclopedia of Herbs & Herbalism. (Illus.). 1979. 25.00 o.p. (ISBN 0-448-15472-2, G&D). Putnam Pub Group.
Stuart, Mark, ed. & intro. by. In the Record: The "Simeon Stylites" Columns of William A. Caldwell. 1972. 22.50x o.p. (ISBN 0-8135-0728-6). Rutgers U Pr.
Stuart, Mary. Both of Me. LC 79-8038. (Illus.). 480p. 1980. 13.95 o.p. (ISBN 0-385-14494-6). Doubleday.
Stuart, Monroe, jt. auth. see Sperling, Abraham.
Stuart, Nik, jt. auth. see Murdock, Tony.
Stuart, R., jt. ed. see Burgoyne, J.
Stuart, R. V., ed. Vacuum Technology, Thin Films, & Sputtering: An Introduction. LC 82-13748. Date not set. 21.00 (ISBN 0-12-674780-6). Acad Pr.
Stuart, Reginald. Bailout: America's Billion Dollar Gamble on the "New" Chrysler Corporation. LC 80-70279. (Illus.). 210p. (Orig.). 1981. pap. 6.95 (ISBN 0-89708-050-5). And Bks.
Stuart, Richard B. Act Thin, Stay Thin. 288p. pap. 3.50 (ISBN 0-515-07118-8). Jove Pubns.
Stuart, Richard B., ed. Behavioral Self-Management. LC 77-23501. 1977. 22.50 o.p. (ISBN 0-87630-148-0). Brunner-Mazel.
Stuart, Robert, jt. auth. see Gregory, Paul.
Stuart, Sally E. Teaching & Reaching. 1980. pap. 9.95 (ISBN 0-87162-243-2, D7790). Warner Pr.
Stuart, Sarah, jt. auth. see Marx, Patricia.
Stuart, V. A. Brave Captains. (Hazard Saga No. 2). 1972. pap. 1.75 o.p. (ISBN 0-523-40598-7). Pinnacle Bks.
--Hazard of Huntress. (Hazard Ser.: No. 4). 224p. 1980. pap. 1.75 o.p. (ISBN 0-686-61708-8). Pinnacle Bks.
--Hazard's Command. (Hazard Ser.: No. 3). 1979. pap. 1.75 o.p. (ISBN 0-523-40530-8). Pinnacle Bks.
Stuart, Vincent, et al, trs. see Diel, Paul.
Stuart, W. J. Forbidden Planet. (Science Fiction Ser.). 1978. lib. bdg. 12.50 o.p. (ISBN 0-8398-2409-2, Gregg). G K Hall.

Stuart-Burchardt, Sandra. Perceptorships in Nursing. 150p. 1983. price not set (ISBN 0-89443-936-7). Aspen Systems.

Stuart-Fox, Martin, ed. Contemporary Laos: Studies in the Politics and Society of the Lao People's Republic. 345p. 27.50 (ISBN 0-312-16676-1). St Martin.

Stuart-Harris, Charles, ed. The Control of Antibiotic-Resistant Bacteria. Harris, David. (The Beecham Colloquia: No. 4). 37.00 (ISBN 0-12-674750-4). Acad Pr.

Stuart-Harris, Charles H. Influenza: The Viruses & the Disease. LC 76-26808. (Illus.). 252p. 1976. 24.50 o.p. (ISBN 0-88416-124-2). Wright-PSG.

Stuart-Kotze, Robin. Introduction to Organizational Behavior: A Situational Approach. (Illus.). 1980. text ed. 22.95 (ISBN 0-8359-3259-1); instrs.' manual avail. (ISBN 0-8359-3260-5). Reston.

Stuart-Stubbs, Basil, jt. auth. see Verner, Coolie.

Stub, Holger R. The Social Consequences of Long Life. 320p. 1982. pap. 16.75x (ISBN 0-398-04723-5). C C Thomas.

Stubbe, John, jt. auth. see Gore, Marvin.

Stubben, D. J. Five Hundred Fifty-Five Death Row. (Illus.). 219p. (Orig.). 1981. pap. 7.95 (ISBN 0-9607868-0-5). Tri State Prom.

Stubbins, J. Social & Psychological Aspects of Disability. 640p. 1977. 26.95 (ISBN 0-8391-1119-3). Univ Park.

Stubbins, William H. Essentials of Technical Dexterity for the Clarinet. 1956. 5.00x (ISBN 0-685-21782-5). Wahr.

--Recital Literature for the Study of the Clarinet, 5 Vols. 1949. 13.00x ea. Wahr.

--The Study of the Clarinet. rev. ed. 1974. 13.00x (ISBN 0-685-42962-8). Wahr.

Stubblebine, Craig W. & Willett, Thomas D. Reaganomics: A Midterm Report. 250p. 1983. 14.95 (ISBN 0-917616-54-5). ICS Pr.

Stubblefield, Al. How to Buy Without Cash & Grow Rich. Writer's Service, Inc., ed. 131p. (Orig.). 1982. pap. 14.95 (ISBN 0-911229-00-0). Writers Serv FL.

Stubblefield, Phillip G., jt. ed. see Naftolin, Frederick.

Stubbs, Bettie. Easy Bible Talks from Common Objects. (Standard Ideas Ser.). (Illus.). 1978. pap. 1.75 o.s.i. (ISBN 0-87239-217-1, 2818). Standard Pub.

Stubbs, David, tr. see Ihara, Saikaku.

Stubbs, F., jt. auth. see Havers, J.

Stubbs, Jean. By Our Beginnings. 1980. pap. 2.50 o.p. (ISBN 0-451-09449-2, E9449, Sig). NAL.

--Imperfect Joy. 1982. pap. 3.50 (ISBN 0-451-11613-5, AE1613, Sig). NAL.

--The Vivian Inheritance. 288p. 1982. 12.95 (ISBN 0-312-85068-9). St Martin.

Stubbs, Joanna. Shetland Peg. (Illus.). (gr. 1-3). 1969. 4.25 o.p. (ISBN 0-571-08322-6). Transatlantic.

Stubbs, Joanna, jt. auth. see Fitzpatrick, Eva.

Stubbs, John C., et al, eds. Federico Fellini: A Guide to References & Resources. 1978. lib. bdg. 32.00 (ISBN 0-8161-7885-2, Hall Reference). G K Hall.

Stubbs, Marcia, jt. auth. see Barnet, Sylvan.

Stubbs, Michael. Language, Schools & Classrooms. 1977. pap. 6.95x (ISBN 0-416-31610-7). Methuen Inc.

Stubbs, Michael & Delamont, Sara, eds. Explorations in Classroom Observation. LC 74-13166. 221p. 1975. 43.95 (ISBN 0-471-83481-5, Pub. by Wiley-Interscience). Wiley.

Stubbs, Michael, jt. ed. see Agnew, Swanzie.

Stubbs, Robert S., jt. auth. see McVay, Kipling L.

Stuchlik, Milan. Life on a Half Share: Mechanisms of Social Recruitment Among the Mapuche of Southern Chile. LC 75-6049. (Illus.). 300p. 1976. 32.50- (ISBN 0-312-48440-2). St Martin.

Stuckenschmidt, Hans H. Arnold Schoenberg. LC 78-10237. (Illus.). 1979. Repr. of 1960 ed. lib. bdg. 17.50x (ISBN 0-313-20762-3, STAS). Greenwood.

Stuckey, Charles. Scottburton Chairs. (Illus.). 1983. price not set. (ISBN 0-917562-25-9). Contemp Arts.

Stuckey, Gilbert B. Evidence for the Law Enforcement Officer. 3rd ed. (Illus.). 1978. text ed. 21.95 (ISBN 0-07-062401-1, G); instructor's manual & key 3.00 (ISBN 0-07-062403-8); study guide avail. (ISBN 0-07-062402-X). McGraw.

--Procedures in the Justice System. 2nd ed. (Public Service Technology Ser.). 280p. 1980. text ed. 19.95 (ISBN 0-675-08173-4). Additional supplements may be obtained from publisher. Merrill.

Stuckey, Joan, jt. auth. see Stuckey, Ronald.

Stuckey, Ronald & Stuckey, Joan. The Lithographs of Stow Wengenroth. 1975. 25.00 o.p. (ISBN 0-517-51769-8). Crown.

--Stow Wengenroth's Lithographs: A Supplement. LC 82-72164. (Illus.). 120p. 1982. 35.00 (ISBN 0-9608834-0-1). Black Oak NY.

Stuckey, Ronald L., ed. see North American Prairie Conference, 6th, Ohio State Univ., Columbus, Ohio, Aug. 12-17, 1978.

Stuckey, W. J. Caroline Gordon. (United States Authors Ser.). lib. bdg. 12.95 (ISBN 0-8057-0332-2, Twayne). G K Hall.

Stucki, Hans-Ulrich. Product Liability: A Manual of Practice in Selected Nations, 2 vols. LC 80-28894. 1980. 100.00 ea. (ISBN 0-379-20705-2). Oceana.

Stucky, Steven. Lutoslawski & His Music. 225p. 1981. 47.50 (ISBN 0-521-22799-2). Cambridge U Pr.

Studders, R. J., jt. auth. see Parker, Rollin J.

Studdert, Richard de C. Selection: The Stress Theory of Evolution. 160p. 1983. 8.00 (ISBN 0-682-49927-7, University). Exposition.

Studebaker, Gerald A. Acoustical Factors Affecting Hearing Aid Performance. 454p. 1980. text ed. 39.95 (ISBN 0-8391-1553-9). Univ Park.

Studebaker, William. Everything Goes Without Saying. 1978. 2.50 o.p. (ISBN 0-917652-07-X). Confluence Pr.

Students, Expressive Arts Dept., Sogeri National High School, Papua New Guinea & Ison, Barry. Pukari-Voices of Papua New Guinea. LC 75-39434. (Illus., Orig.). (gr. 6 up). 1976. pap. 6.95 o.p. (ISBN 0-914488-09-0). Rand-Tofua.

Studer, Ginny L., et al. Humanities in Physical Education. Kneer, Marian, ed. (Basic Stuff Ser.: No. I, 5 of 6). (Orig.). 1981. pap. text ed. 6.25 (ISBN 0-88314-104-3). AAHPERD.

Studer, Mailyn. Precalculus. 1981. text ed. 23.50x (ISBN 0-8162-8540-3); study guide & instr's manual avail. Holden-Day.

Studt, Elliot, et al. C-Unit: Search for Community in Prison. LC 67-31158. 354p. 1968. 10.00x (ISBN 0-87154-850-X). Russell Sage.

Studva, K., jt. ed. see Pilapil, F.

Studva, Kathleen V., jt. auth. see Pilapil, Frediswinda.

Stueart, Robert D. & Eastlick, John T. Library Management. 2nd ed. LC 80-22895. (Library Science Text Ser.). 292p. 1981. text ed. 30.00 (ISBN 0-87287-241-6); pap. text ed. 21.00 (ISBN 0-87287-243-2). Libs Unl.

Stueart, Robert D. & Miller, George. Collection Development in Libraries, Pts. A & B, Vol. 10. LC 79-93165. (Foundations in Library & Information Science Monographs). (Orig.). 1980. Set. lib. bdg. 60.00 (ISBN 0-686-64266-X); lib. bdg. 40.00 ea. Pt. A (ISBN 0-89232-106-7). Pt. B (ISBN 0-89232-162-8). Jai Pr.

Stueart, Robert D., ed. see Chen, Ching-Chih.

Stueart, Robert D., ed. see Gabriel, Michael R. & Roselle, William C.

Stueart, Robert D., ed. see Jenkins, Harold R.

Stueart, Robert D., ed. see Martin, Murray S.

Stueart, Robert D., ed. see Mitchell, Betty Jo, et al.

Stueart, Robert D., ed. see Robinson, Barbara J. & Robinson, J. Cordell.

Stueart, Robert D., ed. see Tanis, Norman E. & Perkins, David L.

Stueart, Robert D., ed. see Tuttle, Marcia & Smith, Lynn.

Stueart, Robert W., ed. see Smith, Lynn S.

Stueck, William W., Jr. The Road to Confrontation: American Policy Toward China & Korea, 1947 - 1950. LC 80-11818. (Illus.). ix, 326p. 1981. 20.00x (ISBN 0-8078-1445-8); pap. 8.95 (ISBN 0-8078-4080-7). U of NC Pr.

Stugard, Christine. Living Bread. (Illus.). 200p. (Orig.). 1983. pap. 4.95 (ISBN 0-88028-023-9). Forward Movement.

Stugrin, Michael. Monarch Notes on Malory's Morte D'Arthur. 1975. pap. 1.50 (ISBN 0-671-00961-3). Monarch Pr.

Stuhlman, Daniel D. Library of Congress Headings for Judaica. LC 82-73398. (Orig.). 1982. pap. 5.00 (ISBN 0-934402-13-2). BYLS Pr.

Stuhlmann, Gunther, ed. see Nin, Anais.

Stuhlmueller, Carroll. Biblical Meditations for Lent. rev. ed. LC 77-91366. 190p. 1978. pap. 3.95 (ISBN 0-8091-2089-5). Paulist Pr.

Stuhlmueller, Carroll, jt. auth. see Senior, Donald.

Stuhmueller, Carroll C. Biblical Meditations for the Easter Season. LC 80-81030. 256p. 1980. pap. 3.95 (ISBN 0-8091-2283-9). Paulist Pr.

Stukane, Eileen, jt. auth. see Lauersen, Niels.

Stuke, J. & Brenig, W., eds. Amorphous & Liquid Semiconductors, 2 vols. LC 74-12437. 1441p. 1974. Set. 145.95 o.s.i. (ISBN 0-470-83485-4). Halsted Pr.

Stulikova, M., et al, trs. see Pribil, R.

Stull, Dalene W. Spatter of Pearls. 1966. 4.00 o.p. (ISBN 0-8233-0102-8). Golden Quill.

Stull, Daniel R., et al. Chemical Thermodynamics of Organic Compounds. LC 68-9250. 865p. 1969. 93.00 (ISBN 0-471-83490-4, Pub. by Wiley-Interscience). Wiley.

Stull, Donald, et al, eds. Anthropology & Public Policy. (Orig.). 1981. pap. 6.00 (ISBN 0-918592-50-X). Policy Studies.

Stull, James B., jt. auth. see Baird, John W.

Stultz, Newell M. Afrikaner Politics in South Africa, 1934-1948. (Perspectives on Southern Africa: Vol. 13). 1974. 31.50x (ISBN 0-520-02452-4). U of Cal Pr.

Stultz, Russell A. The Illustrated CP-M-Wordstar Dictionary. (Illus.). 192p. 1983. pap. 14.95 (ISBN 0-13-450528-X). P-H.

--The Illustrated Word Processing Dictionary. (Illus.). 176p. 1983. 10.95 (ISBN 0-13-450726-6); pap. 8.95 (ISBN 0-13-450718-5). P-H.

Stumbo, C. R. Thermobacteriology in Food Processing. 2nd ed. (Food, Science & Technology Ser.). 1973. 44.50 (ISBN 0-12-675352-0). Acad Pr.

Stumbo, C. R., et al. CRC Handbook of Lethality Guides, 2 vols. 1982. Vol. 1, 560 Pgs. 74.50 (ISBN 0-8493-2961-2); Vol. 2, 544 Pgs. 69.95 (ISBN 0-8493-2963-9). CRC Pr.

Stumm, Werner & Morgan, James J. Aquatic Chemistry: An Introduction Emphasizing Chemical Equilibria in Natural Waters. 2nd ed. LC 80-25333. 780p. 1981. 56.50 (ISBN 0-471-04831-3, Pub. by Wiley-Interscience); pap. 30.50 (ISBN 0-471-09173-1, Pub. by Wiley-Interscience). Wiley.

Stump, Robert W., jt. auth. see Marquardt, Michael.

Stumpf, Carl. Tonpsychologie: Leipzig 1883-1890, 2 vols. Repr. of 1965 ed. 80.00 o.s.i. (ISBN 90-6027-020-7, Pub. by Frits Knuf Netherlands). Pendragon NY.

Stumpf, F. B. Analytical Accoustics. LC 79-88909. 1980. 31.95 (ISBN 0-250-40302-1). Ann Arbor Science.

Stumpf, P. K. & Conn, E. E., eds. The Biochemistry of Plants: A Comprehensive Treatise, Secondary Plant Products, Vol. 7. LC 80-13168. 1981. 85.00 (ISBN 0-12-675407-1); 72.50 set (ISBN 0-12-675407-1). Acad Pr.

Stumpf, P. K. & Hatch, M. D., eds. The Biochemistry of Plants: A Comprehensive Treatise, Photosynthesis, Vol. 8. 1981. 65.00 (ISBN 0-12-675408-X); 55.00 set (ISBN 0-12-675408-X). Acad Pr.

Stumpf, Samuel. Philosophical Problems. 2nd ed. 384p. 1983. pap. text ed. 13.95x (ISBN 0-07-062180-2, C). McGraw.

--Philosophy: History & Problems. 3rd ed. (Illus.). 912p. 1983. text ed. 22.50x (ISBN 0-07-062181-0, C). Mcgraw.

Stumpf, Samuel E. Elements of Philosophy: An Introduction. 1979. text ed. 21.50 (ISBN 0-07-062216-7, C); 15.00 (ISBN 0-07-062217-5). McGraw.

--Philosophy: History & Problems. 1971. text ed. 13.95 (ISBN 0-07-062198-5, C). McGraw.

--Philosophy: History & Problems. 2nd ed. 1977. text ed. 22.50 (ISBN 0-07-062199-3, C). McGraw.

--Socrates to Sartre. 3rd ed. (Illus.). 512p. 1982. 22.50 (ISBN 0-07-062330-9). McGraw.

--Socrates to Sartre. 2nd ed. 544p. 1974. text ed. 21.95 (ISBN 0-07-062326-0, C). McGraw.

Stumpf, Walter, jt. ed. see Roth, Lloyd J.

Stunkel, Kenneth R. Relations of Indian, Greek, & Christian Thought in Antiquity. LC 79-63750. 1979. pap. text ed. 9.50 (ISBN 0-8191-0737-9). U Pr of Amer.

Stuntz, Hugh C. Gringo Yanqui. 192p. (Orig.). 1983. pap. 6.50 (ISBN 0-682-49933-1). Exposition.

Stuper, Andrew J., et al. Computer Assisted Studies of Chemical Structure & Biological Function. LC 78-12337. 220p. 1979. 43.95 (ISBN 0-471-03896-2, Pub. by Wiley-Interscience). Wiley.

Stupka, Arthur. Notes on the Birds of Great Smoky Mountains National Park. LC 63-14134. 1963. pap. 4.95 o.p. (ISBN 0-87049-042-7). U of Tenn Pr.

Sturcken, H. Tracy. Don Juan Manuel. (World Authors Ser.). 1974. lib. bdg. 15.95 (ISBN 0-8057-2590-3, +009). G K Hall.

Sturcken, H. Tracy, jt. auth. see Dalbor, John B.

Sturdevant, Celeste, jt. auth. see Lauffer, Armand.

Sturdevant, Clifford, et al. Art & Science of Operative Dentistry. (Illus.). 1968. text ed. 5.00 (ISBN 0-07-062282-5, HP). McGraw.

Sturdivant, Frederick D., et al. Managerial Analysis in Marketing. 1970. text ed. 18.95x (ISBN 0-673-05938-3). Scott F.

Sturdy, David & Sturdy, Fiona. Historic Monuments of England & Wales. (Illus.). 218p. 1977. 14.50x o.p. (ISBN 0-460-04158-4, J M Dent England England). Biblio Dist.

Sturdy, Fiona, jt. auth. see Sturdy, David.

Sturdy, John, tr. see Schmidt, Werner H.

Sturdza, Michel. Betrayal by Rulers. LC 73-92437. 1976. pap. 4.95 (ISBN 0-88279-122-2). Western Islands.

--Suicide of Europe: Memoirs of Prince Michel Sturdza. LC 68-58294. (Illus.). 1968. 12.95 (ISBN 0-88279-214-8). Western Islands.

Sturge, M. D., jt. auth. see Rashba, E. I.

Sturgeon, C. Eugene, jt. auth. see David, Irwin T.

Sturgeon, Chuck. Train up a Child. Date not set. pap. 1.50 (ISBN 0-89274-120-1). Harrison Hse.

Sturgeon, Foolbert. Best of the Rip Off Press, Vol. 3: The New Adventures of Jesus. (Best of the Rip Off Press Ser.). (Illus.). 96p. (Orig.). 1980. pap. 6.95 (ISBN 0-89620-080-9). Rip Off.

Sturgeon, Kareen B., jt. ed. see Mitton, Jeffry B.

Sturgeon, Kelso. Guide to Sports Betting. 1976. pap. 2.95 (ISBN 0-451-11196-6, AE1196, Sig). NAL.

Sturgeon, Theodore. Case & the Dreamer. (RL 6). pap. 1.50 o.p. (ISBN 0-451-07933-7, W7933, Sig). NAL.

--The Cosmic Rape. (Science Fiction Ser.). 1977. Repr. of 1958 ed. lib. bdg. 10.95 o.p. (ISBN 0-8398-2362-2, Gregg). G K Hall.

--The Dreaming Jewels. 11.00 (ISBN 0-8398-2467-X, Gregg). G K Hall.

--Venus Plus X. 176p. 1976. Repr. of 1960 ed. lib. bdg. 9.95 (ISBN 0-8398-2321-5, Gregg). G K Hall.

Sturges, Clark. Witnesses. 144p. 1974. pap. cancelled (ISBN 0-87709-221-4). Boyd & Fraser.

Sturges, Hollister, III & Weisberg, Gabriel P. Jules Breton & the French Rural Tradition. LC 82-17135. (Illus.). 148p. (Orig.). 1982. 28.50 (ISBN 0-936364-09-2). Joslyn Art.

Sturges, L. Salads-from Southern Kitchens. 1976. 10.00x o.p. (ISBN 0-911202-15-3). Radio City.

Sturges, Paul, jt. ed. see Blaug, Mark.

Sturgill, Claude C., ed. see Rolle, Denys.

Sturgis, Alice F. Learning Parliamentary Procedure. (Illus.). 1953. text ed. 23.95 (ISBN 0-07-062271-X, C). McGraw.

--Sturgis Standard Code of Parliamentary Procedure. 2nd ed. 1966. 19.95 (ISBN 0-07-062272-8, P&RB); text ed. 16.50 (ISBN 0-07-062268-X). McGraw.

--Your Farm Bureau. 1958. text ed. 5.50 (ISBN 0-07-062275-2, P&RB). McGraw.

Sturgis, Russell. Dictionary of Architecture & Building, Biographical & Descriptive, 3 Vols. LC 66-26997. (Illus.). 1966. Repr. of 1902 ed. Set. 79.00x (ISBN 0-8103-3075-X). Gale.

Sturm, James L. & Chotas, James. Stained Glass from Medieval Times to the Present: Treasures to Be Seen in New York. (Illus.). 144p. 1983. 29.95 (ISBN 0-525-20935-2, 2908-8700); pap. 16.95 (ISBN 0-525-47627-X, 01646-490). Dutton.

Sturm, Mary M. Guide to Modern Clothing. 3rd ed. 1973. 20.36 (ISBN 0-07-062293-0, W). McGraw.

Sturm, Mary M. & Grieser, E. H. Guide to Modern Clothing. (American Home & Family Ser.). (First ed. also avail. at same prices). (gr. 10-12). 1968. text ed. 20.36 (ISBN 0-07-062274-4, W); tchrs' manual 1.72 (ISBN 0-07-062226-4). McGraw.

Sturm, Ruth F. Customs Law & Administration, Bdrs. 1 & 2. 3rd ed. 400p. 1982. lib. bdg. 75.00 ea. o.s.i. (ISBN 0-379-20802-4). Oceana.

Sturm, Sara. Lorenzo de' Medici. (World Authors Ser.: Italy: No. 288). 1974. lib. bdg. 12.50 o.p. (ISBN 0-8057-2609-8, Twayne). G K Hall.

Sturma, Michael. Vice in a Vicious Society: Crime & Convicts in Mid-Nineteenth Century New South Wales. LC 82-8636. (Illus.). 224p. 1983. text ed. 32.50x (ISBN 0-7022-1911-8). U of Queensland Pr.

Sturman, Julie & Schults, Dorothy. Breeding Cockatiels. (Illus.). 93p. 1980. 4.95 (ISBN 0-87666-889-9, KW-099). TFH Pubns.

Sturmthal, Adolf. Left of Center: European Labor since World War II. LC 82-11022. 296p. 1983. 21.95 (ISBN 0-252-01008-6). U of Ill Pr.

Sturo, Edmund. Conquering Academic Failure: A Guide for Parents, Students & Educators. LC 81-85805. (Illus.). 112p. 1983. pap. 5.95 (ISBN 0-86666-060-7). GWP.

Sturrock, John, ed. Structuralism & Since. 1980. 18.95x (ISBN 0-19-215839-2). Oxford U Pr.

--Structuralism & Since: From Levi-Strauss to Derrida. 1981. pap. 6.95 (ISBN 0-19-289105-7, GB 661, GB). Oxford U Pr.

Sturrock, John, tr. see Carpentier, Alejo.

Sturrock, P. A., ed. Plasma Astrophysics. (Italian Physical Society: Course 39). 1967. 63.00 (ISBN 0-12-368839-6). Acad Pr.

Sturrock, Peter, ed. Solar Flares. LC 78-73437. 1979. 18.50x (ISBN 0-87081-076-6). Colo Assoc.

Stursberg, Peter. Lester Pearson & the American Dilemma. LC 79-7716. 1980. 19.95 o.p. (ISBN 0-385-13479-7). Doubleday.

Sturt, George. Wheelwright's Shop. 37.50 (ISBN 0-521-06570-4); pap. 11.95 (ISBN 0-521-09195-0). Cambridge U Pr.

Sturtevant, Alfred H. & Beadle, George W. Introduction to Genetics. (Illus.). 1939. pap. 4.50 o.p. (ISBN 0-486-60306-7). Dover.

Sturtevant, Donald, tr. see Breton de Nijs, E.

Sturtevant, Edgar H. The Pronunciation of Greek & Latin. 2d ed. LC 77-1194. (William Dwight Whitney Linguistic Ser.). 1977. Repr. of 1940 ed. lib. bdg. 15.75x (ISBN 0-8371-9516-0, STPRO). Greenwood.

Sturtevant, Edgar H. & Hahn, E. A. Comparative Grammar of the Hittite Language. 1951. 49.50x (ISBN 0-686-51357-6). Elliots Bks.

Sturtevant, Elsje, tr. see Breton de Nijs, E.

Sturtevant, Jane, jt. auth. see Lozano, Francisco.

Sturtevant, William C., jt. ed. see Bucher, Bernadette.

Sturtridge, Gillian, ed. see Wallace, Michael.

Sturzaker, D. & Sturzaker, J. Colour & the Kabbalah. pap. 9.50 (ISBN 0-87728-292-7). Weiser.

Sturzaker, J., jt. auth. see Sturzaker, D.

Stutchkoff, Nahum. Yiddish Thesaurus. 1950. 14.00 o.p. (ISBN 0-914080-41-5). Shulsinger Sales.

Stutman, Fred A. Walk, Don't Run: The Doctor's Book of Walking. LC 79-84815. 97p. 1979. pap. 6.95 (ISBN 0-934232-00-8). Med Manor Bks.

Stuttard, Colins & Rozee, K. R., eds. Plasmids & Transposons: Environmental Efforts & Maintenance Mechanisms. LC 80-338. 1980. 29.50 (ISBN 0-12-675550-7). Acad Pr.

Stutzman, Warren L. & Thiele, Gary A. Antenna Theory & Design. LC 80-23498. 598p. 1981. text ed. 38.50 (ISBN 0-471-04458-X); sol. manual 25.00 (ISBN 0-471-09441-2). Wiley.

Stuvel, Pieke. A Touch of Style: Sewing Simple, Inventive Clothes. (Illus.). 96p. 1981. pap. 6.95 o.p. (ISBN 0-14-046482-4). Penguin.

Stuyvenberg, Van see Van Stuyvenberg.

Stwalley, William C., jt. ed. see Cole, James L.

Stwertka, Albert, jt. auth. see Stwertka, Eve.

Stwertka, Eve & Stwertka, Albert. Genetic Engineering. (Impact Ser.). (Illus.). 96p. (gr. 7 up). 1982. PLB 8.90 (ISBN 0-531-04486-6). Watts.

--Industrial Pollution Poisoning. LC 80-25898. (Impact Bks.). (YA) (gr. 7 up). 1981. 8.90 (ISBN 0-531-04261-8); pap. 3.95 (ISBN 0-531-02138-6). Watts.

--Marijuana. (First Bks.). (Illus.). (gr. 4 up). 1979. PLB 8.90 s&l (ISBN 0-531-02944-1). Watts.
--Population: Growth, Change, & Impact. (Impact Ser.). (Illus.). 96p. (gr. 7 up). 1981. lib. bdg. 8.90 (ISBN 0-531-04350-9). Watts.
Styan, J. L. Dark Comedy: The Development of Modern Comic Tragedy. 2nd ed. LC 68-23185. 42.50 (ISBN 0-521-06572-0); pap. 11.95 (ISBN 0-521-09529-8). Cambridge U Pr.
--Dramatic Experience. 1965. 27.95 (ISBN 0-521-06573-9); pap. 9.95 (ISBN 0-521-09984-6). Cambridge U Pr.
--Elements of Drama. 1960. 37.50 (ISBN 0-521-06574-7); pap. text ed. 10.95 (ISBN 0-521-09201-9). Cambridge U Pr.
--The Shakespeare Revolution. LC 76-3043. (Illus.). 1977. 29.95 (ISBN 0-521-21193-X). Cambridge U Pr.
--The Shakespeare Revolution. LC 76-3043. 292p. Date not set. pap. 8.95 (ISBN 0-521-27328-5). Cambridge U Pr.
Stycos, J. Mayone. Family & Fertility in Puerto Rico: A Study of the Lower Income Group. LC 73-5273. (Illus.). 332p. 1973. Repr. of 1955 ed. lib. bdg. 17.50x (ISBN 0-8371-6886-4, STFF). Greenwood.
Stykolt, S., jt. auth. see Eastman, H. C.
Styles, Jimmie C., jt. auth. see Pace, Denny F.
Styles, Keith. Working Drawings Handbook. 128p. (Orig.). 1982. pap. 22.50 (ISBN 0-89397-118-9). Nichols Pub.
Styles, Margaretta M. On Nursing: Toward a New Endowment. LC 81-16980. (Illus.). 242p. 1982. pap. text ed. 14.95 (ISBN 0-8016-4874-2). Mosby.
Stylianopoulos, Theodore. The Gospel of Christ. 32p. 1981. pap. 1.95 (ISBN 0-916586-84-7). Hellenic Coll Pr.
Styrikovich, M. A., et al. Heat & Mass Transfer Source Book: Fifth All-Union Conference, Minsk, 1976. LC 77-22337. 1977. 42.95x o.s.i. (ISBN 0-470-99234-4). Halsted Pr.
Styron, Rose, jt. tr. see Carlisle, Olga A.
Styron, Thomas, jt. auth. see Johnson, Brooks.
Styron, William. Confessions of Nat Turner. 1968. pap. 2.25 o.p. (ISBN 0-451-07767-9, E7767, Sig). NAL.
--In the Clap Shack & the Long March. pap. 3.50 o.p. (ISBN 0-452-25098-6, 25098, Plume). NAL.
--Lie Down in Darkness. 1978. pap. 6.95 (ISBN 0-452-25305-5, Z5305, Plume). NAL.
--Set This House on Fire. pap. 1.95 o.p. (ISBN 0-451-07637-0, J7637, Sig). NAL.
--Sophie's Choice. 640p. 1982. pap. 3.95 (ISBN 0-553-13545-7). Bantam.
Su, Kendall L. Fundamentals of Circuits, Electronics, & Signal Analysis. LC 77-74147. (Illus.). 1978. text ed. 35.95 (ISBN 0-395-25038-2); solutions manual 7.50 (ISBN 0-395-25039-0). HM.
Suaree, Octavio de la see De la Suaree, Octavio.
Suares, Carlo. The Cipher of Genesis: The Original Code of the Qabala as Applied to the Scriptures. LC 78-58178. 1978. pap. 4.95 o.p. (ISBN 0-394-73631-1). Shambhala Pubns.
Suares, J. C. The Indispensable Cat. LC 82-10512. (Illus.). 1983. 29.95 (ISBN 0-941434-21-4). Stewart Tabori & Chang.
Suares, J. C. & Brown, Gene. Cat Scrapbook. (Illus.). 1982. pap. 5.95 (ISBN 0-452-25360-8, Plume). NAL.
Suares, J. C. & Chwast, Seymour. Literary Cat. 1977. pap. 6.95 o.p. (ISBN 0-425-03537-9, Windhover). Berkley Pub.
Suares, J. C., jt. auth. see Siegel, Richard.
Suares, Jean-Clande & Stephens, Charles. The Illustrated Horse. 1979. 12.95 o.p. (ISBN 0-517-53632-3, Harmony); pap. 6.95 o.p. (ISBN 0-517-53633-1, Harmony). Crown.
Suares, Jean-Claude & Chwast, Seymour. The Illustrated Cat. (Illus.). 1976. 12.95 o.p. (ISBN 0-517-52644-1, Dist. by Crown); pap. 6.95 o.p. (ISBN 0-517-52643-3). Crown.
Suarez & Castroleal. Aprende en Espanol y en Ingles: Readiness Level. (gr. k-1). 1978. cancelled o.p. (ISBN 0-88345-364-9); write for info. tchr's guide o.p. (ISBN 0-88345-365-7); cassettes, teacher's manuals & spirit masters 100.00 o.p. (ISBN 0-685-78815-6). Regents Pub.
Suarez, Andres. Cuba: Castroism & Communism, 1959-1966. (Studies in Communism, Revisionism & Revolution). 1967. 18.00x o.p. (ISBN 0-262-19037-0). MIT Pr.
Suarez, Diamantina V., jt. auth. see Castroleal, Alicia.
Suarez, Ernesto, tr. see Wenger, John C.
Suarez, J. C., ed. The Snoopy Collection. 96p. 1982. pap. 9.95 (ISBN 0-911818-30-8). World Almanac.
Suarez, J. C., jt. ed. see Malone, William E.
Suarez-Murias, Marguerite C. Essays on Hispanic Literature - Ensayos de Literatura Hispana: A Bilingual Anthology. LC 81-43911. Orig. Title: Eng. & Span. 220p. (Orig.). 1982. lib. bdg. 23.00 (ISBN 0-8191-2600-4); pap. text ed. 10.75 (ISBN 0-8191-2601-2). U Pr of Amer.
Suarez-Richard, Frederick. Salud, Amor y Pesetas! Basic Communication in Spanish. 169p. 1980. pap. text ed. 9.95 (ISBN 0-15-578050-6, HC). HarBraceJ.
Sub-Committee on Energy Resources & Electric Power, 12th Session. Proceedings. (Energy Resources Development Ser.: No. 11). pap. 14.50 (ISBN 0-686-92938-1, UN74/2F14, UN). Unipub.
Subak-Sharpe, Gerald E., jt. auth. see Glaser, Arthur.
Subba. Advances in Agriculture Microbiology. 1982. text ed. 89.95 (ISBN 0-408-10848-7). Butterworth.
Subbarao, E. C. & Wallace, W. E., eds. Science & Technology of Rare Earth Materials. 1980. 33.50 (ISBN 0-12-675640-6). Acad Pr.
Subbarao, K., jt. auth. see Anderson, J.
Subba Rao, N. S., ed. Recent Advances in Biological Nitrogen Fixation. 500p. 1980. text ed. 45.00x (ISBN 0-8419-5825-4). Holmes & Meier.
Sube, R., jt. auth. see Eisenreich, G.
Suben, Eric. Elves & the Shoemaker. LC 82-82287. (Little Golden Bk.). (Illus.). 24p. (ps-2). 1983. 0.89 (ISBN 0-307-03076-8, Golden Pr); PLB price not set (ISBN 0-307-60203-6). Western Pr.
Sublette, Walter. The Resurrection on Friday Night. LC 82-75869. 58p. 1977. 11.95 (ISBN 0-8040-0782-9). Swallow.
Subond, Valerie. House at Haunted Inlet. (YA) 1978. 6.95 (ISBN 0-685-87343-9, Avalon). Bouregy.
Subrahmanian, K. K. Construction Labour Market: A Study in Ahmedabad. 184p. 1982. text ed. 15.25x (ISBN 0-391-02721-2, Pub. by Concept India). Humanities.
Subramaniam, K. Brahmin Priest of Tamil Nadu. LC 74-13072. 183p. 1974. 17.95x o.s.i. (ISBN 0-470-83535-4). Halsted Pr.
Subramanian, C. V., ed. Hyphomycetes. 496p. 65.00 (ISBN 0-12-675620-1). Acad Pr.
Subramanian, Gopal & Rhodes, Buck A., eds. Radiopharmaceuticals. LC 75-16093. (Illus.). 571p. 1975. 30.00 (ISBN 0-88416-041-6). Soc Nuclear Med.
Subramanyam, B. R., ed. Computer Applications in Large Scale Power Systems: Proceedings of the Symposium, New Delhi, India, 16-19 August 1979, 3 vols. (Illus.). 1100p. 1982. 205.00 (ISBN 0-08-024450-5). Pergamon.
Subramanyam, Ka N., ed. Contemporary Indian Short Stories. 1982. o. p. 12.50x (ISBN 0-7069-0684-5, Pub. by Vikas India); pap. 3.95 (ISBN 0-7069-1624-7). Advent NY.
Subramanyan, S., jt. auth. see Kothandaraman, C. P.
Subtelny, Stephen & Konigsberg, Irwin R., eds. Determinants of Spatial Organization: Symposium of the Society for Developmental Biology, 37th. LC 78-23508. 1979. 34.00 (ISBN 0-12-612983-5). Acad Pr.
Subtelny, Stephen & Sussex, Ian M., eds. The Clonal Basis of Development. (Thirty Sixth Symposia of the Society for Developmental Biology Ser.). 1979. 34.00 (ISBN 0-12-612982-7). Acad Pr.
Subtelny, Stephen, ed. see Symposium of the Society for Developmental Biology.
Subtle, Susan, et al. The Contest Book. (Illus.). 1979. 12.95 o.p. (ISBN 0-517-53700-1, Harmony); pap. 7.95 o.p. (ISBN 0-517-53701-X). Crown.
Succop, Margaret P. Twenty-Four Sonnets & Other Poems. 1971. 5.00 (ISBN 0-911838-14-7). Windy Row.
Such, Dennis T. Nickel & Chromium Plating. 1972. pap. text ed. 49.95 (ISBN 0-408-00086-4). Butterworth.
Sucha, Peter. Kritischer Rationalismus In Theologischer Prufung. 443p. (Ger.). 1982. write for info. (ISBN 3-8204-5828-X). P Lang Pubs.
Sucharitkul, Somtow. Fire from the Wine-Dark Sea. Stine, Hank, ed. LC 82-12827. (Illus.). 200p. 1983. pap. 5.95 (ISBN 0-89865-252-9, Starblaze). Donning Co.
--Mallworld. LC 81-9827. (Illus., Orig.). 1981. pap. 5.95 (ISBN 0-89865-161-1, Starblaze). Donning Co.
Sucher, Floyd, jt. auth. see Nielsen, Patricia H.
Sucher, Floyd, et al. The Principal's Role in Improving Reading Instruction. (Illus.). 112p. 1981. pap. 11.75x (ISBN 0-398-04123-7). C C Thomas.
Sucher, Harry V. Harley-Davidson: The Milwaukee Marvel. (Illus.). 288p. 1982. 22.95 (ISBN 0-85429-261-6). Haynes Pubns.
Suchet, J. P. Crystal Chemistry & Semiconduction in Transition Metal Binary Compounds. 1971. 67.00 (ISBN 0-12-675650-3). Acad Pr.
--Electrical Conduction in Solid Materials: Physico-Chemical Bases & Possible Applications. 204p. 1975. text ed. 29.00 (ISBN 0-08-018052-3). Pergamon.
Suchlicki, Jaime, ed. Cuba, Castro, & Revolution. LC 76-177899. 1972. 9.95x o.s.i. (ISBN 0-87024-234-2). U of Miami Pr.
Suchman, Edward A. Evaluative Research: Principles & Practice in Public Service & Social Action Programs. LC 67-25913. 186p. 1968. 10.00x (ISBN 0-87154-863-1). Russell Sage.
--Sociology & the Field of Public Health. LC 63-21228. 182p. 1963. pap. 3.00x (ISBN 0-87154-864-X). Russell Sage.
Suchoff, B., jt. auth. see Bartok, B.
Suchoff, Benjamin. Guide to Bartok's "Mikrokosmos". (Music Reprint Ser.). 152p. 1982. Repr. of 1971 ed. lib. bdg. 19.50 (ISBN 0-306-76159-9). Da Capo.
Suchoff, Benjamin, ed. see Bartok, Bela.
Suckling, Colin J., et al. Chemistry Through Models. LC 77-71429. (Illus.). 1978. 49.50 (ISBN 0-521-21661-3). Cambridge U Pr.
--Chemistry Through Models. LC 77-71429. (Illus.). 321p. 1980. pap. 14.95x (ISBN 0-521-29932-2). Cambridge U Pr.
Suda, J. Religions in India: A Study of Their Essential Unity. 1978. text ed. 15.00x (ISBN 0-391-01085-9). Humanities.
Suda, M. & Hayaishi, O. Biological Rythyms & Their Central Mechanism. 1980. 90.00 (ISBN 0-444-80136-7). Elsevier.
Sudarshan, E. C. & Mukunda, N. Classical Dynamics: A Modern Perspective. LC 73-11312. 615p. 1974. 49.95 o.s.i. (ISBN 0-471-83540-4, Pub. by Wiley-Interscience). Wiley.
--Classical Dynamics: A Modern Perspective. LC 82-21237. 630p. 1983. Repr. of 1974 ed. lib. bdg. write for info. (ISBN 0-89874-583-7). Krieger.
Suddaby, Elizabeth & Yarrow, P. J., eds. Lady Morgan in France. 1971. 19.95 o.p. (ISBN 0-85362-103-9, Oriel). Routledge & Kegan.
Suddard, Adrienne, jt. ed. see LeBar, Frank M.
Suddarth, jt. auth. see Brunner.
Suddarth, Doris, jt. auth. see Brunner, Lillian.
Sudhalter, Treva R. Innocent Questions: Feminist Satire, Personal Essays & Genital Fables. 150p. 1982. pap. cancelled (ISBN 0-938604-01-5). Foxmoor.
Sudhof, H., jt. ed. see Schoen, R.
Sudilovsky, A., et al, eds. Predictability in Psychopharmacology: Preclinical & Clinical Correlations. LC 74-14483. 320p. 1975. 34.50 (ISBN 0-89004-017-6). Raven.
Sudman, Seymour. Applied Sampling. (Quantitative Studies in Social Relations Ser.). 1976. 19.50 (ISBN 0-12-675750-X). Acad Pr.
Sudman, Seymour & Bradburn, Norman M. Asking Questions: A Practial Guide to Questionnaire Design. LC 82-48065. (Social & Behavioral Science Ser.). 1982. text ed. 18.95x (ISBN 0-87589-546-8). Jossey Bass.
Sudnow, David. Passing On: The Social Organization of Dying. (Orig.). 1967. pap. 12.95 (ISBN 0-13-652719-1). P-H.
--Pilgrim in the Microworld. 240p. (Orig.). 1983. 15.50 (ISBN 0-446-51261-3). Warner Bks.
--Talk's Body: A Meditation Between Two Keyboards. LC 79-2120. 1979. 7.95 o.p. (ISBN 0-394-50270-1). Knopf.
Sudo, T. & Shimoda, S. Clay & Clay Minerals of Japan. (Developments in Sedimentology: Vol. 6). 1978. 78.25 (ISBN 0-444-99787-3). Elsevier.
Sudo, T., et al. Electron Micrographs of Clay Minerals. (Developments in Sedimentology: Vol. 31). 1981. 64.00 (ISBN 0-444-99751-2). Elsevier.
Sudraka, Kind. Mrcchakatika, the Little Clay Cart. Oliver, Revilo, tr. from Sanskrit. LC 74-14116. (Illinois Studies in Language & Literature: Vol. 23, Nos. 1-2). 250p. 1975. Repr. of 1938 ed. lib. bdg. 17.00x (ISBN 0-8371-7789-8, SULC). Greenwood.
Sudweeks, Deanna. Kitchen Magic. (Illus.). 1977. pap. 7.95 (ISBN 0-89036-121-5). Hawkes Pub Inc.
Sue, D. W., et al. Counseling the Culturally Different: Theory & Practice. 303p. 1981. 24.95x (ISBN 0-471-04218-8, Pub. by Wiley-Interscience). Wiley.
Sue, David, et al. Understanding Abnormal Behavior. 1981. 24.50 (ISBN 0-395-30752-X); instr's manual 2.50 (ISBN 0-395-30753-8). HM.
Sue, Eugene. The Mysteries of Paris, 3 vols. Date not set. Repr. of 1912 ed. price not set (ISBN 0-86527-281-6). Fertig. Postponed.
Sue, John. The How-to Cookbook. (Illus.). 32p. 1982. pap. 6.95 (ISBN 0-399-20890-9, Philomel). Putnam Pub Group.
--The Time to Eat Cookbook. (Illus.). 32p. 1982. pap. 6.95 (ISBN 0-399-20898-4, Philomel). Putnam Pub Group.
Sue, Stanley & Morishima, James K. The Mental Health of Asian Americans: Contemporary Issues in Identifying & Treating Mental Problems. LC 82-48060. (Social & Behavioral Science Ser.). 1982. text ed. 15.95x (ISBN 0-87589-535-2). Jossey Bass.
Sue, Stanley & Moore, Thomas, eds. The Pluralistic Society: A Community Mental Health Perspective. (Community Psychology Ser.: Vol. 9). 256p. 1983. 26.95 (ISBN 0-89885-055-X). Human Sci Pr.
Sue, Stanley & Wagner, Nathaniel N., eds. Asian American Psychological Perspectives. LC 72-84064. 1973. pap. 7.95x (ISBN 0-8314-0033-1). Sci & Behavior.
Suedfeld, Peter. Restricted Environmental Stimulation: Research & Clinical Application. LC 79-26927. (Wiley Series on Personality Processes). 513p. 1980. 33.95x (ISBN 0-471-83536-6, Pub. by Wiley-Interscience). Wiley.
Suelflow, Roy. Christian Churches in Recent Times. 1980. pap. 6.50 (ISBN 0-570-06274-8, 12-2747). Concordia.
Sueltz, Arthur F. Deeper into John's Gospel. LC 78-3353. (Orig.). 1979. pap. 4.95i o.p. (ISBN 0-06-067764-3, RD 273, HarpR). Har-Row.
--Life at Close Quarters. 1982. 6.95 (ISBN 0-8499-0285-1). Word Pub.
Suematsu, Yasuharu & Iga, Ken-Ichi. Introduction to Optical Fiber Communications. LC 81-23064. (Wiley Ser. in Pure Applied Optics). 208p. 1982. 29.95 (ISBN 0-471-09143-X, Pub. by Wiley-Interscience). Wiley.
Suen, Ching Y. & DeMori, Renato, eds. Computer Analysis & Perception: Visual Signals, Vol. 1. 176p. 1982. 57.00 (ISBN 0-8493-6305-5). CRC Pr.
Suenaga, M. Pictorial History of Ancient Japanese Weapons, Armour, & Artifacts. (Illus.). 100p. Date not set. pap. 12.50 (ISBN 0-87556-582-4). Saifer.
Suendermann, J. & Lenz, W., eds. North Sea Dynamics. (Illus.). 670p. 1983. 41.00 (ISBN 0-387-12013-0). Springer-Verlag.
Suendermann, J., jt. ed. see Brosche, F.
Suenens, Leon J. A New Pentecost? 1975. 3.00 (ISBN 0-8164-0276-0). Seabury.
--Your God? 1978. pap. 2.50 (ISBN 0-8164-2192-7). Seabury.
Suenens, Leon-Joseph. Renewal & the Powers of Darkness. 120p. (Orig.). 1983. pap. 4.95 (ISBN 0-89283-125-1). Servant.
Suess, A. R. & Dugger, W. E., Jr. Introduction to Power System. 1976. pap. 8.96 o.p. (ISBN 0-02-829280-4); ed. 2.00tchr's o.p. (ISBN 0-02-829290-1). Glencoe.
Suessmuth, Patrick. Ideas for Training Managers & Supervisors: Useful Suggestions, Activities, & Instruments. LC 77-93408. 328p. 1978. pap. 19.50 (ISBN 0-88390-143-9). Univ Assocs.
Suetonius. Divus Julius Caesar. Butler, H. E. & Cary, M., eds. 1927. 13.95x o.p. (ISBN 0-19-814418-0). Oxford U Pr.
Sueur, Meridel le see Le Sueur, Meridel.
Sueur, Meridel Le see Le Sueur, Meridel.
Sueur, Sadie Le see Le Sueur, Sadie.
Suffet, I. H. Fate of Pollutants in the Air & Water Environments, 2 pts. LC 76-58408. (Advances in Environmental Science & Technology). 1977. Pt. 1, 484. 72.50x (ISBN 0-471-83539-0, Pub. by Wiley-Interscience); Pt. 2, 442. 67.95x (ISBN 0-471-01803-1). Wiley.
Suffet, I. H. & McGuire, M. J., eds. Activated Carbon Absorption or Organics from the Aqueous Phase, 2 vols. LC 79-55147. (Illus.). 1980. 49.95 ea.; Vol. 1. (ISBN 0-250-40269-6); Vol. 2. 49.95 (ISBN 0-250-40297-1). Ann Arbor Science.
Suffling, Ernest. Church Festival Decorations. 2nd enl. ed. LC 74-6266. (Illus.). vi, 156p. 1974. Repr. of 1907 ed. 37.00x (ISBN 0-8103-4015-1). Gale.
Sugano, Satoru, et al. Multiplets of Transition-Metal Ions in Crystals. (Pure & Applied Physics Ser.: Vol. 33). 1970. 63.00 (ISBN 0-12-676050-0). Acad Pr.
Sugar, A. T., tr. see Von Frisch, Karl.
Sugar, Bert, jt. auth. see Speca, Bob, Jr.
Sugar, Bert, ed. Great Baseball Players of the Past: 32 Picture Postcards. (Illus.). 1978. pap. 3.00 (ISBN 0-486-23708-7). Dover.
Sugar, Bert R. The Book of Sports Quotes. (Illus.). 128p. 1981. pap. 5.95 (ISBN 0-8256-3145-9, Quick Fox). Putnam Pub Group.
--Collectibles: The Nostalgia Collectors Bible. 1981. pap. 12.95 (ISBN 0-8256-3149-1, Quick Fox). Putnam Pub Group.
--Five Hundred & Five Boxing Questions Your Friends Don't Answer. 160p. 1982. 9.95 (ISBN 0-8027-7180-7); pap. 6.95 (ISBN 0-8027-7170-X). Walker & Co.
--Sports Collector's Bible. 4th rev. ed. 578p. pap. 12.95 (ISBN 0-672-52741-3). Bobbs.
Sugar, Bert R., jt. auth. see Amazing Randi.
Sugar, Bert R., ed. American & National League Baseball Card Classics. 1982. pap. 2.95 ea. (ISBN 0-486-24308-7). Dover.
Sugar, Max, ed. Adolescent Parenthood. 256p. 1983. text ed. 25.00 (ISBN 0-89335-185-7). SP Med & Sci Bks.
Sugar, Peter F., ed. Ethnic Diversity & Conflict in Eastern Europe. LC 80-12033. 553p. 1980. 27.50 (ISBN 0-87436-297-0). ABC-Clio.
Sugarman, Allan S., jt. auth. see Greenberg, Sidney.
Sugarman, Daniel A. & Hochstein, Rolaine. Seventeen Guide to Knowing Yourself. (gr. 7-12). 1968. 9.95 o.p. (ISBN 0-02-615300-9). Macmillan.
Sugarman, Joan G., jt. auth. see Freeman, Grace.
Sugarman, Joseph. Success Forces. 1980. 9.95 o.p. (ISBN 0-8092-7061-7). Contemp Bks.
Sugarman, Stephen D., jt. auth. see Coons, John E.
Sugden, D. E. & John, B. S. Glaciers & Landscape: A Geomorphological Approach. LC 76-11014. 1976. 24.95x (ISBN 0-470-15113-7). Halsted Pr.
Sugden, David. Arctic & Antarctic: A Modern Geographical Synthesis. LC 82-13788. (Illus.). 480p. 1982. text ed. 35.00x (ISBN 0-389-20298-3). B&N Imports.
Sugden, Howard F. & Wiersbe, Warren W. Confident Pastoral Leadership. Orig. Title: When Pastors Wonder How. (Orig.). 1977. pap. 5.95 (ISBN 0-8024-1598-9). Moody.
Sugden, John. Niccolo Paganini: Supreme Violinist or Devil's Fiddler? (Illus.). 168p. 1982. 16.95 (ISBN 0-686-97237-6). Hippocrene Bks.
--Paganini: His Life & Times. expanded ed. (Life & Times Ser.). (Illus.). 208p. 1980. 12.95 (ISBN 0-87666-642-X, Z-41). Paganiniana Pubns.
Sugerman, A. Arthur, jt. ed. see Tarter, Ralph E.
Sugerman, Daniel, jt. auth. see Hopkins, Jerry.
Sugg, Alfred, tr. see Aeschylus & Sophocles.
Sugg, Joyce, ed. A Packet of Letters: A Selection from the Correspondence of John Henry Newman. (Illus.). 194p. 1983. 19.95 (ISBN 0-19-826442-9). Oxford U Pr.
Sugg, Redding S., Jr. A Painter's Psalm: The Mural in Walter Anderson's Cottage. (Illus.). 1978. 18.95 o.p. (ISBN 0-87870-046-3). Memphis St Univ.
Sugg, Redding S, Jr., jt. auth. see White, Helen.
Sugg, Richard P. Appreciating Poetry. 1975. pap. text ed. 12.95 (ISBN 0-395-19375-3); instr's. manual 1.65 (ISBN 0-395-19373-7). HM.
Suggitt, G., jt. auth. see McArdle, H.

Suggs, M. Jack. Wisdom, Christology, & Law in Matthew's Gospel. LC 75-95930. 1970. text ed. 7.95x o.p. (ISBN 0-674-95375-4). Harvard U Pr.

Sugi, Haruo. Cross Bridge Mechanisms in Muscle Contraction. 690p. 1979. text ed. 84.50 o.p. (ISBN 0-8391-1481-8). Univ Park.

Sugimoto, Masayoshi & Swain, David L. Science & Culture in Traditional Japan: A.D. 600-1854. (East Asian Studies Ser.). 1978. 45.00x o.p. (ISBN 0-262-19155-5). MIT Pr.

Sugimura, A. & Uyeda, S. Island Arcs. LC 77-180008. (Developments in Geotectonics: Vol. 3). (Illus.). 240p. 1973. 61.75 (ISBN 0-444-40970-X). Elsevier.

Sugimura, Takashi, ed. The Nitroquinolines. (Carcinogenesis, A Comprehensive Survey: Vol. 6). 164p. 1981. text ed. 27.50 (ISBN 0-89004-162-8). Raven.

Sugimura, Takashi & Kondo, Sohei, eds. Environmental Mutagens & Carcinogens. LC 82-15231. 784p. 1982. 80.00 (ISBN 0-8451-3007-2). A R Liss.

Sugimura, Yuzo. Chinese Sculpture, Bronzes, & Jades in Japanese Collections. Watson, Burton, tr. (Illus.). 1966. 20.00 o.p. (ISBN 0-8248-0054-0, Eastwest Ctr). UH Pr.

Sugita, Y. Blackie, the Bird Who Could. (gr. k-3). 1975. PLB 5.72 o.p. (ISBN 0-07-061779-1, GB). McGraw.

Sugita, Yutaka. The Flower Family. new ed. (Illus.). 32p. (ps-3). 1975. 5.95 o.p. (ISBN 0-07-061768-6, GB); PLB 5.72 o.p. (ISBN 0-07-061769-4). McGraw.

--Goodnight, One, Two, Three. LC 76-149045. (Illus.). 32p. (ps-2). 6.50 (ISBN 0-87592-022-5). Scroll Pr.

Suh, C. H. & Radcliffe, C. W. Kinematics & Mechanisms Design. LC 77-7102. 434p. 1978. 46.50 o.s.i. (ISBN 0-471-01461-3). Wiley.

Suh, Chul Won. The Creation-Mediatorship of Jesus Christ. (Amsterdam Studies in Theology: Vol. IV). 325p. 1982. pap. text ed. 27.75x (ISBN 90-6203-624-4, Pub. by Rodopi Holland). Humanities.

Suh, Dae-Sook. Korean Communism, Nineteen Forty-Five to Nineteen Eighty: A Reference Guide to the Political System. LC 81-12952. 540p. 1981. text ed. 35.00x (ISBN 0-8248-0740-5). UH Pr.

Suh, N. P. & Tucker, C. L., III, eds. Polymer Processing: Analysis & Innovation. (PED Ser.: Vol. 5). 163p. 1982. 30.00 (H00229). ASME.

Suh, Nam P. & Saka, Nannaji, eds. Fundamentals of Tribology. (Illus.). 1206p. 1980. 92.50x (ISBN 0-262-19183-0). MIT Pr.

Suh, Nam P. & Sung, Nak-Ho, eds. Science & Technology of Polymer Processing: Proceedings of the International Conference on Polymer Processsing. (Illus.). 1979. 60.00x (ISBN 0-262-19179-2). MIT Pr.

Suhadolnik, R. J. Nucleosides As Biological Probes. 346p. 1979. 75.95 (ISBN 0-471-05317-1). Wiley.

Suhadolnik, Robert J. Nucleoside Antibiotics. LC 73-115655. 1970. 35.00 (ISBN 0-471-83543-9, Pub. by Wiley). Krieger.

Suharno, Ignatius & Pike, Kenneth L., eds. From Baudi to Indonesian. 209p. 1976. 5.00x (ISBN 0-88312-765-2); microfiche 3.00x (ISBN 0-88312-348-7). Summer Inst Ling.

Suhl, Harry & Maple, M. Brian, eds. Superconductivity in D & F-Band Metals. LC 80-12907. 1980. 45.50 (ISBN 0-12-676150-7). Acad Pr.

Suhl, Yuri. An Album of the Jews in America. 96p. Repr. 2.95 (ISBN 0-686-95114-X). ADL.

--They Fought Back: The Story of Jewish Resistance in Nazi Europe. 316p. Repr. 7.95 (ISBN 0-686-95093-3). ADL.

Suhl, Yuri, ed. & tr. They Fought Back: The Story of the Jewish Resistance in Nazi Europe. LC 74-26766. (Illus.). 351p. 1975. pap. 7.95 (ISBN 0-8052-0479-2). Schocken.

Suhrke, Astri, jt. auth. see Morrison, Charles E.

Suid, Murray, jt. auth. see Morrow, James.

Suina, Joseph H., jt. auth. see Loughlin, Catherine E.

Suinn, Richard M. Fundamentals of Behavior Pathology. 2nd ed. LC 74-30206. (Series in Psychology). 595p. 1975. text ed. 30.50 (ISBN 0-471-83547-1); avail. tchr's manual (ISBN 0-471-83548-X). Wiley.

--Psychology in Sport: Methods & Applications. LC 79-55482. (Orig.). 1980. pap. text ed. 11.95x (ISBN 0-8087-3532-2). Burgess.

Suire, C., ed. Congres International De Bryologie, Bordeaux 1977: Proceedings. (Bryophytorum Bibliotheca Ser.: No. 13). (Illus.). 1978. lib. bdg. 80.00 (ISBN 3-7682-1163-0). Lubrecht & Cramer.

Suit, Herman D. & Proppe, Karl H. Soft Tissue Sarcomas. (Illus.). 253p. 1983. pap. 100.00 (ISBN 0-08-027468-4, H210, H230). Pergamon.

Suitin, L. Cook Chinese. (Golden Asia Cookbooks). (Illus.). 152p. 1983. pap. 21.95 (ISBN 9971-65-076-2). Hippocrene Bks.

Suk, Julie, jt. ed. see Newman, Anne.

Sukenick, Ronald. Out: A Novel. LC 82-73419. 295p. 1973. 11.95 (ISBN 0-8040-0630-X). Swallow.

Sukhatme, Balkrishna V., jt. auth. see Sukhatme, Pandurang V.

Sukhatme, Pandurang V. & Sukhatme, Balkrishna V. Sampling Theory of Surveys with Applications. facsimile ed. 1970. pap. 13.90x o.p. (ISBN 0-8138-2395-1). Iowa St U Pr.

Sukhwal, Bheru L. South Asia: A Systematic Geographic Bibliography. LC 74-10852. 1974. 35.00 o.p. (ISBN 0-8108-0761-0). Scarecrow.

Suki, Wadi N. The Kidney in Systemic Disease. 2nd ed. (Perspectives in Nephrology & Hypertension Ser.). 660p. 1981. 60.00 (ISBN 0-471-02632-8, Pub. by Wiley Med). Wiley.

Sukiennicki, Wiktor. East Central Europe in World War I: From Foreign Domination to National Freedom. (Brooklyn College Studies on Society in Change). 1050p. 1982. 45.00x (ISBN 0-88033-012-0, Dist. by Columbia University Press). East Eur Quarterly.

Sukijasovic, Miodrag. Yugoslav Foreign Investment at Work: Experiences So Far. 178p. 1970. 12.00 (ISBN 0-379-00476-3). Oceana.

Suksamran, Somboon. Political Buddhism in Southeast Asia: The Role of the Sangha in the Modernization of Thailand. LC 77-77606. (Illus.). 1977. 20.00x (ISBN 0-312-62137-X). St Martin.

Sukus, Jan. My Little Circus. (Put & Play Ser.). (ps). 1981. 4.50 (ISBN 0-307-05101-3, Golden Pr). Western Pub.

Suleiman, Ezra N., ed. Higher Civil Servants in the Policy Making Process. 350p. 1983. text ed. price not set (ISBN 0-8419-0847-8). Holmes & Meier.

Suleiman, Ezra N., jt. ed. see Warnecke, Steven J.

Suleiman, Susan, tr. see Friedlander, Saul.

Sulkin, Sidney. The Secret Seed. 1983. 11.95 (ISBN 0-686-91653-0); pap. 5.95 (ISBN 0-686-97553-7). Dryad Pr.

Sullender, R. Scott. Family Enrichment Workshops: Leader's Manual. 125p. (Orig.). 1982. pap. 12.95 (ISBN 0-940754-17-7). Ed Ministries.

--Family Enrichment Workshops (Participant's Books) 70p. 1982. pap. 7.50 (ISBN 0-940754-16-9). Ed Ministries.

Sullens, Idelle, ed. The Whole Idea Catalog: College Writing Projects. 1971. pap. text ed. 5.95 (ISBN 0-685-55641-7, 31028). Phila Bk Co.

Sullens, Idelle, ed. see Robert Mannyng of Brunne.

Sullerot, Evelyn. Women on Love: Eight Centuries of Feminine Writing. Lane, Helen R., tr. LC 76-51985. (Illus.). 1979. 12.95 o.p. (ISBN 0-385-11247-5). Doubleday.

Sullerot, Evelyne. Woman, Society & Change. Archer, Margaret S., tr. from Fr. LC 78-90234. (Illus., Orig.). 1971. 4.95 o.p. (ISBN 0-07-062336-8, SP); pap. 3.95 (ISBN 0-07-062335-X). McGraw.

Sullivan. Standards & Standardization. 136p. 1983. price not set (ISBN 0-8247-1919-0). Dekker.

Sullivan, Antony. Robert Thomas Bugeaud, France & Algeria 1784-1849: Politics, Power & the Good Society. 1983. 24.50 (ISBN 0-208-01969-3, Archon Bks). Shoe String.

Sullivan, Arthur, jt. auth. see Gilbert, W. S.

Sullivan Assoc. I Can Read, 8 bks. (Bk. 8, 0-8449-2995-6; tchr's. manual 1.25 or free with I Can Read Set). Set. pap. 16.00 (ISBN 0-686-93297-8); Bk. 1. pap. (ISBN 0-686-73683-4); Bk. 2. pap. (ISBN 0-8449-2989-1); Bk. 3. pap. (ISBN 0-8449-2990-5); Bk. 4. pap. (ISBN 0-8449-2991-3); Bk. 5. pap. (ISBN 0-8449-2992-1); Bk. 6. pap. (ISBN 0-8449-2993-X); Bk. 7. pap. (ISBN 0-8449-2994-8). Learning Line.

Sullivan Associates. Programmed Mathematics Series, Bks. 9-15. 2nd ed. Incl. Bk. 9. Consumer Math (ISBN 0-07-062069-5); Bk. 10. Personal Math (ISBN 0-07-062070-9); Bk. 11. More Personal Math (ISBN 0-07-062071-7); Bk. 12. Understanding Algebra (ISBN 0-07-062072-5); Bk. 13. Using Algebra (ISBN 0-07-062073-3); Bk. 14. Using Geometry (ISBN 0-07-062074-1); Bk. 15. Using Trigonometry (ISBN 0-07-062075-X). 1975. 4.60; instr's. guide 9.88 (ISBN 0-07-062076-8); exam pak 32.88 (ISBN 0-07-079360-3). McGraw.

--Programmed Reading, Ser. 1, Bks. 1-7. 2nd ed. 1968. text ed. 5.60 ea. McGraw.

--Read & Think Storybook Series, 15 bks. Bks. 1-7. 8.36 ea. (ISBN 0-686-76801-9, W); Bk. 8-15. 9.72 ea. (ISBN 0-686-76802-7). tchrs. guide 11.76 ea. (ISBN 0-07-063216-2). McGraw.

Sullivan, Barbara. First Born, Second Born. 186p. 1983. pap. 5.95 (ISBN 0-310-60380-3). Chosen Bks Pub.

--A Page a Day for Lent Nineteen Eighty-Three. LC 82-60607. 56p. 1983. pap. 2.50. Paulist Pr.

--A Page a Day for Lent Nineteen Eighty-Two. 100p. (Orig.). 1982. pap. 2.50 o.p. (ISBN 0-8091-2409-2). Paulist Pr.

Sullivan, Barbara, ed. Daily Prayer: Words & Deeds. 56p. pap. 2.50. Paulist Pr.

Sullivan, Barbara P., jt. ed. see Kellogg, Carolyn J.

Sullivan, C., jt. auth. see Perles, B.

Sullivan, Catherine M., jt. auth. see Gilbert, Jeanne G.

Sullivan, Colin E., et al, eds. The Control of Breathing During Sleep. (Reprint of Sleep Journal: Vol. 3, No. 3-4). 256p. 1981. text ed. 33.00 (ISBN 0-89004-652-2). Raven.

Sullivan, Colleen. The Money Market Fund Primer. 192p. 1983. 13.50 (ISBN 0-02-615440-4). Macmillan.

Sullivan, Constance, compiled by. Nude. LC 79-1797. (Illus.). 224p. 1980. 10.95i (ISBN 0-06-012708-2, HarpT). Har-Row.

Sullivan, D. J. Fundamentals of Logic. 1963. text ed. 24.50 (ISBN 0-07-062338-4, C). McGraw.

Sullivan, Daniel J. Small Business Management: A Practical Approach. 470p. 1977. text ed. write for info. o.p. (ISBN 0-697-08013-7). Wm C Brown.

Sullivan, Daniel J. & Lane, Joseph F. Small Business Management: A Practical Approach. 2nd ed. 480p. 1983. text ed. write for info. (ISBN 0-697-08089-7); instr's manual avail. (ISBN 0-697-08181-8). Wm C Brown.

Sullivan, Debbie. Pocketful of Puppets: Activities for the Special Child. Keller, Merily H., ed. (Puppetry in Education Ser.). (Illus.). 48p. (Orig.). 1982. pap. 5.50 (ISBN 0-931044-07-3). Renfro Studios.

Sullivan, Denis G., et al. How America Is Ruled. 550p. 1980. pap. 19.95 (ISBN 0-471-83554-4); tchrs. manual 4.00 (ISBN 0-471-07804-2). Wiley.

--The Politics of Representation: The Democratic Convention 1972. (Orig.). 1974. 17.95 o.p. (ISBN 0-312-62790-4); pap. text ed. 8.95 o.p. (ISBN 0-312-62825-0). St Martin.

Sullivan, Donald. Gambling Times Guide to Winning by Computer. (Illus., Orig.). Date not set. pap. text ed. 3.95 (ISBN 0-89746-018-9). Lyle Stuart.

Sullivan, E. J., jt. auth. see Dorling, T. A.

Sullivan, Edmund P. Collecting Political Americana. (Illus.). 1979. 15.95 o.p. (ISBN 0-517-53618-8). Crown.

Sullivan, Edmund V. Moral Learning. LC 74-31726. 136p. 1975. pap. 3.95 o.p. (ISBN 0-8091-1872-6). Paulist Pr.

Sullivan, Edward D., ed. The Utopian Vision: Dream & Reality. LC 82-50755. (Chataqua Ser.: No. 1). 272p. (Orig.). 1983. 28.00x (ISBN 0-916304-51-5); pap. 10.00x (ISBN 0-916304-52-3). Campanile.

Sullivan, Eleanor, ed. Alfred Hitchcock's Tales to Be Read with Caution. 1979. 9.95 o.s.i. (ISBN 0-8037-0343-0). Davis Pubns.

--Alfred Hitchcock's Tales to Fill You with Fear & Trembling. 1980. 9.95 o.s.i. (ISBN 0-8037-0392-9). Davis Pubns.

--Alfred Hitchcock's Tales to Keep You Spellbound. 1976. 8.95 o.s.i. (ISBN 0-8037-0077-6). Davis Pubns.

--Alfred Hitchcock's Tales to Make Your Blood Run Cold. 1978. 8.95 o.s.i. (ISBN 0-8037-0134-9). Davis Pubns.

--Alfred Hitchcock's Tales to Make Your Hair Stand on End. 348p. 1981. 9.95 o.s.i. (ISBN 0-8037-0028-8). Davis Pubns.

--Alfred Hitchcock's Tales to Make Your Teeth Chatter. 348p. 1980. 9.95 o.s.i. (ISBN 0-8037-0173-X). Davis Pubns.

--Alfred Hitchcock's Tales to Scare You Stiff. 1978. 8.95 o.s.i. (ISBN 0-8037-0135-7). Davis Pubns.

--Alfred Hitchcock's Tales to Send Chills Down Your Spine. 1979. 8.95 o.s.i. (ISBN 0-8037-0342-2). Davis Pubns.

Sullivan, Elizabeth M., jt. ed. see Anderson, Ernest C.

Sullivan, Eugene J. & Suritz, Penelope W. General Education & Associate Degrees: A National Study. 1979. 5.00 o.p. (ISBN 0-686-75228-7). ACE.

Sullivan, Eugene T., jt. ed. see Sullivan, Marilynn C.

Sullivan, F. M., jt. ed. see Barlow, S. M.

Sullivan, F. Russell. Faith & Reason in Kierkegaard. LC 78-60695. 1978. pap. text ed. 8.25 (ISBN 0-8191-0559-7). U Pr of Amer.

Sullivan, Faith. Watchdog. 1982. pap. 11.95 (ISBN 0-07-062355-4). Mcgraw.

--Watchdog. 1983. pap. 2.95 (ISBN 0-686-43067-0, Sig). NAL.

Sullivan, Frances P. Table Talk with the Recent God: Poems & Liturgies. LC 73-92893. 146p. (Orig.). 1974. pap. 4.95 o.p. (ISBN 0-8091-1818-1). Paulist Pr.

Sullivan, Francis A. Charisms & Charismatic Renewal: A Biblical & Theological Study. 182p. 1982. pap. 8.50 (ISBN 0-89283-121-9). Servant.

Sullivan, George. Bart Starr: The Cool Quarterback. (Putnam Sports Shelf Ser.). (Illus.). (gr. 7 up). 1970. PLB 5.49 o.p. (ISBN 0-399-60040-X). Putnam Pub Group.

--Bert Jones: Born to Play Football. LC 77-24906. (Putnam Sports Shelf Ser.). (Illus.). (gr. 6-8). 1977. PLB 5.29 o.p. (ISBN 0-399-61103-7). Putnam Pub Group.

--Better Roller Skating for Boys & Girls. LC 79-22717. (Better Sports Ser.). (Illus.). (gr. 4 up). 1980. PLB 6.95 (ISBN 0-396-07784-6). Dodd.

--Better Soccer for Boys & Girls. LC 77-16869. (Better Sports Ser.). (Illus.). (gr. 4 up). 1978. 6.95 (ISBN 0-396-07533-9). Dodd.

--Better Softball for Boys & Girls. LC 74-25507. (Better Sports Ser.). (gr. 4 up). 1975. 6.95 (ISBN 0-396-07063-9). Dodd.

--Better Swimming for Boys & Girls. LC 82-4992. (Better Sports Ser.). (Illus.). 64p. (gr. 5 up). 1982. PLB 7.95 (ISBN 0-396-08071-5). Dodd.

--Better Weight Training for Boys. LC 82-19871. (Better Sports Ser.). (Illus.). 64p. (gr. 6 up). 1983. PLB 8.95 (ISBN 0-396-08121-5). Dodd.

--Bobby Bonds: Rising Superstar. LC 75-45427. (Putnam Sports Shelf Biography Ser.). 128p. (gr. 5 up). 1976. PLB 5.29 o.p. (ISBN 0-399-61001-4). Putnam Pub Group.

--The Complete Beginner's Guide to Pool & Other Billiard Games. LC 78-60303. 1979. 9.95a o.p. (ISBN 0-385-13337-5); PLB (ISBN 0-385-13338-3). Doubleday.

--Discover Archaeology. LC 79-7223. (Illus.). 1980. 10.95 o.p. (ISBN 0-385-14522-5). Doubleday.

--Football. LC 72-2790. (All Star Sports Ser). (Illus.). 128p. (gr. 4 up). 1972. 5.95 o.s.i. (ISBN 0-695-80035-3); PLB 5.97 o.s.i. (ISBN 0-695-40035-5). Follett.

--Hank Aaron. LC 74-76357. (See & Read Biography Ser.). (Illus.). 64p. (gr. k-3). 1975. PLB 4.49 o.p. (ISBN 0-399-60904-0). Putnam Pub Group.

--Inside Nuclear Submarines. LC 82-45384. (Illus.). 160p. (gr. 7 up). 1982. PLB 10.95 (ISBN 0-396-08093-6). Dodd.

--Larry Csonka: Power & Pride. LC 74-21063. (Putnam Sports Hero Ser.). (gr. 3-5). 1975. PLB 5.49 o.p. (ISBN 0-399-60953-9). Putnam Pub Group.

--Making Money in Autographs. (Illus.). 224p. 1977. 8.95 o.p. (ISBN 0-698-10747-0, Coward). Putnam Pub Group.

--Paddle: The Beginner's Guide to Platform Tennis. LC 75-10478. (Illus.). 224p. 1975. 8.95 o.p. (ISBN 0-698-10693-8, Coward). Putnam Pub Group.

--The Picture Story of Nadia Comaneci. LC 77-21345. (Illus.). 64p. (gr. 3-6). 1977. PLB 6.97 o.p. (ISBN 0-671-32925-1). Messner.

--Plants to Grow Indoors. (Beginning-to-Read Bks). (Illus.). (ps). pap. 1.50 o.s.i. (ISBN 0-695-37114-2). Follett.

--Pro Football's Greatest Upsets. LC 74-163175. (Sports Library Ser.). (Illus.). 96p. (gr. 3-6). 1972. PLB 7.12 (ISBN 0-8116-6662-X). Garrard.

--Roger Staubach: A Special Kind of Quarterback. new ed. (Putnam Sports Shelf Biography Ser.). 160p. (gr. 5 up). 1974. PLB 6.29 o.p. (ISBN 0-399-60910-5). Putnam Pub Group.

--Sports Superstitions. LC 78-62. (Illus.). (gr. 5 up). 1978. 7.95 (ISBN 0-698-20439-5, Coward). Putnam Pub Group.

--This Is Pro Hockey. LC 75-38369. (Illus.). 128p. (gr. 5 up). 1976. 5.95 o.p. (ISBN 0-396-07318-2). Dodd.

--This Is Pro Soccer. LC 78-10729. (Illus.). (gr. 5 up). 1979. 6.95 o.p. (ISBN 0-396-07643-2). Dodd.

--Tom Seaver. (Putnam Sports Shelf). (gr. 5 up). 1971. PLB 6.29 o.p. (ISBN 0-399-60637-8). Putnam Pub Group.

--Track & Field: Secrets of the Champions. LC 79-7508. (Illus.). (gr. 6-9). 1980. 10.95a o.p. (ISBN 0-385-14999-9); PLB 10.95a (ISBN 0-385-15000-8). Doubleday.

--Willie Mays. (Beginning Biography Ser.). (Illus.). 64p. (gr. 2-4). 1973. PLB 5.99 o.p. (ISBN 0-399-60824-9). Putnam Pub Group.

Sullivan, George, jt. auth. see Kirby, George.

Sullivan, George, jt. auth. see Kramp, Harry.

Sullivan, George E. The Complete Book of Baseball Collectibles. LC 82-16357. (Illus.). 268p. 1983. 14.95 (ISBN 0-668-05529-4); pap. 8.95 (ISBN 0-686-43039-5). Arco.

Sullivan, Gertrude A. Teacher As Gift. 64p. 1979. wire coil 5.95 (ISBN 0-697-01729-X). Wm C Brown.

Sullivan, Harry R. Frederic Harrison. (English Authors Ser.: No. 341). 232p. 1983. lib. bdg. 18.95 (ISBN 0-8057-6827-0, Twayne). G K Hall.

--Walter Bagehot. (English Authors Ser.). 1975. lib. bdg. 12.95 (ISBN 0-8057-1018-3, Twayne). G K Hall.

Sullivan, Harry S. Clinical Studies in Psychiatry. Perry, Helen S., ed. (Norton Library Series, N688). 400p. 1973. pap. 7.95 (ISBN 0-393-00688-3). Norton.

--Conceptions of Modern Psychiatry. 1953. 8.50x o.p. (ISBN 0-393-01050-3, Norton Lib); pap. 6.95 (ISBN 0-393-00740-5, Norton Lib). Norton.

Sullivan, Henry W. Juan Del Encina. (World Authors Ser.). 1976. lib. bdg. 15.95 (ISBN 0-8057-6166-7, Twayne). G K Hall.

--Tirso de Molina & the Drama of the Counter Reformation. 1976. pap. text ed. 25.75x o.p. (ISBN 90-6203-399-7). Humanities.

Sullivan, Howard J., jt. auth. see Higgins, Norman.

Sullivan, J. V., jt. auth. see Miller, A. G.

Sullivan, Jack. Elegant Nightmares: The English Ghost Story from le Fanu to Blackwood. LC 77-92258. 155p. 1980. pap. 5.95 (ISBN 0-8214-0569-1, 82-82709). Ohio U Pr.

--Elegant Nightmares: The English Ghost Story from le Fanu to Blackwood. LC 77-92258. 155p. 1978. 12.95x (ISBN 0-8214-0374-5, 82-82691). Ohio U Pr.

Sullivan, James. Fluid Power: Theory & Applications. 2nd ed. (Illus.). 480p. 1975. 25.95 (ISBN 0-87909-272-6); instrs'. manual avail. (ISBN 0-8359-2074-7). Reston.

Sullivan, James A. Fundamentals of Fluid Mechanics. (Illus.). 1978. text ed. 20.95 (ISBN 0-8359-2999-X); solns. manual avail. (ISBN 0-8359-3000-9). Reston.

--Plumbing: Installation & Design. (Illus.). 480p. 1980. text ed. 21.95 (ISBN 0-8359-5552-4); instr's manual avail. (ISBN 0-8359-5553-2). Reston.

--Whitefoot Mouse. (Illus.). 48p. (gr. 2-5). 1975. PLB 4.29 o.p. (ISBN 0-698-30589-2, Coward). Putnam Pub Group.

Sullivan, James L. Juan Testifa De Jesus. Quarles, J. C., tr. from Eng. Orig. Title: John's Witness to Jesus. 128p. 1981. pap. 2.50 (ISBN 0-311-04324-0). Casa Bautista.

Sullivan, Jeremiah J. & Heggelund, Per O. Foreign Investment in the U. S. Fishing Industry. LC 79-2074. (Pacific Rim Research Ser.: No. 3). 208p. 1979. 24.95x (ISBN 0-669-03066-X). Lexington Bks.

Sullivan, Jo. Suspicion. (Harlequin Romances Ser.). 192p. 1983. pap. 1.75 (ISBN 0-373-02544-0). Harlequin Bks.

Sullivan, John. The Big Game: A Game by Game History of Cal-Stanford Football Rivalry 1899 to 1981. LC 82-81807. (Great Rivalry Ser.). (Illus.). 400p. 1982. 14.95 (ISBN 0-88011-067-8). Leisure Pr.

--Modern College Mathematics. (Illus.). 352p. (Orig.). 1979. pap. 5.95 (ISBN 0-06-460174-9, COS 174, COS). B&N NY.

Sullivan, John, jt. auth. see Rajhans, Gyan S.

Sullivan, John, jt. auth. see Simer, Peter.

Sullivan, John, et al. The Funny Side of Football. (Illus.). 92p. (Orig.). 1980. pap. 3.95 o.p. (ISBN 0-89260-141-8). Hwong Pub.

Sullivan, John E. Ideas of Religion: A Prolegomenon to the Philosophy of Religion. LC 79-66230. 1979. pap. text ed. 10.50 (ISBN 0-8191-0808-1). U Pr of Amer.

Sullivan, John L. Introduction to Police Science. 3rd ed. (Illus.). 1976. text ed. 21.95 (ISBN 0-07-062430-5, G); instructor's manual & key 4.50 (ISBN 0-07-062431-3). McGraw.

Sullivan, John W. Aim for a Job in the Iron & Steel Industry. rev. ed. LC 67-12977. (Aim High Vocational Guidance Ser.). (gr. 7-12). 1982. PLB 7.97 (ISBN 0-8239-0427-X). Rosen Pr.

--Beethoven: His Spiritual Development. 1927. pap. 2.25 (ISBN 0-394-70100-3, Vin). Random.

Sullivan, Judith, et al. New Directions in Community Health Nursing. (Illus.). 384p. 1983. text ed. 15.00 o.p. (ISBN 0-86542-004-1). Blackwell Sci.

Sullivan, Katharine. Girls on Parole. LC 73-9259. 243p. 1973. Repr. of 1956 ed. lib. bdg. 15.00x o.p. (ISBN 0-8371-6994-1, SUGP). Greenwood.

Sullivan, Kenneth M. Practical Computer Cost Accounting. 304p. 1983. text ed. 24.95 (ISBN 0-442-27961-2). Van Nos Reinhold.

Sullivan, Linda, ed. Encyclopedia of Governmental Advisory Organizations. 3rd ed. 800p. 1981. 275.00x (ISBN 0-8103-0253-5). Gale.

--New Governmental Advisory Organizations, No. 1. 300p. 1982. pap. 185.00x (ISBN 0-8103-0252-7). Gale.

Sullivan, Louis H. Autobiography of an Idea. (Illus.). 1924. pap. 6.00 (ISBN 0-486-20281-X). Dover.

--Kindergarten Chats. (Illus.). 1980. pap. 5.00 (ISBN 0-486-23812-1). Dover.

Sullivan, M., jt. auth. see Mizrahi, A.

Sullivan, Margaret P., jt. ed. see Van Eys, Jan.

Sullivan, Marianna P. France's Vietnam Policy: A Study in French-American Relations. LC 77-94749. (Contributions in Political Science: No. 12). 1978. lib. bdg. 25.00x (ISBN 0-313-20317-2, SUV/). Greenwood.

Sullivan, Marilynn C. & Sullivan, Eugene T., eds. Celebrate! Wedding Cakes. (Illus.). 192p. 1983. 12.95 (ISBN 0-912696-23-0). Wilton.

Sullivan, Mary C., jt. auth. see Golden, Robert.

Sullivan, Mary W. The V W Connection. 128p. (gr. 5 up). 1981. 9.25 (ISBN 0-525-66701-6, 0898-270). Lodestar Bks.

Sullivan, Maureen, ed. see Cibber, Colley.

Sullivan, Michael. The Cave Temples of Maichishan. LC 69-15829. (Illus.). 1969. 70.00x (ISBN 0-520-01448-0). U of Cal Pr.

--Chinese Landscape Painting in the Sui & T'ang Dynasties. (Illus.). 1980. 42.50x (ISBN 0-520-03558-5). U of Cal Pr.

Sullivan, Michael, jt. auth. see Mizrahi, Abe.

Sullivan, Michael P. International Relations: Theories & Evidence. (Illus.). 400p. 1976. 22.95 (ISBN 0-13-473470-X). P-H.

Sullivan, Molly. Feeling Strong, Feeling Free: Movement Exploration for Young Children. LC 82-61730. 161p. 1982. pap. text ed. 5.50 (ISBN 0-912674-82-2, 100). Natl Assn Child Ed.

Sullivan, Nelson G., jt. auth. see Copeland, Benny R.

Sullivan, Peggy. Carl H. Milam & the American Library Association. 416p. 1976. 20.00 (ISBN 0-8242-0592-8). Wilson.

Sullivan, Peggy & Ptacek, William. Public Libraries: Smart Practices in Personnel. LC 81-15638. 100p. 1982. lib. bdg. 13.50 (ISBN 0-87287-278-5). Libs Unl.

Sullivan, R. S., jt. auth. see Fitzsimmons, J. A.

Sullivan, Richard. Practical Problems in Mathematics for Electronics Technicians. LC 80-70484. (Practical Problems in Mathematics Ser.). (Illus.). 212p. (Orig.). 1982. pap. text ed. 6.80 (ISBN 0-8273-2086-8); instr.'s guide 3.75 (ISBN 0-8273-2087-6). Delmar.

Sullivan, Robert J. Medical Record & Index Systems for Community Practice. LC 78-31817. (Rural Health Center Ser.). (Illus.). 1979. prof ref 18.00x (ISBN 0-88410-540-7); pap. 11.00x (ISBN 0-88410-546-6). Ballinger Pub.

--Withdrawal of Oil & Gas & Subsidence. 7.50 o.p. (ISBN 0-910874-29-8). Legal Bk Co.

Sullivan, Robert J., jt. auth. see Wright, Marion I.

Sullivan, Roger J. Morality & the Good Life: A Commentary on Aristotle's "Nicomachean Ethics". LC 77-13485. 222p. 1980. pap. text ed. 5.95x o.p. (ISBN 0-87870-111-7). Memphis St Univ.

Sullivan, S. Adams. The Fathers Almanac. LC 78-22650. (Illus.). 384p. 1980. pap. 9.95 (ISBN 0-385-13626-9, Dolp). Doubleday.

Sullivan, T. J., et al. Social Problems: Divergent Perspectives. 184p. 1979. 22.95 (ISBN 0-471-02932-7); avail. tchr's manual (ISBN 0-471-08174-4). Wiley.

Sullivan, Terry & Maiken, Peter T. Killer Clown: The John Wayne Gacy Murders. LC 82-82311. (Illus.). 320p. 1982. 14.95 (ISBN 0-448-16600-3, G&D). Putnam Pub Group.

Sullivan, Thomas F. Environmental Statutes, 1982 Edition. 601p. 1982. pap. text ed. 19.95 (ISBN 0-86587-110-8). Gov Insts.

--EPA RCRA Inspection Manuel. 300p. 1982. pap. text ed. 35.00 (ISBN 0-86587-107-8). Gov Insts.

--TSCA Inspection Manuel Part I. 300p. 1982. pap. text ed. 35.00 (ISBN 0-686-38763-5). Gov Insts.

--U. S. Epa Guidebook. (Illus.). 166p. pap. 28.00 (ISBN 0-86587-057-8). Gov Insts.

Sullivan, Tom & Gill, Derek. If You Could See What I Hear. LC 74-1809. (Illus.). 192p. (YA) 1975. 12.45i (ISBN 0-06-014167-0, HarpT). Har-Row.

--If You Could See What I Hear. (YA) (RL 9). 1976. pap. 2.75 (ISBN 0-451-11811-1, AE1811, Sig). NAL.

Sullivan, Vincent see O'Sullivan, Vincent.

Sullivan, Walter. Continents in Motion. LC 73-17315. (Illus.). 432p. 1974. 22.95 (ISBN 0-07-062412-7, GB). McGraw.

Sullivan, Walter, jt. auth. see Core, George.

Sullivan, William F. & Claycombe, W. Wayne. Fundamentals of Forecasting. (Illus.). 1977. pap. 22.95 (ISBN 0-87909-300-5). Reston.

Sullivan, William G., jt. auth. see Claycombe, William W.

Sullivan, William M., jt. ed. see Rabinow, Paul.

Sulliven, R. L., jt. auth. see Flaim, T.

Sullivent, W. B., et al see Wilkes, Charles.

Sulloway, Frank J. Freud, Biologist of the Mind: Beyond the Psychoanalytic Legend. LC 79-7343. 1983. 25.00 o.p. (ISBN 0-465-02559-5); pap. 13.95 (ISBN 0-465-02560-9). Basic.

Sully, Langdon. How to Get Rid of Fleas...Now & Forever. LC 82-99950. (Illus.). 64p. 1982. write for info. (ISBN 0-910877-00-9). Langdon Assocs.

Sully, Melanie A. Continuity & Change in Austrian Socialism: The Eternal Quest for the Third Way. (East European Monographs: No. 114). 320p. 1982. 25.00x (ISBN 0-88033-008-2). East Eur Quarterly.

Sully, Nina. Health. (Science in Today's World Ser.). (Illus.). 72p. (gr. 7-12). 1983. 14.95 (ISBN 0-7134-4447-9, Pub. by Batsford England). David & Charles.

--Looking at the Senses. (Looking at Science Ser.). (Illus.). 48p. (gr. 5-8). 1982. 9.95 (ISBN 0-7134-4059-7, Pub. by Batsford England). David & Charles.

Sulman, Felix G. Short & Long Term Changes in Climate, Vol. I. 224p. 1982. 59.50 (ISBN 0-686-84131-X). CRC Pr.

--Short & Long Term Changes in Climate, Vol. II. 184p. 1982. 59.50 (ISBN 0-8493-6421-3). CRC Pr.

Suls, Jerry & Greenwald, Anthony G., eds. Psychological Perspectives on the Self, Vol. 2. 320p. 1983. text ed. write for info. (ISBN 0-89859-276-3). L Erlbaum Assocs.

Sultan, Paul, jt. auth. see Enos, Darryl.

Sultan, Paul E. The Disenchanted Unionist. LC 73-15320. (Illus.). 272p. 1975. Repr. of 1963 ed. lib. bdg. 17.25x (ISBN 0-8371-7187-3, SUDU). Greenwood.

Sultan, Ralph G. Pricing in the Electrical Oligopoly, Vol. 1: Competition or Collusion. LC 73-93777. 600p. 1974. 25.00x (ISBN 0-87584-110-4). Harvard Busn.

Sultan, Tanvir. INDO-US Relations: A Study of Foreign Policies. 260p. 1982. 29.95 (ISBN 0-940500-82-5, Pub by Depp & Deep India). Asia Bk Corp.

Sultan, William J. Elementary Baking. (Illus.). (gr. 5-9). 1969. text ed. 16.96 (ISBN 0-07-062408-9, G). wkbk. 7.96 (ISBN 0-07-062406-2). McGraw.

--Modern Pastry Chef: Cakes, Pies & Other Baked Goods, Vol. 1. (Illus.). 1977. lib. bdg. 32.50 (ISBN 0-87055-225-2); pap. text ed. 21.50 o.p. (ISBN 0-87055-310-0). AVI.

--Modern Pastry Chef: French Pastries, Cookies, Molded and Frozen Desserts, Vol. 2. (Illus.). 1977. lib. bdg. 21.50 (ISBN 0-87055-226-0); pap. text ed. 21.50 o.p. (ISBN 0-87055-311-9). AVI.

Sulton, Cynthia G. & Wolfe, Randy P. Equal Employment Opportunity & Affirmative Action: A Sourcebook for Court Managers. LC 82-8291. 64p. 1982. 10.00 (ISBN 0-89656-057-0). Natl Ctr St Courts.

Sultz, Harry A., et al, eds. Nurse Practitioners: USA. LC 78-19728. 272p. 1979. 26.95x o.p. (ISBN 0-669-02727-8). Lexington Bks.

Sulzberger, C. L. The American Heritage Picture History of World War II. McCullough, David G., ed. LC 66-24214. (Illus.). 640p. 1966. 12.98 o.p. (ISBN 0-686-65698-9, Pub. by Am Heritage); Vol. 1, 303 Pgs., Vol 2, 345 Pgs. 15.00 o.p. (ISBN 0-8281-0332-1). Crown.

--Fall of Eagles. (Illus.). 1977. 17.95 o.p. (ISBN 0-517-52817-7). Crown.

Sulzberger, Jean. Search: Journey on the Inner Path. LC 78-4430. 1979. pap. 5.95 (ISBN 0-06-067765-1, HarpR); pap. 5.95 (ISBN 0-686-96730-5, RD 271, HarpR). Har-Row.

Sulzner, George T., jt. auth. see Bach, Stanley.

Sumerkin, Alexander, ed. see Tsvetaeva, Marina.

Sumerkin, Alexander, ed. see Tsvetaeva, Marina I.

Sumichrast, Michael & Shafer, Ronald G. The Complete Book of Home Buying: A Consumer's Guide to Housing in the 80's. rev. ed. LC 80-11100. 366p. 1980. 16.95 (ISBN 0-87128-589-4). Dow Jones-Irwin.

Sumiko. My Baby Brother Ned. (Illus.). 32p. (ps-1). 1983. 8.95 (ISBN 0-434-96533-2, Pub. by Heinemann England). David & Charles.

Sumka, Howard J., jt. auth. see Stegman, Michael A.

Summars, Stephanie, ed. Practical Solutions to a Complex Problem: Identification of Multiple Alloantibodies in the Presence of a Strong Cold Autoantibody. Rev ed. 32p. 1979. 8.00 (ISBN 0-685-48761-X). Am Assn Blood.

Summe, Richard, jt. auth. see DeVoney, Chris.

Summe, Richard, intro. by. Expansion & Software Guide for the IBM PC. 264p. 1982. pap. 19.95 (ISBN 0-88022-019-8). Que Corp.

Summer, Charles E., jt. auth. see Hampton, David R.

Summer Institute of Linguistics, jt. auth. see Linguistic Circle of Saigon.

Summer Institute on International & Comparative Law. Lectures on the Conflict of Laws & International Contracts. LC 51-62311. (Michigan Legal Studies). xiv, 200p. 1982. Repr. of 1951 ed. lib. bdg. write for info. (ISBN 0-89941-177-0). W S Hein.

Summer, Rosemary. Thomas Hardy, Psychologist Novelist. 1981. 22.50x (ISBN 0-312-80161-0). St Martin.

Summer School, Babylon, Czechoslovakia, Sept. 1971. Theory of Nonlinear Operators. Kucera, M., ed. 1973. 41.50 (ISBN 0-12-427650-4). Acad Pr.

Summer School on Weak & Electromagnetic Interactions at High Energy, Session XXIX, les Houches, July 5-August 14, 1976. Weak & Electromagnetic Interactions at High Energy: Proceedings. Balian, R., ed. 1978. 106.50 (ISBN 0-7204-0742-7, North-Holland). Elsevier.

Summerall, C. P., 3rd, et al. Monitoring Heart Rhythm. 208p. 1976. 20.00 o.p. (ISBN 0-471-83556-0). Wiley.

Summerall, Charles P. Monitoring Heart Rhythm. 2nd ed. LC 82-7017. 196p. 1982. 19.50 (ISBN 0-471-09958-9, Pub. by Wiley Med). Wiley.

Summerfield, Geoffrey, jt. ed. see Smith, Peter.

Summerfield, Maggie. Compression Tested. 1979. 9.95 o.p. (ISBN 0-07-062573-5, GB). McGraw.

Summerfield, Melvin B., jt. auth. see Stackpole, Edouard A.

Summerhayes, Martha. Vanished Arizona: Recollections of an Army Life of a New England Woman. LC 76-54922. (Beautiful Rio Grande Classics Ser.). 1976. lib. bdg. 12.00 o.s.i. (ISBN 0-87380-120-2). Rio Grande.

Summerlin, Lee R. Chemistry for the Life Sciences. Incl. P. S. Associates. wkbk. 7.00 (ISBN 0-394-32457-9); Hendrickson, William & Healy, Juanita. lab manual 8.00 (ISBN 0-394-32520-6). 631p. 1981. text ed. 22.00 (ISBN 0-394-32215-0). Random.

Summers, Anthony & Mangold, Tom. The File on the Tsar. 1978. pap. 2.50 o.s.i. (ISBN 0-515-04508-X). Jove Pubns.

Summers, Barbara. Working with People: An Introduction to the Caring Professions. 1982. 25.00x (ISBN 0-304-30604-5, Pub. by Cassell England). State Mutual Bk.

Summers, Claude J. Christopher Isherwood. LC 80-5335. (Literature and Life Ser.). 192p. 1980. 11.95 (ISBN 0-8044-2846-8). Ungar.

Summers, Claude J. & Pebworth, Ted-Larry. Ben Jonson. (English Authors Ser.: No. 268). 1979. 12.95 (ISBN 0-8057-6764-9, Twayne). G K Hall.

Summers, Claude J. & Pebworth, Ted-Larry, eds. Classic & Cavalier: Essays on Jonson & the Sons of Ben. LC 82-1882. (Illus.). xvii, 290p. 1982. 24.95x (ISBN 0-8229-3461-2). U of Pittsburgh Pr.

Summers, Clyde W., et al. Statutory Supplement to Cases & Materials on Labor Law. 2nd ed. (University Casebook Ser.). 104p. 1982. pap. text ed. write for info. (ISBN 0-88277-084-5). Foundation Pr.

Summers, D., jt. auth. see Rappoport, L.

Summers, Dennis. HGV Law Guide. 1981. text ed. 15.95 (ISBN 0-408-00569-6). Butterworth.

Summers, Donald B. Chemistry Handbook. (gr. 10-12). 1975. pap. text ed. 6.00x (ISBN 0-88334-054-2). Ind Sch Pr.

Summers, Festus P. William L. Wilson & Tariff Reform: A Biography. LC 74-3627. (Illus.). 288p. 1974. Repr. of 1953 ed. lib. bdg. 19.75x (ISBN 0-8371-7447-3, SUWW). Greenwood.

Summers, Festus P. & Ambler, C. H. West Virginia: The Mountain State. 2nd ed. 1958. text ed. 24.95 (ISBN 0-13-951699-9). P-H.

Summers, Festus P., ed. see Wilson, William L.

Summers, Gene F., ed. Technology & Social Change in Rural Areas. (Rural Studies Ser.). 400p. 1983. softcover 26.50 (ISBN 0-86531-600-7). Westview.

Summers, Gene F. & Selvik, Arne, eds. Nonmetropolitan Industrial Growth & Community Change. LC 78-22652. (Illus.). 288p. 1979. 25.95x (ISBN 0-669-02820-7). Lexington Bks.

Summers, Gene F., et al, eds. Industrial Invasion of Non-Metropolitan America: A Quarter Century of Experience. LC 75-25026. (Special Studies). 1976. 30.00 o.p. (ISBN 0-275-56080-5). Praeger.

Summers, George, et al. Basic Statistics in Business & Economics. 3rd ed. 1981. text ed. 26.95x (ISBN 0-534-00918-2); wkbk. 10.95x (ISBN 0-534-00919-0). Wadsworth Pub.

Summers, George J. Mind Teasers: Logic Puzzles & Games of Deduction. LC 77-79511. (Illus.). (gr. 6 up). 1977. 6.95 o.p. (ISBN 0-8069-4566-4); PLB 6.69 o.p. (ISBN 0-8069-4567-2). Sterling.

Summers, Gerald. The Lure of the Falcon. 288p. 1973. 7.95 o.p. (ISBN 0-671-21577-9). S&S.

Summers, Ian, jt. auth. see Barlowe, Wayne D.

Summers, Ian, ed. Tomorrow & Beyond. LC 78-7119. (Illus.). 160p. 1978. 19.95 (ISBN 0-89480-062-0); pap. 10.95 o.s.i. (ISBN 0-89480-055-8). Workman Pub.

Summers, James L. The Long Ride Home. LC 66-10140. (gr. 9 up). 1966. 3.50 (ISBN 0-664-32389-8). Westminster.

Summers, Jessica de see De Summers, Jessica.

Summers, Joseph H. Heirs of Donne & Jonson. LC 71-129574. 1970. 16.95x (ISBN 0-19-501451-0). Oxford U Pr.

Summers, Montague. A Bibliography of Restoration Drama. 2nd ed. 94p. 1982. 30.00x (ISBN 0-284-98554-6, Pub. by C Skilton Scotland). State Mutual Bk.

--The Gothic Quest. 448p. 1982. 55.00x (ISBN 0-284-79521-6, Pub. by C Skilton Scotland). State Mutual Bk.

--Supernatural Omnibus. 624p. 1982. 22.50 (ISBN 0-575-03120-4, Pub. by Gollancz England). David & Charles.

--Witchcraft & Black Magic. LC 70-174114. (Illus.). 1971. Repr. of 1916 ed. 40.00x (ISBN 0-685-02995-6). Gale.

Summers, Peter G. How to Read a Coat of Arms. 1979. pap. 2.95 (ISBN 0-7199-1025-0). Pendragon Hse.

Summers, Ray. Digno es el Cordero. Lerin, Alfredo, tr. from Eng. Orig. Title: Worthy is the Lamb. 287p. (Sp.). 1981. pap. 4.95 (ISBN 0-311-04305-4). Casa Bautista.

Summers, Robert. Pragmatic Instrumentalism & American Legal Theory (1890-1940) LC 82-71596. 264p. 28.50x (ISBN 0-8014-1511-X). Cornell U Pr.

--The Seeds in the Passes. LC 78-59774. (Scene Award Ser.). (Illus.). 88p. (Orig.). 1979. pap. 3.00 (ISBN 0-685-48676-1). The Smith.

Summers, Robert S. Collective Bargaining & Public Benefit Conferral: A Jurisprudential Critique. (Institute of Public Employment Monograph: No. 7). 80p. 1976. pap. 3.00 (ISBN 0-87546-246-4). ILR Pr.

Summers, Robert S. & Howard, C. Law, Its Nature, Functions & Limits. 2nd ed. (Illus.). 1024p. 1972. text ed. 25.95 (ISBN 0-13-526400-6). P-H.

Summers, Robert S., ed. Essays in Legal Philosophy. (Library Reprint Ser.). 1976. 28.50x (ISBN 0-520-03213-6). U of Cal Pr.

--More Essays in Legal Philosophy: General Assessment of Legal Philosophies. 1971. 21.50x (ISBN 0-520-01971-7). U of Cal Pr.

Summerscale, Peter. The East European Predicament. LC 81-9400. 180p. 1982. 20.00x (ISBN 0-312-22474-5). St Martin.

Summersgill, Harue, tr. see Yamasaki, Toyoko.

Summersgill, Travis, tr. see Yamasaki, Toyoko.

Summerson, John. Georgian London. 3rd ed. (Illus.). 1978. 22.00 (ISBN 0-262-19173-3). MIT Pr.

--Heavenly Mansions. (Illus.). 1963. pap. 6.95 (ISBN 0-393-00210-1, Norton Lib). Norton.

--The Life & Work of John Nash, Architect. (Illus.). 288p. 1980. 37.50x (ISBN 0-262-19190-3). MIT Pr.

--The London Building World of the 1860s. (Walter Neurath Memorial Lecture Ser.: No. 5). (Illus.). 1974. 8.75 o.s.i. (ISBN 0-500-55005-0). Transatlantic.

Summerville, Margaret. Infamous Isabelle. (Orig.). 1980. pap. 1.50 o.s.i. (ISBN 0-440-13867-1). Dell.

--Rogue's Masquerade. 1981. pap. 2.25 o.p. (ISBN 0-380-78469-5, 78469). Avon.

Sumner, Austin J. The Physiology of Peripheral Nerve Disease. (Illus.). 544p. 1980. text ed. 55.00x (ISBN 0-7216-8639-7). Saunders.

Sumner, Benedict H. Peter the Great & the Emergence of Russia. 1962. pap. 3.95 (ISBN 0-02-037760-6, Collier). Macmillan.

Sumner, Charles. The War System of the Commonwealth of Nations. LC 70-137552. (Peace Movement in America Ser). 71p. 1972. Repr. of 1849 ed. lib. bdg. 10.95x (ISBN 0-89198-082-2). Ozer.

Sumner, David S., jt. auth. see Strandness, D. E.

Sumner, E., jt. auth. see Kaufman, L.

Sumner, F., ed. Supercomputer Systems Technology: Design & Application. (Computer State of the Art Report: Ser.10 No.6). (Illus.). 400p. 1982. 445.00 (ISBN 0-08-028569-4). Pergamon.

Sumner, J. S. Principles of Induced Polarization for Geophysical Exploration. (Developments in Economic Geology Ser.: Vol. 5). 1976. 51.00 (ISBN 0-444-41481-9). Elsevier.
Sumner, J. S., jt. auth. see Craighead, J. J.
Sumner, Jeanne, jt. ed. see Insull, Robert.
Sumner, Margaret. Thought for Food. (Illus.). 1981. 15.95x (ISBN 0-19-217690-0); pap. text ed. 7.95 (ISBN 0-19-286003-8). Oxford U Pr.
Sumner, Philip E. & Phillips, Celeste R. Shared Childbirth: A Guide to Family Birth Centers. 1982. pap. 6.95 (ISBN 0-452-25368-3, Z5368, Plume). NAL.
--Shared Childbirth: A Guide to Family Birth Centers. LC 82-6467. (Medical Library). (Illus.). 136p. 1982. pap. 6.95 (ISBN 0-452-25368-3, 4757-0). Mosby.
Sumner, Robert. Make Your Own Camping Equipment. LC 76-4523. (Illus.). 224p. 1976. pap. 6.95 o.p. (ISBN 0-8069-8488-0). Sterling.
Sumner, Robert L. After the Revival--What? 1980. pap. 3.95 (ISBN 0-87398-026-3, Pub. by Bibl Evang Pr). Sword of Lord.
Sumner, William G. Andrew Jackson As a Public Man: What He Was, What Chances He Had, & What He Did with Them. Repr. of 1882 ed. lib. bdg. 15.50x o.p. (ISBN 0-8371-4104-4, SUAJ). Greenwood.
--Earth-Hunger & Other Essays. 404p. 1980. text ed. 29.95 (ISBN 0-87855-323-1); pap. text ed. 6.95 (ISBN 0-87855-705-9). Transaction Bks.
--Earth Hunger & Other Essays. 1913. text ed. 18.50x (ISBN 0-686-83530-1). Elliots Bks.
--Forgotten Man's Almanac: Rations of Common Sense from William Graham Sumner. Keller, A. G., ed. LC 70-141268. 1971. Repr. of 1943 ed. lib. bdg. 19.75x (ISBN 0-8371-5828-1, SUFM). Greenwood.
--Sumner Today. Davie, Maurice, ed. 1940. text ed. 39.50x (ISBN 0-686-83794-0). Elliots Bks.
--What Social Classes Owe to Each Other. 1947. pap. 3.95 (ISBN 0-87004-166-5). Caxton.
--What Social Classes Owe to Each Other. 1925. text ed. 11.00x (ISBN 0-686-83855-6). Elliots Bks.
Sumpter, Jerry L. Civil Trial Strategy & Technique Notebook. 650p. looseleaf bound 148.00 (ISBN 0-935506-02-0). Carnegie Pr.
Sumption, Merle R. & Engstrom, Y. School-Community Relations: A New Approach. 1965. text ed. 25.95 (ISBN 0-07-062288-4, C). McGraw.
Sumrall, Lester. The Gifts & Ministries of the Holy Spirit. 1982. pap. 7.95 (ISBN 0-89274-189-9, HH-189). Harrison Hse.
--My Story to His Glory. 192p. 1983. pap. 4.95 (ISBN 0-8407-5837-5). Nelson.
--Questions & Answers on Demon Powers. (Orig.). 1983. pap. 3.50 (ISBN 0-89274-261-5). Harrison Hse.
--The Reality of Angels. 1982. pap. 3.95 (ISBN 0-8407-5811-1). Nelson.
--Victory & Dominion Over Fear. 103p. 1982. pap. 2.50 (ISBN 0-89274-233-X, HH-233). Harrison Hse.
Sumrall, Velma & Germany, Lucille. Telling the Story of the Local Church: The Who, What, When, Where & Why of Communication. (Orig.). 1979. pap. 5.00 (ISBN 0-8164-2193-5); wkbk. avail. (ISBN 0-685-59466-1). Seabury.
Sun, Grace Y. & Bazan, Nicolas, eds. Neural Membranes. (Experimental & Clinical Neuroscience Ser.). (Illus.). 544p. 1983. 59.50 (ISBN 0-89603-052-0). Humana.
Sun, Kay. Streets Have Eyes. 1983. 9.95 (ISBN 0-533-05107-X). Vantage.
Sun, Rhoda L. Health Services in the People's Republic of China. LC 79-13832. 144p. 1980. text ed. 16.50 (ISBN 0-87073-897-6); pap. text ed. 6.50 o.p. (ISBN 0-87073-898-4). Schenkman.
Sun, Ruth. Personal Bible Study: A How-To. LC 82-7880. 1982. pap. 4.95 (ISBN 0-8024-4574-8). Moody.
Sun, Tsieh. Pathology & Clinical Features of Parasitic Diseases. LC 81-17147. (Masson Monographs in Diagnostic Pathology: Vol. 5). (Illus.). 360p. 1982. lib. bdg. 62.50x (ISBN 0-89352-165-5). Masson Pub.
Sunagel, Lois A. The Amethyst Quest. (YA) 1975. 6.95 (ISBN 0-685-52991-6, Avalon). Bouregy.
--The Shadow of the Needle. (YA) 1976. 6.95 (ISBN 0-685-69052-0, Avalon). Bouregy.
Sun Bear. Buffalo Hearts. 1976. pap. 5.00 (ISBN 0-686-01908-3). Bear Tribe.
Sun Bear & Wabun. The Bear Tribe's Self Reliance Book. 1977. pap. 5.00 (ISBN 0-686-01909-1). Bear Tribe.
Sund, jt. auth. see Bybee, Roger.
Sund, Robert. Ish River. LC 82-73721. 80p. (Orig.). 1983. pap. 7.50 (ISBN 0-86547-102-9). N Point Pr.
Sund, Robert B., jt. auth. see Carin, Arthur A.
Sundaram, P. S., tr. see Bharati, Subramania.
Sundararajan, C., ed. Dynamic Analysis of Pressure Vessel & Piping Components, Series PVP-PB-022, 1977. 1977. pap. text ed. 16.00 o.p. (ISBN 0-685-86860-5, G00122). ASME.
--Reliability & Safety of Pressure Components. (PVP Ser.: Vol. 12). 254p. 1982. 50.00 (H00219). ASME.
Sundararaman, D. Moduli, Deformations & Classifications of Compact, Complex Manifolds. LC 80-20825. (Research Notes in Mathematics Ser.: No. 45). 240p. 1980. pap. text ed. 26.50 (ISBN 0-273-08458-5). Pitman Pub MA.
Sunday Times of London Insight Team, jt. auth. see Linklater.
Sundberg, Norman & Tyler, Leona. Introduction to Clinical Psychology: Perspectives, Issues, & Contributions to Human Service. (Illus.). 512p. 1983. 23.95 (ISBN 0-13-479451-6). P-H.
Sundberg, Norman D. The Assessment of Persons. (Illus.). 1977. 23.95 (ISBN 0-13-049585-9). P-H.
Sundberg, Norman D., et al. Clinical Psychology: Expanding Horizons. 2nd ed. (Century Psychology Ser.). (Illus.). 1973. 24.95x (ISBN 0-13-137877-5). P-H.
Sundberg, Richard J. Chemistry of Indoles. (Organic Chemistry Ser.: Vol. 18). 1970. 67.50 (ISBN 0-12-676950-8). Acad Pr.
Sundberg-Weitman, B. Discrimination on Grounds of Nationality: Free Movement of Workers of Freedom of Establishment Under the EEC Treaty. new ed. 1977. 38.50 (ISBN 0-7204-0477-0, North-Holland). Elsevier.
Sundburg, M. & Goldkuhl, G. Information Systems Developement: A Systematic Approach. 1981. 26.95 (ISBN 0-13-464677-0). P-H.
Sunde, Elrling D. Communication Systems Engineering Theory. LC 78-78477. (Systems Engineering & Analysis Ser). 1969. text ed. 27.50 (ISBN 0-471-83560-9, Pub. by Wiley). Krieger.
Sundeen, Sandra, et al. Nurse-Client Interaction: Implementing the Nursing Process. 2nd ed. LC 80-27585. (Illus.). 252p. 1981. pap. text ed. 14.95 (ISBN 0-8016-4844-0). Mosby.
Sundeen, Sandra J., jt. auth. see Stuart, Gail W.
Sundel, Martin & Sundel, Sandra S. Behavior Modification in the Human Services: A Systematic Introduction to Concepts & Applications. (Illus.). 320p. 1982. 14.95 (ISBN 0-13-073916-2). P-H.
--Behavior Modification in the Human Services: Introduction to Concepts & Applications. LC 74-23342. 283p. 1975. pap. text ed. 11.50x o.p. (ISBN 0-471-83567-6). Wiley.
Sundel, Sandra S., jt. auth. see Sundel, Martin.
Sundelius, Bengt. Managing Transnationalism in Northern Europe. LC 78-59862. (Westview Replica Edition). 1978. lib. bdg. 20.00 (ISBN 0-89158-282-7). Westview.
Sundell, Roger H., jt. auth. see Patrick, J. Max.
Sundemo, Herbert. Revell's Dictionary of Bible Times. 256p. 1979. 9.95 o.p. (ISBN 0-8007-1058-4). Revell.
Sundene Wood, Barbara. Messages Without Words. LC 77-27848. (Read About Sciences Ser.). (Illus.). (gr. k-3). 1978. PLB 13.30 (ISBN 0-8393-0084-0). Raintree Pubs.
Sunderland, E., jt. ed. see Roberts, D. F.
Sunderland, Eric. Elements of Human & Social Geography (Some Anthropological Perspectives) LC 73-10060. 120p. 1973. text ed. 16.25 (ISBN 0-08-017689-5); pap. text ed. 7.00 (ISBN 0-08-017690-9). Pergamon.
Sunderland, Joan. Constable. (Phaidon Color Library). (Illus.). 84p. Date not set. 25.00 (ISBN 0-7148-2158-6, Pub. by Salem Hse Ltd); pap. 17.95 (ISBN 0-7148-2132-2). Merrimack Bk Serv.
Sunderland, John & Witt, Johnfrwd. by. A Checklist of Painters C.1200-1978: Represented in the Witt Library, Courtauld Institute of Art, London. 356p. 1978. lib. bdg. 40.00 o.p. (ISBN 0-7201-0718-0, Pub. by Mansell England). Wilson.
Sunderland, Neil V. Bank Planning Models. 160p. 1977. 75.00x (ISBN 0-7121-5621-6, Pub. by Macdonald & Evans). State Mutual Bk.
Sunderlin, Sylvia, ed. see Association for Childhood Education International.
Sunderman, James F., ed. World War II in the Air: Europe. 360p. 1981. pap. 8.95 o.p. (ISBN 0-442-20045-5). Van Nos Reinhold.
--World War II in the Air: Pacific. 320p. 1981. pap. 8.95 o.p. (ISBN 0-442-20044-7). Van Nos Reinhold.
Sundermeyer, K. Constrained Dynamics, with Applications to Yang-Mills Theory, General Relativity, Classical Spin, Duel String Model. (Lecture Notes in Physics: Vol. 169). 318p. 1983. pap. 13.00 (ISBN 0-686-83753-3). Springer-Verlag.
Sundh, Kerstin. Augusta Can Do Anything. (Illus.). 112p. (gr. 3-6). 1974. PLB 3.96 o.p. (ISBN 0-399-60827-3). Putnam Pub Group.
Sundick, Sherry, jt. auth. see Small, Ruth.
Sundick, Sherry S. Celebration. new ed. (Illus.). 1977. pap. 2.50 (ISBN 0-932044-03-4). M O Pub Co.
--Rebirth. new ed. 1978. pap. 2.00 (ISBN 0-932044-19-0). M O Pub Co.
Sundquist, Eric J. Faulkner: The House Divided. LC 82-8923. 256p. 1983. 16.95q (ISBN 0-8018-2898-8). Johns Hopkins.
Sundquist, James L. Dispersing Population: What America Can Learn from Europe. 290p. 1975. 22.95 (ISBN 0-8157-8214-4); pap. 8.95 (ISBN 0-8157-8213-6). Brookings.
--Dynamics of the Party System: Alignment & Realignment of Political Parties in the United States. 1973. 22.95 (ISBN 0-8157-8216-0); pap. 9.95 (ISBN 0-8157-8215-2). Brookings.
--Making Federalism Work: A Study of Program Coordination at the Community Level. 1969. 22.95 (ISBN 0-8157-8218-7); pap. 8.95 (ISBN 0-8157-8217-9). Brookings.
--Politics & Policy: The Eisenhower, Kennedy, & Johnson Years. LC 68-31837. 1968. 23.95 (ISBN 0-8157-8222-5); pap. 9.95 (ISBN 0-8157-8221-7). Brookings.
Sundstrom, Donald W. & Klei, Herbert E. Wastewater Treatment. LC 78-13058. (Illus.). 1979. 33.95 (ISBN 0-13-945832-8). P-H.
Sundstrom, Lars. The Exchange Economy of Pre Colonial Tropical Africa. LC 74-75014. 1975. 25.00 o.p. (ISBN 0-312-27370-3). St Martin.
Sundstrom, Susan. Understanding Hearing Loss & What Can Be Done To Help. 64p. 1983. pap. text ed. 2.95x (ISBN 0-8134-2266-3). Interstate.
Sundt, Eilert. On Marriage in Norway. Drake, M., tr. from Norwegian. LC 79-42648. 1980. 34.50 (ISBN 0-521-23199-X). Cambridge U Pr.
Sundt, Wilbur A. Naval Science, Vol. 2. LC 78-56425. (Naval Science Ser.). (Illus.). 360p. 1981. 7.95x (ISBN 0-87021-457-8). Naval Inst Pr.
Sung, Betty Lee. A Survey of Chinese-American Manpower & Employment. LC 76-14435. (Special Studies). (Illus.). 1976. 33.95 o.p. (ISBN 0-275-23090-2). Praeger.
Sung, Nak-Ho, jt. ed. see Suh, Nam P.
Sungolowsky, Joseph. Beaumarchais. LC 74-10580. (World Authors Ser.: France: No. 334). 1974. lib. bdg. 13.95 o.p. (ISBN 0-8057-2122-3, Twayne). G K Hall.
Sung See Whai, tr. see Jackins, Harvey.
Sunier, John. The Handbook of Telephones & Accessories. 432p. 1978. 9.95 (ISBN 0-686-98102-2). Telecom Lib.
--Slide, Sound, & Filmstrip Production. (Illus.). 220p. 1981. 15.95 (ISBN 0-240-51074-7). Focal Pr.
Sunners, William. How to Make & Sell Original Crosswords & Other Puzzles. LC 80-52333. (Illus.). 256p. 1981. 13.95 (ISBN 0-8069-4632-6); lib. bdg. 16.79 (ISBN 0-8069-4633-4). Sterling.
Sunnie, D. & Kidd, James W. Poetic Living. 45p. (Orig.). 1982. pap. text ed. 2.50 (ISBN 0-910727-03-1). Golden Phoenix.
Sunnucks, Anne. Encyclopaedia of Chess. 2nd ed. LC 76-106571. (Illus.). 1977. 17.95 o.p. (ISBN 0-312-24710-9). St Martin.
Sunoo, Harold H., ed. Koreans in America. 210p. 1977. 4.00 (ISBN 0-932014-02-X). AKCS.
Sunoo, Harold H. & Kim, Dong S., eds. Korean Women in a Struggle for Humanization. LC 78-58866. 301p. 1978. pap. 6.00 (ISBN 0-932014-00-3). AKCS.
Sunoo, Harold H., jt. ed. see Dong, Wonmo.
Sunset Books & Sunset Magazine, ed. Bedroom & Bath Storage. LC 81-82870. (Illus.). 80p. (Orig.). 1982. pap. 3.95 (ISBN 0-376-01120-3). Sunset-Lane.
--Easy Basics for Good Cooking. LC 82-81368. (Illus.). 192p. (Orig.). 1982. pap. 9.95 (ISBN 0-376-02093-8). Sunset-Lane.
--Favorite Recipes I. 2nd ed. LC 82-81373. 128p. 1982. pap. 5.95 (ISBN 0-376-02177-2). Sunset-Lane.
--Favorite Recipes II. LC 82-81400. (Illus.). 160p. (Orig.). 1982. pap. 5.95 (ISBN 0-376-02154-3). Sunset-Lane.
--Flooring: Do it Yourself. LC 81-82872. (Illus.). 112p. (Orig.). 1982. pap. 4.95 (ISBN 0-376-01141-6). Sunset-Lane.
--Garage, Attic, & Basement Storage. LC 82-81369. (Illus.). 80p. (Orig.). 1982. pap. 3.95 (ISBN 0-376-01199-8). Sunset-Lane.
--Guide to California's Wine Country. LC 82-81743. (Illus.). 160p. (Orig.). 1982. pap. 7.95 o.p. (ISBN 0-376-06945-7). Sunset-Lane.
--Home Lighting. LC 82-81371. (Illus.). 96p. (Orig.). 1982. pap. 4.95 (ISBN 0-376-01312-5). Sunset-Lane.
--Picnics & Tailgate Parties. LC 81-82868. (Illus.). 96p. 1982. pap. 4.95 (ISBN 0-376-02536-0). Sunset-Lane.
--Solar Remodeling. LC 82-81372. (Illus.). 96p. (Orig.). 1982. pap. 4.95 (ISBN 0-376-01534-9). Sunset-Lane.
--Wallcoverings. LC 82-81370. (Illus.). 96p. (Orig.). 1982. pap. 4.95 (ISBN 0-376-01673-6). Sunset-Lane.
--Windows & Skylights. LC 81-82871. (Illus.). 112p. (Orig.). 1982. pap. 4.95 (ISBN 0-376-01751-1). Sunset-Lane.
Sunset Books & Sunset Magazine Editors. Gardener's Answer Book. LC 82-83214. (Illus.). 160p. 1983. pap. 7.95 (ISBN 0-376-03186-7). Sunset-Lane.
--International Vegetarian Cook Book. LC 82-83218. (Illus.). 96p. 1983. pap. 4.95 (ISBN 0-376-02921-8). Sunset-Lane.
Sunset Editors. Add-a-Room. LC 78-53675. (Illus.). 80p. 1978. pap. 3.95 o.p. (ISBN 0-376-01002-9, Sunset Bks). Sunset-Lane.
--African Violets. 5th ed. LC 76-46656. (Illus.). 80p. 1977. pap. 4.95 (ISBN 0-376-03058-5, Sunset Bks). Sunset-Lane.
--Barbecue Cook Book. 5th ed. LC 78-70272. (Illus.). 96p. 1979. pap. 4.95 (ISBN 0-376-02079-2, Sunset Bks). Sunset-Lane.
--Basic Home Wiring Illustrated. LC 76-46662. (Illus.). 88p. 1977. pap. 4.95 (ISBN 0-376-01094-0, Sunset Bks). Sunset-Lane.
--Basic Plumbing Illustrated. LC 82-83221. (Illus.). 96p. 1983. pap. 5.95 (ISBN 0-376-01466-0, Sunset Bks). Sunset-Lane.
--Bedrooms. LC 80-80857. (Illus.). 80p. (Orig.). 1980. pap. 3.95 (ISBN 0-376-01111-4, Sunset Bks). Sunset-Lane.
--Bookshelves & Cabinets. LC 74-76541. (Illus.). 96p. (Orig.). 1974. pap. 5.95 (ISBN 0-376-01085-1, Sunset Bks). Sunset-Lane.
--Breads. 3rd ed. LC 77-72513. (Illus.). 96p. 1977. pap. 4.95 (ISBN 0-376-02746-0, Sunset Bks). Sunset-Lane.
--Cabins & Vacation Houses. 3rd ed. LC 74-20017. (Illus.). 96p. 1975. pap. 2.95 o.p. (ISBN 0-376-01064-9, Sunset Bks). Sunset-Lane.
--Casserole Cook Book. 3rd ed. LC 80-80854. (Illus.). 96p. 1980. pap. 4.95 (ISBN 0-376-02255-8, Sunset Bks). Sunset-Lane.
--Chinese Cook Book. LC 79-88156. (Illus.). 96p. 1979. pap. 4.95 (ISBN 0-376-02302-3, Sunset Bks). Sunset-Lane.
--Convection Oven Cook Book. LC 80-81283. (Illus.). 96p. (Orig.). 1980. pap. 3.95 (ISBN 0-376-02311-2, Sunset Bks.). Sunset-Lane.
--Cooking for Two. LC 77-90722. (Illus.). 80p. 1978. pap. 4.95 (ISBN 0-376-02333-3, Sunset Bks.). Sunset-Lane.
--Crochet. LC 75-6218. (Illus.). 80p. (Orig.). 1975. pap. 4.95 (ISBN 0-376-04134-X, Sunset Bks.). Sunset-Lane.
--Decorating with Plants. LC 79-90333. (Illus.). 80p. 1980. pap. 3.95 (ISBN 0-376-03342-8, Sunset Bks). Sunset-Lane.
--Desert Gardening. LC 67-27445. (Illus.). 96p. 1967. pap. 3.95 (ISBN 0-376-03133-6, Sunset Bks). Sunset-Lane.
--Favorite Recipes. 2nd ed. LC 69-14226. (Illus.). 112p. 1969. pap. 4.95 o.p. (ISBN 0-376-02176-4, Sunset Bks.). Sunset-Lane.
--Fireplaces: How to Plan & Build. 4th ed. LC 79-90337. 96p. 1980. pap. 3.95 (ISBN 0-376-01155-6). Sunset-Lane.
--Food Processor Cook Book. LC 77-90721. (Illus.). 80p. 1978. pap. 4.95 (ISBN 0-376-02403-8, Sunset Bks.). Sunset-Lane.
--Furniture: Easy-to-Make. LC 76-46661. (Illus.). 80p. 1977. pap. 4.95 (ISBN 0-376-01176-9, Sunset Bks). Sunset-Lane.
--Garden & Patio Building Book. LC 82-83219. (Illus.). 112p. 1983. pap. 5.45 (ISBN 0-376-01216-1, Sunset Bks.). Sunset-Lane.
--Gardening in Containers. 3rd ed. LC 76-46651. (Illus.). 80p. 1977. pap. 3.95 (ISBN 0-376-03205-7, Sunset Bks). Sunset-Lane.
--Greenhouse Gardening. LC 75-26490. (Illus.). 96p. 1976. pap. 3.95 (ISBN 0-376-03263-4, Sunset Bks). Sunset-Lane.
--Hawaii: Travel Guide. 5th ed. LC 74-20023. (Illus.). 160p. 1975. pap. 5.95 (ISBN 0-376-06308-4, Sunset Bks.). Sunset-Lane.
--Herbs: How to Grow. LC 73-181520. (Illus.). 80p. (Orig.). 1972. pap. 3.95 (ISBN 0-376-03323-1, Sunset Bks.). Sunset-Lane.
--Hot Tubs, Spas & Home Saunas. LC 78-70274. (Illus.). 80p. 1979. pap. 4.95 (ISBN 0-376-01243-9, Sunset Bks). Sunset-Lane.
--House Plants: How to Grow. 3rd ed. LC 76-7660. (Illus.). 80p. 1976. pap. 4.95 (ISBN 0-376-03336-3, Sunset Bks). Sunset-Lane.
--How to Grow Vegetables & Berries. LC 81-82865. 1982. pap. 4.95 o.p. (ISBN 0-376-03805-5). Sunset-Lane.
--Italian Cook Book. 2nd ed. LC 81-81377. (Illus.). 112p. 1981. pap. 5.95 (ISBN 0-376-02465-8, Sunset Bks.). Sunset-Lane.
--Knitting. LC 76-7659. (Illus.). 80p. 1976. pap. 2.95 o.p. (ISBN 0-376-04432-2, Sunset Bks). Sunset-Lane.
--Landscaping & Garden Remodeling. LC 77-82872. (Illus.). 80p. 1978. pap. 4.95 (ISBN 0-376-03456-4, Sunset Bks.). Sunset-Lane.
--Lawns & Ground Covers. LC 78-70267. (Illus.). 96p. 1979. pap. 4.95 (ISBN 0-376-03507-2, Sunset Bks). Sunset-Lane.
--Mexican Cook Book. LC 77-72511. (Illus.). 96p. 1977. pap. 5.95 (ISBN 0-376-02496-8, Sunset Bks). Sunset-Lane.
--Mexico: Travel Guide. LC 82-83215. (Illus.). 160p. 1983. pap. 7.95 (ISBN 0-376-06458-7, Sunset Bks). Sunset-Lane.
--Microwave Cook Book. LC 80-53481. (Illus.). 96p. 1981. pap. 4.95 (ISBN 0-376-02505-0, Sunset Books). Sunset-Lane.
--Needlepoint. LC 76-46659. (Illus.). 80p. 1977. pap. 4.95 (ISBN 0-376-04585-X, Sunset Bks). Sunset-Lane.
--Orchids: How to Grow. LC 76-46652. (Illus.). 64p. 1977. pap. 4.95 (ISBN 0-376-03555-2, Sunset Bks). Sunset-Lane.
--The Orient: Travel Guide. LC 82-83216. (Illus.). 160p. (Orig.). 1983. pap. 7.95 (ISBN 0-376-06633-4, Sunset Bks.). Sunset-Lane.
--Paneling, Painting & Wallpapering. LC 75-26493. (Illus.). 80p. 1976. pap. 3.95 o.p. (ISBN 0-376-01393-1, Sunset Bks.). Sunset-Lane.
--Pruning Handbook. LC 82-83213. (Illus.). 120p. 1983. pap. 5.95 (ISBN 0-376-03605-2, Sunset Bks.). Sunset-Lane.

--Remodeling Your Home. 3rd ed. LC 78-53674. (Illus.). 96p. 1978. pap. 4.95 (ISBN 0-376-01506-3, Sunset Bks.). Sunset-Lane.
--Roses: How to Grow. 4th ed. LC 79-90334. (Illus.). 96p. 1980. pap. 4.95 (ISBN 0-376-03656-7, Sunset Bks). Sunset-Lane.
--Salads: Favorite Recipes. LC 78-70273. (Illus.). 96p. 1979. pap. 4.95 (ISBN 0-376-02607-3, Sunset Bks.). Sunset-Lane.
--Small-Space Gardens. LC 77-82874. (Illus.). 80p. 1978. pap. 3.95 o.p. (ISBN 0-376-03702-4, Sunset Bks.). Sunset-Lane.
--Solar Heating & Cooling: Homeowner's Guide. LC 78-53673. (Illus.). 96p. 1978. pap. 5.95 (ISBN 0-376-01524-1, Sunset Bks.). Sunset-Lane.
--Southeast Asia: Travel Guide. 2nd ed. LC 74-20024. (Illus.). 176p. 1975. pap. 5.95 o.p. (ISBN 0-376-06763-2, Sunset Bks.). Sunset-Lane.
--Storage. 3rd ed. LC 74-20021. (Illus.). 96p. 1975. pap. 4.95 (ISBN 0-376-01556-X, Sunset Bks.). Sunset-Lane.
--Swimming Pools. 5th ed. LC 80-53488. (Illus.). 128p. 1981. pap. 5.95 (ISBN 0-376-01608-6, Sunset Bks.). Sunset-Lane.
--Tables & Chairs: Easy to Make. LC 75-26492. (Illus.). 80p. 1976. pap. 4.95 (ISBN 0-376-01654-X, Sunset Bks.). Sunset-Lane.
--Tile: Remodeling with. LC 77-90719. (Illus.). 80p. 1978. pap. 5.95 (ISBN 0-376-01674-4, Sunset Bks). Sunset-Lane.
--Vegetable Cook Book. LC 82-83217. (Illus.). 96p. 1983. pap. 4.95 (ISBN 0-376-02904-8, Sunset Bks.). Sunset-Lane.
--Vegetables & Berries: How to Grow. LC 81-82865. (Illus.). 112p. 1982. pap. 4.95 (ISBN 0-376-03805-5, Sunset Bks.). Sunset-Lane.
--Vegetarian Cooking. LC 80-53483. (Illus.). 96p. (Orig.). 1981. pap. 4.95 (ISBN 0-376-02911-0, Sunset Bks.). Sunset-Lane.
--Walks, Walls, & Patio Floors. 3rd ed. LC 72-92521. (Illus.). 96p. 1973. pap. 4.95 (ISBN 0-376-01706-6, Sunset Bks.). Sunset-Lane.
--Western Garden Book: Sunset New. 4th ed. LC 78-70266. (Illus.). 512p. 1979. pap. 12.95 (ISBN 0-376-03890-X, Sunset Bks). Sunset-Lane.
--Wine Country: California. LC 82-81743. (Illus.). 160p. 1982. pap. 7.95 (ISBN 0-376-06945-7, Sunset Bks.). Sunset-Lane.
--Woodcarving Techniques & Projects. LC 72-157174. (Illus.). 80p. 1971. pap. 4.95 (ISBN 0-376-04805-0, Sunset Bks.). Sunset-Lane.
--Woodworking Projects. 2nd ed. LC 75-6222. (Illus.). 96p. 1975. pap. 4.95 (ISBN 0-376-04885-9, Sunset Bks.). Sunset-Lane.

Sunshine, Madeline. Puppy Love. LC 82-83330. (Little Golden Bk.). (Illus.). 24p. (ps-2). 1983. 0.89 (ISBN 0-307-01095-3, Golden Pr). Western Pub.

Suntharalingam, R. Indian Nationalism: An Historical Analysis. 1983. text ed. write for info. (ISBN 0-7069-2106-2, Pub. by Vikas India). Advent NY.

Sun Tzu. The Art of War. Griffith, Samuel B., tr. & intro. by. 1971. pap. 5.95 (ISBN 0-19-501476-6, 361, GB). Oxford U Pr.
--The Art of War. Clavell, James, ed. 1983. 9.95 (ISBN 0-440-00243-5). Delacorte.

Sunwall, James. Chilblains of the Heart. 1983. pap. 2.95 (ISBN 0-939736-38-1). Wings ME.

Suobodova, L. Computer Performance Measurement & Evaluation Methods: Analysis & Applications. (Computer Design & Architecture Ser.: Vol. 2). 1976. text ed. 29.00 (ISBN 0-444-00192-1); pap. text ed. 10.95 (ISBN 0-444-00197-2). Elsevier.

Suojanen, Waino & Henderson, Richard I. The Operating Manager: An Integrative Approach. (Illus.). 480p. 1974. ref. ed. 23.95 (ISBN 0-13-637942-7). P-H.

Super, Charles W., tr. see Weil, Henri.

Super, Donald E. Work Values Inventory: MRC Machine-Scorable Test Booklets. 51.56 (ISBN 0-395-09529-8); directions manual 3.12 (ISBN 0-395-09530-1); examination set pap. 2.16 (ISBN 0-395-09531-X). HM.

Super Horoscope Editors. Super Horoscopes: 1977. Incl. Aries (ISBN 0-448-12006-2); Taurus (ISBN 0-448-12007-0); Gemini (ISBN 0-448-12008-9); Cancer (ISBN 0-448-12009-7); Leo (ISBN 0-448-12010-0); Virgo (ISBN 0-448-12011-9); Libra (ISBN 0-448-12012-7); Scorpio (ISBN 0-448-12013-5); Sagittarius (ISBN 0-448-12014-3); Capricorn (ISBN 0-448-12015-1); Aquarius (ISBN 0-448-12016-X); Pisces (ISBN 0-448-12017-8). (Illus., Orig.). 1976. pap. 1.95 ea. o.p. (G&D). Putnam Pub Group.

Super Horoscope Editors, ed. Super Horoscopes, 1979. Incl. Aries. (ISBN 0-448-14115-9); Taurus. (ISBN 0-448-14116-7); Gemini. (ISBN 0-448-14117-5); Cancer. (ISBN 0-448-14118-3); Leo. (ISBN 0-448-14119-1); Virgo. (ISBN 0-448-14120-5); Libra. (ISBN 0-448-14121-3); Scorpio. (ISBN 0-448-14122-1); Sagittarius. (ISBN 0-448-14123-X); Capricorn. (ISBN 0-448-14124-8); Aquarius. (ISBN 0-448-14125-6); Pisces. (ISBN 0-448-14126-4). (Illus.). 1978. pap. 2.50 ea. o.p. (G&D). Putnam Pub Group.

Super Horoscopes Editors. Super Horoscopes, 1980. Incl. Aries. pap.; Aquarius. pap. (ISBN 0-448-14214-7); Cancer. pap. (ISBN 0-448-14207-4); Capricorn. pap. (ISBN 0-448-14213-9); Gemini. pap. (ISBN 0-448-14206-6); Leo. pap. (ISBN 0-448-14208-2); Libra. pap. (ISBN 0-448-14210-4); Pisces (ISBN 0-448-14215-5); Sagittarius. pap. (ISBN 0-448-14212-0); Scorpio. pap. (ISBN 0-448-14211-2); Taurus. pap. (ISBN 0-448-14205-8); Virgo. pap. (ISBN 0-448-14209-0). 1979. pap. 2.50 ea. o.p. (G&D). Putnam Pub Group.

Super, R. H., ed. see Arnold.

Super, R. H., ed. see Trollope, Anthony.

Superka, Douglas P., jt. auth. see Greenwald, G. Dale.

Supervielle. Le Voleur D'enfants. (Easy Reader, A). pap. 2.95 (ISBN 0-88436-111-X, 40265). EMC.

Supka, Magdolna B. Genre Painting in the Hungarian National Gallery. (Illus.). 1975. 13.00 (ISBN 0-912728-88-4). Newbury Bks.

Supka, Magdolna B., intro. by. Genre Painting in the Hungarian National Gallery. Compton, Agnes, tr. (Illus.). 102p. 1980. 15.95 (ISBN 0-89893-154-1). CDP.

Supovitz, Marjorie, ed. Gyorgy Kepes: The MIT Years: 1945-1977. (Illus.). 1978. pap. 9.95 (ISBN 0-262-61027-2). MIT Pr.

Suppe, F., ed. see Philosophy of Science Association, Biennial Meeting, 1976.

Suppe, Frederick, ed. see Philosophy of Science Biennial Meeting, 1976.

Suppes, Patrick & Morningstar, Mona. Computer-Assisted Instruction at Stanford, 1966-68. 1972. 43.00 (ISBN 0-12-676856-0). Acad Pr.

Suppes, Patrick, jt. auth. see Davidson, Donald.

Suppes, Patrick C., et al. Computer-Assisted Instruction: Stanford's 1965-66 Arithmetic Program. (Illus.). 1968. 43.00 (ISBN 0-12-676850-1). Acad Pr.

Supple, Barry, ed. Essays in British Business History. 1977. 34.50x (ISBN 0-19-877087-1); pap. 17.95x (ISBN 0-19-877088-X). Oxford U Pr.

Supraner, Leon, jt. auth. see Kaminsky, Marc.

Supraner, Robyn. Think About It, You Might Learn Something. LC 73-8752. (Illus.). 112p. (gr. 3-7). 1973. 9.95 (ISBN 0-395-17707-3). HM.
--Would You Rather Be a Tiger? LC 72-7962. (Illus.). 32p. (gr. k-3). 1973. reinforced bdg. 3.95 o.p. (ISBN 0-395-15495-2). HM.

Supree, Burton & Ross, Ann. Bear's Heart: Scenes from the Life of a Cheyenne Artist of One Hundred Years Ago with Pictures by Himself. LC 76-48952. (Illus.). 1977. 12.45i (ISBN 0-397-31746-8, HarpJ). Har-Row.

Suprunenko, Dmitri A. & Tyshkevich, R. I. Commutative Matrices. LC 68-18683. (Orig.). 1968. 29.50 (ISBN 0-12-677049-2); pap. 17.00 (ISBN 0-12-677050-6). Acad Pr.

Sur, A. K. Sex & Marriage in India. 1973. 6.00x o.p. (ISBN 0-8188-1194-3). Paragon.

Suran, A., ed. Immunology of the Eye III: Infection, Inflamation & Allergy. 526p. 1981. pap. 25.00 (ISBN 0-917000-08-0). IRL Pr.

Suran, Bernard G. & Rizzo, Joseph V. Special Children: An Integrative Approach. 1979. text ed. 23.50x (ISBN 0-673-15068-2). Scott F.
--Special Children: An Integrative Approach. 2nd ed. 1983. text ed. 23.95x (ISBN 0-673-15806-3). Scott F.

Surany, Anico. The Golden Frog. (Illus.). (gr. 3-5). 1963. PLB 3.97 o.p. (ISBN 0-399-60199-6). Putnam Pub Group.
--Ride the Cold Wind. (Illus.). (gr. 2-5). 1964. PLB 5.39 o.p. (ISBN 0-399-60535-5). Putnam Pub Group.

Surat, Michele. Angel Child, Dragon Child. (Illus.). 36p. (Orig.). (gr. 1-5). 1983. pap. 4.75 (ISBN 0-940742-07-1). Carnival Pr.

Surber, Jere P., tr. see Hegel, G. W.

Surburg, Raymond F. How Dependable Is the Bible. 1978. pap. 3.95 o.p. (ISBN 0-87981-094-7). Holman.

Sure, Heng & Heng Chau. With One Heart Bowing to the City of Ten Thousand Buddhas, Vol. III. (Illus.). 140p. (Orig.). 1980. pap. 6.00 (ISBN 0-917512-31-6). Buddhist Text.

Surette, Dick, ed. see Fulsher, Keith & Krom, Charles.

Surge, Frank. Famous Spies. LC 68-30569. (Pull Ahead Books). (Illus.). (gr. 5-12). 1969. PLB 4.95g (ISBN 0-8225-0454-5). Lerner Pubns.
--Singers of the Blues. LC 68-30570. (Pull Ahead Bks.). (Illus.). (gr. 5-12). 1969. PLB 4.95g (ISBN 0-8225-0453-7). Lerner Pubns.
--Western Lawmen. LC 68-30568. (Pull Ahead Books). (Illus.). (gr. 5-10). 1969. PLB 4.95g (ISBN 0-8225-0451-0). Lerner Pubns.
--Western Outlaws. LC 68-30567. (Pull Ahead Books). (Illus.). (gr. 5-10). 1969. PLB 4.95g (ISBN 0-8225-0452-9). Lerner Pubns.

Surgenor, Douglas N., ed. The Red Blood Cell, 2 vols. 2nd ed. Vol. 1, 1974. 84.50 (ISBN 0-12-677201-0); Vol. 2, 1975. 85.50 (ISBN 0-12-677202-9); Set. 121.00 (ISBN 0-686-77034-X). Acad Pr.

Suring, Margit L. The Horn-Motif in the Hebrew Bible & Related Ancient Near Eastern Literature & Iconography. (Andrews University Seminary Doctoral Dissertation Ser.). (Illus.). xxvi, 533p. 1982. pap. 9.95 (ISBN 0-943872-36-7). Andrews Univ Pr.

Suritz, Penelope W., jt. auth. see Sullivan, Eugene J.

Surjaatmadja, J. B., jt. auth. see Fitch, E. C.

Surjan, L. & Bodo, G., eds. Borderline Problems in Otorhinolaryngology: Proceedings, 12th World Congress, Budapest, Hungary, June 12-27, 1981. 724p. 1982. 121.00 (ISBN 0-444-90261-9, Excerpta Medica). Elsevier.

Surmanek, Jim. Media Planning: Quick & Easy Guide. LC 80-67810. 1980. pap. text ed. 10.95 (ISBN 0-87251-046-8). Crain Bks.

Surmanek, Jim, jt. auth. see Sissors, Jack Z.

Surmelian, Leon. Apples of Immortality: Folktales of Armenia. LC 82-24260. (Unesco Collection of Representative Works, Series of Translations from the Literature of the Union of Soviet Socialist Republics). (Illus.). 319p. 1983. Repr. of 1968 ed. lib. bdg. 39.75x (ISBN 0-313-23417-5, SUAP). Greenwood.

Surowiecki, Sandra L. Joshua's Day. 2nd ed. LC 77-20479. 27p. (ps-1). 1977. pap. 3.25 (ISBN 0-914996-18-5). Lollipop Power.

Surpateanu, J. P., et al. Structure & Reactivity of Cycloimmonium Ylides. 1977. pap. text ed. 12.75 o.p. (ISBN 0-08-021585-8). Pergamon.

Surplus, Robert W. Alphabet of Music. LC 62-20799. (Musical Books for Young People Ser). (gr. 5-11). 1963. PLB 3.95g o.p. (ISBN 0-8225-0058-2). Lerner Pubns.
--Beat of the Drum. LC 62-20800. (Musical Books for Young People Ser.). (gr. 5-11). 1963. PLB 3.95g (ISBN 0-8225-0059-0). Lerner Pubns.
--Follow the Leader: The Story of Conducting. LC 62-20801. (Musical Books for Young People Ser). (gr. 5-11). 1962. PLB 3.95g (ISBN 0-8225-0054-X). Lerner Pubns.
--Story of Musical Organizations. LC 62-20805. (Musical Books for Young People Ser). (Illus.). (gr. 5-11). 1963. PLB 3.95g (ISBN 0-8225-0060-4). Lerner Pubns.

Surrency, Erwin C., jt. auth. see Moreland, Carroll C.

Surrency, Erwin C., ed. The Marshall Reader. LC 55-11500. (Docket Ser.: Vol. 3). 256p. (Orig.). 1955. 15.00 (ISBN 0-379-11303-1); pap. 2.50 (ISBN 0-685-19007-2). Oceana.

Surrey, M. J. The Analysis & Forecasting of the British Economy. LC 75-171683. (National Institute of Economic & Social Research, Occasional Papers: No. 25). (Illus.). 100p. 1972. 17.95x (ISBN 0-521-09675-8). Cambridge U Pr.

Surrey, M. J. C., ed. Macroeconomic Themes: Edited Readings in Macroeconomics. (Illus.). 1976. text ed. 29.95x o.p. (ISBN 0-19-877059-6); pap. text ed. 15.95x (ISBN 0-19-877060-X). Oxford U Pr.

Surrey, Stanley S., jt. ed. see Andrews, William D.

Surrey, Stanley S., et al. Federal Income Taxation, Cases & Materials Vol. 1: 1982 Supplement. (University Casebook Ser.). 444p. 1982. pap. text ed. write for info. (ISBN 0-88277-085-3). Foundation Pr.

Surtees, R. S. Mr. Sponge's Sporting Tour. (World's Classics Ser.). (Illus.). 1982. pap. 7.95 (ISBN 0-19-281521-0). Oxford U Pr.

Surtees, Virginia, ed. see Ford, Madox B.

Survey Research Center. Minor American National Election Study, 1960. 1968. codebk. write for info. o.p. (ISBN 0-89138-002-7). ICPSR.
--Perceptions of the 1963 Presidential Transition. 1973. codebk. write for info. (ISBN 0-89138-062-0). ICPSR.

Survey Research Center Computer Support Group. Osiris IV: Statistical Analysis & Data Management Software System. 7th ed. LC 79-83781. 394p. 1981. 3-ring binder 20.00x (ISBN 0-87944-232-8); Subroutine Manual, 1979, 162p. 3-ring binder 15.00x (ISBN 0-87944-244-1). Inst Soc Res.

Survey Research Center Staff. Interviewer's Manual. rev. ed. LC 76-630039. 145p. 1976. 20.00x (ISBN 0-87944-195-X); pap. 14.00x (ISBN 0-87944-194-1). Inst Soc Res.

Survey Research Laboratory Univ. of Illinois for National Science Foundation & U. S. Dept. of Energy. Public Reactions to Wind Energy Devices. 203p. 1982. pap. 24.50x (ISBN 0-89934-169-1, W062). Solar Energy Info.

Surwit, Richard S. & Williams, Redford B., Jr., eds. Behavioral Treatment of Disease, Vol. 19. (NATO Conference Ser. III: Human Factors). 482p. 1982. 42.50x (ISBN 0-686-83971-4, Plenum Pr). Plenum Pub.

Suryadinata, Leo. The Pre-World War II Peranakan Chinese Press of Java: A Preliminary Survey. LC 70-635607. (Papers in International Studies: Southeast Asia: No. 18). 1971. 4.00 (ISBN 0-89680-011-3, Ohio U Ctr Intl). Ohio U Pr.

Suryakanta. A Practical Vedic Dictionary. 768p. 1981. 47.00x (ISBN 0-19-561298-1). Oxford U Pr.
--Sanskrit-Hindi-English Dictionary. 1976. 47.50x (ISBN 0-8002-1950-3). Intl Pubns Serv.

Susanne, E. Danish Cookery. 10th ed. 1974. pap. 8.50x o.p. (ISBN 8-7142-7492-2, D708). Vanous.

Suschny, O. Measurement of Atmospheric Radioactivity. (Technical Note Ser.). 1968. pap. 30.00 (ISBN 0-685-22317-5, W64, WMO). Unipub.

Suskind, Robert M., ed. Malnutrition & the Immune Response. LC 75-14589. 483p. 1977. 48.00 (ISBN 0-89004-060-5). Raven.
--Textbook of Pediatric Nutrition. 680p. 1981. text ed. 66.00 (ISBN 0-89004-253-5). Raven.

Suskind, Sigmund, ed. see Stahl, Franklin W.

Suslov, Ilia. Rasskazy Oytovarishche Staline i Drugikh Tovarishchakh: Tales About Com Stalin & Other Comrades. 140p. (Rus.). 1981. pap. 7.50 (ISBN 0-938920-03-0). Hermitage MI.

Susman, Jackwell, jt. ed. see Kittrie, Nicholas N.

Susman, Susan. There's No Such Thing As a Chanukkah Bush, Sandy Goldstein. Tucker, Kathleen, ed. (Illus.). 40p. (gr. 3-7). 1983. PLB 6.95 (ISBN 0-8075-7862-2). A Whitman.

Susnjara, Ken. A Manager's Guide to Industrial Robots. LC 81-86624. (Illus.). 181p. 1982. 24.95 (ISBN 0-86551-018-0). Corinthian.

Sussams, John. How To Write Effective Reports. 160p. 1983. 19.95 (ISBN 0-89397-145-6). Nichols Pub.

Susser, Mervyn. Causal Thinking in the Health Sciences: Concepts & Strategies of Epidemiology. (Illus.). 1973. text ed. 14.95x (ISBN 0-19-501587-8). Oxford U Pr.

Susser, Mervyn W. & Watson, W. Sociology in Medicine. 2nd ed. (Illus.). 1977. pap. text ed. 29.50x (ISBN 0-19-264912-4). Oxford U Pr.

Susser, Samuel M. The Truth About Selling. 1975. pap. 1.75 o.p. (ISBN 0-451-61813-0, ME1813, Ment). NAL.

Sussex, Ian M., jt. ed. see Subtelny, Stephen.

Sussex, J. N., jt. auth. see Glasscote, R. M.

Sussex, James, jt. ed. see Bernstein, Norman.

Sussex, James N., jt. ed. see Busse, Ewald.

Sussex, Margie & Stapleton, John F. The Complete Real Estate Math Book. 320p. 1976. 16.95 o.p. (ISBN 0-13-162354-0). P-H.

Susskind, Charles. Popov & the Beginnings of Radiotelegraphy. LC 62-22310. (History of Technology Monographs). (Illus.). 1962. pap. 3.50 o.p. (ISBN 0-911302-10-7). San Francisco Pr.

Susskind, Charles, jt. auth. see Kurylo, Friedrich.

Sussman, A. S., jt. ed. see Ainsworth, Geoffrey C.

Sussman, Aaron. The Amateur Photographer's Handbook. 8th ed. LC 72-2558. (Illus.). 420p. 1973. 15.34i (ISBN 0-690-05782-2). T Y Crowell.

Sussman, Alan. The Rights of Young People. 1977. pap. 2.50 o.p. (ISBN 0-380-00935-8, 77032, Discus). Avon.

Sussman, Alan & Cohen, Stephan. Reporting Child Abuse & Neglect: Guidelines for Legislation. LC 75-11798. 288p. 1975. prof ref 18.50x (ISBN 0-88410-210-6). Ballinger Pub.

Sussman, Barry. The Great Cover-up: Nixon & the Scandal of Watergate. (RL 10). 1974. pap. 1.95 o.p. (ISBN 0-451-06303-1, J6303, Sig). NAL.

Sussman, Barth J. Shanghai. (Orig.). 1981. pap. 2.75 o.p. (ISBN 0-451-09563-4, E9563, Sig). NAL.

Sussman, Carl, ed. Planning the Fourth Migration: The Neglected Vision of the Regional Planning Association of America. 1976. 20.00x (ISBN 0-262-19148-2). MIT Pr.

Sussman, Ellen & Johnson, Helen. A Sunny Start: Getting Ready for Kindergarten. (Illus.). 44p. (Orig.). (ps). 1983. pap. 5.95 (ISBN 0-933606-20-6, MS-611). Monkey Sisters.

Sussman, Ellen, ed. see Hornnes, Esther & Magos, Eunice.

Sussman, Ellen, ed. see Petreshene, Susan S.

Sussman, Gerald. Overextension University Bulletin: School of Continual Education & Self-Enlargement. LC 82-13860. (Illus.). 64p. 1982. pap. 3.95 (ISBN 0-87131-389-8). M Evans.

Sussman, Gerald E. The Challenge of Integrated Rural Development in India. (Replica Edition). 190p. 1982. pap. 16.00 (ISBN 0-86531-922-7). Westview.

Sussman, Gerald J. A Computer Model of Skill Acquisition. LC 74-30964. (Artificial Inteligence Ser.: Vol. 1). 133p. 1975. 27.50 (ISBN 0-444-00163-8); pap. text ed. 10.95 (ISBN 0-444-00159-X). Elsevier.

Sussman, Jeffrey, jt. auth. see Prudden, Suzy.

Sussman, Marvin, jt. auth. see Rockstein, Morris.

Sussman, Marvin B., ed. Author's Guide to Journals in Sociology & Related Fields. LC 78-1952. (Author's Guide to Journals Ser.). 1978. 19.95 (ISBN 0-917724-03-8, B3). Haworth Pr.
--Marriage & the Family: Current Critical Issues. LC 79-53232. (Collected Essay Ser.). 63p. 1979. pap. 6.95 (ISBN 0-917724-08-9, B8). Haworth Pr.
--Sourcebook in Marriage & the Family. 4th ed. 432p. 1974. pap. text ed. 15.50 (ISBN 0-395-17538-0). HM.

Sussman, Marvin B., jt. ed. see Cates, Judith N.

Sussman, Marvin B., jt. ed. see Cogswell, Betty.

Sussman, Marvin B., jt. ed. see Gross, Harriet.

Sussman, Marvin B., jt. ed. see Kaslow, Florence.

Sussman, Marvin B., jt. ed. see Lein, Laura.

Sussman, Marvin B., et al. The Family & Inheritance. LC 74-104183. 450p. 1970. 13.95x (ISBN 0-87154-873-9). Russell Sage.

Sussman, Marvin B., jt. ed. see McCubbin, Hamilton I.

Sussman, Marvin L., jt. ed. see Rockstein, Morris.

Sussman, Maurice. Developmental Biology: Its Cellular & Molecular Foundations. (Foundations of Modern Biology Ser). (Illus.). 304p. 1973. pap. 11.95 ref. ed. o.p. (ISBN 0-13-208207-1). P-H.

Sussman, Robert W. Primate Ecology: Problem Oriented Field Studies. LC 78-17828. 596p. 1979. text ed. 26.95 (ISBN 0-471-03823-7). Wiley.

Sussman, Varda. Decorated Jewish Oil Lamps. (Illus.). 144p. 1982. text ed. 50.00x (ISBN 0-85668-164-4, 40455, Pub. by Aris & Phillips England). Humanities.

Sussman, Vic. Never Kiss a Goat on the Lips: Tales of a Suburban Homesteader. Stoner, Carol, ed. (Illus.). 288p. 1981. 12.95 o.p. (ISBN 0-87857-346-1); pap. 8.95 o.p. (ISBN 0-87857-347-X). Rodale Pr Inc.

Sussmann, G., jt. auth. see Mayr, D.

Sussmann, Leila. Tales Out of School: Implementing Organizational Change in the Elementary Grades. LC 77-89413. 282p. 1977. 27.95 (ISBN 0-87722-097-2). Temple U Pr.

Sustendal, Pat, illus. Strawberry Shortcake's One-Two-Three. LC 80-85420. (Chunky Bks.). (Illus.). 28p. (ps). 1981. bds. 2.95 (ISBN 0-394-84896-9). Random.

Susuki, Daisetsu T. Mysticism: Christian & Buddhist. 160p. 1982. pap. 5.95 (ISBN 0-04-149053-3). Allen Unwin.

Sutasurya, L. A., jt. auth. see Nieuwkoop, P. D.

Sutch, R., jt. auth. see Ransom, R.

Sutcliff, Rosemary. Brother Dusty-Feet. (Illus.). (gr. 6 up). 1980. Repr. of 1952 ed. 12.95 (ISBN 0-19-271444-9). Oxford U Pr.

--The Light Beyond the Forest. LC 79-23396. 144p. (gr. 4-7). 1980. 10.95 (ISBN 0-525-33665-6, 01063-320). Dutton.

--Simon. (Illus.). (gr. 6 up). 1980. Repr. of 1953 ed. 12.95 (ISBN 0-19-271442-2). Oxford U Pr.

Sutcliffe. Handbook of Emergency Anesthesia. 1983. text ed. price not set (ISBN 0-408-00395-2). Butterworth.

--Plants & Temperature. (Studies in Biology: No. 86). 1978. 5.95 o.p. (ISBN 0-7131-2677-9). Univ Park.

Sutcliffe, Anthony, ed. The Rise of Modern Urban Planning Eighteen Hundred to Nineteen Fourteen. 1980. 30.00 (ISBN 0-312-68430-4). St Martin.

Sutcliffe, Denham, ed. see Robinson, Edwin A.

Sutcliffe, H., jt. auth. see Pass, G.

Sutcliffe, J. F. & Baker, D. A. Plants & Mineral Salts. 1975. 54.00x (ISBN 0-686-84465-3, Pub. by Oxford & I B H India). State Mutual Bk.

Sutcliffe, James. Plants & Temperature. (Studies in Biology: No. 86). 64p. 1978. pap. text ed. 8.95 (ISBN 0-686-43114-6). E Arnold.

Sutcliffe, James & Baker, Dennis. Plants & Minerals Salts. 2nd ed. (Studies in Biology: No. 48). 72p. 1981. pap. text ed. 8.95 (ISBN 0-7131-2831-3). E Arnold.

Sutcliffe, Jill. Boating & Boats. (Local Search Ser.). (Illus.). 1976. 8.95 (ISBN 0-7100-8356-4). Routledge & Kegan.

Suter, Erich. Contracts at Work. 276p. 1982. pap. text ed. 33.50x (ISBN 0-85292-297-3, Pub by Inst Personnel Mgmt England). Renouf.

Suter, H. R. Sachversicherung. 330p. (Ger.). 1982. write for info. (ISBN 3-261-04979-0). P Lang Pubs.

Suter, Peter F., jt. auth. see Ettinger, Stephen J.

Suter, Richard W., jt. auth. see Cook, Stanley J.

Suter, Ronald. Six Answers to the Problem of Taste. LC 79-84279. 1979. pap. text ed. 6.50 (ISBN 0-8191-0726-3). U Pr of Amer.

Sutermeister. People & Productivity. 3rd ed. (Management Ser). 1976. text ed. 23.95 (ISBN 0-07-062367-8, C); pap. text ed. 17.00 (ISBN 0-07-062371-6). McGraw.

Suteyev, V. What Kind of Bird Is That? Ginsburg, Mirra, ed. LC 72-91703. (Illus.). 32p. (ps-2). 1973. reinforced lib. bdg. 5.95 o.p. (ISBN 0-517-50255-0). Crown.

Suther, Judith D., tr. see Obey, Andre.

Sutherland, A. Barter & Coinage of New Zealand. (Illus.). 1983. pap. 10.00 (ISBN 0-942666-16-X). S J Durst.

Sutherland, Anne. Face Values. 288p. 1978. 40.00x (ISBN 0-686-98233-9, Pub. by BBC Pubns). State Mutual Bk.

Sutherland, Arthur E. Church Shall Be Free: A Glance at Eight Centuries of Church & State. LC 65-24000. (Orig.). 1965. pap. 1.95x o.p. (ISBN 0-8139-0232-0). U Pr of Va.

Sutherland, Audrey. Paddling My Own Canoe. LC 78-16374. (Illus.). 1978. 7.95 (ISBN 0-8248-0618-2, Kolowalu Bk). UH Pr.

--Paddling My Own Canoe. LC 78-16374. 1980. pap. 4.95 o.p. (ISBN 0-8248-0699-9). UH Pr.

Sutherland, C. H. The Romans in Spain, 217 B.C.-A.D. 117. LC 82-15846. (Illus.). xi, 264p. 1982. Repr. of 1939 ed. lib. bdg. 45.00x (ISBN 0-313-23745-X, SURS). Greenwood.

Sutherland, C. H. & Carson, R. A. Roman Imperial Coinage, 12 vols. 1977. 1000.00 set (ISBN 0-685-51530-3, Pub by Spink & Son England). S J Durst.

Sutherland, D. S. Igneous Rocks of the British Isles. LC 80-40281. 645p. 1982. 132.00x (ISBN 0-471-27810-6, Pub. by Wiley-Interscience). Wiley.

Sutherland, Donald. The Chouans: The Social Origins of Popular Counter-Revolution in Upper Brittany, 1770-1796. 400p. 1982. 59.00x (ISBN 0-19-822579-2). Oxford U Pr.

Sutherland, Doug, jt. auth. see Hartman, Doug.

Sutherland, Earl W., jt. auth. see Massett, Larry, 3rd.

Sutherland, Efua. The Marriage of Anansewa. (Sun-Lit Ser.). 100p. (Orig.). 1980. 9.00x o.s.i. (ISBN 0-89410-162-5); pap. 5.00x o.s.i. (ISBN 0-89410-163-3). Three Continents.

Sutherland, Efua T. Edufa. 74p. (Orig.). 1979. 9.00 o.s.i. (ISBN 0-89410-116-1, Sun-Lit); pap. 5.00 o.s.i. (ISBN 0-89410-117-X). Three Continents.

Sutherland, G. H. School Certificate History. pap. 9.50x (ISBN 0-392-08457-0, ABC). Sportshelf.

Sutherland, Ivan E. Sketchpad: A Man-Machine Graphical Communication System. LC 79-50557. (Outstanding Dissertations in the Computer Sciences Ser.: Vol. 21). 176p. 1980. lib. bdg. 20.00 o.s.i. (ISBN 0-8240-4411-8). Garland Pub.

Sutherland, J., ed. see Thackeray, William M.

Sutherland, James. The Oxford Book of Literary Anecdotes. 1977. pap. 5.95 o.p. (ISBN 0-671-22744-0, Touchstone Bks). S&S.

Sutherland, James, ed. The Oxford Book of Literary Anecdotes. 1975. 24.95x (ISBN 0-19-812139-3). Oxford U Pr.

Sutherland, James R. & Hurstfield, J., eds. Shakespeare's World. 1964. 15.95 o.p. (ISBN 0-312-71610-9). St Martin.

Sutherland, John. Offensive Literature: Decensorship in Britain, 1960-1982. LC 82-22758. 200p. 1983. text ed. 24.50x (ISBN 0-389-20354-8). B&N Imports.

--Thackeray at Work. (Illus.). 160p. 1974. text ed. 29.50x (ISBN 0-485-11146-2, Athlone Pr). Humanities.

Sutherland, John, ed. see Thackery, William M.

Sutherland, John, ed. see Trollope, Anthony.

Sutherland, John W. Managing Social Service Systems. LC 77-21806. (Illus.). 1977. text ed. 20.00 (ISBN 0-89433-004-7). Petrocelli.

Sutherland, Margaret. Hello, I'm Karen. LC 75-25614. (Illus.). 96p. (gr. k-5). 1976. 4.95 o.p. (ISBN 0-698-20371-2, Coward). Putnam Pub Group.

Sutherland, Margaret B. Everyday Imagining & Education. 1971. 10.25x o.p. (ISBN 0-7100-6995-2). Routledge & Kegan.

Sutherland, N. S. & MacKintosh, N. J. Mechanisms of Animal Discrimination & Learning. LC 79-127705. 1971. 61.00 (ISBN 0-12-677750-0). Acad Pr.

Sutherland, Norman S. Tutorial Essays in Psychology, Vol. 1. 182p. 1977. text ed. 19.95 (ISBN 0-89859-199-6). L Erlbaum Assocs.

Sutherland, Patricia. The Pet Bird Handbook. LC 81-3441. (Illus.). 224p. 1982. 13.95 (ISBN 0-668-05279-1); pap. 6.96 o.p. (ISBN 0-668-05282-1). Arco.

Sutherland, Sarah P. Masques in Jacobean Tragedy. LC 81-69122. 1982. 24.50 (ISBN 0-404-62279-8). AMS Pr.

Sutherland, Theodore J. Spiritism & the Dead. (An Intimate Life of Man Library Bk.). (Illus.). 127p. 1983. Repr. of 1889 ed. 89.75 (ISBN 0-89901-090-3). Found Class Reprints.

Sutherland, Zena. The Arbuthnot Anthology of Children's Literature. 4th ed. 1976. text ed. 24.50x (ISBN 0-673-15000-3). Scott F.

Sutherland, Zena, compiled by. Nursery Rhymes, Songs & Stories. (Illus.). (gr. k-4). 1980. cancelled o.s.i. (ISBN 0-525-66707-5). Lodestar Bks.

Sutherland, Zena, et al. Children & Books. 6th ed. 1981. text ed. 24.50x (ISBN 0-673-15377-0). Scott F.

Sutherland-Holmes, Nancy. The Calico Collection. (Illus.). 10p. 1980. pap. 4.00 (ISBN 0-943574-03-X). That Patchwork.

Suthren, Victor. The Black Cockade: Paul Gallant's Louisburg Command. 256p. 1982. 10.95 (ISBN 0-312-08303-3). St Martin.

Sutin, J., jt. auth. see Carpenter, Malcolm B.

Sutin, Jerome, jt. auth. see Carpenter, Malcolm B.

Sutliff, Mary. Teanaway Country. new ed. LC 79-66697. (Illus., Orig.). 1980. pap. 5.95 (ISBN 0-913140-39-2). Signpost Bk Pub.

Sutlive, Vinson H., Jr., jt. ed. see Lawless, Robert.

Sutnick, Alton I. & Engstrom, Paul F., eds. Oncologic Medicine: Clinical Topics & Practical Management. (Illus.). 1976. 29.50 o.p. (ISBN 0-8391-0883-4). Univ Park.

Sutor, Andrew P. Police Operations-Tactical Approaches to Crimes in Progress. LC 76-16911. (Criminal Justice Ser.). 1976. 15.95; pap. text ed. write for info. (ISBN 0-8299-0609-6); instrs.' manual avail. (ISBN 0-8299-0611-8). West Pub.

Sutow, Wataru. Malignant Solid Tumors of Childhood: A Review. 235p. 1981. text ed. 28.50 (ISBN 0-89004-299-3). Raven.

Sutphin, Florence E. Autobiography by Chucky Woodchuck. (Illus.). (gr. k-3). 1967. 2.75 o.p. (ISBN 0-8158-0192-0). Chris Mass.

Sutphin, Stanley T. Options in Contemporary Theology. 1978. pap. text ed. 9.50 (ISBN 0-8191-0277-6). U Pr of Amer.

Sutro, Alfred, jt. auth. see Meredith, George.

Suttell, Barbara J., jt. auth. see Pascal, Gerald R.

Sutter, Frederick. Samoa: A Photographic Essay. (Illus.). 1971. 18.95 (ISBN 0-87022-778-5). UH Pr.

Sutter, Robert G. The China Quandary: Domestic Determinants of U. S. - China Policy, 1972-1982. 250p. 1983. lib. bdg. 22.50x (ISBN 0-86531-579-5). Westview.

--Chinese Foreign Policy After the Cultural Revolution: 1966-1977. LC 77-7018. (Special Studies on China & East Asia Ser.). 1978. lib. bdg. 24.50x o.p. (ISBN 0-89158-342-4). Westview.

Sutterley, Doris C. & Donnelly, Gloria F., eds. Coping with Stress: A Nursing Perspective. LC 81-17599. 333p. 1982. text ed. 26.50 (ISBN 0-89443-650-3). Aspen Systems.

Suttie, J. W., ed. Vitamin K Metabolism & Vitamin K-Dependent Proteins. 608p. 1979. text ed. 44.50 o.p. (ISBN 0-8391-1540-7). Univ Park.

Suttle, J. Lloyd, jt. ed. see Hackman, J. Richard.

Suttles, Patricia H., et al, eds. Educators Guide to Free Social Studies Materials. 22nd rev. ed. LC 61-65910. 1982. pap. 21.25 (ISBN 0-87708-127-1). Ed Prog.

Sutton, et al. Barron's How to Prepare for the Registered Nurse Licensing Examination. 1983. pap. 6.95 (ISBN 0-8120-2301-3). Barron.

Sutton, Ann. The Structure of Weaving. LC 82-84398. (Illus.). 192p. 1983. 27.95 (ISBN 0-937274-08-9). Lark Bks.

Sutton, Ann & Sutton, Myron. Appalachian Trail: Wilderness on the Doorstep. LC 67-15502. (Illus.). 1967. 11.49i (ISBN 0-397-00459-1); pap. 4.95i (ISBN 0-397-01179-2, LP-104). Har-Row.

--Life of the Desert. (Our Living World of Nature Ser.). (gr. 7 up). 1966. 14.95 (ISBN 0-07-062384-8, P&RB); pap. 12.95 (ISBN 0-07-046002-7). McGraw.

Sutton, Ann, et al. The Crafts of the Weaver. (Illus.). 152p. (Orig.). 1982. 18.50 (ISBN 0-937274-09-7); pap. 12.95 (ISBN 0-937274-10-0). Lark Bks.

Sutton, Anne & Hammond, Peter, eds. Coronation of Richard III: The Extant Documents. 336p. 1982. text ed. 76.00x (Pub. by Sutton England). Humanities.

Sutton, Antony C. The War on Gold. 1977. 12.50 (ISBN 0-89245-008-8). Seventy Six.

Sutton, Audrey L. Bedside Nursing Techniques in Medicine & Surgery. 2nd ed. LC 69-12891. 1969. pap. 12.95 (ISBN 0-7216-8666-4). Saunders.

Sutton, C. J. Economics & Corporate Strategy. LC 79-4198. (Illus.). 1980. 37.50 (ISBN 0-521-22669-4); pap. 11.95 (ISBN 0-521-29610-2). Cambridge U Pr.

Sutton, Caroline. How Do They Do That? Wonders of the Modern World Explained. LC 82-478. (Illus.). 1982. 13.45 (ISBN 0-688-00486-5); pap. 7.50 (ISBN 0-688-01111-X). Morrow.

Sutton, Catherine. The Beagle. 1977. pap. 2.50 (ISBN 0-7028-1045-2). Palmetto Pub.

Sutton, Charles. New York Tombs, Its Secrets & Its Mysteries. Mix, James B. & Mackeever, Samuel A., eds. LC 76-172588. (Criminology, Law Enforcement, & Social Problems Ser.: No. 178). (Illus., Intro. added). 1973. Repr. of 1874 ed. 18.50x (ISBN 0-87585-178-9). Patterson Smith.

Sutton, Clarence W., Jr. Notable Aircraft of the 1930's & How They Were Built, 8 vols. LC 81-90009. (Illus., 140 pages per vol.). 1982. lib. bdg. 350.00 set (ISBN 0-940300-00-1); 45.00 ea. Vol. 1 (ISBN 0-940300-01-X). Vol. 2 (ISBN 0-940300-02-8). Vol. 3 (ISBN 0-940300-03-6). Vol. 4 (ISBN 0-940300-04-4). Vol. 5 (ISBN 0-940300-05-2). Vol. 6 (ISBN 0-940300-06-0). Vol. 7 (ISBN 0-940300-07-9). Sutton Pr.

Sutton, D. F. Financial Management in Hotel & Catering Operations. 252p. 1983. pap. 17.50 (ISBN 0-434-91887-3, Pub. by Heinemann England). David & Charles.

Sutton, Dana F. Self & Society in Aristophanes. LC 80-5235. 125p. 1980. lib. bdg. 17.75 (ISBN 0-8191-1067-1); pap. text ed. 8.25 (ISBN 0-8191-1068-X). U Pr of Amer.

Sutton, Dorothy L., jt. auth. see Whitworth, John R.

Sutton, F. H. A Short Account of Organs Built in England, Eighteen Forty-Seven. (Bibliotheca Organologica: Vol. 55). 113p. 1979. wrappers 20.00 o.s.i. (ISBN 90-6027-354-0, Pub. by Frits Knuf Netherlands). Pendragon NY.

Sutton, Felix. Big Book of Clowns. (Illus.). (gr. k-3). 1966. 1.50 o.s.i. (ISBN 0-448-00345-7, G&D). Putnam Pub Group.

--The Big Book of Wild Animals. (Illus.). 32p. (gr. k-3). 1982. 3.95 (ISBN 0-448-04243-6, G&D). Putnam Pub Group.

--Dogs. (Silver Dollar Library Ser.). (gr. 1-5). 1962. 1.50 o.p. (ISBN 0-448-00320-1, G&D). Putnam Pub Group.

--Horses of America. (Illus.). (gr. 5-9). 1964. PLB 5.69 o.p. (ISBN 0-399-60265-8). Putnam Pub Group.

Sutton, George A. & Ross, Donald M. Rocket Propulsion Elements: An Introduction to the Engineering of Rockets. 4th ed. LC 75-29197. 557p. 1976. 44.95x (ISBN 0-471-83836-5, Pub. by Wiley-Interscience). Wiley.

Sutton, George H., et al, eds. The Geophysics of the Pacific Ocean Basin & Its Margin. LC 75-38816. (Geophysical Monograph Ser.: Vol. 19). (Illus.). 1976. 20.00 (ISBN 0-87590-019-4). Am Geophysical.

Sutton, George M. Fifty Common Birds of Oklahoma & the Southern Great Plains. LC 77-24336. (Illus.). 113p. 1981. pap. 6.95 (ISBN 0-8061-1704-4). U of Okla Pr.

Sutton, H. Eldon. Mutagenic Effects of Environmental Contaminants. (Environmental Science Ser.). 1972. 32.50 (ISBN 0-12-677950-3). Acad Pr.

Sutton, H. Eldon & Wagner, Robert P. Genetics: A Human Concern. 432p. 1984. text ed. 24.95 (ISBN 0-02-418320-2). Macmillan.

Sutton, Hilton. The Devil Ain't What He Used to Be. 80p. (Orig.). 1983. pap. 1.95 (ISBN 0-686-83910-2). Harrison Hse.

--Questions & Answers on Bible Prophecy. 135p. (Orig.). 1982. pap. 2.95 (ISBN 0-89274-253-4). Harrison Hse.

--World War III. 93p. (Orig.). 1982. pap. 2.25 (ISBN 0-89274-192-9, HH-192). Harrison Hse.

Sutton, Jeff. The River. 192p. 1982. pap. 2.25 o.p. (ISBN 0-505-51864-3). Tower Bks.

Sutton, Joan L. & Watson de Barros, Leda. Novia Hoy-Esposa Manana: Guia Para Novias. S. D. de Lerin, Olivia, tr. Orig. Title: Manual das Noivas. 80p. 1980. pap. 2.15 (ISBN 0-311-46056-9, Edit Mundo). Casa Bautista.

Sutton, John. Brush Work on Ceramics with John Sutton. (Illus.). 192p. 1980. 10.00 (ISBN 0-686-36021-4); pap. o.p. (ISBN 0-686-37266-2). Scott Pubns MI.

--Feature That: A Guide to Painting Features. (Illus.). 36p. (Orig.). 1983. pap. write for info. Scott Pubns MI.

Sutton, John R. & Houston, Charles S., eds. Hypoxia: Man at Altitude. LC 81-84773. (Illus., Orig.). 1982. pap. text ed. 24.95 (ISBN 0-86577-048-4). Thieme-Stratton.

Sutton, Joseph A. Magic Carpet: Aleppo in Flatbush: The Story of a Unique Ethnic Jewish Community. 2nd ed. LC 79-65516. (Illus.). 336p. 1981. text ed. 19.95x (ISBN 0-686-27080-0). Thayer-Jacoby.

Sutton, L., ed. see Dunfee, Thomas W., et al.

Sutton, L., ed. see Litka, Michael P.

Sutton, L., ed. see Litka, Michael P. & Inman, James E.

Sutton, L., ed. see Patti, Charles H. & Murphy, John H.

Sutton, L. Paul, jt. auth. see Rich, William D.

Sutton, Larry. The Case of the Smiley Faces. LC 80-69288. (The Carolrhoda Mini-Mysteries Ser.). (Illus.). 32p. (gr. 1-4). 1981. PLB 4.95g (ISBN 0-87614-133-5). Carolrhoda Bks.

Sutton, M. A. The Rise of Physical Chemistry. 1982. 70.00x o.p. (ISBN 0-86127-112-2, Pub. by Avebury Pub England). State Mutual Bk.

Sutton, Margaret. Palace Wagon Family: A True Story of the Donner Party. (Illus.). (gr. 7-11). 1957. PLB 5.69 o.p. (ISBN 0-394-91477-5). Knopf.

Sutton, Max K. R. D. Blackmore. (English Authors Ser.). 1979. lib. bdg. 14.95 (ISBN 0-8057-6756-8, Twayne). G K Hall.

--W. S. Gilbert. (English Authors Ser.). 1975. lib. bdg. 12.95 (ISBN 0-8057-1217-8, Twayne). G K Hall.

Sutton, Myron, jt. auth. see Sutton, Ann.

Sutton, N. G. Injuries of the Spinal Cord: Management of Paraplegia & Tetraplegia. (Illus.). 200p. 1973. 19.95 o.p. (ISBN 0-407-21520-4). Butterworth.

Sutton, Peter & Walsh, Michael. Linguistic Fieldwork Manual. (AIAS New Ser.). 1979. pap. text ed. 7.75x (ISBN 0-391-00992-3). Humanities.

Sutton, Remar. Don't Get Taken Every Time: The Insider's Guide to Buying Your Next Car. 1983. pap. 5.95 (ISBN 0-14-046597-9). Penguin.

Sutton, Richard, jt. ed. see Burbidge, Peter.

Sutton, Robert C., Jr. The Sutton-Taylor Feud. (Illus.). 82p. 1974. 6.95 o.p. (ISBN 0-89015-066-4). Eakin Pubns.

Sutton, S. B., ed. see Olmstead, Frederick L.

Sutton, Weldon L. Sex for the Handicapped Man. Merriman, Christine, ed. (Illus.). 56p. 1981. self-help manual 15.00 (ISBN 0-686-36408-2). W Sutton.

Sutton, William A. The Road to Winesburg: A Mosaic of the Imaginative Life of Sherwood Anderson. LC 73-181997. (Illus.). 1972. 22.50 o.p. (ISBN 0-8108-0312-7). Scarecrow.

Sutton-Smith, Brian. How to Play with Your Children: And When Not to. 1974. pap. 4.95 (ISBN 0-8015-3685-5, 0674-210, Hawthorn). Dutton.

--Play & Learning. 335p. 1980. 23.95x o.p. (ISBN 0-470-26509-4). Halsted Pr.

Sutton-Smith, Brian, jt. auth. see Avedon, Elliott M.

Suval, Judy & Phillips, Patty. How to Start a Window Cleaning Business. 2nd ed. (Illus.). 41p. (Orig.). 1981. pap. 9.95 (ISBN 0-9609532-0-5). I Can See.

Suver, James D. & Neumann, Bruce R. Management Accounting for Health Care Organizations. (Illus.). 300p. 1981. text ed. 27.50 (ISBN 0-930228-16-2). Healthcare Fin Man Assn.

Suvin, Darko, jt. ed. see Mullen, R. D.

Suviranta, Bruno. Theory of the Balance of Trade in England. LC 67-28342. Repr. of 1923 ed. 17.50x (ISBN 0-678-00328-9). Kelley.

Suvorov, L. N. Marxist Philosophy at the Leninist Stage. 245p. 1982. 6.95 (ISBN 0-8285-2424-6, Pub. by Progress Pubs USSR). Imported Pubns.

Suvorov, Viktor. Inside the Soviet Army. (Illus.). 320p. 1983. 15.95 (ISBN 0-02-615500-1). Macmillan.

Suydam, Marilyn, ed. Developing Computational Skills: 1978 Yearbook. LC 77-28831. (Illus.). 256p. 1978. pap. 14.50 (ISBN 0-87353-121-3). NCTM.

Suyin, Han. Lhasa, the Open City: A Journey to Tibet. LC 77-9379. (Illus.). 1977. 7.95 o.p. (ISBN 0-399-12035-1). Putnam Pub Group.

--A Many Splendid Thing. 336p. 1982. pap. 3.95 (ISBN 0-553-22736-X). Bantam.

--My House Has Two Doors. 544p. 1980. 19.95 (ISBN 0-399-12323-7). Putnam Pub Group.

Suzanne. Color: The Essence of You. LC 79-55313. (Illus.). 1980. 65.00 o.p. (ISBN 0-89087-195-7). Celestial Arts.

Suzawa, Gilbert, jt. auth. see Sato, Ryuzo.

Suzuki, D. T., tr. see Lao Tze.

Suzuki, D. T., tr. see Shaku, Soyen.

Suzuki, Daisetz T. The Essentials of Zen Buddhism. Phillips, Bernard, ed. & intro. by. 544p. 1973. Repr. of 1962 ed. lib. bdg. 45.00x (ISBN 0-8371-6649-7, SUEZ). Greenwood.

--Studies in Zen. 1963. pap. 2.75 o.s.i. (ISBN 0-440-58371-3, Delta). Dell.

Suzuki, H. Electronic Absorption Spectra & Geometry of Organic Molecules. 1967. 82.50 (ISBN 0-12-678150-8). Acad Pr.

Suzuki, S., jt. auth. see Notake, Y.

Suzuki, Shinichi. Cello Part, Vol. 1. (Suzuki Cello School Ser.). 24p. (Japanese.). (gr. k-12). 1980. pap. text ed. 5.55 (ISBN 0-87487-257-X). Summy.

--Cello Part, Vol. 3. (Suzuki Cello School Ser.). 32p. (Japanese.). (gr. k-12). 1980. pap. text ed. 5.95 (ISBN 0-87487-259-6). Summy.

--Cello School, Vol. 2. (Suzuki Cello School Ser.). 24p. (Japanese.). (gr. k-12). 1980. pap. text ed. 5.55 (ISBN 0-87487-258-8). Summy.

--Duets for Two Violins. (Suzuki Violin School Ser.). 16p. (Japanese.). (gr. k-12). 1971. pap. text ed. 3.65 (ISBN 0-87487-093-3). Summy.

--Home Concert, Violin Part. (Suzuki Violin School Ser.). 32p. (Japanese.). (gr. k-12). 1972. pap. text ed. 4.95 (ISBN 0-87487-306-1). Summy.

--Nurtured by Love: A New Approach to Education. 2nd ed. Suzuki, Waltraud, tr. LC 79-82726. 1982. 9.95 (ISBN 0-682-47518-1, Banner); pap. 6.95 (ISBN 0-682-49930-7). Exposition.

--Piano Accompaniments, Vol. A. (Suzuki Violin School Ser.). 176p. (Japanese.). 1980. pap. text ed. 15.90 (ISBN 0-87487-227-8). Summy.

--Piano Accompaniments, Vol. B. (Suzuki Violin School Ser.). 192p. (Japanese.). 1980. pap. text ed. 18.40 (ISBN 0-87487-228-6). Summy.

--Piano School, Vol. 2. (Suzuki Piano School Ser.). 24p. (Ger., Fr., Span., & Japanese.). (gr. k-12). 1978. pap. text ed. 4.65 (ISBN 0-87487-161-1). Summy.

--Piano School, Vol. 3. (Suzuki Piano School Ser.). 32p. (Ger., Fr., Span., & Japanese.). (gr. k-12). 1970. pap. text ed. 5.25 (ISBN 0-87487-162-X). Summy.

--Piano School, Vol. 4. (Suzuki Piano School Ser.). 32p. (Ger., Fr., Span., & Japanese.). (gr. 3-12). 1978. pap. text ed. 5.25 (ISBN 0-87487-163-8). Summy.

--Piano School, Vol. 5. (Suzuki Piano School Ser.). 48p. (Japanese.). (gr. 4-12). 1973. pap. text ed. 6.30 (ISBN 0-87487-099-2). Summy.

--Piano School, Vol. 6. (Suzuki Piano School Ser.). 48p. (Japanese.). (gr. 4-12). 1973. pap. text ed. 6.55 (ISBN 0-87487-101-8). Summy.

--Position Etudes. (Suzuki Violin School Ser.). 32p. (Japanese.). (gr. k-12). 1973. pap. text ed. 5.25 (ISBN 0-87487-096-8). Summy.

--Quint Etudes. (Suzuki Violin School Ser.). 48p. (Japanese.). (gr. k-12). 1976. pap. text ed. 6.45 (ISBN 0-87487-095-X). Summy.

--Suzuki Cello School, Cello Part, Vols. 4 & 5. 24p. (gr. k-12). 1982. pap. text ed. write for info. (ISBN 0-87487-266-9). Summy.

--Suzuki Cello School, Cello Part, Vol. 6. 24p. (gr. k-12). 1982. pap. text ed. write for info. (ISBN 0-87487-267-7). Summy.

--Suzuki Cello School, Piano Accompaniment, Vol. 3. 32p. (gr. k-12). 1983. pap. text ed. write for info. (ISBN 0-87487-265-0). Summy.

--Suzuki Cello School, Piano Accompaniment: International Edition. (Suzuki Method Ser.). 1983. pap. text ed. write for info. Summy.

--Suzuki Viola School: Viola Part, Vol. 3. (Suzuki Viola School Ser.). 24p. (gr. k-12). 1983. pap. text ed. write for info. (ISBN 0-87487-243-X). Summy.

--Suzuki Viola School: Viola Part, Vol. 4. (Suzuki Viola School Ser.). 32p. (gr. k-12). 1982. pap. text ed. write for info. (ISBN 0-87487-244-8). Summy.

--Violin School, Vol. 2. (Suzuki Violin School Ser.). 24p. (Ger., Fr., Span., & Japanese.). (gr. k-12). 1978. pap. text ed. 4.65 (ISBN 0-87487-146-8). Summy.

--Violin School, Vol. 3. (Suzuki Violin School Ser.). (Illus.). 24p. (Ger., Fr., Span., & Japanese.). (gr. k-12). 1978. pap. text ed. 4.50 (ISBN 0-87487-148-4). Summy.

--Violin School, Vol. 4. (Suzuki Violin School Ser.). 24p. (Ger., Fr., Span., & Japanese.). (gr. 4-12). 1978. pap. text ed. 4.50 (ISBN 0-87487-150-6). Summy.

--Violin School, Vol. 5. (Suzuki Violin School Ser.). 24p. (Ger., Fr., Span., & Japanese.). (gr. 4-12). 1978. pap. text ed. 4.65 (ISBN 0-87487-152-2). Summy.

--Violin School, Vol. 6. (Suzuki Violin School Ser.). 24p. (Ger., Fr., Span., & Japanese.). (gr. 5-12). 1978. pap. text ed. 4.45 (ISBN 0-87487-154-9). Summy.

--Violin School, Vol. 7. (Suzuki Violin School Ser.). 24p. (Ger., Fr., Span., & Japanese.). (gr. 6-12). 1978. pap. text ed. 4.45 (ISBN 0-87487-156-5). Summy.

--Violin School, Vol. 8. (Suzuki Violin School Ser.). 24p. (Ger., Fr., Span., & Japanese.). (gr. 6-12). 1978. pap. text ed. 4.65 (ISBN 0-87487-158-1). Summy.

--Violin School, Vol. 9. (Suzuki Violin School Ser.). 48p. (Japanese.). (gr. 6-12). 1975. pap. text ed. 5.95 (ISBN 0-87487-225-1). Summy.

--Violin School, Vol. 10. (Suzuki Violin School Ser.). 48p. (Japanese.). (gr. 6-12). 1976. pap. text ed. 6.10 (ISBN 0-87487-226-X). Summy.

Suzuki, Shoichiro & Ueno, Kazue. Illustrated Laboratory Techniques, 3 Vols. 2nd ed. Kosakai, Nozomu, ed. (Illus.). 1981. Set. 29.50 (ISBN 0-686-86116-7). Igaku-Shoin.

Suzuki, T. Physiology of Adrenocortical Secretion. (Frontiers of Hormone Research: Vol. 11). (Illus.). viii, 200p. 1983. 78.00 (ISBN 3-8055-3644-5). S Karger.

Suzuki, Taneko. Fish & Krill Protein: Processing Technology. (Illus.). 260p. 1981. 43.00 (ISBN 0-85334-954-1, Pub. by Applied Sci England). Elsevier.

Suzuki, Teitaro, tr. see Carus, Paul.

Suzuki, Waltraud, tr. see Suzuki, Shinichi.

Suzuki, Yoko. Elegant Crochet Laces. (Illus.). 100p. (Orig.). 1983. pap. 6.95 (ISBN 0-87040-528-4). Kodansha.

Svaglic, Martin J., ed. see Newman, John H.

Svajian, jt. auth. see Cantwell.

Svalastoga, Kaare. On Deadly Violence. 160p. (Orig.). 1982. 21.00 (ISBN 82-00-06071-3). Universitet.

Svara, James H., jt. ed. see Hawley, Willis D.

Svaren, Jacqueline. Written Letters: Twenty-Nine Alphabets for Calligraphers. rev. ed. LC 81-86266. (Illus.). 64p. 1982. pap. 12.95 (ISBN 0-8008-8734-4, Pentalic). Taplinger.

--Written Letters: Twenty-two Alphabets for Calligraphers. LC 74-3159. 64p. (Calligraphy). (gr. 8 up). 1975. spiral bdg. 12.95 o.s.i. (ISBN 0-87027-161-X). Cumberland Pr.

Svarovsky. Solid Liquid Separation. (Chemical Engineering Ser). 1977. 64.95 o.p. (ISBN 0-408-70795-X). Butterworth.

Svartholm, N. Elementary Particle Theory: Relativistic Groups & Analyticity. (Nobel Symposium Ser.). 1969. 59.95x o.s.i. (ISBN 0-470-83842-6). Halsted Pr.

Svaty, V., jt. auth. see Talavasek, O.

Svec, J., jt. auth. see Halek, V.

Svehla, G. Comprehensive Analytical Chemistry, Vol. 7: Thermal Methods in Analytical Chemistry Substoichiometric Analytical Methods. 1976. 93.75 (ISBN 0-444-41166-6). Elsevier.

Svehla, G. & Wilson, C. Comprehensive Analytical Chemistry, Vol. 8: Enzyme Electrodes in Analytical Chemistry. LC 58-10158. 1977. 110.75 (ISBN 0-444-41523-8). Elsevier.

Svehla, G., ed. Comprehensive Analytical Chemistry: Vol. IX-Ultraviolet Photoelectron & Photoion Spectroscopy; Auger Electron Spectroscopy; Plasma Excitation in Spectrochemical Analysis. 1979. 85.00 (ISBN 0-444-41732-X). Elsevier.

--Comprehensive Analytical Chemistry: Vol. 13, Analysis of Complex Hydrocarbon Mixtures, 2 pts. 95.75 ea.; Pt. A: Separation Methods. (ISBN 0-444-99736-9); Pt. B: Group Analysis & Detailed Analysis. (ISBN 0-444-99735-0); Set. 191.50 (ISBN 0-444-99734-2). Elsevier.

--Comprehensive Analytical Chemisty, Vol. 6: Analytical Infrared Spectroscopy. Wilson, C., et al. 1976. 106.50 (ISBN 0-444-41165-8). Elsevier.

--Wilson & Wilson's Comprehensive Analytical Chemistry Vol. 16: Chemical Microscopy, Thermomicroscopy of Organic Compounds. 514p. 1982. 138.50 (ISBN 0-444-41950-0). Elsevier.

Svehla, G. & Wilson, C., eds. Comprehensive Analytical Chemistry, Vol. 11: Applications of Mathematical Statistics in Analytical Chemistry. 1981. 104.25 (ISBN 0-444-41886-5). Elsevier.

--Comprehensive Analytical Chemistry, Vol. 10: Organic Spot Test Analysis. 1980. 85.00 (ISBN 0-444-41859-8). Elsevier.

--Comprehensive Analytical Chemistry, Vol. 12A: Thermal Analysis; Simultaneous Thermoanalytical Examinations by Means of the Derivatograph. 1981. 72.50 (ISBN 0-444-41949-7). Elsevier.

Svehla, G & Wilson, G., eds. Comprehensive Analytical Chemistry, Vol. 14: Ion Exchangers in Analytical Chemistry. 586p. 1982. 117.00 (ISBN 0-444-99717-2). Elsevier.

Svehla, G., ed. see Wilson, C.

Svehla, G., et al. Comprehensive Analytical Chemistry, Vol. 12B: Biochemical & Clinical Applications of Thermometric & Thermal Analysis. 1982. 72.50 (ISBN 0-444-42062-2). Elsevier.

Svehla, Gyula. Automatic Potentiometric Titrations. 1978. text ed. 54.00 (ISBN 0-08-021590-4). Pergamon.

Svejcer, A. D. Contemporary Sociolinguistics. (Linguistic & Literary Studies in Eastern Europe: 15). 300p. 1983. 50.00 (ISBN 90-272151-9-7); pap. 30.00 (ISBN 90-272151-8-9). Benjamins North Am.

Svejcer, A. D. & Nikol'skij, L. B. Introduction to Sociolinguistics. (Linguistic & Literary Studies in Europe: 14). 200p. 1983. 40.00 (ISBN 90-272-1517-0); pap. 20.00 (ISBN 90-272151-6-2). Benjamins North Am.

Svejnar, Jan, jt. ed. see Jones, Derek C.

Svelmoe, Gordon & Svelmoe, Thelma. Notes on Mansaka Grammar. (Language Data Asian-Pacific Ser.: No. 6). 138p. 1974. pap. 3.75x (ISBN 0-88312-206-5); microfiche 2.25x (ISBN 0-88312-306-1). Summer Inst Ling.

Svelmoe, Thelma, jt. auth. see Svelmoe, Gordon.

Svend, Otto S. The Giant Fish & Other Stories. Tate, Joan, tr. from Danish. LC 82-81484. (Illus.). 84p. 1982. 10.95 (ISBN 0-88332-287-0, 8225). Larousse.

Svendsen, Clara. The Life & Destiny of Isak Dinesen. Lasson, Frans, ed. LC 75-40669. (Illus.). 232p. 1976. pap. 15.00 (ISBN 0-226-46916-6, P686, Phoen). U of Chicago Pr.

Svendsen, Louise A. Klee at the Guggenheim Museum. (Illus.). 1977. 9.95 (ISBN 0-89207-006-4). S R Guggenheim.

Svengalis, Cordell M., jt. auth. see Fitch, Robert M.

Svenkerud, A., jt. auth. see Berulfsen, B.

Svennas, Elsie, jt. auth. see Petersen, Grete.

Svensen, C. L., jt. auth. see French, Thomas E.

Svenson, A., jt. auth. see Wigander, K.

Svensson, Arne. Techniques of Crime Scene Investigation. 1980. text ed. 25.95 (ISBN 0-444-00427-0, North Holland). Elsevier.

Svenvold, Mark. Peripheries. (John Doe Poetry Pamphlet Ser.). 15p. (Orig.). 1982. pap. 3.00 (ISBN 0-686-37956-X). J Doe Pr.

Sverdrup, Elise. Norway's Delight: Dishes & Specialties. 6th ed. (Tokens of Norway Ser). (Illus., Orig.). 1968. pap. 9.00x (ISBN 82-518-0089-7). Intl Pubns Serv.

Sverdrup, H., et al. Oceans: Their Physics, Chemistry & General Biology. 1942. ref. ed. 38.95 o.p. (ISBN 0-13-630350-1). P-H.

Svevo, Italo. Further Confessions of Zeno. Johnson, Ben & Furbank, P. N., trs. LC 69-19076. 1969. 28.50x (ISBN 0-520-01436-7); pap. 2.45 (ISBN 0-520-01753-6, CAL226). U of Cal Pr.

Svitak, Ivan. The Dialectic of Common Sense: The Master Thinkers. LC 78-65849. 1979. pap. text ed. 10.50 (ISBN 0-8191-0675-5). U Pr of Amer.

Svobda, Milan, et al. Exercise Physiology. Kneer, Marian E., ed. (Basic Stuff Ser.: No. 1, 1 of 6). (Illus.). 90p. (gr. k up). 1981. pap. text ed. 6.25 (ISBN 0-88314-024-1). AAHPERD.

Svoboda, Antonin & White, Donnamaie E. Advanced Logical Circuit Design Techniques. LC 77-87595. 308p. 1980. lib. bdg. 37.50 o.s.i. (ISBN 0-8240-7014-3, Garland STPM Pr). Garland Pub.

Svoboda, Frederic J. Hemingway & the Sun Also Rises: The Crafting of a Style. LC 82-20026. (Illus.). 216p. 1983. text ed. 19.95x (ISBN 0-7006-0228-3). Univ Pr KS.

Swaab, D. F. & Pevet, P., eds. Chemical Transmission in the Brain: The Role of Amines, Amino Acids & Peptides: Proceedings of the 12th International Summer School of Brain Research, held at the Royal Netherlands Academy of Arts & Sciences, Amsterdam, The Netherlands, Aug. 31-Sept. 4, 1981. (Progress in Brain Research Ser.: Vol. 55). 490p. 1982. 102.25 (ISBN 0-444-80411-0). Elsevier.

Swaab, D. F., ed. see Ninth International Summer School of Brain Research.

Swaan, Wim. The Late Middle Ages: Art & Architecture from 1350 to the Advent of the Renaissance. 1977. 38.50x o.p. (ISBN 0-8014-1141-6). Cornell U Pr.

Swaay, Maarten V. & Lenhert, Donald H. Fundamentals of Microcomputers. 238p. 1982. looseleaf bound 49.95 (ISBN 0-935506-04-7). Carnegie Pr.

Swad, Randy, jt. auth. see Bandy, Dale.

Swadesh, Frances L. Twenty Thousand Years of History: A New Mexico Bibliography. 1973. pap. 4.95 (ISBN 0-913270-14-8). Sunstone Pr.

Swadesh, Morris, jt. auth. see Sapir, Edward.

Swados, Elizabeth. The Girl with the Incredible Feeling. LC 76-21176. 1976. 5.95 o.p. (ISBN 0-89255-009-0). Persea Bks.

Swagler, Roger M. Consumers & the Market: An Introductory Analysis. 1979. pap. 11.95 (ISBN 0-669-01692-6). Heath.

Swai, B., jt. auth. see Temu, A.

Swails, L. F., Jr. The Genus Porella in Latin America. (Illus.). 1970. 16.00 (ISBN 3-7682-0674-2). Lubrecht & Cramer.

Swaim, C. Richard & Mulcahy, Kevin. Public Policy & the Arts. (Special Studies in Public Policy & Public System Management). 300p. 1982. lib. bdg. 26.25 (ISBN 0-86531-115-3); pap. 15.00 (ISBN 0-86531-288-5). Westview.

Swaim, Gary D. Learning Composition Skills. (Language Arts Ser.). 24p. (gr. 4-9). 1980. wkbk. 5.00 (ISBN 0-8209-0316-7, LA-2). ESP.

--Write Right Correctly. (Language Arts Ser.). 24p. (gr. 4-9). 1977. wkbk. 5.00 (ISBN 0-8209-0315-9, LA-1). ESP.

Swain, Brainerd F., jt. ed. see Graber, T. M.

Swain, C., jt. auth. see Buckley, A.

Swain, David L., jt. auth. see Sugimoto, Masayoshi.

Swain, David L., tr. see Yazaki, Takeo.

Swain, Dwight V. Film Scriptwriting. 384p. 1976. 34.95 (ISBN 0-240-50968-4); pap. 12.95 (ISBN 0-240-51198-0). Focal Pr.

Swain, Frederick M. Non-Marine Organic Geochemistry. (Cambridge Earth Science Ser). (Illus.). 1970. 90.00 (ISBN 0-521-07757-5). Cambridge U Pr.

Swain, G. Russian Society Democracy & the Legal Labour Movement 1906-14. 1982. 80.00x (ISBN 0-686-42930-3, Pub. by Macmillan England). State Mutual Bk.

Swain, George F. Conservation of Water By Storage. 1915. text ed. 65.00x (ISBN 0-686-83512-3). Elliots Bks.

Swain, James J., jt. auth. see Biles, William E.

Swain, Kathleen M., jt. ed. see Ingram, William.

Swain, Laurence R., Jr., jt. auth. see Coate, Godfrey T.

Swain, Philip H. & Davis, Shirley M. Remote Sensing: The Quantitative Approach. (Illus.). 1978. text ed. 48.50 (ISBN 0-07-062576-X, C); solutions manual 7.95 (ISBN 0-07-062577-8). McGraw.

Swain, Ralph B. Insect Guide. LC 48-7228. 1948. 10.95 o.p. (ISBN 0-385-06826-3). Doubleday.

Swain, Raymond C. Out of Darkness. 1962. 3.00 o.p. (ISBN 0-8233-0104-4). Golden Quill.

Swaine, Christopher. Birds of Gloucestershire. 256p. 1982. text ed. 16.75x (ISBN 0-86299-012-2, Pub. by Sutton England). Humanities.

Swaine, D. J., jt. ed. see Trudinger, P. A.

Swaine, Lionel. Galatians. 1969. pap. 0.75 o.p. (ISBN 0-685-07636-9, 80726). Glencoe.

Swainson, Charles. A Handbook of Weather Folk-Lore: Being a Collection of Proverbial Sayings in Various Languages Relating to the Weather. LC 73-5513. xii, 275p. 1974. Repr. of 1873 ed. 34.00x (ISBN 0-8103-3980-3). Gale.

Swainson, Nicola. The Development of Corporate Capitalism in Kenya, Nineteen Eighteen to Nineteen Seventy-Seven. 1980. 30.00x (ISBN 0-520-03988-2); pap. 8.95 (ISBN 0-520-04019-8). U of Cal Pr.

Swajeski, Donna, jt. auth. see Jones, Jeanne.

Swales, Martin, ed. Arthur Schnitzler: Professor Bernhardi. LC 73-183731. 153p. 1972. 6.70 o.s.i. (ISBN 0-08-016801-9); pap. 5.15 (ISBN 0-08-016806-X). Pergamon.

Swalin, Richard A. Thermodynamics of Solids. 2nd ed. LC 72-6334. (Science & Technology of Materials Ser.). 387p. 1972. 47.95x (ISBN 0-471-83854-3, Pub. by Wiley-Interscience). Wiley.

Swallow, jt. auth. see Thompson.

Swallow, Alan. An Editor's Essays of Two Decades. LC 82-70480. 401p. 1962. 8.95 (ISBN 0-8040-0073-5). Swallow.

--Nameless Sight: Selected Poems 1937-1956. LC 82-71520. 74p. 1963. pap. 4.95 (ISBN 0-8040-0223-1). Swallow.

Swallow, Alan, ed. Anchor in the Sea: An Anthology of Psychological Fiction. LC 82-70100. 243p. 1947. pap. 5.95x (ISBN 0-8040-0010-7). Swallow.

Swallow, Su. Danny's Class. LC 81-52498. (Starters Ser.). PLB 8.00 (ISBN 0-382-06499-2). Silver.

--The Red Racing Car. LC 80-52531. (Starters Ser.). PLB 8.00 (ISBN 0-382-06502-6). Silver.

Swalm, James. Diagnostic Reading for Your Classroom. (Illus.). 72p. 1975. pap. text ed. 6.00x (ISBN 0-89061-279-X, 429). Jamestown Pubs.

Swami, Shri P., tr. The Geeta. 96p. (Orig.). 1965. pap. 5.95 (ISBN 0-571-06157-5). Faber & Faber.

Swami Akhilananda. Hindu Psychology: Its Meaning for the West. LC 75-17493. (God Ser.: No. 153). (Illus.). 1977. 8.50 (ISBN 0-89007-153-5). C Stark.

Swami Aseshananda. Glimpses of a Great Soul: Reminiscences & Teachings of Swami Saradanada, Direct Disciple to Sri-Ramakrishna & His Definitive Biographer. LC 74-20572. (God Ser.: No. 107). (Illus.). 300p. 1981. 12.00 (ISBN 0-89007-107-1). C Stark.

Swami Jyotir Maya Nanda. Yoga of Divine Love: A Commentary on Narada Bhakti Sutras. 1982. pap. 4.99 (ISBN 0-934664-42-0). Yoga Res Foun.

Swaminathan, C. Science & Integrated Rural Development, Vol. 1. 370p. 1982. text ed. 21.50x (ISBN 0-391-02752-2, Pub. by Concept India). Humanities.

Swaminathan, K., et al, eds. Plough & the Stars: Stories from Tamil in English. 1964. 6.50x o.p. (ISBN 0-210-26880-8). Asia.

Swaminathan, S., ed. Fixed Point Theory & Its Applications. 1976. 27.00 (ISBN 0-12-678650-X). Acad Pr.

Swami Rama. Inspired Thoughts. 250p. (Orig.). 1983. pap. 6.95 (ISBN 0-89389-086-3). Himalayan Intl Inst.

Swami Shraddhananda. The Story of an Epoch: Swami Virajananda & His Times. Swami Shraddhananda, tr. from Bengali. 298p. 1982. pap. text ed. write for info. (ISBN 0-87481-511-8, Pub. by Ramakrishna Math Madras India). Vedanta Pr.

Swami Shri Purohit, tr. The Bhagavad Gita. (Illus.). pap. 5.95 o.p. (ISBN 0-394-72394-5, V-394, Vin). Random.

Swami Vivekananda. Raja-Yoga. LC 55-12231. (Illus.). 320p. 1982. pap. 5.95 o.p. (ISBN 0-911206-23-X). Ramakrishna.

Swamy, Gurushri. International Migrant Workers' Remittances: Issues & Prospects. (Working Paper: No. 481). 64p. 1981. 5.00 (ISBN 0-686-36045-1, WP-0481). World Bank.

Swamy, Gurushri, jt. auth. see Scandizzo, Pasguale L.

Swamy, M. N. & Thulastraman, K. Graphs, Networks & Algorithms. 592p. 1981. 43.50 (ISBN 0-471-03503-3, Pub. by Wiley-Interscience). Wiley.

Swamy, N. V. & Samuel, Mark A. Group Theory Made Easy for Scientists & Engineers. LC 78-11733. 174p. 1979. 30.95x (ISBN 0-471-05128-4, Pub. by Wiley-Interscience). Wiley.
Swamy, S., et al. Percutaneous Angiography. (Illus.). 848p. 1977. photocopy ed. spiral 88.00x (ISBN 0-398-03540-7). C C Thomas.
Swan, jt. auth. see Corday.
Swan, D. K., ed. New Method Supplementary Readers, 8 bks, Stage 1. Incl. Alice in Wonderland. Carroll, Lewis (ISBN 0-582-53414-3). cassette 7.00x (ISBN 0-582-52678-7); Black Beauty. Sewell, Anna (ISBN 0-582-53522-0); Fables & Fairy Tales (ISBN 0-582-52544-6); Five Famous Fairy Tales (ISBN 0-582-53521-2); King Arthur & the Knights of the Round Table (ISBN 0-582-53415-1); More Adventures of Robin Hood. Turvey, John (ISBN 0-582-52656-6); Robin Hood (ISBN 0-582-53412-7); Tales from Hans Anderson. Anderson, Hans C (ISBN 0-582-53410-0); Tales from the East. new ed (ISBN 0-582-53533-6). (English As a Second Language Bk.). 1963-81. pap. 1.75x ea. Longman.
--New Method Supplementary Readers, 15 bks, Stage 2. Incl. Canterbury Tales. Chaucer, Geoffrey (ISBN 0-582-53442-9); Five on a Treasure Island. Blyton, Enid (ISBN 0-582-53443-7); The Greek Heroes (ISBN 0-582-52677-9); Gulliver's Travels. new ed. Swift, Jonathan (ISBN 0-582-53423-2); Kalulu the Hare. Worthington, Frank (ISBN 0-582-53426-7); The Magic Slipper. Milne, B. Lumsden (ISBN 0-582-53531-X); The Mystery of the Island. Verne, Jules (ISBN 0-582-53429-1); Pirates. Swan, D. K (ISBN 0-582-53541-7); The Prince & the Pauper. Twain, Mark (ISBN 0-582-53422-4); Rip Van Winkle & The Legend of Sleepy Hollow. Irving, Washington (ISBN 0-582-53530-1); The Secret Garden. Burnett, Frances H (ISBN 0-582-53417-8); Stories from Ancient China (ISBN 0-582-53438-0); Tales from the Arabian Nights (ISBN 0-582-53437-2); Traveller's Tales from the Odyssey & Baron Munchausen (ISBN 0-582-53424-0); The Wind in the Willows. Graham, Kenneth (ISBN 0-582-52652-3). (English As a Second Language Bk.). 1963-81. pap. 1.90x ea. Longman.
--New Method Supplementary Readers, 13 bks, Stage 3. Incl. As You Like It & Much Ado About Nothing. Shakespeare, William (ISBN 0-582-53449-6); The Blue Lagoon. new ed. Se Vere Stacpoole, H (ISBN 0-582-53540-9); Children of the New Forest. Marryat, Capt (ISBN 0-582-53450-X); Classic Stories from the Ballet (ISBN 0-582-52595-0); Dracula. Stoker, Bram (ISBN 0-582-53523-9); Frankenstein. Shelley, Mary (ISBN 0-582-52546-2); From Earth to Moon. Verne, Jules (ISBN 0-582-53457-7); King of the Undersea City. Toudouza, George J (ISBN 0-582-53451-8); The Last Days of Pompei. Lyston, Lord (ISBN 0-582-53464-X); Monte Cristo. Dumas, Alexandre (ISBN 0-582-53452-6); The Return of Sherlock Holmes. Conan Doyle, Arthur (ISBN 0-582-52411-3); Robinson Crusoe. Defoe, Daniel (ISBN 0-582-53444-5); Stories from Shakespeare (ISBN 0-582-53529-8); The Swiss Family Robinson. Wyss, J. R (ISBN 0-582-53445-3); Tales of Ancient Rome (ISBN 0-582-53460-7); The Young King & Other Stories. Wilde, Oscar (ISBN 0-582-53421-6). (English As a Second Language Bk.). 1963-81. pap. 1.90x ea. (ISBN 0-686-31606-1). Longman.
--New Method Supplementary Readers, 14 bks, Stage 4. Incl. The African Queen. Forester, C. S (ISBN 0-582-53495-X); The Black Tulip. Dumas, Alexandre (ISBN 0-582-53479-8); Call of the Wild. London, Jack (ISBN 0-582-53497-6); Five Great Plays of Shakespeare (ISBN 0-582-53473-9); The Hunchback of Notre Dame. Hugo, Victor (ISBN 0-582-53494-1); Jane Eyre. Bronte, Charlotte (ISBN 0-582-53843-2); The Last of the Mohicans. Cooper, James F (ISBN 0-582-53492-5); Little Women. Alcott, Louisa M (ISBN 0-582-53489-5); Lorna Doone. Blackmore, R. D (ISBN 0-582-53476-3); Moby Dick. Melville, Herman (ISBN 0-582-53418-6); Oliver Twist. Dickens, Charles (ISBN 0-582-53496-8); Stories of Mystery & Immagination. Poe, Edgar A (ISBN 0-582-53471-2); Three Adventures of Sherlock Holmes. Conan Doyle, Arthur (ISBN 0-582-53470-4). (English As a Second Language Bk.). 1963-81. pap. 2.10x ea. Longman.
--New Method Supplementary Readers, 10 bks, Stage 5. Incl. Anna Karenina. Tolstoy, Leo (ISBN 0-582-53517-4); The Black Arrow. Stevenson, Robert L (ISBN 0-582-53503-4); A Christmas Carol & The Cricket on the Hearth. Dickens, Charles (ISBN 0-582-53490-9); David Copperfield. Dickens, Charles (ISBN 0-582-53501-8); Emma. Austen, Jane (ISBN 0-582-53510-7); King Solomon's Mines. Haggard, H. Rider (ISBN 0-582-53502-6); Lord Jim. Conrad, Joseph (ISBN 0-582-53420-8); Seven Detective Stories (ISBN 0-582-53514-X); Singing Wind & Other Short Stories (ISBN 0-582-53491-7); Treasure Island. new ed. Stevenson, Robert L (ISBN 0-582-53504-2); Tom Jones. Fielding, Henry (ISBN 0-582-53516-6); Twelfth Night & The Taming of the Shrew. Shakespeare, William (ISBN 0-582-53519-0). (English As a Second Language Bk.). 1963-81. pap. 2.10x ea. Longman.
--New Method Supplementary Readers: Bestseller Pack, 10 bks. Incl. Alice in Wonderland; Black Beauty; Dracula; Frankenstein; King Arthur & the Knights of the Round Table; The Secret Garden; Oliver Twist; Robin Hood; Seven Detective Stories; Three Adventures of Sherlock Holmes. (English As a Second Language Bk.). 1981. Set. pap. 54.00x (ISBN 0-582-52797-X). Longman.
Swan, Guide. The Journals of Two Poor Dissenters, 1786-1880. 1970. 5.25 o.p. (ISBN 0-7100-6673-2). Routledge & Kegan.
Swan, Helena. Girls' Christian Names, Their History, Meaning & Association. LC 68-17935. 1968. Repr. of 1900 ed. 37.00x (ISBN 0-8103-3135-7). Gale.
Swan, Helena, ed. Who's Who in Fiction: A Dictionary of Noted Names in Novels, Tales, Romances, Poetry & Drama. LC 73-167218. 1975. Repr. of 1906 ed. 42.00x (ISBN 0-8103-4114-X). Gale.
Swan, Henry, jt. auth. see Broster, W. H.
Swan, J. M. & Black, D. S. Organometallics in Organic Synthesis. 1974. pap. 13.95x (ISBN 0-412-10870-4, Pub. by Chapman & Hall). Methuen Inc.
Swan, James A. & Stapp, W. B., eds. Environmental Education: Strategies Toward a More Livable Future. LC 72-98046. 349p. 1974. 17.95x o.p. (ISBN 0-470-83859-0). Halsted Pr.
Swan, Kenneth G. & Swan, Roy C. Gunshot Wounds: Pathophysiology & Management. LC 79-16118. (Illus.). 264p. 1981. 32.00 (ISBN 0-88416-196-X). Wright-PSG.
Swan, L. Alex. Families of Black Prisoners: Survival & Progress. 1981. 18.95 (ISBN 0-8161-8412-7, Univ Bks). G K Hall.
--The Politics of Riot Behavior. LC 79-5510. 1980. pap. text ed. 11.25 (ISBN 0-8191-0905-3). U Pr of Amer.
--Survival & Progress: The Afro-American Experience. LC 80-1197. (Contributions in Afro-American & African Studies: No. 58). (Illus.). xxiii, 251p. 1981. lib. bdg. 27.50x (ISBN 0-313-22480-3, SSU/). Greenwood.
Swan, Lester A. & Papp, Charles S. The Common Insects of North America. LC 75-138765. (Illus.). 752p. 1972. 17.50 o.p. (ISBN 0-06-014181-6, HarpT); lib. bdg. 13.27i (ISBN 0-06-014179-4). Har-Row.
Swan, Malcom, jt. auth. see Donaldson, George.
Swan, Michael. Practical English Usage. 560p. (Orig.). 1980. pap. 9.95x (ISBN 0-19-431185-6). Oxford U Pr.
Swan, Oscar. A Concise Grammer of Polish. LC 77-18467. 1978. pap. text ed. 5.75 o.p. (ISBN 0-8191-0319-5). U Pr of Amer.
Swan, Oscar E. A Concise Grammar of Polish. 2nd ed. LC 82-24835. 192p. (Orig.). 1983. lib. bdg. 19.75 (ISBN 0-8191-3017-6); pap. text ed. 8.75 (ISBN 0-8191-3018-4). U Pr of Amer.
--First Year Polish. xxii, 292p. (Orig.). 1981. pap. text ed. 12.95 o.p. (ISBN 0-89357-090-7). Slavica.
Swan, P. J., jt. auth. see Wegelin, E. A.
Swan, Roy C., jt. auth. see Swan, Kenneth G.
Swan, Sara K. Home-Made Baby Toys. 1977. pap. 4.95 o.p. (ISBN 0-395-25410-8). HM.
Swan, Susan B. A Winterthur Guide to American Needlework. (Winterthur Ser.). (Illus.). 1976. 6.95 o.p. (ISBN 0-517-52785-5). Crown.
Swanberg, Annette, jt. auth. see Charlton, Leigh.
Swanborough, Gordon, jt. auth. see Green, William.
Swan Egan De Butz, pseud. World's Worst Poems. 1978. pap. 1.25 o.s.i. (ISBN 0-8431-0452-X). Price Stern.
Swanfeldt, Andrew. Crossword Puzzle Dictionary. 4th, rev, new ed. LC 76-57994. 1977. 14.37i (ISBN 0-690-00426-5); thumb-indexed 15.34i (ISBN 0-690-01198-9). T y Crowell.
Swank, J. Grant, Jr. One & Two Peter: A Faith for Testing Times. (Beacon Small-Group Bible Studies). 72p. 1982. pap. 2.25 (ISBN 0-8341-0790-2). Beacon Hill.
--Which Way-Now & Forever. (Youth Counselling Ser). 1971. pap. 1.45 (ISBN 0-8341-0076-2). Beacon Hill.
Swank, Roy L. & Pullen, Mary-Helen. The Multiple Sclerosis Diet Book: A Low-Fat Diet for the Treatment of M.S. Heartdisease & Stroke. LC 76-24215. 1977. 14.95 (ISBN 0-385-12092-3). Doubleday.
Swanland, Charles. Basic English for Science & Technology, Vol. 1. LC 80-84178. (B.E.S.T. Ser.). (Illus.). 228p. 1980. pap. text ed. 8.75x (ISBN 0-933662-17-3). Intercult Pr.
--Basic English for Science & Technology, Vol. 2. LC 80-84178. (B.E.S.T. Ser.). 224p. 1980. pap. text ed. 8.75x (ISBN 0-933662-18-1). Intercult Pr.
--Basic English for Science & Technology, Vol. 3. LC 80-84178. (B.E.S.T. Ser.). 266p. 1980. pap. text ed. 8.75x (ISBN 0-933662-19-X). Intercult Pr.
Swann, jt. auth. see Branch.
Swann, Brian. The Runner. LC 79-9366. (Illus., Orig.). 1979. pap. 5.95x (ISBN 0-914140-07-8). Carpenter Pr.
--Smoothing the Ground: Essays on the Native American Oral Literature. 416p. 1983. 12.95x (ISBN 0-520-04902-0); pap. 9.95 (ISBN 0-520-04913-6). U of Cal Pr.
Swann, Brian, tr. see Cattafi, Bartolo.
Swann, Edward. Prelude to Painting Improvement. 64p. 1982. 25.00x (ISBN 0-284-98560-0, Pub. by C Skilton Scotland). State Mutual Bk.
--Sketches for Painting Practice. 48p. 1982. 20.00x (ISBN 0-284-98563-5, Pub. by C Skilton Scotland). State Mutual Bk.
Swann, Gloria H. Increasing Programmer Productivity. 1979. 12.50 o.p. (ISBN 0-07-091046-4, P&RB). McGraw.
--Increasing Programmer's Production Through Logic Development. (Illus.). 1979. text ed. 13.50 (ISBN 0-89433-065-9). Petrocelli.
Swann, Harry K. Dictionary of English & Folk-Names of British Birds. LC 68-30664. 1968. Repr. of 1913 ed. 30.00x (ISBN 0-8103-3340-6). Gale.
Swann, Michael M. Tierra Adentro: Settlement & Society in Colonial Durango. (Dellplain Latin American Studies: No. 10). (Illus.). 450p. 1982. lib. bdg. 20.00 (ISBN 0-86531-399-7). Westview.
Swann, Thomas B. A. A. Milne. (English Authors Ser.: No. 113). lib. bdg. 10.95 o.p. (ISBN 0-8057-1396-4, Twayne). G K Hall.
Swannell, John. Fine Lines. (Illus.). 128p. 1982. 29.50 (Pub. by Quartet Bks). Merrimack Bk Serv.
Swannell, Julia, ed. Little Oxford Dictionary. 5th ed. 1980. 8.95 (ISBN 0-19-861128-5). Oxford U Pr.
Swanney, Pamela J., jt. auth. see Marsh, John S.
Swansburg, Russell C., jt. auth. see Newcomb, Dorothy.
Swanson. Introduction to Home Management. 1981. 21.95x (ISBN 0-02-418500-0). Macmillan.
Swanson, jt. auth. see Cassel.
Swanson, B. Marion & Willis, Diane J. Understanding Expectional Children & Youth. 1979. 22.95 (ISBN 0-395-30754-6); Tchrs Manual 0.80 (ISBN 0-395-30755-4). HM.
Swanson, Betsy. Historic Jefferson Parish. LC 74-23204. (Illus.). 176p. (Orig.). 1975. 22.50 (ISBN 0-88289-048-4). Pelican.
Swanson, Bruce. Eighth Voyage of the Dragon. LC 81-85443. (Illus.). 432p. 1982. 26.95 (ISBN 0-87021-177-3). Naval Inst Pr.
Swanson, Carl B., et al. Cytogenetics: The Chromosome in Division, Inheritance, & Evolution. 2nd ed. (Biology Ser.). (Illus.). 1980. text ed. 31.95 (ISBN 0-13-196618-9). P-H.
Swanson, Carl L., jt. auth. see Sethi, S. Prakash.
Swanson, Carl P. Ever-Expanding Horizons: The Dual Informational Sources of Human Evolution. LC 82-21750. (Illus.). 132p. 1983. lib. bdg. 13.50x (ISBN 0-87023-391-2); pap. 7.50 (ISBN 0-87023-392-0). U of Mass Pr.
Swanson, Carl P. & Webster, Peter. The Cell. 4th ed. (Foundation of Modern Biology Ser). (Illus.). 1977. 16.95 (ISBN 0-13-121707-0); pap. text ed. 18.95 (ISBN 0-13-121699-6). P-H.
Swanson, Charles R., Jr. & Territo, Leonard. Police Administration: Structures, Processes & Behavior. 480p. 1983. text ed. 20.95 (ISBN 0-02-471650-2). Macmillan.
Swanson, Delia. The Nature of Human Communication. Applbaum, Ronald & Hart, Roderick, eds. (MODCOM Modules in Speech Communication Ser.). 1976. pap. text ed. 2.75 (ISBN 0-574-22511-0, 13-5511). SRA.
Swanson, E. Burton, jt. auth. see Mason, Richard H.
Swanson, Edward. A Manual of AACR2 Examples for Technical Reports. 1983. pap. text ed. 7.00 (ISBN 0-936996-15-3). Soldier Creek.
Swanson, Edward, ed. see Olson, Nancy B.
Swanson, Evadene B. Fort Collins Yesterdays. LC 74-83114. (Illus.). 254p. 1975. 12.00 (ISBN 0-9600862-1-8); pap. 8.50 (ISBN 0-9600862-2-6). E Swanson.
Swanson, Frederick J. Music Teaching in the Junior High & the Middle School. LC 72-94283. (Illus.). 304p. 1973. 19.95 (ISBN 0-13-608240-8). P-H.
Swanson, Gloria, jt. auth. see Ott, Virginia.
Swanson, H. Lee & Reinert, Henry R. Teaching Strategies for Children in Conflict: Curriculum, Methods & Materials. LC 79-40. (Illus.). 358p. 1979. pap. text ed. 18.95 (ISBN 0-8016-4106-3). Mosby.
Swanson, Harold D. Human Reproduction: Biology & Social Change. (Illus.). 1974. text ed. 13.95x (ISBN 0-19-501772-2); pap. text ed. 10.95x o.p. (ISBN 0-19-501771-4). Oxford U Pr.
Swanson, Jack W. & Karsh, Jeff. Rail Ventures. 220p. (Orig.). 1982. pap. 14.95 (ISBN 0-9608764-0-5). J W Swanson.
Swanson, James & Kollenborn, Tom. Superstition Mountain: A Ride Through Time. (Illus.). 210p. 1982. Repr. of 1981 ed. 12.95 (ISBN 0-910973-00-8). Arrowhead Pr.
Swanson, James C. Breathing Today, Breathing Tomorrow. LC 82-62910. 68p. 1983. 5.95 (ISBN 0-938232-25-8). Winston-Derek.
Swanson, James W., ed. One Hundred & Forty-Two Ways to Make a Poem. LC 78-15648. (Creative Writing Ser.). 1978. pap. text ed. 5.95 (ISBN 0-88436-499-2). EMC.
Swanson, Jon C. Emigration & Economic Development. LC 79-5155. (Replica Edition Ser.). 125p. 1979. softcover 16.00x (ISBN 0-89158-690-3). Westview.
Swanson, Laura L., jt. auth. see Corbus, Howard F.
Swanson, Lee H. Behavior Modification & Special Education: Perspectives & Trends. 288p. 1978. 29.50 (ISBN 0-8422-5300-9). Irvington.
Swanson, Leonard W. Linear Programming: Basic Theory & Applications. LC 79-10092. (Quantitative Methods for Management Ser.). (Illus.). 1979. 31.95 (ISBN 0-07-062580-8, C); instructor's manual 12.95 (ISBN 0-07-062581-6). McGraw.
Swanson, Leslie C. Canals of Mid-America. (Illus.). 1964. 5.95 o.p. (ISBN 0-911466-16-9). Swanson.
--Covered Bridges in Illinois, Iowa, & Wisconsin. rev. ed. (Illus., Orig.). 1970. pap. 5.95 o.p. (ISBN 0-911466-14-2). Swanson.
--Old Mills in the Midwest. (Illus.). 1963. 5.95 o.p. (ISBN 0-911466-15-0). Swanson.
--Pigeons, Racing Homer Facts & Secrets. 1958. pap. 2.50 o.p. (ISBN 0-911466-17-7). Swanson.
--Pigeons, Racing Homer Topics. 1955. pap. 2.50 o.p. (ISBN 0-911466-18-5). Swanson.
--Rural One-Room Schools of Mid-America. (Illus.). 1976. 5.95 o.p. (ISBN 0-685-66042-7). Swanson.
--Steamboat Calliopes. 1981. pap. 3.00 o.p. (ISBN 0-686-86781-5). Swanson.
Swanson, Maggie, illus. The Curious Little Kitten on the Farm. (Golden Cloth Bks.). (Illus.). 8p. (ps). 1982. cloth pages & cover 3.50 (ISBN 0-307-11506-2, Golden Pr). Western Pub.
Swanson, Marilyn A., jt. auth. see Cinnamon, Pamela A.
Swanson, Mary E., jt. auth. see Foster, Marshall E.
Swanson, R. N. Universities, Academics & the Great Schism. LC 78-56764. (Cambridge Studies in Medieval Life & Thought: 3rd Ser., No. 12). 1979. 42.50 (ISBN 0-521-22127-7). Cambridge U Pr.
Swanson, Reuben J. The Horizontal Line Synopsis of the Gospels. 1979. 23.95 o.p. (ISBN 0-8010-8164-5). Baker Bk.
Swanson, Richard A., jt. auth. see Spears, Betty.
Swanson, Richard W. & Marquardt, Charles E. On Communications: A Fundamental Approach to Reading, Writing, Speaking & Listening. LC 73-7370. (Illus.). 192p. 1974. pap. text ed. 10.95 (ISBN 0-02-478750-7). Macmillan.
Swanson, Robert, illus. The Prisoner of Vega. LC 77-70858. (Star Trek Storybook). (Illus.). (gr. 2-5). 1977. PLB 3.99 (ISBN 0-394-93576-4, BYR); bds. 2.95 o.p. (ISBN 0-394-83576-X). Random.
Swanson, Robert S. Plastic Technology, Basic Materials & Processes: Basic Materials & Processes. (gr. 11-12). 1965. text ed. 16.64 (ISBN 0-87345-483-9). McKnight.
Swanson, Rodney B., jt. auth. see Marshall, Robert H.
Swanson, S. A. & Freeman, M. A., eds. The Scientific Basis of Joint Replacement. LC 76-51524. 182p. 1977. 55.50 (ISBN 0-471-03012-0, Pub. by Wiley Medical). Wiley.
Swanson, Susie. Call Me... Anytime! 208p. (Orig.). 1975. pap. 1.50 o.s.i. (ISBN 0-89083-140-8). Zebra.
Swant, Dale, ed. see Rice, Tom.
Swant, Dale, ed. see Tole World Magazine Staff.
Swanton, John R. Early Account of the Choctaw Indians. LC 67-52261. 1918. pap. 8.00 (ISBN 0-527-00521-5). Kraus Repr.
--Indian Tribes of the American Southwest. (Shorey Indian Ser.). 130p. Repr. of 1952 ed. pap. 8.95 (ISBN 0-8466-0086-2, SJS86). Shorey.
Swanton, M. J., ed. The Dream of the Rood. (Old & Middle English Text Ser.). 1970. pap. 6.00 (ISBN 0-7190-0440-3). Manchester.
Swanwick, Keith & Taylor, Dorothy. Discovering Music: Developing Music Curriculum in Secondary Schools. (Illus.). 144p. 1982. 17.50 (ISBN 0-7134-4065-1, Pub. by Batsford England). David & Charles.
Swanzey, Thomas B., jt. auth. see Lynch, Robert E.
Swarbrick, A. P., ed. Oliver Goldsmith: His Reputation Re-Assessed. 1982. 60.00x o.p. (ISBN 0-86127-213-7, Pub. by Avebury Pub England). State Mutual Bk.
Swarbrick, J. T., ed. see Hassan, E.
Swarbrick, JJ. T. The Australian Weed Control Handbook. 342p. 1981. pap. 11.95 (ISBN 0-686-98296-7, Pub. by Ento Pr Australia). Intl Schol Bk Serv.
Swarc, Michael. Living Polymers & Mechanisms of Anionic Polymerization. (Advances in Polymer Science: Vol. 49). (Illus.). 187p. 1983. 45.00 (ISBN 0-387-12047-5). Springer-Verlag.
Swarthmore College. Catalog of the Friends Historical Library Book & Serial Collections, 6 vols. 1982. Set. lib. bdg. 630.00 (ISBN 0-8161-0376-3, Hall Library). G K Hall.
Swarthout, Charlene R. School Library As Part of the Instructional System. LC 67-10194. 235p. 1967. lib. bdg. 11.00 o.p. (ISBN 0-8108-0026-8). Scarecrow.
Swarthout, Glendon. Luck & Pluck. LC 72-90971. 168p. 1973. 6.95 o.p. (ISBN 0-385-03366-4). Doubleday.
--Skeletons. LC 78-22370. 1979. 10.00 o.p. (ISBN 0-385-12824-X). Doubleday.
Swarthout, Glendon & Swarthout, Kathryn. Cadbury's Coffin. LC 81-43590. (Illus.). 216p. 1982. 12.95 (ISBN 0-385-17578-7). Doubleday.
Swarthout, Kathryn, jt. auth. see Swarthout, Glendon.
Swartout, Robert R., Jr. Mandarins, Gunboats, & Power Politics: Owen Nickerson Denny & International Rivalries in Korea. LC 79-22242. 1980. text ed. 10.75x (ISBN 0-8248-0681-6). UH Pr.

Swartout, Robert R., Jr., ed. Montana Vistas: Selected Historical Essays. LC 81-40522. 292p. (Orig.). 1982. lib. bdg. 23.50 (ISBN 0-8191-2046-4); pap. text ed. 11.50 (ISBN 0-8191-2047-2). U Pr of Amer.

Swartz, C. E. Phenomenal Physics. 741p. 1981. 29.95 (ISBN 0-471-83880-2); avail. tchr's manual (ISBN 0-471-07914-6). Wiley.

Swartz, Clifford E. Used Math for the First Two Years of College Science. (Illus.). 320p. 1973. pap. 13.95 ref. ed. (ISBN 0-13-939736-1). P-H.

Swartz, Delbert. Collegiate Dictionary of Botany. 520p. 1971. 26.50x o.p. (ISBN 0-471-06826-8, Pub. by Wiley-Interscience). Wiley.

Swartz, Fred. The Pentax Guide. (Modern Camera Guide Ser.). (Illus.). 136p. 1980. 11.95 (ISBN 0-8174-2471-7, Amphoto); pap. 7.95 (ISBN 0-8174-2143-2). Watson-Guptill.

Swartz, Harold M., et al, eds. Biological Applications of Electron Spin Resonance. LC 72-39768. 569p. 1972. 54.50 o.p. (ISBN 0-471-83870-5, Pub. by Wiley-Interscience). Wiley.

Swartz, Jon D., jt. auth. see Cleland, Charles C.

Swartz, M. Evelyn, jt. auth. see Rueschhoff, Phil H.

Swartz, Marc J. & Jordan, David K. Anthropology: Perspective on Humanity. LC 74-14449. (Illus.). 735p. 1976. text ed. 22.95 (ISBN 0-471-83869-1); avail. tchr's manual (ISBN 0-471-83871-3). Wiley.

--Culture: The Anthropological Perspective. LC 79-9211. 476p. 1980. pap. text ed. 22.95 (ISBN 0-471-03333-2). Wiley.

Swartz, Mark H., ed. An Introduction to Physical Diagnosis. 394p. 1981. softcover 12.95 (ISBN 0-89004-562-3). Raven.

Swartz, Merlin L., et al. Studies on Islam. 1981. 19.95x (ISBN 0-19-502716-7); pap. 9.95x (ISBN 0-19-502717-5). Oxford U Pr.

Swartz, Morris A. & Moore, Mary E. Medical Emergency Manual. 3rd ed. (Illus.). 195p. 1983. text ed. price not set (ISBN 0-683-07597-7). Williams & Wilkins.

Swartz, Morton N., jt. auth. see Remington, Jack S.

Swartz, Norman, jt. auth. see Bradley, Raymond.

Swartz, O. Nova Genera of Species Plantarum Quae Sub Itinere in Indiam Occidentalem Digessit. 1962. Repr. of 1788 ed. 14.40 (ISBN 3-7682-0120-1). Lubrecht & Cramer.

Swartz, R. Starting Point: A Guide to Basic Writing Skills. 1980. pap. 12.95 (ISBN 0-13-843029-2). P-H.

Swartz, William H., ed. Obstetrics & Gynecology: PreTest Self-Assessment & Review. 2nd ed. (Illus.). 225p. 1982. pap. 11.95 (ISBN 0-07-050975-1). McGraw.

Swartzentruber, James. God Made Me in a Good Way. (God Is Good Ser.). 1976. 2.55 (ISBN 0-686-18183-2). Rod & Staff.

--God Made the Animals. (God Is Good Ser.). 1976. 2.55 (ISBN 0-686-18185-9). Rod & Staff.

--God Made the Firefly. (God Is Good Ser.). 1976. 2.55 (ISBN 0-686-18186-7). Rod & Staff.

--God Made Us in a Wonderful Way. (God Is Good Ser.). 1976. 2.55 (ISBN 0-686-18184-0). Rod & Staff.

--God Makes Seeds That Grow. (God Is Good Ser.). 1976. 2.55 (ISBN 0-686-18182-4). Rod & Staff.

--We Should Be Thankful. (God Is Good Ser.). 1976. 2.55 (ISBN 0-686-18188-3). Rod & Staff.

Swartzentruber, Mrs. James. God Made the Opossum. (God Is Good Ser.). 1976. 2.55 (ISBN 0-686-18187-5). Rod & Staff.

Swartzlander, E. E., Jr., ed. Computer Arithmetic. LC 78-14397. (Benchmark Papers in Electrical Engineering & Computer Science: Vol. 21). 400p. 1979. 56.50 (ISBN 0-87933-350-2). Hutchinson Ross.

Swartzlander, Ellen. Mister Andrews School 1837-1842: Students' Journal Transcript. (Illus.). 126p. 1958. slipcase 2.00 (ISBN 0-910302-07-3). Bucks Co Hist.

Swarup, Ram. Islam Through Sahih Muslim. 224p. 1983. 12.00 (ISBN 0-682-49948-X). Exposition.

Swarupananda, Swami, tr. Bhagavad-Gita, Srimad. (Sanskrit & Eng). 8.95 (ISBN 0-87481-064-7). Vedanta Pr.

Swathmore College. Catalog of the Peace Collection. 1981. lib. bdg. 300.00 (ISBN 0-8161-0377-1, Hall Library). G K Hall.

Swaton, J. Norman. Personal Finance: Getting Along & Getting Ahead. 1980. text ed. 15.95 (ISBN 0-442-28116-1); instr's. manual 3.95 (ISBN 0-442-26236-1). Van Nos Reinhold.

Swaton, J. Norman & Morgan, Loren. Administration of Justice. 2nd ed. 1980. text ed. 15.95 (ISBN 0-442-25789-9); instructor's manual 2.50x (ISBN 0-442-25712-0). Van Nos Reinhold.

Swatridge, Colin & Swatridge, Susan. The Biblio File: An Index of Prose Passages. 354p. 1979. bds. 19.50x o.p. (ISBN 0-631-92640-2, Pub. by Basil Blackwell); pap. 10.50x o.p. (ISBN 0-631-92620-8). Biblio Dist.

Swatridge, Susan, jt. auth. see Swatridge, Colin.

Swatsburg, Peter. Readings in Administration of Special Education. (Special Education Ser.). (Illus., Orig.). 1980. pap. text ed. 15.00 (ISBN 0-89568-193-5). Spec Learn Corp.

Swaybill, Marion L., jt. auth. see Shapiro, Jacqueline R.

Swaybill, Roger. Threads. 1980. 12.95 o.s.i. (ISBN 0-440-08319-2). Delacorte.

Swaybill, Roger E. Final Witness. 256p. 1983. pap. 2.75 (ISBN 0-380-81422-6). Avon.

Swayne, Sam & Swayne, Zoa. Great-Grandfather in the Honey Tree. LC 81-9738. (Illus.). 53p. (gr. 3-5). 1982. pap. 4.95 perfect bdg. (ISBN 0-9608008-0-8). Legacy Hse.

Swayne, Zoa, jt. auth. see Swayne, Sam.

Swazey, Judith P. Chlorpromazine in Psychiatry: A Study of Therapeutic Innovation. 519p. 1974. 30.00x (ISBN 0-262-19130-X). MIT Pr.

Swazey, Judith P., jt. auth. see Wong, Cynthia B.

Swearer, Harvey. Pulse & Switching Circuits. LC 79-117191. (Illus., Orig.). 1970. 8.95 o.p. (ISBN 0-8306-0528-2); pap. 5.95 (ISBN 0-8306-9528-1, 528). TAB Bks.

Swearingen, A. Rodger & Langer, Paul. Red Flag in Japan: International Communism in Action, 1919-1951. LC 68-54440. (Illus.). 1968. Repr. of 1952 ed. lib. bdg. 29.75x (ISBN 0-8371-0242-1, SWRF). Greenwood.

Swearingen, Phyllis van see Van Swearingen, Phyllis.

Swears, Linda. Discovering the Guitar: Teach Yourself to Play. LC 81-38335. (Illus.). 96p. 1981. PLB 8.16 (ISBN 0-688-00718-X); pap. 6.95 (ISBN 0-688-00717-1). Morrow.

Sweat, Clifford H., ed. Morale & Early Adolescent Education: From Apathy to Action. LC 80-80727. 1980. pap. text ed. 4.25x (ISBN 0-8134-2134-9, 2134). Interstate.

Sweazey, George E. Preaching the Good News. 368p. 1976. 19.95 (ISBN 0-13-694802-2). P-H.

Swedberg, Harriett, jt. auth. see Swedberg, Robert W.

Swedberg, Richard. Sociology as Disenchantment: The Evolution of the Work of George Gurvitch. 201p. 1982. text ed. 17.50x (ISBN 0-391-02397-7). Humanities.

Swedberg, Robert W. & Swedberg, Harriett. American Oak Furniture Styles & Prices. pap. 10.95 (ISBN 0-87069-363-8). Wallace-Homestead.

Swedenberg, H. T. see Dryden, John.

Swedenberg, H. T., Jr., ed. England in the Restoration & Early Eighteenth Century: Essays on Culture & Society. LC 72-149943. 272p. 1972. 31.50x (ISBN 0-520-01973-3). U of Cal Pr.

Swedenborg, Emanual. Heaven & Hell. 1976. pap. 1.95 o.p. (ISBN 0-89129-110-5). Jove Pubns.

Swedenborg, Emanuel. Apocalypse Explained, 6 vols. LC 76-46145. 1979. trade ed. 10.00 ea. Vol. 1 (ISBN 0-87785-007-0). Vol. 2 (ISBN 0-87785-008-9). Vol. 3 (ISBN 0-87785-009-7). Vol. 4 (ISBN 0-87785-010-0). Vol. 5 (ISBN 0-87785-011-9). Vol. 6 (ISBN 0-87785-012-7). 57.00 set (ISBN 0-87785-013-5). Swedenborg.

--Arcana Coelestia (Heavenly Secrets, 12 vols. Incl. Trade Edition. 10.00ea. Vol. 1 (ISBN 0-87785-034-8). Vol. 2 (ISBN 0-87785-035-6). Vol. 3 (ISBN 0-87785-036-4). Vol. 4 (ISBN 0-87785-037-2). Vol. 5 (ISBN 0-87785-038-0). Vol. 6 (ISBN 0-87785-039-9). Vol. 7 (ISBN 0-87785-040-2). Vol. 8 (ISBN 0-87785-041-0); Vol. 9 (ISBN 0-87785-042-9). Vol. 10 (ISBN 0-87785-043-7). Vol. 11 (ISBN 0-87785-044-5). Vol. 12 (ISBN 0-87785-045-3). Set. 114.00 (ISBN 0-87785-046-1). LC 63-1828. 1974. Swedenborg.

--Experientiae Spirituales, 6 Vols. 2nd ed. Odhner, John D., ed. 3600p. (Latin.). 1982. Set. 270.00 (ISBN 0-910557-00-4). Acad New Church.

--Heaven & Hell. large print ed. LC 81-52785. 800p. 8.25 (ISBN 0-87785-167-0). Swedenborg.

--Spiritual Life - the Word of God. 0.75 o.p. (ISBN 0-87785-082-8); pap. 0.50 o.p. (ISBN 0-87785-083-6). Swedenborg.

--True Christian Religion, 2 vols. LC 63-1799. 1098p. trade ed. 10.00 ea. Vol. 1 (ISBN 0-87785-087-9). Vol. 2 (ISBN 0-87785-088-7). Set. 19.00 (ISBN 0-87785-089-5); student ed. 6.50 (ISBN 0-686-82980-8). Vol. 1 (ISBN 0-87785-084-4). Vol. 2. pap. 6.00 (ISBN 0-87785-085-2); 11.00 set (ISBN 0-686-82981-6). Swedenborg.

Swedin, Diane, ed. see Shelton, Jack & Juhasz, Jack R.

Swedish Academy of Engineering. Gengas: The Swedish Classic on Wood Powered Vehicles. Reed, Thomas B. & Jantzen, Dan, eds. Geuther, Maria, tr. (Illus.). 329p. 1981. pap. 15.00 (ISBN 0-942914-00-7). Tipi Wkshp Bks.

Swedish International Development Authority, tr. see FAO.

Swedish Telecommunications Administration & LM Ericson Telephone Company. Human Factors in Telecommunications International Symposium, 6th. 1972. 75.00 (ISBN 0-686-37978-0). Info Gatekeepers.

Swedish Trade Council, ed. Swedish Export Directory, 1982. 63rd ed. LC 72-623267. 800p. (Orig.). 1982. pap. 42.50x (ISBN 0-8002-3028-0). Intl Pubns Serv.

Sweedler, M. E., jt. auth. see Chase, U.

Sweeney. A Combat Reporter's Report. LC 80-13654. (gr. 6 up). 1980. PLB 8.90 (ISBN 0-531-04171-9, E20). Watts.

--Disaster. 1981. 8.95 o.p. (ISBN 0-679-20954-9). McKay.

Sweeney & Olivieri. An Introduction to Nursing Research: Research, Measurement, & Computers in Nursing. pap. text ed. 17.50 (ISBN 0-397-54263-1, Lippincott Nursing). Lippincott.

Sweeney, Amin, jt. auth. see Malm, William P.

Sweeney, Dennis J., jt. auth. see Anderson, David R.

Sweeney, Dennis M. & Lyko, James J. Supplement to Practice Manual for Social Security Claims, 1983. 80p. 1983. pap. 15.00 (ISBN 0-686-82489-X, C5-1175). PLI.

Sweeney, G. P., ed. Information & the Transformation of Society: Papers from the First Joint International Conference of the Institute of Information Scientists & the American Society for Information Science, St. Patrick's College, Dublin, Ireland, 28-30 June, 1982. (Contemporary Topics in Information Transfer Ser.: Vol. 2). 368p. 1982. 51.00 (ISBN 0-444-86505-5, North Holland). Elsevier.

Sweeney, James B. A Pictorial History of Sea Monsters & Other Dangerous Marine Life. 1972. 12.95 o.p. (ISBN 0-517-50112-0). Crown.

--True Spy Stories. (Triumph Bks.). (Illus.). 96p. (gr. 7 up). 1981. lib. bdg. 8.90 (ISBN 0-531-04339-8). Watts.

Sweeney, James J., intro. by. Contemporary Spanish Painters: Miro & after-a Selection. LC 75-14854. (Illus.). 64p. 1975. 3.00 (ISBN 0-88397-020-1, Pub. by Intl Exhibit Foun). C E Tuttle.

Sweeney, James S., Jr. Seasonal Star Charts. 24p. (Orig.). 1972. pap. text ed. 8.75 (ISBN 0-8331-1802-1). Hubbard Sci.

Sweeney, John A. The Treasure House of Early American Rooms. (Illus.). 1978. Repr. 5.98 o.p. (ISBN 0-517-24947-2). Crown.

--The Treasure House of Early American Rooms. (Illus.). 1983. 15.95 (ISBN 0-393-01601-3); pap. 9.95 (ISBN 0-393-30039-0). Norton.

--The Treasure House of Early American Rooms. (Illus.). 179p. 1978. 9.00 (ISBN 0-686-36486-4). Md Hist.

Sweeney, Karen O. Nature Runs Wild: True Disaster Stories. (Illus.). (gr. 5-8). 1979. PLB 8.90 s&l (ISBN 0-531-02220-X). Watts.

Sweeney, Louise B. Women Film Directors: Pride & Prejudice of Hollywood. (Illus.). Date not set. 15.00 (ISBN 0-498-02574-8). A S Barnes.

Sweeney, Mary S., ed. see Spencer, Anne M.

Sweeney, Neil R. Managing a Sales Team: Techniques for Field Sales Managers. LC 78-71964. 1978. 15.95 (ISBN 0-86730-502-9). Lebhar Friedman.

--Managing People: Techniques for Food Service Operators. new ed. LC 76-7286. 128p. 1976. pap. 15.95 (ISBN 0-86730-215-1). Lebhar Friedman.

Sweeney, Richard J. Radiographic Artifacts: Their Cause & Control. (Illus.). 263p. 1983. text ed. price not set (ISBN 0-397-50554-X, Lippincott Medical). Lippincott.

Sweeney, Robert D., compiled by. Raising Money Through Gift Clubs: A Survey of Techniques at 42 Institutions. 71p. 1982. 14.50 (ISBN 0-89964-191-1). CASE.

Sweeney, Stephen B., et al. Education for Administrative Careers in Government Service. LC 72-7831. 366p. 1973. Repr. of 1958 ed. lib. bdg. 18.50x (ISBN 0-8371-6535-0, SWAC). Greenwood.

Sweeney, Terrance A. Streets of Anger, Streets of Hope. (Illus.). 256p. (Orig.). 1981. pap. text ed. 8.95 (ISBN 0-86666-032-1). GWP.

Sweeney, Thomas J. Adlerian Counseling. 1975. pap. 2.60 o.p. (ISBN 0-395-20038-5). HM.

--Rural Poor Students & Guidance. (Guidance Monograph). 1971. pap. 2.40 o.p. (ISBN 0-395-12440-9). HM.

Sweeney, Thomas L. & Bhatt, Harasiddhiprasad D., eds. Hazardous Waste Management for the Eighties. LC 82-71532. (Illus.). 553p. 1982. 39.95 (ISBN 0-250-40429-X). Ann Arbor Science.

Sweeney, Wm. J., III, jt. auth. see Caplan, Ronald M.

Sweeny, Z. T. Spirit & the Word. 1982. pap. 3.95 (ISBN 0-89225-264-2). Gospel Advocate.

Sweet. Obstetric Care. 1981. 10.95 (ISBN 0-471-26033-9, Wiley Heyden). Wiley.

Sweet, C. S. see Scriabine, A.

Sweet, Charles F. see Mickelwait, Donald R., et al.

Sweet, Franklyn H., jt. auth. see Wood, Thomas D.

Sweet, Frederick A. Ivan Albright: A Retrospective Exhibition. 2nd ed. LC 64-25439. (Illus.). 59p. 1964. pap. 5.00x (ISBN 0-86559-005-2). Art Inst Chi.

Sweet, Henry. Anglo-Saxon Primer. 9th ed. Davis, Norman, ed. 1953. pap. 5.95x (ISBN 0-19-811178-9). Oxford U Pr.

Sweet, J. P. Revelation. LC 78-26383. (Westminster Pelican Commentaries). 1979. 14.95 (ISBN 0-664-21375-8); softcover 9.95 (ISBN 0-664-24262-6). Westminster.

Sweet, James, jt. ed. see Rindfuss, R. R.

Sweet, James A. Women in the Labor Force. LC 72-7704. (Studies in Population Ser). 1973. 31.50 (ISBN 0-12-785813-X). Acad Pr.

Sweet, John. Designs for Reading: Plays. (Houghton Books in Literature Ser.). pap. text ed. 5.48 (ISBN 0-395-02790-X). HM.

Sweet, John J. Mounting the Threat: The Battle of Bourguebus Ridge. LC 77-73555. (Illus.). 1978. 10.00 o.p. (ISBN 0-89141-026-0). Presidio Pr.

Sweet, Leonard. The Minister's Wife: Her Role in Nineteenth Century American Evangelicalism. 323p. 1983. text ed. 29.95 (ISBN 0-686-83076-8). Temple U Pr.

Sweet, Leonard I. Black Images of America, 1784-1870. (Essays in American History Ser). 1976. pap. text ed. 2.95 o.p. (ISBN 0-393-09195-3). Norton.

Sweet, Ozzie, jt. auth. see Scott, Jack D.

Sweet, Paul R. Friedrich Von Gentz, Defender of the Old Order. Repr. of 1941 ed. lib. bdg. 15.75x (ISBN 0-8371-2560-X, SWFG). Greenwood.

Sweet, Waldo. Artes Latinae, Level II. 203p. 1982. pap. text ed. 5.75x reference notebook (ISBN 0-686-84390-8). Bolchazy-Carducci.

--Artes Latinae, Bk.1 Level 1. 295p. 1982. pap. text ed. 9.95x (ISBN 0-686-84389-4). Bolchazy-Carducci.

--Artes Latinae: Guide to Filmstrip Series. 48p. 1982. pap. text ed. 2.00x (ISBN 0-686-84391-6). Bolchazy-Carducci.

Sweet, Waldo E. & Knudsvig, Glenn M. A Course on Words. 353p. 1982. pap. text ed. 9.95 (ISBN 0-15-515183-5, HC). HarBraceJ.

Sweet, Walter C., jt. auth. see Bates, Robert L.

Sweet, William D., jt. ed. see Schmidek, Henry H.

Sweet, William H., jt. ed. see Schmidek, Henry H.

Sweeting, George. Catch the Spirit of Love. 120p. 1983. pap. 3.95 (ISBN 0-88207-108-4). Victor Bks.

--Como Iniciar la Vida Cristiana. new ed. Clifford, Alec, tr. from Eng. (Span.). 1977. pap. 2.95 (ISBN 0-8024-1615-2). Moody.

--How to Begin the Christian Life. LC 75-31674. 128p. 1976. pap. 2.95 (ISBN 0-8024-3626-9). Moody.

--How to Begin the Christian Life. study ed 7.95 (ISBN 0-8024-3630-7). Moody.

--How to Begin the Christian Life: Leader's Guide. (Leader's Guide Ser.). (Illus.). 1977. pap. 4.95 (ISBN 0-8024-3629-3). Moody.

--How to Witness Successfully. LC 78-1959. 1978. pap. 3.95 (ISBN 0-8024-3791-5). Moody.

--Love Is the Greatest. 144p. 1976. pap. 2.50 o.p. (ISBN 0-8024-5024-5). Moody.

--Special Sermons for Evangelism. LC 82-7999. (Special Sermons Ser.). (Orig.). 1982. pap. 4.95 (ISBN 0-8024-8210-4). Moody.

--Special Sermons for Special Days. LC 77-1218. (Special Sermon Ser.). 1979. pap. 4.95 (ISBN 0-8024-8206-6). Moody.

--Special Sermons on Special Issues. LC 80-26754. (Special Sermon Ser.). 128p. 1981. pap. 4.95 (ISBN 0-8024-8207-4). Moody.

--Talking It Over. LC 79-18375. 1979. lib. bdg. 5.95 kivar (ISBN 0-8024-8529-4). Moody.

Sweeting, M. M., ed. Karst Geomorphology. LC 81-6558. (Benchmark Papers in Geology Ser.: Vol. 59). 448p. 1981. 56.00 (ISBN 0-87933-379-0). Hutchinson Ross.

Sweeting, O. J. Science & Technology of Polymer Films, 2 vols. LC 67-13963. 1968-71. Vol. 1. 63.95 o.p. (ISBN 0-470-83893-0); Vol. 2. 65.50 o.p. (ISBN 0-471-83894-2, Pub. by Wiley-Interscience). Wiley.

Sweetland, Ben. I Can. 1976. pap. 5.00 (ISBN 0-87980-312-6). Wilshire.

Sweetland, James H. A Bibliography of Africana in the Lilly Library. Gosebrink, Jean E., ed. (African Humanities Ser.). 76p. (Orig.). 1977. pap. text ed. 4.00 (ISBN 0-941934-26-8). Ind U Afro-Amer Arts.

Sweetman, David. Women Leaders in African History. 160p. 1982. 30.00x (ISBN 0-435-94479-7, Pub. by Heinemann England). State Mutual Bk.

Sweetman, John. Operation Chastise: The True Story of the Famous Dams Raid. (Illus.). 256p. 1982. 19.95 (ISBN 0-86720-557-1). Sci Bks Intl.

--Saratoga Seventeen Seventy Seven. (Knight's Battles for Wargamers Ser.). (Illus.). 100p. 1973. 3.95 o.p. (ISBN 0-88254-208-7). Hippocrene Bks.

Sweet's Division. The McGraw-Hill Homebook. (Illus.). 1980. 8.95 (ISBN 0-07-062606-5). McGraw.

Sweetser, Marion M. The Sun in the Golden Cup. 5.95 (ISBN 0-8215-9894-5). Sadlier.

Sweetser, Thomas P. Successful Parishes: How They Meet the Challenge of Change. 204p. 1983. pap. 9.95 (ISBN 0-86683-043-7). Winston Pr.

Sweetwood, Hannelore. Clinical Electrocardiography for Nurses. 400p. 1983. price not set (ISBN 0-89443-846-8). Aspen Systems.

Sweezey, Marilyn P., jt. auth. see Massie, Robert.

Sweigart, Stephen. The Anti-Christ. (Parpaglion Poetry Ser.: No. 6). (Illus.). 50p. (Orig.). 1979. 150.00 (ISBN 0-9604252-1-7). Parpaglion.

--Jason: 1970-74. (Parpaglion Poetry Ser.: Nos. 1-5). 50p. (Orig.). 1974. 10.00 (ISBN 0-9604252-0-9). Parpaglion.

Swellengrebel, J. L., jt. auth. see Reiling, J.

Swenarton, Mark. Homes Fit for Heroes. 1981. text ed. 29.00x (ISBN 0-435-32994-4). Heinemann Ed.

Swenberg, C. E., jt. ed. see Damask, A. C.

Swenberg, Charles E., jt. auth. see Pope, Martin.

Swendson. A Couple of Cooks. pap. 5.95 (ISBN 0-686-81678-1). Corona Pub.

Swensen, Clifford, Jr. Approach to Case Conceptualization. (Guidance Monograph). 1968. pap. 2.60 o.p. (ISBN 0-395-09918-8). HM.

Swensen, Philip R., jt. auth. see Randle, Paul A.

Swenson, Allan. Secrets of a Seashore. (Secret of Ser.). (Illus.). 80p. 1981. 6.95 (ISBN 0-930096-27-4); pap. 5.95 (ISBN 0-930096-28-2). G Gannett.

Swenson, Allan, jt. auth. see McTavish, Thistle.

Swenson, Allan A. Allan Swenson's Big Fun to Grow Book. (Illus.). (gr. 3-7). 1980. pap. 3.95 o.p. (ISBN 0-679-12000-9). McKay.
--Plan Your Own Landscape. LC 77-77296. (Illus.). 1978. 12.95 o.p. (ISBN 0-448-14382-8, G&D); pap. 6.95 o.p. (ISBN 0-448-14383-6, Today Press). Putnam Pub Group.
Swenson, Allen. Starting Over. 228p. 1978. 8.95 o.s.i. (ISBN 0-89479-018-8). A & W Pubs.
Swenson, Ana M., tr. see Jauncey, J. H.
Swenson, Ana Maria, tr. see Dolphin, Lambert T.
Swenson, Birgit. Eagle & the Flower. LC 75-30139. 1976. 6.00 o.p. (ISBN 0-913994-22-7). Hippocrene Bks.
Swenson, Dan H. Business Reporting: A Management Tool. 448p. 1983. text ed. write for info. (ISBN 0-574-20675-2, 13-3675); write for info. instr's. guide (ISBN 0-574-20676-0, 13-3676). SRA.
Swenson, Gwen & Cunningham, Susan. The Mid-Life Crisis Cookbook. Rev. ed. (Illus.). 40p. (Orig.). 1982. pap. 4.50 (ISBN 0-9609806-1-X). Mid Life.
Swenson, John. Bill Haley: The Daddy Of Rock & Roll. LC 82-42760. 200p. 1983. 16.95 (ISBN 0-8128-2909-3); pap. 8.95 (ISBN 0-8128-6177-9). Stein & Day.
Swenson, Karen. East-West. 1980. pap. 3.25 o.p. (ISBN 0-917652-23-1). Confluence Pr.
Swenson, Leland C. Theories of Learning: Traditional Perspectives - Contemporary Development. 1979. text ed. 23.95x (ISBN 0-534-00698-1). Wadsworth Pub.
Swenson, Melinda, jt. auth. see Mins, Ferm.
Swenson, Melvin J., ed. Dukes' Physiology of Domestic Animals. 9th rev. ed. (Illus.). 928p. 1977. text ed. 39.50x (ISBN 0-8014-1076-2). Comstock.
Swenson, Peter J. Secrets of Rivers & Streams. Jack, Susan, ed. (Secrets of Ser.). 90p. 1982. pap. 5.95 (ISBN 0-930096-31-2). G Gannett.
Swenson, Philip R., jt. auth. see Rundle, Paul A.
Swenson, S. D. Heating Technology: Principles Equipment & Application. text ed. 23.95 (ISBN 0-534-01481-X, Breton Pubs). Wadsworth Pub.
Swenson, Sally, ed. Native Resource Control & the Multinational Corporate Challenge -- Background Documents. (Illus.). 40p. 1982. pap. 3.50 (ISBN 0-932978-08-8). Anthropology Res.
Swerdloff, Peter. Men & Women. LC 75-10885. (Human Behavior). (Illus.). (gr. 5 up). 1975. PLB 13.28 o.p. (ISBN 0-8094-1925-4, Pub. by Time-Life). Silver.
Swerdlow, Irving. The Public Administration of Economic Development. LC 74-9426. (Special Studies). (Illus.). 426p. 1975. 44.50 o.p. (ISBN 0-275-05730-5). Praeger.
Swerdlow, Joel. Code Z. LC 78-17969. 1979. 9.95 (ISBN 0-399-12291-5). Putnam Pub Group.
Swerdlow, Robert M. The Step-By-Step Guide to Photo-Offset Lithography. (Illus.). 400p. 1982. 23.95 (ISBN 0-13-846584-3). P-H.
Swern, Daniel. Bailey's Industrial Oil & Fat Products, Vol. II. 4th ed. LC 78-31275. 603p. 1982. 65.00 (ISBN 0-471-83958-2, Pub. by Wiley-Interscience). Wiley.
--Bailey's Industrial Oil & Fat Products, Vol. 1. 4th ed. LC 78-31275. 841p. 1979. 75.00 (ISBN 0-471-83957-4, Pub. by Wiley-Interscience). Wiley.
Swern, Daniel, ed. Organic Peroxides, Vol. 1. LC 80-16096. 666p. 1983. Repr. of 1970 ed. lib. bdg. write for info. (ISBN 0-89874-477-6). Krieger.
--Organic Peroxides, Vol. 2. LC 80-16096. 976p. 1983. Repr. of 1971 ed. lib. bdg. write for info. (ISBN 0-89874-478-4). Krieger.
Swetman, Glen R. A Range of Sonnets. 1983. pap. 2.95 (ISBN 0-939736-32-2). Wings ME.
Swetnam, George. Andrew Carnegie. (United States Authors Ser.: No. 355). 1980. lib. bdg. 11.95 o.p. (ISBN 0-8057-7239-1, Twayne). G K Hall.
Swetnam, George & Smith, Helene. A Guidebook to Historic Western Pennsylvania. LC 75-33421. 1976. 14.95 (ISBN 0-8229-3316-0); pap. 6.95 (ISBN 0-8229-5271-8). U of Pittsburgh Pr.
Sweton, Ernest T. Wild Animals at Home. 126p. 1982. Repr. of 1913 ed. lib. bdg. 30.00 (ISBN 0-89760-852-6). Telegraph Bks.
Swets, John & Pickett, Ronald. Evaluation of Diagnostic Systems: Methods from Signal Detection Theory. LC 82-3885. (Cognition & Perception Ser.). 1982. 29.00 (ISBN 0-12-679080-9). Acad Pr.
Swets, John A., ed. Signal Detection & Recognition by Human Observers. LC 64-13225. 702p. 1964. text ed. 29.50 (ISBN 0-471-83970-1, Pub. by Wiley). Krieger.
Swettenham, John. Canada's Atlantic War. 1979. 19.95 (ISBN 0-88866-604-7). Samuel Stevens.
--The Evening of Chivalry. (Canadian War Museum Historical Publications Ser.). (Illus.). 61p. 1975. pap. 3.50 o.p. (ISBN 0-685-53615-7). Samuel Stevens.
Swettenham, John & Wood, H. Silent Witnesses. LC 74-82811. (Illus.). xii, 243p. 1974. 13.95 o.p. (ISBN 0-88866-557-1). Samuel Stevens.
Swettenham, John & Wood, Herbert. Temoins Silencieux. new ed. Gouin, Jacques, tr. from Eng. LC 74-82811. (Illus.). vi, 247p. 1974. 13.95 o.p. (ISBN 0-88866-563-6). Samuel Stevens.
Swettenham, John, ed. see Morton, Desmond.
Swetz, Frank. Mathematics Education in China: Its Growth & Development. 350p. 1974. 20.00x (ISBN 0-262-19121-0). MIT Pr.
--The Mathematics Laboratory in the Elementary School: What? Why? & How? Valenza, Samuel W., Jr., ed. LC 80-81349. (Illus., Orig.). 1981. pap. 7.95 (ISBN 0-936918-03-9). Intergalactic NJ.
Swezey, Kenneth. Formulas, Methods, Tips & Data for Home & Workshop. rev. ed. Scharff, Robert, rev. by. LC 68-54377. (Popular Science Bk.). (Illus.). 1979. 17.26i (ISBN 0-06-014164-6, HarpT). Har-Row.
Swezey, Robert L. Arthritis: Rational Therapy & Rehabilitation. (Illus.). 1978. text ed. 18.95x o.p. (ISBN 0-7216-8690-7). Saunders.
Swezy, Olive, jt. auth. see Kofoid, C. A.
Swiatecka, M. Jadwiga. The Idea of the Symbol: Some Nineteenth Century Comparisons with Coleridge. LC 70-19802. 220p. 1980. 29.95 (ISBN 0-521-22362-8). Cambridge U Pr.
Swidler, Arleen. Woman in a Man's Church. LC 72-86596. 96p. (Orig.). 1972. pap. 1.95 o.p. (ISBN 0-8091-1740-1, Deus). Paulist Pr.
Swidler, Arlene. Human Rights in Religious Traditions. LC 82-15014. 128p. (Orig.). 1982. pap. 8.95 (ISBN 0-8298-0633-4). Pilgrim NY.
Swidler, Arlene, ed. Sister Celebrations: Nine Worship Experiences. LC 74-80414. 96p. (Orig.). 1974. pap. 0.50 o.p. (ISBN 0-8006-1084-9, 1-1084). Fortress.
Swidler, Arlene & Swidler, Leonard, eds. Women Priests: A Catholic Commentary on the Vatican Declaration. LC 77-83572. 372p. 1977. pap. 9.95 o.p. (ISBN 0-8091-2062-3). Paulist Pr.
Swidler, Arlene, tr. see Van Der Meer, Haye S.
Swidler, Leonard. Aufklarung Cathoicism Seventeen Eighty to Eighteen Fifty: Liturgical & Other Reforms in the Catholic Aufklarung. LC 78-2736. 1978. pap. 9.95 (ISBN 0-89130-227-1, 01-00-17). Scholars Pr Ca.
--Biblical Affirmations of Woman. LC 79-18886. 1979. 19.50 (ISBN 0-664-21377-4); softcover 10.95 (ISBN 0-664-24285-5). Westminster.
Swidler, Leonard, ed. Consensus in Theology? A Dialogue with Hans Kung & Edward Schillebeeckx. LC 80-65385. 1980. 12.95 (ISBN 0-664-21379-0); pap. 5.95 (ISBN 0-664-24322-3). Westminster.
--Kung in Conflict. LC 80-2878. 648p. 1981. 17.95 o.p. (ISBN 0-385-17551-5); pap. 8.95 (ISBN 0-385-17552-3). Doubleday.
Swidler, Leonard & Sloyan, Gerard S., eds. The Oberammergau Passionsspiel 1984. 104p. pap. 5.00 (ISBN 0-686-95110-7). ADL.
Swidler, Leonard, jt. auth. see Swidler, Arlene.
Swidler, Leonard, tr. see Van Der Meer, Haye S.
Swiecicka-Ziemianek, Maria. Polish: A Beginner's Guide. 327p. Date not set. with 8 cassettes 149.00x (ISBN 0-88432-099-5, P500). J Norton Pubs.
Swiecicka-Ziemianek, Maria, tr. see Lem, Stanislaw.
Swienciki, Lawrence W. Adventures with Arithmetic, Algebra. (Illus.). 48p. (Orig.). (gr. 7-12). 1974. wkbk. 5.95 (ISBN 0-88488-003-6). Creative Pubns.
--Adventures with Arithmetic, Decimals. (Illus.). 48p. (Orig.). (gr. 7-12). 1974. wkbk. 5.95 (ISBN 0-88488-001-X). Creative Pubns.
--Adventures with Arithmetic, Fractions. (Illus.). 48p. (Orig.). (gr. 7-12). 1974. wkbk. 5.95 (ISBN 0-88488-000-1). Creative Pubns.
--Adventures with Arithmetic, Per Cent. (Illus.). 48p. (Orig.). (gr. 7-12). 1974. wkbk. 5.95 (ISBN 0-88488-002-8). Creative Pubns.
Swierenga, Robert P. Acres for Cents: Delinquent Tax Auctions in Frontier Iowa. LC 75-23868. (Contributions in American History: No. 46). 256p. 1976. lib. bdg. 29.95x (ISBN 0-8371-8167-4, SWA/). Greenwood.
--Dutch Emigrants to the United States, South Africa, South America, & Southeast Asia, 1835-1880: An Alphabetical Listing by Household Heads & Independent Persons. LC 82-23056. 368p. 1983. lib. bdg. 50.00 (ISBN 0-8420-2207-4). Scholarly Res Inc.
--Dutch Immigrants in U.S. Ship Passenger Manifests, 1820-1880: An Alphabetical Listing by Household Heads & Independent Persons, 2 Vols. LC 82-23078. 1328p. 1983. lib. bdg. 125.00 set (ISBN 0-8420-2206-6). Scholarly Res Inc.
--Pioneers & Profits: Land Speculation on the Iowa Frontier. (Illus.). 1968. 7.50x o.p. (ISBN 0-8138-1262-3). Iowa St U Pr.
Swierenga, Robert P., ed. Beyond the Civil War Synthesis: Political Essays of the Civil War Era. LC 75-10046. (Contributions in American History Ser.: No. 44). 348p. 1975. lib. bdg. 29.95x (ISBN 0-8371-7960-2, SWC); pap. 5.95 (ISBN 0-8371-8921-7, SWC). Greenwood.
Swieringa, Robert J. & Moncur, Robert H. Some Effects of Participative Budgeting on Managerial Behavior. 265p. 17.95 (ISBN 0-86641-043-0, 7475). Natl Assn Accts.
Swieringa, Robert J., jt. auth. see Dyckman, Thomas R.
Swierkos, et al. Industrial Arts for Elementary Classrooms. 1973. pap. text ed. 11.04 (ISBN 0-87002-116-8). Bennett IL.
Swift, A. H., jt. auth. see Hohenemser, K. H.
Swift, Bryan. Mission Code: Scorpion. 192p. 1982. pap. 2.25 (ISBN 0-515-06036-4). Jove Pubns.
Swift, D. F., ed. Basic Readings in the Sociology of Education. (Students Library of Education). 1970. pap. 4.75 o.p. (ISBN 0-7100-6793-3). Routledge & Kegan.
Swift, D. J. & Palmer, Harold D., eds. Coastal Sedimentation. LC 78-18696. (Benchmark Papers in Geology Ser.: Vol. 42). 339p. 1978. 48.50 (ISBN 0-87933-330-8). Hutchinson Ross.
Swift, D. J., et al, eds. Shelf Sediment Transport: Process & Pattern. LC 72-88985. (Illus.). 608p. 1973. 63.50 (ISBN 0-12-787495-X). Acad Pr.
Swift, Digby G. Physics for Rural Development: A Sourcebook for Teachers & Extension Workers in Developing Countries. 272p. 1983. 21.90 (ISBN 0-471-10364-0, Pub. by Wiley-Interscience). Wiley.
Swift, Edward. Principia Martindale: A Comedy in Three Acts. LC 82-48150. 320p. 1983. write for info. (ISBN 0-06-015110-2, HarpT). Har-Row.
Swift, Ernest F. Conservation Saga. (Illus.). 1967. 1.50 o.p. (ISBN 0-912186-01-1). Natl Wildlife.
Swift, Hildegarde H. & Ward, Lynd. Little Red Lighthouse & the Great Gray Bridge. LC 42-36286. (Illus.). (gr. k-3). 1942. 8.95 (ISBN 0-15-247040-9, HJ). HarBraceJ.
--The Little Red Lighthouse & the Great Gray Bridge. LC 73-12861. (Illus.). 51p. (gr. k-3). 1974. pap. 1.95 (ISBN 0-15-652840-1, VoyB). HarBraceJ.
Swift, Hugh. The Trekker's Guide to the Himalaya & Karakoram. LC 82-738. (Illus.). 288p. (Orig.). 1982. pap. 10.95 (ISBN 0-87156-295-2). Sierra.
Swift, Jeremy. The Sahara. (The World's Wild Places Ser.). (Illus.). 1978. lib. bdg. 15.96 (ISBN 0-8094-2017-1). Silver.
Swift, Jonathan. Gulliver's Travels. pap. 2.95 (ISBN 0-440-33308-3, LE). Dell.
--Gulliver's Travels. (gr. 4-6). Companion Lib. ed. 2.95 (ISBN 0-448-05810-3, G&D); 2.95 (ISBN 0-448-05461-2); deluxe ed. 8.95 (ISBN 0-448-06010-8). Putnam Pub Group.
--Gulliver's Travels. (Illus.). 1977. 19.95 (ISBN 0-19-519978-2). Oxford U Pr.
--Gulliver's Travels. LC 78-3394. (Raintree's Illustrated Classics). (Illus.). (gr. 5-8). 1978. PLB 13.30 (ISBN 0-8172-1132-2). Raintree Pubs.
--Gulliver's Travels. LC 76-25231. 1981. Repr. of 1726 ed. 70.00x (ISBN 0-8201-1274-7). Schol Facsimiles.
--Gulliver's Travels. McKelvie, Colin, ed. LC 77-77863. 1977. 20.00 (ISBN 0-312-35325-1). St Martin.
--Gulliver's Travels. (Children's Classics Ser.). (gr. 3-6). 1982. 5.95 (ISBN 0-86020-613-0); PLB 11.95 (ISBN 0-88110-064-1); pap. 2.95 (ISBN 0-86020-612-2). EDC.
--Gulliver's Travels & Other Writings. Starkman, Mirian K., ed. (Bantam Classics Ser.). 536p. (gr. 7-12). 1981. pap. 1.75 (ISBN 0-553-21014-9). Bantam.
--Gulliver's Travels & Other Writings. Quintana, Richard, intro. by. 1950. pap. 3.50x (ISBN 0-394-30992-8, T92, Mod LibC). Modern Lib.
--Gulliver's Travels & Other Writings. Quintana, Ricardo, ed. & intro. by. LC 58-6364. Date not set. 6.95 (ISBN 0-394-60479-2). Modern Lib.
--Gulliver's Travels: Movie Tie-In edition. 1983. pap. 2.25 (ISBN 0-14-006507-5). Penguin.
--Gulliver's Travels with the Illustrations of J. J. Grandville. LC 80-22845. (Illus.). 544p. 1981. 25.00 (ISBN 0-915556-09-X); ltd ed. 37.50x (ISBN 0-915556-06-5). Great Ocean.
--Jonathan Swift: Selected Poems. Sisson, C. H., ed. (Fyfield). 1979. pap. 4.95 o.p. (ISBN 0-85635-134-2, Pub. by Carcanet New Pr England). Humanities.
--Jonathan Swift: The Complete Poems. Rogers, Pat, ed. LC 82-13547. (Yale English Poets Ser.). 1120p. 1983. text ed. 45.00 (ISBN 0-300-02966-7); pap. text ed. 14.95x (ISBN 0-300-02967-5). Yale U Pr.
--Poetical Works. Davis, Herbert, ed. (Oxford Standard Authors Ser). 1967. 35.00 (ISBN 0-19-254161-7). Oxford U Pr.
--Selected Poems. 2nd ed. Sisson, C. H., ed. 91p. 1980. pap. text ed. 5.25x (ISBN 0-85635-135-0, Pub. by Carcanet New Pr England); text ed. 7.95x (ISBN 0-85635-134-2). Humanities.
--Tale of a Tub. LC 71-170512. (Foundations of the Novel Ser: Vol. 8). 322p. 1973. Repr. of 1704 ed. lib. bdg. 50.00 o.s.i. (ISBN 0-8240-0520-1). Garland Pub.
--Tale of a Tub, Battle of the Books, & Mechanical Operation of the Spirit. 2nd ed. Guthkelch, A. C. & Smith, D. N., eds. 1958. 42.00x (ISBN 0-19-811404-4). Oxford U Pr.
--Viajes de Gulliver. (Span.). 9.95 (ISBN 84-241-5631-5). E Torres & Sons.
--The Writings of Jonathan Swift. Greenberg, Robert & Piper, William, eds. (Critical Editions Ser.). 500p. 1973. pap. text ed. 10.95x (ISBN 0-393-09415-4). Norton.
Swift, Jonathan see Swan, D. K.
Swift, Kate, jt. auth. see Miller, Casey.
Swift, L. H. Botanical Bibliographies: Guide to Bibliographic Materials Applicable to Botany. 800p. 1974. Repr. of 1970 ed. lib. bdg. 88.00x (ISBN 3-87429-076-X). Lubrecht & Creamer.
Swift, Marlene E. Reflections. 1979. 4.95 o.p. (ISBN 0-533-03786-7). Vantage.
Swift, Mary G. Belles & Beaux on Their Toes: Dancing Stars in Young America. LC 79-6661. 1980. text ed. 22.25 (ISBN 0-8191-0922-3); pap. text ed. 13.50 (ISBN 0-8191-0923-1). U Pr of Amer.
--With Bright Wings: A Book of the Spirit. LC 75-44806. 1976. pap. 5.95 o.p. (ISBN 0-8091-1936-6). Paulist Pr.
Swift, Pat & Mulhern, Maggie. Great Looks: Full-Figured Woman's Guide to Beauty. LC 81-47869. (Illus.). 192p. 1982. 19.95 (ISBN 0-385-17046-7). Doubleday.
Swift, Robert A. NLRB & Management Decision Making, No. 9. LC 74-80052. (Labor Relations & Public Policy Ser.). 146p. 1974. pap. 6.95 (ISBN 0-686-98144-8). Indus Res Unit-Wharton.
Swift, William & Wilson, D. Principles of Finite Mathematics. (Illus.). 1977. ref. ed. 22.95 o.p. (ISBN 0-13-701359-0). P-H.
Swift-Bandini, Nancy. Manual of Neurological Nursing. (Spiral Manual Ser.). 1982. spiralbound 12.95 (ISBN 0-316-82541-7). Little.
Swigart, Edmund K. The Prehistory of the Indians of Western Connecticut. (Occasional Paper Ser.: No. One). 49p. pap. text ed. write for info. (ISBN 0-936322-02-0). Am Indian Arch.
Swigart, Rob. A.K.A. A Cosmic Fable. 1978. 8.95 o.s.i. (ISBN 0-395-26306-9); pap. 4.95 o.s.i. (ISBN 0-395-26384-0). HM.
--The Time Trip. 1979. 8.95 o.s.i. (ISBN 0-395-27756-6); pap. 4.95 o.s.i. (ISBN 0-395-27757-4). HM.
Swiger, Elinor P. Europe for Young Travelers. LC 72-75893. (gr. 4-8). 1972. 5.00 o.p. (ISBN 0-672-51698-5). Bobbs.
--Mexico for Kids. LC 78-156144. (gr. 4-8). 1971. 4.95 o.p. (ISBN 0-672-51539-3). Bobbs.
Swigert, Victoria L., jt. auth. see Farrell, Ronald A.
Swigert, Victoria L., ed. Law & the Legal Process. (Sage Research Progress Series in Criminology: Vol. 28). (Illus.). 160p. 1982. 18.95 (ISBN 0-8039-1900-X); pap. 8.95 (ISBN 0-8039-1901-8). Sage.
Swigg, Richard. Shakespeare's Great Confines. 320p. 1982. text ed. 27.25x (ISBN 0-85635-335-3, Pub. by Carcanet Pr England). Humanities.
Swihart, Judson I. How to Treat Your Family As Well As You Treat Your Friends. LC 82-11234. 1982. pap. 4.95 (ISBN 0-8307-0855-3, 5417605). Regal.
Swihart, Phillip J. How to Live with Your Feelings. 1976. pap. 2.25 o.p. (ISBN 0-87784-321-X). Inter-Varsity.
Swihart, Stanley J. & Hefley, Beryl F. Computer Systems in the Library: Handbook for Manager & Designer. LC 73-603. (Information Sciences Ser.). (Illus.). 338p. 1973. 39.95 (ISBN 0-471-83995-7, Pub. by Wiley-Interscience). Wiley.
Swihart, Stephen D. The Victor Bible Sourcebook. 1977. pap. 5.95 (ISBN 0-88207-802-X). Victor Bks.
Swihart, Thomas L. Astrophysics & Stellar Astronomy. LC 73-603. (Space Science Text Ser.). 299p. 1968. 26.95x o.p. (ISBN 0-471-83990-6, Pub. by Wiley-Interscience). Wiley.
--Journey Through the Universe: An Introduction to Astronomy. LC 77-76343. (Illus.). 1978. text ed. 26.50 (ISBN 0-395-25518-X); instr's. manual 0.50 (ISBN 0-395-25519-8). HM.
Swillens, Stephane & Dumont, Jacques E., eds. Cell Regulation by Intercellular Signals. LC 82-483. (NATO Advanced Study Institutes Ser. A-Life Sciences: Vol. 44). 344p. Date not set. 42.50x (ISBN 0-306-40980-1, Plenum Pr). Plenum Pub.
Swimme, Brian, jt. auth. see Fox, Matt.
Swinbank, C. Packaging of Chemicals & Other Industrial Liquids & Solids. 1973. text ed. 15.95 o.p. (ISBN 0-408-00106-2). Butterworth.
Swinburne, Algernon C. Poems & Ballads & Atalanta in Calydon. Peckham, Morse, ed. LC 79-117333. (Library of Literature Ser). 1970. 10.25 (ISBN 0-672-51119-3); text ed. 3.55 o.p. (ISBN 0-672-61000-0). Bobbs.
--Selected Poems: Swinburne. Findlay, L. M., ed. 274p. 1982. text ed. 14.75x (ISBN 0-85635-137-7, 80706, Pub. by Carcanet New Pr England). Humanities.
--The Swinburne Letters, 6 vols. Lang, Cecil Y., ed. Incl. Vol. 1. 1854-1869. (Illus.). i, 315p. 1959 (ISBN 0-300-00665-9); Vol. 2. 1869-1875. vi, 378p. 1959 (ISBN 0-300-00666-7); Vol. 3. 1875-1877. (Illus.). vii, 335p. 1960. o.p. (ISBN 0-300-00667-5); Vol. 4. 1877-1882. vi, 325p. 1960. pap. o.p. (ISBN 0-300-00668-3); Vol. 5. 1883-1890. (Illus.). vii, 290p. 1962. o.p. (ISBN 0-300-00669-1). 30.00x ea. Yale U Pr.
Swinburne, Algernon C., jt. auth. see Gordon, Mary.
Swinburne, Algernon C., et al, trs. see Villon, Francois.
Swinburne, Bruce R., jt. auth. see Sloan, Blanche C.
Swinburne, Herbert. Design Cost Analysis for Architects & Engineers. (Illus.). 1980. 24.50 (ISBN 0-07-062635-9, P&RB). McGraw.
Swinburne, Irene, jt. auth. see Swinburne, Laurence.
Swinburne, Laurence. Riders on the Wind: Quest, Adventure, Survival Ser. Bennett, Russell, ed. LC 79-21190. (Illus.). 46p. (gr. 4-9). 1982. pap. 7.93g (ISBN 0-8172-2069-0). Raintree Pubs.
Swinburne, Laurence & Swinburne, Irene. America's First Football Game. LC 78-14865. (Famous Firsts Ser.). (Illus.). 1978. lib. bdg. 10.76 (ISBN 0-89547-046-2). Silver.

--Mysterious Buried Treasures. LC 78-811276. (Unsolved Mysteries of the World Ser.). PLB 11.96 (ISBN 0-89547-066-7). Silver.

Swinburne, Richard. Faith & Reason. 1981. 23.00x (ISBN 0-19-824663-3). Oxford U Pr.

--Space & Time. LC 68-16622. 1968. 21.95 (ISBN 0-312-74935-X). St Martin.

--Space & Time. 2nd ed. 1980. 25.00x (ISBN 0-312-74936-8). St Martin.

Swinburne, Richard, ed. Justification of Induction. (Oxford Readings in Philosophy Ser.). 1974. pap. text ed. 8.95x (ISBN 0-19-875029-3). Oxford U Pr.

Swindell, John G. Rudimentary Treatise on Well-Digging, Boring & Pumpwork, Eighteen Forty-Nine. (Illus.). 88p. pap. 12.50. Saifer.

Swindell, K., jt. auth. see Pemberton, P. H.

Swindell, Larry. Charles Boyer: The Reluctant Lover. LC 81-43419. (Illus.). 288p. 1983. 15.95 (ISBN 0-385-17052-1). Doubleday.

Swindell, William, ed. Polarized Light. LC 74-26881. (Benchmark Papers in Optics Ser: No. 1). 418p. 1975. 55.00 (ISBN 0-12-787498-4). Acad Pr.

Swindells, Robert. Norah to the Rescue. (Illus.). (gr. 4-8). 8.50 (ISBN 0-686-77945-2). Putnam Pub Group.

--When Darkness Comes. LC 74-17383. (Illus.). (gr. 7 up). 1975. 7.95 (ISBN 0-688-22016-9); PLB 7.63 (ISBN 0-688-32016-3). Morrow.

Swinden, Patrick. Paul Scott: Images of India. 130p. 1980. 20.00x (ISBN 0-312-59822-X). St Martin.

Swindle, Fay L., jt. auth. see Bachrach, Ann W.

Swindle, Robert E. Business Math Basics. 1979. pap. text ed. 17.95x (ISBN 0-534-00578-0). Kent Pub Co.

--Business Math Basics. 2nd ed. 368p. 1983. pap. text ed. 17.95x (ISBN 0-534-01323-6); write for info. tchr's Ed. Kent Pub Co.

Swindler, D. R. Study of Cranial & Skeletal Material Excavated at Nippur. (Museum Monographs). (Illus.). 40p. 1956. bound 1.50xsoft (ISBN 0-934718-04-0). Univ Mus of U PA.

Swindler, Daris R. A Racial Study of the West Nakanai. (Museum Monographs). (Illus.). 39p. 1962. bound 4.00xsoft (ISBN 0-934718-16-4). Univ Mus of U PA.

Swindler, Daris R. & Wood, Charles D. Atlas of Primate Gross Anatomy. LC 81-19350. 1982. Repr. of 1973 ed. lib. bdg. 39.50 (ISBN 0-89874-321-4). Krieger.

Swindler, W. F. Chronology & Documentary Handbook of the State of Hawaii. LC 74-14838. (State Chronology Ser.: No. 11). 148p. 1978. 8.50 (ISBN 0-379-16136-2). Oceana.

--Chronology & Documentary Handbook of the State of Virginia. LC 78-26655. (Chronologies & Documentary Handbook of the States: No. 46). 148p. 1978. 8.50 (ISBN 0-379-16171-0). Oceana.

Swindler, William F. Sources & Documents of U. S. Constitutions, 10 vols. & vol. 4A. LC 73-170979. 512p. 1973-1979. 45.00 ea. (ISBN 0-379-16175-3). Oceana.

--Sources & Documents of U. S. Constitutions, Vol. 2 of 3. (Federal-Second Ser.). 500p. Date not set. lib. bdg. 50.00 (ISBN 0-379-16188-5). Oceana.

Swindler, William F., ed. Sources & Documents of U. S. Constitutions, Vol. 1 of 3. LC 82-2284. (National Documents: 1492-1800). 493p. 1982. lib. bdg. 50.00 (ISBN 0-379-16187-7). Oceana.

Swindler, William F. & Frech, Mary, eds. Chronology & Documentary Handbook of the State of Connecticut. LC 73-533. (No. 7). 139p. (gr. 9-12). 1973. PLB 8.50 (ISBN 0-379-16132-X). Oceana.

Swindler, William F. & Trover, Ellen L., eds. Chronology & Documentary Handbook of the State of Alabama. LC 72-51. (No. 3). 142p. (gr. 9-12). 1972. PLB 8.50 (ISBN 0-379-16126-5). Oceana.

Swindler, William F., ed. see Vexler, Robert I.

Swindoll, Charles. You & Your Child. LC 77-1692. 1977. 4.95 o.p. (ISBN 0-8407-5118-4); pap. 4.95 (ISBN 0-8407-5616-X). Nelson.

Swindoll, Charles R. Home: Where Life Makes up Its Mind. LC 79-90363. (Illus.). 1979. 13.95 o.p. (ISBN 0-930014-32-4); pap. 9.95 o.p. (ISBN 0-930014-31-6). Multnomah.

--Pasame Otro Ladrillo. 208p. Date not set. 2.95 (ISBN 0-88113-315-9). Edit Betania.

--Standing Out: Being Real in a Phony World. Orig. Title: Home: Where Life Makes Up Its Mind. 105p. 1983. pap. write for info. (ISBN 0-88070-014-9). Multnomah.

--Starting Over: Fresh Hope for the Road Ahead. LC 77-18364. (Illus.). 1978. pap. 4.95 (ISBN 0-930014-19-7). Multnomah.

--Starting Over: Fresh Hope for the Road Ahead. LC 82-24636. 1983. pap. 4.95 (ISBN 0-88070-015-7). Multnomah.

--Strike the Original Match. LC 80-15639. 1980. 7.95 o.p. (ISBN 0-930014-36-7); pap. 4.95 (ISBN 0-930014-37-5); study guide 2.95 (ISBN 0-930014-49-9). Multnomah.

Swindoll, Lucille. Wide My World, Narrow My Bed: Living & Loving the Single Life. LC 82-7890. 220p. (Orig.). 1982. 9.95 (ISBN 0-88070-004-1); pap. 5.95 (ISBN 0-930014-89-8). Multnomah.

Swineford, A., ed. National Conference on Clays & Minerals, 8th: Proceedings. 1961. inquire for price o.p. (ISBN 0-08-009351-5). Pergamon.

Swinehart, Haldon J., ed. Gundrilling, Trepanning, & Deep Hole Machining. rev. ed. LC 67-30124. (Manufacturing Data Ser.). 1967. pap. 8.25x o.p. (ISBN 0-87263-004-8). SME.

Swinehart, James. Organic Chemistry: An Experimental Approach. (Illus., Orig.). 1969. pap. 22.95 (ISBN 0-13-640649-1). P-H.

Swinger, Marlys. Kingdom of God's Justice: As Foretold by Isaiah. 60p. (Choral edition). 1972. pap. 2.50 (ISBN 0-87486-012-1). Plough.

--Sing Through the Day: Ninety Songs for Younger Children. 3rd ed. Society Of Brothers, ed. LC 68-9673. (Illus.). (gr. 5 up). 1968. 11.95 (ISBN 0-87486-005-9). Plough.

Swinger, Peter W. Railway History in Pictures: East Anglia. (Illus.). 96p. 1983. 14.95 o.p. (ISBN 0-7153-8205-5). David & Charles.

Swingewood, Alan, jt. auth. see Laurenson, Diana T.

Swingle, P. G. Management of Power. LC 75-45316. 1976. 12.95 o.p. (ISBN 0-470-15030-0). Halsted Pr.

Swingle, Paul G., ed. Structure of Conflict. (Social Psychology Ser). 1970. 43.00 (ISBN 0-12-679160-0). Acad Pr.

Swinson, D. R. & Swinson, W. R. Rheumatology. 234p. 1980. pap. 21.95 (ISBN 0-471-08341-0, Pub. by Wiley Med). Wiley.

Swinson, W. R., jt. auth. see Swinson, D. R.

Swinton, A. Instructions to Young Naturalists: Fossils. 14.50x (ISBN 0-392-03503-0, SpS). Sportshelf.

Swinton, F. L., jt. auth. see Rowlinson, J.

Swinton, John, jt. ed. see Goldberg, Maxwell H.

Swinton, W. E. Fossil Amphibians & Reptiles. 5th ed. (Illus.). 133p. 1973. pap. 3.25x (ISBN 0-565-00543-X, Pub. by Brit Mus Nat Hist England). Sabbot-Natural Hist Bks.

--Fossil Birds. 3rd ed. (Illus.). 1975. pap. text ed. 3.25x (ISBN 0-565-05397-3, Pub. by Brit Mus Nat Hist). Sabbot-Natural Hist Bks.

Swire, Margaret R., jt. auth. see Kavaler, Florence.

Swirsky, Jessica & Vandergoot, David. A Handbook of Placement Assessment Resources. LC 79-84038. 144p. 1980. 10.00 (ISBN 0-686-38811-9). Human Res Ctr.

Swirsky, Jessica, jt. auth. see Vandergoot, David.

Swischuk, Leonard E. Emergency Radiology of the Acutely Ill or Injured Child. (Illus.). 512p. 1979. 52.00 (ISBN 0-683-08052-0). Williams & Wilkins.

--Plain Film Interpretation in Congenital Heart Disease. 2nd ed. (Illus.). 288p. 1979. pap. 33.00 (ISBN 0-683-08041-5). Williams & Wilkins.

Swisher, Doug & Richards, Carl. Fly Fishing Strategy. (Sportsmen's Classics Ser.). (Illus.). 220p. (YA) 1975. 12.95 o.p. (ISBN 0-517-52371-X). Crown.

--Fly-Fishing Strategy. write for info. N Lyons Bks.

--Selective Trout. (Illus.). 1971. 10.00 o.p. (ISBN 0-517-50304-2); pap. 7.95 o.p. (ISBN 0-517-52133-4). Crown.

--Selective Trout. write for info. N Lyons Bks.

Swisher, Robert K., Jr. Touch Me If You Love Me. (Illus.). 1976. pap. 2.95 (ISBN 0-913270-53-9). Sunstone Pr.

Swisher, Scott N., jt. auth. see Enelow, Allen J.

Swiss Office for the Development of Trade, Geneva. Swiss Export Products & Services Directory, 1983-85. 14th ed. LC 53-19872. 920p. 1982. 65.00x (ISBN 0-8002-3059-0). Intl Pubns Serv.

Swit, David & Hadley, Richard. The Practical Guide to GMP's. 60p. (Orig.). 1982. pap. 38.00 (ISBN 0-914176-17-X). Wash Busn Info.

--Product Survival: Lessons of the Tylenol Terrorism. LC 82-62917. 250p. 1982. pap. 45.00 (ISBN 0-914176-18-8). Wash Busn Info.

Switkin, Abraham. Hand Lettering Today. LC 75-25067. (Illus.). 192p. (YA) 1976. 15.34i (ISBN 0-06-014204-9, HarpT). Har-Row.

Switzer, Donna, jt. auth. see Switzer, Les.

Switzer, Ellen. Dancers! Horizons in American Dance. LC 82-1701. (Illus.). 288p. (gr. 6 up). 1982. 14.95 (ISBN 0-689-30943-0). Atheneum.

--How Democracy Failed. LC 74-19461. (gr. 5 up). 1975. 7.95 o.p. (ISBN 0-689-30459-5). Atheneum.

--There Ought to Be a Law: How Laws Are Made & Work. (Illus.). (gr. 5 up). 1972. 6.95 o.p. (ISBN 0-689-30068-9). Atheneum.

Switzer, George S., jt. auth. see Hurlbut, Cornelius S., Jr.

Switzer, Kathrine & Peterson, James A. Fit to Run: A Conditioning Handbook for Runners. LC 81-85636. (Illus.). 160p. Date not set. pap. 5.95 (ISBN 0-88011-019-8). Leisure Pr. Postponed.

Switzer, Les & Switzer, Donna. The Black Press in South Africa & Lesotho: A Descriptive Bibliographic Guide to African, Coloured & Indian Newspapers, Newsletters, & Magazines, 1836-1976. 1979. lib. bdg. 30.00 (ISBN 0-8161-8174-8, Hall Reference). G K Hall.

Switzer, Richard, jt. auth. see Koon, Helene.

Switzer, Stephen. An Introduction to a General System of Hydrostaticks & Hydraulics Philosophical & Practical. Hunt, John D., ed. LC 79-57002. 499p. 1982. lib. bdg. 88.00 (ISBN 0-8240-0161-3). Garland Pub.

Swokowski, Earl W. Elements of Calculus with Analytic Geometry. (Illus.). 636p. text ed. write for info. (ISBN 0-87150-504-5); tchr's manual 6.00 (ISBN 0-87150-507-X); write for info. calulator wkbk. (ISBN 0-686-64031-4); write for info. test bank (ISBN 0-686-64032-2); solutiions man. 15.00 (ISBN 0-87150-508-8). Prindle.

Swope, Fred C., jt. auth. see Gupton, Oscar W.

Sworder, D. D., ed. Systems & Simulation in the Service of Society. (SCS Simulation Ser.: Vol. 1, No. 2). 30.00 (ISBN 0-686-36655-7). Soc Computer Sim.

Sworder, David D. Optimal Adaptive Control Systems. (Mathematics in Science & Engineering Ser.: Vol. 25). 1966. 38.50 (ISBN 0-12-679550-9). Acad Pr.

Swords, Liam, ed. Irish-French Connection Fifteen Seventy-Eight to Nineteen Seventy-Eight. (Orig.). 1979. pap. text ed. 9.00x (ISBN 0-391-01706-3). Humanities.

Swyhart, B., ed. see Piediscalzi, N., et al.

Syatauw, J. Decisions of the International Court of Justice, a Digest. LC 62-21951. 237p. 1962. 12.00 (ISBN 0-379-00187-X). Oceana.

Sychev, V. V. Complex Thermodynamics Systems. 240p. 1981. 8.00 (ISBN 0-8285-2279-0, Pub. by Mir Pubs USSR). Imported Pubns.

Sydenham, E. A. Historical References on Coins of the Roman Empire. 1968. 20.00 (ISBN 0-685-51527-3, Pub by Spink & Son England). S J Durst.

Sydenham, Edward. The Coinage of the Roman Republic. LC 76-12921. (Illus.). 1976. Repr. of 1952 ed. lib. bdg. 30.00 (ISBN 0-915262-04-5). S J Durst.

Sydenham, M. J. The First French Republic, 1792-1804. 1974. 37.50x (ISBN 0-520-02577-6). U of Cal Pr.

Sydenham, P. H. Handbook of Measurement Science: Theoretical Fundamentals, Vol. 1. LC 81-14628. 654p. 1982. 65.00x (ISBN 0-471-10037-4, Pub. by Wiley-Interscience). Wiley.

Sydenham, Peter H. Basic Electronics for Instrumentation. Davidovici, Sorin, ed. LC 82-80222. 284p. 1982. pap. text ed. 29.95x (ISBN 0-87664-565-1). Instru Soc.

Sydney Labour History Group. What Rough Beast? 276p. 1983. text ed. 29.50 (ISBN 0-86861-332-0). Allen Unwin.

Sydney, Sheldon B. Ignore Your Teeth & They'll Go Away. (Illus.). 128p. 1982. 14.95 (ISBN 0-9607498-0-2). Devida Pubns.

Sydow, H., jt. auth. see Petrak, F.

Syed, Anwar H., ed. Polity: The Journal of the Northeastern Political Science Association. (Illus.). 150p. 15.00 (ISBN 0-686-35921-6). NE Poli Sci.

Syer, John C., jt. auth. see Culver, John H.

Syers, W. E. The Backroads of Texas. LC 79-50253. (Illus.). 176p. 1979. pap. 8.95 (ISBN 0-88415-053-4). Pacesetter Pr.

Syers, William E. The Devil Gun. LC 75-34380. 1976. 8.95 o.p. (ISBN 0-399-11670-2). Putnam Pub Group.

Sykes, A. G. Inorganic Reaction Mechanisms, Vol. 7. 460p. 1982. 250.00x (ISBN 0-85186-315-9, Pub. by Royal Soc Chem England). State Mutual Bk.

Sykes, A. G., ed. Advances in Inorganic & Bioinorganic Mechanisms, Vol. I. (Serial Publication Ser.). 1982. 67.00 (ISBN 0-12-023801-2). Acad Pr.

Sykes, Camilla, tr. see Gary, Romain.

Sykes, Christopher S. Black Sheep. (Illus.). 288p. 1983. 17.75 (ISBN 0-670-17276-6). Viking Pr.

--The Visitor's Book: A Family Album. LC 78-53402. (Illus.). 1978. 25.00 o.p. (ISBN 0-399-12212-5). Putnam Pub Group.

Sykes, D. H. Sidelights on Elizabethan Drama. 1967. Repr. of 1924 ed. text ed. 10.00x o.p. (ISBN 0-391-02050-1). Humanities.

Sykes, Gary, jt. auth. see Schaffarzick, Jon.

Sykes, Greshman. Criminology. (Illus.). 631p. 1978. text ed. 23.95 (ISBN 0-15-516120-2, HC); instructor's manual avail. (ISBN 0-15-516121-0). HarBraceJ.

Sykes, Hope W. Second Hoeing. LC 82-8424. xviii, 309p. 1982. 21.50x (ISBN 0-8032-4136-4, Bison); pap. 7.50 (ISBN 0-8032-9129-9, BB 806). U of Nebr Pr.

Sykes, J. B., ed. The Concise Oxford Dictionary of Current English. 6th ed. 1976. 19.95 o.p. (ISBN 0-19-861121-8); thumb-indexed 24.95 o.p. (ISBN 0-19-861122-6). Oxford U Pr.

Sykes, M. K., et al. Principles of Clinical Measurement. 2nd. ed. (Illus.). 336p. 1981. text ed. 48.50 (ISBN 0-632-00044-9, B 4648-0). Mosby.

Sykes, Marjorie, ed. & tr. see Bhave, Vinoba.

Sykes, S. W. & Clayton, J. P. Christ, Faith & History. LC 70-176257. (Cambridge Studies in Christology). (Illus.). 280p. 1972. 47.50 (ISBN 0-521-08451-2); pap. text ed. 12.95 (ISBN 0-521-29325-1). Cambridge U Pr.

Sykes, Stephen. The Integrity of Anglicanism. 1978. 6.00 (ISBN 0-8164-0405-4). Seabury.

Syles, W. C. Ghost Stories of Texas. 1981. 10.95 (ISBN 0-686-92301-4). Texian.

Sylliiasen, Alice. Retirement Living. 126p. pap. 6.95 (ISBN 0-910303-01-0). Writers Pub Serv.

Sylvander, Carolyn W. James Baldwin. LC 80-5338. (Literature & Life Ser.). 160p. 1981. 11.95 (ISBN 0-8044-2848-4); pap. 4.95 (ISBN 0-8044-6891-5). Ungar.

Sylvester, D. W. Robert Lowe & Education. LC 73-82446. (Cambridge Texts & Studies in the History of Education: No. 15). 260p. 1974. 34.50 (ISBN 0-521-20310-4). Cambridge U Pr.

Sylvester, David W. Captain Cook & the Pacific. Reeves, Marjorie, ed. (Then & There Ser.). (Illus.). 92p. (gr. 7-12). 1971. pap. text ed. 3.10 (ISBN 0-582-20462-3). Longman.

Sylvester, Ed & Klotz, Lynn. The Gene Age: Genetic Engineering & the Coming Biotechnical Revolution. 1982. write for info o.p. HarBraceJ.

Sylvester, Natalie. The Home-Baking Cookbook. LC 73-7494. (Illus.). 304p. 1973. 1.95 (ISBN 0-448-02208-7, 2208, G&D). Putnam Pub Group.

Sylvester, Richard S., ed. English Seventeenth-Century Verse, 2 vols. (Illus.). 720p. 1974. Vol I. pap. 6.95 o.p. (ISBN 0-393-00675-1, Norton Lib); Vol. 2. pap. 7.95 (ISBN 0-393-00676-X). Norton.

Sylvester, Sawyer F., et al. Prison Homicide. LC 77-22698. (Sociomedical Science Ser.). 1977. 12.00x o.s.i. (ISBN 0-470-99181-X). Halsted Pr.

Sylvester, William, tr. see Aeschylus & Sophocles.

Sylvia, J. Gerin. Cast Metals Technology. LC 74-153067. 1972. text ed. 21.95 (ISBN 0-201-07395-1). A-W.

Sylvia, J. Jerry. Pardon My Convicts. 384p. 1983. 15.50 (ISBN 0-682-49962-5). Exposition.

Sylvia, Richard P. Suburban Fire Fighting. (Illus.). 1969. pap. 7.25 (ISBN 0-686-12265-8). Fire Eng.

Sylvia's Home Help Series. Artistic Homes; or, How to Furnish with Taste. Stansky, Peter & Shewan, Rodney, eds. LC 76-17759. (Aesthetic Movement & the Arts & Crafts Movement Ser.). 1978. Repr. of 1881 ed. lib. bdg. 44.00x o.s.i. (ISBN 0-8240-2464-8). Garland Pub.

Sylwester, R. The Puppet & the Word. LC 12-2966. 1982. pap. 4.95 (ISBN 0-570-03873-1). Concordia.

Sym, C. A., tr. see Kolb, Albert.

Sym, C. A., tr. see Pressat, Roland.

Sym, C. A., tr. see Strich, Fritz.

Symbas, Panagiotis N. Traumatic Injuries of the Heart & Great Vessels. (Illus.). 204p. 1972. 19.75x o.p. (ISBN 0-398-02425-1). C C Thomas.

Symcox, Geoffrey, tr. see Soboul, Albert.

Syme, Daniel & Bogot, Howard. Books Are Treasures. (Illus.). 32p. 1982. pap. text ed. 4.00 (ISBN 0-8074-0160-9, 101033). UAHC.

--I'm Growing. (Illus.). 32p. (ps-1). 1982. pap. 4.00 (ISBN 0-8074-0167-6, 101095). UAHC.

Syme, G. J. & Syme, L. A. Social Structure in Farm Animals. LC 78-26088. (Developments in Animal & Veterinary Sciences Ser.: Vol. 4). 1979. 42.75 (ISBN 0-444-41769-9). Elsevier.

Syme, L. A., jt. auth. see Syme, G. J.

Syme, Ronald. Cartier: Finder of the St. Lawrence. (Illus.). (gr. 3-7). 1958. PLB 7.92 (ISBN 0-688-31146-6). Morrow.

--Columbus: Finder of the New World. (Illus.). (gr. 3-7). 1952. PLB 7.63 (ISBN 0-688-31179-2). Morrow.

--De Soto: Finder of the Mississippi. (Illus.). (gr. 3-7). 1957. PLB 8.59 (ISBN 0-688-31224-1). Morrow.

--Geronimo. LC 74-16337. (Illus.). 96p. (gr. 3-7). 1975. 8.95 (ISBN 0-688-22013-4); PLB 8.59 (ISBN 0-688-32013-9). Morrow.

--Greeks Invading the Roman Empire. (Stephen J. Brademas Lectures Ser.). 30p. (Orig.). Date not set. pap. text ed. 2.50 (ISBN 0-916586-86-3). Hellenic Coll Pr.

--John Cabot & His Son Sebastian. LC 70-168477. (Illus.). 96p. (gr. 3-7). 1972. PLB 8.59 (ISBN 0-688-31816-9). Morrow.

--John Fremont: Last American Explorer. LC 74-4198. (Illus.). 192p. (gr. 5-9). 1974. 8.75 (ISBN 0-688-20120-2); PLB 8.40 (ISBN 0-688-30120-7). Morrow.

--Magellan: First Around the World. (Illus.). (gr. 3-7). 1953. PLB 7.92 (ISBN 0-688-31594-1). Morrow.

--Osceola, Seminole Leader. LC 75-22373. (Illus.). 96p. (gr. 3-7). 1976. 8.50 (ISBN 0-688-22054-1); PLB 8.16 (ISBN 0-688-32054-6). Morrow.

--Sallust. (Sather Classical Lectures: No. 33). 1964. 37.50x (ISBN 0-520-01246-1). U of Cal Pr.

Symeonoglou, Sarantis, jt. ed. see Herbert, Kevin.

Symes, Kenneth M. Two Voices: Writing About Literature. LC 75-31015. (Illus.). 320p. 1976. pap. text ed. 10.50 (ISBN 0-395-20607-3). HM.

Symington, Nikki, jt. auth. see Cruz, Manny.

Symmes, ed. Ewbank's Indiana Criminal Law, 2 vols. 1956. with 1981 cum. suppl. 75.00 (ISBN 0-672-84086-3, Bobbs-Merrill Law); 1981 cum. suppl. 40.00 (ISBN 0-672-84282-3). Michie-Bobbs.

Symmes, Daniel, jt. auth. see Morgan, Hal.

Symmes, S. Stowell, ed. Economic Education: Links to the Social Studies. LC 81-82818. 120p. (Orig.). 1981. pap. 6.25 (ISBN 0-87986-041-3). Coun Soc Studies.

Symmons, Arthur. Arthur Symmons: Selected Writings. Holdsworth, Roger, ed. (Fyfield Ser.). 1980. 6.95 o.p. (ISBN 0-85635-087-7, Pub. by Carcanet New Pr England); pap. 4.95 o.p. (ISBN 0-85635-088-5). Humanities.

Symmons, P. M., jt. auth. see Bennett, F. V.

Symmons, P. M., jt. auth. see Hemming, C. F.

Symoens, J. J. & Hooper, S. S. Studies on Aquatic Vascular Plants: Proceedings of the International Colloquium on Aquatic Vascular Plants, Brussels. (Illus.). 424p. 1982. pap. text ed. 40.00x (ISBN 3-87429-202-9). Lubrecht & Cramer.

Symon, Keith R. Mechanics. 3rd ed. LC 75-128910. (Physics & Physical Science Ser). 1971. text ed. 30.95 (ISBN 0-201-07392-7). A-W.

Symon, Lindsay. Neurosurgery. 3rd ed. Rob, Charles & Smith, Rodney, eds. (Operative Surgery Ser). (Illus.). 1979. text ed. 139.95 (ISBN 0-407-00625-7). Butterworth.

Symonds & Zuspan. Clinical Procedures in Obstetrics. (Reproductive Medicine Ser.). 528p. 1983. price not set (ISBN 0-8247-1778-3). Dekker.

Symonds, E. M., jt. auth. see Riley, A.

Symonds, Francis A. John Robert Gregg: The Man & His Work. 1963. 12.35 (ISBN 0-07-062655-3, G). McGraw.

Symonds, John & Grant, Kenneth, eds. Magick. LC 74-24002. (Illus.). 511p. 1981. Repr. of 1973 ed. 25.00 o.p. (ISBN 0-686-81051-1). Weiser.

Symonds, John, ed. see Crowley, Aleister.

Symonds, John A. Shakespere's Predecessors in the English Drama. Repr. of 1900 ed. lib. bdg. 20.75x (ISBN 0-8371-1154-4, SYSH). Greenwood.

--Shelley. 189p. 1983. Repr. of 1879 ed. lib. bdg. write for info. Century Bookbindery.

--Sir Philip Sidney. LC 67-23878. 1968. Repr. of 1886 ed. 30.00x (ISBN 0-8103-3056-3). Gale.

Symonds, Robert W., ed. Ornamental Designs of Chippendale. (Illus.). 1949. 9.50 o.s.i. (ISBN 0-85458-578-8). Transatlantic.

Symonik, jt. auth. see Young, C.

Symons & Westcott, Alvin. Dips 'n' Doodles. LC 74-108726. (Illus.). (gr. 3-5). 1970. PLB 6.75x (ISBN 0-87783-011-8); pap. 2.95x deluxe ed. (ISBN 0-87783-090-8). Oddo.

Symons, A. Symbolist Movement in Literature. LC 79-166209. (Studies in Comparative Literature, No. 35). 1971. lib. bdg. 49.95x (ISBN 0-8383-1316-7). Haskell.

Symons, Arthur. Selected Writing. Holdsworth, Roger, ed. 98p. 1974. text ed. 7.95x (ISBN 0-85635-058-3, Pub. by Carcanet New Pr England); pap. text ed. 5.25x (ISBN 0-85635-059-1). Humanities.

Symons, C., jt. auth. see Westcott, A.

Symons, Donald. The Evolution of Human Sexuality. 1979. 24.95x (ISBN 0-19-502535-0). Oxford U Pr.

--The Evolution of Human Sexuality. 1981. pap. 7.95 (ISBN 0-19-502907-0, GB 638). Oxford U Pr.

Symons, Julian. Bland Beginning. 1979. pap. 1.95i o.p. (ISBN 0-06-080469-6, P 469, PL). Har-Row.

--The Detling Secret. 1982. cancelled (ISBN 0-89919-096-0, Kahn Bks). Ticknor & Fields.

--The Detling Secret. 228p. 1983. 14.75 (ISBN 0-670-27063-6). Viking Pr.

--Mortal Consequences: A History from the Detective Story to the Crime Novel. LC 72-138767. 269p. 1973. pap. 3.95 (ISBN 0-8052-0404-0). Schocken.

--The Plot Against Roger Rider. 192p. 1983. pap. 3.50 (ISBN 0-14-003949-X). Penguin.

--Sweet Adelaide. LC 80-7610. 288p. 1980. 13.41i (ISBN 0-06-014207-3, HarpT). Har-Row.

--The Tell-Tale Heart: The Life & Works of Edgar Allan Poe. LC 77-15881. 1978. 12.45i (ISBN 0-06-014208-1, HarpT). Har-Row.

--The Tigers of Subtopia & other Stories. 221p. 1983. 14.75 (ISBN 0-670-71283-3). Viking Pr.

Symons, Julian & Adams, Tom. Agatha Christie: The Art of Her Crimes, the Paintings of Tom Adams. (Illus.). 144p. 1982. 24.95 (ISBN 0-686-30962-6, An Everest House Book). Dodd.

Symons, Julian, ed. see Collins, Wilkie.

Symons, L. E., ed. Biology & Control of Endoparasites. LC 81-71779. 1982. 36.50 (ISBN 0-12-680120-7). Acad Pr.

Symons, Leslie. Russian Agriculture: A Geographic Survey. (Advanced Economic Geography Ser.). 1972. lib. bdg. 35.00 (ISBN 0-7135-1627-5). Westview.

Symons, Leslie & Dewdney, J. C. The Soviet Union: A Systematic Geography. LC 82-6683. (Illus.). 278p. 1983. text ed. 28.75x (ISBN 0-389-20309-2); pap. text ed. 18.75x (ISBN 0-389-20310-6). B&N Imports.

Symons, Van J. Ch'ing Ginseng Management: Ch'ing Monopolies in Microcosm. LC 80-71096. (Occasional Paper: No. 13). v, 121p. (Orig.). 1981. pap. text ed. 4.00 (ISBN 0-939252-09-0). ASU Ctr Asian.

Symposia in Applied Mathematics-New York-1959. Nuclear Reactor Theory: Proceedings, Vol. 11. Birkhoff, G. & Wigner, E. P., eds. LC 50-1183. 1961. 32.00 (ISBN 0-8218-1311-0, PSAPM-11). Am Math.

Symposia of theZoological Society of London, 43rd. Artificial Breeding of Non-Domestic Animals. Watson, P. F., ed. 1979. 47.00 (ISBN 0-12-613343-3). Acad Pr.

Symposia on Hormones & Cell Regulation (INSERM), France, 1976-79. Hormones & Cell Regulation: Proceedings, Vols. 1-4. Dumont, J. & Nunez, J., eds. 1977-79. Vol. 1. 50.75 (ISBN 0-7204-0622-6, North-Holland); Vol. 2. 71.00 (ISBN 0-7204-0658-7); Vol. 3. 48.00 (ISBN 0-7204-0672-2); Vol. 4. 62.25 (ISBN 0-444-80239-8). Elsevier.

Symposia on Infectious Disease, 7th & 8th, Wilmington, Del., 1970, 1971. Infectious Disease Reviews, Vol. 1. Holloway, William, ed. LC 72-86349. (Illus.). 200p. 1972. 14.95 o.p. (ISBN 0-87993-016-0). Futura Pub.

Symposian Applied Mathematics. Computed Tomography. Shepp, Lawrence A., ed. LC 82-18508. 20.00 (ISBN 0-8218-0033-7, PSAPM-27); pap. 14.00 (ISBN 0-686-84532-3). Am Math.

Symposium at Pittsburgh, Penn., June, 1974. Turbulence in Mixing Operations: Theory & Application to Mixing & Reaction. Brodkey, Robert S., ed. 1975. 45.00 (ISBN 0-12-134450-9). Acad Pr.

Symposium at the Centre for Research in Mathematics, University of Montreal, Sept., 1971. Applications of Number Theory to Numerical Analysis: Proceedings. Zaremba, S. K., ed. 1972. 53.50 (ISBN 0-12-775950-6). Acad Pr.

Symposium at University of Florence, Italy. The Endocrine Function of the Human Testis: Proceedings. James, V. H., et al, eds. 1973. 57.00 (ISBN 0-12-380101-X). Acad Pr.

Symposium, Brussels. Information & Prediction in Science: Proceedings. Dockx, S. & Bernays, P., eds. 1965. 52.50 (ISBN 0-12-219050-5). Acad Pr.

Symposium, Brussels, Nov. 1978. Computer-Aided Design of Digital Electronic Circuits & Systems: Proceedings. Musgrave, G., ed. 1979. 59.75 (ISBN 0-444-85374-X, North Holland). Elsevier.

Symposium, Cornell University, Ithaca, New York, Oct. 1974. Insects, Science, & Society: Proceedings. Pimentel, David, ed. 1975. 35.00 (ISBN 0-12-556550-X). Acad Pr.

Symposium Held at the Mount Desert Island Biological Laboratory, Salisbury Cove, Maine, Sept. 1974. Fluid Environment of the Brain: Proceedings. Cserr, Helen F., et al, eds. 1975. 31.50 (ISBN 0-12-197450-2). Acad Pr.

Symposium Held at the Roche Institute of Molecular Biology, Nutley, New Jersey, May, 1975. Teratomas & Differentiation: Proceedings. Sherman, Michael I. & Solter, Davor, eds. 1975. 34.50 (ISBN 0-12-639550-5). Acad Pr.

Symposium Held at the University of Nebraska Medical School, Omaha, Nebr., May, 1972. The Role of Membranes in Metabolic Regulation: Proceedings. Mehlman, Myron A. & Hanson, Richard W., eds. 1972. 54.00 (ISBN 0-12-487840-7). Acad Pr.

Symposium, Kingston, Jamaica. Hypoglycin: Proceedings. Kean, Eccleston A., ed. (PAABS Symposium Ser.). 1976. 42.00 (ISBN 0-12-404150-7). Acad Pr.

Symposium Lausanne, Switzerland Aug. 16 to 20 1976. Species Concept Hymenomycetes: Proceedings. Clemencon, H., ed. (Bibliotheca Mycologica: No. 61). (Illus.). 1978. pap. text ed. 48.00 (ISBN 3-7682-1173-8). Lubrecht & Cramer.

Symposium, Lyndon Baines Johnson Library. Equal Opportunity in the United States: A Symposium on Civil Rights: Proceedings. LC 73-620057. 185p. 1973. 3.00 (ISBN 0-89940-400-6). LBJ Sch Public Affairs.

Symposium, Michigan, 1965. Fluid Mechanics of Internal Flow: Proceedings. Sovran, Gino, ed. 1967. 56.00 (ISBN 0-444-40553-4). Elsevier.

Symposium, New Delhi, October 1978. Recent Advances in Reproduction & Regulation of Fertility: Proceedings. Talwar, G. P., ed. 1979. 86.50 (ISBN 0-444-80123-5, North Holland). Elsevier.

Symposium, New York, 1972. Neurobiological Aspects of Maturation & Ageing: Proceedings. Ford, ed. (Progress in Brain Research: Vol. 40). 535p. 1973. 131.50 (ISBN 0-444-41130-5, North Holland). Elsevier.

Symposium of Beta-Carbolines & Tetrahydroisoquinolines, La Jolla, Ca., December, 12-13, 1981 & Bloom, Floyd. Beta-Carbolines & Tetrahydroisoquinolines: Proceedings. LC 82-7789. (Progress In Clinical & Biological Research Ser.: Vol. 90). 378p. 1982. 44.00 (ISBN 0-8451-0090-4). A R Liss.

Symposium of the Birth Defects Institute of the New York State Dept. of Health, Second, October, 1971. Heredity & Society. Porter, Ian H., et al, eds. 1973. 32.00 (ISBN 0-12-562850-1). Acad Pr.

Symposium Of The Entymological Society Of America - Atlantic City - 1960. Biological Transmission of Disease Agents: Proceedings. Maramorosch, K., ed. 1962. 32.50 o.p. (ISBN 0-12-470250-3). Acad Pr.

Symposium of the International Society for the Study of Behavioral Development, University of Nijmegen, the Netherlands, July, 1971. Determinants of Behavioral Development. Monks, F. J., et al, eds. 1972. 63.00 (ISBN 0-12-504750-9). Acad Pr.

Symposium of the Society for Developmental Biology. The Cell Surface: Mediator of Developmental Processes, Vol. 38. Subtelny, Stephen & Wessels, Norman K., eds. 1980. 28.50 (ISBN 0-12-612984-3). Acad Pr.

Symposium on Advanced Fibrous Reinforced Composites, San Diego, Ca. Nov. 9-11, 1966. Proceedings. (Science of Advanced Materials & Process Engineering Ser., Vol. 10). 25.00 (ISBN 0-938994-10-7). Soc Adv Material.

Symposium on Advanced Techniques for Material Investigation & Fabrication, Cocoa Beach, Florida. Nov. 5-7, 1968. Proceedings. (Science of Advanced Materials & Process Engineering Ser., Vol. 14). 25.00 (ISBN 0-938994-14-X). Soc Adv Material.

Symposium on Advances in Biomedical Dosimetry, Vienna, 1975. Biomedical Dosimetry: Proceedings. (Illus.). 709p. 1975. pap. 63.50 (ISBN 0-686-93190-4, STI/PUB/401, IAEA). Unipub.

Symposium on Advances in Structural Composites, Anaheim, Ca. Oct. 10-12, 1967. Proceedings. (Science of Advanced Materials & Process Engineering Ser., Vol. 12). 20.00 (ISBN 0-938994-12-3). Soc Adv Material.

Symposium on Anticholinergic Drugs & Brain Functions in Animals & Man - 6th - Washington D. C., 1968. Anticholinergic Drugs & Brain Functions in Animals & Man. Bradley, P. B. & Fink, Max, eds. (Progress in Brain Research: Vol. 28). (Illus.). 1968. 50.75 (ISBN 0-444-40076-1, North Holland). Elsevier.

Symposium on Aquaculture in Africa, Accra, Ghana, 1975. Report. (CIFA Technical Papers: No. 4). 41p. 1975. pap. 7.50 (ISBN 0-686-92794-X, F738, FAO). Unipub.

Symposium on Ballistic Missile & Space Technology, 6th, Los Angeles, 1961. Ballistic Missile & Aerospace Technology: Proceedings, 4 vols. Morrow, C. T., et al, eds. Incl. Vol. 1. Design & Reliability & Invited Addresses (ISBN 0-12-507301-1); Vol. 2. Ballistic Missile & Space Electronics (ISBN 0-12-507302-X); Vol. 3. Propulsion, Space Science & Space Exploration (ISBN 0-12-507303-8); Vol. 4. Re-Entry (ISBN 0-12-507304-6). 1962. each 44.00 (ISBN 0-686-76925-2). Acad Pr.

Symposium on Biochemistry & Biophysics of Mitochondrial Membranes. Biochemistry & Biophysics of Mitochondrial Membranes: Proceedings. Azzone, G. F., ed. 1972. 59.50 (ISBN 0-12-068950-2). Acad Pr.

Symposium on Chemistry of Nucleic Acids Components, Czechoslovakia. Proceedings. (Nucleic Acids Symposium Series: No. 9). 250p. 22.00 (ISBN 0-686-79669-1). IRL Pr.

Symposium on Chemistry of Nucleic Acids Components, Tokyo. Proceedings. (Nucleic Acids Symposium Series: No. 10). 200p. 20.00 (ISBN 0-686-79670-5). IRL Pr.

Symposium on Cropping Systems Research & Development for the Asian Rice Farmer. Proceedings. 454p. 1977. pap. 20.50 (ISBN 0-686-70658-7, R004, IRRI). Unipub.

Symposium on Education & Training in Nutrition in Europe, Bad Homburg, 1959. Report. (FAO Nutrition Meetings Report Ser.: No. 26). 56p. 1960. pap. 4.50 (ISBN 0-686-92825-3, F387, FAO). Unipub.

Symposium on Energistic Materials, Chicago, Ill. May 7-9, 1968. Proceedings. (Science of Advanced Materials & Process Engineering Ser., Vol. 13). 20.00 (ISBN 0-938994-13-1). Soc Adv Material.

Symposium On Energy Metabolism, Troon Scotland, 3d, 1964. Energy Metabolism: Proceedings, No. 11. Blaxter, K. L., ed. 1965. 72.00 o.p. (ISBN 0-12-105550-7). Acad Pr.

Symposium On Ergodic Theory - New Orleans - 1961. Ergodic Theory: Proceedings. Wright, Fred B., ed. 1963. 43.50 (ISBN 0-12-765450-X). Acad Pr.

Symposium on Forest Meteorology, Ottawa, 1978. Proceedings. (WMO Pubns. Ser.: No. 527). 233p. (Eng. & Fr.). 1979. pap. 10.00 (ISBN 0-686-93912-3, WMO). Unipub.

Symposium on Functioning of Terrestrial Ecosystems at Primary Production Level, Copenhagen, 1968. Functioning of Terrestrial Ecosystems at the Primary Production Level. Eckardt, F. E., ed. (Natural Resources Research, Vol. 5). (Illus.). 1968. 31.75 o.p. (ISBN 92-3-000713-7, U259, UNESCO). Unipub.

Symposium on Fundamental Problems in Turbulence & Their Relation to Geophysics. Turbulence in Geophysics. Frenkiel, F. N., ed. LC 62-60082. (Hard cover edition of July 1962, Vol. 67, No. 8, Journal of Geophysical Research). 5.00 o.p. (ISBN 0-87590-200-6). Am Geophysical.

Symposium on Gastric Secretion, Frankfurt Am Main, 1971. Gastric Secretion. Sachs, George, ed. 1972. 54.50 (ISBN 0-12-613750-1). Acad Pr.

Symposium on General Topology & Its Relations to Modern Analysis & Algebra - 2nd - Prague - 1967. Proceedings. Novak, J., ed. 1967. 63.00 (ISBN 0-12-522556-3). Acad Pr.

Symposium on Hydrological Forecasting, Queensland, 1967. Proceedings. 325p. 1969. pap. 32.50 o.p. (ISBN 0-686-94170-5, UNESCO). Unipub.

Symposium on Infectious Disease, 10th, Wilmington, Del., 1973. Infectious Disease Reviews, Vol. 3. Holloway, William J., ed. LC 72-86349. 1974. 16.00 o.p. (ISBN 0-87993-038-1). Futura Pub.

Symposium on Infectious Disease, 9th, Wilmington, Del., 1972. Infectious Disease Reviews, Vol. 2. Holloway, William, ed. LC 72-86349. (Illus.). 1973. 15.75 o.p. (ISBN 0-87993-017-9). Futura Pub.

Symposium On Informational Macromolecules-Rutgers University, 1962. Informational Macromolecules: Proceedings. Vogel, Henry J., et al, eds. 1963. 55.00 (ISBN 0-12-722550-1). Acad Pr.

Symposium on Inhaled Particles & Vapours. Inhaled Particles: Proceedings, Vol. V. Walton, W. H., ed. (Illus.). 900p. 1982. 150.00 (ISBN 0-08-026838-2). Pergamon.

Symposium on Insulin Action, Toronto, 1971. Insulin Action: Proceedings. Fritz, Irving, ed. 1973. 63.50 (ISBN 0-12-268750-7). Acad Pr.

Symposium on Investigations & Resources of the Caribbean Sea & Adjacent Regions (CICAR) Proceedings. (FAO Fisheries Reports: No. 71.2). 353p. 1971. pap. 19.00 (ISBN 0-686-92975-6, F1678, FAO). Unipub.

Symposium On Ionospheric Physics - Alpbach - 1964. High Latitude Particles & the Ionosphere: Proceedings. Maehlum, B., ed. 1965. 58.00 (ISBN 0-12-465550-5). Acad Pr.

Symposium on Land Subsidence, Tokyo, 1969. Land Subsidence, 2 vols. (Illus., Orig.). 1970. Set. pap. 46.25 o.p. (ISBN 92-3-000832-X, U347, UNESCO). Unipub.

Symposium on Land Use in Semi-Arid Mediterranean Climates, Iraklion, 1962. Proceedings. (Arid Zone Research Ser.: No. 26). 170p. (Eng. & Fr.). 1964. pap. 14.75 o.p. (ISBN 0-686-94169-1, UNESCO). Unipub.

Symposium on Materials, 1971, Anaheim, Ca. April 20-23, 1971. Proceedings. (Science of Advanced Materials & Process Engineering Ser., Vol. 16). 25.00 (ISBN 0-938994-15-8). Soc Adv Material.

Symposium on Mechanical Behavior of Materials Under Dynamic Loads, San Antonio, 1967. Proceedings. Lindholm, U. S., ed. (Illus.). 1968. 43.10 o.p. (ISBN 0-387-04263-6). Springer-Verlag.

Symposium on Modelling & Simulation Methodology, Israel, August 1978. Methodology in Systems Modelling & Simulation: Proceedings. Zeigler, B. P., et al, eds. 1979. 76.75 (ISBN 0-444-85340-5, North Holland). Elsevier.

Symposium on Molecular Pharmacology, 3rd, Buffalo 1968, et al. Fundamental Concepts in Drug-Reactor Interaction. Danielli, J. F., ed. 261p. 1970. 48.50 (ISBN 0-12-202350-1). Acad Pr.

Symposium on New Development in Carp & Trout Nutrition, European Inland Fisheries Advisory Commission, 5th Session, Rome, 1968. Proceedings. (FAO-EIFAC Technical Papers: No. 9). 213p. 1969. pap. 14.25 (ISBN 0-686-92982-9, F755, FAO). Unipub.

Symposium on Nucleic Acids, Chemistry, 4th, Kyoto, 1976. Proceedings. (Nucleic Acids Symposium Ser.: No. 2). 156p. 16.00 (ISBN 0-686-70819-9). IRL Pr.

Symposium on Nucleic Acids Chemistry, 5th, Mishima, Japan, 1977. Proceedings. (Nucleic Acids Symposium Ser.: No. 3). 190p. 12.00 (ISBN 0-686-70820-2). IRL Pr.

Symposium on Nucleic Acids Chemistry, 6th, Nagoya, Japan, 1978. Proceedings. (No. 5). 227p. 15.00 (ISBN 0-686-70821-0). IRL Pr.

Symposium on Nucleic Acids Chemistry, 7th, Okayama, Japan, 1979. Proceedings. (Nucleic Acids Symposium Ser.: No. 6). 250p. 16.00 (ISBN 0-686-70822-9). IRL Pr.

Symposium on Photo-Electronic Image Devices - 1st see Marton, L.

Symposium on Photo-Electronic Image Devices - 2nd see Marton, L.

Symposium on Photo-Electronic Image Devices - 3rd see Marton, L.

Symposium on Photo-Electronic Image Devices - 4th see Marton, L.

Symposium on Photo-Electronic Image Devices - 5th see Marton, L.

Symposium on Recent & Fossil Marine Diatoms, First, 1972. Proceedings. Simonsen, R., ed. 1972. 60.00 (ISBN 3-7682-5439-9). Lubrecht & Cramer.

Symposium on Recent & Fossil Marine Diatoms, Second, 1974. Proceedings. Simonsen, R., ed. 1974. 100.00 (ISBN 3-7682-5445-3). Lubrecht & Cramer.

Symposium On Relaxation Methods In Relation To Molecular Structure - Aberystwyth - 1965. Molecular Relaxation Processes: Proceedings. Cross, R. C., ed. 1966. 33.50 o.p. (ISBN 0-12-150450-6). Acad Pr.

Symposium on Saline Water: a Valuable Resource. Saline Water: A Valuable Resource. (Soft cover edition of papers published in a special section of the October 1970 Water Resources Research). pap. 2.00 o.p. (ISBN 0-87590-218-9). Am Geophysical.

Symposium on Solution Mining, 1974. Proceedings. LC 73-94005. 15.00x o.p. (ISBN 0-89520-025-2). Soc Mining Eng.

Symposium on Surface Physics, 3rd, June 26-28,1974. The Solid-Vacuum Interface: Proceedings. Bootsma, G. A. & Geus, J. W., eds. 422p. 1975. Repr. 53.25 (ISBN 0-444-10828-9, North-Holland). Elsevier.

Symposium on Switch Reference & Universal Grammar. Switch Reference & Universal Grammar: Proceedings of a Symposium on Switch Reference & Universal Grammar, Winnipeg, May 1981. Haiman, John & Munro, Pamela, eds. 250p. 1982. 30.00 (ISBN 90-272-2866-3); pap. 20.00 (ISBN 90-272-2862-0). Benjamins North Am.

Symposium on the Chemistry of Nucleic Acids Components, 3rd, Czechoslovakia, 1975. Proceedings. (Nucleic Acids Symposium Ser.: No. 1). 183p. 15.00 (ISBN 0-686-70817-2). IRL Pr.

Symposium on the Chemistry of Nucleic Acids Components, 4th, Czechoslovakia, 1978. Proceedings. (Nucleic Acids Symposium Ser.: No. 4). 250p. 14.00 (ISBN 0-686-70818-0). IRL Pr.

Symposium On The Dynamics Of Fluids And Plasmas. Dynamics of Fluids & Plasmas: Proceedings. Pai, S. I., ed. 1967. 70.00 (ISBN 0-12-544250-5). Acad Pr.

Symposium on the Effects of the Space Enviornment on Materials, St. Louis, Missouri. April 19-21, 1967. Proceedings. (Science of Advanced Materials & Process Engineering Ser., Vol. 11). 20.00 (ISBN 0-938994-11-5). Soc Adv Material.

Symposium on the Major Communicable Fish Diseases in Europe & their Control. Panel Reviews & Relevant Papers. (FAO-EIFAC Technical Papers: No. 17, Suppl. 2). 255p. 1973. pap. 13.75 (ISBN 0-686-92834-2, F759, FAO). Unipub.

Symposium on the Oceanography & Fisheries Resources of the Tropical Atlantic, Abidjan, 1966. Proceedings. LC 55-4606. (Illus.). 1969. 18.75 o.p. (ISBN 92-3-000749-8, U490, UNESCO). Unipub.

Symposium on the Pituitary, Medical College of Georgia, Augusta, Georgia, May 20-22, 1976. Pituitary- A Current Review: Proceedings. Allen, Marshall B., Jr. & Mahesh, Vivenda B., eds. LC 76-53006. 1977. 48.50 (ISBN 0-12-051850-3). Acad Pr.

Symposium on the Role of Snow & Ice in Hydrology, Banff, 1972. Proceedings. (Eng. & Fr., Vol. 1, 827p.; Vol. 2, 656p.). 1973. Set. pap. 33.75 o.p. (ISBN 92-3-001146-0, UNESCO). Unipub.

Symposium on Theory of Argumentation, Groningen, October 11-13, 1978. Argumentation: Approaches to Theory Formation: Proceedings. Marten, J. L. & Barth, E. M., eds. (Studies in Language Companion Ser.: No. 8). 330p. 1982. text ed. 38.00x (ISBN 90-272-3007-2). Benjamins North Am.

Symposium on Thermophysical Properties, 6th. Proceedings. Liley, P. E., ed. 408p. 1973. pap. text ed. 24.50 o.p. (ISBN 0-685-38861-1, G00046). ASME.

Symposium on Thermophysical Properties, 8th. Thermophysical Properties of Fluids: Proceedings, 2 Vols, Vol. 1. 1981. 65.00 (100151). ASME.

--Thermophysical Properties of Solids & of Selected Fluids for Energy Technology: Proceedings, 2 Vols, Vol. 2. 1981. 65.00 (100152). ASME.

Symposium, Scandinavian Logic, 3rd. Proceedings. Kanger, S., ed. LC 74-80113. (Studies in Logic & the Foundation of Mathematics: Vol. 82). 214p. 1975. 28.00 (ISBN 0-444-10679-0, North-Holland). Elsevier.

Symposium Society of Craniofacial Genetics, 4th, San Diego. Ca., June, 1981 & Salinas, Carlos F. Crantofacial Anomalies, New Perspectives: Proceedings. LC 82-7720. (Birth Defects: Original Article Ser.: Vol. 18, No. 1). 172p. 1982. 38.00 (ISBN 0-8451-1046-2). A R Liss.

Symposium, University of California, Santa Barbara, Mar. 1975. Subject & Topic: Proceedings. Li, Charles N., ed. 1976. 48.00 (ISBN 0-12-447350-4). Acad Pr.

Symposium, University of Florida, Gainsville, March, 1975. Chromosomal Proteins & Their Role in the Regulation of Gene Expression: Proceedings. Stein, Gary S. & Kleinsmith, Lewis J., eds. 1975. 32.00 (ISBN 0-12-664750-X). Acad Pr.

Symposium, 2nd, Geneva, Aug 13-17, 1973. Joint IOC-WMO Planning Group for IGOSS (Integrated Global Ocean Station System) Proceedings. 60p. (Orig.). 1974. pap. 5.50 o.p. (ISBN 0-685-40088-3, WMO). Unipub.

Synek, Elmer, jt. auth. see Harwood, Bruce.

Synge, H. Biological Aspect of Rare Plant Conservation (Proceedings of an International Conference Held at King's College, Cambridge, England, July 14-19, 1980) LC 80-42067. 592p. 1981. 81.00 (ISBN 0-471-28004-6, Pub. by Wiley-Interscience). Wiley.

Synge, J. L. Relativity: The General Theory. 1960. 68.00 (ISBN 0-444-10279-5, North-Holland). Elsevier.

--Relativity: The Special Theory. 2nd ed. 1965. 68.00 (ISBN 0-444-10280-9, North-Holland). Elsevier.

--Talking About Relativity. 1971. 35.00 o.p. (ISBN 0-444-10076-8, North-Holland). Elsevier.

Synge, J. M. Kerry & Wicklow. 5.00 o.p. (ISBN 0-8283-1521-3). Branden.

--The Well of the Saints. Grene, Nicholas, ed. (Irish Dramatic Texts Ser.). 1982. 11.95x (ISBN 0-8132-0571-9); pap. 5.95x (ISBN 0-8132-0570-0). Cath U Pr.

Synge, John M. The Collected Works of John Millington Synge, 4 Vols. Skelton, Robin, ed. Incl. Vol. I. The Poems. Skelton, Robin, ed. LC 82-70362. 16.95x (ISBN 0-8132-0563-8); pap. 5.50x (ISBN 0-8132-0562-X); Vol. II. The Prose. Price, Alan, ed. LC 82-70363. 412p. 30.95x (ISBN 0-8132-0565-4); pap. 10.95x (ISBN 0-8132-0564-6); Vol. III. The Plays, Book 1. Saddlemyer, Ann, ed. LC 82-70364. 282p. 21.95x (ISBN 0-8132-0567-0); pap. 8.95x (ISBN 0-8132-0566-2); Vol. IV. The Plays, Book 2. Saddlemyer, Ann, ed. LC 82-70364. 394p. 30.95x (ISBN 0-8132-0569-7); pap. 10.95x (ISBN 0-8132-0568-9). (Illus.). 1982. Cath U Pr.

--Complete Plays of John M. Synge. Incl. Playboy of the Western World; Riders to the Sea; In the Shadow of the Glen; Well of the Saints; Tinker's Wedding; Deirdre of the Sorrows. 1960. pap. 3.95 (ISBN 0-394-70178-X, Vin). Random.

Synge, John M; see Schaff, Harrison H.

Synge, Lanto. Chairs in Color. (Illus.). 185p. 1980. pap. 6.95 o.p. (ISBN 0-7137-1123-X, Pub. by Blandford Pr England). Sterling.

Synge, Patrick M. The Gardens of Britain, One: Devon & Cornwall. 1977. 24.00 o.p. (ISBN 0-7134-0927-4, Pub. by Batsford England). David & Charles.

Synge, Patrick M., jt. auth. see Hay, Roy.

Synge, Ursula. The People & the Promise. LC 74-10661. 192p. (gr. 7-10). 1974. 10.95 (ISBN 0-87599-208-0). S G Phillips.

--Weland: Smith of the Gods. LC 73-5945. (Illus.). 94p. (gr. 7 up). 1973. 10.95 (ISBN 0-87599-200-5). S G Phillips.

Synhorst, Thomas J., ed. see Birmingham, Frederic A.

Synnott, Marcia G. The Half-Opened Door: Discrimination & Admissions at Harvard, Yale, & Princeton, 1900-1970. LC 78-66714. (Contributions in American History: No. 80). (Illus.). 1979. lib. bdg. 29.95x (ISBN 0-313-20617-1, SHO/). Greenwood.

Synott, William R. & Gruber, William H. Information Resource Management: Opportunities & Strategies for the 1980's. LC 81-11388. 356p. 1981. 27.95 (ISBN 0-471-09451-X, Pub. by Wiley-Interscience). Wiley.

Synovitz, R. J., jt. auth. see Schifferes, J. J.

Sypher, F. J. see Prakken, Sarah L.

Sypher, Wylie. The Ethic of Time: Structures of Experience in Shakespeare. LC 76-13844. 1976. 10.95 o.p. (ISBN 0-8264-0100-7). Continuum.

--Loss of the Self: In Modern Literature & Art. LC 78-11790. 1979. Repr. of 1962 ed. lib. bdg. 17.00x (ISBN 0-313-20759-3, SYLS). Greenwood.

Syrett, Harold C., jt. ed. see Sheehan, Donald.

Syrkin, Marie. The State of the Jews. 1980. 15.95 (ISBN 0-915220-60-1). New Republic.

Syrmia, Edmond De see De Syrmia, Edmond.

Syrop, Konrad. Spring in October: The Story of the Polish Revolution 1956. LC 75-35032. (Illus.). 207p. 1976. Repr. of 1958 ed. lib. bdg. 18.50x (ISBN 0-8371-8574-2, SYSO). Greenwood.

Syrquin, Moshe, ed. Trade, Stability, Technology & Equity in Latin America. LC 82-13890. write for info. (ISBN 0-12-680050-2). Acad Pr.

Sysler, Barry & Fox, Eugene R. Life-Time Sports for the College Student: A Behavioral Objective Approach. 3rd ed. (Illus.). 1980. pap. text ed. 9.95 (ISBN 0-8403-0462-5). Kendall-Hunt.

Systech Corporation. Emergency Medical Services Communications Design Manual. 1980. 50.00 (ISBN 0-686-37969-1). Info Gatekeepers.

Sytsma, Curt. The Rhyme & Reason of Curt Sytsma. LC 81-67557. (Illus.). 224p. 1982. 14.95 (ISBN 0-942170-05-9). CSS Pubns.

Syunyaev, R. A., ed. Soviet Scientific Reviews: Astrophysics & Space Physics Reviews, Vol. 1, Section E. 326p. 1981. 85.00 (ISBN 3-7186-0021-8). Harwood Academic.

Syunydev, R., ed. Soviet Scientific Reviews: Section E, Astrophysics & Space Physics Reviews, Vol. 1. 326p. 1981. 85.00 (ISBN 3-7186-0021-8). Harwood Academic.

Syvanen, Bob. Interior Finish. LC 82-8907. (Illus.). 128p. (Orig.). 1982. pap. 7.95 (ISBN 0-914788-56-6). East Woods.

Szabadi, E., et al. Recent Advances in the Pharmacology of Adrenoceptors: Proceedings. 1978. 77.00 (ISBN 0-444-80083-2, Biomedical Pr). Elsevier.

Szabadi, Judit, intro. by. Jozsef Rippl-Ronai. Hoch, Elizabeth, tr. (Illus.). 102p. 1980. 55.00 (ISBN 0-89893-157-6). CDP.

Szabo, Attila & Ostlund, Neil S. Modern Quantum Chemistry: Introduction to Advanced Structure Theory. LC 81-71955. 1982. 39.95 (ISBN 0-02-949710-8). Free Pr.

Szabo, Denis. Criminology & Crime Policy. LC 79-2724. 256p. 1979. 27.95x (ISBN 0-669-03217-4). Lexington Bks.

Szabo, Denis, jt. auth. see Crelinsten, Ronald D.

Szabo, Denis, jt. auth. see Parizeau, Alice.

Szabo, Denis & Katzenelson, Susan, eds. Offenders & Corrections. LC 78-8399. (Praeger Special Studies). 1978. 27.95 o.p. (ISBN 0-03-044236-2). Praeger.

Szabo, Dezso. Medical Colour Photomicrography. LC 67-9684. 1967. 15.00x (ISBN 0-8002-0850-1). Intl Pubns Serv.

Szabo, George. Masterpieces of Italian Drawing in the Robert Lehman Collection: The Metropolitan Museum of Art. (Illus.). 264p. 1983. 50.00 (ISBN 0-933920-35-0). Hudson Hills.

--Medieval Bronzes in America. LC 77-86243. (Illus.). 1983. 89.50 (ISBN 0-913870-54-4). Abaris Bks.

--The Robert Lehman Collection. LC 74-34207. (Illus.). 312p. 1975. pap. 7.50 o.p. (ISBN 0-87099-127-2). Metro Mus Art.

Szabo, LaVerne, jt. auth. see Kaplan, Alex.

Szabo, M. E. Algebra of Proofs. (Studies in Logic & the Foundations of Mathematics: Vol. 88). 1978. 55.50 (ISBN 0-7204-2286-8, North-Holland). Elsevier.

Szabo, Z. G. & Kallo, D., eds. Contact Catalysis, 2 vols. 1976. Set. 138.50 (ISBN 0-444-99852-7). Elsevier.

Szabolcsi, M. Landmark: Hungarian Writers on Thirty Years of History. 8.00x o.p. (ISBN 0-89918-289-5, H289). Vanous.

Szacki, Jerzy. History of Sociological Thought. LC 78-67566. (Contributions in Sociology: No. 35). 1979. lib. bdg. 45.00x (ISBN 0-313-20737-2, SZH/). Greenwood.

Szajkowski. Documents in Communist Affairs, 1977. 1982. text ed. 39.95 (ISBN 0-408-10818-5). Butterworth.

--Documents in Communist Affairs, 1979. 1982. text ed. 52.50 (ISBN 0-408-10819-3). Butterworth.

--Establishment of Marxist Regimes. 1982. text ed. 29.95 (ISBN 0-408-10834-7); pap. text ed. 15.95 (ISBN 0-408-10833-9). Butterworth.

Szajkowski, Bogdan, ed. Documents in Communist Affairs, 1980. LC 81-670203. 570p. 1981. text ed. 47.50x (ISBN 0-89490-063-3). Enslow Pubs.

Szaloki, Z. Textile Processing: Vol. 1: Opening, Cleaning & Picking. 1976. 19.50x (ISBN 0-87245-595-5). Textile Bk.

Szambelan-Strevinsky, Christina. Dark Hour of Noon. LC 81-48601. 224p. (YA) (gr. 7 up). 1982. 10.10i (ISBN 0-397-32013-2, JBL-J); PLB 10.89g (ISBN 0-397-32014-0). Har-Row.

Szanto, George H. Theater & Propaganda. 236p. 1978. 12.50x o.p. (ISBN 0-292-78020-6). U of Tex Pr.

Szanton, Maria C. A Right to Survive: Subsistence Marketing in a Lowland Philippine Town. LC 72-157769. (Illus.). 161p. 1973. 14.95x (ISBN 0-271-00555-6). Pa St U Pr.

Szanton, Peter. Not Well Advised. LC 80-69174. 185p. 1981. 11.95x (ISBN 0-87154-874-7). Russell Sage.

Szara, Stephen, jt. ed. see Braude, Monique C.

Szarkowski, John. American Landscapes: Photographs from the Collection of the Museum of Modern Art. 80p. 1981. 14.95 (ISBN 0-87070-206-8, 037605); pap. 7.95 (ISBN 0-87070-207-6, 037613). NYGS.

--Walker Evans. LC 71-146835. (Illus.). 1971. 19.95 (ISBN 0-87070-312-9, Pub. by Museum Mod Art); pap. 12.95 (ISBN 0-87070-313-7). NYGS.

--William Eggleston's Guide, with Essay by John Szarkowski. 1976. 19.95 (ISBN 0-262-05018-8). MIT Pr.

Szarkowski, John & Hambourg, Maria M. The Work of Atget: The Art of Old Paris, Vol. II. 1982. 40.00 (ISBN 0-87070-212-2, Pub. by Museum Mod Art). NYGS.

Szarnicki, Henry. Michael O'Conner First Catholic Bishop. (Illus.). 1975. pap. 8.95 (ISBN 0-916114-06-6). Wolfson.

Szasz, G. Y., jt. auth. see Gorog, S.

Szasz, Suzanne. Child Photography Simplified. 2nd ed. (Illus.). 1978. pap. 4.95 o.p. (ISBN 0-8174-2141-6, Amphoto); Spanish Ed. pap. 6.95 o.p. (ISBN 0-8174-0327-2). Watson-Guptill.

--Modern Wedding Photography. LC 76-16680. (Illus.). 1976. 12.95 o.p. (ISBN 0-8174-2439-3, Amphoto); pap. 9.95 (ISBN 0-8174-2411-3). Watson-Guptill.

Szasz, Thomas. The Myth of Psychotherapy. 1979. pap. 4.95 o.p. (ISBN 0-385-06663-5, Anch). Doubleday.

Szasz, Thomas S. Ideology & Insanity - Essays on the Psychiatric Dehumanization of Man. LC 72-84397. 1970. pap. 4.95 (ISBN 0-385-02033-3, A704, Anch). Doubleday.

--Law, Liberty & Psychiatry. LC 63-14187. 1968. pap. 6.95 (ISBN 0-02-074770-5, Collier). Macmillan.

--The Myth of Mental Illness: Foundations of a Theory of Personal Conduct. rev. ed. LC 73-14296. 352p. 1974. 14.37i (ISBN 0-06-014196-4, HarpT); pap. 3.50i (ISBN 0-06-080330-4, P-330). Har-Row.

Szatmary, David P. Shays' Rebellion: The Making of an Agrarian Insurrection. LC 79-22522. 1980. lib. bdg. 14.00x o.p. (ISBN 0-87023-295-9). U of Mass Pr.

Szchory, E. Night in Day. 1978. 5.95 o.p. (ISBN 0-533-03656-9). Vantage.

Szczelkun, Stefan A. Survival Scrapbook 1: Shelter. LC 73-82211. (Illus.). 130p. 1973. pap. 4.95 (ISBN 0-8052-0411-3). Schocken.

--Survival Scrapbook 3: Energy. LC 73-82211. (Illus.). 130p. 1974. 8.95x o.p. (ISBN 0-8052-3547-7). Schocken.

Szczypiorski, Andrzej. The Polish Ordeal: The View from Within. Wieniewska, Celina, tr. 154p. 1982. text ed. 17.50x (Pub. by Croom Helm Ltd England). Biblio Dist.

Sze, S. M. Physics of Semiconductor Devices. 2nd ed. LC 81-213. 868p. 1981. 47.50 (ISBN 0-471-05661-8, Pub. by Wiley-Interscience). Wiley.

--Physics of Semiconductor Devices. LC 69-16132. 1969. 46.00 o.p. (ISBN 0-471-84290-7, Pub. by Wiley-Interscience). Wiley.

--VLSI Technology. 672p. 1983. 32.50 (ISBN 0-07-062686-3, C). McGraw.

Szeftel, Marc. The Russian Constitution of April 23, 1906: Political Institutions of the Duma Monarchy. 517p. 1976. write for info. P Lang Pubs.

Szego, G., jt. auth. see Polya, G.

Szego, G. P., jt. ed. see Dixon, L. C.

Szego, Giorgio, ed. New Quantitative Techniques for Economic Analysis: Economic Theory, Econometrics & Mathematical Economics Ser. 1982. 49.50 (ISBN 0-12-680760-4). Acad Pr.

Szego, Giorgio, jt. ed. see Sarnat, Marshall.

Szego, Giorgio P. Portfolio Theory: With Application to Bank Asset. LC 79-8854. (Economic Theory, Econometrics, Mathematical Economics Ser.). 1980. 34.00 (ISBN 0-12-680780-9). Acad Pr.

Szego, Giorgio P., jt. ed. see Sarnat, Marshall S.

Szejtli, J. Cyclodextrins & Their Inclusion Complexes. Nogradi, M. & Horvath, K., trs. from Hungarian. (Illus.). 296p. 1982. 35.00x (ISBN 963-05-2850-9). Intl Pubns Serv.

Szekeley, Edmond B. Death of the New World. (Illus.). 48p. 1973. pap. 4.80 (ISBN 0-89564-026-0). Ibs Intl.

Szekely, A. Latin America & the Development of the Sea. LC 76-40510. 1976. 32.50 (ISBN 0-379-10180-7); Vol. 1 & 2. 75.00 ea.; Rel. 1. 32.00; Rel. 2. 25.00; Set. 150.00. Oceana.

Szekely, Beatrice B., ed. see Markova, A. K.

Szekely, Beatrice B., ed. see Zankov, L. V., et al.

Szekely, Edmond B. Ancient America: Paradise Lost. (Illus.). 96p. 1974. pap. 4.80 (ISBN 0-89564-025-2). IBS Intl.

--Archeosophy: A New Science. (Illus.). 32p. 1973. pap. 4.80 (ISBN 0-89564-057-0). IBS Intl.

--The Art of Study: The Sorbonne Method. (Illus.). 40p. 1973. pap. 3.50 (ISBN 0-89564-065-1). IBS Intl.

--Biogenic Meditation: Biogenic Self-Analysis, Creative Microcosmos. (Illus.). 40p. 1978. pap. 1.80 (ISBN 0-89564-051-1). IBS Intl.

--Biogenic Reducing: The Wonder Week. (Illus.). 56p. 1977. pap. 3.80 (ISBN 0-89564-055-4). IBS Intl.

--The Book of Herbs. (Illus.). 48p. 1981. pap. 2.95 (ISBN 0-89564-044-9). IBS Intl.

--The Book of Minerals. (Illus.). 40p. 1978. pap. 2.95 (ISBN 0-89564-046-5). IBS Intl.

--The Book of the Living Foods. (Illus.). 56p. 1977. pap. 3.50 (ISBN 0-89564-039-2). IBS Intl.

--The Book of Vitamins. (Illus.). 40p. 1978. pap. 2.95 (ISBN 0-89564-045-7). IBS Intl.

--Books, Our Eternal Companions. (Illus.). 48p. 1971. pap. 3.50 (ISBN 0-89564-064-3). IBS Intl.

--Brother Tree. (Illus.). 32p. 1977. pap. 3.50 (ISBN 0-89564-074-0). IBS Intl.

--The Chemistry of Youth. (Search for the Ageless Ser.: Vol. 3). (Illus.). 184p. 1977. pap. 7.50 (ISBN 0-89564-024-4). IBS Intl.

--The Conquest of Death. 68p. 1973. pap. 2.95 (ISBN 0-89564-043-0). IBS Intl.

--Cosmos, Man & Society. 152p. 1973. pap. 5.80 (ISBN 0-89564-070-8). IBS Intl.

--The Cosmotherapy of the Essenes. (Illus.). 64p. 1975. pap. 3.50 (ISBN 0-89564-012-0). IBS Intl.

--Creative Exercises for Health & Beauty. (Illus.). 48p. 1976. pap. 3.50 (ISBN 0-89564-048-1). IBS Intl.

--Creative Work: Karma Yoga. (Illus.). 32p. 1973. pap. 2.95 (ISBN 0-89564-066-X). IBS Intl.

--The Dialectical Method of Thinking. (Illus.). 40p. 1973. pap. 2.95 (ISBN 0-89564-063-5). IBS Intl.

--The Discovery of the Essene Gospel of Peace: The Essenes & the Vatican. (Illus.). 96p. 1977. pap. 4.80 (ISBN 0-89564-004-X). IBS Intl.

--The Ecological Health Garden & the Book of Survival. (Illus.). 80p. 1978. pap. 4.50 (ISBN 0-89564-072-4). IBS Intl.

--The Essene Book of Asha: Journey to the Cosmic Ocean. (Illus.). 140p. 1976. pap. 7.50 (ISBN 0-89564-008-2). IBS Intl.

--The Essene Book of Creation. (Illus.). 86p. 1975. pap. 4.50 (ISBN 0-89564-005-8). IBS Intl.

--The Essene Code of Life. (Illus.). 44p. 1978. pap. 3.50 (ISBN 0-89564-013-9). IBS Intl.

--The Essene Communions with the Infinite. (Illus.). 64p. 1979. pap. 3.95 (ISBN 0-89564-009-0). IBS Intl.

--The Essene Gospel of Peace, Bk. 1. (Illus.). 72p. 1981. pap. 1.00 (ISBN 0-89564-000-7). IBS Intl.

--The Essene Gospel of Peace, Bk. 2. (Illus.). 132p. 1981. pap. 5.80 (ISBN 0-89564-001-5). IBS Intl.

--The Essene Gospel of Peace, Bk. 3: Lost Scrolls of the Essene Brotherhood. (Illus.). 144p. 1981. pap. 5.60 (ISBN 0-89564-002-3). IBS Intl.

--The Essene Gospel of Peace, Bk. 4: Teachings of the Elect. (Illus.). 40p. 1981. pap. 4.50 (ISBN 0-89564-003-1). IBS Intl.

--The Essene Jesus. (Illus.). 72p. 1977. pap. 4.50 (ISBN 0-89564-007-4). IBS Intl.

--The Essene Origins of Christianity. (Illus.). 184p. 1981. pap. 8.50 (ISBN 0-89564-015-5). IBS Intl.

--The Essene Science of Fasting & the Art of Sobriety. (Illus.). 48p. 1981. pap. 3.50 (ISBN 0-89564-011-2). IBS Intl.

--The Essene Science of Life. (Illus.). 64p. 1976. pap. 3.50 (ISBN 0-89564-010-4). IBS Intl.

--The Essene Teachings of Zarathurstra. (Illus.). 32p. 1974. pap. 2.95 (ISBN 0-89564-016-3). IBS Intl.

--The Essene Way: Biogenic Living. (Illus.). 200p. 1981. pap. 8.80 (ISBN 0-89564-019-8). IBS Intl.

--The Essene Way: World Pictures & Cosmic Symbols. (Illus.). 40p. 1978. pap. 1.80 (ISBN 0-89564-050-3). IBS Intl.

--The Essenes, by Josephus & His Contemporaries. (Illus.). 32p. 1981. pap. 2.95 (ISBN 0-89564-014-7). IBS Intl.

--The Evolution of Human Thought. (Illus.). 44p. 1971. pap. 2.50 (ISBN 0-89564-062-7). IBS Intl.

--Father, Give Us Another Chance. (Illus.). 62p. 1969. pap. 6.80 (ISBN 0-89564-071-6). IBS Intl.

--The Fiery Chariots. (Illus.). 96p. 1971. pap. 4.80 (ISBN 0-89564-017-1). IBS Intl.

--The First Essene. (Illus.). 240p. 1981. pap. 9.50 (ISBN 0-89564-018-X). IBS Intl.

--The Game of the Gods. (Illus.). 24p. 1973. pap. 3.95 (ISBN 0-89564-029-5). IBS Intl.

--The Great Experiment. (Search for the Ageless Ser.: Vol. 2). (Illus.). 328p. 1977. pap. 8.80 (ISBN 0-89564-023-6). IBS Intl.

--The Greatness in the Smallness. (Illus.). 192p. 1978. pap. 7.50 (ISBN 0-89564-052-X). IBS Intl.

--Healing Waters. (Illus.). 64p. 1976. pap. 3.50 (ISBN 0-89564-049-X). IBS Intl.

--I Came Back Tomorrow. (Illus.). 32p. 1976. pap. 3.50 (ISBN 0-89564-073-2). IBS Intl.

--The Living Buddha. (Illus.). 70p. 1977. pap. 4.50 (ISBN 0-89564-059-7). IBS Intl.

--Ludwig Van Beethoven: Prometheus of the Modern World. (Illus.). 24p. 1973. pap. 2.95 (ISBN 0-89564-060-0). IBS Intl.

--Man in the Cosmic Ocean. (Illus.). 56p. 1970. pap. 3.50 (ISBN 0-89564-054-6). IBS Intl.

--My Unusual Adventures on the Five Continents in Search for the Ageless. (Search for the Ageless Ser.: Vol. 1). (Illus.). 212p. 1977. pap. 7.80 (ISBN 0-89564-022-8). IBS Intl.

--The New Fire. (Illus.). 140p. 1973. pap. 4.80 (ISBN 0-89564-028-7). IBS Intl.

--Northern Summer. (Illus.). 32p. 1972. pap. 4.80 (ISBN 0-89564-030-9). IBS Intl.

--Pilgrim of the Himalayas. (Illus.). 32p. 1974. pap. 2.95 (ISBN 0-89564-061-9). IBS Intl.

--The Preventive Diet for Heart & Overweight. (Illus.). 48p. 1977. pap. 3.50 (ISBN 0-89564-040-6). IBS Intl.

--Scientific Vegetarianism. (Illus.). 56p. 1977. pap. 2.95 (ISBN 0-89564-041-4). IBs Intl.

--Sexual Harmony. (Illus.). 60p. 1977. pap. 3.50 (ISBN 0-89564-077-5). IBS Intl.

--The Soul of Ancient Mexico. (Illus.). 136p. 1968. pap. 7.50 (ISBN 0-89564-027-9). IBS Intl.

--Talks By Edmond Bordeaux Szekely. 48p. 1972. pap. 2.95 (ISBN 0-89564-067-8). IBS Intl.

--The Teachings of the Essenes from Enoch to the Dead Sea Scrolls. (Illus.). 112p. 1981. pap. 4.80 (ISBN 0-89564-006-6). IBS Intl.

--The Tender Touch: Biogenic Fulfillment. (Illus.). 120p. 1977. text ed. 5.50 (ISBN 0-89564-020-1). IBS Intl.

--Toward the Conquest of the Inner Cosmos. (Illus.). 64p. 1969. pap. 6.80 (ISBN 0-89564-053-8). IBS Intl.

--Treasury of Raw Foods. (Illus.). 48p. 1981. pap. 2.95 (ISBN 0-89564-042-2). IBS Intl.

--The Zend Avesta of Zarathustra. (Illus.). 100p. 1973. pap. 4.80 (ISBN 0-89564-058-9). IBS Intl.

Szekely, Edmond B. & Bordeaux, Norma N. Messengers from Ancient Civilizations. (Illus.). 44p. (gr. 5 up). 1974. pap. 3.50 (ISBN 0-89564-068-6). IBS Intl.

Szekely, Julian. Alternative Energy Sources for the Steel Industry: Proceedings of the Sixth C. C. Furnas Memorial Conference, Vol. 5. 1977. 21.75 o.p. (ISBN 0-8247-6502-8). Dekker.

Szekely, Julian & Themelis, Nickolas J. Rate Phenomena in Process Metallurgy. LC 72-140554. 784p. 1971. 62.50x (ISBN 0-471-84303-2, Pub. by Wiley-Interscience). Wiley.

Szekely, Julian, jt. auth. see Ray, Willis H.

Szekely, Julian, ed. The Steel Industry & the Energy Crises. (C. C. Furnas Memorial Conference Proceedings Ser.: Vol. 3). 136p. 1975. 23.50 o.p. (ISBN 0-8247-6270-3). Dekker.

--The Steel Industry & the Environment. (C. C. Furnas Memorial Conference Proceedings Ser.: Vol. 2). 312p. 1973. 49.50 o.p. (ISBN 0-8247-6040-9). Dekker.

Szekely, Maria. Gene Structure & Organization. Date not set. pap. 6.50x o.p. (ISBN 0-412-22840-8, Pub. by Chapman & Hall). Methuen Inc.

Szekeres, Cyndy. Cyndy Szekeres' ABC. LC 82-839989. (A Golden Sturdy Bk.). (Illus.). 22p. 1983. 3.95 (ISBN 0-307-12120-8, Golden Pr). Western Pub.

--Long Ago. LC 76-56113. (Illus.). 1977. 8.95 (ISBN 0-07-062665-0, GB). McGraw.

Szekeres, L. & Papp, J. Gy., eds. Symposium on Drugs & Heart Metabolism, Vol. 2. (Hungarian Pharmacological Society, First Congress Ser.). (Illus.). 369p. 1973. 25.00x (ISBN 0-8002-3044-2). Intl Pubns Serv.

Szelenyi, Ivan, jt. auth. see Konrad, George.

Szenberg, Michael, et al. Welfare Effects of Trade Restrictions: A Case Study of the U. S. Footwear Industry. 1977. 30.50 (ISBN 0-12-681050-8). Acad Pr.

Szentagothai, J., et al. Regulatory Functions of the CNS- Motion & Organization Principles: Proceedings of the 28th International Congress of Physiological Sciences, Budapest, 1980. LC 80-4188. (Advances in Physiological Sciences: Vol. 1). (Illus.). 300p. 1981. 35.00 (ISBN 0-08-026814-5). Pergamon.

Szentagothai, John & Arbib, Michael A. Conceptual Models of Neural Organization. LC 75-18837. 510p. 1975. text ed. 17.50x o.p. (ISBN 0-262-19144-X). MIT Pr.

Szentirmai, George, ed. Computer Aided Filter Design. LC 73-85482. (Illus.). 448p. 1973. 14.45 (ISBN 0-87942-030-8). Inst Electrical.

Szent-Miklosy, Istvan. Atlantic Union Movement: Significance in World Politics. (Illus.). 264p. 1983. Repr. 17.95x (ISBN 0-685-41740-9). Irvington.

Szeri. Tribology: Friction, Lubrication & Wear. 1980. 42.00 (ISBN 0-07-062663-4). McGraw.

Szerny, Carl, jt. auth. see Mitchell, Alice.

Szewczyk, David M., compiled by. A Calendar of the Peruvian & Other South American Manuscripts in the Philip H. & A. S. W. Rosenbach Foundation, 1536-1914. (Illus.). 190p. 1977. 15.00x (ISBN 0-939084-06-6, Pub. by Rosenbach Mus & Lib). U Pr of Va.

Szewczyk, David M., ed. Peruvian & Other South American Manuscripts in the Rosenbach Foundation: 1536-1914. 1977. 15.00 (ISBN 0-939084-06-6, Dist. by U Pr of Va). Rosenbach Mus and Lib.

--The Vice Royalty & New Spain & Early Independent Mexico: A Guide to Original Manuscripts in the Collections of the Rosenbach Museum & Library. 1981. 17.50 (ISBN 0-939084-00-7, Dist. by U Pr of Va). Rosenbach Mus & Lib.

Szichman, Mario. A las Viente, Veinte-cicno, la senora entro en la Inmortalidad. 292p. (Span.). 1981. pap. 7.50 (ISBN 0-910061-02-5). Ediciones Norte.

Szikla, G. Stereotactic Cerebral Irradiation. (Inserm Symposium Ser.: No. 12). 1980. 63.50 (ISBN 0-444-80180-4). Elsevier.

Szilagye, Robert J. & Monroe, Stanley. The Trident Tragedy. (Orig.). 1983. pap. 3.75 (ISBN 0-440-18769-9). Dell.

Szilagyi, Andrew. Management & Performance. 1981. text ed. 25.95x (ISBN 0-673-16101-3). Scott F.

Szilagyi, Andrew D., Jr. & Wallace, Marc J., Jr. Organizational Behavior & Performance. 2nd ed. 1980. text ed. 24.50x (ISBN 0-673-16124-2). Scott F.

Szilagyi, Andrew D., Jr. & Wallace, Marc J. Organizational Behavior & Performance. 3rd ed. 1983. text ed. 24.95x (ISBN 0-673-16572-8). Scott F.

Szilagyi, Andrew D., Jr. & Wallace, Marc J., Jr. Reader for Organizational Behavior & Performance. 1983. pap. text ed. 12.95x (ISBN 0-673-16573-6). Scott F.

Szilagyi, Andrew D., Jr. & Wallace, Marc J. Readings in Organizational Behavior & Performance. 2nd ed. 1980. pap. text ed. 14.50x (ISBN 0-673-16125-0). Scott F.

Szilagyi, Andrew D., Jr., jt. auth. see Wallace, Marc J., Jr.

Szilard. The Voice of the Dolphins. 1961. pap. 1.95 o.p. (ISBN 0-671-79261-X, Touchstone Bks). S&S.

Szilard, Gertrud W., ed. see Szilard, Leo.

Szilard, Gertrud W., jt. ed. see Weart, Spencer.

Szilard, J. Ultrasonic Testing. LC 80-41592. 648p. 1982. 85.00x (ISBN 0-471-27938-2, Pub. by Wiley-Interscience). Wiley.

Szilard, Leo. Collected Works of Leo Szilard: Scientific Papers. Feld, Bernard T. & Szilard, Gertrud W., eds. 1972. 35.00x (ISBN 0-262-06039-6). MIT Pr.

--Voice of the Dolphins & Other Stories. (Orig.). 1960. 3.95 o.p. (ISBN 0-671-79260-1). S&S.

Szilard, Paula & Woo, Juliana J. The Electric Vegetarian. LC 80-83141. 224p. (Orig.). 1982. pap. 9.95 (ISBN 0-89815-058-2). Ten Speed Pr.

Szilard, Rudolph, ed. Hydromechanically Loaded Shells: Proceedings of the 1971 Symposium of the International Association for Shell Structures. LC 72-93559. (Illus.). 900p. 1973. text ed. 60.00x (ISBN 0-8248-0264-0). UH Pr.

Szilvasy, Linda. The Jeweled Egg. (Illus.). 1976. pap. 9.95 o.s.i. (ISBN 0-8096-1916-4, Assn Pr). Follett.

Szinovacz, Maximiliane. Women's Retirement: Policy Implications of Recent Research. (Sage Yearbooks in Women's Policy Studies). (Illus.). 320p. 1982. 25.00 (ISBN 0-8039-1894-1); pap. 12.50 (ISBN 0-8039-1895-X). Sage.

Szirmai, E., ed. Nuclear Hematology. 1965. 73.00 (ISBN 0-12-681650-6). Acad Pr.

Szirtes, George. November & May. 1981. 11.50 (ISBN 0-436-50998-9, Pub. by Secker & Warburg). David & Charles.

Szitnyay, Z. Hol Van a Nemzet? 1982. 14.00 o.p. (ISBN 0-936398-12-4). Framo Pub.

Szladits, Charles. Guide to Foreign Legal Materials: French, German, Swiss. LC 59-8608. (Parker School Studies in Foreign & Comparative Law). 599p. 1959. 30.00 (ISBN 0-379-11751-7). Oceana.

Szladits, Charles, ed. A Bibliography of Foreign & Comparative Law: Books & Articles in English, 1953-79, Supplements 1972, 73, 74-79, 5 vols., 7 supplements. LC 80-29035. 1978. Vol. 1 & 2; 1953, 1953-59, 1960-65, 1966-71. lib. bdg. 40.00 ea.; Vol. 1-3; 1972-77. 75.00 ea.; Supplements 1972-74. 15.00 ea.; Supplements 1975-76. 17.50 ea.; Supplements 1978-79. 22.50 ea.; Set. write for info. (ISBN 0-379-14040-3). Oceana.

Szladits, Lola L. Documents, Famous & Infamous: Selected from the Berg Collection of English & American Literature. (Illus.). 34p. 1972. pap. 3.00 o.p. (ISBN 0-87104-240-1). NY Pub Lib.

--Independence: A Literary Panorama 1770-1850. LC 75-23262. (Illus.). 72p. (Orig.). 1975. pap. 7.50 o.p. (ISBN 0-87104-260-6). NY Pub Lib.

--New in the Berg Collection 1965-1969. (Illus.). 1971. pap. 3.00 o.p. (ISBN 0-87104-225-8). NY Pub Lib.

--New in the Berg Collection 1970-1972. LC 73-81334. (Illus.). 76p. 1973. pap. 4.00 o.p. (ISBN 0-87104-244-4). NY Pub Lib.

--Nineteen Twenty-Two: a Vintage Year: A Selection of Works from the Berg Collection. (Illus.). 36p. 1972. 5.00 o.p. (ISBN 0-87104-234-7). NY Pub Lib.

--Owen D. Young, Book Collector. LC 74-83044. (Illus.). 48p. 1974. pap. 6.00 o.p. (ISBN 0-87104-253-3). NY Pub Lib.

Szladits, Lola L. & Simmonds, Harvey. Pen & Brush: The Author As Artist: An Exhibition in the Berg Collection. LC 71-92623. (Illus.). 1969. pap. 7.00 (ISBN 0-87104-142-1). NY Pub Lib.

Szladits, Lola L., ed. Charles Dickens, Eighteen Twelve - Eighteen Seventy: An Anthology from Materials in the Berg Collection. LC 77-127001. 1970. 15.00 o.p. (ISBN 0-87104-229-0); pap. 7.00 o.p. (ISBN 0-87104-051-4). NY Pub Lib.

--Other People's Mail: Letters of Men & Women of Letters Selected from the Henry W. & Albert A. Berg Collection of English & American Literature. LC 73-88373. (Illus.). 96p. 1973. pap. 8.50 o.s.i. (ISBN 0-87104-245-2). NY Pub Lib.

Szladits, Lola L. Arrivals in the Berg Collection, 1973-1975. (Illus.). 1976. pap. 4.00 o.p. (ISBN 0-87104-267-3). NY Pub Lib.

Szogyi, Alex, jt. auth. see Mankin, Paul.

Szoka, Kathryn, jt. auth. see Filley, Richard D.

Szostak, John M. & Leighton, Frances S. In the Footsteps of Pope John Paul II. LC 80-20258. 1980. 11.95 o.p. (ISBN 0-13-476002-6). P-H.

Szporluk, Roman. Ukraine: A Brief History. 2nd ed. LC 79-46644. 1982. pap. 6.50 (ISBN 0-686-43265-7). Cataract Pr.

Sztompka, Piotr. Sociological Dilemmas: Toward a Dialectic Paradigm. LC 79-51686. 1979. 28.50 (ISBN 0-12-681860-6). Acad Pr.

--System & Function: Toward a Theory of Society. 1974. 31.50 (ISBN 0-12-681850-9). Acad Pr.

Szucs, E. Similitude & Modelling. LC 79-10177. (Fundamental Studies in Engineering: Vol. 2). 336p. 57.50 (ISBN 0-444-99780-6). Elsevier.

Szuladzinski, Gregory. Dynamics of Structures & Machinery: Problems & Solutions. LC 80-10487. 297p. 1982. 47.95 (ISBN 0-471-09027-1, Pub. by Wiley Interscience). Wiley.

Szulc, Tad, ed. The United States & the Caribbean. LC 79-140265. 1970. 5.95 o.p. (ISBN 0-13-938555-X); pap. 2.45 o.p. (ISBN 0-13-938548-7). Am Assembly.

Szulec, Jeannette A. & Szulec, Z. Syllabus for the Surgeon's Secretary. 3rd ed. (Illus.). 1113p. 1980. 57.50 (ISBN 0-913092-03-7); wholesale, includes shipping 48.50. Medical Arts.

Szulec, Z., jt. auth. see Szulec, Jeannette A.

Szuprowicz, Bohdan O. How to Avoid Strategic Material Shortages Dealing with Cartels, Embargoes & Supply Disruptions. LC 80-24431. 312p. 1981. 32.50 (ISBN 0-471-07843-3, Pub. by Wiley-Interscience). Wiley.

Szuprowicz, Bohdan O. & Szuprowicz, Maria R. Doing Business with People's Republic of China: Industries & Markets. 449p. 1978. 43.95 (ISBN 0-471-03389-8, Pub. by Wiley-Interscience). Wiley.

Szuprowicz, Maria R., jt. auth. see Szuprowicz, Bohdan O.

Szuts, Ete Z., jt. auth. see Fein, Alan.

Szwarc, Michael. Carbanions Living Polymers & Electron Transfer Processes. LC 67-13964. 695p. 1968. 39.00 (ISBN 0-470-84305-5, Pub. by Wiley). Krieger.

Szwed, John F., jt. ed. see Abrahams, Roger D.

Szydlowski, Mary V. Silent Song. LC 79-92184. 192p. 1980. 8.95 o.p. (ISBN 0-89696-070-6, An Everest House Book). Dodd.

Szykitka, Walter, ed. How to Be Your Own Boss: The Complete Handbook for Starting & Running a Small Business. 1978. pap. 6.95 (ISBN 0-452-25303-9, Z5303, Plume). NAL.

Szyliowicz, Joseph S. Technology & International Affairs. 302p. 1981. 32.95 (ISBN 0-03-053321-X). Praeger.

Szymanski, A., jt. ed. see Jakowlew, B.

Szymanski, Albert. Is the Red Flag Flying? The Political Economy of the Soviet Union Today. 236p. (Orig.). 1979. 17.95 (ISBN 0-905762-35-5, Pub. by Zed Pr England); pap. 7.95 (ISBN 0-905762-36-3, Pub. by Zed Pr England). Lawrence Hill.

Szymanski, Jeanette R. Ecrivons les Verbes - Let's Write Verbs. LC 78-60629. 1978. pap. text ed. 9.00 o.p. (ISBN 0-8191-0560-0). U Pr of Amer.

Szymanski, Ladislas, jt. auth. see Goldman, Norma.

Szymanski, Leszek. Kazimierz Pulaski In America: 1777-1779. LC 79-52916. 34.95x (ISBN 0-89370-060-6). Borgo Pr.

Szymanski, Michael, jt. auth. see Hetzel, Otto.

T

T. F. H. Staff & Doherty, Filomena. Pugs. (Illus.). 128p. 1981. 4.95 (ISBN 0-87666-725-6, KW-104). TFH Pubns.

Taaffe, Edward & Gauthier, Howard L. Geography of Transportation. (Foundations of Economic Geography Ser.). (Illus.). 224p. 1973. pap. 12.95 ref. ed. (ISBN 0-13-351387-4). P-H.

Taaffe, Edward J. & Garner, Barry J. The Peripheral Journey to Work: A Geographic Consideration. 125p. 1963. pap. 1.50 (ISBN 0-686-94038-5, Trans). Northwestern U Pr.

Taaffe, Edward J., ed. see Bach, Wilfrid.

Taaffe, Robert N. & Kingsbury, Robert. Atlas of Soviet Affairs. 1983. price not set (ISBN 0-89158-772-1); pap. 6.95 (ISBN 0-89158-898-1). Westview.

Taagepera, Rein, jt. auth. see Misiunas, Romuald J.

Taam, C. T., ed. see Glimm, J., et al.

Tabachnick, B. Robert, jt. auth. see Popkewitz, Thomas S.

Tabachnick, Barbara G. & Fidell, Linda S. Using Multivariate Statistics. 509p. 1982. text ed. 18.95 scp (ISBN 0-06-042045-6, HarpC). Har-Row.

Tabachnick, Stephen E. Charles Doughty. (English Authors Ser.). 1981. lib. bdg. 13.95 (ISBN 0-8057-6790-8, Twayne). G K Hall.

--T. E. Lawrence. (English Authors Ser.). 1978. lib. bdg. 12.95 (ISBN 0-8057-6704-5, Twayne). G K Hall.

Tabachnick, WAlter, jt. ed. see Steiner, Walter.

T. Abajian, James de, ed. Blacks in Selected Newspapers, Censuses & Other Sources, an Index to Names & Subjects. 1977. lib. bdg. 320.00 (ISBN 0-8161-0056-X, Hall Library). G K Hall.

Tabaka-Juedes, Elizabeth. Concept Formation: Steps Up to Language for the Learning Impaired. 56p. 1978. pap. text ed. 7.95 (ISBN 0-88450-770-X, 3082-B). Communication Skill.

Tabakoff, W., ed. Particular Laden Flows in Tubomachinery. 150p. 1982. 30.00 (G00210). ASME.

Tabakov, George A. Medicine in the United States & the Soviet Union. 1962. 5.95 o.p. (ISBN 0-8158-0194-7). Chris Mass.

Tabaraud, M. M. De la Philosophie de la Henriade. Repr. of 1805 ed. 42.00 o.p. (ISBN 0-8287-0800-2). Clearwater Pub.

Tabarly, Eric. Ocean Racing. LC 71-163378. (Illus.). 1972. 10.00 o.p. (ISBN 0-393-03174-8). Norton.

Tabarrok, B., jt. ed. see Rimrott, F. P.

Tabataba'I, Muhammad H., ed. see Muhammad.

Tabb, William K. & Sawers, Larry, eds. Marxism & the Metropolis: New Perspectives in Urban Political Economy. 1978. pap. text ed. 9.95x (ISBN 0-19-502262-9). Oxford U Pr.

Tabberner, Jeffrey, tr. see Delessert, Etienne.

Taber, Anthony. Night Cats. (Illus.). 64p. Date not set. 9.95 (ISBN 0-312-92571-9). Congdon & Weed. Postponed.

Taber, Charles R., jt. ed. see Yamamori, Tetsunao.

Taber, Gladys. Amber, a Very Personal Cat. 160p. 1983. pap. 5.95 (ISBN 0-940160-20-X). Parnassus Imprints.

--Another Path. LC 63-17678. 1963. 9.57i (ISBN 0-397-00260-2). Har-Row.

--The Best of Stillmeadow: A Treasury of Country Living. Colby, Constance T., intro. by. LC 76-20457. (Illus.). 1976. 13.41i (ISBN 0-397-01156-3). Har-Row.

--Conversations with Amber. LC 77-27903. (Illus.). 1978. 8.95i (ISBN 0-397-01260-8). Har-Row.

--Harvest of Yesterdays. LC 75-44003. 1976. 7.95 o.p. (ISBN 0-397-01133-4). Har-Row.

--My Own Cook Book: From Stillmeadow & Cape Cod. LC 72-747. (Illus.). 1972. 8.95i (ISBN 0-397-00877-5). Har-Row.

--Stillmeadow Cook Book. 336p. 1983. pap. 9.95 (ISBN 0-940160-18-8). Parnassus Imprints.

Taber, M. R., jt. auth. see Tedeschi, F. P.

Taber, Margaret R. & Silgalis, Eugene. Electric Circuit Analysis. LC 78-69525. (Illus.). 1980. text ed. 24.95 (ISBN 0-395-26706-4); instr's. manual 1.05 (ISBN 0-395-26707-2). HM.

Taber, Michael, ed. see Castro, Fidel.

Taber, Regi, ed. see Taber, Tom.

Taber, Tom. Where to see Wildlife in California. Taber, Regi, ed. (Illus.). 112p. 1983. pap. write for info (ISBN 0-9609170-1-2). Oak Valley.

Tabor, D. Gases, Liquids & Solids. 2nd ed. LC 78-26451. (Illus.). 1980. 57.50 (ISBN 0-521-22383-0); pap. 16.95 (ISBN 0-521-29466-5). Cambridge U Pr.

Tabor, Edward. Infectious Complications of Blood Tranfusion. 1982. 24.50 (ISBN 0-12-682140-2). Acad Pr.

Tabor, Margaret. The Baker's Daughter. LC 78-25692. 1979. 8.95 o.p. (ISBN 0-698-10973-2, Coward). Putnam Pub Group.

Tabor, Margaret E. Saints in Art. LC 68-18031. (Illus.). 1969. Repr. of 1908 ed. 30.00x (ISBN 0-8103-3076-8). Gale.

Tabor, Michael, ed. see AIP Conference, 88th, La Jolla Institute, 1981.

Tabor, Stephen, jt. auth. see Sagar, Keith.

Tabori, Lena, jt. ed. see Lahr, Jane.

Tabori, Paul. Lily Dale. 256p. 1982. pap. cancelled (ISBN 0-505-51853-8). Tower Bks.

Tacchi, Derek. Ovarian Gynaecology. LC 76-26778. (Illus.). 1976. text ed. 10.00 (ISBN 0-7216-8725-3). Saunders.

Taccola, Mariano. DeMachinis: The Engineering Treatise of 1449, 2 vols. 1971. 272.50x (ISBN 3-920153-05-7). Intl Pubns Serv.

Tacey, William S. Business & Professional Speaking. 4th ed. 1983. pap. text ed. write for info. (ISBN 0-697-04235-9). Wm C Brown.

Talbert, Peter, tr. Tracy Austin: Tennis Wonder. LC 79-11914. (Illus.). (gr. 7-12). 1979. 8.95 (ISBN 0-399-20689-2); pap. 3.95 o.p.- (ISBN 0-399-20729-5). Putnam Pub Group.

Talbert, R J. Timoleon & the Revival of Greek Cicily, 344-317 BC. 248p. 1974. 24.95 (ISBN 0-521-20419-4). Cambridge U Pr.

Talbert, Robert, jt. auth. see Porterfield, Austin.

Talbert, William F. & Old, Bruce S. The Game of Doubles in Tennis. (Illus.). 214p. 1977. 5.95 o.p. (ISBN 0-686-37484-3). USTA.

--The Game of Singles in Tennis. (Illus.). 158p. 1977. 5.95 o.p. (ISBN 0-686-37483-5). USTA.

--Tennis Tactics: Singles & Doubles. LC 82-48137. (Illus.). 256p. 1983. write for info. (ISBN 0-06-015111-0, HarpT). Har-Row.

Talbot. Clinical Rheumatology. 2nd ed. 1981. 32.50 (ISBN 0-444-00634-6, North Holland); pap. 19.95 (ISBN 0-444-00615-X). Elsevier.

Talbot, Alice-Mary M. Faith Healing in Late Byzantium: The Posthumous Miracles of Patriarch Athanasios I of Constaninople by Theoktistos the Stoudite. Vaporis, N. M., ed. (The Archbishop Iakovos Library of Ecclesiastical & Historical Sources). 160p. (Orig.). 1983. 17.00 (ISBN 0-916586-92-8); pap. 12.00 (ISBN 0-916586-93-6). Hellenic College Pr.

Talbot, Antony, ed. Handbook of Doormaking, Windowmaking & Staircasing. LC 79-91389. (Illus.). 256p. 1980. pap. 8.95 (ISBN 0-8069-8896-7). Sterling.

Talbot, Carol. For This I Was Born. (Illus.). 1977. pap. 5.95 o.p. (ISBN 0-8024-2822-3). Moody.

Talbot, Charlene J. The Great Rat Island Adventure. LC 77-1055. (Illus.). (gr. 4-6). 1977. 7.95 o.p. (ISBN 0-689-30596-6). Atheneum.

Talbot, Charles, jt. auth. see Andersson, Christiane.

Talbot, Charles H., tr. see Borresen, Kari E.

Talbot, Clare R. Historic California in Bookplates. (Illus.). xvi, 287p. 1983. Repr. of 1963 ed. 15.95 (ISBN 0-8214-0737-6, 82-85066). Ohio U Pr.

Talbot, Emile J. La Critique Stendhalienne de Balzac a Zola. (Fr.). 20.00 (ISBN 0-917786-14-9). French Lit.

Talbot, Felix F. In Season, & Out. 1977. pap. text ed. 9.50 (ISBN 0-8191-0243-1). U Pr of Amer.

Talbot, George. Philosophy & Unified Science. 1435p. 1982. Repr. of 1978 ed. 36.50 (ISBN 0-941524-18-3). Lotus Light.

Talbot, Gordon. A Study of the Book of Genesis. LC 81-65578. 288p. (Orig.). 1981. pap. 6.95 (ISBN 0-87509-253-5); leader's guide 3.50 (ISBN 0-87509-311-6). Chr Pubns.

Talbot, Gordon G. Overcoming Materialism. LC 76-47341. 1977. pap. 1.95 o.p. (ISBN 0-8361-1810-3). Herald Pr.

Talbot, J., frwd. by see Herr, Stanley S. & Arons, Stephen.

Talbot, Katherine. Lady Molly. 160p. (Orig.). 1983. pap. 1.95 (ISBN 0-446-90762-6). Warner Bks.

--Philippa. 1982. pap. 1.75 (ISBN 0-686-83132-2). Warner Bks.

Talbot, Kathrine, tr. see Riefenstahl, Leni.

Talbot, L. see Von Mises, Richard & Von Karman, Theodore.

Talbot, Michael. Vivaldi. 1983. write for info. U of Wash Pr.

Talbot, Mike & Boyt, David, eds. Alternative Sources of Energy-Wood Energy, No. 57. 1982. pap. 2.95 (ISBN 0-917328-47-7). ASEI.

Talbot, Richard P. The Perfect Wheel: An Illustrated Guide to Bicycle Wheelbuilding. (Illus.). Date not set. 21.00 (ISBN 0-9602418-2-5). Manet Guild. Postponed.

Talbot, Russell. The Shipping Situation Between New York City & Philadelphia: A Survey of the Factors Causing the Growth of Motor Truck Transportation for the Purpose of Presenting Specifications to Be Met in Coordinating Rail & Motor Truck Transportation for Intercity Service. 1931. pap. 32.50x (ISBN 0-685-89782-6). Elliots Bks.

Talbot, Simon. Land Explorers. 1978. 14.95 (ISBN 0-7134-0990-8, Pub. by Batsford England). David & Charles.

Talbot, Steve. Roots of Oppression: The American Indian Question. LC 81-654. 172p. (Orig.). 1981. 14.00 (ISBN 0-7178-0591-3); pap. 4.75 (ISBN 0-7178-0583-2). Intl Pub Co.

Talbot, Strobe. Endgame: The Inside Story of Salt II. 288p. 1980. pap. 5.95xi (ISBN 0-06-131977-5, TB1977, Torch). Har-Row.

Talbot, Strobe, ed. & tr. see Khrushchev, Nikita S.

Talbot, T. Strobe. Endgame: The Inside Story of Salt II. LC 79-2238. 1979. 16.30i (ISBN 0-06-014213-8, HarpT). Har-Row.

Talbot, Toby. Dear Greta Garbo. (gr. 5-9). 1978. 6.95 o.p. (ISBN 0-399-20613-2). Putnam Pub Group.

--Night of the Radishes. (Illus.). (gr. k-3). 1972. PLB 4.29 o.p. (ISBN 0-399-60755-2). Putnam Pub Group.

Talbot, Toby, tr. see Manuel, Don J.

Talbot, Toby, tr. see Ortega & Gasset.

Talbot, Toby, tr. see Paz, Octavio.

Talbot, Tony. Two by Two. (gr. 1-3). 1974. 4.95 o.s.i. (ISBN 0-695-80484-7); lib ed. 4.98 o.s.i. (ISBN 0-695-40484-9). Follett.

Talbott, David N. The Saturn Myth. LC 76-51986. (Illus.). 1980. 15.95 o.p. (ISBN 0-385-11376-5). Doubleday.

Talbott, G. Douglas & Cooney, Margaret. Today's Disease: Alcohol & Drug Dependence. 202p. 1982. pap. 16.75x (ISBN 0-398-04688-3). C C Thomas.

Talbott, John A. & Kaplan, Seymour R., eds. Psychiatric Administration: A Comprehensive Text for the Clinician-Executive. Date not set. price not set (ISBN 0-8089-1529-0). Grune.

Talbott, John A., ed. see Report of a Conference Held in January 1979.

Talbott, Ran, jt. auth. see Heilborn, John.

Talbott, Richard E. & Humphrey, Donald R., eds. Posture & Movement. LC 77-85515. 325p. 1979. text ed. 36.00 (ISBN 0-89004-259-4). Raven.

Talec, Pierre. Christ & the Sacrament Church. 144p. 1983. pap. 9.95 (ISBN 0-8164-2455-1). Seabury.

Taleghani, Sayyid M. Society & Economics in Islam. Campbell, R., tr. from Persian. LC 82-2115. (Contemporary Islamic Thought Ser.). 225p. 1983. 17.95 (ISBN 0-933782-08-X); pap. write for info. (ISBN 0-933782-09-8). Mizan Pr.

Taleqani, Mahmood. Islam & Ownership. Jabbari, Ahmad & Rajaee, Farhang, eds. Jabbari, Ahmad & Rajaee, Farhang, trs. from Persian. 320p. 1982. 22.50 (ISBN 0-939214-14-8); pap. 12.95 (ISBN 0-939214-04-0). Mazda Pubs.

Talfourd, T. N. The Letters & Life of Charles Lamb. 370p. 1982. Repr. of 1911 ed. lib. bdg. 40.00 (ISBN 0-89984-466-9). Century Bookbindery.

Talhami, Ghada H. Suakin & Massawa Under Egyptian Rule, Eighteen Sixty-Five to Eighteen Eighty-Five. LC 79-66418. 1979. pap. text ed. 12.75 (ISBN 0-8191-0828-6). U Pr of Amer.

Taliaferro, Margaret. Real Reason for Christmas. LC 76-55080. 128p. 1982. pap. 5.95 (ISBN 0-385-18106-X, Galilee); prepacks of ten 59.50 (ISBN 0-385-18367-4). Doubleday.

Taliaferro, W. H. & Humphrey, J. H., eds. Advances in Immunology, Vols. 1-30. Incl. Vol. 1. 1961. 48.50 (ISBN 0-12-022401-1); Vol. 2. 1963. 57.00 (ISBN 0-12-022402-X); Vol. 3. Dixon, F. J., Jr. & Humphrey, J. H., eds. 1963. 57.00 (ISBN 0-12-022403-8); Vol. 4. 1964. 57.00 (ISBN 0-12-022404-6); Vol. 5. 1966. 57.00 (ISBN 0-12-022405-4); Vol. 6. 1967. 57.00 (ISBN 0-12-022406-2); Vol. 7. Dixon, F. J., Jr. & Kunkel, Henry G., eds. 1967. 57.00 (ISBN 0-12-022407-0); Vol. 8. 1968. 57.00 (ISBN 0-12-022408-9); Vol. 9. 1968. 57.00 (ISBN 0-12-022409-7); Vol. 10. 1969. 57.00 (ISBN 0-12-022410-0); Vol. 11. 1969. 57.00 (ISBN 0-12-022411-9); Vol. 12. 1970. 57.00 (ISBN 0-12-022412-7); Vol. 13. 1971. 57.00 (ISBN 0-12-022413-5); Vol. 14. 1971. 57.00 (ISBN 0-12-022414-3); Vol. 15. 1972. 57.00 (ISBN 0-12-022415-1); Vol. 16. 1973. 57.00 (ISBN 0-12-022416-X); Vol. 17. 1973. 57.00 (ISBN 0-12-022417-8); Vol. 18. 1974. 57.00 (ISBN 0-12-022418-6); Vol. 19. 1974. 57.00 (ISBN 0-12-022419-4); Vol. 20. 1975. 57.00 (ISBN 0-12-022420-8); Vol. 21. **1975. 57.00 (ISBN 0-12-022421-6); Vol. 22. 1976. 50.00 (ISBN 0-12-022422-4); Vol. 23. 1976. 57.00 (ISBN 0-12-022423-2); Vol. 24. 1976. 57.00 (ISBN 0-12-022424-0); Vol. 25. 1978. 42.00 (ISBN 0-12-022425-9); Vol. 26. Kunkel, Henry G. & Dixon, E. J., eds. 1978. 46.00 (ISBN 0-12-022426-7); Vol. 27. 1979. 43.00 (ISBN 0-12-022427-5); Vol. 28. 1980. 49.50 (ISBN 0-12-022428-3); Vol. 29. 1980. 40.00 (ISBN 0-12-022429-1). LC 61-17057. Vol. 1-24. 57.00 (ISBN 0-686-66773-5). Acad Pr.**

Talkington, Sylvia. ECG: A Pocket Guide. LC 82-71576. (Illus.). 100p. (Orig.). 1982. pap. text ed. 8.95. Wiley.

Talkington, William A., ed. see Cook, Stanley J. & Suter, Richard W.

Talkington, William A., ed. see Gowen, James A.

Talkington, William A., ed. see Langan, John & Nadell, Judith.

Tall, D. O. Functions of a Complex Variable, 2 vols. (Library of Mathematics). 1970. Vol. 1. pap. 2.95 o.p. (ISBN 0-7100-6567-1); Vol. 2. pap. 2.95 o.p. (ISBN 0-7100-6785-2); pap. 6.50 set o.p. (ISBN 0-685-25621-9). Routledge & Kegan.

Tall, D. O., jt. auth. see Stewart, I.

Tall, D. O., jt. auth. see Stewart, I. N.

Tall, David, jt. auth. see Stewart, Ian.

Tall, Lambert, ed. see Wiley, John.

Tall, Lambert, et al. Structural Steel Design. 2nd ed. (Illus.). 875p. 1974. 37.50x o.p. (ISBN 0-471-06674-5). Wiley.

Tallach, John. God Made Them Great. 1978. pap. 4.95 o.p. (ISBN 0-85151-190-2). Banner of Truth.

Tallack, John C. Introduction to Elementary Vector Analysis. 1966. text ed. 17.95x (ISBN 0-521-07999-3). Cambridge U Pr.

Talland, George A. Deranged Memory: A Psychonomic Study of the Amnesic Syndrome. 1965. 49.50 (ISBN 0-12-683150-5). Acad Pr.

Tallarico. Grosset Word Find Book, No. 2. (Basic Activity Bks.). (Illus.). 64p. (gr. 1-7). Date not set. pap. price not set (ISBN 0-448-11827-0, G&D). Putnam Pub Group.

Tallarico, Anthony. More Mystery Picture Puzzles. (Magic Answer Bks.). (Illus.). 64p. (gr. 3-7). 1983. pap. 2.95 (ISBN 0-671-44924-9). Wanderer Bks.

--Mystery Picture Puzzles. (Magic Answer Bks.). (Illus.). 64p. (gr. 3-7). 1983. pap. 2.95 (ISBN 0-671-44923-0). Wanderer Bks.

Tallarico, Tony. The Alphabet Flip Book Game. (Flip Bks.). (Illus.). 9p. (ps). 1981. 3.50 (ISBN 0-448-11497-6, G&D). Putnam Pub Group.

--Animals. (Tote Bks.). (Illus.). 12p. (gr. 3-8). 1982. pap. 3.50 (ISBN 0-89828-300-0). Tuffy Bks.

--The Bobbsey Twins Detective Activity Book: No. 1. (Illus.). (gr. 1-4). 1978. pap. 1.50 (ISBN 0-448-14790-4, G&D). Putnam Pub Group.

--Colors. (Tote Bks.). (Illus.). 12p. (gr. 3-8). 1982. pap. 3.50 (ISBN 0-89828-304-3). Tuffy Bks.

--Giant Apes Activity Book. (Elephant Bks). (Illus.). 1977. pap. 1.25 o.p. (ISBN 0-448-12974-4, G&D). Putnam Pub Group.

--The Giant I Can Draw Everything. Schneider, Meg, ed. (I Can Draw Ser.). (Illus.). 192p. (Orig.). (gr. 3-7). 1982. pap. 4.95 (ISBN 0-671-44459-X). Wanderer Bks.

--Gobble. (Illus.). 24p. (gr. 3-8). 1982. pap. 2.95 (ISBN 0-448-03871-4, G&D). Putnam Pub Group.

--Gobble, Gobble. (Illus.). 24p. (gr. 3-8). 1982. pap. 2.95 (ISBN 0-448-03872-2, G&D). Putnam Pub Group.

--The Great Big Busy Activity Book. (Elephant Bks.). (Illus.). (gr. 1-3). 1978. pap. 2.95 (ISBN 0-448-14615-0, G&D). Putnam Pub Group.

--Grosset Word Find Book: Nos. 1 & 2. (Elephant Bks.). (Illus., Orig.). (gr. k-3). 1975. No. 1. pap. 1.25 o.p. (ISBN 0-448-11826-2, G&D); No. 2. pap. 1.25 o.p. (ISBN 0-448-11827-0). Putnam Pub Group.

--Guide to Drawing Cartoons: A Step by Step Fun Guide. (Elephant Bks). (Illus.). 64p. (gr. 2-7). 1975. pap. 1.95 (ISBN 0-448-11959-5, G&D). Putnam Pub Group.

--Hardy Boys Adventure Activity Book, No. 1. (Activity Bks.). (Illus.). (gr. 3-8). 1977. pap. 1.50 (ISBN 0-448-12872-1, G&D). Putnam Pub Group.

--Hardy Boys Adventure Activity Book, No. 3. (Elephant Bks.). (Illus.). (gr. 3-8). 1978. pap. 1.50 o.s.i. (ISBN 0-448-14770-X, G&D). Putnam Pub Group.

--Hardy Boys Adventure Activity Book: No. 2. (Elephant Bks). (gr. 3-8). 1977. pap. 1.50 (ISBN 0-448-14423-9, G&D). Putnam Pub Group.

--Let's Take a Trip. (Tote Bks.). (Illus.). 12p. (gr. 3-8). 1982. pap. 3.50 (ISBN 0-89828-305-1). Tuffy Bks.

--Metric Man Activity Book. (Elephant Bks). (Illus.). (gr. k-6). 1977. pap. 1.25 (ISBN 0-448-14297-X, G&D). Putnam Pub Group.

--Mini Poster Book. (Elephant Bks.). (Illus.). 64p. (gr. 2-7). 1975. pap. 1.25 o.p. (ISBN 0-448-11960-9, G&D). Putnam Pub Group.

--Monster Hunt. (Video Game Bk.). (Illus.). 16p. (gr. 3-8). 1982. pap. 3.50 (ISBN 0-89828-327-2). Tuffy Bks.

--Nancy Drew Mystery Activity Book, No. 1. (Activity Bks.). (Illus.). (gr. 3-7). 1977. pap. 1.50 (ISBN 0-448-12871-3, G&D). Putnam Pub Group.

--Nancy Drew Mystery Activity Book, No. 2. (Elephant Bks.). (gr. 3-7). 1977. pap. 1.50 (ISBN 0-448-14424-7, G&D). Putnam Pub Group.

--Nancy Drew Mystery Activity Book, No. 3. (Elephant Bks.). (Illus.). (gr. 3-7). 1978. pap. 1.50 o.s.i. (ISBN 0-448-14780-7, G&D). Putnam Pub Group.

--Numbers. (Tote Bks). (Illus.). 12p. (gr. 3-8). 1982. pap. 3.50 (ISBN 0-89828-303-5). Tuffy Bks.

--The Numbers Flip Book Game. (Flip Bks.). (Illus.). 9p. (ps). 3.50 (ISBN 0-448-11498-4, G&D). Putnam Pub Group.

--Rocket Attack. (Video Game Bk.). (Illus.). 16p. (gr. 3-8). 1982. pap. 3.50 (ISBN 0-89828-326-4). Tuffy Bks.

--Santa Claus Activity Book. Duenewald, Doris, ed. (Elephant Books Ser.). (Illus.). (gr. 1-7). 1978. pap. 1.25 (ISBN 0-448-16166-4, G&D). Putnam Pub Group.

--Seasons. (Tote Bks.). (Illus.). 12p. 1982. pap. 3.50 (ISBN 0-89828-301-9). Tuffy Bks.

--Spring Activity Books. Incl. The Fun Activity Book of Spring (ISBN 0-448-12960-4); An Activity Book of Games, Greeting Cards & Posters (ISBN 0-448-12961-2). (Elephant Bks). (Illus.). (gr. 1-6). 1977. pap. 1.25 ea. (G&D). Putnam Pub Group.

--Star Jokes. Duenewald, Doris, ed. LC 78-54178. (Elephant Books Ser.). (Illus.). (gr. 1-7). 1978. pap. 1.95 o.s.i. (ISBN 0-448-14819-6, G&D). Putnam Pub Group.

--Super Jokes. LC 79-51214. (Illus.). (gr. 2-6). 1980. pap. 2.50 (ISBN 0-448-16564-3, G&D). Putnam Pub Group.

--Time Machine. (Video Game Bk.). (Illus.). 16p. (gr. 3-8). pap. 3.50 (ISBN 0-89828-325-6). Tuffy Bks.

--What Time Is It? (Tote Bks.). (Illus.). 12p. (gr. 3-8). 1982. pap. 3.50 (ISBN 0-89828-302-7). Tuffy Bks.

Tallarico, Tony, illus. All Through the Year. (Baby's First Bks.). (Illus.). 14p. (ps). 1980. 1.95 (ISBN 0-448-16278-4, G&D). Putnam Pub Group.

--Colors All Around. (Baby's First Bks.). (Illus.). 14p. (ps). 1980. 1.95 (ISBN 0-448-16270-9, G&D). Putnam Pub Group.

--Look up at the Sky. (Illus.). 14p. (ps). 1982. 2.95 (ISBN 0-448-12308-8, G&D). Putnam Pub Group.

--Na-No, Na-No, the Mork & Mindy Book of Games, Puzzles & Coloring by Number. (Illus.). (gr. 2-6). 1979. pap. 1.25 o.p. (ISBN 0-448-16144-3, G&D). Putnam Pub Group.

--Skitter Bugs. (Baby's First Bks.). (Illus.). 14p. (ps). 1980. 1.95 (ISBN 0-448-16277-6, G&D). Putnam Pub Group.

--Trucks & Cars. (Baby's First Bks.). (Illus.). 14p. (ps). 1980. 1.95 (ISBN 0-448-16275-X, G&D). Putnam Pub Group.

Tallarieo, Tony. Search A Picture Puzzles. (Puzzlebacks Ser.). 64p. (gr. 3-7). 1981. pap. 1.50 o.p. (ISBN 0-671-42656-7). Wanderer Bks.

Tallent, Elizabeth. In Constant Flight. LC 82-48722. 1983. 11.95 (ISBN 0-394-52816-6). Knopf.

Tallent, Norman. Psychological Report Writing. LC 75-33309. (Illus.). 272p. 1976. 25.95 (ISBN 0-13-732503-7). P-H.

--Report Writing in Special Education. (Illus.). 1980. text ed. 22.95 (ISBN 0-13-773606-1). P-H.

Talleur, Richard W. Fly-Fishing for Trout. (Illus.). 272p. pap. 5.95 o.p. (ISBN 0-88317-027-2). Stoeger Pub Co.

Talley, David. Basic Carrier Telephony. 3rd, rev. ed. 218p. 1977. 9.95 (ISBN 0-686-98107-3). Telecom Lib.

--Basic Electronic Switching for Telephone Systems. 240p. 1981. 8.35 (ISBN 0-686-98106-5). Telecom Lib.

--Basic Telephone Switching Systems. 2nd ed. 184p. 1979. 10.50 (ISBN 0-686-98108-1). Telecom Lib.

Tallgrass Research Center Editors. To Build A Still. 28p. 1980. pap. 15.00 (ISBN 0-686-92648-X). Rutan Pub.

Tallman, Albert. End of Cycle. 1967. 4.00 o.p. (ISBN 0-8233-0106-0). Golden Quill.

Tallman, Irving & Marotz-Braden, Ramon, eds. Adolescent Socialization in Cross-Cultural Perspective. (Monograph). Date not set. price not set (ISBN 0-12-683180-7). Acad Pr.

Tallon, Eugene & Gustave, Maurice. Legislation sur le Travail des Enfants dans les Manufactures. (Conditions of the 19th Century French Working Class Ser.). 600p. (Fr.). 1974. Repr. of 1875 ed. lib. bdg. 146.00x o.p. (ISBN 0-8287-0802-9, 1066). Clearwater Pub.

Talmadge, Betty. Lovejoy Plantation Cookbook. 1983. 8.95 (ISBN 0-931948-44-4). Peachtree Pubs.

Talmage, Frank, ed. Disputation & Dialogue: Reading in the Jewish-Christian Encounter. 411p. pap. 9.95 (ISBN 0-686-95168-9). ADL.

Talmage, Harriet. Statistics As a Tool for Educational Practitioners. new ed. LC 75-31312. (Illus.). 264p. 1976. 20.75x (ISBN 0-8211-1905-2); text ed. 18.60x (ISBN 0-685-61060-8). McCutchan.

Talmage, Harriet, ed. Systems of Individualized Education. LC 74-24478. 200p. 1975. 19.95x (ISBN 0-8211-1904-4); text ed. 17.95x (ISBN 0-685-51465-X). McCutchan.

Talmage, James E. Articles of Faith. 1970. black leather ed. 14.50 (ISBN 0-87747-319-6); brown leather ed. 14.50. Deseret Bk.

--Articles of Faith. 537p. pap. 2.50 (ISBN 0-87747-662-4); pap. 11.00 brown leather ed.; black leather ed. 11.00. Deseret Bk.

--Great Apostasy. 6.95 (ISBN 0-87747-384-6). Deseret Bk.

--Jesus the Christ. (Classics in Mormon Literature Ser.). 804p. 1982. 10.95 (ISBN 0-87747-903-8). Deseret Bk.

Talmon, J. L. Origins of Totalitarian Democracy. 1970. pap. 5.95x o.p. (ISBN 0-393-00510-0, Norton Lib). Norton.

Talmor, E. Combustion Hot Spot Analysis for Furnaces & Fired Process Heaters: Prediction, Control & Troubleshooting. 162p. 1982. 33.95 (ISBN 0-87201-362-6). Gulf Pub.

Taloumis, George. House Plants for Five Exposures. 1975. pap. 2.50 (ISBN 0-451-11922-3, AE1922, Sig). NAL.

Talsma, T., jt. ed. see Holmes, J. W.

Talwani, M., jt. auth. see Scrutton, R. A.

Talwani, Manik & Pitman, Walter C., III, eds. Island Arcs, Deep Sea Trenches & Back-Arc Basins, Vol. 1. LC 76-58102. (Maurice Ewing Ser.). 1977. 23.00 (ISBN 0-87590-400-9). Am Geophysical.

Talwani, Manik, et al, eds. Deep Drilling Results in the Atlantic Ocean: Ocean Crust. LC 79-88753. (Maurice Ewing Ser.). 1979. 23.00 (ISBN 0-87590-401-7, ME0200). Am Geophysical.

--Deep Drilling Results in Atlantic Ocean: Continental Margins & Paleoenvironment. LC 79-88754. (Maurice Ewing Ser.). 1979. 23.00 (ISBN 0-87590-402-5, ME0300). Am Geophysical.

Talwar, Bhagat R. The Talwars of Pathan Land & Subhas Chandra's Great Escape. LC 76-902650. 1976. 11.00x o.p. (ISBN 0-88386-848-2). South Asia Bks.

Talwar, G. P., ed. Regulation of Growth & Differentiated Function in Eukaryote Cells. 584p. 1975. text ed. 48.00 (ISBN 0-89004-032-X). Raven.

Talwar, G. P., ed. see Symposium, New Delhi, October 1978.

Tam Al. Vu Van Cuong. Vietnam's War, Nineteen Forty to Nineteen Seventy-Five. 456p. 1983. 26.95 (ISBN 0-686-84319-3). Brunswick Pub.

Tamar, Erika. Blues for Silk Garcia. 160p. 1982. 9.95 (ISBN 0-517-54671-X). Crown.

Tamarin, Alfred. We Have Not Vanished: Eastern Indians of the United States. (Illus.). 128p. (gr. 3-6). 1974. lib. ed. 5.97 o.s.i. (ISBN 0-695-40332-X). Follett.

Tamarin, Alfred & Glubok, Shirley. Ancient Indians of the Southwest. LC 74-33984. 96p. (gr. 4-7). 1975. PLB 7.95 o.p. (ISBN 0-385-09252-0). Doubleday.

--Voyaging to Cathay: Americans in the China Trade. (Illus.). 224p. (gr. 4-6). 1976. 10.00 o.p. (ISBN 0-670-74857-9). Viking Pr.

Tamarin, R. H., ed. Population Regulation. LC 77-16178. (Benchmark Papers in Ecology Ser.: Vol. 7). 389p. 1978. 46.00 (ISBN 0-87933-324-3). Hutchinson Ross.

Tamarkin, Civia, jt. auth. see Collins, Marva.

Tamarkin, Kenneth. Number Power Six: Word Problems. (Number Power Ser.). 160p. (Orig.). 1983. pap. 4.95 (ISBN 0-8092-5515-4). Contemp Bks.

Tamaru, K. & Ichikawa, M. Catalysis by Electron Donor-Acceptor Complexes: Their General Behavior & Biological Roles. LC 75-28051. 1976. 38.95x o.s.i. (ISBN 0-470-84435-3). Halsted Pr.

Tamasi, Barbara. I'll Stop Tomorrow. 1982. 5.95 (ISBN 0-941478-03-3). Paraclete Pr.

Tambasco, Anthony J. The Bible for Ethics: Juan Luis Segundo & First-World Ethics. LC 80-6253. 286p. (Orig.). 1981. lib. bdg. 21.75 (ISBN 0-8191-1556-8); pap. text ed. 11.00 (ISBN 0-8191-1557-6). U Pr of Amer.

Tambiah, S. J. Buddhism & the Spirit Cults in Northeast Thailand. LC 73-108112. (Cambridge Studies in Social Anthropology: No. 2). (Illus.). 1970. 42.50 (ISBN 0-521-07825-3); pap. 17.95 (ISBN 0-521-09958-7). Cambridge U Pr.

--World Conqueror & World Renouncer. LC 76-8290. (Cambridge Studies in Social Anthropology: No. 15). 1976. 59.50 (ISBN 0-521-21140-9); pap. 18.95 (ISBN 0-521-29290-5). Cambridge U Pr.

Tambiah, S. J., jt. auth. see Goody, Jack.

Tamburello, Adolfo. Japan. Nannicini, Giuliana & Bowman, John, eds. Mondadori, tr. from It. LC 71-179262. (Monuments of Civilization Ser.). Orig. Title: Giappone. (Illus.). 192p. 1973. 25.00 (ISBN 0-448-02022-X, G&D). Putnam Pub Group.

Tamelen, E. E. Van see Van Tamelen, E. E.

Tamer, Joanna, ed. see Spivack, Mayer.

Tames, Richard. Cities. Yapp, Malcolm, et al, eds. (World History Ser.). (Illus.). 32p. (gr. 10). 1980. Repr. of 1977 ed. lib. bdg. 6.95 (ISBN 0-89908-140-1); pap. text ed. 2.25 (ISBN 0-89908-115-0). Greenhaven.

--The French Revolution. Killingray, Margaret, et al, eds. (Wolrd History Ser.). (Illus.). 32p. (gr. 10). 1980. Repr. lib. bdg. 6.95 (ISBN 0-89908-136-3); pap. text ed. 2.25 (ISBN 0-89908-111-8). Greenhaven.

--Growing Up in the Nineteen Sixties. (Growing Up Ser.). (Illus.). 72p. (gr. 7-12). 1983. 14.95 (ISBN 0-7134-1342-5, Pub. by Batsford England). David & Charles.

--Japan Today. 16.95x o.p. (ISBN 0-7182-0454-9, SpS). Sportshelf.

--Napoleon. Yapp, Malcolm & Killingray, Margaret, eds. (World History Ser.). (Illus.). (gr. 10). 1980. Repr. of 1977 ed. lib. bdg. 6.95 (ISBN 0-89908-044-8); pap. text ed. 2.25 (ISBN 0-89908-019-7). Greenhaven.

Tamir, A., jt. auth. see Wisniak, J.

Tamir, Batsheva Bonne see Bonne-Tamir, Batsheva & Cohen, Tirza.

Tamir, T., ed. Integrated Optics. (Topics in Applied Physics Ser.: Vol. 7). (Illus.). 1982. pap. 24.50 (ISBN 0-387-09673-6). Springer-Verlag.

Tamke, Susan S. Make a Joyful Noise Unto the Lord: Hymns As a Reflection of Victorian Social Attitudes. LC 76-51693. 209p. 1978. 12.00x (ISBN 0-8214-0371-0, 82-82642); pap. text ed. 5.00x (ISBN 0-8214-0382-6, 82-82659). Ohio U Pr.

Tamkoc, Metin. The Warrior Diplomats: Guardians of the National Security & Modernization of Turkey. LC 73-93301. (Illus.). 1976. 30.00x o.p. (ISBN 0-87480-115-X). U of Utah Pr.

Tamm. Stereochemistry. (New Comprehension Biochemistry Ser.: Vol. 3). 1982. 59.75 (ISBN 0-444-80389-0). Elsevier.

Tamm, Rudra. The Inner Promise. (Illus.). 1974. pap. 4.95 o.p. (ISBN 0-671-21720-8). S&S.

Tammaro, Thom. Evocations. 16p. 1978. pap. 2.95 (ISBN 0-686-32937-6). Barnwood Pr.

Tammaro, Thom, ed. & intro. by see Stafford, William.

Tammuz, Benjamin. Minotaur. 1981. 11.95 (ISBN 0-453-00401-6, H401). NAL.

--Minotaur. 1982. pap. 1.50 (ISBN 0-451-11582-1, AW1582, Sig). NAL.

--Requiem for Na'Aman. Budny, Mildred & Safran, Yehuda, trs. 240p. 1982. 12.95 (ISBN 0-453-00417-2, H417). NAL.

Tan. Principles of Soil Chemistry. (Books in Soil & the Environment). 304p. 1982. 34.50 (ISBN 0-8247-1336-2). Dekker.

Tan, Leong T. & Tan, Margaret Y. Acupuncture Therapy: Current Chinese Practice. 2nd. rev ed. LC 75-30280. (Illus.). 275p. 1976. text ed. 39.95 (ISBN 0-87722-064-6). Temple U Pr.

Tan, Margaret Y., jt. auth. see Tan, Leong T.

Tan, Soo T. College Math for the Managerial & Social Sciences. (Math Ser.). 784p. 1983. text ed. write for info. (ISBN 0-87150-354-9, 2771). Prindle.

--Finite Math for the Managerial & Social Sciences. (Math Ser.). 480p. 1982. text ed. write for info. (ISBN 0-87150-336-0, 2691). Prindle.

Tan, Terry. The Oriental Kitchen. (Golden Asia Cookbooks Ser.). (Illus.). 336p. 1983. 49.50 (ISBN 0-686-42991-5). Hippocrene Bks.

Tana, Tomoe, jt. tr. see Nixon, Lucille M.

Tanabe, H. Equations of Evolution. (Monographs & Studies: No. 6). 260p. 1979. text ed. 49.50 (ISBN 0-273-01137-5). Pitman Pub MA.

Tanabe, Kozo. Solid Acids & Bases: Their Catalytic Properties. 1971. 39.00 (ISBN 0-12-683250-1). Acad Pr.

Tanahashi, Kazuaki. Enku: Sculptor of a Hundred Thousand Buddhas. LC 81-50969. (Illus.). 176p. (Orig.). 1982. pap. 13.95 (ISBN 0-394-74882-4). Shambhala Pubns.

Tanaka, Hideyuki. The Happy Dog. LC 82-72248. (Illus.). 24p. (ps-3). 1983. 6.95 (ISBN 0-689-50259-1, McElderry Bk). Atheneum.

Tanaka, Ikko, ed. Illustration in Japan, Vol. 3. (Illus.). 180p. 1983. 59.50 (ISBN 0-87011-550-2). Kodansha.

Tanaka, K. & Fujita, T. SFM in Cell Biology & Medicine. (International Congress Ser.: Vol. 545). 1981. 101.50 (ISBN 0-444-90191-4). Elsevier.

Tanaka, Sen'o. The Tea Ceremony. (Illus.). 1977. pap. 7.95 o.p. (ISBN 0-517-53039-2, Dist. by Crown). Crown.

--The Tea Ceremony. LC 73-79766. (Illus.). 214p. 1983. pap. 12.95 (ISBN 0-87011-578-2). Kodansha.

Tanaka, Yukiko & Hanson, Elizabeth, eds. This Kind of Woman: Ten Stories by Japanese Women Writers, 1960-1976. LC 81-51332. 320p. 1982. 18.75x (ISBN 0-8047-1130-5). Stanford U Pr.

Tanaquil, Paul. Sotto Voce (Poetry) 1923. text ed. 24.50x (ISBN 0-686-83777-0). Elliots Bks.

Tanara, Milli U. The World of Amphibians & Reptiles. Pleasance, Simon, tr. LC 79-1441. (Abbeville Press Encyclopedia of Natural Science). (Illus.). 256p. 1979. 13.95 (ISBN 0-89659-037-2); pap. 7.95 o. p. (ISBN 0-89659-031-3). Abbeville Pr.

Tan Boon Liang, John. A Bamboo Flower Blooms. 1983. 15.95 (ISBN 0-533-05285-8). Vantage.

Tancer, Jack. Our Reader. (Illus.). 1964. pap. 2.25x (ISBN 0-88323-060-7, 158). Richards Pub.

Tancer, Shoshana B. Economic Nationalism in Latin America: The Quest for Economic Independence. LC 74-30711. (Praeger Special Studies). 272p. 1976. text ed. 24.50 o.p. (ISBN 0-275-05970-7). Praeger.

Tandler, Bernard & Hoppel, Charles L. Mitochondria. (Monographs on the Ultrastructure of Cells & Organisms Ser.). 1972. 21.00 (ISBN 0-12-454143-7). Acad Pr.

Tandon, Prakash. Beyond Punjab: A Sequel to Punjabi Century. LC 73-123620. (Center for South & Southeast Asia Studies, Uc Berkeley). 1971. 28.50x (ISBN 0-520-01759-5). U of Cal Pr.

--Punjabi Century, 1857-1947. 1968. 22.75x o.p. (ISBN 0-520-01252-6); pap. 5.95 (ISBN 0-520-01253-4, CAL164). U of Cal Pr.

--Return to Punjab. 1981. 21.50x (ISBN 0-520-03990-4). U of Cal Pr.

Taneja, Nawal K. Airline Planning: Corporate, Financial, & Marketing. LC 80-8736. 224p. 1982. 27.95x (ISBN 0-669-04346-X). Lexington Bks.

--Airlines in Transition. LC 80-8735. 272p. 1981. 25.95x (ISBN 0-669-04345-1). Lexington Bks.

--The Commercial Airline Industry: Managerial Practices & Policies. LC 76-18052. 368p. 1976. 24.95x (ISBN 0-669-00129-5). Lexington Bks.

--U. S. Airfreight Industry. LC 78-24840. 272p. 1979. 22.95x (ISBN 0-669-02853-3). Lexington Bks.

--U. S. International Aviation Policy. LC 79-3039. 192p. 1980. 23.95x (ISBN 0-669-03320-0). Lexington Bks.

Tanenbaum, A. Structured Computer Organization. 1976. 28.95 (ISBN 0-13-854505-7). P-H.

Tanenbaum, Andrew S. Computer Networks: Toward Distributed Processing Systems. (Illus.). 544p. 1981. text ed. 32.95 (ISBN 0-13-165183-8). P-H.

Tanenbaum, Marc H. Religious Values in an Age of Violence. (Pere Marquette Theology Lectures). 1976. 7.95 (ISBN 0-87462-508-4). Marquette.

Tanenhaus, Joseph, jt. auth. see Grossman, Joel B.

Tanford, Charles. The Hydrophobic Effect: Formation of Micelles & Biological Membranes. 2nd ed. LC 79-13591. 233p. 1980. 24.50x (ISBN 0-471-04893-3, Pub. by Wiley-Interscience). Wiley.

--Physical Chemistry of Macromolecules. LC 61-11511. 710p. 1961. 49.95x (ISBN 0-471-84447-0, Wiley-Interscience). Wiley.

Tanford, J. Alexander & Quinlan, Richard M. Indiana Trial Evidence Manual. 393p. 1982. 30.00 (ISBN 0-87215-497-1). Michie-Bobbs.

Tanford, J. Alexander, jt. auth. see Bocchino, Anthony J.

Tang, P. The New Manual of Kung Fu. 12.95x o.s.i. (ISBN 0-685-63786-7). Wehman.

Tang, W. H., jt. auth. see Ang, A. H.

Tang, Wu. Painting In China Since the Opium Wars. (Illus., Orig.). 1980. pap. 5.00 (ISBN 0-87846-194-9). Mus Fine Arts Boston.

Tangerman, E. J. Capturing Personality in Woodcarving. LC 81-50979. (Illus.). 128p. (Orig.). 1981. pap. 6.95 (ISBN 0-8069-7530-X). Sterling.

--Carving Faces & Figures in Wood. LC 79-91381. (Home Craftsman Bk.). (Illus.). 128p. 1980. pap. 6.95 (ISBN 0-8069-8904-1). Sterling.

--Carving Flora & Fables in Wood. LC 80-54336. (Illus.). 128p. 1981. pap. 6.95 (ISBN 0-8069-8982-3). Sterling.

--Carving Religious Motifs in Wood. LC 80-52321. (Illus.). 128p. 1980. pap. 6.95 (ISBN 0-8069-8938-6). Sterling.

--Carving the Unusual. LC 82-50544. (Illus.). 128p. (Orig.). 1982. pap. 6.95 (ISBN 0-8069-7632-2). Sterling.

--Carving Wooden Animals. LC 79-65080. (Illus.). 1979. pap. 6.95 (ISBN 0-8069-8864-9). Sterling.

--One Thousand New Designs for Whittling & Woodcarving. LC 76-7950. 1976. pap. 10.95 o.p. (ISBN 0-07-062649-9, SP). McGraw.

--Relief Woodcarving. LC 81-85039. (Illus.). 128p. (Orig.). 1982. pap. text ed. 6.95 (ISBN 0-8069-7596-2). Sterling.

Tangerman, Elmer J. Design & Figure Carving. (Illus.). 1940. pap. 4.50 (ISBN 0-486-21209-2). Dover.

Tanghe, J. & Vlaeminck, S., eds. Cities for Living In? A Case for Urbanism & Guidelines for Re-Urbanization. (Illus.). 384p. 1983. 45.00 (ISBN 0-08-025238-9); pap. 22.50 (ISBN 0-08-025237-0). Pergamon.

Tan Huay Peng. Fun with Chinese Characters. (Vol. I). (Illus.). 192p. 1982. pap. 5.95 (ISBN 9971-4-6072-6). Hippocrene Bks.

--Fun with Chinese Characters. (Vol. 2). (Illus.). 160p. 1983. pap. 5.95 (ISBN 0-686-42987-7). Hippocrene Bks.

Tani, Karl, jt. auth. see Counter, Constance.

Tanikawa, Shuntaro. Billy the Kid. Wright, Harold, tr. from Japanese. lmtd. ed. 10.00 (ISBN 0-931460-21-2). Bieler.

Tanimoto, S. & Klinger, A., eds. Structured Computer Vision: Machine Perception Through Hierarchical Computation Structures. LC 80-14878. 1980. 24.00 (ISBN 0-12-683280-3). Acad Pr.

Tanin, O. & Yohan, E. Militarism & Fascism in Japan. LC 72-136553. 320p. 1973. Repr. of 1934 ed. lib. bdg. 18.25x (ISBN 0-8371-5478-2, TAMF). Greenwood.

Tanis, Elliot A., jt. auth. see Hogg, Robert V.

Tanis, Norman E. & Perkins, David L. China in Books: A Basic Bibliograhy in Western Language, Vol. 4. Stueart, Robert D., ed. LC 77-24396. (Foundations in Library & Information Science Ser.). 1979. lib. bdg. 42.50 (ISBN 0-89232-071-0). Jai Pr.

Tanitch, Robert. A Pictorial Companion to Shakespeare. 128p. 1982. 39.00x (Pub. by Muller Ltd). State Mutual Bk.

--A Pictorial Companion to Shakespeare's Plays. (Illus.). 128p. 1983. 15.95 (ISBN 0-584-11027-8, Pub. by Salem Hse Ltd). Merrimack Bk Serv.

Taniuti, T. & Nishihara, K. Nonlinear Waves. Jeffrey, A., ed. (Monographs & Studies: No. 15). 320p. 1983. text ed. price not set (ISBN 0-273-08466-6). Pitman Pub MA.

Tanizaki, Junichiro. Diary of a Mad Old Man. Hibbett, Howard, tr. from Jap. (Perigee Japanese Library). 320p. 1981. pap. 4.95 (ISBN 0-399-50524-5, Perige). Putnam Pub Group.

--The Key. Hibbett, Howard, tr. from Jap. (Perigee Japanese Library). 190p. 1981. pap. 4.95 (ISBN 0-399-50522-9, Perige). Putnam Pub Group.

--Makioka Sisters. 1966. pap. 4.95 o.p. (ISBN 0-448-00190-X, G&D). Putnam Pub Group.

--The Makioka Sisters. Seidensticker, Edward T., tr. from Jap. (Perigee Japanese Library). 538p. 1981. pap. 7.95 (ISBN 0-399-50520-2, Perige). Putnam Pub Group.

--Seven Japanese Tales. Hibbett, Howard, tr. from Jap. (Perigee Japanese Library). 320p. 1981. pap. 5.95 (ISBN 0-399-50523-7, Perige). Putnam Pub Group.

--Some Prefer Nettles. Seidensticker, Edward G., tr. from Jap. (Perigee Japanese Library). 224p. 1981. pap. 4.95 (ISBN 0-399-50521-0, Perige). Putnam Pub Group.

Tank, Kurt L. Gunter Grass. Conway, John, tr. LC 68-31458. (Literature and Life Ser.). 1969. 11.95 (ISBN 0-8044-2863-8); pap. 4.95 (ISBN 0-8044-6892-3). Ungar.

Tank, Ronald W., ed. Environmental Geology: Text & Readings. 570p. 1983. pap. 16.95 (ISBN 0-19-503288-8). Oxford U Pr.

--Focus on Environmental Geology: A Collection of Case Histories & Readings from Original Sources. 3rd ed. (Illus.). 1983. pap. text ed. 14.95x (ISBN 0-19-503142-3). Oxford U Pr.

Tankard, James W., Jr. The Statistical Pioneers. 256p. 1983. 19.95 (ISBN 0-87073-408-3); pap. 11.95 (ISBN 0-87073-409-1). Schenkman.

Tanksley, Perry. Come Share the Joy. (Illus.). 80p. 1979. 7.95 o.p. (ISBN 0-8007-0990-X). Revell.

--Love from the Living Bible. (Illus.). 128p. 1978. 8.95x o.p. (ISBN 0-8007-0965-9). Revell.

Tann, Jennifer, ed. The Selected Papers of Boulton & Watt: Vol. I: the Engine Partnership, 1775-1825. (Illus.). 448p. 1981. 55.00x (ISBN 0-262-02167-6). MIT Pr.

Tannahill, Neal, jt. auth. see Bedichek, Wendell M.

Tannahill, R. Neal. The Communist Parties of Western Europe: A Comparative Study. LC 77-94750. (Contributions in Political Science). 1978. lib. bdg. 29.95x (ISBN 0-313-20318-0, TCP/). Greenwood.

Tannahill, Reay. A Dark & Distant Shore. 608p. 1983. 16.95 (ISBN 0-312-18225-2). St Martin.

--Sex in History. LC 79-15053. 480p. 1982. 17.95 (ISBN 0-8128-2580-2); 11.95 (ISBN 0-8128-6115-9). Stein & Day.

Tannebaum, S. W., ed. Cytochalasins: Biochemical & Cell Biological Aspects. (Frontiers of Biology Ser.: Vol. 46). 1978. 118.50 (ISBN 0-7204-0651-X, North-Holland). Elsevier.

Tannehill, Ivan R. Hurricane Hunters. LC 55-9480. (Illus.). (gr. 9 up). 1955. 4.50 o.p. (ISBN 0-396-03789-5). Dodd.

Tannehill, Robert C., ed. Semeia Twenty: Pronouncement Stories. (Semeia Ser.). 9.95 (ISBN 0-686-96273-7, 06 20 20). Scholars Pr CA.

Tannehill, Victor C. Boomerang: Story of the Three-Hundred & Twentieth Bombardment Group in WW-II. (Illus.). 316p. 1978. Repr. of 1978 ed. 40.00 o.p. (ISBN 0-9605900-0-5, Pub. by Tannehill). Aviation.

--Pilot's Flight Operating Instructions for the B-26 Martin Marauder. LC 81-67414. (Illus.). 72p. 1981. pap. 6.95 (ISBN 0-9605900-1-3). Boomerang.

Tannen, Deborah. Conversational Style. Wallat, Cynthia & Green, Judith, eds. (Language & Learning for Human Service Professions Ser.). 196p. 1983. text ed. 19.95 (ISBN 0-89391-188-7); pap. text ed. 11.50 (ISBN 0-89391-200-X). Ablex Pub.

--Lilika Nakos. (World Autors Ser.). 200p. 1983. lib. bdg. 21.95 (ISBN 0-8057-6524-7, Twayne). G K Hall.

Tannen, Deborah, ed. Coherence in Spoken & Written Discourse. (The Advances in Discourse Processes Ser.: Vol. 12). 1983. text ed. 29.50 (ISBN 0-89391-097-X); pap. text ed. 16.50 (ISBN 0-89391-098-8). Ablex Pub.

Tannen, Mary. Huntley Nutley & the Missing Link. LC 82-18651. (Illus.). 128p. (gr. 3-5). 1983. 9.95 (ISBN 0-394-85759-3); lib. bdg. 9.99 (ISBN 0-394-95759-8). Knopf.

--The Lost Legend of Finn. LC 81-15599. (Illus.). 160p. (gr. 5-8). 1982. PLB 9.99 (ISBN 0-394-95211-1); 9.95 (ISBN 0-686-96764-X). Knopf.

--The Lost Legend of Finn. 160p. 1983. pap. 2.25 (ISBN 0-380-63354-X, Camelot). Avon.

Tannenbaum, Abraham J. Perspectives on Gifted & Talented Education, 6 vols. (Orig.). Set. pap. text ed. 34.95x (ISBN 0-8077-2594-3). Tchrs Coll.

Tannenbaum, Abraham J., ed. see Hagen, Elizabeth.

Tannenbaum, Abraham J., ed. see Hall, Eleanor & Skinner, Nancy.

Tannenbaum, Abraham J., ed. see Lindsey, Margaret.

Tannenbaum, Abraham J., ed. see Morgan, Harry M., et al.

Tannenbaum, Abraham J., ed. see Roedell, Wendy C., et al.

Tannenbaum, Arnold S., et al. Hierarchy in Organizations: An International Comparison. LC 73-20963. (Social & Behavioral Science Ser.). 240p. 1974. 21.95x (ISBN 0-87589-219-1). Jossey-Bass.

Tannenbaum, Beulah & Stillman, Myra. Understanding Sound. (Illus.). 192p. (gr. 9-12). 1973. PLB 7.95 (ISBN 0-07-062866-1, GB). McGraw.

Tannenbaum, Frank. Ten Keys to Latin America. 1966. pap. 4.95 (ISBN 0-394-70312-X, Vin). Random.

--Wall Shadows: A Study in American Prisons. (Criminology, Law Enforcement, & Social Problems Ser.: No. 205). Date not set. Repr. of 1922 ed. cancelled. Patterson Smith.

Tannenbaum, Percy H. & Kostrich, Leslie J. Turned-On TV - Turned-Off Voters: Policy Options for Election Projections. (People & Communication Ser.: Vol. 15). 244p. 1983. 25.00 (ISBN 0-8039-1929-8). Sage.

Tannenbaum, Samuel A. Problems in Shakespeare's Penmanship. (MLA Rev. Fund Ser.: No. 2). 1927. pap. 24.00 (ISBN 0-527-88750-1). Kraus Repr.

Tannenbaum, Steven, et al, eds. see Fish Protein Conference.

Tannenbaum, Steven R. & Wang, Daniel I., eds. Single-Cell Protein II. 1974. text ed. 30.00x (ISBN 0-262-20030-9). MIT Pr.

Tannenbaum, Steven R., jt. ed. see Scanlan, Richard A.

Tannenhauser, Carol, jt. auth. see Tannenhauser, Robert.

Tannenhauser, Robert & Tannenhauser, Carol. Tax Shelters: A Complete Guide. 1980. pap. 3.50 (ISBN 0-451-11832-4, AE1832, Sig). NAL.

--Tax Shelters: An Investment Guide. 1978. 10.95 o.p. (ISBN 0-517-53487-8, Dist. by Crown). Crown.

Tanner. The Prudent Use of Medicine. LC 81-9273. (Library of Health). PLB 18.60 (ISBN 0-8094-3771-6). Silver.

Tanner, Adrian. Bringing Home Animals: Religious Ideology & Mode of Production of the Mistassini Cree Hunters. LC 79-11612. 1979. 26.00x (ISBN 0-312-09633-X). St Martin.

Tanner, Alain, jt. auth. see Berger, John.

Tanner, C. Kenneth & Williams, Earl J. Educational Planning & Decision Making: A View Through the Organizational Process. LC 80-8631. 256p. 1981. 26.95x (ISBN 0-669-04330-3). Lexington Bks.

Tanner, Christine A. & Schneider, Harriet. Developing Tests to Evaluate Student Achievement in Baccalaureate Nursing Programs. 64p. 1979. 5.50 (ISBN 0-686-38293-5, 15-1761). Natl League Nurse.
Tanner, Clara L. Apache Indian Baskets. 204p. 1982. 35.00 (ISBN 0-8165-0778-3). U of Ariz Pr.
--Prehistoric Southwestern Craft Arts. LC 75-19865. (Illus.). 1976. 27.50 (ISBN 0-8165-0582-9); pap. 9.95 o.s.i. (ISBN 0-8165-0416-4). U of Ariz Pr.
--Southwest Indian Craft Arts. LC 66-24299. (Illus.). 1968. 27.50 (ISBN 0-8165-0083-5). U of Ariz Pr.
Tanner, Daniel. Secondary Education: Perspectives & Prospects. (Illus.). 512p. 1972. text ed. 20.95x (ISBN 0-02-418910-3). Macmillan.
Tanner, Daniel & Tanner, Laurel. Curriculum Development: Theory into Practice. 2nd ed. (Illus.). 1980. text ed. 22.95x (ISBN 0-02-418960-X). Macmillan.
Tanner, Don, ed. see Cole, Margaret R.
Tanner, Don, ed. see Popoff, Peter.
Tanner, Don, ed. see Zack, Jinny.
Tanner, Donna M. The Lesbian Couple. LC 77-16720. 160p. 1978. 17.95x (ISBN 0-669-02078-8). Lexington Bks.
Tanner, Fran A. Basic Drama Projects. rev. ed. 1977. lib. bdg. 7.25 o.p. (ISBN 0-931054-00-1). Clark Pub.
Tanner, Hans & Nye, Doug. Ferrari. rev. ed. 540p. 1982. 55.00 (ISBN 0-85429-238-1). Haynes Pubns.
Tanner, Heather & Tanner, Robin. Woodland Plants. LC 82-5558. (Illus.). 216p. 1982. with slipcover 60.00 (ISBN 0-8052-3821-2). Schocken.
Tanner, J. L., jt. auth. see Everard.
Tanner, J. M., jt. auth. see Eveleth, P. B.
Tanner, J. M. & Whitehouse, R. H., eds. Atlas of Children's Growth: Normal Variation & Growth Disorders. LC 77-8381. 206p. 1982. 268.50 (ISBN 0-12-683340-0). Acad Pr.
Tanner, J. M., et al. Assessment of Skeletal Maturity & Prediction of Adult Height: TW 2 Method. 1976. 51.00 o.s.i. (ISBN 0-12-683350-8). Acad Pr.
Tanner, James T. Guide to the Study of Animal Populations. LC 77-13630. 1978. 11.95x (ISBN 0-87049-235-7). U of Tenn Pr.
Tanner, Jerald & Tanner, Sandra. Changing World of Mormonism. LC 79-18311. 1979. 13.95 (ISBN 0-8024-1234-3). Moody.
Tanner, Joseph R. English Constitutional Conflicts of the Seventeenth Century, 1603-1689. LC 82-25122. x, 315p. 1983. Repr. of 1928 ed. lib. bdg. 49.75x (ISBN 0-313-23855-3, TAEN). Greenwood.
--Mister Pepys: An Introduction to the Diary Together with a Sketch of His Later Life. LC 71-110870. 1971. Repr. of 1925 ed. lib. bdg. 16.25x (ISBN 0-8371-4549-X, TAMP). Greenwood.
Tanner, Laurel, jt. auth. see Tanner, Daniel.
Tanner, Leslie. Voices from Women's Liberation. pap. 1.50 (ISBN 0-451-61356-2, ME1356, Ment). NAL.
Tanner, Louise. Dr. I.R.T. LC 75-46634. 256p. 1976. 7.95 o.p. (ISBN 0-698-10730-6, Coward). Putnam Pub Group.
Tanner, Nancy. On Becoming Human. LC 80-21526. (Illus.). 350p. 1981. 32.50 (ISBN 0-521-23554-5); pap. 10.95 (ISBN 0-521-28028-1). Cambridge U Pr.
Tanner, Ogden. The Battle of the Bulge. (World War II Ser.). (Illus.). 1979. lib. bdg. 19.92 (ISBN 0-8094-2531-9); 17.28 (ISBN 0-8094-2532-7). Silver.
--The Canadians. LC 76-26845. (Old West Ser.). (Illus.). (gr. 5 up). 1977. 17.28 (ISBN 0-8094-1543-7, Pub. by Time-Life). Silver.
--Herbs. LC 76-51513. (Time-Life Encyclopedia for Gardening Ser.). (Illus.). (gr. 6 up). 1977. PLB 17.28 (ISBN 0-8094-2551-3, Pub. by Time-Life). Silver.
--The New England Wilds. LC 73-92887. (American Wilderness). (Illus.). (gr. 6 up). 1974. PLB 15.96 (ISBN 0-8094-1230-6, Pub. by Time-Life). Silver.
--The Ranchers. LC 77-85283. (The Old West Ser.). (Illus.). 1977. 17.28 (ISBN 0-686-51080-1). Silver.
--Urban Wilds. LC 75-4116. (American Wilderness Ser.). (Illus.). (gr. 6 up). 1975. PLB 15.96 (ISBN 0-8094-1335-3, Pub. by Time-Life). Silver.
Tanner, Ogden, jt. auth. see Crockett, James U.
Tanner, R., jt. ed. see Kurokawa, K.
Tanner, R. E. The Witch Murders in Sukumaland: A Sociological Commentary. 41p. 1970. 4.50x (ISBN 0-8419-9713-6). Holmes & Meier.
Tanner, Robin, jt. auth. see Tanner, Heather.
Tanner, Sandra, jt. auth. see Tanner, Jerald.
Tanner, Stephen L. Ken Kesey. (United States Authors Ser.). 180p. 1983. lib. bdg. 13.95 (ISBN 0-8057-7385-1, Twayne). G K Hall.
Tanner, T. Saul Bellow. (Writers & Critics Ser.). 1978. 19.75 (ISBN 0-686-82880-1). Chips.
Tanner, Terence A. Frank Waters: A Bibliography. (Illus.). 304p. 1983. 45.00 (ISBN 0-916638-07-3). Meyerbooks.
Tanner, Tony. Thomas Pynchon. 1982. pap. 4.25 (ISBN 0-416-31670-0). Methuen Inc.
Tanner, Tony, ed. see Austen, Jane.
Tanner, Tracy. How to Find a Man...& Make Him Keep You. LC 78-65883. 256p. 1979. 9.95 o.s.i. (ISBN 0-89479-038-2). A & W Pubs.
Tanner, William E., ed. see Burke, Kenneth, et al.
Tanner, William F. Coastal Sedimentology. 315p. 1977. pap. 20.00 (ISBN 0-686-83995-1). FSU Geology.
--Near-Shore Sedimentology. 300p. 1983. pap. 40.00 (ISBN 0-686-83997-8). FSU Geology.
Tanner, William F., ed. Sediment Transport in the Near-Shore Zone. 147p. 1974. pap. 20.00 (ISBN 0-686-83994-3). FSU Geology.
--Shorelines Past & Present, 3 vols. 745p. 1980. pap. 50.00 (ISBN 0-686-83996-X). FSU Geology.
--Standards for Measuring Shoreline Changes. 87p. 1978. pap. 5.00 (ISBN 0-686-36732-4). FSU Geology.
Tannery, Jules & Molk, Jules. Elements de la Theorie des Fonctions Elliptiques, 4 vols. in 2. 2nd ed. LC 70-113152. 1145p. (Fr.). 1972. Set. text ed. 49.50 (ISBN 0-8284-0257-4). Chelsea Pub.
Tannigel, Fritz, jt. auth. see Peinkofer, Karl.
Tanning, Dorothea. Abyss. 1977. pap. 5.00 (ISBN 0-918746-02-7). Standard Edns.
Tanning, Dorothea, tr. see Ernst, Max.
Tanous, Peter. The Earhart Mission. 224p. 1982. 2.75 (ISBN 0-553-20943-4). Bantam.
Tanrock, L. W., ed. see De Sevigne.
Tanselle, G. T., ed. Typee, Omoo, Mardi: Herman Melville. LC 81-18600. 1344p. 1982. 27.50 (ISBN 0-940450-00-3). Literary Classics.
Tanselle, G. Thomas, ed. see Melville, Herman.
Tanselle, Thomas G., ed. see Melville, Herman.
Tansey, Richard G., jt. auth. see De la Croix, Horst.
Tan Sri Haji Khalid. Malaysia: An Anthology. 1978. 6.95 o.p. (ISBN 0-533-03382-9). Vantage.
Tan Sri Lim Swee Aun. Rubber & the Malaysian Economy: Implications of Declining Prices. (Papers in International Studies: Southeast Asia: No. 11). (Illus.). 1969. pap. 4.00 (ISBN 0-89680-005-9, Ohio U Ctr Intl). Ohio U Pr.
Tan Tai Wei. The Worth of Religious Truth-Claims: A Case for Religious Education. LC 81-43864. 128p. (Orig.). 1982. pap. text ed. 8.25 (ISBN 0-8191-2369-2). U Pr of Amer.
Tantillo, Joe. Amazing Ancient Treasures. LC 82-8287. (Illus.). 64p. (gr. 1 up). 1983. pap. 2.95 (ISBN 0-394-85489-6). Pantheon.
Tanz, Christine. Studies in the Acquisition of Deictic Terms. LC 79-12272. (Cambridge Studies in Linguistics: No. 26). (Illus.). 1980. 37.50 (ISBN 0-521-22740-2). Cambridge U Pr.
Tanz, Ralph D., et al, eds. Factors Influencing Myocardial Contractility. 1967. 89.50 (ISBN 0-12-683450-4). Acad Pr.
Tanzer, Herbert & Lyons, Nick. Your Pet Isn't Sick: (He Just Wants You to Think So) 1978. pap. 1.75 o.s.i. (ISBN 0-515-04599-3). Jove Pubns.
Tanzer, J. M., ed. Animal Models in Cariology: Symposium Proceedings. 458p. 25.00 (ISBN 0-917000-09-9). IRL Pr.
Tanzer, Michael. The Race for Resources: Continuing Struggles Over Minerals & Fuels. LC 80-18027. 285p. 1981. 16.00 o.p. (ISBN 0-85345-540-6); pap. 6.50 (ISBN 0-85345-541-4, PB5414). Monthly Rev.
Tanzer, Milt. Commercial Real Estate Desk Book. LC 81-1190. (Illus.). 414p. 1981. 59.00 (ISBN 0-87624-090-2). Inst Busn Plan.
--Converter's Guide to High Profits from Condo & Time Sharing Conversion. LC 81-20262. 278p. 1982. 89.50 (ISBN 0-87624-103-8). Inst Busn Plan.
Tanzi, Vito. Inflation & Personal Income Tax. LC 79-52667. 1980. 32.50 (ISBN 0-521-22987-1). Cambridge U Pr.
Tapahonomito, Luci. Seasonal Woman. 72p. (Orig.). 1982. pap. 5.00 (ISBN 0-940510-04-9). Tooth of Time.
Tapasyananda, Swami, tr. see Vyasa.
Taper, Bernard. Balanchine: A Biography. (Illus.). 352p. 1974. 8.95 o.p. (ISBN 0-02-616260-1). Macmillan.
Taper, L. J., jt. auth. see Ritchey, S. J.
Tapia, Fernando. The Magic Rooster: A Shortcut to Self-Psychotherapy. Martin, Sara H., ed. 1983. 6.95 (ISBN 0-533-05549-0). Vantage.
Tapia, John R. The Indian in the Spanish-American Novel. LC 80-6182. 120p. (Orig.). 1981. lib. bdg. 18.25 (ISBN 0-8191-1428-6); pap. text ed. 8.25 (ISBN 0-8191-1438-3). U Pr of Amer.
--The Spanish Romantic Theater. LC 80-5565. 87p. 1980. lib. bdg. 14.75 (ISBN 0-8191-1276-3); pap. text ed. 7.00 (ISBN 0-8191-1277-1). U Pr of Amer.
Tapia, Juan R. La Tierra Comprometida: Pa' los Gringos Numas? LC 81-40170. (Illus.). 226p. (Orig., Span.). 1982. pap. text ed. 10.75 (ISBN 0-8191-1932-6). U Pr of Amer.
Tapia, Ralph. Theology of Christ: Commentary. 1971. pap. text ed. 6.95 o.p. (ISBN 0-02-829380-0). Glencoe.
Tapiero, C., jt. ed. see Yaron, D.
Tapiero, C. S. Managerial Planning: An Optimum & Stochastic Approach, 2 vols. 668p. 1977. Set. 64.00 (ISBN 0-677-05400-9). Gordon.
Tapinos, Georges & Piotrow, Phyllis. Six Billion People: Demographic Dilemmas & World Politics. (Illus.). 1978. text ed. 15.95x (ISBN 0-07-062876-9, P&RB); pap. 5.95 (ISBN 0-07-062877-7). McGraw.
Taplin, Oliver. Greek Tragedy in Action. 1979. 28.50x (ISBN 0-520-03704-9); pap. 4.95 (ISBN 0-520-03949-1). U of Cal Pr.
Taplow, Alan B. Lao Tzu Talks to "Be". LC 81-70990. (Illus.). 96p. 1983. 10.50 (ISBN 0-941758-00-1, Co-pub Ctr Orient Studies); pap. 5.95 (ISBN 0-941758-01-X). Omlet Pubns.
Tapp, Edwin. Policies of Survival. (Studies in Twentieth Century History). 1979. pap. text ed. 4.50x o.p. (ISBN 0-86863-534-0, 00549). Heinemann Ed.
Tapp, Elizabeth, tr. see Steiner, Rudolf, et al.
Tapp, Jack, ed. Reinforcement. 1969. 60.00 (ISBN 0-12-683650-7). Acad Pr.
Tapp, Michael, tr. see Steiner, Rudolf, et al.
Tapp, Michael, tr. see Steiner, Rudolf.
Tapp, Robert B. Religion Among the Unitarian Universalists: Converts in the Step Father's House. LC 72-82127. (Quantitative Studies in Social Relations Ser). 1973. 35.00 (ISBN 0-12-785824-5). Acad Pr.
Tappan, Frances. Healing Massage Techniques: A Study of Eastern & Western Methods. (Illus.). 1978. ref. ed. 18.95 (ISBN 0-8359-2821-7); pap. 8.95 (ISBN 0-8359-2819-5). Reston.
Tappan, Paul W. Crime, Justice & Correction. (Sociology Ser.). 1960. text ed. 14.95 o.p. (ISBN 0-07-062870-X, C). McGraw.
--Delinquent Girls in Court: A Study of the Wayward Minor Court of New York. LC 69-14950. (Criminology, Law Enforcement, & Social Problems Ser.: No. 67). 1969. Repr. of 1947 ed. 15.00x (ISBN 0-87585-067-7). Patterson Smith.
Tappan, William. Real Estate Exchange & Acquisition Techniques. 1982. pap. 12.95 (ISBN 0-13-762567-7, Reward). P-H.
Tappe, J., jt. auth. see Beyl, F. R.
Tappen, Ruth M. Nursing Leadership: Concepts & Practice. LC 82-22144. (Illus.). 450p. 1983. pap. text ed. 13.95 (ISBN 0-8036-8334-0). Davis Co.
Tapper, Ted. Political Education & Stability: Elite Responses to Political Conflict. LC 75-30817. 288p. 1976. 31.50 o.p. (ISBN 0-471-01361-7, Pub. by Wiley-Interscience). Wiley.
Tappert, Theodore G., ed. & tr. see Spener, Philip J.
Tapscott, Bangs L. Elementary Applied Symbolic Logic. (Illus.). 512p. 1976. text ed. 20.95 (ISBN 0-13-252940-8). P-H.
Tapscott, Don. Office Automation: A User-Driven Method. 264p. 1982. 27.50 (ISBN 0-306-41071-0, Plenum Pr). Plenum Pub.
Tar, Zolton. The Frankfurt School: The Critical Theories of Max Horkheimer & Theodor W. Adorno. LC 77-2353. 243p. 1977. 27.50 o.p. (ISBN 0-471-84536-1, Pub. by Wiley-Interscience). Wiley.
Tarachow, Michael, ed. & intro. by. Toward a Further Definition. LC 76-21409. (Illus.). 1983. 24.00 (ISBN 0-915316-42-0); pap. 12.50 (ISBN 0-915316-41-2). Pentagram.
Tarachow, Mike, tr. see Arbit Books.
Taracido, Frank, tr. see Barber, Cyril J.
Taracido, Frank, tr. see Strauss, Richard.
Taraman, K. CAD-CAM: Meeting Today's Productivity Challenge. 296p. 1982. text ed. 39.00 (ISBN 0-13-110122-6). P-H.
Taran, Isabel C., jt. ed. see Davis, Lisa E.
Taran, Leonardo. Speusippus of Athens: A Critical Study with a Collection of the Related Texts & Commentary. (Philosophia Antiqua: Vol. 39). xxvii, 521p. 1982. pap. write for info. (ISBN 90-04-06505-9). E J Brill.
Taran, Leonardo, ed. see Billings, Grace H.
Taran, Leonardo, ed. see Wilkins, Eliza G.
Taranatha, Lama, ed. History of Buddhism in India. Lama Chimpa, Alaka Chattopadhyaya & Chattopadhyaya, Alalca, trs. from Tibetan. 500p. 1980. Repr. of 1608 ed. text ed. 26.00x (ISBN 0-391-02176-1). Humanities.
Taranfeld, Clancey G. The United States, Soviet Russia, Europe, the Middle East, Israel & the Rigid Pressure of the Kondratieff Cycle. (Illus.). 139p. 1983. 87.75 (ISBN 0-86722-035-X). Inst Econ Pol.
Tarasov, K. I. The Spectroscope. LC 74-13504. 378p. 1974. 53.50 o.p. (ISBN 0-470-84537-6). Krieger.
Tarasov, L. V. Calculus: Basic Concepts for High Schools. 184p. 1982. pap. 3.50 (ISBN 0-8285-2278-2, Pub. by Mir Pubs USSR). Imported Pubns.
Tarasov, L. V., jt. ed. see Gurevich, I. I.
Tarassuk, Leonid & Blair, Claude, eds. The Complete Encyclopedia of Arms & Weapons. LC 80-5922. (Illus.). 544p. 1982. 41.50 (ISBN 0-671-42257-X). S&S.
Tarbert, Gary C., ed. Book Review Index: Annual Clothbound Cumulations, 16 cumulations. Incl. 1965 Cumulation (ISBN 0-8103-0550-X); 1966 Cumulation (ISBN 0-8103-0551-8); 1967 Cumulation (ISBN 0-8103-0552-6); 1968 Cumulation (ISBN 0-8103-0553-4); 1969 Cumulation (ISBN 0-8103-0554-2); 1970 Cumulation (ISBN 0-8103-0555-0); 1971 Cumulation (ISBN 0-8103-0556-9); 1972 Cumulation (ISBN 0-8103-0557-7); 1973 Cumulation (ISBN 0-8103-0560-7); 1974 Cumulation (ISBN 0-8103-0562-3); 1975 Cumulation (ISBN 0-8103-0564-X); 1976 Cumulation (ISBN 0-8103-0566-6); 1977 Cumulation (ISBN 0-8103-0567-4); 1978 Cumulation (ISBN 0-8103-0568-2); 1979 Cumulation (ISBN 0-8103-0569-0); 1980 Cumulation (ISBN 0-8103-0571-2). LC 65-9908. 92.00x ea. (1965-1981). Gale.
--Book Review Index Nineteen Sixty-Nine to Nineteen Seventy-Nine: A Master Cumulation, 7 vols. 4000p. 1980. Set. 600.00x (ISBN 0-8103-0570-4). Gale.
--Children's Book Review Index: A Master Cumulation 1969-1981, 4 vols. 1982. 220.00x (ISBN 0-8103-2045-2). Gale.
--Children's Book Review Index: Annual Clothbound Volumes. LC 75-27408. 58.00x ea.; Annual 1975. (ISBN 0-8103-0626-3); Annual 1976. (ISBN 0-8103-0627-1); Annual 1977. (ISBN 0-8103-0628-X); Annual 1978. (ISBN 0-8103-0629-8); Annual 1979. (ISBN 0-8103-0630-1). Annual 1980 (ISBN 0-8103-0631-X). Annual 1981 (ISBN 0-8103-0632-8). Gale.
Tarbuck, Edward & Lutgens, Fred. Earth Science. 2nd ed. 1979. text ed. 22.95 (ISBN 0-675-08303-6). Additional supplements may be obtained from publisher. Merrill.
Tarbuck, Edward J. & Lutgens, Frederick K. Earth Science. 3rd ed. 544p. 1982. text ed. 24.95 (ISBN 0-675-09921-8). Additional supplements may be obtained from publisher. Merrill.
Tarbuck, Edward J., jt. auth. see Lutgens, Frederick K.
Tarbuck, Kenneth J., ed. see Luxemburg, Rosa & Bukharin, Nikolai.
Tarbush, Mohammad. The Role of the Military in Politics: A Case Study of Iraq to 1941. 220p. 1983. 28.95 (ISBN 0-7103-0036-0). Routledge & Kegan.
Tarcov, Edith, tr. see Melchinger, Siegfried.
Tarczan, Constance. An Educator's Guide to Psychological Tests: Descriptions & Classroom Implications. (Illus.). 128p. 1975. 12.75 o.p. (ISBN 0-398-02427-8); spiral 8.75x (ISBN 0-398-02491-X). C C Thomas.
Tarde, Gabriel. Penal Philosophy. Howell, Rapalje, tr. LC 68-55783. (Criminology, Law Enforcement, & Social Problems Ser.: No. 16). 1968. Repr. of 1912 ed. 26.00x (ISBN 0-87585-016-2). Patterson Smith.
Tardent, P., ed. Developmental & Cellular Biology of Coelenerates. 1980. 77.00 (ISBN 0-444-80221-5). Elsevier.
Tardieu, Jean. Formeries. Mathe, S., tr. from Fr. 1983. 11.00 (ISBN 0-931556-10-4). Translation Pr.
Tardu, Maxime. Human Rights: The International Petition System. LC 79-14453. 1979. Bdrs. 1 & 2. 85.00 ea.; Rel. 2. 85.00; Set. loose-leaf 3 170.00. Oceana.
Tardy, Mary T., ed. The Living Female Writers of the South. LC 75-44070. 1979. Repr. of 1872 ed. 74.00x (ISBN 0-8103-4286-3). Gale.
Target, C. M. The Nun in the Concentration Camp. 1974. pap. 1.55 (ISBN 0-08-017611-9). Pergamon.
Targowski, Andrew. Red Fascism: The Polish Revolution of 1980. LC 82-721719. 210p. 1983. 15.95 (ISBN 0-931494-23-0). Brunswick Pub.
Tarhan, M. Orhan. Catalytic Reactor Design. (Illus.). 352p. 1983. 36.95 (ISBN 0-07-062871-8, P&RB). McGraw.
Tarharka. Black Manhood: The Building of Civilization by the Black Man of the Nile. rev. ed. LC 79-65009. 1979. pap. text ed. 12.50 (ISBN 0-8191-0780-8). U Pr of Amer.
Tari, Mel. Como un Viento Recio. 208p. Date not set. 2.75 (ISBN 0-88113-041-9). Edit Betania.
Tarjan, Armen C. Supplement (1961-1965) to Check List of Plant & Soil Nematodes: A Nomenclatorial Compilation. LC 60-10226. 1967. 6.75 (ISBN 0-8130-0224-9). U Presses Fla.
Tarkenton, Frances. Incredible Fran. Date not set. pap. 4.95 (ISBN 0-911866-92-2). Advocate.
Tarkington, Booth. The Magnificent Ambersons. 1960. 9.00 (ISBN 0-8446-1443-2). Peter Smith.
--Penrod & Sam. 1975. lib. bdg. 16.95 (ISBN 0-89966-179-3). Buccaneer Bks.
--Seventeen. 190p. 1981. lib. bdg. 15.95x (ISBN 0-89966-174-2). Buccaneer Bks.
--The World Does Move. LC 76-8903. 1976. Repr. of 1928 ed. lib. bdg. 19.25x (ISBN 0-8371-8876-8, TAWD). Greenwood.
Tarling, D. H. & Runcorn, S. K., eds. Implications of Continental Drift to the Earth Sciences. 1973. Vol. 1. 1973. 93.00 o.s.i. (ISBN 0-12-683701-5); Vol. 2 1973. 90.00 o.s.i. (ISBN 0-12-683702-3). Acad Pr.
Tarling, Nicholas. Sulu & Sabah: A Study of the British Policy Towards the Philippines & North Borneo from the Late Eighteenth Century. (Illus.). 1978. 39.00x o.p. (ISBN 0-19-580337-X). Oxford U Pr.
Tarling, Nicholas, jt. ed. see Ch'En, Jerome.
Tarling, Peter N. The Burthen, the Risk & the Glory: A Biography of Sir James Brook. 350p. 1982. 39.00 (ISBN 0-19-582508-X). Oxford U Pr.
Tarlock, A. Dan. Water Resource Management: 1983 Supplement. 2nd ed. (University Casebook Ser.). 223p. 1982. pap. text ed. write for info. (ISBN 0-88277-103-5). Foundation Pr.
Tarlow, Eric K., jt. auth. see Clontz, Ralph C., Jr.
Tarlow, Eric K., jt. auth. see Thorndike, David.
Tarlton, Leigh G. The Two Worlds of Coral Harper. LC 82-48758. 160p. (gr. 10 up). 1983. 11.95 (ISBN 0-15-292371-3, HJ). HarBraceJ.
Tarn, William W. Alexander the Great, 2 vols. LC 78-74533. (Illus.). 1979. Vol. 1. 27.95 (ISBN 0-521-22584-1); Vol. 1. pap. 7.95 (ISBN 0-521-29563-7); Vol. 2. 49.50 (ISBN 0-521-22585-X). Cambridge U Pr.
--Hellenistic Civilization. rev. ed. 1961. pap. 7.95 (ISBN 0-452-00597-3, F597, Mer). NAL.
Tarney, J., jt. ed. see Atherton, M. P.

Tarnopol, Lester, ed. Comparative Reading & Learning Difficulties. Tarnopol, Muriel. 576p. 1981. 38.95x (ISBN 0-669-04107-6). Lexington Bks.

Tarnopol, Lester & Tarnopol, Muriel, eds. Brain Function & Reading Disabilities. LC 77-6300. (Illus.). 232p. 1977. pap. 17.95 (ISBN 0-8391-1130-4). Univ Park.

Tarnopol, Muriel see Tarnopol, Lester.

Tarnopol, Muriel, jt. ed. see Tarnopol, Lester.

Tarnor, Norman, jt. auth. see Tarnor, Pearl.

Tarnor, Pearl & Tarnor, Norman. Biddur Program III to Hebrew & Heritage. 128p. 1983. pap. text ed. 3.50 (ISBN 0-87441-359-1). Behrman.

--Siddur Program, II to Hebrew & Heritage. (Illus.). 128p. 1982. pap. text ed. 3.50 (ISBN 0-87441-330-3). Behrman.

Tarnov, Peter. A Cheerful Pessimist. 312p. 1983. pap. 8.00 (ISBN 0-911109-01-3). Oxymora Bk Pr.

--Seven You Will Remember. 176p. 1983. pap. 8.00 (ISBN 0-911109-00-5). Oxymora Bk Pr.

Tarpley, Fred A. From Blinky to Blue-John: A Word Atlas of Northeast Texas. new ed. LC 76-105904. 1970. text ed. 10.95x o.s.i. (ISBN 0-8413-4671-2). University Pr.

Tarpy, Roger & Mayer, Richard. Readings in Learning & Memory. 1979. pap. text ed. 10.95x (ISBN 0-673-15110-7). Scott F.

Tarpy, Roger M. Basic Principles of Learning. 1975. pap. 12.50x (ISBN 0-673-07905-8). Scott F.

--Principles of Animal Learning & Motivation. 1982. text ed. 21.95x (ISBN 0-673-15383-5). Scott F.

Tarpy, Roger M. & Mayer, Richard E. Foundations of Learning & Memory. 1978. text ed. 19.95x (ISBN 0-673-15074-7). Scott F.

Tarquin, Anthony J., jt. auth. see Blank, Leland T.

Tarr, Andrea, jt. auth. see Katz, William A.

Tarr, Bill. One Hundred One Easy-to-Learn Classic Magic Tricks. 1977. pap. 8.95 (ISBN 0-394-72481-X, Vin). Random.

Tarr, F. C. & Centeno, Augusto. A Graded Spanish Review: Grammar with Composition. 2nd ed. (gr. 9-12). 1973. text ed. 18.95 (ISBN 0-13-362160-X). P-H.

Tarr, John C. The History of Written & Printed Letters. 160p. 1982. 70.00x (ISBN 0-284-39192-1, Pub. by C Skilton Scotland). State Mutual Bk.

Tarr, Katherine. Herbs, Helps, & Pressure Points For Pregnancy & Childbirth. (Illus.). 69p. 1981. pap. 3.95 (ISBN 0-9609514-0-7). Sunbeam.

Tarr, Stanley B. & Fay, Clifford T., Jr. Basic Bookkeeping for the Hospitality Industry. (Illus.). 152p. 1975. text ed. 14.95x o.p. (ISBN 0-86612-006-8). Educ Inst Am Hotel.

Tarr, William, jt. auth. see Ross, Barry.

Tarr, Yvonne. The Up-with-Wholesome, Down-with-Store-Bought Book of Recipes & Household Formulas. 1975. pap. 9.95 (ISBN 0-394-73140-9). Random.

Tarr, Yvonne Y. The Great East Coast Seafood Book. LC 81-52921. (Illus.). 408p. (Orig.). 1982. pap. 12.95 (ISBN 0-394-75325-9, Vin). Random.

--The Super Easy-Step-by-Step Winemaking. (Orig.). 1975. pap. 6.95 (ISBN 0-394-72012-1, Vin). Random.

Tarrant, John R. Agricultural Geography: Problems in Modern Geography. 1980. 31.50 (ISBN 0-7153-6286-0). David & Charles.

--Food Policies. LC 79-40740. (Wiley Series on Studies in Environmental Management & Resources Development). 338p. 1980. 57.95 (ISBN 0-471-27656-1, Pub. by Wiley-Interscience). Wiley.

Tarrant, Patrick. Tis Sweet & Sad in an Irish Cottage. 152p. 1982. pap. 4.00 (ISBN 0-9608850-0-5). Tarrant.

Tarrh, John M., jt. auth. see Thome, Richard J.

Tarrow, Norma B. & Lundsteen, Sara W. Activities & Resources for Guiding Young Children's Learning. (Illus.). 336p. (Orig.). 1981. pap. text ed. 13.95x (ISBN 0-07-039108-4). McGraw.

Tarrow, Sidney, et al. Territorial Politics in Industrial Nations. LC 77-83439. (Praeger Special Studies). 1978. 36.95 o.p. (ISBN 0-03-040961-6). Praeger.

Tarschys, Daniel. The Soviet Political Agenda: Problems & Priorities 1950-1970. LC 78-53821. 1979. 27.50 (ISBN 0-87332-119-7). M E Sharpe.

Tarshis, jt. auth. see Ralston.

Tarshis, Barry. The Average American Book. 1981. pap. 2.95 (ISBN 0-451-09486-7, E9486, Sig). NAL.

--How To Write Like a Pro: A Guide to Effective Nonfiction Writing. 192p. 1982. 10.95 (ISBN 0-453-00418-0, H418). NAL.

--Tennis & the Mind. LC 77-76789. 1977. 7.95 o.p. (ISBN 0-689-10749-8). Atheneum.

--What It Costs: The Ultimate Shopper's Guide. LC 77-3233. (Illus.). 1977. 8.95 o.p. (ISBN 0-399-11933-7). Putnam Pub Group.

Tarshis, Barry, jt. auth. see Funk, Peter.

Tarshis, Barry, jt. auth. see Schneider, Allen M.

Tarski, Alfred. Logic, Semantics, Metamathematics. Corcoran, John, ed. Woodger, J. H., tr. from Polish. 1983. lib. bdg. 40.00 o.s.i. (ISBN 0-915144-75-1); pap. text ed. 30.00 o.s.i. (ISBN 0-915144-76-X). Hackett Pub.

Tarsky, Bernard, jt. ed. see White, Leonard.

Tart, Charles T. Altered States of Consciousness. LC 74-189947. 600p. 1972. pap. 8.95 (ISBN 0-385-06728-3, Anch). Doubleday.

--Altered States of Consciousness: A Book of Readings. LC 69-16040. 575p. 1969. 30.95 (ISBN 0-471-84560-4). Wiley.

Tart, Charles T., et al, eds. Mind at Large: Institute of Electrical & Electronic Engineers Symposia on the Nature of Extrasensory Perception. LC 79-9982. 288p. 1979. 29.95 o.p. (ISBN 0-03-050476-7). Praeger.

Tartak, Laura M. Cockatiels. (Illus.). 96p. 4.95 (ISBN 0-87666-885-6, KW-057). TFH Pubns.

Tartakower, A. & Du Mont, J. Five Hundred Master Games of Chess. Incl. Bk. 1. Open Games. 352p. LC 75-11306. 736p. 1975. pap. 8.50 (ISBN 0-486-23208-5). Dover.

Tartar, Brent & Scribner, Robert L., eds. Revolutionary Virginia, The Road to Independence: Independence & the Fifth Convention, 1776, A Documentary Record, Vol. 7. LC 72-96023. (Revolutionary Virginia, the Road to Independence Ser.). 1982. 50.00 (ISBN 0-8139-0968-6). U Pr of Va.

Tarter, jt. auth. see Clark, V. A.

Tarter, Brent, jt. ed. see Scribner, Robert L.

Tarter, Donald E. Turning Behavior Inside Out. LC 79-63749. 1979. pap. text ed. 12.75 (ISBN 0-8191-0736-0). U Pr of Amer.

Tarter, Ralph E. & Sugerman, A. Arthur, eds. Alcoholism: Interdisciplinary Approaches to an Enduring Problem. 880p. 1976. text ed. 35.95 (ISBN 0-201-08146-6, Adv Bk Prog); pap. text ed. 26.50 (ISBN 0-201-08145-8, Adv Bk Prog). A-W.

Tarumoto, David H., ed. High-Performance Review: Audio Equipment & Recordings for the Perceptive Listener, Vol. 1. (Illus.). 580p. 1981-82. pap. 26.00x (ISBN 0-88232-068-8, Pub. by High-Performance Review Pub). Delbridge Pub Co.

--High-Performance Review: Audio Equipment & Recordings for the Perceptive Listener, Vol. 2. (Illus.). 600p. 1983. pap. 26.00x (ISBN 0-88232-083-1, Pub. by High-Performance Review Pub). Delbridge Pub Co.

Tarver, Sara G., jt. auth. see Kneedler, Rebecca D.

Tarzian, Lucy, ed. Progressive Grocer's Marketing Guidebook. LC 68-126162. 1981. 159.00 (ISBN 0-911790-20-9). Prog Grocer.

Tasaki, Hanama. Long the Imperial Way. Repr. of 1950 ed. lib. bdg. 17.50x (ISBN 0-8371-3060-3, TAIM). Greenwood.

Tasch, Paul. Paleobiology of the Invertebrates: Data Retrieval from the Fossil Record. 2nd ed. LC 79-14929. 975p. 1980. text ed. 40.95 (ISBN 0-471-05272-8). Wiley.

Taseer, Salmaan. Bhutto: A Political Biography. 208p. text ed. (ISBN 0-7069-1085-0, Pub. by Vikas India). Advent NY.

Tash, Eli, jt. ed. see Cruickshank, William M.

Tashdijian, A. Vocabulaire d'Accession a l'Information. (Black Africa Ser.). 94p. (Fr.). 1974. Repr. of 1970 ed. lib. bdg. 34.00x o.p. (ISBN 0-8287-0803-7, 71-2004). Clearwater Pub.

Tashjian, Dickran. William Carlos Williams & the American Scene, 1920-1940. LC 78-20657. (Cal. Ser.: No. 420). (Illus.). 1979. 34.50 o.p. (ISBN 0-520-03854-1); pap. 10.95 o.p. (ISBN 0-520-03878-9). U of Cal Pr.

Tashjian, Nouvart. Armenian Lace. Kliot, Jules & Kliot, Kaethe, eds. 36p. 1982. pap. 4.95 (ISBN 0-916896-20-X). Lacis Pubns.

Tashjian, Virginia A. Juba This & Juba That. LC 69-10666. (Illus.). (gr. 1-3). 1969. 8.95 (ISBN 0-316-83230-8). Little.

--With a Deep Sea Smile: Story Hour Stretches for Large or Small Groups. (Illus.). 144p. (gr. 1-3). 1974. pap. 8.95 (ISBN 0-316-83216-2). Little.

Tashman, Leonard J. & Lamborn, Kathleen R. The Ways & Means of Statistics. 527p. 1979. text ed. 22.95 (ISBN 0-15-595132-7, HC); instructor's manual avail. (ISBN 0-15-595133-5); transparency & ditto masters avail. (ISBN 0-15-595134-3). HarBraceJ.

Task Force on Community Residential Services, jt. auth. see American Psychiatric Association.

Task Force on Educational Credit & Credentials. Recommendations on Credentialing Educational Accomplishment. 1978. 1.50 o.p. (ISBN 0-8268-1225-2). ACE.

Task Force on Institutional Evaluation. Evaluation of Archival Institutions: Services, Principles, & Guide to Self-Study. 48p. 1982. pap. text ed. 5.00 (ISBN 0-931828-55-4). Soc Am Archivists.

Task Force, 1974. The Adolescent, Other Citizens, & Their High Schools. 1975. 14.95 (ISBN 0-07-062918-8, P&RB); pap. 2.25 (ISBN 0-07-062920-X). McGraw.

Tasker, G. P. Saint Paul & His Gospel. 87p. 1982. pap. 1.00 (ISBN 0-686-36256-X). Faith Pub Hse.

Tasker, Joe. Savage Arena. (Illus.). 288p. 1982. 18.95 (ISBN 0-312-69984-0). St Martin.

Tasker, Joe, jt. auth. see Boardman, Peter.

Tasker, Ronald R., jt. auth. see Emmers, Raimond.

Tasman, Alice L. Wedding Album. (Illus.). 96p. 1982. 14.95 (ISBN 0-8027-0653-3); pap. 4.95 (ISBN 0-8027-7159-9). Walker & Co.

Tasman, Norma, jt. ed. see Lass, Abraham.

Tasman, William & Shields, Jerry A. Disorders of the Peripheral Fundus. (Illus.). 1980. text ed. 34.50x o.p. (ISBN 0-06-142530-3, Harper Medical). Lippincott.

Tasman, William, jt. ed. see Brown, Gary.

Tassel, Cynthia L. Van see Van Tassel, Dennie & Van Tassel, Cynthia L.

Tassel, Dennie Van see Van Tassel, Dennie.

Tassel, Dennie Van see Van Tassel, Dennie & Van Tassel, Cynthia L.

Tassel, Dennis Van see Van Tassel, Dennis.

Tasso, Torquato. Tasso's Dialogues: A Selection, With the Discourse on the Art of the Dialogue. Lord, Carnes & Trafton, Dain A., trs. LC 81-12937. (Bibliateca Italiana Ser.). 288p. 1983. 18.50x (ISBN 0-520-04464-9). U of Cal Pr.

Tata, J. R. Metamorphosis. Head, J. J., ed. (Carolina Biology Readers Ser.). (Illus.). 16p. 1983. pap. text ed. 1.60 (ISBN 0-89278-246-3). Carolina Biological.

Tata, Robert J. Haiti: Land of Poverty. LC 82-45035. (Illus.). 140p. (Orig.). 1982. PLB 18.75 (ISBN 0-8191-2439-7); pap. text ed. 8.25 (ISBN 0-8191-2440-0). U Pr of Amer.

--Structural Changes in Puerto Rico's Economy 1947-1976. LC 80-19080. (Latin America Ser., Ohio University Papers in International Studies: No. 9). (Illus.). 104p. (Orig.). 1981. pap. 11.75 (ISBN 0-89680-107-1, Ohio U Ctr Intl). Ohio U Pr.

Tataki, A. B. Rhodes: Lindos-Kamiros-Filerimos. (Athenon Illustrated Guides Ser.). (Illus.). 110p. 1983. pap. 14.00 (ISBN 0-686-43397-1, 8248, Pub. by Ekdotike Athenon Greece). Larousse.

Tatalovich, Raymond, jt. auth. see Daynes, Byron W.

Tate, A., jt. auth. see Billington, E. W.

Tate, Allen. Fathers. LC 82-74136. 306p. 1960. pap. 6.95x (ISBN 0-8040-0108-1). Swallow.

--Jefferson Davis. (Lives to Remember Ser.). (gr. 9 up). 1969. PLB 4.97 o.p. (ISBN 0-399-60312-3). Putnam Pub Group.

--Memoirs & Opinions: Nineteen Twenty-Six to Nineteen Seventy-Four. LC 82-73617. 225p. 1975. 12.95 (ISBN 0-8040-0662-8). Swallow.

--The Poetry Reviews of Allen Tate, Nineteen Twenty-Four to Nineteen Forty-Four. Brown, Ashley & Cheney, Frances N., eds. LC 82-12687. (Southern Literary Studies). 216p. 1983. 16.95 (ISBN 0-8071-1057-4). La State U Pr.

Tate, Allen, jt. ed. see Agar, Herbert.

Tate, Allen, ed. see Poe, Edgar Allan.

Tate, Claudia, ed. Black Women Writers At Work. 256p. 1983. 14.95 (ISBN 0-8264-0232-1). Crossroad NY.

Tate, D. The East German Novel: Identity, Community & Continuity, 1945, 1980. 1981. 60.00x o.p. (ISBN 0-86127-211-0, Pub. by Avebury Pub England). State Mutual Bk.

Tate Gallery, ed. Abstraction Catalogue. (Illus.). 128p. 1982. 29.95 o.p. (ISBN 0-8120-5457-1). Barron.

Tate, Gary, ed. Teaching Composition: Ten Bibliographical Essays. LC 76-629. 1976. pap. 12.50x (ISBN 0-912646-16-0). Tex Christian.

Tate, George, jt. auth. see Morton, Arthur L.

Tate, James. Hints to Pilgrims. LC 82-6876. 80p. 1982. lib. bdg. 8.00x (ISBN 0-87023-346-7); pap. 4.00 (ISBN 0-87023-347-5). U of Mass Pr.

--Land of Little Sticks. (Metacom Limited Edition Ser.: No. 4). 20p. 1981. ltd. 25.00x (ISBN 0-911381-03-1). Metacom Pr.

Tate, Joan. Wild Boy. LC 73-5495. (Illus.). 112p. (gr. 5 up). 1973. PLB 9.89 (ISBN 0-06-026097-1, HarpJ). Har-Row.

Tate, Joan, tr. see Ekstrom, Jan.

Tate, Joan, tr. see Lilius, Irmelin S.

Tate, Joan, tr. see Lorentzen, Karin.

Tate, Joan, tr. see Otto, Svend S.

Tate, Joan, tr. see Svend, Otto S.

Tate, M. & Glisson, O. Family Clothing. 1961. 20.95x (ISBN 0-87245-317-0). Textile Bk.

Tate, Mildred T. & Glisson, Oris. Family Clothing. LC 61-15414. 412p. 1961. text ed. 18.50 o.p. (ISBN 0-471-84579-5). Wiley.

Tate, Nicholas. Pizarro & the Incas. Reeves, Marjorie, ed. (Then & There Ser.). (Illus.). 79p. (gr. 7-12). 1981. pap. text ed. 3.10 (ISBN 0-582-20547-6). Longman.

Tate, Sean. Q-Sort as a Needs Assessment Technique. 20p. (Orig.). 1982. pap. 1.00 (ISBN 0-932288-67-7). Ctr Intl Ed U of MA.

Tate, Sharon & Edwards, Mona. The Complete Book of Fashion Illustration. 344p. 1982. text ed. 28.50 scp (ISBN 0-06-046582-4, HarpC). Har-Row.

Tate, Sharon L. Inside Fashion Design. 1977. text ed. 27.00 scp (ISBN 0-06-453504-5, HarpC); instructor's manual avail. (ISBN 0-06-453507-X). Har-Row.

Tate, Thad W., jt. auth. see Williams, D. Alan.

Tate, Thad W., jt. ed. see Short, James R.

Tate, W. E. Parish Chest. 3rd ed. LC 67-28686. (Illus.). 1969. 44.50 (ISBN 0-521-06603-4). Cambridge U Pr.

Tate, William H. A Mariner's Guide to the Rules of the Road. 2nd ed. LC 81-85441. 145p. 1982. 12.95x (ISBN 0-87021-355-5). Naval Inst Pr.

Tatford, E. Patrick. Problems in Gynecology. Fry, J. & Williams, K., eds. (Problems in Practice Ser.: Vol. 9). 175p. 1983. text ed. 16.50 (ISBN 0-8036-8340-5). Davis Co.

Tatford, Frederick. Daniel & His Prophecy. 1980. 9.25 (ISBN 0-86524-045-0, 2702). Klock & Klock.

Tatford, Frederick A. The Minor Prophets, 3 vols. 1214p. 1982. Set. lib. bdg. 44.95 Smythe Sewn (ISBN 0-86524-135-X, 7000). Klock & Klock.

Tatham, C. Ernest. How May I? pap. 1.25 (ISBN 0-937396-20-6). Walterick Pubs.

Tatham, Eddison C., jt. auth. see Sandberg, Karl C.

Tatham, Julie, jt. auth. see Wells, Helen.

Tatlow, Anthony. The Mask of Evil. (European University Studies: Series 18, Comparative Literature, Vol. 12). 1977. 80.00 (ISBN 3-261-02905-6). P Lang Pubs.

Tatlow, Peter, jt. auth. see Temple, Cliff.

Tator, Charles H., ed. Early Management of Acute Spinal Cord Injury. (Seminars in Neurological Surgery Ser.). 459p. 1982. text ed. 57.00 (ISBN 0-89004-675-1). Raven.

Tatro, Earl E., jt. auth. see Anderson, James.

Tatsch, J. H. Coal Deposits: Origin, Evolution, & Present Characteristics. LC 76-28096. (Illus.). 590p. 1980. 156.00 (ISBN 0-912890-13-4). Tatsch.

--Copper Deposits: Origin, Evolution, & Present Characteristics. LC 74-78916. (Illus.). 339p. 1975. 72.00 (ISBN 0-912890-08-8). Tatsch.

--Earthquakes: Cause, Prediction, & Control. LC 75-9305. (Illus.). 451p. 1977. 108.00 (ISBN 0-912890-02-9). Tatsch.

--The Earth's Tectonosphere: Its Past Development & Present Behavior. 2nd ed. LC 74-78917. (Illus.). 468p. 1977. 30.00 (ISBN 0-912890-03-7). Tatsch.

--Geothermal Deposits: Origin, Evolution, & Present Characteristics. LC 75-9303. (Illus.). 292p. 1976. 84.00 (ISBN 0-912890-10-X). Tatsch.

--Gold Deposits: Origin, Evolution, and Present Characteristics. LC 75-1947. (Illus.). 275p. 1975. 72.00 (ISBN 0-912890-07-X). Tatsch.

--Iron Deposits: Origin, Evolution, & Present Characteristics. LC 76-28095. (Illus.). 600p. Date not set. 216.00 (ISBN 0-912890-12-6); prepub. 180.00 (ISBN 0-686-82984-0). Tatsch.

--Mineral Deposits: Origin, Evolution, & Present Characteristics. LC 73-78206. (Illus.). 264p. 1973. 64.00 (ISBN 0-912890-01-0). Tatsch.

--The Moon: Its Past Development & Present Behavior. LC 73-88554. (Illus.). 338p. 1974. 20.00 (ISBN 0-912890-05-3). Tatsch.

--Petroleum Deposits: Origin, Evolution, & Present Characteristics. LC 73-93625. (Illus.). 378p. 1974. 50.00 (ISBN 0-912890-06-1). Tatsch.

--Uranium Deposits: Origin, Evolution, & Present Characteristics. LC 75-9304. (Illus.). 303p. 1976. 96.00 (ISBN 0-912890-11-8). Tatsch.

Tattan, L. A. Publish Yourself without Killing Yourself. 191p. (Orig.). 1981. pap. 9.95 (ISBN 0-937362-01-8). InPrint.

Tattersall, Bob. Decorating. (Tricks of the Trades Ser.). (Illus.). 1978. 10.95 o.s.i. (ISBN 0-7207-1036-7). Transatlantic.

--Flooring. (Tricks of the Trade Ser.). (Illus.). 1978. 10.95 o.p. (ISBN 0-7207-1045-6). Transatlantic.

Tattersall, G. H. The Workability of Concrete. (Illus.). 1976. pap. 12.75x (ISBN 0-7210-1032-6). Scholium Intl.

Tattersall, Ian. Man's Ancestors: An Introduction to Primate & Human Evolution. (Illus.). 1971. pap. 7.50 o.p. (ISBN 0-7195-2188-2). Transatlantic.

Tattersall, Ian, jt. auth. see Eldredge, Niles.

Tattersall, Jill. Damnation Reef. LC 79-10530. 1979. 9.95 o.p. (ISBN 0-688-03475-6). Morrow.

Tattersall, Robert, jt. auth. see Kobberling, J.

Tattum, Delwyn P. Disruptive Pupils in Schools & Units. LC 81-19727. 329p. 1982. 32.95 (ISBN 0-471-10157-5, Pub. by Wiley-Interscience). Wiley.

Tatum, Charles M. Chicano Literature. (United States Authors Ser.). 1982. lib. bdg. 14.95 (ISBN 0-8057-7373-8, Twayne). G K Hall.

Tatum, Charles M., jt. ed. see Hinds, Harold E., Jr.

Tatum, E. L., ed. see Ycas, M.

Tatum, Jack & Kushner, Bill. They Call Me Assassin. LC 79-51202. (Illus.). 1980. 9.95 (ISBN 0-89696-060-9, An Everest House Book). Dodd.

Tatum, Rita. The Alternative House. LC 78-51058. (Illus.). 1978. 12.95 (ISBN 0-89169-509-5); pap. 6.95 (ISBN 0-89169-508-7). Reed Bks.

Tau, Max. Broken Wings. Hein, Ruth, tr. from Ger. LC 82-11032. Orig. Title: Denn uber uns ist der Himmel. 370p. 1982. 14.95 (ISBN 0-88064-005-7). Fromm Intl Pub.

Taub, H., jt. auth. see Millman, Jacob.

Taub, Herbert. Digital Circuits & Microprocessors. (Electrical Engineering Ser.). (Illus.). 608p. 1981. text ed. 32.95x (ISBN 0-07-062945-5); solutions manual 5.00 (ISBN 0-07-062946-3). McGraw.

Taub, Herbert & Schilling, Donald. Digital Integrated Electronics. (E & EE). (Illus.). 1976. text ed. 34.95 (ISBN 0-07-062921-8, C); solutions manual 7.95 (ISBN 0-07-062922-6); ans. bk. 7.95 (ISBN 0-07-062929-3). McGraw.

--Principles of Communication Systems. (Electronic & Electronic Engineering Ser.). 1970. text ed. 38.95 (ISBN 0-07-062923-4, C); solutions manual 13.00 (ISBN 0-07-062924-2); ans. bk. 7.95 (ISBN 0-07-062927-7). McGraw.

Taub, William. Forces of Power. LC 78-68161. (Illus.). 1979. 11.95 o.p. (ISBN 0-448-15775-6, G&D). Putnam Pub Group.

Taube, H. Electron Transfer Reactions of Complex Ions in Solution. (Current Chemical Concepts Ser). 1970. 24.00 (ISBN 0-12-683850-X). Acad Pr.

Taubenfeld, Howard J. & Taubenfeld, Rita F. Sex-Based Discrimination: International Law & Organization, 2 bdrs. LC 78-14809. 1978. loose-leaf 75.00 ea.; Rel. 1. 35.00; Rel. 2. 75.00; Set. 150.00 (ISBN 0-379-10139-4). Oceana.

Taubenfeld, Rita F., jt. auth. see Taubenfeld, Howard J.

Tauber, Gilbert, jt. ed. see Rachlin, Joseph W.

Taubes. Basic Enameling. (The Grosset Art Instruction Ser.: No. 68). (Illus.). 48p. Date not set. pap. price not set (ISBN 0-448-00577-8, G&D). Putnam Pub Group.

Taubes, Frederic. Acrylic Painting for the Beginner. (Illus.). 144p. 1981. pap. 11.95 (ISBN 0-686-83004-0). Watson-Guptill.

--Acrylic Painting for the Beginner. (Illus.). 144p. (gr. 7-9). 1971. 11.95 o.p. (ISBN 0-8230-0061-3). Watson-Guptill.

--Anatomy for Artists. (The Grosset Art Instruction Ser.: No. 66). (Illus.). 48p. 1981. pap. 2.95 (ISBN 0-448-00576-X, G&D). Putnam Pub Group.

--Pen & Ink Drawing. (Grosset Art Introduction Ser.: Vol. 41). pap. 2.95 (ISBN 0-448-00550-6, G&D). Putnam Pub Group.

Taubman. Sources of Inequality in Earnings. LC 75-23117. (Contributions to Economic Analysis: Vol. 96). 273p. 1976. 47.00 (ISBN 0-444-10965-X, North-Holland). Elsevier.

Taubman, Howard. Music on My Beat: An Intimate Volume of Shop Talk. LC 76-57173. 1977. Repr. of 1943 ed. lib. bdg. 18.75x (ISBN 0-8371-9433-4, TAMU). Greenwood.

Taubman, Howard, pref. by. Gatti-Casazza, Giulio: Memories of the Opera. LC 71-183334. (Illus.). 356p. Date not set. Repr. of 1941 ed. price not set. Vienna Hse.

Taubman, Paul J., jt. ed. see Solmon, Lewis C.

Tauc, J., ed. Optical Properties of Solids. (Italian Physical Society: Course 34). 1967. 64.00 (ISBN 0-12-368834-5). Acad Pr.

Tauchert, T. R. Energy Principles in Structural Mechanics. (Illus.). 416p. 1974. text ed. 24.50 o.p. (ISBN 0-07-062925-0, C); solutions avail. o.p. McGraw.

Taulbut, Shaun. How to Play the French Defence. (Illus.). 96p. 1983. pap. 13.50 (ISBN 0-7134-3717-0, Pub. by Batsford England). David & Charles.

Ta'unga. Works of Ta'unga: Records of a Polynesian Traveller in the South Seas, 1833-1896. Crocombe, Ron, ed. (Pacific History Ser.: No. 2). (Illus.). 1968. 7.50x o.p. (ISBN 0-87022-165-5). UH Pr.

Tauraso, Nicola M. & Batzler, L. Richard. Awaken the Genius in Your Child Through Positive Attitude Training. 1981. pap. 9.95 (ISBN 0-935710-01-9). Hidden Valley.

--How to Benefit from Stress. 1979. 12.95 (ISBN 0-935710-00-0). Hidden Valley.

--Manual of Positive Attitude Training Techniques for Children & Young Adults. 1982. 25.00 (ISBN 0-935710-03-5). Hidden Valley.

Taus, Esther R. The Role of the U. S. Treasury in Stabilizing the Economy, 1941-1946. LC 80-5567. (Illus.). 158p. (Orig.). 1982. lib. bdg. 19.00 (ISBN 0-8191-1872-9); pap. text ed. 9.50 (ISBN 0-8191-1873-7). U Pr of Amer.

Tausch, Gerry. Glamour in the Kitchen: Recipes & Memoirs of a West Point Wife. Tausch, Roland D., ed. LC 82-82681. (Illus.). 152p. 1982. 9.95 (ISBN 0-686-82513-6). Gerosota Pub.

Tausch, Roland D., ed. see Tausch, Gerry.

Tausky, Curt. Work Organizations. 2nd ed. LC 77-83435. 1978. pap. text ed. 9.95 (ISBN 0-87581-226-0). Peacock Pubs.

Tausky, Margaret, tr. see Janacek, Leos.

Tausky, Vilem, tr. see Janacek, Leos.

Tauss, Beatrice. King Lear. (Parallel Text Ser.). 1975. pap. 2.95 o.p. (ISBN 0-671-18740-6). Monarch Pr.

Taussig, F. W. The Psychology of Money Making & How to Master It. (The Library of Scientific Psychology). (Illus.). 121p. 1983. 49.85 (ISBN 0-89266-381-2). Am Classical Coll Pr.

Taussig, M. K., ed. see Twentieth Century Fund of Task Force on Policies Toward Veterans.

Taussig, Michael K., jt. auth. see Seneca, Joseph J.

Tausworthe, Robert C. Standardized Development of Computer Software: Part 1, Methods. 1977. Pt. 2, Standards. 27.95 (ISBN 0-13-842195-1); 27.95 (ISBN 0-13-842203-6); comb. set (pts 1&2) 43.90 (ISBN 0-13-842211-7). P-H.

Tavakolian, Susan, ed. Language Acquisition & Linguistic Theory. (Illus.). 304p. 1981. text ed. 22.50x (ISBN 0-262-20039-2). MIT Pr.

Tavard, George H. Dogmatic Constitution on Divine Revelation. LC 66-19148. 96p. pap. 1.95 o.p. (ISBN 0-8091-1549-2). Paulist Pr.

--Images of the Christ: An Enquiry into Christology. LC 81-40582. 134p. (Orig.). 1982. lib. bdg. 19.00 (ISBN 0-8191-2129-0); pap. text ed. 8.25 (ISBN 0-8191-2130-4). U Pr of Amer.

--The Inner Life: Foundations of Christian Mysticism. LC 75-32858. 116p. (Orig.). 1976. pap. 1.95 o.p. (ISBN 0-8091-1927-7, Deus). Paulist Pr.

--The Vision of the Trinity. LC 80-5845. 166p. (Orig.). 1981. lib. bdg. 20.00 (ISBN 0-8191-1412-X); pap. text ed. 9.50 (ISBN 0-8191-1413-8). U Pr of Amer.

Tavares, Suzanne, jt. auth. see Fassman, Paula.

Tavast, R. R., jt. ed. see Csiro, R. W.

Tavel, Charles. The Third Industrial Age: Strategy for Business Survival. 356p. 25.00 (ISBN 0-686-84792-X). Work in Amer.

Tavernier-Courbin, Jacqueline. Critical Essays on Jack London. (Critical Essays in American Literature Ser.). 308p. 1983. lib. bdg. 30.00 (ISBN 0-8161-8465-8). G K Hall.

Tavill, A. S., jt. auth. see Elkeles, R. D.

Tavis, Lee A., ed. Multinational Managers & Poverty in the Third World. LC 82-50288. 1982. text ed. 19.95 (ISBN 0-268-01353-5). U of Notre Dame Pr.

Tavistock Joint Library, London. Catalogue of the Tavistock Joint Library, 2 vols. 1975. Set. lib. bdg. 135.00 (ISBN 0-8161-1167-7, Hall Library). G K Hall.

Tavolga, W. N., ed. Sound Reception in Fishes, 2 vols. LC 76-13525. (Benchmark Papers in Animal Behavior: Vol. 7). 1976. 55.00 (ISBN 0-12-787516-6); Set. sound production in fishes 76.00 (ISBN 0-685-69401-1). Acad Pr.

Tavolga, William N., ed. Sound Production in Fishes, 2 vols. LC 76-28352. (Benchmark Papers in Animal Behavior: Vol. 9). 1977. 48.50 (ISBN 0-12-787515-8); Set. sound reception in fishes 76.00 (ISBN 0-686-85548-5). Acad Pr.

Tavoulareas, William & Kaysen, Carl. A Debate on a Time to Choose: A Critique, A Reply. LC 77-24059. 128p. 1977. prof ref 12.50x (ISBN 0-88410-070-7). Ballinger Pub.

Tavris, Carol. Anger: The Misunderstood Emotion. 1983. 14.95 (ISBN 0-671-25094-9). S&S.

Tavris, Carol & Offir, Carole. The Longest War: Sex Differences in Perspective. (Illus.). 333p. (Orig.). 1977. pap. text ed. 12.95 (ISBN 0-15-551182-3, HC); instructor's manual avail. (ISBN 0-15-551183-1). HarBraceJ.

Tavuchis, Nicholas & Goode, William J. The Family Through Literature. LC 74-8935. (Sociology Ser.). 448p. 1974. pap. text ed. 14.95 (ISBN 0-07-062919-6, C). McGraw.

Tawerilmang, Anthony F., jt. auth. see Sohn, Ho-Min.

Tawes, Avalynne. My Favorite Maryland Recipes. (Illus.). 1964. 11.95 (ISBN 0-394-40175-1). Random.

Tawes, J. Millard. My Favorite Maryland Recipes. (Illus.). 179p. 1964. 9.95 (ISBN 0-686-36746-4). Md Hist.

Tawney. American Labor Movement. 1980. 26.00 (ISBN 0-312-02503-3). St Martin.

Tawney, James, et al. Programmed Environments Curriculum for the Handicapped. (Special Education Ser.). 1979. text ed. 22.95 (ISBN 0-675-08265-X). Additional supplements may be obtained from publisher. Merrill.

Tawney, R. H. History & Society: Essays by R.H. Tawney. Winter, J. M., ed. 1978. 22.50x (ISBN 0-7100-8953-8). Routledge & Kegan.

--Land & Labor in China. LC 77-72070. 1977. Repr. of 1932 ed. pap. 7.95 (ISBN 0-87332-106-5). M E Sharpe.

Tax Foundation, Incorporated. Unemployment Insurance: Trends & Issues. (Research Publication Ser.: No. 35). 88p. (Orig.). 1982. pap. 5.00 (ISBN 0-686-37951-9). Tax Found.

Tax, Meredith. Rivington Street. 1983. pap. 3.95 (ISBN 0-515-07149-8). Jove Pubns.

Taxation Committee of the Patent Law Association of Chicago, ed. Tax Guide for Patents, Trademarks & Copyrights. 1981. 25.00 (ISBN 0-87632-318-2). Boardman.

Taxi, J., ed. Ontogenesis & Functional Mechanisms of Peripheral Synapses. (Inserm Symposia Ser.: Vol. 13). 1980. 67.25 (ISBN 0-444-80246-0). Elsevier.

Tay, Alice E., jt. auth. see Kemenka, Eugene.

Tay, Alice Erh-Soon see Kamenka, Eugene & Erh-Soon Tay, Alice.

Taya, Teizo see Bigman, David.

Taya, Teizo, jt. ed. see Bigman, David.

Tayar, Graham, jt. ed. see Lauwerys, Joseph.

Taybi, Hooshang. Radiology of Syndromes. 2nd ed. 1982. 69.50 (ISBN 0-8151-8741-6). Year Bk Med.

Taylo, Don H. Trade Union Financial Administration. 64p. 1981. 2.85 (ISBN 92-2-102711-2). Intl Labour Office.

Taylor. Digital Filter Design Handbook. (Electrical Engineering & Electronics Ser.: Vol. 12). 1983. price not set (ISBN 0-8247-1357-5). Dekker.

--Draft. LC 80-25660. 1981. 8.90 (ISBN 0-531-02474-1). Watts.

--Emergency Squads. LC 79-28236. (gr. 5 up). 1980. PLB 8.90 (ISBN 0-531-04117-4, A48). Watts.

--Endosseous Dental Implants. (Illus.). 1970. 19.25 o.p. (ISBN 0-407-16770-6). Butterworth.

--The Future of Conflict. 122p. 1983. 6.95 (ISBN 0-03-061951-3). Praeger.

Taylor & Habgood. Scotland in Colour. 24.00 o.p. (ISBN 0-7134-0026-9, Pub. by Batsford England). David & Charles.

Taylor, jt. auth. see Davidson.

Taylor, A. Speaking in Public. 1979. pap. 15.95 (ISBN 0-13-825844-9). P-H.

Taylor, A. & Lay, D. Introduction to Functional Analysis. 2nd ed. 467p. 1980. 34.95 (ISBN 0-471-84646-5). Wiley.

Taylor, A., ed. Muscle Receptors & Movement. Prochazka, A. 1981. text ed. 55.00x (ISBN 0-19-520280-5). Oxford U Pr.

Taylor, A., tr. see Baernreither, Joseph M.

Taylor, A. E., tr. see Aristotle.

Taylor, A. H. & Pocock, M. A. Handbook of Financial Planning & Control. 448p. 1981. text ed. 66.00x (ISBN 0-566-02127-7). Gower Pub Ltd.

Taylor, A. J. Essays in English History. 1983. pap. 5.95 (ISBN 0-14-021862-9, Pelican). Penguin.

--The Second World War: An Illustrated History. LC 74-83095. (Illus.). 1975. 17.50 o.p. (ISBN 0-399-11412-2). Putnam Pub Group.

Taylor, A. J. & Roberts, J. M., eds. Twentieth Century. rev. ed. LC 78-27424. (Illus.). 2700p. 1979. lib. bdg. 532.67 (ISBN 0-8393-6079-7). Raintree Pubs.

Taylor, A. J., jt. ed. see Black, W. A.

Taylor, A., Jr. The Life of my Years. 160p. (Orig.). 1983. pap. 9.95 (ISBN 0-687-21854-3). Abingdon.

Taylor, Abra. Cloud Over Paradise. Date not set. pap. price not set (Harlequin). PB.

Taylor, Alan J. Struggle for Mastery in Europe: 1848-1918. 1954. 39.50x (ISBN 0-19-822101-0); pap. 12.95x (ISBN 0-19-881270-1). Oxford U Pr.

Taylor, Albert J. Passing Your Biennial Flight Review. (Modern Aircraft Ser.). (Illus.). 1978. 8.95 (ISBN 0-8306-9978-3); pap. 4.95 o.p. (ISBN 0-8306-2243-8, 2243). TAB Bks.

Taylor, Albert W. Training-Scientific Basis & Application: A Symposium Conducted by the Canadian Association of Sports Sciences at the Pavillon de l'Education Physique et des Sports, Laval University, Quebec City. (Illus.). 384p. 1972. photocopy ed. spiral 36.75x (ISBN 0-398-02428-6). C C Thomas.

Taylor, Alexander, tr. see Rifbjerg, Klaus.

Taylor, Alexander S. Bibliografa Californica. Basso, Dave, ed. (Great Basin Abstracts Ser.). (Illus.). 110p. 1983. pap. 32.95 (ISBN 0-936332-20-4). Falcon Hill Pr.

--Bibliografa Californica: Supplement. Basso, Dave, ed. (Great Abstracts Ser.). 26p. (Orig.). 1983. pap. text ed. 17.95 (ISBN 0-936332-17-4). Falcon Hill Pr.

Taylor, Alfred E. Aristotle. 1919. pap. 2.50 (ISBN 0-486-20280-1). Dover.

Taylor, Alice H. Rescued from the Dragon. 199p. (Orig.). 1982. pap. 5.25 (ISBN 0-89367-078-2). Light & Life.

Taylor, Alice L., jt. auth. see Hollis, Ernest V.

Taylor, Andrew. Caroling Minuscule. LC 82-23443. 1983. 10.95 (ISBN 0-396-08149-5). Dodd.

Taylor, Angus E. & Mann, Robert W. Advanced Calculus. 3rd ed. LC 81-16141. 732p. 1982. text ed. 31.95 (ISBN 0-471-02566-6); solutions avail. (ISBN 0-471-09918-X). Wiley.

Taylor, Anne. Laurence Oliphant, 1829-1888. (Illus.). 1982. 29.95x (ISBN 0-19-812676-X). Oxford U Pr.

Taylor, Arnold H. Travail & Triumph: Black Life & Culture in the South Since the Civil War. LC 76-5264. (Contributions in Afro-American & African Studies: No. 26). (Orig.). 1976. lib. bdg. 29.95x (ISBN 0-8371-8912-8, TTT/). Greenwood.

--Travail & Triumph: Black Life & Culture in the South Since the Civil War. LC 76-5264. (Contributions in Afro-American & African Studies: No. 26). 1977. pap. text ed. 6.95 (ISBN 0-313-20162-5, TTT/). Greenwood.

Taylor, Arthur. Notes & Tones: Musician-to-Musician Interviews. (Illus.). 320p. 1982. 14.95 (ISBN 0-698-11152-4, Coward). Putnam Pub Group.

--Notes & Tones: Musician-to-Musician Interviews. (Illus.). 320p. 1982. pap. 7.95 (ISBN 0-399-50584-9, Perige). Putnam Pub Group.

Taylor, Arthur J., ed. The Standard of Living in Britain in the Industrial Revolution. (Debates in Economic History Ser.). 271p. 1975. 19.95x (ISBN 0-416-08250-5); pap. 12.95x (ISBN 0-416-08260-2). Methuen Inc.

Taylor, B. The Green Avenue: The Life & Writings of Forrest Reid, 1875-1947. LC 79-41418. 200p. 1980. 32.50 (ISBN 0-521-22801-8). Cambridge U Pr.

Taylor, B., ed. British Planning Databook. (Illus.). 168p. 1983. 40.00 (ISBN 0-08-028170-2). Pergamon.

Taylor, B. N., et al. Fundamental Constants & Quantum Electrodynamics. (Reviews of Modern Physics Monographs). 1969. 26.00 (ISBN 0-12-684050-4). Acad Pr.

Taylor, Barbara. Eve & the New Jerusalem: Socialism & Feminism in the Nineteenth Century. 315p. 1983. pap. 9.95 (ISBN 0-686-37899-7). Pantheon.

Taylor, Barbara H. Mexico: Her Daily & Festive Breads. Lamb, Ruth S., ed. LC 71-99257. (Latin American Books). (Illus., Orig.). 1969. pap. 6.95x (ISBN 0-685-08703-4, Dist. by Ocelot Pr). Creative Pr.

Taylor, Bernard & MacMillan, Keith, eds. Business Policy: Teaching & Research. LC 72-11487. 429p. 1973. 16.00 (ISBN 0-470-84655-0, Pub. by Wiley). Krieger.

Taylor, Bernard, jt. ed. see Farmer, David.

Taylor, Betty W. & Munro, Robert J. American Law Publishing 1860-1900: Readings & Bibliography, 3 vols. 1983. lib. bdg. 300.00x set (ISBN 0-87802-058-6). Glanville.

Taylor, Beverly. Case Studies in Child Development. LC 81-21782. (Psychology Ser.). 256p. 1982. pap. text ed. 11.95 (ISBN 0-534-01152-7). Brooks-Cole.

Taylor, Bob. Sight-Reading Jazz: Melody, Bass Clef Version, Bk. 1. Taylor, Jennifer J., ed. (Illus., Orig.). 1982. pap. text ed. 12.95x (ISBN 0-943950-02-3). Taylor James.

--Sight-Reading Jazz: Melody Treble Clef Version, Bk. 1. Taylor, Jennifer J., ed. (Illus., Orig.). 1982. pap. text ed. 12.95x (ISBN 0-686-37153-4). Taylor James.

Taylor, Brian. Richard Jefferies. (English Authors Ser.). 1982. lib. bdg. 14.95 (ISBN 0-8057-6816-5, Twayne). G K Hall.

Taylor, C. Hegel. LC 74-25642. 700p. 1975. 59.50 (ISBN 0-521-20679-0); pap. 17.95 (ISBN 0-521-29199-2). Cambridge U Pr.

--Hegel & Modern Society. LC 78-54727. (Modern European Philosophy). 1979. 28.95 (ISBN 0-521-22083-1); pap. 7.95 (ISBN 0-521-29351-0). Cambridge U Pr.

--India: Economic Issues in the Power Sector. iii, 175p. 1979. pap. 15.00 (ISBN 0-686-36108-3, RC-7911). World Bank.

Taylor, C. B., jt. auth. see Rider, C. C.

Taylor, C. T. & Silberston, Z. A. The Economic Impact of the Patent System: A Study of the British Experiment. LC 73-77173. (Department of Applied Economics Monographs, No. 23). (Illus.). 400p. 1973. 57.50 (ISBN 0-521-20255-8). Cambridge U Pr.

Taylor, C. W., jt. auth. see Bettey, J. H.

Taylor, C. W., retold by see Hsiung, S. I.

Taylor, Calton, jt. auth. see Belt, Forest.

Taylor, Charles. The Breaking Which Brings Us Anew: Poems. 1978. 3.50 o.p. (ISBN 0-913152-09-9). Folder Edns.

--The China Watchers. (Illus.). 320p. 1982. cancelled (ISBN 0-920510-69-8, Pub. by Personal Lib). Dodd.

Taylor, Charles D. Show of Force. 352p. 1982. pap. 2.95 (ISBN 0-441-76197-6, Pub. by Charter Bks). Ace Bks.

Taylor, Charles F. The Internal-Combustion Engine in Theory & Practice, Vol. 1: Thermodynamics, Fluid Flow, Performance. 2nd ed. 1967. pap. text ed. 16.00x (ISBN 0-262-70015-8). MIT Pr.

--The Internal-Combustion Engine in Theory & Practice, Vol. 2: Combustion, Fuels, Materials, Design. 1968. 55.00x (ISBN 0-262-20013-9); pap. 18.50x (ISBN 0-262-70016-6). MIT Pr.

Taylor, Charles G. & Kane, Jason. Yellowhair. (Custer Monograph: No. 6). 1979. Repr. of 1977 ed. ed. 10.00xlimited (ISBN 0-940696-08-8). Monroe County Lib.

Taylor, Charles L. Gleanings. 1979. 1.75 (ISBN 0-686-28779-7). Forward Movement.

Taylor, Charlotte P. Transforming Schools: A Social Perspective. LC 75-38022. 200p. 1976. 17.95 o.p. (ISBN 0-312-81410-0); pap. text ed. 8.95 o.p. (ISBN 0-312-81445-3). St Martin.

Taylor, Christine M. Returning to Mental Health. 160p. 1981. 29.00x (ISBN 0-85950-307-0, Pub. by Thornes England). State Mutual Bk.

Taylor, Clive R. Hodgkin's Disease & the Lymphomas, Vol. 1. 1977. 24.00 (ISBN 0-904406-48-2). Eden Pr.

--Hodgkin's Disease & the Lymphomas, Vol. 2. LC 78-300154. 1978. 28.80 (ISBN 0-88831-015-3). Eden Pr.

--Hodgkin's Disease & the Lymphomas, Vol. 3. Horrobin, D. F., ed. LC 78-300154. (Annual Research Reviews). 1979. 31.20 (ISBN 0-88831-043-9). Eden Pr.

--Hodgkin's Disease & the Lymphomas, Vol. 4. Horrobin, D. F., ed. LC 78-300154. (Annual Reviews Ser.). 374p. 1981. 38.00 (ISBN 0-88831-089-7). Eden Pr.

Taylor, Coley. Yankee Doodle. 10.00 (ISBN 0-8159-7400-0). Devin.

Taylor, Conway, jt. auth. see Morse, Milton A., Jr.

Taylor, Craig, jt. ed. see Ferguson, James.

Taylor, D. & Thomason, R. Profitable Hotel Reception. (International Series in Hospitality Management). (Illus.). 236p. 1982. 30.00 (ISBN 0-08-026769-6); pap. 14.95 (ISBN 0-08-026768-8). Pergamon.

Taylor, D. A. Introduction to Marine Biology. 336p. 1983. text ed. 49.95 (ISBN 0-408-00586-6); pap. text ed. 29.95 (ISBN 0-408-00585-8). Butterworth.

Taylor, D. H. & Glezen, G. W. Auditing: Integrated Concepts & Procedures. 2nd ed. 931p. 1982. text ed. 29.95 (ISBN 0-471-08166-3); write for info. tchr's. manual (ISBN 0-471-86343-2); write for info. test (ISBN 0-471-87680-1). Wiley.

Taylor, D. R. The Computer in Contemporary Cartography, Vol. 1. LC 79-42727. (Progress in Contemporary Cartography Ser.). 252p. 1980. 49.95 (ISBN 0-471-27699-5). Wiley.

Taylor, D. R., jt. auth. see Stohr, Walter.

Taylor, D. R. F., jt. auth. see Obudho, R. A.

Taylor, D. S. Transistor Circuit Design Tables. (Illus.). 1971. 14.75x o.p. (ISBN 0-408-70146-3). Transatlantic.

Taylor, Daniel M. Explanation & Meaning: An Introduction to Philosophy. LC 73-116837. (Illus.). 1970. 24.95 (ISBN 0-521-07910-1); pap. 7.95 (ISBN 0-521-09617-0). Cambridge U Pr.

Taylor, Danny. Family Literacy: Young Children Learning to Read & Write. 176p. (Orig.). 1983. pap. text ed. 9.00x (ISBN 0-435-08204-3). Heinemann Ed.

Taylor, David. Elementary Blueprint Reading for Machinists. LC 80-65572. (Blueprint Reading Ser.). 145p. 1981. pap. text ed. 7.80 (ISBN 0-8273-1895-2); instr's. guide 3.25 (ISBN 0-8273-1892-8). Delmar.

Taylor, David A. Mind. 240p. 1982. 14.50 (ISBN 0-671-25541-X). S&S.

Taylor, David C. Managing the Serials Explosion: The Issues for Publishers & Librarians. LC 82-14062. (Professional Librarian Ser.). 175p. 1982. text ed. 34.50 professional (ISBN 0-914236-94-6); pap. text ed. 27.50 professional (ISBN 0-914236-54-7). Knowledge Indus.
Taylor, David L. Blueprint Reading for Machinists. LC 82-72423. (Illus.). 208p. 1983. pap. text ed. price not set (ISBN 0-8273-1085-4); price not set instr's guide (ISBN 0-8273-1086-2). Delmar.
--Drill Press Work. LC 79-50536. (Metalworking Ser.). (gr. 8). 1980. pap. text ed. 7.80 (ISBN 0-8273-1823-5); instr's. manual 2.75 (ISBN 0-8273-1824-3). Delmar.
Taylor, David M. & Rock, Maxine. Gut Reactions: How to Handle Stress & Your Stomach. 192p. 1983. pap. 2.95 (ISBN 0-425-05635-X). Berkley Pub.
Taylor, Dawson, jt. auth. see Anthony, Earl.
Taylor, Day. The Black Swan. 1978. pap. 3.95 (ISBN 0-440-10611-7). Dell.
Taylor, Dean W. Endangerment Status of Lupinus Dedeckerae on the Inyo National Forest, California. (Contributions Mono Basin Research Group Ser.). (Illus.). 91p. 1981. pap. 3.25 (ISBN 0-939714-02-7). Mono Basin Res.
--Plant Checklist for the Mono Basin, California. 16p. 1981. pap. 1.25 (ISBN 0-939714-01-9). Mono Basin Res.
--Plant Checklist of the Sweetwater Mountains, Mono County, California. (Contributions Mono Basin Research Group Ser.). (Illus.). 27p. 1982. pap. 3.50 (ISBN 0-939714-05-1). Mono Basin Res.
--Riparian Vegetation of the Eastern Sierra: Ecological Effects of Stream Diversion. (Contributions Mono Basin Research Group Ser.). (Illus.). 56p. 1982. pap. 3.50 (ISBN 0-939714-04-3). Mono Basin Res.
Taylor, Deems. Some Enchanted Evenings: The Story of Rodgers & Hammerstein. LC 73-138132. (Illus.). 244p. 1972. Repr. of 1953 ed. lib. bdg. 18.50x (ISBN 0-8371-5414-6, TAEE). Greenwood.
--The Well Tempered Listener. LC 70-138190. 333p. 1972. Repr. of 1940 ed. lib. bdg. 17.50x (ISBN 0-8371-5647-5, TAWT). Greenwood.
Taylor, Delores A. & Alpert, Stuart W. Continuity & Support Following Residential Treatment. LC 72-92327. 1973. pap. 6.30 (ISBN 0-87868-098-5, I-35). Child Welfare.
Taylor, Desmond, jt. auth. see Hager, Philip.
Taylor, Dick. Colorado Manhunt. 208p. (Orig.). 1982. pap. 2.25 o.s.i. (ISBN 0-8439-1181-6, Leisure Bks). Nordon Pubns.
Taylor, Donald, jt. auth. see Staudt, Thomas A.
Taylor, Dorothy, jt. auth. see Swanwick, Keith.
Taylor, Doug. Pac-Baby's ABC. (Illus.). 1983. pap. 1.50 (ISBN 0-686-43029-8). Crown.
--Pac-Baby's Colors. (Illus.). (ps). 1983. pap. 1.50 (ISBN 0-517-55018-0). Crown.
--Pac-Baby's Shapes. (ps). 1983. pap. 1.50 (ISBN 0-517-55020-2). Crown.
--Pac-Baby's 1-2-3. (Illus.). 1983. pap. 1.50 (ISBN 0-517-55019-9). Crown.
Taylor, Douglas C. Metalworking for the Designer & Technician. LC 78-23346. (Illus.). 132p. 1979. pap. text ed. 15.00x (ISBN 0-910482-86-1). Drama Bk.
Taylor, Duane R. Home Rule in the District of Columbia: The First 500 Days. LC 78-58442. 1978. pap. text ed. 13.25 (ISBN 0-8191-0535-X). U Pr of Amer.
Taylor, E. C. & McKillop, A. Advances in Organic Chemistry: Methods & Results: the Chemistry of Cyclic Enaminonitriles & O-Aminonitriles, Vol. 7. 415p. 1970. 60.00 o.p. (ISBN 0-471-84661-9). Wiley.
Taylor, Ed S., ed. The History of Playing Cards, with Anecdotes of Their Use in Conjuring, Fortune-Telling, & Card-Sharping. LC 72-89739. (YA) 1973. pap. 8.95 (ISBN 0-8048-1026-5). C E Tuttle.
Taylor, Edgar, tr. see Grimm Brothers.
Taylor, Edward. Harmony of the Gospels, 4 Vols. LC 82-5452. 2688p. 1983. Set. 300.00x (ISBN 0-8201-1379-4). Schol Facsimiles.
Taylor, Edward H. Caecilians of the World: A Taxonomic Review. LC 67-14429. (Illus.). 1968. 25.00x o.p. (ISBN 0-7006-0048-5). Univ Pr KS.
Taylor, Edwin F., jt. auth. see French, A. P.
Taylor, Elaine, jt. auth. see Leonard, Jon.
Taylor, Elizabeth A. The Cable Car Murder. large print ed. LC 82-5468. 412p. 1982. Repr. of 1980 ed. 11.95x (ISBN 0-89621-360-9). Thorndike Pr.
--The Cable Car Murder. (Fingerprint Mysteries Ser.). 224p. 1983. pap. 5.95 (ISBN 0-312-11312-9). St Martin.
Taylor, Emilie. Emilie Taylor's Inflation Fighter Meat Book. (Orig.). 1982. pap. 8.95 (ISBN 0-446-97480-3). Warner Bks.
Taylor, Esther. Colorblind. LC 79-19755. 1983. 15.95 (ISBN 0-87949-136-1). Ashley Bks.
Taylor, F., et al. Foundry Engineering. LC 59-11811. 407p. 1959. 39.95 (ISBN 0-471-84843-3). Wiley.
Taylor, F. K. The Concepts of Illness, Disease & Morbus. LC 78-15123. 1979. 22.95 (ISBN 0-521-22433-0). Cambridge U Pr.
Taylor, Florance W. Ball Two. LC 76-165317. (Felipe Adventure Stories Ser). (gr. 2-4). 1971. PLB 3.95g (ISBN 0-8225-0143-0). Lerner Pubns.
--From Texas to Illinois. LC 79-165315. (Felipe Adventure Stories Ser.). (Illus.). (gr. 2-4). 1971. PLB 3.95g (ISBN 0-8225-0141-4). Lerner Pubns.
--Plane Ride. LC 71-165321. (Felipe Adventure Stories Ser.). (Illus.). (gr. 2-4). 1971. PLB 3.95g (ISBN 0-8225-0147-3). Lerner Pubns.
--School Picnic. LC 70-165318. (Felipe Adventure Stories Ser). (Illus.). (gr. 2-4). 1971. PLB 3.95g (ISBN 0-8225-0144-9). Lerner Pubns.
--What Is a Migrant? LC 72-165316. (Felipe Adventure Stories Ser.). (Illus.). (gr. 2-4). 1971. PLB 3.95g (ISBN 0-8225-0142-2). Lerner Pubns.
--Where's Luis. LC 73-165319. (Felipe Adventure Stories Ser). (gr. 2-4). 1971. PLB 3.95g (ISBN 0-8225-0145-7). Lerner Pubns.
Taylor, Florence, compiled by. Thou Art My God. 1977. boxed 8.95 o.p. (ISBN 0-8378-1863-X). Gibson.
Taylor, Florence M. In the Morning, Bread. LC 76-2983. 1976. pap. 4.95 (ISBN 0-87983-135-9). Keats.
Taylor, Frank. The Day a Team Died. 192p. 1983. 23.50x (ISBN 0-392-16929-0, SpS). Sportshelf.
Taylor, Frank J. High Horizons: Daredevil Flying Postmen to Modern Magic Carpet: The United Airlines Story. Rev. ed. (Airlines History Project Ser.). Date not set. price not set (ISBN 0-404-19338-2). AMS Pr.
Taylor, Fred, ed. The Goebbels Diaries, 1939-1941. 384p. 1983. 17.95 (ISBN 0-399-12763-1). Putnam Pub Group.
Taylor, Fred I. & Smith, Steve L. Digital Signal Processing in FORTRAN. LC 75-28940. 432p. 1976. 31.95x (ISBN 0-669-00330-1). Lexington Bks.
Taylor, Fred M., jt. auth. see Lange, Oskar.
Taylor, Frederick L. The Art of War in Italy, 1494-1529. LC 76-84284. (Illus.). 228p. 1973. Repr. of 1921 ed. lib. bdg. 25.00x (ISBN 0-8371-5025-6, TAWI). Greenwood.
Taylor, Frederick W., jt. auth. see Briggs, Geoffrey A.
Taylor, G. Immunology in Medical Practice. LC 74-4592. (Illus.). 390p. 1975. text ed. 10.00 (ISBN 0-7216-8767-9). Saunders.
Taylor, G. J., jt. auth. see Feder, R. F.
Taylor, G. Jeffrey. Volcanoes in Our Solar System. LC 82-19819. (Illus.). 96p. (gr. 5 up). 1983. PLB 10.95 (ISBN 0-396-08118-5). Dodd.
Taylor, G. Thomas, Jr., jt. auth. see Horan, James F.
Taylor, Geoffrey. Principles of Human Nutrition. (Studies in Biology: No. 94). 72p. 1978. pap. text ed. 8.95 (ISBN 0-686-43112-X). E Arnold.
Taylor, Geoffrey & Reeves, Marjorie. The American South Before the Civil War. (Then & There Ser.). (Illus., Orig.). (gr. 7-12). 1975. pap. text ed. 3.10 (ISBN 0-582-20490-9). Longman.
Taylor, George. Mary Wollstonecraft: A Study in Economics & Romance. LC 68-24924. (English Biography Ser., No. 31). (Illus.). 1969. Repr. of 1911 ed. lib. bdg. 41.95 (ISBN 0-8383-0246-7). Haskell.
Taylor, George & Skinner, Andrew. Maps of the Roads of Ireland. (Illus.). 328p. 1983. Repr. of 1783 ed. text ed. 35.00x (ISBN 0-7165-0063-9, Pub. by Irish Academic Pr Ireland). Biblio Dist.
Taylor, George see Jackson, B. D., et al.
Taylor, George A. Managerial & Engineering Economy. 3rd ed. 1975. text ed. 19.95x (ISBN 0-442-24866-0); instructor's manual 2.00x (ISBN 0-442-25743-0). Van Nos Reinhold.
Taylor, George A., jt. ed. see Palumbo, Dennis.
Taylor, George R. The Transportation Revolution, 1815-1860. LC 76-48799. (The Economic History of the United States Ser.). 1977. pap. 10.95 o.p. (ISBN 0-87332-101-4). M E Sharpe.
Taylor, George R., ed. Jackson Versus Biddle's Bank: Struggle Over the Second Bank of the U. S. 2nd ed. (Problems in American Civilization Ser.). 1972. pap. text ed. 5.95 (ISBN 0-669-84491-8). Heath.
--Turner Thesis Concerning the Role of the Frontier in American History. 3rd ed. (Problems in American Civilization Ser.). 1972. pap. text ed. 5.95 (ISBN 0-669-81059-2). Heath.
--The War of Eighteen Twelve: Past Justifications & Present Interpretations. LC 80-12565. (Problems in American Civilization). xii, 114p. 1980. Repr. of 1963 ed. lib. bdg. 18.50x (ISBN 0-313-22356-4, TATW). Greenwood.
Taylor, Gertrude. The Complete Book of Knitting. 304p. 1983. pap. 9.95 (ISBN 0-686-83773-8, ScribT). Scribner.
Taylor, Glenhall. What is Blazers. 1980. pap. 1.50 (ISBN 0-686-37155-0). Eldridge Pub.
Taylor, Gordon R. Biological Time Bomb. 1969. pap. 1.50 o.p. (ISBN 0-451-61457-7, MY1457, Ment). NAL.
--Great Evolution Mystery. LC 82-47535. (Bessie Bks.). (Illus.). 352p. 1983. 20.00 (ISBN 0-06-039013-1, HarpT). Har-Row.
Taylor, H., ed. Edward J. Dent: Selected Essays. LC 78-62111. (Illus.). 1979. 44.50 (ISBN 0-521-22174-9). Cambridge U Pr.
Taylor, H. F., ed. Chemistry of Cements, 2 Vols. 1964. Vol. 1. 70.00 (ISBN 0-12-683901-8); Vol. 2. 70.00 o.s.i. (ISBN 0-12-683902-6). Acad Pr.
Taylor, H. M. Anglo-Saxon Architecture. LC 65-3244. (Illus.). 1978. Vol. 1, 1965. 99.50 (ISBN 0-521-22481-0); Vol. 2. 99.50 (ISBN 0-521-22482-9); Vol. 3. 114.50 (ISBN 0-521-21692-3); Set. 255.00 (ISBN 0-521-21693-1). Cambridge U Pr.
Taylor, H. M. & Taylor, Joan. Anglo-Saxon Architecture, 2 vols. LC 65-3244. (Illus.). 868p. 1981. pap. 42.50 (ISBN 0-521-29914-4). Cambridge U Pr.
Taylor, Halsey P. & Taylor, Sheila F. Read to Write. 1981. pap. text ed. 9.95x (ISBN 0-673-15388-6). Scott F.
Taylor, Harold. On Education & Freedom. LC 53-13096. 320p. 1967. lib. bdg. 7.00x o.p. (ISBN 0-8093-0245-4). S Ill U Pr.
Taylor, Harold L. Making Time Work for You. 1983. pap. 3.25 (ISBN 0-440-16260-2). Dell.
Taylor, Henry O. Ancient Ideals: A Study of Intellectual & Spiritual Growth from Early Times to the Establishment of Christianity, 2 Vols. 430p. 1982. Repr. of 1900 ed. Set. lib. bdg. 100.00 (ISBN 0-686-81834-2). Telegraph Bks.
--Freedom of the Mind in History. Repr. of 1923 ed. lib. bdg. 15.50x (ISBN 0-8371-4352-7, TAMH). Greenwood.
Taylor, Henry T. Know Your Wheels. (Illus.). 51p. (gr. 4-6). 1981. pap. write for info. (ISBN 0-938956-00-0). H T Taylor.
Taylor, Herb. The Sport Diving Catalog: A Comprehensive Guide & Access Book. LC 80-8221. (Illus.). 304p. Date not set. price not set (ISBN 0-06-014898-5, HarpT); pap. 10.95i (ISBN 0-06-090899-8, CN899, HarpT). Har-Row. Postponed.
--Underwater with the Nikonos & Nikon Systems. LC 76-16462. (Illus.). 1976. 10.95 (ISBN 0-8174-2401-6, Amphoto). Watson-Guptill.
Taylor, Herb, et al. Natural Light & Night Photography. LC 81-71223. (Modern Photo Guides Ser.). (Illus.). 120p. (Orig.). 1982. pap. 7.95 (ISBN 0-385-18156-6). Avalon Comm.
Taylor, Herbert J. The Herbert J. Taylor Story. 128p. 1983. pap. 3.95 (ISBN 0-87784-836-X). Inter-Varsity.
Taylor, Hilary. James McNeill Whistler. LC 78-50983. (Illus.). 1978. 22.50 o.p. (ISBN 0-399-12238-9). Putnam Pub Group.
Taylor, Howard & Taylor, Mary G. Hudson Taylor's Spiritual Secret. pap. 3.95 (ISBN 0-8024-0029-9). Moody.
Taylor, Howard & Wade, Thomas. Contemporary Trigonometry. (Illus.). 224p. 1973. text ed. 14.50 o.p. (ISBN 0-07-067640-2, C). McGraw.
Taylor, Howard E., jt. auth. see Wade, Thomas L.
Taylor, Howard F. Balance in Small Groups. LC 77-106005. 368p. 1970. 17.50 (ISBN 0-442-08438-2, Pub. by Van Nos Reinhold). Krieger.
Taylor, Hudson. Union & Communion. 1971. pap. 2.95 (ISBN 0-87123-571-4, 200571). Bethany Hse.
Taylor, Hugh. Golf Dictionary. 7.50x (ISBN 0-392-12072-0, SpS). Sportshelf.
Taylor, Hugh A., ed. The Arrangement & Description of Archival Materials. (ICA Handbook Ser.: Vol. 2). 181p. 1981. 35.00x (ISBN 3-598-20272-5, Pub. by K G Saur). Gale.
Taylor, Ian. Law & Order - Arguments for Socialism. 234p. 1981. text ed. 31.50x (ISBN 0-333-21442-0, 41259, Pub. by Macmillan England). Humanities.
Taylor, Isaac. Names & Their Histories. LC 68-17936. 1969. Repr. of 1898 ed. 40.00x (ISBN 0-8103-4217-0). Gale.
--Words & Places, or Etymological Illustrations of History, Ethnology, & Geography. 4th ed. 1968. Repr. of 1909 ed. 37.00x (ISBN 0-8103-3240-X). Gale.
Taylor, J., jt. auth. see Dobson, R. B.
Taylor, J. C. Gauge Theories of Weak Interactions. LC 75-9092. (Cambridge Monographs on Mathematical Physics: No. 3). (Illus.). 200p. 1976. 49.95 (ISBN 0-521-20896-3); pap. 13.95x (ISBN 0-521-29518-1). Cambridge U Pr.
Taylor, J. G., jt. ed. see Ferrara, S.
Taylor, J. Golden, ed. Literature of the American West. LC 71-132448. 1971. pap. text ed. 15.95 (ISBN 0-395-05458-3). HM.
Taylor, J. H., ed. Molecular Genetics: An Advanced Treatise, 2 pts. (Molecular Biology Ser). Pt. 1, 1962. 59.50 ea. (ISBN 0-12-684401-1). Pt. 1. Pt. 2, 1967. 59.50 (ISBN 0-12-684402-X). Acad Pr.
Taylor, J. Herbert, ed. Selected Papers on Molecular Genetics. (Perspectives in Modern Biology). (Illus., Orig.). 1965. pap. 28.50 (ISBN 0-12-684456-9). Acad Pr.
Taylor, J. R. Model Building for Architects & Engineers. 1971. 29.50 (ISBN 0-07-062938-2, P&RB). McGraw.
Taylor, Jack. One Home Under God. LC 73-91609. 6.95 (ISBN 0-8054-5222-2); study guide 1.95 (ISBN 0-8054-5225-7); guide book 5.00 (ISBN 0-8054-5615-5). Broadman.
Taylor, Jack L. Fundamentals of Marketing: Additional Dimensions, Selections from the Literatures. 2nd ed. 1975. 15.95 (ISBN 0-07-063116-6, C). McGraw.
Taylor, Jack R. La Llave para una Vida de Triunfo. Guzman, Juan P., tr. from Eng. Orig. Title: The Key to Triumphant Living. 240p. 1982. pap. 6.75 (ISBN 0-311-46095-X, Edit Mundo). Casa Bautista.
Taylor, Jack R., jt. auth. see Glisson, Jerry.
Taylor, James C. Technology & Planned Organizational Change. LC 78-161549. 151p. 1971. 12.00x (ISBN 0-87944-003-1). Inst Soc Res.
Taylor, James C. & Bowers, David G. Survey of Organizations. LC 72-619571. 172p. 1972. 16.00x (ISBN 0-87944-124-0). Inst Soc Res.
Taylor, James C., jt. ed. see Davis, Louis E.
Taylor, James R., jt. auth. see Kinnear, Thomas C.
Taylor, Jane. What We Hear. Lawrence, Leslie & Weingartner, Ronald, eds. (Bright Beginnings I). (Illus.). 48p. (Orig.). (gr. k-2). pap. 1.69 (ISBN 0-88049-030-6, 7393). Milton Bradley Co.
--What We See. Lawrence, Leslie & Weingartner, Ronald, eds. (Bright Beginnings I). (Illus.). 48p. (Orig.). (gr. k-2). pap. 1.69 (ISBN 0-88049-029-2, 7392). Milton Bradley Co.
Taylor, Janelle. Brazen Ecstasy. (Orig.). 1983. pap. 3.50 (ISBN 0-8217-1133-4). Zebra.
Taylor, Jean. Plants & Flowers for Lasting Decoration. LC 81-81039. (Illus.). 144p. 1981. 17.95 o.p. (ISBN 0-88332-258-7, 8187). Larousse.
Taylor, Jennifer & Andrews, John. Architecture: A Performing Art. 176p. 69.00x (ISBN 0-7188-2532-2, Pub. by Lutterworth Pr England). State Mutual Bk.
Taylor, Jennifer J., ed. see Taylor, Bob.
Taylor, Jeremy. Dream Work: Techniques for Discovering the Creative Power of Dreams. LC 82-62411. 1983. pap. 8.95 (ISBN 0-8091-2525-0). Paulist Pr.
--The Rule & Exercises of Holy Living. 295p. 1982. Repr. of 1982 ed. lib. bdg. 35.00 (ISBN 0-89984-468-5). Century Bookbindery.
Taylor, Jeremy R. Science Lecture Room. 1967. 32.50 (ISBN 0-521-06612-3). Cambridge U Pr.
Taylor, Jerome, tr. see Chenu, M. D.
Taylor, Jeromr, ed. see Chenu, M. D.
Taylor, Joan. Asking for It. 258p. 1980. 10.95 o.p. (ISBN 0-312-92027-X). St Martin.
Taylor, Joan & Treon, Ray. Success with Ferrets. Van de John, Richard, ed. (Mini Pet Reference Ser.: No. 2). (Illus.). 1977. pap. 3.50 (ISBN 0-915096-05-6). Palmetto Pub.
Taylor, Joan, jt. auth. see Taylor, H. M.
Taylor, Joan Chatfield see Chatfield-Taylor, Joan.
Taylor, Joan J. Bronze Age Goldwork of the British Isles. LC 75-12160. (Gulbenkian Archaeological Ser.). (Illus.). 188p. 1981. 99.00 (ISBN 0-521-20802-5). Cambridge U Pr.
Taylor, John. Atari Four Hundred-Eight Hundred DiskGuide. (DiskGuides Ser.). 32p. (Orig.). 1983. pap. 7.95 (ISBN 0-931988-95-0). Osborne-McGraw.
--Consumer Lending. 1982. text ed. 17.95 (ISBN 0-8359-0929-8); instr's. manual avail. Reston.
--Introduction to Psychology. 1978. pap. text ed. 10.95 (ISBN 0-8403-1890-1). Kendall-Hunt.
Taylor, John & Walls, Jerry C. Cowries. new ed. (Illus.). 1975. 24.95 (ISBN 0-87666-630-6, S101). TFH Pubns.
Taylor, John, jt. auth. see Pronay, Nicholas.
Taylor, John, ed. Believing in the Church: Doctrine Commission of the Church of England. LC 82-80254. 320p. (Orig.). 1982. Repr. of 1981 ed. 15.95 (ISBN 0-8192-1301-2). Morehouse.
Taylor, John, ed. see Jane's Pocket Books.
Taylor, John F. The Hyperactive Child & the Family: The Complete What-to-Do Handbook. LC 79-56871. 256p. 1980. 12.95 (ISBN 0-89696-080-3, An Everest House Book). Dodd.
Taylor, John H., tr. & annotations by. St. Augustine: The Literal Meaning of Genesis, Vol. 1. (Ancient Christian Writers Ser.: Vol. 41). 292p. 1983. 19.95 (ISBN 0-8091-0326-5). Paulist Pr.
--St. Augustine: The Literal Meaning of Genesis, Vol. 2. (Ancient Christian Writers Ser.: Vol. 42). 358p. 1983. 22.95 (ISBN 0-8091-0327-3). Paulist Pr.
Taylor, John L. & Walford, Rex. Learning & the Simulation Game. LC 78-21338. (Illus.). 228p. 1979. 22.00 (ISBN 0-8039-1207-2); pap. 10.95 (ISBN 0-8039-1208-0). Sage.
Taylor, John R. Graham Greene on Film: Collected Film Criticism 1935-1939. LC 72-83894. (Illus.). 1972. 12.50 o.p. (ISBN 0-671-21412-8). S&S.
--How to Start & Succeed in a Business of Your Own. 1978. ref. ed. 18.95 (ISBN 0-8359-2927-2); pap. 7.95 (ISBN 0-8359-2926-4); instrs'. manual avail. (ISBN 0-8359-2928-0). Reston.
--Model Building for Architects & Engineers. 1983. Repr. of 1971 ed. (ISBN 0-89874-424-5). Krieger.
--Scattering Theory. LC 75-37938. 477p. 1972. 31.95x o.p. (ISBN 0-471-84900-6). Wiley.
--Scattering Theory: The Quantum Theory of Nonrelativitistic Collisions. 496p. 1983. Repr. of 1972 ed. text ed. price not set (ISBN 0-89874-607-8). Krieger.
--Strangers in Paradise: The Hollywood Emigres, 1933-1950. LC 82-21312. 256p. 1983. 16.45 (ISBN 0-03-061944-0). HR&W.
Taylor, John S. Commonsense Architecture. (Illus.). 1983. 12.95 (ISBN 0-393-01647-1). Norton.
Taylor, John V. The Go-Between God: The Holy Spirit & the Christian Mission. 1979. pap. 7.95x (ISBN 0-19-520125-6). Oxford U Pr.
--The Primal Vision: Christian Presence Amid African Religion. (Student Christian Movement Press). (Orig.). 1963. pap. text ed. 7.95x (ISBN 0-19-520340-2). Oxford U Pr.
Taylor, John W. Jets. (Everyday Technology Ser.). (Illus.). 64p. 1976. 9.00x o.p. (ISBN 0-460-06433-9, Pub. by J. M. Dent England). Biblio Dist.

Taylor, John W. & Taylor, Michael J. The Encyclopedia of Aircraft. LC 78-53408. (Illus.). 1978. 20.00 o.p. (ISBN 0-399-12217-6). Putnam Pub Group.

Taylor, John W., jt. auth. see Taylor, Michael J.

Taylor, John W., et al. Air Facts & Feats. LC 77-93306. (Guinness Family of Bks). (Illus.). 1978. 19.95 (ISBN 0-8069-0126-8); lib. bdg. 23.59 (ISBN 0-8069-0127-6). Sterling.

Taylor, Joseph L., et al. A Group Home for Adolescent Girls: Practice & Research. LC 76-27209. 1976. pap. 6.95 (ISBN 0-87868-164-7, GH-14). Child Welfare.

Taylor, Joshua C. Learning to Look: A Handbook for the Visual Arts. 2nd ed. LC 80-26251. 186p. 1981. pap. 5.95 (ISBN 0-226-79154-8). U of Chicago Pr.

Taylor, Joshua C. & Peterson, William. Fritz Scholder. LC 82-40345. (Illus.). 296p. 1982. 65.00 (ISBN 0-8478-0456-9). Rizzoli Intl.

Taylor, Joy. Organizing the Open Classroom: A Teacher's Guide to the Integrated Day. LC 72-79765. (Illus.). 120p. 1974. pap. 3.95 (ISBN 0-8052-0445-8). Schocken.

Taylor, Joyce. Notes from a Young Girl Contemplating Suicide. 1980. 3.95 o.p. (ISBN 0-8062-1374-4). Carlton.

Taylor, Joyce & Ballenger, Sally. Neurological Dysfunction & Nursing Interventions. (Illus.). 1980. text ed. 26.50 (ISBN 0-07-063170-0). McGraw.

Taylor, Judy, ed. see Clary, Wayne.

Taylor, Judy, ed. see Johnson, Nancy.

Taylor, Judy, ed. see Lowe, Doug.

Taylor, Judy, ed. see Noll, Paul.

Taylor, K. Stages in Writing. 1973. text ed. 13.95 (ISBN 0-07-062995-1, C); instr's manual 15.00 (ISBN 0-07-062996-X). McGraw.

Taylor, Keith B. & Anthony, Luean E. Clinical Nutrition. (Illus.). 640p. 1983. pap. text ed. 21.95 (ISBN 0-07-063185-9, HP). McGraw.

Taylor, Keith W. The Birth of Vietnam. LC 81-11590. 440p. 1983. text ed. 38.50x (ISBN 0-520-04428-2). U of Cal Pr.

Taylor, Kenneth. Lost on the Trail. (gr. 4-8). 1980. pap. 2.50 (ISBN 0-8423-3843-8). Tyndale.

Taylor, Kenneth N. Almost Twelve. pap. 2.50 (ISBN 0-8423-0060-0). Tyndale.

--Devotions for the Children's Hour. 4.95 (ISBN 0-8024-2211-X); pap. 3.95 (ISBN 0-8024-0061-2). Moody.

--La Evolucion. Ingledew, Robert, tr. from Eng. Orig. Title: Evolution & the High School Student. 64p. 1981. pap. 1.95 (ISBN 0-311-05761-6). Casa Bautista.

--The Living Bible: Holman Illustrated Edition. new ed. LC 73-3323. (Illus.). 1250p. 1973. 13.95 o.p. (ISBN 0-87981-023-8). Holman.

--Living Letters for the Children's Hour. LC 68-26407. (Illus.). 192p. (gr. k-6). 1968. 4.95 o.p. (ISBN 0-8024-4945-X); pap. 3.95 (ISBN 0-8024-0062-0). Moody.

--Living Thoughts for the Children's Hour. LC 72-77943. (Illus.). 128p. (gr. k-6). 1972. 4.95 o.p. (ISBN 0-8024-4876-3); pap. 3.95 (ISBN 0-8024-0121-X). Moody.

--Meditaciones: Devotions for the Children's Hour. (Span). 1954. pap. 3.95 (ISBN 0-8024-5390-2). Moody.

--Stories for the Children's Hour. rev. ed. LC 68-26408. (Illus.). (gr. k-6). 5.95 o.p. (ISBN 0-8024-8326-7); pap. 2.95 (ISBN 0-8024-0063-9). Moody.

--Taylor's Bible Story Book. rev. ed. 1976. 15.95 (ISBN 0-8423-2302-3). Tyndale.

Taylor, Kenneth N., tr. New Life: Living New Testament. 1976. pap. 2.95 (ISBN 0-8423-4680-5). Tyndale.

Taylor, Kenneth R. What High School Students Should Know about Creation. (YA) (gr. 9-12). 1983. pap. 2.50 (ISBN 0-8423-7872-3). Tyndale.

--What High School Students Should Know about Evolution. 70p. (YA) (gr. 9-12). 1983. pap. 2.50 (ISBN 0-8423-7873-1). Tyndale.

Taylor, L. Urbanized Society. 1980. text ed. 19.95x o.p. (ISBN 0-673-16330-X). Scott F.

Taylor, L. A. Footnote to Murder. 192p. 1983. 12.95 (ISBN 0-8027-5486-4). Walker & Co.

Taylor, L. B. The New Right. (Impact Ser.). 96p. (gr. 7 up). 1981. lib. bdg. 8.90 (ISBN 0-531-04337-1). Watts.

--Story of Evolution. LC 80-52126. (YA) (gr. 7 up). 1981. PLB 10.90 (ISBN 0-531-09180-5). Watts.

Taylor, L. B., Jr. Haunted House. Schneider, Meg, ed. (Chiller Ser.). 128p. (Orig.). (gr. 3-7). 1983. pap. 3.95 (ISBN 0-671-46282-2). Wanderer Bks.

--Haunted Houses. (Chiller Ser.). 128p. (gr. 8-12). 1983. PLB 8.79 (ISBN 0-671-46783-2). Messner.

--The Nuclear Arms Race. (Impact Bks). (Illus.). 112p. (gr. 7 up). 1982. PLB 8.90 (ISBN 0-531-04401-7). Watts.

--Rescue! True Stories of Heroism. (Illus.). (gr. 7-9). 1980. pap. 1.50 o.p. (ISBN 0-671-29989-1). Archway.

--Space: Battleground of the Future? (Impact Ser.). 128p. (gr. 7 up). 1983. PLB 8.90 (ISBN 0-531-04546-3). Watts.

--Spotlight on Scott Baio, Clark Brandon, Leif Garret & John Schneider. Barish, Wendy, ed. (Illus.). 144p. (gr. 3 up). 1982. pap. 2.95 (ISBN 0-671-45212-6). Wanderer Bks.

Taylor, L. J., jt. auth. see Ayliffe, G. A.

Taylor, L. J., ed. British Librarianship & Information Work, 1976-1980. 1982. Vol. 1, 304p. write for info. (ISBN 0-85365-763-7, Pub. by Lib Assn England); Vol. 2, 304p. write for info. (ISBN 0-85365-825-0). Oryx Pr.

--A Librarian's Handbook, Vol. 1. 1977. pap. 55.25x o.p. (ISBN 0-85365-079-9, Pub. by Lib Assn England). Oryx Pr.

Taylor, L. Lowry. Speak English, Wkbk. 6. (Speak English Ser.). (Illus.). 64p. (Orig.). 1983. pap. text ed. 4.95 (ISBN 0-88499-662-X). Inst Mod Lang.

Taylor, Lance. Macro Models for Developing Countries. (Economic Handbook Ser.). (Illus.). 1979. text ed. 28.50 (ISBN 0-07-063135-2, C). McGraw.

--Structuralist Macroeconomics: Applicable Models for the Third World. 1983. text ed. 18.95x (ISBN 0-465-08239-4). Basic.

Taylor, Laurie. Changing the Past. LC 81-83881. (Minnesota Voices Project Ser.: No. 6). (Illus.). 72p. 1981. pap. 3.00 (ISBN 0-89823-029-2). New Rivers Pr.

Taylor, Lawrence. Eyewitness Identification. 304p. 1982. 35.00 (ISBN 0-686-84228-6). Michie-Bobbs.

--Witness Immunity. 176p. 1983. 16.75x (ISBN 0-398-04765-0). C C Thomas.

Taylor, Lester. Telecommunications Demand: A Survey & Critique. 232p. 1980. prof ref 35.00x (ISBN 0-88410-496-6). Ballinger Pub.

Taylor, Lily R. The Divinity of the Roman Emperor. LC 32-22470. (APA Philological Monographs Reprints). 1981. pap. 22.50 (ISBN 0-686-31379-8, 40-00-01). Scholars Pr CA.

--Party Politics in the Age of Caesar. (Sather Classical Lectures: No. 22). 1949. pap. 7.95x (ISBN 0-520-01257-7, CAMPUS53). U of Cal Pr.

Taylor, Linda, jt. auth. see Adelman, Howard S.

Taylor, Linda J. Henry James,1816-1916: A Reference Guide. 1982. lib. bdg. 42.50 (ISBN 0-8161-7874-7, Hall Reference). G K Hall.

Taylor, Lisa, ed. Urban Open Spaces. (Illus.). 1980. pap. 9.95 (ISBN 0-8478-0304-X). Rizzoli Intl.

Taylor, Lloyd C., Jr. Margaret Ayer Barnes. (United State Authors Ser.). 1974. lib. bdg. 13.95 (ISBN 0-8057-0037-4, Twayne). G K Hall.

Taylor, Loretta, jt. auth. see Silvey, Linda.

Taylor, Louis. Bits-Their History, Use & Misuse. pap. 5.00 (ISBN 0-87980-231-6). Wilshire.

Taylor, Lowry L. Speak English, Wkbk. 4. (Speak English Ser.). (Illus.). 64p. (Orig.). 1983. pap. text ed. 4.95 (ISBN 0-88499-658-1). Inst Mod Lang.

Taylor, Lyn P. & Tom, Gary F. Electromyometric Biofeedback Therapy. (Illus.). 1981. text ed. 28.00 (ISBN 0-686-36334-5). BATI.

Taylor, Lynda, jt. auth. see Worthington, Bonnie.

Taylor, M. Anarchy & Cooperation. LC 75-12589. 151p. 1976. 34.95 (ISBN 0-471-84647-3, Pub. by Wiley-Interscience). Wiley.

--Coverdale on Management. 1982. 19.00 (ISBN 0-434-90275-6, Pub. by Heinemann). David & Charles.

Taylor, M. A. Technology of Textile Properties: An Introduction. 26.00x (ISBN 0-87245-608-0). Textile Bk.

Taylor, Marcia W. A Computer Simulation of Innovative Decision-Making in Organizations. LC 78-56051. 1978. pap. text ed. 8.25 (ISBN 0-8191-0517-1). U Pr of Amer.

Taylor, Margot W., ed. see Marcon, Mike.

Taylor, Mark. Shakespeare's Darker Purpose: A Question of Incest. LC 81-69124. (Studies in the Renaissance). 216p. 1982. 24.00 (ISBN 0-404-62277-1). AMS Pr.

Taylor, Mark, ed. see Will, Paul J., et al.

Taylor, Mark C. Deconstructing Theology. (American Academy of Religion Studies in Religion Series Co-Published with Scholars Press). 176p. 1983. 12.95 (ISBN 0-8245-0533-6). Crossroad NY.

--Deconstructing Theology. LC 82-5970. (AAR Studies in Religion). 152p. 1982. 12.95 (ISBN 0-89130-582-3, 01-00-28). Scholars Pr CA.

Taylor, Mark C., ed. Unfinished... Essays in Honor of Ray L. Hart. (JAAR Thematic Studies). 1981. pap. 13.50 (ISBN 0-686-87092-1, 01-24-81). Scholars Pr CA.

Taylor, Mark C., et al. Religion & the Human Image. (Illus.). 1977. pap. text ed. 14.95 (ISBN 0-13-773424-7). P-H.

Taylor, Martha & Marks, Morton. Aphasia Rehabilitation Manual & Therapy Kit. 1959. 49.95 (ISBN 0-07-062948-X, HP). McGraw.

Taylor, Mary A. Aloha to Love. Bd. with Hawaiian Interlude. 1982. pap. 2.75 (ISBN 0-451-11470-1, AE1470, Sig). NAL.

--Bittersweet Love. 1978. pap. 1.50 o.p. (ISBN 0-451-08404-7, W8404, Sig). NAL.

Taylor, Mary Ann. Aloha to Love. (Orig.). 1979. pap. 1.75 o.p. (ISBN 0-451-08765-8, E8765, Sig). NAL.

--Capture My Love. 1977. pap. 1.50 o.p. (ISBN 0-451-07755-5, W7755, Sig). NAL.

Taylor, Mary C. A History of the Foundations of Catholicism in Northern New York. LC 77-359034. (Monograph Ser.: No. 32). (Illus.). 13.50x (ISBN 0-930060-12-1). US Cath Hist.

Taylor, Mary G., jt. auth. see Taylor, Howard.

Taylor, Mary L., jt. ed. see Lowenstein, Janet.

Taylor, Maureen. Writing to Communicate: A Rhetoric, Reader, & Handbook for College Writers. 392p. 1982. pap. text ed. 13.95x (ISBN 0-534-01196-9). Wadsworth Pub.

Taylor, Maxwell D. Uncertain Trumpet. LC 74-7540. 203p. 1974. Repr. of 1960 ed. lib. bdg. 20.50x (ISBN 0-8371-7577-1, TAUT). Greenwood.

Taylor, May. Notre Dame Recipe Book. 14.50 (ISBN 0-392-01654-0, LTB). Sportshelf.

Taylor, Mendell. Every Day with the Psalms. 1972. 5.95 (ISBN 0-8341-0258-7). Beacon Hill.

Taylor, Mendell L. Every Day with Paul. 1978. 6.95 (ISBN 0-8341-0529-2). Beacon Hill.

Taylor, Michael. Community, Anarchy & Liberty. LC 82-1173. 150p. 1982. 24.50 (ISBN 0-521-24621-0); pap. 8.95 (ISBN 0-521-27014-6). Cambridge U Pr.

--Fantastic Flying Machines. (Illus.). 144p. 1982. 12.95 (ISBN 0-86720-552-0). Sci Bks Intl.

Taylor, Michael & Mondey, David. Giants in the Sky. (Illus.). 216p. 1982. 17.95 (ISBN 0-86720-626-8). Sci Bks Intl.

Taylor, Michael, jt. auth. see McDermott, Phillip.

Taylor, Michael & Thrift, Nigel, eds. The Geography of the Multinationals: Studies in the Spatial Development & Economic Consequences of Multinational Corporations. LC 82-6002. 352p. 1982. 35.00x (ISBN 0-312-32176-7). St Martin.

Taylor, Michael, jt. ed. see Lomas, Charles W.

Taylor, Michael, jt. auth. see Mondey, David.

Taylor, Michael J. & Taylor, John W. Helicopters of the World. 2nd rev. ed. LC 79-303153. 1978. 13.50x (ISBN 0-7110-0685-7). Intl Pubns Serv.

Taylor, Michael J., jt. auth. see Taylor, John W.

Taylor, Michael J., ed. Planemakers: 1 Boeing. (Planemakers Ser.). (Illus.). 160p. 1982. 17.95 (ISBN 0-86720-554-7). Sci Bks Intl.

Taylor, Norman. God-Given Promises: Meet Every Need. LC 82-61861. 152p. pap. 3.95 (ISBN 0-87808-192-5). William Carey Lib.

Taylor, Norman B. & McPhedran, Margaret G. Basic Physiology & Anatomy. (Illus.). 1965. 6.95 o.p. (ISBN 0-399-40002-8). Putnam Pub Group.

Taylor, P., ed. Essays on Political Education. 201p. 1977. write for info. (ISBN 0-905273-03-6, Pub. by Taylor & Francis); pap. write for info. (ISBN 0-905273-04-4). Intl Pubns Serv.

Taylor, P. H. & Reid, W. A., eds. Curriculum, Culture & Classroom: Trends in Curriculum Studies. (General Ser.). 1980. pap. text ed. cancelled o.p. (ISBN 0-85633-163-5, NFER). Humanities.

Taylor, Pamela, ed. Notebooks of Leonardo Da Vinci. pap. 5.95 (ISBN 0-452-25283-0, Z5283, Plume). NAL.

Taylor, Pat E. A Foot in a Field of Men: Short Stories. 132p. pap. write for info. o.p. (ISBN 0-941720-12-8). Slough Pr TX.

Taylor, Paula. Cancer. (Sun Signs). (Illus.). (gr. 4-12). 1978. PLB 6.95 (ISBN 0-87191-644-4); pap. 3.25 (ISBN 0-89812-074-8). Creative Ed.

--Capricorn. (Sun Signs Ser.). (Illus.). (gr. 4-12). 1978. PLB 6.95 (ISBN 0-87191-650-9); pap. 3.25 (ISBN 0-89812-080-2). Creative Ed.

--Gemini. (Sun Signs Ser.). (Illus.). (gr. 4-12). 1978. PLB 6.95 (ISBN 0-685-86765-X); pap. 3.25 (ISBN 0-89812-073-X). Creative Ed.

--Gymnastics' Happy Superstar: Olga Korbut. (The Allstars Ser.). (Illus.). (gr. 2-6). 1977. PLB 6.95 (ISBN 0-87191-581-2); pap. 3.25 op. (ISBN 0-89812-197-3). Creative Ed.

--Henry Kissinger. LC 74-32470. (Creative Education Closeup Bk.). (Illus.). 32p. (gr. 3-6). 1975. PLB 7.95 (ISBN 0-87191-422-0). Creative Ed.

--Leo. (Sun Signs Ser.). (Illus.). (gr. 4-12). 1978. PLB 6.95 (ISBN 0-87191-645-2); pap. 3.25 (ISBN 0-89812-075-6). Creative Ed.

--Sagittarius. (Sun Signs Ser.). (Illus.). (gr. 4 up). 1978. PLB 6.95 (ISBN 0-87191-649-5); pap. 3.25 (ISBN 0-89812-079-9). Creative Ed.

Taylor, Peter. Australia: The/First Twelve Years. (Illus.). 220p. 1982. text ed. 25.00x (ISBN 0-86861-268-5). Allen Unwin.

Taylor, Peter J. Quantitative Methods in Geography: An Introduction to Spatial Analysis. LC 75-26097. (Illus.). 384p. 1977. text ed. 24.95 o.p. (ISBN 0-395-18699-4). HM.

Taylor, Peter J., jt. auth. see Archer, John C.

Taylor, Peter J., jt. auth. see Burnett, Alan D.

Taylor, Peter J., jt. auth. see Gudjin, Graham.

Taylor, Philip. Distant Magnet: European Immigration to the USA. 1972. pap. 4.95xi o.p. (ISBN 0-06-131656-3, TB1656, Torch). Har-Row.

Taylor, Philip A. A New Dictionary of Economics. 2nd ed. 321p. (Orig.). 1969. pap. 10.00 (ISBN 0-7100-7812-9). Routledge & Kegan.

Taylor, Philip A., ed. Industrial Revolution in Britain: Triumph or Disaster. rev. ed. (Problems in European Civilization Ser.). 1970. pap. text ed. 5.50 o.p. (ISBN 0-669-51847-6). Heath.

--Origins of the English Civil War: Conspiracy, Crusade, or Class Conflict. (Problems in European Civilization Ser.). 1960. pap. text ed. 5.50 o.p. (ISBN 0-669-24174-1). Heath.

Taylor, Philip H. & Reid, W. A. The English Sixth Form: A Case Study in Curriculum Research. (International Library of Sociology). 1974. 14.00 o.p. (ISBN 0-7100-7832-3). Routledge & Kegan.

Taylor, Philip M. The Projection of Britain: British Overseas Publicity & Propaganda 1919-1939. LC 80-42291. 384p. 1981. 49.50 (ISBN 0-521-23843-9). Cambridge U Pr.

Taylor, Phillip. Nonstate Actors in International Politics: From Transregional to Substate Organizations. 280p. (Orig.). 1982. lib. bdg. 30.00 (ISBN 0-86531-344-X); pap. text ed. 13.95 (ISBN 0-86531-345-8). Westview.

--When Europe Speaks with One Voice: The External Relations of the European Community. LC 78-57767. (Contributions in Political Science: No. 22). 1979. lib. bdg. 27.50x (ISBN 0-313-20614-7, TES/). Greenwood.

Taylor, Phillip H., jt. auth. see Cangelosi, Vincent E.

Taylor, R. The Neglected Hardy: Thomas Hardy's Lesser Novels. 1982. 59.00x (ISBN 0-686-42949-4, Pub. by Macmillan England). State Mutual Bk.

--The Politics of the Soviet Cinema: Nineteen Seventeen to Nineteen Twenty-Nine. LC 78-67809. (International Studies). 1979. 32.50 (ISBN 0-521-22290-7). Cambridge U Pr.

Taylor, R., ed. George Washington Wilson. (Illus.). 224p. 1982. 39.00 (ISBN 0-08-025760-7). Pergamon.

Taylor, R. B., et al, eds. Fundamentals of Family Medicine. (Illus.). 488p. 1983. pap. 34.50 (ISBN 0-387-90705-X). Springer-Verlag.

Taylor, R. D. The Book where Michael meets the Royal Street Elves & Learns about Whales & Whale Oil, the Electric Light, the Ostrich, & the Two-Headed Sea Serpent. LC 78-55985. (Illus.). 1978. 6.95 (ISBN 0-931604-00-1); pap. 3.95 (ISBN 0-686-99866-9). Curbstone Pub NY TX.

Taylor, R. D., ed. see Little, Geraldine.

Taylor, R. D., ed. see Wevill, David.

Taylor, R. E., ed. Family Medicine-Principles & Practice. 2nd ed. (Illus.). 2021p. 1983. 69.50 (ISBN 0-387-90718-1). Springer-Verlag.

Taylor, R. E. & Meighan, Clement W., eds. Chronologies in New World Archaeology. (Studies in Archaeology Ser). 1978. 64.50 (ISBN 0-12-685750-4). Acad Pr.

Taylor, R. G. Geology of Tin Deposits. LC 79-12323. (Developments in Economic Geology Ser.: Vol. 11). 1979. 76.75 (ISBN 0-444-41805-9). Elsevier.

Taylor, R. H. Magnetic Ions in Metals: A Review of Thier Study by Electron Spin Resonance. LC 76-53798. 1977. 24.95x o.p. (ISBN 0-470-99024-4). Halsted Pr.

Taylor, R. J. Food Additives. LC 79-42729. (The Institution of Environmental Sciences Ser.). 126p. 1980. 34.95 (ISBN 0-471-27684-7, Pub. by Wiley Interscience); pap. 16.95 (ISBN 0-471-27683-9). Wiley.

Taylor, R. P. Programming Primer: A Graphic Introduction to Computer Programming with BASIC & PASCAL. LC 81-2209. 1982. 17.95 (ISBN 0-201-07400-1). A-W.

Taylor, Ralph & Brooks, Bearl. No American Indians. (Social Studies Ser.). 24p. (gr. 4-6). 1979. wkbk. 5.00 (ISBN 0-8209-0240-3, SS-7). ESP.

Taylor, Ray, et al. Britain's Planning Heritage. 1981. 27.50x (ISBN 0-686-96951-0, Pub. by Royal Town England). State Mutual Bk.

Taylor, Rex & Gilmore, Anne, eds. Current Trends in British Gerontology. 230p. 1982. text ed. 35.00x (ISBN 0-566-00495-X). Gower Pub Ltd.

Taylor, Richard. Introductory Readings in Metaphysics. 1979. pap. text ed. 14.95 (ISBN 0-13-502302-5). P-H.

--Metaphysics. 3rd ed. 160p. 1983. pap. 8.50 (ISBN 0-686-82032-0). P-H.

--Understanding the Elements of Literature. LC 81-9295. 256p. 1982. 19.95x (ISBN 0-312-83216-8). St Martin.

Taylor, Richard K. Blockade! Guide to Nonviolent Intervention. LC 76-30600. 193p. (Orig.). 1977. 6.95x o.p. (ISBN 0-88344-036-9); pap. 2.95x o.p. (ISBN 0-88344-037-7). Orbis Bks.

Taylor, Richard K., jt. auth. see Sider, Ronald J.

Taylor, Richard S. La Vida Disciplinada. 144p. Date not set. 2.25 (ISBN 0-88113-341-8). Edit Betania.

Taylor, Rob. The Breach: Kilimanjaro & the Conquest of Self. (Illus.). 1981. 14.95 (ISBN 0-698-11086-2, Coward). Putnam Pub Group.

Taylor, Robert. Bible Baseball. pap. 3.95 (ISBN 0-8024-0211-9). Moody.

--Lord Salisbury. LC 75-7711. (British Political Biography Ser.). 250p. 1975. 17.95 o.p. (ISBN 0-312-49875-6). St Martin.

--Workers & the New Depression. 224p. 1982. text ed. 27.75x (ISBN 0-333-19295-8, Pub. by Macmillan England); pap. text ed. 18.95x (ISBN 0-333-33411-6). Humanities.

Taylor, Robert, jt. ed. see Bogue, Allan G.

Taylor, Robert B. Dr. Taylor's Self-Help Medical Guide. 1977. 9.95 o.p. (ISBN 0-87000-370-4, Arlington Hse). Crown.

--Dr. Taylor's Self-Help Medical Guide. 1978. pap. 2.50 (ISBN 0-451-09274-0, E9274, Sig). NAL.

Taylor, Robert E., ed. see Evans, Rupert & Herr, Edward.

Taylor, Robert G. Cripple Creek Mining District. LC 75-135193. (Indiana University Geographic Monograph Ser., Vol. 1). (Illus.). 180p. 1973. 10.00 o.s.i. (ISBN 0-910584-20-6); pap. 7.00 o.s.i. (ISBN 0-910584-66-4). Filter.

Taylor, Robert J. Colonial Connecticut: A History. LC 79-1099. (A History of the American Colonies Ser.). 1979. lib. bdg. 30.00 (ISBN 0-527-18710-0). Kraus Intl.

Taylor, Robert L. Niagara. LC 79-21620. 1980. 13.95 (ISBN 0-399-12432-2). Putnam Pub Group.

--Roaring in the Wind: Being a History of Alder Gulch Montana, in Its Great & Its Shameful Days. LC 77-16509. 1978. 10.95 (ISBN 0-399-12089-0). Putnam Pub Group.

--W. C. Fields: His Follies & Fortunes. (Illus.). 1967. pap. 1.25 (ISBN 0-451-50653-7, CY653, Sig Classics). NAL.

Taylor, Robert R. The Word in Stone: The Role of Architecture in the Nationalist Socialist Ideology. (Illus.). 1974. 38.50x (ISBN 0-520-02193-2). U of Cal Pr.

Taylor, Rodney L. The Cultivation of Sagehood As a Religious Goal in Neo-Confucianism: A Study of Selected Writings of Kao P'an-Lung (1562-1626) LC 78-18685. 1978. pap. 9.95 (ISBN 0-89130-239-5, 01-01-22). Scholars Pr Ca.

Taylor, Roger. Beyond Art: What Art Is & Might Become If Freed from Cultural Elitism. LC 81-157244. 192p. 1981. 26.50x (ISBN 0-389-20205-3). B&N Imports.

Taylor, Roger C. The Elements of Seamanship. LC 82-80400. (Illus.). 192p. 1982. 12.95 (ISBN 0-87742-153-6). Intl Marine.

Taylor, Ron. Fifty Facts About Animals. (Fifty Facts About Ser.). (Illus.). 32p. (gr. 4-6). 1983. PLB 8.90 (ISBN 0-531-09208-9). Watts.

--Fifty Facts About Speed & Power. (Fifty Facts About Ser.). (Illus.). 32p. (gr. 4-6). 1983. PLB 8.90 (ISBN 0-531-09211-9). Watts.

--How the Body Works. Moore, Linda, ed. (Full Color Fact Books). (Illus.). 32p. (gr. 4-12). 1982. PLB 7.95 (ISBN 0-8219-0012-9, 35544). EMC.

--Man & Technology. LC 80-50332. (World of Knowledge Ser.). lib. bdg. 16.72 (ISBN 0-382-06409-7). Silver.

Taylor, Ron, jt. auth. see Teel, Leonard R.

Taylor, Ronald B. Sweatshops in the Sun: Child Labor on the Farm. LC 72-6233. 288p. 1973. 6.95 o.p. (ISBN 0-8070-0516-9). Beacon Pr.

Taylor, Ronald C., jt. auth. see Gordon, Adrian H.

Taylor, Ross, jt. auth. see Levinson, A. A.

Taylor, S. J. Introduction to Measure & Integration. LC 73-84325. 272p. 1975. pap. text ed. 16.95x (ISBN 0-521-09804-1). Cambridge U Pr.

Taylor, S. J., jt. auth. see Kingman, John F.

Taylor, S. M., jt. auth. see Dear, M. J.

Taylor, Samuel G., 3rd, ed. Oncology. (Medical Examination Review Bk. Ser.: Vol. 29). 1973. spiral bdg. 23.00 (ISBN 0-87488-146-3). Med Exam.

Taylor, Samuel W. Family Kingdom. 350p. 1974. 9.95 (ISBN 0-914740-14-8). Western Epics.

Taylor, Selwyn & Cotton, Leonard. A Short Textbook of Surgery. 5th ed. LC 82-73297. (Illus.). 631p. 1983. pap. text ed. 16.50x (ISBN 0-668-05740-8, 5740). Arco.

Taylor, Serge. Making Bureaucracies Think: The Evironmental Impact Statement Strategy of Administrative Reform. LC 81-84456. 320p. 1983. pap. 29.50x (ISBN 0-8047-1152-6). Stanford U Pr.

Taylor, Sheila F., jt. auth. see Taylor, Halsey P.

Taylor, Simon, ed. The Anglo-Saxon Chronicle: 4 MS B. 96p. 1983. text ed. 30.00x (ISBN 0-85991-104-7, Pub by Boydell & Brewer). Biblio Dist.

Taylor, Simon W. & Lucie-Smith, Edward, eds. French Poetry Today: A Bilingual Anthology. LC 71-163335. 1972. 10.00x o.p. (ISBN 0-8052-3426-8). Schocken.

Taylor, Simon W., tr. see Artaud, Antonin.

Taylor, Simon W., tr. see Breton, Andre.

Taylor, Simon W., tr. see Jarry, Alfred.

Taylor, Simon W., tr. see Vian, Boris.

Taylor, Steve. Durkeheim & the Study of Suicide. (Contemporary Social Theory Ser.). 240p. 1982. 35.00x (ISBN 0-333-28645-6, Pub. by Macmillan England). State Mutual Bk.

--Durkheim & the Study of Suicide. LC 82-6001. 240p. 1982. 22.50x (ISBN 0-312-22266-1). St Martin.

Taylor, Steven J., jt. auth. see Bogdan, Robert.

Taylor, Stuart R. Planetary Science: A Lunar Perspective. (Illus.). 512p. 1982. 39.95X (ISBN 0-942862-00-7). Lunar & Planet Inst.

Taylor, Sybil. Ireland's Pubs. (Illus., Orig.). 1983. pap. 6.95 (ISBN 0-14-006488-5). Penguin.

Taylor, Sydney. All-of-a-Kind Family. (Illus.). (gr. 4-6). 1951. trade ed. 4.95 (ISBN 0-695-80280-1); PLB 5.97 o.s.i. (ISBN 0-695-40280-3). Follett.

--All-Of-A-Kind Family Downtown. (gr. 3-6). 1973. pap. 1.75 (ISBN 0-440-42032-6, YB). Dell.

--All-of-a-Kind Family Downtown. LC 70-184789. (Illus.). 160p. (gr. 5 up). 1972. 2.49 (ISBN 0-695-80308-5); PLB 4.95 (ISBN 0-695-40308-7). Follett.

--Dog Who Came to Dinner. (Beginning-to-Read Ser.). (Illus.). (gr. 1-3). 1966. PLB 4.39 (ISBN 0-695-42086-0, Dist. by Caroline Hse); pap. 1.95 (ISBN 0-695-32086-6). Follett.

--Ella of All of a Kind Family. (Illus.). (gr. 4-7). 1978. 9.95 (ISBN 0-525-29238-1, 0966-290). Dutton.

--More All-Of-A-Kind Family. (Illus.). (gr. 4-6). 1954. 4.95 o.s.i. (ISBN 0-695-85880-7); lib. ed. 4.98 o.s.i. (ISBN 0-695-45880-9). Follett.

Taylor, T. G. The Importance of Vitamins to Human Health. 194p. 1979. text ed. 18.95 o.p. (ISBN 0-8391-1461-3). Univ Park.

Taylor, T Geoffrey. Nutrition & Health. (Studies in Biology: No. 141). 64p. 1982. pap. text ed. 8.95 (ISBN 0-7131-2840-2). E Arnold.

Taylor, T. H., jt. ed. see Hemming, C. F.

Taylor, T. N., jt. ed. see Dilcher, D. L.

Taylor, Theodore. The Cay. (gr. 3 up). 1977. pap. 1.95 (ISBN 0-380-00142-X, 53165-8, Camelot). Avon.

--H.M.S. Hood vs. Bismarck: The Battleship Battle. 144p. 1982. pap. 2.25 (ISBN 0-380-81174-X, 81174, Flare). Avon.

--Trouble with Tuck. LC 80-707. 96p. (gr. 4-6). 1981. 9.85a (ISBN 0-385-17774-7); PLB (ISBN 0-385-17775-5). Doubleday.

--The Trouble with Tuck. 120p. (gr. 5 up). 1983. pap. 2.25 (ISBN 0-380-62711-6, Camelot). Avon.

Taylor, Theodore B., jt. auth. see Willrich, Mason.

Taylor, Thomas. Christ Revealed. LC 79-10885. 1979. Repr. of 1635 ed. 44.00x (ISBN 0-8201-1334-4). Schol Facsimiles.

--Dans le Filet de L'Oiseleur. Cosson, Annie, ed. Luc-Barbier, Jean, tr. from Eng. 152p. 1981. pap. 2.00 (ISBN 0-8297-1103-1). Life Pubs Intl.

--An Exposition of Titus. 1970. 20.75 (ISBN 0-86524-027-2, 5601). Klock & Klock.

--The Theoretic Arithmetic of the Pythagoreans. LC 82-83818. 1983. pap. 12.50 (ISBN 0-87728-558-6). Weiser.

--Theoretic Arithmetic of the Pythagoreans. pap. 12.50 (ISBN 0-686-43261-4). Philos Res.

Taylor, Thomas N. Paleobotany: An Introduction to Fossil Plant Biology. (Illus.). 576p. 1981. 37.50x (ISBN 0-07-062954-4). McGraw.

Taylor, Tom. Of Wrath & Praise. LC 80-29453. 224p. (Orig.). 1981. pap. 4.50 (ISBN 0-8024-9249-5). Moody.

Taylor, Trevor. Defense, Technology & International Integration. 290p. 1982. 30.00x (ISBN 0-312-19115-4). St Martin.

Taylor, V. J. How to Build Period Country Furniture. LC 79-3731. (Illus.). 1980. 10.00 o.p. (ISBN 0-8128-2696-5); pap. 4.95 (ISBN 0-8128-6047-0). Stein & Day.

Taylor, Verta, jt. auth. see Richardson, Laurel W.

Taylor, Victor J. Constructing Modern Furniture. LC 79-91383. (Home Craftsman Bk.). (Illus.). 144p. 1980. pap. 6.95 (ISBN 0-8069-8888-6). Sterling.

Taylor, Vincent, intro. by. The Gospel According to St. Mark: The Greek Text. 2nd ed. 20.00 o.p. (ISBN 0-312-34055-9). St Martin.

Taylor, Virginia, tr. see Guzman, Martin L.

Taylor, Virginia H. The Franco-Texan Land Company. (M. K. Brown Range Life Ser.: No. 7). (Illus.). 345p. 1969. 15.00 o.p. (ISBN 0-292-78417-1). U of Tex Pr.

Taylor, W. Carey. Es Su Salvacion Eterna? Marsili, Juan, tr. from Port. 1979. pap. 2.25 (ISBN 0-311-09068-0). Casa Bautista.

Taylor, W. H., ed. see Kuttner, Henry.

Taylor, W. H., ed. see Priestley, J. B.

Taylor, W. H., ed. see Tyrer, Walter.

Taylor, W. I. & Battersby, A. R., eds. Oxidative Coupling of Phenols. (Organic Substances of Natural Origin Ser: Vol. 1). 1967. 69.00 o.p. (ISBN 0-8247-1657-4). Dekker.

Taylor, W. R. The Marine Algae of Florida: With Special Reference to Dry Tortugas. (Bibl. Phyco.: Vol.2). 1967. Repr. of 1928 ed. 48.00 (ISBN 3-7682-0504-5). Lubrecht & Cramer.

Taylor, Walter K. Laboratory Instructions for General Zoology. (Illus.). 1978. pap. text ed. 11.95x (ISBN 0-02-419790-4). Macmillan.

Taylor, Welford D. Amelie Rives (Princess Troubetzkoy) (United States Authors Ser.). 1971. lib. bdg. 13.95 (ISBN 0-8057-0625-9, Twayne). G K Hall.

--Sherwood Anderson. LC 77-6948. (Literature and Life Ser.). 1977. 11.95 (ISBN 0-8044-2861-1). Ungar.

Taylor, Willard H. Beacon Bible Expositions. (Beacon Bible Exposition Ser.: Vol. 8). 228p. 1981. 6.95 (ISBN 0-8341-0734-1). Beacon Hill.

Taylor, Willard H., ed. see Airhart, Arnold E.

Taylor, Willard H., ed. see Greathouse, Willam M.

Taylor, Willard H., ed. see Martin, Sydney.

Taylor, Willard H., ed. see Purkiser, W. T.

Taylor, Willard H., ed. see Welch, Reuben.

Taylor, Willard H., ed. see Young, Samuel.

Taylor, William. Heading for Change: The Management of Innovation in the Large Secondary School. (Orig.). 1973. 11.25x o.p. (ISBN 0-7100-7426-3); pap. 6.50 o.p. (ISBN 0-7100-7427-1). Routledge & Kegan.

Taylor, William & Braswell, Michael. Issues in Police & Criminal Psychology. LC 78-61915. 1978. pap. text ed. 11.50 (ISBN 0-8191-0624-0). U Pr of Amer.

Taylor, William see Simon, Brian.

Taylor, William J., Jr. & Maaranen, Steven A., eds. The Future of Conflict in the Nineteen Eighties. LC 82-48474. 1983. write for info. (ISBN 0-669-06145-X). Lexington Bks.

Taylor, William N. Anabolic Steroids & the Athlete. LC 82-17269. (Illus.). 128p. 1982. pap. 13.95x (ISBN 0-89950-055-2). McFarland & Co.

--Marathon Running: A Medical Science Handbook. (Illus.). 112p. 1982. pap. 12.95x (ISBN 0-89950-054-4). McFarland & Co.

Taylor, William R. Marine Algae of the Eastern Tropical & Sub-Tropical Coasts of the Americas. LC 59-9736. (Illus.). 1960. 39.50x (ISBN 0-472-08841-6). U of Mich Pr.

--Marine Algae of the Northeastern Coast of North America. 2nd rev. ed. LC 57-7103. (Illus.). 1957. 35.00x (ISBN 0-472-08840-8). U of Mich Pr.

--Sydney Pollack. (Filmmakers Ser.). 1981. lib. bdg. 14.95 (ISBN 0-8057-9279-1, Twayne). G K Hall.

Taylor-Gordon, Elaine, jt. auth. see Murphy, Patricia.

Taylor-Hyler, Ariel. Numerology: Its Facts & Secrets. 1958. 8.95 (ISBN 0-910140-17-0). Anthony.

Taylour, William. The Myceneans. rev. ed. (Ancient Peoples & Places Ser.). (Illus.). 1983. 19.95 (ISBN 0-500-02103-1). Thames Hudson.

Taymor, R., jt. ed. see Hoffman, I.

Taynton, Mark & Slik, Sheila T. Successful Kennel Management. 3rd ed. LC 66-25954. (Illus.). 250p. 1982. pap. 12.95 (ISBN 0-910210-01-2). Beech Tree.

Taynton, Mark & Slik, Shelia. Here We Go Again. LC 82-811215. 206p. 1982. soft cover 9.95 (ISBN 0-910210-02-0). Beech Tree.

Taynton, Mark, jt. auth. see Pisano, Beverly.

Tazewell, Charles. The Littlest Angel. 32p. (gr. k-6). 1980. pap. cancelled o.s.i. (ISBN 0-89542-922-5); pap. 3.25 o.s.i. (ISBN 0-89542-923-3). Ideals.

--Littlest Snowman. (Nursery Treasure Bks.). (gr. k-3). 1967. 1.95 (ISBN 0-448-04225-8, G&D). Putnam Pub Group.

Tazieff, Haroun. The Making of the Earth. 1975. pap. 3.95 (ISBN 0-86000-032-X). Gordon-Cremonesi.

Tchadaief, Pierre. Oeuvres Choisies, Publiees pour la Premiere Fois par Gagarin. (Nineteenth Century Russia Ser.). 209p. (Fr.). 1974. Repr. of 1862 ed. lib. bdg. 59.50x o.p. (ISBN 0-8287-0807-X, R52). Clearwater Pub.

Tchekhov, Anton. Plays & Stories. 1974. Repr. of 1937 ed. 8.95x (ISBN 0-460-00941-9, Evman). Biblio Dist.

Tchemerzine, Avenir. Bibliographie D'editions Originales & Rares D'auteurs Francais Des XVe, XVIe, XVIIe, XVIIIe Siecles Contenant Environ 6,000 Fac-Similes De Titres & Gravures. LC 73-87061. (Illus.). 420p. (Fr., Originally published in 10 vols. & reprinted in reduced format in 1 vol.). 1973. Repr. of 1927 ed. 160.00x (ISBN 0-914146-02-5). Somerset Hse.

Tchernavin, Tatiana. My Childhood in Siberia. (Illus.). 1972. 5.95x o.p. (ISBN 0-19-917020-7). Oxford U Pr.

Tchistyakova, Tanya, tr. see Ginsburg, Lev.

Tchividjian, Gigi. A Woman's Quest for Serenity. LC 80-25103. 160p. 1981. 8.95 o.p. (ISBN 0-8007-1183-1). Revell.

Tchobanoglous, George, jt. auth. see Metcalf & Eddy, Inc.

Tchobanoglous, George, ed. see Metcalf & Eddy Inc.

Tchobanoglous, George, et al. Solid Wastes: Engineering Principles & Management Issues. (Illus.). 1977. text ed. 37.50 (ISBN 0-07-063235-9, C); solutions manual 13.50 (ISBN 0-07-063236-7). McGraw.

Tchobanoglous, George, et al, eds. Wastewater Management: A Guide to Information Sources. LC 74-11570. (Man & the Environment Information Guide Ser.: Vol. 2). 260p. 1976. 42.00x (ISBN 0-8103-1338-3). Gale.

Tchoume, Mezan. Etude de la Vegetation Adventice des Palmeraies. (Black Africa Ser.). 93p. (Fr.). 1974. Repr. of 1968 ed. lib. bdg. 34.00x o.p. (ISBN 0-8287-0808-8, 71-2018). Clearwater Pub.

Tchudi, Stephen. The Burg-O-Rama Man. LC 82-14075. 192p. (YA) (gr. 7 up). 1983. 13.95 (ISBN 0-440-00833-6). Delacorte.

Teacher & Cookman. The Family Car Songbook. 96p. (Orig.). (gr. 4-12). 1983. lib. bdg. 12.90 (ISBN 0-89471-213-6); pap. 3.95 (ISBN 0-89471-212-8). Running Pr.

Teacher, Lawrence, ed. The Gardener's Notebook: A Personal Journal. (Illus.). 96p. (Orig.). 1983. lib. bdg. 12.90 (ISBN 0-89471-205-5); pap. 4.95 (ISBN 0-89471-204-7). Running Pr.

Teacher Services Committee. Handbook on Teacher Renewal & Development. 1981. pap. 6.75 (ISBN 0-934338-46-9). NAIS.

Teachers & Writers Collaborative, ed. Five Tales of Adventure: Collection of Stories by Children. (Orig.). 1975. pap. 4.00 (ISBN 0-915924-04-8). Tchrs & Writers Coll.

Teachers College Library. Bibliographic Guide to Education: Nineteen Seventy-Eight. (Library Catalogs-Bibliographic Guides). 1979. lib. bdg. 75.00 o.p. (ISBN 0-8161-6852-0, Biblio Guides). G K Hall.

Tead, Ordway. College Teaching & College Learning. 1949. 19.50x (ISBN 0-685-69874-2). Elliots Bks.

Teague, Bob. Super-Spy K-Thirteen in Outer Space. LC 79-7213. (Illus.). (gr. 1-3). 1980. 9.95a (ISBN 0-385-14314-1); PLB o.p. (ISBN 0-385-14315-X). Doubleday.

Teague, Kathleen. What Happened to Hector? LC 73-22078. (Easy Venture Ser). (Illus.). 32p. (gr. k-2). 1974. PLB 6.69 (ISBN 0-8116-6050-8). Garrard.

Teague, Richard D., ed. see Wildlife Society, Inc.

Teague, Robert & Erickson, Clint, eds. Computers & Society: A Reader. LC 74-4279. 350p. 1974. pap. text ed. 12.95 (ISBN 0-8299-0021-7). West Pub.

Teague, S. J. Microform Librarianship. 2nd ed. (Illus.). 1979. 22.95 (ISBN 0-408-70930-8). Butterworth.

Teal, Larry. Art of Saxophone Playing. (Illus.). 1963. pap. text ed. 12.50 (ISBN 0-87487-057-7). Summy.

Teal, Thomas, tr. see Nilsson, Birgit.

Teale, A. E. Kantian Ethics. LC 74-30981. 328p. 1975. Repr. of 1951 ed. lib. bdg. 19.25x (ISBN 0-8371-7940-8, TEKE). Greenwood.

Teale, Edwin W. Photographs of American Nature. LC 72-5876. (Illus.). 1972. 17.50 o.p. (ISBN 0-396-06713-1). Dodd.

Teale, Edwin W. & Zwinger, Ann. A Conscious Stillness: Two Naturalists on Thoreau's River. LC 81-48153. (Illus.). 224p. 1982. 18.22i (ISBN 0-06-015002-5, HarpT). Har-Row.

Teare, B. R., jt. auth. see Ver Planck, Dennistown W.

Teare, Iwan D. & Peet, Mary M. Crop Water Relations. LC 82-8671. 541p. 1983. 55.00 (ISBN 0-471-04630-2, Pub. by Wiley-Interscience). Wiley.

Tearle, Barbara, ed. Index to Legal Essays. 352p. 1982. 40.00 (ISBN 0-7201-1653-8, Pub. by Mansell England). Wilson.

Tearney, A., jt. ed. see Krajicek, M.

Teasdale, Wayne. Essays in Mysticism. 196p. 1982. pap. 8.95 (ISBN 0-941850-02-1). Sunday Pubn.

Tebbel, John. The Media in America. 1976. pap. 2.50 o.p. (ISBN 0-451-61451-8, ME1451, Ment). NAL.

Tebble, R. S., jt. auth. see Kalvius, G. M.

Tebeaux, Elizabeth, jt. auth. see Lawrence, Nelda R.

Tebeaux, W. Gene, jt. auth. see Pierce, R. C.

Teberosky, Ana, jt. auth. see Ferreiro, Emilia.

Tec, Leon. The Fear of Success. 1978. pap. 3.50 (ISBN 0-451-12311-5, AE2311, Sig). NAL.

--Targets. 1982. pap. 2.50 (ISBN 0-451-11277-6, AE1277, Sig). NAL.

--Targets: How to Set Goals for Yourself--& Reach Them. LC 78-20190. (Illus.). 192p. 1980. 11.49i (ISBN 0-06-014241-3, HarpT). Har-Row.

Tec, Nechama. Dry Tears. 216p. 1982. 12.95 (ISBN 0-686-97032-2). Wildcat Pubs.

Technical Conference British Pump Manufacturers' Assn. 4th, Pumps & Progress: Proceedings. 174p. 1975. 70.00x (ISBN 0-686-97042-X, Pub. by BHRA Fluid England). State Mutual Bk.

Technical Conference on Fish Finding, Purse Seining & Aimed Trawling, Reykjavik, 1970. Report. (FAO Fisheries Reports: No. 110). 47p. 1971. pap. 7.50 (ISBN 0-686-93069-X, F1699, FAO). Unipub.

Technical Conference on Fishery Management & Development, Vancouver, 1973. Report. (FAO Fisheries Reports: No. 134). 83p. 1973. pap. 7.50 (ISBN 0-686-93091-6, F785, FAO). Unipub.

Technical Conference on Fishery Products, Tokyo, 1973. Report. (FAO Fisheries Reports: No. 146). 59p. 1974. pap. 7.50 (ISBN 0-686-93977-8, F789, FAO). Unipub.

Technical Consultation of the Official Contacts of the Countries Participating in the Market Information Service for Fish Products in the Latin American Region, Panama, 1979. Report. (FAO Fisheries Reports: No. 216). 31p. 1979. pap. 7.50 (ISBN 0-686-94004-0, F1829, FAO). Unipub.

Technical Consultation on the Latin American Lake Industry, Montevideo, Uruguay, 1977. Report. (FAO Fisheries Reports: No. 203). 76p. 1978. pap. 7.50 (ISBN 0-686-94000-8, F1484, FAO). Unipub.

Technical Preservation Services Division, U. S. Department of the Interior. Respectful Rehabilitation: Answers to Your Questions about Old Buildings. (Illus.). 192p. (Orig.). 1982. pap. 9.95 (ISBN 0-89133-103-4). Preservation Pr.

Technical Staff of the Solarex Corp. Making & Using Electricity from the Sun. (Illus.). 1979. 7.95 o.p. (ISBN 0-8306-9833-7); pap. 6.95 (ISBN 0-8306-9812-4, 1118). TAB Bks.

Technology Assessment Office, U. S. Congress. Energy from Biological Processes: Vol. 1, Energy from Biological Processes; Vol. 2, Technical & Environmental Analyses, 2 Vols. 429p. 1982. pap. 44.50 set (ISBN 0-89934-124-1, B-023). Solar Energy Info.

Technology Proceedings, Seminar III. Uranium Resource. Morse, Jerome G., ed. (Illus.). 408p. (Orig.). 1980. pap. 16.00 (ISBN 0-918062-38-1). Colo Sch Mines.

Teclaff, Ludwik A. & Utton, Albert E. International Groundwater Law. LC 81-3964. 490p. 1981. lib. bdg. 50.00 (ISBN 0-379-20718-4). Oceana.

Teclaff, Ludwik A., jt. ed. see Utton, Albert E.

Teclaff, Ludwipk A. & Utton, Albert E., eds. International Environmental Law. LC 73-15198. (Special Studies). 262p. 1974. text ed. 25.00 o.p. (ISBN 0-275-08630-5). Praeger.

Tedd, L. A. Introduction to Computer-Based Library Systems. 1977. 29.95 (ISBN 0-471-26034-7, Wiley Heyden). Wiley.

Tedd, Lucy A. The Teaching of On-Line Cataloguing & Searching & the Use of New Technology in UK Schools of Librarianship & Information Science. 126p. 1981. pap. 40.00x (ISBN 0-905984-67-6, Pub. by Brit Lib England). State Mutual Bk.

Tedder, Arthur W. Air Power in War. LC 75-7243. (Illus.). 124p. 1975. Repr. of 1948 ed. lib. bdg. 19.75x (ISBN 0-8371-8103-8, TEAP). Greenwood.

Tedder, J. M., jt. auth. see Nonhebel, D. C.

Tedder, J. M., et al, eds. Basic Organic Chemistry, Pt. 5. LC 73-14384. 646p. 1975. pap. 31.95 (ISBN 0-471-85016-0, Pub. by Wiley-Interscience). Wiley.

Tedder, John M., et al. Basic Organic Chemistry, Pt. 4. LC 66-17112. 528p. (Pub. by Wiley-interscience). 1972. 29.95 (ISBN 0-471-85010-1). Wiley.

Teddlie, Tillit S. Great Christian Hymnal. 1965. 3.95 (ISBN 0-89137-600-3). Quality Pubns.

Tedeschi, Cesare G., et al, eds. Forensic Medicine, 3 vols. LC 74-4593. (Illus.). 1680p. 1977. Vol. 1. 35.50x (ISBN 0-7216-8772-5); Vol. 2. 25.00x (ISBN 0-7216-8773-3); Vol. 3. 28.50 (ISBN 0-7216-8774-1); 89.00x (ISBN 0-7216-8771-7). Saunders.

Tedeschi, David H. & Tedeschi, Ralph E., eds. Importance of Fundamental Principles in Drug Evaluation. LC 68-56046. (Illus.). 509p. 1968. 34.50 (ISBN 0-911216-05-7). Raven.

Tedeschi, F. P. & Taber, M. R. Solid State Electronics. LC 75-27996. 1976. pap. 12.00 (ISBN 0-8273-1171-0); instructor's guide 2.75 (ISBN 0-8273-1172-9). Delmar.

Tedeschi, Frank P. The Active Filter Handbook. (Illus.). 1979. 10.95 (ISBN 0-8306-9788-8); pap. 8.95 (ISBN 0-8306-1133-9, 1133). TAB Bks.

--How To Design, Build, & Use Electronic Control Systems. (Illus.). 308p. 1981. 13.95 o.p. (ISBN 0-8306-9844-2); pap. 10.95 (ISBN 0-8306-1229-7). TAB Bks.

Tedeschi, Frank P. & McIntyre, Raymond W. Three Hundred Three Dynamic Electronic Circuits. (Illus.). 1978. 9.95 (ISBN 0-8306-9908-2); pap. 6.95 o.p. (ISBN 0-8306-1060-X, 1060). TAB Bks.

Tedeschi, James T. & Lindskold, Svern. Social Psychology, Interdependence, Interaction, & Influence. LC 75-38883. 705p. 1976. write for info. (ISBN 0-471-85017-9, Pub. by Wiley-Interscience). Wiley.

Tedeschi, James T., ed. Impression Management Theory & Social Psychological Research. 1981. 32.50 (ISBN 0-12-685180-8). Acad Pr.

Tedeschi, Ralph E., jt. ed. see Tedeschi, David H.

Tedeschi, Richard, ed. see Gide, Andre.

Tedesco, Dominick, jt. auth. see Fuori, William M.

Tedesco, Eleanor & Mitchell, Robert. Administrative Office Management: Systems & Services. 752p. 1983. text ed. write for info. (ISBN 0-471-09062-X). Wiley.

Tedesco, Mary M. Del see Del Tedesco, Mary M.

Tedford, Alberta & Van Hoozer, Helen. Pharmacology: A Self-Instructional Approach. (Illus.). 1980. pap. text ed. 22.50 (ISBN 0-07-063385-1). McGraw.

Tedlock, Barbara, jt. ed. see Tedlock, Dennis.

Tedlock, Dennis. The Spoken Word & the Work of Interpretation. LC 82-40489. (Illus.). 400p. 1983. 35.00x (ISBN 0-8122-7880-1); pap. 14.95x (ISBN 0-8122-1143-X). U of Pa Pr.

Tedlock, Dennis & Tedlock, Barbara, eds. Teachings from the American Earth: Indian Religion & Philosophy. (Illus.). 304p. 1976. pap. 7.95 (ISBN 0-87140-097-9). Liveright.

Tedlock, Ernest. You See I Don't Forget, Selected Poems & Stories. Elder, Gary, ed. LC 80-12807. 1980. pap. 4.95 (ISBN 0-914974-22-X). Holmgangers.

Tedlock, Ernest W., ed. Dylan Thomas: The Legend & the Poet. LC 72-9050. 283p. 1975. Repr. of 1961 ed. lib. bdg. 19.00x (ISBN 0-8371-6564-4, TEDT). Greenwood.

Tedlow, Richard S. Public Relation & Business, Nineteen Hundred to Nineteen Fifty. Porter, Glenn, ed. (Industrial Development & the Social Fabric). (Orig.). 1979. lib. bdg. 36.00 (ISBN 0-89232-095-8). Jai Pr.

Tedone, David. Practical Publicity: How to Boost Any Cause. (Illus.). 176p. 1983. 12.95 (ISBN 0-916782-36-0); pap. 8.95 (ISBN 0-916782-35-2). Harvard Common Pr.

Tee, Lim H. Malaysia. (World Bibliographical Ser.: No. 12). 1983. write for info. (ISBN 0-903450-23-2). ABC-Clio.

Teece, David J. Multinational Corporation & the Resource Cost of International Technology Transfer. LC 76-26053. 152p. 1976. prof ref 22.50x (ISBN 0-88410-053-7). Ballinger Pub.

Teece, David J., jt. ed. see Griffin, James M.

Teed, Jack H. Gunships: The Killing Zone. 1983. pap. 2.50 (ISBN 0-8217-1130-X). Zebra.

Teed, Lee B. Woman, You Are the Expert: A Guide to Confirming & Enhancing Your Sexuality. LC 79-92664. 1980. pap. 3.95 o.p. (ISBN 0-930626-06-0). Psych & Consul Assocs.

Teegarden, Kenneth L. We Call Ourselves Disciples. 2nd ed. 116p. 1983. pap. 5.95 (ISBN 0-8272-4215-8). Bethany Pr.

Teeguarden, Iona M. The Acupressure Way of Health: Jin Shin Do. (Illus., Orig.). 1978. pap. 11.50 (ISBN 0-87040-421-0). Japan Pubns.

Teel, Leonard R. & Taylor, Ron. Into the Newsroom: An Introduction to Journalism. (Illus.). 224p. 1983. 14.95 (ISBN 0-13-477133-8); pap. 7.95 (ISBN 0-13-477125-7). P-H.

Teel, Leonard R., jt. auth. see Calderon, Erma.

Teer, F. & Spence, J. D. Political Opinion Polls. 1973. text ed. 11.50x o.p. (ISBN 0-09-115230-5, Hutchinson U Lib); pap. text ed. 6.50x o.p. (ISBN 0-09-115231-3). Humanities.

Tees, David W. & Hawk, Curtis E. Municipal Personnel Systems Training Program, 6 modules. 209p. 1979. Set. 55.00 (ISBN 0-936440-23-6). Inst Urban Studies.

Tees, David W. & Stanford, Jay G. A Code Enforcement Handbook for Municipal Officials. 239p. 1973. 5.00 (ISBN 0-936440-38-4). Inst Urban Studies.

--Handbook for Interlocal Contracting in Texas. 239p. 8.00 (ISBN 0-936440-38-4). Inst Urban Studies.

Tees, David W. & Wilkes, Stanley W., Jr. The Private Connection. 75p. (Orig.). 1982. pap. 10.00 (ISBN 0-936440-42-2). Inst Urban Studies.

Teeter, Don E. The Acoustic Guitar: Adjustment, Care, Maintenance, & Repair, Vol. II. LC 79-5962. (Illus.). 202p. 1980. 24.95 (ISBN 0-8061-1607-2). U of Okla Pr.

Teeters, J. L., jt. auth. see Ranucci, E. R.

Teets, Robert. Construction Management for the Subcontractor. 1976. 27.50 (ISBN 0-07-063387-8, P&RB). McGraw.

Teff, Harvey, jt. auth. see Roshier, Bob.

Teffeteller, Gordon L. The Surpriser: The Life of Rowland, Lord Hill. LC 81-72058. (Illus.). 272p. 1983. 32.50 (ISBN 0-87413-212-6). U Delaware Pr.

Teffi, Nadezhda. All About Love. Goldstein, Darra, tr. from Rus. 144p. Date not set. 15.00 (ISBN 0-88233-792-0); pap. 6.50 (ISBN 0-88233-793-9). Ardis Pubs.

Tefft, Bonnie, jt. auth. see Tefft, Gary T.

Tefft, Gary T. & Tefft, Bonnie. Price Guide to Red Wing Potters & Their Wares. 16p. 1981. 1.50 (ISBN 0-9606730-2-4). Locust Ent.

Tefft, Stanton K., ed. Secrecy: A Crosscultural Perspective. LC 79-25454. 351p. 1980. text ed. 34.95 (ISBN 0-87705-442-8); pap. text ed. 16.95 (ISBN 0-87705-443-6). Human Sci Pr.

Teg, William. Almuchicoitt. 1950. 4.00 o.p. (ISBN 0-8158-0196-3). Chris Mass.

--Vikings & Vagabonds. 1955. 3.00 o.p. (ISBN 0-8158-0197-1). Chris Mass.

Tega, Vasile G., ed. Management & Economics Journals: An International Selection. LC 76-4578. (Management Information Guide Ser.: No. 33). 1977. 42.00x (ISBN 0-8103-0833-9). Gale.

Tegeler, Philip D., jt. auth. see Cole, Roland J.

Tegg, William. Knot Tied: Marriage Ceremonies of All Nations. LC 75-99073. 1970. Repr. of 1877 ed. 42.00x (ISBN 0-8103-3585-9). Gale.

--The Last Act: Being the Funeral Rites of Nations & Individuals. LC 72-10592. (Illus.). 404p. 1973. Repr. of 1876 ed. 37.00x (ISBN 0-8103-3172-1). Gale.

Tegner, Bruce. Black Belt Karate, Judo & Jujitsu: Advanced Techniques. 2nd, rev. ed. LC 80-11673. (Illus., Orig.). 1980. pap. 3.95 o.p. (ISBN 0-87407-033-3, T-33). Thor.

--Bruce Tegner's Complete Book of Jujitsu. LC 77-5023. (Illus.). 1977. 7.95 (ISBN 0-87407-516-5, C16); pap. 5.95 (ISBN 0-87407-027-9, T27). Thor.

--Bruce Tegner's Complete Book of Self-Defense. LC 74-28358. (Illus.). 1975. 7.95 (ISBN 0-87407-510-6); pap. 5.95 (ISBN 0-87407-030-9, T-30). Thor.

--Instant Self-Defense. (Illus.). 1965. pap. 2.95 o.p. (ISBN 0-448-01359-2, G&D). Putnam Pub Group.

--Judo: Beginner to Black Belt. 2nd, Rev. ed. McGrath, Alice, ed. LC 82-796. (Illus.). 207p. 1982. 10.95 (ISBN 0-87407-521-1, C-21); pap. 6.95 (ISBN 0-87407-041-4, T-41). Thor.

--Savate. 3rd rev. ed. (Illus.). 128p. 1983. pap. 3.95 (ISBN 0-87407-042-2, T-2). Thor.

--Self-Defense: A Basic Course. LC 79-13556. (Illus.). 1979. 5.95 (ISBN 0-87407-517-3); pap. 3.95 (ISBN 0-87407-031-7). Thor.

--Stick Fighting: Self-Defense. LC 70-109225. (Illus.). 128p. 1972. pap. 3.95 (ISBN 0-87407-020-1, T-20). Thor.

--Stick Fighting, Sport Forms: Stick Fencing, Sword Stick, Staff Sport Fighting. LC 72-91387. (Illus.). 127p. (Orig.). 1973. pap. 2.95 o.p. (ISBN 0-87407-021-X). Thor.

Tegner, Bruce & McGrath, Alice. Self-Defense for Your Child: Practical Defenses & Assault-Prevention. LC 76-1856. (Illus.). 127p. (Orig.). 1976. 4.95 o.p. (ISBN 0-87407-514-9); pap. 2.95 (ISBN 0-87407-024-4, T-24). Thor.

--Survival. 224p. 1983. pap. 3.95 (ISBN 0-553-20825-X). Bantam.

Tehama County Library. List of Northern California Holdings, Tehama County Library as of January 1, 1977. 1977. 4.50 (ISBN 0-686-38942-5). Assn NC Records.

Teich, Albert H., ed. Technology & Man's Future. 3rd ed. 350p. 1981. text ed. 15.95x (ISBN 0-312-78997-1); pap. text ed. 8.95x (ISBN 0-312-78996-3). St Martin.

Teichert, Curt, jt. ed. see Moore, Raymond C.

Teichert, Curt, et al, eds. Paleontology in China, 1979. (Special Paper Ser.: No. 187). (Illus.). 1981. 44.00x (ISBN 0-8137-2173-3). Geol Soc.

Teichert, Marilyn, tr. see Couer de Jesus d' Elbee, Jean du.

Teichler-Zallen, Doris & Clements, Colleen D. Science & Morality: New Directions in Bioethics. LC 80-8926. 320p. 1982. 26.95x (ISBN 0-669-04406-7). Lexington Bks.

Teichmann, Howard. Fonda: My Life. large type ed. LC 82-5983. (Illus.). 697p. 1982. Repr. of 1981 ed. 13.95 (ISBN 0-89621-370-6). Thorndike Pr.

--Fonda: My Life As Told to Howard Teichmann. 1981. 15.95 (ISBN 0-453-00402-4, H402). NAL.

Teicholz, Eric. McGraw-Hill A-E Computer Systems Update: Selecting & Acquiring a Low-Cost CAD System for Design & Drafting. 280p. 1983. 240.00 (ISBN 0-07-063402-5, P&RB). McGraw.

Teichova, Alice. An Economic Background to Munich. LC 72-89811. (Soviet & East European Studies). (Illus.). 300p. 1974. 47.50 (ISBN 0-521-20065-2). Cambridge U Pr.

Teika, Fujiwara. Fujiwara Teika's "Superior Poems of Our Time". A Thirteenth Century Poetic Treatise & Sequence. Brower, R. H. & Miner, E., trs. 1967. 10.00x (ISBN 0-8047-0171-7). Stanford U Pr.

Teilhard De Chardin, Pierre. Human Energy. LC 79-139231. (Helen & Kurt Wolff Bk). 1971. 5.95 o.p. (ISBN 0-15-142390-3). HarBraceJ.

--Let Me Explain. Demoulin, J. P., ed. 1972. pap. 3.95 o.p. (ISBN 0-06-061800-0, RD-42, HarpR). Har-Row.

--Phenomenon of Man. pap. 5.95i (ISBN 0-06-090495-X, CN495, CN). Har-Row.

Teilhet-Fisk, Jehane. Paradise Reviewed: An Interpretation of Gauguin's Polynesian Symbolism. Foster, Stephen C., ed. LC 82-4904. (Studies in Fine Arts: The Avant-Garde: No. 31). 1983. 39.95 (ISBN 0-8357-1334-2). Univ Microfilms.

Teiser, Ruth & Harroun, Catherine. Winemaking in California. 1982. 24.95 (ISBN 0-07-063401-7). McGraw.

Teissier, B. see Zariski, Oscar.

Teitelbaum, Harry. How to Write Book Reports. (How To Ser.). 112p. (Orig.). 1982. pap. 4.95 (ISBN 0-671-18727-9). Monarch Pr.

--How to Write Theses. (How to Ser.). (gr. 12 up). 1975. pap. 1.95 o.p. (ISBN 0-671-18726-0). Monarch Pr.

Teitelbaum, Lee. Standards Relating to Counsel for Private Parties. (Juvenile Justice Standards Project Ser.). 240p. 1980. 20.00x (ISBN 0-88410-215-7); pap. 10.00x (ISBN 0-88410-817-1). Ballinger Pub.

Teitelbaum, Lee E., jt. auth. see Stapleton, W. Vaughan.

Teitelbaum, Lee E. & Gough, Aidan, eds. Beyond Control: Status Offenders in the Juvenile Court. LC 76-30285. 352p. 1977. prof ref 17.50x (ISBN 0-88410-202-5); pap. 10.95x (ISBN 0-88410-212-2). Ballinger Pub.

Teitelman, Edward & Longstreth, Richard W. Architecture in Philadelphia: A Guide. (Illus.). 304p. 1974. pap. 9.95 (ISBN 0-262-70021-2). MIT Pr.

Teitlebaum, Harry. How to Write Book Reports. (How to Ser.). 1975. pap. 4.95 o.p. (ISBN 0-671-45895-7, 18727). Monarch Pr.

Teitler, Risa. Amazon Parrots, Taming. (Illus.). 1979. 4.95 (ISBN 0-87666-881-3, KW-039). TFH Pubns.

--Budgerigars, Taming & Training. (Illus.). 96p. 1979. 4.95 (ISBN 0-87666-887-2, KW-070). TFH Pubns.

--Cockatoos, Taming & Training. (Illus.). 96p. 1980. 4.95 (ISBN 0-87666-888-0, KW-071). TFH Pubns.

--Lovebirds, Taming & Training. (Illus.). 1979. 4.95 (ISBN 0-87666-988-7, KW-038). TFH Pubns.

--Macaws: Taming & Training. (Illus.). 1979. 4.95 (ISBN 0-87666-884-8, KW-054). TFH Pubns.

--Taming & Training African Grey Parrots. (Illus.). 1979. 4.95 (ISBN 0-87666-994-1, KW025). TFH Pubns.

--Taming & Training Conures. (Illus.). 96p. 1981. 4.95 (ISBN 0-87666-842-2, KW-139). TFH Pubns.

--Taming & Training Ringneck Parakeets. (Illus.). 96p. 1981. 4.95 (ISBN 0-87666-822-8, KW-145). TFH Pubns.

--Training & Taming Cockatiels. (Illus.). 1979. 4.95 (ISBN 0-87666-981-X, KW-001). TFH Pubns.

Teixeira, Francisco Gomes see Gomes Teixeira, Francisco.

Teja, Ed & Gonnella, Gary. Voice Technology. 1983. text ed. 19.95 (ISBN 0-8359-8417-6). Reston.

Tejada-Flores, Lito. Backcountry Skiing: The Sierra Club Guide to Skiing off the Beaten Track. LC 81-8958. (Outdoor Activities Guides Ser.). (Illus.). 288p. 1981. pap. 8.95 (ISBN 0-87156-287-1). Sierra.

Tekaat, Leonard C. Inflation, the Economy Killer: How to Create, Control & Stop High Inflation. LC 81-81954. 184p. (Orig.). 1982. pap. 9.95 (ISBN 0-942368-21-5). Intl Econ Pubns.

Tekeuchi, Kei, et al. The Foundations of Multivariate Analysis: A Unified Approach by Means of Projection onto Linear Subspaces. 400p. 1982. 24.95x o.p. (ISBN 0-470-27311-9). Halsted Pr.

Tekippe, Terry J., ed. Papal Infallibility: An Application of Lonergan's Theological Method. LC 82-23837. 416p. (Orig.). 1983. lib. bdg. 27.50 (ISBN 0-8191-2995-X); pap. text ed. 15.75 (ISBN 0-8191-2996-8). U Pr of Amer.

Tel Aviv University Conference on Erythropoiesis, July, 1970, Petah Tikva. Erythropoiesis: Regulatory Mechanisms & Developmental Aspects. Matoth, Yehuda, ed. 1972. 39.50 (ISBN 0-12-480250-8). Acad Pr.

Telander, Marcie, et al. Acting Up! An Innovative Approach to Creative Drama for Older Adults. 186p. 1982. pap. 12.95 (ISBN 0-88020-108-8). Coach Hse.

Telang, K. T., tr. from Sanscrit. The Anugita. LC 81-50202. (Secret Doctrine Reference Ser.). 176p. 1981. Repr. of 1882 ed. 9.00 (ISBN 0-913510-40-8). Wizards.

Telecom Library Research Group. Telecom Library Guide to Key Systems & Mini-PBXs. 156p. 1981. 75.00 (ISBN 0-686-98036-0). Telecom Lib.

Telecommunications Policy Research Conference, Annual 10th. Proceedings. Gandy, Oscar, et al, eds. 256p. 1983. text ed. 24.95 (ISBN 0-89391-195-X). Ablex Pub.

Telek, Lehel & Graham, Horace D. Leaf Protein. (Illus.). 1983. lib. bdg. 85.00 (ISBN 0-87055-412-3). AVI.

Teleki, G., jt. ed. see Fricke, W.

Teleki, Geza, et al. Aerial Apes: Gibbons of Asia. LC 78-10721. (Illus.). (gr. 1-3). 7.50 o.p. (ISBN 0-698-20477-8, Coward). Putnam Pub Group.

Teleki, Gloria R. Collecting Traditional American Basketry. (Illus.). 1979. pap. 8.95 (ISBN 0-525-47553-2). Dutton.

Telemaque, Eleanor W. Haiti Through Its Holidays. (Illus.). 59p. (gr. 4-6). 1980. 7.50 o.p. (ISBN 0-914110-08-X). Blyden Pr.

Telfair. The Adventures of Justin Clay. 182p. 1981. pap. 3.95 (ISBN 0-9609502-0-6). Perilous Pr.

Telfer, Daniel. Guilty Ones. Date not set. pap. 2.50 o.p. (ISBN 0-451-09569-3, E9569, Sig). NAL.

Telfer, Elizabeth. Happiness. LC 79-16373. 1980. 22.50 (ISBN 0-312-36171-8). St Martin.

Telford, Charles W. & Sawrey, James. The Exceptional Individual. 3rd ed. LC 76-44470. (Illus.). 1977. ref. ed. 24.95 (ISBN 0-13-293837-5). P-H.

Telford, Ira, jt. auth. see Christensen, John B.

Telford, Kenneth, tr. see Aristotle.

Telford, W. M., et al. Applied Geophysics. LC 74-16992. (Illus.). 700p. 1975. 99.50 (ISBN 0-521-20670-7); pap. 29.95x (ISBN 0-521-29146-1). Cambridge U Pr.

Tell, G., jt. auth. see Coute, A.

Teller, Edward. The Pursuit of Simplicity. LC 80-82499. 1980. 10.95 (ISBN 0-932612-03-2); pap. 6.95 (ISBN 0-686-36902-5). Pepperdine U Pr.

Teller, Edward & Brown, Allen. The Legacy of Hiroshima. LC 75-23264. 325p. 1975. Repr. of 1962 ed. lib. bdg. 19.25x (ISBN 0-8371-8344-8, TELH). Greenwood.

Teller, Edward, et al. Education of the Scientist in a Free Society. Drought, A. Bernard, ed. 1959. pap. 7.95 (ISBN 0-87462-412-6). Marquette.

Teller, Virginia & White, Sheila J., eds. Studies in Child Language & Multilingualism. LC 80-16810. (Annals of the New York Academy of Sciences: Vol. 345). 187p. 1980. 30.00x (ISBN 0-89766-078-1); pap. 30.00x (ISBN 0-89766-079-X). NY Acad Sci.

Teller, Woolsey & Gauvin, Marshall. Hell, A Christian Doctrine. (Illus.). 47p. 1983. pap. 3.00 (ISBN 0-910309-01-9). Am Atheist.

Telleria, M. T. Contribucion al Estudio de los Aphyllophorales Espanoles: With Key to Species in English. (Bibliotheca Mycologica: No. 74). (Illus.). 474p. (Span.). 1981. lib. bdg. 40.00x (ISBN 3-7682-1274-2). Lubrecht & Cramer.

Tellier. Size Effects of Thin Films. (Thin Films Science & Technology Ser.: Vol. 2). 1982. 68.00 (ISBN 0-444-42106-8). Elsevier.

Tello, Carlos, jt. ed. see Reynolds, Clark W.

Telman, Judith, et al. Sex Education for Today's Child: A Guide for Modern Parents. pap. 6.95 o.s.i. (ISBN 0-695-81170-3). Follett.

Teluk, John, jt. auth. see Katsaros, Thomas.

Temam, R., jt. auth. see Ekeland, I.

Teman, R. Navier-Stokes Equations. 2nd ed. LC 79-15106. (Studies Inmathematics & Its Applications: Vol. 2). 520p. 1979. 85.00 (ISBN 0-444-85307-3, North Holland); pap. 38.50 (ISBN 0-444-85308-1, North-Holland). Elsevier.

Tembrock, jt. auth. see Schmidt.

Temes, Gabor & Lapatra, Jack. Introduction to Circuit Synthesis. 1977. text ed. 36.50 (ISBN 0-07-063489-0, C); solutions manual 25.00 (ISBN 0-07-063490-4). McGraw.

Temes, Gabor C. & Mitra, Sanjit K., eds. Modern Filter Theory & Design. 566p. 1973. 49.50x (ISBN 0-471-85130-2, Pub. by Wiley-Interscience). Wiley.

Temes, Lloyd. Communication Electronics for Technicians. 400p. 1974. text ed. 24.95 (ISBN 0-07-063487-4, G). McGraw.

--Electronic Circuits for Technicians. 2nd ed. (Illus.). 1977. text ed. 22.95 (ISBN 0-07-063492-0, G); answers 1.50 (ISBN 0-07-063493-9). McGraw.

--Schaum's Outline of Electronic Communication. (Schaum Outline Ser.). (Illus.). 1979. pap. 6.95 (ISBN 0-07-063495-5, SP). McGraw.

Temes, Terry L. The Inner I. 75p. (Orig.). 1983. pap. 4.00 (ISBN 0-682-49936-6). Exposition.

Temime, Emile, jt. auth. see Broue, Pierre.

Temkin, Samuel. Elements of Acoustics. LC 80-24416. 515p. 1981. text ed. 39.95 (ISBN 0-471-05990-0). Wiley.

Temkin, Sara, jt. auth. see Myers, Alpha.

Temko, Florence. Chinese Papercuts: Their Story & How to Make & Use Them. LC 82-12854. (Illus.). 168p. (Orig.). 1982. pap. 10.95 (ISBN 0-8351-0999-2). China Bks.

--Elementary Art Games & Puzzles. LC 81-18789. 223p. 1982. 13.50 (ISBN 0-13-252965-3, Parker). P-H.

--Folk Crafts for World Friendship. LC 76-4215. (gr. 3-5). 1976. 14.95 o.p. (ISBN 0-385-11115-0). Doubleday.

Tempelton, Darlene. Woman in Yorkist England. LC 79-19011. (Woman in History Ser.: Vol. 16). (Illus.). 100p. 1983. 18.95 (ISBN 0-86663-051-1); pap. 15.95 (ISBN 0-86663-052-X). Ide Hse.

Temperley, H. N., ed. Combinatorics: Proceedings of the British Combinatorial Conference, 8th, University College, Swansea, 1981. LC 81-10007. (London Mathematical Society Lecture Note Ser.: No. 52). (Illus.). 200p. 1981. pap. 24.50 (ISBN 0-521-28514-3). Cambridge U Pr.

Temperley, H. W. History of Serbia. LC 68-9592. 1969. Repr. of 1917 ed. 22.50x (ISBN 0-86527-097-X). Fertig.

Temperley, Mary S., jt. auth. see Rivers, Wilga M.

Temperley, Nicholas. The Music of the English Parish Church, 2 vols. LC 77-84811. (Cambridge Studies in Music). (Illus.). 1980. Vol. 1. 84.50 (ISBN 0-521-22045-9); Vol. 2. 44.50 (ISBN 0-521-22046-7). Cambridge U Pr.

Temperley, Nocholas, ed. William Sterndale Bennett, Three Symphonies (3,4,5) (The Symphony 1720-1840 Series E: Vol. 7). 1982. lib. bdg. 90.00 (ISBN 0-8240-3813-4). Garland Pub.

Tempest, D. W. see Rose, A. H., et al.

Temple. Real Estate Finance in California. 2nd ed. 1981. text ed. 26.50x (ISBN 0-673-16524-8). Scott F.

Temple, C. Chemistry of Heterocyclic Compounds: Tnazoles One Two Four, Vol. 37. 791p. 1981. 224.50x o.p. (ISBN 0-471-04656-6, Pub. by Wiley-Interscience). Wiley.

Temple, Cliff. Daley Thompson. (Profiles Ser.). (Illus.). 64p. (gr. 4-6). 1983. 7.95 (ISBN 0-241-10932-9, Pub. by Hamish Hamilton England). David & Charles.

--The Marathon Made Easier. LC 82-71258. 192p. 1982. 12.95 (ISBN 0-689-11336-6). Atheneum.

Temple, Cliff & Tatlow, Peter. Gymnastics for Girls. (Pelham Pictorial Sports Instruction Ser.). (Illus.). 1978. 12.50 o.s.i. (ISBN 0-7207-1013-8). Transatlantic.

Temple, Douglas. Creative Home Financing: You Can Buy A House, Condo or Co-op In Today's Market. 288p. 1982. 13.95 (ISBN 0-698-11127-3, Coward). Putnam Pub Group.

Temple, Douglas M. Real Estate Investment for the '80s. 336p. 1982. pap. cancelled (ISBN 0-8092-7023-4). Contemp Bks.

Temple, E. A History of Manuscripts Illuminated in the British Isles: Anglo-Saxon Manuscripts 900-1066, Vol. 2. (Illus.). 1976. 74.00x (ISBN 0-19-921009-8). Oxford U Pr.

Temple, Nigel. John Nash & the Village Picturesque. (Illus.). 172p. 1982. text ed. 31.25x (ISBN 0-904387-24-0); pap. text ed. 12.50x (ISBN 0-86299-007-6). Humanities.

Temple, Philip. Ways to the Wilderness: Great New Zealand Walking Tracks. (Illus.). 168p. 1977. 25.00x (ISBN 0-7233-0537-4). Intl Pubns Serv.

Temple, Ruth Z. & Tucker, Martin A., eds. Modern British Literature, 3 vols. LC 65-28048. (Library of Literary Criticism Ser.). 120.00 (ISBN 0-8044-3275-9); vol. IV supplement 45.00 (ISBN 0-686-76910-4). Ungar.

Temple, Stanley A., ed. Bird Conservation, No. 1. 192p. 1983. write for info. (ISBN 0-299-08984-3). U of Wis Pr.

Temple, William. Religious Experience. Baker, A. E., ed. 275p. 1959. 9.95 (ISBN 0-227-67579-7). Attic Pr.

--What Christians Stand For in the Secular World. Sherman, Franklin, ed. LC 65-21081. (Facet Bks.). (Orig.). 1965. pap. 0.50 o.p. (ISBN 0-8006-3021-1, 1-3021). Fortress.

Templer, J. C. Further Listening Comprehension Tests. 1972. pap. text ed. 3.50x (ISBN 0-435-28728-1); tchr's ed. 5.00x (ISBN 0-435-28729-X). Heinemann Ed.

--Listening Comprehension Tests. 1974. pap. text ed. 3.50x (ISBN 0-435-28736-2); tchr's ed. 5.00x (ISBN 0-435-28737-0); tape of sel. tests 28.00x (ISBN 0-435-28727-3); cassette of sel. tests 22.00x (ISBN 0-435-28747-8). Heinemann Ed.

Templeton, Bryce, jt. ed. see Samph, Thomas.

Templeton, Darlene & Ude, Arthur. Woman in Medieval England. LC 79-19011. (Woman in History Ser.: Vol. 13). (Illus.). 1983. 15.95 (ISBN 0-86663-057-0); pap. 9.95 (ISBN 0-86663-058-9). Ide Hse.

Templeton, David H. & Somorjai, G. A., eds. Low Energy Electron Diffraction. pap. 5.00 (ISBN 0-686-60375-3). Polycrystal Bk Serv.

Templeton, J. G., jt. auth. see Chaudhry, M. L.

Templeton, Larry D. The Stars of Childsland. (Illus.). 22p. (gr. k-3). 1982. pap. 1.98 (ISBN 0-9608914-0-4). L D Templeton.

Templeton, Lee. Cannon Boy of the Alamo. 1977. 6.95 (ISBN 0-89015-085-0). Eakin Pubns.

Templin, Kevin J. Finality Testament: Book of Life. cancelled o.s.i. (ISBN 0-8062-1679-4). Carlton.

Temu, A. & Swai, B. Historians & Africanist History: A Critique. 206p. (Orig.). 1982. 20.00 (ISBN 0-905762-78-9, Pub. by Zed Pr England); pap. 8.95 (ISBN 0-905762-79-7, Pub. by Zed Pr England). Lawrence Hill.

Ten, C. L. Mill on Liberty. 1980. 38.50x (ISBN 0-19-824643-9); pap. 14.95x (ISBN 0-19-824644-7). Oxford U Pr.

Tenant, Rose. Persian Cats & Other Longhairs. 14.50x (ISBN 0-392-09009-0, SpS). Sportshelf.

Tenaza, Richard. Penguins. (gr. 4 up). 1980. PLB 8.90 (ISBN 0-531-04104-2). Watts.

Ten Boom, Corrie. Cada Nuevo Dia. Clifford, Alejandro, tr. from Eng. 224p. 1981. pap. 4.50 (ISBN 0-311-40043-4, Edit Mundo). Casa Bautista.

--Each New Day. 1977. 9.95 o.p. (ISBN 0-8007-0894-6); pap. 2.95 (ISBN 0-8007-8403-0, Spire Bks). Revell.

--In My Father's House. (Illus.). 192p. 1976. pap. 5.95 (ISBN 0-8007-5002-0, Power Bks). Revell.

--A Tramp Finds a Home. 1977. pap. 1.50 o.p. (ISBN 0-8007-8368-9, Spire Bks). Revell.

Ten Boom, Corrie see Boom, Corrie T.

Ten Boom, Corrie, et al. The Hiding Place. 1974. pap. 2.95 (ISBN 0-8007-8156-2, Spire Bks); pap. 2.50 movie ed. (ISBN 0-8007-8219-4); 0.79 (ISBN 0-8007-8502-9). Revell.

TenBrink, Terry. Evaluation: A Practical Guide for Teachers. (Illus.). 512p. 1974. text ed. 32.50 (ISBN 0-07-063497-1, C); instructor's manual 14.95 (ISBN 0-07-063498-X). McGraw.

Ten Broek, Jacobus. Family Law & the Poor: Essays. Handler, Joel F., ed. LC 70-150918. 220p. 1971. lib. bdg. 25.00x (ISBN 0-8371-5817-6, HFL/). Greenwood.

Ten Cate, A. Richard. Oral Histology: Development, Structure & Function. LC 79-18620. (Illus.). 472p. 1980. text ed. 37.95 (ISBN 0-8016-4886-6). Mosby.

Tenenbaum, Aaron, jt. auth. see Augenstein, Moshe.

Tenenbaum, Aaron M., jt. auth. see Augenstein, Moshe.

Tenenbaum, Edward A. National Socialism vs. International Capitalism. 1942. text ed. 39.50x (ISBN 0-686-83630-8). Elliots Bks.

Tenenbaum, Frances, jt. auth. see Meras, Phyllis.

Tenenti, Alberto. Piracy & the Decline of Venice, Fifteen Eighty to Sixteen Fifteen. Pullan, Janet & Pullan, Brian, trs. (Illus.). 1967. 32.50x (ISBN 0-520-01263-1). U of Cal Pr.

Teng, Wayne C. Foundation Design. (Illus.). 1962. ref. ed. 33.95 (ISBN 0-13-329805-1). P-H.

Tengbom, Luvenre, jt. auth. see Tengbom, Mildred.

Tengbom, M. Help for Families of the Terminally Ill. (Trauma Bks.: Ser. 2). 1983. pap. 2.50 ea. (ISBN 0-570-08256-0); Set. pap. 9.15. Concordia.

Tengbom, Mildred. The Bonus Years. LC 74-14180. 160p. (Orig.). 1975. pap. 3.95 o.p. (ISBN 0-8066-1463-3, 10-0782). Augsburg.

--I Wish I Felt Good All the Time. 128p. (Orig.). 1983. pap. 4.95 (ISBN 0-87123-281-2). Bethany Hse.

--Is Your God Big Enough? LC 72-90261. 128p. (Orig.). 1973. pap. 2.95 o.p. (ISBN 0-8066-1308-4, 10-3403). Augsburg.

--No Greater Love. (Greatness with Faith Ser.). (Illus.). (gr. 5-8). 1978. 4.95 (ISBN 0-570-07878-4, 39-1203); pap. 3.50 (ISBN 0-570-07883-0, 39-1213). Concordia.

Tengbom, Mildred & Tengbom, Luvenre. Bible Readings for Families. LC 80-65542. 112p. (Orig.). 1980. pap. 3.50 (ISBN 0-8066-1787-X, 10-0677). Augsburg.

Tengrove, Chris, jt. auth. see Butler, Dougal.

Teng Ssu-Ya. Historiography of the Taiping Rebellion. LC 63-1158. (East Asian Monographs: No. 14). 1962. pap. 11.00x (ISBN 0-674-39451-8). Harvard U Pr.

Tengstrom, Emin, jt. auth. see Benner, Margareta.

Tenjack, Martha, tr. see Roy, Kristina.

Ten Kate, Lambert. Aenleiding Tot de Kennisse van het Verhevene Deel der Nederduitsche Sprake, 2 vols. (Linguistics, 13th-18th Centuries Ser). (Fr.). 1974. Repr. of 1723 ed. Set. lib. bdg. 369.00 o.p. (ISBN 0-8287-0810-X). Clearwater Pub.

Tennaille, Mabel, jt. auth. see Bergeret, Annie.

Tennant, Alan & Werler, John E. The Snakes of Texas: A Field Guide. (Illus.). 384p. Date not set. text ed. (ISBN 0-292-77559-8); pap. (ISBN 0-292-77560-1). U of Tex Pr.

Tennant, Emma. The Bad Sister. LC 78-17366. 1978. 8.95 o.p. (ISBN 0-698-10940-6, Coward). Putnam Pub Group.

--The Bad Sisters. 176p. 1980. pap. 1.95 o.s.i. (ISBN 0-380-48280-0, 48280). Avon.

--The Last of the Country House Murders: A Novel of Science Fiction. (YA) 1976. 7.95 o.p. (ISBN 0-525-66490-4). Lodestar Bks.

Tennant, F. R. The Origin & Propagation of Sin: Being the Hulsean Lectures Delivered Before the University of Cambridge, in 1901-2. 235p. 1982. Repr. of 1908 ed. lib. bdg. 50.00 (ISBN 0-89987-822-9). Darby Bks.

--Philosophical Theology, 2 vols. LC 29-3316. (Library Editions Ser). 1969. Vol. 1. 64.50 (ISBN 0-521-07431-2); Vol. 2. 47.50 (ISBN 0-521-07434-7). Cambridge U Pr.

Tennant, P. F. Ibsen's Dramatic Technique. 1965. Repr. of 1948 ed. text ed. 15.00x (ISBN 0-391-00471-9). Humanities.

Tenneco Oil Company. Operators Handbook. 208p. 1961. 14.95x (ISBN 0-87201-643-9). Gulf Pub.

Tennekes, Hendrik & Lumley, John L. First Course in Turbulence. 1972. 22.50x (ISBN 0-262-20019-8). MIT Pr.

Tennenbaum, Frances. Over Fifty-Five Is Not Illegal. 1979. 14.95 (ISBN 0-395-27595-4); pap. 7.95 o.s (ISBN 0-395-27936-4). HM.

Tennenbaum, Silvia. Yesterday's Streets. 576p. 1982. pap. 3.95 (ISBN 0-345-30030-0). Ballantine.

Tennent, R. Principles of Programming Languages. 1981. 26.95 (ISBN 0-13-709873-1). P-H.

Tennessen, Ralph. Winds of Hope. 1979. 4.50 o.p. (ISBN 0-533-03219-9). Vantage.

Tenney, Merill E., tr. Diccionario Biblico. (Spanish Bks.). (Span.). 1979. 4.00 (ISBN 0-8297-0540-6); pap. 2.75 (ISBN 0-8297-0534-1). Life Pubs Intl.

Tenney, Merrill C. Nuestro Nuevre Testamente-New Testament Survey. 1963. 11.95 (ISBN 0-8024-9200-2). Moody.

--Quien Manda en Tu Vida? Carrodeguas, Andy & Marosi, Esteban, eds. Mercado, Benjamin, tr. 174p. (Span.). 1981. pap. 2.00 (ISBN 0-8297-1261-5). Life Pubs Intl.

Tenney, Merrill C., jt. auth. see Packer, J. I.

Tenney, Merrill C., ed. Bible - the Living Word of Revelation. kivar 4.95 o.p. (ISBN 0-310-33141-2). Zondervan.

Tenney, Thomas A. Mark Twain: A Reference Guide. 1977. lib. bdg. 52.00 (ISBN 0-8161-7966-2, Hall Reference). G K Hall.

Tennican, Michael L. Convertible Debentures & Related Securities: Findings from Some Theoretical, Empirical & Interview Investigations. LC 74-20369. 360p. 1975. text ed. 18.00x (ISBN 0-87584-111-2). Harvard Busn.

Tennison, B. R. Sheaf Theory. LC 74-31791. (London Mathematical Society Lecture Note Ser.: No. 20). 120p. 1976. pap. 19.95 (ISBN 0-521-20784-3). Cambridge U Pr.

Tennissen, A. Nature of Earth Materials. 1974. ref. ed. 24.95 (ISBN 0-13-610501-7). P-H.

Tennissen, Anthony C. Colorful Mineral Identifier. LC 72-151706. (Illus.). (gr. 10 up). 1971. 9.95 (ISBN 0-8069-3040-3); PLB 9.29 o.p. (ISBN 0-8069-3041-1). Sterling.

--Nature of Earth Materials. (Illus.). 448p. 1983. prof. ref. 21.95 (ISBN 0-13-610527-0). P-H.

Tennissen, Anthony T., ed. see Schumann, Walter.

Tennov, Dorothy. Super Self: A Woman's Guide to Self-Management. 1978. pap. 1.95 o.s.i. (ISBN 0-515-04510-1). Jove Pubns.

Tennyson, Alfred. Alfred Tennyson: "In Memoriam", "Maud", & Other Poems. Jump, John D., ed. (Rowman & Littlefield University Library). 237p. 1974. 8.50x o.p. (ISBN 0-87471-592-X); pap. 4.00x (ISBN 0-87471-593-8). Rowman.

--Idylls of the King & a Selection of Poems. pap. 2.25 (ISBN 0-451-51644-3, CE1644, Sig Classics). NAL.

Tennyson, Alfred L. A Choice of Tennyson's Verse. Cecil, David, ed. 144p. 1971. pap. 4.95 (ISBN 0-571-09184-9). Faber & Faber.

--Poems & Plays. Warren, T. Herbert & Page, Frederick, eds. (Oxford Paperbacks Ser: No. 261). 1971. pap. 9.50x o.p. (ISBN 0-19-281115-0, OX261). Oxford U Pr.

Tennyson, Brian D. Canadian Relations with South Africa: A Diplomatic History. 254p. (Orig.). 1982. lib. bdg. 23.50 (ISBN 0-8191-2632-2); pap. text ed. 11.50 (ISBN 0-8191-2633-0). U Pr of Amer.

Tennyson, Elizabeth J., jt. ed. see Tennyson, G. B.

Tennyson, G. B. & Tennyson, Elizabeth J., eds. Index to Nineteenth-Century Fiction: 1945-1975, Vols. 1-30. 1978. 28.50x (ISBN 0-520-03334-5). U of Cal Pr.

Tennyson, Hallam. Alfred Lord Tennyson: A Memoir by His Son, 4 Vols. Repr. of 1899 ed. Set. lib. bdg. 43.00x o.p. (ISBN 0-8371-0680-X, TEAT). Greenwood.

Tennyson, Hallam, ed. Studies in Tennyson. LC 79-55520. 244p. 1981. text ed. 27.50x (ISBN 0-389-20236-3). B&N Imports.

Tennyson, Noel, illus. Santa Is Coming. LC 80-54768. (Shape Bks.). (Illus.). 24p. (ps-k). 1981. spiral plastic bdg. 2.95 (ISBN 0-394-84797-0). Random.

Tennyson, W. Wesley & Hansen, L. Sunny. Career Development Education: A Program Approach for Teachers & Counselors. 1980. Repr. of 1975 ed. 7.75 (ISBN 0-686-36410-4, 72213); nonmembers 8.75 (ISBN 0-686-37309-X). Am Personnel.

Tenorio, Jo Ann see Zimmerman, Elwood C. & Hardy, D. Elmo.

Tenquist, D. W., et al. University Optics, 2 vols. 1970. Set. 114.00x (ISBN 0-677-62090-X); Vol. 1, 350p. 65.00x (ISBN 0-677-62070-5); Vol. 2, 382p. 65.00x (ISBN 0-677-62080-2). Gordon.

Tent, James F. Mission on the Rhine: Reeducation & De-Nazification in American-Occupied Germany. 344p. 1983. lib. bdg. 26.00x (ISBN 0-226-79357-5); pap. text ed. 12.95x (ISBN 0-226-79358-3). U of Chicago Pr.

Tentler, Leslie W. Wage-Earning Women: Industrial Work & Family Life in the United States, 1900-1930. 280p. 1982. pap. 7.95 (ISBN 0-19-503211-X, GB). Oxford U Pr.

Tenzer, Jeff, jt. auth. see Long, Jerry.

Teodoro, Luis V., ed. Out of This Struggle: The Filipinos in Hawaii. LC 81-714. (Illus.). 116p. 1981. 10.95 (ISBN 0-8248-0747-2). UH Pr.

Teodosiu, C. Elastic Models Crystal Defects. (Illus.). 340p. 1982. pap. 25.80 (ISBN 0-387-11226-X). Springer-Verlag.

TePaske, John J. & Klein, Herbert S. The Royal Treasuries of the Spanish Empire in America, 3 vols. LC 82-2457. 1982. Set. 125.00 (ISBN 0-8223-0486-4); Vol. I: Peru, 590 p. 55.00 (ISBN 0-8223-0530-5); Vol. II: Peru (Bolivia), 446 p. 45.00 (ISBN 0-686-81650-1); Vol. III: Chile & the Rio de la Plata, 434 p. 45.00 (ISBN 0-8223-0532-1). Duke.

Teple, Edwin R. see Labor Law Group.

Teple, Edwin R., ed. see Labor Law Group.

Teplick, J. G. & Haskin, Marvin E. Roentgenologic Diagnosis. 3rd ed. LC 75-10390. (Illus.). 1976. text ed. 95.00x (ISBN 0-7216-8792-X); Vol.I. 50.00 (ISBN 0-7216-8789-X); Vol. II. 50.00 (ISBN 0-7216-8790-3). Saunders.

Teplick, J. George & Haskin, Marvin E. Surgical Radiology: A Complement in Radiology & Imaging to the Sabiston-Davis-Christopher Textbook of Surgery, 3 vols. (Illus.). 1152p. 1981. text ed. Vol. 1. 72.00x (ISBN 0-7216-8781-4); Vol. 2. text ed. 72.00 (ISBN 0-7216-8782-2); Vol. 3. text ed. 80.00 (ISBN 0-7216-8791-1); Set. 224.00 (ISBN 0-7216-8783-0). Saunders.

Teplitz, Doris, ed. Electromagnetism: Paths to Research. 375p. 1982. 55.00x (ISBN 0-306-41047-8, Plenum Pr). Plenum Pub.

Teplitz, Paul V., jt. auth. see Markham, Jesse W.

Teply, Larry. Legal Research & Citation Exercises. (American Casebook Ser.). 364p. 1982. Tchrs.' Manual Answer Key avail. (ISBN 0-314-65786-X). West Pub.

Teply, Larry L. Legal Research & Citation: Programmed Materials. 326p. 1982. 9.95 (ISBN 0-314-65784-3). West Pub.

Tepper, Albert. Speech Communication: Theory & Practice. 1978. pap. text ed. 7.95 (ISBN 0-8403-1931-2). Kendall-Hunt.

Tepper, Ruth L. The Sherlock Holmes Crossword Puzzle Book. (Illus.). 1977. pap. 2.95 (ISBN 0-517-53101-1, C N Potter Bks). Crown.

Tepper, Sheri S. King's Blood Four. 1983. pap. 2.50 (ISBN 0-441-44524-1, Pub. by Ace Science Fiction). Ace Bks.

Tepping, Benjamin J., jt. auth. see Cernea, Michael M.

Terada, Kazuo, ed. Excavations at Huacaloma in the North Highlands of Peru, 1979: Report No. 2 of the Japanese Scientific Expedition to Nuclear America. (Illus.). 300p. 1982. text ed. 79.50 (ISBN 0-86008-315-2, Pub. by U of Tokyo Japan). Columbia U Pr.

Teran, Lisa St. Aubin De see St. Aubin de Teran, Lisa.

Teranishi, Roy & Barrera-Benitez, Heriberto, eds. Quality of Selected Fruits & Vegetables of North America. (ACS Symposium Ser.: No. 170). 1981. write for info. (ISBN 0-8412-0662-7). Am Chemical.

Terasaki, Etsuko see Shan, Han.

Terasaki, Paul, ed. Blood Transfusion & Transplantation. 178p. 1982. 39.50 (ISBN 0-8089-1522-3). Grune.

Terauchi, E., jt. auth. see Neilon, J. R.

Terban, Marvin. In a Pickle & other Funny Idioms. (Illus.). 64p. (gr. 1-4). 1983. 11.50 (ISBN 0-89919-153-3, Clarion); pap. 3.95 (ISBN 0-89919-164-9). HM.

Tercentenary of Scientific Hydrology, Paris, 1974. Three Centuries of Scientific Hydrology, 1674-1974: Papers. 123p. (Eng, Fr, Span. & Rus.). 1974. pap. 9.50 (ISBN 0-686-94189-6, U680, UNESCO). Unipub.

Terenius, L., jt. ed. see Van Ree, J. M.

Teresa of Avila, St. Way of Perfection. pap. 4.95 (ISBN 0-385-06539-6, D176, Im). Doubleday.

Teresa Of Calcutta, Mother A Gift for God. LC 74-4628. (Illus.). 96p. 1974. 6.95i o.p. (ISBN 0-06-068231-0, HarpR). Har-Row.

Teresi, Dick & Colligan, Doug. The Cyclist's Manual. LC 80-85520. (Illus.). 1981. 13.95 (ISBN 0-8069-5562-7); lib. bdg. 13.29 (ISBN 0-8069-5563-5). Sterling.

Teresinski, Michael F. & Cheremisinoff, Paul N. Industrial Respiratory Protection. LC 82-72859. (Illus.). 200p. 1983. 27.50 (ISBN 0-250-40587-3). Ann Arbor Science.

Ter Haar, D. Elements of Hamiltonian Mechanics. 2nd ed. 1971. pap. 16.25 (ISBN 0-08-016726-8). Pergamon.

Ter Haar, D. & Scully, M. O., eds. Willis E. Lamb, Jr. A Festschrift on the Occasion of His 65th Birthday. (Physics Reports Reprint Book: Vol. 3). 1979. 72.50 (ISBN 0-444-85253-0, North Holland). Elsevier.

Ter Haar, D., ed. see Kapitza, P. L.

Ter Horst, J. F. Gerald Ford: Past... Present... Future. LC 74-82727. 1974. 11.95 o.p. (ISBN 0-89388-191-0). Okpaku Communications.

TerHorst, Jerald F., jt. auth. see Albertazzie, Ralph.

Ter Horst, Robert. Calderon: The Secular Plays. LC 80-5183. 264p. 1982. 21.50x (ISBN 0-8131-1440-3). U Pr of Ky.

Terhune, Albert P. The Further Adventures of Lad. 1983. pap. 2.25 (ISBN 0-686-43017-4). NAL.

--Lad of Sunnybank. 1980. pap. 2.25 (ISBN 0-451-12087-6, AE2087, Sig). NAL.

Terhune, Frances, ed. Florida Statistical Abstract, 1982. (Illus.). 704p. (LC A67-7393). 1982. casebound 25.00x (ISBN 0-8130-0745-3); pap. 17.00 (ISBN 0-8130-0746-1). U Presses Fla.

Terkel, Studs. Division Street: America. 1975. pap. 3.50 o.p. (ISBN 0-380-00279-5, 55723, Discus). Avon.

Terkel, Studs, et al. Envelopes of Sound: The Art of Oral History. 2nd ed. Grele, Ronald, ed. 1983. 12.95t (ISBN 0-913750-23-9); pap. write for info (ISBN 0-913750-24-7); 2 cass. of panel discussions 17.95 (ISBN 0-685-51815-9). Precedent Pub.

Terkel, Susan N. Yoga Is for Me. LC 81-18623. (Sports for Me Bks.). (Illus.). 48p. (gr. 2-5). 1982. PLB 6.95g (ISBN 0-8225-1098-7). Lerner Pubns.

Terlecki, Tymon. Stanislaw Wyspianski. (World Authors Ser.). 166p. 1983. lib. bdg. 18.95 (ISBN 0-8057-6521-2, Twayne). G K Hall.

Terleckyj, Nestor E. Improvements in the Quality of Life: Estimates of Possibilities in the United States, 1974-1983. LC 74-82709. 297p. 1977. 15.00 (ISBN 0-89068-009-4). Natl Planning.

Terlouw, Jan. Winter in Wartime. LC 75-41345. 144p. (gr. 7-12). 1976. PLB 7.95 (ISBN 0-07-063504-8, GB). McGraw.

Terman, F. E., ed. see Millman, Jacob & Halkias, Christos.

Terme, J. F. & Monfalcon, J. B. Histoire des Enfants Trouves, Nouvelle Edition Revue et Augmentee. (Conditions of the 19th Century French Working Class Ser.). 497p. 1974. Repr. of 1840 ed. lib. bdg. 124.00 o.p. (ISBN 0-8287-0811-8, 1163). Clearwater Pub.

Terminello, Joanne, ed. Energy Directory 1983. LC 74-79869. 250.00 (ISBN 0-89947-014-9). EIC Intell.

Ternay, Andrew L., Jr. Contemporary Organic Chemistry. LC 75-8187. (Illus.). 1010p. 1976. text ed. 23.50 (ISBN 0-7216-8794-6); student guide 6.25 (ISBN 0-7216-3832-5). HR&W.

Ternberg, Jessie L., et al. A Handbook for Pediatric Surgery. (Illus.). 212p. 1979. pap. 12.95 (ISBN 0-683-08150-0). Williams & Wilkins.

Terpstra. International Marketing. 3rd ed. 624p. 1983. 25.95 (ISBN 0-03-062736-2). Dryden Pr.

Terpstra, Dan, jt. auth. see Levy, George C.

Terpstra, P. & Codd, L. W. Crystallometry. 1961. 64.00 (ISBN 0-12-685250-2). Acad Pr.

Terr, Leonard. Sitting in Our Treehouse Waiting for the Apocalypse. 63p. 1975. 3.50 (ISBN 0-87886-064-9). Ithaca Hse.

Terrace, Vincent, jt. auth. see Parish, James R.

Terras, Victor. Belinskij & Russian Literary Criticism: The Heritage of Organic Aesthetics. LC 73-2050. 316p. 1974. 37.50 (ISBN 0-299-06350-X). U of Wis Pr.

--A Karamazov Companion: Commentary on the Genesis, Language, & Style of Dostoevsky's Novel. 496p. 1981. 30.00 (ISBN 0-299-08310-1); pap. text ed. 12.50 (ISBN 0-299-08314-4). U of Wis Pr.

Terrass & Comfort. Teaching Occupational Home Economics. 1979. 13.96 (ISBN 0-87002-282-2). Bennett IL.

Terrell, jt. auth. see Daniel.

Terrell, Carroll F. A Companion to the Cantos of Ezra Pound, Volume I, (Cantos 1-71) 800p. 1980. 34.50x (ISBN 0-520-03687-5). U of Cal Pr.

Terrell, Carroll F., ed. Basil Bunting: Man & Poet. (Man & Poet Ser.). (Illus.). 450p. (Orig.). 1981. 25.00 (ISBN 0-915032-51-1); pap. 12.95 (ISBN 0-686-73366-5). Natl Poet Foun.

Terrell, Dahlia, ed. The Crayon Miscellany. (Critical Editions Program). 1979. 27.50 (ISBN 0-8057-8518-3, Twayne). G K Hall.

Terrell, David, jt. auth. see Cave, Frank.

Terrell, Elizabeth. Games They Paid Michael to Play. LC 79-14344. 1983. 16.95 (ISBN 0-87949-149-3). Ashley Bks.

Terrell, James C., jt. auth. see Daniel, Wayne W.

Terrell, John, jt. auth. see Leonard, Anne.

Terrell, M. E. Professional Food Preparation. 2nd ed. 741p. 1979. 32.95 (ISBN 0-471-85202-3). Wiley.

Terrell, Margaret E., jt. auth. see Kotschevar, Lendal H.

Terrell, Robert W. Soil 'neath My Feet. 1979. 5.50 o.p. (ISBN 0-533-03950-9). Vantage.

Terrell, T. see Karshen, S.

Terrell, Timothy P., jt. auth. see Freed, Daniel J.

Terrell, Tracy D. & Salgues de Cargill, Maruxa. Linguistica Aplicada: A la Ensenanza Del Espagnol a Anglohablantes. LC 78-21016. 218p. 1979. pap. text ed. 17.95 (ISBN 0-471-03946-2). Wiley.

Terrell, Tracy David, jt. auth. see Barrutia, Richard.

Terrell, Trevor J. An Introduction to Digital Filters. LC 79-25409. 1980. 34.95x o.p. (ISBN 0-470-26909-X). Halsted Pr.

Terres, John, ed. see Rue, Leonard L., 3rd.

Terreur, Marc La see Halpenny, Francess.

Terrill, Rose. Mao: A Biography. LC 79-1687. 1980. 18.22i (ISBN 0-06-014243-X, HarpT); pap. 6.95i (ISBN 0-06-090859-9, CN-859). Har-Row.

Terrill, Ross. Eight Hundred Million: The Real China. 1972. pap. 2.95 o.s.i. (ISBN 0-440-52267-6, Delta). Dell.

--The Future of China. 1978. 11.95 o.s.i. (ISBN 0-440-02499-4). Delacorte.

--The Future of China. 1978. pap. 4.95 o.s.i. (ISBN 0-440-52612-4, Delta). Dell.

Terrill, Ross, ed. The China Difference. LC 78-2179. 1979. 14.37i (ISBN 0-06-014249-9, HarpT); pap. 5.95 (ISBN 0-06-090757-6, CN-757). Har-Row.

Terrill, Tom E. The Tariff, Politics, & American Foreign Policy, 1874-1901. LC 72-140921. (Contributions in American History Ser.: No. 31). 1973. lib. bdg. 29.95x (ISBN 0-8371-5819-2, TTP/). Greenwood.

Terris, Susan. The Chicken Pox Papers. 1978. pap. 1.50 o.p. (ISBN 0-440-41402-4, YB). Dell.

--No Scarlet Ribbons. 176p. (gr. 5 up). 9.95 (ISBN 0-374-35353-0). FS&G.

--No Scarlet Ribbons. 160p. 1983. pap. 2.25 (ISBN 0-380-62844-9, Flare). Avon.

Terris, Virginia R., ed. Woman in America: A Guide to Information Sources. LC 73-17564. (American Studies Information Guide Ser.: Vol. 7). 1980. 42.00x (ISBN 0-8103-1268-9). Gale.

Territo, Leonard, jt. auth. see Swanson, Charles R., Jr.

Territorial Bureau of Immigration. The Resources of New Mexico. LC 73-80703. 76p. 1973. Repr. of 1881 ed. lib. bdg. 7.50x (ISBN 0-88307-504-0); pap. 0.75 (ISBN 0-88307-503-2). Gannon.

Terruwe, Anna A., jt. auth. see Baars, Conrad W.

Terry. Plaid for Principles of Management. 3rd ed. 1978. 5.95 o.p. (ISBN 0-256-02134-1, 11-0757-03). Dow Jones-Irwin.

Terry & Rue. Principles of Management. 4th ed. (Plaid Ser.). 1982. pap. 8.95 (ISBN 0-87094-338-3). Dow Jones-Irwin.

Terry, Ann. Children's Poetry Preferences: A National Survey of Upper Elementary Grades. LC 74-77997. 72p. 1974. pap. 3.95 o.p. (ISBN 0-8141-0660-9); pap. 2.90 members o.p. (ISBN 0-686-86387-9). NCTE.

Terry, Ann, jt. auth. see Fischer, Carol.

Terry, Ann, jt. auth. see Fisher, Carol.

Terry, Charles, tr. see Higuchi, Tadahiko.

Terry, Charles E. & Pellens, Mildred. Opium Problem. LC 76-108232. (Criminology, Law Enforcement, & Social Problems Ser.: No. 115). (Illus., With a new preface by Charles Winick & a new intro. by John C. Ball). 1970. Repr. of 1928 ed. 40.00x (ISBN 0-87585-115-0). Patterson Smith.

Terry, Charles S. Music of Bach. (Illus.). 1933. pap. 2.95 (ISBN 0-486-21075-8). Dover.

Terry, Charles S., tr. see Mori, Masahiro.

Terry, Ellen. The Story of My Life. LC 82-3330. 248p. 1982. 12.95x (ISBN 0-8052-3814-X); pap. 6.95 (ISBN 0-8052-0721-X). Schocken.

Terry, Garth M., jt. ed. see Jones, Malcolm V.

Terry, George R. & Rue, Leslie W. Supervision. Rev. ed. (Plaid Ser.). 141p. 1983. pap. 6.95 (ISBN 0-256-02718-8). Dow Jones-Irwin.

Terry, Gloria, jt. auth. see Reber, Ralph W.

Terry, Hazelmai M., jt. auth. see Snyder, Bernadette M.

Terry, Jack. The Way to Happiness in Your Home: Bible Study on Family Living. 36p. 1982. pap. 3.50 (ISBN 0-939298-06-6). J M Prods.

Terry, James W., et al. Physical Activity for All Ages: The Concepts Approach. 272p. (Orig.). 1979. pap. text ed. 11.95 (ISBN 0-8403-2498-7, 40249801). Kendall-Hunt.

Terry, Margaret. The Last of April. 1982. 6.95 (ISBN 0-686-84164-6, Avalon). Bouregy.

Terry, Mary. Homecraft. pap. 7.50x (ISBN 0-392-03257-0, ABC). Sportshelf.

Terry, Patricia, jt. ed. see Caws, Mary Ann.

Terry, R., et al, eds. Neural Aging & Its Implications in Human Neurological Pathology. (Aging Ser.: Vol. 18). 258p. 1982. text ed. 31.00 (ISBN 0-89004-677-8). Raven.

Terry, R. C. Anthony Trollope: The Artist in Hiding. (Illus.). 286p. 1977. 20.00x o.p. (ISBN 0-87471-875-9). Rowman.

Terry, Robert A., jt. ed. see Kay, Robert S.

Terry, Robert D., jt. auth. see Katzman, Robert.

Terry, Sheila G., et al. Children: Their Growth & Development. (Careers in Home Economics Ser.). (Illus.). 1979. pap. text ed. 11.96 (ISBN 0-07-063731-8, G); tchr's manual & key 4.00 (ISBN 0-07-063733-4); wkbk. 5.96 (ISBN 0-07-063732-6). McGraw.

Terry, W. Clinton, III. Teaching Religion: The Secularization of Religion Instruction in a West German School System. LC 80-5569. 208p. 1981. lib. bdg. 20.75 (ISBN 0-8191-1366-2); pap. text ed. 10.50 (ISBN 0-8191-1367-0). U Pr of Amer.

Terry, Walter. Frontiers of Dance: The Life of Martha Graham. LC 75-9871. (Women of America Ser.). (Illus.). 160p. (gr. 5-9). 1975. 12.95 o.p. (ISBN 0-690-00920-8, TYC-J). Har-Row.

Tersac, Helene. The Animals' Ball. cloth 17.95 (ISBN 0-914676-95-4). Green Tiger Pr.

Terschluse, Marilyn, ed. see Stafford, Marilyn.

Tersine, Richard J. Materials Management & Inventory Systems. LC 76-477. 1976. text ed. 24.95 (ISBN 0-444-00186-7, North Holland). Elsevier.

Tertz, Abram & Sinyavsky, Andrei. The Trail Begins on Socialist Realism. Hayward, Max & Denis, George, trs. 220p. 1982. pap. 6.95 (ISBN 0-520-04677-3). U of Cal Pr.

Terwilliger, Robert E. & Holmes, Urban T. To Be a Priest: Perspectives on Vocation & Ordination. 192p. (Orig.). 1975. pap. 4.95 (ISBN 0-8164-2592-2, 8164-2592-2). Seabury.

Terwoord, Carole A., jt. auth. see Spragens, William C.

Terzaghi, Karl. Theoretical Soil Mechanics. 510p. 1943. 46.95 (ISBN 0-471-85305-4, Pub. by Wiley-Interscience). Wiley.

Terzaghi, Karl & Peck, R. B. Soil Mechanics in Engineering Practice. 2nd ed. LC 67-17356. 729p. 1967. 43.95x (ISBN 0-471-85273-2, Pub. by Wiley-Interscience). Wiley.

Terzi, M. Genetics & the Animal Cell. LC 73-14385. 272p. 1974. 36.75 o.p. (ISBN 0-471-85343-7, Pub. by Wiley-Interscience). Wiley.

Terzian, James A., jt. ed. see Hill, Rolla B.

Terzian, Yervant & Bilson, Elizabeth, eds. Cosmology & Astrophysics: Essays in Honor of Thomas Gold on His 60th Birthday. (Illus.). 168p. 1982. 22.50x (ISBN 0-8014-1497-0). Cornell U Pr.

Teschner, Richard V. see Blansitt, Edward L., Jr.

Teselkin, A. S. Old Javanese: Kawi. Echols, John M., ed. & tr. 107p. 1972. pap. 3.50 o.p. (ISBN 0-87763-006-2). Cornell Mod Indo.

Tesich, Steve. Division Street & Other Plays. LC 81-83750. 1982. 17.95 (ISBN 0-933826-28-1); pap. 6.95 (ISBN 0-933826-29-X). Performing Arts.

Teskey, A. Plantanov & Fedorov: The Influence of Religious Philosophy Upon a Soviet Writer. 1981. 60.00x o.p. (ISBN 0-86127-214-5, Pub. by Avebury Pub England). State Mutual Bk.

Teskey, F. N. Principles of Text Processing. (Computers & Their Applications Ser.). 180p. 1982. 49.95X (ISBN 0-470-27335-6). Halsted Pr.

Teski, Marea. Living Together: An Ethnography of a Retirement Hotel. LC 79-88268. 1979. pap. text ed. 9.25 (ISBN 0-8191-0769-7). U Pr of Amer.

Tesla, N. Experiments with Alternate Currents of High Potential & High Frequency. (Illus.). 1979. Repr. of 1904 ed. 15.00 (ISBN 0-686-77985-1). Heinman.

Teslik, Kennan L. Congress, The Executive Branch, & Special Interests: The American Response to the Arab Boycott of Israel. LC 81-20338. (Contributions in Political Science Ser.: No. 80). 296p. 1982. lib. bdg. 29.95 (ISBN 0-313-23120-6, TCE/). Greenwood.

Tesmer, Irving H., ed. Colossal Cataract: The Geological History of Niagara Falls. LC 80-26858. (Illus.). 210p. 1981. 39.50x (ISBN 0-87395-522-6); pap. 10.95x (ISBN 0-87395-523-4). State U NY Pr.

Tessier, Claudia J. The Surgical Word Book. LC 81-40485. 507p. pap. text ed. 17.50 (ISBN 0-7216-8805-5). Saunders.

Tessier, Paul A. Plastic Surgery of the Orbit & Eyelids. Wolfe, S. Anthony, tr. LC 80-29032. (Illus.). 320p. 1981. 62.50x (ISBN 0-89352-041-1). Masson Pub.

Tessier, Thomas. The Nightwalker. 1981. pap. 2.50 o.p. (ISBN 0-451-09720-3, E9720, Sig). NAL.

--Phantom. LC 82-71058. 256p. 1982. 13.95 (ISBN 0-689-11328-5). Atheneum.

Tessler, Richard & Goldman, Howard. The Chronically Mentally Ill: Assessing Community Support Programs. LC 82-3884. 240p. 1982. prof ref 27.50x (ISBN 0-88410-379-X). Ballinger Pub.

Tessman, Jack. My Back Doesn't Hurt Anymore. (Illus.). 1980. pap. 6.95 (ISBN 0-8256-3175-0, Quick Fox). Putnam Pub Group.

Testa, Fulvio. If You Take a Paintbrush: A Book of Colors. LC 82-45512. (Illus.). 32p. (ps-2). 1983. 10.95 (ISBN 0-8037-3829-3, 01063-320). Dial Bks Young.

--If You Take a Pencil. LC 82-1505. 32p. (ps-2). 1982. 10.95 (ISBN 0-8037-4023-9). Dial.

--Never Satisfied. (Illus.). 32p. (gr. 1-4). 1982. lib. bdg. 10.95 (ISBN 0-571-12513-1). Faber & Faber.

Testa, Fulvio & Burgess, Anthony. The Land Where the Ice Cream Grows. LC 78-14714. 32p. 1979. PLB 6.95a o.s.i. (ISBN 0-385-15023-7). Doubleday.

Testa, R. B., ed. Aerostructures, Selected Papers of Nicholas J. Hoff. LC 77-164024. 1974. 34.00 (ISBN 0-08-016834-5). Pergamon.

Tester, Jefferson W., jt. auth. see Milora, Stanley L.

Tester, Sylvia R. Billy's Basketball. LC 76-15632. (Kids in Sports Ser.). (Illus.). (gr. 1-3). 1976. PLB 5.95 (ISBN 0-913778-57-5); pap. 2.75 (ISBN 0-89565-124-6). Childs World.

--Carla-Too-Little. LC 76-16020. (Kids in Sports Ser.). (Illus.). (gr. 1-3). 1976. PLB 5.95 (ISBN 0-913778-56-7); pap. 2.75 (ISBN 0-89565-122-X). Childs World.

--Chase! LC 80-14509. (Picture Word Bks.). (Illus.). 32p. (ps-2). 1980. 7.95g (ISBN 0-516-06439-8). Childrens.

--Family! LC 80-12373. (Picture Word Bks.). (Illus.). 32p. (ps-2). 1980. 7.95g (ISBN 0-516-06440-1). Childrens.

--Frustrated. LC 79-23804. (What Does It Mean? Ser.). (Illus.). (ps-2). 1980. PLB 5.95 (ISBN 0-89565-110-6). Childs World.

--The Great Big Boat. LC 79-12176. (Bible Story Books). (Illus.). (ps-3). 1979. PLB 6.50 (ISBN 0-89565-087-8). Childs World.

--Jealous. LC 79-24042. (What Does It Mean? Ser.). (Illus.). 32p. (ps-2). 1980. 7.95g (ISBN 0-516-06446-0). Childrens.

--Jealous. LC 79-24042. (What Does It Mean? Ser.). (Illus.). (ps-2). 1980. PLB 5.95 (ISBN 0-89565-111-4). Childs World.

--Learning About Ghosts. LC 81-7697. (The Learning About Ser.). (Illus.). 48p. (gr. 2-6). 1981. 9.25 (ISBN 0-516-06533-5); pap. 3.95 (ISBN 0-516-46533-3). Childrens.

--Magic Monsters' Halloween. LC 79-25183. (Magic Monsters Ser.). (Illus.). 32p. (ps-3). 1980. 8.65g (ISBN 0-516-06465-7). Childrens.

--Magic Monsters Learn About Weather. LC 79-24826. (Magic Monsters Ser.). (Illus.). 32p. (ps-3). 1980. 8.65g (ISBN 0-516-06464-9). Childrens.

--Parade! LC 80-12389. (Picture Word Bks.). (Illus.). 32p. (ps-2). 1980. 7.95g (ISBN 0-516-06441-X). Childrens.

--Sad. LC 79-26252. (What Does It Mean? Ser.). (Illus.). (ps-2). 1980. 7.95g (ISBN 0-516-06448-7). Childrens.

--Sad. LC 79-26252. (What Does It Mean? Ser.). (Illus.). (ps-2). 1980. PLB 5.95 (ISBN 0-89565-112-2). Childs World.

--Traffic Jam! LC 80-16303. (Picture Word Bks.). (Illus.). 32p. (ps-2). 1980. 7.95g (ISBN 0-516-06442-8). Childrens.

--The World into Which Jesus Came. LC 82-9430. (Illus.). 96p. 1982. PLB 12.95 (ISBN 0-89565-232-3, 4951, Pub. by Childs World). Standard Pub.

Tetel, Marcel. Montaigne. (World Authors Ser.). 1974. lib. bdg. 12.95 o.p. (ISBN 0-8057-2623-3, Twayne). G K Hall.

Tetelman, A. S. & McEvily, A. J. Fracture of Structural Materials. LC 67-12573. (Wiley Series on the Science & Technology of Materials Ser.). 697p. 1967. 49.95x o.p. (ISBN 0-471-85350-X, Pub. by Wiley-Interscience). Wiley.

Tether, Ivan J. Government Procurement & Operations. LC 77-333. (Environmental Law Institute State & Local Energy Conservation Project Ser.). 1977. prof ref 17.50x (ISBN 0-88410-057-X). Ballinger Pub.

Tether, Philip, jt. auth. see Ingle, Stephen.

Teti, Frank & Moline, Karen. Streisand: Through the Lens. 144p. (Orig.). 1982. pap. 9.95 (ISBN 0-933328-42-7). Delilah Bks.

Tetrazzini, Louisa, jt. auth. see Caruso, Enrico.

Tetreault, Wilfred F. & Clements, Robert W. Starting Right in Your New Business. LC 80-66118. (Illus.). 242p. 1980. 7.95x (ISBN 0-937152-01-3). Am Busn Consult.

Tets, Gerard F. Van see Van Tets, Gerard F.

Tetsmann, A. & Lind, H. Yachting Dictionary. 192p. 1980. 50.00x (ISBN 0-686-82331-1, Pub. by Collets). State Mutual Bk.

Tetzlaff, Daniel B. Shining Brass: The Story of the Trumpet & Other Brass. LC 62-20804. (Musical Books for Young People Ser). (Illus.). (gr. 5-11). 1963. PLB 3.95g (ISBN 0-8225-0061-2). Lerner Pubns.

Tetzleff, Judith & Nama, Prabharathie G. How to Examine Your Breasts: A Guide to Breast Health Care. (Illus.). 1981. pap. 1.00 (ISBN 0-686-84300-2). Budlong.

Teufel, Manfred. Das Nachste Dorf Liegt in America: Waterville-eine kleine Gemeinde zwischen Marginalitat und Anpassung. 279p. 1982. write for info (ISBN 3-8204-5803-4). P Lang Pubs.

Teukolsky, Saul A., jt. auth. see Shapiro, Stuart L.

Teune, Henry, jt. auth. see Przeworski, Adam.

Tevesz, M. J. S., jt. ed. see McCall, P. L.

Tevis, Walter. The Man Who Fell to Earth. (Science Fiction Ser.). 10.00 o.p. (ISBN 0-8398-2438-6, Gregg). G K Hall.

--The Queen's Gambit. LC 82-15058. 328p. 1983. 13.95 (ISBN 0-394-52801-8). Random.

--The Steps of the Sun. LC 81-43899. 264p. Date not set. cancelled (ISBN 0-385-17037-8). Doubleday. Postponed.

Tew, Brian. The Evolution of the International Monetary System, 1945-81. 2nd ed. 250p. 1982. pap. text ed. 15.00 (ISBN 0-686-84477-7). Sheridan.

Tew, Marzee K. Country Style Romance. (YA) 1979. 6.95 (ISBN 0-686-59786-9, Avalon). Bouregy.

--Fireside Love. (YA) 1979. 6.95 (ISBN 0-685-95870-1, Avalon). Bouregy.

Tew, Marzee King. Pearl of Great Price. (YA) 1978. 6.95 (ISBN 0-685-87347-1, Avalon). Bouregy.

Tewalt, Susan J., et al. Geological Circular 82-2: Detailed Evaluation of Two Texas Lignite Deposits of Fluvial & Deltaic Origins. (Illus.). 12p. 1982. Repr. 1.00 (ISBN 0-686-37546-7). U of Tex Econ Geology.

Tewari, S. C. Indo-US Relations: 1947-1976. 1977. text ed. 12.50x o.p. (ISBN 0-391-01001-8). Humanities.

Tewarson, Reginald P. Sparse Matrices. (Mathematics in Science & Engineering Ser.: Vol. 99). 1973. 31.00 (ISBN 0-12-685650-8). Acad Pr.

Tewary, V. K. Mechanics of Fibre Composites. LC 77-29117. 1978. 18.95x o.p. (ISBN 0-470-99240-9). Halsted Pr.

Teweles, Richard J. & Bradley, Edward S. The Stock Market. 4th ed. LC 82-8535. 474p. 1982. 24.95 (ISBN 0-471-08588-X). Wiley.

Teweles, Richard J., et al. The Commodity Futures Game: Who Wins? Who Loses? Why? (Illus.). 544p. 1974. 36.95 (ISBN 0-07-063726-1, P&RB). McGraw.

Tewinkel, Joseph M. Built Upon the Cornerstone. LC 80-65148. (Illus.). 178p. (Orig.). 1980. 4.75 (ISBN 0-87509-280-2); Leader's Guide. 2.95 (ISBN 0-87509-286-1). Chr Pubns.

Tewksbury, M. G., jt. auth. see Fenn, H. C.

Tewksbury, M. Gardner. Character Text for Speak Chinese. 3.25 (ISBN 0-686-15214-X). Far Eastern Pubns.

--Speak Chinese. 6.95 (ISBN 0-686-09997-4); tapes avail. (ISBN 0-686-09998-2). Far Eastern Pubns.

Tewksbury, M. Gardner, jt. auth. see Fenn, Henry C.

Tewksbury, M. Gardner, ed. see Fenn, Henry, et al.

Texas Attorneys or Professors of Law. Creditors' Rights in Texas, 2 Vols. 2nd ed. Cook, Eugene A., ed. LC 80-620019. 1311p. 1982. 135.00 set (ISBN 0-938160-24-9, 6325). State Bar TX.

Texas Instruments. Sourcebook for Programmable Calculators. 1979. 26.95 (ISBN 0-07-063746-6, P&RB). McGraw.

Texas Instruments Engineering Staff. The Linear Control Circuits Data Book. 2nd, rev. ed. LC 79-92000. 416p. 1980. pap. 3.90 (ISBN 0-89512-104-2, LCC4781). Tex Instr Inc.

--The Optoelectronics Data Book for Design Engineers. 5th ed. LC 78-65638. 408p. 1977. pap. 11.50 (ISBN 0-89512-102-6, LCC4410). Tex Instr Inc.
--Sixteen Bit Microprocessor Systems. (Illus.). 592p. 1982. 45.00 (ISBN 0-07-063760-1, P&RB). McGraw.
--The TTL Data Book for Design Engineers. 2nd ed. 832p. 1981. text ed. 14.95 (ISBN 0-89512-111-5, LOC4112). Tex Instr Inc.
Texas Instruments Inc. Circuit Design for Audio, AM-FM & TV. (Illus.). 1967. 38.50 (ISBN 0-07-063740-7, P&RB). McGraw.
--Designing with TTL Integrated Circuits. 1971. 49.90 (ISBN 0-07-063745-8, P&RB). McGraw.
--Digital-Integrated-Circuit, Operational-Amplifier & Optoelectronic Circuit Design. (Illus.). 1976. 37.25 (ISBN 0-07-063753-9, P&RB). McGraw.
--Electronic Power Control & Digital Techniques. (Illus.). 1976. 39.50 (ISBN 0-07-063752-0, P&RB). McGraw.
--M O S, Special-Purpose Bipolar Integrated-Circuits & R-F Power Transistor Circuit Design. (Illus.). 1976. 29.50 (ISBN 0-07-063751-2, P&RB). McGraw.
Texas Instruments, Inc. Microprocessors-Microcomputers-System Design. (Texas Instruments Bk. Ser.). (Illus.). 1980. 26.95 (ISBN 0-07-063758-X, P&RB). McGraw.
--Power-Transistor & TTL Integrated-Circuit Applications. (Texas Instruments Ser.). (Illus.). 1977. 29.50 (ISBN 0-07-063754-7, P&RB). McGraw.
Texas Instruments Inc. Solid State Communications: Design of Communications Equipment Using Semiconductors. (Texas Instruments Electronics Ser.). 1966. 47.25 (ISBN 0-07-063739-3, P&RB). McGraw.
--Transistor Circuit Design. (Illus.). 1963. 49.00 (ISBN 0-07-063737-7, P&RB). McGraw.
Texas Instruments Inc. Engineering Staff. The Interface Circuits Data Book for Design Engineers. 2nd ed. LC 81-51166. 752p. 1981. pap. 16.00 (ISBN 0-89512-109-3, LCC5921). Tex Instr Inc.
Texas Instruments, Inc. Engineering Staff. The Line Driver & Line Receiver Data Book for Design Engineers Nineteen Eighty-One. rev. ed. LC 80-54794. 296p. 1981. pap. write for info. o.p. (ISBN 0-89512-106-9, LCCJ290A). Tex Instr Inc.
Texas Instruments Learning Center. Understanding Solid-State Electronics. 3rd ed. LC 78-57025. (Understanding Ser.). (Illus.). 272p. 1978. pap. text ed. 6.95 (ISBN 0-89512-018-6, LCB-3361). Tex Instr Inc.
Texas Instruments Learning Center Staff. Programming Discovery in TI LOGO Student Guide. Rev. ed. (Illus.). 32p. (gr. 3-10). 1982. pap. text ed. 5.95 (ISBN 0-89512-067-4). Tex Instr Inc.
--Texas Instruments Awareness Program for Children: Activity Book. Rev. ed. (Illus.). 40p. (gr. 3-10). 1982. pap. text ed. 5.95 (ISBN 0-89512-068-2). Tex Instr Inc.
Texas Instruments Learning Center Staff & Texas Instruments Personal Computer Division Staff. User's Reference Guide. rev. ed. LC 81-51829. (Texas Instruments Home Computer User Software Ser.). 200p. 1981. pap. 9.95 loose leaf three hole punched (ISBN 0-89512-048-8). Tex Instr Inc.
Texas Instruments Personal Computer Division Staff, jt. auth. see Texas Instruments Learning Center Staff.
Texas Press Women's Assn. Texas Press Women's Cookbook. LC 75-26425. (Illus.). 190p. (Orig.). 1976. pap. 4.95 o.p. (ISBN 0-914872-05-2, Co-Pub Lone Star Publishers). Austin Pr.
Textbook Committee of Barbering. Advanced Textbook of Barbering & Men's Hairstyling. 1969. 12.95 o.p. (ISBN 0-87350-101-2); pap. (ISBN 0-87350-102-0). Milady.
Textile World. Leaders in the Textile Industry. 1979. 31.95 o.p. (ISBN 0-07-063721-0, P&RB). McGraw.
Textor, Robert B., ed. Cultural Frontiers of the Peace Corps. (Illus.). 1966. Repr. 20.00x (ISBN 0-262-20008-2). MIT Pr.
Tey, Josephine. The Daughter of Time. 220p. 1976. lib. bdg. 14.95x (ISBN 0-89966-184-X). Buccaneer Bks.
Teynac, Francoise & Nolot, Pierre. Wallpaper: A History. Morgan, Conway L., tr. from Fr. LC 81-86461. (Illus.). 250p. 1982. 50.00 (ISBN 0-8478-0434-8). Rizzoli Intl.
Tezak, E. J. Exam Reviews in Beauty Salon Management. 1980. 4.30 (ISBN 0-87350-125-X). Milady.
--Successful Salon Management for Cosmetology Students. 1980. 9.90 (ISBN 0-87350-123-3); wkbk. 4.83 (ISBN 0-87350-124-1). Milady.
Tezak, Mark R., jt. auth. see Culbertson, Robert G.
TFH Publications Staff. Bulldogs. (Illus.). 125p. 1980. 4.95 (ISBN 0-87666-714-0, KW-101). TFH Pubns.
T.F.H. Staff. Scottish Terrier. (Illus.). 128p. 1982. 4.95 (ISBN 0-87666-728-0, KW-103). TFH Pubns.
T. Fujii & Channing, C. P. Non-Steroidal Regulations in Reproductive Biology & Medicine: Proceedings of a Satellite Symposium to the 8th International Congress of Pharmacology, Tokyo, 26-27 July 1981, Vol. 34. (Illus.). 266p. 1982. 54.00 (ISBN 0-08-027976-7, H130); firm 27.00 (ISBN 0-686-97505-7). Pergamon.
Thabault, George, ed. see Raymond, Dick.
Thacher, Amos B. Turkoman Rugs. (Illus.). 1982. 38.00x (ISBN 0-87556-623-5). Saifer.
Thacker, Christopher. The Wilderness Pleases: The Origins of Romanticism. LC 82-10769. 288p. 1983. 27.50x (ISBN 0-312-87960-1). St Martin.
Thacker, Ronald. Accounting Principles. 2nd ed. (Illus.). 1979. text ed. 25.95 (ISBN 0-13-002766-9). P-H.
Thacker, Ronald J. Introduction to Modern Accounting. 3rd ed. (Illus.). 1977. pap. text ed. 25.95 (ISBN 0-13-487736-5); study guide 12.95 (ISBN 0-13-487710-1); working papers 12.95 (ISBN 0-13-488064-1). P-H.
Thacker, Ronald J. & Smith, Richard L. Modern Management Accounting. (Illus.). 1977. 19.95 (ISBN 0-87909-504-0); instrs'. manual o.p. avail. (ISBN 0-87909-503-2). Reston.
Thacker, Ronald J., jt. auth. see Ellis, Loudell O.
Thackeray, Helen & Brown, Beth. Mormon Family Cookbook. LC 82-73085. (Illus.). 180p. 1982. 12.95 (ISBN 0-87747-930-5). Deseret Bk.
Thackeray, Milton G., jt. auth. see Skidmore, Rex A.
Thackeray, W. M. see Eyre, A. G.
Thackeray, William. Henry Esmond. 1982. pap. 10.00 (ISBN 0-686-98202-9, Pub. by Pan Bks). State Mutual Bk.
Thackeray, William M. The Book of Snobs. Sutherland, J., ed. LC 78-54067. 1978. 25.00 (ISBN 0-312-09011-0). St Martin.
--Rose & the Ring. (Illus.). 1947. 30.00 o.p. (ISBN 0-87598-006-6). Pierpont Morgan.
--Vanity Fair. 1962. pap. 4.50 (ISBN 0-451-51726-1, CE1726, Sig Classics). NAL.
Thackery, Milton G. & Skidmore, Rex A. Introduction to Mental Health: Field & Practice. (P-H Series in Social Work Practice). (Illus.). 1979. text ed. 22.95 (ISBN 0-13-487801-9). P-H.
Thackery, William M. The History of Henry Esmond. Sutherland, John & Greenfield, Michael, eds. (English Library). 1977. pap. 4.95 (ISBN 0-14-043049-0). Penguin.
Thackrah, J. R. Making of the Yorkshire Dales. 160p. 1982. 50.00x (ISBN 0-86190-070-7, Pub. by Moorland). State Mutual Bk.
Thackray, Arnold. John Dalton: Critical Assessments of His Life & Science. LC 72-75403. (Monographs in the History of Science). (Illus.). 216p. 1972. 12.50x (ISBN 0-674-47525-9). Harvard U Pr.
Thackray, Arnold, jt. auth. see Morrell, Jack.
Thackray, Patricia. Amazing Mumford Forgets the Magic Words. (A Young Reader Ser.). (Illus.). 24p. (gr. k-3). 1979. PLB 5.00 (ISBN 0-307-60178-1, Golden Pr). Western Pub.
--Big Bird Gets Lost. (Scratch & Sniff Sesame Street Bk.). (Illus.). (gr. k-2). 1978. 5.95 (ISBN 0-307-13524-1, Golden Pr); PLB 10.69 (ISBN 0-307-63739-5). Western Pub.
Thackston, W. M., Jr. The Tales of the Prophets of al'Kisa'i. (International Studies & Translations Program). 1978. 25.00 (ISBN 0-8057-8160-9, Twayne). G K Hall.
Thaden, Edward C. Russia & the Balkan Alliance of Nineteen Twelve. LC 64-8086. 1965. 18.75x (ISBN 0-271-73099-4). Pa St U Pr.
Thadepalli, Haragopal. Infectious Diseases: Focus on Clinical Diagnosis. 1979. pap. 27.50 (ISBN 0-87488-830-1). Med Exam.
Thakkur, Chandrasekhar. Introduction to Ayurveda: The Science of Life. rev. ed. LC 74-75522. 1974. 8.95 (ISBN 0-88231-057-7). ASI Pubs Inc.
Thakur, Baleshwar. Urban Settlements in Eastern India: A History of Yaks-Their Culture, Customs & Odors. 1980. text ed. 21.00x (ISBN 0-391-01926-0). Humanities.
Thakur, Manab, jt. auth. see Carby, Keith.
Thakurdas, Frank. German Political Idealism. 368p. 1980. text ed. 23.50x (ISBN 0-391-01796-9). Humanities.
Thakurx, Upendra. Madhubani Paintings. 158p. 1982. text ed. 37.50x (ISBN 0-391-02411-6, Pub. by Macmillan England). Humanities.
Thal, Herbert V., ed. see Bulwer-Lytton, Edward.
Thal, Herbert Van see Broughton, Rhoda.
Thale, Mary. The Autobiography of Francis Place 1771-1854. LC 78-174265. (Illus.). 344p. 1972. 42.50 (ISBN 0-521-08399-0). Cambridge U Pr.
Thaler, George J. Design of Feedback Systems. LC 72-93614. (Illus.). 350p. 1973. text ed. 42.00 (ISBN 0-12-787531-X). Acad Pr.
Thaler, George J., ed. Automatic Control: Classical Linear Theory. LC 74-2469. (Benchmark Papers in Electrical Engineering & Computer Science Ser: Vol. 7). 448p. 1975. 54.00 (ISBN 0-12-787530-1). Acad Pr.
Thaler, Mike. The Chocolate Marshmelephant Sundae. LC 78-58566. (Illus.). (gr. 4-6). 1978. PLB 5.90 s&l (ISBN 0-531-02244-7). Watts.
--The Moon & the Balloon. (Illus.). 32p. (ps-3). 1982. 9.95 (ISBN 0-8038-4744-0). Hastings.
--My Puppy. LC 79-2681. (Illus.). 32p. (ps-2). 1980. 5.95i (ISBN 0-06-026078-5, HarpJ); PLB 8.89 (ISBN 0-06-026079-3). Har-Row.
--The Pac Man Riddle & Joke Book. (Illus.). (gr. 3 up). 1982. pap. 1.95 (ISBN 0-671-46185-0). Archway.
--PAWS: Cat Riddles, Cat Jokes & Catoons. (Illus.). (gr. 3 up). 1982. pap. 1.95 (ISBN 0-671-45287-8). Archway.
--Riddle Rainbow. (Illus.). 128p. (gr. 2-7). 1983. PLB 8.95 (ISBN 0-8038-6368-3). Hastings.
--Scared Silly. (Illus.). 1982. pap. 1.95 (ISBN 0-380-80291-0, 80291, Camelot). Avon.
--Yellow Brick Toad: Funny Frog Cartoons, Riddles & Silly Stories. (Illus.). (gr. 3-5). 1980. pap. 1.50 (ISBN 0-671-56035-2). Archway.
Thales. Revelations of the Nameless One: An Interpretation of the "T" Tarot. (Illus.). 100p. (Orig.). 1982. pap. 5.95 (ISBN 0-935548-07-6). Santarasa Pubns.
Thaller, M. Instrument Development Inquiry. 2nd ed. (No. 232). 1977. pap. 15.00 (ISBN 0-685-77319-1, W65, WMO). Unipub.
Thampan, P. K. Handbook of Coconut Palm. 311p. 1981. 63.00x (ISBN 0-686-84455-6, Pub. by Oxford & I B H India). State Mutual Bk.
Thane, Elswyth. Dawns Early Light. 352p. 1982. pap. 2.95 (ISBN 0-553-22581-2). Bantam.
ThanWi, A. A. Holy Quran: Arabic-Urdu. 14.95 (ISBN 0-686-83593-X). Kazi Pubns.
Thao. Phenomenologie & Materialisme Dialectique. (Reimpressions Ser.). 370p. (Fr.). 1971. 24.00x (ISBN 0-677-50615-5). Gordon.
Thapar, Romesh. An Indian Future. 164p. 1981. 16.95 (ISBN 0-940500-89-2, Pub by Pubs Allied India). Asia Bk Corp.
Thapar, Romila. From Lineage to State: Social Formations of the Mid-First Millenium B.C. in the Ganges Valley. 1982. pap. 15.00x (ISBN 0-19-561394-5). Oxford U Pr.
Tharaud, Ross. Openings. 63p. 1976. 3.50 (ISBN 0-87886-076-2). Ithaca Hse.
Tharn, John. Baseball's Dream Team. 192p. 1982. pap. 2.25 (ISBN 0-448-16922-3, Pub. by Tempo). Ace Bks.
Tharp, C. Patrick & Lecca, Pedro J. Pharmacy Management for Students & Practitioners. 2nd ed. LC 79-10786. (Illus.). 226p. 1979. pap. text ed. 18.95 o.p. (ISBN 0-8016-4898-X). Mosby.
Tharp, Gerald D. Experiments in Physiology. 4th. ed. 1980. pap. text ed. 11.95x (ISBN 0-8087-3610-8). Burgess.
Tharp, Paul M. Tested to Be Trusted. 1979. 5.95 o.p. (ISBN 0-533-04119-8). Vantage.
Tharp, Roland G., jt. auth. see Watson, David L.
Tharpe, Jac L., ed. Tennessee Williams: Thirteen Essays. LC 80-12805. 300p. 1980. pap. text ed. 2.00 o.p. (ISBN 0-87805-118-X). U Pr of Miss.
Tharpe, Josephine M., jt. auth. see Reichmann, Felix.
Thatcher, David S., jt. auth. see Gooch, Bryan N.
Thatcher, Mary, ed. Cambridge South Asian Archive. 360p. 1974. 20.00x o.p. (ISBN 0-7201-0364-9, Pub. by Mansell England). Wilson.
Thatcher, Rebecca. Academic Skills: A Handbook for Working Adults Returning to School. 1976. pap. 1.50 (ISBN 0-87546-248-0). ILR Pr.
Thatcher, Robert W. & John, E. Roy. Functional Neuroscience: Foundations of Cognitive Processes, Vol. 1. 400p. 1977. text ed. 29.95 (ISBN 0-89859-141-4). L Erlbaum Assocs.
Thaves, Bob. Frank & Ernest. 64p. 1983. pap. 3.95 (ISBN 0-03-063552-7). HR&W.
Thaxter, R. Contribution Towards a Monograph of the Laboulbeniaceae. (Illus.). 1971. 160.00 (ISBN 3-7682-0708-0). Lubrecht & Cramer.
Thaxter, Rosamond. Sandpiper: The Life & Letters of Celia Thaxter. (Illus.). 364p. 8.50 (ISBN 0-686-84142-5). Down East.
Thaxton, Nolan A., jt. auth. see Bucher, Charles A.
Thaxton, Nolan A., jt. ed. see Bucher, Charles A.
Thaxton, Ralph. China Turned Rightside Up: Revolutionary Legitimacy in the Peasant World. LC 82-40165. (Illus.). 312p. 1983. text ed. 27.50x (ISBN 0-300-02707-9). Yale U Pr.
--China Turned Rightside Up: Revolutionary Legitimacy in the Peasant World. 27.50 (ISBN 0-686-42817-X). Yale U Pr.
Thayer, Calvin G. Ben Jonson: Studies in the Plays. (Illus.). 1966. Repr. of 1963 ed. 13.95x o.p. (ISBN 0-8061-0555-0). U of Okla Pr.
Thayer, D. W., ed. Microbial Interaction with the Physical Environment. LC 75-20439. (Benchmark Papers in Microbiology Ser: Vol. 9). 431p. 1975. 48.50 (ISBN 0-12-787536-0). Acad Pr.
Thayer, Ernest L. Casey at the Bat. 8.00 (ISBN 0-8446-5613-5). Peter Smith.
--Casey at the Bat: A Ballad of the Republic, Sung in the Year 1888. LC 77-21199. (Illus.). (gr. k-5). 1980. 7.95 (ISBN 0-698-20457-3, Coward); pap. 3.95 (ISBN 0-698-20486-7). Putnam Pub Group.
Thayer, George. Who Shakes the Money Tree? American Campaign Financing Practices from 1789 to the Present. 1974. pap. 2.95 o.p. (ISBN 0-671-21913-8, Touchstone Bks). S&S.
Thayer, H. S. see Dewey, John.
Thayer, H. S., ed. Pragmatism: The Classic Writings. LC 82-2944. 400p. 1982. lib. bdg. 18.50 (ISBN 0-915145-38-3); pap. text ed. 7.95 (ISBN 0-915145-37-5). Hackett Pub.
Thayer, James E. The Deep Structure of the Sentence in Sara-Ngambay Dialogues. (Linguistics & Related Fields Ser.: No. 57). 1978. 10.00x (ISBN 0-88312-071-2); microfiche 3.00x (ISBN 0-88312-470-X). Summer Inst Ling.
Thayer, James S. The Earhart Betrayal. 1980. 10.95 (ISBN 0-399-12485-3). Putnam Pub Group.
--The Hess Cross. LC 77-9017. 1977. 8.95 o.p. (ISBN 0-399-12082-3). Putnam Pub Group.
--The Stettin Secret. LC 78-27527. 1979. 9.95 (ISBN 0-399-12313-X). Putnam Pub Group.
Thayer, Jane. Applebaums Have a Robot! LC 79-28065. (Illus.). 32p. (gr. k-3). 1980. 9.75 (ISBN 0-688-22231-5); PLB 9.36 (ISBN 0-688-32231-X). Morrow.
--Clever Raccoon. LC 80-23119. (Illus.). 32p. (gr. k-3). 1981. 8.95 (ISBN 0-688-00238-2); PLB 8.59 (ISBN 0-688-00239-0). Morrow.
--Gus & the Baby Ghost. LC 76-161874. (Illus.). 32p. (ps-3). 1972. PLB 9.12 (ISBN 0-688-31369-8). Morrow.
--Gus Was a Christmas Ghost. LC 77-101707. (Illus.). (ps-3). 1970. 7.25 o.p. (ISBN 0-688-21370-7); PLB 9.12 (ISBN 0-688-31370-1). Morrow.
--Gus Was a Gorgeous Ghost. (Illus.). (ps-3). 1978. 8.75 (ISBN 0-688-22133-5); PLB 8.40 (ISBN 0-688-32133-X). Morrow.
--Gus Was a Mexican Ghost. (Illus.). 32p. (ps-3). 1974. 9.50 (ISBN 0-688-20104-0); PLB 9.12 (ISBN 0-688-30104-5). Morrow.
--I Don't Believe in Elves. LC 74-32045. (Illus.). 32p. (ps-3). 1975. o.s. 7.25 (ISBN 0-688-22030-4); PLB 9.12 (ISBN 0-688-32030-9). Morrow.
--The Little House: A New Math Story-Game. (Illus.). (ps-1). 1972. PLB 8.16 (ISBN 0-688-30051-0). Morrow.
--Mister Turtle's Magic Glasses. LC 74-118284. (Illus.). (ps-3). 1971. 8.95 (ISBN 0-688-21650-1). Morrow.
--The Mouse on the Fourteenth Floor. (Illus.). (ps-3). 1977. 9.50 (ISBN 0-688-22094-0); PLB 9.12 (ISBN 0-688-32094-5). Morrow.
--The Popcorn Dragon. (Illus.). (ps-3). 1953. PLB 8.16 (ISBN 0-688-31630-1). Morrow.
--Puppy Who Wanted a Boy. (Illus.). (ps-3). 1958. PLB 9.12 (ISBN 0-688-31631-X). Morrow.
--Quiet on Account of Dinosaur. (Illus.). (ps-3). 1964. PLB 9.12 (ISBN 0-688-31632-8). Morrow.
--Rockets Don't Go to Chicago, Andy. (Illus.). (ps-3). 1967. 8.75 (ISBN 0-688-21660-9). Morrow.
--Try Your Hand. LC 79-18608. (Illus.). 32p. (gr. k-3). 1980. 8.75 (ISBN 0-688-22215-3); PLB 8.40 (ISBN 0-688-32215-8). Morrow.
--Where Is Squirrel? LC 78-31611. (Illus.). 32p. (gr. k-3). 1979. 8.75 (ISBN 0-688-22192-0); PLB 8.40 (ISBN 0-688-32192-5). Morrow.
Thayer, Joseph H. Thayer's Greek-English Lexicon of the New Testament. LC 78-67264. 1978. pap. 16.95 (ISBN 0-8054-1376-6). Broadman.
Thayer, Louis, ed. Fifty Strategies for Experiential Learning: Book One. LC 75-27735. Orig. Title: Affective Education, Strategies for Experiential Learning. 230p. 1976. pap. 15.95 (ISBN 0-88390-108-0). Univ Assocs.
--Fifty Strategies for Experiential Learning: Book Two. LC 80-54160. 336p. (Orig.). 1981. pap. 15.95 (ISBN 0-88390-164-1). Univ Assocs.
Thayer, Lynn W. Church Music Handbook. 9.95 o.p. (ISBN 0-310-36880-4). Zondervan.
Thayer, Marion P. Tom Sawyer Notes. (Orig.). 1967. pap. 2.50 (ISBN 0-8220-1301-0). Cliffs.
Thayer, Nancy. Bodies & Souls. LC 82-45126. 360p. 1983. 15.95 (ISBN 0-385-18166-3). Doubleday.
--Stepping. LC 79-7214. 1980. 12.95 o.p. (ISBN 0-385-15203-5). Doubleday.
--Stepping. 1983. pap. 2.95 (ISBN 0-425-06002-0). Berkley Pub.
--The Women at the Waters' Edge. large print ed. LC 82-3365. 559p. 1982. Repr. of 1981 ed. 13.95 (ISBN 0-89621-353-6). Thorndike Pr.
Thayer, Philip & Gumpertz, Robert. From Fiddletown to Tuba City. LC 82-60063. (Illus.). 96p. 1982. 3.95 (ISBN 0-89480-172-4). Workman Pub.
Thayer, Theodore. As We Were: The Story of Old Elizabethtown, Vol. 13. (Illus.). 280p. 1964. 17.95 (ISBN 0-686-81820-2). NJ Hist Soc.

The, Lian & Van Der Veur, Paul W. Treasures & Trivia: Dissertations on Southeast Asia. LC 68-66324. (Papers in International Studies: Southeast Asia: No. 1). 1968. pap. 9.00 (ISBN 0-89680-000-8, Ohio U Ctr intl). Ohio U Pr.
--The Verhandelingen Van Het Bataviaasch Genootschap. LC 73-620033. (Papers in International Studies: Southeast Asia: No. 26). (Illus.). 1973. pap. 7.00x o.p. (ISBN 0-89680-014-8, Ohio U Ctr Intl). Ohio U Pr.
Thear, Katie. The Family Smallholding. (Illus.). 168p. 1983. 22.50 (ISBN 0-7134-1935-0, Pub. by Batsford England); pap. 14.95 (ISBN 0-7134-1936-9, Pub. by Batsford England). David & Charles.
Theatre Craft Editors see Smith, C. Ray.
Theberge, James D., jt. ed. see Salisbury, William T.
Theberge, James D., et al. Latin America: Struggle for Progress, Vol. 14. LC 75-44723. 1976. 19.95x (ISBN 0-669-00428-6). Lexington Bks.
Theberge, Leonard, ed. The Judiciary in a Democratic Society. LC 77-25740. 240p. 1979. 18.95x (ISBN 0-669-01508-3). Lexington Bks.
Theberge, Leonard J. TV Coverage of the Oil Crises: How Well Was the Public Served? (Illus.). 150p. 1982. cancelled (ISBN 0-08-029372-7, K110). Pergamon.
Theberge, Leonard J., ed. TV Coverage of the Oil Crises: How Well Was the Public Served, 3 Vols. Incl. Vol. I: A Qualitative Analysis. Media Institute. (Illus.). 73p. 1982; Vol. II: A Quantitative Analysis. Media Institute. (Illus.). 81p. 1982; Vol. III: An Economist's Perspective. Hazlett, Thomas W. 59p. 1982. LC 81-86030. (Orig.). Set. pap. 12.95 (ISBN 0-937790-12-5). Media Inst.
Thee, Marek, jt. ed. see Eide, Asbjorn.
Theertha, Rama. Pilgrimage & Spiritual Advancement. 23p. 1982. write for info. (ISBN 0-937698-02-4). Golden Mean.
Theil, H. Applied Economic Forecasting. 1971. 44.00 (ISBN 0-444-10283-3, North-Holland). Elsevier.
--Statistical Decomposition Analysis. (Studies in Mathematical & Managerial Economics: Vol. 14). 1972. 37.25 (ISBN 0-444-10378-3, North-Holland). Elsevier.
--System-Wide Explorations in International Economics, Input-Output Analysis, & Marketing Research. (Lectures in Economics Ser.: Vol. 2). 139p. 1980. 30.00 (ISBN 0-444-85377-4). Elsevier.
Theil, H., et al. International Consumption Comparisons: A System-Wide Approach. (Studies in Mathematics & Managerial Economics: Vol. 30). 200p. 1982. 55.50 (ISBN 0-444-86312-5). Elsevier.
Theil, Henri. Introduction to Econometrics. LC 77-14972. (Illus.). 1978. ref. 27.95 (ISBN 0-13-481028-7). P-H.
--Principles of Econometrics. LC 78-118626. (Illus.). 736p. 1971. 35.95x (ISBN 0-471-85845-5). Wiley.
--The Theory & Measurement of Consumer Demand, Vol. 2. LC 74-84206. (Studies in Mathematical & Managerial Economics: Vol. 21). 335p. 1976. 23.25 (ISBN 0-444-10913-7, North-Holland); pap. 18.75 (ISBN 0-444-10971-4). Elsevier.
Theissen, F. Die Gattung Asterina: In Systematischer Darstellung. 1968. pap. 16.00 (ISBN 3-7682-0545-2). Lubrecht & Cramer.
Theissen, Frank & Dales, Dave. Automotive Steering, Suspension, & Braking Systems: Principles & Service. 1982. text ed. 19.95 (ISBN 0-8359-0291-9); pap. text ed. 17.95 (ISBN 0-8359-0290-0); instrs.' manual free (ISBN 0-8359-0292-7). Reston.
--Diesel Fundamentals: Principles & Service. 1982. text ed. 23.95 (ISBN 0-8359-1284-1); instrs' manual avail. (ISBN 0-8359-1285-X). Reston.
Theissen, Gerd. The Miracle Stories of the Early Christian Tradition. Riches, John, ed. McDonagh, Francis, tr. LC 82-48546. 416p. 1983. text ed. 27.95 (ISBN 0-8006-0700-7). Fortress.
--Sociology of Early Palestinian Christianity. Bowden, John, tr. from Ger. LC 77-15248. 144p. 1978. pap. 4.95 (ISBN 0-8006-1330-9, 1-1330). Fortress.
Thelen, David. The New Citizenship: Origins of Progressivism in Wisconsin, 1885-1900. LC 79-158075. 350p. 1972. 20.00x (ISBN 0-8262-0111-3). U of Mo Pr.
Thelen, David P. Robert La Follette & the Insurgent Spirit. 208p. 1976. 7.50 (ISBN 0-316-83927-2); pap. 5.95 (ISBN 0-316-83925-6). Little.
Thelen, James, jt. auth. see Sentlowitz, Michael.
Thelin, John R. The Cultivation of Ivy: A Saga of the College in America. LC 76-9682. 96p. 1976. text ed. 12.95x (ISBN 0-87073-376-1). Schenkman.
Thelning, K. Steel & Its Heat Treatment: Bofors Handbook. 564p. 1975. 69.95 o.p. (ISBN 0-408-70651-1). Butterworth.
Thelwall, John. The Peripatetic, 3 vols. in 2. Reiman, Donald H., ed. LC 75-31262. (Romantic Context Ser.: Poetry 1789-1830). 1978. Set. lib. bdg. 47.00 o.s.i. (ISBN 0-8240-2208-4). Garland Pub.
Themelis, Nickolas J., jt. auth. see Szekely, Julian.
Themelis, Petros G. The Delphi Museum. (Athenon Illustrated Guides Ser.). (Illus.). 104p. 1983. pap. 10.00 (ISBN 0-88332-299-4, Pub. by Ekdotike Athenon Greece). Larousse.
Themerson, Stefan. Professor MMAA's Lecture. LC 74-21585. 226p. 1975. 14.95 (ISBN 0-87951-029-3). Overlook Pr.
Theng, B. K. Formation & Properties of Clay-Polymer Complexes. (Developments in Soil Science: Vol. 9). 1979. 70.25 (ISBN 0-444-41706-0). Elsevier.
Theobald, John, tr. from Fr. The Lost Wine: Seven Centuries of French into English Lyrical Poetry. (Illus.). 600p. 1982. 25.00 o.s.i. (ISBN 0-914676-36-9, Star & Eleph Bks). Green Tiger Pr.
Theobald, Robert. Alternative Future for America II: Essays & Speeches. rev.& enl. ed. LC 82-70050. Orig. Title: Alternative Future for America. 199p. 1970. 8.95x o.p. (ISBN 0-8040-0002-6); pap. 5.95x (ISBN 0-8040-0003-4). Swallow.
--An Alternative Future for America's Third Century. LC 82-74003. 266p. 1976. pap. 5.95x (ISBN 0-8040-0725-X). Swallow.
--Avoiding Nineteen Eighty-Four: Moving Toward Interdependence. LC 82-75448. xvi, 114p. 1982. 18.95 (ISBN 0-8040-0400-5); pap. 8.95 (ISBN 0-8040-0429-3). Swallow.
--Economizing Abundance: A Noninflationary Future. LC 82-73310. 151p. 1970. pap. 4.95x (ISBN 0-8040-0611-3). Swallow.
Theobald, Robert & Scott, J. M. TEG's Nineteen Ninety-Four: An Anticipation of the Near Future. LC 82-72502. 210p. 1972. 8.95x (ISBN 0-8040-0509-5); pap. 3.95 o.s.i. (ISBN 0-8040-0510-9). Swallow.
Theobald, Robert, ed. Middle Class Support: A Route to Socioeconomic Security. LC 82-73328. 199p. 1972. pap. 5.95x (ISBN 0-8040-0612-1). Swallow.
Theobald, Robert A. Final Secret of Pearl Harbor. pap. 6.95 (ISBN 0-8159-5503-0). Devin.
Theobald, William F. Evaluation of Recreation & Park Programs. LC 78-24227. 204p. 1979. 29.50 (ISBN 0-471-01797-3). Wiley.
Theobald-Neal, Vickie. Daddy, What Did You Do to Me. 1983. 14.95 (ISBN 0-87949-221-X). Ashley Bks.
Theobaldus of Provins Saint. Two Old French Poems on Saint Thibaut. Hill, Raymond T., ed. 1936. text ed. 9.50x (ISBN 0-686-83834-3). Elliots Bks.
Theocritus. Poems, 2 Vols. Gow, A. S., tr. 1952. Set. 135.00 (ISBN 0-521-06616-6). Cambridge U Pr.
--Poems. Dover, K. J., ed. LC 73-163889. (Classical Ser). 1972. text ed. 12.95x o.p. (ISBN 0-312-79555-6). St Martin.
Theodor, Oskar. An Illustrated Catalogue of the Rothschild Collection of Nycteribiidae (Diptera) in the British Museum (Natural History) (Illus.). viii, 506p. 1967. 81.50x (ISBN 0-565-00655-X, Pub. by British Mus Nat Hist England). Sabbot-Natural Hist Bks.
Theodore, Chris A. Managerial Statistics: A Unified Approach. 499p. 1982. 23.95x (ISBN 0-534-01093-8). Kent Pub Co.
Theodore, Louis & Buonicore, Anthony J., eds. Air Pollution Control Equipment: Selection, Design, Operation & Maintenance. (Illus.). 640p. 1982. text ed. 39.95 (ISBN 0-13-021154-0). P-H.
Theodorson, Achilles A., jt. auth. see Theodorson, George A.
Theodorson, Achilles G., jt. auth. see Theodorson, George A.
Theodorson, George A. & Theodorson, Achilles G. Modern Dictionary of Sociology. LC 69-18672. 1969. 14.37i (ISBN 0-690-55058-8, TYC-T). T Y Crowell.
Theodorson, George A. & Theodorson, Achilles A. A Modern Dictionary of Sociology. (Everyday Handbooks). 469p. pap. 5.95 (ISBN 0-06-463483-3). B&N NY.
Theodorson, George A., ed. Urban Patterns: Studies in Human Ecology. rev. ed. LC 81-83145. (Illus.). 475p. 1982. 22.50x (ISBN 0-271-00297-2). Pa St U Pr.
Theoharis, Alan, jt. auth. see Dubofsky, Melvyn.
Theoharis, Athan. Spying on Americans: Political Surveillance from Hoover to the Huston Plan. LC 78-12037. 331p. 1978. 29.95 (ISBN 0-87722-141-3). Temple U Pr.
--The Yalta Myths: An Issue in U. S. Politics, 1945-1955. LC 70-105269. 280p. 1970. 16.00x (ISBN 0-8262-0088-5). U of Mo Pr.
Theoharis, Athan, ed. Beyond the Hiss Case: The FBI, Congress, & the Cold War. 350p. 1982. 24.95 (ISBN 0-87722-241-X). Temple U Pr.
Theordore, Frederick & Bloomfield, Stephen. Allergy & Immunology of the Eye. 200p. 1983. lib. bdg. price not set (ISBN 0-683-08175-6). Williams & Wilkins.
Theorell, Tores, jt. auth. see De Faire, Ulf.
Theran. Leonard's Annual Index of Art Auctions. Date not set. 175.00 (ISBN 0-686-43126-X). Apollo.
Therborn, Goran. What Does the Ruling Class Do When It Rules? 290p. 1980. pap. 8.75 (ISBN 0-8052-7080-9, Pub. by NLB). Schocken.
Therese of Lisieux, St. Autobiography of Saint Therese of Lisieux: The Story of a Soul. 1957. pap. 3.95 (ISBN 0-385-02903-9, D56, Im). Doubleday.
Theriault, Jean Y. & Jennings, Joseph. Full-Contact Karate. (Illus.). 192p. (Orig.). 1983. pap. 7.95 (ISBN 0-8092-5597-9). Contemp Bks.
Therien, Normand, ed. Simulating the Environment Impact of a Large Hydroelectric Project. (SCS Simulation Ser.: Vol. 9, No. 2). 30.00 (ISBN 0-686-36677-8). Soc Computer Sim.
Theriot, David. Leola et la Pirogue. (Illus.). 39p. (Fr.). (gr. 3). 1979. pap. text ed. 1.25x (ISBN 0-911409-03-3). Natl Mat Dev.
--Les Trois Petits Amis et La Decouverte du Gumbo. (Illus.). 41p. (Fr.). (gr. 3). 1979. pap. 1.25x (ISBN 0-911409-04-1). Natl Mat Dev.
Theriot, Jude. La Meilleure de la Louisiane: The Best of Louisiana. (Illus.). 361p. 1983. Repr. of 1980 ed. spiral 10.95 (ISBN 0-88289-407-2). Pelican.
Theroux, Alexander. Master Snickup's Cloak. LC 79-1799. (Illus.). 1979. 7.95i (ISBN 0-06-014283-9, HarpT); lib. bdg. 7.89 (ISBN 0-06-014284-7). Har-Row.
--Three Wogs. LC 75-137019. 1972. 9.95 (ISBN 0-87645-055-9). Gambit.
Theroux, Gary, jt. auth. see Gilbert, Bob.
Theroux, Paul. The London Embassy. LC 82-15663. 288p. 1983. 13.95 (ISBN 0-395-33107-2). HM.
--The Mosquito Coast. 384p. 1983. pap. 3.95 (ISBN 0-380-61945-8, 61945-8). Avon.
Theroux, Rosemary & Tingley, Josephine. The Care of Twin Children: A Common Sense Guide for Parents. 2nd ed. Keith, Louis G., ed. (Twin Care Ser.). (Illus.). 150p. 1983. pap. 14.95 (ISBN 0-932254-04-7); text ed. 7.95 (ISBN 0-932254-03-9). Ctr Multiple Birth.
Thesen, Arne, ed. Computer Methods in Operations Research. (Operations Research & Industrial Engineering Ser). 1978. 21.51 (ISBN 0-12-686150-1). Acad Pr.
Thesen, Karen. Country Remedies. LC 78-24701. (Illus.). 1979. pap. 4.95i o.p. (ISBN 0-06-090687-1, CN687, CN). Har-Row.
Theurer, Martin, tr. see Storette, Ronald F.
Thew, Carol L., jt. ed. see Johnson, Carolyn E.
Thews, G., jt. ed. see Schmidt, R. F.
Thiagarajan, Sivasailam & Stolovitch, Harold D. Games with the Pocket Calculator. 47p. (gr. 3 up). 1976. pap. 3.95 o.p. (ISBN 0-918398-19-3). Dilithium Pr.
Thibault, John C. The Mystery of Ovid's Exile. 1964. 26.00x (ISBN 0-520-01265-8). U of Cal Pr.
Thibault, L., ed. Advances In Bioengineering, 1982. 1982. 40.00 (H00247). ASME.
Thibaut, J. & Walker, L. Procedural Justice: A Psychological Analysis. LC 75-15944. 1975. text ed. 9.95x o.p. (ISBN 0-470-85868-0); pap. 4.95 o.p. (ISBN 0-470-85869-9). Halsted Pr.
Thibaut, John & Walker, Laurens. Procedural Justice: A Psychological Analysis. LC 75-15944. 150p. 1975. 5.50 (ISBN 0-470-85868-0, Pub. by Wiley). Krieger.
Thibaut, John, et al. Contemporary Topics in Social Psychology. 1976. pap. text ed. 12.50x (ISBN 0-673-15310-X). Scott F.
Thibaut, John W. & Kelley, Harold H. Social Psychology of Groups. LC 59-11813. (Illus.). 313p. 1959. 28.50x (ISBN 0-471-85866-8). Wiley.
Thibaut, John W., jt. auth. see Kelley, Harold H.
Thibert, Marguerite. Le Feminisme Dans le Socialisme Francais De Eighteen Thirty a Eighteen Fifty. (Perspectives in European History: No. 30). (Fr.). Repr. of 1926 ed. lib. bdg. 27.50x (ISBN 0-87991-822-5). Porcupine Pr.
Thibodaux Service League Members. Louisiana Legacy: A Rich Tradition of Artistry with Food & Joy in Life. Lynch, Gloria E. & Silverberg, Katherine D., eds. LC 82-50498. (Illus.). 288p. 1982. 11.95 (ISBN 0-9608800-0-3). Thibodaux.
Thibodeau, Gary A., jt. auth. see Anthony, Catherine P.
Thibodeau, J. A. & Hawkins, J. W. Primary Care Nursing: Crises Model in Client Management. LC 82-2728. (Nursing Ser.). 300p. 1982. pap. text ed. 19.95 (ISBN 0-534-01148-9). Brooks-Cole.
Thibodeau, Janice A. Nursing Models, Analysis & Evaluation. LC 82-5794. (Nursing Ser.). 300p. 1982. pap. text ed. 10.95 (ISBN 0-534-01149-7). Brooks-Cole.
Thibodeau, Lynn, ed. Remember, Remember. LC 77-95171. 1978. 8.95 (ISBN 0-89310-033-1); pap. 3.95 o.p. (ISBN 0-89310-034-X). Carillon Bks.
Thibodeaux, Louis J. Chemodynamics: Environmental Movement of Chemicals in Air, Water, & Soil. LC 78-31637. 501p. 1979. 47.50x (ISBN 0-471-04720-1, Pub. by Wiley-Interscience). Wiley.
Thie, Paul R. An Introduction to Linear Programming & Game Theory. LC 78-15328. 335p. 1979. text ed. 27.95 (ISBN 0-471-04248-X); tchr's. manual 9.00x (ISBN 0-471-04267-6). Wiley.
Thiebault, Andre. Kites & Other Wind Machines. LC 82-50554. (Illus.). 96p. 1982. 10.95 (ISBN 0-8069-5465-5); lib. bdg. 13.29. Sterling.
Thiebaux, Marcelle. Ellen Glasgow. LC 81-70128. (Literature and Life Ser.). 230p. 1982. 14.50 (ISBN 0-8044-2872-7). Ungar.
Thiede, H., ed. see Miller, R. K.
Thiede, Jan. Mamakuu's Family: An Elephant Herd. LC 76-27288. (Illus.). (gr. 2-6). 1976. 6.95 o.p. (ISBN 0-698-20387-9, Coward). Putnam Pub Group.
Thiele, Colin. The Shadow on the Hills. LC 77-118929. 1978. 10.53i (ISBN 0-06-026126-9, HarpJ); PLB 7.89 o.p. (ISBN 0-06-026127-7). Har-Row.
Thiele, Edwin. The Mysterious Numbers of the Hebrew Kings. 256p. 1982. 12.95 (ISBN 0-310-36010-2). Zondervan.
Thiele, Gary A., jt. auth. see Stutzman, Warren L.
Thiele, Steven. Yugul: An Arnhem Land & Gattle Station. 73p. (Orig.). 1982. pap. text ed. 9.95 (ISBN 0-86784-007-2, 1189, Pub. by ANUP Australia). Bks Australia.
Thielicke, Helmut. Between Heaven & Earth. Doberstein, J. W., tr. from Ger. 192p. 1978. Repr. 12.95 (ISBN 0-227-67726-9). Attic Pr.
--Christ & the Meaning of Life. Doberstein, J. W., tr. from Ger. 186p. 1978. Repr. 12.95 (ISBN 0-227-67684-X). Attic Pr.
--Encounter with Spurgeon. Doberstein, J. W., tr. from Ger. 284p. 1978. Repr. 12.95 (ISBN 0-227-67655-6). Attic Pr.
--The Ethics of Sex. Doberstein, J. W., tr. from Ger. 340p. 1964. 12.95 (ISBN 0-227-67656-4). Attic Pr.
--How the World Began. Doberstein, J. W., tr. from Ger. 308p. 1978. Repr. 12.95 (ISBN 0-227-67484-7). Attic Pr.
--Living with Death. Bromiley, Geoffrey W., tr. 205p. 1983. 11.95 (ISBN 0-8028-3572-4). Eerdmans.
--Man in God's World. Doberstein, J. W., tr. from Ger. 224p. 1978. Repr. 12.95 (ISBN 0-227-67709-9). Attic Pr.
--The Prayer That Spans the World. Doberstein, J. W., tr. from Ger. 160p. 1978. Repr. 12.95 (ISBN 0-227-67671-8). Attic Pr.
--The Waiting Father. Doberstein, J. W., tr. from Ger. 192p. 1978. Repr. 12.95 (ISBN 0-227-67634-3). Attic Pr.
Thielking, William B. Quintillius: The Star That Shone. (gr. 3-6). 1974. 3.50 (ISBN 0-8358-0311-2). Upper Room.
Thieme, Darius L., ed. see United States Library of Congress. Music Division.
Thieme, J. G. Coconut Oil Processing. (Illus., Orig.). 1968. pap. 4.50 o.p. (ISBN 0-685-20806-0, F96, FAO). Unipub.
Thier, Herbert D. Teaching Elementary School Science: A Laboratory Approach. LC 78-113717. (Illus.). 1970. text ed. 15.95 o.p. (ISBN 0-669-51805-0). Heath.
Thierauf, Robert J. Decision Support Systems for Effective Planning & Control: A Case Study Approach. (Illus.). 672p. 1982. text ed. 32.00 (ISBN 0-13-198234-6); instr. man. free (ISBN 0-13-198242-7). P-H.
--Distributed Processing Systems. (Illus.). 1978. 25.95 (ISBN 0-13-216507-4). P-H.
--Effective Information Systems Management. 368p. 1982. text ed. 22.95 (ISBN 0-675-09988-9). Merrill.
--An Introductory Approach to Operations Research. LC 77-23031. (Series on Management & Administration). 412p. 1978. text ed. 29.95x o.p. (ISBN 0-471-03125-9). Wiley.
--An Introductory Approach to Operations Research. LC 82-7835. 428p. 1982. Repr. of 1982 ed. lib. bdg. 28.95 (ISBN 0-89874-503-9). Krieger.
--Systems Analysis & Design of Real-Time Management Information Systems. LC 74-28368. (Illus.). 624p. 1975. ref. ed. 29.95 (ISBN 0-13-881219-5). P-H.
Thierauf, Robert J. & Klekamp, Robert C. Decision Making Through Operations Research. 2nd ed. LC 74-19473. (Management & Administration Ser). 650p. 1975. 34.95x (ISBN 0-471-85861-7); instructors manual 8.50x (ISBN 0-471-85856-0); Wiley.
Thierauf, Robert J. & Niehaus, John F. An Introduction to Data Processing for Business. LC 79-20568. 366p. 1980. text ed. 30.95 (ISBN 0-471-03439-8); tchrs' manual 9.00 (ISBN 0-471-03440-1); study guide 11.50 (ISBN 0-471-07870-0). Wiley.
Thierauf, Robert J. & Reynolds, George W. Systems Analysis & Design: A Case Study Approach. 1980. text ed. 18.95 (ISBN 0-675-08172-6). Additional supplements may be obtained from publisher. Merrill.
Thierauf, Robert J., et al. Management Principles & Practices: A Contingency & Questionnaire Approach. LC 77-23297. (Management & Administration Ser.). 819p. 1977. text ed. 29.95 o.p. (ISBN 0-471-29504-3); tchr's manual 8.00 o.p. (ISBN 0-471-03728-1). Wiley.
Thiers, Adolphe. The Mississippi Bubble: A Memoir of John Law. Fisk, Frank S., ed. Fiske, Frank S., tr. LC 69-19685. xii, 338p. Repr. of 1859 ed. lib. bdg. 20.50x (ISBN 0-8371-0681-8, THMB). Greenwood.
Thiers, Bruce H., jt. ed. see Dobson, Richard L.
Thiers, Harry D. Mushrooms of California I: The Genus Amanita. (Illus.). 60p. (Orig.). 1982. pap. 4.45x (ISBN 0-916422-24-0). Mad River.

Thiery, Avocat. Eloge De J. J. Rousseau, Qui a Concouru Pour le Prix D'eloquence De L'Academie Francaise, En L'annee 1791. (Rousseauism: 1788-1797). (Fr.). 1978. Repr. of 1791 ed. lib. bdg. 30.50x o.p. (ISBN 0-8287-0817-7). Clearwater Pub.

Thies, Dagmar. Cat Breeding. Ahrens, Christa, tr. from Ger. (Illus.). 128p. 1980. text ed. 4.95 (ISBN 0-87666-863-5, KW065). TFH Pubns.

--Cat Care. Madero, Thomas P., tr. from Ger. Orig. Title: Katzenhaltung, Katzenpflege. (Illus.). 96p. 1980. 4.95 (ISBN 0-87666-862-7, KW 064). TFH Pubns.

Thies, James B., jt. auth. see Ferrara, William L.

Thies, Wallace J. When Governments Collide: Coercion & Diplomacy in the Vietnam Conflict, 1964-1968. 500p. 1980. 28.50x (ISBN 0-520-03962-9). U of Cal Pr.

Thiesen, Eva. Textos Folkloricos De los Bora. (Comunidades y Culturas Peruanas: No. 2). 1975. 2.65x (ISBN 0-88312-648-6); microfiche 1.50 (ISBN 0-88312-498-X). Summer Inst Ling.

Thiesse, James L. Plumbing Fundamentals. (Contemporary Construction Ser.). (Illus.). 192p. (gr. 10-12). 1981. 17.96 (ISBN 0-07-064191-9, G); tchr's manual 2.00 (ISBN 0-07-064192-7). McGraw.

Thiessen, Delbert D. Gene Organization & Behavior. 1971. pap. text ed. 7.95x (ISBN 0-685-69592-1). Phila Bk Co.

Thiessen, Diane, jt. auth. see Matthias, Margaret.

Thiessen, Frank & Dales, D. N. Automotive Engines & Related Systems: Principles & Service. (Illus.). 1981. text ed. 19.95 (ISBN 0-8359-0280-3); pap. 17.95 (ISBN 0-8359-0279-X); instr's manual free (ISBN 0-8359-0281-1). Reston.

Thiessen, Frank J. & Dales, Davis. Automotive Principles & Service. (Illus.). 1980. text ed. 23.95 (ISBN 0-8359-0287-0); free instrs'. manual (ISBN 0-8359-0288-9). Reston.

Thiessen, Henry C. Introduction to the New Testament. 1943. 10.95 (ISBN 0-8028-3259-8). Eerdmans.

Thiessen, John C. Pastoring the Smaller Church. kivar 5.95 (ISBN 0-310-36901-0). Zondervan.

Thiffault, Mark. Bicycle Digest. 1973. pap. 5.95 o.s.i. (ISBN 0-695-80398-0). Follett.

Thigpen, Corbett & Cleckley, Hervey M. Three Faces of Eve. 24.50 (ISBN 0-911238-51-4). Regent House.

Thigpen, M. Elton & Maw-Cheng Yang. International Cotton Market Prospects. (Working Paper: No. 2). v, 67p. 1978. 5.00 (ISBN 0-686-36096-6, CP-0002). World Bank.

Thijssen, H. O., ed. Liber Amicorum Presented to Prof. Dr. Wm. Penn. (Journal: Diagnostic Imaging: Vol. 52, No. 2-3). (Illus.). ii, 108p. 1983. pap. 45.50 (ISBN 3-8055-3671-2). S Karger.

Thijsson, J. M. Ultrasonic Tissue Characterization. 1983. 34.50 (ISBN 90-247-2757-X, Pub. by Martinus Nijhoff Netherlands). Kluwer Boston.

Thill, Carol J. Creative Writing. 218p. 1982. pap. text ed. 10.95x (ISBN 0-911337-00-8). Acad Pub Amer.

Thimann, Kenneth V., jt. auth. see Langenheim, Jean H.

Thimm, Alfred L. The False Promise of Codetermination. LC 80-8422. 320p. 1980. 29.95x (ISBN 0-669-04108-4). Lexington Bks.

Thimm, B. M. Brucellosis: Distribution in Man, Domestic & Wild Animals. (Sitzungsberichte der Heidelberger Akademie der Wissenschaften Ser., Mathematisch-Naturwissenschaftliche Klasse, 1981; Supplement.). (Illus.). 64p. 1982. 20.00 (ISBN 0-387-11232-4). Springer-Verlag.

Thimm, Franz. Spanish Quickly: Easy Method. pap. 2.95 (ISBN 0-685-22113-X); 2.95 (ISBN 0-686-66566-X). Wehman.

Thio, Alex. Deviant Behavior. LC 77-90439. (Illus.). 1978. text ed. 21.95 (ISBN 0-395-25323-3); instr's. manual 1.00 (ISBN 0-395-25324-1). HM.

--Deviant Behavior. 2nd ed. 480p. 1983. text ed. 22.95 (ISBN 0-395-32584-6); write for info. instr's manual (ISBN 0-395-32585-4). HM.

Thiong'O, Ngugi Wa. Petals of Blood. 1978. pap. 7.75 (ISBN 0-525-04195-8, 0752-230). Dutton.

Third European Congress. Prenatal Diagnosis. Murken, J. D., et al, eds. (Illus.). 416p. 1979. pap. text ed. 49.00 o.p. (ISBN 0-88416-291-5). Wright-PSG.

Thirkell, Angela. August Folly. LC 80-7835. 312p. 1980. pap. 2.50i o.p. (ISBN 0-06-080525-0, P 525, PL). Har Row.

--Before Lunch. LC 40-6709. 1979. pap. 2.25i o.p. (ISBN 0-06-080498-X, P 498, PL). Har-Row.

--The Brandons. LC 39-27473. 1979. pap. 2.25i o.p. (ISBN 0-06-080497-1, P 497, PL). Har-Row.

--High Rising. LC 80-7833. (Barsetshire Ser.). 296p. 1980. pap. 2.50i o.p. (ISBN 0-06-080524-2, P 524, PL). Har-Row.

Thirlwall, A. P., ed. Keynes & International Monetary Relations: The Second Keynes Seminar Held at University of Kent at Canterbury, 1974. LC 75-44515. 115p. 1976. 15.95 o.p. (ISBN 0-312-45255-1). St Martin.

Thiroux, Jacques P. Ethics: Theory & Practice. 2nd ed. 392p. 1980. pap. text ed. 13.95 (ISBN 0-02-470220-X). Macmillan.

Thirring, Hans. Energy for Man: Windmills to Nuclear Power. LC 68-9715. (Illus.). 1968. Repr. of 1958 ed. lib. bdg. 19.00x (ISBN 0-8371-0247-2, THEM). Greenwood.

Thirring, W. A Course in Mathematical Physics IV: Quantum Mechanics of Large Systems. (Illus.). 290p. 1983. 32.00 (ISBN 0-387-81701-8). Springer-Verlag.

Thirsk, H. R. & Harrison, J. A. A Guide to the Study of Electrode Kinetics. 1972. 28.00 o.s.i. (ISBN 0-12-687750-5). Acad Pr.

Thirsk, J., ed. Agrarian History of England & Wales, Vol. 4: 1500-1640. 97.50 (ISBN 0-521-06617-4). Cambridge U Pr.

Thirsk, Joan. English Peasant Farming: The Agrarian History of Lincolnshire from Tudor to Recent Times. (Methuen Library Reprint Ser.). (Illus.). 368p. 1981. 46.00x (ISBN 0-416-30530-X). Methuen Inc.

Thirwall, A. P. Inflation, Savings & Growth in Developing Countrie. 272p. 1975. 26.00 (ISBN 0-312-41615-6). St Martin.

Thiry, Paul. Eskimo Artifacts. LC 77-14553. (Illus.). 1978. 19.95 (ISBN 0-87564-016-8). Superior Pub.

Thiselton-Dyer, Thomas F. British Popular Customs, Present & Past. LC 67-23908. (Social History Reference Ser.). (Illus.). 1968. Repr. of 1876 ed. 34.00x (ISBN 0-8103-3261-2). Gale.

--English Folk-Lore. LC 75-150242. Repr. of 1878 ed. 37.00x (ISBN 0-8103-3680-4). Gale.

--Folk-Lore of Plants. LC 68-22054. 1968. Repr. of 1889 ed. 34.00x (ISBN 0-8103-3554-9). Gale.

--Folk-Lore of Women As Illustrated by Legendary & Traditionary Tales, Folk-Rhymes, Proverbial Sayings, Superstitions Etc. LC 68-24475. 1968. Repr. of 1906 ed. 30.00x (ISBN 0-8103-3555-7). Gale.

Thisse. Locational Analysis of Public Facilities. (Studies in Mathematics & Mangerial Economics: Vol. 31). Date not set. 64.00 (ISBN 0-444-86486-5). Elsevier.

Thistlethwaite, F. The Great Experiment. (Illus.). 1977. pap. 12.95 (ISBN 0-521-29224-7). Cambridge U Pr.

Thistlethwaite, Linda L., jt. auth. see Snouffer, Nancy K.

Thivolet, Jean & Schmitt, Daniel, eds. Cutaneous Immopathology. 506p. 1978. pap. text ed. 20.50 (ISBN 2-85598-175-1). Masson Pub.

Thoburn, John. Multinational Mining & Development: A Study of the Tin Industry. 192p. 1981. text ed. 34.25x (ISBN 0-566-00417-8). Gower Pub Ltd.

Thoburn, John T. Primary Commodity Exports & Economic Development: Theory, Evidence, & a Study of Malaysia. LC 76-26337. 310p. 1977. 44.95x (ISBN 0-471-99441-3, Pub. by Wiley-Interscience). Wiley.

Thoday, J. M. see Demerec, M.

Thoday, J. M., jt. ed. see Thompson, James N.

Thode, Bradley R. Materials Processing. LC 80-70702. (Industrial Arts Ser.). (Illus.). 306p. 1982. text ed. 17.60 (ISBN 0-8273-1767-0); instr's. manual 3.25 (ISBN 0-8273-1768-9). Delmar.

Thodes, Sonya & Wilson, Josleen. Surviving Family Life: The Seven Crises of Living Together. 300p. 1981. 13.95 (ISBN 0-399-12507-8). Putnam Pub Group.

Thoenen, T., jt. auth. see Malmfors, T.

Thoerner. Etudes sur la Question de l'Abolition du Servage en Russie. (Nineteenth Century Russia Ser.). 360p. (Fr.). 1974. Repr. of 1859 ed. lib. bdg. 93.00x o.p. (ISBN 0-8287-0818-5, R82). Clearwater Pub.

Thoinan, E. Les Hotteterre et les Chedeville Eighteen & Ninety Four. (The Flute Library: Vol. 19). 37.50 o.s.i. (ISBN 90-6027-355-9, Pub. by Frits Knuf Netherlands). Pendragon NY.

Thoinan, E., jt. auth. see Nuitter, C.

Tholfsen, Trygve R. Sir James Kay-Shuttleworth on Popular Education. LC 73-15046. 1974. text ed. 10.00 (ISBN 0-8077-2402-5); pap. text ed. 5.00x (ISBN 0-8077-2411-4). Tchrs Coll.

Thollander, Earl. Back Roads of California: 65 New Trips Along Country Roads. (Illus.). 1983. 19.95 (ISBN 0-517-54966-2, C N Potter Bks); pap. 9.95 (ISBN 0-517-54967-0). Crown.

--Back Roads of New England. Rev. ed. (Illus.). 224p. 1982. 19.95 (ISBN 0-517-54712-0, C N Potter); pap. 10.95 (ISBN 0-517-54595-0, C N Potter Bks). Crown.

--Back Roads of Oregon. (Illus.). 1979. 14.95 (ISBN 0-517-53069-4, C N Potter); pap. 9.95 (ISBN 0-517-53781-8, C N Potter Bks). Crown.

--Back Roads of Washington. (Illus.). 208p. 1981. 17.95 (ISBN 0-517-54269-2, C N Potter); pap. 9.95 (ISBN 0-517-54270-6, C N Potter Bks). Crown.

--Earl Thollander's Back Roads of California. 1983. 19.95 (C N Potter Bks); pap. 9.95. Crown.

Tholstrup, Knud. Why Put up with Inflation? 32p. 1961. pap. 0.25 (ISBN 0-911312-44-7). Schalkenbach.

Thom, Derrick J. The Niger-Nigerian Boundary: 1890-1906. LC 75-620024. (Papers in International Studies: Africa: No. 23). (Illus.). 1975. pap. 4.75 (ISBN 0-89680-056-3, Ohio U Ctr Intl). Ohio U Pr.

Thom, Gary B. The Human Nature of Social Maladies: Alienation, Anomie, Ambivalence. 200p. 1983. text ed. 23.95x (ISBN 0-86598-105-1). Allanheld.

--The Human Nature of Social Maladies: Alienation, Anomie, Ambivalence. 200p. 1983. text ed. 23.95x (ISBN 0-86598-105-1). Rowman.

Thom, H. C. Some Methods of Climatological Analysis. (Technical Note Ser.). 1966. pap. 9.00 (ISBN 0-685-22341-8, W50, WMO). Unipub.

Thom, Martin, tr. see Safouan, Moustafa.

Thom, Robert. Children of the Ladybug: A Drama in 2 Acts. 1956. 19.50x (ISBN 0-685-69875-0). Elliots Bks.

Thoma, Henry F. The American Prospect: Insights into Our Next One Hundred Years. 1977. o.s. 7.95 (ISBN 0-395-25354-3); pap. 3.95 (ISBN 0-395-25405-1). HM.

Thoma, Kurt H. Oral Surgery, 2 Vols. 5th ed. LC 69-15220. (Illus.). 1264p. 1969. Set. 79.50 o.p. (ISBN 0-8016-4915-3). Mosby.

Thoma, R. W., ed. Industrial Microbiology. (Benchmark Papers in Microbiology: Vol. 12). 1977. 55.50 (ISBN 0-12-787540-9). Acad Pr.

Thoman, Frances & Nelson, Meryl. The Golden This & That. Sing, Shirley, ed. (Illus.). 20p. (Orig.). 1982. pap. cancelled (ISBN 0-941900-04-5). This N That.

--The This from That Craftbook. Sing, Shirley, ed. (Illus.). 40p. (Orig.). 1981. pap. 3.00 (ISBN 0-941900-02-9). This N That.

Thoman, Frances, jt. auth. see Nelson, Meryl.

Thoman, Richard S. The United States & Canada: Present & Future. (Geography Ser.). 1978. text ed. 23.95 (ISBN 0-675-08410-5). Additional supplements may be obtained from publisher. Merrill.

Thoman, Richard S. & Corbin, Peter. The Geography of Economic Activity. rev. 3rd ed. LC 74-5756. (Illus.). 528p. 1974. text ed. 35.95 (ISBN 0-07-064207-9, C); instructor's manual 15.00 (ISBN 0-07-029635-9). McGraw.

Thomann, Robert V. Systems Analysis & Water Quality Management. 286p. 1974. text ed. 34.50 (ISBN 0-07-064214-1, C). McGraw.

Thomas, ed. Teen-Age Wild Animal Stories. (gr. 6-10). 1966. PLB 6.19 o.p. (ISBN 0-8313-0048-5). Lantern.

Thomas, A. D. Zeta-Functions: An Introduction to Algebraic Geometry. (Research Notes in Mathematics Ser.: No. 12). 230p. 1977. pap. text ed. 21.95 (ISBN 0-273-01038-7). Pitman Pub MA.

Thomas, A. D. & Wood, G. V. Group Tables. (Shiva Mathematics Ser.). 190p. 31.50 (ISBN 0-906812-04-6, Pub. by Shiva Pub England); pap. text ed. 16.50 (ISBN 0-906812-02-X). Imprint Edns.

Thomas, A. J., Jr., jt. auth. see Van Wynen Thomas, Ann.

Thomas, A. P., jt. tr. see Von Brandenstein, C. G.

Thomas, Aaron J. & Thomas, Ann. Dominican Republic Crisis, 1965. Carey, John, ed. LC 67-14395. (Hammarskjold Fourm Ser.: No. 9). 164p. 1967. 10.00 (ISBN 0-379-11809-2). Oceana.

Thomas, Adin B. Stock Control in Manufacturing Industries. 2nd ed. 240p. 1980. text ed. 16.25 (ISBN 0-566-02140-4). Gower Pub Ltd.

Thomas, Alan. Time in a Frame: Photography & the Nineteenth-Century Mind. LC 77-75294. (Illus.). 1977. 17.95 o.p. (ISBN 0-8052-3674-0). Schocken.

Thomas, Alan G. Great Books & Book Collectors. LC 74-77298. (Illus.). 280p. 1975. 35.00 o.p. (ISBN 0-399-11367-3). Putnam Pub Group.

Thomas, Alastair H., jt. auth. see Elder, Neil.

Thomas, Alexander, jt. ed. see Chess, Stella.

Thomas, Alexander, et al. Behavioral Individuality in Early Childhood. LC 79-16817. (Illus.). 1980. Repr. of 1963 ed. lib. bdg. 19.75x (ISBN 0-313-22049-2, THBI). Greenwood.

Thomas, Alfred. I Have Roads to Take & Decisions to Make. 31p. (gr. 7-12). 1981. pap. 2.25; 2.50. Synod NC Church.

Thomas, Alfred B. Alonso De Posada Report, Sixteen Eighty-Six: A Description of the Area of the Present Southern United States in the Late 17th Century. LC 82-15017. (The Spanish Borderlands Ser.: Vol. 4). (Illus.). 72p. (Orig.). 1982. pap. text ed. 8.95x (ISBN 0-933776-10-1). Perdido Bay.

Thomas, Alstair H., ed. see Patterson, William F.

Thomas & Leeds. Skiiers Directory & Almanac: 1983. 1982. pap. 3.95 (ISBN 0-686-82385-0). Dell.

Thomas, Ann. Creation. (Aglow Bible Study: Bk. 1). 64p. 1973. 2.95 o.p. (ISBN 0-930756-02-9, 4220-1). Women's Aglow.

Thomas, Ann, jt. auth. see Thomas, Aaron J.

Thomas, Ann Van Wynen see Van Wynen Thomas, Ann & Thomas, A. J., Jr.

Thomas, Anna. The Vegetarian Epicure, Bk 2. LC 77-16685. (Illus.). 1978. 12.50 (ISBN 0-394-41363-6); pap. 7.95 (ISBN 0-394-73415-7). Knopf.

Thomas, Antony, jt. auth. see Lloyd, Richard.

Thomas, Art. Fencing Is for Me. LC 81-20716. (Sports for Me Bks.). (Illus.). 48p. (gr. 2-5). 1982. PLB 6.95g (ISBN 0-8225-1129-0). Lerner Pubns.

--Merry-Go-Rounds. LC 81-3825. (Carolrhoda on My Own Bks.). (Illus.). 48p. (gr. k-3). 1981. PLB 6.95g (ISBN 0-87614-168-8, AACR2). Carolrhoda Bks.

Thomas, Art & Blackburn, Emily. Horseback Riding Is for Me. LC 80-13081. (Sports for Me Bks.). (Illus.). (gr. 2-5). 1981. PLB 6.95g (ISBN 0-8225-1092-8). Lerner Pubns.

Thomas, Art & Storms, Laura. Boxing Is for Me. LC 80-20086. (Sports for Me Bks.). (Illus.). (gr. 2-5). 1982. PLB 6.95g (ISBN 0-8225-1133-9). Lerner Pubns.

Thomas, Audrey C. Munchmeyer & Prospero on the Island. LC 75-161252. 1972. 5.95 o.p. (ISBN 0-672-51432-X). Bobbs.

Thomas, Barry. Building the Herreshoff Dinghy: The Manufacturer's Method. (Illus.). 72p. 1983. pap. 5.95 (ISBN 0-8289-0508-8). Greene.

Thomas, Benjamin P. Abraham Lincoln: A Biography. 1968. Repr. of 1965 ed. 7.95 (ISBN 0-394-60468-7). Modern Lib.

Thomas, Bill & Thomas, Phyllis. Natural New York. 320p. 1983. 17.95 (ISBN 0-03-057554-0); pap. 10.95 (ISBN 0-03-057553-2). HR&W.

Thomas, Bill, jt. auth. see Karsk, Roger.

Thomas, Bob. Golden Boy: The Untold Story of William Holden. (Illus.). 1983. 16.95 (ISBN 0-312-33697-7). St Martin.

Thomas, Brinley. Migration & Economic Growth: A Study of Great Britain & the Atlantic Economy. 2nd ed. LC 79-171684. (Illus.). 1972. 57.50 (ISBN 0-521-08566-7). Cambridge U Pr.

Thomas, C. K., jt. auth. see Sastry, N. S.

Thomas, C. William & Henke, Emerson O. Auditing: Theory & Practice. 992p. 1983. text ed. 29.95x (ISBN 0-534-01388-0). Kent Pub Co.

Thomas, Carol G. The Earliest Civilizations: Ancient Greece & the Near East, 3000-200 B. C. LC 82-45051. (Illus.). 220p. (Orig.). 1982. lib. bdg. 23.00 (ISBN 0-8191-2598-9); pap. text ed. 10.75 (ISBN 0-8191-2599-7). U Pr of Amer.

Thomas, Carol G., jt. ed. see Griffeth, Robert.

Thomas, Carol H. & Thomas, James L., eds. Bilingual Special Education Resource Guide. LC 82-8149. 192p. 1982. lib. bdg. 25.00 (ISBN 0-89774-008-4). Oryx Pr.

--Library Services for the Handicapped Adult: Survey & Resources. LC 82-2544. 176p. 1982. lib. bdg. 25.00 (ISBN 0-89774-007-6). Oryx Pr.

--Sports Splash: A Handbook of Reading Activities for Use With Children. (A Fun with Reading Bk.). (Illus., Orig.). 1983. pap. 18.50 (ISBN 0-89774-000-9). Oryx Pr.

Thomas, Carolyn B., jt. auth. see Cass, Loretta K.

Thomas, Carolyn E. Sport in a Philosophic Context. LC 82-12662. 250p. (Orig.). 1983. pap. price not set (ISBN 0-8121-0871-X). Lea & Febiger.

Thomas, Charles I. Ophthalmology. 4th ed. (Medical Examination Review Book: Vol. 15). 1980. pap. 24.00 (ISBN 0-87488-115-3). Med Exam.

Thomas, Charles L. Catalytic Processes & Proven Catalysts. 1970. 54.50. Acad Pr.

Thomas, Charles W. & Hepburn, John R. Crime, Criminal Law & Criminology. 600p. 1983. pap. text ed. write for info. (ISBN 0-697-08220-2); instrs' manual avail. Wm C Brown.

Thomas, Charles W., jt. auth. see Peterson, David M.

Thomas, Clayton L., ed. Taber's Cyclopedic Medical Dictionary. 14th ed. LC 80-16588. (Illus.). 1818p. 1981. 15.95x (ISBN 0-8036-8307-3); Thumb-indexed Edition. text ed. 18.95x. Davis Co.

Thomas, Colin J., jt. auth. see Herbert, David T.

Thomas Cook, Inc. & Norback & Co., Inc. Thomas Cook Travel Guide to New York. (Orig.). Date not set. pap. 3.95 (ISBN 0-440-18889-X). Dell. Postponed.

--The Thomas Cook Travel Guide to San Francisco. Date not set. pap. 3.95 (ISBN 0-440-18896-2). Dell. Postponed.

--The Thomas Cook Travel Guide to Tokyo. Date not set. pap. 3.95 (ISBN 0-440-18901-2). Dell. Postponed.

--Thomas Cook Travel Guide to Toronto. (Orig.). Date not set. pap. 3.95 (ISBN 0-440-18897-0). Dell. Postponed.

Thomas, Craig. Firefox. 1982. pap. 3.50 (ISBN 0-686-97809-9). Bantam.

--Sea Leopard. 1982. pap. 3.50 (ISBN 0-553-20903-5). Bantam.

Thomas, D. Learn BASIC: A Guide to Programming the Texas Instruments Professional Compact Computer. 256p. 1983. 9.95 (ISBN 0-07-064257-5, GB). McGraw.

--Learn BASIC: A Guide to Programming the Texas Instruments Professional Compact Computer 40 (Texas Instruments Edition) 256p. 1983. write for info. (ISBN 0-07-064258-3, GB). McGraw.

Thomas, D., jt. auth. see Davia, N. C.

Thomas, D. G. Introduction to Warp Knitting. 1971. 18.00x (ISBN 0-87245-410-X). Textile Bk.

Thomas, D. H. & Davia, N. C. Komara Miniskimm ER: An Assessment of Performance, 1980. 1981. 30.00x (ISBN 0-686-97102-7, Pub. by W Spring England). State Mutual Bk.

Thomas, D. M. Ararat. 192p. 1983. 13.50 (ISBN 0-670-13009-5). Viking Pr.

--Selected Poems. 128p. 1983. 15.75 (ISBN 0-670-70396-6). Viking Pr.

--Selected Poems. 130p. 1983. pap. 7.95 (ISBN 0-14-042306-0). Penguin.

Thomas, D. M., tr. see Akhmatova, Anna.

Thomas, D. M., tr. see Pushkin, Alexander.

Thomas, D. M., tr. see Yevtushenko, Yevgeny.

Thomas, D. O. see Peach, Bernard.

Thomas, D. T. Engineering Electromagnetics. 416p. 1973. text ed. 33.00 (ISBN 0-08-016778-0). Pergamon.

Thomas, D. Winton, ed. Archaeology & Old Testament Study. 1967. 37.50x (ISBN 0-19-813150-X). Oxford U Pr.

Thomas, Dana L. Lords of the Land: The Triumphs & Scandals of America's Real Estate Barons--from Early Times to the Present. 1977. 9.95 o.p. (ISBN 0-399-11641-9). Putnam Pub Group.

--The Media Moguls: From Joseph Pulitzer to William S. Paley: the Wheelings & Dealings of America's News Merchants. 264p. 1981. 14.95 (ISBN 0-399-12218-4). Putnam Pub Group.

Thomas, David. Book of Proverbs, 2 Vols. in One. (Kregel Bible Classics Ser.). 836p. 1983. Repr. of 1885 ed. 18.95 (ISBN 0-8254-3813-6). Kregel.

--Naturalism & Social Science. LC 79-14223. (Themes in Social Sciences Ser.). 1980. 38.50 (ISBN 0-521-22821-2); pap. 13.95 (ISBN 0-521-29660-9). Cambridge U Pr.

--Notes & Queries on Linguistic Analysis. (Language Data, Asian-Pacific Ser.: No. 10). 121p. 1974. pap. 3.25x (ISBN 0-88312-210-3); microfiche 2.25x (ISBN 0-88312-310-X). Summer Inst Ling.

Thomas, David, ed. Horse Stories. (gr. 5-7). 1964. pap. 2.25 (ISBN 0-671-44201-5). Archway.

Thomas, David, jt. ed. see Gregerson, Kenneth.

Thomas, David, et al see Linguistic Circle of Saigon & Summer Institute of Linguistics.

Thomas, David A. Crete Nineteen Forty-One: The Battle at Sea. (Illus.). 1980. pap. 7.50 (ISBN 0-686-91772-3). Heinman.

Thomas, David B., jt. auth. see Peterson, Donald R.

Thomas, David D. Chrau Grammar. LC 77-127332. (Oceanic Linguistics Special Publications: No. 7). (Orig.). 1971. pap. 7.00x (ISBN 0-87022-788-2). UH Pr.

Thomas, David D. see Linguistic Circle of Saigon & Summer Institute of Linguistics.

Thomas, David G. User's Reference Guide: A Complete Owner's Manual for the TI Programmable 88. 448p. 1982. 15.00 o.p. (ISBN 0-89512-054-2). Tex Instr Inc.

Thomas, David J., ed. A Regional History of the Railways of Great Britain, 5 vols. Incl. Vol. 1. The West Country. rev ed. Thomas, David J. 214p. 1966. o.p. (ISBN 0-678-05731-1); Vol. 2. Southern England. 3rd ed. White, H. P. 218p. 1970. o.p. (ISBN 0-678-05657-9); Vol. 3. Greater London. White, H. P. 227p. 1963. o.p. (ISBN 0-678-05732-X); Vol. 4. North East England. Hoole, K. 237p. 1965. o.p. (ISBN 0-678-05733-8); Vol. 5. The Eastern Counties. Gordon, Donald I. LC 76-385595. (Illus.). 256p. 1968. 12.95x (ISBN 0-678-05734-6). Kelley.

Thomas, David M., ed. Marital Spirituality. LC 78-69753. (Marriage & Family Living in Depth Bk.). 1978. pap. 2.45 o.p. (ISBN 0-87029-139-4, 20222-6). Abbey.

Thomas, David O. The Honest Mind: The Thought & Work of Richard Price. 1977. text ed. 55.00x (ISBN 0-19-824571-8). Oxford U Pr.

Thomas, David S. & Bermont, Hubert. Getting Published. 1974. pap. 4.95i (ISBN 0-06-090382-1, CN382, CN). Har-Row.

Thomas, Dawn C. I Love My Cat. (Illus.). 1982. pap. write for info (ISBN 0-9610186-0-7). Boojum Pr.

Thomas, Denis. Picasso & His Art. (The Artist & His Art Ser.). (Illus.). 128p. 1981. 9.98 o.p. (ISBN 0-89196-092-9, Bk Value Intl). Quality Bks IL.

Thomas, Dian. Roughing It Easy. (Illus.). 248p. 1976. pap. 3.50 (ISBN 0-446-30643-6). Warner Bks.

--Roughing It Easy, Two. (Illus.). 224p. (Orig.). 1978. pap. 3.50 (ISBN 0-446-30644-4). Warner Bks.

--Today's Tips for Easy Living. 160p. 1982. pap. 5.95 (ISBN 0-89586-167-4). H P Bks.

Thomas, Diane C. How to Save Money on Your Business Rent: A Tenant's Guide to Office & Retail Leasing. LC 79-84224. 1979. 14.95 o.p. (ISBN 0-933690-00-2). Peachtree Park.

Thomas, Donald. Robert Browning: A Life Within Life. 352p. 1983. 18.75 (ISBN 0-670-60090-3). Viking Pr.

--State Trials, 2 vols. Incl. Vol. 1. Treason & Libel (ISBN 0-7100-7325-9); Vol. 2. The Public Conscience (ISBN 0-7100-7326-7). (Illus.). 1972. Set. 35.00x o.p. (ISBN 0-685-25617-0); 20.00 ea. o.p. Routledge & Kegan.

--Swinburne: The Poet of His World. 1979. 17.95x (ISBN 0-19-520136-1). Oxford U Pr.

--Welcome to the Grand Hotel. 68p. 1975. 12.50 (ISBN 0-7100-8104-9). Routledge & Kegan.

Thomas, Donald R. The Schools Next Time: Explorations in Educational Sociology. 192p. 1973. pap. text ed. 7.95 o.p. (ISBN 0-07-064245-1, C). McGraw.

Thomas, Donald W. Semiotics 1: Signs, Language & Reality. 2nd ed. (Illus.). 239p. (Orig.). 1980. pap. text ed. 7.95 (ISBN 0-536-03240-8); handbk., 78p. 2.95 (ISBN 0-536-03250-5). Ginn Custom.

--Semiotics 2: Communication in Man & Beast. (Illus.). 248p. (Orig.). 1983. pap. text ed. 10.95 (ISBN 0-536-03133-9). Ginn Custom.

--Semiotics 3: Communication, Codes & Culture. (Illus.). 58p. (Orig.). 1982. pap. text ed. 3.95 (ISBN 0-536-03997-6). Ginn Custom.

--Semiotics 4: Language in the Making. (Illus., Orig.). 1983. pap. text ed. 4.00x (ISBN 0-536-04041-9). Ginn Custom.

Thomas, Dorothy, jt. ed. see Gregerson, Marilyn.

Thomas, Dorothy S. The Salvage. 1975. Repr. of 1952 ed. 37.50x (ISBN 0-520-02915-1). U of Cal Pr.

Thomas, Dorothy S. & Nishimoto, Richard. The Spoilage: Japanese-American Evacuation & Resettlement During World War Two. (California Library Reprint Ser.). 1974. Repr. 32.50x (ISBN 0-520-02637-3). U of Cal Pr.

Thomas, Dylan. Early Prose Writings. Davies, Walford, ed. LC 70-159741. 1972. 10.00 o.p. (ISBN 0-8112-0395-6). New Directions.

--Letters to Vernon Watkins. Watkins, Vernon, intro. by. LC 82-15823. (Illus.). 145p. 1982. Repr. of 1957 ed. lib. bdg. 25.00x (ISBN 0-313-23746-8, THLV). Greenwood.

--Rebecca's Daughters. LC 82-7986. (Illus.). 160p. 1982. Repr. 8.50 (ISBN 0-8112-0852-4). New Directions.

Thomas, E., et al. From Single Cells to Plants. (Wykeham Science Ser.: No. 38). 188p. 1975. 9.95x (ISBN 0-8448-1453-9). Crane Russak Co.

Thomas, E. J. Understanding & Experiencing Prayer. (Lets Discuss It Ser.). pap. 0.95 (ISBN 0-88172-130-1); pap. 9.50 o.p. Believers Bkshelf.

Thomas, Earl W. A Grammar of Spoken Brazilian Portuguese. LC 74-16228. 192p. 1975. pap. text ed. 7.95x (ISBN 0-8265-1197-X). Vanderbilt U Pr.

Thomas, Edith. Eve & the Others. Eirinberg, Estelle, tr. from Fr. LC 75-36694. 125p. 1976. case bound 6.95 (ISBN 0-916868-01-X); pap. 3.50. Continent Edns.

Thomas, Edward. From Quarks to Quasars. 1977. pap. text ed. 13.25x (ISBN 0-485-12024-0, Athlone Pr). Humanities.

--The Icknield Way. 320p. 1982. 30.00x (ISBN 0-7045-0407-3, Pub. by Wildwood House). State Mutual Bk.

--In Pursuit of Spring. 302p. 1982. 30.00x (ISBN 0-7045-0423-5, Pub. by Wildwood House). State Mutual Bk.

Thomas, Edwin J., ed. New Models of Social Service Research. (Journal of Social Service Research Ser.: Vol. 2, No. 1). 140p. (Orig.). 1979. pap. text ed. 10.00 (ISBN 0-917724-71-2, B71). Haworth Pr.

Thomas, Elaine. A Grammatical Description of the Engenni Language. (Publications in Linguistics & Related Fields: No. 60). 191p. 1978. pap. 9.75x (ISBN 0-88312-074-7); 2.25 (ISBN 0-686-86780-7). Summer Inst Ling.

Thomas, Elaine & Benton, C. E. Safe Chain Saw Design. 1983. write for info. (ISBN 0-938830-02-3). Inst Product.

Thomas, Elbert D. Chinese Political Thought: A Study Based Upon the Theories of the Principal Thinkers of the Chou Period. LC 68-23333. 1968. Repr. of 1927 ed. lib. bdg. 18.75x (ISBN 0-8371-0248-0, THCP). Greenwood.

Thomas, Emory M. American War & Peace, Eighteen Sixty to Eighteen Seventy-Seven. (Illus.). 240p. 1973. pap. 14.95 (ISBN 0-13-032391-8). P-H.

--Confederate Nation Eighteen Sixty-One to Eighteen Sixty-Five. Commager, Henry S. & Morris, Richard B., eds. LC 76-26255. (New American Nation Ser.). (Illus.). 1979. 16.30xi (ISBN 0-06-014252-9, HarpT); pap. 6.95xi (ISBN 0-06-131965-1). Har-Row.

--The Confederate State of Richmond: A Biography of the Capital. (Illus.). 237p. 1971. 15.00 o.p. (ISBN 0-292-70085-7). U of Tex Pr.

Thomas, Sr. Evangeline, ed. Women's Religious History Sources. 400p. 1983. 65.00 (ISBN 0-8352-1681-0). Bowker.

Thomas, F. Richard. Literary Admirers of Alfred Stieglitz. LC 82-10543. 116p. 1983. price not set (ISBN 0-8093-1097-X). S Ill U Pr.

Thomas Foundation. Keys to Understanding & Teaching Your Bible. (Illus.). 1983. pap. 5.95 (ISBN 0-8407-5826-X). Nelson.

Thomas, Frank & Johnston, Ollie. Disney Animation: The Illusion of Life. LC 81-12699. (Illus.). 576p. 1981. text ed. 59.95 (ISBN 0-89659-232-4); collector's edition 125.00 (ISBN 0-89659-233-2). Abbeville Pr.

Thomas, Frank, jt. auth. see Gooden, George.

Thomas, G. & Finney, R. Elements of Calculus & Analytic Geometry. 4th ed. (gr. 11-12). 1981. text ed. 24.00 (ISBN 0-201-07664-0, Sch Div); cancelled tchrs' commentary (ISBN 0-201-07665-9); solns. manual s.p. 25.00 (ISBN 0-201-07666-7); self study manual 8.40 (ISBN 0-201-07667-5). A-W.

Thomas, Gail, ed. see Layard, et al.

Thomas, Gareth & Goringe, Michael J. Transmission Electron Microscopy of Materials. LC 79-449. 388p. 1979. 36.95x (ISBN 0-471-12244-0, Pub. by Wiley-Interscience). Wiley.

Thomas, Geoffrey, jt. ed. see Barnaby, Frank.

Thomas, Geoffrey, jt. ed. see Davies, Bruce.

Thomas, George B., Jr. Elements of Calculus. 3rd ed. (gr. 11-12). 1976. text ed. 24.00 (ISBN 0-201-07549-0, Sch Div); Tchr's. Commentary 9.72 (ISBN 0-201-07547-4); Solutions Manual 25.20 (ISBN 0-201-07545-8). A-W.

Thomas, George B., Jr. & Finney, Ross L. Calculus & Analytic Geometry. 5th ed. LC 78-55832. (Illus.). 1979. Combined Ed. text ed. 33.95 (ISBN 0-201-07540-7); Pt. 1. 24.95 (ISBN 0-201-07541-5); Pt. 2. 23.95 (ISBN 0-201-07542-3); avail. Gill: student suppl. 10.95 (ISBN 0-201-07543-1); avail. Weir: self study guide 10.95 (ISBN 0-201-07655-1); solmano 13.95 (ISBN 0-201-07544-X). A-W.

Thomas, George H. Building the Universal Pillartool. (Illus.). 144p. (Orig.). 1982. pap. 10.50x (ISBN 0-85242-785-9). Intl Pubns Serv.

Thomas, George L., Jr Goldfish Pools, Water Lilies & Tropical Fish. (Illus.). 1965. 19.95 (ISBN 0-87666-080-4, H919). TFH Pubns.

Thomas, Gerald W., et al. Food & Fiber for a Changing World. 2nd ed. 1982. 12.50x (ISBN 0-8134-2154-3). Interstate.

Thomas Graham Memorial Symposium. Diffusion Processes: Proceedings. Sherwood, J. N., ed. 1971. Set. 175.00 (ISBN 0-677-14260-9); Vol. 1. 92.00 (ISBN 0-677-14820-8); Vol. 2, 444p. 103.00 (ISBN 0-677-14830-5). Gordon.

Thomas, Graham S. Climbing Roses: Old & New. (Illus.). 208p. 1983. text ed. 21.95x (ISBN 0-460-04604-7, Pub by J. M. Dent England). Biblio Dist.

Thomas, H. Electronic Vest Pocket Reference Book. 1969. 6.95 (ISBN 0-13-252361-2). P-H.

Thomas, H. C., jt. auth. see Meites, Louis.

Thomas, H. R. Better Understanding. (Better Ser.). (Illus.). (gr. 9 up). 10.50x (ISBN 0-392-02268-0, SpS). Sportshelf.

Thomas, H. Randolph, jt. ed. see Willenbrock, Jack H.

Thomas, Helen. Time & Again: Memoirs & Letters. Thomas, Myfanwy, ed. (Essay & Prose Ser.). (Illus.). 159p. 1978. 11.95x (ISBN 0-85635-243-8, Pub. by Carcanet New Pr England). Humanities.

Thomas, Helen S. An Enterlude Called Lusty Iuuentus. Liuely Describing the Frailtie of Youth, or Nature Prone to Vyce: By Grace & Good Councell Traynable to Vertue, by R. Wever, An Old Spelling Critical Edition. LC 80-9008. (Garland English Texts Ser.). 1982. lib. bdg. 35.00 (ISBN 0-8240-9406-9). Garland Pub.

Thomas, Henry H. The Engineering of Large Dams. LC 75-15886. 777p. 1976. 2 vol. set 189.00x (ISBN 0-471-01528-8, Pub. by Wiley-Interscience). Wiley.

Thomas, Hilah F. & Keller, Rosemary S., eds. Women in New Worlds: Vol. 1. LC 81-7984. (Historical Perspectives on the Wesleyan Tradition Ser.). 448p. (Orig.). 1981. pap. 18.95 (ISBN 0-687-45968-0). Abingdon.

Thomas, Hilary. Complete Games of Mikhail Tal, 1967-1973. LC 79-16617. 1980. 12.95 o.p. (ISBN 0-668-04832-8, 4832-8). Arco.

--Complete Games of Mikhail Tal, 1974-1980. LC 81-65573. 160p. 1981. (ISBN 0-668-05265-1, 5265). Arco.

Thomas, Hilary, ed. Complete Games of Mikhail Tal, 1960-1966. LC 79-50276. 1979. 12.95 o.p. (ISBN 0-668-04772-0, 4772-0). Arco.

Thomas, Homer L. Near Eastern Mediterranean & European Chronology: The Historical, Archaeological Radiocarbon Pollenanalytical & Geochronological Evidence, 2 vols. (Studies in Mediterranean Archaeeolgy Ser: No. Xvii,). (Illus.). 1967. Set. pap. text ed. 30.00x (ISBN 0-686-77194-X). Vol. 1 (ISBN 9-1850-5816-5). Vol. 2 (ISBN 9-1850-5817-3). Humanities.

Thomas, Howard, jt. auth. see Hertz, David.

Thomas, Howard, jt. auth. see Hertz, David B.

Thomas, Hugh. Cuba: The Pursuit of Freedom, 1762-1969. LC 65-20442. (Illus.). 1971. 33.65i (ISBN 0-06-014259-6, HarpT). Har-Row.

--A History of the World. LC 79-1688. (Illus.). 1979. 19.18i (ISBN 0-06-014281-2, HarpT). Har-Row.

Thomas, Ianthe. Hi, Mrs. Mallory! LC 78-3013. (Illus.). (gr. k-3). 1979. 7.95i o.p. (ISBN 0-06-026128-5, HarpJ); PLB 9.89 (ISBN 0-06-026129-3). Har-Row.

--Lordy, Aunt Hattie. LC 72-9857. (Illus.). (ps-3). 1973. 9.57i (ISBN 0-06-026114-5, HarpJ). Har-Row.

--The Time Junkie. LC 78-52821. (gr. 7 up). Date not set. 6.95cancelled o.p. (ISBN 0-15-288191-3). HarBraceJ.

--Walk Home Tired Billy Jenkins. LC 73-5497. (Illus.). (gr. 4-6). 1974. PLB 9.89 (ISBN 0-06-026109-9, HarpJ). Har-Row.

Thomas, J., jt. ed. see Cohen, L.

Thomas, J. A. Textbook of Roman Law. 1976. text ed. 38.50 (ISBN 0-7204-0513-0, North-Holland); pap. text ed. 21.00 (ISBN 0-7204-0517-3). Elsevier.

Thomas, J. Alan, jt. ed. see Dreeben, Robert.

Thomas, J. B. Shop Boy: An Autobiography. 182p. 1983. 13.95 (ISBN 0-7100-9347-0). Routledge & Kegan.

Thomas, J. B., jt. ed. see Kassam, S. A.

Thomas, J. D. The Message of the New Testament Romans. LC 82-70933. (Way of Life Ser.: 166). (Illus.). 108p. 1982. pap. 3.95 (ISBN 0-89112-166-8). Bibl Res Pr.

Thomas, J. D., jt. auth. see Griffiths, P. J.

Thomas, J. E. English Prison Officer since Eighteen Fifty: A Study in Conflict. (International Library of Social Policy). 1972. 24.00x (ISBN 0-7100-7280-5). Routledge & Kegan.

Thomas, J. F., jt. auth. see Bennet, D.

Thomas, J. Heywood. Paul Tillich. Nineham, D. E. & Robertson, E. H., eds. LC 66-11072. (Makers of Contemporary Theology Ser). 1966. pap. 1.99 (ISBN 0-8042-0678-3). John Knox.

Thomas, J. M. & Lambert, R. M. Characterization of Catalysts. LC 80-40961. 324p. 1981. 52.95x (ISBN 0-471-27874-2, Pub. by Wiley-Interscience). Wiley.

Thomas, J. M., et al, eds. see Royal Society of London.

Thomas, J. W., tr. from Ger. The Best Novellas of Medieval Germany. (Studies in German Literature, Linguistics, & Culture: Vol. 17). (Illus.). 160p. 1983. 15.00x (ISBN 0-938100-10-6). Camden Hse.

Thomas, J. W., tr. see Hartman, Von Aue.

Thomas, J. W., tr. see Hartmann Von Aue.

Thomas, James A. Holy War. 1974. 8.95 o.p. (ISBN 0-87000-215-5, Arlington Hse). Crown.

--Symbolic Logic. (Philosophy Ser.). 1977. text ed. 14.95 (ISBN 0-675-08558-6). Additional supplements may be obtained from publisher. Merrill.

Thomas, James L. Nonprint Production for Students, Teachers, & Media Specialists: A Step-by-Step Guide. 180p. 1982. lib. bdg. 22.50 (ISBN 0-87287-337-4). Libs Unl.

--Turning Kids on to Print Using Nonprint. LC 78-9075. (Illus.). 168p. 1978. lib. bdg. 18.50 (ISBN 0-87287-184-3). Libs Unl.

Thomas, James L. & Loring, Ruth. Motivating Children & Young Adults to Read. 2nd ed. 1983. price not set (ISBN 0-89774-046-7). Oryx Pr.

Thomas, James L., jt. auth. see Brizendine, Nancy H.

Thomas, James L., ed. Cartoons & Comics in the Classroom: A Reference for Teachers & Librarians. LC 82-17957. 182p. 1983. lib. bdg. 18.50 (ISBN 0-87287-357-9). Libs Unl.

--Nonprint in the Secondary Curriculum: Readings for Reference. LC 81-18596. 215p. 1982. text ed. 19.50 (ISBN 0-87287-274-2). Libs Unl.

Thomas, James L., jt. ed. see Thomas, Carol H.

Thomas, Jane R. Elizabeth Catches a Fish. LC 76-28318. (Illus.). (gr. 1-4). 1976. 6.95 (ISBN 0-395-28827-4, Clarion). HM.

Thomas, Jean. Devil's Ditties: Being Stories of the Kentucky Mountain People, Told by Jean Thomas, with the Songs They Sing. LC 75-16369. (Illus.). viii, 180p. 1976. Repr. of 1931 ed. 40.00x (ISBN 0-8103-3999-4). Gale.

Thomas, Jeff. Oregon Rock: A Climber's Guide. (Illus.). 132p. (Orig.). 1983. pap. 7.95 (ISBN 0-89886-040-7). Mountaineers.

Thomas, John. Leonardo Da Vinci. LC 57-6244. (Illus.). (gr. 6-10). 1957. 9.95 o.s.i. (ISBN 0-87599-112-2). S G Phillips.

--Rise of the Staffordshire Potteries. LC 69-17618. (Illus.). 1971. lib. bdg. 20.00x o.p. (ISBN 0-678-07750-9). Kelley.

Thomas, John A. & Keenan, Edward J. Handbook of Endocrine Pharmacology. 1983. 25.00 (ISBN 0-8067-1901-X). Urban & S.

Thomas, John A., jt. ed. see Singhal, Radhey L.

Thomas, John L. Alternative America: Henry George, Edward Bellamy, Henry Demarest Lloyd & the Adversary Tradition. (Illus.). 416p. 1983. 25.00x (ISBN 0-674-01676-9). Harvard U Pr.

Thomas, John M., jt. auth. see Slater, Barbara R.

Thomas, Joseph. Universal Pronouncing Dictionary of Biography & Mythology, 2 vols. LC 79-167222. 1976. Repr. of 1870 ed. Set. 196.00x (ISBN 0-8103-4221-9). Gale.

Thomas, Joseph see Brehier, Emile.

Thomas, Josephine H., jt. ed. see Harrington, Mildred P.

Thomas, Judith, jt. auth. see Gagne, Danai A.

Thomas, Justine & King, David. Santa Fe the City Different. (Illus.). 48p. (Orig.). 1979. pap. 4.95 (ISBN 0-913270-21-0). Sunstone Pr.

Thomas, K., ed. Housewife Guide to Meat. pap. 5.00x (ISBN 0-392-06207-0, SpS). Sportshelf.

Thomas, Kas. Personal Aircraft Maintenance. (Aviation Ser.). (Illus.). 256p. 1980. 21.95 (ISBN 0-07-064241-9, P&RB). McGraw.

Thomas, Kathleen. Nifkin. LC 82-45375. (Illus.). 160p. (gr. 3-6). 1982. PLB 8.95 (ISBN 0-396-08089-8). Dodd.

--Out of the Bug Jar. (Illus.). 128p. (gr. 3-6). 1981. PLB 7.95 (ISBN 0-396-07992-X). Dodd.

Thomas, Keith, ed. see Barnes, Johnathan.

Thomas, Keith, ed. see Burke, Peter.

Thomas, Keith, ed. see Carpenter, Humphrey.

Thomas, Keith, ed. see Dawson, Raymond.

Thomas, Keith, ed. see Drake, Stiliman.

Thomas, Keith, ed. see Griffin, Jasper.

Thomas, Keith, ed. see Hare, R. M.

Thomas, Keith, ed. see Howard, Jonathan.

Thomas, Keith, jt. ed. see Pennington, Donald.

Thomas, L. C. Interpretation of the Infrared Spectra of Organophosphorus Compounds. 1974. 83.00 (ISBN 0-471-26036-3, Wiley Heyden). Wiley.

--New Chemical Structure. 1982. text ed. 36.95 (ISBN 0-471-26112-2, Pub. by Wiley-Interscience). Wiley.

Thomas, L. C. & Chamberlin, G. J. Colorimetric Chemical Analytical Methods. 9th ed. LC 79-56635. 626p. 1980. 113.95x (ISBN 0-471-27605-7, Pub. by Wiley-Interscience). Wiley.

Thomas, L. C., jt. auth. see Getz, M. E.

Thomas, L. C., ed. see Carrick, A.

Thomas, L. C., ed. see Tromp, S. W.

Thomas, L. J. An Introduction to Mining: Exploration, Feasibility, Extraction, Rock Mechanics. LC 73-14857. 1977. pap. 24.95 o.p. (ISBN 0-470-99220-4). Halsted Pr.

Thomas, L. Joseph, jt. auth. see Dyckman, Thomas.

Thomas, L. Joseph, jt. auth. see Dyckman, Thomas R.

Thomas, L. Murray, jt. auth. see Gurdjian, E. Stephen.

Thomas, L. W., jt. auth. see Ouellette, Robert P.

Thomas, Leslie. Bare Nell. LC 78-3960. 1978. 8.95 o.p. (ISBN 0-312-06641-4). St Martin.

Thomas, Leslie G. One Hundred Sermons: Outlines. 7.50 (ISBN 0-89225-136-0). Gospel Advocate.

Thomas, Lewis. The Medusa & the Snail. (General Ser.). 1979. lib. bdg. 10.95 (ISBN 0-8161-3013-2, Large Print Bks). G K Hall.

--The Youngest Science: Notes of a Medicine Watcher. (Alfred P. Sloan Foundation Ser.). 300p. 1983. 14.75 (ISBN 0-670-79533-X). Viking Pr.

Thomas, Linda. Caring & Cooking for the Allergic Child. rev. ed. LC 79-91379. (Illus.). 144p. 1980. 12.95 (ISBN 0-8069-5552-X); lib. bdg. 15.69 (ISBN 0-8069-5553-8); pap. 6.95 (ISBN 0-8069-8906-8). Sterling.

Thomas, Lindon. Fundamentals of Heat Transfer. (Illus.). 1980. text ed. 33.95 (ISBN 0-13-339903-6). P-H.

Thomas, Lisa. So Narrow the Bridge & Deep the Water. LC 80-52865. 156p. 1980. pap. 4.95 (ISBN 0-931188-08-3). Seal Pr WA.

Thomas, Lloyd B. Money, Banking, & Economic Activity. 2nd ed. (Illus.). 576p. 1982. text ed. 23.95 (ISBN 0-13-599985-5). P-H.

Thomas, Lloyd B., Jr. Money, Banking & Economic Activity. (Illus.). 1979. ref. 21.00 o.p. (ISBN 0-13-599969-3). P-H.

Thomas, Lowell. Good Evening Everybody. (General Ser.). 1980. lib. bdg. 15.95 (ISBN 0-8161-3024-8, Large Print Bks). G K Hall.

Thomas, Lynn. The Backpacking Woman. LC 80-15275. 288p. (Orig.). 1980. pap. 7.95 (ISBN 0-385-15303-1, Anch). Doubleday.

Thomas, M. A Guide to the Preparation of Civil Engineering Drawings. 1982. 65.00x (ISBN 0-333-28081-4, Pub. by Macmillan England). State Mutual Bk.

Thomas, M. Donald. Your School: How Well is it Working. 73p. 1982. 3.50 (ISBN 0-934460-18-3). NCCE.

Thomas, M. G. Export Marketing (Spanish) 102p. 1978. pap. text ed. 8.95x (ISBN 0-582-35159-6). Longman.

Thomas, M. K., jt. auth. see Hare, F. K.

Thomas, M. V. Techniques in Calcium Research. (Biological Techniques Ser.). 26.50 (ISBN 0-12-688680-6). Acad Pr.

Thomas, Mai, ed. Grannies' Remedies. (Illus.). 1967. 4.95 o.p. (ISBN 0-685-11958-0). Heineman.

Thomas, Marlo, et al. Free to Be... You & Me. LC 73-14784. (Illus.). 144p. 1974. 10.95 (ISBN 0-07-064223-0, GB); pap. 7.95 (ISBN 0-07-064224-9). McGraw.

Thomas, Marvin. Architectural Working Drawings. (Illus.). 1978. 24.50 (ISBN 0-07-064240-0, P&RB). McGraw.

Thomas, Mary. Mary Thomas's Book of Knitting Patterns. (Illus.). 9.50 (ISBN 0-8446-4611-3). Peter Smith.

--Mary Thomas's Knitting Book. (Illus.). 9.00 (ISBN 0-8446-4617-2). Peter Smith.

Thomas, Mary, ed. see American School of Needlework.

Thomas, Melvin, jt. ed. see Immerzeel, George.

Thomas, Michael. Studien Zur Short Story Als Fiktional-Narrative Textform und die Moglichkeiten Einer Typenbildung. 390p. (Ger.). 1982. write for info. (ISBN 3-8204-6267-8). P Lang Pubs.

Thomas, Michael, jt. auth. see Boot, Adrian.

Thomas, Michael M. Someone Else's Money. 384p. 1982. 14.95 (ISBN 0-671-43302-4). S&S.

Thomas, Millard. Home from Seven North. LC 81-83739. 1983. 15.00 (ISBN 0-87212-158-5). Libra.

Thomas, Myfanwy, ed. see Thomas, Helen.

Thomas, Nancy, tr. see Solzhenitsyn, Alexander.

Thomas, Nicholas. Guide to Prehistoric England. 1977. 27.00 o.p. (ISBN 0-7134-3267-5, Pub. by Batsford England); pap. 12.50 (ISBN 0-7134-3268-3, Pub. by Batsford England). David & Charles.

Thomas, Nigel. City Rider: How to Survive with Your Bike. (Illus.). 160p. 1981. pap. 10.95 (ISBN 0-241-10575-7, Pub. by Hamish Hamilton England). David & Charles.

--The French Foreign Legion. LC 77-283. (History Makers Ser.). (Illus.). (YA) 1977. 6.95 o.p. (ISBN 0-312-30465-X). St Martin.

Thomas, Noel. The Narrative Works of Guenter Grass: A Critical Interpretation. (German Language & Literature Monographs: 12). 370p. 1983. 38.00 (ISBN 90-272-4005-1). Benjamins North Am.

Thomas, Norman. Great Dissenters. 1970. pap. 3.95x o.p. (ISBN 0-393-00529-1, Norton Lib). Norton.

Thomas, Norman & Wilson, Edmund. Who Killed Carlo Tresca? Mope, Warren, ed. 36p. 1983. pap. 3.95x (ISBN 0-911687-00-9). Mountain Laurel.

Thomas, Norman, jt. auth. see Laidler, Harry W.

Thomas, Norman C. Rule Nine: Politics, Administration & Civil Rights. (Orig.). 1966. pap. text ed. 2.95 (ISBN 0-685-19764-6). Phila Bk Co.

Thomas, Norman C. & Lamb, Karl A. Congress: Politics & Practice. (Orig.). 1964. pap. text ed. 3.40x (ISBN 0-685-19714-X). Phila Bk Co.

Thomas, Norman C. & Stoerker, Fredrick C. Your American Government. LC 79-26788. 1980. text ed. 22.95 (ISBN 0-471-03031-7); write for info tchr's ed (ISBN 0-471-06330-4); study guide (ISBN 0-471-07907-3). Wiley.

Thomas, Norman M. Is Conscience a Crime? LC 77-137554. (Peace Movement in America Ser). Orig. Title: The Conscientious Objector in America. xiii, 303p. 1972. Repr. of 1927 ed. lib. bdg. 19.95x (ISBN 0-89198-084-9). Ozer.

--The Prerequisites for Peace. LC 78-13967. 1978. Repr. of 1959 ed. lib. bdg. 17.00x (ISBN 0-313-20732-1, THPP). Greenwood.

Thomas, Owen. Metaphor & Related Subjects. (Orig.). 1969. pap. text ed. 2.25 (ISBN 0-685-19745-X). Phila Bk Co.

Thomas, Owen G. Introduction to Theology. 2nd ed. LC 82-61890. 304p. 1983. pap. 12.95 (ISBN 0-8192-1319-5). Morehouse.

Thomas, P. D. G., jt. ed. see Simmons, R. C.

Thomas, Pamela, ed. see Ritter, Lawrence S. & Honig, Donald.

Thomas, Paul. Karl Marx & the Anarchists. 448p. 1980. 25.00 (ISBN 0-7100-0427-3). Routledge & Kegan.

Thomas, Paul H., ed. see Gentry, Howard S. & Thomson, Paul H.

Thomas, Paul I. How to Estimate Building Losses & Construction Costs. 3rd ed. (Illus.). 1976. 18.00 o.p. (ISBN 0-13-405886-0, Parker). P-H.

Thomas, Paul I. & Reed, Prentiss B., Sr. Adjustment of Property Losses. 4th ed. (Illus.). 1977. text ed. 25.90 (ISBN 0-07-064215-X, G); instructor's manual & key 6.15 (ISBN 0-07-064216-8). McGraw.

Thomas, Peter. Working with Acrylics: An Introductory Course for Schools. (Technical Drawing Ser.). (gr. 11-12). 1979. 24.00x o.p. (ISBN 0-435-75980-9); information cards 10.00x o.p. (ISBN 0-435-75981-7). Heinemann Ed.

Thomas, Peter D. Lord North. LC 75-29819. (British Political Biography Ser.). 175p. 1975. 22.50 (ISBN 0-312-49840-3). St Martin.

Thomas, Philip A., ed. Law in the Balance: Legal Services in the 1980s. (Law in Society Ser.). 256p. 1981. text ed. 40.00x (ISBN 0-85520-444-3, Pub. by Martin Robertson Co); pap. text ed. 9.95x (ISBN 0-85520-482-6). Biblio Dist.

Thomas, Philippe & Destang, Francoise. Please, Lord. (Rejoice Ser.). (ps). pap. 0.35 o.p. (ISBN 0-8091-6513-9). Paulist Pr.

Thomas, Phyllis, jt. auth. see Thomas, Bill.

Thomas, R. H. & Bullivant, K. Literature in Upheaval. 1974. 17.00 (ISBN 0-7190-0576-0). Manchester.

Thomas, R. Murray. Comparing Theories of Child Development. 1978. text ed. 26.95x (ISBN 0-534-00591-8). Wadsworth Pub.

Thomas, R. P., jt. auth. see North, D. C.

Thomas, R. S. H'm. 1973. 4.95 o.p. (ISBN 0-312-35595-5). St Martin.

Thomas, R. T. Britain & Vichy: The Dilemma of Anglo-French Relations, 1940-42. (The Making of the Twentieth Century Ser.). 1979. 22.50 (ISBN 0-312-09822-7). St Martin.

Thomas, R. W., ed. see Jones, C. E.

Thomas, Ralph. Handbook of Fictitious Names. LC 70-90248. 1969. Repr. of 1868 ed. 34.00x (ISBN 0-8103-3145-4). Gale.

Thomas, Ray. Planting & Growing a Fundamental Church. 1979. 7.95 (ISBN 0-89265-055-9). Randall Hse.

Thomas, Rick. The Money Manager: A Personal Finance Simulation. 1983. ring binder 74.95 (ISBN 0-88408-166-4); pap. 5.95 student manual (ISBN 0-88408-167-2). Sterling Swift.

Thomas, Robert & Gundry, Stanley. A Harmony of the Gospels. LC 78-16048. 1978. 13.95 (ISBN 0-8024-3413-4). Moody.

Thomas, Robert C., ed. New Research Centers: Interedition Supplements to Research Centers. 4th ed. LC 60-14807. 300p. 1982. 160.00x (ISBN 0-8103-0451-1). Gale.

--Research Centers Directory: A Guide to University-Related & Other Non-Profit Research Organizations Established on a Permanent Basis & Carrying on Continuing Research Programs. 7th ed. 1300p. 1982. 180.00x (ISBN 0-8103-0455-4). Gale.

Thomas, Robert C. & Ruffner, James A., eds. New Research Centers: A Periodic Supplement to Research Centers Directory. 250p. 1982. 160.00x (ISBN 0-8103-0457-0). Gale.

Thomas, Robert C. & Watkins, Michelle, eds. Research Centers Directory. 8th ed. 1200p. 1983. 200.00x (ISBN 0-8103-0458-9). Gale.

Thomas, Robert C., jt. ed. see Kruzas, Anthony T.

Thomas, Robert C., jt. ed. see Ruffner, Frederick G., Jr.

Thomas, Robert C., et al, eds. National Directory of Newsletters & Reporting Services, 4 pts. 2nd ed. LC 77-99180. 669p. 1981. pap. 95.00x (ISBN 0-8103-0676-X). Gale.

Thomas, Robert N. & Hunter, John M., eds. Internal Migration Systems in the Developing World: With Special Reference to Latin America. 1980. lib. bdg. 19.95 (ISBN 0-8161-8414-3, Univ Bks). G K Hall.

Thomas, Roger W. After the Spirit Comes. LC 77-83659. 1979. pap. 1.95 (ISBN 0-87239-194-9, 40049). Standard Pub.

Thomas, Rosie. Love's Choice. (Avon Romance Ser.). 352p. 1982. pap. 2.95 (ISBN 0-380-61713-7). Avon.

Thomas, Ross. The Mordida Man. 1983. pap. 2.95 (ISBN 0-425-05330-X). Berkley Pub.

--The Mordida Man. 1981. 13.95 o.p. (ISBN 0-671-42186-7). S&S.

Thomas, Roy, ed. Insurance Information Sources. LC 75-137575. (Management Information Guide Ser.: No. 24). 1971. 42.00x (ISBN 0-8103-0824-X). Gale.

Thomas, Ruth. Broadcasting & Democracy in France. LC 77-90540. (International & Comparative Broadcasting Ser.). 223p. 1977. 24.95 (ISBN 0-87722-110-3). Temple U Pr.

Thomas, Sari. Communication Theory & Interpersonal Interaction. 308p. 1983. text ed. 29.50 (ISBN 0-89391-134-8). Ablex Pub.

--Studies in Mass Communication. (Studies in Mass Communication & Technology). 308p. 1983. text ed. 29.50 (ISBN 0-89391-133-X). Ablex Pub.

Thomas, Sari, ed. Film-Culture: Explorations of Cinema in Its Social Context. LC 81-23254. 281p. 1982. 17.50 (ISBN 0-8108-1519-2); pap. 8.50 (ISBN 0-8108-1520-6). Scarecrow.

Thomas, Stephen C. Foreign Intervention & China's Industrial Development, 1870-1911. (Replica Edition). 200p. 1982. lib. bdg. 19.00x o.p. (ISBN 0-86531-912-X). Westview.

Thomas, Stephen N. Practical Reasoning in Natural Language. (Illus.). 352p. 1981. pap. text ed. 14.95 (ISBN 0-13-692137-X). P-H.

Thomas, Sydney F., jt. auth. see Weigen, John F.

Thomas, T. A. Technical Illustration. 3rd ed. (Illus.). 1978. pap. text ed. 22.95 (ISBN 0-07-064228-1, G). McGraw.

Thomas Telford Editorial Staff, Ltd. A Century of Soil Mechanics. 490p. 1980. 35.00x (ISBN 0-901948-15-2, Pub. by Telford England). State Mutual Bk.

Thomas, Terry. At Least We Were Married. 156p. (gr. 10 up). 1973. Repr. pap. 2.95 o.p. (ISBN 0-310-36932-0). Zondervan.

Thomas, Tony. The Films of Olivia de Havilland. (Illus.). 256p. 1983. 18.95 (ISBN 0-8065-0805-1). Citadel Pr.

Thomas, Tony, jt. auth. see Fawcett, Edmund.

Thomas, Tracy Y. Concepts from Tensor Analysis & Differential Geometry. 2nd ed. (Mathematics in Science & Engineering: Vol. 1). 1965. 31.50 o.p. (ISBN 0-12-688462-5). Acad Pr.

--Plastic Flow & Fracture in Solids. (Mathematics in Science & Engineering Ser: Vol. 2). 1961. 46.50 (ISBN 0-12-688450-1). Acad Pr.

Thomas, Ulrich. Applemouse. (Illus.). 40p. (gr. 5 up). 1972. 5.95 o.p. (ISBN 0-8090-2005-X, Terra Magica); 5.95 o.p. Hill & Wang.

Thomas, Ursula & Twaddell, Freeman. Lesestoff. Incl. Physik & Chemie. LC 76-11313 (ISBN 0-299-07194-4); Mensch & Gesellschaft. LC 46-1323 (ISBN 0-299-07184-7); Literatur. LC 76-11317 (ISBN 0-299-07174-X); Biologie. LC 76-11322 (ISBN 0-299-07164-2). 1977. pap. text ed. 6.00 ea. U of Wis Pr.

Thomas, Vaughan. Basketball: Techniques & Tactics. (Illus.). 256p. 1972. 13.95 o.p. (ISBN 0-571-09523-2). Faber & Faber.

Thomas, Violet S. & Schubert, Dexter R. Records Management: Systems & Administration. 416p. 1983. text ed. 20.95 (ISBN 0-471-09094-8); write for info. (ISBN 0-471-89473-7). Wiley.

Thomas, Vivien, ed. see Drayton, Michael.

Thomas, W. H. Principles of Theology. (Canterbury Bks.). pap. 8.95 o.p. (ISBN 0-8010-8844-5). Baker Bk.

Thomas, W. I. Mystery of Godliness. 1964. pap. 3.50 (ISBN 0-310-33252-4). Zondervan.

Thomas, W. I., et al see Bernard, William S.

Thomas, W. L., jt. auth. see Spencer, J. E.

Thomas, W. O., jt. auth. see Meurig, H.

Thomas, Wayne. Bail Reform in America. 1977. 25.75x (ISBN 0-520-03131-8). U of Cal Pr.

Thomas, William A., ed. Law & Science: An Essential Alliance. (Special Study). 150p. 1983. lib. bdg. 16.50 (ISBN 0-86531-442-X). Westview.

Thomas, William E. Backstage Broadway: Careers in the Theater. LC 80-10393. (Career Bks.). (Illus.). 160p. (gr. 7 up). 1980. PLB 7.79 o.p. (ISBN 0-671-33002-0). Messner.

--So You Want to Be a Dancer. LC 78-26247. (Illus.). 128p. (gr. 4 up). 1979. PLB 8.79 o.p. (ISBN 0-671-32993-6). Messner.

Thomas, William I. Unadjusted Girl, with Cases & Standpoint for Behavior Analysis. LC 69-14951. (Criminology, Law Enforcement, & Social Problems Ser.: No. 26). 1969. Repr. of 1923 ed. 12.00x (ISBN 0-87585-026-X). Patterson Smith.

Thomas, William I., et al. Old World Traits Transplanted. (Criminology, Law Enforcement, & Social Problems Ser). 1975. 30.00x (ISBN 0-87585-125-8); pap. 7.50x (ISBN 0-87585-905-4). Patterson Smith.

Thomas, William K. History & Evolution of Metered Postage. 1962. 4.75 o.p. (ISBN 0-686-09667-3). Am Philatelic.

Thomas, William L., jt. auth. see Barham, Jerry N.

Thomas, William S. Field Book of Common Mushrooms. rev ed. (Putnam's Nature Field Bks.). (Illus.). 1948. 6.95 o.p. (ISBN 0-399-10285-X). Putnam Pub Group.

Thomas Aquinas. The Grace of Christ. (Summa Theologial Ser.: Vol. 49). 1974. 16.95 (ISBN 0-07-002024-8). McGraw.

Thomas A'Kempes. Imitation of Christ. 3.50 (ISBN 0-448-01644-3, G&D). Putnam Pub Group.

Thomas A Kempis. The Imitation of Christ. 1976. 7.95 o.p. (ISBN 0-385-12313-2). Doubleday.

Thomas A Kempis, Saint Imitation of Christ. 1959. 2.25 o.p. (ISBN 0-685-43925-9, 80955). Glencoe.

--Imitation of Christ. Sherley-Price, Leo, tr. (Classics Ser.). (Orig.). 1952. pap. 3.95 (ISBN 0-14-044027-5). Penguin.

Thomas Aquinas. Activity & Contemplation. (Summa Theologial Ser.). 1966. 12.95 (ISBN 0-07-002021-3). McGraw.

--Charity. (Summa Theologial Ser.: Vol. 34). 1975. 19.95 (ISBN 0-07-002009-4). McGraw.

--Courage. (Summa Theologial Ser.: Vol. 42). 1966. 11.95 (ISBN 0-07-002017-5). McGraw.

--Effects of Sin, Stain & Guilt. (Summa Theological Ser.: Vol. 27). 1974. 14.95 (ISBN 0-07-002002-7). McGraw.

--Faith. (Summa Theologial Ser.: Vol. 31). 1975. 19.95 (ISBN 0-07-002006-X). McGraw.

--The Passion of Christ. (Summa Theologial Ser.: Vol. 54). 1965. 11.95 (ISBN 0-07-002029-9). McGraw.

--The Trinity. (Summa Theologial Ser.: Vol. 6). 1964. 12.95 (ISBN 0-07-001981-9). McGraw.

Thomas Aquinas, Saint Providence & Predestination: Questions 5 & 6 of "Truth". Mulligan, Robert W., tr. 154p. 1961. pap. 5.95 (ISBN 0-89526-937-6). Regnery-Gateway.

--Saint Thomas Aquinas: On Charity. Kendzierski, Lotti H., tr. (Medieval Philosophical Texts in Translation: No. 10). 1960. pap. 7.95 (ISBN 0-87462-210-7). Marquette.

--Saint Thomas Aquinas: On Spiritual Creatures. Fitzpatrick, Mary C., tr. (Medieval Philosophical Texts in Translation: No. 5). 1949. pap. 7.95 (ISBN 0-87462-205-0). Marquette.

Thomas Aquinas, St. Selected Writings of St. Thomas Aquinas. Goodwin, Robert P., tr. Incl. The Principles of Nature; On Being & Essence; On the Virtues in General; On Free Choice. LC 65-26529. (Orig.). 1965. pap. 3.50 (ISBN 0-672-60469-8, LLA217). Bobbs.

--Summa Theologiae, Vol. 1: The Existence of God. Gilby, Thomas, ed. LC 70-84399. pap. 4.95 (ISBN 0-385-02768-0, Im). Doubleday.

--Summa Theologiae, Vol. 48: The Incarnate Word. 1976. 21.95 (ISBN 0-07-002023-X, P&RB). McGraw.

Thomasma, David, jt. auth. see Bergsma, Jurrit.

Thomasma, David C., jt. auth. see Pellegrino, Edmund D.

Thomasma, Kenneth. Naya Nuki: Girl Who Ran. (Voyager Ser.). (Orig.). 1983. pap. 2.95 (ISBN 0-8010-8868-2). Baker Bk.

Thomason, Burke C. Making Sense of Reification: Alfred Schultz & Constructionist Theory. 200p. 1982. text ed. 31.50x (ISBN 0-391-02350-0). Humanities.

Thomason, Michael. Handbook of Solid State Devices: Characteristics & Applications. (Illus.). 1979. ref. 20.00 (ISBN 0-8359-2761-X). Reston.

Thomason, Michael G., jt. auth. see Gonzalez, Rafael C.

Thomason, Myron M. Thomason's Guide to Special Education: A Handbook of Materials & Evaluation Instruments for Special Education. 1978. pap. text ed. 8.45x (ISBN 0-932950-01-9). Athena Pubns.

Thomason, Nevada. Circulation Systems for School Media Centers. (Illus.). 250p. 1983. lib. bdg. 23.50 (ISBN 0-87287-370-6). Libs Unl.

Thomason, R., jt. auth. see Taylor, D.

Thomason, Richmond H. Symbolic Logic: An Introduction. (Illus.). 1970. text ed. 22.95x (ISBN 0-02-420210-X). Macmillan.

Thome, Richard J. & Tarrh, John M. MHD & Fusion Magnets: Field & Force Design Concepts. LC 81-19666. 360p. 1982. 38.95x (ISBN 0-471-09317-3, Pub. by Wiley-Interscience). Wiley.

Thomen, Harold O., compiled by. Supplement to the Index of Congressional Committee Hearings Prior to January 3, 1935. LC 73-7481. 1973. lib. bdg. 35.00x (ISBN 0-8371-5909-1, CHI/). Greenwood.

Thomis, Malcolm & Grimmett, Jennifer. Women in Protest Eighteen Hundred to Eighteen Fifty. LC 81-21290. 166p. 1982. 25.00x (ISBN 0-312-88746-9). St Martin.

Thomis, Malcolm I. The Luddites: Machine-Breaking in Regency England. LC 72-80042. (Studies in the Libertarian & Utopian Tradition). (Illus.). 196p. 1972. pap. 3.95 o.p. (ISBN 0-8052-0369-9). Schocken.

Thomison, Dennis, jt. auth. see Schlachter, Gail.

Thomlinson, Ralph. Sociological Concepts & Research: Acquisition, Analysis, & Interpretation of Social Information. LC 81-40782. 192p. 1981. pap. text ed. 8.25 (ISBN 0-8191-1805-2). U Pr of Amer.

Thomopoulos, N. Applied Forecasting Methods. 1980. 27.95 (ISBN 0-13-040139-0). P-H.

Thompson. The Hitchhikers. (Triumph Bks.). (gr. 6 up). 1980. PLB 8.90 (ISBN 0-531-04115-8, B17). Watts.

--Regulatory Policy & Practices. 270p. 1982. 28.95 (ISBN 0-03-062178-X). Praeger.

--Shakespeare's Chaucer. 252p. 1982. 45.00x (ISBN 0-85323-463-9, Pub. by Liverpool Univ England). State Mutual Bk.

Thompson & Cox. Steps to Better Health: Common Problems & What to Do About Them. 1983. pap. 9.95 (ISBN 0-8359-7077-9). Reston.

Thompson & Swallow. Animals Around Us. (Animal World Books). (gr. 3-6). 1978. 10.95 (ISBN 0-686-36301-9, Usborne-Hayes). EDC.

Thompson, jt. auth. see Harwood.

Thompson, A. Economics of the Firm: Theory & Practice. 3rd ed. 1981. 25.95 (ISBN 0-13-231423-1). P-H.

Thompson, A. M. Bibliography of Nursing Literature: Eighteen Fifty-Nine to Nineteen Sixty. 1969. 61.00x (ISBN 0-85365-470-0, Pub. by Lib Assn England). Oryx Pr.

Thompson, A. W. A. B. Simpson: His Life & Work. rev. ed. (Illus.). 228p. 1960. pap. 5.50 (ISBN 0-87509-044-3). Chr Pubns.

Thompson, Adell. Biology, Zoology, & Genetics: Evolution Model vs. Creation Model. LC 82-21995. (Illus.). 144p. (Orig.). 1983. lib. bdg. 18.00 (ISBN 0-8191-2921-6); pap. text ed. 8.25 (ISBN 0-8191-2922-4). U Pr of Amer.

Thompson, Alec, jt. auth. see Stearn, Jess.

Thompson, Allan. The Dynamics of the Industrial Revolution. LC 73-82224. 224p. 1973. text ed. 17.95 o.p. (ISBN 0-312-22330-7). St Martin.

Thompson, Ann M. & Wood, Marcia D. Management Strategies for Women: Self-Tests, Helpful Hints, Wit & Wisdom & Superb Management Strategies for Woman. 1982. pap. 5.95 (ISBN 0-671-25477-4, Touchstone Bks). S&S.

Thompson, Arthur R. & Harker, Laurence A. Manual of Hemostasis & Thrombosis. 3rd ed. LC 82-14871. (Illus.). 219p. 1982. pap. text ed. 8.95 (ISBN 0-8036-8481-9). Davis Co.

Thompson, B. A., jt. auth. see Belson, W. A.

Thompson, Barbara, tr. see Duby, Georges.

Thompson, Bard. Renaissance & Reformation. (Texts & Studies in Religion). (Orig.). Date not set. price not set (ISBN 0-88946-915-6). E Mellen. Postponed.

Thompson, Bill. The Basic of China Painting. (Illus.). 234p. 1976. 10.00 (ISBN 0-686-36015-X); pap. o.p. (ISBN 0-686-37260-3). Scott Pubns MI.

--China Painting With Bill Thompson. (Illus.). 192p. 1978. 10.00 (ISBN 0-686-36017-6); pap. o.p. (ISBN 0-686-37262-X). Scott Pubns MI.

--The Fundamentals of Hobby Ceramics. (Illus.). 218p. 1975. 10.00 (ISBN 0-686-36013-3); pap. o.p. (ISBN 0-686-37258-1). Scott Pubns MI.

--How to Create Great Informal Portraits: How to Take Dynamic, Professional Quality Photos in Your Own Home. (Illus.). 144p. (Orig.). 1982. 14.95 (ISBN 0-8174-4000-3, Amphoto); pap. 8.95 (ISBN 0-8174-4001-1). Watson-Guptill.

--The Technique of Hobby Ceramics. (Illus.). 159p. 1977. 10.00 (ISBN 0-686-36011-7); pap. o.p. (ISBN 0-686-37256-5). Scott Pubns MI.

Thompson, Bob. Guide to California. (The American Express Pocket Guides Ser.). (Illus.). 1983. 7.95 (ISBN 0-671-45374-2). S&S.

Thompson, Brenda & Giesen, Rosemary. Bones & Skeletons. LC 76-22420. (The First Fact Books). (Illus.). (gr. k-3). 1977. PLB 4.95g (ISBN 0-8225-1352-8). Lerner Pubns.

--Famous Planes. LC 76-22426. (First Fact Books Ser). (Illus.). (gr. k-3). 1977. PLB 4.95g (ISBN 0-8225-1354-4). Lerner Pubns.

--Flags. LC 76-22431. (First Fact Books Ser). (Illus.). (gr. k-3). 1977. PLB 4.95g (ISBN 0-8225-1355-2). Lerner Pubns.

--Gold & Jewels. LC 76-22437. (First Fact Books Ser). (Illus.). (gr. k-3). 1977. PLB 4.95g (ISBN 0-8225-1356-0). Lerner Pubns.

Thompson, Brenda & Overbeck, Cynthia. Animal Attackers. LC 76-22414. (First Fact Books Ser). (Illus.). (gr. k-3). 1977. PLB 4.95g (ISBN 0-8225-1351-X). Lerner Pubns.

--The Children's Crusade. LC 76-22469. (First Fact Books Ser). (Illus.). (gr. k-3). 1977. PLB 4.95g (ISBN 0-8225-1353-6). Lerner Pubns.

--The Great Wall of China. LC 76-22443. (First Fact Books Ser). (Illus.). (gr. k-3). 1977. PLB 5.95g (ISBN 0-8225-1218-1). Lerner Pubns.

--Monkeys & Apes. LC 76-22474. (First Fact Books Ser). (Illus.). (gr. k-3). 1977. PLB 4.95g (ISBN 0-8225-1358-7). Lerner Pubns.

--The Winds That Blow. LC 76-62984. (First Facts Books Ser). (Illus.). (gr. k-3). 1977. PLB 4.95g (ISBN 0-8225-1366-8). Lerner Pubns.

Thompson, Bruce. Black Walnut for Profit. 285p. 1978. pap. 12.95x (ISBN 0-917304-40-3). Timber.

--Black Walnut for Profit: A Guide to Risks & Rewards. (Illus.). 285p. 1976. 9.95 o.p. (ISBN 0-686-69373-6); pap. 7.95 o.s.i. (ISBN 0-917304-40-3). Walnut AZ.

--Franz Grillparzer. (World Authors Ser.). lib. bdg. 15.95 (ISBN 0-8057-6481-X, Twayne). G K Hall.

--Syrup Trees. Motsinger, Marilyn, ed. LC 78-63316. (Illus.). 1978. pap. 6.95 o.s.i. (ISBN 0-931318-00-9). Walnut AZ.

Thompson, Bryan, jt. auth. see Sinclair, Robert.

Thompson, C. J. Hand of Destiny: The Folk-Lore & Superstition of Everyday Life. LC 70-125600. 1970. Repr. of 1932 ed. 40.00x (ISBN 0-8103-3419-4). Gale.

--Love, Marriage & Romance in Old London. LC 70-76076. (Illus.). 1971. Repr. of 1936 ed. 27.00x (ISBN 0-8103-3211-6). Gale.

--The Lure & Romance of Alchemy. LC 76-167224. (Illus.). vi, 249p. 1975. Repr. of 1932 ed. 34.00x (ISBN 0-8103-4000-3). Gale.

--Magic & Healing. LC 73-2850. (Illus.). 176p. 1973. Repr. of 1947 ed. 34.00x (ISBN 0-8103-3275-2). Gale.

--Mysteries & Secrets of Magic. LC 78-174119. (Tower Bks). (Illus.). 1971. Repr. of 1928 ed. 42.00x (ISBN 0-8103-3213-2). Gale.

--Mysteries of History, with Accounts of Some Remarkable Characters & Charlatans. LC 76-164056. (Tower Bks). 1971. Repr. of 1928 ed. 34.00x (ISBN 0-8103-3908-0). Gale.

--Mystery & Art of the Apothecary. LC 78-89294. (Illus.). 1971. Repr. of 1929 ed. 37.00x (ISBN 0-8103-3210-8). Gale.

--The Mystery & Lore of Apparitions, with Some Account of Ghosts, Spectres, Phantoms & Boggarts in Early Times. LC 70-167225. (Illus.). 331p. 1975. Repr. of 1930 ed. 34.00x (ISBN 0-8103-3981-1). Gale.

--Mystery & Lure of Perfume. LC 74-75789. 1969. Repr. of 1927 ed. 30.00x (ISBN 0-8103-3842-4). Gale.

--Mystery & Romance of Astrology. LC 71-89295. 1969. Repr. of 1929 ed. 34.00x (ISBN 0-8103-3146-2). Gale.

--The Mystic Mandrake. LC 74-19199. (Illus.). 253p. 1975. Repr. of 1934 ed. 37.00x (ISBN 0-8103-4138-7). Gale.

--Quacks of Old London. LC 75-89296. (Tower Bks). (Illus.). 1971. Repr. of 1929 ed. 37.00x (ISBN 0-8103-3212-4). Gale.

Thompson, Carlos. The Assassination of Winston Churchill. 1978. text ed. cancelled o.p. (ISBN 0-901072-01-X). Humanities.

Thompson, Carolyn, jt. auth. see Thompson, W. Oscar, Jr.

Thompson, Carroll. The Bruises of Satan. 1982. 2.95 (ISBN 0-89985-986-0). Christ Nations.

Thompson, Carroll J. The Miracle of Holistic Healing. 1982. pap. 9.95 (ISBN 0-87949-203-1). Ashley Bks.

Thompson, Charles H. Fundamentals of Pipe Drafting. LC 58-13471. 66p. 1958. pap. 11.50x (ISBN 0-471-85998-2, Pub. by Wiley-Interscience). Wiley.

Thompson, Chris. Care & Repair of Small Marine Diesels. 144p. 1982. 40.00x o.p. (ISBN 0-229-11635-3, Pub. by Granada England). State Mutual Bk.

Thompson, Clem W. Manual of Structural Kinesiology. 9th ed. LC 81-1675. (Illus.). 142p. 1981. pap. text ed. 14.95 (ISBN 0-8016-4940-4). Mosby.

Thompson, D., ed. see Sampson, George.

Thompson, D. A. Recovering From Divorce. (Counseling Guides Ser.). 96p. (Orig.). 1982. pap. 4.95 Oversize (ISBN 0-87123-476-9, 210476). Bethany Hse.

Thompson, D. N. & Leighton, D. S., eds. Canadian Marketing: Problems & Prospects. LC 72-12416. 300p. 1973. 8.95 o.p. (ISBN 0-471-86000-X, Pub. by Wiley-Interscience). Wiley.

Thompson, D. V., Jr., tr. see Cennini, C. D'Andrea.

Thompson, Daniel C. Private Black Colleges at the Crossroads. LC 72-841. (Contributions in Afro-American & African Studies: No. 13). 1973. lib. bdg. 29.95x (ISBN 0-8371-6410-9, TBC/). Greenwood.

Thompson, D'Arcy W. On Growth & Form, 2 Vols. 1952. Set. 130.00 (ISBN 0-521-06622-0). Cambridge U Pr.

--On Growth & Form. abr. ed. Bonner, John T., ed. 55.00 (ISBN 0-521-06623-9); pap. 16.95 (ISBN 0-521-09390-2). Cambridge U Pr.

Thompson, David. Overexposures: The Crisis in American Filmmaking. 333p. 1981. pap. 8.95 (ISBN 0-688-00489-X). Quill NY.

Thompson, David L. Mummy Portraits in the J. Paul Getty Museum. LC 82-81303. 70p. 1982. pap. 16.95 (ISBN 0-89236-038-0). J P Getty Mus.

Thompson, David W. The Manager: Understanding & Influencing Behavioral Change. Grammentine, Ray, ed. LC 74-18628. 290p. 1974. text ed. 12.00 (ISBN 0-915064-00-6). Bradford Pr.

--Managing People: Influencing Behavior. LC 77-15993. 158p. 1978. pap. text ed. 10.45 o.p. (ISBN 0-8016-4933-1). Mosby.

Thompson, Dennis F. Democratic Citizen. LC 76-128633. (Illus.). 1970. 29.95 (ISBN 0-521-07963-2). Cambridge U Pr.

Thompson, Denys. The Uses of Poetry. LC 77-82517. 1978. 39.50 (ISBN 0-521-21804-7); pap. 13.95 (ISBN 0-521-29287-5). Cambridge U Pr.

Thompson, Denys & Tunnicliffe, Stephen. Reading & Discrimination. 175p. 1979. 12.95 o.s.i. (ISBN 0-7011-2359-1); pap. 6.95 o.s.i. (ISBN 0-7011-2360-5). Transatlantic.

Thompson, Denys, ed. Children As Poets. 1972. pap. text ed. 12.00x o.p. (ISBN 0-435-14893-1). Heinemann Ed.

--Directions in the Teaching of English. LC 60-19383. 1969. 16.95 (ISBN 0-521-07512-2); pap. 6.95 (ISBN 0-521-09595-6). Cambridge U Pr.

Thompson, Donald A. Cardiovascular Assessment: Guide for Nurses & Other Health Professionals. LC 80-26489. (Illus.). 238p. 1981. pap. text ed. 14.95 (ISBN 0-8016-4954-4). Mosby.

Thompson, Dorothea. Creative Decorations with Dried Flowers. rev. ed. (Illus.). 160p. 1972. 7.95 (ISBN 0-8208-0033-3). Hearthside.

Thompson, Dorothy, jt. ed. see Epstein, James.

Thompson, E. A. Human Evolutionary Trees. LC 75-2739. (Illus.). 160p. (Orig.). 1975. pap. 24.95x (ISBN 0-521-09945-5). Cambridge U Pr.

Thompson, E. P. Beyond the Cold War: A New Approach to the Arms Race & Nuclear Annihilation. LC 82-47896. 1982. 15.00 (ISBN 0-394-52796-8); pap. 5.95 (ISBN 0-394-71218-8). Pantheon.

--The Poverty of Theory & Other Essays. LC 78-26899. 1980. pap. 6.50 (ISBN 0-85345-491-4). Monthly Rev.

--Writing by Candlelight. (Illus.). 286p. 1981. pap. 6.95 (ISBN 0-85345-576-7, PB5767, Pub. by Merlin England). Monthly Rev.

Thompson, E. P., et al. Exterminism & Cold War. 352p. 1982. 27.50 (ISBN 0-8052-7130-9, Pub. by NLB England); pap. 9.50 (ISBN 0-8052-7131-7, Pub. by NLB England). Schocken.

Thompson, E. V. Chase the Wind. LC 77-1844. 352p. 1977. 9.95 o.p. (ISBN 0-698-10822-1, Coward). Putnam Pub Group.

--Harvest of the Sun. LC 78-14992. 1979. 9.95 o.p. (ISBN 0-698-10931-7). Putnam Pub Group.

Thompson, Earl. Caldo Largo. (Orig.). 1977. pap. 2.95 (ISBN 0-451-12157-0, AE2157, Sig). NAL.

--Caldo Largo. 1976. 8.95 (ISBN 0-399-11862-4). Putnam Pub Group.

--The Devil to Pay. 1982. pap. 3.95 (ISBN 0-451-11909-6, AE1909, Sig). NAL.

--Garden of Sand. 1975. pap. 3.95 (ISBN 0-451-08039-4, E8039, Sig). NAL.

--Tattoo. 1975. pap. 3.95 (ISBN 0-451-11157-5, AE1157, Sig). NAL.

Thompson, Edith M. & Thompson, William L. Beaver Dick: The Honor & the Heartbreak. Jones, Jean R., ed. 186p. 1982. 20.00 (ISBN 0-936204-26-5); pap. 10.00 (ISBN 0-936204-25-7). Jelm Mtn.

Thompson, Edward. Four Short Plays. (Orig.). 1980. pap. text ed. 5.00x o.p. (ISBN 0-435-23956-2). Heinemann Ed.

Thompson, Edward J. Rabindranath Tagore: Poet & Dramatist. LC 75-3743. (Illus.). 330p. 1975. Repr. of 1948 ed. lib. bdg. 21.00x (ISBN 0-8371-8065-1, THRT). Greenwood.

Thompson, Edward P. Making of the English Working Class. 1966. pap. 9.95 (ISBN 0-394-70322-7, Vin). Random.

Thompson, Edward V. & Ceckler, William H. Introductory Chemical Engineering. (Illus.). 1977. text ed. 34.00 (ISBN 0-07-064396-2, C); solutions manual 25.00 (ISBN 0-07-064397-0). McGraw.

Thompson, Eleanor D. Pediatric Nursing: An Introductory Text. 400p. 1981. pap. text ed. 14.95x (ISBN 0-7216-8843-8). Saunders.

--Pediatrics for Practical Nurses. 3rd ed. LC 75-40640. (Illus.). 380p. 1976. text ed. 8.95 o.p. (ISBN 0-7216-8842-X). Saunders.

Thompson, Emmanuel B. Drug Screening: Fundamentals of Drug Evaluation Techniques in Pharmacology. LC 80-83409. (Illus.). 325p. (Orig.). 1983. text ed. price not set (ISBN 0-932126-06-5); pap. text ed. price not set (ISBN 0-932126-07-3). Graceway.

Thompson, Enid T. Local History Collections: A Manual for Librarians. LC 77-28187. (Illus.). 1978. pap. 7.95 (ISBN 0-910050-33-3). AASLH.

Thompson, Ernest. On Golden Pond. LC 79-12879. 1979. 7.95 o.p. (ISBN 0-396-07710-2). Dodd.

--The West Side Waltz: A Play in 3/4 Time. LC 82-2501. 198p. 1982. 11.95 (ISBN 0-396-08061-8). Dodd.

Thompson, Ernest T. Through the Ages: A History of the Christian Church. (Orig.). 1965. pap. 4.50 o.p. (ISBN 0-8042-9040-7). John Knox.

Thompson, Evelina, et al. Pitman Secretarial Shorthand for Colleges with Student's Transcript. LC 77-80300. 1978. pap. 18.00 o.p. (ISBN 0-8224-2121-6); instr's handbk. & supplementary dictation o.p. 8.80 o.p. (ISBN 0-8224-2123-2). Pitman Learning.

Thompson, Ewa M. Witold Gombrowicz. (World Authors Ser.). 1979. lib. bdg. 15.95 (ISBN 0-8057-6351-1, Twayne). G K Hall.

Thompson, F. V; see Bernard, William S.

Thompson, Flora. Still Glides the Stream. (Illus.). 1981. 15.95x (ISBN 0-19-217414-2). Oxford U Pr.

Thompson, Frances. Point Lobos: An Illustrated Walker's Handbook. LC 80-82176. (Illus.). 112p. 1980. pap. 5.00 (ISBN 0-9604542-0-9). Inkstone Books.

Thompson, Francis. Hound of Heaven & Other Poems. pap. 2.50 (ISBN 0-8283-1440-3, 10, IPL). Branden.

--Literary Criticisms. Connolly, Terence L., ed. LC 74-30927. 1975. Repr. of 1948 ed. lib. bdg. 37.00x o.p. (ISBN 0-8371-7888-6, THLC). Greenwood.

--Murder & Mystery in the Highlands. (Illus.). 1978. 12.50 o.p. (ISBN 0-7091-6370-3). Transatlantic.

--The Uists & Barra. LC 74-81056. (Islands Ser). (Illus.). 192p. 1974. 16.95 o.p. (ISBN 0-7153-6676-9). David & Charles.

Thompson, Frank. Scotland. 160p. 1983. pap. 9.95 (ISBN 0-7063-6218-7, Pub. by Auto Assn-British Tourist Authority England). Merrimack Bk Serv.

Thompson, Frank H., Jr. Jungle Notes. (Orig.). 1970. pap. 2.25 (ISBN 0-8220-0699-5). Cliffs.

Thompson, Frank J. Health Policy & the Bureaucracy: Politics & Implementation. 252p. 1981. 27.50x (ISBN 0-262-20041-4). MIT Pr.

--Health Policy & the Bureaucracy: Politics & Implementation. 352p. 1983. pap. text ed. 10.95x (ISBN 0-262-70024-7). MIT Pr.

Thompson, Frank J., ed. Classics of Public Personnel Policy. LC 79-15423. (Classics Ser.). (Orig.). 1979. pap. 11.00x (ISBN 0-935610-07-3). Moore Pub IL.

Thompson, Frank, Jr. Nineteen Eighty-Four Notes. (Orig.). 1967. pap. 2.50 (ISBN 0-8220-0899-8). Cliffs.

Thompson, Frank T. William A. Wellman. (Filmmakers Ser.: No. 4). 339p. 1983. 22.50 (ISBN 0-8108-1594-X). Scarecrow.

Thompson, Fred, jt. auth. see Stanbury, W. T.

Thompson, Fred, Jr. What the Bible Says about Heaven & Hell. (What the Bible Says Ser.). 400p. 1982. 13.50 o.s.i. (ISBN 0-89900-081-9). College Pr Pub.

Thompson, G A., ed. The Technical College Library: A Primer for Its Development. 144p. 1969. 10.50 (ISBN 0-233-96100-3, 05824-6, Pub. by Gower Pub by England). Lexington Bks.

Thompson, G. G., jt. auth. see Brackbill, Yvonne.

Thompson, G. L., jt. auth. see Morgenstern, Oskar.

Thompson, G. V., ed. Space Research & Technology. 225p. 1962. 52.00x (ISBN 0-677-11910-0). Gordon.

Thompson, Gene E. & Handelman, Ira. Health Data & Information Management. (Illus.). 1978. 34.95 (ISBN 0-409-95008-4). Butterworth.

Thompson, George A. Some Dreams Die: Utah's Ghost Towns & Lost Treasures. Brown, Marc, ed. (Illus.). 200p. (Orig.). 1982. pap. 10.00 (ISBN 0-942688-01-5). Dream Garden.

Thompson, George A., Jr. Comparative & European Literature: An Annotated Guide to Reference Materials. LC 82-40253. (Illus.). 400p. 1983. 40.00 (ISBN 0-8044-3281-3). Ungar.

Thompson, George C. & Brady, Gerald P. Shortened CPA Law Review. 5th ed. (Business Ser.). 560p. 1980. text ed. 22.95x (ISBN 0-686-69155-5). Kent Pub Co.

Thompson, George G., ed. Social Development & Personality. LC 77-146673. (Readings in Educational Research Ser.). 1971. 30.75 (ISBN 0-471-86005-0); text ed. 28.00 ten or more copies (ISBN 0-685-52962-2). McCutchan.

Thompson, George H., et al, eds. Comprehensive Management of Cerebral Palsy. Date not set. price not set (ISBN 0-8089-1504-5). Grune.

Thompson, Gerald & Oxford Scientific Films Members. Focus on Nature. (Illus.). 184p. 1983. cancelled (ISBN 0-87663-423-4). Universe.

Thompson, Gerald E. Linear Programming: An Elementary Introduction. LC 79-89205. 1979. pap. text ed. 12.50 o.p. (ISBN 0-8191-0799-9). U Pr of Amer.

--Management Science: An Introduction to Modern Quantitative Analysis & Decision Making. LC 82-13071. 466p. 1982. Repr. of 1976 ed. lib. bdg. 26.50 (ISBN 0-89874-547-0). Krieger.

--Management Science: Introduction to Modern Quantitative Analysis & Decision Making. 1976. text ed. 25.95 (ISBN 0-07-064360-1, C); instr's manual 5.50 (ISBN 0-07-064361-X). McGraw.

Thompson, Geraldine B. Sing a New Song. 1982. 10.95 (ISBN 0-533-05461-3). Vantage.

Thompson, Ginnie. Favorite Illustrations from Children's Classics in Counted Cross-Stitch. LC 76-18404. (Dover's Needlework Ser). (Illus., Orig.). 1977. pap. 0.95 (ISBN 0-486-23394-4). Dover.

Thompson, Grant P. Building to Save Energy-Legal & Regulatory Approaches. LC 79-11754. (Environmental Law Institute State & Local Energy Conservation Project). (Illus.). 288p. 1980. prof ref 22.50x (ISBN 0-88410-059-6). Ballinger Pub.

Thompson, H. Pelagic Tunicates of Australia. 1982. 30.00x (ISBN 0-686-97903-6, Pub. by CSIRO Australia). State Mutual Bk.

Thompson, H. Stanley, et al. Topics in Neuro-Ophthalmology. (Handbook in Ophthalmology Ser.). (Illus.). 392p. 1979. 43.50 o.p. (ISBN 0-683-08178-0). Williams & Wilkins.

Thompson, Harwood & Ellis. Florida Real Estate Resource Book. 1978. pap. 12.95 ref. ed. (ISBN 0-87909-739-6). Reston.

Thompson, Helen. Journey Toward Wholeness: A Jungian Model of Adult Spiritual Growth. LC 81-83184. 96p. (Orig.). 1982. pap. 4.95 (ISBN 0-8091-2422-X). Paulist Pr.

Thompson, Henry O., jt. auth. see Thompson, Joyce B.

Thompson, Henry O., ed. The Global Congress of the World's Religions. LC 82-73565. (Conference Ser.: No. 15). (Orig.). 1982. pap. text ed. write for info. (ISBN 0-932894-15-1). Unif Theol Seminary.

Thompson, Henry O., jt. ed. see Wynne, Edward J., Jr.

Thompson, Herbert, jt. ed. see Griffith, F. L.

Thompson, Holland. Age of Invention. 1921. text ed. 8.50x (ISBN 0-686-83456-9). Elliots Bks.

--New South. 1919. text ed. 8.50x (ISBN 0-686-83648-0). Elliots Bks.

Thompson, Homer C. & Kelly, William C. Vegetable Crops. 5th ed. (Agricultural Sciences Ser.). (Illus.). 1957. text ed. 36.00 (ISBN 0-07-064418-7, C). McGraw.

Thompson, Howard E., jt. ed. see Krajewski, Lee J.

Thompson, Hugo W. Love-Justice. 1970. 6.95 o.p. (ISBN 0-8158-0032-0); pap. 3.95 o.p. (ISBN 0-8158-0242-0). Chris Mass.

Thompson, Hunter S. Fear & Loathing in Las Vegas. (Illus.). 224p. 1982. pap. 2.95 (ISBN 0-446-31030-1). Warner Bks.

--The Great Shark Hunt. 704p. 1982. pap. 4.50 (ISBN 0-446-31034-4). Warner Bks.

--Hell's Angels: The Motor Cycle Gangs. 1967. 8.95 o.p. (ISBN 0-394-42819-6); pap. 2.95 (ISBN 0-394-30113-7). Random.

Thompson, Ida. The Audubon Society Field Guide to North American Fossils. LC 81-84772. (Illus.). 1982. 12.50 (ISBN 0-394-52412-8). Knopf.

Thompson, J. Foundations of Vocational Education: Social & Philosophical Concepts. (Illus.). 1973. ref. ed. 24.95 (ISBN 0-13-330068-4). P-H.

Thompson, J., jt. auth. see Vane, H.

Thompson, J. A., jt. ed. see Bratcher, R. G.

Thompson, J. Dana, jt. ed. see Glantz, Micheal H.

Thompson, J. E. Four Miscellaneous Papers on Mayans. (Chicago Field Museum of Natural History Fieldiana Anthropology Ser). 1927. pap. 69.00 (ISBN 0-527-01877-5). Kraus Repr.

Thompson, J. F., ed. Numerical Grid Generation: Proceedings of the Symposium on the Numerical Generation of Curvilenear Coordinate Systems & Use in the Numerical Solution of Partial Differential Equations, Nashville, Tennessee, April 13-16, 1982. 944p. 1982. 95.00 (ISBN 0-444-00757-1, North Holland). Elsevier.

Thompson, J. H. Canadian Textiles. (Illus.). 22.50x (ISBN 0-87245-322-7). Textile Bk.

--Czechoslovak Textiles. (Illus.). 22.50x (ISBN 0-87245-323-5). Textile Bk.

Thompson, J. M. Instabilities & Catastrophes in Science & Engineering. 226p. 1982. 34.95x (ISBN 0-471-09973-2, Pub. by Wiley-Interscience); pap. 19.95x (ISBN 0-471-10071-4). Wiley.

Thompson, J. M. & Hunt, G. W. General Theory of Elastic Stability. LC 73-8199. 322p. 1973. 61.95x (ISBN 0-471-85991-5, Pub. by Wiley-Interscience). Wiley.

Thompson, J. R., ed. see Poe, Edgar A.

Thompson, Jack, jt. auth. see Miller, Albert.

Thompson, Jack C., jt. auth. see Miller, Albert.

Thompson, Jacqueline. Image Impact for Men. (Illus.). 288p. 1983. 14.95 (ISBN 0-89479-120-6). A & W Pubs.

--The Very Rich Book: America's Supermillionaires & Their Money - Where They Got It, How They Spend It. LC 81-14135. (Illus.). 432p. 1981. pap. 6.95 (ISBN 0-688-00805-4). Quill NY.

Thompson, Jacqueline A., ed. Directory of Personal Image Consultants, 1982-1983. rev. ed. (Orig.). 1982. pap. 17.50 (ISBN 0-685-96267-9). Edit Services.

Thompson, James. The End of Libraries. 1983. 17.50 (ISBN 0-85157-349-5, Pub. by Bingley England). Shoe String.

Thompson, James C. & Vidmer, Richard. Administrative Science & Politics in the U.S.S.R. & the U. S. Soviet Responses to American Management Techniques 1917 - Present. (Illus.). 224p. 1983. text ed. 25.95x (ISBN 0-686-78904-0). J F Bergin.

Thompson, James D. & Vroom, Victor H., eds. Organizational Design & Research: Approaches to Organizational Design & Methods of Organizational Research. LC 70-137859. 1971. pap. text ed. 5.95x (ISBN 0-8229-5222-X). U of Pittsburgh Pr.

Thompson, James J. Tried as by Fire: Southern Baptists & the Religious Controversies of the 1920's. LC 82-8056. 188p. 1982. 13.95x (ISBN 0-86554-032-2). Mercer Univ Pr.

Thompson, James M. Tabulation Typing. 1955. text ed. 7.48 (ISBN 0-07-064452-7, G). McGraw.

Thompson, James M., jt. auth. see Dallas, Richard J.

Thompson, James N. & Thoday, J. M., eds. Quantitative Genetic Variation. LC 79-9917. 1979. 29.50 (ISBN 0-12-688850-7). Acad Pr.

Thompson, James R. Leigh Hunt. (English Authors Ser.). 1977. lib. bdg. 13.95 (ISBN 0-8057-6679-0, Twayne). G K Hall.

Thompson, Janice & Lewis, Naomi. Marco Polo & Wellington. (ps-1). 1983. 9.95 (ISBN 0-686-38877-1, Pub. by Chatto & Windus). Merrimack Bk Serv.

--Marco Polo & Wellington: Search for Solomon. (Illus.). 32p. (ps-1). 1983. laminated boards 9.95 (ISBN 0-224-02036-6, Pub by Jonathan Cape). Merrimack Bk Serv.

Thompson, Jay. I Am Also a You. (Illus.). 1971. pap. 2.95 (ISBN 0-517-50343-3, C N Potter, C N Potter Bks). Crown.

Thompson, Jean. Brother of the Wolves. LC 78-18014. (gr. 4-6). 1978. 9.75 (ISBN 0-688-22168-8); PLB 9.36 (ISBN 0-688-32168-2). Morrow.

--Don't Forget Michael. LC 79-16637. (Illus.). 64p. (gr. k-3). 1979. 8.75 (ISBN 0-688-22196-3); PLB 8.40 (ISBN 0-688-32196-8). Morrow.

--House of Tomorrow. LC 67-10491. 1967. 13.41i (ISBN 0-06-014262-6, HarpT). Har-Row.

--My Wisdom. 384p. 1982. 15.95 (ISBN 0-531-09870-2). Watts.

Thompson, Jerry. My Life in the Klan. 320p. 1982. 14.95 (ISBN 0-399-12695-3). Putnam Pub Group.

Thompson, Jerry D. Vaqueros in Blue & Gray. (Illus.). 1977. 9.50 o.s.i. (ISBN 0-686-21182-0); deluxe ed. 35.00 (ISBN 0-686-21183-9). Presidial.

Thompson, Joan. Interesting Times. 322p. 1981. 12.95 o.p. (ISBN 0-312-41914-7). St Martin.

Thompson, John. Country Bed & Breakfast Places in Canada. 4th ed. 350p. 1982. pap. 8.95 (ISBN 0-88879-049-X, Pub. by Deneau Publishers). Berkshire Traveller.

--Nelson: Hero of Trafalgar. (Lives to Remember Ser). (Illus.). (gr. 6 up). 1969. PLB 4.97 o.p. (ISBN 0-399-60486-3). Putnam Pub Group.

--On Lips of Living Men. 13.50 (ISBN 0-392-08541-0, ABC). Sportshelf.

Thompson, John, ed. New Zealand Literature to Nineteen Seventy-Seven: A Guide to Information Sources. LC 74-11537. (American Literature, English Literature, & World Literature in English Information Guide Ser.: Vol. 30). 250p. 1980. 42.00x (ISBN 0-8103-1246-8). Gale.

Thompson, John C. A Reader's Guide to Fifty British Plays: 1660-1900. (Reader's Guide Ser.). 448p. 1980. 22.50x (ISBN 0-389-20139-1). B&N Imports.

Thompson, John D. Applied Health Services Research. LC 75-12482. (Illus.). 224p. 1977. 21.95x o.p. (ISBN 0-669-00028-0). Lexington Bks.

Thompson, John K. Financial Policy, Inflation & Economic Development: The Mexican Experience, Vol. 16. Altman, Edward I. & Walter, Ingo, eds. LC 77-7787. (Contemporary Studies in Economic & Financial Analysis). 1979. lib. bdg. 36.00 (ISBN 0-89232-084-2). Jai Pr.

Thompson, John N. Interaction & Coevolution. LC 82-11026. 179p. 1982. 27.50 (ISBN 0-471-09022-0, Pub. by Wiley-Interscience). Wiley.

Thompson, John O., ed. Monty Python: Complete & Utter Theory of the Grotesque. (Illus.). 58p. 1982. pap. 7.95 (ISBN 0-85170-119-1). NY Zoetrope.

Thompson, John T. Policymaking in American Public Education: A Framework for Analysis. LC 75-5841. (Illus.). 304p. 1975. 22.95 (ISBN 0-13-685370-6). P-H.

Thompson, John W. & Slauson, Nedra, eds. Index to Illustrations of the Natural World: Where to Find Pictures of the Living Things of North America. 265p. 1981. Repr. of 1980 ed. price not set (ISBN 0-208-01911-1, Lib Prof Pubns). Shoe String.

Thompson, John W., compiled by. Index to Illustrations of the Natural World: Where to Find Pictures of the Living Things of North America. Slauson, Nedra, ed. 29.95 o.p. (ISBN 0-915794-12-8). Gaylord Prof Pubns.

Thompson, Jonathan. Ferrari Turbo. (Illus.). 1982. 24.95 (ISBN 0-85045-465-4, Pub. by Osprey England). Motorbooks Intl.

Thompson, Jonathan, ed. Ferrari Album, No. 2. 96p. 1981. pap. 16.95 (ISBN 0-940014-02-5). Color Market.

--Ferrari Album, No. 3. (Illus.). 96p. 1982. pap. 16.95 (ISBN 0-940014-03-3). Color Market.

Thompson, Joseph R. & Hasso, Anton N. Correlative Sectional Anatomy of the Head & Neck: A Color Atlas, Vol. I. LC 79-19978. (Illus.). 446p. 1979. text ed. 176.00 o.p. (ISBN 0-8016-4934-X). Mosby.

Thompson, Joseph W. Selling: A Managerial & Behavioral Science Analysis. 2nd ed. (Illus.). 600p. 1973. text ed. 26.50 (ISBN 0-07-064378-4, C); instructor's manual 15.95 (ISBN 0-07-064379-2). McGraw.

Thompson, Joyce. Willie & Phil. 1980. pap. 1.95 o.p. (ISBN 0-380-75804-0, 75804). Avon.

Thompson, Joyce B. & Thompson, Henry O. Ethics in Nursing. 1981. pap. text ed. 13.95x (ISBN 0-02-420690-3). Macmillan.

Thompson, Julia. Assessment of Fluency in School-Age Children. (Illus.). 192p. 1982. text ed. 32.50x (ISBN 0-8134-2240-X). Interstate.

Thompson, Julian. The Grounding of Group Six. 304p. 1983. pap. 2.50 (ISBN 0-380-83386-7, Flare). Avon.

Thompson, Juliet. Diary of Juliet Thompson. 1983. 14.95 (ISBN 0-933770-27-8). Kalimat.

Thompson, June M. & Bowers, Arden C. Clinical Manual of Health Assessment. LC 79-28832. (Illus.). 476p. 1980. pap. text ed. 21.95 (ISBN 0-8016-4935-8). Mosby.

Thompson, Kay. Eloise. LC 55-11039. (Illus.). (gr. k-6). 1969. 11.50 (ISBN 0-671-22350-X). S&S.

Thompson, Keith P., jt. auth. see Holt, Dennis M.

Thompson, Kenneth. Auguste Comte: The Foundation of Sociology. LC 75-12566. 1975. 27.95x o.s.i. (ISBN 0-470-85988-1). Halsted Pr.

--Emile Durkheim. (Key Sociologists Ser.). 1982. pap. 3.95x (ISBN 0-85312-419-1, Pub. by Tavistock England). Methuen Inc.

Thompson, Kenneth & Myers, Robert J., eds. Truth & Tragedy: A Tribute to Hans J. Morganthau. LC 76-56206. 1977. 20.00 (ISBN 0-915220-21-0, 23036). New Republic.

Thompson, Kenneth R., jt. auth. see Luthans, Fred.

Thompson, Kenneth W. American Diplomacy & Emergent Patterns. LC 82-23862. 294p. 1983. pap. text ed. 11.50 (ISBN 0-8191-2935-6). U Pr of Amer.

--The American Presidency, Vol. I: Principles & Problems. LC 82-45217. 84p. (Orig.). 1982. lib. bdg. 17.75 (ISBN 0-8191-2549-0); pap. text ed. 6.50 (ISBN 0-8191-2550-4). U Pr of Amer.

--American Values Projected Abroad, Vol. II: Political Traditions & Contemporary Problems. LC 82-40160. 140p. (Orig.). 1982. lib. bdg. 18.75 (ISBN 0-8191-2588-1); pap. text ed. 8.00 (ISBN 0-8191-2589-X). U Pr of Amer.

--Foreign Assistance: A View from the Private Sector. LC 82-25091. 170p. 1983. pap. text ed. 8.75 (ISBN 0-8191-2713-2). U Pr of Amer.

--Interpreters & Critics of the Cold War. LC 78-57575. 1978. pap. text ed. 7.25 (ISBN 0-8191-0504-X). U Pr of Amer.

--Political Realism & the Crisis of World Politics: An American Approach to Foreign Policy. LC 82-45061. 270p. 1982. pap. text ed. 10.75 (ISBN 0-8191-2352-8). U Pr of Amer.

--The Virginia Papers on the Presidency: The White Burkett Miller Center Forums, 1979, Vol. 1. LC 79-66241. 1979. pap. text ed. 6.75 (ISBN 0-8191-0819-7). U Pr of Amer.

--The Virginia Papers on the Presidency, Volume IX: The White Burkett Miller Center Forums, 1981, Pt. V. LC 79-66241. 90p. (Orig.). 1982. lib. bdg. 16.75 (ISBN 0-8191-2425-7); pap. text ed. 6.00 (ISBN 0-8191-2426-5). U Pr of Amer.

--Winston Churchill's World View: Statesmanship & Power. LC 82-4699. 368p. 1983. text ed. 25.00x (ISBN 0-8071-1045-0). La State U Pr.

Thompson, Kenneth W., ed. Herbert Butterfield: The Ethics of History & Politics. LC 79-5375. 1979. text ed. 14.50 (ISBN 0-8191-0875-8); pap. text ed. 8.00 (ISBN 0-8191-0876-6). U Pr of Amer.

--The Moral Imperatives of Human Rights: A World Survey. LC 79-3736. 1980. text ed. 19.75 (ISBN 0-8191-0920-7); pap. text ed. 9.25 (ISBN 0-8191-0921-5). U Pr of Amer.

--The Roosevelt Presidency: Four Intimate Perspectives of FDR. LC 82-17479. (Portraits of American Presidents Ser.: Vol. I). 100p. 1983. lib. bdg. 17.25 (ISBN 0-8191-2827-9); pap. text ed. 6.50 (ISBN 0-8191-2828-7). U Pr of Amer.

--Ten Presidents & the Press. LC 82-20293. (American Presidents & the Press Ser.). 128p. (Orig.). 1983. lib. bdg. 17.50 (ISBN 0-8191-2877-5); pap. text ed. 7.25 (ISBN 0-8191-2878-3). U Pr of Amer.

--The Virginia Papers of the Presidency, Vol. V: The White Burkett Miller Center Forums, 1981, Pt. 1. 91p. 1981. lib. bdg. 13.75 (ISBN 0-8191-1502-9); pap. text ed. 6.00 (ISBN 0-8191-1503-7). U Pr of Amer.

--The Virginia Papers on the Presidency: The White Burkett Miller Center Forums, 1980, Part II, Vol. IV. LC 80-5576. 110p. 1980. lib. bdg. 14.50 (ISBN 0-8191-1201-1); pap. text ed. 6.75 (ISBN 0-8191-1202-X). U Pr of Amer.

--Virginia Papers on the Presidency: The White Burkett Miller Center Forums, Nineteen Seventy-Nine, Vol. II. LC 79-66241. 152p. 1980. 14.50 (ISBN 0-8191-0997-5); pap. 6.75 (ISBN 0-8191-0998-3). U Pr of Amer.

--The Virginia Papers on the Presidency: Vol. III, The White Burkett Miller Center Forums, 1980, Pt. 1. LC 79-66241. 133p. 1980. lib. bdg. 14.50 (ISBN 0-8191-1120-1); pap. text ed. 6.75 (ISBN 0-8191-1121-X). U Pr of Amer.

--The Virginia Papers on the Presidency: Vol. VI--the White Burkett Miller Center Forums, 1981, Part II. LC 79-66241. 128p. 1981. lib. bdg. 13.75 (ISBN 0-8191-1544-4); pap. text ed. 6.25 (ISBN 0-8191-1604-1). U Pr of Amer.

--The Virginia Papers on the Presidency, Vol VII: The White Burkett Miller Center Forums, 1981, Part III. LC 79-66241. 104p. 1982. lib. bdg. 15.75 (ISBN 0-8191-1901-6); pap. text ed. 7.00 (ISBN 0-8191-1902-4). U Pr of Amer.

--The Virginia Papers on the Presidency, Vol. VIII: The White Burkett Miller Center Forums, 1981, Part IV. LC 79-66241. 104p. 1982. lib. bdg. 18.75 (ISBN 0-8191-1951-2); pap. text ed. 7.00 (ISBN 0-8191-1952-0). U Pr of Amer.

--The Virginia Papers on the Presidency, Vol. X: The White Burkett Miller Center Forums, 1982, Pt. 1. LC 79-66241. 114p. (Orig.). 1983. lib. bdg. 16.50 (ISBN 0-8191-2823-6); pap. text ed. 6.25 (ISBN 0-8191-2824-4). U Pr of Amer.

Thompson, Kenneth W., ed. see Coll, Alberto R.

Thompson, Kenneth W., jt. ed. see Halle, Louis J.

Thompson, Kenneth W., jt. ed. see Morgenthau, Hans J.

Thompson, Kristin, jt. auth. see Bordwell, David.

Thompson, L. General Mathematics with Applications. 1976. 11.76 (ISBN 0-02-829390-8); tchr's ed. 15.98 (ISBN 0-02-829400-9); solns. manual avail. Glencoe.

--The Slow Learner. 1978. pap. text ed. 10.50x o.p. (ISBN 0-86863-255-4, 00552). Heinemann Ed.

Thompson, Laurence G., tr. see Briere, O.

Thompson, Laurie. Stig Dagerman. (World Authors Ser.: No. 676). 166p. 1983. lib. bdg. 19.95 (ISBN 0-8057-6523-9, Twayne). G K Hall.

Thompson, Lawrence C., jt. ed. see Jenner, Philip N.

Thompson, Lawrence S. Bibliography of British & American Drama of the Nineteenth & Twentieth Centuries. 1975. lib. bdg. 28.50 (ISBN 0-8161-7842-9, Hall Reference). G K Hall.

--The New Sabin, Vol. 8. 419p. 1981. 30.00x (ISBN 0-87875-217-X); index 10.00 (ISBN 0-87875-218-8). Whitston Pub.

--The New Sabin: Entries, Vol. 7. 345p. 1980. 25.00x (ISBN 0-87875-183-1); index o.p. 7.50 (ISBN 0-686-65245-2). Whitston Pub.

Thompson, Leonard. Survival in Two Worlds: Moshoeshoe of Lesotho 1786-1870. (Illus.). 1975. pap. 14.95x (ISBN 0-19-822702-7). Oxford U Pr.

Thompson, Leonard L. Introducing Biblical Literature: A More Fantastic Country. LC 78-6632. (Illus.). ref. ed. 20.95 (ISBN 0-13-498824-8). P-H.

Thompson, Lida F., jt. auth. see Byrne, Majorie L.

Thompson, Lida F., et al. Sociology: Nurses & Their Patients in a Modern Society. 9th ed. LC 74-34417. 280p. 1975. text ed. 10.95 o.p. (ISBN 0-8016-4942-0). Mosby.

Thompson, Linda J., jt. auth. see Johnson, Marlys C.

Thompson, Linda L. Consumer Mathematics. LC 76-4003. 470p. 1978. text ed. 11.76 (ISBN 0-02-479280-2); tchrs. manual 3.90 (ISBN 0-02-479300-0); wkbk. 4.59 (ISBN 0-02-479290-X); solutions key 2.49 (ISBN 0-686-65782-9). Glencoe.

Thompson, Lloyd J. Reading Disability: Developmental Dyslexia. (Illus.). 228p. 1974. pap. 10.75x (ISBN 0-398-03123-1). C C Thomas.

Thompson, Louis M. & Troeh, Frederic. Soil & Soil Fertility. 3rd ed. LC 72-2473. (Agricultural Sciences Ser.). (Illus.). 512p. 1972. text ed. 29.95 (ISBN 0-07-064410-1, C). McGraw.

Thompson, Louis M. & Troeh, Frederick. Soils & Soil Fertility. 4th ed. (Ag Ser.). (Illus.). 1977. text ed. 31.00 (ISBN 0-07-064411-X, C). McGraw.

Thompson, M., ed. IFDC Annual Report 1980. (Circular Ser.: S-4). (Illus.). 60p. (Orig.). 1982. pap. 4.00 (ISBN 0-88090-030-X). Intl Fertilizer.

Thompson, M., jt. ed. see Fletcher, C.

Thompson, M., tr. see Belozerskaya-Bulgakova, L. E.

Thompson, M. K., ed. IFDC Annual Report, 1981. (Circular Ser.: S-5). 60p. (Orig.). 1982. pap. text ed. 4.00. Intl Fertilizer.

Thompson, M. W. Defects & Radiation Damage in Metals. LC 69-10434. (Cambridge Monographs on Physics). (Illus.). 1969. 67.50 (ISBN 0-521-07068-6); pap. 19.50x (ISBN 0-521-09865-3). Cambridge U Pr.

Thompson, Malcolm H., jt. auth. see Jastrow, Robert.

Thompson, Margaret J. Workbook in the Calculation of Solutions & Dosage for Student Nurses. 80p. 1982. pap. text ed. 5.95 (ISBN 0-8403-2744-7). Kendall-Hunt.

Thompson, Margurite. Martin Luther King Jr. A Story For Children. 24p. 1983. 3.00 (ISBN 0-912444-25-8). Gaus.

Thompson, Marie K., ed. see McCune, Donald L.

Thompson, Marie K., ed. see Winterborn, Benjamin.

Thompson, Mark S. Decision Analysis for Program Evaluation. 424p. 1982. prof ref 35.00x (ISBN 0-88410-865-1). Ballinger Pub.

Thompson, Maynard, jt. auth. see Maki, Daniel.

Thompson, Maynard, jt. auth. see Maki, Daniel P.

Thompson, Michael, tr. see Aoki, Hiroyuki.

Thompson, Michael E. W. Situation & Theology: Old Testament Interpretations of the Syro-Euphramite War. 1983. text ed. 25.95x (ISBN 0-686-42730-0, Pub. by Almond Pr England); pap. text ed. 12.95x (ISBN 0-907459-15-3, Pub. by Almond Pr England). Eisenbrauns.

Thompson, Morton. Not As a Stranger. (RL 6). 1975. pap. 3.50 o.p. (ISBN 0-451-07991-4, AE1050, Sig); pap. 1.50 o.p. (ISBN 0-451-09507-3, W9507). NAL.

Thompson, Neil. A Closer Look at Horses. LC 78-4834. (Closer Look at Ser.). (Illus.). (gr. 4 up). 1978. PLB 9.40 (ISBN 0-531-01428-2, Gloucester Pr); pap. 1.95 o.p. (ISBN 0-531-02486-5). Watts.

Thompson, Norma H. & Cole, Bruce, eds. The Future of Jewish-Christian Relations. 1982. 10.95 (ISBN 0-915744-27-9); pap. 8.95 (ISBN 0-915744-28-7). Character Res.

Thompson, P. A. Compressible Fluid Dynamics. (Control Systems Engineering Ser.). 1971. text ed. 44.00 (ISBN 0-07-064405-5, C). McGraw.

Thompson, Paul. The Edwardians: The Remaking of British Society. LC 75-10897. (Illus.). 396p. 1975. 15.00x o.p. (ISBN 0-253-31941-2). Ind U Pr.

--The Lorenzaccio Story. 72p. (Orig.). 1981. pap. 4.95 (ISBN 0-686-98033-6). Pluto Pr.

--Nutrition. (First Bks.). 72p. 1981. lib. bdg. 8.90 (ISBN 0-531-04328-2). Watts.

--Our Common History. 334p. 1982. text ed. 19.95x (ISBN 0-391-02606-2). Humanities.

--The Voice of the Past: Oral History. 1978. text ed. 12.95x o.p. (ISBN 0-19-215833-3); pap. text ed. 6.95x (ISBN 0-19-289102-2, OPB). Oxford U Pr.

Thompson, Paul D. Gases & Plasmas. (Introducing Modern Science Ser.). (Illus.). (gr. 7-9). 1966. 5.95 o.p. (ISBN 0-397-30868-X, HarpJ). Har-Row.

Thompson, Paul E. & Werbel, Leslie M. Antimalarial Agents: Chemistry & Pharmacology. 1972. 64.00 (ISBN 0-12-688950-3). Acad Pr.

Thompson, Paul H., jt. auth. see Ritchie, J. B.

Thompson, Philip. Stranger In Town: A Guide to Taverns in Oregon & Southwest Washington. 1983. pap. 4.95 (ISBN 0-932576-14-1). Breitenbush Pubns.

Thompson, Philip & Davenport, Peter, eds. The Dictionary of Graphic Images. 288p. 1980. 30.00 (ISBN 0-312-20108-7). St Martin.

Thompson, Phyllis. Artichoke & Other Poems. LC 75-76763. 1969. 6.00 (ISBN 0-87022-791-2). UH Pr.
--Each to Her Post. 1982. pap. 3.95 (ISBN 0-340-26933-2). OMF Bks.

Thompson, Phyllis F. Sodbuster: Five Stories of Church Planters. (Home Mission Graded Ser.). (Illus.). 136p. Date not set. pap. 2.50 (ISBN 0-937170-50-X). Home Mission.

Thompson, R. & Casey, R. Perspectives for Peas & Lupins As Protein Crops. 1983. 54.50 (ISBN 90-247-2792-8, Pub. by Martinus Nijhoff Netherlands). Kluwer Boston.

Thompson, R., ed. Energy & Chemistry. 368p. 1982. 55.00x (ISBN 0-85186-845-2, Pub. by Royal Soc Chem England). State Mutual Bk.

Thompson, R. A. The Practice of Clinical Immunology. 2nd ed. (Current Topics in Immunology: Vol. 1). (Illus.). 1979. pap. 24.95 (ISBN 0-8151-8784-X). Year Bk Med.
--Techniques in Clinical Immunology. 2nd. ed. (Illus.). 252p. 1981. pap. text ed. 34.00 (ISBN 0-632-00723-0, B 4948-X). Mosby.

Thompson, R. L., jt. auth. see Bauer, C. E.

Thompson, Ralph B., ed. Florida Statistical Abstract, 1981. (Bureau of Economic & Business Research Ser.). 1981. write for info. o.p. (ISBN 0-8130-0715-1); pap. write for info. o.p. (ISBN 0-8130-0716-X). U Presses Fla.

Thompson, Raymond & Daly, Treve. The Number to Call Is... 288p. 1981. pap. 2.50 o.p. (ISBN 0-380-53769-5, 53769). Avon.

Thompson, Raymond H. Gordon R. Dickson: A Primary & Secondary Bibliography. 1983. lib. bdg. 27.50 (ISBN 0-8161-8363-5, Hall Reference). G K Hall.

Thompson, Richard. An Introduction to Physical Signs. (Illus.). 232p. 1981. pap. text ed. 19.95 (ISBN 0-632-00054-6, B 4943-9). Mosby.

Thompson, Richard A., ed. New Perspectives in Cerebral Localization. (Barrow Neurological Institute Ser.). 264p. 1981. text ed. 32.50 (ISBN 0-89004-663-8). Raven.

Thompson, Richard A. & Green, J. R., eds. Infectious Diseases of the Central Nervous System. LC 74-79192. (Advances in Neurology Ser: Vol. 6). 296p. 1974. 38.00 (ISBN 0-911216-82-0). Raven.
--Stroke. LC 75-25129. (Advances in Neurology Ser.: Vol. 16). 250p. 1977. 27.50 (ISBN 0-89004-098-2). Raven.

Thompson, Richard A. & Green, John R., eds. Complications of Nervous System Trauma. LC 78-52425. (Advances in Neurology Ser.: Vol. 22). 345p. 1979. text ed. 38.00 (ISBN 0-89004-295-0). Raven.
--Critical Care of Neurologic & Neurosurgical Emergencies. 252p. 1979. text ed. 25.00 (ISBN 0-89004-401-5). Raven.
--Neoplasia in the Central Nervous System. LC 75-25113. (Advances in Neurology Ser.: Vol. 15). 394p. 1976. 45.50 (ISBN 0-89004-058-3). Raven.

Thompson, Richard E. Helping Hospital Trustees Understand Physicians. LC 79-21428. 96p. (Orig.). 1979. pap. 15.00 (ISBN 0-87258-287-6, AHA-196115). Am Hospital.

Thompson, Richard F., et al, eds. Neural Mechanisms of Goal-Directed Behavior & Learning. LC 79-6775. 1980. 54.50 (ISBN 0-12-688980-5). Acad Pr.

Thompson, Robert. What Comes After Pentecost. 1982. pap. 6.95 (ISBN 0-686-95485-8). Omega Pubns Or.

Thompson, Robert & Cornet, Joseph. The Four Moments of the Sun. LC 81-14033. (Illus.). pap. 19.95 (ISBN 0-89468-003-X). Natl Gallery Art.

Thompson, Robert C. & Yaqub, Adil. Introduction to Linear Algebra. 1970. text ed. 14.95x o.p. (ISBN 0-673-05950-2). Scott F.

Thompson, Robert F. Flash of the Spirit: African Art & Culture in the New World. (Illus.). 1981. 19.95 (ISBN 0-394-50515-8). Random.

Thompson, Robert G. BASIC: A First Course. (Data Processing Ser.). (Illus.). 352p. 1981. text ed. 16.95 (ISBN 0-675-08057-6). Additional supplements may be obtained from publisher. Merrill.

Thompson, Robert J., Jr. & O'Quinn, Aglaia N. Developmental Disabilities: Etiologies, Manifestations, Diagnoses & Treatment. (Illus.). 1979. text ed. 24.95x (ISBN 0-19-502421-4); pap. text ed. 14.95x (ISBN 0-19-502422-2). Oxford U Pr.

Thompson, Robert W. How to Barter for Fun & Profit. 1983. 6.95 (ISBN 0-533-05642-X). Vantage.

Thompson, Roger. Women in Stuart England & America: A Comparative Study. 1974. 17.50x o.p. (ISBN 0-7100-7822-6). Routledge & Kegan.

Thompson, Roger, jt. ed. see Allen, H. C.

Thompson, Russell E. Precalculus Mathematics: A Short Course. LC 82-13366. 200p. (Orig.). 1982. pap. text ed. 10.00 (ISBN 0-8191-2634-9). U Pr of Amer.

Thompson, Russell G., jt. ed. see Thrall, Robert M.

Thompson, Ruth H., ed. see Hunt, Harrison J.

Thompson, Samuel W. & Luna, Lee G. An Atlas of Artifacts: Encountered in the Preparation of Microscopic Tissue Sections. (Illus.). 208p. 1978. 27.75x (ISBN 0-398-03624-1). C C Thomas.

Thompson, Sandra see Hopper, Paul.

Thompson, Silvanus P. The Life of Lord Kelvin, 2 vols. 2nd ed. LC 75-45133. (Illus.). 1977. text ed. 49.50 set (ISBN 0-8284-0292-2). Chelsea Pub.
--Michael Faraday: His Life & Work. 2nd ed. Date not set. 14.95 (ISBN 0-8284-0311-2). Chelsea Pub.

Thompson, Snook P. The Private Life of Petty Officer F.D.R. Perdue & His Report on Segregation & Integration. 1983. 7.85 (ISBN 0-533-05457-5). Vantage.

Thompson, Stephanie. Clothes & Ornaments. LC 78-64657. (Fact Finders Ser.). (Illus.). 1979. PLB 8.00 (ISBN 0-382-06239-6). Silver.
--Shops & Markets. LC 78-64655. (Fact Finders Ser.). (Illus.). 1979. PLB 8.00 (ISBN 0-686-51131-X). Silver.

Thompson, Steven. Countdown to China. 304p. 1982. pap. 2.95 (ISBN 0-446-90647-6). Warner Bks.

Thompson, Stith. The Folktale. 1977. 28.50x (ISBN 0-520-03359-0); pap. 8.95 (ISBN 0-520-03537-2). U of Cal Pr.

Thompson, T. E. Nudibranchs. (Illus., Orig.). 1976. pap. 9.95 (ISBN 0-87666-459-1, PS-696). TFH Pubns.

Thompson, Terry & O'Malley, Jeanne. Training the Performance Horse. 1979. 10.53i (ISBN 0-397-01371-X). Har-Row.

Thompson, Thea. Edwardian Childhoods. (Illus.). 256p. 1981. 27.50 (ISBN 0-7100-0676-4); pap. 13.95 (ISBN 0-7100-9335-7). Routledge & Kegan.

Thompson, Theodore R. Intensive Care of Newborn Infants: A Practical Manual. (Illus.). 414p. spiral bdg. 29.50 (ISBN 0-8166-1090-8). U of Minn Pr.

Thompson, Thomas. Celebrity. 640p. 1983. pap. 3.95 (ISBN 0-446-30238-4). Warner Bks.

Thompson, Thomas M. From Error-Correcting Codes Through Spere Packing to Simple Groups. (Carus Monograph: No. 21). Date not set. text ed. price not set (ISBN 0-88385-023-0). Math Assn.

Thompson, Toby. Positively Main Street: An Unorthodox View of Bob Dylan. 1971. 5.95 o.p. (ISBN 0-698-10305-X, Coward). Putnam Pub Group.

Thompson, Tom. Organizational TV News. LC 80-81874. (Illus.). 217p. (Orig.). 1980. pap. 16.95x (ISBN 0-935608-00-1); pap. text ed. 16.95x (ISBN 0-686-96788-7). Media Concepts.

Thompson, Tommy. Script Letter: Its Form, Construction & Application. 9.00 (ISBN 0-8446-3068-3). Peter Smith.
--Script Lettering for Artists. rev. ed. (Illus.). 1955. pap. 3.50 (ISBN 0-486-21311-0). Dover.

Thompson, Travis & Dews, Peter B., eds. Advances in Behavioral Pharmacology. Vol. 1. 1977. 32.50 (ISBN 0-12-004701-2); lib. ed. 43.50 (ISBN 0-12-004770-5); microfiche 21.00 (ISBN 0-12-004771-3). Acad Pr.
--Advances in Behavioral Pharmacology, Vol. 2. LC 74-10187. 1979. 29.50 (ISBN 0-12-004702-0); library ed. 39.00 (ISBN 0-12-004772-1); microfiche 19.50 (ISBN 0-12-004773-X). Acad Pr.

Thompson, Travis & Dockens, William S., eds. Application of Behaviour Modification. 1975. 62.00 (ISBN 0-12-689550-3). Acad Pr.

Thompson, Travis & Grabowski, John, eds. Behavior Modification of the Mentally Retarded. 2nd ed. (Illus.). 576p. 1977. text ed. 24.95x (ISBN 0-19-502052-9); pap. text ed. 14.95x (ISBN 0-19-502053-7). Oxford U Pr.

Thompson, Treva L. The Comprehensive System Procedure Desk Book. LC 82-80832. 350p. Date not set. 24.95 (ISBN 0-942898-01-X). Halpern & Simon.
--Information Processing Job Description for Personnel Officers. LC 82-83717. 100p. Date not set. 10.50 (ISBN 0-942898-03-6). Halpern & Simon.
--Systems Project Management: Principles & Guidelines. LC 82-80833. 200p. Date not set. 14.50 (ISBN 0-942898-00-1). Halpern & Simon.
--VSAM Performance & System Fine-Tuning Quick Reference Handbook. LC 82-83606. 150p. Date not set. 17.50 (ISBN 0-942898-02-8). Halpern & Simon.

Thompson, Van, jt. auth. see Simonsen, Richard.

Thompson, Victor H. Eudora Welty: A Reference Guide. 1976. lib. bdg. 19.50 o.p. (ISBN 0-8161-7801-1, Hall Reference). G K Hall.

Thompson, Virginia & Adloff, Richard. The French Pacific Islands: French Polynesia & New Caledonia. LC 71-138634. (Illus.). 1971. 47.50x (ISBN 0-520-01843-5). U of Cal Pr.

Thompson, Virginia, ed. see Shulte, Albert P. & Choate, Stuart A.

Thompson, Vivian L. George Washington. (Beginning Biography Ser.). (Illus.). (gr. k-3). 1964. PLB 5.99 o.p. (ISBN 0-399-60195-3). Putnam Pub Group.
--Hawaiian Tales of Heroes & Champions. LC 72-151757. (Illus.). 128p. (gr. 3-6). 1971. PLB 7.95 (ISBN 0-8234-0192-8). Holiday.
--The Horse That Liked Sandwiches. (See & Read Storybooks). (Illus.). (gr. k-3). 1962. PLB 4.49 o.p. (ISBN 0-399-60264-X). Putnam Pub Group.

Thompson, W. Oscar, Jr. & Thompson, Carolyn. Concentric Circles of Concern. LC 81-67488. 1981. 6.95 (ISBN 0-8054-6233-3). Broadman.

Thompson, W. S. & Whelpton, P. K. Population Trends in the United States. (Demographic Monographs). 428p. 1969. 58.00 (ISBN 0-677-02370-7). Gordon.

Thompson, W. Scott, ed. National Security in the 1980's: From Weakness to Strength. LC 80-80648. 524p. (Orig.). 1980. text ed. 19.95 (ISBN 0-87855-412-2); pap. text ed. 8.95 (ISBN 0-917616-38-3). ICS Pr.
--National Security in the 1980's: From Weakness to Strength. 524p. 1980. text ed. 19.95 (ISBN 0-87855-398-3); pap. text ed. 8.95 (ISBN 0-917616-38-3). Transaction Bk.
--The Third World: Premises of U. S. Policy. 2nd ed. 350p. 1983. text ed. 22.50 (ISBN 0-917616-58-8); pap. text ed. 8.95 (ISBN 0-917616-57-X). ICS Pr.
--The Third World: Premises of U.S. Policy. LC 78-67593. 334p. 1978. pap. 7.95 o.p. (ISBN 0-917616-30-8). ICS Pr.

Thompson, Waite & Gottleib, Richard M. The Santa Fe Guide. Hausman, Gerald, ed. LC 80-18575. (Illus.). 64p. (Orig.). 1980. pap. 4.50 (ISBN 0-913270-89-X). Sunstone Pr.

Thompson, Wayne C. Western Europe, 1982. Dostert, Pierre E., ed. (The World Today Ser.). (Illus.). 368p. 1982. pap. text ed. 8.00 (ISBN 0-943448-05-0). Stryker-Post.

Thompson, William. Music for Listeners. (Illus.). 1978. text ed. 20.95 (ISBN 0-13-608026-X); records 18.95 (ISBN 0-13-608018-9). P-H.

Thompson, William, jt. auth. see Palmer, Monte.

Thompson, William B., jt. auth. see Simon, Albert.

Thompson, William F. & Karanganis, Jerome J. Choice Over Chance: Options for Economic & Energy Futures. 304p. 1981. 27.95 (ISBN 0-03-059554-1); pap. 11.95 (ISBN 0-03-059556-8). Praeger.

Thompson, William I. The Imagination of an Insurrection: Dublin, Easter 1916. 288p. 1982. pap. 7.95 (ISBN 0-940262-02-9). Lindisfarne Pr.
--Quetzalcoatl: The Flight of the Serpent. LC 82-84052. 80p. (Orig.). 1983. pap. 6.95 (ISBN 0-940262-03-7). Lindisfarne Pr.

Thompson, William L., jt. auth. see Thompson, Edith M.

Thompson, William P. Orientation in Science. LC 82-20189. 480p. (Orig.). 1983. lib. bdg. 28.50 (ISBN 0-8191-2885-6); pap. text ed. 16.75 (ISBN 0-8191-2886-4). U Pr of Amer.

Thompson, William R., jt. auth. see Fuller, John L.

Thomsen, Charles B. CM: Developing, Marketing & Delivering Construction Management Services. (Illus.). 192p. 1982. 27.95x (ISBN 0-07-064490-X). McGraw.

Thomsen, Gregory & McInerny, Paul M. An Accent Guide: 151 Tax Deductions You Can Take. (Orig.). 1982. pap. 3.50 (ISBN 0-915708-14-0). Cheever Pub.

Thomsen, Moritz. Farm on the River of Emeralds. 1978. 10.95 o.p. (ISBN 0-395-26311-5). HM.

Thomsen, Robert. Bill W. 15.95 o.p. (ISBN 0-686-92062-7). Hazelden.

Thomsen, Russel J., jt. auth. see Popp, Lothar.

Thomsen, Russell J. Medical Wisdom from the Bible. Date not set. pap. 1.95 (ISBN 0-8007-8370-0, Spire Bks). Revell.

Thomsett, Karin. Verses, Rhymes, & Other Nonsense. 1979. 5.50 o.p. (ISBN 0-533-04196-1). Vantage.

Thomson. Museum Environment: Control for Preservation. LC 78-40366. 1978. 59.95 (ISBN 0-408-70792-5). Butterworth.
--Teaching Patient Care. 1981. 9.95 (ISBN 0-471-26039-8, Wiley Heyden). Wiley.

Thomson, A. D. & Cotton, R. E. Lecture Notes on Pathology. (Illus.). 880p. 1982. pap. text ed. 35.00 (ISBN 0-632-00032-5, B4798-3). Mosby.

Thomson, A. M., jt. auth. see Roberts, D. F.

Thomson, A. W. The Grievance Procedure in the Private Sector. 1974. pap. 2.00 (ISBN 0-87546-249-9). ILR Pr.

Thomson, A. W. J. Introduction to Collective Bargining in Higher Education. (Key Issues Ser.: No. 16). 40p. 1974. pap. 2.00 (ISBN 0-87546-250-2). ILR Pr.

Thomson, Andrew & Warner, Malcolm. The Behavioural Sciences & Industrial Relations. 202p. 1981. text ed. 35.50 (ISBN 0-566-00383-X). Gower Pub Ltd.

Thomson, Arthur. Handbook of Anatomy for Art Students. 5th ed. (Illus.). 11.50 (ISBN 0-8446-3069-1). Peter Smith.

Thomson, Barry, photos by. The Enchanted Light: Images of the Grand Canyon. 1979. pap. 7.00 (ISBN 0-89734-050-7). Mus Northern Ariz.

Thomson, C. Theoretical Chemistry, Vol. 4. 189p. 1982. 140.00x (ISBN 0-85186-784-7, Pub. by Royal Soc Chem England). State Mutual Bk.

Thomson, Charles M. Fundamentals of Electronics. 1979. 22.95 (ISBN 0-13-338103-X). P-H.
--Mathematics for Electronics. (Illus.). 560p. 1976. text ed. 21.95x (ISBN 0-13-562629-3). P-H.

Thomson, D. F., ed. Catullus: A Critical Edition. LC 77-26314. xv, 205p. 1978. 18.00x (ISBN 0-8078-1323-0). U of NC Pr.

Thomson, D. F., tr. see Erasmus, Desiderius.

Thomson, D. M., ed. Assessment of Immune Status by the Leukocyte Adherence Inhibition Test. LC 82-3984. 380p. 1982. 45.00 (ISBN 0-12-689750-6). Acad Pr.

Thomson, Daisy. Journey to Love. 1978. pap. 1.25 o.p. (ISBN 0-515-04479-2). Jove Pubns.

Thomson, David. England in the Twentieth Century, 1914-63. lib. bdg. 11.50x (ISBN 0-88307-269-6). Gannon.
--Language. LC 75-24866. (Human Behavior). (Illus.). (gr. 5 up). 1975. PLB 13.28 (ISBN 0-685-72980-X, Pub. by Time-Life). Silver.
--Two Frenchmen. LC 75-8806. 255p. 1975. Repr. of 1951 ed. lib. bdg. 16.00x (ISBN 0-8371-8115-1, THTWF). Greenwood.

Thomson, David & Evans, George E. The Leaping Hare. (Illus.). 7.95 (ISBN 0-571-09559-3); pap. 4.95 (ISBN 0-571-10630-7). Faber & Faber.

Thomson, David B. In the Shining Mountains: A Would-Be Mountain Man in Search of the Wilderness. LC 79-2126. (Illus.). 1979. 10.95 o.p. (ISBN 0-394-42755-6). Knopf.

Thomson, Derick. An Introduction to Gaelic Poetry. LC 73-86601. 319p. 1974. 10.00 o.p. (ISBN 0-312-42735-2). St Martin.

Thomson, Donald A., et al. Reef Fishes of the Sea of Cortez: The Rocky Shore Fishes of the Gulf of California. LC 78-18835. 302p. 1979. 49.95 (ISBN 0-471-86162-6, Pub. by Wiley-Interscience). Wiley.

Thomson, Donald F. Kinship & Behavior in North Queensland: A Preliminary Account of Kinship & Social Organization on Cape York Peninsula. Scheffler, H. W., ed. (AIAS Social Anthropology Ser.: No. 7). (Illus.). 1972. pap. text ed. 8.50x (ISBN 0-85575-026-X). Humanities.

Thomson, Elizabeth H., jt. auth. see Fulton, John F.

Thomson, Ernie. It's a Baby. LC 80-925. pap. 2.99 o.s.i. (ISBN 0-385-17128-5). Doubleday.

Thomson, F. J. Elsevier's Dictionary of Financial Terms. LC 79-11810. 496p. (Eng., Ger., Span., Fr., Ital., Dutch.). 1980. 113.00 (ISBN 0-444-41775-3). Elsevier.

Thomson, F. P. Tapestry: Mirror of History. 1980. 14.95 o.p. (ISBN 0-517-53415-0). Crown.

Thomson, George H., ed. see Forster, E. M.

Thomson, George L. Traditional Irish Recipes. (Illus.). 1982. pap. 9.95 (ISBN 0-88289-339-4, Pub. by Canongate Pub Scotland). Pelican.

Thomson, George M. The Ball at Glenkerran. 229p. 1983. 16.95 (ISBN 0-436-52044-3, Pub by Secker & Warburg). David & Charles.

Thomson, H. Douglas. Masters of Mystery: A Study of the Detective Story. LC 77-92479. (Illus.). 1978. pap. 4.00 o.p. (ISBN 0-486-23606-4). Dover.

Thomson, Helen. Fibres & Fabrics of Today. 3rd ed. 1974. pap. text ed. 6.00x o.p. (ISBN 0-435-42302-9). Heinemann Ed.
--Working with Fibres & Fabrics. 1967. pap. text ed. 2.50x o.p. (ISBN 0-435-42880-2). Heinemann Ed.

Thomson, Hugh G., jt. auth. see Kernahan, Desmond A.

Thomson, J. Walt Whitman: The Man & the Poet. LC 71-163457. (Studies in Whitman, No. 28). 1971. Repr. of 1910 ed. lib. bdg. 32.95x (ISBN 0-8383-1319-1). Haskell.

Thomson, J., ed. A Guide to Instrument Design. 456p. 1963. write for info. (ISBN 0-85066-006-8, Pub. by Taylor & Francis). Intl Pubns Serv.

Thomson, J. Arthur. Concerning Evolution. 1925. text ed. 32.50x (ISBN 0-686-83508-5). Elliots Bks.

Thomson, J. H., jt. auth. see Smith, F. Graham.

Thomson, J. K. Clermont-De-Lodeve, 1633-1789: Fluctuations in the Prosperity of a Languedocian Cloth-Making Town. LC 81-12222. (Illus.). 520p. 1982. 59.50 (ISBN 0-521-23951-6). Cambridge U Pr.

Thomson, J. R. An Introduction to Seed Technology. LC 79-4412. 252p. 1979. 69.95x o.s.i. (ISBN 0-470-26644-9). Halsted Pr.

Thomson, J. R., ed. Advances in Research & Technology of Seeds, Pt. 2. 1977. pap. 15.00 (ISBN 90-220-0606-9, PDC13, Pub. by PUDOC). Unipub.
--Advances in Research & Technology of Seeds, Pt. 3. 1978. pap. 16.00 (ISBN 90-220-0649-2, PDC14, Pub. by PUDOC). Unipub.

Thomson, J. S. International Book of Honor. 1000p. 1983. 95.00 (ISBN 0-934544-24-7). Am Biog Inst.

Thomson, J. S., ed. American Registry Series. 900p. 1981. 40.00 o.p. (ISBN 0-934544-11-5). Am Biog Inst.
--The American Registry Series--First Selected Edition. LC 79-56931. 700p. 1983. 49.95x (ISBN 0-934544-11-5, Pub. by Intl Biog). Biblio Dist.
--The Biographical Roll of Honor, Vol. I. 1000p. 1983. 150.00 (ISBN 0-934544-25-5). Am Biog Inst.
--Community Leaders & Noteworthy Americans. 10th rev. ed. LC 74-111336. (Community Leaders & Noteworthy Americans Ser.). 1979. 39.95 o.p. (ISBN 0-934544-02-6). Am Biog Inst.
--Community Leaders of America. 11th rev. ed. LC 74-111336. (Community Leaders & Noteworthy Americans Ser.). 1981. 39.95 o.p. (ISBN 0-934544-09-3). Am Biog Inst.
--Personalities of America, First Edition. LC 79-51997. (Illus.). 1982. 55.00 o.p. (ISBN 0-934544-06-9). Am Biog Inst.
--Personalities of the South. 11th ed. LC 73-4535. 382p. 1981. 54.95x (ISBN 0-934544-04-2, Pub. by Intl Biog Ctr). Biblio Dist.
--Personalities of the West & Midwest, Sixth Edition. rev. ed. LC 68-56857. (Personalities of the West & Midwest Ser.). 1979. 39.95 o.p. (ISBN 0-934544-07-7). Am Biog Inst.
--Personalities of the West & Midwest. 7th rev. ed. LC 68-56857. 1982. 54.95x o.p. (ISBN 0-934544-08-5). Am Biog Inst.

--The Registry of American Achievement. 2nd ed. (American Registry Ser.). 1983. 100.00 (ISBN 0-686-81733-8). Am Biog Inst.

--Two Thousand Notable Americans. 1000p. 1982. 125.00 (ISBN 0-934544-23-9). Am Biog Inst.

Thomson, J. W. The Lichen Genus Physcia in North America. (Illus.). 1963. pap. 24.00 (ISBN 3-7682-5407-0). Lubrecht & Cramer.

Thomson, James. The Seasons. Sanbrook, James, ed. (Oxford English Texts). (Illus.). 1981. 110.00x (ISBN 0-686-80318-3). Oxford U Pr.

Thomson, James & Roberts, Henry D. The Seasons. 184p. 1982. Repr. of 1939 ed. lib. bdg. 30.00 (ISBN 0-89987-820-2). Darby Bks.

Thomson, James C., Jr., et al. Sentimental Imperialists. LC 79-1689. 347p. 1982. pap. 6.68i (ISBN 0-06-090970-6, CN 970, CN). Har-Row.

Thomson, James W. An Introduction to the Fundamentals of Financial Analysis for Business Students. LC 79-8512. 1979. pap. text ed. 13.50 (ISBN 0-8191-0872-3). U Pr of Amer.

Thomson, John. China & It's People in Early Photographs. (Photography Ser.). (Illus.). 320p. 1983. pap. 12.95 (ISBN 0-486-24393-1). Dover.

Thomson, John M. A Distant Music: The Life & Times of Alfred Hill 1870-1960. (Illus.). 1982. 39.00 (ISBN 0-19-558051-6). Oxford U Pr.

--Recorder Profiles. 1972. pap. 9.00 (ISBN 0-901938-09-2, 75-A11330). Eur-Am Music.

Thomson, John W., jt. auth. see Holmes, Lowell D.

Thomson, Joseph J. Electricity & Matter. 1911. text ed. 32.50x (ISBN 0-686-83533-6). Elliots Bks.

Thomson, June. Alibi in Time. (Crime Club Ser.). 192p. 1980. 10.95 o.p. (ISBN 0-385-17075-0). Doubleday.

--Portrait of Lilith. LC 82-45503. (Crime Club Ser.). 192p. 1983. 11.95 (ISBN 0-385-18335-6). Doubleday.

Thomson, Kenneth, jt. auth. see McGill, Angus.

Thomson, Norman, jt. auth. see Easton, Brian.

Thomson, Patricia. The Victorian Heroine: A Changing Ideal, 1837-1873. LC 73-19303. 1978. Repr. of 1956 ed. lib. bdg. 17.25x (ISBN 0-8371-7118-0, THVH). Greenwood.

Thomson, Paul H. Macadamia Handbook. 60p. 1983. pap. 5.00 (ISBN 0-9602066-3-9). Bonsall Pub.

Thomson, Paul H., jt. auth. see Gentry, Howard S.

Thomson, Paul H., ed. see Koch, Frank D.

Thomson, Philip. The Grotesque. (Critical Idiom Ser.). 1979. pap. 4.95x (ISBN 0-416-08180-0). Methuen Inc.

Thomson, Robb W., jt. auth. see Wert, Charles A.

Thomson, Robert. Bill W. LC 74-1861. (Illus.). 382p. 1975. 17.26i (ISBN 0-06-014267-7, HarpT). Har-Row.

--The Grosset Encyclopedia of Natural Medicine. LC 79-56186. (Illus.). 1980. pap. 9.95 (ISBN 0-448-14897-8, G&D). Putnam Pub Group.

--The Marquesas: Their Description & Early History. 2nd ed. (Monograph Ser.: No. 2). pap. 6.95 (ISBN 0-939154-05-6). Inst Polynesian.

--Natural Medicine. 1978. 10.95 o.p. (ISBN 0-07-064513-2, GB). McGraw.

--Source & Guide to the Western Tradition of Natural Hearing: The Tibb System. 400p. (Orig.). 1983. pap. 12.95 (ISBN 0-89281-042-4). Destiny Bks.

Thomson, Robert P., jt. auth. see Hyman, Ronald T.

Thomson, Rodney M. Manuscripts from St. Albans Abbey, 1066-1235, 2 vols. 302p. 1982. text ed. 120.00x set (ISBN 0-85991-085-7, Pub. by Boydell & Brewer). Biblio Dist.

Thomson, S. J., jt. ed. see Lenihan, J. M.

Thomson, Sarah K. Interlibrary Loan Policies Directory. LC 74-32182. 496p. 1975. 9.00 o.p. (ISBN 0-8389-0197-2). ALA.

Thomson, T., ed. see Tait, Malcolm.

Thomson, Tom. Ideas from Chemistry. (Science Modules Ser.). (gr. 7-8). 1973. pap. text ed. 7.84 (ISBN 0-201-07578-4, Sch Div); tchr's manual 3.48 (ISBN 0-201-07579-2). A-W.

Thomson, Virgil. Musical Scene. Repr. of 1945 ed. lib. bdg. 17.50x (ISBN 0-8371-0684-2, THMS). Greenwood.

Thomson, W. T. Agricultural Chemicals, Book 3: Miscellaneous Chemicals. Rev. ed. 175p. 1980-81. 13.50 (ISBN 0-913702-08-0). Thomson Pub CA.

Thomson, W. T., jt. auth. see Page, B. G.

Thomson, William. Theory of Vibrations with Applications. 2nd ed. (Illus.). 608p. 1981. text ed. 34.95 (ISBN 0-13-914523-0). P-H.

Thomson, William, ed. see Gillett, Dorothy.

Thomson, William E. Introduction to Music Reading: Concepts & Applications. 2nd ed. 320p. 1980. pap. text ed. 14.95x (ISBN 0-534-00817-8). Wadsworth Pub.

Thomson, William J. Te Pito Te Henua, or Easter Island. (The Americas Collection Ser.). (Illus.). 108p. 1982. pap. 14.95 (ISBN 0-936332-14-X). Falcon Hill Pr.

Thomson, William P. The Little General & the Rousay Crofters. 248p. 1981. text ed. 37.50x (ISBN 0-686-86095-0, Pub. by Donald Scotland). Humanities.

Thonner, F. The Flowering Plants of Africa: An Analytical Key to the Genera of African Phanerogams. 1962. Repr. of 1916 ed. 72.00 (ISBN 3-7682-0118-X). Lubrecht & Cramer.

Thonssen, Lester see Braden, Waldo W. & Peterson, Owen.

Thonssen, Lester, et al. Speech Criticism. 2nd ed. 590p. 1981. Repr. of 1970 ed. text ed. 25.00 (ISBN 0-89874-247-1). Krieger.

Thorbjarnarson, Bjorn. Surgery of the Biliary Tract. LC 74-25482. (Mpcs Ser.: Vol. 16). (Illus.). 166p. 1975. text ed. 18.00 o.p. (ISBN 0-7216-8858-6). Saunders.

--Surgery of the Biliary Tract. 2nd ed. (Major Problems in Surgery Ser.: Vol. 16). (Illus.). 265p. 1982. 29.50 (ISBN 0-7216-8853-5). Saunders.

Thorburn, Anna H. & Turner, P. Living Salt Free...& Easy. 1976. pap. 2.25 (ISBN 0-451-12091-4, AE2091, Sig). NAL.

Thorburn, Craig. Teknologi Kampungan: A Compendium of Indonesian Indigenous Technologies. Darrow, Ken & Stanley, Bill, eds. (Illus.). 154p. 1982. pap. 5.00 (ISBN 0-917704-16-9). Volunteers Asia.

Thorburn, H. Party Politics in Canada. 4th ed. 1979. pap. 10.95 (ISBN 0-13-652602-0). P-H.

Thoreau, Henry D. The Annotated Walden. Stern, Philip V., ed. (Illus.). 512p. 1971. 15.00 o.p. (ISBN 0-517-50402-2, C N Potter Bks). Crown.

--Civil Disobedience. Brown, Edmund R., ed. (International Pocket Library). pap. 3.00 (ISBN 0-686-77251-2). Branden.

--The Illustrated World of Thoreau. Chapnick, Howard, ed. LC 73-15134. (Illus.). 192p. 1976. pap. 6.95 o.p. (ISBN 0-448-12590-0, G&D). Putnam Pub Group.

--In the Woods & Fields of Concord: Selections From the Journals of Henry David Thoreau. Harding, Walter, ed. (Illus.). 176p. 1982. pap. 6.95 (ISBN 0-87905-090-X). Peregrine Smith.

--Journal 2: Eighteen Forty-Two to Eighteeen Forty-Eight. Sattelmeyer, Robert, ed. LC 78-70325. (The Writings of Henry D. Thoreau Ser.). (Illus.). 600p. 1983. 22.50x (ISBN 0-691-06186-6). Princeton U Pr.

--Portable Thoreau. rev. ed. Bode, Carl, ed. (Viking Portable Library: No. 31). 1977. pap. 6.95 (ISBN 0-14-015031-5, P31). Penguin.

--Thoreau: Selected Writings. Leary, Lewis, ed. LC 58-5337. (Crofts Classics Ser.). 1958. pap. text ed. 3.25x (ISBN 0-88295-099-1). Harlan Davidson.

--Thoreau's Guide to Cape Cod. Adams, Alexander B., ed. (Illus.). 1962. pap. 7.50 (ISBN 0-8159-6904-X). Devin.

--Walden. Bd. with On the Duty of Civil Disobedience. 1962. pap. 2.95 (ISBN 0-02-054720-X, 05472, Collier). Macmillan.

--Walden & Other Writings. New ed. Atkinson, Brooks, ed. 1981. pap. 3.95x (ISBN 0-394-30935-9, T35, Mod LibC). Modern Lib.

--What Befell at Mrs. Brook's. LC 72-13329. (Seedling Bks.). (Illus.). 32p. (gr. 2-6). 1974. PLB 4.95g (ISBN 0-8225-0284-4). Lerner Pubns.

Thoreau, Henry D. & Krutch, Joseph W. Walden & Other Writings. (Bantam Classics Ser.). 435p. (YA) (gr. 9-12). 1981. pap. 1.75 (ISBN 0-553-21012-2). Bantam.

Thoreau, Henry D; see Brown, Edmund R.

Thoreau, Henry David. Walden & Other Writings. Atkinson, Brooks, ed. & intro. by. 7.95 (ISBN 0-394-60421-0). Modern Lib.

Thorell, Jan I. & Larson, Steven M. Radioimmunoassay & Related Techniques: Methodology & Clinical Applications. LC 77-23927. (Illus.). 298p. 1978. 24.50 o.p. (ISBN 0-8016-4944-7). Mosby.

Thorelli, Hans & Thorelli, Sarah. Consumer Information Systems & Consumer Policy. LC 76-48925. 432p. 1977. prof ref 25.00x (ISBN 0-88410-271-8). Ballinger Pub.

Thorelli, Sarah, jt. auth. see Thorelli, Hans.

Thoret, Jacques, jt. auth. see Ferrair, Antoine.

Thoret, Jean-Claude. Les Djimini: Elements d'Organisation Sociale. (Black Africa Ser.). 173p. (Fr.). 1974. Repr. of 1969 ed. lib. bdg. 51.00x o.p. (ISBN 0-8287-0819-3, 71-2016). Clearwater Pub.

Thorgerson, Storm & Dean, Roger, eds. Album Cover Album, Vol. 2. (Illus.). 160p. (Orig.). 1982. pap. 14.95 (ISBN 0-89104-312-8, A & W Visual Library). A & W Pubs.

Thorlin, Anders. Ideas for Woodturning. (Creative Handcrafts Ser.). (Illus.). 128p. 1980. 13.95 (ISBN 0-13-450361-9, Spec); pap. 5.95 (ISBN 0-13-450353-8). P-H.

Thorn, et al, eds. Harrison's Principles of Internal Medicine. 8th ed. (Illus.). 1976. text ed. 45.00 1 vol. ed. o.p. (ISBN 0-07-064518-3, 64518-3, HP); text ed. 55.00 2 vol. ed. o.p. (ISBN 0-07-064519-1, 64519-1). McGraw.

Thorn, Colin E. Space & Time in Geomorphology. (The Binghamton' Symposia in Geomorphology, International Ser.: No. 12). (Illus.). 350p. 1982. text ed. 45.00x (ISBN 0-04-551056-3). Allen Unwin.

Thorn, Ian. Frankenstein Meets Wolfman. Schroeder, Howard, ed. LC 81-9902. (Monsters Ser.). (Illus.). 48p. (gr. 3-5). 1981. PLB 7.95 (ISBN 0-89686-188-0); pap. text ed. 3.50 (ISBN 0-89686-191-0). Crestwood Hse.

Thorn, John. A Century of Baseball Lore. (Illus.). 240p. (Orig.). 1976. pap. 3.95 o.s.i. (ISBN 0-89104-226-1, A & W Visual Library). A & W Pubs.

--The Relief Pitcher: Baseball's New Hero. 1979. 10.95 o.p. (ISBN 0-525-19048-1). Dutton.

Thorn, John, ed. The Armchair Quarterback. (Illus.). 320p. 1982. 19.95 (ISBN 0-684-17657-2, ScribT). Scribner.

Thorn, Richard S. Introduction to Money & Banking. LC 75-34099. 544p. 1976. text ed. 16.95x o.p. (ISBN 0-06-046614-6). Kelley.

Thorn, Richard S., ed. Monetary Theory & Policy. LC 81-43023. 702p. 1981. lib. bdg. 28.50 (ISBN 0-8191-1623-8); pap. text ed. 16.50 (ISBN 0-8191-1624-6). U Pr of Amer.

Thornberg, Kathy. The Whole Teacher. LC 76-52301. 1976. pap. text ed. 14.95 (ISBN 0-89334-005-7). Humanics Ltd.

Thornberry, Richard P. Designing Stair Pressurization Systems. Date not set. 4.65 (ISBN 0-686-37668-4, TR 82-4). Society Fire Protect.

Thornberry, Terence P. & Sagarin, Edward, eds. Images of Crime: Offenders & Victims. LC 73-21460. (Special Studies). (Illus.). 150p. 1974. 26.95 o.p. (ISBN 0-275-28871-4). Praeger.

Thornborough, Laura. Great Smoky Mountains. rev. ed. (Illus.). 1962. 8.50 (ISBN 0-87049-034-6). U of Tenn Pr.

Thornburg, Hershel D. Development in Adolescence. 2nd ed. LC 81-7753. 1982. text ed. 22.95 (ISBN 0-8185-0448-X); test items avail. (ISBN 0-685-55265-9). Brooks-Cole.

Thornburg, Max W., et al. Turkey, an Economic Appraisal. LC 68-8074. (Illus.). 1968. Repr. of 1949 ed. lib. bdg. 19.00x (ISBN 0-8371-0250-2, THEA). Greenwood.

Thornburg, Newton. Dreamland. 1983. 14.95 (ISBN 0-87795-444-5). Arbor Hse.

Thornbury, William D. Principles of Geomorphology. 2nd ed. LC 68-8323. 594p. 1969. text ed. 32.95x (ISBN 0-471-86197-9). Wiley.

Thorndike, David & Tarlow, Eric K. Consumer Credit Computation & Compliance Guide with Annual Percentage Rate Tables. LC 80-52857. pap. 48.50 (ISBN 0-88262-511-X). Warren.

Thorndike, Eard L. & Bergman, Elsie O. Adult Learning. 335p. Repr. of 1928 ed. lib. bdg. 50.00 (ISBN 0-89987-821-0). Darby Bks.

Thorndike, Edward L. Selected Writings from a Connectionist's Psychology. Repr. of 1949 ed. lib. bdg. 18.50x (ISBN 0-8371-2570-7, THWP). Greenwood.

--A Teacher's Word Book of the Twenty Thousand Words Found Most Frequently & Widely in General Reading for Children & Young People. rev. ed. LC 73-5527. 182p. 1975. Repr. of 1932 ed. 40.00x (ISBN 0-8103-4108-5). Gale.

Thorndike, R. L. & Hagen, E. P. Measurement & Evaluation in Psychology & Education. 4th ed. 693p. 1977. 27.95 (ISBN 0-471-86366-1). Wiley.

--Perspectives in Measurement & Evaluation: A Study Guide. 153p. 1977. 10.95 (ISBN 0-471-02190-3). Wiley.

Thorndike, R. M. Correlational Procedures for Research. LC 76-8462. 340p. 1978. 21.50x o.p. (ISBN 0-470-15090-4). Halsted Pr.

Thorndike, Robert L. Applied Psychometrics. LC 81-81699. 1982. 26.95 (ISBN 0-395-30077-0). HM.

Thorndike, Robert L., ed. Educational Measurement. 2nd ed. 1971. 35.00 o.p. (ISBN 0-8268-1271-6). ACE.

Thorndike, Susan. The Electric Radish & Other Jokes. LC 79-6981. (Illus.). 1979. pap. 3.50 o.p. (ISBN 0-385-14753-8, Zephyr). Doubleday.

Thorne, Anne. Spectrophysics. 1974. 32.00x o.p. (ISBN 0-412-12510-2, Pub. by Chapman & Hall); pap. 22.95x (ISBN 0-412-12520-X). Methuen Inc.

Thorne, Barrie. Language & Sex. Henley, Nancy, ed. 1975. 14.95 (ISBN 0-88377-043-1). Newbury Hse.

Thorne, Christopher. Allies of a Kind: The United States, Britain, & the War Against Japan, 1941-1945. LC 79-14921. (Illus.). 1979. pap. 12.95 (ISBN 0-19-520173-6, GB 585, GB). Oxford U Pr.

Thorne, Christopher, ed. see Nicholls, A. J.

Thorne, G. D. Understanding the Mentally Retarded. 1965. 14.95 (ISBN 0-07-064526-4, HP). McGraw.

Thorne, Ian. Ancient Astronauts. Schroeder, Howard, ed. LC 78-7973. (Search for the Unknown Ser.). (Illus.). (gr. 4). 1978. PLB 6.95 (ISBN 0-913940-86-0); pap. 3.50 (ISBN 0-89686-007-8). Crestwood Hse.

--The Bermuda Triangle. Schroeder, Howard, ed. LC 78-5626. (Search for the Unknown Ser.). (Illus.). (gr. 4). 1978. PLB 6.95 (ISBN 0-913940-81-X); pap. 3.50 (ISBN 0-89686-002-7). Crestwood Hse.

--Big Foot. Schroeder, Howard, ed. LC 78-5358. (Search for the Unknown Ser.). (Illus.). (gr. 4). 1978. PLB 6.95 (ISBN 0-913940-82-8); pap. 3.50 (ISBN 0-89686-003-5). Crestwood Hse.

--The Blob. Schroeder, Howard, ed. (Monsters Ser.). (Illus.). 48p. (Orig.). (gr. 4-8). 1982. PLB 7.95 (ISBN 0-89686-212-7); pap. 3.50 (ISBN 0-89686-215-1). Crestwood Hse.

--Creature from the Black Lagoon. Schroeder, Howard, ed. LC 81-12468. (The Monsters Ser.). (Illus.). 48p. (Orig.). (gr. 3-5). 1981. PLB 7.95 (ISBN 0-89686-187-2); pap. 3.50 (ISBN 0-89686-190-2). Crestwood Hse.

--The Deadly Mantis. Schroeder, Howard, ed. (Monsters Ser.). (Illus.). 48p. (Orig.). (gr. 4-8). 1982. PLB 7.95 (ISBN 0-89686-214-3); pap. 3.50 (ISBN 0-89686-217-8). Crestwood Hse.

--Dracula. LC 76-51145. (Monster Ser.). (Illus.). (gr. 4-5). 1977. PLB 7.95 (ISBN 0-913940-67-4); pap. 3.50 (ISBN 0-913940-74-7). Crestwood Hse.

--Frankenstein. LC 76-51144. (Monster Ser.). (Illus.). (gr. 4-5). 1977. PLB 7.95 (ISBN 0-913940-66-6); pap. 3.50 (ISBN 0-913940-73-9). Crestwood Hse.

--Godzilla. LC 76-51148. (Monster Ser). (Illus.). (gr. 4-5). 1977. PLB 7.95 (ISBN 0-913940-68-2); pap. 3.50 (ISBN 0-913940-75-5). Crestwood Hse.

--It Came from Outer Space. Schroeder, Howard, ed. (Monsters Ser.). (Illus.). 48p. (Orig.). (gr. 4-8). 1982. PLB 7.95 (ISBN 0-89686-213-5); pap. 3.50 (ISBN 0-89686-216-X). Crestwood Hse.

--King Kong. LC 76-51147. (Monster Ser.). (Illus.). (gr. 4-5). 1977. PLB 7.95 (ISBN 0-913940-69-0); pap. 3.50 (ISBN 0-913940-76-3). Crestwood Hse.

--The Loch Ness Monster. Schroeder, Howard, ed: LC 78-6193. (Search for the Unknown Ser.). (Illus.). (gr. 4). 1978. PLB 6.95 (ISBN 0-913940-83-6); pap. 3.50 (ISBN 0-89686-004-3). Crestwood Hse.

--Mad Scientists. LC 76-51149. (Monster Ser.). (Illus.). (gr. 4-5). 1977. PLB 7.95 (ISBN 0-913940-70-4); pap. 3.50 (ISBN 0-913940-77-1). Crestwood Hse.

--Monster Tales of Native Americans. Schroeder, Howard, ed. LC 78-5234. (Search for the Unknown Ser.). (Illus.). (gr. 4). 1978. PLB 6.95 (ISBN 0-913940-85-2); pap. 3.50 (ISBN 0-89686-006-X). Crestwood Hse.

--The Mummy. Schroeder, Howard, ed. LC 81-12481. (The Monster Ser.). (Illus.). 48p. (Orig.). (gr. 3-5). 1981. PLB 7.95 (ISBN 0-89686-186-4); pap. text ed. 3.50 (ISBN 0-89686-189-9). Crestwood Hse.

--UFOs. Schroeder, Howard, ed. LC 78-6529. (Search for the Unknown Ser.). (Illus.). (gr. 4). 1978. PLB 6.95 (ISBN 0-913940-84-4); pap. 3.50 (ISBN 0-89686-005-1). Crestwood Hse.

--The Wolf Man. LC 76-51146. (Monster Ser.). (Illus.). (gr. 4-5). 1977. PLB 7.95 (ISBN 0-913940-71-2); pap. 3.50 (ISBN 0-913940-78-X). Crestwood Hse.

Thorne, Mrs. James W. American Rooms in Miniature. 7th ed. (Illus.). 74p. 1941. pap. 3.95 (ISBN 0-86559-001-X). Art Inst Chi.

--European Rooms in Miniature. 6th ed. (Illus.). 62p. 1948. pap. 3.95 (ISBN 0-86559-002-8). Art Inst Chi.

Thorne, Jean W. Rodeo! LC 76-5641. (Winners Circle Ser.). (gr. 4-5). 1976. PLB 7.95 (ISBN 0-913940-42-9). Crestwood Hse.

Thorne, Jenny. My Uncle. LC 81-22786. (Illus.). 32p. (ps-3). 9.95 (ISBN 0-689-50233-8, McElderry Bk). Atheneum.

Thorne, Leon. Out of the Ashes. 1976. Repr. 6.95 o.p. (ISBN 0-8197-0394-X). Bloch.

Thorne, Nicola. Cashmere. (Illus.). 408p. 1982. 18.95 (ISBN 0-385-17644-9). Doubleday.

--The Perfect Wife & Mother. 266p. 1981. 11.95 o.p. (ISBN 0-312-60077-1). St Martin.

--Sisters & Lovers. LC 80-509. 600p. 1981. 14.95 o.p. (ISBN 0-385-15857-2). Doubleday.

Thorne, Ramsay. Renagade No. 3: Fear Merchant. (Orig.). 1980. pap. 2.25 (ISBN 0-446-30774-2). Warner Bks.

--Renegade No. Nine: Hell Raider. 208p. (Orig.). 1981. pap. 2.25 (ISBN 0-446-30777-7). Warner Bks.

--Renegade No. 11: Citadel of Death. 192p. (Orig.). 1981. pap. 2.25 (ISBN 0-446-30778-5). Warner Bks.

--Renegade, No. 14: Harvest of Death. 192p. 1982. pap. 1.95 (ISBN 0-446-30124-8). Warner Bks.

--Renegade, No. 15: Terror Trail. 192p. 1982. pap. 2.25 (ISBN 0-446-30125-6). Warner Bks.

--Renegade, No. 16: Mexican Marauder. 192p. (Orig.). 1983. pap. 2.25 (ISBN 0-446-30255-4). Warner Bks.

--Renegade, No. 17: Slaughter in Sinaloa. 192p. (Orig.). 1983. pap. 2.25 (ISBN 0-446-30257-0). Warner Bks.

--Renegade, No. 18: Cavern of Doom. 192p. (Orig.). 1983. pap. 2.25 (ISBN 0-446-30258-9). Warner Bks.

--Renegade No. 19: Hellfire in Honduras. 192p. (Orig.). 1983. pap. 2.25 (ISBN 0-446-30630-4). Warner Bks.

--Renegade No. 2: Blood Runner. (Orig.). 1979. pap. 2.25 (ISBN 0-446-30780-7). Warner Bks.

--Renegade No. 5: Macumba Killer. 224p. (Orig.). 1980. pap. 2.25 (ISBN 0-446-30775-0). Warner Bks.

--Renegade No. 7: Death in High Places. 192p. (Orig.). 1981. pap. 2.25 (ISBN 0-446-30776-9). Warner Bks.

--Renegade No. 8: Over the Andes to Hell. 192p. (Orig.). 1981. pap. 2.25 (ISBN 0-446-30781-5). Warner Bks.

--Renegade N0. 12: Badlands Brigade. 224p. (Orig.). 1982. pap. 2.25 (ISBN 0-446-30779-3). Warner Bks.

Thorne, Robert, ed. Fugitive Facts. 2nd ed. LC 69-19882. 1969. Repr. of 1889 ed. 37.00x (ISBN 0-8103-3750-9). Gale.

Thorne, S., ed. Developments in Food Preservation, Vol. 1. 1981. 67.75 (ISBN 0-85334-979-7, Pub. by Applied Sci England). Elsevier.

Thorne, Samuel E., jt. ed. see Berkowitz, David S.

Thorne, Samuel E., ed. see Constable, Robert.

Thorne, Samuel E., ed. see Robinson, Henry, et al.

Thorner, Michael O., et al. Bromocriptine: A Clinical & Pharmacologica Review. 189p. 1980. text ed. 26.50 (ISBN 0-89004-419-8). Raven.

Thornes, John, jt. ed. see Embleton, Clifford.

Thorne-Thomsen, Kathleen & Brownridge, Linda. Why the Cake Won't Rise & the Jelly Won't Set: A Complete Guide to Avoiding Kitchen Failures. LC 78-6997. (Illus.). 224p. 1979. 10.95 o.s.i. (ISBN 0-89479-036-6). A & W Pubs.

Thornhill, Alan, jt. auth. see Muggeridge, Malcolm.

Thornhill, John. Person & the Group. 1967. 6.75 o.p. (ISBN 0-685-07658-X, 80730). Glencoe.

Thornley, G. C. Elementary Scientific English Practice. 1975. pap. text ed. 3.10x (ISBN 0-582-52183-1). Longman.

Thornley, Margo L. Every Child Can Learn-Something. LC 73-81605. (Illus.). 1973. pap. 6.50x o.p. (ISBN 0-87562-043-4). Spec Child.

Thornton, A. P. For the File on Empire. 1969. 23.00 (ISBN 0-312-29785-8). St Martin.

Thornton, Alice B. How Come You're Not Married. 1966. 5.95 o.p. (ISBN 0-8158-0200-5). Chris Mass.

Thornton, Andre & Janssen, Al. Triumph Born of Tragedy. LC 82-82812. 176p. (Orig.). 1983. pap. 4.95 (ISBN 0-89081-367-1). Harvest Hse.

Thornton, C. S. & Bromley, S. C., eds. Vertebrate Regeneration. LC 73-13830. (Benchmark Papers in Biological Concepts Ser). 528p. 1973. text ed. 58.50 (ISBN 0-12-787544-1). Acad Pr.

Thornton, Carol A. Look into the Facts: Multiplication & Division. Gregory, John, ed. (Illus.). (gr. 2-6). 1977. wkbk. set of 5 9.95 (ISBN 0-88488-063-X); wkbk. set of 30 51.95 (ISBN 0-88488-156-3); tchr's ed. 5.25 (ISBN 0-88488-075-3). Creative Pubns.

Thornton, Carol A. & Noxon, Cathy. Look into the Facts-Addition & Subtraction. Gregory, John, ed. (Illus.). (gr. 2-6). 1977. wkbk set of 5 9.95 (ISBN 0-88488-064-8); wkbk. set of 30 51.95 (ISBN 0-88488-155-5); tchr's ed. 5.25 (ISBN 0-88488-074-5). Creative Pubns.

Thornton, Carol A., jt. auth. see Bley, Nancy S.

Thornton, Earl A., jt. auth. see Huebner, Kenneth H.

Thornton, Emma S., jt. auth. see Adams, Pauline.

Thornton, Francis J. The Snake Harvest. LC 77-20651. 1978. 9.95 o.p. (ISBN 0-698-10904-X, Coward). Putnam Pub Group.

Thornton, George C., 3rd & Oetting, Eugene R. Exercises in Psychological Testing. 2nd ed. 341p. 1982. pap. text ed. 15.50 scp (ISBN 0-06-044909-8, HarpC); instr's. manual avail. (ISBN 0-06-364895-4). Har-Row.

Thornton, Henry D. The Metaphysics of the Womb. (Illus.). 141p. 1981. 49.85 o.p. (ISBN 0-89266-271-9). Am Classical Coll Pr.

Thornton, J. A. Adverse Reactions to Anesthetic Drugs. (Monographs in Anaesthesiology: Vol. 8). 1981. 91.50 (ISBN 0-444-80213-4). Elsevier.

--Techniques of Anaesthesia: With Management of the Patient & Intensive Care. 1974. 29.95x o.p. (ISBN 0-412-12280-4, Pub. by Chapman & Hall). Methuen Inc.

Thornton, J. Quinn. Camp of Death: The Donner Party Mountain Camp, 1846-47. Jones, William R., ed. 1978. pap. 5.95 (ISBN 0-89646-037-1). Outbooks.

Thornton, James E. Design of a Computer: The Control Data 6600. 1970. text ed. 25.50x (ISBN 0-673-05953-7). Scott F.

Thornton, James W., Jr. The Community Junior College. 3rd ed. LC 74-37647. 304p. 1972. text ed. 25.95x (ISBN 0-471-86530-3). Wiley.

Thornton, John. The Kingdom of Kongo: Civil War & Transition, 1641-1718. LC 82-70549. (Illus.). 224p. 1983. 25.00 (ISBN 0-299-09290-9). U of Wis Pr.

Thornton, John L. Medical Books, Libraries & Collectors. 464p. 1966. 41.00 (ISBN 0-233-95501-1, 05825-4, Pub. by Gower Pub Co England). Lexington Bks.

Thornton, Kelsey, ed. see Clare, John.

Thornton, Mary C. The Church & Freemasonry in Brazil, 1872-1875. LC 73-2647. 287p. 1973. Repr. of 1948 ed. lib. bdg. 19.25x (ISBN 0-8371-6816-3, THCF). Greenwood.

Thornton, Maurice, tr. see Gourfinkel, Nina.

Thornton, P. A., jt. auth. see Colangelo, V.

Thornton, Pat, jt. auth. see Odmark, Leif.

Thornton, Penny. Synastry: A Comprehensive Guide to the Astrology of Relationships. 160p. 1983. pap. 8.95 (ISBN 0-85030-276-5). Newcastle Pub.

Thornton, Peter. Baroque & Rococo Silks. 1965. 33.00 o.p. (ISBN 0-571-06315-2). Faber & Faber.

Thornton, R. H. British Shipping. 2nd ed. (English Institution Ser). 1959. 32.50 (ISBN 0-521-06626-3). Cambridge U Pr.

Thornton, R. K., ed. see Gurney, Ivor.

Thornton, Richard C. China: A Political History. 500p. (Orig.). 1981. lib. bdg. 32.50 (ISBN 0-86531-197-8); pap. 15.00 (ISBN 0-86531-198-6). Westview.

Thornton, Robert J. Space, Time & Culture Among the Iraq of Tanzania. LC 79-6793. (Studies in Anthropology Ser.). 1980. 32.50 (ISBN 0-12-690580-0). Acad Pr.

Thornton, William E., et al. Delinquency & Justice. 1981. text ed. 18.95x o.p. (ISBN 0-673-15225-1). Scott F.

Thornton, Willis. Almanac for Americans. LC 70-175784. (Illus.). viii, 418p. 1973. Repr. of 1941 ed. 40.00x (ISBN 0-8103-3276-0). Gale.

Thorogood, Bernard. A Guide to the Book of Amos. LC 76-48551. 1977. pap. 3.95 o.p. (ISBN 0-8170-0725-3). Judson.

Thorou, L., jt. auth. see Heilbroner, R.

Thorp, Edward O. Elementary Probability. LC 75-45419. 162p. 1977. Repr. of 1966 ed. text ed. 9.50 o.p. (ISBN 0-88275-389-4). Krieger.

Thorp, James H. & Gibbons, J. Whitfield, eds. Energy & Environmental Stress in Aquatic Systems: Proceedings. LC 78-27913. (DOE Symposium Ser.). 876p. 1978. pap. 30.00 (ISBN 0-87079-115-X, CONF-771114); microfiche 4.50 (ISBN 0-87079-191-5, CONF-771114). DOE.

Thorp, Margaret. Female Persuasion: Six Strong-Minded Women. 1949. text ed. 16.50x (ISBN 0-686-83549-2). Elliots Bks.

Thorp, R. & Bunker, R. Crow Killer: Jeremiah Johnson. (RL 10). pap. 1.50 (ISBN 0-451-09366-6, W9366, Sig). NAL.

Thorp, Roderick. Jenny & Barnum. 384p. 1981. 14.95 o.p. (ISBN 0-385-15058-X). Doubleday.

Thorp, Rosemary & Whitehead, Lawrence, eds. Inflation & Stabilisation in Latin America. LC 79-11887. 1980. text ed. 37.50x (ISBN 0-8419-0512-6). Holmes & Meier.

Thorp, Willard. American Writing in the Twentieth Century. LC 59-14739. (Library of Congress Ser. in American Civilization). 1960. 18.50x o.p. (ISBN 0-674-02951-8). Harvard U Pr.

Thorp, Willard, intro. by. Four Classic American Novels. Incl. Scarlet Letter. Hawthorne, Nathaniel; Adventures of Huckleberry Finn. Twain, Mark; Red Badge of Courage. Crane, Stephan; Billy Budd. Melville, Herman. 1969. pap. 3.95 (ISBN 0-451-51765-2, CL1765, Sig Classics). NAL.

Thorpe, Don. Amphoto Guide to Available Light Photography. (Amphoto Guide Ser.). (Illus.). 1980. 10.95 o.p. (ISBN 0-8174-2477-6, Amphoto); pap. 7.95 (ISBN 0-8174-2149-1). Watson-Guptill.

Thorpe, Earl E. Eros & Freedom in Southern Life & Thought. LC 78-15170. 1979. Repr. of 1967 ed. lib. bdg. 19.75x (ISBN 0-313-21112-4, THEF). Greenwood.

Thorpe, Elliott R. East Wind, Rain: The Intimate Account of an Intelligence Officer in the Pacific 1939-49. LC 69-12586. 1969. 7.95 o.p. (ISBN 0-87645-020-6). Gambit.

Thorpe, Frances & Pronay, Nicholas. British Official Films in the Second World War: A Descriptive Catalog. 321p. 1980. 45.00 (ISBN 0-903450-27-5). ABC-Clio.

Thorpe, Geoffrey L. & Burns, Laurence E. The Agoraphobic Syndrome: Behavioral Approaches to Evaluation & Treatment. 200p. 1983. 34.95x (ISBN 0-471-10495-7, Pub. by Wiley-Interscience). Wiley.

Thorpe, J. Book of Hillman Imp & Singer Chamois. (Illus.). pap. 5.00x (ISBN 0-392-02318-0, SpS). Sportshelf.

Thorpe, John. Book of Reliant. pap. 5.00x (ISBN 0-392-02335-0, SpS). Sportshelf.

--Exogeny. LC 81-50230. 64p. 1981. pap. 5.00 (ISBN 0-917588-04-5). Trike.

Thorpe, Kay. A Man of Means. (Harlequin Presents Ser.). 192p. 1983. pap. 1.75 (ISBN 0-373-10573-8). Harlequin Bks.

--Master of Morley. (Harlequin Presents Ser.). 192p. 1983. pap. 1.95 (ISBN 0-373-10597-5). Harlequin Bks.

Thorpe, L., ed. see Rothwell, W. & Barron, W. R.

Thorpe, Malcolm R., ed. Organic Adaptation to Environment. 1924. 39.50x (ISBN 0-685-69877-7). Elliots Bks.

Thorpe, R. S. Andesites: Orogenic Andesites & Related Rocks. LC 80-42307. 724p. 1982. 83.95x (ISBN 0-471-28034-8, Pub. by Wiley-Interscience). Wiley.

Thorpe, Sylvia A., tr. see Ramon Y Cajal, Santiago.

Thorpe, W. H. The Origins & Rise of Ethology. 186p. 1979. 23.95 (ISBN 0-03-053251-5). Praeger.

Thorpe, William H. Science, Man, & Morals. LC 76-14962. (Illus.). 1976. Repr. of 1965 ed. lib. bdg. 16.00x (ISBN 0-8371-8143-7, THSMM). Greenwood.

Thorson, James, ed. see Smollett, Tobias G.

Thorson, James L., ed. see Smollett, Tobias G.

Thorson, Thomas L. Biopolitics. LC 81-43504. 224p. 1982. Repr. of 1970 ed. lib. bdg. 23.00 (ISBN 0-8191-2139-8); pap. text ed. 11.00 (ISBN 0-8191-2140-1). U Pr of Amer.

Thorsson, Edred. Futhark: A Handbook of Rune Magic. Date not set. pap. 8.95 (ISBN 0-87728-548-9). Weiser.

Thorsten, Geraldine, jt. auth. see Weideger, Paula.

Thorstenson, Clark T., jt. auth. see Heaton, Israel C.

Thorton, J. A. Lake McIlwaine: The Eutrophication & Recovery of a Tropical African Man-Made Lake. 1982. text ed. 49.50 (ISBN 90-6193-102-9, Pub. by Junk Pubs Netherlands). Kluwer Boston.

Thorton, J. C., ed. see Voltaire, Francois M. De.

Thorup, Penny L., jt. auth. see Little, Billie.

Thouless, D. J. The Quantum Mechanics of Many-Body Systems. 2nd ed. (Pure & Applied Physics Ser.: Vol. 11). 1972. 48.00 (ISBN 0-12-691560-1). Acad Pr.

Thouless, R. H. An Introduction to the Psychology of Religion. 3rd ed. LC 76-184142. 160p. 1972. pap. 34.50 (ISBN 0-521-08149-1); pap. 9.95 (ISBN 0-521-09665-0). Cambridge U Pr.

Thourlby, William. You Are What You Wear. (Illus.). 1980. pap. 2.95 (ISBN 0-451-12195-3, AE2195, Sig). NAL.

Thrall, Robert M. & Thompson, Russell G., eds. Large-Scale Energy Models: Prospects & Potential. (AAAS Selected Synposium 73). 350p. 1982. lib. bdg. 25.00x (ISBN 0-86531-408-X). Westview.

Thrall, Robert M., jt. ed. see Cobb, Loren.

Thrall, Robert M., jt. ed. see Tsokos, Chris P.

Thran, P. & Brockhuizen, S., eds. Agro-Climatic Atlas of Europe. (Agro-Ecological Atlas Ser.: Vol. 1). 1965. 202.25 (ISBN 0-444-40569-0). Elsevier.

Thran, P., jt. ed. see Broekhuizen, S.

Thrane, Carl. Friedrich Kuhlau. (Facsimilies of Early Biographies Ser.: Vol. 6). iv, 110p. 17.50 o.s.i. (ISBN 90-6027-356-7, Pub. by Frits Knuf Netherlands). Pendragon NY.

Thrane, T. Referential-Semantic Analysis. LC 79-17405. (Cambridge Studies in Linguistics Monograph: No. 28). 1980. 44.50 (ISBN 0-521-22791-7). Cambridge U Pr.

Thrapp, Dan L. General Crook & the Sierra Madre Adventure. (Illus.). 1977. pap. 5.95 o.p. (ISBN 0-8061-1370-7). U of Okla Pr.

Thrash, Agatha & Thrash, Calvin. Nutrition for Vegetarians. (Illus.). 155p. 1982. pap. 8.95 (ISBN 0-942658-03-5). Yuchi Pines.

Thrash, Agatha M. & Thrash, Calvin L., Jr. The Animal Connection: Cancer & Other Diseases from Animals & Foods of Animal Origin. 262p. (Orig.). 1983. pap. write for info. (ISBN 0-942658-04-3). Yuchi Pines.

Thrash, Agatha M., jt. auth. see Austin, Phylis A.

Thrash, Calvin, jt. auth. see Thrash, Agatha.

Thrash, Calvin L., Jr., jt. auth. see Thrash, Agatha M.

Thrasher, Crystal. Between Dark & Daylight. LC 79-12423. 192p. (gr. 4-8). 1979. 10.95 (ISBN 0-689-50150-1, McElderry Bk). Atheneum.

--End of a Dark Road. LC 82-3958. 228p. (gr. 3-7). 10.95 (ISBN 0-689-50250-8, McElderry Bk). Atheneum.

Thrasher, Jean H., jt. auth. see Franklin, Jack L.

Threlfall, A. J. Design Charts for Water Retaining Structures: BS 5337. (Viewpoint Publication Ser). (Illus.). 1978. pap. text ed. 16.50x (ISBN 0-7210-1104-7). Scholium Intl.

Threlfall, W., jt. auth. see Seifert, Herbert.

Threlkeld, James L. Thermal Environmental Engineering. 2nd ed. 1970. ref. ed. 33.95 (ISBN 0-13-914721-7). P-H.

Thresher, Ronald E. Reef Fish: Behaviors & Ecology on the Reef & in the Aquarium. LC 79-28234. (Major Ser.). 1980. 17.95 (ISBN 0-915096-09-9). Palmetto Pub.

Thrift, Nigel, jt. auth. see Parkes, Don.

Thrift, Nigel, jt. ed. see Taylor, Michael.

Thring, M. W. Man, Machines & Tomorrow. (Illus.). 142p. 1973. 15.00 o.p. (ISBN 0-7100-7555-3). Routledge & Kegan.

Thring, M. W., ed. Engineering: An Outline for the Intending Student. (Outlines Ser). 150p. 1972. 8.25 o.p. (ISBN 0-7100-7403-4); pap. 3.95 o.p. (ISBN 0-7100-7404-2). Routledge & Kegan.

Thro, Linus J. History of Philosophy in the Making: A Symposium of Essays to Honor Professor James D. Collins on His 65th Birthday By His Colleagues & Friends. LC 81-43840. 340p. (Orig.). 1982. lib. bdg. 25.00 (ISBN 0-8191-2658-6); pap. text ed. 12.75 (ISBN 0-8191-2659-4). U Pr of Amer.

Throckmorton, Burton H., Jr. Adopted in Love: Contemporary Studies in Romans. LC 77-22143. 1978. pap. 1.00 (ISBN 0-8164-1230-8). Seabury.

Throckmorton, Tom, jt. auth. see MacDonald, Kenneth.

Thron, W. J., jt. auth. see Jones, William B.

Throop, Sara & Hunter, Kathryn. Service Occupations. 1974. wkbk. 3.25x (ISBN 0-88323-114-X, 202). Richards Pub.

Thrope, Sidney C. Standard Teachers Guide for Beauty Culture. 1976. 16.75 (ISBN 0-87350-066-0). Milady.

Throsby, D. C. & Withers, G. A. The Economics of the Performing Arts. LC 79-5104. (Illus.). 1979. 40.00x (ISBN 0-312-23438-4). St Martin.

Thrower, James R., jt. auth. see Marcus, Abraham.

Thrower, N. Maps & Man: An Examination of Cartography in Relation to Culture & Civilization. 1972. pap. 12.95 (ISBN 0-13-555953-7). P-H.

Thrower, Norman, ed. see General Drafting Co.

Thrower, Norman J., ed. The Compleat Plattmaker: Essays on Chart, Map, & Globe-Making in England in the 17th & 18th Centuries. LC 77-78415. 1979. 29.50x (ISBN 0-520-03522-4). U of Cal Pr.

Thrower, Norman J. & Bradbury, D. E., eds. Chile-California Mediterranean Scrub Atlas. (U.S.-T.B.P. Synthesis Ser.: Vol. 2). 1977. 49.50 (ISBN 0-12-787550-6). Acad Pr.

Thrower, Peter A., ed. Chemistry & Physics of Carbon, Vol. 18. (Illus.). 208p. 1983. 45.00 (ISBN 0-8247-1740-6). Dekker.

Thrower, W. R. Life at Sea in the Age of Sail. (Illus.). 190p. 1972. 17.75x o.p. (ISBN 0-8476-1377-1). Rowman.

Thrush, John C. & Smith, Philip R. Japan's Economic Growth & Educational Change: 1950-1970. LC 79-55704. (Orig.). 1980. 9.95 o.p. (ISBN 0-935662-00-6); pap. 4.95x (ISBN 0-935662-01-4). EBHA Pr.

Thubron, Colin. The Ancient Mariners. LC 80-24182. (Seafarers Ser.). PLB 19.92 (ISBN 0-8094-2739-7). Silver.

--Istanbul. (The Great Cities Ser.). (Illus.). 1978. lib. bdg. 12.00 (ISBN 0-8094-2336-7). Silver.

--Jerusalem. (The Great Cities Ser.). (Illus.). (gr. 6 up). 1976. 10.00 (ISBN 0-8094-2251-4, Pub by Time-Life). Silver.

Thucydides. Histories. Marchant, E. C., ed. (Classical Ser). Bk. 2. 5.95x o.p. (ISBN 0-312-80395-8). St Martin.

--History of the Peloponnesian War. Livingstone, Richard, ed. (Illus.). 1960. pap. 7.95x (ISBN 0-19-500218-0). Oxford U Pr.

--The Peloponnesian War. New ed. Crawley, Richard, tr. Bd. wit. 1981. pap. 4.95x (ISBN 0-394-30951-0, T51, Mod LibC). Modern Lib.

--The Peloponnesian War. rev. ed. Warner, Rex, tr. (Classic Ser.). (Orig.). 1954. pap. 5.95 (ISBN 0-14-044039-9). Penguin.

Thuesen, G. J., jt. auth. see Fabrycky, W. J.

Thuesen, G. J., jt. auth. see Fabrycky, Walter J.

Thulastraman, K., jt. auth. see Swamy, M. N.

Thum, Marcella. Blazing Star. 384p. (Orig.). 1983. pap. 2.95 (ISBN 0-449-20095-7, Crest). Fawcett.

Thumann, Albert. Handbook of Energy Audits. 2nd ed. (Illus.). 440p. 1983. text ed. 36.00 (ISBN 0-915586-76-2); pap. text ed. 20.00 (ISBN 0-915586-75-4). Fairmont Pr.

--Plant Engineers & Managers Guide to Energy Conservation: The Role of the Energy Manager. 2nd ed. 272p. 1982. text ed. 24.95 (ISBN 0-442-28414-4). Van Nos Reinhold.

--The Waste Heat Recovery Handbook. 250p. 1983. text ed. 36.00 (ISBN 0-915586-64-9). Fairmont Pr.

Thumm, Ulrich. Peru: Major Development Policy Issues & Recommendations. vii, 220p. 1981. pap. 10.00 (ISBN 0-686-36099-0, RC-8102). World Bank.

Thumm, Walter, jt. auth. see Tilley, Donald E.

Thun, R. E. see Hass, Georg, et al.

Thurber, Carol C. Calypso Cookbook by the Mad Hatter. Young, Billie, ed. LC 73-83918. 1974. 7.95 o.s.i. (ISBN 0-87949-014-4). Ashley Bks.

Thurber, James. Credos & Curios. LC 82-48236. 192p. 1983. pap. 4.76i (ISBN 0-06-091018-6, CN 1018, CN). Har-Row.

--Fables for Our Time. LC 82-48237. (Illus.). 128p. 1983. pap. 3.80i (ISBN 0-06-090999-4, CN 999, CN). Har-Row.

--Fables for Our Time & Famous Poems Illustrated. (Illus.). 160p. 1974. pap. 1.95 (ISBN 0-06-080319-3, P319, PL). Har-Row.

--The Great Quillow. LC 75-6613. (Illus.). 54p. (gr. 2-3). 1975. pap. 1.95 (ISBN 0-15-636490-5, VoyB). HarBraceJ.

--The Last Flower. 1977. Repr. of 1939 ed. lib. bdg. 16.95x (ISBN 0-89244-057-0). Queens Hse.

--Let Your Mind Alone. 1977. Repr. of 1937 ed. lib. bdg. 17.95x (ISBN 0-89244-058-9). Queens Hse.

--Many Moons. LC 43-51250. (Illus.). 47p. (gr. 3-7). 1973. pap. 3.95 (ISBN 0-15-656980-9, VoyB). HarBraceJ.

--The Middle-Aged Man on the Flying Trapeze. 1977. Repr. of 1935 ed. lib. bdg. 17.95x (ISBN 0-89244-059-7). Queens Hse.

--My Life & Hard Times. (Illus.). 128p. 1973. pap. 2.84i (ISBN 0-06-080290-1, P290, PL). Har-Row.

--Thirteen Clocks. (Illus.). (gr. 5 up). 1950. 8.95 o.p. (ISBN 0-671-72100-3). S&S.

--Thurber Album. 1965. pap. 4.95 o.p. (ISBN 0-671-21015-7, Fireside). S&S.

--Thurber Carnival. 1957. 6.95 (ISBN 0-394-60474-1). Modern Lib.

--Thurber Country. 1960. pap. 2.95 o.p. (ISBN 0-671-72901-2, Fireside). S&S.

--Thurber Country. 1982. Repr. of 1953 ed. 16.50 (ISBN 0-671-45931-7, Touchstone Bks); pap. 5.95 (ISBN 0-671-45930-9). S&S.

--White Deer. LC 45-35191. (Illus.). (gr. 6 up). 1968. pap. 2.95 (ISBN 0-15-696264-0, Harv). HarBraceJ.

Thurber, Kenneth J & Masson, G. M. Distributed Processor Communication Architecture. LC 79-1563. (Illus.). 288p. 1979. 26.95x (ISBN 0-669-02914-9). Lexington Bks.

Thurber, Kenneth J. & Patton, Peter C. Computer-System Requirements: Techniques & Examples. LC 79-7184. 128p. 1982. 15.95x (ISBN 0-669-02958-0). Lexington Bks.

--Data Structures & Computer Architecture. LC 76-12688. 224p. 1977. 23.95x (ISBN 0-669-00723-4). Lexington Bks.

Thureau, P. & Lecler, D. An Introduction to the Principles of Vibrations of Linear Systems. Grosjean, J., tr. 144p. 1981. 30.00x (ISBN 0-85950-465-4, Pub. by Thornes England). State Mutual Bk.

Thuret, G., jt. auth. see Bornet, E.

Thurian, Max. Our Faith: Basic Christian Belief. Chisholm, Emily, tr. from Fr. LC 82-72008. 192p. 1982. 12.95 (ISBN 0-8245-0547-6). Crossroad NY.

Thurkauf, Ernest A. One Small Lifetime. 1983. 11.95 (ISBN 0-533-05508-3). Vantage.

Thurley, Geoffrey. The American Moment: American Poetry in the Mid-Century. LC 77-91071. 1978. 25.00 (ISBN 0-312-02884-9). St Martin.

--The Dickens Myth: Its Genesis & Structure. LC 76-5957. 380p. 1976. 18.95 o.p. (ISBN 0-312-19985-6). St Martin.

Thurley, Geoffrey, tr. see Esenin, Sergei.

Thurlimann, Bruno & Furler, Rene. Strength of Brick Walls Under Enforced End Rotation. (IBA Ser.: No. 89). 14p. 1979. pap. text ed. 4.95x (ISBN 3-7643-1108-8). Birkhauser.

Thurlow, Edward. Moonlight: The Doge's Daughter, Ariadne, Carmen Britanicum. Reiman, Donald H., ed. LC 75-31266. (Romantic Context Ser.: Poetry 1789-1830). 1978. Repr. of 1814 ed. lib. bdg. 47.00 o.s.i. (ISBN 0-8240-2212-2). Garland Pub.

Thurlow, Richard C., jt. ed. see Lunn, Kenneth.

Thurman, Anne & Piggins, Carol Ann. Drama Activities with Older Adults: A Handbook for Leaders. (Activities, Adaptation & Aging Ser.: Vol. 2, Nos. 2-3). (Illus.). 176p. 1982. text ed. 16.95 (ISBN 0-86656-167-6, B167). Haworth Pr.

Thurman, Evelyn. A Pioneer Civil War Story for Molly & Ben. (Illus.). 1979. 4.50 o.p. (ISBN 0-533-03848-0). Vantage.

Thurman, Harold V. Essentials of Oceanography. 512p. 1983. text ed. 19.95 (ISBN 0-675-20031-8). Merrill.

--Introductory Oceanography. 3rd ed. (Illus.). 596p. 1981. text ed. 25.95 (ISBN 0-675-08058-4). Additional supplements may be obtainedfrom publisher. Merrill.

Thurman, Ronald G., et al, eds. Alcohol & Aldehyde Metabolizing Systems, 3 vols. (Johnson Foundation Colloquia Ser.). 1974-78. Vol. 1. 50.50 (ISBN 0-12-691450-8); Vol. 2. 54.00 (ISBN 0-12-691402-8); Vol. 3, 1977. 54.00 (ISBN 0-12-691403-6); Set. 112.00 (ISBN 0-686-77325-X). Acad Pr.

Thurmer, Tressa E., jt. auth. see Pisano, Beverly.

Thurmond, Nancy M. Happy Mother, Happy Child. 386p. (Orig.). 1982. pap. 7.95 (ISBN 0-8423-1305-2). Tyndale.

Thurner, Cass. Deep in Debt Valley. LC 78-74744. 1979. 6.00 o.p. (ISBN 0-915854-12-0); pap. 5.00 o.p. (ISBN 0-915854-16-3). Friend Freedom.

Thurneysen, Eduard. Sermon on the Mount. LC 64-12625. 1964. pap. 1.95 o.p. (ISBN 0-8042-3448-5). John Knox.

Thurnwald, R. Banaro Society: Social Organization & Kinship System of a Tribe in the Interior of New Guinea. LC 19-10227. 1916. pap. 15.00 (ISBN 0-527-00515-0). Kraus Repr.

Thurow, jt. auth. see Heilbroner.

Thurow, Glen E. Abraham Lincoln & American Political Religion. LC 76-12596. 1976. 29.50x (ISBN 0-87395-334-7). State U NY Pr.

Thurow, Harold F. Real Estate Law of Texas. 10th rev. ed. (Orig.). 1982. 14.95x (ISBN 0-914696-15-7); pap. 12.95 (ISBN 0-914696-16-5). Hemphill.

Thurow, L., jt. auth. see Heilbroner, R.

Thurow, Lester, jt. auth. see Heilbroner, Robert.

Thurow, Lester C. Generating Inequality: Mechanisms of Distribution in the U. S. Economy. LC 75-7264. 1975. 10.95x o.s.i. (ISBN 0-465-02670-2); pap. 6.95x o.s.i. (ISBN 0-465-02668-0). Basic.

--Poverty & Discrimination. (Studies in Social Economics). 1969. 12.95 (ISBN 0-8157-8444-9). Brookings.

Thurow, Lester C., jt. auth. see Heilbroner, Robert L.

Thurow, Raymond C. Atlas of Orthodontic Principles. 2nd ed. LC 77-7096. (Illus.). 420p. 1977. text ed. 38.50 o.p. (ISBN 0-8016-4951-X). Mosby.

Thursland, Arthur L. Work Measurement: A Guidebook to Word Processing Management. 2nd ed. 1981. text ed. 45.00 (ISBN 0-935220-01-1). IIWPA.

Thurston, D. B. Design for Safety. LC 79-25241. 1980. 19.50 (ISBN 0-07-064554-X). McGraw.

Thurston, David B. Design for Flying. (Illus.). 1978. 24.50 (ISBN 0-07-064553-1, P&RB). McGraw.

--Home Built Aircraft. (Illus.). 224p. 1981. 27.75 (ISBN 0-07-064552-3, P&RB). McGraw.

Thurston, Gavin. Great Thames Disaster. (Illus.). 17.50 (ISBN 0-392-03131-0, SpS). Sportshelf.

Thurston, Jarvis A. Reading Modern Short Stories. 1955. pap. 10.95x (ISBN 0-673-05419-5). Scott F.

Thurston, Mark. How to Interpret Your Dreams. 1978. pap. 6.95 (ISBN 0-87604-107-1). ARE Pr.

Thurston, Mark, jt. auth. see Puryear, Herbert B.

Thurston, Mark A. Understand & Develop Your ESP: Based on the Edgar Cayce Readings. (Illus.). 80p. 1977. pap. 2.95 book only (ISBN 0-87604-097-0); pap. 8.98 tape & book set (ISBN 0-87604-146-2); tape only 5.98 (ISBN 0-686-66266-0). ARE Pr.

Thurston, R. see Mason, Warren P.

Thurston, R. N. see Mason, Warren P.

Thurston, Robert. Alicia II. LC 77-28897. 1978. 10.95 o.p. (ISBN 0-399-12219-2, Pub. by Berkley). Putnam Pub Group.

--Set of Wheels. 288p. (Orig.). 1983. pap. 2.50 (ISBN 0-425-05820-4). Berkley Pub.

Thurston, Robert, jt. auth. see Larson, Glen A.

Thurston, Robert, jt. ed. see Mason, Warren.

Thut, I. N. & Adams, D. K. Educational Patterns in Contemporary Societies. (Foundations in Education Ser.). 1964. text ed. 14.95 o.p. (ISBN 0-07-064556-6, C). McGraw.

Thuvenet, Renee, ed. see Olivier, Tanya.

Thwaite, Anthony. Larkin at Sixty. 144p. 1982. 15.95 (ISBN 0-571-11878-X). Faber & Faber.

Thwaite, Anthony, jt. tr. see Bownas, Geoffrey.

Thwaite, Jean & Smith, Susan. Chef's Secrets from Great Restaurants in California. (Chef's Secrets Cookbooks Ser.). (Illus.). 270p. 1983. 11.95 (ISBN 0-939944-24-3). Marmac Pub.

--Chef's Secrets from Great Restaurants in Louisiana: 1984 World Exposition Edition. (Chef's Secrets Cookbooks Ser.). (Illus.). 270p. 1983. 11.95 (ISBN 0-939944-25-1). Marmac Pub.

--Chef's Secrets from Great Restaurants in Pennsylvania. (Chef's Secrets Cookbooks Ser.). (Illus.). 270p. 1983. 11.95 (ISBN 0-939944-26-X). Marmac Pub.

Thwaite, Jean & Nicholson, Diana, eds. Chefs' Secrets from Great Restaurants in Georgia. (Cookbook Ser.). (Illus.). 248p. 11.95 (ISBN 0-939944-06-5). Marmac Pub.

Thwaites, C. J. Capillary Joining-Brazing & Soft Soldering. (Materials Science Research Studies Ser.). 211p. 1982. 29.95x (ISBN 0-471-10167-2, Pub. by Res Stud Pr). Wiley.

Thwaites, Thomas. Fifty Hikes in Western Pennsylvania: Walks & Day Hikes from the Laurel Highlands to Lake Erie. LC 82-25277. (Fifty Hikes Ser.). (Illus.). 224p. 1983. pap. 8.95 (ISBN 0-942440-10-2). Backcountry Pubns.

Thwaites, Tom. Fifty Hikes in Central Pennsylvania. LC 78-71141. (Fifty Hikes Ser.). (Illus.). 1979. pap. 7.95 (ISBN 0-89725-002-8). Backcountry Pubns.

Thwing, Annie H. Crooked & Narrow Streets of the Town of Boston, 1630-1822. LC 74-129974. (Illus.). 1970. Repr. of 1920 ed. 34.00x (ISBN 0-8103-3538-7). Gale.

Thygerson, A. L. Accidents & Disasters: Causes & Countermeasures. (Illus.). 1977. 19.95x (ISBN 0-13-000968-7). P-H.

Thygerson, Alton L. The First Aid Book. (Illus.). 288p. 1982. 12.95 (ISBN 0-13-318006-9). P-H.

--First Aid Practices: Study Guide. (Illus.). 1978. 10.95 (ISBN 0-13-317958-3). P-H.

--Safety: Concepts & Instruction. 2nd ed. (Illus.). 160p. 1976. pap. text ed. 10.95 (ISBN 0-13-785733-0). P-H.

Thypin, Marilyn & Glasner, Lynne. Good Buy! (Buying Home Furnishings) LC 79-9367. (Consumer Education Ser.: No. 2). (Orig.). (gr. 9-12). 1980. pap. text ed. 3.95 (ISBN 0-88436-519-0). EMC.

--The Growth of the United States. (Illus.). 96p. (Orig.). 1982. pap. text ed. 4.95 (ISBN 0-941342-03-4). Entry Pub.

--Health Care for the Wongs (Obtaining Medical Aid) LC 79-17188. (Consumer Education Ser.: No. 2). (Orig.). (gr. 9-12). 1980. pap. text ed. 3.95 (ISBN 0-88436-513-1). EMC.

--A History of the United States, 4 Bks. (Illus.). 96p. 1982. pap. text ed. 19.80 set (ISBN 0-941342-00-X); tchr's guide 2.00 (ISBN 0-941342-05-0). Entry Pub.

--Leases & Landlords. LC 79-9391. (Consumer Education Ser.: No. 2). (Orig.). (gr. 9-12). 1980. pap. text ed. 3.95 (ISBN 0-88436-515-8). EMC.

--More Food for Our Money: Food Planning, Buying, Nutrition. LC 78-13591. (Consumer Education Ser.). 1979. pap. text ed. 3.95 (ISBN 0-88436-502-6). EMC.

--Put Your Money Down: Buying on Credit. LC 78-12666. (Consumer Education Ser.). 1979. pap. text ed. 3.95 (ISBN 0-88436-510-7). EMC.

--State Your Claim! (Consumer Redress) LC 79-9559. (Consumer Education Ser.: No. 2). (Orig.). (gr. 9-12). 1980. pap. text ed. 3.95 (ISBN 0-88436-517-4). EMC.

--Try It on: Buying Clothing. LC 78-12440. (Consumer Education Ser.). 1979. pap. text ed. 3.95 (ISBN 0-88436-508-5). EMC.

--Wheels & Deals: Buying a Car. LC 78-12466. (Consumer Education Ser.). 1979. pap. text ed. 3.95 (ISBN 0-88436-506-9). EMC.

--When Things Don't Work: Appliance Buying, Repairs, Warranties. LC 78-14349. (Consumer Education Ser.). 1979. pap. text ed. 3.95 (ISBN 0-88436-504-2). EMC.

Tibawi, A. L. A Modern History of Syria: Including Lebanon & Palestine. (Illus.). 1970. 10.95 o.p. (ISBN 0-312-54005-1). St Martin.

Tibbetts, A. M. Working Papers: A Teacher's Observations on Composition. 1981. pap. text ed. 10.95x (ISBN 0-673-15490-4). Scott F.

Tibbetts, A. M. & Tibbetts, Charlene. Strategies of Rhetoric. 3rd ed. 1979. pap. text ed. 13.50x (ISBN 0-673-15179-4). Scott F.

--Strategies of Rhetoric. 4th ed. 1983. pap. text ed. 13.95x (ISBN 0-673-15626-5). Scott F.

--Strategies of Rhetoric with Handbook. 3rd ed. 1979. text ed. 15.50x (ISBN 0-673-15178-6). Scott F.

--Strategies of Rhetoric with Handbook. 4th ed. 1983. text ed. 14.95x (ISBN 0-673-15627-3). Scott F.

Tibbetts, Arnold M. To the Point: Efficient & Attractive Writing...for Almost Any Audience. 1983. pap. text ed. 6.95x (ISBN 0-673-15491-2). Scott F.

Tibbetts, Charlene, jt. auth. see Tibbetts, A. M.

Tibbits, Donald F. Language Disorders in Adolescents. LC 82-71669. (Cliffs Speech & Hearing Ser.). 120p. (Orig.). 1982. pap. text ed. 4.95 (ISBN 0-8220-1832-2). Cliffs.

Tibbits, Patricia, jt. auth. see Johnson, Robert M.

Tibbitts, Clark, ed. see Conference on Aging, 2nd, University of Michigan.

Tibbitts, John C. Guide for Insulator Collectors, with Prices, 3 Vols. LC 67-28696. (Illus.). 1967-1969. pap. 4.00 ea.; Vol. 1. pap. 12.00 set (ISBN 0-911508-10-4); Vol. 2. pap. (ISBN 0-911508-05-8); Vol. 3 With Index For Set. pap. (ISBN 0-911508-06-6). Little Glass.

Tibbitts, T. & Kozlowski, T. K., eds. Controlled Environment Guidelines for Plant Research. LC 79-23521. 1980. 28.50 (ISBN 0-12-690950-4). Acad Pr.

Tibble, Anne, ed. see Clare, John.

Tibble, J. W., ed. The Extra Year: The Raising of the School Leaving Age. 1970. 7.50x o.p. (ISBN 0-7100-6883-2); pap. 4.50 o.p. (ISBN 0-7100-6884-0). Routledge & Kegan.

--The Future of Teacher Education. 1971. 18.95x (ISBN 0-7100-7189-2). Routledge & Kegan.

--An Introduction to the Study of Education: An Outline for the Intending Student. (Outlines Ser). 1971. pap. 3.75 o.p. (ISBN 0-7100-7081-0). Routledge & Kegan.

Tibbs, Hardwin. The Future of Light. 112p. 1981. 12.00x o.p. (ISBN 0-7224-0196-5, Pub. by Watkins England). State Mutual Bk.

Tibbs, John F. The Aulacanthidae (Radiolaria: Phaeodaria) of the Antarctic Seas: Paper 2 in Biology of the Antarctic Seas V. Pawson, David L., ed. (Antarctic Research Ser.: Vol. 23). 1976. pap. 19.25 (ISBN 0-87590-126-3). Am Geophysical.

Tibbs, Thomas S. Affect-Effect. (Illus.). 13p. 1969. 3.00x (ISBN 0-686-99832-4). La Jolla Mus Contemp Art.

--Root. (Illus.). 12p. 1969. 2.00x (ISBN 0-686-99830-8). La Jolla Mus Contemp Art.

Tibell, G., ed. see International Conference on High-Energy Physics & Nuclear Structure, 5th.

Tiberghien, J. & Carlstedt, G., eds. Microprocessors & Their Applications. Lewi, J. 1980. 64.00 (ISBN 0-444-85390-1). Elsevier.

Tibi, Bassam, ed. Arab Nationalism: A Critical Inquiry. 1980. 25.00 (ISBN 0-312-04716-9). St Martin.

Tiblier, Henry, jt. auth. see Fay, Cornelius R.

Tibullus. Poems of Tibullus. Dunlop, Philip, tr. (Classics Ser.). 1972. pap. 4.95 (ISBN 0-14-044266-9). Penguin.

Tiburzi, D. James, jt. auth. see Dolgin, Robert M.

Tice, George. Urban Romantic: The Photographs of George Tice. LC 81-81447. (Illus.). 128p. 1982. 50.00 (ISBN 0-87923-413-X); limited ed. 300.00 (ISBN 0-87923-414-8). Godine.

Ticer, James W. Radiographic Technique in Small Animal Practice. LC 74-24520. (Illus.). 350p. 1975. text ed. 35.00 o.p. (ISBN 0-7216-8860-8). Saunders.

Tichauer, E. R. The Biochemical Basis of Ergonomics: Anatomy Applied to the Design of Work Situations. LC 77-28807. 99p. 1978. 18.00x (ISBN 0-471-03644-7, Pub. by Wiley-Interscience). Wiley.

Tichenor, Tom. Christmas Tree Crafts. LC 75-15777. (Illus.). 112p. (gr. 5 up). 1975. 9.57 (ISBN 0-397-31637-2, HarpJ); pap. 3.95 (ISBN 0-397-31638-0, LSC-38). Har-Row.

Tichenor, Trebor J. Ragtime Rarities. LC 74-28941. (Illus.). 320p. (Orig.). 1975. pap. 8.95 (ISBN 0-486-23157-7). Dover.

Tichumanatman, D. Letters on Creativity: A Universalist Guidebook. 1982. pap. 5.00 (ISBN 0-686-37641-2). All In All.

--Raising the Roof: The Transformation of Being. 1979. 10.00 (ISBN 0-533-04228-3). All In All.

Tichy, H. Effective Writing for Engineers-Managers-Scientists. LC 66-21062. 337p. 1966. 25.95 (ISBN 0-471-86778-0, Pub. by Wiley-Interscience). Wiley.

Tichy, M. & Rakosnik, J. Plastic Analysis of Concrete Frames: With Particular Reference to Limit States Des. Dagmar, et al, trs. from Czech. (Illus.). 320p. 1977. text ed. 40.00x (ISBN 0-569-08199-8, Pub. by Collets England). Scholium Intl.

Tichy, Monique K. Health Care Teams: An Annotated Bibliography. LC 74-14674. (Special Studies). 190p. 1974. 26.95 o.p. (ISBN 0-275-05750-X). Praeger.

Tichy, Noel M. Managing Strategic Change: Technical Political & Cultural Dynamics. (Organization Assessment & Change Ser.). 375p. 1983. 27.95x (ISBN 0-471-86559-1, Pub. by Wiley-Interscience). Wiley.

Tichy, William. Poisons, Antidotes & Anectodes. LC 76-51188. (Illus.); (gr. 7 up). 1977. 8.95 o.p. (ISBN 0-8069-3738-6); PLB 8.29 o.p. (ISBN 0-8069-3739-4). Sterling.

Tick, Judith. American Women Composers Before 1870. Buelow, George, ed. LC 82-2694. (Studies in Musicology: No. 57). 1983. 39.95 (ISBN 0-8357-1326-1, Pub. by UMI Res Pr). Univ Microfilms.

Tickell, Jerrard. See How They Run. LC 36-7793. 320p. 1975. Repr. of 1936 ed. 7.50x o.p. (ISBN 0-7182-0903-6). Intl Pubns Serv.

Tickle, John. Discovering the Bible: 8 Simple Keys for Learning & Praying. 1978. pap. 3.95 leader's guide, Bk. 1 (ISBN 0-89243-074-5); leader's guide, bk. 2 2.95 (ISBN 0-89243-141-5). Liguori Pubns.

Tickle, Phyllis. Tobias and the Angels: Or, Puppeteers for Our Lady. 96p. (Orig.). 1982. pap. text ed. 2.95 (ISBN 0-918518-23-7). St Luke TN.

Ticktin, Max, tr. see Harkabi, Yehoshafat.

Tidall, Harriet. The Handloom Weaves. LC 57-49779. (Shuttle Craft Guild Monograph: No. 33). (Illus.). 38p. pap. 7.45 (ISBN 0-916658-00-7). HTH Pubs.

Tidball, Derek. An Introduction to the Sociology of the New Testament. 168p. pap. text ed. 9.95 (ISBN 0-85364-301-6). Attic Pr.

Tidball, Harriet. Brocade. LC 68-5499. (Shuttle Craft Guild Monographs: No. 22). (Illus.). 50p. 1967. pap. 8.75 (ISBN 0-916658-22-8). HTH Pubs.

--Build or Buy a Loom, Pt. 1. Bd. with Pt. 2. Patterns for Pick-Ups. LC 76-24013. (Shuttle Craft Guild Monographs: No. 23). (Illus.). 38p. 1968. pap. 7.45 (ISBN 0-916658-23-6). HTH Pubs.

--Color & Dyeing. LC 76-24007. (Shuttle Craft Guild Monograph: No. 16). (Illus.). 53p. 1965. pap. 8.75 (ISBN 0-916658-16-3). HTH Pubs.

--Contemporary Costume: Strictly Handwoven. LC 76-24014. (Shuttle Craft Guild Monograph: No. 24). (Illus.). 44p. 1968. pap. 8.75 (ISBN 0-916658-24-4). HTH Pubs.

--Contemporary Tapestry. LC 76-24004. (Shuttle Craft Guild Monograph: No. 12). (Illus.). 46p. 1964. pap. 8.75 (ISBN 0-916658-12-0). HTH Pubs.

--The Double Weave, Plain & Patterned. LC 61-669. (Shuttle Craft Guild Monograph: No. 1). (Illus.). 34p. 1960. pap. 6.95 (ISBN 0-916658-01-5). HTH Pubs.

--Handwoven Specialties. LC 76-24003. (Shuttle Craft Guild Monograph: No. 11). (Illus.). 38p. 1964. pap. 6.95 (ISBN 0-916658-11-2). HTH Pubs.

--Merry Christmas, Handweavers. LC 76-24002. (Shuttle Craft Guild Monograph: No. 10). (Illus.). 29p. 1963. pap. 6.45 (ISBN 0-916658-10-4). HTH Pubs.

--Mexican Motifs. LC 76-23998. (Shuttle Craft Guild Monographs: No. 6). (Illus.). 22p. 1962. pap. 6.45 (ISBN 0-916658-06-6). HTH Pubs.

--Peru: Textiles Unlimited. LC 76-24015. (Shuttle Craft Guild Monograph: No. 25). (Illus.). 36p. 1968. pap. 10.95 set (ISBN 0-916658-25-2). HTH Pubs.

--Peru: Textiles Unlimited, Part II. LC 76-24015. (Shuttle Craft Guild Monograph: No. 26). (Illus.). 46p. 1969. pap. 10.95 set (ISBN 0-916658-26-0). HTH Pubs.

--Summer & Winter. LC 76-24010. (Shuttle Craft Guild Monograph: No. 19). (Illus.). 58p. 1966. pap. 8.45 (ISBN 0-916658-19-8). HTH Pubs.

--Supplementary Warp Patterning. LC 76-24008. (Shuttle Craft Guild Monograph: No. 17). (Illus.). 46p. pap. 7.95 (ISBN 0-916658-17-1). HTH Pubs.

--Surface Interest: Textiles of Today. LC 61-2332. (Shuttle Craft Guild Monograph: No. 2). (Illus.). 21p. 1961. pap. 6.45 (ISBN 0-916658-02-3). HTH Pubs.

--Textile Structures & Analysis. LC 76-24009. (Shuttle Craft Guild Monograph: No. 18). (Illus.). 31p. 1966. pap. 6.95 (ISBN 0-916658-18-X). HTH Pubs.

--Thomas Jackson, Weaver. LC 76-24005. (Shuttle Craft Guild Monograph: No. 13). (Illus.). 37p. 1964. pap. 7.45 (ISBN 0-916658-13-9). HTH Pubs.

--Two-Harness Textiles: The Loom-Controlled Weaves. LC 76-24011. (Shuttle Craft Guild Monograph: No. 20). (Illus.). 30p. 1967. pap. 7.45 (ISBN 0-916658-20-1). HTH Pubs.

--Two-Harness Textiles: The Open-Work Weaves. LC 76-24012. (Shuttle Craft Guild Monographs: No. 21). (Illus.). 38p. pap. 7.45 (ISBN 0-916658-21-X). HTH Pubs.

--Undulating Weft Effects. LC 76-24001. (Shuttle Craft Guild Monographs: No. 9). (Illus.). 25p. 1963. pap. 6.95 (ISBN 0-916658-09-0). HTH Pubs.

--The Weaver's Book of Scottish Tartans. LC 76-23997. (Shuttle Craft Guild Monograph: No. 5). (Illus.). 46p. 1962. pap. 6.95 (ISBN 0-916658-05-8). HTH Pubs.

--Weaving Inkle Bands. LC 76-24016. (Shuttle Craft Guild Monograph: No. 27). (Illus.). 40p. 1969. pap. 8.45 (ISBN 0-916658-27-9). HTH Pubs.

--Woolens & Tweeds. LC 62-698. (Shuttle Craft Guild Monograph: No. 4). (Illus.). 46p. 1961. pap. 6.95 (ISBN 0-916658-04-X). HTH Pubs.

Tidball, Harriet, jt. auth. see Harvey, Virginia I.

Tidball, Harriet, ed. see Collingwood, Peter.

Tidestrom, I. Flora of Utah & Nevada. 1969. pap. 24.00 (ISBN 3-7682-0625-4). Lubrecht & Cramer.

Tidmarsh, I., tr. see Shingarev, A. I.

Tidmarsh, I., tr. see Zhdanov, Andrei.

Tidsworth, Floyd, Jr. Planting & Growing Missions. LC 79-89866. 1979. pap. 5.95 (ISBN 0-87716-108-9, Pub. by Moore Pub Co). F Apple.

Tidwell. Famafess Teacher Manual: Available to Professors Only. 1974. tchr's manual 7.50 o.p. (ISBN 0-685-05643-0); wkbk 5.00 o.p. (ISBN 0-685-05644-9). Assn Sch Busn.

--Financial & Managerial Accounting for Elementary & Secondary School Systems. 19.95 (ISBN 0-685-57171-8). Assn Sch Busn.

Tidwell, et al. Guidelines to Establish a Certificate of Conformance Program for Financial Reporting by School Systems. (Research Bulletin: No. 14). pap. 1.00 o.p. (ISBN 0-685-57176-9). Assn Sch Busn.

--Models of Financial Reporting by School Systems: Michigan Tech Workshop Papers. 1975. 25.00 ea. o.p. Assn Sch Busn.

--School (K-12) Accounting, Junior & Community College Accounting: Principles & Procedures. (Research Bulletin: No. 9). pap. 0.69 (ISBN 0-685-57181-5). Assn Sch Busn.

Tidwell, Charles A., jt. auth. see Schaller, Lyle E.

Tidwell, J. B. Geografia Biblica. Pierson, Carlos C., tr. (Illus.). 144p. (Sp.). 1982. pap. 5.50 (ISBN 0-311-15031-4). Casa Bautista.

Tidwell, Victor H., jt. auth. see Raby, William.

Tidy, Bill. Robbie & the Blobbies. (Illus.). 40p. (gr. 2-5). 1983. 8.95 (ISBN 0-434-96620-7, Pub. by Heinemann England). David & Charles.

Tidy, Michael & Leeming, Donald. History of Africa Eighteen-Forty to Nineteen-Fourteen, Vol. 1. (Illus.). 188p. 1981. 21.50x (ISBN 0-8419-0661-0, Africana); pap. text ed. 12.50x (ISBN 0-686-96740-2). Holmes & Meier.

Tiechert, Curt, jt. ed. see Robison, Richard A.

Tieck, Johann L. Letters of Ludwig Tieck, Hitherto Unpublished, 1792-1853. Zeydel, Edwin H., et al, eds. LC 73-9682. (MLA Gen. Ser.: No. 7). 636p. 1973. Repr. of 1937 ed. 45.00 (ISBN 0-527-90100-8). Kraus Repr.

Tiedebohl, Harriet, jt. auth. see Doolittle, Rosalie.

Tiedman, Gary, jt. auth. see Hawkins, Richard.

Tiedt, I. & Tiedt, S. Contemporary English in the Elementary School. 2nd ed. 1975. 23.95 (ISBN 0-13-169961-X). P-H.

Tiedt, Iris M. Exploring Books with Children. LC 78-69530. (Illus.). 1979. text ed. 20.95 (ISBN 0-395-25498-1). HM.

Tiedt, Iris M. & Bruemmer, S. Suzanne. Teaching Writing in K-8 Classrooms: The Time Has Come. (Illus.). 1983. pap. 16.95 (ISBN 0-13-896290-1). P-H.

Tiedt, S., jt. auth. see Tiedt, I.

Tiegs, Cheryl. The Way to Natural Beauty. (Illus.). 1980. 15.95 o.p. (ISBN 0-671-24894-4). S&S.

--The Way to Natural Beauty. (Illus.). 288p. 1983. pap. 8.95 (ISBN 0-671-47245-3, Fireside). S&S.

Tiel, Helmut. Digging in: Selected Prose Poems. 1979. pap. 4.95 (ISBN 0-931958-01-6). Apeiron Pr.

Tiemeyer, Raymond. Ordination of Women. 1970. 1.00 o.p. (ISBN 0-8066-1013-1, 10-4815). Augsburg.

Tiempo, Edilberto K. Finalities: A Novelette & 5 Short Stories. 132p. (Orig.). 1982. pap. 6.00x (ISBN 0-686-37685-4, Pub. by New Day Philippines). Cellar.

Tiempo, Edith. The Tracks of Babylon & Other Poems. 1966. pap. 0.75 o.p. (ISBN 0-8040-0293-2). Swallow.

Tien, Chang-Lim & Lienhard, John H. Statistical Thermodynamics. (McGraw-Hill Hemisphere Ser. in Thermal & Fluids Engineering). 1979. pap. 35.00 (ISBN 0-07-064570-1, C); solutions manual 5.95 (ISBN 0-07-064571-X). McGraw.

Tien, Doong, ed. see Low, Jennie.

Tien, H. Yuan, ed. Population Theory in China. LC 79-57159. 136p. 1980. 22.50 (ISBN 0-87332-174-X). M E Sharpe.

Tien, Hung-Mao, ed. Mainland China, Taiwan, & U. S. Policy. LC 82-14155. 212p. 1983. 25.00 (ISBN 0-89946-151-4). Oelgeschlager.

Tien, John K., et al, eds. Alloy & Microstructural Design. 1976. 64.00 (ISBN 0-12-690850-8). Acad Pr.

T'ien Chun, see Hsiacd Chun, pseud.

Tienhoven, Ari Van. Reproductive Physiology of Vertebrates. 2nd ed. (Illus.). 560p. 1982. 47.50x (ISBN 0-8014-1281-1). Cornell U Pr.

Tien-Mo Shih, ed. Numerical Properties & Methodologies in Heat Transfer: Proceedings of the Second Annual Symposium. LC 82-6187. (Computational Methods in Mechanics & Thermal Sciences Ser.). (Illus.). 1983. text ed. 69.50 (ISBN 0-89116-257-7). Hemisphere Pub.

Tiepolo, Giovanni D., illus. Picturesque Ideas on the Flight into Egypt. LC 72-90171. (Illus.). 64p. 1972. 5.00 (ISBN 0-87099-121-3). Metro Mus Art.

Tier, Lynne L. & Roberts, Barbara D. Teaching & Evaluation in the Classroom. 73p. 1980. 5.95 (ISBN 0-686-38252-8, 23-1826). Natl League Nurse.

Tierney, Ariel. Sultry Nights, No. 74. 1982. pap. 1.75 (ISBN 0-515-06685-0). Jove Pubns.

Tierney, Brian. Ockham, the Conciliar Theory, & the Canonists. Oberman, Heiko A., ed. LC 74-157547. (Facet Bks). (Orig.). 1971. pap. 1.00 o.p. (ISBN 0-8006-3064-5, 1-3064). Fortress.

Tierney, Brian & Painter, Sidney. Western Europe in the Middle Ages, 300-1475. 3rd ed. 1978. text ed. 22.00 (ISBN 0-394-32180-4). Random.

Tierney, Brian, ed. The Middle Ages: Sources of Medieval History, Vol. 1. 3rd ed. 1978. pap. text ed. 7.95 o.p. (ISBN 0-394-32151-0). Knopf.

Tierney, Brian, et al. Ancient Science. 1968. pap. text ed. 1.25x (ISBN 0-685-55647-6, 30802). Phila Bk Co.

--Great Issues on Western Civilization Since 1500. 1967. pap. text ed. 6.95x (ISBN 0-685-55642-5, 30563). Phila Bk Co.

--Outbreak of the First World War. 1968. pap. text ed. 3.00 (ISBN 0-394-32061-1, RanC). Random.

Tierney, Brian, et al, eds. The Bolshevik Revolution: Why Did It Succeed? 3rd ed. (Historical Pamphlets). 1977. pap. text ed. 1.95x o.p. (ISBN 0-394-32062-X). Random.

--English Liberalism: The New Democratic Way? 3rd ed. (Historical Pamphlets). 1977. pap. text ed. 1.95x o.s.i. (ISBN 0-394-32060-3). Random.

--Martin Luther--Reformer or Revolutionary? 3rd ed. (Historical Pamphlets). 1977. pap. text ed. 1.95x o.s.i. (ISBN 0-394-32055-7). Random.

--The Origins of the French Revolution: Popular Misery, Social Ambitions, or Philosophical Ideas? 3rd ed. (Historical Pamphlets). 1977. pap. text ed. 2.95x (ISBN 0-394-32058-1). Random.

Tierney, Hanne. Where's Your Baby Brother, Becky Bunting? (gr. 1-3). 1979. 7.95 (ISBN 0-385-08653-9); PLB o.p. (ISBN 0-385-08654-7). Doubleday.

Tierney, John J., Jr. Somozas & Sadinistas: The U.S. & Nicaragua in the Twentieth Century. LC 82-8112. (Illus.). 95p. (Orig.). 1982. pap. 5.00 (ISBN 0-943624-19-3). Coun Inter-Am.

Tierney, Kevin. Darrow: A Biography. LC 78-3319. (Illus.). 1979. 17.26i (ISBN 0-690-01408-2). T Y Crowell.

Tierney, Richard L., jt. auth. see Smith, David C.

Tierney, Tom. American Family of the Colonial Era: Paper Dolls in Full Color. (Illus.). 32p. (Orig.). (gr. 3 up). 1983. pap. 3.00 (ISBN 0-486-24394-X). Dover.

--Catsnips: Cat Paper Dolls. 32p. 1983. pap. 4.95 (ISBN 0-943392-12-8). Tribeca Comm.

--Cut & Assemble a Toy Theater: The Nutcracker Ballet. 32p. 1981. pap. 3.95 (ISBN 0-486-24194-7). Dover.

--Great Empresses & Queens Paper Dolls in Full Color. 32p. 1982. pap. 3.00 (ISBN 0-486-24268-4). Dover.

--Great Fashion Designs of the Belle Epoque: Paper Dolls in Full Color. (Illus.). 32p. (gr. 5 up). Date not set. pap. 3.50 (ISBN 0-486-24425-3). Dover.

--Isadora Duncan, Martha Graham & Other Stars of the Modern Dance Paper Dolls in Full Color. (Illus.). 32p. (Orig.). (gr. 9 up). 1983. pap. 3.50 (ISBN 0-486-24490-3). Dover.

--Judy Garland Paper Dolls in Full Color. (Illus.). 32p. (Orig.). pap. 3.50 (ISBN 0-486-24404-0). Dover.

--Marilyn Monroe Paper Dolls. 32p. 1979. pap. 2.75 (ISBN 0-486-23769-9). Dover.

--Nancy Reagan Fashion Paper Dolls in Full Color. (Illus.). 32p. (Orig.). (gr. 4 up). 1893. pap. 3.50 (ISBN 0-486-24474-1). Dover.

--Pavlova & Nijinsky Paper Dolls in Full Color. (Illus.). 32p. (Orig.). 1981. pap. 3.50 (ISBN 0-486-24093-2). Dover.

--Ready-to-Use Illustrations of Children (Clip Art) (Pictorial Archive Ser.). (Illus.). 64p. (Orig.). 1983. pap. 2.95 (ISBN 0-486-24405-9). Dover.

--Vivien Leigh Paper Dolls in Full Cover. 32p. 1981. pap. 3.00 (ISBN 0-486-24207-2). Dover.

Tierney, William F. Modern Upholstering Methods. (gr. 9 up). 1965. text ed. 18.64 (ISBN 0-87345-482-0). McKnight.

Tierra, Michael, ed. Way of Herbs. 1983. pap. 3.50 (ISBN 0-686-37705-2). WSP.

Tiersten, Irene. Among Friends: The Stories of Five Women. LC 82-5783. 256p. 1982. 13.95 (ISBN 0-312-03138-6). St Martin.

Tietjen, Mary L. The Bethlehem Tree: A Family Advent Resource Book. LC 76-9364. 136p. 1976. pap. 4.50 o.p. (ISBN 0-8091-1949-8). Paulist Pr.

--Holy Days & Holidays: Activities, Crafts & Stories for Children. LC 82-62416. 1983. pap. 2.95 (ISBN 0-8091-2531-5). Paulist Pr.

--Summer Savory: A Family Resource Book. LC 77-78961. 112p. 1977. pap. 3.95 o.p. (ISBN 0-8091-2034-8). Paulist Pr.

Tietze, Andreas, ed. see Komurjian, Eremya.

Tietze, Christopher. Induced Abortion: A World Review, 1981. 5th ed. LC 81-4986. 113p. (Orig.). 1983. pap. text ed. 6.00 (ISBN 0-87834-047-5). Population Coun.

Tiffany, Francis. Dorothea Lynde Dix. LC 70-145702. 1971. Repr. of 1918 ed. 42.00x (ISBN 0-8103-3655-3). Gale.

Tiffany, James R. & Moss, Robert A. The Exer-Trail Guide to Total Fitness. LC 81-85970. (Illus.). 128p. 1982. pap. 5.95 (ISBN 0-88011-026-0). Leisure Pr.

Tiffany, Lawrence P, et al. Detection of Crime: Stopping & Questioning, Search & Seizure, & Encouragement & Entrapment. 286p. 1967. pap. 7.95 o.p. (ISBN 0-316-84532-9). Little.

Tiffany, Sharon. Women, Work & Motherhood: The Power of Female Sexuality in the Workplace. 148p. 1982. 11.95 (ISBN 0-13-962092-3); pap. 5.95 (ISBN 0-13-962084-2). P-H.

Tiffany, Sharon W., ed. Women & Society: An Anthropological Reader. 1979. 20.95 (ISBN 0-920792-01-4). Eden Pr.

Tiffany, William R. & Carrell, James. Phonetics: Theory & Application. 2nd ed. (Speech Ser.). (Illus.). 1977. text ed. 27.50 (ISBN 0-07-064575-2, C). McGraw.

Tiffin, Robert, jt. auth. see Diamond, Dorothy.

Tiger, Edith, ed. In Re Alger Hiss, Vol. I. (American Century Ser.). 438p. 1979. pap. 8.95 (ISBN 0-8090-0143-8, AmCen); 17.50 (ISBN 0-8090-5808-1). Hill & Wang.

Tiger, Lionel. Optimism. 1980. 4.95 o.p. (ISBN 0-671-25395-6, Touchstone). S&S.

Tiger, R. P., jt. auth. see Entelis, S. G.

Tiger, Virginia. William Golding: The Dark Fields of Discovery. (Critical Appraisals Ser.). 240p. 1974. text ed. 15.00x o.p. (ISBN 0-7145-1012-2). Humanities.

Tigerman, Stanley. Versus: An American Architect's Alternatives. LC 81-86435. (Illus.). 224p. 1982. 35.00 (ISBN 0-8478-0429-1); pap. 19.95 (ISBN 0-8478-0433-X). Rizzoli Intl.

Tigerman, Stanley & Lewin, Susan Grant. The California Condition: A Pregnant Architecture. Adler, Sebastian J., frwd. by. LC 82-83257. (Illus.). 104p. (Orig.). pap. 14.85 (ISBN 0-934418-15-2). La Jolla Mus Contemp Art.

Tighe, Donald J., jt. auth. see Casty, Alan.

Tighe, Freida. Journey to the Top of the Divide. pap. 4.50x (ISBN 0-686-82443-1). Golden Bell.

Tighe, Mary Ann & Lang, Elizabeth E. Art America. (Illus.). 1977. 29.00 (ISBN 0-07-064607-4, C); pap. 15.95 (ISBN 0-07-064601-5). McGraw.

Tighe, Ruth, ed. see ASIS Annual Meeting 38th.

Tighe, Thomas J., ed. Perception, Cognition & Development: Interactional Analyses. Shepp, Bryan E. 400p. 1983. text ed. 39.95 (ISBN 0-89859-254-2). L Erlbaum Assocs.

Tigner, Marcy. Little Marcy & Her Friends. LC 80-80092. (Orig.). 1980. pap. 1.25 o.p. (ISBN 0-89081-229-2). Harvest Hse.

--Little Marcy Loves Jesus. (Orig.). 1980. pap. 1.25 o.p. (ISBN 0-89081-227-6). Harvest Hse.

Tignor, Robert L., jt. auth. see Collins, Robert O.

Tigunait, Pandit R. Seven Systems of Indian Philosophy: A Survey. LC 81-85537. 250p. (Orig.). 1983. pap. write for info. (ISBN 0-89389-076-6). Himalayan Intl Inst.

Tihany, Leslie C. The History of Middle Europe: From the Earliest Times to the Age of the World Wars. LC 75-25945. 1976. 25.00x (ISBN 0-8135-0814-2). Rutgers U Pr.

Tihomirov, V. M., jt. auth. see Ioffe, A. D.

Tijssen & Halprin. Familial Brain Tumours. 1982. 54.50 (ISBN 90-247-2691-3, Pub. by Martinus Nijhoff Netherlands). Kluwer Boston.

Tikhonov, A. N., et al, eds. Mathematical Models & Numerical Methods. (Banach Center Publications Ser.: Vol. III). 391p. 1978. 60.00x (ISBN 0-8002-2268-7). Intl Pubns Serv.

Tikhonov, V. N. Analytical Chemistry of Aluminum. LC 72-4102. (Analytical Chemistry of the Elements Ser.). 250p. 1973. 52.95 o.p. (ISBN 0-470-86787-6). Halsted Pr.

Til, John Van, jt. ed. see Smith, David H.

Til, Jon Van see Van Til, Jon.

Til, William Van see Van Til, William.

Tilak, B. V., jt. auth. see Weinberg, N. L.

Tilberg, JoAnne Van see Van Tilburg, JoAnne & Meighan, Clement W.

Tilburg, JoAnne Van see Van Tilburg, JoAnne.

Tilbury, R. H., ed. Developments in Food Preservatives, Vol. 1. 1980. 39.00 (ISBN 0-85334-918-5, Pub. by Applied Sci England). Elsevier.

Tilden, Bill. How to Play Better Tennis. (Illus.). 144p. 1950. pap. 2.95 o.p. (ISBN 0-686-37461-4). USTA.

--Match Play & the Spin of the Ball. 2nd ed. LC 76-333. (Illus.). 1969. pap. 3.95 o.p. (ISBN 0-8046-1771-6). Kennikat.

Tilden, J. The Myxophyceae of North America & Adjacent Regions. (Bibl. Phyco.: Vol. 4). (Illus.). 1968. pap. 32.00 (ISBN 3-7682-0546-0). Lubrecht & Cramer.

Tilden, J. W. Butterflies of the San Francisco Bay Region. (California Natural History Guides: No. 12). (Illus.). 1965. 14.95x o.p. (ISBN 0-520-03101-6); pap. 2.65 o.s.i. (ISBN 0-520-01268-2). U of Cal Pr.

Tilden, William T., 2nd. Match Play & the Spin of the Ball. LC 75-33763. (Illus.). 1975. 6.95 (ISBN 0-405-06679-1). Ayer Co.

Tileston, Mary W. Great Souls at Prayer. 366p. 1980. Repr. of 1898 ed. 9.50 (ISBN 0-227-67474-X). Attic Pr.

Tileston, Mary W., ed. Daily Strength for Daily Needs. 1959. 2.95 (ISBN 0-448-01639-7, G&D). Putnam Pub Group.

--Joy & Strength. 1959. 2.95 o.p. (ISBN 0-448-01648-6, G&D). Putnam Pub Group.

Tiley, Nancy A. Discovering DNA. 304p. 1983. text ed. 16.95 (ISBN 0-442-26260-4). Van Nos Reinhold.

Tilke, M., jt. auth. see Bruhn, W.

Tilkian, Sarko M. & Conover, Mary B. Clinical Implications of Laboratory Tests. 3rd ed. (Illus.). 494p. 1983. pap. text ed. 13.95 (ISBN 0-8016-4960-9). Mosby.

Till, Geoffrey. Maritime Strategy & the Nuclear Age. 220p. 1982. 60.00x (ISBN 0-333-26109-7, Pub. by Macmillan England). State Mutual Bk.

Till, Irene, jt. auth. see Hamilton, Walton.

Till, Nicholas. Debussy: His Life & Times. (Illus.). 150p. 1983. 16.95 (ISBN 0-88254-808-5, Pub. by Midas Bks England). Hippocrene Bks.

Till, Roger. Statistical Methods for the Earth Scientist: An Introduction. LC 73-22704. 1978. pap. 24.95x (ISBN 0-470-26340-7). Halsted Pr.

Till, William C. & Luxon, James T. Integrated Circuits: Materials, Devices & Fabrication. (Illus.). 512p. 1982. 34.95 (ISBN 0-13-469031-1). P-H.

Tillapaugh, Frank R. The Church Unleashed: Getting God's People Out Where the Needs Are. LC 82-9783. 1982. pap. 5.95 (ISBN 0-8307-0823-5, 5416300). Regal.

Tillee, Sandee W. Lord, I've Been in Hell So Long. 1978. pap. 2.50x o.p. (ISBN 0-8358-0375-9). Upper Room.

Tiller, Ann Q. The University As an Agent of Community Development in Brazil with Emphasis on the Crutac Program. 200p. 1977. pap. text ed. 9.00 o.p. (ISBN 0-8191-0312-8). U Pr of Amer.

Tiller, D. J., jt. auth. see Loblay, R. H.

Tiller, David J., jt. auth. see McGovern, Vincent J.

Tiller, Terence, ed. see Dante Alighieri.

Tiller, Veronica E. The Jicarilla Apache Tribe: A History, 1846-1970. LC 82-6973. (Illus.). 265p. 1983. 23.95x (ISBN 0-8032-4409-6). U of Nebr Pr.

Tillery, Dale. Distribution & Differentiation of Youth: A Study of Transition from School to College. LC 73-9578. 192p. 1973. prof ref 16.50 (ISBN 0-88410-152-5). Ballinger Pub.

Tillett, Leslie. Plant & Animal Alphabet Coloring Book. (Illus.). 1982. text ed. 1.75 (ISBN 0-486-23898-9). Dover.

Tilley, Donald E. Contemporary College Physics. LC 78-57146. 1979. pap. text ed. 28.95 (ISBN 0-8053-9290-4); instr's guide 6.95 (ISBN 0-8053-9291-2). Benjamin-Cummings.

--University Physics for Science & Engineering. LC 75-14974. 1976. 29.95 (ISBN 0-8465-7536-1); instr's guide 3.75 (ISBN 0-8465-7537-X). Benjamin-Cummings.

Tilley, Donald E. & Thumm, Walter. Physics for College Students. LC 72-89140. 800p. 1974. 29.95 (ISBN 0-8465-7538-8). Benjamin-Cummings.

--Physics for College Students. alt. ed. 1976. 29.95 (ISBN 0-8465-7534-5); 3.95 o.p. instr's guide (ISBN 0-8465-7533-7). Benjamin-Cummings.

Tillich, Paul. Courage to Be. (Terry Lectures Ser.). 1952. 17.50x (ISBN 0-300-00990-9); pap. 4.95 (ISBN 0-300-00241-6, Y11). Yale U Pr.

--Dynamics of Faith. pap. 3.95xi (ISBN 0-06-130042-X, TB42, Torch). Har-Row.

--A History of Christian Thought. 1972. pap. 10.75 (ISBN 0-671-21426-8, Touchstone Bks). S&S.

--Protestant Era. abr ed. Adams, James L., tr. 1957. pap. 7.50x (ISBN 0-226-80342-2, P19, Phoen). U of Chicago Pr.

--The Socialist Decision. Sherman, Franklin, tr. from Ger. LC 82-21913. 224p. 1983. pap. text ed. 9.75 (ISBN 0-8191-2911-9). U Pr of Amer.

--Systematic Theology: Life & the Spirit History & the Kingdom of God, Vol. 3. LC 51-2235. 1976. pap. 9.95 (ISBN 0-226-80339-2, P706, Phoen). U of Chicago Pr.

--Theology of Culture. Kimball, Robert C., ed. 1964. pap. 6.95 (ISBN 0-19-500711-5, GB). Oxford U Pr.

Tillin, Alma M. & Quinly, William J. Standards for Cataloging Nonprint Materials. 4th ed. LC 75-38605. 898p. 1976. pap. 8.95 (ISBN 0-89240-000-5). Assn Ed Comm Tech.

Tilling, Thomas, jt. auth. see Donoghue, William E.

Tilling, Thomas, jt. auth. see Toney, Albert.

Tillion, Diana R., jt. auth. see Hoopes, David T.

Tillion, Germaine. France & Algeria. Howard, Richard, tr. 1976. Repr. of 1961 ed. lib. bdg. 15.50x (ISBN 0-8371-8859-8, TIFN). Greenwood.

Tillman, Albert. The Program Book for Recreation Professionals. LC 72-87825. 236p. 1973. text ed. 14.95 (ISBN 0-87484-189-5). Mayfield Pub.

Tillman, David, jt. ed. see Sarkanen, Kyosti V.

Tillman, David A., jt. auth. see Anderson, Larry L.

Tillman, David A., jt. ed. see Sarkanen, Kyosti V.

Tillman, Dick & Powlison, Dave. The New Laser Sailing. (Illus.). 160p. 1983. 14.95 (ISBN 0-914814-32-X). Sail Bks.

Tillman, Kenneth G., jt. auth. see Camaione, David N.

Tillman, Murray, et al. Learning to Teach. 1976. pap. 14.95 (ISBN 0-669-84848-4); instr's manual 1.95 (ISBN 0-669-98079-X). Heath.

Tillman, William A., jt. auth. see Maston, T. B.

Tillmann, H. Pope Innocent III. (Europe in the Middle Ages Selected Studies: Vol. 12). 1979. 64.00 (ISBN 0-444-85137-2, North-Holland). Elsevier.

Tillotson, Delight M., jt. auth. see Butnarescu, Glenda F.

Tillotson, Geoffrey. A View of Victorian Literature. 1978. 25.00x (ISBN 0-19-812044-3). Oxford U Pr.

Tilly, Bertha, ed. see Virgil.

Tilly, C., jt. auth. see Shorter, E.

Tilly, Charles. From Mobilization to Revolution. LC 77-79468. (Illus.). 1978. pap. text ed. 15.95 (ISBN 0-201-07571-7). A-W.

Tillyard, Eustace M. Essays: Literary & Educational. LC 78-2020. 1978. Repr. of 1962 ed. lib. bdg. 20.00x (ISBN 0-313-20359-8, TIEL). Greenwood.

Tilman, H. W. In Mischief's Wake. 1972. 9.50 o.p. (ISBN 0-370-01377-8). Transatlantic.

Tilney-Basset, R. A., jt. auth. see Kirk, J. T.

Tilp, Frederick. This Was Potomac River. (Illus.). 358p. 1978. 26.00 (ISBN 0-686-36783-9). Md Hist.

Tilson, Ann & Weiss, Carol H. The Mail Order Food Guide. 1977. 10.95 o.p. (ISBN 0-671-22810-2); pap. 4.95 o.p. (ISBN 0-671-23077-8). S&S.

Tilson, M. David, jt. auth. see Wright, Hastings K.

Tilth. The Future Is Abundant: A Guide to Sustainable Agriculture in the Pacific Northwest. Korn, Larry, ed. LC 82-10351. (Illus.). 192p. (Orig.). 1982. pap. 11.95 (ISBN 0-931380-01-4). Tilth.

Tilton, Dennis. Taking the Stand. LC 81-5453. 1981. pap. 9.95 (ISBN 0-686-85964-2). Film Communicators.

Tilton, Helga, ed. Deutsch Mit Emil. 1980. pap. text ed. 7.95x (ISBN 0-393-95111-1). Norton.

Tilton, John E. The Future of Nonfuel Minerals. 1977. 12.95 (ISBN 0-8157-8460-0). Brookings.

Timagenis. International Control of Marine Pollution, Vols. 1-2. LC 80-124574. 64p. 1980. 37.50 ea. Vol. 1 (ISBN 0-379-20685-4). Vol. 2 (ISBN 0-379-20686-2). Oceana.

Timar, Janos. Planning the Labor Force in Hungary. LC 66-20465. 1966. 22.50 (ISBN 0-87332-015-8). M E Sharpe.

Timasheff, Nicholas S. Religion in Soviet Russia, Nineteen Seventeen to Nineteen Forty-Two. LC 78-23615. 1979. Repr. of 1942 ed. lib. bdg. 17.00x (ISBN 0-313-21040-3, TIRS). Greenwood.

Timasheff, S. & Fasman, G., eds. Subunits in Biological Systems, Pt. A. (Biological Macromolecules Ser: Vol. 5). 1971. 59.50 o.p. (ISBN 0-8247-1187-4). Dekker.

Timasheff, S. N. & Fasman, G. D., eds. Structure & Stability of Biological Macromolecules. (Biological Macromolecules Ser: Vol. 2). 1969. 75.00 o.p. (ISBN 0-8247-1670-1). Dekker.

--Subunits in Biological Systems, Pt. C. (Biological Macromolecules Ser.: Vol. 7). 376p. 1975. 59.50 o.p. (ISBN 0-8247-6279-7). Dekker.

Timasheff, Serge, jt. ed. see Fasman, Gerald D.

Timber Engineering Company. Timber Design & Construction Handbook. 1956. 55.00 (ISBN 0-07-064606-6, P&RB). McGraw.

Timberg, Bernard, jt. ed. see Lawrence, John S.

Timberlake, Charles & Greenwood, Larry. How to Search for Information: A Beginner's Guide to the Literature of Sociology. (Basic Tools Ser.: No. 2). 80p. (Orig.). 1983. pap. text ed. write for info (ISBN 0-938376-01-2). Willowood Pr.

Timberlake, Karen. Chemistry. 2nd ed. 1979. text ed. 24.50 scp o.p. (ISBN 0-06-163409-3, HarpC); inst. manual avail. o.p. (ISBN 0-06-163412-3); scp lab manual 8.95 o.p. (ISBN 0-06-163411-5); scp study guide 8.50 o.p. (ISBN 0-06-163410-7). Har-Row.

Timberlake, Karen C. Chemistry. 3rd ed. 604p. 1983. text ed. 23.50 scp (ISBN 0-06-046632-4, HarpC); instr's manual avail. (ISBN 0-06-366621-9); scp lab manual 8.50 (ISBN 0-06-046631-6); scp study guide 8.50 (ISBN 0-06-046629-4). Har-Row.

Timberlake, Linda H. Barney's Gift. (Illus.). 48p. (Orig.). (gr. 1-3). 1982. pap. 6.50 (ISBN 0-87397-244-9). Strode.

Timberlake, P. H. Review of the Species of Exomalopsis Occurring in North America (Hymenoptera, Anthophoridae) (Publications in Entomology Ser.: Vol. 86). 164p. 1980. 21.50x (ISBN 0-520-09606-1). U of Cal Pr.

--Supplementary Studies on the Systematics of the Genus Perdita (Hymenoptera, Andrenidae, Part II. (U. C. Publications in Entomology Ser.: Vol. 85). 1980. pap. 13.00x (ISBN 0-520-09605-3). U of Cal Pr.

Timbrell, J. A. Principles of Biochemical Toxicology. 240p. 1982. 88.00x (ISBN 0-85066-221-4, Pub. by Taylor & Francis). State Mutual Bk.

Timbs, John. Clubs & Club Life in London with Anecodotes of Its Famous Coffee-Houses, Hostelries, & Taverns from the Seventeenth Century to the Present Time. LC 66-28045. 1967. Repr. of 1872 ed. 30.00x (ISBN 0-8103-3262-0). Gale.

--Curiosities of London. rev. ed. LC 68-22056. 1968. Repr. of 1867 ed. 45.00x (ISBN 0-8103-3497-6). Gale.

--English Eccentrics & Eccentricities. LC 69-18076. 1969. Repr. of 1875 ed. 37.00x (ISBN 0-8103-3556-5). Gale.

--Historic Ninepins. LC 68-22057. 1969. Repr. of 1869 ed. 34.00x (ISBN 0-8103-3539-5). Gale.

--Romance of London. LC 68-22058. 1968. Repr. of 1865 ed. 63.00x (ISBN 0-8103-3498-4). Gale.

--The Romance of London: Historic Sketches, Remarkable Duels, Notorious Highwaymen, Rogueries, Crimes, & Punishments, & Love & Marriage. 509p. 1982. Repr. lib. bdg. 50.00 (ISBN 0-89984-469-3). Century Bookbindery.

--Things Not Generally Known. Wells, David A., ed. LC 68-30584. 1968. Repr. of 1857 ed. 42.00x (ISBN 0-8103-3101-2). Gale.

Time & Life Editors, ed. New Living Spaces. LC 72-72104. (Home Repair & Improvement). (Illus.). (gr. 7 up). 1977. PLB 15.96 (ISBN 0-8094-2375-8, Pub by Time-Life). Silver.

Time Life Bks Editors. The Boat. LC 74-19438. (Time Life Library of Boating). (Illus.). (gr. 6 up). 1975. PLB 22.60 (ISBN 0-8094-2101-1). Silver.

--Boat Handling. LC 74-29194. (Time Life Library of Boating). (Illus.). (gr. 6 up). 1975. PLB 22.60 (ISBN 0-8094-2105-4). Silver.

--Classic Techniques. LC 73-85529. (Art of Sewing Ser.). (Illus.). 208p. (gr. 6 up). 1973. lib. bdg. 11.97 o.p. (ISBN 0-8094-1703-0). Silver.

--Creative Design. LC 74-29449. (Art of Sewing Ser.). (Illus.). 208p. (gr. 6 up). 1975. lib. bdg. 11.97 o.p. (ISBN 0-8094-1743-X). Silver.

Time-Life Book Editors. Breads. LC 80-22396. (Good Cook Ser.). PLB 19.96 (ISBN 0-8094-2901-2). Silver.

Time-Life Books. Kitchens & Bathrooms. LC 77-83171. (Home Repairs & Improvement Ser.). (Illus.). 1977. lib. bdg. 15.96 (ISBN 0-8094-2387-1). Silver.

Time Life Books, ed. Basic Tailoring. LC 74-80076. (Art of Sewing Ser.). (gr. 6 up). 1974. lib. bdg. 11.97 o.p. (ISBN 0-8094-1719-7, Pub. by Time-Life). Silver.

--The Classic Boat. LC 76-55862. (Library of Boating). (Illus.). (gr. 6 up). 1977. PLB 22.60 (ISBN 0-8094-2145-3, Pub. by Time-Life). Silver.

Time-Life Books, ed. A Commonsense Guide to Sex, Birth, & Babies. (Library of Health Ser.). 1983. lib. bdg. 18.60 (ISBN 0-8094-3827-5). Silver.

Time Life Books, ed. The Community. LC 76-20311. (Human Behavior). (Illus.). (gr. 5 up). 1976. PLB 13.28 (ISBN 0-8094-1959-9, Pub. by Time-Life). Silver.

--Cruising. LC 75-27445. (Library of Boating Ser.). (gr. 6 up). 1975. PLB 22.60 (ISBN 0-8094-2121-6, Pub. by Time-Life). Silver.

--Cruising Grounds. LC 76-9629. (Library of Boating Ser.). (Illus.). (gr. 6 up). 1976. PLB 22.60 (ISBN 0-8094-2133-X, Pub. by Time-Life). Silver.

Time-Life Books, ed. Dried Beans & Grains. 176p. 1982. 13.95 (ISBN 0-8094-2920-9). Time-Life.

--Heating & Cooling. LC 77-80200. (Home Repair & Improvement Ser.). (Illus.). (gr. 7 up). 1977. PLB 15.96 (ISBN 0-8094-2379-0, Pub. by Time-Life). Silver.

Time Life Books, ed. Maintenance. LC 75-18911. (Library of Boating Ser.). (Illus.). (gr. 6 up). 1975. PLB 22.60 (ISBN 0-8094-2117-8, Pub. by Time-Life). Silver.

--Masonry. LC 76-25711. (Home Repair & Improvement). (Illus.). (gr. 7 up). 1976. PLB 15.96 (ISBN 0-8094-2363-4, Pub. by Time-Life). Silver.

--Offshore-Cruising Navigation Racing. LC 76-417. (Library of Boating Ser.). (Illus.). (gr. 6 up). 1976. PLB 22.60 (ISBN 0-685-73295-9, Pub. by Time-Life). Silver.

--Paint & Wallpaper. LC 76-3377. (Home Repair & Improvement). (Illus.). (gr. 7 up). 1976. PLB 15.96 (ISBN 0-8094-2355-3, Pub. by Time-Life). Silver.

--Plumbing. LC 76-46139. (Home Repair & Improvement). (Illus.). (gr. 7 up). 1976. PLB 15.96 (ISBN 0-8094-2367-7, Pub. by Time-Life). Silver.

--Racing. LC 75-34791. (Library of Boating Ser.). (Illus.). (gr. 6 up). 1976. PLB 22.60 (ISBN 0-8094-2125-9, Pub. by Time-Life). Silver.

--Seamanship. LC 75-651. (Library of Boating Ser.). (gr. 6 up). 1975. PLB 22.60 (ISBN 0-8094-2109-7, Pub. by Time-Life). Silver.

--Space & Storage. LC 75-34852. (Home Repair & Improvement). (Illus.). (gr. 7 up). 1976. PLB 15.96 (ISBN 0-8094-2351-0, Pub. by Time-Life). Silver.

--Terrines, Pates & Galantines. LC 81-21310. (Illus.). 176p. 1982. 13.95 (ISBN 0-8094-2925-X). Time-Life.

Time-Life Books, ed. Volcano. LC 81-18539. (Planet Earth Ser.: No. 2). (Illus.). 1982. 9.95 (ISBN 0-8094-4304-X). Time-Life.

Time Life Books, ed. Weatherproofing. LC 76-55869. (Home Repair & Improvement Ser.). (Illus.). (gr. 7 up). 1977. PLB 15.96 (ISBN 0-8094-2371-5, Pub. by Time-Life). Silver.

Time-Life Books Editors. Advertising Giveaways to Baskets. LC 77-99201. (The Encyclopedia of Collectibles Ser.). (Illus.). 1978. lib. bdg. 15.62 (ISBN 0-8094-2751-6). Silver.

--Beads to Boxes. LC 78-50707. (The Encyclopedia of Collectibles Ser.). (Illus.). 1978. lib. bdg. 15.96 (ISBN 0-8094-2755-9). Silver.

--Buttons to Chess Sets. LC 78-54098. (The Encyclopedia of Collectibles Ser.). (Illus.). 1978. lib. bdg. 15.96 (ISBN 0-8094-2759-1). Silver.

--Children's Books to Comics. LC 77-99201. (The Encyclopedia of Collectibles Ser.). (Illus.). 1978. lib. bdg. 15.96 (ISBN 0-8094-2763-X). Silver.

--Cookbooks to Detective Fiction. LC 77-99201. (The Encyclopedia of Collectibles Ser.). (Illus.). 1978. lib. bdg. 15.96 (ISBN 0-8094-2767-2). Silver.

--Dogs to Fishing Tackle. (The Encyclopedia of Collectibles Ser.). (Illus.). 1978. lib. bdg. 15.96 (ISBN 0-8094-2771-0). Silver.

--Folk Art to Horse-Drawn Carriages. (The Encyclopedia of Collectibles Ser.). (Illus.). 1979. lib. bdg. 15.96 (ISBN 0-8094-2775-3). Silver.

--Inkwells to Lace. LC 77-99201. (The Encyclopedia of Collectibles Ser.). (Illus.). 1979. lib. bdg. 15.96 (ISBN 0-686-50979-X). Silver.

--Lalique to Masks. (The Encyclopedia of Collectibles Ser.). (Illus.). 1979. lib. bdg. 15.96 (ISBN 0-8094-2783-4). Silver.

--Matchsafes to Nursing Bottles. (The Encyclopedia of Collectibles Ser.). (Illus.). 1979. lib. bdg. 15.96 (ISBN 0-8094-2787-7). Silver.

--Modern American Painting: 1900 - 1970. LC 72-131017. (Library of Art Ser.). (Illus.). (gr. 6 up). 1970. 19.92 (ISBN 0-8094-0287-4, Pub. by Time-Life). Silver.

--Oak Furniture to Pharmacist's Equipment. (The Encyclopedia of Collectibles Ser.). (Illus.). 1979. lib. bdg. 15.96 (ISBN 0-8094-2791-5). Silver.

--Phonographs to Quilts. (The Encyclopedia of Collectibles Ser.). (Illus.). 1979. lib. bdg. 15.96 (ISBN 0-8094-2795-8). Silver.

--Sports Afloat. LC 76-17459. (Library of Boating Ser.). (gr. 6 up). 1976. PLB 22.60 (ISBN 0-8094-2129-1, Pub. by Time-Life). Silver.

--Volcano. LC 81-18539. (Planet Earth Ser.). lib. bdg. 19.92 (ISBN 0-8094-4305-8, Pub. by Time-Life). Silver.

--The Wholesome Diet. LC 81-8987. (Library of Health). lib. bdg. 18.60 (ISBN 0-8094-3767-8). Silver.

Time-Life Books Editors, ed. How Things Work in Your Home. LC 74-24853. (Illus.). 1979. pap. 7.95 o.p. (ISBN 0-448-16542-2, G&D). Putnam Pub Group.

Time-Life Editors. The Handy Boatman. LC 76-26732. (Time-Life Library of Boating). 1976. lib. bdg. 22.60 (ISBN 0-8094-2141-0). Silver.

--Time-Life Holiday Cookbook. LC 76-10075. 1976. lib. bdg. 22.60 (ISBN 0-8094-1932-7). Silver.

Time-Life Editors, ed. Decorating with Plants. (Encyclopedia of Gardening Ser.). (Illus.). 1978. 11.95 (ISBN 0-8094-2579-3). Time-Life.

--Gardening under Lights. (The Encyclopedia of Gardening Ser.). (Illus.). 1978. 11.95 (ISBN 0-8094-2570-X). Time-Life.

Time-Life Television. Birds of Field & Forest. LC 77-5596. (Wild World of Animals Ser.). (gr. 5 up). 1977. PLB 12.00 (ISBN 0-913948-13-6). Silver.

Time Periodicals Ltd., ed. Straits Times Directory of Singapore. LC 75-940975. 948p. 1980. 58.50x (ISBN 0-8002-2750-6). Intl Pubns Serv.

Timerding, H. Emil. Geometrie der Krafte. (Bibliotheca Mathematica Teubneriana, 33). (Ger). Repr. of 1908 ed. 28.00 (ISBN 0-384-60640-7). Johnson Repr.

Timerlake, Richard H., Jr. & Selby, Edward B., Jr. Money & Banking. 1972. 16.95x o.p. (ISBN 0-534-00108-4). Wadsworth Pub.

Timerman, Jacobo. The Longest War: Israel in Lebanon. Acoca, Miguel, tr. from Span. LC 82-48584. 167p. 1982. 11.95 (ISBN 0-394-53022-5). Knopf.

--The Longest War: Israel in Lebanon. LC 82-20208. 192p. 1983. pap. 2.95 (Vin). Random.

--Preso Sin Nombre, Celda Sin Numero. LC 80-2715. (Span.). 1981. pap. write for info (ISBN 0-394-70778-8). Knopf.

Timiras, Paola, jt. auth. see Sherwood, Nancy.

Timko, Michael & Kaplan, Fred, eds. Dickens Studies Annual: Essays on Victorian Fiction, Vol. 10. (Illus.). 1982. 32.50 (ISBN 0-404-18530-4). AMS Pr.

Timm, Henry C., jt. auth. see Timm, Joan S.

Timm, Joan S. & Timm, Henry C. Athena's Mirror: Moral Reasoning in Poetry, Short Story & Drama. 1983. write for info. (ISBN 0-915744-34-1). Character Res.

Timm, Paul R. Functional Business Presentations: Getting Across. (Illus.). 192p. 1981. pap. text ed. 13.95 (ISBN 0-13-331470-7). P-H.

--Managerial Communication: A Finger on the Pulse. (Illus.). 1980. text ed. 20.95 (ISBN 0-13-549824-4). P-H.

Timm, Paul R. & Jones, Christopher G. Business Communication: Getting Results. 312p. 1983. 22.95 (ISBN 0-13-091793-1). P-H.

Timm, Paul R. & Peterson, Brent D. People at Work: Human Relations in Organizations. (Illus.). 508p. 1982. text ed. 22.95 (ISBN 0-314-63296-4). West Pub.

Timmer, W. J. The Human Side of Agriculture: Theory & Practice of Agricultural Extension. LC 80-53419. 223p. 1982. 10.00 (ISBN 0-533-04849-4). Vantage.

Timmerhaus, Klaus, jt. auth. see Peters, Max S.

Timmerman, E. H. Practical Reservoir Engineering, Vol. 1. 365p. 1981. 59.95x (ISBN 0-87814-168-5). Pennwell Books Division.

--Practical Reservoir Engineering, Vol. 2. 367p. 1982. 59.95x (ISBN 0-87814-181-2). Pennwell Books Division.

Timmerman, John. Shaper. 176p. 1983. 9.95 (ISBN 0-310-60390-0). Chosen Bks Pub.

Timmerman, John J. Markings on a Long Journey: Selections from the writing of John J. Timmerman. Mulder, Rodney J. & Timmerman, John J., eds. 320p. (Orig.). 1982. pap. 9.95 (ISBN 0-8010-8867-4). Baker Bk.

Timmerman, John J., ed. see Timmerman, John J.

Timmermann, Tim & Blecha, Diane. Modern Stress: The Needless Killer. 176p. 1982. pap. text ed. 13.95 (ISBN 0-8403-2722-6). Kendall-Hunt.

Timmermann, Waltraud. Studien Zur Allegorischen Bildlichkeit In Den Parabolae Bernhards Von Clairvaux. 305p. (Ger.). 1982. write for info. (ISBN 3-8204-6274-0). P Lang Pubs.

Timmermans, Felix. The Perfect Joy of St. Francis. 280p. 1974. pap. 4.50 (ISBN 0-385-02378-2, Im). Doubleday.

Timmermans, Jean. Physico-Chemical Constants of Pure Organic Compounds, Vol. 2. 2nd ed. 1965. 93.00 (ISBN 0-444-40572-0). Elsevier.

Timmins, Robert S., jt. ed. see Baddour, Raymond F.

Timmins, Samuel, ed. see British Association For The Advancement Of Science - Committee On Local Industries.

Timmis, Gerald C., et al, eds. Cardiovascular Review 1983. (Monograph). 1982. 29.50. Acad Pr.

Timmons, Bascom N. The Man & the Statesman. LC 74-31366. (Illus.). 414p. 1975. Repr. of 1956 ed. lib. bdg. 27.50x o.p. (ISBN 0-8371-7925-4, TIJJ). Greenwood.

Timmons, Tim. Loneliness Is Not a Disease. (Epiphany Bks.). 1983. pap. 2.25 (ISBN 0-345-30509-4). Ballantine.

--Maximum Marriage. 1977. pap. 4.95 o.p. (ISBN 0-8007-5003-9, Power Bks). Revell.

--Maximum Marriage. rev. & updated ed. 160p. pap. 5.95 (ISBN 0-8007-5106-X, Power Bks). Revell.

--Stress in the Family: How to Live Through It. LC 87-81649. 160p. (Orig.). 1982. pap. 5.95 (ISBN 0-89081-359-0). Harvest Hse.

Timmons, W. H. The Anglo-American Advance into Texas, 1810-1830. (Illus.). 46p. 1982. pap. text ed. 1.95x (ISBN 0-89641-103-6). American Pr.

Timms, Art. Finding Out About Aircraft. (Finding-Out Bks.). (Illus.). 64p. (gr. 4-9). 1983. PLB 8.951 (ISBN 0-89490-077-3). Enslow Pubs.

Timms, Duncan. Urban Mosaic: Towards a Theory of Residential Differentiation. LC 70-123665. (Geographical Studies: No. 2). (Illus.). 1971. 45.50 (ISBN 0-521-07964-0); pap. 14.95 (ISBN 0-521-09988-9). Cambridge U Pr.

Timms, Moira & Zar, Zachariah. Natural Sources Vitamin B-17. 4.95x o.p. (ISBN 0-89087-217-1). Cancer Control Soc.

Timms, Noel. Recording in Social Work. (Library of Social Work). 1972. 14.95x (ISBN 0-7100-7288-0); pap. 6.95 (ISBN 0-7100-7289-9). Routledge & Kegan.

--Social Work Values: An Inquiry. 200p. (Orig.). 1983. pap. price not set (ISBN 0-7100-9404-3). Routledge & Kegan.

Timms, Noel & Timms, Rita. Dictionary of Social Welfare. 228p. 1982. 19.95 (ISBN 0-7100-9084-6). Routledge & Kegan.

Timms, Noel, jt. auth. see Mayer, John E.

Timms, Noel, ed. The Receiving End: Consumer Accounts of Social Help for Children. 102p. 1973. 9.95 (ISBN 0-7100-7549-9). Routledge & Kegan.

--Social Welfare: Why & How. (International Library of Welfare & Philosophy). 306p. 1980. 30.00 (ISBN 0-7100-0615-2). Routledge & Kegan.

Timms, P. L., jt. auth. see Powell, P.

Timms, Rita, jt. auth. see Timms, Noel.

Timms, W. W. & Pulgar, M. Advanced Spanish Course. 1971. pap. text ed. 5.50x (ISBN 0-582-36480-9). Longman.

Timofeyev, T., jt. auth. see Fedoseyev, P.

Timofiewitch, Wladimir. The Chiesa Del Redentore. LC 74-113199. (Corpus Palladianum, Vol. 3). (Illus.). 1972. 42.50x (ISBN 0-271-00090-2). Pa St U Pr.

Timoney, R. F., jt. auth. see Deasy, P. B.

Timoney, R. F., jt. ed. see Deasy, P. B.

Timoshenko, S., et al. Vibration Problems in Engineering. 4th ed. LC 74-6191. 521p. 1974. text ed. 38.95x (ISBN 0-471-87315-2). Wiley.

Timoshenko, Stephen P. History of Strength of Materials: With a Brief Account of the History of Theory of Elasticity & Theory of Structure. (Illus.). 452p. 1983. pap. 8.95 (ISBN 0-486-61187-6). Dover.

Timoshenko, Stephen P. & Gere, J. Theory of Elastic Stability. 2nd ed. (Engineering Societies Monographs). (Illus.). 1961. text ed. 43.95 (ISBN 0-07-064749-6, C). McGraw.

Timoshenko, Stephen P. & Goodier, J. N. Theory of Elasticity. 3rd ed. (Engineering Societies Monographs Ser). (Illus.). 1969. text ed. 44.50 (ISBN 0-07-064720-8, C). McGraw.

Timoshenko, Stephen P. & Woinowsky-Krieger, S. Theory of Plates & Shells. 2nd ed. (Engineering Societies Monographs). (Illus.). 1959. text ed. 46.50 (ISBN 0-07-064779-8, C). McGraw.

Timoshenko, Stephen P. & Young, D. H. Theory of Structures. 2nd ed. (Illus.). 1965. text ed. 39.50 (ISBN 0-07-064868-9, C). McGraw.

Timpanaro, Sebastiano. The Freudian Slip: Psychoanalysis & Textual Criticism. 1976. 15.00 (ISBN 0-8052-7015-9, Pub. by NLB). Schocken.

--On Materialism. 1976. 14.00x (ISBN 0-8052-7015-9, Pub. by NLB). Schocken.

Timpane, Michael P., ed. The Federal Interest in Financing Schooling. LC 78-5563. (Rand Educational Policy Study Ser.). 320p. 1978. prof ref 18.50x (ISBN 0-88410-184-3). Ballinger Pub.

Timpane, P. Michael, jt. ed. see Pechman, Joseph A.

Timpane, P. Michael, jt. ed. see Rivlin, Alice M.

Tinao, D., et al, trs. see Brister, C. W.

Tinbergen, B. J., jt. ed. see Krol, B.

Tinbergen, B. J., ed. see Second International Symposium on Nitrite in Meat Products, Zeist, the Netherlands, 7-10 Sept. 1976.

Tinbergen, Elisabeth A., jt. auth. see Tinbergen, Niko.

Tinbergen, J. Income Differences. (Professor Dr. F. De Vries Lectures: Vol. 10). 1976. pap. 18.75 (ISBN 0-444-11054-2, North-Holland). Elsevier.

--Income Distribution. LC 74-30921. 170p. 1975. 30.00 (ISBN 0-444-10832-7, North-Holland). Elsevier.

--Shaping the World Economy: Suggestions for an International Economic Policy. 1962. pap. 7.00 (ISBN 0-527-02836-3). Kraus Repr.

Tinbergen, Jan. Centralization & Decentralization in Economic Policy. LC 81-2723. (Contributions to Economic Analysis Ser.: No. 6). 80p. 1981. Repr. of 1954 ed. lib. bdg. 19.25x (ISBN 0-313-23077-3, TICD). Greenwood.

--The Rio Report: Reshaping the International Order: a Report to the Club of Rome Coordinator. 1977. pap. 2.50 o.p. (ISBN 0-451-07708-3, E7708, Sig). NAL.

Tinbergen, N. Social Behavior in Animals. 1965. pap. 8.95x (ISBN 0-412-20000-7, Pub. by Chapman & Hall England). Methuen Inc.

Tinbergen, Niko. Animal Behavior. rv. ed. LC 80-52120. (Life Nature Library). (Illus.). (gr. 5 up). 1980. PLB 13.40 o.p. (ISBN 0-8094-3891-7, Pub. by Time-Life). Silver.
--Animal Behavior. (Young Readers Library). (Illus.). 1977. lib. bdg. 6.80 (ISBN 0-8094-1352-3). Silver.
--Herring Gull's World. 1971. pap. 3.95xi o.p. (ISBN 0-06-131594-X, TB1594, Torch). Har-Row.
Tinbergen, Niko & Tinbergen, Elisabeth A. Autistic Children: New Hope for Cure. (Illus.). 380p. 1983. text ed. 39.50x (ISBN 0-04-157010-3). Allen Unwin.
Tindale, Norman B. Aboriginal Tribes of Australia: Their Terrain, Environmental Controls, Distribution, Limits, & Proper Names. (Illus.). 1975. 110.00x (ISBN 0-520-02005-7). U of Cal Pr.
Tindall, A. R., jt. auth. see Guthrie, D. M.
Tindall, George T. & Collins, William F., eds. Clinical Management of Pituitary Discorders. (Seminars in Neurological Surgery). 468p. 1979. 53.50 (ISBN 0-89004-362-0). Raven.
Tindall, Gillian. City of Gold: The Biography of Bombay. 1981. 40.00x (ISBN 0-686-82399-0, Pub. by M Temple Smith). State Mutual Bk.
--Fields Beneath. (Illus.). 225p. 1982. pap. 7.95 (ISBN 0-686-83176-4, Pub. by Granada England). Academy Chi Ltd.
Tindall, H. D. & Sai, F. A. Fruits & Vegetables in West Africa. (Orig.). 1971. pap. 11.00 (ISBN 92-5-100062-X, F201, FAO). Unipub.
Tindall, Jemima. Scottish Island Hopping. (Travel Ser.). (Illus.). 320p. 1981. pap. 14.95 o.s.i. (ISBN 0-88254-590-6). Hippocrene Bks.
Tindall, Jemina. Scottish Island Hopping. 2nd ed. (Handbooks for the Independent Traveller). (Illus.). 320p. 1982. pap. 12.94 (ISBN 0-686-43004-2, Regnary Gateway). Hippocrene Bks.
Tindall, Richard S. A., ed. Therapeutic Apheresis & Plasma Perfusion. LC 82-17236. (Progress in Clinical & Biological Research Ser.: Vol. 106). 492p. 1982. 48.00 (ISBN 0-8451-0106-4). A R Liss.
Tindall, William Y. James Joyce: His Way of Interpreting the Modern World. LC 79-17220. 1979. Repr. of 1950 ed. lib. bdg. 16.25x (ISBN 0-313-22033-6, TIJA). Greenwood.
--The Joyce Country. new ed. LC 72-83501. (Illus.). 182p. 1972. pap. 6.95 (ISBN 0-8052-0347-8). Schocken.
--The Literary Symbol. LC 58-6957. (Midland Bks.: No. 7). 288p. 1958. pap. 2.95x o.p. (ISBN 0-253-20007-5). Ind U Pr.
Tindell-Hopwood, A. & Hollyfield, J. P. Fossil Mammals of Africa, No. 8: An Annotated Bibliography of the Fossil Mammals of Africa 1742-1950. 194p. 1954. pap. 21.50x (ISBN 0-565-00179-5). Sabbot-Natural Hist Bks.
Tine, Robert. State of Grace. 264p. 1980. 10.95 o.p. (ISBN 0-670-66851-6). Viking Pr.
Tiner, John H. The Seven Day Mystery. (Voyager Ser.). 176p. (Orig.). (gr. 6-10). 1981. pap. 3.50 (ISBN 0-8010-8856-9). Baker Bk.
--They Followed Jesus: Word Search Puzzles. 48p. pap. 1.50 (ISBN 0-87239-586-3). Standard Pub.
Tinervia, J., jt. auth. see Love, C.
Tinervia, Joseph, ed. see Camp, Sue C.
Tinervia, Joseph, ed. see Fruehling, Rosemary T. & Bouchard, Sharon.
Tinervia, Joseph, ed. see Sabin, William A.
Ting, I. P. & Jennings, Bill, eds. Deep Canyon: A Desert Wilderness for Science. LC 76-12717. 1976. 7.95 (ISBN 0-942290-02-X). Boyd Deep Canyon.
Ting, Irwin P. Plant Physiology. LC 80-16448. (Illus.). 635p. 1981. text ed. 29.95 (ISBN 0-201-07406-0). A-W.
Ting, Irwin P. & Gibbs, Martin, eds. Crassulacean Acid Metobolism. 316p. 1982. pap. 15.00 (ISBN 0-943088-00-3). Am Soc of Plant.
Tingay, Graham, ed. see Tacitus.
Tingay, Lance. Guinness Book of Tennis Facts & Feats. (Illus.). 256p. 1983. 19.95 (ISBN 0-85112-268-X, Pub. by Guinness Superlatives England); pap. 12.95 (ISBN 0-85112-289-2, Pub. by Guinness Superlatives England). Sterling.
Tingey, Henry, jt. auth. see Gulezian, Ronald.
Tingle, Dolli. And Now You're a New Mom. 1982. 3.95 (ISBN 0-8378-1913-X). Gibson.
--Expecting? LC 68-21794. (Illus.). 1968. 3.95 (ISBN 0-8378-1912-1). Gibson.
--Hello, Daddy! 1978. 3.95 (ISBN 0-8378-1911-3). Gibson.
--Look Who's a Grandma. LC 74-148610. (Illus.). 1971. 3.95 (ISBN 0-8378-1992-X). Gibson.
Tingle, Dolli, compiled by. Going to Be a Bride. LC 75-98695. (Illus.). 1970. 3.95 (ISBN 0-8378-1991-1). Gibson.
Tingley, Donald F., ed. Social History of the United States: A Guide to Information Sources. LC 78-13196. (American Government & History Information Guide Ser: Vol. 3). 1979. 42.00x (ISBN 0-8103-1366-9). Gale.
Tingley, Donald F., jt. ed. see Tingley, Elizabeth.
Tingley, Elizabeth & Tingley, Donald F., eds. Women & Feminism in American History: A Guide to Information Sources. LC 80-19793. (American Government & History Information Guide Ser.: Vol. 12). 289p. 1981. 42.00x (ISBN 0-8103-1492-4). Gale.
Tingley, Josephine, jt. auth. see Theroux, Rosemary.
Tingley, Katherine. The Wisdom of the Heart: Katherine Tingley Speaks. Small, W. Emmett, ed. LC 78-65338. 1978. pap. 5.75 (ISBN 0-913004-33-2). Point Loma Pub.
Tingley, Katherine, jt. auth. see De Purucker, G.
Tingsten, Herbert. Victoria & the Victorians. (Illus.). 1972. 15.00 o.s.i. (ISBN 0-440-09423-2, Sey Lawr). Delacorte.
Tingy, Frederick. Continental Car Holidays. 11.50x (ISBN 0-392-06093-0, SpS). Sportshelf.
Tinic, Seha M. & West, Richard R. Investing in Securities: An Efficient Markets Approach. LC 78-55833. 1979. text ed. 26.95 (ISBN 0-201-07631-4); instr's manual avail. (ISBN 0-201-07632-2). A-W.
Tinker, C. B., ed. see Arnold, Matthew.
Tinker, Chauncey B. Good Estate of Poetry. 1929. text ed. 9.50x (ISBN 0-686-83561-1). Elliots Bks.
Tinker, Edward L. Lafcadio Hearn's American Days. LC 71-99064. (Library of Lives & Letters). (Illus.). 1970. Repr. of 1924 ed. 37.00x (ISBN 0-8103-3366-X). Gale.
Tinker, Hugh. The Banyan Tree: Overseas Emigrants from India, Pakistan & Bangladesh. 1977. 12.95x o.p. (ISBN 0-19-215946-1). Oxford U Pr.
Tinker, Irene & Buvinic, Mayra, eds. The Many Facets of Human Settlement: Science & Society. LC 77-6307. 1977. text ed. 140.00 (ISBN 0-08-021994-2). Pergamon.
Tinker, Irene, et al, eds. Women & World Development. LC 76-20602. 1976. 31.95 o.p. (ISBN 0-275-56520-3). Praeger.
Tinker, J. & Rapin, M., eds. Care of the Critically Ill Patient. (Illus.). 1150p. 1983. 124.00 (ISBN 0-387-11289-8). Springer-Verlag.
Tinker, Jack & Porter, Susan W. Intensive Therapy Nursing. 304p. 1980. pap. text ed. 19.95 (ISBN 0-7131-4347-9). E Arnold.
Tinker, Miles A. & McCullough, Constance M. Teaching Elementary Reading. 4th ed. (Illus.). 640p. 1975. 24.95x (ISBN 0-13-892083-4). P-H.
Tinker, Richard, ed. see Ramamurti, C. C.
Tinkham, Charles W. Boston & Five Islands: A Retrospective. LC 80-69866. (Illus.). 166p. (Orig.). 1981. pap. 17.95 (ISBN 0-89272-109-X, PIC478). Down East.
Tinkham, M. Superconductivity. (Documents on Modern Physics Ser.). 90p. 1965. 21.00 (ISBN 0-677-00065-0). Gordon.
Tinkham, Michael. Group Theory & Quantum Mechanics. (International Series in Pure & Applied Physics). 1964. text ed. 44.50 (ISBN 0-07-064895-6, C). McGraw.
Tinkham, Sandra S., ed. Catalog of Ceramics & Glass. (Index of American Design Ser.: Pt. 8). (Orig.). 1979. pap. 36.00x (ISBN 0-914146-77-7); incl. color microfiche 745.00x (ISBN 0-914146-76-9). Somerset Hse.
--Catalog of Domestic Utensils. (Index of American Design Ser.: Pt. 5). (Orig.). 1979. pap. 30.00x (ISBN 0-914146-71-8); incl. color microfiche 595.00x (ISBN 0-914146-70-X). Somerset Hse.
--Catalog of Furniture & Decorative Accessories. (Index of American Design Ser.: Pt. 6). (Orig.). 1979. pap. 36.00x (ISBN 0-914146-73-4); incl. color microfiche 690.00x (ISBN 0-914146-72-6). Somerset Hse.
--Catalog of Textiles, Costume & Jewelry. (Index of American Design Ser.: Pt. 1). (Orig.). 1979. pap. 36.00x (ISBN 0-914146-63-7); incl. color microfiche 828.00x (ISBN 0-914146-62-9). Somerset Hse.
--Catalog of the Art & Design of Utopian & Religious Communities. (Index of American Design Ser.: Pt. 2). (Orig.). 1979. pap. 26.00x (ISBN 0-914146-65-3); incl. color microfiche 690.00x (ISBN 0-914146-64-5). Somerset Hse.
--Catalog of Tools, Hardware, Firearms, & Vehicles. (Index of American Design Ser.: Pt. 4). (Orig.). 1979. pap. 36.00x (ISBN 0-914146-69-6); incl. color microfiche 312.00x (ISBN 0-914146-68-8). Somerset Hse.
--The Consolidated Catalog to the Index of American Design. (Index of American Design Ser.). 1979. 95.00x (ISBN 0-914146-95-5); incl. color microfiche 4750.00x (ISBN 0-914146-94-7). Somerset Hse.
Tinkleman, Murray. Rodeo: The Great American Sport. (Illus.). 1982. 8.59 (ISBN 0-688-00841-0); lib. bdg. 7.00 (ISBN 0-688-01194-2). Greenwillow.
Tinkler, Hugh. Race, Conflict & the International Order: From Empire to United Nations. LC 77-79017. (The Making of the 20th Century Ser.). (Illus.). 1977. 22.50x (ISBN 0-312-66130-4). St Martin.
Tinnell, Richard W. Television Symptom Diagnosis. 1977. instructor's manual 6.67 (ISBN 0-672-97618-8); student manual 11.95 (ISBN 0-672-97617-X). Bobbs.
--Television Symptom Diagnosis. 2nd ed. 1977. pap. 12.95 (ISBN 0-686-82336-2). Sams.
Tinnell, Roger D. An Annotated Discography of Music in Spain before 1650. xvi, 146p. 1980. 12.00 (ISBN 0-942260-09-0). Hispanic Seminary.
Tinney, James S. & Rector, Justine J. Issues & Trends in Afro-American Journalism. LC 80-6074. 371p. 1980. lib. bdg. 23.25 (ISBN 0-8191-1352-2); pap. text ed. 13.75 (ISBN 0-8191-1353-0). U Pr of Amer.
Tinoco, Ignacio, Jr., et al. Physical Chemistry: Principles & Applications in Biological Sciences. LC 77-25417. 1978. text ed. 29.95 (ISBN 0-13-665901-2); solutions 7.95 (ISBN 0-13-665919-5). P-H.
Tinsley, Elizabeth, ed. see Byalin, Joan.
Tinsley, Ian J. Chemical Concepts in Pollutant Behavior. LC 78-24301. (Environmental Science & Technology Ser.). 265p. 1979. 39.00x (ISBN 0-471-03825-3, Pub. by Wiley-Interscience). Wiley.
Tinsley, J. D., jt. ed. see Johnson, D. C.
Tinsley, James A. Texas Society of Certified Public Accountants. rev. ed. (Illus.). 216p. 1983. Repr. of 1962 ed. 24.95x (ISBN 0-89096-152-2). Tex A&M Univ Pr.
Tinsley, Royal L., Jr., et al, trs. see Wunderlich, Christof.
Tinsley, Russell. All About Small-Game Hunting in America. (Stoeger Books). 1977. pap. 5.95 o.s.i. (ISBN 0-695-80849-4). Follett.
--Hunting the Whitetailed Deer. rev. ed. LC 65-14986. (Funk & W Bk.). (Illus.). 1977. 11.49i (ISBN 0-308-10326-2); pap. 4.50i (ISBN 0-308-10327-0, TYC-T). T Y Crowell.
Tint, Herbert. France Since Nineteen Eighteen. 2nd ed. 1980. 25.00 (ISBN 0-312-30315-7). St Martin.
--French Foreign Policy since the Second World War. LC 72-83418. 1973. 22.50 (ISBN 0-312-30485-4). St Martin.
Tintner, Gerhard & Sengupta, Jati K. Stochastic Economics: With Applications of Stochastic Processes, Control & Programming. 1972. 46.00 (ISBN 0-12-691650-0). Acad Pr.
Tintoretto. Drawings. DeLogu, Giuseppe, ed. Bargellini, Clara, tr. LC 68-27838. (Great Masters of Drawing Ser). (Illus.). 1969. pap. 2.50 o.p. (ISBN 0-486-21992-5). Dover.
Tiphaigne De La Roche, C. F. Amilec: Ou la Graine d'Hommes Qui Sert a Peupler les Planets par L'a. D. P. (Utopias in the Enlightenment Ser.). 416p. (Fr.). 1974. Repr. of 1754 ed. lib. bdg. 105.50 o.p. (ISBN 0-8287-0821-5, 027). Clearwater Pub.
--L'Empire de Zaziris sur les Humains ou la Zazirocratie. (Utopias in the Enlightenment Ser.). 137p. (Fr.). 1974. Repr. of 1761 ed. lib. bdg. 43.50x o.p. (ISBN 0-8287-0822-3, 036). Clearwater Pub.
--Giphantie. (Utopias in the Enlightenment Ser.). 354p. (Fr.). 1974. Repr. of 1760 ed. lib. bdg. 91.50x o.p. (ISBN 0-8287-0823-1, 015). Clearwater Pub.
Tiphaigne De La Roche, Charles-Francois. Historie Des Galligenes, Ou Memoire De Duncan. Repr. of 1765 ed. 55.50 o.p. (ISBN 0-8287-0824-X). Clearwater Pub.
Tipler, Frank J., ed. Essays in General Relativity. LC 80-517. 1980. 34.50 (ISBN 0-12-691380-3). Acad Pr.
Tipler, Paul A. Modern Physics. 2nd ed. LC 77-58725. 1977. text ed. 26.95x (ISBN 0-87901-088-6). Worth.
--Physics. 2nd ed. LC 81-70205. (Illus.). xxiv, 1078p. 1982. Vol. 1 Chpts. 1-19. 19.95 (ISBN 0-87901-182-3); Vol. 2 Chpts. 20-37. 19.95 (ISBN 0-87901-183-1); text ed. 33.95 (ISBN 0-87901-135-1); study guide 10.95 (ISBN 0-87901-180-7). Worth.
Tipling, Carmen, et al. Three Caribbean Plays. Hill, Errol, ed. (Horizons Ser.). (Illus.). 117p. (Orig.). (gr. 8-12). 1979. pap. 5.00 o.s.i. (ISBN 0-582-76548-X). Three Continents.
Tipp, G. & Watson, V. J. Polymeric Surfaces for Sports & Recreation. 1982. 49.25 (ISBN 0-85334-980-0, Pub. by Applied Sci England). Elsevier.
Tippah County Historical & Genealogical Society. The History of Tippah County, Mississippi. (Illus.). 722p. Date not set. Repr. of 1981 ed. 55.00 (ISBN 0-88107-000-9). Natl ShareGraphics.
Tippens, Paul E. Applied Physics. 2nd ed. (Illus.). 1978. text ed. 24.50 (ISBN 0-07-064961-8, G); instructor's & solution manual 8.00 (ISBN 0-07-064962-6); study guide 8.95 (ISBN 0-07-064963-4). McGraw.
--Basic Technical Physics. LC 82-7182. 512p. 1983. text ed. 15.95x (ISBN 0-07-064971-5, C); instr's. manual 7.95 (ISBN 0-07-064972-3). Mcgraw.
Tipper, C., jt. ed. see Bamford, C.
Tipper, C. F., ed. Oxidation & Combustion Reviews, Vol. 6. LC 65-12562. 240p. 1973. 34.00 (ISBN 0-444-41104-6). Elsevier.
Tipper, C. F., jt. ed. see Bamford, C. H.
Tippert-Neilson, Terry E. & Behler, Donna M. Pediatric Nurse Practitioner: Certification Review. 304p. 1983. 17.95 (ISBN 0-471-86411-0, Pub. by Wiley Med.). Wiley.
Tippett, Alan R. Church Growth & the Word of God. 1970. pap. 1.95 o.p. (ISBN 0-8028-1328-3). Eerdmans.
Tippett, Maria. Emily Carr: A Biography. (Illus.). 1979. 19.95x (ISBN 0-19-540314-2). Oxford U Pr.
Tippette, Giles. Austin Davis. 1980. pap. 1.95 o.s.i. (ISBN 0-440-14430-2). Dell.
--The Mercenaries. (YA) 1976. 8.95 o.s.i. (ISBN 0-440-05579-2, E Friede). Delacorte.
--Wilson's Choice. (Orig.). 1981. pap. 1.95 o.s.i. (ISBN 0-440-19518-7). Dell.
Tippett-Neilson, Terry E. & Behler, Donna M. Adult Nurse Practitioner Certification Review. 352p. 1983. 17.95 (ISBN 0-471-86410-2, Pub. by Wiley Med.). Wiley.
Tippit, Sammy. Reproduced by Permission of the Author. 144p. 1979. pap. 3.95 (ISBN 0-88207-579-9). Victor Bks.
Tippit, Sammy & Jenkins, Jerry. You Me He. 1978. pap. 3.50 (ISBN 0-88207-766-X). Victor Bks.
Tips, Charles. Frisbee by the Masters. LC 76-55832. (Illus., Orig.). 1977. pap. 5.95 o.p. (ISBN 0-89087-142-6). Celestial Arts.
Tips, Charles & Roddick, Dan. Frisbee Disc Sports & Games. LC 78-67849. (Illus.). 1979. pap. 5.95 o.p. (ISBN 0-89087-233-3). Celestial Arts.
Tipson, R. Stuart & Horton, Derek, eds. Advances in Carbohydrate Chemistry & Biochemistry, Vol. 41. (Serial Publication). Date not set. price not set (ISBN 0-12-007241-6); price not set Lib. ed. (ISBN 0-12-007294-7). Acad Pr.
Tipson, R. Stuart, jt. ed. see Townsend, Leroy B.
Tipson, R. Stuart, jt. ed. see Zorback, W. Werner.
Tipson, Stuart & Horton, D., eds. Advances in Carbohydrate Chemistry & Biochemistry, Vol. 40. 402p. 1982. 65.00 (ISBN 0-12-007240-8); lib. ed. 84.50 (ISBN 0-12-007292-0); Microfiche 45.50 (ISBN 0-12-007293-9). Acad Pr.
Tipson, Stuart, jt. ed. see Horton, Derek.
Tipton, I. C., ed. Locke on Human Understanding: Selected Essays. 1977. pap. text ed. 8.95x (ISBN 0-19-875039-0). Oxford U Pr.
Tipton (Iowa) Woman's Club. How Iowa Cooks. LC 82-9070. 268p. 1983. spiral bdg. 9.95 (ISBN 0-88289-321-1). Pelican.
Tipton, Steven M., jt. ed. see Douglas, Mary.
Tiptree, James, Jr Ten Thousand Light-Years from Home. (Science Fiction Ser.). 328p. 1976. Repr. of 1973 ed. lib. bdg. 13.50 o.p. (ISBN 0-8398-2322-3, Gregg). G K Hall.
Tiranti, John. Glass Fibre for Schools. (gr. 9-12). 1972. 8.95 o.s.i. (ISBN 0-85458-330-0); pap. 4.95 o.s.i. (ISBN 0-85458-340-8). Transatlantic.
Tirard, H. M., tr. see Erman, Adolf.
Tiratsoo, E. N. Oilfields of the World. 2nd ed. 400p. 1976. 42.50x (ISBN 0-87201-630-7). Gulf Pub.
Tiratsoo, E. N., jt. auth. see Hobson, G. D.
Tirion, Wil. Sky Atlas 2000.0 Color. 1981. spiral bound 34.95 (ISBN 0-933346-33-6, 46336). Sky Pub.
--Sky Atlas 2000.0 Desk: Black Stars on White Backround. (Illus.). 1981. 15.95 (ISBN 0-933346-31-X). Sky Pub.
--Sky Atlas 2000.0 Field: White Stars on Black Backround. (Illus.). 1981. 15.95 (ISBN 0-933346-32-8, 46328). Sky Pub.
--Sky Atlas 2000.0: Twenty-Six Star Charts Covering Both Hemispheres. LC 81-52999. (Illus.). 26p. 1981. 34.95 (ISBN 0-521-24467-6). Cambridge U Pr.
Tiritilli, Robert A., jt. auth. see Hellman, Charles S.
Tirner, Peter, tr. see Niedermayer, Franz.
Tirro, Frank. Jazz: A History. (Illus.). 1977. 22.95 (ISBN 0-393-02194-7); text ed. 16.95x (ISBN 0-393-09078-7). Norton.
Tirso De Molina. Venganza De Tamar. Paterson, A. K., ed. text ed. 27.50x (ISBN 0-521-07205-0). Cambridge U Pr.
Tiruchelvan, Nellan, jt. ed. see Gunatilleke, Godfrey.
Tisa, John, ed. The Palette & the Flame: Posters of the Spanish Civil War. LC 77-16602. 1979. 17.50 (ISBN 0-7178-0496-8). Intl Pub Co.
Tiscareno, Froylan, jt. tr. see Del Barco, Miguel.
Tischler, Alice. Fifteen Black American Composers: A Bibliography of Their Works. LC 81-1162. (Detroit Studies in Music Bibliography Ser.: No. 45). 1981. 19.75 (ISBN 0-686-81287-5). Info Coord.
Tischler, Hans. The Earliest Motets (to ca. 1270) A Complete Comparative Edition, 3 vols. LC 78-15005. 1982. Set. 425.00 (ISBN 0-300-01534-8); Vol. 1, 856 pp. write for info. (ISBN 0-300-02918-7); Vol. 2, 636 pp. write for info. (ISBN 0-300-02919-5); Vol. 3, 256 pp. write for info. (ISBN 0-300-02920-9). Yale U Pr.
Tischler, Hans, tr. see Apel, Willi.
Tischler, Morris. Experiments in General & Biomedical Instrumentation. Haas, Mark, ed. (Illus.). 176p. 1980. pap. text ed. 12.95x (ISBN 0-07-064781-X, G). McGraw.
--Experiments in Telecommunications. Haas, Mark, ed. (Linear Integrated Circuit Applications Ser.). (Illus.). 176p. (gr. 12 up). 1980. pap. text ed. 11.95x (ISBN 0-07-064782-8). McGraw.
--Tischler: Experiments in Amplifiers, Filters, Oscillators. Haas, Mark, ed. (Linear Integrated Circuit Applications). (Illus.). 176p. 1981. pap. text ed. 11.95x (ISBN 0-07-064780-1). McGraw.
Tischler, Nancy M. Black Masks: Negro Characters in Modern Southern Fiction. LC 68-8187. 1969. 16.50x (ISBN 0-271-00082-1). Pa St U Pr.
--Dorothy L. Sayers: A Pilgrim Soul. LC 79-87739. 1980. 4.49 (ISBN 0-8042-0882-4). John Knox.
Tisdall, Caroline. Joseph Beuys. (Illus.). 1979. 40.00 o.p. (ISBN 0-500-09136-6). Thames Hudson.
Tisdall, Patricia. Agents of Change: The Development & Practice of Management Consultancy. (Illus.). 192p. 1983. 24.95 (ISBN 0-434-91961-6, Pub. by Heinemann England). David & Charles.
Tisdall, William. Hindustani Conversation Grammar. 27.50 (ISBN 0-8044-0723-1). Ungar.
--Modern Persian Conversation Grammar. LC 58-14432. 30.00 (ISBN 0-8044-0714-2). Ungar.
Tisdell, Clem. Wild Pigs: Environmental Pest or Economic Resource? (Illus.). 288p. 1982. 29.00 (ISBN 0-08-024820-9). Pergamon.

Tisdell, Clem, jt. auth. see Hartley, Keith.

Tisdell, F. Science & Technology Policy: Priorities of Governments. LC 80-41228. 210p. 1981. 27.00x (ISBN 0-412-23320-7, Pub. by Chapman & Hall). Methuen Inc.

Tise, Larry E., jt. ed. see Crow, Jeffrey J.

Tisi, Gennaro M. Pulmonary Physiology in Clinical Medicine. (Illus.). 280p. 1980. lib. bdg. 29.95 (ISBN 0-683-08250-7). Williams & Wilkins.

Tisljarlentulis, G., jt. ed. see Feinendegen, L. E.

Tiso, Francis & Catholic Heritage Press. A Young Person's Book of Catholic Signs & Symbols. LC 81-43459. 128p. 1982. pap. 3.50 (ISBN 0-385-17951-0, Im). Doubleday.

Tiso, Francis, et al, eds. Aging: Spiritual Perspectives. 320p. 1982. pap. 9.95 (ISBN 0-941850-03-X). Sunday Pubn.

Tissier, Pierre. The Government of Vichy. LC 74-65. 347p. 1974. Repr. of 1942 ed. lib. bdg. 18.50x (ISBN 0-8371-7372-8, TIGV). Greenwood.

Tissot, B. Petroleum Formation & Occurrence: A New Approach to Oil & Gas Exploration. (Illus.). 1978. 39.50 o.p. (ISBN 0-387-08698-6). Springer-Verlag.

Titard, Pierre L. Managerial Accounting: An Introduction. 704p. 1983. text ed. 26.95 (ISBN 0-03-061556-9). Dryden Pr.

Titchener, Edward B. Textbook of Psychology. LC 80-14831. (Hist. of Psych. Ser.). Repr. of 1910 ed. 65.00x (ISBN 0-8201-1354-9). Schol Facsimiles.

Titchett, Kenneth J., ed. Europe & the World: The External Relations of the Common Market. LC 75-45817. 220p. 1976. 22.50 (ISBN 0-312-26845-9). St Martin.

Titchmarsh, Edward C. Theory of Functions. 2nd ed. 1939. 19.95x (ISBN 0-19-853349-7). Oxford U Pr.

Titcomb, Margaret. Native Use of Fish in Hawaii. 2nd ed. 1972. pap. 3.95 (ISBN 0-8248-0592-5). UH Pr.

--Native Use of Marine Invertebrates in Old Hawaii. 1979. pap. text ed. 6.95x o.p. (ISBN 0-8248-0715-4). UH Pr.

Tite, C. G. Impeachment & Parlimentary Judicature in Early Stuart England. (University of London Historical Studies: No. 37). 256p. 1974. text ed. 46.25x (ISBN 0-485-13137-4, Athlone Pr). Humanities.

Tite, Graham. Buildings of Britain, 1550-1750: South East England. 160p. 1982. 50.00x (ISBN 0-86190-064-2, Pub. by Moorland). State Mutual Bk.

Titelbaum, Olga A., tr. see Sivachev, Nikolai V. & Yakovlev, Nikolai N.

Titherington, D. & Rimmer, J. G. Applied Mechanics. 2nd ed. 192p. Date not set. 9.00 (ISBN 0-07-084659-6). McGraw.

Titl, A. see Singh, M. G.

Titler, Dale. Haunted Treasures: True Tales of Ghosts & Gold. (Treehouse Bks.). (Illus.). (gr. 4-8). 1981. pap. 2.95 (ISBN 0-13-384230-4). P-H.

Titley, E. B. Church, State, & the Control of Schooling in Ireland, 1900-1944. 232p. 1983. 27.50x (ISBN 0-7735-0394-3). McGill-Queens U Pr.

Titli, A., jt. auth. see Bernussou, J.

Titlow, Richard E. Americans Import Merit: Origins of the United States Civil Service System & the Influence of the British Model. LC 78-65352. 1978. pap. text ed. 14.00 (ISBN 0-8191-0655-0). U Pr of Amer.

Titman, Fred. Talk of the Double. 10.50 (ISBN 0-392-07146-0, SpS). Sportshelf.

Titow, J. Z. Winchester Yields: A Study in Medieval Agricultural Productivity. LC 72-171685. (Cambridge Studies in Economic History). 1972. 32.50 (ISBN 0-521-08349-4). Cambridge U Pr.

Titow, W. V. & Lenham, B. J. Reinforced Thermoplastics. LC 75-16335. 295p. 1975. 49.95 o.s.i. (ISBN 0-470-87518-6). Halsted Pr.

Tittle, Carol K., jt. ed. see Jaeger, Richard M.

Tittler, Robert. Nicholas Bacon: The Making of a Tudor Statesman. LC 75-36976. (Illus.). 255p. 1976. 15.00x (ISBN 0-8214-0225-0, 82-82303). Ohio U Pr.

Titunik, Irwin R., jt. ed. see Matejka, Ladislav.

Titus, E. & Galdone, Paul. Anatole & the Pied Piper. 1979. 9.95 (ISBN 0-07-064897-2, GB). McGraw.

Titus, Elizabeth A., ed. see Johnson, O.

Titus, Eve. Anatole & the Cat. (Illus.). (gr. k-3). 1957. PLB 7.95 (ISBN 0-07-064910-3, GB). McGraw.

--Anatole & the Piano. (gr. k-3). 1966. PLB 7.95 (ISBN 0-07-064892-1, GB). McGraw.

--Anatole & the Thirty Thieves. (Anatole Ser). (Illus.). (gr. k-3). 1969. PLB 5.72 o.p. (ISBN 0-07-064888-3, GB). McGraw.

--Basil & the Lost Colony. (Illus.). (gr. 3-6). 1978. pap. 1.50 (ISBN 0-671-41602-2). Archway.

--Basil & the Pygmy Cats. (Illus.). (gr. 3-6). 1973. pap. 1.95 (ISBN 0-671-45531-1). Archway.

--Basil in Mexico. (Illus.). (gr. 3-6). 1977. pap. 1.75 (ISBN 0-671-42421-1). Archway.

--Basil in Mexico. LC 75-10827. (gr. 4-6). 1976. 7.95 (ISBN 0-07-064898-0, GB); PLB 7.95 (ISBN 0-07-064900-6). McGraw.

--Basil of Baker Street. (Illus.). (gr. 3-6). 1970. pap. 1.75 (ISBN 0-671-41729-0). Archway.

Titus, Eve & Galdone, Paul. Basil of Baker Street. (gr. 3-6). 1958. PLB 8.95 o.p. (ISBN 0-07-064907-3, GB). McGraw.

Titus, Harold & Smith, Marilyn. Living Issues in Philosophy. 7th ed. 576p. 1979. text ed. 15.95 (ISBN 0-442-25820-8). Van Nos Reinhold.

Titus, Harold H. & Hepp, Maylon H. The Range of Philosophy: Introductory Reading. 3rd ed. 1975. text ed. 8.95 (ISBN 0-442-25821-6). Van Nos Reinhold.

Titus, Harold H. & Keeton, Morris T. Ethics for Today. 5th ed. 1973. text ed. 13.95 (ISBN 0-442-25803-8). Van Nos Reinhold.

Titus, Jonathan & Larsen, David. Eighty Eighty A Cookbook. 1980. pap. 15.95 (ISBN 0-672-21697-3). Sams.

Titus, Warren I. Winston Churchill. (U. S. Authors Ser.: No. 43). 13.95 o.p. (ISBN 0-8057-0144-3, Twayne). G K Hall.

Titus, Warren I., Jr. John Fox. (United States Authors Ser.). 13.95 (ISBN 0-8057-0272-5, Twayne). G K Hall.

Titus, William A. Wisconsin Writers. LC 77-145704. 1974. Repr. of 1930 ed. 42.00x (ISBN 0-8103-3658-8). Gale.

Tivey, L. J. The Politics of the Firm. LC 78-9796. 1979. 25.00x (ISBN 0-312-62879-X). St Martin.

Tivy, J. & O'Hare, G. Human Impact on the Ecosystem. LC 81-82809. (Conceptual Frameworks in Geography Ser.). (Illus.). 240p. (Orig.). 1982. text ed. 19.95x (ISBN 0-05-003203-8); pap. text ed. 10.95 (ISBN 0-686-36898-3). Longman.

Tiwari, S. C., jt. ed. see Singh, Indera P.

Tixier, P. Bryogeographie-Du Mont Bokor (Cambodge) 1979. (Bryophytorum Bibliotheca 18). (Illus.). 1979. pap. text ed. 16.00x (ISBN 3-7682-1227-0). Lubrecht & Cramer.

--Contribution a L'etude du Genre Colo-Lejeuna. Les Colclejeuniceas de Nouvelles Caledonie. (Illus.). 1979. pap. text ed. 12.00x (ISBN 3-7682-1230-0). Lubrecht & Cramer.

Tizard, Ian R. An Introduction to Veterinary Immunology. LC 77-72794. (Illus.). 1977. text ed. 26.00x o.p. (ISBN 0-7216-8868-3). Saunders.

Tjalsma, R. C. & Lohmann, G. P. Paleocene-Eocene Bathyal & Abyssal Foraminifera from the Atlantic Basin. (Micropaleontology Special Publications Ser.: No. 4). 1982. 45.00 (ISBN 0-686-84256-1). Am Mus Natl Hist.

Tjalsma, William, tr. see Shafarevich, Igor.

Tjalve, E. Short Course in Industrial Design. (Illus.). 1979. pap. text ed. 24.95 (ISBN 0-408-00388-X). Butterworth.

Tjosvold, Dean & Johnson, David W. Productive Conflict Management: Perspectives for Organizations. 224p. 1983. 18.95x (ISBN 0-8290-1266-4). Irvington.

Tjosvold, Dean & Tjosvold, Mary. Working with the Mentally Handicapped in Their Residences. (Illus.). 256p. 1981. text ed. 19.95 (ISBN 0-02-932490-4). Free Pr.

Tjosvold, Mary, jt. auth. see Tjosvold, Dean.

Tjur, Tue. Probability Based on Random Measures. LC 80-40503. (Wiley Series in Probability & Mathematical Statistics Ser.). 232p. 1980. 55.95x (ISBN 0-471-27824-6, Pub. by Wiley-Interscience). Wiley.

Tlali, Miriam. Muriel at Metropolitan. 190p. (Orig.). 1979. 9.00 o.s.i. (ISBN 0-89410-101-3); pap. 5.00 o.s.i. (ISBN 0-89410-100-5). Three Continents.

Toalson, Robert F., jt. auth. see Rodney, Lynn S.

Toates, Frederick M. Animal Behaviour: A Systems Approach. LC 79-41485. 299p. 1980. 55.95 (ISBN 0-471-27724-X); pap. 21.95x (ISBN 0-471-27723-1). Wiley.

Tobach, Ethel, et al. Biopsychology of Development. 1971. 67.50 (ISBN 0-12-691750-7). Acad Pr.

Tobak, Sandy B. & Lukatsky, Debbie. The Jewish American Princess Handbook. (Illus.). 144p. (Orig.). 1982. pap. 4.95 (ISBN 0-943084-02-4). Print Mat.

Tobe, John. How to Conquor Arthritis. 1976. 11.95x (ISBN 0-686-37944-6). Cancer Control Soc.

Tobe, John H. Cataract Glaucoma & Other Eye Disorders: Prevention & Cure. 1973. 10.95x (ISBN 0-685-72762-9, Pub. by Provoker). Formur Intl.

Toben, Bob. Home of the Stars: The Illustrated Story of the Universe & Its Beginnings. (Illus.). 192p. 1982. pap. 8.95 (ISBN 0-525-47629-6, 0869-260). Dutton.

Tobey, B. Go Down There & Make Them Laugh: Cartoons from the New Yorker. (Illus.). 128p. Date not set. 12.95 (ISBN 0-89479-107-9). A & W Pubs. Postponed.

Tobey, G. E., et al. Operational Amplifiers: Design & Application. 42.25 (ISBN 0-07-064917-0, P&RB). McGraw.

Tobey, Jeremy L. The History of Ideas: A Bibliographical Introduction, 2 vols. 320p. 1975-76. Vol. 1 Classical Antiquity. text ed. 26.25 o.p. (ISBN 0-87436-143-5, LC 74-83160); text ed. 28.75 o.p. (ISBN 0-686-31713-0). ABC-Clio.

Tobias, Andrew. Fire & Ice: The Story of Charles Revson-the Man Who Built the Revlon Empire. (Illus.). 288p. 1983. pap. 6.95 (ISBN 0-688-01887-4). Quill NY.

--Getting by on One Hundred Thousand Dollars a Year & Other Sad Tales. 1980. 10.95 o.p. (ISBN 0-671-25518-5). S&S.

--The Invisible Bankers: Everything the Insurance Industry Never Wanted You to Know. LC 81-18564. 1982. 15.50 (ISBN 0-671-22849-8, Linden). S&S.

Tobias, Art, tr. see Shan, Han.

Tobias, Charles & Drasdo, Harold, eds. The Mountain Spirit. 264p. 1983. pap. 25.00 (ISBN 0-87951-168-0). Overlook Pr.

Tobias, Charles W., jt. ed. see Gerischer, Heinz.

Tobias, Charles W., ed. see Gerischer, Heinz.

Tobias, Cornelius see Lawrence, John H. & Hamilton, J. G.

Tobias, Cornelius A. see Lawrence, John H. & Hamilton, J. G.

Tobias, J. J. Crime & Police in England Seventeen Hundred to Nineteen Hundred. LC 78-27882. 1979. 26.00 (ISBN 0-312-17201-X). St Martin.

Tobias, Jean T. Love, Life & Laughter. LC 72-93577. 64p. 1973. 4.00 (ISBN 0-911838-31-7). Windy Row.

Tobias, Jerry V., ed. Foundations of Modern Auditory Theory, 2 vols. LC 78-91432. 1970-72. Vol. 1. 65.00 (ISBN 0-12-691901-1); Vol. 2. 65.00 (ISBN 0-12-691902-X). Acad Pr.

Tobias, Marc W. Police Communications. (Illus.). 650p. 1974. 39.50x (ISBN 0-398-02970-9); pap. 27.75x (ISBN 0-398-02994-6). C C Thomas.

Tobias, P. V., jt. ed. see Leakey, L. S.

Tobias, Richard C. The Art of James Thurber. LC 68-20938. vi, 196p. 1969. 13.50x (ISBN 0-8214-0058-4, 82-80646). Ohio U Pr.

--T. E. Brown. (English Authors Ser.). 1978. 13.95 (ISBN 0-8057-6682-0, Twayne). G K Hall.

Tobias, Richard C. & Zolbrod, Paul G., eds. Shakespeare's Late Plays: Essays in Honor of Charles Crow. LC 74-27704. xiv, 235p. 1974. 14.00x (ISBN 0-8214-0178-5, 82-81750). Ohio U Pr.

Tobias, S. A. & Koenigsbergen, T. Proceedings of the Seventeenth International Machine, Tool, Design & Research Conference. 1978. 134.95 o.s.i. (ISBN 0-470-99076-7). Halsted Pr.

Tobias, S. A. & Koenigsberger, F., eds. Proceedings of the Thirteenth International Machine Tool Design & Research Conference. LC 73-2955. 1973. 129.95 o.s.i. (ISBN 0-470-87529-1). Halsted Pr.

Tobias, S. A., ed. see International Machine Tool Design & Research Conference, 15th.

Tobias, S. A., ed. see International Machine Tool Design & Research Conference, 20th.

Tobias, S. A., jt. ed. see Koenigsberger, T.

Tobias, Sheila. Overcoming Math Anxiety. (Illus.). 288p. 1980. pap. 6.95 (ISBN 0-395-29088-0). HM.

--Overcoming Math Anxiety. (Illus.). 1978. 13.95 (ISBN 0-393-06439-5). Norton.

Tobias, Sheila & Goudinoff, Peter. What Kinds of Guns Are They Buying for Your Butter? A Beginner's Guide to Defense, Weaponry, & Military Spending. LC 82-12565. (Illus.). 320p. 1982. 15.95 (ISBN 0-688-01374-0). Morrow.

Tobias, Tobi. Arthur Mitchell. LC 74-13730. (Biography Ser.). (Illus.). (gr. 1-5). 1975. PLB 10.89 (ISBN 0-690-00662-4, TYC-J). Har-Row.

--Chasing the Goblins Away. LC 77-75041. (Illus.). (ps-3). 1977. 6.95 o.p. (ISBN 0-7232-6144-X). Warne.

--The Dawdlewalk. LC 81-21666. (Illus.). 32p. (ps-3). 1983. PLB 8.95 (ISBN 0-87614-204-8). Carolrhoda Bks.

--A Day off. (Illus.). 32p. (ps-3). 1973. PLB 5.69 o.p. (ISBN 0-399-60762-5). Putnam Pub Group.

--How We Got Our First Cat. (gr. 1-3). 1980. 6.90 o.p. (ISBN 0-531-02870-4, G35); PLB 7.90 (ISBN 0-531-04173-5, F20). Watts.

--Moving Day. LC 75-22275. (Illus.). 36p. (gr. k-2). 1976. 4.95 (ISBN 0-394-83115-2); PLB 6.99 (ISBN 0-394-93115-7). Knopf.

--Petey. LC 76-25515. (Illus.). (gr. k-4). 1978. 8.95 o.p. (ISBN 0-399-20555-1). Putnam Pub Group.

--The Quitting Deal. (Puffin Ser.). (gr. 6-9). 1979. pap. 2.25 o.p. (ISBN 0-14-050347-1, Puffin). Penguin.

Tobin, Catherine. Math Study Skills Student Text. Marshak, David & Morimoto, Kigo, eds. 1982. pap. 5.00 (ISBN 0-88210-123-4). Natl Assn Principals.

--Math Study Skills Teacher's Guide. Marshak, David & Morimoto, Kigo, eds. 1981. pap. text ed. 4.00 (ISBN 0-88210-124-2). Natl Assn Principals.

Tobin, Charles E. & Jacobs, John J. Shearer's Manual of Human Dissection. 6th ed. (Illus.). 352p. 1981. pap. text ed. 22.00 (ISBN 0-07-064926-X). McGraw.

Tobin, Des, jt. auth. see Griffin, Graeme M.

Tobin, Helen M. & Wise, Pat S. The Process of Staff Development: Components for Change. 2nd ed. LC 78-31459. (Illus.). 248p. 1979. text ed. 22.95 (ISBN 0-8016-4996-X). Mosby.

Tobin, James, ed. New Macroeconomics, Prices, & Quantities: Essays in Memory of Arthur M. Okun. LC 82-45981. 300p. 1983. 26.95 (ISBN 0-8157-8486-4); pap. 9.95 (ISBN 0-8157-8485-6). Brookings.

Tobin, Joseph R. How to Improvise Piano Accompaniments. 1956. 8.50 (ISBN 0-19-321800-3). Oxford U Pr.

Tobin, McLean. The Black Female Ph.D. Education & Career Development. LC 80-5578. 133p. 1980. lib. bdg. 17.75 (ISBN 0-8191-1312-3); pap. text ed. 8.25 (ISBN 0-8191-1313-1). U Pr of Amer.

Tobin, Richard J. The Social Gamble: Determining Acceptable Levels of Air Control. LC 78-19229. 192p. 1979. 19.95x o.p. (ISBN 0-669-02468-6). Lexington Bks.

Tobin, Sheldon, jt. auth. see Lieberman, Morton.

Tobin, Terence. James Bridie. (English Authors Ser.). 1980. 14.95 (ISBN 0-8057-6786-X, Twayne). G K Hall.

Tobin, William J. Basic Injection Molding & Basic Trouble Shooting, 2 vols. (Illus.). 127p. 1981. Repr. of 1977 ed. Set. 29.50 (ISBN 0-938648-11-X). T-C Pubns CA.

--Moldeamiento De Inyeccion Basico & Problemas Basico De Disparar, 2 vols. Leguizamon, Martha & Sharon, Elizabeth, trs. Orig. Title: Basic Injection Molding & Basic Trouble Shooting. (Illus.). 128p. (Span.). 1981. Repr. of 1978 ed. Set. 31.50 (ISBN 0-938648-12-8). T-C Pubns CA.

--Quality Control Manual for Injection Molding. 85p. 1978. 31.50 (ISBN 0-938648-13-6). T-C Pubns CA.

Tobler, John & Grundy, Stuart. The Record Producers. (Illus.). 256p. 1983. 19.95 (ISBN 0-312-66593-8); pap. 10.95 (ISBN 0-312-66594-6). St Martin.

--The Record Producers. 1982. 35.00x (ISBN 0-563-17958-9, BBC Pubns). State Mutual Bk.

Toboldt, Bill. Auto Body Repairing & Repainting. rev. ed. LC 82-14320. (Illus.). 256p. 1982. text ed. 12.00 (ISBN 0-87006-423-1). Goodheart.

--Diesel: Fundamentals Service & Repair. LC 82-14320. (Illus.). 348p. 1983. text ed. 14.00 (ISBN 0-87006-423-1). Goodheart.

--Diesel: Fundamentals, Service, Repair. Rev. ed. LC 82-14319. (Illus.). 1983. text ed. 14.00 (ISBN 0-87006-424-X). Goodheart.

--Fix Your Chevrolet. rev. ed. LC 62-12426. (Illus.). 384p. 1981. 8.00 (ISBN 0-87006-329-4). Goodheart.

--Fix Your Ford. rev. ed. (Illus.). 416p. 1981. 8.00 (ISBN 0-87006-330-8). Goodheart.

Toboldt, William K. & Johnson, Larry. Automotive Encyclopedia. rev. ed. LC 80-27699. (Illus.). 816p. 1981. text ed. 17.60 (ISBN 0-87006-314-6). Goodheart.

Tobriner, Stephen. The Genesis of Noto: An Eighteenth-Century Sicilian City. LC 77-78417. (Illus.). 252p. 1982. 95.00x (ISBN 0-520-03526-7). U of Cal Pr.

Toby, Jackson, ed. see Parsons, Talcott.

Tocchini, John J., ed. Restorative Dentistry. (Illus.). 1967. 33.00 (ISBN 0-07-064929-4, HP). McGraw.

Tocci, Lisa, et al. Oil Industry U. S. A. 1983. 1982. 75.00 (ISBN 0-686-84378-9). Oil Daily.

Tocci, Ronald & Laskowski, Lester. Microprocessors & Microcomputers: Hardware & Software. 2nd ed. (Illus.). 416p. 1982. 23.95 (ISBN 0-13-581322-0); solutions manual avail. P-H.

Tocci, Ronald J. Fundamentals of Electronic Devices. 3rd ed. 480p. 1982. text ed. 23.95 (ISBN 0-675-09887-4). Additional supplements may be obtained from publisher. Merrill.

--Fundamentals of Electronic Devices. 2nd ed. Oppenheimer, Samuel L., ed. (Technology Ser.). (Illus.). 496p. 1975. text ed. 23.95 (ISBN 0-675-08771-6). Additional supplements may be obtained from publisher. Merrill.

--Fundamentals of Pulse & Digital Circuits. 2nd ed. (Electronics Technology Ser.). 1977. text ed. 23.95 (ISBN 0-675-08492-X). Additional supplements may be obtained from publisher. Merrill.

--Fundamentals of Pulse & Digital Circuits. 3rd ed. 1983. text ed. 22.95 (ISBN 0-675-20033-4). Additional supplements may be obtained from publisher. Merrill.

--Introduction to Electric Circuit Analysis. 1973. text ed. 26.95x (ISBN 0-675-08985-9). Additional supplements may be obtained from publisher. Merrill.

--Introduction to Electric Circuit Analysis. 2nd ed. 1983. text ed. 25.95 (ISBN 0-675-20002-4). Additional supplements may be obtained from publisher. Merrill.

Tocci, Ronald J. & Laskowski, Lester P. Microprocessors & Microcomputers: Hardware & Software. (Illus.). 1979. text ed. 20.95 o.p. (ISBN 0-13-581330-1). P-H.

Tocci, Ronale J. Electronic Devices: Conventional Flow Version. 3rd ed. 1983. text ed. 23.95 (ISBN 0-675-20063-6). Merrill.

Toch, Hans & Grant, J. Douglas. Change Through Participation: Humanizing Human Service Settings. (Library of Social Research). (Illus.). 240p. 1982. 22.00 (ISBN 0-8039-1886-0); pap. 10.95 (ISBN 0-8039-1887-9). Sage.

Toch, Hans, jt. ed. see Johnson, Robert.

Toch, Henry. Economics for Professional Studies. 240p. 1979. 29.00x (ISBN 0-7121-0568-9, Pub. by Macdonald & Evans). State Mutual Bk.

Toches, Nick. Hellfire. (Orig.). 1982. pap. 6.95 (ISBN 0-440-53549-2, Dell Trade Pbks). Dell.

Tochigi, K., jt. auth. see Kojima, K.

Tocqueville, Alexis. Alexis de Tocqueville on Democracy, Revolution, & Society. Stone, John, et al, eds. LC 79-21204. (Heritage of Sociology Ser.). 392p. 1982. pap. 7.95 (ISBN 0-226-80527-1). U of Chicago Pr.

Tocqueville, Alexis De. Democracy in America, 2 vols. Bradley, Phillips, ed. (American Past Ser). 1944. Vol. 1. pap. 3.95 (ISBN 0-394-70110-0, Vin); Vol. 2. pap. 4.95 (ISBN 0-394-70111-9). Random.

--Rapport Fait au Nom de la Commission Chargee d'Examiner la Proposition de M. De Tracy, Relative aux Esclaves des Colonies...Seance du 23 Juillet, 1839. (Slave Trade in France Ser., 1744-1848). 98p. (Fr.). 1974. Repr. lib. bdg. 35.00x o.p. (ISBN 0-8287-0825-8, TN 144). Clearwater Pub.

Tocqueville, Alexis De see De Tocqueville, Alexis.

Tod, Osma G. & Benson, Oscar H. Weaving with Reeds & Fibers. Orig. Title: Hand Weaving with Reeds & Fibers. (Illus.). 224p. 1975. pap. 3.50 (ISBN 0-486-23143-7). Dover.

Toda, K., jt. auth. see Driscoll, Lucy.

Toda, M., et al. Statistical Physics I: Equilibrium Statistical Mechanics. (Spinger Series in Solid-State Sciences: Vol. 30). (Illus.). 270p. 1983. 34.00 (ISBN 0-387-11460-2). Springer-Verlag.

Todaro, Martin T., jt. auth. see Cartier, Francis A.

Todd, Ann. The Eighth Veil. (Illus.). 220p. 1981. 14.95 o.s.i. (ISBN 0-399-12662-7). Putnam Pub Group.

Todd, Arthur C. Cornish Miner in America. (Illus.). 1968. 15.00 o.p. (ISBN 0-87062-063-0). A H Clark.

Todd, C. D. Zener & Avalanche Diodes. LC 77-120709. 1970. 21.50 o.p. (ISBN 0-471-87605-4, Pub. by Wiley). Krieger.

Todd, Charles B. In Olde Connecticut. LC 68-26612. 1968. Repr. of 1906 ed. 30.00x (ISBN 0-8103-3540-9). Gale.

--In Olde Massachusetts: Sketches of Old Times & Places During the Early Days of the Commonwealth. LC 77-99060. 1971. Repr. of 1907 ed. 30.00x (ISBN 0-8103-3775-4). Gale.

Todd, Charles L. & Blackwell, Russell T. Language & Value. 1969. lib. bdg. 29.95x (ISBN 0-8371-1494-2, TOL/). Greenwood.

Todd, David. Experimental Organic Chemistry. (Illus.). 1979. pap. 21.95 (ISBN 0-13-294660-2). P-H.

Todd, David K. Groundwater Hydrology. 2nd ed. LC 80-11831. 535p. 1980. 39.95x (ISBN 0-471-87616-X). Wiley.

Todd, David K., jt. ed. see Giefer, Gerald J.

Todd, Douglas C. Whippet. rev ed. LC 62-14986. (Illus.). 1961. 8.95 o.p. (ISBN 0-668-00948-9). Arco.

Todd, Frank S. Sea World Book of Penguins. LC 86-25588. (Illus.). 96p. (gr. 4-6). 1981. 9.95 (ISBN 0-15-271949-0, HJ). HarBraceJ.

Todd, H. N., jt. auth. see Rickmers, A. D.

Todd, Harry F. & Ruffini, Julio L., eds. Teaching Medical Anthropology. 1979. pap. 5.00 (ISBN 0-686-36582-8). Am Anthro Assn.

Todd, Helen. Mary Musgrove: Georgia Indian Princess. LC 80-54424. 148p. 1981. pap. 4.49 (ISBN 0-9605514-0-9). Seven Oaks GA.

--Psychic Powers. (Theosophical Manual: No. 11). 1975. pap. 2.50 (ISBN 0-913004-38-3). Point Loma Pub.

Todd, Helen, ed. see Benjamin, Elsie.

Todd, Helen, ed. see De Purucker, G.

Todd, Helen, ed. see De Purucker, G. & Tingley, Katherine.

Todd, Helen, ed. see Edge, Henry T.

Todd, Helen, ed. see Greenwalt, Emmett A.

Todd, Helen, ed. see Ross, Lydia.

Todd, Helen, ed. see Ryan, Charles J.

Todd, Helen, jt. ed. see Small, W. Emmett.

Todd, Helen, ed. see Van Pelt, G.

Todd, Helen, ed. see Van Pelt, Gertrude W.

Todd, Helen, ed. see Wright, L. L.

Todd, Helen, ed. see Wright, Leoline L.

Todd, Helen, ed. see Wright, Leoline L., et al.

Todd, Hollis N. Photographic Sensitometry: A Self-Teaching Text. LC 76-22657. (Photographic Science & Technology & the Graphic Arts Ser.). 225p. 1976. 27.50x (ISBN 0-471-87649-6, Pub. by Wiley-Interscience). Wiley.

Todd, I. P. Colon, Rectum & Anus. 3rd ed. (Operative Surgery Ser.). 1977. 125.00 (ISBN 0-407-00606-0). Butterworth.

Todd, Ian. The Prehistoric of Central Anatolia I: The Neolithic Period. (Studies in Mediterranean Archaeology: Vol. LX). 177p. 1981. pap. text ed. 45.00x (ISBN 91-85058-87-4, Pub. by Astroms, Sweden). Humanities.

Todd, J. F., jt. ed. see Price, D.

Todd, J. P. & Ellis, H. B. An Introduction to Thermodynamics of Engineering Technologists. 469p. 1981. text ed. 27.95 (ISBN 0-471-05300-7); solutions manual 10.00 (ISBN 0-471-09794-2). Wiley.

Todd, Jane. The Pressure Cookbook. (Illus.). 128p. 1981. 7.95 o.p. (ISBN 0-686-73562-5, 8184). Larousse.

Todd, Janet, ed. Bibliography of Women & Literature. 550p. 1983. text ed. 75.00x (ISBN 0-8419-0693-9). Holmes & Meier.

--Jane Austen. (Women & Literature Ser.: No. 3). (Orig.). 1983. text ed. price not set (ISBN 0-8419-0863-X); pap. text ed. price not set (ISBN 0-8419-0864-8). Holmes & Meier.

--Men by Women. LC 80-20702. (Women & Literature Ser.: Vol. II). 270p. 1982. text ed. 29.50x (ISBN 0-8419-0732-3); pap. text ed. 19.50x (ISBN 0-8419-0733-1). Holmes & Meier.

--Women Writers Talking. 200p. 1983. 24.50x (ISBN 0-8419-0756-0); pap. 9.95 (ISBN 0-686-81247-6). Holmes & Meier.

Todd, Janet M., jt. auth. see Marshall, Madeleine F.

Todd, John & Todd, Nancy J. Tomorrow Is Our Permanent Address. LC 78-2171. (Lindisfarne Bk.). (Illus.). 1979. pap. 4.95i o.p. (ISBN 0-06-090712-6, CN712, CN). Har-Row.

--Tomorrow Is Our Permanent Address. LC 78-2171. (Lindisfarne Bk.). (Illus.). 1980. 16.30i (ISBN 0-06-014319-3, HarpT); pap. 4.95xi (ISBN 0-06-090712-6, CN-712). Har-Row.

Todd, John, jt. auth. see Yeric, Jerry L.

Todd, John E. Frederick Law Olmstead. (World Leaders Ser.). 1982. lib. bdg. 13.95 (ISBN 0-8057-7729-6, Twayne). G K Hall.

Todd, Judith. The Right to Say No. LC 72-93680. 224p. 1973. 7.95 o.p. (ISBN 0-89388-066-3). Okpaku Communications.

Todd, Kathleen. Snow. (Illus.). (ps-3). Date not set. 7.95 (ISBN 0-201-16280-6). A-W.

Todd, Loreto. Pidgins & Creoles. (Language & Society Ser.). 1974. 12.00x (ISBN 0-7100-7865-X); pap. 6.95 (ISBN 0-7100-7927-3). Routledge & Kegan.

--Tortoise the Trickster: And Other Folktales from Cameroon. LC 79-64121. (Illus.). (gr. k-5). 1979. 8.95x o.p. (ISBN 0-8052-3725-9). Schocken.

Todd, Loreto, jt. auth. see O'Donnell, W. R.

Todd, Mabel E. The Hidden You. LC 76-49251. (Illus.). 248p. pap. 7.50 o.p. (ISBN 0-87127-096-X). Dance Horiz.

Todd, Malcolm. The Coritani. (Peoples of Roman Britain Ser.). 1973. text ed. 17.50x o.p. (ISBN 0-7156-0649-2). Humanities.

Todd, Michael, Jr. & Todd, Susan M. A Valuable Property: The Life Story of Michael Todd. (Illus.). 1983. 16.95 (ISBN 0-87795-491-7). Arbor Hse.

Todd, Nancy, ed. The Journal of the New Alchemists, No. 6. LC 78-945501. (Illus.). 1980. 15.95 (ISBN 0-8289-0366-2); pap. 9.95 o.p. (ISBN 0-8289-0367-0). Greene.

Todd, Nancy J., jt. auth. see Todd, John.

Todd, Patrick. A Fire by the Tracks. 70p. 1983. 12.50 (ISBN 0-8142-0343-4). Ohio St U Pr.

Todd, Paul. Do You Know the Church? LC 76-27402. 102p. (Orig.). 1977. pap. 1.75 o.p. (ISBN 0-8189-1140-9, Pub. by Alba Bks). Alba.

Todd, Peter, pseud. The Adventures of Herlock Sholmes. LC 76-7154. 1976. 10.00 o.p. (ISBN 0-89296-000-0). Mysterious Pr.

Todd, Ralph, jt. auth. see Costley, Dan L.

Todd, Robert M. Sopwith Camel Fighter Ace. LC 78-72947. (Illus.). 1978. softcover 6.95 o.p. (ISBN 0-939440-04-0). AJAY Ent.

Todd, Ruthven, ed. see Gilchrist, Alexander.

Todd, Susan M., jt. auth. see Todd, Michael, Jr.

Todd, V. E. & Heffernan, H. Years Before School: Guiding Preschool Children. 3rd ed. 1977. text ed. 22.95x (ISBN 0-02-420880-9). Macmillan.

Todd, Virgil H. Prophet Without Portfolio. LC 77-178202. 165p. 1972. 4.95 o.p. (ISBN 0-8158-0270-6). Chris Mass.

Todd, Vivian E. Aid in Early Childhood Education. (Illus.). 224p. 1973. text ed. 12.95x (ISBN 0-02-420900-7). Macmillan.

Todd, W. E. Clyde. Birds of the Labrador Peninsula. LC 80-66715. (Illus.). 1980. 85.00x (ISBN 0-931130-06-9). Buteo.

Todd, William. Hoskins: The Artist as Terrorist. (Illus.). 180p. (Orig.). 1982. pap. 4.50 (ISBN 0-686-36933-5). Ehling Clifton Bks.

Todd, William B., ed. Guy of Warwick. (Illus.). 192p. 1968. Repr. of 1959 ed. 10.00x o.p. (ISBN 0-292-73427-1). U of Tex Pr.

Todhunter, Isaac. History of the Calculus of Variations in the Nineteenth Century. LC 61-18586. 18.50 (ISBN 0-8284-0164-0). Chelsea Pub.

--History of the Mathematical Theory of Probability. LC 51-146. 1949. 17.95 (ISBN 0-8284-0057-1). Chelsea Pub.

Todorov. Clinical Neurology. 1983. price not set (ISBN 0-86577-084-0). Thieme-Stratton.

Todorov, Nikolai. The Balkan City, Fourteen Hundred to Nineteen Hundred: Its Socioeconomic & Demographic Development. (Publications in Russia & Eastern Europe of the School of International Studies: No. 12). 500p. 1983. 30.00 (ISBN 0-295-95897-9). U of Wash Pr.

Todorov, Tzvetan. Symbolism & Interpretation. Porter, Catherine, tr. from Fr. LC 82-5078. 160p. 1982. 19.50 (ISBN 0-8014-1269-2). Cornell U Pr.

Todorov, Tzvetan, ed. French Literary Theory Today: A Reader. 250p. 1982. 39.50 (ISBN 0-521-23036-5); pap. 9.95 (ISBN 0-521-29777-X). Cambridge U Pr.

Toebes, G. H. & Sheppard, A., eds. Reservoir Systems Operations. LC 81-70788. 600p. 1982. pap. text ed. 40.00 (ISBN 0-87262-288-6). Am Soc Civil Eng.

Toelken, Barre. The Dynamics of Folklore. LC 78-69536. (Illus.). 1979. text ed. 18.50 (ISBN 0-395-27068-5); instr's. manual 0.50 (ISBN 0-395-27069-3). HM.

Toenniessen, G. H., jt. auth. see Staples, R. C.

Toepfer, Thomas. American Beer Can Encyclopedia. (Illus.). pap. 7.95 (ISBN 0-89145-189-7). Wallace-Homestead.

Toepke, U. P. EEC Competition Law: Business Issues & Legal Principles in Common Market Antitrust Cases. 925p. 1982. text ed. 115.00x (ISBN 0-471-09366-1). Ronald Pr.

Toeplitz, Otto, jt. auth. see Hellinger, Ernst.

Toer, Pramoedya A. The Fugitive. Aveling, Harry, tr. (Writing in Asia Ser.). 1975. pap. text ed. 4.50x (ISBN 0-686-66065-X, 00208). Heinemann Ed.

Toews, John B. Czars, Soviets & Mennonites. LC 81-71490. 221p. 1982. pap. 10.95 (ISBN 0-87303-064-8). Faith & Life.

Toews, John E. Hegelianism: The Path Toward Dialectic Humanism, 1805 to 1841. LC 80-16370. 512p. 1981. 44.50 (ISBN 0-521-23048-9). Cambridge U Pr.

Toews, Margaret P. Paul & the Unfriendly Town. (Arch Bks: No. 13). (Illus.). 32p. (ps-3). 1976. pap. 0.89 (ISBN 0-570-06102-4, 59-1220). Concordia.

Toffler, Alvin. Future Shock. 1970. 17.45 (ISBN 0-394-42586-3). Random.

--Previews & Premises. 192p. 1983. 11.95 (ISBN 0-688-01910-2). Morrow.

--The Third Wave. 544p. 1980. 14.95 (ISBN 0-686-98076-X). Telecom Lib.

Toga, Carl J., et al. Geriatric Dentistry: Clinical Application of Selected Biomedical & Psychosocial Topics. LC 78-24646. 288p. 1979. 25.95x (ISBN 0-669-02806-1). Lexington Bks.

Toghill, Jeff. Knots & Splices. (Illus.). 64p. (Orig.). 1979. pap. 4.00 (ISBN 0-589-50079-1, Pub. by Reed Books Australia). C E Tuttle.

--Trailer Sailers. (Illus.). 1977. pap. 8.00 (ISBN 0-589-07218-8, Pub. by Reed Books Australia). C E Tuttle.

Toglia, Michael P. & Battig, William F. Handbook of Semantic Word Norms. LC 78-6556. 160p. 1978. text ed. 24.95 (ISBN 0-89859-297-6). L Erlbaum Assocs.

Togliatti, Palmiro. Lectures on Fascism. LC 75-35674. 1976. 6.95 (ISBN 0-7178-0429-1); pap. 2.95 (ISBN 0-7178-0430-5). Intl Pub Co.

Tognoni, G. C., et al, eds. Epidemiological Impact of Psychotropic Drugs: Proceedings of the International Seminar on Epidemiological Impact of Psychotropic Drugs, Milan, Italy, 24-26 June, 1981. (Clinical Pharmacology & Drug Epidemiology Ser.: Vol. 3). 398p. 1982. 71.00 (ISBN 0-444-80388-2). Elsevier.

Tognoni, Gianni, et al, eds. Frontiers in Therapeutic Drug Monitoring: Pharmacology-Clinical Chemistry. (Monographs of the Mario Negri Institute for Pharmacological Research). 200p. 1980. text ed. 23.50 (ISBN 0-89004-508-9). Raven.

Tohei, Koichi. The Book of "Ki": Co-Ordinating Body and Mind in Daily Life. LC 76-29340. (Illus.). 128p. 1976. pap. 8.95 (ISBN 0-87040-379-6). Japan Pubns.

--Kiatsu. (Illus.). 180p. 1983. pap. text ed. 11.95 (ISBN 0-87040-511-X). Japan Pubns.

Tohen, Alfonso. Manual of Mechanical Orthopaedics. (Illus.). 340p. 1973. 18.75x (ISBN 0-398-02614-9). C C Thomas.

Toit, Brian M. Du see Du Toit, Brian M.

Toker, Cyril. Tumors: An Atlas of Differential Diagnosis. (Illus.). 1983. price not set (ISBN 0-8391-1812-0, 17914). Univ Park.

Tokheim, Roger. Digital Electronics. Schuler, Charles A., ed. (Basic Skills in Electricity & Electronics Ser). (Illus.). 1979. pap. text ed. 13.96 (ISBN 0-07-064954-5, G); activities manual 10.96 (ISBN 0-07-064955-3); tchr's manual 2.00 (ISBN 0-07-064956-1). McGraw.

Tokheim, Roger L. Schaum's Outline of Digital Principles. (Illus., Orig.). 1980. pap. 6.95 (ISBN 0-07-064928-6, SP). McGraw.

Toklas, Alice B. Staying on Alone: Letters of Alice B. Toklas. Burns, Edward, ed. 1982. pap. 8.95 (ISBN 0-87140-131-2). Liveright.

Tokmakoff, George. P. A. Stolypin & the Third Duma: An Appraisal of the Three Major Issues. LC 81-40349. (Illus.). 258p. (Orig.). 1982. lib. bdg. 23.00 (ISBN 0-8191-2058-8); pap. text ed. 11.50 (ISBN 0-8191-2059-6). U Pr of Amer.

Tokson, Elliot. The Popular Image of the Black Man in English Drama, 1550-1688. 1982. lib. bdg. 18.95 (ISBN 0-8161-8392-9, Univ Bks). G K Hall.

Toksoz, M. N. & Uyeda, S. Oceanic Ridges & Arcs: Geodynamic Processes. (Developments in Geotectonics Ser.: Vol. 14). 1980. 30.00 (ISBN 0-444-41839-3). Elsevier.

Tolan, Fred, jt. ed. see Alaska Magazine Publishers.

Tolan, Stephaie. Grandpa & Me. (gr. 6 up). 1982. pap. 1.95 o.p. (ISBN 0-440-43260-X, YB). Dell.

Tolan, Stephanie S. The Great Skinner Strike. LC 82-17992. 120p. (gr. 7 up). 1983. 8.95 (ISBN 0-02-789360-X). Macmillan.

Toland, Drexel & Strong, Susan. Hospital-Based Medical Office Buildings. (Illus.). 260p. (Orig.). 1981. 45.00 (ISBN 0-87258-297-3, AHA-145138). Am Hospital.

Toland, John. Dillinger Days. (Illus.). 1963. 15.00 o.p. (ISBN 0-394-42221-X). Random.

--Infamy: Pearl Harbor & Its Aftermath. (Illus.). 384p. 1983. pap. 3.95 (ISBN 0-425-05991-X). Berkley Pub.

--Letters to Serena. Wellek, Rene, ed. LC 75-11259. (British Philosophers & Theologians of the 17th & 18th Centuries: Vol. 58). 1977. Repr. of 1704 ed. lib. bdg. 42.00 o.s.i. (ISBN 0-8240-1809-5). Garland Pub.

--Lettres Philosophiques sur l'Origine des Prejuges du Dogme. (Holbach & His Friends Ser). 271p. (Fr.). 1974. Repr. of 1768 ed. lib. bdg. 73.00x o.p. (ISBN 0-8287-0826-6, 1543). Clearwater Pub.

--Le Nazareen ou le Christianisme des Juifs, des Gentils et des Mahometans. (Holbach & His Friends Ser). 315p. (Fr.). 1974. Repr. of 1777 ed. lib. bdg. 83.00x o.p. (ISBN 0-8287-0827-4, 1563). Clearwater Pub.

Tolbert, Audrey S. Four Plays. 1981. cancelled 4.95 (ISBN 0-8062-1664-6). Carlton.

Tolbert, E. L. Counseling for Career Development. 2nd ed. LC 79-89452. (Illus.). 352p. 1980. text ed. 21.95 (ISBN 0-395-28251-9); instr's. manual 1.00 (ISBN 0-395-28252-7). HM.

--Introduction to Counseling. 2nd ed. (Education Ser). (Illus.). 512p. 1971. text ed. 15.95 o.p. (ISBN 0-07-064935-9, C). McGraw.

Tolbert, N. E. & Osmond, C. B., eds. Photorespiration in Marine Plants. (Illus.). 139p. 1976. 7.50 (ISBN 0-686-37454-1). Sabbot-Natural Hist Bks.

Tole World Magazine Staff. Tole World Cook Book. Swant, Dale, ed. (Illus.). 220p. (Orig.). 1982. pap. 9.95 (ISBN 0-943470-02-1). Daisy Pub WA.

Toledano, Ralph De see De Toledano, Ralph.

Toledano, Roulhac, ed. see Wilson, Samuel, Jr. & Lemann, Bernard.

Toledano, Roulhac, et al. New Orleans Architecture, Vol. 4: Creole Faubourgs. LC 74-16744. (New Orleans Architecture Ser.). (Illus.). 192p. 1974. 22.50 (ISBN 0-88289-037-9). Pelican.

Toledo-Pereyra, Luis. Basic Concepts of Organ Procurement Perfusion & Perservation in Transplantation. 39.50 (ISBN 0-12-692680-8). Acad Pr.

Tolert, E L., ed. An Introduction to Guidance: The Professional Counselor. 2nd ed. 1982. text ed. 17.95 (ISBN 0-316-84992-8); tchrs.' manual avail. (ISBN 0-316-84993-6). Little.

Tolf, Robert. Discover Florida: A Guide to Unique Sites & Sights. (Illus.). 143p. pap. 5.95 (ISBN 0-686-84224-3). Banyan Bks.

--Discover Fort Lauderdale's Top Twelve Attractions. (Florida Keepsake Ser.: No. 1). (Illus.). 28p. Date not set. 3.00 (ISBN 0-686-84227-8). Banyan Bks.

--Discover Fort Lauderdale's Top Twelve Restaurants. (Florida Keepsake Ser.: No. 2). (Illus.). 28p. 3.00 (ISBN 0-686-84230-8). Banyan Bks.

Tolf, Robert W. Country Inns of the Old South. LC 78-11262. (Illus.). 1978. pap. 4.95 o.p. (ISBN 0-89286-144-4). One Hund One Prods.

Tolis, George, et al, eds. Clinical Neuroendocrinology: A Pathophysiological Approach. LC 78-64844. 492p. 1979. text ed. 55.00 (ISBN 0-89004-355-8). Raven.

Tolk, N. H., et al, eds. Desorption Induced by Electron Transitions, DIET I. (Springer Ser. in Chemical Physics: Vol. 24). (Illus.). 305p. 1983. 29.50 (ISBN 0-387-12127-7). Springer-Verlag.

Tolkien, J. R. The Old English Exodus. Turville-Petre, Joan, ed. 1982. 19.95x (ISBN 0-19-811177-0). Oxford U Pr.

Tolkien, J. R. R. Mr. Bliss. 1983. 11.95 (ISBN 0-395-32936-1). HM.

Toll, Robert. On with the Show! The First Century of American Show Business. LC 75-46355. (Illus.). 1976. 25.00x (ISBN 0-19-502057-X). Oxford U Pr.

Toll, Robert C. Blacking up: The Minstrel Show in Nineteenth-Century America. LC 74-83992. (Illus.). 1977. pap. 7.95 (ISBN 0-19-502172-X, 489, GB). Oxford U Pr.

--The Entertainment Machine: American Show Business in the Twentieth Century. LC 81-16930. (Illus.). 1982. 29.95 (ISBN 0-19-503081-8). Oxford U Pr.

Toll, William. The Making of an Ethnic Middle Class: Portland Jewry Over Four Generations. LC 82-655. (Modern Jewish History Ser.). (Illus.). 200p. 1982. 39.50x (ISBN 0-87395-609-5); pap. 12.95x (ISBN 0-87395-610-9). State U NY Pr.

--The Resurgence of Race: Black Social Theory from Reconstruction to the Pan-African Conferences. 288p. 1979. 29.95 (ISBN 0-87722-167-7). Temple U Pr.

Tollar, Jerry R., jt. ed. see Greenwood, Michael.

Tolle, Gordon J. Human Nature Under Fire: The Political Philosophy of Hannah Arendt. LC 81-43723. 180p. (Orig.). 1982. lib. bdg. 22.00 (ISBN 0-8191-2560-1); pap. text ed. 10.00 (ISBN 0-8191-2561-X). U Pr of Amer.

Tolle, Leon J., Jr. Floral Arts for Religious Events. LC 68-20196. (Illus.). 1969. 8.95 (ISBN 0-8208-0062-7). Hearthside.

Tollefson, James W. The Language Situation & Language Policy in Slovenia. LC 80-5579. 296p. 1981. lib. bdg. 20.75 (ISBN 0-8191-1570-3); pap. text ed. 11.00 (ISBN 0-8191-1571-1). U Pr of Amer.

Tollenaere, J. P., et al. Atlas of the Three-Dimensional Structure of Drugs. (Janssen Research Foundation Ser.: Vol. 1). 322p. 1979. 40.50 (ISBN 0-444-80145-6, North Holland). Elsevier.

Toller, C. Van see Van Toller, C.

Tollers, Vincent L., ed. Bibliography of Matthew Arnold, 1932-1970. 1974. 18.75x (ISBN 0-271-01113-0). Pa St U Pr.

Tolles, Bryant F., Jr. & Tolles, Carolyn K. New Hampshire Architecture: An Illustrated Guide. LC 78-63586. (Illus.). 420p. 1979. text ed. 25.00x (ISBN 0-87451-165-8); pap. 9.95 (ISBN 0-87451-167-4). U Pr of New Eng.

Tolles, Carolyn K., jt. auth. see Tolles, Bryant F., Jr.

Tolles, Frederick B. James Logan & the Culture of Provincial America. Handlin, Oscar, ed. LC 77-2783. (The Library of American Biography). 1978. Repr. of 1957 ed. lib. bdg. 20.50x o.p. (ISBN 0-313-20197-8, TOJL). Greenwood.
Tolley, George, et al. Elements of Environmental Analysis. (Environmental Policy Ser.: Vol. I). 224p. 1981. prof ref 22.50x (ISBN 0-88410-625-X). Ballinger Pub.
Tolley, George S. & Graves, Philip E., eds. Environmental Policy, Vol. II. 456p. 1982. prof ref 40.00x (ISBN 0-88410-626-8). Ballinger Pub.
Tolley, George S. & Havelick, Joseph, Jr., eds. Environmental Policy Vol. IV: Solid Wastes. 1983. prof ref 22.50x (ISBN 0-88410-627-6). Ballinger Pub.
Tolley, George S. & Vaughan, Roger J., eds. Environmental Policy Vol. V: Recreation & Aesthetics. 1983. prof ref 22.50x (ISBN 0-88410-628-4). Ballinger Pub.
Tolley, George S., ed. see Conference on Income Support Policies for the Aging-University of Chicago.
Tolley, George S., et al. Electric Energy Availability & Regional Growth. LC 76-20748. 1977. prof ref 20.00x (ISBN 0-88410-609-8). Ballinger Pub.
--Urban Growth Policy in a Market Economy. LC 78-8838. (Studies in Urban Economics). 1979. 24.50 (ISBN 0-12-692850-9). Acad Pr.
Tolley, George S., et al, eds. Environmental Policy Vol. III: Water Quality. 1983. prof ref 22.50x (ISBN 0-88410-632-2). Ballinger Pub.
Tolley, Howard B., Jr. Children & War: Political Socialization to International Conflict. LC 72-90521. (Illus.). 274p. 1973. pap. text ed. 7.95x (ISBN 0-8077-2280-4). Tchrs Coll.
Tolley, Kemp. Cruise of the Lanikai. LC 82-8980. 360p. 1982. Repr. of 1973 ed. lib. bdg. 19.50 (ISBN 0-89874-526-8). Krieger.
Tollini, Helio, jt. auth. see Schuh, G. Edward.
Tollison, C. David. Headache: A Multimodel Program for Relief. LC 82-50550. 128p. 1982. 12.95 (ISBN 0-8069-5572-4); lib. bdg. 15.69 (ISBN 0-8069-5573-2); pap. 6.95 (ISBN 0-8069-7648-9). Sterling.
--Managing Chronic Pain: A Patient's Guide. LC 81-85035. (Illus.). 144p. 1982. 12.95 (ISBN 0-8069-5570-8); lib. bdg. 15.69 (ISBN 0-8069-5571-6). Sterling.
Tollison, Robert D., jt. auth. see Wagner, Richard E.
Tollison, Robert D., ed. The Political Economy of Antitrust: Principal Paper by William Baxter. LC 80-7928. 160p. 1980. 18.95x (ISBN 0-669-03876-8). Lexington Bks.
Tollison, Robert D., jt. auth. see Wagner, Richard E.
Tolliver, Robert E., jt. auth. see Anthony, Michael J.
Tolliver, Ruby C. Decision at Brushycreek. (Orig.). (gr. 7-12). 1983. pap. 4.95 (ISBN 0-8054-7318-1). Broadman.
Tolman, Ruth. Charm Teacher's Manual, 6 pts. Incl. Pt. 1. Visual Poise. 1972 (ISBN 0-87350-156-X); Pt. 2. Wardrobe Planning. 1974 (ISBN 0-87350-157-8); Pt. 3. Personal Grooming. 1972 (ISBN 0-87350-158-6); Pt. 4. Body Perfection. 1974 (ISBN 0-87350-159-4); Pt. 5. Social Graces. 1974 (ISBN 0-87350-160-8); Pt. 6. Success Insurance. (Beauty Culture or General Edition). 1962 (ISBN 0-87350-161-6). 1972. 10.35 ea.; Set. 25.00 (ISBN 0-87350-177-2). Milady.
--A Woman's Guide to Business & Social Success. rev. ed. 1982. 15.95 o.p. (ISBN 0-87350-182-9). Milady.
Tolmie, J., jt. auth. see Birch, A.
Tolnay, Stewart E., jt. auth. see McFalls, Joseph A.
Tolner, J. The Gnu Book. 90p. (Orig.). 1983. pap. 5.95 (ISBN 0-939722-17-8). Pressworks.
Toloudis, Constantin. Jacques Audiberti. (World Authors Ser.). 1980. lib. bdg. 15.95 (ISBN 0-8057-6392-9, Twayne). G K Hall.
Tolson, Andrew. The Limits of Masculinity. LC 78-69630. 1979. 11.49i (ISBN 0-06-014333-9, HarpT). Har-Row.
Tolson, Melvin B. Caviar & Cabbage: Selected Columns by Melvin B. Tolson from the Washington Tribune, 1937-1944. Farnsworth, Robert M., ed. LC 81-10480. 272p. text ed. 20.00x (ISBN 0-8262-0348-5). U of Mo Pr.
--Harlem Gallery: Book I, the Curator. 1971. lib. bdg. 10.95 (ISBN 0-8057-5808-9, Twayne). G K Hall.
--Libretto for the Republic of Liberia. 1971. lib. bdg. 5.50 o.p. (ISBN 0-8057-5813-5, Twayne). G K Hall.
Tolstoi, Alexei N. Aelita or, The Decline of Mars. Fetzer, Leland, tr. from Rus. 140p. 1983. 15.00 (ISBN 0-88233-788-2); pap. 4.50 (ISBN 0-88233-789-0). Ardis Pubs.
Tolstoi, L. N. A Captive in the Caucasus. Shoenberg, Zlata & Domb, Jessie, trs. from Russian. (Bilingual Ser.). (Illus.). 1945. 5.00 (ISBN 0-911268-45-6). Rogers Bk.
Tolstoy. Chozjain I Rabotnik. (Easy Reader, C). pap. 3.95 (ISBN 0-88436-054-7, 65252). EMC.
Tolstoy, Alexandra. I Worked For the Soviet. 1934. text ed. 39.50x (ISBN 0-686-83576-X). Elliots Bks.
Tolstoy, Alexei. Aelita. Bouis, Antonina W., tr. from Rus. (Best of Soviet Science Fiction Ser.). 156p. 1981. 11.95 o.p. (ISBN 0-02-619200-4). Macmillan.
Tolstoy, Ivan. James Clerk Maxwell: A Biography. (Illus.). viii, 192p. 1983. lib. bdg. 17.00x (ISBN 0-226-80785-1); pap. 6.95 (ISBN 0-226-80787-8). U of Chicago Pr.
--Wave Propagation. (Earth & Planetary Science Ser.). (Illus.). 416p. 1973. text ed. 29.95 o.p. (ISBN 0-07-064944-8, C). McGraw.
Tolstoy, L. Childhood, Adolescence, Youth. 456p. 1981. 7.50 (ISBN 0-8285-2241-3, Pub. by Progress Pubs USSR). Imported Pubns.
--Resurrection. 585p. 1972. 6.95 (ISBN 0-8285-1060-1, Pub. by Progress Pubs USSR). Imported Pubns.
Tolstoy, Leo. Anna Karenin. rev. ed. Edmonds, Rosemary, tr. from Rus. (Classics Ser.). 1954. pap. 4.95 (ISBN 0-14-044041-0). Penguin.
--Anna Karenin, T. V. Edition. 1977. pap. 3.95 o.p. (ISBN 0-14-004498-1). Penguin.
--Anna Karenina. Carmichael, Joel, tr. from Russian. (Bantam Classics Ser.). 873p. (Orig.). (gr. 9-12). 1981. pap. 2.75 (ISBN 0-553-21034-3). Bantam.
--Anna Karenina. Magarshac, David, tr. pap. 2.75 (ISBN 0-451-51540-4, CE 1540, Sig Classics). NAL.
--Anna Karenina. Kent & Berberova, eds. Garnett, Constance, tr. 9.95 (ISBN 0-394-60448-2). Modern Lib.
--Death of Ivan Ilych & Other Stories. Maude, Aylmer, tr. 1960. pap. 1.95 (ISBN 0-451-51676-1, CJ1676, Sig Classics). NAL.
--The Death of Ivan Ilyich. Solotaroff, Lynn, tr. (Bantam Classics Ser.). 134p. (gr. 9-12). 1981. pap. 1.95 (ISBN 0-553-21035-1). Bantam.
--Master & Man. Aitken, Eleanor, ed. LC 70-77293. 1969. text ed. 14.95x (ISBN 0-521-07466-5). Cambridge U Pr.
--Papa Panov's Special Day. (Illus.). (gr. 1-4). 1978. 2.95 o.p. (ISBN 0-89191-139-1). Cook.
--Resurrection. Traill, Vera, tr. (Orig.). pap. 3.95 (ISBN 0-451-51689-3, CE1689, Sig Classics). NAL.
--Short Novels. Simmons, Ernest J., ed. & intro. by. LC 65-12448. 6.95 (ISBN 0-394-60482-2). Modern Lib.
--War & Peace. Constance, Garnett, tr. 1931. 9.95 (ISBN 0-394-60475-X). Modern Lib.
--War & Peace. Dunnigan, Ann, tr. (Orig.). 1968. pap. 4.95 (ISBN 0-451-51661-3, CE1661, Sig Classics). NAL.
--War & Peace, 1 vol. ed. 1982. pap. 8.95 (ISBN 0-14-044417-3). Penguin.
Tolstoy, Leo see Swan, D. K.
Tolstoy, Tatiana. Tolstoy Remembered. LC 77-16266. 1978. 14.95 o.p. (ISBN 0-07-064940-5, GB). McGraw.
Tom, Gary F., jt. auth. see Taylor, Lyn P.
Tom, M. E. El see El Tom, M. E.
Tom Stained Glass Artisans. Challenging Projects in Stained Glass. LC 82-18437. (Illus.). 1983. pap. 7.95 (ISBN 0-668-05581-2). Arco.
Tom Studio Artisans. Getting Started in Stained Glass. LC 82-18438. (Illus.). 144p. 1983. pap. 7.95 (ISBN 0-668-05577-4). Arco.
Toma, David & Brett, Michael. Toma: The Compassionate Cop. (Illus.). 224p. 1973. 6.95 o.p. (ISBN 0-399-11277-4). Putnam Pub Group.
Tomabechi, Yoko. Catalogue of Artifacts in the Babylonian Collection of the Lowe Museum of Anthropology. LC 81-71739. (Bibliotheca Mesopotamica Ser.: Vol. 16). (Illus.). viii, 65p. (Orig.). 1983. write for info. (ISBN 0-89003-107-X); pap. write for info. (ISBN 0-89003-106-1). Undena Pubns.
Tomacci, Toni M., jt. auth. see Kelley, Barbara.
Tomain, Joseph P. & Hollis, Shelia S. Energy Decision Making: The Interaction Law & Policy. LC 81-47747. 224p. 1983. 24.95x (ISBN 0-669-04800-3). Lexington Bks.
Tomalin, Ruth. W. H. Hudson: A Biography. 321p. 1982. 24.95 (ISBN 0-571-10599-8). Faber & Faber.
Toman, W. An Introduction to Psychoanalytic Theory of Motivation. 1976. text ed. 20.00 (ISBN 0-08-009485-6). Pergamon.
Tomas, Jason & Shilton, Peter. Peter Shilton: The Magnificent Obession. (Illus.). 256p. 1982. 19.95 (ISBN 0-437-17430-1, Pub. by World's Work). David & Charles.
Tomasch, E. J. & Larmer, Oscar. A Foundation for Expressive Drawing. 2nd ed. 224p. 1983. pap. text ed. 16.95x (ISBN 0-8087-2076-7). Burgess.
Tomasello, Len, jt. auth. see Segal, Marilyn.
Tomasi, Lydio F., ed. see Annual Legal Conference on the Representation of Aliens 1978-1981.
Tomasi, Silvano M., ed. see Center for Migration Studies.
Tomasino, Joseph, jt. auth. see Vasi, Susanne.
Tomasson, Richard, ed. Comparative Social Research: Annual, Vol. 3. 350p. (Orig.). 1980. 42.50 (ISBN 0-89232-150-4). Jai Pr.
Tomasson, Richard F. Sweden, Prototype of Modern Society: Perspectives from Classical Sociology. pap. text ed. 4.95x (ISBN 0-394-30793-3). Phila Bk Co.
Tomasson, Richard F., ed. Comparative Social Research Annual, Vol. 2. 347p. 1979. 42.50 (ISBN 0-89232-112-1). Jai Pr.
--Comparative Social Research Annual, Vol. 4. 350p. 1981. 42.50 (ISBN 0-686-73774-1). Jai Pr.
--Comparative Studies in Sociology: An Annual Compilation of Research, Vol. 1. 1978. lib. bdg. 42.50 (ISBN 0-89232-025-7). Jai Pr.
Tomassoni, Mark, jt. ed. see Leeper, John.
Tomb, David A. Child Psychiatry & Behavioral Pediatrics Case Studies. (Case Studies Ser.). 1982. pap. text ed. 22.50 (ISBN 0-87488-100-5). Med Exam.
Tombaugh, Clyde W. & Moore, Patrick. Out of the Darkness: The Planet Pluto. (Illus.). 1981. pap. 3.50 o.p. (ISBN 0-451-61997-8, ME1997, Ment). NAL.
Tomberlin, James E., ed. Agent, Language, & the Structure of the World: Essays Presented to Hector-Neri Casteneda with His Replies. LC 82-15805. 536p. 1983. lib. bdg. 50.00 (ISBN 0-686-83517-4); pap. text ed. 25.00 (ISBN 0-915145-54-5). Hackett Pub.
Tombs, Robert. The War Against Paris, 1871. LC 80-42024. (Illus.). 272p. 1981. 47.50 (ISBN 0-521-23551-0); pap. 15.95 (ISBN 0-521-28784-7). Cambridge U Pr.
Tomczak, S. P. Successful Consulting for Engineers & Data Processing Professionals. 337p. 1982. text ed. 39.95x (ISBN 0-471-86135-9). Ronald Pr.
Tomczak, Starr L. Corporate Finance Agreements, 2 vols. 1500p. 1982. Set. 120.00x o.p. (ISBN 0-07-064945-6). McGraw.
Tomek, Ivan. Introduction to Computer Organization. (Illus.). 200p. 1981. text ed. 25.95x (ISBN 0-914894-08-0). Computer Sci.
Tomes, John. Belgium & Luxembourg. 6th ed. (Blue Guides Ser.). (Illus.). 1983. 25.50 (ISBN 0-393-01656-0); pap. 14.95 (ISBN 0-393-30063-3). Norton.
Tomes, Margot. Wanda Gag's the Six Swans. (gr. 4-8). pap. 8.95 (ISBN 0-686-96195-1, Coward). Putnam Pub Group.
Tomes, Margot, jt. auth. see Gag, Wanda.
Tomescu, Ioan. Introduction to Combinatorics. Lloyd, E. Keith, ed. Rudeanu, S., tr. from Romanian. (Illus.). 250p. 1975. text ed. 30.00x (ISBN 0-569-08057-6, Pub. by Collets England). Scholium Intl.
Tomeski, Edward & Lazarus, Harold. People-Oriented Computer Systems: The Computer in Crisis. LC 74-12208. 300p. 1975. 15.95 o.p. (ISBN 0-442-28556-6). Krieger.
Tomeski, Edward A. Fundamentals of Computers in Business: A Systems Approach. LC 78-54208. 1979. text ed. 22.95x (ISBN 0-8162-8733-3); instructor's manual 6.00 (ISBN 0-8162-8734-1). Holden-Day.
Tomeski, Edward A. & Kleinschmidt, William. Fundamentals of Computers in Business: A Systems Approach (Student Study Guide) 1979. 8.50 (ISBN 0-8162-8735-X). Holden-Day.
Tomeski, Edward A., et al. People-Oriented Computer Systems: The Computer in Transition. rev. ed. LC 81-14304. 320p. 1983. Repr. of 1975 ed. write for info (ISBN 0-89874-385-0). Krieger.
Tometsko, Andrew M. & Richard, Frederic M., eds. Applications of Photochemistry in Probing Biological Targets. LC 80-15368. (Annals of the New York Academy of Sciences: Vol. 346). 502p. 1980. 100.00x (ISBN 0-89766-080-3); pap. 100.00x (ISBN 0-89766-081-1). NY Acad Sci.
Tomikel, John. A Summary of Earth Processes & Environments. LC 74-28957. 1975. pap. 8.00 (ISBN 0-910042-19-5). Allegheny.
Tomimoto, Kenkichi, jt. auth. see Sanders, Herbert H.
Tominberg, Larry. Using Your Textbook: Social Studies. (Study Skills Ser.). 1982. wkbk. 4.75 (ISBN 0-9602800-9-X). Comp Pr.
Tomioka, Seishiro & Tomoika, Ellen M. Planned Unit Developments: Design & Regional Impact. 272p. 1983. 25.00x (ISBN 0-471-08595-2, Pub. by Wiley-Interscience). Wiley.
Tomita, Jun & Tomita, Noriko. Japanese Ikat Weaving: The Techniques of Kasuri. 128p. 1982. pap. 10.95 (ISBN 0-7100-9043-9). Routledge & Kegan.
Tomita, Noriko, jt. auth. see Tomita, Jun.
Tomizuka, Carl & Emrick, Roy, eds. Physics of Solids at High Pressures. 1965. 68.50 (ISBN 0-12-693850-4). Acad Pr.
Tomkins, Calvin. World of Marcel Duchamp. LC 66-28544. (Library of Art Ser.). (Illus.). (gr. 6 up). 1966. 19.92 (ISBN 0-8094-0265-3, Pub. by Time-Life). Silver.
Tomkins, Cyril, et al. An Economic Analysis of the Financial Leasing Industry. 1979. text ed. 34.25x (ISBN 0-566-00316-3). Gower Pub Ltd.
Tomkins, J., jt. ed. see Kidman, A. D.
Tomkins, Jasper. Nimby. (Illus.). pap. 7.95 o.p. (ISBN 0-914676-83-0, Star & Eleph Bks). Green Tiger Pr.
Tomkins, Mary E. Ida M. Tarbell. LC 73-2293. (U. S. Authors Ser.: No. 247). 184p. 1974. lib. bdg. 10.95 o.p. (ISBN 0-8057-0714-X, Twayne). G K Hall.
Tomkins, Reginald, jt. auth. see Popovych, Orest.
Tomko, J., jt. auth. see Bartfai, P.
Tomkys, W. H., jt. auth. see Plumpton, C.
Tomlin, Evelyn, jt. auth. see Erickson, Helen.
Tomlin, Gwynne, jt. auth. see Cherry, Joetta.
Tomlin, Pinky. The Object of My Affection: An Autobiography. LC 80-5938. (Illus.). 300p. 1981. 14.95 (ISBN 0-8061-1719-2). U of Okla Pr.
Tomlinson, Charles. In Black & White: The Graphics of Charles Tomlinson. (Illus.). 1979. 7.95 o.p. (ISBN 0-85635-117-2, Pub. by Carcanet New Pr England). Humanities.
--Poetry & Metamorphosis. LC 82-19893. 112p. Date not set. 19.95 (ISBN 0-521-24848-5). Cambridge U Pr.
Tomlinson, Charles, ed. The Oxford Book of Verse in English Translation. 1980. 37.50x (ISBN 0-19-214103-1). Oxford U Pr.
Tomlinson, Charles, ed. see Hobbs, A. C.
Tomlinson, Charles, tr. see Paz, Octavio.
Tomlinson, H. The Divination of Disease. 1980. 12.95x o.p. (ISBN 0-8464-1006-0). Beekman Pubs.
--Norman Douglas. LC 74-1189. (English Biography Ser., No. 31). 1974. lib. bdg. 43.95x (ISBN 0-8383-1804-5). Haskell.
Tomlinson, Henry. Thomas Hardy. LC 70-160129. (Studies in Thomas Hardy, No. 14). 1971. lib. bdg. 40.95x (ISBN 0-8383-1283-7). Haskell.
Tomlinson, Hugh, jt. auth. see Deleuze, Gilles.
Tomlinson, Jim. Problems of British Economic Policy, 1870-1945. 1981. 22.00x (ISBN 0-416-30430-3); pap. 9.95x (ISBN 0-416-30440-0). Methuen Inc.
Tomlinson, Kerry. Night Letter. (Illus.). 36p. (Orig.). 1982. 7.00 (ISBN 0-930012-29-1). Mudborn.
Tomlinson, M. An Introduction to the Chemistry of Benzenoid Components. 1971. 24.00 (ISBN 0-08-015659-2); pap. 10.75 o.p. (ISBN 0-08-016921-X). Pergamon.
Tomlinson, M. A. The Glorious Church of God. 1968. pap. 3.50 (ISBN 0-934942-06-4). White Wing Pub.
Tomlinson, M. J. Foundation Design & Construction. 4th ed. (Civil Engineering Ser.). 793p. 1980. text ed. 55.00 (ISBN 0-273-08455-0); 43.95 (ISBN 0-273-08456-9). Pitman Pub MA.
--Pile Design & Construction Practice. (Viewpoint Ser.). (Illus.). 1981. 57.50x (ISBN 0-7210-1013-X). Scholium Intl.
Tomlinson, P. B. Anatomy of the Monocotyledons, Vol. 7: Helobiae (Alismatidae) (Including the Seagrasses) (Illus.). 576p. 1982. text ed. 98.00x (ISBN 0-19-854502-9). Oxford U Pr.
Tomlinson, P. B. & Zimmermann, M. H., eds. Tropical Trees As Living Systems. LC 77-8579. (Illus.). 1978. 80.00 (ISBN 0-521-21686-9). Cambridge U Pr.
Tomlinson, R. A. Epidauros. (Illus.). 96p. 1982. pap. text ed. 21.00x (ISBN 0-246-11404-5, Pub. by Granada England). Humanities.
--Epiduaros. (Illus.). 96p. 1983. 12.50 (ISBN 0-292-72044-0). U of Tex Pr.
--Greek Sanctuaries. LC 76-27588. (Illus.). 1977. 19.95x o.p. (ISBN 0-312-34930-0). St Martin.
Tomlinson-Keasey, Carol. Child's Eye View. 1980. 11.95 o.p. (ISBN 0-312-13245-X). St Martin.
Tomoika, Ellen M., jt. auth. see Tomioka, Seishiro.
Tomori, S. H. The Morphology & Syntax of Present-Day English: An Introduction. 1977. pap. text ed. 10.00x o.p. (ISBN 0-435-92894-5). Heinemann Ed.
Tomory, Edith. A History of Fine Arts in India & the West. (Illus.). 532p. 1982. text ed. 45.00x (ISBN 0-686-42713-0, Pub. by Orient Longman Ltd India). Apt Bks.
Tomory, Peter. Catalog of the Italian Paintings Before 1800. LC 76-730. (Illus.). 198p. 1976. 19.50 (ISBN 0-916758-01-X). Ringling Mus Art.
Tomory, William M. Frank O'Connor. (English Authors Ser.). 1980. lib. bdg. 11.95 (ISBN 0-8057-6789-4, Twayne). G K Hall.
Tomovic, Rajko & Karplus, Walter J. High-Speed Analog Computers. 1970. pap. 3.50 o.p. (ISBN 0-486-62564-8). Dover.
Tomozawa, Minoru, jt. ed. see Herman, Herbert.
Tompert, Ann. Charlotte & Charles. LC 78-26363. (Illus.). (gr. k-3). 1979. PLB 8.95g o.p. (ISBN 0-517-53660-9). Crown.
--The Clever Princess. LC 77-72559. (Illus.). 39p. (gr. k-4). 1977. 6.75 (ISBN 0-914996-15-0); pap. 3.25 (ISBN 0-914996-13-4). Lollipop Power.
--It May Come in Handy Someday. LC 74-19487. (Illus.). 48p. (gr. 4-6). 1975. 5.95 o.p. (ISBN 0-07-064932-4, GB); PLB 5.72 o.p. (ISBN 0-07-064933-2). McGraw.
--Three Foolish Tales. LC 78-12637. (Illus.). (gr. k-3). 1979. reinforced lib. bdg. 6.95 o.p. (ISBN 0-517-53595-5). Crown.
Tompkins, Dorothy, jt. auth. see Homebook, Beeton.
Tompkins, Dorothy C. Administration of Criminal Justice, Nineteen Forty-Nine-Nineteen Fifty-Six: A Selected Bibliography. LC 77-108219. (Criminology, Law Enforcement, & Social Problems Ser.: No. 102). 1970. Repr. of 1956 ed. 24.00x (ISBN 0-87585-102-9). Patterson Smith.
--Sources for the Study of the Administration of Criminal Justice, 1938 - 1948: A Selected Bibliography. LC 73-108218. (Criminology, Law Enforcement, & Social Problems Ser.: No. 101). 1970. Repr. of 1949 ed. 24.00x (ISBN 0-87585-101-0). Patterson Smith.
Tompkins, Iverna. The Worth of a Woman. 1978. pap. 4.95 (ISBN 0-88270-256-4, Pub. by Logos). Bridge Pub.
Tompkins, James A. & Moore, James M. Computer Aided Layout: A User's Guide. 1978. pap. text ed. 16.00 (ISBN 0-89806-003-6, 119); pap. text ed. 8.00 members. Inst Indus Eng.
Tompkins, Jim. The Trinity. (Illus.). 160p. 1983. 15.00x (ISBN 0-9609824-0-X). Yossarian Pub.
Tompkins, Keitha, jt. ed. see Capouya, Emile.
Tompkins, Peter. Secrets of the Great Pyramid. LC 74-88639. (Illus.). 1971. 25.00i (ISBN 0-06-014327-4, CN-631, HarpT); pap. 8.95i. Har-Row.
Tompkins, Peter & Bird, Christopher. The Secret Life of Plants. LC 72-9160. (Illus.). 416p. 1973. 12.95i (ISBN 0-06-014326-6, HarpT). Har-Row.

Tompkins, Phillip K. Communication as Action: An Introduction to Rehtoric & Communication. 272p. 1982. text ed. 15.95x (ISBN 0-534-01157-8). Wadsworth Pub.

Tompkins, Stuart R. The Russian Intelligentsia: Makers of the Revolutionary State. LC 75-36516. 282p. 1976. Repr. of 1957 ed. lib. bdg. 20.00x (ISBN 0-8371-8641-2, TORI). Greenwood.

Tompkins, W. & Webster, J., eds. Design of Microcomputer-Based Medical Instrumentation. 1981. 33.95 (ISBN 0-13-201244-8). P-H.

Toms, Agnes. Eat, Drink & Be Healthy. 1968. pap. 1.50 o.s.i. (ISBN 0-515-04606-X). Jove Pubns.

--The Joy of Eating Natural Foods. (Illus.). 7.95 (ISBN 0-8159-5900-1). Devin.

Tomsic, F. German-Slovene Dictionary. 989p. (Ger. & Slovene.). 1980. 49.95 (ISBN 0-686-97384-4, M-9696). French & Eur.

Tomson, Tommy. Jesuit Gold of Lower California. 1983. 12.95 (ISBN 0-533-05331-5). Vantage.

Ton, Mary E. The Flames Shall Not Consume You. 1983. pap. 5.95 (ISBN 0-89191-556-7, 55566). Cook.

Tonca, Eugenia, jt. auth. see Matasa, Claudius.

Toncre, Emery. The Action Step Plan to Owning & Operating a Successful Business. (Illus.). 228p. 1983. 15.95 (ISBN 0-13-003327-8); pap. 6.95 (ISBN 0-13-003319-7). P-H.

Tondro, Terry J. Connecticut Land Use Regulation. LC 79-68712. 356p. (Orig.). 1979. pap. text ed. 10 (ISBN 0-939328-02-X). U Conn Sch Law.

Tone, Teone. Lady on the Line. 304p. (Orig.). 1983. pap. 2.75 (ISBN 0-449-12449-5, GM). Fawcett.

Toner, P. G., et al. The Digestive System: An Ultrastructural Atlas & Review. (Illus.). 1971. 38.50 o.p. (ISBN 0-407-14850-7). Butterworth.

Toner, Peter G., jt. ed. see McLay, A. L.

Toner, Richard, jt. auth. see Whitwell, J. C.

Tonetti, Claretta. Luchino Visconti. (Filmmakers Ser.). 219p. 1983. lib. bdg. 24.00 (ISBN 0-8057-9289-9, Twayne). G K Hall.

Toney, Albert & Tilling, Thomas. Winning Investments in High-Tech. 1983. 14.95 (ISBN 0-671-46235-0). S&S.

Toney, Anthoney. Painting & Drawing: Discovering Your Own Visual Language. LC 77-11873. (Illus.). 1978. pap. 8.95 o.p. (ISBN 0-13-648105-1, Spec). P-H.

Toney, Anthony. One Hundred Fifty Masterpieces of Drawing. (Illus., Orig.). 1963. pap. 6.00 (ISBN 0-486-21032-4). Dover.

Tong, Hollington K., jt. ed. see China Ministry of Information.

Tong, L. S. Boiling Crisis & Critical Heat Flux. LC 72-600190. (AEC Critical Review Ser.). 89p. 1972. pap. 10.25 (ISBN 0-87079-154-0, TID-25887); microfiche 4.50 (ISBN 0-87079-155-9, TID-25887). DOE.

Tong, L. S. & Weisman, Joel. Thermal Analysis of Pressurized Water Reactors. 2nd, rev. ed. Wallin, Diane, ed. LC 79-54237. (Monograph). 1979. 39.50 (ISBN 0-89448-019-7, 300015). Am Nuclear Soc.

Tong, Pin & Rossettos, John N. Finite-Element Method: Basic Technique & Implementation. LC 76-7453. 1976. text ed. 21.50x (ISBN 0-262-20032-5). MIT Pr.

Tong, Y. L. Probability Inequalities in Multivariate Distribution. LC 79-27077. (Probability & Mathematical Statistics Ser.). 1980. 34.00 (ISBN 0-12-694950-6). Acad Pr.

Tonge, Frederic M. & Feldman, Julian. Computing: An Introduction to Procedure & Procedure-Followers. (Illus.). 336p. 1975. text ed. 27.95 (ISBN 0-07-064947-2, C); instructors' manual 3.00 (ISBN 0-07-064946-4). McGraw.

Tonge, W. L. The Mending of Minds: Psychiatric Illness & its Treatment: A Guide for Families. 1970. 26.00x (ISBN 0-686-97122-1, Pub. by Phillimore England). State Mutual Bk.

Tongue, Ruth L. The Chime Child: Or, Somerset Singers - Being an Account of Some of Their Songs Collected Over Sixty Years. LC 68-77292. x, 102p. Repr. of 1968 ed. 30.00x (ISBN 0-8103-5022-X). Gale.

Tonies, C., jt. auth. see Jensen, R.

Tonkin, Jim. The Book of Hereford. 1981. 39.50x o.p. (ISBN 0-86023-010-4, Pub. by Barracuda England). State Mutual Bk.

Tonkin, Peter. Killer. LC 79-1482. 1979. 9.95 (ISBN 0-698-10974-0, Coward). Putnam Pub Group.

--Killer. 1980. pap. 2.50 o.p. (ISBN 0-451-09241-4, E9241, Sig). NAL.

Tonn, Katie. I Ran Away from Home Last Week. (Uplook Ser.). 1975. pap. 0.75 o.p. (ISBN 0-8163-0174-3, 09107-4). Pacific Pr Pub Assn.

Tonndorf, Juergen, ed. Physiological Acoustics. LC 81-6488. (Benchmark Papers in Acoustics Ser.: Vol. 15). 416p. 1981. 49.00 (ISBN 0-87933-404-5). Hutchinson Ross.

Tonne. Principles of Business Education. 4th ed. 1970. 18.30 (ISBN 0-07-064968-5, G). McGraw.

Tonne, Herbert A., et al. Methods of Teaching Business Subjects. 3rd ed. 1965. text ed. 18.30 (ISBN 0-07-064953-7, G). McGraw.

Tonnelat, Marie A. Einstein's Theory of Unified Fields. 198p. 1966. 60.00x (ISBN 0-677-00810-4). Gordon.

--Principles of Electromagnetism & Relativity. 488p. 1966. 100.00x (ISBN 0-677-01220-9). Gordon.

Tonner, Leslie. Female Complaints. 272p. 1983. pap. 2.95 (ISBN 0-345-30775-5). Ballantine.

Tonnies, Ferdinand. Custom: An Essay on Social Codes. LC 61-9175. 1971. pap. 5.95 (ISBN 0-89526-990-2). Regnery-Gateway.

Tonry, Don. Sports Illustrated Tumbling. LC 82-47537. (Sports Illustrated Ser.). (Illus.). 192p. 1983. pap. 5.72i (ISBN 0-06-090984-6, CN984, CN). Har-Row.

--Sports Illustrated Tumbling. (Sports Illustrated Ser.). (Illus.). 192p. 1983. write for info. (ISBN 0-06-015022-X, HarpT). Har-Row.

--Sports Illustrated Women's Gymnastics: The Floor Exercise Event. (Sports Illustrated Bks.). (Illus.). 1980. 8.95i o.p. (ISBN 0-690-01909-2); pap. 5.95i (ISBN 0-690-01907-6). T Y Crowell.

--Sports Illustrated Women's Gymnastics: The Vaulting, Balance Beam, & Uneven Parallel Bars Events. (Sports Illustrated Bks.). (Illus.). 192p. 1980. 8.95i o.p. (ISBN 0-690-01908-4); pap. 5.95i (ISBN 0-690-01906-8). T Y Crowell.

Tonry, Michael & Morris, Norval, eds. Crime & Justice: An Annual Review of Research, Vol. 4. LC 82-13435. 344p. 1983. 25.00 (ISBN 0-226-80797-5). U of Chicago Pr.

Tonso, William R. Gun & Society: The Social & Existential Roots of the American Attachment to Firearms. LC 81-40261. 378p. (Orig.). 1982. lib. bdg. 26.50 (ISBN 0-8191-2378-1); pap. text ed. 14.25 (ISBN 0-8191-2379-X). U Pr of Amer.

Tonsor, Stephen. Tradition & Reform in Education. LC 73-82779. 262p. 1974. 17.00x (ISBN 0-87548-124-8). Open Court.

Tontsch. Fundamental Circuit Analysis. rev. ed. 512p. 1982. text ed. write for info. (ISBN 0-574-21570-0, 13-4570); write for info. sol manual (ISBN 0-574-21572-7, 13-4572). SRA.

Toogood, Alan. Propagation. LC 80-6164. (Illus.). 336p. 1982. pap. 12.95 (ISBN 0-8128-6149-3). Stein & Day.

Toohey, Barbara, jt. auth. see Biermann, June.

Toohey, Catherine, jt. auth. see Polkingharn, Anne T.

Tooker, Elisabeth. Iroquois Ceremonial of Midwinter. LC 70-119873. (New York State Studies). (Illus.). 1970. 14.95x (ISBN 0-8156-2149-3). Syracuse U Pr.

Tookey, Douglas, ed. Physical Distribution for Export. (Illus.). 215p. 1971. text ed. 21.00x o.p. (ISBN 0-8464-1267-5). Beekman Pubs.

Tool, Marc R. The Discretionary Economy. LC 78-17977. 1979. pap. text ed. 14.50x (ISBN 0-673-16158-7). Scott F.

Toole, Amy L. & Boehm, Ellen. Off to a Good Start: Four Hundred Sixty-Four Readiness Activities for Reading, Math Social Studies, & Science. (Illus.). 224p. 1983. 16.95 (ISBN 0-8027-9179-4). Walker & Co.

Toole, Blanche. Sabine County Marriages, 1875-1900, 1900-1910, Prior to 1875. LC 82-84531. 150p. (Orig.). 1983. pap. 12.50 (ISBN 0-911317-08-2). Ericson Bks.

Toole, James F. & Patel, Aneel N. Cerebrovascular Disorders. 2nd ed. (Illus.). 384p. 1973. text ed. 29.00 o.p. (ISBN 0-07-064970-7, HP). McGraw.

Toole, John K. A Confederacy of Dunces. LC 80-8922. 416p. 1982. pap. 3.95 (ISBN 0-394-17969-2, B-474, BC). Grove.

Toole, K. Ross. Montana: An Uncommon Land. (Illus.). 1977. Repr. of 1959 ed. 16.95 (ISBN 0-8061-0427-9). U of Okla Pr.

--Twentieth-Century Montana: A State of Extremes. LC 75-177348. (Illus.). 278p. (Orig.). 1983. pap. 12.95 (ISBN 0-8061-1826-1). U of Okla Pr.

Tooley, Desmond. Production Control Systems & Records. 2nd ed. 168p. 1981. text ed. 45.75x (ISBN 0-566-02253-2). Gower Pub Ltd.

Tooley, M. J., jt. auth. see Kidson, C.

Tooley, Ronald V. Some English Books with Coloured Plates. LC 75-162521. 1971. Repr. of 1935 ed. 37.00x (ISBN 0-8103-3762-2). Gale.

Toomay, John C. Radar Principles for the Non-Specialist. (Engineering Ser.). 173p. 1982. 21.95 (ISBN 0-534-97943-2). Lifetime Learn.

Toomay, Melinda, jt. auth. see Geiskopf, Susann.

Toombs, G. A., ed. see Stafl, Milos.

Toombs, Lawrence E., jt. auth. see Blakely, Jeffry A.

Toomer, Jean see Harrison, Paul C.

Toomey, Lauren, ed. see Muhaiyaddeen, Bawa M.

Toon. God Here & Now: The Christian View of God. 1979. pap. 2.95 (ISBN 0-8423-1046-0). Tyndale.

Toon, Peter & Martin, Peter, eds. Evangelical Theology, Eighteen Thirty-Three to Eighteen Fifty-Six: A Response to Tractarianism. LC 79-16701. (New Foundations Theological Library Ser.). 254p. 12.95 (ISBN 0-8042-3703-4). John Knox.

Toon, Peter, ed. see Avis, Paul D.

Toon, Peter, ed. see Carson, D. A.

Toon, Peter, jt. ed. see Martin, Ralph.

Toon, Peter, ed. see Owen, John.

Toon, Thomas E. The Politics of Early Old English Sound Change. (Quantitative Analyses of Linguistic Structure Ser.). Date not set. price not set (ISBN 0-12-694980-8). Acad Pr.

Toonder, Jan G., jt. auth. see West, John A.

Toops, Connie M. The Alligator-Monarch of the Everglades. LC 79-51891. 64p. Date not set. pap. 1.95 (ISBN 0-686-84286-3). Banyan Bks.

Toor, Ruth & Weisburg, Hilda K. The Complete Book of Forms for Managing the School Library Media Center. 256p. 1982. comb-bound 34.50x (ISBN 0-87628-229-X). Ctr Appl Res.

--Library Media Specialist's Daily Plan Book. 256p. 1982. spiral wire 16.50X (ISBN 0-87628-534-5). Ctr Appl Res.

Toorn, Pieter C. van den see Van den Toorn, Pieter C.

Tootelain, Dennis H. & Gaedeke, Ralph M. Small Business Management: Operations & Profile. 1980. text ed. 24.50x (ISBN 0-673-16145-5); o.p. instructor's manual (ISBN 0-87620-824-3); 13.95x (ISBN 0-673-16144-7). Scott F.

Tootelian, Dennis, jt. ed. see Gaedeke, Ralph M.

Tootelian, Dennis H., jt. auth. see Gaedeke, Ralph M.

Toothill, Harry. With Adams Through Japan. (Illus.). (gr. 7 up). 12.75x (ISBN 0-392-01833-0, LTB). Sportshelf.

Toothman, John M. Conducting the Small Group Experience. LC 78-59854. 1978. pap. 8.00 (ISBN 0-8191-0554-6). U Pr of Amer.

Top, Franklin & Wehrle, Paul. Communicable & Infectious Diseases. 8th ed. LC 76-25892. (Illus.). 808p. 1976. 48.50 o.p. (ISBN 0-8016-5007-0). Mosby.

Topal, Judit. The Southern Cemetery of Matricia. 106p. 1981. 90.00x (ISBN 0-569-08702-3, Pub. by Collets). State Mutual Bk.

Topalian, Elyse. V. I. Lenin. (Impact Biography Ser.). (Illus.). 128p. (gr. 7 up). 1983. PLB 8.90 (ISBN 0-531-04589-7). Watts.

Topchiev, A., et al. Alkylation with Olefins. 1964. 18.30 (ISBN 0-444-40579-8). Elsevier.

Topham, J., ed. Modern Metaphysical Lyrics. LC 81-12695. 24p. (Orig.). 1983. pap. 3.95 (ISBN 0-933486-37-5, Academic Poetry Pr.). Am Poetry Pr.

--Paradise Lost: A Continuation. LC 82-3947. 64p. (Orig.). 1983. pap. 6.95 (ISBN 0-933486-35-9, Academic Poetry Pr.). Am Poetry Pr.

--Twentieth Century Sonnets. 44p. Date not set. pap. 3.95 (ISBN 0-933486-43-X); pap. text ed. 3.95 (ISBN 0-933486-42-1). Am Poetry Pr.

Topham, J., ed. see Facos, James.

Topham, J., ed. see Hollis, Jocelyn.

Topham, J., ed. see McAfee, John P., et al.

Topham, J., ed. see Maiman, Joan M., et al.

Topham, J., ed. see Sikora, Mieczyslaw S.

Topkins, Robert M. Marriage & Death Notices from the Western Carolinian (Salisbury, North Carolina) 1820-1842: An Indexed Abstract. LC 82-20495. 264p. 1983. Repr. of 1975 ed. 22.50 (ISBN 0-87152-367-1). Reprint.

Toplin, Robert B. Freedom & Prejudice: The Legacy of Slavery in the United States & Brazil. LC 80-656. (Contributions in Afro-American & African Studies: No. 56). xxvi, 134p. 1981. lib. bdg. 25.00x (ISBN 0-313-22008-5, TFP/). Greenwood.

--Unchallenged Violence: An American Ordeal. LC 75-72. 1975. lib. bdg. 29.95x (ISBN 0-8371-7748-0, TLV/). Greenwood.

Topliss, John G., ed. Quantitative Structure-Activity Relationships of Drugs. Date not set. price not set (ISBN 0-12-695150-0). Acad Pr.

Topliss, W. S. The Optical Dispensing & Workshop Practice. 1975. 39.95 o.p. (ISBN 0-407-00025-9). Butterworth.

Topol, Allan. A Woman of Valor. LC 79-20186. 1980. 10.95 o.p. (ISBN 0-688-03578-7). Morrow.

Topolski, Diane F., jt. auth. see Silver, Jeffery H.

Toponce, Alexander. Reminiscences of Alexander Toponce. LC 71-145507. (Illus.). 1971. 7.95x o.p. (ISBN 0-8061-0954-8). U of Okla Pr.

Topp. Scientific Basis for Nuclear Waste Management. (Materials Research Society Symposia Ser.: Vol. 6). 1982. 95.00 (ISBN 0-444-00699-0). Elsevier.

Topp, Sylvia, jt. auth. see Kupferberg, Tuli.

Topper, Michael A., jt. auth. see Ewen, Dale.

Topper, Suzanne. The Fruit Cookbook. 1973. pap. 3.45 o.p. (ISBN 0-380-01202-2, 15818). Avon.

Topping, Donald. Spoken Chamorro: With Gramatical Notes & Glossary. 2nd ed. LC 80-14596. (PALI Language Texts: Micronesia). 376p. (Orig.). 1980. pap. text ed. 9.00x (ISBN 0-8248-0417-1). UH Pr.

Topping, Donald M. Chamorro Reference Grammar. LC 72-98012. (PALI Language Texts: Micronesian). 296p. 1973. pap. text ed. 8.00x (ISBN 0-8248-0269-1). UH Pr.

Topping, Donald M., et al. Chamorro-English Dictionary. LC 74-16907. (PALI Language Texts: Micronesian). 420p. (Orig.). 1975. pap. text ed. 8.00x (ISBN 0-8248-0353-1). UH Pr.

Topping, Ruth, jt. auth. see Worthington, George E.

Topping, Victor & Dempsey, S. J. Transportation: A Survey of Current Methods of Study & Instruction & of Research & Experimentation. 1926. pap. 37.50x (ISBN 0-686-51321-5). Elliots Bks.

Topsfield, L. T. Troubadours & Love. LC 74-14440. (Illus.). 304p. 1975. 44.50 (ISBN 0-521-20596-4); pap. 12.95 (ISBN 0-521-09897-1). Cambridge U Pr.

Toraldo Di Francia, G. Investigation of the Physical World. LC 80-12791. (Illus.). 480p. 1981. 65.00 (ISBN 0-521-23338-0); pap. 19.95 (ISBN 0-521-29925-X). Cambridge U Pr.

Torbe, Mike & Medway, Peter. The Climate for Learning. LC 82-14768. 160p. 1982. pap. 7.45 (ISBN 0-86709-041-3, Pub. by Writers & Readers). Boynton Cook Pub.

Torbert, William R. Creating a Community of Inquiry: Conflict, Collaboration, Transformation. LC 76-7457. (Individuals, Groups & Organizations Ser.). 184p. 1976. 34.95x (ISBN 0-471-01655-1, Pub. by Wiley-Interscience). Wiley.

Torbet, Laura & Hatton, Hap. Helpful Hints for Hard Times. 288p. 1982. 15.95 (ISBN 0-87196-617-4); pap. 7.95 (ISBN 0-87196-672-7). Facts on File.

Torbet, Laura, jt. auth. see Bach, George R.

Torbet, Laura, jt. auth. see Brill, Allen.

Torbet, Laura, jt. auth. see Nicholson, Luree.

Torbet, Robert G. A History of the Baptists. rev. ed. LC 63-8225. 592p. 1973. 19.95 (ISBN 0-8170-0074-7). Judson.

Torbiorn, I. Living Abroad: Personal Adjustment & Personnel Policy in the Overseas Setting. 200p. 1982. text ed. 32.00x (ISBN 0-471-10094-3, Pub. by Wiley-Interscience). Wiley.

Torchio, Menico. The World Beneath the Sea. (The World of Nature Ser.). (Illus.). 128p. 1973. 4.98 o.p. (ISBN 0-517-12041-0). Crown.

Torda, Clara. Information Processing: The Central Nervous System & the Computer. Walters, ed. 157p. 1982. pap. 9.50 (ISBN 0-686-35738-8). Walters Pub.

Tordoff, William, ed. Government & Politics in Zambia. LC 73-86660. (Perspectives on Southern Africa Ser). 1975. 35.75x (ISBN 0-520-02593-8). U of Cal Pr.

Tordoir, jt. auth. see Van Heemstra-Lequir, A. H.

Tordoir, W. F. & Van Hemstra-Lequin, E. A., eds. Field Worker Exposure During Pesticide Application. (Studies in Environmental Science: Vol. 7). 1980. 47.00 (ISBN 0-444-41879-2). Elsevier.

Torelli, Mario. Typology & Structure of Roman Historical Reliefs. (Jerome Lectures Fourteenth Ser.). 1982. text ed. 25.00x (ISBN 0-472-10014-9). U of Mich Pr.

Torg, R. & Puthoff, H. Mindreach: Scientists Look at Psychic Ability. 1978. pap. 4.95 o.s.i. (ISBN 0-440-55665-1, Delta). Dell.

Torgersen, Don. Elephant Herds & Rhino Horns. LC 81-10158. (Animal Safari Nature Library). (Illus.). (gr. 4 up). 1982. PLB 9.95g (ISBN 0-516-00652-5); pap. 3.95 (ISBN 0-516-40652-3). Childrens.

--Giraffe Hooves & Antelope Horns. LC 81-15508. (Animal Safari Nature Library). (Illus.). (gr. 4 up). 1982. PLB 9.95g (ISBN 0-516-00655-X); pap. 3.95 (ISBN 0-516-40655-8). Childrens.

--Killer Whales & Dolphin Play. LC 81-15480. (Animal Safari Nature Library). (Illus.). (gr. 4 up). 1982. PLB 9.95g (ISBN 0-516-00653-3); pap. 3.95 (ISBN 0-516-40653-1). Childrens.

--The Last Days of Gorlock the Dragon. LC 81-38551. (Troll & Gnome Stories Ser.). (Illus.). 32p. (gr. k-4). 1982. PLB 8.65 (ISBN 0-516-03743-9); pap. text ed. 2.95 (ISBN 0-516-43743-7). Childrens.

--Lion Prides & Tiger Tracks. LC 81-10074. (Animal Safari Nature Library). (Illus.). (gr. 4 up). 1982. PLB 9.95g (ISBN 0-516-00654-1); pap. 3.95 (ISBN 0-516-40654-X). Childrens.

--The Secret of Cathedral Lake: Troll & Gnome Stories. LC 81-3877. (Illus.). 32p. (gr. k-4). 1981. PLB 9.25 (ISBN 0-516-03742-0); pap. 2.95 (ISBN 0-516-43742-9). Childrens.

Torgersen, Eric. Ethiopia. 1977. pap. 3.50 (ISBN 0-914610-06-6). Hanging Loose.

Torgerson, Paul E. & Weinstock, Irwin T. Management: An Integrated Approach. LC 71-162354. (Illus.). 1972. text ed. 22.00 o.p. (ISBN 0-13-548396-4). P-H.

Torgerson, Peter G. Torrek & the Elfin Girl: (Troll & Gnome Stories) LC 81-10047. (Illus.). 32p. (gr. k-4). 1981. PLB 9.25 (ISBN 0-516-03741-2); pap. 2.95 (ISBN 0-516-43741-0). Childrens.

Torgerson, Warren S. Theory & Method of Scaling. LC 58-10812. (Illus.). 1958. 33.50x (ISBN 0-471-87945-2). Wiley.

Torgeson, Dewayne C., ed. Fungicides: An Advanced Treatise, Vols. 1-2. 1969. Vol. 1. 78.50 (ISBN 0-12-695601-4); Vol. 2. 85.00 (ISBN 0-12-695602-2). Acad Pr.

Torgeson, Roy. Chrysalis Ten. LC 81-640147. (Science Fiction Ser.). 192p. 1983. 11.95 (ISBN 0-385-17598-1). Doubleday.

Torgoff, Martin, ed. The Complete Elvis. LC 81-71011. (Illus.). 256p. (Orig.). 1982. 24.95 (ISBN 0-933328-28-1); pap. 13.95 (ISBN 0-933328-20-6). Delilah Bks.

Torgoff, Martin, ed. see Amazing Randi & Sugar, Bert R.

Torines, John B. The Packer Legend: An Inside Look. (Illus.). 251p. 1982. deluxe ed. 24.95 (ISBN 0-910937-00-1). Laranmark.

Torky, Mohamed A. El see Correa, Hector & El Torky, Mohamed A.

Torloni, H., jt. auth. see Scarff, R. W.

Tormey, John. Emotional Child Abuse: Don't Hurt Your Child! LC 78-73622. (Illus.). 1979. pap. 1.95 o.p. (ISBN 0-8189-1158-1, 158, Pub. by Alba Bks). Alba.

Tormey, John C. Tell Me Again You Love Me. LC 75-44675. (Illus.). 128p. 1976. pap. 1.65 o.p. (ISBN 0-8189-1128-X, Pub. by Alba Bks). Alba.

--What's Cooking in the Priesthood? LC 74-28963. (Illus.). 128p. 1975. pap. 1.25 o.p. (ISBN 0-8189-1120-4, Pub. by Alba Bks). Alba.

Tornabene, Lyn. Long Live the King: A Biography of Clark Gable. LC 76-43227. (Illus.). 1977. 10.95 (ISBN 0-399-11863-2). Putnam Pub Group.

Tornatzky, Louis G. Innovation & Social Process: A National Experiment in Implementing Social Technology. LC 80-36809. (Pergamon Policy Studies on Politics, Policy & Modeling). 150p. 1981. 25.00 (ISBN 0-08-026303-8). Pergamon.

Torney, John A., Jr. & Clayton, Robert D. Aquatic Organization & Management. 190p. 1981. pap. text ed. 10.95x (ISBN 0-8087-3624-8). Burgess.

Torney, Judith, et al. Civic Education in Ten Countries: An Empirical Study. LC 75-42147. (International Studies in Evaluation: Vol. 6). 1976. pap. 35.95x o.p. (ISBN 0-470-14989-2). Halsted Pr.

Torney, Judith V., et al. Civic Education in Ten Countries. LC 75-42147. 341p. 1975. pap. 21.50 o.p. (ISBN 0-470-14989-2, Pub. by Wiley). Krieger.

Torney-Purta, Judith, jt. ed. see Branson, Margaret S.

Torng. Switching Circuits: Theory & Logic Design. 1976. 25.95 (ISBN 0-201-07576-8). A-W.

Tornya, Rheba de see Poshek, Neila & De Tornya, Rheba.

Toro, V. Del see Del Toro, V.

Toro, Vincent Del see Del Toro, Vincent.

Torosian, Martin. Securities Transfer: Principles & Procedures. 4th ed. LC 82-14245. 368p. 1982. 25.00 (ISBN 0-13-799072-3). NY Inst Finance.

Torp, Jens, jt. auth. see Marcussen, Henrik.

Torp, Thaddeus L., ed. see Strindberg, August & Ibsen, Henrik.

Torrance, E. Paul. The Search for "Satori" & Creativity. LC 79-65469. 1979. pap. 9.50 (ISBN 0-930222-04-0). Creat Educ Found.

Torrance, G. F. see Barth, Karl.

Torrance, Kenneth, jt. auth. see Midgley, Derek.

Torrance, Thomas F. Apocalypse Today. 192p. 1960. 10.95 (ISBN 0-227-67405-7). Attic Pr.

--Calvin's Doctrine of Man. LC 77-5615. 1977. Repr. lib. bdg. 17.50x (ISBN 0-8371-9639-6, TOCD). Greenwood.

--Divine & Contingent Order. 176p. 1981. 29.95x (ISBN 0-19-826658-8). Oxford U Pr.

--Space, Time & Incarnation. 1978. pap. 4.95 (ISBN 0-19-520082-9, GB562, GB). Oxford U Pr.

--Theological Science. 1978. pap. 7.95 (ISBN 0-19-520083-7, GB563, GB). Oxford U Pr.

Torre, Frank D. Woodworking for Kids. LC 77-76264. (gr. 3-7). 1978. 7.95a (ISBN 0-385-11430-3); PLB (ISBN 0-385-11431-1). Doubleday.

Torre, Joe & Ryan, Nolan. Pitching & Hitting. Cohen, Joel, ed. LC 77-23327. (Illus.). 1977. 7.95 o.p. (ISBN 0-13-676205-0). P-H.

Torre, K. W. Von Della see Von Dalla Torre, K. W. & Harms, H.

Torre, Susana, ed. Women in American Architecture: A Historic & Contemporary Perspective. (Illus.). 1977. 25.00 (ISBN 0-8230-7485-4, Whitney Lib). Watson-Guptill.

Torre Bueno, Laura De La see Graham, Munir & De la Torre Bueno, Laura.

Torrence, Kathy. An Art Noveau Album. (Illus.). 80p. 1981. pap. 10.95 (ISBN 0-525-47635-0). Dutton.

Torrence, Rosemary. Mending Our Nets. 176p. 1980. 10.95 (ISBN 0-697-01757-5). Wm C Brown.

Torrens, I. M., jt. auth. see Chadderton, L. T.

Torrens, Ian. Changing Structures in the World Oil Market. (The Atlantic Papers: No. 41). 43p. (Orig.). 1981. pap. text ed. 6.50 (ISBN 0-86598-049-7). Allanheld.

Torrens, Ian M. Interatomic Potentials. 1972. 48.50 (ISBN 0-12-695850-5). Acad Pr.

Torrens, P. R., jt. auth. see Williams, S. J.

Torrents, J. M. Abandoned Spouse. 1969. 5.75 o.p. (ISBN 0-685-07605-9, 80734). Glencoe.

Torres, Angel. The Baseball Bible. LC 81-81949. (Illus.). 480p. 1983. pap. 14.95 (ISBN 0-86666-080-1). GWP.

Torres, Elena, tr. see Jacobson, R. E.

Torres, Esther Z. De see Borges, Jorge L. & De Torres, Esther Z.

Torres, F. F., jt. ed. see Encarnacas, J.

Torres, Francisco R. Spanish-Espanol-English: Determinos Medicos. pap. 60.95 o.p. (ISBN 84-205-0455-6). Larousse.

Torres, Gertrude & Kelley, Jean. Curriculum Revision in Baccalaureate Nursing Education. (Faculty-Curriculum Development Ser.: Pt. VI). 49p. 1975. 4.25 (ISBN 0-686-38270-6, 15-1576). Natl League Nurse.

Torres, Gertrude & Lynch, Eleanor A. Unifying the Curriculum: The Integrated Approach. (Faculty-Curriculum Development Ser.: Pt. IV). 46p. 1974. 3.95 (ISBN 0-686-38268-4, 15-1552). Natl League Nurse.

Torres, Gertrude & Stanton, Marjorie. Curriculum Process in Nursing: A Guide to Curriculum Development. (Illus.). 208p. 1982. 18.95 (ISBN 0-13-196261-2). P-H.

Torres, Gertrude & Yura, Helen. Conceptual Framework-Its Meaning & Function. (Faculty-Curriculum Development Ser.: Pt. III). 56p. 1975. 4.50 (ISBN 0-686-38267-6, 15-1558). Natl League Nurse.

Torres, Gertrude J., jt. auth. see Lynch, Eleanor A.

Torres, Gertrude J., jt. auth. see Yura, Helen.

Torres, Lillian S. & Moore, Carol M. Basic Medical Techniques & Patient Care for Radiologic Technologists. LC 78-10520. 1978. 16.75 o.p. (ISBN 0-397-54222-4, Lippincott Medical). Lippincott.

Torres, Miguel. Wines & Vineyards of Spain. 200p. 1982. 19.95 (ISBN 0-932664-27-X). Wine Appreciation.

Torres, Sergio, jt. ed. see Appiah-Kubi, Kofi.

Torres, Sergio, jt. ed. see Fabella, Virginia.

Torres, Victor. El Hijo de La Calle Tenebrosa. 160p. Date not set. 2.25 (ISBN 0-88113-100-8). Edit Betania.

Torres-Gil, Fernando M. Politics of Aging Among Elder Hispanics. LC 82-16067. 230p. (Orig.). 1983. lib. bdg. 23.00 (ISBN 0-8191-2756-6); pap. text ed. 10.75 (ISBN 0-8191-2757-4). U Pr of Amer.

Torres-Metzgar, Joseph V. Below the Summit. LC 76-41036. 1976. pap. 5.00 (ISBN 0-89229-005-6). Tonatiuh-Quinto Sol Intl.

Torres-Reyes, Ricardo, jt. auth. see Manucy, Albert.

Torres-Rioseco, Arturo. New World Literature: Tradition & Revolt in Latin America. LC 82-20961. 250p. 1983. Repr. of 1949 ed. lib. bdg. 29.75x (ISBN 0-313-23444-2, TRNW). Greenwood.

Torrey, A. Holy Spirit: Who He Is & What He Does. 208p. 1927. 11.95 (ISBN 0-8007-0139-9). Revell.

Torrey Botanical Club, N.Y. Annual Index to Botanical Literature: 1979. 1980. lib. bdg. 130.00 (ISBN 0-8161-0369-0, Hall Library). G K Hall.

Torrey, Charles C. Chronicler's History of Israel: Chronicles-Ezra-Nehemiah Restored to It's Original Form. 1954. text ed. 11.50x (ISBN 0-686-37866-0). Elliots Bks.

Torrey, Charles G. Apocalypse of John. 1958. text ed. 29.50x (ISBN 0-686-83474-7). Elliots Bks.

Torrey, John G. Development in Flowering Plants. (Orig.). 1967. pap. text ed. 8.95x (ISBN 0-02-420960-0). Macmillan.

Torrey, Norman L., jt. auth. see Fellows, Otis E.

Torrey, R. A. Como Obtener la Plenitud Del Poder. Rivas, Jose G., tr. from Eng. Orig. Title: How to Obtain Fullness of Power. 112p. (Span.). 1980. pap. 2.20 (ISBN 0-311-46083-6). Casa Bautista.

--How to Obtain Fullness of Power. 96p. 1982. pap. text ed. 2.95 (ISBN 0-88368-116-1). Whitaker Hse.

--Revival Addresses. 282p. 1974. Repr. of 1903 ed. 10.95 (ISBN 0-227-67808-7). Attic Pr.

Torrey, Reuben A. How to Pray. pap. 2.95 (ISBN 0-8024-3709-5). Moody.

--Preguntas Practicas y Dificiles. Orig. Title: Practical & Perplexing Questions Answered. (Span). 1909. pap. 2.95 (ISBN 0-8024-6810-1). Moody.

Torrey, S., ed. Adhesive Technology: Developments Since 1977. LC 79-25936. (Chemical Technology Review Ser.: No. 148). (Illus.). 500p. 1980. 54.00 (ISBN 0-8155-0787-9). Noyes.

--Coal Ash Utilization-Fly Ash, Bottom Ash & Slag. LC 78-62525. (Pollution Technology Review: No. 48). (Illus.). 1979. 39.00 o.p. (ISBN 0-8155-0722-4). Noyes.

--Edible Oils & Fats: Developments Since 1978. LC 82-19091. (Food Technology Review: No. 57). (Illus.). 402p. 1983. 44.00 (ISBN 0-8155-0923-5). Noyes.

--Pre-emergence Herbicides: Recent Advances. LC 82-7954. (Chemical Technology Rev. 211). (Illus.). 335p. 1983. 48.00 (ISBN 0-8155-0914-6). Noyes.

Torrey, Theodore W. & Feduccia, Alan. Morphogenesis of the Vertebrates. 4th ed. LC 78-17196. 1979. 30.95 (ISBN 0-471-03232-8). Wiley.

Torrie, James H., jt. auth. see Steel, Robert G.

Torrington, Derek. Comparative Industrial Relations in Europe. LC 78-1359. (Contributions in Economics & Economic History: No. 21). 1978. lib. bdg. 29.95x (ISBN 0-313-20366-0, TCI/). Greenwood.

Torrington, Derek & Hitner, Trevor. Management & the Multi-Racial Work Force. 117p. 1982. text ed. 34.00x (ISBN 0-566-00585-9). Gower Pub Ltd.

Torrington, Derek, jt. auth. see Cooper, Cary.

Torrington, William, ed. House of Lords Sessional Papers, 1714-1805, 60 vols. LC 70-141328. 1972. 75.00 ea. (ISBN 0-379-20014-7); Vols. 1-4 & index. 100.00 ea. (ISBN 0-379-20015-5). Oceana.

Torshen, K. P. The Mastery Approach to Competency - Based Education. 1977. 25.00 (ISBN 0-12-696050-X). Acad Pr.

Torsoli, A. & Lucchelli, P. E. Further Experience with H-Receptor Antagonists in Peptic Ulcer Disease & Progress in Histamine Research. (International Congress Ser.: Vol. 521). 1980. 69.00 (ISBN 0-444-90147-7). Elsevier.

Torssell, Kurt. Natural Product Chemistry: A Mechanistic & Biosynthetic Approach to Secondary Metabolism. 1982. 54.95 (ISBN 0-471-10378-0, Pub. by Wiley-Interscience). Wiley.

Tort, Patrick & Desalmand, Paul. Sciences Humaines et Philosophie en Afrique: La Difference Culturelle. (Illus.). 399p. (Orig., Fr.). 1978. pap. text ed. 21.00 (ISBN 2-218-04222-3). Intl Pubns Serv.

Tortora. Principios de Anatomia y Fisiolologia. 3rd ed. 1983. pap. text ed. write for info. (ISBN 0-06-317153-8, Pub. by HarLA Mexico). Har-Row.

--Principios de Fisiocogia Humana. (Span.). 1983. pap. text ed. price not set (ISBN 0-06-317149-X, Pub. by HarLA Mexico). Har-Row.

Tortora, et al. Microbiology: An Introduction. 1982. 29.95 (ISBN 0-8053-9310-2, 39310); instr's guide 4.95 (ISBN 0-8053-9311-0); study guide 8.95 (ISBN 0-8053-9312-9). Benjamin-Cummings.

Tortora, Daniel F. The Right Dog For You: Choosing a Breed that Matches Your Personality, Family & Lifestyle. (Illus.). 384p. 1983. pap. 8.95 (ISBN 0-671-47247-X, Fireside). S&S.

Tortora, Gerard. Principles of Human Anatomy. 2nd ed. (Illus.). 1980. text ed. 29.00 scp o.p. (ISBN 0-06-046637-5, HarpC); instrs,. manual avail. o.p. (ISBN 0-06-366636-7). Har-Row.

Tortora, Gerard J. Principles of Human Anatomy. 3rd ed. 704p. 1983. text ed. 30.50 scp (ISBN 0-06-046634-0, HarpC); instr's. manual avail. (ISBN 0-06-366638-3); scp learning guide 9.50 (ISBN 0-06-045291-9). Har-Row.

Tortora, Gerard J. & Anagnostakos, Nicholas P. Laboratory Exercises in Anatomy & Physiology with Cat Dissections. 1980. pap. text ed. 15.95x (ISBN 0-8087-3609-4). Burgess.

--Principles of Anatomy & Physiology. 3rd ed. (Illus.). 826p. 1981. text ed. 30.95 scp (ISBN 0-06-046642-1, HarpC); scp learning guide 13.50 (ISBN 0-06-045289-7); instr. manual avail. (ISBN 0-06-366637-5); test bank avail. (ISBN 0-06-362582-2); transparencies avail. (ISBN 0-06-362581-4). Har-Row.

Tortora, Phyllis G. Understanding Textiles. 2nd ed. 1982. text ed. 22.95 (ISBN 0-02-420870-1). Macmillan.

Tortoriello, Thomas R. & DeWine, Sue. Communication in the Organization: An Applied Approach. 1978. pap. text ed. 19.95 (ISBN 0-07-064989-8, C); instr's. manual 15.00 (ISBN 0-07-064990-1). McGraw.

Tosaw, Richard T. D. B. Cooper... Dead or Alive? LC 82-90414. (Illus., Orig.). Date not set. pap. 4.50 (ISBN 0-9609016-0-4). Tosaw.

Tosches, Nick. Country: The Biggest Music in America. 1979. pap. 5.95 o.s.i. (ISBN 0-440-51440-1, Delta). Dell.

--Hellfire: The Jerry Lee Lewis Story. LC 81-12460. (Illus.). 263p. 12.95 o.s.i. (ISBN 0-440-03546-5). Delacorte.

--Rear View. (Illus.). 96p. (Orig.). 1981. pap. 8.95 (ISBN 0-933328-06-0). Delilah Bks.

Tosco, Uberto. World of Mushrooms. (World of Nature Ser.). 1973. 4.98 o.p. (ISBN 0-517-12039-9, Bounty Books). Crown.

--The World of Wildflowers & Trees. (The World of Nature Ser.). (Illus.). 128p. 1973. 4.98 o.p. (ISBN 0-517-12037-2, Bounty Books). Crown.

Tosh & Ordway. Real Estate Math Made Easy. 1981. text ed. 17.95 (ISBN 0-8359-6556-2); instr's. manual o.p. free (ISBN 0-8359-6557-0). Reston.

Tosh, Dennis S. & Furukawa, James. Narello-Guide to Examinations & Careers in Real Estate. (Illus.). 1979. text ed. 13.95 (ISBN 0-8359-4872-2); pap. text ed. 8.95 (ISBN 0-8359-4871-4). Reston.

Toshihiko, Shimada, et al. Japan's Road to the Pacific War: The China Quagmire. Morley, James W., ed. Crowley, James B., tr. from Japanese. (Studies of the East Asian Institute). 508p. 1983. 30.00x (ISBN 0-231-05522-6). Columbia U Pr.

Tosi, Henry L. Readings in Management: Contingencies, Structure & Process. LC 76-5292. (Illus.). 1976. pap. text ed. 16.95x (ISBN 0-471-06235-9). Wiley.

--Theories of Organization. LC 75-17063. (Illus.). 160p. 1975. pap. text ed. 13.50x (ISBN 0-471-06237-5). Wiley.

Tosi, Henry L. & Carroll, Stephen J. Management: Contingencies, Structure & Process. 2nd ed. LC 75-43280. (Series in Critical Sociologies). (Illus.). 608p. 1976. text ed. 26.95 (ISBN 0-471-07884-0). Wiley.

Tosi, Henry L., jt. auth. see Carroll, Stephen J.

Tosi, Henry L. & Hamner, W. Clay, eds. Organizational Behavior & Management: A Contingency Approach. 3rd ed. LC 77-77475. (Series in Critical Sociologies). 1977. pap. text ed. 20.95 (ISBN 0-471-08504-9). Wiley.

Tosi, M. P., jt. auth. see March, N. H.

Tosi, Pietro F. Observations on the Florid Song. 2nd ed. Repr. of 1743 ed. 37.50 (ISBN 0-384-60980-5). Johnson Repr.

Tosi, Umberto, jt. auth. see Sakhorov, Valdimir.

Toskes, P. The Digestive System: Disease, Diagnosis, Treatment. (Clinical Monographs Ser.). (Illus.). 1975. pap. 7.95 o.p. (ISBN 0-87618-063-2). R J Brady.

Toskes, P. P. Antibiotic Therapy. (Clinical Monographs Ser.). (Illus.). 1974. pap. 7.95 o.p. (ISBN 0-87618-061-6). R J Brady.

Toski, Bob & Aultman, Dick. Bob Toski's Complete Guide to Better Golf. LC 75-39958. (Illus.). 1980. pap. 10.95 (ISBN 0-689-70592-1). Atheneum.

Tosteson, D. C. & Ovchinnikov, Yu. A., eds. Membrane Transport Processes, Vol. 2. LC 76-19934. 468p. 1977. 48.00 (ISBN 0-89004-174-1). Raven.

Totemeyer, Gerhard. Namibia Old & New: Traditional & Modern Leaders in Ovamboland. LC 78-50675. (Illus.). 1978. 26.00x (ISBN 0-312-55877-5). St Martin.

Totenham, Kathrine. All About the Lurcher. (All About Ser.). (Illus.). 150p. 1983. 12.95 (ISBN 0-7207-1441-9, Pub by Michael Joseph). Merrimack Bk Serv.

Toth, A. G. Legal Protection of Individuals in the European Communities, Vols. 1 & 2. 1978. Vol. 1: The Individual & Community Law. 38.50 (ISBN 0-444-85044-9, North-Holland); Vol. 2: Remedies & Procedures. 72.50 (ISBN 0-444-85045-7); Set. 93.75 (ISBN 0-444-85046-5). Elsevier.

Toth, Louis E. Transition Metal Carbides & Nitrides. (Refractory Materials Ser.: Vol. 7). 1971. 54.00 (ISBN 0-12-695950-1). Acad Pr.

Toth, Marian D. Tales From Thailand: Folklore, Culture, & History. LC 77-125563. (Illus.). 184p. 1983. 14.50 (ISBN 0-8048-0563-6). C E Tuttle.

Toth, Max. Pyramid Power. (Illus.). 257p. pap. 2.95 (ISBN 0-686-33187-7, Warner-Destiny). Inner Tradit.

--Pyramid Prophecies. (Illus.). 368p. pap. 2.50 (ISBN 0-686-33188-5, Warner-Destiny). Inner Tradit.

Toth, Michael A. The Theory of the Two Charismas. LC 81-40054. 204p. (Orig.). 1982. lib. bdg. 23.00 (ISBN 0-8191-2011-1); pap. text ed. 10.50 (ISBN 0-8191-2012-X). U Pr of Amer.

Toth, Robin & Hostage, Jacqueline. Does Your Lunch Pack Punch For the Crunch & Munch Bunch? LC 82-24512. (Illus.). 160p. 1983. pap. 6.95 (ISBN 0-932620-20-5). Betterway Pubns.

Toth, Robin H. Naturally It's Good...I Cooked It Myself. 176p. 1982. 9.95 (ISBN 0-932620-09-4, Pub. by Betterway Publications). Berkshire Traveller.

Totman, Conrad. The Collapse of the Tokugawa Bakufu: Eighteen Sixty-Two to Eighteen Sixty-Eight. LC 79-22094. (Illus.). 1980. text ed. 25.00x (ISBN 0-8248-0614-X). UH Pr.

--Japan Before Perry: A Short History. (Illus.). 275p. 1982. 20.00x (ISBN 0-520-04132-1); pap. 6.95 (ISBN 0-520-04134-8). U of Cal Pr.

Tottel, R. Tottel's Miscellany, 1557-1587, 2 Vols. rev. ed. Rollins, Hyder E., ed. LC 64-22722. 1965. Set. boxed 40.00x (ISBN 0-674-89610-6). Harvard U Pr.

Totten, George O., III, jt. ed. see Schmidhauser, John R.

Totten, Herman L., jt. ed. see Cassata, Mary B.

Tottenham, Katharine. Horse & Pony Breeding Explained. LC 78-9001. (Horseman's Handbook Ser.). (Illus.). 1979. 7.95 o.p. (ISBN 0-668-04580-9); pap. 3.95 (ISBN 0-668-04584-1). Arco.

Tottenham, Katherine & Nicholas, Anna K. This Is the Jack Russell Terrier. (Illus.). 192p. 1982. 19.95 (ISBN 0-87666-746-9, H-1053). TFH Pubns.

Totterdell, B., et al, eds. The Effective Library. 1976. 34.50x o.p. (ISBN 0-85365-248-1, Pub. by Lib Assn England). Oryx Pr.

Tottie, Malcolm, jt. ed. see Sjoqvist, Folke.

Tottle, C. R. Encyclopedia of Metallurgy & Materials. (Illus.). 800p. 1983. text ed. 85.00x (ISBN 0-911378-45-6). Sheridan.

Tottress, Richard E. Twenty-Five Silver "A" Broadcasts. 1979. 6.50 o.p. (ISBN 0-533-03714-X). Vantage.

Tou, J. T. & Gonzalez, R. C. Pattern Recognition Principles: Applied Mathematics & Computation Ser. 2nd ed. 1975. text ed. 34.50 (ISBN 0-201-07587-3); instr's man. 4.50 (ISBN 0-201-07588-1). A-W.

Tou, Julius. Optimum Design of Digital Control Systems Via Dynamic Programming. (Mathematics in Science & Engineering: Vol. 10). 1963. 38.50 (ISBN 0-12-696250-2). Acad Pr.

--Software Engineering, Vols. 1-2. 1970. Vol. 1. 44.00 (ISBN 0-12-696201-4); Vol. 2. 50.50 (ISBN 0-12-696202-2). Acad Pr.

Tou, Julius T., ed. Applied Automata Theory. LC 68-26634. (Electrical Science Ser). 1969. 63.50 (ISBN 0-12-696230-8). Acad Pr.

Touche Ross & Co. Controlling Assets & Transactions in Hospitals: How to Improve Internal Accounting Control. Rev. ed. (Illus.). 108p. 1982. pap. 9.95 (ISBN 0-930228-17-0). Healthcare Fin Man Assn.

Touchie-Specht, Phyllis, jt. auth. see Kefgen, Mary.

Touchstone, Billie L. Redneck Country Cookin' 100p. (Orig.). 1982. pap. 3.95 (ISBN 0-941186-03-2). Twin Oaks LA.

Touchstone, J. C. Practice of Thin Layer Chromatography. 2nd ed. 432p. 1983. 40.00x (ISBN 0-471-09766-7, Pub. by Wiley-Interscience). Wiley.

Touchstone, J. C. & Sherma, J. Densitometry in Thin Layer Chromatography: Practice & Applications. 747p. 1979. text ed. 58.50 (ISBN 0-471-88041-8, Pub. by Wiley Interscience). Wiley.

Touchstone, Joseph C. Advances in Thin Layer Chromatography: Clinical & Environmental Applications. LC 81-23146. 544p. 1982. text ed. 55.00x (ISBN 0-471-09936-8, Pub. by Wiley-Interscience). Wiley.

Touchstone, Joseph C. & Dobbins, Murrell F. Practice of Thin Layer Chromatography. LC 77-22075. 383p. 1978. 40.00x (ISBN 0-471-88042-6, Pub. by Wiley-Interscience). Wiley.

Touchstone, Joseph C. & Rogers, Dexter. Thin Layer Chromatography: Quantitative Environmental & Clinical Applications. LC 80-36871. 561p. 1980. 57.95x (ISBN 0-471-07958-8, Pub. by Wiley-Interscience). Wiley.

Touchstone, Joseph C., ed. Quantitative Thin Layer Chromatography. LC 72-13689. 330p. 1973. 44.00x (ISBN 0-471-88040-X, Pub. by Wiley-Interscience). Wiley.

Toudouza, George J see Swan, D. K.

Tougas, Gerard. History of French-Canadian Literature. 2nd ed. Cook, Alta L., tr. from Fr. LC 76-7977. 1976. Repr. of 1966 ed. lib. bdg. 20.00x (ISBN 0-8371-8858-X, TOHF). Greenwood.

Tough, Allen. The Adult's Learning Projects. 2nd ed. 1979. 16.95 (ISBN 0-89384-045-9). Learning Concepts.

Touhey, John C. Student Study Guide to the Child. 1980. 9.95 (ISBN 0-8053-9012-X). Benjamin Cummings.

Toulfanidis, Nick. Fundamentals of Ionizing Radiation Measurements. (Illus.). 592p. 1983. text ed. 39.95x (ISBN 0-07-065397-6, C). McGraw.

Touliatos, John & Compton, Norma. Approaches to Child Study. 336p. (Orig.). 1983. text ed. write for info (ISBN 0-8087-3636-1). Burgess.

Toulmin, Stephen. The Philosophy of Science. 1977. pap. 3.95xi (ISBN 0-06-130513-8, TB513, Torch). Har-Row.

--The Return to Cosmology: Postmodern Science & the Theology of Nature. 224p. 1982. 17.95 (ISBN 0-520-04295-6). U of Cal Pr.

Toulmin, Stephen, et al. An Introduction to Reasoning. 1979. text ed. 20.95x (ISBN 0-02-421030-7). Macmillan.

Toulmin, Stephen E. Foresight & Understanding: An Enquiry into the Aims of Science. LC 81-13446. 115p. 1982. Repr. of 1961 ed. lib. bdg. 20.75x (ISBN 0-313-23345-4, TOFO). Greenwood.

Touloukian, R. J. Pediatric Trauma. 646p. 1978. 84.00 (ISBN 0-471-01500-8, Pub. by Wiley Med). Wiley.

Touloukian, U. S. & Ho, C. Y. Physical Properties of Rocks & Minerals, Vol. II. (M-H-CINDAS Data Series on Material Properties). (Illus.). 576p. 1981. text ed. 47.50 (ISBN 0-07-065032-2). McGraw.

Touloukian, Y. S. & Ho, C. Y. Properties of Nonmetallic Fluid Elements, Vol. III. (M-H-CINDAS Data Series on Material Properties). 224p. 1981. text ed. 36.50 (ISBN 0-07-065033-0). McGraw.

--Properties of Selected Ferrous Alloying Elements, Vol. III. (M-H-CINDAS Data Series on Material Properties). 288p. 1981. text ed. 36.50 (ISBN 0-07-065034-9). McGraw.

--Thermal Accommodation & Adsorption Coefficients of Gases, Vol. II-1. 1st ed. (McGraw-Hill-CINDAS Data Ser. on Material Properties). 448p. (Orig.). 1981. 45.50 (ISBN 0-07-065031-4). McGraw.

Toulouse, Gerard, jt. auth. see Pfeuty, Pierre.

Toulous-Latrec, Henri de. Great Lithographs of Toulouse-Lautrec Including 8 in Full Color. (Fine Art, History of Art Ser.). (Illus.). 104p. (Orig.). Date not set. pap. 6.95 (ISBN 0-486-24359-1). Dover.

Touraine. Transplantation & Clinical Immunology, No. 11. (Symposia Foundation Merieux Ser.: Vol. 3). 1980. 66.50 (ISBN 0-444-90118-3). Elsevier.

Touraine, ed. Transplantation & Clinical Immunology, No. 12. (Symposia Foundation Merieux Ser.: Vol. 4). 1981. 55.75 (ISBN 0-444-90184-1). Elsevier.

Touraine, Alain. The Voice & the Eye: The Analysis of Social Movements. Duff, Alan, tr. from Fr. Orig. Title: Le Voix et le Regard. 1981. 39.50 (ISBN 0-521-23874-9); pap. 14.95 (ISBN 0-521-28271-3). Cambridge U Pr.

Touraine, J. L. Bone Marrow Transplantation in Europe. (Symposia Foundation Merieux: Vol. 2). 1980. 50.25 (ISBN 0-444-90113-2). Elsevier.

Touraine, J. L., ed. Bone Marrow Transplantation Two. (Symposia Fondation Merieux: Vol. 6). 1981. 57.50 (ISBN 0-444-90204-X). Elsevier.

--Transplantation & Clinical Immunology: Proceedings of the International Course, 13th, Lyon, June 15-17, 1981, No. XIII. (Symposia Foundation Merieux 1981 Ser.: Vol. 7). 284p. 1982. 55.50 (ISBN 0-444-90205-8). Elsevier.

Tourangeau, Kevin. Strategy Management: How to Plan, Execute & Control Strategic Plans for Your Business. 256p. 1980. 21.00 (ISBN 0-07-065043-8, P&RB). McGraw.

Tourda, Wayne F. Basic Aikido. (Illus.). 77p. (Orig.). 1981. pap. text ed. 8.00 (ISBN 0-942728-03-3). Custom Pub Co.

Tourda, Wayne F. & Dye, David A. Intermediate Aikido. 97p. (Orig.). 1982. pap. 15.00 (ISBN 0-686-38101-7). Aikido Fed.

Toure, Ahmed S. Africa on the Move. 612p. 1981. 30.00x o.p. (ISBN 0-901787-50-7, Pub. by Panaf Bks England). State Mutual Bk.

Toure, H. Pain. 1981. 8.90 (ISBN 0-531-02203-X). Watts.

Tourette, Jacquelin La see La Tourrette, Jacqueline.

Tourgueniev, Nicolas I. Un Dernier Mot sur l'Emancipation des Serfs en Russie. (Nineteenth Century Russia Ser.). 114p. (Fr.). 1974. Repr. of 1860 ed. lib. bdg. 38.50x o.p. (ISBN 0-8287-0828-2, R61). Clearwater Pub.

--La Russie et les Russes, 3 vols. (Nineteenth Century Russia Ser.). (Fr.). 1974. Repr. of 1847 ed. Set. lib. bdg. 402.50x o.p. (ISBN 0-8287-0829-0). Vol. 1 (R56). Vol. 2 (R57). Vol. 3 (R58). Clearwater Pub.

Tourlakis. Computability. 1983. text ed. 27.95 (ISBN 0-8359-0876-3). Reston.

Tourney, Leonard. Low Treason. 228p. 1983. 12.95 (ISBN 0-525-24153-1, 01258-370). Dutton.

--The Player's Boy Is Dead. LC 80-7611. 208p. 1980. 12.45i (ISBN 0-06-014341-X, HarpT). Har-Row.

Tourney, Leonard D. Joseph Hall. (English Authors Ser.). 1979. lib. bdg. 14.95 (ISBN 0-8057-6740-1, Twayne). G K Hall.

Tournier, Jacques M. Extermination as a Policy of Political & Military Power in Nazi Germany & the Middle East. (The Great Currents of History Library Book). (Illus.). 135p. 1983. 87.45 (ISBN 0-86722-020-1). Inst Econ Pol.

Tournier, Paul. The Adventure of Living. 4.95 o.p. (ISBN 0-686-92278-6, 6306). Hazelden.

--Escape from Loneliness. LC 61-14599. 1976. pap. 6.95 (ISBN 0-664-24592-7). Westminster.

--Guilt & Grace. LC 62-7305. 1962. 11.95i o.p. (ISBN 0-06-068330-9, HarpR). Har-Row.

--Meaning of Gifts. LC 63-19172. 1963. 4.75 (ISBN 0-8042-2124-3); pap. 1.95 (ISBN 0-8042-3604-6). John Knox.

--Meaning of Persons. 1957. 7.95i o.p. (ISBN 0-06-068370-8, HarpR); pap. 2.50 o.p. (ISBN 0-685-11826-6, P-304, HarpR). Har-Row.

--The Meaning of Persons. LC 57-9885. 244p. 1982. pap. 6.95 (ISBN 0-686-97228-7, HarpR). Har-Row.

--Seasons of Life. 1976. pap. 1.25 o.s.i. (ISBN 0-89129-170-9). Jove Pubns.

--The Strong & the Weak. LC 63-8898. 1976. pap. 6.95 (ISBN 0-664-24745-8). Westminster.

--To Resist or Surrender. LC 64-16248. 1977. pap. 0.95 (ISBN 0-8042-3663-1). John Knox.

--To Understand Each Other. 4.75 o.p. (ISBN 0-686-92408-8, 6290). Hazelden.

Tournier, Paul, et al. Are You Nobody? LC 66-21649. (Orig.). 1966. pap. 2.95 (ISBN 0-8042-3356-X). John Knox.

Tournier, T. H., jt. auth. see Hanzowat, M.

Tourret. International Symposium on Rolling Contact Fatigue. 1977. 83.00x (ISBN 0-471-25823-7). Wiley.

--Performance & Testing of Gear Oils & Transmission Fluids. 1981. 114.00 (ISBN 0-471-26058-4, Wiley Heyden). Wiley.

--Performance Testing of Hydraulic Fluids. 1979. 83.00 (ISBN 0-471-26059-2, Wiley Heyden). Wiley.

Tourtellot, Arthur B. An Anatomy of American Politics: Innovation Versus Conservatism. LC 72-139153. 349p. 1972. Repr. of 1950 ed. lib. bdg. 17.00x (ISBN 0-8371-5769-2, TOAP). Greenwood.

Touschek, B., ed. Physics with Intersecting Storage Rings. (Italian Physical Society: Course 46). 1971. 76.50 (ISBN 0-12-368846-9). Acad Pr.

Tousimis, A. J. see Marton, L.

Toussaint, Charmian E. The Trusteeship System of the United Nations. LC 75-27689. 1976. Repr. of 1956 ed. lib. bdg. 20.25x (ISBN 0-8371-8460-6, TOTS). Greenwood.

Toussaint, W. D., jt. auth. see Bishop, Charles E.

Toussoun, T. A., et al, eds. Root Diseases & Soil-Borne Pathogens. LC 73-84531. (Illus.). 1970. 57.50x (ISBN 0-520-01582-7). U of Cal Pr.

Tout, T. F., ed. see Hovell, Mark.

Toutenburg, Helge. Prior Information in Linear Models. (Series in Probability & Mathematical Statistics-Tracts on Probability & Statistics Section). 192p. 1982. 39.95x (ISBN 0-471-09974-0, Pub. by Wiley-Interscience). Wiley.

Toutenburg, Helge, jt. auth. see Bibby, John.

Touval, Saadia. The Peace Brokers: Mediators in the Arab-Israeli Conflict, 1948-1979. (Illus.). 370p. 1982. 25.00 (ISBN 0-686-97790-4). Princeton U Pr.

Tov, Emanual. The Septuagint Translation of Jeremiah & Baruch: A Discussion of an Early Revision of the IXX of Jeremiah 29-52 & Baruch 1: 1-3: 8. LC 75-43872. (Harvard Semitic Monographs). 1976. 9.00 (ISBN 0-89130-070-8, 06-02-08). Scholars Pr Ca.

Tova. No More Wrinkles: Facial Exercises for Men & Women. (Illus.). 1981. pap. 1.95 (ISBN 0-399-50515-6, Perige). Putnam Pub Group.

Tovatt see Carlsen, G. Robert, et al.

Tovatt, A., jt. auth. see Carlsen, G. Robert.

Tovey, Donald F. Essays in Musical Analysis, 6 vols. Incl. Vol. 1. Symphonies 1. 1982. 22.50x (ISBN 0-19-315146-4); pap. 12.50x (ISBN 0-19-315147-2); Vol. 2. Symphonies 2, Variations & Orchestral Polyphony. 1982. pap. 9.95 (ISBN 0-19-315138-3); o.p. (ISBN 0-19-315148-0); Vol. 3. Concertos. 1936. 7.50x (ISBN 0-19-315129-4); pap. 6.95 (ISBN 0-686-96828-X); Vol. 4. Illustrative Music. 1936. pap. 6.95 (ISBN 0-19-315140-5); Vol. 5. Vocal Music. 1937. pap. 12.50x (ISBN 0-19-315141-3); Vol. 6. Miscellaneous Notes, Glossary, Index. 1939. pap. 6.95 (ISBN 0-19-315142-1). (Illus.). 22.50. Oxford U Pr.

--Essays in Musical Analysis: Concertos & Choral Works. 448p. 1981. 22.50x (ISBN 0-19-315148-0); pap. 12.50x (ISBN 0-19-315149-9). Oxford U Pr.

Tovey, Doreen. A Comfort of Cats. (Illus.). 181p. 1980. 9.95 o.p. (ISBN 0-312-15088-1). St Martin.

Tovey, John. Weaves & Pattern Drafting. 1969. pap. 5.95 o.p. (ISBN 0-442-28565-5). Van Nos Reinhold.

Tovias, Alfred. Tariff Preferences in Mediterranean Diplomacy. LC 77-12265. 1978. 20.00x (ISBN 0-312-78550-X). St Martin.

Tow, William T., jt. ed. see Stuart, Douglas T.

Towbin, Richard B. Endocardial Cushion Defects: Embryology, Anatomy & Angiography. 280p. 1983. 32.50 (ISBN 0-87527-252-5). Green.

Towe, Kenneth M., jt. auth. see Hubley, Faith.

Towe, William H. Barriers to Black Political Participation in North Carolina. 1972. 3.00 (ISBN 0-686-37999-3). Voter Ed Proj.

Tower, D. B., ed. The Nervous System, 3 vols. Incl. Vol. 1. Basic Neurosciences. 752p. 22.00 (ISBN 0-89004-075-3); Vol. 2. Clinical Neurosciences. 556p. 22.00 (ISBN 0-89004-076-1); Vol. 3. Human Communication & Its Disorders. 576p. 22.00 (ISBN 0-89004-077-X). LC 75-33499. 1800p. 1975. Set. 65.50 (ISBN 0-685-61107-8). Raven.

Tower Publishing Company. Maine Marketing Directory 1980. 1982. pap. write for info. Tower Pub Co.

--New Hampshire Marketing Directory Nineteen Eighty. 1982. pap. 11.95 o.p. Tower Pub Co.

Tower, Samuel A. Makers of America: Stamps That Honor Them. LC 77-26060. (Illus.). 96p. (gr. 5 up). 1978. PLB 7.29 o.p. (ISBN 0-671-32869-7). Messner.

Tower, Stuarrt F. Hear O' Isreal. LC 82-82557. (Illus.). 100p. 1983. 8.95 (ISBN 0-86666-132-8). GWP.

Towers, Bernard. Teilhard De Chardin. Nineham, D. E. & Robertson, E. H., eds. LC 66-15515. (Makers of Contemporary Theology Ser). (Orig.). 1966. pap. 3.95 o.p. (ISBN 0-8042-0723-2). John Knox.

Towers, Bernard, jt. auth. see Lewis, John.

Towers, J. Role Playing for Managers. 1974. text ed. 37.00 (ISBN 0-08-017827-8); pap. text ed. 23.00 (ISBN 0-08-018984-9). Pergamon.

Towers, Robert. The Summoning. LC 82-48686. 288p. 1983. 13.41i (ISBN 0-06-015168-4, HarpT). Har-Row.

Towers, T. D. Towers' International Microprocessor Selector. (Illus.). 160p. vinyl 19.95 (ISBN 0-8306-1716-7, 1516). TAB Bks.

Towill, Denis R. Coefficient Plane Models for Control System Analysis & Design. LC 80-41695. (Mechanical Engineering Research Studies: Vol. 1). 271p. 1981. 49.95x (ISBN 0-471-27955-2, Pub. by Wiley-Interscience). Wiley.

Towle, Albert. A Paguran Adventure. 1978. 7.50 o.p. (ISBN 0-533-03635-6). Vantage.

Towle, Charlotte. Common Human Needs. rev. ed. LC 65-22393. 174p. 1965. pap. 5.50x (ISBN 0-87101-014-3, CBO-014-I). Natl Assn Soc Wkrs.

Towle, Laird C., ed. see Mayhew, Catherine M.

Towle, Maxine, jt. auth. see Lietz, Jeremy J.

Towler, Robert. Homo Religiosus: Sociological Problems in the Study of Religion. LC 74-78939. 206p. 1974. 17.95 o.p. (ISBN 0-312-38920-5). St Martin.

Towles, Martin F. Practical Accounting Systems & Procedures. (Illus.). 1977. 32.95 o.p. (ISBN 0-13-689208-6, Busn). P-H.

Towlmin, Stephen, jt. auth. see Janik, Allan.

Town, H. C. & Moore, H. Inspection Machines: Measuring Systems & Instruments. 1978. 22.00 (ISBN 0-7134-0795-6, Pub. by Batsford England); pap. 12.50 (ISBN 0-7134-0796-4). David & Charles.

Towne, Mary. Boxed In. LC 81-43875. 160p. (gr. 4-6). 1982. 9.13i (ISBN 0-690-04239-6, TYC-J); PLB 9.89g (ISBN 0-690-04240-X). Har-Row.

--Paul's Game. (YA) (gr. 7-12). 1983. pap. 2.50 (ISBN 0-440-96633-7, LFL). Dell.

--Paul's Game. LC 82-72750. 192p. (gr. 7 up). 1983. 13.95 (ISBN 0-440-07039-2). Doubleday.

Towne, Peter. George Washington Carver. LC 74-34296. (Biography Ser.). (Illus.). 40p. (gr. 1-4). 1975. PLB 9.89 o.p. (ISBN 0-690-00777-9, TYC-J). Har-Row.

Towner, George. The Architecture of Knowledge. LC 80-5127. 220p. 1980. text ed. 20.00 (ISBN 0-8191-1049-3); pap. text ed. 10.50 (ISBN 0-8191-1050-7). U Pr of Amer.

Townes, C. H. & Miles, P. A., eds. Quantum Electronics & Coherent Light. (Italian Physical Society: Course 31). 1965. 63.00 (ISBN 0-12-368831-0). Acad Pr.

Townes, Henry & Townes, Marjorie. A Revision of the Serphidae (Hymenoptera) (Memoir Ser.: No. 32). (Illus.). 541p. 48.00 (ISBN 0-686-30277-X). Am Entom Inst.

Townes, Marjorie, jt. auth. see Townes, Henry.

Townley, Helen M. Systems Analysis for Information Retrieval. 128p. 1978. 26.50 (ISBN 0-233-96920-9, 05826-2, Pub. by Gower Pub Co England). Lexington Bks.

Townley, Helen M. & Gee, Ralph D. Thesaurus-Making: Grow Your Own Word-Stock. 206p. 1980. 30.50 (ISBN 0-233-97225-0, 05828-9, Pub. by Gower Pub Co England). Lexington Bks.

Townley, James, ed. see Maimonides, Moses.

Townley, John. Love Cycles. 196p. 1983. 7.95 (ISBN 0-89281-029-7). Destiny Bks.

Townley, Marjorie, jt. auth. see Scarlett, Frank.

Townley, Mary. Another Look, 3 levels. (Townley Art Project Ser.). (gr. k-2). 1978. Level A. pap. text ed. 7.32 (ISBN 0-201-07646-2, Sch Div); Level B. pap. text ed. 7.32 (ISBN 0-201-07647-0); Level C. pap. text ed. 7.32 (ISBN 0-201-07648-9); 24.44 o.p. tchr's ed. (ISBN 0-201-07649-7); Levels A,B,C. Tchr. Guides 10.68 (7656,7657,7658); Intermediate Level. 3.80 (7661,7662,7663). A-W.

Townroe, P. M. & Roberts, N. J. Local External Economies for British Manufacturing Industry. 192p. 1980. text ed. 34.25x (ISBN 0-566-00391-0). Gower Pub Ltd.

Townroe, Peter. The Industrial Movement: Experience in the United States & the United Kingdom. 1979. text ed. 41.00x (ISBN 0-566-00279-5). Gower Pub Ltd.

Townroe, Peter M. Location Factors for Industry Decentralizing from Metropolitan Sao Paulo, Brazil. LC 82-8664. (World Bank Staff Working Papers: No. 517). (Orig.). 1982. pap. write for info. (ISBN 0-8213-0005-9). World Bank.

Towns, Elmer L. Say-It-Faith. 1982. pap. 4.95 (ISBN 0-8423-5825-0). Tyndale.

Towns, Elmer L. & Barber, Cyril L. Successful Church Libraries. 1971. pap. 3.50 o.p. (ISBN 0-8010-8768-6). Baker Bk.

Townsend, A. A. The Structure of Turbulent Shear Flow. 2nd ed. LC 79-8526. (Cambridge Monographs on Mechanics & Applied Mathematics). (Illus.). 441p. 1980. pap. 24.95x (ISBN 0-521-29819-9). Cambridge U Pr.

--The Structure of Turbulent Shear Flow. 2nd ed. LC 74-14441. (Monographs on Mechanics & Applied Mathematics). 300p. 1975. 82.50 (ISBN 0-521-20710-X). Cambridge U Pr.

Townsend, Alan R. The Impact of Recession: On Industry, Employment & the Regions, 1976-1981. 224p. 1983. text ed. 30.00x (ISBN 0-7099-2417-8, Pub. by Croom Helm Ltd England). Biblio Dist.

Townsend, Carl. CP-M Database Management. 300p. 1983. pap. 19.95 (ISBN 0-88056-082-7). Dilithium Pr.

--CP-M Wordprocessing Systems. 300p. 1983. pap. text ed. 19.95 (ISBN 0-88056-104-1). Dilithium Pr.

--How to Get Started with MSDOS. 230p. 1983. pap. 13.95 (ISBN 0-88056-086-X). Dilithium Pr.

--Practical Guide to CP-M. Barry, Tim, ed. (CP-M Ser.: No. 2). 250p. 1983. pap. 14.95 (ISBN 0-88056-077-0). Dilithium Pr.

Townsend, Carolynn. Nutrition & Diet Modifications. 3rd ed. LC 78-74166. (Health Occupations Ser.). (gr. 9). 1980. pap. text ed. 12.60 (ISBN 0-8273-1324-1); instr.'s guide 2.75 (ISBN 0-686-85868-9). Delmar.

Townsend, Charles. Continuing with Russian. 1970. text ed. 16.50 o.p. (ISBN 0-07-065115-9, C); 4.50 o.p. instructor's manual (ISBN 0-07-065117-5). McGraw.

Townsend, Charles E. Russian Word-Formation, Corrected Reprint. c ed. 1975. soft cover 11.95 (ISBN 0-89357-023-0). Slavica.

Townsend, Charles E., tr. The Memoirs of Princess Natal'ja Borisovna Dolgorukaja. (Illus.). viii, 146p. (Eng.). 1977. pap. 9.95 (ISBN 0-89357-044-3). Slavica.

Townsend, Colin R. Ecology of Streams & Rivers. (Studies in Biology: No. 122). 64p. 1980. pap. text ed. 8.95 (ISBN 0-7131-2804-6). E Arnold.

Townsend, Derek. Practical Guide to Holiday Family Movies. 11.50x (ISBN 0-392-09401-0, SpS). Sportshelf.

Townsend, Doris M. How to Cook With Herbs, Spices & Flavorings. 160p. 1982. pap. 6.95 (ISBN 0-89586-192-5). H P Bks.

Townsend, Duane E., jt. auth. see Morrow, C. Paul.

Townsend, George. Campaigns of a Non-Combatant. (Collector's Library of the Civil War). 1983. 26.60 (ISBN 0-8094-4250-7). Silver.

--Everything You Wanted TO Know About American Watches & Didn't Know Who to Ask. 1974. 8.00 (ISBN 0-913902-38-1). Heart Am Pr.

--Watch That Made the Dollar Famous. 1974. 8.00 (ISBN 0-913702-39-0). Heart Am Pr.

Townsend, James R. Political Participation in Communist China. (Center for Chinese Studies, UC Berkeley). 1967. 28.50x (ISBN 0-520-01279-8); pap. 7.50x (ISBN 0-520-01416-2, CAMPUS83). U of Cal Pr.

--Politics in China. 2nd ed. 380p. 1980. pap. text ed. 10.95 (ISBN 0-316-85131-0). Little.

--The Revolutionization of Chinese Youth: A Study of Chung-Kuo Ch'ing-Nien. LC 67-65707. (China Research Monographs: No. 1). 71p. 1967. pap. 3.00 o.s.i. (ISBN 0-912966-02-5). IEAS.

Townsend, James R., jt. auth. see Bush, Richard C.

Townsend, James R. & Bush, Richard C., eds. People's Republic of China: A Basic Handbook. 2nd, rev. ed. (Illus., Orig.). 1981. pap. text ed. 4.50 (ISBN 0-936876-13-1). Learn Res Intl Stud.

Townsend, Jimmy. It's True What They Say about Dixie. 1981. 8.95 (ISBN 0-932298-18-4). Copple Hse.

Townsend, John. Oman: The Making of a Modern State. LC 76-62532. 1977. 25.00x (ISBN 0-312-58432-6). St Martin.

Townsend, John R. Goodnight Prof Dear. (gr. 9 up). 1977. pap. 1.25 o.p. (ISBN 0-440-92884-2, LFL). Dell.

--The Islanders. LC 81-47105. 256p. (YA) (gr. 7 up). 1981. 12.95i (ISBN 0-397-31940-1, JBL-J); PLB 9.89g (ISBN 0-397-31959-2). Har-Row.

--Kate & the Revolution. LC 81-48605. 224p. (YA) (gr. 7 up). 1983. 11.06i (ISBN 0-397-32015-9, JBL-J); PLB 11.89g (ISBN 0-397-32016-7). Har-Row.

--Noah's Castle. 1978. pap. 1.75 o.p. (ISBN 0-440-96445-8, LFL). Dell.

--Written for Children: An Outline of English-Language Children's Literature. (Illus.). 1974. pap. 8.00 (ISBN 0-87675-278-4). Horn Bk.

Townsend, John R., ed. Modern Poetry. LC 73-7736. 224p. (gr. 7 up). 1974. 12.95 (ISBN 0-397-31477-9, HarpJ). Har-Row.

Townsend, Joseph. A Dissertation on the Poor Laws: By a Well-Wisher to Mankind. 1971. 23.75x (ISBN 0-520-01700-5). U of Cal Pr.

Townsend, Joyce C. Bureaucratic Politics in American Decision Making: Impact on Brazil. LC 81-48681. 210p. 1983. lib. bdg. 22.50 (ISBN 0-8191-2706-X); pap. text ed. 11.50 (ISBN 0-8191-2707-8). U Pr of Amer.

Townsend, Leroy B. & Tipson, R. Stuart, eds. Nucleic Acid Chemistry: Improved & New Synthetic Procedures, Methods & Techniques, 2 pts. LC 77-22816. 1177p. 1978. Set. 140.95x (ISBN 0-471-04738-4, Pub. by Wiley-Interscience); Pt. I. 63.50 o.p. (ISBN 0-471-88090-6); Pt. II. 63.50 (ISBN 0-471-04680-9). Wiley.

Townsend, P., jt. auth. see Bosanquet, N.

Townsend, P., ed. Concepts of Poverty. 1970. 22.95 (ISBN 0-444-19640-4). Elsevier.

Townsend, P. D. & Kelly, J. C. Colour Centres & Imperfections in Insulators & Semiconductors. 39.00x (ISBN 0-686-96992-8, Pub. by Scottish Academic Pr Scotland). State Mutual Bk.

Townsend, Peter. The Girl in the White Ship. LC 82-3110. 224p. 1983. 15.95 (ISBN 0-03-057787-X). HR&W.

Townsend, Peter, jt. ed. see Walker, Alan.

Townsend, Rochelle, tr. Russian Short Stories. 300p. 1983. Repr. of 1924 ed. pap. text ed. 4.50x (ISBN 0-460-01758-6, Pub by Evwan). Biblio Dist.

Townsend, Sallie & Ericson, Virginia. The Sea Cook: Or How to Have Superb Meals Afloat Without Becoming a Galley Slave. 2nd ed. LC 76-19080. (Funk & W Bk.). (Illus.). 1977. 9.95i (ISBN 0-308-10268-1); pap. 4.95i (ISBN 0-308-10269-X). T y Crowell.

Townsend, W. C. Handbook of Homophones. 121p. 1975. pap. 1.50x (ISBN 0-88312-772-5); microfiche 2.25x (ISBN 0-88312-350-9). Summer Inst Ling.

Townsent. Digital Computer & Design. 2nd ed. 1982. text ed. 39.95 (ISBN 0-408-01158-0); pap. text ed. 24.95 (ISBN 0-408-01155-6). Butterworth.

Townshend, Charles. The British Campaign in Ireland, Nineteen Nineteen to Nineteen Twenty-One. (Oxford Historical Monographs). (Illus.). 1978. pap. 15.95x (ISBN 0-19-821874-5). Oxford U Pr.

Townshend, George. The Mission of Baha'u'llah and Other Literary Pieces. 1952. 6.95 (ISBN 0-85398-021-7, 331-018-10, Pub. by G Ronald England). Baha'i.

Townshend, J. R., ed. Terrain Analysis & Remote Sensing. (Illus.). 240p. (Orig.). 1981. text ed. 45.00x (ISBN 0-04-551036-9); pap. text ed. 24.95x (ISBN 0-04-551037-7). Allen Unwin.

Townshend, John N., jt. auth. see Ram, James.

Townson, Duncan. Alexander. Killingray, Margaret, et al, eds. (World History Ser.). (Illus.). 32p. (gr. 10). 1980. Repr. of 1977 ed. lib. bdg. 6.95 (ISBN 0-89908-039-1); pap. text ed. 2.25 (ISBN 0-89908-014-6). Greenhaven.

--Spices & Civilizations. Yapp, Malcolm, et al, eds. (World History Ser.). (Illus.). (gr. 10). 1980. Repr. of 1977 ed. lib. bdg. 6.95 (ISBN 0-89908-029-4); pap. text ed. 2.25 (ISBN 0-89908-004-9). Greenhaven.

Townsend, Peter. Time & Chance. (Illus.). 317p. 1978. 10.95 o.p. (ISBN 0-458-93710-X). Methuen Inc.

Toy, Barbara. Rendezvous in Cyprus. (Illus.). 147p. 1972. 10.00 o.p. (ISBN 0-7195-2074-6). Transatlantic.

Toy, Gerald. Cracked Lens at Sundown. Lenahan, Sheila, ed. & illus. (Illus.). 22p. 1982. pap. 3.00 (ISBN 0-911017-00-3). Seacliffe.

Toy, Wing N., jt. auth. see Kraft, George D.

Toye, Clive. Soccer. 2nd rev. ed. (First Bks.). (Illus.). (gr. 4-6). 1979. PLB 8.90 s&l (ISBN 0-531-02936-0). Watts.

Toye, F. J. Public Expenditure & Indian Development Policy, 1960-1970. LC 80-41011. 284p. 1981. 44.50 (ISBN 0-521-23081-0). Cambridge U Pr.

Toye, Kenneth. Regional French Cookery. (Illus.). 1979. 13.50 o.p. (ISBN 0-7153-6327-1). David & Charles.

Toye, William. The Loon's Necklace. (Illus.). 1977. 7.95 (ISBN 0-19-540278-2). Oxford U Pr.

Toynbee, Arnold. Civilization on Trial. Bd. with World & the West. pap. 4.95 o.p. (ISBN 0-452-00453-5, F453, Mer). NAL.

--The Greeks & Their Heritages. 1981. 22.50x (ISBN 0-19-215256-4). Oxford U Pr.

--Lectures on the Industrial Revolution of the Eighteenth Century in England: Popular Addresses, Notes & Other Fragments. 282p. 1982. Repr. of 1908 ed. lib. bdg. 40.00 (ISBN 0-89984-470-7). Century Bookbindery.

Toynbee, Arnold J. Acquaintances. 1967. 18.95x (ISBN 0-19-500189-3). Oxford U Pr.

--Cities on the Move. 1970. 15.95x (ISBN 0-19-501244-5). Oxford U Pr.

--Experiences. 1969. 22.50x (ISBN 0-19-500194-X). Oxford U Pr.

--An Historian's Approach to Religion. 2nd ed. 1979. 22.50x (ISBN 0-19-215260-2). Oxford U Pr.

--Mankind & Mother Earth: A Narrative History of the World. (Illus.). 1976. 35.00x (ISBN 0-19-215257-2). Oxford U Pr.

--A Study of History. (Royal Institute of International Affairs). 1954. Vols. 1-6. o.p.; Vols. 7-10. 65.00 o.p. maroon cloth (ISBN 0-19-519689-9); Vols. 11-12 (vol. 11 o.p.) maroon cloth 22.50x (ISBN 0-19-500197-4). Oxford U Pr.

--A Study of History. abr. ed. Somervell, D. C., ed. Incl. Vols. 1-6. 1947. 22.50x (ISBN 0-19-500198-2); Vols. 7-10. 1957. 22.50x (ISBN 0-19-500199-0). (Royal Institute of International Affairs Ser). Oxford U Pr.

--A Study of History, 2 Vols. 1939. Vol. 4. text ed. 37.50x (ISBN 0-19-215211-4); Vol. 5. text ed. 37.50x (ISBN 0-19-215212-2). Oxford U Pr.

--Surviving the Future. 1971. 18.95x (ISBN 0-19-501505-3). Oxford U Pr.

Toynbee, J. M. Death & Burial in the Roman World. Scullard, H. H., ed. LC 77-120603. (Aspects of Greek & Roman Life Ser). (Illus.). 336p. 1971. 24.50x (ISBN 0-8014-0593-9). Cornell U Pr.

Toynbee, Margaret & Young, Peter. Cropredy Bridge, Sixteen Forty-Four. 1980. 21.00x (ISBN 0-900093-17-X, Pub. by Peter Dix). State Mutual Bk.

Toynbee, Margaret, jt. auth. see Smith, Geoffrey R.

Toynbee, Paget. Dante Studies & Researches. LC 78-118417. 1971. Repr. of 1902 ed. 14.00 o.p. (ISBN 0-8046-1194-7). Kennikat.

Toyne, Peter. Organization, Location & Behavior: Decision Making in Economic Geography. LC 73-22708. 285p. 1974. 24.95x o.s.i. (ISBN 0-470-88100-3). Halsted Pr.

Toyoda, Takeshi, jt. ed. see Hall, John W.

Tozer, A. W. Christ, the Eternal Son. Smith, G. B., ed. 136p. 1982. pap. 3.50 mm (ISBN 0-87509-230-6). Chr Pubns.

--Echoes from Eden. Smith, Gerald B., ed. LC 1-67321. (Tozer Pulpit: Vol. 8). 121p. (Orig.). 1981. 2.95 (ISBN 0-87509-227-6). Chr Pubns.

--Gems from Tozer. 96p. 1979. pap. 2.25 (ISBN 0-87509-163-6). Chr Pubns.

--How to Be Filled with the Holy Spirit. 58p. pap. 1.25 (ISBN 0-87509-187-3). Chr Pubns.

--I Call It Heresy. pap. 2.50 (ISBN 0-87509-209-8). Chr Pubns.

--I Talk Back to the Devil. Smith, Gerald B., ed. Orig. Title: Tozer Pulpit, Vol. 4. Twelve Sermons on Spiritual Perfection. 144p. (Orig.). 1972. pap. 2.95 (ISBN 0-87509-206-3). Chr Pubns.

--Paths to Power. 64p. pap. 1.25 (ISBN 0-87509-190-3). Chr Pubns.

--Renewed Day by Day: Three Hundred & Sixty Five Daily Devotions. 1981. 12.95 o.p. (ISBN 0-8010-8861-5). Baker Bk.

--That Incredible Christian. 1978. pap. 2.95 (ISBN 0-8423-7025-0). Tyndale.

--That Incredible Christian. 135p. 1964. 4.95 (ISBN 0-87509-196-2); pap. 3.25 (ISBN 0-87509-197-0); 2.50 (ISBN 0-87509-250-0). Chr Pubns.

--The Tozer Pulpit, 8 vols. Smith, Gerald B., ed. Incl. Vol. 1. Selected Quotations from the Sermons of A. W. Tozer. 158p. 1967. pap. 3.50 (ISBN 0-87509-199-7); Vol. 2. Ten Sermons on the Ministry of the Holy Spirit. 146p. 1968. pap. 3.50 (ISBN 0-87509-178-4); Vol. 3. Ten Sermons from the Gospel of John. 167p. 1970. pap. 3.50 (ISBN 0-87509-202-0); Vol. 4. Twelve Sermons on Spiritual Perfection. 144p. 1972. 5.95 (ISBN 0-87509-204-7); Vol. 5. Twelve Sermons in Peter's First Epistle. 159p. 1974. 5.95 (ISBN 0-87509-207-1); Vol. 6. Twelve Messages on Well-Known & Favorite Bible Texts. 174p. 1975. 5.95 (ISBN 0-87509-210-1); Vol. 7. Twelve Sermons Relating to the Life & Ministry of the Christian Church. 1978. 5.95 (ISBN 0-87509-213-6); Vol. 8. Ten Sermons on the Voices of God Calling Man. 5.95 (ISBN 0-87509-225-X). pap. Chr Pubns.

--Who Put Jesus on the Cross. 1976. pap. 3.25 (ISBN 0-87509-212-8). Chr Pubns.

--Worship: The Missing Jewel of the Evangelical Church. 30p. 1979. bklet 1.00 (ISBN 0-87509-219-5). Chr Pubns.

Tozer, A. W. & Smith, G. B. When He Is Come. Orig. Title: Tozer Pulpit, Vol. 2: Ten Sermons on the Ministry of the Holy Spirit. 146p. (Orig.). 1980. pap. 3.50 (ISBN 0-87509-221-7). Chr Pubns.

Tozer, A. W., ed. The Christian Book of Mystical Verse. 1975. Repr. 5.50 (ISBN 0-87509-181-4). Chr Pubns.

Tozer, Aiden W. Born after Midnight. 4.95 (ISBN 0-87509-257-8); pap. 3.25 (ISBN 0-87509-258-6); pap. 2.50 mass mkt (ISBN 0-87509-167-9). Chr Pubns.

--God Tells the Man Who Cares. Bailey, Anita, ed. 1970. 4.95 (ISBN 0-87509-184-9); pap. 3.25 (ISBN 0-87509-185-7); mass market ed. 2.95 (ISBN 0-87509-220-9). Chr Pubns.

--Let My People Go. pap. 4.25 (ISBN 0-87509-189-X). Chr Pubns.

--Man, the Dwelling Place of God. 4.95 (ISBN 0-87509-188-1); pap. 3.25 (ISBN 0-87509-165-2); mass market 2.95 (ISBN 0-87509-166-0). Chr Pubns.

--Of God & Men. 4.95 (ISBN 0-87509-168-7); pap. 3.25 (ISBN 0-87509-193-8); mass market 2.95 (ISBN 0-87509-254-3). Chr Pubns.

--Pursuit of God. 4.95 (ISBN 0-87509-191-1); pap. 3.25 (ISBN 0-87509-192-X); 2.95 (ISBN 0-87509-223-3). Chr Pubns.

--Renewed Day by Day. LC 80-69301. 380p. 12.95 (ISBN 0-87509-252-7); pap. 8.25 kivar (ISBN 0-87509-292-6). Chr Pubns.

--Root of the Righteous. 4.95 (ISBN 0-87509-194-6); pap. 3.25 (ISBN 0-87509-195-4); mass market 2.95 (ISBN 0-87509-224-1). Chr Pubns.

--Wingspread. pap. 3.95 (ISBN 0-87509-218-7). Chr Pubns.

Tozer, Alden W. The Pursuit of God. 128p. pap. 1.95 (ISBN 0-8007-8404-9, Spire Bks). Revell.

Tozoni, O. V. & Kaye, A. A. Mathematical Models for the Evaluation of Electric & Magnetic Fields. 338p. 1970. 78.00x (ISBN 0-677-61780-1). Gordon.

Tozzini & Reeves. Endocrine Physiopathology of the Ovary. 1980. 62.75 (ISBN 0-444-80214-2). Elsevier.

Trabucchi, Marco, jt. ed. see Costa, Erminio.

Trabucci, M., jt. ed. see Costa, E.

Trace, Arthur. Christianity & the Intellectuals. 208p. (Orig.). 1982. 12.95 (ISBN 0-89385-019-5); pap. 4.95 (ISBN 0-89385-018-7). Sugden.

Trace, Arthur S. What Ivan Knows That Johnny Doesn't. LC 78-622. 1978. Repr. of 1961 ed. lib. bdg. 20.00x (ISBN 0-313-20276-1, TRWI). Greenwood.

Tracey, Steve, jt. auth. see Carr, Pat.

Trachenberg, Alan. The Incorporation of America: Culture & Society in the Guilded Age. 1982. 12.95 (ISBN 0-8090-5827-8); pap. 6.95 (ISBN 0-8090-0145-4). Hill & Wang.

Tracht, Myron E., et al, eds. Digestive System Basic Sciences. (Basic Science Review Bks.). 1973. spiral bdg. 8.00 o.p. (ISBN 0-87488-215-X). Med Exam.

Trachtenberg, Alan. Hart Crane: A Collection of Critical Essays. (Twentieth Century Views Ser.). 224p. 1981. 13.95 (ISBN 0-13-383935-4, Spec); pap. 5.95 (ISBN 0-13-383927-3). P-H.

Trachtenberg, Alan, jt. auth. see Gross, Theodore L.

Trachtenberg, Paul. Short Changes for Loretta. 64p. 1982. pap. 4.00x (ISBN 0-916156-62-1). Cherry Valley.

Trachtman, Paul. The Gunfighters. LC 74-80284. (Old West Ser.). (gr. 5 up). 1974. 17.28 (ISBN 0-8094-1481-3, Pub. Time-Life). Silver.

Traci, Philip, jt. auth. see Felheim, Marvin.

Tracton, Ken. The BASIC Cookbook. (Illus.). 1978. 10.95 (ISBN 0-8306-9901-5); pap. 5.95 (ISBN 0-8306-1055-3, 1055). TAB Bks.

--Fifty Seven Practical Programs & Games in BASIC. (Illus.). 210p. 1978. 11.95 (ISBN 0-8306-9987-2); pap. 7.95 (ISBN 0-8306-1000-6, 1000). TAB Bks.

--IC Function Locator. 1978. 8.95 o.p. leatherette (ISBN 0-8306-8960-5); pap. 5.95 (ISBN 0-8306-7960-X, 960). TAB Bks.

--The Most Popular Subroutines in BASIC. (Illus.). 1979. 12.95 (ISBN 0-8306-9740-3); pap. 7.95 (ISBN 0-8306-1050-2, 1050). TAB Bks.

--Programmer's Guide to LISP. (Illus.). 1979. 13.95 (ISBN 0-8306-9761-6); pap. 8.95 (ISBN 0-8306-1045-6, 1045). TAB Bks.

--Twenty-Four Tested Ready-to-Run Game Programs in BASIC. (Illus.). 1978. 11.95 (ISBN 0-8306-9876-0); pap. 9.95 (ISBN 0-8306-1085-5, 1085). TAB Bks.

Tracy, David. Blessed Rage for Order: The New Pluralism in Theology. 1979. pap. 9.95 (ISBN 0-8164-2202-8). Seabury.

Tracy, David & Cobb, John B., Jr. Talking About God: Doing Theology in the Context of Modern Pluralism. 144p. 1983. 6.95 (ISBN 0-8164-2458-6). Seabury.

Tracy, David & Lash, Nicholas. Cosmology & Theology. (Concilium 1983: Vol. 166). 128p. (Orig.). 1983. pap. 6.95 (ISBN 0-8164-2446-2). Seabury.

Tracy, Diane & Warren, Roger G. Mosby's Fundamentals of Animal Health Technology: Small Animal Surgical Nursing. (Illus.). 347p. 1983. pap. text ed. 17.95 (ISBN 0-8016-5399-1). Mosby.

Tracy, Dick, jt. auth. see Scannell, Dale.

Tracy, Jack. The Encyclopaedia Sherlockiana. 1979. pap. 7.95 o.p. (ISBN 0-380-46490-X, 46490). Avon.

Tracy, John A. Fundamentals of Financial Accounting. 2nd ed. 1978. text ed. 32.95 (ISBN 0-471-88160-0); study guide o.p. 10.95x (ISBN 0-471-88161-9); tchrs. manual o.p. 14.95 (ISBN 0-471-02293-4); working papers o.p. 11.95 (ISBN 0-471-88162-7). Wiley.

--Fundamentals of Management Accounting. LC 75-26988. 565p. 1976. text ed. 25.95 o.p. (ISBN 0-471-88151-1, Pub. by Wiley-Hamilton). Wiley.

--How to Read a Financial Report: Wringing Cash Flow & Other Vital Signs Out of the Numbers. LC 79-18853. 156p. 1980. 24.95 (ISBN 0-471-05712-6, Pub. by Wiley-Interscience). Wiley.

Tracy, Joseph. Pilot's Sketchbook. LC 80-66116. 1982. pap. 14.95 (ISBN 0-8168-7408-5); deluxe ed. 37.50 autographed & numbered ltd. ed. (ISBN 0-686-82847-X). Aero.

Tracy, Lane, jt. auth. see Peterson, Richard B.

Tracy, Larry J. The Art & Skill of Real Estate & Time Share Selling. 1982. 9.95 (ISBN 0-933984-03-0). Tracy Pub.

Tracy, Lorna. Amateur Passions: Love Stories? 206p. 1983. pap. 6.95 (ISBN 0-86068-198-X, Virago Pr). Merrimack Bk Serv.

Tracy, Marian, ed. Favorite American Regional Recipes; by Leading Food Editors. LC 76-24563. (Cookbook Ser). 320p. 1976. pap. 3.50 o.p. (ISBN 0-486-23415-0). Dover.

Tracy, Marion. Real Food: Simple, Sensuous, & Splendid, a Treasury of over 230 Favorite Recipes. 1978. 14.95 o.p. (ISBN 0-670-59030-4). Viking Pr.

Tracy, Mark. Secrets of the Great Italian Dames at the Court of the De'Medicis. (The Memoirs Collections of Significant Historical Personalities Ser.). (Illus.). 119p. 1983. Repr. of 1916 ed. 89.75 (ISBN 0-89901-085-7). Found Class Reprints.

Tracy, Robert. Trollope's Later Novels. LC 76-55572. 1978. 28.50x (ISBN 0-520-03407-4). U of Cal Pr.

Tracy, Susie, jt. auth. see Moon, Susan E.

Tracy, Thomas & Ward, James O. The Morrow Book of Havens & Hideaways: A Guide to America's Unique Lodgings. LC 79-27951. (Illus.). 448p. 1980. 12.95 (ISBN 0-688-03622-8); pap. 6.95 (ISBN 0-688-08622-5, Quill). Morrow.

Tracy, Thomas, ed. see Moscow, Henry.

Trader Vic, see Bergeron, Victor J.

Traetta, John & Traetta, MaryJean. Gymnastics Basics. (Illus.). 48p. (ps-7). 1983. pap. 3.95 (ISBN 0-13-371740-2). P-H.

Traetta, MaryJean, jt. auth. see Traetta, John.

Traffic World, ed. Traffic World's Questions & Answers, Vol. 28. 576p. 1982. text ed. write for info. (ISBN 0-87408-024-X). Traffic Serv.

Trafford, Abigail. Crazy Time: Predictable Stages of Divorce. LC 82-47864. 256p. 1982. 12.45i (ISBN 0-06-015047-5, HarpT). Har-Row.

Trafton, Dain A., tr. see Tasso, Torquato.

Trafzer, Clifford, jt. auth. see Scheuerman, Richard.

Trafzer, Clifford E. The Kit Carson Campaign: The Last Great Navajo War. LC 81-40283. (Illus.). 288p. 1982. 16.95 (ISBN 0-8061-1683-8). U of Okla Pr.

Trager, Brahna. Home Health Care & National Health Policy. LC 80-15988. (Home Health Care Services Quarterly Monograph: Vol. 1, No. 2). 111p. 1980. text ed. 14.95 (ISBN 0-917724-20-8, B20); pap. text ed. cancelled (ISBN 0-917724-21-6). Haworth Pr.

Trager, Edith C. PD's in Depth. (Orig.). (gr. 9-12). 1982. pap. 4.95 (ISBN 0-87789-215-6, 1600); write for info. cassettes (ISBN 0-87789-216-4, 1601). Eng Language.

Trager, Edith C. & Henderson, Sara C. Pronunciation Drills for Learners of English. 1956. Repr. text ed. 5.50 (ISBN 0-87789-008-0); cassette tapes 70.00 (ISBN 0-87789-124-9). Eng Language.

Trager, James. Letters from Sachiko. LC 82-43512. 224p. 1982. 12.95 (ISBN 0-689-11337-4). Atheneum.

Trager, Philip, et al. Wesleyan Photographs. Scully, Vincent & Green, Samuel, eds. LC 81-21853. 1982. 39.95 (ISBN 0-8195-5063-9); Ltd. ed. 250.00x (ISBN 0-686-92012-0); pap. 19.95 (ISBN 0-8195-6073-1). Wesleyan U Pr.

Trahair, N. S. The Behaviour & Design of Steel Structures. 1977. pap. 25.00x (ISBN 0-412-14900-1, Pub. by Chapman & Hall). Methuen Inc.

Traherne, Thomas. Selected Writings. Davis, Dick, ed. (Fyfield Ser.). 128p. 1981. pap. 4.95 o.p. (ISBN 0-85635-231-4, Pub. by Carcanet New Pr England). Humanities.

Trail, Ronald, ed. Patterns in Clause, Sentence & Discourse in Selected Languages in India & Nepal, 4 vols. (Publications in Linguistics Ser.: No. 41). pap. 35.50x set (ISBN 0-88312-047-X); Pt. 1. pap. 9.00x (ISBN 0-88312-048-8); Pt. 2. pap. 10.00x (ISBN 0-88312-049-6); Pt. 3. pap. 9.50x (ISBN 0-88312-050-X); Pt. 4. pap. 7.00x (ISBN 0-88312-051-8); Pt. 1. microfiche 3.75x (ISBN 0-88312-448-3); Pt. 2. microfiche 5.25x (ISBN 0-88312-449-1); Pt. 3. microfiche 3.75x (ISBN 0-88312-450-5); Pt. 4. microfiche 3.00 (ISBN 0-88312-487-4). Summer Inst Ling.

Trail, Ronald L. A Grammar of Lamani. (Publications in Linguistics & Related Fields Ser.: No. 24). 225p. 1970. pap. 4.50x (ISBN 0-88312-026-7); microfiche 3.00x (ISBN 0-88312-426-2). Summer Inst Ling.

Trail, W. The Literary Characteristics & Achievements of the Bible. 335p. 1983. Repr. of 1863 ed. lib. bdg. 85.00 (ISBN 0-89984-471-5). Century Bookbindery.

Trailer Life, ed. Trailer Life's RV Campground & Services Directory 1983. (Illus.). 1300p. 1983. 11.95 (ISBN 0-934798-32-X). TL Enterprises.

Trailer Life Editors. Trailer Life's RV Campground & Services Directory. (Illus.). 1400p. 1982. 10.95 o.p. (ISBN 0-934798-04-4). TL Enterprises.

Traill, Henry D. Coleridge. LC 67-23874. 1968. Repr. of 1884 ed. 34.00x (ISBN 0-8103-3052-0). Gale.

Traill, Vera, tr. see Tolstoy, Leo.

Train, John. Preserving Capital & Making It Grow. 1983. 14.95 (ISBN 0-517-54766-X, C N Potter Bks). Crown.

--Remarkable Names of Real People. 1981. pap. 2.95 (ISBN 0-517-54303-6, C N Potter Bks). Crown.

--Remarkable Names of Real People. (Illus.). 1977. 5.95 o.p. (ISBN 0-517-53130-5, C N Potter Bks). Crown.

--Remarkable Occurrences. (Illus.). 1978. 5.95 (ISBN 0-517-53505-X, C N Potter Bks). Crown.

--Remarkable Relatives. (Illus.). 64p. 1981. 5.95 (ISBN 0-517-54542-X, C N Potter Bks). Crown.

--Remarkable Words: With Astonishing Origins. (Clarkson N. Potter Bks.). 1980. 5.95 (ISBN 0-517-54185-8, C N Potter Bks). Crown.

Train, John, compiled by. Even More Remarkable Names. (Illus.). 1979. 5.95 (ISBN 0-517-53694-3, C N Potter Bks). Crown.

Traina, Richard, jt. auth. see Rappaport, Armin.

Trainor, F. R. Introductory Phycology. LC 77-26663. 1978. text ed. 31.50 (ISBN 0-471-88190-2). Wiley.

Trainor, William T., jt. ed. see Young, Louise B.

Traister. Blueprint Reading for the Building Trades. (Illus.). 1980. 18.95 o.p. (ISBN 0-8359-0514-4); pap. 14.95 (ISBN 0-8359-0513-6). Reston.

Traister, John. Mechanical Specifications for Building Construction. (Illus.). 224p. 1980. text ed. 19.00 (ISBN 0-8359-4318-6). Reston.

Traister, John & Traister, Robert. Treasure Hunter's Handbook. (Illus.). 1977. 8.95 (ISBN 0-8306-7996-0); pap. 4.95 (ISBN 0-8306-6996-5, 996). TAB Bks.

Traister, John, ed. see Wahl, Paul.

Traister, John E. Design & Application of Security-Fire-Alarm Systems. (Illus.). 176p. 1981. 16.75 (ISBN 0-07-065114-0). McGraw.

--Do-It-Yourselfer's Guide to Modern Energy-Efficient Heating & Cooling Systems. (Illus.). 1978. 9.95 o.p. (ISBN 0-8306-7903-0); pap. 5.95 o.p. (ISBN 0-8306-6903-5, 903). TAB Bks.

--Electrical Design for Building Construction. 1976. 36.50 (ISBN 0-07-065127-2, P&RB). McGraw.

--Handbook of Electrical Systems Design Practices. (Illus.). 1978. text ed. 21.95 (ISBN 0-87909-348-X). Reston.

--Handbook of Modern Electrical Wiring. (Illus.). 1979. text ed. 19.95 (ISBN 0-8359-2754-7). Reston.

--Handbook of Power Generation: Transformers & Generators. (Illus.). 272p. 1982. 19.95 (ISBN 0-13-380816-5). P-H.

--How to Build Your Own Boat from Scratch. 1978. pap. 6.95 o.p. (ISBN 0-8306-7923-5, 923). TAB Bks.

--How to Buy & Sell Used Guns. 192p. (Orig.). 1982. pap. 9.95 (ISBN 0-88317-114-7). Stoeger Pub Co.

Traister, John E., jt. auth. see Chapman, Keeler C.

Traister, Robert, jt. auth. see Traister, John.

Traister, Robert J. DC Power Supplies: Application & Theory. (Illus.). 1979. text ed. 18.95 (ISBN 0-8359-1275-2). Reston.

Trakl, Georg. Georg Trakl: A Profile. Graziano, Frank, ed. Mandel, S. & Iverson, R., trs. from Ger. 160p. (Orig.). 1983. 16.00 (ISBN 0-937406-28-7); pap. 6.50 (ISBN 0-937406-27-9). Logbridge-Rhodes.

Trakman, Leon E. The Law Merchant: The Evolution of Commercial Law. LC 82-15067. xi, 195p. 1983. text ed. 35.00x (ISBN 0-8377-1207-6). Rothman.

Trall, Russell. Scientific Basis of Vegetarianism. 1970. 2.50x (ISBN 0-686-37947-0). Cancer Control Soc.

Trambley, Estela P. Rain of Scorpions. LC 75-37178. 1975. pap. 6.50 (ISBN 0-89229-001-3). Tonatiuh-Quinto Sol Intl.

Tramonte, Bob. Fat Like Me: A Satire on Dieting. 1982. pap. 3.95 o.p. (ISBN 0-686-34594-0). Caroline Hse.

Tranbarger, Charlotte. Love Beyond Yesterday. 1982. 6.95 (ISBN 0-686-84174-3, Avalon). Bouregy.

--Rules of the Heart. 1982. pap. 6.95 (ISBN 0-686-84743-1, Avalon). Bouregy.

Transamerica Delaval Inc. Transamerica Delaval Engineering Handbook. 4th ed. Welch, Harry & Crawford, Harold B., eds. (Illus.). 640p. 1983. 39.50 (ISBN 0-07-016250-6, P&RB). McGraw.

Transitour, Inc. The Streetcar Guide to Uptown New Orleans. Raarup, Peter, ed. (Illus.). 128p. pap. 5.95 (ISBN 0-686-82700-7). Pelican.

Transportation Division. Transportation Libraries in the U. S. & Canada: A Directory. 3rd ed. LC 77-17615. 1978. 8.75 (ISBN 0-87111-233-7). SLA.

Transue, Ralph E. Impact of Modern Electronics on Fire Protection. Date not set. 3.35 (ISBN 0-686-37670-6, TR 82-6). Society Fire Protect.

Tranter, C. J. Integral Transforms in Mathematical Physics. 3rd ed. 1971. pap. 9.95x o.p. (ISBN 0-412-20860-1, Pub. by Chapman & Hall). Methuen Inc.

Tranter, John. The Livin' Is Easy. 12.50 (ISBN 0-392-03808-0, ABC). Sportshelf.

Tranter, William, jt. auth. see Ziemer, Rodger E.

Trap, Charles, ed. see Hofacker, Winfried & Floegel, Ekkehard.

Trapeznikov, S. P. Leninism & the Agrarian & Peasant Question, 2 vols. 1114p. 1981. Set. 15.95 (ISBN 0-8285-2491-2, Pub. by Progress Pubs USSR). Imported Pubns.

Trapido, Barbara. Brother of the More Famous Jack. LC 82-70236. 220p. 1982. 12.95 (ISBN 0-670-19246-5). Viking Pr.

Trapmore, Alison. Color Printing. (Photographer's Library Ser.). (Illus.). 168p. 1983. pap. 12.95 (ISBN 0-240-51113-1). Focal Pr.

Trapnell, Coles. Teleplay: An Introduction to Television Writing. 256p. 1974. pap. text ed. 7.95 (ISBN 0-8015-7486-2, 0772-230, Hawthorn). Dutton.

Trapnell, D. H., ed. see Ansell, G.

Trapnell, D. H., ed. see Ngan, H. & James, K. W.

Trapnell, David H., ed. see Evans, K. T. & Gravelle, I. H.

Trapnell, David H., ed. see Russell, J. G.

Trapnell, David H., ed. see Wright, F. W.

Trapp, Maria A. Sound of Music: Story of the Trapp Family Singers. 1966. pap. 1.95 o.p. (ISBN 0-440-99032-7, LFL). Dell.

--Story of the Trapp Family Singers. (Illus.). (gr. 7-9). 1949. 10.00 o.p. (ISBN 0-397-00018-9, HarpJ). Har-Row.

Trapp, Maria von see Von Trapp, Maria.

Trapp, Maria Von see Von Trapp, Maria.

Trappl, R. Progress in Cybernetics & Systems Research, Vol. 8. 1982. 110.00 (ISBN 0-07-065068-3). McGraw.

Trappl, R., ed. Cybernetics & Systems Research: Proceedings of the Sixth European Meeting, Organized by the Austrian Society for Cybernetic Studies, University of Vienna, 1982. 984p. 1982. 127.75 (ISBN 0-444-86488-1, North Holland). Elsevier.

Trappl, Robert, ed. Cybernetics: Theory & Applications. (Illus.). 600p. 1983. text ed. 80.00 (ISBN 0-89116-128-7). Hemisphere Pub.

Trappl, Robert, et al, eds. Progress in Cybernetics & Systems Research, 5 vols. Incl. Vol. 1. General Systems, Engineering Systems, Biocybernetics & Neural Systems. 24.50x o.s.i. (ISBN 0-470-88475-4); Vol. 2. Socio-Economic Systems, Cognition & Learning, Systems Education, Organization & Management. 24.50x o.s.i. (ISBN 0-470-88476-2); Vol. 3. General Systems Methodology, Fuzzy Mathematics & Fuzzy Systems, Biocybernetics & Theoretical Neurobiology. 40.00x o.s.i. (ISBN 0-470-26371-7); Vol. 4. Cybernetics of Cognition & Learning, Structure & Dynamics of Socioeconomic Systems, Health Care Systems, Engineering Systems Methodology. 40.00x o.s.i. (ISBN 0-470-99380-4); Vol. 5. Organization & Management, Organic Problem-Solving in Management System Approach in Urban & Regional Planning, Computer Performance, Control & Evaluation of Computer Linguistics. 50.00x o.s.i. (ISBN 0-470-26553-1). LC 75-6641. 1975-79. Halsted Pr.

Trasatti, S. Electrodes of Conductive Metallic Oxides, 2 Pts. (Studies in Physical & Theoretical Chemistry: VOl. 11). 1980. Pt. A. 76.75 (ISBN 0-444-41912-8); Pt. B. 76.75 (ISBN 0-444-41988-8). Elsevier.

Traschen, Isadore, jt. auth. see Frakes, James R.

Trask. They Shall Call Me Trask. LC 81-80158. 160p. 1983. pap. 7.95 (ISBN 0-86666-008-9). GWP.

Trask, Anne E., jt. auth. see Gross, Neal.

Trask, David F. General Tasker Howard Bliss & the "Sessions of the World", 1919. LC 66-30495. (Transactions Ser.: Vol. 56, Pt. 8). 1966. pap. 1.00 o.p. (ISBN 0-87169-568-5). Am Philos.

Trask, Richard, jt. auth. see Emmerling, Mary.

Trask, Willard R., tr. see Corbin, Henry.

Trattner, Walter I. Social Welfare or Social Control? Some Historical Reflections on "Regulating the Poor". LC 82-15901. 176p. 1983. text ed. 14.95x (ISBN 0-87049-374-4); pap. text ed. 7.95x (ISBN 0-87049-375-2). U of Tenn Pr.

Traub, Barbara F. The Matrushka Doll. LC 79-9807. 1979. 12.50 o.p. (ISBN 0-399-90044-6, Marek). Putnam Pub Group.

Traub, J. F. & Wozniakowski, H. A General Theory of Optimal Algorithms. LC 79-8859. (ACM Monograph). 1980. 41.50 (ISBN 0-12-697650-3). Acad Pr.

Traub, J. F., ed. Algorithms & Complexity: New Directions & Recent Results. 1976. 41.50 (ISBN 0-12-697540-X). Acad Pr.

--Analytic Computational Complexity. 1976. 26.50 (ISBN 0-12-697560-4). Acad Pr.

--Complexity of Sequential & Parallel Numerical Algorithms. 1973. 34.50 (ISBN 0-12-697550-7). Acad Pr.

Traub, Stuart H. & Little, Craig B., eds. Theories of Deviance. 2nd ed. LC 79-91105. 400p. 1980. pap. text ed. 12.95 (ISBN 0-87581-247-3). Peacock Pubs.

Trauger, Wilmer K. Language Arts in Elementary Schools. 1963. text ed. 10.95 o.p. (ISBN 0-07-065139-6, C). McGraw.

Traugott, John. Tristram Shandy's World: Sterne's Philosophical Rhetoric. LC 76-102551. 1970. Repr. of 1954 ed. 9.00x o.p. (ISBN 0-8462-1484-9). Russell.

Trause, Mary Anne, jt. auth. see Reukauf, Diane.

Trauth, Mary P. Italo-American Diplomatic Relations, Eighteen Sixty-One to Eighteen Eighty-Two: The Mission of George Perkins Marsh, First American Minister to the Kingdom of Italy. LC 79-25192. 190p. 1980. Repr. of 1958 ed. lib. bdg. 19.00x (ISBN 0-313-22143-X, TRIA). Greenwood.

Trautman, Joanne, jt. ed. see Nicolson, Nigel.

Trautman, R., ed. see Owens, W.

Trautmann, Frederic. The Voice of Terror: A Biography of Johann Most. LC 79-8279. (Contributions in Political Science: No. 42). (Illus.). xxv, 288p. 1980. lib. bdg. 29.95 (ISBN 0-313-22053-0, TVT). Greenwood.

Trautmann, Joanne, jt. ed. see Nicolson, Nigel.

Trautmann, Joanne, ed. see Woolf, Virginia.

Travelaid Staff. Travelaid Guide to Greece. (Travelaid Guides Ser.). (Illus., Orig.). 1978. pap. 5.95 o.p. (ISBN 0-8467-0435-8, Pub. by Two Continents). Hippocrene Bks.

Travell, Janet G. & Simons, David G. Myofacial Pain & Dysfunction: The Trigger Point Manual. (Illus.). 568p. 1983. price not set o.p. (ISBN 0-683-08366-X). Williams & Wilkins.

Traven, B. The Death Ship. LC 72-96593. 384p. 1973. Repr. of 1934 ed. 12.00 o.s.i. (ISBN 0-88208-034-2). Lawrence Hill.

--Treasure of Sierra Madre. 1968. pap. 1.25 o.p. (ISBN 0-451-06857-2, Y6857, Sig). NAL.

Traven, Beatrice. The Complete Book of Natural Cosmetics. (Illus.). 160p. 1974. 8.95 o.p. (ISBN 0-671-21769-0). S&S.

Traver, Gayle A. Respiratory Nursing: The Science & the Art. LC 81-16285. 474p. 1982. 19.95 (ISBN 0-471-04539-X, Pub. by Wiley Med). Wiley.

Traver, Robert. Anatomy of a Murder. 2.95 o.p. (ISBN 0-89559-009-3). Green Hill.

--Anatomy of A Murder. 448p. 1983. pap. 7.95 (ISBN 0-312-03356-7). St Martin.

--Trout Magic. (Sportsmen's Classics Ser.). (Illus.). 220p. 1974. 7.50 o.p. (ISBN 0-517-51604-7). Crown.

Travers, David. Preparing Design Office Brochures: A Handbook. 2nd ed. (Illus.). 1982. pap. 10.75 (ISBN 0-931228-08-5). Arts & Arch.

Travers, Henry J. Organizations: Size & Intensity. LC 78-52294. 1978. pap. text ed. 7.25 (ISBN 0-8191-0483-3). U Pr of Amer.

Travers, Jeffrey, jt. auth. see Pizer, Stuart A.

Travers, John F. Educational Psychology. 1979. pap. text ed. 20.95 scp o.p. (ISBN 0-06-046655-3, HarpC); inst. manual avail. o.p. (ISBN 0-06-366648-0); scp study guide 8.95 o.p. (ISBN 0-06-046652-9). Har-Row.

--The Growing Child: An Introduction to Child Development. 2nd ed. 1982. text ed. 21.95x (ISBN 0-673-16022-X). Scott F.

Travers, Linda R. Writings of Linda. 1983. 6.95 (ISBN 0-533-05525-3). Vantage.

Travers, P. L. The Complete Mary Poppins, 4 vols. 1976. 17.25 (ISBN 0-15-619810-X, VoyB). HarBraceJ.

--Mary Poppins Opens the Door. LC 75-30697. (Illus.). 239p. (gr. 4-6). 1976. pap. 4.95 (ISBN 0-15-657692-9, VoyB). HarBraceJ.

Travers, P. L. & Moore-Betty, Maurice. Mary Poppins in the Kitchen. LC 77-17764. (Illus.). (gr. 1 up). 1978. pap. 1.95 (ISBN 0-15-657688-0, VoyB). HarBraceJ.

--Mary Poppins in the Kitchen: A Cookery Book with a Story. LC 75-10131. (Illus.). 128p. (gr. k up). 1975. 6.95 o.p. (ISBN 0-15-252898-9, HJ). HarBraceJ.

Travers, Pamela. Mary Poppins. rev. ed. LC 81-7273. (Illus.). 206p. (gr. 4-6). 1981. 12.95 (ISBN 0-15-252408-8, HJ). HarBraceJ.

Travers, Pamela L. Mary Poppins. rev. ed. LC 81-7273. (Illus.). (gr. 4-6). 12.95 o.p. (ISBN 0-15-252408-8, HJ); pap. 3.95 o.p. (ISBN 0-15-252409-6). HarBraceJ.

--Mary Poppins Comes Back. LC 74-17258. (Illus.). 268p. (gr. 4 up). 1975. pap. 4.95 (ISBN 0-15-657683-X, VoyB). HarBraceJ.

Travers, Robert M. How Research Has Changed American Schools: A History from 1840 to the Present. (Illus.). xii, 600p. 1983. lib. bdg. 25.00 (ISBN 0-686-38132-7). Mythos Pr.

--Introduction to Educational Research. 4th ed. (Illus.). 1978. text ed. 22.95x (ISBN 0-02-421370-5, 42137). Macmillan.

Travers, Robert M. & Cooke, Jacqueline. Making of a Teacher. 1975. pap. 6.95x (ISBN 0-02-421340-3). Macmillan.

Traversi, Derek. The Literary Imagination: Studies in Dante, Chaucer & Shakespeare. LC 81-50650. 272p. 1982. 29.50 (ISBN 0-87413-198-7). U Delaware Pr.

--T. S. Eliot: The Longer Poems. LC 76-18793. 1976. 10.00 o.p. (ISBN 0-15-191380-3, HB346). HarBraceJ.

Traversie, Rick. Trails from Cheyenne River. 1981. pap. 1.50 (ISBN 0-912678-51-8). Greenfld Rev Pr.

Travis. Interval on Symi. 1971. 5.95 (ISBN 0-686-84078-X). Gambit.

--Interval on Symi. 1971. 5.95 (ISBN 0-87645-034-6). Gambit.

Travis, Carole, ed. see Standing Conference on Library Materials on Africa.

Travis, Charles, jt. auth. see Rosenberg, Jay F.

Travis, Curtis C. & Etnier, Elizabeth L., eds. Health Risks of Energy Technologies. (AAAS Selected Symposium: No. 82). 291p. 1982. lib. bdg. 25.00 (ISBN 0-86531-520-5). Westview.

Travis, Edward L. Speech Pathology. 331p. 1982. Repr. of 1931 ed. lib. bdg. 75.00 (ISBN 0-89984-467-7). Century Bookbindery.

Travis, Gretchen. Two Spruce Lane. LC 74-30587. 1975. 7.95 o.p. (ISBN 0-399-11514-5). Putnam Pub Group.

Travis, John W. A Guide to Restringing. 2nd ed. Travis, Michael R., ed. LC 82-60057. (Illus.). 1982. 35.00x; pap. 30.00x (ISBN 0-9600394-5-7). Travis.

Travis, L. D., jt. auth. see Anderson, Charles.

Travis, Lee E., ed. Handbook of Speech Pathology & Audiology. LC 74-146360. (Orig.). 1971. 69.95 (ISBN 0-13-381764-4). P-H.

Travis, Marlene, ed. see McIlroy, Gary.

Travis, Michael R., ed. see Travis, John W.

Travnikar, Rock. The Blessing Cup. 64p. (Orig.). 1979. pap. 2.25 (ISBN 0-912228-60-1). St Anthony Mess Pr.

Trawick, Buckner B. Bible As Literature: Old Testament & the Apocrypha. 2nd ed. 1970. pap. 5.95 (ISBN 0-06-460056-4, CO 56, COS). B&N NY.

--Bible As Literature: The New Testament. 2nd ed. (Orig.). 1968. pap. 3.95 (ISBN 0-06-460057-2, CO 57, COS). B&N NY.

Trawicki, D. J., jt. auth. see Beyer, R.

Trawicki, Donald, jt. auth. see Beyer, Robert.

Traxel, Robert G. Manager's Guide to Successful Job Hunting. (Illus.). 1978. 15.95 o.p. (ISBN 0-07-065096-9, P&RB). McGraw.

Traxler, Arthur E. Introduction to Testing & the Use of Test Results in Public Schools. LC 71-98241. (Illus.). 113p. Repr. of 1953 ed. lib. bdg. 17.75x (ISBN 0-8371-4043-9, TRIT). Greenwood.

Traylor, Melvin A., Jr., jt. auth. see Paynter, Raymond A., Jr.

Traynham, James G. Organic Nomenclature: A Programmed Introduction. 2nd ed. 1980. pap. text ed. 11.95 (ISBN 0-13-640771-4). P-H.

Traynor, Mark & Seide, Diane. Mark Traynor's Beauty Book. LC 79-7881. (Illus.). 256p. 1980. 11.95 o.p. (ISBN 0-385-14775-9). Doubleday.

Treacy, Margaret, jt. auth. see Stroup, Marjory.

Treacy, Margaret, ed. Pretransfusion Testing for the '80s. 139p. 1980. 21.00 (ISBN 0-914404-56-3). Am Assn Blood.

Treacy, Margaret & Bertsch, Judith, eds. Selecting Policies & Procedures for the Transfusion Service. 127p. 1982. 19.00 (ISBN 0-914404-75-X); non-members 21.00 (ISBN 0-686-83045-8). Am Assn Blood.

Treacy, Sean. A Smell of Broken Glass. 2.95 o.p. (ISBN 0-85468-457-3). David & Charles.

Treadgold, Donald W. The Great Siberian Migration. LC 75-25498. 1976. Repr. of 1957 ed. lib. bdg. 21.00x (ISBN 0-8371-8427-4, TRSM). Greenwood.

--A History of Christianity. LC 78-78118. 277p. (Orig.). 1979. 27.50 (ISBN 0-913124-35-4); pap. 8.95 (ISBN 0-686-96806-9). Nordland Pub.

Treadgold, Mary. Journey from the Heron. 160p. (gr. 5 up). 1983. 9.95 (ISBN 0-224-01970-8, Pub by Jonathan Cape). Merrimack Bk Serv.

Treadgold, Warren T. The Byzantine State Finances in the Eighth & Ninth Centuries. (East European Monographs: No. 121). 280p. 1982. 22.50x (ISBN 0-88033-014-7). East Eur Quarterly.

Treadle, John, jt. auth. see Brearley, Alan.

Treadway, John D. The Falcon & the Eagle: Montenegro & Austria-Hungary, 1908-1914. LC 81-82728. (Illus.). 324p. 1983. 18.00 (ISBN 0-911198-65-2). Purdue.

Treadway, Sandra G., ed. Journals of the Council of the State of Virginia: 1788-1791, Vol. 5. 400p. 1982. 10.00 (ISBN 0-88490-096-7). VA State Lib.

Treadwell, Hugh W., ed. see Reeve, Kay A.

Treadwell, Jimmie. My Victory or Defeat. 1979. 4.95 o.p. (ISBN 0-533-03397-7). Vantage.

Treager, Irwin. Aircraft Gas Turbine Engine Technology. 2nd ed. (Illus.). 1978. pap. text ed. 27.50 (ISBN 0-07-065158-2, G). McGraw.

Trease, Geoffrey. Popinjay Stairs: An Historical Adventure About Samuel Pepys. LC 74-30873. (gr. 3-6). 1982. 9.95 (ISBN 0-8149-0758-X). Vanguard.

Treasure, G. R. Cardinal Richelieu and the Development of Absolutism. LC 76-183397. 1972. text ed. 17.95 o.p. (ISBN 0-312-12040-0). St Martin.

Treasure, Geoff. The Most Unforgettable Character You'll Ever Meet. 1977. pap. 2.95 o.p. (ISBN 0-8024-5625-1). Moody.

Treasure, Geoffrey. Cardinal Richelieu & the Development of Absolutism. 316p. 1982. 30.00x (ISBN 0-7136-1287-8, Pub. by Shepheard-Walwyn England). State Mutual Bk.

--Cardinal Richelieu & the Development of Absolutism. 316p. 1982. 7.50 (ISBN 0-85683-065-8, Pub. by Shepheard-Walwyn). Flatiron Book Dist.

Treasurer, Kim. The Nolans. (Illus.). 128p. (gr. 6 up). 1983. 9.95 (ISBN 0-88254-736-4, Pub. by Midas Bks England). Hippocrene Bks.

Treat, Lawrence. A Special Kind of Crime. LC 81-43452. (Crime Club Ser.). 192p. 1982. 10.95 (ISBN 0-385-17993-6). Doubleday.

Treat, Roger. The Encyclopedia of Football. 16th rev. ed. Palmer, Pete, ed. (Illus.). 1979. pap. 11.95 (ISBN 0-385-15091-1, Dolp). Doubleday.

Trebach, Arnold S. The Heroin Solution. LC 81-15993. 352p. 1982. 24.95x (ISBN 0-300-02773-7). Yale U Pr.

Trebaticka, Heather, tr. see Dekan, Jan.

Trebbi, Diana, jt. auth. see Shaughnessy, Edward J.

Trebesch, Karsten. Organisation Development in Europe, 2 vols. 1628p. 1981. Set. 150.00 (ISBN 0-7121-5612-7, Pub. by Macdonald & Evans). State Mutual Bk.

Treble, Henry A. Classical & Biblical Reference Book. (YA) (gr. 9 up). 1959. 6.00 o.p. (ISBN 0-7195-1426-6). Transatlantic.

Treble, J. H. Urban Poverty in Britain, Eighteen Thirty to Nineteen Sixty. 1979. 42.50 o.p. (ISBN 0-7134-1906-7, Pub. by Batsford England). David & Charles.

--Urban Poverty in Britain, 1830-1914. 1979. 26.00x (ISBN 0-312-83463-2). St Martin.

Treble, Rosemary. Van Gogh & His Art. (The Artist & His Art Ser.). (Illus.). 128p. 1981. 9.98 o.p. (ISBN 0-89196-090-2, Bk Value Intl). Quality Bks IL.
Tredell, Nicolas. The Novels of Colin Wilson. LC 82-13913. (Critical Studies Ser.). 158p. 1982. text ed. 26.50x (ISBN 0-389-20280-0). B&N Imports.
Tree, Christina & Jennison, Peter S. Vermont: An Explorer's Guide. 256p. (Orig.). 1983. pap. 9.95 (ISBN 0-88150-002-X). Countryman.
Tree, Cornelia. Child of the Night. 1983. pap. 2.95 (ISBN 0-553-23054-9). Bantam.
Treece, Eleanor W. & Treece, James W., Jr. Elements of Research in Nursing. 3d ed. LC 81-14149. (Illus.). 424p. 1982. pap. text ed. 16.95 (ISBN 0-8016-5109-3). Mosby.
Treece, Henry. Further Adventures of Robinson Crusoe. LC 58-9623. (Illus.). (gr. 7-11). 1958. 10.95 (ISBN 0-87599-116-5). S G Phillips.
--Men of the Hills. LC 58-5448. (Illus.). (gr. 6-9). 1958. 10.95 (ISBN 0-87599-115-7). S G Phillips.
--Ride into Danger. LC 59-12203. (Illus.). (gr. 7-10). 1959. 10.95 (ISBN 0-87599-113-0). S G Phillips.
--Road to Miklagard. LC 57-12280. (Illus.). (gr. 6-10). 1957. 10.95 (ISBN 0-87599-118-1). S G Phillips.
--Viking's Dawn. LC 56-9962. (Illus.). (gr. 7-9). 1956. 10.95 (ISBN 0-87599-117-3). S G Phillips.
Treece, James W., Jr., jt. auth. see Treece, Eleanor W.
Treece, Patricia. A Man for Others: Maximilian Kolbe in the Words of Those Who Knew Him. LC 82-48404. (Illus.). 192p. 1983. 12.45i (ISBN 0-06-067069-X, HarpR). Har-Row.
Treen, David C., ed. Can You Afford This House? (Republican Study Committee Papers Ser.). 1978. pap. 2.95 o.p. (ISBN 0-916054-72-1). Caroline Hse.
Trees, H. L. Van see Van Trees, Harry L.
Trees, Harry L. Van see Van Trees, Harry L.
Trees, Harry L. van see Van Trees, Harry L.
Trees, James Van see Van Trees, James & Wolenik, Robert.
Treese, Glenn J. Van see Van Treese, Glenn J.
Treffinger, D. J., et al, eds. Handbook on Teaching Educational Psychology. 1977. 28.50 (ISBN 0-12-697750-X). Acad Pr.
Trefil, James S. Introduction to the Physics of Fluids & Solids. 320p. 1975. text ed. 30.00 (ISBN 0-08-018104-X). Pergamon.
--The Unexpected Vista: A Physicist's View of Nature. (Illus.). 256p. 14.95 (ISBN 0-684-17869-9, ScribT). Scribner.
Trefil, James S., jt. auth. see Rood, Robert T.
Trefousse, Hans, ed. see McPherson, Edward.
Trefren, Doris. From Headhunters to Hallelujahs. LC 80-69540. 190p. (Orig.). 1980. pap. 3.95 (ISBN 0-89957-047-X). AMG Pubs.
Trefry, D. & Trefry, J. F. Kuman Language Course. 133p. 1967. pap. 2.05 o.p. (ISBN 0-88312-781-4); microfiche 2.25 o.p. (ISBN 0-88312-399-1). Summer Inst Ling.
Trefry, J. F., jt. auth. see Trefry, D.
Tregarthen, Timothy D. Food, Fuel, & Shelter: A Watershed Analysis of Land-Use Trade-Offs in a Semi-Arid Region. LC 77-19355. (Westview Special Studies in Natural Resources & Energy Management Ser.). 1978. lib. bdg. 20.00x o.p. (ISBN 0-89158-070-0). Westview.
Tregellas, W. Michael & Wallas, Charles H., eds. Prenatal & Perinatal Immunohematology. (Illus.). 117p. 1981. 21.00 (ISBN 0-914404-66-0). Am Assn Blood.
Tregle, J. G., Jr., ed. see Hutchins, Thomas.
Treglown, Jeremy. Spirit of Wit. 90p. 1982. 25.00 (ISBN 0-208-02012-8, Archon Bks). Shoe String.
Tregoe, Benjamin, jt. auth. see Kepner, Charles H.
Tregoe, Benjamin B. & Zimmerman, John W. Top Management Strategy. 1983. pap. price not set (ISBN 0-671-25402-2, Touchstone Bks). S&S.
Tregoe, Benjamin B., jt. auth. see Kepner, Charles H.
Treharne, R. E., ed. see Muir, Ramsey.
Treharne, R. F. The Baronial Plan of Reform, 1258-1263. 1932. 31.00 (ISBN 0-7190-0397-0). Manchester.
Treher, Charles H. & Barba, Preston A. Snow Hill Cloister: Bd. with Dialect Poems of Ralph Funk, Vol. II. LC 68-59437. 1969. 20.00 (ISBN 0-911122-25-7). Penn German Soc.
Treherne, J. E. Neurochemistry of Arthropods. (Cambridge Monographs in Experimental Biology: No. 14). 1966. 32.50 (ISBN 0-521-08555-1); pap. 12.95 (ISBN 0-521-06645-X). Cambridge U Pr.
Treherne, J. E. see Beament, J. W., et al.
Treherne, J. E., et al, eds. Advances in Insect Physiology, Vol. 16. (Serial Publication). 368p. 1982. 55.00 (ISBN 0-12-024216-8). Acad Pr.
Treiman, D. J., ed. Occupational Prestige in Comparative Perspective. (Quantitative Studies in Social Discontinuity Ser.). 1977. 29.50 (ISBN 0-12-698750-5). Acad Pr.
Treitel, Sven, jt. auth. see Robinson, Enders A.
Trejo, Arnulfo D., ed. Bibliografia Chicana: A Guide to Information Sources. LC 74-11562. (Ethnic Studies Information Guide: Vol. 1). 240p. 1975. 42.00x (ISBN 0-8103-1311-1). Gale.
Trelawny, John E. Records of Shelley, Byron. 1983. pap. 4.95 (ISBN 0-14-043088-1). Penguin.
Trelease, Allen W. White Terror: The Ku Klux Klan Conspiracy & Southern Reconstruction. LC 78-12864. 1979. Repr. of 1972 ed. lib. bdg. 45.00x (ISBN 0-313-21168-X, TRWT). Greenwood.
Trelease, Richard N., et al. Biology One Hundred One Laboratory Manual. 1982. pap. text ed. 4.50 (ISBN 0-8403-2745-5). Kendall-Hunt.
--Biology One Hundred Two Laboratory Manual. 1982. pap. text ed. 9.95 (ISBN 0-8403-2763-3). Kendall-Hunt.
Trelease, Sam F. How to Write Scientific & Technical Papers. 1969. pap. 5.95x (ISBN 0-262-70004-2). MIT Pr.
Trelease, W. The American Oaks. (Plant Monograph Ser.). (Illus.). 1969. 60.00 (ISBN 3-7682-0600-9). Lubrecht & Cramer.
--A Revision of the American Species of Epilobium Occurring North of Mexico. 1977. Repr. of 1891 ed. 10.00 (ISBN 3-7682-0600-9). Lubrecht & Cramer.
Trelford, Donald, ed. Sunday Best from the Observer. 224p. 1981. 16.50 o.p. (ISBN 0-575-03071-2, Pub. by Gollancz England). David & Charles.
--Sunday Best Two: Selections from the London Observer. 256p. 1982. 17.50 (ISBN 0-575-03190-5, Pub. by Gollancz England). David & Charles.
Trell, Max, jt. auth. see Foster, Hal.
Treloar, L. R. G. The Physics of Rubber Elasticity. 3rd ed. (Monographs on the Physics & Chemistry of Materials). (Illus.). 1975. 65.00x (ISBN 0-19-851355-0). Oxford U Pr.
Tremaine, Jennie. Ginny. (Orig.). 1980. pap. 1.50 o.s.i. (ISBN 0-440-12820-X). Dell.
--Molly. (Orig.). 1980. pap. 1.50 o.s.i. (ISBN 0-440-15856-7). Dell.
--Polly. (Orig.). 1980. pap. 1.50 o.s.i. (ISBN 0-440-17033-8). Dell.
--Poppy. (Candlelight Regency Ser.: No. 704). (Orig.). 1982. pap. 1.75 o.s.i. (ISBN 0-440-16969-0). Dell.
--Susie. (Candlelight Edwardian Special Ser.: No. 685). 256p. (Orig.). 1981. pap. 1.75 o.s.i. (ISBN 0-440-18391-X). Dell.
--Tilly. (Candlelight Romance Ser.). (Orig.). 1981. pap. 1.50 o.s.i. (ISBN 0-440-18637-4). Dell.
Tremaine, Jennie, ed. Lucy. (Orig.). 1980. pap. 1.50x o.s.i. (ISBN 0-440-15609-2). Dell.
Tremayne, Archibald. Records From Erech, Time of Cyrus & Cambyses. 1926. text ed. 29.50x (ISBN 0-686-83726-6). Elliots Bks.
Tremayne, Nicholas. Golf: How to Become a Champ. (Illus.). 1976. pap. 5.95 o.p. (ISBN 0-86002-129-7). Transatlantic.
Tremayne, Peter. The Ants. 1980. pap. 1.75 o.p. (ISBN 0-451-09163-9, J9163, Sig). NAL.
Tremblay, J. P. & Manohar, R. Discrete Mathematical Structures with Applications to Computer Science. (Computer Science Ser.). (Illus.). 544p. 1975. text ed. 33.95 (ISBN 0-07-065142-6, C); instructor's manual 7.95 (ISBN 0-07-065144-2). McGraw.
Tremblay, J. P. & Sorenson, P. G. An Introduction to Data Structures with Applications. 2nd ed. 736p. 1982. 22.00x (ISBN 0-07-065157-4). McGraw.
--An Introduction to Data Structures with Applications: Computer Science Ser. 1976. text ed. 32.95 (ISBN 0-07-065150-7, C); instr's. manual 25.00 (ISBN 0-07-065151-5). McGraw.
--The Theory & Practice of Compiler Writing. Date not set. price not set (ISBN 0-07-065161-2); supplementary materials avail. McGraw.
Tremblay, Jean P. & Bunt, Richard B. Structured Fortran WATFIV-S Programming. 1979. pap. text ed. 18.95 (ISBN 0-07-065171-X). McGraw.
--Structured Pascal. 448p. 1980. pap. text ed. 19.95 (ISBN 0-07-065159-0, C). McGraw.
--Structured PL-One (PL-C) Programming. 1979. pap. text ed. 18.95x (ISBN 0-07-065173-6). McGraw.
Tremblay, Jean-Paul & Bunt, Richard B. Introduction to Computer Science: An Algorithmic Approach. (Illus.). 1979. text ed. 28.95 (ISBN 0-07-065163-9, C); instructor's manual 15.00 (ISBN 0-07-065164-7). McGraw.
--An Introduction to Computer Science: An Algorithmic Approach, Short Edition. Stewart, Charles E., ed. (Illus.). 432p. 1980. text ed. 23.95 (ISBN 0-07-065167-1, C). McGraw.
Tremblay, Remi. Un Revenant. (Novels by Franco-Americans in New England 1850-1940 Ser.). 348p. (Fr.). (gr. 10 up). 1980. pap. 4.50x (ISBN 0-911409-21-1). Natl Mat Dev.
Tremblay, Sharyn F., jt. auth. see Wills, Sheryle L.
Tremblay, Sharyn F., jt. ed. see Wills, Sheryle L.
Tremens, Del. A Very Young Housewife. LC 79-17808. (Bogus Bks). (Orig.). 1979. pap. 5.95 o.p. (ISBN 0-916782-18-2). Harvard Common Pr.
Tremewan, Phillip, jt. auth. see Horrocho, Roger.
Treml, Vladimir, jt. auth. see Woll, Josephine.
Treml, Vladimir G. Alcohol in the U.S.S.R. A Statistical Study. (Duke Press Policy Studies). 200p. 1982. 27.75 (ISBN 0-8223-0484-8). Duke.
Treml, Vladimir G., ed. Studies in Soviet Input-Output Analysis. LC 77-2739. (Praeger Special Studies). 1977. 53.95 o.p. (ISBN 0-275-56550-5). Praeger.
Tremonger. Basic Stress Analysis. 1982. text ed. 19.95 (ISBN 0-408-01113-0). Butterworth.
Tremont, Stuart. How Even a Superficial Knowledge of Charts May Help You to Double, Treble, Quadruple your Stock Market Profits. (New Stock Market Library Book). (Illus.). 67p. (Orig.). 1983. pap. 6.95 (ISBN 0-89266-389-8). Am Classical Coll Pr.
Tremonte, Julia. The Devil's House. (Orig.). 1979. pap. 1.50 o.p. (ISBN 0-523-40709-2). Pinnacle Bks.
Tremper, Andra & Diebert, Linda. What's New at the Zoo, Kangaroo? (ps-6). 1982. 7.95 (ISBN 0-86653-083-5, GA 429). Good Apple.
Trench, Richard C. Commentary on the Epistle to the Seven Churches. 1978. 8.50 (ISBN 0-86524-113-9, 6601). Klock & Klock.
Trench, William F. & Kolman, Bernard. Answers to Selected Problems in Multi-Variable Calculus with Linear Algebra & Series. 1972. 3.50 (ISBN 0-12-699056-5). Acad Pr.
--Multivariable Calculus with Linear Algebra & Series. 758p. 1972. text ed. 27.00 o.s.i. (ISBN 0-12-699050-6). Acad Pr.
Trenchard, Warren C. Ben Sira's View of Women: A Literary Analysis. LC 82-16755. (Brown Judaic Studies: No. 38). 352p. 1982. pap. 15.75 (ISBN 0-89130-593-9, 14-00-38). Scholars Pr CA.
Trencher, Barbara R. Child's Play: An Activities & Materials Handbook. LC 76-46501. (gr. 3 up). 1976. pap. text ed. 14.95 (ISBN 0-89334-003-0). Humanics Ltd.
Trend, M. G. Housing Allowances for the Poor: A Social Experiment. LC 78-52057. (A Westview Replica Edition Ser.). 1978. softcover 32.50 o.p. (ISBN 0-89158-057-3). Westview.
Trendall, A. D. & Cambitoglou, A. The Red-Figured Vases of Apulia, 2 Pts, Vol. 2. (Monographs on Classical Archaeology). (Illus.). 1982. 160.00 set (ISBN 0-19-813219-0). Oxford U Pr.
Trenhaile, John. A Man Called Kyril. 288p. 1983. 12.95 (ISBN 0-312-92515-8). Congdon & Weed.
Trenkle, Clare. You. 1966. text ed. 7.95x (ISBN 0-88323-086-0, 182); wkbk. 2.75 (ISBN 0-88323-087-9, 183). Richards Pub.
Trenn. Transmutation: Natural & Artificial. 1981. cloth 29.95 (ISBN 0-471-26105-X, Wiley Heyden); pap. 19.95 (ISBN 0-471-26106-8). Wiley.
Trenn, T. J. Radioactivity & Atomic Theory. LC 75-19168. 517p. 1975. 40.25 o.p. (ISBN 0-470-88520-3). Krieger.
Trenn, Thaddeus J. America's Golden Bough: Science, Polity, & the Public. LC 82-18873. 196p. 1983. text ed. 25.00 (ISBN 0-89946-160-3). Oelgeschlager.
Trenner, Richard, ed. E. L. Doctorow: Essays & Conversations. 286p. 1983. 14.95 (ISBN 0-86538-023-6); pap. 8.95 (ISBN 0-86538-024-4). Ontario Rev NJ.
Trennert, Robert A., Jr. Alternative to Extinction: Federal Indian Policy & the Beginning of the Reservation System, 1846-51. LC 74-83203. 272p. 1975. 24.95 (ISBN 0-87722-030-1). Temple U Pr.
Trent, E. M. Metal Cutting. 1977. 39.95 (ISBN 0-408-10603-4). Butterworth.
Trent, William P. William Gilmore Simms. Repr. of 1892 ed. lib. bdg. 16.25x (ISBN 0-8371-1171-4, TRWS). Greenwood.
Trenton, Patricia & Hassrick, Peter H. The Rocky Mountains: A Vision for Artists in the Nineteenth Century. LC 82-21879. (Illus.). 440p. 1983. 65.00 (ISBN 0-8061-1808-3). U of Okla Pr.
Trenton, Rudolph W. Basic Economics. 4th ed. 1978. pap. text ed. 17.95 (ISBN 0-13-059139-4). P-H.
Treon, Ray, jt. auth. see Taylor, Joan.
Trepp, Leo. Judaism: Development & Life. 2nd ed. 1974. pap. text ed. 8.95x o.p. (ISBN 0-8221-0114-9). Dickenson.
Trepper, Leopold. The Great Game. LC 76-7537. 1977. 10.95 o.p. (ISBN 0-07-065146-9, GB). McGraw.
Tresemer, David. The Scythe Book: Mowing Hay, Cutting Weeds, & Harvesting Small Grains with Hand Tools. (Illus.). 128p. 1982. pap. 6.95 (ScribT). Scribner.
--Splitting Firewood. (Illus.). 160p. 1982. pap. 6.95 (ScribT). Scribner.
Treshow, Michael. Environment & Plant Response. 1970. text ed. 33.95 (ISBN 0-07-065134-5, C). McGraw.
--The Human Environment. (Population Biology Ser.). 1976. text ed. 21.00 (ISBN 0-07-065136-1, C). McGraw.
Tresler, Kathleen M. Clinical Laboratory Tests: Significance & Nursing Implications. (Illus.). 496p. 1982. 17.95 (ISBN 0-13-137760-4). P-H.
Tresolini, Rocco J., jt. auth. see Shapiro, Martin.
Tressell, Robert. The Ragged Trousered Philanthropists. LC 62-11421. (Leo Huberman People's Library). 1978. pap. 7.50 (ISBN 0-85345-457-4, PB 457-4). Monthly Rev.
Tressler, Arthur, ed. Science Year, The World Book Science Annual. LC 65-21776. (Illus.). (YA) (gr. 7-12). 1979. lib. bdg. write for info. o.p. (ISBN 0-7166-0580-5). World Bk.
Tressler, Arthur G., jt. ed. see World Book Inc.
Trester, H. Supervision of the Offender. 1981. 19.95 (ISBN 0-13-876938-9). P-H.
Trester, Kenneth R. The Compleat Option Player. 2nd ed. (Illus.). 316p. 1981. 16.95 (ISBN 0-9604914-0-6). Investrek.
Trethowan, W. H., jt. auth. see Enoch, M. D.
Tretiak, O. J., jt. auth. see Huang, T. S.
Tretkoff, M. see Siegel, C. L.
Tretter, Steven A. Introduction to Discrete-Time Signal Processing. LC 76-25943. 1976. text ed. 39.95x (ISBN 0-471-88760-9). Wiley.
Treuch, Herbert, tr. from Rus. see Merejkowski, Dmitri.
Trevarrow, W. M. The Book of Free Books. LC 79-54261. (Illus.). 156p. (Orig.). 1979. pap. 4.95 o.p. (ISBN 0-89196-042-2, Domus Bks). Quality Bks IL.
Trevathan, Robert E. Tracking the Bar-J Gold. (YA) 1978. 6.95 (ISBN 0-685-05593-0, Avalon). Bouregy.
Trevelyan, E., ed. Digest of the Decisions of the Supreme Court of Kenya in the Exercise of Its Criminal Revisional Jurisdiction in the Years 1897-1964. 102p. 1966. 12.00 (ISBN 0-379-00335-X). Oceana.
Trevelyan, G. M. England under the Stuarts. 21st ed. 1966. pap. 16.95x (ISBN 0-416-69240-0). Methuen Inc.
Trevelyan, George M. English Revolution, Sixteen Eighty-Eight to Sixteen Eighty-Nine. (YA) (gr. 9 up). 1965. pap. 5.95 (ISBN 0-19-500263-6, GB). Oxford U Pr.
--Lord Grey of the Reform Bill, Being the Life of Charles, Second Earl Grey. Repr. of 1920 ed. lib. bdg. 19.75x (ISBN 0-8371-4553-8, TRLG). Greenwood.
Trevelyan, George O. The Life & Letters of Lord MaCaulay. 1978. pap. 14.95 o.p. (ISBN 0-19-822487-7). Oxford U Pr.
Trevelyan, Humphrey. Living with the Communists: China 1953-1955 Soviet Union 1962-5. LC 70-167958. 1971. 7.95 (ISBN 0-87645-054-0). Gambit.
--Middle East in Revolution. LC 70-121353. 1970. 7.95 (ISBN 0-87645-033-8). Gambit.
Trevelyan, Humphry. Goethe & the Greeks. LC 81-3908. 368p. 1981. 49.50 (ISBN 0-521-24137-5); pap. 17.95 (ISBN 0-521-28471-6). Cambridge U Pr.
Trever, John C. Scrolls from Qumran Cave I: The Great Isaiah Scroll the Order of the Community, the Pesher to Habakkuk (color) 163p. 1972. text ed. 30.00x (ISBN 0-89757-002-2, Am Sch Orient Res). Eisenbrauns.
Treverton, Gregory, ed. Energy & Security. LC 80-67838. (Adelphi Library: Vol. 1). 172p. 1981. text ed. 28.50x (ISBN 0-916672-71-9). Allanheld.
Treverton, Gregory F. The "Dollar Drain" & American Forces in Germany: Managing the Political Economics of Alliance. LC 76-51689. xvi, 226p. 1978. 14.00x (ISBN 0-8214-0368-0, 82-82618). Ohio U Pr.
Treves, Francois. Basic Linear Partial Differential Equations. 1975. 57.00 (ISBN 0-12-699440-4). Acad Pr.
--Topological Vector Spaces, Distributions & Kernels. 1967. 63.00 (ISBN 0-12-699450-1). Acad Pr.
Treves, Frederick. Highways & Byways of Dorset. 376p. 1982. 30.00x (ISBN 0-7045-0430-8, Pub. by Wildwood House). State Mutual Bk.
Treves, Giuliana A. The Golden Ring: The Anglo-Florentines, 1847-1862. Sprigge, Sylvia, tr. from Ital. 221p. 1982. Repr. of 1956 ed. lib. bdg. 45.00 (ISBN 0-89760-897-6). Telegraph Bks.
Treves, S., jt. auth. see Schneider, P. B.
Treves, Yvain M., ed. see AIP Conference, 88th, La Jolla Institute, 1981.
Trevino, Alejandro. El Predicador: Platicas a Mis Estudiantes. 155p. 1982. pap. 2.95 (ISBN 0-311-42016-8). Casa Bautista.
Trevino, Alejandro, tr. see Harvey, H.
Trevino, Alejandro, tr. see Pendleton, J. M.
Trevino, Lee & Blair, Sam. They Call Me Super Mex. 200p. 1983. 12.95 (ISBN 0-394-52336-9). Random.
Trevisick, Charles. The Care & Training of Talking Birds. Foyle, Christina, ed. (Foyle's Handbks). 1971. 2.25 (ISBN 0-685-55816-9). Palmetto Pub.
Trevithick, J. A. & Mulvey, C. The Economics of Inflation. LC 75-256. 184p. 1975. 29.95 o.p. (ISBN 0-470-88775-3); pap. 16.95x o.p. (ISBN 0-470-26894-8). Halsted Pr.
Trevor, Aston, et al. Social Relations & Ideas. LC 82-9727. (Past & Present Publications). 352p. Date not set. price not set (ISBN 0-521-25132-X). Cambridge U Pr.
Trevor, M. D. The Development of Gymnastic Skills: A Scheme of Work for Teachers. (Development Skills Ser.). (Illus.). 64p. 1981. pap. 5.95x o.p. (ISBN 0-631-12577-9, Pub. by Basil Blackwell England). Biblio Dist.
Trevor, Toms. The ZX 81 Pocketbook. 1982. text ed. 18.95 (ISBN 0-8359-9525-9); lib. bdg. 10.95 (ISBN 0-8359-9524-0). Reston.
Trevor-Roper, Hugh. Princes & Artists: Patronage & Ideology at Four Habsburg Courts, 1517-1633. LC 75-34681. (Illus.). 176p. 1977. 20.00i (ISBN 0-06-014362-2, HarpT). Har-Row.
Trevor-Roper, Hugh, ed. The Final Entries, 1945: The Diaries of Joseph Goebbels. LC 78-6707. (Illus.). 1978. 14.95 (ISBN 0-399-12116-1). Putnam Pub Group.
Trevor-Roper, Hugh, ed. see Macaulay, Thomas.
Trew, Anthony. Sea Fever. 229p. 1981. 9.95 o.p. (ISBN 0-312-70813-0). St Martin.
Trew, Antony. Running Wild. 256p. 1983. 13.95 (ISBN 0-312-69601-9). St Martin.

Trewartha, Glenn. The Earth's Problem Climates. 2nd ed. LC 80-5120. (Illus.). 340p. 1981. 25.00 (ISBN 0-299-08230-X). U of Wis Pr.

Trewartha, Glenn T. Introduction to Climate. 4th ed. (Geography Ser.). (Maps). 1968. text ed. 21.50 (ISBN 0-07-065148-5, C). McGraw.

--Japan: A Geography. rev. ed. (Illus.). 662p. 1965. 25.00 (ISBN 0-299-03440-2); pap. 12.50 (ISBN 0-299-03444-5). U of Wis Pr.

Trewartha, Glenn T. & Horn, Lyle H. An Introduction to Climate. 5th ed. (McGraw-Hill Ser. in Geography). (Illus.). 1980. Repr. text ed. 29.95 (ISBN 0-07-065152-3). McGraw.

Trewartha, Glenn T., et al. Elements of Geography. 5th ed. 1967. text ed. 34.95 (ISBN 0-07-065155-8, C). McGraw.

--Fundamentals of Physical Geography. 3rd ed. (Illus.). 1976. text ed. 27.50 (ISBN 0-07-065183-3, C). McGraw.

Trexler, Edgar R. Mission in a New World. LC 76-62613. (Orig.). 1977. pap. 0.50 (ISBN 0-8006-1257-4). Fortress.

Trexler, Pat. Pat's Pointers: The Needlepoint Handbook. 200p. 1982. 15.00 (ISBN 0-8362-2500-7); pap. 6.95 (ISBN 0-8362-2502-3). Andrews & McMeel.

Treybal, Robert E. Mass Transfer Operations. 3rd ed. (Chemical Engineering Ser.). (Illus.). 1979. text ed. 38.50x (ISBN 0-07-065176-0, C); 19.00 (ISBN 0-07-065177-9). McGraw.

Trezel, Roger, jt. auth. see Reese, Terence.

Trezel, S., jt. auth. see Reese, T.

Trezise, Philip H. The Atlantic Connection. 200p. 1975. pap. 5.95 (ISBN 0-8157-8527-5). Brookings.

--Rebuilding Grain Reserves: Toward an International System. 1976. pap. 5.95 (ISBN 0-8157-8529-1). Brookings.

Trezise, Philip H., ed. The European Monetary System: Its Promise & Prospects. LC 79-55581. 96p. 1979. pap. 5.95 (ISBN 0-8157-8531-3). Brookings.

Trezza, Alphonse E., ed. see Library Equipment Institute, New York, July 7-9, 1966.

Triandis, Harry C. Attitude & Attitude Change. LC 76-140555. (Foundations of Social Psychology Ser). (Illus.). 1971. pap. text ed. 13.95x (ISBN 0-471-88831-1). Wiley.

Triandis, Harry C., ed. Analysis of Subjective Culture. LC 74-178910. (Comparative Studies in Behavioral Science Ser). 1972. 34.50 o.p. (ISBN 0-471-88905-9, Pub. by Wiley-Interscience). Wiley.

Trias, Eugenio. Philosophy & Its Shadow. Krabbenhoft, Kenneth, tr. LC 82-12803. (European Perspectives Ser.). 160p. 1983. text ed. 20.00x (ISBN 0-231-05288-X). Columbia U Pr.

Tribbe, Frank C. Portrait of Jesus? The Illustrated Story of the Shroud of Turin. 176p. 1983. 17.95 (ISBN 0-8128-2904-2). Stein & Day.

Tribe, Carol. Profile of Three Theories: Erikson, Maslow, Piaget. 120p. 1982. pap. text ed. 5.95 (ISBN 0-8403-2800-1). Kendall-Hunt.

--Self World Understanding: Analysis & Observation Manual. 1979. pap. text ed. 5.95 (ISBN 0-8403-2084-1). Kendall-Hunt.

Tribe, David. Questions of Censorship. LC 73-86068. 362p. 1974. 18.95 o.p. (ISBN 0-312-66045-6). St Martin.

Tribe, Ian. The Plant Kingdom. LC 70-120438. (Illus.). 160p. 1976. Repr. of 1970 ed. 0.99 o.p. (ISBN 0-448-12483-1, G&D); lib. bdg. 6.99 o.p. (ISBN 0-448-13363-6). Putnam Pub Group.

Tribe, Keith. Land, Labour & Economic Discourse. 1978. 22.00x (ISBN 0-7100-0002-2); pap. 10.00 (ISBN 0-7100-0003-0). Routledge & Kegan.

Tribe, Lawrence H., et al, eds. When Values Conflict: Essays on Environmental Analysis, Discourse & Decision. LC 75-45448. (American Academy of Arts and Sciences Ser.). 200p. 1976. text ed. 20.00x prof ref (ISBN 0-88410-431-1). Ballinger Pub.

Tribe, M. A., et al. Dynamic Aspects of Cells. LC 75-46198. (Basic Biology Course: Bk.3). (Illus.). 112p. 1976. 39.50 (ISBN 0-521-21175-1); pap. 13.95 (ISBN 0-521-21176-X). Cambridge U Pr.

--Ecological Principles. (Basic Biology Course Ser.: Bk. 4). (Illus.). 1976. 49.50 (ISBN 0-521-20658-8); pap. 15.95 (ISBN 0-521-20638-3). Cambridge U Pr.

--Enzymes. LC 75-14642. (Cambridge Biology Course Ser.: Bk. 7). (Illus.). 128p. 1975. 39.50 (ISBN 0-521-20870-X); limp bdg. 12.95x (ISBN 0-521-20960-9). Cambridge U Pr.

--Hormones Book. LC 77-87396. (Basic Biology Course Ser.: Bk. 11). 1979. 39.50 (ISBN 0-521-21371-1); pap. 15.95 (ISBN 0-521-21370-3); film strip 19.95x (ISBN 0-521-22956-1). Cambridge U Pr.

--Metabolism & Mitochondria. LC 75-25427. (Basic Biology Course Ser.: Bk. 8). (Illus.). 160p. 1976. 39.50 (ISBN 0-521-20952-8); pap. 15.95 (ISBN 0-521-20953-6). Cambridge U Pr.

--Nerves & Muscle. LC 76-55511. (Basic Biology Course Ser.: Bk. 10). (Illus.). 1977. 39.50 (ISBN 0-521-21369-X); pap. 13.95x (ISBN 0-521-21368-1). Cambridge U Pr.

--Photosynthesis. LC 75-12162. (Basic Biology Course Ser: Bk. 6). (Illus.). 88p. (Prog. Bk.). 1975. text ed. 29.95 (ISBN 0-521-20820-3); pap. text ed. 11.95x (ISBN 0-521-20821-1). Cambridge U Pr.

--Protein Synthesis. LC 76-2260. (Basic Biology Course Ser.: Bk. 9). (Illus.). 120p. 1976. 34.50 (ISBN 0-521-21092-5); pap. 13.95 (ISBN 0-521-21093-3). Cambridge U Pr.

--Cell Membranes. LC 75-7217. (Basic Biology Course Ser: Bk. 5). (Illus.). 84p. 1976. text ed. 32.50 (ISBN 0-521-20737-1); pap. text ed. 11.95 (ISBN 0-521-20738-X). Cambridge U Pr.

--Electron Microscopy & Cell Structure. LC 75-6284. (Basic Biology Course Ser.: Bk. 2). (Illus.). 120p. 1975. 39.50 (ISBN 0-521-20657-X); pap. 13.95x (ISBN 0-521-20557-3); film 19.95 (ISBN 0-521-20907-2); tape commentary for film 22.50 (ISBN 0-521-20965-X). Cambridge U Pr.

--Light Microscopy. (Basic Biology Course Ser: Bk. 1). (Illus.). 128p. 1975. 39.50 (ISBN 0-521-20656-1); pap. text ed. 13.95 (ISBN 0-521-20556-5). Cambridge U Pr.

--Case Studies in Genetics. LC 77-75778. (Basic Biology Course Ser.: Bk. 12). (Illus.). 1977. 34.50 (ISBN 0-521-21373-8); pap. 13.95x (ISBN 0-521-21372-X). Cambridge U Pr.

Tribe, Michael A. & Morgan, Andrew J. Evolution & Eudaroyotic Cells. (Studies in Biology: No. 131). 64p. 1981. pap. text ed. 8.95 (ISBN 0-7131-2821-6). E Arnold.

Tribolet, J. Seismic Applications of Homomorphic Signal Processing. 1979. 34.00 (ISBN 0-13-779801-6). P-H.

Tribus, Myron, jt. ed. see Levine, Raphael D.

Tributsch, Helmut. How Life Learned to Live: Adaptation in Nature. Varon, Miriam, tr. from Ger. (Illus.). 264p. 1983. 13.95 (ISBN 0-262-20045-7). MIT Pr.

Tricart, J. The Landforms of the Humid Tropics, Forests, & Savannas. 1973. 21.50 o.p. (ISBN 0-312-46550-5). St Martin.

Tricart, J. & Cailleux. An Introduction to Climatic Geomorphology. 1973. 21.50 o.p. (ISBN 0-312-42630-5). St Martin.

Trice, Harrison M. Alcoholism in Industry. 1.25 o.p. (ISBN 0-686-92157-7, 9040). Hazelden.

Trice, Harrison M. & Roman, Paul M. Spirits & Demons at Work: Alcohol & Other Drugs on the Job. 2nd ed. LC 78-23804. 294p. 1979. pap. 8.95 (ISBN 0-87546-072-0). ILR Pr.

Trice, Harrison M., jt. auth. see Ritzer, George.

Trice, Harrison M., jt. auth. see Roman, Paul M.

Trice, J. E., jt. auth. see Medjati, Z. M.

Trick, Timothy N. An Introduction to Circuit Analysis. LC 77-10843. 1978. 35.95 (ISBN 0-471-88850-8); solutions manual avail. (ISBN 0-471-03041-4). Wiley.

Tricker, B. J., jt. auth. see Tricker, R. A.

Tricker, R. A. Introduction to Meteorological Optics. 1971. 28.95 (ISBN 0-444-19700-1). Elsevier.

Tricker, R. A. & Tricker, B. J. Science of Movement. 1967. 22.00 (ISBN 0-444-19803-2). Elsevier.

Tricker, R. I. Management Information & Control Systems. 1975. 74.95x (ISBN 0-471-88855-9). Wiley.

Tricker, R. I. & Boland, Richard. Management Information & Control Systems. 2nd ed. LC 82-7056. 346p. 1982. 41.95 (ISBN 0-471-10450-7, Pub. by Wiley-Interscience); pap. text ed. 19.95 (ISBN 0-471-90020-6). Wiley.

Tricker, R. I., ed. The Individual, the Enterprise & the State. LC 77-78350. 1977. 23.95x o.s.i. (ISBN 0-470-99211-5). Halsted Pr.

Trickett, Edison J., jt. auth. see O'Neil, Patrick.

Tricky Ricky. Wordy Gurdy. Weigle, Oscar, ed. (Elephant Books Ser.). (Illus.). 1978. pap. 1.25 o.s.i. (ISBN 0-448-16164-8, G&D). Putnam Pub Group.

Triebel, H. Interpolation Theory: Function Spaces, Differential Operators. (North-Holland Mathematical Library: Vol. 18). 1978. 93.75 (ISBN 0-7204-0710-9, North-Holland). Elsevier.

Triebel, Hans. Fourier Analysis. LC 77-555434. 1977. pap. 9.50x o.p. (ISBN 0-8002-0808-0). Intl Pubns Serv.

Triebel, Walter A. & Chu, Alfred E. Handbook of Semiconductor & Bubble Memories. (Illus.). 448p. 1982. 26.95 (ISBN 0-13-381251-0). P-H.

Triem, Eve. Midsummer Rites. 12p. (Orig.). 1982. 5.00 (ISBN 0-686-38173-4). Seal Pr WA.

Triennial World Congress World Association of Societies of Pathology (Anatomic & Clinical) Laboratory Medicine, Jerusalem, Israel, XIth, 20-25 Sept. 1981. Advances in Pathology (Anatomic & Clinical) Laboratory Medicine: Proceedings, Vol. I. Levy, E., ed. (Illus.). 542p. 1982. 120.00 (ISBN 0-08-028878-2); 250.00 (ISBN 0-08-029777-3); 200.00 (ISBN 0-08-028859-6). Pergamon.

Trier, Carola S. Excercise: What It Is, What It Does. (Illus.). (gr. 1-4). 1982. 6.50 (ISBN 0-688-00950-6); PLB 5.71 (ISBN 0-688-00951-4). Greenwillow.

Trier, James R., jt. auth. see Beck, William C.

Trieschmann, jt. auth. see Rodda.

Trieschmann, James S., jt. auth. see Rodda, Williams H.

Triffin, Robert. Our International Monetary System. 1968. pap. text ed. 4.50x (ISBN 0-394-30714-3). Phila Bk Co.

Trifilo, S. Samuel, ed. see Gorostiza, C.

Trifonov, Yuri. Another Life: The House on the Embankment. Glenny, Michael, tr. 1983. 13.95 (ISBN 0-671-24266-0). S&S. Postponed.

Triger, David R. Practical Management of Liver Disease. (Illus.). 256p. 1981. text ed. 21.50 (ISBN 0-632-00719-2, B 5129-8). Mosby.

Trigg, Emma G. Paulownia Tree. 1969. 4.00 o.p. (ISBN 0-8233-0141-9). Golden Quill.

Trigg, R. Reason & Commitment. LC 72-89806. 192p. 1973. 24.95 (ISBN 0-521-20119-5); pap. 7.95 (ISBN 0-521-09784-3). Cambridge U Pr.

Trigg, Roger. The Shaping of Man: Philosophical Aspects of Sociobiology. LC 82-16868. 208p. 1983. 14.95 (ISBN 0-8052-3840-9). Schocken.

Trigger, Bruce G. The Late Nubian Settlement at Arminna West. (Pubns of the Penn-Yale Expedition to Egypt: No. 2). 1967. 16.00x (ISBN 0-686-17768-1). Univ Mus of U PA.

Triggle, D. J., et al, eds. Cholinergic Ligand Interactions. 1971. 34.00 (ISBN 0-12-700450-5). Acad Pr.

Triggs, James M. Piper Cub Story. 1963. 8.95 o.p. (ISBN 0-8306-9927-9); pap. 4.95 o.p. (ISBN 0-8306-2227-6, 2227). TAB Bks.

Triggs, Matt. Christmas Tree Taxation. LC 82-62548. 75p. 1982. pap. 25.00 (ISBN 0-910744-06-8). Media Awards.

Trigoboff, Joseph. Streets. LC 73-138846. 1970. 4.00 (ISBN 0-911838-07-4). Windy Row.

Trikha, M. Robert Frost: Poetry of Clarifications. 224p. 1982. text ed. 11.00x (ISBN 0-391-02751-4, Pub. by Heinemann India). Humanities.

Trillin, Calvin. Third Helpings. LC 82-19517. 192p. 1983. 12.95 (ISBN 0-89919-173-8). Ticknor & Fields.

--Uncivil Liberties. LC 82-48713. 228p. 1983. pap. 7.95 (ISBN 0-385-18764-5, Anch). Doubleday.

Trilling, L. see Von Mises, Richard & Von Karman, Theodore.

Trilling, Lionel. Selected Short Stories of John O'Hara. LC 56-8834. Date not set. 6.95 (ISBN 0-394-60494-6). Modern Lib.

Trilling, Lionel, ed. see Arnold, Matthew.

Trilling, Lionel, ed. see Austen, Jane.

Trilling, Richard J. Party Image & Electoral Behavior. LC 76-24794. 234p. 1976. 23.50x o.p. (ISBN 0-471-88935-0, Pub. by Wiley-Interscience). Wiley.

--Party Image & Electoral Behavior. LC 76-24794. 250p. Repr. of 1976 ed. text ed. 23.50 (ISBN 0-471-88935-0). Krieger.

Trim, Donald W. Calculus & Analytic Geometry. LC 82-16287. (Illus.). 960p. 1983. text ed. write for info. (ISBN 0-201-16270-9). A-W.

Trim, J. L. & Kneebone, P. English Pronunciation Illustrated. LC 74-25643. (Illus.). 96p. 1975. pap. text ed. 4.95x (ISBN 0-521-20634-0); cassette 1 13.95 (ISBN 0-521-20766-5); cassette 2 13.95x (ISBN 0-521-20767-3). Cambridge U Pr.

Trimble, Bjo. On the Good Ship Enterprise: My 15 Years With Star Trek. Stine, Hank, ed. LC 82-9709. (Illus.). 224p. (Orig.). 1982. pap. 5.95 (ISBN 0-89865-253-7). Donning Co.

Trimble, M. R. Post-Traumatic Neurosis: From Railway Spine to Whiplash. 1981. 33.75x (ISBN 0-471-09975-9, Pub. by Wiley-Interscience). Wiley.

Trimble, Michael R. Neuropsychiatry. LC 80-40766. 287p. 1981. 42.95x (ISBN 0-471-27827-0, Pub. by Wiley-Interscience). Wiley.

Trimble, R. Thomas, et al. Childhood. Kneer, Marion, ed. (Basic Stuff Ser.: No. II, 2 of 3). (Illus.). 92p. (Orig.). 1981. pap. text ed. 6.25 (ISBN 0-88314-022-5). AAHPERD.

Trimble, Stephen. Timpanogos Cave: A Window into the Earth. Priehs, T. J. & Dodson, Carolyn, eds. LC 82-61192. 1983. pap. price not set (ISBN 0-911408-64-9). SW Pks Mnmts.

Trimby, Elisa see Moore, Clement C.

Trimby, Robin. Soccer Techniques & Tactics. LC 77-3390. (Illus.). 1977. 5.95 (ISBN 0-668-04266-4); pap. 3.95 o.p. (ISBN 0-668-04272-9). Arco.

Trimingham, J. Spencer. History in Two Dimensions: A Christian Interpretation of History as Being an Equation Between Time & Eternity. 1983. 11.95 (ISBN 0-533-05395-1). Vantage.

--History of Islam in West Africa. (Oxford Paperbacks Ser). 1970. pap. 6.95x (ISBN 0-19-285038-5). Oxford U Pr.

--Sufi Orders in Islam. 1971. 32.50x (ISBN 0-19-826524-7). Oxford U Pr.

Trimm, D. L. Design of Industrial Catalysts. (Chemical Engineering Monographs: Vol. 11). 1980. 59.75 (ISBN 0-444-41906-3). Elsevier.

Trimmer. Understanding & Servicing Alarms. 1981. text ed. 21.95 (ISBN 0-409-95045-9). Butterworth.

Trimmer & Hairston. The Riverside Reader, Vol.II. 1982. pap. text ed. 10.95 (ISBN 0-686-84581-1, EN76); instr's. manual with test items avail. (EN77). HM.

Trimmer, Eric. Having a Baby. (Illus.). 142p. 1981. pap. 9.95 (ISBN 0-312-36436-9). St Martin.

Trimmer, Eric J. The Visual Dictionary of Sex. LC 77-73126. (Illus.). 1977. 25.00 o.s.i. (ISBN 0-89479-006-4); deluxe ed. 35.00 slipcased o.s.i. (ISBN 0-89479-011-0). A & W Pubs.

Trimmer, John W. How to Avoid Huge Ships: Or I Never Met A Ship I Liked. LC 82-61398. (Illus.). 112p. 1982. pap. 9.95 (ISBN 0-88100-019-1). Natl Writ Pr.

Trimmer, Joseph & Hairston, Maxine. The Riverside Reader, Vol. 2. 576p. 1982. pap. text ed. 9.95 (ISBN 0-395-32639-7); write for info. instr's. manual (ISBN 0-395-32640-0). HM.

Trimmer, Joseph F. The National Book Awards for Fiction: An Index to the First Twenty-Five Years. 1978. lib. bdg. 38.00 (ISBN 0-8161-7898-4, Hall Reference). G K Hall.

Trimmer, Sarah. Fabulous Histories, Designed for the Instruction of Children, Respecting Their Treatment of Animals, Repr. Of 1786 Ed. Bd. with The Dairyman's Daughter. Richmond, Legh. Repr. of 1810 ed. LC 75-32147. (Classics of Children's Literature, 1621-1932; Vol. 13). 1976. PLB 38.00 o.s.i. (ISBN 0-8240-2261-0). Garland Pub.

Trimpi, Wesley. Muses of One Mind: The Literary Analysis of Experience & Its Continuity. LC 82-61389. 450p. 1983. 40.00x (ISBN 0-691-06568-3). Princeton U Pr.

Trinci, A. P., jt. ed. see Burnett, J. H.

Trinder, Barrie. The Making of the Industrial Landscape. (Illus.). 288p. 1982. text ed. 24.95x (ISBN 0-460-04427-3, Pub. by J. M. Dent England). Biblio Dist.

Trine, Ralph W. What All the World's A-Seeking. LC 73-83946. (Pivot Family Readers Ser). 176p. 1973. pap. 1.25 o.p. (ISBN 0-87983-053-0). Keats.

Trinius, K. B. Species Graminum Iconibus et Descriptionbus Illustravit, 3 vols. in 1. (Illus.). 1970. Repr. of 1836 ed. 110.00 (ISBN 3-7682-0669-6). Lubrecht & Cramer.

Trinkaus, Erick, ed. The Sanidar Neandertals. (Monograph). Date not set. price not set (ISBN 0-12-700550-1). Acad Pr.

Trinkaus, J. P. Cells into Organs: The Forces That Shape the Embryo. 1969. pap. 13.95x ref. ed. o.p. (ISBN 0-13-121640-6). P-H.

Trinks, W. Industrial Furnaces, 2 vols. Incl. Vol. 1. Principals of Design & Operation. 5th ed. 486p. 1961 (ISBN 0-471-89034-0); Vol. 2. Fuels, Furnace Types & Furnace Equipment: Their Selection & Influence Upon Furnace Operation. 4th ed. 358p. 1967 (ISBN 0-471-89068-5). LC 61-11493. 52.50x ea. (Pub. by Wiley-Interscience). Wiley.

Trinterud, Leonard J., ed. Elizabethan Puritanism. (Library of Protestant Thought). 1971. 22.50x (ISBN 0-19-501281-X). Oxford U Pr.

Triola, Mario F. Elementary Statistics. 2nd ed. 21.95 (ISBN 0-8053-9320-X); answer book 4.95 (ISBN 0-8053-9307-2). Benjamin-Cummings.

--Mathematics & the Modern World. 2nd ed. LC 77-99264. 1978. 23.95 (ISBN 0-8053-9301-3); instr's guide 5.95 (ISBN 0-8053-9303-X). Benjamin-Cummings.

Triparthi, B. D. Nature of Sociological Theories: The Action Approach. 1979. text ed. 14.75x (ISBN 0-391-01040-9). Humanities.

Tripathy, K. C. Lithic Industries in India: A Study of South Western Orissa. 190p. 1980. text ed. 13.00x (ISBN 0-391-02139-7). Humanities.

Triplett, Frank. Life, Times & Treacherous Death of Jesse James. Snell, Joseph, ed. LC 70-75734. (Illus.). 344p. 1970. 16.95 o.p. (ISBN 0-8040-0187-1, SB); limited ed. 30.00 o.p. (ISBN 0-8040-0188-X). Swallow.

Triplett, Robert. Stagefright: Letting It Work for You. LC 82-14205. (Illus.). 208p. 1983. 17.95 (ISBN 0-88229-720-1). Nelson-Hall.

Tripodi, Tony & Fellin, Phillip. The Assessment of Social Research. 2nd ed. LC 82-81419. 210p. 1983. pap. text ed. 12.50x (ISBN 0-87581-285-6). Peacock Pubs.

Tripodi, Tony, et al. Differential Social Program Evaluation. LC 77-83401. 1978. pap. text ed. 8.95 (ISBN 0-87581-227-9). Peacock Pubs.

Tripp, Alice. Basic Mechanism of Congestive Heart Failure. 1978. pap. text ed. 9.95 (ISBN 0-07-065223-6, HP). McGraw.

--Basic Mechanisms of Endocrine Dysfunction. (Illus.). 1978. pap. text ed. 7.95 o.p. (ISBN 0-07-065221-X, HP). McGraw.

--Basic Mechanisms of Inflammation. (Illus.). 1978. pap. text ed. 7.95 (ISBN 0-07-065222-8, HP). McGraw.

--Basic Pathophysiological Mechanism of Shock. (Illus.). 1978. pap. text ed. 9.95 (ISBN 0-07-065224-4, HP). McGraw.

Tripp, C. A. Homosexual Matrix. LC 75-6987. 336p. 1975. 11.95 (ISBN 0-07-065201-5, GB). McGraw.

Tripp, D. W., jt. auth. see Stone, R. H.

Tripp, Edward, ed. Meridian Handbook of Classical Mythology. pap. 7.95 (ISBN 0-452-00582-5, F582, Mer). NAL.

Tripp, Jenny. The Man Who Was Left For Dead. Bennett, Russell, ed. LC 79-21519. (Quest, Adventure, Survival Ser.). (Illus.). 46p. (gr. 4-9). 1982. pap. 7.93g (ISBN 0-8172-2064-X). Raintree Pubs.

Tripp, Maggie, ed. Woman in the Year Two Thousand. 352p. 1976. pap. 2.25 o.p. (ISBN 0-440-39709-X, LE). Dell.

Tripp, Rhoda T., ed. International Thesaurus of Quotations. LC 73-106587. 1970. 14.37i (ISBN 0-690-44584-9); 15.34i (ISBN 0-690-44585-7). T Y Crowell.

Tripp, Robert M., ed. The Best of Micro Series, Vol. 1. 176p. 1978. pap. 6.00 o.p. (ISBN 0-938222-00-7). Micro Ink.

--The Best of Micro Series, Vol. 2. 224p. 1979. 8.00 o.p. (ISBN 0-938222-02-3). Micro Ink.

--The Best of Micro Series, Vol. 3. 320p. 1980. pap. 10.00 o.p. (ISBN 0-938222-04-X). Micro Ink.

Tripp, Robert M., ed. see Micro Ink, Inc.

Tripp, Susan M. Ervin see Ervin-Tripp, Susan M.

Tripp, Wallace. A Great Big Ugly Man Came Up & Tied His Horse to Me: A Book of Nonsense Verse. (Illus.). 48p. (gr. k-12). 1973. 7.95 (ISBN 0-316-85280-5); pap. 3.95 (ISBN 0-316-85281-3). Little.

--Sir Toby Jingle's Beastly Journey. LC 75-10455. (Illus.). 32p. (ps-4). 1976. 7.95 o.p. (ISBN 0-698-20340-2, Coward). Putnam Pub Group.

Trippensee. Wildlife Management, 2 vols. Incl. Vol. 1. Upland Game & General Principles. text ed. 38.50 (ISBN 0-07-065195-7); Vol. 2. Furbearers, Waterfowl & Fish. text ed. 19.50 (ISBN 0-07-065196-5). (American Forestry Ser., C). McGraw.

Trisco, Robert, jt. auth. see Ellis, John T.

Trisler, Hank. No Bull Selling. 192p. 1982. 12.95 (ISBN 0-8119-0484-9). Fell.

Trismegistus, Hermes. Hermetica: Introduction, Texts & Translations, Vol. 1. Scott, Walter, tr. LC 82-11991. 553p. (Orig.). 1982. pap. 15.00 (ISBN 0-87773-764-9). Great Eastern.

Trissel. Handbook of Injectable Drugs. 1981. 12.00 (ISBN 0-686-43120-0); pap. 10.00 (ISBN 0-686-43121-9). Elsevier.

Trissel, L. A. Pocket Guide to Injectable Drugs. 159p. 1981. pap. text ed. 13.50 (ISBN 0-471-09131-6, Pub. by Wiley Med). Wiley.

Trissel, Lawrence A. Handbook on Injectable Drugs. 2nd ed. 630p. 1980. pap. 25.00 o.p. (ISBN 0-930530-14-4). Am Soc Hosp Pharm.

Tristan, Flora. The Workers' Union. Livingston, Beverly, tr. LC 82-1891. 188p. 1983. 14.95 (ISBN 0-252-00921-5). U of Ill Pr.

Triston, H. U. Men in Cages. LC 70-174122. (Illus.). 1971. Repr. of 1938 ed. 37.00x (ISBN 0-8103-3801-7). Gale.

Trites, A. A. The New Testament Concept of Witness. LC 76-11067. (Society for New Testament Studies Monograph: No. 31). 1977. 52.50 (ISBN 0-521-21015-1). Cambridge U Pr.

Trites, R. Hyperactivity in Children. 256p. 1979. text ed. 27.95 (ISBN 0-8391-1400-1). Univ Park.

Tri T. Ha. Solid-State Microwave Amplifier Design. LC 81-21. 326p. 1981. 39.50x o.p. (ISBN 0-471-08971-0). Wiley.

Tritonio, Antonio M., jt. auth. see Conti, Natale.

Tritten, Kurt. European Banks 1981. 328p. 1981. 110.00x (ISBN 0-7121-5613-5, Pub. by Macdonald & Evans). State Mutual Bk.

Tritton, S. M. Guide to Better Wine & Beer Making for Beginners. 157p. 1969. pap. 2.95 (ISBN 0-486-22528-3). Dover.

Trivedi, P. K., jt. auth. see Rowley, J. C.

Trivedi, P. S., jt. auth. see Pandey, S. N.

Trivedi, R. D. Iconography of Parvati. 1982. 18.00x (ISBN 0-686-97040-3, Pub. by Agam). South Asia Bks.

Trivelpiece, Alvin W., jt. auth. see Krall, Nicholas A.

Trivers, Mildred. If You Want a Modern Mother. 40p. (Orig.). 1981. pap. 4.95 (ISBN 0-935306-10-2). Barnwood Pr.

Trivett, Daphne & Trivett, John. Time for Clocks. LC 78-4782. (Illus.). (gr. 2-5). 1979. PLB 10.89 (ISBN 0-690-03896-8, TYC-J). Har-Row.

Trivett, John, jt. auth. see Trivett, Daphne.

Trivisone, Margaret, jt. auth. see Sentlowitz, Michael.

Trjapitzin, V., jt. auth. see Gordh, Gordon.

Trnkova, V., jt. auth. see Pultr, A.

Trobisch, Walter. I Loved a Girl. LC 75-12281. 128p. 1975. pap. 4.95i (ISBN 0-06-068443-7, RD 352, HarpR). Har-Row.

--Love Is a Feeling to Be Learned. 1968. pap. 2.50 (ISBN 0-87784-314-7). Inter-Varsity.

--The Misunderstood Man. 96p. (Orig.). 1983. pap. 3.95 (ISBN 0-87784-302-3). Inter-Varsity.

Trobridge, George. Swedenborg: Life & Teaching. 1976. pap. 1.95 o.s.i. (ISBN 0-89129-058-3). Jove Pubns.

Trobridge, Gerry. Conversation with a World Voyager. 3.00 o.s.i. (ISBN 0-685-32968-2). Seven Seas.

Trocke, John K., jt. auth. see Downey, W. David.

Trocme, Andre. Jesus & the Nonviolent Revolution. Shenk, Michel, tr. from Fr. LC 73-9934. (Christian Peace Shelf Ser.). 296p. 1982. 9.95 (ISBN 0-8361-3320-X). Herald Pr.

Troeger, Jack. From Rift to Drift: Iowa's Story in Stone. (Illus.). 120p. 1983. 12.50 (ISBN 0-8138-1521-5). Iowa St U Pr.

Troeger, Thomas H. Are You Saved? Answers to the Awkward Question. LC 79-14402. 1979. pap. 6.95 (ISBN 0-664-24267-7). Westminster.

Troeger, W. E. Optical Determination of Rock-Forming Minerals. Part I: Determinative Tables. Hoffman, C., tr. from Ger. (Illus.). 1979. lib. bdg. 20.50 (ISBN 3-5106-5311-4). Lubrecht & Cramer.

Troeh, Frederic, jt. auth. see Thompson, Louis M.

Troeh, Frederick, jt. auth. see Thompson, Louis M.

Troeh, Frederick R., et al. Soil & Water Conservation. Troeh, Miriam, ed. (Illus.). 1980. text ed. 30.00 (ISBN 0-13-822155-3). P-H.

Troeh, Miriam, ed. see Troeh, Frederick R., et al.

Troelstra, A. S. Choice Sequences: A Chapter of Intuitionistic Mathematics. (Oxford Logic Guides Ser.). 1977. 29.95x (ISBN 0-19-853163-X). Oxford U Pr.

Troelstra, A. S. & Van Dalen, D., eds. The L. E. J. Brouwer Centenary Symposium: Proceedings of the Conference Held at Noordwijkerhout, June 1981. (Studies in Logic & the Foundations of Mathematics: Vol. 110). 456p. 1982. 68.00 (ISBN 0-444-86494-6, North Holland). Elsevier.

Troelstrup, Arch W. The Consumer in American Society: Personal & Family Finance. 5th ed. (Finance Ser.). (Illus.). 704p. 1974. text ed. 14.95 o.p. (ISBN 0-07-065210-4, C). McGraw.

Troelstrup, Archibald & Hall, E. Carl. The Consumer in American Society: Personal & Family Finance. 6th ed. (Illus.). 1978. text ed. 24.95 (ISBN 0-07-065215-5, C); instr's. manual 18.95 (ISBN 0-07-065216-3); study guide 9.00 (ISBN 0-07-065219-8). McGraw.

Troen, Philip & Nankin, Howard, eds. The Testis in Normal & Infertile Men. LC 76-19852. 592p. 1977. 53.50 (ISBN 0-89004-129-6). Raven.

Trofimov, V., intro. by. Stepan Erzia. Vezey, V., tr. (Illus.). 153p. 1980. 17.95 (ISBN 0-89893-060-X). CDP.

Troike, Rudolph C. Research Evidence for the Effectiveness of Bilingual Education. LC 79-103425. 22p. 1978. pap. 2.25 (ISBN 0-89763-006-8). Natl Clearinghse Bilingual Ed.

Troike, Rudolph C., et al. Assessing Successful Strategies in Bilingual Vocational Training Programs. LC 82-167587. 256p. (Orig.). 1981. pap. 11.25 (ISBN 0-89763-061-0). Natl Clearinghse Bilingual Ed.

Troike, Rudolph D., jt. ed. see Abraham, Roger D.

Troike, Rudpolph, jt. auth. see Macdonald, Ross.

Troise, Joe. Cherries & Lemons. 1980. pap. 1.95 o.p. (ISBN 0-446-90547-X). Warner Bks.

--Drive It till It Drops: Keep Your Car Running Forever. LC 80-123393. (Illus.). 1980. pap. 4.95 (ISBN 0-89708-024-6). And Bks.

Trojan, Paul K., jt. auth. see Flinn, Richard A.

Trojanowicz, Robert & Dixon, Samuel. Criminal Justice & the Community. (Illus.). 464p. 1974. ref. ed. 21.95x (ISBN 0-13-193557-7). P-H.

Trojcak, Doris A. Science with Children. (Illus.). 1979. text ed. 26.50 (ISBN 0-07-065217-1, C). McGraw.

Troll, Christian. Sayyid Ahmad Khan: A Reinterpretation of Muslim Theology. 1978. text ed. 17.75x (ISBN 0-7069-0626-8). Humanities.

Troll, Christian W., ed. Islam in India-Studies & Commentaries: Vol. 1, The Akbar Mission & Miscellaneous Studies. 240p. 1982. text ed. 32.50x (ISBN 0-7069-1889-4, Pub. by Vikas India). Advent NY.

Troll, Lillian E. Continuations: Adult Development & Aging. LC 81-10272. (Psychology Ser.). 970p. 1982. text ed. 22.95 (ISBN 0-8185-0484-6). Brooks-Cole.

Troll, Lillian E., et al. Families in Later Life. 1979. pap. 9.95x (ISBN 0-534-00613-2). Wadsworth Pub.

Troller, John A., ed. Sanitation in Food Processing. LC 82-16291. (Food Science & Technology Ser.). Date not set. price not set (ISBN 0-12-700660-5). Acad Pr.

Trollope, A. North America, 2 Vols. 1049p. 1981. 50.00x (ISBN 0-686-97617-7, Pub. by Dawson). State Mutual Bk.

Trollope, Anthony. Bearchester Towers & the Warden. Bd. with Warden. (YA) 1950. pap. 4.95x (ISBN 0-394-30937-5, T37, Mod LibC). Modern Lib.

--Can You Forgive Her? (World's Classics Ser.: No. 468). (Illus.). 17.95 o.p. (ISBN 0-19-250468-1). Oxford U Pr.

--Can You Forgive Her? Wall, Stephen, ed. (English Library Ser). 1978. pap. 5.95 (ISBN 0-14-043086-5). Penguin.

--Castle Richmond. Wolff, Robert L., ed. (Ireland Nineteenth Century Fiction Ser. 2: Vol. 55). 912p. 1979. lib. bdg. 32.00 o.s.i. (ISBN 0-8240-3504-6). Garland Pub.

--Christmas at Thompson Hall. Shannon, John K., ed. (Harting Grange Library Ser.). (Illus.). 1978. 8.95 (ISBN 0-932282-07-5); lib. bdg. 9.95 o.p. (ISBN 0-932282-09-1). Caledonia Pr.

--The Duke's Children. (Illus.). 1973. 15.00 o.p. (ISBN 0-19-254616-3). Oxford U Pr.

--The Eustace Diamonds. Gill, Stephen & Sutherland, John, eds. (English Library Ser). 1978. pap. 5.95 (ISBN 0-14-043041-5). Penguin.

--Framley Parsonage. 1978. pap. 3.25x (ISBN 0-460-01181-2, Evman). Biblio Dist.

--The Kellys & the O'Kelleys. (World's Classics Ser: No. 341). 1975. 13.95 o.p. (ISBN 0-19-250341-3). Oxford U Pr.

--The Kellys & the O'Kellys. Wolff, Robert L., ed. (Ireland Nineteenth Century Fiction - Ser. Two: Vol. 54). 888p. 1979. lib. bdg. 32.00 o.s.i. (ISBN 0-8240-3503-8). Garland Pub.

--Marion Fay. Super, R. H., ed. LC 82-7036. (Illus.). 465p. 1982. pap. 12.95 (ISBN 0-932282-18-0). Caledonia Pr.

--Marion Fay: A Novel. Super, R. H., ed. LC 82-7036. (Illus.). 464p. 1982. text ed. 25.00x (ISBN 0-472-10013-0). U of Mich Pr.

--The Pallisers: The Six Famous Parliamentary Novels. abr. ed. Hardwick, Michael, ed. LC 74-79479. 437p. 1975. 8.95 o.p. (ISBN 0-698-10622-9, Coward). Putnam Pub Group.

--Phineas Finn. 17.95 o.p. (ISBN 0-19-250447-9, WC447). Oxford U Pr.

--Phineas Redux. (World's Classics Ser.: No. 450). 14.95x (ISBN 0-19-250450-9). Oxford U Pr.

--Thackeray. LC 67-23880. 1968. Repr. of 1879 ed. 27.00x (ISBN 0-8103-3060-1). Gale.

--The Way We Live Now. (Illus.). 416p. 1982. pap. 7.95 (ISBN 0-486-24360-5). Dover.

--The Way We Live Now. Sutherland, John, ed. (World's Classics Ser.). 1982. pap. 9.95 (ISBN 0-19-281576-8). Oxford U Pr.

Trollope, Frances M. Father Eustace: A Tale of the Jesuits. Wolff, Robert L., ed. LC 75-448. (Victorian Fiction Ser.). 1975. Repr. of 1847 ed. lib. bdg. 66.00 o.s.i. (ISBN 0-8240-1528-2). Garland Pub.

--The Vicar of Wrexhill. Wolff, Robert L., ed. LC 75-486. (Victorian Fiction Ser.). 1975. Repr. of 1837 ed. lib. bdg. 66.00 o.s.i. (ISBN 0-8240-1563-0). Garland Pub.

Trombetta, M. BASIC for Students: With Applications. 1981. pap. 13.95 (ISBN 0-201-07611-X). A-W.

Trombley, Charles. Released to Reign. LC 79-90266. 1979. pap. 3.95 (ISBN 0-89221-064-8). New Leaf.

Trombly, Catherine A. Occupational Therapy for Physical Dysfunction. 2nd ed. (Illus.). 536p. 1982. text ed. 29.00 (ISBN 0-683-08387-2). Williams & Wilkins.

Tromlitz, J. G. Ausfuhrlicher und Grundlicher Unterricht Die Flote Zu Spielen. (The Flute Library: Vol. 1). 60.00 o.s.i. (ISBN 90-6027-358-3, Pub. by Frits Knuf Netherlands); wrappers 45.00 o.s.i. (ISBN 90-6027-357-5). Pendragon NY.

Tromovitch, jt. auth. see Stegman.

Tromp, S. W. Biometeorology. Thomas, L. C., ed. 352p. 1980. 42.95x (ISBN 0-471-26062-2, Pub. by Wiley Heyden). Wiley.

Tromp, S. W. & Bouma, J. J., eds. Biometeorology Survey, 2 vols. 437p. 1980. 110.00x (ISBN 0-471-26066-5, Pub. by Wiley Heyden). Wiley.

--Biometeorology Survey Part A: Human Biometeorology, 2 vols. (Biometeorology Survey Ser.). 257p. 1980. 76.00x (ISBN 0-471-26063-0, Pub. by Wiley Heyden). Wiley.

--Biometeorology Survey, Part B: Animal Biometeorology, 2 vols. (Biometeorology Survey Ser.). 180p. 1980. 61.95x (ISBN 0-471-26064-9, Pub. by Wiley Heyden). Wiley.

Trompf, G. W. The Idea of Historical Recurrence in Western Thought: From Antiquity to the Reformation. 1979. 36.00x (ISBN 0-520-03479-1). U of Cal Pr.

Tronick, Edward Z., ed. Social Interchange in Infancy: Affect, Cognition & Communication. (Illus.). 240p. 1982. 29.95 (ISBN 0-8391-1510-5, 17493). Univ Park.

Tropp, Barbara. The Modern Art of Chinese Cooking. LC 82-8143. (Illus.). 544p. 1982. 24.95 (ISBN 0-688-00566-7). Morrow.

Troppman, R. J., jt. auth. see Fuoss, D. E.

Troppmann, Robert J., jt. auth. see Fuoss, Donald E.

Trosclair. A Cajun Night Before Christmas. Jacobs, Howard, ed. Rice, James. (Illus.). 48p. (gr. 6-12). 1973. 7.95 (ISBN 0-88289-002-6). Pelican.

Troskolanski, A. T. Dictionary of Hydraulic Machinery. (Eng. & Ger. & Span. & Fr. & Ital. & Rus.). Date not set. 117.00 (ISBN 0-444-99728-8). Elsevier.

Trossbach, J. E. Fourteen Generations of Trossbach's, 1470-1982. 4th ed. 130p. 1982. 16.00 (ISBN 0-686-43300-9). J E Trossbach.

Trost, Arty & Rauner, Judy A. Gaining Momentum for Board Action. LC 82-17202. (Illus.). 104p. (Orig.). 1983. pap. 10.50x (ISBN 0-9604594-1-3). Marlborough Pubns.

Trost, Barry M. & Melvin, Lawrence S., Jr. Sulfer Ylides: Emerging Synthetic Intermediates. (Organic Chemistry Ser.). 1975. 59.50 (ISBN 0-12-701060-2). Acad Pr.

Trost, Lucille W. The Amazing World of American Birds. (Illus.). 1975. PLB 6.59 o.p. (ISBN 0-399-60949-0). Putnam Pub Group.

--Biography of a Cottontail. (Nature Biography Ser.). (Illus.). (gr. 2-5). 1971. PLB 5.49 o.p. (ISBN 0-399-60058-2). Putnam Pub Group.

--Lives & Deaths of a Meadow. (Illus.). 96p. (gr. 5 up). 1973. PLB 4.69 o.p. (ISBN 0-399-60835-4). Putnam Pub Group.

Trost, Stanley R. Doing Business with SuperCalc. 300p. 1983. pap. text ed. 12.95 (ISBN 0-89588-095-4). Sybex.

--Doing Business with VisiCalc. LC 82-50622. 260p. 1982. pap. 11.95 (ISBN 0-89588-086-5, V104). Sybex.

Trost, Stanley R. & Pomernacki, Charles. VisiCalc for Science & Engineering. 225p. 1983. pap. text ed. 13.95 (ISBN 0-89588-096-2). Sybex.

Trotman, Edward R. Dyeing & Chemical Technology of Textile Fibres. 5th ed. 1976. 75.00x (ISBN 0-87245-570-X). Textile Bk.

--Textile Scouring & Bleaching, 1968. 1969. 33.00x (ISBN 0-87245-366-9). Textile Bk.

Trotman, R. E. Technological Aids to Microbiology. 96p. 1978. pap. text ed. 16.95 (ISBN 0-7131-4293-6). E Arnold.

Trotsky, Leon. My Life: Authorized Translation & Edition. 9.00 (ISBN 0-8446-0944-7). Peter Smith.

--Russian Revolution: The Overthrow of Tzarism & the Triumph of the Soviets. abr. ed. LC 59-6990. 1959. pap. 7.95 (ISBN 0-385-09398-5, A170, Anch). Doubleday.

--Writings of Leon Trotsky Nineteen Thirty-Four to Nineteen Thirty-Five. Breitman, George & Scott, Beverly, eds. LC 73-80226. 1972. lib. bdg. 30.00 (ISBN 0-87348-194-1). Path Pr NY.

--Writings of Leon Trotsky, 1933-34. Breitman, George & Scott, Bev, eds. Wright, John G., et al, trs. from Rus. & Fr. LC 73-80226. 356p. 1972. cloth 30.00 (ISBN 0-87348-213-1). Path Pr NY.

Trott, P. E., jt. auth. see Bedborough, D. R.

Trotta, Maurice S. Handling Grievances: A Guide for Management & Labor. LC 76-42311. 184p. 1976. 12.50 (ISBN 0-87179-237-0). BNA.

Trottenberg, U., jt. ed. see Hackbusch, W.

Trotter, Ann. Britain & East Asia, 1933 to 1937. LC 74-76581. (International Studies). (Illus.). 292p. 1975. 37.50 (ISBN 0-521-20475-5). Cambridge U Pr.

Trotter, Hale, jt. auth. see Williamson, Richard.

Trotter, S. E. A Primer on Establishing & Financing a Business. 1977. pap. text ed. 5.75 (ISBN 0-8191-0337-3). U Pr of Amer.

Trotter, Sharland, jt. auth. see Chu, Franklin D.

Trotter, W. Five Letters on Worship & Ministry. 39p. pap. 0.60 (ISBN 0-88172-128-X). Believers Bkshelf.

Trotter, Wilfred. Instincts of the Herd in Peace & War. 2nd ed. LC 74-19217. 264p. 1975. Repr. of 1923 ed. 34.00x (ISBN 0-8103-4090-9). Gale.

Trotter, Wilfrid P. The Royal Navy in Old Photographs. LC 75-2890. 1975. 12.50 o.p. (ISBN 0-87021-959-6). Naval Inst Pr.

Trotzer, James P. The Counselor & the Group: Integrating Theory, Training & Practice. LC 77-7306. (Illus.). 1977. text ed. 17.95 (ISBN 0-8185-0233-9). Brooks-Cole.

Trouchaud, J. P. Bilan de l'Operation Secteurs Pilotes en Moyenne Cote d'Ivoire, 2 vols. (Black Africa Ser.). 415p. (Fr.). 1974. Repr. of 1968 ed. Set. lib. bdg. 562.50 o.p. (ISBN 0-8287-0834-7). Vol. 1 (71-2039). Vol. 2 (71-2040). Clearwater Pub.

--Essai de Division Regionale En Cote d'Ivoire. (Black Africa Ser.). 193p. (Fr.). 1974. Repr. of 1968 ed. lib. bdg. 56.00x o.p. (ISBN 0-8287-0835-5, 71-2037). Clearwater Pub.

--Propositions pour un Cadre Regional de Planification En Cote d'Ivoire Travaux Preparatoires au Plan, 1971-1975. (Black Africa Ser.). 50p. (Fr.). 1974. Repr. of 1970 ed. lib. bdg. 29.00x o.p. (ISBN 0-8287-0836-3, 71-2038). Clearwater Pub.

--Zone Rurale de San Pedro. Enquetes Demographiques. (Black Africa Ser.). 36p. (Fr.). 1974. Repr. of 1969 ed. 20.00x o.p. (ISBN 0-8287-0837-1, 71-2062). Clearwater Pub.

Troughton, J. & Donaldson, L. A. Probing Plant Structures. 1972. 11.95 o.p. (ISBN 0-07-065260-0). McGraw.

Troughton, M. J. Canadian Agriculture. (Geography of World Agriculture Ser.: Vol. 10). (Illus.). 355p. 1982. 42.50x (ISBN 963-05-2653-0). Intl Pubns Serv.

Troung Tien Dat. The Red Dragon. 1983. 15.95 (ISBN 0-533-05578-4). Vantage.

Troup. Workboats. 1980. write for info. o.p. (ISBN 0-85501-212-9). Wiley.

Troup, K. D. Workboats. 300p. 1982. text ed. 62.95x (ISBN 0-471-26067-3, Pub. by Wiley Heyden). Wiley.

Trout, Andrew. Colbert Jean-Baptiste. (World Leaders Ser.). 1978. lib. bdg. 13.95 (ISBN 0-8057-7715-6, Twayne). G K Hall.

Trout, Andrew P., jt. auth. see Jennings, Robert M.

Trout, Charles H. Boston, the Great Depression, & the New Deal. LC 76-47439. (Urban Life in America Ser.). (Illus.). 1977. 19.95x (ISBN 0-19-502190-8). Oxford U Pr.

Trout, Jack & Ries, Al. Positioning: The Battle for Your Mind. 256p. 1982. pap. 3.95 (ISBN 0-446-30800-5). Warner Bks.

Trout, Jack, jt. auth. see Ries, Al.

Trout, John M. The Voyage of Prudence: The World View of Alan of Lille. LC 79-66473. 1979. pap. text ed. 9.75 (ISBN 0-8191-0840-5). U Pr of Amer.

Troutman, Andria P. & Lichtenberg, Betty K. Mathematics: A Good Beginning. 2nd ed. LC 81-17997. (Mathematics Ser.). 1982. pap. text ed. 19.95 (ISBN 0-8185-0492-7). Brooks-Cole.

Troutman, Anne, jt. auth. see Alberto, Paul.

Troutman, Richard C. Microsurgery of the Anterior Segment of the Eye: The Cornea, Vol. 2. LC 74-12453. (Illus.). 358p. 1977. 59.50 o.p. (ISBN 0-8016-5106-9). Mosby.

--Microsurgery of the Anterior Segment of the Eye: Volume I: Introduction & Basic Techniques. LC 74-12453. 324p. 1974. 56.50 o.p. (ISBN 0-8016-5107-7). Mosby.

Troutner, Joanne J. The Media Specialist, The Microcomputer, & the Curriculum. 175p. 1983. lib. bdg. 19.50 (ISBN 0-87287-367-6). Libs Unl.

Trouton, Ruth. Peasant Renaissance in Yugoslavia, 1900-1950. LC 72-11339. 344p. 1973. Repr. of 1952 ed. lib. bdg. 18.25x (ISBN 0-8371-6662-4, TRPR). Greenwood.

Trover, Ellen L., jt. ed. see Swindler, William F.

Trow, Jo Anne J., jt. auth. see Moore, Kathryn M.

Trow, W. Clark & Haddan, Eugene E., eds. Psychological Foundations of Educational Technology. LC 75-35605. 410p. 1976. 24.95 (ISBN 0-87778-086-2); pap. 19.95 (ISBN 0-87778-092-7). Educ Tech Pubn.

Trowbridge. Crowns of the British Empire. (Illus.). 170p. 5.00 o.p. (ISBN 0-87637-202-7). Hse of Collectibles.

Trowbridge, Keith. Resort Timesharing. 1982. 10.95 (ISBN 0-671-43984-7). S&S.

Trowell, H. C. Kwashiokor. (Nutrition Foundations' Reprint Ser.). 1982. 35.00 (ISBN 0-12-701150-1). Acad Pr.

Troxel, Terrie E., jt. auth. see Breslin, Cormick.

Troxel, Terrie E., jt. auth. see Breslin, Cormick L.

Troxell, George E., et al. Composition & Properties of Concrete. 2nd ed. LC 68-13104. (Series in Civil Engineering). 1968. text ed. 35.00 (ISBN 0-07-065286-4, C). McGraw.

Troxell, Mary D. Fashion Merchandising. 2nd ed. 1976. text ed. 18.05 (ISBN 0-07-065278-3, G); instructor's manual & key 4.95 (ISBN 0-07-065279-1). McGraw.

Troxell, Mary D. & Stone, Elaine. Fashion Merchandising. 3rd ed. LC 80-25077. (Gregg McGraw-Hill Marketing Ser.). (Illus.). 480p. 1981. 18.95 (ISBN 0-07-065280-5); instr's manual & key 4.95 (ISBN 0-07-065281-3). McGraw.

Troy, jt. auth. see Epstein.

Troy, Amanda. Double Deception. 192p. 1982. pap. 1.75. Jove Pubns.

Troy, Carol, jt. auth. see Milinaire, Catherine.

Troy, Helen, jt. ed. see Jones, Donald G.

Troy, Kathryn. Annual Survey of Corporate Contributions: 1980 Edition. LC 76-24946. (Report No. 779). (Illus.). 51p. (Orig.). 1980. pap. 15.00 (ISBN 0-8237-0215-4). Conference Bd.

Troy, Leo. Almanac of Business & Industrial Financial Ratios: 1981-1982 Edition. LC 72-181403. 373p. 1982. 16.00 (ISBN 0-13-022749-8, Busn). P-H.

Troy, Mark L. Mummeries of Ressurection: The Cycle of Osiris in Finnegan's Wake. (Studie Anglistica Upsaliensia Ser.: No. 26). 1976. pap. text ed. 10.50x o.p. (ISBN 0-686-86103-5). Humanities.

Troyat, Henri. Alexander of Russia: Napoleon's Conqueror. 320p. 1983. 17.95 (ISBN 0-525-24144-2, 01743-520). Dutton.

--La Tete Sur les Epaules. (Easy Readers, C). (Illus.). pap. text ed. 3.95 (ISBN 0-88436-285-X). EMC.

Troyen, Carol. The Boston Tradition: American Paintings from the Museum of Fine Arts, Boston. LC 80-69210. (Illus.). 216p. (Orig.). 1980. pap. 19.95 (ISBN 0-917418-66-2). Am Fed Arts.

Troyepolsky, Gavriil. Beem. Bouis, Antonina W., tr. from Rus. LC 78-2072. 1978. 10.53i (ISBN 0-06-014348-7, HarpT). Har-Row.

Troyer, Terry L. Amish Life Style Illustrated. LC 82-90105. (Illus.). 96p. (gr. 6-12). 1982. 19.95 (ISBN 0-943314-00-3). TLT.

Troyer, Warner. Divorced Kids: Children of Divorce Speak Out & Give Advice to Mother, Fathers, Lovers, Stepparents, Brother & Sisters, Boyfriends & Girlfriends, Each Other. LC 79-3531. 180p. 1980. Repr. of 1979 ed. 8.95 (ISBN 0-15-125748-5). HarBraceJ.

Troyes, Chretien de see De Troyes, Chretien.

Troyes, Chretien De see De Troyes, Chretien.

Troyka, Lynn Q. Structured Reading. (Illus.). 1978. pap. text ed. 13.95 (ISBN 0-13-854513-8). P-H.

Troyka, Lynn Q. & Nudelman, Jerrold. Steps in Composition: Alternate. 2nd ed. (Illus.). 1979. pap. text ed. 13.95 (ISBN 0-13-846550-9). P-H.

--Taking Action: Writing, Reading, Speaking & Listening Through Simulation Games. (Illus.). 176p. 1975. pap. text ed. 10.95 (ISBN 0-13-882571-8). P-H.

Troyna, Barry, jt. auth. see Cashmore, Ernest.

Trozan, Peter A. Social Security Overpayments: Do I Really Have to Pay Them Back? LC 82-16594. 160p. (Orig.). 1982. pap. write for info. (ISBN 0-9608154-0-6). Red Tape.

Truax, Carol. The Woman's Day Buffet Cookbook. Date not set. pap. 6.95 (ISBN 0-449-90076-2, Columbine). Fawcett.

Trubetzkoy, N. S. Principles of Phonology. Baltaxe, Christiane A., tr. LC 68-16112. 1969. 40.00x (ISBN 0-520-01535-5). U of Cal Pr.

Trubner, Nikolaus. Trubner's Bibliographical Guide to American Literature. 1966. Repr. of 1859 ed. 47.00x (ISBN 0-8103-3315-5). Gale.

Trubo, Richard, jt. auth. see Behrstock, Barry.

Trubowitz, Sidney. Handbook for Teaching in the Ghetto School. 176p. 4.95 (ISBN 0-686-95033-X); pap. 2.25 (ISBN 0-686-99452-3). ADL.

Truby, David. Take a Trip to Australia. LC 80-52721. (Take a Trip Ser.). (gr. 1-3). 1981. PLB 8.40 (ISBN 0-531-00988-2). Watts.

Truckenbrodt, Erich A., jt. auth. see Schlichting, Hermann T.

Trudeau, G. Doonesbury. 1971. 5.95 (ISBN 0-07-065294-5, GB). McGraw.

Trudeau, Garry. It's Supposed to Be Yellow, Pinhead: Selected Cartoons from Ask for May, Settle for June, Vol. 1. 128p. 1983. pap. 2.25 (ISBN 0-449-20193-7, Crest). Fawcett.

--The Wreck of the Rusty Nail. LC 82-83139. 128p. 1983. pap. 5.25 (ISBN 0-03-061732-4). HR&W.

Trudel, Marcel see Halpenny, Francess.

Trudgill, P. The Social Differentiation of English in Norwich. LC 73-77178. (Cambridge Studies in Liguistics: No. 13). 208p. 1974. 37.50 (ISBN 0-521-20264-7); pap. text ed. 15.95 (ISBN 0-521-29745-1). Cambridge U Pr.

Trudgill, P., jt. auth. see Chambers, J. K.

Trudgill, Peter. Coping with America: A Beginner's Guide to the U. S. A. (Illus.). 158p. 1982. text ed. 17.95 (ISBN 0-631-12557-4, Pub. by Basil Blackwell England); pap. text ed. 5.95 (ISBN 0-631-12969-3, Pub. by Basil Blackwell England). Biblio Dist.

Trudgill, Peter & Hannah, Jean. International English: A Guide to the Varieties of Standard English. 144p. 1982. pap. text ed. 9.95 (ISBN 0-7131-6362-3). E Arnold.

Trudgill, Peter, jt. auth. see Hughes, Arthur.

Trudgill, Peter, ed. see Milroy, Lesley.

Trudgill, Stephen A. Soil & Vegetation Systems. (Contemporary Problems in Geography Ser.). (Illus.). 1977. 33.00x (ISBN 0-19-874058-1); pap. 11.95x (ISBN 0-19-874059-X). Oxford U Pr.

Trudinger, N. S., jt. auth. see Gilbarg, D.

Trudinger, P., jt. auth. see Roy, A. B.

Trudinger, P. A. & Swaine, D. J., eds. Biogeochemical Cycling of Mineral-Forming Elements. LC 79-21297. (Studies in Environmental Science: Vol. 3). 616p. 1979. 106.50 (ISBN 0-444-41745-1). Elsevier.

True, D. L., jt. ed. see Meighan, Clement.

True, Dan. A Family of Eagles. LC 79-92193. (Illus.). 224p. 1980. 12.95 (ISBN 0-89696-078-1, An Everest House Book). Dodd.

True, Frederick W. The Whalebone Whales of the Western North Atlantic. (Illus.). 360p. 1983. Repr. of 1904 ed. text ed. 35.00x (ISBN 0-87474-922-0). Smithsonian.

True, June A. Finding Out: Conduction & Evaluating Social Research. 448p. 1982. pap. text ed. 16.95x (ISBN 0-534-01168-3). Wadsworth Pub.

True, Michael. Homemade Social Justice. LC 82-7291. 174p. (Orig.). 1982. pap. 6.95 (ISBN 0-8190-0648-3, FC142). Fides Claretian.

Trueba, H. Bilingual Bicultural Education for the Spanish Speaking in the U. S., A Bibliography. 1977. pap. 6.80x (ISBN 0-87563-130-4). Stipes.

Trueba, Henry T. & Barnett-Mizrahi, Carol, eds. Bilingual Multicultural Education & the Professional: From Theory to Practice. 1979. pap. text ed. 19.95 (ISBN 0-88377-138-1). Newbury Hse.

Trueba, Henry T., et al, eds. Culture & the Bilingual Classroom: Studies in Classroom Ethnography. (Bilingual Multicultural Education Ser.). 288p. (Orig.). 1981. pap. text ed. 19.95 (ISBN 0-88377-182-9). Newbury Hse.

Trueblood, Benjamin F. The Development of the Peace Idea & Other Essays. LC 70-137555. (Peace Movement in America Ser). xxviii, 244p. 1972. Repr. of 1932 ed. lib. bdg. 16.95x (ISBN 0-89198-085-7). Ozer.

Trueblood, David E. La Iglesia un Companerismo Incendiario. Velasquez, Roger, tr. from Eng. Orig. Title: The Incendiary Fellowship. 114p. (Span.). 1981. pap. 4.75 (ISBN 0-311-17022-6, Edit Mundo). Casa Bautista.

Trueblood, Elton. Abraham Lincoln: Theologian of American Anguish. LC 72-79955. 160p. 1973. 8.95i o.p. (ISBN 0-06-068511-5, HarpR). Har-Row.

--While It is Day. 163p. 1983. pap. write for info. (ISBN 0-932970-36-2). Yokefellow Pr.

Trueblood, Kenneth N., jt. auth. see Glusker, Jenny P.

Trueblood, Mark & Genet, Russell M. Microcomputer Control of Telescopes. LC 82-84768. 220p. (Orig.). 1983. pap. 24.95 (ISBN 0-911351-02-7). Fairborn Observ.

Trueblood, Paul G. Lord Byron. 2nd ed. (English Authors Ser.). 1977. lib. bdg. 11.95 (ISBN 0-8057-6694-4, Twayne). G K Hall.

Trueman, E. The Locomotion of Soft-Bodied Animals. (Contemporary Biology Ser). 208p. 1978. pap. text ed. 14.95 o.p. (ISBN 0-444-19510-6). Univ Park.

Trueman, E. R., jt. ed. see Elder, H. Y.

Truesdale, Richard, jt. auth. see MacGregor, Bruce A.

Truesdell, C. An Idiot's Fugitive Essays on Science: Methods, Criticism, Training, Circumstances. (Illus.). 350p. 1983. 30.00 (ISBN 0-387-90703-3). Springer-Verlag.

Truesdell, C. & Muncaster, R. G. Fundamentals of Maxwell's Kinetic Theory of a Simple Monatomic Gas: Treated As a Branch of Rational Mechanics. (Pure & Applied Mathematics Ser.). 1980. 67.50 (ISBN 0-12-701350-4). Acad Pr.

Truesdell, C., ed. Continuum Mechanics, 4 vols. Incl. Vol. 1. Mechanical Foundations of Elasticity. 324p. 1966. 40.00x (ISBN 0-677-00820-1); Vol. 2. Rational Mechanics of Materials. 446p. 1965. 47.00x (ISBN 0-677-00830-9); Vol. 3. Foundations of Elasticity Theory. 320p. 1965. 43.00x (ISBN 0-677-00840-6); Vol. 4. Problems of Nonlinear Elasticity. 276p. 1965. 40.00x (ISBN 0-677-00850-3). (International Science Review Ser.). (Illus.). 1965. Gordon.

Truesdell, Clifford A. Unified Theory of Special Functions. 1948. pap. 16.00 (ISBN 0-527-02734-0). Kraus Repr.

Truett, Dale B., jt. auth. see Truett, Lila F.

Truett, Lila F. & Truett, Dale B. Economics. (Illus.). 938p. 1982. text ed. 23.95 (ISBN 0-314-63298-0). West Pub.

--Macroeconomics. (Illus.). 580p. 1982. pap. text ed. 14.95 (ISBN 0-314-63302-2). West Pub.

--Microeconomics. (Illus.). 596p. 1982. pap. text ed. 14.95 (ISBN 0-314-63304-9). West Pub.

Truex, James E., ed. The Second Coastal Archaeology Reader: Nineteen Hundred to the Present. (Readings in Long Island Archaeology & Ethnohistory Ser.: Vol. V). (Illus.). 312p. 1982. pap. 16.00 (ISBN 0-686-97475-1). Ginn Custom.

Truex, R. C. & Carpenter, M. B. Human Neuroanatomy. 6th ed. 1981. 40.00x o.p. (ISBN 0-686-72952-8, Pub. by Oxford & IBH India). State Mutual Bk.

Truex, Raymond C., jt. ed. see Buchheit, William.

Truffaut, Francois. Hitchcock. 1969. pap. 10.75 (ISBN 0-671-20346-0, Touchstone Bks). S&S.

--Jules & Jim. LC 68-27592. (Film Scripts Modern Ser). 1968. pap. 2.95 o.p. (ISBN 0-671-20089-5, Touchstone Bks). S&S.

Truffaut, Francois, pref. by see Almendros, Nestor.

Truffaut, Francois, ed. see Bazin, Andre.

Truitt, Anne. Daybook: The Journal of an Artist. 1982. 14.95 (ISBN 0-394-52398-9). Pantheon.

Truitt, Deborah, ed. Dolphins & Porpoises: A Comprehensive, Annotated Bibliography of the Smaller Cetacea. LC 73-19803. 584p. 1974. 74.00x (ISBN 0-8103-0966-1). Gale.

Truitt, G. A. The Ten Commandments: Learning about God's Law. (Concept Bks.: Ser. 4). 1983. pap. 3.50 (ISBN 0-570-08527-6). Concordia.

Truitt, Gloria. Animals. Mahany, Patricia, ed. (Nature Riddle Coloring Bks.). (Illus.). 16p. (Orig.). (ps-4). 1982. pap. 0.89 (ISBN 0-87239-597-9, 2384). Standard Pub.

--Birds. Mahany, Patricia, ed. (Nature Riddle Coloring Bks.). (Illus.). 16p. (Orig.). (ps-4). 1982. pap. 0.89 (ISBN 0-87239-598-7, 2385). Standard Pub.

--Foods. Mahany, Patricia, ed. (Nature Riddle Coloring Bks.). (Illus.). 16p. (Orig.). (ps-4). 1982. pap. 0.89 (ISBN 0-87239-599-5, 2386). Standard Pub.

--God's Creatures & Creations. Mahany, Patricia, ed. (Nature Riddle Coloring Bks.). (Illus.). 16p. (Orig.). (ps-4). 1982. pap. 0.89 (ISBN 0-87239-600-2, 2387). Standard Pub.

--People of the New Testament: Arch Book Supplement. 1983. pap. 0.89 (ISBN 0-570-06173-3). Concordia.

--People of the Old Testament: Arch Book Supplement. 1983. pap. 0.89 (ISBN 0-570-06172-5). Concordia.

Truitt, John. Telesearch: Direct Dial the Best Job of Your Life. LC 82-15714. 160p. 1983. 11.95 (ISBN 0-87196-900-9). Facts on File.

Truitt, Velma S. On the Hoof in Nevada. (Illus.). 1950. 95.00 (ISBN 0-913814-06-7). Nevada Pubns.

Truitt, Willis H., jt. auth. see Gould, James A.

Trull, Joe E. Forty Object Sermons for Children. (Object Lesson Ser.). 96p. 1975. pap. 3.50 (ISBN 0-8010-8831-3). Baker Bk.

Trullinger, Theo C. The Robin Who Could Not Sing. 1978. 4.50 o.p. (ISBN 0-533-02988-0). Vantage.

Truman, D. E. The Biochemistry of Cytodifferentiation. LC 73-21785. 122p. 1974. text ed. 17.95x o.p. (ISBN 0-470-89190-4). Halsted Pr.

Truman, D. E. see Yeoman, M. M.

Truman, D. E., jt. ed. see Clayton, R. M.

Truman, Harry S. The Autobiography of Harry S. Truman. Ferrell, Robert H., ed. LC 80-66304. 1980. 10.95 (ISBN 0-87081-090-1); pap. 4.95 (ISBN 0-87081-091-X). Colo Assoc.

Truman, Margaret. Murder in the Smithsonian. 1983. 14.50 (ISBN 0-87795-475-5). Arbor Hse.

--Murder in the Supreme Court. (General Ser.). 1983. lib. bdg. 15.50 (ISBN 0-8161-3516-9, Large Print Bks). G K Hall.

Trumble, Stephen. The Bright Edge: A Guide to the National Parks of the Colorado Plateau. 1979. pap. 4.95 (ISBN 0-89734-048-5). Mus Northern Ariz.

Trump, jt. auth. see Bray.

Trump, B. F. Diagnostic Electron Microscopy, Vol. 3. (Diagnostic Electron Microscopy Ser.). 536p. 1980. 80.00 (ISBN 0-471-05150-0, Pub. by Wiley-Interscience). Wiley.

Trump, B. F. & Jones, R. T. Diagnostic Electron Microscopy, Vol. 1. (Diagnostic Electron Microscopy Ser.). 346p. 1978. text ed. 65.00 (ISBN 0-471-89196-7, Pub. by Wiley Med). Wiley.

Trump, Barbara. Forgiven Love. LC 79-84793. (Orig.). 1979. pap. 2.25 o.p. (ISBN 0-89877-010-6). Jeremy Bks.

Trump, Benjamin F., jt. auth. see Cowley, R. Adams.

Trump, Benjamin F. & Arstila, A. U., eds. Pathobiology of Cell Membranes, 2 vols, Vol. 1. 1975. 69.00 (ISBN 0-12-701501-9). Acad Pr.

--Pathobiology of Cell Membranes, Vol. 3. Date not set. price not set (ISBN 0-12-701503-5). Acad Pr.

Trump, Benjamin F. & Jones, Raymond T., eds. Diagnostic Electron Microscopy, Vol. 4. (Diagnostic Electron Microscopy Ser.). 544p. 1983. 65.00 (ISBN 0-471-05149-7, Pub. by Wiley Med). Wiley.

Trumpower, Bernard L., ed. Function of Quinones in Energy Conserving Systems. 1982. 74.50 (ISBN 0-12-701280-X). Acad Pr.

Trumpy, Bob & Mefford, Bill. Trump! LC 79-20367. (Illus.). 1979. pap. 5.95 o.p. (ISBN 0-89865-019-4). Donning Co.

Trunber, Henry & Rathbun, William. Treasures of Asian Art from the Idemitsu Collection. LC 81-52557. (Illus.). 204p. 1981. pap. 13.95 (ISBN 0-932216-06-4). Seattle Art.

Trundell. Questions & Answers: Color TV. 3rd ed. (Illus.). 1983. pap. write for info. (ISBN 0-408-01305-2). Focal Pr.

Trundle. People of the World. (People of the World Ser.). (gr. 4-9). 1978. 6.95 (ISBN 0-86020-210-0, Usborne-Hayes); PLB 9.95 (ISBN 0-88110-116-8); pap. 3.95 (ISBN 0-86020-189-9). EDC.

Trundle, jt. auth. see King.

Trungpa, Chogyam, jt. auth. see Fremantle, Francesca.

Trunk, Isaiah. Jewish Responses to Nazi Persecution. LC 78-6378. 384p. 1981. pap. 10.95 (ISBN 0-8128-6103-5). Stein & Day.

--Jewish Responses to Nazi Persecution. 1978. 15.95 o.p. (ISBN 0-8128-2500-4). Stein & Day.

--Jewish Responses to Nazi Persecution. (Illus.). 371p. Repr. 13.00 (ISBN 0-686-95071-2). ADL.

Trunkey, Donald T. & Lewis, Frank R., Jr., eds. Current Therapy of Trauma & Emergency Medicine. 300p. 1983. text ed. 36.00 (ISBN 0-941158-12-8, D5152-2). Mosby.

Trupin, Judy. A Concoctionist Cookbook. 1982. pap. 4.50 (ISBN 0-934834-32-6). White Pine.

Truscott, Alan. Contract Bridge. LC 81-44. 96p. 1982. 8.95 (ISBN 0-8119-0422-9). Fell.

Truscott, Alan, ed. see Wei, C. C.

Truse, Kenneth. Benny's Magic Baking Pan. LC 73-22077. (Easy Venture Ser). (Illus.). 32p. (gr. k-2). 1974. PLB 6.69 (ISBN 0-8116-6062-1). Garrard.

Trusky, Tom, ed. see Church, Peggy P.

Trusky, Tom, ed. see Flanner, Hildegarde.

Trusky, Tom, ed. see Greasybear, Charley J.

Trusky, Tom, ed. see Walsh, Marnie.

Trusler, Ivan & Ehret, Walter. Functional Lessons in Singing. 2nd ed. LC 73-180598. (Illus.). 240p. 1972. pap. 18.95 ref. ed. (ISBN 0-13-331801-X). P-H.

Truss, Jan. Bird at the Window. LC 79-1999. 224p. (gr. 7 up). 1980. 8.95 o.p. (ISBN 0-06-026137-4, HarpJ); PLB 8.79 (ISBN 0-06-026138-2). Har-Row.

Trussel, Patricia & Brandt, Anne. Using Nursing Research: Discovery, Analysis & Interpretation. LC 80-84150. 240p. 1981. Repr. 21.50 (ISBN 0-913654-70-1, 654701). Aspen Systems.

Trussler, S., jt. auth. see Leeming, G.

Trussler, Simon. Plays of John Osborne: An Assessment. 1969. pap. text ed. 7.50x (ISBN 0-575-00267-0). Humanities.

Trussler, Simon, jt. auth. see Leeming, Glenda.

Trussler, Simon, ed. New Theatre Voices of the Seventies: Interviews from "Theatre Quarterly" 1970-1980. 192p. 1981. 22.00x (ISBN 0-413-48920-5); pap. 11.95 (ISBN 0-413-48930-2). Methuen Inc.

--The Royal Shakespeare Company, 1981-82: A Complete Record of the Year's Work. (Illus.). 1982. pap. text ed. 12.95 (ISBN 0-9505057-4-9, Pub. by Royal Shakespeare England). Advent NY.

Trusted, Jennifer. Logic of Scientific Inference: An Introduction. (Modern Introductions to Philosophy Ser.). 144p. 1980. text ed. 20.00x (ISBN 0-333-26669-2); pap. text ed. 10.00x o. p. (ISBN 0-333-26670-6). Humanities.

Trustees of the British Museum (Natural History) Report on the British Museum (Natural History) 1978-1980. (Illus.). x, 167p. 1981. pap. 18.75 (ISBN 0-565-00842-0, Pub. by Brit Mus Nat Hist England). Sabbot-Natural Hist Bks.

Trusty, Francis M., ed. Administering Human Resources: A Behavioral Approach to Educational Administration. LC 71-146311. (Orig.). 1971. 22.00x (ISBN 0-8211-1903-6); text ed. 20.20x (ISBN 0-685-04200-6). McCutchan.

Trutter, Edith E., jt. auth. see Trutter, John T.

Trutter, John T. & Trutter, Edith E. The Governor Takes a Bride: The Celebrated Marriage of Cora English & John R. Tanner, Governor of Illinois, 1897-1901. LC 77-7643. (Illus.). 82p. 1977. pap. 3.95x o.p. (ISBN 0-8093-0825-8). S Ill U Pr.

Truxal, J. G., ed. see Motil, John M.

Truxal, John G. Control Engineers Handbook: Servomechanics, Regulators & Automatic Feedback Control Systems. (Chemical Engineering Ser.). 1958. 49.50 o.p. (ISBN 0-07-065308-9, P&RB). McGraw.

--Introductory System Engineering. (Electronic Systems Ser). (Illus.). 640p. 1972. text ed. 39.95 (ISBN 0-07-065317-8, C); solutions manual 9.50 (ISBN 0-07-065318-6). McGraw.

Truxal, John G., jt. auth. see Piel, E. Joseph.

Truzzi, Marcello, ed. Sociology: The Classic Statements. 1971. pap. text ed. 12.00 (ISBN 0-394-31280-5, RanC). Random.

Truzzi, Marcello, jt. ed. see Chamelin, Neil C.

Tryckare Co. Antique Locomotives Coloring Book. (Illus.). Date not set. pap. 2.25 (ISBN 0-486-23293-X). Dover.

Tryckare, Tre. Historic Sailing Ships Coloring Book. (Illus.). 48p. (Orig.). (gr. 3 up). 1982. pap. 2.50 (ISBN 0-486-23584-X). Dover.

Trygstad, Louise, jt. auth. see Jasmin, Sylvia.

Tryman, Mfanya D. Afro-American Mass Political Integration: A Casual & Deductive Model. 238p. (Orig.). 1982. lib. bdg. 21.50 (ISBN 0-8191-2645-4); pap. text ed. 10.75 (ISBN 0-8191-2646-2). U Pr of Amer.

Tryon, Alice, jt. auth. see Tryon, Rolla.

Tryon, Rolla & Tryon, Alice. Ferns & Allied Plants: With Special Reference to Tropical America. (Illus.). 896p. 1982. 148.00 o.p. (ISBN 0-387-90672-X). Springer-Verlag.

Tryon, Thomas. Kingdom Come. LC 81-48119. Date not set. 17.50 (ISBN 0-394-52389-X). Knopf. Postponed.

Trypanosomiasis Seminar, jt. auth. see Baker, John R.

Trythall, Anthony J. Boney Fuller: Soldier, Strategist & Writer, 1878-1966. 1977. 27.50 (ISBN 0-8135-0844-4). Rutgers U Pr.

Trytten, John M. Ten Steps for Boosting Your Sales Right Now. 1975. pap. 6.95 (ISBN 0-686-98287-8). Sales & Mktg.

Trzyna, Thaddeus C. California Environmental Directory: A Guide to Organizations & Resources. 3rd ed. LC 77-642158. (California Information Guides). (Illus.). 134p. (Orig.). 1980. pap. text ed. 18.50x (ISBN 0-912102-53-5). Cal Inst Public.

Trzyna, Thaddeus C., et al. Preserving Agricultural Land: An International Annotated Bibliography. LC 81-21629. (Environmental Studies: No. 7). 100p. (Orig.). 1981. pap. 25.00x (ISBN 0-912102-59-4). Cal Inst Public.

Trzyna, Thomas N., et al, eds. Careers for Humanities-Liberal Arts Majors: A Guide to Programs & Resources. 2nd ed. LC 80-50352. 188p. 1980. pap. 17.50 (ISBN 0-9604078-0-4). Weatherford.

Tsai, Christiana. Jewels from the Queen of the Dark Chamber. LC 82-12544. 128p. 1982. pap. 3.95 (ISBN 0-8024-4336-2). Moody.

Tsai, Fong Y. & Hieshima, Grant B. Neuroradiology of Head Trauma. (Illus.). 1983. price not set (ISBN 0-8391-1776-0, 13668). Univ Park.

Tsai, S. C. Fundamentals of Coal Benefication & Utilization. (Coal Science & Technology Ser.: Vol. 2). 1982. 83.00 (ISBN 0-444-42082-7). Elsevier.

Tsalf, A. Combined Properties of Conductors: An Aid for Calculation of Thermal Processes in Electrical & Heat Engineering. (Physical Science Data Ser.: No. 9). 1981. 110.75 (ISBN 0-686-80759-6). Elsevier.

Tsao, G. T., jt. ed. see Perlman, D.

Tscharnuter, Ingrid, jt. auth. see Scherzer, Alfred L.

Tschebotarioff, Gregory P. Foundations, Retaining & Earth Structures: The Art of Design Construction & Its Scientific Basis in Soil Mechanics. 2nd ed. (Illus.). 704p. 1973. 37.95 (ISBN 0-07-065377-1, P&RB). McGraw.

Tschirgi, Daniel. Politics of Indecision. 368p. 1983. 24.95 (ISBN 0-03-062361-8). Praeger.

Tschirhart, William, jt. auth. see Munem, Mustafa.

Tschirky, Oscar. Oscar of the Waldorf's Cookbook. 907p. 1973. Repr. of 1896 ed. 15.00 o.p. (ISBN 0-486-20790-0). Dover.

Tschudy, Robert H. & Scott, Richard A., eds. Aspects of Palynology: An Introduction to Plant Microfossils in Time. LC 73-84968. 510p. 1969. 70.95 (ISBN 0-471-89220-3, Pub. by Wiley-Interscience). Wiley.

Tschuppik, Karl. Ludendorff: The Tragedy of a Military Mind. Johnston, W. H., tr. from Ger. LC 74-14118. (Illus.). 1975. Repr. of 1932 ed. lib. bdg. 18.50x (ISBN 0-8371-7788-X, TSLU). Greenwood.

Tsederberg, N. V. Thermal Conductivity of Gases & Liquids. 1965. 19.50x o.s.i. (ISBN 0-262-20004-X). MIT Pr.

Tselementes, Nicholas. Greek Cookery. 3rd ed. 1956. 6.00 (ISBN 0-685-09035-3). Divry.

Tselikov, A. I. Theory of Lengthwise Rolling. 342p. 1981. 10.00 (ISBN 0-8285-2181-6, Pub. by Mir Pubs USSR). Imported Pubns.

Tseng, Sally C. LC Rule Interpretations of AACR2, 1978-1982. LC 82-10353. 360p. 1982. 16.50 (ISBN 0-8108-1572-9); update CSB No. 17 10.00. Scarecrow.

Tseng, Wen-Shing, et al, eds. Adjustment in Intercultural Marriage. 1977. pap. text ed. 5.00x (ISBN 0-8248-0579-8). UH Pr.

Tseng Yu-Ho. Some Contemporary Elements in Classical Chinese Art. LC 63-17008. (Illus., Orig.). 1963. pap. 4.95 (ISBN 0-87022-812-9). UH Pr.

Tseng-Tseng Yu, Leslie see Yu, Leslie Tseng-Tseng & Tuchman, Gail S.

Tsharner, Renata Von see Fleming, Ronald L. & Von Tsharner, Renata.

Tsichritzis, Dennis & Klug, Anthony, eds. The ANSI-X3-SPARC DBMS Framework Report of the Study Group on Database Management Systems. (Illus.). xii, 19p. 1978. saddle-stitch 8.00 (ISBN 0-88283-013-9). AFIPS Pr.

Tsichritzis, Dennis C. & Lochovsky, F. H. Data Base Management Systems. 1977. text ed. 25.00 (ISBN 0-12-701740-2). Acad Pr.

Tsichritzis, Dionysios C. & Bernstein, Philip. Operating Systems. (Computer Science & Applied Mathematics Ser.). 298p. 1974. 26.00 (ISBN 0-12-701750-X). Acad Pr.

Tsien, Richard W., jt. ed. see Stevens, Charles F.

Tsien, Tsuen-Hsuin & Chen, James K. China: An Annotated Bibliography of Bibliographies. 1978. lib. bdg. 49.00 (ISBN 0-8161-8086-5, Hall Reference). G K Hall.

Tsien, Tsuen-hsuin, jt. ed. see Roy, David T.

Tsintsadze, Vakhtang, jt. auth. see Mepisashvilli, Rusudan.

Tsipis, Kosta, et al. The Future of the Sea-Based Deterrent. 1974. 17.50x (ISBN 0-262-06049-3); pap. 4.95x (ISBN 0-262-56012-7). MIT Pr.

Tsirpanlis, C. N. Ecumenical Consensus On the Church, the Sacraments, the Minstry & Reunion. 37p. 1980. pap. 1.50 (ISBN 0-686-36333-7). EO Pr.

Tsirpanlis, Constance N. The Anthropology of Saint John of Damascus. 64p. 1980. pap. 3.00 (ISBN 0-686-36332-9). EO Pr.

--The Liturgical & Mystical Theology of Nicolas Cabasilas. 2nd ed. 103p. 1979. pap. 6.99 (ISBN 0-686-36328-0). EO Pr.

--The Trinitarian & Mystical Theology of St. Symeon the New Theologian. 42p. 1981. pap. 2.00 (ISBN 0-686-36331-0). EO Pr.

Ts'o. Basic Principles of Nucleic Chemistry. 1974. Vol. 1. subscription 55.50 68.00 (ISBN 0-12-701901-4); Vol. 2, 1974. subscription 52.00 64.00 (ISBN 0-12-701902-2). Acad Pr.

Tso, Lin. Complete Investor's Guide to Listed Options: Calls & Puts. 240p. 1981. 19.95 (ISBN 0-13-161216-6, Spec); pap. 11.95 (ISBN 0-13-161208-5). P-H.

Tso, Paul O. The Molecular Biology of the Mammalian Genetic Apparatus, 2 vols. Incl. Vol. 1. 93.75 (ISBN 0-7204-0625-0); Vol. 2. 68.00 (ISBN 0-7204-0626-9). 1977. Set. 101.50 (North-Holland). Elsevier.

Tso, Tien C. Physiology & Biochemistry of Tobacco Plants. LC 79-178259. (Illus.). 393p. 1972. text ed. 61.00 (ISBN 0-87933-000-7). Hutchinson Ross.

Tsokos, C. P. & Shimi, I. N., eds. Theory & Application of Reliability: With Emphasis on Bayesian & Nonparametric Methods, 2 vols. 1977. Vol. 1. 49.50 (ISBN 0-12-702101-9); Vol. 2. 50.50 (ISBN 0-12-702102-7). Acad Pr.

Tsokos, Chris P. Mainstreams of Finite Mathematics with Applications. (Mathematics Ser.). 1978. text ed. 20.95 (ISBN 0-675-08436-9). Additional supplements may be obtained from publisher. Merrill.

Tsokos, Chris P. & Padgett, W. J. Random Integral Equations with Applications to Life Sciences & Engineering. 1974. 52.50 (ISBN 0-12-702150-7). Acad Pr.

Tsokos, Chris P., jt. auth. see Milton, J. Susan.

Tsokos, Chris P. & Thrall, Robert M., eds. Decision Information. 1979. 48.50 (ISBN 0-12-702250-3). Acad Pr.

Tsokos, J. O., jt. auth. see Milton, J. S.

Tsoukalis, Loukas & White, Maureen. Japan & Western Europe: Conflict & Cooperation. LC 82-6031. 1982. 25.00 (ISBN 0-686-81980-2). St Martin.

Tsow, Ming. A Day with Ling. (Illus.). 32p. (gr. 1-3). 1982. 7.95 (ISBN 0-241-10833-0, Pub. by Hamish Hamilton England). David & Charles.

Tsuang, Ming T. & VanderMey, Randall. Genes & the Mind: Inheritance of Mental Illness. (Illus.). 1980. text ed. 15.95x (ISBN 0-19-261268-9). Oxford U Pr.

Tsubaki, T. & Irukayama, K., eds. Minamata Disease: Methylmercury Poisoning in Minamata & Nigata, Japan. 1977. 85.75 (ISBN 0-444-99816-0). Elsevier.

Tsuboi, Sakae. Twenty-Four Eyes. Miura, Akira, tr. from Japanese. LC 82-51098. Orig. Title: Nijushi no Hitomi. 256p. 1983. pap. 6.50 (ISBN 0-8048-1462-7). C E Tuttle.

Tsuchiya, K., et al. Cadmium Studies in Japan: A Review. 1978. 102.25 (ISBN 0-444-80049-2). Elsevier.

Tsuchiya, M., et al. Collagen Degradation & Mammalian Collagenase. (International Congress Ser.: No. 601). Date not set. 61.75 (ISBN 0-444-90292-9). Elsevier.

Tsuchiya, M., et al, eds. Basic Aspects of Microcirculation: Proceedings of the International Symposium, Tokyo, July 26, 1981. (International Congress Ser.: No. 578). 404p. 1982. 93.00 (ISBN 0-444-90256-2, Excerpta Medica). Elsevier.

Tsui, Kitty. The Words of a Woman Who Breathes Fire. 80p. 1983. pap. 5.00 (ISBN 0-933216-06-8). Spinsters Ink.

Tsuji, Masatugu. Potential Theory in Modern Function Theory. 2nd ed. LC 74-4297. 600p. 1975. text ed. 23.50 (ISBN 0-8284-0281-7). Chelsea Pub.

Tsukada, Y. & Agranoff, B. W. Neurobiological Basis of Learning & Memory. 260p. 1980. text ed. 39.95 (ISBN 0-471-05148-9, Pub. by Wiley Med). Wiley.

Tsukada, Y., ed. Genetic Approaches to Development Neurobiology. 269p. 1983. 43.00 (ISBN 0-387-11872-1). Springer-Verlag.

Tsukui, J. & Murakami, Y. Turnpike Optimality in Input-Output Systems: Theory & Application for Planning. (Contributions to Economic Analysis Ser.: Vol. 122). 1979. 44.75 (ISBN 0-444-85221-2, North Holland). Elsevier.

Tsukui, Nobuko. Ezra Pound & Japanese Noh Plays. LC 82-23833. 132p. (Orig.). 1983. lib. bdg. 18.75 (ISBN 0-8191-2987-9); pap. text ed. 8.25 (ISBN 0-8191-2988-7). U Pr of Amer.

Tsunoda, S., et al, eds. Brassica Crops & Wild Allies. 360p. 1980. 38.00x (ISBN 0-89955-211-0, Pub. by Japan Sci Soc Japan). Intl Schol Bk Serv.

Tsuru, Shigego. The Mainsprings of Japanese Growth: A Turning Point. (Atlantic Papers: No. 76/3). (Orig.). 1977. pap. text ed. 4.75x (ISBN 0-686-83621-9). Allanheld.

Tsurumi, Yoshi. The Japanese Are Coming: A Multinational Spread of Japanese Firms. LC 76-23262. 384p. 1976. prof ref 25.00x (ISBN 0-88410-651-9). Ballinger Pub.

--Multinational Management: Business Strategy & Government Policy. 622p. 1976. prof ref 19.50x (ISBN 0-88410-297-1). Ballinger Pub.

Tsushima, Yuko. Child of Fortune. Harcourt, G., tr. from Japanese. LC 82-48168. 176p. 1983. 14.95 (ISBN 0-87011-532-4). Kodansha.

Tsutakawa, Mayumi & Lau, Alan C., eds. Turning Shadows into Light. (Illus.). 104p. (Orig.). 1982. pap. 9.95 (ISBN 0-9608280-0-1). Young Pine Pr.

Tsutsui, Minoru, jt. auth. see Nakamura, Akira.

Tsutsui, Minoru, jt. ed. see Becker, Ernest I.

Tsuzaki, Stanley M. & Reinecke, John E. English in Hawaii: An Annotated Bibliography. (Oceanic Linguistics Special Publications: No. 1). 1966. pap. text ed. 4.00x (ISBN 0-87022-815-3). UH Pr.

Tsuzuki, C. Edward Carpenter: Eighteen Forty-Four to Nineteen Twenty Nine. LC 80-40152. 240p. 1980. 39.50 (ISBN 0-521-23371-2). Cambridge U Pr.

Tsvetaeva, Marina. Marina Tsvetaeva: Stikhotvoreniia i poemy v 5-i tomakh, 5 vols. Sumerkin, Alexander, ed. LC 80-51177. (Orig., Rus.). 1980. Set. pap. write for info. (ISBN 0-89830-016-9); Vol. 1, 1980. pap. 25.00 (ISBN 0-89830-017-7); Vol. 2, 1982. pap. 25.00 (ISBN 0-89830-018-5); Vol. 3. pap. write for info. (ISBN 0-89830-019-3); Vol. 4. pap. write for info. (ISBN 0-89830-020-7); Vol. 5. pap. write for info. (ISBN 0-89830-021-5). Russica Pubs.

Tsvetaeva, Marina I. Izbrannaya Proza V Dvukh Tomakh, 2 vols. Sumerkin, Alexander, ed. LC 78-68928. (Rus.). 1979. Set. pap. 35.00 (ISBN 0-89830-004-5). Russica Pubs.

Tsvetayeva, Marina. Selected Poems of Marina Tsvetayeva. rev. ed. Feinstein, Elaine, tr. from Rus. 1982. pap. 11.95x (ISBN 0-19-211894-3). Oxford U Pr.

Tsypkin, Ya. Z. Adaptation & Learning in Automatic Systems. Nikolic, S. J., tr. LC 78-129017. (Mathematics in Science & Engineering Ser.: Vol. 73). 1971. 56.50 (ISBN 0-12-702050-0). Acad Pr.

Tsypkin, Ya Z. Foundations of the Theory of Learning Systems. (Mathematics in Science & Engineering Ser.). 1973. 43.00 (ISBN 0-12-702060-8). Acad Pr.

Tsytovich, N. A. Mechanics of Frozen Ground. 1975. 45.00 o.p. (ISBN 0-07-065410-7, P&RB). McGraw.

Tu, A. T. Raman Spectroscopy in Biology: Principles & Applications. 448p. 1982. text ed. 65.00x (ISBN 0-471-07984-7, Pub. by Wiley-Interscience). Wiley.

Tu, Anthony T. Survey of Contemporary Toxicology, Vol. 2. LC 79-25224. 248p. 1982. 55.00 (ISBN 0-471-06352-5, Pub. by Wiley-Interscience). Wiley.

--Venoms: Chemistry & Molecular Biology. LC 76-30751. 560p. 1977. 65.95x (ISBN 0-471-89229-7, Pub. by Wiley-Interscience). Wiley.

Tu, Anthony T., ed. Survey of Contemporary Toxicology, Vol. 1. LC 79-25224. 357p. 1980. 54.00x (ISBN 0-471-04085-1, Pub. by Wiley-Intersience). Wiley.

Tu, K. N., jt. auth. see Ho, P. S.

Tu, K. N., jt. ed. see Herman, H.

Tu, Wei-Ming. Centrality & Commonality: An Essay on Chung-Yung. LC 76-17054. (Society for Asian & Comparative Philosophy Monograph: No.3). 200p. 1976. pap. text ed. 6.00x (ISBN 0-8248-0447-3). UH Pr.

--Neo-Confucian Thought in Action: Wang Yang-Ming's Youth. 1976. 28.50x (ISBN 0-520-02968-2). U of Cal Pr.

Tuan Yi-Fu. Topophilia: A Study of Environmental Perception, Attitudes & Values. (Illus.). 272p. 1974. pap. text ed. 14.95 (ISBN 0-13-925230-4). P-H.

Tuazon & Schaffer. The New Comprehensive A-Z Crossword Dictionary. 1982. pap. 3.95 (ISBN 0-380-50492-8, 50492). Avon.

Tuazon, Redentor M. & Schaffer. The New Comprehensive A-Z Crossword Dictionary. LC 72-79971. 600p. 1973. 5.95 (ISBN 0-448-01525-0, G&D). Putnam Pub Group.

Tubb, E. C. The Coming Event. 1982. pap. 2.25 (ISBN 0-87997-725-6, UW1725). DAW Bks.

--Earth Is Heaven. (Dumarest of Terra Ser.: No. 27). 160p. 1982. pap. 2.25 (ISBN 0-87997-786-8, UE1786). DAW Bks.

--Iduna's Universe: Dumarest of Terra. (Science Fiction Ser.). (Orig.). 1979. pap. 1.75 o.p. (ISBN 0-87997-500-8, UE1500). Daw Bks.

--Incident on Ath: Dumarest, No. 18. (Science Fiction Ser). (Orig.). 1978. pap. 2.50 (UE1668). DAW Bks.

--Technos. (Dumarest of Terra Ser.: No. 7). 1982. pap. 2.25 (ISBN 0-441-79976-0, Pub. by Ace Science Fiction). Ace Bks.

--Veruchia. (Dumarest of Terra Ser.: No. 8). 160p. 1982. pap. 2.25 (ISBN 0-441-86181-4, Pub. by Ace Science Fiction). Ace Bks.

--The Winds of Gath. (Dumarest of Terra Ser.: No. 4). 192p. 1982. pap. 2.50 (ISBN 0-441-89302-3, Pub. by Ace Science Fiction). Ace Bks.

Tubbs, D. B. Art & the Automobile. (Illus.). 1979. 14.95 o.p. (ISBN 0-448-16425-6, G&D). Putnam Pub Group.

Tubbs, N. & London, P. S. Topical Reviews in Accident Surgery, Vol. 1. (Topical Reviews Ser.). (Illus.). 240p. 1980. text ed. 29.00 (ISBN 0-7236-0534-3). Wright-PSG.

--Topical Reviews in Accident Surgery, Vol. 2. (Topical Reviews Ser.). (Illus.). 272p. 1982. case bdg. 32.00 (ISBN 0-7236-0614-5). Wright-PSG.

Tubbs, Stewart L. & Moss, Sylvia. Human Communication. 3rd ed. 414p. 1980. text ed. 15.00 (ISBN 0-394-32411-0). Random.

--Interpersonal Communication. 2nd ed. 299p. 1981. pap. text ed. 11.95 (ISBN 0-394-32684-9). Random.

Tuberculosis Association of India. Textbook of Tuberculosis. 2nd rev. ed. 620p. 1982. 85.00x (ISBN 0-686-94063-6, Pub. by Garlandfold England). State Mutual Bk.

Tubesing, Donald A. Kicking Your Stress Habits. 1982. pap. 3.50 (ISBN 0-451-11834-0, AE1834, Sig). NAL.

Tubesing, Richard. Architectural Preservation & Urban Renovation: An Annotated Bibliography of U. S. Congressional Documents. LC 81-48417. 500p. 1982. lib. bdg. 60.00 (ISBN 0-8240-9386-0). Garland Pub.

Tubis, Manuel & Wolf, Walter. Radiopharmacy. LC 75-28385. 911p. 1976. 108.50 (ISBN 0-471-89227-0, Pub. by Wiley-Interscience). Wiley.

Tucan, Fawwaz & Wedde, Ian, trs. from Arabic. Mahmoud Darwish: Selected Poems. (Translation Ser.). 1979. 6.95 o.p. (ISBN 0-85635-064-8, Pub. by Carcanet New Pr England). Humanities.

Tuccille, Jerome. Dynamic Investing. rev. ed. 1982. pap. 2.50 (ISBN 0-451-11625-9, AE1625, Sig). NAL.

--Everything the Beginner Needs to Know to Invest Shrewdly: A Step-by-Step Guide to the Basics of Financial Growth. 192p. 1979. pap. 5.29i (ISBN 0-06-463476-0, EH 476, EH). B&N NY.

--Inside the Underground Economy. 158p. 1982. pap. 2.50 (ISBN 0-451-11648-8, AE1648, Sig). NAL.

--Mind Over Money: Why Most People Lose Money in the Stock Market & How You Can Become a Winner. LC 79-22813. 1980. 8.95 o.p. (ISBN 0-688-03595-7). Morrow.

--The Optimist's Guide to Making Money in the 1980's. LC 78-14771. 1978. 7.95 o.p. (ISBN 0-688-03387-3); pap. 4.95 o.p. (ISBN 0-688-08387-0). Morrow.

--Who's Afraid of 1984? The Case for Optimism. 256p. 1975. 7.95 o.p. (ISBN 0-87000-308-9, Arlington Hse). Crown.

Tuccillo, John. Housing & Investment in an Inflationary World: Theory & Evidence. (Illus.). 55p. (Orig.). 1980. pap. text ed. 5.50 (ISBN 0-87766-281-9). Urban Inst.

Tuccillo, John & Weicher, John. Local Mortgage Revenue Bonds: Economic & Financial Impacts. (Illus.). 46p. (Orig.). 1979. pap. text ed. 4.00 (ISBN 0-87766-252-5). Urban Inst.

Tuccillo, John & Villani, Kevin, eds. House Prices & Inflation. LC 81-53062. 175p. 1981. text ed. 21.00 (ISBN 0-87766-306-8, URI 33300). Urban Inst.

Tucek, S. Acetylcholine Synthesis in Neurons. 259p. 1978. 47.00x (ISBN 0-412-15030-1, Pub. by Chapman & Hall England). Methuen Inc.

Tucek, S., et al, eds. see International Conference on the Synapse, Czechoslovakia, May, 1978.

Tuchak, Vladimir, jt. auth. see Bergson, Anika.

Tuchak, Vladimir see Bergson, Anika.

Tuchman, Barbara. Practicing History: Selected Essays. 1982. pap. 7.95 (ISBN 0-345-30363-6). Ballantine.

Tuchman, Barbara W. Guns of August. (Illus.). (gr. 9 up). 1962. 19.95 (ISBN 0-02-620310-3). Macmillan.

Tuchman, Gail S., jt. auth. see Yu, Leslie Tseng-Tseng.

Tuchman, Gaye, et al, eds. Hearth & Home: Images of Women in the Mass Media. 1978. text ed. 19.95x (ISBN 0-19-502351-X); pap. text ed. 6.95x (ISBN 0-19-502352-8). Oxford U Pr.

Tuchman, Maurice, jt. ed. see Barron, Stephanie.

Tuchman, Phyllis. George Segal. (Modern Masters Ser.). (Illus.). 128p. 1983. 24.95 (ISBN 0-89659-328-2); pap. 16.95 (ISBN 0-89659-329-0). Abbeville Pr.

Tuck. A Guide to Seabirds of Ocean Routes. 23.95 (ISBN 0-686-42755-6, Collins Pub England). Greene.

Tuck, Anthony. Richard the Second & the English Nobility. LC 73-89995. 256p. 1974. 18.95 o.p. (ISBN 0-312-68215-8). St Martin.

Tuck, B., jt. ed. see Makram-Ebeid, S.

Tuck, Charles A., Jr., ed. NFPA Inspection Manual. 5th ed. LC 76-5194. (Illus.). 387p. 1982. 20.00 (ISBN 0-87765-239-2, SPP-11C). Natl Fire Prot.

Tuck, Donald H. Encyclopedia of Science Fiction & Fantasy, Vol. 3. LC 73-91828. 1983. 30.00 (ISBN 0-911682-26-0). Advent.

Tuck, Mary. How Do We Choose. (Essential Psychology Ser.). 1976. pap. 4.50x (ISBN 0-416-82000-X). Methuen Inc.

Tuck, William P. Knowing God: Religious Knowledge in the Theology of John Baillie. LC 78-52865. 1978. pap. text ed. 8.25 (ISBN 0-8191-0484-1). U Pr of Amer.

Tucker. Atlantic Alliance & Its Critics. 204p. 1983. 24.95 (ISBN 0-03-062888-1); pap. 12.75 (ISBN 0-03-063352-4). Praeger.

Tucker, Abraham. The Light of Nature Pursued, 7 vols. Wellek, Rene, ed. LC 75-11262. (British Philosophers & Theologians of the 17th & 18th Centuries: Vol. 60). 1977. Repr. of 1805 ed. Set. lib. bdg. 231.00 o.s.i. (ISBN 0-8240-1811-7); lib. bdg. 42.00 ea. o.s.i. Garland Pub.

Tucker, Allen B., Jr. Programming Languages. (Computer Science Ser.). (Illus.). 1977. text ed. 33.95 (ISBN 0-07-065415-8, C). McGraw.

--Text Processing: Algorithms, Languages, & Applications. LC 79-23130. (Computer Science & Applied Mathematics Ser.). 1979. 17.50 (ISBN 0-12-702550-2). Acad Pr.

Tucker, Bernard L., ed. Second Clinical Conference on Congential Heart Disease. 448p. 1982. 29.50 (ISBN 0-8089-1507-X). Grune.

Tucker, Bettie C. The Children's Rhyming Bible. Smith, Dale R. & Petrikovic, John J., eds. (Illus.). 300p. (Orig.). (gr. k-12). 1982. pap. 7.95 (ISBN 0-9608780-0-9). Rainbows End.

Tucker, Billy, jt. auth. see Hagin, Josef.

Tucker, C. L., III, jt. ed. see Suh, N. P.

Tucker, C. M. The Taxonomy of the Genus Phytophtora. (Illus.). 24.00 (ISBN 3-7682-0515-0). Lubrecht & Cramer.

Tucker, Cathy, ed. see Chevalier, Christa.

Tucker, Cathy, ed. see Henriod, Lorraine.

Tucker, Charles O., jt. auth. see Hess, Herbert J.

Tucker, David. Marxism & Individualism. 1980. 27.50 (ISBN 0-312-51839-0). St Martin.

Tucker, David M. Black Pastors & Leaders: The Memphis Clergy, 1819-1972. LC 75-1248. 176p. 1975. 9.95x o.p. (ISBN 0-87870-024-2). Memphis St Univ.

--Memphis Since Crump: Bossism, Blacks, & Civic Reformers, 1948-1968. LC 79-12211. (Illus.). 1980. 12.50 (ISBN 0-87049-282-9). U of Tenn Pr.

Tucker, Dennis & Caruthers, Madeline. Taking Care of Eyeglasses. (Project MORE Daily Living Skills Ser.). 32p. 1979. Repr. of 1976 ed. pap. text ed. 5.95 (ISBN 0-8331-1238-4). Hubbard Sci.

Tucker, Don H., ed. Vector & Operator Valued Measures & Applications. 1974. 48.50 (ISBN 0-12-702450-6). Acad Pr.

Tucker, Eric. Another Way Out. LC 81-85735. 80p. 1983. pap. 4.95 (ISBN 0-86666-057-7). GWP.

Tucker, Gabe, jt. auth. see Crumbaker, Marge.

Tucker, Gail. Oscar the Oil Rig Meets Tuckee the Tug. 1982. 4.95 (ISBN 0-533-05364-1). Vantage.

Tucker, Gardiner. Toward Rationalizing Allied Weapons Production. (The Atlantic Papers: No. 76/1). 54p. (Orig.). 1976. pap. text ed. 4.75 (ISBN 0-686-83681-2). Allanheld.

Tucker, Gary J., jt. auth. see Pincus, Jonathan H.

Tucker, Gene & Knight, Douglas, eds. Humanizing America's Iconic Book. LC 82-836. (SBL Biblical Scholarship in North America Ser.). 188p. 1982. 29.95 (ISBN 0-89130-570-X, 06-11-06); pap. 17.50 (ISBN 0-686-42952-4). Scholars Pr CA.

Tucker, Gene M., ed. see Robertson, David.

Tucker, George. A Voyage to the Moon. 1975. Repr. of 1827 ed. lib. bdg. 13.00 (ISBN 0-8398-2315-0, Gregg). G K Hall.

Tucker, George H. Virginia Supernatural Tales: Ghosts, Witches & Eerie Doings. LC 77-12746. (Illus.). 1977. pap. 4.95 o.p. (ISBN 0-915442-40-X). Donning Co.

Tucker, Gilbert M. Your Money & What to Do With It. 1960. 9.95 (ISBN 0-8159-7401-9). Devin.

Tucker, Gordon, jt. auth. see Gibbons, Euell.

Tucker, H., ed. see IFIP Workshop on Methodology in Computer Graphics, France, May 1976.

Tucker, Howard F. Automatic Transmissions. LC 78-62623. (gr. 7-12). 1980. pap. text ed. 16.00 (ISBN 0-8273-1648-8); instructor's guide 2.75 (ISBN 0-8273-1649-6). Delmar.

Tucker, J. W. & Rampton, V. W. Microwave Ultrasonics in Solid State Physics. 1973. 60.50 (ISBN 0-444-10385-6, North-Holland). Elsevier.

Tucker, James C. & Wentworth, Anna. Goatie. (Illus.). 24p. (Orig.). (gr. 2-8). 1982. pap. 2.95 (ISBN 0-910341-00-1). Blackwater Pub Co.

Tucker, James F. Essentials of Economics. LC 74-12097. (Illus.). 384p. 1974. pap. 13.95 o.p. (ISBN 0-13-285858-4). P-H.

Tucker, Jan L., jt. ed. see Mehlinger, Howard D.

Tucker, John M., jt. ed. see Gleaves, Edwin S.

Tucker, Karl & Jensen, Clayne. Skiing: Exploring Sports Ser. 3rd ed. 90p. 1983. pap. write for info. (ISBN 0-697-09964-4). Wm C Brown.

Tucker, Karl & Jensen, Clayne R. Skiing. 4th ed. (Physical Education Activities Ser.). 110p. 1983. pap. text ed. write for info. (ISBN 0-697-07210-X). Wm C Brown.

Tucker, Kathleen, ed. see Hopkins, Lee B.

Tucker, Kathleen, ed. see Osborn, Lois.

Tucker, Kathleen, ed. see Simon, Norma.

Tucker, Kathleen, ed. see Susman, Susan.

Tucker, Kathleen, ed. see Van Steenwyk, Elizabeth.

Tucker, Kathy, ed. see Girard, Linda.

Tucker, Kenneth. A Bibliography of Writings by & About John Ford & Cyril Tourneur. 1977. lib. bdg. 15.00 o.p. (ISBN 0-8161-7834-8, Hall Reference). G K Hall.

Tucker, Kerry. Greetings from Los Angeles: A Visit to the City of Angels in Postcards. (Illus.). 112p. (Orig.). 1982. pap. 8.95 (ISBN 0-942820-00-2). Steam Pr MA.

Tucker, Lewis R., jt. auth. see Jain, Subhash C.

Tucker, Louis L. Cincinnati. Lord, Clifford, ed. LC 68-9258. (YA) 1969. pap. 2.95 o.p. (ISBN 0-8077-2283-9). Tchrs Coll.

Tucker, Louis L; see Weaver, Glenn.

Tucker, Martin. Joseph Conrad. LC 75-37265. (Literature and Life Ser.). 1980. 11.95 (ISBN 0-8044-2928-6). Ungar.

Tucker, Martin A., jt. ed. see Temple, Ruth Z.

Tucker, Maurice E. A Field Description of Sedimentary Rocks. LC 81-6539. (Geological Society of London Handbook Ser.). 112p. 1982. pap. 12.95X (ISBN 0-470-27239-2). Halsted Pr.

Tucker, N., ed. Suitable for Children? Controversies in Children's Literature. 39.00x (ISBN 0-686-97022-5, Pub. by Scottish Academic Pr Scotland). State Mutual Bk.

Tucker, Nancy B. Patterns in the Dust: Chinese-American Relations & the Recognition Controversy, 1949-1950. Leuchtenburg, William E., ed. (Contemporary American History Ser.). 400p. 1983. text ed. 30.00 (ISBN 0-231-05362-2); pap. 15.00 (ISBN 0-231-05363-0). Columbia U Pr.

Tucker, Nicholas. The Child & the Book: A Psychological & Literary Exploration. LC 80-49883. 275p. 1981. 32.50 (ISBN 0-521-23251-1); pap. 11.95 (ISBN 0-521-27048-0). Cambridge U Pr.

Tucker, Nicholas, ed. Suitable for Children? Controversies in Children's Literature. 1976. 27.50x (ISBN 0-520-03236-5). U of Cal Pr.

Tucker, Patsy M. Carolina Treasures. LC 78-78073. (Illus.). 1979. 7.95 (ISBN 0-87716-099-6, Pub. by Moore Pub Co). F Apple.

Tucker, R. H., et al. Global Geophysics. 1970. 21.95 (ISBN 0-444-19648-X). Elsevier.

Tucker, Raymond, et al. Research in Speech Communication. (Ser. in Speech Communication). (Illus.). 352p. 1981. text ed. 25.95 (ISBN 0-13-774273-8). P-H.

Tucker, Richard, jt. ed. see Alatis, James E.

Tucker, Richard P., jt. auth. see Richards, John F.

Tucker, Robert C. Philosophy & Myth in Karl Marx. 2nd ed. LC 70-180022. 250p. 1972. 39.50 (ISBN 0-521-08455-5); pap. 10.95 (ISBN 0-521-09701-0). Cambridge U Pr.

Tucker, Robert W. The Inequality of Nations. LC 76-9673. 1979. pap. 7.95 (ISBN 0-465-03246-X, CN5046). Basic.

--The Just War: A Study in Contemporary American Doctrine. LC 78-14322. 1979. Repr. of 1960 ed. lib. bdg. 20.75x (ISBN 0-313-20621-X, TUJW). Greenwood.

Tucker, Spencer. Handbook of Business Formulas & Controls. (Illus.). 1979. 34.95 (ISBN 0-07-065421-2, P&RB). McGraw.

Tucker, Spencer A. Pricing for Higher Profit. 1966. 31.00 (ISBN 0-07-065419-0, P&RB). McGraw.

Tucker, Stefan F. & Cowan, Martin B., eds. Real Estate Income Taxation 1982. 816p. 1982. 48.00 (ISBN 0-88262-829-1). Warren.

Tucker, Susan M. & Bryant, Sandra. Fetal Monitoring & Fetal Assessment in High Risk Pregnancy. LC 77-19098. 156p. 1978. pap. text ed. 14.95 (ISBN 0-8016-5121-2). Mosby.

Tucker, Susie I. Enthusiasm: A Study of a Word & Its Relatives. LC 79-161296. 1972. 39.50 (ISBN 0-521-08263-3). Cambridge U Pr.

Tucker, W. Leon. Studies in Ephesians. 1983. pap. 3.95 (ISBN 0-8254-3828-4). Kregel.

Tucker, Wallace A. Radiation Processes in Astrophysics. LC 75-29236. 311p. 1975. pap. 7.95x (ISBN 0-262-70010-7). MIT Pr.

Tucker, Wilson. The Year of the Quiet Sun. 1979. lib. bdg. 14.95 (ISBN 0-8398-2529-3, Gregg). G K Hall.

Tuckerman. Book of the Artists. Date not set. 25.00 (ISBN 0-686-43151-0). Apollo.

Tuckerman, E. Collected Lichenological Papers, 2 vols. Culberson, W. L., ed. 1964. Vol. 1. 40.50 (ISBN 3-7682-0221-6); Vol. 2. 48.60 (ISBN 3-7682-0222-4); Set. 79.20 (ISBN 3-7682-0220-8). Lubrecht & Cramer.

Tuckerman, Murray M. & Turco, Salvatore J. Human Nutrition. LC 82-13033. (Illus.). 376p. 1983. write for info (ISBN 0-8121-0853-1). Lea & Febiger.

Tuckett, David, ed. An Introduction to Medical Sociology. 1976. 27.95x o.p. (ISBN 0-422-74510-3, Pub. Ty Tavistock England); pap. 16.50x (ISBN 0-422-74320-8, Pub. by Tavistock). Methuen Inc.

Tuckett, David & Kaufert, Joseph M., eds. Basic Readings in Medical Sociology. 1978. pap. text ed. 13.95x (ISBN 0-422-76290-3, Pub. by Tavistock England). Methuen Inc.

Tuckey, John S., ed. see Twain, Mark.

Tuckman, Bruce W. Conducting Educational Research. 2nd ed. (Illus.). 479p. 1978. text ed. 20.95 (ISBN 0-15-512981-3, HC). HarBraceJ.

Tucks, E., jt. auth. see Roy, Ranjan.

Tuden, Arthur, jt. ed. see Rubin, Vera.

Tudor, Andre. Image & Influence: Studies in the Sociology of Film. LC 74-26212. 256p. 1975. text ed. 19.95 o.p. (ISBN 0-312-40915-X). St Martin.

Tudor, Bethany. Drawn from New England: A Portrait in Words & Pictures. LC 79-14230. (Illus.). 1979. 10.95 o.p. (ISBN 0-399-20835-6, Philomel). Putnam Pub Group.

--Samuel's Treehouse. LC 78-12087. (Illus.). 32p. (ps-3). 1979. 6.95 o.s.i. (ISBN 0-529-05435-3, Philomel); PLB 6.99 o.s.i. (ISBN 0-529-05522-8). Putnam Pub Group.

Tudor, Dean & Tudor, Nancy. Black Music. LC 78-15563. (American Popular Music on Elpee Ser). 1979. lib. bdg. 22.50 (ISBN 0-87287-147-9). Libs Unl.

--Grass Roots Music. LC 78-31686. (American Popular Music on Elpee). 367p. 1979. lib. bdg. 25.00 (ISBN 0-87287-133-9). Libs Unl.

--Jazz. LC 78-11737. (American Popular Music on Elpee Ser). 1979. lib. bdg. 23.50 (ISBN 0-87287-148-7). Libs Unl.

Tudor, Dean, jt. auth. see Armitage, Andrew D.

Tudor, Mary J. Child Development. 544p. 1981. text ed. 29.95 (ISBN 0-07-065412-3, HP). McGraw.

Tudor, Nancy, jt. auth. see Tudor, Dean.

Tudor, Nancy, jt. ed. see Armitage, Andrew D.

Tudor, Tasha. A Book of Christmas. (Illus.). 1979. 6.95 o.p. (ISBN 0-529-05532-5, Philomel). Putnam Pub Group.

--Dolls' Christmas. LC 59-12744. (Illus.). (gr. k-3). 1950. 6.95g (ISBN 0-8098-1026-3); pap. 3.95 (ISBN 0-8098-2912-6). McKay.

--Mother Goose. LC 58-58523. (Illus.). (gr. k-3). 1944. 8.95g (ISBN 0-8098-1901-5). McKay.

--Take Joy: The Tasha Tudor Christmas Book. LC 66-10645. (Illus.). 1966. 10.95 (ISBN 0-399-20766-X, Philomel); PLB 10.99 (ISBN 0-399-61169-X). Putnam Pub Group.

--Tasha Tudor's Five Senses. (Illus.). 24p. (ps-3). Date not set. price not set (ISBN 0-448-40550-4, G&D). Putnam Pub Group.

--A Tasha Tudor's Sampler: A Tale for Easter Pumpkin Moonshine the Dolls' Christmas. (gr. k-3). 1977. 9.95 (ISBN 0-679-20412-1). McKay.

Tudor, Tasha, illus. First Poems of Childhood. (Illus.). 24p. (ps-3). Date not set. price not set (ISBN 0-448-40505-9, G&D). Putnam Pub Group.

--The Lord Is My Shepherd: The Twenty-Third Psalm. LC 79-27134. 32p. (gr. 2 up). 1980. 6.95 (ISBN 0-399-20756-2, Philomel). Putnam Pub Group.

Tueleners, T. Beginning Karate. 6.95x (ISBN 0-685-63744-1). Wehman.

Tuell, Anne K. John Sterling: Representative Victorian. 1949. text ed. 49.50x (ISBN 0-686-83598-0). Elliots Bks.

Tuer, Andrew W. One Thousand Quaint Cuts from Books of Other Days. LC 68-31097. 1968. Repr. of 1886 ed. 34.00x (ISBN 0-8103-3494-1). Gale.

--Pages & Pictures from Forgotten Children's Books. LC 68-31096. (Illus.). 1969. Repr. of 1899 ed. 34.00x (ISBN 0-8103-3488-7). Gale.

--Stories from Old-Fashioned Children's Books, Brought Together & Introduced to the Reader. LC 68-31438. 1968. Repr. of 1899 ed. 34.00x (ISBN 0-8103-3489-5). Gale.

Tuer, David F. & Bolz, Roger W. Robotics Sourcebook & Dictionary. 304p. 1983. 29.95 (ISBN 0-8311-1152-6). Indus Pr.

Tuerck, David G., ed. The Political Economy of Advertising. 1978. 15.25 (ISBN 0-8447-2120-4); pap. 4.75 (ISBN 0-8447-2110-7). Am Enterprise.

Tuexen, R. Pflanzengesellschaften Westdeutschlands. 1970. Repr. of 1937 ed. 10.00 (ISBN 3-7682-0702-1). Lubrecht & Cramer.

Tuexen, R. & Schwabe-Braun, Angelika, eds. Internationale Vereinigung Fuer Vegetationskunde: Berichte der Internationalen Symposien: Vegetation Als Anthrop-Oekologischer Gegenstand (1971) Gefaehrdete Vegetation und Ihre Erhaltung (1972) (Illus.). 662p. (Ger.). 1981. lib. bdg. 80.00x (ISBN 3-7682-1311-0). Lubrecht & Cramer.

Tufayl, Ibn. Hayy Ibn Yaqzan. Goodman, Lenn E., tr. (International Studies & Translations Ser.). 1972. lib. bdg. 7.50 o.p. (ISBN 0-8057-5677-9, Twayne). G K Hall.

Tuffet-Anghileri, Anne M., jt. ed. see Anghileri, Leopold J.

Tufte, Edward, ed. Electoral Reform. 1974. pap. 6.00 (ISBN 0-918592-07-0). Policy Studies.

Tufte, Edward R. Data Analysis for Politics & Policy. (Illus.). 192p. 1974. pap. text ed. 12.95 (ISBN 0-13-197525-0). P-H.

Tufty, Barbara. Cells: Units of Life. (Illus.). (gr. 5 up). 1973. PLB 5.89 o.p. (ISBN 0-399-60798-6). Putnam Pub Group.

Tugarinov, A. I., ed. Recent Contributions to Geochemistry & Analytical Chemistry. Slutzkin, D., tr. from Rus. LC 74-8165. 694p. 1976. 98.95 o.s.i. (ISBN 0-470-89228-5). Halsted Pr.

Tugendhat, Ernst. Traditional & Analytical Philosophy: Lectures on the Philosophy of Language. Gorner, P. A., tr. from Ger. LC 81-15509. 450p. (Eng.). 1982. 49.50 (ISBN 0-521-22236-2). Cambridge U Pr.

Tuggle, Diane. Spencer's Toothbrush. LC 80-54611. (Illus.). 72p. (Orig.). (gr. k-6). Date not set. pap. 4.95 (ISBN 0-932238-08-4). Avant Bks. Postponed.

Tuggle, Francis D. Organizational Processes. Mackenzie, Kenneth D., ed. LC 77-86001. (Organizational Behavior Ser.). (Illus.). 1978. pap. text ed. 13.95x (ISBN 0-88295-455-5). Harlan Davidson.

Tuggle, H. David & Griffin, P. Bion, eds. Lapakahi, Hawaii: Archaeological Studies. (Social Science & Linguistics Institute Special Publications). (Illus.). 380p. 1973. pap. 8.00x (ISBN 0-8248-0246-2). UH Pr.

Tuggle, Joyce, jt. auth. see McCarthy, Nancy M.

Tuggle, Sharon. Assembler Language Programming: Systems-360 & 370. LC 74-84276. 400p. 1975. pap. text ed. 18.95 (ISBN 0-574-19160-7, 13-4015); instr's guide avail. (ISBN 0-574-19161-5, 13-4016). SRA.

Tuggy, David H. & Brockway, Earl. Studies in Uto-Aztecan Grammar Vol. 2: Modern Aztec Grammatical Sketches, 4 vols. Langacker, Ronald W., ed. LC 78-56488. (Publications in Linguistics: No. 56). 380p. 1979. pap. text ed. 13.50 Set (ISBN 0-88312-072-0); microfiche 3.75. Summer Inst Ling.

Tugwell, Rexford. The Emerging Constitution. LC 73-6316. (Illus.). 1974. 20.00i (ISBN 0-06-128225-1). Har-Row.

Tugwell, Simon, ed. Early Dominicans, Selected Writings. (The Classics of Western Spirituality Ser.). 400p. 1982. 13.95 (ISBN 0-8091-0325-7); pap. 9.95 (ISBN 0-8091-2414-9). Paulist Pr.

Tuite, Don. Electronic Experimenter's Guidebook. LC 74-14322. (Illus.). 182p. 1974. 7.95 o.p. (ISBN 0-8306-4540-3); pap. 4.95 o.p. (ISBN 0-8306-3540-8, 540). TAB Bks.

Tukey, J. W. Convergence & Uniformity in Topology. 1940. pap. 12.00 (ISBN 0-527-02718-9). Kraus Repr.

Tukey, John W. Exploratory Data Analysis. LC 76-5080. (Illus.). 1977. 27.95 (ISBN 0-201-07616-0). A-W.

Tukey, John W., jt. auth. see Mosteller, Frederick.

Tulane. Catalog of the Latin American Library of the Tulane University Library: Third Supplement, 2 vols. 1978. Set. lib. bdg. 260.00 (ISBN 0-8161-0005-5, Hall Library). G K Hall.

Tulane University, New Orleans. Catalog of the Latin American Library of the Tulane University Library, 9 vols. 1970. Set. lib. bdg. 855.00 (ISBN 0-8161-0894-3, Hall Library). G K Hall.

--Catalog of the Latin American Library of the Tulane University Library, First Supplement, 2 vols. 1973. Set. lib. bdg. 240.00 (ISBN 0-8161-0914-1, Hall Library). G K Hall.

--Catalog of the Latin American Library of the Tulane University Library, Second Supplement. 1975. lib. bdg. 240.00 (ISBN 0-8161-1052-2, Hall Library). G K Hall.

Tulchin, Joseph S., ed. Hemispheric Perspectives on the United States: Papers from the New World Conference. LC 77-87973. (Contributions in American Studies: No. 36). 1978. lib. bdg. 35.00x (ISBN 0-313-20053-X, TUH/). Greenwood.

Tuleja, Tad, jt. auth. see Samtur, Susan.

Tulku, Tarthang. Crystal Mirror, Vol. I. (Illus.). 1971. pap. 4.95 o.p. (ISBN 0-913546-04-6). Dharma Pub.

Tulku, Tarthang, ed. Nyringma Edition of the sDe-dge bKa-gyur & bsTun-gyur, 120 vols. (Tibetan Buddhist Canon). 65000p. 1981. Set. 1500.00 (ISBN 0-89800-129-3). Dharma Pub.

Tull, Donald S. & Hawkins, Del I. Marketing Research: Measurement & Method. 2nd ed. (Illus.). 1980. text ed. 26.95x (ISBN 0-02-421760-3). Macmillan.

Tullar, Richard M. The Human Species: Its Nature, Evolution & Ecology. (Illus.). 1976. pap. text ed. 23.95 (ISBN 0-07-065423-9, C); instr's. manual 15.00 (ISBN 0-07-065424-7). McGraw.

Tuller, Martin A. Acid-Base Homeostasis & Its Disorders. 98p. 1971. spiral bdg. 7.00 o.p. (ISBN 0-87488-601-5). Med Exam.

Tullis, James E., jt. auth. see Burns, George W.

Tullius, John, jt. auth. see Burwash, Peter.

Tulloch, D. S. Physical Fundamentals of Materials Science. 193p. 1971. 9.95 o.p. (ISBN 0-408-70097-1). Butterworth.

Tulloch, John. Australian Cinema: Industry, Narrative & Meaning. (Studies in Society: No. 11). 264p. 1982. text ed. 28.50x (ISBN 0-86861-076-3); pap. text ed. 12.50 (ISBN 0-686-82849-6). Allen Unwin.

Tullock, Gordon, jt. auth. see McKenzie, Richard.

Tullock, Gordon & Wagner, Richard, eds. Deductive Models in Policy Analysis. new ed. 1977. pap. 6.00 (ISBN 0-918592-20-8). Policy Studies.

--Policy Analysis & Deductive Reasoning. LC 77-18380. (Policy Studies Organization Ser.). 224p. 1978. 21.95x (ISBN 0-669-02080-X, Pub. by Transaction Bks). Lexington Bks.

Tully, Alice, jt. auth. see Tully, Marianne.

Tully, Andrew. Inside the F.B.I. LC 80-14092. 240p. 1980. 12.95 o.p. (ISBN 0-07-065425-5, GB). McGraw.

--The Secret War Against Dope. 320p. 1973. 7.95 o.p. (ISBN 0-698-10532-X, Coward). Putnam Pub Group.

Tully, Gordon. Sun-Pulse II: Solar Heating Systems Program. (Illus.). 1979. 125.00 (ISBN 0-07-065442-5, P&RB). McGraw.

Tully, Gordon F. Solar Heating Systems: Analysis & Design with the Sun-Pulse Method. (Energy Learning Systems Bks.). (Illus.). 232p. 1981. 27.50 (ISBN 0-07-065441-7). McGraw.

Tully, J. A Discourse on Property. LC 79-15989. 1980. 29.95 (ISBN 0-521-22830-1). Cambridge U Pr.

Tully, James. A Discourse on Property: John Locke & His Adversaries. 208p. 1983. pap. 9.95 (ISBN 0-521-27140-1). Cambridge U Pr.

Tully, James, ed. see Locke, John.

Tully, Marianne. Dread Diseases. (First Bks). (Illus.). (gr. 4-6). 1978. PLB 8.90 s&l (ISBN 0-531-01406-1). Watts.

Tully, Marianne & Tully, Alice. Heart Disease. (gr. 4 up). 1980. PLB 8.90 (ISBN 0-531-04163-8). Watts.

Tully, Marianne & Tully, Mary A. Facts About the Human Body. LC 76-54752. (First Bks.). (Illus.). (gr. 4-6). 1977. PLB 8.90 s&l (ISBN 0-531-00395-7). Watts.

Tully, Mary A., jt. auth. see Tully, Marianne.

Tully, Mary Jo. Blessed Be. 96p. 1982. pap. 3.50 (ISBN 0-697-01822-9). Wm C Brown.

--Church: A Faith Filled - People. 96p. 1982. pap. 3.50 (ISBN 0-697-01823-7). Wm C Brown.

--A Family Book of Praise. (Illus.). 128p. (Orig.). 1980. 8.95 (ISBN 0-8215-6543-5); pap. 5.95 (ISBN 0-8215-6542-7). Sadlier.

--Psalms: Faith Songs for the Faith-Filled. 96p. 1982. pap. 3.50 (ISBN 0-697-01824-5). Wm C Brown.

Tully, Mary Jo & Hirstein, Sandra J. Focus on Believing. (Light of Faith Ser.). (Orig.). (gr. 3). 1981. pap. text ed. 3.20 (ISBN 0-697-01767-2); tchrs.' ed. 10.95 (ISBN 0-697-01768-0); tests 12.95 (ISBN 0-697-01829-6). Wm C Brown.

--Focus on Belonging. (Light of Faith Ser.). (Orig.). (gr. 2). 1981. pap. text ed. 2.80 (ISBN 0-697-01765-6); tchrs.' ed. 10.95 (ISBN 0-697-01766-4); tests 12.95 (ISBN 0-697-01828-8). Wm C Brown.

--Focus on Celebrating. (Light of Faith Ser.). (Orig.). (gr. 5). 1981. pap. text ed. 3.20 (ISBN 0-697-01771-0); tchr's ed 10.95 (ISBN 0-686-69655-7); tests 12.95 (ISBN 0-697-01831-8). Wm C Brown.

--Focus on Living. (Light of Faith Ser.). (Orig.). (gr. 4). 1981. pap. text ed. 3.20 (ISBN 0-697-01769-9); tchrs.' ed. 10.95 (ISBN 0-697-01770-2); tests 12.95 (ISBN 0-697-01830-X). Wm C Brown.

--Focus on Loving. (Light of Faith Ser.). (Orig.). (gr. 1). 1981. pap. text ed. 2.80 (ISBN 0-697-01763-X); tchrs.' ed. 10.95 (ISBN 0-697-01764-8); tests 12.95 (ISBN 0-697-01827-X). Wm C Brown.

Tully, Shawn, jt. auth. see McCurdy, Doug.

Tulman, Michael M., jt. auth. see Felmeister, Charles J.

Tulving, Endel. Elements of Episodic Memory. (Oxford Psychology Ser.). 400p. 1982. 29.95 (ISBN 0-19-852102-2). Oxford U Pr.

Tulving, Endel & Donaldson, Wayne, eds. Organization of Memory. 1972. 49.50 (ISBN 0-12-703650-4). Acad Pr.

Tuma, David T. & Reif, F., eds. Problem Solving & Education: Issues in Teaching & Research. LC 79-22461. 224p. 1980. text ed. 19.95x (ISBN 0-89859-008-6). L Erlbaum Assocs.

Tuma, Elias H. Twenty-Six Centuries of Agrarian Reform: A Comparative Analysis. (Near Eastern Center, UCLA). 1965. 30.00x (ISBN 0-520-01286-0). U of Cal Pr.

Tuma, Elias H. & Darin-Drabkin, H. The Economic Case for Palestine. LC 77-25974. 1978. 20.00 (ISBN 0-312-22734-5). St Martin.

Tuma, J. J. Advanced Structural Analysis. (Schaum's Outline Ser). pap. 8.95 (ISBN 0-07-065426-3, SP). McGraw.

--Engineering Mathematics Handbook. 1970. 18.50 o.p. (ISBN 0-07-065430-1, P&RB). McGraw.

--Engineering Mathematics Handbook. 2nd ed. 1979. text ed. 31.25 (ISBN 0-07-065429-8). McGraw.

--Handbook of Physical Calculations. 1975. 32.50 o.p. (ISBN 0-07-065438-7, P&RB). McGraw.

--Structural Analysis. (Schaum's Outline Ser). 1969. pap. 8.95 (ISBN 0-07-065422-0, SP). McGraw.

Tuma, Jan J. Handbook of Physical Calculations. 2nd ed. (Illus.). 512p. 1982. 39.95 (ISBN 0-07-065439-5). McGraw.

--Technology Mathematics Handbook. LC 74-26962. 384p. 1975. 23.50 (ISBN 0-07-065431-X, P&RB). McGraw.

Tuma, June M. Handbook for the Practice of Pediatric Psychology. LC 81-11567. (Personality Processes Ser.). 356p. 1982. 35.50x (ISBN 0-471-06284-7, Pub. by Wiley-Interscience). Wiley.

Tumarkin, Nina. Lenin Lives! The Lenin Cult in Soviet Russia. (Illus.). 384p. 1983. 20.00 (ISBN 0-674-52430-6). Harvard U Pr.

Tumber, Howard. Television & the Riots. 54p. 1981. pap. 5.50 (ISBN 0-85170-120-5). NY Zoetrope.

Tumblin, Charles R. Construction Cost Estimates. LC 79-16376. (Ser. on Practical Construction Guides). 406p. 1980. 35.95x (ISBN 0-471-05699-5, Pub. by Wiley-Interscience). Wiley.

Tumin, M. Social Stratification: The Form & Functions of Inequality. 1967. 9.95 (ISBN 0-13-818591-3). P-H.

Tumin, Melvin M. Caste in a Peasant Society. LC 75-29328. (Illus.). 300p. 1975. Repr. of 1952 ed. lib. bdg. 20.75x (ISBN 0-8371-8390-1, TUPS). Greenwood.

Tumin, Melvin M. & Plotch, Walter, eds. Pluralism in a Democratic Society. 248p. pap. 4.95 (ISBN 0-686-95022-4). ADL.

Tummala, Krishna K., ed. Administrative Systems Abroad. LC 82-16130. (Illus.). 386p. 1983. lib. bdg. 25.50 (ISBN 0-8191-2734-5); pap. text ed. 14.00 (ISBN 0-8191-2735-3). U Pr of Amer.

Tumulty, Philip A. The Effective Clinician: His Methods & Approach to Diagnosis & Care. LC 73-77942. 379p. 1973. text ed. 15.00 o.p. (ISBN 0-7216-8915-9). Saunders.

Tunberg, Karl & Tunberg, Terence. Master of Rosewood. (Orig.). 1980. pap. 2.50 o.p. (ISBN 0-446-91134-8). Warner Bks.

--The Quest of Ben Hur. pap. 2.95 o.p. (ISBN 0-446-93278-7). Warner Bks.

Tunberg, Terence, jt. auth. see Tunberg, Karl.

Tunbridge, David, ed. Notes on Clinical Methods. 120p. pap. 5.95 (ISBN 0-7190-0851-4). Manchester.

Tuncel, Selim, jt. auth. see Parry, William.

Tuncer, Baran, jt. auth. see Krueger, Anne O.

Tune, G. S., jt. auth. see Davies, D. R.

Tung, P. C. & Pollard, D. E. Colloquial Chinese. (Colloquial Ser.). 300p. (Orig.). 1982. pap. 9.50 (ISBN 0-7100-0891-0); cassette 11.95. Routledge & Kegan.

Tung, P. P., et al. Fracture & Failure: Analyses, Mechanisms & Applications. 1981. 40.00 (ISBN 0-87170-113-8). ASM.

Tung, Rosalie L. Chinese Industrial Society After Mao. LC 81-47183. 384p. 1982. 28.95x (ISBN 0-669-04565-9). Lexington Bks.

--U. S. - China Trade Negotiations. (Pergamon Policy Studies on Business & Economics Ser.). 245p. 1982. 32.50 (ISBN 0-08-027187-1). Pergamon.

Tung, William L. The Chinese in America 1820-1974: A Chronology & Fact Book. LC 74-3116. (Ethnic Chronology Ser.: No. 14). 150p. (gr. 9 up). 1974. text ed. 8.50 (ISBN 0-379-00510-7). Oceana.

Tunick, Barry, jt. auth. see Bursztyn, Sylvia.

Tunis, Edwin. Colonial Craftsmen: The Beginnings of American Industry. LC 75-29612. (Illus.). 160p. (gr. 7 up). 1976. 16.95 (ISBN 0-690-01062-1, TYC-J). Har-Row.

--Colonial Living. LC 75-29611. (Illus.). 160p. (gr. 7 up). 1976. 16.95 (ISBN 0-690-01063-X, TYC-J). Har-Row.

--Frontier Living. LC 75-29639. (Illus.). 168p. (gr. 7 up). 1976. 16.95 (ISBN 0-690-01064-8, TYC-J). Har-Row.

--Indians. rev. ed. LC 78-60175. (Illus.). (gr. 5 up). 1979. Repr. of 1959 ed. 16.95 (ISBN 0-690-03806-2, TYC-J); PLB 16.89 (ISBN 0-690-01283-7). Har-Row.

--Oars, Sails & Steam: A Picture Book of Ships. LC 76-25453. (Illus.). (gr. 6 up). 1977. 16.95 (ISBN 0-690-01284-5, TYC-J). Har-Row.

--The Tavern at the Ferry. LC 73-4488. (Illus.). 128p. (gr. 5 up). 1973. 16.95 (ISBN 0-690-00099-5, TYC-J). Har-Row.

--Wheels: A Pictorial History. LC 76-25809. (Illus.). (gr. 6 up). 1977. 16.95 (ISBN 0-690-01341-8, TYC-J). Har-Row.

--The Young United States 1783 to 1830. LC 75-29613. (Illus.). 160p. (gr. 7 up). 1976. 16.95 (ISBN 0-690-01065-6, TYC-J). Har-Row.

Tunis, John R. Go, Team, Go. (gr. 7 up). 1954. 9.50 (ISBN 0-688-21349-9). Morrow.

--Silence Over Dunkerque. (Illus.). (gr. 7 up). 1962. PLB 10.08 (ISBN 0-688-31760-X). Morrow.

Tunison, jt. auth. see Corman.

Tunley, David. Couperin. LC 81-71302. (BBC Music Guides Ser.). 104p. (Orig.). 1983. pap. 5.95 (ISBN 0-295-95924-X). U of Wash Pr.

Tunley, David see Callaway, Frank.

Tunnadine, David & Green, Roger. Unwanted Pregnancy: Accident or Illness. (Illus.). 1979. text ed. 22.00x o.p. (ISBN 0-19-261136-4). Oxford U Pr.

Tunnessen, Walter W. Signs & Symptoms in Pediatrics. 624p. 1983. text ed. write for info (ISBN 0-397-50556-6, Lippincott Medical). Lippincott Medical.

Tunney, Christopher. Exploring the Midnight World. LC 78-67837. (Explorer Books). (Illus.). (gr. 3-5). 1979. 2.95 (ISBN 0-531-09131-7, Warwick Press); PLB 7.90 s&l (ISBN 0-531-09116-3). Watts.

Tunnicliff, C. F. Sketches of Bird Life. (Illus.). 146p. 1982. 24.95 (ISBN 0-8230-4856-X). Watson-Guptill.

Tunnicliffe, Stephen, jt. auth. see Thompson, Denys.

Tunstall, J. P. & King, W. J. The Gumbia Cotton Handbook. 1979. 40.00x (ISBN 0-85135-100-X, Pub. by Centre Overseas Research). State Mutual Bk.

Tunstall, Jeremy & Walker, David. Media Made in California: Hollywood, Politics, & the News. (Illus.). 1981. 18.95 (ISBN 0-19-502922-4). Oxford U Pr.

Tunyogi, Andrew C. Divine Struggle for Human Salvation: Biblical Convictions in Their Historical Settings. LC 78-65852. 1979. pap. text ed. 17.50 (ISBN 0-8191-0676-3). U Pr of Amer.

Tuohy, William S., jt. auth. see Fagen, Richard R.

Tuomi & Vayrynen. Militarization & Arms Production. LC 82-16882. 320p. 1983. 30.00x (ISBN 0-312-53255-5). St Martin.

Tuominen, Arvo P. The Bells of the Kremlin: An Experience in Communism. Heiskanen, Piltti, ed. Leino, Lily, tr. from Finnish. LC 82-17647. 320p. 1983. 20.00 (ISBN 0-87451-249-2). U Pr of New Eng.

Tuomola, Olli, ed. International TV & Video Guide 1983. (International TV & Video Guide Ser.). (Illus.). 87p. 1982. pap. 9.95 (ISBN 0-900730-10-2). NY Zoetrope.

Tupa, D. D. An Investigation of Certain Chaetophoralean Algae. 1974. 48.00 (ISBN 3-7682-5446-1). Lubrecht & Cramer.

Tuplin, W. A: The Steam Locomotive. 1980. text ed. 20.75x (ISBN 0-239-00198-2). Humanities.

Tupou Posesi Fanua. Po Fananga - Folk Tales of Tonga. LC 74-34532. (Illus.). 96p. (Orig., Tongan-Eng.). 1975. pap. 5.95 o.s.i. (ISBN 0-914488-04-X). Rand-Tofua.

Tupper, Allan & Doern, G. Bruce, eds. Public Corporations & Public Policy in Canada. 398p. 1981. pap. text ed. 16.95x (ISBN 0-920380-51-4, Inst Res Pub Canada). Renouf.

Tupper, Ben. Canon Guide. (Illus.). 1978. 10.95 o.p. (ISBN 0-8174-2454-7, Amphoto); pap. 5.95 o.p. (ISBN 0-8174-2129-7). Watson-Guptill.

Turakka, H. & Van der Kleijn, E., eds. Progress in Clinical Pharmacy, Vol. 3. 1981. 61.50 (ISBN 0-444-80338-6). Elsevier.

Turan, P. Topics in Number Theory. (Colloquia Mathematica Societatis Janos Bolyai: Vol. 13). 1976. 68.00 (ISBN 0-7204-0454-1, North-Holland). Elsevier.

Turausky, Dianne. Errands. (Oral Language Development Ser.). (Illus.). 16p. (Orig.). (gr. 3-6). 1983. write for info wkbk. (ISBN 0-88084-038-2). Alemany Pr.

Turbak, Gary. Traveler's Guide to Montana. (Illus.). 256p. 1983. pap. 7.95 (ISBN 0-934318-14-X). Falcon Pr MT.

Turban, Ephraim, et al. Cost Containment in Hospitals. LC 80-13272. 648p. 1980. text ed. 57.50 (ISBN 0-89443-279-6). Aspen Systems.

Turbayne, Colin M., ed. see Berkeley, George.

Turbervile, George, tr. see Baptista Mantuanus.

Turberville, George. Epitaphes, Epigrams, Songs & Sonets. LC 77-16311. 1977. Repr. of 1576 ed. lib. bdg. 53.00x (ISBN 0-8201-1303-4). Schol Facsimiles.

Turbeville, Deborah. Women on Women. LC 78-70395. (Illus.). 164p. 1979. 22.50 o.s.i. (ISBN 0-89479-040-4). A & W Pubs.

Turbill, Jan, ed. No Better Way to Teach Writing. 96p. (Orig.). 1982. pap. text ed. 6.00x (ISBN 0-909955-39-5, 00568). Heinemann Ed.

Turbo, Richard, jt. auth. see Behrstock, Barry.

Turbott, E. G., ed. see Buller, Walter L.

Turchi, Boone A. The Demand for Children: The Economics of Fertility in the United States. LC 75-22111. 256p. 1975. prof ref 20.00x (ISBN 0-88410-353-6). Ballinger Pub.

Turcic, Lawrence, jt. auth. see Bean, Jacob.

Turco, Lewis. American Still-Lifes. LC 81-80751. (Illus.). 78p. 1981. 12.00 (ISBN 0-686-71742-2); pap. 7.95 (ISBN 0-686-77405-1). Mathom.

--Awaken, Bells Falling: Poems, 1959-1967. LC 68-21677. (Literary Frontiers Ser: No. 4). 67p. (Orig.). 1968. pap. 5.95 (ISBN 0-8262-0068-0). U of Mo Pr.

--Book of Forms: A Handbook of Poetics. 1968. pap. 5.25 (ISBN 0-525-47209-6, 0510-150). Dutton.

--A Cage of Creatures. (Illus.). 1979. pap. 3.50 (ISBN 0-686-52326-1); pap. 6.50 signed (ISBN 0-918092-08-6). Tamarack Edns.

--The Compleat Melancholick. 1983. price not set (ISBN 0-931460-12-3); pap. price not set (ISBN 0-931460-15-8). Bieler.

Turco, Salvatore J., jt. auth. see Tuckerman, Murray M.

Turcotte, Donald L. & Schubert, Gerald. Geodynamics: Application of Continuum Physics to Geological Problems. LC 81-15965. 450p. 1982. text ed. 30.95x (ISBN 0-471-06018-6). Wiley.

Turekian, Karl K., jt. auth. see Skinner, Brian J.

Turell, Ebenezer. The Life & Character of the Reverend Benjamin Colman, D. D. LC 72-4539. 256p. 1972. Repr. of 1749 ed. 33.00x (ISBN 0-8201-1104-X). Schol Facsimiles.

Turfler, Katherine, tr. see Oksaar.

Turgenev, Ivan. Fathers & Sons. Makanowitzky, Barbara, tr. from Russian. (Bantam Classics Ser.). 208p. (Orig.). (gr. 9-12). 1981. pap. 1.95 (ISBN 0-553-21036-X). Bantam.

--First Love. Berlin, Isaiah, tr. Bd. with A Fire at Sea. Berlin, Isaiah, tr. 1982. 14.95 (ISBN 0-686-82588-8). Viking Pr.

--Home of the Gentry. Freeborn, Richard, tr. (Classics Ser.). (Orig.). 1970. pap. 3.95 (ISBN 0-14-044224-3). Penguin.

Turgenev, Ivan see Bond, Otto F., et al.

Turgenev, Ivan S. Mumu. Domb, J. & Shoenberg, Z., trs. from Rus. (Harrap's Bilingual Ser.). 96p. 1946. 5.00 (ISBN 0-911268-54-5). Rogers Bk.

Turgeon, A. J. & Giles, Floyd. Turfgrass Management. (Illus.). 1980. text ed. 20.95 (ISBN 0-8359-7885-0); instrs' manual avail. Reston.

Turgeon, Charles, jt. auth. see Turgeon, Charlotte.

Turgeon, Charlotte. Favorite Meals from Williamsburg. Sheppard, Donna C., ed. LC 82-4518. (A Menu Cookbook). (Illus.). 156p. 1982. pap. 5.95 (ISBN 0-87935-067-9). Williamsburg.

--Of Cabbages & Kings Cookbook. LC 77-85390. (Illus.). 160p. 1977. 8.95 (ISBN 0-89387-014-5, Co-Pub. by Sat Eve Post). Curtis Pub Co.

Turgeon, Charlotte & Saturday Evening Post Editors. The Saturday Evening Post All-American Cookbook. rev. ed. LC 81-65814. (Illus.). 320p. 1981. 14.95 (ISBN 0-89387-058-7, Co-Pub. by Sat Eve Post). Curtis Pub Co.

--The Saturday Evening Post Small-Batch Canning & Freezing Cookbook. LC 78-53040. (Illus.). 160p. 1978. 8.95 (ISBN 0-89387-020-X, Co-Pub. by Sat Eve Post); pap. 4.95 (ISBN 0-686-36893-2). Curtis Pub Co.

Turgeon, Charlotte & Turgeon, Charles. The Saturday Evening Post Time to Entertain Cookbook. LC 78-73386. 240p. 1978. 9.95 o.p. (ISBN 0-89387-025-0, Co-Pub. by Sat Eve Post). Curtis Pub Co.

Turgeon, Charlotte, ed. Holiday Magazine Award Cookbook. LC 76-41562. 464p. 1976. 12.50 o.p. (ISBN 0-89387-002-1, Co-Pub by Sat Eve Post). Curtis Pub Co.

Turgeon, Charlotte, ed. see Montagne, Prosper.

Turgeon, Lynn. The Advanced Capitalist System: A Revisionist View. LC 80-51202. 192p. 1980. 15.00 o.p. (ISBN 0-87332-171-5); pap. 8.95 (ISBN 0-87332-172-3). M E Sharpe.

Turgot, A. B. Oeuvres et Documents le Concernant: 1913-1923. 345.00 o.p. (ISBN 0-8287-0838-X). Clearwater Pub.

Turi. Thermal Analysis in Polymer Characterization. 1981. 35.95 (ISBN 0-471-26192-0, Wiley Heyden). Wiley.

Turi, Johan O. Turi's Book of Lappland. (Illus.). 1966. pap. text ed. 15.00x (ISBN 0-391-02064-1). Humanities.

Turi, Leonard F. OEM & Turnkey Contracts. 178p. 1982. 59.95 (ISBN 0-935506-09-8). Carnegie Pr.

Turiello, Edmund. A Beginners Planbook in Architecture & Building Construction. pap. 15.00 o.s.i. (ISBN 0-8283-1337-7). Branden.

Turin, H. J., et al. Atlas of the Carbid Beetles of the Netherlands. 1977. 27.00 (ISBN 0-7204-8326-3, North Holland). Elsevier.

Turitz, Evelyn, jt. auth. see Turitz, Leo.

Turitz, Leo & Turitz, Evelyn. Jews in Early Mississippi. LC 82-25093. (Illus.). 144p. (Orig.). 1983. 20.00x (ISBN 0-87805-178-3). U Pr of Miss.

Turk, Amos, jt. auth. see Green, Michael E.

Turk, Amos, et al. Introduction to Chemistry. LC 68-14653. 1968. text ed. 22.00 (ISBN 0-12-703850-7). Acad Pr.

Turk, Christopher & Kirkman, John. Effective Writing. 1982. 23.00x (ISBN 0-419-11670-2, Pub. by E & FN Spon); pap. 9.95 (ISBN 0-419-11680-X). Methuen Inc.

Turk, D. E. Verzeichniss der Musikalischen und Andern Bucher. (Auction Catalogues of Music Ser.: Vol. 3). Date not set. Repr. of 1973 ed. wrappers 25.00 o.s.i. (ISBN 90-6027-361-3; Pub. by Frits Knuf Netherlands). Pendragon NY.

Turk, Daniel G. Anweisung Zum Generalbass-Spielen. Repr. of 1971 ed. wrappers 35.00 o.s.i. (ISBN 90-6027-137-8, Pub. by Frits Knuf Netherlands). Pendragon NY.

--School of Clavier Playing; or, Instructions in Playing the Clavier for Teachers & Students. Haggh, Raymond H., tr. LC 81-14626. xxxvi, 564p. 1982. 50.00x (ISBN 0-8032-2316-1). U of Nebr Pr.

--Von Den Wichtigsten Pflichten Eines Organisten. (Bibliotheca Organologica: Vol. 5). Date not set. Repr. of 1966 ed. wrappers 27.50 o.s.i. (ISBN 90-6027-027-4, Pub. by Frits Knuf Netherlands). Pendragon NY.

Turk, Dennis & Meichenbaum, Donald. Pain & Behavioral Medicine. LC 82-11695. (Clinical & Psychology & Psychotherapy Ser.). 422p. 1983. 25.00x (ISBN 0-89862-002-3). Guilford Pr.

Turk, Frederick J. Financial Management for the Arts. Rev. ed. 1983. 17.50 (ISBN 0-915400-40-5); pap. text ed. 12.50 (ISBN 0-915400-41-3). Am Council Arts.

Turk, Hanne. A Lesson for Max. LC 82-61833. (Max the Mouse Ser.). (Illus.). 24p. 1983. pap. 2.95 (ISBN 0-907234-23-2). Neugebauer Pr.

--Max the Artlover. LC 82-61832. (Max the Mouse Ser.). (Illus.). 24p. 1983. pap. 2.95 (ISBN 0-907234-25-9). Neugebauer Pr.

--Rainy Day Max. LC 82-61834. (Max the Mouse Ser.). (Illus.). 24p. 1982. pap. 2.95 (ISBN 0-907234-24-0). Neugebauer Pr.

Turk, Hanne, illus. Max Versus the Cube. (A Max the Mouse Bk.). (Illus.). 28p. 1982. pap. 2.95 (ISBN 0-907234-19-4). Neugebauer Pr.

--The Rope Skips Max. (Max the Mouse Bk.). (Illus.). 28p. 1980. pap. 2.95 (ISBN 0-907234-20-8). Neugebauer Pr.

--A Surprise for Max. (A Max the Mouse Bk.). (Illus.). 28p. (Orig.). pap. 2.95 (ISBN 0-907234-18-6). Neugebauer Pr.

Turk, J. Delayed Hypersensitivity. 3rd ed. (Research Monographs in Immunology: Vol. 1). 1980. 78.50 (ISBN 0-444-80163-4). Elsevier.

Turk, Laurel H. & Espinosa, Aurelio M., Jr. Mastering Spanish. 3rd ed. 1979. text ed. 18.95 (ISBN 0-669-01712-4); wkbk. 7.95x (ISBN 0-669-01714-0); tapes-reels 35.00 (ISBN 0-669-01716-7); transcripts 1.95 (ISBN 0-669-01715-9); demonstration & tape 1.95 (ISBN 0-669-01718-3). Heath.

--Mastering Spanish. 4th ed. 1983. lib. bdg. 19.95 (ISBN 0-669-05395-3); pap. 7.95 (ISBN 0-669-05396-1). Heath.

Turk, Laurel H., et al. Foundation Course in Spanish. 5th ed. (Illus.). 432p. 1981. text ed. 21.95 (ISBN 0-669-02637-9); wkbk. 8.95 (ISBN 0-669-02638-7); answer keys with tests 1.95 (ISBN 0-669-02639-5); tapescript avail. (ISBN 0-669-02640-9); reels set of 15 60.00 (ISBN 0-669-02641-7); cassettes set of 15 25.00 (ISBN 0-669-02643-3); demo tape avail. (ISBN 0-669-02644-1). Heath.

Turk, Michael H. Occupational Medicine: Surveillance, Diagnosis & Treatment. F & S Press Book, ed. 1982. prof ref 34.95x (ISBN 0-86621-005-9). Ballinger Pub.

Turk, Peter B., jt. auth. see Jugenheimer, Donald W.

Turkensteen, L. J. Partial Resistance of Tomatoes Against Phytophthora Infestans, the Late Blight Fungus. new ed. (Illus.). 88p. 1974. pap. 16.00 (ISBN 90-220-0497-X, PDC112, Pub. by PUDOC). Unipub.

Turkerich, I. B., ed. see Chernyshevsky, Nikolai G.

Turkle, Brinton. The Adventures of Obadiah. (Illus.). 40p. (gr. k-3). 1983. pap. cancelled (ISBN 0-14-050392-7, Puffin). Penguin.

--Deep in the Forest. (Illus.). (ps-1). 1976. 9.95 (ISBN 0-525-28617-9, 0966-290). Dutton.

Turkle, Thomas, ed. see Hays, Edward.

Turko, L. & Pekalski, A., eds. Developments in the Theory of Fundamental Interactions. (Studies in High Energy Physics: Vol. 3). 1981. 52.00 (ISBN 0-686-86032-2). Harwood Academic.

Turkova, J. Affinity Chromatography. (Journal of Chromatography Library: Vol. 12). 1978. 83.00 (ISBN 0-444-41605-6). Elsevier.

Turleau, Catherine, jt. auth. see De Grouchy, Jean.

Turley, C. David, jt. ed. see Brenchley, David L.

Turley, Raymond. Understanding the Structure of Scientific & Technical Literature: A Visual Approach. 176p. 1983. write for info. (ISBN 0-85157-368-1, Pub. by Bingley England). Shoe String.

Turley, William S., ed. Vietnamese Communism in Comparative Perspective. (A Westview Replica Edition Ser.). 200p. 1980. lib. bdg. 26.50 (ISBN 0-89158-773-X). Westview.

Turman, James C., jt. ed. see Tyson, Pete.

Turmeau De La Morandiere. Appel Des Etrangers Dans Nos Colonies. Repr. of 1763 ed. 16.50 o.p. (ISBN 0-8287-0840-1). Clearwater Pub.

Turn, Rein & Roth, Alexander D., eds. Supporting Documents: Transborder Data Flows: Concerns in Privacy Protection & Free Flow of Information, Vol. II. 300p. 1979. pap. 28.75 (ISBN 0-88283-024-4). AFIPS Pr.

Turn, Rein, ed. see Report of the AFIPS Panel on Transborder Data Flow.

Turnage, Anne S., jt. auth. see Turnage, Mac N.

Turnage, Mac N. & Turnage, Anne S. More Than You Dare Ask: The First Year of Living with Cancer. LC 75-32940. 1976. 3.99 (ISBN 0-8042-1129-9). John Knox.

--People, Families, & God. LC 76-12400. 1981. pap. 3.95 (ISBN 0-8042-8077-0). John Knox.

Turnage, Thomas W., jt. auth. see Horton, David L.

Turnball, Yvonne. Living Cookbook. 396p. 1983. looseleaf bdg. 14.95 (ISBN 0-686-42983-4). Bethany Hse.

Turnbul, Coulson. Sema-Kanda: Threshold Memories. 254p. 11.50 (ISBN 0-686-38234-X). Sun Bks.

Turnbull, A. B. Government Budgeting & PPBS: A Programmed Introduction. 1970. pap. 17.95 (ISBN 0-201-07615-2). A-W.

Turnbull, Agnes S. Gown of Glory. (General Ser.). 1982. lib. bdg. 15.95 (ISBN 0-8161-3475-8, Large Print Bks). G K Hall.

Turnbull, Ann & Turnbull, H. R. Parents Speak Out: Views from the Other Side of the Two-Way Mirror. 1978. pap. 9.95 (ISBN 0-675-08385-0). Merrill.

Turnbull, Ann P., et al. Developing & Implementing Individualized Education Programs. 2nd ed. 384p. 1982. pap. text ed. 16.95 (ISBN 0-675-09908-0). Merrill.

Turnbull, Bob. Calling Angel One. 1976. pap. 4.95 (ISBN 0-931608-82-1). Omega Pubns Or.

--How to Handle Your Hassles & Hurts. 1979. pap. 2.95 (ISBN 0-89728-065-2). Omega Pubns Or.

Turnbull, Bob & Turnbull, Yvonne. Free to be Fit. 160p. (Orig.). 1982. pap. 3.95 (ISBN 0-87123-165-4, 210165). Bethany Hse.

Turnbull, Colin. Forest People. (Illus.). 1961. 10.95 o.p. (ISBN 0-671-26650-0, Touchstone Bks); pap. 4.95 o.p. (ISBN 0-671-20031-3). S&S.

Turnbull, Colin M. The Human Cycle. 320p. (Orig.). 1983. 14.95 (ISBN 0-671-22620-7). S&S.

--Lonely African. 1968. pap. 7.75 (ISBN 0-671-20069-0, Touchstone Bks). S&S.

Turnbull, Colin M., ed. Africa & Change. 1973. text ed. 11.95x (ISBN 0-685-84260-6). Phila Bk Co.

Turnbull, D. E. Fluid Power Engineering. 1975. pap. 19.95 o.p. (ISBN 0-408-00199-2). Butterworth.

Turnbull, Eleanor L., tr. Contemporary Spanish Poetry: Selections from Ten Poets. Repr. of 1945 ed. lib. bdg. 19.00x (ISBN 0-8371-0689-3, TUSP). Greenwood.

Turnbull, Gerry. Official Star Trek Catalog. 1977. pap. 6.95 o.p. (ISBN 0-448-14053-5, G&D). Putnam Pub Group.

Turnbull, H. R., jt. auth. see Turnbull, Ann.

Turnbull, J. G., et al. Economic & Social Security. 4th ed. 728p. 1973. 24.95 o.p. (ISBN 0-471-06643-5, Pub. by Wiley-Interscience). Wiley.

Turnbull, John G. Labor-Management Relations. LC 49-48994. (Social Science Research Council Bulletin: No. 61). 1949. pap. 4.00 (ISBN 0-527-03289-1). Kraus Repr.

Turnbull, Krista J., jt. auth. see Hacker, Katherine F.

Turnbull, Murray, ed. see Haar, Francis.

Turnbull, Peter. Dead Knock. 208p. 1983. 10.95 (ISBN 0-312-18499-9). St Martin.

Turnbull, Ralph G., jt. ed. see Whyte, Alexander.

Turnbull, Robert G., jt. ed. see Machamer, Peter K.

Turnbull, Stephen. The Samurai-a Military History. LC 76-50595. 1977. 22.95 o.p. (ISBN 0-02-620540-8, 62054). Macmillan.

Turnbull, Yvonne. The Living Cookbook. 1981. 14.95 (ISBN 0-86694-089-8). Omega Pubns Or.

Turnbull, Yvonne, jt. auth. see Turnbull, Bob.

Turndorf, Herman & Chalon, Jack. Circulatory Control & Management, Vol. I. (Current Problems in Anesthesiology Ser.). (Illus.). 300p. 1980. lib. bdg. cancelled o.p. (ISBN 0-683-08473-9). Williams & Wilkins.

Turndorf, Herman, jt. auth. see Cottrell, James E.

Turnebe, Odet De see De Turnebe, Odet.

Turnell, Martin. Art of French Fiction. LC 59-9491. 1968. pap. 2.95 o.p. (ISBN 0-8112-0211-9, NDP251). New Directions.

--Classical Moment: Studies of Corneille, Moliere, & Racine. LC 79-138601. (Illus.). 1971. Repr. of 1948 ed. lib. bdg. 17.75x (ISBN 0-8371-5803-6, TUCM). Greenwood.

Turnell, Martin, tr. see Revel, Jean-Francois.

Turner. Electronic Engineers Reference Book. 5th ed. 1983. text ed. price not set. Butterworth.

Turner & Horn. Multiple Lines Insurance Production. 1981. 15.00 o.p. (ISBN 0-686-95944-2). IIA.

Turner, jt. auth. see Battie.

Turner, jt. auth. see Meek.

Turner, A. C. Traveller's Health Guide. 2nd ed. 188p. 1980. 7.95 (ISBN 0-903909-08-1). Bradt Ent.

Turner, A. C., et al. The Determination of Environmental Lead Near Works & Roads in Conjunction with the EEC Blood-Level Survey: 1978-9, 1980. 1981. 70.00x (ISBN 0-686-97055-1, Pub. by W Spring England). State Mutual Bk.

Turner, A. Simon & McIlwraith, C. Wayne. Techniques in Large Animal Surgery. LC 81-18654. (Illus.). 333p. 1982. text ed. 49.50 (ISBN 0-8121-0828-0). Lea & Febiger.

Turner, Alford E., ed. The Earps Talk. LC 80-65456. (Illus.). 193p. 1979. 15.50 (ISBN 0-932702-05-8); collector's ed. 75.00 (ISBN 0-932702-06-6); pap. 8.95 (1982) (ISBN 0-932702-13-9). Creative Texas.

Turner, Ann. The Way Home. 160p. (gr. 7 up). 1982. 8.95 (ISBN 0-517-54426-1). Crown.

Turner, Anthony & Brown, Christopher. Burgundy. 1977. 22.50 (ISBN 0-7134-0889-8, Pub by Batsford, England). David & Charles.

Turner, Arlin. Nathaniel Hawthorne: A Biography. (Illus.). 1980. 25.00x (ISBN 0-19-502547-4). Oxford U Pr.

Turner, B. L. Once Beneath the Forest: Prehistoric Terracing in the Rio Bec Region of the Maya Lowlands. (Dellplain Latin American Studies: No. 13). 160p. 1983. lib. bdg. 15.00 (ISBN 0-86531-536-1). Westview.

Turner, B. L., II & Harrison, Peter D., eds. Pulltrouser Swamp: Ancient Maya Habitat, Agriculture, & Settlement in Northern Belize. (Texas Pan American Ser.). (Illus.). 296p. text ed. 22.50x (ISBN 0-292-75067-6). U of Tex Pr.

Turner, Barry & Nordquist, Gunilla. The Other European Community: Integration & Cooperation in Nordic Europe. LC 81-58946. 190p. 1982. 22.50x (ISBN 0-312-58946-8). St Martin.

Turner, Bryan S. & Hepworth, Mike. Confession: Studies in Deviance & Society. 220p. 1983. 19.95 (ISBN 0-7100-9198-2). Routledge & Kegan.

Turner, C. E. Personal & Community Health. 14th rev. ed. LC 79-129655. (Illus.). 491p. 1971. text ed. 11.95 o.p. (ISBN 0-8016-5126-3). Mosby.

Turner, C. M., jt. auth. see Rowley, J. E.

Turner, C. M. D., jt. auth. see Rowley, J. E.

Turner, Carann G., ed. Proceedings of the Fourteenth Annual Conference: APLIC International. LC 76-643241. 159p. (Orig.). 1982. pap. text ed. 14.00 (ISBN 0-933438-06-0). APLIC Intl.

Turner, Charles. The Celebrant. 150p. 1982. 8.95 (ISBN 0-89283-154-5). Servant.

Turner, Clair E. Planning for Health Education in Schools. 1966. 6.00 o.p. (ISBN 92-3-100626-6, U452, UNESCO). Unipub.

Turner, D. R., jt. auth. see Risdon, R. A.

Turner, Darwin, jt. ed. see Sekora, John.

Turner, Darwin T. Black American Literature: Essays, Poetry, Fiction, Drama. 1970. pap. text ed. 14.95x (ISBN 0-675-09278-7). Merrill.

Turner, David R. Assistant Accountant, Junior Accountant, Account Clerk. 2nd ed. LC 79-83163. 1969. pap. 8.00 (ISBN 0-668-00056-2). Arco.

--Beginning Office Worker. 9th ed. LC 79-18112. (Arco Civil Service Test Tutor Ser.). 224p. (Orig.). 1980. pap. 8.00 o.p. (ISBN 0-668-04849-2, 4849-2). Arco.

--Detective Investigator. LC 74-24565. 160p. (Orig.). 1975. pap. 8.00 (ISBN 0-668-03738-5). Arco.

--File Clerk. 6th ed. LC 77-22297. (Orig.). 1977. pap. 6.00 o.p. (ISBN 0-668-04377-6). Arco.

--Homestudy Course for Civil Service Jobs. 5th ed. LC 76-1309. 1976. lib. bdg. 8.50 o.p. (ISBN 0-668-00138-0); pap. 8.00 (ISBN 0-668-01587-X). Arco.

--Practice for Navy Placement Tests. LC 77-19033. 1978. lib. bdg. 12.00 o.p. (ISBN 0-668-04594-9); pap. text ed. 6.00 o.p. (ISBN 0-668-04560-4). Arco.

--Preliminary Practice for the High School Equivalency Diploma Test. 5th ed. LC 75-34848. (gr. 9-12). 1972. pap. 6.00 o.p. (ISBN 0-668-01441-5). Arco.

--Supervising Clerk (Income Maintenance) LC 73-76272. 256p. 1973. pap. 6.00 o.p. (ISBN 0-668-02879-3). Arco.

--Teacher of Common Branches. LC 64-24631. (Orig.). 1971. pap. 6.00 o.p. (ISBN 0-668-00770-2). Arco.

--Teacher of Industrial Arts: Junior High School & High School. (Orig.). 1970. pap. 6.00 o.p. (ISBN 0-668-01307-9). Arco.

--Tractor Operator. LC 80-11822. 224p. 1980. pap. cancelled o.p. (ISBN 0-668-04971-5, 4971-5). Arco.

Turner, Denys. Marxism & Christianity. LC 82-22713. 250p. 1983. text ed. 25.00x (ISBN 0-389-20351-3). B&N Imports.

Turner, Derek. The Black Death. Reeves, Marjorie, ed. (Then & There Ser.). (Illus.). 96p. (gr. 7-12). 1978. pap. text ed. 3.10 (ISBN 0-582-20544-1). Longman.

Turner, Diana O. African Needlepoint Designs. LC 75-21352. (Needlepoint Ser.). (Illus.). 48p. (Orig.). 1976. pap. 2.95 (ISBN 0-486-23244-1). Dover.

Turner, Dixie M. A Jungian Psychoanalytic Interpretation of William Faulkner's "As I Lay Dying". LC 80-5582. 107p. 1981. lib. bdg. 18.75 (ISBN 0-8191-1452-9); pap. text ed. 8.25 (ISBN 0-8191-1451-0). U Pr of Amer.

Turner, Don. Custer's First Massacre: The Battle of the Washita. 40p. 1968. pap. 1.00 (ISBN 0-912996-01-3). Humbug Gulch Pr.

--The Life & Castle of Stephen W. Dorsey. 34p. 1967. pap. 1.00 (ISBN 0-912996-00-5). Humbug Gulch Pr.

--The Massacre of Gov. Bent. 40p. 1969. pap. 1.50 (ISBN 0-912996-02-1). Humbug Gulch Pr.

--A Plea for the Heroes: Theodore Roosevelt & the Rough Riders. LC 70-183773. 41p. 1971. 5.00 (ISBN 0-912996-03-X). Humbug Gulch Pr.

Turner, Donald, jt. auth. see Areeda, Philip.

Turner, Donald F., jt. auth. see Areeda, Phillip E.

Turner, Dorothea. Jane Mander. (World Authors Ser.). lib. bdg. 15.95 (ISBN 0-8057-2576-8, Twayne). G K Hall.

Turner, Dorothy B. Crown of Life. (Orig.). pap. 2.00 (ISBN 0-685-08697-6). Creative Pr.

--Earn As You Learn Writing. (Orig.). pap. 3.00 (ISBN 0-685-08698-4). Creative Pr.

--How to Gain Health, Happiness, Prosperity. (Orig.). pap. 2.00 (ISBN 0-685-08700-X). Creative Pr.

Turner, E. G., tr. see Menander.

Turner, Edward R. Practice for Clerical, Typing & Stenographic Tests. 5th ed. LC 77-2822. 208p. (Orig.). 1977. lib. bdg. 9.00 o.p. (ISBN 0-668-04324-5); pap. 5.00 (ISBN 0-668-04297-4). Arco.

Turner, Elizabeth, ed. Chemistry for Medical Technologists: PreTest Self-Assessment & Review. (Illus.). 200p. (Orig.). 1981. pap. 9.95 o.p. (ISBN 0-07-051655-3). McGraw.

Turner, Eric. Introduction to Brass. (The Victoria & Albert Museum Introductions to the Decorative Arts Ser.). (Illus.). 48p. 1982. 9.95 (ISBN 0-88045-007-X). Stemmer Hse.

Turner, Ernest S. Boys Will Be Boys. LC 76-175338. (Illus.). 1977. Repr. of 1948 ed. 37.00x (ISBN 0-8103-4091-7). Gale.

Turner, F. H. Concrete & Cryogenics. (Viewpoint Publication Ser.). (Illus.). 125p. 1979. pap. text ed. 32.50x (ISBN 0-7210-1124-1, Pub by C&CA London). Scholium Intl.

Turner, F. H., tr. see Guyon, Y.

Turner, F. H., tr. see Petzold, A. & Rohrs, M.

Turner, Francis J. Metamorphic Petrology. 2nd ed. LC 79-27496. (International Earth & Planetary Sciences Ser.). (Illus.). 512p. 1980. text ed. 45.00 (ISBN 0-07-065501-4, C). McGraw.

--Metamorphic Petrology: Mineralogical & Field Aspects. LC 67-28087. (International Earth & Planetary Science Ser). (Illus.). 1968. text ed. 39.95 (ISBN 0-07-065500-6, C). McGraw.

Turner, Francis J. & Verhoogen, Jean. Igneous & Metamorphic Petrology. 2nd ed. (International Science in the Earth & Planetary Sciences Ser.). 1960. text ed. 49.95 (ISBN 0-07-065579-0, C). McGraw.

Turner, Francis J. & Weiss, Lionel. Structural Analysis of Metamorphic Tectonites. (International Series in the Earth & Planetary Sciences). 1963. text ed. 49.95 (ISBN 0-07-065574-X, C). McGraw.

Turner, Francis J., ed. Differential Diagnosis & Treatment in Social Work. 3rd, rev. ed. LC 82-48390. 1983. 24.95 (ISBN 0-02-932990-6). Free Pr.

--Social Work Treatment: Interlocking Theoretical Approaches. 2nd ed. LC 78-73027. 1979. text ed. 19.95 (ISBN 0-02-932920-5). Free Pr.

Turner, Frederick. A Double Shadow. LC 77-17938. 1978. 7.95 (ISBN 0-399-12150-1, Pub. by Berkley). Putnam Pub Group.

Turner, Frederick C. & Miguens, Jose E., eds. Juan Peron & the Reshaping of Argentina. LC 82-4870. (Pitt Latin American Ser.). (Illus.). 360p. 1983. text ed. 24.95 (ISBN 0-8229-3464-7). U of Pittsburgh Pr.

Turner, Frederick J. The Frontier in American History. LC 75-22065. 400p. 1976. Repr. of 1920 ed. 14.50 (ISBN 0-88275-347-9). Krieger.

Turner, G. Alan. Heat & Concentration Waves: Analysis & Applications. 1972. 43.00 (ISBN 0-12-704050-1). Acad Pr.

Turner, G. P. Introduction to Paint Chemistry. 2nd ed. 1980. 24.95x (ISBN 0-412-16180-X, Pub. by Chapman & Hall); pap. 12.50x (ISBN 0-412-16190-7). Methuen Inc.

Turner, Geoffrey. Indians of North America. (Illus.). 1979. 14.95 (ISBN 0-7137-0843-3, Pub. by Blandford Pr England). Sterling.

Turner, George A. Witnesses of the Way. 176p. (Orig.). 1981. pap. 3.95 (ISBN 0-8341-0692-2). Beacon Hill.

Turner, George E., jt. auth. see Price, Michael H.

Turner, George T., ed. see Perry, Elliot.

Turner, Gerard L. Antique Scientific Instruments. (Illus.). 176p. 1980. 12.95 o.p. (ISBN 0-7137-0923-5, Pub. by Blandford Pr England). Sterling.

Turner, Gladys T. Papa Babe's Stamp Collection. (Illus.). 100p. (gr. 1-8). 1983. 5.50 (ISBN 0-682-49944-7). Exposition.

Turner, Glen. The Social World of the Comprehensive School: How Pupils Adapt. 160p. 1983. text ed. 23.50x (ISBN 0-7099-2424-0, Pub. by Croom Helm Ltd England). Biblio Dist.

Turner, Gwyn. The Complete Home Astrologer. 110p. (Orig.). 1979. pap. 8.95 (ISBN 0-7100-0130-4). Routledge & Kegan.

Turner, H. A., et al. Management Characteristics & Labour. LC 77-76076. (DAE Papers in Industrial Relations Ser.: No. 3). (Illus.). 1977. 14.50 o.p. (ISBN 0-521-21734-2); pap. 9.95 (ISBN 0-521-29245-X). Cambridge U Pr.

Turner, H. Newton & Young, S. S. Quantitative Genetics in Sheep Breeding. 1982. 95.00x (ISBN 0-686-97901-X, Pub. by CSIRO Australia). State Mutual Bk.

Turner, Harold. Bibliography of New Religious Movements in Primal Societies: Volume I: Black Africa. 1977. lib. bdg. 25.00 o.p. (ISBN 0-8161-7927-1, Hall Reference). G K Hall.

Turner, Harold W. Religious Innovation in Africa: Collected Essays on New Religious Movements. 1979. lib. bdg. 31.00 (ISBN 0-8161-8303-1, Hall Reference). G K Hall.

Turner, Harry. Triad Optical Illusions & How to Design Them. LC 77-81212. (Illus.). 1977. pap. 2.50 (ISBN 0-486-23549-1). Dover.

Turner, Henry & Vieg, J. Government & Politics of California. 4th ed. 1971. text ed. 10.95 (ISBN 0-07-065580-4, C); pap. text ed. 10.50 (ISBN 0-07-065581-2); 3.95 o.p. instructor's manual (ISBN 0-07-065582-0). McGraw.

Turner, Henry E. & Montefiore, Hugh. Thomas & the Evangelists. LC 63-59763. (Studies in Biblical Theology: No. 35). 1962. 8.45x (ISBN 0-8401-4035-5); pap. 7.95x (ISBN 0-8401-3035-X). Allenson-Breckinridge.

Turner, Herbert A., et al. Labor Relations in the Motor Industry. LC 67-83828. 1967. 25.00x (ISBN 0-678-06027-4). Kelley.

Turner, Hunter H., Jr. The Little Lighthouse. 1983. 4.95 (ISBN 0-533-05425-7). Vantage.

Turner, J. Lloyd George's Secretariat. LC 79-50510. (Studies in the History & Theory of Politics). 1980. 32.50 (ISBN 0-521-22370-9). Cambridge U Pr.

Turner, J. C., jt. auth. see Shippen, J. M.

Turner, J. Clifford. Voice & Speech in the Theatre. pap. 13.50x (ISBN 0-7136-2209-1, SpS). Sportshelf.

--Voice & Speech in the Theatre. 3rd ed. Morrison, Malcolm, rev. by. (Theatre & Stage Ser.). 146p. 1982. pap. 13.50 (ISBN 0-7136-2209-1). Sportshelf.

Turner, J. D. & Rushton, J., eds. Education for the Professionals. 1976. 14.00 (ISBN 0-7190-0641-4). Manchester.

--Teacher in a Changing Society. 1974. 12.50 (ISBN 0-7190-0566-3). Manchester.

Turner, J. D., jt. ed. see Rushton, J.

Turner, J. E., jt. auth. see Morgan, K. Z.

Turner, J. Howard. Care & Operation of Small Engines, Vol. 2. 4th ed. 8.95 o.p. (ISBN 0-914452-23-1). Green Hill.

--Maintenance & Repair of Small Engines. 10.95 o.p. (ISBN 0-914452-24-X). Green Hill.

Turner, J. S. Bouyancy Effects in Fluids. LC 72-76085. (Cambridge Monographs on Mechanics & Applied Mathematics). (Illus.). 350p. 1973. 54.50 (ISBN 0-521-08623-X). Cambridge U Pr.

--Buoyancy Effects in Fluids. LC 79-7656. (Cambridge Monographs on Mechanics & Applied Mathematics). (Illus.). 1980. pap. 21.95 (ISBN 0-521-29726-5). Cambridge U Pr.

Turner, James. Sceptered Isle. 13.95 o.p. (ISBN 0-416-00301-X). Methuen Inc.

Turner, James, jt. auth. see Turner, Mary D.

Turner, Johanna. Psychology for the Classroom. 1977. pap. 14.95x (ISBN 0-416-76800-8). Methuen Inc.

Turner, John E., et al. Community Development & Rational Choice: A Korean Study. (Monograph Ser. in World Affairs: Vol. 20, Bk. 1). 120p. (Orig.). 1983. pap. 5.00 (ISBN 0-87940-072-2). U of Denver Intl.

Turner, John H. London, Brighton & South Coast Railway, Vol. 1. 1977. 31.50 (ISBN 0-7134-0275-X, Pub. by Batsford England). David & Charles.

--London, Brighton & South Coast Railway, Vol. 2. 1978. 31.50 (ISBN 0-7134-1198-8, Pub. by Batsford England). David & Charles.

Turner, John J., Jr., jt. ed. see Lane, Roger.

Turner, Jonathan H. Patterns of Social Organizations: A Survey of Social Institutions. rev. ed. (McGraw-Hill Series in Sociology). (Illus.). 448p. 1972. text ed. 33.50 (ISBN 0-07-065560-X, C). McGraw.

--Sociology: Studying the Human System. 2nd ed. 1981. text ed. 21.95x o.p. (ISBN 0-673-16324-5). Scott F.

Turner, June, jt. auth. see Arbit, Naomi.

Turner, Justin G. & Turner, Linda L., eds. Mary Todd Lincoln: Her Life & Letters. 1972. 17.50 o.p. (ISBN 0-394-46643-8). Knopf.

Turner, Kermit. Rebel Powers. LC 79-2429. (gr. 9 up). 1979. 8.95 o.p. (ISBN 0-7232-6171-7). Warne.

Turner, L. C. Origins of the First World War. (Foundations of Modern History Ser.). (Illus.). 120p. 1970. pap. text ed. 3.95x (ISBN 0-393-09947-4). Norton.

Turner, L. C., ed. see Von Mellenthin, F. W.

Turner, L. W. Electronic Engineer's Reference Book. 4th ed. 1976. text ed. 105.00 (ISBN 0-408-00168-2). Butterworth.

Turner, Lana. Lana: The Lady, the Legend, the Truth. 352p. 1982. 14.95 (ISBN 0-525-24106-X, 01451-440). Dutton.

Turner, Lawrence E. & Howson, Rosemary J. Basic BASIC for Basic Beginners. x, 293p. 1982. pap. text ed. 8.95 (ISBN 0-943872-82-0). Andrews Univ Pr.

Turner, Linda. A Persistent Flame. (Superromance Ser.). 295p. 1983. pap. 2.95 (ISBN 0-373-70065-2, Pub. by Worldwide). Harlequin Bks.

Turner, Linda L., jt. ed. see Turner, Justin G.

Turner, Louis & Ash, John. The Golden Hordes: International Tourism & the Pleasure Periphery. LC 76-25498. (Illus.). 1977. 10.00 o.p. (ISBN 0-312-33740-X). St Martin.

Turner, Lynn W. The Ninth State: New Hampshire's Formative Years. LC 82-13386. (Illus.). 530p. 1983. 19.95x (ISBN 0-8078-1541-1). U of NC Pr.

Turner, M. R. Nutrition & Lifestyles. 1980. 41.00 (ISBN 0-85334-874-X, Pub. by Applied Sci England). Elsevier.

Turner, Margery J. New Dance: Approaches to Nonliteral Choreography. 1976. 12.95 (ISBN 0-8229-3215-6); pap. 4.95x (ISBN 0-8229-5269-6). U of Pittsburgh Pr.

Turner, Mary. Slaves & Missionaries: The Disintegration of Jamaican Slave Society, 1787-1834. LC 82-6983. (Blacks in the New World Ser.). 240p. 1982. 25.95 (ISBN 0-252-00961-4). U of Ill Pr.

Turner, Mary D. & Turner, James. Making Your Own Baby Food. rev. ed. LC 76-25808. (Illus.). 1977. 6.95 o.s.i. (ISBN 0-911104-89-5); pap. 3.95 o.p. (ISBN 0-911104-90-9). Workman Pub.

Turner, Mason. RX: Applause-Biography of a Blind Performer. 1983. pap. 5.95 (ISBN 0-8283-1879-4). Branden.

Turner, Michael. The Vice President as Policy Maker: Rockefeller in the Ford White House. LC 81-20301. (Contributions in Political Science Ser.: No. 78). 296p. 1982. lib. bdg. 29.95 (ISBN 0-313-23229-6, TUV). Greenwood.

Turner, Michael L. Index & Guide to the Lists of the Publications of Richard Bentley & Son 1829-1898. 388p. 1974. PLB 35.00x (ISBN 0-914146-10-6); with lists on microfiche 205.00x (ISBN 0-914146-15-7). Somerset Hse.

Turner, Michael R. Nutrition & Health. LC 82-70. 270p. 1982. 42.00 (ISBN 0-8451-3006-4). A R Liss.

Turner, Myron. Things That Fly. LC 82-75885. vi, 61p. 1978. 7.95 (ISBN 0-8040-0783-7); pap. 4.95 (ISBN 0-8040-0826-4). Swallow.

Turner, N., jt. auth. see Stevens, W. C.

Turner, N. C. & Kramer, P. J. Adaptation of Plants to Water & High Temperature Stress. 482p. 1980. text ed. 49.95x (ISBN 0-471-05372-4, Pub. by Wiley-Interscience). Wiley.

Turner, Nicholas. Handbook for Biblical Studies. LC 82-7111. 156p. 1982. pap. 6.95 (ISBN 0-664-24436-X). Westminster.

Turner, P. Continental Red Beds. (Developments in Sedimentology Ser.: Vol. 29). 1980. 68.00 (ISBN 0-444-41908-X). Elsevier.

Turner, P., jt. auth. see Thorburn, Anna H.

Turner, P. D. Oil Palm Diseases, & Disorders. (Illus.). 1981. 59.00x (ISBN 0-19-580468-6). Oxford U Pr.

Turner, P. R., ed. Topics in Numerical Analysis: Proceedings, S.E.R.C. Summer School, Lancaster, 1981. (Lecture Notes in Mathematics Ser.: Vol. 965). 202p. 1983. pap. 11.00 (ISBN 0-387-11967-1). Springer-Verlag.

Turner, Paige. The Littler Fiddler: How A Mouse Makes His Way in Music City U. S. A. (Illus.). 34p. (gr. 3-6). 1983. pap. 3.95 (ISBN 0-9606284-4-4). Gibraltar.

Turner, Paul. Tennyson. (Routledge Author Guides Ser.). 1980. 16.00 (ISBN 0-7100-0475-3); pap. 7.95. Routledge & Kegan.

Turner, Paul, jt. auth. see Silverstone, Trevor.

Turner, Paul, tr. see Lucian.

Turner, Peter, jt. ed. see Osman, Colin.

Turner, R. C., jt. auth. see Lewis, John P.

Turner, R. E. & Betts, D. S. Introductory Statistical Mechanics. 39.00x (ISBN 0-686-97006-3, Pub. by Scottish Academic Pr Scotland). State Mutual Bk.

Turner, R. H., et al, eds. Annual Review of Sociology, Vol. 8. LC 75-648500. (Illus.). 1982. text ed. 22.00 (ISBN 0-8243-2208-8). Annual Reviews.

Turner, R. Kerry & Collis, Clive. Economics of Planning. LC 77-71241. 1977. 18.95x (ISBN 0-312-23440-6). St Martin.

Turner, R. Kerry, jt. ed. see O'Riordan, Timothy.

Turner, R. W., ed. The Grants Register: Postgraduate Awards for the English-Speaking World. 553p. 1971. 15.00x o.p. (ISBN 0-312-34300-0). St Martin.

Turner, Ralph & Killian, Lewis. Collective Behavior. 2nd ed. (Illus.). 480p. 1972. text ed. 22.95 (ISBN 0-13-140657-4). P-H.

Turner, Ralph B. Analytical Biochemistry of Insects. LC 76-54362. 1977. 57.50 (ISBN 0-444-41539-4). Elsevier.

Turner, Ralph H. Family Interaction. LC 71-118627. (Illus.). 505p. 1970. 30.95 (ISBN 0-471-89300-5). Wiley.

Turner, Ralph H., jt. auth. see Rosenberg, Morris.

Turner, Ralph R. & Reese, Hayne W., eds. Life-Span Developmental Psychology: Intervention. 1980. 28.00 (ISBN 0-12-704150-8). Acad Pr.

Turner, Richard. The Eye of the Needle: Toward Participatory Democracy in South Africa. LC 77-16301. 208p. (Orig.). 1978. pap. 5.95 o.p. (ISBN 0-88344-122-5). Orbis Bks.

--Focus on Sports: Photographing Action. (Illus.). 160p. 1975. pap. 7.95 o.p. (ISBN 0-8174-0577-1, Amphoto). Watson-Guptill.

Turner, Richard D. & Waranch, Seeman. Multiple-Lines Insurance Protection. LC 81-80772. 704p. 1981. pap. text ed. 17.00 (ISBN 0-89462-007-X). IIA.

Turner, Robert F. The War Powers Resolution: Its Implementation in Theory & Practice. (Philadelphia Policy Papers). (Orig.). 1983. pap. 3.95 (ISBN 0-910191-06-9). For Policy Res.

Turner, Roderick & Scheller, Arnold, eds. Revision Total Hip Arthoplasty. 412p. 1982. 59.50 (ISBN 0-8089-1466-9). Grune.

Turner, Roland. The Grants Register: Nineteen Seventy-Nine to Nineteen Eighty-One. 800p. 1979. 26.50 o.p. (ISBN 0-312-34406-6). St Martin.

Turner, Roland, ed. The Grants Register, 1977-1979. LC 77-12055. 1976. 25.00 o.p. (ISBN 0-312-34405-8). St Martin.

--The Grants Register, 1979-1981. 6th ed. 1979. 26.50x o.p. (ISBN 0-312-34406-6). St Martin.

Turner, Ronald C. Real-Time Programming with Microcomputers. LC 77-80773. 192p. 1978. 21.95x (ISBN 0-669-01666-7). Lexington Bks.

Turner, Rufus. Electronic Conversions, Symbols, & Formulas. LC 75-31464. (Illus.). 224p. 1975. 8.95 o.p. (ISBN 0-8306-5750-9); pap. 8.95 (ISBN 0-8306-4750-3, 750). TAB Bks.

--Impedance. LC 75-41733. (Illus.). 196p. 1976. 11.95 (ISBN 0-8306-6829-2); pap. 5.95 o.p. (ISBN 0-8306-5829-7, 829). TAB Bks.

Turner, S. M., et al. Handbook of Clinical Behavior Therapy. 765p. 1981. 45.00x (ISBN 0-471-04178-5, Pub. by Wiley-Interscience). Wiley.

Turner, Stephen. Our Noisy World. LC 79-13210. (Illus.). 64p. (gr. 3-5). 1979. PLB 6.97 o.p. (ISBN 0-671-32987-1). Messner.

Turner, Stephen J., jt. auth. see Meek, Gary E.

Turner, Stephen P. Sociological Explanation As Translation. (American Sociological Association Rose Monographs Ser.). 195p. 1980. 19.95 (ISBN 0-521-23030-6); pap. 7.95 (ISBN 0-521-29773-7). Cambridge U Pr.

Turner, Steve & Weed, Frank. Conflict in Organizations: Practical Guidelines Any Manager Can Use. (Illus.). 192p. 1983. 14.95 (ISBN 0-13-167395-5); pap. 6.95 (ISBN 0-13-167387-4). P-H.

Turner, Susan. Bouquets, Brambles, & Buena Vista or "Down Home". LC 76-7852. 1976. 4.95 (ISBN 0-87397-094-2). Strode.

--Wheels & Grindstones. 1980. pap. 4.95 (ISBN 0-87397-180-9). Strode.

Turner, Terisa, jt. ed. see Nore, Peter.

Turner, Victor. The Forest of Symbols: Aspects of Ndembu Ritual. LC 67-12308. (Illus.). 405p. 1967. 29.95x (ISBN 0-8014-0432-0); pap. 7.95x (ISBN 0-8014-9101-0, CP101). Cornell U Pr.

--Process, Performance & Pilgramage: A Study in Comparative Symbology. (Ranchi Anthropology Ser.: 1). 164p. 1979. 15.00x (ISBN 0-8002-2307-1). Intl Pubns Serv.

--Process, Performance & Pilgrimage. 1979. text ed. 13.00x (ISBN 0-391-01929-5). Humanities.

Turner, Victor, ed. Celebration: Studies in Festivity & Ritual. (Illus.). 1982. text ed. 25.00x (ISBN 0-87474-920-4); pap. 9.95x (ISBN 0-87474-919-0). Smithsonian.

Turner, W. B. & Aldridge, D. C. Fungal Metabolities, Vol. II. 1982. 80.00 (ISBN 0-12-704556-2). Acad Pr.

Turner, W. C. & Malloy, J. F. Thermal Insulation Handbook. 1981. 64.50 (ISBN 0-07-039805-4). McGraw.

Turner, W. D., ed. Solar Engineering, 1982. 603p. 1982. 85.00 (H00212). ASME.

Turner, Wayne C., ed. Energy Management Handbook. LC 81-10351. 714p. 1982. 55.00x (ISBN 0-471-08252-X, Pub. by Wiley-Interscience). Wiley.

Turner, Wayne C., et al. Introduction to Industrial & Systems Engineering. (P-H Ser. in Industrial & Systems Engineering). (Illus.). 1978. ref. ed. 26.95x (ISBN 0-13-484543-9). P-H.

Turner, Wesley. The War of Eighteen Twelve. (Focus on Canadian History Ser.). (Illus.). (gr. 6-10). 1982. PLB 7.90 o.p. (ISBN 0-531-04574-9). Watts.

Turner, Wesley B. Life in Upper Canada. (gr. 6-10). 1980. PLB 8.40 (ISBN 0-531-00447-3). Watts.

Turner, William. Book of Wines. LC 41-26942. 1980. Repr. of 1568 ed. 28.00x (ISBN 0-8201-1200-3). Schol Facsimiles.

Turner, William A. Epilepsy: A Study of the Idiopathic Disease. LC 73-82850. 289p. 1973. Repr. of 1907 ed. 12.00 (ISBN 0-911216-62-6). Raven.

Turner, William C., III & Turner, William C., IV. Thermal Insulation for Residences & Buildings: Economic Design for Comfort & Safety in Homes & Buildings. Date not set. write for info. (ISBN 0-88275-985-X). Krieger.

Turner, William O. Ride the Vengeance Trail. 192p. (Orig.). 1982. pap. 2.25 (ISBN 0-425-05755-0). Berkley Pub.

Turner, Wilson G. Maya Design Coloring Book. (Illus.). 48p. (Orig.). (gr. 1-6). 1980. pap. 2.25 (ISBN 0-486-24047-9). Dover.

Turney, Alan, tr. see Soseki, Natsume.

Turney, C. & Cairns, L. G. The Practicum in Teacher Education: Research, Practice & Supervision. (Illus.). 208p. 1983. pap. 22.00 (ISBN 0-424-00096-2, Pub. by Sydney U Pr). Intl Schol Bk Serv.

Turney-High, Harry H. Ethnography of the Kutenai. LC 41-16930. 1941. pap. 23.00 (ISBN 0-527-00555-X). Kraus Repr.

--The Flathead Indians of Montana. LC 38-6188. Repr. of 1937 ed. pap. 12.00 (ISBN 0-527-00547-9). Kraus Repr.

Turnock, D. Scotland's Highlands & Islands. (Problem Regions of Europe Ser.). (Illus.). 1973. pap. text ed. 5.95x o.p. (ISBN 0-19-913102-3). Oxford U Pr.

Turnock, David. The Historical Geography of Scotland Since 1707. LC 82-1175. (Cambridge Studies in Historical Geography: No. 2). (Illus.). 346p. 1982. 49.50 (ISBN 0-521-24453-6). Cambridge U Pr.

Turnor, C. Frank. Across the Medicine Line. 1973. 5.95 (ISBN 0-7710-8616-4). Jefferson Natl.

Turnovsky, S. J. Macroeconomic Analysis & Stabilization Policy. LC 76-46862. (Illus.). 1977. 52.50 (ISBN 0-521-21520-X); pap. 19.95 (ISBN 0-521-29187-9). Cambridge U Pr.

Turnovsky, Stephen J., jt. auth. see Pitchford, J. D.

Turnquist, Jeanette, jt. auth. see Birkey, Verna.

Turoff, Murray, jt. auth. see Hiltz, Starr R.

Turoff, Murray, jt. ed. see Linstone, Harold A.

Turok, Ben. Revolutionary Thought in the Twentieth Century. 360p. (Orig.). 1980. 35.00 (ISBN 0-905762-42-8, Pub. by Zed Pr England); pap. 9.95 (ISBN 0-905762-43-6, Pub. by Zed Pr England). Lawrence Hill.

Turok, Ben, ed. Development in Zambia: A Reader. 272p. 1981. pap. 11.00 (ISBN 0-905762-08-8, Pub. by Zed Pr England). Lawrence Hill.

Turov, E. A. Physical Properties of Magnetically Ordered Crystals. Scripta Technica, tr. 1965. 48.00 (ISBN 0-12-704950-9). Acad Pr.

Turovsky, Paul, jt. ed. see Wilkie, James W.

Turow, Scott. One "L". LC 76-57246. 1977. 8.95 (ISBN 0-399-11932-9). Putnam Pub Group.

Turpin, Allan. The Old Man's Darling. LC 76-41336. 1977. 7.95 o.p. (ISBN 0-698-10804-3, Coward). Putnam Pub Group.

Turpin, Barbara H., jt. auth. see Turpin, John C.

Turpin, James W. God As Man & Man As God. 1980. 5.95 o.p. (ISBN 0-8062-1392-2). Carlton.

Turpin, John. John Hogan: Irish Neoclassical Sculptor in Rome 1800-1858. (Illus.). 216p. 1983. text ed. 25.00x (ISBN 0-7165-0212-7, Pub by Irish Academic Pr Ireland). Biblio Dist.

Turpin, John C. & Turpin, Barbara H. A Positive Approach to Personal Growth. (Illus.). 158p. (Orig.). 1981. pap. text ed. 7.95 (ISBN 0-939506-00-9). Turpin & Assocs.

Turpin, Waters, jt. auth. see Ford, Aaron N.

Turpin, William N. Soviet Foreign Trade: Purpose & Performance. LC 76-47337. 192p. 1977. 18.95x o.p. (ISBN 0-669-01143-6). Lexington Bks.

Turro, James C. Reflections: Path to Prayer. LC 72-75632. 96p. 1972. 7.50 o.p. (ISBN 0-8091-8754-X). Paulist Pr.

Turro, Nicholas J. Modern Molecular Photochemistry. 1981. pap. 18.95 (ISBN 0-8053-9354-4, 39). Benjamin-Cummings.

--Modern Molecular Photochemistry. LC 78-57151. 1978. 29.95 (ISBN 0-8053-9353-6). Benjamin-Cummings.

Tur-Sinai, N. H. The Book of Job. rev. ed. 672p. 1982. Repr. of 1967 ed. text ed. 18.00 (ISBN 965-17-0009-2). Ridgefield Pub.

Turski, W. M. Computer Programming Methodology. 1977. 49.95x (ISBN 0-471-26068-1, Pub. by Wiley Heyden). Wiley.

Turtle, William J. Dr. Turtle's Babies. 336p. 1983. pap. 3.95 (ISBN 0-446-31065-4). Warner Bks.

Turtledove, Harry, tr. The Chronicle of Theophanes: An English Translation of Anni Mundi 6095-6305 (A.D.602-813), with an Introduction & Notes. LC 82-4861. (Middle Ages Ser.). (Orig.). 1982. 25.00x (ISBN 0-8122-7842-9); pap. 8.95x (ISBN 0-8122-1128-6). U of Pa Pr.

Turvey, Celia see Allen, W. S.

Turvey, John see Swan, D. K.

Turvey, Ralph. Demand & Supply. 2nd ed. (Illus.). 128p. 1980. text ed. 19.95x (ISBN 0-04-330302-1); pap. text ed. 6.95x (ISBN 0-04-330303-X). Allen Unwin.

Turville-Petre, E. E. Scaldic Poetry. 1976. 24.95x o.p. (ISBN 0-19-812517-8). Oxford U Pr.

Turville-Petre, E. Gabriel. The Heroic Age of Scandinavia. LC 75-8176. 1976. Repr. of 1951 ed. lib. bdg. 16.00x (ISBN 0-8371-8128-3, TUHA). Greenwood.

Turville-Petre, E. O., ed. Viga-Blum Saga. 2nd ed. (Illus.). 1960. text ed. 24.95x o.p. (ISBN 0-19-811117-7). Oxford U Pr.

Turville-Petre, Joan, ed. see Tolkien, J. R.

Turyn, Anne. Volunteer: A Photo Novel. (Illus.). 32p. (Orig.). 1982. pap. 5.50 (ISBN 0-939784-04-1). CEPA Gallery.

Tushingham, A. D. The Excavations at Dibon (Dhiban) in Moab: The Third Campaign 1952-53. (American Schools of Oriental Research Ser.: Vol. 40). 172p. 1972. text ed. 6.00x (ISBN 0-89757-040-5, Am Sch Orient Res). Eisenbrauns.

Tushman, Michael. Organizational Change: An Exploratory Study & Case History. LC 73-620201. (ILR Paperback Ser.: No. 15). 120p. 1974. pap. 6.75 (ISBN 0-87546-055-0); pap. 9.75 special hard bdg. o.s.i. (ISBN 0-87546-285-5). ILR Pr.

Tusiani, Joseph, tr. see Michelangelo.

Tuska, Jon & Piekarski, Vicki. Encyclopedia of Frontier & Western Fiction. (Illus.). 384p. 1983. 24.95 (ISBN 0-07-065587-1, P&RB). McGraw.

Tuska, Jon, ed. The American West in Fiction. 1982. pap. 3.95 (ISBN 0-451-62086-0, ME2086, Ment). NAL.

Tussac, R. De see De Tussac, R.

Tusselman, Goldie. Bazoomericks. (Limericklets Ser.: No. 9). (Illus.). 1982. pap. 1.25 (ISBN 0-938338-20-X). Winds World Pr.

--Bazoomericks II. (Illus.). 1982. pap. 1.25 (ISBN 0-938338-21-8). Winds World Pr.

--Bazoomericks III. (Limericklets Ser.: No. 11). pap. 1.25 (ISBN 0-938338-22-6). Winds World Pr.

Tussie, Diana. Latin America in the World Economy. LC 82-47501. 213p. 1982. 25.00x (ISBN 0-312-47333-8). St Martin.

Tussing, A. Dale. Poverty & the Dual Economy. 224p. (Orig.). 1975. 17.95 o.p. (ISBN 0-312-63315-7); pap. text ed. 8.95 o.p. (ISBN 0-312-63350-5). St Martin.

Tussing, Lyle. Psychology for Better Living. LC 59-14126. (Illus.). 1959. text ed. 18.50x o.p. (ISBN 0-471-89397-8). Wiley.

Tussing, Ruth-Elaine see Alden, Douglas W., et al.

Tussing, Ruth-Elaine, et al see Alden, Douglas W., et al.

Tussman, Joseph. Government & the Mind. LC 77-74796. 1977. 12.95x (ISBN 0-19-502230-0). Oxford U Pr.

--Obligation & the Body Politic. LC 60-15099. 1968. pap. 5.95 (ISBN 0-19-500785-9, GB). Oxford U Pr.

Tustin, Frances. Autistic States in Children. (Illus.). 376p. 1981. 27.50x (ISBN 0-7100-0763-9). Routledge & Kegan.

Tustison, F. E. & Ruehl, P. W. Electrical Essentials for the Practical Shop. (Illus., Orig.). 1967. pap. 2.50 o.p. (ISBN 0-02-829520-X, 82952). Glencoe.

Tustison, F. E., et al. Metalwork Essentials. rev. ed. 1962. 6.00 o.p. (ISBN 0-02-829540-4). Glencoe.

Tutchings, Terrence R. Rhetoric & Reality: Presidential Commissions & the Making of Public Policy. (Illus.). 190p. 1979. lib. bdg. 24.00 (ISBN 0-89158-657-1). Westview.

Tuthill, Arthur H., et al. Corrosion Resistance of Alloys to Bleach Plant Environment. (TAPPI PRESS Reports). (Illus.). 199p. 1980. pap. 69.95 (ISBN 0-89852-384-2, 01-01-RO84). TAPPI.

Tuthill, Marge. Art For Children's Liturgy: What You Need & How To Do It. LC 82-60855. 1982. pap. 4.95 (ISBN 0-8091-2478-5). Paulist Pr.

Tutin, T. G., et al. Flora Europaea. Incl. Vol. 1. Lycopodiaceae to Plantanaceae. 1964. 105.00 (ISBN 0-521-06661-1); Vol. 2. Rosaceae to Umbelliferae. 1968. 105.00 (ISBN 0-521-06662-X); Vol. 3. Diapseniaceae to Myoporaceae. 105.00 (ISBN 0-521-08489-X); Vol. 4. Plantaginaceae to Compositae (& Rubiaceae) 1976. 105.00 (ISBN 0-521-08717-1); Vol. 5. Alismataceae to Orchidaceae. 1980. 115.00 (ISBN 0-521-20108-X). LC 64-24315. Cambridge U Pr.

Tutorow, Norman E., compiled by. The Mexican-American War: An Annotated Bibliography. LC 80-1789. (Illus.). xxix, 427p. 1981. lib. bdg. 45.00x (ISBN 0-313-22181-2, TMA/). Greenwood.

Tutte, W. T. Introduction to the Theory of Matroids. LC 77-135060. (Modern Analytic & Computational Methods in Science & Mathematics: Vol. 37). 96p. 1971. 21.95 (ISBN 0-444-00096-8, North Holland). Elsevier.

Tutte, W. T., ed. Recent Progress in Combinatorics: Proceedings. 1969. 63.50 (ISBN 0-12-705150-3). Acad Pr.

Tuttle, Anthony. Steve Cauthen: Boy Jockey. LC 77-16770. (Illus.). (gr. 3-6). 1978. 7.95 o.p. (ISBN 0-399-20631-0). Putnam Pub Group.

Tuttle, David. Circuits. (Electronic Science). (Illus.). 1977. text ed. 24.95 o.p. (ISBN 0-07-065591-X, C); solutions manual 5.95 o.p. (ISBN 0-07-065592-8). McGraw.

Tuttle, Donald, jt. ed. see Maginn, John.

Tuttle, Gene. Buckshot Bite. 1982. 6.95 (ISBN 0-686-84171-9, Avalon). Bouregy.

--Cattleman's War. (YA) 1981. 6.95 (ISBN 0-686-74801-8, Avalon). Bouregy.

--Revenge in Peace Valley. 1982. pap. 6.95 (ISBN 0-686-84729-6, Avalon). Bouregy.

--Rusty Colt of the Cross L. 192p. (YA) 1975. 6.95 (ISBN 0-685-51771-3, Avalon). Bouregy.

--The Silver Cowboy. 1981. pap. 6.95 (ISBN 0-686-84688-5, Avalon). Bouregy.

Tuttle, Jack L. Dogs Need Our Love. 1983. 10.95 (ISBN 0-87212-163-1). Libra.

Tuttle, Lisa. Familiar Spirits. 208p. (Orig.). 1983. pap. 2.95 (ISBN 0-425-05854-9). Berkley Pub.

Tuttle, Marcia & Smith, Lynn. Introduction to Serials Management, Vol. 11. Stueart, Robert D., ed. LC 81-81658. (Foundations in Library & Information Sciences). 250p. 1981. 42.50 (ISBN 0-89232-107-5). Jai Pr.

Tuttle, Michael D. Practical Business Math. 3rd ed. 450p. 1982. pap. text ed. write for info. (ISBN 0-697-08187-7); instructor's edition avail. (ISBN 0-697-08188-5). Wm C Brown.

--Practical Business Math: A Performance Approach. 3rd ed. 475p. 1982. pap. text ed. write for info. (ISBN 0-697-08187-7); instrs.' manual avail. (ISBN 0-697-08188-5). Wm C Brown.

Tuttle, Michael D. & Walls, Elizabeth. Accounting: A Basic Approach. 352p. 1981. text ed. write for info. (ISBN 0-697-08048-X); instr.'s manual avail. (ISBN 0-697-08053-6); study wkbk avail. (ISBN 0-697-08054-4); practice set a avail. (ISBN 0-697-08055-2); practice set b avail. (ISBN 0-697-08058-7); avail. solutions manual practice set a (ISBN 0-697-08060-9); avail. soltions manual practice set b (ISBN 0-697-08061-7). Wm C Brown.

Tuttle, Sharon. My Little Animal Babies. (Put & Play Ser.). 1981. 4.50 (ISBN 0-307-05100-5, Golden Pr). Western Pub.

Tuttle, W. C. Thunderbird Range. 256p. (YA) 1974. 6.95 (ISBN 0-685-39470-0, Avalon). Bouregy.

Tuttle, Wainwright. There's Something Wrong with Our Money. (Illus.). 139p. (Orig.). (gr. 11-12). 1982. pap. 3.57 (ISBN 0-9609494-0-2). Jebco Bks.

Tuttle, William M., Jr. Race Riot: Chicago in the Red Summer of 1919. LC 71-130983. (Illus.). 1970. 8.95 (ISBN 0-689-10372-7); pap. text ed. 6.95x (ISBN 0-689-70287-6, NL30). Atheneum.

Tuttleton, James W. Thomas Wentworth Higginson. (United States Authors Ser.). 1978. lib. bdg. 13.95 (ISBN 0-8057-7236-7, Twayne). G K Hall.

Tutu, Desmond. Crying in the Wilderness. 125p. (Orig.). 1982. pap. 5.95 (ISBN 0-8028-1940-0). Eerdmans.

Tutuola, Amos. My Life in the Bush of Ghosts. 1962. pap. 6.95 (ISBN 0-394-17324-4, E559, Ever). Grove.

Tuve, George L. Energy, Environment, Population & Food: Our Four Interdependent Crises. LC 76-40351. 1976. 44.95x (ISBN 0-471-02091-5, Pub. by Wiley-Interscience); pap. 13.50 o.p. (ISBN 0-471-02090-7). Wiley.

Tuve, George L. & Domholdt, L. C. Engineering Experimentation. rev. ed. 1966. text ed. 38.95 (ISBN 0-07-065595-2, C). McGraw.

Tuveson, Ernest L. Redeemer Nation: The Idea of America's Millenial Role. LC 68-14009. (Midway Reprint Ser.). 1980. pap. 11.00x (ISBN 0-226-81921-3). U of Chicago Pr.

Tuyl, Barbara Van see Johnson, Pat & Van Tuyl, Barbara.

Tuyl, Barbara Van see Van Tuyl, Barbara.

Tuzin, Donald F. The Ilahita Arapesh: Dimensions of Unity. 1976. 39.50x (ISBN 0-520-02860-0). U of Cal Pr.

--The Voice of the Tambaran: Truth & Illusion in Ilahita Arapesh Religion. 350p. 1980. 28.50x (ISBN 0-520-03964-5). U of Cal Pr.

TV Vet. Illustrated Textbook of Cat Diseases. (Illus.). 191p. 1981. 12.95 (ISBN 0-87666-865-1, PS-771). TFH Pubns.

Tvardovsky, Alexander. Tyrokin & the Stove Makers. Rudolf, Anthony, tr. from Rus. (Translation Ser.). 1979. 6.95 o.p. (ISBN 0-85635-066-4, Pub. by Carcanet New Pr England). Humanities.

Tveten, John L. Coastal Texas: Water, Land, & Wildlife. LC 82-40317. (The Louise Lindsey Merrick Texas Environment Ser.: No. 5). (Illus.). 122p. 1982. 29.95 (ISBN 0-89096-138-7). Tex A&M Univ Pr.

Twaddell, Freeman, jt. auth. see Thomas, Ursula.

Twaddle, Andrew C. Sickness Behavior & the Sick Role. 1979. lib. bdg. 18.00 (ISBN 0-8161-9006-2, Univ Bks). G K Hall.

Twaddle, W. Old Dunstable. 64p. 1982. 25.00x (ISBN 0-900804-08-4, Pub. by White Crescent England). State Mutual Bk.

Twain. Creating Change in Social Settings: Planned Program Development. 224p. 1983. 25.95 (ISBN 0-03-062391-X). Praeger.

Twain, Mark. The Adventures of Huckleberry Finn. 292p. (Incl. criticisms, background material, biography). (gr. 7-12). pap. 1.75 (ISBN 0-553-21079-3, 12349-1). Bantam.

--The Adventures of Huckleberry Finn. (Hardy Boys' Favorite Classics). (Illus.). (gr. 6-9). 1978. 2.95 (ISBN 0-448-14922-2, G&D). Putnam Pub Group.

--Adventures of Huckleberry Finn. (Illus.). (gr. 4-6). Companion Lib. ed. o.s.i. 2.95 (ISBN 0-448-05451-5, G&D); lib. bdg. 5.95 il. jr. o.p. (ISBN 0-448-05800-6); deluxe ed. 8.95 (ISBN 0-448-06000-0); pap. 4.95 (ISBN 0-448-11002-4); 5.95 (ISBN 0-686-85988-X). Putnam Pub Group.

--Adventures of Huckleberry Finn. holiday ed. (Illus.). Repr. of 1884 ed. 11.49i (ISBN 0-06-014376-2, HarpT); lib. bdg. 9.87 o.p. (ISBN 0-06-014377-0). Har-Row.

--Adventures of Huckleberry Finn. (Classics Edition). pap. 1.50i (ISBN 0-06-080612-5, HC612, PL). Har-Row.

--The Adventures of Huckleberry Finn. Eyre, A. G., ed. (Longman Simplified English Ser.). (Illus.). 110p. 1978. pap. 2.15x (ISBN 0-582-52824-0). Longman.

--Adventures of Huckleberry Finn. 1962. pap. 1.95 o.p. (ISBN 0-02-045550-X, Collier). Macmillan.

--Adventures of Huckleberry Finn. (YA) (RL 7). 1971. pap. 1.50 (ISBN 0-451-51673-7, CW1673, Sig Classics). NAL.

--The Adventures of Huckleberry Finn. 1982. Repr. lib. bdg. 18.95x (ISBN 0-89967-047-4). Harmony Raine.

--Adventures of Huckleberry Finn. 1983. pap. 2.25 (ISBN 0-14-035007-1, Puffin). Penguin.

--The Adventures of Tom Sawyer. Spector, Robert D., ed. (Bantam Classics Ser.). 232p. (Incl. essay & discussion). (gr. 7 up). 1981. pap. 1.50 (ISBN 0-553-21001-7). Bantam.

--The Adventures of Tom Sawyer. (Hardy Boys' Favorite Classics). (Illus.). (gr. 6-9). 1978. 2.95 (ISBN 0-448-14921-4, G&D). Putnam Pub Group.

--Adventures of Tom Sawyer. (Illus.). (gr. 4-6). illus. jr. lib. o.p. 5.95 (ISBN 0-448-05802-2, G&D); companion lib. o.s.i. 2.95 (ISBN 0-448-05452-3); deluxe ed. 8.95 (ISBN 0-448-06002-7); pap. 4.95 (ISBN 0-448-11002-4). Putnam Pub Group.

--Adventures of Tom Sawyer. holiday ed. (Illus.). 11.49i (ISBN 0-06-014465-3, HarpT); PLB 7.87 o.p. (ISBN 0-06-014427-0). Har-Row.

--The Adventures of Tom Sawyer. Incl. The Adventures of Huckleberry Finn. (RL 7). 1979. pap. 2.95 (ISBN 0-451-51613-3, CL1613, Sig Classics). NAL.

--The Adventures of Tom Sawyer. LC 78-2796. (Raintree's Illustrated Classics). (Illus.). (gr. 5-8). 1978. PLB 13.30 (ISBN 0-8172-1130-6). Raintree Pubs.

--The Adventures of Tom Sawyer. LC 81-40324. (The Mark Twain Library). (Illus.). 250p. 1983. 13.50 (ISBN 0-520-04559-9); pap. 2.95 (ISBN 0-686-82992-1, CAL 556). U of Cal Pr.

--The Adventures of Tom Sawyer. Barish, Wendy, ed. (Illus.). 288p. 1982. 14.95 (ISBN 0-671-43791-7). Wanderer Bks.

--The Adventures of Tom Sawyer. 1982. Repr. lib. bdg. 17.95 (ISBN 0-89967-046-6). Harmony Raine.

--Adventures of Tom Sawyer. 1983. pap. 2.25 (ISBN 0-14-035003-9, Puffin). Penguin.

--The Adventures of Tom Sawyer & Huckleberry Finn. (gr. 3 up). Date not set. price not set (ISBN 0-448-41100-8, G&D). Putnam Pub Group.

--Autobiography of Mark Twain. Neider, Charles, ed. (Illus.). 1959. 20.00i (ISBN 0-06-014368-1, HarpT). Har-Row.

--The Boys' Ambition: Life on the Mississippi; an Excerpt from the Book by Mark Twain. LC 72-12489. (Seedling Bks.). (Illus.). 32p. (gr. 2-6). 1975. PLB 4.95g (ISBN 0-8225-0283-6). Lerner Pubns.

--The Comic Mark Twain Reader: The Most Humorous Selections from His Stories, Sketches, Novels, Travel Books & Speeches. LC 76-23785. 1977. 14.95 (ISBN 0-385-11334-X). Doubleday.

--Complete Humorous Sketches & Tales of Mark Twain. LC 61-6503. 1961. 14.95 (ISBN 0-385-01094-X). Doubleday.

--A Connecticut Yankee in King Arthur's Court. 274p. (gr. 9-12). 1981. pap. 1.75 (ISBN 0-553-21003-3). Bantam.

--Great Short Works of Mark Twain. Kaplan, Justin, ed. 1967. pap. 3.50i (ISBN 0-06-083075-1, P3075, PL). Har-Row.

--Huckleberry Finn. (Childrens Illustrated Classics Ser). (Illus.). 338p. 1977. Repr. of 1955 ed. 10.00x (ISBN 0-460-05031-1, Pub. by J. M. Dent England). Biblio Dist.

--Huckleberry Finn. Carnell, Corbin S., ed. (Graded Readers for Students of English Ser.). (Illus.). 1979. pap. text ed. 3.50 o.p. (ISBN 0-89285-151-1). English Lang.

--Innocents Abroad. pap. 3.95 (ISBN 0-451-51753-9, CE1753, Sig Classics). NAL.

--King Leopold's Soliloquy. Heym, Stefan, ed. (Illus.). 1970. pap. 1.25 o.p. (ISBN 0-7178-0114-4). Intl Pub Co.

--Letters from the Earth. Devoto, Bernard, ed. 240p. 1974. pap. 3.37i (ISBN 0-06-080331-2, P331, PL). Har-Row.

--Life on the Mississippi. (Bantam Classics Ser.). 312p. (gr. 7-12). 1981. pap. 1.75 (ISBN 0-553-21002-5). Bantam.

--Mark Twain on Man & Beast. Smith, Janet, ed. LC 72-78319. 258p. 1972. o. p. 7.95 (ISBN 0-88208-007-5); pap. 8.95 (ISBN 0-88208-008-3). Lawrence Hill.

--Mark Twain on the Damned Human Race. Smith, Janet, ed. (Orig.). 1962. pap. 6.95 (ISBN 0-8090-0054-7, AmCen). Hill & Wang.

--Mark Twain's Correspondence with Henry Huttleston Rogers, 1893-1909. Leary, Lewis, ed. LC 68-23900. (Mark Twain Papers). 1969. 44.50x (ISBN 0-520-01467-7). U of Cal Pr.

--Mark Twain's Hannibal, Huck & Tom. Blair, Walter, ed. LC 69-10575. (Mark Twain Papers). 1969. 37.50x (ISBN 0-520-01501-0). U of Cal Pr.

--Mark Twain's Letters from Hawaii. Day, A. Grove, ed. LC 74-31359. (Pacific Classics Ser.: No. 5). 320p. 1975. pap. 4.95 (ISBN 0-8248-0288-8). UH Pr.

--Mark Twain's Mysterious Stranger Manuscripts. Gibson, William M., ed. LC 69-10576. (Mark Twain Papers). 1969. 37.50x (ISBN 0-520-01473-1); pap. 8.95x (ISBN 0-520-01661-0). U of Cal Pr.

--Mark Twain's Notebooks & Journals, 1855-1873, Vol. 1. Anderson, Frederick, et al, eds. 700p. 1976. 42.50x (ISBN 0-520-02326-9). U of Cal Pr.

--Mark Twain's Notebooks & Journals, 1877-1883, Vol. 2. Anderson, Frederick, et al, eds. 700p. 1976. 42.50x (ISBN 0-520-02542-3). U of Cal Pr.

--Mark Twain's Satires & Burlesques. Rogers, Franklin R., ed. (Mark Twain Papers). 1967. 24.95 o.s.i. (ISBN 0-520-01081-7). U of Cal Pr.

--Mark Twain's "Which Was the Dream?" & Other Symbolic Writings of the Later Years. Tuckey, John S., ed. (Mark Twain Papers). 1966. 40.00x (ISBN 0-520-01285-2). U of Cal Pr.

--Mississippi Writings. Cardwell, Guy, ed. LC 82-9917. 1087p. 1982. 27.50 (ISBN 0-940450-07-0). Literary Classics.

--The Mysterious Stranger: No. 44. LC 81-40326. (The Mark Twain Library). 200p. 1982. 13.50 (ISBN 0-520-04544-0, CAL 538); pap. 3.95 (ISBN 0-520-04545-9). U of Cal Pr.

--A Pen Warmed-up in Hell: Mark Twain in Protest. Anderson, Frederick, ed. & intro. by. LC 70-181606. 160p. 1972. 12.45i (ISBN 0-06-010117-2, HarpT); pap. 4.95i (ISBN 0-06-090678-2, CN-678). Har-Row.

--Prince & the Pauper. (gr. 4-6). companion lib. ed. 2.95 (ISBN 0-448-05477-9, G&D). Putnam Pub Group.

--Prince & the Pauper. holiday ed. (Illus.). Repr. of 1881 ed. lib. bdg. 10.89i (ISBN 0-06-014406-8, HarpT). Har-Row.

--Prince & the Pauper. (RL 6). 1964. pap. 1.95 (ISBN 0-451-51777-6, CJ1777, Sig Classics). NAL.

--The Prince & the Pauper. (Bantam Classics Ser.). 219p. (gr. 4-12). 1982. pap. 1.75 (ISBN 0-553-21090-4). Bantam.

--Prince & the Pauper. Bd. with Connecticut Yankee. 1982. pap. 3.50 (ISBN 0-451-51628-1, CE1628, Sig Classics). NAL.

--Pudd'nhead Wilson. (Bantam Classics Ser.). 1981. pap. 1.75 (ISBN 0-553-21004-1). Bantam.

--Pudd'nhead Wilson. pap. 1.75 (ISBN 0-451-51743-1, CE1743, Sig Classics). NAL.

--Roughing It. LC 28-1234. (Illus.). Repr. of 1875 ed. 11.49i (ISBN 0-06-014420-3, HarpT). Har-Row.

--Roughing It. (RL 10). pap. 2.95 (ISBN 0-451-51658-3, CE1658, Sig Classics). NAL.

--Roughing It. (Classics of the Old West Ser.). 1982. lib. bdg. 17.28 (ISBN 0-8094-3995-6). Silver.

--Simon Wheeler, Detective. Rogers, Franklin R., ed. LC 63-18140. (Levy Pub. Ser.: No. 2). 1965. 15.00 (ISBN 0-87104-161-8). NY Pub Lib.

--Tom Sawyer Abroad. (Illus.). (gr. 4-6). companion lib. ed. 2.95 (ISBN 0-448-05478-7, G&D). Putnam Pub Group.

--Tom Sawyer Detective. (Illus.). (gr. 4-6). companion lib. ed. 2.95 (ISBN 0-448-05479-5, G&D). Putnam Pub Group.

Twain, Mark & Warner, Charles D. Gilded Age. pap. 3.50 (ISBN 0-451-51542-0, CE1542, Sig Classics). NAL.

Twain, Mark see Allen, W. S.

Twain, Mark see Eyre, A. G.

Twain, Mark see Swan, D. K.

Twaite, James A. & Monroe, Jane A. Introductory Statistics. 1979. text ed. 21.95x (ISBN 0-673-15097-6). Scott F.

Twarog, B. M., et al, eds. Basic Biology of Muscles: A Comparative Approach. (Society of General Physiologists Ser.: Vol. 37). 448p. 1982. text ed. 70.00 (ISBN 0-89004-799-5). Raven.

Tway, Eileen, ed. Reading Ladders for Human Relations. 1981. pap. 9.95 (ISBN 0-8268-1414-X). NCTE.

Tweddle, David A., jt. auth. see Ainscow, Mel.

Twedt, Dik W. Survey of Marketing Research, 1978. 1978. 15.00 (ISBN 0-87757-119-8). Am Mktg.

Tweeddale, J. Welding & Fabrication. 1969. 10.00 (ISBN 0-444-19756-7). Elsevier.

Tweedie. The Arabian Horse: His Country & People. (Arab Background Ser.). 1972. 30.00x (ISBN 0-86685-170-4). Intl Bk Ctr.

Tweedie & Wilkinson. The Butterflies & Moths of Britain & Europe. pap. 8.95 (ISBN 0-686-42746-7, Collins Pub England). Greene.

Tweedie, Donald. Christian & Sex. 1965. pap. 1.50 o.p. (ISBN 0-8010-8808-9). Baker Bk.

Tweedie, Michael. Atlas of Insects. LC 73-12022. (John Day Bk.). (Illus.). 128p. 1974. 14.37i (ISBN 0-381-98258-0). T Y Crowell.

Tweedsmuir, Lord. The Country Life Picture Book Scotland. (Illus.). 1983. 19.95 (ISBN 0-393-01734-6, Pub. by Country Life). Norton.

Twelveponies, Mary. There are No Problem Horses, Only Problem Riders. 1982. 17.95 (ISBN 0-395-32558-7); pap. 8.95 (ISBN 0-686-83173-X). HM.

Twenhofel, William H., jt. auth. see Shrock, Robert R.

Twentieth Centrury Fund, Inc. Law Enforcement: The Federal Role, Report of the Twentieth Century Fund Task Force on the Law Enforcement Assistance Administration. LC 76-12526. 1976. text ed. 8.95 (ISBN 0-07-065627-4, P&RB); pap. text ed. 3.95 o.p. (ISBN 0-686-76807-8). McGraw.

Twentieth Century Fund. Abuse on Wall Street: Conflicts of Interest in the Securities Markets. LC 79-8295. (Illus.). 1980. lib. bdg. 39.95 (ISBN 0-89930-001-4, TWC/, Quorum). Greenwood.

--Commission on Campaign Costs in the Electronic Era. Voters' Time. 1969. pap. 2.00 (ISBN 0-527-02840-1). Kraus Repr.

Twentieth Century Fund, Inc. Building a Broader Market: Report of the Twentieth Century Fund Task Force on the Municipal Bond Market. LC 76-28368. 1976. 7.95 o.p. (ISBN 0-07-065629-0, P&RB); pap. 3.95 o.p. (ISBN 0-07-065630-4). McGraw.

--Rights in Conflict: Report of the Twentieth Century Fund Task Force on Justice, Publicity & the First Amendment. LC 75-43831. 1976. text ed. 6.95 o.p. (ISBN 0-07-065625-8, P&RB); pap. text ed. 3.95 o.p. (ISBN 0-07-065626-6). McGraw.

Twentieth Century Fund of Task Force on Policies Toward Veterans. Those Who Served. Taussig, M. K., ed. 1974. pap. 5.00 (ISBN 0-527-02854-1). Kraus Repr.

Twentieth Century Fund. Task Force on Financing Congressional Campaigns. Electing Congress: The Financial Dilemma. Rosenbloom, D. L., ed. LC 74-14390. 1970. pap. 5.00 (ISBN 0-527-02852-5). Kraus Repr.

Twentieth Century Fund. Task Force on Labor Disputes in Public Employment. Pickets at City Hall. LC 73-9638. 53p. 1973. Repr. of 1970 ed. pap. 7.00 (ISBN 0-527-91350-2). Kraus Repr.

Twichell, Heath, Jr. Allen: The Biography of an Army Officer 1859-1930. 1974. 30.00 (ISBN 0-8135-0778-2). Rutgers U Pr.

Twidale, C. R. Granite Landforms. 372p. 1982. 115.00 (ISBN 0-444-42116-5). Elsevier.

--Structural Landforms. (Geomorphology Ser.: Vol. 5). 1971. 20.00x (ISBN 0-262-20018-X). MIT Pr.

Twiggs, Robert D. Pan-African Language in the Western Hemisphere. LC 72-94707. (Illus.). 280p. 1973. 9.75 o.p. (ISBN 0-8158-0301-X). Chris Mass.

Twiname, Eric. The Rules Book: 1981,1984 Int'l Yacht Racing Rules. (Illus.). 156p. 1981. 7.95 (ISBN 0-914814-28-1). Sail Bks.

--Sail, Race & Win. (Illus.). 154p. 1982. 11.95 (ISBN 0-914814-34-6). Sail Bks.

--Start to Win. 2nd ed. Sambrooke-Sturgess, Gerald, ed. (Illus.). 220p. 1983. 19.95 (ISBN 0-229-11688-4, Pub. by Adlard Coles). Sheridan.

Twing, J. W. The Receptionist. 160p. 1983. 7.96 (ISBN 0-07-065641-X, G). McGraw.

Twing, J. W., jt. auth. see Morrison, Peter.

Twing, J. W., jt. auth. see Morrison, Phyllis.

Twining, James E., jt. auth. see Giroux, James A.

Twining, William & Miers, David. How to Do Things with Rules: A Primer of Interpretation. (Law in Context Ser). xvii, 270p. 1976. text ed. 16.00x o.p. (ISBN 0-297-77132-9). Rothman.

--How to Do Things with Rules: A Primer of Interpretation. 2nd ed. xx, 387p. 1982. text ed. 37.50x (ISBN 0-297-78083-2). Rothman.

Twinn, Michael. Lady Who Loved Animals. (Illus.). 32p. 1981. 5.50 (ISBN 0-85953-121-X, Pub. by Child's Play England). Playspaces.

Twinn, Michael, illus. Going Shopping. (Nursery Ser.). 8p. 1977. 2.00 (ISBN 0-85953-072-8, Pub. by Child's Play England). Playspaces.

--I Go to Nursery School. (Nursery Ser.). 8p. 1977. 2.00 (ISBN 0-85953-070-1, Pub. by Child's Play England). Playspaces.

--My Baby Brother. (Nursery Ser.). (Illus.). 8p. 1977. 2.00 (ISBN 0-85953-068-X, Pub. by Child's Play England). Playspaces.

--Transport. (Concertina Ser.). (Illus.). 12p. (Orig.). 1977. 4.50 (ISBN 0-85953-006-X, Pub. by Child's Play England). Playspaces.

--A Visit to the Doctor. (Nursery Ser.). (Illus., Orig.). 1977. 2.00 (ISBN 0-85953-067-1, Pub. by Child's Play England). Playspaces.

Twiss, Brian C., ed. The Managerial Implications of Microelectronics. 200p. 1981. 17.50x (ISBN 0-8448-1406-7). Crane-Russak Co.

--Social Forecasting for Company Planning. 200p. 1982. 16.50x (ISBN 0-8448-1396-6). Crane-Russak Co.

Twitchell, Mary. Wood Energy: A Practical Guide to Heating with Wood. 1978. pap. 8.95 o.p. (ISBN 0-88266-145-0). Garden Way Pub.

Twitchett, Carol C., ed. Harmonization in the EEC. 1980. 30.00 (ISBN 0-312-36309-5). St Martin.

Twitchett, D., ed. Cambridge History of China: Sui & T'ang China, Vol. 3: 589-906 A.D., Part 1. LC 76-29852. (Illus.). 1979. 89.50 (ISBN 0-521-21446-7). Cambridge U Pr.

Twitchett, Denis. Printing & Publishing in Medieval China. (Illus.). 72p. 1983. pap. 14.50 (ISBN 0-913720-08-9, Sandstone). Beil F C.

Twitchett, Kenneth J. The Evolving United Nations. LC 70-178037. 1971. 17.95 o.p. (ISBN 0-312-27335-5). St Martin.

Twitchett, Kenneth J., jt. auth. see Cosgrove, Carol A.

Twohig, Elizabeth S. The Megalithic Art of Western Europe. (Illus.). 1981. 145.00x (ISBN 0-19-813193-3). Oxford U Pr.

Twombly, Gerald & Kennedy, Timothy. A Taste of Grace, Vol. 1. (Illus.). 182p. 1982. pap. 7.50 (ISBN 0-910219-04-4). Little People.

Twombly, Gerald H. An Analytical Survey of the Bible. pap. 5.95 (ISBN 0-88469-120-9). BMH Bks.

Twombly, Robert C. Frank Lloyd Wright: His Life & His Architecture. LC 78-9466. 444p. 1979. 29.95 (ISBN 0-471-03400-2, Pub. by Wiley-Interscience). Wiley.

Twomey, Jeremiah J. The Pathophysiology of Human Immunologic Disorders. LC 82-8675. (Illus.). 280p. 1982. 39.50 (ISBN 0-8067-1921-4). Urban & S.

Twomey, Mark J. A Parade of Saints. LC 82-202387. (Illus.). 300p. 1983. pap. 8.50 (ISBN 0-8146-1275-X). Liturgical Pr.

Twomey, S. Introduction to the Mathematics of Inversion in Remote Sensing & Indirect Measurements. (Developments in Geomathematics Ser.: Vol. 3). 1977. 81.00 (ISBN 0-444-41547-5, North Holland). Elsevier.

Twomley, Dale E. Parochiaid & the Courts. (Andrews University Monographs, Studies in Education: Vol. 2). x, 165p. 1979. 3.95 (ISBN 0-943872-51-0). Andrews Univ Pr.

Twyne, Thomas, tr. see Petrarca, Francesco.

Tyabji, Surayya. Mirch Masala. 92p. 1981. pap. text ed. 3.95x (ISBN 0-86131-205-8, Pub. by Orient Longman Ltd India). Apt Bks.

Tyack, David B. Turning Points in American Educational History. 1967. pap. 23.95x (ISBN 0-471-00596-7). Wiley.

Tyack, Geoffrey. Buildings of Britain, 1550-1750: South Midlands. 160p. 1982. 50.00x (ISBN 0-86190-063-4, Pub. by Moorland). State Mutual Bk.

Tyack, Jim. Rented Tuxedo. 1976. 4.00 (ISBN 0-686-81973-X); signed ed. 10.00. Street Pr.

Tyagaraja. Spiritual Heritage of Tyagaraja. Ramanujachari, C., tr. (Sanskrit, Telegu & Eng.). 6.95 o.p. (ISBN 0-87481-440-5). Vedanta Pr.

Tyagisananda, Swami, tr. see Narada.

Tyberg, Judith M. Sanskrit Keys to the Wisdom-Religion. 180p. 1976. pap. 5.00 (ISBN 0-913004-29-4). Point Loma Pub.

Ty-Casper, Linda. The Hazards of Distance: A Novel. 111p. 1982. pap. 6.50 (ISBN 0-686-37014-7, Pub. by New Day Philippines). Cellar.

Tydeman, W. The Theatre in the Middle Ages. LC 77-85683. (Illus.). 1979. 47.50 (ISBN 0-521-21891-8); pap. 11.95 (ISBN 0-521-29304-9). Cambridge U Pr.

Tydeman, William, ed. Oscar Wilde: Comedies. 1981. pap. 25.00x (ISBN 0-686-91716-2, Pub. by Macmillan England). State Mutual Bk.

Tydeman, William & Heath, Michael, eds. Six Christmas Plays. 1971. text ed. 4.50x o.p. (ISBN 0-435-23730-6); pap. text ed. 4.00x o.p. (ISBN 0-435-23731-4). Heinemann Ed.

Tydings, Kenneth S. Candid Wedding Photography Guide. 1959. pap. 2.95 o.p. (ISBN 0-8174-0217-9, Amphoto). Watson-Guptill.

--Portrait Photography. (Illus.). 1960. pap. 2.95 o.p. (ISBN 0-8174-0268-3, Amphoto). Watson-Guptill.

Tydings, Kenneth S. & Tydings, Shirley C. The Photo-Visual Guide to Yashica Twin-Lens Reflex Cameras. (Illus.). 128p. 1972. pap. 2.95 o.p. (ISBN 0-8174-0175-X, Amphoto). Watson-Guptill.

Tydings, Shirley C., jt. auth. see Tydings, Kenneth S.

Tyers, Rodney, jt. ed. see Chisholm, Anthony H.

Tykhy, Oleksiy. Reflections. LC 82-50026. (Ukrainian Ser.). 79p. 1982. pap. 3.95 (ISBN 0-914834-49-5). Smoloskyp.

Tyl, Noel. Guide to the Principles & Practices of Astrology. 1979. 17.95 (ISBN 0-686-43166-9). Llewellyn Pubns.

Tyldesley, W. R. Oral Medicine. (Illus.). 1981. pap. text ed. 24.95x (ISBN 0-19-261275-1). Oxford U Pr.

Tyler. Image of America. 1981. 13.95 (ISBN 0-686-84618-4, Nonpareil Bks). Godine.

Tyler, jt. auth. see Watts.

Tyler, Anne. Celestial Navigation. 256p. 1983. pap. 3.50 (ISBN 0-446-31169-3). Warner Bks.

--Dinner at the Homesick Restaurant. LC 81-13694. 1982. 13.50 (ISBN 0-394-52381-4). Knopf.

--Dinner at the Homesick Restaurant. (General Ser.). 1982. lib. bdg. 15.95 (ISBN 0-8161-3438-3, Large Print Bks). G K Hall.

--Dinner at the Homesick Restaurant. 320p. 1983. pap. 3.50 (ISBN 0-425-05999-5). Berkley Pub.

--Earthly Possessions. 224p. 1983. pap. 2.95 (ISBN 0-446-31171-5). Warner Bks.

--If Morning Ever Comes. 272p. 1983. pap. 3.50 (ISBN 0-425-06140-X). Berkley Pub.

--Morgan's Passing. (General Ser.). 1980. lib. bdg. 16.95 (ISBN 0-8161-3131-7, Large Print Bks). G K Hall.

--Searching for Caleb. 320p. 1983. pap. 3.50 (ISBN 0-425-06137-X). Berkley Pub.

Tyler, C., jt. auth. see Gee, E. A.

Tyler, Chaplin, jt. auth. see Gee, Edwin A.

Tyler, David. Electrical & Electronic Applications, No. 2. (Technician Ser.). (Illus.). 1980. 17.50 (ISBN 0-408-00412-6). Butterworth.

Tyler, Dick, jt. auth. see Columbu, Franco.

Tyler, E. J. American Clocks for the Collector. (Illus.). 224p. 1981. pap. 13.50 (ISBN 0-525-47682-2, 01311-390). Dutton.

--Clock Types. LC 82-15358. (Illus.). 160p. 1982. 17.95x (ISBN 0-582-50308-6). Longman.

Tyler, Edward J. Estimating Electrical Construction. 272p. 1983. pap. 19.00 (ISBN 0-910460-99-X). Craftsman.

Tyler, Francine. Great American Etchings, 1870-1900: 122 Plates. (Fine Art Ser.). (Illus.). 160p. (Orig.). 1983. pap. 8.95 (ISBN 0-486-24388-5). Dover.

Tyler, Gary R., jt. auth. see Coleman, Arthur.

Tyler, H. Richard & Dawson, David, eds. Current Neurology, Vol. 2. (Illus.). 531p. 1979. 50.00 (ISBN 0-471-09497-8, Pub. by Wiley Med). Wiley.

Tyler, Henry M., ed. Selections from the Greek Lyric Poets. 1983. 25.00 (ISBN 0-89241-363-8); pap. 12.50 (ISBN 0-89241-120-1). Caratzas Bros.

Tyler, J. E. The New Tolkien Companion. 672p. 1980. pap. 7.95 (ISBN 0-380-46904-9, 63743). Avon.

Tyler, J. E. A. Tolkien Companion. 1977. pap. 7.95 (ISBN 0-380-00901-3, 63743-X). Avon.

Tyler, Jenny & Watts, Lisa. Children's Book of the Seas. LC 77-15549. (Children's Guides Ser.). (Illus.). (gr. 3 up). 1978. PLB 7.95 (ISBN 0-88436-464-X). EMC.

Tyler, Jenny, jt. auth. see Watts, Lisa.

Tyler, John E., ed. Light in the Sea. (Benchmark Paper in Optics Ser.: Vol. 3). 1977. 51.00 (ISBN 0-12-787595-6). Acad Pr.

Tyler, Leona, jt. auth. see Walsh, W. Bruce.

Tyler, Leona, jt. auth. see Sundberg, Norman.

Tyler, Leona E. Individual Differences: Abilities & Motivational Directions. (Illus.). 1974. pap. 14.95 (ISBN 0-13-458042-7). P-H.

--Work of the Counselor. 3rd ed. 1969. 24.95x (ISBN 0-13-965087-3). P-H.

Tyler, Lyon G. England in America, 1580-1652. Repr. of 1904 ed. lib. bdg. 16.50x o.p. (ISBN 0-8371-1634-1, TYEA). Greenwood.

Tyler, M. L. Homoeopathic Drug Pictures. 1978. 20.00 (ISBN 0-85032-021-6, Pub. by C. W. Daniels). Formur Intl.

Tyler, Martin. The Decisive Speculative Significance of the Last of the Elliott Waves Upon the Future Course of the Stock Market. 131p. 1983. 79.85 (ISBN 0-89266-399-5). Am Classical Coll Pr.

Tyler, Michael J. Frogs. (Illus.). 256p. 1983. pap. 12.50 (ISBN 0-00-216450-7, Pub. by W Collins Australia). Intl Schol Bk Serv.

Tyler, Parker. Chaplin: Last of the Clowns. (Illus.). 248p. 1972. pap. 3.95 (ISBN 0-8180-0703-6). Horizon.

--A Pictorial History of Sex in Films. (Illus.). 1976. pap. 9.95 (ISBN 0-8065-0540-0). Citadel Pr.

Tyler, Paul E., ed. Biologic Effects of NonIonizing Radiation. (Annals of the New York Academy of Sciences: Vol. 247). 1975. 64.75x (ISBN 0-89072-761-9). NY Acad Sci.

Tyler, Ralph, ed. From Youth to Constructive Adult Life: The Role of the Public School. LC 77-95249. (National Society for the Study of Education, Series on Contemp. Educ. Issues). 1978. 19.00 (ISBN 0-8211-1907-9); text ed. 17.25 ten copies (ISBN 0-685-04972-8). McCutchan.

Tyler, Ralph W. Prospects for Research & Development in Education. new ed. LC 75-36111. 190p. 1978. 19.00x (ISBN 0-8211-1906-0); text ed. 17.25x (ISBN 0-685-61058-6). McCutchan.

Tyler, Ralph W. & Wolf, Richard M. Crucial Issues in Testing. LC 73-20855. 1974. 18.50x (ISBN 0-8211-1714-9); text ed. 16.95x (ISBN 0-685-42643-2). McCutchan.

Tyler, Richard, jt. auth. see Columbu, Franco.

Tyler, Richard H., ed. Current Neurology. Dawson, David M. (Current Neurology Ser.: Vol. 1). 499p. 1978. 50.00 (ISBN 0-471-09521-4, Pub. by Wiley Med). Wiley.

Tyler, Robert L. Rebels of the Woods: The I.W.W. in the Pacific Northwest. LC 68-1776. 1967. pap. 7.50 (ISBN 0-87114-018-7). U of Oreg Bks.

Tyler, Ron, ed. Posada's Mexico. LC 79-22460. (Illus.). xii, 316p. 1979. pap. 18.00 (ISBN 0-8444-0315-6). Lib Congress.

Tyler, Royall. Algerine Captive. LC 67-10272. 1967. Repr. of 1797 ed. 50.00x (ISBN 0-8201-1046-9). Schol Facsimiles.

--Verse of Royall Tyler. Peladeau, Marius B., ed. LC 68-14026. 1968. 13.95 (ISBN 0-8139-0235-5). U Pr of Va.

Tyler, Stephen A. The Said & the Unsaid: Mind Meaning & Culture. 1978. 43.00 (ISBN 0-12-705550-9). Acad Pr.

Tyler, T. Texas. Remember Me. 1981. cancelled 5.95 (ISBN 0-8062-1746-4). Carlton.

Tyler, W. T. Rogue's March. LC 82-47544. 352p. 1982. 14.37i (ISBN 0-06-015048-3, HarpT). Har-Row.

Tyler, William G. The Brazilian Industrial Economy. LC 79-5440. 160p. 1981. 19.95x (ISBN 0-669-03448-7). Lexington Bks.

--Issues & Prospects for New International Economic Order. LC 77-78367. (Illus.). 208p. 1977. 21.95x o.p. (ISBN 0-669-01445-1). Lexington Bks.

Tyler, Zack. Foxx! (Orig.). 1981. pap. 1.95 o.s.i. (ISBN 0-440-12742-4). Dell.

Tylman, Stanley D. & Malone, William F. Tylman's Theory & Practice of Fixed Prosthodontics. 7th ed. LC 78-17821. 744p. 1978. text ed. 44.95 (ISBN 0-8016-5166-2). Mosby.

Tylor, Edward. The Origins of Culture. (Primitive Culture - Part 1). 10.00 (ISBN 0-8446-0945-5). Peter Smith.

Tylor, Edward B. Anahuac or Mexico & the Mexicans Ancient & Modern. LC 66-29078. 1970. Repr. of 1861 ed. text ed. 17.00x o.p. (ISBN 0-391-01956-2). Humanities.

Tymieniecka, A. T. The Phenomenology of Man & the Human Condition. 1983. lib. bdg. 69.50 (ISBN 90-277-1447-9, Pub. by Reidel Holland). Kluwer Boston.

Tymn, Marshall B. The Year's Scholarship in Science Fiction, Fantasy & Horror Literature, 1980. (Annotated Bibliography of Scholarly Bks.: No. 1). 80p. (Orig.). 1983. pap. 6.00x (ISBN 0-87338-279-X). Kent St U Pr.

Tymn, Marshall B. & Schlobin, Roger C. The Year's Scholarship in Science Fiction & Fantasy, 1976-1979, Vol. 40. (The Serif Series of Bibliographies & Checklists). 200p. 1983. 22.50x (ISBN 0-87338-257-9). Kent St U Pr.

Tymn, Marshall B., compiled by. The Teacher's Guide to Fantastic Literature. (Illus., Orig.). 1983. write for info. (ISBN 0-916732-61-4); pap. text ed. write for info. (ISBN 0-916732-60-6). Starmont Hse.

Tymon, Frank & Tymon, Tim. How to Program Computer Games for Fun & Profit. 300p. 1983. pap. price not set. Dilithium Pr.

Tymon, Tim, jt. auth. see Tymon, Frank.

Tyms, James D. The Rise of Religious Education Among Negro Baptists. LC 79-66419. 1979. pap. text ed. 14.75 (ISBN 0-8191-0827-8). U Pr of Amer.

--Spiritual (Religious) Values in the Black Poet. 1977. 10.75 o.p. (ISBN 0-8191-0296-2). U Pr of Amer.

Tynan, D. M. Leonardo Da Vinci. (History First Ser.). (gr. 3-4). 1977. pap. text ed. 15.95 (ISBN 0-521-21209-X). Cambridge U Pr.

Tynan, Kenneth. Show People. 1980. 11.95 o.p. (ISBN 0-671-25012-4). S&S.

Tyndall, John. Sound. rev. 3rd ed. Repr. of 1903 ed. lib. bdg. 18.50x (ISBN 0-8371-2255-4, TYS). Greenwood.

Tyndalo, Vassili, jt. auth. see Rinaldi, Augusto.

Tyne, C. H. Van see Van Tyne, C. H. & Leland, W. G.

Tyne, C. H. Van see Webster, Daniel.

Tyne, Claude H. Van see Van Tyne, Claude H.

Tyne, Josselyn Van see Van Tyne, Josselyn & Berger, Andrew J.

Tyner, Fay S., et al. Fundamentals of EEG Technology, Vol. 1. 400p. 1982. 35.00 (ISBN 0-89004-385-X). Raven.

Tyner, Wallace E., et al. Western Coal: Promise or Problem? LC 78-3005. (Illus.). 208p. 1978. 23.95x (ISBN 0-669-02320-5). Lexington Bks.

Tyran, Michael R. Product Cost Estimating & Pricing: A Computerized Approach. LC 82-3753. 367p. 1982. 49.50 (ISBN 0-13-724039-2, Busn). P-H.

Tyras, G. Radiation & Propagation of Electromagnetic Waves. (Electrical Science Ser). 1969. 63.50 (ISBN 0-12-705650-5). Acad Pr.

Tyrell, Arthur. The Basics of Reprography. (Reprographic Library). 1972. 12.50 (ISBN 0-8038-0733-3). Hastings.

Tyrell, R. Emmett, ed. The Future That Doesn't Work: Social Democracy's Failures in Britain. LC 82-21929. 216p. (Orig.). 1983. pap. text ed. 8.95 (ISBN 0-8191-2740-X). U Pr of Amer.

Tyrell, R. Emmett, Jr. Public Nuisances. LC 78-19940. 1979. 11.95 o.s.i. (ISBN 0-465-06772-7). Basic.

Tyrer. Drugs in Psychiatric Practice. 1982. text ed. 59.95 (ISBN 0-407-02212-0). Butterworth.

Tyrer & Lee. Synopsis of Occupational Medicine. 192p. 1979. pap. 16.00 (ISBN 0-7236-0513-0). Wright-PSG.

Tyrer, J. H., jt. ed. see Eadis, M. J.

Tyrer, John H. & Eadie, Mervyn J. Clinical & Experimental Neurology, Vol. 18. 248p. text ed. 57.00 (ISBN 0-686-37437-1). Wright-PSG.

Tyrer, Peter. The Role of Bodily Feelings in Anxiety. (Maudsley Monographs: Vol. 23). (Illus.). 1976. text ed. 18.00x o.p. (ISBN 0-19-712145-4). Oxford U Pr.

Tyrer, Walter. Such Friends Are Dangerous. Barzun, J. & Taylor, W. H., eds. LC 81-47390. (Crime Fiction 1950-1975 Ser.). 224p. 1982. lib. bdg. 14.95 (ISBN 0-8240-4974-8). Garland Pub.

Tyrkiel, E. F. Dictionary of Physical Metallurgy. (Eng. & Ger. & Fr. & Pol. & Rus.). 1978. 85.00 (ISBN 0-444-99810-1). Elsevier.

Tyrmand, Leopold. The Liberal Culture. cancelled. Green Hill.

Tyrnauer, Gabrielle, jt. auth. see Stasny, Charles.

Tyroler, Else. Sewing Pants for Women. 3.50 (ISBN 0-8208-0324-3). Hearthside.

Tyrrell, Bernard J. Christotherapy II: A New Horizon for Counselors, Spiritual Directors & Seekers of Healing & Growth in Christ. 1982. 12.95 (ISBN 0-8091-0332-X); pap. 8.95 (ISBN 0-8091-2482-3). Paulist Pr.

Tyrrell, G. W. Principles of Petrology. 1978. pap. 14.95x (ISBN 0-412-21500-4, Pub. by Chapman & Hall England). Methuen Inc.

Tyrrell, Ian R. Sobering Up: From Temperance to Prohibition in Antebellum America, Eighteen Hundred to Eighteen Sixty. LC 78-22132. (Contributions in American History: No. 82). 1979. lib. bdg. 29.95x (ISBN 0-313-20822-0, TYT/). Greenwood.

Tyrrell, J. A. & Semple, J. G. Generalized Clifford Parallelism. LC 74-134625. (Tracts in Mathematics Ser.: No. 61). 1971. 24.95 (ISBN 0-521-08042-8). Cambridge U Pr.

Tyrrell, John. Leos Janacek: Kat'a Kabanova. LC 81-38505. (Cambridge Opera Handbooks). (Illus.). 190p. 1982. 24.95 (ISBN 0-521-23180-9); pap. 9.95 (ISBN 0-521-29853-9). Cambridge U Pr.

Tyrrell, Joseph M. Louis XI. (World Leaders Ser.). 1980. lib. bdg. 12.95 (ISBN 0-8057-7728-8, Twayne). G K Hall.

Tyrrell, R. W. The Work of the Television Journalist. (Library of Film & Television Practice). 176p. 1972. 21.95 o.p. (ISBN 0-240-51051-8). Focal Pr.

Tyrrell, Robert. Work of the T V Journalist. 2nd ed. (Library of Film & Television Practice). (Illus.). 184p. 1981. 27.95 (ISBN 0-240-51051-8). Focal Pr.

--Work of the Television Journalist. 2nd ed. LC 80-41970. 200p. 1981. 27.95 o.p. (ISBN 0-240-51051-8). Focal Pr.

Tyrrell, Robert Y., ed. Cicero in His Letters. 1983. 11.50 (ISBN 0-89241-347-6). Caratzas Bros.

Tyrrell, Ronald, et al. Growing Pains in the Classroom: A Guide for Teachers of Adolescents. (Illus.). 368p. 1977. text ed. 15.95 (ISBN 0-87909-312-9). Reston.

Tyshkevich, R. I., jt. auth. see Suprunenko, Dmitri A.

Tysoe, B. A. Construction Costs & Price Indices: Description & Use. 1981. 25.00x (ISBN 0-419-11930-2, Pub. by E & FN Spon). Methuen Inc.

Tyson, Alan, ed. Beethoven Studies III. LC 77-30191. (Illus.). 256p. 1982. 49.50 (ISBN 0-521-24131-6). Cambridge U Pr.

Tyson, Carl N. The Red River in Southwestern History. LC 81-40292. (Illus.). 240p. 1981. 16.95 (ISBN 0-8061-1659-5). U of Okla Pr.

Tyson, J., tr. see Vydra, F., et al.

Tyson, James L. Target America. LC 80-54762. 284p. 1981. 12.95 (ISBN 0-89526-671-7). Regnery-Gateway.

Tyson, Joseph B. A Study of Early Christianity. Scott, Kenneth J., ed. (Illus.). 448p. 1973. text ed. 23.95x (ISBN 0-02-421900-2). Macmillan.

Tyson, Laura D. The Yugoslav Economic System & Its Performance in the Nineteen Seventies. LC 80-24650. (Research Ser.: No. 44). x, 115p. 1980. pap. 5.50x (ISBN 0-87725-144-4). U of Cal Intl St.

Tyson, Laura D., jt. ed. see Neuberger, Egon.

Tyson, Martha E. A Brief Account of the Settlement of Ellicott's Mills. 63p. 6.00 (ISBN 0-686-36839-8). Md Hist.

Tyson, Pete. Handball. LC 73-141160. (Physical Education Ser). (Illus.). 1972. pap. text ed. 7.95x (ISBN 0-673-16192-7). Scott F.

Tyson, Pete & Turman, James C., eds. The Handball Book. LC 82-81813. (Illus.). 224p. (Orig.). 1983. pap. 9.95 (ISBN 0-88011-065-1). Leisure Pr.

Tyson, Russ. Philosopher's Scrap Book. 10.50 (ISBN 0-392-09382-0, ABC). Sportshelf.

Tyson-Flyn, Juanita, ed. see Joers, Lawrence.

Tyssot De Patot, Simon. La Vie, les Aventures et le Voyage de Groenland du R. P. Cordelier Pierre de Mesange, 2 vols. (Utopias in the Enlightenment Ser.). 571p. (Fr.). 1974. Repr. of 1720 ed. lib. bdg. 152.50x set o.p. (ISBN 0-8287-0842-8). Vol. 1 (022). Vol. 2 (023). Clearwater Pub.

--Voyages et Aventures de Jacques Masse. (Utopias in the Enlightenment Ser.). 515p. (Fr.). 1974. Repr. of 1710 ed. lib. bdg. 127.50x o.p. (ISBN 0-8287-0843-6, 021). Clearwater Pub.

Tytell, J. & Jaffe, Harold, eds. Affinities: A Short Story Anthology. 468p. 1976. pap. 6.95 (ISBN 0-690-05248-0, HarpC). Har-Row.

Tytler, I. F., et al. Vehicles & Bridging. (Brassey's Battlefield Weapons Systems & Technology: Vol. 1). 160p. 1983. 26.01 (ISBN 0-08-028322-5); pap. 13.01 (ISBN 0-08-028323-3). Pergamon.

Tzafestas. Simulation of Distributed-Parameter & Large-Scale Systems. 1980. 64.00 (ISBN 0-444-85447-9). Elsevier.

Tzafestas, S. G. Optimization & Control of Dynamic Operational Research Models. (Systems & Control Ser.: Vol. 4). 1982. 64.00 (ISBN 0-444-86380-X). Elsevier.

Tzafestas, S. G., ed. Distributed Parameter Control Systems: Theory & Application. (International Series on Systems & Control: Vol. 6). 525p. 1982. 60.00 (ISBN 0-08-027624-5). Pergamon.

Tzonchev, et al. Radiology of Joint Disease. (Illus.). 1973. 49.95 o.p. (ISBN 0-407-90050-0). Butterworth.

Tzonis, Alexander. Towards a Non-Oppressive Environment. LC 79-189033. 1978. 12.50x (ISBN 0-262-20038-4); pap. 4.95x (ISBN 0-262-70018-2). MIT Pr.

U

U-Bild Enterprises. Patterns for Better Living, 1983-84 Edition. 112p. 1982. pap. 2.95 (ISBN 0-910495-00-9). U-Bild.

--Wood Ornaments & Creche. 24p. 1982. pap. 3.50 (ISBN 0-910495-01-7). U-Bild.

U. S.-Japan Seminar or Inelastic Light Scattering, Santa Monica, California. January 22-25, 1979. Inelastic Light Scattering: Proceedings. Burstein, E. & Kawamura, H., eds. 124p. 1980. 29.50 (ISBN 0-08-025425-X). Pergamon.

Ubaldi, V., jt. auth. see Altenberg, G. A.

Ubbelohde, A. R. The Molten State of Matter: Melting & Crystal Structure. LC 77-28300. 454p. 1979. 107.95x (ISBN 0-471-99626-2). Wiley.

Ubbelohde, Carl. American Colonies & the British Empire, 1607-1763. 2nd ed. LC 75-17525. (AHM American History Ser,). 1975. pap. text ed. 6.95x (ISBN 0-88295-767-8). Harlan Davidson.

Ubbelohde, Carl, et al, eds. A Colorado Reader. rev. ed. 300p. 1982. 14.95 (ISBN 0-87108-238-1); pap. 8.95 (ISBN 0-87108-239-X). Pruett.

Ubell, Alvin & Bittman, Sam. Recipes for Home Repair. 288p. 1976. pap. 3.95 o.p. (ISBN 0-452-25209-1, Z5209, Plume). NAL.

Uberall, Herbert. Electron Scattering from Complex Nuclei Pts. A & B. (Pure & Applied Physics Ser: Vol. 25). 1971. Pt. A. 60.00 (ISBN 0-12-705701-3); Pt. B. 58.00 (ISBN 0-12-705702-1); Set. 93.00 (ISBN 0-685-02415-6). Acad Pr.

Uberoi, Chanchal, jt. auth. see Hasegawa, Akira.

Uberoi, Pritam. Non-Vegetarian Indian Cookery. 203p. (Orig.). 1981. pap. 9.95x (ISBN 0-940500-62-0, Pub by S Chand India). Asia Bk Corp.

--Pure Vegetarian Indian Cookery. 167p. 1981. pap. 9.95 (ISBN 0-940500-61-2, Pub. by Sterling India). Asia Bk Corp.

Uchendu, V. C., ed. Education & Politics in Tropical Africa. 1980. 35.00 (ISBN 0-914970-33-X). Conch Mag.

Uchenick, Joel, jt. auth. see Dinkelspiel, John R.

Uchida, Yoshiko. Desert Exile: The Uprooting of a Japanese American Family. LC 81-16187. (Illus.). 160p. 1982. 13.95 (ISBN 0-295-95898-7). U of Wash Pr.

--The Magic Listening Cap: More Folk Tales from Japan. LC 55-5240. (Illus.). (gr. 4-6). 1965. pap. 1.95 (ISBN 0-15-655119-5, VoyB). HarBraceJ.

--The Sea of Gold & Other Tales from Japan. (Children's Literature Ser.). 1980. PLB 8.95 o.p. (ISBN 0-8398-2613-3, Gregg). G K Hall.

Uchiyama, Kosho. Refining Your Life: From the Zen Kitchen to Enlightenment. Wright, Tom, tr. LC 82-20295. 136p. 1983. pap. 9.95 (ISBN 0-8348-0179-5). Weatherhill.

Uchtmann, Donald L. & Looney, J. W. Agricultural Law: Principles & Cases. (Illus.). 688p. 1981. text ed. 33.50 (ISBN 0-07-065746-7, C). McGraw.

Ucker, A. Applied Combinatorics. 385p. 1980. text ed. 26.50x o.p. (ISBN 0-471-04766-X). Wiley.

Ucko, David. Living Chemistry. 1977. text ed. 21.75 (ISBN 0-12-705950-4); lab manual 7.50 (ISBN 0-12-705956-3); transparency masters 3.00 (ISBN 0-686-96639-2); tchr's guide 3.50 (ISBN 0-12-705957-1). Acad Pr.

Ucko, P. J. Anthropomorphic Figurines. 1968. 70.00x (ISBN 0-686-98308-4, Pub. by Royal Anthro Ireland). State Mutual Bk.

UCLA Applied Health Professions Project & Pattison, J. Behrens. Dental Hygiene: The Detection & Removal of Calculus. LC 72-96758. (Illus.). 208p. 1973. pap. text ed. 17.95 (ISBN 0-87909-185-1). Reston.

UCLA Extension. Regulation & the Accounting Profession. Buckley, John W. & Weston, J. Fred, eds. LC 79-28661. (The UCLA Conference Ser.). 245p. 1980. 27.95 (ISBN 0-534-97983-1). Lifetime Learn.

Udall, jt. auth. see Smurthwaite.

Udall, Lee, jt. auth. see Wilson, Joseph T.

Udall, Nicholas. Roister Doister: Written before 1553. Arber, Edward, ed. pap. 12.50 (ISBN 0-87556-340-6). Saifer.

Ude, Arthur, jt. auth. see Templeton, Darlene.

Udell, Gerald G. & Baker, Kenneth G. How to Assess Before You Invest: Pies IV-Preliminary Innovation (self) Evaluation System. rev. ed. LC 82-88234. Orig. Title: Pies II-Manual for Innovation Evaluation. (Illus.). 242p. 1982. pap. 16.50 (ISBN 0-943812-00-3). Locus.

Udell, James & Bernstein, Bruce. Salaries: Nineteen Eighty-Two. 328p. 1982. ref 45.00x (ISBN 0-88410-860-0). Ballinger Pub.

Udell, James, jt. auth. see Bernstein, Bruce.

Udell, Jon G. The Economics of the American Newspaper. (Illus.). 1978. 12.95 (ISBN 0-8038-1932-3); pap. text ed. 5.95 (ISBN 0-8038-1933-1). Hastings.

Udell, Jon G. & Laczniak, Gene R. Marketing in an Age of Change: An Introduction. LC 80-19923. (Marketing Ser.). 577p. 1981. text ed. 26.50 (ISBN 0-471-08169-8); avail. tchrs'. ed. (ISBN 0-471-08184-1); test file avail. (ISBN 0-471-08187-6); study guide avail. (ISBN 0-471-08183-3). Wiley.

Udell, Rochelle. How to Eat an Artichoke: And Other Trying, Troublesome, Hard-To-Get-At Foods. (Illus.). 128p. 1982. 4.95 (ISBN 0-399-12677-5). Putnam Pub Group.

Udell, Rochelle, jt. auth. see Stein, Frances P.

Udell, William L., jt. auth. see Franke, Lois.

Udenfriend, Sidney. Fluorescence Assay in Biology & Medicine, 2 Vols. (Molecular Biology: Vol. 3). (Illus.). Vol. 1, 1962. 57.50 (ISBN 0-12-705850-8); Vol. 2. 59.50 (ISBN 0-12-705802-8). Acad Pr.

Udintsev, G. B., jt. ed. see Vinogradov, A. P.

Udis, Bernard. From Guns to Butter: Technology Organizations & Reduced Military Spending in Western Europe. LC 77-14569. 376p. 1978. prof ref 25.00x (ISBN 0-88410-657-8). Ballinger Pub.

Udo, Reuden K. The Human Geography of Tropical Africa. 256p. 1982. pap. 39.00x (ISBN 0-435-95919-0, Pub. by Heinemann England). State Mutual Bk.

Udoguchi, T. & Griffin, D. S., eds. Elevated Temperature Design Symposium, 1976. 1976. pap. text ed. 6.00 o.p. (ISBN 0-685-72345-3, G00104). ASME.

Udovitch, Abraham L., jt. auth. see Valensi, Lucette.

Udris, jt. auth. see Bacham.

Udry, J. Richard & Huyck, Earl E., eds. Demographic Evaluation of Domestic Family Planning Programs. LC 75-4661. 144p. 1975. prof ref 16.00 (ISBN 0-88410-355-2). Ballinger Pub.

Udry, Janice M. Oh No, Cat! (Illus.). (gr. k-2). 1977. 6.95 o.p. (ISBN 0-698-20368-2, Coward). Putnam Pub Group.

Udvardy, M. D. Audubon Society Guide to North American Birds: Western Region. 1977. 12.50 (ISBN 0-394-41410-1). Knopf.

Udwadia, Farokh E., jt. ed. see Vakil, Rustom J.

Ueberle, Jerrie K., jt. auth. see Click, Marilyn J.

Uecker, Bob & Herskowitz, Mickey. The Catcher in the Wry. 192p. 1982. 12.95 (ISBN 0-399-12586-8). Putnam Pub Group.

--Catcher in the Wry: Outrageous But True Stories of Baseball. 240p. 1983. pap. 3.50 (ISBN 0-515-07254-0). Jove Pubns.

Ueda, Kunihiro, jt. ed. see Hayaishi, Osamu.

Ueda, Makoto. Matsuo Basho. LC 82-48165. 202p. 1983. pap. 4.95 (ISBN 0-87011-553-7). Kodansha.

--Modern Japanese Poets & the Nature of Literature. LC 82-60487. 432p. 1983. 28.50x (ISBN 0-8047-1166-6). Stanford U Pr.

Ueda, R., ed. see International Spring School on Crystal Growth, 2nd, Japan, 1974.

Ueda, Reed, jt. auth. see Glazer, Nathan.

Uehara, Toyoaki & Kiyose, Gisaburo N. Fundamentals of Japanese. LC 73-21245. (East Asian Ser.). 608p. 1975. pap. 17.50x o.p. (ISBN 0-253-32523-4). Ind U Pr.

Uehling, Theodore E., Jr., jt. ed. see French, Peter A.

Uekusa, Masu, jt. auth. see Caves, Richard E.

Uellner, W. Fungorum Libri Bibliothecae Joachim Schliemann. (Books & Prints of 4 Centuries). 1976. 24.00 (ISBN 3-7682-1075-8). Lubrecht & Cramer.

Uemura, T., et al. Neuro-Otological Examination. (Illus.). 188p. 1977. text ed. 59.50 o.p. (ISBN 0-8391-0887-7). Univ Park.

Ueno, Kazue, jt. auth. see Suzuki, Shoichiro.

Ueno, Keihei, jt. auth. see Cheng, K. L.

Uffelman, Larry K. Charles Kingsley. (English Authors Ser.). 1979. 13.95 (ISBN 0-8057-6752-5, Twayne). G K Hall.

Uffenbeck, John E. Hardware Interfacing with the TRS-80. 01/1983 ed. (Illus.). 240p. text ed. 19.95 (ISBN 0-13-383877-3); pap. 13.95 (ISBN 0-13-383869-2). P-H.

--Introduction to Electronics: Devices & Circuits. (Illus.). 432p. 1982. 24.95 (ISBN 0-13-481507-6). P-H.

Ugalde, Sharon K. Gabriel Celaya. (World Authors Ser.). 1978. 15.95 (ISBN 0-8057-6324-4, Twayne). G K Hall.

Ugarte, Francisco. Espana y Su Civilizacion. 2nd ed. LC 64-23908. 1965. 10.95 (ISBN 0-672-63165-2). Odyssey Pr.

Ugi, Ivar. Isonitrile Chemistry. (Organic Chemistry Ser.: Vol. 20). 1971. 54.50 (ISBN 0-12-706150-9). Acad Pr.

Uglow, Jennifer S., ed. The International Dictionary of Women's Biography. LC 82-7417. (Illus.). 534p. 1983. 27.50 (ISBN 0-8264-0192-9). Continuum.

Ugural, Ansel C. Stresses in Plates & Shells. (Illus.). 352p. 1981. text ed. 37.50x (ISBN 0-07-065730-0, C); solutions manual 15.00 (ISBN 0-07-065731-9). McGraw.

Uhde, W. Van Gogh. (Phaidon Color Library). (Illus.). 84p. 1983. pap. 17.95 (ISBN 0-7148-2161-6, Pub. by Salem Hse Ltd). Merrimack Bk Serv.

Uher, Vladimir, jt. auth. see Pavlik, Milan.

Uhl, Joseph N., jt. auth. see Kohls, Richard L.

Uhl, Kenneth P., jt. auth. see Schoner, Bertram.

Uhl, Kenneth P., jt. auth. see Schoner, Bertran.

Uhl, Laura C., jt. auth. see Houghtalen, Esther G.

Uhl, Marjorie V. Madame Alexander Dolls Are Made With Love. Ltd. ed. (Illus.). 164p. 40.00 (ISBN 0-9608590-1-2). From Me.

--Madame Alexander Dolls on Review. LC 81-90052. (Illus.). 231p. 1981. 29.95 (ISBN 0-9608590-0-4). From Me.

Uhl, Vincent & Gray, Joseph B., eds. Mixing: Theory & Practice, 2 Vols. 1966-67. 59.00 ea. Vol. 1 (ISBN 0-12-706601-2). Vol. 2 (ISBN 0-12-706602-0). Acad Pr.

Uhlein, Gabriele. Meditations with TM Hildegrade of Bingen. LC 82-73363. (Meditations with TM). 128p. (Orig.). 1982. pap. 6.95 (ISBN 0-939680-12-2). Bear & Co.

Uhlendorf, Bernhard A., tr. see Baurmeister, Carl L.

Uhler, Horace S. Original Tables to One Hundred & Thirty-Seven Decimal Places of Natural Logarithms for Factors of the Form One Plus N Ten Minus P Enhanced by Auxiliary Tables of Logarithms of Small Integers. 1942. pap. 32.50x (ISBN 0-685-89769-9). Elliots Bks.

Uhlich, Richard. Twenty Minutes to Live. Uhlich, Richard, ed. (Bluejeans Paperback Ser.). (Illus., Orig.). (gr. 7-12). 1978. pap. text ed. 1.25 o.p. (ISBN 0-8374-0044-9). Xerox Ed Pubns.

Uhlich, Richard, ed. see Carlson, Diane.

Uhlich, Richard, ed. see Carlson, Gordon.

Uhlich, Richard, ed. see Hogan, Elizabeth.

Uhlich, Richard, ed. see Otfinoski, Steven.

Uhlich, Richard, ed. see Sorensen, Robert.

Uhlig, H., ed. System & Theory of Geosciences, 2 pts. 103p. 1975. Vol. 1. pap. text ed. 24.00 (ISBN 0-08-019664-0); Pt. 2. pap. text ed. 24.00 (ISBN 0-08-019670-5). Pergamon.

Uhlig, Herbert H. Corrosion & Corrosion Control: An Introduction to Corrosion Science & Engineering. 2nd ed. LC 71-162425. 419p. 1971. 40.50x (ISBN 0-471-89563-6, Pub. by Wiley-Interscience). Wiley.

--Corrosion Handbook. 1188p. 1948. 65.95x (ISBN 0-471-89562-8, Pub. by Wiley-Interscience). Wiley.

Uhlig, R. P., ed. Computer Message Systems. 1981. 53.25 (ISBN 0-444-86253-6). Elsevier.

Uhlig, Ronald P. & Farber, David J. The Office of the Future. 378p. 1979. 35.00 (ISBN 0-686-98082-4). Telecom Lib.

Uhlman, Fred. Reunion. 1977. 6.95 (ISBN 0-374-24951-2). FS&G.

--Reunion. 1978. pap. 2.95 (ISBN 0-14-004790-5). Penguin.

Uhlman, Thomas M. Racial Justice: Black Judges & Defendants in an Urban Trial Court. LC 78-19569. 144p. 1979. 16.95x o.p. (ISBN 0-669-02625-5). Lexington Bks.

Uhlmann, D. K., jt. ed. see Simmons, J. H.

Uhlmann, D. R. & Kreidl, N. J., eds. Glass: Science & Technology: Vol. 1: Glass Systems & Glass Ceramics. 424p. 1983. price not set (ISBN 0-12-706701-9); price not set subscription price. Acad Pr.

--Glass: Science & Technology, Vol. 5, Elasticity & Strength in Glasses. 1980. 40.00 (ISBN 0-12-706705-1). Acad Pr.

Uhlmann, Dietrich. Hydrobiology: A Text for Engineers & Scientists. LC 77-24258. 1979. 61.95x (ISBN 0-471-99557-6, Pub. by Wiley-Interscience). Wiley.

Uhlmann, L., jt. auth. see Ray, G. F.

Uhr, Carl G. Economic Doctrines of Knut Wicksell. (Institute of Business & Economic Research UC Berkeley). 1960. 44.00x (ISBN 0-520-01290-9). U of Cal Pr.

Uhr, Jonathan W. & Landy, Maurice, eds. Immunologic Intervention. (Perspectives in Immunology Ser.). 1972. 49.50 (ISBN 0-12-706950-X). Acad Pr.

Uhr, Leonard, ed. Algorithm-Structured Computer Arrays & Networks: Architectures & Processes for Images, Percepts, Models, Information. Date not set. price not set (ISBN 0-12-706960-7). Acad Pr.

Uhrig, Robert E., ed. Neutron Noise, Waves & Pulse Propagation: Proceedings. LC 66-60048. (AEC Symposium Ser.). 788p. 1967. pap. 27.75 (ISBN 0-87079-290-3, CONF-660206); microfiche 4.50 (ISBN 0-87079-291-1, CONF-660206). DOE.

--Noise Analysis in Nuclear Systems: Proceedings. (AEC Symposium Ser.). 518p. 1964. pap. 21.00 (ISBN 0-87079-292-X, TID-7679); microfiche 4.50 (ISBN 0-87079-293-8, TID-7679). DOE.

Uhthoff, H. K., ed. Current Concepts of External Fixation of Fractures. (Illus.). 460p. 1982. 59.00 (ISBN 0-387-11314-2). Springer-Verlag.

Uiker, John J., jt. auth. see Shigley, Joseph E.

Uitert, Evert van see Van Uitert, Evert.

Ujka, Mary. The Cross Gives Me Courage. 132p. (Orig.). 1983. pap. 5.95 (ISBN 0-87973-618-6, 618). Our Sunday Visitor.

Ukers, William H. All About Coffee. LC 71-178659. (Illus.). 1975. Repr. of 1935 ed. 74.00x (ISBN 0-8103-4092-5). Gale.

Ukrainka, Lesia. Spirit of Flame. Cundy, Percival, tr. from Slavic. LC 76-147225. (Illus.). 1970. Repr. of 1950 ed. lib. bdg. 16.25x (ISBN 0-8371-5990-3, UKSF). Greenwood.

Ulack, Richard, jt. auth. see Raitz, Karl B.

Ulam, Adam. Fall of the American University. 217p. 1972. 16.00x (ISBN 0-912050-20-9, Library Pr). Open Court.

Ulam, Adam B. Bolsheviks. 1968. pap. 8.95 (ISBN 0-02-038100-X, Collier). Macmillan.

--Dangerous Relations: The Soviet Union in World Politics, 1970-1982. 320p. 1983. 25.00 (ISBN 0-19-503237-3). Oxford U Pr.

--Titoism & the Cominform. LC 70-100246. 1971. Repr. of 1952 ed. lib. bdg. 17.50x (ISBN 0-8371-3404-8, ULTC). Greenwood.

--The Unfinished Revolution. 1979. lib. bdg. 27.50 (ISBN 0-89158-485-4); pap. 11.00 (ISBN 0-89158-496-X). Westview.

Ulam, S. M. Adventures of a Mathematician. LC 75-20133. (Illus.). 320p. 1983. pap. 7.95 (ISBN 0-684-15064-6, SL728, ScribT). Scribner.

Ulam, Stanislaw M. Stanislaw Ulam: Sets, Numbers & Universes: Selected Works. Beyer, William, et al, eds. LC 73-21686. 654p. 1974. 45.00x (ISBN 0-262-13094-7). MIT Pr.

Ulanoff, Stanley M. Fighter Pilot. rev. ed. (Illus.). 394p. 1983. pap. 19.95 (ISBN 0-668-05399-2, 5399-2). Arco.

Ulanov, Ann & Ulanov, Barry. Primary Speech: A Psychology of Prayer. LC 81-85328. 192p. 1982. 9.95 (ISBN 0-8042-1134-5). John Knox.

--Religion & the Unconscious. LC 75-16302. 288p. 1975. 13.95 (ISBN 0-664-20799-5). Westminster.

Ulanov, Barry. A Handbook of Jazz. LC 74-10018. 248p. 1975. Repr. of 1957 ed. lib. bdg. 18.75x (ISBN 0-8371-7659-X, ULHJ). Greenwood.

Ulanov, Barry, jt. auth. see Hall, James B.

Ulanov, Barry, jt. auth. see Ulanov, Ann.

Ulanov, Barry, tr. from Lat. Prayers of St. Augustine. 160p. 1983. pap. price not set (ISBN 0-8164-2454-3). Seabury.

Ulc, Otto. The Judge in a Communist State: A View from Within. LC 71-141382. xiv, 307p. 1972. 14.00x (ISBN 0-8214-0091-6, 82-80968). Ohio U Pr.

Ulehla, Ivan, et al. Optical Model of the Atomic Nucleus. Alter, G., tr. 1965. 34.00 (ISBN 0-12-707450-3). Acad Pr.

Ulenberg, G. H., ed. European Brewery Convention: 18th International Congress, Copenhagen 1981. 800p. 80.00 (ISBN 0-904147-30-4). IRL Pr.

Ulene, Art & Feldman, Sandy. Help Yourself to Health: A Health Information & Services Directory. 1980. 19.95 (ISBN 0-399-12474-8, Perige); pap. 10.95 (ISBN 0-399-50465-6). Putnam Pub Group.

Ulett, G. A., jt. ed. see Steinhilber, R. M.

Ulett, George A. Principles & Practice of Physiologic Acupuncture. 240p. 1982. 42.50 (ISBN 0-87527-309-2). Green.

Ulett, George A. & Smith, Kathleen. A Synopsis of Contemporary Psychiatry. 6th ed. LC 79-14554. (Illus.). 436p. 1979. pap. text ed. 18.95 (ISBN 0-8016-5176-X). Mosby.

Ulibarri, George. Documenting Alaska: A Guide to National Archives Relating to Alaska. (Illus.). 300p. 25.00 (ISBN 0-686-83926-9). U of Alaska Pr.

Ulibarri, Sabine R. Mi Abuela Fumaba Puros. (Illus.). 1977. pap. 6.00 (ISBN 0-88412-105-4). Tonatiuh-Quinto Sol Intl.

Ulich, Robert. Fundamentals of Democratic Education: An Introduction to Educational Philosophy. Repr. of 1940 ed. lib. bdg. 16.00x (ISBN 0-8371-3015-8, ULDE). Greenwood.

Ullman, Betty E. The Voluptuaries. LC 78-2187. 1978. 8.95 (ISBN 0-399-12084-X). Putnam Pub Group.

Ullman, James M. & Bercoon, Norman. How to Build a Fortune with an IRA. 144p. 1982. pap. 7.95 (ISBN 0-02-008800-0). Macmillan.

Ullman, James R. The Day on Fire. 1978. pap. 2.50 o.p. (ISBN 0-380-38430-2, 38430). Avon.

Ullman, Jeffrey. Principles of Database Systems. 2nd ed. 1982. text ed. 24.95 (ISBN 0-914894-36-6). Computer Sci.

Ullman, Jeffrey D. Programming Systems. LC 75-374. (Illus.). 336p. 1976. text ed. 25.95 (ISBN 0-201-07654-3). A-W.

Ullman, Jeffrey D., jt. auth. see Aho, Alfred V.

Ullman, Jeffrey D., jt. auth. see Hopcroft, John E.

Ullman, John E., ed. Social Costs in Modern Society: A Qualitative & Quantitative Assessment. LC 82-18590. (Illus.). 272p. 1983. lib. bdg. 29.95 (ISBN 0-89930-019-7, USC/, Quorum). Greenwood.

Ullman, Michael. Jazz Lives. (Illus.). 1980. 9.95 (ISBN 0-915220-51-2). New Republic.

--Jazz Lives: Portraits in Words & Pictures. 244p. 1981. pap. 6.95 (ISBN 0-8256-3253-6, Quick Fox). Putnam Pub Group.

--Jazz Lives: Portraits in Words & Pictures. 256p. 1982. 5.95 (ISBN 0-399-50687-X, Perige). Putnam Pub Group.

Ullman, Montague & Zimmerman, Nan. Working with Dreams. 1979. 11.95 o.s.i. (ISBN 0-440-09282-5). Delacorte.

Ullman, Neil R. Elementary Statistics: An Applied Approach. LC 77-10828. 1978. text ed. 23.95 (ISBN 0-471-02105-9). wkbk & study guide 10.95 (ISBN 0-471-03209-3). Wiley.

Ullman, Pierre L. Mariano de Larra & Spanish Political Rhetoric. (Illus.). 440p. 1971. 35.00 (ISBN 0-299-05750-X). U of Wis Pr.

Ullman, Ralph, jt. auth. see Stratmann, William C.

Ullman, Richard, jt. auth. see Dunn, Robert.

Ullman-Margalit, Edna. The Emergence of Norms. (Clarendon Library of Logic & Philosophy). (Illus.). 1978. 35.00x (ISBN 0-19-824411-8). Oxford U Pr.

Ullmann, John. Quantitative Methods in Management. (Schaum's Outline Ser). 256p. (Orig.). 1976. pap. 6.95 (ISBN 0-07-065742-4, SP). McGraw.

Ullmann, John E., ed. The Suburban Economic Network: Economic Activity, Resource Use, & the Great Sprawl. LC 76-12883. (Special Studies). 1977. 33.95 o.p. (ISBN 0-275-23560-2). Praeger.

Ullmann, John E., jt. ed. see Mauss, Evelyn A.

Ullmann, Leonard & Krasner, Leonard. A Psychological Approach to Abnormal Behaviour. 2nd ed. LC 74-28271. 832p. 1975. text ed. 29.95 (ISBN 0-13-732545-2). P-H.

Ullmann, Leonard P. Research in Clinical Psychology: Effective Coping Through Data Collection. (Pergamon General Psychology Ser.). 325p. 1984. write for info. (ISBN 0-08-025945-6); pap. write for info. (ISBN 0-08-025944-8). Pergamon.

Ullmann, Walter. A Short History of the Papacy in the Middle Ages. 1974. pap. 14.95x (ISBN 0-416-74970-4). Methuen Inc.

Ulloth, Dana R. & Klinge, Peter L. Mass Media: Past, Present, & Future. (Illus.). 400p. 1983. pap. text ed. 12.95 (ISBN 0-314-69683-0). West Pub.

Ullrich, Helen D., ed. Health Maintenance Through Food & Nutrition: A Guide to Information Sources. (Health Affairs Information Guide Ser.: Vol. 7). 350p. 1981. 42.00x (ISBN 0-8103-1500-9). Gale.

Ullyet, Kenneth. Ham Radio. LC 76-54072. 1977. 14.95 o.p. (ISBN 0-7153-7247-5). David & Charles.

Ullyett, Kenneth. The Eleven Hundred Companion. 12.50x (ISBN 0-392-05851-0, SpS). Sportshelf.

Ullyot, Joan. Running Free: A Book for Women Runners & Their Friends. (Illus.). 1980. 10.95 (ISBN 0-399-12492-6). Putnam Pub Group.

Ullyot, Joan L. Running Free: A Book for Women Runners & Their Friends. (Illus.). 288p. 1982. pap. 4.95 (ISBN 0-399-50580-6, Perige). Putnam Pub Group.

Ulman, Michael, tr. see Vakhtin, Boris.

Ulmer, L. The Bible That Wouldn't Burn. 1983. pap. 3.50 (ISBN 0-570-03634-8). Concordia.

Ulmer, Louis. What's the Matter with Job. (Arch Bks.: Set 11). (Illus.). 32p. (gr. 1-4). 1974. pap. 0.89 (ISBN 0-570-06080-X, 59-1200). Concordia.

Ulmer, Louise. Elijah & the Wicked Queen. (Arch Bks: NO. 13). (Illus.). 32p. (ps-4). 1976. pap. 0.89 (ISBN 0-570-06101-6, 59-1219). Concordia.

--Jesus' Twelve Disciples: Arch Bks. 1982. pap. 0.89 (ISBN 0-570-06160-1, 59-1307). Concordia.

--The Man Who Learned to Give. (Arch Book Series Fourteen). (gr. k-2). 1977. pap. 0.89 (ISBN 0-570-06109-1, 59-1227). Concordia.

--The Son Who Said He Wouldn't. (Arch Bks.: No. 18). 1981. pap. 0.89 (ISBN 0-570-06145-8, 59-1262). Concordia.

Ulmer, Louise & Meyer, Sheila. Theatrecraft for Church & School. LC 82-62453. (Illus.). 75p. 1983. pap. text ed. write for info. (ISBN 0-916260-00-3). Meriwether Pub.

Ulmer, Lousie. A Teacher's Guide to Using Arch Books with Children. 1982. pap. 4.95 (ISBN 0-570-04065-5, 56-1369). Concordia.

Ulmer, Raymond A. On the Development of a Token Economy Mental Hospital Treatment Program. LC 75-37984. (Clinical Psychology Ser.). 1976. 17.95x o.s.i. (ISBN 0-470-01393-1). Halsted Pr.

Ulmsten, U., ed. Female Stress Incontinence. (Contributions to Gynecology & Obstetrics: Vol. 10). (Illus.). viii, 120p. 1983. pap. 57.50 (ISBN 3-8055-3665-8). S Karger.

Ulph, Owen. The Leather Throne. 400p. 1983. 16.00 (ISBN 0-9604402-7-5); ltd. signed ed. 45.00 (ISBN 0-9604402-8-3). Dream Garden.

Ulrich, Celeste. The Social Matrix of Physical Education. Nixon, John E., ed. LC 79-18190. 1980. Repr. of 1968 ed. lib. bdg. 18.25x (ISBN 0-313-22099-9, ULSM). Greenwood.

--To Seek & Find. 184p. 1977. text ed. 9.95x (ISBN 0-88314-196-5, 240-25860). AAHPERD.

Ulrich, Heinz. How to Prepare Your Own High Intensity Resume. newly rev. combined ed. 224p. 1983. 16.95 (ISBN 0-13-430603-1); pap. 7.95 (ISBN 0-13-430595-7). P-H.

Ulrich, Henri. Cycloaddition Reactions of Heterocumulenses. (Organic Chemistry Ser.: Vol. 9). 1967. 59.50 (ISBN 0-12-708250-6). Acad Pr.

Ulrich, Homer & Pisk, Paul A. History of Music & Musical Style. (Illus.). 1963. text ed. 21.95 (ISBN 0-15-537720-5, HC). HarBraceJ.

Ulrich, Laurel T. Good Wives: Image & Reality in the Lives of Women in Northern New England, 1650-1750. LC 81-18589. (Illus.). 1982. 17.50 (ISBN 0-394-51940-X). Knopf.

Ulrich, Roger E., et al. Control of Human Behavior, Vol. 1: Expanding the Behavioral Laboratory. 1966. pap. 9.95x o.p. (ISBN 0-673-05484-5). Scott F.

--Control of Human Behavior, Vol. 2: From Cure to Prevention. 1970. pap. 10.95x (ISBN 0-673-05965-0). Scott F.

--Control of Human Behavior, Vol. 3: Behavior Modification in Education. 1974. pap. 10.95x (ISBN 0-673-07621-0). Scott F.

Ulrich, William, jt. auth. see Lambert, Karel.

Ulseth, Shannon. Antique Children's Fashions. 126p. 1982. pap. 12.95 (ISBN 0-87588-192-0). Hobby Hse.

Ultan, Lloyd, ed. see Mead, Edna.

Ultan, Lloyd, et al. Devastation-Resurrection: The South Bronx. LC 79-54730. 1979. pap. 12.00 (ISBN 0-89062-139-X, Pub by Bronx Museum Arts). Pub Ctr Cult Res.

Ulyatt, Kenneth. North Against the Sioux. (Illus.). (gr. 3-5). 1978. pap. 1.50 o.p. (ISBN 0-14-030406-1, Puffin). Penguin.

--Outlaws. LC 77-10127. (Illus.). 128p. (gr. 4-8). 1978. 9.57i (ISBN 0-397-31773-5, JBL-J). Har-Row.

Uman, Martin A. Introduction to Plasma Physics. (Illus.). 1964. text ed. 18.50 o.p. (ISBN 0-07-065744-0, C). McGraw.

Uman, Myron F. Introduction to the Physics of Electronics. 1974. 32.95 (ISBN 0-13-492702-8). P-H.

Umbach, Arnold, jt. auth. see Peery, Rex.

Umbdenstock, Richard J. So You're on the Hospital Board! 1981. pap. 7.50 (ISBN 0-87258-351-1, AHA-196119). Am Hospital.

Umbers, I. G. CRT-TV Displays in the Control of Process Plant: A Review of Applications & Human Factors Design Criteria, 1976. 1981. 30.00x (ISBN 0-686-97052-7, Pub. by W Spring England). State Mutual Bk.

--A Review of Human Factors Data on Imput Devices used for Process Computer Communication, 1977. 1981. 40.00x (ISBN 0-686-97156-6, Pub. by W Spring England). State Mutual Bk.

Umbreit, John. Physical Disabilities & Health Conditions: An Introduction. 484p. 1983. text ed. 29.95 (ISBN 0-675-20045-8). Merrill.

Umeasiegbu, Rems N. Words Are Sweet: Igbo Stories & Storytelling. xv, 140p. 1982. pap. write for info. (ISBN 90-04-06794-9). E J Brill.

Umeasiegbu, Rems Nna. The Way We Lived. (African Writers Ser.). 1969. pap. text ed. 3.50x (ISBN 0-435-90061-7). Heinemann Ed.

Umezawa, H. Index of Antibiotics from Actinomycetes, Vol. II. 1466p. 1979. text ed. 99.95 (ISBN 0-8391-1347-1). Univ Park.

Umezawa, H., ed. Index of Antibiotics from Actinomycetes, Vol. I. (Illus.). 954p. 1967. text ed. 99.95 o.p. (ISBN 0-8391-0000-0). Univ Park.

Umezawa, H. & Hooper, I. R., eds. Aminoglycoside Antibiotics. (Handbook of Experimental Pharmacology Ser.: Vol. 62). (Illus.). 400p. 1982. 125.00 (ISBN 0-387-11532-3). Springer-Verlag.

Umezawa, Hamad, et al, eds. Bioactive Peptides Produced by Microorganisms. LC 78-11402. 1979. 59.95x o.s.i. (ISBN 0-470-26562-0). Halsted Pr.

Umezawa, Hamao, ed. see International Congress On Chemotherapy- 6th.

Umezsiva, H. & Matsujoto, H. Thermo Fields Dynamics & Condensed States. Date not set. 117.00 (ISBN 0-444-86361-3). Elsevier.

Umhoefer, Jim. Guide to Wisconsin's Parks, Forests, Recreation Areas, & Trails. LC 82-3608. (Illus.). 80p. (Orig.). 1982. pap. 7.95 (ISBN 0-942802-00-4). Northword.

Umland, Samuel J. Call of the Wild & White Fang Notes. 70p. (Orig.). 1982. pap. text ed. 2.50 (ISBN 0-8220-0279-5). Cliffs.

--Frankenstein Notes. 71p. (Orig.). 1982. pap. text ed. 2.50 (ISBN 0-8220-0498-4). Cliffs.

Umlas, Joel & Silvergleid, Arthur, eds. Transfusion for Patients with Selected Clinical Problems. 224p. 1982. 25.00 (ISBN 0-914404-76-8); non-members 27.00 (ISBN 0-686-83044-X). Am Assn Blood.

Umlas, Joel, jt. ed. see Berkman, Eugene.

Umlauf Lane, Hana, ed. World Almanac Book of Who. 352p. (Orig.). 1980. pap. 5.95 o.p. (ISBN 0-911818-11-1). World Almanac.

Umobuarie, David. Black Justice. (Three Crown Books Ser.). (Orig.). 1976. pap. 8.95x o.p. (ISBN 0-19-575232-5). Oxford U Pr.

Umstead, Douglas R. Ugo Foscolo. (World Authors Ser.). 15.95 (ISBN 0-8057-2320-X, Twayne). G K Hall.

Unada. Andrews Amazing Boxes. (See & Read Storybook Ser.). (Illus.). (gr. 1-3). 1971. PLB 4.49 o.p. (ISBN 0-399-60025-6). Putnam Pub Group.

Unada, G. Ricky's Boots. (See & Read Storybook Ser). (Illus.). (gr. 1-3). 1970. PLB 3.96 o.p. (ISBN 0-399-60534-7). Putnam Pub Group.

Unamuno, M. de see De Unamuno, M.

Unamuno, Miguel, et al. Dos Novelas Cortas. LC 61-14661. (Span). 1975. pap. 9.50x (ISBN 0-471-00597-5). Wiley.

Unamuno, Miguel de see De Unamuno, Miguel.

Unamuno, Miguel De see De Unamuno, Miguel.

Unanue, Emil, jt. auth. see Benacerraf, Baruj.

Unanue, Emil R. & Rosenthal, Alan S., eds. Macrophage Regulation of Immunity. LC 79-24609. 1980. 31.00 (ISBN 0-12-708550-5). Acad Pr.

Unbehaun, Laraine, et al. Principles of Biology Laboratory Manual. 222p. (Orig.). 1980. pap. text ed. 11.95x (ISBN 0-8087-2115-1). Burgess.

Undell. Study Guide to Accompany Marketing in an Age of Change. 298p. 1981. pap. text ed. 9.50x o.p. (ISBN 0-471-08183-3). Wiley.

Underdown, B., jt. auth. see Galutier, M. W.

Underdown, B., jt. auth. see Glautier, M. W.

Underhay, Ernest, jt. auth. see Hudson, Travis.

Underhill, Alice, ed. see Christ Episcopal Church.

Underhill, Evelyn. Abba. 96p. 1982. pap. 1.65 (ISBN 0-88028-020-4). Forward Movement.

--Mysticism. 1961. pap. 7.95 (ISBN 0-525-47073-5, 0772-230). Dutton.

--Mysticism. 1955. pap. 7.95 (ISBN 0-452-00575-2, F575, Mer). NAL.

--Mystics of the Church. 260p. 1975. 12.95 (ISBN 0-227-67820-6). Attic Pr.

--Practical Mysticism. 1960. pap. 4.75 (ISBN 0-525-47049-2, 0461-140). Dutton.

--Worship. LC 78-20499. 1980. Repr. of 1937 ed. 26.50 (ISBN 0-88355-874-2). Hyperion Conn.

Underhill, Frank P. Physiology of the Amino Acids. 1915. text ed. 32.50x. Elliots Bks.

Underhill, J. E. Wild Berries of the Pacific Northwest. (Illus.). 128p. 5.95 o.s.i. (ISBN 0-919654-06-1). Superior Pub.

Underhill, Lonnie E. The First Arizona Volunteer Infantry, 1865-1866. New ed. (Orig.). 1983. write for info. collector's edition (ISBN 0-933234-08-2); pap. write for info. (ISBN 0-933234-09-0). Roan Horse.

Underhill, Lonnie E., ed. Arizona Quarterly Illustrated, 1880-1881: A Reprint With Introduction & Index. New ed. Orig. Title: Arizona Quarterly Illustrated. (Orig.). 1983. pap. write for info. (ISBN 0-933234-06-6); write for info. collector's edition (ISBN 0-933234-07-4). Roan Horse.

--Index to the Tombstone, Arizona, Weekly Nugget. New ed. (Orig.). 1982. pap. 5.00 (ISBN 0-933234-10-4). Roan Horse.

--Tombstone, Arizona, 1880 Business & Professional Directory. LC 82-551. (Illus.). vi, 38p. (Orig.). pap. 20.00 (ISBN 0-933234-04-X); collector's ed. 45.00 (ISBN 0-933234-05-8). Roan Horse.

Underhill, Richard G., et al. Diagnosing Mathematical Difficulties. (Elementary Education Ser.: No. C22). 408p. 1980. text ed. 20.95 (ISBN 0-675-08195-5). Merrill.

Underhill, Robert. Turkish Grammar. LC 75-46535. 1976. text ed. 25.00x (ISBN 0-262-21006-1). MIT Pr.

Underhill, Robert G. Teaching Elementary School Mathematics. 2nd ed. (Elementary Education Ser.). 1977. text ed. 19.95 (ISBN 0-675-08541-1). Additional supplements may be obtained from publisher. Merrill.

--Teaching Elementary School Mathematics. 3rd ed. 1981. text ed. 19.95 (ISBN 0-675-09998-6). Additional supplements may be obtained from publisher. Merrill.

Underhill, Robert J. Methods of Teaching Elementary School Mathematics. new ed. (Elementary Education Ser). 224p. 1975. pap. text ed. 7.95x (ISBN 0-675-08780-5); media: audiocassettes & filmstrips o.s.i. 495.00 (ISBN 0-675-08781-3). Additional supplements may be obtained from publisher. Merrill.

Underhill, Roy. The Woodwright's Companion: Exploring Traditional Woodcraft. LC 82-20077. (Illus.). 225p. 1982. 19.95 (ISBN 0-8078-1540-3); pap. 12.95 (ISBN 0-8078-4095-5). U of NC Pr.

Underhill, Rueben L. From Cowhides to Golden Fleece: A Narrative of California, 1832-1858. (Illus.). 226p. Date not set. pap. cancelled (ISBN 0-934136-18-1). Western Tanager. Postponed.

Underhill, Ruth M. Autobiography of a Papago Woman. LC 37-22775. 1936. pap. 13.00 (ISBN 0-527-00545-2). Kraus Repr.

--The Navajos. LC 59-5996. (The Civilization of the American Indian Ser.: Vol. 43). (Illus.). 288p. 1983. pap. 9.95 (ISBN 0-8061-1816-4). U of Okla Pr.

--Red Man's America: A History of Indians in the United States. rev. ed. LC 79-171345. 398p. 1971. pap. 9.95 (ISBN 0-226-84165-0, P437, Phoen). U of Chicago Pr.

--Singing for Power: The Song Magic of the Papago Indians of Southern Arizona. (Library Reprint Ser.). 1977. 19.50x (ISBN 0-520-03310-8); pap. 2.95 (ISBN 0-520-03280-2). U of Cal Pr.

Underhill, Ruth M., et al. Rainhouse & Ocean: Speeches for the Papago Year. LC 79-66733. (Illus.). vi, 154p. 1979. pap. 12.95x (ISBN 0-89734-029-9). Mus Northern Ariz.

Underhill, Sandra L. & Woods, Susan L. Cardiac Nursing. (Illus.). 976p. 1982. text ed. 35.00 (ISBN 0-397-54275-5, Lippincott Nursing). Lippincott.

Underhill, W. Vance. Introduction to Analysis. LC 80-5584. 432p. 1980. pap. text ed. 14.00 (ISBN 0-8191-1205-4). U Pr of Amer.

Underkoffler, Milton. Introduction to Structured Programming with Pascal. 376p. 1983. pap. text ed. write for info. (ISBN 0-87150-394-8, 8040). Prindle.

Underwager, Ralph C. I Hurt Inside: A Christian Psychologist Helps You Understand & Overcome Feelings of Fear, Frustration, & Failure. LC 72-90265. (Study of Generations Paperbacks Ser). 104p. 1973. pap. 4.50 (ISBN 0-8066-1312-2); study guide 00.30 (10-3186). Augsburg.

Underwood, Arthur L., jt. auth. see Day, R. A., Jr.

Underwood, Barbara & Underwood, Betty. Hostage to Heaven. 1979. 10.95 o.p. (ISBN 0-517-53875-X, C N Potter Bks). Crown.

Underwood, Barbara A., ed. Nutrition Intervention Strategies in National Development. 394p. 1983. price not set (ISBN 0-12-709080-0). Acad Pr.

Underwood, Benton & Shaughnessy, John J. Experimentation in Psychology. LC 74-31157. 236p. 1975. text ed. 22.95 o.p. (ISBN 0-471-89636-5). Wiley.

Underwood, Benton J. Attributes of Memory. 1983. 21.95x (ISBN 0-673-15798-9). Scott F.

--Experimental Psychology. 2nd ed. (Illus.). 1966. 24.95 (ISBN 0-13-295113-4); wkbk. - problems in experimental design & influence 6.95 (ISBN 0-13-295147-9). P-H.

--Experimentation in Psychology. corrected ed. 244p. 1983. Repr. of 1975 ed. text ed. price not set (ISBN 0-89874-605-1). Krieger.

Underwood, Betty, jt. auth. see Underwood, Barbara.

Underwood, Bob A. Lunker! (Illus.). 1978. pap. 6.95 o.s.i. (ISBN 0-695-80922-9). Follett.

Underwood, C. G. Leif Garrett Scrapbook. j ed. (Illus.). 192p. (Orig.). 1980. pap. 2.50 o.p. (ISBN 0-523-41104-9). Pinnacle Bks.

Underwood, Camila K. Where to Go & What to Do in South Carolina. 1983. pap. 4.95 (ISBN 0-87844-049-6). Sandlapper Pub Co.

Underwood, Diane. Reflections in My River. 1980. 4.50 o.p. (ISBN 0-8062-1066-4). Carlton.

Underwood, E. J. Trace Elements in Human & Animal Nutrition. 4th ed. 1977. 59.50 (ISBN 0-12-709065-7). Acad Pr.

Underwood, Edna W. Famous Stories from Foreign Countries: Austrian, Armenian, Bohemian, Czech, Dutch, Finnish, Hungarian, Norwegian. pap. 3.00 (ISBN 0-8283-1433-0, IPL34, IPL). Branden.

Underwood, J. A., tr. see Segalen, Victor.

Underwood, Jane H. Human Variation & Human Microevolution. (Illus.). 1979. pap. 13.95 (ISBN 0-13-447573-9). P-H.

Underwood, John & Williams, Ted. Ted Williams Fishing "The Big Three". 192p. 1982. 15.95 (ISBN 0-671-24400-0). S&S.

Underwood, John, jt. auth. see Williams, Ted.

Underwood, John C. Literature & Insurgency. 1914. 15.00x (ISBN 0-8196-0160-8). Biblo.

Underwood, John W. Acrobats in the Sky: Aerobatics Since 1913. 1972. pap. 7.95 (ISBN 0-911834-08-7, Pub. by Collinwood). Aviation.

--Stinsons: Air Pioneers & Aircraft. LC 69-17708. (Illus.). 1976. pap. 8.95 (ISBN 0-911834-06-0, Pub. by Collingwood). Aviation.

Underwood, Jon, ed. see Christie, Les.

Underwood, Jon, ed. see Staton, Knofel.

Underwood, Lamar, ed. Lamar Underwood's Bass Almanac. LC 79-3898. (Illus.). 1979. 15.95 o.p. (ISBN 0-385-15348-1, NLB); pap. 12.95 (ISBN 0-385-15349-X). Doubleday.

Underwood, Michael. The Hand of Fate. 196p. 1982. 10.95 (ISBN 0-312-35740-0). St Martin.

Underwood, Pat. Landscapes of Maderia. 2nd ed. 64p. (gr. 3-4). 1981. pap. 7.95 (ISBN 0-9506942-0-7). Bradt Ent.

Underwood, Ralph. Ask Me Another Riddle. LC 76-14690. (Elephant Books Ser). (Illus.). (gr. k-7). 1976. pap. 4.95 o.p. (ISBN 0-448-12689-3, G&D). Putnam Pub Group.

--Tell Me Another Joke. (Illus.). (gr. 4-6). 1964. 4.95 o.p. (ISBN 0-448-02578-7, G&D, 3231-7). Putnam Pub Group.

Underwood, Tim & Miller, Chuck, eds. Fear Itself: The Horror Fiction of Stephen King. 256p. 1982. 13.95 (ISBN 0-934438-59-5). Underwood-Miller.

Underwood, Virginia & Kett, Merriellyn. College Writing Skills. 2nd ed. 320p. 1981. pap. text ed. 12.95 (ISBN 0-675-08046-0); audio-cassettes 125.00 set (ISBN 0-675-08031-2). Additional supplements may be obtained from publisher. Merrill.

Underwood, Virginia, jt. auth. see Kett, Merriellyn.

UNDP-FAO Pelagic Fishery Investigation Project FIRS IND-75-038, 1977. Report of Acoustic Survey Along the Southwest of India, November 1976: Phase II, Progress Report. (Fisheries Papers: No. 6). 50p. 1977. pap. 7.50 (ISBN 0-686-93083-5, F1826, FAO). Unipub.

UNDP-FAO Seminar on Methodology of Planning Land & Water Development Projects, Bucharest, 1961. Planning Methodology Seminar: Report. (Irrigation & Drainage Papers: No. 11). 132p. 1972. pap. 9.00 (ISBN 0-686-92783-4, F980, FAO). Unipub.

Undset, Sigrid. Happy Times in Norway. Birkeland, Joran, tr. from Norwegian. LC 79-9997. (Illus.). 1979. Repr. of 1942 ed. lib. bdg. 20.75x (ISBN 0-313-21267-8, UNHT). Greenwood.

--The Master of Hestviken. 1978. pap. 9.95 (ISBN 0-452-25383-7, Z5383, Plume). NAL.

Unell, Barbara. Kansas City Kids Catalog. 96p. (Orig.). (gr. 4 up). 1980. pap. 6.00 (ISBN 0-8309-0286-4). Ind Pr MO.

UNESCO. Human Rights, Comments & Interpretations: A Symposium. LC 72-9595. 287p. 1973. Repr. of 1949 ed. lib. bdg. 17.50x (ISBN 0-8371-6589-X, HRCI). Greenwood.

--Interrelations of Cultures: Their Contribution to International Understanding. LC 72-88956. (Illus.). 1971. Repr. of 1953 ed. lib. bdg. 16.25x (ISBN 0-8371-3153-7, UNCU). Greenwood.

--Paris Cumulative Index to English Translations, 1948-1968, 2 vols. 1973. lib. bdg. 410.00 (ISBN 0-8161-1042-5, Hall Library). G K Hall.

--Seven Hundred Science Experiments for Everyone. rev. ed. LC 64-10638. (Illus.). (gr. 5-9). 1958. 10.95a (ISBN 0-385-05275-8); PLB (ISBN 0-385-06354-7). Doubleday.

UNESCO General Conference, 17th, Paris, 1972. Records: Reports, Programme Commissions, Administrative Comission, Legal Committee, Vol. 2. 207p. (Orig.). 1974. pap. 9.75 (ISBN 92-3-101156-1, U533, UNESCO). Unipub.

UNESCO General Conference, 19th, 1976. Records: Vol. 2, Proceedings, 2 Pts. pap. 37.25 (ISBN 92-3-001620-9, U895, UNESCO). Unipub.

UNESCO General Conference, 20th, 1978. Records: Vol. 2, Reports. pap. 11.50 (ISBN 92-3-101756-X, U966, UNESCO). Unipub.

UNESCO Regional Conference of Ministers Responsible for Science & Technology Policy. Science, Technology & Government Policy: A Ministerial Conference for Europe & North America (Minespol II) (Science Policy Studies & Documents: No. 44). 183p. 1979. pap. 7.50 (ISBN 0-686-94186-1, U943, UNESCO). Unipub.

UNESCO-United Nations Educational, Scientific & Cultural Organization (Paris) Statistical Yearbook (UNESCO) 1981. 17th ed. LC 65-3517. 1280p. 1981. 104.00x o.p. (ISBN 92-3-001965-8). Intl Pubns Serv.

Ungar, Frederick, ed. Austria in Poetry & History. LC 82-40525. 450p. (Bilingual Volume). Date not set. 20.00 (ISBN 0-8044-2941-3). Ungar. Postponed.

Ungar, Peter C. Hematology. (Medical Examination Review Book: Vol. 32). 1982. 24.00 (ISBN 0-87488-148-X). Med Exam.

Ungaro, Dan, jt. auth. see Borba, Michele.

Ungaro, Peter C. Hematologic Diseases - New Directions in Therapy. 2nd ed. 1979. pap. 21.50 (ISBN 0-87488-682-1). Med Exam.

--Medical Examination Review: Hematology, Vol. 32. 2nd ed. 1982. pap. text ed. 24.00 (ISBN 0-87488-148-X). Med Exam.

Unger, A. L. The Totalitarian Party. LC 73-93786. (International Studies). 290p. 1974. 34.50 (ISBN 0-521-20427-5). Cambridge U Pr.

Unger, Carl. Cosmic Understanding. 1982. pap. 1.95 (ISBN 0-916786-62-5). St George Bk Serv.

--The Language of the Consciousness Soul. 1983. 25.00x (ISBN 0-916786-56-0); pap. 16.95 (ISBN 0-916786-57-9). St George Bk Serv.

--Life Forces from Anthroposophy. 1982. pap. 1.95 (ISBN 0-916786-63-3). St George Bk Serv.

--Steiner's Theosophy: Notes on the Book "Theosophy". 1982. Repr. 5.95 (ISBN 0-916786-64-1). St George Bk Serv.

Unger, David, tr. see Alexander, Vicente.

Unger, E. A. & Ahmed, Nasir. Computer Science Fundamentals: An Algorithmic Approach Via Structured Programming. 1979. text ed. 20.95 (ISBN 0-675-08301-X). Additional supplements may be obtained from publisher. Merrill.

Unger, Irwin. American History,Two (from 1865) (College Outline Ser.). pap. 4.95 o.p. (ISBN 0-671-08052-0). Monarch Pr.

Unger, J. H., ed. Lit Survey of Communications Satellite System & Technology. LC 75-39326. 1976. 23.95 (ISBN 0-87942-067-7). Inst Electrical.

Unger, Jim. Apart from a Little Dampness, Herman, How's Everything Else? LC 75-1664. (Alligator Bks). (Illus.). 96p. 1975. pap. 2.50 o.s.i. (ISBN 0-8362-0622-3). Andrews & McMeel.

Unger, Jonathan. Education Under Mao. (Studies of the East Asian Institute). 360p. 1982. 24.00x (ISBN 0-231-05298-7); pap. 12.50x (ISBN 0-231-05299-5). Columbia U Pr.

Unger, June D. & Shaffer, Katherine A. Ear, Nose & Throat Radiology. LC 74-113034. (Advanced Exercises in Diagnostic Radiology Ser.: Vol. 14). (Illus.). 174p. 1980. pap. text ed. 17.50x (ISBN 0-7216-8946-9). Saunders.

Unger, Leo, tr. see Hilbert, David.

Unger, Leonard. Eliot's Compound Ghost: Influence & Confluence. LC 81-47173. 140p. 1982. 12.95x (ISBN 0-271-00292-1). Pa St U Pr.

Unger, Merrill. Unger's Bible Dictionary (Thumb Indexed Edition) 1961. 28.95 (ISBN 0-8024-9036-0). Moody.

Unger, Merrill F. Archaeology & the New Testament. (Illus.). 1962. 13.95 (ISBN 0-310-33380-6). Zondervan.

--The Baptism & Gifts of the Holy Spirit. LC 74-2931. 192p. 1974. pap. text ed. 5.95 (ISBN 0-8024-0467-7). Moody.

--Demons in the World Today. pap. 5.95 (ISBN 0-8423-0661-7). Tyndale.

--Manual Biblico de Unger: Unger's Bible Handbook. 960p. 1975. 11.95 (ISBN 0-8024-5244-2). Moody.

--Unger's Bible Commentary: Genesis-Song of Solomon, Vol. 1. 360p. 1981. text ed. 21.95 (ISBN 0-8024-9028-X). Moody.

--Unger's Bible Handbook. LC 66-16224. 1966. 9.95 (ISBN 0-8024-9039-5). Moody.

--Unger's Commentary on the Old Testament: Vol. 2 (Isaiah-Malachi) LC 81-2542. 1000p. 1982. 21.95 (ISBN 0-8024-9029-8). Moody.

Unger, Peter. Ignorance. 1975. pap. 9.50x (ISBN 0-19-824417-7). Oxford U Pr.

Unger, Rhoda K. & Denmark, Florence L. Woman: Dependent or Independent Variable? LC 75-765161. 848p. 1975. 29.95 (ISBN 0-88437-000-3). Psych Dimensions.

Unger, Stephen H. Asynchronous Sequential Switching Circuits. LC 70-88320. 290p. 1969. 17.50 o.p. (ISBN 0-471-89632-2). Krieger.

Unger, Steven, ed. The Destruction of American Indian Families. LC 76-24533. 1977. pap. 4.25 (ISBN 0-686-24119-3). Assn Am Indian.

Ungerer, Tomi. One, Two, Where's My Shoe. LC 64-12811. (Illus.). (gr. k-1). 1964. PLB 10.89 (ISBN 0-06-026241-9, HarpJ). Har-Row.

Unger-Hamilton, Clive. Keyboard Instruments. (Illus.). 128p. 1981. 19.95 (ISBN 0-89893-505-9); pap. 10.95 (ISBN 0-89893-303-X). CDP.

Ungers, O. M. Architecture as Theme. LC 82-60199. (Illus.). 128p. 1982. pap. 25.00 (ISBN 0-8478-5363-2). Rizzoli Intl.

Ungerson, Clare & Karn, Valerie, eds. The Consumer Experience of Housing. 224p. 1980. text ed. 44.50x (ISBN 0-566-00359-7). Gower Pub Ltd.

Ungnad, Arthur. Babylonian Letters of the Hammurabi Period. (Publications of the Babylonian Section: Vol. 7). (Illus.). 50p. 1915. soft bound 7.00x (ISBN 0-686-11921-5). Univ Mus of U PA.

Ungnade, Herbert E. Guide to the New Mexico Mountains. enl. & rev. 2nd ed. LC 72-80752. (Illus.). 235p. 1972. 7.50 o.p. (ISBN 0-8263-0241-6); pap. 6.95 (ISBN 0-8263-0242-4). U of NM Pr.

Ungson, Gerardo R. & Braunstein, Daniel N. Decision Making: An Interdisciplinary Inquiry. 400p. 1982. text ed. 29.95x (ISBN 0-534-01161-6). Kent Pub Co.

Unibook Staff. Mexico: The Macmillan Concise Illustrated Encyclopedia. Rubio, Pascal O., 3rd, ed. (Illus.). 416p. 1981. cancelled o.p. (ISBN 0-02-620910-1). Macmillan.

Union for Radical Political Enconomics (URPE), ed. Crisis in the Public Sector: A Reader. LC 80-8936. 1981. pap. 7.50 (ISBN 0-85345-575-9, PB5759). Monthly Rev.

Union for Radical Political Science. Reading Lists in Radical Social Science. LC 81-86025. 360p. (Orig.). 1982. pap. 10.00 (ISBN 0-85345-616-X, PB616X). Monthly Rev.

Union of International Organizations, ed. Annual International Congress Calendar, 1982. 22nd ed. LC 60-1648. (Orig.). 1982. pap. 47.50x (ISBN 0-686-83039-3). Intl Pubns Serv.

Union Theological Seminary. Library. Alphabetical Arrangement of Main Entries from the Shelf List of the Union Theological Seminary Library, 10 Vols. 1960. Set. 1360.00 (ISBN 0-8161-0595-2, Hall Library). G K Hall.

Union Theological Seminary Library. Shelf List of the Union Theological Seminary Library (New York), 10 vols. 1960. Set. lib. bdg. 950.00 (ISBN 0-8161-0499-9, Hall Library). G K Hall.

Unispace International Round Table, New York, 8-10 March 1982. Alternative Space Futures & the Human Condition: Proceedings. Karnik, K., ed. 180p. 1982. 20.00 (ISBN 0-08-029969-5). Pergamon.

Unitas, John & Dintiman, George B. Improving Health & Performance in the Athlete. LC 79-12459. (Illus.). 1979. 9.95 o.p. (ISBN 0-13-452607-4). P-H.

United Business Service, ed. Successful Investing. rev. ed. 1983. pap. 14.95 (ISBN 0-671-46734-4). S&S.

United Business Services, ed. Successful Investing. 1979. 14.95 o.p. (ISBN 0-671-24604-6). S&S.

United Ministries in Education Health & Human Values Program, jt. auth. see Harron, Frank.

United Nations. Demographic Year Book 1980. 65.00 (ISBN 0-686-84891-8, E/F.81.XIII.1). UN.

--Demographic Yearbook, 1980. 32nd ed. LC 50-641. (Illus.). 973p. 1982. 65.00x (ISBN 0-8002-3062-0). Intl Pubns Serv.

--Disarmament: A Periodic Review by the United Nations, Vol. V, No. 1. 1982. 5.00 (ISBN 0-686-84895-0, E.82.IX.5). UN.

--Economic & Social Survey of Asia & the Pacific. new ed. 1980. pap. 11.00 (ISBN 0-686-84897-7, E.81.II.F.1). UN.

--Economic & Social Survey of Asia & the Pacific, 1977. 31st ed. LC 76-643956. (Illus.). 104p. (Orig.). 1982. pap. 8.00x (ISBN 0-8002-1057-3). Intl Pubns Serv.

--Economic Bulletin for Asia & the Pacific. Vol. 29, No. 2. pap. 11.00 (ISBN 0-685-20773-0, E.79.II.F.9); Vol. 30, No. 1. pap. 9.00 (ISBN 0-686-66557-0, E, 80.II.F.13); Vol. 30, No. 2. 8.00 (ISBN 0-686-86823-4, E, 81.II.F.5); Vol. 31, No. 1. 10.00 (E.81.II.F.12). UN.

--Economic Bulletin for Europe. Vol. 31. pap. 13.00 o.p. (ISBN 0-685-20774-9, E.80.II.E.2); Vol. 30, No. 1. pap. 10.00 o.p. (ISBN 0-686-66558-9, E.79.II.E.2 O.P.). Vol. 30, No.2 (E, 79, II, E, 10). Vol. 31 No. 2. 7.00 o.p. (ISBN 0-686-86824-2, E,80,II,E,3); Vol. 32. 5.00 o.p. (ISBN 0-686-91543-7, E,81,II,E,12); 9.00 o.p. (ISBN 0-686-96910-3). UN.

--Economic Survey of Europe. 1980. pap. 17.00 (ISBN 0-686-84901-9, E.81.II.E.1). UN.

--Economic Survey of Europe in 1979. 32nd ed. LC 48-10193. (Illus.). 227p. (Orig.). 1982. pap. 17.00x (ISBN 0-8002-1062-X). Intl Pubns Serv.

--Economic Survey of Latin America 1979. LC 50-3616. (Illus.). 534p. (Orig.). 1981. pap. 29.00x (ISBN 0-8002-1069-7). Intl Pubns Serv.

--How to Plan & Conduct Model U. N. Meetings. LC 75-14173. 1961. 7.50 o.p. (ISBN 0-379-00114-4). Oceana.

--Statistical Yearbook for Asia & the Pacific-Annuaire Statistique pour l'Asie et le Pacifique 1979. 12th ed. LC 76-641968. (Illus.). 536p. (Orig.). 1981. pap. 30.00x (ISBN 0-8002-1084-0). Intl Pubns Serv.

--Statistical Yearbook, 1979-1980. cloth 60.00 (ISBN 0-685-77573-9, E/F.81.XVII.1). UN.

--World Energy Supplies, 1973-1978. 20.00 o.p. (ISBN 0-685-20781-1, E.79.XVII.13). UN.

--Yearbook National Accounts Statistics, 1980, 3 vols. Set. 125.00 (ISBN 0-686-81292-1, E.82.XVII.6). UN.

--Yearbook of Industrial Statistics, 1979: Vol. 1-General Industrial Statistics. 13th ed. LC 76-646970. (Illus.). 603p. 1981. 45.00x (ISBN 0-8002-1140-5). Intl Pubns Serv.

--Yearbook of Industrial Statistics 1980. 14th ed. Incl. Vol. I. General Industrial Statistics. 613p. 45.00x (ISBN 0-8002-1142-1); Vol. II. Commodity Production Data, 1971-1980. 750p. 45.00x (ISBN 0-8002-1143-X). LC 76-646970. (Illus.). 1982. Intl Pubns Serv.

--Yearbook of National Accounts Statistics, 1979, 2 vols. 23rd ed. LC 58-3718. (Illus.). 1980. Set. 70.00x o.p. (ISBN 0-8002-1123-5). Intl Pubns Serv.

--Yearbook of National Accounts Statistics, 1980, 2 Vols. 24th ed. LC 58-3718. (Illus.). 2337p. 1982. Set. 125.00x (ISBN 0-8002-1124-3). Intl Pubns Serv.

--Yearbook of the United Nations 1979, Vol. 33. LC 47-7191. 1294p. 1982. 72.00x (ISBN 0-8002-3038-8). Intl Pubns Serv.

United Nations, ed. Analysis of Exploration & Mining Technology for Manganese Nodules, Vol. 2. (Seabed Minerals Ser.). 120p. 1983. 26.00x (ISBN 0-939144-06-9); lib. bdg. 34.95. Crane-Russak Co.

--Analysis of Processing Technology for Manganese Nodules, Vol. 3. (Seabed Minerals Ser.). 90p. 1983. 26.00x (ISBN 0-8448-1431-8). Crane-Russak Co.

--Assessment of Manganese Nodule Resources, Vol. 1. (Seabed Minerals Ser.). 120p. 1983. 26.00x (ISBN 0-8448-1428-8). Crane-Russak Co.

--Petroleum Exploration Strategies in Developing Countries. 300p. 1983. 33.00x (ISBN 0-8448-1434-2). Crane-Russak Co.

--Statistical Yearbook for Asia & the Pacific 1980: Annuaire Statistique Pour L'Asie et le Pacifique. 13th ed. LC 76-641968. 526p. (Orig.). 1981. pap. 33.00x (ISBN 0-8002-3008-6). Intl Pubns Serv.

--World Economic Survey, 1981-82. LC 48-1401. (Illus.). 97p. (Orig.). 1981. pap. 9.00x (ISBN 0-8002-1110-3). Intl Pubns Serv.

United Nations Asian & Pacific Development Inst., ed. Local Level Planning & Rural Development: Alternative Strategies. 409p. 1980. text ed. 21.50x (ISBN 0-391-02171-0, Pub. by Concept India). Humanities.

United Nations Assn. of the U.S.A. Issues Before the Thirty-Seventh General Assembly of the United Nations. Puchala, Donald J., ed. 168p. 1982. 17.95 (ISBN 0-669-06398-3). Lexington Bks.

United Nations Conference on New & Renewable Sources of Energy, Nairobi, 1981. Report. 126p. 1981. pap. 11.00 (ISBN 0-686-94412-7, UN81/1/24, UN). Unipub.

United Nations Conference on Technical Co-Operation Among Developing Countries. Report. pap. 5.50 (ISBN 0-686-94387-2, UN78/2A11, UN). Unipub.

United Nations Congress on the Prevention of Crime & the Treatment of Offenders, 5th. Report. pap. 7.00 (ISBN 0-686-94409-7, UN76/4/2, UN). Unipub.

United Nations Department of International Economic & Social Affairs, Ocean Economics & Technology Branch. Coastal Area Management & Development. 196p. 1982. 40.00 (ISBN 0-08-023393-7). Pergamon.

United Nations Economic & Social Council. Transport of Dangerous Goods. 2nd, rev. ed. LC 82-81841. (Illus.). 462p. 1982. loose-leaf 35.00 (ISBN 0-940394-04-9). INTEREG.

United Nations Economic Commission for Europe. Combined Production of Electric Power & Heat: Proceedings of a Seminar Organized by the Committee on Electric Power of the United Nations Economic Commission for Europe, Hamburg, FR Germany, 6-9 November 1978. LC 80-755. (Illus.). 150p. 1980. 34.00 (ISBN 0-08-025677-5). Pergamon.

United Nations Economic Commission for Europe, Geneva, Switzerland. Energy Modelling Studies & Conservation: Proceedings of a Seminar of the United Nations Economic Commission for Europe, Washington, D. C. 24-28 March 1980. (Illus.). 600p. 1982. 95.00 (ISBN 0-08-027416-1). Pergamon.

United Nations, Economic Commission for Latin America. Latin American Initialisms & Acronyms-Lista De Siglas Latinoamericanas: Document E-CN, 12-Lib. 3. LC 73-81473. 146p. 1973. Repr. of 1970 ed. 12.50x o.p. (ISBN 0-87917-035-2). Ethridge.

United Nations Economic Commission for Western Asia, Natural Resources, Science & Technology Division. Technology Transfer & Change in the Arab World: Proceedings of a Seminar, Beirut, Oct. 1977. Zahlan, A. B., ed. 1979. text ed. 77.00 (ISBN 0-08-022435-0). Pergamon.

United Nations Educational Scientific & Cultural Organization. Democracy in a World of Tensions: A Symposium. McKeon, Richard, ed. Repr. of 1951 ed. lib. bdg. 20.75x (ISBN 0-8371-2303-8, DEWT). Greenwood.

--International Directory of New & Renewable Energy Information Sources & 467p. 1983. pap. text ed. 35.00 (ISBN 0-89553-142-9). Am Solar Energy.

United Nations Educational, Scientific & Cultural Organization. UNESCO Yearbook on Peace & Conflict Studies, 1980. 384p. 1981. lib. bdg. 30.00 (ISBN 0-313-22922-8, UN80). Greenwood.

United Nations Educational, Scientific, & Cultural Organzation. Unesco Yearbook on Peace & Conflict Studies 1981. (United Nations Educational, Scientific & Cultural Organization Annuals Ser.). (Illus.). 576p. 1982. lib. bdg. 35.00 (ISBN 0-313-22923-6, UN81). Greenwood.

United Nations Educational, Scientific & Cultural Organization. World Directory of National Science Policy-Making Bodies: Vol. 2, Asia & Oceania. 1968. 9.50 (ISBN 92-3-000688-2, U721, UNESCO). Unipub.

United Nations Environment Programme. Biotechnology & Waste Treatment: Proceedings of a Workshop Sponsored by the United Nations Environment Programme Held at the University of Waterloo, Canada, 27-31 July, 1981. Moo-Young, M., ed. 84p. 1982. 35.00 (ISBN 0-08-028784-0). Pergamon.

United Nations Expert Group Meeting. Barrier Free Design. (Illus.). 40p. 1975. 5.00 (ISBN 0-686-94881-5). Rehab Intl.

United Nations-FAO Committee on Food Aid Policies & Programmes, 2nd Session, Rome, 1976. World Food Programme: Report. (FAO Development Documents: No. 34). 56p. 1976. pap. 7.50 (ISBN 0-686-93068-1, F1184, FAO). Unipub.

United Nations-FAO Committee on Food Aid Policies & Programmes, 7th Session, Rome, 1979. World Food Programme: Report. (FAO Development Documents: No. 63). 54p. 1979. pap. 7.50 o.p. (ISBN 0-686-93073-8, F1839, FAO). Unipub.

United Nations Institute for Training & Research. Alternative Strategies for Desert Development & Management: Proceedings of an International Conference, Sacramento California, June 1977, 4 pts. Incl. Vol. I. Energy & Minerals. 320p. 45.00 (ISBN 0-08-022402-4); Vol. II. Agriculture. 264p. 40.00 (ISBN 0-08-022403-2); Vol. III. Water. 504p. 70.00 (ISBN 0-08-022404-0); Vol. IV. Desert Management. 488p. 65.00 (ISBN 0-08-022405-9). LC 81-23433. (Environmental Sciences & Application Ser.: Vol. 3). 1576p. 1979. Set. 200.00 (ISBN 0-08-022401-6, G135). Pergamon.

United Nations Institute for Training & Research (UNITAR) Long Term Energy Resources, Vol. 1. 816p. 1981. text ed. 55.00 (ISBN 0-273-08531-X). Pitman Pub MA.

--Long Term Energy Resources, Vol. 2. 768p. 1981. text ed. 55.00 (ISBN 0-273-08532-8). Pitman Pub MA.

--Long Term Energy Resources, Vol. 3. 656p. 1981. text ed. 55.00 (ISBN 0-273-08533-6). Pitman Pub MA.

United Nations Library, Geneva, ed. League of Nations & United Nations Monthly List of Selected Articles - Cumulative, 1920-1970, 14 vols. Incl. Legal Questions, 2 vols (ISBN 0-379-14156-6); Political Questions, 6 vols (ISBN 0-379-14155-8); Economic Questions, 6 vols. 1974 (ISBN 0-379-14157-4). 65.00 ea., 50.00 ea. if bought in complete set (ISBN 0-379-14150-7). Oceana.

United Nations Regional Cartographic Conference for Asia & the Far East, 8th, Bangkok, 1977. Technical Papers (Map Supplement, Vol. 2. 1981. pap. 2.00 (ISBN 0-686-94261-2, UN81/1/6, UN). Unipub.

United Nations Water Conference. Report. pap. 8.50 (ISBN 0-686-94398-8, 77.II.A.12, UN). Unipub.

U. S. Arms Control & Disarmament Agency. World Military Expenditures & Arms Transfers, 1969-1978. LC 82-81820. 1982. write for info. (ISBN 0-89138-934-2, ICPSR 7964). ICPSR.

U. S. Army. Counter Sniper Guide. (Illus.). 28p. 1977. pap. 5.00 o.p. (ISBN 0-87364-069-1). Paladin Ent.

United States Army, Continental Army. General Orders of George Washington: Commander-in-Chief of the Army of Revolution Issued at Newburgh on the Hudson, 1782-1783. new ed. Boynton, Edward C., ed. LC 73-16354. (Illus.). 160p. 1974. Repr. of 1883 ed. 11.50 (ISBN 0-916346-04-8). Harbor Hill Bks.

U. S. Army Natick Laboratories. Glossary of Environmental Terms (Terrestrial) LC 73-2851. 149p. 1973. Repr. of 1968 ed. 34.00x (ISBN 0-8103-3277-9). Gale.

United States Atomic Energy Commission, ed. In the Matter of J. Robert Oppenheimer. 1971. 23.00x o.s.i. (ISBN 0-262-21003-7); pap. 9.95x (ISBN 0-262-71002-1). MIT Pr.

United States Atomic Energy Commission. Reactor Handbook, 2 vols. 2nd ed. Incl. Vol. 1. Materials. 1223p. 1960. 75.95 o.s.i. (ISBN 0-470-71082-9); Vol. 3, Pt. A. Physics. 313p. 1962. 38.50 o.s.i. (ISBN 0-470-71148-5); Vol. 3, Pt. B. Shielding. 287p. 1962. 33.95 o.s.i. (ISBN 0-470-71150-7). Pub. by Wiley-Interscience). Wiley.

United States Bureau of Labor Statistics. The Gift of Freedom: A Study of the Economic & Social Status of Wage Earners in the United States. LC 78-10339. (Illus.). 1978. Repr. of 1949 ed. lib. bdg. 17.50x (ISBN 0-313-20687-2, USGF). Greenwood.

--History of Wages in the United States from Colonial Times to 1928 with Supplement, 1929-1933. LC 67-13749. 1966. Repr. of 1934 ed. 44.00x (ISBN 0-8103-3363-5). Gale.

U. S. Bureau of Labor Statistics. Productivity: A Bibliography, November, 1957. Spatz, Laura, ed. LC 75-16611. 182p. 1975. Repr. of 1958 ed. lib. bdg. 17.00x (ISBN 0-8371-8255-7, SPPR). Greenwood.

U. S. Bureau of the Census. Catalogs of the Bureau of the Census Library: First Supplement, 5 vols. (Library Catalogs Bib.Guides). 1979. Set. lib. bdg. 595.00 (ISBN 0-8161-0296-1, Hall Library). G K Hall.

--Population & Manpower of China: An Annotated Bibliography. LC 68-55103. (Illus.). 1968. Repr. of 1958 ed. lib. bdg. 16.00x (ISBN 0-8371-0691-5, POMA). Greenwood.

U. S. Bureau of the Census (Washington, D.C.) Catalogs of the Bureau of the Census Library, 20 vols. 1976. Set. 1800.00 (ISBN 0-8161-0050-0, Hall Library). G K Hall.

U. S. Children's Bureau. Handbook for Recreation. rev. 1959 ed. LC 74-174126. (Children's Bureau Publication Ser.: No. 231). (Illus.). x, 148p. 1975. Repr. of 1960 ed. 31.00x (ISBN 0-8103-4001-1). Gale.

U. S. Commissioner of Education. Public Libraries in the United States of America: Their History, Condition & Management, 3 Vols. 1971. Repr. of 1876 ed. Set. 60.00x o.p. (ISBN 0-87471-738-8); Part 1 (in 2 Vols.: Vol. 1-525p., Vol. 2-662p.) 40.00x o.p. (ISBN 0-87471-012-X); Part 2 (vol. 3 Only-262p.) 20.00x o.p. (ISBN 0-87471-313-7). Rowman.

United States Congress House Committee on the Judiciary. The Antitrust Laws: A Basis for Economic Freedom. LC 78-11628. 1978. Repr. of 1959 ed. lib. bdg. 16.00x (ISBN 0-313-20693-7, USAN). Greenwood.

U. S. Congress, House Committee on Agriculture. Food Costs-Farm Prices: A Compilation or Information Relating to Agriculture. (Illus.). x, 114p. 1973. Repr. of 1970 ed. 30.00x (ISBN 0-8103-3278-7). Gale.

U. S. Congress - Joint Economic Committee. Economic Policy in Western Europe: Report on Conferences in Western Europe. LC 68-55109. (Illus.). 1968. Repr. of 1959 ed. lib. bdg. 20.00x (ISBN 0-8371-0709-1, EOPW). Greenwood.

U. S. Congress-Senate. Presidential Vetoes. LC 68-55111. (Illus.). 1968. Repr. of 1961 ed. lib. bdg. 18.00x (ISBN 0-8371-0703-2, PRVE). Greenwood.

U. S. Congress - Senate Committee on the Judiciary. Juvenile Delinquency: Treatment & Rehabilitation of Juvenile Drug Addicts. LC 68-55116. (Illus.). 1968. Repr. of 1957 ed. lib. bdg. 19.75x (ISBN 0-8371-2335-6, JUDT). Greenwood.

U. S. Congress - Senate Committee on Foreign Relations. Review of the United Nations Charter. LC 68-55114. (Illus.). 1968. lib. bdg. 19.00x (ISBN 0-8371-3170-7, UNNC). Greenwood.

U. S. Department of Agriculture. Climate & Man: Nineteen Forty-One Yearbook of Agriculture, House Document No. 27, 77th Congress, 1st Session. LC 74-6297. 1248p. 1975. Repr. of 1941 ed. 86.00x (ISBN 0-8103-4016-X). Gale.

--Common Weeds of the United States. 1970. pap. 7.50 (ISBN 0-486-20504-5). Dover.

United States Department of Agriculture. The World Food Situation: Prospects to 1985, 2 vols. 1976. 37.50 o.p. (ISBN 0-379-00573-5). Oceana.

U. S. Department of Commerce. Foreign Business Practices: Materials on Practical Aspects of Exporting, International Licensing & Investing. 1981. 50.00 (ISBN 0-686-37967-5). Info Gatekeepers.

U. S. Department of Energy. Solar Energy for Agriculture & Industrial Process Heat: Program Summary. 91p. 1979. pap. 14.95x o.s.i. (ISBN 0-930978-26-9, D-005). Solar Energy Info.

U. S. Department of Energy Experts. Energy & Land Use. (U. S. Energy Special Ser.). (Illus.). 312p. 1982. text ed. 25.00 (ISBN 0-686-97468-9). Abt Bks.

--Energy & Water Resources. (U. S. Energy Ser.). (Illus.). 464p. 1982. 25.00 (ISBN 0-89011-573-7). Abt Bks.

--Energy Technologies & the Environment. (U. S. Energy Ser.). (Illus.). 520p. 1982. 25.00 (ISBN 0-89011-578-8). Abt Bks.

U. S. Department of Health, Education & Welfare, Washington, D. C. Author-Title Catalog of the Department Library: First Supplement. Incl. Author-Title Catolog, 7 vols. lib. bdg. 735.00 (ISBN 0-8161-1109-X). 1973 (Hall Library). G K Hall.

U. S. Department of Health, Education & Welfare Washington D. C. Author-Title Catalog of the Department Library, 29 vols. 1965. Set. 2755.00 (ISBN 0-8161-0717-3, Hall Library). G K Hall.

U. S. Department of Health, Education and Welfare, Washington, D. C. Subject Catalog of the Department Library, 20 Vols. 1965. Set. 1800.00 (ISBN 0-8161-0234-1, Hall Library). G K Hall.

U. S. Department of Health, Education, & Welfare, Washington, D. C. Subject Catalog of the Department Library: First Supplement, 4 vols. 1973. Set. 420.00 (ISBN 0-8161-1109-X, Hall Library). G K Hall.

U. S. Department of Health, Education, & Welfare. Work in America: Report of a Special Task Force to the Secretary of Health, Education, & Welfare. 262p. 1973. pap. 4.95x (ISBN 0-262-58023-3). MIT Pr.

U. S. Department of Housing and Urban Development, Washington, D. C. Dictionary Catalog of the United States Department of Housing & Urban Development Library & Information Division, 19 vols. 1972. Set. lib. bdg. 1805.00 (ISBN 0-8161-1007-7, Hall Library). G K Hall.

--Dictionary Catalog of the United States Department of Housing & Urban Development Library & Information Division, First Supplement, 2 vols. 1974. Set. lib. bdg. 210.00 (ISBN 0-8161-1135-9, Hall Library). G K Hall.

U. S. Department of Housing & Urban Development in Cooperation with the U. S. Department of Energy. Passive Solar Homes. (Illus.). 284p. (Orig.). 1982. pap. 12.95 (ISBN 0-89696-161-3, An Everest House Book). Dodd.

U. S. Department of Labor. Washington D. C. Catalog of the United States Department of Labor Library (Washington, D.C., 38 vols. 1975. Set. lib. bdg. 3800.00 (ISBN 0-8161-1165-0, Hall Library). G K Hall.

U. S. Department Of State. United States Policy in the Middle East, September 1956-June 1957: Documents. LC 68-55122. (Illus.). 1968. Repr. of 1957 ed. lib. bdg. 20.75x (ISBN 0-8371-0707-5, USPM). Greenwood.

U. S. Department Of State - Office Of Public Affairs. Korea, Nineteen Forty-Five to Nineteen Forty-Eight: A Report on Political Development & Economic Resources with Selected Documents. LC 68-55125. (Illus.). 1968. Repr. of 1948 ed. lib. bdg. 15.50x (ISBN 0-8371-1731-3, KORE). Greenwood.

U. S. Department of the Interior - U. S. Geological Survey, Washington, D. C. Catalog of the United States Geological Survey Library, 25 vols. 1964. Set. lib. bdg. 2375.00 (ISBN 0-8161-0712-2, Hall Library). G K Hall.

U. S. Department of the Interior - U. S. Geological Survey, Washington D. C. Catalog of the United States Geological Survey Library - Supplement 1, 11 vols. 1972. Set. 1155.00 (ISBN 0-8161-0876-5, Hall Library). G K Hall.

U. S. Department of the Interior - U. S. Geological Survey, Washington, D. C. Catalog of the United States Geological Survey Library: 2nd Suppl, 4 vols. 1975. Set. lib. bdg. 420.00 (ISBN 0-8161-1031-X, Hall Library). G K Hall.

U. S. Department of the Interior, Washington, D. C. Catalog of the United States Geological Survey 3rd Suppl, 6 vols. 1976. lib. bdg. 630.00 (ISBN 0-8161-0051-9, Hall Library). G K Hall.

--Dictionary Catalog of the Department Library, 37 Vols. 1967. Set. 3515.00 (ISBN 0-8161-0715-7, Hall Library). G K Hall.

U. S. Department of the Interior Washington D.C. Dictionary Catalog of the Department Library, Fourth Suppl, 8 vols. 1975. Set. lib. bdg. 790.00 (ISBN 0-8161-0016-0, Hall Library). G K Hall.

U. S. Department of the Interior, Federal Water Pollution Control Administration, Committee on Water Quality Criteria, 1968. Facsimile of Section Three: Fish, Other Aquatic Life, & Wildlife - Report. (FAO Fisheries Technical Papers: No. 94). 113p. 1969. pap. 7.50 (ISBN 0-686-92755-9, F1744, FAO). Unipub.

U. S. Dept. of Agriculture. Vacation Homes & Cabins: Sixteen Complete Plans. (USDA Material Ser.). (Illus.). 1978. pap. 4.50 (ISBN 0-486-23631-5). Dover.

U. S. Dept of Agriculture Research Service Staff. Index-Catalogue of Medical & Veterinary Zoology, No. 24. 1983. Set. pap. text ed. 295.00x (ISBN 0-89774-051-3). Vol. 1 (ISBN 0-89774-052-1). Vol. 2 (ISBN 0-89774-053-X). Vol. 3 (ISBN 0-89774-054-8). Vol. 4 (ISBN 0-89774-055-6). Vol. 5 (ISBN 0-89774-056-4). Vol. 6A (ISBN 0-89774-057-2). Vol. 6B (ISBN 0-89774-058-0). Vol. 6C. (ISBN 0-89774-059-9); Vol. 7. (ISBN 0-89774-060-2) Oryx Pr.

U. S. Dept. of Commerce. A Basic Guide to Exporting. 1981. 50.00 (ISBN 0-686-37968-3). Info Gatekeepers.

U. S. Dept. of Energy & Institute of Real Estate Management. No-Cost Low-Cost Energy Conservation Measures for Multifamily Housing. Kirk, Nancye J., ed. (Illus.). 36p. (Orig.). 1981. pap. 6.95 (ISBN 0-912104-58-9). Inst Real Estate.

U. S. Dept. of Forestry. Encyclopedia of Wood. LC 77-7728. (Illus.). 384p. 1980. pap. 13.95 (ISBN 0-8069-8890-8). Sterling.

U. S. Dept of Justice, Bureau of Justice Statistics. Survey of Inmates of State Correctional Facilities, 1979. 1982. write for info. (ISBN 0-89138-941-5). ICPSR.

U. S. Dept. Of State. Catalog of Treaties, Eighteen Fourteen to Nineteen Eighteen. 716p. 1964. Repr. of 1919 ed. 50.00 (ISBN 0-379-00237-X). Oceana.

--Correspondence Concerning Claims Against Great Britain, 7 vols. LC 6-9813. 1976. Set. 313.00 (ISBN 0-527-91930-6). Kraus Repr.

U. S. Environmental Data Service. Weather Atlas of the United States. LC 74-11931. 1975. 56.00x (ISBN 0-8103-1048-1). Gale.

U. S. Federal Emergency Relief Administration & U.S. Works Progress Administration. Subject Index of Research Bulletins & Monographs Issued by Federal Emergency Relief Administration & Works Progress Administration, Division of Social Research. LC 75-45297. (U.S. Government Documents Program Ser.). (Illus.). 110p. 1976. Repr. of 1937 ed. lib. bdg. 15.75x (ISBN 0-8371-8716-8, USSP). Greenwood.

U. S. Federal Works Agency. Final Report on the WPA Program, 1935-1943. LC 75-35362. (U.S. Government Documents Program Ser.). 145p. 1976. Repr. of 1947 ed. lib. bdg. 17.25x (ISBN 0-8371-8600-5, USWP). Greenwood.

U. S. Forest Products Laboratory. Wood Engineering Handbook. LC 82-7610. 1982. 29.95 (ISBN 0-13-962449-X, Busn). P-H.

United States Geographic Board. Sixth Report of the United States Geographic Board: 1890-1932. LC 67-8571. 1967. Repr. of 1933 ed. 42.00x (ISBN 0-685-11676-X). Gale.

U. S. Geological Survey. Geology of Washington. (Reprint: No. 12). Repr. 0.50 (ISBN 0-686-36916-5). Geologic Pubns.

United States Immigration Commission. Dictionary of Races or Peoples. LC 68-30665. 1969. Repr. of 1911 ed. 30.00x (ISBN 0-8103-3364-3). Gale.

United States Institute of Inter-American Affairs. Paraguayan Rural Life, Survey of Food Problems, 1943-1945. Reh, Emma, et al, eds. LC 75-90733. (Illus.). 130p. 1975. Repr. of 1946 ed. lib. bdg. 17.25x (ISBN 0-8371-4047-1, PARL). Greenwood.

United States Library of Congress. Statistical Bulletins: An Annotated Bibliography of the General Statistical Bulletins of Major Political Subdivisions of the World. LC 78-9897. 1978. Repr. of 1954 ed. lib. bdg. 15.50x (ISBN 0-313-20677-5, CASB). Greenwood.

--Statistical Yearbooks: An Annotated Bibliography of the General Statistical Yearbooks of Major Political Subdivisions of the World. LC 78-10213. 1978. Repr. lib. bdg. 16.25x (ISBN 0-313-20676-7, CAST). Greenwood.

U. S. Library Of Congress - Census Library Project. Catalog of United States Census Publications, 1790-1945. LC 68-55126. (Illus.). 1968. Repr. of 1950 ed. lib. bdg. 17.50x (ISBN 0-8371-0714-8, USCP). Greenwood.

U. S. Library Of Congress - General Reference And Bibliography Division. Current National Bibliographies. LC 68-55128. (Illus.). 1968. Repr. of 1955 ed. lib. bdg. 16.00x (ISBN 0-8371-0716-4, CUNB). Greenwood.

--Guide to Soviet Bibliographies: A Selected List of References. LC 68-55130. (Illus.). 1968. Repr. of 1950 ed. lib. bdg. 16.00x (ISBN 0-8371-0717-2, GUSB). Greenwood.

U. S. Library Of Congress-General Reference & Bibliography Division. Iran: A Selected & Annotated Bibliography. LC 68-55131. (Illus.). 1968. Repr. of 1951 ed. lib. bdg. 15.50x (ISBN 0-8371-0718-0, IRSB). Greenwood.

U. S. Library of Congress, General Reference & Bibliography Division. Sixty American Poets, Eighteen Ninety-Six to Nineteen Forty-Four. rev. ed. LC 73-5993. xii, 155p. Repr. of 1954 ed. 30.00x (ISBN 0-8103-3365-1). Gale.

U. S. Library Of Congress - Legislative Reference Service. Trends in Economic Growth: A Comparison of the Western Powers & the Soviet Bloc. LC 69-10166. (Illus.). 1969. Repr. of 1955 ed. lib. bdg. 19.75x (ISBN 0-8371-0720-2, ULSB). Greenwood.

United States Library of Congress Map Division. Civil War Maps: An Annotated Lists of Maps & Atlases in Map Collections of Library of Congress. Stephenson, Richard W., compiled by. LC 78-14050. 1978. Repr. of 1961 ed. lib. bdg. 18.50x (ISBN 0-313-20683-X, STWM). Greenwood.

United States Library of Congress. Music Division. African Music: A Brief Annotated Bibliography. Thieme, Darius L., ed. LC 78-17849. 1978. Repr. of 1964 ed. lib. bdg. 18.50x (ISBN 0-313-20543-4, USAM). Greenwood.

U. S. Library Of Congress - Orientalia Division. Arabian Peninsula: A Selected, Annotated List of Periodicals, Books & Articles in English. LC 68-55135. (Illus.). 1968. Repr. of 1951 ed. lib. bdg. 17.50x (ISBN 0-8371-0943-4, ARPE). Greenwood.

--Southeast Asia: An Annotated Bibliography of Selected Reference Sources. LC 68-55136. (Illus.). 1968. Repr. of 1964 ed. lib. bdg. 19.25x (ISBN 0-8371-0712-1, SOEA). Greenwood.

U. S. Library Of Congress - Processing Department. British Manuscripts Project: A Checklist of the Microfilm Prepared in England & Wales for the American Council of Learned Societies 1941-1945. LC 68-55138. (Illus.). 1968. Repr. of 1955 ed. lib. bdg. 20.75x (ISBN 0-8371-0713-X, BRMP). Greenwood.

U. S. Library of Congress. Science Policy Reseach Division, 95th Congress, 1st Session 1977, et al. State Legislature Use of Information Technology. LC 78-18915. (House Document Ser.: No. 271). 1978. Repr. of 1977 ed. lib. bdg. 18.75x (ISBN 0-313-20519-1, CHSL). Greenwood.

U. S. National Committee on Rock Mechanics, 15th, South Dakota School of Mines & Technology, Sept. 1973 & American Society of Civil Engineers. Application of Rock Mechanics: Proceedings. Haskins, Earl R., Jr., ed. 672p. 1976. text ed. 27.00 o.p. (ISBN 0-87262-154-5). Am Soc Civil Eng.

U. S. National Congress of Applied Mechanics, 9th. Proceedings. 480p. 1982. 75.00 (H00228). ASME.

U. S. National Oceanic & Atmospheric Administration. The Complete Underwater Diving Manual. (Nautical Ser.). (Illus.). 1971. pap. 12.50 (ISBN 0-679-50826-0). McKay.

United States. Nautical Almanac Office & Gale Research Company. Sunrise & Sunset Tables for Key Cities & Weather Stations in the United States. LC 76-24796. 1977. 58.00x (ISBN 0-8103-0464-3). Gale.

U. S. Naval Institute. U. S. Naval Institute Cumulative Index Eighteen Seventy-Four to Nineteen Seventy-Seven. 384p. 1982. 18.95x (ISBN 0-87021-025-4). Naval Inst Pr.

U. S. Naval Photographic Interpretation Center. Antarctic Bibliography. LC 68-55142. (Illus.). 1968. Repr. of 1951 ed. lib. bdg. 20.50x (ISBN 0-8371-0723-7, ANBI). Greenwood.

U. S. Navy. Basic Electronics. (Illus.). 1962. pap. 8.50 (ISBN 0-486-21076-6). Dover.

U. S. Navy (Bureau of Naval Personnel) Basic Data Processing. (Illus.). 1963. pap. 3.00 o.p. (ISBN 0-486-20229-1). Dover.

U. S. Navy Bureau of Naval Personnel. Basic Machines & How They Work. LC 77-153739. 1971. lib. bdg. 11.50x (ISBN 0-88307-633-0). Gannon.

U. S. Office Of Business Economics. Personal Income by States Since 1929: A Supplement to the Survey of Current Business. Schwartz, Charles F. & Graham, Robert E., Jr., eds. Repr. of 1956 ed. lib. bdg. 20.75x (ISBN 0-8371-2492-1, PEIS). Greenwood.

U. S. Office Of Education. Accreditation in Higher Education. Blauch, Lloyd E., ed. Repr. of 1959 ed. lib. bdg. 19.00x (ISBN 0-8371-2277-5, ACHE). Greenwood.

--Bibliography of Research Studies in Education, Nineteen Twenty-Six to Nineteen Forty, 4 vols. LC 74-1124. 4801p. 1974. Repr. of 1928 ed. Set. 258.00x (ISBN 0-8103-0975-0). Gale.

U. S. Office of Personnel Management. Problems on the Job: A Supervisor's Guide to Coping. 1.50 (ISBN 0-89486-085-2). Hazelden.

United States Pharmacopeial Convention, Inc. Drug Information for the Health Care Provider, Vol. 1. 1982. 24.95 (ISBN 0-686-37168-2). USPC.

U. S. Post Office Department. Street Directory of the Principal Cities of the United States: Embracing Letter-Carrier Offices Established to April 30, 1908. 5th ed. LC 76-179692. 904p. Repr. of 1908 ed. 65.00x (ISBN 0-8103-3072-5). Gale.

U. S. Public Health Service. Air Pollution in Donora: An Analysis of the Extreme Effects of Smog. 1970. Repr. of 1949 ed. 21.00 o.p. (ISBN 0-08-022310-9). Pergamon.

U. S. Senate, Committee on the Judiciary, 89th Congress, 1st Session. Morgenthau Diary (China, 2 vols. in 1. LC 70-167844. (FDR & the Era of the New Deal Ser.). 1693p. 1974. Repr. of 1965 ed. Set. lib. bdg. 165.00 (ISBN 0-306-70332-7). Da Capo.

U. S. Specialty Group on Infrared Detectors. Infrared Detectors. Moss, T. S. & Wolfe, W. L., eds. 1976. text ed. write for info. (ISBN 0-08-020548-8). Pergamon.

United States Superintendent of Documents. Decennial Cumulative Index 1941-1950 to United States Government Publications Monthly Catalog, 2 Vols. LC 77-84611. 1972. Repr. of 1953 ed. 88.00x (ISBN 0-8103-3361-9). Gale.

U. S. Synchronized Swimming. U. S. Synchronized Swimming Rulebook, 1983. 125p. (Orig.). pap. 5.00 (ISBN 0-911543-00-7). US Synch Swim.

U. S. Tariff Commission. Postwar Developments in Japan's Foreign Trade. Repr. of 1958 ed. lib. bdg. 19.00x (ISBN 0-8371-2503-0, PODJ). Greenwood.

United States Trademark Association. Trademark Law Handbook: 1981-82. 1981-82. pap. 19.50 (ISBN 0-87632-402-2). Boardman.

U. S. War Department. Dictionary of Spoken Russian: Russian-English: English-Russian. 1959. pap. 8.95 (ISBN 0-486-20496-0). Dover.

--A Phrase & Sentence Dictionary of Spoken Spanish. LC 58-14487. 1958. lib. bdg. 13.50x (ISBN 0-88307-580-6). Gannon.

United States, 66th Congress, House of Representatives, 1st. Session. Case of Victor L. Berger of Wisconsin, 2 vols. LC 78-39129. (Civil Liberties in American History Ser). 1972. Repr. of 1920 ed. lib. bdg. 125.00 (ISBN 0-686-96699-6). Vol. 1 (ISBN 0-306-70465-X). Vol. 2 (ISBN 0-306-70466-8). Set. lib. bdg. 65.50 ea. vol. (ISBN 0-686-57599-7). Da Capo.

United Synagogue, jt. auth. see Silverman, Morris.

United Technical Publications Staff. Modern Guide to Digital Logic: Processors, Memories & Interfaces. LC 75-20846. 294p. 1976. 9.95 o.p. (ISBN 0-8306-6709-1); pap. 7.95 (ISBN 0-8306-5709-6, 709). TAB Bks.

Universal House of Justice. The Baha'i World: An International Record 1968-1973, Vol. XV. (Illus.). 1976. 19.50 o.s.i. (ISBN 0-85398-059-4, 233-015). Baha'i.

Universal House of Justice Staff. Baha'i Holy Places at the World Centre. LC 78-15959. 1968. 3.95 o.p. (ISBN 0-87743-066-7, 215-002). Baha'i.

Universal Training Systems Staff. How to Develop & Conduct Successful in-Company Training Program. 1972. 71.50 (ISBN 0-85013-037-9). Dartnell Corp.

Universite Laval,Centre d'Etudes Nordiques, Quebec. Bibliographie de la Peninsule du Quebec-Labrador, 2 Vols. Cooke, Alan & Caron, Fabien, eds. 1968. Set. 190.00 (ISBN 0-8161-0758-0, Hall Library). G K Hall.

University Aviation Association. Collegiate Aviation Directory: A Guide to College Level Aviation-Aerospace Study. Schukert, Michael A., ed. 128p. 1982. pap. text ed. 2.55 (ISBN 0-8403-2876-1). Kendall-Hunt.

University of Abidjan. Vocabulaire Essential de l'Enseignement Primaire, 2 vols. (Black Africa Ser.). 223p. (Fr.). 1974. Repr. of 1970 ed. lib. bdg. 75.50x o.p. (ISBN 0-8287-0844-4, 71-2001). Clearwater Pub.

University of Arizona Library, ed. The Arizona Index: A Subject Index to Periodical Articles About the State, 2 vols. 1978. lib. bdg. 170.00 (ISBN 0-8161-0090-X, Hall Library). G K Hall.

University of British Columbia, August 1981 & Caves, D. W. The Impact of Regulation & Ownership on Economic Efficiency - U. S. & Canadian Railroads: Proceedings. 57p. 1981. pap. 3.50 (ISBN 0-686-94051-2, Trans). Northwestern U Pr.

University Of California - Berkeley. Bancroft Library, Catalog of Printed Books, 22 Vols. 1964. Set. 1980.00 (ISBN 0-8161-0678-9, Hall Library). G K Hall.

--Bancroft Library, Catalog of Printed Books. First Suppl. 1969. 6 Vols. lib. bdg. 630.00 set (ISBN 0-8161-0837-4, Hall Library); Second Suppl. 1974, 6 Vols. lib. bdg. 720.00 (ISBN 0-8161-0853-6). G K Hall.

--Bancroft Library, Index to Printed Maps. 1964. lib. bdg. 60.00 (ISBN 0-8161-0704-1, Hall Library); First Suppl., 1975, 1 Vol. 105.00 (ISBN 0-8161-1172-3). G K Hall.

--Dictionary Catalog of the Giannini Foundation of Agricultural Economics Library, 12 vols. 1971. 1140.00 (ISBN 0-8161-0908-7, Hall Library). G K Hall.

--Dictionary Catalog of the Water Resources Center Archives, 5 vols. 1970. lib. bdg. 475.00 (ISBN 0-8161-0884-6, Hall Library); first suppl. (1971) 110.00 (ISBN 0-8161-0895-1); second suppl. (1972 110.00 (ISBN 0-8161-0983-4). G K Hall.

University of California, Berkeley. Dictionary Catalog of the Water Resources Center Archives, Fourth Suppl. 942p. 1975. lib. bdg. 110.00 (ISBN 0-8161-0002-0, Hall Library). G K Hall.

University of California - Berkeley. East Asiatic Library, 2 pts. Incl. Pt. 1. Author-Title Catalog, 13 vols. Set. lib. bdg. 1235.00 (ISBN 0-8161-0801-3); Pt. 2. Subject Catalog, 6 vols. Set. lib. bdg. 570.00 (ISBN 0-8161-0128-0). 1968 (Hall Library). G K Hall.

University of California, Berkeley. East Asiatic Library. Incl. Author Catalog, First Supplement, 2 Vols. 230.00 (ISBN 0-8161-0842-0); Subject Catalog, First Supplement, 2 vols. lib. bdg. 230.00 (ISBN 0-8161-0129-9). 1973. lib. bdg. 230.00 (ISBN 0-686-76995-3, Hall Library). G K Hall.

University of California, Berkeley Institute of Governmental Studies Library. Subject Catalog of the Institute of Governmental Studies Library, 26 Vols. 1970. Set. 2470.00 (ISBN 0-8161-0907-9, Hall Library). G K Hall.

University of California, Berkeley, Library. Guide to Special Collections. Phillips, Audrey E., ed. LC 73-9572. 1973. 11.00 o.p. (ISBN 0-8108-0657-6). Scarecrow.

University of California, Berkeley, Water Resources Center. Dictionary Catalog of the Water Resources Center Archives: Sixth Supplement, 2 vols. 1978. Set. lib. bdg. 250.00 (ISBN 0-8161-0244-9, Hall Library). G K Hall.

University of California, Davis, ed. Biomass Alcohol for California: a Potential for the 1980's: Proceedings. 52p. 1980. Repr. pap. 14.95x (ISBN 0-89934-059-8, B002). Solar Energy Info.

University of California - San Diego. Catalogs of the Scripps Institution of Oceanography Library, 4 pts. Incl. Pt. 1. Author-Title Catalog, 7 vols. 1970. Set. 640.00 (ISBN 0-8161-0860-9); Pt. 2. Subject Catalog, 2 vols. 1970. Set. 190.00 (ISBN 0-8161-0112-4); Pt. 3. Shelf List, 2 vols. 1970. Set. 175.00 (ISBN 0-8161-0113-2); Pt. 4. Shelf List of Documents, Reports & Translations Collection. 1970. 90.00 (ISBN 0-8161-0114-0). Hall Library). G K Hall.

--Catalogs of the Scripps Institution of Oceanography Library, First Supplement to Pt. 1, Author-Title Catalog, 3 vols. 1973. 315.00 (ISBN 0-8161-0897-8, Hall Library). G K Hall.

--Catalogs of the Scripps Institution of Oceanography Library, First Supplement to Pts. 2-4, Subject Catalog, Shelf List, Shelf List of Documents & Reports. 1974. 105.00 (ISBN 0-8161-1144-8, Hall Library). G K Hall.

University of Chicago. Catalog of the Oriental Institute Library, Supplement I, Vol. 1. 1977. lib. bdg. 105.00 (ISBN 0-8161-0067-5, Hall Library). G K Hall.

--Catalogs of the Far Eastern Library, 6 vols. 1973. Set. lib. bdg. 790.00 (ISBN 0-8161-1119-7, Hall Library). G K Hall.

University Of Colorado Department Of Philosophy. Readings on Fascism & National Socialism. LC 82-71819. 112p. (Orig.). 1952. pap. 4.95x (ISBN 0-8040-0259-2). Swallow.

University Of Edinburgh - Department Of Social Anthropology Staff. African Urbanization: A Bibliography. 2nd ed. (African Bibliography Ser., Ser. B: Special Subjects). 1972. 15.00x o.p. (ISBN 0-85302-038-8). Intl Pubns Serv.

University of Geneva. Archives Jean Piaget: Catalog of the Jean Piaget Archives. 1975. lib. bdg. 35.00 (ISBN 0-8161-1184-7, Hall Library). G K Hall.

University of Guelph. Biophysics Handbook I: Lab Manual. 208p. 1982. pap. text ed. 8.95 (ISBN 0-8403-2815-X). Kendall-Hunt.

University of Hawaii Ethnic Studies Oral History Project, ed. Uchinanchu: A History of Okinawans in Hawaii. 696p. 1982. 25.00 o.p. (ISBN 0-8248-0749-9, Ethnic Stud Oral Hist). UH Pr.

University of Hawaii, Honolulu. Sinclair Library: Dictionary Catalog of the Hawaiian Collection, 4 vols. 1963. Set. lib. bdg. 340.00 (ISBN 0-8161-0650-9, Hall Library). G K Hall.

University of Hawaii Music Project & Burton, Leon. Comprehensive Musicianship Through Classroom Music: Zone 2, Hawaii. (gr. 2-3). 1972. Bk. A. text ed. 5.32 o.p. (ISBN 0-201-00785-1, Sch Div); Bk. B. text ed. 7.12 (ISBN 0-201-00856-4); tchr's bk. for bk. A o.p. 12.52 (ISBN 0-201-00788-6); tchr's bk. for bk. B 12.52 (ISBN 0-201-00857-2). A-W.

University of Illinois at Urbana-Champaign - University Library. Catalog of the Rare Book Room, 11 vols. 1972. Set. 1090.00 (ISBN 0-8161-0938-9, Hall Library). G K Hall.

University of Illinois at Urbana-Champaign - Library. Mereness Calendar: Federal Documents on the Upper Mississippi Valley, 1780-1890, 13 vols. 1971. Set. 1470.00 (ISBN 0-8161-0915-X, Hall Library). G K Hall.

University of Illinois, Communications Library. Catalog of the Communications Library, 3 vols. 1975. Set. lib. bdg. 285.00 (ISBN 0-8161-1174-X, Hall Library). G K Hall.

University of London. Dictionary Catalogue of the London School of Hygiene & Tropical Medicine, 7 Vols. 1965. Set. lib. bdg. 590.00 (ISBN 0-8161-0703-3, Hall Library); serials catalogue. 35.00 (ISBN 0-8161-0182-5); 1st suppl. (1971) 105.00 (ISBN 0-8161-0821-8). G K Hall.

University of London, Institute of Education. Catalogue of the Comparative Education Library, 1st Suppl, 3 vols. 1974. Set. lib. bdg. 315.00 (ISBN 0-8161-0988-5, Hall Library). G K Hall.

--Catalogue of the Comparative Education Library. (Library Catalogs-Bib. Guides). 1971. lib. bdg. 550.00 six reels (ISBN 0-8161-0923-0, Hall Library). G K Hall.

University Of London-Institute Of Historical Research. Corrections & Additions to the Dictionary of National Biography Cumulated from the Bulletin of the Institute of Historical Research Covering the Years 1923-1963. 1966. lib. bdg. 75.00 (ISBN 0-8161-0723-8, Hall Library). G K Hall.

University Of London Library. Palaeography Collection, 2 Vols. 1968. Set. 160.00 (ISBN 0-8161-0789-0, Hall Library). G K Hall.

University of London - School of Oriental & African Studies. Library Catalogue of the School of Oriental & African Studies, 28 Vols. 1963. Set. 2560.00 (ISBN 0-8161-0635-5, Hall Library); First Suppl. 1968 16 Vols. 1680.00 (ISBN 0-8161-0734-3). G K Hall.

--Library Catalogue of the School of Oriental & African Studies: 2nd Supplement, 16 vols. 1973. Set. lib. bdg. 1680.00 (ISBN 0-8161-0841-2, Hall Library). G K Hall.

University of London - Warburg Institute. Catalog of the Warburg Institute Library, 12 Vols. 2nd rev. ed. 1967. Set. 990.00 (ISBN 0-8161-0744-0, Hall Library). G K Hall.

University of Michigan. Catalogs of the Asia Library, the University of Michigan, 25 vols. 1978. Set. 2350.00 (ISBN 0-8161-0096-9, Hall Library). G K Hall.

University of Michigan, Ann Arbor, William L. Clements Library. Author-Title & Chronological Catalogs of Americana, 1493-1860, in the William L. Clements Library, 7 vols. 1970. Set. 620.00 (ISBN 0-8161-0874-9, Hall Library). G K Hall.

University of Mid-America. A Distance Learning - Independent Study Course: Accounting. 5th ed. 1982. 12.95x (ISBN 0-07-065771-8); instr's. guide 2.50 (ISBN 0-07-065772-6). McGraw.

University of Missouri School of Journalism, jt. auth. see National Press Photographers Association.

University of Oregon. Didactics & Mathematics. 1978. 16.50 (ISBN 0-88488-088-5). Creative Pubns.

--Geometry & Visualization. 1978. 45.95 (ISBN 0-88488-091-5). Creative Pubns.

--Mathematics in Science & Society. 1978. 35.50 (ISBN 0-88488-092-3). Creative Pubns.

--Number Sense & Arithmetic Skills. 1978. 45.95 (ISBN 0-88488-089-3). Creative Pubns.

--Ratio, Proportion & Scaling. 1978. 35.95 (ISBN 0-88488-090-7). Creative Pubns.

--Statistics & Information Organization. (gr. 5-9). 1978. 45.95 (ISBN 0-88488-093-1). Creative Pubns.

University Of Pennsylvania. Catalog of the Edgar Fahs Smith Memorial Collection in the History of Chemistry. 1960. 85.00 (ISBN 0-8161-0522-7, Hall Library). G K Hall.

--Catalog of the Programmschriften Collection. 1961. 65.00 (ISBN 0-8161-0558-8, Hall Library). G K Hall.

University of Sheffield 8-9 April 1976 Conference. Hydraulic Cement Pastes, Their Structure & Properties: Proceedings. (Illus.). 1976. pap. 32.50x (ISBN 0-7210-1047-4). Scholium Intl.

University Of Singapore Library. Catalogue of the Singapore-Malaysia Collection. 1968. lib. bdg. 125.00 (ISBN 0-8161-0818-8, Hall Library). G K Hall.

University of Southampton Faculty Committee. Digest of World Shipping Law. LC 79-18789. 1979. looseleaf 85.00 (ISBN 0-379-10165-3). Oceana.

University of Southern California. Author-Title & Subject Catalogs of the Ethel Percy Andrus Gerontology Center, 2 vols. 1976. Set. lib. bdg. 190.00 (ISBN 0-8161-1095-6, Hall Library). G K Hall.

University of Tennessee. International Energy Symposium Series: World Energy Production & Productivity, Vol. I. 448p. 1981. Professional Ref. 28.50x (ISBN 0-88410-649-7). Ballinger Pub.

University of Texas, Austin. Catalog of the Latin American Collection of the University of Texas Library: Second Supplement, 3 vols. 1973. Set. lib. bdg. 325.00 (ISBN 0-8161-0979-6, Hall Library). G K Hall.

University of Texas Library, Austin. Catalog of the Latin American Collection of the University of Texas Library, First Supplement, 5 vols. 1971. 525.00 (ISBN 0-8161-0889-7, Hall Library). G K Hall.

University of Virginia Hospital Circle. The Monticello Cook Book. 1950. 5.50 (ISBN 0-685-47899-8). Dietz.

University of Wales Press. A Dictionary of the Welsh Language: Part 31. Bevan, G. A., ed. 63p. 1982. pap. text ed. 8.00 (ISBN 0-686-81869-5). Verry.

University of Western Ontario Philosophy Colloquim, 4th. Agent, Action, & Reason: Proceedings. Binkley, Robert, et al, eds. LC 71-151360. 1971. 17.50x o.p. (ISBN 0-8020-1732-0). U of Toronto Pr.

University of Wisconsin. Center for Health Sciences. Strategies to Promote Self-Management of Chronic Disease. LC 82-11533. 128p. 1982. pap. 14.00 (ISBN 0-87258-380-5, AHA-070150). Am Hospital.

University of Wisconsin, Madison. School of Pharmacy. Catalogs of the F. B. Power Pharmaceutical Library, 4 vols. 1976. Set. lib. bdg. 380.00 (ISBN 0-8161-0021-7, Hall Library). G K Hall.

University of Wurzburg, Library. Katalog der Sammlung Schoenlein Catalog of the Schonleiniana Collection. 1972. lib. bdg. 55.00 (ISBN 0-8161-1017-4, Hall Reference). G K Hall.

Unkelbach, Kurt. Best of Breeds Guide: For Young Dog Lovers. LC 77-13346. (Illus.). (gr. 6-12). 1978. 7.95 (ISBN 0-399-20622-1). Putnam Pub Group.

--Catnip: Selecting & Training Your Cat. (Illus.). (gr. 3-7). pap. 1.50 o.p. (ISBN 0-13-121178-1). P-H.

Unnevehr, Laurian, jt. auth. see Bovet, David.

Unnewehr, L. E. & Nasar, S. A. Electric Vehicle Technology. LC 81-21909. 232p. 1982. 44.95x o.p. (ISBN 0-471-08378-X, Pub. by Wiley-Interscience). Wiley.

Unnewehr, L. E., jt. auth. see Nasar, S. A.

Unnithan, T. K. & Singh, Y. Tradition of Nonviolence in East & West. 468p. 1973. text ed. 12.50x (ISBN 0-391-00309-7). Humanities.

Unno, Mitsuko, tr. see Gluck, Cellin & Takeda, Yasushi.

Unruh, David. Invisible Lives: Social Worlds of the Aged. (Sociological Observations Ser.: Vol. 14). (Illus.). 200p. 1982. 22.00 (ISBN 0-8039-1954-9); pap. 10.95 (ISBN 0-8039-1955-7). Sage.

Unruh, Glenys G. Responsive Curriculum Development: Theory & Action. LC 74-24476. (Illus.). 250p. 1975. 21.75x (ISBN 0-8211-2002-6); text ed. 19.50x (ISBN 0-685-51462-5). McCutchan.

Unschuld, Paul. Medical Ethics in Imperial China: A Study in Historical Anthropology. LC 78-80479. (Comparative Studies of Health Systems & Medical Care). 1979. 21.50x (ISBN 0-520-03543-7). U of Cal Pr.

Unseld, Charles T., jt. auth. see Farhar-Pilgrim, Barbara.

Unseld, D. W. German-English, English-German Medical Dictionary. rev. & enl. 8th ed. 1982. 35.00 (ISBN 3-8047-0661-4). Heinman.

Unseld, Dieter. Medical Dictionary of the English & German Languages: Medizinisches Worterbuch der Deutschen und Englischen Sprache. 8th ed. 593p. 1982. 30.00x (ISBN 0-686-43337-8). Intl Pubns Serv.

Unstead. See Inside a Castle. 1979. 9.40 (ISBN 0-531-09119-8). Watts.

Unstead, R. J. History of the Modern World. Incl. World War One. LC 72-92427 (ISBN 0-382-06091-1); The Twenties. LC 72-92427 (ISBN 0-382-06094-6); The Thirties. LC 72-92430 (ISBN 0-382-06095-4); World War Two. LC 72-92428 (ISBN 0-382-06093-8); Turn of the Century. LC 74-26174 (ISBN 0-382-06096-2); The Forties & Fifties. LC 74-31819 (ISBN 0-382-06097-0); The Sixties. LC 75-18048 (ISBN 0-382-06098-9). (Illus.). (gr. 4 up). 13.00 (ISBN 0-686-57850-3, Pub. by Macdonald Ed). Silver.

--A Pictorial History, 8 vols. Incl. Vol. 1. Invaded Island. LC 78-169914. 1972 (ISBN 0-382-06063-6); Vol. 2. Kings, Barons, & Serfs. LC 71-169915. 1972 (ISBN 0-382-06064-4); Vol. 3. Years of the Sword. LC 75-169916. 1972 (ISBN 0-382-06065-2); Vol. 4. Struggle for Power. LC 72-172430. 1972 (ISBN 0-382-06066-0); Vol. 5. Emerging Empire. LC 76-172431. 1972 (ISBN 0-382-06067-9); Vol. 6. Freedom & Revolution. LC 70-172432. 1972 (ISBN 0-382-06068-7); Vol. 7. Age of Machines. LC 73-172433. 1973 (ISBN 0-382-06069-5); Vol. 8. Incredible Century. LC 77-172434. 1975 (ISBN 0-382-06070-9). (Illus.). (gr. 4 up). 11.96 (ISBN 0-685-36802-5). Silver.

Unsworth. Effects of Gaseous Air Pollution in Agriculture & Horticulture. 1982. text ed. 89.95 (ISBN 0-686-37584-X). Butterworth.

Unsworth, Barry. The Rage of the Vulture. 443p. 1983. 15.95 (ISBN 0-395-32526-9). HM.

Unsworth, Walt. Walking & Climbing. (Local Search Ser). (Illus.). (gr. 6-11). 1977. 8.95 (ISBN 0-7100-8596-6). Routledge & Kegan.

Unterberger, Betty M. America's Siberian Expedition, 1918-1920: A Study of National Policy. LC 69-14128. 1969. Repr. of 1956 ed. lib. bdg. 15.75x (ISBN 0-8371-0726-1, UNSE). Greenwood.

Unterecker, John. Stone. LC 76-26078. 64p. 1977. pap. 3.95 (ISBN 0-8248-0492-9). UH Pr.

Unterecker, John, jt. ed. see Stewart, Frank.

Unterkoefler, Ernest L. & Harsanyi, Dr. Andrew, eds. Unity We Seek: A Statement by the Roman Catholic-Presbyterian-Reformed Consultation. (Orig.). 1977. pap. 4.95 (ISBN 0-8091-2027-5). Paulist Pr.

Unterman, Alan. The Wisdom of the Jewish Mystics. LC 76-7933. (The Wisdom Books). 1976. 6.50 o.s.i. (ISBN 0-8112-0624-6); pap. 2.45 o.s.i. (ISBN 0-8112-0625-4, NDP423). New Directions.

Untermann, Juergen & Brogyanyi, Bela, eds. Das Germanische & die Rekonstruktion der Indogermanischen Grundsprache: Akten des Freiburger Kolloquiums der Indogermanischen Gesellschaft, Freiburg, Februar, 1981. (Current Issues in Linguistics Theory: 22). 200p. 1983. 20.00 (ISBN 90-272-3515-5). Benjamins North Am.

Untermeyer, Jean S., tr. see Broch, Hermann.

Untermeyer, Louis. Pour toi. (Illus., Fr.). 1968. 1.95 o.p. (ISBN 0-88332-128-9, 4420). Larousse.

Untermeyer, Louis, ed. Love Sonnets. LC 73-85859. (Illus.). 48p. 1974. 3.95 o.p. (ISBN 0-517-51313-7, Harmony); pap. 2.50 o.p. (ISBN 0-517-51314-5). Crown.

--A Treasury of Great Poems. Incl. Vol. 1. Chaucer to Burns; Vol. 2. Wordsworth to Dylan Thomas. 1955-64. 2 vols. in 1 29.95 o.p. (ISBN 0-671-75010-0). S&S.

Untersee, Philip A., jt. auth. see Curtiss, Ellen T.

Unterweiser, P. M., jt. auth. see Hutchings, F. R.

Unterweiser, P. M., ed. Case Histories in Failure Analysis. 1979. 75.00 (ISBN 0-87170-078-6). ASM.

Unthoff, H. K., ed. Current Concept of Internal Fixation of Fractures. (Illus.). 460p. 1980. 59.00 (ISBN 0-387-09846-1). Springer-Verlag.

Untracht, Oppi. Jewelry Concepts & Technology. LC 80-2637. (Illus.). 864p. 1982. 60.00; 60.00 (ISBN 0-686-82900-X). Doubleday.

--Metal Techniques for Craftsmen. LC 65-16397. 1968. 29.95 (ISBN 0-385-03027-4). Doubleday.

Unus, Iabal & Beekun, Rifeek. A Management Guide for Islamic Associations. LC 82-70349. 175p. 1982. pap. 6.00 (ISBN 0-89259-026-2). Am Trust Pubns.

Unwin, David. Introductory Spatial Analysis. (Illus.). 1982. 27.00x (ISBN 0-416-72190-7); pap. 12.95x (ISBN 0-416-72200-8). Methuen Inc.

Unwin, Derick & McAleese, Ray, eds. The Encyclopaedia of Educational Media Communications & Technology. LC 78-26988. 1979. lib. bdg. 65.00x (ISBN 0-313-20921-9, UNE/). Greenwood.

Unwin, Raymond. Legacy of Raymond Unwin: A Human Pattern for Planning. Creese, Raymond, ed. 1967. 22.50x (ISBN 0-262-03022-5). MIT Pr.

U. O. H. Jung, ed. Reading: A Symposium. (Language Teaching Methodology Ser.). (Illus.). 96p. 1982. pap. 9.50 (ISBN 0-08-028614-3, S220); pap. 4.75 firm (ISBN 0-686-97497-2). Pergamon.

Upadhyay, V. S., jt. auth. see Vidyarthi, L. P.

Upadhyaya, G. S & Dube, R. K. Problems in Metallurgical Thermodynamics & Kinetics. LC 77-7376. 1977. text ed. 28.00 o.s.i. (ISBN 0-08-020865-7); pap. text ed. 14.50 (ISBN 0-08-020864-9). Pergamon.

Upchurch, Boyd. Slave Stealer. 1969. pap. 1.95 o.p. (ISBN 0-451-07879-9, J7879, Sig). NAL.

Upchurch, Michael. Jamboree. 166p. 1982. pap. 2.75 (ISBN 0-441-38219-3, Pub. by Charter Bks). Ace Bks.

Upcraft, M. Lee. Learning to Be a Resident Assistant: A Manual for Effective Participation in the Training Program. LC 82-48075. (Higher Education Ser.). 1982. pap. text ed. 10.95x (ISBN 0-87589-539-5). Jossey Bass.

--Residence Hall Assistants in College: A Guide to Selection, Training & Supervision. LC 82-48075. 1982. text ed. 19.95x (ISBN 0-87589-538-7). Jossey Bass.

Update Publicare Research Staff. Almost Free Cookbooks & Recipes Update: Notebook of Back Issues. 35p. 1983. pap. text ed. 8.00 (ISBN 0-686-38886-0). Update Pub Co.

--Barter Update: Notebook of Back Issues. 35p. 1983. pap. text ed. 8.00 (ISBN 0-686-38888-7). Update Pub Co.

--Boombusinesses U.S.A. Update: Notebook of Back Issues. 35p. 1983. 8.00 (ISBN 0-686-38889-5). Update Pub Co.

--Continuing Education Alternatives Update: Notebook of Back Issues. 35p. 1983. pap. text ed. 8.00 (ISBN 0-686-38892-5). Update Pub Co.

--Guide for the Unemployed Update: Notebook of Back Issues. 35p. 1983. pap. text ed. 8.00 (ISBN 0-686-38893-3). Update Pub Co.

--Recycling Update: Notebook of Back Issues. 35p. 1983. pap. text ed. 8.00 (ISBN 0-686-38894-1). Update Pub Co.

--Refunding Update: Notebook of Back Issues. 35p. 1983. pap. text ed. 8.00 (ISBN 0-686-38895-X). Update Pub Co.

--Self Employment Update: Notebook of Back Issues. 35p. 1983. pap. text ed. 8.00 (ISBN 0-686-38897-6). Update Pub Co.

--Telemarketing Update: Notebook of Back Issues. 35p. 1983. pap. text ed. 8.00 (ISBN 0-686-38921-2). Update Pub Co.

Update Publicare Staff. Small Press Update: Notebook of Back Issues. 35p. 1983. pap. text ed. 8.00 (ISBN 0-686-38898-4). Update Pub Co.

Update Publishing Staff. The Update Directory of Updating Newsletters. 25p. 1983. pap. text ed. 8.95 (ISBN 0-686-38859-3). Update Pub Co.

Updegraffe, Imelda & Updegraffe, Robert. Continents & Climates. (Turning Points Ser.). (Illus.). 24p. 1983. pap. 3.50 (ISBN 0-14-049188-0, Puffin). Penguin.

--Earthquakes & Volcanoes. (Turning Points Ser.). (Illus.). 24p. 1983. pap. 3.50 (ISBN 0-14-049190-2, Puffin). Penguin.

--Mountains & Valleys. (Turning Points Ser.). (Illus.). 24p. 1983. pap. 3.50 (ISBN 0-14-049189-9, Puffin). Penguin.

--Rivers & Lakes. (Turning Points Ser.). (Illus.). 24p. 1983. pap. 3.50 (ISBN 0-14-049192-9, Puffin). Penguin.

--Seas & Oceans. (Turning Points Ser.). (Illus.). 24p. 1983. pap. 3.50 (ISBN 0-14-049193-7, Puffin). Penguin.

--Weather. (Turning Points Ser.). (Illus.). 24p. 1983. pap. 3.50 (ISBN 0-14-049191-0, Puffin). Penguin.

Updegraffe, Robert, jt. auth. see Updegraffe, Imelda.

Updike, John. Bech: A Book. 1970. 13.95 (ISBN 0-394-41638-4). Knopf.

--Bech is Back. LC 82-161. (Illus.). 224p. 1982. 13.95 (ISBN 0-394-52806-9); Ltd. ed. 50.00 (ISBN 0-394-52849-2). Knopf.

--The Carpentered Hen. LC 81-48133. 112p. 1982. 11.50 (ISBN 0-394-52394-6). Knopf.

--The Chaste Planet. write for info. (ISBN 0-911381-00-7). Metacom Pr.

--Museums & Women & Other Stories. (Illus.). 1972. 15.00 (ISBN 0-394-48173-9). Knopf.

--Music School. 1966. 12.50 (ISBN 0-394-43727-6). Knopf.

--Rabbit Is Rich. LC 81-1287. 480p. 1981. ltd. ed. 40.00 o.p. (ISBN 0-394-52047-5); 13.95 o.p. (ISBN 0-394-52087-4). Knopf.

--Tossing & Turning. 1977. 11.50 (ISBN 0-394-41090-4). Knopf.

Updike, John, et al see Allen, W. S.

Upfield, Arthur. The Bone Is Pointed. LC 75-46003. (Crime Fiction Ser). 1976. Repr. of 1938 ed. lib. bdg. 17.50 o.s.i. (ISBN 0-8240-2395-1). Garland Pub.

Upfield, Arthur W. Death of a Lake. 192p. 1983. pap. 2.95 (ISBN 0-686-83690-1, ScribT). Scribner.

--The House of Cain. Farmer, Philip Jose, intro. by. (Illus.). 296p. 1983. Repr. of 1928 ed. 20.00x (ISBN 0-9609986-0-8). D McMillan.

--Murder Down Under. 304p. 1983. pap. 3.50 (ISBN 0-686-83687-1, ScribT). Scribner.

Upham, T. C. Life, Religious Opinions & Experience of Madame Guyon. 617p. 1961. Repr. of 1905 ed. 10.00 (ISBN 0-227-67521-5). Attic Pr.

Upham, Thomas. Abridgement of Mental Philosophy. LC 79-10925. (History of Psychology Ser.). 1979. Repr. of 1861 ed. lib. bdg. 60.00x (ISBN 0-8201-1331-X). Schol Facsimiles.

Upham, Thomas C. The Manual of Peace, Embracing 1. Evils & Remedies of War, 2. Suggestions on the Law of Nations, 3. Consideration of a Congress of Nations. LC 79-143433. (Peace Movement in America Ser). 408p. 1972. Repr. of 1836 ed. lib. bdg. 22.95x (ISBN 0-89198-086-5). Ozer.

Uphaus, Suzanne H. John Updike. LC 79-48076. (Literature & Life Ser.). 160p. 1980. 11.95 (ISBN 0-8044-2934-0); pap. 4.95 (ISBN 0-8044-6945-8). Ungar.

Uphof, J. C. Dictionary of Economic Plants. 2nd, rev. & enl. ed. 1968. 28.00 (ISBN 3-7682-0001-9). Lubrecht & Cramer.

Uphoff, Norman T., jt. auth. see Ilchman, Warren F.

Upledger, John & Vredevoogd, Jon. Craniosacral Therapy. (Illus.). 381p. 1983. 39.95 (ISBN 0-939616-01-7). Eastland.

Upp, Robert D., jt. auth. see Paust, Jordan L.

Uppal, J. S. India's Economic Problems. 1975. text ed. 19.95 (ISBN 0-07-096624-9, C). McGraw.

Uppal, J. S., jt. auth. see Pettengill, Robert B.

Uppal, J. S., ed. India's Economic Problems: An Analytical Approach. 2nd ed. LC 78-62033. 1979. 26.00x (ISBN 0-312-41409-9). St Martin.

Uppal, Jogindar S. Economic Development in South Asia. LC 76-28131. 1977. text ed. 18.95 (ISBN 0-312-23030-3); pap. text ed. 9.95 (ISBN 0-312-23065-6). St Martin.

Upshur, Carole. How to Set up a Non-Profit Organization. 252p. 1982. 18.95 (ISBN 0-13-433755-7); pap. 9.95 (ISBN 0-13-433748-4). P-H.

Upson, Norma S. The Bean Cookbook: Dry Legume Cookery. 132p. (Orig.). 1982. pap. 6.95 (ISBN 0-914718-72-X). Pacific Search.

Upton & Upton. Photography. 2nd ed. 1981. pap. text ed. 19.95 (ISBN 0-316-88747-1). Little.

Upton, Albert. Design for Thinking: A First Book in Semantics. rev. ed. LC 61-14653. (Illus.). xii, 240p. 1973. pap. text ed. 6.95x (ISBN 0-87015-207-6). Pacific Bks.

Upton, Emory. Armies of Asia & Europe. Repr. of 1878 ed. lib. bdg. 18.50x (ISBN 0-8371-0727-X, UPAA). Greenwood.

Upton, G., ed. Physical & Creative Activities for the Mentally Handicapped. LC 77-82519. (Illus.). 1979. 16.95 (ISBN 0-521-21778-4). Cambridge U Pr.

Upton, Graham J. The Analysis of Cross-Tabulated Data. LC 78-4210. (Probability & Mathematical Statistics: Applied Section Ser.). 1978. 49.95x (ISBN 0-471-99659-9, Pub. by Wiley-Interscience). Wiley.

Upton, John, tr. see Benitez, Fernando.

Upton, M. Agricultural Production Economics & Resource-Use. (Illus.). 1976. 45.00x o.p. (ISBN 0-19-859452-6). Oxford U Pr.

Upton, Mark. Dark Summer. LC 78-1044. 1979. 9.95 o.p. (ISBN 0-698-10957-0, Coward). Putnam Pub Group.

--The Dream Lover. LC 77-10107. 1978. 8.95 o.p. (ISBN 0-698-10855-8, Coward). Putnam Pub Group.

Upton, Martin. Farm Management in Africa: The Principles of Production & Planning. 1973. 47.50x o.p. (ISBN 0-19-215646-2). Oxford U Pr.

Upton, Robert. A Golden Fleecing. 256p. 1981. pap. 2.50 o.p. (ISBN 0-523-41535-4). Pinnacle Bks.

--A Golden Fleecing. LC 79-16585. 1979. 9.95 o.p. (ISBN 0-312-33730-2). St Martin.

--Who'd Want to Kill Old George? LC 76-44560. 1976. 7.95 o.p. (ISBN 0-399-11867-5). Putnam Pub Group.

Uquahart, Ian A., jt. auth. see Manaka, Yoshio.

Ural, Oktay. Construction of Lower-Cost Housing. LC 79-15561. (Practical Construction Guides Ser.). 1980. 35.95x (ISBN 0-471-89643-8, Pub. by Wiley-Interscience). Wiley.

Uranga, Raul R., jt. auth. see Pavlic, Breda.

Urbach, Reinhard. Arthur Schnitzler. Daviau, Donald, tr. LC 73-178165. (Literature and Life Ser.). (Illus.). 1973. 11.95 (ISBN 0-8044-2936-7). Ungar.

Urban, E. K., jt. ed. see Brown, L.

Urban, G. R., ed. Communist Reformation: Nationalism, Internationalism, & Change in the World Communist Movement. LC 79-5326. 1979. 25.00 (ISBN 0-312-15280-9). St Martin.

--Toynbee on Toynbee: A Conversation Between Arnold J. Toynbee & G. R. Urban. 1974. 14.95x (ISBN 0-19-501739-0). Oxford U Pr.

Urban, George. Hazards of Learning: A Symposium on the Crisis of the University. LC 76-3094. 316p. 1976. 21.00x (ISBN 0-87548-339-9). Open Court.

--Stalinism. LC 82-10759. 400p. 1982. 25.00x (ISBN 0-312-75515-5). St Martin.

Urban, Glen & Hauser, John R. Design & Marketing of New Products. (Illus.). 1980. 28.00 (ISBN 0-13-201269-3); text ed. 27.00 student ed. (ISBN 0-686-96832-8). P-H.

Urban, Hugh B., jt. auth. see Ford, Donald H.

Urban, Ivan & Philippe, Richard. A Stereotaxic Atlas of the New Zealand Rabbit's Brain. (Illus.). 92p. 1972. photocopy ed. spiral 11.75x (ISBN 0-398-02431-6). C C Thomas.

Urban, JoDeen A. Regional Instability & Expatriate Labor in the Persian Gulf. 1983. 9.50 (ISBN 0-8315-0186-3). Speller.

Urban, L., jt. auth. see Price, J.

Urban Land Institute. Parking Requirements for Shopping Centers. Incl. Summary Recommendations. 23p. pap. 17.50 (ISBN 0-87420-604-9, P32); Summary Recommendations & Research Study Report. LC 81-70789. 136p. pap. 30.00 (ISBN 0-87420-605-7, P33). (Illus.). 1982. pap. Urban Land.

Urban, Linwood P. & Walton, Douglas, eds. The Power of God: Readings on Omnipotence & Evil. 1979. text ed. 10.95x o.p. (ISBN 0-19-502201-7); pap. text ed. 7.95x (ISBN 0-19-502202-5). Oxford U Pr.

Urban, Michael E. The Ideology of Administration: American & Soviet Cases. LC 81-9035. 190p. 1982. 34.50x (ISBN 0-87395-556-0); pap. 10.95x (ISBN 0-87395-557-9). State U NY Pr.

Urban, Peter. Karate Dojo: Traditions & Tales of a Martial Art. LC 67-20952. 1967. 8.25 (ISBN 0-8048-0334-X). C E Tuttle.

Urban, Wayne J. Why Teachers Organized. 228p. 1982. 18.95 (ISBN 0-8143-1714-6). Wayne St U Pr.

Urban, William. The Livonian Crusade. LC 81-40365. (Illus.). 572p. (Orig.). 1981. lib. bdg. 30.50 (ISBN 0-8191-1683-1); pap. text ed. 19.75 (ISBN 0-8191-1684-X). U Pr of Amer.

--The Prussian Crusade. LC 80-5647. 469p. 1980. lib. bdg. 26.25 (ISBN 0-8191-1278-X); pap. text ed. 16.75 (ISBN 0-8191-1279-8). U Pr of Amer.

Urban, William L., jt. tr. see Smith, Jerry C.

Urbanick, Byron, jt. auth. see Helsel, Jay.

Urcia, Ingeborg. All About Rex Cats. (Illus.). 9.95 (ISBN 0-87666-858-9). TFH Pubns.

Urdang. Urdang Dictionary of Current Medical Terms. LC 80-22916. 455p. 1981. 19.95 (ISBN 0-471-05853-X, Pub. by Wiley Med). Wiley.

Urdang, Constance. Only the World. LC 82-20062. (Pitt Poetry Ser.). 1983. 10.95 (ISBN 0-8229-3477-9); pap. 4.95 (ISBN 0-8229-5349-8). U of Pittsburgh Pr.

Urdang, Elliott B., tr. see Caraion, Ion.

Urdang, Laurance, ed. Allusions, Cultural, Literary, Biblical, & Historical: A Thematic Dictionary. 1982. 48.00x (ISBN 0-8103-1124-0). Gale.

Urdang, Laurence. The Basic Book of Synonyms & Antonyms. 1978. pap. 2.75 (ISBN 0-451-11716-6, AE1716, Sig). NAL.

--Modifiers. 205p. 1982. 54.00x (ISBN 0-8103-1195-X). Gale.

--The World Almanac Dictionary of Dates. 320p. 1982. 8.95 (ISBN 0-911818-26-X). World Almanac.

Urdang, Laurence, ed. Dictionary of Advertising Terms. LC 76-45506. (Orig.). 1979. pap. text ed. 15.95 (ISBN 0-87251-042-5). Crain Bks.

--Suffixes: And Other Word-Final Elements of English. 320p. 1982. 54.00x (ISBN 0-8103-1123-2). Gale.

--Twentieth-Century American Nicknames. 398p. 1979. 21.00 (ISBN 0-8242-0642-8). Wilson.

--Verbatim: A Language Quarterly, 4 vols. 1100p. 1982. 20.00x ea. Gale.

Urdang, Laurence, jt. ed. see LaRoche, Nancy.

Urdang, Lawrence & Hoequist, Charles, Jr., eds. Ologies & Isms: A Thematic Dictionary. 2nd ed. 365p. 1981. 70.00x (ISBN 0-8103-1055-4). Gale.

Ure. Elizabethan & Jacobean Drama. 262p. 1982. 50.00x (ISBN 0-85323-142-7, Pub. by Liverpool Univ England). State Mutual Bk.

--Yeats & Anglo-Irish Literature. 216p. 1982. 50.00x (ISBN 0-85323-322-5, Pub. by Liverpool Univ England). State Mutual Bk.

Ure, A. M., jt. auth. see Ottaway, J. M.

Ure, Ian. Ure's Truly. 15.00x (ISBN 0-392-07485-0, SpS). Sportshelf.

Ure, Peter. Yeats the Playwright: A Commentary on Character & Design in the Major Plays. 1963. cased 16.00x o.p. (ISBN 0-7100-2351-0). Routledge & Kegan.

Ureta, Floreal, tr. see Maston, T. B.

URI Department of Ocean Engineering. Model-Predicted Tidal Current Charts, Long Island Sound to Buzzards Bay. (Marine Bulletin Ser.: No. 30). 28p. 1979. 2.00 (ISBN 0-938412-25-6, P771). URI Mas.

Uri, Noel D. Demensions of Energy Economics, Vol. 32. Altman, Edward I. & Walter, Ingo, eds. LC 1-81656. (Contemporary Studies in Economic & Financial Analysis). 275p. 1981. 45.00 (ISBN 0-89232-226-8). Jai Pr.

Uri, Pierre. North-South: Developing a New Relationship. (The Atlantic Papers: No. 75/6). 58p. (Orig.). 1976. pap. text ed. 4.75x (ISBN 0-686-83679-0). Allanheld.

Uribe, M. Tecnicas Modernas De Archivo. (Span). 1960. 8.95 o.p. (ISBN 0-07-066079-4, G). McGraw.

Urick, Kevin. Snow World. LC 82-51026. 477p. 1983. 16.95 (ISBN 0-917976-16-9). White Ewe.

Urick, R. J. Principles of Underwater Sound. 2nd ed. 1975. text ed. 45.75 (ISBN 0-07-066086-7, P&RB). McGraw.

Urick, Robert J. Principles of Underwater Sound. 3rd, rev. ed. (Illus.). 352p. 1983. 45.75 (ISBN 0-07-066087-5, P&RB). McGraw.

Uricoechea, Fernando. The Patrimonial Foundations of the Brazilian Bureaucratic State. 248p. 1980. 25.75x (ISBN 0-520-03853-3). U of Cal Pr.

Urioste, George L., ed. Hijos de Pariya Qaqa: La tradicion oral de Waru Chiri (Mitologia, ritual y costumbres) (Foreign & Comparative Studies Program, Latin American Ser.: No. 6). (Orig.). 1983. pap. write for info. (ISBN 0-915984-97-0). Syracuse U Foreign Comp.

Uris, Auren. Executive Interviewer's Deskbook. 210p. 1978. 59.95 (ISBN 0-87201-395-2). Gulf Pub.

--Mastering the Art of Dictation. 146p. (Orig.). 1980. pap. 9.95 (ISBN 0-87201-171-2). Gulf Pub.

Uris, Leon. Armageddon. LC 64-16837. 1964. 17.95 (ISBN 0-385-00356-0). Doubleday.

--Battle Cry. 1953. 9.95 o.p. (ISBN 0-399-10072-5). Putnam Pub Group.

--Exodus. LC 62-16691. 1958. 19.95 (ISBN 0-385-05082-8). Doubleday.

--Mila Eighteen. LC 61-9562. 14.95 (ISBN 0-385-02076-7). Doubleday.

--Q. B. Seven. LC 70-129894. 14.95 (ISBN 0-385-03452-0). Doubleday.

--Topaz. 1967. 9.95 o.p. (ISBN 0-07-066102-2, GB). McGraw.

--Trinity. LC 75-14844. 384p. 1976. 19.95 (ISBN 0-385-03458-X). Doubleday.

Urizar, Rodrigo E. & Largent, Jill A. Pediatric Nephrology. (New Directions in Therapy Ser.). 1982. text ed. 50.00 (ISBN 0-87488-846-8). Med Exam.

Urli, N. B. & Corbett, J. W., eds. Radiation Effects in Semiconductors 1976. (Conference Ser.: Vol. 31). (Illus.). 1977. lib. bdg. 42.00x cancelled o.p. (ISBN 0-85498-121-7). Am Inst Physics.

Urlin, Ethel L. Festivals, Holy Days & Saints Days. LC 70-89301. (Illus.). 1971. Repr. of 1915 ed. 40.00x (ISBN 0-8103-3745-2). Gale.

--Short History of Marriage: Marriage Rites, Customs, & Folklore in Many Countries in All Ages. LC 69-16071. 1969. Repr. of 1913 ed. 34.00x (ISBN 0-8103-3569-7). Gale.

Urmi-Koenig, K. Bluetentragende Spross-Systeme Einiger Chenopodiaceae. (No.63, Dissertationes Botanica). (Illus.). 240p. pap. text ed. 20.00x (ISBN 3-7682-1322-6). Lubrecht & Cramer.

Urmson, J. O. Philosophical Analysis: Its Development Between the Two World Wars. 1956. pap. 5.95x (ISBN 0-19-500277-6, OPB). Oxford U Pr.

Urofsky, Melvin I. Lows D. Brandeis & the Progressive Tradition. (Library of American Biography). 1980. pap. text ed. 5.95 (ISBN 0-316-88788-9). Little.

Urquhart, Fred & Gordon, Giles. Modern Scottish Short Stories. 224p. (Orig.). 1982. pap. 6.95 (ISBN 0-571-11953-0). Faber & Faber.

Urquhart, James. John Paul Jones: Bicentennial Salute & Souvenir from Great Britain. (Illus.). 140p. (Orig.). 1982. pap. 18.00x (ISBN 0-9507033-4-6). J Russell.

Urquhart, Jane M., jt. auth. see Engeln, Oscar Dedrich Von.

Urquhart, John. Wonders of Prophecy. pap. 4.75 (ISBN 0-87509-155-5). Chr Pubns.

Urquhart, Kenneth T., ed. see Foster, William L.

Urquhart, Lena M. Cold Snows of Carbonate. (Illus.). 1967. pap. 1.00x (ISBN 0-87315-004-X). Golden Bell.

Urquhart, Leonard C. Civil Engineering Handbook. 4th ed. 1959. 58.00 (ISBN 0-07-066148-0, P&RB). McGraw.

Urquhart, R. M. Scottish Burgh & County Heraldry. LC 72-12491. (Illus.). 272p. 1973. 41.00x (ISBN 0-8103-2005-3). Gale.

Urquidi, Marjory M., tr. see Cardoso, Fernando E. & Faletto, Enzo.

Urrets-Zavalia, A. Diabetic Retinopathy. 125p. 1977. 29.00x (ISBN 0-89352-003-9). Masson Pub.

Urrutia, Lawrence. Philip Guston Recent Work. (Illus.). 6p. 1971. 0.25x (ISBN 0-686-99827-8). La Jolla Mus Contemp Art.

--Projections: Antimaterialism. (Illus.). 20p. 1970. 5.00x (ISBN 0-686-99828-6). La Jolla Mus Contemp Art.

Urry, James, jt. ed. see Barwick, Diane.

Urry, John. The Anatomy of Capitalist Societies: The Economy, Civil Society & the State. (Contemporary Social Theory Ser.). 178p. 1981. pap. text ed. 32.50x (ISBN 0-333-29430-0, Pub. by Macmillan England); pap. text ed. 15.00x (ISBN 0-391-02255-5). Humanities.

--Reference Groups & the Theory of Revolution. (International Library of Sociology). 256p. 1973. 21.95x (ISBN 0-7100-7541-3). Routledge & Kegan.

--Reference Groups & the Theory of Revolution. (International Library of Sociology). 1978. pap. 7.95 (ISBN 0-7100-8899-X). Routledge & Kegan.

Urry, John, jt. auth. see Keat, Russell.

Ursin, Edmund, jt. auth. see Krier, James E.

Ursin, H. & Murison, R., eds. Biological & Physical Basis of Psychosomatic Disease: Based on Papers Presented at a Conference on Psychological Load & Stress in the Work Environment, Bergen, Norway, 1980. (Illus.). 304p. 1982. 60.00 (ISBN 0-08-029774-9). Pergamon.

Ursin, Michael J. Life in & Around the Freshwater Wetlands. LC 74-13632. (Apollo Eds.). (Illus.). 192p. 1975. pap. 2.95i (ISBN 0-8152-0378-0, A-378). T Y Crowell.

Ursus, Thomas O., jt. ed. see Von Heitlinger, E. I.

Urton, Gary. At the Crosswords of the Earth & the Sky: An Andean Cosmology. (Latin American Monograph Ser.: No. 55). (Illus.). 268p. 1981. text ed. 30.00x (ISBN 0-686-86815-3). U of Tex Pr.

Urushnizaki, I., jt. ed. see Aoki, T.

Urvater, Michele. Fine Fresh Food--Fast. LC 82-48679. (Illus.). 80p. 1983. 8.61i (ISBN 0-06-015170-6, HarpT). Har-Row.

--Fine Fresh Food-Fast. Atcheson, Richard, ed. LC 81-68836. (Great American Cooking Schools Ser.). (Illus.). 84p. 1981. pap. 6.95 (ISBN 0-941034-02-X). I Chalmers.

Urvater, Michele, jt. auth. see Liederman, David.

Urwick, L., jt. ed. see Fox, Elliot M.

Urwin, G. C., ed. Humorists of the Eighteenth Century. (gr. 9-12). 1969. 3.50 o.p. (ISBN 0-7195-1432-0). Transatlantic.

Urwin, George G., ed. Taste for Living: Young People in the Modern Novel. (gr. 9-12). text ed. 4.95x o.p. (ISBN 0-693-11717-6). Transatlantic.

Urwin, Gregory J. Custer Victorious: The Civil War Battles of General George Armstrong Custer. LC 81-65873. (Illus.). 312p. 1982. 29.50 (ISBN 0-8386-3113-4). Fairleigh Dickinson.

Ury, Marian, tr. Tales of Times Now Past: Sixty-Two Stories from a Medieval Japanese Collection. 1979. 10.95 (ISBN 0-520-03864-9). U of Cal Pr.

Ury, William, jt. auth. see Fisher, Roger.

U.S. Cartridge Company. U. S. Cartridge Company's Collection of Firearms. (Illus.). 6.00 (ISBN 0-87364-230-9). Paladin Pr.

U.S. Department of Agriculture. Handbook of the Nutritional Contents of Foods. LC 75-2616. (Illus.). 192p. 1975. pap. 5.50 (ISBN 0-486-21342-0). Dover.

U.S. Department of the Interior (Washington, D.C.) Biographical & Historical Index of American Indians & Persons Involved in Indian Affairs, 8 Vols. 1966. 820.00 (ISBN 0-8161-0716-5, Hall Library). G K Hall.

U.S. Department of Transportation Contract DOT-OS-60163, Feb. 29 - March 1, 1976 & Moses, Leon N. Regulatory Reform & the Federal Aviation Act of 1975: Report No. DOT-TST-76-59. 182p. 1976. pap. 1.50 (ISBN 0-686-94047-4, Trans). Northwestern U Pr.

US Dept. of War. Dog Team Transportation Basic Field Manual. facs. ed. (Shorey Lost Arts Ser.). 84p. Repr. of 1941 ed. pap. 6.95 (ISBN 0-8466-6048-2, SJU48). Shorey.

U.S. Senate Commiteee on Corporate Ownership. Structure of Corporate Concentration: A Staff Study, 2 Vols. LC 81-83840. (Corporate Ownership & Control in the United States: Congressional Investigation Ser.). 1981. Repr. of 1980 ed. lib. bdg. 32.00 per vol. (ISBN 0-89941-109-6). W S Hein.

U.S. Senate Committee on Corporate Ownership. Corporate Ownership & Control. LC 81-83885. (Corporate Ownership & Control in the United States: Congressional Investigation Ser.). 1981. Repr. of 1975 ed. Set. lib. bdg. 32.50 (ISBN 0-89941-109-6). W S Hein.

--Disclosure of Corporate Ownership: Corporate Ownership & Control in the United States. LC 81-83883. (Congressional Investigations Ser.). 1981. Repr. of 1974 ed. lib. bdg. 32.50 (ISBN 0-89941-109-6). W S Hein.

--Institutional Investors Common Stock Holdings & Voting Rights. LC 81-83884. (Corporate Ownership & Control in the United States: Congressional Investigation Ser.). 1981. lib. bdg. 32.50 (ISBN 0-89941-109-6). W S Hein.

U.S. Senate Committeeon Corporate Ownership. Institutional Investor Study Report of the Secruities & Exchange Commission, 5 Vols. & Supp. Vols. I, II, Summary Vol. LC 81-83839. (Corporate Ownership & Control in the United States: Congressional Investigation Ser.). 1981. Repr. of 1971 ed. Set. lib. bdg. 32.50 (ISBN 0-89941-109-6). W S Hein.

U.S. Works Progress Administration, jt. auth. see U. S. Federal Emergency Relief Administration.

Usami, T., jt. auth. see Lapwood, E. R.

Usborne, Richard. Dr. Sir Pelham Wodehouse Old Boy. (Wodehouse Monograph: No. 1). 34p. (Orig.). 1978. pap. 14.50 (ISBN 0-87008-100-4). Heineman.

Usborne, Richard, jt. auth. see Donaldson, Frances.

Uscinski, Barry J. The Elements of Wave Propagation in Random Media. (Illus.). 1977. text ed. 38.50x (ISBN 0-07-066650-4, C). McGraw.

Usdin & Kvetnansky. Catecholamines & Stress: Recent Advances. (Developments in Neuroscience Ser.: Vol. 8). 1980. 79.25 (ISBN 0-444-00402-5). Elsevier.

Usdin, E. Biochemistry of S Adenosylmethionine & Related Compounds. 1982. 195.00x (ISBN 0-686-42937-0, Pub. by Macmillan England). State Mutual Bk.

Usdin, E. & Weiner, N. Function & Regulation of Monoamine Enzymes: Basic & Clinical Aspects. 1982. 159.00x (ISBN 0-686-42941-9, Pub. by Macmillan England). State Mutual Bk.

Usdin, Earl & Bunney, William E. Neuroreceptors Basic & Clinical Aspects. LC 80-40962. 279p. 1981. 67.95x (ISBN 0-471-27876-9, Pub. by Wiley-Interscience). Wiley.

Usdin, Earl, ed. Neuropsychopharmacology of Monoamines & Their Regulatory Enzymes. LC 74-77231. (Advances in Biochemical Psychopharmacology Ser: Vol. 12). 530p. 1974. 45.50 (ISBN 0-911216-77-4). Raven.

Usdin, Earl, et al. Enzymes & Neurotransmitters in Mental Disease: Based on a Symposium Held at the Technion Faculty of Medicine, Haifa, Israel August 28-30 1979. LC 80-40130. 650p. 1980. text ed. 114.95x (ISBN 0-471-27791-6, Pub. by Wiley-Interscience). Wiley.

Usdin, Earl, et al, eds. Endorphins in Mental Health Research. Bunney, William E., Jr. (Illus.). 1979. text ed. 59.00x (ISBN 0-19-520110-8). Oxford U Pr.

Usdin, Gene & Lewis, Jerry M., eds. Psychiatry in General Medical Practice. (Illus.). 1979. text ed. 29.00 (ISBN 0-07-066670-9, HP). McGraw.

Usdin, Gene, jt. ed. see Lewis, Jerry M.

Uselding, Paul, ed. Research in Economic History, Vol. 1. 350p. (Orig.). 1976. lib. bdg. 45.00 (ISBN 0-89232-001-X). Jai Pr.

--Research in Economic History, Vol. 3. 378p. 1979. 40.00 (ISBN 0-89232-056-7). Jai Pr.

--Research in Economic History, Vol. 4. (Orig.). 1979. lib. bdg. 42.50 (ISBN 0-89232-080-X). Jai Pr.

--Research in Economic History, Vol. 5. (Orig.). 1980. lib. bdg. 42.50 (ISBN 0-89232-117-2). Jai Pr.

--Research in Economic History, Vol. 6. 325p. 1981. 42.50 (ISBN 0-89232-119-9). Jai Pr.

--Research in Economic History, Vol. 7. 350p. 1981. 47.50 (ISBN 0-89232-198-9). Jai Pr.

--Research in Economic History: An Annual Compilation of Research, Vol. 2. LC 76-13771. (Orig.). 1977. lib. bdg. 40.00 (ISBN 0-89232-036-2). Jai Pr.

Ushenko, Andrew P. Power & Events: An Essay on Dynamics in Philosophy. Repr. of 1946 ed. lib. bdg. 17.00x (ISBN 0-8371-1041-6, USPE). Greenwood.

Usher, Dan. The Price Mechanism & the Meaning of National Income Statistics. LC 79-11629. (Illus.). 1979. Repr. of 1968 ed. lib. bdg. 20.50x (ISBN 0-313-21466-2, USPR). Greenwood.

Usher, Don. Rich & Poor Countries: A Study in the Problems of Comparison of Real Incomes. (Institute of Economic Affairs, Eaton Papers Ser.: No. 9). (Orig.). pap. 1.95 o.p. (ISBN 0-255-69540-3); 2.50 o.p. Transatlantic.

Usher, Harlan. Retire, Quit, or Get Fired! But Live It Up! (Illus., Orig.). 1983. 13.95 (ISBN 0-937428-18-3); pap. 8.95 (ISBN 0-937428-17-5). Ell Ell Diversified.

Usher, Harlan & Ell Ell Diversified, Inc. How to Get a Job -- with "No Experience" or "Not Enough". 3rd ed. LC 81-3266. (Illus.). 128p. 1981. 10.95 (ISBN 0-937428-15-9); pap. 7.95 (ISBN 0-937428-14-0); pap. text ed. 6.95 o. p. (ISBN 0-937428-16-7). Ell Ell Diversified.

Usher, John. European Court Practice. (European Practice Books). 300p. 1983. lib. bdg. 50.00 (ISBN 0-379-20714-1). Oceana.

Usher, M. B. Biological Management & Conservation. 1973. 29.95x o.p. (ISBN 0-412-11330-9, Pub. by Chapman & Hall). Methuen Inc.

Usher, M. B. & Ocloo, J. K. The Natural Resistance of Eighty-Five West African Hardwood Timbers to Attack by Termites & Micro-Organisms. 1979. 35.00x (ISBN 0-85135-103-4, Pub. by Centre Overseas Research). State Mutual Bk.

Usher, Michael & Bormuth, Robert. Experiencing Life Through Mathematics, Vol. 2. (Illus.). (gr. 9-12). 1980. pap. text ed. 4.92x (ISBN 0-913688-20-7); tchr's ed. 8.00x (ISBN 0-913688-21-5). Pawnee Pub.

Usherwood, Stephen. The Great Enterprise: The History of the Spanish Armada. 192p. 1982. 39.00x (ISBN 0-7135-1309-8, Pub. by Bell & Hyman England). State Mutual Bk.

Usigli, Rodolfo. Corona de Sombra. Ballinger, Rex E., ed. (Illus.). (gr. 10-12). 1961. pap. text ed. 12.95 (ISBN 0-13-173146-7). P-H.

Usinger, Robert L. Life of Rivers & Streams. (Illus.). 1967. 14.95 (ISBN 0-07-066690-3, P&RB); pap. 3.95 subs. (ISBN 0-07-046008-6). McGraw.

Usinger, Robert L., jt. auth. see Storer, Tracy I.

Usinger, Robert L., ed. Aquatic Insects of California, with Keys to North American Genera & California Species. (Illus.). 1956. 38.50x (ISBN 0-520-01293-3). U of Cal Pr.

Uslan, Michael, ed. see Goldwater, John.

Uslander, Arlene S. Out of the Frying Pan, onto the Floor. LC 79-51204. 1979. 8.95 o.p. (ISBN 0-89696-065-X, An Everest House Book). Dodd.

Uslenghi, Piergiorgio. Nonlinear Electromagnetics. 1980. 34.50 (ISBN 0-12-709660-4). Acad Pr.

Uslenghi, Piergiorgio L., ed. Electromagnetic Scattering. 1978. 54.00 (ISBN 0-12-709650-7). Acad Pr.

Uspensky, Boris. A Poetics of Composition: The Structure of the Artist Text & Typology of a Compositional Form. Zavarin, Valentina & Wittig, Susan, trs. from Rus. 199p. 1983. 27.75x (ISBN 0-520-02309-9); pap. 7.95 (ISBN 0-520-02309-9, CAL 596). U of Cal Pr.

Uspensky, James V. Theory of Equations. (Illus.). 1958. pap. 4.95 (ISBN 0-07-066736-5, SP). McGraw.

Ussher, Arland. From a Dark Lantern: A Journal. Parisious, Roger N., et al, eds. 1978. text ed. 45.50x o.p. (ISBN 0-391-01594-X). Humanities.

USSR Ministry of Defense, ed. Whence the Threat to Peace. 2nd ed. (Illus.). 1982. pap. 1.95 (ISBN 0-8285-9077-X, Pub. by Military Pubs USSR). Imported Pubns.

USTA Education & Research Center. College Tennis Guide. 35p. 1982-83. 3.00 (ISBN 0-938822-22-5). USTA.

--Directory of Tennis Programs for Seniors. 19p. 1981. 1.00 (ISBN 0-938822-19-5). USTA.

--Directory of Tennis Programs for the Disabled. 40p. 1982. 2.00 (ISBN 0-938822-18-7). USTA.

--Financing Public Tennis Courts. Rev. ed. 88p. 1979. 2.50 (ISBN 0-938822-21-7). USTA.

Ustinov, D. F. Serving the Homeland & the Cause of Communism. (World Leaders Speeches & Writings Ser.). 96p. 1982. 30.00 (ISBN 0-08-028174-5). Pergamon.

Ustinov, Peter. My Russia. (Illus.). 224p. 1983. 19.45i (ISBN 0-316-89052-9). Little.

Uston, Ken. Ken Ustson's Home Video 1983. 1982. pap. 2.95 (ISBN 0-451-12010-8, AE2010, Sig). NAL.

--Million Dollar Blackjack. (Illus.). 330p. 1982. 18.95 (ISBN 0-914314-08-4). Lyle Stuart.

Uszler, J. Michael, jt. ed. see Greenfield, Larry D.

Uta-Renate Blumenthal. God & Atheism: A Philosophical Approach to the Problem of God. 1979. 19.95x (ISBN 0-8132-0549-2). Cath U Pr.

Uta-Renate Blumenthal, ed. Carolingian Essays: Andrew W. Mellon Lectures in Early Christian Studies. 1983. 24.95 (ISBN 0-8132-0579-4). Cath U Pr.

Utas, Bo. A Persian Sufi Poem: Vocabulary & Terminology. Concordance, Frequency Word-List, Statistical Survey, Arabic Loan-Words & Sufi-Religious Terminology in Tariq Ut-Tajqiq. (Scandinavian Institute of Asian Studies Monographs: No. 36). 1978. pap. text ed. 13.75x o.p. (ISBN 0-7007-0116-8). Humanities.

Utian, Wulf H., jt. ed. see Van Keep, Pieter A.

Utley, Joe R. Pathophysiology & Techniques of Cardiopulmonary Bypass, Vol. II. (Illus.). 274p. 1983. lib. bdg. price not set (ISBN 0-683-08502-6). Williams & Wilkins.

Utley, Joe R. & Ashleigh, E. A. Pathophysiology & Techniques of Cardiopulmonary Bypass, Vol. I. (Illus.). 216p. 1982. lib. bdg. 38.00 (ISBN 0-683-08501-8). Williams & Wilkins.

Utley, Jon B. The Inflation Survival Manual. 300p. Date not set. cancelled o.p. (ISBN 0-89803-042-0). Caroline Hse.

Utley, Robert M. Custer & the Great Controversy: The Origin & Development of a Legend. LC 62-19153. (Illus.). 8.95 (ISBN 0-87026-053-7). Westernlore.

--Frontier Regulars: The U. S. Army & the Indian, 1866-1891. LC 77-74430. (Wars of the United States Ser.). (Illus.). 476p. 1977. pap. 6.95x o.p. (ISBN 0-253-28150-4). Ind U Pr.

--Indian, Soldier & Settler. 85p. 1979. pap. 3.95 (ISBN 0-931056-01-2). Jefferson Natl.

Uttal, William R. An Autocorrelation Theory of Form Detection. LC 75-4911. 1975. 12.95x o.s.i. (ISBN 0-470-89654-X). Halsted Pr.

--Cellular Neurophysiology & Integration: An Interpretive Introduction. LC 75-4673. 1975. 14.95x o.s.i. (ISBN 0-470-89655-8). Halsted Pr.

--Visual Form Detection in Three Dimensional Space. (MacEachram Lectures). 160p. 1983. text ed. write for info. (ISBN 0-89859-289-5). L Erlbaum Assocs.

Utter, Ethel C. Parliamentary Law at a Glance. 1928. 4.95 (ISBN 0-8092-8891-5). Contemp Bks.

Utter, Robert P. Pearls & Pepper: (Hardy, DeFoe, Richardson) 1924. 14.50x (ISBN 0-686-51285-5). Elliots Bks.

Uttley, Alison. Stories for Christmas. Lines, Kathleen, ed. (Illus.). 128p. 1977. 10.95 o.p. (ISBN 0-571-11074-6). Faber & Faber.

--Stories for Christmas. Lines, Kathleen, selected by. (gr. k-3). 1982. pap. 2.95 (ISBN 0-14-031349-4, Puffin). Penguin.

--A Traveller in Time. (Illus.). 331p. (gr. 3-7). 1981. 8.95 (ISBN 0-571-06182-6). Faber & Faber.

Uttley, David. Marlborough in Colour. 64p. 1982. text ed. 13.75x (ISBN 0-86299-033-5, Pub. by Sutton England). Humanities.

Utton, Albert E., jt. auth. see Teclaff, Ludwik A.

Utton, Albert E. & Mead, Walter J., eds. U. S. Energy Policy: Errors of the Past, Proposals for the Future. 280p. prof ref 25.00x (ISBN 0-88410-085-5). Ballinger Pub.

Utton, Albert E. & Teclaff, Ludwik A., eds. Water in a Developing World: The Management of a Critical Resource. (Special Studies in Natural Resources & Energy Management). 1978. softcover 20.00 (ISBN 0-89158-050-6). Westview.

Utton, Albert E., jt. ed. see Teclaff, Ludwipk A.

Utton, Albert E., et al, eds. Natural Resources for a Democratic Society: Public Participation in Decision-Making. LC 76-15363. (Special Studies on Natural Resources Management Ser). 1976. pap. text ed. 10.50 o.p. (ISBN 0-89158-110-3); pap. text ed. 12.00 o.p. (ISBN 0-89158-110-3). Westview.

Utton, M. A. Diversification & Competition. LC 79-11664. (NIESR, Occasional Papers: No. 31). 1979. 21.95 (ISBN 0-521-22725-9). Cambridge U Pr.

--The Political Economy of Big Business. LC 82-10739. 272p. 1982. 32.50x (ISBN 0-312-62255-4). St Martin.

Utz. A Delightful Day with Bella Ballet. LC 75-190267. (Illus.). (gr. 2-3). 1972. PLB 6.75x (ISBN 0-87783-056-8); pap. 2.95x deluxe ed. (ISBN 0-87783-089-4). Oddo.

--The Houndstooth Check. LC 79-190268. (Illus.). (gr. 2-3). 1972. PLB 6.75x (ISBN 0-87783-057-6); pap. 2.95x deluxe ed. (ISBN 0-87783-095-9). Oddo.

--The King, the Queen, & the Lima Bean. LC 73-93020. (Illus.). (gr. k-3). 1974. PLB 6.75x (ISBN 0-87783-121-1); pap. 2.95x deluxe ed. (ISBN 0-87783-122-X). Oddo.

--The Simple Pink Bubble That Ended the Trouble with Jonathan Hubble. LC 78-190273. (gr. 2-3). 1972. PLB 6.75x (ISBN 0-87783-062-2); pap. 2.95x deluxe ed. (ISBN 0-87783-108-4). Oddo.

Utz, Peter. The Home Video Users Encyclopedia, 2 vols. (Illus.). 608p. 1983. 29.95 set (ISBN 0-13-394544-8); Vol. 1. pap. 16.95 (ISBN 0-13-394536-7); Vol. 2. pap. 9.95 (ISBN 0-13-394528-6). P-H.

--Video User's Handbook. rev. ed. LC 79-379. (Video Bookshelf Ser.). (Illus.). 410p. 1980. text ed. 24.95x (ISBN 0-914236-78-4). Knowledge Indus.

--Video User's Handbook. 2nd ed. (Illus.). 496p. 1982. 24.95 (ISBN 0-13-941880-6); pap. 14.95 (ISBN 0-13-941872-5). P-H.

--Video User's Handbook. 2nd ed. (Illus.). 1982. text ed. 24.95 (ISBN 0-13-941880-6, Spec); pap. 14.95 (ISBN 0-13-941872-5). P-H.

--Video User's Handbook. 2nd ed. (Illus.). 500p. 1982. 24.95 (ISBN 0-686-42869-2). Knowledge Indus.

Uusitalo, Liisa. Consumer Behavior & Environmental Quality. LC 82-10686. 156p. 1982. 25.00x (ISBN 0-312-16606-0). St Martin.

Uvarov, B. P. Grasshoppers & Locusts: A Handbook of General Acridology, 2 Vols. Vol. 1, 1966. 50.00x (ISBN 0-521-06669-7, Pub. by Centre Overseas Research); Vol. 2, 1977. 70.00x (ISBN 0-85135-072-0, Pub. by Centre Overseas Research). State Mutual Bk.

Uvarov, B. P. & Chapman, E. Observations on the Moroccan Locust (Dociostaurus Maroccanus Thunberg) in Cyprus, 1950. 1951. 35.00x (ISBN 0-85135-039-9, Pub. by Centre Overseas Research). State Mutual Bk.

Uvezian, Sonia. The Book of Salads. LC 77-23838. (Illus.). 1977. pap. 6.95 (ISBN 0-89286-126-6). One Hund One Prods.

--The Complete International Appetizer CookBook. LC 82-40015. 288p. 1983. 14.95 (ISBN 0-8128-2877-1). Stein & Day.

--The Complete International Sandwich Book. 284p. 1982. 17.95 (ISBN 0-686-38086-X). Stein & Day.

--Complete International Sandwich Cookbook. LC 80-5715. 288p. 1981. 17.95 (ISBN 0-8128-2787-2). Stein & Day.

Uwechue, Ralph. Know Africa, 3 Vols. Incl. Vol. 1. Africa Today; Vol. 3. Makers of Modern Africa; Vol. 3. Africa Who's Who. 3290p. 1981. 250.00 set (ISBN 0-686-42731-9, Pub. by Africa Journal Limited). Gale.

Uyanga, Joseph T. A Geography of Rural Development in Nigeria. LC 79-9601. 188p. 1980. pap. text ed. 9.75 (ISBN 0-8191-0956-8). U Pr of Amer.

Uyeda, S., jt. auth. see Sugimura, A.

Uyeda, S., jt. auth. see Toksoz, M. N.

Uyeda, S., et al, eds. Geodynamics of the Western Pacific. (Advances in Earth & Planetary Sciences Ser.: Pt. 6). 592p. 1980. 49.50x (ISBN 0-89955-315-X, Pub. by Japan Sci Soc Japan). Intl Schol Bk Serv.

Uyehara, Cecil H., ed. United States-Japan Technological Exchange Symposium: Sponsored by the Japan-American Society of Washington, 1981. LC 82-40064. 142p. (Orig.). 1982. PLB 19.00 (ISBN 0-8191-2423-0); pap. text ed. 8.25 (ISBN 0-8191-2424-9). U Pr of Amer.

Uyttenbroeck, Frans. Gynecologic Surgery: Treatment of Complications & Prevention of Injuries. LC 80-80968. 288p. 1980. 34.25x (ISBN 0-89352-088-8). Masson Pub.

Uzawa, Hirofumi, jt. ed. see Stiglitz, Joseph E.

Uzkan, T., ed. Flows in Internal Combustion Engines. 1982. 24.00 (H00245). ASME.

Uzoigwe, Godfrey N. Uganda: The Dilemma of Nationhood. LC 74-81845. 1983. 20.00 (ISBN 0-88357-037-8). NOK Pubs.

V

Vable, D. The Arya Samaj: Hindu without Hinduism. 1983. text ed. write for info. (ISBN 0-7069-2131-3, Pub. by Vikas India). Advent NY.

Vacano, Otto-Wilhelm Von see Von Vacano, Otto-Wilhelm.

Vacca, Richard & O'Brien, Stephen. The Supreme Court & the Religion-Education Controversy: A Tightrope to Entanglement. LC 74-14961. 1974. 12.00 (ISBN 0-87716-056-2, Pub. by Moore Pub Co). F Apple.

Vacca, Richard S. & Hudgins, H. C. Liability of School Officials & Administrators for Civil Rights Torts. 327p. 1982. 20.00 (ISBN 0-87215-561-7). Michie-Bobbs.

Vacca, Richard T. Content Area Reading. 1981. text ed. 18.95 (ISBN 0-316-89488-5). Little.

Vaccara, Beatrice N. Employment & Output in Protected Manufacturing Industries. LC 79-27932. (Illus.). x, 107p. 1980. Repr. of 1960 ed. lib. bdg. 19.25x (ISBN 0-313-22302-5, VAEO). Greenwood.

Vaccaro, Michael A., illus. The Happy World of Strawberry Shortcake. LC 80-53104. (Board Bks.). (Illus.). 14p. (ps). 1981. boards 3.50 (ISBN 0-394-84734-2). Random.

Vachek, Josef, ed. Praguiana: Basic & Less Known Aspects of the Prague Linguistic School. (Linguistic & Literary Studies in Eastern Europe: 12). 250p. 1983. 32.00 (ISBN 90-272-1514-6). Benjamins North Am.

Vachon, Andre see Halpenny, Francess.

Vachon, Brian. Writing for Regional Publications. LC 79-9381. 203p. 1979. 11.95 o.p. (ISBN 0-911654-73-9). Writers Digest.

Vachss, Andrew H. & Bakal, Yitzhak. The Life-Style Violent Juvenile: The Secure Treatment Approach. LC 77-2520. 512p. 1979. 27.95x (ISBN 0-669-01515-6). Lexington Bks.

Vacquier, Victor. Geomagnetism in Marine Geology. (Elsevier Oceanography Ser.: Vol. 6). 1972. 51.00 (ISBN 0-444-41001-5). Elsevier.

Vactor, David Van see Van Vactor, David & Moore, Katherine D.

Vaenius, Otho V. Amorum Emblemata....Emblemes of Love. Orgel, Stephen, ed. LC 78-68196. (Philosophy of Images Ser.: Vol. 9). (Illus.). 1980. lib. bdg. 66.00 o.s.i. (ISBN 0-8240-3683-2). Garland Pub.

Vaeth, J. M. Conservation Surgery & Radiation Therapy in the Treatment of Operable Breast Cancer. (Frontiers of Radiation Therapy & Oncology: Vol. 17). (Illus.). viii, 156p. 1982. 85.25 (ISBN 3-8055-3560-0). S Karger.

Vafai, G. H. see Keesee, Allen P.

Vagg, Daphne. Flower Arrangements Through the Year. (Illus.). 64p. 1983. pap. 4.95 (ISBN 0-7134-3732-4, Pub. by Batsford England). David & Charles.

--Flowers for the Table. (Illus.). 120p. 1983. 22.50 (ISBN 0-7134-4176-3, Pub. by Batsford England). David & Charles.

Vagg, Peter R., jt. ed. see Spielberger, Charles D.

Vaghn, Jim. Jumbo Geometry Yearbook. (Jumbo Math Ser.). 96p. (gr. 10). 1981. wkbk. 14.00 (ISBN 0-8209-0039-7, JMY-10). ESP.

Vago, Robert, ed. see CUNY Linguistics Conference on Vowel Harmony, May 14, 1977.

Vagts, Detlev F., jt. auth. see Steiner, Henry J.

Vahanian, Gabriel. God & Utopia. LC 77-24029. 1977. 3.00 (ISBN 0-8164-0358-9). Seabury.

Vahey, Esther J. Micro Wave the Easy Way Vol. II. (Audio Cassette Cooking School Library). 16p. 1982. pap. text ed. 12.95x. Cuisine Con.

Vahey, Esther J., jt. auth. see Lefebvre, G. G.

Vai, Marjorie, jt. auth. see Ferreira, Linda A.

Vaid, K. N. State & Labour in India. 10.00x o.p. (ISBN 0-210-26949-9). Asia.

Vaid, Krishna B. Steps in Darkness. 151p. 1972. pap. 2.75 (ISBN 0-88253-120-4). Ind-US Inc.

Vaid, Sudesh. The Divided Mind: Studies in Defoe & Richardson. 1980. text ed. 12.25x (ISBN 0-391-01729-2). Humanities.

Vaidyanathaswamy, R. Set Topology. 2nd ed. LC 60-8968. 14.95 (ISBN 0-8284-0139-X). Chelsea Pub.

Vail, Harley W. When Harley Heard from Heaven. LC 82-72633. 84p. 1982. pap. 2.95 (ISBN 0-9609096-0-5). Bethel Pub Or.

Vail, Linda. Fool's Paradise. (Candlelight Ecstasy Ser.: No. 160). (Orig.). 1983. pap. 1.95 (ISBN 0-440-12852-8). Dell.

Vail, Priscilla L. Clear & Lively Writing: Language Games & Activities for Everyone. LC 80-54818. 269p. 1981. 14.95 (ISBN 0-8027-0682-7). Walker & Co.

--The World of the Gifted Child. 1980. pap. 4.95 (ISBN 0-14-005546-0). Penguin.

Vail, Priscilla L., jt. auth. see Migdail, Sherry R.

Vail, Van Horn & Sparks, Kimberly. Modern German. 2nd ed. (Illus.). 560p. 1978. text ed. 18.95 (ISBN 0-15-561316-2, HC); tapes 300.00 (ISBN 0-15-561317-0); cassettes 125.00 (ISBN 0-15-561318-9). HarBraceJ.

Vail, Van Horn, jt. auth. see Sparks, Kimberly.

Vaillancourt, Jean-Guy. Papal Power: A Study of Vatican Control Over Lay Catholic Elites. 375p. 1980. 18.95 (ISBN 0-520-03733-2). U of Cal Pr.

Vaillancourt, Sarah. Perspectives Francaises, No. 1. LC 80-12737. (Illus.). 1981. text ed. 10.95 (ISBN 0-88436-754-1, 40450); pap. text ed. 7.50 (ISBN 0-88436-755-X, 40250). EMC.

--Perspectives Francaises, No. 2. LC 81-3311. (Illus.). 400p. (Fr.). 1982. text ed. 11.70 (ISBN 0-88436-756-8, 40451); pap. text ed. 7.95 (ISBN 0-88436-757-6, 40251). EMC.

Vailland, Roger. Turn of the Wheel. Wiles, Peter, tr. from Fr. LC 77-20080. 1978. Repr. of 1962 ed. lib. bdg. 18.25x (ISBN 0-313-20014-9, VATW). Greenwood.

Vaillant, George E. The Natural History of Alcoholism. (Illus.). 384p. 1983. text ed. 25.00x (ISBN 0-674-60375-3). Harvard U Pr.

Vainio, H., et al. Occupational Cancer & Carcinogenesis. 1981. 49.50 (ISBN 0-07-066798-5). McGraw.

Vainio, Harri, jt. ed. see Sorsa, Marja.

Vainshtein, B. K. Structure Analysis by Electron Diffraction. 1964. inquire for price. (ISBN 0-08-010241-7). Pergamon.

Vainshtein, Boris K. Diffraction of X-Rays by Chain Molecules. 1966. 95.75 (ISBN 0-444-40588-7). Elsevier.

Vainshtein, Sevyan. Nomads of South Siberia: The Pastoral Economies of Tuva. Humphrey, Caroline, ed. Colenso, M., tr. from Russian. LC 78-504728. (Studies in Social Anthropology: No. 25). 1981. 42.50 (ISBN 0-521-22089-0). Cambridge U Pr.

Vairasse D'Allais, Denis. Histoire des Sevarambes, Peuples Qui Habitent une Partie du Troisieme Continent Communement Appele la Terre Australe, 4 vols. (Utopias in the Enlightenment Ser.). (Fr.). 1974. Repr. of 1677 ed. Set. lib. bdg. 370.00x o.p. (ISBN 0-8287-0845-2). Clearwater Pub.

Vaitsos, Constantine, jt. ed. see Seers, Dudley.

Vaitukaitis. Clinical Reproductive Neuroendocrinology. (Current Endocrinology Ser.: Vol. 5). 1982. 39.95 (ISBN 0-444-00657-5). Elsevier.

Vaizey, J. & Chesswas, J. D. The Costing of Educational Plans. (Fundamentals of Educational Planning Ser.: No. 6). 63p. 1967. pap. 6.00 o.p. (ISBN 92-803-1011-9, UNESCO). Unipub.

Vaizey, John, ed. Economic Sovereignty & Regional Policy. LC 74-22003. 1975. 39.95x o.p. (ISBN 0-470-89777-5). Halsted Pr.

Vaizey, Marina. One Hundred Masterpieces of Art. LC 79-64170. 1979. 14.95 (ISBN 0-399-12394-6); pap. 7.95 (ISBN 0-399-50398-6, Perigee). Putnam Pub Group.

Vaizey, Marina, jt. auth. see Lawrence, Lee.

Vajda, David. Arkansas. 1982. 1.00 (ISBN 0-686-37512-2). Ptolemy Brown.

--Lucretius: A Cognac Carnation. 14p. 1982. 1.00 (ISBN 0-686-37503-3). Ptolemy Brown.

Vajda, M., ed. Le Tournant Du Siecle Des Lumieres 1780-1820. (Comparative Literature Ser.: No. 3). 684p. (Fr.). 1982. text ed. 39.50x (ISBN 0-686-43088-3, Pub. by Kultura Pr Hungary). Humanities.

Vajda, Mihaly. Fascism As a Mass Movement. LC 76-19160. 1976. 18.95 (ISBN 0-312-28350-4). St Martin.

--The State & Socialism. 160p. 1981. 25.00x (ISBN 0-312-75603-8). St Martin.

Vajda, S. Linear Programming: Algorithms & Applications. 1981. pap. 10.95x (ISBN 0-412-16430-2, Pub. by Chapman & Hall). Methuen Inc.

--Mathematics of Manpower Planning. LC 77-26104. 1978. 53.95x (ISBN 0-471-99627-0, Pub. by Wiley-Interscience). Wiley.

--Probabilistic Programming. (Probability & Mathematical Statistics Ser.). 1972. 24.00 (ISBN 0-12-710150-0). Acad Pr.

Vajda, Steven, jt. auth. see Lederman, Walter.

Vajpeyi, Kailash. The Science of Mantras: A Manual of Happiness & Prosperity. 128p. 1980. 14.25x o.p. (ISBN 0-391-02213-X). Humanities.

Vajrathon, Mallica, jt. ed. see Stokland, Torill.

Vakar, Gertrude, ed. see Vygotsky, Lev S.

Vakhtin, Boris. The Sheep-Skin Coat & an Absolutely Happy Village. Dessaix, Robert & Ulman, Michael, trs. from Rus. Date not set. 15.00 (ISBN 0-686-82227-7); pap. 6.00 (ISBN 0-686-82228-5). Ardis Pubs.

Vakil, C. N. Poverty & Planning. LC 73-19310. 357p. 1974. Repr. of 1963 ed. lib. bdg. 19.00x (ISBN 0-8371-7320-5, VAPP). Greenwood.

Vakil, Chandulal N., jt. auth. see Nanavati, Manilal B.

Vakil, Rustom J. & Udwadia, Farokh E., eds. Diagnosis & Management of Medical Emergencies. 2nd ed. (Illus.). 1977. 24.00x o.p. (ISBN 0-19-261118-6). Oxford U Pr.

Valadon-Reeves, Christine. Rendez-Vous Avec la France: Langue Idiomatique et Culture. 152p. 1982. pap. text ed. 7.95 (ISBN 0-88377-220-5). Newbury Hse.

Valasek, V. F. Diagnostic Tests & Nursing Implications. 704p. 1983. 13.95x (ISBN 0-07-066805-1). McGraw.

Valaskakis, Kimon, et al. The Conserver Society: A Blueprint for the Future. LC 77-90868. 1979. 19.18i (ISBN 0-06-014489-0, HarpT). Har-Row.

--The Conserver Society: A Workable Alternative for the Future. LC 77-90868. 1979. pap. 4.95i o.p. (ISBN 0-06-090671-5, CN-671, CN). Har-Row.

Valckenaer, L. C. Observationes Academicae. (Linguistics, 13th-18th Centuries Ser.). 97p. (Fr.). 1974. Repr. of 1805 ed. lib. bdg. 34.50x o.p. (ISBN 0-8287-0846-0, 5053). Clearwater Pub.

Valcour, Vanessa. Play it by Heart. (Second Chance at Love Ser.: No. 121). 1983. pap. 1.75 (ISBN 0-515-07209-5). Jove Pubns.

Valdemi, Maria. Demon Lover. 320p. (Orig.). 1981. pap. 2.95 o.p. (ISBN 0-523-48012-1). Pinnacle Bks.

Valdes, Alberto, ed. Food Security for Developing Countries. 350p. 1981. lib. bdg. 27.50 (ISBN 0-86531-071-8). Westview.

Valdes, Ivy. It Happened in Spain & Christina's Fantasy. 1978. pap. 1.75 o.p. (ISBN 0-451-07983-3, E7983, Sig). NAL.

Valdes, Nelson P., ed. see Castro, Fidel.

Valdivia, Manual. Topics in Locally Convex Spaces. 1982. 64.00 (ISBN 0-444-86418-0). Elsevier.

Valdman, Albert. Introduction to French Phonology & Morphology. LC 76-1888. 1976. pap. text ed. 11.95 (ISBN 0-88377-054-7). Newbury Hse.

--Trends in Language Teaching. 1966. pap. 15.95 o.p. (ISBN 0-07-066812-4, C). McGraw.

Valdoni, Pietro. Abdominal Surgery: An Atlas of Operative Techniques. Nardi, George, tr. LC 75-40641. (Illus.). 1976. text ed. 70.00 o.p. (ISBN 0-7216-8950-7). Saunders.

Vale, Adrian. Radio Controlled Model Aircraft. (Illus.). 181p. (Orig.). 1979. pap. 10.50x o.p. (ISBN 0-905418-04-2). Intl Pubns Serv.

Vale, Eugene. The Technique of Screen & Television Writing. 302p. 1983. 15.95 (ISBN 0-13-901793-3); pap. 6.95 (ISBN 0-13-901785-2). P-H.

--The Thirteenth Apostle. 352p. 1983. pap. 7.95 (ISBN 0-9609674-0-0). Jubilee Pr.

Vale, J. & Cox, B. Drugs & the Eye. 1978. 24.95 (ISBN 0-407-00128-X). Butterworth.

Vale, J. A. & Meredeth, T. J., eds. Poisoning: Diagnosis & Treatment. 190p. 1980. 38.00 (ISBN 0-906141-81-8, Pub. by Update Pubns England); pap. 31.00 (ISBN 0-906141-82-6). Kluwer Boston.

Vale, Juliet. Edward III & Chivalry: Chivalric Society & Its Context, 1270-1350. 256p. 1983. text ed. 49.50x (ISBN 0-85115-170-1, Pub. by Boydell & Brewer). Biblio Dist.

Vale, M. G. Charles the Seventh. Ross, Charles, ed. LC 74-79775. (The French Monarchs Ser). (Illus.). 1974. 40.00x (ISBN 0-520-02787-6). U of Cal Pr.

Vale, Michael, tr. see Martin, Helmut.

Vale, Michael, tr. see Saffioti, Heleieth.

Vale, Michel & Steinke, Rudolf, eds. Germany Debates Security: The NATO Alliance at the Crossroads. Vale, Michel, tr. from Ger. 228p. 1983. 25.00 (ISBN 0-87332-243-6). M E Sharpe.

Vale, Michel, tr. see Fernandes, Florestan.

Vale, Michel, tr. see Komarov, Boris.

Vale, Michel, tr. see Markova, A. K.

Vale, Michel, tr. see Schulz, Eberhard, et al.

Vale, Michel, tr. see Vale, Michel & Steinke, Rudolf.

Vale, Michel, tr. see Wolter, Ulf.

Vale, Michel, tr. see Yanowitch, Murray.

Vale, Michel, et al, trs. see Experience & the Future Discussion Group.

Vale, V., ed. see Ballard, J. G.

Vale, Vale, ed. Re-Search: Industrial Culture Handbook. 96p. 1983. pap. 6.95 (ISBN 0-940642-07-7). Re-Search Prods.

--Re-Search: Sex & Control. 96p. 1983. pap. write for info. (ISBN 0-940642-06-9). Re-Search Prods.

--Re-Search: William S. Burroughs, Brion Gysin, Throbbing Gristle. (Illus.). 96p. 1982. pap. 5.95 (ISBN 0-940642-05-0). Re-Search Prods.

Valen, Henry. Norwegian Election Study, 1965. 1976. codebk. write for info. (ISBN 0-89138-155-4). ICPSR.

Valen, Henry, tr. see Allardt, Erik & Andre, Nils.

Valencak, Hannelore. A Tangled Web. Crampton, Patricia, tr. from Ger. (gr. 7-9). 1978. 9.75 (ISBN 0-688-22169-6); PLB 9.36 (ISBN 0-688-32169-0). Morrow.

--When Half-Gods Go. Crampton, Patricia, tr. from Ger. LC 76-6140. 192p. (Orig.). (gr. 7 up). 1976. 9.50 (ISBN 0-688-22077-0); PLB 9.12 (ISBN 0-688-32077-5). Morrow.

Valencia & Bacon. En Marcha. 1982. pap. text ed. 18.95 (ISBN 0-686-84593-5, SN30); instr's. ed. 19.95 (ISBN 0-686-84594-3, SN27); write for info. supplementary materials. HM.

Valencia, B. Michael, jt. auth. see Jackson, Michael P.

Valencia, M., ed. Hydrocarbon Potential of the South China Sea: Possibilities of Joint Development: Proceedings of the EAPI/CCOP Workshop, East-West Center, Honolulu, Hawaii, USA. 260p. 1982. 24.00 (ISBN 0-08-028692-5). Pergamon.

Valencia, Pablo & Bacon, Susan. En Marcha: Espanol Para Niveles Intermedios. 384p. 1982. pap. text ed. 19.95 (ISBN 0-395-32741-5); write for info. supplementary materials. HM.

Valency, Maurice. The Breaking String: The Plays of Anton Chekhov. LC 82-3369. (The Making of Modern Drama Ser.: Vol. 2). 344p. 1983. 20.00x (ISBN 0-8052-3809-3); pap. 9.95x (ISBN 0-8052-0716-3). Schocken.

--The Cart & the Trumpet: The Plays of George Benard Shaw. LC 82-16954. (Volume III of the Making of Modern Drama Ser.). 488p. 1983. 22.00 (ISBN 0-8052-3832-8); pap. 11.95 (ISBN 0-8052-0740-6). Schocken.

--The End of the World: An Introduction to Contemporary Drama. 1980. 25.00x (ISBN 0-19-502639-X). Oxford U Pr.

--The Flower & the Castle. LC 82-5528. (The Making of Modern Drama Ser.: Vol. I). 460p. 1982. 20.00x (ISBN 0-8052-3819-0); pap. 9.95 (ISBN 0-8052-0727-9). Schocken.

--In Praise of Love: An Introduction to the Love Poetry of the Renaissance. LC 82-3376. 336p. 1982. 18.95x (ISBN 0-8052-3808-5); pap. 9.95 (ISBN 0-8052-0715-5). Schocken.

Valency, Maurice J. The Cart & the Trumpet: The Plays of George Bernard Shaw. 1973. 25.00x (ISBN 0-19-501636-X). Oxford U Pr.

Valensi, Lucette & Udovitch, Abraham L. The Last Arab Jews: The Communities of Jerba. (Social Orders: A Series of Tracts & Monographs). 1983. write for info. (ISBN 3-7186-0135-4). Harwood Academic.

Valenstein, Elliot S. Brain Control: A Critical Examination of Brain Stimulation & Psychosurgery. LC 73-13687. (Illus.). 407p. 1973. 29.95 (ISBN 0-471-89784-1, Pub. by Wiley-Interscience); pap. 18.95 (ISBN 0-471-03328-6). Wiley.

--Brain Stimulation & Motivation: Research & Commentary. 1973. pap. 8.95x (ISBN 0-673-05443-8). Scott F.

Valenstein, Suzanne & Meech-Pekarik, Julia. Metropolitan Museum of Art, New York. LC 80-82645. (Oriental Ceramics Ser.: Vol. 11). (Illus.). 200p. 1982. 68.00 (ISBN 0-87011-450-6). Kodansha.

Valenta, Lubomir & Afrasiabe, A. Ali. Handbook of Endocrine & Metabolic Emergencies. 1981. pap. text ed. 21.00 (ISBN 0-87488-597-3). Med Exam.

Valente, Michael F. Sex: The Radical View of a Catholic Theologian. 1970. pap. 2.95 o.p. (ISBN 0-685-03349-X, 80737). Glencoe.

Valente, William D. Law in the Schools. (Educational Administration Ser.: No. C21). 580p. 1980. text ed. 23.95 (ISBN 0-675-08165-3). Merrill.

Valenti, Dan, jt. auth. see Coleman, Ken.

Valenti, Helena. Vamos a Ver. 1972. pap. 4.95 (ISBN 0-912022-31-0). EMC.

Valentin, L. Subatomic Physics: Nuclei & Particles, 2 vols. 1981. Set. 106.50 (ISBN 0-444-86117-3); Vols. 1 & 2. 59.75 ea. Elsevier.

Valentine, Alan & Valentine, Lucia. The American Academy in Rome, 1894-1969. LC 72-92663. 200p. 1973. 15.00 (ISBN 0-8139-0444-7). U Pr of Va.

Valentine, Bethanie. Picture Stories for Speech Correction, Set 1. 1972. text ed. 9.95x (ISBN 0-8134-1443-1). Interstate.

Valentine, C. G., jt. auth. see Woolman, M.

Valentine, D. Eugene, jt. auth. see Furgis, Ellen V.

Valentine, D. H., ed. Taxonomy, Phytogeography & Evolution. 1972. 68.50 o.s.i. (ISBN 0-12-710250-7). Acad Pr.

Valentine, D. W. Fractional Currency of the United States. LC 80-70058. 1981. Repr. of 1920 ed. softcover 10.00 (ISBN 0-915262-59-2). S J Durst.

Valentine, E. R. Conceptual Issues in Psychology. 224p. 1982. text ed. 25.00x (ISBN 0-04-150079-2); pap. text ed. 9.95x (ISBN 0-04-150080-6). Allen Unwin.

Valentine, Foy. Layman's Bible Book Commentary: Hebrews, James, 1 & 2 Peter, Vol.23. LC 79-56863. 1981. 4.75 (ISBN 0-8054-1193-3). Broadman.

Valentine, Frederick A. Convex Sets. LC 75-12753. 248p. 1976. Repr. of 1964 ed. 14.00 o.p. (ISBN 0-88275-289-8). Krieger.

Valentine, G. H. Chromosome Disorders: An Introduction for Clinicians. 3rd ed. (Illus.). 1975. 17.50 o.p. (ISBN 0-397-58185-8, Lippincott Medical). Lippincott.

Valentine, Grant M. Non-Metallic Minerals, Pt. 1. (Illus.). 258p. 1960. 3.00 (ISBN 0-686-34693-9). Geologic Pubns.

Valentine, James W. Evolutionary Paleoecology of the Marine Biosphere. (Illus.). 512p. 1973. ref. ed. 31.95 o.p. (ISBN 0-13-293720-4). P-H.

Valentine, James W., jt. auth. see Ayala, Francisco J.

Valentine, Lucia, jt. auth. see Valentine, Alan.

Valentine, W. H. Copper Coins of India. 1978. 22.00 (ISBN 0-685-51122-7, Pub by Spink & Son England). S J Durst.

--Modern Copper Coins of the Muhammaden State. 1978. 22.00 (ISBN 0-686-50090-3, Pub. by Spink & Son England). S J Durst.

Valentine-Millstein, Bethanie. Picture Stories for Speech Correction, Set 2. 1978. text ed. 9.95x (ISBN 0-8134-2010-5). Interstate.

Valenza, Samuel W., Jr. Conceptual Mathematics. (Illus.). (gr. 9-12). 1976. pap. 9.50 (ISBN 0-936918-02-0). Intergalactic NJ.

--The Professor Googol Flying Time Machine & Atomic Space Capsule Math Primer. 3rd ed. (Illus.). 196p. (gr. 7-12). 1974. 10.95 (ISBN 0-936918-00-4). Intergalactic NJ.

Valenza, Samuel W., Jr., jt. ed. see Gagliardi, Richard L.

Valenza, Samuel W., Jr., ed. see Swetz, Frank.

Valenzuela, Luisa. Cambio de armas. (Span.). 1982. pap. 7.00 (ISBN 0-910061-10-6). Ediciones Norte.

--The Lizard's Tail. Rabassa, Gregory, tr. from Spanish. 1983. 12.50 (ISBN 0-374-18994-3). FS&G.

Valeo, Francis R. & Morrison, Charles E., eds. The Japanese Diet & the U. S. Congress. 300p. 1982. lib. bdg. 12.00x (ISBN 0-86531-469-1). Westview.

Valeri, C. R., et al. Red Cell Freezing. 95p. 1973. 10.00 o.p. (ISBN 0-914404-02-4). Am Assn Blood.

Valeriano Bolzani, Giovanni P. Hieroglyphica. LC 75-27864. (Renaissance & the Gods Ser.: Vol. 17). (Illus.). 1977. Repr. of 1602 ed. lib. bdg. 73.00 o.s.i. (ISBN 0-8240-2069-3). Garland Pub.

Vales, Pedro A., jt. ed. see Riedel, Marc.

Vales, Robert L. Peter Pindar (John Wolcot) (English Authors Ser.: No. 155). 1974. lib. bdg. 7.95 o.p. (ISBN 0-8057-1443-X, Twayne). G K Hall.

Valeton, I. Bauxites. LC 70-151740. (Developments in Soil Science Ser.: Vol. 1). (Illus.). 233p. 1972. 80.50 (ISBN 0-444-40888-6). Elsevier.

Valett, Robert. Developing Cognitive Abilities: Teaching Children to Think. LC 77-9912. (Illus.). 272p. 1978. pap. text ed. 11.45 o.p. (ISBN 0-8016-5213-8). Mosby.

Valett, Robert E. Case Studies in Special Education: A Prescriptive Approach. 78p. 1982. pap. text ed. 9.50 (ISBN 0-89106-019-7, 7989). Consulting Psychol.

Valetutti, Peter J., jt. ed. see Haslam, Robert H.

Valfells, Sigrid & Cathey, James F. Old Icelandic: An Introductory Course. 1981. text ed. 36.50x (ISBN 0-19-811172-X); pap. text ed. 17.95x (ISBN 0-19-811173-8). Oxford U Pr.

Valid, N. Mechanics of Continuous Media & Analyses of Structures, Vol. 26. (North Holland Series in Applied Mathematics & Mechanics). 1982. 59.75 (ISBN 0-444-86150-5). Elsevier.

Valin, Jonathan. Dead Letter. 224p. 1982. pap. 2.50 (ISBN 0-380-61366-2, 61366). Avon.

--Natural Causes. 256p. 1983. 12.95 (ISBN 0-312-92560-3). Congdon & Weed.

Valins, Stuart, jt. auth. see Baum, Andrew.

Valiron, Georges. Theory of Integral Functions. LC 51-7375. 14.95 (ISBN 0-8284-0056-3). Chelsea Pub.

Valis, Noel M. The Decadent Vision in Leopoldo Alas. LC 80-24108. xvi, 215p. 1981. 17.50 (ISBN 0-8071-0769-7). La State U Pr.

Valis, Wayne, ed. The Future under President Reagan. 1981. 12.95 o.p. (ISBN 0-87000-504-9, Arlington Hse). Crown.

Valk, Barbara G., ed. Hispanic American Periodicals Index, 1977. LC 75-642408. 1980. lib. bdg. 125.00x (ISBN 0-87903-402-5). UCLA Lat Am Ctr.

--Hispanic American Periodicals Index, 1978. LC 75-642408. 1981. lib. bdg. 125.00 (ISBN 0-87903-404-1). UCLA Lat Am Ctr.

Valk, J. Computed Tomography & Cerebral Infarctions. 190p. 1980. 32.50 (ISBN 0-89004-646-8). Raven.

Valkenburg, M. E. Van see Cruz, Jose B. & Van Valkenburg, M. E.

Valkenburg, M. E. Van see Van Valkenburg, M.

Valkenburg, M. E. Van see Van Valkenburg, M. E.

Valkovic, Vlado. Trace Elements in Petroleum. 269p. 1978. 34.95x (ISBN 0-87814-084-0). Pennwell Book Division.

Vall, Mark Van De see Van De Vall, Mark.

Vallacher, Robin R., jt. auth. see Wegner, Daniel M.

Vallacher, Robin R., jt. ed. see Wegner, Daniel M.

Vallance, Elizabeth. Women in the House: A Study of Women Members of Parliament. (Illus.). 212p. 1979. 30.00x (ISBN 0-485-11186-1); pap. text ed. 12.50x (ISBN 0-485-11229-9). Humanities.

Vallance, Elizabeth, jt. auth. see Eisner, Elliot W.

Vallance, Theodore & Sabre, Ru Michael. Mental Health Services in Transition: A Policy Sourcebook. LC 81-6805. 304p. 1982. 29.95 (ISBN 0-87705-700-1). Human Sci Pr.

Vallandro, L. Dicionario Ingles-Portugues. 1174p. (Eng. & Port.). 1979. 39.95 (ISBN 0-686-97639-8, M-9210). French & Eur.

--Dicionario Ingles-Portugues, Portugues-Ingles. 981p. (Eng. & Port.). 1980. 39.95 (ISBN 0-686-97640-1, M-9213). French & Eur.

Vallarino, L., jt. auth. see Quagliano, James.

Vallarino, L. M., et al. Chemistry. 15.20 (ISBN 0-07-051025-3, W); tchrs' guide 8.84 (ISBN 0-07-051026-1); tests 44.20 (ISBN 0-07-051028-8). McGraw.

--Chemistry in the Laboratory. 1976. 4.48 (ISBN 0-07-051027-X, W). McGraw.

Vallas, Leon. Cesar Franck. LC 73-5210. (Illus.). 283p. 1973. Repr. of 1951 ed. lib. bdg. 18.25x (ISBN 0-8371-6873-2, VACF). Greenwood.

Vallat, F. A. International Law & the Practitioner. LC 66-19474. (Melland Schill Lectures). 159p. 1966. 13.50 (ISBN 0-379-11906-4). Oceana.

Vallat, Jean M., jt. auth. see Vital, Claude.

Valldejuli, Carmen A. Puerto Rican Cookery. (Illus.). 389p. 1983. Repr. of 1977 ed. 11.95 (ISBN 0-88289-411-0). Pelican.

Valle, Luis Gonzalez Del see Shaw, Bradley & Gonzalez-Del Valle, Luis.

Valle, Roger V., tr. see Ramm, Bernard.

Valle, Stephen K. Alcoholism Counseling: Issues for an Emerging Profession. (Illus.). 184p. 1979. 19.75x (ISBN 0-398-01952-5). C C Thomas.

Valle, Teresa La see Ralph, Margaret.

Vallecorsa, Ada, jt. auth. see Zigmond, Naomi.

Vallee, Jacques, jt. auth. see Johansen, Robert.

Valle-Inclan, Ramon. The Pleasant Memoirs of the Marquis De Bradomin. Heywood Broun, May & Walsh, Thomas, trs. from Span. LC 76-28508. 1983. Repr. of 1924 ed. 15.00x (ISBN 0-86527-294-8). Fertig.

Vallejo, Ceasar. The Mayakovsky Case. Scully, James, ed. Schaaf, Richard, tr. LC 82-2544. (Art on the Line Ser.). 48p. (Orig.). 1982. pap. 3.00 (ISBN 0-915306-31-X). Curbstone.

Vallejo, Cesar. Cesar Vallejo: The Complete Posthumous Poetry. Eshleman, Clayton & Barcia, Jose R., trs. from Span. LC 77-93472. 1978. 20.00 o.p. (ISBN 0-686-82993-X); pap. 6.95 (ISBN 0-520-04099-6). U of Cal Pr.

Vallentin, Antonina. This I Saw: The Life & Times of Goya. Woods, Katherine W., tr. from Fr. LC 78-152612. (Illus.). 371p. Repr. of 1949 ed. lib. bdg. 19.75x (ISBN 0-8371-6047-2, VATI). Greenwood.

Vallentine, John F. & Sims, Phillip L., eds. Range Science: A Guide to Information Sources. (Natural World Information Guide Ser.: Vol. 2). 250p. 1980. 42.00x (ISBN 0-8103-1420-7). Gale.

Valle-Riestra, J. Frank. Project Evaluation in the Chemical Process Industries. (Chemical Engineering Ser.). (Illus.). 736p. 1983. text ed. 33.50 (ISBN 0-07-066840-X, C); write for info. solutions manual (ISBN 0-07-066841-8). McGraw.

Valles, Jorge. How to Live with an Alcoholic. 2.75 o.p. (ISBN 0-686-92098-8). Hazelden.

Vallet, H. Lawrence & Porter, Ian H., eds. Genetic Mechanisms of Sexual Development. LC 78-25762. (Birth Defects Institute Symposium Ser.: No. 7). 1979. 30.00 (ISBN 0-12-710550-6). Acad Pr.

Vallette, Rebecca M. Modern Language Testing: A Handbook. 2nd ed. LC 76-49392. 347p. (Orig.). 1977. pap. text ed. 10.95 (ISBN 0-15-561926-8, HC). HarBraceJ.

Valletuhi, Peter J., jt. auth. see Bender, Michael.

Valletutti & Cristoplos, F., eds. Interdisciplinary Approaches to Human Services. (Illus.). 454p. 1977. pap. text ed. 22.95 (ISBN 0-8391-1164-9). Univ Park.

Valletutti, J. & Bender, Michael. Teaching Interpersonal & Community Living Skills: A Curriculum Model for Handicapped Adolescents & Adults. 288p. 1982. pap. text ed. 19.95 (ISBN 0-8391-1748-5, 18341). Univ Park.

Valletutti, P. Individualizing Educational Objectives & Programs: A Modular Approach. 296p. 1979. pap. text ed. 14.95 (ISBN 0-8391-1265-3). Univ Park.

Valletutti, Peter J., jt. auth. see Bender, Michael.

Vallianatos, E. G. Fear in the Countryside: The Control of Agricultural Resources in the Poor Countries by Non-Peasant Elites. LC 76-14355. 1976. prof ref 22.50x (ISBN 0-88410-298-X). Ballinger Pub.

Vallier, Dora. Henri Rousseau. (Q. L. P. Ser.). (Illus.). 1979. pap. 7.95 (ISBN 0-517-53697-8). Crown.

Vallier, Jane. Poet on Demand: The Life, Letters, & Works of Celia Thaxter. Randall, Peter, ed. LC 81-67591. 267p. 1982. lib. bdg. 14.95 (ISBN 0-89272-136-7, PIC485); pap. 9.95 (ISBN 0-89272-130-8, PIC484). Down East.

Vallier, Jean, tr. see Dr. Suess.

Vallieres, William De La see De La Vallieres, William.

Vallings, H. G. Mechanisation in Building. 2nd ed. (Illus.). 1976. 39.00 (ISBN 0-85334-651-8, Pub. by Applied Sci England). Elsevier.

Vallins, G. H. The Pattern of English. (Andre Deutsch Language Library). 1977. lib. bdg. 11.50 o.p. (ISBN 0-233-95538-0). Westview.

Valmai, Fenster. Guide to American Literature. 250p. 1983. lib. bdg. 23.50 (ISBN 0-87287-373-0). Libs Unl.

Valmiki. Ramayana. 3rd ed. Rajagopalachari, Chakravarti, ed. & tr. from Tamil. 320p. (Orig.). 1980. pap. 6.50 (ISBN 0-934676-17-8). Greenlf Bks.

Valnet, Jean. The Practice of Aromatherapy: Holistic Health & the Essential Oils of Flowers & Herbs. (Illus.). 279p. 1982. pap. 8.95 (ISBN 0-89281-026-2). Destiny Bks.

Valois, Ninette de see De Valois, Ninette.

Valsangkar, K, et al. Aspects of Political Theory. (Illus.). 292p. 1981. pap. text ed. 8.95x (ISBN 0-86131-108-6, Pub. by Orient Longman Ltd India). Apt Bks.

Valtin, Heinz, ed. see International Symposium on the Brattleboro Rat, Sept. 4-7, 1981.

Valyi, L. Atom & Ion Sources. LC 76-44880. 1978. 105.95x (ISBN 0-471-99463-4, Pub. by Wiley-Interscience). Wiley.

Valzelli, L., jt. ed. see Essman, W. B.

Valzelli, Luigi. Psychobiology of Aggression & Violence. 262p. 1981. text ed. 28.50 (ISBN 0-89004-403-1). Raven.

Valzey, John, jt. auth. see Norris, Keith.

Vambe, Lawrence. From Rhodesia to Zimbabwe. LC 75-20354. (Illus.). 1976. 12.95 (ISBN 0-8229-3317-9). U of Pittsburgh Pr.

--An Ill-Fated People: Zimbabwe Before & After Rhodes. LC 72-87477. 1973. 12.95 (ISBN 0-8229-3256-3). U of Pittsburgh Pr.

Vambery, Robert G. Capital Investment Control in the Air Transport Industry. LC 76-49506. 395p. 1976. lib. bdg. 39.00x (ISBN 0-379-00588-3). Oceana.

Vamos, Mara S., tr. see Dorian, Emil.

Van World Editors. Do-It-Yourselfer's Guide to Van Conversion. (Illus.). 1977. 8.95 o.p. (ISBN 0-8306-7992-8); pap. 6.95 o.p. (ISBN 0-8306-6992-2, 992). TAB Bks.

Vana, Zdenek. The World of the Ancient Slavs. Gottheinerova, Till, tr. (Illus.). 240p. 1983. 35.00 (ISBN 0-686-43100-6, Co-publication with Orbis Pub). Wayne St U Pr.

Van Acht, R., jt. auth. see Scheurwater, W.

Van Acht, R. J. see Acht, R. J. van, et al.

Van Ackeren, Ruth, jt. auth. see Richards, Bartlett, Jr.

Vanags, Patricia. Imperial Rome. (Civilization Library). (Illus.). (gr. 5-8). 1979. PLB 9.40 s&l (ISBN 0-531-01445-2, Gloucester Press). Watts.

Van Aken, A. Encyclopedia of Classical Mythology. 1965. pap. 2.45 o.p. (ISBN 0-13-275362-6, S97, Spec). P-H.

Van Allen, James A. Origins of Magnetospheric Physics. 128p. 1983. text ed. 19.95x (ISBN 0-87474-940-9). Smithsonian.

VanAllen, Leroy C. & Mallis, A. George. The Comprehensive Catalog & Encyclopedia of U.S. Morgan & Peace Silver Dollars. LC 76-18299. (Illus.). 1976. 29.95 (ISBN 0-668-04021-1). Arco.

Van Allen, Rodger, ed. American Religious Values & the Future of America. LC 76-15894. 224p. 1978. 12.95x o.p. (ISBN 0-8006-0486-5, 1-486). Fortress.

Van Alsburg, Chris. The Wreck of the Zephyr. LC 82-23371. (Illus.). 32p. 1983. pap. text ed. 14.95 (ISBN 0-395-33075-0). HM.

Van Alstyne, Richard W. The Rising American Empire. (Illus.). 240p. 1974. pap. 5.95x (ISBN 0-393-00750-2). Norton.

Van Amerongen, C., tr. see Bruggeling, Ir A.

Van Amersfoort, Hans. Immigration & the Formation of Minority Groups: The Dutch Experience 1945-1975. LC 81-18097. (Illus.). 192p. 1982. 34.50 (ISBN 0-521-23293-7). Cambridge U Pr.

Van Antwerp, Margaret A., ed. Dictionary of Literary Biography Documentary: An Illustrated Chronicle, Vol. 1. (Dictionary of Literary Biography Ser.). (Illus.). 440p. 1982. 74.00x (ISBN 0-8103-1112-7). Gale.

Van Antwerp, Margret A., ed. Dictionary of Literary Biography Documentary Series, Vol. 1. LC 82-1105. 432p. 1982. 74.00x (ISBN 0-686-98301-7). Gale.

Van Apeldoorn, G. Jan. Perspectives on Drought & Famine in Nigeria. (Illus.). 192p. 1982. text ed. 22.50x (ISBN 0-04-301135-7). Allen Unwin.

Van Arsdale, Mary G. A Guide to Family Financial Counseling. LC 81-71909. (The Dorsey Professional Ser.). 400p. 1982. 29.95 (ISBN 0-87094-324-3). Dow Jones-Irwin.

Van Arsdale, Robert S. The Unknown Domestic Life of Primitive Men & Women. (The Great Currents of History Library Bks). (Illus.). 147p. 1983. 67.45 (ISBN 0-89266-384-7). Am Classical Coll Pr.

Van Arsdale, Tom, et al. Our Basketball Lives. (Putnam Sports Shelf Ser.). 224p. (gr. 5 up). 1973. PLB 4.97 o.p. (ISBN 0-399-60792-7). Putnam Pub Group.

Van Arsdell, Paul M. Corporation Finance: Policy, Planning, Administration. LC 68-13475. 1739p. 1968. 49.95 o.p. (ISBN 0-471-06579-X). Ronald Pr.

Van Asbeck, W. Bitumen In Hydraulic Engineering, Vol. 2. 1964. 32.70 (ISBN 0-444-40590-9). Elsevier.

Van Assche, C., ed. Agricultural Aspects of Soil Disinfestation. (Agro-Ecosystems Ser.: Vol. 1, No. 3). (Proceedings). 1974. 20.50 (ISBN 0-686-43413-7). Elsevier.

--Agro-Ecological Aspects of Soil Disinfestation. (Agro-Ecosystems Ser.: Vol. 1, No. 2). 1974. 18.00 (ISBN 0-686-43414-5). Elsevier.

Vanasse, Debra L., jt. auth. see Hyska, June E.

Vanasse, Robert W. Statistical Sampling for Auditing & Accounting Decisions: A Simulation. 2nd ed. 1976. text ed. 9.95 (ISBN 0-07-066851-5, C); instructor's manual 5.50 (ISBN 0-07-066852-3). McGraw.

Van Atta, Dale, jt. auth. see Bradlee, Ben, Jr.

Van Atta, Frieda. Eighth Grade: How to Help. 1.00 ea. o.p. Gr. 6 (ISBN 0-394-40976-0). Gr. 7 (ISBN 0-394-40977-9). Gr. 8 (ISBN 0-394-40978-7). Random.

Vanatta, John C. & Fogelman, Morris J. Moyer's Fluid Balance: A Clinical Manual. 3rd ed. (Illus.). 1982. pap. 14.95 (ISBN 0-8151-8963-X). Year Bk Med.

Vanatta, John C., et al. Oxygen Transport, Hypoxia, & Cyanosis. (Illus.). 130p. 1974. pap. 13.95 o.p. (ISBN 0-87618-001-2). R J Brady.

Van Atta, Robert E. Instrumental Methods of Analysis for Laboratory Technicians. 1982. pap. text ed. 20.50 (ISBN 0-89917-374-8). TIS Inc.

Van Atta, Winfred. The Adam Sleep. 192p. 1981. pap. 2.25 o.s.i. (ISBN 0-380-53744-3, 53744). Avon.

--Adam Sleep. LC 79-7781. (Crime Club Ser.). 1980. 10.95 o.p. (ISBN 0-385-06897-2). Doubleday.

Van Auken, Philip M., jt. auth. see Sexton, Donald L.

Van Becker, David, jt. auth. see Van Becker, Nell S.

Van Becker, Nell S. & Van Becker, David. Journal to Essay: A Sequential Program in Composition. 192p. 1982. pap. text ed. 12.95 (ISBN 0-8403-2719-6). Kendall-Hunt.

Van Beeck, Frans J. Grounded in Love: Sacramental Theology in an Ecumenical Perspective. LC 81-40117. 162p. (Orig.). 1982. lib. bdg. 20.75 (ISBN 0-8191-2040-5); pap. text ed. 9.75 (ISBN 0-8191-2041-3). U Pr of Amer.

Van Beek, Wil see Beek, Wil van.

VanBekkum, D. W., ed. The Biological Activity of Thymic Hormones. LC 75-17617. 1975. 44.95 o.s.i. (ISBN 0-470-89835-6). Halsted Pr.

Van Bekkum, O. & De Vries, H. Radiation Chimeras. 1967. 61.00 (ISBN 0-12-710350-3). Acad Pr.

VanBelle, Harry. Basic Intent & Therapeutic Approach of Carl R. Rogers: A Study of His View of Man in Relation to His View of Therapy, Personality & Interpersonal Relations. pap. 11.95x (ISBN 0-88906-109-2). Wedge Pub.

Van Belle, O.. C., ed. see Bottcher, C. J., et al.

Van Bemmel, J. H., ed. see IFPtC4 Working Conference, Amsterdam, 1976.

Van Bemmelen, W. Geodynamic Models. (Developments in Geotectonics: Vol. 2). 1972. 56.00 (ISBN 0-444-40967-X). Elsevier.

Vanbery, Armin. Scenes from the East: Through the Eyes of a European Traveller in the 1860's. Kortvelyessy, Eniko & Gaster, Bertha, trs. from Hungarian. (Illus.). 418p. (Orig.). 1979. pap. 8.50x (ISBN 963-13-0832-4). Intl Pubns Serv.

VanBiervliet, Alan & Sheldon-Wildgen, Jan. Liability Issues in Community-Based Programs: Legal Principles, Problem Areas, & Recommendations. LC 81-245. 224p. 1981. pap. text ed. 13.95 (ISBN 0-933716-08-7). P H Brookes.

Van Blankenburg, Quirinus see Blankenburg, Quirinus Van.

Van Boer, Bertil H., Jr., jt. ed. see Bengtsson, Ingmar.

Van Brabant, J. M. Socialist Economic Integration. LC 79-23766. (Soviet & East European Studies). (Illus.). 275p. 1980. 39.50 (ISBN 0-521-23046-2). Cambridge U Pr.

Van Bragt, Jan see Nishitani, Keiji.

Van Breemen, Peter G. As Bread That Is Broken. 5.95 (ISBN 0-87193-052-8). Dimension Bks.

--Called by Name. 6.95 (ISBN 0-87193-094-3). Dimension Bks.

Vanbreuseghem, R., et al. Practical Guide to Medical & Veterinary Mycology. LC 77-94829. (Illus.). 288p. 1978. text ed. 55.25x (ISBN 0-89352-018-7). Masson Pub.

Van Bruggen, Theodore. The Vascular Plants of South Dakota. (Illus.). 564p. 1976. pap. text ed. 10.50x (ISBN 0-8138-0650-X). Iowa St U Pr.

Van Brunt, H. L. For Luck: Poems 1962-1977. LC 77-80342. (Poetry Ser). 1977. pap. 4.95 (ISBN 0-915604-12-4). Carnegie-Mellon.

--Uncertainties. LC 68-22913. (Illus.). 4.50 (ISBN 0-912292-00-8); pap. 2.25 (ISBN 0-912292-01-6). The Smith.

Van Brunt, Leroy B. Applied ECM, Vol. 2. EW Engineering Inc., ed. LC 78-50538. (Illus.). 1982. 43.00 (ISBN 0-931728-01-0). EW Eng.

Van Buitenen, J. A., jt. auth. see Deutsch, Eliot.

Van Buitenen, J. A., tr. see Dimmitt, Cornelia.

Van Buren, J. M., jt. ed. see Sandri, C.

Van Buren, Martin. Metrics for Architects, Designers & Builders. 192p. 1982. text ed. 18.95 (ISBN 0-442-28889-1). Van Nos Reinhold.

Van Buren, Paul M. The Burden of Freedom: Americans & the God of Israel. 1976. 1.00 (ISBN 0-8164-0318-X). Seabury.

Van Buskirk, Robert & Bauer, Fred. Tailwind: My Story. 1983. 8.95 (ISBN 0-8499-0341-6). Word Bks.

Van Buuren, Catherine. The Buke of the Sevyne Sagis: A Middle Scots Version of the Seven Sages of Rome. (Germanic & Anglistic Studies of the University of Leiden: Vol. 20). (Illus.). xii, 463p. 1982. pap. write for info. (ISBN 90-04-06753-1). E J Brill.

Van Caenegem, R. C. The Birth of the English Common Law. LC 72-89812. 150p. 1973. 29.95 (ISBN 0-521-20097-0). Cambridge U Pr.

--Guide to the Sources of Medieval History. (Europe in the Middle Ages - Selected Studies: Vol. 2). 1978. 63.00 (ISBN 0-7204-0743-5, North-Holland). Elsevier.

Van Camp, Diana. Basic Skills Nutrition Workbook: Grade 2. (Basis Skills Workbooks). 32p. (gr. 2). 1982. tchrs' ed. 0.99 (ISBN 0-8209-0408-2, NW-C). ESP.

--Basic Skills Nutrition Workbook: Grade 3. (Basic Skills Workbooks). 32p. (gr. 3). 1982. tchrs' ed. 0.99 (ISBN 0-8209-0409-0, NW-D). ESP.

--Basic Skills Nutrition Workbook: Grade 6. (Basic Skills Workbooks). 32p. (gr. 6). 1982. tchrs' ed. 0.99 (ISBN 0-8209-0412-0, NW-G). ESP.

--Jumbo Human Body Yearbook: Grade 5. (Jumbo Human Body Ser.). 96p. (gr. 5). 1980. 14.00 (ISBN 0-8209-0070-2, JHBY 5). ESP.

--Jumbo Human Body Yearbook: Grade 6. (Jumbo Human Body Ser.). 96p. (gr. 6). 1980. 14.00 (ISBN 0-8209-0071-0, JHBY 6). ESP.

--Jumbo Human Body Yearbook: Grade 7. (Jumbo Human Body Ser.). 96p. (gr. 7). 1980. 14.00 (ISBN 0-8209-0072-9, JHBY 7). ESP.

--Jumbo Human Body Yearbook: Grade 8. (Jumbo Human Body Ser.). 96p. (gr. 8). 1982. 14.00 (ISBN 0-8209-0073-7, JHBY 8). ESP.

--Jumbo Nutrition Yearbook: Grade 2. (Jumbo Nutrition Ser.). 96p. (gr. 2). 1981. 14.00 (ISBN 0-8209-0041-9, JNY 2). ESP.

Van Camp, Diana see Camp, Diana Van.

VanCamp, Marilyn. Jumbo Nutrition Yearbook: Grade 3. (Jumbo Nutrition Ser.). 96p. (gr. 3). 1981. 14.00 (ISBN 0-8209-0042-7, JNY 3). ESP.

Van Campen, Shirley. Hawaii: A Woman's Guide. 150p. 1979. pap. 5.95 o.p. (ISBN 0-916032-07-8). Chicago Review.

Van Carlton, Doren, et al. Land & Leisure: Concepts & Methods in Outdoor Recreation. 2nd ed. 317p. 1979. pap. 9.95x (ISBN 0-416-71840-X). Methuen Inc.

Vance, Adrian. Audio Visual Production. (Illus.). 1979. 16.95 (ISBN 0-8174-2480-6, Amphoto); pap. 9.95 o.p. (ISBN 0-8174-2152-1). Watson-Guptill.

Vance Bibliographics. Index to Architecture: Bibliography A 637-A 876 (January 1982-December 1982) 1983. pap. 10.50 (ISBN 0-88066-327-8, A 877). Vance Biblios.

Vance Bibliographies. Index to Public Administration: Bibliography P 877- P 1116 (January 1982-December 1982) (Public Administration Ser.). 78p. 1983. pap. 12.00 (ISBN 0-88066-347-2). Vance Biblios.

Vance Bibliographies Staff. Author Index to Public Administration: Bibliography P1 to P1000 (June 1978-July 1982) (Public Administration Ser.: Bibliography P-1060). 63p. 1982. pap. 9.75 (ISBN 0-88066-210-7). Vance Biblios.

--Subject Index to Public Administration Series: Bibliography P1 to P1000 (June 1978-July 1982) (Public Administration Ser.: Bibliography P1061). 139p. 1982. pap. 18.00 (ISBN 0-88066-211-5). Vance Biblios.

--Title Index to Public Administration Series: Bibliography P1 to P1000 (June 1978-July 1982) (Public Administration Ser.: Bibliography P-1059). 57p. 1982. pap. 8.25 (ISBN 0-88066-199-2). Vance Biblios.

Vance, Charles C. Boss Psychology: Help Your Boss Make You a Success. 1975. 3.25 (ISBN 0-07-066871-X, P&RB). McGraw.

--Manager Today, Executive Tomorrow. LC 82-14865. 240p. 1983. Repr. of 1974 ed. lib. bdg. write for info. (ISBN 0-89874-554-3). Krieger.

Vance, Cyrus. The Choice is Ours. 1983. price not set (ISBN 0-671-44339-9). S&S.

Vance, Edward F. Coupling to Shielded Cables. LC 78-16186. 1978. 29.95x (ISBN 0-471-04107-6, Pub. by Wiley-Interscience). Wiley.

Vance, Eleanor G., ed. see Sewell, Anna.

Vance, J. E. & Warner, J. C. Uranium Technology. (National Nuclear Energy Ser.: Div. VII, Vol. 2A). 231p. 1951. pap. 20.50 (ISBN 0-87079-227-X, TID-5231); microfilm 4.50 (ISBN 0-87079-463-9, TID-5231). DOE.

Vance, Jack. The Dragon Masters. 128p. 1976. Repr. of 1962 ed. lib. bdg. 9.95 o.p. (ISBN 0-8398-2323-1, Gregg). G K Hall.

--Dust of Far Suns. (Science Fiction Ser.). 1981. pap. 1.75 o.p. (ISBN 0-87997-588-1, UE1588). Daw Bks.

--The Eyes of the Overworld. (Science Fiction Ser.). Repr. of 1966 ed. lib. bdg. 11.00 o.p. (ISBN 0-8398-2366-5, Gregg). G K Hall.

--The Face. (Science Fiction Ser.). (Orig.). 1979. pap. 1.95 o.p. (ISBN 0-87997-498-2, UJ1498). Daw Bks.

--The Five Gold Bands. (Science Fiction Ser.). 1980. pap. 1.95 o.p. (ISBN 0-87997-518-0, UJ1518). DAW Bks.

--The Gray Prince. 1983. pap. 2.25 (ISBN 0-87997-716-7, UE1716). DAW Bks.

--The Languages of Pao. (Science Fiction Ser.). pap. 1.75 o.p. (ISBN 0-87997-541-5, UE541). DAW Bks.

--Lyonesse. 448p. (Orig.). 1983. pap. 6.95 (ISBN 0-425-05873-5). Berkley Pub.

--Maske: Thaery. 1977. pap. 1.50 o.p. (ISBN 0-425-03503-4, Medallion). Berkley Pub.

--Maske: Thaery. 224p. 1983. pap. 2.50 (ISBN 0-425-05934-0). Berkley Pub.

--Solar Wind. (Paper Tiger Ser.). (Illus.). 96p. 1980. pap. 6.98 (ISBN 0-399-50498-2, Perige). Putnam Pub Group.

--To Live Forever. 1982. pap. 2.25 (ISBN 0-87997-787-6, UE1787). DAW Bks.

--Vandals of the Void. 1979. lib. bdg. 9.50 (ISBN 0-8398-2517-X, Gregg). G K Hall.

Vance, Joel M. Upland Bird Hunting. LC 80-5886. (Illus.). 311p. 1982. 17.95 (ISBN 0-525-93234-8, Outdoor Life Bk). Dutton.

Vance, Lee W. Tracing your Philippine Ancestors, 3 vols. (Illus.). 771p. 1980. 42.50 set (ISBN 0-9608528-0-8); pap. 28.50 set (ISBN 0-9608528-4-0). Philippine Anc.

--Tracing Your Philippine Ancestors, 3 vols. Set. pap. 28.50 (ISBN 0-9608528-4-0). Vol. 1 (ISBN 0-9608528-1-6). Vol. 2 (ISBN 0-9608528-2-4). Vol. 3 (ISBN 0-9608528-3-2). Philippine Anc.

--Tracing Your Phillippine Ancestors. 42.50 (ISBN 0-9608528-0-8). Philippine Anc.

Vance, Malcolm. The Movie Ad Book. (Illus.). 160p. 1981. 19.95 (ISBN 0-89893-503-2); pap. 9.95 (ISBN 0-89893-301-3). CDP.

Vance, Mary. Industrial Waste Disposal: A Bibliography. (Public Administration Ser.: Bibliography). 1982. pap. 8.25 (ISBN 0-88066-153-4). Vance Biblios.

--Mortgage & Construction Finance: A Bibliography. (Architecture Ser.: Bibliography A-778). 57p. 1982. pap. 8.25 (ISBN 0-88066-202-6). Vance Biblios.

--New Publications for Architecture Libraries. (Architecture Ser.: Bibliography A-816). 1982. pap. 7.50 (ISBN 0-88066-201-8). Vance Biblios.

--Reinforced Concrete: A Bibliography. (Architecture Ser.: Bibliography A 838). 48p. 1982. pap. 7.50 (ISBN 0-88066-248-4). Vance Biblios.

Vance, William E. Death Stalks the Cheyenne Trail. LC 80-926. (Double D Western Ser.). 192p. 1980. 10.95 o.p. (ISBN 0-385-15518-2). Doubleday.

Vance, Wilson J. Stone's River: Turning Point of the Civil War. 1982. pap. text ed. 25.00 (ISBN 0-87556-584-0). Saifer.

Vancil, Chris. Algebra & Trigonometry. 544p. 1983. text ed. 21.95 (ISBN 0-02-422400-6). Macmillan.

Vancil, Richard F. Financial Executive's Handbook. LC 69-15541. 1970. 45.00 (ISBN 0-87094-008-2). Dow Jones-Irwin.

Vancil, Richard F., jt. auth. see Lorange, Peter.

Van Cise, Jerrold G. & Lifland, William T. Understanding the Antitrust Laws. 8th ed. LC 80-83813. 377p. 1980. text ed. 35.00 (ISBN 0-686-69172-5, B1-1276). PLI.

Van Cleaf, David W., jt. auth. see Brooks, Douglas M.

Van Cleave, Charles. Late Somatic Effects of Ionizing Radiation. LC 68-62106. (AEC Technical Information Center Ser.). 310p. 1968. pap. 15.75 (ISBN 0-87079-253-9, TID-24310); microfiche 4.50 (ISBN 0-87079-254-7, TID-24310). DOE.

Van Cleve, Spike. Forty Years' Gatherin's. LC 77-71679. (Illus.). 1977. 12.95 (ISBN 0-913504-39-4). Lowell Pr.

Van Cleve, Thomas C. The Emperor Frederick Second of Hohenstaufen, Immutator Mundi. (Illus.). 1972. 42.00x o.p. (ISBN 0-19-822513-X). Oxford U Pr.

Van Clief, Ron. The Manual of the Martial Arts: An Introduction to the Combined Techniques of Karate, Kung-Fu, Tae Kwon Do, & Aiki-Jitsu for Everyone. (Illus.). 1981. 14.95 (ISBN 0-89256-204-8); pap. 9.95 (ISBN 0-686-96859-X). Rawson Wade.

Van Clief, Sylvia, jt. auth. see Heide, Florence P.

Van Corstanje. Francis: Bible of the Poor. 1977. 5.95 o.p. (ISBN 0-8199-0661-1). Franciscan Herald.

Vancouver Planning Dept., ed. Signs in Vancouver. 1974. pap. 5.00 o.p. (ISBN 0-685-51830-2). Signs of Times.

Van Creveld, Martin L. Hitler's Strategy Nineteen Forty to Nineteen Forty-One: The Balkan Clue. LC 72-97885. (International Studies). (Illus.). 272p. 1973. 29.95 (ISBN 0-521-20143-8). Cambridge U Pr.

--Supplying War. LC 77-5550. 1979. pap. 11.95 (ISBN 0-521-29793-1). Cambridge U Pr.

--Supplying War: Logistics from Wallenstein to Patton. LC 77-5550. (Illus.). 1977. 34.50 (ISBN 0-521-21730-X). Cambridge U Pr.

Van Croonenburg, Englebert J. Gateway to Reality: An Introduction to Philosophy. LC 82-13712. 164p. 1982. pap. text ed. 10.00 (ISBN 0-8191-2635-7). U Pr of Amer.

Van Daele, A. Continuous Crossed Products & Type 111 von Neumann Algebras. LC 77-91096. (London Mathematical Society Lecture Note Ser.: No. 31). 1978. 14.95 (ISBN 0-521-21975-2). Cambridge U Pr.

Van Dalen, D. & Lascar, D., eds. Logic Colloquium 1980: Papers Intended for the European Meeting of the Association for Symbolic Logic. (Studies in Logic & the Foundations of Mathematics: Vol. 108). 342p. 1982. 51.00 (ISBN 0-444-86465-2, North Holland). Elsevier.

Van Dalen, D., jt. ed. see Troelstra, A. S.

Van Dalen, D. B. Understanding Educational Research. 4th ed. 1978. text ed. 26.50 (ISBN 0-07-066883-3). McGraw.

Van Dalen, Deobold B. & Bennett, Bruce. World History of Physical Education: Cultural, Philosophical & Comparative. 2nd ed. 1971. ref. ed. 25.95x (ISBN 0-13-967919-7). P-H.

Van Dalen, J. T., jt. ed. see Lessell, S.

Van Dallen, H. & Zeigler, L. Introduction to Political Science: People, Politics, & Perception. 1977. pap. 13.95 (ISBN 0-13-493205-6). P-H.

Van Dam, H., jt. ed. see Frampton, P. H.

Van Dam, K. & Van Gelder, B. F., eds. Structure & Function of Energy-Transducing Membranes: Proceedings of a Workshop, Amsterdam, August, 1977. (BBA Library: Vol. 14). 1978. 77.00 (ISBN 0-444-80019-0, North Holland). Elsevier.

Vandam, Leroy D., jt. auth. see Volpitto, Perry P.

Van Dan, B. The Ethnic Phenomenon. 1982. 19.95 (ISBN 0-444-01550-7). Elsevier.

Van Deburg, William L. The Slave Drivers: Black Agricultural Labor Supervisors in the Antebellum South. LC 78-59261. (Contributions in Afro-American & African Studies: No. 43). 1979. lib. bdg. 25.00x (ISBN 0-313-20610-4, VSD/). Greenwood.

Van Deenen, L. L., jt. ed. see Florkin, M.

Van De Hulst, H. C. Multiple Light Scattering: Tables, Formulas & Applications, Vol.1. LC 79-51687. 1980. 38.50 (ISBN 0-12-710701-0). Acad Pr.

Van de John, Richard, ed. see Taylor, Joan & Treon, Ray.

Vande Kempe, Hendrika & Malony, H. Newton. Psychology & Theology: A Bibliography of Historical Bases for the Integration of Psychology & Theology. LC 82-49045. (Bibliographies in the History of Psychology & Psychiatry Ser.). (Orig.). 1983. lib. bdg. 65.00 (ISBN 0-527-92779-1). Kraus Intl.

Vande Kieft, Ruth M. Eudora Welty. (United States Authors Ser.). 1962. lib. bdg. 11.95 (ISBN 0-8057-0776-X, Twayne). G K Hall.

Van D'Elden, Karl H. & Kirchow, Evelyn. Was Deutsche Lesen. 192p. (Orig., Ger.). 1973. text ed. 13.95 (ISBN 0-07-066935-X, C). McGraw.

Van De Leuv, John H., ed. see American College of Emergency Physicians.

Vandell, Frank J. Police Training for Tough Calls: Discretionary Situations. 140p. 1980. pap. 9.95 o.p. (ISBN 0-686-64815-3). Carrollton Pr.

Vandeman, G. Is Anybody Driving. LC 75-11469. (Stories That Win Ser.). 1975. pap. 0.95 o.p. (ISBN 0-8163-0175-1, 12523-7). Pacific Pr Pub Assn.

Vandeman, G. E. Psychic Roulette. 1973. pap. 3.95 o.p. (ISBN 0-8163-0136-0, 16693-4). Pacific Pr Pub Assn.

Vandenberg, Arthur H., Jr. & Morris, Joe A. The Private Papers of Senator Vandenberg. LC 74-15561. (Illus.). 599p. 1975. Repr. of 1952 ed. lib. bdg. 32.50x o.p. (ISBN 0-8371-7829-0, VAPR). Greenwood.

Vandenberg, Edwin J., jt. ed. see Price, Charles C.

Vandenberg, M., jt. auth. see Gage, Michael.

Vandenberg, Philipp. The Curse of the Pharaohs. Weyr, Tom, tr. LC 75-830. (Illus.). 1975. 9.95i (ISBN 0-397-01035-4). Har-Row.

Vandenberge, Peter N. The Historical Directory of the Reformed Church in America. 1978. pap. 17.95 (ISBN 0-8028-1746-7). Eerdmans.

Vandenbergh, John G., ed. Pheromones & Reproduction in Mammals. LC 82-22776. Date not set. price not set (ISBN 0-12-710780-0). Acad Pr.

Van Den Bergh, T. Trade Unions: What Are They? LC 79-97952. 1970. write for info. (ISBN 0-08-006517-1); pap. write for info. (ISBN 0-08-006516-3). Pergamon.

Vandenberghe, J. P., jt. auth. see Chaballe, L. Y.

Van Den Berghe, Pierre L., jt. auth. see Colby, Benjamin N.

Van Den Berghe, Pierre L., ed. The Liberal Dilemma in South Africa. LC 79-10341. 1979. 25.00x (ISBN 0-312-48246-9). St Martin.

Vandenbosch, Amry. United Nations: Background, Organization, Functions, Activities. Repr. of 1952 ed. lib. bdg. 16.00x (ISBN 0-8371-4050-1, VAUN). Greenwood.

Van Den Bosch, Robert. The Pesticide Conspiracy. LC 77-12885. (Orig.). 1980. pap. 4.95 o.p. (ISBN 0-385-15792-4, Anch). Doubleday.

Vandenbosch, Robert & Huizenga, John R. Nuclear Fission. 1973. 63.50 (ISBN 0-12-710850-5). Acad Pr.

Van Den Bosch, Robert see Nouwen, Henri J. & Gaffney, Walter J.

Van Den Bossche, ed. Comparative Biochemistry of Parasites. 1972. 56.00 (ISBN 0-12-711050-X). Acad Pr.

Van den Bossche, H. Host Invader Interplay. (Janssen Research Foundations Ser.: Vol. 2). 1981. 101.50 (ISBN 0-444-80284-3). Elsevier.

Van Den Bossche, H. & Van Den Bossche, H., eds. Symposium on Biochemistry of Parasites & Host Parasitic Relationships: Proceedings, Second International Symposium, 1976. 1977. 86.00 (ISBN 0-7204-0592-0, North Holland). Elsevier.

Van den Brock, A. A., jt. ed. see Nieuwenhuis, Paul.

VandenBroeck, A., tr. see Schwaller de Lubicz, R. A.

VandenBroeck, Andre, tr. see Schwaller de Lubicz, R. A.

VandenBroeck, G., tr. see Schwaller de Lubicz, R. A.

VandenBroeck, Go, tr. see Schwaller de Lubicz, R. A.

Van Den Bruck, Arthur Moeller see Moeller Van Den Bruck, Arthur.

Vandenburg, Mary Lou. Help! Emergencies That Could Happen to You, & How to Handle Them. LC 75-7007. (Medical Books for Children). (Illus.). 72p. (gr. 4-7). 1975. PLB 3.95g (ISBN 0-8225-0020-5). Lerner Pubns.

Vandenburgh, Jane, ed. see Hamamura, John & Hamamura, Susan.

Vandenbusche, D. & Myers, R. Marble Colorado. pap. 5.95x (ISBN 0-686-82442-3). Golden Bell.

Van Den Doel, H. Democracy & Welfare Economics. LC 78-21160. 1979. 34.50 (ISBN 0-521-22568-X); pap. 10.95 (ISBN 0-521-29555-6). Cambridge U Pr.

Van Den Essen, A. R. & Levelt, A. H. Irregular Singularities in Several Variables. LC 82-18161. (Memoirs of the American Mathematical Society Ser.: No. 270). 4.00 (ISBN 0-8218-2270-5, MEMO/270). AM Math.

Vanden Eynden, Charles, jt. auth. see Eggan, Lawrence C.

Van Den Handel, J. Selected Papers in Physics in Honor of C. J. Gorter. 1976. 30.00 (ISBN 0-444-10616-2, North-Holland). Elsevier.

Van Den Hengel, John W. see Den Hengel, John W. Van.

Van den Hoek, C. Revision of the European Species of Cladophora. (Illus.). 1976. Repr. of 1963 ed. lib. bdg. 46.00x (ISBN 3-87429-112-X). Lubrecht & Cramer.

Van den Kerkhoff, Harry P. Abandoned. 1983. 7.95 (ISBN 0-533-05627-6). Vantage.

Van den Toorn, Pieter C. The Music of Igor Stravinsky. LC 82-2560. (Composers of the Twentieth Century Ser.). 536p. 1983. text ed. 35.00x (ISBN 0-300-02693-5). Yale U Pr.

Van den Werve, jt. auth. see Hue.

Vander, A. J., et al. Human Physiology: The Mechanisms of Body Function. 2nd ed. 1975. 19.50 o.p. (ISBN 0-07-066954-6, C); instructor's manual 5.50 o.p. (ISBN 0-07-066955-4); wkbk. 6.95 o.p. (ISBN 0-07-066956-2). McGraw.

Vander, Arthur, et al. Human Physiology. 3rd ed. (Illus.). 736p. 1980. text ed. 29.00 (ISBN 0-07-066961-9, C); instr's. manual 10.95 (ISBN 0-07-066955-4); wkbk. study guide 12.95 (ISBN 0-07-066963-5). McGraw.

Vander, Arthur J. Renal Physiology. 2nd ed. (Illus.). 1980. pap. text ed. 14.95 (ISBN 0-07-066958-9). McGraw.

Vander, Arthur J., jt. auth. see Luciano, Dorothy S.

Van Der, Veur Paul W. see The, Lian & Van Der Veur, Paul W.

Van der Awevera, Johan, ed. The Semantics of Determiners. 320p. 1980. text ed. 34.50 o.p. (ISBN 0-8391-1627-6). Univ Park.

Vanderbauwhede, A. Local Bifurcation & Symmetry. (Research Notes in Mathematics Ser.: No. 75). 320p. 1982. pap. text ed. 23.95 (ISBN 0-273-08569-7). Pitman Pub MA.

Van der Beist. Analysis of High Temperature Materials. Date not set. 53.50 (ISBN 0-85334-172-9). Elsevier.

Vanderbilt, Amy see Baldridge, Letitia.

Vanderbilt, Arthur T. The Challenge of Law Reform. LC 76-3784. 194p. 1976. Repr. of 1955 ed. lib. bdg. 18.50x (ISBN 0-8371-8809-1, VALR). Greenwood.

Vanderbilt, Byron M. Inventing: How the Masters Did It. LC 74-14959. 1974. 12.95 (ISBN 0-87716-054-6, Pub. by Moore Pub Co). F Apple.

Vanderburgh, Rosamond M., jt. auth. see Salerno, Nan F.

Van der Eyken, Willem. The Education of Three to Eight Year Olds in Europe in the Eighties. (NFER European Trends Reports). 168p. 1982. pap. text ed. 11.75x (ISBN 0-85633-237-2, NFER). Humanities.

Vanderford, Jennifer. Joy Cometh in the Morning. LC 82-83503. (Illus.). 160p. 1983. pap. 4.95 (ISBN 0-89081-364-7). Harvest Hse.

Van Der Geest, Bans. Presence in the Pulpit: The Impact of Personality in Preaching. Stott, Doug, tr. LC 81-82352. 1982. pap. 12.95 (ISBN 0-8042-1897-8). John Knox.

Vandergoot, David. Placement in Rehabilitation. 252p. 1979. pap. text ed. 15.95 (ISBN 0-8391-1439-7). Univ Park.

Vandergoot, David & Avellani, Pamela B. A Compendium of Placement-Related Literature. LC 78-62048. 352p. 1978. 9.25 (ISBN 0-686-43001-8). Human Res Ctr.

Vandergoot, David & Jacobsen, Richard J. New Directions for Placement-Related Research & Practice in the Rehabilitation Process. LC 79-105250. 44p. 1977. 4.75 (ISBN 0-686-38812-7). Human Res Ctr.

Vandergoot, David & Swirsky, Jessica. A Review of Placement Services Within a Comprehensive Rehabilitation Framework: Technical Report. LC 78-72067. 60p. 1979. 5.25 (ISBN 0-686-38819-4). Human Res Ctr.

Vandergoot, David, jt. auth. see Engelkes, James R.

Vandergoot, David, jt. auth. see Swirsky, Jessica.

Vander Goot, Mary see Goot, Mary V.

Vandergraft, James S. Introduction to Numerical Computations. (Computer Science & Applied Mathematics Ser.). 1978. 32.50 (ISBN 0-12-711350-9). Acad Pr.

Vandergraft, James S., ed. Introduction to Numerical Computations. LC 82-16252. (Computer Science & Applied Mathematics Ser.). 369p. 1983. price not set (ISBN 0-12-711356-8). Acad Pr.

Vandergriff, Aola. Daughters of the Opal Skies. 496p. (Orig.). 1982. pap. 3.50 (ISBN 0-446-30564-2). Warner Bks.

--Daughters of the Southwind. 544p. (Orig.). 1982. pap. 3.50 (ISBN 0-446-30561-8). Warner Bks.

--Daughters of the Wild Country. 496p. (Orig.). 1982. pap. 3.50 (ISBN 0-446-30562-6). Warner Bks.

Vandergrift, Kay. The Teaching Role of the School Media Specialist. (School Media Centers: Focus on Issues & Trends: No. 3). 1979. pap. 6.00 (ISBN 0-8389-3222-3). ALA.

Vanderheiden, G. Non-Vocal Communication Resource Book. 314p. 1978. text ed. 19.95 (ISBN 0-8391-1252-1). Univ Park.

Vanderheiden, Gregg C. & Grilley, Kate, eds. Non-Vocal Communication Techniques & Aids for the Severely Physically Handicapped. (Illus.). 246p. 1976. pap. 19.95 (ISBN 0-8391-0952-0). Univ Park.

Vanderhoeven, P. I., jt. ed. see Meighan, Clement W.

Van der Houwen, P. Construction of Integrated Formulas for Initial Value Problems. 1976. 64.00 (ISBN 0-444-10903-X). Elsevier.

Van der Hulst, Harry & Smith, Norval, eds. The Structure of Phonological Representation: Pt. Two. 265p. 1983. 35.00x (ISBN 90-70176-59-9); pap. 21.00x (ISBN 90-70176-58-0). Foris Pubns.

Van de Riet, R. P. Distributed Data Sharing Systems. 1982. 42.75 (ISBN 0-444-86374-5). Elsevier.

Van Der Kamp, Leo. J., jt. ed. see De Gruijter, Dato N.

Van Der Kamp, Leo J., et al, eds. Psychometrics for Educational Debates. LC 79-4308. 1980. 66.95x (ISBN 0-471-27596-4, Pub. by Wiley-Interscience). Wiley.

Vander Klay, Grace. Bible Puzzle Fun. (Pelican Activity Ser.). 32p. (gr. 5-7). 1976. pap. 0.89 o.p. (ISBN 0-8010-9267-1). Baker Bk.

Van der Kleijn, E. & Jonkers, J. R. Clinical Pharmacy. 1977. 62.50 (ISBN 0-444-80007-7). Elsevier.

Van der Kleijn, E., jt. ed. see Turakka, H.

Van Der Klip, Rita. Crochet. (Illus.). 1977. 6.95 o.p. (ISBN 0-8467-0240-1, Pub. by Two Continents). Hippocrene Bks.

VanderKolk, Charles J. Assessment & Planning with the Visually Impaired. 232p. 1981. text ed. 17.95 (ISBN 0-8391-1629-2). Univ Park.

Van der Korst, J. K. see Korst, J. K.

Van Der Kulk, W., jt. auth. see Schouten, Jan A.

Vanderlaan, Roger F. Persuasion. LC 81-71065. 185p. (Orig.). Date not set. pap. 11.95 (ISBN 0-942060-00-8). El Camino.

Vanderleest, Henry W. & Johnston, Michael L. Cases in Transportation Management. (Illus.). 104p. (Orig.). 1983. pap. text ed. 5.95x (ISBN 0-88133-011-6). Waveland Pr.

Van Der Leeuw, Gerardus. Religion in Essence & Development, 2 vols. 11.00 ea. (ISBN 0-8446-1457-2). Peter Smith.

Van der Linden, G. A., ed. APL Eighty: Proceedings of the International APL Congress, Leiden, June 1980. 1980. 51.00 (ISBN 0-444-86015-0). Elsevier.

Van Der Linder, Frank. The Real Reagan. 11.95 o.p. (ISBN 0-686-73298-7). Morrow.

Van Der Lingen, Gerrit J., ed. Diagenesis of Deep-Sea Biogenic Sediments. LC 77-7496. (Benchmark Papers in Geology: Vol. 40). 1977. 53.50 (ISBN 0-12-787646-4). Acad Pr.

Vanderlip, D. George. Christianity According to John. LC 74-34585. 1975. 10.00 (ISBN 0-664-20737-5). Westminster.

Van Der Lyn, Edita. Akitas. (Illus.). 128p. 1981. 4.95 (ISBN 0-87666-710-8, KW-107). TFH Pubns.

--Dachshunds. (Illus.). 128p. 1980. 4.95 (ISBN 0-87666-704-3, KW-085). TFH Pubns.

Van Der Maas. Interpretation of Infrared Spectra: An Audio Visual Program. 1979. 297.00 (ISBN 0-471-26072-X, Wiley Heyden). Wiley.

Van der Maas, J. H. Basic Infrared Spectroscopy. 2nd ed. 1972. 38.00x (ISBN 0-471-26070-3, Pub. by Wiley Heyden); pap. 29.95 (ISBN 0-471-26069-X). Wiley.

Van Der Marck, Jan. Christo: Collection on Loan from the Rothschild Bank Art Gallery, Zurich. LC 81-84093. (Illus.). 144p. 1981. pap. 19.95x (ISBN 0-934418-12-8). La Jolla Mus Contemp Art.

--Herbert Bayer: From Type to Landscape - Designs, Projects, & Proposals, 1923-73. (Illus.). 55p. 1977. pap. 10.00x o.p. (ISBN 0-87451-982-9). U Pr of New Eng.

Van der Marel, R. & Beutelspacher, H. Atlas of Infrared Spectroscopy of Clay Minerals & Their Admixtures. 1976. 106.50 (ISBN 0-444-41187-9). Elsevier.

Van der Mass, Ed, tr. see Roberts, David.

Van Der Meer, Atie, jt. auth. see Van Der Meer, Ron.

Van Der Meer, Dennis, jt. auth. see Loehr, James E.

Van Der Meer, Haye S. Women Priests in the Catholic Church? A Theological-Historical Investigation. Swidler, Leonard & Swidler, Arlene, trs. from Ger. LC 73-79480. Orig. Title: Priestertum der Frau? 230p. 1973. 12.95 (ISBN 0-87722-059-X). Temple U Pr.

Van der Meer, J. H., jt. auth. see Van Leeuwen Boomkamp, C.

Van Der Meer, Ron & Van Der Meer, Atie. Funny Fingers. (Illus.). 14p. (ps). 1983. finger-hole cards in box 8.95 (ISBN 0-434-97104-9, Pub. by Heinemann England). David & Charles.

Van Der Meid, Louise B. Cats. (Orig.). pap. 2.95 (ISBN 0-87666-173-8, M503). TFH Pubns.

--Siamese Cats. (Orig.). pap. 2.95 (ISBN 0-87666-183-5, M509). TFH Pubns.

Van Der Meijden, R. Systematics & Evolution of Xantophyllum: Polygalaceae. (Leiden Botanical Ser.: Vol. 7). (Illus.). vii, 159p. 1982. pap. write for info. (ISBN 90-04-06594-6). E J Brill.

Van Der Merwe, Alwyn, ed. Old & New Questions in Physics, Cosmology, Philosophy, & Theoretical Biology: Essays in Honor of Wolfgang Yourgrau. 905p. 1983. 95.00x (ISBN 0-306-40962-3, Plenum Pr). Plenum Pub.

Van Der Merwe, H. W. The Future of the University in Southern Africa. Welsh, David, ed. LC 78-60638. 1978. 26.00x (ISBN 0-312-31484-1). St Martin.

Van der Meulen, Jan & Price, Nancy W. The West Portals of Chartres Cathedral, I: The Iconology of the Creation. LC 80-5586. 1981. lib. bdg. 22.25 (ISBN 0-8191-1402-2); pap. text ed. 11.50 (ISBN 0-8191-1403-0). U Pr of Amer.

Vander Meulen, S. V., jt. auth. see Lindsey, C. H.

Vandermey, H. Ronald, jt. ed. see Cohen, Gary G.

VanderMey, Randall, jt. auth. see Tsuang, Ming T.

Van Der Molen, H. J. & Klopper, A., eds. Hormonal Factors in Fertility, Infertility & Contraception: Proceedings of the Tenth Meeting of the International Study Group for Steroid Hormones, Rome, December 2-4, 1981. (International Congress Ser.: No. 580). 318p. 1982. 86.00 (ISBN 0-444-90258-9, Excerpta Medica). Elsevier.

Vander Mrck, J., jt. auth. see Hedberg, G.

Vandermyn, Gaye, jt. auth. see LeMoine, Suzanne.

Van Der Noot, Jan see Noot, Jan Van Der.

Van der Pijl, L. Principles of Dispersal in Higher Plants. 2nd ed. LC 72-83445. (Illus.). 170p. 1972. 17.90 o.p. (ISBN 0-387-05881-8). Springer-Verlag.

Van Der Plank, J. E. Plant Diseases: Epidemics & Control. 1964. 46.00 (ISBN 0-12-711450-5). Acad Pr.

Van Der Plas, Leendert. Identification of Detrital Feldspars. (Developments in Sedimentology: Vol. 6). 1966. 76.75 (ISBN 0-444-40597-6). Elsevier.

Van Der Poel, Jean, ed. see Smuts, J. C.

Van Der Post, Laurens. A Far-off Place. LC 74-7632. 1974. 7.95 o.p. (ISBN 0-688-00286-2). Morrow.

--The Lost World of the Kalahari. LC 77-4292. (Illus.). 1977. pap. 3.95 o.p. (ISBN 0-15-653706-0, Harv). HarBraceJ.

--Yet Being Someone Other. 352p. 1983. Repr. 14.95 (ISBN 0-688-01843-2). Morrow.

Vanders, Iris & Kerr, Paul F. Mineral Recognition. LC 66-25223. 1967. 37.95 (ISBN 0-471-90295-0, Pub. by Wiley-Interscience). Wiley.

Van Dersal, William R. The Successful Supervisor: In Government & Business. 3rd, rev. ed. LC 73-4134. (Illus.). 220p. 1974. 12.45xi (ISBN 0-06-014487-4, HarpT). Har-Row.

Vander Shrier, Nettie. The Golden Thread. 169p. 1983. pap. 2.95 (ISBN 0-8024-0173-2). Moody.

Van der Smissen, Betty. Bibliography of Research: Organized Camping, Environmental Education, Adventure Activities, Interpretative Services, Outdoor Recreation Users & Programming. 266p. (Orig.). 1982. pap. 17.50. Am Camping.

Van der Spoel, S. & Pierrot-Bults, A. C., eds. Zoogeography & Diversity in Plankton. LC 79-9494. 410p. 1979. 82.95x o.p. (ISBN 0-470-26798-4). Halsted Pr.

Van Der Spuy, H. I., ed. The Psychology of Apartheid: A Psychosocial Perspective on South Africa. LC 78-63064. 1978. pap. text ed. 7.75 o.p. (ISBN 0-8191-0610-0). U Pr of Amer.

Van der Starre, H., ed. see International Symposium on Olfaction & Taste, 7th, the Netherlands 1980.

Van Dertang, Ger, jt. auth. see Van Maarseveen, Henc.

Van der Veen, B., et al, eds. A Bibliography of Frisian Dictionaries. 100p. 1983. 12.00 (ISBN 0-686-36290-X). Benjamins North Am.

Vanderveen, B. H. & Miller, D. N., eds. Commercial Vehicles. (Illus.). 10.95x o.p. (ISBN 0-8464-0259-9). Beekman Pubs.

Vandervelde, G. Original Sin: Two Major Trends in Contemporary Roman Catholic Reinterpretation. LC 81-40000. 364p. 1982. lib. bdg. 25.75 (ISBN 0-8191-1849-4); pap. text ed. 14.00 (ISBN 0-8191-1850-8). U Pr of Amer.

Vandervell, T. & Witham, H. Figure Skating: 1880. (Illus.). 200p. Date not set. pap. 12.50 (ISBN 0-87556-583-2). Saifer.

Van Der Ven, A. H. Introduction to Scaling. 301p. 1980. 44.95x (ISBN 0-471-27686-3, Pub. by Wiley-Interscience). Wiley.

Vanderver, Timothy A., Jr. Federal Lands Notebook. 250p. 1981. 48.00 (ISBN 0-686-38760-0). Gov Insts.

Van der Veur, Paul W. Freemasonry in Indonesia from Radermacher to Soekanto, 1762-1961. LC 76-620040. (Papers in International Studies: Southeast Asia: No. 40). (Illus.). 1976. pap. 4.00 (ISBN 0-89680-026-1, Ohio U Ctr Intl). Ohio U Pr.

Van Der Veur, Paul W., jt. auth. see The, Lian.

Van Der Vlugt, Ebed. Asia Aflame. (Illus.). 5.00 (ISBN 0-8159-5015-2). Devin.

Van der Voort, G. F. Metallurgy. 608p. 1983. 28.95x (ISBN 0-07-066970-8). McGraw.

Vandervoort, Tom. Sailing Is for Me. LC 81-3726. (Sports for Me Bks.). (Illus.). (gr. 2-5). 1981. PLB 6.95g (ISBN 0-8225-1128-2, AACR2). Lerner Pubns.

Van der Waay, D. & Verhoef, J. New Criteria for Antimicrobial Therapy: Maintenance of Digestive Tract Colonization Resistance. (International Congress Ser.: Vol. 477). 1980. 50.25 (ISBN 0-444-90096-9). Elsevier.

Vanderwalker, F. N. Wood Finishing. rev. ed. LC 76-21190. (Illus.). 408p. 1980. pap. 7.95 (ISBN 0-8069-8798-7). Sterling.

Vanderwarker, Peter. Boston Then & Now: Sixty-Five Boston Sites Photographed in the Past & Present. LC 81-17385. (Illus.). 128p. 1982. pap. 6.95 (ISBN 0-486-24312-5). Dover.

Van der Wee, Hermann & Vinogradov, Vladimir A., eds. Fifth International Conference of Economic History, 3 vols. 1898p. 1979. 130.00x (ISBN 90-279-3158-5). Mouton.

Vanderweide, Harry. Maine Fishing Maps: Rivers & Streams. (Illus.). 96p. (Orig.). 1983. pap. 7.95 (ISBN 0-89933-038-X). DeLorme Pub.

Van der Werf, Tjeerd. Cardiovascular Pathophysiology: A Book of Parents & Professionals. (Illus.). 1980. 21.95x (ISBN 0-19-261153-4); pap. text ed. 13.95x (ISBN 0-19-261229-8). Oxford U Pr.

Van Der Werff, A. & Huls, H. Diatomeenflora van Nederland, 10 fasc. in one vol. 1976. Repr. looseleaf binder 112.00x (ISBN 3-87429-113-8). Lubrecht & Cramer.

Vander Werff, Fred, jt. auth. see Wilson, Doug.

Vanderwood, Paul J. Night Riders of Reelfoot Lake. LC 79-91959. (Illus.). 1980. pap. 6.95 o.p. (ISBN 0-87870-196-6). Memphis St Univ.

Vanderwood, Paul J., ed. Juarez. (Wisconsin-Warner Screenplay Ser.). (Illus.). 128p. 1983. text ed. 17.50 (ISBN 0-299-08740-9); pap. 6.95 (ISBN 0-299-08744-1). U of Wis Pr.

Vander Zanden, James. Educational Psychology. 640p. 1980. pap. text ed. 16.00 (ISBN 0-394-32186-3). Random.

Vander Zanden, James W. Social Psychology. 2nd ed. 524p. 1981. text ed. 21.00 (ISBN 0-394-32427-7). Random.

--Sociology. 4th ed. LC 78-14447. 1979. text ed. 23.95 (ISBN 0-471-04341-9); tchrs manual o.p. (ISBN 0-471-04846-1); study guide avail. (ISBN 0-471-04845-3); tchr's. manual journal entries o.p.- avail. (ISBN 0-471-05813-0). Wiley.

Van der Ziel, Aldert. The Natural Sciences & the Christian Message. LC 60-9802. 259p. 1976. Repr. of 1960 ed. lib. bdg. 16.00x (ISBN 0-8371-7941-6, VANS). Greenwood.

--Noise in Measurements. LC 76-12108. 228p. 1976. 32.50x (ISBN 0-471-89895-3, Pub. by Wiley-Interscience). Wiley.

--Nonlinear Electronic Circuits. LC 76-48145. 1977. 29.95x (ISBN 0-471-02227-6, Pub. by Wiley-Interscience). Wiley.

--Solid State Physical Electronics. 3rd ed. (Illus.). 544p. 1976. 31.95 (ISBN 0-13-821603-7). P-H.

Van Der Zouwen, J., jt. ed. see Dijkstra, W.

Van Der Zouwen, J. see Geyer, R. F. & Zouwen, J. van der.

Van Deurs, George see Deurs, George van.

Van Deursen, A. Illustrated Dictionary of Bible Manners & Customs. (Illus.). 1967. pap. 4.75 (ISBN 0-8022-1762-1). Philos Lib.

Van De Vall, Mark. Labor Organizations: A Macro & Micro Sociological Comparison. 1970. 34.50 (ISBN 0-521-07637-4). Cambridge U Pr.

Van Devanter, Lynda & Morgan, Christopher. Home Before Morning: The Story of an Army Nurse in Vietnam. 1983. 16.95 (ISBN 0-8253-0132-7). Beaufort Bks NY.

Van de Vate, Dwight, Jr. Romantic Love: A Philosophical Inquiry. LC 81-47171. 176p. 1981. 16.75x (ISBN 0-271-00288-3). Pa St U Pr.

Van De Vate, Dwight, Jr., ed. Persons, Privacy & Feeling: Essays in the Philosophy of Mind. LC 78-110147. 1970. 8.95x o.p. (ISBN 0-87870-004-8). Memphis St Univ.

Van de Velde, Paul, jt. auth. see Steininger, G. Russell.

Van de Ven, Andrew H. & Ferry, Diane L. Measuring & Assessing Organizations. LC 79-20003. (Organizational Assessment & Change Ser.). 1980. 39.50x (ISBN 0-471-04832-1, Pub. by Wiley-Interscience). Wiley.

Van De Ven, Andrew H. & Joyce, William F., eds. Perspectives on Organization Design & Behavior. LC 81-11550. (Wiley Ser. on Organizational Assessment & Change). 486p. 1981. 33.95x (ISBN 0-471-09358-0, Pub. by Wiley-Interscience). Wiley.

Van de Ven, Nicole, jt. ed. see Russell, Diana E.

Van De Voorde, Annouk M. Calorie Watchers Cookbook. Walsh, Jackie, ed. LC 78-74603. (Illus.). 1979. pap. 4.95 o.p. (ISBN 0-911954-50-3). Nitty Gritty.

VandeWalle, L. J. Efficient Materials & Coatings Applications for Improved Design & Corrosion Resistance. 1981. 37.00 (ISBN 0-87170-107-3). ASM.

--Residual Stress for Designers & Metallurgists. 1981. 44.00 (ISBN 0-87170-106-5). ASM.

Van De Wetering, Janwillem. The Maine Massacre. (General Ser.). 1979. lib. bdg. 13.95 (ISBN 0-8161-6753-2, Large Print Bks). G K Hall.

Van de Wetering, Janwillen. The Butterfly Hunter. 1982. 12.95 (ISBN 0-686-94092-X). HM.

Vandi, Abdulai. A Model of Mass Communications & National Development: A Liberian Perspective. LC 79-89253. 1979. pap. text ed. 10.75 (ISBN 0-8191-0812-X). U Pr of Amer.

Van Dihn, jt. ed. see Sigham.

Van Dijk, T. A. Pragmatics of Language & Literature. LC 75-31589. (Studies in Theoretical Poetics: Vol. 2). 236p. 1976. pap. 38.50 (ISBN 0-444-10897-1, North-Holland). Elsevier.

Van Dine, S. S. The Benson Murder Case. 1980. lib. bdg. 10.95 (ISBN 0-8398-2553-6, Gregg). G K Hall.

--The Bishop Murder Case. 1980. lib. bdg. 10.95 (ISBN 0-8398-2557-9, Gregg). G K Hall.

--The Canary Murder Case. 1980. lib. bdg. 10.95 (ISBN 0-8398-2554-4, Gregg). G K Hall.

--The Greene Murder Case. 1980. lib. bdg. 10.95 (ISBN 0-8398-2555-2, Gregg). G K Hall.

--The Kennel Murder Case. 1980. lib. bdg. 10.95 (ISBN 0-8398-2558-7, Gregg). G K Hall.

--The Scarab Murder Case. 1980. lib. bdg. 10.95 (ISBN 0-8398-2556-0, Gregg). G K Hall.

VanDine, Stephen, et al. Restraining the Wicked: The Incapacitation of the Dangerous Criminal. (Illus.). 160p. 1979. 17.95x (ISBN 0-669-01774-4). Lexington Bks.

Vandiver, Frank E. Jubal's Raid: General Early's Famous Attack on Washington in 1864. LC 73-19432. (Illus.). 198p. 1974. Repr. of 1960 ed. lib. bdg. 15.50x (ISBN 0-8371-7332-9, VAJR). Greenwood.

Vandiver, Frank E., jt. auth. see Sommers, Richard J.

Vandiver, James V. Criminal Investigation: A Guide to Techniques & Solutions. LC 82-10554. 408p. 1983. 27.50 (ISBN 0-8108-1576-1). Scarecrow.

Vandiver, Trish, jt. auth. see Husain, Syed Arshad.

Vandivert, Rita & Vandivert, William. To The Rescue: Seven Heroes of Conservation. LC 82-6890. (Illus.). 128p. (gr. 7). 1982. PLB 9.95 (ISBN 0-7232-6215-2). Warne.

Vandivert, William, jt. auth. see Vandivert, Rita.

Vandoni, C. E., ed. Eurographics Eighty. 1980. 44.75 (ISBN 0-444-86107-6). Elsevier.

Vandonne, Maurice. The Fully Illustrated Book of Old & Romantic Europe. (The Masterpieces of World Architecture Library). (Illus.). 89p. 1983. 91.75 (ISBN 0-89901-095-4). Found Class Reprints.

Van Door, G. & Perlman, M., eds. Health, Economics & Health Economics: Contributions to Economic Analysis, Vol. 137. 1981. 47.00 (ISBN 0-444-86210-2). Elsevier.

Van Dooren, Ingrid, jt. auth. see Pinxten, Rik.

Van Doorn, J. Disequilibrium Economics. LC 75-19139. 96p. 1976. pap. text ed. 10.95 o.p. (ISBN 0-470-89902-6). Halsted Pr.

Van Dop, H., jt. ed. see Nieuwstadt, F.

Van Dore, Wade. Richard Eberhart: Poet of Life in Death. 12p. (Orig.). 1982. pap. 1.50 (ISBN 0-934996-17-2). Am Stud Pr.

Van Doren, Carl. Three Worlds. LC 77-14329. 1977. Repr. of 1936 ed. lib. bdg. 22.00x o.p. (ISBN 0-8371-9831-3, VATH). Greenwood.

Van Doren, Carl, ed. The Portable Swift. 1956. pap. 14.95 (ISBN 0-670-68720-0). Viking Pr.

Van Doren, Carl, intro. by see Prokosch, Frederic.

Van Doren, Carl C. Many Minds. LC 73-17657. 242p. 1975. Repr. of 1924 ed. lib. bdg. 17.00x (ISBN 0-8371-7261-6, VAMM). Greenwood.

Van Doren, Carlton, et al, eds. Land & Leisure: Concepts & Methods in Outdoor Recreation. 2nd ed. LC 77-94184. (Maaroufa Press Geography Ser.). (Illus.). 1979. pap. text ed. 7.95x (ISBN 0-88425-010-5). Maaroufa Pr.

Van Doren, Charles, jt. auth. see Adler, Mortimer J.

Van Doren, Charles, jt. auth. see Roske, Ralph J.

Van Doren, Mark. The Essays of Mark Van Doren: Nineteen Twenty-Four to Nineteen Seventy-Two. Claire, William, ed. LC 79-8411. (Contributions in American Studies: No. 47). (Illus.). xxv, 270p. 1980. lib. bdg. 29.95x (ISBN 0-313-22098-0, CEV/). Greenwood.

--Henry David Thoreau. LC 61-12121. 1961. Repr. of 1916 ed. 8.00x o.p. (ISBN 0-8462-0290-5). Russell.

--Nathaniel Hawthorne. LC 72-7878. (American Men of Letters Ser.). (Illus.). 285p. 1973. Repr. of 1949 ed. lib. bdg. 19.75x (ISBN 0-8371-6552-0, VANH). Greenwood.

Van Doren, Mark, ed. The Portable Walt Whitman. 1974. pap. 14.95 (ISBN 0-670-76411-6). Viking Pr.

Van Doren, Mark, ed. see Bartram, William.

Van Doren, V. E., jt. ed. see Devreese, J. T.

Van Dorsten, Jan, ed. see Sidney, Philip.

Van Druten, John. I Am a Camera: A Play in Three Acts. LC 71-152613. (Illus.). 1971. Repr. of 1952 ed. lib. bdg. 18.00x (ISBN 0-8371-6048-0, VAIC). Greenwood.

Van Duijvenbooden, W., et al, eds. Quality of Groundwater. (Studies in Environment Science: Vol. 17). 1981. 149.00 (ISBN 0-444-42022-3). Elsevier.

Van Dusen, C. Raymond & Van Smith, Howard. The New Speech-o-Graham: Technique for Persuasive Public Speaking. 264p. 1983. pap. 5.95 (ISBN 0-13-615732-7). P-H.

Van Dusen, Gerald C. William Starbuck Mayo. (United States Authors Ser.). 1979. lib. bdg. 13.95 (ISBN 0-8057-7278-2, Twayne). G K Hall.

Van Dusen, Raymond. Speech Program for Stroke Patients. (Royal Court Reports: No. 2). (Illus.). 52p. (Orig.). 1982. pap. 3.00 (ISBN 0-686-38376-1). Royal Court.

Van Dusen, William D., et al. The Guide to Implementing Financial Aid Data Processing Systems. 56p. (Orig.). 1980. pap. 8.95 o.p. (ISBN 0-87447-134-6). College Bd.

--Planning for a Statewide Educational Information Center Network. 1978. pap. 4.00 o.p. (ISBN 0-87447-070-6, 237406); 2.00, 25 or more copies o.p. (ISBN 0-686-52319-9). College Bd.

Van Duym, A. V., tr. see DeJong, Dola.
Van Duyn, A. V., tr. see DeJong, Dola.
Van Duyn, H., jt. auth. see Cobb, W. A.
Van Duyn, J. The DP Professional's Guide to Writing Effective Technical Communications. 224p. 1982. 22.95 o.p. (ISBN 0-471-06643-5, Pub. by Wiley-Interscience). Wiley.
--The DP Professional's Guide to Writing Effective Technical Communications. 218p. 1982. text ed. 22.95x (ISBN 0-471-05843-2). Ronald Pr.
Van Duyn, Janet. The Greeks. (Library of the Early Civilizations Ser.). (Illus.). 192p. (gr. 10 up). 1972. PLB 9.95 (ISBN 0-07-067038-2, 67038, GB). McGraw.
Van Duyn, Mona. Letters from a Father & Other Poems. LC 81-70068. 1982. 11.95 (ISBN 0-689-11286-6); pap. 6.95 (ISBN 0-689-11287-4). Atheneum.
Van Duyse, Florimond see Duyse, Florimond van.
Van Dyke, Henry, jt. auth. see Garbee, Ed.
Van Dyke, John M. Jury Selection Procedures: Our Uncertain Commitment to Representative Juries. LC 76-43342. 448p. 1977. prof ref 22.50x (ISBN 0-88410-237-8). Ballinger Pub.
Van Dyke, M. & Wehausen, J. V., eds. Annual Review of Fluid Mechanics, Vol. 14. LC 74-80866. (Illus.). 1982. text ed. 22.00 (ISBN 0-8243-0714-3). Annual Reviews.
Van Dyke, Robert E., ed. see Baker, Ray J.
Van Dyke Hubbard, Cortlandt, jt. auth. see Eberlein, H. D.
Van Dyne, Susan, ed. Woman's Voices in American Poetry: The Beauty of Inflections or the Beauty of Innuendoes. 54p. 1981. pap. 3.50 (ISBN 0-87391-024-9). Smith Coll.
Vane, H. & Thompson, J. An Introduction to Macroeconomic Policy. 317p. 1982. text ed. 27.50x (ISBN 0-7108-0130-0, Pub. by Harvester England). Humanities.
Vane, John R. & Bergstrom, Sune, eds. Prostacyclin. LC 78-601200. 466p. 1979. text ed. 51.00 (ISBN 0-89004-330-2). Raven.
Van Eck, G. H. see Eck, G. H. van, Jr.
Van Eeden, Frederik. Deeps of Deliverance. Robinson, Margaret, tr. LC 74-8923. (International Studies & Translations Ser.). 1974. lib. bdg. 10.95 o.p. (ISBN 0-8057-3419-8, Twayne). G K Hall.
--Paul's Awakening. Lake, H. S., tr. from Dutch. LC 78-70615. 1983. pap. 6.95 (ISBN 0-86164-106-X, Pub. by Momenta Pub Ltd). Hunter Hse.
Van Eemeren, Grootendorst. Regels voor Redilijke Discussies. 496p. (Dutch.). Date not set. 19.50x (ISBN 0-686-37587-4); pap. price not set. Foris Pubns.
Van Egmond, J., et al, eds. Information Systems for Patient Care: Proceedings of the IFIP Working Conference on Information Systems for Patient Care Review, Analysis & Evaluation. 1976. 57.50 (ISBN 0-7204-0463-0, North-Holland). Elsevier.
Van Ek, J. A. The Threshold Level for Modern Language Learning in Schools. (Applied Linguistics & Language Study Ser.). 1978. pap. text ed. 10.75 (ISBN 0-582-55700-3). Longman.
Vanek, Miroslav & Cratty, Bryant J. Psychology & the Superior Athlete. (Illus.). 1970. text ed. 15.95x (ISBN 0-02-422670-X). Macmillan.
Van Elliot, Mai see Elliot, Mai Van.
Van Erk, Rien. Oscilloscopes: Functional Operation & Measuring Examples. 1978. 30.50 (ISBN 0-07-067050-1, P&RB). McGraw.
Van Ess, Donald H. The Heritage of Musical Style. LC 80-6235. 384p. 1981. lib. bdg. 30.75 (ISBN 0-8191-1667-X); pap. text ed. 19.50 (ISBN 0-8191-1668-8). U Pr of Amer.
Van Ess, Dorothy. Pioneers in the Arab World. 1974. pap. 4.95 (ISBN 0-8028-1585-5). Eerdmans.
Van Esterik, Penny. Ban Chiang Pottery. Kern, Dick, ed. & illus. (Papers in International Studies: Southeast Asia Ser.: No. 55). (Orig.). 1979. pap. cancelled o.p. (ISBN 0-89680-078-4, Ohio U Ctr Intl). Ohio U Pr.
--Cognition & Design Production in Ban Chiang Pottery. LC 81-11172. (Southeast Asia Ser.: No. 58). (Illus.). 88p. 1981. pap. text ed. 12.00 (ISBN 0-89680-078-4, Ohio U Ctr Intl). Ohio U Pr.
--Women of Southeast Asia: Illinois University Center For SEAsian Studies. (Occasional Paper Ser.: No. 9). viii, 274p. (Orig.). 1982. pap. 14.00 (Pub. by U Cal S&SE Asian Stud); pap. text ed. 14.00 (ISBN 0-686-38779-1). Cellar.
Vanet, Alain, et al. Larousse Light French Cooking. LC 80-14934. (Illus.). 320p. 1981. 15.95 o.p. (ISBN 0-07-067056-0). McGraw.
Van Every, Dale & Messner, Julian. The Captive Witch. 320p. 1982. pap. 3.50 (ISBN 0-553-22523-5). Bantam.
--The Shining Mountains. 320p. 1982. pap. 3.25 (ISBN 0-553-20671-0). Bantam.
Van Every, Edward. Sins of New York As "Exposed" by the Police Gazette. LC 70-174130. (Illus.). 299p. 1976. Repr. of 1930 ed. 37.00x (ISBN 0-8103-4038-0). Gale.
Van Every Frost, Joan. Kings of the Sea. 640p. (Orig.). 1982. pap. 3.50 (ISBN 0-686-98392-0, Crest). Fawcett.
Van Eyke, Daniel K., jt. auth. see Carr, Robert K.
Van Eys, Jan, ed. Research on Children: Medical Imperatives, Ethical Quandaries & Legal Constraints. LC 77-25235. 1977. pap. 13.95 (ISBN 0-8391-1191-6). Univ Park.
Van Eys, Jan & Sullivan, Margaret P., eds. Status of the Curability of Childhood Cancers. (M. D. Anderson Clinical Conferences on Cancer: 24th). 350p. 1980. text ed. 37.50 (ISBN 0-89004-478-3). Raven.
Vanezis, P. N. Makarios: Pragmatism V. Idealism. (Illus.). 203p. 1975. 9.95 o.p. (ISBN 0-200-72207-7). Transatlantic.
Van Fleet, David, jt. auth. see Albanse, Robert.
Van Fleet, James K. Extraordinary Healing Secrets from a Doctor's Private Files. 1976. 14.95 o.p. (ISBN 0-13-298190-4, Parker). P-H.
--Van Fleet's Master Guide for Managers. 1978. 18.95 o.p. (ISBN 0-13-940452-X, Parker). P-H.
Van Fredenberg, D. Probate Guide for Washington. 2nd ed. 100p. 1980. 9.95 (ISBN 0-88908-715-6); probate forms 6.50 (ISBN 0-686-35989-5). Self Counsel Pr.
Van Fredenberg, D. see Fredenberg, D. Van.
Van Furth, R. Developments in Antibiotic Treatment of Respiratory Infections. 1982. 39.50 (ISBN 90-247-2493-7, Pub by Martinus Nijhoff Netherlands). Kluwer Boston.
Van Gelder, B. F., jt. ed. see Van Dam, K.
Vanger, Milton I. The Model Country: Jose Batlle y Ordonez of Uruguay, 1907-1915. LC 80-50489. (Illus.). 448p. (Orig.). 1980. text ed. 30.00x (ISBN 0-87451-184-4). U Pr of New Eng.
Van Gerpen, Maurice. Privileged Communication & the Press: The Citizen's Right to Know Versus the Law's Right to Confidential News Source Evidence. LC 78-55334. (Contributions in Political Science: No. 19). 1979. lib. bdg. 27.50x (ISBN 0-313-20523-X, VGP/). Greenwood.
Vangheli, Spiridon. Meet Guguze. 1977. PLB 5.95 (ISBN 0-201-08056-7, 8056). A-W.
Van Ghent, Dorothy. The English Novel: Form & Function. pap. 6.50xi (ISBN 0-06-131050-6, TB1050, Torch). Har-Row.
--Keats: The Myth of the Hero. Robinson, Jeffrey C. ed. LC 82-61391. 328p. 1983. 25.00x (ISBN 0-691-06569-1). Princeton U Pr.
Van Ginneken, Jaap. The Rise & Fall of Lin Piao. 1977. pap. 2.50 o.p. (ISBN 0-380-00988-9, 32656, Discus). Avon.
Van Ginneken, Wouter. Socio-Economic Groups & Income Distribution in Mexico. 1980. 30.00x (ISBN 0-312-73941-9). St Martin.
Van Ginneken, Wouter & Garzuel, Michel. Unemployment in France, the Federal Republic of Germany & the Netherlands: A Survey of Trends, Causes & Policy Options. iii, 116p. (Orig.). 1982. pap. 10.00 (ISBN 92-2-103032-6). Intl Labour Office.
Van Gogh, Vincent. Dear Theo: The Autobiography of Vincent Van Gogh. Stone, Irving, ed. 1969. pap. 2.95 (ISBN 0-451-09598-7, E9598, Sig). NAL.
--Van Gogh. (Art Library Ser.: Vol. 2). pap. 3.50 (ISBN 0-448-00453-4, G&D). Putnam Pub Group.
Van Golf-Racht, T. Fundamentals of Fractures Reservoir Engineering. (Developments in Petroleum Science Ser.: Vol. 12). 1982. 85.00 (ISBN 0-444-42046-0). Elsevier.
Van Greenaway, Peter. Manrissa Man. 192p. 1982. 17.50 (ISBN 0-575-03100-X, Pub. by Gollancz England). David & Charles.
Van Gulik, Robert. Emperor's Pearl. 1982. 3.50 (ISBN 0-434-82559-X, Pub. by Heinemann). David & Charles.
--Lacquer Screen. 1982. 3.50 (ISBN 0-434-82560-3, Pub. by Heinemann). David & Charles.
Van Gunsteren, Herman R. The Quest for Control: A Critique of the Rational-Central-Planning Approach in Public Affairs. LC 75-19228. 162p. 1976. 34.95x (ISBN 0-471-89920-8, Pub. by Wiley-Interscience). Wiley.
Vanhaelst, L., jt. ed. see Pinchera, A.
Van Halm, John. The Development of Special Libraries As an International Phenomenon. LC 78-13188. (State of-the-Art Review Ser.: No. 4). 1979. pap. 15.00 (ISBN 0-87111-245-0). SLA.
Van Halsema, Thea. Three Men Came to Heidelberg. (Christian Biography Ser.). 96p. 1982. pap. 3.95 (ISBN 0-8010-9289-2). Baker Bk.
Van Harssel, Jan. Tourism: An Exploration. (Illus.). 384p. 1982. pap. text ed. 18.00 (ISBN 0-935920-00-5). Natl Pub BlacK Hills.
Van Harten, A., jt. auth. see Eckhaus, W.
Van Harten, A. M., jt. auth. see Broertjes, C.
Van Hasselt, Carlos, jt. auth. see Schatborn, Peter.
Van Hattum, Rolland J. Communication Disorders. (Illus.). 1980. text ed. 24.95x (ISBN 0-02-422730-7). Macmillan.
Van Hecke, G. American-Belgian Private International Law. LC 68-21377. (Bilateral Studies in Private International Law: No. 17). 127p. 1968. 15.00 (ISBN 0-379-11417-8). Oceana.
Van Heemstra-Lequir, A. H. & Tordoir. Education & Safe Handling in Pesticide Application. (Studies in Environmental Science: Vol. 18). 1982. 64.00 (ISBN 0-444-42041-X). Elsevier.
Van Hemstra-Lequin, E. A., jt. ed. see Tordoir, W. F.
Van Heurck, H. A. A Treatise on the Diatomacea. 1962. Repr. of 1896 ed. 48.00 (ISBN 3-7682-0116-3). Lubrecht & Cramer.
Van Heurck, Jan. Couples Therapy. LC 79-89946. Orig. Title: Therapie der Zweierbeziehung. (Orig.). Date not set. p.n.s. (ISBN 0-89793-029-0). Hunter Hse.
Van Heurck, Jan, tr. see Pieper, Josef.
Van Heurck, Jan, tr. see Richter, Horst E.
Van Heurck, Jan, tr. see Von der Grun, Max.
Van Heurck, Jan, tr. see Wolf, Christa.
Van Heurn, J. see Heurn, J. van.
Van Heyningen, jt. auth. see Cohen.
Van Hiatsma, Julia, jt. auth. see Van Hiatsma, Willard.
Van Hiatsma, Willard & Van Hiatsma, Julia. A Hierarchical Sketch of Mixe As Spoken in San Jose el Paraiso. (Publications in Linguistics & Related Fields Ser: No. 44). 198p. 1975. pap. 8.50x (ISBN 0-88312-054-2); microfiche 3.00x (ISBN 0-88312-454-8). Summer Inst Ling.
Van Hise, Charles R. Conservation & Regulation in the United States During the World War. LC 74-75243. (The United States in World War 1 Ser). 242p. 1974. Repr. of 1917 ed. lib. bdg. 14.95x (ISBN 0-89198-108-X). Ozer.
Van Hoeven, James W. Piety & Patriotism. 1976. pap. 4.95 (ISBN 0-8028-1663-0). Eerdmans.
Van Hof, M. W. & Mohn, G., eds. Recovery from Brain Damage. (Developments in Neuroscience Ser.: Vol. 13). 1982. 82.00 (ISBN 0-444-80394-7). Elsevier.
Van Holde, K. Physical Biochemistry. 1971. pap. 14.95 ref. ed. (ISBN 0-13-665877-6). P-H.
Van Holst, Auke. Physical Education Curriculum for Elementary Grades, Grade One. (Orig.). 1980. pap. text ed. 7.95 (ISBN 0-8403-2137-6). Kendall-Hunt.
--Physical Education Curriculum for Elementary Grades, Grade Three. (Orig.). 1980. pap. text ed. 7.95 (ISBN 0-8403-2139-2). Kendall-Hunt.
--Physical Education Curriculum for Elementary Grades, Grade Two. (Orig.). 1980. pap. text ed. 7.95 (ISBN 0-8403-2138-4). Kendall-Hunt.
--Physical Education Curriculum for Elementary Grades, Kindergarten. (Orig.). 1980. pap. text ed. 7.95 (ISBN 0-8403-2136-8). Kendall-Hunt.
Van Hook, Jay M., ed. see Ellul, Jacques, et al.
VanHoose, William H. & Worth, Maureen R. Adulthood in the Life Cycle. 396p. 1982. pap. text ed. write for info. (ISBN 0-697-06552-9). Wm C Brown.
Van Hoose, William H. & Worth, Maureen R. Counseling Adults: A Developmental Approach. LC 81-10159. (Counseling Ser.). 370p. 1982. text ed. 17.95 (ISBN 0-8185-0502-8). Brooks-Cole.
Van Hoozer, Helen, jt. auth. see Tedford, Alberta.
Van Horn, Carl E. Policy Implementation in the Federal System: National Goals & Local Implementors. LC 78-19929. (Illus.). 192p. 1979. 22.95x (ISBN 0-669-02435-X). Lexington Bks.
Van Horn, James. The Community Orchestra: A Handbook for Conductors, Managers, & Boards. LC 78-60531. (Illus.). 1979. lib. bdg. 25.00x (ISBN 0-313-20562-0, VCO/). Greenwood.
Van Horn, James C., jt. auth. see Lee, Sang M.
Van Horn, Royal. Computer Programming for Kids & Other Beginners, Radio Shack Color Computer. (Orig.). 1983. pap. text ed. 9.95 (ISBN 0-88408-163-X). Sterling Swift.
--Computer Programming for Kids & Other Beginners, TRS-80 Model III. (Orig.). 1983. pap. text ed. 9.95 (ISBN 0-88408-162-1). Sterling Swift.
--Teaching Computer Programming to Kids & Other Beginners: A Teacher's Manual. 1982. ringbinder 9.95 (ISBN 0-88408-154-0). Sterling Swift.
Van Horne, James C. Financial Management & Policy. 6th ed. (Illus.). 832p. 1983. 26.95 (ISBN 0-13-316026-2). P-H.
--Fundamentals of Financial Management. 4th ed. (Illus.). 1980. text ed. 25.95 (ISBN 0-13-339408-5); study guide 9.95 (ISBN 0-13-339424-7). P-H.
--Fundamentals of Financial Management. 5th ed. (Illus.). 640p. 1983. 25.95 (ISBN 0-13-339465-4); study guide 9.95 (ISBN 0-13-339499-9). P-H.
Van House, Nancy A. Public Library User Fees: The Use & Finance of Public Libraries. LC 82-11741. (Contributions in Librarianship & Information Science Ser.: No. 43). (Illus.). 160p. 1983. lib. bdg. 27.50 (ISBN 0-313-22753-5, DPU/). Greenwood.
Van Houten, Franklyn B., ed. Ancient Continental Deposits. (Bench Mark Papers in Geology Ser.). 1977. 51.054 (ISBN 0-12-787650-2). Acad Pr.
Van Houten, Lois. Behind the Door. (Stone Country Poetry Ser.: No. 1). (Illus.). 1976. pap. text ed. 3.00 o.p. (ISBN 0-930020-00-6). Stone Country.
--The Woman Who Warped with Doors. LC 77-76421. (Stone Country Poetry Ser.: No. 3). (Illus.). 1977. pap. 4.00 o.p. (ISBN 0-930020-02-2). Stone Country.
Van Houtte, J. A. An Economic History of the Low Countries 800-1800. LC 77-81397. (Illus.). 1977. 28.50x (ISBN 0-312-23320-5). St Martin.
Vanhoutte, P. M., jt. ed. see Shepherd, J. T.
Vanhoutte, Paul M., jt. auth. see Shepherd, John T.
Vanhoutte, Paul M. & Leusen, Isadore, eds. Vasodilatation. 552p. 1981. 61.50 (ISBN 0-89004-602-6). Raven.
Vanhoutte, Paul M., jt. ed. see DeClerck, Fred.
Van Huss, Wayne D., et al. Physical Activity in Modern Living. 2nd ed. LC 69-10722. 1969. pap. text ed. 13.95 (ISBN 0-13-665513-0). P-H.
Vanicek, P. & Krakiwsky, E. J. Geodesy: The Concepts. 1982. 117.00 (ISBN 0-444-86149-1). Elsevier.
Vanier, Jean. Be Not Afraid. 160p. 1975. pap. 5.95 (ISBN 0-8091-1885-8). Paulist Pr.
--Eruption to Hope. pap. 4.95 o.p. (ISBN 0-8091-1560-3). Paulist Pr.
Van Impe, Rexella. Satisfied. 160p. 1983. pap. 4.95 (ISBN 0-8407-5841-3). Nelson.
Van Iterson, S. R. In the Spell of the Past. LC 74-31022. 192p. (gr. 7 up). 1975. PLB 8.59 (ISBN 0-688-32023-6). Morrow.
--The Spirits of Chocamata. (gr. 7 up). 1977. 8.95 (ISBN 0-688-22108-4); lib. bdg. 8.59 (ISBN 0-688-32108-9). Morrow.
--Village of Outcasts. LC 74-168478. 240p. (gr. 7 up). 1972. PLB 8.59 (ISBN 0-688-31988-2). Morrow.
Van Kaam, Adrian. A Light to the Gentiles. rev. ed. 9.95 o.p. (ISBN 0-87193-084-6). Dimension Bks.
--Looking for Jesus. pap. 4.95 casebound (ISBN 0-87193-064-1); 7.95. Dimension Bks.
Van Kamm, Adrian & Healy, Kathleen. The Demon & the Dove: Personality Growth Through Literature. LC 82-20173. 308p. 1983. pap. text ed. 11.50 (ISBN 0-8191-2897-X). U Pr of Amer.
Van Kamm, Adrian & Muto, Susan A. Creative Formation of Life & World. LC 82-16014. 462p. 1983. lib. bdg. 29.75 (ISBN 0-8191-2708-6); pap. text ed. 17.25 (ISBN 0-8191-2709-4). U Pr of Amer.
Van Kampen, N. G. Stochastic Models in Physics & Chemistry. 1982. 76.75 (ISBN 0-444-86200-5). Elsevier.
Van Kampen, V. Dizionario Italiano-Olandese, Olandese-Italiano. 486p. (Ital. & Dutch.). 1980. leatherette 5.95 (ISBN 0-686-97344-5, M-9171). French & Eur.
Vankat, John L. The Natural Vegetation of North America. LC 78-31264. 1979. text ed. 15.95 (ISBN 0-471-01770-1). Wiley.
Van Keep, Pieter A. & Utian, Wulf H., eds. The Controversial Climacteric. (Illus.). 200p. 1982. text ed. 25.00 (ISBN 0-85200-410-9, Pub. by MTP Pr England). Kluwer Boston.
Van Kesteren, Aloysius, jt. ed. see Schmid, Herta.
Van Kirk, Sylvia. Many Tender Ties: Women in Fur-Trade Society, Sixteen Seventy to Eighteen Seventy. LC 82-40457. (Illus.). 303p. 1983. 22.50x (ISBN 0-8061-1842-3); pap. 9.95x (ISBN 0-8061-1847-4). U of Okla Pr.
Van Kleek, Peter E., jt. auth. see Visick, H. E.
Van Kranendonk. Intermolecular Spectroscopy & Dynamical Properties of Dense Systems. (Enrico Fermi Summer School Ser.: Vol. 75). 1980. 100.00 (ISBN 0-444-85460-6). Elsevier.
Van Kranendonk, Jan. Solid Hydrogen: Theory of the Properties of Solid H2, HD, & D2. 300p. 1982. 39.50x (ISBN 0-306-41080-X, Plenum Pr). Plenum Pub.
Van Krevelen. Coal: Topology, Chemistry, Physics & Constitution. (Coal Science & Technology Ser.: Vol. 3). 1981. 95.75 (ISBN 0-444-40600-X). Elsevier.
Van Krevelen, D. W. Properties of Polymers: Their Estimation & Correlation with Chemical Structure. 2nd ed. 1976. 117.00 (ISBN 0-444-41467-3). Elsevier.
Van Landingham, S. Catalogue of the Fossil & Recent Genera & Species of Diatoms & Their Synonyms: Suppl. Taxa, Additions & Corrections, Pt. 8. 1979. lib. bdg. 40.00 (ISBN 3-7682-0478-2). Lubrecht & Cramer.
Van Landingham, S. L. Catalogue of the Fossil & Recent Genera & Species of Diatoms & Their Synonyms-Part 7: Rhoicosphenia Through Zygoceros. 1979. lib. bdg. 40.00x (ISBN 3-7682-0477-4). Lubrecht & Cramer.
--Catalogue of the Fossil & Recent Genera & Species of Diatoms & Their Synonyms. Incl. Pt. 1. Acanthoceras - Bacillaria. 1967 (ISBN 3-7682-0471-5); Pt. 2. Bacteriastrum - Coscinodiscus. 1968 (ISBN 3-7682-0472-3); Pt. 3. Coscinophaena - Fibula. 1969 (ISBN 3-7682-0473-1); Pt. 4. Fragilaria - Maunema. 1971 (ISBN 3-7682-0474-X). pap. 40.00 ea. (ISBN 0-686-22227-X). Lubrecht & Cramer.
--Catalogue of the Fossil & Recent Genera & Species of Diatoms & Their Syhonyms: Navicula, Pt. 5. 2963p. 1975. text ed. 40.00x (ISBN 3-7682-0475-8). Lubrecht & Cramer.
--Catalogue of the Fossil & Recent Genera & Species of Diatoms & Their Synonyms: Neidium-Rhocicosigma, Pt. 6. 3605p. 1978. text ed. 40.00x (ISBN 3-7682-0476-6). Lubrecht & Cramer.
--Miocene Non-Marine Diatoms from the Yakima Region in South Central Washington. (Illus.). 1965. pap. 16.00 (ISBN 3-7682-5414-3). Lubrecht & Cramer.
--Paleoecology & Microfloristics of Miocene Diatomites from the Otis Basin-Juntura Region of Harney & Malheur Counties, Oregon. (Illus.). 1967. pap. 16.00 (ISBN 3-7682-5426-7). Lubrecht & Cramer.
Van Leeuwen, Jean. The Great Cheese Conspiracy. (gr. 2-6). 1973. pap. 1.75 (ISBN 0-440-13080-8, YB). Dell.
Van Leeuwen, Louis Th., ed. see Howard, Ronald L.
Van Leeuwen, Mary S. The Sorcerer's Apprentice: A Christian Looks at the Changing Face of Psychology. 144p. (Orig.). 1982. pap. 5.95 (ISBN 0-87784-398-8). Inter-Varsity.
Vanleeuwen, W. A., jt. auth. see De Groot, S. R.

Van Leeuwen Bookmkamp, C. & Van der Meer, J. H. The Carl Van Leeuwen Boomkamp Collection of Musical Instruments. (Haags Gemeente Museum Ser.). 1971. 25.00 o.s.i. (ISBN 90-6027-150-5, Pub. by Frits Knuf Netherlands). Pendragon NY.

Van Leewen, Eva C. Sterne's 'Journal to Eliza' A Semiological & Linguistic Approach to the Text. (Studies & Texts in English: No. 2). 240p. (Orig.). 1981. pap. 22.00 (ISBN 3-87808-442-0). Benjamins North Am.

Van Lelyveld, H. & Zoeteman, B. C. Water Supply & Health: Proceedings. (Studies in Environmental Science: Vol. 12). 1981. 68.00 (ISBN 0-444-41960-8). Elsevier.

Van Lennep, J. D. Etymologicum Linguae Graecae, 2 vols. (Linguistics, 13th-18th Centuries Ser.). (Fr.). 1974. Repr. of 1790 ed. Set. lib. bdg. 337.50x o.p. (ISBN 0-8287-0849-5). Clearwater Pub.

--Praelectiones Academicae de Analogia Linguae Graecae, Sive Rationum Analogicarum Linguae Graecae Expositio. (Linguistics, 13th-18th Centuries Ser.). 520p. (Latin.). 1974. Repr. of 1805 ed. lib. bdg. 128.50x o.p. (ISBN 0-8287-0850-9, 5057). Clearwater Pub.

Van Leuven, Edwin P. General Trade Mathematics. 2nd ed. 1952. text ed. 18.88 (ISBN 0-07-067079-X, W). McGraw.

Van Lier, H. N. Determination of Planning Capacity & Layout Criteria of Outdoor Recreation Projects. 168p. 1974. 30.00 (ISBN 90-220-0445-7, PDC25, Pub. by Pudoc). Unipub.

Van Linden, Philip. The Gospel According to Mark, No. 2. Karris, Robert J., ed. LC 82-20356. (Collegeville Bible Commentary Ser.). (Illus.). 96p. 1983. pap. 2.50 (ISBN 0-8146-1302-0). Liturgical Pr.

Van Lint, J. H., jt. auth. see Cameron, P. J.

Van Lint, V. A., et al. Mechanisms of Radiation Effects in Electronic Materials, Vol. 1. LC 79-9083. 1980. 37.95x (ISBN 0-471-04106-8, Pub. by Wiley-Interscience). Wiley.

Vanlonkhuyzen, John H., jt. auth. see Nielsen, Kaj L.

Van Loon, Antonia. Sunshine & Shadow. large print ed. LC 82-3278. 568p. 1982. Repr. of 1981 ed. 12.95 (ISBN 0-89621-359-5). Thorndike Pr.

Van Loon, J. H. & Staudt, F. J., eds. Ergonomics in Tropical Agriculture & Forestry: Proceedings. 136p. 1979. pap. 14.00 (ISBN 0-686-93162-9, PDC148, Pudoc). Unipub.

Van Loon, M., ed. see Liebowitz, Harold.

Van Loon, M. N. Korucutepe. (Studies in Ancient Civilization: Vol. 3). 1980. 191.50 (ISBN 0-444-85284-0). Elsevier.

--Korucutepe, Vol. 1. LC 74-83722. (Studies in Ancient Civilization Ser.: Vol. 2). 246p. 1975. 85.00 (ISBN 0-444-10677-4, North-Holland). Elsevier.

Van Loon, M. N., ed. Korucutepe, Vol. 2: Final Report on the Excavations of the Universities of Chicago, Calif. (Los Angeles) & Amsterdam in Keban Reservoir, Eastern Anatolia, 1968-1970. (Studies in Ancient Civilization: Vol. 3). 1978. 123.50 (ISBN 0-7204-0531-9, North-Holland). Elsevier.

Van Lustbader, Eric. The Sunset Warrior. 1978. pap. 1.50 o.s.i. (ISBN 0-515-04714-7). Jove Pubns.

Van Lustbader, Eric see Lustbader, Eric Van.

Vanmaanen, jt. auth. see Manning.

Van Maanen, John. Varieties of Qualitative Research. (Studying Organization: Innovations in Methodology Ser.). 168p. 1982. 17.95 (ISBN 0-8039-1869-0); pap. 7.95 (ISBN 0-8039-1870-4). Sage.

Van Maarseveen, Henc & Van Dertang, Ger. Written Constitutions, a Computerized Comparative Study. 335p. 1978. 37.50 (ISBN 0-379-20361-8). Oceana.

Van Maercke & Van Moer, eds. Stomach Diseases: Current Status. (International Congress Ser.: Vol. 555). 1981. 85.00 (ISBN 0-444-90228-7). Elsevier.

Van Mansum, C. J. Elsevier's Dictionary of Building Construction. (Eng. & Fr. & Dutch & Ger., Polyglot). 1959. 97.75 (ISBN 0-444-40601-8). Elsevier.

Van Marck, E. E., jt. ed. see Gigase, P. L.

VanMeer, Mary, ed. Free Campgrounds, USA. LC 81-15126. (Illus.). 631p. 1982. pap. 8.95 o.p. (ISBN 0-914788-46-9). East Woods.

--Free Campgrounds, USA. rev. ed. 600p. 1983. pap. 9.95 (ISBN 0-914788-69-8). East Woods.

Van Meter, Donald, jt. auth. see Sharkansky, Ira.

Van Meter, Margaret, ed. Managing the Critically Ill Effectively. (Illus.). 250p. 1982. pap. 16.95 (ISBN 0-87489-274-0). Med Economics.

Van Meter, Margaret, ed. see Yacone, Linda A.

Van Meurs, A. P. Petroleum Economics & Offshore Mining Legislation. 1971. 56.00 (ISBN 0-444-40889-4). Elsevier.

Van Middelkoop, J. H. Physiological & Genetical Aspects of Egg Production in White Plymouth Rock Pullets. (Illus.). 76p. 1978. pap. 13.75 (ISBN 90-220-0495-3, PDC65, Pub. by Pudoc). Unipub.

Van Mieghen, J. see Landsberg, H. E.

Van Miert, A. S., ed. Trends in Veterinary Pharmacology & Toxicology. (Developments in Animal & Veterinary Science: Vol. 6). 1980. 64.00 (ISBN 0-444-41878-4). Elsevier.

Van Moer, jt. ed. see Van Maercke.

Vann, James Allen. The Swabian Kreis: Institutional Growth in the Holy Roman Empire, 1648-1715. write for info. P Lang Pubs.

Vann, Richard T. Social Development of English Quakerism 1655-1755. LC 79-78524. 1969. 14.00x o.p. (ISBN 0-674-81290-5). Harvard U Pr.

Van Name, Frederick W. & Flory, David. Elementary Physics. 2nd ed. (Illus.). 352p. 1974. ref. ed. 20.95 (ISBN 0-13-259515-X); pap. 4.95 study guide & wkbk. (ISBN 0-13-259523-0). P-H.

Vannatta, Dennis. H. E. Bates. (English Authors Ser.). 177p. 1983. lib. bdg. 17.95 (ISBN 0-8057-6844-0, Twayne). G K Hall.

Van Ness, Bethann. The Bible Story Book. LC 63-9758. 1963. 14.95 (ISBN 0-8054-4402-5). Broadman.

Van Ness, Bethann & De Clemente, Elizabeth M. Historias De Toda la Biblia. Orig. Title: A Bible Story Book. (Illus.). 684p. 1979. pap. 19.95 (ISBN 0-311-03600-7). Casa Bautista.

Van Ness, H. C. Understanding Thermodynamics. 1969. text ed. 13.95 o.p. (ISBN 0-07-067091-9, C); pap. 2.95 o.p. (ISBN 0-07-067090-0). McGraw.

--Understanding Thermodynamics. 103p. 1983. pap. 4.00 (ISBN 0-486-63277-6). Dover.

Van Ness, H. C. & Abbott, M. M. Classical Thermodynamics of Non-Electrolyte Solutions. (Chemical Engineering Ser.). (Illus.). 480p. 1982. text ed. 39.50x (ISBN 0-07-067095-1); solns. manual 20.00 (ISBN 0-07-067096-X). McGraw.

VanNess, H. C., jt. auth. see Abbott, M. M.

VanNess, H. C., jt. auth. see Smith, J. M.

Van Ness, Lottye G. The Cookie Connection. LC 81-81356. 315p. (Orig.). 1981. pap. 7.95 laminated (ISBN 0-9608648-0-6, CC-2). Van Ness LOTCO.

Van Ness, Peter. Revolution & Chinese Foreign Policy: Peking's Support for Wars of National Liberation. (Center for Chinese Studies UC Berkeley). 1970. 38.50x (ISBN 0-520-01583-5); pap. 8.45x (ISBN 0-520-02055-3, CAMPUS63). U of Cal Pr.

Vannette, Walter M., jt. auth. see Wood, John J.

Vann Hunter, Mary. Sassafras. 288p. 1981. pap. 2.75 o.p. (ISBN 0-523-41476-5). Pinnacle Bks.

Van Nieberg, Camilla. English Verbs. (Blue Book Ser). pap. 1.25 o.p. (ISBN 0-671-18108-4). Monarch Pr.

Van Niel, Robert. Survey of Historical Source Materials in Java & Manila. LC 72-132554. (Asian Studies at Hawaii Ser.: No. 5). (Orig.). 1971. pap. text ed. 8.00x (ISBN 0-87022-841-2). UH Pr.

Vannier, M. Physical Activities for the Handicapped. 1977. 22.95 (ISBN 0-13-665638-2). P-H.

Van Nieuwenhuijze, C. A. see Nieuwenhuijze, C. A. van.

Van Nieuwenhuizen, P. & Freidman, D. Z. Supergravity. 1980. 64.00 (ISBN 0-444-85438-X). Elsevier.

Van Nooten, B. A., jt. auth. see Emeneau, Murray B.

Van Nooten, Barend A. Mahabharata. (World Authors Ser.). lib. bdg. 13.95 (ISBN 0-8057-2564-4, Twayne). G K Hall.

Van Norman, Richard W. Experimental Biology. 2nd ed. LC 74-105444. 1970. ref. ed. 19.95 o.p. (ISBN 0-13-294710-2). P-H.

Van Nostran, William. The Nonbroadcast Television Writer's Handbook. (Video Bookshelf Ser.). 1983. text ed. 29.95 (ISBN 0-914236-82-2). Knowledge Indus.

Van Nostrand, A. D. & Knoblauch, C. H. The Process of Writing: Discovery & Control. LC 81-83449. 1982. 9.95 (ISBN 0-395-31755-X); Instr's. manual 1.00 (ISBN 0-395-31756-8). HM.

Van Nostrand, Frederic. Mars Through the Signs. 64p. 1982. pap. 4.95 (ISBN 0-940058-05-7). Clancy Pubns.

Van Nostrand, Jeanne. The First Hundred Years of Painting in California 1775-1875. LC 80-50443. (Illus.). 1980. 75.00 (ISBN 0-910760-10-1). J Howell.

Van Note, Gene. Catch an Angel's Wing. 76p. 1979. pap. 1.95 (ISBN 0-8341-0559-4). Beacon Hill.

--How to Lead a Small Group Bible Study. 51p. pap. 1.75 (ISBN 0-686-30686-4). Beacon Hill.

--John, Vol. 1. (Beacon Small Group Bible Studies). 68p. (Orig.). 1980. pap. 2.25 (ISBN 0-8341-0651-5). Beacon Hill.

--Ministering to Single Adults. 109p. 1978. pap. 2.95 (ISBN 0-8341-0556-X). Beacon Hill.

Van Nouhuys, C. Dominant Exudative Vitroretinopathy & Other Vascular Disorders of the Peripheral Retina. 1982. 83.00 (ISBN 90-6193-805-8, Pub. by Junk Pubs Netherlands). Kluwer Boston.

Vannoy, Russell. Sex Without Love: A Philosophical Exploration. LC 79-57534. 226p. 1980. text ed. 14.95 (ISBN 0-87975-128-2); pap. text ed. 8.95 (ISBN 0-87975-129-0). Prometheus Bks.

Van Olphen, H. An Introduction to Clay Colloid Chemistry. 2nd ed. LC 77-400. 1977. 46.00x (ISBN 0-471-01463-X, Pub. by Wiley-Interscience). Wiley.

Van Olphen, H., ed. International Clay Conference, 1981: Proceedings of the VII International Clay Conference, Bologna & Pavia, Italy, September 6-12, 1981. (Developments in Sedimentology Ser.: No. 35). 828p. 1982. 85.00 (ISBN 0-444-42096-7). Elsevier.

Van Onselen, Charles. Studies in the Social & Economic History of the Witwatersrand 116-1914: New Babylon, Vol. 1. (Illus.). 1982. 35.00x (ISBN 0-582-64382-1); pap. 10.95x (ISBN 0-582-64383-X). Longman.

--Studies in the Social & Economic History of the Witwatersrand 116-1914: New Nineveh, Vol. 2. (Illus.). 288p. 1982. 35.00x (ISBN 0-582-64384-8); pap. 10.95x (ISBN 0-582-64385-6). Longman.

Van Oosting, James. The Business Report: Writer, Reader & Text. (Illus.). 320p. 1983. pap. 13.95 (ISBN 0-13-107581-0). P-H.

Vanorden, Bianca. Water Music. LC 58-10887. 1958. 3.95 o.p. (ISBN 0-15-195015-6). HarBraceJ.

Van Orden, Naola & Steed, S. Paul. The Bio-Plan for Lifetime Weight Control. 256p. 1983. pap. 10.95 (ISBN 0-385-27665-6). Dial.

Van Orden, Phyllis J. The Collection Program in Elementary & Middle Schools: Concepts, Practices, & Information Sources. LC 82-15325. (Library Science Text Ser.). 301p. 1982. text ed. 18.50 (ISBN 0-87287-335-8). Libs Unl.

Van Orman, H. A. Estimating for Residential Construction. LC 76-14083. 1978. pap. text ed. 16.00 (ISBN 0-8273-1605-4); instr.'s guide 4.25 (ISBN 0-8273-1606-2). Delmar.

Van Osdol, William R. & Shane, Don G. An Introduction to Exceptional Children. 3rd ed. 480p. 1982. pap. text ed. write for info. (ISBN 0-697-06061-6); instrs.' manual avail. (ISBN 0-697-06062-4). Wm C Brown.

Van Oudenaren, John. The United States & Europe: Issues to Resolve. (Seven Springs Studies). 1981. pap. 3.00 (ISBN 0-943006-02-3). Seven Springs.

Vanous, Jan, jt. auth. see Marrese, Michael.

Van Over, Raymond. Eastern Mysticism: The Near East & India, Vol.1. 1977. pap. 2.50 o.p. (ISBN 0-451-61575-1, ME1575, Ment). NAL.

--Taoist Tales. 1973. pap. 2.95 (ISBN 0-451-62107-7, ME2107, Ment). NAL.

Van Over, Raymond, ed. I Ching. rev ed. (Orig.). 1971. pap. 3.50 (ISBN 0-451-62138-7, ME2138, Ment). NAL.

Vanoverbergh, Morice. Isneg-English Vocabulary. (Oceanic Linguistics Special Publications: No. 11). 600p. 1972. pap. 12.00x (ISBN 0-8248-0235-7). UH Pr.

Van Oyen, Hendrik. Affluence & the Christian. Sherman, Franklin, ed. Clarke, Frank, tr. LC 66-24863. (Facet Bks.). 1966. pap. 0.50 o.p. (ISBN 0-8006-3034-3, 1-3034). Fortress.

Van Oystaeyen, F., jt. auth. see Nastasescu, C.

Van Pelt, Ethel. Silver Threads to Love. 192p. (YA) 1976. 6.95 (ISBN 0-685-62628-8, Avalon). Bouregy.

Van Pelt, G. Hierarchies: The Cosmic Ladder of Life. Small, W. Emmett & Todd, Helen, eds. (Theosophical Manual: No. 9). 1975. pap. 2.00 (ISBN 0-913004-23-5). Point Loma Pub.

--Man's Divine Parentage & Destiny: The Great Rounds & Races. Small, W. Emmett & Todd, Helen, eds. (Theosophical Manual: No. 7). 64p. 1975. pap. 2.00 (ISBN 0-913004-24-3, 913004-24). Point Loma Pub.

Van Pelt, G. W. The Archaic History of the Human Race. (Study Ser.: No. 3). 1980. pap. 2.00 (ISBN 0-913004-36-7). Point Loma Pub.

Van Pelt, Gertrude W. The Doctrine of Karma. Small, W. Emmett & Todd, Helen, eds. (Theosophical Manual: No. 3). 64p. 1975. pap. 2.00 (ISBN 0-913004-16-2). Point Loma Pub.

Van Peteghem, C., jt. auth. see Roncucci, R.

Van Poolen, H. K., et al. Fundamentals of Enhanced Oil Recovery. 176p. 1980. 39.95x (ISBN 0-87814-144-8). Pennwell Pub.

Van Powell, Nowland. The American Navies of the Revolutionary War. (Illus.). 128p. 1974. 20.00 o.p. (ISBN 0-399-11183-2). Putnam Pub Group.

Van Praagh, G. Chemistry by Discovery. (gr. 8-12). 5.95 o.p. (ISBN 0-7195-1439-8). Transatlantic.

Van Pragg, H. M., jt. auth. see Mendlewicz, J.

Van Raalte, Joan, jt. auth. see Stewart, Arlene.

Van Rede, C., jt. auth. see Cocks, Leslie V.

Van Ree, J. M. & Terenius, L., eds. Characteristics & Functions of Opioids. (Proceedings). 1978. 87.50 (ISBN 0-444-80076-X). Elsevier.

Van Reine, W. F. Prud'Homme. A Taxonomic Revision of the European Sphacelariaceae: Sphacelariales, Phaeophyceae. (Leiden Botanical Ser.: Vol. 6). (Illus.). ix, 293p. 1982. pap. write for info (ISBN 90-04-06597-0). E J Brill.

Van Reine, W. F. Prud'Homme see Van Reine, W. F. Prud'Homme.

Vanrell, Bartholomew. Psychotherapy with Spiritual Orientation in Clinical Settings: Transcendental Therapy. 60p. Date not set. 10.00 (ISBN 0-89697-032-9). Intl Univ MO.

Van Rens & Kayser, F. H. Local Antibiotic Treatment in Osteomyelitis & Soft Tissue Infections. (International Congress Ser.: Vol. 556). 1981. 38.50 (ISBN 0-444-90222-8). Elsevier.

Van Rensselaer, Mrs. John K. Prophetical, Educational & Playing Cards. LC 77-78249. (Illus.). 1971. Repr. of 1912 ed. 37.00x (ISBN 0-8103-3867-X). Gale.

Van Rensselaer, Mariana G. Book of American Figure Painters. Weinberg, H. Barbara, ed. LC 75-28875. (Art Experience in Late 19th Century America Ser.: Vol. 11). (Illus.). 1976. Repr. of 1886 ed. lib. bdg. 72.50 o.s.i. (ISBN 0-8240-2235-1). Garland Pub.

Van Rensselaer, Phillip. A Million Dollar Baby: The Life Story of Barbara Hutton. 1979. 10.95 (ISBN 0-399-12366-0). Putnam Pub Group.

Van Rijn, Rembrandt. Rembrandt: The Etchings. LC 77-87012. (Illus.). 1977. 29.95 o.p. (ISBN 0-8467-0411-0, Pub. by Two Continents); pap. 22.50 (ISBN 0-8467-0414-5). Hippocrene Bks.

Van Rijsbergen, C. J. Information Retrieval. 2nd ed. 1981. pap. text ed. 19.95 (ISBN 0-408-70951-0). Butterworth.

Van Riper, Charles. A Career in Speech Pathology. LC 78-9678. 1979. pap. 12.95 ref. (ISBN 0-13-114769-2). P-H.

Van-Riper, Charles. My Father, Doctor Van. Carter, James L., ed. LC 81-83254. (Illus.). 9p. 1982. 5.95x. Longyear Res.

Van Riper, Charles. My Father, Doctor Van. 1982. 5.95 (ISBN 0-938746-05-7). Marquette Cnty Hist.

--The Nature of Stuttering. 2nd ed. (Illus.). 496p. 1982. 24.95 (ISBN 0-13-610709-5). P-H.

--Speech Corrections: Principles & Methods. 6th ed. (Illus.). 1978. ref. ed. 24.95 (ISBN 0-13-829523-9). P-H.

--The Treatment of Stuttering. (Illus.). 464p. 1973. 25.95 (ISBN 0-13-930594-7). P-H.

Van Riper, Guernsey. Babe Ruth. new ed. (Childhood of Famous Americans Ser.). (Illus.). 204p. (Orig.). (gr. 2 up). 1983. pap. 3.95 (ISBN 0-672-52754-5). Bobbs.

--Knute Rockne. new ed. (Childhood of Famous Americans Ser.). (Illus.). 204p. (Orig.). (gr. 2 up). 1983. pap. 3.95 (ISBN 0-672-52753-7). Bobbs.

Van Riper, Guernsey, Jr. Game of Basketball. LC 67-15026. (Sports Library). (Illus.). (gr. 3-6). 1968. PLB 7.12 (ISBN 0-8116-6657-3). Garrard.

--Golfing Greats: Two Top Pros. LC 74-16266. (Sports Library Ser). (Illus.). 96p. (gr. 3-6). 1975. PLB 7.12 (ISBN 0-8116-6669-7). Garrard.

--Lou Gehrig: One of Baseball's Greatest. (Childhood of Famous Americans Ser.). (gr. 3-8). 1982. pap. 3.95 (ISBN 0-686-95257-X). Bobbs.

Van Riper, Peter. On Blank Pages. 64p. (Orig.). 1982. pap. 7.00 (ISBN 0-940170-07-8). Open Bk Pubns.

Van Rjndt, Philippe. Blueprint. LC 77-2934. 1977. 8.95 o.p. (ISBN 0-399-12002-5). Putnam Pub Group.

--Samaritan. LC 82-9695. 406p. 1983. 16.95 (ISBN 0-385-27221-9). Dial.

Van Rosevelt, Frans, tr. see Nieuwenhuys, Rob.

Van Rosevelt, Frans, tr. see Van Schendel, Arthur.

Van Rossum, Rex. Your Book of Athletics. (gr. 7 up). 1964. 3.25 o.p. (ISBN 0-685-20653-X). Transatlantic.

Van Royen, P. Alpine Flora of New Giunea, 4 vols. Incl. Vol. 1. General Part. 1980. lib. bdg. 40.00; Vol. 2. Taxonomic Part II: Cupressaceae to Poaceae. 1980. lib. bdg. 120.00 (ISBN 3-7682-1244-0); Vol. 3. Taxonomic Part 2: Winteraceae to Polygonaceae. 1982. lib. bdg. 120.00 (ISBN 3-7682-1245-9); Vol. 4. Taxonomic Part 3: Fagaceae to Asteraceae. 1983. lib. bdg. 100.00 (ISBN 3-7682-1246-7). 400.00 set (ISBN 3-7682-1247-5). Lubrecht & Cramer.

--The Alpine Flora of New Guina: Taxonomic Part: Winteraceae to Polygonaceae. (Illus.). 1169p. 1982. lib. bdg. 135.00x o.p. (ISBN 3-7682-1245-9). Lubrecht & Cramer.

--The Alpine Flora of New Guinea, Vol. 1: General Part. (Illus.). 418p. 1980. PLB 40.00x (ISBN 0-686-35956-9). Lubrecht & Cramer.

--The Alpine Flora of New Guinea, Vol. 2: Taxonomic Pt. 1-Cupressaceae to Poaceae. (Illus.). 1232p. 1980. PLB 120.00x (ISBN 3-7682-1244-0). Lubrecht & Cramer.

--The Orchids of the High Mountains of New Guinea. (Illus.). 784p. 1980. 80.00 (ISBN 3-7682-1261-0). Lubrecht & Cramer.

Van Ryn, August. Luke, Meditations. 1953. 3.25 (ISBN 0-87213-888-7). Loizeaux.

Van Ryzin, John, jt. auth. see Robbins, Herbert.

Van Ryzin, Jr. Cutting a Record in Nashville. (Triumph Bks.). (gr. 7 up). 1980. PLB 8.90 (ISBN 0-531-04114-X, A38). Watts.

Van Ryzin, Lani. Disco. (Concise Guides). (Illus.). (gr. 6 up). 1979. PLB 8.90 s&l (ISBN 0-531-02891-7). Watts.

Van Santvoord, George. Lives, Times & Judical Services of the Chief Justices of the Supreme Court of the United States. 2nd ed. Mersky, Roy M. & Jacobstein, J. Myron, eds. LC 76-52305. (Classics in Legal History Reprint Ser.: Vol. 30). 740p. 1977. Repr. of 1882 ed. lib. bdg. 30.00 (ISBN 0-89941-029-4). W S Hein.

Van Schendel, Arthur. John Company. Beekman, E. M., ed. Van Rosevelt, Frans, tr. from Dutch. LC 82-21877. (Library of the Indies). Orig. Title: Jan Compagie. 224p. 1983. lib. bdg. 16.00x (ISBN 0-87023-383-1). U of Mass Pr.

Van Schendel, W. Peasant Mobility. (Studies in Developing Countries: No. 26). 372p. 1981. text ed. 25.75x (41317, Pub. by Van Gorcum Holland). Humanities.

Van Schendelen, M. P., jt. auth. see Herman, V.

Van Schouten, Joop. Sailing in Glass. (Illus.). 96p. 1983. 12.95 (ISBN 0-914814-37-0). Sail Bks.

Van Scotter, Richard D., et al. Foundations of Education: Social Perspective. (Illus.). 1979. text ed. 22.95 (ISBN 0-13-329268-1). P-H.

Van Scoy-Mosher, Michael B. Medical Oncology: Controversies in Cancer Treatment. 1981. lib. bdg. 49.95 (ISBN 0-8161-2159-1, Pub. by Hall Medical). G K Hall.

Van Scyoc, Sydney J. Bluesong. 272p. (Orig.). 1983. pap. 4.95 (ISBN 0-425-05881-6). Berkley Pub.
--Cloudcry. 224p. 1983. pap. 2.50 (ISBN 0-425-05864-6). Berkley Pub.
Vanselow & England, eds. Chemistry & Physics of Solid Surfaces, Vol. III. 352p. 1982. 44.95 (ISBN 0-8493-0128-9). CRC Pr.
Van Seters, John. In Search of History: Historiography in the Ancient World & the Origins of Biblical History. LC 82-48912. 272p. 1983. text ed. 30.00x (ISBN 0-300-02877-6). Yale U Pr.
Van Sickle, Larry. Teaching Poor Kids to Labor: The American Dream & the Impact of Class. 240p. 1983. text ed. 19.95x (ISBN 0-8290-1294-X). Irvington.
Van Sickle, Sylvia. First Reference Library, 50 bks, Bks. 1-25. Incl. Rivers & River Life (ISBN 0-356-03790-8); Snakes & Lizards. (ISBN 0-356-03791-6); Roads & Highways (ISBN 0-356-03792-4); Ports & Harbors (ISBN 0-356-04027-5); Bridges & Tunnels (ISBN 0-356-04028-3); Towns & Cities (ISBN 0-356-04029-1); Horses & Ponies (ISBN 0-356-04030-5); Airplanes & Balloons (ISBN 0-356-04031-3); The Story of Cars. (ISBN 0-356-04032-1); Mountains (ISBN 0-356-04099-2); Electricity (ISBN 0-356-04100-X); Television (ISBN 0-356-04101-8); Photography (ISBN 0-356-04102-6); The Jungle (ISBN 0-356-04275-8); The Dog Family (ISBN 0-356-04276-6); Gypsies & Nomads. (ISBN 0-356-04277-4); Ballet & Dance (ISBN 0-356-04278-2); Paper & Printing. (ISBN 0-356-04279-0); Food & Drink (ISBN 0-356-04280-4); Cloth & Weaving (ISBN 0-356-04281-2); Lakes & Dams (ISBN 0-356-04282-0); Building (ISBN 0-356-04283-9); Butterflies & Moths (ISBN 0-356-04284-7); Vanishing Animals (ISBN 0-356-04614-1); Animals That Burrow (ISBN 0-356-04615-X). **(Illus., Minimum order: 20 books). (gr. 1-4). 1976. PLB 10.25 ea. o.p. Raintree Pubs.**
--First Reference Library, Bks. 26-50. Incl. Spiders (ISBN 0-356-03669-3); Pirates & Buccaneers (ISBN 0-356-03670-7); Size (ISBN 0-356-03671-5); Fire (ISBN 0-356-03672-3); Weather (ISBN 0-356-03673-1); Deserts (ISBN 0-356-03674-X); Skyscrapers (ISBN 0-356-03675-8); Monkeys & Apes (ISBN 0-356-03676-6); Trains & Railroads (ISBN 0-356-03677-4); Trees & Woods (ISBN 0-356-03678-2); Cowboys (ISBN 0-356-03783-5); Time & Clocks (ISBN 0-356-03784-3); Light & Color (ISBN 0-356-03785-1); Birds & Migration (ISBN 0-356-03786-X); The Universe (ISBN 0-356-03787-8); Farms & Farmers. (ISBN 0-356-03788-6); Rocks & Mining. (ISBN 0-356-03789-4); Fuel & Energy (ISBN 0-356-04616-8); Animals with Shells (ISBN 0-356-04617-6); The Theater (ISBN 0-356-04618-4); Health & Disease (ISBN 0-356-04619-2); Pollution (ISBN 0-356-04620-6); The Movies. o.p.; Signals & Messages (ISBN 0-356-04622-2); Fishing. (ISBN 0-356-04623-0). (Illus.). (gr. 1-4). 1976. PLB 10.25 ea. o.p. Raintree Pubs.
Vansina, Jan. Kingdoms of the Savanna. (Illus.). 374p. 1966. pap. 12.50 (ISBN 0-299-03664-2). U of Wis Pr.
Van Slyke, Helen. All Visitors Must Be Announced. LC 72-76215. 408p. 1972. 14.95 (ISBN 0-385-01612-3). Doubleday.
--Always is Not Forever. 480p. 1982. pap. 3.50 (ISBN 0-446-31009-3). Warner Bks.
--The Best People. 288p. 1982. pap. 3.50 (ISBN 0-446-31010-7). Warner Bks.
--The Best Place to Be. 480p. 1982. pap. 3.50 (ISBN 0-446-31011-5). Warner Bks.
--The Heart Listens. 576p. 1982. pap. 3.50 (ISBN 0-446-31012-3). Warner Bks.
--The Mixed Blessing. 512p. 1982. pap. 3.50 (ISBN 0-446-31013-1). Warner Bks.
--A Necessary Woman. 448p. 1982. pap. 3.50 (ISBN 0-446-31015-8). Warner Bks.
--No Love Lost. LC 79-26056. 1980. 12.45 (ISBN 0-690-01897-5). Har-Row.
--Public Smiles, Private Tears. large type ed. LC 82-10341. 540p. 1982. Repr. of 1982 ed. 13.95 (ISBN 0-89621-376-5). Thorndike Pr.
--The Rich & the Righteous. 1982. pap. 3.50 (ISBN 0-446-31016-6). Warner Bks.
--Sisters & Strangers. large print ed. LC 82-3361. 667p. 1982. 13.95 (ISBN 0-89621-356-0). Thorndike Pr.
--Sisters & Strangers. 416p. 1982. pap. 3.50 (ISBN 0-446-31018-2). Warner Bks.
Van Slyke, Helen & Ashton, Sharon. The Santa Ana Wind. 256p. 1982. pap. 3.50 (ISBN 0-446-31017-4). Warner Bks.
Van Slyke, Helen & Elward, James. Public Smiles, Private Tears. 1983. pap. 3.95 (ISBN 0-686-43028-X). Bantam.
Van Slyke, L. L. & Price, W. V. Cheese. (Illus.). 522p. 1980. 35.00 o.p. (ISBN 0-917930-21-5); lib. bdg. 28.00 (ISBN 0-917930-31-2); pap. 18.00 (ISBN 0-917930-51-7); pap. text ed. 14.00x (ISBN 0-917930-11-8). Ridgeview.
Van Smith, Howard, jt. auth. see Van Dusen, C. Raymond.
Van Soest, Peter J. Nutritional Ecology of the Ruminant. LC 81-83655. 375p. 1982. 30.00x (ISBN 0-9601586-0-X). O & B Bks.
Van Son, L. George, ed. Video in Health. LC 81-13706. (Video Bookshelf Ser.). (Illus.). 231p. 1981. Professional 29.95 (ISBN 0-914236-69-5). Knowledge Indus.
VanSpanckeren, Kathryn, jt. ed. see Morace, Robert A.
Van Spronsen, C. J., ed. see EUROMICRO Symposium on Microprocessing & Microprogramming, 8th, 1982.
Van Stan, Ina. Textiles from Beneath the Temple of Pachacamac, Peru. (Museum Monographs). (Illus.). 91p. 1967. bound 5.00xsoft (ISBN 0-934718-22-9). Univ Mus of U PA.
Van Stee, Ethard W., ed. Cardiovascular Toxicology. (Target Organ Toxicology Ser.). 400p. 1982. text ed. 54.50 (ISBN 0-89004-576-3). Raven.
Van Steenberghen, Fernand. Aristotle in the West: The Origins of Latin Aristotelianism. Johnston, Leonard, tr. 1970. Repr. of 1955 ed. text ed. 11.00x o.p. (ISBN 0-391-00049-7). Humanities.
Vansteenkiste, G. C. System Simulation in Water Resources. 1976. 76.75 (ISBN 0-444-11093-3, North-Holland). Elsevier.
Vansteenkiste, G. C., ed. Modelling, Identification & Control in Environmental Systems. 1979. 104.75 (ISBN 0-444-85180-1, North Holland). Elsevier.
Van Steenwyk, Elizabeth. Behind the Scenes at the Amusement Park. Tucker, Kathleen, ed. (Behind the Scenes Ser.). (Illus.). 48p. (gr. 2-7). 1983. PLB 9.25 (ISBN 0-8075-0605-2). A Whitman.
--Illustrated Skating Dictionary for Young People. (Illus.). (gr. 4 up). 1979. pap. 2.50 o.p. (ISBN 0-13-451260-X). P-H.
--Presidents at Home. LC 80-36864. (Illus.). 128p. (gr. 4-6). 1980. PLB 8.29 o.p. (ISBN 0-671-34008-5). Messner.
Van Stijgeren, E., ed. Recent Advances In Pipe Support Design. (PVP Ser.: Vol. 68). 115p. 1982. 30.00 (H00225). ASME.
--Special Applications in Piping Dynamic Analysis. (PVP Ser.: Vol. 67). 80p. 1982. 20.00 (H00224). ASME.
Van Stijgeren, E & Krawzya, L., eds. Practical Considerations In Piping Analysis. (PVP Ser.: Vol. 69). 181p. 1982. 34.00 (H00226). ASME.
Van Stockum, Hilda, tr. see Broger, Achim.
Van Stone, James W. Athapaskan Adaptations: Hunters & Fishermen of the Subarctic Forests. LC 73-89518. (Worlds of Man Ser.). 176p. 1974. text ed. 12.95x (ISBN 0-88295-610-8); pap. text ed. 6.95x (ISBN 0-88295-611-6). Harlan Davidson.
Van Stone, John C. Dialysis & Treatment of Renal Insufficency. write for info (ISBN 0-8089-1566-5). Grune.
Vanstone, W. H. The Risk of Love. 1978. 9.95x (ISBN 0-19-520053-5). Oxford U Pr.
Van Straaten, Zac, ed. Basic Concepts in Philosophy. 1982. 24.95x (ISBN 0-19-570288-3). Oxford U Pr.
Van Straaten, Zak, ed. Philosophical Subjects: Essays Presented to P. F. Strawson. 1980. 37.50x (ISBN 0-19-824603-X). Oxford U Pr.
Van Strum, Carol. A Bitter Fog: Herbicides & Human Rights. LC 82-16821. 320p. 1983. 14.95 (ISBN 0-87156-329-0). Sierra.
Van Stuyvenberg. Margarine: An Economic, Social & Scientific History, 1869-1969. 366p. 1982. 49.00x (ISBN 0-85323-130-3, Pub. by Liverpool Univ England). State Mutual Bk.
Van Swearingen, Phyllis. Bits of Americana: Whirly Girlys to Country Gossip. (Illus.). 80p. 1982. 5.50 (ISBN 0-682-49939-0). Exposition.
Van Tamelen, E. E., ed. Bioorganic Chemistry, 2 vols. Incl. Vol. 1. Enzyme Action. 1977. 61.00 (ISBN 0-12-714301-7); Vol. 2. 1978. by subscription 54.00 64.00 (ISBN 0-12-714302-5). Acad Pr.
Van Tassel, Cynthia L., jt. auth. see Van Tassel, Dennie.
Van Tassel, Dennie. Basic-Pack Statistics Programs. (Ser. in Personal Computing). (Illus.). 240p. 1981. pap. text ed. 19.95 (ISBN 0-13-066381-6). P-H.
Van Tassel, Dennie & Van Tassel, Cynthia L. The Compleat Computer. 2nd ed. 280p. 1983. pap. text ed. write for info. (ISBN 0-574-21415-1, 13-4415). SRA.
VanTassel, Dennie L. Introductory Cobol. LC 78-54210. 1979. pap. text ed. 16.50x (ISBN 0-8162-9133-0). Holden-Day.
Van Tassel, Dennis. The Complete Computer. LC 75-31760. (Illus.). 250p. 1976. pap. text ed. 9.95 (ISBN 0-574-21060-1, 13-4060). SRA.
Van Tets, Gerard F. Comparative Study of Some Social Communication Patterns in the Pelecaniformes. American Ornithologists' Union, ed. 88p. 1965. 3.50 (ISBN 0-943610-02-8). Am Ornithologists.
Van Thal, Herbert, ed. Edward Lear's Journals: A Selection. 260p. 1982. Repr. of 1952 ed. lib. bdg. 35.00 (ISBN 0-8495-3401-1). Arden Lib.
Van Thal, Herbert, ed. see Broughton, Rhoda.
Van Til, Cornelius. A Survey of Christian Epistemology. 1967. kivar 5.00 (ISBN 0-87552-495-8). Presby & Reformed.
Van Til, John see Smith, David H. & Til, John Van.
Van Til, Jon. Living with the Energy Shortfall: The Future of American Towns & Cities. 225p. (Orig.). 1982. lib. bdg. 25.00 (ISBN 0-86531-135-8); pap. text ed. 10.00 (ISBN 0-86531-136-6). Westview.
Van Til, William. Curriculum: Quest for Relevance. 2nd ed. LC 79-144319. 400p. 1974. pap. text ed. 17.50 (ISBN 0-395-17787-1). HM.
--Education: A Beginning. 2nd ed. 624p. 1974. text ed. 24.50 (ISBN 0-395-17576-3); instr's manual 1.65 (ISBN 0-395-17850-9). HM.
--Secondary Education: School & Community. LC 77-76861. (Illus.). 1978. text ed. 21.95 (ISBN 0-395-25751-4); instr's manual 1.00 (ISBN 0-395-25764-6). HM.
Van Tilburg, JoAnne. Ancient Images on Stone: Rock Art of the Californians. LC 82-84337. (Illus.). 128p. 1983. pap. 20.00 (ISBN 0-917956-40-0). UCLA Arch.
Van Tilburg, JoAnne & Meighan, Clement W., eds. Prehistoric Indian Rock Art: Issues & Concerns. (Monograph: No. XIX). (Illus.). 66p. 1981. pap. text ed. 6.00 (ISBN 0-917956-24-9). UCLA Arch.
Van Toller, C. The Nervous Body: An Introduction to the Autonomic Nervous System & Behaviour. LC 78-16758. 1979. 46.95 (ISBN 0-471-99703-X); pap. 18.95x (ISBN 0-471-99729-3, Pub. by Wiley-Interscience). Wiley.
Vanton, Monte. Marriage: Grounds for Divorce. 1979. 10.00 o.p. (ISBN 0-671-24803-0). S&S.
Van Trees, H. L., ed. Satellite Communications. LC 78-65704. 1979. 51.95 (ISBN 0-87942-121-5). Inst Electrical.
Van Trees, Harry L. Detection, Estimation & Modulation Theory, 2 pts. Incl. Pt. 1. Detection, Estimation & Linear Modulation Theory. 697p. 1968. 48.95x (ISBN 0-471-89955-0); Pt. 3. Radar-Sonar Signal Processing & Gaussian Signals in Noise. 626p. 1971. 64.95 (ISBN 0-471-89958-5). LC 67-23331. (Illus.). Wiley.
Van Trees, Harry L., ed. Satellite Communications. LC 78-65704. (A Volume in the IEEE Press Selected Reprint Ser). 1980. 51.95x (ISBN 0-471-06101-8, Pub. by Wiley-Interscience); pap. 35.95 (ISBN 0-471-06100-X, Pub. by Wiley-Interscience). Wiley.
--Satellite Communications. 665p. 1979. 46.00 (ISBN 0-686-98093-X). Telecom Lib.
Van Trees, James & Wolenik, Robert. A Buyer's Guide to Home Computers. 288p. (Orig.). 1983. pap. 3.75 (ISBN 0-523-41992-9). Pinnacle Bks.
Van Treese, Glenn J. D'Alembert & Frederick the Great: A Study of Their Relationship. Matczak, Sebastian A., ed. LC 73-82788. (Philosophical Questions Ser.: No. 9). 191p. 1974. 18.00x (ISBN 0-912116-11-0). Learned Pubns.
Vantuono, William. The Pearl Poems: An Omnibus Edition. LC 82-21026. 500p. 1983. lib. bdg. 60.00 (ISBN 0-8240-5450-4). Garland Pub.
Van Turnhout, J., jt. ed. see Fillard, J. P.
Van Tuyl, Barbara. The Betrayal of Bonnie. (Orig.). (RL 5). 1975. pap. 1.95 (ISBN 0-451-11980-0, AJ1980, Sig). NAL.
--Bonnie & the Haunted Farm. (Orig.). (RL 5). 1974. pap. 1.75 (ISBN 0-451-11184-2, AE1184, Sig). NAL.
--Select, Buy, Train & Care for Your Own Horse. Johnson, Patricia H., ed. 1969. 5.95 o.p. (ISBN 0-448-01736-9, G&D). Putnam Pub Group.
Van Tuyl, Barbara, jt. auth. see Johnson, Pat.
Van Tyne, C. H. & Leland, W. G. Guide to the Archives of the Government of the United States in Washington. 2nd enl. ed. 1907. 32.00 (ISBN 0-527-00681-5). Kraus Repr.
Van Tyne, C. H., ed. see Webster, Daniel.
Van Tyne, Claude H. American Revolution, Seventeen Seventy-Six to Seventeen Eighty-Three. Repr. of 1905 ed. lib. bdg. 17.50x o.p. (ISBN 0-8371-1875-1, VAAR). Greenwood.
--Causes of the War of Independence. 9.50 (ISBN 0-8446-1459-9). Peter Smith.
Van Tyne, Josselyn & Berger, Andrew J. Fundamentals of Ornithology. 2nd. ed. LC 75-20430. 808p. 1976. 44.95x (ISBN 0-471-89965-8, Pub. by Wiley-Interscience). Wiley.
Van Uitert, Evert. Van Gogh Drawings. LC 78-4361. (Illus.). 228p. 1979. 15.95 (ISBN 0-87951-085-4). Overlook Pr.
Van Vactor, David & Moore, Katherine D. Every Child May Hear. LC 80-12222. 1960. pap. 7.50x (ISBN 0-87049-030-3). U of Tenn Pr.
Van Valkenburg, M. Linear Circuits. (Illus.). 448p. 1982. 29.95 (ISBN 0-13-536722-0). P-H.
Van Valkenburg, M. E. Network Analysis. 3rd ed. (Illus.). 699p. 1974. 32.95 (ISBN 0-13-611095-9). P-H.
Van Valkenburg, M. E., jt. auth. see Cruz, Jose B.
Van Valkenburg, M. E., ed. Circuit Theory: Foundations & Classical Contributions. LC 74-2475. (Benchmark Papers in Electrical Engineering & Computer Science Ser.: Vol. 8). 464p. 1974. text ed. 55.50 (ISBN 0-12-787660-X). Acad Pr.
Van Vechten, B. D. The First Year of Forever. LC 82-45171. 224p. 1982. 12.95 (ISBN 0-689-11317-X). Atheneum.
Van Vechten, Carl. The Dance Photography of Carl Van Vechten. LC 81-51117. (Dance Horizons Bk.). 1981. 29.95 (ISBN 0-872680-4). Macmillan.
--Parties. 1977. pap. 1.95 o.p. (ISBN 0-380-00986-2, 32631, Bard). Avon.
--Sacred & Profane Memories. LC 78-27584. 1979. Repr. of 1932 ed. lib. bdg. 20.75x (ISBN 0-313-20835-2, VVSP). Greenwood.
Van Vlaanderen, Edward, ed. Molecular Biology & Cardiovascular Disease: New Directions in Research & Therapy for the 1980's. 1981. text ed. 4.00 (ISBN 0-89004-671-9). Raven.
Van Vlack, Lawrence H. Elements of Materials Science & Engineering. 4th ed. LC 79-19352. (Metallurgy & Materials Ser.). 1980. text ed. 27.95 (ISBN 0-201-08090-7). A-W.
--A Textbook of Materials Technology. LC 70-190614. 1973. text ed. 25.95 (ISBN 0-201-08066-4); instructor's manual 3.95 (ISBN 0-201-08067-2). A-W.
Van Vleck, Jane, ed. see Olson, Jim.
Van Vleck, John H. Theory of Electric & Magnetic Susceptibilities. (International Series of Monographs on Physics). (Illus.). 1932. pap. 42.50x (ISBN 0-19-851243-0). Oxford U Pr.
Van Vliet, J., jt. ed. see De Bakker, J. W.
Van Vogt, A. E. The Battle of Forever. 1982. pap. 2.25 (ISBN 0-87997-758-2, UE1758). DAW Bks.
--The Darkness on Diamondia. 1982. pap. 2.25 (ISBN 0-87997-724-8, UE1724). DAW Bks.
--Earth Factor X. (Science Fiction Ser.). 1978. pap. 1.50 o.p. (ISBN 0-87997-412-5, UW1412). DAW Bks.
--Lost: Fifty Sun. (Daw Science Fiction Ser.). Orig. Title: Book of Van Vogt. 1979. pap. 1.75 o.p. (ISBN 0-87997-491-5, UE1491). Daw Bks.
--The Players of Null-A. (Science Fiction Ser.). 1977. Repr. of 1948 ed. lib. bdg. 10.00 o.p. (ISBN 0-8398-2352-5, Gregg). G K Hall.
--Slan. Del Rey, Lester, ed. LC 75-439. (Library of Science Fiction). 1975. lib. bdg. 17.50 o.s.i. (ISBN 0-8240-1441-3). Garland Pub.
Van Vooren, Monique. Night Sanctuary. 1983. pap. 3.95 (ISBN 0-686-43054-9, Sig). NAL.
Van Voorhis, S. N., ed. Microwave Receivers. (Illus.). 8.50 (ISBN 0-8446-3106-X). Peter Smith.
Van Voorst, Dick. Corrugated Carton Crafting. LC 71-90803. (Little Craft Book Ser). (Illus.). (gr. 5 up). 1969. 5.95 o.p. (ISBN 0-8069-5138-9); PLB 6.69 o.p. (ISBN 0-8069-5139-7). Sterling.
Van Voorthuijsen, A. M. World Collectors Annuary, 32 vols. write for info. vols. 1-32, 1946-1980; vol. 33, 1981 100.00 (ISBN 0-685-52513-9). Heinman.
Van Voorthuijsen, J. J. World Collectors Index, 1946-1972, with Supplements 1978-81: An Alphabetical Index to Volumes 1-33 of World Collectors Annuary. 1976. 60.00 (ISBN 90-70139-01-4). Heinman.
Van Voorthuizen, A. E., ed. Fourth Generation Cat Scanning. (International Congress Ser.: Vol. 524). 1980. 29.00 (ISBN 0-444-90166-3). Elsevier.
Van Vorst, W. D., ed. see World Hydrogen Energy Conference, Fourth.
Van Voss, M. Heerma. Agypten, die 21: Dynastie. (Iconography of Relifions Ser.: XVI/9). (Illus.). viii, 18p. 1982. pap. write for info. (ISBN 90-04-06826-0). E J Brill.
Van Vuuren, Nancy. The Subversion of Women As Practiced by Churches, Witch-Hunters, & Other Sexists. LC 73-5874. 1973. 5.95 o.s.i. (ISBN 0-664-20972-6). Westminster.
Van Wade, David & Van Wade, Sarah. Second Chance. LC 75-20899. 1975. 4.95 (ISBN 0-88270-137-1, Pub. by Logos); pap. 4.95 (ISBN 0-88270-138-X). Bridge Pub.
Van Wade, Sarah, jt. auth. see Van Wade, David.
Van Walsum-Quispel, J. see Walsum-Quispel, J. van.
Van Way, Charles W. & Buerk, Charles A. Surgical Skills in Patient Care. LC 78-4198. 174p. 1978. pap. text ed. 19.95 (ISBN 0-8016-5214-6). Mosby.
Van Wazer, John R. & Absar, Ilyas. Electron Densities in Molecules & Molecular Orbitals. (Physical Chemistry Ser.). 1975. 32.00 (ISBN 0-12-714550-8). Acad Pr.
Van Well, Sr. Mary Stanislaus. Educational Aspects of the Missions of the Southwest. 1942. pap. 7.95 (ISBN 0-87462-438-X). Marquette.
Van Wert, William F. The Film Career of Alain Robbe-Grillet. 1977. lib. bdg. 22.00 (ISBN 0-8161-7992-1, Hall Reference). G K Hall.
--The Film Career of Alain Robbe-Grillet. (Orig.). 1979. pap. 7.80 o.p. (ISBN 0-913178-59-4, Pub. by Two Continents). Hippocrene Bks.
Van Wezel, Antonius L., jt. ed. see Mizrahi, Avshalom.
Van Wezel, Ru see Wezel, Ru van.
Van Wijnbergen, S. see Wijnbergen, S. Van.
Van Wimersma, Greidanus, jt. ed. see Gispen, W. H.
Van Winkle, jt. auth. see Heyne.
Van Winkle, Matthew. Distillation. (Chemical Engineering Ser.). 1967. text ed. 39.50 (ISBN 0-07-067195-8, C). McGraw.
Van Winkle, Walton, jt. auth. see Peacock, Erle E.
Van Woerkom, Dorothy. Alexandra the Rock-Eater. LC 77-13778. (gr. k-3). 1978. 6.95 o.p. (ISBN 0-394-83536-0); 7.99 (ISBN 0-394-93536-5). Knopf.
--Becky & the Bear. LC 74-16628. (See & Read Storybooks). (Illus.). 48p. (gr. 1-3). 1975. PLB 6.29 o.p. (ISBN 0-399-60924-5). Putnam Pub Group.
--Journeys to Bethlehem. (Illus.). 48p. (gr. 1-3). 1974. 7.95 (ISBN 0-570-03432-9, 56-1187). Concordia.
--Wake up & Listen. (Illus.). 48p. 1976. 4.95 o.p. (ISBN 0-570-03257-1, 15-2165). Concordia.
Van Wormer, Joe. How to Be a Wildlife Photographer. (Illus.). 160p. (gr. 7 up). 1982. 10.95 (ISBN 0-525-66772-5, 01063-320). Lodestar Bks.
--World of the American Elk. LC 77-86080. (Illus.). 1969. 8.95i (ISBN 0-397-00621-7). Har-Row.
--World of the Canada Goose. LC 68-24138. (Living World Books Ser). (Illus.). (gr. 4-9). 1968. PLB 7.82 o.p. (ISBN 0-397-00931-3). Har-Row.

--World of the Pronghorn. LC 69-14340. (Living World Books Ser). (Illus.). (gr. 4-9). 1969. PLB 7.82 o.p. (ISBN 0-397-00625-X). Har-Row.

Van Wyk Smith, M. Drummer Hodge: The Poetry of the Anglo-Boer War, 1899-1902. 1978. 37.50x (ISBN 0-19-812082-6). Oxford U Pr.

Van Wylen, G. J., jt. auth. see Sonntag, R. E.

Van Wylen, Gordon J. & Sonntag, Richard E. Fundamentals of Classical Thermodynamics. 2nd ed. LC 72-1297. (Thermal & Transport Sciences Ser.). (Illus.). 724p. 1973. text ed. 33.95x (ISBN 0-471-90227-6). Wiley.

--Fundamentals of Classical Thermodynamics: SI Version. 2nd rev. ed. LC 76-2405. 1976. text ed. 33.95 (ISBN 0-471-04188-2); solutions manual 9.00 (ISBN 0-471-04519-5); Arabic Translation avail. Wiley.

Van Wylen, Gordon J., jt. auth. see Sonntag, Richard E.

Van Wynen Thomas, Ann & Thomas, A. J., Jr. The War Making Powers of the President. 180p. 1982. 15.00 (ISBN 0-87074-185-3). SMU Press.

Van Wyngarden, Carole. The Gentle Way. (Freya Ser.). (Accordion fold design). 1974. 2.00 (ISBN 0-686-09140-X). Merging Media.

Van Zant, Nancy P. Selected U.S. Government Series: A Guide for Public & Academic Libraries. LC 77-10337. 1978. 15.00 (ISBN 0-8389-0252-9). ALA.

Van Zanten, Ann, jt. auth. see Chappell, Sally.

Van Zanten, David. Architectural Polychromy of the Eighteen Thirties. LC 76-23648. (Outstanding Dissertations in the Fine Arts: Second Series-Nineteenth Century). (Illus.). 1977. Repr. of 1970 ed. lib. bdg. 63.00 o.s.i. (ISBN 0-8240-2733-7). Garland Pub.

Van Zeggeren, F. & Storey, S. H. Computation of Chemical Equilibria. LC 78-92255. (Illus.). 1970. 37.50 (ISBN 0-521-07630-7). Cambridge U Pr.

Van Zeller, Hubert. The Trodden Road. 173p. 1982. 4.00 (ISBN 0-8198-7326-8, SP0773); pap. 3.00 (ISBN 0-8198-7327-6). Dghtrs St Paul.

Van Zile, Judy. The Japanese Bon Dance in Hawaii. (Illus.). 96p. 1982. pap. 5.95 (ISBN 0-916630-27-7). Pr Pacifica.

Van Zuylan, Guirne. Gourmet Cooking for Everyone. 1969. 7.95 o.p. (ISBN 0-571-08714-0). Transatlantic.

Van Zuylen, Guirne. Eating with Wine. (Illus.). 1972. 8.95 o.p. (ISBN 0-571-09958-0). Transatlantic.

Van Zwanenberg, R. M. see Zwanenberg, R. M. van & King, Anne.

Van Zwienen, John. Pivot. 1980. 2.25 o.s.i. (ISBN 0-515-05639-1). Jove Pubns.

Van Zyl Slabbert, F. & Welsh, David. South Africa's Options. 1979. 20.00x (ISBN 0-312-74696-2). St Martin.

--South Africa's Options: Strategies for Sharing Power. 210p. 1982. 30.00x (ISBN 0-86036-117-9, Pub. by Collins England). State Mutual Bk.

Vapnik, Vladimir N. Estimation of Dependences Based on Empirical Data Dependences. (Springer Series in Statistics). (Illus.). 432p. 1982. 56.00 (ISBN 0-387-90733-5). Springer-Verlag.

Vaporis, N. M., intro. by see Moskos, C. C., Jr. & Papajohn, J. C.

Vaporis, N. M., ed. see Patsavos, L. J. & Charles, G. J.

Vaporis, N. M., ed. see Talbot, Alice-Mary M.

Vapp, Malcolm. The Enlightenment. Killingray, Margaret, et al, eds. (Greenhaven World History Ser.). (Illus.). 32p. (gr. 10). 1980. lib. bdg. 6.95 (ISBN 0-89908-225-4); pap. text ed. 2.25 (ISBN 0-89908-200-9). Greenhaven.

Vara, Albert C. Food & Beverage Industries: A Bibliography & Guidebook. LC 70-102058. (Management Information Guide Ser.: No. 16). 1970. 42.00x (ISBN 0-8103-0816-9). Gale.

Varacalli, Joseph A. Toward the Establishment of Liberal Catholicism in America. LC 82-23811. 326p. (Orig.). 1983. lib. bdg. 23.75 (ISBN 0-8191-2974-7); pap. text ed. 13.00 (ISBN 0-8191-2975-5). U Pr of Amer.

Varadan. Problems in Elastic Wave Scattering & Propagation. LC 81-70871. 200p. 1982. 39.95 (ISBN 0-250-40534-2). Ann Arbor Science.

Varadarajian, V. S. Lie Groups, Lie Algebras, & Their Representations. (Modern Analysis Ser.). 496p. 1974. ref. ed. 32.95 (ISBN 0-13-535732-2). P-H.

Varadpande, M. L. Religion & Theatre in India. 100p. 1982. text ed. 10.00x (ISBN 0-391-02794-8). Humanities.

Varberg, Dale, jt. auth. see Fleming, Walter.

Varberg, Dale E., jt. auth. see Fleming, Walter.

Varble, Dale. Cases in Marketing Management. (Business Ser.). 272p. 1976. pap. text ed. 12.50 (ISBN 0-675-08638-8). Additional supplements may be obtained from publisher. Merrill.

Varcop, L., jt. auth. see Dolezal, R.

Vardaman, G. T. & Vardaman, P. B. Successful Writing: A Short Course for Professionals. 1977. 55.95x (ISBN 0-471-02428-7). Wiley.

Vardaman, George T. & Vardaman, Patricia B. Communication in Modern Organizations. LC 82-12694. 534p. 1982. Repr. of 1973 ed. lib. bdg. 32.50 (ISBN 0-89874-537-3). Krieger.

Vardaman, James M. Tree Farm Business Management. 2nd ed. LC 78-1610. 1978. 22.95x (ISBN 0-471-07263-X, Pub. by Wiley-Interscience). Wiley.

Vardaman, Jerry. La Arqueologia y la Palabra Viva. Benlliure, F., tr. Orig. Title: Archeology & the Living Word. 137p. 1976. pap. 3.25 (ISBN 0-311-03649-X). Casa Bautista.

Vardaman, P. B., jt. auth. see Vardaman, G. T.

Vardaman, Patricia B., jt. auth. see Vardaman, George T.

Vardeman, Robert E. Cenotaph Road. 1983. pap. 2.75 (ISBN 0-441-09845-2, Pub. by Ace Science Fiction). Ace Bks.

Vardey, Lucinda, jt. auth. see Bowman, Sarah.

Vardi, Joseph & Avi-Itzhak, Benjamin. Electric Energy Generation: Economics, Reliability & Rates. 192p. 1981. text ed. 27.50x (ISBN 0-262-22024-5). MIT Pr.

Vardys, V. Stanley & Misiunas, Romuald J., eds. The Baltic States in Peace & War, 1917-1945. LC 77-88472. 1978. 18.95x (ISBN 0-271-00534-3). Pa St U Pr.

Varela, jt. auth. see De La Portilla.

Varenhorst, Barbara B. Real Friends: Becoming the Friend You'd Like to Have. LC 82-48412. (Illus.). 160p. (Orig.). 1983. pap. 5.72 (ISBN 0-06-250890-3, HarpR). Har-Row.

Varenne, Herve. Americans Together: Structured Diversity in a Midwestern Town. LC 77-10109. 1977. pap. text ed. 10.95x (ISBN 0-8077-2519-6). Tchrs Coll.

--The Rhetorical Structuring of American Daily Conversations: Culturally Patterned Conflicts in a Suburban High School. 250p. 1983. text ed. 24.50x (ISBN 0-8290-1288-5). Irvington.

Varennes De Mondasse. La Decouverte de l'Empire de Cantahar. (Utopias in the Enlightenment Ser.). 383p. (Fr.). 1974. Repr. of 1730 ed. lib. bdg. 98.00x o.p. (ISBN 0-8287-0853-3, 005). Clearwater Pub.

Varese, Louise, tr. see Michaux, Henri.

Varese, Louise, tr. see Stendhal.

Varey, Simon, ed. Lord Bolingbroke: Contributions to the Craftsman. 1982. 39.95 (ISBN 0-19-822386-2). Oxford U Pr.

Varg, Paul A. The Making of a Myth: The United States & China, Eighteen Ninety-Seven to Nineteen Twelve. LC 79-25619. 184p. 1980. Repr. of 1968 ed. lib. bdg. 20.25x (ISBN 0-313-22125-1, VAMA). Greenwood.

--New England & Foreign Relations, 1789-1850. LC 82-40338. 272p. 1982. text ed. 18.00x (ISBN 0-87451-224-7). U Pr of New Eng.

Varga, Eugen. Two Systems: Socialist Economy & Capitalist Economy. Arnot, R. Page, tr. LC 68-30830. (Illus.). 1968. Repr. of 1939 ed. lib. bdg. 18.25x (ISBN 0-8371-0257-X, VATS). Greenwood.

Varga, Judy. Circus Cannonball. LC 74-26796. (Illus.). 32p. (gr. k-3). 1975. 7.75 o.p. (ISBN 0-688-22026-6); PLB 9.12 (ISBN 0-688-32026-0). Morrow.

--The Crow Who Came to Stay. (Illus.). (ps-3). 1967. 9.95 (ISBN 0-688-21203-4); PLB 9.55 (ISBN 0-688-31203-9). Morrow.

--Once-a-Year Witch. (Illus.). 32p. (ps-3). 1973. PLB 9.55 (ISBN 0-688-31777-4). Morrow.

Varga, R. S., jt. ed. see Saff, E. B.

Varga, Richard S. Functional Analysis & Approximation Theory in Numerical Analysis. (CBMS Regional Conference Ser.: Vol. 3). iii, 76p. (Orig.). 1971. pap. text ed. 7.00 (ISBN 0-89871-003-0). Soc Indus-Appl Math.

--Matrix Iterative Analysis. 1962. ref. ed. 24.95 (ISBN 0-13-565507-2). P-H.

Varga, Sarah S., jt. auth. see Bennett, L. Claire.

Vargaftik, N. B. Handbook of Physical Properties of Liquids & Gases: Pure Substances & Mixtures. 2nd ed. LC 82-25857. 1983. text ed. 59.95 (ISBN 0-89116-356-5). Hemisphere Pub.

Vargas, Alberto & Austin, Reid. Vargas. (Illus.). 128p. 1978. 17.95 (ISBN 0-517-53047-3); pap. 9.95 (ISBN 0-517-53048-1). Crown.

Vargas, Carlos A., tr. see Keller, Phillip.

Vargas, Glenn & Vargas, Martha. Diagrams For Faceting, Vol. II. (Illus.). 1983. 15.00 (ISBN 0-686-82596-9). Glenn Vargas.

Vargas, Martha, jt. auth. see Vargas, Glenn.

Vargas-Llosa, Mario. Aunt Julia & the Scriptwriter. Lane, Helen R., tr. from Span. 1982. 16.95 (ISBN 0-374-10691-6). FS&G.

Vargas Llosa, Mario. Captain Pantoja & the Special Service. Christ, Ronald & Kolovakos, Gregory, trs. LC 76-26280. Orig. Title: Special Brigade. 1978. 11.49i (ISBN 0-06-014494-7, HarpT). Har-Row.

--Conversation in the Cathedral. Rabassa, Gregory, tr. LC 74-1892. 608p. 1983. cancelled (ISBN 0-06-014502-1, HarpT). Har-Row.

--The Cubs & Other Stories. Christ, Ronald & Kolovakos, Gregory, trs. from Span. LC 78-20217. 1979. 11.49i (ISBN 0-06-014491-2, HarpT). Har-Row.

--The Green House. Rabassa, Gregory, tr. LC 68-28227. 405p. 1983. 19.23i o.p. (ISBN 0-06-014503-X, HarpT). Har-Row.

--The Time of the Hero. Kemp, Lysander, tr. from Span. LC 65-14204. 1979. pap. 5.95i o.p. (ISBN 0-06-090652-9, CN 652, CN). Har-Row.

Vargh, George. Pharmacoangiography in the Diagnosis of Tumours. Kerner, Nora, tr. from Hungarian. (Illus.). 253p. 1981. 35.00x (ISBN 963-05-2912-2). Intl Pubns Serv.

Vargo, Richard J. & Dierks, Paul A. Readings & Cases in Governmental & Nonprofit Accounting. LC 82-70506. 272p. 1983. pap. text ed. 13.95x (ISBN 0-931920-37-X). Dame Pubns.

Vargoshe, Richard & Steinberg, Peter. The Household Book of Animal Medicine. 208p. 1980. 14.95 (ISBN 0-13-392670-2, Spec); pap. 6.95 (ISBN 0-13-395863-9). P-H.

Varian, Hal E. Microeconomic Analysis. 1978. pap. text ed. 20.95x (ISBN 0-393-09036-1); pap. text ed. 7.95x exercise application (ISBN 0-393-95078-6). Norton.

Varian, Hal R. Microeconomic Analysis. 2nd ed. 1983. write for info (ISBN 0-393-95282-7); write for info Exercises & applications (ISBN 0-393-95330-0). Norton.

Varlamova, Inna. A Counterfeit Life. Lowe, David, tr. from Rus. 107p. Date not set. lib. bdg. 15.00 (ISBN 0-88233-823-4); pap. price not set (ISBN 0-88233-824-2). Ardis Pubs.

Varlejs, Jana & DeProspo, Ernest, eds. The Economics of Information. LC 82-14842. 92p. 1982. pap. 9.95x (ISBN 0-89950-059-5). McFarland & Co.

Varlet, Jean-Francois. Declaration Solennelle des Droits De l'Homme Dans l'Etat Social. (Fr.). 1977. lib. bdg. 13.75x o.p. (ISBN 0-8287-0854-1); pap. text ed. 3.75x o.p. (ISBN 0-685-75742-0). Clearwater Pub.

Varley, Allen, ed. Who's Who in Ocean Freshwater Science. 336p. 165.00x (ISBN 0-686-75643-6, Pub. by Longman). Gale.

Varley, Desmond. Seven: The Number of Creation. (Illus.). 1977. 16.50 o.s.i. (ISBN 0-7135-1947-9). Transatlantic.

Varley, John. Millennium. 1983. pap. 6.95 (ISBN 0-425-06250-3). Berkley Pub.

--Wizard. 1980. 12.95 (ISBN 0-399-12472-1). Putnam Pub Group.

Varma, Baidya N., ed. The New Social Sciences. LC 75-35358. (Contributions in Sociology Ser.: No. 18). 320p. 1976. lib. bdg. 29.95x (ISBN 0-8371-8591-2, VSS/). Greenwood.

Varma, Monika, tr. see Jayadeva.

Varma, Ravi & Hrubesh, Lawrence W. Chemical Analysis by Microwave Rotational Spectroscopy. LC 78-17415. (Chemical Analysis Series of Monographs on Analytical Chemistry & Its Application). 1979. 31.50 o.p. (ISBN 0-471-03916-0, Pub. by Wiley-Interscience). Wiley.

--Chemical Analysis by Microwave Rotational Spectroscopy. LC 78-17415. 218p. Repr. of 1979 ed. text ed. 31.50 (ISBN 0-471-03916-0). Krieger.

Varma, S. P. Modern Political Theory. 1976. 15.95x o.p. (ISBN 0-7069-0369-2, Pub. by Vikas India). Advent NY.

--Modern Political Theory. 2nd ed. xvii, 426p. 1982. text ed. 27.50 (ISBN 0-7069-1380-9, Pub. by Vikas India). Advent NY.

Varma, Ved P. & Williams, Philip, eds. Piaget: Psychology & Education. 1977. pap. text ed. 9.95 (ISBN 0-87581-220-1, 220). Peacock Pubs.

Varmus, Harold & Levine, Arnold J., eds. Readings in Tumor Virology. LC 82-72707. 700p. 1983. 39.50X (ISBN 0-87969-157-3). Cold Spring Harbor.

Varnedor, Kirk, illus. Northern Light: Realism & Symbolism in Scandinavian Painting, 1880-1910. 240p. 1982. pap. 17.95 (ISBN 0-686-82279-X). Bklyn Mus.

Varner, Jane T. Word Processing Operations: Document Preparation. 352p. 1982. pap. text ed. 17.95 write for info. (ISBN 0-574-20630-2, 13-3630); working papers 5.95 (ISBN 0-574-20631-0, 13-3632); Legal & Medical - Technical Applications 5.95 (ISBN 0-574-20632-9, 13-3670). SRA.

Varner, Jeannette, ed. see Garcilaso de la Vega.

Varner, Jeannette, tr. see Garcilaso de la Vega.

Varner, John, ed. see Garcilaso de la Vega.

Varner, Velmer. The Animal Frolic. 1967. PLB 4.69 o.p. (ISBN 0-399-60027-2). Putnam Pub Group.

Varney, Glenn H. Individual Performance Planning. 30p. 1974. pap. 6.50 (ISBN 0-686-05626-4). Mgmt Advisory.

--Management by Objectives Workbook. 1974. pap. 6.50 (ISBN 0-686-38067-3). Mgmt Advisory.

Varney, Wilbur R., jt. auth. see Clark, Donald S.

Varnum, Charles & Carroll, John M. I, Varnum: The Autobiographical Reminiscences of Custer's Chief of Scouts. LC 82-70693. (Hidden Springs of Custeriana: VII). (Illus.). 194p. 1982. 45.00 (ISBN 0-87062-142-4). A H Arthur.

Varnusz, Egon. Selected Games of Lajos Portisch. Crane, Keith, tr. LC 78-10319. (Illus.). 1979. 12.95 o.p. (ISBN 0-668-04722-4). Arco.

Varon, Bension. Zaire: Current Economic Situation & Constraints. v, 191p. 1980. pap. 15.00 (ISBN 0-686-36127-X, RC-8005). World Bank.

Varon, Miriam, tr. see Tributsch, Helmut.

Vartanian, Aram. Diderot & Descartes: A Study of Scientific Naturalism in the Enlightment. LC 75-18406. (History of Ideas Series: No. 6). 336p. 1975. Repr. of 1953 ed. lib. bdg. 19.25x (ISBN 0-8371-8337-5, VADD). Greenwood.

Varty, Kenneth. Reynard the Fox: A Study of the Fox in Medieval English Art. 1967. text ed. 25.00x o.p. (ISBN 0-391-01055-7, Leicester). Humanities.

Varute, A. T. & Bhatia, K. S. Cell Structure & Function. 1976. 17.50x o.p. (ISBN 0-7069-0461-3, Pub. by Vikas India). Advent NY.

Varwell, D. W. Police & the Public. 128p. 1978. 30.00x (ISBN 0-7121-1683-4, Pub. by Macdonald & Evans). State Mutual Bk.

Vas, Irwin E., ed. Wind Energies, 3 Vols. (Supplement to Progress in Solar Energy Ser.). 1982. pap. text ed. 148.00X (ISBN 0-89553-056-2). Am Solar Energy.

--Wind Energy: Progress in Solar Energy, Supplements, Vol. I. (SERI Ser.). 550p. 1982. pap. text ed. 55.00x (ISBN 0-89553-061-9). Am Solar Energy.

--Wind Energy: Progress in Solar Energy, Supplements, Vol. II. (SERI Ser.). 726p. 1982. pap. text ed. 58.00x (ISBN 0-89553-062-7). Am Solar Energy.

--Wind Energy: Progress in Solar Energy, Supplements, Vol. III. (SERI Ser.). 322p. 1982. pap. text ed. 36.00x (ISBN 0-89553-063-5). Am Solar Energy.

Vasa, Stanley F., jt. auth. see Stellern, John.

Vasari, Giorgio. Lives of Painters, Sculptors & Architects, Vol. 2. 1980. Repr. of 1963 ed. 9.95x (ISBN 0-460-00785-8, Evman). Biblio Dist.

--Lives of Painters, Sculptors & Architects, Vol. 3. 1980. Repr. of 1963 ed. 9.95x (ISBN 0-460-00786-6, Evman). Biblio Dist.

--Lives of the Painters, Sculptors & Architects, Vol. 1. 1980. Repr. of 1963 ed. 9.95x (ISBN 0-460-00784-X, Evman). Biblio Dist.

--Lives of the Painters, Sculptors & Architects, Vol. 4. 1980. Repr. of 1963 ed. 9.95x (ISBN 0-460-00787-4, Evman). Biblio Dist.

--Vite de'piu eccellenti architetti, pittori, et scultori italiani, 2 vols. (Documents of Art & Architectural History, Ser. 1: Vol. 1). (Ital.). 1980. Repr. of 1550 ed. Set. 85.00x (ISBN 0-89371-101-2). Broude Intl Edns.

Vasarinsh. Clinical Dermatology: Diagnosis & Treatment. 1982. text ed. 49.95 (ISBN 0-409-95013-0). Butterworth.

Vasconcellos, John. A Liberating Vision: Politics for Growing Humans. LC 79-16778. 1979. pap. 3.00 o.p. (ISBN 0-915166-16-X). Impact Pubs Cal.

Vasconcelos, G., ed. Anaesthesiology. (International Congress Ser.: No. 387). (Abstracts). 1976. pap. 28.50 (ISBN 0-444-15220-2). Elsevier.

Vasconcelos, Jose. A Mexican Ulysses, an Autobiography. Crawford, W. Rex, tr. LC 72-6215. 288p. 1972. Repr. of 1963 ed. lib. bdg. 18.75x (ISBN 0-8371-6477-X, VAMU). Greenwood.

Vasconcelos, W. V. Divisor Theory in Module Categories. (Mathematics Studies: Vol. 14). 120p. 1974. pap. text ed. 23.25 (ISBN 0-444-10737-1, North-Holland). Elsevier.

Vasey, Lloyd R., ed. ASEAN & a Positive Strategy for Foreign Investment. 1978. pap. text ed. 8.00x o.p. (ISBN 0-8248-0621-2). UH Pr.

--Pacific Asia & U. S. Policies: A Political-Economic-Strategic Assessment. 1978. pap. text ed. 8.00x o.p. (ISBN 0-8248-0624-7). UH Pr.

Vashista, jt. auth. see Kalia.

Vasi, Susanne & Tomasino, Joseph. Exercises in Spanish. new ed. 200p. (gr. 11-12). 1980. pap. 3.75 (ISBN 0-88345-421-1, 18638); cassettes 25.00 (ISBN 0-686-70158-5). Regents Pub.

Vasil, Indra K. Plant Improvement & Somatic Cell Genetics - Symposium. 1982. 22.00 (ISBN 0-12-714980-5). Acad Pr.

Vasil, Indra K., ed. International Review of Cytology: Supplement 11, Part A: Perspectives in Plant Cell & Tissue Culture. (Serial Pub.). 1980. 34.00 (ISBN 0-12-364371-6). Acad Pr.

--International Review of Cytology: Supplement 11, Part B: Advances in Plant Cell & Tissue Culture. (Serial Pub.). 1980. 34.00 (ISBN 0-12-364372-4). Acad Pr.

Vasil, Raj K. Ethnic Politics in Malaysia. (Illus.). 234p. 1980. text ed. 19.50x (ISBN 0-391-01770-5). Humanities.

Vasil'chenko, I. T. Novitates Systematicae: Plantarum Vascularium 1972, Vol. 9. 378p. 1978. 82.00 (ISBN 0-686-84461-0, Pub. by Oxford & I B H India). State Mutual Bk.

Vasil chenko, J. T. Novitates Systematicae: Plantarum Vascularium 1971, Vol. 8. 342p. 1978. 77.00x (ISBN 0-686-84460-2, Pub. by Oxford & I B H India). State Mutual Bk.

Vasil'Ev, L. A. Schlieren Methods. 1968. 44.95x o.s.i. (ISBN 0-470-90335-X). Halsted Pr.

Vasil eva, E. K. The Young People of Leningrad: School & Work Options & Attitudes. Schultz, Arlo A. & Smith, Andrew J., trs. from Russian. LC 75-46109. 220p. 1976. 27.50 (ISBN 0-87332-077-8). M E Sharpe.

Vasiliev, Alexander A. History of the Byzantine Empire, 324-1453, 2 Vols. (Illus., Orig.). 1952. pap. 9.95 ea.; Vol. 1, 382p. (ISBN 0-299-80925-0); Vol. 2, 478p. (ISBN 0-299-80926-9). U of Wis Pr.

Vasiliev, J. M. & Gelfand, I. M. Neoplastic & Normal Cells in Culture. LC 80-40075. (Developmental & Cell Biology: No. 8). (Illus.). 300p. 1981. 85.50 (ISBN 0-521-23149-3). Cambridge U Pr.

Vasils, Theodora, tr. see Kazantzakis, Nikos.

Vasistha, K. K. Teacher Education in India: A Study in New Dimensions. 1979. text ed. 14.25x (ISBN 0-391-01841-8). Humanities.

Vasko, Donna M. I'd Rather Be Flying. 112p. pap. 6.95 (ISBN 0-942032-03-9). Calligrafree.
Vasquez, E., jt. auth. see Zambrano, E.
Vasquez, Guillermo H. Lo Que los Padres y Maestros Deben Saber Acerca De las Drogas. 128p. 1978. pap. 1.20 (ISBN 0-311-46080-1). Casa Bautista.
Vasquez, John A. The Power of Power Politics: A Critique. (Illus.). 300p. Date not set. 27.50 (ISBN 0-8135-0919-X). Rutgers U Pr.
Vasquez, John A., jt. auth. see Mansbach, Richard W.
Vasquez, Richard. Chicano. 1971. pap. 1.75 o.s.i. (ISBN 0-380-01095-X, 35147). Avon.
Vass, George. Reggie Jackson: From Superstar to Candy Bar. LC 78-21511. (Sport Stars Ser.). (Illus.). 48p. (gr. 2-6). 1979. PLB 7.95 (ISBN 0-516-04303-X); pap. 2.50 (ISBN 0-516-44303-8). Childrens.
Vassale, Mario, ed. Cardiac Physiology for the Clinician. 1976. 40.00 (ISBN 0-12-715050-1). Acad Pr.
Vassalle, Mario, jt. auth. see Levy, Matthew N.
Vasse, William W., jt. auth. see Edwards, John H.
Vassi. Erotic Comedies. 1982. 16.95 (ISBN 0-686-94129-2); pap. 8.98 (ISBN 0-531-07433-1). Watts.
Vassi, Marco. The Erotic Comedies. LC 81-85723. 224p. 16.95 (ISBN 0-932966-20-9); pap. 8.95 (ISBN 0-932966-21-7). Permanent Pr.
Vassil, Thomas V., jt. auth. see Balgopal, Pallassana R.
Vassos, Basil H. & Ewing, Galen W. Analog & Digital Electronics for Scientists. 2nd ed. LC 79-16700. 1980. 28.50x (ISBN 0-471-04345-1, Pub. by Wiley-Interscience). Wiley.
--Electroanalytical Chemistry. 332p. 1983. 35.00 o.p. (ISBN 0-471-09028-X, Pub. by Wiley-Interscience). Wiley.
Vasta, Ross F., jt. auth. see Whitehurst, Grover J.
Vastenhoud, Jim, ed. World DX Guide. 1978. pap. 14.95 o.p. (ISBN 0-8230-5892-1, Billboard Bks). Watson-Guptill.
Vasto, Lanza Del see Del Vasto, Lanza.
Vasto, Lanzo Del see Del Vasto, Lanzo.
Vastyan, James E., ed. see Jones, Samuel & Luchsinger, Arlene E.
Vastyan, James E., ed. see Kay, Ronald D.
Vastyan, James E., ed. see Sanders, Donald H.
Vastyan, James E., ed. see Siewiorek, Daniel P. & Barbacci, Mario.
Vasu, Nagendranath. The Archaeological Survey of Mayurabhanja. (Illus.). 160p. 1981. Repr. text ed. 59.00x (ISBN 0-391-02262-8, Pub. by Concept India). Humanities.
Vasu-Bandhu. Wei Shih Er Shih Lun: Or, the Treatise in Twenty Stanzas on Representation Only. 1938. pap. 10.00 (ISBN 0-527-02687-5). Kraus Repr.
Vasudevamoorthy, M. Social Action. 1966. pap. 3.50x o.p. (ISBN 0-210-22644-7). Asia.
Vatcher, William H., Jr. Panmunjom: The Story of the Korean Military Armistice Negotiations. LC 72-14001. (Illus.). 322p. 1973. Repr. of 1958 ed. lib. bdg. 18.25x (ISBN 0-8371-6743-4, VAPA). Greenwood.
Vate, Dwight Van De see Van de Vate, Dwight, Jr.
Vate, Dwight Van De see Van De Vate, Dwight, Jr.
Vatican Council Two. Declaration on Christian Education. Hurley, Mark, ed. LC 66-19151. 160p. (Orig.). 1966. pap. 1.95 o.p. (ISBN 0-8091-1534-4). Paulist Pr.
--Declaration on Religious Freedom. Stransky, Thomas F., ed. LC 67-16718. 192p. 1967. pap. 1.95 o.p. (ISBN 0-8091-1536-0). Paulist Pr.
--Decree on the Apostolate of the Laity. Sheerin, John, ed. LC 66-19149. 94p. (Orig.). 1966. pap. 1.95 o.p. (ISBN 0-8091-1537-9). Paulist Pr.
--Decree on the Pastoral Office of Bishops. Onclin, Willy, ed. LC 67-28693. 142p. 1967. pap. 1.95 o.p. (ISBN 0-8091-1538-7). Paulist Pr.
--Decree on the Renewal of Religious Life. Baum, Gregory, ed. LC 66-19150. 96p. 1966. pap. 1.95 o.p. (ISBN 0-8091-1540-9). Paulist Pr.
Vatican Curators. The Vatican: Spirit & Art of Christian Rome. 1983. 75.00 (ISBN 0-686-42994-X). Abrams.
Vatikiotis, P. J. Nasser & His Generation. LC 78-9765. 1978. 27.50x (ISBN 0-312-55938-0). St Martin.
Vatsal, Tulsi. Indian Political History: From the Marathas to Modern Times. (Illus.). v, 225p. 1982. pap. text ed. 7.95x (ISBN 0-686-42712-2, Pub. by Orient Longman Ltd India). Apt Bks.
Vatsyayan, Kapila. Dance in Indian Painting. 204p. 1981. text ed. 110.00x (ISBN 0-391-02236-9, Pub. by Abhinav India). Humanities.
--Traditional Indian Theatre: Multiple Stream. (Illus.). 230p. 1980. 16.95 (ISBN 0-940500-28-0, Pub. by National Bk India). Asia Bk Corp.
Vatsyayana. Kama Sutra of Vatsyayana: Classic Hindu Treatise on Love & Social Conduct. Burton, Sir Richard, tr. 1964. pap. 3.75 (ISBN 0-525-47139-1, 0364-110). Dutton.
Vatter, Harold G. The Drive to Industrial Maturity: The U. S. Economy, 1860-1914. LC 75-16970. (Contributions in Economics & Economic History: No. 13). (Illus.). 368p. 1976. lib. bdg. 29.95x (ISBN 0-8371-8180-1, VIM/); pap. text ed. 6.95 (ISBN 0-8371-8930-6, VIM/). Greenwood.
Vaubel, E., jt. auth. see Gabka, J.
Vaubel, George D. Municipal Home Rule in Ohio. LC 78-52029. 1978. Repr. of 1977 ed. lib. bdg. 27.50 (ISBN 0-930342-58-5). W S Hein.
Vauclair, Marguerite. Guest Houses, Bed & Breakfasts, Inns & Hotels in Newport, R. I. Peeples, Bill, ed. LC 82-90154. (Illus.). 1982. pap. 3.75x (ISBN 0-9608536-0-X). Port Quarters.
Vaughan. German Romanticism & English Art. LC 79-10621. 1979. 60.00x (ISBN 0-300-02194-1). Yale U Pr.
Vaughan, Alan. The Edge of Tomorrow: How to Foresee & Fulfill Your Future. 1982. 13.95 (ISBN 0-698-11090-0, Coward). Putnam Pub Group.
--Incredible Coincidence: The Baffling World of Synchronicity. 1979. 12.45i (ISBN 0-397-01351-5). Har-Row.
Vaughan, Alden. American Genesis: Captain John Smith & the Founding of Virginia. 1975. 6.95 (ISBN 0-316-89808-2); pap. text ed. 5.95 (ISBN 0-316-89807-4). Little.
Vaughan, Alden T. Narratives of North American Indian Captivity: A Selective Bibliography. LC 82-48771. 100p. 1983. lib. bdg. 18.00 (ISBN 0-8240-9222-8). Garland Pub.
--New England Frontier: Puritans & Indians 1620-1675. rev. ed. 1980. pap. 7.95 (ISBN 0-393-00950-5). Norton.
Vaughan, Alden T. & Richter, Daniel K. Crossing the Cultural Divide: Indians & New Englanders, 1605-1763. 76p. 1980. pap. 5.00 o.p. (ISBN 0-912296-48-8, Dist. by U Pr of Va). Am Antiquarian.
Vaughan, Alden T., ed. America Before the Revolution: 1725-1775. (Eyewitness Accounts of American History). (Orig.). (YA) (gr. 9-12). 1967. pap. 3.45 o.p. (ISBN 0-13-023945-3, Spec). P-H.
Vaughan, Alden T., compiled by. The American Colonies in the Seventeenth Century. LC 78-151118. (Goldentree Bibliographies in American History Ser.). (Orig.). 1971. 12.95x (ISBN 0-88295-529-2); pap. 6.95x o.p. (ISBN 0-88295-528-4). Harlan Davidson.
Vaughan, B. W. Planning in Education. LC 77-82520. (Illus.). 1979. 32.50 (ISBN 0-521-21817-9); pap. 13.95 (ISBN 0-521-29285-9). Cambridge U Pr.
Vaughan, Betty A. Folk Art Painting: A Bit of the Past & Present. (Illus.). 52p. 1981. pap. 7.95 (ISBN 0-9605172-0-0). BETOM Pubns.
Vaughan, Curtis. Acts - a Study Guide Commentary. 160p. (Orig.). 1974. pap. 4.95 (ISBN 0-310-33513-2). Zondervan.
Vaughan, David J. & Craig, James R. Mineral Chemistry of the Metal Sulfides. LC 76-62585. (Earth Science Ser.). (Illus.). 1978. 65.00 (ISBN 0-521-21489-0). Cambridge U Pr.
Vaughan, David J., jt. auth. see Craig, James R.
Vaughan, Edwin C. Some Desperate Glory: The Diary of a Young Officer, 1917. Date not set. cancelled o.p. (ISBN 0-686-86744-0). Shoe String.
Vaughan, Emmett J. & Elliot, Curtis M. Fundamentals of Risk & Insurance. 2nd ed. LC 77-18769. (Wiley-Hamilton Series in Risk & Insurance). 1978. text ed. 28.95x o.p. (ISBN 0-471-90353-1); tchrs'. manual o.p. avail. o.p. (ISBN 0-471-02164-4). Wiley.
Vaughan, Emmett J. & Elliott, Curtis M. Fundamentals of Risk & Insurance. 3rd ed. LC 81-48188. 673p. 1982. text ed. 28.95 (ISBN 0-471-09951-1); tchrs'. ed. 20.00 (ISBN 0-471-86338-6). Wiley.
Vaughan, Frances E. Awakening Intuition. LC 77-27685. 1979. pap. 4.95 (ISBN 0-385-13371-5, Anch). Doubleday.
Vaughan, Frederick. The Tradition of Political Hedonism from Hobbes to J. S. Mill. xii, 271p. 1982. 25.00 (ISBN 0-8232-1077-4); pap. 12.00 (ISBN 0-8232-1078-2). Fordham.
Vaughan, Henry. Henry Vaughan: Selected Poems. Shaw, Robert B., ed. (Fyfield Ser.). 1976. 7.95x (ISBN 0-85635-138-5, Pub. by Carcanet New Pr England); pap. text ed. 5.25x (ISBN 0-85635-139-3). Humanities.
Vaughan, Henry H. Welsh Proverbs with English Translations. LC 68-17945. (Eng. & Welsh.). 1969. Repr. of 1889 ed. 37.00x (ISBN 0-8103-3205-1). Gale.
Vaughan, J., jt. auth. see Jones, L.
Vaughan, James A., jt. auth. see Bass, Bernard M.
Vaughan, Janet. The Physiology of Bone. 3rd ed. (Illus.). 1981. PLB 49.00x (ISBN 0-19-857584-X). Oxford U Pr.
Vaughan, Jenny. Anna & the Moon Queen. LC 80-52516. (Starters Ser.). PLB 8.00 (ISBN 0-382-06507-7). Silver.
--The Easter Book. LC 80-83362. (Illus.). 48p. (gr. 1-6). 1982. 4.95 (ISBN 0-448-11541-7, G&D); lib. bdg. 10.15 (ISBN 0-448-13492-6). Putnam Pub Group.
--Zoo for Sale. (Starters Ser.). PLB 8.00 (ISBN 0-382-06494-1). Silver.
Vaughan, Linda K. & Stratton, Richard. Canoeing & Sailing. (Physical Education Activities Ser). 80p. 1970. pap. text ed. write for info. (ISBN 0-697-07023-9); tchrs.' manual avail. (ISBN 0-697-07222-3). Wm C Brown.
Vaughan, Louise. Lovequest. (Orig.). pap. 2.25 (ISBN 0-515-04696-5). Jove Pubns.
Vaughan, M., jt. auth. see Beech, H. R.
Vaughan, Michael, ed. see Braithewaite, Walter.
Vaughan, Michalina & Archer, Margaret. Social Conflict & Educational Change in England & France, 1789-1848. LC 70-155581. (Illus.). 1971. 37.50 (ISBN 0-521-08190-4). Cambridge U Pr.
Vaughan, P. H. Meaning of Bama in the Old Testament. LC 73-89004. (Society for Old Testament Study Monographs: No. 3). (Illus.). 96p. 1974. 27.95 (ISBN 0-521-20425-9). Cambridge U Pr.
Vaughan, R. C. The Hardy-Littlewood Method. (Cambridge Tracts in Mathematics: No. 80). 160p. 1981. 36.50 (ISBN 0-521-23439-5). Cambridge U Pr.
Vaughan, Richard. Matthew Paris. LC 78-73130. (Studies in Medieval Life & Thought: Vol. 6). (Illus.). 1979. 37.50 (ISBN 0-521-22612-0); pap. 12.95 (ISBN 0-521-29575-0). Cambridge U Pr.
--Mulcarrey's Ridge. 1980. 6.95 (ISBN 0-8062-1341-8). Carlton.
Vaughan, Richard, ed. Post-War Integration in Europe. LC 76-14513. (Documents of Modern History Ser.). 1976. 25.00 (ISBN 0-312-63245-2). St Martin.
Vaughan, Robert. The Brave & the Lonely. 1982. pap. 3.50 (ISBN 0-440-00649-X, Emerald). Dell.
--Divine Wind. (The Wartorn Ser.: No. 3). (Orig.). 1983. pap. 3.50 (ISBN 0-440-01992-3). Dell.
--Masters & Martyrs. 320p. 1983. pap. 3.50 (ISBN 0-440-06370-1, Emerald). Dell.
Vaughan, Roger J., jt. ed. see Tolley, George S.
Vaughan, Thomas & Crownhart-Vaughan, E. A. Voyage of Enlightenment: Malaspina on the Northwest Coast, 1791-1792. LC 77-88147. (North Pacific Studies Series Three). (Illus.). 72p. 1977. pap. 3.95 (ISBN 0-295-95957-6, Pub by Oreg Hist Soc). U of Wash Pr.
Vaughan, Thomas & O'Donnell, Terence. Portland: An Informal History & Guide. 2nd, rev. ed. (Illus.). 1983. pap. 6.95 (ISBN 0-87595-101-5, Western Imprints). Oreg Hist Soc.
Vaughan, Thomas, et al. Mount St. Helens Remembered. (Illus.). 224p. (Orig.). 1983. price not set (ISBN 0-87595-110-4, Western Imprints); pap. price not set (ISBN 0-87595-111-2, Western Imprints). Oreg Hist Soc.
Vaughan, Victor C., III, et al. Nelson Textbook of Pediatrics. 11th ed. LC 77-16959. (Illus.). 1979. text ed. 62.50 (ISBN 0-7216-9019-X). Saunders.
Vaughan, Virginia C. Weakley County. Crawford, Charles, ed. (Tennessee County History Ser.: No. 92). (Illus.). 144p. 1983. 12.50 (ISBN 0-87870-188-5). Memphis St Univ.
Vaughan, William. German Romantic Painting. LC 80-13170. (Illus.). 288p. 1982. 50.00x (ISBN 0-300-02387-1); pap. 16.95 (ISBN 0-300-02917-9). Yale U Pr.
Vaughan-Jackson. Drawing for Boys. (The Grosset Art Instruction Ser.: No. 13). (Illus.). 48p. Date not set. pap. 2.95 (ISBN 0-448-00522-0, G&D). Putnam Pub Group.
--Drawing for Girls. (The Grosset Art Instruction Ser.: No. 30). (Illus.). 48p. Date not set. pap. 2.95 (ISBN 0-448-00539-5, G&D). Putnam Pub Group.
Vaughan-Thomas, Wynford. Wales. 224p. 1983. pap. 12.95 (ISBN 0-7181-2251-8, Pub by Michael Joseph). Merrimack Bk Serv.
Vaughan Williams, Ralph. The Making of Music. LC 76-1009. (Illus.). 61p. 1976. Repr. of 1955 ed. lib. bdg. 19.75x (ISBN 0-8371-8771-0, WIMM). Greenwood.
Vaughan Williams, Ralph & Holst, Gustav. Heirs & Rebels: Letters Written to Each Other & Occasional Writings on Music. Vaughan Williams, Ursula & Holst, Imogen, eds. LC 80-12245. (Illus.). xiii, 111p. 1980. Repr. of 1959 ed. lib. bdg. 18.25x (ISBN 0-313-22384-X, VWHR). Greenwood.
Vaughan Williams, Ralph, ed. see Dearmer, Percy.
Vaughan Williams, Ursula, ed. see Vaughan Williams, Ralph & Holst, Gustav.
Vaughn, C. Dennis. A Move to Basketball. 1979. 4.95 o.p. (ISBN 0-533-04083-3). Vantage.
Vaughn, Charles L. Franchising. 2nd & rev. ed. LC 78-24841. (Illus.). 304p. 1979. 24.95x (ISBN 0-669-02852-5). Lexington Bks.
Vaughn, David, jt. ed. see Clarke, Mary.
Vaughn, Donald E., jt. auth. see Aby, Carroll, Jr.
Vaughn, Donald E., Jr., jt. ed. see Aby, Carroll D.
Vaughn, J. Basic Skills Mathematics Workbook: Grade 9. (Basic Skills Workbooks). 32p. (gr. 9). 1982. tchrs' ed. 0.99 (ISBN 0-8209-0396-5, MW-J). ESP.
Vaughn, Jack A. Drama A to Z: A Handbook. LC 78-4298. 1978. 11.95 (ISBN 0-8044-2937-5); pap. 5.95 (ISBN 0-8044-6946-6). Ungar.
--Early American Dramatists: From the Beginnings to 1900. LC 80-53703. (Literature and Life Ser.). (Illus.). 224p. 1981. 11.95 (ISBN 0-8044-2940-5). Ungar.
--Shakespeare's Comedies. LC 79-48080. (Literature and Life Ser.). (Illus.). 190p. 1980. 14.50 (ISBN 0-8044-2938-3). Ungar.
--Shakespeare's Comedies. LC 79-48080. (Literature & Life Ser.). (Illus.). 249p. 1983. pap. 6.95 (ISBN 0-8044-6947-4). Ungar.
Vaughn, James E. Basic Skills Vocabulary Workbook: Junior High. (Basic Skills Workbooks). 32p. (gr. 7-9). 1982. wkbk. 0.99 (ISBN 0-8209-0383-3, VW-H). ESP.
--Basic Skills Vocabulary Workbook: Senior High. (Basic Skills Workbooks). 32p. (gr. 9-12). 1982. wkbk. 0.99 (ISBN 0-8209-0384-1, VW-I). ESP.
--Impact: Grades Eleven to Twelve. (Impact Ser.). 24p. 1979. wkbk. 5.00 (ISBN 0-8209-0350-7, IM-1112). ESP.
--Impact: Grades Five to Six. (Impact Ser.). 24p. 1979. wkbk. 5.00 (ISBN 0-8209-0348-5, IM-56). ESP.
--Impact: Grades Seven to Eight. (Impact Ser.). 24p. 1979. wkbk. 5.00 (ISBN 0-8209-0349-3, IM-78). ESP.
--Impact: Grades Three to Four. (Impact Ser.). 24p. 1979. wkbk. 5.00 (ISBN 0-8209-0347-7, IM-34). ESP.
Vaughn, Jesse W. The Battle of Platte Bridge. (Illus.). 1964. 9.95 o.p. (ISBN 0-8061-0592-5). U of Okla Pr.
Vaughn, Jim. Basic Skills Mathematics Workbook: Grade 2. (Basic Skills Workbooks). 32p. (gr. 2). 1982. tchrs' ed. 0.99 (ISBN 0-8209-0389-2, MW-C). ESP.
--Basic Skills Mathematics Workbook: Grade 3. (Basic Skills Workbooks). 32p. 1982. tchrs' ed. 0.99 (ISBN 0-8209-0390-6, MW-D). ESP.
--Basic Skills Mathematics Workbook: Grade 4. (Basic Skills Workbooks). 32p. (gr. 4). tchrs' ed. 0.99 (ISBN 0-8209-0391-4, MW-E). ESP.
--Basic Skills Mathematics Workbook: Grade 5. (Basic Skills Worrkbooks). 32p. (gr. 5). 1982. tchrs' ed. 0.99 (ISBN 0-8209-0392-2, MW-F). ESP.
--Basic Skills Mathematics Workbook: Grade 6. (Basic Skills Workbooks). 32p. (gr. 6). tchrs' ed. 0.99 (ISBN 0-8209-0393-0, MW-G). ESP.
--Basic Skills Mathematics Workbook: Grade 7. (Basic Skills Workbooks). 32p. (gr. 7). 1982. tchrs' ed. 0.99 (ISBN 0-8209-0394-9, MW-H). ESP.
--Basic Skills Mathematics Workbook: Grade 8. (Basic Skills Workbooks). 32p. (gr. 8). 1982. tchrs' ed. 0.99 (ISBN 0-8209-0395-7, MW-I). ESP.
--Basic Skills Workbooks: Grade 10. (Basic Skills Workbooks). 32p. (gr. 10). 1982. wkbk. 0.99 (ISBN 0-8209-0397-3, MW-K). ESP.
--Jumbo Algebra Yearbook. (Jumbo Math Ser.). 96p. (gr. 9). 1981. wkbk. 14.00 (ISBN 0-8209-0038-9, JMY-9). ESP.
--Jumbo Early Childhood Readiness Yearbook. (Jumbo Social Studies Ser.). 96p. (gr. k). 1982. wkbk. 14.00 (ISBN 0-8209-0074-5, JECR-R). ESP.
--Jumbo Math Yearbook: Grade 2. (Jumbo Math Ser.). 96p. (gr. 2). 1980. 14.00 (ISBN 0-8209-0031-1, JMY 2). ESP.
--Jumbo Math Yearbook: Grade 3. (Jumbo Math Ser.). 96p. (gr. 3). 1978. 14.00 (ISBN 0-8209-0032-X, JMY 3). ESP.
--Jumbo Math Yearbook: Grade 4. (Jumbo Math Ser.). 96p. (gr. 4). 1978. 14.00 (ISBN 0-8209-0033-8, JMY 4). ESP.
--Jumbo Math Yearbook: Grade 5. (Jumbo Math Ser.). 96p. (gr. 5). 1978. 14.00 (ISBN 0-8209-0034-6, JMY 5). ESP.
--Jumbo Math Yearbook: Grade 6. (Jumbo Math Ser.). 96p. (gr. 6). 1978. 14.00 (ISBN 0-8209-0035-4, JMY 6). ESP.
--Jumbo Math Yearbook: Grade 7. (Jumbo Math Ser.). 96p. (gr. 7). 1978. 14.00 (ISBN 0-8209-0036-2, JMY 7). ESP.
--Jumbo Math Yearbook: Grade 8. (Jumbo Math Ser.). 96p. (gr. 8). 1979. 14.00 (ISBN 0-8209-0037-0, JMY 8). ESP.
--Jumbo Vocabulary Development Yearbook: Grade 7. (Jumbo Vocabulary Ser.). 96p. (gr. 7-9). 1981. 14.00 (ISBN 0-8209-0056-7, JVDY J). ESP.
--Jumbo Vocabulary Development Yearbook: Grade 10. (Jumbo Vocabulary Ser.). 96p. (gr. 10-12). 1981. 14.00 (ISBN 0-8209-0057-5, JVDY S). ESP.
Vaughn, Lewis. Chilton's Home Energy Saving Guide. LC 80-70335. 256p. 1982. 15.95 (ISBN 0-8019-7231-0); pap. 10.95 (ISBN 0-8019-7019-9). Chilton.
Vaughn, Percy J., jt. auth. see Buskirk, Richard H.
Vaughn, Robert G. Conflict-of-Interest Regulation in the Federal Executive Branch. (Illus.). 208p. 1979. 21.95x o.p. (ISBN 0-669-02776-6). Lexington Bks.
--The Spoiled System: A Call For Civil Service Reform. 360p. 1975. 12.95 (ISBN 0-686-36544-5). Ctr Responsive Law.
Vaughn, Ruth. Letters In A Lock Box. 1982. pap. 3.95 (ISBN 0-87162-254-8, WP#D5180). Warner Pr.
--More Skits That Win. 1977. pap. 2.50 (ISBN 0-310-33671-6). Zondervan.
--To Be a Girl, to Be a Woman. 160p. (gr. 9-12). 1982. 8.95 (ISBN 0-8007-1328-1). Revell.
--What's a Mother to Say? 1982. pap. 2.95 (ISBN 0-87162-241-6, D8824). Warner Pr.
Vaughn, Sally N. The Abbey of Bec & the Anglo-Norman State 1034 to 1136. 176p. 1981. 40.00x (ISBN 0-85115-140-X, Pub. by Boydell & Brewer). Biblio Dist.
Vaughn, Thomas & Holm, Bill. Soft Gold: The Fur Trade & Cultural Exchange on the Northwest Coast of America. (Illus.). 320p. 1982. 29.95 (ISBN 0-295-96002-7, Pub. by Oreg Hist Soc). U of Wash Pr.
Vaughn, William P. The Antimasonic Party in the United States, 1826-1843. LC 82-40180. 208p. 1982. 16.00x (ISBN 0-8131-1474-8). U Pr of Ky.
Vaughn-Roberson, Courtney & Vaughn-Roberson, Glen. City in the Osage Hills: A History of Tulsa, Oklahoma. (Illus.). 1983. price not set (ISBN 0-87108-644-1). Pruett.

Vaughn-Roberson, Glen, jt. auth. see Vaughn-Roberson, Courtney.

Vaught, Carl G. The Quest for Wholeness. LC 81-18365. 224p. 1982. 34.50x (ISBN 0-87395-593-5); pap. 10.95x (ISBN 0-87395-594-3). State U NY Pr.

Vaught, Carl J., ed. Essays in Metaphysics. LC 71-121785. 1970. 16.95x (ISBN 0-271-00123-2). Pa St U Pr.

Vaught, John. Rebel Coach: My Football Family. LC 78-171535. (Illus.). 1971. 9.95 o.p. (ISBN 0-87870-008-0). Memphis St Univ.

Vautier, Ghislaine. The Shining Stars: Greek Legends of the Zodiac. McLeish, Kenneth, adapted by. LC 81-10161. (Illus.). 32p. 1981. 10.95 (ISBN 0-521-23886-2). Cambridge U Pr.

Vautier, Ghislaine & McLeish, Kenneth. The Way of the Stars: Greek Legends of the Constellations. (Illus.). 32p. Date not set.. 9.95 (ISBN 0-521-25061-7). Cambridge U Pr.

Vaux, Roland de see De Vaux, Roland.

Vavoulis, Alexander & Colver, A. Wayne, eds. Science & Society: Selected Essays. LC 66-15005. 1966. pap. text ed. 7.50x (ISBN 0-8162-9172-1). Holden-Day.

Vavra, Michael H. Aero-Thermodynamics & Flow in Turbomachines. LC 74-9545. 626p. 1974. Repr. of 1960 ed. 35.50 (ISBN 0-88275-189-1). Krieger.

Vavra, Robert. Felipe the Bullfighter. LC 68-10006. (Illus.). (gr. 4-6). 4.95 (ISBN 0-15-227510-X, HJ); PLB 4.95 (ISBN 0-15-227511-8). HarBraceJ.

Vawter, Bruce. Amos, Hosea, Micah, with Introduction to Classical Prophecy. 1982. 8.95 (ISBN 0-89453-242-1); pap. 5.95 (ISBN 0-686-32763-2). M Glazier.

--Four Gospels: An Introduction, 2 vols. LC 67-10408. 1969. pap. 4.95 vol. I o.p. (ISBN 0-385-01479-1, Im); volume II o.p. 3.50 o.p. (ISBN 0-385-06557-4, 255A). Doubleday.

--Job & Jonah: Questioning the Hidden God. LC 82-62413. 1983. pap. 5.95 (ISBN 0-8091-2524-2). Paulist Pr.

Vay, David Le see Roth, Joseph.

Vayda, Andrew P., ed. Environment & Cultural Behavior: Ecological Studies in Cultural Anthropology. (Texas Press Sourcebooks in Anthropology: No. 8). 503p. 1976. pap. 9.95x (ISBN 0-292-72019-X). U of Tex Pr.

Vayhinger, John M. Before Divorce. Hulme, William E., ed. LC 72-171512. (Pocket Counsel Bks). 56p. 1972. pap. 1.75 o.p. (ISBN 0-8006-1106-3, 1-1106). Fortress.

Vayrynen, jt. auth. see Tuomi.

Vaz, E. Aspects of Deviance. 1976. pap. 10.95 (ISBN 0-13-049304-X). P-H.

Vazquez, Adolfo Sanchez. Art & Society: Essays in Marxist Aesthetics. Riofrancos, Maro, tr. from Span. LC 72-92025. (Modern Reader Paperbacks). 288p. 1974. pap. 5.95 o.p. (ISBN 0-85345-327-6, PB3276). Monthly Rev.

Vazquez, J. C. & Lebon, G., eds. Stability of Thermodynamic Systems, Barcelona, Spain, 1981: Proceedings. (Lecture Notes in Physics: Vol. 164). 321p. 1982. text ed. 17.50 (ISBN 0-387-11581-1). Springer-Verlag.

VDE Berlin. Human Factors in Telecommunications International Symposium, 4th. 1968. 75.00 (ISBN 0-686-37974-8). Info Gatekeepers.

Vdovenko, V. M. & Dubasov, Yu V. Analytical Chemistry of Radium. Mandel, N., tr. from Rus. LC 74-30131. (Analytical Chemistry of Elements Ser.). 198p. 1925. 54.95 o.s.i. (ISBN 0-470-90488-7). Halsted Pr.

Veal, F. J. Economics of Producing Certain Chemicals from Cellulose: A Review of Recent Literature, 1979. 1981. 80.00x (ISBN 0-686-97066-7, Pub. by W Spring England). State Mutual Bk.

--Methane from Sorted Domestic Refuse: An Economic Assessment, 1977. 1981. 40.00x (ISBN 0-686-97114-0, Pub. by W Spring England). State Mutual Bk.

--Methane from Sorted Domestic Refuse: A Re-appraisal, 1979. 1982. 40.00x (ISBN 0-686-97117-5, Pub. by W Spring England). State Mutual Bk.

Veaner, Allen B. Evaluation of Micropublications. LC 73-138700. (LTP Publication: No. 17). 1971. pap. 5.00 (ISBN 0-8389-3128-6). ALA.

Vears. Microelectronics Systems One: Checkbook. 1981. text ed. 19.95 (ISBN 0-408-00638-2). Butterworth.

Veasey, William. Blue Ribbon Pattern Series, Bk. 1: Full Size Decorative Patterns. (Illus.). 63p. 1982. 14.95 (ISBN 0-916838-71-4). Schiffer.

--Head Patterns. (Blue Ribbon Pattern Ser.: Book III). (Illus.). 64p. 1983. pap. 14.95 (ISBN 0-916838-78-1). Schiffer.

--Miniature Decoy Patterns. (Blue Ribbon Pattern Ser.: Bk. II). (Illus.). 64p. (Orig.). 1983. pap. 14.95 (ISBN 0-916838-77-3). Schiffer.

--Song Bird Patterns. (Blue Ribbon Pattern Series: Bk. IV). (Illus.). 64p. 1983. pap. 14.95 (ISBN 0-916838-79-X). Schiffer.

Veasey, William & Hull, Cary S. Waterfowl Carving, Blue Ribbon Techniques. LC 82-50616. (Illus.). 272p. 1982. 35.00 (ISBN 0-916838-67-6). Schiffer.

Veatch, et al. Key Words to Reading: The Language Experience Approach. 2nd ed. (Elementary Reading Ser.). 1979. pap. text ed. 10.95 (ISBN 0-675-08363-X). Merrill.

Veatch, Deborah. How to Get the Job you Really Want. 174p. 1982. pap. text ed. 10.95x (ISBN 0-913072-50-8). Natl Assn Deaf.

Veatch, H. C. Pulse & Switching Circuit Action. 1971. text ed. 23.95 (ISBN 0-07-067386-1, G); answers 1.50 (ISBN 0-07-067387-X). McGraw.

--Pulse & Switching Circuit Measurements. 1971. 14.95 (ISBN 0-07-067382-9, G). McGraw.

--Transistor Circuit Action. 2nd ed. (Illus.). 1976. text ed. 19.95 (ISBN 0-07-067383-7, G); answers 1.50 (ISBN 0-07-067388-8). McGraw.

Veatch, Henry. Realism & Nominalism Revisited. (Aquinas Lecture Ser.). 1954. 7.95 (ISBN 0-87462-119-4). Marquette.

Veatch, Henry B. Rational Man: A Modern Interpretation of Aristotelian Ethics. LC 62-16161. (Midland Bks.: No. 71). 228p. 1962. pap. 5.00x (ISBN 0-253-20071-7). Ind U Pr.

Veatch, Henry C., ed. Electrical Circuit Action. LC 77-22049. 1978. text ed. 22.95 (ISBN 0-574-21510-7, 13-4510); answer book 2.25 (ISBN 0-574-21511-5, 13-4511). SRA.

Veatch, Jeannette. Reading in the Elementary Schools. 2nd ed. LC 78-14722. 628p. 1978. text ed. 24.95 (ISBN 0-471-06884-5). Wiley.

Veatch, Robert M. Case Studies in Medical Ethics. 1977. 20.00x (ISBN 0-674-09931-1); pap. 10.00x (ISBN 0-674-09932-X). Harvard U Pr.

Veatch, Robert M. & Branson, Roy, eds. Ethics and Health Policy. LC 76-3741. 352p. 1976. prof ref 22.50x (ISBN 0-88410-137-1). Ballinger Pub.

Veatch, Robert M., jt. ed. see Levine, Carol.

Veazie, Walter & Connolly, Thomas. Marketing of Information Analysis Center Products & Services. 1971. 6.50 (ISBN 0-685-33434-1). Am Soc Info Sci.

Veblen, Thorstein. Engineers & the Price System. (Social Science Classics Ser.). 151p. 1983. pap. 12.95 (ISBN 0-87855-915-9). Transaction Bks.

--The Theory of Business Enterprise. 420p. 1978. 29.95 (ISBN 0-87855-311-8); pap. 4.95 (ISBN 0-87855-699-0). Transaction Bks.

Veblen, Thorstein B. Essays, Reviews & Reports. Dorfman, Joseph, ed. LC 72-13590. 1973. 37.50x (ISBN 0-678-00960-0). Kelley.

Vecchio, Giorgio del. Formal Basis of Law. (Modern Legal Philosophy Ser.: Vol. 10). lvii, 412p. 1969. Repr. of 1914 ed. 20.00x (ISBN 0-8377-2700-6). Rothman.

--Justice: An Historical & Philosophical Essay. Campbell, A. H., ed. Guthrie, Lady, tr. from Fr. 263p. 1982. Repr. of 1953 ed. lib. bdg. 26.00x (ISBN 0-8377-1231-9). Rothman.

Vecellio, Cesare. Vecellio's Renaissance Costume Book. LC 76-55952. (Pictorialarchive Ser.). (Illus.). 1977. pap. 6.00 (ISBN 0-486-23441-X). Dover.

Vechten, Carl Van see Van Vechten, Carl.

Vecsey, Christopher & Venables, Robert W., eds. American Indian Environments: Ecological Issues in Native American History. LC 80-26458. (Illus.). 236p. 1980. text ed. 22.00x (ISBN 0-8156-2226-0); pap. text ed. 9.95x (ISBN 0-8156-2227-9). Syracuse U Pr.

Vecsey, George. Baseball's Most Valuable Players. (Major League Baseball Library: No. 5). (Illus.). (gr. 5-9). 1966. 2.50 o.p. (ISBN 0-394-80185-7, BYR); PLB 3.69 (ISBN 0-394-90185-1). Random.

Vecsey, George, jt. auth. see Lynn, Loretta.

Veda, jt. auth. see Samskrti.

Veda, Makoto. Matsuo Basho. (World Authors Ser.: No. 102). 13.95 o.p. (ISBN 0-8057-2116-9, Twayne). G K Hall.

Vedder, Alan C. Furniture of Spanish New Mexico. LC 76-50322. (Illus.). 96p. 1977. 12.95 (ISBN 0-913270-67-9). Sunstone Pr.

Vedder, E. P., Jr. The Man of God. (Let's Discuss It Ser.). pap. 0.95 (ISBN 0-88172-129-8); pap. 9.50 o.p. Believers Bkshelf.

Vedder, Enrique C. Breve Historia De los Bautistas Hasta 1900. Barocio, Teofilo, tr. Repr. of 1978 ed. 4.50 (ISBN 0-311-15039-X). Casa Bautista.

Vedder, Eugene P., Jr., jt. auth. see Bennett, Gordon H.

Vedder, K., jt. ed. see Jungnickel, D. H.

Vedder, O. F., jt. auth. see Keating, J. M.

Vedder, Richard, jt. ed. see Klingaman, David.

Vedral, Joyce. I Dare You. 144p. (gr. 7 up). 11.95 (ISBN 0-03-061266-7). HR&W.

Vedrinne, J., jt. ed. see Soubrier, J. P.

Vedung, Evert. Political Reasoning. (Illus.). 224p. 1982. 22.50 (ISBN 0-8039-1815-1). Sage.

Veen, B. van der see Van der Veen, B., et al.

Veenhius, A. A., jt. auth. see Pipe, G. R.

Veenker, Wolfgang. Vogul Suffixes & Pronouns. LC 77-625112. (Uralic & Altaic Ser: Vol. 110). (Orig.). 1969. pap. text ed. 5.50x o.p. (ISBN 0-87750-044-4). Res Ctr Lang Semiotic.

Veer, Florine De see De Veer, Florine.

Veer, Yajan. The Language of the Atharva-Veda. 1979. text ed. 17.25x (ISBN 0-391-01853-1). Humanities.

Veer Reddy, G. P., jt. auth. see Pardee, Arthur B.

Vega, Jose E. Education, Politics, & Bilingualism in Texas. 262p. (Orig.). 1983. lib. bdg. 21.50 (ISBN 0-8191-2985-2); pap. text ed. 11.50 (ISBN 0-8191-2986-0). U Pr of Amer.

Vega, Jose L. Cesar Vallejo en Trilce. LC 79-26380. (Coleccion UPREX, 60 Ser.: Estudios Literarios). ix, 132p. Date not set. pap. write for info. (ISBN 0-8477-0060-7). U of PR Pr.

Vega, Lope De see De Vega, Lope.

Vega, Sara L. De La see De La Vega, Sara L. & Parr, Carmen S.

Vegh, jt. auth. see Layer.

Vegh, Elizabeth de see DeVegh, Elizabeth.

Vegh, Janos. Sixteenth Century German Panel Paintings. 2nd, Rev. ed. Horn, Susanna, tr. from Hungarian. LC 77-357632. 133p. 1972. 13.50x (ISBN 963-13-1280-1). Intl Pubns Serv.

Veglahn, Nancy. Coils, Magnets & Rings: Michael Faraday's World. LC 76-14385. (Science Discovery Book). (Illus.). (gr. 2-6). 1976. 6.95 (ISBN 0-698-20384-4, Coward). Putnam Pub Group.

--Dance of the Planets: The Universe of Nicolaus Copernicus. LC 78-8615. (Science Discovery Bks). (Illus.). (gr. 2-6). 1979. PLB 5.99 (ISBN 0-698-30693-7, Coward). Putnam Pub Group.

--Getting to Know the Missouri River. (Getting to Know Ser.). (Illus.). 72p. (gr. 3-4). 1972. PLB 3.97 o.p. (ISBN 0-698-30445-4, Coward). Putnam Pub Group.

--The Mysterious Rays: Marie Curie's World. LC 77-8361. (Science Discovery Book Ser.). (Illus.). (gr. 3-6). 1977. PLB 5.99 (ISBN 0-698-30681-3, Coward). Putnam Pub Group.

Vehling, Joseph D., ed. & tr. see Apicius.

Veiga, John F. & Yanouzas, John N. The Dynamics of Organization Theory: Gaining a Macro Perspective. (Illus.). 1979. text ed. 17.50 o.s.i. (ISBN 0-8299-0182-5); insts.' manual avail. o.s.i. (ISBN 0-8299-0578-2). West Pub.

Veiga, Jose J. The Three Trials of Manirema. Bird, Pamela G., tr. 160p. 1982. 13.95 (ISBN 0-7206-0552-0, Pub. by Peter Owen). Merrimack Bk Serv.

Veiga-Pires, J. A. & Grainger, Ronald G., eds. Pioneers in Angiography: The Portugese School of Angiography. (Illus.). 131p. 1981. text ed. 24.95 (ISBN 0-85200-448-6, Pub. by MTP Pr England). Kluwer Boston.

--Pioneers in Radiology. 1982. text ed. 19.50 (ISBN 0-686-37440-1, Pub. by MTP Pr England). Kluwer Boston.

Veiga-Pires, J. A., jt. ed. see Oliva, L.

Veigel, Jon M., jt. ed. see Rich, Daniel.

Veigh, Gretchen. Physical Therapy in the Home: Management, Evaluation & Treatment of Patients. (Illus.). 150p. 1983. 17.50 (ISBN 0-932426-27-1). Trado-Medic.

Veilleux, Armand. Pachomian Koinonia Third: Instructions, Letters & Other Writings, No. 47. (Cistercian Studies). 1983. 29.95 (ISBN 0-87907-847-2); pap. 10.00 (ISBN 0-87907-947-9). Cistercian Pubns.

Veinott, Cyril G. Computer-Aided Design of Electric Machinery. (Monographs in Modern Electrical Technology). (Illus.). 168p. 1973. 20.00x (ISBN 0-262-22016-4). MIT Pr.

--Fractional & Subfractional Horsepower Electric Motors. 3rd ed. LC 79-85117. (Illus.). 1970. 42.50 (ISBN 0-07-067390-X, P&RB). McGraw.

Veirs, Christina, et al, eds. see Hausauer, Nancy.

Veis. Chemistry & Biology of Mineralized Connective Tissue. (Developments in Biochemistry Ser.: Vol. 22). 1981. 100.00 (ISBN 0-444-00678-8). Elsevier.

Veis, A., ed. Biological Polyelectrolytes. (Biological Macromolecules Ser: Vol. 3). 1970. 46.50 o.p. (ISBN 0-8247-1706-6). Dekker.

Veis, Arthur. Macromolecular Chemistry of Gelatin. (Molecular Biology: Vol. 5). 1964. 59.00 (ISBN 0-12-715450-7). Acad Pr.

Veis, G., ed. Use of Artificial Satellites for Geodesy. 1963. 49.00 (ISBN 0-444-10296-5). Elsevier.

Veit, Fritz. Community College Library. LC 72-843. (Contributions in Librarianship & Information Science Ser.: No. 14). (Illus.). 221p. 1975. lib. bdg. 25.00x (ISBN 0-8371-6412-5, VEJ/). Greenwood.

Veit, Lawrence A. Economic Adjustment to an Energy-Short World. (Atlantic Papers Ser.: No. 38). 78p. 1980. write for info. o.p. (ISBN 0-916672-78-6). Allanheld.

--India's Second Revolution: The Dimension of Development. LC 76-853. (Illus.). 1976. 15.95 o.p. (ISBN 0-07-067395-0, P&RB). McGraw.

Veit, Richard C. Little Writing Book: The Cases for Rhetorical Expression. 128p. 1982. pap. text ed. 7.50 (ISBN 0-13-538041-3). P-H.

Veitch, B. & Harms, T. Cook & Learn: A Child's Cookbook. (ps-4). 1981. Kit, includes Cookbook & Tchrs. Guide 11.50 (ISBN 0-201-09430-4, Sch Div); tchr's guide free o.p.; recipe step book 17.50 (ISBN 0-201-09426-6); cook & learn teacher guide 7.41 (ISBN 0-201-09424-X, 9424); tchrs' guide 3.50 (ISBN 0-201-09425-8). A-W.

Veitch, Carol & Boklage, Cecilia. Literature Puzzles for Elementary & Middle Schools. 120p. 1983. pap. text ed. 12.50 (ISBN 0-87287-363-3). Libs Unl.

Veitch, John. The History & Poetry of the Scottish Border: Their Main Features & Relations. 356p. 1982. lib. bdg. 125.00 (ISBN 0-89760-930-1). Telegraph Bks.

Veitch, John, tr. see Descartes, Rene.

Veith, Ilza, tr. The Yellow Emperor's Classic of Internal Medicine. 1966. 28.50x (ISBN 0-520-01296-8); pap. 7.95 (ISBN 0-520-02158-4, CAL238). U of Cal Pr.

Veith, Richard H. Multinational Computer Nets: The Case of International Banking. 160p. 1981. 21.95x (ISBN 0-669-04092-4). Lexington Bks.

Velasco, ed. Arterial Hypertension: Proceedings, Caracas, Aug-Sept. 1979. (International Congress Ser.: No. 496). 1980. 74.00 (ISBN 0-444-90123-X). Elsevier.

Velasco, Jesus-Agustin S. Impacts of Mexican Oil Policy on Economic & Political Development. LC 82-47787. 1983. write for info. (ISBN 0-669-05592-1). Lexington Bks.

Velasco, Manuel. Arterial Hypertension. (International Congress Ser.: No. 410). 1978. 33.50 (ISBN 0-444-15260-1). Elsevier.

Velasquez, Carmen C. Digenetic Trematodes of Philippine Fishes. 1975. 6.65x (ISBN 0-8248-0444-9). UH Pr.

Velasquez, Manuel G. Business Ethics: Concepts & Cases. 416p. 1982. pap. 18.95 (ISBN 0-13-096008-X). P-H.

Velasquez, Roger, tr. see Trueblood, David E.

Velazquez, Clara V. English As a Second Language, Vol. I. 240p. 1982. pap. text ed. 12.95 (ISBN 0-8403-2859-1). Kendall-Hunt.

Velchak, John H. My Name Is Not Bob Loblaw. LC 76-62480. 1977. 10.95 (ISBN 0-87949-071-3). Ashley Bks.

Velde, B. Clays & Clay Minerals in Natural & Synthetic Systems. LC 76-40462. (Developments in Sedimentology: No. 21). (Illus.). 1978. 34.25 (ISBN 0-444-41505-X). Elsevier.

Veley, Charles. Night Whispers. LC 79-8946. 1980. 10.95 o.p. (ISBN 0-385-15124-1). Doubleday.

Veley, Victor F. Third Class FCC License Study Guide. (Illus.). 1977. 9.95 (ISBN 0-8306-7893-X); pap. 6.95 o.p. (ISBN 0-8306-6893-4, 893). TAB Bks.

Veley, Victor F., jt. auth. see Dulin, John J.

Veley, Victory & Dulin, John. Lab Experiments for Modern Electronics: A First Course. (Illus.). 256p. 1983. pap. text ed. 13.95 (ISBN 0-13-593103-7). P-H.

Velez-Ibanez, Carlos. Bonds of Mutual Trust: The Cultural Systems of Rotating Credit Associations Among Urban Mexicans & Chicanos. (Illus.). 185p. 1983. 22.50 (ISBN 0-8135-0952-1). Rutgers U Pr.

Velez-Ibanez, Carlos G. Rituals of Marginality: Politics, Process, & Culture Change in Central Urban mexico, 1969-1974. LC 82-19964. (Illus.). 270p. 1983. text ed. 27.50x (ISBN 0-520-04839-3). U of Cal Pr.

Velie, L. Desperate Bargain. 1977. 10.00 (ISBN 0-07-067392-6). McGraw.

Velie, Lester. Murder Story: A Tragedy of Our Time. (Illus.). 352p. 1983. 15.95 (ISBN 0-02-621720-1). Macmillan.

Velikhov, E. P. Molecular Gas Lasers. 266p. 1981. pap. 8.00 (ISBN 0-8285-2280-4, Pub. by Mir Pubs USSR). Imported Pubns.

Velikovsky, Immanuel. Stargazers & Gravediggers: Memoirs to Worlds in Collision. LC 82-14463. 320p. 1983. 14.95 (ISBN 0-688-01545-X). Morrow.

Vella, Dorothy, jt. auth. see Vella, Walter F.

Vella, Walter F. & Vella, Dorothy. Chaiyo! King Vajiravudh & the Development of Thai Nationalism. LC 78-1060. 1978. text ed. 20.00x (ISBN 0-8248-0493-7). UH Pr.

Vella, Walter F., ed. Aspects of Vietnamese History. (Asian Studies at Hawaii Ser.: No. 8). 230p. (Orig.). 1973. pap. text ed. 8.00x (ISBN 0-8248-0236-5). UH Pr.

Vella, Walter F., ed. see Coedes, G.

Vellaccio, Frank, jt. auth. see Kemp, Daniel S.

Vellacott, P. Ironic Drama. LC 74-19522. 276p. 1975. 37.50 (ISBN 0-521-20590-5); pap. 12.95 (ISBN 0-521-09896-3). Cambridge U Pr.

Vellis, Jean de see Perez-Polo, J. Regino & De Vellis, Jean.

Vellucci, Augusto, jt. auth. see Nuzzolo, Luccio.

Vellutino, Frank R. Dyslexia: Theory & Research. (Illus.). 1979. 27.50x (ISBN 0-262-22021-0); pap. 12.50x (ISBN 0-262-72007-8). MIT Pr.

Velo, G. P., ed. Trends in Inflammation Research One. (Agents & Actions Supplement Ser.: Vol. 7). 362p. 1980. text ed. 98.10x (ISBN 3-7643-1177-0). Birkhauser.

Velo-news Editors. Ten Years of Championship Bicycle Racing. (Illus.). 128p. (Orig.). 1983. specialty trade 14.95 (ISBN 0-686-42828-5). Velo-News.

Veltri, John. Architectural Photography. (Illus.). 256p. 1974. 19.95 o.p. (ISBN 0-8174-0556-9, Amphoto). Watson-Guptill.

Velz, Clarence J. Applied Stream Sanitation. LC 71-120710. (Environmental Science & Technology Ser). 1970. 71.95x (ISBN 0-471-90525-9, Pub. by Wiley-Interscience). Wiley.

Vemuri, V. Modeling of Complex Systems. (Operation Research & Industrial Engineering). 1978. text ed. 34.00 (ISBN 0-12-716550-9). Acad Pr.

Vemuri, V. & Karplus, Walter. Digital Computer Treatment of Partial Differential Equations. (Illus.). 480p. 1981. text ed. 32.95 (ISBN 0-13-212407-6). P-H.

Ven, Andrew H. Van de see Van de Ven, Andrew H. & Ferry, Diane L.

Venable, Emerson. Poets of Ohio. LC 73-18459. 1974. Repr. of 1909 ed. 45.00x (ISBN 0-8103-3622-7). Gale.

Venable, Frank R., ed. Full Colour Reproductions of Some of the Greatest Paintings of Profane & Divine Love. (A Promotion of the Arts Library Bk.). 98p. 1983. 68.45 (ISBN 0-86650-052-9). Gloucester Art.

Venable, Wallace, jt. auth. see Plants, Helen.

Venables, Hubert, ed. The Frankenstein Diaries. LC 80-14806. (Illus.). 128p. 1980. 10.00 o.p. (ISBN 0-670-32710-7). Viking Pr.

Venables, P. H. & Christie, M. J., eds. Research in Psychophysiology. LC 74-18266. 444p. 1975. 89.95x (ISBN 0-471-90555-0, Pub. by Wiley-Interscience). Wiley.

Venables, Peter H., jt. ed. see Martin, Irene.

Venables, Robert W., jt. ed. see Vecsey, Christopher.

Ve Nard, Victor. All America is Ours. (Illus.). 70p. (Orig.). 1982. pap. 4.95 (ISBN 0-9610342-0-3). Ve Nard Pubs.

Vence, Celine & Courtine, Robert J. The Grand Masters of French Cuisine: Five Centuries of Great Cooking. LC 78-57581. (Illus.). 1978. 25.00 o.p. (ISBN 0-399-12220-6). Putnam Pub Group.

Vendelin, George D. Design of Amplifiers & Oscillators by the S-Parameter Method. LC 81-13005. 190p. 1982. 27.50x (ISBN 0-471-09226-6, Pub. by Wiley-Interscience). Wiley.

Venditti, Arnaldo. The Loggia del Capitaniato. LC 74-113200. (Corpus Palladianum, Vol. 4). (Illus.). 1972. 42.50x (ISBN 0-271-00089-9). Pa St U Pr.

Venedikov, Ivan & Gerassimov, Todor. Thracian Art Treasures. 388p. 1979. 69.00x (ISBN 0-686-97596-0, Pub. by Collet's). State Mutual Bk.

Venema, Jack E. & Waldman, John. English Made Simple Jr. Series. pap. 4.50 (ISBN 0-385-00986-0, Made). Doubleday.

Venet, Luc, tr. see SATPREM.

Veney, James E., jt. auth. see Kaluzny, Arnold D.

Vengris, Jonas. Lawns. Rev. ed. LC 82-82822. (Illus.). 250p. 1982. pap. 15.50 (ISBN 0-913702-19-6). Thomson Pub CA.

--Lawns -- Basic Factors, Construction & Maintenance of Fine Turf Areas. rev. ed. 10.00 o.p. (ISBN 0-913702-05-6). Thomson Pub CA.

Vengroff, Richard. Development Administration at the Local Level: The Case of Zaire. (Foreign & Comparative Studies Program, African Ser.: No. 40). (Illus.). 1983. pap. price not set (ISBN 0-915984-63-6). Syracuse U Foreign Comp.

Veniard, John. Fly Tying Problems. write for info. N Lyons Bks.

Veniard, John & Downs, Donald. Fly-Tying Problems & Their Answers. (Illus.). 124p. 1972. 5.95 o.p. (ISBN 0-517-50787-0). Crown.

Venieris, Y. P. & Sebold, F. D. Macroeconomic, Models & Policy. 1977. 34.95 (ISBN 0-471-90560-7). Wiley.

Venikov, V. A. Transient Processes in Electrical Power Systems. 501p. 1977. 12.00 (ISBN 0-8285-0699-X, Pub. by Mir Pubs USSR). Imported Pubns.

Venkatacharya, ed. The Sahityakantakoddhara. 64p. 1980. 9.95 o.p. (ISBN 0-89684-250-9, Pub. by Motilal Banarsidass India). Orient Bk Dist.

Venkataraman, G., et al. Dynamics of Perfect Crystals. 1975. 50.00x (ISBN 0-262-22019-9). MIT Pr.

Venkataraman, K. The Analytical Chemistry of Synthetic Dyes. LC 76-39881. 1977. 90.50x (ISBN 0-471-90575-5, Pub. by Wiley-Interscience). Wiley.

Venkataraman, K., jt. auth. see Kumar, Sushil.

Venkataraman, Krishnasami, ed. The Chemistry of Synthethic Dyes, 8 vols. Incl. Vol. 1. 1952. 82.00 (ISBN 0-12-717001-4); Vol. 2. 1952. 82.00 (ISBN 0-12-717002-2); Vol. 3. 1970. 71.50 o.s.i. (ISBN 0-12-717003-0); Vol. 4. 1971. 82.00 (ISBN 0-12-717004-9); Vol. 5. 1971. 89.00 (ISBN 0-12-717005-7); Vol. 6. 1972. 82.00 (ISBN 0-12-717006-5); Vol. 7. 1974. 82.00 (ISBN 0-12-717007-3); Vol. 8. 1978. 82.00 (ISBN 0-12-717008-1). (Organic & Biological Chemistry Ser.). Set. 472.50. Acad Pr.

Venkataramani, M. S. The American Role in Pakistan. 480p. 1982. text ed. 36.75x (ISBN 0-391-02764-6, 40389, Pub. by Radiant Pub India). Humanities.

--The Sunny Side of F.D.R. LC 75-181688. 292p. 1973. 16.00x (ISBN 0-8214-0107-6, 82-81107). Ohio U Pr.

Venkatarman, S. A Treatise on Hindu Law. (Orient Longman Law Library). 550p. 1980. pap. text ed. 18.95x (ISBN 0-86131-211-2, Pub. by Orient Longman Ltd India). Apt Bks.

Venkatesan, K., jt. auth. see Mathews, P. M.

Venkatesananda, Swami. The Enlightened Living. 1978. pap. 2.95 (ISBN 0-89684-202-9). Orient Bk Dist.

--Yoga. (Illus., Orig.). Date not set. pap. 8.95 canceled (ISBN 0-89407-021-5). Strawberry Hill.

Venn, John. Logic of Chance. 4th ed. LC 62-11698. 14.95 (ISBN 0-8284-0173-X). Chelsea Pub.

--The Principles of Inductive Logic. 2nd ed. LC 72-119162. Orig. Title: The Principles of Empirical, or Inductive Logic. 624p. 1973. 25.00 (ISBN 0-8284-0265-5). Chelsea Pub.

--Symbolic Logic. 2nd ed. LC 79-119161. 1971. text ed. 19.50 (ISBN 0-8284-0251-5). Chelsea Pub.

Vennard, E. Electric Power Business. 2nd ed. 1970. 33.95 (ISBN 0-07-067399-3, P&RB). McGraw.

--Government in the Power Business. LC 68-13105. (Illus.). 1968. 22.95 (ISBN 0-07-067396-9, G). McGraw.

Vennard, Edwin. Management of the Electric Energy Business. LC 79-696. (Illus.). 1979. 35.75 (ISBN 0-07-067402-7). McGraw.

Vennard, John K. & Street, Robert L. Elementary Fluid Mechanics. 5th ed. LC 74-31232. 740p. 1975. text ed. 32.95x o.p. (ISBN 0-471-90587-9). Wiley.

--Elementary Fluid Mechanics: SI Edition. 5th ed. LC 76-4885. 1976. 36.95 (ISBN 0-471-90589-5) (ISBN 0-685-68753-8). Wiley.

Venn-Brown, Janet, ed. For a Palestinian: A Memorial to Wael Zuaiter. (Illus.). 200p. 1983. write for info. (ISBN 0-7103-0039-5, Kegan Paul). Routledge & Kegan.

Vennemann, T., jt. auth. see Bartsch, R.

Vennewitz, Leila, tr. see Boll, Heinrich.

Vennewitz, Leila, tr. see Born, Nicolas.

Ven Nicole Van, de see Russell, Diana E. & Van de Ven, Nicole.

Venning, Ralph. The Plague of Plagues. 1965. pap. 2.95 (ISBN 0-686-77102-8). Banner of Truth.

Vennum, Thomas, Jr. The Ojibwa Dance Drum: Its History & Construction. (Folklife Ser.: Vol. 2). (Illus.). 320p. (Orig.). 1983. pap. 12.50x (ISBN 0-87474-941-7). Smithsonian.

Venolia, Jan. Better Letters: A Handbook of Business & Personal Correspondence. LC 82-80209. 160p. 1982. 9.95 (ISBN 0-89815-065-5); pap. 5.95 (ISBN 0-89815-064-7); spiral bdg. 7.95 (ISBN 0-89815-066-3). Ten Speed Pr.

--Write Right! LC 82-80234. 128p. 6.95 (ISBN 0-89815-062-0); pap. 3.95 (ISBN 0-89815-061-2); spiral bdg. 4.95 (ISBN 0-89815-063-9). Ten Speed Pr.

Ventafridda, Vittorio, jt. ed. see Bonica, John J.

Vente, Maarten A. Vijf Eeuwen Zwolse Orgels Fourteen Forty-Seven to Nineteen Seventy-One. (Bibliotheca Organologica: Vol. 49). 22.50 o.s.i. (ISBN 90-6027-240-4, Pub. by Frits Knuf Netherlands). Pendragon NY.

Ventolo, William L. Residential Construction. 212p. 1979. pap. 17.95 o.s.i. (ISBN 0-695-81407-9). Follett.

Ventris, M. & Chadwick, J. Documents in Mycenaean Greek. 2nd ed. (Illus.). 600p. 1973. 120.00 (ISBN 0-521-08558-6). Cambridge U Pr.

Ventry, I. M., jt. auth. see Chaiklin, J. B.

Ventry, Ira M. & Schiavetti, Nicholas. Evaluating Research in Speech Pathology & Audiology: A Guide for Clinicians & Students. (Speech-Language Pathology & Audiology Ser.). (Illus.). 1980. text ed. 23.95 (ISBN 0-201-08194-6). A-W.

Ventry, Lord & Kolesnik, Eugene M. Airship Saga. 192p. 1983. 16.95 (ISBN 0-7137-1001-2, Pub. by Blandford Pr England). Sterling.

Ventura, Piero. Man & the Horse. (Illus.). 80p. 1982. 11.95 (ISBN 0-399-20842-9). Putnam Pub Group.

Ventura, Sylvia M. Mauro Mendez: From Journalism to Diplomacy. (Illus.). 1979. text ed. 15.00x (ISBN 0-8248-0651-4); pap. text ed. 11.50x (ISBN 0-8248-0656-5). UH Pr.

Venturi, Franco. Italy & the Enlightenment: Studies in a Cosmopolitan Century. Woolf, Stuart, ed. LC 72-77153. 302p. 1972. 14.50x o.p. (ISBN 0-8147-8752-5). NYU Pr.

--Roots of Revolution: A History of the Populist & Socialist Movements in Nineteenth-Century Russia. Haskell, Francis, tr. xxxviii, 850p. 1960. pap. 14.95 (ISBN 0-226-85270-9). U of Chicago Pr.

--Studies in Free Russia. Walsby, Fausta S., tr. from Ital. LC 81-23149. 1982. lib. bdg. 27.50x (ISBN 0-226-85272-5). U of Chicago Pr.

Venturi, Ken & Barkow, Al. The Venturi Analysis: Learning Better Golf from the Champions. LC 80-69389. 160p. 1982. 14.95 (ISBN 0-689-11145-2); pap. 9.95 (ISBN 0-689-70633-2, 286). Atheneum.

Venturi, Rauch & Scott Brown. Venturi, Rauch & Scott Brown. (Architecture Ser.: Bibliography A 840). 63p. 1982. pap. 9.75 (ISBN 0-88066-250-6). Vance Biblios.

Venturi, Robert, et al. Learning from Las Vegas. rev. ed. 1977. 22.50x (ISBN 0-262-22020-2); pap. 9.95 (ISBN 0-262-72006-X). MIT Pr.

Venugopalan, M., jt. ed. see Veprek, S.

Venulet, J., et al, eds. Standardizing Methods of Assessing Causality of Adverse Drug Reactions. 1982. 29.50 (ISBN 0-12-717350-1). Acad Pr.

Venus, Jill, jt. auth. see Causton, David.

Venus, Jill C., jt. auth. see Causton, David R.

Venuti, Lawrence, tr. & intro. by see Buzzati, Dino.

Venzio, Dick De see DeVenzio, Dick.

Vepa, Ram K. Small Industry in the Eighties. 450p. 1982. text ed. write for info. (ISBN 0-7069-1964-5, Pub. by Vikas India). Advent NY.

Veprek, S. & Venugopalan, M., eds. Plasma Chemistry, Vol. IV. (Topics in Current Chemistry Ser.: Vol. 107). (Illus.). 186p. 1983. 34.00 (ISBN 0-387-11828-4). Springer-Verlag.

Vera, Hernan. Professionalization & Professionalism of Catholic Priests. LC 82-6886. (Social Sciences Monographs: No. 68). (Illus.). xii, 116p. 1982. pap. 7.00x (ISBN 0-8130-0713-5). U Presses Fla.

Verakis, jt. auth. see Nagy.

Verba, S., et al. Participation & Political Equality. LC 77-88629. (Illus.). 1978. 37.50 (ISBN 0-521-21905-1); pap. 12.95 (ISBN 0-521-29721-4). Cambridge U Pr.

Verba, Sidney, jt. auth. see Almond, Gabriel.

Verba, Sidney, jt. auth. see Almond, Gabriel A.

Verba, Sidney, jt. auth. see Prewitt, Kenneth.

Verba, Sidney, jt. ed. see Almond, Gabriel A.

Verba, Sidney, jt. ed. see Knorr, Klaus E.

Verbeke, Gerard. The Presence of Stoicism in Medieval Thought. 1982. 11.95x (ISBN 0-8132-0572-7); pap. 6.95x (ISBN 0-8132-0573-5). Cath U Pr.

VerBerg, Kenneth, jt. auth. see Press, Charles.

Verbic, S. Yugoslavin Mining Dictionary: English-Serbo-English. 527p. 1981. pap. text ed. 25.00x (ISBN 0-89918-783-8). Vanous.

Verbist, J., jt. ed. see Caudano, R.

Verbruggen & Veys. Degenerative Joint Diseases. (International Congress Ser.: No. 573). 1982. 64.00 (ISBN 0-444-90250-3). Elsevier.

Verbruggen, Hugo, jt. auth. see Pearsall, Mile D.

Verbruggen, J. F. The Art of Warfare in Western Europe During the Middle Ages. new ed. (Europe in the Middle Ages Ser.: Vol. 1). 1977. 57.50 (ISBN 0-444-10968-4, North-Holland). Elsevier.

Verbsky, Ray & Williams, Don. The Gay Print & Coloring Book. 1980. 7.95 o.p. (ISBN 0-937520-00-4). Green Hill.

Verburg, K., jt. auth. see Press, C.

VerBurg, Kenneth, jt. auth. see Press, Charles.

Verby, John. How to Talk to Doctors. LC 75-42924. (Illus.). 1977. pap. 1.75 o.p. (ISBN 0-668-03956-6). Arco.

Verby, John E. Family Practice Specialty Board Recertification Review. 3rd ed. 1978. spiral bdg. 23.00 (ISBN 0-87488-309-1). Med Exam.

Vercel, Roger. Bertrand of Brittany: Biography of Messire du Guesclin. Saunders, M., tr. 1934. text ed. 39.50x (ISBN 0-686-83487-9). Elliots Bks.

--Tides of Mont St. Michel. Wells, Warre B., tr. Repr. of 1938 ed. lib. bdg. 15.50x (ISBN 0-8371-4052-8, VEMM). Greenwood.

Verchot, Louis. Word Processors Worldwide: Opportunities & Pitfalls. (Illus.). 575p. 1983. 1800.00 (ISBN 0-910211-01-9). Laal Co.

Vercoutter, Jean. The Image of the Black in Western Art: From the Pharaohs to the Fall of the Roman Empire. LC 76-25772. 1976. 70.00 (ISBN 0-688-03086-6). Morrow.

Vercoutter, Jean, jt. auth. see M'Bow, Amadou-Mahtar.

Verder, M. Thermal Methods of Oil Recovery. (Fr.). 1984. 24.59 (ISBN 0-87201-866-0). Gulf Pub.

Verderber, Kathleen S., jt. auth. see Verderber, Rudolph F.

Verderber, Rudolph F. & Verderber, Kathleen S. Inter-Act: Using Interpersonal Communication Skills. 2nd ed. 368p. 1980. pap. text ed. 12.95x (ISBN 0-534-00785-6). Wadsworth Pub.

Verdeyen, Joseph T. Laser Electronics. (Illus.). 480p. 1981. 35.00 (ISBN 0-13-485201-X). P-H.

Verdi, Giuseppe. Aida: Opera Guide & Libretto. Bleiler, Ellen, tr. (Illus., Orig.). 1962. pap. 2.25 o.s.i. (ISBN 0-486-20405-7). Dover.

--Verdi's Aida. 96p. (Orig.). 1983. pap. 1.95 (ISBN 0-486-24459-8). Dover.

--Verdi's Rigoletto. (Opera Libretto Ser.). 64p. (Orig.). 1983. pap. 1.95 (ISBN 0-486-24497-0). Dover.

Verdier, M. Borehole Geology. 228p. cancelled (ISBN 0-87201-082-1). Gulf Pub.

Verdina, Joseph. Geometry. new ed. (Mathematics Ser). (Illus.). 400p. 1975. text ed. 17.95x (ISBN 0-675-08738-4). Additional supplements may be obtained from publisher. Merrill.

Verdon, Thomas A., Jr. Nuclear Medicine for the General Physician. LC 78-26954. (Illus.). 244p. 1980. 26.00 (ISBN 0-88416-206-0). Wright-PSG.

Verdu, Alfonso. Early Buddhist Philosophy in Light of the Four Noble Truths. LC 79-66172. 1979. pap. text ed. 10.50 (ISBN 0-8191-0189-3). U Pr of Amer.

Verduin, John R., jt. auth. see Miller, Harry G.

Verduin, John R., Jr. Curriculum Building for Adult Learning. LC 79-23111. 187p. 1980. 13.50x (ISBN 0-8093-0960-2). S Ill U Pr.

Verdy Du Vernois, Julius A. Von see Von Verdy Du Vernois, Julius A.

Verey, David. Cotswold Churches. 189p. 1982. pap. text ed. 9.00x (ISBN 0-904387-78-X, 61040, Pub. by Sutton England). Humanities.

Verey, David & Welander, David. Gloucester Cathedral. 160p. 1981. text ed. 15.75x (ISBN 0-904387-40-2, Pub. by Sutton England); pap. text ed. 8.50x (ISBN 0-904387-34-8). Humanities.

Verga, Giovanni. Cavalleria Rusticana, & Other Stories. Lawrence, D. H., tr. from It. LC 75-9590. 301p. 1975. Repr. of 1928 ed. lib. bdg. 17.75x (ISBN 0-8371-8105-4, VECR). Greenwood.

--The House by the Medlar Tree. Mosbacher, Eric, tr. from It. LC 75-11490. 247p. 1975. Repr. of 1953 ed. lib. bdg. 20.75x (ISBN 0-8371-8205-0, VEMT). Greenwood.

--Little Novels of Sicily. Lawrence, D. H., tr. LC 75-11483. 226p. 1975. Repr. of 1953 ed. lib. bdg. 15.75x (ISBN 0-8371-8199-2, VENS). Greenwood.

--Mastro-Don Gesuald. 1979. 21.50x (ISBN 0-520-03598-4). U of Cal Pr.

--She-Wolf & Other Stories. new, enl. ed. Cecchetti, Giovanni, tr. & intro. by. LC 79-181437. 1973. pap. 3.25 o.p. (ISBN 0-520-02153-3, CAL17). U of Cal Pr.

Vergani, Luisa. Divine Comedy: Inferno Notes. (Orig.). 1969. pap. 2.75 (ISBN 0-8220-0391-0). Cliffs.

--Prince Notes. (Orig.). 1967. pap. 2.50 (ISBN 0-8220-1093-3). Cliffs.

Vergara, Lisa. Rubens & the Poetics of Landscape. LC 81-11385. (Illus.). 228p. 1982. 35.00x (ISBN 0-300-02508-4). Yale U Pr.

Vergara, William C. Science in Everyday Life. LC 79-3405. (Illus.). 1980. 14.37i (ISBN 0-06-014474-2, HarpT). Har-Row.

Vergers, Charles A. Handbook of Electrical Noise: Measurement & Technology. (Illus.). 1979. 10.95 o.p. (ISBN 0-8306-9807-8); pap. 6.95 (ISBN 0-8306-1132-0, 1132). TAB Bks.

Vergez, Robert. Okumura Masanobu: Early Ukiyo-e Master. LC 82-48780. (Great Japanese Art Ser.). (Illus.). 48p. 1983. 18.95 (ISBN 0-87011-564-2). Kodansha.

Verghese, K. E. Slow Flows the Pampa. 238p. 1982. text ed. 15.25x (ISBN 0-391-02724-7, Pub. by Concept). Humanities.

Vergneaud, J. R. Grammaire Formelle: Constructions Causatives et Constructions Relatives en Francais. (Linguisticae Investigationes Supplementa: 10). 500p. 1983. 50.00 (ISBN 90-272-3114-1). Benjamins North Am.

Vergo, Peter, ed. see Kandinsky, Wassily.

Vergun, Dimitry, jt. auth. see Ambrose, James.

Verhalen, Philip A. Faith in a Secularized World. LC 75-46067. 180p. 1976. pap. 3.95 o.p. (ISBN 0-8091-1937-4). Paulist Pr.

Verhelst, Wilbert. Sculpture: Tools, Materials, & Techniques. (Illus.). 304p. 1973. ref. ed. 24.95 (ISBN 0-13-796615-6). P-H.

Ver Hoef, jt. auth. see Kutrth.

Verhoef, J., jt. auth. see Van der Waay, D.

Verhoef, J., ed. Infections in the Immuno-Compromised Host. (Developments in Immunology Ser.: Vol. 11). 1981. 50.75 (ISBN 0-444-80287-8). Elsevier.

Verhoeven, John D. Fundamentals of Physical Metallurgy. LC 75-4600. 567p. 1975. text ed. 42.95x (ISBN 0-471-90616-6). Wiley.

Verhoogen, Jean, jt. auth. see Turner, Francis J.

Veri, Anthony. The New Moral Code of Action for the Large Corporation's Executive. (Illus.). 1977. 49.50 (ISBN 0-89266-068-6). Am Classical Coll Pr.

Verissimo, Erico. Consider the Lillies of the Field. Karnoff, Jean N., tr. Repr. of 1947 ed. lib. bdg. 15.75x (ISBN 0-8371-2320-8, VELF). Greenwood.

--Rest Is Silence. Kaplan, L. C., tr. Repr. of 1946 ed. lib. bdg. 19.00x (ISBN 0-8371-2318-6, VERS). Greenwood.

Verkade, John G., jt. ed. see Quin, Louis D.

Verkamp, Bernard J. The Indifferent Mean: Adiaphorism in the English Reformation to 1554. LC 77-13672. (Studies in the Reformation: Vol. 1). 1977. 15.00x (ISBN 0-8214-0387-7, 82-82808, Co-Pub by Wayne State). Ohio U Pr.

Verkest, Susan. Crocheting Christmas Ornaments: Complete Instructions for 13 Projects. (Knitting, Crocheting, Tatting Ser.). (Illus.). 32p. (Orig.). 1982. pap. 1.95 (ISBN 0-486-24351-6). Dover.

Verkler, Linda & Zempel, Edward. Convection Oven Cooking. (Orig.). 1983. pap. 8.95 (ISBN 0-88289-377-7). Pelican.

Verkler, R. C., jt. auth. see Pegels, C. Carl.

Verkruijsse, H. D., jt. auth. see Bradsma, L.

Verleger, Phillip K., Jr. Oil Markets in Turmoil: An Economic Analysis. 328p. 1982. prof ref 27.50x (ISBN 0-88410-867-8). Ballinger Pub.

Verma, Bhagwati C. Chitralekha. Karki, Chandra B., tr. 1966. pap. 2.50 (ISBN 0-88253-198-0). Ind-US Inc.

Verma, G. K., et al. Illusion & Reality in Indian Secondary Education. 1979. text ed. 28.50x (ISBN 0-566-00292-2). Gower Pub Ltd.

Verma, Gajendra K. & Beard, Ruth M. What Is Educational Research? Perspectives on Techniques of Research. 224p. 1981. text ed. 33.75x (ISBN 0-566-00323-6); pap. text ed. 15.75x (ISBN 0-566-00429-1). Gower Pub Ltd.

Verma, Gajendra K. & Bagley, Christopher, eds. Race, Education & Identity. LC 78-2981. 1979. 24.00x (ISBN 0-312-66134-7). St Martin.

Verma, H. S. Post Independence Change in Rural India: A Pilot Study of an Uttar Pradesh Village. 92p. 1981. text ed. 11.75x (ISBN 0-391-02278-4, Pub. by Concept India). Humanities.

Verma, Harish L. & Gross, Charles W. Introduction to Quantitative Methods: A Managerial Emphasis. LC 77-21089. 1978. text ed. 34.95 (ISBN 0-471-02610-7); tchrs. manual o.p. 8.00 (ISBN 0-471-02495-3, Pub. by Wiley-Hamilton). Wiley.

Verma, Kiran, jt. auth. see Shuttleworth, Riley.

Verma, Rajendra. Man & Society in Tagore & Eliot. 188p. 1982. text ed. 15.75x (ISBN 0-391-02464-7). Humanities.

--Time & Poetry in Eliot's Four Quartets. 1979. text ed. 13.00x (ISBN 0-391-00769-6). Humanities.

Verma, Som P. Art & Material Culture in the Paintings of Akbar's Court. (Illus.). 1978. text ed. 23.50x (ISBN 0-7069-0595-4). Humanities.

Vermaseren, M. J. Corpus Cultus Cybelae Attidisque CCCA II: Graecia atque Insulae. (Etudes Preliminaires aux Religions Orientales dans l'Empire Romain Ser.: Vol. 50). (Illus.). xxxi, 278p. 1982. write for info. (ISBN 90-04-06499-0). E J Brill.

--Mithriaca III: The Mithraeum at Marino. (Etudes Preliminaires aux Religions Orientales dans l'Empire Romain Ser.: Vol. 16). (Illus.). xiii, 105p. 1982. write for info. (ISBN 90-04-06500-8). E J Brill.

Vermaseren, Maarten J., jt. auth. see Bianchi, Ugo.

Vermeersch, LaVonne F. & Southwick, Charles E. Practical Problems in Mathematics for Graphic Arts. Rev. ed. LC 82-72128. (Illus.). 176p. 1983. pap. text ed. 7.00 (ISBN 0-8273-2100-7); Instr's Guide avail. (ISBN 0-8273-2101-5). Delmar.

Vermes, Pamela. Buber on God & the Perfect Man. Neusner, J., et al, eds. LC 80-23406. (Brown Judaic Studies). 1981. 15.00 (ISBN 0-89130-426-6, 14-00-13); pap. 10.50 (ISBN 0-89130-427-4). Scholars Pr CA.

Vermeule, Cornelius. Greek, Etruscan & Roman Art: The Classical Collection of the Museum of Fine Arts, Boston. 4th, rev. ed. (Illus.). 290p. 1972. pap. 5.95 (ISBN 0-87846-169-8). Mus Fine Arts Boston.

Vermeule, Emily. Aspects of Death in Early Greek Art & Poetry. LC 76-55573. (Sather Classical Lectures: Vol. 46). 1979. 37.50x (ISBN 0-520-03405-8); pap. 7.95 (ISBN 0-520-04404-5). U of Cal Pr.

Vermeule, Emily T. see Euripides.

Vermeulen, A. & Exley, D., eds. Androgens in Normal & Pathological Conditions. (International Congress Ser.: No. 101). (Proceedings). 1966. 14.75 (ISBN 90-219-0053-X, Excerpta Medica). Elsevier.

Vermilye, Jerry. The Films of the Thirties. LC 82-12965. 288p. 1982. 18.95 (ISBN 0-8065-0807-8). Citadel Pr.

Vernadakis, Antonia, jt. ed. see Prasad, Kedar N.

Vernadakis, Nikos. Econometric Models for the Developing Economies: A Case Study of Greece. LC 78-61886. (Praeger Special Studies). 1979. 24.95 o.p. (ISBN 0-03-047231-8). Praeger.

Vernadsky, George. History of Russia. rev. ed. (Illus.). 1961. 35.00x o.p. (ISBN 0-300-01010-9); pap. 10.95x (ISBN 0-300-00247-5, Y43). Yale U Pr.

--The Origins of Russia. LC 75-11804. (Illus.). 354p. 1975. Repr. of 1959 ed. lib. bdg. 20.75x (ISBN 0-8371-8052-X, VEOR). Greenwood.

Vernan, Ivan R., jt. auth. see Berkman, Harold W.

Vernberg, F. J., jt. auth. see Vernberg, W. B.

Vernberg, F. John & Vernberg, Winona B., eds. Pollution & Physiology of Marine Organisms. 1974. 42.50 (ISBN 0-12-718250-0). Acad Pr.

Vernberg, W. B. & Vernberg, F. J. Environmental Physiology of Marine Animals. LC 70-183485. (Illus.). 346p. 1972. 30.00 o.p. (ISBN 0-387-05721-8). Springer-Verlag.

Vernberg, Winona B., jt. ed. see Vernberg, F. John.

Vernberg, Winona B., et al. Marine Pollution: Functional Responses. LC 79-10451. 1979. 26.50 (ISBN 0-12-718260-8). Acad Pr.

Vernberg, Winona B., et al, eds. Physiological Mechanisms of Marine Pollutant Toxicity. 1982. 45.00 (ISBN 0-12-718460-0). Acad Pr.

Verne. De la Terre a la Lune. (Easy Reader, C). 1970. pap. 3.95 (ISBN 0-88436-048-2, 40275). EMC.

Verne, Etienne, jt. auth. see Illich, Ivan.

Verne, Jules. An Antarctic Mystery. (Science Fiction Ser.). 368p. 1975. Repr. of 1899 ed. lib. bdg. 15.00 o.p. (ISBN 0-8398-2316-9, Gregg). G K Hall.

--Around the World in Eighty Days. (Classics Ser). (gr. 8 up). 1964. pap. 1.50 (ISBN 0-8049-0024-8, CL-24). Airmont.

--From the Earth to the Moon. (Childrens Illustrated Classics Ser.). (Illus.). 192p. 1975. Repr. of 1970 ed. 9.00x o.p. (ISBN 0-460-05088-5, Pub. by J. M. Dent England). Biblio Dist.

--Journey to the Centre of the Earth. (Childrens Illustrated Classics Ser). (Illus.). 255p. 1973. Repr. of 1970 ed. 9.00x o.p. (ISBN 0-460-05084-2, Pub. by J. M. Dent England). Biblio Dist.

--Twenty Thousand Leagues under the Sea. (Classics Ser). (gr. 8 up). 1964. pap. 1.50 (ISBN 0-8049-0012-4, CL-12). Airmont.

--Twenty Thousand Leagues under the Sea. (Literature Ser.). (gr. 7-12). 1970. pap. text ed. 4.42 (ISBN 0-87720-740-2). AMSCO Sch.

--Twenty Thousand Leagues Under the Sea. (gr. 3 up). Date not set. price not set (ISBN 0-448-41109-1, G&D). Putnam Pub Group.

--Twenty Thousand Leagues under the Sea. annotated ed. Miller, Walter J., ed. (Illus.). 1977. pap. 7.95 o.p. (ISBN 0-452-00474-8, F474, Mer). NAL.

--Twenty Thousand Leagues under the Sea. Brunetti, Mendor T., tr. (Orig.). 1969. pap. 1.95 (ISBN 0-451-51584-6, CJ1584, Sig Classics). NAL.

--Twenty Thousand Leagues under the Sea. 1981. pap. 2.50 (ISBN 0-671-43473-X, Timescape). PB.

--Twenty Thousand Leagues under the Sea. (gr. 9-12). pap. 2.50 o.p. (ISBN 0-671-48826-0, Timescape). PB.

--Twenty Thousand Leagues under the Sea. new ed. Binder, Otto, ed. LC 73-75466. (Now Age Illustrated Ser.). (Illus.). 64p. (Orig.). (gr. 5-10). 1973. 5.00 (ISBN 0-88301-222-7); pap. 1.95 (ISBN 0-88301-104-2); student activity bk. 1.25 (ISBN 0-88301-180-8). Pendulum Pr.

--Twenty Thousand Leagues Under the Sea. Bonner, Anthony, tr. (Bantam Classics Ser.). 384p. (Fr.). (gr. 6-12). 1981. pap. 1.75 (ISBN 0-686-81836-9). Bantam.

--Voyage to the Moon. (Illus.). 1977. 4.95 o.p. (ISBN 0-517-52851-7, Harmony). Crown.

Verne, Jules see Allen, W. S.

Verne, Jules see Eyre, A. G.

Verne, Jules, jt. auth. see Poe, Edgar Allan.

Verne, Jules see Swan, D. K.

Verne, Julio. Viaje a la Luna. (Span.). 9.95 (ISBN 84-241-5635-8). E Torres & Sons.

Verner, Bill & Skowrup, Drew. Racquetball. LC 77-89923. (Illus.). 110p. 1977. pap. 4.95 (ISBN 0-87484-426-6). Mayfield Pub.

Verner, Clara. Velma. new ed. 1973. 3.95 (ISBN 0-8341-0081-9). Beacon Hill.

Verner, Coolie & Stuart-Stubbs, Basil. The Northpart of America. 500.00 (ISBN 0-384-64300-0). Johnson Repr.

Verner, Elizabeth O. The Stonewall Ladies. 1963. 10.00 (ISBN 0-937684-07-4). Tradd St Pr.

Verneuil, Louis. The Fabulous Life of Sarah Bernhardt. Boyd, Ernest, tr. from Fr. LC 70-138134. (Illus.). 312p. 1972. Repr. of 1942 ed. lib. bdg. 17.75x (ISBN 0-8371-5707-2, VESB). Greenwood.

Verniani, F. Structure & Dynamics of the Upper Atmosphere. (Developments in Atmospheric Sciences: Vol. 1). 1974. 113.00 (ISBN 0-444-41105-4). Elsevier.

Vernick, Judy & Nesgoda, John. American English Sounds & Spellings for Beginning ESL Students. (Piit Series in English as a Second Language). 1980. pap. text ed. 7.95x (ISBN 0-8229-8208-0, Pub. by U Ctr Intl St). U of Pittsburgh Pr.

Vernois, Julius A. Von Verdy Du see Von Verdy Du Vernois, Julius A.

Vernon, Ann. Help Yourself to a Heathier You. LC 80-5125. 186p. 1980. pap. text ed. 9.50 (ISBN 0-8191-1048-5). U Pr of Amer.

Vernon, Arthur. The History & Romance of the Horse. LC 70-185379. (Illus.). xviii, 525p. 1975. Repr. of 1939 ed. 40.00x (ISBN 0-8103-3982-X). Gale.

Vernon, Glenn M. Symbolic Aspects of Interaction. LC 78-69837. 1978. pap. text ed. 10.25 o.p. (ISBN 0-8191-0581-3). U Pr of Amer.

--A Time to Die. 1977. 8.75 (ISBN 0-8191-0126-5). U Pr of Amer.

Vernon, Glenn M. & Cardwell, Jerry D. Social Psychology: Shared, Symboled, Situated Behavior. LC 80-5967. (Illus.). 580p. (Orig.). 1981. lib. bdg. 30.50 (ISBN 0-8191-1700-5); pap. text ed. 19.75 (ISBN 0-8191-1701-3). U Pr of Amer.

Vernon, Grenville. Yankee Doodle-Doo: A Collection of Songs of the Early American Stage. LC 73-78662. 1972. Repr. of 1927 ed. 37.00x (ISBN 0-8103-3872-6). Gale.

Vernon, Ida W. Pedro De Valdivia, Conquistador of Chile. (Illus.). Repr. of 1946 ed. lib. bdg. 17.75x (ISBN 0-8371-1034-3, TLVV). Greenwood.

Vernon, John. The Grandfather Clock Maintenance Manual. (Illus.). 104p. 1983. 14.95 (ISBN 0-7153-8438-4). David & Charles.

Vernon, K. D., ed. Use of Management & Business Literature. 400p. 1975. 24.95x o.p. (ISBN 0-408-70690-2). Butterworth.

Vernon, Leo P. & Seely, G. R. Chlorophylls: Physical, Chemical & Biological Properties. 1966. 77.00 (ISBN 0-12-718650-6). Acad Pr.

Vernon, Louise A. A Heart Strangely Warmed. LC 75-11767. (Illus.). 128p. (YA) 1975. 4.95 (ISBN 0-8361-1768-9); pap. 3.25 (ISBN 0-8361-1769-7). Herald Pr.

--Thunderstorm in Church. LC 74-5009. (Illus.). 128p. (gr. 4-9). 1974. pap. 3.25 (ISBN 0-8361-1740-9). Herald Pr.

Vernon, Magdalen D. Human Motivation. LC 69-14396. 1969. 32.50 (ISBN 0-521-07419-3); pap. 10.95 (ISBN 0-521-09580-8, 580). Cambridge U Pr.

--Reading & Its Difficulties: A Psychological Study. LC 73-153013. 1971. 29.95 (ISBN 0-521-08217-X). Cambridge U Pr.

Vernon, Marjorie. Roses Out of Reach. (Aston Hall Romances Ser.). 192p. (Orig.). 1981. pap. 1.75 o.p. (ISBN 0-523-41127-8). Pinnacle Bks.

Vernon, Philip E. Intelligence & Cultural Environment. (Illus.). 275p. 1972. pap. 7.95x o.p. (ISBN 0-416-65800-8). Methuen Inc.

--Personality Assessment. (Methuen's Manuals of Psychology Ser.). 1979. pap. 11.95x (ISBN 0-422-72560-9, Pub. by Tavistock England). Methuen Inc.

Vernon, Raymond. Two Hungry Giants: The United States & Japan in the Quest for Oil & Ores. (Center for International Affairs). (Illus.). 192p. 1983. text ed. 16.00x (ISBN 0-674-91470-8). Harvard U Pr.

Vernon, Raymond, jt. auth. see Wells, Louis T.

Vernon, Raymond & Aharoni, Yair, eds. State-Owned Enterprise in the Western Economics. 1980. 30.00 (ISBN 0-312-75623-2). St Martin.

Vernon, Sidney. The Adolescent Drug-Sex-Crime Matter: Common Sense About the National Defense. 1982. pap. 0.99 (ISBN 0-943150-02-7). Rovern Pr.

--Happiness, Drug-Crime & the Law. Salter, Thomas, ed. (Illus.). 100p. 1983. 9.95 (ISBN 0-943150-04-3); pap. 5.95 (ISBN 0-943150-05-1). Rovern Pr.

--Totemics Incorporated. Salter, Thomas, ed. (Illus.). 50p. (Orig.). 1983. pap. 6.95 (ISBN 0-943150-03-5). Rovern Pr.

Vernon, Thomas S. A Philosophy of Language Primer. LC 80-489. 136p. 1980. text ed. 18.00 (ISBN 0-8191-1023-X); pap. text ed. 8.25 (ISBN 0-8191-1024-8). U Pr of Amer.

Vernon, Walter M. Introductory Psychology. 3rd ed. 1980. 21.95 (ISBN 0-395-30845-3); Tchrs Manual 1.00 (ISBN 0-395-30846-1); Test Manual 1.00 (ISBN 0-395-30847-X). HM.

Vernon-Harcourt, Tony. Rewarding Management 1982. 4th ed. 148p. (Orig.). 1981. pap. text ed. 38.50x (ISBN 0-566-02327-X). Gower Pub Ltd.

Vernon-Roberts, B. The Macrophage. LC 72-184141. (Biological Structure & Function Ser.: No. 2). (Illus.). 280p. 1972. 55.00 (ISBN 0-521-08481-4). Cambridge U Pr.

Vernor, James D. An Introduction to Risk Management in Property Development. LC 81-51564. (Development Component Ser.). (Illus.). 20p. 1981. pap. 10.00 (ISBN 0-87420-602-2, D18). Urban Land.

Verny, Thomas & Kelly, John. The Secret Life of the Unborn Child. 256p. 1982. pap. 6.93 (ISBN 0-440-58238-5, Delta). Dell.

Vero, Radu. Airbrush: The Complete Studio Handbook. Wood, Barbara, ed. (Illus.). 192p. 1983. 24.95 (ISBN 0-8230-0166-0). Watson-Guptill.

Veroff, Joanne B., jt. auth. see Veroff, Joseph.

Veroff, Joseph & Dawan, Elizabeth. Americans View Their Mental Health, 1976. LC 82-80684. 1982. write for info. (ISBN 0-89138-939-3). ICPSR.

Veroff, Joseph & Veroff, Joanne B. Social Incentives: A Life-Span Developmental Approach. LC 79-8872. 1980. 26.50 (ISBN 0-12-718750-2). Acad Pr.

Veroff, Joseph, et al. The Inner American: A Self-Portrait from 1957-1976. LC 80-68187. 492p. 1981. 36.00 (ISBN 0-465-03293-1). Basic.

Veron, Enid, ed. Humor in America: An Anthology. 350p. 1976. pap. text ed. 10.95 (ISBN 0-15-540475-X, HC). HarBraceJ.

Veronesi. Tetanus. (Symposia Foundation Merieux Ser.: Vol. 5). 1981. 50.75 (ISBN 0-444-90203-1). Elsevier.

Veronis, A. Microprocessors: Design & Applications. 1978. 23.00 (ISBN 0-87909-493-1). Reston.

Veronis, Andrew. Integrated Circuit Fabrication Technology. (Illus.). 1978. text ed. 23.95 (ISBN 0-8359-3092-0); students manual avail. Reston.

Ver Planck, Dennistown W. & Teare, B. R. Engineering Analysis. LC 54-8420. 1954. 40.50x (ISBN 0-471-90618-2). Wiley.

Verral, Charles S. Babe Ruth: Sultan of Swat. LC 75-38825. (Sports Series). (Illus.). 96p. (gr. 3-6). 1976. PLB 7.12 (ISBN 0-8116-6679-4). Garrard.

--Casey Stengel: Baseball's Great Manager. LC 78-6894. (Sports Ser.). (Illus.). (gr. 3-6). 1978. PLB 7.12 (ISBN 0-8116-6683-2). Garrard.

--Popeye & the Haunted House. (Wonder Bks). (Illus.). 24p. (ps-1). 1980. 0.79 (ISBN 0-686-64623-1, 500-0, G&D). Putnam Pub Group.

--Popeye Climbs a Mountain. (Wonder Bks.). (Illus.). 24p. 1980. 0.79 (ISBN 0-686-64624-X, 502-6). Putnam Pub Group.

--Popeye Goes Fishing. (Wonder Bks.). (Illus.). 24p. (ps-1). 1980. 0.79 (ISBN 0-686-64625-8, 508-5, G&D). Putnam Pub Group.

Verrier, Anthony. Through the Looking Glass. 1983. 18.00x (ISBN 0-393-01648-X). Norton.

Verrier, Michelle. Fantin-Latour. (Illus.). 1978. pap. 6.95 o.p. (ISBN 0-517-53414-2, Harmony). Crown.

--The Orientalists. LC 79-64345. (Illus.). 1979. pap. 8.95 o.p. (ISBN 0-8478-0228-0). Rizzoli Intl.

Verriest, G. Colour Vision Deficiencies VI. 1982. text ed. 99.50 (ISBN 90-6193-729-9, Pub. by Junk Pubs Netherlands). Kluwer Boston.

Verrill, Addison E. Bermuda Islands: An Account of Their Scenery, Climate, Productions, Etc. 1903. pap. text ed. 49.50x (ISBN 0-686-83486-0). Elliots Bks.

Verruijt, A. Grounderwater Flow. 2nd ed. (Illus.). 145p. 1982. text ed. 33.50x (ISBN 0-333-32958-9); pap. text ed. 17.50 (ISBN 0-333-32959-7). Scholium Intl.

Verschoth, Anita. One, Two, Ski, the Easy American Way. LC 76-25989. (Illus.). (gr. 6 up). 1976. 6.95 o.p. (ISBN 0-399-20576-4). Putnam Pub Group.

Verschueren, Jef. Pragmatics: An Annotated Bibliography. (Library & Information Sources in Linguistics Ser.). xvi, 270p. 1978. 30.00 (ISBN 90-272-0995-2, 4). Benjamins North Am.

Verseghy, K. Gattung Ochrolechia. 1962. pap. 16.00 (ISBN 3-7682-5401-1). Lubrecht & Cramer.

Versenyi, Laszlo. Holiness & Justice: An Interpretation of Plato's "Euthyphro". LC 81-43830. 164p. 1982. lib. bdg. 21.25 (ISBN 0-8191-2316-1); pap. text ed. 10.00 (ISBN 0-8191-2317-X). U Pr of Amer.

Versenyi, Lazslo. Socratic Humanism. LC 78-23762. 1979. Repr. of 1963 ed. lib. bdg. 18.50x (ISBN 0-313-20716-X, VESH). Greenwood.

Verser, Trudy G., jt. auth. see Maier, Norman R.

Versey-Fitzgerald, D. F. The Vegetation of the Outbreak Areas of the Red Locust (Nomadacris Septemfasciata Serville in Tanganyika & Northern Rhodesia) 1955. 35.00x (ISBN 0-85135-014-3, Pub by Centre Overseas Research). State Mutual Bk.

Vershel, Allen. Your Future in Dentistry. LC 77-114127. (Career Guidance Ser). 1971. pap. 3.95 o.p. (ISBN 0-668-02239-6). Arco.

--Your Future in Dentistry. rev ed. LC 79-92459. (Careers in Depth Ser). (Illus.). (gr. 7up). 1978. PLB 5.97 o.p. (ISBN 0-8239-0450-4). Rosen Pr.

Versluysen, Eugene. The Political Economy of International Finance. 350p. 1981. 26.00x (ISBN 0-312-62235-X). St Martin.

Versteeg, C. Pectinesterases From the Orange Fruit: Their Purification, General Characteristics & Juice Cloud Destablizing Properties. 109p. 1979. pap. 16.00 o.p. (ISBN 0-686-93173-4, 0709-X, Pudoc). Unipub.

Versteegh, Cornelis H., et al, eds. The History of Linguistics in the Near East. (Studies in the History of Linguistics: No. 28). vi, 270p. 1983. 36.00 (ISBN 90-272-4509-6). Benjamins North Am.

Verster, J. F. XL Muzikale Boekmerken Met Een Opgave Van Meer Dan CCC Spreuken, Die Op Dit Soort Van Boekmerken Voorkomen. wrappers 30.00 o.s.i. (ISBN 90-6027-362-1, Pub. by Frits Knuf Netherlands). Pendragon NY.

Ver Straten, Charles A. How To Start Lay Shepherding Ministries. 120p. 1983. pap. 5.95 (ISBN 0-8010-9290-6). Baker Bk.

Vert, P. & Aranda, J. V., eds. Proceedings of the Third International Colloquium of Developmental Pharmacology, Nancy, June 1981: Developmental Pharmacology & Therapeutics, Vol. 4, Suppl. 1, 1982. 232p. 1982. pap. 43.25 (ISBN 3-8055-3476-0). S Karger.

Vertes, A., et al. Mossbauer Spectroscopy. LC 79-199. (Studies in Physical & Theoretical Chemistry: Vol. 5). 416p. 1980. 70.25 (ISBN 0-444-99782-2). Elsevier.

Vertrees, J. D. Japanese Maples. LC 77-18737. (Illus.). 1978. 40.00 (ISBN 0-917304-09-8). Timber.

Vervalin, Charles H., ed. Communication & the Technical Professional. 140p. (Orig.). 1981. pap. 17.95 (ISBN 0-87201-133-X). Gulf Pub.

--Fire Protection Manual for Hydrocarbon Processing Plants, Vol. 1. 2nd ed. 484p. 1973. 49.95x (ISBN 0-87201-286-7). Gulf Pub.

Vervliet, H. D. Annual Bibliography of the History of the Printed Book & Libraries. 1983. lib. bdg. 85.00 (ISBN 0-686-37696-X, Pub. by Martinus Nijhoff Netherlands). Kluwer Boston.

Vervoren, Thora & Oppeneer, Joan. Workbook of Solutions & Dosage of Drugs, Including Arithmetic. 11th ed. (Illus.). 202p. 1980. pap. text ed. 12.50 (ISBN 0-8016-0236-X). Mosby.

Vervoren, Thora M., jt. auth. see Oppeneer, Joan E.

Verway, David I., ed. Michigan Statistical Abstract. 17th ed. 1983. pap. 15.50 (ISBN 0-686-83168-3). WSU Bur Bus Res.

--Michigan Statistical Abstract. 16th ed. LC 56-62855. 876p. 1982. pap. 15.50 (ISBN 0-942650-00-X). WSU Bur Bus Res.

Verwer, George. Veintinueve Soldados de Plomo. 112p. Date not set. 1.95 (ISBN 0-88113-331-0). Edit Betania.

Verwey, Gerlof. Economist's Handbook: A Manual of Statistical Sources. LC 74-157492. 1971. Repr. of 1934 ed. 56.00x (ISBN 0-8103-3728-2). Gale.

Verwoerdt, Adrian. Clinical Geropsychiatry. 2nd ed. 353p. 1981. lib. bdg. 37.00 o.p. (ISBN 0-683-08592-1). Williams & Wilkins.

Very, Alice, jt. auth. see Brown, Edmund R.

Very, Frank W. Luminiferous Ether. (Orig.). 1919. pap. 1.00 o.p. (ISBN 0-8283-1189-7). Branden.

--Lunar & Terrestrial Albedoes. (Orig.). pap. 1.00 o.p. (ISBN 0-8283-1188-9). Branden.

--Radiant Properties of the Earth. pap. 1.00 o.p. (ISBN 0-8283-1190-0). Branden.

Veryan, Patricia. Married Past Redemption. 320p. 1983. 13.95 (ISBN 0-312-51615-0). St Martin.

--Nanette. 288p. 1981. 11.95 o.s.i. (ISBN 0-8027-0664-9). Walker & Co.

--Some Brief Folly. 352p. 1982. pap. 2.95 (ISBN 0-449-24544-6, Crest). Fawcett.

Verzello, J. R. & Reutter, J. This Is Data Processing: Systems & Concepts. 560p. 1982. 21.95x (ISBN 0-07-067325-X); study guide 10.95x (ISBN 0-07-067326-8). McGraw.

Verzijl, J. J. Production Planning & Information Systems. LC 76-7906. 1976. 34.95x o.p. (ISBN 0-470-90620-0). Halsted Pr.

Vesaas, Tarjei & Rokkan, Elizabeth. The Bleaching Yard. 156p. 1982. 14.95 (ISBN 0-7206-0560-1, Pub. by Peter Owen). Merrimack Bk Serv.

Vesell & Braude. Interactions of Drug Abuse, Vol. 281. 1976. 32.00 (ISBN 0-89072-027-4). NY Acad Sci.

Veselov, M. G., ed. Methods of Quantum Chemistry. Scripta Technica, tr. 1966. 36.50 (ISBN 0-12-719450-9). Acad Pr.

Veselovsky, Zdenek, jt. auth. see Hanzak, Jan.

Vesely, Anton. Kawasaki KDX 80-420 Singles 1979-1981. Jorgensen, Eric, ed. (Illus.). 200p. (Orig.). 1981. pap. 10.95 (ISBN 0-89287-338-8, M446). Clymer Pubns.

--Kawasaki KX 80-450 Piston Port 1974-1981. Jorgensen, Eric, ed. (Illus.). 216p. (Orig.). 1981. pap. text ed. 10.95 (ISBN 0-89287-337-X, M445). Clymer Pubns.

--Kawasaki KZ500 & 550 Fours 1979-1981 Service Repair Performance. Wauson, Sydnie A., ed. (Illus.). 268p. (Orig.). 1982. pap. 10.95 (ISBN 0-89287-363-9). Clymer Pubns.

Vesely, Anton & Wauson, Sydnie. Kawasaki Jet Ski 1976-1981 Service-Repair-Maintenance. (Illus.). 164p. (Orig.). 1982. pap. 10.95 (ISBN 0-89287-354-X, X956). Clymer Pubns.
Vesentini, E., jt. auth. see Franzoni, T.
Veseth, Michael. Introductory Macroeconomics. 432p. 1981. 13.75 (ISBN 0-12-719552-1). Acad Pr.
Veseth, Michael, ed. Introductory Economics. LC 80-617. 1981. 21.00 (ISBN 0-12-719565-3). Acad Pr.
Vesey, Caulean. Write Your Way to Success with the Paragraph System. (Illus.). 206p. (Orig.). 1982. pap. 9.95 (ISBN 0-9609582-0-7). Excel Pr.
Vesey, Godfrey, ed. Impressions of Empiricism: Royal Institute of Philosophy Lectures, 1974-75, Vol. 9. LC 75-37030. 256p. 1976. 23.00 (ISBN 0-312-41055-7). St Martin.
--Understanding Wittgenstein. LC 74-75012. (Royal Institute of Philosophy Lectures, 1972-73 Ser.: Vol. 7). 288p. 1974. 22.50 (ISBN 0-312-83230-3). St Martin.
Vesiland, P., et al. Unit Operations in Resource Recovery Engineering. (Illus.). 1980. text ed. 34.95 (ISBN 0-13-937953-3). P-H.
Vesilind, P. Aarne. Environmental Engineering. LC 81-70872. 1982. 29.95 (ISBN 0-250-40422-2). Ann Arbor Science.
--Treatment & Disposal Wastewater Sludges. rev. ed. LC 78-71431. (Illus.). 1979. 39.95 (ISBN 0-250-40290-4). Ann Arbor Science.
Vesilind, P. Aarne & Minear, Roger A. Register of Environmental Engineering Graduate Programs. LC 81-65712. 1000p. 1981. text ed. 49.95 (ISBN 0-250-40461-3). Ann Arbor Science.
Vesilind, P. Aarne & Peirce, Jeffrey J. Environmental Pollution & Control. LC 82-48648. (Illus.). 375p. Date not set. pap. 14.95 (ISBN 0-250-40619-5). Ann Arbor Science.
Vesilind, P. Aarne, ed. see Klee, Albert J.
Vesme, Alexandre De see Massar, Phyllis D. & De Vesme, Alexandre.
Vesper, Karl H., ed. Frontiers of Entrepreneurship Research: 1982. 634p. 1982. pap. 25.00 (ISBN 0-910897-02-6). Babson College.
Vessa, Al. Classroom Guitar, 4 vols. Vessa, Virginia, ed. (Illus., 40p ea.). 1972-75. pap. text ed. 1.68 ea. (ISBN 0-915816-18-0). Vol. 1 (ISBN 0-915816-15-6). Vol. 2 (ISBN 0-915816-16-4). Vol. 3 (ISBN 0-915816-17-2). Vol. 4. Coast Pubns NY.
--Melody & Chord Guitar, 5 phases. Vessa, Virginia, ed. (Illus., 48p ea.). 1972. pap. text ed. 1.98 ea.; Phase 1. (ISBN 0-915816-05-9); Phase 2. (ISBN 0-915816-06-7); Phase 3. (ISBN 0-915816-07-5); Phase 4. (ISBN 0-915816-08-3); Phase 5. (ISBN 0-915816-09-1). Coast Pubns NY.
Vessa, Virginia, ed. see Vessa, Al.
Vest, Charles M. Holographic Interferometry. LC 78-14883. (Wiley Series in Pure & Applied Optics). 1979. 46.95x (ISBN 0-471-90683-2, Pub. by Wiley-Interscience). Wiley.
Vestal, Katherine W. Pediatric Critical Care Nursing. LC 80-22913. 450p. 1981. 24.50 (ISBN 0-471-05674-X, Pub. by Wiley Med). Wiley.
Vestal, R. E., ed. Drug Therapy in the Elderly. 300p. 1982. text ed. write for info. (ISBN 0-86792-008-4, Pub by Adis Pr Australia). Wright-PSG.
Vestal, Stanley. The Missouri. LC 44-5196. (Illus.). viii, 368p. 1964. pap. 9.95 (ISBN 0-8032-5207-2, BB 186, Bison). U of Nebr Pr.
--Short Grass Country. Repr. of 1941 ed. lib. bdg. 15.00 o.p. (ISBN 0-8371-2978-8, VESG). Greenwood.
Vestal, Stanley, ed. see Seger, John H.
Vested, I. M. The Confidential Memos of I. M. Vested. LC 82-60688. 208p. 1983. pap. 2.95 (ISBN 0-86721-231-4). Playboy Pbks.
Vestergaard, K., jt. auth. see Foelsch, D.
Vestermark, Mary J., jt. auth. see Johnson, Dorothy E.
Vetter, H., jt. ed. see Belcher, E. H.
Vetter, Harold J. Language Behavior & Communication: An Introduction. LC 68-57969. 1969. text ed. 12.50 (ISBN 0-87581-012-8). Peacock Pubs.
Vetter, Harold J., jt. auth. see Smith, Barry D.
Vetter, J. L., ed. Adding Nutrients to Foods: Where Do We Go from Here? LC 81-71373. 152p. 1982. pap. text ed. 20.00 (ISBN 0-913250-25-2). Am Assn Cereal Chem.
Vetter, Klaus J. Electrochemical Kinetics Theoretical Aspects. 1967. 63.50 (ISBN 0-12-720250-1). Acad Pr.
Vetter, M. & Maddison, R. Data Base Design Methodology. 1980. 32.95 (ISBN 0-13-196535-2). P-H.
Vetterli, Richard. Orrin Hatch: Challenging the Washington Establishment. LC 82-61024. (Illus.). 204p. 1982. 10.95 (ISBN 0-89526-629-6). Regnery-Gateway.
Vetterling-Braggin, Mary, ed. Femininity, Masculinity, & Androgyny: A Modern Philosophical Discussion. LC 81-19365. (Quality Paperback: No. 399). 336p. (Orig.). 1982. pap. text ed. 8.95 (ISBN 0-8226-0399-3). Littlefield.
--Femininity", "Masculinity", & "Androgyny". A Modern Philosophical Discussion. 336p. 1982. text ed. 22.50x (ISBN 0-8476-7070-8). Rowman.
Vetterling-Braggin, Mary, et al, eds. Feminism & Philosophy. (Quality Paperback Ser: No. 335). 1977. pap. 8.95 (ISBN 0-8226-0335-7). Littlefield.
--Sexist Language: A Modern Philosophical Analysis. LC 80-26263. 342p. 1981. 15.00x (ISBN 0-8476-6293-4). Rowman.
Vettorazzi, G., ed. International Regulatory Aspects for Pesticide Chemicals, Vol. II. 256p. 1982. 77.00 (ISBN 0-8493-5608-3). CRC Pr.
Vettorazzi, Gaston. Handbook of International Food Regulatory Toxicology, 2 vols. Incl. Vol. 1: Evaluations. 176p. 1980 (ISBN 0-89335-086-9); Vol. 2: Profiles. 256p. 1981. text ed. 30.00 ea. Spectrum Pub.
Vevers, Gwynne. Animal Colors. (Studies in Biology: No. 146). 64p. 1982. pap. text ed. 8.95 (ISBN 0-7131-2858-5). E Arnold.
--Birds & Their Nests. new ed. LC 72-11452. (Illus.). 32p. (gr. 3-7). 1973. PLB 5.72 o.p. (ISBN 0-07-067414-0, GB). McGraw.
--Fishes. LC 75-26667. (Illus.). 48p. (gr. 4-9). 1976. PLB 6.95 o.p. (ISBN 0-07-067420-5, GB). McGraw.
--Octopus, Cuttlefish & Squid. LC 77-25083. (New Biology Ser.). (Illus.). 1978. 7.95 (ISBN 0-07-067405-1, GB). McGraw.
Vevers, Gwynne, tr. see Brunner, Gerhard.
Vevers, Gwynne, tr. see Jocher, Willy.
Vevers, Gwynne, tr. see Wachtel, Hellmuth.
Vevers, Gwynne, tr. see Wickler, Wolfgang.
Vexler, R. I. Idaho Chronology & Factbook, Vol. 12. LC 78-6092. (Chronologies & Documentary Handbook of the States). 141p. 1978. 8.50 (ISBN 0-379-16137-0). Oceana.
--Illinois Chronology & Factbook, Vol. 13. LC 78-6661. (Chronologies & Documentary Handbook of the States). 145p. 1978. 8.50 (ISBN 0-379-16138-9). Oceana.
--Indiana Chronology & Factbook, Vol. 14. LC 78-6941. (Chronologies & Documentary Handbook of the States). 149p. 1978. 8.50 (ISBN 0-379-16139-7). Oceana.
--Iowa Chronology & Factbook, Vol. 15. LC 78-6076. (Chronologies & Documentary Handbook of the States). 145p. 1978. 8.50 (ISBN 0-379-16140-0). Oceana.
--Kansas Chronology & Factbook, Vol. 16. LC 78-6554. (Chronologies & Documentary Handbook of the States). 145p. 1978. 8.50 (ISBN 0-379-16141-9). Oceana.
--Kentucky Chronology & Factbook, Vol. 17. LC 78-6667. (Chronologies & Documentary Handbook of the States). 145p. 1978. 8.50 (ISBN 0-379-16142-7). Oceana.
--Louisiana Chronology & Factbook, Vol. 18. LC 78-6086. (Chronologies & Documentary Handbook of the States). 145p. 1978. 8.50 (ISBN 0-379-16143-5). Oceana.
--Maine Chronology & Factbook. LC 78-6942. (Chronologies & Documentary Handbook of the States). 141p. 1978. 8.50 (ISBN 0-379-16144-3). Oceana.
--Maryland Chronology & Factbook, Vol. 20. LC 78-6558. (Chronologies & Documentary Handbook of the States). 147p. 1978. 8.50 (ISBN 0-379-16145-1). Oceana.
--New Mexico Chronology & Factbook, Vol. 31. LC 78-64403. (Chronologies & Documentary Handbook of the States). 148p. 1978. 8.50 (ISBN 0-379-16156-7). Oceana.
--North Carolina Chronology & Factbook, Vol. 33. LC 78-64405. (Chronologies & Documentary Handbook of the States). 151p. 1978. 8.50 (ISBN 0-379-16158-3). Oceana.
--North Dakota Chronology & Factbook, Vol. 34. LC 78-64411. (Chronologies & Documentary Handbook of the States). 148p. 1978. 8.50 (ISBN 0-379-16159-1). Oceana.
--Ohio Chronology & Factbook, Vol. 35. LC 78-64407. (Chronologies & Documentary Handbook of the States). 151p. 1978. 8.50 (ISBN 0-379-16160-5). Oceana.
--Oklahoma Chronology & Factbook, Vol. 36. LC 78-26885. (Chronologies & Documentary Handbook of the States). 146p. 1978. 8.50 (ISBN 0-379-16161-3). Oceana.
--Oregon Chronology & Factbook, Vol. 37. LC 78-25839. (Chronologies & Documentary Handbook of the States). 146p. 1978. 8.50 (ISBN 0-379-16162-1). Oceana.
--Pennsylvania Chronology & Factbook, Vol. 38. LC 78-21054. (Chronologies & Documentary Handbook of the States). 149p. 1978. 8.50 (ISBN 0-379-16163-X). Oceana.
--Rhode Island Chronology & Factbook, Vol. 39. LC 78-26348. (Chronologies & Documentary Handbook of the States). 150p. 1978. 8.50 (ISBN 0-379-16164-8). Oceana.
--South Carolina Chronology & Factbook, Vol. 40. LC 78-26305. (Chronologies & Documentary Handbook of the States). 147p. 1978. 8.50 (ISBN 0-379-16165-6). Oceana.
--South Dakota Chronology & Factbook, Vol. 41. LC 78-26887. (Chronologies & Documentary Handbook of the States). 148p. 1978. 8.50 (ISBN 0-379-16166-4). Oceana.
--Tennessee Chronology & Factbook, Vol. 42. LC 78-26261. (Chronologies & Documentary Handbook of the States). 145p. 1978. 8.50 (ISBN 0-379-16167-2). Oceana.
--Texas Chronology & Factbook, Vol. 43. LC 78-26888. (Chronologies & Documentary Handbook of the States). 152p. 1978. 8.50 (ISBN 0-379-16168-0). Oceana.
--Utah Chronology & Factbook, Vol. 44. LC 78-21310. (Chronologies & Documentary Handbook of the States). 148p. 1978. 8.50 (ISBN 0-379-16169-9). Oceana.
--Vermont Chronology & Factbook. LC 78-26322. (Chronologies & Documentary Handbook of the States). 148p. 1978. 8.50 (ISBN 0-379-16170-2). Oceana.
--Washington Chronology & Factbook, Vol. 47. LC 78-26886. (Chronologies & Documentary Handbook of the States). 151p. 1978. 8.50 (ISBN 0-379-16172-9). Oceana.
--West Virginia Chronology & Factbook, Vol. 48. LC 78-21049. (Chronologies & Documentary Handbook of the States). 150p. 1978. 8.50 (ISBN 0-379-16173-7). Oceana.
--Wyoming Chronology & Factbook, Vol. 50. LC 78-26251. (Chronologies & Documentary Handbook of the States). 150p. 1978. 8.50 (ISBN 0-379-16189-3). Oceana.
Vexler, Robert I. Chronologies & Documentary Handbooks of the States. Swindler, William F., ed. Incl. Massachusetts. LC 78-15807 (ISBN 0-379-16146-X); Michigan. LC 78-15754 (ISBN 0-379-16147-8); Minnesota. LC 78-15236 (ISBN 0-379-16148-6); Mississippi. LC 78-16013 (ISBN 0-379-16149-4); Missouri. LC 78-16072 (ISBN 0-379-16150-8); Montana. LC 78-16163 (ISBN 0-379-16151-6); Nebraska. LC 78-16164 (ISBN 0-379-16152-4); Nevada. LC 78-16166 (ISBN 0-379-16153-2); New Hampshire. LC 78-16165 (ISBN 0-379-16154-0); New Jersey. LC 78-15751 (ISBN 0-379-16155-9). (gr. 9-12). 1978. 7.50 ea. Oceana.
--England 1485-1973: A Chronology & Fact Book. LC 73-17607. (World Chronology Ser.). 186p. 1974. lib. bdg. 8.50x (ISBN 0-379-16306-3). Oceana.
--France Fifteen Eighty-Nine to Nineteen Seventy-Four: A Chronology & Fact Book. LC 75-34433. (World Chronology Ser.). 183p. 1977. 8.50x. Oceana.
--Germany Fourteen Fifteen to Nineteen Seventy-Two: A Chronology & Fact Book. LC 73-7792. (World Chronology Ser.). 184p. 1973. lib. bdg. 8.50x (ISBN 0-379-16305-5). Oceana.
--Scandinavia, Denmark, Norway, Sweden 1319-1974: A Chronology & Fact Book. LC 76-37538. (World Chronology Ser.). 185p. 1977. 8.50x (ISBN 0-379-16314-4). Oceana.
--The Vice-Presidents & Cabinet Members: Biographical Sketches Arranged Chronologically by Administration, 2 vols. LC 75-28085. 1975. text ed. 60.00 set (ISBN 0-686-96824-7); Vol. 1. text ed. (ISBN 0-379-12089-5); Vol. 2. text ed. (ISBN 0-379-12090-9). Oceana.
Veys, jt. auth. see Verbruggen.
Vezda, A., jt. auth. see Poelt, J.
Vezeris, Olga, ed. see Bell, Terrel H.
Vezey, V., tr. see Trofimov, V.
Veziroglu, T. N., ed. see World Hydrogen Energy Conference, Fourth.
Veziroglu, T. Nejat, ed. Alternative Energy Sources IV, 8 vols. Incl. Vol. 1. Solar Collectors-Storage. 1982 (ISBN 0-250-40554-7); Vol 2. Solar Heating-Cooling-Desalination. 1982 (ISBN 0-250-40555-5); Vol. 3. Solar Power-Applications-Alcohols. 1982 (ISBN 0-250-40556-3); Vol. 4. Indirect Solar-Wind-Geothermal. 1982 (ISBN 0-250-40557-1); Vol. 5. Nuclear-Hydrogen-Biogas. 1982 (ISBN 0-250-40558-X); Vol. 6. Hydrocarbon Technology-Environment. 1982 (ISBN 0-250-40559-8); Vol. 7. Energy Conservation-Management-Education. 1982 (ISBN 0-250-40560-1); Vol. 8. Energy Programs-Policy-Economics. 1982 (ISBN 0-250-40561-X). LC 82-71533. (Illus.). Set. 510.00 (ISBN 0-250-40553-9); 85.00 ea. Ann Arbor Science.
--Energy Conservation: Proceedings of the Energy Research & Development Administration Conference Held at the University of Miami, Dec. 1975. 1977. pap. text ed. 120.00 (ISBN 0-08-022134-3). Pergamon.
--Remote Sensing: Energy Related Studies. LC 75-23018. 491p. 1975. 39.50x o.s.i. (ISBN 0-470-90665-0). Halsted Pr.
--Solar Energy: International Progress: Proceedings of the International Symposium-Workshop on Solar Energy, 16-22 June 1978, Cairo, Egypt, 4 vols. 355.00 (ISBN 0-08-025077-7); pap. 200.00 o.p. (ISBN 0-08-025078-5). Pergamon.
--Thermal Sciences Sixteen: Proceedings of the Sixteenth Southeastern Seminar, 2 Vols. (Illus.). 1983. Set. 195.00 (ISBN 0-89116-319-0). Hemisphere Pub.
Veziroglu, T. Nejat, ed. see International Conference on Alternative Energy Sources, 3rd, Miami Beach, 1980.
Vezmer, G. Nueva Enciclopedia Medica. 820p. (Span.). 1980. leather 95.00 (ISBN 0-686-97434-4, S-34777). French & Eur.
Via, Dan O. The Time It Is: A Play About Jesus. LC 82-45056. 106p. (Orig.). 1982. PLB 17.75 (ISBN 0-8191-2483-4); pap. text ed. 6.25 (ISBN 0-8191-2484-2). U Pr of Amer.
Via, Mariano F. La see Hill, Rol la B. & La Via, Mariano F.
Via, Richard A. English in Three Acts. (Culture Learning Institute Monographs). 220p. 1976. pap. text ed. 5.95x (ISBN 0-8248-0380-9, Eastwest Ctr). UH Pr.
Vialls, Christine. The Industrial Revolution Begins. LC 81-13714. (Cambridge Topic Bks.). (Illus.). 52p. (gr. 6 up). 1982. PLB 6.95g (ISBN 0-8225-1223-8). Lerner Pubns.
Viamonte, M., jt. auth. see Wilkins, R. A.
Vian, Boris. The Empire Builders. Taylor, Simon W., tr. (Illus.). 1967. pap. 2.95 o.s.i. (ISBN 0-394-17344-9, E414, Ever). Grove.
Viana, Luis D., jt. auth. see Diaz, Joaquin.
Vianello, Gianni, ed. Pubblicita in Italia, 1977-1978: Advertising in Italy. LC 77-72963. (Illus.). 1978. 30.00 (ISBN 0-910158-36-3). Art Dir.
Viano, Emilio C., ed. Victims & Society. 2nd ed. LC 76-11949. 1980. pap. text ed. 16.50x (ISBN 0-916965-46-5). Visage Pr.
Viatte, Francoise, jt. auth. see Bacou, Roseline.
Viatte, Francoise, jt. auth. see Goguel, Catherine M.
Vicari, Andrew. The Bedouin. (Illus.). 128p. 1983. 50.00 (ISBN 0-7103-0028-X, Kegan Paul). Routledge & Kegan.
Vicente, Jesus, et al, eds. Clinical Oncology: The Foundations of Current Patient Management. LC 80-80729. (Cancer Management Series: Vol. 4). (Illus.). 224p. 1980. 45.75x (ISBN 0-89352-083-7). Masson Pub.
Vichas, Robert P. New Encyclopedia Dictionary of Systems & Procedures. LC 82-11275. 680p. 1983. 65.00 (ISBN 0-13-612705-3, Busn). P-H.
Vichenevetsky, Robert. Computer Methods for Partial Differential Equations: Elliptical Equations & the Finite Element Method, Vol. 1. (Illus.). 400p. 1981. text ed. 32.95 (ISBN 0-13-165233-8). P-H.
Vichnevetsky, R. & Bowles, J. B. Fourier Analysis of Numerical Approximations of Hyperbolic Equations. LC 81-85699. (SIAM Studies in Applied Mathematics: No. 5). xii, 140p. 1982. 21.50 (ISBN 0-89871-181-9). Soc Indus Appl Math.
Vick, Ann, ed. The Cama-I Book. LC 82-45127. (Illus.). 416p. 1983. 19.95 (ISBN 0-385-15522-0, Anchor Pr); pap. 9.95 (ISBN 0-385-15212-4, Anch). Doubleday.
Vick, Marie & Cox, Rosann M. A Collection of Dances for Children. 1970. wallet 10.95x (ISBN 0-8087-2207-7). Burgess.
Vicker, Denise. God, Let Me Out of This Marriage. LC 80-83459. 160p. 1981. pap. 4.95 (ISBN 0-89221-080-X). New Leaf.
Vickerman, R. W. Spatial Economic Behavior: The Microeconomic Foundations of Urban & Transport Economics. LC 79-25872. 200p. 1980. 26.00x (ISBN 0-312-75022-6). St Martin.
Vickers, B. W., ed. see Hooker, Richard.
Vickers, Betty & Vincent, Bill. Swimming. (Exploring Sports Ser.). 1983. pap. write for info (ISBN 0-697-09977-6). Wm C Brown.
Vickers, Brian. Francis Bacon & Renaissance Prose. LC 68-22664. (Illus.). 1968. 57.50 (ISBN 0-521-06709-X, X). Cambridge U Pr.
--Rhetoric Revalued: Papers from the International Society for the History of Rhetoric. 288p. 1983. 16.00 (ISBN 0-86698-020-2). Medieval & Renaissance NY.
Vickers, Hugo. Debrett's Book of the Royal Wedding. LC 80-54659. (Illus.). 176p. 1981. 19.95 o.p. (ISBN 0-670-60997-8, Studio). Viking Pr.
Vickers, James E. Coriolanus Notes: Bound with Timon of Athens Notes. (Orig.). 1981. pap. 2.50 (ISBN 0-8220-0012-1). Cliffs.
--Julius Caesar Notes. (Orig.). 1980. pap. 2.95 (ISBN 0-8220-0020-2). Cliffs.
Vickers, M. D., jt. ed. see Prys-Roberts, C.
Vickers, Michael, jt. auth. see Post, Kenneth.
Vickers, Ralph. Beyond Beginning BASIC. 300p. 1983. pap. 12.95 (ISBN 0-88056-126-2). Dilithium Pr.
Vickers, Roy. Department of Dead Ends: Fourteen Detective Stories. 1978. pap. 4.50 (ISBN 0-486-23669-2). Dover.
--The Sole Survivor & the Kynsard Affair. 192p. 1982. pap. 3.95 (ISBN 0-486-24433-4). Dover.
Vickers, Stephen, jt. auth. see Line, Maurice B.
Vickers, William T., jt. ed. see Hames, Raymond B.
Vickery, B. C. Classification & Indexing in Science. 3rd ed. 228p. 1975. 27.95 o.p. (ISBN 0-408-70662-7). Butterworth.
Vickery, D. M. Triage: Problem Oriented Sorting of Patients. (Illus.). 1976. pap. 17.95 o.p. (ISBN 0-87618-133-7). R J Brady.
Vickery, Olga W., jt. auth. see Hoffman, Frederick J.
Vickery, Walter N. Alexander Pushkin. (World Authors Ser.: 06052204x). lib. bdg. 12.95 (ISBN 0-8057-2726-4, Twayne). G K Hall.
Vickery, Walter N., jt. ed. see McLean, Hugh.
Vickets, Geoffrey. Responsibilities its Sources & Limits. (Systems Inquiry Ser.). 142p. (Orig.). 1980. pap. text ed. 8.95 (ISBN 0-686-36603-4). Intersystems Pubns.
Vickman, Thomas. Financial Officer's Manual & Guide. LC 82-15793. 400p. 1982. text ed. 89.50 (ISBN 0-87624-151-8). Inst Busn Plan.
Vico, Giambattista. Principi di Scienza Nuova d'Intorno alla Comune Natura delle Nazioni. (Linguistics, 13th-18th Centuries Ser.). 546p. (Ital.). 1974. Repr. of 1744 ed. lib. bdg. 134.50x o.p. (ISBN 0-8287-0858-4, 5056). Clearwater Pub.

Vicomterie De Saint-Sanson. Les Droits Du Peuple Sur L'assemblee Nationale. (Rousseauism, 1788-1797). 1978. Repr. lib. bdg. 62.00x o.p. (ISBN 0-8287-0859-2). Clearwater Pub.

Victor, Buzz, jt. auth. see Cornwell, Richard E.

Victor, Edward. Electricity. (Beginning Science Books). (Illus.). (gr. 2-4). 1967. 2.50 o.s.i. (ISBN 0-695-82166-0); PLB 3.39 o.s.i. (ISBN 0-695-42166-2). Follett.

--Friction. (Illus.). (gr. 2-4). 1961. 4.39 (ISBN 0-695-43205-2). Follett.

--Science for the Elementary School. 4th ed. (Illus.). 1980. text ed. 24.95x (ISBN 0-02-422900-8). Macmillan.

Victor, Jeffrey S. Human Sexuality: A Social Psychological Approach. (Sociology Ser.). 1980. pap. text ed. 18.95 (ISBN 0-13-447474-0). P-H.

Victor, Joan B. Shells Are Skeletons. LC 75-23258. (Let's Read & Find Out Science Book Ser.). (Illus.). (gr. k-3). 1977. 10.89 (ISBN 0-690-01038-9, TYC-J). Har-Row.

Victor, John. Everything You Always Wanted to Understand about Personal Computers: But Did Not Know How to Ask. 1982. pap. 9.95 (ISBN 0-686-81780-X); pap. 19.95 audio & cassette (ISBN 0-686-81781-8). Devin.

Victor, Kathleen. Captive Desire. 304p. 1982. pap. 2.95 (ISBN 0-86721-205-5). Playboy Pbks.

Victor, M., jt. auth. see Adams, R. D.

Victor, M., jt. auth. see Gardner, Thomas J.

Victor, Paul see Allen, W. S.

Victoria And Albert Museum & Bolingbroke, J. M. Carolian Fabrics Ser. (World's Heritage of Woven Fabrics). (Illus.). 1969. 22.50x (ISBN 0-87245-391-X). Textile Bk.

Victoria, British Columbia, jt. auth. see Provincial Archives.

Victoria, Pablo. Foundations of Economic Development: Intelligence vs. Capital. (Illus.). 128p. 1983. 7.50 (ISBN 0-682-49932-3). Exposition.

Victor-Rood, Juliette. Say It in Hungarian. (Say It In Ser.). (Illus.). 224p. (Orig.). 1983. pap. 2.95 (ISBN 0-486-24423-7). Dover.

Vida, Ginny, ed. Our Right to Love: A Lesbian Resource Book. LC 77-20184. 1978. 12.95 o.p. (ISBN 0-13-644401-6); pap. 10.95 (ISBN 0-13-644393-1). P-H.

Vida, Julius A. Chemistry & Pharmacology of Androgens & Anabolic Agents. 1969. 59.00 (ISBN 0-12-721850-5). Acad Pr.

Vidal, C. & Pacault, A., eds. Nonlinear Phenomena in Chemical Dynamics: Proceedings. (Springer Series in Synergetics: Vol. 12). (Illus.). 280p. 1982. 33.00 (ISBN 0-387-11294-4). Springer-Verlag.

Vidal, Gore. Creation. 1981. ltd. ed. 45.00 (ISBN 0-394-50015-6). Random.

--Julian. LC 64-15048. 1970. Repr. of 1964 ed. 3.95 o.s.i. (ISBN 0-394-60395-8, M395). Modern Lib.

--Julian. 1977. pap. 5.95 (ISBN 0-394-72101-2, Vin). Random.

--Messiah. 13.00 (ISBN 0-8398-2599-4, Gregg). G K Hall.

--The Second American Revolution. LC 82-40425. 288p. 1983. pap. 5.95 (ISBN 0-394-71379-6, Vin). Random.

--The Second American Revolution: And Other Essays, 1976-1982. 1982. 15.00 (ISBN 0-394-52265-6). Random.

Vidal, P. Non-Linear Sampled Data Systems - Exercises & Problems. (Information & Systems Theory Ser.). 112p. 1972. 32.00x (ISBN 0-677-30500-1). Gordon.

--Systems Echantillonnes Nonlineaires - Exercises et Problemes: Exercises et Problemes. (Theorie des Systemes Ser.). 124p. (Fr.). 1970. 35.00 (ISBN 0-677-50500-0). Gordon.

Vidal, Paul, tr. see Aikman, Lonnelle.

Vidali, Vittorio. Diary of the Twentieth Congress of the Communist Party of the Soviet Union. Cattonar, Nell & Elliot, A. M., trs. from Italian. 204p. (Orig.). 1983. pap. 8.95 (ISBN 0-88208-134-9). Lawrence Hill.

Vidal-Naquet, P., jt. auth. see Austin, M. M.

Vidaver, Doris & Sherry, Pearl A. Arch of a Circle. LC 82-79754. (Illus.). 143p. 1981. 7.95 (ISBN 0-8040-0807-8); pap. 3.95 (ISBN 0-8040-0808-6). Swallow.

Videback. Spleen in Health & Disease. 1983. 49.95 (ISBN 0-8151-9004-2). Year Bk Med.

Videla, E. Your First Goldfish. (Illus.). 32p. 1982. 3.95 (ISBN 0-87666-574-1, ST-002). TFH Pubns.

Videla, E., illus. Your First Aquarium. (Illus.). 32p. 1982. 3.95 (ISBN 0-87666-548-2, ST001). TFH Pubns.

--Your First Budgie. (Illus.). 32p. 3.95 (ISBN 0-87666-868-6, ST-003). TFH Pubns.

Vider, Manuel. Mind & Heart in Verse. LC 78-51264. 1979. 4.50 o.p. (ISBN 0-533-03606-2). Vantage.

Vidger, Leonard V. Borrowing & Lending on Residential Property: Fundamentals for Homeowners, Investors, & Students. LC 77-9996. (Illus.). 304p. 1981. 25.95x (ISBN 0-669-01643-8). Lexington Bks.

Vidler, A. R. Soundings: Essays Concerning Christian Understanding. 1962. 39.50 (ISBN 0-521-06710-3); pap. 11.95x (ISBN 0-521-09373-2). Cambridge U Pr.

--Variety of Catholic Modernists. (Sarum Lectures in the University of Oxford for the Year 1968-69). 1970. 39.50 (ISBN 0-521-07649-8). Cambridge U Pr.

Vidmer, Richard, jt. auth. see Thompson, James C.

Vido, Alfredo De see De Vido, Alfredo.

Vidyarthi. The Tribal Culture of India. Date not set. text ed. price not set (ISBN 0-391-01167-7). Humanities.

Vidyarthi, L. P. The Rise of Anthropology in India: A Social Science Orientation, 2 vols. Incl. Vol. I. The Tribal Dimensions; Vol. II. The Rural Urban & Other Dimensions. 1979. Set. 42.00x (ISBN 0-391-01086-7). Humanities.

--Rise of World Anthropology. 180p. 1979. text ed. 10.00x (ISBN 0-391-01784-5). Humanities.

--The Sacred Complex in Hindu Gaya. 2nd ed. 264p. 1980. pap. text ed. 11.75x (ISBN 0-391-02214-8). Humanities.

--The Sacred Complex of Kashi. 1979. text ed. 18.25x (ISBN 0-391-01856-6). Humanities.

--Trends in World Anthropology. 112p. 1979. text ed. 9.00x (ISBN 0-391-01783-7). Humanities.

Vidyarthi, L. P. & Upadhyay, V. S. The Kharia: Then & Now. 296p. 1980. text ed. 16.00x (ISBN 0-391-01838-8, Pub. by Concept India). Humanities.

Vidyarthi, L. P., ed. Tribal Development & Its Administration. 388p. 1981. text ed. 13.00x (ISBN 0-391-02281-4, Pub. by Concept India). Humanities.

Vidyarthi, L. P., et al. Changing Dietary Patterns & Habits. 1979. text ed. 15.75x (ISBN 0-391-01928-7). Humanities.

Vidyarthi, R. B. Early Indian Religious Thought. LC 76-904388. 1976. 13.50x o.p. (ISBN 0-88386-874-1). South Asia Bks.

Vidyasagar, M., jt. auth. see Desoer, C. A.

Vidyasagar, M., jt. ed. see Aggarwal, J. K.

Vidyasagara, Isvarchandra & Podder, Arabinda. Marriage of Hindu Widows. LC 76-900930. 1975. 8.00x o.p. (ISBN 0-88386-738-9). South Asia Bks.

Vieg, J., jt. auth. see Turner, Henry.

Vieg, John A. Progress Versus Utopia. 5.75x o.p. (ISBN 0-210-27035-7). Asia.

Viega-Pires, ed. Intervention Radiology. (International Congress Ser.: Vol. 522). 1981. 79.75 (ISBN 0-444-90165-5). Elsevier.

Viegas, Leslie A. The Feasibility of Contracting Separately for Data Collection in a Revalution Project. (Lincoln Institute Monograph: No. 77-5). 1977. pap. 1.50 o.p. (ISBN 0-686-20035-7). Lincoln Inst Land.

Viehe, H. G., jt. auth. see Bohme, H.

Viehe, H. G., ed. Chemistry of Acetylenes. 1969. 135.00 o.p. (ISBN 0-8247-1675-2). Dekker.

Viehe, H. G., jt. ed. see Bohme, H.

Vieira, Nelson H., tr. see Santareno, Bernardo.

Viemeister, Peter. Microcars. (Illus.). 136p. (Orig.). (gr. 4 up). 1982. pap. 8.95 (ISBN 0-9608598-0-2). Hamiltons.

Vienna Institute for Comparative Economic Studies, ed. COMECON Foreign Trade Data 1981. LC 82-47960. 455p. 1982. lib. bdg. 45.00 (ISBN 0-313-23629-1, VI481). Greenwood.

Vienne', Augustus. The Power of Auto-Suggestion & How to Master it for the Energizing of One's Life. (Illus.). 121p. 1983. 39.75 (ISBN 0-89920-053-2). Am Inst Psych.

Vierck, Charles J., jt. auth. see French, Thomas E.

Viereck, George S. & Eldridge, Paul. My First Two Thousand Years. 1983. price not set (ISBN 0-911378-16-2). Sheridan.

Viereck, Peter R. Conservatism: From John Adams to Churchill. LC 78-827. 1978. Repr. of 1956 ed. lib. bdg. 19.00x (ISBN 0-313-20263-X, VICO). Greenwood.

--Conservatism Revisited: With the Addition of "The New Conservatism-What Went Wrong". rev. enl. ed. LC 78-831. 1978. Repr. of 1962 ed. lib. bdg. 19.25x (ISBN 0-313-20299-0, VICR). Greenwood.

Vierke, Jorg. Dwarf Cichlids. Ahrens, Christa, tr. from Ger. (Illus.). 1979. 4.95 (ISBN 0-87666-509-1, KW-005). TFH Pubns.

Viersma, T. J. Analysis Synthesis & Design Hydraulic Servosystem & Pipelines. (Studies in Mechanical Engineering: Vol. 1). 1980. 61.75 (ISBN 0-444-41869-5). Elsevier.

Viertel, Arthur T. Trees, Shrubs, & Vines: A Pictorial Guide to the Ornamental Woody Plants of the Northern United States, Exclusive of Conifers. (Illus.). 1970. pap. 7.95x (ISBN 0-8156-0068-2). Syracuse U Pr.

Viertel, John, tr. see Habermas, Jurgen.

Viertel, Joyce, ed. see Graves, William W.

Viertel, Weldon. La Biblia y su Interpretacion. Orig. Title: The Bible & Its Interpretation. 208p. Date not set. pap. write for info. (ISBN 0-311-03670-8). Casa Bautista.

Viertel, Weldon, ed. see Graves, William W.

Viete, Francois. The Analytic Art. Witmer, T. Richard, tr. from Fr. & Lat. LC 82-21381. (Illus.). 300p. 1983. 45.00X (ISBN 0-87338-282-X). Kent St U Pr.

Vieth, W. R., et al, eds. Biochemical Engineering. (Annals of the New York Academy of Sciences: Vol. 326). (Orig.). 1979. pap. 57.00x (ISBN 0-89766-020-X). NY Acad Sci.

Vietor, Jack. Time Out. 208p. 1982. 13.95 (ISBN 0-8168-9025-0). Aero.

Vietor, Joan E., jt. auth. see Singleton, Ralph S.

Vieux, Jacques. The One Night Girl. 65p. (Orig.). 1980. pap. 2.95 o.p. (ISBN 0-89260-184-1). Hwong Pub.

Vigdorchik, Michael. Submarine Permafrost on the Alaskan Continental Shelf. (Westview Special Studies in Earth Science). 1979. lib. bdg. 26.00 (ISBN 0-89158-659-8). Westview.

Vigdorchik, Michael & Ives, Jack. Arctic Pleistocene History & the Development of Submarine Permafrost. LC 79-13561. (Westview Special Studies in Earth Science). 286p. 1980. lib. bdg. 39.00 (ISBN 0-89158-658-X). Westview.

Vigersky, Robert A. Anorexia Nervosa. LC 76-57005. 408p. 1977. 34.50 (ISBN 0-89004-185-7). Raven.

Vigfusson, Robin. Expensive Habits. LC 82-60689. 288p. 1983. pap. 3.25 (ISBN 0-86721-232-2). Playboy Pbks.

Vigier, Francois. Change & Apathy: Liverpool & Manchester During the Industrial Revolution. (Illus.). 1970. 17.50x (ISBN 0-262-22012-1). MIT Pr.

Vigil, Constance C. Fallow Land. 5.00 o.p. (ISBN 0-685-47523-9). Branden.

Vigil, James D. From Indians to Chicanos: A Sociocultural History. LC 80-18539. (Illus.). 245p. pap. text ed. 15.50 (ISBN 0-8016-5230-8). Mosby.

Vigil, Maurilio. Chicano Politics. 1977. pap. text ed. 11.75 (ISBN 0-8191-0110-9). U Pr of Amer.

--Los Patrones: Profiles of Hispanic Political Leaders in New Mexico History. LC 79-6813. 179p. 1980. 20.00 (ISBN 0-8191-0962-2); pap. 9.50 (ISBN 0-8191-0963-0). U Pr of Amer.

Viglielmo, V. H., tr. see Nishida, Kitaro.

Viglielmo, V. H., tr. see Soseki, Natsume.

Viglino, Giovanni. Intermediate Algebra. 1980. text ed. 23.95x (ISBN 0-02-423000-6). Macmillan.

Vigman, Fred K. Beauty's Triumph. 1966. 4.00 o.p. (ISBN 0-8158-0204-8). Chris Mass.

--Fateful Subversion of the American Economy. 1971. 6.50 o.p. (ISBN 0-8158-0256-0). Chris Mass.

--Winding Down & Selling Out the United States, the Course of an Historical Self-Destruct. 250p. 1973. 6.50 o.p. (ISBN 0-8158-0308-7). Chris Mass.

Vigna, Judith. Daddy's New Baby. (Concept Books). (gr. k-4). 8.25 (ISBN 0-686-36215-2). Whitman Pub.

Vignes, Jacques. The Rage to Survive. Voukitchevitch, Mihailo, tr. LC 75-23312. (Illus.). 1976. 6.95 o.p. (ISBN 0-688-02992-2). Morrow.

Vigny, Alfred De see De Vigny, Alfred.

Vigor, P. H. Soviet Blitzkrieg Theory. LC 82-10421. 200p. 1983. 22.50x (ISBN 0-312-74755-1). St Martin.

Vigorelli, Giancarlo see Marchione, Margherita & Scalia, S. Eugene.

Vigram, George V. The Englishman's Greek Concordance of the New Testament. rev. ed. 1982. pap. 29.95 (ISBN 0-8054-1388-X). Broadman.

Vikan, Gary. Byzantine Pilgrimage Art. (Byzantine Collection Publications Ser.: No. 5). (Illus.). 52p. 1982. pap. 4.50x (ISBN 0-88402-113-0). Dumbarton Oaks.

Viksnins, George J. Financial Deepening in the ASEAN Counties. 96p. (Orig.). 1980. pap. 7.50x (ISBN 0-8248-0745-6). UH Pr.

Viladas, Joseph M. The Book of Survey Techniques. LC 82-90995. 278p. 1982. write for info. three-ring binder (ISBN 0-911397-00-0). Havemeyer Bks.

Vilain, Raymond & Michon, Jacques. Plastic Surgery of the Hand & Pulp. LC 78-61477. (Illus.). 184p. 1979. 36.00 (ISBN 0-89352-037-3). Masson Pub.

Vilakazi, Absolom L., et al. Africa's Rough Road: Problems of Change & Development. 1977. pap. text ed. 11.00 (ISBN 0-8191-0113-3). U Pr of Amer.

Vilar, Pierre. A History of Gold & Money 1450-1920. (Illus.). 1976. 21.00 o.p. (ISBN 0-902308-18-1, Pub. by NLB). Schocken.

--Spain: A Brief History. 2nd ed. 1977. text ed. 16.50 o.p. (ISBN 0-08-021462-2); pap. text ed. 6.25 (ISBN 0-08-021461-4). Pergamon.

Vilas, Charles H. Saga of Direction. (Illus.). 1978. 12.95 (ISBN 0-915160-20-X). Seven Seas.

Vilazon. Critical Care Medicine. (International Congress Ser.: No. 499). 1979. 21.50 (ISBN 0-444-90107-8). Elsevier.

Vilcek, Jan, et al, eds. Regulatory Functions of Interferons, Vol. 350. LC 80-25207. (Annals of the New York Academy of Sciences). 641p. 1980. 126.00x (ISBN 0-89766-089-7); pap. 126.00x (ISBN 0-89766-090-0). NY Acad Sci.

Vile, Richard. Apple II Programmer's Handbook. (Illus.). 276p. 1982. 24.95 (ISBN 0-13-039206-5); pap. 16.95 (ISBN 0-13-039198-0). P-H.

Vilenkin, N. Y. Combinatorics. 1971. 42.00 (ISBN 0-12-721940-4). Acad Pr.

Vilhjalmsson, Thor. The Deep Blue Sea: Pardon the Ocean. 57p. 1981. pap. 6.00 (ISBN 0-910477-01-9). LoonBooks.

Vill, V. I. Friction Welding of Metals. (Eng.). 1962. 18.00 (ISBN 0-685-65943-7). Am Welding.

Villa, Leo & Gray, Tony. Record Breakers: Sir Malcolm & Donald Campbell Land & Water Speed Kings of the 20th Century. 1971. 9.50 o.p. (ISBN 0-685-04861-6). Transatlantic.

Villa, Susie H. One Hundred Armenian Tales. 602p. 1982. 19.95 (ISBN 0-8143-1282-9); pap. 11.95 (ISBN 0-8143-1736-7). Wayne St U Pr.

Villa, Susie H. & Matossian, Mary K. Armenian Village Life Before 1914. (Illus.). 220p. 1982. 15.95X (ISBN 0-686-87029-8). Wayne St U Pr.

Villadsen, John & Michelson, Michael. Solution of Differential Equation Models for Polynomial Approximation. LC 77-4331. (Illus.). 1977. 37.95 (ISBN 0-13-822205-3). P-H.

Villagran, M. C. Vegetationsgeschichtliche und Pflanzensoziologische Untersuchungen Im Vicente Perez Nationalpark: Chile. (Dissertationes Botanicae: No. 54). (Illus.). 166p. (Ger.). 1981. pap. text ed. 20.00x (ISBN 3-7682-1265-3). Lubrecht & Cramer.

Villa Havelin, Jim La see La Villa Hauelin, Jim.

Villalobos, Fernando, tr. see Bergey, Alyce.

Villani, Jim & Sayre, Rose, eds. Science Fiction. (Pig Iron Ser.: No. 10). (Illus.). 96p. (Orig.). 1982. pap. 5.95 (ISBN 0-917530-18-7). Pig Iron Pr.

--Surrealism. (Pig Iron Ser.: No. 11). (Illus.). 96p. (Orig.). 1983. pap. text ed. 5.95 (ISBN 0-917530-19-5). Pig Iron pr.

Villani, Kevin, jt. ed. see Tuccillo, John.

Villano, Caesar. Food Service Management & Control: The Profitable Approach. (Orig.). 1977. 19.95 (ISBN 0-86730-210-0). Lebhar Friedman.

Villanucci, Robert & Avtgis, Alexander. Electronic Shop Fabrication: A Basic Course. (Illus.). 272p. 1982. 18.95 (ISBN 0-13-251959-3). P-H.

Villanueva, Aggie, jt. auth. see Lawrence, Deborah.

Villard, Fanny G., ed. William Lloyd Garrison on Nonresistance Together with a Personal Sketch by His Daughter and a Tribute by Leo Tolstoi. LC 74-137556. (Peace Movement in America Ser). xii, 79p. 1972. Repr. of 1924 ed. lib. bdg. 9.95x (ISBN 0-89198-087-3). Ozer.

Villard, Kenneth L. & Whipple, Leland. Beginnings in Relational Communication. LC 75-33845. 275p. 1976. pap. text ed. 18.95x o.p. (ISBN 0-673-15728-8). Scott F.

Villareal, Ruben L. Tomatoes in the Tropics. (IADS Development-Oriented Ser.). 200p. 1980. lib. bdg. 25.00 (ISBN 0-89158-989-9). Westview.

Villarello, Ildefonso, tr. see Dana, H. E.

Villarello, Ildefonso, tr. see Olson, Natanael.

Villari, Luigi. Italian Foreign Policy Under Mussolini. 1956. 8.00 (ISBN 0-8159-5820-X). Devin.

Villarreal, Herman. Hypertension. LC 81-4952. (Perspectives in Nephrology & Hypertension Ser.). 320p. 1981. 42.95 (ISBN 0-471-07900-6, Pub. by Wiley Med). Wiley.

Villars, Elizabeth. The Normandie Affair. LC 81-43727. 336p. 1982. 15.95 (ISBN 0-385-17652-X). Doubleday.

--The Rich Girl. LC 77-5347. 1977. 9.95 o.p. (ISBN 0-698-10786-1, Coward). Putnam Pub Group.

--The Very Best People. LC 78-26160. 1979. 9.95 o.p. (ISBN 0-698-10980-5, Coward). Putnam Pub Group.

Villasenor, Emma Z., tr. see Eudaly, Maria S. De.

Villasenor, Laura, tr. see De Oca, Marco A.

Villasenor, Laura, tr. see Montes De Oca, Marco A.

Villauet, Nicolas. Relation des Cotes d'Afrique Appelees Guinee: Avec la Description du Pays, Moeurs et Facons de Vivre des Habitants, des Productions de la Terre et des Marchandises Qu'On en Apporte, avec les Remarques Historiques sur les Cotes. (Bibliotheque Africaine Ser.). 460p. (Fr.). 1974. Repr. of 1969 ed. lib. bdg. 115.00 o.p. (ISBN 0-8287-0862-2, 72-2108). Clearwater Pub.

Villazon, ed. Critical Care Medicine: Proceedings, 1979. (International Congress Ser.: Vol. 503). 1981. 58.50 (ISBN 0-444-90128-0). Elsevier.

Villee, Claude A., et al, eds. Respiratory Distress Syndrome: Based on a Conference at Dedham, Mass.,May,1973. 1973. 42.00 (ISBN 0-12-722350-9). Acad Pr.

Villee, Dorothy B. Human Endocrinology: A Developmental Approach. LC 73-91280. (Illus.). 479p. 1975. 20.00 o.p. (ISBN 0-7216-9041-6). Saunders.

Villegas, Joseph E. Brazil As a Model for Developing Countries. LC 78-68605. 1979. 5.95 o.p. (ISBN 0-533-04176-7). Vantage.

Villella, Joseph A. The Hospitality Industry-the World of Food Service. (Illus.). 352p. 1975. text ed. 21.95 (ISBN 0-07-067450-7, G); instructor's manual & key 4.50 (ISBN 0-07-067451-5). McGraw.

Villemain. Tableau de l'Etat Actuel de l'Instruction Primaire en France. (Conditions of the 19th Century French Working Class Ser.). 116p. (Fr.). 1974. Repr. of 1841 ed. lib. bdg. 39.00x o.p. (ISBN 0-8287-0863-0, 1110). Clearwater Pub.

Villeneuve, N. De. Le Voyager Philosophe dans un Pais Inconnu aux Habitants de la Terre, 2 vols. (Utopias in the Enlightenment Ser.). 753p. (Fr.). 1974. Repr. of 1761 ed. Set. lib. bdg. 193.00x o.p. (ISBN 0-8287-0864-9). Vol. 1 (034). Vol. 2 (035). Clearwater Pub.

Villeneuve-Bargemont, Alban De see De Villeneuve-Bargemont, Alban.

Villere, Sidney L. Jacques Philippe Villere, First Native Born Governor of Louisiana: 1816-1820. LC 82-112474. (Illus.). 1981. 10.00x (ISBN 0-917860-06-3). Historic New Orleans.

Villerme, Louis-Rene. Des Associations Ouvrieres. (Conditions of the 19th Century French Working Class Ser.). 104p. 1974. Repr. of 1849 ed. lib. bdg. 36.00 o.p. (ISBN 0-8287-0866-5, 1101). Clearwater Pub.

--Des Prisons. (Conditions of the 19th Century French Working Class Ser.). 203p. (Fr.). 1974. Repr. of 1820 ed. lib. bdg. 58.00x o.p. (ISBN 0-8287-0867-3, 1098). Clearwater Pub.
--Sur les Cites Ouvrieres. (Conditions of the 19th Century French Working Class Ser.). 32p. (Fr.). 1974. Repr. of 1850 ed. lib. bdg. 23.50x o.p. (ISBN 0-8287-0868-1, 1111). Clearwater Pub.
--Tableau de l'Etat Physique et Moral des Ouvriers Employes dans les Manufactures de Cotton, de Laine et ! De Soie, 2 vols. (Conditions of the 19th Century French Working Class Ser.). 455p. 1974. Repr. of 1840 ed. lib. bdg. 249.75x o.p. (ISBN 0-8287-0869-X, 1060-1). Clearwater Pub.
Villers, M., et al. Lexique de Prevention des Accidents. 137p. (Eng. & Fr.). 1980. pap. 4.95 (ISBN 0-686-97398-4, M-9225). French & Eur.
Villet, Barbara. Blood River: The Passionate Saga of South Africa's Afrikaners & of Life in Their Embattled Land. (Illus.). 320p. 1982. 16.95 (ISBN 0-89696-034-X, An Everest House Book). Dodd.
Villette, Ch. De. Memoires et Anecdotes, Pour Servir a L'histoire De M. De Voltaire. Repr. of 1779 ed. 35.00 o.p. (ISBN 0-8287-0870-3). Clearwater Pub.
Villette, Charles-Michel. Protestation D'un Serf Du Mont-Jura, Contre L'assemblee Des Notables. Repr. of 1789 ed. 5.00 o.p. (ISBN 0-8287-0871-1). Clearwater Pub.
Villiard, Paul. Collecting Stamps. LC 73-10950. 208p. (gr. 5-7). 1974. PLB 8.95 o.p. (ISBN 0-385-08677-6). Doubleday.
Villiers. Dormancy & the Survival of Plants. (Studies in Biology: No. 57). 72p. 1975. pap. text ed. 8.95 (ISBN 0-7131-2517-9). E Arnold.
Villiers, Arnold. Routledge's Complete Letter Writer: For Ladies & Gentlemen in Society, in Love & in Business. rev. ed. 1965. pap. 3.00 o.p. (ISBN 0-7100-2238-7). Routledge & Kegan.
Villiers, George. The Rehearsal, Sixteen Seventy-One. Arber, EDward, ed. 132p. pap. 15.00 (ISBN 0-87556-342-2). Saifer.
Villiers, Gerard De see De Villiers, Gerard.
Villiers, Guy. The British Heavy Horse. (Illus.). 1978. 12.00 o.p. (ISBN 0-214-20095-7). Transatlantic.
Villiers de l'Isle Adam. Tomorrow's Eve. Adams, Robert M., tr. & intro. by. LC 82-13411. 280p. 1982. 17.95 (ISBN 0-252-00942-8). U of Ill Pr.
Villiers du Terrage, Marc de see De Villiers du Terrage, Marc.
Villines, W., jt. auth. see Hickey, H.
Villines, William M., Jr., jt. auth. see Hickey, Henry V.
Villiod, Eugene. How They Cheat You at Cards. Barnhart, Russell, tr. from Fr. LC 77-20642. (Illus.). 192p. 1979. pap. 4.95 (ISBN 0-89650-750-5). Gamblers.
Villoldo, Alberto, jt. auth. see Krippner, Stanley.
Villon, Francois. Book of Francois Villon: The Little Testament & Ballads. Swinburne, Algeron C., et al, trs. pap. 2.50 international pocket library (ISBN 0-8283-1425-X). Branden.
Villot, Rhondi. Her Secret Self. (Sweet Dreams Ser.: No. 25). 1982. pap. 1.95 (ISBN 0-553-22543-X). Bantam.
Vilmorin-Andrieux, MM. The Vegetable Garden. LC 81-50300. 620p. 1981. pap. 11.95 (ISBN 0-89815-041-8). Ten Speed Pr.
Vilnay, Zev. Guide to Israel, 1981. 21st, rev. ed. LC 66-33490. (Illus.). 662p. 1980. 10.00x o.p. (ISBN 0-8002-2854-5). Intl Pubns Serv.
--Legends of Judaea & Samaria. new ed. LC 74-22895. (The Sacred Land Ser.: Vol. 2). (Illus.). 328p. 1976. 7.50 o.p. (ISBN 0-8276-0064-X, 371). Jewish Pubn.
Vilquin, Jean-Claude, jt. ed. see Issacharoff, Michael.
Vinacke, W. Edgar. The Psychology of Thinking. 2nd ed. 640p. 1974. text ed. 34.95 (ISBN 0-07-067486-8, C). McGraw.
Vinal, George W. Storage Batteries. 4th ed. LC 54-12826. 1955. 43.95x (ISBN 0-471-90816-9, Pub. by Wiley-Interscience). Wiley.
Vinaver, Eugene, ed. see Malory, Thomas.
Vinaver, Martin. La Vida De los Novios: The Life of Two Sweethearts. (Illus.). 128p. 4.00 (ISBN 0-912528-05-2). John Muir.
Vinayshil, Gautam, jt. ed. see Yadava, J. S.
Vincard, Pierre. Les Ouvriers de Paris: Alimentation. (Conditions of the 19th Century French Working Class Ser.). 381p. (Fr.). 1974. Repr. of 1863 ed. lib. bdg. 97.50x o.p. (ISBN 0-8287-0873-8, 1075). Clearwater Pub.
Vince, John. Old Farms: An Illustrated Guide. LC 82-10698. (Illus.). 160p. (Orig.). 1983. pap. 11.95 (ISBN 0-8052-0729-5). Schocken.
Vince, Michael. In the New District. 64p. 1982. pap. text ed. 7.00x (ISBN 0-85635-368-X, 80025, Pub. by Carcanet New Pr England). Humanities.
--The Orchard Well. (Poetry Ser.). 1979. pap. 4.95 o.p. (ISBN 0-85635-248-9, Pub. by Carcanet New Pr England). Humanities.
Vincelli, M., jt. ed. see Bologna, G.
Vincent, Alan. Molecular Symmetry & Group Theory: A Programmed Introduction to Chemical Application. LC 76-26095. 1977. pap. 24.95x o.p. (ISBN 0-471-01867-8); pap. 14.95x (ISBN 0-471-01868-6, Pub. by Wiley-Interscience). Wiley.
Vincent, Benjamin. A Dictionary of Biography: Past & Present, Containing the Chief Events in the Lives of Eminent Persons of All Ages & Nations. LC 77-174132. 641p. 1974. Repr. of 1877 ed. 68.00x (ISBN 0-8103-3983-8). Gale.
Vincent, Bill, jt. auth. see Vickers, Betty.
Vincent, Colin A., jt. ed. see Kertes.
Vincent, David, ed. Testaments of Radicalism: Memoirs of Working Class Politicians 1790-1885. LC 77-377253. 1977. 17.50x (ISBN 0-905118-01-4). Intl Pubns Serv.
Vincent, E. R., tr. see Abba, Giuseppe C.
Vincent, Harold. Sonship Training. 64p. (Orig.). 1980. pap. 1.50 o.p. (ISBN 0-89841-009-6). Zoe Pubns.
Vincent, J. M. Nitrogen Fixation in Legumes. 1982. 27.95 (ISBN 0-12-721980-3). Acad Pr.
Vincent, Jack E. Project Theory: Interpretations & Policy Relevance. LC 78-59172. 1978. pap. text ed. 12.50 (ISBN 0-8191-0551-1). U Pr of Amer.
--Understanding International Relations. 1978. pap. text ed. 16.00 (ISBN 0-8191-0538-4). U Pr of Amer.
Vincent, Joan. A Bond of Honor. (Orig.). 1980. pap. 1.50 o.s.i. (ISBN 0-440-10858-6). Dell.
--The Curious Rogue. (Orig.). 1981. pap. 1.50 o.s.i. (ISBN 0-440-11186-2). Dell.
--The Education of Joanne. 1980. pap. 1.50 o.s.i. (ISBN 0-440-12303-8). Dell.
--Rescued by Love. (Orig.). 1981. pap. 1.50 o.s.i. (ISBN 0-440-17433-3). Dell.
--A Scheme for Love. (Orig.). 1980. pap. 1.50 o.s.i. (ISBN 0-440-18387-1). Dell.
--Teso in Transformation: Peasantry & Class in Colonial Uganda, 1890-1927. LC 80-28813. 320p. 1982. 28.50x (ISBN 0-520-04163-1). U of Cal Pr.
--Thomasina. (Orig.). 1980. pap. 1.50 o.s.i. (ISBN 0-440-18844-X). Dell.
Vincent, John M. Costume & Conduct in the Laws of Basel, Bern & Zurich, 1370-1800. Repr. of 1935 ed. lib. bdg. 18.50x (ISBN 0-8371-2363-1, VILB). Greenwood.
Vincent, John P., ed. Advances in Family Intervention, Assessment & Theory, Vol. 1. (Orig.). 1980. lib. bdg. 40.00 (ISBN 0-89232-137-7). Jai Pr.
--Advances in Family Intervention Assessment & Theory, Vol. 2. 300p. 1981. 40.00 (ISBN 0-89232-192-X). Jai Pr.
Vincent, M. O. God, Sex & You. (Trumpet Bks). 1976. pap. 1.75 o.p. (ISBN 0-87981-058-0). Holman.
--God, Sex & You. 1976. pap. 1.75 o.s.i. (ISBN 0-89129-191-1). Jove Pubns.
Vincent, Marvin. Word Studies in the New Testament, 4 Vols. 1957. 49.95 (ISBN 0-8028-8083-5). Eerdmans.
Vincent, Monica. A Woman's Place? (Longman Structural Readers Ser.: Stage 4). 1982. pap. 1.75x (ISBN 0-582-52410-5). Longman.
Vincent, Monica see Allen, W. S.
Vincent, Nigel & Harris, Martin, eds. Studies in the Romance Verb: Essays Offered to Joe Cremona on the Occasion of His 60th Birthday. 250p. 1982. text ed. 32.00 (ISBN 0-7099-2602-2, Pub. by Croom Helm Ltd England). Biblio Dist.
Vincent, Theodore G., ed. Voices of a Black Nation: Political Journalism in the Harlem Renaissance. LC 72-85094. 1973. 10.00 (ISBN 0-87867-034-3); pap. 4.95 o.p. (ISBN 0-87867-035-1). Ramparts.
Vincent, Thomas L. & Grantham, Walter J. Optimality in Parametric Systems. LC 81-1870. 243p. 1981. 34.50x (ISBN 0-471-08307-0, Pub. by Wiley-Interscience). Wiley.
Vincenti, W. G. & Kruger, C. H. Introduction to Physical Gas Dynamics. LC 75-5806. 556p. 1975. Repr. of 1965 ed. 33.50 (ISBN 0-88275-309-6). Krieger.
Vincenti, Walter G., jt. auth. see Rosenberg, Nathan.
Vincenzi, Frank F., jt. ed. see Watterson, D. Martin.
Vince-Prue, Daphne. Photoperiodism in Plants. (European Biology Ser). 424p. 1975. text ed. 49.95 (ISBN 0-07-084048-2, C). McGraw.
Vinci, Leonardo Da see Da Vinci, Leonardo.
Vinck, Catherine De see De Vinck, Catherine.
Vinck, Jose De see De Vinck, Jose.
Vinck, Jose De see Raya, Joseph & De Vinck, Jose.
Vincze, I., jt. auth. see Sarkadi, K.
Vine, Louis D. Your Dog, His Health & Happiness: The Breeder's & Pet Owners Guide to Better Dog Care. LC 72-88607. 446p. 1973. pap. 4.95 o.p. (ISBN 0-668-02876-9). Arco.
Vine, Louis L. Breeding, Whelping & Natal Care of Dogs. LC 77-1817. 1977. 6.95 (ISBN 0-668-04152-8); pap. 2.50 (ISBN 0-668-04160-9). Arco.
Vine, Victor T. Le see Le Vine, Victor T.
Viner, Jacob. The Customs Union Issue. 1950. 10.00 (ISBN 0-910136-01-7). Anderson Kramer.
Vines, Harriet M., jt. auth. see Austin, Margaret F.
Vines, Jerry. I Shall Return: Jesus. 1977. pap. 3.95 (ISBN 0-88207-702-3). Victor Bks.
--Interviews with Jesus. LC 80-69241. 1981. 3.95 (ISBN 0-8054-5180-3). Broadman.
Vines, Robert A. Trees of East Texas. (Illus.). 556p. 1977. text ed. 0.00 o.p.; pap. 9.95 (ISBN 0-292-78017-6). U of Tex Pr.
Vines, Robert F., jt. ed. see Carter, William C.
Vines, Sherard. Course of English Classicism: From the Tudor to the Victorian Age. LC 70-91351. 1969. Repr. of 1930 ed. 8.50x (ISBN 0-87753-041-6). Phaeton.
Viney, Elliott & Nightingale, Pamela. Old Aylesbury. 100p. 1982. 25.00x (ISBN 0-900804-21-1, Pub. by White Crescent England). State Mutual Bk.
Viney, Linda L. Images of Illness. 256p. 1983. text ed. 17.50 (ISBN 0-89874-612-4). Krieger.
Viney, N. J., jt. auth. see Bailey, J. C.
Viney, Wayne, et al, eds. The History of Psychology: A Guide to Information Sources. LC 79-9044. (Psychology Information Guide Ser.: Vol. 1). 1979. 42.00x (ISBN 0-8103-1442-8). Gale.
Vineyard, Ben S., jt. auth. see Kimbrell, Grady.
Vineyard, Sue. Beyond Banquets, Plaques & Pins: Creative Ways to Recognize Volunteers & Staff. 2nd ed. (Illus.). 24p. 1981. pap. text ed. 3.50 (ISBN 0-911029-01-X). Heritage Arts.
--Finding Your Way Through the Maze of Volunteer Management. (Illus.). 68p. (Orig.). 1981. pap. text ed. 4.95 (ISBN 0-911029-00-1). Heritage Arts.
Vinge, Joan. Outcasts of Heavens Belt. 1982. pap. 2.50 (ISBN 0-451-11653-4, AE1653, Sig). NAL.
Vinge, Joan D. Return of the Jedi. LC 82-20538. (Movie Storybooks). (Illus.). 64p. (gr. 3-8). 1983. PLB 7.99 (ISBN 0-394-95624-9); pap. 6.95 (ISBN 0-394-85624-4). Random.
Vinge, Vernor see Martin, George R.
Vingoe, Frank J. Clinical Psychology & Medicine: An Interdisciplnary Approach. (Illus.). 1981. text ed. 45.00x (ISBN 0-19-261219-0). Oxford U Pr.
Vinh, N. X. Optimal Trajectories in Atmospheric Flight. (Studies in Astronautics: Vol. 2). 1982. 85.00 (ISBN 0-444-41961-6). Elsevier.
Vining, Elizabeth G. Flora: A Biography. LC 66-12343. (Illus.). 1966. 4.95i (ISBN 0-397-00427-3). Har-Row.
--Windows for the Crown Prince: An American Woman's Four Years As Private Tutor to the Crown Prince of Japan. (Illus.). (gr. 7-9). 1952. 11.06i (ISBN 0-397-00037-5). Har-Row.
Vinken, P. J. & Bruyn, G. W., eds. Handbook of Clinical Neurology, Vol. 42: Neurogenetic Directory, Pt. 1. 1981. 172.50 (ISBN 0-7204-7242-3, North-Holland). Elsevier.
Vinnichenko, N. K. & Gorelik, A. G., eds. Advances in Satellite Meteorology, Vol. 2. Levi, M., tr. from Rus. 1974. text ed. 33.95 o.s.i. (ISBN 0-470-90836-X). Halsted Pr.
Vinogradov, A. P. & Udintsev, G. B., eds. The Rift Zones of the World Oceans. Kaner, N., tr. from Rus. LC 75-16178. 503p. 1975. 89.95 o.s.i. (ISBN 0-470-90838-6). Halsted Pr.
Vinogradov, V. V. Vinogradov: History of the Russian Literary Language from the 17th to the 19th Centuries. LC 69-16108. 304p. 1969. 20.00x o.p. (ISBN 0-299-05260-5). U of Wis Pr.
Vinogradov, Vladimir A., jt. ed. see Van der Wee, Hermann.
Vinokur, G. O. Russian Language: A Brief History. Forsyth, J., ed. LC 70-127238. (Illus.). 1971. 29.95 (ISBN 0-521-07944-6). Cambridge U Pr.
Vinokurov, Evgeny. The War Is Over. Rudolf, Anthony & Weissbort, Daniel, trs. from Rus. (Translation Ser.). 1979. 7.95 o.p. (ISBN 0-902145-39-8, Pub. by Carcanet New Pr England). Humanities.
Vinoly, Alberto, ed. Pequeno diccionario de sinonimos, ideas afines y contrarios. (Span.). 1979. pap. 7.95 (ISBN 8-4307-7052-6). Larousse.
Vinovskis, Maris A., ed. Studies in American Historical Demography. LC 78-25611. (Studies in Population Ser.). 1979. Repr. 19.50 (ISBN 0-12-722050-X). Acad Pr.
Vinovskis, Maris A., jt. ed. see Schneider, Carl.
Vinsant, Marielle & Spence, Martha I. Commonsense Approach to Coronary Care: A Program. 3rd ed. LC 80-36795. 350p. 1981. pap. text ed. 16.95 (ISBN 0-8016-5235-9). Mosby.
Vinson, Jack R. & Chou, Tsu-Wei. Composite Materials & Their Use in Structures. (Illus.). xii, 438p. 1974. 71.75 (ISBN 0-85334-593-7, Pub. by Applied Sci England). Elsevier.
Vinson, James, ed. Contemporary Novelists of the English Language. 1500p. 1972. 30.00x o.p. (ISBN 0-312-16730-X, C47100). St Martin.
Vinson, James & Kirkpatrick, D. L., eds. Twentieth-Century Romance & Gothic Writers. 898p. 1982. 75.00x (ISBN 0-8103-0226-8, Pub. by Macmillan England). Gale.
--Twentieth-Century Western Writers. 1000p. 1983. 75.00x (ISBN 0-8103-0227-6, Pub. by Macmillan England). Gale.
Vinson, James & Kirkpatrick, Daniel, eds. Contemporary Dramatists. 3rd ed. LC 82-22994. 1024p. 1982. 55.00x (ISBN 0-312-16664-8). St Martin.
Vinson, Jim & Kirkpatrick, Daniel, eds. Contemporary Poets. 3rd ed. (Contemporary Writers Ser.). 1900p. 1980. lib. bdg. 60.00x (ISBN 0-312-16835-7). St Martin.
Vintage Image, et al. Central Coast Wine Tour. 112p. 1983. pap. 3.95 (ISBN 0-932664-33-4). Wine Appreciation.
--Sonoma-Mendocino Wine Tour. 112p. 1983. pap. 3.95 (ISBN 0-932664-32-6). Wine Appreciation.
Vinter, R. B., jt. auth. see Aubin, J. P.
Vinton, Dearing see Dryden, John.
Vinton, Dearing A. see Dryden, John.
Vinton, Iris. Look Out for Pirates. LC 61-7790. (Illus.). (gr. 1-2). 1961. PLB 5.99 (ISBN 0-394-90022-7). Beginner.
Vinton, Jean, jt. ed. see Manning, William.
Vinycomb, John. Fictitious & Symbolic Creatures in Art with Special Reference to Their Use in British Heraldry. LC 76-89300. (Illus.). 1969. Repr. of 1906 ed. 34.00x (ISBN 0-8103-3147-0). Gale.
Vinz, Mark & Ray, Grayce, eds. Dakota Territory: A Ten Year Anthology. 147p. 1982. pap. 9.75 (ISBN 0-911042-26-1). N Dak Inst.
Viola, Herman J. The Indian Legacy of Charles Bird King. LC 76-15022. (Illus.). 162p. 1981. Repr. of 1976 ed. 25.00 (ISBN 0-87474-943-3, 82-87724). Ohio U Pr.
--Thomas L. McKenney: Architect of America's Early Indian Policy, 1816-1830. LC 82-73666. (Illus.). 365p. 1974. 15.00 (ISBN 0-8040-0668-7). Swallow.
Viola, Jerome. Painting & Teaching of Philip Pearlstein. (Illus.). 168p. (Orig.). 1982. 29.95 (ISBN 0-8230-3862-9). Watson-Guptill.
Violette, Paul E. Shelling in the Sea of Cortez. LC 64-8861. (Illus., Orig.). 1964. 6.50 (ISBN 0-912762-13-6); pap. 2.50 (ISBN 0-912762-12-8). King.
Violi, Paul. Splurge. LC 81-8911. 81p. (Orig.). 1982. pap. 5.00 (ISBN 0-915342-35-9). SUN.
Viorst, Judith. How Did I Get to Be Forty... & Other Atrocities. 1976. 8.95 (ISBN 0-671-22366-6). S&S.
--It's Hard to Be Hip Over Thirty & Other Tragedies of Married Life. 1980. 4.95 o.p. (ISBN 0-453-00276-5, H276). NAL.
--Love & Guilt & the Meaning of Life, Etc. 1979. 5.95 o.p. (ISBN 0-671-22869-2). S&S.
--People & Other Aggravations. 112p. 1973. pap. 1.50 (ISBN 0-451-11366-7, AW1366, Sig). NAL.
--The Village Square. (Illus.). 1967. pap. 2.95 o.p. (ISBN 0-698-10481-1, Coward). Putnam Pub Group.
Viorst, Judith & Lober, Arnold. I'll Fix Anthony. (ps-3). 1983. pap. 2.95 (ISBN 0-689-70761-4, A-137, Aladdin). Atheneum.
Viorst, Milton. Fire in the Streets: America in the Nineteen Sixties. 1981. pap. 10.75 (ISBN 0-671-42814-4, Touchstone Bks). S&S.
Viosinet, D., jt. auth. see Jensen, C.
Viotti, R., jt. ed. see Friedjung, M.
Virbila, Sherry. Cooks' Marketplace: San Francisco Bay Area Sourcebook. LC 82-7839. (Illus.). 276p. (Orig.). pap. 8.95 (ISBN 0-89286-198-3). One Hund One Prods.
Virbila, Sherry, ed. see Sousanis, Marti E.
Virga, Patricia H. The American Opera to 1790. Buelow, George, ed. LC 82-15950. (Studies in Musicology: No. 61). 414p. 1982. 49.95 (ISBN 0-8357-1374-1). Univ Microfilms.
Virga, Vincent. A Comfortable Corner. 1982. pap. 3.50 (ISBN 0-380-80895-1, 80895). Avon.
Virgil. Aeneid Book VIII. Gransden, K. W., ed. LC 76-12729. (Cambridge Greek & Latin Classics Ser.). (Illus.). 1976. 29.95 (ISBN 0-521-21113-1); pap. 11.50 (ISBN 0-521-29047-3). Cambridge U Pr.
--The Aeneid of Virgil. Mandelbaum, Allan, tr. from Latin. (Bantam Classics Ser.). 416p. (gr. 9-12). 1981. pap. text ed. 2.95 (ISBN 0-553-21041-6). Bantam.
--The Aeneid of Virgil: A Verse Translation. Mandelbaum, Allen, tr. (Illus.). 1982. pap. 10.95 (ISBN 0-520-04550-5, CAL 566). U of Cal Pr.
--Appendix Vergiliana. Clausen, W. V., et al, eds. (Oxford Classical Texts Ser). 1966. 15.95x (ISBN 0-19-814648-5). Oxford U Pr.
--Bucolics et Georgica. Page, T. E., ed. Incl. Georgics. (Classical Ser.). 386p. (Lat.). 1969. text ed. 16.95 (ISBN 0-312-84910-9). St Martin.
--Ciris: A Poem Attributed to Virgil. Lyne, R. O., ed. LC 77-80845. (Classical Texts & Commentaries Ser.: No. 20). (Illus.). 1978. 65.00 (ISBN 0-521-21727-X). Cambridge U Pr.
--Eclogues. Coleman, Robert, ed. LC 76-16917. (Cambridge Greek & Latin Classics Ser.). 1977. 42.00 (ISBN 0-521-20082-2); pap. 13.95 (ISBN 0-521-29107-0). Cambridge U Pr.
--The Georgics. Wells, Robert, ed. 95p. 1982. text ed. 12.50x (ISBN 0-85635-338-8, 60776, Pub. by Carcanet New Pr England). Humanities.
--The Georgics. Wilkinson, L. P., tr. 1983. pap. 3.95 (ISBN 0-14-044414-9). Penguin.
--Opera, 2 vols. LC 75-27849. (Renaissance & the Gods Ser.: Vol. 7). (Illus.). 1977. Repr. of 1544 ed. Set. lib. bdg. 146.00 o.s.i. (ISBN 0-8240-2056-1); lib. bdg. 73.00 ea. o.s.i. Garland Pub.
--Selections from Aeneid II. Craddock, C. H., ed. (Cambridge Latin Texts Ser.). 1975. pap. 3.50 (ISBN 0-521-20827-0). Cambridge U Pr.
--Selections from Aeneid IV. (Cambridge Latin Texts Ser.). 1977. limp bdg 3.50 (ISBN 0-521-21581-1). Cambridge U Pr.
--Selections from Aeneid VI. Haward, Anne, ed. LC 82-12760. (Cambridge Latin Texts Ser.). 64p. Date not set. pap. 2.95 (ISBN 0-521-28694-8). Cambridge U Pr.
--Story of Camilla. Tilly, Bertha, ed. text ed. 5.50 (ISBN 0-521-06701-4). Cambridge U Pr.
--Virgil Selections from Aeneid VIII. Craddock, C. H., ed. (Cambridge Latin Texts Ser.). 48p. 1973. pap. 3.50 (ISBN 0-521-20280-9). Cambridge U Pr.
Virgil M. Hancher Auditorium, The University of Iowa. Entertaining Arts: Menus & Recipes from Performers & Patrons. LC 82-81567. (Illus.). 258p. 1982. spiral bdg. 14.70 (ISBN 0-941016-06-4). Penfield.

Virgin Books, ed. The Illustrated Book of Rock Records. (Illus.). 192p. (Orig.). 1982. pap. 5.95 (ISBN 0-933328-27-3). Delilah Bks.

Virgines, George. Western Legends & Lore. (Illus.). 128p. 1983. 12.95 (ISBN 0-686-81870-9); pap. 6.95 (ISBN 0-686-81871-7). Pine Mntn.

Virginia. Calendar of Virginia State Papers & Other Manuscripts Preserved in the Capitol at Richmond, 1652-1869, 11 Vols. 1875-1893. Set. 606.00 (ISBN 0-527-02388-4). Kraus Repr.

Virginia Association of Legal Secretaries. Handbook for Legal Secretaries in Virginia. 2nd ed. 364p. 1980. with 1977 suppl. o.p. 30.00 (ISBN 0-87215-174-3); suppl seperately 12.50 (ISBN 0-87215-267-7). Michie-Bobbs.

Virginia Historic Landmarks Commission. Historic American Buildings Survey, Virginia Catalog: A List of Measured Drawings, Photographs, & Written Documentation in the Survey. LC 74-7402. (Illus.). 461p. 1975. 14.95 (ISBN 0-8139-0518-4); pap. 7.95x (ISBN 0-8139-0708-X). U Pr of Va.

Virmani, Arvind. The Nature of Credit Markets in Less Developed Countries: A Framework for Policy Analysis. LC 82-11087. (World Bank Staff Working Papers: No. 524). (Orig.). 1982. pap. text ed. 5.00 (ISBN 0-8213-0019-9). World Bank.

Virmaux, Alain, ed. see Colette.

Virmaux, Odette, ed. see Colette.

Virta, Nikolai E. Alone. Shartse, O., tr. from Rus. LC 75-39018. (Soviet Literature in English Translation Ser.). (Illus.). 451p. Repr. of 1957 ed. cancelled o.p. (ISBN 0-88355-419-4). Hyperion-Conn.

Virtue Magazine, ed. Everyday Spice. 2nd ed. LC 82-81674. 142p. 1983. pap. cancelled (ISBN 0-89081-328-0). Harvest Hse.

Visaria, Pravin. Incidence of Poverty & the Characteristics of the Poor in Peninsular Malaysia, 1973. (Working Paper: No. 460). viii, 213p. 1981. 5.00 (ISBN 0-686-36044-3, WP-0460). World Bank.

--Size of Land Holding, Living Standards & Employment in Rural Western India, 1972-73. (Working Paper: No. 459). 117p. 1981. 5.00 (ISBN 0-686-36047-8, WP-0459). World Bank.

Viscardi, Henry, Jr. & Friedman, Irving M. A Study of Workmen's Compensation In Relation To Sheltered Workshops. 68p. 1971. 1.50 (ISBN 0-686-38807-0). Human Res Ctr.

Vischer, Lukas, ed. Growth In Agreement: Reports & Agreed Statements of Interconfessional Conversations at World Level. 1982. pap. 14.95 (ISBN 0-8091-2497-1). Paulist Pr.

Viscione, Jerry. Financial Analysis: Principles & Procedures. LC 76-13794. (Illus.). 1977. pap. text ed. 12.95 (ISBN 0-395-24455-2); instr's manual with solutions 1.65 (ISBN 0-395-24454-4). HM.

Viscione, Jerry & Aragon, George. Cases in Financial Management. LC 79-87854. 1980. text ed. 23.95 (ISBN 0-395-26715-3); instr's. manual 3.25 (ISBN 0-395-26716-1). HM.

Viscusi, Margo. Literacy for Working: Functional Literacy in Rural Tanzania. (Educational Studies & Documents, No. 5). (Illus.). 57p. (Orig.). 1972. pap. 2.50 o.p. (ISBN 92-3-100905-2, U360, UNESCO). Unipub.

Viscusi, W. Kip. Risk by Choice: Regulating Health & Safety in the Workplace. (Illus.). 216p. 1983. text ed. 18.50x (ISBN 0-674-77302-0). Harvard U Pr.

--Welfare of the Elderly: An Economic Analysis & Policy Prescription. LC 78-31223. (Urban Research Ser.). 1979. 31.95x (ISBN 0-471-01506-7, Pub. by Wiley-Interscience). Wiley.

Viscusi, W. Kip, jt. auth. see Berkman, Richard L.

Vishniac, Roman. Polish Jews: A Pictorial Record. LC 65-25413. (Illus.). 1968. 12.00 (ISBN 0-8052-3205-2); pap. 4.95 (ISBN 0-8052-0360-5). Schocken.

Vishniac, W., ed. see C.O.S.P.A.R., 11th Plenary Meeting, Tokyo, 1968.

Vishniac, W., ed. see C.O.S.P.A.R., 12th Meeting, Prague, 1969.

Vishwanathan, K. S. Many Electron Problem. 10.00x o.p. (ISBN 0-310-26904-0). Asia.

Visick, H. E. & Van Kleek, Peter E. Menu Planning: A Blueprint for Better Profits. (Illus.). 176p. 1973. pap. text ed. 11.95 (ISBN 0-07-067063-3, G). McGraw.

Visick, Mary. The Genesis of Wuthering Heights. 88p. 1982. Repr. of 1967 ed. lib. bdg. 40.00 (ISBN 0-89760-929-8). Telegraph Bks.

Visick, W. Pat see Senior, Patrick, pseud.

Visigli, R. El Gesticulador: Pieza Para Demagogos En Tres Actos. Ballinger, R., ed. (Span.). 1963. 11.95 (ISBN 0-13-273771-X). P-H.

Visitatio Organorum. Feestbundel voor Maarten Albert Vente, Aangeb. T.G.V.Z. 65e verjaardag, onder red. v. Albert Dunning, 2 vols. (Illus.). 675p. 87.50 o.s.i. (ISBN 90-6027-402-4, Pub. by Frits Knuf Netherlands); wrappers 70.00 o.s.i. (ISBN 90-6027-401-6, Pub. by Frits Knuf Netherlands). Pendragon NY.

Visiting Nurse Assoc. of New Haven, CT. Child Health Conference: Nurses' Resource Manual. (League Exchange Ser.: No. 101). 127p. 1975. 6.50 (ISBN 0-686-38202-1, 21-1502). Natl League Nurse.

Visiting Nurse Association, Inc., of Burlington, VT. The Problem-Oriented System in a Home Health Agency: A Training Manual. (League Exchange Ser.: No. 103). 127p. 1974. 5.95 (ISBN 0-686-38191-2, 21-1554). Natl League Nurse.

Viskochil, Karen, jt. ed. see Karni, Karen.

Visscher, Michel De see De Visscher, Michel.

Visse & Hanbery. Elements of Income Tax, 1981. 400p. 1981. pap. text ed. 14.95 o.p. (ISBN 0-8302-2435-1). Scott F.

Visser, David, ed. Theatre Facts Eighty. 68p. (Orig.). 1981. pap. 5.00 (ISBN 0-930452-17-8). Theatre Comm.

Visser, H. The Quanity of Money. LC 75-4762. 294p. 1974. 13.95 o.p. (ISBN 0-470-90845-9, Pub. by Wiley). Krieger.

--The Quantity of Money. LC 75-4762. 294p. 1975. text ed. 22.95x o.p. (ISBN 0-470-90845-9). Halsted Pr.

Visser, Vivien, tr. see Dulieu, Jean.

Visser't Hooft, W. A. The Fatherhood of God in an Age of Emancipation. LC 82-13404. 180p. 1983. pap. 7.95 (ISBN 0-664-24462-9). Westminster.

Visson, Lynn. A Complete Russian Cookbook: A Heritage Preserved. 400p. 1982. lib. bdg. 15.95 (ISBN 0-88233-788-2); pap. 10.00 o.p. (ISBN 0-88233-789-0). Ardis Pubs.

Vistnes, Lars M., et al. Plastic & Reconstructive Surgery. 2nd ed. Laub, Donald R. & Ott, Richard F., eds. (Medical Examination Review Ser.: Vol. 27). 1977. spiral bdg. 26.00 (ISBN 0-87488-129-3). Med Exam.

Viswanathan, M., jt. ed. see Podolsky, Stephen.

Viswanathan, S. The Shakespeare Play As Poem. LC 79-41618. 250p. 1980. 29.95 (ISBN 0-521-22547-7). Cambridge U Pr.

Vita, Vincent T. De see DeVita, Vincent T., Jr. & Hellman, Samuel.

Vita-Finzi, Claudio. Mediterranean Valleys: Geological Change in Historical Times. LC 69-10341. (Illus.). 1969. 34.50 (ISBN 0-521-07355-3). Cambridge U Pr.

Vital, Claude & Vallat, Jean M. Ultrastructural Study of the Human Diseased Peripheral Nerve. LC 80-81988. (Illus.). 200p. 1980. 40.50 (ISBN 0-89352-096-9). Masson Pub.

Vital, David. The Origins of Zionism. (Illus.). 1975. 14.95x (ISBN 0-19-827439-4); pap. 12.95x (ISBN 0-686-77121-4). Oxford U Pr.

Vital Issues Editor & Bradley, Bill. The Olympic Games: What's to Become of Them? (Vital Issues, Vol. XXIX 1979-80: No. 7). 0.50 (ISBN 0-686-81612-9). Ctr Info Am.

Vitale, Anthony J. Swahili Syntax. 260p. 1981. 36.00x (ISBN 0-686-33150-8); pap. 21.00x (ISBN 0-686-33151-6). Foris Pubns.

Vitale, B. Bibliography on Heavy Mesons & Hyperons. 1950. 17.00 (ISBN 0-7204-0069-4, North Holland). Elsevier.

Vitale, Frank. Individualized Fitness Programs. 1973. ref ed. 17.95 (ISBN 0-13-457002-2); pap. text ed. 12.95 (ISBN 0-13-456996-2). P-H.

Vitale, Philip. Basic Tools of Research. rev. ed. LC 74-8827. (gr. 9-12). 1979. pap. text ed. 3.50 (ISBN 0-8120-0627-5). Barron.

Vitarelli, Robert. Fun with Magic Tricks. (Elephant Bks.). (gr. 1-6). 1977. pap. 1.25 o.s.i. (ISBN 0-448-14452-2, G&D). Putnam Pub Group.

Vitek, Antonin V., jt. auth. see Horak, M.

Vitek, Donna K. Dangerous Embrace. (Candlelight Ecstasy Ser.: No. 136). (Orig.). 1983. pap. 1.95 (ISBN 0-440-12162-0). Dell.

Vitek, John D., jt. ed. see Coates, Donald R.

Viteles, Harry. A History of the Co-Operative Movement in Israel. Incl. Bk. 1. The Evolution of the Co-Operative Movement. 252p. 1966. o.p. (ISBN 0-85303-052-9); Bk. 2. The Evolution of the Kibbutz Movement. 749p. 1967. o.p. (ISBN 0-85303-053-7); Bk. 3. An Analysis of the Four Sectors of the Kibbutz Movement. 751p. 1968. o.p. (ISBN 0-85303-010-3); Bk. 4. Co-Operative Smallholders Settlements: The Moshav Movement. 405p. 1968. (ISBN 0-85303-012-X); Bk. 5. Workers Producers Transportation & Service Co-Operatives. 414p. 1968. (ISBN 0-85303-013-8); Bk. 6. Central Agricultural Co-Operatives. 750p. 1970. (ISBN 0-85303-031-6); Bk. 7. Consumers Co-Operative. 348p. 1970. (ISBN 0-85303-034-0); 140.00x set. 20.00x ea. (Pub. by Vallentine Mitchell England). Biblio Dist.

Vitelli, James R. Randolph Bourne. (United States Authors Ser.). 1981. lib. bdg. 13.95 (ISBN 0-8057-7337-1, Twayne). G K Hall.

--Van Wyck Brooks. (U. S. Authors Ser.: No. 134). 1969. lib. bdg. 10.95 o.p. (ISBN 0-8057-0096-X, Twayne). G K Hall.

--Van Wyck Brooks: A Reference Guide. 1977. lib. bdg. 13.95 (ISBN 0-8161-7978-6, Hall Reference). G K Hall.

Viterbi, A. Principles of Coherent Communication. (Systems Science Ser.). 1966. text ed. 39.50 (ISBN 0-07-067515-5, C). McGraw.

Viterbi, Andrew J. & Omura, James K. Principles of Digital Communication & Coding. (Electrical Engineering Ser.). (Illus.). 1979. text ed. 42.50 (ISBN 0-07-067516-3, C). McGraw.

Vitetta, Ellen S., ed. B & T Cell Tumors: Symposium. LC 82-13948. 583p. 1982. 52.00 (ISBN 0-12-722380-0). Acad Pr.

Vithoulkas, George. Homeopathy: Medicine of the New Man. LC 77-29272. 1979. lib. bdg. 7.95 o.p. (ISBN 0-668-04577-9, 4577); pap. 3.95 (ISBN 0-668-04581-7). Arco.

Vitis, A. A. De see De Vitis, A. A.

Vitkovitch, D. Experimental Methods of Field Analysis. 1966. 19.95x o.p. (ISBN 0-442-09032-3). Van Nos Reinhold.

Vitro Laboratories. Reliability & Maintainability of Solar System Components. (Progress in Solar Energy Ser.: Suppl.). 100p. 1983. pap. text ed. 10.50 (ISBN 0-89553-134-8). Am Solar Energy.

--Solar Energy Performance History Information Ser. Vol. 4, Performance of Active Solar Space Heating Systems, Comparitive Report; Vol. 5, Performance of Solar Hot Water Systems, Comaparitive Report; Vol. 6, Performance of Active Solar Space Cooling Systems, Comparitive Report. 610p. 1983. pap. 69.50 (ISBN 0-89934-200-0, H-045). Solar Energy Info.

Vitruvius. Ten Books on Architecture. Morgan, Morris H., tr. (Illus.). pap. text ed. 5.00 (ISBN 0-486-20645-9). Dover.

Vitry, Aubert De. & Philbert, Francois J. Rousseau a L'assemblee Nationale. (Rousseauism, 1788-1797). 1978. Repr. lib. bdg. 87.00x o.p. (ISBN 0-8287-0040-0). Clearwater Pub.

Vitt, Dale H. A Revision of the Genus Orthotricham in North America, North of Mexico. (Bryophytorum Bibliotheca: No. 1). (Illus.). 24.00 (ISBN 3-7682-0825-7). Lubrecht & Cramer.

Vitt, Joseph E., jt. auth. see Stout, Gary.

Vittitow, M. L. Christians Celebrate. pap. 5.50 (ISBN 0-87509-297-7). Chr Pubns.

Vittorini, Domenico. The Age of Dante. LC 75-10219. (Illus.). 188p. 1975. Repr. of 1957 ed. lib. bdg. 17.75x (ISBN 0-8371-8175-5, VIAD). Greenwood.

Vittorini, Elio. The Dark & the Light: Erica & la Garibaldina, Two Short Novels. Keene, Frances, tr. LC 77-23993. 1977. Repr. of 1961 ed. lib. bdg. 17.25x (ISBN 0-8371-9780-5, VIDL). Greenwood.

Vitulli, William F. Growth Squirt. 1979. 6.95 o.p. (ISBN 0-533-03767-0). Vantage.

Vivante, Paolo. The Epithets in Homer: A Study in Poetic Values. LC 82-4856. 224p. 1982. text ed. 22.00x (ISBN 0-300-02708-7). Yale U Pr.

--The Homeric Imagination: A Study of Homer's Poetic Perception of Reality. 215p. 1983. Repr. of 1970 ed. text ed. 22.50x (ISBN 0-8290-1296-6). Irvington.

Vivas. Fundamentos de Correspondencia Comercial. 1970. 5.45 (ISBN 0-07-067525-2, G). McGraw.

Vivekananda, Swami. Complete Works of Swami Vivekananda, 8 vols. pap. 55.00x (ISBN 0-87481-176-7). Vedanta Pr.

--In Search of God & Other Poems. pap. 3.75 (ISBN 0-87481-121-X). Vedanta Pr.

--Karma-Yoga & Bhakti-Yoga. LC 55-8657. 336p. 1982. pocket ed. 5.95 (ISBN 0-911206-07-8); pap. 5.95 large size (ISBN 0-911206-22-1). Ramakrishna.

--Letters of Swami Vivekananda. 2nd ed. 7.95 o.s.i. (ISBN 0-87481-093-0); pap. 6.75 o.s.i. (ISBN 0-87481-192-9). Vedanta Pr.

--Selections from Swami Vivekananda. 10.00x (ISBN 0-87481-094-9); pap. 6.95 (ISBN 0-87481-174-0). Vedanta Pr.

--Teachings of Swami Vivekananda. 1971. pap. 3.95 (ISBN 0-87481-134-1). Vedanta Pr.

Vivelo, Frank. The Hero of Western Botswana: Aspects of Change in a Group of Bantu-Speaking Cattle Herders. (AES Ser.). (Illus.). 1977. text ed. 23.95 (ISBN 0-8299-0057-8). West Pub.

Vivelo, Frank R. Cultural Anthropology Handbook. (Illus.). 1977. pap. text ed. 16.95 (ISBN 0-07-067530-9, C). McGraw.

Viveros-Long, Anamaria, jt. auth. see Bohen, Halcyone H.

Vives, Juan L. Vives, On Education: A Translation of the "De Tradendis Disciplinis" of Juan Luis Vives. 497p. 1971. Repr. of 1913 ed. 20.00x o.p. (ISBN 0-87471-009-X). Rowman.

Vivian, John. Wood Heat. new & improved ed. 1978. 12.95 (ISBN 0-87857-241-4); pap. 9.95 o.p. (ISBN 0-87857-242-2). Rodale Pr Inc.

Vivian, Katherine, tr. see Orbeliani, Sulkhan-Saba.

Vivian, V. Eugene, ed. see Dixon, Eustace A.

Vivien, Renee. The Muse of the Violets. Kroger, Catharine & Porter, Margaret, trs. LC 77-77988. 1982. 4.00 o.p. (ISBN 0-930044-07-X). Naiad Pr.

Vivo, G. Hugo. El Crecimiento de las Empresas en los Estados Unidos y en la America Latina: Un Estudio Comparativo. LC 81-70693. 121p. (Orig., Span.). 1982. pap. 9.95 (ISBN 0-89729-306-1). Ediciones.

Vixen, Richard M. Deep Foot. LC 77-79739. (Illus.). 1978. pap. 3.00 (ISBN 0-930182-02-2). Avant-Garde CR.

--Deeper Foot. LC 77-79740. (Illus.). 1978. pap. 3.00 (ISBN 0-930182-03-0). Avant-Garde CR.

--The Game of Orgy. LC 77-93805. (Illus.). 1978. pap. 2.95 (ISBN 0-930182-04-9). Avant-Garde CR.

--The Magic Carpet & the Cement Wall. LC 77-93804. (Illus.). (gr. 3-10). 1978. 8.75 (ISBN 0-930182-06-5); pap. 5.50 (ISBN 0-930182-05-7). Avant-Garde CR.

Vixman, Rachel, ed. see Robert, Henry M.

Vizard, David. How to Modify Your Mini. LC 76-57811. (Illus.). 1977. pap. 9.95 (ISBN 0-912656-47-6). H P Bks.

--How to Rebuild Small Block Chevys. LC 78-52275. (Illus.). 1978. pap. 9.95 (ISBN 0-912656-66-2). H P Bks.

Vizetelly, Frank H. Desk-Book of Errors in English. LC 74-3021. 1974. Repr. of 1920 ed. 34.00x (ISBN 0-8103-3637-5). Gale.

--How to Use English. 658p. 1982. Repr. of 1933 ed. lib. bdg. 45.00 (ISBN 0-8495-5532-9). Arden Lib.

--The Preparation of Manuscripts for the Printer. 148p. 1982. Repr. of 1905 ed. lib. bdg. 25.00 (ISBN 0-8495-5531-0). Arden Lib.

Vizetelly, Frank H. & De Bekker, Leander J. Desk-Book of Idioms & Idiomatic Phrases in English Speech & Literature. LC 73-121208. 1970. Repr. of 1923 ed. 42.00x (ISBN 0-8103-3291-4). Gale.

Vlaanderen, Edward van see Van Vlaanderen, Edward.

Vlack, Lawrence H. Van see Van Vlack, Lawrence H.

Vladeck, Bruce C. Unloving Care: The Nursing Home Tragedy. LC 79-3076. 305p. 1980. 13.95 (ISBN 0-465-08880-5, CN-5072); pap. 7.95 (ISBN 0-465-08881-3). Basic.

Vladimir, Koziakin. The Amazing Amazeman: In a Super Maze Adventure. 112p. 1982. pap. 1.95 (ISBN 0-380-81547-8, 81547). Avon.

Vladimirov, V. S. & Steklov Institute of Mathematics, Academy of Sciences, U S S R, Vol. 136. International Conference on Mathematical Problems of Quantum Field Theory & Quantum Statistics, II: Fields & Particles. LC 78-6757. 80.00 (ISBN 0-8218-3036-8, STEKLO-136). Am Math.

Vlaeminck, S., jt. ed. see Tanghe, J.

Vlasopolos, Anca. The Symbolic Method of Coleridge, Baudelaire, & Yeats. 232p. 1983. 17.95 (ISBN 0-8143-1730-8). Wayne St U Pr.

Vlasova, ed. see Andreichina, K., et al.

Vlasto, A. P. Entry of the Slavs into Christendom: An Introduction to the Medieval History of the Slav. LC 70-98699. 1970. 52.50 (ISBN 0-521-07459-2). Cambridge U Pr.

Vleck, John H. Van see Van Vleck, John H.

Vleck, Van Jane see Olson, Jim.

Vlieger, M. de see De Vlieger, M.

Vlietstra, J. Ship Operations Automation III. (Computer Applications in Shipping & Shipbuilding Ser.: Vol. 7). 1980. 59.75 (ISBN 0-444-86033-9). Elsevier.

Vlietstra, J., jt. auth. see Aune, A. B.

Vlisidis, Angelina C., jt. auth. see Schaller, Waldemar T.

Vlitos, Roger. Taking Photos. LC 80-52198. (Whizz Kids Ser.). 8.00 (ISBN 0-382-06458-5). Silver.

Vlodaver, Zeev, et al. Coronary Arterial Variations in the Normal Heart & in Congenital Heart Disease. 1975. 31.50 (ISBN 0-12-722450-5). Acad Pr.

Vlugt, Ebel Van Der see Van Der Vlugt, Ebed.

V Nandini Rao, jt. auth. see VV Prakasa Rao.

Vobis, G. Bau und Entwicklung der Flechtenpycnidien und Ihrer Goniedien. (Bibliotheca Lichenologica: No. 14). 200p. (Ger.). 1981. pap. text ed. 20.00x (ISBN 3-7682-1270-X). Lubrecht & Cramer.

Vocational Research Group. Concise Occupational Reference Handbook. 350p. 1983. pap. 11.95 (ISBN 0-910164-01-0). Assoc Bk.

Vocino, Thomas & Rabin, Jack. Contemporary Public Administration. 490p. 1981. text ed. 20.95 (ISBN 0-15-513682-8, HC); instr's. manual 1.95 (ISBN 0-15-513683-6). HarBraceJ.

Vocke, Harold. The Lebanese Civil War. LC 78-50674. (Illus.). 1978. 16.95 (ISBN 0-312-47733-3). St Martin.

Voe, Thomas F De see De Voe, Thomas F.

Voegeli, H. E., jt. auth. see Sachs, G.

Voegelin, Eric. From Enlightenment to Revolution. Hallowell, John H., ed. LC 74-81864. ix, 307p. 1975. 18.50 (ISBN 0-8223-0326-4); pap. 9.75 (ISBN 0-8223-0478-3). Duke.

--Science, Politics & Gnosticism. LC 68-14367. 128p. 4.95 (ISBN 0-89526-964-3). Regnery-Gateway.

Voehl, Dick, jt. auth. see Bellak, Rhoda.

Voelcker, Hunce. The Hart Crane Voyages. 3.50 (ISBN 0-917996-00-3). Panjandrum.

--Logan. 3.00 (ISBN 0-917996-02-X). Panjandrum.

--Parade of Gumdrop Prose. 3.00 (ISBN 0-917996-04-6). Panjandrum.

--Sillycomb. 1973. 4.95 (ISBN 0-915572-10-9). Panjandrum.

--Songs for the Revolution. 3.00 (ISBN 0-917996-03-8). Panjandrum.

--Within the Rose. (Illus.). 60p. 1976. 4.50 (ISBN 0-915572-19-2). Panjandrum.

Voelpel, Jack. Word Retrieval Handbook. 82p. (Orig.). 1983. pap. 4.95 (ISBN 0-940534-02-9). Beekman Hill.

Voelter, W. & Wunsch, E., eds. Chemistry of Peptides & Proteins, Vol. 1. xv, 533p. 1982. 98.00x (ISBN 3-11-008604-2). De Gruyter.

Voge, Marietta, jt. auth. see Markell, Edward K.

Vogel, A. I. Elementary Practical Organic Chemistry: Pt. 2, Qualitative Organic Analysis. 2nd ed. 1966. 19.95x o.s.i. (ISBN 0-471-90963-7). Halsted Pr.

Vogel, Alfred. Swiss Nature Doctor. 1982. 3.95 (ISBN 0-686-36009-5). Bioforce of America.

Vogel, Andreas. Klimabedingungen und Stickstoff-Versorgung von Wiesengesellschaften verschiedener Hoehenstufen des Westharzes. (Dissertationes Botanicae: Vol. 60). (Illus.). 168p. (Ger.). 1981. pap. text ed. 16.00x (ISBN 3-7682-1299-8). Lubrecht & Cramer.

Volpe, Peter E. Man, Nature, & Society: An Introduction to Biology. 2nd ed. 650p. 1979. text ed. write for info. o.p. (ISBN 0-697-04568-4); instr's manual avail. o.p. (ISBN 0-697-04726-1); lab. manual avail. o.p. (ISBN 0-697-04569-2); study guide avail. o.p. (ISBN 0-697-04571-4). Wm C Brown.

Volpe, Richard, et al, eds. Maltreatment of the School-Aged Child. LC 79-3581. 224p. 1980. 20.95x (ISBN 0-669-03463-0). Lexington Bks.

Volpe, Robert, jt. auth. see Adams, Laurie.

Volpe, S. P. Construction Management Practices. 181p. 1972. 24.50x o.p. (ISBN 0-471-91010-4). Wiley.

--Construction Management Practices. 181p. Repr. of 1972 ed. text ed. 24.50 (ISBN 0-471-91010-4). Krieger.

Volpe, Stanley U. This Is the Boxer. 12.95 (ISBN 0-87666-254-8, PS610). TFH Pubns.

Volper, jt. auth. see Hacker.

Volpicelli, Luigi, jt. ed. see Bereday, George Z.

Vol'pin, M. E., ed. Chemistry Reviews. Gingold, Kurt, tr. from Russian. (Soviet Scientific Reviews, Section B: Vol. 4). 378p. 1982. 157.00 (ISBN 0-686-84005-4). Harwood Academic.

--Soviet Scientific Reviews: Chemistry Reviews, Vol. 3, Section B. 307p. 1981. 83.00 (ISBN 3-7186-0057-9). Harwood Academic.

Volpin, M. E., ed. Soviet Scientific Reviews Chemistry Reviews, Vol. 4, Section B. Date not set. write for info. (ISBN 3-7186-0057-9). Harwood Academic.

Volpitto, Perry P. & Vandam, Leroy D. The Genesis of Contemporary American Anesthesiology. (Illus.). 256p. 1982. 29.75x (ISBN 0-398-04715-4). C C Thomas.

Volsky, Paula. The Curse of the Witch-Queen. 384p. (Orig.). 1982. pap. 2.95 (ISBN 0-345-29520-X, Del Rey). Ballantine.

Volta, Alessandro G. Opere, 7 vols. (Sources of Science Ser.). Repr. of 1929 ed. Set. 315.00 (ISBN 0-384-64900-9). Johnson Repr.

Voltaire. Candide. Bair, Lowell, tr. from Fr. (Bantam Classics Ser.). (Illus.). 122p. (gr. 8-12). 1981. pap. 1.75 (ISBN 0-553-21028-9). Bantam.

--Candide & Other Tales. Smollett, Tobias, tr. 1983. pap. text ed. 4.50x (ISBN 0-460-01936-8, Pub. by Evman England). Biblio Dist.

--Mahomet the Prophet, or Fanaticism. Myers, Robert L., tr. LC 64-15701. (Milestones of Thought Ser.). pap. 3.95 (ISBN 0-8044-6960-1). Ungar.

--Peter the Great. Jenkins, M. F., tr. LC 81-72050. 340p. 1983. 37.50 (ISBN 0-8386-3148-7). Fairleigh Dickinson.

--Traite de Metaphysique. (Modern French Text Ser.). 1937. pap. write for info. (ISBN 0-7190-0166-8). Manchester.

Voltaire, compiled by. Evangile de la Raison: Ouvrage Posthume de M. D. M....y. (Holbach & His Friends Ser). 256p. (Fr.). 1974. Repr. of 1764 ed. lib. bdg. 70.00x o.p. (ISBN 0-8287-1370-7, 1554). Clearwater Pub.

Voltaire, F. M. Candide: Bilingual Edition. Gay, Peter, ed. LC 63-10683. 300p. (Fr. & Eng.). 1969. pap. 8.95 (ISBN 0-312-85190-1). St Martin.

Voltaire, Francois M. Candide & Other Writings. Block, Haskell M., ed. (YA) 1964. pap. 3.95x (ISBN 0-394-30964-2, T64, Mod LibC). Modern Lib.

Voltaire, Francois M. De. Candide, & Other Tales. Thorton, J. C., ed. Smollett, tr. 1971. Repr. of 1937 ed. 9.95x (ISBN 0-460-00936-2, Evman). Biblio Dist.

Voltaire, Francois M. De see De Voltaire, Francois M.

Voltaire, Francois M. de see Voltaire, Francois M. De.

Volten, Peter M. E. Brezhnev's Peace Program: A Study of Domestic Political Process & Power. (Replica Edition). (Illus.). 368p. 1982. lib. bdg. 24.50 (ISBN 0-86531-910-3). Westview.

Volterra, Enrico & Gaines, J. H. Advanced Strength of Materials. 1971. ref. ed. 32.95 (ISBN 0-13-013854-1). P-H.

Voltmer, Edward F., et al. The Organization & Administration of Physical Education. 5th ed. (Illus.). 1979. ref. 22.95 (ISBN 0-13-641100-2). P-H.

Voltz, Jeanne. The Los Angeles Times Natural Foods Cookbook. 1975. pap. 3.50 (ISBN 0-451-11237-7, AE1237, Sig). NAL.

Volunteer Lawyers for the Arts, jt. ed. see Council of New York Law Associates.

Volz, Carl A. Church of the Middle Ages. LC 72-99217. (Church in History Ser). 1978. pap. 4.95 (ISBN 0-570-06270-5, 12-2725). Concordia.

--Faith & Practice in the Early Church. LC 82-72654. 224p. 1983. pap. 9.95 (ISBN 0-8066-1961-9, 10-2177). Augsburg.

Von Allman, Marie, jt. auth. see Nemiro, Beverly.

Von Allmen, et al. Roles in the Liturgical Assembly. O'Connell, Matthew J., tr. from Fr. (Orig.). 1981. pap. 14.95 (ISBN 0-916134-44-X). Pueblo Pub Co.

Vonalt, Larry P., ed. Poems of Lord Vaux. LC 60-8071. 30p. 1960. 3.95 o.p. (ISBN 0-8040-0250-9). Swallow.

Von Arx, J. A. A Revision of the Fungi Described As Gloesporium. 1970. 32.00 (ISBN 3-7682-0667-X). Lubrecht & Cramer.

Von Arx, J. A. see Arx, J. A. von.

Von Arx, William S. An Introduction to Physical Oceanography. (Illus.). 1962. 28.50 (ISBN 0-201-08174-1, Adv Bk Prog). A-W.

Von Aulock, W. H. see Marton, L.

Von Aulock, Wilhelm H., ed. Handbook of Microwave Ferrite Materials. (Illus.). 1965. 58.50 (ISBN 0-12-723350-4). Acad Pr.

Von Balthasar, Hans. The Threefold Garland. Leiva, Erasmo, tr. from Ger. LC 81-83569. 146p. (Orig.). 1982. pap. 6.95 (ISBN 0-89870-015-9). Ignatius Pr.

Von Balthasar, Hans Urs see Balthasar, Hans Urs von.

Von Baravalle, Hermann. Rudolf Steiner As Educator. pap. 1.50 o.p. (ISBN 0-916786-24-2, Pub by St George Books). St George Bk Serv.

Von Barghahn, Barbara. Philip IV of Spain: His Art Collections at the Buen Retiro Palace, a Hapsburg "Versailles". LC 80-67180. (Illus.). 701p. 1980. lib. bdg. 29.50 o.p. (ISBN 0-8191-1208-9). U Pr of Amer.

Von Bekesy, Georg. Experiments in Hearing. LC 77-4715. 756p. 1980. Repr. of 1960 ed. lib. bdg. 35.00 (ISBN 0-88275-552-8). Krieger.

Von Bergen, W. Wool Handbook, Vol. 2, Pt. 2. 115.00x (ISBN 0-87245-526-2). Textile Bk.

Von Bergen, Werner, ed. Wool Handbook. 3rd ed. LC 63-11600. (Illus.). 1963-70. Vol. 2, Pt. 1. 89.00 o.p. (ISBN 0-471-91015-5); Vol. 2, Pt. 2. 115.00x (Pub. by Wiley-Interscience). Wiley.

Von Bernhard, Buelow. Imperial Germany. LC 77-127900. Repr. of 1914 ed. 21.00 (ISBN 0-404-01228-0). AMS Pr.

Von Bertholdi, Franz W. Considerations on the Phenomenon of Italian Fascism & the Evaluation of the Principle of Authority. (The Great Currents of History Library Bks). (Illus.). 137p. 1983. 77.55 (ISBN 0-89266-382-0). Am Classical Coll Pr.

Von Beyme, Klaus, ed. Policy Making in the German Democratic Republic. LC 82-5544. 220p. 1982. 25.00x (ISBN 0-312-62032-2). St Martin.

Von Bieberstein, F. Marschall. Flora Taurico Caucasicia, Exhibens Stirpes Phaenogamas, in Charsoneso Taurica & Regionibus Caucasicis Sponte Cresentes, 3vols. in 2. 1972. 160.00 (ISBN 3-7682-0762-5). Lubrecht & Cramer.

Von Bock, Maria P. Reminiscences of My Father, Peter A. Stolypin: An Annotated Translation from the Russian. Patoski, Margaret, tr. from Rus. LC 75-16442. 1970. 11.00 o.p. (ISBN 0-8108-0331-3). Scarecrow.

Von Bohm-Bawerk, Eugen see Bohm-Bawerk, Eugen Von.

Von Bonin, Gerhardt see Bonin, Gerhardt Von.

Von Bothmer, Dietrich & Mertens, Joan R. The Search for Alexander: Supplement to the Catalogue. Howard, Kathleen, ed. (Illus.). 24p. 1982. pap. 3.95 (ISBN 0-686-82670-1). Metro Mus Art.

Von Brand, T. Biochemistry & Physiology of Parasites. 1979. 107.75 (ISBN 0-444-80073-5). Elsevier.

Von Brandenstein, C. G. Names & Substance of the Australian Subsection System. LC 82-4869. (Illus.). 208p. 1983. lib. bdg. 20.00x (ISBN 0-226-86481-2). U Of Chicago Pr.

Von Brandenstein, C. G. & Thomas, A. P., trs. Taruru: Aboriginal Song Poetry from the Pilbara. 150p. 1975. 7.50x (ISBN 0-8248-0363-9). UH Pr.

Von Brandt, Andres. Fish Catching Methods of the World. 1981. pap. (FNB). Unipub.

Von Brandt, Andres see Brandt, Andres von.

Von Braun, Wernher & Ordway, Frederick I., 3rd. History of Rocketry & Space Travel. rev. ed. LC 74-13813. (Illus.). 320p. 1975. 28.80i (ISBN 0-690-00588-1). T Y Crowell.

Von Braun, Wernher & Ordway, Frederick I., III. The Rockets Red Glare. LC 75-6162. 224p. 1976. 12.95 o.p. (ISBN 0-385-07847-1). Doubleday.

Von Breman, L., et al. Economic Evaluation of Fertilizer Supply Strategies for the Asean Region: A Linear Programming Approach. McCune, D. L., intro. by. (Technical Bulletins Ser.: T-21). (Illus.). 72p. (Orig.). 1981. pap. 4.00 (ISBN 0-88090-020-2). Intl Fertilizer.

Von Bulow, Marie, ed. Hans Von Bulow: The Early Correspondence. Bache, Constance, tr. LC 71-163788. 266p. Date not set. Repr. of 1869 ed. price not set. Vienna Hse.

Von Buttlar, Johannes. Time Slip Dreams: A Parallel Reality. Fry, Nicholas, tr. 192p. 1982. 11.95 (ISBN 0-283-98505-4, Pub. by Sidgwick & Jackson). Merrimack Bk Serv.

Von Canon, Claudia. The Inheritance. ed. LC 82-23418. 224p. (gr. 7 up). 1983. 10.95 (ISBN 0-395-33891-3). HM.

--The Moonclock. (General Ser.). 1979. lib. bdg. 10.95 (ISBN 0-8161-3008-6, Large Print Bks). G K Hall.

Von Clausewitz, Carl. On War. 1982. pap. 4.95 (ISBN 0-14-044427-0). Penguin.

Von Clausewitz, Karl. War, Politics & Power. Collins, Edward M., tr. 304p. 1962. pap. 5.95 (ISBN 0-89526-999-6). Regnery-Gateway.

Von Cranach, M. Goal-Directed Action. (European Monographs Social Psychology: No. 30). 1982. 46.00 (ISBN 0-12-724760-2). Acad Pr.

Von Cranach, Mario, ed. The Analysis of Action: Recent Theoretical & Empirical Advances. Harre, Rom. LC 81-12304. (European Studies in Social Psychology). (Illus.). 400p. 1982. 49.50 (ISBN 0-521-24229-0); pap. 16.95 (ISBN 0-521-28644-1). Cambridge U Pr.

Von Cube, Hans L. & Staimle, Fritz. Heat Pump Technology. Goodall, E. G., tr. 1981. text ed. 49.95 (ISBN 0-408-00497-5, Newnes-Butterworth). Butterworth.

Von Dalla Torre, K. W. & Harms, H. Register to "Genera Siphonogamarum". 1958. Repr. of 1907 ed. 24.00 (ISBN 3-7682-0072-8). Lubrecht & Cramer.

Von Damm, Helene. Sincerely, Ronald Reagan. LC 76-3355. 176p. 1976. pap. 1.95 o.p. (ISBN 0-916054-05-5). Green Hill.

Von Daniken, Eric. Signs of the Gods. (Illus.). 239p. 1980. 10.95 (ISBN 0-399-12559-0). Putnam Pub Group.

Von Daniken, Erich. Chariots of the Gods? abr. ed. LC 73-87579. (gr. 6 up). 1974. 7.95 o.p. (ISBN 0-399-20392-3). Putnam Pub Group.

--Chariots of the Gods: Unsolved Mysteries of the Past. (Illus.). 1970. 8.95 o.s.i. (ISBN 0-399-10128-4). Putnam Pub Group.

--Gods from Outer Space: Return to the Stars or Evidence of the Impossible. (Illus.). 1971. 6.50 o.p. (ISBN 0-399-10344-9). Putnam Pub Group.

--The Gold of the Gods. (Illus.). 457p. 1973. 6.95 o.p. (ISBN 0-399-11208-1). Putnam Pub Group.

--In Search of Ancient Gods: My Pictorial Evidence for the Impossible. LC 73-93725. (Illus.). 256p. 1974. 8.95 o.p. (ISBN 0-399-11346-0). Putnam Pub Group.

--Pathways to the Gods: The Stones of Kiribati. Heron, Michael, tr. from Ger. (Illus.). 288p. 1982. 16.95 (ISBN 0-399-12751-8). Putnam Pub Group.

Von Dechend, Hertha, jt. auth. see De Santillana, Giorgio.

Von Del Chamberlain. When Stars Came Down to Earth: Cosmology of the Skidi Pawnee Indians of North America. LC 82-16390. (Ballena Press Anthropological Papers: No. 26). (Illus.). 260p. (Orig.). 1982. pap. 17.95 (ISBN 0-87919-098-1). Ballena Pr.

Von den Driesch, Angela. A Guide to the Measurement of Animal Bones from Archaeological Sites. LC 76-49773. (Peabody Museum Bulletins: No. 1). (Illus.). 1976. pap. text ed. 10.00x (ISBN 0-87365-950-3). Peabody Harvard.

Von Der Borch, C. C., ed. Synthesis of Deep Sea Drilling Results in the Indian Ocean. (Oceanography Ser.: Vol. 21). 1978. 57.50 (ISBN 0-444-41675-7). Elsevier.

Von der Grun, Max. Howl Like the Wolves: Growing up in Nazi Germany. Van Heurck, Jan, tr. from Ger. LC 80-19144. Orig. Title: Wie War das Eigentlich? (Illus.). 288p. (gr. 7-9). 1980. 11.75 (ISBN 0-688-22252-8); PLB 11.28 (ISBN 0-688-32252-2). Morrow.

Von der Mehden, Fred R. Religion & Nationalism in Southeast Asia: Burma, Indonesia, & the Philippines. (Illus.). 272p. 1963. pap. 6.95 (ISBN 0-299-02944-1). U of Wis Pr.

Von Doenhoff, Albert E., jt. auth. see Abbott, Ira H.

VonDoenhoff, Richard A., ed. Versatile Guardian: Research in Naval History. LC 79-15678. 1979. 17.50 (ISBN 0-88258-078-7). Howard U Pr.

Von Dorotka Bagnell, Prisca, ed. Gerontology & Geriatrics Collections. LC 82-11697. (Special Collections Ser.: Vol. 1, No. 3 & 4). 181p. 1982. 29.95 (ISBN 0-917724-53-4, B53). Haworth Pr.

Von Dorp, Rolf, tr. see Myrdal, Jan.

Von Dreele, W. H. If Liberals Had Feathers. 2nd ed. LC 67-30829. 1967. pap. 3.75 (ISBN 0-8159-5802-1). Devin.

Voneche, J. Jacques, jt. ed. see Gruber, Howard E.

Von Eckardt, Wolf. Back to the Drawing Board: Planning for Livable Cities. LC 78-12257. (Illus.). 1978. 10.00 (ISBN 0-915220-45-8). New Republic.

--Live the Good Life! Creating a Human Community Through the Arts. LC 82-6753. (Illus.). 129p. (Orig.). 1982. pap. 7.50 (ISBN 0-915400-24-3). Am Council Arts.

Von Egidy, T. & Gonnenweir, F., eds. Neutron-Capture Gamma-Ray Spectroscopy. 1982. 90.00x o.p. (ISBN 0-85498-153-5, Pub. by A Hilger). State Mutual Bk.

Von Eichborn, Reinhart. Economic Dictionary, 2 Vols. 4th ed. Incl. Vol. 1. English-German; Vol. 2. German-English. 1975. 160.00x set o.p. (ISBN 0-8464-0349-8). Beekman Pubs.

Von Elbe, Guenther, jt. auth. see Lewis, Bernard.

Von Elgg, Y. A., jt. ed. see Feldbrugge, J. T.

Von Engeln, Oscar D. Finger Lakes Region: Its Origin & Nature. (Illus.). 1961. 12.95 o.p. (ISBN 0-8014-0437-1). Cornell U Pr.

Von Engeln, Oscar Dedrich see Engeln, Oscar Dedrich Von & Urquhart, Jane M.

Von Erdberg, Eleanor. Chinese Influence on European Garden Structures. (Illus.). 1936. 87.50x (ISBN 0-686-51351-7). Elliots Bks.

Von Eschen, Jessie M. Pot of Gold. 1983. 7.95 (ISBN 0-8062-2135-6). Carlton.

Von Eschenbach, Wolfram see Eschenbach, Wolfram Von.

Von Euler. Release & Uptake Functions in Adrenergic Nerve Granules. 110p. 1982. 50.00x (ISBN 0-85323-084-6, Pub. by Liverpool Univ England). State Mutual Bk.

Von Euler, Ulf S. & Eliasson, Rune, eds. Prostaglandins. 1968. 32.00 (ISBN 0-12-724950-8). Acad Pr.

Von Euler, Ulf S. & Pernow, Bengt, eds. Substance P. LC 76-52600. (Nobel Symposium Ser: No. 37). 360p. 1977. 34.50 (ISBN 0-89004-100-8). Raven.

Von Filek, Werner. Frogs in the Aquarium. new ed. Orig. Title: Frosche im Aquarium. (Illus.). 96p. (Orig.). 1973. pap. 7.95 (ISBN 0-87666-191-6, PS690). TFH Pubns.

Von Franz, Marie-Louise. Individuation in Fairytales. (No. 12). 189p. 1977. pap. 10.00 (ISBN 0-88214-112-0). Spring Pubns.

--An Introduction to the Interpretation of Fairy Tales. (Seminar Ser.: No. 1). 160p. 1970. pap. text ed. 8.50 (ISBN 0-88214-101-5). Spring Pubns.

--Patterns of Creativity Mirrored in Creation Myths. (Seminar Ser: No. 6). 250p. 1972. pap. text ed. 12.50 (ISBN 0-88214-106-6). Spring Pubns.

--Projection & Re-Collection in Jungian Psychology: Reflections of the Soul. Kennedy, William H., tr. from Ger. (The Reality of the Psyche Ser.). Orig. Title: Spiegelungen der Seele: Projektion und Innere Sammlung. 264p. 1980. 18.00x (ISBN 0-87548-357-7). Open Court.

--A Psychological Interpretation of the Golden Ass of Apuleius. (Seminar Ser.: No. 3). 224p. 1970. pap. text ed. 13.50 (ISBN 0-88214-103-1). Spring Pubns.

--Shadow & Evil in Fairytales. (Seminar Ser., No. 9). 284p. 1974. pap. 13.50 (ISBN 0-88214-109-0). Spring Pubns.

--Time: Patterns of Flow & Return. (Illus.). 1979. pap. 8.95 (ISBN 0-500-81016-8). Thames Hudson.

Von Franz, Mary-Louise. Problems of the Feminine in Fairytales. (Seminar Ser: No. 5). 194p. 1972. pap. text ed. 9.50 (ISBN 0-88214-105-8). Spring Pubns.

Von Fraunhofer, J. A. Scientific Aspects of Dental Materials. 1975. 49.95 o.p. (ISBN 0-407-00001-1). Butterworth.

Von Freyhold, Karl F., illus. The Rabbit Book. Morgenstern, Christian. (Illus.). 8.95 (ISBN 0-914676-43-1); pap. 5.95 (ISBN 0-914676-38-5). Green Tiger Pr.

Von Frisch, Karl. Twelve Little Housemates. Sugar, A. T., tr. LC 78-40341. 1979. text ed. 17.00 (ISBN 0-08-021959-4); pap. text ed. 7.75 (ISBN 0-08-021958-6). Pergamon.

Von Furer-Haimendorf, Christoph. Himalayan Traders. LC 75-755. (Illus.). 325p. 1975. 21.50 o.p. (ISBN 0-312-37310-4). St Martin.

--South Asian Societies: A Study of Values & Social Controls. 1979. text ed. 15.00x (ISBN 0-391-01192-8). Humanities.

Von-Furer-Haimendorf, Christoph, ed. Contributions to the Anthropology of Nepal. 260p. 1974. text ed. 34.00x (ISBN 0-85668-021-4, Pub. by Aris & Phillips England); pap. text ed. 18.00x (Pub. by Aris & Phillips England). Humanities.

Von Furer-Haimendorf, Christopher. Tribes of India: The Struggle for Survival. LC 80-28647. (Illus.). 360p. 1982. 29.95x (ISBN 0-520-04315-4). U of Cal Pr.

Von Furstenberg, Egon & Fisher, Karen. The Power Look at Home: Decorating for Men. LC 79-26436. (Illus.). 1980. 25.00 o.p. (ISBN 0-688-03599-X). Morrow.

Von Furstenberg, George M., ed. Capital Investment & Saving Volume III: Capital, Efficiency, & Growth. LC 79-26371. 584p. 1980. prof ref 39.50x (ISBN 0-88410-677-2). Ballinger Pub.

--Capital Investment & Saving, Volume I: Social Security Versus Private Saving. LC 79-16389. 456p. 1979. prof ref 39.50x (ISBN 0-88410-675-6). Ballinger Pub.

--Capital Investment & Saving Volume II: The Government & Capital Formation. 560p. 1980. prof ref 39.50x (ISBN 0-88410-676-4). Ballinger Pub.

Von Gabain, A., et al, eds. Turkologie. (Handbuch der Orientalistik Ser.). ix, 471p. 1982. pap. write for info. (ISBN 90-04-06555-5). E J Brill.

Von Gentz, Friedrich see Gentz, Friedrich Von.

VonGlahn, Gerhard. Law Among Nations: An Introduction to Public Law. 4th ed. 810p. 1981. text ed. 29.95 (ISBN 0-02-423160-6). Macmillan.

Von Glehn, M. E., tr. see Hiller, Ferdinand.

Von Gleich, C. C. see Gleich, C. C. von.

Von Gleich, C. C. see Gleich, C. C. Von.

Von Gnielinski, Stefan, ed. Liberia in Maps. LC 72-80411. (Graphic Perspectives of Developing Countries Ser.). (Illus.). 111p. 1972. text ed. 35.00x (ISBN 0-8419-0126-0, Africana). Holmes & Meier.

Von Goethe, J. W. Novellen, Tales & Entertainments. Flatauer, Susanne, tr. 224p. 1982. 50.00x (ISBN 0-284-98634-8, Pub. by C Skilton Scotland). State Mutual Bk.

Von Goethe, J. W. & Steiner, Rudolf. The Fairy Tale of the Green Snake & the Beautiful Lily. 2nd ed. LC 78-73644. 72p. (Orig.). 1981. pap. 3.50 (ISBN 0-89345-203-3, Steinerbks). Garber Comm.

Von Goethe, Johann W. Faust, Part One. Morgan, B. Q., ed. LC 47-26635. (Crofts Classics Ser.). 1946. pap. text ed. 3.25x (ISBN 0-88295-038-X). Harlan Davidson.

--Italian Journey: 1786-1788. Auden, W. H. & Mayer, Elizabeth, trs. from Ger. LC 81-86248. 528p. 1982. pap. 16.50 (ISBN 0-86547-076-6). N Point Pr.
--Sorrows of Young Werther. Mayer, Elizabeth, et al, trs. Bd. with Novella. 1973. pap. 3.95 (ISBN 0-394-71958-1, Vin). Random.
--Sorrows of Young Werther & Selected Writings. Hutter, Catherine, tr. (Orig.). 1962. pap. 2.95 (ISBN 0-451-51736-9, CE1736, Sig Classics). NAL.
Von Goethe, Johann W. & Steiner, Rudolf. Goethe's Fairy Tale of the Green Snake & the Beautiful Lily. Carlyle, Thomas & Bittleston, Adam, trs. from Ger. LC 78-73644. (Illus.). 69p. 1979. pap. 4.00 (ISBN 0-8334-1769-X, Pub. by Steinerbooks NY). Anthroposophic.
Von Goethe, Rudolf Wolfgang see Von Goethe, Johann W. & Steiner, Rudolf.
Von Grimmelshausen, H. J. see Grimmelshausen, H. J. Von.
Von Gronicka, Andre. Thomas Mann: Profile & Perspectives. (Orig.). 1971. pap. text ed. 3.95x (ISBN 0-685-04770-9). Phila Bk Co.
Von Gronicka, Andre & Bates-Yakobson, Helen. Essentials of Russian. 4th ed. 1964. text ed. 20.95 (ISBN 0-13-287706-6). P-H.
Von Grunebaum, G. E., ed. see Giorgio Levi Della Vida Conference-2nd-los Angeles-1969.
Von Gunden, Heidi. The Music of Pauline Oliveros. LC 82-21443. 206p. 1983. 15.00 (ISBN 0-8108-1600-8). Scarecrow.
Von Haag, Michael. Egypt. LC 77-70186. (Countries Ser.). (Illus.). 1977. PLB 12.68 (ISBN 0-382-06112-8). Silver.
Von Hagen, Victor. Maya, Land of the Turkey & the Deer. (Illus.). 1960. PLB 5.91 o.p. (ISBN 0-529-03567-7, 1888W, Philomel). Putnam Pub Group.
Von Hagen, Victor W., ed. see Prescott, William H.
Von Hartmann, Eduard. Philosophy of the Unconscious: Speculative Results According to the Inductive Method of Physical Science. LC 76-108843. 368p. 1931. Repr. lib. bdg. 40.50x o.p. (ISBN 0-8371-3732-2, HAPH). Greenwood.
Von Heidenstam, Verner. Sweden's Laureate: Selected Poems of Verner Von Heidenstam. Stork, Charles W., tr. from Swedish. 1919. text ed. 29.50x (ISBN 0-686-83798-3). Elliots Bks.
Von Heider, W. M. Come unto These Yellow Sands. LC 79-55739. 1983. 14.95 (ISBN 0-89742-031-4). Celestial Arts.
Von Heimendahl, Manfred & Wolff, U. Electron Microscopy of Materials: An Introduction. LC 79-6810. 1980. 27.50 (ISBN 0-12-725150-2). Acad Pr.
Von Heitlinger, E. I. & Ursus, Thomas O., eds. New Poets Two. (Annual New Poets Anthologies Ser.). 114p. 1983. lib. bdg. 22.95 (ISBN 0-910691-01-0). Ursus Pr.
Von Hellborn, Heinrich K. The Life of Franz Schubert, 2 vols. Coleridge, A. D., tr. LC 73-163791. Date not set. Repr. of 1869 ed. price not set. Vienna Hse.
Von Hentig, Hans. Punishment: Its Origin, Prupose, & Psychology. LC 74-172566. (Criminology, Law Enforcement, & Social Problems Ser.: No. 147). 270p. (With new intro. & index). 1973. Repr. of 1937 ed. 16.00x (ISBN 0-87585-147-9). Patterson Smith.
Von Hentig, Hans see Hentig, Hans Von.
Von Hildebrand, D. see Hildebrand, D. Von.
Von Hildebrand, Dietrich. Ethics. LC 72-83947. Orig. Title: Christian Ethics. 1973. 7.50 o.p. (ISBN 0-8199-0445-7). Franciscan Herald.
Von Hindenburg, Paul. Out of My Life, 2 vols. in 1. Holt, F. A., tr. from Ger. LC 74-22303. 1983. Repr. of 1921 ed. 23.00 (ISBN 0-86527-146-1). Fertig.
Von Hippel, Arthur R., ed. Dielectric Materials & Applications. 1966. pap. 9.95x student ed. (ISBN 0-262-72002-7). MIT Pr.
--Molecular Designing of Materials & Devices. 1965. 35.00x (ISBN 0-262-22006-7). MIT Pr.
Von Hippel, Ursula. The Craziest Halloween. (Illus.). (gr. 1-3). 1957. PLB 4.99 (ISBN 0-698-30059-9, Coward). Putnam Pub Group.
--Toute Ma Famille. (Illus., Fr). (gr. k-3). 1967. PLB 3.49 o.p. (ISBN 0-698-30373-3, Coward). Putnam Pub Group.
Von Hirsch, Andrew & Hanrahan, Kathleen. The Question of Parole: Retention, Reform or Abolition? LC 78-21131. 208p. 1979. prof ref 16.50x (ISBN 0-88410-796-5). Ballinger Pub.
Von Hoelscher, Russ. How to Acheive Total Sucess. 348p. 1983. 11.95 (ISBN 0-940398-07-9). Profit Ideas.
Von Hoelscher, Russ, jt. auth. see Sterne, George.
Von Hofmannsthal, Hugo, jt. auth. see Strauss, Richard.
Von Holst, H. V. Country & Suburban Homes of the Prairie School Period: 408 Examples, Photographs & Floor Plans. (Architecture Ser.). (Illus.). 128p. 1983. pap. 5.95 (ISBN 0-486-24373-7). Dover.
Von Horvath, Odon. Don Juan Comes Back from the War. Hampton, Christopher, tr. 64p. 1978. pap. 5.95 (ISBN 0-571-11301-X). Faber & Faber.
Von Huegel, Friedrich see Hugel, Friedrich Von.
Von Hugel, F. see Hugel, F. von.
Von Humboldt, Wilhelm. Limits of State Action. Burrow, J. W., ed. LC 70-75824. (Cambridge Studies in the History & Theory of Politics). 1969. 27.95 (ISBN 0-521-07656-0). Cambridge U Pr.
Vonk. Art & Antique World Wide. 1981. 35.00 (ISBN 90-7041-371-X). Apollo.
Von Kahler, Erich. Man the Measure: A New Approach to History. (Historiography: Interdisciplinary Studies: No. 3). 700p. Repr. of 1943 ed. lib. bdg. 37.50x (ISBN 0-87991-102-6). Porcupine Pr.
Von Karman, Theodore, jt. ed. see Von Mises, Richard.
Von Karolyi, Ilona, jt. auth. see Allen, Rex W.
Von Kaulla, K. N. & Davidson, J. F., eds. Synthetic Fibrinolytic Thrombolytic Agents: Chemical, Biochemical, Pharmacological & Clinical Aspects. (Illus.). 528p. 1975. 46.75x o.p. (ISBN 0-398-02927-X). C C Thomas.
VON Keitzell, F. By Many Infallible Proofs. 76p. pap. 3.95 (ISBN 0-88172-137-9). Believers Bkshelf.
Vonkhury, Alexander. Business Speculation: Ideas, Guidelines, Techniques. (Illus., Orig.). lib. bdg. 21.00x (ISBN 0-935402-13-6); pap. 19.00 (ISBN 0-935402-14-4). Intl Comm Serv.
Von Kietzel, F. Behold the Lamb of God. 4.95x (ISBN 0-88172-136-0). Believers Bkshelf.
Von Kleist, Heinrich. An Abyss Deep Enough: The Letters of Heinrich Von Kleist with a Selection of Essays & Anecdotes. Miller, Philip B., ed. & tr. LC 78-16900. 288p. 1982. 16.95 (ISBN 0-525-05479-0, 01646-490). Dutton.
--The Broken Jug. Jones, R., tr. from Ger. (Classics of Drama in English Translation Ser.). 1977. pap. 6.50 (ISBN 0-7190-0667-8). Manchester.
Von Klenze, Camillo see Klenze, Camillo Von.
Von Koch, H., ed. see Conference on Instruments & Measurements.
Von Krafft-Ebbing, Richard see Krafft-Ebbing, Richard Von.
Von Kreisler, Max. The Pillagers. LC 79-6180. (Double D Western Ser.). 192p. 1982. 10.95 (ISBN 0-385-15519-0). Doubleday.
Von Krusenstierna, Sten, ed. Services of Our Lady. 70p. 1982. pap. text ed. write for info. St Alban Pr.
Von Kuehnelt-Leddihn, Erik. The Intelligent American's Guide to Europe. (Illus.). 1979. 20.00 o.p. (ISBN 0-87000-419-0, Arlington Hse). Crown.
Von Lang, Jochen & Sibyll, Claus. The Secretary, Martin Bormann: The Man Who Manipulated Hitler. Armstrong, Christa & White, Peter, trs. from Ger. LC 81-80847. (Illus.). x, 430p. 1981. pap. 9.95 (ISBN 0-8214-0615-9, 82-83988). Ohio U Pr.
Von Lang, Jochen, ed. Eichmann Interrogated: Transcripts from the Archives of the Israeli Police. Manheim, Ralph, tr. from German. 1983. 15.50 (ISBN 0-374-14666-7). FS&G.
Von Laue, Max. Theory of Superconductivity. 1952. 28.50 (ISBN 0-12-726556-2). Acad Pr.
Von Leyden, W. Hobbes & Locke: The Politics of Freedom & Obligation. 272p. 1981. 25.00x (ISBN 0-312-38824-1). St Martin.
Von Liebenstein-Kurtz, Ruth F. Das Subventionierte Englische Theatre. (Tuebinger Beitraege zur Anglistik Ser.: No. 2). 428p. (Orig., Ger.). 1981. pap. 24.80 (ISBN 3-87808-949-X). Benjamins North Am.
Von Maltitz, F. Living & Learning in Two Languages: Bilingual-Bicultural Education in the U.S. 1975. 16.95 (ISBN 0-07-067609-7, P&RB). McGraw.
Von Maltitz, Frances. The Rhone: River of Contrasts. (Rivers of the World Ser.). (Illus.). (gr. 4-7). 1965. PLB 3.98 (ISBN 0-8116-6364-7). Garrard.
Von Marion Beaujean, Herausgegeben, ed. Metropolitan Libraries on Their Way Into the 80's. 1982. 27.00 (ISBN 0-686-97275-9, Pub. by K G Saur). Shoe String.
Von Marx, Bomer. Three Star Cuisine: A Nobleman in the Kitchen. McCully, H., ed. (Illus.). 1966. 4.95 o.p. (ISBN 0-685-11986-6). Heineman.
Von Matuschka, A. G. Boronizing. 100p. 1981. text ed. 29.95x (ISBN 0-471-25867-9, Pub. by Wiley-Interscience). Wiley.
Von Mauntz, Alfred. Heraldik in Diensten der Shakespeare-Forschung. LC 68-57296. 1969. Repr. of 1903 ed. 34.00x (ISBN 0-8103-3886-6). Gale.
Von Mellenthin, F. W. Panzer Battles: A Study of the Employment of Armor in the Second World War. Turner, L. C., ed. Betzler, H., tr. (Illus.). 1971. 17.95 o.p. (ISBN 0-8061-0342-6). U of Okla Pr.
--Panzer Battles: A Study of the Employment of Armor in the Second World War. Turner, L. C., ed. Betzler, H., tr. from Ger. (Illus.). 383p. 1982. pap. 12.95 (ISBN 0-8061-1802-4). U of Okla Pr.
Von Mises, Ludwig. The Anti-Capitalistic Mentality. LC 56-12097. 140p. 1981. pap. 6.00 (ISBN 0-910884-14-5). Libertarian Press.
--A Critique of Interventionism. 1977. 8.95 o.p. (ISBN 0-87000-382-8, Arlington Hse). Crown.
--Ludwig Von Mises: Notes & Recollections. LC 76-29877. 200p. 1978. 9.95 (ISBN 0-910884-04-8). Libertarian Press.
--Planning for Freedom. new ed. LC 62-14881. 192p. 1979. pap. 5.00 o.p. (ISBN 0-910884-02-1). Libertarian Press.
Von Mises, Richard & Von Karman, Theodore, eds. Advances in Applied Mechanics. Incl. Vol. 1. 1948. 58.00 (ISBN 0-12-002001-7); Vol. 2. 1951. 58.00 (ISBN 0-12-002002-5); Vol. 3. 1953. 58.00 (ISBN 0-12-002003-3); Vol. 4. Dryden, H. L., et al, eds. 1956. 58.00 (ISBN 0-12-002004-1); Vol. 5. 1958. 58.00 (ISBN 0-12-002005-X); Vol. 6. 1960. 58.00 (ISBN 0-12-002006-8); Vol. 7. 1962. 58.00 (ISBN 0-12-002007-6); Vol. 8. 1964. 58.00 (ISBN 0-12-002008-4); Vol. 9. Kuerti, G., ed. 1966. 58.00 (ISBN 0-12-002009-2); Vol. 10. Fascicle 1. 1967. 11.00 (ISBN 0-12-002091-2); Vol. 11. Chia-Sun Yih, ed. 1971. 58.00 (ISBN 0-12-002011-4); Vol. 12. 1972. 58.00 (ISBN 0-12-002012-2); Vol. 13. 1973. 63.00 (ISBN 0-12-002013-0); Vol. 16. Yih, Chia-Shun, ed. 1976. 67.50 (ISBN 0-12-002016-5); lib ed 87.00 (ISBN 0-12-002043-2); microfiche 48.50 (ISBN 0-686-66621-6); Vol. 17. Yih, Chia-Shun, ed. 1977. 67.50 (ISBN 0-12-002017-3); lib. ed 87.00 (ISBN 0-12-002045-9); microfiche 48.50 (ISBN 0-12-002046-7); Vol. 18. Yih, Chia-Shun, ed. 1979. 57.00 (ISBN 0-12-002018-1); **lib. ed. 74.00 (ISBN 0-12-002047-5); 41.50 (ISBN 0-12-002048-3). LC 48-8503. Acad Pr.**
--Advances in Applied Mechanics: Supplements. Incl. Suppl. 1. Rarefied Gas Dynamics: Proceedings. International Symposium on Rarefied Gas Dynamics - 2nd. Talbot, L., ed. 1961 (ISBN 0-12-002061-0); Suppl. 2. Rarefied Gas Dynamics: Proceedings. International Symposium on Rarefied Gas Dynamics - 3rd. Laurmann, John A., ed. 1963. Vol. 1-2. Vol. 1 (ISBN 0-12-002067-X). Vol. 2 (ISBN 0-12-002068-8); Suppl. 3. Rarefied Gas Dynamics: Proceedings. International Symposium on Rarefied Gas Dynamics - 4th. De Leeuw, J. H., ed. 1965-66. Vol. 1 (ISBN 0-12-002074-2). Vol. 2. 24.00 (ISBN 0-12-002075-0); Suppl. 4. Rarefied Gas Dynamics: Proceedings. International Symposium on Rarefied Gas Dynamics - 5th. Brundin, C. L., ed. 1967. Vol. 1-2. Vol. 1 (ISBN 0-12-002081-5). Vol. 2 (ISBN 0-12-002082-3); Suppl. 5. Rarefied Gas Dynamics: Proceedings. International Symposium on Rarefied Gas Dynamics - 6th. Trilling, L. & Wachman, H., eds. 1967-69. Vols. 1-2. Vol. 1 (ISBN 0-12-002085-8). Vol. 2 (ISBN 0-12-002086-6). Suppls. 1-5. 67.50 ea. Acad Pr.
Von Mohrenschildt, Dimitri see Mohrenschildt, Dimitri Von.
Von Moos, Stanislaus. Le Corbusier: Elements of a Synthesis. 1979. 35.00x (ISBN 0-262-22023-7). MIT Pr.
Vonnegut, Kurt. Jailbird. 1980. pap. 3.50 (ISBN 0-440-15447-2). Dell.
--Jailbird. 1980. lib. bdg. 13.95 (ISBN 0-8161-3022-1, Large Print Bks). G K Hall.
--Palm Sunday: An Autobiographical Collage. 1981. 13.95 o.s.i. (ISBN 0-440-06593-3). Delacorte.
--Slapstick or Lonesome No More. 1978. pap. 7.95 (ISBN 0-440-58009-9, Delta). Dell.
--The Vonnegut Statement. Klinkowitz, Jerome & Somer, John, eds. (Orig.). 1973. pap. 3.95 o.s.i. (ISBN 0-440-59236-4, Delta). Dell.
Vonnegut, Kurt, Jr. Breakfast of Champions. 320p. pap. 3.25 (ISBN 0-440-13148-0). Dell.
--God Bless You, Mr. Rosewater. LC 65-16434. 1974. pap. 8.95 (ISBN 0-440-52929-8, Delta). Dell.
--Happy Birthday, Wanda June. 1974. pap. 6.95 (ISBN 0-440-53422-4, Delta). Dell.
--Player Piano. 320p. pap. 3.50 (ISBN 0-440-17037-0). Dell.
Von Netzer, U. Induktion der Primordienbildung bei dem Basidiomyceten Pleurotus ostreatus. (Bibliotheca Mycologica Ser.: No. 62). (Illus.). 1978. pap. text ed. 10.00 (ISBN 3-7682-1185-1). Lubrecht & Cramer.
Von Neumann, J. Functional Operators, Vol. 2, Geometry Of Orthogonal Spaces. (Annals of Mathematics Studies). Repr. of 1950 ed. pap. 12.00 (ISBN 0-527-02738-3). Kraus Repr.
Von Neumann, John see Neumann, John Von.
Von Noorden. Burian-Von Noordens Binocular Vision & Ocular Motility: Theory & Management of Strabismus. 2nd ed. LC 79-19275. 520p. 1979. 67.50 (ISBN 0-8016-0898-8). Mosby.
Von Noorden, Gunter K. Atlas of Strabismus. 4th ed. (Illus.). 256p. 1983. text ed. 35.00 (ISBN 0-8016-5053-7). Mosby.
Von Oppen, Beate Ruhm see Adenauer, Konrad.
Von Pivka, Otto. Napoleon's German Allies, Vol. 1. (Men-at-Arms Ser.). (Illus.). 40p. 1976. pap. 7.95 o.p. (ISBN 0-85045-211-2). Hippocrene Bks.
Von Rad, Gerhard. Old Testament Theology, 2 Vols. LC 62-7306. Vol. 1. 14.95xiea. (ISBN 0-06-068930-7, HarpR). Vol. 2 (ISBN 0-06-068931-5, HarpR). Har-Row.
Von Raumer, Frederick. England in Eighteen Thirty Five, 3 vols. 960p. 1971. Repr. of 1836 ed. 84.00x (ISBN 0-7165-1780-9, Pub. by Irish Academic Pr). Biblio Dist.
Von Regel, C., jt. auth. see Von Wiesner, J.
Von Sachs, Julius see Sachs, Julius Von.
Von Savigny, Friedrich Carl. Private International Law, & the Retrospective Operation of Statutes: A Treatise on the Conflict of Laws & the Limits of Their Operation in Respect of Place & Time. rev. 2nd ed. Guthrie, William, tr. from Ger. LC 72-190293. xii, 568p. 1972. Repr. of 1880 ed. lib. bdg. 25.00x o.p. (ISBN 0-8377-2604-2). Rothman.
Von Schardt, Emma see Kohler, Carl.
Von Scharnhorst, Gerhard J. Briefe. Linnebach, Karl, ed. 600p. 1980. lib. bdg. 40.00 (ISBN 3-601-00262-0). Kraus Intl.
Von Schweinitz, L. D. Synopsis Fungorum Carolinea Superioris. 1976. Repr. of 1822 ed. 16.00 (ISBN 3-7682-1065-0). Lubrecht & Cramer.
Von Schwind, J. Geophysical Fluid Dynamics for Oceanographers. 1980. 34.00 (ISBN 0-13-352591-0). P-H.
Von Seidlein, Cornelia, illus. My Album. (Coppenrath Ser.). (Illus.). 44p. (ps). 1983. 14.95 (ISBN 0-914676-79-2, Star & Eleph Bks). Green Tiger Pr.
--My Calendar Book. (Coppenrath Ser.). (Illus.). 50p. (ps). 1983. 14.95 (ISBN 0-88138-008-3, Star & Eleph Bks). Green Tiger Pr.
--My First Book. (Coppenrath Ser.). (Illus.). 32p. (ps). 1983. 14.95 (ISBN 0-914676-80-6, Star & Eleph Bks). Green Tiger Pr.
Von Siebold, Philipp F. Flora Japonica. 1976. 1535.00 (ISBN 0-384-64940-8). Johnson Repr.
--Nippon. 1975. 2750.00 (ISBN 0-384-64942-4). Johnson Repr.
Von Sivers, Marie Steiner see Steiner, Rudolf & Steiner-von Sivers, Marie.
Von Sivers Steiner, Marie see Steiner, Rudolf & Steiner Von Sivers, Marie.
Von Speyr, Adrienne. The Cross: Word & Sacrament. Harrison, Graham, tr. from Ger. LC 82-83496. Orig. Title: Kreuzeswort und Sakrament. 63p. (Orig., Eng.). 1983. pap. price not set (ISBN 0-89870-021-3). Ignatius Pr.
Von Stackelberg, Mark, jt. auth. see Schmidt, Helmut.
Von Staden, Heinrich see Giamatti, A. Bartlett.
Von Staden, Wendelgard. Darkness Over the Valley. 1982. pap. 4.95 (ISBN 0-14-006316-1). Penguin.
Von Stroheim, Erich. Greed. (Film Scripts-Classic Ser.). 1970. pap. 4.95 o.p. (ISBN 0-671-20614-1, Touchstone Bks). S&S.
Von Trapp, Maria. Maria. 1974. pap. 2.75 o.p. (ISBN 0-380-00783-5, 56267). Avon.
--Yesterday Today & Forever. LC 75-32010. 1977. pap. 2.50 (ISBN 0-89221-035-4). New Leaf.
Vontress, Clemmont E. Counseling Negroes. (Guidance Monograph). 1971. pap. 2.40 o.p. (ISBN 0-395-12048-9, 9-78857). HM.
Von-Tschudi, John J., jt. auth. see Rivero, Mariano E.
Von Tsharner, Renata, jt. auth. see Fleming, Ronald L.
Vontver, Louis A. Obstetrics & Gynecology Review. 3rd ed. LC 82-8773. (Illus.). 320p. 1983. pap. text ed. 10.00 (ISBN 0-668-05484-0, 5484). Arco.
Von Vacano, Otto-Wilhelm. Etruscans in the Ancient World. Ogilvie, Sheilia A., tr. (Illus.). 1960. 22.50 (ISBN 0-312-26635-9). St Martin.
Von Verdy Du Vernois, Julius A. With the Royal Headquarters in Eighteen Seventy to Eighteen Seventy-One. LC 68-54812. (Illus.). 1968. Repr. of 1897 ed. lib. bdg. 16.00x (ISBN 0-8371-0392-4, VERH). Greenwood.
Von Welanetz, Diana & Von Welanetz, Paul. The Von Welanetz Guide to Ethnic Ingredients. LC 82-10470. (Illus.). 496p. 1982. 20.00 (ISBN 0-87477-225-7). J P Tarcher.
Von Welanetz, Paul, jt. auth. see Von Welanetz, Diana.
Von Werder, Klaus, jt. ed. see Fahlbusch, Rudolf.
Von Westenholz, C. Differential Forms in Mathematical Physics. rev. ed. (Studies in Mathematics & its Applications: Vol. 3). 1981. 89.50 (ISBN 0-444-85435-5, North Holland); pap. 40.50 (ISBN 0-444-85437-1). Elsevier.
Von Westernhagen, Curt. The Forging of the "Ring". Whittall, Arnold & Whittall, Mary, trs. LC 76-7140. (Illus.). 1976. 37.50 (ISBN 0-521-21293-6). Cambridge U Pr.
--Wagner: A Bibliography, 2 vols. LC 77-88680. (Illus.). 1979. Vol. 1 (1813-64) 37.50 (ISBN 0-521-21930-2); Vol. 2 (1864-83) 37.50 (ISBN 0-521-21932-9); 64.50 set (ISBN 0-521-08774-0). Cambridge U Pr.
--Wagner: A Biography, 1813 to 1833. Whittall, Mary, tr. LC 78-2397. (Illus.). 720p. 1981. pap. 15.95 (ISBN 0-521-28254-3). Cambridge U Pr.
Von Wiese, B., ed. Deutsche Gedichte: Von Den Anfaengen Bis Zur Gegenwart. (Ger). 1981. 13.95 (ISBN 3-513-53200-8). Schoenhof.
Von Wieser, Friedrich. Social Economics. Hinrichs, A. F., tr. LC 67-20930. Repr. of 1927 ed. 27.50x (ISBN 0-678-00274-6). Kelley.
Von Wiesner, J. & Von Regel, C. Die Rohstoffe Des Pflanzenreichs, 7 pts. 5th ed. Incl. Pt. 1. Tanning Materials (Gerbstoffe) Endres, H., et al. (Eng. & Ger.). 1962. 32.00 (ISBN 3-7682-0111-2); Pt. 2. Antibiotiques (Antibiotica) Hagemann, G. (Fr.). 1964. 38.00 (ISBN 3-7682-0170-8); Pt. 3. Organic Acids. Whitting, G. C. 1964. 27.20 (ISBN 3-7682-0244-5); Pt. 4. Insecticides. Fuell, A. J. 1965. 32.00 (ISBN 3-7682-0259-3); Pt. 5. Glykoside. Zechner, L. 1966. 32.00 (ISBN 3-7682-0298-4); Pt. 6. Staerke. Samecl, E. & Bling, M. (Illus.). 1966. 32.00 (ISBN 3-7682-0186-4); Pt. 7. Aetherische Oele. Bournot, K. & Weber, M. (Illus.). 1968. 32.00 (ISBN 3-7682-0562-2). Lubrecht & Cramer.
Von Wilkens, Leonie. Mansions in Miniature: Four Centuries of Dolls' Houses. Orig. Title: Das Puppenhaus. (Illus.). 252p. 1980. 50.00 o.p. (ISBN 0-670-45410-9, Studio). Viking Pr.

Von Winning, Hasso. Pre-Columbian Art of Mexico & Central America. LC 68-13065. (History of World Architecture Ser.). (Illus.). 1968. 45.00 o.p. (ISBN 0-8109-0423-3); ltd. ed. leather bd 125.00 (ISBN 0-8109-4751-X). Abrams.

Von Wright, G. H. see Wright, G. H. von.

Von Wright, G. H., ed. see Wittgenstein, Ludwig.

Von Wright, Georg H., jt. auth. see Malcolm, Norman.

Von Wuthenau, Alexander. Terracotta Pottery in Pre-Columbian, Central, & South America. (Art of the World Library). (Illus.). 1970. 6.95 o.p. (ISBN 0-517-50855-9). Crown.

--Unexpected Faces in Ancient America. (Illus.). 197p. 1975. 12.95 o.p. (ISBN 0-517-51657-8). Crown.

Von Zittel, K. A. History of Geology & Paleontology. Olgivie-Gordon, Maria M., tr. 1962. Repr. of 1901 ed. 20.00 (ISBN 3-7682-7100-5). Lubrecht & Cramer.

--Text-Book of Palaeontology, 3 vols. Eastmann, C. R. & Woodward, A. Smith, eds. Incl. Vol. 2. Vertebrates I: Pisces, Amphibia, Reptile, Aves. 20.00 (ISBN 3-7682-7100-5); Vol. 3. Mammalia. 16.00 (ISBN 3-7682-7103-X). 1964. Set. 85.00 (ISBN 3-7682-7100-5). Lubrecht & Cramer.

Von Zitzewitz, M. Florence & Tuscany. 190p. 1982. pap. 9.95 (ISBN 0-933982-28-3, Lascelles). Bradt Ent.

VonZweck, Dina. Woman's Day Dictionary of Furniture. 1983. pap. 4.95 (ISBN 0-8065-0842-6). Citadel Pr.

--Woman's Day Dictionary of Glass. 1983. pap. 4.95 (ISBN 0-8065-0841-8). Citadel Pr.

Voogl, H. J. de see Schroeder, F. H. & De Voogl, H. J.

Voorehoeve, H. C. & Bennett, Gordon H. El Bautismo. 2nd ed. Bautista, Sara, tr. from Eng. (La Serie Diamante). 36p. (Span.). 1982. pap. 0.85 (ISBN 0-942504-06-2). Overcomer Pr.

Vooren, Monique van see Van Vooren, Monique.

Voorhees, Jerry L. Classifying Flute Fingering Systems of the Nineteenth & Twentieth Centuries. (The Flute Library: Vol. 15). (Illus.). 100p. 1980. 32.50 o.s.i. (ISBN 90-6027-366-4, Pub. by Frits Knuf Netherlands); 22.50 o.s.i. (ISBN 90-6027-365-6). Pendragon NY.

Voorhees, Mary M. Lilting Lyrics II. LC 82-90625. 88p. 1983. 6.95 (ISBN 0-533-05545-8). Vantage.

Voorhies, Barbara, jt. ed. see Stark, Barbara L.

Voorhis, Horace J. Confessions of a Congressman. Repr. of 1947 ed. lib. bdg. 16.00x o.p. (ISBN 0-8371-2383-6, VOCO). Greenwood.

Voorhis, S. N. Van see Van Voorhis, S. N.

Voorst, Dick Van see Van Voorst, Dick.

Voorthuijsen, A. M. Van see Van Voorthuijsen, A. M.

Vopat, W. A., jt. auth. see Skrotzki, Bernhardt G.

Vorce, Eleanor. Teaching Speech to Deaf Children. LC 74-81230. 1974. pap. text ed. 9.95 (ISBN 0-88200-067-5, A2319). Alexander Graham.

Vorderwinkler, jt. auth. see Axelrod.

Vorderwinkler, W., jt. auth. see Axelrod, Herbert.

Vorderwinkler, W., jt. auth. see Axelrod, Herbert R.

Vore, Nicholas De see De Vore, Nicholas.

Vorgrimler, Herbert. Karl Rahner: His Life, Thought & Works. pap. 1.95 o.p. (ISBN 0-8091-1609-X). Paulist Pr.

Vorherr, Helmuth. The Breast: Morphology & Lactation. 1974. 51.00 (ISBN 0-12-728050-2). Acad Pr.

Vorndran, B. J., jt. auth. see Winn, Charles S.

Vorndran, Barbara S. & Litchfield, Carolyn. General Merchandise Retailing. Lynch, Richard, ed. (Career Competencies in Marketing). (Illus.). (gr. 11-12). 1978. pap. text ed. 9.32 (ISBN 0-07-067625-9, G); tchr's manual & key 4.50 (ISBN 0-07-067626-7). McGraw.

Vorndran, Richard A., ed. see Hand, William P. & Williams, Gerald.

Vorndran, Richard A., ed. see Hinerman, Ivan D.

Vorndran, Richard A., ed. see Hopkins, Charles R., et al.

Vorndran, Richard A., ed. see Miller, Rex & Culpepper, Fred.

Vorren, Ornulf, jt. ed. see Hultkrantz, Ake.

Vorres, Karl S., ed. Rare Earth Research, Vol. 2. (Rare Earth Research Ser.). 770p. 1965. 156.00 (ISBN 0-677-10130-9). Gordon.

Vorster, D. J., ed. The Human Biology of Environmental Change. 206p. 1972. pap. write for info. (ISBN 0-85066-092-0, Pub. by Taylor & Francis). Intl Pubns Serv.

Vorzimmer, Peter J. Charles Darwin, the Years of Controversy. the Origin of Species & Its Critics, 1859-82. LC 78-118377. 300p. 1970. 17.95 (ISBN 0-87722-001-8). Temple U Pr.

Vos, Geerhardus. The Pauline Eschatology. (Twin Brooks Ser.). 1979. pap. 10.95 (ISBN 0-8010-9279-5). Baker Bk.

Vos, Howard. Archaeology in Bible Lands. LC 77-2981. (Illus.). 1977. 11.95 (ISBN 0-8024-0289-5). Moody.

--Galatians. (Everyman's Bible Commentary Ser.). 1970. pap. 4.50 (ISBN 0-8024-2048-6). Moody.

Vos, Howard F. Genesis. (Everyman's Bible Commentary Ser.). 1982. pap. 4.50 (ISBN 0-8024-2001-X). Moody.

--Matthew: A Study Guide Commentary. (Study Guide Commentary Ser.). 1979. pap. 4.95 (ISBN 0-310-33883-2). Zondervan.

Vos, Howard F., jt. auth. see Pfeiffer, Charles F.

Vos, Raymond de see De Vos, Raymond.

Vosburgh, John. The Land We Live on: Restoring Our Most Valuable Resource. (New Conservation Ser). (Illus.). (gr. 6-9). 1971. PLB 4.49 o.p. (ISBN 0-698-30211-7, Coward). Putnam Pub Group.

Vose, Holly, jt. auth. see Raymo, Anne.

Voskuil, Dennis. Mountains into Goldmines: Robert Schuller & the Gospel of Success. 176p. 1983. 12.95 (ISBN 0-8028-3573-2). Eerdmans.

Voss, Gilbert L. Seashore Life of Florida & the Caribbean. LC 80-20172. (Illus.). 199p. Date not set. pap. 8.95 (ISBN 0-686-84302-9). Banyan Bks.

Voss, Hans-Georg & Keller, Heide, eds. Curiosity & Exploration: Theories & Results. LC 82-22705. Date not set. price not set (ISBN 0-12-728080-4). Acad Pr.

Voss, Harwin L., jt. auth. see Shepard, Jon M.

Voss, J. Color Patterns of African Cichlids. Orig. Title: Les Livrees Ou Patrons De Coloration Chezles Poissons Chichlides Africains. (Illus.). 128p. 1980. 9.95 (ISBN 0-87666-503-2, PS-755). TFH Pubns.

Voss, Thomas M. Antique American Country Furniture. LC 82-48009. (Illus.). 384p. 1983. pap. 7.95 (ISBN 0-06-464061-2, BN 4061). B&N NY.

--Antique American Country Furniture: A Field Guide. LC 77-15898. (Illus.). 1978. 11.49i (ISBN 0-397-01219-5); pap. 7.95i (ISBN 0-397-01267-5, LP-124). Har-Row.

Voss, Tom. Bargain Hunter's Guide to Used Furniture. (Orig.). 1980. pap. 7.95 o.s.i. (ISBN 0-440-50464-3, Delta). Dell.

Vossler, Otto. Jefferson & the American Revolutionary Ideal. Philippon, Catherine & Wishy, Bernard, trs. LC 79-6726. 1980. pap. text ed. 11.25 (ISBN 0-8191-0941-X); lib. bdg. 20.75 (ISBN 0-8191-0938-X). U Pr of Amer.

Voss M. Heerma, Van see Van Voss, M. Heerma.

Vot, Andre Le see Le Vot, Andre.

Votaw, Clyde W. Gospels & Contemporary Biographies in the Greco-Roman World. LC 79-135748. (Facet Bks.). 72p. 1970. pap. 0.50 o.p. (ISBN 0-8006-3061-0, 1-3061). Fortress.

Votaw, Dow. Legal Aspects of Business Administration. 3rd ed. 1969. text ed. 25.95 (ISBN 0-13-527531-8). P-H.

Votaw, Dow, jt. auth. see Epstein, Edward.

Voth, Alden H. Moscow Abandons Israel for the Arabs: Ten Crucial Years in the Middle East. LC 80-5478. 275p. 1980. lib. bdg. 20.50 (ISBN 0-8191-1111-2); pap. text ed. 11.25 (ISBN 0-8191-1112-0). U Pr of Amer.

Voth, Anne. Women in the New Eden. LC 82-24793. (Illus.). 224p. (Orig.). 1983. lib. bdg. 21.50 (ISBN 0-8191-2917-8); pap. text ed. 10.75 (ISBN 0-8191-2918-6). U Pr of Amer.

Voth, H. R. Traditions of the Hopi. (Chicago Field Museum of Natural History Fieldiana Anthropology Ser). 1905. pap. 36.00 (ISBN 0-527-01868-6). Kraus Repr.

Voth, H. R., jt. auth. see Dorsey, G. A.

Voth, Norma J. Festive Breads of Christmas. LC 82-15731. 104p. (Orig.). 1983. pap. 3.25 (ISBN 0-8361-3319-6). Herald Pr.

Vouga, Daniel. Oudot. (Q L P Art Ser). (Illus.). 6.95 o.p. (ISBN 0-517-03725-4). Crown.

Vouk, V. see Friberg, L., et al.

Voukitchevitch, Mihailo, tr. see Vignes, Jacques.

Voulgaropoulos, Emmanuel, jt. auth. see Breakey, Gail F.

Vourakis, Christine, jt. auth. see Bennett, Gerald.

Vowles, Bernard, tr. see Lindroth, Stan, et al.

Vox, Valentine. I Can See Your Lips Moving. (Illus.). 176p. 1983. 31.50 (ISBN 0-7182-5870-3, Pub. by Kaye & Ward). David & Charles.

Voyat, Gilbert, ed. The World of Henri Wallon. LC 81-66757. 329p. 1983. 30.00 (ISBN 0-87668-434-7). Aronson.

Voyce, Pamela, jt. auth. see Cairoli, Oscar.

Voyles, J. Bruce, jt. auth. see Parker, James F.

Voyles, Jean, jt. auth. see Bonner, William H.

Voynich, E. L., tr. see Opienski, Henryk.

Voynick, Stephen M. The Mid-Atlantic Treasure Coast: The Romance & Reality of Coin Beaches & Treasure Shipwrecks. LC 82-18846. (Illus.). 224p. (Orig.). 1983. pap. 9.95 (ISBN 0-912608-16-1). Mid Atlantic.

Voynow, Zina, jt. auth. see Leyda, Jay.

Voysey, A. Looking at the Countryside. (Local Search Ser.). 1971. 7.50 o.p. (ISBN 0-7100-7141-8). Routledge & Kegan.

Vozar, Joe. Morton the Bird. 1980. 4.00 o.p. (ISBN 0-8062-1083-4). Carlton.

Vozoff, Kate, ed. see Schneider, Jerome.

Vraciu, Robert A., jt. ed. see Bisbee, Gerald E., Jr.

Vrana, Ralph. PITH: Short, Original Sayings for All Occasions. LC 81-85755. (Illus.). 100p. (Orig.). 1982. pap. 10.00 (ISBN 0-935320-06-7). San Luis Quest.

Vrana, Stan A. Interviews & Conversations with Twentieth Century Authors Writing in English: An Index. LC 82-3275. 259p. 1982. 16.00 (ISBN 0-8108-1542-7). Scarecrow.

Vrbova, G., et al. Nerve-Muscle Interaction. 1978. 55.00x (ISBN 0-412-15720-9, Pub. by Chapman & Hall). Methuen Inc.

Vredeman De Vries, Jan. Perspective. pap. 3.95 (ISBN 0-486-20186-4). Dover.

Vredenburgh, Larry. Basic Exploration Geology. 1982. 36.00 (ISBN 0-89419-251-5). Inst Energy.

Vredevoe, Donna L., et al. Concepts of Oncology Nursing. (Illus.). 400p. 1981. text ed. 22.95 (ISBN 0-13-166587-1). P-H.

Vredevoogd, Jon, jt. auth. see Upledger, John.

Vree, Dale. On Synthesizing Marxism & Christianity. LC 76-27706. 1976. 30.95x (ISBN 0-471-01603-9, Pub. by Wiley-Interscience). Wiley.

Vreeken, Elizabeth. Boy Who Would Not Say His Name. (Beginning-to-Read Bks). (gr. 2-4). PLB 4.39 (ISBN 0-695-40814-3, Dist. by Caroline Hse); pap. 1.95 (ISBN 0-695-30814-9). Follett.

--One Day Everything Went Wrong. (Beginning-to-Read Bks). (Illus.). (ps). pap. 1.95 (ISBN 0-695-36550-9, Dist. by Caroline Hse). Follett.

Vreeland, Helen K., ed. see Austin, Mary S.

Vreeland, Herbert H., 3rd. Mongol Community & Kinship Structure. LC 72-12334. (Illus.). 327p. 1973. Repr. of 1962 ed. lib. bdg. 19.25x (ISBN 0-8371-6734-5, VRMC). Greenwood.

Vreeland, R. Become Financially Independent: An Investment Plan That Really Works. 1978. 11.95 (ISBN 0-13-073635-X, Spec); pap. 5.95 (ISBN 0-13-073627-9, Spec). P-H.

Vreuls, Diane. Sums: A Looking Game. 1977. PLB 7.95 o.p. (ISBN 0-670-68325-6). Viking Pr.

Vriends, Matthew, jt. auth. see Naether, Carl.

Vriends, Matthew M. Encyclopedia of Lovebirds: And Other Dwarf Parrots. (Illus.). 1978. 14.95 (ISBN 0-87666-972-0, H-1014). TFH Pubns.

--Encyclopedia of Softbilled Birds. (Illus.). 221p. 1980. 19.95 (ISBN 0-87666-891-0, H-1026). TFH Pubns.

--Handbook of Canaries. (Illus.). 351p. 1980. 14.95 (ISBN 0-87666-876-7, H-994). TFH Pubns.

--Parakeets of the World. (Illus.). 1979. 19.95 (ISBN 0-87666-999-2, H-101). TFH Pubns.

--Starting an Aviary. (Illus.). 255p. 1981. 14.95 (ISBN 0-87666-898-8, H-1032). TFH Pubns.

Vriends, Matthew M. & Axelrod, Herbert R. Parrots. (Illus.). 1979. 4.95 (ISBN 0-87666-995-X, KW-032). TFH Pubns.

Vriends, Matthew M. & Bleher, Petra. Dwarf Parrots. (Illus.). 1979. 4.95 (ISBN 0-87666-996-8, KW-033). TFH Pubns.

Vriends, Matthew M. & Feyerabend, Cessa. Breeding Budgerigars. (Illus.). 1978. pap. 7.95 (ISBN 0-87666-970-4, PS-761). TFH Pubns.

Vriends, Matthew M., jt. auth. see Feyerabend, Cessa.

Vriends, Matthew M., jt. auth. see Harman, Ian.

Vriends, Matthew M., jt. auth. see Schneider, Earl.

Vriends, Matthew M., jt. ed. see Feyerabend, Cessa.

Vries, A. De see De Vries, A.

Vries, Barend A. de. Export Promotion Policies. (Working Paper: No. 313). v, 75p. 1979. 5.00 (ISBN 0-686-36207-1, WP-0313). World Bank.

--Philippines: Industrial Development Strategy & Policies. ix, 301p. 1980. pap. 20.00 (ISBN 0-686-36116-4, RC-8007). World Bank.

Vries, Egbert De see De Vries, Egbert & Casanova, P. Gonzales.

Vries, H. De see Van Bekkum, O. & De Vries, H.

Vries, H. P. De see De Vries, H. P. & Rodriguez-Novas, J.

Vries, J. De see De Vries, J.

Vries, Jan De see De Vries, Jan.

Vries, Jose de. The World Sugar Economy: An Econometric Analysis of Long-Term Developments. (Working Paper: No. 5). vii, 124p. 1980. 5.00 (ISBN 0-686-36097-4, CP-0005). World Bank.

Vries, Madeline De see De Vries, Madeline & Weber, Eric.

Vries, Pieter A. De see DeVries, Pieter A. & Shapiro, Stephen R.

Vries, Tom De see De Vries, Tom.

Vries, W. R. de see De Vries, W. R. & Dornfield, D. A.

Vroman, Barbara F., jt. auth. see Dopp, Peggy H.

Vroman, Leo & Leonard, Edward F., eds. The Behavior of Blood & Its Components at Interface, Vol. 283. (Annals of the New York Academy of Sciences). 1977. 43.00x (ISBN 0-89072-029-0). NY Acad Sci.

Vroman, Wayne. Wage Inflation: Prospects for Deceleration. LC 82-84713. (Changing Domestic Priorities Ser.). 56p. (Orig.). 1983. pap. 5.95 (ISBN 0-87766-320-3). Urban Inst.

Vroom, Victor H. Work & Motivation. LC 82-9963. 344p. 1982. lib. bdg. 27.50 (ISBN 0-89874-527-6). Krieger.

Vroom, Victor H., jt. ed. see Thompson, James D.

Vrooman, Christine W. Willowby's World of Unicorns. Kane, Sandy & Ogden, Peggy, eds. (Willowby's World Ser.). (Illus.). 32p. (gr. 2-6). 1982. pap. 1.75 (ISBN 0-910349-00-2). Cloud Ten.

Vrooman, David M., jt. auth. see Boling, Edwin T.

Vroon, P. A. Intelligence: On Myths & Measurements. (Advances in Psychology Ser.: Vol. 3). 1980. 34.00 (ISBN 0-444-85465-7). Elsevier.

Vryonis, S., Jr., ed. The Past in Medieval & Modern Greek Culture. LC 78-18624. (Byzantine kai Metabyzantina Ser.: Vol. 1). (Illus.). vii, 288p. 1978. 32.00x (ISBN 0-89003-026-X); pap. 26.00x (ISBN 0-89003-027-8). Undena Pubns.

Vryonis, Speros, ed. Islam & Cultural Change in the Middle Ages: Fourth Giogio Levi Della Vida Biennial Conference, May 11-13, 1973 (University of California, Los Angeles) 150p. (Orig.). pap. 45.00x (ISBN 3-447-01608-6). Intl Pubns Serv.

Vryonis, Speros, Jr. A Brief History of the Greek-American Community of St. George, Memphis, Tennessee 1962-1982. LC 82-50980. (Byzantina Kai Metabyzantina Ser.: Vol. 3). 130p. 1982. 17.50x (ISBN 0-89003-126-6); pap. 12.50x (ISBN 0-89003-127-4). Undena Pubns.

--Studies on Byzantium, Seljuks, & Ottomans: Reprinted Studies. LC 81-51168. (Byzantina kai Metabyzantina Ser.: Vol. 2). x, 343p. 1981. 26.00x (ISBN 0-89003-072-3); pap. 19.50x (ISBN 0-89003-071-5). Undena Pubns.

Vuchic, Vukan. Urban Public Transportation. (Illus.). 672p. 1981. text ed. 41.95 (ISBN 0-13-939496-6). P-H.

Vucinich, Wayne S. At the Brink of War & Peace: The Tito-Stalin Split in Historic Perspective. (Brooklyn College Studies on Society in Change). 384p. 1982. 27.50x (ISBN 0-914710-98-2). East Eur Quarterly.

Vucinich, Wayne S., ed. At the Brink of War & Peace: The Tito-Stalin Split in a Historic Perspective. 384p. 1982. 27.50 (ISBN 0-686-82240-4). Columbia U Pr.

Vuilleumier, Marion R. Meditations in the Mountains. 128p. (Orig.). 1983. pap. 6.95 (ISBN 0-687-24260-6). Abingdon.

Vukov, Konstantin. Physics & Chemistry of Sugar-Beet in Sugar Manufacture. LC 76-7400. 1977. 95.75 (ISBN 0-444-99836-5). Elsevier.

Vukovic, V. The Art of Attack in Chess. 1965. 26.00 (ISBN 0-08-011197-1); pap. text ed. 11.95 (ISBN 0-08-011196-3). Pergamon.

Vulliamy, Graham & Lee, Ed, eds. Pop Music in School. 2nd ed. LC 79-7708. (The Resources of Music Ser.: No. 13). (Illus.). 1980. 24.95 (ISBN 0-521-22930-8); pap. 9.95 (ISBN 0-521-29727-3). Cambridge U Pr.

--Pop Rock & Ethnic Music in Schools. LC 81-9967. (Resources of Music Ser.). (Illus.). 224p. 1982. 18.95 (ISBN 0-521-23341-0); pap. 9.95 (ISBN 0-521-29927-6). Cambridge U Pr.

Vuuren, Nancy Van see Van Vuuren, Nancy.

VV Prakasa Rao & V Nandini Rao. Marriage, the Family & Women in India. 1982. 19.50x (ISBN 0-8364-0850-0); text ed. 14.00x (ISBN 0-686-97658-4). South Asia Bks.

Vyas, R. N., jt. auth. see Bhattacharya, A. N.

Vyasa. Mahabharata. 6th ed. Rajagopalachari, Chakravarti, ed. Rajagopalachari, Chakravarti & Rao, N. R., trs. from Tamil. 332p. 1980. pap. 6.50 (ISBN 0-934676-16-X). Greenlf Bks.

--Srimad Bhagavata, Vol. I. Tapasyananda, Swami, tr. from Sanskrit. 455p. 1983. 25.00x (ISBN 0-87481-516-9). Vedanta Pr.

--Srimad Bhagavata, Vol. II. Tapasyananda, Swami, tr. from Sanskrit. 492p. 1983. 25.00x (ISBN 0-87481-517-7). Vedanta Pr.

--Srimad Bhagavata, Vol. III. Tapasyananda, Swami, tr. from Sanskrit. 447p. 1983. 25.00x (ISBN 0-87481-518-5). Vedanta Pr.

--Srimad Bhagavata, Vol. IV. Tapasyananda, Swami, tr. from Sanskrit. 1983. 25.00x (ISBN 0-87481-519-3). Vedanta Pr.

Vyasulu, Vinod, ed. Technological Choice in the Indian Environment. 351p. 1980. 44.95x (ISBN 0-940500-59-0, Pub. by Sterling India). Asia Bk Corp.

Vyden. Post Myocardial Infarction Management & Rehabilitation. (Cardiology Ser.). 544p. 1983. price not set (ISBN 0-8247-1799-6). Dekker.

Vydra, F., et al. Electrochemical Stripping Analysis. Tyson, J., tr. LC 76-10946. (Series on Analytical Chemistry). 1977. 76.95 o.p. (ISBN 0-470-15131-5). Halsted Pr.

Vye, George & Grossman, Stewart. Cooking with Grass. LC 75-39089. (Illus.). 128p. (Orig.). 1976. pap. 3.95 o.p. (ISBN 0-8467-0151-0, Pub. by Two Continents). Hippocrene Bks.

Vygotsky, Lev S. Thought & Language. Vakar, Gertrude, ed. Hanfmann, Eugenia, tr. 1962. 17.50x (ISBN 0-262-22003-2); pap. 4.95 (ISBN 0-262-72001-9). MIT Pr.

Vylder, Stephan de see De Vylder, Stephan.

Vyn, Kathleen. The Prairie Community. LC 78-6732. (Illus.). 64p. (gr. 3-5). 1978. PLB 6.97 o.p. (ISBN 0-671-32924-3). Messner.

--Spring in the High Sierras. LC 79-25450. (Illus.). 64p. (gr. 3-5). 1980. PLB 6.97 o.p. (ISBN 0-671-33084-5). Messner.

Vysny, P. Neo-Slavism & the Czechs, 1898-1914. LC 76-4239. (Soviet & East European Studies). (Illus.). 1977. 47.50 (ISBN 0-521-21230-8). Cambridge U Pr.

Vy Thi Be, jt. auth. see Freiberger, Nancy.

Vyverberg, Henry. The Living Tradition: Art, Music & Ideas in the Western World. (Illus.). 385p. 1978. pap. text ed. 17.95 (ISBN 0-15-551125-4, HC); 40 slides avail. (ISBN 0-685-87940-2). HarBraceJ.

Vyvyan, John. The Dark Face of Science. 207p. 1972. 8.75 o.p. (ISBN 0-7181-0879-5). Transatlantic.

W

W. Foulsham & Co. The Bumper Book of Things a Boy Can Make. (Illus.). 1978. pap. 8.95 (ISBN 0-8306-1090-1, 1090). TAB Bks.
Waage, Karl M., jt. auth. see Dunbar, Carl O.
Waagenaar, Sam. The Pope's Jews. (Illus.). 500p. 1974. 27.50x (ISBN 0-912050-49-7, Library Pr). Open Court.
Waal, Frans de see De Waal, Frans.
Waal, Hugo De see Faber, Heije.
Waal, M. de see De Waal, M.
Waar, Bob, jt. auth. see Fisher, Bill.
Waard, J. De see De Waard, J. & Nida, E. A.
Waard, J. de see De Waard, J. & Smalley, W. A.
Waard, Jan de see Borg, Albert J. & De Waard, Jan.
Waay, D. Van der see Van der Waay, D. & Verhoef, J.
Wabe, Stuart. Manpower Changes in the Engineering Industry. (Illus.). 141p. 1977. 33.50x (ISBN 0-686-94838-6). Intl Ideas.
Waber, Bernard. Bernard. (gr. k-3). 1982. PLB 10.20 (ISBN 0-395-31865-3); 9.95. HM.
--Cheese. LC 67-24665. (Illus.). (gr. 5 up). 1967. 1.50 o.p. (ISBN 0-395-07162-3). HM.
--Just Like Abraham Lincoln. (Illus.). (gr. 1-5). 1964. reinforced bdg. 6.95 o.p. (ISBN 0-395-20107-1). HM.
--Lyle & the Birthday Party. (Illus.). (gr. k-3). 1966. reinforced bdg. 10.95 (ISBN 0-395-15080-9). HM.
Wabun, jt. auth. see Sun Bear.
Waby, Marian. Montevalle: The Story of a Dream Come True. (Illus.). 100p. 1975. pap. 4.00 (ISBN 0-686-14546-1). M Waby.
Wace, Alan J. Nomads of the Balkans. 1973. Repr. 19.00x (ISBN 0-685-30613-5). Biblo.
Wace, Henry, jt. auth. see Brewer, J. S.
Wace, Robert & Layamon. Arthurian Chronicles: A Paraphrase of Wace's "Roman De Brut". Mason, Eugene, tr. 1976. 8.95x (ISBN 0-460-00578-2, Evman); pap. 3.50x (ISBN 0-460-01578-8, Evman). Biblio Dist.
Wach, Joachim. Understanding & Believing: Essays. Kitagawa, Joseph M., ed. LC 75-31987. 204p. 1976. Repr. of 1968 ed. lib. bdg. 15.50x (ISBN 0-8371-8488-6, WAUB). Greenwood.
Wacher, John. The Towns of Roman Britain. LC 73-91663. (Illus.). 1975. 50.00x (ISBN 0-520-02669-1). U of Cal Pr.
Wachman, H. see Von Mises, Richard & Von Karman, Theodore.
Wachorst, Wyn. Thomas Alva Edison: An American Myth. (Illus.). 256p. 1981. 15.00 (ISBN 0-262-23108-5). MIT Pr.
Wachs, Harry, jt. auth. see Furth, Hans D.
Wachs, Martin. Transportation for the Elderly: Changing Lifestyles, Changing Needs. 1979. 29.75x (ISBN 0-520-03691-3). U of Cal Pr.
Wachsmann, Konrad, jt. ed. see Malcolmson, Reginald.
Wachsmuth, Guenther. The Life & Work of Rudolf Steiner: From the Turn of the Century to His Death. 2nd ed. Wanamaker, Olim D. & Raab, Reginald, trs. from Ger. LC 82-82476. (Steinerbooks Spiritual Science Library). (Illus.). 644p. 1982. Repr. of 1955 ed. 30.00 (ISBN 0-89345-036-7). Garber Comm.
Wachspress, Eugene L. A Rational Finite Element Basis. (Mathematics in Science & Engineering Ser.). 1975. 35.50 (ISBN 0-12-728950-X). Acad Pr.
Wachtel, Chuck. Joe the Engineer. LC 82-14227. 221p. 1983. 11.95 (ISBN 0-688-01548-4). Morrow.
Wachtel, Erna & Loken, Newton C. Girls' Gymnastics. rev ed. LC 63-19163. (gr. 6 up). 1967. 8.95 (ISBN 0-8069-4310-6); PLB 10.99 (ISBN 0-8069-4311-4). Sterling.
Wachtel, Hellmuth. Aquarium Ecology. Vevers, Gwynne, tr. from Ger. (Illus.). 128p. 1973. pap. 14.95 (ISBN 0-87666-024-3, PS-694). TFH Pubns.
Wachtel, L. John. How to Buy Land. LC 81-85032. (Illus.). 128p. 1982. 13.95 (ISBN 0-8069-7156-8); lib. bdg. 16.79 (ISBN 0-8069-7157-6); pap. 7.95 (ISBN 0-8069-7602-0). Sterling.
Wachtel, Paul. Crises in the Economic & Financial Structure. LC 81-48391. (A Salomon Brothers Center Bk.). (Illus.). 368p. 1982. 33.95x (ISBN 0-669-05360-0). Lexington Bks.
Wachtel, Stephen, ed. H-Y Antigen & the Biology of Sex Determination. Date not set. price not set (ISBN 0-8089-1514-2). Grune.
Wachter, H. & Curtius, H. C., eds. Biochemical & Clinical Aspects of Pteridines, Vol. 1. (Illus.). 373p. 1982. 75.00x (ISBN 0-686-82599-3). De Gruyter.
Wachter, Michael L. & Wachter, Susan M. Toward a New U. S. Industrial Policy? LC 81-16060. 536p. 1983. pap. 12.95x (ISBN 0-8122-1142-1). U of Pa Pr.
Wachter, P. & Boppart, H., eds. Valence Instabilities: Proceedings of the International Conference on Valence Instabilities, Zurich, Switzerland, April, 1982. 98p. 1982. 61.75 (North Holland). Elsevier.
Wachter, Susan M., jt. auth. see Wachter, Michael L.
Wackenheim, A. Radiodiagnosis of the Vertebrae in Adults: 125 Exercises for Students & Practitioners. (Exercises in Radiological Diagnosis Ser.). (Illus.). 176p. 1983. pap. 14.80 (ISBN 0-387-11681-8). Springer-Verlag.
Wacker, Charles H. Lasers: How They Work. new ed. (How It Works Ser.). (Illus.). 96p. (gr. 6 up). 1973. PLB 4.79 o.p. (ISBN 0-399-60841-9). Putnam Pub Group.
Wacker, Hansjorg, ed. Continuation Methods. 1978. 34.00 (ISBN 0-12-729250-0). Acad Pr.
Wacker, R. Fred. Ethnicity, Pluralism, & Race: Race Relations Theory in America Before Myrdal. LC 82-11687. (Contributions in Sociology Ser.: No. 42). 160p. 1983. lib. bdg. 27.50 (ISBN 0-313-23580-5, WER/). Greenwood.
Wackerbarth, Marjorie & Graham, Lillian S. Games for All Ages. (Direction Bks.). (Orig.). 1973. pap. 4.50 (ISBN 0-8010-9536-0). Baker Bk.
Wackerman, Albert E., et al. Harvesting Timber Crops. 2nd ed. (American Forestry Ser.). 1966. text ed. 20.00 o.p. (ISBN 0-07-067638-0, C). McGraw.
Wacziarg, Francis & Nath, Aman. Rajasthan: The Painted Walls of Shekhavati. (Illus.). 120p. 1983. 35.00 (ISBN 0-8390-0309-9). Allanheld & Schram.
Wada, Juhn, ed. Modern Perspectives in Epilepsy. 1978. 16.00 (ISBN 0-88831-017-X). Eden Pr.
Wada, Juhn, ed. see Epilepsy International Symposium, 10th.
Wada, Juhn A., ed. Kindling Two. 374p. 1981. 41.50 (ISBN 0-89004-630-1). Raven.
Wada, Y., et al, eds. Charge Storage, Charge Transport & Electrostatics & Their Applications. LC 79-20991. (Studies in Electrical & Electronic Engineering: Vol. 2). 460p. 1980. 72.50 (ISBN 0-444-99769-5). Elsevier.
Wada, Yoshiko. Shibori: Japanese Shaped Resist Dyeing. LC 82-48789. (Illus.). 296p. 1983. 65.00 (ISBN 0-87011-559-6). Kodansha.
Waddams, Herbert. The Church & Man's Struggle for Unity. 1973. pap. 5.95 o.p. (ISBN 0-7137-0480-2). Transatlantic.
Waddell, Charles. Faith, Hope & Luck: A Sociological Study of Children Growing Up With a Life-Threatening Illness. LC 82-24871. 104p. (Orig.). 1983. lib. bdg. 18.75 (ISBN 0-8191-3011-7); pap. text ed. 8.25 (ISBN 0-8191-3012-5). U Pr of Amer.
Waddell, H. Poetry in the Dark Ages. (Studies in Poetry, No. 38). 1948. pap. 9.95x (ISBN 0-8383-0079-0). Haskell.
Waddell, Heather. London Art Guide. 1981. 5.95 (ISBN 0-9507160-4-9, Pub. by Art Guide England). Morgan.
Waddell, Helen. Stories from Holy Writ. LC 74-25538. 280p. 1975. Repr. of 1949 ed. lib. bdg. 18.25x (ISBN 0-8371-7872-X, WAHW). Greenwood.
Waddell, Jack O. & Everett, Michael W., eds. Drinking Behavior Among Southwestern Indians: An Anthropological Perspective. 1980. 16.50xo.s.i. (ISBN 0-8165-0676-0); pap. 9.50x (ISBN 0-8165-0615-9). U of Ariz Pr.
Waddell, Joseph J. Practical Quality Control for Concrete. LC 76-56855. (Illus.). 1978. Repr. of 1962 ed. lib. bdg. 21.50 (ISBN 0-88275-508-0). Krieger.
Waddell, Joseph J., ed. Concrete Construction Handbook. 2nd ed. LC 73-17385. 960p. 1974. 58.00 (ISBN 0-07-067654-2, P&RB). McGraw.
Waddell, Marie L., et al. Twenty Patterns for Successful Writing: The Sentence. new ed. LC 70-184892. (gr. 9-12). 1983. pap. text ed. 3.95 (ISBN 0-8120-2269-6). Barron.
Wadden, Douglas, jt. ed. see Berger, Paul.
Wadden, Paul. Stork Tracks. pap. 2.00 (ISBN 0-686-84330-4, NAIKU14). Juniper Pr WI.
Wadden, Richard A. Energy Utilization & Environmental Health: Methods for Prediction & Evaluation of Impact on Human Health. LC 78-9688. 216p. Repr. of 1978 ed. text ed. 29.50 (ISBN 0-686-84496-3). Krieger.
Wadden, Richard A. & Scheff, Peter A. Indoor Air Pollution: Characterization, Prediction & Control. (Environmental Science & Technology: A Wiley Interscience Series of Texts & Monographs). 213p. 1983. 39.95x (ISBN 0-471-87673-9, Pub. by Wiley-Interscience). Wiley.
Waddington, C. H. The Man-Made Future. LC 77-29043. 1978. 25.00 (ISBN 0-312-51045-4). St Martin.
Waddington, Conrad H., jt. ed. see Jantsch, Erich.
Waddington, D. & Herlevich, F. Ann. Evaluation of Pumps & Motors for PV Water Pumping Systems. (Progress in Solar Energy Supplements SERI Ser.). 150p. 1983. pap. text ed. 13.50x (ISBN 0-89553-081-3). Am Solar Energy.
Waddington, Lawrence C. Criminal Evidence. 1978. text ed. 20.95x (ISBN 0-02-479510-0). Macmillan.
Waddington, Margaret. Reading Between the Lions. LC 82-72480. (Illus.). 64p. (Orig.). 1982. pap. 4.95 (ISBN 0-914960-39-3). Academy Bks.
Waddington, Raymond B., jt. ed. see Sloan, Thomas O.
Waddy, Charis. The Muslim Mind. 2nd ed. LC 82-7778. (Illus.). 232p. 1983. 25.00x (ISBN 0-582-78346-1); pap. 7.95x (ISBN 0-582-78345-3). Longman.
Waddy, Lawrence. Mayor's Race. LC 80-81489. 260p. pap. text ed. 3.95 o.p. (ISBN 0-89882-009-X). Lane & Assoc.
--Symphony. LC 80-81488. 222p. pap. text ed. 3.95 o.p. (ISBN 0-89882-008-1). Lane & Assoc.
Wade. Special Effects in the Camera. (Photographer's Library). (Illus.). 1983. pap. 12.95x (ISBN 0-240-51184-0). Focal Pr.
Wade, Alex & Ewenstein, Neal. Thirty Energy-Efficient Houses You Can Build. 1977. 16.95 o.p. (ISBN 0-87857-203-1); pap. 12.95 (ISBN 0-87857-191-4). Rodale Pr Inc.
Wade, Allen. Football (Soccer) Association Guide to Training & Coaching. 1982. 17.95 (ISBN 0-434-83550-1, Pub. by Heinemann). David & Charles.
Wade, Bonnie. Music in India: The Classical Traditions. 1979. 16.95 (ISBN 0-13-607036-1); pap. 13.95 (ISBN 0-13-607028-0). P-H.
Wade, Bonnie C. Tegotomono: Music for Japanese Koto. LC 75-5265. (Contributions in Intercultural & Comparative Studies: No. 2). 1976. lib. bdg. 29.95x (ISBN 0-8371-8908-X, WTM/). Greenwood.
Wade, Bonnie C., ed. Performing Arts in India: Essays on Music, Dance & Drama. LC 82-20141. (Monograph Ser.: No. 21). (Illus.). 270p. 1983. lib. bdg. 21.75 (ISBN 0-8191-2872-4); pap. text ed. 11.00 (ISBN 0-8191-2873-2). U Pr of Amer.
Wade, Carlson. Brand-Name Handbook of Protein, Calories & Carbohydrates. 1977. 8.95 o.p. (ISBN 0-13-081307-9, Parker). P-H.
--Natural Hormones: Secret of Youthful Health. 3.95x (ISBN 0-13-609958-0). Cancer Control Soc.
--Natural Hormones: The Secret of Youthful Health. 1972. 12.95 (ISBN 0-13-609941-6, Reward); pap. 4.95 (ISBN 0-13-609958-0). P-H.
--The Yeast Flakes Cookbook. 1973. pap. 1.25 o.s.i. (ISBN 0-515-02904-1). Jove Pubns.
Wade, Carlson, jt. auth. see Banik, Allan E.
Wade, Charles E. John Pym. LC 79-110880. (Illus.). 1971. Repr. of 1912 ed. lib. bdg. 17.00x (ISBN 0-8371-4561-9, WAJP). Greenwood.
Wade, Charles G. Contemporary Chemistry: A Chemical & Physical Approach. (Illus.). 1976. text ed. 22.95 (ISBN 0-02-423650-0). Macmillan.
Wade, Charles R., ed. see Belove, Charles, et al.
Wade, David Van see Van Wade, David & Van Wade, Sarah.
Wade, Edwin L. & Strickland, Rennard. As in a Vision: Masterworks of American Indian Art. LC 82-40456. (Illus.). 144p. (Orig.). 1983. pap. 19.95 (ISBN 0-8061-1841-5). U of Okla Pr.
Wade, Francis C. The Catholic University & the Faith. (Aquinas Lecture Ser.). 1978. 7.95 (ISBN 0-87462-143-7). Marquette.
--John of Saint Thomas: Outlines of Formal Logic. 2nd ed. (Medieval Philosophical Texts in Translation: No. 8). 1962. pap. 7.95 (ISBN 0-87462-208-5). Marquette.
Wade, Graham. Traditions of the Classical Guitar. 270p. 1982. pap. 9.95 (ISBN 0-686-83101-2). Riverrun NY.
Wade, H. W. Administrative Law. 4th ed. (Clarendon Law Ser). 1977. 44.00x o.p. (ISBN 0-19-876070-1). Oxford U Pr.
--Administrative Law. 5th ed. 1982. 55.00 (ISBN 0-19-876138-4); pap. 29.95 (ISBN 0-19-876139-2). Oxford U Pr.
Wade, H. W., jt. auth. see Schwartz, Bernard.
Wade, Harlan. L' Eau. Potvin, Claude & Potvin, Rose-Ella, trs. from Eng. (A Book About Ser.). Orig. Title: Water. (Illus., Fr.). (gr. k-3). 1979. PLB 10.25 o.p. (ISBN 0-8172-1465-8). Raintree Pubs.
--Electricity. rev. ed. LC 78-26825. (A Book About Ser.). (Illus.). (gr. k-3). 1979. PLB 10.25 o.p. (ISBN 0-8172-1537-9). Raintree Pubs.
--Le Levier. Potvin, Claude & Potvin, Rose-Ella, trs. from Eng. (A Book About Ser.). Orig. Title: The Lever. (Illus., Fr.). (gr. k-3). 1979. PLB 10.25 o.p. (ISBN 0-8172-1464-X). Raintree Pubs.
--Sound. rev. ed. LC 78-20961. (A Book About Ser.). (Illus.). (gr. k-3). 1979. PLB 10.25 o.p. (ISBN 0-8172-1525-5). Raintree Pubs.
--Springs. rev. ed. LC 78-21066. (A Book About Ser.). (Illus.). (gr. k-3). 1979. PLB 10.25 o.p. (ISBN 0-8172-1529-8). Raintree Pubs.
--La Vitesse. Potvin, Claude & Potvin, Rose-Ella, trs. from Eng. (A Book About Ser.). Orig. Title: Speed. (Illus., Fr.). (gr. k-3). 1979. PLB 10.25 o.p. (ISBN 0-8172-1454-2). Raintree Pubs.
--Water. rev. ed. LC 78-21290. (A Book About Ser.). (Illus.). (gr. k-3). 1979. PLB 10.25 o.p. (ISBN 0-8172-1539-5). Raintree Pubs.
--Wood. rev. ed. LC 78-21060. (A Book About Ser.). (Illus.). (gr. k-3). 1979. PLB 10.25 o.p. (ISBN 0-8172-1532-8). Raintree Pubs.
Wade, Henry. The Duke of York's Steps. LC 81-48023. 350p. 1982. pap. cancelled o.p. (ISBN 0-06-080588-9, P-588, PL). Har-Row.
--A Dying Fall. LC 80-8719. 256p. 1981. pap. 2.84i (ISBN 0-06-080543-9, P543, PL). Har-Row.
Wade, Herb. Building Underground: The Design & Construction Handbook for Earth-Sheltered Houses. Balitas, Maggie, ed. (Illus.). 320p. (Orig.). 1983. 19.95 (ISBN 0-87857-421-2, 04-000-0); pap. 14.95 (ISBN 0-87857-422-0, 04-000-1). Rodale Pr Inc.
Wade, Herbert, et al, eds. Passive Solar: Subdivisions, Windows, Underground. 1983. text ed. 15.00x (ISBN 0-89553-057-0). Am Solar Energy.
Wade, Jack W., Jr. When You Owe the IRS. (Illus.). 192p. 1983. 12.95 (ISBN 0-02-622230-2, Collier). Macmillan.
Wade, Jennifer. The Singing Wind. LC 77-23984. 1977. 8.95 o.p. (ISBN 0-698-10857-4, Coward). Putnam Pub Group.
Wade, John. History of the Middle & Working Classes. LC 66-18321. Repr. of 1833 ed. 35.00x (ISBN 0-678-00173-1). Kelley.
--Portrait Photography. (Photographer's Library Ser.). (Illus.). 168p. 1982. pap. 12.95 (ISBN 0-240-51111-5). Focal Pr.
--A Short History of the Camera. LC 79-670346. (Illus., Orig.). 1979. pap. text ed. 12.50x o.p. (ISBN 0-85242-640-2). Intl Pubns Serv.
--A Treatise on the Police and Crimes of the Metropolis. LC 71-129306. (Criminology, Law Enforcement, & Social Problems Ser.: No. 128). 410p. (With intro. added). 1972. Repr. of 1829 ed. 18.00x (ISBN 0-87585-128-2). Patterson Smith.
Wade, John S., tr. see Burssens, Gaston.
Wade, Joseph D. Sexuality, Chastity, & Personal Hangups. LC 72-83554. 188p. 1972. pap. 1.25 o.p. (ISBN 0-8189-0199-3, Pub. by Alba Bks). Alba.
Wade, Judy, jt. auth. see Hudson, Val.
Wade, Kevin. Key Exchange. 96p. 1982. pap. 2.50 (ISBN 0-380-61119-8, 61119-8, Discus). Avon.
Wade, L. G. Compendium of Organic Synthetic Methods, Vol. 4. 497p. 26.95 (ISBN 0-471-04923-9, Pub. by Wiley-Interscience). Wiley.
Wade, L. G. & O'Donnell, M. J., eds. Annual Reports in Organic Synthesis, Vol. 11. (Serial Publication). 1981. 24.00 (ISBN 0-12-040811-2). Acad Pr.
Wade, L. G., Jr. & O'Donnell, Martin J., eds. Annual Reports in Organic Synthesis, Vol. 10. 1980. 27.00 (ISBN 0-12-040810-4). Acad Pr.
Wade, Larry, jt. ed. see Samuels, Warren.
Wade, Larry L., jt. ed. see Samuels, Warren J.
Wade, Leroy, jt. auth. see Hegedus, Louis S.
Wade, N. A., jt. auth. see Wallace, J. E.
Wade, Nicholas. The Art & Science of Visual Illusions. (International Library of Psychology). (Illus.). 224p. 1983. 40.00 (ISBN 0-7100-0868-6). Routledge & Kegan.
--The Ultimate Experiment. 2nd ed. 1979. pap. 7.95 o.s.i. (ISBN 0-8027-7149-1). Walker & Co.
--The Ultimate Experiment: Man Made Evolution. LC 76-52575. (Illus.). 1977. 8.95 o.s.i. (ISBN 0-8027-0572-3). Walker & Co.
Wade, Nicholas, jt. auth. see Broad, William.
Wade, Richard. Companion Guide to the Loire. (Illus.). 352p. 1983. 15.95 (ISBN 0-13-154526-4); pap. 7.95 (ISBN 0-13-154518-3). P-H.
Wade, Richard C. Slavery in the Cities: The South, Eighteen Twenty to Eighteen Sixty. 1967. pap. 8.95 (ISBN 0-19-500755-7, GB). Oxford U Pr.
Wade, Richard C., ed. Cities in American Life. LC 73-132975. (Life in America Ser). (Illus.). (gr. 9-10). 1971. pap. 7.68 (ISBN 0-395-11207-9). HM.
Wade, Richard C. & Anderson, Howard R., eds. Negro in American Life. (Life in America Ser). (gr. 9-12). 1970. pap. 7.68 (ISBN 0-395-03147-8). HM.
Wade, S. J., jt. tr. see Kendzierski, Lottie.
Wade, Sarah Van see Van Wade, David & Van Wade, Sarah.
Wade, Theodore E., Jr., et al. School at Home: A Guide for Parents Teaching Their Own Children. rev. ed. 275p. 1983. 11.00 (ISBN 0-930192-12-5); pap. 7.95 (ISBN 0-930192-13-3). Gazelle Pubns.
Wade, Thomas, jt. auth. see Taylor, Howard.
Wade, Thomas L. & Taylor, Howard E. Fundamental Mathematics. 4th ed. (Illus.). 608p. 1974. text ed. 28.50 (ISBN 0-07-067652-6, C); instr's. manual 10.95 (ISBN 0-07-067657-7). McGraw.
Wade, Torlen L., jt. auth. see Brooks, Edward F.
Wadekin, Karl-Eugen. Agrarian Policies in Communist Europe: A Critical Introduction, Vol. 1. Jacobs, Everett M., ed. LC 79-55000. (Studies in East European & Soviet Russian Agrarian Policy: Vol. 1). 336p. 1982. text ed. 24.95x (ISBN 0-916672-40-9); pap. 11.45x (ISBN 0-86598-084-5). Allanheld.
--The Private Sector in Soviet Agriculture. 2nd enl. & rev ed. Karcz, George, ed. Bush, Keith, tr. from Ger. LC 76-95322. Orig. Title: Privatproduzenten in der Sowjetischen Landwirtschaft. 350p. 1973. 42.50x (ISBN 0-520-01558-4). U of Cal Pr.
Wadell, Heather see Lyzell, Richard.
Wademan, Victor. Money-Making Advertising: Guide to Advertising That Sells. LC 80-19059. 142p. 1981. 20.95x (ISBN 0-471-06276-6, Pub. by Ronald Pr). Wiley.
--Riskfree Advertising: How to Come Close to It. LC 77-8083. (Series on Marketing Management). 1977. 22.50 (ISBN 0-471-02714-6, Pub. by Wiley-Interscience). Wiley.
Wadeson, Harriet. Art Psychotherapy. LC 79-21440. (Ser. on Personality Processes). 1980. 32.95x (ISBN 0-471-06383-5, Pub. by Wiley-Interscience). Wiley.
Wadhwa, D. C., jt. auth. see Rothermund, D.
Wadhwa, Kamlesh K. Minority Safeguards in India: Constitutional Provisions & Their Implementation. LC 75-901908. 1975. 14.00x o.p. (ISBN 0-88386-607-2). South Asia Bks.
Wadley, James, jt. auth. see Juergensmeyer, Julian.

Wadley, Nicholas. Cezanne & His Art. (The Artist & His Art Ser.). (Illus.). 128p. 1981. 9.98 o.p. (ISBN 0-89196-093-7, Bk Value Intl). Quality Bks IL.

Wadley, Susan, jt. auth. see Jacobson, Doranne.

Wadlington, Walter, et al. Cases & Materials on Children in the Legal System. LC 82-21114. (University Casebook Ser.). 965p. 1982. text ed. write for info. (ISBN 0-88277-101-9); write for info. tchr's manual (ISBN 0-88277-125-6). Foundation Pr.

Wadman, Robert C., et al. Law Enforcement Supervision: A Case Study Approach. (Criminal Justice Ser.). 1975. pap. text ed. 11.50 o.s.i. (ISBN 0-8299-0631-2). West Pub.

Wadsworth, Charles, compiled by. Root & Sky: Poetry from the Plays of Christopher Fry. (Illus.). 136p. 1976. ltd. ed. 250.00 o.p. (ISBN 0-87923-187-4). Godine.

Wadsworth, Charles E. & Wadsworth, Jean G., eds. Roots & Sky: Poetry from the Plays of Christopher Fry. (Illus., Ltd. ed. 220 copies, printed by C. E. Wadsworth). special bdg. 250.00 (ISBN 0-930954-17-3); limited ed. 28 copies avail. Tidal Pr.

Wadsworth, Gladys, jt. auth. see Kendall, Florence P.

Wadsworth, Jean G., jt. ed. see Wadsworth, Charles E.

Wadsworth, Joseph A., jt. auth. see King, John H.

Wadsworth, Philip A. Moliere & the Italian Theatrical Tradition. 15.00 (ISBN 0-686-38458-X). French Lit.

Waechter, Friedrich K. Three Is Company. Allard, Harry, tr. LC 79-7790. (Illus.). (gr. k-3). 1980. 9.95a o.p. (ISBN 0-385-14632-9); PLB 9.95a (ISBN 0-385-14633-7). Doubleday.

Waehrer, Helen Y., jt. auth. see Glazer, Nona Y.

Waelbrock, J. The Models of Project Link. (Contributions to Economic Analysis: Vol. 102). 1976. 55.50 (ISBN 0-7204-0514-9, North-Holland). Elsevier.

Waelbroeck, J. L., jt. auth. see Ginsburgh, V. A.

Waelti-Walters, Jennifer. Fairy Tales & the Female Imagination. 225p. 1982. 14.95 (ISBN 0-920792-07-3). Eden Pr.

Waelti-Walters, Jennifer R. J. M. G. Leclezio. (World Author Ser.). 1977. lib. bdg. 15.95 (ISBN 0-8057-6266-3, Twayne). G K Hall.

Waesche, James. Baltimore, Annapolis & Chesapeake County Guidebook. (Illus.). 160p. 1976. pap. 4.95 (ISBN 0-686-36501-1). Md Hist.

Wafer, James W. Drippings from a Churn: Unique Views of Education. 256p. 1983. 11.50 (ISBN 0-682-49926-9). Exposition.

Waffle, Harvey W. Architectural Drawing. rev. ed. 1962. 9.00 o.p. (ISBN 0-02-829660-5). Glencoe.

Wagai & Omoto, eds. Ultrasound in Medicine & Biology. (International Congress Ser.: Vol. 505). 1980. 69.00 (ISBN 0-444-90138-8). Elsevier.

Wagar, W. Warren. Terminal Visions: The Literature of Last Things. LC 81-48625. 256p. 1982. 24.50 (ISBN 0-253-35847-7). Ind U Pr.

Wagar, W. Warren, ed. The Secular Mind: Transformations of Faith in Modern Europe. LC 81-20019. 275p. 1982. text ed. 35.00x (ISBN 0-8419-0766-8). Holmes & Meier.

Wage, J. L. How to Use the Telephone in Selling. 1974. 17.95x o.p. (ISBN 0-8464-0497-4). Beekman Pubs.

Wagener, Hans. The German Baroque Novel. (World Authors Ser.: Germany: No. 229). lib. bdg. 10.95 o.p. (ISBN 0-8057-2356-0, Twayne). G K Hall.

Wagener, Jerrold L. Principles of Fortran Seventy-Seven Programming. LC 79-17421. 1980. pap. text ed. 19.95 (ISBN 0-471-04474-1); tchr's manual 5.50x (ISBN 0-471-07831-X). Wiley.

Wagenfeld, Morton, jt. ed. see Robin, Stanley.

Wagenfeld, Morton O. & Lemkau, Paul V., eds. Public Mental Health. (Studies in Community Mental Health). (Illus.). 288p. 1982. 25.00 (ISBN 0-8039-1120-3); pap. 12.50 (ISBN 0-8039-1224-2). Sage.

Wagenhauser, F. J. Principles of Antirheumatic Therapy. (Illus.). 46p. Date not set. pap. text ed. 9.50 (ISBN 3-456-81204-3, Pub. by Hans Huber Switzerland). J K Burgess.

Wagenheim, Kal, tr. see Zeno-Gandia, Manuel.

Wageningen Symposium, 1969. Water in the Unsaturated Zone: Proceedings, 2 Vols. 1969. 54.00 (ISBN 92-3-000733-1, U714, UNESCO). Unipub.

Wagenknecht, Edward. Gamaliel Bradford. (Twayne's United States Authors Ser.). 1982. lib. bdg. 15.95 (ISBN 0-8057-7355-X, Twayne). G K Hall.

--The Novels of Henry James. LC 82-40280. 250p. 1983. 18.50 (ISBN 0-8044-2959-6). Ungar.

--A Pictorial History of New England. (Illus.). 352p. 1976. 12.95 o.p. (ISBN 0-517-52346-9). Crown.

Wagenknecht, Edward, ed. Chaucer: Modern Essays in Criticism. (Orig.). 1959. pap. 9.95 (ISBN 0-19-500683-6, GB). Oxford U Pr.

--Fireside Book of Christmas Stories. (gr. 3-9). 1963. 8.95 (ISBN 0-448-01027-5, G&D). Putnam Pub Group.

Wagenknecht, Edward C. Ambassadors for Christ: Seven American Preachers. 1972. 15.95x (ISBN 0-19-501520-7). Oxford U Pr.

--James Russell Lowell: Portrait of a Many-Sided Man. (Portraits of American Writers Ser). 1971. 15.95x (ISBN 0-19-501376-X). Oxford U Pr.

--Merely Players. (Illus.). 1966. 16.95x (ISBN 0-8061-0717-0). U of Okla Pr.

--Ralph Waldo Emerson: Portrait of a Balanced Soul. 1974. 17.95x (ISBN 0-19-501766-8). Oxford U Pr.

--William Dean Howells: The Friendly Eye. LC 70-83055. 1969. 17.95x (ISBN 0-19-500649-6). Oxford U Pr.

Wagennar, Willem A., jt. ed. see Wertheim, Alexander H.

Wagenvoord, James. Auction Notes. 160p. Date not set. pap. cancelled (ISBN 0-312-06062-9); pap. cancelled (ISBN 0-312-06063-7). St Martin.

--Diet & Exercise Diary. (Illus.). 160p. 1981. 6.95 o.p. (ISBN 0-312-20996-7). St Martin.

--Doubleday Wine Companion, 1983. LC 81-43751. (Illus.). 160p. 1983. 16.95 (ISBN 0-385-18516-2). Doubleday.

--Golf Diary. (Illus.). 160p. 1981. 6.95 o.p. (ISBN 0-312-33806-6). St Martin.

--Photography Notes. (Illus.). 160p. 1981. 6.95 o.p. (ISBN 0-312-60840-3). St Martin.

--The Swim Book. LC 79-5381. (Illus.). 288p. 1980. 14.95 o.p. (ISBN 0-672-52622-0). Bobbs.

--Tennis Notes, Vol. 3. (Illus.). 160p. 1981. 6.95 o.p. (ISBN 0-312-79104-6). St Martin.

--The Wine Diary. 160p. 1979. 8.95 o.p. (ISBN 0-672-52619-0). Bobbs.

Wagenvoord, James, jt. auth. see Irwin, Yukiko.

Wagenvoord, James, ed. Women: A Book for Men. 1979. pap. 7.95 o.p. (ISBN 0-380-42994-2, 76018). Avon.

Wagenvoort, C. A. & Wagenvoort, Noeke. Pathology of Pulmonary Hypertension. LC 76-39782. (Wiley Ser. in Clinical Cardiology). 345p. 1977. text ed. 41.95 o.p. (ISBN 0-471-91355-3, Pub. by Wiley Medical). Wiley.

Wagenvoort, Hendrik. Roman Dynamism: Studies in Ancient Roman Thought Language & Custom. LC 74-30929. 1976. Repr. of 1947 ed. lib. bdg. 16.25x (ISBN 0-8371-7887-8, WARD). Greenwood.

Wagenvoort, Noeke, jt. auth. see Wagenvoort, C. A.

Wagenvourd, James. The Wine Book. 144p. 1980. 12.95 (ISBN 0-8256-3193-9, Quick Fox); 13 copy prepack 155.40 (ISBN 0-8256-3195-5). Putnam Pub Group.

Wages, Jack D. Seventy-Five Writers of the Colonial South: A Reference Guide. 1979. lib. bdg. 30.00 (ISBN 0-8161-7979-4, Hall Reference). G K Hall.

Wagg, Susan. Percy Erskine Nobbs: Architect, Artist Craftsman-Architecte, Artiste, Atrisan. (Illus.). 114p. 1982. pap. 12.95 (ISBN 0-7735-0395-1). McGill-Queens U Pr.

Waggoner, D. R., jt. auth. see Diamond, R. B.

Waggoner, D. R., jt. auth. see Diamond, R. D.

Waggoner, Donald R. Granular Urea: Advantages & Processes. (Technical Bulletin - T-1). (Illus.). 12p. (Orig.). 1975. pap. 5.00x o.p. (ISBN 0-88090-000-8). Intl Fertilizer.

Waggoner, Hyatt H., ed. see Hawthorne, Nathaniel.

Waggoner, Laurence W., jt. auth. see Kahn, Douglas A.

Waggoner, Lawrence, jt. auth. see Kahn, Douglas.

Waggoner, Lawrence W., jt. auth. see Kahn, Douglas A.

Waggoner, Susan, jt. auth. see Dietrich, John.

Wa-Githumo, Mwangi. Land & Nationalism: The Impact of Land Expropriation & Land Grievances Upon the Rise & Development of Nationalist Movements in Kenya, 1885-1939. LC 80-5589. 502p. 1981. lib. bdg. 27.50 (ISBN 0-8191-1491-X); pap. text ed. 17.25 (ISBN 0-8191-1492-8). U Pr of Amer.

Wagley, Charles. Economics of a Guatemalan Village. LC 41-19381. 1941. pap. 10.00 (ISBN 0-527-00557-6). Kraus Repr.

Wagman, jt. ed. see Weinstein.

Wagman, G. H. & Weinstein, M. J. Chromatography of Antibiotics. LC 72-97439. 256p. 1973. 58.25 o.p. (ISBN 0-444-41106-2). Elsevier.

Wagman, Michael. The Far Horizons. 1980. 12.95 o.s.i. (ISBN 0-440-02815-9). Delacorte.

Wagman, Richard J. New Complete Medical & Health Encyclopedia, 4 vols. LC 8393009976000006. 1977. Set. lib. bdg. 66.60 (ISBN 0-89434-007-7). Purnell Ref Bks.

--The New Concise Family Health & Medical Guide. 400p. 1972. 12.95 (ISBN 0-385-08075-1). Doubleday.

Wagman, Robert J., jt. auth. see Engelmayer, Sheldon D.

Wagner, jt. auth. see Moffett.

Wagner, A. F. & Folkers, K. Vitamins & Coenzymes. LC 74-30499. 552p. 1975. Repr. of 1964 ed. 29.50 (ISBN 0-88275-258-8). Krieger.

Wagner, Augusta. Labor Legislation in China. LC 78-22780. (The Modern Chinese Economy Ser.). 301p. 1980. lib. bdg. 33.00 o.s.i. (ISBN 0-8240-4283-2). Garland Pub.

Wagner, Bernard M. & Fleischmajer, Paul. Connective Tissue & Diseases of Connective Tissue. (International Academy of Pathology: No. 24). (Illus.). 246p. 1983. lib. bdg. price not set (ISBN 0-683-08601-4). Williams & Wilkins.

Wagner, Betty J., jt. auth. see Moffett, James.

Wagner, Betty Jane, jt. auth. see Moffett, James.

Wagner, C. F. & Evans, R. D. Symmetrical Components. LC 82-14051. 454p. 1982. Repr. of 1933 ed. lib. bdg. 27.50 (ISBN 0-89874-556-X). Krieger.

Wagner, C. Peter. Our Kind of People: The Ethical Dimensions of Church Growth in America. LC 77-15754. 1979. pap. 9.50 (ISBN 0-8042-0838-7). John Knox.

Wagner, C. Peter, et al. Unreached Peoples, Eighty-One. (Orig.). 1981. pap. 8.95 (ISBN 0-89191-331-9). Cook.

Wagner, Candy & Marquez, Sandra. Cooking Texas Style: A Heritage of Traditional Recipes. (Illus.). 1983. 12.95 (ISBN 0-292-71082-8). U of Tex Pr.

Wagner, Carol F., jt. auth. see Wagner, Edwin E.

Wagner, Charles F. & Evans, R. D. Symmetrical Components. (Illus.). 1933. text ed. 33.50 (ISBN 0-07-067660-7, C). McGraw.

Wagner, Charles R. The CPA & the Computer Fraud. LC 77-90861. (Illus.). 176p. 1979. 18.95x (ISBN 0-669-02079-6). Lexington Bks.

Wagner, D. R. Cruisin' at the Limit: Selected Poems 1968-78. Robertson, Kirk, ed. LC 82-72997. (Windriver Ser.). 120p. (Orig.). 1982. pap. 7.95 (ISBN 0-916918-20-3); pap. 25.00 signed ed. (ISBN 0-916918-21-1). Duck Down.

Wagner, David K., et al, eds. Year Book of Emergency Medicine 1983. 1983. 40.00 (ISBN 0-686-83756-8). Year Bk Med.

Wagner, Edward W., tr. see Lee, Ki-Baik.

Wagner, Edwin E. & Wagner, Carol F. The Interpretation of Projective Test Data: Theoretical & Practical Guidelines. (Illus.). 362p. 1981. pap. text ed. 35.50x (ISBN 0-398-04602-6). C C Thomas.

Wagner, Eileen N. For the Sake of Argument: Writing Editorials & Position Papers. LC 79-64515. 1979. pap. text ed. 10.25 (ISBN 0-8191-0763-8). U Pr of Amer.

Wagner, F. E., jt. ed. see Shenoy, G. K.

Wagner, F. J. J. H. Shorthouse. (English Authors Ser.). 1979. 14.95 (ISBN 0-8057-6729-0, Twayne). G K Hall.

Wagner, Galen S. Myocardial Infarction. 1982. 69.50 (ISBN 90-247-2513-5, Pub. by Martinus Nijhoff Netherlands). Kluwer Boston.

Wagner, Gary. Publicity Forum. 1977. pap. 6.95 (ISBN 0-913046-06-X). Public Relations.

Wagner, Geoffrey. Wyndham Lewis: A Portrait of the Artist As the Enemy. LC 72-12320. 363p. 1973. Repr. of 1957 ed. lib. bdg. 18.75x (ISBN 0-8371-6692-6, WAWK). Greenwood.

Wagner, George. Practical Truths from Israel's Wanderings. 384p. 1983. Repr. of 1862 ed. 12.95 (ISBN 0-8254-4017-3). Kregel.

Wagner, Gerard, jt. auth. see Koch, Elisabeth.

Wagner, Gunther. An Exegetical Bibliography of the New Testament: Vol. 1-Matthew & Mark. (Bibliographical Tools for New Testament Studies). 320p. 1983. 35.00x (ISBN 0-86554-013-6). Mercer Univ Pr.

Wagner, H. R. Rise of Fernando Cortes. 1944. 56.00 (ISBN 0-527-19733-5). Kraus Repr.

Wagner, H. R., tr. Discovery of New Spain in Fifteen Eighteen by Juan De Grijalva. Repr. of 1942 ed. 13.00 (ISBN 0-527-19731-9). Kraus Repr.

--Discovery of Yucatan by Francisco Hernandez De Cordoba. Repr. of 1942 ed. 21.00 (ISBN 0-527-19732-7). Kraus Repr.

Wagner, Harold A. As I Lived It: An Autobiographical History of the YMCA of Los Angeles, 1925-1966. LC 79-50564. (Illus.). 1979. 10.00 o.p. (ISBN 0-87062-129-7). A H Clark.

Wagner, Harvey M. Principles of Management Science: With Applications to Executive Decisions. 2nd ed. (Illus.). 576p. 1975. 29.95 (ISBN 0-13-709535-X). P-H.

--Principles of Operations Research with Applications to Managerial Decisions. 2nd ed. (Illus.). 1088p. 1975. 33.95 (ISBN 0-13-709592-9). P-H.

Wagner, Henry N., jt. auth. see Dibos, Pablo E.

Wagner, Henry W., jt. auth. see DeLand, Frank H.

Wagner, Hilda S., jt. auth. see Ecroyd, Donald.

Wagner, Hilmar. The Social Psychology of Adolescence. 1977. pap. text ed. 11.50 o.p. (ISBN 0-8191-0488-4). U Pr of Amer.

--The Wagner Report: Readings for Teachers & Parents. 1976. pap. text ed. 7.50 (ISBN 0-8191-0032-3). U Pr of Amer.

Wagner, Jenny. Aranea. LC 78-55212. (Illus.). 32p. (gr. k-2). 1978. 8.95 (ISBN 0-02-792390-8). Bradbury Pr.

--The Bunyip of Berkeley's Creek. LC 77-73826. (Illus.). 32p. (ps-2). 1977. 9.95 (ISBN 0-02-792490-4). Bradbury Pr.

--John Brown, Rose & the Midnight Cat. LC 77-76836. (Illus.). 32p. (ps-2). 1978. 9.95 (ISBN 0-02-792470-X). Bradbury Pr.

Wagner, Jon, ed. Sex Roles in Contemporary American Communes. LC 81-47571. 256p. 1982. 17.50x (ISBN 0-253-35187-1). Ind U Pr.

Wagner, Joseph E., jt. auth. see Harkness, John E.

Wagner, Joseph F. Band Scoring. (Music Ser.). 1960. text ed. 15.95 o.p. (ISBN 0-07-067658-5, C). McGraw.

Wagner, Karl E. Bloodstone. 304p. 1975. pap. 2.95 (ISBN 0-446-30629-0). Warner Bks.

--Dark Crusade. 224p. (Orig.). 1983. pap. 2.95 (ISBN 0-446-30679-7). Warner Bks.

--Darkness Weaves. (Orig.). 1983. pap. 2.95 (ISBN 0-446-30653-3). Warner Bks.

--In a Lonely Place. 288p. 1983. pap. 2.95 (ISBN 0-446-30534-0). Warner Bks.

Wagner, Kurt J. & Imber, Gerald. Beauty by Design: A Complete Look at Cosmetic Surgery. (Illus.). 1979. 7.95 o.p. (ISBN 0-07-067671-2, GB). McGraw.

Wagner, Leopold. Manners, Customs & Observances. LC 68-22059. 1968. Repr. of 1894 ed. 30.00x (ISBN 0-8103-3097-0). Gale.

--More About Names. LC 68-17937. 1968. Repr. of 1893 ed. 37.00x (ISBN 0-8103-3099-7). Gale.

--Names & Their Meanings, A Book for the Curious. LC 68-22060. 1968. Repr. of 1893 ed. 34.00x (ISBN 0-8103-3098-9). Gale.

Wagner, Linda W. Ellen Glasgow: Beyond Convention. LC 82-2067. 160p. 1982. text ed. 15.95x (ISBN 0-292-72039-4). U of Tex Pr.

--Ernest Hemingway: A Reference Guide. 1977. lib. bdg. 24.00 (ISBN 0-8161-7976-X, Hall Reference). G K Hall.

Wagner, Linda W. & Mead, C. David. Introducing Poems. 416p. 1976. pap. text ed. 13.50 scp (ISBN 0-06-046875-0, HarpC); instr's. manual avail. (ISBN 0-06-367021-6). Har-Row.

Wagner, Linda W., ed. William Carlos Williams: A Reference Guide. 1978. lib. bdg. 19.50 o.p. (ISBN 0-8161-7977-8, Hall Reference). G K Hall.

Wagner, M. Wilhelm, jt. auth. see Mohan, Rakesh.

Wagner, Manfred, ed. see Bontinck-Kueffel, Irmgard.

Wagner, Marsden & Wagner, Mary. The Danish National Child Care System: A Successful System As Model for the Reconstruction of American Child Care. LC 75-33183. 200p. 1976. lib. bdg. 20.00 o.p. (ISBN 0-89158-008-5). Westview.

Wagner, Marsha L. Wang Wei. (World Authors Ser.). 1981. lib. bdg. 15.95 (ISBN 0-8057-6448-8, Twayne). G K Hall.

Wagner, Martha, jt. auth. see Norton, Reggi.

Wagner, Mary, jt. auth. see Wagner, Marsden.

Wagner, Mary M., ed. Care of the Burn-Injured Patient: A Multidisciplinary Involvement. 310p. 1981. 25.00 (ISBN 0-88416-249-4). Wright-PSG.

Wagner, Melinda B. Metaphysics in Midwestern America. 275p. 1983. 17.50x (ISBN 0-8142-0346-9). Ohio St U Pr.

Wagner, Michael J. Machine Language Disk I-O & Other Mysteries. (TRS-80 Information Ser.: Vol. V). 272p. (Orig.). 1982. pap. 29.95 (ISBN 0-936200-06-5). IJG Inc.

Wagner, Miriam M., jt. auth. see Lee, Mabel.

Wagner, Nathaniel N., jt. ed. see Sue, Stanley.

Wagner, Peter C. Stop the World I Want to Get on. 144p. 1980. pap. 3.95 o.p. (ISBN 0-87808-740-0). William Carey Lib.

Wagner, Philip, tr. see Geipel, Robert.

Wagner, Philip M. Wine-Grower's Guide. rev ed. (Illus.). 1965. 13.50 (ISBN 0-394-40183-2). Knopf.

Wagner, R. Helping the Wordblind: Effective Intervention Techniques for Overcoming Reading Problems in Older Students. 1976. 16.50 (ISBN 0-685-73730-6). P-H.

Wagner, R. J. & Abbott, R. Tucker. Standard Catalog of Shells. new ed. LC 77-88916. (Illus.). 1978. buckram looseleaf 55.00 (ISBN 0-915826-03-8); Supplement 1 looseleaf incl. (ISBN 0-915826-04-6); Supplement 2 incl. (ISBN 0-915826-10-0). Am Malacologists.

Wagner, R. P. Genetics & Metabolism. 2nd ed. LC 63-18630. 673p. 1964. 21.50 (ISBN 0-471-91412-6, Pub. by Wiley). Krieger.

Wagner, R. P., et al. Introduction to Modern Genetics. 573p. 1980. text ed. 28.95x (ISBN 0-471-91430-4). Wiley.

--Answers to Introduction to Modern Genetics. 73p. 1980. pap. text ed. 3.95x o.p. (ISBN 0-471-07915-4). Wiley.

Wagner, Richard. Ancient Ships & Boats to Color, Cut-Out & Float: P S S Coloring Experience. (Illus.). (gr. 1-4). 1978. pap. 1.95 o.s.i. (ISBN 0-8431-0467-8). Price Stern.

--The Diary of Richard Wagner. Bergfeld, J., ed. Bird, G., tr. LC 79-56128. 224p. 1980. 16.95 (ISBN 0-521-23311-9). Cambridge U Pr.

--Logengrin in Full Score. (Music Scores & Music to Play Ser.). 295p. 1982. pap. 12.95 (ISBN 0-486-24335-4). Dover.

--Three Wagner Essays. Jacobs, Robert L., tr. (Eulenburg Music Ser.). (Illus.). 127p. 1982. pap. text ed. 15.00 (ISBN 0-903873-56-7). Da Capo.

--Wagner on Music & Drama. Goldman, Albert & Sprinchorn, Evert, eds. (Music Ser.). 447p. 1981. Repr. of 1964 ed. lib. bdg. 39.50 (ISBN 0-306-76109-2). Da Capo.

--Works of Richard Wagner, 10 Vols. in 7. Balling, Michael, ed. LC 72-75306. (Music Ser). (Ger). 1971. Repr. of 1912 ed. Set. lib. bdg. 525.00 (ISBN 0-306-77250-7); lib. bdg. 85.00 ea. Da Capo.

Wagner, Richard, jt. ed. see Tullock, Gordon.

Wagner, Richard E. & Tollison, Robert D. Balanced Budgets, Fiscal Responsibility, & the Constitution. (Cato Public Policy Research Monograph Ser.: No. 1). 64p. (Orig.). 1980. pap. 4.00x o.p. (ISBN 0-932790-12-7). Cato Inst.

--Balanced Budgets, Fiscal Responsibility & the Constitution. 109p. 1982. pap. 6.00 (ISBN 0-932790-36-4). Cato Inst.

Wagner, Robert P., jt. auth. see Sutton, H. Eldon.

Wagner, Robert P., ed. Genes & Proteins. LC 75-8851. (Benchmark Papers in Genetics Ser: Vol. 2). 395p. 1975. 54.00 (ISBN 0-12-787710-X). Acad Pr.

Wagner, Robin S. Sarah T. Portrait of a Teen-Age Alcoholic. 1.50 o.p. (ISBN 0-686-92249-2, 5015). Hazelden.

Wagner, Rudolph F. Dyslexia & Your Child: A Guide for Teachers & Parents. rev. ed. LC 78-4740. (Illus.). 1979. 12.45i (ISBN 0-06-014583-8, HarpT). Har-Row.

Wagner, Sally R. That Word is Liberty: A Biography of Matilda Joslyn Gage. 1983. write for info (ISBN 0-8093-1086-4); pap. write for info (ISBN 0-8093-1087-2). S Ill U Pr.

Wagner, Sharon. Charade of Love. (Orig.). 1982. pap. 1.95 o.p. (ISBN 0-451-11286-5, AJ1286, Sig). NAL.

--Gypsy & Nimblefoot. (Gypsy Bks.). (gr. 4 up). 1978. pap. 1.50 (ISBN 0-307-21545-8, Golden Pr); Golden Pr. PLB 5.52 (ISBN 0-307-61545-6). Western Pub.

--Gypsy from Nowhere. (Gypsy Bks.). (gr. 4 up). 1978. pap. 1.50 (ISBN 0-307-21509-1, Golden Pr); Golden Pr. PLB 5.52 (ISBN 0-686-77044-7). Western Pub.

--Jaquelle's Shadow. (Adventures in Love Ser.: No. 28). 1982. pap. 1.75 (ISBN 0-451-11707-7, AE1707, Sig). NAL.

--Journey to Paradise. (Adentures in Love Ser.: No. 34). 1982. pap. 1.95 (ISBN 0-451-11841-3, Sig). NAL.

--New Dream for Kendra. (Adventures in Love Ser.: No. 24). 1982. pap. 1.75 (ISBN 0-451-11705-0, AE1705, Sig). NAL.

Wagner, Sheldon L. Clinical Toxicology of Agricultural Chemicals. LC 82-14421. (Illus.). 306p. 1983. 28.00 (ISBN 0-8155-0930-8). Noyes.

Wagner, Thomas A. Kognitive Problemlosungsbarrieren Bei Entscheidungsprozessen In der Unternehmung. vi, 250p. (Ger.). 1982. write for info. (ISBN 3-8204-5774-7). P Lang Pubs.

Wagner, Walter. Solomon: Man of Peace. LC 74-77634. 290p. pap. text ed. 3.25 cancelled (ISBN 0-89081-316-7, 3167). Harvest Hse.

Wagner, Walter F., Jr. More Houses Architects Design for Themselves. Archirtectural Record, ed. (Illus.). 1982. 29.95 (ISBN 0-07-002365-4). McGraw.

Wagner, Walter F., Jr., ed. see Architectural Record Magazine.

Wagner, Willis H. Modern Carpentry. LC 79-11956. 1979. text ed. 16.00 (ISBN 0-87006-274-3); wkbk. 3.80 (ISBN 0-87006-282-4). Goodheart.

--Modern Woodworking. LC 80-18994. (Illus.). 1980. text ed. 15.00 (ISBN 0-87006-301-4); wkbk. 3.80 (ISBN 0-87006-300-6). Goodheart.

Wagniere, J. L., jt. auth. see Longchamp, S. G.

Wagoner, David. Baby, Come on Inside. LC 68-23743. 256p. 1968. 4.95 o.p. (ISBN 0-374-10785-8). FS&G.

Wagoner, Harless D. U. S. Machine Tool Industry from 1900 to 1950. 1968. 30.00x (ISBN 0-262-23030-5). MIT Pr.

Wagoner, Jean B. Jane Addams: Little Lame Girl. LC 62-9250. (Childhood of Famous Americans Ser.). (Illus.). (gr. 3-7). 1944. 3.95 o.p. (ISBN 0-672-50087-6). Bobbs.

--Martha Washington: America's First, First Lady. LC 59-12849. (Childhood of Famous Americans Ser.). (gr. 3-8). 1983. pap. 3.95 (ISBN 0-686-95262-6). Bobbs.

Wagoner, Jennings L., Jr., jt. ed. see Mosher, Edith K.

Wagoner, Joseph K., jt. ed. see Saffotti, Umberto.

Wagoner, R. & Goldsmith, D. Cosmic Horizons: Understanding the Universe. 1982. 18.95 (ISBN 0-7167-1417-5); pap. 9.95 (ISBN 0-7167-1418-3). W H Freeman.

Wagonseller, Bill R. & McDowell, Richard L. Tip-Teaching Involved Parenting: A Total Workhop. LC 82-80624. (Illus.). 273p. (Orig.). 1982. pap. 44.95 3-ring binder (ISBN 0-87822-262-6, 2626). Res Press.

Wagstaff, J. M. The Development of Rural Settlements: A Study of the Helos Plain in Southern Greece. 1981. 60.00x o.p. (ISBN 0-86127-302-8, Pub. by Avebury Pub England). State Mutual Bk.

--The Development of Rural Settlements: A Study of the Helos Plain in Southern Greece. 166p. 1982. pap. text ed. 23.95x (ISBN 0-86127-302-8, Pub. by Avebury England). Humanities.

Wagstaff, Lanny. Little Restaurants of San Diego. (Illus.). 1977. 2.25 o.s.i. (ISBN 0-913290-07-6). Camaro Pub.

Wah, Yeo K. see Yeo Kim Wah.

Wahab, A. Shadowless Prophet of Islam. 5.50 o.p. (ISBN 0-686-18427-0). Kazi Pubns.

Wahba, Magdi. English-French-Arabic Dictionary of Political Idioms. 35.00x (ISBN 0-86685-118-6). Intl Bk Ctr.

Waheeduddin. The Benefactor. pap. 4.75 (ISBN 0-686-18425-4). Kazi Pubns.

Wahl, Edward C. Geothermal Energy Utilization. LC 77-546. 1977. 47.95x (ISBN 0-471-02304-3, Pub. by Wiley-Interscience). Wiley.

Wahl, Jahn. Mooga Mega Mekki. LC 73-16818. (Lead-off Books Ser.). (Illus.). 48p. (gr. 2-4). 1974. 4.95 (ISBN 0-87955-111-9). O'Hara.

Wahl, Jan. Crazy Brobobalou. (Illus.). 64p. (gr. 2-5). 1973. PLB 4.69 o.p. (ISBN 0-399-60846-X). Putnam Pub Group.

--Dracula's Cat. LC 77-27051. (Illus.). (ps-3). 1981. 6.95 (ISBN 0-13-218933-X); pap. 2.50 (ISBN 0-13-218925-9). P-H.

--Five in the Forest. (Picture Bk). (Illus.). 48p. (gr. k-3). 1974. 4.95 o.s.i. (ISBN 0-695-80446-4); lib. ed. 4.98 o.s.i. (ISBN 0-695-40446-6). Follett.

--How the Children Stopped the Wars. (Illus.). 96p. (gr. 3-6). 1972. pap. 1.50 (ISBN 0-380-01271-5, 45815-2, Camelot). Avon.

--Juan Diego & the Lady-la Dama y Juan Diego. (Illus.). 48p. (Eng. & Span.). (gr. 2-5). 1974. PLB 5.29 o.p. (ISBN 0-399-60845-1). Putnam Pub Group.

--May Horses. LC 68-20105. (Illus.). (ps-3). 1969. 4.95 o.s.i. (ISBN 0-440-05507-5, Sey Lawr); PLB 4.58 o.s.i. (ISBN 0-440-05516-4, Sey Lawr). Delacorte.

--More Room for the Pipkins. (Illus.). 32p. (ps-7). 1983. 7.95 (ISBN 0-13-601146-2). P-H.

--The Muffletumps Christmas Party. (Picture Bk). (Illus.). 32p. (gr. k-3). 1975. 5.95 o.s.i. (ISBN 0-695-80617-3); PLB 5.97 o.s.i. (ISBN 0-695-40617-5). Follett.

--The Muffletumps' Halloween Scare. (Illus.). (ps-3). 6.95 o.s.i. (ISBN 0-695-80754-4); lib. bdg. 4.65 (ISBN 0-695-40754-6). Follett.

--Old Hippo's Easter Egg. LC 79-9199. (Illus.). 32p. (gr. k-3). 1980. pap. 3.50 (ISBN 0-15-668452-7, VoyB). HarBraceJ.

--Plesant Fieldmouse's Halloween Party. LC 73-88814. (Illus.). 32p. (gr. k-3). 1974. 5.95 o.p. (ISBN 0-399-20395-8). Putnam Pub Group.

--The Teeny, Tiny Witches. LC 78-15657. (Illus.). (gr. 1-4). 1979. 6.95 o.p. (ISBN 0-399-20682-5). Putnam Pub Group.

Wahl, John R., ed. see Rossetti, Dante G.

Wahl, Nicholas. The Fifth Republic: France's New Political System. LC 78-24135. 1979. Repr. of 1959 ed. lib. bdg. 16.00x (ISBN 0-313-21217-1, WAFI). Greenwood.

Wahl, Paul. Gun Trader's Guide. (Illus.). 392p. pap. 9.95 o.p. (ISBN 0-88317-097-3). Stoeger Pub Co.

--Gun Trader's Guide. 10th ed. Traister, John, ed. 416p. 1982. pap. 10.95 (ISBN 0-88317-113-9). Stoeger Pub Co.

Wahl, Thomas. How Jesus Came. (Illus.). 48p. (gr. k-3). 1981. 11.95 (ISBN 0-916134-51-2). Pueblo Pub Co.

Wahlberg, Rachel C. Jesus According to a Woman. LC 74-27461. 112p. 1975. pap. 2.95 (ISBN 0-8091-1861-0). Paulist Pr.

Wahle, Ted, ed. see Linke, Frances.

Wahlke, John & Eulau, Heinz. Legislative Behavior Study, 1959. 1974. codebk. write for info. (ISBN 0-89138-120-1). ICPSR.

Wahlke, John C., ed. Causes of the American Revolution. 3rd ed. (Problems in American Civilization Ser.). 1973. pap. text ed. 5.95 (ISBN 0-669-82685-5). Heath.

Wahloo, Per, jt. auth. see Sjowall, Maj.

Wahlroos, Sven. Family Communication. 1976. pap. 1.95 o.p. (ISBN 0-451-07067-4, J7067, Sig). NAL.

Wahlster, W., ed. Artificial Intelligence, Bad Honnef, FRG 1982: Proceedings. (Informatik Fachberichte Ser.: Vol. 58). 246p. 1983. pap. 14.00 (ISBN 0-387-11960-4). Springer-Verlag.

Wahlstrom, Eric H., tr. see Aulen, Gustaf E.

Wahlstrom, Ernest E. Optical Crystallography. 5th ed. LC 78-13695. 488p. 1979. text ed. 31.95 (ISBN 0-471-04791-0). Wiley.

Wahner, Heinz W., jt. ed. see Scott, George P.

Wahrman, Ralph, jt. auth. see Denisoff, R. Serge.

Waicukauski, Ronald J., ed. Law & Amateur Sports. LC 82-47773. 320p. 1983. 32.50 (ISBN 0-253-13730-6). Ind U Pr.

Waidelich, W., ed. Optoelectronics in Medicine: Proceedings of the Fifth International Congress LASER 81. (Illus.). 239p. 1982. pap. 25.80 (ISBN 0-387-10968-4). Springer-Verlag.

Waidson, H. M. German Short Stories, Vol. 1. 1900-1945, Vol. 2. 1945-1955, Vol. 3. 1955-1965. Vol. 1. text ed. 5.50 (ISBN 0-521-06717-0); Vol. 2. text ed. 5.25 o.p. (ISBN 0-521-06718-9); Vol. 3. text ed. 6.50 (ISBN 0-521-07180-1). Cambridge U Pr.

Waidson, H. M., rev. by see Bennett, E. K.

Waidson, H. M., tr. Alfons Paquet, Prophecies. LC 82-84465. (Studies in German Literature, Linguistics, & Culture: Vol. 10). (Illus.). xx, 120p. 1983. 13.95x (ISBN 0-938100-08-4). Camden Hse.

Wailes, P. C., et al. Organmetallic Chemistry of Titanium, Zirconium, & Hafnium. 1974. 60.00 (ISBN 0-12-730350-2). Acad Pr.

Wailes, Rex. Windmills in England: A Study of Their Origin, Development & Future. 48p. 1982. 25.00x (ISBN 0-284-40007-6, Pub. by C Skilton Scotland). State Mutual Bk.

Wain, Barry, ed. see Allen, Thomas W.

Wain, Eirian, ed. see Chapman, George.

Wain, Harold J., ed. Treatment of Pain. LC 81-65783. 350p. 1982. 30.00 (ISBN 0-87668-607-2). Aronson.

Wain, John. A House for the Truth: Critical Essays. 1973. 11.95 o.p. (ISBN 0-670-38015-6). Viking Pr.

Wain, John, ed. Interpretations: Essays on Twelve English Poems. 2nd ed. 256p. 1972. 21.50x (ISBN 0-7100-7385-2); pap. 7.95 (ISBN 0-7100-7386-0). Routledge & Kegan.

--Shakespeare: Othello. 1981. pap. 15.00x (ISBN 0-686-97823-4, Pub. by Macmillan England). State Mutual Bk.

Waine, A., jt. auth. see Bartram, G.

Waine, Anthony, jt. ed. see Bartram, Graham.

Wainer, Howard & Messick, Samuel, eds. Principles of Modern Psychological Measurement: A Festschrift for Frederic M. Lord. 366p. 1983. text ed. price not set (ISBN 0-89859-277-1). L Erlbaum Assocs.

Wainhouse, Austryn, ed. see Sade, Marquis De.

Wainhouse, Austryn, tr. see Sade, Marquis De.

Wainio, E. A. Monographia Cladoniarum Universalis, 3 vols. 1278p. (Lat. & Fr.). 1978. Set. lib. bdg. 160.00x (ISBN 3-87429-135-9). Lubrecht & Cramer.

Wainio, Walter W. Mammalian Mitochondrial Respiratory Chain. (Molecular Biology Ser). 1971. 66.50 (ISBN 0-12-730650-1). Acad Pr.

Wainright, Aristides. The Curse of the Arabs & the Ethical Deterioration of the State of Israel. (Illus.). 117p. 1983. 77.85 (ISBN 0-86722-036-8). Inst Econ Pol.

Waintraub, Jack L., jt. auth. see Seidman, Arthur H.

Wainwright, Arthur. Beyond Biblical Criticism: Encountering Jesus Christ in the Scripture. LC 81-85327. 153p. 1982. pap. 9.95 (ISBN 0-8042-0007-6). John Knox.

Wainwright, David. Broadwood by Appointment: A History. (Illus.). 360p. 1983. text ed. 30.00x (ISBN 0-87663-419-6). Universe.

Wainwright, Frederick T. Problem of the Picts. Repr. of 1955 ed. lib. bdg. 19.75x (ISBN 0-8371-3381-5, WAPI). Greenwood.

Wainwright, Geoffrey. Doxology: The Praise of God in Worship, Doctrine, & Life. 1980. 29.95x (ISBN 0-19-520192-2). Oxford U Pr.

--Eucharist & Eschatology. 1981. 16.95x (ISBN 0-19-520248-1); pap. text ed. 7.95 (ISBN 0-19-520249-X). Oxford U Pr.

Wainwright, Geoffrey, jt. ed. see Jones, Cheslyn.

Wainwright, Jeffrey. Heart's Desire. (Poetry Ser.). 1979. 6.95 o.p. (ISBN 0-85635-238-1, Pub. by Carcanet New Pr England). Humanities.

Wainwright, John. Dominoes. 224p. 1980. 8.95 o.p. (ISBN 0-312-21668-8). St Martin.

--Duty Elsewhere. 1982. 15.00x (ISBN 0-686-97824-2, Pub. by Macmillan England). State Mutual Bk.

--Man of Law. 224p. 1981. 9.95 o.p. (ISBN 0-312-51088-8). St Martin.

--Take Murder. 176p. 1981. 9.95 o.p. (ISBN 0-312-78357-4). St Martin.

--Their Evil Ways. 256p. 1983. 10.95 (ISBN 0-312-79526-2). St Martin.

Wainwright, William J., jt. ed. see Rowe, William L.

Waisbren, Burton. The Family First Aid Handbook. (Good Health Ser.). (Illus.). 1978. pap. 2.95 (ISBN 0-448-14645-2, G&D). Putnam Pub Group.

Waisbren, Burton A. Critical Care Manual: A Systems Approach Method. 2nd ed. 1977. pap. 20.00 o.p. (ISBN 0-87488-983-9). Med Exam.

Waismann, Friedrich. How I See Philosophy. Harre, R., ed. LC 68-12306. 1968. 17.95 o.p. (ISBN 0-312-39515-9). St Martin.

--Principles of Linguistic Philosophy. Harre, R., ed. 1965. 22.50 (ISBN 0-312-64610-0); pap. 8.95 (ISBN 0-312-64575-9). St Martin.

Waismann, Friedrich see Grassl, Wolfgang.

Wait, George W. New Jersey's Money. Bartle, Dorothy B., ed. LC 76-3234. 1977. 17.50 (ISBN 0-932828-03-5). Newark Mus.

Wait, James. Geo-Electromagnetism. 1982. 34.00 (ISBN 0-12-730880-6). Acad Pr.

Wait, John V., jt. auth. see Korn, Granino A.

Wait, John V., et al. Introduction to Operational & Amplifier Theory Applications. (Illus.). 480p. 1975. text ed. 37.00 (ISBN 0-07-067765-4, C); solutions manual 25.00 (ISBN 0-07-067766-2). McGraw.

Wait, Minnie W. & Leonard, Merton C. Among Flowers & Trees with the Poets or the Plant Kingdom in Verse: A Practical Cyclopedia for Lovers of Flowers. 415p. 1982. Repr. of 1901 ed. lib. bdg. 45.00 (ISBN 0-89760-020-7). Telegraph Bks.

Wait, Peter, tr. see Dupeux, Georges.

Wait, R. The Numerical Solution of Algebraic Equations. LC 78-21869. 1979. 32.95x (ISBN 0-471-99755-2, Pub. by Wiley-Interscience). Wiley.

Wait, R. A., jt. auth. see Mitchell, A. R.

Wait, R. J. The Background to Shakespeare's Sonnets. LC 72-79480. 208p. 1972. 9.50x o.p. (ISBN 0-8052-3470-5). Schocken.

Wait, Walter K. & Nelson, Ben A., eds. The Star Lake Archaeological Project: Anthropology of a Headwaters Area of Chaco Wash, New Mexico. LC 81-13596. (Publications in Archaeology Ser.). (Illus.). 480p. 1983. 18.95x (ISBN 0-8093-0949-1). S Ill U Pr.

Waite, A. E. Secret Tradition in Alchemy. 128p. 1982. pap. 24.50 (ISBN 0-7224-0129-9). Robinson & Watkins.

Waite, A. E., tr. see Levi, Eliphas.

Waite, Arthur E. Alchemists Through the Ages. LC 76-130814. (Spiritual Science Library). (Illus.). 320p. 1981. 15.00x (ISBN 0-89345-018-9, Steinerbks); pap. cancelled (ISBN 0-8334-1704-5). Garber Comm.

--The Hermetic Museum, Restored & Enlarged. LC 73-76951. 1982. Repr. of 1893 ed. write for info. (ISBN 0-87728-578-0). Weiser.

--The Quest of the Golden Stairs: A Mystery of Kinghood in Faerie. LC 80-19659. 176p. 1980. Repr. of 1974 ed. lib. bdg. 11.95x (ISBN 0-89370-628-0). Borgo Pr.

--Real History of the Rosicrucians. LC 76-53632. (Illus.). 456p. 1977. pap. 11.00 (ISBN 0-89345-019-7). Garber Comm.

--Real History of the Rosicrucians. LC 76-53632. (Illus.). 454p. 1975. pap. 11.00 o.p. (ISBN 0-89345-019-7, Steinerbks). Garber Comm.

--Real History of the Rosicrucians. (Steiner Books Spiritual Science Library). (Illus.). 456p. 1982. Repr. of 1977 ed. lib. bdg. 17.00 (ISBN 0-89345-018-9). Garber Comm.

--Real History of the Rosicrucians. LC 76-53632. (Illus.). 456p. 1982. pap. 11.00 (ISBN 0-89345-019-7, Steinerbks). Garber Comm.

--The Turba Philosophorum. LC 73-76950. 211p. 1982. Repr. of 1896 ed. write for info o.s.i. (ISBN 0-87728-139-4). Weiser.

Waite, David H., jt. auth. see Neher, William W.

Waite, Diana S. & Cawley, Frederick D., eds. Farmsteads & Market Towns: A Handbook for Preserving the Cultural Landscape. (Illus.). 50p. (Orig.). 1982. pap. 4.00 (ISBN 0-942000-00-5). Pres League NYS.

--A Primer: Preservation for the Property Owner. (Illus.). 35p. (Orig.). 1978. pap. 3.00 (ISBN 0-942000-01-3). Pres League NY

Waite, Helen E. How Do I Love Thee. (gr. 7-11). 1953. 6.25 (ISBN 0-8255-9050-7). Macrae.

--Valiant Companions. (gr. 7-11). 1959. 6.25 (ISBN 0-8255-9060-4). Macrae.

Waite, M., jt. auth. see Kamins, S.

Waite, Mitch & Arca, Julie. Wordprocessing Primer. 192p. 1982. pap. 14.95 (ISBN 0-07-067761-1, P&RB). McGraw.

Waite, Mitch, jt. auth. see Fox, David.

Waite, Mitch, jt. auth. see Morgan, Chris.

Waite, Mitchell, jt. auth. see Fox, David.

Waite, Robert G. Psychopathic God: Adolf Hitler. LC 76-43484. (Illus.). 1977. 14.50 o.s.i. (ISBN 0-465-06743-3). Basic.

--The Psychopathic God: Adolf Hitler. (Illus.). 1978. pap. 2.95 o.p. (ISBN 0-451-08078-5, E8078, Sig). NAL.

Waite, Thomas D. & Freeman, Neil J. Mathematics of Environmental Processes. LC 76-25770. 192p. 1977. 21.95x o.p. (ISBN 0-669-00979-2). Lexington Bks.

Waite, William M. Implementing Software for Non-Numeric Applications. (Automatic Computation Ser). (Illus.). 400p. 1973. ref. ed. 26.95x (ISBN 0-13-451898-5). P-H.

Waitley, Douglas. The Roads We Traveled: An Amusing History of the Automobile. LC 78-21082. (Illus.). 224p. (gr. 7 up). 1979. PLB 8.29 o.p. (ISBN 0-671-32911-1). Messner.

Waitley, Douglas, jt. auth. see Ogilvie, Bruce.

Waits, Bert K., jt. auth. see Hart, William L.

Waitt, Ian, jt. ed. see Gray, Lynton.

Waitzkin, Howard. The Second Sickness: Contradictions of Capitalist Health Care. (Illus.). 320p. 1982. text ed. 19.95 (ISBN 0-02-933750-X). Free Pr.

Wakabayashi, J. F., tr. see Ozima, Minoru.

Wakao, N. & Kaguei, S. Heat & Mass Transfer in Packed Beds. (Topics in Chemical Engineering Ser.: Vol. 1). 360p. 1982. write for info. Gordon.

Wake, Clive, tr. see Ousmane, Sembene.

Wake, Clive, tr. see Sembene, Ousmane.

Wake, Clive, tr. see Senglor, Leopold S.

Wake, Harry S. To Make A Double Bass. (Illus.). 100p. 1982. pap. 29.50x (ISBN 0-9607048-6-8). H S Wake.

Wake, W. C. Adhesion & the Formation of Adhesives. 2nd ed. (Illus.). 326p. 1982. 49.25 (ISBN 0-85334-134-6, Pub. by Applied Sci England). Elsevier.

--Adhesion & the Formulation of Adhesives. 1976. 45.00 (ISBN 0-85334-660-7, Pub. by Applied Sci England). Elsevier.

--Developments in Adhesives, Vol. 1. 1977. 57.50 (ISBN 0-85334-749-2, Pub. by Applied Sci England). Elsevier.

Wake, W. C. & Wootton, D. B., eds. Textile Reinforcement of Elastomers. (Illus.). xiii, 271p. 1982. 49.25 (ISBN 0-85334-998-3, Pub. by Applied Sci England). Elsevier.

Wakefield, Dan. Starting Over. 352p. 1982. pap. 3.50 (ISBN 0-440-38301-3, LE). Dell.

--Under the Apple Tree. 1983. pap. price not set (ISBN 0-440-19402-4). Dell.

--Under the Apple Tree. (General Ser.). 1983. lib. bdg. 16.50 (ISBN 0-8161-3474-X, Large Print Bks). G K Hall.

Wakefield, Ernest H. The Consumer's Electric Car. LC 76-50984. 1977. softcover 15.95 (ISBN 0-250-40240-8). Ann Arbor Science.

Wakefield, Frances & Harkins, Dorothy. Track & Field: Fundamentals for Girls & Women. 4th ed. LC 77-170. 284p. 1977. 11.50 o.p. (ISBN 0-8016-5328-2). Mosby.

Wakefield, Hugh. Nineteenth Century British Glass. 2nd ed. (Monographs on Glass). (Illus.). 176p. 1982. 49.95 (ISBN 0-571-18054-X). Faber & Faber.

Wakefield, Jay S., ed. see Weed, Lawrence L.

Wakefield, Lucille, jt. auth. see Bass, Mary Ann.

Wakefield, Robert. Schwiering & the West. new ed. LC 73-77752. (Illus.). 1973. 40.00 (ISBN 0-87970-128-5). North Plains.

Wakefield, Robert S. Plymouth Colony Marriages to 1650. Sherman, Ruth W., ed. Bd. with Mary Chilton's Title to Celebrity. Libby, Charles T. LC 78-50608. 1978. 7.00x (ISBN 0-930272-02-1). RI Mayflower.

Wakefield, Robert S. & Sherman, Ruth W. Index to Wills in R. I. Genealogical Register. 64p. (Orig.). 1982. pap. 4.00x (ISBN 0-910233-00-4). Plymouth Col.

Wakeford, John see Littlejohn, Gary, et al.

Wakeley, John H., jt. auth. see Smith, Henry C.

Wakelin, L. R. Home Electrical Repairs. (Invest in Living Ser.). (Illus.). 1977. pap. 6.25x o.p. (ISBN 0-7158-0491-X). Intl Pubns Serv.

Wakelin, Martyn F. English Dialects: An Introduction. 1972. pap. text ed. 14.75x (ISBN 0-485-12020-8, Athlone). Humanities.

Wakelyn, Jon L. The Politics of a Literary Man: William Gilmore Simms. LC 72-845. (Contributions in American Studies: No. 5). 256p. 1973. lib. bdg. 29.95x (ISBN 0-8371-6414-1, WPL/). Greenwood.

Wakeman, Frederic & Grant, Carolyn. Conflict & Control in Late Imperial China. LC 73-87247. 400p. 1976. 38.50x (ISBN 0-520-02597-0). U of Cal Pr.

Wakeman, Fredric, Jr., ed. Ming & Qing Historical Studies in the People's Republic of China. (China Research Monographs: No. 17). 1981. pap. 8.00x (ISBN 0-912966-27-0). IEAS.

Wakeman, Geoffrey. Victorian Book Illustration. LC 72-14042. (Illus.). 200p. 1973. 40.00x (ISBN 0-8103-2008-8). Gale.

Wakeman, John, ed. World Authors: 1950-1970. 1593p. 1975. 70.00 (ISBN 0-8242-0419-0). Wilson.

--World Authors: 1970-1975. 893p. 1979. 48.00 (ISBN 0-8242-0641-X). Wilson.

Wakeman, R. Filtration Post-Treatment Processes. LC 75-31613. (Chemical Engineering Monographs: Vol. 2). 149p. 1975. 38.50 (ISBN 0-444-41391-X). Elsevier.

Wakeman, R. J., ed. Progress in Filtration & Separation, Vol. 1. 1979. 64.00 (ISBN 0-444-41819-9). Elsevier.

Wakeman, T. J. Modern Agricultural Mechanics. LC 76-28839. 1977. 22.50 (ISBN 0-8134-1851-8); text ed. 16.95x. Interstate.

Wakerly, John. Logic Design Projects Using Standard Integrated Circuits. LC 76-5471. 250p. 1976. text ed. 15.95x (ISBN 0-471-91705-2). Wiley.

Wakerly, John F. Microcomputer Architecture & Programming. LC 80-29060. 692p. 1981. text ed. 32.95 (ISBN 0-471-05232-9); tchr's manual avail. (ISBN 0-471-86574-5). Wiley.

Wakil, Salih J., ed. Lipid Metabolism, Vol. 1. 1970. 66.00 (ISBN 0-12-730950-0). Acad Pr.

Wakin, Edward. Monday Morality: Right & Wrong in Daily Life. LC 80-80871. 96p. (Orig.). 1980. pap. 3.95 o.p. (ISBN 0-8091-2317-7). Paulist Pr.

Wakin, Malham M., ed. War, Morality & the Military Profession. 531p. 1979. lib. bdg. 31.00 (ISBN 0-89158-670-9); pap. 13.50 (ISBN 0-89158-661-X). Westview.

Wakita, Osamu A. & Linde, Richard M. The Professional Practice of Architectural Detailing. LC 77-7658. 1977. 28.95x (ISBN 0-471-91715-X); tchrs'. manual 3.00x (ISBN 0-471-04173-4). Wiley.

Wakoman, R. J., ed. Progress in Filtration & Separation, Vol. 2. 1982. 66.00 (ISBN 0-444-42006-1). Elsevier.

Wakoski, Diane. Dancing on the Grave of a Son of a Bitch. 140p. (Orig.). 1980. 14.00 (ISBN 0-87685-180-4); pap. 5.00 (ISBN 0-87685-179-0). Black Sparrow.

--Greed, Pts. 5-7. 45p. (Orig.). 1976. pap. 10.00 o.p. (ISBN 0-87685-095-6). Black Sparrow.

--The Lady Who Drove Me to the Airport. (Metacom Limited Edition Ser.: No. 6). 16p. 1982. ltd. 25.00x (ISBN 0-911381-05-8). Metacom Pr.

--Towards a New Poetry. (Poets on Poetry Ser.). 1979. pap. 7.95 (ISBN 0-472-06307-3). U of Mich Pr.

--Trilogy. LC 73-10548. 192p. 1974. pap. 3.95 (ISBN 0-385-09010-2). Doubleday.

--Waiting for the King of Spain. 157p. (Orig.). 1980. 14.00 (ISBN 0-87685-294-0); pap. 5.00 (ISBN 0-87685-293-2). Black Sparrow.

Wakowski, Diane. Motorcycle Betrayal Poems. 1972. pap. 2.95 o.p. (ISBN 0-671-21429-2, Touchstone Bks). S&S.

Waksh, James E. Eighteen Forty-Eight Austrian Revolutionary Broadsides & Pamphlets: A Catalogue of the Collection at the Houghton Library, Harvard University. 1976. lib. bdg. 25.00 (ISBN 0-8161-7870-4, Hall Reference). G K Hall.

Walbank. The Awful Revolution: The Decline of the Roman Empire in the West. 154p. 1982. pap. 40.00x (ISBN 0-85323-040-4, Pub. by Liverpool Univ England). State Mutual Bk.

Walbank, F. W. The Hellenistic World. (Fontana History of the Ancient World Ser.). 256p. 1981. text ed. 35.00x (ISBN 0-391-02302-0, Pub. by Harvester England). Humanities.

--A Historical Commentary on Polybius: Commentary on Bks. VII-XVIII. 59.00x (ISBN 0-19-814173-4). Oxford U Pr.

--A Historical Commentary on Polybius: Vol. 1, Commentary Books I-IV, Vol. 1. (Illus.). 1957. text ed. 59.00x o.p. (ISBN 0-19-814152-1). Oxford U Pr.

--Polybius. LC 72-189219. (Sather Classical Lectures, No. 42). 1973. 22.50x o.p. (ISBN 0-520-02190-8). U of Cal Pr.

Walberg, Herbert, jt. ed. see Amick, Daniel J.

Walberg, Herbert J. Evaluating Educational Performance. LC 73-17613. 1974. 24.25x (ISBN 0-685-42644-0); text ed. 22.00x (ISBN 0-685-42645-9). McCutchan.

Walberg, Herbert J., ed. Educational Environments & Effects: Evaluation, Policy, & Productivity. LC 78-62101. (Education Ser). 1979. 21.25 (ISBN 0-8211-2259-2); 10 or more copies 19.25 ea. (ISBN 0-685-65115-0). McCutchan.

--Improving Educational Standards & Productivity: The Research Basis for Policy. LC 81-83251. (NSSE, Education Ser.). 376p. 1982. 21.00x (ISBN 0-8211-2260-6); text ed. 19.00x (ISBN 0-686-97397-6). McCutchan.

Walberg, Herbert J., jt. ed. see Peterson, Penelope L.

Walberg, Herbert J., jt. ed. see Spodek, Bernard.

Walch, Timothy & Sedlak, Michael W., eds. American Educational History: A Guide to Information Sources. LC 80-19646. (American Government & History Information Guide Ser.: Vol. 10). 265p. 1981. 42.00x (ISBN 0-8103-1478-9). Gale.

Walcha, Otto. Meissen Porcelain. (Illus.). 514p. 1981. 60.00 (ISBN 0-399-11749-0). Putnam Pub Group.

Walchars, John. The Unfinished Mystery. (Orig.). 1978. pap. 5.95 (ISBN 0-8164-2184-6). Seabury.

Walcher, Dwain N. & Kretchmer, Norman, eds. Food, Nutrition & Evolution: Food As an Environmental Factor in the Genesis of Human Variability. LC 81-12422. (Illus.). 248p. 1981. lib. bdg. 46.75 (ISBN 0-89352-158-2). Masson Pub.

Walcher, Dwain N. & Peters, Donald L., eds. Early Childhood: The Development of Self-Regulatory Mechanisms. 1971. 39.50 (ISBN 0-12-731750-3). Acad Pr.

Walcher, Dwain N., et al, eds. Mutations: Biology & Society. Barnett, Henry L. & Kretchmer, Norman. LC 78-63411. (Illus.). 432p. 1978. 36.50x (ISBN 0-89352-020-9). Masson Pub.

Walcoff, Carol & Ouellette, Robert P. Techniques for Managing Technological Innovation: Overcoming Process Barriers. LC 82-72860. (Illus.). 151p. 1982. 18.75 (ISBN 0-250-40603-9). Ann Arbor Science.

Walcott, Charles C., ed. see Melville, Herman.

Walcott, Derek. Dream on Monkey Mountain & Other Plays. 326p. 1970. pap. 8.95 (ISBN 0-374-50860-7, N390). FS&G.

--The Fortunate Traveller. LC 81-9865. 98p. 1982. 11.95 (ISBN 0-374-15765-0); pap. 7.25 (ISBN 0-374-51744-4). FS&G.

--Midsummer. 1983. 10.50 (ISBN 0-374-20884-0). FS&G.

--Selected Poems. 85p. 1964. 4.95 o.p. (ISBN 0-374-25880-5). FS&G.

--The Star-Apple Kingdom. LC 78-11323. 98p. 1979. 10.00 (ISBN 0-374-26974-2); pap. 5.95 (ISBN 0-374-51532-8). FS&G.

Wald, Abraham. Statistical Decision Functions. LC 77-113154. 1971. Repr. of 1950 ed. text ed. 9.95 (ISBN 0-8284-0243-4). Chelsea Pub.

Wald, Alan M. The Revolutionary Imagination: The Poetry & Politics of John Wheelwright & Sherry Mangan. LC 82-8498. 370p. 1983. 28.00x (ISBN 0-8078-1535-7). U of NC Pr.

Wald, Esther. The Remarried Family: Challenge & Promise. LC 80-205980. 254p. 1981. 19.95 (ISBN 0-87304-184-4); pap. 14.95 (ISBN 0-87304-183-6). Family Serv.

Wald, Kenneth D. Crosses on the Ballot: Patterns of British Voter Alignment Since 1885. LC 82-61392. 290p. 1983. 25.00x (ISBN 0-691-07652-9). Princeton U Pr.

Wald, Michael, jt. auth. see Burt, Robert A.

Wald, Robert, illus. Introduction to Jewelry Casting. 1974. pap. 7.95 o.s.i. (ISBN 0-8096-1885-0, Assn Pr). Follett.

Wald, Susan, tr. see Anselme, Michel.

Wald, Susan, tr. see Lamblin, Simone.

Waldbaum, Jane C. Metalwork from Sardis: The Finds Through 1974. (Archaeological Exploration of Sardis Monographs: No. 8). (Illus.). 280p. 1983. text ed. 40.00x (ISBN 0-674-57070-7). Harvard U Pr.

Waldbott, George L. Health Effects of Environmental Pollutants. 2nd ed. LC 77-26880. (Illus.). 350p. 1978. pap. text ed. 18.95 (ISBN 0-8016-5331-2). Mosby.

Waldcock, H. see Royal Institute of International Affairs.

Walde, Leonard O. Productivity & the Self-Fulfilling Prophecy: The Pygmalion Effect. (Illus.). 1978. leader's guide 10.00 o.p. (ISBN 0-07-067774-3, T&D); wkbk-op 6.95 o.p. (ISBN 0-07-067773-5). McGraw.

Waldegrave, Caroline, jt. auth. see Leith, Prudence.

Waldeland, Lynne. John Cheever. (United States Authors Ser.). 1979. lib. bdg. 11.95 (ISBN 0-8057-7251-0, Twayne). G K Hall.

Waldemar, Carla. Dining In--Minneapolis-St. Paul, Vol. II. (Dining In--Ser.). 210p. 1982. pap. 8.95 (ISBN 0-89716-120-3). Peanut Butter.

Walden, Amelia. Go, Phillips, Go! LC 73-15959. (gr. 6 up). 1974. 6.50 o.s.i. (ISBN 0-664-32541-6). Westminster.

--Play Ball, McGill! LC 72-76437. 192p. (gr. 6 up). 1972. 4.95 o.s.i. (ISBN 0-664-32516-5). Westminster.

--To Catch a Spy. LC 64-11048. (gr. 7-10). 1964. 5.50 o.s.i. (ISBN 0-664-32329-4). Westminster.

--Valerie Valentine Is Missing. LC 76-152337. (gr. 7 up). 1971. 4.75 o.s.i. (ISBN 0-664-32496-7). Westminster.

--Where Is My Heart? LC 60-5205. (gr. 9 up). 1960. 4.95 o.s.i. (ISBN 0-664-32228-X). Westminster.

--Where Was Everyone When Sabrina Screamed? LC 72-13458. 160p. (gr. 7 up). 1973. 4.95 o.s.i. (ISBN 0-664-32525-4). Westminster.

Walden, Daniel, ed. Studies in American Jewish Literature: Issac Bashevis Singer, Vol. 1, A Mosaic of Jewish Writers, Vol. 2. 326p. 1982. pap. 25.00x ea. (ISBN 0-686-97287-2). State U NY Pr.

Walden, David B., ed. Maize Breeding & Genetics. LC 78-6779. 1978. 70.00x (ISBN 0-471-91805-9, Pub. by Wiley-Interscience). Wiley.

Walden, Russell, ed. The Open Hand: Essays on Le Corbusier. LC 76-40046. 1977. 32.50x (ISBN 0-262-23074-7); pap. 8.95 (ISBN 0-262-73062-6). MIT Pr.

Waldenstrom, Jan G. Paraneoplasia: Biological Signals in the Diagnosis of Cancer. LC 78-18494. 1978. text ed. 72.95x (ISBN 0-471-03490-8, Pub. by Wiley Medical). Wiley.

Walder, Eugene. How to Get Out of an Unhappy Marriage. LC 78-15554. 1978. 9.95 (ISBN 0-399-12221-4). Putnam Pub Group.

Walder, Loretta. Pass This Bar: A Readiness Guide for Bar Examination Preparation. 90p. 1982. 19.95 o.p. (ISBN 0-686-93883-6). Wiley.

--Pass This Bar: A Readiness Guide for Bar Examination Preparation. 1982. pap. 9.95 (ISBN 0-471-89877-5). Wiley.

Waldfogel, Diana, jt. ed. see Rosenblatt, Aaron.

Waldhauer, Fred D. Feedback. LC 81-13104. 651p. 1982. 47.50x (ISBN 0-471-05319-8, Pub. by Wiley Interscience). Wiley.

Waldhausl, W. Diabetes, Nineteen Seventy-Nine. (International Congress Ser.: Vol. 500). 1980. 134.00 (ISBN 0-444-90121-3). Elsevier.

Waldheim, Kurt. The Challenge of Peace. LC 79-91079. Date not set. 12.95 (ISBN 0-448-15171-5, G&D). Putnam Pub Group. Postponed.

Waldhorn, Arthur & Zeiger, Arthur. English Made Simple. rev. ed. LC 80-2631. 1981. pap. 4.50 (ISBN 0-385-17483-7, Made). Doubleday.

Waldhorn, Judith, jt. auth. see Olwell, Carol.

Waldinger, Renee & Corbiere-Gille, Gisele. Promenades. Litteraires & Grammaticales. 1966. text ed. 12.95x o.p. (ISBN 0-669-28662-1); tapes. 6 reels o. p. 30.00 o.p. (ISBN 0-669-33977-6). Heath.

Waldman, Anne. Life Notes. LC 72-86553. 1973. pap. 3.95 o.p. (ISBN 0-672-51779-5). Bobbs.

Waldman, Anne, ed. Baby Breakdown. LC 73-125999. 1970. 5.00 o.p. (ISBN 0-672-51335-8). Bobbs.

Waldman, Diane. Kenneth Noland: A Retrospective. (Illus.). 160p. 20.00 o.p. (ISBN 0-8109-1353-4). Abrams.

--Mark Rothko, Nineteen Three to Nineteen Seventy: A Retrospective. LC 78-58411. (Illus.). 30.00 (ISBN 0-89207-014-5); pap. 17.95 (ISBN 0-686-96878-6). S R Guggenheim.

--Twentieth-Century American Drawing: Three Avant-Garde Generations. LC 75-45506. (Illus.). 127p. 1976. soft cover 6.50 o.p. (ISBN 0-89207-001-3). S R Guggenheim.

--Willem De Kooning in East Hampton. LC 77-93652. 1978. soft cover 11.50 o.p. (ISBN 0-89207-011-0). S R Guggenheim.

Waldman, Don E. Antitrust Action & Market Structure. LC 78-8813. (Illus.). 208p. 1978. 22.95x (ISBN 0-669-02401-5). Lexington Bks.

Waldman, Guido, tr. see Ariosto, Ludovico.

Waldman, John. Rapid Reading Made Simple. LC 80-2632. pap. 4.50 (ISBN 0-385-17484-5, Made). Doubleday.

Waldman, John, jt. auth. see Venema, Jack E.

Waldman, Milton. The Omnibus Book of Travellers' Tales: Being the History of Exploration Told by the Explorers. 864p. 1982. Repr. of 1931 ed. lib. bdg. 50.00 (ISBN 0-8495-5663-5). Arden Lib.

Waldman, S. & Goldstein, M., eds. The Black Book Nineteen Eighty-Three. (Illus.). 1175p. 1983. 70.00 (ISBN 0-916098-11-7). Friendly Pubns.

Waldman, S., jt. ed. see Goldstein, M.

Waldman, Stu & Goldstein, Marty. Creative Black Book, 1982. 12th ed. 1982. comb bdg 45.00x o.p. (ISBN 0-916098-06-0). Friendly Pubns.

Waldmann, Hermann, jt. auth. see Lefkovitz, Ivan.

Waldmann, Thomas, jt. ed. see Rothschild, Marcus A.

Waldner, George, ed. see Jansen, Mariuse, et al.

Waldo, Kay C., jt. auth. see MacKenzie, Alec.

Waldo, Myra. The Great International Barbeque Book. LC 78-8654. 1978. 10.95 o.p. (ISBN 0-07-067777-8, GB). McGraw.

--Myra Waldo's Chinese Cookbook. LC 68-17205. 192p. 1972. pap. 2.95 (ISBN 0-02-010420-0, Collier). Macmillan.

--Myra Waldo's Travel Guide to the South Pacific, 1981. (Illus.). 382p. 1982. pap. 10.95 (ISBN 0-02-099000-6, Collier). Macmillan.

--The Prime of Life & How to Make It Last. 1980. 14.95 o.p. (ISBN 0-02-622690-1). Macmillan.

Waldock, Arthur J. Sophocles the Dramatist. pap. 9.95 (ISBN 0-521-09374-0). Cambridge U Pr.

Waldock, H. see Royal Institute of International Affairs.

Waldock, Humphrey, ed. The British Year Book of International Law, 1972-1973, Vol. 46. 1975. 94.00x (ISBN 0-19-214662-9). Oxford U Pr.

Waldock, Humphrey, ed. see Brierly, James L.

Waldron, Ann. True or False? Amazing Art Forgeries. (Illus.). 160p. 1983. PLB 10.95 (ISBN 0-8038-7220-8); pap. 6.95 (ISBN 0-8038-7229-1). Hastings.

Waldron, M. B. Sintering. 1978. 42.95 (ISBN 0-471-26075-4, Wiley Heyden). Wiley.

Waldron, Maggie. Barbeque & Smoke Cookery. rev. ed. (Illus.). 192p. 1983. pap. 7.95 (ISBN 0-89286-211-4). One Hund One Prods.

--Fire & Smoke. LC 78-6621. (Illus.). 1978. pap. 4.95 o.p. (ISBN 0-89286-136-3). One Hund One Prods.

--Strawberries. LC 77-2126. (The Edible Garden Ser.). (Illus.). 1977. pap. 2.50 o.s.i. (ISBN 0-89286-112-6). One Hund One Prods.

Waldron, R. A. Ferrites: An Introduction for Microwave Engineers. LC 61-13474. 265p. 1961. 14.00 (ISBN 0-442-09267-9, Pub. by Van Nos Reinhold). Krieger.

--Sense & Sense Development. rev. ed. (Andre Deutsch Language Library). 1979. 36.75 (ISBN 0-233-95948-3). Westview.

--Theory of Waveguides & Cavities. 134p. 1969. 32.00x (ISBN 0-677-61480-2). Gordon.

Waldron, Ronald, jt. ed. see Andrew, Malcolm.

Waldron, Ronald J., et al. The Criminal Justice System: An Introduction. 2nd ed. LC 79-65288. (Illus.). 1980. text ed. 21.95 (ISBN 0-395-28669-7); instr's. manual 1.00 (ISBN 0-395-28668-9); 6.50 (ISBN 0-395-29304-9). HM.

Waldrop, Keith, tr. see Acker, Kathy & Cherches, Peter.

Waldrop, Rosmarie. Camp Printing. 1970. pap. 5.00 (ISBN 0-930900-42-1). Burning Deck.

Waldrop, Rosmarie, tr. see Jabes, Edmond.

Waldrop, Ruth W. Alabama Authors. 151p. (Orig.). 1980. pap. 7.95 (ISBN 0-87397-182-5). Strode.

Waldrop, Victor H., ed. Ranger Rick's Wonder Book. LC 82-60673. (Illus.). 96p. (gr. 2-7). 1982. 9.95 o.p. (ISBN 0-912186-44-5). Natl Wildlife.

Wale. Tidy's Massage & Remedial Exercise. 11th ed. 520p. 1968. 21.50 (ISBN 0-7236-0458-4). Wright-PSG.

Wale, William, ed. What Great Men Have Said About Great Men. LC 68-17944. 1968. Repr. of 1902 ed. 34.00x (ISBN 0-8103-3195-0). Gale.

Walecka, J. Dirk, jt. auth. see Fetter, Alexander L.

Walen, Susan R., et al. A Practitioner's Guide to Rational-Emotive Therapy. 1980. text ed. 19.95x (ISBN 0-19-502667-5); pap. 10.95x (ISBN 0-19-502668-3). Oxford U Pr.

Wales, Charles E., et al. Guided Engineering Design: An Introduction to Engineering Calculations. 432p. 1974. pap. text ed. 12.95 o.s.i. (ISBN 0-8299-0001-2); instrs.' manual avail. o.s.i. (ISBN 0-8299-0005-5). West Pub.

--Guided Engineering Design: An Introduction to Engineering Calculations. 2nd ed. (Illus.). 432p. 1980. pap. text ed. 17.95 (ISBN 0-8299-0353-4); project bk. 11.95 (ISBN 0-8299-0378-X). West Pub.

--Guided Engineering Design Projects Book. 138p. 1974. 9.95 o.s.i. (ISBN 0-8299-0002-0). West Pub.

Wales, Nym & San, Kim. Song of Ariran: A Korean Communist in the Chinese Revolution. LC 72-75808. (Illus.). 1973. 7.95 o.p. (ISBN 0-87867-021-1); pap. 6.95 (ISBN 0-87867-022-X). Ramparts.

Wales, Roger J & Walker, Edward. New Approaches to Language Mechanisms: A Collection of Psycholinguistic Studies. LC 76-22710. (North-Holland Linguistic Ser.: Vol. 30). (Illus.). 1976. pap. 38.50 (ISBN 0-7204-0523-8, North-Holland). Elsevier.

Wales, Susan R. & DiGiuseppe, Raymond. A Practitioner's Guide to Rational-Emotive Therapy. 12.50 (ISBN 0-686-36784-7); pap. 8.95 (ISBN 0-686-37355-3). Inst Rat Liv.

Wales Tourist Board. Mid Wales: A Tourist Guide. (Illus.). 80p. 1982. pap. 2.95 o.p. (ISBN 0-900784-73-3, Pub. by Auto Assn-British Tourist Authority England). Merrimack Bk Serv.

--North Wales: A Tourist Guide. rev. ed. (Illus.). 84p. 1981. pap. 2.95 o.p. (ISBN 0-900784-71-7, Pub. by Auto Assn-British Tourist Authority England). Merrimack Bk Serv.

Waley, Arthur. Japanese Poetry: The Uta. LC 75-29338. 112p. 1976. pap. 2.95 (ISBN 0-8248-0405-8, Eastwest Ctr). UH Pr.

--The No Plays of Japan. LC 75-28969. 1976. pap. 6.75 (ISBN 0-8048-1198-9). C E Tuttle.

--The Poetry & Career of Li Po. (Ethical & Religious Classics of East & West Ser.). 1951. 13.50 o.p. (ISBN 0-04-895012-2). Allen Unwin.

--Three Ways of Thought in Ancient China. xv, 216p. 1982. pap. 5.95 (ISBN 0-8047-1169-0, SP-46). Stanford U Pr.

Waley, Arthur, tr. The Tale of Genji. 8.95 (ISBN 0-394-60405-9). Modern Lib.

Waley, Arthur, tr. see Confucius.

Waley, Arthur D., ed. Chinese Poems. 1982. pap. 5.95 (ISBN 0-04-895021-1). Allen Unwin.

Waley, D. Italian City Republics. (Illus., Orig.). 1969. pap. 3.95 o.p. (ISBN 0-07-067805-7, SP). McGraw.

Waley, Daniel P., jt. auth. see Hearder, H.

Waleys, Thomas. Metamorphosis Ovidiana Moraliter... Explanata Libellus. Orgel, Stephen, ed. LC 78-68208. (Philosophy of Images: Vol. 1). 1979. lib. bdg. 66.00 o.s.i. (ISBN 0-8240-3675-1). Garland Pub.

Walf, Knut, jt. ed. see Huizing, Peter.

Walfman, Walt & Fasold, Ralph W. The Study of Social Dialects in American English. 272p. 1974. ref. ed. 15.95 (ISBN 0-13-858787-6). P-H.

Walford, A. J. Walford's Guide to Reference Material, Vol. 2. 4th ed. 1982. lib. bdg. 64.50x (ISBN 0-85365-564-2, Pub. by Lib Assn England). Oryx Pr.

--Walford's Guide to Reference Material: Volume 1, Science & Technology, 1980. 4th ed. 712p. 1980. 60.00 (ISBN 0-85365-611-8, Pub. by Lib Assn England). Oryx Pr.

--Walford's Guide to Reference Material: Volume 3, Generalities, Languages, the Arts & Literature. 3rd ed. 720p. 1977. 40.00 (ISBN 0-85365-409-3, Pub. by Lib Assn England). Oryx Pr.

--Wolford's Concise Guide to Reference Material. 434p. 1981. 50.00x (ISBN 0-85365-882-X, Pub. by Lib Assn England). State Mutual Bk.

Walford, D. E., ed. see Cooper, A. A.

Walford, J., ed. Developments in Food Colours, Vol. 1. 1980. 45.00 (ISBN 0-85334-881-2, Pub. by Applied Sci England). Elsevier.

Walford, Naomi, tr. see Diehl, Charles.

Walford, Naomi, tr. see Lagerkvist, Par.

Walford, Rex, jt. auth. see Taylor, John L.

Walford, Roy L. Maximum Life Span. (Illus.). 1983. 15.00x (ISBN 0-393-01649-8). Norton.

Walgenbach, Paul H., et al. Financial Accounting: An Introduction. 3rd ed. 1982. text ed. 23.95 (ISBN 0-15-527381-7, HC); study guide by Imogene Posey 8.95 (ISBN 0-15-527383-3); working papers 9.95 (ISBN 0-15-527387-6); practice sets a & b 5.95 ea.; solutions manual for practice sets avail. (ISBN 0-15-527386-8); achievement tests avail. (ISBN 0-15-527388-4); key to tests avail. (ISBN 0-15-527389-2); overhead transparencies of solutions to problems avail. (ISBN 0-15-527382-5); checklist of key figures avail. (ISBN 0-15-527391-4). HarBraceJ.

--Principles of Accounting. 2nd ed. 1065p. 1980. text ed. 24.95 o.p. (ISBN 0-15-571336-1, HC); study guide by Imogene Posey 8.95 o.p. (ISBN 0-686-64998-2); solutions manual avail. o.p.; practice set A, practice set A with business papers, practice sets B & C & solutions manual 5.95 ea. o.p.; working papers. set 1 8.95 o.p. (ISBN 0-15-571347-7); working papers set 2 8.95 o.p. (ISBN 0-15-571348-5); test item file, achievement tests & ans. key avail. o.p.; transparencies avail. o.p. HarBraceJ.

Walheim, Lance, jt. auth. see Stebbins, Robert L.

Walhout, Donald. A Festival of Aesthetics. 1978. pap. text ed. 10.25 o.p. (ISBN 0-8191-0643-7). U Pr of Amer.

--Send My Roots Rain: A Study of Religious Experience in the Poetry of Gerard Manley Hopkins. LC 80-23549. xii, 203p. 1981. 16.95x (ISBN 0-8214-0565-9, 82-83566). Ohio U Pr.

Walicki, Andrzei. The Slavophile Controversy: History of a Conservative Utopia in Nineteenth Century Russian Thought. Andrews, Hilda, tr. from Polish. 1975. 62.00x (ISBN 0-19-822507-5). Oxford U Pr.

Walicki, Andrzej. A History of Russian Thought: From the Enlightenment to Marxism. Andrews-Rusiecka, Hilda, tr. from Polish. LC 78-66181. xviii, 456p. 1979. 25.00x (ISBN 0-8047-1026-0, SP 89); pap. 10.95 (ISBN 0-8047-1132-1). Stanford U Pr.

--Philosophy & Romantic Nationalism: The Case of Poland. (Illus.). 1982. 34.50x (ISBN 0-19-827250-2). Oxford U Pr.

Waliszewski, Kazimierz. Peter the Great. Loyd, Mary, tr. Repr. of 1897 ed. lib. bdg. 20.00x (ISBN 0-8371-0734-2, WAPG). Greenwood.

Walker. Basic Statistics. 1983. text ed. write for info. (ISBN 0-408-01107-6). Butterworth.

--Electronic Security Systems. 1983. text ed. price not set (ISBN 0-408-01160-2). Butterworth.

--Export Practice & Documentation. 2nd ed. 1977. 29.95 (ISBN 0-408-00271-9). Butterworth.

Walker, jt. ed. see Rhodes.

Walker, A. L., et al. How to Use Adding & Calculating Machines. 3rd ed. 1967. text ed. 11.24 (ISBN 0-07-067823-5, G); tchr's manual 5.95 (ISBN 0-07-067824-3). McGraw.

Walker, A. N., jt. auth. see Brailsford, D. F.

Walker, Alan. Franz Liszt: The Virtuoso Years, Eighteen Eleven to Eighteen Forty-Seven. LC 82-47821. 1983. 25.00 (ISBN 0-394-52540-X). Knopf.

--The New Evangelism. 112p. 1975. pap. 3.25 o.p. (ISBN 0-687-27736-1). Abingdon.

--Unqualified & Underemployed: Handicapped Young People & the Labour Market. 240p. 1981. 39.00x (ISBN 0-333-32189-8, Pub. by Macmillan England). State Mutual Bk.

Walker, Alan, ed. & pref. by. The Chopin Companion: Profiles of the Man & the Musician. Orig. Title: Frederick Chopin, Profiles of the Man & the Musician. (Illus.). 336p. 1973. pap. 7.95 (ISBN 0-393-00668-9). Norton.

Walker, Alan & Townsend, Peter, eds. Community Care: The Family the State & Social Policy. 236p. 1982. text ed. 19.95x (ISBN 0-85520-455-9, Pub. by Martin Robertson England). Biblio Dist.

Walker, Alexander. An Account of a Voyage to the North West Coast of America in 1785 & 1786. Fisher, Robin & Bumsted, J. M., eds. LC 82-2823. (Illus.). 319p. 1982. 24.95 (ISBN 0-295-95930-4). U of Wash Pr.

--Stanley Kubrick Directs. enl. ed. LC 77-153692. (Illus.). 304p. 1972. pap. 8.95 (ISBN 0-15-684892-9, Harv). HarBraceJ.

Walker, Alf. The Art & Craftsmanship of Fly Fishing. (Illus.). 272p. 1981. 19.95 (ISBN 0-920510-52-3, Pub. by Personal Lib). Dodd.

Walker, Alice. Langston Hughes, American Poet. LC 73-9565. (Biography Ser). (Illus.). 40p. (gr. 2-5). 1974. PLB 10.89 (ISBN 0-690-00219-X, TYC-J). Har-Row.

Walker, Anthony R. Farmers in the Hills: Upland Peoples of North Thailand. (East Asian Folklore & Social Life Monographs: Vol. 105). 211p. 1981. 15.00 (ISBN 0-89986-336-1). Oriental Bk Store.

Walker, Arthur, et al, eds. How to Use Adding & Calculating Machines. 4th ed. (gr. 9-12). 1978. softcover text 11.24 (ISBN 0-07-067825-1, G); tchr's manual & key 5.95 (ISBN 0-07-067826-X). McGraw.

Walker, Arthur L., Jr. Educating for Christian Missions. LC 80-68751. (Orig.). 1981. pap. 5.95 (ISBN 0-8054-6934-6). Broadman.

Walker, Ashley, jt. auth. see Walker, Taiko.

Walker, B. H., jt. ed. see Huntley, B. J.

Walker, B. J. & Blake, Ian F. Computer Security & Protection Structures. 1977. 29.50 (ISBN 0-12-787718-5). Acad Pr.

Walker, B. J., ed. Management of Semi-Arid Ecosystems. (Developments in Agricultural & Managed-Forest Ecology Ser.: Vol. 7). 398p. 1980. 76.75 (ISBN 0-444-41759-1). Elsevier.

Walker, Barbara G. Charted Knitting Designs: A Treasury of Knitting Patterns. (Illus.). 304p. 1982. pap. 13.95 (ISBN 0-684-17462-6, ScribT). Scribner.

--Knitting from the Top. (Illus.). 128p. 1982. pap. 9.95 (ISBN 0-684-17669-6, ScribT). Scribner.

Walker, Benjamin. Tantrism: Its Secret Principles & Practices. 176p. 1983. pap. 8.95 (ISBN 0-85030-272-2). Newcastle Pub.

Walker, Braz. All About Cichlids. (Illus., Orig.). 1978. pap. 7.95 (ISBN 0-87666-472-9, PS-751). TFH Pubns.

--Angelfish. (Illus.). 1974. 7.95 (ISBN 0-87666-755-8, PS-711). TFH Pubns.

--Sharks & Loaches. (Illus.). 160p. 1974. 9.95 (ISBN 0-87666-779-5, PS-718). TFH Pubns.

--Tropical Fish Identifier. LC 78-126851. (Illus.). (gr. 10 up). 1971. 9.95 (ISBN 0-8069-3714-9); PLB 12.49 (ISBN 0-8069-3715-7). Sterling.

Walker, Brian M. Shadows on Glass: A Portfolio of Early Ulster Photography. (Illus.). 140p. 1982. 18.00 (ISBN 0-904651-14-2, Pub. by Salem Hse Ltd). Merrimack Bk Serv.

Walker, Bruce J., et al, eds. An Assessment of Marketing Thought & Practice: Proceedings of the Educators' Conference, 1982. LC 82-6693. (Illus.). 465p. (Orig.). 1982. pap. text ed. 30.00 (ISBN 0-87757-158-9). Am Mktg.

Walker, Bryce. The Armada. LC 80-24182. (Seafarers Ser.). PLB 19.92 (ISBN 0-8094-2698-6). Silver.

--Earthquake. 1982. 9.95 (ISBN 0-8094-4300-7). Time-Life.

--Earthquake. LC 81-16662. (Planet Earth Ser.). lib. bdg. 19.92 (ISBN 0-8094-4301-5, Pub. by Time-Life). Silver.

--Fighting Jets. (Epic of Flight Ser.). 1983. lib. bdg. 19.96 (ISBN 0-8094-3363-X, Pub. by Time-Life). Silver.

--The Great Divide. LC 73-81327. (American Wilderness Ser). (Illus.). (gr. 6 up). 1973. lib. bdg. 15.96 (ISBN 0-8094-1185-7, Pub. by Time-Life). Silver.

Walker, C. E., ed. The Handbook of Clinical Psychology: Theory, Research & Practice, Vol. I. (The Dorsey Professional Ser.). 425p. 1983. 35.00 (ISBN 0-87094-319-7). Dow Jones-Irwin.

--The Handbook of Clinical Psychology: Theory, Research & Practice, Vol. II. (The Dorsey Professional Ser.). 425p. 1983. 35.00 (ISBN 0-87094-411-8). Dow Jones-Irwin.

Walker, C. Eugene & Roberts, Michael C. Handbook of Clinical Child Psychology. (Personality Processes Ser.). 1600p. 1983. 65.00x (ISBN 0-471-09036-0, Pub. by Wiley-Interscience). Wiley.

Walker, C. Eugene, et al. Clinical Procedures for Behavior Therapy. (Illus.). 464p. 1981. text ed. 24.95 (ISBN 0-13-137794-9). P-H.

Walker, C. J. Principles of Cost Accounting. 3rd ed. 352p. 1982. pap. text ed. 23.50x (ISBN 0-7121-1757-1). Intl Ideas.

Walker, C. T. Geochemistry of Boron. LC 75-4645. (Benchmark Papers in Geology Ser: Vol. 23). 457p. 1975. 60.50 (ISBN 0-12-787719-3). Acad Pr.

Walker, Carroll. Norfolk: A Pictoral History. LC 75-16407. (Illus.). 1975. 15.95 (ISBN 0-915442-03-5). Donning Co.

--Norfolk: A Tricentennial Pictorial History. 2nd ed. Friedman, Donna R., ed. LC 80-39668. (Illus.). 208p. 1981. 17.95 (ISBN 0-89865-129-8). Donning Co.

Walker, Charles. Authentick Memoirs of... Sally Salisbury, Vol. 41. Shugrve, Michael, ed. Incl. The Agreeable Caledonian. Haywood, Eliza. LC 79-170557. (Foundations of the Novel Ser.). 1973. Repr. of 1723 ed. lib. bdg. 50.00 o.s.i. (ISBN 0-8240-0553-8). Garland Pub.

Walker, Charles A. Applications of Pharmacokinetics to Patient Care. 192p. 1982. 29.95 (ISBN 0-03-061504-6). Praeger.

Walker, Charles A. & Gould, Leroy C., eds. Too Hot to Handle?: Social & Policy Issues in the Management of Radioactive Wastes. LC 82-20000. (Yale Fastback Ser.: No. 26). 240p. 1983. text ed. 20.00 (ISBN 0-300-02899-7); pap. 5.95 (ISBN 0-300-02993-4). Yale U Pr.

Walker, Charles R. Toward the Automatic Factory: A Case Study of Men & Machines. LC 76-45083. (Illus.). 1977. Repr. of 1957 ed. lib. bdg. 21.00x (ISBN 0-8371-9301-X, WATA). Greenwood.

Walker, Charls E., jt. ed. see Baughn, William H.

Walker, D. & West, R. G., eds. Studies in the Vegetation History of the British Isles. 85.00 (ISBN 0-521-07565-3). Cambridge U Pr.

Walker, D. C., ed. Origins of Optical Activity in Nature. (Studies in Physical & Theoretical Chemistry: Vol. 7). 261p. 1979. 51.00 (ISBN 0-444-41841-5). Elsevier.

Walker, D. F. Planning Industrial Development. 350p. 1980. 64.95x (ISBN 0-471-27621-9, Pub. by Wiley-Interscience). Wiley.

Walker, Dale. Buckey O'Neill: The Story of a Rough Rider. 220p. 1983. pap. 9.50 (ISBN 0-8165-0805-4). U of Ariz Pr.

Walker, David. Big Ben. LC 74-82477. (Illus.). (gr. 3-7). 1969. 5.95 o.p. (ISBN 0-395-07167-4). HM.

--Energy, Plants & Man: An Introduction to Photosynthesis in C3, C4 & CAM Plants. (Readers in Plant Productivity Ser.). (Illus.). 1979. pap. text ed. 8.95x (ISBN 0-906527-00-7). Intl Ideas.

--Moving Out. LC 75-31971. (Virginia Commonwealth Univ. Contemporary Poetry Ser.). 70p. 1976. 8.95x (ISBN 0-8139-0657-1). U Pr of Va.

Walker, David, jt. auth. see Tunstall, Jeremy.

Walker, David, jt. ed. see Spearritt, Peter.

Walker, David, jt. ed. see Megarry, Jacquetta.

Walker, David A. The IEA Six Subject Survey: An Empirical Study of Education in Twenty-One Countries. LC 75-43262. 285p. 1976. pap. text ed. 25.00 o.p. (ISBN 0-470-15009-2, Pub. by Wiley). Krieger.

Walker, David B. Toward a Functioning Federalism. 1981. text ed. 13.95 (ISBN 0-316-91835-0); pap. text ed. 9.95 (ISBN 0-316-91836-9). Little.

Walker, David F., jt. ed. see Collins, Lyndhurst.

Walker, David M. Principles of Scottish Private Law, Vol. II. 3rd ed. 680p. 1983. 55.00 (ISBN 0-19-876133-3). Oxford U Pr.

--Principles of Scottish Private Law, Vol. 1. 1982. 58.00 (ISBN 0-19-876132-5). Oxford U Pr.

Walker, Deward E., Jr. Myths of Idaho Indians. rev. ed. LC 79-57484. (Gem Bk. & Anthropological Monograph). (Illus.). 188p. (Orig.). 1980. pap. 10.95 (ISBN 0-89301-066-9). U Pr of Idaho.

--Myths of Idaho Indians. 1979. 10.95 (ISBN 0-89301-066-9). U Pr of Idaho.

Walker, Diana. Mother Wants a Horse. LC 77-11553. (gr. 5 up). 1978. 8.61i (ISBN 0-200-00179-5, AbS-J); PLB 9.89 (ISBN 0-200-00181-7). Har-Row.

--Mother Wants a Horse. (gr. 5 up). 1979. pap. 1.95 o.p. (ISBN 0-06-440101-4, Trophy). Har-Row.

Walker, Donald B., jt. auth. see Kratcoski, Peter C.

Walker, Doris. Dana Point Harbor - Capistrano Bay: Home Port for Romance. 2nd ed. LC 80-53180. (Illus.). 264p. 1982. 39.95 (ISBN 0-9606476-1-9). To-the-Point.

Walker, Dorothea. Sheila Kaye-Smith. (English Authors Ser.). 1980. lib. bdg. 14.95 (ISBN 0-8057-6777-0, Twayne). G K Hall.

Walker, Dorothy C. Off the Stove! The Eat-Without-Heat Food Book. 1978. pap. 3.95 (ISBN 0-915162-48-2). Westland Pubns.

Walker, E. N., jt. auth. see Wendt, N.

Walker, Edward. Hot Bread, Crawdads & Other ANA. LC 82-90120. (Illus.). 200p. (Orig.). 1982. pap. 12.50 (ISBN 0-943486-00-9). Hedgehog Pr.

Walker, Edward, jt. auth. see Wales, Roger J.

Walker, Edward, ed. Explorations in the Biology of Language. LC 78-18352. (Higher Mental Processes Ser.). (Illus.). 256p. 1980. text ed. 25.00x (ISBN 0-262-23110-7, Pub. by Bradford). MIT Pr.

Walker, Edward, et al. Readings in American Public Opinion. 369p. 1968. pap. 10.50 (ISBN 0-442-26610-3, Pub. by Van Nos Reinhold). Krieger.

Walker, Edward, jt. ed. see Mehler, Jacques.

Walker, Edward L., ed. see Heimstra, Norman & McFarling, Leslie H.

Walker, Elizabeth N. Paper Tiger. (Finding Mr. Right Ser.). 256p. 1983. pap. 2.75 (ISBN 0-380-81620-2, 81620-2). Avon.

Walker, Eric. Scott's Fiction & the Picturesque. (Salzburg - Romantic Reassessment Ser.: No. 108). 79p. 1982. pap. text ed. 25.00x (ISBN 0-391-02739-5, Pub. by Salzburg Austria). Humanities.

Walker, Eric A. British Empire: Its Structure & Spirit, 1497-1953. 2nd ed. 1953. text ed. 39.50x (ISBN 0-686-83494-1). Elliots Bks.

Walker, Ernest W. & Petty, J. William, II. Financial Management of the Small Firm. LC 78-873. (Illus.). 1978. ref. 22.95 (ISBN 0-13-316091-2). P-H.

Walker, Ernest W., ed. The Dynamic Small Firm: Selected Readings. LC 74-14491. (Illus.). 484p. 1975. pap. text ed. 10.00 (ISBN 0-914872-03-6). Austin Pr.

Walker, F. Deauville. William Carey. 256p. 1980. pap. 3.95 o.p. (ISBN 0-8024-9562-1). Moody.

Walker, Forrest A. The Civil Works Administration. Freidel, Frank, ed. LC 78-62516. (Modern American History Ser.: Vol. 18). 1979. lib. bdg. 23.00 o.s.i. (ISBN 0-8240-3641-7). Garland Pub.

Walker, Franklin. San Francisco's Literary Frontier. LC 74-8955. (Americana Library Ser.: No. 10). (Illus.). 480p. 1969. 12.50 (ISBN 0-295-95025-0, AL10); pap. 3.95 o.p. (ISBN 0-295-95096-X). U of Wash Pr.

Walker, Franklin, ed. see Conrad, Joseph.

Walker, Fred M., jt. auth. see Johnson, Glen R.

Walker, G. Soviet Book Publishing Policy. LC 77-12543. (Soviet & East European Studies). (Illus.). 1978. 29.95 (ISBN 0-521-21843-8). Cambridge U Pr.

Walker, G. W., jt. auth. see Kuspira, John.

Walker, George E., jt. ed. see Foner, Philip S.

Walker, George F. A Slice of Country Life, Nineteen Two to Nineteen Fifteen. (Illus., Orig.). 1983. pap. 7.95 (ISBN 0-89407-037-1). Strawberry Hill.

Walker, Gregory, ed. Official Publications of the Soviet Union & Eastern Europe: 1945-1980. 624p. 1982. 64.00 (ISBN 0-7201-1641-4). Mansell.

Walker, Greta. Walt Disney. LC 76-54835. (Beginning Biography Ser.). (Illus.). (gr. k-3). 1977. PLB 5.99 o.p. (ISBN 0-399-61021-9). Putnam Pub Group.

Walker, H. F. & Fitzgibbon, W. E., eds. Nonlinear Diffusion. LC 77-8501. (Research Notes in Mathematics Ser: No. 14). (Illus.). pap. cancelled o.p. (ISBN 0-8224-1066-4, 1066). Pitman Pub MA.

Walker, H. F., jt. ed. see Fitzgibbon, W. E.

Walker, H. Kenneth, jt. auth. see Hurst, J. Willis.

Walker, H. Kenneth, et al. Applying the Problem-Oriented System. LC 73-13868. 488p. 1973. 29.00 (ISBN 0-8463-0103-2). Krieger.

Walker, H. Lynn, jt. auth. see Charudattan, R.

Walker, H. Thomas & Montgomery, Paula K. Teaching Media Skills: An Instructional Program for Elementary & Middle School Students. LC 76-30605. 1977. lib. bdg. 19.50 (ISBN 0-87287-135-5). Libs Unl.

Walker, Hallam. Moliere. (World Authors Ser.). lib. bdg. 12.50 (ISBN 0-8057-2620-9, Twayne). G K Hall.

Walker, Henry M. Problems for Computer Solution Using BASIC. (Orig.). 1980. pap. text ed. 13.95 (ISBN 0-316-91834-2). Little.

--Problems for Computer Solutions Using FORTRAN. (Orig.). 1980. pap. text ed. 13.95 (ISBN 0-316-91833-4). Little.

Walker, Hill M. & McConnell, Scott. The Walker Social Skills Curriculum: ACEPTS. 250p. (Orig.). 1983. pap. text ed. write for info. (ISBN 0-936104-30-9, 0370). Pro Ed.

Walker, Howard E. Teaching Yourself to Teach. 1983. kit 13.95 (ISBN 0-687-41137-8); wkbk. 1.50 (ISBN 0-687-41138-6). Abingdon.

Walker, Hubert. Preventive Maintenance Apparatus. (Illus.). 1968. pap. 4.00 o.p. (ISBN 0-686-12266-6). Fire Eng.

Walker, Hugh. Army of Darkness. (Science Fiction Ser.). 1979. pap. 1.50 o.p. (ISBN 0-87997-438-9, UW1438). DAW Bks.

Walker, Irma. Surrender. (Love & Life Romance Ser.). 176p. (Orig.). 1983. pap. 1.75 (ISBN 0-345-30450-0). Ballantine.

Walker, J. Walker's Rhyming Dictionary of the English Language: In Which the Whole Language is Arranged According to its Terminations. rev. & enl. ed. 558p. 1979. Repr. of 1924 ed. 14.95 (ISBN 0-7100-2247-6). Routledge & Kegan.

Walker, J. I. Psychiatric Emergencies: Intervention & Resolution. (Illus.). 288p. 1983. pap. text ed. 19.50 (ISBN 0-397-50495-0, Lippincott Medical). Lippincott.

Walker, J. N. Attacking the King. 1977. pap. 9.95 o.p. (ISBN 0-19-217557-2). Oxford U Pr.

--First Steps in Chess. (Chess Bks). (Illus.). 1979. pap. 12.50 (ISBN 0-19-217580-7). Oxford U Pr.

Walker, J. Samuel. Henry A. Wallace & American Foreign Policy. LC 75-44658. (Contributions in American History: No.50). 240p. (Orig.). 1976. lib. bdg. 25.00x (ISBN 0-8371-8774-5, WHW/). Greenwood.

Walker, Jacilyn G. & DeHaven, Martha L. Texas Conservation Guide for Municipal Services. 133p. 1977. 6.00 (ISBN 0-936440-18-X). Inst Urban Studies.

Walker, James C., jt. auth. see Goody, Richard.

Walker, James D., ed. Local History: America's Collective Memory. (National Archives Conference Ser.). 1983. 17.50 (ISBN 0-88258-106-6). Howard U Pr.

Walker, James W. Human Resource Planning. (Management Ser.). (Illus.). 1980. text ed. 23.50x (ISBN 0-07-067840-5, C). McGraw.

Walker, James W. & Lazer, Harriet L. The End of Mandatory Retirement: Implications for Management. LC 78-13692. 1978. 20.95 o.p. (ISBN 0-471-04417-2, Pub. by Wiley-Interscience). Wiley.

Walker, James W., jt. auth. see Price, Karl F.

Walker, Janet, ed. see Brayer, Yves & Faxon, Alicia.

Walker, Janet, ed. see Forbes, Crosby H.

Walker, Janet, ed. see Niemeijer, J. W. & De Groot, Irene.

Walker, Janet M., ed. see Fletcher, Hans.

Walker, Janet M., ed. see Guibert, Herve.

Walker, Jearl. The Flying Circus of Physics. LC 75-5670. 224p. 1975. 13.50x (ISBN 0-471-91808-3). Wiley.

--The Flying Circus of Physics with Answers. LC 77-5670. 1977. text ed. 14.50 (ISBN 0-471-02984-X); Arabic translation avail. Wiley.

Walker, Jerry L., et al, eds. Your Reading: A Booklist for Junior High Students. 5th ed. LC 75-21358. 440p. (gr. 7-9). 1975. pap. 4.20 o.p. (ISBN 0-8141-5937-0); pap. 3.00 members o.p. (ISBN 0-686-86493-X). NCTE.

Walker, Jim, jt. auth. see Roy, Willy.

Walker, Jim, ed. see Moffat, Bruce.

Walker, Joan, jt. auth. see Walker, Morton.

Walker, Joanna, et al. The New Doberman Pinscher. Rev. ed. LC 81-6600. 352p. 1981. 12.95 o.p. (ISBN 0-87605-113-1). Howell Bk.

Walker, Joe & Walker, W. Gary. Create a Superhero. (gr. 4-9). 1981. 7.95 (ISBN 0-86653-003-7, GA231). Good Apple.

Walker, John. Experts' Choice: One Hundred Years of the Art Trade. LC 92-19596. (Illus.). 208p. 1983. text ed. 35.00 (ISBN 0-941434-31-1, 0031). Stewart Tabori & Chang.

Walker, John & Walker, Katharine. The Walker Washington Guide. rev. ed. LC 75-4256. Orig. Title: The Washington Guidebook. (Illus.). 288p. (Orig.). 1981. pap. 4.95 (ISBN 0-915472-02-3). Guide Pr.

Walker, John C. Plant Pathology. 3rd ed. (Agricultural Sciences Ser.). (Illus.). 1968. text ed. 49.95 (ISBN 0-07-067860-X, C). McGraw.

Walker, John R. Arc Welding. (Illus.). 128p. 1981. pap. text ed. 6.00 (ISBN 0-87006-328-6). Goodheart.

--Bank Costs for Decision Making. LC 77-103701. 1970. 27.00 (ISBN 0-87267-016-3). Bankers.

--Biology of Plant Phenolics. (Studies in Biology: No. 54). 64p. 1975. pap. text ed. 8.95 (ISBN 0-7131-2480-6). E Arnold.

--Exploring Drafting. LC 81-20003. (Illus.). 320p. 1982. text ed. 11.96 (ISBN 0-87006-406-1); wkbk. 5.28 (ISBN 0-87006-295-6); metric wkbk. 5.28 (ISBN 0-87006-242-5). Goodheart.

--Exploring Metalworking. LC 75-31808. 1976. text ed. 12.00 (ISBN 0-87006-199-2); wkbk. 3.80 (ISBN 0-87006-169-0). Goodheart.

--Exploring Metric Drafting. LC 79-24019. (Illus.). 320p. 1980. text ed. 12.80 (ISBN 0-87006-289-1). Goodheart.

--Exploring Power Technology. rev. ed. LC 81-2904. (Illus.). 240p. 1981. text ed. 12.00 (ISBN 0-87006-323-5); wkbk. 3.80 (ISBN 0-87006-333-2). Goodheart.

--Graphic Arts Fundamentals. LC 79-24182. (Illus.). 320p. 1980. 13.20 (ISBN 0-87006-288-3); wkbk 3.80 (ISBN 0-87006-303-0). Goodheart.

--Machining Fundmentals. LC 81-6745. 512p. 1981. 16.96 (ISBN 0-87006-331-6); 3.80 (ISBN 0-87006-332-4). Goodheart.

--Metal Projects, Bk. 1. (Illus.). 1966. pap. 5.40 (ISBN 0-87006-153-4). Goodheart.

--Metal Projects, Bk. 3. LC 77-21602. (Illus.). pap. 5.40 (ISBN 0-87006-238-7). Goodheart.

--Modern Metalworking. LC 81-6736. (Illus.). 520p. 1981. 16.96 (ISBN 0-87006-334-0); wkbk. 3.80 (ISBN 0-87006-335-9). Goodheart.

Walker, Judith. Education in Two Languages: A Guide for Bilingual Teachers. LC 78-65847. 1979. pap. text ed. 7.50 (ISBN 0-8191-0674-7). U Pr of Amer.

Walker, Juliet E. Free Frank: A Black Pioneer on the Antebellum Frontier. LC 82-40181. (Illus.). 272p. 1983. 20.00x (ISBN 0-8131-1472-1). U Pr of Ky.

Walker, Katharine, jt. auth. see Walker, John.

Walker, Katherine S. De Basil's Ballets Russes. LC 82-16339. 317p. 1983. 19.95 (ISBN 0-689-11365-X). Atheneum.

Walker, Katherine S. & Woodcock, Sarah. The Royal Ballet. (Quality Paperbacks Ser.). (Illus.). 144p. 1982. pap. 10.95 (ISBN 0-306-80176-0). Da Capo.

Walker, Katherine S., jt. auth. see Butler, Joan.

Walker, Keith M. Applied Mechanics for Engineering Technology. 2nd ed. (Illus.). 1978. 22.95 (ISBN 0-87909-025-1). Reston.

Walker, L., jt. auth. see Thibaut, J.

Walker, Laurens, jt. auth. see Thibaut, John.

Walker, Leo. The Big Band Almanac. (Illus.). 1978. pap. 9.95 o.p. (ISBN 0-517-53756-7). Crown.

Walker, Les. Housebuilding for Children. LC 76-47220. (Illus.). 176p. 1977. 13.95 (ISBN 0-87951-059-5). Overlook Pr.

Walker, Leslie J., tr. see Machiavelli, Niccolo.

Walker, Lewis, jt. auth. see Hunt, Chester L.

Walker, Louisa. Graded Lessons in Macrame, Knotting & Netting. Orig. Title: Varied Occupations in String Work. (Illus.). 254p. 1896. pap. 4.50 (ISBN 0-486-22754-5). Dover.

Walker, Lucye. Daystar. 1978. 4.00 o.p. (ISBN 0-682-49009-1). Exposition.

Walker, M., jt. auth. see Weinstein, S.

Walker, Malcolm T. Politics & the Power Structure: A Rural Community in the Dominican Republic. LC 72-89624. 1972. text ed. 12.95x (ISBN 0-8077-2302-9). Tchrs Coll.

Walker, Marcia J. & Brodsky, Stanley L., eds. Sexual Assault: The Victim & the Rapist. LC 75-24560. (Illus.). 208p. 1976. 19.95x o.p. (ISBN 0-669-00196-1). Lexington Bks.

Walker, Margaret. The Daemonic Genius of Richard Wright. 576p. 1983. 15.95 (ISBN 0-88258-029-9). Howard U Pr.

Walker, Margaret, jt. auth. see Giovanni, Nikki.

Walker, Mark. The Great Halloween Book. LC 82-184276. (Illus.). 160p. 1983. pap. 6.95 (ISBN 0-89709-038-1). Liberty Pub.

Walker, Martin. The Money Soldiers. LC 79-7882. 1980. 11.95 o.p. (ISBN 0-385-15601-4). Doubleday.

--Powers of the Press: Twelve of the World's Influential Newspapers. 416p. 1983. 20.00 (ISBN 0-8298-0659-8). Pilgrim NY.

Walker, Mary Lou. Basic Skills Music Workbook. (Basic Skills Workbooks). 32p. (gr. 3-5). 1983. 0.99 (ISBN 0-8209-0543-7, MUW-2). ESP.

--Exercises in Bass Clef. (Music Ser.). 24p. (gr. 4 up). 1980. wkbk. 5.00 (ISBN 0-8209-0282-9, MU-11). ESP.

--Exercises in Treble Clef. (Music Ser.). 24p. (gr. 2-6). 1980. wkbk. 5.00 (ISBN 0-8209-0275-6, MU-4). ESP.

--Harmony, Chords, & Scales. (Music Ser.). 24p. (gr. 3 up). 1980. wkbk. 5.00 (ISBN 0-8209-0279-9, MU-8). ESP.

--Introduction to Bass Clef. (Music Ser.). 24p. (gr. 3 up). 1980. wkbk. 5.00 (ISBN 0-8209-0281-0, MU-10). ESP.

--Music Notation. (Music Ser.). 24p. (gr. 1 up). 1980. wkbk. 5.00 (ISBN 0-8209-0277-2, MU-6). ESP.

--Music Signs. (Music Ser.). 24p. (gr. 1 up). 1980. wkbk. 5.00 (ISBN 0-8209-0276-4, MU-5). ESP.

--Musical Puzzles. (Music Ser.). 24p. (gr. 3 up). 1980. wkbk. 5.00 (ISBN 0-8209-0280-2, MU-9). ESP.

--Rhythm, Time, & Value. (Music Ser.). 24p. (gr. 3 up). 1980. wkbk. 5.00 (ISBN 0-8209-0278-0, MU-7). ESP.

--Treble Clef & Notes. (Music Ser.). 24p. (gr. 1 up). 1980. wkbk. 5.00 (ISBN 0-8209-0274-8, MU-3). ESP.

Walker, Matthew. Down Below: Aboard the World's Classic Yachts. LC 80-12327. (Illus.). 136p. 1980. 18.95 (ISBN 0-87701-137-0). Chronicle Bks.

Walker, Mildred. Winter Wheat. LC 44-40006. (gr. 10 up). 1966. pap. 3.95 (ISBN 0-15-697225-5, Harv). HarBraceJ.

Walker, Mort. We're All in the Same Boat, Beetle Bailey, No. 7. 128p. (gr. 2 up). 1982. pap. 1.75 (ISBN 0-686-81833-4, Pub. by Tempo). Ace Bks.

Walker, Mort & Brown, Dik. Hi & Lois: Beware Children at Play. (Hi and Lois Ser.). 128p. (gr. 5 up). pap. 1.50 (ISBN 0-448-14051-9, G&D). Putnam Pub Group.

Walker, Morton. Total Health: The Holistic Alternative to Traditional Medicine. LC 78-57412. 1979. 9.95 o.p. (ISBN 0-89696-010-2, An Everest House Book). Dodd.

--Your Guide to Foot Health. LC 77-185299. (Illus.). 224p. 1972. pap. 1.65 o.p. (ISBN 0-668-02594-8). Arco.

Walker, Morton & Gordon, Garry. The Chelation Answer: How to Prevent Hardening of the Arteries & Rejuvenate Your Cardiovascular System. LC 82-11344. 256p. 1982. 14.95 (ISBN 0-87131-373-1). M Evans.

Walker, Morton & Walker, Joan. Sexual Nutrition: The Ultimate Program for a Lifetime of Sexual Health. 288p. 1983. 16.95 (ISBN 0-698-11199-0, Coward). Putnam Pub Group.

Walker, Morton, jt. auth. see Donsbach, Kurt.

Walker, Morton, jt. auth. see Douglass, William C.

Walker, N., tr. see Sinnecker, Herbert.

Walker, N., et al. Legal Pitfalls in Architecture, Engineering & Building Construction. 1979. 22.95 o.p. (ISBN 0-07-067851-0, P&RB). McGraw.

Walker, N. W. Colon Health: The Key to a Vibrant Life. (Illus.). 1979. pap. 3.95 o.s.i. (ISBN 0-695-81269-6). Follett.

--Raw Vegetables Juices. 4.95x (ISBN 0-89019-033-X). Cancer Control Soc.

Walker, Nancy P. Southern Legacies. Stone, Nancy W. & Stone, William E., eds. (Illus.). 256p. 1982. pap. 9.95 (ISBN 0-939114-75-5). Wimmer Bks.

Walker, Nigel. Morale in the Civil Service: A Study of the Desk Worker. LC 76-49867. (Illus.). 1977. Repr. of 1962 ed. lib. bdg. 20.25x (ISBN 0-8371-9397-4, WAMCS). Greenwood.

Walker, Norman W. Pure & Simple Natural Weight Control. LC 81-11080. 1981. pap. 4.95 (ISBN 0-89019-078-X). O'Sullivan Woodside.

Walker, Orville C. & Pope, Jack, eds. Appellate Procedure in Texas. 2nd ed. LC 79-620000. 864p. 1979. 75.00 (ISBN 0-938160-20-6, 6343). State Bar TX.

Walker, P. D. & Foster, W. H. Bacterial Vaccine Production. 1981. pap. write for info. x o.p. (ISBN 0-471-28014-3, Pub. by Wiley-Interscience). Wiley.

Walker, P. L. An Introduction to Complex Analysis. LC 74-24686. 141p. 1974. 24.95x o.p. (ISBN 0-470-91807-1). Halsted Pr.

Walker, Percy. Lost in the Cosmos. 1983. 16.50 (ISBN 0-374-19165-4). FS&G.

Walker, R. Water Supply Treatment & Distribution. (Illus.). 1978. 31.95 (ISBN 0-13-946004-7). P-H.

Walker, R. D., jt. auth. see Krebs, R. D.

Walker, R. G. Industrial Heat Exchangers. 1982. 41.50 (ISBN 0-07-067814-6). McGraw.

Walker, R. J. Algebraic Curves. LC 78-11956. 1979. pap. 13.00 o.p. (ISBN 0-387-90361-5). Springer-Verlag.

Walker, Ralph. Hobby Gunsmithing. 1972. pap. 6.95 o.s.i. (ISBN 0-695-80361-1). Follett.

Walker, Ralph C. Kant. 1982. pap. 9.50 (ISBN 0-7100-0009-X). Routledge & Kegan.

Walker, Ralph T. Black Powder Gunsmithing. (Illus.). 288p. 1978. pap. 8.95 o.p. (ISBN 0-695-80943-1). DBI.

--Black Powder Gunsmithing. 1978. pap. 6.95 o.s.i. (ISBN 0-695-80659-9). Follett.

Walker, Richard & Walker, Robert. Exploring Photography. LC 82-21006. (Illus.). 1983. text ed. 12.80 (ISBN 0-87006-430-4); write for info. wkbk.; write for info. (ISBN 0-87006-432-0). Goodheart.

Walker, Robert. Rachmaninoff: His Life & Times. expanded ed. (Illus.). 138p. 1981. Repr. of 1980 ed. 12.95 (ISBN 0-87666-582-2, Z-51). Paganiniana Pubns.

Walker, Robert, jt. auth. see Walker, Richard.

Walker, Robert H. American Studies Abroad. LC 75-16963. (Contributions in American Studies: No. 22). (Illus.). 1975. lib. bdg. 22.50x (ISBN 0-8371-7951-3, WAS/). Greenwood.

Walker, Robert H., ed. American Studies: Topics & Sources. LC 75-35675. (Illus.). 320p. (Orig.). 1976. lib. bdg. 35.00x (ISBN 0-8371-8559-9, WBE/). Greenwood.

--Everyday Life in the Age of Enterprise. (Everyday Life in America Ser.). (Illus.). (gr. 7 up). 1967. 6.75 o.p. (ISBN 0-399-20047-9). Putnam Pub Group.

--The Reform Spirit in America: A Documentation of the Pattern of Reform in the American Republic. 1976. 15.00 o.p. (ISBN 0-399-11651-6). Putnam Pub Group.

Walker, Robert H., jt. ed. see Kellogg, Jefferson B.

Walker, Robert L., jt. auth. see Mathews, Jon.

Walker, Robert W. Daniel Webster Jones & the Wrongway Railway. (gr. 11 up). Date not set. 7.95 (ISBN 0-916392-96-1). Oak Tree Pubns.

Walker, Roberta, jt. auth. see Esch, Robert.

Walker, Ronald G. Infernal Paradise: Mexico & the Modern English Novel. LC 75-46046. 1978. 30.00x (ISBN 0-520-03197-0). U of Cal Pr.

Walker, Roy. The Molecular Biology of Enzyme Synthesis: Regulatory Mechanisms of Enzyme Adaptation. 400p. 1983. 49.95x (ISBN 0-471-06051-8, Pub. by Wiley-Interscience). Wiley.

Walker, S., jt. ed. see Straughan, B. P.

Walker, Samuel. A Critical History of Police Reform. LC 76-53866. 224p. 1977. 22.95x o.p. (ISBN 0-669-01292-0). Lexington Bks.

Walker, Samuel E. Popular Justice: A History of American Criminal Justice. 1980. 16.95x (ISBN 0-19-502655-1); pap. text ed. 6.95x (ISBN 0-19-502654-3). Oxford U Pr.

Walker, Sandy & Rainwater, Clarence. Solarization. (Illus.). 160p. 1974. 14.95 o.p. (ISBN 0-8174-0561-5, Amphoto). Watson-Guptill.

Walker, Sheila S. The Religious Revolution in the Ivory Coast: The Prophet Harris & the Harrist Church. LC 81-13010. (Studies in Religion). xvii, 206p. 1983. 29.95x (ISBN 0-8078-1503-9). U of NC Pr.

Walker, Shoshana. Haggadah. 104p. 1982. 24.95 (ISBN 965-220-017-4, Carta Maps & Guides Pub Isreal). Hippocrene Bks.

Walker, Stephen. Animal Thought. (International Library of Psychology Ser.). 280p. 1982. 35.00 (ISBN 0-7100-9037-4). Routledge & Kegan.

Walker, Stephen, jt. auth. see Barton, Len.

Walker, Steven F. Theocritus. (World Authors Ser.). 1980. lib. bdg. 14.95 (ISBN 0-8057-6451-8, Twayne). G K Hall.

Walker, Stuart. Tactics of Small Boat Racing. (Illus.). 1966. 18.95 (ISBN 0-393-03132-2). Norton.

Walker, T. A Guide for Using the Foreign Exchange & Market. LC 80-21975. 372p. 1981. 29.95x (ISBN 0-471-06254-5, Ronald Pr). Wiley.

Walker, Taiko & Walker, Ashley. Hold the Horse. 1983. 7.95 (ISBN 0-533-05225-4). Vantage.

--The Man in the Black Square & Hotels Aren't for Sleeping. LC 79-56882. 338p. 1982. 7.95 (ISBN 0-533-04549-5). Vantage.

Walker, Theodore D. Perspective Sketches. 4th, rev ed. LC 75-551. (Illus.). 1982. 22.75 (ISBN 0-914886-13-4); pap. 16.75 (ISBN 0-914886-14-2). PDA Pubs.

Walker, Thomas G., jt. auth. see Ippolito, Dennis S.

Walker, Thomas H. & Montgomery, Paula K. Teaching Library Media Skills: An Instructional Program for Elementary & Middle School Students. 2nd ed. 1983. lib. bdg. 19.50 (ISBN 0-87287-365-X). Libs Unl.

Walker, Thomas W. Nicaragua: A Profile. (Nations of Contemporary Latin America). 128p. 1982. lib. bdg. 20.00X (ISBN 0-89158-940-6); pap. 10.95X (ISBN 0-86531-273-7). Westview.

Walker, Thomas W., ed. see Frei, Eduardo.

Walker, W. C. Print Quality Factor Classification. (TAPPI PRESS Reports). (Illus.). 16p. 1979. pap. 4.95 (ISBN 0-89852-379-6, 01-01-R079). TAPPI.

Walker, W. C., et al. Print Quality Evaluation: A Bibliography. Ray, C. T. & Fetsko, J. M., eds. (TAPPI PRESS Reports Ser.). 63p. 1973. pap. 19.95 (ISBN 0-89852-350-8, 01-01-R050). TAPPI.

Walker, W. Gary, jt. auth. see Walker, Joe.

Walker, Walter. A Dime to Dance By. LC 82-48688. 256p. 1983. 14.37 (ISBN 0-06-015145-5, HarpT). Har-Row.

Walker, Westbrook A. Visual Concept of Astronomy. Chow, Brian G., rev. by. 46p. (Orig.). pap. text ed. 6.50 (ISBN 0-686-37061-9). Trippensee Pub.

Walker, Wilfred, ed. Metallogeny & Global Tectonics. LC 76-3605. (Benchmark Papers in Geology Ser.: Vol. 29). 425p. 1976. 55.50 (ISBN 0-12-787720-7). Acad Pr.

Walker, William & Lonnroth, Mans. Nuclear Power Struggles: Industrial Competition & Proliferation Control. (Illus.). 192p. 1983. text ed. 24.00x (ISBN 0-04-338104-9). Allen Unwin.

Walker, William B. Industrial Innovation & International Trading Performance, Vol. 15. Altman, Edward V. & Walter, Ingo, eds. LC 77-7777. (Contemporary Studies in Economic & Financial Analysis). 1979. lib. bdg. 34.00 (ISBN 0-89232-083-4). Jai Pr.

Walker, Williston. Coming of Yale to New Haven. 1917. pap. text ed. 9.50x (ISBN 0-686-83506-9). Elliots Bks.

Walker, Williston, jt. auth. see Smyth, Norman.

Walkerly. The Motor Industry As a Career. 13.50x o.p. (ISBN 0-392-05929-0, SpS). Sportshelf.

Walkerly, Ronald. Sports Cars Today. 14.50x (ISBN 0-392-06014-0, SpS). Sportshelf.

Walkers, J. O., ed. Spraying Systems for the Nineteen Eighties: Proceedings. (BCPC Monograph: No. 24). 317p. pap. 38.75 o.p. (ISBN 0-901436-61-5, CAB). Unipub.

Walker's Manual Inc. Walker's Manual of Western Corporations: 72nd Annual Edition, 2 vols. LC 10-19951. 1650p. 1980. Set. 182.00 o.p. (ISBN 0-916234-05-3). Walkers Manual.

Walker's Manual Incorporated. Walker's Manual of Western Corporations: 71st Annual Edition, 2 vols. LC 10-19951. 1979. 158.00 o.p. (ISBN 0-916234-04-5). Walkers Manual.

Walker-Smith, John. Diseases of the Small Intestine in Childhood. 2nd ed. 428p. 1979. text ed. 54.50 o.p. (ISBN 0-272-79533-X). Univ Park.

Walking Night Bear. How the Creator Gave Us the Herbs. (Illus.). 48p. (gr. 3-6). 1983. lib. bdg. price not set (ISBN 0-943986-22-2); pap. 5.95 (ISBN 0-943986-21-4). Gold Circle.

Walkington, Thomas. Optick Glasse of Humors. LC 81-16630. 1982. Repr. of 1631 ed. 30.00x (ISBN 0-8201-1371-9). Schol Facsimiles.

Walkov, Samuel. Understanding your Car. 1979. pap. 9.95 (ISBN 0-672-21623-X). Sams.

Walkowitz, Daniel J., jt. ed. see Frisch, Michael H.

Walkowitz, Judith. Prostitution & Victorian Society: Women, Class & the State. LC 79-21050. 347p. 1982. pap. 9.95 (ISBN 0-521-27064-2). Cambridge U Pr.

Walkowitz, Judith R. Prostitution & Victorian Society. LC 79-21050. 368p. 1980. 27.95 (ISBN 0-521-22334-2). Cambridge U Pr.

Walkup, Kathleen, ed. see Steinberg, Lois.

Wall, Barbara, tr. see Carretto, Carlo.

Wall, Bernard. Alessandro Manzoni. 1954. 29.50 (ISBN 0-686-51343-6). Elliots Bks.

Wall, Bernard, tr. see Moravia, Alberto.

Wall, C. Edward, ed. Public Affairs Information Service: Cumulative Author Index 1965-1969. LC 70-143248. (Cumulative Author Index Ser.: No. 3). 100.00 (ISBN 0-87650-014-9). Pierian.

Wall, C. T., ed. Homological Groups Theory. LC 78-74013. (London Mathematical Society Lecture Note: No. 36). 1980. pap. 44.50 (ISBN 0-521-22729-1). Cambridge U Pr.

Wall, Clifford N., et al. Physics Laboratory Manual. 3rd ed. 1972. pap. text ed. 13.95 (ISBN 0-13-674101-0). P-H.

Wall, Edward B. How We Do It: Student Selection at the Nation's Most Prestigious Colleges. rev., 2nd ed. 1982. pap. 1.50 (ISBN 0-917760-35-2). Octameron Assocs.

Wall, Elizabeth S. Computer Alphabet Book. 2nd ed. LC 78-78391. (Beginning Computer Literacy Ser.). (Illus.). (gr. 2-5). 1982. lib. bdg. 9.95x (ISBN 0-9602314-0-4). Bayshore Bks.

Wall, George B. Is God Really Good? Conversations with a Theodicist. LC 82-24854. 130p. (Orig.). 1983. pap. text ed. 8.25 (ISBN 0-8191-3032-X). U Pr of Amer.

Wall, H. S. Analytic Theory of Continued Fractions. LC 66-24296. 17.50 (ISBN 0-8284-0207-8). Chelsea Pub.

Wall, Hershel P. Pediatrics. 5th ed. LC 61-66847. (Medical Examination Review Book: Vol. 11A). 1980. pap. 14.95 (ISBN 0-87488-111-0). Med Exam.

Wall, Irwin M. French Communism in the Era of Stalin: The Quest for Unity & Integration, 1945-1962. LC 82-20970. (Contributions in Political Science Ser.: No. 97). 280p. 1983. lib. bdg. 29.95 (ISBN 0-313-23662-3, WFC/). Greenwood.

Wall, J. Charles. Devils. LC 69-16798. 1969. Repr. of 1904 ed. 34.00x (ISBN 0-8103-3541-7). Gale.

Wall, James D., ed. Environmental Management Handbook for Hydrocarbon Processing Industries. 224p. (Orig.). 1980. pap. 19.95x (ISBN 0-87201-265-4). Gulf Pub.

Wall, James T. From the Law of Moses to the Magna Carta: Essays in Ancient & Medieval History. LC 79-66236. 1979. pap. text ed. 8.25 (ISBN 0-8191-0801-4). U Pr of Amer.

--Manifest Destiny Denied: America's First Intervention in Nicaragua. LC 81-40586. 215p. 1981. lib. bdg. 21.75 (ISBN 0-8191-1972-5); pap. text ed. 10.75 (ISBN 0-8191-1973-3). U Pr of Amer.

Wall, James T., ed. The Landscape of American History: Essays in Memorium to Richard W. Griffin. LC 79-89255. 1979. pap. text ed. 9.50 o.p. (ISBN 0-8191-0811-1). U Pr of Amer.

Wall, Jesse D. Introductory Physics: A Problem-Solving Approach. 1977. text ed. 21.95 (ISBN 0-669-00188-0). Heath.

Wall, Joseph F. Andrew Carnegie. LC 74-83056. 1970. 35.00x (ISBN 0-19-501282-8). Oxford U Pr.

--Policies & People. LC 79-11636. (Illus.). 1979. 14.95 o.p. (ISBN 0-13-684019-1). P-H.

Wall, Kevin. Relation in Hegel. LC 82-23775. 118p. 1983. pap. text ed. 8.50 (ISBN 0-8191-2976-3). U Pr of Amer.

Wall, Muriel. Sens-ational Travel. (Illus.). write for info. ICA Pubs.

Wall, Muriel, ed. Directory of Intercultural Education Newsletters: Third Annual, 1983. 80p. 1982. pap. text ed. 10.00 (ISBN 0-941472-01-9). ICA Pubs.

Wall, Norbert, jt. auth. see Creedy, Judith.

Wall, O. A. Sex & Sex Worship in the World. (Illus.). 1980. text ed. 33.50x (ISBN 0-391-01863-9). Humanities.

Wall, Patrick D., jt. auth. see Melzack, Ronald.

Wall, R., jt. ed. see Laslett, P.

Wall, Richard, et al, eds. Family Forms in Historic Europe. LC 82-4376. 626p. Date not set. 64.50 (ISBN 0-521-24547-8). Cambridge U Pr.

Wall, Robert. Airliners. (Illus.). 256p. 1981. 27.95 o.p. (ISBN 0-13-021105-2). P-H.

--Bristol Channel Pleasure Steamers. (Illus.). 1973. 6.50 o.p. (ISBN 0-7153-6069-8). David & Charles.

--Introduction to Mathematical Linguistics. LC 75-38044. (Illus.). 304p. 1972. ref. ed. 21.95 (ISBN 0-13-487496-X). P-H.

Wall, Robert E. Birthright: (Volume III, The Canadians) 300p. 1982. 16.95 (ISBN 0-920510-64-7, Pub. by Personal Lib). Dodd.

--Blackrobe. 368p. 16.95 o.p. (ISBN 0-920510-27-2, Pub. by Personal Lib). Dodd.

--Blackrobe. (The Canadians Ser.: Vol. I). 384p. 1981. 16.95 (ISBN 0-920510-27-2, Pub. by Personal Lib). Dodd.

--Bloodbrothers. (The Canadians Ser.: Vol. II). 324p. 1981. 16.95 (ISBN 0-920510-45-0, Pub. by Personal Lib). Dodd.

--Patriots. (The Canadians Ser.: No. IV). 288p. 1982. pap. 3.50 (ISBN 0-553-22686-X). Bantam.

Wall, Shavaun M. & Hixenbaugh, Paula. WISC-R Administration & Scoring: Handbook of Training Exercises. (Professional Handbook Ser.). 220p. 1983. 24.50 (ISBN 0-87424-178-2). Western Psych.

Wall, Stephen, ed. see Trollope, Anthony.

Wall, Thomas F. Medical Ethics: Basic Moral Issues. LC 80-5592. 180p. 1980. lib. bdg. 19.25 (ISBN 0-8191-1142-2); pap. text ed. 9.75 (ISBN 0-8191-1143-0). U Pr of Amer.

Wall, W. D. & Williams, H. L. Longitudinal Studies & the Social Sciences. Mitchell, Jeremy, ed. pap. text ed. 4.00x o.p. (ISBN 0-435-82847-9). Heinemann Ed.

Walla, Feroze R. Satyajit Ray's Art. 132p. 1980. 15.95 (ISBN 0-89684-260-6, Pub. by Clarion India). Orient Bk Dist.

Wallace & Pitz. Mathematics for Business with Machine Applications. 448p. 1977. text ed. 19.00x (ISBN 0-7715-0901-4); tchr's. manual with text solutions 13.40x (ISBN 0-7715-0902-2); tchr's. ed., wkbk. 1 11.15x (ISBN 0-7715-0904-9); tchr's. ed., wkbk. 2 12.95x (ISBN 0-7715-0906-5); wkbk. 1, units 1-9 5.15x (ISBN 0-7715-0903-0); wkbk. 2, units 10-22 5.95x (ISBN 0-7715-0905-7). Forkner.

Wallace, A. F. Perspectives on Anthropology 1976. 1977. pap. 4.00 (ISBN 0-686-36566-6). Am Anthro Assn.

Wallace, A. H. Guy de Maupassant: (World Authors Ser.). 1973. lib. bdg. 11.95 (ISBN 0-8057-2602-0, Twayne). G K Hall.

Wallace, Alfred R. Narrative of Travels on the Amazon & Rio Negro, with an Account of the Native Tribes, & Observations on the Climate, Geology, & Natural History of the Amazon Valley. LC 68-55226. (Illus.). 1969. Repr. of 1889 ed. lib. bdg. 17.25x (ISBN 0-8371-1641-4, WARN). Greenwood.

Wallace, Alfred-Russel. La Selection Naturelle, Essais. Repr. of 1872 ed. 121.00 o.p. (ISBN 0-8287-0878-9). Clearwater Pub.

Wallace, Alison, jt. auth. see Rees, Stuart.

Wallace, Amy, jt. auth. see Wallechinsky, David.

Wallace, Angelo. Automotive Literature Index: 1977-1981. 327p. pap. 24.95 (ISBN 0-9606804-4-6). Wallace Pub.

Wallace, Angelo, tr. from Ital. Ferrari 246 GT-GTS: Repair & Workshop Manual. 225p. wkbk. 60.00 (ISBN 0-9606804-0-3). Wallace Pub.

Wallace, Anthony F. The Death & Rebirth of the Seneca. 416p. 1972. pap. 5.95 (ISBN 0-394-71699-X, Vin). Random.

--Rockdale: The Growth of an American Village in the Early Industrial Revolution. (Illus.). 576p. 1980. pap. 8.95 (ISBN 0-393-00991-2). Norton.

Wallace, Arthur. LDS Roots in Egypt. 63p. 1981. pap. 3.50 (ISBN 0-937892-08-4). LL Co.

Wallace, Arthur & Ford, Audrey. The Roots of King Tutankhamun. (Illus.). 16p. 1980. pap. 1.95 (ISBN 0-686-32534-6). LL Co.

Wallace, Arthur & Wallace, Elna. Arthur Wallace's Punch Bowl. (Illus.). 64p. 1983. pap. 5.00 (ISBN 0-937892-10-6). LL Co.

Wallace, Arthur, ed. see Sety, Omm & El Zeini, Hanny.

Wallace, B., jt. auth. see Harding, T.

Wallace, Barbara B. Julia & the Third Bad Thing. LC 75-2965. (Illus.). 64p. (gr. 2-4). 1975. 5.95 o.s.i. (ISBN 0-695-80590-8); PLB 5.97 o.s.i. (ISBN 0-695-40590-X). Follett.

--Miss Switch to the Rescue. LC 81-10916. (Illus.). 144p. (gr. 4-6). 1983. 9.95g (ISBN 0-687-27077-4). Abingdon.

--Palmer Patch. LC 76-2185. (Illus.). 128p. (gr. 3-6). 1976. 5.95 o.s.i. (ISBN 0-695-80668-8); lib. ed. 5.97 o.s.i. (ISBN 0-695-40668-X). Follett.

--The Secret Summer of L. E. B. LC 73-93557. (Illus.). 192p. (gr. 3-6). 1974. 5.95 o.s.i. (ISBN 0-695-80481-2); lib. bdg. 5.97 o.s.i. (ISBN 0-695-40481-4). Follett.

--The Trouble with Miss Switch. (Illus.). (gr. 3-5). 1981. pap. 1.95 (ISBN 0-671-46394-2). Archway.

--Victoria. (gr. 5 up). 1972. PLB 5.97 o.s.i. (ISBN 0-695-40322-2). Follett.

Wallace, Bell. Fly Fishing Digest. (DBI Bks). 1973. pap. 4.95 o.s.i. (ISBN 0-695-80325-5). Follett.

Wallace, Betty J. Pronunciation of American English for Teachers of English As a Second Language. 1951. 3.95x (ISBN 0-685-21797-3). Wahr.

Wallace, Bill. A Dog Called Kitty. LC 80-16293. 160p. (gr. 5-9). 1980. 9.95 (ISBN 0-8234-0376-9). Holiday.

Wallace, Bill C., jt. auth. see Kirk, Robert H.

Wallace, Bruce & Srb, Adrian M. Adaption. LC 77-18812. (Foundations of Modern Biology Ser.). 1978. Repr. of 1964 ed. lib. bdg. 17.25x (ISBN 0-313-20212-5, WAAD). Greenwood.

Wallace, Bruce, ed. Genetics, Evolution, Race, Radiation, Biology: Essays in Social Biology, Vol. 2. LC 79-167789. 1972. pap. text ed. 13.95x (ISBN 0-13-351155-3). P-H.

Wallace, Bruce, jt. ed. see Hecht, Max K.

Wallace, C. M. The Design of Biographia Literaria. 176p. 1983. text ed. 25.00 (ISBN 0-04-800016-7). Allen Unwin.

Wallace, Carol McD. & Wiley, Mason. Welcome to Mount Merry College. 1982. 4.95 (ISBN 0-399-50615-2, Perige). Putnam Pub Group.

Wallace, Cornelia. C'nelia. LC 75-35835. 240p. 1976. 7.95 o.p. (ISBN 0-87981-047-5). Holman.

Wallace, Cynthia D. Legal Control of the Multinational Enterprise. 1982. lib. bdg. 58.50 (ISBN 90-247-2668-9, Pub. by Martinus Nijhoff Netherlands). Kluwer Boston.

Wallace, Dan, ed. see Hall, Walter.

Wallace, Dan, ed. see Logsdon, Gene.

Wallace, Dan, ed. see Sanders, William.

Wallace, David R. The Klamath Knot. LC 82-3237. (Illus.). 160p. 1983. 14.95 (ISBN 0-87156-316-9). Sierra.

Wallace, Douglass W., jt. auth. see Bird, Roy D.

Wallace, Duane C. Thermodynamics of Crystals. LC 71-161495. 1972. 52.95 o.p. (ISBN 0-471-91855-5, Pub. by Wiley-Interscience). Wiley.

Wallace, Edwin R. Dynamic Psychiatry in Theory & Practice. LC 82-14880. 407p. 1983. text ed. 30.00 (ISBN 0-8121-0856-6). Lea & Febiger.

Wallace, Elna, jt. auth. see Wallace, Arthur.

Wallace, Forrest & Cross, Gilbert. The Game of Wine. (Illus.). 400p. 1977. pap. 7.95 (ISBN 0-06-465079-0, BN 5079, BN). B&N NY.

Wallace, Frank R. Neo-Tech II. (Neo-Tech Discovery Ser.: Vol. 2). 480p. 1981. 78.50 (ISBN 0-911752-36-6); pap. 68.50 (ISBN 0-911752-35-8). I & O Pub.

--Poker: A Guaranteed Income for Life. rev. & expanded ed. 1977. 10.00 o.p. (ISBN 0-517-53017-1). Crown.

--Poker Power. Date not set. (ISBN 0-911752-28-5). I & O Pub. Postponed.

--Psychuous Sex. LC 75-24723. 1976. 78.50 (ISBN 0-911752-21-8); flexible bdg. 68.50 (ISBN 0-911752-20-X). I & O Pub.

Wallace, Frank R. & Savage, Eric. Poker Troubleshooting Guide & Answer Book. 1983. 250.00 (ISBN 0-911752-26-9). I & O Pub.

Wallace, Frank R., et al. The Neo-Tech Discovery. (Illus.). 1980. 100.00 (ISBN 0-911752-33-1); pap. 88.50 (ISBN 0-911752-34-X). I & O Pub.

--Neocheating, the Unbeatable Weapon in Poker, Blackjack, Bridge, & Gin. LC 79-92518. (Illus.). 1980. 68.50 (ISBN 0-911752-27-7); pap. 48.50 (ISBN 0-911752-29-3). I & O Pub.

Wallace, George & Wallace, Inger. Authentic Mexican Cooking. rev. ed. LC 72-177202. 181p. 1982. pap. 5.95 (ISBN 0-911954-70-8). Nitty Gritty.

Wallace, George J. & Mahan, Harold D. An Introduction to Ornithology. 3rd ed. (Illus.). 1974. text ed. 24.95x (ISBN 0-02-423980-1). Macmillan.

Wallace, Gerald M. & Kauffman, James M. Teaching Children with Learning Problems. 2nd ed. (Special Education Ser.). 1978. text ed. 22.95 (ISBN 0-675-08425-3). Merrill.

Wallace, Gordon. Random Journey: Selections from the Notebook of a Longtime Wanderer. 1978. 8.95 o.p. (ISBN 0-533-03737-9). Vantage.

--The Valiant Heart. 201p. 1982. 12.95 (ISBN 0-942078-01-2). R Tanner Assocs Inc.

Wallace, Grocet. The New York Historical Society's Dictionary of Artists in America, 1564-1860. 1979. 65.00 (ISBN 0-686-43145-6). Apollo.

Wallace, H. Vertebrate Limb Regeneration. LC 80-40963. 276p. 1981. 61.95x (ISBN 0-471-27877-7, Pub. by Wiley-Interscience). Wiley.

Wallace, Helen M., et al. Maternal & Child Health Practices: Problems, Resources, & Methods of Delivery. 2nd ed. LC 82-6884. (Wiley Series in Health Services). 861p. 1982. 30.00 (ISBN 0-471-86720-9, Pub. by Wiley Med). Wiley.

Wallace, Hugh A. & Martin, J. R. Asphalt Pavement Engineering. 1967. 39.50 (ISBN 0-07-067923-1, P&RB). McGraw.

Wallace, Ian. Nothing Quite Like It. (Illus.). 256p. 1982. 22.50 (ISBN 0-241-10853-5, Pub. by Hamish Hamilton England). David & Charles.

Wallace, Inger, jt. auth. see Wallace, George.

Wallace, Irving. Chapman Report. pap. 2.95 (ISBN 0-451-09456-5, E9456, Sig). NAL.

--Fabulous Showman. pap. 2.95 (ISBN 0-451-11385-3, AE1385, Sig). NAL.

--The Prize. pap. 2.95 (ISBN 0-451-09455-7, E9455, Sig). NAL.

--Sins of Philip Fleming. 1968. pap. 1.50 o.p. (ISBN 0-451-07672-9, W7672, Sig). NAL.

--Special People, Special Times. 192p. (Orig.). 1981. pap. 2.25 o.p. (ISBN 0-523-48001-6). Pinnacle Bks.

--Three Sirens. 1971. pap. 3.50 (ISBN 0-451-11359-4, AE1359, Sig). NAL.

--Twenty-Seventh Wife. 1971. pap. 2.25 o.p. (ISBN 0-451-08069-6, E8069, Sig). NAL.

Wallace, Irving, jt. auth. see Wallechinsky, David.

Wallace, Irving, et al. The Intimate Sex Lives of Famous People. (Illus.). 1981. 14.95 o.s.i. (ISBN 0-440-04152-X). Delacorte.

--The People's Almanac Presents the Book of Lists, No. 2. 560p. 1982. pap. 3.50 (ISBN 0-553-13101-X). Bantam.

Wallace, J. E. & Wade, N. A. Review Questions in Analytical Toxicology. LC 82-70669. 200p. (Orig.). 1982. pap. text ed. 17.50 (ISBN 0-931890-09-8). Biomed Pubns.

Wallace, J. G., jt. auth. see Klahr, D.

Wallace, James. Psalms 23. 1981. pap. 3.95 (ISBN 0-934942-23-4). White Wing Pub.

Wallace, James A. Preaching Through the Saints. LC 82-7745. 80p. 1982. pap. 2.50 (ISBN 0-8146-1271-7). Liturgical Pr.

Wallace, Joanne. Image of Loveliness. (Illus.). 160p. 1978. 9.95 (ISBN 0-8007-0963-2). Revell.

Wallace, John. Control in Conflict. LC 82-72227. (Orig.). 1983. pap. 4.95 (ISBN 0-8054-3001-6). Broadman.

Wallace, John, jt. auth. see Margulies, Newton.

Wallace, John M. Destiny His Choice: The Loyalism of Andrew Marvell. LC 68-10334. 1968. 44.50 (ISBN 0-521-06725-1); pap. 13.50 (ISBN 0-521-28042-7). Cambridge U Pr.

Wallace, Joyce. A Closer Walk. LC 82-99994. 128p. 1982. pap. 4.50 (ISBN 0-686-38098-3). Foun Christ Serv.

Wallace, Karl R., jt. auth. see Bryant, Donald C.

Wallace, Lew. Ben Hur. De Reedy, Ginette D., tr. (Biblioteca de Libros Condensados). 1981. pap. 1.75 (ISBN 0-311-37012-8). Casa Bautista.

--Ben-Hur. pap. 3.50 (ISBN 0-451-11661-5, AE1661, Sig). NAL.

Wallace, Marc J., jt. auth. see Szilagyi, Andrew D., Jr.

Wallace, Marc J., Jr. & Fay, Charles H. Compensation Theory & Practice. 304p. 1982. pap. text ed. 11.95x (ISBN 0-534-01399-6). Kent Pub Co.

Wallace, Marc J., Jr. & Szilagyi, Andrew D., Jr. Managing Behavior in Organizations. 1982. text ed. 23.50x (ISBN 0-673-16008-4). Scott F.

Wallace, Marc J., Jr., jt. auth. see Szilagyi, Andrew D., Jr.

Wallace, Marc J., Jr., et al. Administering Human Resources. 568p. 1982. text ed. 24.95 (ISBN 0-394-32262-2); wkbk 15.95 (ISBN 0-394-32863-9). Random.

Wallace, Marie, jt. auth. see Sloane, Richard.

Wallace, Martin. One Hundred Irish Lives. (Illus.). 168p. (Orig.). 1983. cancelled (ISBN 0-7153-8331-0). David & Charles.

--One Hundred Irish Lives. LC 82-24289. (Illus.). 168p. 1983. text ed. 17.50x (ISBN 0-389-20364-5). B&N Imports.

Wallace, Mary E. & Wallace, Robert. Opera Scenes for Class & Stage. LC 78-11095. 314p. 1979. 19.95x (ISBN 0-8093-0903-3). S Ill U Pr.

Wallace, Mary L. Spelling. Raygor, Alton, ed. (Communication Skills Ser.). 288p. 1981. pap. text ed. 11.95 (ISBN 0-07-067901-0, C). McGraw.

Wallace, Michael. Teaching Vocabulary, No. 10. Geddes, Marion & Sturtridge, Gillian, eds. (Practical Language Teaching Ser.). 144p. (Orig.). 1983. pap. text ed. 7.50x (ISBN 0-435-28974-8). Heinemann Ed.

Wallace, P., tr. see Gall, J. C.

Wallace, P. R., ed. Superconductivity: McGill Summer School Proceedings, 2 vols. 1969. Vol. 1, 544p. 111.00x (ISBN 0-677-13810-5); Vol. 2, 420p. 86.00x (ISBN 0-677-13820-2); Set. 178.00x (ISBN 0-677-13210-7). Gordon.

Wallace, Pamela. Malibu Colony. 320p. (Orig.). 1980. pap. 2.75 o.p. (ISBN 0-523-40873-0). Pinnacle Bks.

Wallace, Patricia, jt. auth. see Brown, Thomas S.

Wallace, Phyllis A., ed. Women in the Workplace. 246p. 1982. 21.95 o.p. (ISBN 0-86569-069-3); pap. 12.95 (ISBN 0-86569-096-0). Auburn Hse.

Wallace, Phyllis A. & LaMond, Annette M., eds. Women, Minorities, & Discrimination. LC 76-53903. (Illus.). 224p. 1977. 22.95x o.p. (ISBN 0-669-01282-3). Lexington Bks.

Wallace, Phyllis A., et al. Black Women in the Labor Force. 192p. 1980. text ed. 16.50x (ISBN 0-262-23103-4). MIT Pr.

Wallace, Ralph G., jt. auth. see Houghton, Diane.

Wallace, Ralph J. What Does He Mean by "A Little While?". (Orig.). 1981. pap. 4.95 (ISBN 0-937172-30-8). JLJ Pubs.

Wallace, Randall. The Russian Rose. 324p. 1980. 11.95 (ISBN 0-399-12536-1). Putnam Pub Group.

--So Late into the Night. LC 82-45834. 336p. 1983. 15.95 (ISBN 0-385-18440-9). Doubleday.

Wallace, Robert. The Gamblers. LC 78-12281. (The Old West Ser.). (Illus.). 1978. 17.96 (ISBN 0-8094-2310-3). Silver.

--The Grand Canyon. LC 71-179463. (American Wilderness Ser). (Illus.). (gr. 6 up). 1972. lib. bdg. 15.96 (ISBN 0-8094-1145-8, Pub. by Time-Life). Silver.

--Hawaii. LC 73-179462. (American Wilderness Ser). (Illus.). (gr. 6 up). 1973. lib. bdg. 15.96 (ISBN 0-8094-1177-6, Pub. by Time-Life). Silver.

--How They Do It. (Illus.). 1980. pap. 4.95 (ISBN 0-688-08718-3). Quill NY.

--The Italian Campaign. LC 78-52857. (World War II Ser.). (Illus.). 1978. lib. bdg. 19.92 (ISBN 0-8094-2503-3). Silver.

--The Miners. LC 76-15917. (The Old West). (Illus.). (gr. 5 up). 1976. 17.28 (ISBN 0-8094-1539-9, Pub. by Time-Life). Silver.

--Rise of Russia. LC 67-18419. (Great Ages of Man). (Illus.). (gr. 6 up). 1967. 11.97 o.p. (ISBN 0-8094-0375-7, Pub. by Time-Life). Silver.

--Swimmer in the Rain. LC 78-74988. (Poetry Ser.). 1979. 8.95 o.p. (ISBN 0-915604-56-6); pap. 4.50 (ISBN 0-915604-57-4). Carnegie-Mellon.

--World of Bernini. LC 70-122329. (Library of Art Ser.). (Illus.). (gr. 6 up). 1970. 19.92 (ISBN 0-8094-0286-6, Pub. by Time-Life). Silver.

--World of Leonardo. LC 66-24104. (Library of Art Ser.). (Illus.). (gr. 6 up). 1966. 19.92 (ISBN 0-8094-0263-7, Pub. by Time-Life). Silver.

--World of Rembrandt. LC 68-22321. (Library of4Art Ser.). (Illus.). (gr. 6 up). 1968. 19.92 (ISBN 0-8094-0273-4, Pub. by Time-Life). Silver.

--World of Van Gogh. LC 70-78988. (Library of Art Ser.). (Illus.). (gr. 6 up). 1969. 19.92 (ISBN 0-8094-0280-7, Pub. by Time-Life). Silver.

Wallace, Robert, jt. auth. see Cloke, Marjane.

Wallace, Robert, jt. auth. see Wallace, Mary E.

Wallace, Robert A. Animal Behavior: Development, Ecology, Evolution. LC 78-11616. 1979. text ed. 27.50x (ISBN 0-673-16243-5). Scott F.

--Biology: The World of Life. 3rd ed. 1981. text ed. 25.50x (ISBN 0-673-16245-1). Scott F.

--Ecology & Evolution of Animal Behavior. 2nd ed. 1979. pap. text ed. 16.50x (ISBN 0-673-16246-X). Scott F.

--The Genesis Factor. LC 79-65876. 1979. 9.95 o.p. (ISBN 0-688-03536-1). Morrow.

Wallace, Robert A. & King, Jack L. Biology: The Science of Life. 1981. text ed. 31.95x (ISBN 0-673-15591-9). Scott F.

Wallace, Roberta & Heiss, Marie L. Staff Manual for Teaching Patients about Rheumatoid Arthritis. LC 78-20816. (Illus.). 472p. 1979. pap. 39.75 o.p. (ISBN 0-87258-252-3, 070112). Am Hospital.

Wallace, Roberta, et al. Staff Manual for Teaching Patients about Rheumatoid Arthritis. LC 82-8727. (Illus.). 524p. 1982. 47.50 (ISBN 0-87258-374-0, AHA-070123). Am Hospital.

Wallace, Ronald. Plums, Stones, Kisses, & Hooks. LC 80-15970. 80p. (Orig.). 1983. pap. 5.95 (ISBN 0-8262-0400-7). U of Mo Pr.

Wallace, Ronald S. Calvin's Doctrine of the Christian Life. xvi, 349p. 1982. pap. 13.95 (ISBN 0-939404-03-6). Geneva Divinity.

--Calvin's Doctrine of the Word & Sacraments. xii, 253p. 1982. pap. 12.95 (ISBN 0-939404-02-8). Geneva Divinity.

Wallace, Ruth A. & Wolf, Alison. Contemporary Sociological Theory. LC 79-13971. (Sociology Ser.). (Illus.). 1980. text ed. 22.95 (ISBN 0-13-170506-7). P-H.

Wallace, Sally F. Practically Painless English. (English Composition Ser.). 1979. pap. text ed. 10.95 (ISBN 0-13-692194-9). P-H.

Wallace, Samuel E. After Suicide. LC 73-9793. 269p. 1973. 21.95 o.p. (ISBN 0-471-91865-2, Pub. by Wiley-Interscience). Wiley.

Wallace, Samuel E., ed. Total Institutions. 198p. 1971. pap. 3.95x (ISBN 0-87855-057-7); 9.95. Transaction Bks.

Wallace, W. Development of the Chlorinity-Salinity Concept in Oceanography. LC 72-97440. (Elsevier Oceanography Ser.: Vol. 7). 240p. 1974. 64.00 (ISBN 0-444-41118-6). Elsevier.

Wallace, W. E. Rare Earth Intermetallics. (Materials Science Ser.). 1973. 55.00 (ISBN 0-12-732850-5). Acad Pr.

Wallace, W. E., jt. ed. see Subbarao, E. C.

Wallace, W. Stewart, ed. Macmillan Dictionary of Canadian Biography. 3rd ed. 1963. 20.00 o.p. (ISBN 0-312-50260-5). St Martin.

Wallace, Walter L., jt. auth. see Conyers, James E.

Wallace, Willard M; see Weaver, Glenn.

Wallace, William A. Causality & Scientific Explanation: Classical & Contemporary Science, Vol. 2. 432p. 1981. lib. bdg. 25.50 (ISBN 0-8191-1480-4); pap. text ed. 15.50 (ISBN 0-8191-1481-2). U Pr of Amer.

--Causality & Scientific Explanation: Medieval & Early Classical Science, Vol. 1. 298p. 1981. lib. bdg. 21.75 (ISBN 0-8191-1478-2); pap. text ed. 11.50 (ISBN 0-8191-1479-0). U Pr of Amer.

--From a Realist Point of View: Essays on the Philosophy of Science. LC 79-66154. 1979. pap. text ed. 13.75 (ISBN 0-8191-0797-2). U Pr of Amer.

Wallace, William J., jt. auth. see Ingmanson, Dale E.

Wallace, William S. Dictionary of North American Authors Deceased Before 1950. LC 68-19955. 1968. Repr. of 1951 ed. 40.00x (ISBN 0-8103-3153-5). Gale.

Wallace, Wyss. The Complete Guide to the Ferrari 308 Series. (Illus.). 96p. 1982. 14.95 (ISBN 0-901564-58-3, Pub. by Dalton England). Motorbooks Intl.

Wallace-Hadrill, D. S. Christian Antioch: A Study of Early Christian Thought in the East. 240p. 1982. 29.95 (ISBN 0-521-23425-5). Cambridge U Pr.

Wallace-Hadrill, J. M. The Long-Haired Kings & Other Studies in Frankish History. (Medieval Academy Reprints for Teaching Ser.). 272p. 1982. pap. 8.50 (ISBN 0-8020-6500-7). U of Toronto Pr.

Wallach, Anne T. Women's Work. 1982. pap. 3.95 (ISBN 0-451-11610-0, AE1610, Sig). NAL.

Wallach, Donald F. Proteins of Animal Cell Plasma Membranes, Vol. 2. Horrobin, D. F., ed. (Annual Research Reviews). 1979. 28.00 (ISBN 0-88831-048-X). Eden Pr.

Wallach, Edward E. & Kempers, Roger D. Modern Trends in Infertility & Conception Control, Vol. 2. 480p. 1982. text ed. 32.50x (ISBN 0-06-142605-9, Harper Medical). Lippincott.

Wallach, Geraldine P., jt. auth. see Butler, Katherine G.

Wallach, Ira. Hopalong-Freud & Other Parodies. 1965. pap. 1.50 o.p. (ISBN 0-486-21547-4). Dover.

Wallach, Janet. Working Wardrobe: Affordable Clothes that Work for You. 200p. (Orig.). 1982. pap. 8.95 (ISBN 0-446-37253-6). Warner Bks.

Wallach, Mark I. & Bracker, Jon. Christopher Morley. (United States Authors Ser.). 1976. lib. bdg. 13.95 (ISBN 0-8057-7178-6, Twayne). G K Hall.

Wallach, P. I. Architecture: Drafting & Design, Study Guide. 1972. 6.28 (ISBN 0-07-067933-9, W). McGraw.

Wallach, Paul. Guide to the Restaurants of Northern California. (Illus.). 600p. 1983. pap. 9.95 (ISBN 0-932948-04-9). Am Guide Pubns.

--Guide to the Restaurants of Southern California. (Illus.). 768p. 1983. pap. 9.95 (ISBN 0-932948-03-0). Am Guide Pubns.

Wallach, Paul & Hepler, Don. Reading Construction Drawings: Trade Edition. (Illus.). 320p. 1980. 24.95 (ISBN 0-07-067940-1, P&RB). McGraw.

Wallach, Paul, jt. auth. see Hepler, Donald.

Wallach, Paul I. & Hepler, Donald E. Reading Construction Drawings. (Illus.). 1979. pap. text ed. 15.95 (ISBN 0-07-067935-5, G). McGraw.

Wallach, Robert C., jt. auth. see Watson, Rita E.

Wallach, Theresa. Easy Motorcycle Riding. rev. enlarged ed. LC 78-57787. (Illus.). 1978. 8.95 (ISBN 0-8069-4134-0); lib. bdg. 10.99 (ISBN 0-8069-4135-9). Sterling.

--Easy Motorcycle Riding. LC 82-19322. (Illus.). 160p. 1983. pap. 4.95 (ISBN 0-8069-7712-4). Sterling.

Wallack, F. Bradford. The Epochal Nature of Process in Whitehead's Metaphysics. LC 79-22898. 1980. 44.50x (ISBN 0-87395-404-1); pap. 14.95x (ISBN 0-87395-454-8). State U NY Pr.

Wallack, Stanley S. & Kretz, Sandra E. Rural Medicine: Obstacles & Solutions for Self-Sufficiency, LC 79-48057. (The University Health Policy Consortium Ser.). (Illus.). 208p. 1981. 22.95x (ISBN 0-669-03691-9). Lexington Bks.

Wallant, Edward L. The Human Season. LC 60-10923. 192p. 1973. pap. 1.65 (ISBN 0-15-642330-8, Harv). HarBraceJ.

--The Tenants of Moonbloom. LC 63-13501. 245p. 1973. pap. 3.50 (ISBN 0-15-688535-2, Harv). HarBraceJ.

Wallas, Charles H. & Muller, Victor H., eds. The Hospital Transfusion Committee. 100p. 1982. 16.00 (ISBN 0-914404-78-4); non-members 18.00 (ISBN 0-686-83042-3). Am Assn Blood.

Wallas, Charles H., jt. ed. see Tregellas, W. Michael.

Wallas, Charles H., jt. ed. see Banzhaf, Jane C.

Wallat, Cynthia, jt. ed. see Green, Judith.

Wallat, Cynthia, ed. see Tannen, Deborah.

Wallbank, T. Walter, et al. Civilization Past & Present. 7th ed. 1976. Bk. 2. pap. 12.50x (ISBN 0-673-15079-8). Scott F.

--Civilization Past & Present, Vol. 1. 8th ed. 1981. pap. text ed. 17.95x (ISBN 0-673-15235-9). Scott F.

--Civilization Past & Present, Vol. 2. 8th ed. 1981. pap. text ed. 17.95x (ISBN 0-673-15236-7). Scott F.

--Civilization Past & Present: Prehistory to 1650. 5th ed. 1979. Vol. 1. pap. text ed. 16.50x (ISBN 0-673-15246-4). Scott F.

--Civilization Past & Present: 1650 to the Present. 5th ed. 1979. Vol. 2. pap. text ed. 16.50x (ISBN 0-673-15247-2). Scott F.

--Western Civilization: People & Progress, 2 vols. Incl. Vol. 1. Ancient World to 1750 (ISBN 0-673-15082-8); Vol. 2. 1650 to the Present (ISBN 0-673-15083-6). 1977. pap. 10.95x ea. Scott F.

--Western Civilization: People & Progress. 1977. pap. 17.95x (ISBN 0-673-15081-X). Scott F.

--Civilization Past & Present. 5th ed. 1978. 26.50x (ISBN 0-673-07951-1). Scott F.

--Civilization Past & Present: Special Printing. 5th ed. 1982. text ed. 26.50x (ISBN 0-673-15624-9). Scott F.

--Studying Civilization. 5th ed. 1978. pap. 7.95x (ISBN 0-673-15125-5). Scott F.

Wallbridge, David, jt. auth. see Davis, Madeleine.

Wallechinsky, David & Wallace, Amy. The Book of Lists, No. 3. 512p. 1983. 15.95 (ISBN 0-688-01647-2). Morrow.

Wallechinsky, David & Wallace, Irving. The People's Almanac, No. 3. 736p. 1982. 4.50 (ISBN 0-553-20924-8). Bantam.

--The People's Almanac Presents the Book of Lists 3. (Book of Lists Ser.). 1981. pap. write for info. (ISBN 0-553-01352-1). Bantam.

Wallen, C. C., ed. Climates of Northern & Western Europe. (World Survey of Climatology: Vol. 5). 1971. 98.00 (ISBN 0-444-40705-7). Elsevier.

Wallen, C. C., jt. ed. see Landsberg, H. E.

Wallen, I. Eugene, jt. ed. see Llano, George A.

Wallenburg. Placental Transfer Primates. 300p. 1982. 56.50 (ISBN 0-03-063036-3). Praeger.

Wallender, Harvey W. Technology Transfer & Management in the Developing Countries: Company Cases & Policy Analysis in Brazil, Kenya, Korea, Peru, & Tanzania. LC 79-12745. 320p. 1979. reference 23.50 o.p. (ISBN 0-88410-372-2). Ballinger Pub.

Wallendorf, M., jt. auth. see Zaltman, G.

Wallendorf, Melanie & Zaltman, Gerald. Readings in Consumer Behavior: Individuals, Groups & Organizations. LC 78-13228. (Marketing Ser.). 1979. pap. text ed. 25.95 (ISBN 0-471-03021-X). Wiley.

Wallenfeldt, E. C. American Higher Education: Servant of the People or of Special Interests? LC 82-15837. (Contributions to the Study of Education: No. 9). 256p. 1983. lib. bdg. 29.95 (ISBN 0-313-23469-8). Greenwood.

Wallenius, Anna B. Libraries in East Africa. LC 70-163924. 200p. 1971. text ed. 25.00x (ISBN 0-8419-0091-4, Africana). Holmes & Meier.

Wallenstein, Gerd. International Telecommunication Agreements, 2 vols. LC 77-72058. (International Telecommunications Agreements Ser.). 1977. Set. 175.00 (ISBN 0-379-10045-2). Oceana.

Waller, Adrian. Adrian Waller's Guide to Music. (Quality Paperback: No. 296). (Illus.). 156p. (Orig.). 1975. pap. 3.95 (ISBN 0-8226-0296-2). Littlefield.

--Theatre on a Shoestring. (Quality Paperback: No. 295). 158p. (Orig.). 1975. pap. 3.95 (ISBN 0-8226-0295-4). Littlefield.

Waller, Derek J. Kiangsi Soviet Republic: Mao & the National Congresses of 1931 & 1934. (China Research Monographs: No. 10). 1973. pap. 5.00x (ISBN 0-912966-11-4). IEAS.

Waller, Edmund. Poems. Drury, G. Thorn, ed. Repr. of 1893 ed. lib. bdg. 16.00x (ISBN 0-8371-0735-0, WAEW). Greenwood.

Waller, F. G. Biographisch Woordenboer Van Noord Nederlandsche Graveurs. (Illus.). 377p. 1974. Repr. 58.00 (ISBN 0-8390-0145-2). Allanheld & Schram.

Waller, G. F. Dreaming America: Obsession & Transcendence in the Fiction of Joyce Carol Oates. LC 78-16141. 1979. 17.50x (ISBN 0-8071-0478-7). La State U Pr.

Waller, Gary. Impossible Futures Indelible Pasts. 80p. 1983. pap. 5.95 (ISBN 0-686-38735-X). Kellner-McCaffery.

Waller, George M., ed. Pearl Harbor: Roosevelt & the Coming of the War. 3rd ed. (Problems in American Civilization Ser.). 1976. pap. text ed. 5.95 (ISBN 0-669-98376-4). Heath.

--Puritanism in Early America. 2nd ed. (Problems in American Civilization Ser). 1973. pap. text ed. 5.95 (ISBN 0-669-82719-3). Heath.

Waller, George R. & Dermer, Otis C. Biochemical Applications of Mass Spectrometry: First Supplementary Volume. 1980. 199.50x (ISBN 0-471-03810-5, Pub. by Wiley-Interscience). Wiley.

Waller, George R., ed. Biochemical Applications of Mass Spectrometry. LC 78-158529. 1972. 120.50x (ISBN 0-471-91900-4, Pub. by Wiley-Interscience). Wiley.

Waller, Hannah, tr. see Eckart, Richard.

Waller, Irene. Fine-Art Weaving. (Illus.). 144p. 1980. 22.50 (ISBN 0-7134-0412-4, Pub. by Batsford England). David & Charles.

Waller, J. M., jt. auth. see Hill, D. S.

Waller, Leslie. Blood & Dreams. 1982. pap. 3.25 (ISBN 0-515-06426-2). Jove Pubns.

--Blood & Dreams. 396p. 1980. 12.95 (ISBN 0-399-12564-7). Putnam Pub Group.

--The Brave & the Free. 1980. pap. 2.50 o.s.i. (ISBN 0-440-10915-9). Dell.

--Family. 1969. pap. 1.50 o.p. (ISBN 0-451-06537-9, W6537, Sig). NAL.

--Trocadero. 1978. 12.95 o.s.i. (ISBN 0-440-09073-3). Delacorte.

Waller, P. P., jt. auth. see Obudho, R. A.

Waller, Ray A., jt. auth. see Martz, Harry F.

Waller, T. G. & Mackinnon, G. E., eds. Reading Research: Advances in Theory & Practice, Vol. 2. (Serial Publication). 1981. 24.50 (ISBN 0-12-572302-4). Acad Pr.

Waller, T. Gary & Mackinnon, G. E., eds. Reading Research: Advances in Theory & Practice, Vol. 1. 1979. 26.50 (ISBN 0-12-572301-6). Acad Pr.

Wallerstein, I. The Capitalist World Economy. LC 78-1161. (Studies in Modern Capitalism). 1979. 54.50 (ISBN 0-521-22085-8); pap. 13.95 (ISBN 0-521-29358-8). Cambridge U Pr.

Wallerstein, Immanuel, ed. Labor in the World Social Structure. (Explorations in the World Economy Ser.: Vol. 2). (Illus.). 272p. 1983. 25.00 (ISBN 0-8039-1922-0). Sage.

--On the European Workers' Movement. (Contemporary Marxism Ser.). 100p. 1980. pap. 5.00 (ISBN 0-89935-011-9). Synthesis Pubns.

Wallerstein, Immanuel, ed. see De Braganca, Aquino.

Wallerstein, Immanuel, ed. see De Branganca, Aquino.

Wallerstein, Judith S. & Kelly, Joan B. Surviving the Breakup: How Children & Parents Cope with Divorce. LC 79-5199. 448p. 1980. 18.50 o.s.i. (ISBN 0-465-08341-2). Basic.

--Surviving the Breakup: How Children & Parents Cope with Divorce. 1982. pap. 8.95 (ISBN 0-465-08339-0). Basic.

Wallerstein, Mitchel B. Food for War - Food for Peace: U. S. Food Aid in a Global Context. 320p. 1980. text ed. 32.50x (ISBN 0-262-23106-9). MIT Pr.

Walley, B. H. Handbook of Office Management. 2nd ed. 297p. 1982. text ed. 35.75x (Pub. by Busn Bks England). Renouf.

Walley, David. No Commercial Potential: The Saga of Frank Zappa Then & Now. (Illus.). 192p. 1980. pap. 6.95 (ISBN 0-525-93153-8, 0674-210). Dutton.

Walley, Dean. For You...Because You're My Friend. 1977. pap. 5.50 (ISBN 0-8378-5005-3). Gibson.

--Friendship Is a Very Special Thing. 1979. pap. 5.50 (ISBN 0-8378-5032-0). Gibson.

--Our Love Is. 1977. pap. 4.95 o.p. (ISBN 0-8378-5004-5). Gibson.

Walley, Joyce I. Writing Implements & Accessories: From the Roman Stylus to the Typewriter. LC 75-7563. (Illus.). 176p. 1975. 31.00x (ISBN 0-8103-2017-7). Gale.

Walley, Ronald. Eyes to See; & Ears to Hear: The Way of Concious Love. 1979. 7.95 o.p. (ISBN 0-533-04025-6). Vantage.

Wallgren, Mark. The Beatles on Record. LC 82-10305. (Illus.). 336p. Date not set. pap. 9.95 (ISBN 0-671-45682-2, Fireside). S&S.

Wallich, Christine. State Finances in India. LC 82-11087. (World Bank Staff Working Papers: No. 523). (Orig.). 1982. pap. 3.00 (ISBN 0-8213-0013-X). World Bank.

Wallich, Henry C. The Cost of Freedom: A New Look at Capitalism. LC 78-27775. 1979. Repr. of 1960 ed. lib. bdg. 17.95x (ISBN 0-313-20935-9, WACF). Greenwood.

--Monetary Policy & Practice: A View from the Federal Reserve Board. LC 81-47648. 416p. 1981. 20.95x (ISBN 0-669-04712-0). Lexington Bks.

Wallich, Henry C. & Adler, John H. Public Finance in a Developing Country: El Salvador, a Case Study. LC 68-8339. (Illus.). 1968. Repr. of 1951 ed. lib. bdg. 17.00x (ISBN 0-8371-0259-6, WAPF). Greenwood.

Wallin, Cheryl W. The Lane County Kid's Book: Stories to 1900. (Illus.). 96p. 1982. pap. write for info. (ISBN 0-9607040-0-0). Silver Pennies.

Wallin, Diane, ed. see Tong, L. S. & Weisman, Joel.

Wallin, Douglas. Basics of Underwater Photography. (Illus.). 128p. 1975. 7.95 (ISBN 0-8174-0578-X, Amphoto). Watson-Guptill.

Wallin, Luke. Blue Wings. LC 81-21562. 224p. (gr. 6-8). 1982. 9.95 (ISBN 0-02-792400-9). Bradbury Pr.

--The Redneck Poacher's Son. LC 80-26782. 224p. (gr. 7 up). 1981. 10.95 (ISBN 0-02-792480-7). Bradbury Pr.

--The Slavery Ghosts. 144p. (gr. 5-7). 1983. 10.95 (ISBN 0-02-792380-0). Bradbury Pr.

Wallin, S. C., jt. auth. see Clayton, P.

Walling, Ardyce. What Do You Know? LC 78-65187. 1979. 6.50 o.p. (ISBN 0-533-04074-4). Vantage.

Walling, Donovan R. Complete Book of School Public Relations an Administrator's Manual & Guide. LC 82-12340. 222p. 1982. 17.50 (ISBN 0-13-158337-9, Busn). P-H.

Walling, George W. Recollections of a New York Chief of Police with Historic Supplement of the Denver Police. LC 70-129311. (Criminology, Law Enforcement, & Social Problems Ser.: No. 133). (Illus.). 682p. (With intro. & index added). 1972. Repr. of 1890 ed. 18.50x (ISBN 0-87585-133-9). Patterson Smith.

Walling, William A. Mary Shelley. (English Authors Ser.). lib. bdg. 11.95 (ISBN 0-8057-1484-7, Twayne). G K Hall.

Wallinger, D. C. The Marriage & Other Traumas. 1978. 4.95 o.p. (ISBN 0-533-03898-7). Vantage.

Wallington, C. E. Meteorology for Glider Pilots. 3rd ed. (Illus.). 331p. 1980. 30.00 (ISBN 0-7195-3303-1). Transatlantic.

Wallington, Clint, ed. see Merrill, Irving R. & Drob, Harold A.

Wallis, Arthur. El Ayuno Escogido por Dios. 176p. Date not set. 2.50 (ISBN 0-88113-006-0). Edit Betania.

--Desafio a Triunfar. 128p. 1983. 1.95 (ISBN 0-88113-000-1). Edit Betania.

--Orad en el Espiritu. LC 82-23203. 144p. 1983. 2.95 (ISBN 0-88113-240-3). Edit Betania.

Wallis, Betty, jt. auth. see Wallis, Charles.

Wallis, Celestina, et al. Anushka's Complete Body Makeover Book. (Illus.). 224p. 1981. 14.95 (ISBN 0-399-12579-5). Putnam Pub Group.

Wallis, Charles & Wallis, Betty. Our Christian Home & Family: An Illustrated Treasury of Inspirational Quotations, Poems & Prayers. LC 82-47758. (Illus.). 1982. 14.37i (ISBN 0-06-069009-7, HarpR). Har-Row.

Wallis, Charles G., et al, trs. see Pico Della Mirandola, Giovanni.

Wallis, Charles L. American Epitaphs, Grave & Humorous. (Illus.). 320p. 1973. pap. 3.00 o.p. (ISBN 0-486-20263-1). Dover.

Wallis, Charles L., ed. Funeral Encyclopedia. (Source Bks for Ministers Ser.). 1973. pap. 5.95 o.p. (ISBN 0-8010-9539-5). Baker Bk.

--The Ministers Manual, Nineteen Eighty-Three. LC 25-21658. 288p. 1982. 9.57i (ISBN 0-06-069027-5, HarpR). Har-Row.

Wallis, Charles L., compiled by. Treasure Chest. LC 65-15395. (Illus.). 1965. 12.95i (ISBN 0-06-069010-0, HarpR); deluxe ed. 17.95i (ISBN 0-06-069011-9); deluxe ed. 17.95i (white) (ISBN 0-06-069051-8). Har-Row.

Wallis, Charles L., ed. see Allen, Charles L.

Wallis, Frank A. The History of Pagan Architecture. (An Essential Knowledge Library Bk.). (Illus.). 117p. 1983. Repr. of 1908 ed. 78.45 (ISBN 0-89901-097-0). Found Class Reprints.

Wallis, Graham. One-Dimensional Two-Phase Flow: The First Complete Account of John Paul Jones' Greatest Battle. (Illus.). 1969. 43.50 (ISBN 0-07-067942-8, C). McGraw.

Wallis, J. Software Portability. 1982. 100.00x (ISBN 0-333-31035-7, Pub. by Macmillan England). State Mutual Bk.

Wallis, J. H. Challenge of Middle Age. 1972. 8.50 o.p. (ISBN 0-7100-2250-6). Routledge & Kegan.

Wallis, Jim. Call to Conversion. LC 80-8901. 192p. 1981. 9.95i o.p. (ISBN 0-06-069237-5, HarpR). Har-Row.

--Jim Wallis Revive Us Again: A Sojourner's Story. Raines, Robert A., ed. 192p. 1983. text ed. 9.95 (ISBN 0-687-36173-7). Abingdon.

Wallis, Jim, ed. Waging Peace: A Handbook for the Struggle Against Nuclear Arms. LC 82-47759. 224p. (Orig.). 1982. pap. 4.67i (ISBN 0-06-069240-5, HarpR). Har-Row.

Wallis, John. Thinking About Retirement. LC 72-652. 120p. 1975. text ed. 21.00 (ISBN 0-08-018269-0); pap. text ed. 8.75 (ISBN 0-08-018268-2). Pergamon.

Wallis, Julia, jt. auth. see Constantine, John.

Wallis, R. T. Neoplatonism. (Classical Life & Letters Ser.). 224p. 1983. pap. text ed. 12.00x (ISBN 0-7156-1218-2, Pub. by Duckworth England). Biblio Dist.

Wallis, Roy. Salvation & Protest: Studies of Social & Religious Movements. 1979. 26.00x (ISBN 0-312-69834-8). St Martin.

Wallis, Roy, jt. ed. see Morley, Peter.

Wallman, Jeffrey M., jt. auth. see Jeier, Thomas.

Wallman, Sandra, ed. Perceptions of Development. LC 76-46863. (Perspectives on Development: No. 6). 1977. 29.95 (ISBN 0-521-21498-X). Cambridge U Pr.

Wallmann, Jeffrey. The Manipulator. 368p. 1982. pap. 3.25 (ISBN 0-380-81166-9, 81166). Avon.

Wallmann, Jeffrey M. Brand of the Damned. (Bronc: No. 1). 192p. 1982. pap. 1.95 o.s.i. (ISBN 0-8439-0983-8, Leisure Bks). Nordon Pubns.

Wallner, Linda, ed. Recipes for Leftovers. 64p. 1975. pap. 2.95 (ISBN 0-89821-006-2). Reiman Assoc.

Wallner, S. J. Friendly Little Hobo. LC 68-56814. (Illus.). (gr. 2-4). PLB 6.75x (ISBN 0-87783-013-4); pap. 2.95x deluxe ed. (ISBN 0-87783-092-4). Oddo.
--Hans & The Golden Stirrup. LC 68-56815. (Illus.). (gr. 2-3). PLB 6.75x (ISBN 0-87783-016-9); pap. 2.95x deluxe ed. (ISBN 0-87783-093-2). Oddo.
Wallo, Olav. The New Complete Norwegian Elkhound. 2nd ed. (Complete Breed Book Ser.). (Illus.). 1982. 14.95 o.p. (ISBN 0-87605-243-X). Howell Bk.
Wallraff, Gunter. The Undesirable Journalist. LC 78-70935. 192p. 1979. 15.00 (ISBN 0-87951-095-1). Overlook Pr.
--Wallraff: The Undesirable Journalist. Gooch, Steve & Knight, Paul, trs. LC 78-70935. 192p. pap. 6.95 (ISBN 0-87951-169-9). Overlook Pr.
Walls, Elizabeth, jt. auth. see Tuttle, Michael D.
Walls, H. J. & Attridge, G. G. Basic Photo Science: How Photography Works. rev. ed. (Illus.). 1977. 29.95 (ISBN 0-240-50945-5). Focal Pr.
Walls, Ian. Modern Greenhouse Methods: Flowers & Plants. 220p. 1982. 31.00x (ISBN 0-584-10386-7, Pub. by Muller Ltd). State Mutual Bk.
--Modern Greenhouse Methods: Vegetables. 220p. 1982. 31.00x (ISBN 0-584-10388-3, Pub. by Muller Ltd). State Mutual Bk.
Walls, Jerry. Cone Shells: A Synopsis of the Living Conidae. (Illus.). 1979. 39.95 (ISBN 0-87666-628-4, S-102). TFH Pubns.
Walls, Jerry C., jt. auth. see Taylor, John.
Walls, Jerry G. Conchs, Tibias, & Harps. (Illus.). 192p. 1980. 14.95 (ISBN 0-87666-629-2, S-103). TFH Pubns.
--Fishes of the Northern Gulf of Mexico. (Illus.). 432p. 1975. 14.95 (ISBN 0-87666-445-1, H960). TFH Pubns.
--Shell Collecting. (Illus.). 96p. 1981. 4.95 (ISBN 0-87666-631-4, KW-130). TFH Pubns.
--Starting with Marine Invertebrates. (Illus.). 160p. (Orig.). 1974. 12.95 (ISBN 0-87666-767-1, PS-729). TFH Pubns.
Walls, Jerry G., ed. The Encyclopedia of Marine Invertebrates. (Illus.). 736p. 1982. 49.95 (ISBN 0-87666-495-8, H-951). TFH Pubns.
Walls, Sara, ed. see Porter, Benjamin F.
Wallwork, John N. Desert Soil Fauna. 304p. 1982. 37.50 (ISBN 0-03-055306-7). Praeger.
Walmais. Crazy Animal Stories. 1982. 9.95 (ISBN 0-07-015198-9). McGraw.
Walmsley, Julian. The Foreign Exchange Handbook: A User's Guide. 425p. 1983. 39.95x (ISBN 0-471-86388-2, Pub. by Wiley-Interscience). Wiley.
Walmsley, R. Peterloo. 1969. 25.00 (ISBN 0-7190-0392-X). Manchester.
Walne, Damien & Flory, Joan. The Lady Said Come to Lourdes. (Illus.). 1978. pap. 3.95 o.p. (ISBN 0-8199-0753-7). Franciscan Herald.
Walne, Shirley. The Poodle. 1977. pap. 2.50 (ISBN 0-7028-1064-9). Palmetto Pub.
Waloff, N., jt. auth. see Richards, O. W.
Waloff, Z. Field Studies on Solitary & Transient Desert Locusts in the Red Sea Area. 1963. 35.00 (ISBN 0-85135-040-2, Pub. by Centre Overseas Research). State Mutual Bk.
--Some Temporal Characteristics of Desert Locust Plagues. 1976. 35.00x (ISBN 0-85135-075-5, Pub. by Centre Overseas Research). State Mutual Bk.
--The Upsurges & Recessions of the Desert Locust Plague: An Historical Survey. 1968. 35.00x (ISBN 0-85135-041-0, Pub. by Centre Overseas Research). State Mutual Bk.
Waloff, Z. & Rainey, R. C. Field Studies on Factors Affecting the Displacement of Desert Locust Swarms in Eastern Africa. 1951. 35.00x (ISBN 0-85135-042-9, Pub. by Centre Overseas Research). State Mutual Bk.
Waloff, Z., jt. auth. see Rainey, R. C.
Walowit, J. A. & Anno, J. N. Modern Developments in Lubrication Mechanics. (Illus.). x, 244p. 1975. 51.25 (ISBN 0-85334-592-9, Pub. by Applied Sci England). Elsevier.
Walpole, Horace. Castle of Otranto. 1963. pap. 2.95 (ISBN 0-02-055200-9, Collier). Macmillan.
--The Castle of Otranto. Lewis, W. S. & Reed, Joseph W., Jr., eds. (World's Classics Ser.). 1982. pap. 3.95 (ISBN 0-19-281606-3). Oxford U Pr.
--The Castle of Otranto: A Gothic Story. Lewis, W. S., ed. (Oxford Paperbacks Ser: No. 187). (Illus.). 1974. pap. 5.95x o.p. (ISBN 0-19-281047-2). Oxford U Pr.
--Correspondence with George Montague 1st & 2nd, 2 vols. Lewis, W. S. & Brown, R. S., Jr., eds. (Horace Walpole's Correspondence Ser.). (Illus.). 1941. 50.00x ea. Vol. 9 (ISBN 0-300-00694-2). Vol. 10 (ISBN 0-300-00695-0). Yale U Pr.
--Horace Walpole's Fugitive Verses. Lewis, W. S., ed. (Miscellaneous Antiquities Ser.: No. 5). 1931. text ed. 65.00x Ltd. Ed. (ISBN 0-686-83569-7). Elliots Bks.
--The Yale Edition of Horace Walpole's Correspondence, Vol. 43. Martz, Edwine M. & McClure, Ruth K., eds. LC 65-11182. 408p. 1983. text ed. 65.00x (ISBN 0-300-02711-7). Yale U Pr.
--The Yale Edition of Horace Walpole's Correspondence, Vols. 44-48. Smith, Warren H. & Martz, Edwine M., eds. LC 65-11182. 424p. 1983. text ed. 325.00x (ISBN 0-300-02718-4). Yale U Pr.
Walpole, Ronald E. Elementary Statistical Concepts. (Illus.). 288p. 1976. text ed. 20.95x (ISBN 0-02-424090-7). Macmillan.
--Introduction to Statistics. 3rd ed. 1982. text ed. 24.95x (ISBN 0-02-424150-4). Macmillan.
Walpole, Ronald E. & Meyers, Raymond. Probability & Statistics for Engineers & Scientists. 2nd ed. (Illus.). 512p. 1978. text ed. 29.95x (ISBN 0-02-424110-5, 42411). Macmillan.
Walpole, Ronald E., jt. auth. see Freund, John E.
Walpole, Ronald N. The Old French Johannis Translation of the Pseudo-Turpin Chronicle: A Critical Edition. 1976. 40.00x (ISBN 0-520-02707-8); suppl. 50.00x (ISBN 0-520-02840-6). U of Cal Pr.
Walpot, Peter. True Surrender & Christian Community of Goods, 1521-1578. 1957. pap. 1.95 (ISBN 0-87486-205-1). Plough.
Walras, L. Les Associations Populaires de Consommation, de Production et de Credit. (Conditions of the 19th Century French Working Class Ser.). 300p. (Fr.). 1974. Repr. of 1865 ed. lib. bdg. 80.00 o.p. (ISBN 0-8287-0879-7, 1077). Clearwater Pub.
Walraven & Harding. Manual of Advanced Prehospital Care. 2nd ed. (Illus.). 416p. 1983. pap. text ed. 19.95 (ISBN 0-89303-252-2). R J Brady.
Walrod, Michael R. Discourse Grammar in Ga'dang. Davis, Irvine & Poulter, Virgil, eds. LC 79-66350. (Publications in Linguistics: No. 63). (Illus.). 117p. 1979. pap. text.ed. 8.00 (ISBN 0-88312-077-1); microfiche 2.25 (ISBN 0-686-82707-4). Summer Inst Ling.
Walsberg, Glenn E. The Ecology & Energetics of Contrasting Social Systems in the Phainopepia. (Publications in Zoology: Vol. 108). 1977. 13.00x (ISBN 0-520-09562-6). U of Cal Pr.
Walsby, Fausta S., tr. see Venturi, Franco.
Walsdorf, John J. William Morris in Private Press & Limited Editions: A Descriptive Bibliography of Books by & about William Morris. 1983. price not set (ISBN 0-89774-041-6). Oryx Pr.
Walser, Richard. Young Readers' Picturebook of Tar Heel Authors. 5th & rev. ed. (Illus.). 1981. pap. 1.00 (ISBN 0-86526-184-9). NC Archives.
Walser, Richard, ed. North Carolina Miscellany. vii, 275p. 1962. 9.95 o.p. (ISBN 0-8078-0842-3). U of NC Pr.
Walser, Robert. Jakob von Gunten. Middleton, Christopher, tr. from Ger. 154p. 1969. 10.95x (ISBN 0-292-70015-6); pap. 0.00 o.p. U of Tex Pr.
--Selected Stories. Middleton, Christopher, tr. 200p. 1982. 15.50 (ISBN 0-374-25901-1). FS&G.
Walsh, A. E. & Paxton, John. Competition Policy: European & International Trends & Practices. LC 74-33134. 200p. 1975. 26.00 (ISBN 0-312-15540-9). St Martin.
Walsh, Ann, jt. ed. see Pearson, J. D.
Walsh, Anne B. A Gardening Book: Indoors & Outdoors. LC 75-28272. (Illus.). 112p. (gr. 4-7). 1976. 6.95 o.p. (ISBN 0-689-50042-4, McElderry Bk). Atheneum.
Walsh, Annmarie H. The Public's Business: The Politics & Practices of Government Corporations. LC 77-15595. 456p. 1978. 25.00x (ISBN 0-262-23086-0); pap. 9.95x (ISBN 0-262-73055-3). MIT Pr.
Walsh, Anthony. Human Nature & Love: Biological, Intrapsychic & Social-Behavioral Perspectives. LC 80-6176. 342p. 1981. lib. bdg. 23.00 (ISBN 0-8191-1532-0); pap. text ed. 13.25 (ISBN 0-8191-1533-9). U Pr of Amer.
Walsh, Anthony & McNulty, James G. The Urinary Tract. LC 76-26383. (Advanced Exercises in Diagnostic Radiology Ser.: Vol. 10). 1977. text ed. 12.95x o.p. (ISBN 0-7216-9112-9). Saunders.
Walsh, Barry & Douglas, Peter. Fitness the Footballer's Way. (Illus., Orig.). 1978. pap. 2.95 o.p. (ISBN 0-8467-0428-5, Pub. by Two Continents). Hippocrene Bks.
--Getting Fit the Hard Way. (Illus.). 1981. 12.50 o.p. (ISBN 0-7137-1086-1, Pub. by Blandford Pr England). Sterling.
Walsh, Bill, jt. ed. see NFL.
Walsh, Chad. Doors into Poetry. 2nd ed. 1970. pap. text ed. 11.95 (ISBN 0-13-218727-2). P-H.
--End of Nature. LC 72-70605. 104p. 1969. 6.50 (ISBN 0-8040-0100-6). Swallow.
--From Utopia to Nightmare. 191p. 1962. 10.00 (ISBN 0-89366-131-7). Ultramarine Pub.
--Hang Me Up My Begging Bowl. LC 82-75034. viii, 98p. 1981. 12.95x (ISBN 0-8040-0351-3); pap. 7.95 (ISBN 0-8040-0358-0). Swallow.
--The Psalm of Christ: Forty Poems on the Twenty-Second Psalm. LC 82-5566. (Wheaton Literary Ser.). 80p. 1982. pap. 4.95 (ISBN 0-87788-700-4). Shaw Pubs.
--A Rich Feast: Encountering the Bible from Genesis to Revelation. LC 80-8356. 192p. 1981. 9.95i o.p. (ISBN 0-06-069249-9, HarpR). Har-Row.
Walsh, Charles V. & Marks, Leonard. Firefighting Strategy & Leadership. 2nd ed. (Illus.). 1976. text ed. 22.95 (ISBN 0-07-068026-4, G); instructor's manual 4.50 (ISBN 0-07-068027-2). McGraw.
Walsh, Charlie. My Summer Vacation Poetry. Marron, John, ed. (Orig.). 1978. pap. 5.00 (ISBN 0-918842-00-X). So&So Pr.
Walsh, D P. Shoplifting: Controlling a Major Crime. (Illus.). 159p. 1978. text ed. 25.00x o.p. (ISBN 0-8419-5044-X). Holmes & Meier.
Walsh, Diana C., jt. ed. see Egdaul, Richard H.
Walsh, Donald, ed. see Martinez Sierra, Gregorio.
Walsh, Donald D., ed. see Goytortua, Jesus.
Walsh, Donald D., tr. from Span. see Neruda, Pablo.
Walsh, Donald D., tr. from Sp. & see Neruda, Pablo.
Walsh, Edward. Classic Racing Cars. (Illus.). 224p. 1982. pap. 5.95 (ISBN 0-668-05226-0). Arco.
Walsh, Eleanor & Hardy, Merrill. Golf. 1980. pap. text ed. 7.95x (ISBN 0-673-16190-0). Scott F.
Walsh, Ellen S. Theodore All Grown up. LC 80-2244. 32p. (gr. 2-3). 1981. 8.95a o.p. (ISBN 0-385-15868-8); PLB 8.95a (ISBN 0-385-15869-6). Doubleday.
Walsh, Francis J., Jr. Identifying Accounting Principles: The Process of Developing Financial Reporting Standards & Rules in the United States. (Report Ser.: No. 762). (Orig.). 1979. pap. 10.00 (ISBN 0-8237-0198-0). Conference Bd.
Walsh, Froma, ed. Normal Family Processes. LC 81-7197. (Guilford Family Therapy Ser.). 486p. 1982. 25.00 (ISBN 0-89862-051-1). Guilford Pr.
Walsh, G. R. Methods of Optimization. LC 74-20714. 200p. 1975. 43.95x o.p. (ISBN 0-471-91922-5); pap. 21.95x (ISBN 0-471-91924-1, Pub. by Wiley-Interscience). Wiley.
Walsh, Gordon see Allen, W. S.
Walsh, Henry L. Hallowed Were the Gold Dust Trails: The Story of the Pioneer Priests of Northern California. LC 46-2126. 559p. 1982. lib. bdg. 44.95x (ISBN 0-89370-717-1). Borgo Pr.
Walsh, Huber M. Introducing the Young Child to the Social World. (Illus.). 1980. text ed. 19.95x (ISBN 0-02-424200-4). Macmillan.
Walsh, J., jt. ed. see Delves, L. M.
Walsh, J. Martyn, jt. auth. see Lindberg, Stanley W.
Walsh, Jack. The Night on Fire: The First Complete Account of John Paul Jones' Greatest Battle. LC 77-26762. 1978. 9.95 o.p. (ISBN 0-07-067952-5, GB). McGraw.
Walsh, Jackie, ed. see Boyd, Ina C.
Walsh, Jackie, ed. see Pappas, Lou S.
Walsh, Jackie, ed. see Simmons, Bob & Simmons, Coleen.
Walsh, Jackie, ed. see Van De Voorde, Annouk M.
Walsh, James & Walsh, Phyllis A. Golden Retrievers. (Illus.). 128p. 1980. 4.95 (ISBN 0-87666-678-0, KW 067). TFH Pubns.
Walsh, James, jt. auth. see Gourlay, Alastair.
Walsh, James, ed. Pre-Reformation English Spirituality. LC 65-12885. 1966. 20.00 o.p. (ISBN 0-8232-0655-6). Fordham.
Walsh, James E., ed. Mazarinades: A Catalogue of the Collection of 17th Century French Civil War Tracts in the Houghton Library, Harvard University. 1976. lib. bdg. 35.00 (ISBN 0-8161-7871-2, Hall Reference). G K Hall.
Walsh, James J. Cures: The Story of Cures That Failed. LC 70-137343. 1971. Repr. of 1923 ed. 37.00x (ISBN 0-8103-3773-8). Gale.
Walsh, James J., jt. ed. see Hyman, Arthur.
Walsh, James P; see Weaver, Glenn.
Walsh, John. Management Tactics: Short Cases in Operational Management. (Illus.). 1979. 11.50 (ISBN 0-07-067963-0); instr's. manual 11.95 (ISBN 0-07-067964-9). McGraw.
--Presenting Poetry. 1973. pap. text ed. 4.00x o.p. (ISBN 0-435-18920-4). Heinemann Ed.
Walsh, John A., ed. see Morse, Albert L.
Walsh, John E. Humanistic Culture Learning: An Introduction. LC 78-26859. 1979. pap. text ed. 8.50x (ISBN 0-8248-0637-9, Eastwest Ctr). UH Pr.
--Intercultural Education in the Community of Man. LC 72-93149. 236p. 1973. 12.00x (ISBN 0-8248-0260-8, Eastwest Ctr). UH Pr.
Walsh, John E., Jr., jt. auth. see Smith, Shea.
Walsh, John Evangelist. One Day at Kitty Hawk. LC 75-12740. (Illus.). 352p. (YA) 1975. 12.45i (ISBN 0-690-00103-7). T Y Crowell.
Walsh, Joseph. Massachusetts Legal Forms-Corporations. 175p. 1983. write for info. looseleaf binder (ISBN 0-88063-015-9). Butterworth Legal Pubs.
Walsh, Joy, ed. see Fried, Emanuel.
Walsh, Judith. Growing up in British India: Indian Autobiographies on Childhood & Education under the Raj. 190p. 1983. text ed. 27.50x (ISBN 0-8419-0734-X). Holmes & Meier.
Walsh, Ken. The Backpacker's Guide to Europe. (Illus.). 288p. (Orig.). 1982. pap. 4.95 (ISBN 0-8329-0270-5). New Century.
Walsh, Kevin & Cowles, Milly. Developmental Discipline. LC 82-13305. 264p. (Orig.). 1982. pap. 9.95 (ISBN 0-89135-032-2). Religious Educ.
Walsh, L. A. & Dorr, E. L. Physical Distribution. (Occupational Manuals & Projects in Marketing). 1969. text ed. 7.68 (ISBN 0-07-067955-X, G). McGraw.
Walsh, L. A., jt. auth. see Winn, Charles S.
Walsh, L. A., et al. Selling Farm & Garden Supplies. 10.04 (ISBN 0-07-067960-6, G); tchr's manual & key 4.95 (ISBN 0-07-067961-4). McGraw.
Walsh, L. S. International Marketing. 2nd ed. 256p. 1981. pap. text ed. 11.95x (ISBN 0-7121-0943-9, Pub. by Macdonald & Evans England). Intl Ideas.
--International Marketing. 272p. 1981. 30.00x (ISBN 0-7121-0968-4, Pub. by Macdonald & Evans). State Mutual Bk.
Walsh, Lawrence, jt. auth. see Ertel, Kenneth.
Walsh, Leo M, jt. ed. see Larson, William E.
Walsh, M. Understanding Computers: What Managers & Users Need to Know. 266p. 1982. pap. 14.95 (ISBN 0-471-87417-5, Pub. by Wiley-Interscience). Wiley.
Walsh, M., ed. War & the Human Race. 1971. 6.90 (ISBN 0-444-40901-7). Elsevier.
Walsh, M. M. B. The Four-Colored Hoop. LC 75-34381. 1976. 7.95 (ISBN 0-399-11732-6). Putnam Pub Group.
Walsh, Marcus, ed. see Gay, John.
Walsh, Marcus, ed. see Smart, Christopher.
Walsh, Margaret. The Rise of the Midwestern Meat Packing Industry. LC 82-40184. 192p. 1982. 14.50x (ISBN 0-8131-1473-X). U Pr of Ky.
Walsh, Marilyn, jt. auth. see Edelhertz, Herbert.
Walsh, Marilyn E. The Fence: A New Look at the World of Property Theft. LC 76-5266. (Contributions in Sociology Ser.: No. 21). (Illus., Orig.). 1976. lib. bdg. 25.00x (ISBN 0-8371-8910-1, WTF/). Greenwood.
Walsh, Marnie. A Taste of the Knife. 3rd ed. Trusky, Tom, ed. LC 76-15877. (Modern & Contemporary Poets of the West). (Orig.). 1976. pap. 3.00 (ISBN 0-916272-03-6). Ahsahta Pr.
Walsh, Mary A. & Sickles, Margaret. How to Read the Bible. LC 82-61467. 140p. Date not set. pap. 6.95 (ISBN 0-87973-619-4, 619). Our Sunday Visitor. Postponed.
Walsh, Michael, jt. auth. see Sutton, Peter.
Walsh, Michael, et al, eds. Barron's Regents Exams & Answers Chemistry. rev. ed. LC 57-58729. 300p. (gr. 10-12). 1982. pap. text ed. 4.50 (ISBN 0-8120-3163-6). Barron.
Walsh, Michael A., jt. auth. see Ahuja, Hira N.
Walsh, Michelle, jt. auth. see Bernhard, Linda A.
Walsh, Myles E. Information Management Systems: Virtual Storage. (Illus.). 1979. text ed. 19.95 (ISBN 0-8359-3075-0). Reston.
--Understanding Computers: What Managers & Users Need to Know. LC 80-20547. 266p. 1981. 23.95x (ISBN 0-471-08191-4, Pub. by Wiley-Interscience). Wiley.
Walsh, Patricia B. Growing Through Time: An Intoduction to the Psychology of Adult Life. LC 82-14590. (Psychology Ser.). 400p. 1982. pap. text ed. 16.95 (ISBN 0-534-01214-0). Brooks-Cole.
Walsh, Phyllis A., jt. auth. see Walsh, James.
Walsh, Richard. Charleston's Sons of Liberty: A Study of the Artisans, 1763-1789. LC 59-15684. (Illus.). xii, 166p. 1968. 12.95x (ISBN 0-87249-072-6); pap. 2.25x o.p. (ISBN 0-87249-001-7). U of SC Pr.
Walsh, Richard, jt. auth. see Vogel, Jerome.
Walsh, Richard, ed. Mind & Spirit of Early America: Sources in American History, 1607-1789. LC 80-5704. 442p. 1980. lib. bdg. 25.25 (ISBN 0-8191-1239-9); pap. text ed. 13.50 (ISBN 0-8191-1240-2). U Pr of Amer.
Walsh, Roger N., jt. ed. see Shapiro, Deane H., Jr.
Walsh, Ruth M. & Birkin, Stanley J., eds. Business Communications: An Annotated Bibliography. LC 79-8296. 1980. lib. bdg. 45.00x (ISBN 0-313-20923-5, WBW/). Greenwood.
--Job Satisfaction & Motivation: An Annotated Bibliography. LC 78-67915. 1979. lib. bdg. 45.00x (ISBN 0-313-20635-X, WJS/). Greenwood.
Walsh, Sheila. The Golden Songbird. 1975. pap. 1.75 o.p. (ISBN 0-451-08155-2, E8155, Sig). NAL.
--A Highly Respectable Marriage. 1982. pap. 2.25 (ISBN 0-451-11830-8, AE1830, Sig). NAL.
--Lord Gilmore's Bride. (Orig.). 1979. pap. 1.75 o.p. (ISBN 0-451-08600-7, E8600, Sig). NAL.
--Madalena. (Orig.). 1977. pap. 1.75 o.p. (ISBN 0-451-09332-1, E9332, Sig). NAL.
Walsh, Stephen. Bartok Chamber Music. LC 81-71299. (BBC Music Guides Ser.). (Illus.). 88p. (Orig.). 1983. pap. 5.95 (ISBN 0-295-95922-3). U of Wash Pr.
Walsh, Thomas, tr. see Valle-Inclan, Ramon.
Walsh, Thomas P. & Northouse, Cameron. John Barth, Jerzy Kosinski & Thomas Pynchon. 1978. lib. bdg. 16.00 (ISBN 0-8161-7910-7, Hall Reference). G K Hall.
Walsh, Thomas P., jt. auth. see Northouse, Cameron.
Walsh, Vincent M. The Kingdom at Hand. 340p. pap. 6.00 (ISBN 0-943374-00-6). Key of David.
Walsh, W. Bruce & Tyler, Leona. Tests & Measurements. 3rd ed. (Foundations of Modern Psychology Ser.). (Illus.). 1979. ref. o.p. 12.95 (ISBN 0-13-911859-4); pap. 10.95 ref. ed. (ISBN 0-13-911842-X). P-H.
Walsh, W. Bruce & Osipow, Samuel H., eds. Handbook of Vocational Psychology: Applications, Vol. 2. 1983. text ed. write for info. (ISBN 0-89859-286-0). L Erlbaum Assocs.
--Handbook of Vocational Psychology: Foundations, Vol. 1. 375p. 1983. text ed. write for info. (ISBN 0-89859-285-2). L Erlbaum Assocs.
Walsh, William. D. J. Enright: Poet of Humanism. LC 73-90814. 120p. 1974. 19.95 (ISBN 0-521-20383-X). Cambridge U Pr.
--Introduction to Keats. 1981. 14.95x o.p. (ISBN 0-416-30490-7); pap. 6.95x (ISBN 0-416-30500-8). Methuen Inc.
--R. K. Narayan: A Critical Appreciation. LC 82-40320. (Illus.). 192p. 1983. lib. bdg. 12.50x (ISBN 0-226-87213-0). U of Chicago Pr.

Walsh, William H. Introduction to Philosophy of History. 3rd rev. ed. 1967. text ed. 7.50x o.p. (ISBN 0-391-00672-X); pap. text ed. 7.50x o.p. (ISBN 0-391-02163-X). Humanities.

--Metaphysics. LC 66-26470. (Orig.). 1966. pap. 2.25 o.p. (ISBN 0-15-659305-X, Harv). HarBraceJ.

Walsh, William M. Counseling Children & Adolescents. new ed. LC 75-5097. 424p. 1976. 23.25x o.p. (ISBN 0-8211-2253-3); text ed. 20.95x o.p. (ISBN 0-685-61056-X). McCutchan.

Walsh, William S. Curiosities of Popular Customs. LC 66-23951. 1966. Repr. of 1898 ed. 61.00x (ISBN 0-8103-3008-3). Gale.

--Handy Book of Curious Information, Comprising Strange Happenings in the Life of Men & Animals, Odd Statistics, Extraordinary Phenomena & Out of the Way Facts Concerning the Wonderlands of the Earth. LC 68-30583. 1970. Repr. of 1913 ed. 62.00x (ISBN 0-8103-3100-4). Gale.

--Handy-Book of Literary Curiosities. LC 68-24370. 1966. Repr. of 1892 ed. 67.00x (ISBN 0-8103-0162-8). Gale.

--Heroes & Heroines of Fiction, 2 vols. LC 66-29782. 1966. Repr. of 1915 ed. 40.00x ea. Vol. 1, Classical (ISBN 0-8103-0167-9). Vol. 2, Modern (ISBN 0-8103-0163-6). Gale.

--Story of Santa Klaus: Told for Children of All Ages, from Six to Sixty. LC 68-58166. (Holiday Ser). (Illus.). 1970. Repr. of 1909 ed. 37.00x (ISBN 0-8103-3370-8). Gale.

Walsh, William Thomas. Our Lady of Fatima. pap. 4.50 (ISBN 0-385-02869-5, D1, Im). Doubleday.

Walshaw. SI Calculations in Engineering Science. 1977. 6.95 o.p. (ISBN 0-408-00284-0). Butterworth.

Walshe, G. Recent Trends in Monopoly in Great Britain. (Illus.). 132p. 1974. 18.95 (ISBN 0-521-09863-7). Cambridge U Pr.

Walshe, M. O. Introduction to the Scandinavian Languages. (Andre Deutsch Language Library). 1977. lib. bdg. 11.50 o.p. (ISBN 0-233-95754-5). Westview.

Walston, jt. auth. see Walston, Betty J.

Walston, Betty J. & Walston. The Nurse Assistant in Long Term Care: A New Era. LC 80-12308. (Illus.). 204p. 1980. pap. text ed. 12.95 (ISBN 0-8016-5355-X). Mosby.

Walsum-Quispel, J. van. Tina's Island Home. LC 71-99920. (Illus.). 36p. (gr. k-5). 5.75 (ISBN 0-87592-053-5). Scroll Pr.

Walt, Alexander J. & Wilson, Robert F., eds. Management of Trauma: Pitfalls & Practice. LC 74-22475. (Illus.). 626p. 1975. text ed. 30.00 o.p. (ISBN 0-8121-0318-1). Lea & Febiger.

Walt Disney Productions. The Aristocats. LC 73-15626. (Illus.). 48p. 1974. 4.95 (ISBN 0-394-82553-5, BYR); PLB 4.99 o.p. (ISBN 0-394-92553-X). Random.

--Black Hole. (Young Reader). 24p. (ps-3). 1980. PLB 5.00 (ISBN 0-307-60105-6, Golden Pr). Western Pub.

--Goofy's Book of Colors. LC 82-18630. (Disney's Wonderful World of Reading: No. 52). (Illus.). 32p. 1983. 4.95 (ISBN 0-394-85734-8); PLB 4.99 (ISBN 0-394-95734-2). Random.

--How to Draw Mickey Mouse. Klimo, Kate, ed. (Mickey's Drawing Class Ser.). (Illus.). 64p. 1982. pap. 3.95 (ISBN 0-671-44493-X, Little Simon). S&S.

--If I Met Winnie the Pooh. LC 77-95424. (Stretch Books). (Illus.). (gr. k-2). 1978. 2.95 (ISBN 0-448-16150-8, G&D). Putnam Pub Group.

--Mickey's Counting Book. LC 82-18554. (Disney's Wonderful World of Reading: No. 51). (Illus.). 32p. (ps-1). 1983. 4.95 (ISBN 0-394-85735-6); PLB 4.99 (ISBN 0-394-95735-0). Random.

--Walt Disney Productions Presents "The Black Hole". LC 79-10622. (Walt Disney's Wonderful World of Reading: No. 47). (Illus.). (ps-3). 1979. 4.95 (ISBN 0-394-84279-0, BYR); PLB 4.99 o.p. (ISBN 0-394-94279-5). Random.

--Walt Disney Productions Presents "the Rescuers". LC 76-54412. (Disney's Wonderful World of Reading: No. 37). (Illus.). (ps-2). 1977. 4.95 o.p. (ISBN 0-394-83456-9, BYR); PLB 4.99 (ISBN 0-394-93456-3). Random.

--Walt Disney's Pinocchio. (Disney's Wonderful World of Reading Ser: No. 10). (Illus.). (ps-3). 1973. 4.95 (ISBN 0-394-82626-4, BYR); PLB 4.99 o.p. (ISBN 0-394-92626-9). Random.

--Walt Disney's The Brave Little Tailor. LC 74-1253. (Disney's Wonderful World of Reading Ser.: No. 18). (Illus.). 48p. (ps-3). 1974. 4.95 (ISBN 0-394-82559-4, BYR); PLB 4.99 (ISBN 0-394-92559-9). Random.

Walt Disney Productions, illus. Bambi's Forest Friends. (Golden Cloth Bks.). (Illus.). 8p. (ps). 1982. cloth pages & cover 3.50 (ISBN 0-307-11501-1, Golden Pr). Western Pub.

--Walt Disney Character Tubby Book. (Tubby Bks.). (Illus.). 10p. (ps). 1980. vinyl book 3.50 (ISBN 0-671-41334-1, Pub. by Windmill). S&S.

Walt Disney Studio. Bambi's Fragrant Forest. (Golden Scratch & Sniff Bks). (Illus.). 32p. (gr. k-1). 1975. 5.95 o.p. (ISBN 0-307-13530-6, Golden Pr); PLB 9.92 o.p. (ISBN 0-307-63530-9). Western Pub.

--Pooh Sleepytime Stories. (A Golden Story Book Ser.). (Illus.). (gr. k-3). 1979. PLB 10.69 (ISBN 0-307-63735-2, Golden Pr); pap. 4.95 (ISBN 0-307-13735-X). Western Pub.

Walt Disney Studios. How to Draw Donald Duck. Klimo, Kate, ed. (Mickey's Drawing Class Ser.). (Illus.). 64p. 1982. pap. 3.95 (ISBN 0-671-44494-8, Little Simon). S&S.

--If I Met Mickey Mouse. Duenewald, Doris, ed. LC 77-95423. (Illus.). 1978. 2.95 (ISBN 0-448-16151-6, G&D). Putnam Pub Group.

Walter. Skeletal Muscle Pharmacology. 1982. 102.25 (ISBN 0-444-90226-0). Elsevier.

Walter, A. H. Biodeterioration of Materials. 514p. 1972. 84.95x o.s.i. (ISBN 0-470-91925-6, BC25 16). Halsted Pr.

Walter, Arline, jt. auth. see Bohl, Marilyn.

Walter, Bob J. The Territorial Expansion of the Nandi of Kenya, 1500-1905. LC 79-633595. (African Ser.). (Illus.). 37p. 1970. pap. 3.00x o.s.i. (ISBN 0-89680-042-3, Ohio U Ctr Intl). Ohio U Pr.

Walter, Carol & Miller, Lenore. Moving Free: A Total Program of Post-Mastectomy Exercises. LC 80-2735. (Illus.). 1981. pap. 9.95 (ISBN 0-672-52686-7). Bobbs.

Walter, D. & Brazier, M., eds. Advances in EEG Analysis. 1969. 14.75 (ISBN 0-444-40693-X). Elsevier.

Walter, Daniel. Spasmic Vistas. (Illus.). 1974. pap. 3.00 (ISBN 0-686-22348-9). Oll Korrect.

Walter, David. Great Adventurers. LC 79-64163. (Adventures in History Ser.). PLB 12.68 (ISBN 0-382-06295-7). Silver.

Walter, Doris R., et al, eds. Hine's Insurance Adjusters: 1982-83 Edition. 46th ed. (Illus.). 84p. 1982. 12.00x (ISBN 0-910911-01-0). Hines Legal Direct.

Walter, E. Identifiability of State Space Models: With Applications to Transformation Systems. (Lecture Notes in Biomathematics Ser.: Vol. 46). 202p. 1983. pap. 13.50 (ISBN 0-387-11590-0). Springer-Verlag.

Walter, Edward. The Immorality of Limiting Growth. LC 81-166. 220p. 1981. 39.50x (ISBN 0-87395-478-5); pap. 11.95x (ISBN 0-87395-479-3). State U NY Pr.

Walter, Ernest. Technique of the Film Cutting Room. rev. 2nd ed. (Library of Communication Techniques). (Illus.). 1973. 21.95 o.p. (ISBN 0-240-50657-X). Focal Pr.

Walter, Eugene. American Cooking: Southern Style. LC 76-144345. (Foods of the World Ser.). (Illus.). (gr. 6 up). 1971. lib. bdg. 17.28 (ISBN 0-8094-0078-2, Pub. by Time-Life). Silver.

Walter, Fogg. One Thousand Sayings of History: Presented as Pictures in Prose. 915p. 1982. Repr. of 1929 ed. lib. bdg. 50.00 (ISBN 0-89984-208-9). Century Bookbindery.

Walter, George W. The Loomis Gang. Rev. Ed. ed. 1982. Repr. of 1953 ed. 9.95 (ISBN 0-932052-29-0). North Country.

--Sinners & Saints. 1973. 6.95 (ISBN 0-932052-31-2). North Country.

Walter, Gordon A. & Marks, Stephen E. Experimental Learning & Change: Theory Design & Practice. 600p. 1981. 27.95x (ISBN 0-471-08355-0, Pub. by Wiley-Interscience). Wiley.

Walter, H. Vegetation of the Earth: In Relation to Climate & the Eco-Physiological Conditions. Wieser, J., tr. LC 72-85947. (Heidelberg Science Library: Vol. 15). (Illus.). xvi, 240p. 1973. pap. 17.00 (ISBN 0-387-90404-2). Springer-Verlag.

Walter, Henriette, jt. auth. see Martinet, Andre.

Walter, I. & Murray, T. Handbook of International Business. 1981. 55.00x (ISBN 0-471-07949-9, Pub. by Wiley-Interscience). Wiley.

Walter, I., jt. ed. see Jensen, F. B.

Walter, Ingo. International Economics. 3rd ed. LC 80-21541. 510p. 1981. text ed. 27.95 (ISBN 0-471-04957-3). Wiley.

Walter, Ingo, jt. auth. see Gladwin, Thomas N.

Walter, Ingo, ed. Studies in International Environmental Economics. LC 75-38614. 364p. 1976. 45.50 o.p. (ISBN 0-471-91927-6, Pub. by Wiley-Interscience). Wiley.

Walter, Ingo, ed. see Ahlers, David M.

Walter, Ingo, ed. see Ahmad, Jaleel.

Walter, Ingo, ed. see Allen, Loring.

Walter, Ingo, ed. see Altman, Edward I., et al.

Walter, Ingo, ed. see Balbkins, Nicholas.

Walter, Ingo, ed. see Bierwag, G. O.

Walter, Ingo, ed. see Bloch, Ernest & Schwartz, Robert A.

Walter, Ingo, ed. see Dreyer, Jacob S.

Walter, Ingo, ed. see Fewings, David R.

Walter, Ingo, ed. see Ghatak, Subrata.

Walter, Ingo, ed. see Gladwin, Thomas N.

Walter, Ingo, ed. see Hallwood, Paul.

Walter, Ingo, ed. see Hunt, Lacy H.

Walter, Ingo, ed. see Kaufman, George G.

Walter, Ingo, ed. see Kobrin, Stephen J.

Walter, Ingo, ed. see Levich, Richard M.

Walter, Ingo, ed. see Newfarmer, Richard.

Walter, Ingo, ed. see Oh, John.

Walter, Ingo, ed. see Oldfield, George S., Jr.

Walter, Ingo, ed. see Parry, Thomas G.

Walter, Ingo, ed. see Pastre, Oliver.

Walter, Ingo, ed. see Ramsey, James B.

Walter, Ingo, ed. see Roxburgh, Nigel.

Walter, Ingo, ed. see Sciberras, Edmond.

Walter, Ingo, ed. see Sinkey, Joseph F., Jr.

Walter, Ingo, ed. see Stapleton, Richard.

Walter, Ingo, ed. see Thompson, John K.

Walter, Ingo, ed. see Uri, Noel D.

Walter, Ingo, ed. see Walker, William B.

Walter, Ingo I. see Ramsey, James B.

Walter, James E. Piedmont College Graduates Make Good. 1982. 10.00 (ISBN 0-533-05277-7). Vantage.

Walter, John B. An Introduction to the Principles of Disease. LC 76-27063. (Illus.). 1977. text ed. 18.95 o.p. (ISBN 0-7216-9114-5). Saunders.

Walter, Juelich. Higher Taxa of Basidiomycetes. (Bibliotheca Mycologica Ser.: No. 85). (Illus.). 486p. 1981. lib. bdg. 60.00x (ISBN 3-7682-1324-2). Lubrecht & Cramer.

Walter, M. R. Stromatolites. (Developments in Sedimentology Ser.: Vol. 20). 1976. 136.25 (ISBN 0-444-41376-6). Elsevier.

Walter, Marion I. & Brown, Stephen I. The Art of Problem Posing. (Problem Solving Ser.). (Illus.). 250p. (Orig.). 1983. pap. text ed. write for info. (ISBN 0-89168-052-7). Franklin Inst Pr.

Walter, Mildred P. The Girl on the Outside. LC 82-267. 160p. (gr. 6 up). 1982. 9.50 (ISBN 0-688-01438-0). Lothrop.

Walter, Richard. Anson's Voyage Round the World in the Years 1740-44 with an Account of the Last Capture of a Manila Galleon. LC 73-85692. (Illus.). 1974. Repr. of 1928 ed. 6.00 o.p. (ISBN 0-486-22993-9). Dover.

Walter, Rita, et al. No Shadow of Turning. LC 78-20105. 9.95 o.p. (ISBN 0-385-14710-4). Doubleday.

Walter, Roderich, ed. Neurophysins: Carriers of Peptide Hormones. (Annals of the New York Academy of Sciences: Vol. 248). 512p. 1975. 61.00x (ISBN 0-89072-002-9). NY Acad Sci.

Walter, Susan, jt. auth. see Choate, Pat.

Walters. The Language Pathology. 16.95 (ISBN 0-471-26076-2, Wiley Heyden). Wiley.

Walters, ed. see Torda, Clara.

Walters, A. & Elphick, eds. Biodeterioration of Materials. 1968. 63.50 (ISBN 0-444-20033-9). Elsevier.

Walters, A. A. Costs & Scale of Bus Services. (Working Paper: No. 325). iv, 49p. 1979. 3.00 (ISBN 0-686-36225-X, WP-0325). World Bank.

Walters, A. A., ed. see Wood, J. H.

Walters, A. H. Biodeterioration Investigation Techniques. 1977. 67.75 o.s.i. (ISBN 0-85334-696-8). Elsevier.

Walters, A. H., et al, eds. Biodeterioration of Materials, Vols. 1 & 2. 1968-72. Vol. 1: Microbiological & Allied Aspects. 96.50 (ISBN 0-85334-623-2); Vol.2: Biodynamic Effects of Messinian Salinity. 96.50 (ISBN 0-85334-538-4). Elsevier.

Walters, Barbara. How to Talk with Practically Anybody about Practically Anything. LC 82-45618. 216p. 1983. pap. 6.95 (ISBN 0-385-18334-8, Dolp). Doubleday.

Walters, C. Glenn & Bergiel, Blaise J. Marketing Channels. 2nd ed. 1982. text ed. 25.50x (ISBN 0-673-16014-9). Scott F.

Walters, David R. Physical & Sexual Abuse of Children: Causes & Treatment. LC 75-1940. 196p. 1976. 12.95x (ISBN 0-253-34490-5); pap. 5.95x (ISBN 0-253-34491-3). Ind U Pr.

Walters, David W. Real Estate Exchanges. LC 81-11406. (Real Estate Professional Practioners: A Wiley Ser.). 205p. 1982. 33.95x (ISBN 0-471-08083-7). Ronald Pr.

Walters, Derek. Chemistry. (Science World Ser.). 40p. (gr. 4 up). 1983. PLB 8.90 (ISBN 0-531-04581-1). Watts.

Walters, Derek, ed. Your Future Revealed by the Maj Jongg. 192p. 1983. pap. 9.95 (ISBN 0-85030-290-0). Newcastle Pub.

Walters, Dorothy. Flannery O'Connor. (United States Authors Ser.). 1971. lib. bdg. 11.95 (ISBN 0-8057-0556-2, Twayne). G K Hall.

Walters, Dorothy, jt. ed. see Konek, Carol.

Walters, Douglas B., ed. Safe Handling of Chemical Carcinogens, Mutagens Teratogens & Highly Toxic Substances. LC 79-88922. 1980. Vol. 1. 49.95 (ISBN 0-250-40303-X); Vol. 2. 49.95 (ISBN 0-250-40354-4). Ann Arbor Science.

Walters, Elsa H. & Castle, E. B. Principles of Education. 1967. pap. text ed. 8.95x o.p. (ISBN 0-04-370018-7). Allen Unwin.

Walters, F. Studies of Some of Robert Browning's Poems. LC 79-184648. (Studies in Browning, No. 4). 180p. 1972. Repr. of 1893 ed. lib. bdg. 49.95x (ISBN 0-8383-1380-9). Haskell.

Walters, Glenn & Robin, Donald. Classics in Marketing. LC 77-27511. 1978. pap. text ed. 14.50x (ISBN 0-673-16078-5). Scott F.

Walters, H. B. Church Bells of Wiltshire. 12.50x o.p. (ISBN 0-87556-401-1). Saifer.

Walters, Idwal, tr. see Roberts, Kate.

Walters, James, jt. auth. see Stinnett, Nick.

Walters, Janet L. Nurse Karen Comes Home. (YA) 1981. 6.95 (ISBN 0-686-74792-5, Avalon). Bouregy.

Walters, K. Rheometry. 1975. 45.00x (ISBN 0-412-12090-9, Pub. by Chapman & Hall England). Methuen Inc.

Walters, K. D., jt. auth. see Monsen, R. J.

Walters, Kenneth. Rheometry: Industrial Applications. LC 80-40956. (Materials Science Research Studies). 418p. 1980. 79.95x (ISBN 0-471-27878-5, Pub. by Res Stud Pr). Wiley.

Walters, L. R., jt. auth. see Freeman, S. T.

Walters, Leroy. Bibliography of Bioethics, Vol. 8. 1982. lib. bdg. 55.00x (ISBN 0-02-933780-1). Free Pr.

Walters, LeRoy, jt. auth. see Beauchamp, Tom L.

Walters, Leroy, ed. Bibliography of Bioethics, 6 vols. LC 75-4140. 60.00x ea.; Vol. 1 1975. (ISBN 0-8103-0978-5); Vol. 2 1976. (ISBN 0-8103-0980-7); Vol. 3 1977. (ISBN 0-8103-0982-3); Vol. 4 1978. (ISBN 0-8103-0983-1); Vol. 5 1979. Vol. 6 1980. (ISBN 0-8103-0987-4). Gale.

--Bibliography of Bioethics, Vol. 7. 375p. 1981. 55.00 (ISBN 0-02-933770-4). Free Pr.

--Bibliography of Bioethics, Vol. 8. 1982. 60.00 (ISBN 0-686-83896-3). Macmillan.

Walters, Michael. Birds of the World. (Illus.). 704p. 1980. 60.00 (ISBN 0-87666-894-5, H-1022). TFH Pubns.

Walters, Michael E. Restoring Personal Meaning in Reading Instruction: American Education's Greatest Need. 45p. (Orig.). 1983. pap. text ed. 8.00 (ISBN 0-910609-03-9). Reading Tutor.

Walters, Michelle S. Maryland Pet Profiles. LC 82-61528. (Illus.). 224p. 1982. pap. 10.95 (ISBN 0-686-38107-6). Maryland Pub.

Walters, Peter. The Text of the Septuagint: Its Corruption & Their Emendations. Gooding, D. W., ed. LC 74-161292. (Illus.). 440p. 1972. 79.50 (ISBN 0-521-07977-2). Cambridge U Pr.

Walters, R., jt. auth. see Blake, O.

Walters, R. R. Ludlow's Mill. 304p. (Orig.). 1981. pap. 2.75 o.p. (ISBN 0-523-48006-7). Pinnacle Bks.

Walters, Richard P. Forgive & Be Free: Healing the Wounds of Past & Present. 144p. 1983. pap. 4.95 (ISBN 0-310-42611-1). Zondervan.

Walters, Robert. Managing Tax in Your Business. 226p. 1982. text ed. 36.75x (ISBN 0-09-147350-0, Pub. by Busn Bks England). Renouf.

Walters, Robert E. Science Experiments for Elementary Schools. 187p. 1977. pap. text ed. 9.50 (ISBN 0-8191-0204-0). U Pr of Amer.

Walters, Robert S., jt. auth. see Blake, David H.

Walters, Ronald G. American Reformers Eighteen Fifteen to Eighteen Sixty. 256p. 1978. 8.95 (ISBN 0-8090-2557-4); pap. 5.95 (ISBN 0-8090-0130-6). Hill & Wang.

Walters, S. M., jt. auth. see Perring, F. H.

Walters, Sally, jt. auth. see Roth, Mark.

Walters, Susan, ed. Canadian Almanac & Directory, 1981. 1094p. 1981. 39.00x (ISBN 0-8103-1186-0, Pub. by Copp Clark Pitman). Gale.

Walters, Thomas. Always Next August. LC 77-82881. (Illus.). 1977. 7.95 (ISBN 0-87716-073-2, Pub. by Moore Pub Co). F Apple.

Walters, Thomas M. Seeing in the Dark. LC 72-90710. (Illus.). 70p. 1973. 7.95 (ISBN 0-87716-036-8, Pub. by Moore Pub Co). F Apple.

Walters, Thomas N. Randolph Silliman Bourne: Education Through Radical Eyes. LC 81-84208. 108p. 1982. pap. text ed. 7.00 (ISBN 0-89080-007-3). Mercer Hse.

Walters, Thomas N., jt. auth. see Stein, Allen F.

Walters, William & Singer, Peter. Test Tube Babies. 160p. 1982. 16.95x (ISBN 0-19-554342-4); pap. 8.95 (ISBN 0-19-554340-8). Oxford U Pr.

Walters, William, Jr. The Practice of Real Estate Management: For the Experienced Property Manager. Kirk, Nancye J., ed. LC 79-84053. 464p. 1979. 22.95 (ISBN 0-912104-37-6). Inst Real Estate.

Walthall, Hugh. Ladidah. LC 78-11954. 52p. 1978. 3.50 (ISBN 0-87886-100-9). Ithaca Hse.

Walthall, Wylie A. Getting into Business. 2nd ed. 1979. pap. text ed. 13.50 scp o.p. (ISBN 0-06-389126-3, HarpC); avail. instr. manual o.p. (ISBN 0-06-377917-X). Har-Row.

Walthall, Wylie A. & Wirth, Michael J. Getting into Business. 3rd ed. 368p. 1983. pap. text ed. 13.50 scp (ISBN 0-06-046895-5, HarpC); instr's. manual avail. (ISBN 0-06-366992-7). Har-Row.

Waltham, A. C. The World of Caves. LC 75-37228. (Illus.). 1976. 12.95 o,p. (ISBN 0-399-11733-4). Putnam Pub Group.

Walthe, Franz. Sons of Vernon Hill. 1983. 15.95 (ISBN 0-533-05078-2). Vantage.

Walther, Carl F. Proper Distinction Between Law & Gospel. Dau, W. H., tr. 1929. 13.95 (ISBN 0-570-03248-2, 15-1601). Concordia.

Walther, Clara M. The Little Lamb's First Christmas. 1978. 4.50 o.p. (ISBN 0-533-03430-2). Vantage.

Walther, Fritz R., et al. Gazelles & Their Relatives. LC 82-22245. (Animal Behavior, Ecology, Conservation & Management Ser.). (Illus.). 239p. 1983. 28.00 (ISBN 0-8155-0928-6). Noyes.

Walther, Herbert, ed. Hitler. (Illus.). 256p. 1982. 12.98 (ISBN 0-8119-0518-7, Pub. by Bison Bks). Fell.

Walther, Mina. Tide Lines. Curtis, Jim, ed. 224p. 1982. pap. 5.97 (ISBN 0-910713-00-6). Lindsay News.

Waltman, Stephen R. & Krupin, Theodore. Complications in Opthalmic Surgery. (Illus.). 333p. 1980. text ed. 47.50 o.p. (ISBN 0-397-50441-1, Lippincott Medical). Lippincott.

Walton, A. G. Polypeptide & Protein Structure. 1982. 39.50 (ISBN 0-444-00407-6). Elsevier.
Walton, A. G., ed. Recombinant DNA: Proceedings. 1982. 78.75 (ISBN 0-444-42039-8). Elsevier.
--Structure & Properties of Amorphous Polymers. (Studies in Physical & Theoretical Chemistry: Vol. 10). 1980. 53.25 (ISBN 0-444-41905-5). Elsevier.
Walton, A. G., ed. see Cleveland Symposium on Macromolecules, 1st, Case Western Reserve Univ., Oct. 1976.
Walton, Alan G. & Blackwell, John. Biopolymers. (Molecular Biology Ser). 1973. 75.00 (ISBN 0-12-734350-4). Acad Pr.
Walton, Alan H., tr. The Essential Works of Charles Baudelaire. 272p. 1982. 60.00x (ISBN 0-284-98609-7, Pub. by C Skilton Scotland). State Mutual Bk.
Walton, Alan J. Three Phases of Matter. 2nd ed. (Illus.). 1982. 41.00x (ISBN 0-19-851957-5); pap. 18.95x (ISBN 0-19-851953-2). Oxford U Pr.
Walton, Alfred G. Lyrics for Living. 1963. 2.75 o.p. (ISBN 0-8233-0110-9). Golden Quill.
Walton, Anne. Molecular & Crystal Structure Models. LC 78-40227. 1978. 34.95x o.s.i. (ISBN 0-470-26356-3). Halsted Pr.
Walton, Brian G. & Higgins, William R. The Greek & Roman Worlds. LC 80-5791. (Illus.). 716p. 1980. pap. text ed. 20.50 (ISBN 0-8191-1254-2). U Pr of Amer.
Walton, Craig & Anton, John P., eds. Philosophy & the Civilizing Arts: Essays Presented to Herbert W. Schneider. LC 73-92907. xxii, 508p. 1974. 18.00x (ISBN 0-8214-0145-9, 82-81487). Ohio U Pr.
Walton, David. The Focalguide to Photographing Plants & Flowers. (Focalguide Ser.). (Illus.). 1979. pap. 7.95 (ISBN 0-240-50999-4). Focal Pr.
Walton, Douglas. The Ad Hominem Fallacy: A Study in the Logical Pragmatics of Criticism. (Pragmatics & Beyond IV: No. 4). 120p. 1983. pap. 16.00 (ISBN 90-272252-4-9). Benjamins North Am.
Walton, Douglas, jt. ed. see Urban, Linwood P.
Walton, Douglas N. Ethics of Withdrawal of Life-Support Systems: Case Studies on Decision Making in Intensive Care. LC 82-15662. (Contributions in Philosophy: No. 23). 288p. 1983. lib. bdg. 29.95x (ISBN 0-313-23752-2, R726). Greenwood.
Walton, G., jt. auth. see Shepherd, J. F.
Walton, G. M. & Shepherd, J. F. The Economic Rise of Early America. LC 78-13438. (Illus.). 1979. 32.50 (ISBN 0-521-22282-6); pap. 8.95 (ISBN 0-521-29433-9). Cambridge U Pr.
Walton, Gary M., ed. Regulatory Change in an Atmosphere of Crisis: Current Implications of the Roosevelt Years. LC 79-23164. 1979. 23.00 (ISBN 0-12-733950-7). Acad Pr.
Walton, H., ed. Programs for Network Analysis. LC 76-360389. 50p. 1974. pap. 22.50x o.p. (ISBN 0-85012-124-8). Intl Pubns Serv.
Walton, H. F., ed. Ion-Exchange Chromatography. LC 75-31610. (Benchmark Papers in Analytical Chemistry Ser.: Vol. 1). 400p. 1976. 56.00 (ISBN 0-12-787725-8). Acad Pr.
Walton, Hanes, Jr. Political Philosophy of Martin Luther King Jr. LC 76-111260. (Contributions in Afro-American & African Studies: No. 10). 137p. 1971. lib. bdg. 29.95x (ISBN 0-8371-4661-5, Pub. by Negro U Pr); pap. 4.95 (ISBN 0-8371-8931-4, WMK/). Greenwood.
Walton, Izaak & Cotton, Charles. The Compleat Angler. Buxton, John, ed. (World's Classics Ser.). (Illus.). 384p. 1982. pap. 4.95 o.p. (ISBN 0-19-281511-3). Oxford U Pr.
Walton, J. K., jt. auth. see Marshall, J. D.
Walton, J. Michael. Greek Theatre Practice. LC 79-8580. (Contributions in Drama & Theatre Studies: No. 3). (Illus.). viii, 237p. 1980. lib. bdg. 27.50x (ISBN 0-313-22043-3, WGT/). Greenwood.
Walton, Jeremy. Capri. (Illus.). 304p. 1982. 29.95 (ISBN 0-85429-279-9). Haynes Pubns.
--Fiat X1-9. (AutoHistory Ser.). (Illus.). 136p. 1982. 14.95 (ISBN 0-85045-456-5, Pub. by Osprey England). Motorbooks Intl.
--Lotus Esprit: Mid-Engined S1, S2, S2.2, S3 & Turbo. (AutoHistory Ser.). (Illus.). 136p. 1982. 14.95 (ISBN 0-85045-460-3, Pub. by Osprey England). Motorbooks Intl.
Walton, Joan M., jt. auth. see Stevens, Rolland E.
Walton, John B. Business Profitability Data 1982. (Annual Publication). 170p. (Orig.). 1982. pap. 12.00 (ISBN 0-939356-02-3). Weybridge.
Walton, John H. Jonah: A Bible Study Commentary. 80p. (Orig.). 1982. pap. 3.95 (ISBN 0-310-36303-9). Zondervan.
Walton, Kathy, ed. AWP Catalogue of Writing Programs. 3rd. ed. LC 80-67017. 120p. 1980. pap. 6.00x (ISBN 0-936266-01-5). Assoc Writing Progs.
Walton, Lew & Douglass, Herb. How to Survive the Eighties. 108p. 1982. pap. text ed. 1.25 (ISBN 0-8163-0491-2). Pacific Pr Pub Assn.
Walton, Marilyn. Tea & Whoppers. (Karen & Gwendolyn at Ser.: No. 1). (Illus.). 32p. (Orig.). (ps-4). 1983. pap. 4.75 (ISBN 0-940742-06-3). Carnival Pr.
Walton, Nancy. Famous Pioneers. (Social Studies). 24p. (gr. 5-9). 1979. wkbk. 5.00 (ISBN 0-8209-0253-5, SS-20). ESP.
Walton, Mrs. O. F. Christie's Old Organ. rev. ed. Wright, Christopher, ed. 1982. 4.95 (ISBN 0-88270-532-6). Bridge Pub.
Walton, Paul, jt. auth. see Gamble, Andrew.
Walton, Peggy J. The Nursing Curriculum Outline Study Guide. pap. text ed. 27.50 (ISBN 0-911067-00-0). Health Ed Train.
Walton, Richard A., jt. auth. see Cotton, F. Albert.
Walton, Richard E. & McKensie, R. B., eds. Behavioral Theory of Labor Negotiation. (Economics Handbook Ser.). (Illus.). 1965. text ed. 33.00 (ISBN 0-07-068049-3, C). McGraw.
Walton, Robert C., ed. Over There: European Reactions to Americans in World War I. LC 72-174163. (Primary Sources in American History Ser.). text ed. 12.95 (ISBN 0-88295-790-2); pap. text ed. 6.95 (ISBN 0-88295-791-0). Harlan Davidson.
Walton, S., jt. auth. see Ell, P. J.
Walton, Thomas F. Communications & Data Management. Buckley, John W., ed. LC 76-10264. 1976. 36.95x (ISBN 0-471-91935-7, Pub. by Wiley-Interscience). Wiley.
Walton, Todd. Forgotten Impulses. 1981. pap. 2.75 o.p. (ISBN 0-451-09802-1, E9802, Sig). NAL.
--Louie & Women. 192p. 1983. 12.95 (ISBN 0-525-24167-1, 01258-370). Dutton.
Walton, W. C. Groundwater Resource Evaluation. 1970. text ed. 26.50 o.p. (ISBN 0-07-068051-5, C). McGraw.
Walton, W. H., ed. see Symposium on Inhaled Particles & Vapours.
Waltz, Alan K. To Proclaim the Faith. 144p. 1983. pap. 3.95 (ISBN 0-687-42252-3). Abingdon.
Waltz, J. R. & Inbau, F. E. Medical Jurisprudence. 1971. 23.50 (ISBN 0-02-424430-9). Macmillan.
Waltz, Jon R. & Kaplan, John. Evidence: Making the Record. LC 82-13634. (University Casebook Ser.). 83p. 1982. pap. text ed. write for info. (ISBN 0-88277-075-6). Foundation Pr.
Waltz, Julie. Food Habit Management: A Comphrensive Guide to Dietary Change. Ainsworth, Fay & Sommerman, Susan, eds. 1982. instrs.' edition 16.95 (ISBN 0-931836-01-8, 384 PP.); student edition 14.95 (ISBN 0-931836-00-X, 352 PP.). Northwest Learn.
Waltz, Kenneth N. Theory of International Politics. LC 78-62549. (Political Science Ser.). (Illus.). 1979. pap. text ed. 12.95 (ISBN 0-201-08349-3). A-W.
Waltzer, Herbert. Job of Academic Department Chairman. 1975. 2.25 o.p. (ISBN 0-8268-1343-7). ACE.
Walum, Laurel R. Dynamics of Sex & Gender. LC 80-52468. 1977. pap. 11.95 o.p. (ISBN 0-395-30848-8). HM.
Walvin, J. Slavery & British Society 1780-1838. 1982. 65.00x (ISBN 0-686-42927-3, Pub. by Macmillan England). State Mutual Bk.
Walvin, James. The Black Presence: A Documentary History of the Negro in England 1555-1860. LC 75-169829. (Sourcebooks in Negro History Ser). 228p. 1972. 8.50x o.p. (ISBN 0-8052-3434-9). Schocken.
Walvin, James, jt. auth. see Royle, Edward.
Walvin, James & Edwards, Paul, eds. Black Personalities in the Era of the Slave Trade. 256p. 1983. text ed. 27.50x (ISBN 0-8071-1053-1). La State U Pr.
Walvoord, John. Daniel. LC 75-123161. 1970. 13.95 (ISBN 0-8024-1752-3). Moody.
--Matthew: Thy Kingdom Come. 1974. pap. 7.95 (ISBN 0-8024-5189-6). Moody.
Walvoord, John F. Jesus Christ Our Lord. LC 70-80941. 318p. 1974. pap. text ed. 7.95 (ISBN 0-8024-4326-5). Moody.
--Philippians: Joy & Peace. (Everyman's Bible Commentary). 1971. pap. 4.50 (ISBN 0-8024-2050-8). Moody.
--Prophetic Trilogy. 1982. 15.85 o.p. (ISBN 0-310-34148-5). Zondervan.
--Prophetic Trilogy: The Nations in Prophecy, the Church in Prophecy, Israel in Prophecy. pap. 15.85 (ISBN 0-310-34148-5). Zondervan.
--Revelation of Jesus Christ. LC 66-16227. 1966. 13.95 (ISBN 0-8024-7310-5). Moody.
Walvoord, John F. & Zuck, Roy B. The Bib Sac Reader. (Orig.). 1983. pap. 7.95 (ISBN 0-8024-0459-6). Moody.
Walworth, Clarence A. The Oxford Movement in America. LC 77-150436. (Monograph Ser.: No. 30). (Illus.). 1974. Repr. of 1895 ed. 12.00x (ISBN 0-930060-10-5). US Cath Hist.
Walworth, Dan. Automobile Accident. (Illus.). 72p. 1978. pap. 4.00 (ISBN 0-686-82500-4). Cave Canem Bks.
Walworth, Ralph. Subdue the Earth. 1977. pap. 3.95 o.s.i. (ISBN 0-440-58295-4, Delta). Dell.
Walz, Alfred. Boundary Layers of Flow & Temperature. Oser, Hans J., tr. (Illus.). 1969. 32.50x (ISBN 0-262-23035-6). MIT Pr.
Walz, Daniel A. & McCoy, Lowell E., eds. Contributions to Hemostasis, Vol. 370. 856p. 1981. 161.00x (ISBN 0-89766-129-X); pap. 159.00x (ISBN 0-89766-130-3). NY Acad Sci.
Walz, Edgar. Church Business Methods: A Handbook for Pastors & Leaders of the Congregation. LC 79-100492. (Orig.). 1970. pap. 4.50 (ISBN 0-570-03106-0, 12-2330). Concordia.
Walz, Eugene P. Franscois Truffaut: A Guide to References & Resources. 356p. 1982. lib. bdg. 35.00 (ISBN 0-8161-8337-6, Hall Reference). G K Hall.
Walz, Lila. The Mysteries of the "Talking" Animals. LC 79-17127. (Unsolved Mysteries of the World Ser.). 11.96 (ISBN 0-89547-077-2). Silver.
Walzer, M., ed. Regicide & Revolution: Speeches Made at the Trial of Louis XVI. Rothstein, Marian, tr. from Fr. (Studies in the History & Theory of Politics). 219p. 1974. 27.95 (ISBN 0-521-20370-8). Cambridge U Pr.
Walzer, Mary M. Handbook of Needlepoint Stitches. 1976. pap. 4.95 o.p. (ISBN 0-442-29176-0). Van Nos Reinhold.
Walzer, Michael. Obligations: Essays on Disobedience, War, & Citizenship. LC 70-111489. 1982. 14.00x (ISBN 0-674-63000-9); pap. 6.95x (ISBN 0-674-63025-4). Harvard U Pr.
--The Spheres of Justice: A Defense of Pluralism & Equality. LC 82-72409. 356p. 1983. 19.95 (ISBN 0-465-08190-8). Basic.
Walzer, Michael & Kantowicz, E. The Politics of Ethnicity. (Dimensions in Ethnicity Ser.). 160p. 1982. pap. text ed. 5.95x (ISBN 0-674-68753-1). Harvard U Pr.
Walzer, S. M., tr. see Wellhausen, Julius.
Wambach, Helen. Reliving Past Lives: The Evidence Under Hypnosis. LC 77-11805. (Illus.). 1978. 11.49i (ISBN 0-06-014513-7, HarpT). Har-Row.
Wambaugh, Joseph. The Delta Star. 288p. 1983. 15.95 (ISBN 0-688-01912-9). Morrow.
Wampler, Ralph L. Forced Pooling! A Guide for Oklahoma Mineral Owners. 1982. pap. write for info. (ISBN 0-943264-01-4). San Anselmo Pub.
Wamser, Carl C., jt. auth. see Harris, J. Milton.
Wamsley, James S. The Crafts of Williamsburg. LC 82-1305. (World of Williamsburg Ser.). (Illus.). 80p. (Orig.). 1982. 9.95 (ISBN 0-87935-064-4); pap. 5.95 (ISBN 0-87935-065-2). Williamsburg.
Wan, Thomas T., et al. Promoting the Well-being of the Elderly: A Community Diagnosis. LC 82-9209. 248p. 1982. text ed. 29.95 (ISBN 0-917724-38-0, B38); pap. text ed. 14.95 (ISBN 0-917724-39-9, B39). Haworth Pr.
Wanamaker, Olim D., tr. see Wachsmuth, Guenther.
Wanandi, Jusuf, jt. ed. see Scalapino, Robert A.
Wanczek, K. P., jt. auth. see Hartmann, H.
Wanderer, Zev & Cabot, Tracy. Letting Go: A Twelve Week Personal Action Program to Overcome a Broken Heart. 1979. pap. 3.95 (ISBN 0-446-30704-1). Warner Bks.
Wanderer, Dr. Zev & Cabot, Tracy. Letting Go: A Twelve Week Personal Action Program to Overcome a Broken Heart. LC 77-26616. 1978. 9.95 (ISBN 0-399-12136-6). Putnam Pub Group.
Wanderer, Dr. Zev & Fabian, Erika. Making Love Work: New Techniques in the Art of Staying Together. 1979. 10.95 (ISBN 0-399-12427-6). Putnam Pub Group.
Wandor, Michelene. Plays by Women, Vol. 1. 1982. pap. 8.50 (ISBN 0-413-50020-9). Methuen Inc.
--Understudies: Theatre & Sexual Politics. 80p. 1981. pap. 6.95 (ISBN 0-413-40060-3). Methuen Inc.
Wandruszka, Adam. The House of Habsburg: Six Hundred Years of a European Dynasty. Epstein, Cathleen & Epstein, Hans, trs. LC 75-5004. 212p. 1975. Repr. of 1964 ed. lib. bdg. 17.75x (ISBN 0-8371-7928-9, WAHH). Greenwood.
Wandtner, Reinhard. Indikatoreigenschaften der Vegetation von Hochmooren der BR Deutschland fuer Schwermetallimmissionen. (Dissertationes Botanicae: Vol. 59). (Illus.). 190p. (Ger.). 1981. pap. text ed. 16.00x (ISBN 0-686-30972-3). Lubrecht & Cramer.
Wandycz, Piotr S. Czechoslovak-Polish Confederation & the Great Powers, 1940-1943. LC 79-4543. (Slavic & East European Ser.). 1979. Repr. of 1956 ed. lib. bdg. 18.25x (ISBN 0-313-21251-1, WACP). Greenwood.
Waner, Wallace. Troubleshooting Solid State Circuits & Systems. (Illus.). 1979. 21.95 (ISBN 0-8359-7855-9). Reston.
Wang. Radiation Therapy of Head & Neck Neoplasms. 736p. 1983. text ed. 39.50 (ISBN 0-7236-7049-8). Wright-PSG.
Wang, C. H. The Bell & the Drum: A Study of Shih Ching As Formulaic Poetry. (Illus.). 1975. 28.50x (ISBN 0-520-02441-9). U of Cal Pr.
Wang, C. K. Intermediate Structural Analysis. (Illus.). 768p. 1982. 37.50x (ISBN 0-07-068135-X); solns. manual 22.00 (ISBN 0-07-068136-8). McGraw.
Wang, Chih H. & Willis, David L. Radiotracer Methodology in the Biological Environmental & Physical Sciences. (Illus.). 512p. 1975. 32.95 (ISBN 0-13-752212-6). P-H.
Wang, Chu-Kia & Salmon, Charles G. Reinforced Concrete Design. 3rd ed. 918p. 1979. text ed. 38.50 scp (ISBN 0-7002-2514-5, HarpC); solutions manual avail. (ISBN 0-06-367019-4). Har-Row.
Wang, Daniel I., jt. ed. see Tannenbaum, Steven R.
Wang, Daniel I., et al. Fermentation & Enzyme Technology. LC 78-7596. (Techniques in Pure & Applied Microbiology Ser.). 1979. 37.95x (ISBN 0-471-91945-4, Pub. by Wiley-Interscience). Wiley.
Wang, Darsan. The Stationary Front. 1983. 6.95 (ISBN 0-533-04588-6). Vantage.
Wang, F. P., ed. Impurity Doping Processes in Silicon. (Materials Processing, Theory & Practices: Vol. 2). 1982. 119.25 (ISBN 0-444-86095-9). Elsevier.
Wang, Fred. The Lady in the Painting. 4.00 (ISBN 0-686-09944-3); tapes avail. (ISBN 0-686-09945-1). Far Eastern Pubns.
Wang, Fun-Den, et al, eds. Water Jet Symposium: Proceedings. (Illus.). 260p. 1982. pap. text ed. 32.50 (ISBN 0-918062-48-9). Colo Sch Mines.
Wang, George C., ed. Economic Reform in the PRC: In Which China's Economists Make Known What Went Wrong, Why & What Should Be Done About It. (WVSS on China & East Asia Ser.). 130p. 1982. lib. bdg. 17.00 (ISBN 0-86531-348-2); pap. 8.95 (ISBN 0-86531-349-0). Westview.
Wang, Hao. Logic, Computers & Sets. LC 70-113155. Orig. Title: Survey of Mathematical Logic. 1970. Repr. of 1962 ed. text ed. 24.95 (ISBN 0-8284-0245-0). Chelsea Pub.
Wang, Herbert, jt. auth. see Simmons, Gene.
Wang, Hsuan-Hsien, jt. auth. see Hershey, Daniel.
Wang, J. Y., et al. Exploring Man's Environment. 1973. pap. text ed. 12.50 o.p. (ISBN 0-8465-3051-1). Benjamin-Cummings.
Wang, James C. Contemporary Chinese Politics. (Illus.). 1980. pap. text ed. 14.95 (ISBN 0-13-169987-3). P-H.
--The Cultural Revolution in China: An Annotated Bibliography. LC 75-24099. (Reference Library of Social Science: Vol. 16). 250p. 1975. lib. bdg. 28.50 o.s.i. (ISBN 0-8240-9973-7). Garland Pub.
Wang, Jaw-Kai & Hagan, Ross E. Irrigated Rice Production Systems. (Tropical Agriculture Ser.). 1980. lib. bdg. 38.00 (ISBN 0-89158-486-2). Westview.
Wang, Jaw-Kai, ed. Taro: A Review of "Colocasia Esculenta" & Its Potentials. LC 82-21903. (Illus.). 416p. 1983. text ed. 35.00x (ISBN 0-8248-0841-X). UH Pr.
Wang, John L., jt. ed. see Hawkes, Susan.
Wang, K. D. Mineral Resources & Basic Industries in the People's Republic of China. LC 76-27652. 1977. lib. bdg. 25.00 o.p. (ISBN 0-89158-204-5). Westview.
Wang, Lawrence & Hudson, Jack W., eds. Strategies in Cold: Natural Torpidity & Thermogenesis. 1978. 51.00 (ISBN 0-12-734550-7). Acad Pr.
Wang, N. T., ed. Taxation & Development. LC 75-27023. (Special Studies). 1976. 33.95 o.p. (ISBN 0-275-56010-4). Praeger.
Wang, Peter, ed. see Automation Technology Symposium.
Wang, Peter C., ed. Graphical Representation of Multivariate Data. 1978. 27.00 (ISBN 0-12-734750-X). Acad Pr.
Wang, Peter C., et al, eds. Information Linkage Between Applied Mathematics & Industry. 1979. 50.00 (ISBN 0-12-734250-8). Acad Pr.
Wang, Ping'Chun. Numerical & Matrix Methods in Structural Mechanics, with Applications to Computers. LC 66-11529. 1966. 52.50x (ISBN 0-471-91950-0, Pub. by Wiley-Interscience). Wiley.
Wang, Robert. The Qabalistic Tarot. (Illus.). 320p. Date not set. pap. text ed. write for info. (ISBN 0-87728-520-9). Weiser.
Wang, Tong-Eng. Economic Policies & Price Stability in China. LC 80-620008. (China Research Monographs: No. 16). (Illus.). 1980. pap. 8.00x (ISBN 0-912966-24-6). IEAS.
Wang, Virginia, jt. ed. see D'Onofrio, Carol.
Wang, Y. J., ed. see Hartman, Howard L., et al.
Wang, Yang-ming. The Philosophical Letters of Wang Yang-Ming. Ching, Julia, ed. & tr. from Chinese. LC 72-12715. (Asian Publications Ser.: No. 1). (Illus.). xxviii, 148p. 1973. 17.95x o.s.i. (ISBN 0-87249-265-6). U of SC Pr.
Wangara, Harun K., jt. ed. see Alhamsi, Ahmed.
Wang Chi-Chen, tr. Contemporary Chinese Stories. LC 69-14137. 1969. Repr. of 1944 ed. lib. bdg. 20.50x (ISBN 0-8371-0738-5, WACS); pap. 4.95 (ISBN 0-8371-8943-8, WAC). Greenwood.
Wang Chi-Kao. Dissolution of the British Parliament 1832-1931. LC 79-127433. (Columbia University Studies in the Social Sciences: No. 396). Repr. of 1934 ed. 12.50 (ISBN 0-404-51396-4). AMS Pr.
Wang Chi-Teh. Applied Elasticity. (Illus.). 1953. text ed. 39.00 (ISBN 0-07-068125-2, C). McGraw.
Wang Chu-Kia. Statically Indeterminate Structures. (Illus.). 1953. text ed. 36.00 (ISBN 0-07-068130-9, C). McGraw.
Wange, Willy B., jt. auth. see Huberty, Ernst.
Wangerin, W., Jr. & Jennings, A. God, I've Gotta Talk to You. (Arch Bk.). (Illus.). 32p. (gr. k-4). 1974. pap. 0.89 (ISBN 0-570-06086-9, 59-1301). Concordia.
Wangerin, Walter, Jr. The Baby God Promised. (Arch Bks: No. 13). (Illus.). 32p. (ps-4). 1976. pap. 0.89 (ISBN 0-570-06105-9, 59-1223). Concordia.
--Book of the Dun Cow. LC 77-25641. 1978. 8.61i (ISBN 0-06-026346-6, HarpJ); PLB 8.89 (ISBN 0-06-026347-4). Har-Row.
--The Book of the Dun Cow. 1982. pap. 2.50 (ISBN 0-671-83217-4, Timescape). PB.
--The Glory Story. (Arch Bks.: Set 11). (Illus.). 32p. (gr. 1-4). 1974. pap. 0.89 (ISBN 0-570-06083-4, 59-1203). Concordia.
--A Penny Is Everything. (Arch Bks.: Set 11). (Illus.). 32p. (gr. 1-4). 1974. pap. 0.89 (ISBN 0-570-06084-2, 59-1204). Concordia.
Wan-go Weng & Boda, Yang. The Palace Museum, Peking: Treasures of the Forbidden City. (Illus.). 320p. 1982. 65.00 (ISBN 0-8109-1477-8). Abrams.

Wangsness, Ronald K. Electromagnetic Fields. LC 78-15027. 1979. text ed. 32.95x (ISBN 0-471-04103-3); solutions manual 7.75x (ISBN 0-471-05936-6). Wiley.

Wang-Wei. Poems of Wang-Wei. Robinson, G. W., tr. (Classics Ser.). 1974. pap. 4.95 (ISBN 0-14-044296-0). Penguin.

Wangyal, Geshe, tr. from Tibetan. The Door of Liberation: Essential Teachings of the Tibetan Buddhist Tradition. LC 78-61176. (Illus.). 249p. (Orig.). 1982. pap. 7.95 (ISBN 0-87773-785-1). Great Eastern.

Wanielista, Martin P. Stormwater Management: Quantity & Quality. LC 78-62292. 1978. 47.50 (ISBN 0-250-40261-0). Ann Arbor Science.

Wanielista, Martin P. & Eckenfelder, W. W., Jr., eds. Advances in Water & Wastewater Treatment: Biological Nutrient Removal. LC 78-67495. (Illus.). 1979. 37.50 o.p. (ISBN 0-250-40282-3). Ann Arbor Science.

Wanjohi, Gerald, tr. see Erny, Pierre.

Wank, Solomon, ed. Doves & Diplomats: Foreign Offices & Peace Movements in Europe & America in the 20th Century. LC 77-20278. (Contributions in Political Science: No. 4). (Illus.). 1978. lib. bdg. 29.95x (ISBN 0-313-20027-0, WDD/). Greenwood.

Wanless, P. T. & Forrester, D. A., eds. Readings in Inflation Accounting. LC 79-40741. 1979. 53.95x (ISBN 0-471-27657-X, Pub. by Wiley-Interscience). Wiley.

Wann, Brian. The Fox & the Buffalo. 12p. (Orig.). pap. 2.50 (ISBN 0-88138-003-2, Pub. by Envelope Bks). Green Tiger Pr.

Wannamaker, Bruce. God's Care Is Everywhere. LC 82-7244. (Illus.). 32p. (ps-k). 1982. text ed. 4.95 (ISBN 0-89693-202-8). SP Pubns.

--We Visit the Farm. LC 76-15975. (Going Places Ser.). (Illus.). (ps-3). 1976. 5.95 (ISBN 0-913778-43-5). Childs World.

--We Visit the Zoo. LC 76-15639. (Going Places Ser.). (Illus.). (ps-3). 1976. PLB 5.95 (ISBN 0-913778-61-3). Childs World.

Wannamaker, Lewis W. & Matsen, John M., eds. Streptococci & Streptococcal Diseases. 1972. 69.00 (ISBN 0-12-734950-2). Acad Pr.

Wannan, Bill, jt. auth. see Prior, Tom.

Wannen, Bill. Fair Go Spinner. (Illus.). 13.50 (ISBN 0-392-02836-0, ABC). Sportshelf.

Wanner, Criag. Introduction to Statistics for Management & Policy Analysis. 370p. 1983. text ed. 28.50x (ISBN 0-8290-1280-X); pap. text ed. 14.95 (ISBN 0-8290-1281-8). Irvington.

Wanner, Eric & Gleitman, Lila R., eds. Language Acquisition: The State of the Art. LC 82-4407. (Illus.). 528p. 1982. 49.50 (ISBN 0-521-23817-X); pap. 17.95 (ISBN 0-521-28238-1). Cambridge U Pr.

Wannier, George H. Elements of Solid State Theory. LC 79-99504. 280p. Repr. of 1959 ed. lib. bdg. 15.50x (ISBN 0-8371-3030-1, WASS). Greenwood.

Wanniski, Jude. The Way the World Works: How Economics Fail--& Succeed. rev. ed. 1983. pap. 8.25 (ISBN 0-671-43862-X, Touchstone Bks). S&S.

Wannon, Bill. Marcus Clarke Reader. 13.50 (ISBN 0-392-03890-0, ABC). Sportshelf.

Wanscher, J. H., jt. auth. see Kornup, A.

Want, E. Cleve, jt. auth. see Burt, Forest D.

Wantland, William C. Foundations of the Faith. LC 82-61889. 176p. (Orig.). 1983. pap. 6.95 (ISBN 0-8192-1320-9). Morehouse.

Wantz, Molly, jt. auth. see Engs, Ruth.

Wan-Z-Xian. Lie Algebras. LC 74-13832. 244p. 1975. text ed. 40.00 (ISBN 0-08-017952-5). Pergamon.

Warach, Marie N. I Like Red. LC 78-72123. (Illus.). (ps). 1979. 6.75 (ISBN 0-89799-116-8); pap. 3.50 (ISBN 0-89799-002-1). Dandelion Pr.

Waranch, Seeman, jt. auth. see Turner, Richard D.

Warbeke, John M. Power of Art. 1951. 6.00 o.p. (ISBN 0-8022-1807-5). Philos Lib.

Warburg, Gabriel. Islam, Nationalism & Communism in a Traditional Society: The Case of Sudan. 253p. 1978. 29.50x (ISBN 0-7146-3080-2, F Cass Co). Biblio Dist.

Warburg, Sandol S. On the Way Home. LC 73-6578. (Illus.). 144p. (gr. 5 up). 1973. 4.95 o.p. (ISBN 0-395-17510-0). HM.

Warburton, A. B., jt. auth. see Bunn, D. S.

Warburton, Annie O. Melody Writing & Analysis. LC 78-5698. viii, 188p. 1978. Repr. of 1960 ed. lib. bdg. 19.00x (ISBN 0-313-20426-8, WAMW). Greenwood.

Warburton, David M. Brain, Behavior & Drugs: Introduction to the Neurochemistry of Behaviour. LC 74-20789. 280p. 1975. 46.00 o.p. (ISBN 0-471-91991-8, Pub. by Wiley-Interscience). Wiley.

Warburton, David M., jt. auth. see Hamilton, Vernon.

Warburton, Minnie. Mykonos. LC 79-67. 1979. 9.95 o.p. (ISBN 0-698-10922-8, Coward). Putnam Pub Group.

Warby, Marjorie. To Love a Stranger. (Aston Hall Romances Ser.). 192p. (Orig.). 1981. 1.50 o.p. (ISBN 0-523-41126-X). Pinnacle Bks.

Warch, Willard F., jt. auth. see Melcher, Robert A.

Ward. Developments in Oriented Polymers, Vol. 1. 1982. 53.50 (Pub. by Applied Sci England). Elsevier.

Ward, Alan J. The Easter Rising: Revolution & Irish Nationalism. LC 79-55729. (Europe Since 1500 Ser.). (Illus., Orig.). 1980. pap. text ed. 8.95x (ISBN 0-88295-803-8). Harlan Davidson.

Ward, Albert. Book Production, Fiction, & the German Reading Public. (Eng. & Ger.). 1974. text ed. 26.00x o.p. (ISBN 0-19-818157-4). Oxford U Pr.

Ward, Alfred C. Specimens of English Dramatic Criticism: 17th-20th Centuries. LC 73-138605. 1971. Repr. of 1945 ed. lib. bdg. 19.75x (ISBN 0-8371-5545-2, WASE). Greenwood.

Ward, Annie, jt. ed. see Peterson, Donovan.

Ward, Arthur A., Jr., jt. ed. see Lockard, Joan S.

Ward, Brian. The Ear & Hearing. LC 80-54826. (The Human Body Ser.). (Illus.). 48p. (gr. 4 up). 1981. lib. bdg. 8.90 (ISBN 0-531-04289-8). Watts.

--The Eye & Sight. LC 80-54827. (The Human Body Ser.). (Illus.). 48p. (gr. 4 up). 1981. lib. bdg. 8.90 (ISBN 0-686-76379-3). Watts.

--Food & Digestion. LC 82-50057. (The Human Body Ser.). (Illus.). 48p. (gr. 4 up). 1982. PLB 8.90 (ISBN 0-531-04458-0). Watts.

--The Heart & Blood. (The Human Body Ser.). (Illus.). 48p. (gr. 4 up). 1982. PLB 8.90 (ISBN 0-531-04357-6). Watts.

--The Lungs & Breathing. (The Human Body Ser.). (Illus.). 48p. (gr. 4 up). 1982. PLB 8.90 (ISBN 0-531-04358-4). Watts.

--Skeleton & Movement. (The Human Body Ser.). (Illus.). 48p. (gr. 4 up). 1981. lib. bdg. 8.90 (ISBN 0-531-04291-X). Watts.

--Touch, Taste & Smell. LC 82-50058. (The Human Body Ser.). (Illus.). 48p. (gr. 4 up). 1982. PLB 8.90 (ISBN 0-531-04460-2). Watts.

Ward, Brian R. Birth & Growth. (The Human Body Ser.). (Illus.). 48p. (gr. 4 up). 1983. PLB 8.90 (ISBN 0-531-04459-9). Watts.

--Body Maintenance. (The Human Body Ser.). (Illus.). 48p. (gr. 4 up). 1983. PLB 8.90 (ISBN 0-531-04457-2). Watts.

Ward, Brice. Digital Electronics: Principles & Practice. LC 73-178689. (Illus.). 1972. 12.95 o.p. (ISBN 0-8306-2585-2); pap. 8.95 (ISBN 0-8306-1585-7, 585). TAB Bks.

--Microprocessor-Microprograming Handbook. LC 75-31466. (Illus.). 294p. 1975. 12.95 o.p. (ISBN 0-8306-5785-1); pap. 9.95 (ISBN 0-8306-4785-6, 785). TAB Bks.

Ward, Bryan. Hospital. LC 78-61228. (Careers Ser.). (Illus.). 1978. PLB 12.68 (ISBN 0-382-06194-2). Silver.

Ward, C. M. Sermons from Luke. 96p. (Orig.). 1983. pap. 2.25 (ISBN 0-89274-260-7). Harrison Hse.

Ward, C. S. Anaesthetic Equipment: Physical Principles & Maintenance. (Illus.). 1975. text ed. 32.50 o.p. (ISBN 0-02-859670-6, Pub. by Bailliere-Tindall). Saunders.

Ward, Catherine E., tr. see Hernandez, Jose.

Ward, Charlotte R. This Blue Planet: Introduction to Physical Science. 417p. 1972. text ed. 17.95 (ISBN 0-316-92230-7); instuctor's Manual avail. (ISBN 0-316-92222-6). Little.

Ward, Colin. Anarchy in Action. 152p. pap. 3.50 (ISBN 0-900384-20-4). Left Bank.

Ward, Colin & Fyson, Anthony. Streetwork: The Exploding School. 150p. 1974. 16.95x (ISBN 0-7100-7683-5); pap. 7.95 (ISBN 0-7100-7702-5). Routledge & Kegan.

Ward, Dan S. Dawn the Chosen. LC 82-62334. 200p. 1983. 13.95 (ISBN 0-911631-03-8). Pub Ward Inc.

Ward, David. T. S. Eliot: Between Two Worlds. 314p. 1973. 24.00x (ISBN 0-7100-7638-X). Routledge & Kegan.

Ward, David, ed. Geographic Perspectives on America's Past: Readings on the Historical Geography of the United States. (Illus.). 1979. pap. text ed. 10.95x (ISBN 0-19-502353-6). Oxford U Pr.

Ward, David, jt. auth. see Easterlin, Richard A.

Ward, David A. & Schoen, Kenneth F. Confinement in Maximum Custody: New Last-Resort Prisons in the United States & Western Europe. LC 78-24630. 224p. 1981. 23.95x (ISBN 0-669-02799-5). Lexington Bks.

Ward, David A., jt. ed. see Cressey, Donald R.

Ward, Dennis, jt. auth. see Jones, D.

Ward, Dennis M. Applied Digital Electronics. 408p. 1981. text ed. 22.95 (ISBN 0-675-09925-0). Additional supplements may be obtained from publisher. Merrill.

Ward, Dwayne. Toward a Critical Political Economy: A Critique of Liberal & Radical Economic Thought. LC 76-29795. (Illus.). 1977. pap. 14.50x (ISBN 0-673-16179-X). Scott F.

Ward, Ed. Michael Bloomfield: The Rise & Fall of an American Guitar Hero. (Illus.). 1983. pap. 7.95 (ISBN 0-89524-157-9, #8605). Cherry Lane.

Ward, Eddie L. Poet's Last Stand Before the Vanguard. 1979. 4.95 o.p. (ISBN 0-533-04257-7). Vantage.

Ward, Edmund. The Main Chance. 1977. 7.95 o.p. (ISBN 0-698-10816-7, Coward). Putnam Pub Group.

Ward, Elaine. After My House Burned Down. 88p. (Orig.). 1982. pap. 6.95 (ISBN 0-940754-11-8). Ed Ministries.

--Be & Say a Fingerplay. 71p. (Orig.). 1982. pap. 5.95 (ISBN 0-940754-12-6). Ed Ministries.

--Being-in-Creation. 80p. (Orig.). 1983. pap. 9.95 (ISBN 0-940754-14-2). Ed Ministries.

--Feelings Grow Too! 81p. (Orig.). 1981. pap. 9.95 (ISBN 0-940754-07-X). Ed Ministries.

--Growing Roots & Wings: A Guide to Teaching Children "Roots & Wings". (Orig.). 1983. pap. write for info. (ISBN 0-377-00131-7). Friend Pr.

--Roots & Wings. (Orig.). (gr. 1-6). 1983. pap. write for info. (ISBN 0-377-00130-9). Friend Pr.

Ward, Elaine M. A Beautiful Valentine. (The Story Tree Ser.). (Illus.). 64p. (Orig.). (ps). 1981. pap. 1.95 (ISBN 0-89505-073-0). Argus Comm.

Ward, Elizabeth, jt. auth. see Silver, Alain.

Ward, Eric F. Beginning Statistics for Psychology Students. 3rd ed. 1980. pap. text ed. 7.25x- (ISBN 0-89917-305-5). TIS Inc.

Ward, Estolv E. The Gentle Dynamiter: A Biography of Tom Mooney. LC 82-80645. (Illus.). 350p. 1983. 15.00 (ISBN 0-87867-089-0); pap. 6.95 (ISBN 0-686-97941-9). Ramparts.

Ward, F. A. Primer of Hematology. 1971. 6.95 o.p. (ISBN 0-407-62506-2). Butterworth.

Ward, Frances. Keep the Fruit on the Table. 48p. 1982. pap. 1.95 (ISBN 0-88144-006-X, CPS-006). Christian Pub.

Ward, George A., ed. see Curwen, Samuel.

Ward, Gerald M. Energy Impacts Upon Future Livestock Production. (Special Study in Agriculture-Aquaculture Science & Policy). 250p. 1982. lib. bdg. 30.00 (ISBN 0-86531-286-9). Westview.

Ward, H. Snowden, ed. see Berry, James.

Ward, Harry M. & Greer, Harold E., Jr. Richmond During the Revolution, 1775-1783. LC 77-22586. 205p. 1977. 10.95 (ISBN 0-8139-0715-2). U Pr of Va.

Ward, Hiley. Feeling Good About Myself. LC 82-25613. 180p. (gr. 5-9). 1983. price not set (ISBN 0-664-32704-4). Westminster.

Ward, I. M., ed. Structure & Properties of Oriented Polymers. LC 74-26599. 500p. 1975. 79.95 o.s.i. (ISBN 0-470-91996-5). Halsted Pr.

Ward, I. M., jt. ed. see Ciferri, A.

Ward, Ian & Watts, Denis. Athletics for Student & Coach. (Illus.). 180p. 1976. 14.00 o.p. (ISBN 0-7207-0881-8). Transatlantic.

Ward, Ian M. Mechanical Properties of Solid Polymers. LC 79-149575. 1972. 62.95x (ISBN 0-471-91995-0, Pub. by Wiley-Interscience). Wiley.

Ward, J. M. Hiram Abiff. 7.95x o.p. (ISBN 0-685-21968-2). Wehman.

Ward, J. Neville. The Use of Praying. 1977. 9.95x (ISBN 0-19-520106-X); pap. 5.95 (ISBN 0-19-519959-6). Oxford U Pr.

Ward, J. T. Popular Movements. LC 73-110257. (Problems in Focus Ser). 1970. 22.50x (ISBN 0-312-63035-2). St Martin.

Ward, Jack A. & Hetzel, Howard R. Biology: Today & Tomorrow. (Illus.). 1980. text ed. 22.50 (ISBN 0-8299-0310-0); study guide 7.95 (ISBN 0-8299-0335-6); instrs.' manual avail. (ISBN 0-8299-0579-0). West Pub.

Ward, James. Historic Ornament: A Treatise on Decorative Art & Architectural Ornament. (Illus.). 858p. 1983. pap. 9.95 (ISBN 0-686-38395-8). Tanager Bks.

Ward, James A. J. Edgar Thomson, Master of the Pennsylvania. LC 79-6569. (Contributions in Economics & Economic History: No. 33). (Illus.). xviii, 265p. 1980. lib. bdg. 29.95x (ISBN 0-313-22095-6, WJE/). Greenwood.

Ward, James A., jt. auth. see Ingle, H. L.

Ward, James O., jt. auth. see Tracy, Thomas.

Ward, Joanne, jt. auth. see Ward, John.

Ward, John. The Arkansas Rockefeller. LC 75-5354. 1978. 19.50 (ISBN 0-8071-0253-9). La State U Pr.

Ward, John & Ward, Joanne. The Wide Mouth Frog. (Illus.). 26p. 1981. pap. 2.50x (ISBN 0-910195-01-3). Genesis Pubns.

Ward, John M. James Macarthur: Colonial Conservative 1798-1867. 345p. 1982. 52.00 (ISBN 0-424-00087-3, Pub. by Sydney U Pr). Intl Schol Bk Serv.

Ward, John O., ed. see Scholes, Percy A.

Ward, John R. Meetings by Telephone. (Illus.). 57p. 1980. pap. 3.75x (ISBN 0-910195-00-5). Genesis Pubns.

Ward, John R., jt. auth. see Strum, Robert D.

Ward, John T. Meetings by Telephone. 55p. 1980. 3.25 (ISBN 0-686-98119-7). Telecom Lib.

Ward, John W. Andrew Jackson: Symbol for an Age. (YA) (gr. 9 up). 1962. pap. 6.95 (ISBN 0-19-500699-2, GB). Oxford U Pr.

Ward, Keith. The Concept of God. LC 74-82271. 256p. 1975. 22.50 (ISBN 0-312-15925-0). St Martin.

Ward, Leslie. Forty Years of Spy. LC 70-81512. 1969. Repr. of 1915 ed. 40.00x (ISBN 0-8103-3575-1). Gale.

Ward, Lester F. Dynamic Sociology, 2 Vols. LC 8-31367. (American Studies). Repr. of 1883 ed. Set. 65.00 (ISBN 0-384-65763-X). Johnson Repr.

Ward, Lynd. God's Man: A Novel in Woodcuts. LC 77-91889. (Illus.). 1978. 7.95 o.p. (ISBN 0-312-33100-2); pap. 4.95 o.p. (ISBN 0-312-33101-0). St Martin.

--The Silver Pony. LC 72-5402. (Illus.). 192p. (gr. k-3). 1973. 12.95 (ISBN 0-395-14753-0). HM.

Ward, Lynd, jt. auth. see Swift, Hildegarde H.

Ward, Maisie. The Tragi-Comedy of Pen Browning. LC 72-1865. (Illus.). 1972. 8.50x (ISBN 0-8362-0494-8, Pub by Browning Inst). Pub Ctr Cult Res.

Ward, Margaret E. Rolf Hochhuth. (World Authors Ser.). 1977. lib. bdg. 15.95 (ISBN 0-8057-6300-7, Twayne). G K Hall.

Ward, Marjorie. The Blessed Trade. 1972. 15.00x o.p. (ISBN 0-7181-0951-1). Transatlantic.

Ward, Martha E. Steve Carlton: Star Southpaw. LC 74-21079. (Putnam Sports Shelf). (gr. 6-8). 1975. PLB 6.29 o.p. (ISBN 0-399-60934-2). Putnam Pub Group.

Ward, Mary A. & Barbaresi, Sara M. How to Raise & Train a Beagle. 1966. pap. 2.95 (ISBN 0-87666-242-4, DS1004). TFH Pubns.

Ward, Matthew, tr. see Barthes, Ronald.

Ward, Morris A. The Clean Water Act: The Second Decade. 54p. (Orig.). 1982. pap. write for info. (ISBN 0-9609130-0-9). E B Harrison.

Ward, Nick. Giant. (Umbrella Books). (Illus.). 30p. (ps). 1983. bds. 5.95 (ISBN 0-19-278201-0, Pub by Oxford U Pr Childrens). Merrimack Bk Serv.

Ward, Norman, rev. by see Dawson, Robert M.

Ward, P., jt. auth. see Magor, J. T.

Ward, Patricia A. Farm Journal's Best-Ever Cookies. LC 80-948. (Illus.). 1980. 14.95 (ISBN 0-385-17146-3). Doubleday.

Ward, Peter. The Adventures of Charles Darwin: A Story of the Beagle Voyage. LC 81-21751. (Illus.). 96p. (gr. 9-12). 1982. 7.95 (ISBN 0-521-24510-9). Cambridge U Pr.

Ward, Phebe. Terminal Education in the Junior College. 282p. 1982. Repr. of 1947 ed. lib. bdg. 30.00 (ISBN 0-8495-5662-7). Arden Lib.

Ward, Philip. Albania: A Travel Guide. (Oleander Travel Bks.: Vol. 10). (Illus.). 160p. 1983. 26.50 (ISBN 0-906672-41-4); pap. 16.00 (ISBN 0-906672-42-2). Oleander Pr.

--Collected Poems. 1960. 3.95 (ISBN 0-902675-40-0). Oleander Pr.

--Indonesian Traditional Poetry. 1975. 13.50 (ISBN 0-902675-49-4). Oleander Pr.

--The Oxford Companion to Spanish Literature. 1978. 35.00 (ISBN 0-19-866114-2). Oxford U Pr.

--Touring Lebanon. (Illus.). 1971. 9.50 o.p. (ISBN 0-571-09433-3). Transatlantic.

Ward, Philip, ed. see Burton, Richard F.

Ward, Philip, tr. see Gomez de la Serna, Ramon.

Ward, Phillip. Touring Libya: The Southern Provinces. 8.50 o.p. (ISBN 0-571-08703-5). Transatlantic.

--Touring Libya: The Western Provinces. 8.50 o.p. (ISBN 0-571-08667-5). Transatlantic.

Ward, R. E. May I Kill You? Draft-Dodging & Military Escape Stories, A Collection. (Illus.). 156p. (Orig.). 1982. pap. 5.00 (ISBN 0-9610280-1-7). Reward Pub.

Ward, R. S. see Hughston, L. P.

Ward, Rhode, tr. see Narramore, Clyde & Narramore, Ruth.

Ward, Richard & McDowell, Ernest R. North American P-51 BC Mustang. LC 71-93927. (Arco-Aircam Aviation Ser., No. 5). 1969. pap. 2.95 o.p. (ISBN 0-668-02101-2). Arco.

Ward, Richard, jt. auth. see Hooten, Ted.

Ward, Richard, jt. auth. see Hooton, Ted.

Ward, Richard, jt. auth. see Shores, Christopher F.

Ward, Richard A. The Economics of Health Resources. 150p. 1975. 10.25 (ISBN 0-686-68580-6, 14914). Healthcare Fin Man Assn.

Ward, Robert E. Japan's Political System. 2nd ed. (Illus.). 1978. 11.95 (ISBN 0-13-509588-3). P-H.

Ward, Robert E. & Shulman, Frank J. Allied Occupation of Japan: 1945-52. LC 73-8772. 170p. 1974. pap. text ed. 50.00 o.p. (ISBN 0-8389-0127-1). ALA.

Ward, Roy C. Floods: A Geographical Perspective Paper. (Focal Problems in Geography Ser.). 244p. 1980. pap. text ed. 16.95x o.p. (ISBN 0-470-26965-0). Halsted Pr.

Ward, Russell. Man Makes History. 10.50x (ISBN 0-392-03842-0, ABC). Sportshelf.

Ward, Ruth. Encouragement: A Wife's Special Gift. 1979. pap. 2.50 (ISBN 0-8010-9634-0). Baker Bk.

--Yes, I'll Teach--Now What? LC 81-70171. (Illus.). 95p. (Orig.). 1982. pap. 4.75 (ISBN 0-87509-313-2); Leader's guide. 3.50 (ISBN 0-87509-315-9). Chr Pubns.

Ward, Sheila A. Dippitidy Doo: Songs & Activities for Children. (English As a Second Language Bk.). (Illus.). 32p. (gr. 1-5). 1980. pap. text ed. 3.50x activity bk. (ISBN 0-582-51005-8); tchr's guide 2.75x (ISBN 0-582-51004-X); cassette 12.50x (ISBN 0-582-51006-6); record 13.50x (ISBN 0-582-51007-4). Longman.

Ward, Sol A. & Litchfield, Thorndike. Cost Control in Design & Construction. (Illus.). 1980. 24.50 (ISBN 0-07-068139-2). McGraw.

Ward, Stanley. Vergil's Lovers. 49p. (Orig.). 1982. pap. 4.00 (ISBN 0-942626-01-X). Quincunx.

Ward, T. S. The Distribution of Consumer Goods. LC 73-84321. (Dept. of Applied Economics, Occasional Papers: No. 38). (Illus.). 250p. 1973. 34.50 (ISBN 0-521-20145-4); pap. 16.95 (ISBN 0-521-09791-6). Cambridge U Pr.

Ward, W. F. & White, L. W. East Africa: A Century of Change, 1870-1970. LC 70-161232. 1972. text ed. 19.50x (ISBN 0-8419-0079-5, Africana); pap. text ed. 15.50x (ISBN 0-8419-0092-2, Africana). Holmes & Meier.

Ward, W. R., ed. Early Victorian Methodism: The Correspondence of the Jabez Bunting, 1830-1858. 1976. 35.00x o.p. (ISBN 0-19-713140-9). Oxford U Pr.

Ward, William B. Divine Physician. rev. ed. LC 53-11762. (Orig.). 1957. pap. 3.25 (ISBN 0-8042-2316-5). John Knox.

--Toward Responsible Discipleship. LC 61-7078. (Orig.). 1961. pap. 1.49 (ISBN 0-8042-4049-3); leader's guide o.p. 1.00 (ISBN 0-8042-4050-7). John Knox.

--When You're Married. (Orig.). 1947. pap. 1.95 (ISBN 0-8042-2604-0). John Knox.

Ward, William S. Literary Reviews in British Periodicals, 1798-1820, 2 vols. LC 72-2308. (Library of Humanities Reference Bks.: No. 9). Set. lib. bdg. 80.00 o.s.i. (ISBN 0-8240-0512-0). Garland Pub.

Ward, Winifred. Playmaking with Children from Kindergarten Through Junior High School. 2nd ed. (Illus.). 1957. text ed. 18.95 (ISBN 0-13-683888-X). P-H.

Warde, Alan. Consensus & Beyond: The Development of Labour Party Strategy since the Second World War. 240p. 1982. 25.00 (ISBN 0-7190-0849-2). Manchester.

Warde, John, ed. Make It! Don't Buy It: Home Furnishings & Accessories to Make from Wood, Metal & Fabric. (Illus.). 464p. 1983. 24.95 (ISBN 0-87857-450-6, 14-013-0). Rodale Pr Inc.

Wardell, David B., jt. auth. see Brown, James R.

Wardell, Sandra C. Acute Intervention: Nursing Process Throughout the Life Span. (Illus.). 1979. text ed. 19.95 (ISBN 0-8359-0133-5); pap. text ed. 14.95 (ISBN 0-8359-0132-7); instrs'. manual o.p. avail. (ISBN 0-8359-0134-3). Reston.

Warden, Carol D., jt. auth. see Lewis, Marti.

Warden, Rob & Griffin, Dick, eds. Done in a Day: One Hundred Years of Great Writing from the Chicago Daily News. LC 82-74177. 473p. 1977. 16.95 (ISBN 0-8040-0755-1); pap. 8.95 (ISBN 0-8040-0756-X). Swallow.

Warden, Rob & Groves, Martha, eds. Murder Most Foul: And Other Great Crime Stories from the World Press. LC 82-75901. (Illus.). x, 348p. 1980. 18.00 (ISBN 0-8040-0796-9). Swallow.

Warder, Anthony K., ed. New Paths in Buddhist Research. LC 82-83594. 128p. 1983. 12.95 (ISBN 0-89386-008-5); pap. 7.95 (ISBN 0-89386-009-3). Acorn NC.

Wardhaugh, K. & Ashour, Y. Experiments on the Incubation & Hopper Development Periods of the Desert Locust (Schistocerca) Gregaria Forskal) in Saudi Arabia. 1969. 35.00x (ISBN 0-85135-048-8, Pub. by Centre Overseas Research). State Mutual Bk.

Wardhaugh, Ronald. Introduction to Linguistics. 2nd ed. (Illus.). 1977. pap. text ed. 18.95 (ISBN 0-07-068152-X, C). McGraw.

Wardhaugh, Ronald & Brown, H. Douglas, eds. A Survey of Applied Linguistics. LC 75-31053. 1976. pap. 12.50x (ISBN 0-472-08959-5). U of Mich Pr.

Wardian, Jeanne, jt. auth. see Andrews, J. Austin.

Wardlaw, Alastair, jt. ed. see Primrose, S. B.

Wardlaw, Don M., ed. Preaching Biblically. 180p. (Orig.). 1983. pap. price not set (ISBN 0-664-24478-5). Westminster.

Wardlaw, Grant. Political Terrorism: Theory, Tactics & Counter-Measures. LC 82-9431. (Illus.). 256p. Date not set. 29.50 (ISBN 0-521-25032-3); pap. 9.95 (ISBN 0-521-27147-9). Cambridge U Pr.

Wardlaw, Ralph. Book of Proverbs, 3 Vol. 1981. Set. 45.00 (ISBN 0-86524-042-6, 2001). Klock & Klock.

Wardle, David. English Popular Education: Seventeen Eighty to Nineteen Seventy. 2nd ed. LC 75-41713. 208p. 1976. 24.95 (ISBN 0-521-21202-2); pap. 9.95 (ISBN 0-521-29073-2). Cambridge U Pr.

--The Rise of the Schooled Society: The History of Formal Schooling in England. 190p. 1974. 14.95x (ISBN 0-7100-7717-3). Routledge & Kegan.

Wardle, M. E., jt. auth. see Bolt, Albert B.

Wardle, Patricia. Victorian Lace. Date not set. 21.95 (ISBN 0-903585-13-8). Robin & Russ.

Wardle, Patricia, tr. see Bing, Valetyn & Braet Von Uberfeldt, Jan.

Wardle, Ralph M., ed. Godwin & Mary: Letters of William Godwin & Mary Wollstonecraft. LC 76-13032. (Illus.). x, 125p. 1977. 9.50x (ISBN 0-8032-0901-0); pap. 2.65x (ISBN 0-8032-5852-6, BB 631, Bison). U of Nebr Pr.

Wardley, R. C. & Crowther, J. R. The Elisa: Enzyme-Linked Immunosorbent Assay in Veterinary Research & Diagnosis. 1982. 54.50 (ISBN 90-247-2769-3, Pub. by Martinus Nijhoff Netherlands). Kluwer Boston.

Wardley-Smith, J. The Control of Oil Pollution. 272p. 1983. 40.00x (ISBN 0-8448-1439-3). Crane-Russak.

Wardman, Alan. Religion & Statecraft among the Romans. 288p. 1982. text ed. 26.25x (ISBN 0-246-11743-5, Pub. by Granada England). Humanities.

--Rome's Debt to Greece. LC 76-41575. 1977. 16.95x o.p. (ISBN 0-312-69230-7). St Martin.

Ward-Perkins, J. B. Roman Imperial Architecture. (Pelican History of Art Ser.: No. 45). 1981. 35.00 (ISBN 0-670-60349-X). Viking Pr.

Wardwell, Allen, intro. by. Handbook of the Mr & Mrs John D. Rockefeller. 3rd ed. LC 81-7905. (Illus.). 112p. 1981. pap. 6.50 (ISBN 0-87848-059-5). Asia Soc.

Ware, Alan. The Logic of Party Democracy. LC 78-1109. 1979. 20.00x (ISBN 0-312-49450-5). St Martin.

Ware, Archimandrite K., jt. tr. see Mary, Mother.

Ware, Edith E. Business & Politics in the Far East. 1932. text ed. 47.50x (ISBN 0-686-83497-6). Elliots Bks.

Ware, George W. Pesticides: Theory & Applications. LC 82-7412. (Illus.). 291p. 1982. pap. text ed. write for info. (ISBN 0-7167-1416-7). W H Freeman.

Ware, George W. & McCollum, J. P. Producing Vegetable Crops. 3rd ed. (Illus.). (gr. 9-12). 1980. 19.35 (ISBN 0-8134-2083-0); text ed. 14.50x. Interstate.

Ware, Gilbert & Hill, Herbert, eds. From the Black Bar: Voices for Equal Justice. (New Perspectives on Black America). 356p. 1976. 10.00 o.p. (ISBN 0-399-11463-7). Putnam Pub Group.

Ware, Henry. Memoirs of the Reverend Noah Worcester, D. D. LC 78-137557. (Peace Movement in America Ser). xii, 155p. 1972. Repr. of 1844 ed. lib. bdg. 12.95x (ISBN 0-89198-088-1). Ozer.

Ware, James H., Jr. Not with Words of Wisdom: Performative Language & Liturgy. LC 80-6239. 252p. (Orig.). 1981. lib. bdg. 22.50 (ISBN 0-8191-1706-4); pap. text ed. 11.50 (ISBN 0-8191-1707-2). U Pr of Amer.

Ware, James R., tr. see Confucius.

Ware, John P., jt. auth. see Duncan, Roger F.

Ware, Kay, jt. auth. see Kottmeyer, William A.

Ware, L. A. Learn Sanskrit Through Stories. 1979. pap. 2.00 (ISBN 0-87481-487-1). Vedanta Pr.

Ware, Leon. Delta Mystery. LC 74-6441. (gr. 6-9). 1974. 5.50 o.s.i. (ISBN 0-664-32553-X). Westminster.

Ware, M. J., jt. auth. see Salthouse, J. A.

Ware, Marsha, jt. auth. see Notelowitz, Morris.

Ware, Porter & Lockard, Thaddeus. P. T. Barnum Presents Jenny Lind. LC 80-1150. 320p. 1980. 22.50x (ISBN 0-8071-0687-9). La State U Pr.

Ware, Susan. Holding Their Own: American Women in the 1930s. (History of American Women in the 20th Century Ser.). 1982. lib. bdg. 15.00 (ISBN 0-8057-9900-1, Twayne). G K Hall.

Ware, William R. The American Vignola: A Guide to the Making of Classical Architecture. (Illus.). 1977. pap. 6.95 (ISBN 0-393-00839-8, Norton Lib). Norton.

Wareing, P. F., ed. Plant Growth Substances. 1982. write for info. (ISBN 0-12-735380-1). Acad Pr.

Wares, Alan C. & Wares, Iris M. Punctuation, Proofreading & Printing: How to Prepare a Manuscript for Publication. rev. ed. 1975. pap. 1.75 o.p. (ISBN 0-88312-798-9); microfiche 1.50 o.p. (ISBN 0-88312-491-2). Summer Inst Ling.

Wares, Iris M., jt. auth. see Wares, Alan C.

Warfel, Harry R. Language: A Science of Human Behavior. LC 62-9619. 1962. 20.00x (ISBN 0-8201-1047-7). Schol Facsimiles.

Warfel, M. C. & Waskey, Frank H. The Professional Food Buyer. LC 75-46108. 1979. 26.00 (ISBN 0-8211-2254-1); ten or more copies 23.50 ea. McCutchan.

Warfel, William B. Handbook of Stage Lighting Graphics. LC 73-16421. (Illus.). 50p. 1974. pap. 5.95x (ISBN 0-910482-47-0). Drama Bk.

Warfield, B. B. Counterfeit Miracles. 1976. pap. 5.95 (ISBN 0-85151-166-X). Banner of Truth.

--Faith & Life. 1974. pap. 5.95 (ISBN 0-85151-188-0). Banner of Truth.

Warfield, Gerald. The Investor's Guide to Stock Quotations: And Other Financial Listings. LC 82-47539. (Illus.). 416p. 1983. pap. 10.53i (ISBN 0-06-091036-4, CN 1036, CN). Har-Row.

--The Investor's Guide to Stock Quotations: And Other Financial Listings. (Illus.). 416p. 1983. 25.00 (ISBN 0-06-015050-5, HarpT). Har-Row.

Warfield, John N. Societal Systems: Planning, Policy, & Complexity. LC 76-25908. (Systems Engineering & Analysis Ser.). 1976. 52.50x (ISBN 0-471-01569-5, Pub. by Wiley-Interscience). Wiley.

Warfield, Ronald G. & Juillerat, Lee. Crater Lake. LC 82-82579. (The Story Behind the Scenery Ser.). (Illus.). 48p. (Orig.). 1982. 7.95 (ISBN 0-916122-80-8); pap. 3.00 (ISBN 0-916122-79-4). KC Pubns.

Warga, J. Optimal Control of Differential & Functional Equations. 1972. 64.00 (ISBN 0-12-735150-7). Acad Pr.

Warga, Richard G. Personal Awareness: A Psychology of Adjustment. 2nd ed. LC 78-69531. (Illus.). 1979. pap. text ed. 15.95 (ISBN 0-395-26795-1); instr's. manual 1.20 (ISBN 0-395-26796-X). HM.

--Personal Awareness: A Psychology of Adjustment. 3rd ed. LC 82-81113. 528p. 1982. text ed. 21.95 (ISBN 0-395-32586-2). HM.

Wargo, Louis G., Jr., jt. auth. see Jaberg, Gene.

Wargo, Robert, tr. see Nakamura, Hiroshi.

Warham, John. Technique of Bird Photography. 4th ed. (Illus.). 304p. 1983. 39.95 (ISBN 0-240-51084-4). Focal Pr.

--Technique of Wildlife Cinematography. (Illus.). 224p. 1966. 24.95 (ISBN 0-240-50640-5). Focal Pr.

Warhol, Andy. Andy Warhol's Exposures. (Illus.). 1979. 25.00 (ISBN 0-448-12850-0, G&D); pap. 12.50 (ISBN 0-448-12658-3). Putnam Pub Group.

Warhurst, John. Jobs or Dogma: The Industrial Assistance Commission & Australian Politics. LC 82-8653. (Policy, Politics, & Administration Ser.). (Illus.). 255p. 1983. text ed. 19.50x (ISBN 0-7022-1850-2); pap. text ed. 8.50x (ISBN 0-7022-1982-7). U of Queensland Pr.

Warin, Robert P. & Champion, Robert H. Urticaria. LC 73-89192. (Major Problems in Dermatology Ser.: Vol. 1). (Illus.). 185p. 1974. text ed. 9.00 (ISBN 0-7216-9111-0). Saunders.

Waring, Alan J., jt. auth. see Barnes, John E.

Waring, Dennis. Making Folk Instruments in Wood. LC 81-50985. (Illus.). 160p. (Orig.). 1981. pap. 8.95 (ISBN 0-8069-7540-7). Sterling.

Waring, George H. Horse Behavior. LC 82-19083. (Animal Behavior, Ecology, Conservation & Management Ser.). (Illus.). 292p. 1983. 35.00 (ISBN 0-8155-0927-8). Noyes.

Waring, Gilchrist. The City of Once Upon a Time. 1946. 5.00 o.p. (ISBN 0-685-47898-X). Dietz.

Waring, H. Color-Change Mechanisms of Coldblooded Vertebrates. 1963. 36.00 o.p. (ISBN 0-12-735450-6). Acad Pr.

Waring, Janet. Early American Stencils on Walls & Furniture. (Illus.). 12.50 (ISBN 0-8446-3138-8). Peter Smith.

Waring, Richard H., ed. see Biology Colloquium, 40th, Oregon State University, 1979.

Waring, Walter. Thomas Carlyle. (English Author Ser.). 1978. 12.95 (ISBN 0-8057-6710-X, Twayne). G K Hall.

Waring, William W. & Jeansonne, Louis O. Practical Manual of Pediatrics: A Pocket Reference for Those Who Treat Children. 2nd ed. LC 81-14148. (Illus.). 483p. 1982. pap. text ed. 13.95 (ISBN 0-8016-5347-9). Mosby.

Waringhien, Gaston, ed. Plena Ilustrita Vortaro De Esperanto. 2nd ed. (Illus., Esperanto.). 1981. 54.00x (ISBN 0-685-71608-2, 1069). Esperanto League North Am.

Wark & Mogen. Read, Underline, Review: A Method for More Efficient Learning. (Basic Skills System). 1970. text ed. 13.50 (ISBN 0-07-051375-9). McGraw.

Wark, David M., jt. auth. see Raygor, Alton L.

Wark, Edna. Drawn Fabric Embroidery. 1979. 24.00 o.p. (ISBN 0-7134-1476-6, Pub. by Batsford England). David & Charles.

Wark, K. R. Elizabethan Recusancy in Cheshire. 1971. 18.50 (ISBN 0-7190-1154-X). Manchester.

Wark, Kenneth. Thermodynamics. 3rd ed. (Illus.). 1977. text ed. 33.50 (ISBN 0-07-068280-1, C); solutions manual 25.00 (ISBN 0-07-068281-X). McGraw.

--Thermodynamics. (Illus.). 1249p. 1983. text ed. 34.50c (ISBN 0-07-068284-4, C); solns. manual 15.00 (ISBN 0-07-068285-2). McGraw.

Wark, Robert R. British Portrait Drawings 1600-1900: Twenty-Five Examples from the Huntington Collection. LC 82-9315. (Illus.). 64p. (Orig.). 1982. pap. 5.00 (ISBN 0-87328-123-3). Huntington Lib.

--Sir Joshua Reynolds: Discourses on Art. LC 74-17647. (Paul Mellon Center for Studies in British Art Ser.). (Illus.). 384p. 1981. pap. 40.00x o.p. (ISBN 0-300-01823-1); pap. 14.95x (ISBN 0-300-02775-3, Y-411). Yale U Pr.

Warkentin, John, jt. auth. see Harris, R. Cole.

Warkentin, Marjorie. Ordination: A Biblical-Historical View. 188p. (Orig.). 1982. pap. 7.95 (ISBN 0-8028-1941-9). Eerdmans.

Warkentin, Viola, jt. auth. see Whittaker, Arabelle.

Warkov, Seymour. Energy Policy in the United States: Social & Behavioral Dimensions. LC 78-8454. (Praeger Special Studies). 1978. 29.95 o.p. (ISBN 0-03-043486-6). Praeger.

--Lawyers in the Making. LC 79-26229. (National Opinion Research Center Monographs in Social Research: No. 7). (Illus.). 1980. Repr. of 1965 ed. lib. bdg. 20.00x (ISBN 0-313-22215-0, WALM). Greenwood.

Warkov, Seymour & Meyer, Judith W. Solar Diffusion & Public Incentives. LC 81-47000. (Illus.). 176p. 1982. 20.95x (ISBN 0-669-04510-1). Lexington Bks.

Warlick, Harold C., Jr. How to Be a Minister & a Human Being. 128p. 1982. pap. 7.95 (ISBN 0-8170-0961-2). Judson.

Warman, E. A., jt. ed. see Greenaway, D. S.

Warman, E. A., jt. ed. see Sata, T.

Warme, Paul. BASEX. LC 79-775. 1979. pap. 8.00 (ISBN 0-07-068290-9, BYTE Bks). McGraw.

Warmington, C., et al. Organizational Behavior & Performance. 1978. 19.95 (ISBN 0-87909-594-6). Reston.

Warmke, Germaine L. & Abbott, R. Tucker. Caribbean Seashells: A Guide to the Marine Mollusks of Puerto Rico & Other West Indian Islands, Bermuda & the Lower Florida Keys. LC 74-20443. (Illus.). 352p. 1975. pap. 6.00 o.p. (ISBN 0-486-21359-5). Dover.

Warmke, Roman F., et al. The Study & Teaching of Economics. (Social Science Seminar, Secondary Education Ser.: No. C28). 168p. 1980. pap. text ed. 7.95 (ISBN 0-675-08166-1). Merrill.

Warmus, William, jt. auth. see Buechner, Thomas.

Warne, Frank J. The Immigrant Invasion. LC 78-145494. (The American Immigration Library). 418p. 1971. Repr. of 1913 ed. lib. bdg. 21.95x (ISBN 0-89198-027-X). Ozer.

--The Slav Invasion & the Mine Workers: A Study in Immigration. LC 71-145495. (The American Immigration Library). 218p. 1971. Repr. of 1904 ed. lib. bdg. 10.95x o.s.i. (ISBN 0-89198-028-8). Ozer.

Warnecke, Steven J. & Suleiman, Ezra N., eds. Industrial Policies in Western Europe. LC 75-23998. 266p. 1975. text ed. 36.95 o.p. (ISBN 0-275-01670-6). Praeger.

Warner, A. R., jt. auth. see Brown, K. W.

Warner, Anne R., ed. Innovations in Community Health Nursing: Health Care Delivery in Shortage Areas. LC 77-20114. 1978. pap. text ed. 9.50 o.p. (ISBN 0-8016-5350-9). Mosby.

Warner, Blaine, jt. auth. see Leonard, John.

Warner, Carmen G. Conflict Intervention in Social-Domestic Violence. (Illus.). 256p. 1981. text ed. 19.95 (ISBN 0-87619-855-8); pap. text ed. 13.95 (ISBN 0-87619-854-X). R J Brady.

--Emergency Care: Assessment & Intervention. 3rd ed. LC 81-189985. (Illus.). 693p. 1983. pap. text ed. 24.95 (ISBN 0-8016-5352-5). Mosby.

--Rape & Sexual Assault: Management & Intervention. LC 79-24643. 364p. 1980. text ed. 32.50 (ISBN 0-89443-172-2). Aspen Systems.

Warner, Carmen G., jt. auth. see Kravis, Thomas C.

Warner, Carmen G., et al, eds. Emergency Care: Assessment & Intervention. 2nd ed. LC 77-18285. (Illus.). 538p. 1978. 21.95 o.p. (ISBN 0-8016-4744-4). Mosby.

Warner, Charles D., jt. auth. see Twain, Mark.

Warner, Charles D., et al, eds. Biographical Dictionary & Synopsis of Books, Ancient & Modern. LC 66-4326. Repr. of 1902 ed. 45.00x (ISBN 0-8103-3023-7). Gale.

Warner, Charles K. The Winegrowers of France & the Government Since 1875. LC 74-14029. 303p. 1975. Repr. of 1960 ed. lib. bdg. 19.00x (ISBN 0-8371-7779-0, WAWF). Greenwood.

Warner, D. Michael & Griffith, John R. Exercises in Quantitative Techniques for Hospital Planning & Control. LC 74-28899. 150p. 1974. pap. text ed. 15.00 o.p. (ISBN 0-914904-45-0); pap. 10.00 o.p. (ISBN 0-914904-07-8). Health Admin Pr.

Warner, Denis & Warner, Peggy. The Sacred Warriors. 272p. 1982. 24.95 (ISBN 0-442-25418-0). Van Nos Reinhold.

Warner, Dorothy D. Adapting American Antiques. 1971. 8.95 o.p. (ISBN 0-685-03345-7, 80740). Glencoe.

Warner-Eddison Associates. Words That Mean Business: Three Thousand Terms for Access to Business Information. 235p. 1981. 49.95 (ISBN 0-918212-55-3). Neal-Schuman.

Warner, Emily H., jt. auth. see McGuire, Jerry.

Warner, Ezra J. & Yearns, W. B. Biographical Register of the Confederate Congress. LC 74-77329. (Illus.). 352p. 1975. 25.00x (ISBN 0-8071-0092-7). La State U Pr.

Warner, Frank M. & McNeary, M. Applied Descriptive Geometry. 5th ed. (Illus.). 1959. text ed. 22.95 (ISBN 0-07-068298-4, C) (ISBN 0-07-068296-8). McGraw.

Warner, Frank W. Foundations of Differentiable Manifolds & Lie Groups. 1971. 27.50x (ISBN 0-673-05737-2). Scott F.

Warner, Gerald. Homelands of the Clans. 320p. 1983. 19.95 (ISBN 0-00-411128-1, Collins Pub England). Greene.

--Tales of the Scottish Highlands. 192p. 1982. 11.50 (ISBN 0-85683-060-7, Pub. by Shepheard-Walwyn); pap. 5.95 (ISBN 0-85683-061-5). Flatiron Book Dist.

Warner, Gertrude C. Schoolhouse Mystery. LC 65-23889. (Boxcar Children Mysteries-Pilot Bk.). (Illus.). 128p. (gr. 3-7). 1965. 7.50g (ISBN 0-8075-7262-4). A Whitman.

Warner, Horace E. The Ethics of Force. LC 71-137558. (The Peace Movement in America Ser). v, 126p. 1972. Repr. of 1905 ed. lib. bdg. 11.95x (ISBN 0-89198-089-X). Ozer.

Warner, J. C., jt. auth. see Vance, J. E.

Warner, J. C., et al, eds. Metallurgy of Uranium & Its Alloys. (National Nuclear Energy Ser.: Div. IV, Vol. 12). 208p. 1953. pap. 19.00 (ISBN 0-87079-273-3, NNES-IV-12A); microfilm 4.50 (ISBN 0-87079-453-1, NNES-IV-12A). DOE.

Warner, Joan. Business Calculator Operations. 2nd ed. 1982. pap. text ed. 15.95 (ISBN 0-8359-0576-4); solutions manual avail. (ISBN 0-8359-0577-2). Reston.

Warner, Joan E. Business English for Careers. (Illus.). 464p. 1980. text ed. 16.95 (ISBN 0-8359-0572-1); instrs. manual avail. Reston.

Warner, Jonathan H., jt. auth. see Jenkins, Michael D.

Warner, Ken. Handloader's Digest Bullet & Powder Update. 96p. 1980. pap. 4.95 o.s.i. (ISBN 0-695-81418-4). Follett.

Warner, Ken, ed. Gun Digest 1980. 34th ed. (Illus.). 448p. 1979. pap. 9.95 o.s.i. (ISBN 0-695-81309-9). Follett.

Warner, Kerstin P. Thomas Otway. (English Authors Ser.). 1982. lib. bdg. 15.95 (ISBN 0-8057-6733-9, Twayne). G K Hall.

Warner, Laverne & Berry, Paulette. Tunes for Tots. (ps-2). 1982. 7.95 (ISBN 0-86653-077-0, GA 414). Good Apple.

Warner, M., jt. auth. see Edelstein, J. D.

Warner, Malcolm. Organizational Choice & Constraint. (Approaches to the Sociology of Enterprise Behavior). (Illus.). 1978. 25.95x o.p. (ISBN 0-566-00180-2, 01619-5, Pub. by Saxon Hse England). Lexington Bks.

Warner, Malcolm, jt. auth. see Thomson, Andrew.

Warner, Marina. Alone of All Her Sex: The Myth & the Cult of the Virgin Mary. LC 82-40051. (Illus.). 448p. 1983. pap. 9.95 (ISBN 0-394-71155-6, Vin). Random.

--Queen Victoria's Sketchbook. (Illus.). 1979. 17.95 o.p. (ISBN 0-517-53936-5). Crown.

--The Skating Party. LC 82-73007. 192p. 1983. 10.95 (ISBN 0-689-11368-4). Atheneum.

Warner, Oliver. Captain Cook & the South Pacific. LC 63-19987. (American Heritage Junior Library). 154p. (YA) (gr. 7 up). 1963. 9.95i o.p. (ISBN 0-06-026355-5, HarpJ); PLB 14.89 (ISBN 0-06-026356-3). Har-Row.

Warner, Paul & Dublin, Lewis. Economics. (Blue Books Ser.). pap. 1.25 o.p. (ISBN 0-671-18114-9). Monarch Pr.

Warner, Peggy, jt. auth. see Warner, Denis.

Warner, Peter O. Analysis of Air Pollutants. LC 75-26685. (Environmental Science & Technology Ser.). 329p. 1976. 33.00 o.p. (ISBN 0-471-92107-6, Pub. by Wiley-Interscience). Wiley.

Warner, Ralph & Ihara, Toni. Twenty-Nine Reasons Not to Go to Law School. LC 82-99889. 128p. 1982. pap. 4.95 (ISBN 0-917316-49-5). Nolo Pr.

Warner, Raynor M., et al. New Profits from Old Buildings: Private Enterprise Approaches to Making Preservation Pay. (Illus.). 1979. 29.95 (ISBN 0-07-068315-8). McGraw.

Warner, Rebecca & Wolfe, Sidney M. Off Diabetes Pills: A Diabetic's Guide to Longer Life. 121p. 1982. 3.50 (ISBN 0-686-96258-3). Pub Citizen Health.

Warner, Rex, tr. see Augustine, Saint.

Warner, Rex, tr. see Thucydides.

Warner, Richard. APGA Licensure Committee Action Packet, 1979. 5.00 (ISBN 0-686-36561-5, 72129); nonmembers 6.75 (ISBN 0-686-37328-6). Am Personnel.

--Napoleon's Enemies. (Illus.). 1977. 14.95 o.p. (ISBN 0-85045-172-8). Hippocrene Bks.

Warner, Richard, Jr. & Brooks, David K., Jr., eds. Counselor Licensure-Issues & Perspectives: A Book of Readings. 8.50 (ISBN 0-686-36430-9, 72140); nonmembers 9.25 (ISBN 0-686-37316-2). Am Personnel.

Warner, Richard W., jt. auth. see Hansen, James C.

Warner, Sam B., Jr. The Urban Wilderness: A History of the American City. (Illus.). 384p. (Incl. bibliographic essay). 1973. pap. text ed. 13.50 scp (ISBN 0-06-046909-9, HarpC). Har-Row.

Warner, Sam B., Jr., ed. Planning for a Nation of Cities. (Orig.). 1966. pap. 3.95x (ISBN 0-262-73013-8). MIT Pr.

Warner, Samuel J. Self-Realization & Self-Defeat. LC 66-24911. 1966. pap. 12.50 (ISBN 0-394-62434-3, E453, Ever). Grove.

Warner, Steven D. & Schweer, Kathryn D., eds. Author's Guide to Journals in Nursing & Related Fields. (Author's Guide to Journals Ser.). 1982. 24.95 (ISBN 0-917724-11-9, B11). Haworth Pr.

Warner, Sylvia T. Collected Poems: Sylvia Townsend Warner. Harman, Claire, ed. 320p. 1983. 26.00 (ISBN 0-670-74993-1). Viking Pr.

--Kingdoms of Elfin. 1978. pap. 4.95 o.s.i. (ISBN 0-440-54499-8, Delta). Dell.

Warner, Val, ed. Charlotte Mew: Collected Poems & Prose. 446p. 1983. pap. 10.95 (ISBN 0-86068-223-4, Virago Pr). Merrimack Bk Serv.

Warner, Val, ed. see Mew, Charlotte.

Warner, Val, tr. see Corbiere.

Warner, Val, tr. see Corbiere, Tristan.

Warner, W. Lloyd. Black Civilization: A Social Study of an Australian Tribe. rev. ed. (Illus.). 10.00 (ISBN 0-8446-0954-4). Peter Smith.

Warner, W. Lloyd & Lunt, Paul S. The Status System of a Modern Community. LC 73-8153. (Illus.). 246p. 1973. Repr. of 1942 ed. lib. bdg. 16.00x (ISBN 0-8371-6959-3, WASM). Greenwood.

Warner, William. Distant Water: The Fate of the North Atlantic Fisherman. (Illus.). 352p. 1983. 17.45i (ISBN 0-316-92328-1). Little.

Warner, William L. Social Life of a Modern Society. 1941. text ed. 20.00x (ISBN 0-686-83769-X). Elliots Bks.

--Social Systems of American Ethnic Groups. LC 75-31425. (Yankee City Series: Vol. 3). (Illus.). 318p. 1976. Repr. of 1945 ed. lib. bdg. 38.00x (ISBN 0-8371-8502-5, WAAE). Greenwood.

--Social Systems of American Ethnic Groups. 1945. text ed. 25.00x (ISBN 0-686-83770-3). Elliots Bks.

Warner, William L. & Low, J. O. The Social System of the Modern Factory. LC 75-31426. (Yankee City Series: Vol. 4). 245p. 1976. Repr. lib. bdg. 19.25x (ISBN 0-8371-8503-3, WAMF). Greenwood.

Warner, William L., jt. auth. see Low, J. D.

Warner, William L., et al. Democracy in Jonesville: A Study in Quality & Inequality. LC 76-2034. 313p. 1976. Repr. of 1949 ed. lib. bdg. 20.00x (ISBN 0-8371-8741-9, WADJ). Greenwood.

Warner, William W. Beautiful Swimmers. 304p. 1976. pap. 3.50 (ISBN 0-686-36788-X). Md Hist.

Warnes, A. M. Geographical Perspectives on the Elderly. 478p. 1982. 46.95x (ISBN 0-471-09976-7, Pub. by Wiley-Interscience). Wiley.

Warnicke, Retha M. Women of the English Renaissance & Reformation. LC 82-12180. (Contributions in Women's Studies: No. 38). 224p. 1983. lib. bdg. 29.95 (ISBN 0-313-23611-9, HQ1596). Greenwood.

Warnke, James R. Balustrades & Gingerbread: Key West's Handcrafted Homes & Buildings. LC 78-15247. (Illus.). 1978. pap. 7.95 o.s.i. (ISBN 0-916224-43-0). Banyan Bks.

Warnken, Kelly, ed. The Directory of Fee-Based Information Services 1980-81. LC 76-55469. 1982. pap. 12.95 o.p. (ISBN 0-936288-00-0). Info Alternative.

Warnock, Connie. My Song... 1978. 4.95 o.p. (ISBN 0-533-03275-X). Vantage.

Warnock, G. J. Morality & Language. LC 82-18171. 240p. 1983. text ed. 35.00x (ISBN 0-389-20349-1). B&N Imports.

--Object of Morality. 1971. pap. 10.95x (ISBN 0-416-29900-8). Methuen Inc.

Warnock, Geoffrey J., ed. see Austin, John L.

Warnock, Mary, ed. see Mill, John S.

Warnock, Robert. Representative Modern Plays: American. 1952. pap. 9.95x (ISBN 0-673-05420-9). Scott F.

--Representative Modern Plays: British. 1953. pap. 9.95x (ISBN 0-673-05417-9). Scott F.

--Representative Modern Plays: Ibsen to Tennessee Williams. 1964. pap. 9.95x (ISBN 0-673-05415-2). Scott F.

Warnock, Robert, jt. auth. see Anderson, George K.

Warnod, Jeanine. Suzanne Valadon. (Illus.). 1981. 7.95 (ISBN 0-517-54499-7). Crown.

Warns, Johannes. Baptism. 1980. 13.25 (ISBN 0-86524-063-9, 9402). Klock & Klock.

Warr, P. Personal Goals & Work Design. 1976. 49.95x (ISBN 0-471-92095-9). Wiley.

Warr, Peter, et al. Developing Employee Relations. 216p. 1978. text ed. 26.75x (ISBN 0-566-00209-4). Gower Pub Ltd.

Warrack, B. D., jt. auth. see Naimpally, S. A.

Warrack, John. Carl Maria Von Weber. 2nd ed. LC 76-12915. (Illus.). 1976. 44.50 (ISBN 0-521-21354-1); pap. 15.95 (ISBN 0-521-29121-6). Cambridge U Pr.

--Tchaikovsky Symphonies & Concertos. LC 78-105437. (BBC Music Guides Ser.: No. 16). (Illus.). 56p. 1971. pap. 1.95 o.p. (ISBN 0-295-95109-5). U of Wash Pr.

Warren. Operating Theatre Nursing. 280p. 1983. pap. text ed. 16.95 (ISBN 0-06-318240-8, Pub. by Har-Row Ltd England). Har-Row.

Warren & Stone. Federal Income Taxation, 1982 Supplement. 1982. pap. 6.95 (ISBN 0-316-09690-3). Little.

Warren, jt. auth. see Kirby, Anthony J.

Warren, Andrew, jt. auth. see Cooke, Ronald U.

Warren, Austin. New England Saints. LC 76-28302. 1976. Repr. of 1956 ed. lib. bdg. 14.50x o.p. (ISBN 0-8371-9086-X, WANE). Greenwood.

Warren, B. A. & Jeynes, B. J. Basic Histology: A Review with Questions and Explanations. 1983. pap. write for info. (ISBN 0-316-92358-3). Little.

Warren, Barbara L. Capture Creativity. 40p. (gr. k-12). 1982. pap. 69.95 (ISBN 0-88450-200-7, 47000). Communication Skill.

Warren, Beatrice. Hood River Nurse. 1983. 6.95 (ISBN 0-686-84189-1, Avalon). Bouregy.

--Nurse in Yosemite. 1982. pap. 6.95 (ISBN 0-686-84747-4, Avalon). Bouregy.

--Nurse Paula's New Look. 1982. 6.95 (ISBN 0-686-84178-6, Avalon). Bouregy.

--Occupational Health Nurse. 1981. pap. 6.95 (ISBN 0-686-84684-2, Avalon). Bouregy.

Warren, Beverly C. Invitation to a Waltz. LC 82-45563. (Starlight Romance Ser.). 192p. 1983. 11.95 (ISBN 0-385-18398-4). Doubleday.

Warren, Bob & Model Railroader Staff, eds. Seven Hundred Sixty Four Helpful Hints for Model Railroaders. LC 65-22095. (Illus.). 64p. 1965. pap. 5.00 (ISBN 0-89024-505-3). Kalmbach.

Warren, Bruce, jt. ed. see Sears, M.

Warren, Bruce A. & Wunsch, Carl, eds. Evolution of Physical Oceanography: Scientific Surveys in Honor of Henry Stommel. 664p. 1980. 40.00x (ISBN 0-262-23104-2). MIT Pr.

Warren, David. Blindness & Early Childhood Development. LC 77-3245. 1977. 5.75 o.p. (ISBN 0-89128-074-X). Am Foun Blind.

--The Great Escaper. LC 78-26629. (Raintree Great Adventures). (Illus.). (gr. 3-6). 1979. PLB 12.85 (ISBN 0-8393-0152-9). Raintree Pubs.

--Natural Bone. LC 78-31612. (Ithaca House Fiction Ser.). 143p. 1978. 5.50 (ISBN 0-87886-095-9). Ithaca Hse.

--The World According to Two Feathers. (Ithaca House Fiction Ser.). 71p. 1973. 4.95 (ISBN 0-87886-029-0); pap. 2.95 (ISBN 0-87886-030-4). Ithaca Hse.

Warren, David G. A Legal Guide for Rural Health Programs. LC 78-27621. (Rural Health Center Ser.). (Illus.). 224p. 1979. prof ref 20.00x (ISBN 0-88410-538-5); pap. 11.95x (ISBN 0-88410-544-X). Ballinger Pub.

--Problems in Hospital Law. 3rd. ed. LC 78-15865. 339p. 1978. text ed. 26.00 (ISBN 0-89443-045-9). Aspen Systems.

Warren, Dennis M., jt. auth. see Grindal, Bruce T.

Warren, Donald R., ed. History, Education, & Public Policy: Recovering the American Educational Past. LC 77-95251. (National Society for the Study of Education, Series on Contemp. Educ. Issues). 1978. 22.00 (ISBN 0-8211-2258-4); text ed. 20.20 ten copies (ISBN 0-685-04973-6). McCutchan.

Warren, E. Kirby. Long Range Planning: Executive Viewpoint. 1966. ref. ed. 18.95 (ISBN 0-13-540187-9). P-H.

Warren, E. Kirby, jt. auth. see Newman, William H.

Warren, Earl. The Public Papers of Chief Justice Earl Warren. Christman, Henry M., ed. LC 74-10019. 237p. 1974. Repr. of 1959 ed. lib. bdg. 17.00x (ISBN 0-8371-7654-9, WAPP). Greenwood.

Warren, Edward H. Corporate Advantages Without Incorporation. LC 29-9601. x, 1012p. 1982. Repr. of 1929 ed. lib. bdg. 40.00 (ISBN 0-89941-162-2). W S Hein.

Warren, Frank A. Liberals & Communism: The "Red Decade" Revisited. LC 75-45488. 276p. 1976. Repr. of 1966 ed. lib. bdg. 18.50x (ISBN 0-8371-8738-9, WALC). Greenwood.

Warren, George. Dominant Species. Freas, Polly & Freas, Kelly, eds. LC 78-15343. (Illus.). 1979. pap. 4.95 o.p. (ISBN 0-915442-63-9, Starblaze). Donning Co.

Warren, Gloria K., jt. auth. see Stead, Evelyn S.

Warren, Harris G. Paraguay: An Informal History. LC 82-15519. (Illus.). xii, 393p. 1982. Repr. of 1949 ed. lib. bdg. 45.00x (ISBN 0-313-23651-8, WARP). Greenwood.

Warren, Henry. Artistic Anatomy of the Human Figure. (A Human Development Library Bk.). (Illus.). 131p. 1983. 47.85 (ISBN 0-86650-053-7). Gloucester Art.

Warren, Henry C. Olympic. LC 82-82580. (The Story Behind the Scenery Ser.). (Illus.). 64p. (Orig.). 1982. lib. bdg. 7.95 (ISBN 0-916122-78-6); pap. 3.50 (ISBN 0-916122-77-8). KC Pubns.

Warren, James R. & McCoy, William R. Highlights of Seattle's History. (History Ser.). (Illus.). 50p. (Orig.). pap. 2.95 (ISBN 0-686-83960-9). Hist Soc Seattle.

Warren, James V., ed. Cardiovascular Physiology. LC 74-26568. (Benchmark Papers in Human Physiology Ser: No. 4). 1975. 59.50 (ISBN 0-12-787730-4). Acad Pr.

Warren, Jean. Super Snacks. (Illus.). 64p. (Orig.). 1982. pap. 3.95 (ISBN 0-686-82677-9). Warren Pub.

Warren, Jim C., Jr., ed. National Computer Conference '78 Personal Computing Digest. (Illus.). iv, 425p. 1978. pap. 14.00 (ISBN 0-88283-011-2). AFIPS Pr.

Warren, Kenneth. North-East England. (Problem Regions in Europe Ser). (Illus.). 1973. pap. 6.95x o.p. (ISBN 0-19-913099-X). Oxford U Pr.

Warren, Kenneth F. Administrative Law in the American Political System. (Illus.). 650p. 1982. text ed. 24.95 (ISBN 0-314-63306-5). West Pub.

Warren, Kenneth S. Schistosomiasis: The Evolution of a Medical Literature 1852-1972. 1200p. 1974. 65.00x (ISBN 0-262-23057-7). MIT Pr.

Warren, Kenneth S. & Purcell, Elizabeth F., eds. The Current Status & Future Of Parasitology. LC 81-84673. (Illus.). 298p. 1982. pap. 10.00 (ISBN 0-914362-37-2). J Macy Foun.

Warren, Mame, jt. auth. see Warren, Marion E.

Warren, Marion E. & Warren, Mame. An Annapolis Portrait, Eighteen Fifty-Nine to Nineteen-Ten: The Train's Done Been & Gone. (Illus.). 96p. 1976. 19.95 (ISBN 0-686-36489-9). Md Hist.

Warren, Martyn. Financial Management for Farmers: The Basic Techniques of Money-Farming. 288p. 1982. 55.00X (ISBN 0-09-148930-X, Pub. by Hutchinson); pap. 40.00x (ISBN 0-09-148931-8). State Mutual Bk.

Warren, Mary A. Personhood. 1982. pap. write for info. (ISBN 0-918528-15-1). Edgepress.

Warren, Mary P. Lord, I'm Back Again: Story Devotions for Girls. LC 81-65651. 112p. (Orig.). 1981. pap. 3.50 (ISBN 0-8066-1887-6, 10-4098). Augsburg.

Warren, Mary P. & Mathews. Boy with a Sling. LC 65-15143. (Arch Bks: Set 2). 1965. pap. 0.89 (ISBN 0-570-06012-5, 59-1116). Concordia.

Warren, Mary P. & Rada. Little Boat That Almost Sank. LC 64-23371. (Arch Bks: Set 2). 1965. pap. 0.89 (ISBN 0-570-06010-9, 59-1111). Concordia.

Warren, Mary P. & Wind, Betty. Lame Man Who Walked Again. (Arch Bks: Set 3). 1966. laminated bdg. 0.89 (ISBN 0-570-06020-6, 59-1129). Concordia.

Warren, Mercy Otis. Plays & Poems of Mercy Otis Warren. LC 80-16625. 1980. 45.00x (ISBN 0-8201-1344-1). Schol Facsimiles.

Warren, Mervyn A. Black Preaching: Truth & Soul. 1977. pap. text ed. 9.00 (ISBN 0-8191-0173-7). U Pr of Amer.

Warren, Michael. A Future for Youth Catechesis. LC 75-9234. 120p. 1975. pap. 1.95 o.p. (ISBN 0-8091-1883-1, Deus). Paulist Pr.

--Resources for Youth Ministry. pap. 2.95 o.p. (ISBN 0-8091-2083-6). Paulist Pr.

Warren, Michael, ed. Youth Ministry: A Book of Readings. pap. 2.95 o.p. (ISBN 0-8091-2018-6). Paulist Pr.

Warren, Michael M. Genitourinary Differential Diagnosis. (Illus.). 284p. 1982. lib. bdg. 32.00 (ISBN 0-683-08801-7). Williams & Wilkins.

Warren, Neil C. Make Anger Your Ally: Harnessing Our Most Baffling Emotion. LC 82-45933. 216p. 1983. 13.95 (ISBN 0-385-18788-2). Doubleday.

Warren, Nigel. Small Motor Cruisers. (Illus.). 253p. 1976. 18.50 o.s.i. (ISBN 0-229-11537-3). Transatlantic.

Warren, Rachel L. Type-Specimens of Birds in the British Museum (Natural History) Vol. 1, Non-Passerines. ix, 320p. 1966. pap. 30.00x (ISBN 0-565-00651-7, Pub. by Brit Mus Nat Hist). Sabbot-Natural Hist Bks.

Warren, Rachel L. & Harrison, C. J. Type-Specimens of Birds in the British Museum (Natural History) Vol. 3, Systematic Index. xi, 76p. 1973. pap. 13.50x (ISBN 0-565-00716-5, Pub. by Brit Mus Nat Hist). Sabbot-Natural Hist Bks.

Warren, Rachel M. & Harrison, C. J. Type Specimens of Birds in the British Museum (Natural History) Vol. 2, Passerines. vi, 628p. 1971. pap. 60.00x (ISBN 0-565-00691-6, Pub. by Brit Mus Nat Hist). Sabbot-Natural Hist Bks.

Warren, Richard. Twelve Dynamic Bible Study Methods. 252p. 1980. pap. 7.95 (ISBN 0-88207-815-1). Victor Bks.

Warren, Robert P. All the King's Men. 512p. 1982. 5.95 o.p. (ISBN 0-15-604762-4, Harv). HarBraceJ.

--The Legacy of the Civil War. 120p. 1983. pap. 4.95x (ISBN 0-674-52175-7). Harvard U Pr.

--Now & Then: Poems, 1976-1978. 1978. 11.95 (ISBN 0-394-50164-0); pap. 5.95 (ISBN 0-394-73515-3); 15.00 o.p. ltd. ed. (ISBN 0-394-50220-5). Random.

Warren, Robert P. & Brooks, Cleanth. Understanding Fiction. 3rd ed. 1979. pap. text ed. 11.95 (ISBN 0-13-936690-3). P-H.

Warren, Robert P., jt. auth. see Brooks, Cleanth.

Warren, Robert P. & Erskine, Albert, eds. Short Story Masterpieces. pap. 3.50 (ISBN 0-440-37864-8, LE). Dell.

Warren, Robert Penn. Katherine Anne Porter: A Collection of Critical Essays. (Twentieth Century Views Ser.). 1978. 12.95 (ISBN 0-13-514679-8, Spec); pap. 3.95 (ISBN 0-13-514661-5). P-H.

Warren, Roger G. Mosby's Fundamentals of Animal Health Technology: Small Animal Anesthesia. LC 82-6421. (Illus.). 367p. 1983. pap. text ed. 17.95 (ISBN 0-8016-5398-3). Mosby.

Warren, Roger G., jt. auth. see Giovanoni, Richard.

Warren, Roger G., jt. auth. see Kleine, Lawrence J.

Warren, Roger G., jt. auth. see Tracy, Diane.

Warren, Roland L. The Community in America. 3rd ed. 1978. 22.95 (ISBN 0-395-30765-1). HM.

--New Perspectives on the American Community. 3rd ed. 1977. pap. 13.95 o.p. (ISBN 0-395-30763-5). HM.

Warren, Roland L., jt. auth. see Perlman, Robert.

Warren, Ruth. The First Book of Modern Greece. LC 66-10130. (First Bks). (Illus.). 88p. (gr. 4-6). 1972. PLB 7.90 (ISBN 0-531-00544-5). Watts.

--Modern Greece. rev. ed. (First Bks.). (Illus.). (gr. 4 up). 1979. PLB 8.90 s&l (ISBN 0-531-02934-4). Watts.

--A Pictorial History of Women in America. LC 74-83212. (Illus.). 256p. (gr. 5 up). 1975. 7.95 o.p. (ISBN 0-517-51845-7). Crown.

Warren, S. Chemistry of the Carbonyl Group: A Programmed Approach to Reaction Mechanism Chemistry. LC 74-670. 128p. 1974. 13.95x o.p. (ISBN 0-471-92104-1, Pub. by Wiley-Interscience). Wiley.

Warren, Sandra. If I Were a Road. (gr. 1-6). 1981. 5.95 (ISBN 0-86653-010-X, GA 238). Good Apple.

--If I Were a Table. (gr. 1-6). 1982. 5.95 (ISBN 0-86653-089-4, GA 440). Good Apple.

Warren Spring Laboratory, ed. Evaluation of Infrared Line Scan (IRLS) & Side-Looking Airborne Radar (SLAR) over Controlled Oil Spills in the North Sea, 1979. 1981. 45.00x (ISBN 0-686-97070-5, Pub. by W Spring England). State Mutual Bk.

--Odours Control: A Concise Guide, 1980. 1981. 85.00x (ISBN 0-686-97135-3, Pub. by W Spring England). State Mutual Bk.

--Thesaurus of Terms for Indexing the Literature of Minerals Processing & Metals Extraction, 1974. 1981. 75.00x (ISBN 0-686-97151-5, Pub. by W Spring England). State Mutual Bk.

Warren, Steven F., jt. ed. see Rogers-Warren, Ann.

Warren, Stuart. Designing Organic Syntheses: A Programmed Introduction to the Synthon Approach. LC 77-15479. 1978. 14.95x (ISBN 0-471-99612-2, Pub. by Wiley-Interscience). Wiley.

--Organic Synthesis: The Disconnection Approach. 1983. 34.95x (ISBN 0-471-10160-5, Pub. by Wiley-Interscience); wkbk. avail. (ISBN 0-471-90082-6). Wiley.

Warren, Sukanya & Mellen, Francis. Gurudev: The Life of Yogi Amrit Desai. 116p. 1982. pap. 6.95 (ISBN 0-940258-07-2). Kripalu Pubns.

Warren, T. Herbert, ed. see Tennyson, Alfred L.

Warren, Thomas B. Logic & the Bible. 1983. write for info (ISBN 0-934916-01-2). Natl Christian Pr.

Warren, Thomas B. & Elkins, Garland, eds. The Home As God Would Have It & Contemporary Attacks Against It. 1979. pap. 10.95 (ISBN 0-934916-34-9). Natl Christian Pr.
--The Living Messages of the Books of the New Testament. 1976. 11.95 o.p. (ISBN 0-934916-35-7). Natl Christian Pr.
--Sermon on the Mount. 1982. 14.95 (ISBN 0-934916-00-4). Natl Christian Pr.
Warren, Thomas F., jt. auth. see Davis, Gary A.
Warren, Tully E. Senior Citizens & Political Power: What's the Situation? (Vital Issues, Vol. XXVIII 1978-79: No. 1). 0.50 (ISBN 0-686-81616-1). Ctr Info Am.
Warren, Virgil. What the Bible Says about Salvation. LC 82-73345. (What the Bible Says Ser.). 640p. 1982. 13.50 (ISBN 0-89900-088-6). College Pr Pub.
Warren, W. L. Henry Second. (English Monarchs Ser.). 1973. 45.00x (ISBN 0-520-02282-3); pap. 8.95 (ISBN 0-520-03494-5). U of Cal Pr.
--King John. rev. ed. (Campus Ser.: No. 209). (Illus.). 362p. 1982. pap. 8.95 (ISBN 0-520-03643-3, CAL 574). U of Cal Pr.
Warren, W. Preston. Roy Wood Sellars. (World Leaders Ser). 1975. lib. bdg. 13.95 (ISBN 0-8057-3719-7, Twayne). G K Hall.
Warren, William L; see Weaver, Glenn.
Warren, William M., jt. ed. see Rubin, Neville.
Warren Bailey, Zeila, jt. auth. see Hayne, Arlene.
Warren-Boulton, Frederick. Vertical Control of Markets: Business & Labor Practices. LC 77-9618. 240p. 1977. prof ref 22.50x (ISBN 0-88410-040-5). Ballinger Pub.
Warren-Roberts, Mary P. Great Escape. (Arch Bks: Set 3). 1966. laminated bdg. 0.89 (ISBN 0-570-06016-8, 59-1125). Concordia.
Warren-Wind. Great Surprise. LC 63-23147. (Arch Bks: Set 1). (gr. 5 up). 1964. 0.89 (ISBN 0-570-06002-8, 59-1105). Concordia.
Warrick, Donald & Zawacki, Robert. Supervision Management: Understanding Behavior & Managing for Results. 496p. Date not set. pap. text ed. 18.50 scp (ISBN 0-06-046942-0, HarpC). Har-Row. Postponed.
Warrick, Louis F. see Food Processors Institute.
Warrick, Patricia, jt. auth. see Katz, Harvey A.
Warrick, Patricia S. The Cybernetic Imagination in Science Fiction. 1980. 16.50 (ISBN 0-262-23100-X). MIT Pr.
Warrick, Ruth & Preston, Don. The Confessions of Phoebe Tyler. LC 80-18272. 1980. 9.95 o.p. (ISBN 0-13-167403-X). P-H.
Warrin, George E., jt. auth. see Lopez, Ulises M.
Warriner, Doreen. Land Reform & Development in the Middle East. LC 75-31476. (Illus.). 238p. 1976. Repr. of 1962 ed. lib. bdg. 17.00x (ISBN 0-8371-8530-0, WALR). Greenwood.
Warring, R. H. A Beginner's Guide to Designing & Building Transistor Radios. (Illus.). (gr. 10). 1978. 7.95 (ISBN 0-8306-7958-8); pap. 4.95 (ISBN 0-8306-1023-5, 1023). TAB Bks.
--A Beginner's Guide to Making Electronic Gadgets. 1977. 9.95 o.p. (ISBN 0-8306-7958-8); pap. 5.95 o.p. (ISBN 0-8306-6958-2, 958). TAB Bks.
--Filters & Filtration Handbook. 300p. 1982. 57.95x (ISBN 0-87201-283-2). Gulf Pub.
--Fluids for Power Systems. (Illus.). 1970. 42.50x (ISBN 0-85461-040-5). Intl Ideas.
--Handbook of Valves, Piping & Pipelines. 1982. 65.00x (ISBN 0-87201-885-7). Gulf Pub.
--Power Tools. (Illus.). 5.50x (ISBN 0-392-04277-0, LTB). Sportshelf.
--Understanding Digital Electronics. 128p. 1982. 39.00x (ISBN 0-7188-2521-7, Pub. by Lutterworth Pr England). State Mutual Bk.
Warrington, A. R. Protective Relays: Their Theory & Practice, 2 vols. Incl. Vol. 1, 2nd ed. LC 70-385616. 484p. 1968. text ed. 44.95x (ISBN 0-412-09060-0); Vol. 2, 3rd ed. 434p. 1978. 44.95x (ISBN 0-412-15380-7). Pub. by Chapman & Hall England). Methuen Inc.
Warrington, Janet. Sweet & Natural: Desserts without Sugar, Honey, Molasses, or Artifical Sweeteners. LC 82-4962. 1982. 16.95 (ISBN 0-89594-073-6); pap. 7.95 (ISBN 0-89594-072-8). Crossing Pr.
Warrington, John, ed. The Paston Letters, 2 vols. in 1. 1978. Repr. of 1975 ed. 14.95x (ISBN 0-460-00752-1, Evman). Biblio Dist.
Warrington, John, ed. see Smith, William.
Warrior, Betsy, ed. Battered Women's Directory. 8th ed. Orig. Title: Working on Wife Abuse. (Illus.). 200p. 1982. pap. 9.50 (ISBN 0-9601544-5-0). B Warrior.
Warshauer, W., jt. auth. see Gross, M. J.
Warshauer, William, jt. auth. see Gross, Malvern J.
Warshaw. Biological Basis of Reproductive & Developmental Medicine. Date not set. price not set (ISBN 0-444-00764-4). Elsevier.
Warshaw, John H. One of Jackson's Foot Cavalry. (Collector's Library of the Civil War). 26.60 (ISBN 0-8094-4216-7). Silver.
Warshaw, Joseph B. & Hobbins, John. Perinatal Medicine in Primary Practice. 1982. 34.95 (ISBN 0-201-08294-2, Med-Nurse). A-W.
Warshaw, M., jt. auth. see Kubler-Ross, Elisabeth.
Warshofsky, Fred, jt. auth. see Stevens.
Warshow, David, ed. California: A Guide: An Illustrated History of the World's Largest University & its Environment. (Illus.). 220p. 1982. 6.95 (ISBN 0-87297-055-8). Diablo.
Warsoff, Louis A. Equality & the Law. LC 75-136089. 324p. 1975. Repr. of 1938 ed. lib. bdg. 27.50x (ISBN 0-8371-5239-9, WAEL). Greenwood.
Warson, Sydnie A., ed. AMC Jeep CJ-5, CJ-6, CJ-7: 1968-1981. (Orig.). pap. 11.95 (ISBN 0-89287-364-7). Clymer Pubns.
--Dodge Aries & Plymouth Reliant: 1981-1982. (Orig.). pap. 11.95 (ISBN 0-89287-360-4). Clymer Pubns.
--GMC J Cars: Buick Skylark, Cadillac Cimarron, Chevrolet Cavalier, Oldsmobile Firenza, Pontiac J-2000. (Orig.). pap. 11.95 (ISBN 0-89287-362-0). Clymer Pubns.
Wartak, Joseph. Clinical Pharmacokinetics: A Modern Approach to Individualized Drug Therapy. (Clinical Pharmacology & Therapeutics Ser.: Vol. 2). 232p. 1983. 35.00 (ISBN 0-03-062652-8). Praeger.
--Drug Dosage & Administration: Modern Theory & Practice. (Illus.). 208p. 1983. pap. text ed. 32.50 (ISBN 0-8391-1786-8, 19445). Univ Park.
Warters, Jane. Techniques of Counseling. 2nd ed. (Guidance Counseling & Student Personnel in Education). (Illus.). 1964. text ed. 22.00 o.p. (ISBN 0-07-068381-6, C). McGraw.
Warth, Robert D. Joseph Stalin. (World Leaders Series -Spain: No. 10). 1969. lib. bdg. 9.95 o.p. (ISBN 0-8057-3080-X, Twayne). G K Hall.
--Leon Trotsky. (World Leaders Ser.). 1977. lib. bdg. 11.95 (ISBN 0-8057-7720-2, Twayne). G K Hall.
Wartofsky, L. The Endocrine System: Disease, Diagnosis, Treatment. (Clinical Monographs Ser.). (Illus.). 1973. pap. 7.95 o.p. (ISBN 0-87618-060-8). R J Brady.
Wartofsky, M. W., ed. see Colloquim for the Philosophy of Science, Boston, 1969-1972.
Wartofsky, Marx. Feuerbach. LC 76-9180. 480p. 1982. pap. 14.95 (ISBN 0-521-28929-7). Cambridge U Pr.
Wartofsky, Marx, jt. auth. see Cohen, Robert.
Wartofsky, Marx, jt. auth. see Cohen, Robert S.
Wartofsky, Marx W., jt. auth. see Gould, Carol C.
Warton, Thomas. History of English Poetry, 4 Vols in 3. (Classics in Art & Literary Criticism Ser.). Repr. of 1774 ed. Set. 95.00 (ISBN 0-384-65930-6). Johnson Repr.
Wartski, Maureen C. The Lake is on Fire. 1982. pap. 2.25 (ISBN 0-451-11942-8, Sig Vista). NAL.
--A Long Way from Home. 1982. pap. 1.75 (ISBN 0-451-11434-5, AE1434, Vista). NAL.
--A Long Way From Home. 1982. pap. 1.75 (ISBN 0-451-11434-5, Sig Vista). NAL.
--My Brother Is Special. (YA) 1981. pap. 1.95 (ISBN 0-451-12036-1, AJ2036, Sig). NAL.
--My Brother Is Special. LC 78-23999. 1979. 8.95 (ISBN 0-664-32644-7). Westminster.
Warwick, Alan. With Whymper in the Alps. (Illus.). (gr. 7 up). 12.75x (ISBN 0-392-01945-0, LTB). Sportshelf.
--With Younghusband in Tibet. (Illus.). (gr. 7 up). 12.75x (ISBN 0-392-05624-0, SpS). Sportshelf.
Warwick, Donald P. Bitter Pills: Population Policies & Their Implementation in Eight Developing Countries. LC 81-21758. (Illus.). 256p. 1982. 24.95 (ISBN 0-521-24347-5). Cambridge U Pr.
Warwick, Donald P. & Lininger, Charles A. The Sample Survey: Theory & Practice. (Illus.). 384p. 1975. text ed. 27.50 (ISBN 0-07-068396-4, C); pap. text ed. 16.50 (ISBN 0-07-068395-6). McGraw.
Warwick, E. J. & Legates, J. E. Breeding & Improving of Farm Animals. 7th ed. (Agricultural Sciences Ser). (Illus.). 1979. text ed. 34.00 (ISBN 0-07-068375-1, C). McGraw.
Warwick, Roger, jt. auth. see Williams, Peter L.
Warwick, Roger & Williams, Peter L., eds. The Gray's Anatomy. 35th ed. LC 72-97718. (Illus.). 1500p. 1973. 39.50 (ISBN 0-7216-9127-7). Saunders.
Warwick, Ronald, jt. ed. see Paolucci, Anne.
Wasan, M. T. Parametric Estimation. 1970. text ed. 29.95 (ISBN 0-07-068400-6, C). McGraw.
--Stochastic Approximation. LC 69-11150. (Cambridge Tracts in Mathematics & Mathematical Physics). (Illus.). 1969. 39.50 (ISBN 0-521-07368-5). Cambridge U Pr.
Wasburn, Philo. Political Sociology: Approaches, Concepts, Hypotheses. (Illus.). 384p. 1982. 22.95 (ISBN 0-13-684860-5). P-H.
Wasby, Stephen, ed. Civil Liberties & Free Speech Policy. 1975. pap. 6.00 (ISBN 0-918592-13-5). Policy Studies.
Wasby, Stephen, jt. ed. see Grumm, John.
Wasby, Stephen L. Civil Liberties: Policy & Policy Making. 271p. 1976. pap. 9.95 (ISBN 0-8093-0817-7). Lexington Bks.
Wasby, Stephen L., jt. ed. see Grumm, John G.
Waseda, Yoshio. The Structure of Non-Crystalline Materials. (Illus.). 304p. 1980. text ed. 53.50 (ISBN 0-07-068426-X, C). McGraw.
Wasendorf, Russell R. Facts on Futures: Essentials of Commodity Trading. 300p. Date not set. price not set (ISBN 0-87094-292-1). Dow Jones-Irwin. Postponed.
Waser, Jurg, et al. Chem One. 2nd ed. Ricci, Jay, ed. (Illus.). 1980. text ed. 29.95 (ISBN 0-07-068432-4, C); instr's manual 26.95 (ISBN 0-07-068433-2); study guide 14.50 (ISBN 0-07-068434-0); solns. manual & suppl. materials 14.00 (ISBN 0-07-068436-7). McGraw.
Waser, P., ed. Cholinergic Mechanisms. LC 74-14485. 573p. 1975. 49.50 (ISBN 0-89004-009-5). Raven.
Waser, P., jt. ed. see Akert, K.
Washabaugh, William, jt. ed. see Woolford, Ellen.
Washam, Veronica, jt. auth. see Bilotto, Gerardo.
Washbourn, Penelope. Becoming Woman: The Quest for Spiritual Wholeness in Female Experience. LC 76-9948. 1979. pap. 6.95i (ISBN 0-06-069261-8, RD 256, HarpR). Har-Row.
Washbourn, Penelope, ed. Seasons of Woman: Song, Poetry, Ritual, Prayer, Myth, Story. LC 78-3359. (Illus.). 128p. (Orig.). 1982. pap. 4.76i (ISBN 0-06-250930-6, HarpR). Har-Row.
Washbrook, D. A. The Emergence of Provincial Politics: The Madras Presidency, 1870 to 1920. LC 75-36292. (South Asian Studies: No. 18). (Illus.). 368p. 1976. 49.50 (ISBN 0-521-20982-X). Cambridge U Pr.
Washburn, A. Periglacial Processes & Environments. 1973. 30.00 (ISBN 0-312-60095-X). St Martin.
Washburn, David E. The Peoples of Pennsylvania: An Annotated Bibliography of Resource Materials. LC 80-14437. 1981. text ed. 14.95x (ISBN 0-8229-4206-2). U of Pittsburgh Pr.
Washburn, Dorothy, ed. Hopi Kachina: Spirit of Life. California Academy of Sciences. (Illus.). 160p. (Orig.). 1980. pap. 19.95 (ISBN 0-295-95751-4, Pub. by Calif Acad Sci). U of Wash Pr.
Washburn, John M. Reason vs. the Sword: A Treatise. LC 75-137559. (Peace Movement in America Ser.). 470p. 1972. Repr. of 1873 ed. lib. bdg. 24.95x (ISBN 0-89198-090-3). Ozer.
Washburn, Mark. The Armageddon Game. LC 76-58425. 1977. 8.95 o.p. (ISBN 0-399-11934-5). Putnam Pub Group.
--Distant Encounters: The Exploration of Jupiter & Saturn. LC 82-47659. (Illus.). 296p. 1983. 22.95 (ISBN 0-15-125744-2, Harv); pap. 12.95 (ISBN 0-15-626108-1). HarBraceJ.
--Mars at Last! LC 77-8509. 1977. 8.95 o.p. (ISBN 0-399-11935-3). Putnam Pub Group.
Washburn, S. L. & Moore, Ruth. Ape into Human: A Study of Human Evolution. 2nd ed. (Illus.). 194p. 1980. pap. text ed. 6.95 (ISBN 0-316-92374-5). Little.
Washburn, Stanley. American Eyewitness: The Russo-Japanese War 1905. 1983. 12.95 (ISBN 0-8315-0140-5). Speller.
Washburn, Wilcomb E. The Indian in America. LC 74-1870. (New American Nation Ser.). (Illus.). 318p. (YA) 1975. 19.18xi06979488x (ISBN 0-06-014534-X, HarpT). Har-Row.
Washburn, Wilcomb E., ed. A Narrative of the Lord's Wonderful Dealings with John Marrant, a Black, Repr. Of 1785. Bd. with A Very Remarkable Narrative of Luke Swetland, Who Was Taken Captive Four Times in the Space of Fifteen Months. Repr. of 1785 ed. 1875 ed. with additions incl. (ISBN 0-8240-1641-6); Edward Merrifield: The Story of the Captivity & Rescue from the Indians of Luke Swetland. Merrifield, Edward. Repr. of 1915 ed; A Surprising Account of the Captivity & Escape of Philip M'Donald & Alexander M'Leod of Virginia from the Chickkemogga Indians. Repr. of 1786 ed. 1794 ed. incl. (ISBN 0-685-63633-X); A Surprising Account of the Discovery of a Lady Who Was Taken by the Indians in the Year 1777, & After Making Her Escape, She Retired to a Lonely Cave, Where She Lived Nine Years. in: Bickerstaff's Almanack for the Year...1788. Repr. of 1787 ed. 1794 ed. incl. (ISBN 0-685-63634-8). (Narratives of North American Indian Captivities Ser.). 1979. lib. bdg. 44.00 (ISBN 0-8240-1641-6). Garland Pub.
Washburne, Randel. The Coastal Kayaker: Kayak Camping on the Alaska & B.C. Coast. (Illus.). 248p. (Orig.). 1983. pap. 9.95 (ISBN 0-914718-80-0). Pacific Search.
Washington, Allyn J. Basic Technical Mathematics. 3rd ed. LC 77-71469. 1978. pap. text ed. 25.95 (ISBN 0-8053-9520-2); instr's guide 9.95 (ISBN 0-8053-9522-9). Benjamin-Cummings.
--Basic Technical Mathematics with Calculus. 3rd ed. LC 77-71470. 1978. pap. text ed. 27.95 (ISBN 0-8053-9521-0); instr's guide 9.95 (ISBN 0-8053-9522-9). Benjamin-Cummings.
--Basic Technical Mathematics with Calculus: Metric Version. 3rd ed. LC 77-71471. 1978. pap. text ed. 27.95 (ISBN 0-8053-9523-7); instr's guide 8.95 (ISBN 0-8053-9524-5). Benjamin-Cummings.
--An Introduction to Calculus with Applications. LC 71-187928. 352p. 1972. text ed. 21.95 (ISBN 0-8465-8611-8). Benjamin-Cummings.
--Introduction to Trigonometry. (Modules in Technical Mathematics: No. 3). 1974. 7.95 (ISBN 0-8465-8615-0). Benjamin-Cummings.
--Mathematics: A Developmental Approach. LC 78-65558. 1979. 20.95 (ISBN 0-8053-9527-X); instr's guide 3.95 (ISBN 0-8053-9528-8). Benjamin-Cummings.
--Technical Calculus with Analytical Geometry. 2nd ed. 1980. 23.95 (ISBN 0-8053-9519-9); instr's guide 4.95 (ISBN 0-8053-9533-4). Benjamin-Cummings.
Washington, Allyn J. & Edmond, Carolyn E. Plane Trigonometry. LC 76-7883. 1977. 21.95 (ISBN 0-8465-8622-3); instr's guide 8.95 (ISBN 0-8465-8623-1). Benjamin-Cummings.
Washington, Allyn J., et al. Essentials of Basic Mathematics. 3rd ed. 1981. 20.95 (ISBN 0-8053-9529-6). Benjamin-Cummings.
Washington, Booker T. & Park, Robert E. The Man Farthest Down: A Record of Observation & Study in Europe. (Social Science Classics, Black Classics). 1983. pap. 19.95 (ISBN 0-87855-933-7). Transaction Bks.
Washington, D.C. Chapter, Social Science Group, et al. A Sampler of Forms for Special Libraries. LC 81-8747. (Illus.). 212p. 1982. spiral bdg. 26.00 (ISBN 0-87111-262-0). SLA.
Washington Gashol Commission Staff. The American Artichoke, Vol. 1. (The Weed That Whips OPEC). 113p. 1981. pap. 10.00 (ISBN 0-939864-00-2). Wash Gasohol.
Washington, Gregory. C. I. Lewis' Theory of Meaning & Theory of Value. 1978. pap. text ed. 6.75 (ISBN 0-8191-0388-8). U Pr of Amer.
Washington, Harold R. Communication Skills & the Lawyering Process. LC 82-71697. 140p. (Orig.). 1983. pap. text ed. 12.00x (ISBN 0-86733-024-4). Assoc Faculty Pr.
Washington International Arts Letter Editors, jt. auth. see Millsaps, Daniel.
Washington, Jerome. A Bright Spot in the Yard: Stories & Notes from a Prison Journal. 112p. 1981. 13.95 (ISBN 0-89594-063-9); pap. 5.95 (ISBN 0-89594-064-7). Crossing Pr.
Washington, Mary Helen, ed. Black-Eyed Susans: Classic Stories by & About Black Women. LC 75-6169. 200p. 1975. pap. 4.50 (ISBN 0-385-09043-9, Anch). Doubleday.
Washington Opera Womens Committee, ed. The Washington Cookbook. 200p. 1982. pap. write for info. (ISBN 0-9610542-0-4). Wash Opera.
Washington Post Writers Group. The Editorial Page. 1977. pap. text ed. 11.95 (ISBN 0-395-24015-8). HM.
Washington, R. O. Program Evaluation in the Human Services. LC 80-5479. 283p. 1980. lib. bdg. 20.75 (ISBN 0-8191-1105-8); pap. text ed. 11.75 (ISBN 0-8191-1106-6). U Pr of Amer.
Washington, Ray. Cracker Florida. 160p. 1982. pap. 7.95 (ISBN 0-686-84275-8). Banyan Bks.
Washington Researchers. European Markets: A Guide to Company & Industry Information Sources. 500p. 1983. pap. text ed. 150.00 (ISBN 0-934940-17-7). Wash Res.
Washington, Robert O., jt. auth. see Meenaghan, Thomas M.
Washington, Rosemary G. Cross-Country Skiing is for Me. LC 82-7225. (Sports for Me Bks.). (Illus.). 48p. (gr. 2-5). 1982. PLB 6.95g (ISBN 0-8225-1126-6). Lerner Pubns.
--Gymnastics Is for Me. LC 79-4496. (Sports for Me Bks.). (Illus.). (gr. 2-5). 1979. PLB 6.95g (ISBN 0-8225-1078-2). Lerner Pubns.
--Softball Is for Me. LC 81-15562. (Sports for Me Bks.). (Illus.). 48p. (gr. 2-5). 1982. PLB 6.95g (ISBN 0-8225-1130-4). Lerner Pubns.
Washington, Sybil D., jt. auth. see Norris, Clarence.
Washington, William D. & Beckoff, Samuel, eds. Black Literature: An Anthology of Black Writers. pap. 3.95 o.p. (ISBN 0-671-18701-5). Monarch Pr.
Washington, Willie, III. This. 1979. 4.50 o.p. (ISBN 0-533-03728-X). Vantage.
Washizu, Kyuichiro. Variational Methods in Elasticity & Plasticity. 2nd ed. 1975. text ed. 69.00 (ISBN 0-08-017653-4). Pergamon.
Washnis, George J. Productivity Improvement Handbook for State & Local Government. LC 80-11254. 1492p. 1980. 75.00x (ISBN 0-471-04638-8, Pub. by Wiley-Interscience). Wiley.
Wasiloff, T. Machine Shop Safety Kit: Set 1. 1974. Kit Set. 315.00 (ISBN 0-07-079410-3, G); instr's manual 4.50 (ISBN 0-07-068419-7); wkbk. 12.50 (ISBN 0-07-068413-8). McGraw.
--OXY-Acetylene Welding Safety. 1974. Kit. 110.00 (ISBN 0-07-079412-X, G); wkbk. 7.95 (ISBN 0-07-068418-9). McGraw.
Wasiolek, Edward, jt. auth. see Bauer, Raymond A.
Waskey, Frank H., jt. auth. see Warfel, M. C.
Wasko, Janet. Movies & Money: Financing the American Film Industry. (Communication & Information Science Ser.). 1982. text ed. 27.50 (ISBN 0-89391-108-9); pap. text ed. 14.95 (ISBN 0-89391-131-3). Ablex Pub.
Waskow, Arthur I. Godwrestling. LC 78-54389. 1978. 9.95 o.p. (ISBN 0-8052-3691-0). Schocken.
--Godwrestling. LC 78-54389. 208p. 1980. pap. 4.95 o.p. (ISBN 0-8052-0645-0). Schocken.
Wasks, Janet, jt. ed. see Mosoo, Vincent.
Wasley, John. Beginner's Guide to Photography. 1974. 20.00 o.p. (ISBN 0-7207-0696-3). Transatlantic.
--Black & White Photography. (Photographer's Library). (Illus.). 168p. 1983. pap. 12.95 (ISBN 0-240-51117-4). Focal Pr.
Wasley, John & Hill, Ron. A Guide to Hi-Fi. 1977. 15.00 o.p. (ISBN 0-7207-0906-7). Transatlantic.
Wasmuth, Eleanor. What's That Noise? (Illus.). 10p. (ps-3). 1981. 3.50 (ISBN 0-448-46825-5, G&D). Putnam Pub Group.

Wasmuth, Eleanor, illus. Look at the Seashore. (Illus.). 14p. (ps). 1982. 2.95 (ISBN 0-448-12309-6, G&D). Putnam Pub Group.

Wasmuth, W. & Greerhalgh, L. Effective Supervision: Developing Your Skills Through Critical Incidents. 1979. pap. 16.95 (ISBN 0-13-246462-4). P-H.

Wason, P. C., jt. ed. see Johnson-Laird, P. N.

Wasen, Peter, ed. Dynamics of Writing. 94p. 6.00 (ISBN 0-686-95308-8); members 5.00 (ISBN 0-686-99491-4). NCTE.

Wason, Sandy, jt. ed. see Grierson, Herbert J.

Wasow, Mona. Coping with Schizophrenia. LC 81-86713. 12.95 (ISBN 0-8314-0062-5); pap. 8.95 (ISBN 0-686-82342-7). Sci & Behavior.

Wasp, Edward J., et al. Solid-Liquid Flow Slurry Pipeline Transportation. 240p. 1979. 44.95x (ISBN 0-87201-809-1). Gulf Pub.

Wass, Alonzo. Data Book for Residential Contractors & Estimators. (Illus.). 1979. 20.95 (ISBN 0-87909-177-0). Reston.

--Estimating Residential Construction. (Illus.). 1980. text ed. 23.95 (ISBN 0-13-289942-6). P-H.

--Methods & Materials of Residential Construction. 2nd ed. LC 76-39990. 1977. ref. ed. 22.95 (ISBN 0-87909-488-5); text ed. 17.95 (ISBN 0-686-96868-9). Reston.

--Understanding Construction Law. 1982. text ed. 18.95 (ISBN 0-8359-8021-9). Reston.

Wass, Alonzo & Sanders, Gordon. Materials & Procedures for Residential Construction. (Illus.). text ed. 20.95 (ISBN 0-8359-4284-8). Reston.

Wass, H. & Corr, C. A. Helping Children Cope with Death. 1982. 32.00 (ISBN 0-07-068427-8). McGraw.

Wass, Hannelore & Corr, Charles A., eds. Childhood & Death. LC 82-23365. (Death, Education, Aging, & Health Care). (Illus.). 400p. 1983. text ed. 24.50 (ISBN 0-89116-320-4). Hemisphere Pub.

Wass, Hennelore. Dying: Facing the Facts. (Illus.). 1979. text ed. 32.50 (ISBN 0-07-068438-3, HP); pap. text ed. 15.95 (ISBN 0-07-068437-5). McGraw.

Wass, Stan & Alvord, David W. Twenty-Five Ski Tours in Connecticut. LC 78-56107. (Twenty-Five Ski Tours Ser.). (Illus.). 128p. 1978. pap. 4.95 (ISBN 0-912274-95-6). Backcountry Pubns.

Wasser, Clinton H. see Scott, Thomas G.

Wasser, Samuel K., ed. Social Behavior of Female Vertebrate. LC 82-11602. write for info. (ISBN 0-12-735950-8). Acad Pr.

Wasserberger, Jonathan & Eubanks, David H. Advanced Paramedic Procedures: A Practical Approach. LC 76-25886. (Illus.). 154p. 1977. pap. 11.95 o.p. (ISBN 0-8016-5351-7). Mosby.

Wasserberger, Jonathan & Eubanks, David. Practical Paramedic Procedures. 2nd ed. LC 81-458. (Illus.). 222p. 1981. 14.95 (ISBN 0-8016-5353-3). Mosby.

Wasserman, A. I., jt. ed. see Schneider, H. J.

Wasserman, A. I., jt. ed. see Weber, H.

Wasserman, Edward & Gromisch, Donald S. Survey of Clinical Pediatrics. 7th ed. (Illus.). 560p. 1981. text ed. 34.00 (ISBN 0-07-068431-6, HP). McGraw.

Wasserman, Elga, et al, eds. Women in Academia: Evolving Policies Toward Equal Opportunities. LC 74-1734. (Special Studies). (Illus.). 188p. 1975. 26.95 o.p. (ISBN 0-275-09530-4). Praeger.

Wasserman, G. B. Politics of Decolonization. LC 75-2735. (African Studies: No. 17). (Illus.). 224p. 1976. 37.50 (ISBN 0-521-20838-6). Cambridge U Pr.

Wasserman, Gary. The Basics of American Politics. 3rd ed. 1982. pap. text ed. 10.95 (ISBN 0-316-92425-3); tchrs'. manual avail. (ISBN 0-316-92426-1). Little.

Wasserman, George R. John Dryden. (English Authors Ser.). 1964. lib. bdg. 12.95 (ISBN 0-8057-1176-7, Twayne). G K Hall.

--Roland Barthes. (World Authors Ser.). 13.95 (ISBN 0-8057-6456-9, TWayne). G K Hall.

--Samuel "Hudibras" Butler. (English Author Ser.). 1976. lib. bdg. 13.95 (ISBN 0-8057-6667-7, Twayne). G K Hall.

Wasserman, Gerald S. Color Vision: An Historical Introduction. LC 78-5346. (Wiley Ser. in Behavior). 1978. 35.00x (ISBN 0-471-92128-9, Pub. by Wiley-Interscience). Wiley.

Wasserman, Harry, jt. auth. see Bubis, Gerald B.

Wasserman, Julian N., jt. auth. see Clark, Susan L.

Wasserman, Julian N. & Linsley, Joy L., eds. Edward Albee: An Interview & Essays. 184p. 1983. text ed. 18.00 (ISBN 0-8156-8106-2); pap. text ed. 10.00 (ISBN 0-8156-8107-0). U of St Thomas.

Wasserman, Lou. Raise & Show Guppies. (Illus.). 1977. pap. 6.95 (ISBN 0-87666-453-2, PS-738). TFH Pubns.

Wasserman, Mark, jt. auth. see Keen, Benjamin.

Wasserman, Miriam. School Fix, NYC, U. S. A. 1971. pap. 3.95 o.p. (ISBN 0-671-21070-X, Touchstone Bks). S&S.

Wasserman, Paul. Law & Legal Information Directory. 2nd ed. 580p. 1982. 148.00x (ISBN 0-8103-0172-5). Gale.

--Librarian & the Machine. LC 65-25320. 1965. 22.00x (ISBN 0-8103-0164-4). Gale.

Wasserman, Paul, ed. Awards, Honors & Prizes: International & Foreign, Vol.2. 5th ed. LC 78-16691. (Vol. 2). 600p. 1982. PLB 98.00x (ISBN 0-8103-0379-5). Gale.

--Awards, Honors & Prizes: United States & Canada, Vol. 1. 5th ed. 600p. 1982. 90.00x (ISBN 0-8103-0380-9). Gale.

--Catalog of Museum Publications & Media. 2nd ed. LC 79-22633. 1980. 210.00x (ISBN 0-8103-0388-4). Gale.

--Commodity Prices: A Source Book & Index. LC 73-19898. 200p. 1974. 36.00x (ISBN 0-8103-0369-8). Gale.

--Consultants & Consulting Organizations Directory. 5th ed. 1000p. 1982. 235.00x (ISBN 0-686-71974-3). Gale.

--Speakers & Lecturers: How to Find Them, 2 vols. 2nd ed. 350p. 1981. Set. 115.00x (ISBN 0-8103-0393-0). Gale.

--Training & Development Organizations Directory. 2nd ed. 1980. 180.00x (ISBN 0-8103-0314-0). Gale.

--Training & Development Organizations Directory. 3rd ed. 1982. 190.00x (ISBN 0-8103-0432-5). Gale.

--Who's Who in Consulting, 3 pts. 1982. Set. pap. 130.00x (ISBN 0-8103-0361-2). Gale.

Wasserman, Paul & Bernero, Jacqueline, eds. Statistics Sources. 7th ed. 975p. 1982. 150.00x (ISBN 0-8103-0399-X). Gale.

Wasserman, Paul & Herman, Esther, eds. Festivals Sourcebook: A Reference Guide to Fairs, Festivals, & Celebrations. 1st ed. LC 76-48852. 1977. 90.00x (ISBN 0-8103-0311-6). Gale.

--Library Bibliographies & Indexes: A Subject Guide to Resource Material Available from Libraries, Information Centers, Library Schools, & Library Associations in the U. S. & Canada. LC 74-26741. xii, 301p. 1975. 74.00x (ISBN 0-8103-0390-6). Gale.

Wasserman, Paul & Kaszubski, Marek, eds. Law & Legal Information Directory: A Guide to National & International Organizations, Bar Associations, Federal Court System, Federal Regulatory Agencies, Law Schools, Continuing Legal Education, Scholarships & Grants, Awards & Prizes, Special Libraries, Information Systems & Services, Research Centers, Etc. 800p. 1980. 135.00 o.p. (ISBN 0-8103-0169-5). Gale.

Wasserman, Paul & McLean, Janice, eds. New Consultants, Periodical Supplement for Consultants & Consulting Organizations Directory: Four Issues Covering the Period Between Editions, Issue 1. 5th ed. 1979. 200.00x (ISBN 0-8103-0351-5). Gale.

--Who's Who in Consulting: A Reference Guide to Professional Personnel Engaged in Consultation for Business, Industry & Government. 2nd ed. LC 73-16373. 1973. 130.00x (ISBN 0-8103-0360-4). Gale.

Wasserman, Paul & Morgan, Jean, eds. Consumer Sourcebook, 2 vols. 3rd ed. 1800p. 1981. Set. 115.00x (ISBN 0-8103-0383-3). Gale.

--Ethnic Information Sources of the United States: A Guide to Organizations, Agencies, Foundations, Institutions, Media, Commercial & Trade Bodies, Government Programs, Research Institutes, Libraries & Museums, Etc. 2nd ed. LC 76-4642. 350p. 1981. 100.00x (ISBN 0-8103-0367-1). Gale.

Wasserman, Paul & Wasserman, Steven R., eds. Recreation & Outdoor Life Directory. LC 79-4594. 500p. 1979. 86.00x (ISBN 0-8103-0315-9). Gale.

Wasserman, Paul, ed. see Change Institute. University of Maryland.

Wasserman, Paul, et al, eds. Encyclopedia of Business Information Sources. 4th, rev. ed. LC 79-24771. 1980. 130.00x (ISBN 0-8103-0368-X). Gale.

--Encyclopedia of Geographic Information Sources. 3rd ed. LC 78-55032. 1978. 70.00x (ISBN 0-8103-0374-4). Gale.

--LIST: Library & Information Services Today, Vol. 5. LC 74-7634. 633p. 1975. 65.00x (ISBN 0-8103-0387-6). Gale.

--LIST: Library & Information Services Today, an International Registry of Research & Innovation, Vol. 4. LC 74-7634. 548p. 1974. 65.00x (ISBN 0-8103-0386-8). Gale.

--Learning Independently: A Directory of Self-Instruction Resources, Including Correspondence Courses, Programmed Learning Products, Audio Cassettes, Multi-Media Kits & Conversational Learning Materials Such As Books Intended for Non-Formal Education. 2nd ed. 452p. 1982. 140.00x (ISBN 0-8103-0318-3). Gale.

Wasserman, Pauline & Wasserman, Sheldon. A Guide to Fortified Wines. LC 82-62295. (Illus.). 200p. 1983. pap. 9.95 (ISBN 0-910793-01-8). Marlborough Pr.

Wasserman, Rosanne, ed. see Ainworth, Maryan W. & Brealy, John.

Wasserman, Rosanne, ed. see O'Neill, John P.

Wasserman, Rosanne, ed. see Pekarik, Andrew J.

Wasserman, Rosanne, ed. see Takeshi, Nagatake.

Wasserman, Rosanne, ed. see Watts, Edith.

Wasserman, Sheldon, jt. auth. see Wasserman, Pauline.

Wasserman, Steven R., ed. Lively Arts Information Directory. 800p. 1982. 98.00x (ISBN 0-8103-0320-5). Gale.

Wasserman, Steven R., jt. ed. see Wasserman, Paul.

Wassermann, Jacob. Caspar Hauser. 1956. 6.95 o.s.i. (ISBN 0-87140-818-X). Liveright.

Wasserstein, Bernard. Britain & the Jews of Europe 1939-1945. 1979. 22.50x (ISBN 0-19-822600-4). Oxford U Pr.

Wasserstein, Bruce. Corporate Finance Law: A Guide for the Executive. 1979. 28.95 (ISBN 0-07-068423-5, P&RB). McGraw.

Wassersug, Joseph D. Jarm-How to Jog with Your Arms to Live Longer. LC 81-10919. 1983. 12.95 (ISBN 0-87949-197-3). Ashley Bks.

Wassink, Jan, jt. auth. see Gildart, R. C.

Wassmer, S. J. Christian Ethics Today. 1969. pap. text ed. 4.95 o.p. (ISBN 0-02-829680-X). Glencoe.

Wasson, Ben. Count No'Count: Flashbacks to Faulkner. (Center for the Study of Southern Culture Ser.). (Illus.). 208p. 1983. 12.95 (ISBN 0-87805-162-7). U Pr of Miss.

Wasson, John, et al. The Common Symptom Guide. 368p. (Orig.). 1975. pap. text ed. 12.95 (ISBN 0-07-068435-9, HP). McGraw.

Wasson, John M. Subject & Structure: An Anthology for Writers. 7th ed. 1981. pap. text ed. 11.95 (ISBN 0-316-92423-7); tchr's manual avail. (ISBN 0-316-92424-5). Little.

Wasson, R. Gordon. The Wonderous Mushroom: Mycolatry in Mesoamerica. LC 79-26895. (Illus.). 178p. 1980. 14.95-op (ISBN 0-07-068441-3); deluxe ed. 525.00 (ISBN 0-07-068442-1); pap. 10.95-op (ISBN 0-07-068443-X). McGraw.

Wasson, Valentina P. The Chosen Baby. 3rd ed. Coalson, Glo, tr. LC 76-41391. 1977. 7.64i (ISBN 0-397-31738-7, HarpJ). Har-Row.

Waswo, Ann. Japanese Landlords: The Decline of a Rural Elite. 1977. 23.50x (ISBN 0-520-03217-9). U of Cal Pr.

Watabe, Masakazu & Gilbert, Kent S. Japanese: A Graded Approach to Reading, Writing & Vocabulary Building. 336p. 1983. 18.50 (ISBN 0-8048-1448-1). C E Tuttle.

Watanabe, F. Philosophy & Its Development in the Nikayas & Abhidharma. 250p. Date not set. 15.00 (ISBN 0-89581-157-X). Lancaster-Miller.

Watanabe, M. S. Knowing & Guessing: A Quantitative Study of Inference & Information. 1969. 39.95 o.p. (ISBN 0-471-92130-0, Pub. by Wiley-Interscience). Wiley.

Watanabe, Ruth T. Introduction to Music Research. 1967. 19.95 (ISBN 0-13-489641-6). P-H.

Watanabe, S., jt. auth. see Ikeda, N.

Watanabe, S., ed. Frontiers of Pattern Recognition. 1972. 54.50 (ISBN 0-12-737140-0). Acad Pr.

--Methodologies of Pattern Recognition. 1969. 62.00 (ISBN 0-12-737150-8). Acad Pr.

Watanabe, Shigeo. Get Set! Go! (I Can Do It All by Myself). (Illus.). 32p. 1981. 6.95 (ISBN 0-399-20780-5, Philomel); lib. bdg. 6.99g (ISBN 0-399-61175-4). Putnam Pub Group.

--How Do I Put It on? LC 79-12714. (I Can Do It All by Myself Ser.). (Illus.). (gr. 2-4). 1979. 6.95 (ISBN 0-399-20761-9, Philomel); PLB 6.99 (ISBN 0-399-61166-5). Putnam Pub Group.

--I Can Ride It! (I Can Do It All By Myself Bks.). (Illus.). 32p. 1982. 7.95 (ISBN 0-399-20867-4, Philomel); PLB 7.99 (ISBN 0-399-61194-0). Putnam Pub Group.

--I'm the King of the Castle. (I Can Do It All By Myself Bks.). (Illus.). 32p. 1982. 7.95 (ISBN 0-399-20868-2, Philomel); PLB 7.99 (ISBN 0-399-61195-9). Putnam Pub Group.

--What a Good Lunch! LC 79-19535. (I Can Do It All by Myself Bks.). (Illus.). 28p. (ps). 1980. 6.95 (ISBN 0-399-20811-9, Philomel); PLB 6.99 o.p. (ISBN 0-399-61181-9). Putnam Pub Group.

--Where's My Daddy? (Illus.). 32p. 1982. 7.95 (ISBN 0-399-20899-2, Philomel). Putnam Pub Group.

Watanabe, Yuichi. Wally the Whale Who Loved Balloons. Ooka, Diane, tr. from Japanese. (Illus.). 1982. 8.95 (ISBN 0-89346-150-4). Heian Intl.

Watanade, Tokuji & Kishi, Asako. The Book of Soybeans: Nature's Miracle Protein. LC 81-80832. (Illus.). 192p. 1982. pap. 12.95 (ISBN 0-686-97678-9). Kodansha.

Watchman, Paul, jt. ed. see Robson, Peter.

Watchman, T. S. A Quem Enviarei. (Port.). 1980. pap. 1.20 (ISBN 0-8297-0652-6). Life Pubs Intl.

Watchman Nee. The Messenger of the Cross. Kaung, Stephen, tr. (Orig.). 1980. pap. text ed. 3.10 (ISBN 0-935008-50-0). Christian Fellow Pubs.

Watchorn, G. W. Medical Calculations for Nurses. 2nd ed. 84p. 1976. pap. 2.95 (ISBN 0-571-04915-X). Faber & Faber.

Wateman, Arthur E. Susan Glaspell. (United States Auhtors Ser.). 14.95 (ISBN 0-8057-0328-4, Twayne). G K Hall.

Water, Michael. Fish Light. 55p. 1975. 3.50 (ISBN 0-87886-068-1). Ithaca Hse.

Water Pollution Control Federation, jt. auth. see American Society of Civil Engineers.

Water Pollution Control Federation, ed. see Research Symposia-53rd Conference, 80.

Water Pollution Control Federation, et al. Glossary: Water & Wastewater Control Engineering. 440p. 1981. 25.00 (ISBN 0-686-36997-1, M0022). Water Pollution.

Water Pollution Control Federation. History of the Water Pollution Control Federation 1928-1977. 320p. Date not set. pap. 5.00 (ISBN 0-943244-28-5). Water Pollution.

--Industrial Wastes Symposia: Proceedings. Date not set. pap. 20.00 o.p. (ISBN 0-686-30423-3). Water Pollution.

--Laboratory Management. (Manual of Pratice System Management Ser.: No. 1). (Illus.). 56p. 1981. 8.00 (ISBN 0-686-36998-X). Water Pollution.

--Pretreatment of Industrial Waste. (Manual of Practice Facilities Development Ser.: No. 3). (Illus.). 157p. 1981. 14.00 (ISBN 0-686-36999-8). Water Pollution.

--Salaries of Wastewater Personnel. (Illus.). 50p. 1980. 12.50 (ISBN 0-686-37000-7, E0299). Water Pollution.

Water Pollution Control Federation, et al. Waste Stabilization Ponds Training Package. (Illus.). 1981. 16.00 (ISBN 0-686-37001-5, E0360). Water Pollution.

Water Pollution Control Federation. Wastewater Sampling for Process & Quality Control, 1980: Manual of Practice, Operation & Maintenance - I. 101p. Date not set. pap. 12.00 (ISBN 0-943244-21-8). Water Pollution.

Water Pollution Control Federation Staff. Design & Construction of Sanitary & Storm Sewers ('69) (Manual of Practice Ser.: No. 9). Date not set. 17.00 (ISBN 0-943244-09-9). Water Pollution.

Water Research Enter. Water Purification in the EEC. LC 77-5475. 1977. pap. write for info. o.p. (ISBN 0-08-021225-5). Pergamon.

Waterbury Clock Co. Waterbury Clocks: The Complete Illustrated Catalog of 1983. 2nd ed. (Illus.). 128p. 1983. pap. 5.00 (ISBN 0-486-24460-1). Dover.

Waterbury, John. The Egypt of Nasser & Sadat: The Political Economy of Two Regimes. LC 82-61393. (Princeton Studies on the Near East). (Illus.). 496p. 1983. 45.00x (ISBN 0-691-07650-2); pap. 12.50 (ISBN 0-691-10147-7). Princeton U Pr.

Waterbury, John & Mallakh, Ragaei E. The Middle East in the Coming Decade: From Wellhead to Well-Being. (Council on Foreign Relations 1980's Project Ser.). 1978. text ed. 14.95x (ISBN 0-07-068445-6, P&RB); pap. 5.95 (ISBN 0-07-068446-4). McGraw.

Waterbury, Ruth & Arceri, Gene. Elizabeth Taylor: Her Loves, Her Future. 1982. pap. 3.50 (ISBN 0-553-22613-4). Bantam.

Waterfield, Gordon. Sultans of Aden. 1970. 10.00 o.p. (ISBN 0-7195-1793-1). Transatlantic.

Waterfield, Robin A., tr. see Plato.

Waterford, Giles. Faces. LC 82-3935. (Looking At Art Ser.). (Illus.). 48p. 1982. 11.95 (ISBN 0-689-50251-6, McElderry Bk). Atheneum.

Waterford, Van. All About Telephones. 190p. 1978. 5.95 (ISBN 0-686-98101-4). Telecom Lib.

Waterhouse. Abingdon Clergy Income Tax Guide, 1983: For 1982 Returns. Rev. ed. 96p. (Orig.). 1983. pap. 4.95 (ISBN 0-687-00384-9). Abingdon.

Waterhouse, E. The Dictionary of British Eighteenth Century Painters in Oils & Crayons. 79.50 o.p. (ISBN 0-686-95482-3). Antique Collect.

Waterhouse, James. Water Engineering for Agriculture. (Illus.). 368p. 1981. 45.00 (ISBN 0-7134-1409-X, Pub. by Batsford England). David & Charles.

Waterhouse, Keith, tr. see De Filippo, Eduardo.

Waterhouse, Philip. Managing the Learning Process. (Illus.). 191p. 1983. pap. 13.50 (ISBN 0-686-84664-8). Nichols Pub.

Waterhouse, R. B. Fretting Fatigue. 1981. 45.00 (ISBN 0-85334-932-0, Pub. by Applied Sci England). Elsevier.

Waterhouse, Robert, jt. auth. see Clifford, John.

Waterloo, Stanley. Armageddon. (Science Fiction Ser.). 280p. 1976. Repr. of 1898 ed. lib. bdg. 13.00 o.p. (ISBN 0-8398-2348-7, Gregg). G K Hall.

Waterlow, Charlotte & Evans, Archibald. Europe, Nineteen Forty-Five to Nineteen Seventy. 1975. pap. text ed. 7.95x o.p. (ISBN 0-423-89250-9). Methuen Inc.

Waterlow, J. C. & Stephen, J. M. Nitrogen Metabolism in Man. 1982. 100.50 (ISBN 0-85334-991-6, Pub. by Applied Sci England). Elsevier.

Waterlow, Sarah. Nature, Change, & Agency in Aristotle's Physics: A Philosophical Study. 1982. 29.95x (ISBN 0-19-824653-6). Oxford U Pr.

--Passage & Possibility: A Study of Aristotle's Modal Concepts. 1982. 24.50x (ISBN 0-19-824656-0). Oxford U Pr.

Waterman & Andrews. Designing Short-Term Instructional Programs. 1979. 4.00 (ISBN 0-686-38072-X). Assn Tchr Ed.

Waterman, Andrew. Out for the Elements. 151p. 1981. pap. text ed. 8.50x (ISBN 0-85635-377-9, 90190, Pub. by Carcanet New Pr England). Humanities.

--Over the Wall. 80p. (Orig.). 1980. pap. text ed. 7.96x (ISBN 0-85635-230-6, Pub. by Carcanet New Pr England). Humanities.

Waterman, Arthur. Chronology of American Literary History. LC 74-94878. 1970. pap. text ed. 3.50x (ISBN 0-675-09407-0). Merrill.

Waterman, Don & Hayes-Roth, Rick, eds. Pattern-Directed Inference Systems. 1978. 54.00 (ISBN 0-12-737550-3). Acad Pr.

Waterman, Isaac. The Ultimate Goals of Israel's World Policies. (Illus.). 117p. 1983. 87.85 (ISBN 0-86722-017-1). Inst Econ Pol.

Waterman, John T. Leibniz & Ludolf on Things Linguistic: Excerpts from Their Correspondence, (1688-1703) (Publications in Linguistics: No. 88). 1978. pap. 14.00x (ISBN 0-520-09586-3). U of Cal Pr.

Waterman, Leroy. Religion Faces the World Crisis. 1943. 3.75x (ISBN 0-685-21800-7). Wahr.

Waterman, Peter, jt. ed. see Gutkind, Pete C. W.

Waterman, Peter, jt. ed. see Gutkind, Peter C. W.
Waterman, Robert H., Jr., jt. auth. see Peters, Thomas J.
Waterman, T. H., ed. The Physiology of Crustacea, 2 vols. Incl. Vol. 1. Metabolism & Growth. 1960. 72.00 (ISBN 0-12-737601-1); Vol. 2. Sense Organs, Integration & Behavior. 1961. 72.00 (ISBN 0-12-737602-X). Set. 103.00 (ISBN 0-686-76924-4). Acad Pr.
Waterman, V. Ann. Surface Pattern Design. (Illus.). 104p. (Orig.). 1983. 16.95 (ISBN 0-8038-6779-4). Hastings.
Waterman, William H. The Long & Narrow Road. 1983. 10.00 (ISBN 0-533-05572-5). Vantage.
Waters, Alice L. The Chez Panisse Menu Cookbook. (Illus.). 1982. 16.95 (ISBN 0-394-51787-3). Random.
Waters, Andrew W. All the U. S. Air Force's Airplanes 1907-1980. (Illus.). 1983. 30.00 (ISBN 0-88254-582-5). Hippocrene Bks.
Waters, Anthony. An Introduction to Deductive Argument Analysis. LC 81-40311. (Illus.). 286p. (Orig.). 1982. lib. bdg. 23.00 (ISBN 0-8191-2095-2); pap. text ed. 11.50 (ISBN 0-8191-2096-0). U Pr of Amer.
Waters, Clara E. A Handbook of Legendary & Mythological Art. 520p. 1983. pap. 9.50 (ISBN 0-88072-013-1). Tanager Bks.
Waters, Donald J. Strange Ways & Sweet Dreams: Afro-American Folklore from the Hampton Institute. 466p. 1983. lib. bdg. 49.95 (ISBN 0-8161-9022-4, Univ Bks). G K Hall.
Waters, Ethel & Michel, Charles. His Eye Is on the Sparrow. 1972. pap. 2.95 o.p. (ISBN 0-515-06738-5). Jove Pubns.
Waters, Frank. Book of the Hopi. (Illus.). 1977. pap. 4.95 o.p. (ISBN 0-14-004527-9). Penguin.
--Man Who Killed the Deer. LC 82-71264. 266p. 1942. 9.95 o.p. (ISBN 0-8040-0193-6); pap. 6.95 (ISBN 0-8040-0194-4). Swallow.
--Masked Gods: Navaho & Pueblo Ceremonialism. LC 82-71280. 438p. 1950. 16.95 (ISBN 0-8040-0196-0); pap. 8.95 (ISBN 0-8040-0641-5). Swallow.
--Mexico Mystique: The Coming Sixth World of Consciousness. LC 82-73625. (Illus.). 326p. 1975. 15.95 (ISBN 0-8040-0663-6, SB). Swallow.
--Midas of the Rockies: The Story of Stratton & Cripple Creek. LC 82-72908. 347p. 1972. pap. 7.95 (ISBN 0-8040-0591-5, SB). Swallow.
--Mountain Dialogues. LC 82-75083. x, 237p. 1981. 15.95 (ISBN 0-8040-0361-0, SB). Swallow.
--People of the Valley. LC 82-71652. 201p. 1941. 10.95 (ISBN 0-8040-0242-8, SB); pap. 6.95 (ISBN 0-8040-0243-6). Swallow.
--Pikes Peak: A Family Saga. LC 82-72460. 743p. 1971. 15.95 (ISBN 0-8040-0503-6, SB). Swallow.
--Pumpkin Seed Point: Being Within the Hopi. LC 82-71769. 175p. 1973. 9.95 (ISBN 0-8040-0255-X); pap. 5.95 (ISBN 0-8040-0635-0). Swallow.
--To Possess the Land: A Biography of Arthur Rochford Manby. LC 82-73526. (Illus.). 287p. 1973. 12.95 (ISBN 0-8040-0647-4, SB). Swallow.
--The Woman at Otowi Crossing: A Novel. LC 82-72312. 300p. 1981. pap. 8.95 (ISBN 0-8040-0415-3, SB). Swallow.
--The Yogi of Cockroach Court. LC 82-73336. 277p. 1947. pap. 6.95 (ISBN 0-8040-0613-X, SB). Swallow.
Waters, Frank, ed. see Evans-Wentz, W. Y.
Waters, John F. Camels: Ships of the Desert. LC 73-14514. (A Let's Read-&-Find-Out Science Bk.). (Illus.). (ps-3). 1974. 8.95 o.p. (ISBN 0-690-00394-3, TYC-J); PLB 10.89 (ISBN 0-690-00395-1). Har-Row.
--Crime Labs: The Science of Forensic Medicine. LC 78-23890. (Impact Ser.). (Illus.). (gr. 7 up). 1979. PLB 8.90 s&l (ISBN 0-531-02286-2). Watts.
--Fishing. LC 77-12679. (First Bks.). (Illus.). (gr. 4-6). 1978. PLB 8.90 s&l (ISBN 0-531-01407-X). Watts.
--Hungry Sharks. LC 72-7563. (A Let's-Read-&-Find-Out Science Bk). (Illus.). 40p. (ps-3). 1974. PLB 10.89 (ISBN 0-690-01121-0, TYC-J). Har-Row.
--A Jellyfish Is Not a Fish. LC 77-26594. (Let's-Read-&-Find-Out Bk.). (Illus.). (gr. k-3). 1979. 10.53i (ISBN 0-690-03888-7, TYC-J); PLB 9.89 (ISBN 0-690-03889-5). Har-Row.
--Summer of the Seals. LC 78-6712. (Illus.). (gr. 3-6). 1978. 6.95 o.p. (ISBN 0-7232-6155-5). Warne.
Waters, Kathleen & Murphy, Gretchen. Medical Records in Health Information. LC 79-18793. 706p. 1979. text ed. 34.95 (ISBN 0-89443-157-9). Aspen Systems.
--Systems Analysis & Computer Application in Health Information Management. LC 82-18468. 4449p. 1982. 29.95 (ISBN 0-89443-838-7). Aspen Systems.
Waters, Kenneth H. Reflection Seismology. 2nd ed. LC 80-26042. 453p. 1981. 49.95x (ISBN 0-471-08224-4, Pub. by Wiley-Interscience). Wiley.
--Reflection Seismology: A Tool for Energy Resource Exploration. LC 77-10837. 1978. 34.95 o.p. (ISBN 0-471-03186-0, Pub. by Wiley-Interscience). Wiley.
Waters, Les. The Union of Christmas Island Workers. 184p. 1983. text ed. 27.50x (ISBN 0-86861-221-9). Allen Unwin.
Waters, Michael. Not Just Any Death. (American Poets Continuum Ser.: No. 4). 1979. 10.00 (ISBN 0-918526-23-X); pap. 5.00 (ISBN 0-918526-24-8). BOA Edns.
Waters, Roger. Pink Floyd Lyric Book. (Illus.). 96p. (Orig.). 1983. pap. 6.95 (ISBN 0-7137-1280-5, Pub. by Blandford Pr England). Sterling.
Waters, Verle, jt. auth. see Peterson, Carol J.
Waters, Virginia. Color Us Rational. (Illus.). pap. 4.95 (ISBN 0-686-36811-8). Inst Rat Liv.
--Rational Stories for Children. pap. 8.00 (ISBN 0-686-36825-8). Inst Rat Liv.
Waterson, A. P. Introduction to Animal Virology. 2nd ed. LC 68-18347. (Illus.). 1968. 27.95 (ISBN 0-521-06957-2, 2). Cambridge U Pr.
Waterson, A. P. & Wilkinson, L. An Introduction to the History of Virology. LC 77-17892. (Illus.). 1978. 42.50 (ISBN 0-521-21917-5). Cambridge U Pr.
Waterson, D. B. & Arnold, John. Biographical Register of the Queensland Parliament 1930-1980. new ed. 144p. (Orig.). 1982. pap. text ed. 13.95 (ISBN 0-7081-1957-3, 1243, Pub. by ANUP Australia). Bks Australia.
Waterson, Natalie & Snow, Catherine, eds. The Development of Communication. LC 77-27237. 1978. 64.95x (ISBN 0-471-99628-9, Pub. by Wiley-Interscience). Wiley.
Waterton, Charles. Wanderings in South America. Phelps, Gilbert, intro. by. (Illus.). 257p. 1974. 15.00x o.p. (ISBN 0-85314-155-X). Transatlantic.
Wates, Nick. The Battle for Tolmers Square. (Orig.). 1976. pap. 7.95 (ISBN 0-7100-8448-X). Routledge & Kegan.
Wathen, James F. Is the Order of St. John Masonic? 84p. 1973. pap. 3.50 (ISBN 0-686-81626-9). TAN Bks Pubs.
Watherwax, Richard, jt. auth. see Bissell, LeClair.
Wathey, Richard B., jt. auth. see Cuskey, Walter R.
Wa Thiong'O, Ngugi. Homecoming. LC 72-96592. 176p. 1973. 6.50 o.s.i. (ISBN 0-88208-035-0); pap. 5.95 (ISBN 0-88208-036-9). Lawrence Hill.
Watkin, D. The Triumph of the Classical. LC 77-12164. (Illus.). 1977. 17.50 (ISBN 0-521-21854-3); pap. 10.95 (ISBN 0-521-29292-1). Cambridge U Pr.
Watkin, David. Athenian Stuart: Pioneer of the Greek Revival, Vol. 1. (Studies in Architecture Ser.). (Illus.). 128p. 1982. text ed. 21.95x (ISBN 0-04-720026-X); pap. 9.95 (ISBN 0-04-720027-8). Allen Unwin.
--The English Vision. LC 82-47548. (Icon Editions). (Illus.). 256p. 1982. 52.88i (ISBN 0-06-438875-1, HarpT). Har-Row.
--Morality & Architecture: The Development of a Theme in Architectural History & Theory from the Gothic Revival to the Modern Movement. 1978. pap. 12.95x (ISBN 0-19-817350-4). Oxford U Pr.
Watkin, Donald M. Handbook of Nutrition, Health, & Aging. LC 82-14450. 290p. 1983. 32.00 (ISBN 0-8155-0929-4). Noyes.
Watkin, T. G. Nature of Law. (European Studies in Law: Vol. 9). 1980. 44.75 (ISBN 0-444-85422-3). Elsevier.
Watkin, V. E., tr. see Steiner, Rudolf.
Watkins, Alan. Brief Lives. (Illus.). 224p. 1982. 22.50 (ISBN 0-241-10890-X, Pub by Hamish Hamilton England). David & Charles.
Watkins, Anthony, jt. auth. see Reese, Terence.
Watkins, Arthur M. Building or Buying the High-Quality House at Lowest Cost. LC 62-11435. (Illus.). pap. 3.50 o.p. (ISBN 0-385-01195-4, C374, Dolp). Doubleday.
Watkins, Bruce O. & Meador, Roy. Technology & Human Values: Collision & Solution. 1977. softcover 11.95 (ISBN 0-250-40241-6). Ann Arbor Science.
Watkins, David W., jt. auth. see Stanski, Donald R.
Watkins, Derek. Close-Ups. (Photographer's Library). (Illus.). 1983. pap. 12.95x (ISBN 0-240-51188-3). Faber & Faber.
--SLR Photography. LC 76-54090. 1977. 17.50 (ISBN 0-7153-7301-3). David & Charles.
Watkins, Derry, jt. auth. see Clegg, Peter.
Watkins, Floyd C. Then & Now: The Personal Past in the Poetry of Robert Penn Warren. LC 81-51016. 200p. 1982. 15.00x (ISBN 0-8131-1456-X). U Pr of Ky.
Watkins, Floyd C. & Dillingham, William B. Practical English Handbook. 6th ed. 1982. pap. 9.50 (ISBN 0-395-31734-7). HM.
--Practical English Workbook. 2nd ed. 1982. pap. 8.95 (ISBN 0-686-84826-8); instrs' manual 1.00 (ISBN 0-686-84827-6). HM.
Watkins, Floyd C., et al. Practical English Workbook. LC 77-75888. 1978. pap. 7.95 o.p. (ISBN 0-395-25830-8); Tchrs Manual 0.45 o.p. (ISBN 0-395-25831-6). HM.
--Practical English Workbook. 312p. 1982. pap. text ed. 8.95 (ISBN 0-395-33187-0); write for info. instr's. manual (ISBN 0-395-33186-2). HM.
Watkins, Frederick, jt. auth. see Kramnick, Isaac.
Watkins, G. M. Compendium of Cotton Diseases. LC 80-85457. (Compendia Ser.: No. 5). (Illus.). 95p. 1981. saddle stitched 12.00 (ISBN 0-89054-031-4). Am Phytopathol Soc.
Watkins, Helen H., jt. auth. see Watkins, John G.
Watkins, Jean. My Father Is a Priest. LC 78-65691. 1979. 5.95 o.p. (ISBN 0-533-04113-9). Vantage.
Watkins, John G. & Watkins, Helen H. Ego-States & Hidden Observers & the Women in Black & the Lady in White. (Sound Seminars Ser.). 1980. transcript & 2 tapes 29.50x (ISBN 0-88432-065-0, 29400-29401). J Norton Pubs.
Watkins, Josephine E. Fairchild's Who's Who in Fashion. 1975. 10.00 o.p. (ISBN 0-87005-143-1). Fairchild.
Watkins, K. W. Britain Divided. LC 75-36364. 270p. 1976. Repr. of 1963 ed. lib. bdg. 17.50x (ISBN 0-8371-8627-7, WABD). Greenwood.
Watkins, L. H. Environmental Impact of Roads & Traffic. 1981. 57.50 (ISBN 0-85334-963-0, Pub. by Applied Sci England). Elsevier.
Watkins, Mary M. Waking Dreams. 1977. pap. 3.45i o.p. (ISBN 0-06-090586-7, CN586, CN). Har-Row.
Watkins, Michelle, jt. ed. see Thomas, Robert C.
Watkins, Miles A., et al. Alternative Three. 1979. pap. 2.25 o.s.i. (ISBN 0-380-44677-4, 44677). Avon.
Watkins, Owen. The Puritan Experience: Studies in Spiritual Autobiography. LC 70-150987. 1972. 12.00x o.p. (ISBN 0-8052-3425-X). Schocken.
Watkins, Paul. British Crafts. (Golden Hart Guides Ser.). (Illus.). 96p. 1983. pap. 3.95 (ISBN 0-283-98914-9, Pub by Sidgwick & Jackson). Merrimack Bk Serv.
--Historic English Inns. (Golden Hart Guides Ser.). (Illus.). 96p. 1983. pap. 3.95 (ISBN 0-283-98915-7, Pub by Sidgwick & Jackson). Merrimack Bk Serv.
--Oxford. (Golden Hart Guides Ser.). (Illus.). 96p. 1983. pap. 3.95 (ISBN 0-283-98907-6, Pub by Sidgwick & Jackson). Merrimack Bk Serv.
--Traditional Britain. (Golden Hart Guides Ser.). (Illus.). 96p. 1983. pap. 3.95 (ISBN 0-283-98913-0, Pub by Sidgwick & Jackson). Merrimack Bk Serv.
--X Devon. (Golden Hart Guides Ser.). (Illus.). 96p. 1983. pap. 3.95 (ISBN 0-283-98911-4, Pub by Sidgwick & Jackson). Merrimack Bk Serv.
Watkins, Peter & Hughes, Erica. A Book of Prayer. (Julia MacRae Ser.). 128p. (gr. 7 up). 1983. 10.95 (ISBN 0-531-04578-1, MacRae). Watts.
Watkins, R. P. Computer Problem Solving. LC 79-22235. 172p. 1980. Repr. of 1974 ed. lib. bdg. 10.50 (ISBN 0-89874-058-4). Krieger.
Watkins, Robert. Something Here Might Help. 1980. 4.50 o.p. (ISBN 0-8062-1355-8). Carlton.
Watkins, Ruel D. Romeo Judas. 1983. 6.95 (ISBN 0-533-05243-2). Vantage.
Watkins, Sam R. Co. Aytch. 1982. 20.00 (ISBN 0-686-91697-2). Pr of Morningside.
Watkins, Susan. Conversations with Seth, Vol. 1. 384p. 1982. pap. 4.50 o.p. (ISBN 0-13-172007-4). P-H.
--Conversations with Seth, Vol. 2. 384p. 1982. pap. 5.95 (ISBN 0-13-172080-5). P-H.
Watkins, Susan M. Conversations with Seth, Vol. 1. LC 80-17760. 1980. 10.95 o.p. (ISBN 0-13-172007-4). P-H.
Watkins, Vernon, intro. by see Thomas, Dylan.
Watkins, W. B. Shakespeare & Spencer. LC 81-43798. 350p. (Orig.). 1982. lib. bdg. 24.25 (ISBN 0-8191-2418-4); pap. text ed. 12.25 (ISBN 0-8191-2610-1). U Pr of Amer.
Watkins, Wayne. Hypothalamic Releasing Factors, Vol. 1. 1977. 19.20 (ISBN 0-88831-002-1). Eden Pr.
--Hypothalamic Releasing Factors, Vol. 3. Horrobin, D. F., ed. (Annual Research Reviews Ser.). 1979. 20.00 (ISBN 0-88831-046-3). Eden Pr.
Watkins, Wayne B. Hypothalamic Releasing Factors, Vol. 2. Horrobin, David F., ed. (Annual Research Reviews Ser.). 1978. 21.60 (ISBN 0-88831-033-1). Eden Pr.
Watkins, William J. Suburban Wilderness. (Illus.). 192p. 1981. 9.95 (ISBN 0-399-12552-3). Putnam Pub Group.
Watkins, William J. & Cavalieri, Grace. Per-Se Award Plays, 1969: Special Issue 5. 38p. pap. 1.00 o.p. (ISBN 0-912292-06-7). The Smith.
Watkinson, R. J., ed. Developments in Biodegradation of Hydrocarbons, Vol. 1. (Illus.). 1978. text ed. 49.25x (ISBN 0-85334-751-4, Pub. by Applied Sci England). Elsevier.
Watling, Dick. Birds of Figi, Tonga & Somoa. (Illus.). 1983. 45.00 (ISBN 0-686-38392-3). Tanager Bks.
Watling, Roy & Gregory, Norma. Census Catalogue of World Members of the Bolbitiaceae. (Bibliotheca Mycologica). 300p. 1981. lib. bdg. 32.00x (ISBN 3-7682-1279-3). Lubrecht & Cramer.
Watney, Bernard. English Blue & White Porcelain of the Eighteenth Century. 2nd ed. 258p. 1973. 29.95 (ISBN 0-571-04796-3). Faber & Faber.
Watney, John. Cruising in British & Irish Waters. (Illus.). 224p. 1983. 23.95 (ISBN 0-7153-8402-3). David & Charles.
Watrasiewicz, B. M. & Rudd, M. J. Laser Doppler Measurements. 256p. 1975. 16.95 o.p. (ISBN 0-408-70684-8). Butterworth.
Watrous, Hilda. The County Between the Lakes: A Public History of Seneca County, 1876-1982. (Illus.). 430p. 1983. deluxe ed. 18.75 deluxe (ISBN 0-932334-61-X). Heart of the Lakes.
Watrous, James. Craft of Old Master Drawings. (Illus.). 184p. 1957. 17.50 (ISBN 0-299-01421-5); pap. text ed. 15.00 (ISBN 0-299-01425-8). U of Wis Pr.
Watson. Aesop's Fable. (Animal Story Book). (gr. k-4). 1982. 5.95 (ISBN 0-86020-668-8, Usborne-Hayes); PLB 8.95 (ISBN 0-88110-093-5); pap. 2.95 (ISBN 0-86020-667-X). EDC.
--Construction Cost Estimating. 1983. write for info. (ISBN 0-07-068450-2). McGraw.
--The Shop. (Picture Word Books). (gr. k-2). 1980. 5.95 (ISBN 0-86020-393-X, Usborne-Hayes); PLB 8.95 (ISBN 0-88110-069-2); pap. 2.95 (ISBN 0-86020-390-5). EDC.
--Sixty-Seven Ready-to-Run Programs in BASIC, Graphics, Home & Business, Education, Games. 182p. 1981. 13.95 (ISBN 0-8306-9660-1); pap. 7.95 (ISBN 0-8306-1195-9, 1195). TAB Bks.
Watson, jt. auth. see Brown.
Watson, ed. see Grosicki.
Watson, A. Diplomacy: The Dialogue Between the States. 240p. 1982. 19.95 (ISBN 0-07-068461-8). McGraw.
Watson, A., jt. auth. see Robinson, G. N.
Watson, Alan D. Bertie County: A Brief County. (Illus.). 89p. 1982. pap. 2.00 o.p. (ISBN 0-86526-194-6). Natl Wildlife.
--Society in Colonial North Carolina. (Illus.). 1982. pap. 1.00 (ISBN 0-86526-103-2). NC Archives.
Watson, Aldren A. Hand Tools: Their Ways & Workings. (Illus.). 424p. 1982. 29.95 (ISBN 0-393-01654-4). Norton.
Watson, Andrew. Living in China. (Littlefield Adams Quality Paperbacks Ser.: No. 327). (Illus.). 1977. pap. 3.95 (ISBN 0-8226-0327-6). Littlefield.
--With Wellesley to Madras. (Illus.). (gr. 7 up). 12.75x (ISBN 0-392-01931-0, LTB). Sportshelf.
Watson, Andrew, ed. Mao Zedong & the Political Economy of the Border Region. LC 78-67434. (Publications of the Contemporary China Institute). (Illus.). 1980. 32.50 (ISBN 0-521-22551-5); pap. 12.95 (ISBN 0-521-29547-5). Cambridge U Pr.
Watson, B. W., ed. IEE Medical Electronics Monographs. Incl. Vol. 1. Monographs 1-6. 1971. 22.00 (ISBN 0-901223-07-7); Vol. 2. Monographs 7-12. Hill, D. W., ed. 1974. 23.00 (ISBN 0-901223-51-4); Vol. 3. Monographs 13-17. Hill, D. W., ed. 1975. 30.00 (ISBN 0-901223-77-8); Vol. 4. Monographs 18-22. Hill, D. W., ed. 1976. 38.50 (ISBN 0-901223-84-0); Vol. 5. Monographs 23-27. Hill, D. W., ed. 1977. 38.50 (ISBN 0-901223-98-0). (Illus., Pub. by Peregrinus England). Inst Elect Eng.
Watson, Bruce W. Red Navy at Sea: An Interpretive History of Soviet Naval Operations, 1956-1979. 1982. 27.50 (ISBN 0-86531-204-4). Westview.
Watson, Burton, tr. see Sugimura, Yuzo.
Watson, Charles C., jt. auth. see Rudd, Dale F.
Watson, Charles N., Jr. The Novels of Jack London: A Reappraisal. LC 82-70548. 324p. 1983. 19.95 (ISBN 0-299-09300-X). U of Wis Pr.
Watson, CLyde. Applebet. (Illus.). 32p. (ps up). 1982. 10.95 (ISBN 0-374-30384-3). FS&G.
--Binary Numbers. LC 75-29161. (Young Math Ser.). (Illus.). (gr. 1-4). 1977. PLB 10.89 (ISBN 0-690-00993-3, TYC-J). Har-Row.
--Catch Me & Kiss Me & Say It Again. LC 78-17644. (Illus.). (gr. 1-12). 1978. 8.95 (ISBN 0-529-05436-1, Philomel); PLB 8.99 (ISBN 0-529-05438-8). Putnam Pub Group.
--Hickory Stick Rag. LC 75-6607. (Illus.). 40p. (gr. k up). 1976. 5.95i o.p. (ISBN 0-690-00959-3, TYC-J); PLB 8.89 (ISBN 0-690-00960-7). Har-Row.
--Midnight Moon. LC 78-26376. (Illus.). (ps-3). 1979. 6.95 o.p. (ISBN 0-529-05526-0, Philomel); PLB 6.99 o.p. (ISBN 0-529-05527-9). Putnam Pub Group.
Watson, Colin. Charity Ends at Home. (Murder Ink Ser.: No. 59). 1983. pap. 2.75 (ISBN 0-440-11187-0). Dell.
--It Shouldn't Happen to a Dog. LC 76-45534. 1977. 7.95 o.p. (ISBN 0-399-11881-0). Putnam Pub Group.
--Plaster Sinners. LC 80-1989. (Crime Club Ser.). 192p. 1981. 10.95 o.p. (ISBN 0-385-17338-5). Doubleday.
--Whatever's Been Going on at Mumblesby? LC 82-45550. (Crime Club Ser.). 192p. 1983. 11.95 (ISBN 0-385-18382-8). Doubleday.
Watson, D. Richard Wagner: A Biography. 384p. 1983. 8.95 (ISBN 0-07-068479-0, GB). McGraw.
Watson, D. M. Paleontology & Modern Biology. 1951. text ed. 39.50x (ISBN 0-686-83673-1). Elliots Bks.
Watson, D. R. The Life & Times of Charles I. Fraser, Antonia, ed. (Kings & Queens of England Ser.). (Illus.). 224p. 1972. text ed. 17.50x (ISBN 0-297-99436-0, Pub. by Weidenfeld & Nicolson England). Biblio Dist.
Watson, David. Called & Committed: World-Changing Discipleship. LC 82-824. 240p. 1982. cloth 9.95 (ISBN 0-87788-100-6). Shaw Pubs.
--Caring for Strangers: An Introduction to Practical Philosophy for Students of Social Administration. (International Library of Welfare & Philosophy). 144p. 1980. 21.95 (ISBN 0-7100-0390-0); pap. 10.00 (ISBN 0-7100-0391-9). Routledge & Kegan.
--Is Anyone There? And Does It Really Matter? LC 80-25032. 108p. 1981. pap. 3.95 (ISBN 0-87788-395-5). Shaw Pubs.
--Psychology: What It Is & How to Use It. 1978. text ed. 21.50 scp (ISBN 0-06-389140-9, HarpC); instr's. manual avail. (ISBN 0-06-377966-8). Har-Row.
Watson, David L. & Tharp, Roland G. Self Directed Behavior: Self-Modification for Personal Adjustment. 3rd ed. LC 80-24411. 300p. 1981. text ed. 14.95 (ISBN 0-8185-0443-9). Brooks-Cole.

Watson, David L. & Brown, A. W., eds. Pesticide Management & Insecticide Resistance. 1977. 46.00 (ISBN 0-12-738650-5). Acad Pr.
Watson, Derek. Bruckner. (Master Musicians Ser.: No. M171). (Illus.). 1975. pap. 7.95 (ISBN 0-8226-0708-5). Littlefield.
Watson, Diane, jt. auth. see Rambo, Beverly J.
Watson, Don A. Construction Materials & Processes. 2nd ed. LC 77-612. (Illus.). 1978. pap. text ed. 26.95 (ISBN 0-07-068471-5, G). McGraw.
Watson, Donald. Energy Conservation Through Building Design. 1979. 29.50 (ISBN 0-07-068460-X, P&RB). McGraw.
Watson, Donald & Labs, Kenneth. Climatic Design: Energy Efficient Buildings Principles & Practices. (Illus.). 288p. 1983. 29.95 (ISBN 0-07-068478-2, P&RB). McGraw.
Watson, Donald A. Specifications Writing for Architects & Engineers. (Illus.). 1964. 14.95 o.p. (ISBN 0-07-068473-1, G). McGraw.
Watson, Donald S. & Getz, Malcolm. Price Theory & Its Uses. 5th ed. LC 80-82461. (Illus.). 480p. 1981. text ed. 23.95 (ISBN 0-395-30056-8); instr's manual 1.00 (ISBN 0-395-30057-6). HM.
--Price Theory in Action. 4th ed. LC 81-80260. 448p. 1981. pap. text ed. 15.50 (ISBN 0-395-30058-4). HM.
Watson, Donald S., jt. auth. see Burns, Arthur E.
Watson, E. Elaine. I Wish, I Wish. Mahany, Patricia, ed. (Happy Day Bks.). (Illus.). 24p. (ps-2). 1983. 1.29 (ISBN 0-87239-637-1, 3557). Standard Pub.
Watson, E. W. & Blanco, Miquel A. Cuatro Dramas De Navidad. 1981. pap. 0.80 (ISBN 0-311-08224-6). Casa Bautista.
Watson, Elbert. Senators from Alabama. 1981. 12.95 o.p. (ISBN 0-87397-081-0). Strode.
Watson, Elizabeth E. All About Hands. LC 81-50676. (A Happy Day Bk.). (Illus.). 24p. (Orig.). (ps-1). 1981. pap. 1.29 (ISBN 0-87239-460-3, 3593). Standard Pub.
--Busy Feet. LC 81-50674. (A Happy Day Bk.). (Illus.). 24p. (Orig.). (ps-1). 1981. pap. 1.29 (ISBN 0-87239-461-1, 3594). Standard Pub.
--God Didn't Put Elephants in Trees. LC 81-65800. (gr. k-3). 1981. 5.95 (ISBN 0-8054-4267-7). Broadman.
--God Knows You. LC 81-50678. (A Happy Day Bk.). (Illus.). 24p. (Orig.). (ps-1). 1981. pap. 1.29 (ISBN 0-87239-463-8, 3596). Standard Pub.
--God Made the Sea, the Sand & Me. (gr. k-3). 1979. 4.95 (ISBN 0-8054-4254-5). Broadman.
--Where Are You, God? (Illus.). 1977. bds. 4.50 (ISBN 0-8054-4235-9). Broadman.
Watson, Emmett, jt. auth. see Brewster, David.
Watson, F. R. Developments in Mathematics Teaching. (Changing Classroom). 1976. text ed. 9.75x o.p. (ISBN 0-7291-0085-5); pap. text ed. 4.75x o.p. (ISBN 0-7291-0080-4). Humanities.
Watson, Foster. Luis Vivies, el Gran Valenciano. 1922. pap. 3.00 (ISBN 0-87535-013-5). Hispanic Soc.
Watson, Francis B., jt. auth. see Fahy, Everett.
Watson, Francis M. Political Terrorism: The Threat & the Response. LC 75-28548. 1976. 10.00 o.p. (ISBN 0-88331-078-3). Luce.
Watson, G. A. Approximation Theory & Numerical Methods. 229p. 1980. 29.95x (ISBN 0-471-27706-1, Pub. by Wiley-Interscience). Wiley.
Watson, G. A., jt. auth. see Gourlay, A. R.
Watson, G. Llewellyn. Social Theory & Critical Understanding. 336p. (Orig.). 1982. lib. bdg. 24.00 (ISBN 0-8191-2590-3); pap. text ed. 12.75 (ISBN 0-8191-2591-1). U Pr of Amer.
Watson, Gail C. Cooking Naturally for Pleasure & Health. (The G-Jo Institute Fabulous Foods Ser.). (Illus.). 272p. (Orig.). 1983. case 12.95 (ISBN 0-916878-16-3). Falkynor Bks.
Watson, Gary. Free Will. 200p. 1982. pap. 7.95 (ISBN 0-19-875054-4). Oxford U Pr.
Watson, George & McGaw, Dickinson. Statistical Inquiry: Elementary Statistics for the Political, Social & Policy Sciences. LC 79-12109. 1980. text ed. 25.95x (ISBN 0-471-02087-7); tchrs'. manual o.p. avail. (ISBN 0-471-05730-4). Wiley.
Watson, George, jt. auth. see McGaw, Dickinson L.
Watson, George, ed. Concise Cambridge Bibliography of English Literature, 600-1950. 2nd ed. (Orig.). 1965. 49.50 (ISBN 0-521-04504-5); pap. 15.95 (ISBN 0-521-09265-5). Cambridge U Pr.
--New Cambridge Bibliography of English Literature. Incl. 600-1600. 1973. Vol. 1. 135.00 (ISBN 0-521-20004-0); 1660-1800. Vol. 2. 125.00 (ISBN 0-521-07934-9); 1800-1900. Vol. 3. 135.00 (ISBN 0-521-07255-7); 1900-1950. Willison, I., ed. 1972. Vol. 4. 135.00 (ISBN 0-521-08535-7); Index. Pickles, J. D., compiled by. 1976. 44.50 (ISBN 0-521-21310-X). LC 73-82455. (Illus.). Set. 450.00 (ISBN 0-521-08761-9). Cambridge U Pr.
--The Shorter New Cambridge Bibliography of English Literature. 850p. 1981. 79.95 (ISBN 0-521-22600-7). Cambridge U Pr.
Watson, George E. Birds of the Antarctic & Sub-Antarctic. LC 75-34547. (Antarctic Research Ser.: Vol. 24). (Illus.). 1975. 18.00 (ISBN 0-87590-124-7). Am Geophysical.
Watson, George N. Theory of Bessel Functions. pap. text ed. 32.50 (ISBN 0-521-09382-1). Cambridge U Pr.
Watson, George N., jt. auth. see Whittaker, Edmund T.
Watson, Glegg, jt. auth. see Davis, George.
Watson, Godfrey. Goodwife Hot & Others: Northumberland's Past As Shown in Its Place Names. 1970. 10.50 o.p. (ISBN 0-85362-090-3, Oriel). Routledge & Kegan.
Watson, H. J. Modern Gear Production. 1970. inquire for price o.p. (ISBN 0-08-015835-8). Pergamon.
Watson, H. J., jt. auth. see Gallagher, C. A.
Watson, H. W. & McGuinn, S. German in the Office. pap. text ed. 5.25x (ISBN 0-582-35256-8). Longman.
Watson, Harry L. An Independent People: The Way We Lived in North Carolina, 1770-1820. Nathans, Sydney, ed. LC 82-20098. (The Way We Lived in North Carolina Ser.). (Illus.). viii, 118p. 1983. 11.95 (ISBN 0-8078-1550-0); pap. 6.95 (ISBN 0-8078-4102-1). U of NC Pr.
Watson, Hilary. The Book of Maidstone. 1981. 39.50x o.p. (ISBN 0-86023-121-6, Pub. by Barracuda England). State Mutual Bk.
--Winter's Crimes Fourteen. 224p. 1983. 11.95 (ISBN 0-312-88241-6). St Martin.
Watson, Hugh J. Computer Simulation in Business. LC 80-20612. 358p. 1981. text ed. 28.95x (ISBN 0-471-03638-2). Wiley.
Watson, J. Book of Stamps & Collecting. (Illus.). 24.95. StanGib Ltd.
Watson, J., jt. auth. see McCormack, R. M.
Watson, J. B. Psychology from the Standpoint of a Behaviourist. Wolfe, Joseph, ed. (Classics of Psychology & Psychiatry Ser.). 464p. 1983. Repr. of 1919 ed. write for info. (ISBN 0-904014-44-4). F Pinter Pubs.
Watson, J. K. Applications of Magnetism. LC 79-20882. 1980. 36.50x (ISBN 0-471-03540-8, Pub. by Wiley-Interscience). Wiley.
Watson, J. P., jt. auth. see Shepherd, Eric.
Watson, J. R. Wordsworth's Vital Soul: The Sacred & Profane in Wordsworth's Poetry. 259p. 1982. text ed. 30.00x (ISBN 0-391-02563-5). Humanities.
Watson, J. Richard, jt. auth. see Messenger, Nigel P.
Watson, J. S., tr. see Cicero.
Watson, J. W. & O'Riordan, T. American Environment: Perceptions & Policies. LC 73-21939. 352p. 1976. 38.45 o.p. (ISBN 0-471-92221-8, Pub. by Wiley-Interscience); pap. 22.25 o.p. (ISBN 0-471-92222-6). Wiley.
Watson, J. Wreford. The United States. (Geography for Advanced Study Ser.). (Illus.). 304p. 1983. text ed. 45.00x (ISBN 0-582-30004-5); pap. text ed. 19.95x (ISBN 0-582-30005-3). Longman.
Watson, James D. Double Helix. (Illus.). 1969. pap. 2.95 (ISBN 0-451-62172-7, ME2172, Ment). NAL.
--Double Helix: Being a Personal Account of the Discovery of the Structure of DNA. LC 68-11211. (Illus.). 1968. 7.95 (ISBN 0-689-10285-2); pap. 5.95 (ISBN 0-689-70602-2, 261). Atheneum.
Watson, James L. Asian & African Systems of Slavery. 1980. 33.00x (ISBN 0-520-04031-7). U of Cal Pr.
--Emigration & the Chinese Lineage: The 'Mans' in Hong Kong & London. 1975. 28.50x (ISBN 0-520-02647-0). U of Cal Pr.
Watson, Jane W. Alternate Energy Sources. LC 78-10872. (First Bks.). (Illus.). (gr. 4 up). 1979. PLB 8.90 s&l (ISBN 0-531-02252-8). Watts.
--Canada: Giant Nation of the North. LC 68-11035. (Living in Today's World Ser). (Illus.). (gr. 3-6). 1968. PLB 7.99 (ISBN 0-8116-6858-4). Garrard.
--The Case of the Semi-Human Beans. LC 78-13247. (Illus.). (gr. 4-7). 1979. 7.95 (ISBN 0-698-20476-X, Coward). Putnam Pub Group.
--The Case of the Vanishing Spaceship. 120p. 1982. 8.95 (ISBN 0-698-20547-2, Coward). Putnam Pub Group.
--Dance to a Happy Song. LC 72-10602. (Venture Ser). (Illus.). 40p. (gr. 1). 1973. PLB 6.69 (ISBN 0-8116-6730-8). Garrard.
--Deserts of the World: Future Threat or Promise? (Illus.). 136p. (gr. 10-12). 1981. 13.95 (ISBN 0-399-20785-6, Philomel). Putnam Pub Group.
--India Celebrates! LC 72-10743. (Around the World Holiday Ser.). (Illus.). 96p. (gr. 4-7). 1974. PLB 7.12 (ISBN 0-8116-4950-4). Garrard.
--The Indus: South Asia's Highway of History. LC 71-95747. (Rivers of World Ser.). (Illus.). (gr. 4-7). 1970. PLB 3.98 (ISBN 0-8116-6373-6). Garrard.
--Iran: Crossroads of Caravans. LC 66-10160. (Developing Countries Ser.). (gr. 3-6). 1966. PLB 7.99 (ISBN 0-8116-6851-7). Garrard.
--The Mysterious Gold & Purple Box. LC 72-3803. (Venture Ser.). (Illus.). 64p. (gr. 2). 1972. PLB 6.89 (ISBN 0-8116-6971-8). Garrard.
--Parade of Soviet Holidays. LC 73-12785. (Around the World Holidays Ser). (Illus.). 96p. (gr. 4-7). 1974. PLB 7.12 (ISBN 0-8116-4951-2). Garrard.
--The People's Republic of China: Red Star of the East. rev. ed. LC 81-910. (Illus.). 112p. (gr. 4). Date not set. lib. bdg. 7.99 (ISBN 0-8116-6864-9). Garrard.
--The Soviet Union: Land of Many Peoples. LC 72-14255. (Living in Today's World Ser). (Illus.). 112p. (gr. 3-6). 1973. PLB 7.99 (ISBN 0-8116-6862-2). Garrard.
--Tanya & the Geese. LC 74-7360. (Venture Ser). (Illus.). 64p. (gr. 2). 1974. PLB 6.89 (ISBN 0-8116-6977-7). Garrard.
--The Volga. (Rivers of the World Ser.). PLB 12.68 (ISBN 0-382-06373-2). Silver.
--The Volga: Russia's River of Five Seas. LC 72-172118. (Rivers of the World Ser.). (Illus.). (gr. 4-7). 1972. PLB 3.98 (ISBN 0-8116-6375-2). Garrard.
Watson, Jane W., ed. Castles in Spain. LC 72-132850. (Myths & Legends Ser.). (Illus.). (gr. 4-7). 1971. PLB 3.98 o.p. (ISBN 0-8116-4207-0). Garrard.
--Rama of the Golden Age. LC 70-126415. (Illus.). (gr. 4-7). 1971. PLB 3.98 (ISBN 0-8116-4206-2). Garrard.
Watson, Janet. Rocks & Minerals. 2nd rev. ed. (Introducing Geology Ser.). (Illus.). pap. text ed. 5.95x (ISBN 0-04-551031-8). Allen Unwin.
Watson, Janet, jt. auth. see Read, H. H.
Watson, Jean. Sounds, Sounds, All Around. (Illus.). 16p. 1983. Repr. of 1981 ed. pap. 0.99 (ISBN 0-86683-706-X). Winston Pr.
--Watchmaker's Daughter: The Life of Corrie ten Boom for Young People. (Illus.). 160p. (gr. 5-8). 1983. pap. 5.95 (ISBN 0-8007-5116-7, Power Bks). Revell.
Watson, John. The Philosophy of Kant Explained. Beck, Lewis W., ed. LC 75-32047. (Philosophy of Immanual Kant Ser.: Vol. 11). 1977. Repr. of 1908 ed. lib. bdg. 40.00 o.s.i. (ISBN 0-8240-2335-8). Garland Pub.
Watson, John C. Patient Care & Special Procedures in Radiologic Technology. 4th ed. LC 74-1115. 200p. 1974. text ed. 17.95 o.p. (ISBN 0-8016-5358-4). Mosby.
Watson, John L. English One: P-K4. 1979. 22.50 o.p. (ISBN 0-7134-2085-5, Pub. by Batsford England). David & Charles.
--English Two: N-KB3 Systems. 1979. 19.95 o.p. (ISBN 0-7134-2087-1, Pub. by Batsford England). David & Charles.
Watson, K. L. Slate Waste: Engineering & Environmental Aspects. 1980. 39.00 (ISBN 0-85334-880-4, Pub. by Applied Sci England). Elsevier.
Watson, K. M. & Nuttall, J. Topics in Several Particle Dynamics. LC 67-13836. 1967. write for info. Holden-Day.
Watson, Katherine, tr. see Schneeberger, Pierre-F.
Watson, Lillian E. Light from Many Lamps. 1951. 12.95 (ISBN 0-671-42300-2). S&S.
Watson, Lyall. Sea Guide to Whales of the World: A Complete Guide to the World's Living Whales, Dolphins & Porpoises. (Illus.). 304p. 1981. 18.95 (ISBN 0-525-93202-X, 03519-1060). Dutton.
Watson, M., jt. ed. see Hayward, J.
Watson, Margaret. Greenwood County Sketches: Old Roads & Early Families. LC 70-142447. (Illus.). 1982. 25.00 (ISBN 0-87921-066-4); pap. 16.95 (ISBN 0-87921-069-9). Attic Pr.
Watson, Margaret, jt. auth. see Forrest, Jane.
Watson, Mary A. & Whitlock, Flint. Breaking the Bonds: The Realities of Sexually Open Relationships. 203p. (Orig.). 1982. pap. 4.95 (ISBN 0-686-36694-8). BMI.
Watson, Miller. Basic Dog Training. (Illus.). 1979. 4.95 (ISBN 0-87666-673-X, KW-022). TFH Pubns.
Watson, N. & Janota, M. S. Turbocharging the Internal Combustion Engine. 608p. 1982. 84.95 (ISBN 0-471-87072-2, Pub. by Wiley-Interscience). Wiley.
--Turbocharging the Internal Combustion Engine. 1982. 125.00x (ISBN 0-333-24290-4, Pub. by Macmillan England). State Mutual Bk.
Watson, Nancy, jt. auth. see Anderson, Gary.
Watson, Nancy D. The Birthday Goat. LC 73-3389. (Illus.). 40p. (ps-3). 1974. 6.95i o.p. (ISBN 0-690-00145-2, TYC-J); PLB 8.89 (ISBN 0-690-00146-0). Har-Row.
Watson, P. F., ed. see Symposia of theZoological Society of London, 43rd.
Watson, Patty J. Archeology of the Mammoth Cave Area. 1974. 32.50 (ISBN 0-12-785927-6). Acad Pr.
Watson, Pauline. Curley Cat Baby-Sits. LC 77-1589. (Let Me Read Ser.). (Illus.). 32p. (gr. 1-4). 1977. pap. 2.95 (ISBN 0-15-622700-2, VoyB). HarBraceJ.
Watson, Percy. Building the Medieval Cathedrals. LC 78-56794. (Cambridge Topic Bks). (Illus.). (gr. 5-10). 1978. PLB 6.95g (ISBN 0-8225-1213-0). Lerner Pubns.
Watson, Peter. Twins: An Uncanny Relationship? 208p. 1983. pap. 6.95 (ISBN 0-8092-5649-5). Contemp Bks.
Watson, Peter G. & Hazleman, Brian L. The Sclera & Systemic Disorders. LC 76-26776. (Major Problems in Ophthalmology Ser.: Vol. 2). (Illus.). 1976. text ed. 10.00 (ISBN 0-7216-9134-X). Saunders.
Watson, Peter G., jt. auth. see Mathies, M. Lorraine.
Watson, Philip. Light Fantastic. LC 82-80989. (Science Club Ser.). (Illus.). 48p. (gr. 3-6). 1983. PLB 8.16 (ISBN 0-688-00969-7); pap. 5.25 (ISBN 0-688-00975-1). Lothrop.
--Liquid Magic. LC 82-80988. (Science Club Ser.). (Illus.). 48p. (gr. 3-6). 1983. PLB 8.16 (ISBN 0-688-00967-0); pap. 5.25 (ISBN 0-688-00974-3). Lothrop.
--Super Motion. LC 82-80990. (Science Club Ser.). (Illus.). 48p. (gr. 3-6). 1983. PLB 8.16 (ISBN 0-688-00971-9); pap. 5.25 (ISBN 0-688-00976-X). Lothrop.
Watson, Philip S., jt. ed. see Rupp, E. Gordon.
Watson, R. The Presidential Contest with a Guide to the Nineteen Eighty Race. 159p. 1980. pap. text ed. 9.95 (ISBN 0-471-05642-1). Wiley.
Watson, R. W. Time Sharing Design Concepts. 1970. text ed. 22.95 o.p. (ISBN 0-07-068465-0, C). McGraw.
Watson, Richard. An Apology for Christianity in a Series of Letters Addressed to Edward Gibbon. Wellek, Rene, ed. LC 75-25132. (British Philosophers & Theologians of the 17th & 18th Centuries Ser.). 1977. lib. bdg. 42.00 o.s.i. (ISBN 0-8240-1765-X). Garland Pub.
--The Runner. 1982. 8.95 o.p. (ISBN 0-686-34664-5). Caroline Hse.
Watson, Richard A. Promise & Performance of American Democracy: Brief Edition. 4th ed. LC 80-54436. 640p. 1981. text ed. 17.95 (ISBN 0-471-07964-2). Wiley.
Watson, Richard A. & Fitzgerald, Michael R. Promise & Performance of American Democracy: National Editon. 4th ed. LC 80-54436. 720p. 1981. text ed. 18.95 (ISBN 0-471-08380-1). Wiley.
--Promise & Performance of American Democracy: State Edition. 4th ed. 824p. 1981. text ed. 22.50 (ISBN 0-471-08381-X). Wiley.
Watson, Richard L., Jr. The Development of National Power: The United States 1900-1919. LC 82-20175. 380p. 1983. pap. text ed. 13.75 (ISBN 0-8191-2856-2). U Pr of Amer.
Watson, Rita E. & Wallach, Robert C. New Choices, New Chances: A Woman's Guide to Conquering Cancer. 273p. 1983. pap. 6.95 (ISBN 0-686-42921-4). St Martin.
Watson, Robert. Night-Blooming Cactus. LC 80-65999. 1980. 10.00 (ISBN 0-689-11090-1); pap. 5.95 (ISBN 0-689-11091-X). Atheneum.
--Rumours of Fulfilment. 224p. 1982. 14.95 (ISBN 0-434-84201-X, Pub by Heinemann, England). David & Charles.
Watson, Robert, jt. auth. see Langford, Herbert G.
Watson, Robert I. Basic Writings in the History of Psychology. (Illus.). 1979. text ed. 22.50x (ISBN 0-19-502443-5); pap. text ed. 11.95x (ISBN 0-19-502444-3). Oxford U Pr.
--Great Psychologists: From Aristotle to Freud. 2nd ed. LC 68-15731. 1968. pap. 9.95 o.p. (ISBN 0-397-47239-0). Har-Row.
Watson, Robert I. & Lindgren, Henry C. Psychology of the Child & the Adolescent. 4th ed. (Illus.). 1979. text ed. 24.95x (ISBN 0-02-424600-X); study guide avail.; instrs'. manual avail. Macmillan.
Watson, S. R., ed. The Practice of Decision Making. 100p. 1983. 15.50 (ISBN 0-08-028162-1). Pergamon.
Watson, Sara R. V. Sackville-West. (English Authors Ser.: No. 134). lib. bdg. 10.95 o.p. (ISBN 0-8057-1472-3, Twayne). G K Hall.
Watson, Scott. Platonic Love. 105p. 1981. pap. 6.25 (ISBN 0-919888-41-0). Crossing Pr.
Watson, Stanley W. & Levin, Jack, eds. Endotoxins & Their Detection with the Limulus Amebocyte Lysate Test. LC 82-8967. (Progress in Clinical & Biological Research Ser.: Vol. 93). 438p. 1982. 44.00 (ISBN 0-8451-0093-9). A R Liss.
Watson, Sterling. Weep No More My Brother. LC 77-28354. 1978. 8.95 o.p. (ISBN 0-688-03311-3). Morrow.
Watson, Stewart C., ed. Joint Sealing & Bearing Systems for Concrete Structures. (SP-70: Vol. 1). (Orig.). 1981. pap. 79.95 (ISBN 0-686-95239-1). ACI.
Watson, Thomas & Davidson, Jeffrey. Hazardous Wastes Handbook. 4th ed. 500p. 1982. Wkbk. 95.00 (ISBN 0-86587-097-7). Gov Insts.
Watson, V. J., jt. auth. see Tipp, G.
Watson, W., jt. auth. see Susser, Mervyn W.
Watson, W. A. Numerical Analysis. 240p. 1981. pap. text ed. 13.95 (ISBN 0-7131-2817-8). E Arnold.
Watson, W. E. Cell Biology of Brain. 1976. 52.00x (ISBN 0-412-11950-1, Pub. by Chapman & Hall England). Methuen Inc.
Watson, Wendy. Has Winter Come? LC 77-18863. (Illus.). (ps-3). 1978. 6.95 (ISBN 0-529-05439-6, Philomel); PLB 6.99 (ISBN 0-399-61189-4). Putnam Pub Group.
--Has Winter Come? (Illus.). (gr. 1-4). 1981. 3.95 (ISBN 0-399-20799-6, Philomel). Putnam Pub Group.
--Jamie's Story. (Illus.). 32p. (gr. 1-4). 1981. 6.95 (ISBN 0-399-20789-9, Philomel); lib. bdg. 6.99 (ISBN 0-399-61177-0). Putnam Pub Group.
Watson, Wilbur H. Aging & Social Behavior: An Introduction to Social Gerontology. LC 81-14728. (Nursing Ser.). 819p. 1982. text ed. 20.95 (ISBN 0-8185-0487-0). Brooks-Cole.
Watson, Wilbur H. & Maxwell, Robert J. Human Aging & Dying: A Study in Sociocultural Gerontology. LC 76-28130. 1977. text ed. 13.95x o.p. (ISBN 0-312-39690-2); pap. text ed. 7.95x o.p. (ISBN 0-312-39725-9). St Martin.
Watson, Wilbur H., ed. Older Women: Illness, Aging & Folk Medicine. 1983. price not set. Transaction Bks.
Watson, William. Advanced Textile Design. 4th ed. 1976. 56.95x (ISBN 0-87245-505-X). Textile Bk.
--Ancient Chinese Bronzes. 2nd ed. (Illus.). 250p. 1977. 30.95 (ISBN 0-571-04917-6). Faber & Faber.
--Textile Design & Colour. 7th ed. 1975. 56.95x (ISBN 0-87245-506-8). Textile Bk.

--Watson's Textile Design & Color. 7th ed. Grosicki, Z. J., ed. 1977. text ed. 49.95 (ISBN 0-408-70515-9). Butterworth.

Watson, William C. Physiological Psychology: An Introduction. LC 80-82838. (Illus.). 592p. 1981. text ed. 25.50 (ISBN 0-395-30221-8); instr's. manual 1.00 (ISBN 0-395-30222-6); study guide 5.95 (ISBN 0-395-30223-4). HM.

Watson de Barros, Leda, jt. auth. see Sutton, Joan L.

Watson-Gegeo, Karen A. & Seaton, S. Lee, eds. Adaptation & Symbolism: Essays on Social Organization. 1978. pap. text ed. 10.00x (ISBN 0-8248-0559-3, Eastwest Ctr). UH Pr.

Watson-Strome, Celia. The Drum & the Melody. LC 82-50630. (Illus.). 72p. (Orig.). 1983. 3.50 (ISBN 0-912292-72-5). The Smith.

Watt, Alan. Evolution of Australian Foreign Policy (1938-1965) 49.50 (ISBN 0-521-06747-2); pap. 14.95 (ISBN 0-521-09552-2). Cambridge U Pr.

Watt, Alec. Barnes & Noble Thesaurus of Geology. (Illus.). 192p. (gr. 11-12). 1983. 13.41i (ISBN 0-06-015177-3); pap. 6.68i (ISBN 0-06-463579-1). B&N NY.

Watt, Alexander. The Art of Papermaking. (Illus.). 240p. Date not set. pap. 20.00 (ISBN 0-87556-581-6). Saifer.

Watt, D. Pocket Guide to... PASCAL. 64p. 1982. spiral bdg. 6.95 (ISBN 0-201-07748-5). A-W.

Watt, D. C. Personalities & Policies. LC 75-5005. 275p. 1975. Repr. of 1965 ed. lib. bdg. 17.25x (ISBN 0-8371-7692-1, WAPPO). Greenwood.

Watt, David A., jt. auth. see Findlay, William.

Watt, Donald C. Too Serious a Business: European Armed Forces & the Coming of the Second World War. LC 74-82853. 1975. 27.50x (ISBN 0-520-02829-5). U of Cal Pr.

Watt, E. D. Authority. LC 82-42542. 140p. 1982. 19.95x (ISBN 0-312-06121-8). St Martin.

Watt, Francis. The Law's Lumber Room. LC 72-96203. 166p. 1973. Repr. of 1896 ed. lib. bdg. 18.50x (ISBN 0-912004-08-8). W W Gaunt.

--The Law's Lumber Room, Second Series. LC 72-96204. viii, 202p. 1973. Repr. of 1898 ed. lib. bdg. 18.75x (ISBN 0-912004-09-6). W W Gaunt.

Watt, Homer A., et al. Outlines of Shakespeare's Plays. rev. ed. (Orig.). 1969. pap. 4.95 (ISBN 0-06-460025-4, CO 25, COS). B&N NY.

Watt, Ian. Conrad in the Nineteenth Century. 1980. 17.95 (ISBN 0-520-03683-2); pap. 7.95 (ISBN 0-520-04405-3). U of Cal Pr.

--The Rise of the Novel: Studies in Defoe, Richardson & Fielding. 1957. 24.50x (ISBN 0-520-04656-0); pap. 5.95 (ISBN 0-520-01318-2). U of Cal Pr.

Watt, Ian, ed. British Novel: Scott Through Hardy. LC 72-96559. (Goldentree Bibliographies in Language & Literature Ser.). (Orig.). 1973. pap. 12.95x (ISBN 0-88295-533-0). Harlan Davidson.

Watt, J. A. Church & the Two Nations in Medieval Ireland. LC 72-120196. (Cambridge Studies in Medieval Life & Thought: Vol. 3). (Illus.). 1970. 44.50 (ISBN 0-521-07738-9). Cambridge U Pr.

Watt, James, jt. auth. see Silver, Robert S.

Watt, Jean, tr. see Dermenghem, Emile.

Watt, Jean M., tr. see Dermenghem, Emile.

Watt, Jill. Grannie Loosley's Kitchen Album. 129p. 1982. 12.95 o.p. (ISBN 0-283-98704-9, Pub. by Sidgwick & Jackson). Merrimack Bk Serv.

Watt, Kenneth E. Ecology & Resource Management. (Population Biology Ser.). 1967. text ed. 34.95 (ISBN 0-07-068573-8, C). McGraw.

--Principles of Environmental Science. (Illus.). 1972. text ed. 39.95 (ISBN 0-07-068575-4, C). McGraw.

Watt, Kenneth E., et al. The Unsteady State: Environmental Problems, Growth, & Culture. LC 77-3879. 1977. 15.00x (ISBN 0-8248-0480-5, Eastwest Ctr). UH Pr.

Watt, N. F., jt. auth. see White, R. W.

Watt, Richard M. Bitter Glory: Poland & Its Fate, 1918-1939. 1982. 20.00 (ISBN 0-671-45379-3); pap. 8.25 (ISBN 0-671-45378-5). S&S.

Watt, Robert. Bibliography of Robert Watt. LC 68-28119. 1968. Repr. of 1950 ed. 30.00x (ISBN 0-8103-3323-6). Gale.

Watt, Roderick, ed. see Schnurre, Wolfdietrich.

Watt, Ruth. Love Unveiled. 192p. (YA) 1976. 6.95 (ISBN 0-685-62025-5, Avalon). Bouregy.

Watt, Ruth M. And the Piper Played. (YA) 1979. 6.95 (ISBN 0-685-90720-1, Avalon). Bouregy.

Watt, W. Montgomery. Muhammad at Medina. 1981. Repr. of 1956 ed. 37.50x (ISBN 0-19-577307-1). Oxford U Pr.

--Muhammad: Prophet & Statesman. 1974. pap. 6.95 (ISBN 0-19-881078-4, GB409, GB). Oxford U Pr.

Watt, W. S. Cicero: Epistulae, Vol. I. 2nd ed. (Oxford Classical Texts Ser.). 1982. 19.50x (ISBN 0-19-814660-4). Oxford U Pr.

Wattel, Jan. Geographical Differentiation in the Genus Accipiter. (Illus.). 231p. 1973. 17.50 (ISBN 0-686-35802-3). Nuttall Ornithological.

Wattenberg, Ben J., jt. auth. see Scammon, Richard M.

Wattenmaker, Richard J. & Young, Christopher R. Alexander Calder. (Illus.). 48p. (Orig.). 1983. pap. 5.50 (ISBN 0-939896-05-2). Flint Inst Arts.

Watters, David & Watters, Nancy. An English-Kham, Kham-English Glossary. 126p. 1973. pap. 2.00x (ISBN 0-88312-756-3); 2.25. Summer Inst Ling.

Watters, Elsie M., ed. Facts & Figures on Government Finance. 21st biennial ed. LC 44-7109. 328p. (Orig.). pap. 15.00x (ISBN 0-686-30844-1). Tax Found.

Watters, Garnette & Courtis, S. A. Picture Dictionary for Children. (Illus.). (gr. 1-3). pap. 3.95 (ISBN 0-448-14002-0, G&D). Putnam Pub Group.

Watters, Gary Z. Modern Analysis & Control of Unsteady Flow in Pipelines. LC 77-92597. 1979. 39.95 (ISBN 0-250-40228-9). Ann Arbor Science.

Watters, John. Cobol Programming. (Computer Programming Ser). 1970. 10.00x o.p. (ISBN 0-435-77803-X). Intl Pubns Serv.

Watters, Nancy, jt. auth. see Watters, David.

Watters, Pat & Cleghorn, Reese. Climbing Jacob's Ladder: The Arrival of Negroes in Southern Politics. LC 67-20324. 1970. pap. 2.95 (ISBN 0-15-618105-3, Harv). HarBraceJ.

Watterson, D. Martin & Vincenzi, Frank F., eds. Calmodulin & Cell Functions, Vol. 356. LC 80-29310. (Annals of the New York Academy of Sciences). 446p. 1980. 88.00x (ISBN 0-89766-101-X); pap. 86.00x (ISBN 0-89766-102-8). NY Acad Sci.

Watterson, John S. Thomas Burke Restless Revolutionary. LC 79-3875. 302p. 1980. text ed. 21.25 (ISBN 0-8191-0943-6); pap. text ed. 11.75 (ISBN 0-8191-0944-4). U Pr of Amer.

Watt-Evans, Lawrence. The Sword of Bheleu. 288p. 1983. pap. 2.50 (ISBN 0-345-30777-1, Del Rey). Ballantine.

Wattles, Gurdon H. Survey Drafting-Drafting Practices in Surveying & Engineering Offices. 2nd ed. LC 81-52885. 382p. 1981. problems with answers 24.00x (ISBN 0-9606962-0-2). Wattles Pubns.

--Writing Legal Descriptions in Conjunction with Survey Boundary Control. 2nd ed. LC 78-68650. 346p. 1979. Repr. of 1976 ed. 21.00 (ISBN 0-9606962-8-8). Wattles Pubns.

--Writing Legal Descriptions in Conjunction with Survey Boundary Control, Court Case References. LC 78-68650. 346p. 1979. problems with answers 21.00x (ISBN 0-9606962-8-8). Wattles Pubns.

Wattles, Gurdon H., jt. auth. see Wattles, William C.

Wattles, William C. & Wattles, Gurdon H. Land Survey Descriptions. 10th ed. LC 74-78750. 144p. 1974. 9.00 (ISBN 0-9606962-3-7). Wattles Pubns.

Watts & Tyler. The Earth. (Children's Guides Ser.). (gr. 3-6). 1976. pap. 3.95 (ISBN 0-686-36414-7, Usborne-Hayes). EDC.

Watts, A. E., tr. from Latin. The Metamorphoses of Ovid. LC 80-36845. (Illus.). 432p. 1980. pap. 12.50 (ISBN 0-86547-019-7). N Point Pr.

Watts, A. Faulkner. Black Rebels on the Spanish Main. Date not set. price not set (ISBN 0-914110-07-1). Blyden Pr.

Watts, Alan. Meditation. 1976. pap. 2.95 o.s.i. (ISBN 0-515-05842-4). Jove Pubns.

--Play to Live. Watts, Mark, ed. LC 82-72606. 100p. (Orig.). 1982. pap. text ed. 5.95 (ISBN 0-89708-098-X). And Bks.

--Uncarved Block, Unbleached Silk. 120p. 1978. 20.00 o.s.i. (ISBN 0-89104-103-6, A & W Visual Library); pap. 10.00 o.s.i. (ISBN 0-89104-102-8, A & W Visual Library). A & W Pubs.

--The Way of Liberation: Essays & Lectures on the Transformation of the Self. Watts, Mark, ed. Shropshire, Rebecca, tr. LC 82-21917. 128p. 1983. pap. 8.95 (ISBN 0-8348-0181-7). Weatherhill.

Watts, Alan W. Beat Zen, Square Zen & Zen. 1959. pap. 1.00 o.p. (ISBN 0-87286-051-5). City Lights.

--The Meaning of Happiness: The Quest for Freedom of the Spirit in Modern Psychology & the Wisdom of the East. 1979. pap. 4.95i (ISBN 0-06-090676-6, CN 676, CN). Har-Row.

--The Supreme Identity. 1972. pap. 3.95 (ISBN 0-394-71835-6, Vin). Random.

--This Is It. 1972. pap. 2.95 (ISBN 0-394-71904-2, Vin). Random.

Watts, C. T., ed. Joseph Conrad's Letters to R. B. Cunninghame Graham. LC 69-16288. (Illus.). 1969. 42.50 (ISBN 0-521-07213-1). Cambridge U Pr.

Watts, Cedric. R. B. Cunninghae Graham. (English Authors Ser.). 155p. 1983. lib. bdg. 18.95 (ISBN 0-8057-6843-2, Twayne). G K Hall.

Watts, Charles, jt. auth. see Hall, Jerry.

Watts, Cynthia. Just Right for You. (Hello World Ser.). 1977. pap. 1.65 o.p. (ISBN 0-8163-0284-7). Pacific Pr Pub Assn.

Watts, D. G. The Learning of History. (Students Library of Education). 128p. 1972. 12.95x (ISBN 0-7100-7433-6). Routledge & Kegan.

Watts, David. Handbook of Medical Treatment. 17th ed. 500p. 1983. pap. text ed. 12.95 (ISBN 0-930010-07-8). Jones Med.

Watts, Denis, jt. auth. see Ward, Ian.

Watts, Donald G. Future of Statistics: Proceedings. 1968. 58.50 (ISBN 0-12-738750-1). Acad Pr.

Watts, Donald G., jt. auth. see Jenkins, Gwilym M.

Watts, Edith. A Young Person's Guide to European Arms & Armor in the Metropolitan Museum of Art. Wasserman, Rosanne, ed. (Illus.). 40p. (Orig.). (gr. 7-8). 1982. pap. 1.95 (ISBN 0-87099-282-1). Metro Mus Art.

Watts, Emily S. The Businessman in American Literature. LC 81-21977. 192p. 1982. text ed. 16.00x (ISBN 0-8203-0616-9). U of Ga Pr.

Watts, Eugene J. The Social Bases of City Politics: Atlanta, 1865-1903. LC 77-94756. (Contributions in American History: No. 73). 1978. lib. bdg. 25.00x (ISBN 0-313-20322-9, WTS/). Greenwood.

Watts, Frances B. Tales of Mr. Cinnamon. LC 81-65813. (The Saturday Evening Post Read-to-Me Ser.). (Illus.). 96p. (ps up). 1981. 7.95 (ISBN 0-89387-053-6, Co-Pub by Sat Eve Post). Curtis Pub Co.

Watts, Gilbert S. The Complete Guide for the Everyday Use of Gardeners, Fruit Growers, Poultrymen & Farmers on the Marketing of Their Products Directly to the Consumer. (Illus.). 156p. Date not set. Repr. of 1926 ed. deluxe ed. 59.85 (ISBN 0-89901-013-X). Found Class Reprints.

--How to Make a Million Dollars from a Fruit & Vegetables Roadside Market. (Illus.). 1977. Repr. 54.15 (ISBN 0-89266-054-6). Am Classical Coll Pr.

Watts, H. D. The Large Industrial Enterprise: Some Spatial Perspectives. (Geography & Environment Ser.). (Illus.). 303p. 1980. 44.00x o.p. (ISBN 0-7099-0267-0, Pub. by Croom Helm Ltd England). Biblio Dist.

Watts, Harold H. Aldous Huxley. (English Authors Ser.). 1969. lib. bdg. 11.95 (ISBN 0-8057-1284-4, Twayne). G K Hall.

Watts, Harold W. & Rees, Albert, eds. The New Jersey Income Maintenance Experiment. (Institute for Research on Poverty Monograph Ser.: Vols. 2 & 3). 1977. Vol. 2. 29.50 (ISBN 0-12-738502-9); Vol. 3. 29.50 (ISBN 0-12-738503-7). Acad Pr.

Watts, Harris. The Programme-Maker's Handbook or Goodbye Totter TV. (Illus.). 230p. (Orig.). 1982. text ed. 20.90 (ISBN 0-9507582-1-3); pap. text ed. 12.50 (ISBN 0-9507582-0-5). Kumarian Pr.

Watts, Henry E. Life of Miguel De Cervantes. LC 79-141743. 1971. Repr. of 1891 ed. 24.00x (ISBN 0-8103-3631-6). Gale.

Watts, Isaac. Reliquiae Juveniles: Miscellaneneous Thoughts in Prose & Verse. LC 68-17018. 1968. Repr. of 1734 ed. 43.00x (ISBN 0-8201-1049-3). Schol Facsimiles.

Watts, John R. Evaporated Air Conditioning. 2nd ed. (Illus.). 300p. 1983. 26.95 (ISBN 0-8311-1151-8). Indus Pr.

Watts, L., III. Fine Art of Baseball: A Complete Guide to Strategy, Skills, & Systems. 2nd ed. (Illus.). 1973. 19.95 (ISBN 0-13-316968-5). P-H.

Watts, Lisa & Tyler, Jenny. The Children's Book of the Earth. LC 77-13212. (Children's Guides). (Illus.). (gr. 3 up). 1978. PLB 7.95 (ISBN 0-88436-466-6). EMC.

Watts, Lisa, jt. auth. see Tyler, Jenny.

Watts, Mark, ed. see Watts, Alan.

Watts, Martin, jt. auth. see Coulthard, Alfred J.

Watts, Martin, jt. auth. see Major, J. Kenneth.

Watts, Michael J. Silent Violence: Food, Famine, & Peasantry in Northern Nigeria. LC 82-13384. (Illus.). 500p. 1983. text ed. 38.50x (ISBN 0-520-04323-5). U of Cal Pr.

Watts, Murray, jt. auth. see Burbridge, Paul.

Watts, Nita, ed. Economic Relations Between East & West. (International Economics Association Publications). 1979. 40.00x (ISBN 0-312-23508-9). St Martin.

Watts, Oswald M., ed. Reed's Nautical Almanac & Coast Pilot for 1982. 2nd ed. 862p. Date not set. pap. cancelled o.p. (ISBN 0-686-92023-6). Western Marine Int.

Watts, Pauline M. Nicolaus Cusanus: A Fifteenth-Century Vision of Man. (Studies in the History of Christian Thought: Vol. 30). (Illus.). ix, 248p. 1982. write for info. (ISBN 90-04-06581-4). E J Brill.

Watts, R. K. Point Defects in Crystals. LC 76-43013. 1977. 35.50 o.p. (ISBN 0-471-92280-3, Pub by Wiley-Interscience). Wiley.

Watts, R. O. & McGee, I. J. Liquid State Chemical Physics. LC 76-21793. 1976. 35.50 o.p. (ISBN 0-471-91240-9, Pub. by Wiley-Interscience). Wiley.

Watts, Richard J. Elementary Principles of Diffusion Theory & the Chain Reaction. (Illus.). 307p. (Orig.). 1982. pap. 25.00x (ISBN 0-9609112-0-0). Desperation Pr.

Watts, Thomas D., Jr. & Wright, Roosevelt. Black Alcoholism: Toward a Comprehensive Understanding. (Illus.). 272p. 1983. 26.75x (ISBN 0-398-04743-X). C C Thomas.

Watts, Thomas M., jt. auth. see Dickey, John W.

Watts, W., jt. auth. see Knipe, A. C.

Watts, W. E., jt. auth. see Knipe, A. C.

Watts, Wayne. The Gift of Giving. LC 82-61301. 128p. 1982. pap. 2.95 (ISBN 0-89109-491-1). NavPress.

Watts, William, et al. Japan, Korea & China: American Perceptions & Policies. LC 78-7128. 176p. 1979. 19.95x (ISBN 0-669-02470-8). Lexington Bks.

Watts, William B., jt. auth. see Eldridge, Benjamin P.

Watzlawick, Paul. How Real Is Real? Confusion, Disinformation, Communication. 1977. pap. 4.95 (ISBN 0-394-72256-6, Vin). Random.

Watznauer, A. Dictionary of Geosciences, 2 vols. (Eng. & Ger.). Date not set. English-German. 57.50 (ISBN 0-444-99702-4); German-English. 57.50 (ISBN 0-444-99701-6). Elsevier.

Wauck, LeRoy A., ed. see Godin, Andre.

Waud, Roger N. Economics. (Illus.). 1980. text ed. 17.95 scp o.p. (ISBN 0-06-046963-3, HarpC); scp study guide 9.95 o.p. (ISBN 0-06-046987-0); instrs. manual & test bk. avail. avail. o.p. (ISBN 0-06-367024-0); transparencies avail. o.p. (ISBN 0-06-367026-7). Har-Row.

--Economics. 2nd ed. 912p. 1983. text ed. 25.50 scp (ISBN 0-06-046953-6, HarpC); instr's manual & transparency masters avail. (ISBN 0-06-367017-8). scp study guide 8.50 (ISBN 0-06-046983-8); test bank avail. (ISBN 0-06-367018-6). Har-Row.

--Macroeconomics. (Illus.). 1980. pap. text ed. 16.95 scp o.p. (ISBN 0-06-046965-X, HarpC); scp study guide 7.95 o.p. (ISBN 0-06-046989-7). Har-Row.

--Macroeconomics. 2nd ed. 512p. 1983. pap. text ed. 16.50 scp (ISBN 0-06-046951-X, HarpC); scp study guide 6.50 (ISBN 0-06-046985-4). Har-Row.

--Microeconomics. (Illus.). 1980. pap. text ed. 17.95 scp o.p. (ISBN 0-06-046966-8, HarpC); scp study guide 7.95 o.p. (ISBN 0-06-046988-9). Har-Row.

--Microeconomics. 2nd ed. 448p. 1983. pap. text ed. 16.50 scp (ISBN 0-06-046952-8, HarpC); scp study guide 6.50 (ISBN 0-06-046984-6). Har-Row.

Wauer, Roland H. Naturalist's Big Bend. LC 78-21776. (Illus.). 158p. 1980. 10.45 (ISBN 0-89096-069-0); pap. 6.95 o.p. (ISBN 0-89096-070-4). Tex A&M Univ Pr.

Waugh, Albert E. Sundials: Theory & Construction. (Orig.). 1973. pap. 4.00 (ISBN 0-486-22947-5). Dover.

Waugh, Alec. The Mule on the Minaret. 506p. 1965. 6.95 o.p. (ISBN 0-374-21596-0). FS&G.

--Wines & Spirits. LC 68-55300. (Foods of the World Ser). (Illus.). (gr. 6 up). 1968. lib. bdg. 17.28 (ISBN 0-8094-0061-8, Time-Life). Silver.

Waugh, Carol-Lynn. Petite Portraits. 224p. 1982. pap. 12.95 (ISBN 0-87588-190-4). Hobby Hse.

Waugh, Carol-Lynn R., et al. Show Business is Murder. 256p. (Orig.). 1983. pap. 2.75 (ISBN 0-380-81554-0). Avon.

Waugh, Carol-Lynne R. Octagonal Houses of Maine. (Illus.). 64p. 1982. 22.00 (ISBN 0-88014-045-3). Mosaic Pr OH.

Waugh, Carol W. & LaBelle, Judith L. Quilter's Precises Yardage Guide. (Illus.). 144p. 1983. pap. 4.95 (ISBN 0-8329-0275-6). New Century.

Waugh, Charles G. & Greenberg, Martin H. Baseball Three Thousand. 240p. (gr. 7 up). 1981. 12.50 (ISBN 0-525-66732-6, 01214-360). Lodestar Bks.

Waugh, Charles G., ed. see Asimov, Isaac.

Waugh, Charles G., jt. ed. see Asimov, Isaac.

Waugh, Charles G., ed. see Gardner, Erle S.

Waugh, Charles G., jt. ed. see Greenberg, Martin H.

Waugh, Earle H. & Prithipaul, K. Dad, eds. Native Religious Traditions. 244p. 1979. pap. text ed. 7.00x o.p. (ISBN 0-919812-10-4, Pub. by Wilfrid Laurier U Pr Canada). Humanities.

Waugh, Evelyn. Brideshead Revisited. 1982. 9.95 (ISBN 0-316-92627-2); pap. 4.95 (ISBN 0-316-92634-5). Little.

--Brideshead Revisited. 1982. 20.00 (ISBN 0-316-92582-9). Little.

--Charles Ryder's Schooldays & Other Stories. 1982. 12.95 (ISBN 0-316-92638-8); pap. 5.95 (ISBN 0-316-92639-6). Little.

--Tourist in Africa. LC 76-30533. (Illus.). 1977. Repr. of 1960 ed. lib. bdg. 18.25x (ISBN 0-8371-9358-3, WATAF). Greenwood.

Waugh, Hal & Keim, Charles J. Fair Chase with Alaskan Guides. LC 72-83636. (Illus.). 206p. 1972. pap. 5.95 (ISBN 0-88240-010-X). Alaska Northwest.

Waugh, Hillary. The Doria Rafe Case. (Raven House Mysteries Ser.). 224p. 1982. pap. cancelled (ISBN 0-373-63043-3, Pub. by Worldwide). Harlequin Bks.

Waugh, J. S., ed. Advances in Magnetic Resonance. Vol. 1, 1966. 60.00 (ISBN 0-12-025501-4); Vol. 2, 1967. 64.00 (ISBN 0-12-025502-2); Vol. 3, 1968. 64.00 (ISBN 0-12-025503-0); Vol. 4, 1970. 64.00 (ISBN 0-12-025504-9); Vol. 5, 1971. 64.00 (ISBN 0-12-025505-7); Vol. 6, 1973. 64.00 (ISBN 0-12-025506-5); Vol. 7, 1974. 64.00 (ISBN 0-12-025507-3); Vol. 8, 1976. 54.00 (ISBN 0-12-025508-1); Vol. 9, 1977. 60.50 (ISBN 0-12-025509-X). Acad Pr.

--Advances in Magnetic Resonance, Vol. 11. Date not set. price not set (ISBN 0-12-025511-1); price not set lib. ed. (ISBN 0-12-025580-4); price not set microfiche (ISBN 0-12-025581-2). Acad Pr.

Waugh, John, ed. Advances in Magnetic Resonance, Vol. 10. 196p. 1982. 35.00 (ISBN 0-12-025510-3); lib. ed. 45.50 (ISBN 0-12-025578-2); microfiche 24.50 (ISBN 0-12-025579-0). Acad Pr.

Waugh, Kenneth, jt. auth. see Bush, Wilma J.

Waugh, Kenneth W., jt. auth. see Bush, Wilma J.

Waugh, Linda R. Melody of Language. 392p. 1979. text ed. 34.50 o.p. (ISBN 0-8391-1557-1). Univ Park.

Waughfield, Claire, jt. auth. see Kalman, Natalie.

Wauquier, A. & Rolls, E. T., eds. Brain Stimulation Reward. 1976. 127.00 (ISBN 0-7204-0587-4, North-Holland). Elsevier.

Wauson, Sydnie, jt. auth. see Vesely, Anton.

Wauson, Sydnie A., jt. auth. see Ahlstrand, Alan.

Wauson, Sydnie A., ed. see Pegal, Alfred A.

Wauson, Sydnie A., ed. see Scott, Ed.

Wauson, Sydnie A., ed. see Vesely, Anton.

Wavell, Bruce B. The Living Logos: A Philosophico Religious Essay in Free Verse. LC 77-18478. 1978. pap. text ed. 9.00 o.p. (ISBN 0-8191-0324-1). U Pr of Amer.

Wawersik, J., jt. ed. see Rugheimer, E.

Wawn, Brian. The Economics of ASEAN Countries. LC 82-5958. 1983. 27.50x (ISBN 0-312-23673-5). St Martin.

Wawn, William T. The South Sea Islanders & the Queensland Labour Trade. new ed. Corris, Peter, ed. & intro. by. LC 73-78979. (Pacific History Ser.: No. 5). 529p. 1973. text ed. 17.50x (ISBN 0-8248-0282-9). UH Pr.

Wawrytko, Sandra A. The Undercurrent of Feminine Philosophy in Eastern & Western Thought. LC 81-40591. 382p. (Orig.). 1982. lib. bdg. 25.25 (ISBN 0-8191-2067-7); pap. text ed. 14.00 (ISBN 0-8191-2068-5). U Pr of Amer.

Wax, Murray L. Indian-Americans: Unity & Diversity. LC 71-146886. (Ethnic Groups in American Life Ser). 1971. pap. 10.95 ref. ed. (ISBN 0-13-456970-9). P-H.

Wax, Murray L., ed. When Schools Are Desegregated: Problems & Possibilities for Students, Educators, Parents & the Community. LC 79-66449. 300p. write for info cancelled (ISBN 0-87855-376-2). Transaction Bks.

Wax, Murray L. & Cassell, Joan, eds. Federal Regulations: Ethical Issues & Social Research. (AAAS Selected Symposium: No. 36). 1979. lib. bdg. 20.00 (ISBN 0-89158-487-0). Westview.

Waxman, Bruce, jt. auth. see Stacy, Ralph W.

Waxman, Chaim I., jt. ed. see Maier, Joseph B.

Waxman, Meyer, et al. Blessed Is the Daughter. 8th ed. LC 65-12053. (Illus.). 1980. 13.95 (ISBN 0-88400-064-8). Shengold.

Waxman, Stephanie. Growing Up-Feeling Good: A Child's Introduction to Sexuality. 1979. 9.95 (ISBN 0-915572-41-9); pap. 5.95 (ISBN 0-915572-35-4). Panjandrum.

Waxman, Stephen G., ed. Physiology & Pathobiology of Axons. LC 77-17751. 462p. 1978. 45.00 (ISBN 0-89004-215-2). Raven.

Waxman, Stephen G. & Murdoch, Ritchie J., eds. Demyelinating Diseases: Basic & Clinical Electrophysiology. (Advances in Neurology Ser.: Vol. 31). 544p. 1982. 66.00 (ISBN 0-89004-625-5). Raven.

Way & Lee. The Anatomy of the Horse: A Pictorial History. (Illus.). 214p. 1965. text ed. 22.00 o.p. (ISBN 0-397-50142-0, Lippincott Medical). Lippincott.

Way, Charles W. Van see Van Way, Charles W. & Buerk, Charles A.

Way, Eric J. Mathematics for Operators. LC 81-68898. (Illus.). 106p. 1981. pap. text ed. 16.95 (ISBN 0-250-40502-4). Ann Arbor Science.

Way, H. Frank. Liberty in the Balance. 5th, rev. ed. (Foundations of American Government & Political Science Ser.). 144p. 1981. pap. text ed. 10.95 (ISBN 0-07-068661-0, C). McGraw.

Way, Jean, ed. see Davidson, Roger & Oleszek, Walter.

Way, Jean, ed. see Dodd, Lawrence D. & Oppenheimer, Bruce I.

Way, Margaret. Hunter's Moon. (Harlequin Romances Ser.). 192p. 1983. pap. 1.75 (ISBN 0-373-02556-4). Harlequin Bks.

--Pres Des Cascades D'Argent. (Collection Harlequin Ser.). 192p. 1983. pap. 1.95 (ISBN 0-373-49332-0). Harlequin Bks.

--The Silver Veil. (Harlequin Romances Ser.). 192p. 1983. pap. 1.75 (ISBN 0-373-02539-4). Harlequin Bks.

--Spellbound. (Harlequin Romances Ser.). 192p. 1983. pap. 1.75 (ISBN 0-373-02537-8). Harlequin Bks.

Way, Olivia R., jt. auth. see Jones, Cornelia.

Way, Peter. Icarus. LC 79-25792. 1980. 10.95 o.p. (ISBN 0-698-11030-7, Coward). Putnam Pub Group.

--A Perfect State of Health. LC 77-18497. 145p. 1972. 6.95 (ISBN 0-89388-039-6). Okpaku Communications.

Way, Peter, jt. auth. see Carter, Ron.

Way, Robert. The Garden of the Beloved. 80p. 1983. pap. 3.95 (ISBN 0-8091-2534-X). Paulist Pr.

Way, Wendy L. & Nitzke, Susan A. Techniques for Meeting Nutrition Education Needs. 1981. 4.00 (ISBN 0-686-34525-8). Home Econ Educ.

Way, Zilla S., et al. Tracings of Shadow & Sunlight. Phifer, Keith R., ed. LC 78-61715. (Illus.). 1978. pap. 2.95 (ISBN 0-930678-03-6). Key Ray Pub.

Wayburn, Peggy. Adventuring in Alaska: The Ultimate Travel Guide to the Great Land. LC 81-18222. (Illus.). 320p. (Orig.). 1982. pap. 10.95 (ISBN 0-87156-299-5). Sierra.

Wayembergh, Josse, jt. auth. see Bring, Mitchell.

Wayman, Frank W., jt. auth. see Stockton, Ronald R.

Wayman, P. Reports on Astronomy. 1982. 67.50 (ISBN 90-277-1423-1, Pub. by Reidel Holland). Kluwer Boston.

Waymat, E. C. Portable Beach Incinerator, 1977. 1981. 25.00x (ISBN 0-686-97141-8, Pub. by W Spring England). State Mutual Bk.

Waymouth, John F. Electric Discharge Lamps. 384p. 1971. text ed. 22.50x (ISBN 0-262-23048-8). MIT Pr.

Wayne, Bennett. Women in the White House: Four First Ladies. LC 75-20388. (Target Ser). (Illus.). 168p. (gr. 5-12). 1976. PLB 7.99 (ISBN 0-8116-4915-6). Garrard.

Wayne, Bennett, ed. Adventurers in Buckskin. LC 72-6741. (Target Ser.). (Illus.). 168p. (gr. 5-12). 1973. PLB 7.99 (ISBN 0-8116-4900-8). Garrard.

--Big League Pitchers & Catchers. LC 73-17166. (Target Ser). (Illus.). 168p. (gr. 5-12). 1974. PLB 7.99 (ISBN 0-8116-4907-5). Garrard.

Wayne, Bennett, ed. & commentary by. Black Crusaders for Freedom. LC 74-3154. (Target Bks). (Illus.). 168p. (gr. 5-12). 1974. PLB 7.99 (ISBN 0-8116-4910-5). Garrard.

Wayne, Bennett, ed. The Founding Fathers. LC 74-19112. (Target Books Ser.). (Illus.). 168p. (gr. 5-12). 1975. PLB 7.99 (ISBN 0-8116-4912-1). Garrard.

--Four Women of Courage. LC 74-13482. (Target Books Ser). (Illus.). 168p. (gr. 5-12). 1975. PLB 7.99 (ISBN 0-8116-4911-3). Garrard.

Wayne, Bennett, ed. & commentary by. Heroes of the Home Run. LC 73-6750. (Target Ser.). (Illus.). 168p. (gr. 5-12). 1973. PLB 7.99 (ISBN 0-8116-4903-2). Garrard.

Wayne, Bennett, ed. Hockey Hotshots. LC 76-47478. (Target). (Illus.). (gr. 3-4). 1977. lib. bdg. 7.99 (ISBN 0-8116-4917-2). Garrard.

--Indian Patriots of the Eastern Woodlands. LC 75-20048. (Target Ser). (Illus.). 168p. (gr. 5-12). 1976. PLB 7.99 (ISBN 0-8116-4916-4). Garrard.

--Indian Patriots of the Great West. LC 73-17110. (Target Ser). (Illus.). 168p. (gr. 5-12). 1974. PLB 7.99 (ISBN 0-8116-4906-7). Garrard.

--Let's Hear It for America: Symbols, Songs, & Celebrations. LC 74-18342. (Target Ser). (Illus.). 168p. (gr. 5-12). 1975. PLB 7.99 (ISBN 0-8116-4913-X). Garrard.

--Men of the Wild Frontier. LC 73-13615. (Target Ser.). (Illus.). 168p. (gr. 5-12). 1974. PLB 7.99 (ISBN 0-8116-4905-9). Garrard.

Wayne, Bennett, ed. & commentary by. The Super Showmen. LC 74-2282. (Target Bks). (Illus.). 168p. (gr. 5-12). 1974. PLB 7.99 (ISBN 0-8116-4909-1). Garrard.

Wayne, Bennett, ed. Three Jazz Greats. LC 72-6801. (Target Ser.). (Illus.). 168p. (gr. 5-12). 1973. PLB 7.99 (ISBN 0-8116-4901-6). Garrard.

Wayne, Bennett, ed. & commentaries by. Women Who Dared to Be Different. LC 72-6802. (Target Ser.). (Illus.). 168p. (gr. 5-12). 1973. PLB 7.99 (ISBN 0-8116-4902-4). Garrard.

Wayne, Bennett, ed. Women with a Cause. LC 75-4971. (Target Ser.). (Illus.). 168p. (gr. 5-12). 1975. PLB 7.99 (ISBN 0-8116-4914-8). Garrard.

Wayne, Jennifer. Sprout. LC 75-41341. (Illus.). (gr. 4-6). 1976. PLB 6.95 o.p. (ISBN 0-07-068695-5, GB). McGraw.

--Sprout's Window Cleaner. LC 75-41342. (Illus.). (gr. 4-6). 1976. PLB 6.95 o.p. (ISBN 0-07-068697-1, GB). McGraw.

Wayne, Jerry. The Bad Back Book. LC 82-62473. 1983. pap. 6.95 (ISBN 0-918024-25-0). Ox Bow.

Wayne, Lea A. Computer Recognition of Speech. (Speech Technology Ser.). (Illus.). 450p. 1982. 79.00 (ISBN 0-686-37642-0); student ed. 54.00 (ISBN 0-686-37643-9). Speech Science.

Wayne, Michael. The Reshaping of Plantation Society: The Natchez District, 1860-1880. xviii, 272p. 1983. 22.50x (ISBN 0-8071-1050-7). La State U Pr.

Wayne, Roy. Apache Rifles. 1982. 6.95 (ISBN 0-686-84161-1, Avalon). Bouregy.

--Apache Scout. 1981. pap. 6.95 (ISBN 0-686-84683-4, Avalon). Bouregy.

--Trail to Mesilla. (YA) 1979. 6.95 (ISBN 0-685-95880-9, Avalon). Bouregy.

Wayne, Stephen J. The Legislative Presidency. 1978. pap. text ed. 11.95 scp (ISBN 0-06-046964-1, HarpC). Har-Row.

Wayne, Stephen J., jt. ed. see Edwards, George C., III.

Waynick, A. H., ed. Geomagnetism & Aeronomy. LC 65-60042. (Antarctic Research Ser.: Vol. 4). 1965. 13.00 (ISBN 0-87590-104-2). Am Geophysical.

Ways, New. Homosexuality & the Catholic Church. 1983. write for info. (ISBN 0-88347-149-3). Thomas More.

Waz, Joe, jt. auth. see Simon, Sam.

Waz, Joseph & Sirico, Louis J. Reverse the Charges: How to Save Dollars on Your Phone Bill. 1981. pap. 6.00 o.s.i. (ISBN 0-9603466-6-X). NCCB.

Wazer, John R. Van see Van Wazer, John R. & Absar, Ilyas.

Wcela, Emil A., ed. see O'Grady, John F.

Wead, George & Lellis, Geore. Film: Form & Function. LC 80-82804. (Illus.). 512p. 1981. pap. text ed. 15.50 (ISBN 0-395-29740-0). HM.

Wead, George & Lellis, George, eds. The Film Career of Buster Keaton. 1977. lib. bdg. 15.00 o.p. (ISBN 0-8161-7923-9, Hall Reference). G K Hall.

Weagraff, Patrick J. & Lynn, James J. Communications at Work. Herr, Edwin L., ed. (Cooperative Work Experience Education for Careers Program). (Illus.). (gr. 11-12). 1976. pap. text ed. 7.96 (ISBN 0-07-028333-8, G); tchrs manual & key 3.50 (ISBN 0-07-028334-6). McGraw.

--Making Decisions Work. Herr, Edwin L., ed. (Cooperative Work Experience Education for Careers Program Ser.). (Illus.). (gr. 11-12). 1976. pap. text ed. 7.96 (ISBN 0-07-028329-X, G); tchrs manual & key 3.50 (ISBN 0-07-028330-3). McGraw.

Weale, Anne. Flora. 512p. 1983. pap. 3.95 (ISBN 0-373-97004-8). Harlequin Bks.

Weale, B. L. Indiscreet Letters From Peking. 322p. 1983. Repr. of 1907 ed. text ed. 25.00x (ISBN 0-7165-2047-8, Pub. by Irish Academic Pr England). Biblio Dist.

Weale, Margaret. The Slimmer's Microwave Cookbook. (Illus.). 120p. (Orig.). 1983. 17.50 (ISBN 0-7153-8392-2). David & Charles.

Weale, Margaret, tr. see France, Anatole.

Weale, Mary Jo, et al. Environmental Interiors. 1982. text ed. 25.95x (ISBN 0-02-424850-9). Macmillan.

Weale, R. A. Focus on Vision. (Illus.). 208p. 1983. pap. text ed. 15.00x (ISBN 0-674-30701-1). Harvard U Pr.

Weales, Gerald C. Religion in Modern English Drama. LC 75-45367. 317p. 1976. Repr. of 1961 ed. lib. bdg. 20.00x (ISBN 0-8371-8735-4, WEME). Greenwood.

Wear, Jennifer & Holmes, King. How to Have Intercourse Without Getting Screwed. LC 76-41190. 1976. pap. 5.95 (ISBN 0-914842-12-9). Madrona Pubs.

Wearing, J. P. The London Stage 1910-1919: A Calendar of Plays & Players, 2 Vols. LC 82-19190. 1388p. 1982. Set. 65.00 (ISBN 0-8108-1596-6). Scarecrow.

Wearing, J. P., jt. ed. see Conolly, Leonard W.

Weart, Edith L. The Story of Your Blood. (Health Bks.). (Illus.). (gr. 4-7). 1960. PLB 6.99 (ISBN 0-698-30332-6, Coward). Putnam Pub Group.

--The Story of Your Bones. (Health Bks.). (Illus.). (gr. 4-7). 1966. 6.99 (ISBN 0-698-30333-4, Coward). Putnam Pub Group.

--The Story of Your Brain & Nerves. (Health Bks.). (Illus.). (gr. 4-7). 1961. PLB 6.99 (ISBN 0-698-30334-2, Coward). Putnam Pub Group.

--The Story of Your Glands. (Health Bks.). (Illus.). (gr. 4-7). 1962. PLB 6.59 o.p. (ISBN 0-698-30335-0, Coward). Putnam Pub Group.

--The Story of Your Respiratory System. (Health Bks.). (Illus.). (gr. 4-7). 1964. 6.99 (ISBN 0-698-30336-9, Coward). Putnam Pub Group.

--The Story of Your Skin. LC 69-12662. (Health Bks.). (Illus.). (gr. 4-7). 1970. 6.99 (ISBN 0-698-30338-5, Coward). Putnam Pub Group.

Weart, Spencer & Szilard, Gertrud W., eds. Leo Szilard: His Version of the Facts. Selected Recollections & Correspondence. (Illus.). 1978. 22.50x (ISBN 0-262-19168-7); pap. 7.95x (ISBN 0-262-69070-5). MIT Pr.

Weathby, W. J. The Moondancers. (Orig.). 1983. pap. 3.50 (ISBN 0-440-06189-X). Dell.

Weatherall, D. J. & Clegg, J. B. The Thalassaemia Syndromes. 3rd. ed. (Illus.). 888p. 1981. text ed. 92.50 (ISBN 0-632-00084-8, B 5364-9). Mosby.

Weatherall, D. J., et al, eds. Advances in Red Blood Cell Biology. 441p. 1982. text ed. 53.00 (ISBN 0-89004-755-3). Raven.

--The Oxford Textbook of Medicine, 2 vols. (Illus.). 2700p. 1983. Set. 85.00 (ISBN 0-19-261159-3). Oxford U Pr.

Weatherall, David J. Medicine Nineteen Seventy-Eight. LC 78-58440. 1978. 24.50 o.p. (ISBN 0-471-04888-7, Pub. by Wiley Medical). Wiley.

Weatherby, Meredith, tr. see Mishima, Yukio.

Weatherby, W., jt. ed. see Ottley, R.

Weatherby, W. J. Squaring Off: Mailer vs. Baldwin. 1977. 9.95 o.p. (ISBN 0-442-80449-0). Van Nos Reinhold.

Weatherford, Gary & Brown, Lee, eds. Water & Agriculture in the Western U. S. Conservation, Reallocation, & Markets. (Water Policy & Management Ser.). (Illus.). 300p. 1982. lib. bdg. 25.00 (ISBN 0-86531-367-9). Westview.

Weatherford, Roy. Philosophical Foundations of Probability Theory. (International Library of Philosophy). 304p. 1982. 25.00 (ISBN 0-7100-9002-1). Routledge & Kegan.

Weatherford De Ruiz, L. M., compiled by. La Navidad. 192p. (Span.). 1981. pap. 2.75 (ISBN 0-311-08207-6). Casa Bautista.

Weatherhead, A. Kingsley. The British Dissonance: Essays on Ten Contemporary Poets. LC 82-17319. 224p. 1983. text ed. 21.00x (ISBN 0-8262-0391-4). U of Mo Pr.

Weatherhead, A. Kingsley, jt. ed. see Greenfield, Stanley B.

Weatherhead, K. G. FRP Technology. 1980. 69.75 (ISBN 0-85334-886-3, Pub. by Applied Sci England). Elsevier.

Weatherhead, Leslie. Will of God. 1976. pap. 1.25 o.s.i. (ISBN 0-89129-165-2). Jove Pubns.

Weatherhead, Leslie D. The Will of God. (Festival Books). 1976. pap. 2.25 (ISBN 0-687-45600-2). Abingdon.

Weatherhill, Craig. Belerion: Ancient Sites of Land's End. 96p. 1980. 15.00x o.p. (ISBN 0-906720-01-X, Pub. by Hodge England). State Mutual Bk.

Weatherill, Stephen. Goosey Goosey Gander. (Illus.). 32p. (ps-1). 1983. 3.45. Greenwillow.

Weatherley, M. L. The National Survey of Smoke & Sulphur Dioxide: Quality Control & the Air Sampling Arrangements, 1979. 1981. 50.00x (ISBN 0-686-97121-3, Pub. by W Spring England). State Mutual Bk.

Weatherley, Richard A. Reforming Special Education: Policy Implementation from State Level to Street Level. 1979. text ed. 19.95x (ISBN 0-262-23094-1). MIT Pr.

Weatherman, H. M. Book One, Price Trends. (Illus.). 144p. 1983. pap. 5.50 (ISBN 0-913074-18-7). Weatherman.

--Price Trends 1981. (Illus.). 144p. 1981. pap. 5.50 o.p. (ISBN 0-913074-15-2). Weatherman.

Weatherman, Hazel M. Colored Glassware of the Depression Era, Bk. 1. (Illus.). 240p. 1970. 12.00 (ISBN 0-913074-00-4). Glassbooks MO.

--Colored Glassware of the Depression Era, Bk. 2. (Illus.). 400p. 1983. 25.00 (ISBN 0-913074-04-7). Glassbooks MO.

--The Decorated Tumbler. (Illus.). 160p. 1978. pap. 15.00 (ISBN 0-913074-11-X). Glassbooks MO.

--Decorated Tumbler "PriceGuy". 128p. 1979. pap. 3.75 o.p. (ISBN 0-913074-13-6). Weatherman.

--Decorated Tumbler "PriceGuy". 128p. 1983. pap. 4.00 (ISBN 0-913074-19-5). Weatherman.

--Fostoria: Its First Fifty Years. (Illus.). 352p. 18.00 (ISBN 0-913074-02-0). Glassbooks MO.

--Fostoria: Its First Fifty Years. (Illus.). 320p. 1972. 18.00 (ISBN 0-913074-02-0). Weatherman.

--Fostoria Price Watch: Third. (Illus.). 152p. 1983. pap. 6.00 (ISBN 0-913074-16-0). Glassbooks MO.

--Price Guide to the Decorated Tumbler. (Illus.). 128p. 1983. pap. 4.00 (ISBN 0-913074-19-5). Glassbooks MO.

--Price Trends, Bk. 1. (Illus.). 144p. 1983. pap. 5.50 (ISBN 0-913074-15-2). Glassbooks MO.

--Price Trends Two. (Illus.). 304p. 1982. pap. 10.50 (ISBN 0-913074-17-9). Glassbooks MO.

Weathermen, Hazel M. Book Two Price Trends. (Illus.). 288p. 1979. pap. 9.50 o.p. (ISBN 0-913074-12-8). Weatherman.

--Book Two, Price Trends. (Illus.). 304p. 1982. pap. 10.50 (ISBN 0-913074-17-9). Weatherman.

Weathers, Thomas & Hunter, Claud. Fundamentals of Electricity & Automotive Electrical Systems. (Illus.). 256p. 1981. pap. 17.95 (ISBN 0-13-337030-5). P-H.

Weathers, Tom & Hunter, Claud. Diesel Engines for Automobiles & Small Trucks. 300p. 1981. text ed. 19.95 (ISBN 0-8359-1288-4); instr's. manual free (ISBN 0-8359-1289-2). Reston.

Weathers, Wesley W. Birds of Southern California's Deep Canyon. LC 82-13382. (Illus.). 267p. 1983. 35.00x (ISBN 0-520-04754-0). U of Cal Pr.

Weathers, Willie T., jt. auth. see Cox, Virginia D.

Weathers, Winston. An Alternative Style: Options in Compostition. LC 80-18325. 144p. 1980. text ed. 6.25 (ISBN 0-8104-6130-7). Boynton Cook Pubs.

--The Broken Word: Communication Pathos in Modern Literature. 240p. 1981. 39.00 (ISBN 0-686-86001-2). Gordon.

--The Tyger. LC 72-84930. (Literary Casebook Ser.). 1969. pap. text ed. 3.50x (ISBN 0-675-09443-7). Merrill.

Weathers, Winston & Winchester, Otis. The New Strategy of Style. 2nd ed. 1978. pap. text ed. 17.95x (ISBN 0-07-068692-0, C). McGraw.

Weathersby, Robert W. Joseph Holt Ingraham. (United States Authors Ser.). 1980. lib. bdg. 13.95 (ISBN 0-8057-7302-9, Twayne). G K Hall.

Weave, C. P. & Weaver, C. R. Steam on Canals. (Illus.). 96p. (Orig.). 1983. 16.50 (ISBN 0-7153-8218-7). David & Charles.

Weaver. Electoral & Electronic Clocks & Watches. 1982. text ed. 29.95 (ISBN 0-408-01140-8). Butterworth.

Weaver, jt. auth. see Hudson.

Weaver, A. David, ed. Lameness in Cattle. 2nd ed. (Illus.). 480p. 1981. text ed. 43.00 (ISBN 0-686-97937-0, Lippincott Medical). Lippincott.

Weaver, Ann A. & Hudson, Margaret W. I Want a Job. 1964. pap. 2.75x (ISBN 0-88323-047-X, 146). Richards Pub.

--On the Job. 1965. pap. 2.50x o.p. (ISBN 0-88323-059-3, 157). Richards Pub.

Weaver, Ann A., jt. auth. see Hudson, Margaret W.

Weaver, Barbara N. & Bishop, Wiley L. The Corporate Memory: A Profitable, Practical Approach to Information Management & Retention. LC 74-7410. (Systems & Controls for Financial Management Ser.). 257p. 1974. 29.50 o.p. (ISBN 0-471-92323-0, Pub. by Wiley-Interscience). Wiley.

Weaver, Betsy & Frederick, Gary E. Hands, Horses & Engines: A Centennial History of the Baltimore County Fire Service. Campbell, Colin A., ed. (Illus.). 160p. 1982. 16.95 (ISBN 0-9608952-0-5). Baltimore CFSCC.

Weaver, Bob, jt. auth. see Nash, Bruce.

Weaver, C. E. & Beck, K. C. Miocene of the South East United States: A Model for Chemical Sedimentation in a Peri-Marine Environment. (Developments in Sedimentology: Vol. 22). 1977. 51.00 (ISBN 0-444-41568-8). Elsevier.

Weaver, C. R., jt. auth. see Weave, C. P.

Weaver, Carolyn. The Crisis in Social Security: Economic & Political Origins. (Duke Press Policy Studies). 248p. 1982. 36.75 (ISBN 0-8223-0474-0). Duke.

Weaver, Clifford L. & Babcock, Richard F. City Zoning. LC 79-90347. 328p. (Orig.). 1980. pap. 18.95 (ISBN 0-918286-17-4). Planners Pr.

Weaver, Clyde, jt. auth. see Friedmann, John.

Weaver, Constance, jt. auth. see Malmstrom, Jean.

Weaver, Constance, ed. Using Junior Novels to Develop Language & Thought: Five Integration Teaching Guides. 75p. 4.00 (ISBN 0-686-95325-8); members 3.50 (ISBN 0-686-99496-5). NCTE.

Weaver, D. H. Transparencies for Accounting: Systems & Procedures. 4th ed. Date not set. 110.00 (ISBN 0-07-086512-4). McGraw.

Weaver, D. H., jt. auth. see Grubbs, R.

Weaver, D. H., jt. auth. see Winger, F. E.

Weaver, D. H., et al. Accounting: Systems & Procedures, 3 pts. 4th ed. 608p. 1982. Set. 15.60 (ISBN 0-07-069320-X). McGraw.

--Accounting: Systems & Procedures. 4th ed. 1982. evaluation manual 1.32 (ISBN 0-07-069340-4). McGraw.

--Accounting: Systems & Procedures, Pt. 1 - Elements of Financial Records. 4th ed. 256p. 1982. 6.40 (ISBN 0-07-069321-8); learning guide & working papers 5.60 (ISBN 0-07-069330-7). working papers & chapter problems 3.36 (ISBN 0-07-069324-2). McGraw.

--Accounting: Systems & Procedures, Pt. 2 - Accounting Subsystems. 4th ed. LC 81-12335. 224p. 1982. 6.40 (ISBN 0-07-069322-6); learning guide & working papers 6.04 (ISBN 0-07-069331-5); tchr's ed. working papers & Chapter problems 10.00 (ISBN 0-07-069328-5); working papers & chapter problems 3.16 (ISBN 0-07-069325-0). McGraw.

--Accounting: Systems & Procedures, Pt. 3 - Special Accounting Systems & Procedures. 4th ed. LC 81-12335. 192p. 1982. 6.40 (ISBN 0-07-069323-4, G); learning guide & working papers 6.04 (ISBN 0-07-069332-3). working papers & chapter problems 3.92 (ISBN 0-07-069326-9). McGraw.

--Allen Electronic Service Accounting Application. 2nd ed. 1973. 5.86 (ISBN 0-07-068740-4, G); key 3.50 (ISBN 0-07-068741-2). McGraw.

--Jeans Plus Accounting Application. 168p. 1982. 6.36 (ISBN 0-07-069335-8). McGraw.

--Kenna's Carpet Mart Accounting Application. 4th ed. 168p. 1982. 6.60 (ISBN 0-07-069336-6). McGraw.

--Accounting: Systems & Procedures, Advanced Course. 1982. 17.32 (ISBN 0-07-068931-8); accounting application 6.64 (ISBN 0-07-068933-4). McGraw.

Weaver, David H. Videotex Journalism: Teletext, Viewdata, & the News. 160p. 1983. text ed. write for info. (ISBN 0-89859-263-1). L Erlbaum Assocs.

Weaver, David H. & Hanna, J. Marshall. Accounting Ten-Twelve, Part 1: Elements of Financial Records. 3rd ed. (Illus.). (gr. 10-12). 1976. pap. text ed. 6.40 (ISBN 0-07-068901-6, G); indiv. lrng. guides 6.64 (ISBN 0-07-068904-0); working papers & chapter problems 3.80 (ISBN 0-07-068907-5). McGraw.

--Accounting Ten-Twelve, Part 2: Accounting Systems & Procedures. 3rd ed. (Illus.). (gr. 10-12). 1976. pap. text ed. 6.40 (ISBN 0-07-068902-4, G); individualized learning guides 6.64 (ISBN 0-07-068905-9); working papers & chapters problems 3.80 (ISBN 0-07-068908-3). McGraw.

--Accounting Ten-Twelve, Part 3: Business Data Processing. 3rd ed. (Illus.). (gr. 10-12). 1977. pap. text ed. 6.40 (ISBN 0-07-068903-2, G); learning guides 6.64 (ISBN 0-07-068906-7); tchng suggestions, tests & key 6.64 (ISBN 0-07-068924-5); working papers & chap. problems 4.28 (ISBN 0-07-068921-0). McGraw.

Weaver, David H., et al. Home Heating Company: Accounting Application for Accounting 10-12 Ser, Pt. 2, Accounting Systems & Procedures. 3rd ed. 1978. 7.28 (ISBN 0-07-068917-2, G); key 3.50 (ISBN 0-07-068918-0). McGraw.

Weaver, Donald B. & Baird, Julia L. How to Do a Literature Search in Psychology. (Illus.). 56p. (Orig.). 1982. pap. text ed. 6.95 (ISBN 0-9609182-0-5). Resource Pr.

Weaver, Earl & Stainback, Berry. It's What You Learn After You Know It All That Counts. Rev. ed. 1983. pap. 8.95 (ISBN 0-671-47239-9, Fireside). S&S.

Weaver, F. W., ed. Somerset Medieval Wills. (Illus.). 1226p. 1982. text ed. 59.00x (ISBN 0-86299-022-X, Pub. by Sutton England). Humanities.

Weaver, Frank P., jt. auth. see Sheldon, Charles H.

Weaver, Gerald L. Structural Detailing for Technicians. (Illus.). 256p. 1974. pap. 21.50 (ISBN 0-07-068712-9, G). McGraw.

Weaver, Glenn, ed. The Connecticut Revolutionary Series, 30 vols. Incl. Vol. 1. Connecticut Joins the Revolution. Barrow, Thomas C; Vol. 2. Connecticut in the Continental Congress. Collier, Christopher; Vol. 3. Connecticut's Revolutionary War Leaders. Callahan, North; Vol. 4. Connecticut's Black Soldiers, 1775-1783. White, David O; Vol. 5. Connecticut: The Provisions State. Destler, Chester M; Vol. 6. Connecticut's Loyalists. East, Robert A; Vol. 7. Connecticut Education in the Revolutionary Era. Frost, J. William; Vol. 8. Connecticut's Seminary of Sedition: Yale College. Tucker, Louis L; Vol. 9. Connecticut's War Governor: Jonathan Trumbull. Roth, David M; Vol. 10. Connecticut Attacked: A British Viewpoint, Tryon's Raid on Danbury. McDevitt, Robert; Vol. 11. Connecticut's First Family: William Pitkin & His Connections. Daniels, Bruce C; Vol. 12. Connecticut Signer: William Williams. Stark, Bruce P; Vol. 13. Connecticut's Revolutionary Cavalry: Sheldon's Horse. Hayes, John T; Vol. 14. **Connecticut's Revolutionary Press. Cutler, Charles L; Vol. 15. Connecticut Women in the Revolutionary Era. Fennelly, Catherine; Vol. 16. Connecticut Art & Architecture: Looking Backwards Two Hundred Years. Warren, William L; Vol. 17. Connecticut's Loyalist Gadfly: the Reverend Samuel Andrew Peters. Cohen, Sheldon S; Vol. 18. Connecticut's Colonial & Continental Money. Parker, Wyman W; Vol. 19. Connecticut Revolutionary: Eliphalet Dyer. Willingham, William F; Vol. 20. Connecticut Congressman: Samuel Huntington, 1731-1796. Gerlach, Larry R; Vol. 21. Connecticut Society in the Revolutionary Era. Main, Jackson T; Vol. 22. Connecticut's Hero: Israel Putnam. Niven, John; Vol. 23. Connecticut Congregationalists in the Era of the American Revolution. Meyer, Freeman; Vol. 24. Connecticut's Cannon: The Salisbury Iron Furnace in the American Revolutionary. Rome, Adam; Vol. 25. Connecticut's Nationalist Revolutionary: Jonathan Trumbull, Jr. Ifkovic, John; Vol. 26. Connecticut's Dark Star of the Revolution: General Benedict Arnold. Wallace, Willard M; Vol. 27. Connecticut Science, Technology, & Medicine in the Era of the American Revolution. Kuslan, Louis L; Vol. 28. Connecticut Anglicans in the Revolutionary Era: A Study in Communal Tensions. Steiner, Bruce E; Vol. 29. Connecticut Industry & the Revolution. Walsh, James P. 1978. 3.50 ea. Conn Hist Com.**

Weaver, Gordon. The American Short Story, 1945-1980: A Critical History. (Critical History of the Modern Short Story Ser.). 208p. 1983. lib. bdg. 17.95 (ISBN 0-8057-9350-X, Twayne). G K Hall.

Weaver, Harriet. Redwood Country: A Pictorial Guide Through California's Magnificent Redwood Forests. rev. ed. (Illus., Orig.). 1983. pap. 8.95 (ISBN 0-87701-279-2). Chronicle Bks.

Weaver, Harriett E. Adventures in the Redwoods. LC 75-3912. (Illus.). 1982. pap. 4.95 o.p. (ISBN 0-87701-060-9). Chronicle Bks.

--Frosty: A Raccoon to Remember. (gr. 5-7). 1974. pap. 1.95 (ISBN 0-671-42094-1). Archway.

Weaver, Helen, jt. auth. see Brau, Jean-Louis.

Weaver, Helen, tr. see Piaget, Jean & Inhelder, Barbel.

Weaver, Horace R., ed. The International Lesson Annual 1982-83: A Comprehensive Commentary on the International Sunday School Lessons. (Orig.). 1982. pap. 4.95 (ISBN 0-687-19146-7). Abingdon.

Weaver, Horace R. & Laymon, Charles M., eds. The International Lesson Annual, 1983-84. 448p. (Orig.). 1983. pap. 5.95 (ISBN 0-687-19147-5). Abingdon.

Weaver, James & Jameson, Kenneth. Economic Development: Competing Paradigms. LC 80-6257. (Illus.). 138p. (Orig.). 1981. lib. bdg. 18.75 (ISBN 0-8191-1770-6); pap. text ed. 8.25 (ISBN 0-8191-1771-4). U Pr of Amer.

Weaver, John L. Grizzly Bears. LC 82-45378. (Skylight Bk.). (Illus.). 64p. (gr. 2-5). 1982. PLB 7.95 (ISBN 0-396-08084-7). Dodd.

Weaver, John T. Twenty Years of Silents, Nineteen Hundred & Eight to Nineteen Twenty-Eight. LC 73-157729. 514p. 1971. lib. bdg. 23.00 o.p. (ISBN 0-8108-0401-8). Scarecrow.

Weaver, Lydia & Morrow, Gray. Barbara Cartland Romances. (Illus.). 128p. 1981. pap. 4.95 (ISBN 0-8256-3239-0, Quick Fox); 10 copy prepack 49.50 (ISBN 0-8256-3256-0). Putnam Pub Group.

Weaver, Lynn E., ed. Reactor Kinetics & Control: Proceedings. (AEC Symposium Ser.). 593p. 1964. pap. 22.75 (ISBN 0-87079-333-0, TID-7662); microfiche 4.50 (ISBN 0-87079-334-9, TID-7662). DOE.

Weaver, Lynn E., jt. ed. see Hetrick, David L.

Weaver, M. William Carlos Williams. LC 77-149431. (Illus.). 1977. 39.50 (ISBN 0-521-08072-X); pap. 10.95 (ISBN 0-521-29195-X). Cambridge U Pr.

Weaver, Martha. Black Beauty. 1969. pap. 3.25x (ISBN 0-88323-005-4, 106); tchr's manual free (ISBN 0-88323-006-2, 107). Richards Pub.

Weaver, Martha & Prevo, Helen. Good Literature for Slow Readers, 10 vols. Incl. Beautiful Joe; Heidi; Swiss Family Robinson; The Prince & the Pauper; Ivanhoe; Freckls; Treasure Island; Little Women; Tom Sawyer; Twenty-Thousand Leagues Under the Sea. (Illus.). 1967. fabrikoid 89.50x set (ISBN 0-88323-032-1, 130). Richards Pub.

Weaver, Maureen. Viewpoints: A Directory of Major Newspapers & Their Op-Ed Pollicies. 32p. 1983. pap. 2.00 (ISBN 0-910175-03-9). Campaign Political.

Weaver, P. R. Familia Caesaris: A Social Study of the Emperor's Freedmen & Slaves. LC 76-171686. (Illus.). 1972. 47.50 (ISBN 0-521-08340-0). Cambridge U Pr.

Weaver, Paul H. see Commission on Critical Choices.

Weaver, Peter A. You, Inc. A Detailed Escape Route to Being Your Own Boss. LC 72-97094. 312p. 1975. pap. 4.95 o.p. (ISBN 0-385-09895-2, Dolp). Doubleday.

Weaver, Phyllis A., jt. auth. see Resnick, Lauren B.

Weaver, Rachel L. Bulletin Board Sketches. pap. 3.70 (ISBN 0-686-32319-X). Rod & Staff.

Weaver, Rex. Behold: New Holland! 8.50 (ISBN 0-392-16428-0, ABC). Sportshelf.

Weaver, Richard L. Understanding Public Communication. (Illus.). 352p. 1983. pap. text ed. 13.95 (ISBN 0-13-936740-3). P-H.

Weaver, Richard L., jt. auth. see Hybels, Saundra.

Weaver, Richard L., II. Understanding Interpersonal Communication. 2nd ed. 1981. pap. text ed. 13.50x (ISBN 0-673-15436-X). Scott F.

Weaver, Richard M. The Ethics of Rhetoric. LC 53-8796. 234p. pap. 4.95 (ISBN 0-89526-998-8). Regnery-Gateway.

--Ideas Have Consequences. LC 29-18915. (Midway Reprint Ser.). 1948. pap. 9.00x (ISBN 0-226-87679-9). U of Chicago Pr.

Weaver, Rip. Blueprint Reading Basics. 296p. 1982. text ed. 16.95 (ISBN 0-87201-075-9). Gulf Pub.

--Modern Basic Drafting. 2nd ed. (Illus.). 392p. 1979. 19.95x (ISBN 0-87201-059-7); wkbks. 9.95x ea.; Wkbk. 1. (ISBN 0-87201-055-4); Wkbk 2. (ISBN 0-87201-056-2); Instructor's Manual. Gulf Pub.

--Piper's Pocket Handbook. 127p. 1979. pap. 9.95 (ISBN 0-87201-701-X). Gulf Pub.

--Process Piping Drafting. 2nd. ed. 270p. 1975. 19.95x (ISBN 0-87201-761-3). Gulf Pub.

--Process Piping Drafting Workbook. (Illus.). 84p. 1977. 11.95 (ISBN 0-87201-762-1). Gulf Pub.

--Structural Drafting. (Illus.). 206p. 1977. 16.95x (ISBN 0-87201-810-5). Gulf Pub.

--Structural Drafting Workbook. (Illus.). 112p. 1980. pap. text ed. 7.95 (ISBN 0-686-70161-5). Gulf Pub.

Weaver, Robert, ed. Canadian Short Stories. pap. 7.50x (ISBN 0-19-540134-4). Oxford U Pr.

--Canadian Short Stories. (Ser. 3). 1978. pap. 7.95x (ISBN 0-19-540291-X). Oxford U Pr.

Weaver, Robert B. The Birth of Our Nation & Foundation of Our Republic: An Analysis & Interpretation of the Declaration of Independence & the Constitution. 84p. (gr. 11-12). 1974. pap. 1.25 o.s.i. (ISBN 0-912530-13-8); test 0.10 o.s.i. (ISBN 0-686-77027-7). Patriotic Educ.

Weaver, Robert J. Grape Growing. LC 76-22753. 1976. 27.50x (ISBN 0-471-92324-9, Pub. by Wiley-Interscience). Wiley.

Weaver, Ruth C., compiled by. Reverend John McMillan. (Illus.). 174p. 1981. pap. text ed. 7.00 (ISBN 0-9607168-0-7). R C Weaver.

Weaver, Suzanne. Decision to Prosecute: Organization & Public Policy in the Antitrust Division. 208p. 1977. 17.50x (ISBN 0-262-23085-2); pap. 5.95x (ISBN 0-262-73053-7). MIT Pr.

Weaver, Suzanne, jt. auth. see Moynihan, Daniel P.

Weaver, Thomas & White, Douglas. The Anthropology of Urban Environments, No. 11. 1972. pap. 2.50 (ISBN 0-686-36584-4). Am Anthro Assn.

Weaver, Thomas, jt. auth. see Hoebel, E. Adamson.

Weaver, Thomas, et al, eds. To See Ourselves: Anthropology & Modern Social Issues. 1973. pap. 10.95x o.p. (ISBN 0-673-07780-2). Scott F.

Weaver, W. Timothy. The Contest for Educational Resources: Equity & Reform in a Meritocratic Society. LC 81-47332. (Illus.). 208p. 1981. 23.95x (ISBN 0-669-04586-1). Lexington Bks.

Weaver, Warren, jt. auth. see Shannon, Claude E.

Weaver, William, tr. see Bassani, Giorgio.

Weaver, William, tr. see Calvino, Italo.

Weaver, William, tr. see Eco, Umberto.

Weaver, William, tr. see Moravia, Alberto.

Weaver, William, Jr., jt. auth. see Gere, James M.

Weaver, William W. Sauerkraut Yankees: Pennsylvania German Food & Foodways. LC 82-40488. (Illus.). 224p. (Orig.). 1983. 25.00x (ISBN 0-8122-7868-2); pap. 12.50 (ISBN 0-8122-1145-6). U of Pa Pr.

Weaver, William W., ed. see Lea, Elizabeth E.

Webb & Gehrke, eds. Exploratory Field Experience. 1981. 2.50 (ISBN 0-686-38073-8). Assn Tchr Ed.

Webb, A. N. Edition of the Cartulary of Burscough Priory. 1970. 27.00 (ISBN 0-7190-1152-3). Manchester.

Webb, Augustus D. New Dictionary of Statistics: A Complement to the Fourth Edition of Mulhall's Dictionary of Statistics. LC 68-18017. 1971. Repr. of 1911 ed. 56.00x (ISBN 0-8103-3988-9). Gale.

Webb, Barbara, jt. ed. see Cook, Peter.

Webb, Beatrice. My Apprenticeship. LC 79-15437. 1980. 54.50 (ISBN 0-521-22941-3); pap. 16.95 (ISBN 0-521-29731-1). Cambridge U Pr.

--Our Partnership. Drake, Barbara & Cole, Margaret, eds. LC 75-28806. (Illus.). 608p. 1975. Repr. of 1948 ed. 37.50 (ISBN 0-521-20852-1). Cambridge U Pr.

Webb, Beatrice, jt. auth. see Webb, Sidney.

Webb, Beatrice & MacKenzie, Jeanne, eds. The Diary of Beatrice Webb: Glitter Around & Darkness Within, 1873-1892, Vol. 1. (Illus.). 432p. 1982. text ed. 25.00x (ISBN 0-674-20287-2, Belknap Pr). Harvard U Pr.

Webb, Bernard L. & Launie, J. J. Insurance Company Operations, 2 Vols. 2nd ed. LC 81-66113. 935p. 1981. Vol. 1. text ed. 18.00 (ISBN 0-89463-024-5); Vol. 2. text ed. 18.00 (ISBN 0-89463-025-3). Am Inst Property.

Webb, Bernard L., et al. Insurance Company Operations. 1978. write for info. o.p. (CPCU 5). IIA.

Webb, Chris. Be Your Own Car Mechanic. (Illus.). 176p. 1976. pap. 7.50 o.p. (ISBN 0-86002-150-5). Transatlantic.

Webb, D. A., jt. auth. see McDowell, R. B.

Webb, D. R. & Papadakis, C. N., eds. Small Hydro Power Fluid Machinery. 1982. 40.00 (H00233). ASME.

Webb, David A. & Scannell, Mary J. Flora of Connemara & the Burren. LC 82-4425. (Illus.). 320p. Date not set. 69.50 (ISBN 0-521-23395-X). Cambridge U Pr.

Webb, David M. The Old Woman and the Bird. LC 79-55781. (Illus.). 45p. (gr. 3-8). 1983. 7.95 (ISBN 0-935054-04-9). Webb-Newcomb.

Webb, David R., ed. Immunopharmacology & the Regulation of Leukocyte Function. (Immunology Ser.: Vol. 19). (Illus.). 312p. 1982. 45.00 (ISBN 0-8247-1707-4). Dekker.

Webb, Dean, jt. ed. see Odden, Allan.

Webb, Douglas, jt. auth. see Eason, Thomas S.

Webb, Eugene J. & Campbell, Donald T. Nonreactive Measures in the Social Science. 2nd ed. 1981. 13.50 (ISBN 0-395-30767-8). HM.

Webb, Frank. Watercolor Energies. (Illus.). 176p. 1983. 22.50 (ISBN 0-89134-054-8); pap. 14.95 (ISBN 0-89134-055-6). North Light Pub.

Webb, G. A. Nuclear Magnetic Resonance, Vol. 10. 372p. 1982. 199.00x (ISBN 0-85186-332-9, Pub. by Royal Soc Chem England). State Mutual Bk.

Webb, G. A., jt. ed. see Mooney, E. F.

Webb, George E. Tree Rings & Telescopes: The Scientific Career of A. E. Douglass. 250p. 1983. 19.50x (ISBN 0-8165-0798-8). U of Ariz Pr.

Webb, George J., jt. auth. see Mason, Lowell.

Webb, Iris, ed. The Complete Guide to Flower & Foliage Arrangement. (Illus.). 256p. 1979. 24.95 (ISBN 0-385-15119-5). Doubleday.

Webb, J. A., jt. auth. see Moore, P. D.

Webb, J. D., ed. Noise Control in Industry. 1976. 32.00x (ISBN 0-419-11220-0, Pub. by E & FN Spon). Methuen Inc.

Webb, J. F. Age of Bede. 1983. pap. price not set (ISBN 0-14-044437-8). Penguin.

Webb, J. L. Enzyme & Metabolic Inhibitors, 3 vols. Incl. Vol. 1. General Principles of Inhibition. 1963 (ISBN 0-12-739201-7); Vol. 2. Malonate, Analogs, Dehydroacetate, Sulfhydryl Reagents, o-Iodosobenzoate, Mercurials. 1966 (ISBN 0-12-739202-5); Vol. 3. Iodoacetate, Meleate, N-Ethylmaleimide, Alloxan, Quinones, Arsenicals. 1966 (ISBN 0-12-739203-3). 91.50 ea. Acad Pr.

Webb, J. T. Coral 66 Programming. 1978. 19.50x (ISBN 0-85012-193-0). Intl Pubns Serv.

Webb, James. The Harmonious Circle. LC 77-16261. (Illus.). 1980. 19.95 (ISBN 0-399-11465-3). Putnam Pub Group.

--The Occult Establishment. LC 75-22157. (Illus.). 535p. 1976. 27.50x (ISBN 0-912050-56-X, Library Pr). Open Court.

--The Occult Underground. LC 73-22458. (Illus.). 395p. 1974. 24.50x (ISBN 0-912050-46-2, Library Pr). Open Court.

Webb, James T. & McNamara, Kathleen T. Configural Interpretations of the MMPI & CPI. 76p. 1981. pap. write for info. Ohio Psych Pub.

Webb, James T. & Meckstroth, Betty. Guiding the Gifted Child. LC 82-9939. 262p. 1982. pap. 11.95 (ISBN 0-910707-00-6). Ohio Psych Pub.

Webb, James W. & Green, A. Wigfall, eds. William Faulkner of Oxford. LC 65-23763. (Illus.). 1965. pap. 4.95x o.p. (ISBN 0-8071-0143-5). La State U Pr.

Webb, John N. & Brown, Malcolm. Migrant Families. LC 76-165605. (Research Monograph Ser.: Vol. 18). (Illus.). xxx, 192p. 1971. Repr. of 1938 ed. lib. bdg. 25.00 (ISBN 0-306-70350-5). Da Capo.

Webb, John N., jt. auth. see Brown, Malcolm.

Webb, John W., jt. auth. see Broek, C. M.

Webb, Kempton, jt. auth. see James, Preston E.

Webb, Lance. How Bad are Your Sins? 224p. (Orig.). Date not set. pap. 3.95 (ISBN 0-687-17520-8, Festival). Abingdon.

--How Good are your Virtues? 176p. (Orig.). 1983. pap. 3.50 (ISBN 0-687-17528-3, Festival). Abingdon.

Webb, Lesley. Making a Start on Child Study. 92p. (Orig.). 1975. pap. 6.25x o.p. (ISBN 0-631-16480-4, Pub. by Basil Blackwell England). Biblio Dist.

--Purpose & Practice in Nursery Education. 188p. 1974. pap. 9.25x o.p. (ISBN 0-631-15240-7, Pub. by Basil Blackwell). Biblio Dist.

Webb, Linda J., et al, eds. DSM-III Training Program for Health Professionals. LC 81-10174. 176p. 1981. text ed. 15.00 (ISBN 0-87630-279-7); pap. text ed. 10.95 a guide to clinical use (ISBN 0-87630-293-2); per slide set 150.00x (ISBN 0-87630-281-9); per videotape set 200.00x (ISBN 0-87630-280-0); complete pkg. set 350.00x (ISBN 0-87630-282-7). Brunner-Mazel.

Webb, Lucas. The Attempted Assassination of John F. Kennedy. LC 76-40282. 1976. lib. bdg. 9.95x (ISBN 0-89370-104-1); pap. 3.95x (ISBN 0-89370-204-8). Borgo Pr.

Webb, M. Chemistry, Biochemistry & Biology of Cadmium. (Topics in Environmental Health Ser.: Vol. 2). 1980. 96.75 (ISBN 0-444-80109-X). Elsevier.

Webb, M. J. & Holtje, H. Mechanical Technician's Handbook. 1982. 35.00 (ISBN 0-07-068802-8). McGraw.

Webb, Mark, jt. auth. see Leiter, Michael P.

Webb, Mena. The Curious Wine. LC 78-77149. 1969. 8.95 (ISBN 0-87716-006-6, Pub. by Moore Pub Co). F Apple.

Webb, R. H. & Wilshire, H. G., eds. Environmental Effects of Off-Road Vehicles: Impact & Management in Arid Regions. (Springer Series on Environmental Management). (Illus.). 560p. 1983. 49.80 (ISBN 0-387-90737-8). Springer-Verlag.

Webb, Ralph, Jr. Interpersonal Speech Communication: Principles & Practices. (Illus.). 320p. 1975. pap. text ed. 19.95 (ISBN 0-13-475103-5). P-H.

Webb, Richard C., jt. auth. see Pfeffermann, Guy P.

Webb, Richard C., jt. ed. see Frank, Charles R., Jr.

Webb, Robert A., ed. The Washington Post Deskbook on Style. 1978. 8.95-op (ISBN 0-07-068397-2, GB); pap. 5.95 (ISBN 0-07-068398-0). McGraw.

Webb, Robert L., jt. auth. see Frank, Stuart M.

Webb, Robert N. America Is Also Irish. (America Is Also Ser.). (Illus.). 128p. (gr. 5 up). 1973. PLB 4.97 o.p. (ISBN 0-399-60809-5). Putnam Pub Group.

Webb, Ross A. Benjamin Helm Bristow: Border State Politician. LC 74-80089. (Illus.). 384p. 1969. 14.50x o.p. (ISBN 0-8131-1182-X). U Pr of Ky.

Webb, Samuel C. Managerial Economics. LC 75-31039. (Illus.). 608p. 1976. text ed. 26.95 (ISBN 0-395-20589-1); solutions manual 2.95 (ISBN 0-395-20590-5). HM.

Webb, Sharon. Earthchild. LC 82-1791. 216p. 1982. 11.95 (ISBN 0-689-30945-7, Argo). Atheneum.

Webb, Shelia. Paper: The Continuous Thread. LC 82-12840. (Themes in Art Ser.). (Illus.). 72p. (Orig.). 1983. pap. 6.95x (ISBN 0-910386-69-2, Pub. by Cleveland Mus Art). Ind U Pr.

Webb, Sheyann & Nelson, Rachel W. Selma, Lord, Selma: Girlhood Memories of the Civil Rights Days. LC 80-24049. (Illus.). 164p. 1980. pap. 4.95 (ISBN 0-688-08744-2). Quill NY.

Webb, Sidney & Webb, Beatrice. A Constitution for the Socialist Commonwealth of Great Britain. LC 75-28805. 416p. 1975. Repr. of 1920 ed. 29.95 (ISBN 0-521-20851-3). Cambridge U Pr.

--Methods of Social Study. LC 75-22553. 304p. 1975. Repr. of 1931 ed. 29.95 (ISBN 0-521-20850-5). Cambridge U Pr.

Webb, Sidney, ed. Seasonal Trades. LC 79-1597. 1983. Repr. of 1912 ed. 27.50 (ISBN 0-88355-902-1). Hyperion Conn.

Webb Society & Jones, Kenneth G., eds. Webb Society Deep-Sky Observer's Handbook: Galaxies, Vol. IV. LC 77-359099. 296p. 1981. pap. 15.95x (ISBN 0-89490-050-1). Enslow Pubs.

--Webb Society Deep-Sky Observer's Handbook: Clusters of Galaxies, Vol. V. LC 78-31260. 241p. 1982. pap. 16.95x (ISBN 0-89490-066-8). Enslow Pubs.

--Webb Society Deep-Sky Observer's Handbook: Double Stars, Vol. I. LC 78-31260. 1979. pap. 7.95x (ISBN 0-89490-027-7). Enslow Pubs.

--Webb Society Deep-Sky Observer's Handbook: Planetary & Gaseous Nebulae, Vol. II. LC 78-31260. 1979. pap. 9.95x (ISBN 0-89490-028-5). Enslow Pubs.

Webb, Suzanne S. Prose That Works. 288p. 1982. text ed. 8.95 (ISBN 0-15-597882-9, HC). HarBraceJ.

Webb, Terry, jt. auth. see Gibb, Allan.

Webb, Terry & Quince, Thelma, eds. Small Business Research: The Development of Entrepreneurs. 218p. 1982. text ed. 34.00x (ISBN 0-566-00381-3). Gower Pub Ltd.

Webb, Vincent J., jt. auth. see Roberg, Roy R.

Webb, W. B. Biological Rhythms, Sleep & Performance. 248p. 1982. 34.95x (ISBN 0-471-10047-1, Pub. by Wiley-Interscience). Wiley.

Webb, Walter F. Foreign Land Shells. (Illus.). 1948. 7.95 (ISBN 0-910872-13-9). Lee Pubns.

--Geographic Guide to Sea Shells. (Illus.). 6.95 (ISBN 0-910872-14-7). Lee Pubns.

--Handbook for Shell Collectors. 16th rev. ed. (Illus.). 12.00 (ISBN 0-910872-11-2). Lee Pubns.

--United States Mollusca. (Illus.). 7.95 (ISBN 0-910872-12-0). Lee Pubns.

Webb, Walter P. Divided We Stand: The Crisis of a Frontierless Democracy. LC 79-1598. 1983. Repr. of 1944 ed. 16.00 (ISBN 0-88355-903-X). Hyperion Conn.

--Great Plains. 1957. pap. 4.95 o.p. (ISBN 0-448-00029-6, G&D). Putnam Pub Group.

--An Honest Preface & Other Essays. LC 74-15562. 216p. 1975. Repr. of 1959 ed. lib. bdg. 14.00x o.p. (ISBN 0-8371-7828-2, WEHP). Greenwood.

--Talks on Texas Books: A Collection of Book Reviews. Friend, Llerena B., ed. LC 76-84083. 1970. 6.00 o.p. (ISBN 0-87611-024-3). Tex St Hist Assn.

Webb, Wheaton P. The Heart Has Its Seasons: A Sourcebook of Christmas Meditations. LC 82-3898. 96p. (Orig.). 1982. pap. 5.95 (ISBN 0-687-16800-7). Abingdon.

Webb, Wilfred M. The Heritage of Dress: Being Notes on the History & Evolution of Clothes. LC 70-141749. (Illus.). 1971. Repr. of 1912 ed. 34.00x (ISBN 0-8103-3398-8). Gale.

Webb, Willard. Crucial Moments of the Civil War. (Illus.). 350p. 1983. Repr. 17.50x (ISBN 0-685-41737-9). Irvington.

Webb, William S. Indian Knoll. LC 73-18473. (Illus.). 280p. 1974. Repr. of 1946 ed. 16.50x (ISBN 0-87049-150-4). U of Tenn Pr.

Webb, Willis L. Structure of the Stratosphere & Mesosphere. (International Geophysics Ser.: Vol. 9). 1966. 63.00 (ISBN 0-12-739850-3). Acad Pr.

Webb, Wilse B. Sleep: An Active Process (Research & Commentary) 160p. 1973. pap. 8.95x (ISBN 0-673-07704-7). Scott F.

--Sleep: The Gentle Tyrant. (Illus.). 192p. 1976. 9.95 o.p. (ISBN 0-13-812933-9, Spec); pap. 3.95 o.p. (ISBN 0-13-812925-8). P-H.

Webber, B. M., jt. auth. see Mayfield, J. M.

Webber, Diane, jt. auth. see Webber, Joe.

Webber, Frederick R. Church Symbolism: An Explanation of the More Important Symbols of the Old & New Testament, the Primitive, the Mediaeval & the Modern Church. rev. 2nd ed. LC 79-107627. (Illus.). 1971. Repr. of 1938 ed. 47.00x (ISBN 0-8103-3349-X). Gale.

Webber, Irma. It Looks Like This. 1983. 5.50 (ISBN 0-686-84075-5); pap. 4.00 (ISBN 0-686-84076-3). Intl Gen Semantics.

Webber, Jeanette & Grumman, Joan. Woman As Writer. (Illus., LC 77-074379). 1978. pap. text ed. 13.50 (ISBN 0-395-26438-3). HM.

Webber, Joe & Webber, Diane. Naked & Together. 9.95 (ISBN 0-910550-06-9). Elysium.

Webber, Michael. Impact of Uncertainty on Location. 368p. 1972. 20.00x (ISBN 0-262-23054-2). MIT Pr.

Webber, N. B. Fluid Mechanics for Civil Engineers. 354p. 1971. pap. 12.95x (ISBN 0-412-10600-0, Pub. by Chapman & Hall England). Methuen Inc.

Webber, Patrick J., ed. High Altitude Geocology. (AAAS Selected Symposium Ser.: No. 12). (Illus.). 1979. lib. bdg. 23.50 o.p. (ISBN 0-89158-440-4). Westview.

Webber, R. World List of National Newspapers. 1977. 19.95 o.p. (ISBN 0-408-70817-4). Butterworth.

Webber, Robert. Worship Old & New. 256p. 1982. 11.95 (ISBN 0-310-36650-X). Zondervan.

Webber, Robert E. The Moral Majority: Right or Wrong? LC 81-66611. 190p. 1981. 9.95 (ISBN 0-89107-226-8, Crossway Bks). Good News.

Webber, Robert P. Precalculus: An Elementary Functions Approach. LC 78-10882. 1979. text ed. 22.95 (ISBN 0-8185-0292-4). Brooks-Cole.

Webber, Ross A., ed. see Hampton, David R. & Summer, Charles E.

Webber, Roy. County Cricket Champion. 10.50 (ISBN 0-392-07082-0, SpS). Sportshelf.

Webber, T. G. Coloring of Plastics. 220p. 1979. 34.95x (ISBN 0-471-92327-3, Pub. by Wiley-Interscience). Wiley.

Webber, Thomas L. Deep Like the Rivers: Education in the Slave Quarter Community,1831-1865. 1978. 19.95 o.p. (ISBN 0-393-05685-6); pap. 5.95 (ISBN 0-393-00998-X). Norton.

Webber, Toni. Ponies & Riding. LC 80-50944. (Whizz Kids Ser.). 8.00 (ISBN 0-382-06436-4). Silver.

Webber, Winslow L. Books about Books. LC 73-18456. 1974. Repr. of 1937 ed. 40.00x (ISBN 0-8103-3690-1). Gale.

Weber, et al. Forkner Shorthand for Colleges. LC 81-67853. 300p. 1982. text ed. 10.72x (ISBN 0-912036-23-0); instr's manual 6.96x (ISBN 0-686-83216-7); skill builder 6.36x (ISBN 0-912036-45-1); (18 cassettes) 300.00x (ISBN 0-912036-47-8). Forkner.

Weber, Alfred. Farewell to European History: or, the Conquest of Nihilism. Hull, R. F., ed. LC 76-52396. 1977. Repr. of 1948 ed. lib. bdg. 17.00x (ISBN 0-8371-9447-4, WEFA). Greenwood.

Weber, Arnold R. In Pursuit of Price Stability: The Wage Price Freeze of 1971. LC 73-11346. (Studies in Wage-Price Policy). 137p. 1973. 14.95 (ISBN 0-8157-9264-6); pap. 5.95 (ISBN 0-8157-9263-8). Brookings.

Weber, Arnold R. & Mitchell, Daniel J. B. The Pay Board's Progress: Wage Controls in Phase II. (Studies in Wage-Price Policy). 1978. 24.95 (ISBN 0-8157-9266-2); pap. 10.95 (ISBN 0-8157-9265-4). Brookings.

Weber, Arnold R., jt. auth. see Shultz, George.

Weber, Arnold R., jt. ed. see Hartman, Robert W.

Weber, Brom see Crane, Hart.

Weber, Bruce & Howell, Robert E., eds. Coping with Rapid Growth in Rural Communities. (Replica Edition Ser.). (Illus.). 315p. 1982. lib. bdg. 23.50 (ISBN 0-86531-905-7). Westview.

Weber, C. A., jt. auth. see Poull, Jean.

Weber, Carl, ed. Heiner Muller: Five Plays. 1983. 18.95 (ISBN 0-933826-44-3); pap. 7.95 (ISBN 0-933826-45-1). Performing Arts.

Weber, Carl J., ed. see Hardy, Thomas.

Weber, Charles. Arthritis As a Chronic Potassium Deficiency. Rev. ed. 63p. 1981. pap. 8.00 (ISBN 0-9610114-0-8). Kalium.

Weber, Darrell J. & Hess, W. M. The Fungal Spore: Form & Function. LC 75-38889. 895p. 1976. 46.75 o.p. (ISBN 0-471-92332-X, Pub. by Wiley-Interscience). Wiley.

Weber, Darrell J., ed. The Fungal Spore: Form & Function. LC 75-3889. 912p. 1976. 52.50 (ISBN 0-686-74188-9). Krieger.

Weber, David C., jt. auth. see Rogers, Rutherford D.

Weber, David J. Suffix-As-Operator Analysis & the Grammar of Successive Encoding in Llacon (Huanuco) Quechua. (Documentos Del Trabajo (Peru): No. 13). 1976. pap. 2.85x (ISBN 0-88312-646-X); microfiche 2.25 (ISBN 0-88312-479-3). Summer Inst Ling.

--Los Sufijos Posesivos En el Quechua Del Huallaga (Huanuco) (Documentos Del Trabajo (Peru): No. 12). 1976. pap. 2.25x o. p. (ISBN 0-88312-647-8); microfiche 1.50 (ISBN 0-88312-497-1). Summer Inst Ling.

Weber, Diana. Presuposiciones de Preguntas en el Quechua de Huanuco. (Documentos Del Trabajo (Peru): No. 8). 14p. 1976. pap. 1.50 (ISBN 0-88312-796-2); microfiche 1.50 (ISBN 0-88312-489-0). Summer Inst Ling.

Weber, Edwin J., jt. auth. see Weber, Gloria Hansen.

Weber, Eric. Getting Together. 1977. Repr. text ed. 11.95 (ISBN 0-914094-04-1). Symphony.

--How to Pick up Girls. rev. ed. 1980. text ed. 12.95 (ISBN 0-914094-00-9). Symphony.

--How to Pick up Girls: Summer Edition. 1979. pap. 6.95 (ISBN 0-914094-12-2). Symphony.

--Meeting People: 101 Best Opening Lines. 1983. pap. 2.95 (ISBN 0-517-54954-9, Harmony). Crown.

--One Hundred Best Opening Lines. 1977. pap. 7.95 (ISBN 0-914094-02-5). Symphony.

--Separate Vacations. 1979. pap. 2.50 o.p. (ISBN 0-380-47266-X, 47266). Avon.

Weber, Eric & Cochran, Molly. How to Pick Up Women. 1980. text ed. 12.95 (ISBN 0-914094-14-9). Symphony.

Weber, Eric & Miller, Judi. Shy Persons Guide to a Happier Love Life. Repr. of 1979 ed. text ed. 11.95 (ISBN 0-914094-17-3). Symphony.

Weber, Eric & Simring, Steven S. How to Win Back the One You Love. 192p. 1983. 11.95 (ISBN 0-02-624700-3). Macmillan.

Weber, Eric, jt. auth. see De Vries, Madeline.

Weber, Eric, et al. Inner Looks. 1977. text ed. 11.95 (ISBN 0-914094-06-8). Symphony.

Weber, Eugen. The Nationalist Revival in France. (California Library Reprint: No. 7). 1968. 33.00x (ISBN 0-520-01321-2). U of Cal Pr.

--The Western Tradition: From the Ancient World to Louis 14th. 3rd ed. LC 72-172911. 1972. pap. text ed. 13.95 (ISBN 0-669-81166-1). Heath.

--The Western Tradition: From the Enlightenment to the Present. 3rd ed. LC 72-172911. 1972. pap. text ed. 9.95x o.p. (ISBN 0-669-81158-0). Heath.

--The Western Tradition: From the Renaissance to the Present. 3rd ed. LC 72-172911. 1971. pap. text ed. 13.95 (ISBN 0-669-81141-6). Heath.

Weber, Eugen, jt. ed. see Rogger, Hans.

Weber, Eugen, tr. see Guillaumin, Emile.

Weber, Eugene, ed. Twentieth Century Europe. 1980. pap. text ed. 6.95 (ISBN 0-88273-199-8). Forum Pr IL.

Weber, Eugene, jt. ed. see Spaethling, Robert.

Weber, Fritz W. Elsevier's Dictionary of High Vacuum Science & Technology. (Eng., Ger., Fr., Ital., Span. & Rus.). 1968. 106.50 (ISBN 0-444-40625-5). Elsevier.

Weber, G. P., et al, eds. Word Is Life. Incl. Bk. 1. Live. pap. 2.40 o.p. (ISBN 0-02-649550-3, 64955); Bk. 2. Grow. pap. 2.40 o.p. (ISBN 0-02-649590-2, 64959); Bk. 3. Act (ISBN 0-02-649630-5, 64963); Bk. 4. Unite. pap. 3.60 o.p. (ISBN 0-02-649670-4, 64967); Bk. 5. Believe. pap. 3.60 o.p. (ISBN 0-02-649710-7, 64971); Bk. 6. Hear. pap. 3.80 o.p. (ISBN 0-02-649750-6, 64975); Bk. 7. Think. pap. 4.68 o.p. (ISBN 0-02-649790-5, 64979); Bk. 8. Seek. pap. 4.68 o.p. (ISBN 0-02-649830-8, 64983). 1973. Bks. 1-8. pap. 2.00 ea. activity bk. o.p.; Bks. 1-8. pap. 0.68 ea. parent's handbk. o.p.; Bks. 1-8. tchr's annotated ed. -school 8.00 ea. o.p.; Bks. 1-8. tchr's annotated ed. -ccd 8.00 ea. o.p. tchr's enrichment section 2.48 o.p. (ISBN 0-02-648870-1, 64887); Bks 1-6. scope & sequence chart 0.80 o.p. (ISBN 0-02-649540-6, 64954). Glencoe.

Weber, Gerard P. Growth in the Eucharist. 2nd ed. 1978. pap. 2.64 o.s.i. (ISBN 0-02-647430-1); tchrs. ed. 4.80 o.s.i. (ISBN 0-02-647440-9); parent handbook 1.76 o.s.i. (ISBN 0-02-647450-6). Benziger Pub Co.

Weber, Gerard P. & Killgallon, James J. Growth in Peace: Level A. (gr. 3-5). 1975. pap. 2.48 o.s.i. (ISBN 0-02-647870-6); tchrs. ed. 4.80 o.s.i. (ISBN 0-02-647880-3); parent guide 1.84 o.s.i. (ISBN 0-02-647890-0). Benziger Pub Co.

--Growth in Reconciliation. 1976. pap. 2.96 o.s.i. (ISBN 0-02-647370-4); tchrs. ed. 4.80 o.s.i. (ISBN 0-02-647380-1); parent guide 1.84 o.s.i. (ISBN 0-02-647390-9). Benziger Pub Co.

--Growth in the Spirit: Preparation for Confirmation. 2nd ed. 1977. 2.96 o.s.i. (ISBN 0-02-648060-3); tchrs. manual 1.60 o.s.i. (ISBN 0-02-648180-4); tchrs. ed. 4.80 o.s.i. (ISBN 0-02-648070-0). Benziger Pub Co.

Weber, Gerard P., et al. Come Children Hear Me. 2nd ed. (The Word Is Life Ser.). (ps). 1977. 3.28 o.s.i. (ISBN 0-02-658050-0); tchrs. ed. 4.92 o.s.i. (ISBN 0-02-658060-8). Benziger Pub Co.

--Growth in Love. 1976. pap. 2.28 o.s.i. (ISBN 0-02-658010-1); tchrs. ed 3.44 o.s.i. (ISBN 0-02-658020-9); parent ed. 1.76 o.s.i. (ISBN 0-02-658030-6). Benziger Pub Co.

--Seek. 2nd ed. (The Word Is Life Ser.). (gr. 8). 1979. 3.80 o.p. (ISBN 0-02-658800-5); tchrs. ed. 8.00 o.p. (ISBN 0-02-658810-2); family handbook 0.64 o.p. (ISBN 0-02-658850-1). Benziger Pub Co.

Weber, Gloria H., et al. Notetaking & Study Skills. (gr. 10-12). 1977. 9.52 (ISBN 0-912036-27-3); wkbk. 4.80 (ISBN 0-912036-28-1); instrs'. manual 3.44x (ISBN 0-912036-29-X); profile pkg. of 25 o.p. 7.52 (ISBN 0-912036-30-3); tape library (6 cassettes) 81.00x (ISBN 0-912036-43-5). Forkner.

Weber, Gloria Hansen & Weber, Edwin J. Guided Study in Forkner Shorthand. 1974. pap. 4.72x (ISBN 0-912036-21-4); theory tapes (18 cassettes) 320.00x (ISBN 0-912036-84-2). Forkner.

Weber, H. & Wasserman, A. I., eds. Issues in Data Base Management. LC 79-10481. 1979. 47.00 (ISBN 0-444-85316-2, North Holland). Elsevier.

Weber, H. E. Die Gattung Rubus L. (Rosaceae) im nordwestlichen Europa vom Nordwestdeutschen Tiefland bis Skandinavien mit besonderer Berucksichtigung Schleswig-Holsteins. (Illus.). 1973. 60.00 (ISBN 3-7682-0858-3). Lubrecht & Cramer.

Weber, H. R., et al. Festschrift Heinrich Weber. LC 71-125926. 1971. Repr. of 1912 ed. text ed. 29.50 (ISBN 0-8284-0246-9). Chelsea Pub.

Weber, Hans, jt. auth. see Bloomberg, Marty.

Weber, Hans-Ruedi. Experiments with Bible Study. LC 82-13398. 336p. 1983. pap. 12.95 (ISBN 0-664-24461-0). Westminster.

--Salty Christians. 1963. pap. 1.95 (ISBN 0-8164-2062-9). Seabury.

Weber, Harry B. see Wieczynski, Joseph L.

Weber, Heidi, jt. auth. see Platt, John.

Weber, Heinrich. Lehrbuch der Algebra, Vols. 1, 2, & 3. 3rd ed. LC 61-6890. 1979. Repr. of 1962 ed. Set. text ed. 95.00 (ISBN 0-8284-0144-6). Chelsea Pub.

Weber, Helen I. Nursing Care of the Elderly. (Illus.). 240p. 1980. text ed. 13.95 o.p. (ISBN 0-8359-5035-2); pap. 13.95 (ISBN 0-8359-5034-4). Reston.

Weber, Henri. Nicaragua: The Sandinist Revolution. 144p. 1982. 15.00 (ISBN 0-8052-7117-1, Pub. by NLB England); pap. 5.95 (ISBN 0-8052-7118-X). Schocken.

Weber, J., jt. ed. see May, R.

Weber, J. R. How to Use Your TRS-80 Model II Computer. LC 80-70467. (WSI's How to Use Your Microcomputer Ser.). 300p. (gr. 10-12). 1982. cancelled (ISBN 0-938862-00-6); pap. 13.95 (ISBN 0-938862-01-4). Weber Systems.

--User's Guide to PET-CBM Computers. LC 80-70466. (WSI's How to Use Your Microcomputer Ser.). 320p. (gr. 10-12). 1982. cancelled (ISBN 0-9604892-7-4); pap. 13.95 (ISBN 0-9604892-8-2). Weber Systems.

Weber, James A. Power Grab: The Conserver Cult & the Coming Energy Catastrophe. 1980. 12.95 o.p. (ISBN 0-87000-453-0, Arlington Hse). Crown.

Weber, Jeffrey R. Accounts Payable System for Micro-Computers: Installation Guide & Disks. (WSI's Computerized Accounting System Ser.). 100p. 1983. 99.95 (ISBN 0-938862-06-5). Weber Systems.

--Accounts Receivable System for Micro-Computers: Installation Guide & Disks. (WSI's Computerized Accounting System Ser.). 100p. 1983. 99.95 (ISBN 0-938862-07-3). Weber Systems.

--C-BASIC Simplified. LC 82-70598. (WSI's How to Use Your Microcomputer). 1982. pap. 13.95 (ISBN 0-938862-10-3). Weber Systems.

--Camera Repair Simplified. LC 80-65475. 112p. (Orig.). 1980. pap. text ed. 14.95 (ISBN 0-9604892-0-7). Weber Systems.

--Computerized Accounts Payable System: For Microcomputers. LC 82-70699. (WSI's Computerixed Accounting System Ser.). 196p. 1983. pap. 19.95 (ISBN 0-9604892-5-8). Weber Systems.

--Computerized General Ledger System: For Microcomputers. LC 80-70435. (WSI's Computerized Accounting System Ser.). 196p. 1983. pap. 19.95 (ISBN 0-9604892-6-6). Weber Systems.

--Computerized Payroll System: For Microcomputers. (WSI's Computerized Accounting System Ser.). 196p. 1982. pap. 19.95 cancelled (ISBN 0-9604892-3-1). Five Arms Corp.

--CP-M Simplified. LC 81-66910. (WSI's How to Use Your Microcomputer Ser.). 300p. (Orig.). (gr. 10-12). 1982. cancelled (ISBN 0-938862-04-9); pap. 13.95 (ISBN 0-938862-05-7). Weber Systems.

--General Ledger System for Micro-Computers: Installation Guide & Disks. (IDM's Computerized Accounting System Ser.). 100p. 1983. 99.95 (ISBN 0-938862-08-1). Weber Systems.

--Payroll System for Micro-Computers: Installation Guide & Disks. 100p. 1982. cancelled (ISBN 0-938862-09-X). Five Arms Corp.

--Users Guide to the IBM Personal Computer. (WSI's How to Use Your Microcomputer Ser.). (Illus.). 300p. 1982. pap. 13.95 (ISBN 0-938862-13-8). Weber Systems.

--User's Guide to the Timex-Sinclair ZX-81. (WSI's How to Use Your Microcomputer Ser.). 280p. (Orig.). 1983. pap. cancelled (ISBN 0-938862-27-8). Weber Systems.

--Users Handbook to IBM Basic. (WSI's How to Use Your Microcomputer Ser.). 300p. 1982. pap. text ed. 13.95 (ISBN 0-938862-14-6). Weber Systems.

--WSI's Accounts Receivable System: For Microcomputers. (WSI's Computerized Accounting System Ser.). 196p. 1982. pap. 19.95 (ISBN 0-9604892-4-X). Weber Systems.

Weber, Jeffrey R. & Chen, Daniel. BASIC Programs You Can Use. (WSI's How to Use Your Microcomputer Ser.). 280p. 1983. pap. text ed. 13.95 (ISBN 0-938862-11-1). Weber Systems.

--BASIC Programs You Can Use: CP-M Edition. (WSI's How to Use Your Microcomputer Ser.). 250p. 1983. pap. 13.95 (ISBN 0-938862-25-1). Weber Systems.

--BASIC Programs You Can Use: IBM PC Edition. (WSI's How to Use Your Microcomputer Ser.). 250p. 1983. pap. 13.95 (ISBN 0-938862-24-3). Weber Systems.

--BASIC Programs You Can Use: Sinclair ZX81 Edit. (WSI's How to Use Your Microcomputer Ser.). 250p. 1983. pap. 13.95 (ISBN 0-938862-26-X). Weber Systems.

Weber, Jon N., ed. Geochemistry of Germanium. LC 73-12621. (Benchmark Papers in Geology Ser). 480p. 1974. text ed. 59.00 (ISBN 0-12-787740-1). Acad Pr.

Weber, Josef. The Dog in Training. 1939. 17.50 o.p. (ISBN 0-686-19922-7). Quest Edns.

Weber, Joseph, ed. Lasers, 2 Vols. (International Science Review Ser). 1968. Vol. 1, 838p. 129.00 (ISBN 0-677-00880-5); Vol. 2, 760p. 129.00 (ISBN 0-677-00890-2). Gordon.

Weber, Karl. The Art of Test Taking. 256p. (gr. 9-10). Date not set. pap. price not set Cancelled (ISBN 0-8120-2493-1). Barron.

Weber, Ken. Canoeing Massachusetts, Rhode Island & Connecticut. LC 79-90812. (Illus.). 1980. pap. 6.95 (ISBN 0-89725-009-5). Backcountry Pubns.

--Twenty-Five Walks in Rhode Island. LC 77-90853. (Twenty-Five Walks Ser.). (Illus.). 118p. 1978. 10.00 o.p. (ISBN 0-912274-88-3); pap. 4.95 (ISBN 0-912274-84-0). Backcountry Pubns.

Weber, L. J. Christianity & War: Religious Ideas & Political Consequences. 1971. pap. 3.50 o.p. (ISBN 0-685-01114-3, 80985). Benziger Pub Co.

Weber, Lavern J., ed. Aquatic Toxicology, Vol. I. 236p. 1982. text ed. 30.00 (ISBN 0-89004-439-2). Raven.

Weber, Lillian. The English Infant School & Informal Education. LC 71-167910. 1971. pap. 6.95 o.p. (ISBN 0-13-281287-8, Pub. by P-H). Workshop Ctr.

Weber, M. see Von Wiesner, J. & Von Regel, C.

Weber, Marianne. Max Weber: A Biography. Zohn, Harry, ed. & tr. LC 74-23904. 719p. 1975. 34.95 o.p. (ISBN 0-471-92333-8, Pub. by Wiley-Interscience). Wiley.

Weber, Marsha I., jt. auth. see Montero, Darell.

Weber, Max. The Agrarian Sociology of Ancient Civilizations. 1976. 20.00 o.p. (ISBN 0-8052-7021-3, Pub. by NLB). Schocken.

--From Max Weber: Essays in Sociology. Gerth, Hans H. & Mills, C. Wright, trs. 1946. pap. 9.95x (ISBN 0-19-500462-0). Oxford U Pr.

--General Economic History. LC 79-412. (Social Science Classics Ser.). 438p. 1981. text ed. 29.95 (ISBN 0-87855-317-7); pap. 9.95 (ISBN 0-87855-690-7). Transaction Bks.

--Rational & Social Foundations of Music. Martindale, Don, et al, trs. LC 56-12134. (Arcturus Books Paperbacks). 1969. pap. 6.95 o.p. (ISBN 0-8093-0355-8). S Ill U Pr.

--Religion of China. 1968. 14.95 (ISBN 0-02-934440-9). Free Pr.

--Sociology of Religion. Fischoff, Ephraim, tr. 1964. pap. 6.95x (ISBN 0-8070-4193-9, BP189). Beacon Pr.

--Theory of Social & Economic Organization. Parsons, Talcott, tr. 1947. 17.95 (ISBN 0-02-934920-6); pap. text ed. 9.95 (ISBN 0-02-934930-3). Free Pr.

Weber, Nancy. Lily, Where's Your Daddy? LC 79-28346. 270p. 1980. 10.95 (ISBN 0-399-90075-6, Marek). Putnam Pub Group.

Weber, Nelva M. How to Plan Your Own Home Landscape. LC 75-33535. (Illus.). 320p. 1976. 13.95 o.p. (ISBN 0-685-62625-3). Bobbs.

Weber, O., ed. Audiovisual Market Place A Multimedia Guide 1981: A Multimedia Guide. 11th ed. LC 69-18201. 1981. pap. 32.50 o.p. (ISBN 0-8352-1333-1). Bowker.

--Magazine Industry Market Place--1982: The Directory of American Periodical. 730p. 1981. pap. 37.50 o.p. (ISBN 0-8352-1362-5). Bowker.

Weber, Otto. Foundations of Dogmatics, Vol. 2. Guder, Darrell L., tr. from Ger. 736p. 1983. 31.00 (ISBN 0-8028-3564-3). Eerdmans.

Weber, Patricia. My Way. (Illus.). 30p. (Orig.). 1979. pap. text ed. 3.95 (ISBN 0-686-96468-3, 7915). DOK Pubs.

Weber, R. David. Energy Information Guide, 3 vols. LC 82-8729. Vol. I: General & Alternative Energy Sources 1982 442 pgs. text ed. 39.95 (ISBN 0-87436-317-9); Vol. II: Nuclear & Electric Power 1982. text ed. 39.95 (ISBN 0-87436-342-X); Vol. III: Fossil Fuels 1983. text ed. write for info. (ISBN 0-87436-343-8). ABC-Clio.

Weber, Robert L., jt. auth. see Shive, John N.

Weber, Robert L., jt. auth. see Strother, G. K.

Weber, Robert L. A Random Walk in Science: An Anthology. LC 74-75874. (Illus.). 206p. 1974. 16.50x o.s.i. (ISBN 0-8448-0574-2). Crane-Russak Co.

Weber, Robert L., et al. College Physics. 5th ed. (Illus.). 704p. 1974. text ed. 27.00 o.p. (ISBN 0-07-068827-3, C). McGraw.

Weber, Ronald. The Literature of Fact: Literary Nonfiction in American Writing. LC 80-16323. viii, 181p. 1980. 15.95x (ISBN 0-8214-0558-6, 82-83533). Ohio U Pr.

Weber, Rudolf, ed. Biochemistry of Animal Development, 3 vols. Incl. Vol. 1. Descriptive Biochemistry of Early Development. 1965. 65.00 (ISBN 0-12-740601-8); Vol. 2. Biochemical Control Mechanisms & Adaptations in Development. 1967. 56.00 (ISBN 0-12-740602-6); Vol. 3. 1975. 61.00 (ISBN 0-12-740603-4). Set. 136.50 (ISBN 0-686-76923-6). Acad Pr.

Weber, Samuel, tr. see Adorno, Theodor W.

Weber, Shierry, tr. see Adorno, Theodor W.

Weber, Theodore R. Foreign Policy Is Your Business. LC 74-37769. (Christian Ethics for Modern Man Ser.). (Illus.). 128p. (Orig.). 1972. pap. 1.95 o.p. (ISBN 0-8042-9091-1). John Knox.

Weber, Thomas. Northern Railroads in Civil War, Eighteen Sixty-One to Eighteen Sixty-Five. Repr. of 1952 ed. lib. bdg. 18.25x (ISBN 0-8371-3549-4, WERR). Greenwood.

Weber, Thomas W. An Introduction to Process Dynamics & Control. LC 73-2678. 434p. 1973. 43.95x (ISBN 0-471-92330-3, Pub. by Wiley-Interscience). Wiley.

Weber, W. A. & Wetmore, C. M. Catalogue of Lichens of Australia: Exclusive of Tasmania. 1972. 16.00 (ISBN 3-7682-5441-0). Lubrecht & Cramer.

Weber, W. J., jt. auth. see Mancy, K. H.

Weber, Walter J. Diseases Transmitted by Rats & Mice. LC 82-50537. (Illus.). 182p. (Orig.). 1982. pap. text ed. 13.50 (ISBN 0-913702-18-8). Thomson Pub CA.

Weber, Walter J., Jr. Physicochemical Processes for Water Quality Control. LC 77-37026. (Environmental Science & Technology Ser). 640p. 1972. 49.95x (ISBN 0-471-92435-0, Pub. by Wiley-Interscience). Wiley.

Weber, William A. Theodore D. A. Cockerell: Letters from West Cliff, Colorado, 1887-1889. 1978. pap. 7.95 (ISBN 0-87081-122-3). Colo Assoc.

Weber, William H., III. Socioeconomic Methods in Educational Analysis. LC 74-28195. (Illus.). 125p. 1975. text ed. 14.95x (ISBN 0-8077-2449-1); pap. text ed. 8.95x (ISBN 0-8077-2448-3). Tchrs Coll.

Weber, William P. Silicon Reagents for Organic Synthesis. (Reactivity & Structure: Vol. 14). 450p. 1982. 100.00 (ISBN 0-387-11675-3). Springer-Verlag.

Weberman, Alan J., jt. auth. see Canfield, Michael.

Webern, Anton. Letters to Hildegard Jone & Josef Humplik. Polnauer, Josef, ed. Cardew, Cornelius, tr. Orig. Title: Briefe an Hildegard Jone und Josef Humplik. 1967. pap. 11.00 (ISBN 3-7024-0031-1, 50 14230). Eur-Am Music.

--The Path to the New Music. Reich, Willi, ed. Black, Leo, tr. from Ger. pap. 8.25 (ISBN 3-7024-0030-3, 47-12947). Eur-Am Music.

Weber-Stadelmann, W., ed. Adriamycin & Derivatives in Gastrointestinal Cancer. (Beitraege zur Onkologie. Contributions to Oncology Ser.: Vol. 15). (Illus.). vi, 144p. 1983. pap. 58.75 (ISBN 3-8055-3689-5). S Karger.

Webman, Jerry A. Reviving the Industrial City: The Politics of Urban Renewal in Lyon & Birmingham. 208p. 1982. 25.00 (ISBN 0-8135-0947-5). Rutgers U Pr.

Webman, Jerry A., jt. auth. see Nathan, Richard P.

Webster & Anderson. Gems. 4th ed. 1983. text ed. price not set (ISBN 0-408-01148-3). Butterworth.

Webster, ed. see Sophocles.

Webster, Brenda. Blake's Prophetic Psychology. (Illus.). 336p. 1983. 27.50 (ISBN 0-8203-0658-4). U of Ga Pr.

Webster, Bryce & Perry, Robert. The Complete Social Security Handbook. LC 81-19443. 1983. 24.95 (ISBN 0-89696-121-4, An Everest House Book); pap. 12.95 (ISBN 0-89696-147-8). Dodd.

Webster, C. A. Introduction to Pascal. 1976. 15.00 o.p. (ISBN 0-85501-225-0). Wiley.

Webster, Charles. From Paracelsus to Newton: Magic & the Making of Modern Science. LC 82-4586. (Illus.). 120p. Date not set. price not set (ISBN 0-521-24919-8). Cambridge U Pr.

Webster, Charles, ed. Biology, Medicine & Society Eighteen Forty to Nineteen Forty. LC 80-41752. (Past & Present Publications Ser.). 344p. 1981. 39.50 (ISBN 0-521-23770-X). Cambridge U Pr.

--Health, Medicine & Mortality in the Sixteenth Century. LC 78-73234. (Cambridge Monographs on the History of Medicine). (Illus.). 1979. 49.50 (ISBN 0-521-22643-0). Cambridge U Pr.

--Samuel Hartlib & the Advancement of Learning. LC 73-93713. (Cambridge Texts & Studies in the History of Education: No. 7). 1970. 24.95 (ISBN 0-521-07715-X). Cambridge U Pr.

Webster, Charles E., jt. auth. see Greenberg, Edward.

Webster, Clarence M. Town Meeting Country. Repr. of 1945 ed. lib. bdg. 15.00x o.p. (ISBN 0-8371-2979-6, WETM). Greenwood.

Webster, D. Robert, jt. ed. see Foust, Cleon H.

Webster, Daniel. Letters. Van Tyne, C. H., ed. LC 68-57645. (Illus.). 1969. Repr. of 1902 ed. lib. bdg. 22.75x o.p. (ISBN 0-8371-4467-1, WELE). Greenwood.

--The Papers of Daniel Webster: Correspondence, Volume 1, 1798-1824. Wiltse, Charles M. & Moser, Harold D., eds. LC 73-92705. (Papers of Daniel Webster: Series 1, Correspondence). (Illus.). 544p. 1974. text ed. 40.00x (ISBN 0-87451-096-1). U Pr of New Eng.

--The Papers of Daniel Webster: Correspondence, Vol. 2, 1825-1829. Wiltse, Charles M. & Moser, Harold D., eds. LC 73-92705. (The Papers of Daniel Webster: Series 1, Correspondence). (Illus.). 587p. 1976. text ed. 40.00x (ISBN 0-87451-120-8). U Pr of New Eng.

--The Papers of Daniel Webster: Correspondence, Vol. 5, 1840-1843. Moser, Harold D., ed. LC 73-92705. (Papers of Daniel Webster; Series 1, Correspondence). (Illus.). 618p. 1982. 40.00x (ISBN 0-87451-231-X). U Pr of New Eng.

--The Papers of Daniel Webster: Legal Papers, Vol. 1, The New Hampshire Practice. Konefsky, Alfred S. & King, Andrew J., eds. LC 73-92705. (Papers of Daniel Webster: Series 2, Legal Papers). 600p. 1982. 35.00x (ISBN 0-87451-232-8). U Pr of New Eng.

--The Papers of Daniel Webster: Legal Papers, Vol. 2, The Boston Practice. Konefsky, Alfred S. & King, Andrew J., eds. LC 73-92705. (Papers of Daniel Webster; Series 2, Lega; Papers). 700p. 1983. 30.00x (ISBN 0-87451-240-9). U Pr of New Eng.

Webster, David. How to Do a Science Project. LC 73-12214. (First Bks). (Illus.). 72p. (gr. 4 up). 1974. PLB 8.90 (ISBN 0-531-00817-7). Watts.

Webster, Donald H. & Zibell, Wilfried. Inupiat Eskimo Dictionary. LC 76-632478. Orig. Title: Inupiat Dialect of Eskimo. (Illus.). 212p. (Eng., Eskimo.). 1970. pap. 2.20 (ISBN 0-88312-377-0); microfiche 3.00. Summer Inst Ling.

Webster, Douglas B. & Webster, Molly. Comparative Vertebrate Morphology. 1974. text ed. 29.50 (ISBN 0-12-740850-9). Acad Pr.

Webster, Frederick E. Industrial Marketing Strategy. LC 78-26599. (Marketing Management Ser.). 1979. 21.95 (ISBN 0-471-04879-8). Ronald Pr.

--Industrial Marketing Strategy. (Marketing Management Ser.). 279p. 1979. 21.95x (ISBN 0-471-04879-8, Pub. by Wiley-Interscience). Wiley.

Webster, Frederick E., Jr., jt. auth. see Davis, Kenneth R.

Webster, Gordon L., jt. auth. see Charbonneau, Harvey C.

Webster, Grady L., jt. auth. see Deghan, Bijan.

Webster, Graham. Boudica: The British Revolt Against Rome A.D. 60. 1978. 31.50 o.p. (ISBN 0-7134-1064-7, Pub. by Batsford England). David & Charles.

--The Cornovii. (Peoples of Roman Britain Ser.). 1975. text ed. 17.50x o.p. (ISBN 0-7156-0832-0). Humanities.

--Practical Archaeology: An Introduction to Archaeological Field Work Excavations. LC 74-82133. 1975. 22.50 (ISBN 0-312-63455-2). St Martin.

Webster, Harriet, jt. auth. see Webster, Jonanthan.

Webster, Harriet, jt. auth. see Webster, Jonathan.

Webster, Hutton. Rest Days, the Christian Sunday, the Jewish Sabbath & Their Historical & Anthropological Prototypes. LC 68-58165. 1968. Repr. of 1916 ed. 42.00x (ISBN 0-8103-3342-2). Gale.

Webster, J. Automotive Fundamentals for the Consumer. 1976. pap. 7.96 (ISBN 0-02-829750-4). Glencoe.

--Reading Matters: A Practical Philosophy. 208p. Date not set. 11.00 (ISBN 0-07-084134-9). McGraw.

Webster, J., jt. ed. see Tompkins, W.

Webster, J. B. & Boahen, A. A. Revolutionary Years: West Africa Since 1800. 343p. 1967. 8.50x (ISBN 0-582-60246-7). Intl Pubns Serv.

Webster, James A., Jr. Real Estate Law in North Carolina. 1971. with 1977 suppl. 40.00 o.p. (ISBN 0-87215-122-0); 1977 suppl. separately 15.00 o.p. (ISBN 0-87215-289-8). Michie-Bobbs.

Webster, Jan. Colliers Row. LC 77-3961. 1977. 8.95i (ISBN 0-397-01228-4). Har-Row.

--Colliers Row. 1978. pap. 2.25 o.p. (ISBN 0-446-82582-4). Warner Bks.

Webster, Jay. Auto Mechanics. LC 79-2488. 576p. (gr. 10-12). 1980. text ed. 17.40 (ISBN 0-02-829770-9); instrs'. manual 9.60 (ISBN 0-02-829780-6); auto shop act. guide 5.40 (ISBN 0-02-829790-3). Glencoe.

--Principles of Automatic Transmissions. rev. & enl. ed. LC 79-51618. (Illus.). 1980. pap. 6.95x (ISBN 0-911168-43-5). Prakken.

Webster, Jean. Daddy-Long-Legs. 160p. 1982. 1.95 (ISBN 0-553-20908-6). Bantam.

--Dear Enemy. 1980. PLB 9.95 (ISBN 0-8398-2614-1, Gregg). G K Hall.

Webster, John. The Devil's Law-Case. Shirley, Frances A., ed. LC 72-179813. (Regents Renaissance Drama Ser). xxvi, 149p. 1972. 13.95x (ISBN 0-8032-0296-2). U of Nebr Pr.

--Introduction to Fungi. 2nd ed. LC 79-52856. (Illus.). 1980. 85.50 (ISBN 0-521-22888-3); pap. 22.95x (ISBN 0-521-29699-4). Cambridge U Pr.

Webster, John, tr. see Esser, Karl.

Webster, John B., et al. A Bibliography on Kenya. (Foreign & Comparative Studies-Eastern African Bibliographic Ser.: No. 2). 461p. 1967. pap. 8.00x o.p. (ISBN 0-686-70995-0). Syracuse U Foreign Comp.

Webster, John G. Medical Instrumentation: Application & Design. LC 77-76419. (Illus.). 1978. pap. text ed. 38.95 (ISBN 0-395-25411-6); solutions manual 8.50 (ISBN 0-395-25412-4). HM.

Webster, John G., jt. auth. see Jacobson, Bertil.

Webster, John G., jt. ed. see Cook, Albert M.

Webster, Jonanthan & Webster, Harriet. Eighteen: The Teenage Catalog. LC 76-8070. 1976. pap. 7.95 o.p. (ISBN 0-8256-3066-5, Quick Fox). Putnam Pub Group.

Webster, Jonathan & Webster, Harriet. The Underground Marketplace: A Guide to New England & the Middle Atlantic States. LC 80-54401. 176p. 1981. 12.50x (ISBN 0-87663-348-3); pap. 6.95 (ISBN 0-87663-555-9). Universe.

Webster, Marie D. Quilts: Their Story & How to Make Them. LC 75-174137. (Tower Bks). (Illus.). xviii, 178p. 1972. Repr. of 1915 ed. 34.00x (ISBN 0-8103-3111-X). Gale.

Webster, Mary E. Love's Dark Wilderness. (YA) 1980. 6.95 (ISBN 0-686-73918-3, Avalon). Bouregy.

Webster, Molly, jt. auth. see Webster, Douglas B.

Webster, Murray, Jr. & Sobieszek, Barbara. Sources of Self Evaluation: A Formal Theory of Significant Others & Social Influence. LC 74-5066. 189p. 1974. 26.95 o.p. (ISBN 0-471-92440-7, Pub. by Wiley-Interscience). Wiley.

Webster, Nancy, jt. auth. see Wittemann, Betsy.

Webster, Nesta H. Secret Societies & Subversive Movements. 419p. 1972. pap. 6.00 (ISBN 0-913022-05-5). Angriff Pr.

Webster, Noah. Collection of Essays & Fugitive Writings on Moral, Historical, Political, & Literary Subjects. LC 77-22094. 1977. Repr. of 1790 ed. 50.00x (ISBN 0-8201-1297-6). Schol Facsimiles.

Webster, Norman. City People, City Life. LC 72-13894. (Discovery Today's China Ser.). (Illus.). (gr. 3-8). 1973. pap. 3.95 (ISBN 0-912022-45-0). EMC.

--Posters & Pedicarts. LC 72-13815. (Discovering Today's China Ser.). (Illus.). (gr. 3-8). 1973. PLB 4.95 o.p. (ISBN 0-912022-49-3); pap. 3.95 (ISBN 0-912022-43-4). EMC.

--Stubborn Land. LC 72-13913. (Discovering Today's China Ser.). (Illus.). (gr. 3-8). 1973. PLB 4.95 o.p. (ISBN 0-912022-34-5); pap. 3.95 (ISBN 0-912022-46-9). EMC.

--Youth on the March. LC 72-13932. (Discovering Today's China Ser.). (Illus.). (gr. 3-8). 1973. PLB 4.95 o.p. (ISBN 0-912022-33-7); pap. 3.95 (ISBN 0-912022-44-2). EMC.

Webster, Paula, jt. auth. see Gilbert, Lucy.

Webster, Peter, jt. auth. see Swanson, Carl P.

Webster, Richard A. Industrial Imperialism in Italy, 1908-1915. LC 74-76393. 480p. 1975. 42.50x (ISBN 0-520-02724-8). U of Cal Pr.

Webster, Richard C. & Smith, Richard C., eds. Consultations on the Aging Face. (Illus.). 224p. 1983. lib. bdg. write for info. Masson Pub.

Webster, Richard J. Philadelphia Preserved: Catalog of the Historic American Buildings Survey. LC 76-18669. (Illus.). 512p. 1976. 29.95 (ISBN 0-87722-089-1). Temple U Pr.

Webster, Susan, jt. auth. see Phillips, Ralph.

Webster, T. B. From Mycenae to Homer: A Study in Early Greek Literature & Art. (Illus.). 1977. Repr. of 1958 ed. 28.50x o.p. (ISBN 0-87471-882-1). Rowman.

Webster, Thomas B. Greece: The Age of Hellenism. (Art of the World Library). (Illus.). 1966. 6.95 o.p. (ISBN 0-517-50841-9). Crown.

Webster, Tony. Microcomputer Buyer's Guide. 2nd ed. (Illus.). 352p. 1983. pap. text ed. 19.95 (ISBN 0-07-068959-8, P&RB). McGraw.

Webster, Vera. Plant Experiments. LC 82-9448. (New True Bks.). (Illus.). (gr. k-4). 1982. PLB 9.25g (ISBN 0-516-01638-5). Childrens.

--Science Experiments. LC 82-4429. (New True Bks.). (gr. k-4). 1982. PLB 9.25g (ISBN 0-516-01646-6). Childrens.

Wechsberg, Joseph. Cooking of Vienna's Empire. LC 68-25883. (Foods of the World Ser.). (Illus.). (gr. 6 up). 1968. PLB 17.28 (ISBN 0-8094-0059-6, Time-Life). Silver.

--The Danube. LC 79-4720. (Great Rivers of the World Ser.). (Illus.). 1979. 14.95 o.p. (ISBN 0-88225-273-9). Newsweek.
--Dream Towns of Europe. LC 76-6037. (Illus.). 1976. 17.50 o.p. (ISBN 0-399-11783-0). Putnam Pub Group.
Wechsberg, Joseph & Witzmann, Reingard. The Imperial Style: Fashions of the Hapsburg Era. Cone, Polly, ed. (Illus.). 116p. 1980. 22.50 (ISBN 0-87099-232-5). Metro Mus Art.
Wechsler, Ben L., jt. auth. see Smith, William A., Jr.
Wechsler, Ben L., jt. auth. see Whitehouse, Gary E.
Wechsler, David. The Selected Papers of David Wechsler. 1974. 32.50 (ISBN 0-12-741250-6). Acad Pr.
Wechsler, Harold. The Qualified Student: A History of Selective College Admission in America. LC 76-47692. 1977. 29.95 o.p. (ISBN 0-471-92441-5, Pub. by Wiley-Interscience). Wiley.
Wechsler, Henry & Gale, Barbara. Medical School Admissions: A Strategy for Success. 1983. pap. 12.95 prof ref (ISBN 0-88410-915-1). Ballinger Pub.
Wechsler, Henry, ed. Minimum-Drinking-Age Laws: An Evaluation. LC 79-3133. 208p. 1980. 21.95x (ISBN 0-669-03380-4). Lexington Bks.
Wechsler, Henry, et al. The Social Context of Medical Research. Cahill, George F., Jr., ed. 360p. 1981. prof ref 29.50x (ISBN 0-88410-730-2). Ballinger Pub.
Wechsler, Henry, et al, eds. Social Work Research in the Human Services. 2nd ed. LC 81-1760. 368p. 1981. text ed. 34.95 (ISBN 0-89885-038-X); pap. text ed. 14.95 (ISBN 0-89885-039-8). Human Sci Pr.
Wechsler, Herman J. Great Prints & Printmakers. LC 77-73921. (Illus.). 1977. 35.00 o.p. (ISBN 0-8148-0682-1). L Amiel Pub.
Wechsler, James A. Age of Suspicion. LC 72-152616. 1971. Repr. of 1953 ed. lib. bdg. 17.00x (ISBN 0-8371-6051-0, WEAG). Greenwood.
--Labor Baron: A Portrait of John L. Lewis. LC 72-143312. 278p. 1972. Repr. of 1944 ed. lib. bdg. 17.50x (ISBN 0-8371-5968-7, WELB). Greenwood.
Wechsler, Louis K. Benjamin Franklin. LC 76-2679. (World Leader Ser.: No. 56). 1976. lib. bdg. 8.50 o.p. (ISBN 0-8057-7667-2, Twayne). G K Hall.
--College Entrance Examinations. LC 73-104077. pap. 5.95 o.p. (ISBN 0-06-460408-X, CO 408, CO). B&N NY.
Wechsler, Susan. Low Fire Ceramics. (Illus.). 184p. 1981. 24.95 o.p. (ISBN 0-8230-2885-2); pap. 14.95 (ISBN 0-8230-2886-0). Watson-Guptill.
Weck, J. Dictionary of Forestry. (Eng. & Ger. & Fr. & Span. & Rus.). 1966. 106.50 (ISBN 0-444-40626-3). Elsevier.
Wecklein, N., ed. Prometheus Bound, & the Fragments of Prometheus Loosed. 1981. 25.00 (ISBN 0-89241-358-1); pap. 12.50 (ISBN 0-89241-126-0). Caratzas Bros.
Weckselmann, David & Bevan, Elizabeth. Tunde et Ses Amis, 2 bks. 1962-65. text ed. 2.50 ea. Vol. 1 (ISBN 0-521-06757-X). Vol. 2 (ISBN 0-521-06758-8). Cambridge U Pr.
Weckstein, Joyce R. Get Fit & Play Racquetball. LC 82-82295. (Illus.). 100p. (Orig.). 1982. pap. 4.95 (ISBN 0-9600980-2-X). J R Weckstein.
Wecter, Dixon. When Johnny Comes Marching Home. Repr. of 1944 ed. lib. bdg. 20.00x o.p. (ISBN 0-8371-2795-5, WEJM). Greenwood.
Wedberg, Anders. A History of Philosophy: Antiquity & the Middle Ages, Vol. 1. 200p. 1982. 24.50 (ISBN 0-19-824639-0); pap. 9.95x (ISBN 0-19-824691-9). Oxford U Pr.
--A History of Philosophy: Volume 2: The Modern Age to Romanticism. (Illus.). 227p. 1982. 24.50 (ISBN 0-19-824640-4); pap. 9.95 (ISBN 0-19-824692-7). Oxford U Pr.
Wedde, Horst, ed. Adequate Modeling of Systems: Proceedings of the International Working Conference on Model Realism, Bad Honnef, Federal Republic of Germany, April 20-23, 1982. 300p. cancelled (ISBN 0-08-029415-4). Pergamon.
Wedde, Ian, jt. tr. see Tucan, Fawwaz.
Weddell, H. A. Chloris Andina: Essai d'une Flore de la Region alpine des Cordilleres de l'Amerique du Sud, 2 vols. in 1. (Illus.). 1972. 100.00 (ISBN 3-7682-0729-3). Lubrecht & Cramer.
Wedderburn, Dorothy & Crompton, Rosemary. Worker's Attitudes & Technology. LC 70-183225. (Cambridge Papers in Sociology: No. 2). (Illus.). 143p. 1972. 21.00 o.p. (ISBN 0-521-07432-0); pap. 9.95x (ISBN 0-521-09711-8). Cambridge U Pr.
Wedderburn, Dorothy, ed. Poverty, Inequality & Class Structure. LC 73-80479. (Illus.). 232p. 1974. 34.50 (ISBN 0-521-20153-5); pap. 10.95 (ISBN 0-521-09823-8). Cambridge U Pr.
Wedderspoon, A. G., ed. Religious Education, Nineteen Forty-Four to Nineteen Eighty-Four. 238p. 1966. 5.00 (ISBN 0-87921-063-X); pap. 3.00 (ISBN 0-87921-064-8). Attic Pr.
Wedding, Dan & Corsini, Raymond J. Great Cases in Psychotherapy. LC 78-61878. 1979. pap. text ed. 10.95 (ISBN 0-87581-234-1). Peacock Pubs.
Wedding, Mary E., jt. auth. see Gylys, Barbara A.
Weddington, D. Patterns for Practical Communications: Composition Package. 1977. text ed. 250.00 (ISBN 0-13-653881-9); tchrs manual 11.00 (ISBN 0-13-653865-7). P-H.
--Patterns for Practical Communications: Sentence Package. 1977. text ed. 250.00 (ISBN 0-13-653790-1); script sentences 14.95 (ISBN 0-13-653816-9). P-H.
Weddington, Doris C. Patterns for Practical Communications: Lesson Sheets-Composition. 1976. pap. text ed. 8.95 (ISBN 0-13-653832-0). P-H.
--Patterns for Practical Communications: Script Composition. 1977. pap. text ed. 14.95 (ISBN 0-13-653840-1). P-H.
Weddle, Perry. Argument: A Guide to Critical Thinking. 1977. pap. text ed. 14.50 (ISBN 0-07-068961-X, C). McGraw.
Wedeck, Harry E. Classics of Greek Literature. LC 63-11490. 1963. 6.00 o.p. (ISBN 0-8022-1826-1). Philos Lib.
--A Treasury of Witchcraft. 271p. 1983. pap. 4.95 (ISBN 0-8065-0038-7). Citadel Pr.
Wedel, Alton. The Mighty Word. (Preacher's Workshop Ser.). 48p. 1977. pap. 2.50 (ISBN 0-570-07400-2, 12-2672). Concordia.
Wedel, Erwin, jt. auth. see Gajek, Bernhard.
Wedell, K. Learning & Perceptual: Motor Disabilities in Children. LC 72-8617. 136p. 1973. 25.95x (ISBN 0-471-92442-3, Pub. by Wiley-Interscience). Wiley.
--Orientation in Special Education. LC 74-6660. 220p. 1975. 42.95x o.p. (ISBN 0-471-92443-1, Pub. by Wiley-Interscience). Wiley.
Wedemeyer, Albert C. Wedemeyer Reports! 10.00 o.p. (ISBN 0-8159-7204-0); pap. 5.95 (ISBN 0-8159-7216-4). Devin.
Wedertz, Frank S. Mono Diggings. 1977. 12.95 OSI (ISBN 0-912494-28-X); pap. 10.95 (ISBN 0-912494-29-8). Chalfant Pr.
Wedge, Bryant M., ed. see Yale University Division of Student Mental Hygiene Staff.
Wedge, George A. Applied Harmony, 2 bks. 1930. Bk. 1. pap. 9.95 (ISBN 0-02-872760-6); Bk. 2. pap. 6.95 (ISBN 0-02-872770-3). Schirmer Bks.
Wedge, Peter, jt. auth. see Essen, Juliet.
Wedgewood, C. V. The Thirty Years War. 542p. 1981. pap. 10.95 (ISBN 0-416-32020-1). Methuen Inc.
Wedgewood, Cicely V. World of Rubens. LC 67-27679. (Library of Ar4 Ser.). (Illus.). (gr. 6 up). 1967. 19.92 (ISBN 0-8094-0269-6, Pub. by Time-Life). Silver.
Wedgeworth, Robert, ed. ALA Yearbook 1976. LC 76-647548. 1976. text ed. 55.00 (ISBN 0-8389-0223-5). ALA.
--ALA Yearbook 1977. LC 76-647548. 1977. text ed. 55.00 (ISBN 0-8389-0233-2). ALA.
--ALA Yearbook 1978. LC 76-647548. 1978. text ed. 55.00 (ISBN 0-8389-0261-8). ALA.
--ALA Yearbook 1979. LC 76-647548. 1979. text ed. 55.00 (ISBN 0-8389-0292-8). ALA.
--ALA Yearbook, 1982. 432p. 1982. lib. bdg. 60.00 (ISBN 0-8389-0350-9). ALA.
Wedgwood, Cicely V. Richelieu & the French Monarchy. 1962. pap. 4.95 (ISBN 0-02-038240-5, Collier). Macmillan.
--Strafford Fifteen Ninty-Three to Sixteen Forty-One. Repr. of 1935 ed. lib. bdg. 17.75x (ISBN 0-8371-4566-X, WEST). Greenwood.
Wedgwood, Julia, tr. see Steiner, Rudolf & Steiner-von Sivers, Marie.
Wedgwood, Ralph J., et al. Infections in Children. 1623p. 1982. text ed. 95.00x (ISBN 0-06-142645-8, Harper Medical). Lippincott.
Wedlock, Bruce D. & Roberge, James K. Electronic Components & Measurements. 1969. ref. ed. 26.95 (ISBN 0-13-250464-2). P-H.
Wedlock, Bruce D., jt. auth. see Senturia, Stephen D.
Wedlock, D. J., jt. ed. see Phillips, G. O.
Wedwick, Daryl M., jt. auth. see Lee, Briant H.
Wee, Hermann Van Der see Van der Wee, Hermann & Vinogradov, Vladimir A.
Wee, James L. Studies on the Synuraceae (Chrysophyceae) of Iowa. (Bibliotheca Phycologica 62 Ser.). 184p. (Orig.). 1982. pap. text ed. 20.00x (ISBN 3-7682-1341-2). Lubrecht & Cramer.
Weeber, Stanley C., jt. auth. see Roebuck, Julian.
Weed, Frank, jt. auth. see Turner, Steve.
Weed, Lawrence L. Managing Medicine. 3rd ed. Wakefield, Jay S., ed. (Illus.). 250p. 1983. pap. 20.00 (ISBN 0-917054-18-0). Med Communications.
Weed, Libby, jt. auth. see Weed, Michael.
Weed, Michael & Weed, Libby. Bible Handbook: A Guide for Basic Bible Learning. LC 73-91023. 1978. student's ed. 5.95 (ISBN 0-8344-0101-0). Sweet.
Weed, Mike & Willis, Wendell. Basic Christian Beliefs, Part 1. (Living Word Paperback Ser.). pap. 2.95 ea; Pt. 1 1971. pap. (ISBN 0-8344-0085-5); Pt. 2 1973. pap. o. p. (ISBN 0-8344-0091-X). Sweet.
Weeden, Hester E., ed. see Schuster, Edgar H.
Weeden, Hester E., ed. see Stanford, Gene.
Weedman, Jane. Samuel R. Delany. LC 81-21673. (Starmont Reader's Guide Ser.: No. 9). 64p. 1982. Repr. lib. bdg. 10.95x (ISBN 0-89370-040-1). Borgo Pr.
Weedman, Jane B. Reader's Guide to Samuel R. Delany. Schlobin, Roger C., ed. LC 82-5545. (Reader's Guides to Contemporary Science Fiction & Fantasy Authors Ser.: Vol. 10). (Illus., Orig.). 1982. 10.95x (ISBN 0-916732-28-2); pap. text ed. 4.95x (ISBN 0-916732-25-8). Starmont Hse.
Weedon, Syd. Portfolio of Unknown Persons. 16p. 1982. pap. 1.00 (ISBN 0-686-37939-X). Samisdat.
Weedon, William B. Economic & Social History of New England 1620-1789, 2 Vols. 1963. Set. text ed. 25.00x o.p. (ISBN 0-391-00493-X). Humanities.
Weedy, B. M. Electric Power Systems. 3rd ed. LC 79-40081. 33.95x (ISBN 0-471-27584-0, Pub. by Wiley-Interscience). Wiley.
--Underground Transmission of Electric Power. 294p. 1979. text ed. 59.95x (ISBN 0-471-27700-2, Pub. by Wiley-Interscience). Wiley.
Weegee, pseud. Weegee's People. LC 75-4846. (Illus.). 242p. 1975. Repr. of 1946 ed. lib. bdg. 18.50 (ISBN 0-306-70723-3). Da Capo.
Weekes, A. J., jt. auth. see Cooper, R. A.
Weekes, Richard V., ed. Muslim Peoples: A World Ethnographic Survey. LC 77-84759. (Illus.). 1978. lib. bdg. 45.00x (ISBN 0-8371-9880-1, WMW/). Greenwood.
Weekley, Ernest. Jack & Jill: A Study in Our Christian Names. LC 74-148925. 1974. Repr. of 1939 ed. 30.00x (ISBN 0-8103-3649-9). Gale.
--Something About Words. 233p. 1982. Repr. of 1935 ed. lib. bdg. 35.00 (ISBN 0-89760-942-5). Telegraph Bks.
Weekly, James. The Tangerine Flavored Peanut Butter Gang: Your Family Growth Workbook. Meyer, Sheila, ed. LC 82-62574. (Illus.). 145p. (Orig.). 1983. pap. text ed. write for info. (ISBN 0-916260-21-6). Meriwether Pub.
Weekly Newspaper Workers World Staff. What Is Marxism All About. 51p. 1976. pap. 1.50 (ISBN 0-89567-015-1). WV Pubs.
Weeks, Albert, jt. auth. see London, Herbert I.
Weeks, Christoper, jt. auth. see Bourne, Michael.
Weeks, David, tr. see Dumezil, Georges.
Weeks, Francis W. & Locker, Kitty O. Business Writing Cases & Problems. 162p. 1980. pap. text ed. 4.80x (ISBN 0-87563-193-2). Stipes.
Weeks, Gerald R. & L'Abate, Luciano. Paradoxical Psychotherapy: Theory & Technique. LC 81-17083. 288p. 1982. 20.00 (ISBN 0-87630-289-4). Brunner-Mazel.
Weeks, J. Devereux. Personal Liability of Public Officials Under Federal Law. LC 80-13271. 17p. 1981. pap. 3.25 (ISBN 0-89854-068-2). U of GA Inst Govt.
Weeks, J. Devereux & Slawsky, Norman L. Section Five, U. S. Voting Rights Act of 1965: Changes That Require Federal Approval. 55p. (Orig.). 1981. pap. 6.50 (ISBN 0-89854-073-9); updated insert 1.00. U of GA Inst Govt.
Weeks, Jane, jt. auth. see Spitz, Bruce.
Weeks, Jeffery, jt. auth. see Cook, Chris.
Weeks, Jim. Oklahoma Football. 1982. 10.95 o.p. (ISBN 0-87397-238-4). Strode.
--The Sooners: A Story of Oklahoma Football. Rev. & enl. ed. LC 74-84330. (College Sports Ser.). Orig. Title: Oklahoma Football. 1982. 10.95 (ISBN 0-87397-238-4). Strode.
Weeks, John. Assault from the Sky: A History of Airborne Warfare. LC 78-53430. (Illus.). 1978. 20.00 o.p. (ISBN 0-399-12222-2). Putnam Pub Group.
--The Pyramids. LC 76-22457. (Cambridge Topic Bks.). (Illus.). (gr. 5-10). 1977. PLB 6.95g (ISBN 0-8225-1209-2). Lerner Pubns.
Weeks, John & Elliot, Jeffrey M. A Superman of Letters: R. Reginald & the Borgo Press. LC 80-11112. (Borgo Reviews Ser.: Vol. 10). 64p. 1983. lib. bdg. 9.95x (ISBN 0-89370-811-9); pap. 3.95x (ISBN 0-89370-911-5). Borgo Pr.
Weeks, John, jt. auth. see Hogg, Ivan V.
Weeks, John, jt. ed. see Hogg, Ian.
Weeks, John R. Population: An Introduction to Concepts & Issues. 2nd ed. 1978. text ed. 22.95x (ISBN 0-534-00921-2). Wadsworth Pub.
--Teenage Marriages: A Demographic Analysis. LC 76-5330. (Studies in Population & Urban Demography Ser.: No. 2). (Illus.). 192p. (Orig.). 1976. lib. bdg. 25.00x (ISBN 0-8371-8898-9, WTM/). Greenwood.
Weeks, Kent R. The Classic Christian Townsite at Arminna West. (Pubns of the Penn-Yale Expedition to Egypt: No. 3). 1967. 14.00x (ISBN 0-686-17769-X). Univ Mus of U PA.
Weeks, Lewis, jt. auth. see Anderson, Odin.
Weeks, Lewis E., jt. auth. see Berman, Howard W.
Weeks, Lewis E. & Griffith, John R., eds. Progressive Patient Care: An Anthology. (Illus.). 385p. 1964. pap. text ed. 25.00 o.p. (ISBN 0-914904-22-1). Health Admin Pr.
Weeks, Lewis E., jt. ed. see Berman, Howard J.
Weeks, Paul M. Acute Bone & Joint Injuries of the Hand & Wrist: A Clinical Guide to Management. LC 80-24813. (Illus.). 299p. 1980. text ed. 42.50 (ISBN 0-8016-5373-8). Mosby.
Weeks, Robert L. As a Master of Clouds. (Chapbk Ser.). 1979. pap. 3.00 (ISBN 0-685-85408-6). Juniper Pr WI.
Weeks, Rupert. Pachee Goyo: History & Legends from the Shoshone. (Orig.). 1981. 12.00 (ISBN 0-936204-29-X); lib. bdg. 12.00; pap. 6.00 (ISBN 0-936204-16-8). Jelm Mtn.
Weeks, Thelma E. Born to Talk. 1979. pap. 7.95 o.p. (ISBN 0-88377-153-5). Newbury Hse.
Weeks, Walter. Antenna Engineering. 1968. text ed. 39.50 (ISBN 0-07-068970-9, C); solutions manual 7.95 (ISBN 0-07-068971-7). McGraw.
Weeks, William H., et al, eds. A Manual of Structured Experiences for Cross-Cultural Learning. LC 79-100422. 117p. 1977. pap. text ed. 5.95x (ISBN 0-933934-05-X). Intercult Pr.
Weelan, Guy. J. M. W. Turner. Paris, I. Mark, tr. (Illus.). 171p. 1983. 60.00 (ISBN 0-933516-51-7). Alpine Fine Arts.
Weels, Betty. A Dream Come True. (Harlequin Romance Ser.). 192p. 1983. pap. 1.75 (ISBN 0-373-02550-5). Harlequin Bks.
Weems, David B. How to Design, Build & Test Complete Speaker Systems. (Illus.). 1978. 10.95 (ISBN 0-8306-9897-3); pap. 7.95 o.p. (ISBN 0-8306-1064-2, 1064). TAB Bks.
Weems, Edward, ed. A Texas Christmas. (Illus.). 245p. 1983. price not set (ISBN 0-939722-19-4). Pressworks.
Weenolsen, Hebe. The Forbidden Mountain. LC 82-14302. 288p. 1983. 13.95 (ISBN 0-688-01630-8). Morrow.
Weerasinghe, R. M. A Cosmic Struggle. 1983. 10.95 (ISBN 0-533-05679-9). Vantage.
Weerts, Richard K., ed. Original Manuscript Music for Wind & Percussion Instruments. 2nd ed. LC 73-76728. 42p. 1973. 2.00x (ISBN 0-940796-11-2, 1033). Music Ed.
Wees, Stephen J. Practical Points in Rheumatology. 1982. pap. text ed. 24.95 (ISBN 0-87488-701-1). Med Exam.
Weese, Gene De see DeWeese, Gene.
Weesner, Gail, ed. American Cookery by Amelia Simmons, Orphan. LC 82-60671. 75p. 1982. pap. text ed. 4.95 (ISBN 0-937672-11-4). Rowan Tree.
Weg, Ruth B., ed. Sexuality in the Later Years: Roles & Behavior. LC 82-11395. write for info. (ISBN 0-12-741320-0). Acad Pr.
Wegelin, C. American Novel: Background Readings & Criticism. LC 76-136274. 1972. pap. text ed. 6.95 o.s.i. (ISBN 0-02-934590-1). Free Pr.
Wegelin, E. A. & Swan, P. J. Management of Sites & Services Housing Schemes: The Asian Experience. 220p. 1983. 24.95 (ISBN 0-471-90072-9, Pub. by Wiley Interscience). Wiley.
Wegen, Ron. Billy Gorilla. LC 82-17934. (Illus.). 32p. (gr. k-3). 1983. 10.50 (ISBN 0-688-01985-4); PLB 10.08 (ISBN 0-688-01986-2). Lothrop.
Wegen, Ronald. The Sky Dragon. (ps-3). 1982. 9.50 (ISBN 0-688-01144-6); PLB 8.59 (ISBN 0-688-01146-2). Greenwillow.
Wegener, O. H. Whole Body Computerized Tomography. (Illus.). viii, 400p. 1983. 49.25 (ISBN 3-8055-2773-X). S Karger.
Weger, Jackie. A Strong & Tender Thread. (American Romance Ser.). 192p. 1983. pap. 2.25 (ISBN 0-373-16005-4). Harlequin Bks.
Weggalaer, Jan. Amsterdam: Capital City of the Netherlands. (Q Books: Famous Cities). (Illus.). (gr. 3-6). 1978. 3.95 o.p. (ISBN 0-8467-0446-3, Pub. by Two Continents). Hippocrene Bks.
Wegman, David H., jt. ed. see Levy, Barry S.
Wegner, Daniel M. & Vallacher, Robin R. Implicit Psychology: An Introduction to Social Cognition. (Illus.). 1978. 17.95x (ISBN 0-19-502228-9); pap. text ed. 9.95x (ISBN 0-19-502229-7). Oxford U Pr.
Wegner, Daniel M. & Vallacher, Robin R., eds. The Self in Social Psychology. (Illus.). 1980. text ed. 18.95x (ISBN 0-19-502647-0); pap. text ed. 9.95x (ISBN 0-19-502648-9). Oxford U Pr.
Wegner, Hart, ed. Der Blaue Engel. 214p. (Ger.). 1982. pap. text ed. 8.95 (ISBN 0-15-517350-2, HC). HarBraceJ.
Wegner, O. H., jt. ed. see Felix, R. E.
Wegner, P. Programming with ADA: An Introduction by Means of Graduated Examples. 1980. 19.95 (ISBN 0-13-730697-0). P-H.
Wegner, Peter, ed. Research Directions in Software Technology. (MIT Computer Science & Artificial Intelligence Ser.: No. 2). (Illus.). 1979. text ed. 35.00x (ISBN 0-262-23090-9). MIT Pr.
Wegner, Robert & Sayles, Leonard. Cases in Organizational & Administrative Behavior. LC 71-158913. 1972. pap. text ed. 13.95 (ISBN 0-13-118562-4). P-H.
Wegner, Robert, ed. Land Development Decision-Making: Special Training in Zoning, Teamwork, Policy Making, Land Management, Citizen Participation, & Land Development Planning. 160p. 1979. 120.00 (ISBN 0-936440-10-4). Inst Urban Studies.
Wehausen, J. V., jt. ed. see Dyke, Van M.
Wehausen, J. V., jt. ed. see Van Dyke, M.
Wehle, Mary M. Financial Management for Arts Organizations. 175p. 1975. pap. 13.50x (ISBN 0-915440-01-6, Pub by A.A.R.I.). Pub Ctr Cult Res.
--Financial Practice for Performing Arts Companies: A Manual. 167p. 1977. pap. 13.50x (ISBN 0-915440-05-9, Pub by A.A.R.I.). Pub Ctr Cult Res.
Wehman. Recreation Programming for Developmentally Disabled Persons. 300p. 1978. pap. text ed. 15.95 (ISBN 0-8391-1295-5). Univ Park.
Wehman, Paul & McLaughlin, Phillip J. Program Development in Special Education. (Illus.). 464p. 1980. text ed. 23.50x (ISBN 0-07-068991-1, C). McGraw.
Wehman, Paul & Schleien, Stuart. Leisure Programs for Handicapped Persons: Adaptations, Techniques & Curriculum. 288p. 1981. pap. text ed. 16.95 (ISBN 0-8391-1643-8). Univ Park.

Wehmeyer, L. E. A Revision of Melanconis, Pseudovalva, Prostecium & Titania. (Univ. of Michigan Studies: No. 14). (Illus.). 1941. Repr. 20.00 (ISBN 3-7682-0929-6). Lubrecht & Cramer.

Wehmeyer, Lewis E. The Pyrenomycetous Fungi. (Mycologia Memoir: No. 6). 1975. text ed. 32.00 (ISBN 3-7682-0967-9). Lubrecht & Cramer.

Wehmeyer, Lillian B. Images in a Crystal Ball: World Futures in Novels for Young People. LC 80-26892. 211p. 1981. lib. bdg. 19.50 (ISBN 0-87287-219-X). Libs Unl.

--The School Librarian As Educator. LC 76-41303. 266p. 1976. lib. bdg. 18.50x o.p. (ISBN 0-87287-165-7). Libs Unl.

--The School Librarian As Educator. 2nd ed. 320p. 1983. lib. bdg. 22.50 (ISBN 0-87287-372-2). Libs Unl.

Wehner, Walter L. Humanism & the Aesthetic Experience: Eduaction of the Sensibilities. 1977. pap. text ed. 8.25 (ISBN 0-8191-0311-X). U Pr of Amer.

--Rhythmic Sightsinging. LC 78-66281. 1979. pap. text ed. 8.50 (ISBN 0-8191-0687-9). U Pr of Amer.

Wehr, M. Russell, et al. Physics of the Atom. 3rd ed. LC 77-77752. (Physics Ser.). (Illus.). 1978. text ed. 25.95 (ISBN 0-201-08587-9). A-W.

Wehr, Paul. Like a Mustard Seed. LC 82-81963. (Illus.). 120p. 1982. 14.00 (ISBN 0-913122-37-8). Mickler Hse.

Wehrle, Paul, jt. auth. see Top, Franklin.

Wehrle, Pauline, tr. see Steiner, Rudolf.

Wehrli. Totem Tales: Beaver. (gr. 3-8). 1979. pap. 1.95 coloring bk. (ISBN 0-918146-10-0). Peninsula WA.

--Totem Tales: Giant Rock Oyster. (gr. 3-8). 1979. pap. 1.95 coloring bk. (ISBN 0-918146-12-7). Peninsula WA.

--Totem Tales: Raven & Sun. (gr. 3-8). 1979. pap. 1.95 coloring bk. (ISBN 0-918146-11-9). Peninsula WA.

--Totem Tales: The Dogfish. (gr. 3-8). 1979. pap. 1.95 coloring bk. (ISBN 0-918146-14-3). Peninsula WA.

--Totem Tales: The Old Witch. (gr. 3-8). 1979. pap. 1.95 coloring bk. (ISBN 0-918146-13-5). Peninsula WA.

--Totem Tales: Thunderbird. (gr. 3-8). 1979. pap. 1.95 coloring bk. (ISBN 0-918146-09-7). Peninsula WA.

Wehrli, Christoph. Mittelaterliche Uberlieferungen Von Dagobert I. 386p. (Ger.). 1982. write for info (ISBN 3-261-04914-6). P Lang Pubs.

Wehrli, F. & Wirthlin, T. Interpretation of Carbon-13 NMR Spectra. 1976. 42.95 (ISBN 0-471-26078-9, Wiley Heyden). Wiley.

Wehrli, K. Division. (Michigan Arithmetic Program Ser.). (gr. 4). 1976. wkbk. 8.00 (ISBN 0-89039-180-7). Ann Arbor Pubs.

Wehrli, Kitty. Addition, Ten to Twenty. (Michigan Arithmetic Program Ser.). (gr. 2). 1977. wkbk. 8.00 (ISBN 0-89039-105-X). Ann Arbor Pubs.

--Listening Experiences (Primary) (Illus.). 60p. (gr. 1). 1981. 4.00 (ISBN 0-686-84636-2); tchr's script 1.00. Ann Arbor Pubs.

--Math Readiness Workbook: Math Readiness Pretest Manual. (Michigan Arithmetic Program Ser.). (Illus.). (gr. k-3). 1978. 1.00 (ISBN 0-89039-241-2); 1.00 (ISBN 0-89039-238-2). Ann Arbor Pubs.

--Michigan Arithmetic Program, Multiplication, Level 2: Reusable Edition. (gr. 3). 1975. 8.00 (ISBN 0-89039-132-7). Ann Arbor Pubs.

--Multiplication, Level 1: Reusable Edition. (Michigan Arithmetic Program Ser.). (gr. 3). 1975. Repr. wkbk 8.00 (ISBN 0-89039-094-0). Ann Arbor Pubs.

--Numbers & Numerals. (Michigan Arithmetic Program). (ps-2). 1976. 1.00x (ISBN 0-89039-199-8); wkbk. 6.00 (ISBN 0-89039-102-5). Ann Arbor Pubs.

--Subtraction 10-0. (Michigan Arithmetic Program Ser.). (gr. 2-3). 1976. wkbk. 8.00 (ISBN 0-89039-176-9). Ann Arbor Pubs.

--Subtraction 20-10, Levels 1 & 2. (Michigan Arithmetic Program). (gr. 2-3). 1976. Level 1. wkbk 8.00 ea. (ISBN 0-89039-178-5). Level 2 (ISBN 0-89039-220-X). Ann Arbor Pubs.

--A Teachers' Script A: Numbers & Numerals, Addition 0-10, Addition 10-20, Multiplication. (Michigan Arithmetic Program). 162p. 1974. 5.00x (ISBN 0-89039-115-7). Ann Arbor Pubs.

--Teachers' Script B: Subtraction 10-0, Subtraction 20-10, Division. (Michigan Arithmetic Program). 146p. 1974. tchrs. ed 5.00x (ISBN 0-89039-116-5). Ann Arbor Pubs.

--Visual & Transfer Skill Mastery, 2 levels. (Michigan Arithmetic Program Ser.). 1976. wkbk. 8.00 ea.; Level 1. (ISBN 0-89039-948-4); Level 2. write for info (ISBN 0-89039-850-X). Ann Arbor Pubs.

Wehrly, Max. Mobile Homes, 2 pts. LC 72-79132. (Illus.). 80p. 1972. Set. pap. 5.00, Pt. II (Pt. I out of print) (ISBN 0-87420-068-7). An Analysis Of Characteristics. An Analysis Of Communities. Urban Land.

Wehry, E. L. Modern Fluorescence Spectroscopy. 713p. 1976. text ed. 178.00x (ISBN 0-471-26079-7, Pub. by Wiley-Interscience). Wiley.

Wei, B. C., jt. ed. see Pugh, C. E.

Wei, C. C. The Precision Bidding System in Bridge. Truscott, Alan, ed. (Illus.). 116p. 1973. pap. 3.00 (ISBN 0-486-21171-1). Dover.

Wei, James, et al. The Structure of the Chemical Processing Industries: Function & Economics. (Chemical Engineering Series). (Illus.). 1978. text ed. 36.95 (ISBN 0-07-068985-7, C). McGraw.

Wei, Tan Tai. The Concept of Education, Educational Conceptions, & Liberal Education. LC 77-18470. 1978. pap. text ed. 8.25 (ISBN 0-8191-0418-3). U Pr of Amer.

Weich, I. Edward. Real Estate. (Orig.). 1967. pap. 4.95 (ISBN 0-06-460060-2, CO 60, COS). B&N NY.

Weicher, John, jt. auth. see Tuccillo, John.

Weicher, John, et al. Rental Housing: Is There a Crisis? LC 81-53063. 113p. 1981. text ed. 16.50 (ISBN 0-87766-307-6, URI 33400). Urban Inst.

Weicher, John C. & Yap, Lorene. Metropolitan Housing Needs for the 1980's. LC 81-70526. 138p. text ed. 16.50 (ISBN 0-87766-308-4, URI 33500). Urban Inst.

Weichert, Charles K. Anatomy of the Chordates. 4th ed. 1970. text ed. 32.50 (ISBN 0-07-069007-3, C). McGraw.

--Representative Chordates. 2nd ed. (Zoological Ser.). (Illus.). 1961. text ed. 16.95 (ISBN 0-07-068984-9, C). McGraw.

Weichert, Charles K. & Presch, William. Elements of Chordate Anatomy. 4th ed. (Illus.). 608p. 1975. text ed. 32.50 (ISBN 0-07-069008-1, C). McGraw.

Weichmann, Louis J. A True History of the Assassination of Abraham Lincoln & of the Conspiracy of 1865. Risvold, Floyd E., ed. 1977. Repr. of 1975 ed. 16.95 (ISBN 0-394-49319-2, Vin). Random.

Weick, Carl. Applied Electronics. 1976. text ed. 22.95 (ISBN 0-07-069012-X, G). McGraw.

Weideger, Paula & Thorsten, Geraldine. Traveling with Your Pet. 1973. 7.95 o.p. (ISBN 0-671-21449-7); pap. 2.95 o.s.i. (ISBN 0-671-21756-9). S&S.

Weidemann, Alfred M. Plants of the Oregon Coastal Dunes. 1969. pap. text ed. 6.20X (ISBN 0-88246-117-6). Oreg St U Bkstrs.

Weidemann, K. Eine Probe Unserer Kuns Zu Zeigen (to Show a Sample of Our Art) (Illus., Ger.). ltd. edition 22.50 o.p. (ISBN 0-685-26822-5). Museum Bks.

Weidenaar, Dennis J. & Weiler, Emanuel. Economics: An Introduction to the World Around You. 3rd ed. LC 82-11477. 512p. Date not set. pap. text ed. 17.95 (ISBN 0-201-08271-3). A-W.

Weidenbaum, M. Business, Government, & the Public. 2nd ed. 1981. 21.00 (ISBN 0-13-099325-5). P-H.

Weidenfeld, Sheila R. First Lady's Lady: With the Fords at the White House. LC 78-10662. (Illus.). 1979. 11.95 (ISBN 0-399-12292-3). Putnam Pub Group.

Weidenhan, Joseph L. Baptismal Names. 4th ed. LC 68-26618. 1968. Repr. of 1931 ed. 40.00x (ISBN 0-8103-3136-5). Gale.

Weidenmuller, H. A., jt. auth. see Norenberg, W.

Weider, Ben. The Murder of Napoleon. 304p. 1982. 14.95 (ISBN 0-312-92548-4). Congdon & Weed.

Weider, Betty & Weider, Joe. The Weider Book of Bodybuilding for Women. (Illus.). 160p. 1981. 14.95 (ISBN 0-8092-5907-9); pap. 7.95 (ISBN 0-8092-5906-0). Contemp Bks.

Weider, Betty, jt. auth. see Weider, Joe.

Weider, Joe. The Best of Joe Weider's Muscle & Fitness Bodybuilding Nutrition & Training Programs. (Illus.). 1981. 12.95 (ISBN 0-8092-5917-6); pap. 7.95 (ISBN 0-8092-5916-8). Contemp Bks.

--The Best of Joe Weider's Muscle & Fitness Champion Bodybuilders' Training Strategies & Routines. (Illus.). 128p. 1982. 15.50 (ISBN 0-8092-5752-1); pap. 7.95 (ISBN 0-8092-5751-3). Contemp Bks.

--The Best of Joe Weider's Muscle & Fitness Training Tips & Routines. (Illus.). 1981. 12.95 (ISBN 0-8092-5911-7); pap. 7.95 (ISBN 0-8092-5910-9). Contemp Bks.

--The Best of Joe Weider's Muscle & Fitness: The World's Leading Bodybuilders Answer Your Questions. (Illus.). 1981. 12.95 (ISBN 0-8092-5914-1); pap. 6.95 (ISBN 0-8092-5912-5). Contemp Bks.

--Bodybuilding: The Weider Approach. (Illus.). 224p. 1981. 17.50 (ISBN 0-8092-5909-5); pap. 8.95 (ISBN 0-8092-5908-7). Contemp Bks.

--More Bodybuilding Nutrition & Training Programs. 160p. 1982. cancelled (ISBN 0-8092-5595-2); pap. 7.95 (ISBN 0-8092-5619-3). Contemp Bks.

--More Training Tips & Routines. (Illus.). 160p. Date not set. cancelled (ISBN 0-8092-5594-4); pap. 7.95 (ISBN 0-8092-5618-5). Contemp Bks.

--Muscle & Fitness: Champion Bodybuilders' Training Strategies & Routines. 1982. 15.50 (ISBN 0-8092-5752-1); pap. 7.95 (ISBN 0-8092-5751-3). Contemp Bks.

--The Weider System of Bodybuilding. Reynolds, Bill, ed. (Illus.). 224p. (Orig.). 1983. 17.95 (ISBN 0-8092-5561-8); pap. 8.95 (ISBN 0-8092-5559-6). Contemp Bks.

--Women's Weight Training & Bodybuilding Tips & Routines. 7.95 (ISBN 0-686-93942-5). Contemp Bks.

Weider, Joe & Weider, Betty. The Best of Joe Weider's Muscle & Fitness Women's Weight Training & Bodybuilding Training Tips & Routines. (Illus.). 128p. 1982. 15.50 (ISBN 0-8092-5755-6); pap. 7.95 (ISBN 0-8092-5754-8). Contemp Bks.

Weider, Joe, jt. auth. see Weider, Betty.

Weidhorn, Manfred. Sir Winston Churchill. (English Authors Ser.). 1979. lib. bdg. 12.95 (ISBN 0-8057-6760-6, Twayne). G K Hall.

Weidler, Roy. Numerology for Pleasure. 1961. pap. 2.00 (ISBN 0-910140-18-9). Anthony.

Weidman, Jerome. Counselors-at-Law. LC 78-14712. 408p. 1980. 12.95 o.p. (ISBN 0-385-12880-0). Doubleday.

--The Temple. 448p. 1976. 9.95 o.p. (ISBN 0-671-22100-0). S&S.

Weidman, M. L., ed. Charting the Course. pap. 2.25 (ISBN 0-87509-062-1). Chr Pubns.

Weidman, Mavis. Junior Worker's Handbook. pap. 2.25 (ISBN 0-87509-098-2). Chr Pubns.

Weidmann, M. J., jt. auth. see Hume, D. A.

Weidner, Edward W. Intergovernmental Relations As Seen by Public Officials. LC 73-16645. (Intergovernmental Relations in the U.S., Research Monograph: No. 9). 162p. 1974. Repr. of 1960 ed. lib. bdg. 18.50x (ISBN 0-8371-7209-8, WEIR). Greenwood.

Weidner, Edward W., ed. see Hutchins, John G. B.

Weidner, James H. Rusky-Poetry & Prose Vignettes. LC 80-68817. 104p. (Orig.). 1980. pap. 5.95x (ISBN 9-0701-7619-X). Foris Pubns.

Weidner, Richard T., jt. auth. see Carr, Herman Y.

Weier, Elliot T., et al. Botany: An Introduction to Plant Biology. 6th ed. LC 81-10304. 720p. 1982. text ed. 26.95 (ISBN 0-471-01561-X); 8.95 (ISBN 0-471-08519-7). Wiley.

Weigand, Dennis A. Dermatology Continuing Education Review. 2nd. ed. Olson, Robert L., ed. 1980. pap. 20.00 (ISBN 0-87488-341-5). Med Exam.

Weigand, Dennis A., ed. Dermatology. 4th ed. (Medical Examination Review Book: Vol. 21). 1980. pap. 24.00 (ISBN 0-87488-127-7). Med Exam.

Weigand, George. Getting Ready for College: How to Settle Down & Make the Grade. 1984. pap. text ed. 3.50 (ISBN 0-8120-2080-4). Barron.

--How to Succeed in High School & Score High on College Entrance Examinations. rev. ed. LC 79-140632. (gr. 9-12). 1979. pap. 3.50 (ISBN 0-8120-2478-8). Barron.

Weigand, Hermann J. Critical Probings: Essays in European Literature. Goldsmith, Ulrich K., ed. 310p. Date not set. price not set. P Lang Pubs.

Weigand, J., ed. Implementing Teacher Competencies: Positive Approaches to Personalizing Education. 1977. pap. text ed. 17.95 (ISBN 0-13-451930-2). P-H.

Weigand, James E., ed. Developing Teacher Competencies. LC 70-149972. (Illus.). 1971. pap. text ed. 17.95 (ISBN 0-13-205278-4). P-H.

Weigel, James, Jr. Mythology. 210p. 1973. pap. 3.95 (ISBN 0-8220-0865-3). Cliffs.

--Pickwick Papers Notes. (Orig.). 1970. pap. 2.25 (ISBN 0-8220-1021-6). Cliffs.

--Tale of Two Cities Notes. (Orig.). 1969. pap. 2.50 (ISBN 0-8220-1255-3). Cliffs.

Weigel, John A. B.F. Skinner. (World Leaders Ser.). 1977. lib. bdg. 11.95 (ISBN 0-8057-7713-X, Twayne). G K Hall.

--Colin Wilson. (English Authors Ser.). 1975. lib. bdg. 12.95 (ISBN 0-8057-1575-4, Twayne). G K Hall.

--Lawrence Durrell. (English Authors Ser.: No. 29). 1965. lib. bdg. 12.95 o.p. (ISBN 0-8057-1180-5, Twayne). G K Hall.

Weigel, Tom. Twenty Four Haiku After the Japanese. Owen, Maureen, ed. (Summer Ser.). 1982. pap. 3.00 (ISBN 0-686-43221-5). Telephone Bks.

Weigen, John F. & Thomas, Sydney F. Complications of Diagnostic Radiology. (Illus.). 576p. 1973. 35.75x o.p. (ISBN 0-398-02501-0). C C Thomas.

Weiger, John G. Cristobal de Virues. (World Authors Ser.: No. 497 (Spain)). 1978. 15.95 (ISBN 0-8057-6338-4, Twayne). G K Hall.

--The Individuated Self: Cervantes & the Emergence of the Individual. LC 78-13019. xvi, 183p. 1979. 13.95x (ISBN 0-8214-0396-6, 82-82873). Ohio U Pr.

--The Valencian Dramatists of Spain's Golden Age. (World Authors Ser.). 1976. lib. bdg. 15.95 (ISBN 0-8057-6219-1, Twayne). G K Hall.

Weigert, Andrew J. Life & Society: A meditation on the Social Thought of Jose Ortega y Gassett. 250p. 1983. text ed. 19.95x (ISBN 0-8290-1278-8). Irvington.

Weigh, Iris. Someone to Love. (Aston-Hall Romances Ser.). 192p. (Orig.). 1981. pap. 1.75 o.p. (ISBN 0-523-41131-6). Pinnacle Bks.

Weight, Harold, ed. see Bagley, Helen G.

Weight, Lucile, ed. see Bagley, Helen G.

Weightman, Doreen, tr. see Levi-Strauss, Claude.

Weightman, John. Concept of the Avant-Garde. 323p. 1973. 21.00x (ISBN 0-912050-40-3, Library Pr). Open Court.

Weightman, John, tr. see Levi-Strauss, Claude.

Weigl, Bruce, ed. see Smith, Dave J.

Weigl, Etta R. Meltwater. LC 82-60191. (Illus.). 80p. 1982. 10.95 (ISBN 0-9608824-0-5); pap. 5.95 (ISBN 0-9608824-1-3). Stereopticon Pr.

Weigle, Luther A. American Idealism. 1928. text ed. 22.50x (ISBN 0-686-83462-3). Elliots Bks.

Weigle, Marta. Brothers of Light, Brothers of Blood: The Penitentes of the Southwest. LC 75-21188. (Illus.). 300p. 1976. 14.95 o.p. (ISBN 0-8263-0400-1). U of NM Pr.

--A Penitente Bibliography. LC 75-40839. 176p. 1976. pap. 8.50x o.p. (ISBN 0-8263-0401-X). U of NM Pr.

--The Penitentes of the Southwest. LC 78-131971. (Illus.). 48p. 1980. lib. bdg. 8.95 (ISBN 0-941270-01-7); pap. 2.95 (ISBN 0-941270-00-9). Ancient City Pr.

Weigle, Marta & Fiore, Kyle. Santa Fe & Taos: The Writer's Era, 1916-1941. LC 81-71485. (Illus.). 220p. 1982. 15.95 (ISBN 0-941270-08-4). Ancient City Pr.

Weigle, Marta & Larcombe, Claudia, eds. Hispanic Arts & Ethohistory in the Southwest: New Papers Inspired by the Work of E. Boyd. LC 82-74221. (A Spanish Colonial Arts Society Book). (Illus.). 350p. 1983. 35.00 (ISBN 0-941270-14-9); pap. 20.00 (ISBN 0-941270-13-0). Ancient City Pr.

Weigle, Oscar. Jokes & Riddles. (Elephant Activity Bks.). (Illus.). 128p. (gr. k-3). 1975. pap. 1.25 (ISBN 0-448-11884-X, G&D). Putnam Pub Group.

--Jokes, Riddles, Funny Stories. (Illus.). (gr. 4-6). 1959. 4.95 (ISBN 0-448-02892-1, G&D). Putnam Pub Group.

--Short Tales for Sleepyheads. LC 78-54177. (Elephant Books Ser.). (Illus.). (gr. k-3). pap. 3.95 (ISBN 0-448-16165-6, G&D). Putnam Pub Group.

--Treasury of Bedtime Stories. LC 69-17269. (Juvenile Fiction Ser.). 160p. (gr. k-3). 1975. pap. 2.95 (ISBN 0-448-11908-0, G&D). Putnam Pub Group.

Weigle, Oscar, ed. Great Big Joke & Riddle Book. LC 79-129734. (Illus.). 224p. (gr. 1-5). 1981. 6.95 (ISBN 0-448-02584-1, G&D); PLB 10.15 (ISBN 0-448-03167-1). Putnam Pub Group.

Weigle, Oscar, adapted by. Puppet Storybooks, 6 bks. Incl. Cinderella (ISBN 0-448-09747-8); Goldilocks & the Three Bears (ISBN 0-448-09748-6); Little Red Riding Hood (ISBN 0-448-09749-4); Mother Goose; Pinocchio (ISBN 0-448-09752-4); The Three Little Pigs (ISBN 0-448-09746-X). (Illus.). (ps). 1980. 2.95 ea. (G&D). Putnam Pub Group.

Weigle, Oscar, compiled by. Walt Disney's World of Riddles. LC 78-71307. (gr. 2 up). 1979. 5.95 (ISBN 0-448-16827-8, G&D); PLB 10.15 (ISBN 0-448-13127-7, Today Pr). Putnam Pub Group.

Weigle, Oscar, ed. see Tricky Ricky.

Weigley, Emma S., jt. auth. see Robinson, Corinne H.

Weigley, Russell F. Towards an American Army. LC 74-5785. 297p. 1974. Repr. of 1962 ed. lib. bdg. 20.25x (ISBN 0-8371-7499-6, WETA). Greenwood.

Weigley, Russell F., ed. New Dimensions in Military History: An Anthology. LC 76-4159. 432p. 1976. 14.95 o.p. (ISBN 0-89141-002-3). Presidio Pr.

Weigner, Gladys, jt. auth. see Moosbrugger, Bernhard.

Weigold, Erich, ed. see AIP Conference, 86th, Adelaide, Australia, 1982.

Weihaupt, John G. Exploration of the Oceans: An Introduction to Oceanography. 1979. text ed. 26.95x (ISBN 0-02-425040-6). Macmillan.

Weihofen, Henry. Legal Services & Community Mental Health Centers. 74p. 1969. pap. 3.00 o.p. (ISBN 0-685-24859-3, P229-0). Am Psychiatric.

Weihrauch. Esophageal Manometry: Methods & Clinical Practice. LC 81-11430. (Illus.). 144p. 1981. text ed. 22.50 (ISBN 0-8067-2151-0). Urban & S.

Weihrich, Heinz, jt. auth. see O'Donnell, Harold K.

Wei-Hsun Fu, Charles & Wing-tsit, Chan, eds. Guide to Chinese Philosophy. 1978. lib. bdg. 30.00 (ISBN 0-8161-7901-8, Hall Reference). G K Hall.

Weiker, Walter F. The Turkish Revolution, Nineteen Sixty to Nineteen Sixty-One: Aspects of Military Politics. LC 79-27852. (Illus.). viii, 172p. 1980. Repr. of 1963 ed. lib. bdg. 19.25x (ISBN 0-313-22303-3, WETR). Greenwood.

Weikert, Heidrun-Edda. Tom Stoppards Dramen. (Tuebinger Beitrae zur Anglistik: 4). 350p. 1982. pap. 25.50 (ISBN 3-87808-570-2). Benjamins North Am.

Weil, A. Adeles & Algebraic Groups. (Progress in Mathematics Ser.: Vol. 23). 126p. 1982. text ed. 10.00x (ISBN 3-7643-3092-9). Birkhauser.

Weil, Andrew & Rosen, Winifred. Chocolate to Morphine: Understanding Mind-Active Drugs. LC 82-12112. (Illus.). 250p. 1983. 14.95 (ISBN 0-395-33108-0); pap. 8.95 (ISBN 0-686-42997-4). HM.

Weil, Ann. John Philip Sousa: Marching Boy. LC 59-12856. (Childhood of Famous Americans Ser.). (Illus.). (gr. 3-7). 1959. 3.95 o.p. (ISBN 0-672-50107-4). Bobbs.

Weil, C., jt. ed. see Sen, R. N.

Weil, G. L. Trade Policy in the 70's: A New Round. LC 73-4787. 1969. pap. 2.00 (ISBN 0-527-02784-7). Kraus Repr.

Weil, Henri. The Order of Words in the Ancient Languages Compared with That of the Modern Languages. Super, Charles W., tr. (Amsterdam Classics in Linguistics Ser.). xxxix, 114p. 1978. 21.00 (ISBN 90-272-0975-8, 14). Benjamins North Am.

Weil, Lisl. The Foolish King. LC 82-4640. (Illus.). 32p. (gr. k-3). 1982. 9.95 (ISBN 0-02-792570-6). Macmillan.

--Gillie & the Flattering Fox. LC 77-21248. (Illus.). (ps-2). 1978. 7.95 o.p. (ISBN 0-689-30637-7). Atheneum.
--I, Christopher Columbus. LC 82-16323. (Illus.). 48p. (gr. k-4). 1983. 10.95 (ISBN 0-689-30965-1). Atheneum.
Weil, Louis, jt. auth. see Price, Charles P.
Weil, Mark S. Baroque Theatre & Stage Design. 44p. 1983. pap. 5.00 (ISBN 0-936316-04-7). Washington U Gallery.
Weil, Marsha & Joyce, Bruce. Information Processing Models of Teaching: Expanding Your Teaching Repertoire. LC 77-5414. (Illus.). 1978. ref. ed. o.p. 17.95 (ISBN 0-13-464552-9); pap. text ed. 16.95 (ISBN 0-13-464545-6). P-H.
--Social Models of Teaching: Expanding Your Teaching Repetoire. LC 77-5448. (Illus.). 1978. 20.95 (ISBN 0-13-815944-0); pap. 16.95 (ISBN 0-13-815936-X). P-H.
Weil, Marsha, jt. auth. see Joyce, Bruce R.
Weil, Martin. Bichon Frise. (Illus.). 128p. 1981. 4.95 (ISBN 0-87666-739-6, KW 140). TFH Pubns.
--Mynahs. (Illus.). 96p. 1981. 4.95 (ISBN 0-87666-890-2, KW-120). TFH Pubns.
--Puli. (Illus.). 128p. 1982. 4.95 (ISBN 0-87666-740-X, KW-141). TFH Pubns.
--Saint Bernards. (Illus.). 1982. 4.95 (ISBN 0-87666-727-2, KW-109). TFH Pubns.
--Silky Terriers. (Illus.). 128p. 1981. 4.95 (ISBN 0-87666-730-2, KW-115). TFH Pubns.
Weil, N. A. see Ordway, Frederick I., 3rd.
Weil, R., jt. auth. see Davidson, S.
Weil, Roman, jt. auth. see Davidson, Sidney.
Weil, Simone. Lectures on Philosophy. Price, H., tr. from Fr. LC 77-26735. 1978. 32.95 (ISBN 0-521-22005-X); pap. 8.95 (ISBN 0-521-29333-2). Cambridge U Pr.
--The Notebooks, 2 vols. 1976. 16.95 ea. o.p.; Vol. 1. (ISBN 0-7100-8522-2); Vol 2. (ISBN 0-7100-8523-0); 32.00 set o.p. (ISBN 0-686-68038-3). Routledge & Kegan.
--Waiting for God. pap. 5.29i (ISBN 0-06-090295-7, CN295, CN). Har-Row.
Weil, Stephen E. Beauty & the Beasts: On Museums, Art, the Law, & the Market. 304p. 1983. text ed. 17.50x (ISBN 0-87474-958-1); pap. text ed. 9.95x (ISBN 0-87474-957-3). Smithsonian.
Weil, Susanne & Singer, Barry. Steppin' Out: A Guide to Live Music in Manhattan. LC 79-23812. (Illus.). 160p. 1980. pap. 7.95 (ISBN 0-914788-24-8). East Woods.
Weiland, R. G. & Woytek, S. J. Mathematics in Living, 4 bks. Incl. Bk. I. Buying. 1979 (ISBN 0-87108-152-0); Bk. II. Wages & Budgets. 1979 (ISBN 0-87108-153-9); Bk. III. Banking & Loans. 1970. 3.50 o.p. (ISBN 0-87108-154-7); Bk. IV. Credit, Loans & Taxes. 1974. 2.95 o.p. (ISBN 0-87108-179-2). (Illus.). 1970. pap. text ed. 3.50x o.p. (ISBN 0-686-86672-X); ans. bk. 4.95x o.p. (ISBN 0-87108-156-3). Pruett.
Weilbacher, William M. Advertising in Business & Society. 1979. 24.95x (ISBN 0-02-425100-3). Macmillan.
--Choosing an Ad Agency. 192p. 1983. pap. price not set (ISBN 0-87251-083-2). Crain Bks.
--Marketing Management Cases: Planning & Executing Marketing Strategy. 3rd ed. (Illus.). 1980. pap. text ed. 11.95x (ISBN 0-02-425070-8). Macmillan.
Weiler, Emanuel, jt. auth. see Weidenaar, Dennis J.
Weiler, Kathi, jt. auth. see Kernicki, Jeanette.
Weiler, Lawrence D., jt. ed. see Platt, Alan.
Weiler, Lawrence D., ed. see Stanford Arms Control Group.
Weill, Francis W. Ultrasonography of Digestive Diseases. LC 77-13046. (Illus.). 1978. 57.50 o.p. (ISBN 0-8016-5374-6). Mosby.
Weill, Gus. The Fuhrer Seed. LC 79-385. 1979. 9.95 o.p. (ISBN 0-688-03452-7). Morrow.
Weimar, Karl S. & Hoffmeister, Werner G. Practice & Progress: A German Grammar for Review & Reference. 1970. text ed. 21.95x (ISBN 0-471-00619-X); tapes avail. (ISBN 0-471-00621-1). Wiley.
Weimer, Anne, jt. auth. see Weimer, Wayne.
Weimer, Arthur M., et al. Real Estate. 7th ed. LC 77-79170. 1978. text ed. 28.95x o.p. (ISBN 0-471-06878-0). Wiley.
Weimer, David L. Improving Prosecution? The Inducement & Implementation of Innovations for Prosecution Management. LC 79-6190. (Contributions in Political Science: No. 49). (Illus.). xv, 237p. 1980. lib. bdg. 27.50x (ISBN 0-313-22247-9, WEP/). Greenwood.
--The Strategic Petroleum Reserve: Planning, Implementation, & Analysis. LC 82-6184. (Contributions in Economics & Economic History Ser.: No. 48). (Illus.). 256p. 1982. lib. bdg. 29.95 (ISBN 0-313-23404-3, WPO/). Greenwood.
Weimer, H. & Weimer, N. Yareba-English Dictionary. 525p. 1974. pap. 6.50 o.s.i. (ISBN 0-7263-0283-X); 5.25 o.s.i. (ISBN 0-88312-726-1). Summer Inst Ling.
Weimer, N., jt. auth. see Weimer, H.
Weimer, R. J., et al. Tectonic Influence on Sedimentation, Early Cretaceous, East Flank Powder River Basin, Wyoming & South Dakota. (Colorado School of Mines Quarterly: Vol. 77, No. 4). (Illus.). 95p. 1982. pap. text ed. 12.00 (ISBN 0-686-82131-9). Colo Sch Mines.
Weimer, Wayne & Weimer, Anne. Arithmetic Readiness Inventory. (Elementary Education Ser.). 1977. pap. text ed. 8.95 (ISBN 0-675-08546-2). Merrill.
Wein, Horst. Science of Hockey. 2nd ed. Belchamber, David, tr. (Illus.). 22.00 o.s.i. (ISBN 0-7207-1149-5). Transatlantic.
Wein, Ross W. & MacLean, David A. The Role of Fire in Northern Circumpolar Ecosystems (Scope 18) 350p. 1983. 54.95x (ISBN 0-471-10222-9, Pub. by Wiley-Interscience). Wiley.
Weinacht, R., jt. auth. see Gilbert, R.
Weinandt, Elwyn. Johann Pezel: A Thematic Catalogue. (Thematic Catalogue Ser.). 141p. 1983. lib. bdg. 52.00 (ISBN 0-918728-23-1). Pendragon NY.
Weinbaum, Batya. Picture of Patriarchy. 200p. 1982. 17.50 (ISBN 0-89608-161-3); pap. 7.00 (ISBN 0-89608-162-1). South End Pr.
Weinbaum, Martin, jt. auth. see Chew, Helena.
Weinbaum, Martin, ed. The London Eyre of Twelve Seventy-Six. 1976. 50.00 (ISBN 0-686-96609-0, Pub by London Rec Soc England). State Mutual Bk.
Weinbaum, Stanley G. Martian Odyssey, & Other Science Fiction Tales. LC 73-13269. (Illus.). 604p. 1974. 16.50 (ISBN 0-88355-123-3); pap. 5.75 o.p. (ISBN 0-88355-152-7). Hyperion Conn.
Weinber, jt. auth. see Bell.
Weinberg, Alvin M., ed. see Institute for Energy Analysis.
Weinberg, Arthur & Weinberg, Lila. Clarence Darrow: The Sentimental Rebel. 1980. 17.95 (ISBN 0-399-11936-1). Putnam Pub Group.
Weinberg, B. French Realism: The Critical Reaction, 1830-1870. (MLA Gen. Ser.: No. 5). 1937. pap. 23.00 (ISBN 0-527-95200-1). Kraus Repr.
Weinberg, Bernard. A History of Literary Criticism in the Italian Renaissance. LC 60-5470. (Midway Reprint Ser.). 348p. 1974. pap. 17.50 ea.; Vol. 1. (ISBN 0-226-88554-2); Vol. 2. o.s.i. (ISBN 0-226-88555-0). U of Chicago Pr.
Weinberg, Bernd, jt. auth. see Shedd, Donald P.
Weinberg, Bernd, ed. Reading in Speech Following Total Laryngectomy. 600p. 1980. pap. text ed. 19.95 (ISBN 0-8391-1570-9). Univ Park.
Weinberg, Bernd & Meitus, Irv J., eds. AN Introduction to Diagnosis of Speech & Language Disorders. 1983. pap. text ed. price not set (ISBN 0-8391-1810-4, 18430). Univ Park.
Weinberg, Carole, ed. see Gower, John.
Weinberg, Charles, jt. auth. see Lovelock, Christopher.
Weinberg, Charles B., jt. auth. see Lovelock, Christopher H.
Weinberg, Daniel, jt. auth. see Friedman, Joseph.
Weinberg, Daniela. Peasant Wisdom: Cultural Adoption in a Swiss Village. (Illus.). 226p. 1975. 32.50x (ISBN 0-520-02789-2). U of Cal Pr.
Weinberg, Daniela, jt. auth. see Weinberg, Gerald M.
Weinberg, Edgar. Labour-Management Cooperation for Productivity. (Work in America Institute Studies in Productivity). 1983. 35.00 (ISBN 0-08-029511-8). Pergamon.
Weinberg, Eli. Portrait of a People. (Illus.). 200p. 1982. pap. 8.95 (ISBN 0-904759-42-3, Pub. by Intl Defence England). Lawrence Hill.
Weinberg, Elizabeth A. The Development of Sociology in the Soviet Union. (International Library of Sociology). 188p. 1975. 19.95x (ISBN 0-7100-7876-5). Routledge & Kegan.
Weinberg, George. The Pliant Animal. 256p. 1981. 10.95 o.p. (ISBN 0-312-61751-8). St Martin.
--Society & the Healthy Homosexual. 160p. 1983. pap. 5.95 (ISBN 0-312-73851-X). St Martin.
Weinberg, George H., et al. Statistics: An Intuitive Approach. 4th ed. 384p. 1980. text ed. 20.95 (ISBN 0-8185-0426-9). Brooks-Cole.
Weinberg, Gerald, ed. see Marcus, Robert.
Weinberg, Gerald M. An Introduction to General Systems Thinking. LC 74-26689. (Systems Engineering & Analysis Ser.). 279p. 1975. 29.95x (ISBN 0-471-92563-2, Pub. by Wiley-Interscience). Wiley.
Weinberg, Gerald M. & Weinberg, Daniela. On the Design of Stable Systems: A Companion Volume to an Introduction to General Systems Thinking. LC 79-13926. (Systems Engineering & Analysis Ser.). 1980. 29.95x (ISBN 0-471-04722-8, Pub. by Wiley-Interscience). Wiley.
Weinberg, Gerald M., et al. High Level COBOL Programming. 1977. text ed. 25.95 (ISBN 0-316-92846-1). Little.
Weinberg, Gerhard L. The Foreign Policy of Hitler's Germany: Diplomatic Revolution in Europe, 1933-1936. LC 70-124733. xii, 398p. 1970. pap. 10.95 (ISBN 0-226-88513-5). U of Chicago Pr.
--World in the Balance: Behind the Scenes of World War II. LC 81-51606. (Tauber Institute Ser.). (Illus.). 185p. 1981. text ed. 12.50x (ISBN 0-87451-216-6); pap. text ed. 5.50x (ISBN 0-87451-217-4). U Pr of New Eng.
Weinberg, H. Barbara, ed. see Jarves, James J.
Weinberg, H. Barbara, ed. see Van Rensselaer, Mariana G.
Weinberg, Herman G. Coffee, Brandy & Cigars: A Kaleidoscope of the Arts & that Strange Thing Called Life. 96p. 1982. write for info.; pap. write for info. Anthology Film.
--A Manhattan Odyssey: A Memoir. (Illus.). 206p. 1982. write for info.; pap. write for info. Anthology Film.
Weinberg, Joel S. College Reading: Skills & Practice. LC 77-78585. (Illus.). 1978. text ed. 13.50 spiral bdg. (ISBN 0-395-25319-5); instr's manual 0.50 (ISBN 0-395-25320-9). HM.
Weinberg, Judith W., jt. auth. see Weinberg, Lee S.
Weinberg, Julius R. Ideas & Concepts. (Aquinas Lectures Ser). 1970. 7.95 (ISBN 0-87462-135-6). Marquette.
Weinberg, Lee S. & Weinberg, Judith W. Law & Society: An Interdisciplinary Introduction. LC 80-5229. 495p. 1980. pap. text ed. 22.75 (ISBN 0-8191-1055-8). U Pr of Amer.
Weinberg, Leonard B. After Mussolini: Italian Neo-Fascism & the Nature of Fascism. LC 79-8511. 1979. pap. text ed. 7.25 (ISBN 0-8191-0870-7). U Pr of Amer.
Weinberg, Lila, jt. auth. see Weinberg, Arthur.
Weinberg, Louis. Network Analysis & Synthesis. LC 75-11929. 708p. 1975. Repr. of 1962 ed. 38.50 (ISBN 0-88275-321-5). Krieger.
Weinberg, M. A Chance to Learn. LC 76-4235. (Illus.). 1977. 42.50 (ISBN 0-521-21303-7); pap. 10.95 (ISBN 0-521-29128-3). Cambridge U Pr.
Weinberg, Martha W. Managing the State. 1977. text ed. 17.50x (ISBN 0-262-23077-1); pap. text ed. 6.95x (ISBN 0-262-73048-0). MIT Pr.
Weinberg, Martha W., jt. ed. see Burnham, Walter D.
Weinberg, Martin, jt. auth. see Rubington, Earl.
Weinberg, Martin S., jt. auth. see Bell, Alan P.
Weinberg, Martin S., et al, eds. The Solution of Social Problems: Five Perspectives. 2nd ed. 1981. pap. text ed. 8.95x (ISBN 0-19-502787-6). Oxford U Pr.
Weinberg, Meyer. Integrated Education: A Reader. 448p. 1968. pap. text ed. 6.95x o.p. (ISBN 0-02-478800-7, 47880). Glencoe.
--The Search for Quality Integrated Education: Policy & Research on Minority Students in School & College. LC 82-12016. (Contributions to the Study of Education: No. 7). (Illus.). 320p. 1983. lib. bdg. 35.00 (ISBN 0-313-23714-X, LC214). Greenwood.
Weinberg, N. L. & Tilak, B. V. Technique of Electroorganic Synthesis: Scale-up & Engineering Aspects. LC 75-18447. (Techniques of Chemistry Ser.). 536p. 1982. 85.00x (ISBN 0-471-06359-2, Pub. by Wiley-Interscience). Wiley.
Weinberg, Nathan G. Preservation in American Towns & Cities. (Illus.). 1979. lib. bdg. 23.50 (ISBN 0-89158-488-9). Westview.
Weinberg, Norbert. The Essential Torah. 1973. 8.95 o.s.i. (ISBN 0-8197-0282-X). Bloch.
Weinberg, Norman & Colletti, Paul J. Real Estate Review's New York Guide to Real Estate Licensing Examination for Salespersons. LC 79-56597. 344p. 1982. text ed. 23.95 (ISBN 0-471-87756-5); write for info. tchr's ed. (ISBN 0-471-89518-0). Wiley.
Weinberg, Norman, et al. Real Estate Review's New York Guide to Real Estate Licensing Examination for Salespersons. LC 79-56597. 344p. 1980. text ed. 18.50 o.p. (ISBN 0-88262-403-2). Warren.
Weinberg, Norman L., ed. Technique of Electroorganic Synthesis. LC 73-18447. (Techniques of Chemistry Ser.). 928p. Repr. of 1974 ed. text ed. 74.50 (ISBN 0-686-84485-8). Krieger.
Weinberg, Robert & Caldwell, Patsy. Health Related Fitness: Theory & Practice. (Illus.). 176p. pap. text ed. 9.95 (ISBN 0-88136-001-5). Jostens.
Weinberg, Roy D. Family Planning & the Law. 2nd ed. LC 68-21374. (Legal Almanac Ser.: No. 18). (Illus.). 121p. 1979. 5.95 (ISBN 0-379-11111-X, LA). Oceana.
Weinberg, Samuel, et al. Color Atlas of Pediatric Dermatology. (Illus.). 256p. 1975. 75.00 (ISBN 0-07-069015-4, HP). McGraw.
Weinberg, Sanford, jt. auth. see Colburn, William.
Weinberg, Sanford, ed. Messages: A Reader in Human Communication. 3rd ed. 321p. 1980. pap. text ed. 8.95 o.p. (ISBN 0-394-32431-5). Random.
Weinberg, Sharon L. & Goldberg, Kenneth P. Basic Statistics for Education & the Behavioral Sciences. LC 78-56433. (Illus.). 1979. text ed. 24.50 (ISBN 0-395-26853-2); instr's. manual 1.00 (ISBN 0-395-26854-0). HM.
Weinberg, Steven. Gravitation & Cosmology; Principles & Applications of the General Theory of Relativity. LC 78-37175. 750p. 1972. 40.95x (ISBN 0-471-92567-5). Wiley.
Weinberg, Thomas S. Gay Men, Gay Selves: The Social Construction of Homosexual Identities. 225p. 1983. text ed. 19.95x (ISBN 0-8290-1275-3). Irvington.
Weinberg, Victor. Structured Analysis. (Illus.). 1980. text ed. 29.95 (ISBN 0-13-854414-X). P-H.
--Structured Analysis. LC 78-105808. 344p. 1979. pap. 23.00 (ISBN 0-917072-05-7). Yourdon.
Weinberger, Caspar see Seabury, Paul, et al.
Weinberger, Emily K., jt. auth. see Krawitt, Laura P.
Weinberger, Hans F. First Course in Partial Differential Equations: With Complex Variables & Transform Methods. 1965. 36.50x (ISBN 0-471-00623-8). Wiley.
--Variational Methods for Eigenvalue Approximation: Proceedings. (CBMS Regional Conference Ser.: Vol. 15). v, 160p. (Orig.). 1974. pap. text ed. 16.50 (ISBN 0-89871-012-X). Soc Indus-Appl Math.
Weinberger, J., ed. see Bacon, Francis.
Weinberger, Lilla G., jt. auth. see Leckart, Bruce.
Weinberger, Marvin I. & Greevy, Doug, eds. PAC Directory. LC 82-11480. 1472p. 1982. ref 185.00x (ISBN 0-88410-856-2). Ballinger Pub.
Weinberger, Michael J. Estate & Gift Tax After Erta: A Successor to the 1977 Estate & Gift Tax After Tax Reform. 431p. 1982. text ed. 50.00 (ISBN 0-686-97905-2, D3-0152). PLI.
Weinberger, Norman S. Encyclopedia of Comparative Letterforms for Artists & Designers. LC 79-158572. 396p. 1971. 24.95 (ISBN 0-910158-01-0). Art Dir.
Weinberger, P. E. Perspectives on Social Welfare: An Introductory Anthology. 2nd ed. 1974. pap. 14.95x (ISBN 0-02-425160-7). Macmillan.
Weinberger, Philip R., jt. auth. see Sicard, Gerald L.
Weine, Franklin S. Endodontic Therapy. 3rd ed. LC 81-14194. (Illus.). 692p. 1982. text ed. 43.95 (ISBN 0-8016-5380-0). Mosby.
Weine, Ruth, ed. see Curran, June.
Weine, Ruth, ed. see Helmlinger, Trudy.
Weine, Ruth, ed. see Hyde, Marj.
Weiner. Phonological Process Analysis. 222p. 1978. pap. text ed. 19.95 (ISBN 0-8391-1300-5). Univ Park.
Weiner, jt. auth. see Brownstein.
Weiner, Albert. Doctor Weiner's Miracle Diet for Health & Longevity. 1978. 9.95 o.p. (ISBN 0-13-217109-0, Parker). P-H.
Weiner, Annette B. Women of Value, Men of Renown: New Perspectives in Trobriand Exchange. (Illus.). 321p. 1976. text ed. 20.00x o.p. (ISBN 0-292-79004-X). U of Tex Pr.
--Women of Value, Men of Renown: New Perspectives in Trobriand Exchange. (Texas Press Sourcebooks in Anthropology: No. 11). (Illus.). 321p. 1983. pap. text ed. 8.95x (ISBN 0-292-79019-8). U of Tex Pr.
Weiner, Elliot, jt. auth. see Aero, Rita.
Weiner, Hannah. Code Poems. 32p. 1982. 3.95 (ISBN 0-940170-03-5). Open Bk Pubns.
Weiner, Harvey S. & Palmer, Rose W. The Writing Lab. 2nd ed. 216p. 1980. pap. text ed. 20.95 (ISBN 0-02-472410-6). Macmillan.
Weiner, Henry & Wermuth, Bendicht, eds. Enzymology of Carbonyl Metabolism: Aldehyde Dehydrogenase & Carbonyl Reductase. LC 82-20381. (Progress in Clinical & Biological Research Ser.: Vol. 114). 430p. 1982. 44.00 (ISBN 0-8451-0114-5). A R Liss.
Weiner, Herbert, et al, eds. Brain, Behavior, & Bodily Disease. (Association of Research in Nervous & Mental Disease (ARNMD) Research Publications Ser.: Vol. 59). 388p. 1980. text ed. 47.50 (ISBN 0-89004-480-5). Raven.
Weiner, Howard D. Introductory Structured Cobol: A Programming Approach. 550p. 1983. pap. text ed. write for info. o.p. (ISBN 0-697-08149-4); write for info instr's manual o.p. (ISBN 0-697-08170-2); write for info. wkbk o.p. (ISBN 0-697-08171-0). Wiley.
Weiner, Howard L. The Children's Ward. 264p. 1980. 11.95 (ISBN 0-399-12509-4). Putnam Pub Group.
Weiner, Howard L., et al. Pediatric Neurology for the House Officer. 2nd ed. (House Officer Ser.). (Illus.). 227p. 1982. pap. text ed. 9.95 (ISBN 0-683-08903-X). Williams & Wilkins.
Weiner, Hyman J., et al. Mental Health Care in the World of Work. 1973. 8.95 o.s.i. (ISBN 0-8096-1863-X). Follett.
Weiner, I. B., jt. auth. see Exner, J. E.
Weiner, Irving B. Child & Adolescent Psychopathology. LC 81-21930. 529p. 1982. pap. text ed. 23.95 (ISBN 0-471-04709-0). Wiley.
--Clinical Methods in Psychology. LC 75-28366. (Personality Processes Ser). 678p. 1976. 45.95x (ISBN 0-471-92576-4, Pub. by Wiley-Interscience). Wiley.
--Principles of Psychotherapy. LC 74-26830. (Personality Processes Ser). 352p. 1975. 34.95x (ISBN 0-471-92569-1, Pub. by Wiley-Interscience). Wiley.
--Psychodiagnosis in Schizophrenia. LC 66-26761. 573p. 1966. 35.95x (ISBN 0-471-92570-5). Wiley.
--Psychological Disturbance in Adolescence. (Personality Processes Ser.). 400p. 1970. 37.95x (ISBN 0-471-92568-3, Pub. by Wiley-Interscience). Wiley.
Weiner, Irving B. & Elkind, David. Readings in Child Development. LC 79-23636. 518p. 1980. Repr. of 1972 ed. lib. bdg. 20.50 (ISBN 0-89874-105-X). Krieger.
Weiner, Irving B., jt. auth. see Elkind, David.
Weiner, J. S., jt. auth. see Collins, K. J.
Weiner, J. S. & Weiner, J. S., eds. Physiological Variation & Its Genetic Basis: Proceedings, Vol. 17. (Society for the Study of Human Biology, Symposia). 1977. 29.95x o.s.i. (ISBN 0-470-99314-6). Halsted Pr.
Weiner, Jerome H., jt. auth. see Boley, Bruno A.
Weiner, Joe, jt. ed. see Edholm, Otto.
Weiner, M., jt. auth. see Brownstein, S.
Weiner, M. B., jt. auth. see Starr, B. D.

Weiner, Marcella B., et al. Working with the Aged. (Illus.). 1978. pap. 13.95 ref. ed. (ISBN 0-13-967570-1). P-H.

Weiner, Melissa R. & Ruffner, Budge. Arizona Territorial Cookbook: The Food & Lifestyles of a Frontier. Browder, Robyn, ed. LC 82-2489. (Regional Cookbook Ser.). (Illus.). 232p. Date not set. pap. 8.95 (ISBN 0-89865-312-6, AACR2). Donning Co.

Weiner, Michael. The People's Herbal. (Orig.). 1981. pap. 8.95 cancelled o.p. (ISBN 0-446-97574-5). Warner Bks.

--Vital Signs. (Illus.). 128p. (Orig.). 1983. pap. 8.95 (ISBN 0-932238-20-3). Avant Bks.

Weiner, Michael A. The People's Herbal: A Complete Family Guide for All Ages to Safe Home Remedies. LC 82-80371. 227p. 1983. 14.95 (ISBN 0-399-50772-8, Perigee); pap. 7.95 (ISBN 0-399-50756-6). Putnam.

--Way of the Sceptical Nutritionist. 256p. 1981. 12.95 (ISBN 0-02-625620-7). Macmillan.

--Weiner's Herbal. LC 78-26616. (Illus.). 1979. 18.95 (ISBN 0-8128-2586-1); pap. 11.95 (ISBN 0-8128-6023-3). Stein & Day.

Weiner, Mitchel. Barron's Verbal Aptitude Workbook for College Entrance Examinations. rev. ed. (gr. 10-12). 1983. pap. text ed. 5.95 (ISBN 0-8120-2434-6). Barron.

--English Vocabulary Card Guide. (Vocabulary Card Guide Ser.). 12p. (gr. 9-12). 1983. pap. 2.95 (ISBN 0-8120-5475-X). Barron.

Weiner, Mitchel, jt. auth. see Brownstein, Samuel C.

Weiner, Myron F. The Psychotherapeutic Impasse. 1982. text ed. 19.95 (ISBN 0-02-934620-7). Free Pr.

--Therapist Disclosure: The Use of Self in Psychotherapy. 1978. 23.95 (ISBN 0-409-95070-X). Butterworth.

--Therapist Disclosure: The Use of Self in Psychotherapy. 2nd ed. 1983. 24.95 (ISBN 0-8391-1792-2, 19135). Univ Park.

Weiner, N., jt. auth. see Usdin, E.

Weiner, Neal O. & Schwartz, David M. The Interstate Gourmet: California & the Pacific Northwest, Vol. 3. (Illus.). 288p. 1983. pap. 5.95 (ISBN 0-671-44994-X). Summit Bks.

--The Interstate Gourmet: Mid-Atlantic States, Vol. 2. (Illus.). 256p. 1983. pap. 5.95 (ISBN 0-671-44993-1). Summit Bks.

--The Interstate Gourmet: New England, Vol. 1. 1982. pap. write for info. (ISBN 0-671-44992-3). Summit Bks.

Weiner, Norbert. Norbert Wiener: Collected Work: Vol. 1 Mathematical Philosophy & Foundations, Potential Theory, Brownian Movement, Wiener Integrals, Ergodic & Chaos Theories, Turbulence & Statistical Mechanics. Masani, P., ed. LC 74-17362. (Mit Mathematicians of Our Time Ser.). 1975. text ed. 55.00x (ISBN 0-262-23070-4). MIT Pr.

--Norbert Wiener: Collected Work: Vol. 2 Generalized Harmonic Analysis & Tauberian Theory, Classical Harmonic & Complex Analysis. Masani, P., ed. (Mathematicians of Our Time Ser.). 1979. 55.00x (ISBN 0-262-23092-5). MIT Pr.

Weiner, Norman L. The Roles of the Police in Urban Society: Conflicts & Consequences. LC 76-14958. 1976. pap. text ed. 4.95 o.p. (ISBN 0-672-61365-4). Bobbs.

Weiner, Rex & Stillman, Deanne. Woodstock Census. Date not set. pap. 5.95 (ISBN 0-449-90036-3, Columbine). Fawcett.

Weiner, Richard. Professional's Guide to Public Relations Services. 4th ed. LC 74-30735. 1980. 60.00x (ISBN 0-913046-10-8, Richard Weiner Inc.). Gale.

--Professional's Guide to Publicity. 2nd, rev. ed. LC 78-52626. 176p. 1981. 9.50 (ISBN 0-913046-07-8). Public Relations.

--Syndicated Columnists. 3rd ed. LC 78-64585. 1979. 15.00 (ISBN 0-913046-10-8). Public Relations.

Weiner, Samuel, jt. ed. see Robins, Philip K.

Weiner, Seymoure. How to Stop Inflation Without A Recession. 64p. 1982. 7.95 (ISBN 0-89962-300-X). Todd & Honeywell.

Weiner, Sheila L. Ajanta: Its Place in Buddhist Art. (Illus.). 1977. 37.50x (ISBN 0-520-02878-3). U of Cal Pr.

Weiner, Solomon. Clear & Simple Guide to Business Letter Writing. 1978. pap. 6.95 (ISBN 0-671-47090-6). Monarch Pr.

Weiner, Walter. So Call It a Mitzvah. 1978. 6.00 o.p. (ISBN 0-682-49116-0). Exposition.

Weiner, William J. Neurology for the Non-Neurologist. (Illus.). 426p. 1981. pap. text ed. 17.25 (ISBN 0-06-142654-7, Harper Medical). Lippincott.

Weinfield, Barbara A., jt. ed. see Cummings, William W.

Weingart, J., jt. auth. see Energy Development International.

Weingarten, Arthur. The Sky Is Falling. (Orig.). 1977. 10.00 o.p. (ISBN 0-448-14411-5, G&D). Putnam Pub Group.

Weingarten, Carol-Grace, jt. auth. see Sherwen, Laurie N.

Weingarten, Henry. The Study of Astrology, Vol. II. 1983. pap. 7.95 (ISBN 0-88231-030-5). ASI Pubs Inc.

Weingarten, Ralph. Die Hilfeleistung der Westlichen Welt bei der Deutschen Judenfrage: Das "Intergovernmental Committee on Political Refugees" 1938-1939. 232p. Date not set. price not set (ISBN 3-261-04939-1). P Lang Pubs.

Weingarten, Roger, jt. ed. see Bellamy, Joe D.

Weingarten, Samuel. Response in Reading. 1969. pap. text ed. 5.50 (ISBN 0-685-19701-8). Phila Bk Co.

Weingarten, Violet. The Jordan: River of the Promised Land. LC 67-10039. (Rivers of the World Ser.). (Illus.). (gr. 4-7). PLB 3.98 (ISBN 0-8116-6368-X). Garrard.

Weingartner, Charles, jt. auth. see Postman, Neil.

Weingartner, James J. Crossroads of Death: The Story of the Malmedy Massacre & Trial. LC 77-91771. 1979. 21.50x (ISBN 0-520-03623-9). U of Cal Pr.

Weingartner, Ronald, ed. see Bizer, Linda & Nathan, Beverly.

Weingartner, Ronald, ed. see Kinsman, Barbara.

Weingartner, Ronald, ed. see Taylor, Jane.

Weingartt, Eleanor. The Elements of Dental Materials: Study Guide. 3rd ed. 1977. pap. text ed. 8.95 (ISBN 0-7216-9165-X). Saunders.

Weingast, David E. We Elect a President. rev. ed. LC 77-2658. (Illus.). 256p. (gr. 7 up). 1977. PLB 8.29 o.p. (ISBN 0-671-32839-5). Messner.

Weingatner, Charles, jt. auth. see Postman, Neil.

Weingerb, N. L. see Weissberger, A.

Weingrad, Bracha. Dani on the Kibbutz. (Illus.). 24p. (Eng. Hebrew.). 1982. 5.00 (ISBN 0-686-38115-7). K Sefer.

Weinheimer, B., jt. ed. see Emrich, D.

Weinhold, Barry & Elliott, Lynn C. Transpersonal Communication. LC 79-10871. (Illus.). 1979. text ed. 9.95 o.p. (ISBN 0-13-930396-0, Spec); pap. 4.95 o.p. (ISBN 0-13-930388-X). P-H.

Weinhold, Barry, jt. auth. see Andresen, Gail.

Weinhold, Barry K. & Andersen, Gail. Threads: Unraveling the Mysteries of Adult Life. LC 78-31870. 1979. pap. 9.95 o.p. (ISBN 0-399-90049-7, Marek). Putnam Pub Group.

Weinhouse, Sidney, jt. auth. see Klein, George.

Weinig, Sr. Mary. Coventry Patmore. (English Authors Ser.). lib. bdg. 14.95 (ISBN 0-8057-6767-3, Twayne). G K Hall.

Weininger, Jean, jt. auth. see Briggs, George M.

Weininger, Otto. Out of the Minds of Babes: The Strength of Children's Feelings. (Illus.). 226p. 1982. 22.75x (ISBN 0-398-04577-1). C C Thomas.

--The Sexual Psychology of Males & Females: Intimate Life of Man Lib. (Illus.). 101p. 1983. 51.85 (ISBN 0-686-84793-8). Am Inst Psych.

Weinland, James D. How to Study. pap. 3.00 (ISBN 0-8283-1441-1). Branden.

Weinman, David & Kursham, Barbara. VAX BASIC. 1982. text ed. 21.95 (ISBN 0-8359-8239-4); pap. text ed. 14.95 (ISBN 0-8359-8238-6). Reston.

Weinman, David & Ristic, Miodrag. Infectious Blood Diseases of Man & Animals, 2 Vols. LC 68-18685. 1968. Vol. 1. subscription 77.00 77.00 (ISBN 0-12-742501-2); Vol. 2. subscription 83.50 83.50 (ISBN 0-12-742502-0). Acad Pr.

Weinmann, Karl. History of Church Music. LC 78-31681. 1979. Repr. of 1910 ed. lib. bdg. 18.25x (ISBN 0-8371-4363-2, WEHC). Greenwood.

Weinrach, Stephen G. Career Counselling: Theoretical & Practical Perspectives. (Illus.). 1979. text ed. 24.00 (ISBN 0-07-069017-0, C). McGraw.

Weinraub, Bernard. Bylines. LC 80-3000. 372p. 1983. 17.95 (ISBN 0-385-17000-9). Doubleday.

Weinrauch, J. Donald & Piland, William E. Applied Marketing Principles. (Illus.). 1979. ref. 20.95 (ISBN 0-13-041103-5). P-H.

Weinreb, Eva L. Anatomy & Physiology. 896p. 1982. text ed. write for info. (ISBN 0-201-08852-5). A-W.

Weinreb, Lloyd L. The Law of Criminal Investigation. 216p. 1982. text ed. 17.50x (ISBN 0-88410-838-4). Ballinger Pub.

Weinreich, Uriel. College Yiddish; an Introduction to the Yiddish Language & to Jewish Life & Culture. 5th ed. LC 76-88208. 399p. 1979. 12.00 (ISBN 0-914512-04-8). Yivo Inst.

--Modern English-Yiddish, Yiddish-English Dictionary. 1968. 44.95 (ISBN 0-07-069038-3, P&RB). McGraw.

--Modern English-Yiddish Yiddish-English Dictionary. LC 77-76038. 1978. pap. 18.95 (ISBN 0-8052-0575-6). Schocken.

--Modern English-Yiddish, Yiddish-English Dictionary. LC 67-23848. 789p. 1968. write for info (ISBN 0-914512-25-0). Yivo Inst.

Weinreich-Haste, Helen & Locke, Don. Morality in the Making: Thought, Action & the Social Context. (Developmental Psychology Ser.). 300p. 1983. 35.95 (ISBN 0-471-10423-X, Pub. by Wiley Interscience). Wiley.

Weinrich, A. K. Mucheke: Race, Status & Politics in a Rhodesian Community. LC 76-62524. 1977. pap. text ed. 19.95x (ISBN 0-8419-0299-2, Africana). Holmes & Meier.

Weinrich, William C. Spirit & Martyrdom: A Study of the Work of the Holy Spirit in Contexts of Persecution & Martyrdom in the New Testament & Early Christian Literature. LC 80-5597. 334p. (Orig.). 1981. lib. bdg. 22.25 (ISBN 0-8191-1655-6); pap. text ed. 12.25 (ISBN 0-8191-1656-4). U Pr of Amer.

Weinsier, Roland L. Handbook of Clinical Nutrition: Clinician's Manual for the Diagnosis & Management of Nutritional Problems. LC 80-20161. (Illus.). 231p. 1981. pap. text ed. 12.95 (ISBN 0-8016-5406-8). Mosby.

Weinstein, John M., jt. ed. see Kennedy, Robert.

Weinstein. Pneumonias. (Seminars in Infections Disease Ser.: Vol. 4). 1983. price not set (ISBN 0-86577-091-3). Thieme-Stratton.

Weinstein & Wagman, eds. Antibiotics: Isolation, Separation & Purification. (Journal of Chromatography Library Ser.: Vol. 15). 1978. 98.00 (ISBN 0-444-41727-3). Elsevier.

Weinstein, Alan, jt. auth. see Marsden, Jerrold.

Weinstein, Alexander & Stenger, William. Methods of Intermediate Problems for Eigenvalues. (Mathematics in Science & Engineering Ser.: Vol. 89). 1972. 43.50 (ISBN 0-12-742450-4). Acad Pr.

Weinstein, Allen. Freedom & Crisis: An American History, 2 vols. 3rd ed. 1981. Vol. 1, 498p. pap. text ed. 15.00; Vol. 2, 539p. pap. text ed. 15.00. Random.

Weinstein, Allen & Wilson, R. Jackson. Freedom & Crisis, 2 vols. 2nd ed. 1978. Single Vol. pap. text ed. 24.00 (ISBN 0-394-32415-3); pap. 15.00 ea.; Vol. 1. (ISBN 0-394-32611-3); Vol. 2. (ISBN 0-394-32612-1); wkbks. 4.95 ea. (ISBN 0-394-32294-0); Vol. 1. 4.95 o.p. wkbk. for Vol. II (ISBN 0-686-96858-1). Vol. 2 (ISBN 0-394-32295-9). Random.

Weinstein, Allen, ed. Origins of Modern America, 1860-1900. (Orig.). 1970. pap. text ed. 3.95x (ISBN 0-685-19750-6). Phila Bk Co.

Weinstein, Allen & Gatell, Frank O., eds. Segregation Era, Eighteen Sixty Three to Nineteen Fifty Four. (gr. 9-12). 1970 (ISBN 0-19-500657-7). pap. 6.95x (ISBN 0-19-501099-X). Oxford U Pr.

Weinstein, Alvin S., et al. Products Liability & the Reasonably Safe Product: A Guide for Management, Design & Marketing. LC 78-8749. 1978. 27.95x (ISBN 0-471-03904-7, Pub. by Wiley-Interscience). Wiley.

Weinstein, Barbara. The Amazon Rubber Boom, 1850-1920. LC 82-80926. (Illus.). 376p. 1983. 29.50x (ISBN 0-8047-1168-2). Stanford U Pr.

Weinstein, Bob. Breaking Into Modeling: A Guide for Beginners. LC 82-20630. (Illus.). 160p. (gr. 10-12). 1983. PLB 12.95 (ISBN 0-668-05597-9); pap. 7.95 (ISBN 0-668-05600-2). Arco.

--Your Career in Public Relations. LC 82-3891. (Arco's Career Guidance Ser.). 128p. 1982. lib. bdg. 7.95 (ISBN 0-668-05555-3); pap. 4.50 (ISBN 0-668-05562-6). Arco.

--Your Money Hang-Ups. 162p. 1982. 7.95 o.p. (ISBN 0-471-09599-0). Wiley.

Weinstein, Boris, ed. Chemistry & Biochemistry of Amino Acids, Peptides & Proteins, Vol. 4. 1977. 57.50 o.p. (ISBN 0-8247-6604-0). Dekker.

Weinstein, Brian. Gabon: Nation-Building on the Ogooue. (Illus.). 1967. 20.00x (ISBN 0-262-23023-2). MIT Pr.

Weinstein, Deena. Bureaucratic Opposition: Challenging Abuses at the Workplace. (Pergamon Policy Studies). 1979. 19.00 (ISBN 0-08-023903-X); pap. 6.95 (ISBN 0-08-023902-1). Pergamon.

Weinstein, Donald & Bell, Rudolph M. Saints & Society: The Two Worlds of Western Christendom, 1000 to 1700. LC 82-6972. (Illus.). 1983. 25.00 (ISBN 0-226-89055-4). U of Chicago Pr.

Weinstein, Edwin A. & Friedland, Robert P., eds. Hemi-Inattention & Hemisphere Specialization. LC 77-5278. (Advances in Neurology Ser.: Vol. 18). 170p. 1977. 17.00 (ISBN 0-89004-115-6). Raven.

Weinstein, Franklin B. U. S. - Japan Relations & the Security of East Asia: The Next Decade. LC 77-13752. (Special Studies on International Relations & U. S. Foreign Policy Ser.). 1978. lib. bdg. 14.00x o.p. (ISBN 0-89158-053-0); softcover 12.95 (ISBN 0-89158-067-0). Westview.

Weinstein, Franklin B. & Kamiya, Fuji, eds. The Security of Korea: U. S. & Japanese Perspectives on the Nineteen Eighties. (Westview Special Studies in International Relations). 260p. 1980. lib. bdg. 24.00 (ISBN 0-89158-668-7); pap. text ed. 9.50 (ISBN 0-89158-758-6). Westview.

Weinstein, Fred & Platt, Gerald M. The Wish To Be Free: Society, Psyche, & Value Change. LC 71-83291. 1969. 29.75x (ISBN 0-520-01398-0); pap. 0.85x o.p. (ISBN 0-520-02493-1). U of Cal Pr.

Weinstein, Grace, jt. auth. see Yelon, Stephen L.

Weinstein, Harel & Green, Jack P., eds. Quantum Chemistry in Biomedical Sciences, Vol. 367. 552p. 1981. 108.00x (ISBN 0-89766-121-4); pap. 108.00x (ISBN 0-89766-122-2). NY Acad Sci.

Weinstein, Jack B., et al. Cases & Materials on Evidence. 7th ed. LC 82-21049. (University Casebook Ser.). 1543p. 1982. text ed. write for info. (ISBN 0-88277-074-8). Foundation Pr.

Weinstein, Joshua. When Religion Comes to School. LC 78-78402. 1979. pap. text ed. 8.00 (ISBN 0-8191-0711-5). U Pr of Amer.

Weinstein, L. Albertovich. Theory of Diffraction & the Factorization Method: Generalized Wiener-Hopf Technique. Beckmann, Petr, tr. LC 79-95852. (Electromagnetics Ser.: Vol. 3). (Illus.). 1969. 25.00x (ISBN 0-911762-05-1). Golem.

Weinstein, Leo. Hippolyte Taine. (World Authors Ser.). lib. bdg. 15.95 (ISBN 0-8057-2878-3, Twayne). G K Hall.

Weinstein, M. J., jt. auth. see Wagman, G. H.

Weinstein, M. N. Some Recovery & Macroeconomic Impacts of the National Industrial Recovery Act: 1933-35. (Studies in Mathematical & Managerial Economics: Vol. 6). 1981. 32.00 (ISBN 0-444-86007-X). Elsevier.

Weinstein, Martin. Uruguay: The Politics of Failure. LC 74-19809. (Illus.). 1975. lib. bdg. 25.00x (ISBN 0-8371-7845-2, WPF/). Greenwood.

Weinstein, Martin E., ed. Northeast Asian Security after Vietnam. LC 82-1909. 192p. 1982. 17.50 (ISBN 0-252-00966-5). U of Ill Pr.

Weinstein, Michael. Examples of Groups. LC 76-51379. 1977. 14.00 (ISBN 0-936428-01-5); pap. 9.00 (ISBN 0-936428-00-7). Polygonal Pub.

Weinstein, Michael A. Philosophy, Theory, & Method in Contemporary Political Thought. 1971. text ed. 10.95x (ISBN 0-673-07610-5). Scott F.

--The Polarity of Mexican Thought. LC 76-23159. 1977. 15.95x (ISBN 0-271-01232-3). Pa St U Pr.

--The Wilderness & the City: American Classical Philosophy as a Moral Quest. LC 82-4769. 176p. 1982. lib. bdg. 17.50x (ISBN 0-87023-375-0). U of Mass Pr.

Weinstein, Michael A., jt. auth. see Grundy, Kenneth W.

Weinstein, Robert A. & Booth, Larry. Collection, Use, & Care of Historical Photographs. LC 76-27755. (Illus.). 1977. 19.00 (ISBN 0-910050-21-X). AASLH.

Weinstein, Robert A., jt. auth. see Belous, Russell E.

Weinstein, Robert V. Jobs for the Twenty-First Century. (Illus.). 192p. 1983. pap. 6.95 (ISBN 0-02-082560-9, Collier). Macmillan.

Weinstein, S. & Walker, M. Annual Accounting Review, Vol. 2. 282p. 1980. lib. bdg. 55.00 (ISBN 0-686-60584-5). Harwood Academic.

Weinstein, Warren, ed. Soviet & Chinese Aid to Africa. LC 74-3512. (Special Studies). (Illus.). 316p. 1975. 37.95 o.p. (ISBN 0-275-09050-7). Praeger.

Weinstock, E. B. A Poem in Your Eye: An Introductory to the Art of Seeing, Through Poetry. LC 78-56918. 1978. pap. text ed. 8.00 (ISBN 0-8191-0523-6). U Pr of Amer.

Weinstock, E. B. & Arthur, Robert P. New Gothic Restaurant. 1978. pap. text ed. 9.75 (ISBN 0-8191-0369-1). U Pr of Amer.

Weinstock, Herbert, tr. see Chavez, Carlos.

Weinstock, Irwin T., jt. auth. see Torgerson, Paul E.

Weintraub, jt. ed. see Aldington, Richard.

Weintraub, A. Psychorheumatologie. (Illus.). viii, 92p. 1983. 11.50 (ISBN 3-8055-3628-3). S Karger.

Weintraub, Benjamin & Resnick, Alan N. Bankruptcy Law Manual. LC 80-52860. 1980. 56.00 (ISBN 0-88262-494-6). Warren.

Weintraub, E. Roy. Mathematics for Economists: An Integrated Approach. LC 82-4244. 250p. 1982. 16.95 (ISBN 0-521-24535-4). Cambridge U Pr.

--Microfoundations. LC 78-16551. (Cambridge Surveys of Economic Literature Ser.). 1979. 32.50 (ISBN 0-521-22305-9); pap. 10.95 (ISBN 0-521-29445-2). Cambridge U Pr.

Weintraub, Karl J. Visions of Culture: Voltaire, Guizot, Burckhardt, Lamprecht, Huizinga, Ortega y Gasset. LC 66-13893. 1966. 15.00x o.p. (ISBN 0-226-89088-0). U of Chicago Pr.

Weintraub, Michael I. Hysterical Conversion Reaction: A Guide to Diagnosis & Treatment. (Illus.). 185p. 1983. text ed. 25.00 (ISBN 0-89335-178-4). SP Med & Sci Bks.

Weintraub, Rodelle. Fabian Feminist: Bernard Shaw and Woman. LC 76-41698. 1977. 17.95x (ISBN 0-271-01235-8). Pa St U Pr.

Weintraub, Rodelle, jt. auth. see Weintraub, Stanley.

Weintraub, Rodelle, ed. see Lawrence, T. E.

Weintraub, Sam & Cowan, Robert J., eds. Vision-Visual Perception. (Annotated Bibliography Ser.). 93p. (Orig.). 1982. pap. text ed. 4.50 (ISBN 0-87207-339-4, 339). Intl Reading.

Weintraub, Sidney. Our Stagflation Malaise: Ending Inflation & Unemployment. LC 80-39658. 208p. 1981. lib. bdg. 25.00 (ISBN 0-89930-005-7, WCA/, Quorum). Greenwood.

Weintraub, Sidney, jt. auth. see Cline, William R.

Weintraub, Sidney & Goodstein, Marvin, eds. Reaganomics in the Stagflation Economy. LC 82-60305. (Post Keynesian Economics Ser.). 200p. (Orig.). 1983. 20.00x (ISBN 0-8122-7858-5); pap. 7.95x (ISBN 0-8122-1133-2). U of Pa Pr.

Weintraub, Sidney & Lambert, Richard D., eds. Income Inequality. LC 73-78959. (Annals of the American Academy of Political & Social Science: No. 409). 300p. 1973. 15.00 (ISBN 0-87761-169-6); pap. 7.95 (ISBN 0-87761-168-8). Am Acad Pol Soc Sci.

Weintraub, Sidney & Purvis, Hoyt, eds. Foreign Economic Decisionmaking: Case Studies from the Johnson Administration & Their Implications. (Policy Research Project Report Ser.: No. 54). 300p. 1983. 9.00 (ISBN 0-89940-656-4). L B J Sch Pub Aff.

Weintraub, Stanley. Aubrey Beardsley: Imp of the Perverse. LC 75-27231. (Illus.). 480p. 1976. 18.95x (ISBN 0-271-01215-3); pap. 10.00 (ISBN 0-271-01216-1). Pa St U Pr.

--Shaw. (The Annual of Bernard Shaw Studies Ser.: Vol. 2). (Illus.). 224p. 1982. 16.95x (ISBN 0-271-00305-7). Pa St U Pr.

--War in the Wards. LC 76-51509. (Illus.). 1977. 8.95 o.p. (ISBN 0-89141-012-0). Presidio Pr.

Weintraub, Stanley & Weintraub, Rodelle. Lawrence of Arabia-the Literary Impulse. LC 74-27195. 184p. 1975. 15.00x (ISBN 0-8071-0152-4). La State U Pr.

Weintraub, Stanley, ed. British Dramatists Since World War II, 2 vols. (Dictionary of Literary Biography Ser.: Vol. 13). (Illus.). 1982. 148.00x (ISBN 0-686-94167-5). Gale.

--Modern British Dramatists, 1900 to 1945, 2 vols. (Dictionary of Literary Biography Ser.: Vol. 10). (Illus.). 645p. 1982. Set. 148.00x (ISBN 0-8103-0937-8). Gale.

Weintraub, Stanley, ed. see Lawrence, T. E.

Weintraub, Stanley, ed. see Shaw, George B.

Weintritt, Donald J., jt. auth. see Cowan, Jack C.

Weintz, Caroline & Weintz, Walter. The Discount Guide for Travelers over 55. rev. ed. LC 80-83630. 256p. 1983. pap. 5.95 (ISBN 0-525-93281-X, 0577-180). Dutton.

Weintz, Walter, jt. auth. see Weintz, Caroline.

Weinzinger, Anita. Graves As a Critic. (Salzburg - Poetic Drama Ser.: No. 79). 141p. 1982. pap. text ed. 25.00x (ISBN 0-391-02803-0, Pub. by Salzburg Austria). Humanities.

Weir. Handbook of Experimental Immunology: Application of Immunological Methods, Vol. 3. 3rd ed. 1978. pap. 41.50 (ISBN 0-8016-5395-9, Blackwell Scientific). Mosby.

Weir, A. J. General Integration & Measure. LC 73-91620. (Illus.). 344p. 1974. 39.95 (ISBN 0-521-20407-0); pap. 14.95 (ISBN 0-521-29715-X). Cambridge U Pr.

--Lebesgue Integration & Measure. LC 72-83584. (Illus.). 220p. (Orig.). 1973. 39.95 (ISBN 0-521-08728-7); pap. 14.95x (ISBN 0-521-09751-7). Cambridge U Pr.

Weir, Albert E., ed. see Bachmann, Alberto.

Weir, D. M., ed. Handbook of Experimental Immunology: Cellular Immunology, Vol. 2. 3rd ed. 1978. pap. 41.50 (ISBN 0-8016-5395-9, Blackwell Scientific). Mosby.

Weir, J. E., ed. see Baxter, James K.

Weir, LaVada. Breaking Point. LC 74-641. (Laurie Newman Adventures Ser.). 32p. (gr. 3-9). 1974. 6.95 (ISBN 0-87191-337-2). Creative Ed.

--Chaotic Kitchen. LC 74-858. (Laurie Newman Adventures Ser). 32p. (gr. 3-9). 1974. 6.95 (ISBN 0-87191-334-8). Creative Ed.

--Edge of Fear. LC 74-859. (Laurie Newman Adventures Ser). 32p. (gr. 3-9). 1974. 6.95 (ISBN 0-87191-338-0). Creative Ed.

--The Horse-Flambeau. LC 74-860. (Laurie Newman Adventures Ser). 32p. 1974. 6.95 (ISBN 0-87191-335-6). Creative Ed.

--Laurie Loves a Horse. LC 74-643. (Laurie Newman Adventures Ser). 32p. (gr. 7-9). 1974. 6.95 (ISBN 0-87191-352-6). Creative Ed.

--A Long Distance. LC 74-971. (Laurie Newman Adventures Ser). 32p. (gr. 3-9). 1974. 6.95 (ISBN 0-87191-333-X). Creative Ed.

--Men! LC 74-974. (Laurie Newman Adventures Ser). 32p. (gr. 3-9). 1974. 6.95 (ISBN 0-87191-336-4). Creative Ed.

--The New Girl. LC 74-824. (Laurie Newman Adventures Ser). 32p. (gr. 3-9). 1974. 6.95 (ISBN 0-87191-351-8). Creative Ed.

--The Roller Skating Book. LC 79-19653. (Illus.). 128p. (gr. 4 up). 1979. PLB 8.29 o.p. (ISBN 0-671-33048-9). Messner.

--Skateboards & Skateboarding: The Complete Beginner's Guide. LC 76-51296. (Illus.). 128p. (gr. 4 up). 1977. PLB 7.79 o.p. (ISBN 0-671-32828-X). Messner.

Weir, M. D. Hewitt-Nachbin Spaces. LC 74-28991. (Mathematics Studies Ser: Vol. 17). 270p. 1975. pap. 44.25 (ISBN 0-444-10860-2, North-Holland). Elsevier.

Weir, Marie. Woman's Hockey for the '70's. (Illus.). 1974. 15.95x o.p. (ISBN 0-7182-0978-8, Sps). Sportshelf.

Weir, Mary. House Recycling: The Best Real Estate Opportunity for the 80's. (Illus.). 160p. 1982. 11.95 (ISBN 0-8092-5941-9); pap. 6.95 (ISBN 0-8092-5940-0). Contemp Bks.

Weir, Mary, jt. auth. see Weir, Sam.

Weir, Maurice D. Calculus by Calculator: Solving Single-Variable Calculus Problems with the Programable Calculator. (Illus.). 387p. 1982. 22.95 (ISBN 0-13-111930-3); pap. 15.95 (ISBN 0-13-111922-2). P-H.

Weir, Robert. Colonial South Carolina-A History. LC 82-48990. (A History of the American Colonies Ser.). (Orig.). 1983. lib. bdg. 30.00 (ISBN 0-527-18721-6). Kraus Intl.

Weir, Sam & Weir, Mary. How We Made a Million Dollars Recycling Great Old Houses. 1980. pap. 8.95 (ISBN 0-8092-7426-4). Contemp Bks.

Weir, Tom. Scottish Islands. LC 76-8618. (Leisure & Travel Ser.). (Illus.). 128p. 1976. 7.50 o.p. (ISBN 0-7153-7214-9). David & Charles.

Weir, William & Abata, Russell M. Dealing with Depression. 144p. 1982. pap. 3.50 (ISBN 0-89243-170-9). Liguori Pubns.

Weis, Charles M., ed. see Boswell, James.

Weis, Elisabeth, ed. The National Society of Film Critics on the Movie Star. LC 81-65278. (Illus.). 1981. 25.00 (ISBN 0-670-49187-X); pap. 12.95 o.p. (ISBN 0-686-86859-5). Viking Pr.

Weis, Elisabeth, jt. ed. see Byron, Stuart.

Weis, Elizabeth, ed. The National Society of Film Critics on the Movie Star. 400p. pap. cancelled o.s.i. (ISBN 0-686-32110-3). Penguin.

Weis, Erich, jt. auth. see Schoffer, Herbert.

Weis, Lois, jt. ed. see Apple, Michael.

Weis, Norm. The Starduster. LC 80-11068. (Illus.). 1980. 9.95 o.p. (ISBN 0-13-842914-6). P-H.

Weis, S. F., et al. Foundations of Occupational Home Economics. 1981. 3.00 (ISBN 0-686-34526-6, A261-08446). Home Econ Educ.

Weisband, Edward, jt. auth. see Franck, Thomas M.

Weisband, Edward, jt. ed. see Franck, Thomas M.

Weisberg, Arthur. The Art of Wind Playing. LC 74-33818. 1975. 11.95 (ISBN 0-02-872800-9). Schirmer Bks.

Weisberg, Gabriel P., jt. auth. see Sturges, Hollister, III.

Weisberg, Gabriel P., ed. The European Realist Tradition. LC 81-48399. (Illus.). 256p. 1983. 25.00x (ISBN 0-253-32084-4). Ind U Pr.

Weisberg, Herbert, jt. auth. see Niemi, Richard.

Weisberg, Joseph S. Meteorology. 2nd ed. (Illus.). 432p. 1981. text ed. 25.95 (ISBN 0-395-29516-5); instr's manual 1.00 (ISBN 0-395-29517-3). HM.

Weisberg, Joseph S. & Parish, Howard I. Introductory Oceanography. (Illus.). 288p. 1974. text ed. 27.50 (ISBN 0-07-069046-4, C); instructor's manual 9.95 (ISBN 0-07-069047-2). McGraw.

Weisberg, Leon A. & Strub, Richard L. Essentials of Clinical Neurology. 1983. pap. text ed. 14.95 (ISBN 0-8391-1778-7, 17817). Univ Park.

Weisberg, Leon A., et al. Cerebral Computed Tomography: A Text Atlas. LC 77-11357. (Illus.). 1978. text ed. 35.00x o.p. (ISBN 0-7216-9167-6). Saunders.

Weisberg, S., jt. auth. see Cook, R. D.

Weisberger, B. A. From Sea to Shining Sea. 1981. 22.12 (ISBN 0-07-069099-5); tchr's guide 13.60 (ISBN 0-07-069100-2). McGraw.

Weisberger, Bernard A. Age of Steel & Steam, Eighteen Seventy-Seven to Eighteen Ninety. LC 63-8572. (Life History of the United States Ser.). (Illus.). (gr. 5 up). 1974. PLB 10.60 (ISBN 0-8094-0556-3, Pub. by Time-Life). Silver.

--The Impact of Our Past: A History of the United States. 2nd ed. LC 75-1342. (Illus.). 832p. (gr. 7-12). 1976. text ed. 23.40 (ISBN 0-07-069086-3, W); study guide 4.88 (ISBN 0-07-069105-3); tchr's. ed. 25.08 (ISBN 0-07-069087-1); study guide 9.64 (ISBN 0-07-069106-1). McGraw.

--Reaching for Empire, 1890-1901. LC 63-8572. (Life History of the United States). (Illus.). (gr. 5 up). 1974. lib. bdg. 10.60 o.s.i. (ISBN 0-8094-0557-1, Pub. by Time-Life). Silver.

--Reporters for the Union. LC 76-56346. (Illus.). 1977. Repr. of 1953 ed. lib. bdg. 19.50x o.p. (ISBN 0-8371-9340-0, WERE). Greenwood.

Weisberger, Bernard A. & Josephy, Alvin M. The Embattled Peace. LC 81-20495. Date not set. 24.95 (ISBN 0-8281-1163-4); until Dec. 31, 1982 19.95 (ISBN 0-686-86925-7); deluxe ed. price not set (ISBN 0-8281-1164-2). Am Heritage. Postponed.

Weisberger, Bernard A. & Landcaster, Gerald. The Impact of Our Past: A History of the United States. (Illus.). 816p. (gr. 7-8). 1971. text ed. 23.60 (ISBN 0-07-069052-9, W); tchr's ed. 25.32 (ISBN 0-07-069064-2); webster master tests 56.90 (ISBN 0-07-069067-7). McGraw.

Weisbord, Marvin. Basic Photography. (Illus.). 1973. 4.95 o.p. (ISBN 0-8174-0423-6, Amphoto). Watson-Guptill.

Weisbord, Robert G. Ebony Kinship: Africa, Africans & the Afro-American. LC 72-847. (Contributions in Afro-American & African Studies: No. 14). 256p. 1974. lib. bdg. 18.95 (ISBN 0-8371-6416-8, WEA&, Pub. by Negro U Pr); pap. 6.95 (ISBN 0-8371-7340-X, WBC/). Greenwood.

--Genocide? Birth Control & the Black American. LC 75-13531. 219p. 1975. lib. bdg. 25.00x (ISBN 0-8371-8084-8, WBC). Greenwood.

Weisbord, Robert G. & Stein, Arthur. Bittersweet Encounter: The Afro-American & the American Jew. LC 72-127828. (Contributions in Afro-American & African Studies: No. 5). 1970. 27.50 (ISBN 0-8371-5093-0, Pub. by Negro U Pr). Greenwood.

Weisbrod, Alain, jt. auth. see Kern, Raymond.

Weisbrod, Burton A. The Voluntary Non-Profit Sector: An Economic Analysis. LC 77-9132. 208p. 1977. 21.95x o.p. (ISBN 0-669-01772-8). Lexington Bks.

Weisbrod, Harry, et al. Wage-Hour & Employment Practices Manual for the Multihousing Industry. Schleker, Peggy J., ed. LC 78-70825. 210p. 1979. 19.95 (ISBN 0-912104-37-6). Inst Real Estate.

Weisbrot, Robert. Father Divine & the Struggle for Racial Equality. Meier, August, ed. LC 82-2644. (Blacks in the New World Ser.). (Illus.). 272p. 1983. 17.50 (ISBN 0-686-84862-4). U of Ill Pr.

Weisburd, Claudia. Raising Your Own Livestock. (Illus.). 1980. 15.95 (ISBN 0-13-752758-6, Spec); pap. 7.95 (ISBN 0-13-752741-1). P-H.

Weisburg, Hilda K., jt. auth. see Toor, Ruth.

Weischedel, Randall. The Joy of Ascension. LC 82-7349. (Illus.). 160p. 1983. 8.95 (ISBN 0-87516-499-4). De Vorss.

Weise, Frieda O., ed. Health Statistics: A Guide to Information Sources. LC 80-12039. (Health Affairs Information Guide Ser.: Vol. 4). 1980. 42.00x (ISBN 0-8103-1412-6). Gale.

Weisel, Marion, tr. see Wiesel, Elie.

Weisenberg, Matisyohu, et al. The Control of Pain. 320p. Date not set. 12.50 o.p. (ISBN 0-88437-003-8). Psych Dimensions.

Weisenfeld, Murray. Runner's Repair Manual. 192p. 1981. pap. 5.95 (ISBN 0-312-69597-7). St Martin.

Weiser, Artur. Psalms: A Commentary. LC 62-16760. (Old Testament Library). 1962. 24.95 (ISBN 0-664-20418-X). Westminster.

Weiser, Frederick S., jt. auth. see Wood, Ralph C.

Weiser, Frederick S. & Heaney, Howell J., eds. The Pennsylvania German Fraktur Collection of The Free Library of Philadelphia, 2 vols. Neff, Larry M., tr. from Ger. LC 76-13357. 1976. Set. 60.00 o.p. (ISBN 0-686-79896-1). Vol. 1 (ISBN 0-911122-32-X). Vol. 2 (ISBN 0-911122-33-8). Penn German Soc.

Weiser, Frederick S., jt. ed. see Neff, Larry M.

Weiser, Frederick S., jt. tr. see Hinke, William J.

Weiser, H., jt. auth. see Folomkina, S.

Weiser, Russell S. see Myrvik, Quentin N.

Weisfelder, Richard F. The Basotho Monarchy: A Spent Force or a Dynamic Political Factor. LC 72-619651. (African Ser.: No. 16). (Illus.). 1972. pap. 7.00x (ISBN 0-89680-049-0, Ohio U Ctr Intl). Ohio U Pr.

--Defining National Purpose in Lesotho. LC 72-630647. (Papers in International Studies: Africa: No. 3). (Illus.). 1969. pap. 3.25 (ISBN 0-89680-037-7, Ohio U Ctr Intl). Ohio U Pr.

Weisfeldt, Myron L., ed. The Aging Heart: Its Function & Response to Stress. (Aging Ser.: Vol. 12). 335p. 1980. 35.00 (ISBN 0-89004-307-8, 382). Raven.

Weisgal, Meyer. So Far: The Autobiography of Meyer Weisgal 1894-1977. (Illus.). 404p. 1978. 14.95 (ISBN 0-686-77352-7). Transaction Bks.

Weisgal, Meyer W., ed. The Letters & Papers of Chaim Weizmann, 23 vols. Incl. Vol. 1 (ISBN 0-87855-194-8); Vol. 2 (ISBN 0-87855-195-6); Vol. 3 (ISBN 0-87855-196-4); Vol. 4 (ISBN 0-87855-197-2); Vol. 5 (ISBN 0-87855-198-0); Vol. 6 (ISBN 0-87855-199-9); Vol. 7 (ISBN 0-87855-200-6); Vol. 8 (ISBN 0-87855-224-3); Vol. 9 (ISBN 0-87855-249-9); Vol. 10 (ISBN 0-87855-250-2); Vol. 11 (ISBN 0-87855-251-0); Vol. 12 (ISBN 0-87855-252-9); Vol. 13 (ISBN 0-87855-253-7); Vol. 14. July 29-December 1930 (ISBN 0-87855-254-5); Vol. 15. January1931-June 1933 (ISBN 0-87855-255-3); Vol. 16. July 1933-August 1935 (ISBN 0-87855-256-1); Vol. 17. August 1935-December 1936 (ISBN 0-87855-257-X); Vol. 18. January 1937-December 1938 (ISBN 0-87855-258-8); Vol. 19 (ISBN 0-87855-259-6); Vol. 20 (ISBN 0-87855-260-X); Vol. 21 (ISBN 0-87855-261-8). Set. casebound 500.00 (ISBN 0-87855-222-7); 24.95 ea. Transaction Bks.

Weisgard, Leonard. The Athenians: In the Classical Period. (Life Long Ago Ser). (Illus.). (gr. 5-8). 1963. PLB 4.69 o.p. (ISBN 0-698-30019-X, Coward). Putnam Pub Group.

--The First Farmers: In the New Stone Age. (Life Long Ago Ser). (Illus.). (gr. 5-8). 1966. PLB 5.49 o.p. (ISBN 0-698-30083-1, Coward). Putnam Pub Group.

--My First Picture Book. (Nursery Treasure Bks.). (Illus.). (ps). 1964. 1.95 (ISBN 0-448-04209-6, G&D). Putnam Pub Group.

--Treasures to See: A Museum Picture-Book. LC 56-10739. (Illus.). (gr. k-3). 1956. 6.95 o.p. (ISBN 0-15-290337-2, HJ). HarBraceJ.

Weisgard, Leonard, illus. Big Book of Nursery Tales. (Nursery Treasure Bks.). (Illus.). (ps). 1962. 1.50 o.s.i. (ISBN 0-448-04201-0, G&D). Putnam Pub Group.

--My First Picture Book. (Illus.). 32p. (ps-1). 1982. 3.95 (ISBN 0-448-04246-0, G&D). Putnam Pub Group.

--Nursery Tales. (Illus.). 32p. (ps-1). 1982. 3.95 (ISBN 0-448-04244-4, G&D). Putnam Pub Group.

Weisgerber, Jean. Faulkner & Dostoevsky: Influence & Confluence. McWilliams, Dean, tr. from Fr. LC 72-85537. xxii, 383p. 1974. 18.00x (ISBN 0-8214-0149-1, 82-81529). Ohio U Pr.

Weisgerber, Robert A., ed. Perspectives in Individualized Learning. LC 78-138641. (Illus.). 1971. pap. text ed. 10.95 (ISBN 0-87581-077-2). Peacock Pubs.

Weishahn, Mel W., jt. auth. see Gearheart, Bill R.

Weisheit, Eldon. Excuse Me, Sir. LC 78-139996. 1971. 3.95 o.p. (ISBN 0-570-03009-9, 6-1145). Concordia.

--God's Promise for Children: Object Lessons on Old Testament Texts. LC 81-65656. (Series B). 128p. (Orig.). 1981. pap. 4.50 (ISBN 0-8066-1892-2, 10-2693). Augsburg.

Weising, Edward F. & Weising, Gwen. Singleness: An Opportunity for Growth & Fulfillment. LC 82-80197. (Radiant Life Ser.). 128p. (Orig.). 1982. pap. 2.50 (ISBN 0-88243-901-4, 02-0901); teacher's ed. 3.95 (ISBN 0-88243-196-X, 32-0196). Gospel Pub.

--Singleness: An Opportunity for Growth & Fulfillment. 2.50 (ISBN 0-686-97217-1, 02-0901). Gospel Pub.

Weising, Gwen, jt. auth. see Weising, Edward F.

Weisinger, Hendrie & Lobsenz, Norman. Nobody's Perfect. 288p. 1983. pap. 3.50 (ISBN 0-446-30575-8). Warner Bks.

Weisinger, Hendrie & Lobsenz, Norman M. Nobody's Perfect. LC 81-52013. 1981. 12.95 (ISBN 0-936906-07-3). Stratford Pr.

Weisinger, Thelma. One Thousand & One Valuable Things You Can Get Free. (Things You Can Get Free Ser.: No. 12). 224p. 1982. pap. 2.95 (ISBN 0-553-22662-2). Bantam.

Weiskel, Thomas. The Romantic Sublime: Studies in the Structure & Psychology of Transcendence. 232p. 1976. text ed. 16.00x (ISBN 0-8018-1770-6). Johns Hopkins.

Weiskopf, Herm. His Five Smooth Stones. (Illus.). 160p. 1982. 8.95 (ISBN 0-8007-1324-9). Revell.

Weiskopf, Tom. Go for the Flag. 1969. pap. 5.25 (ISBN 0-8015-3018-0, 0510-150, Hawthorn). Dutton.

Weiskrantz, L., jt. ed. see Broadbent, D. E.

Weisman, Avery D. Coping with Cancer. (Illus.). 1979. pap. 12.95 (ISBN 0-07-069009-X, HP). McGraw.

Weisman, Dale, ed. see Wevill, David.

Weisman, Herman. Technical Report Writing. 2nd ed. (Speech Ser). 192p. 1975. pap. text ed. 11.95 (ISBN 0-675-08791-0). Merrill.

Weisman, Herman M. Basic Technical Writing. 4th ed. 1980. text ed. 16.95 (ISBN 0-675-08146-7). Merrill.

--Information Systems, Services & Centers. LC 72-1156. (Information Sciences Ser.). 265p. 1972. 22.95 o.p. (ISBN 0-471-92645-0, Pub. by Wiley-Interscience). Wiley.

Weisman, Joel, jt. auth. see Gottfried, Byron S.

Weisman, Joel, jt. auth. see Tong, L. S.

Weisman, Joel, ed. Elements of Nuclear Reactor Design. 526p. 1983. text ed. 34.50 (ISBN 0-89874-518-7). Krieger.

Weisman, John. Dark Room. 1981. pap. 2.50 o.p. (ISBN 0-686-69806-1, E9724, Sig). NAL.

--Evidence. 1981. pap. 2.95 o.p. (ISBN 0-451-09892-7, E9892, Sig). NAL.

--Watchdogs. 288p. 1983. 15.75 (ISBN 0-670-75022-0). Viking Pr.

Weismantel, Guy E., ed. Paint Handbook. (Illus.). 741p. 1981. 41.25 (ISBN 0-07-069061-8). McGraw.

Weisner, L. Telegraph & Data Transmission Over Shortwave Radio Links. 1981. 38.00 (ISBN 0-471-26085-1, Wiley Heyden). Wiley.

Weiss. Home Maintenance. (gr. 9-12). 1978. text ed. 15.20 (ISBN 0-87002-199-0); student guide 3.52 (ISBN 0-87002-239-3); tchr's guide free. Bennett IL.

--Home Maintenance. rev. ed. 1983. text ed. 15.20 (ISBN 0-87002-386-1). Bennett IL.

--Working Places. 1980. 17.95 o.p. (ISBN 0-312-88646-2); pap. 8.95 o.p. (ISBN 0-312-88985-2). St Martin.

Weiss & Mann. Human Biology & Behavior. 3rd ed. 1981. text ed. 19.95 (ISBN 0-316-92891-7); tchr's manual avail. (ISBN 0-316-92892-5). Little.

Weiss, jt. auth. see Smith.

Weiss, Alfred, ed. Computer Methods for the Eighties, in the Mineral Industry. LC 79-52274. (Illus.). 975p. 1979. text ed. 55.00x (ISBN 0-89520-257-3). Soc Mining Eng.

Weiss, Ann E. The American Congress. LC 77-21818. (Illus.). 96p. (gr. 4-6). 1977. PLB 7.29 o.p. (ISBN 0-671-32845-X). Messner.

--The American Presidency. LC 75-43763. (Illus.). 96p. (gr. 4-6). 1976. PLB 7.29 o.p. (ISBN 0-671-32765-8). Messner.

--Party Politics, Party Problems. LC 79-7831. (Illus.). 160p. (gr. 7 up). 1980. 10.95 (ISBN 0-690-04072-5, TYC-J); PLB 8.79 (ISBN 0-690-04073-3). Har-Row.

--Polls & Surveys: A Look at Public Opinion Research. (Impact Bks.). (Illus.). (gr. 7 up). 1979. PLB 8.90 s&l (ISBN 0-531-02859-3). Watts.

--What's That You Said. LC 79-3767. (Let-Me-Read Ser.). (Illus.). 48p. (gr. k-3). 1980. 6.95 (ISBN 0-15-295525-9, HJ); pap. 2.25 (ISBN 0-15-696119-9, VoyB). HarBraceJ.

Weiss, Ann E., jt. auth. see Weiss, Malcolm E.

Weiss, Bernard, jt. ed. see Merigan, William.

Weiss, C., ed. see Basar, E.

Weiss, Carol, ed. Research Utilization. 1976. pap. text ed. 6.00 (ISBN 0-918592-14-3). Policy Studies.

Weiss, Carol H. Evaluation Research: Methods of Assessing Program Effectiveness. (Methods of Social Science Ser). (Illus.). 176p. 1972. pap. text ed. 13.95 (ISBN 0-13-292193-6). P-H.

Weiss, Carol H., jt. auth. see Tilson, Ann.

Weiss, Carol H., ed. Using Social Research for Public Policy-Making. LC 75-42954. (Policy Studies Organization Ser.). 272p. 1977. 23.95x o.p. (ISBN 0-669-00498-7). Lexington Bks.

Weiss, Curtis E. & Lillywhite, Herold S. Communicative Disorders: Prevention & Early Intervention. 2nd ed. LC 80-27134. (Illus.). 267p. 1981. pap. text ed. 15.50 (ISBN 0-8016-5389-4). Mosby.

Weiss, Curtis E. & Lillywhite, Herolds. Clinical Management of Articulation Disorders. LC 80-17348. (Illus.). 303p. 1980. pap. text ed. 15.50 (ISBN 0-8016-5391-6). Mosby.

Weiss, D., jt. auth. see Kuhn, G.

Weiss, D. G. & Gorio, A., eds. Axioplasmic Transport in Physiology & Pathology. (Proceedings in Life Science Ser.). (Illus.). 220p. 1983. 32.00 (ISBN 0-387-11663-X). Springer-Verlag.

Weiss, D. W., ed. Immunological Parameters of Host - Tumor Relationships, Vol. 4. 1977. 43.50 (ISBN 0-12-743554-9). Acad Pr.

Weiss, Daniel, et al, eds. The Critic Agonistes. 1983. write for info. U of Wash Pr.

Weiss, David, ed. Immunological Parameters of Host-Tumor Relationship, Vol. 5. 1979. 32.50 (ISBN 0-12-743555-7). Acad Pr.

Weiss, Dieter G., ed. Axioplasmic Transport. (Proceedings in Life Sciences Ser.). (Illus.). 477p. 1982. 62.00 (ISBN 0-387-11662-1). Springer-Verlag.

Weiss, E. Cohomology of Groups. (Pure & Applied Mathematics Ser.: Vol. 34). 1969. 53.50 (ISBN 0-12-742750-3). Acad Pr.

Weiss, E. & Weiss, H. Catering Handbook. 23.95x (ISBN 0-911202-04-8). Radio City.

Weiss, E. A., jt. auth. see Computer Usage Co., Inc.

Weiss, E. A., jt. auth. see Computer Usage Company Inc.

Weiss, Eberhard. Input-Output Modellgenerator. 284p. 1982. write for info. (ISBN 3-8204-5808-5). P Lang Pubs.

Weiss, Edda. Deutsch: Entdecken Wir Es! Saslow, Joan, ed. (Illus., Ger.). (gr. 9). 1980. text ed. 17.32 (ISBN 0-07-069211-4); tchrs.' ed. 19.12 (ISBN 0-07-069212-2); wkbk. 5.32 (ISBN 0-07-069213-0); tests 63.52 (ISBN 0-07-069214-9); filmstrips 146.52 (ISBN 0-07-097813-1); tapes 520.60 (ISBN 0-07-097811-5); cassettes 275.28 (ISBN 0-07-097812-3). McGraw.

--Deutsch: Entdecken Wir Es, Level 1. (Learning German the Modern Way). (Illus.). 368p. (gr. 9). 1972. text ed. 18.72 (ISBN 0-07-069075-8, W); tchr's. ed. 19.80 (ISBN 0-07-069076-6); wkbk. 5.64 (ISBN 0-07-069077-4); cassettes 552.00 (ISBN 0-07-097807-7); filmstrips 138.00 (ISBN 0-07-097801-8); tapes 527.40 (ISBN 0-07-097800-X); test pkg. 74.08 (ISBN 0-07-069078-2). McGraw.

--Deutsch: Erleben Wir Es! 2nd ed. Saslow, Joan, ed. LC 80-16484. (Illus.). 344p. (Ger.). (gr. 10). 1980. text ed. 17.56 (ISBN 0-07-069215-7, W); tchrs. ed. 19.96 (ISBN 0-07-069216-5); wkbk. 5.32 (ISBN 0-07-069217-3); tests 84.36 (ISBN 0-07-069218-1); tapes 358.12 (ISBN 0-07-097815-8); cassettes 339.00 (ISBN 0-07-097816-6); filmstrips 142.20 (ISBN 0-07-097817-4). McGraw.

--Deutsch: Erleben Wir Es, Level 2. LC 72-8377. (Learning German the Modern Way Ser.). (Illus.). 418p. (gr. 10-12). 1973. text ed. 18.88 (ISBN 0-07-069081-2, W); tchr's. ed. 19.92 (ISBN 0-07-069082-0); wkbk. 5.68 (ISBN 0-07-069083-9); cassettes 504.88 (ISBN 0-07-097808-5); filmstrips 138.00 (ISBN 0-07-097806-9); tapes 611.40 (ISBN 0-07-097805-0); test pkg. 88.88 (ISBN 0-07-069084-7). McGraw.

Weiss, Edmond H. The Writing System for Engineers & Scientists. LC 81-775. (Illus.). 288p. 1982. text ed. 19.95 (ISBN 0-13-971606-8). P-H.

Weiss, Edward. The Queen & I: A Manual for the Beginning Beekeeper. LC 77-3779. (Illus.). 1978. 12.45i (ISBN 0-06-014578-1, HarpT). Har-Row.

Weiss, Edward C., ed. The Many Faces of Information Science. LC 77-12103. (AAAS Selected Symposium Ser.: No. 3). (Illus.). 1978. lib. bdg. 16.00 o.p. (ISBN 0-89158-430-7). Westview.

Weiss, Edwin. Algebraic Number Theory. 2nd ed. LC 76-5803. xii, 275p. 1976. 14.95 (ISBN 0-8284-0293-0). Chelsea Pub.

Weiss, Elizabeth & Wolfson, Rita P. The Gourmet's Low-Cholesterol Cookbook. 1980. pap. 2.25 (ISBN 0-515-05690-1, V3458). Jove Pubns.

Weiss, Ellen. The Angry Book Starring Temper Tantrum Turtle. LC 82-50433. (Sweet Pickles Mini-Storybooks). (Illus.). 32p. (ps-4). 1983. pap. 1.25 (ISBN 0-394-85541-8). Random.

--The Messy Book Starring Goof-Off Goose. LC 82-50432. (Sweet Pickles Mini-Storybooks). (Illus.). 32p. (ps-4). 1983. pap. 1.25 (ISBN 0-394-85545-0). Random.

--Millicent Maybe. LC 78-13144. (Easy-Read Story Bks.). (Illus.). (gr. k-3). 1979. PLB 8.60 (ISBN 0-531-02299-4). Watts.

--The Muppets on the Road. LC 81-11978. (Muppet Press Bks.). (Illus.). 48p. (gr. 1-6). 1983. pap. 4.50 (ISBN 0-394-85103-X). Random.

--Pigs in Space. LC 82-16578. (Muppet Press Bks.). (Illus.). 32p. (gr. 1-6). 1983. pap. 1.95 (ISBN 0-394-85730-5). Random.

Weiss, Eric, ed. see Computer Usage Co., Inc.

Weiss, Frederick G., ed. see Hegel, G. W.

Weiss, H., jt. auth. see Weiss, E.

Weiss, Harold & McGrath, J. B. Technically Speaking: Oral Communication for Engineers, Scientists & Technical Personnel. 1963. 26.00x (ISBN 0-07-069085-5, C). McGraw.

Weiss, Harry B. A Book about Chapbooks: The People's Literature of Bygone Times. LC 69-20399. (Illus.). x, 149p. Repr. of 1969 ed. 34.00x (ISBN 0-8103-5028-9). Gale.

Weiss, Harvey. How to Run a Railroad: Everything You Need to Know about Model Trains. LC 76-18128. (Illus.). 96p. (gr. 4-7). 1983. pap. 4.76i (ISBN 0-690-04329-5, TYC-J). Har-Row.

--Ship Models & How to Build Them. LC 72-7562. (Illus.). (gr. 5-9). 1973. 10.95i o.p. (ISBN 0-690-73270-8, TYC-J). Har-Row.

Weiss, Harvey J., ed. Platelets: Pathophysiology & Antiplatelet Drug Therapy. 178p. 1982. 22.00 (ISBN 0-8451-0217-6). A R Liss.

Weiss, Harvey R., jt. ed. see Merrill, Gary F.

Weiss, Herman, jt. auth. see Davis, Julie.

Weiss, J. D. Better Buildings for the Aged. 1971. 39.50 o.p. (ISBN 0-07-069071-5, P&RB). McGraw.

Weiss, Jacqueline S. Prizewinning Books for Children: Themes & Stereotypes in U.S. Prizewinning Prose Fiction for Children. LC 82-48624. (Libraries & Librarianship Special Ser.). 1983. write for info. (ISBN 0-669-06352-5). Lexington Bks.

Weiss, Jeffrey. Free Things for Campers: And Others Who Love the Outdoors. Osborn, Susan, ed. LC 81-15405. (Free Things! A Bargain Hunter's Bonzana Ser.). (Illus.). 127p. 1982. pap. 4.95 (ISBN 0-399-50605-5, Perige). Putnam Pub Group.

--Lofts. (Illus.). 1979. 14.95 o.p. (ISBN 0-393-01290-5); pap. 7.95 (ISBN 0-393-00945-9). Norton.

--Outdoor Places. 1980. 12.95 o.p. (ISBN 0-393-01365-0); pap. 7.95 (ISBN 0-393-00976-9). Norton.

Weiss, Jeffrey & Gault, Lila. Small Houses. (Illus.). 96p. 1983. pap. 7.95 (ISBN 0-446-97346-7). Warner Bks.

Weiss, Jeffrey & Wise, Herbert. Good Lives. LC 77-78527. (Illus.). 1977. text ed. cancelled (ISBN 0-8256-3080-0, Quick Fox); pap. 6.95 (ISBN 0-686-96802-6, 030080). Putnam Pub Group.

Weiss, Jeffrey, jt. auth. see Wise, Herbert H.

Weiss, Jeffrey, ed. see Hamburger, Robert & Stern, Susan.

Weiss, Jeffrey, ed. see Saxton, Martha.

Weiss, John. Advanced Bass Fishing. (Illus.). 1978. pap. 5.95 o.s.i. (ISBN 0-695-80934-2). Follett.

Weiss, Justin L., jt. auth. see Grunebaum, Henry.

Weiss, K. M. & Ballonoff, P. A., eds. Demographic Genetics. LC 75-31580. (Benchmark Papers in Genetics: Vol. 3). 414p. 1975. 51.00 (ISBN 0-12-787745-2). Acad Pr.

Weiss, Ken & Goodgold, Ed. To Be Continued...a Complete Guide to Over Two-Hundred Twenty Motion Picture Serials with Sound Tracks. (Illus.). 1972. 12.95 o.p. (ISBN 0-517-50340-9). Crown.

Weiss, Leatie. Funny Feet. (Easy-Read Story Books Ser.). (Illus.). (gr. k-3). 1978. PLB 8.60 s&l (ISBN 0-531-01348-0). Watts.

Weiss, Leon. Cells & Tissues of the Immune System: Structure, Functions, Interactions. (Foundations of Immunology Ser). (Illus.). 1972. ref. ed. 23.95x o.p. (ISBN 0-13-121772-0). P-H.

--Histology. 5th ed. Date not set. 49.50 (ISBN 0-444-00716-4). Elsevier.

Weiss, Leon & Greep, Roy O. Histology. 4th ed. LC 76-42251. (Illus.). 1977. text ed. 55.00 (ISBN 0-07-069091-X, HP). McGraw.

Weiss, Leonard. Economics & Society. 2nd ed. LC 80-26631. 600p. 1981. text ed. 24.95 (ISBN 0-471-03160-7). Wiley.

Weiss, Leonard & Gilbert, Harvey. Pulmonary Metastasis. 1978. lib. bdg. 37.50 (ISBN 0-8161-2107-9, Hall Medical). G K Hall.

Weiss, Leonard & Gilbert, Harvey A. Lymphatic System Metastasis. 1980. lib. bdg. 55.00 (ISBN 0-8161-2142-7, Hall Medical). G K Hall.

Weiss, Leonard & Strickland, Allyn. Regulation: A Case Approach. (Illus.). 1976. pap. text ed. 15.00 (ISBN 0-07-069097-9, C). McGraw.

Weiss, Leonard, ed. Ordinary Differential Equations: The 1971 NRL-MRC Conference. 1972. 57.00 (ISBN 0-12-743650-2). Acad Pr.

Weiss, Leonard & Gilbert, Harvey A., eds. Brain Metastasis. 1980. lib. bdg. 55.00 (ISBN 0-8161-2119-2, Hall Medical). G K Hall.

Weiss, Leonard A., jt. auth. see Cavender, Nancy M.

Weiss, Leonard W. Case Studies in American Industry. 3rd ed. LC 78-31149. (Introduction to Economics Ser.). 1980. pap. text ed. 17.95 (ISBN 0-471-03159-3). Wiley.

Weiss, Lionel, jt. auth. see Turner, Francis J.

Weiss, Louis, jt. auth. see Bozimo, Henry T.

Weiss, M., jt. auth. see Ramirez, E. V.

Weiss, Malcolm E. Blindness. LC 80-14059. (gr. 4 up). 1980. PLB 8.90 (ISBN 0-531-02939-5). Watts.

--Six Hundred & Sixty-Six Jellybeans! All That? An Introduction to Algebra. LC 75-9528. (Young Math Ser.). (Illus.). 40p. (gr. k-3). 1976. 10.89 (ISBN 0-690-00914-3, TYC-J). Har-Row.

--Solomon Grundy, Born on Oneday: A Finite Arithmetic Puzzle. LC 76-26560. (Young Math Ser.). (Illus.). (gr. k-3). 1977. PLB 10.89 (ISBN 0-690-01275-6, TYC-J). Har-Row.

--What's Happening to Our Climate? LC 78-15684. (Illus.). 96p. (gr. 4-6). 1978. PLB 7.29 o.p. (ISBN 0-671-32846-8). Messner.

Weiss, Malcolm E. & Weiss, Ann E. The Vitamin Puzzle. LC 75-45293. (Illus.). 96p. (gr. 3-6). 1976. PLB 7.29 o.p. (ISBN 0-671-32777-1). Messner.

Weiss, Martin D. The Great Money Panic: A Guide for Survival & Action. (Illus.). 256p. 1981. 14.95 (ISBN 0-87000-502-2, Arlington Hse). Crown.

Weiss, Martin H. Clinical Neurosurgery, Vol. 29. (Congress of Neurological Surgeons). (Illus.). 809p. 1982. 48.00 (ISBN 0-683-02024-2). Williams & Wilkins.

Weiss, Max L., jt. auth. see Kelly, Paul J.

Weiss, Milton. Songs, Psalms, Poetry & Prose. 1978. 4.95 o.p. (ISBN 0-533-03374-8). Vantage.

Weiss, N. A. & Yoseloff, M. L. Finite Mathematics. LC 74-20001. (Illus.). ix, 628p. 1975. text ed. 22.95x (ISBN 0-87901-039-8). Worth.

Weiss, Nancy. Charles Francis Murphy, Eighteen Fifty-Eight-Nineteen Twenty-Four: Respectability & Responsibility in Tammany Politics. LC 67-21037. (Edwin H. Land Prize Essays). 1968. 2.00 o.s.i. (ISBN 0-87391-012-5). Smith Coll.

Weiss, Neil & Hassett, Matthew. Introductory Statistics. LC 80-23520. (Statistics Ser.). (Illus.). 672p. 1981. text ed. 23.95 (ISBN 0-201-09507-6); instr's manual (ISBN 0-201-09508-4). A-W.

Weiss, Nicki. Chuckie. (Illus.). (ps-3). 1982. 8.50 (ISBN 0-688-00670-1); PLB 7.63 (ISBN 0-688-00671-X). Greenwillow.

--Hank & Oogie. LC 81-7136. (Illus.). 32p. (gr. k-3). 1982. 8.00 (ISBN 0-688-00928-X); PLB 7.63 (ISBN 0-688-00936-0). Greenwillow.

Weiss, Norman. Memoirs of a Millman, Vol. 1. 245p. 1982. text ed. 12.00 (ISBN 0-686-43344-0). Maywood Pub.

Weiss, P. Adhesion & Cohesion. 1962. 34.25 (ISBN 0-444-40627-1). Elsevier.

Weiss, Paul. Modes of Being. LC 57-11877. (Arcturus Books Paperbacks). 626p. 1968. pap. 11.95 (ISBN 0-8093-0294-2). S Ill U Pr.

--Privacy. LC 81-21513. 368p. 1983. write for info (ISBN 0-8093-1066-X). S Ill U Pr.

--Reality. LC 67-11699. 318p. 1967. lib. bdg. 11.95x o.p. (ISBN 0-8093-0243-8). S Ill U Pr.

--Religion & Art. (Aquinas Lecture). 1963. 7.95 (ISBN 0-87462-128-3). Marquette.

Weiss, Paul, ed. see Peirce, Charles S.

Weiss, Paul A. Dynamics of Development: Experiments & Inferences. LC 68-23476. (Illus.). 1968. 38.50 (ISBN 0-12-742850-X). Acad Pr.

Weiss, Peg, ed. Adelaide Alsop Robineau: Glory in Porcelain. LC 81-9107. (Illus.). 235p. 1981. 55.00 o.p. (ISBN 0-8156-2249-X); pap. 21.95 o.p. (ISBN 0-8156-0171-9). Syracuse U Pr.

Weiss, Phyllis R. Guide to Use of Speech Improvement: Do-It-Yourself. (Illus., Orig.). 1981. pap. text ed. 39.50 incl. 3 audio cassettes (ISBN 0-88432-075-8, 23639). J Norton Pubs.

Weiss, R., ed. Quarterly Review of Literature. (Poetry Series Four: Vol. 23). 340p. 1982. 20.00 (ISBN 0-686-36879-7); pap. 10.00 (ISBN 0-686-37365-0). Quarterly Rev.

Weiss, R. J. X-Ray Determination of Electron Distribution. Wohlforth, E. P., ed. (Selected Topics in Solid State Physics: Vol. 6). 1966. 21.50 (ISBN 0-444-10305-8, North-Holland). Elsevier.

Weiss, Rita. The Artist's & Craftsman's Guide to Reducing, Enlarging & Transferring Designs. (General Crafts Ser.). 64p. (Orig.). Date not set. pap. 3.25 (ISBN 0-486-24142-4). Dover. Postponed.

--Christmas Needlepoint Designs. LC 74-21224. (Illus.). 48p. 1975. pap. 1.75 (ISBN 0-486-23161-5). Dover.

--Early American Iron-on Transfer Patterns for Crewel & Embroidery. (Needlework Ser.). pap. 1.95 (ISBN 0-486-23162-3). Dover.

--Needlepoint Designs After Illustrations by Beatrix Potter. LC 75-9177. (Illus.). 32p. (Orig.). 1976. pap. 1.75 (ISBN 0-486-20218-6). Dover.

Weiss, Rita, ed. Easy-to-Make Patchwork Quilts: Step-by-Step Instructions & Full-Size Templates for 12 Quilts. (Illus.). 1978. pap. 3.50 (ISBN 0-486-23641-2). Dover.

Weiss, Robert H., jt. auth. see Field, John P.

Weiss, Robert M., ed. Conant Controversy in Teacher Education. (Orig.). 1969. pap. text ed. 3.95x (ISBN 0-685-19713-1). Phila Bk Co.

Weiss, Robert R. & Pexton, Myron R. Dr. Pexton's Guide for the Expectant Father. 1970. 5.95 o.p. (ISBN 0-8158-0230-7). Chris Mass.

Weiss, Robert S. Marital Separation: Managing After a Marriage Ends. LC 74-78307. 1977. pap. 6.95 o.s.i. (ISBN 0-465-09723-5, CN-5023). Basic.

Weiss, Robert S., jt. auth. see Parkes, Colin M.

Weiss, Robert S., ed. Loneliness. 240p. 1974. pap. 6.95x (ISBN 0-262-73041-3). MIT Pr.

Weiss, Robin A., et al, eds. RNA Tumor Viruses: Molecular Biology of Tumor Viruses. LC 81-69062. (Cold Spring Harbor Monographs: Vol. 10C). 1396p. 1982. 125.00 (ISBN 0-87969-132-8). Cold Spring Harbor.

Weiss, Ruth, jt. auth. see Arnold, Guy.

Weiss, Sharon W., jt. auth. see Enzinger, Franz M.

Weiss, Shirley F., jt. ed. see Chapin, F. Stuart, Jr.

Weiss, Sholom M., jt. auth. see Kulikowski, Casimir A.

Weiss, Stanley, jt. auth. see Singer, Stuart R.

Weiss, Stephen, jt. auth. see Dougan, Clark.

Weiss, Stephen, jt. auth. see Maitland, Terrence.

Weiss, Stephen M., et al, eds. Perspectives on Behavioral Medicine Nineteen Eighty, Vol. I. LC 80-2577. (Serial Publication). 1981. 39.50 (ISBN 0-12-532101-5). Acad Pr.

Weiss, Theodore. Recoveries: A Poem. 80p. 1982. 11.95 (ISBN 0-02-625810-2); pap. 6.95 (ISBN 0-02-071050-X). Macmillan.

Weiss, Theodore J. Food Oils & Their Uses. (Illus.). 1970. lib. bdg. 27.50 o.p. (ISBN 0-87055-093-4). AVI.

--Foods Oils & Their Uses. 2nd ed. (Illus.). 1983. text ed. 27.50 (ISBN 0-87055-420-4). AVI.

Weiss, Thomas G. & Jennings, Anthony. More for the Least? Prospects for Poorest Countries in the Eighties. LC 82-48170. 208p. 1982. 24.95x (ISBN 0-669-06009-7). Lexington Bks.

Weiss, Ulrich & Edwards, John. Biosynthesis of Aromatic Compounds. LC 78-1496. 1980. 51.50x (ISBN 0-471-92690-6, Pub by Wiley-Interscience). Wiley.

Weiss, Volker, jt. ed. see Burke, John J.

Weiss, Volker, jt. ed. see Kula, Eric.

Weiss, W. H. The Supervisor's Problem Solver. 240p. 1983. 15.95 (ISBN 0-8144-5754-1). Am Mgmt.

Weissbach, Herbert & Kunz, Robert. Dimension in Health Research: Search for the Medicines of Tomorrow. 1978. 24.50 (ISBN 0-12-744260-X). Acad Pr.

Weissbach, Herbert & Pestka, Sidney, eds. Protein Biosynthesis. (Molecular Biology Ser.). 1977. 79.50 (ISBN 0-12-744250-2). Acad Pr.

Weissberg, Michael. Dangerous Secrets: Maladaptive Responses to Stress. 256p. 1983. 14.95 (ISBN 0-393-01732-X). Norton.

Weissberg, Michael P., jt. auth. see Dubovsky, Steven L.

Weissberg, Robert. Public Opinion & Popular Government. (Illus.). 320p. 1976. pap. 13.95 (ISBN 0-13-737908-0). P-H.

Weissberg, Robert, jt. auth. see Jacob, Herbert.

Weissberger, A. Technique of Organic Chemistry. Incl. Vol. 2. Catalytic, Photochemical & Electrolytic Reactions. 2nd ed. 1956. 53.50 o.s.i. (ISBN 0-470-92862-X); Vol. 3, Pt. 2. Laboratory Engineering. 1957. 36.95 o.p. (ISBN 0-470-92928-6). (All other vols. in set o.p., Pub. by Wiley-Interscience). Wiley.

--Techniques of Chemistry Separation & Purification. 3rd ed. Edwards, Perry, ed. LC 77-114920. (Techniques of Chemistry Ser.: Vol. 12). 1978. 69.50x (ISBN 0-471-02655-7, Pub. by Wiley-Interscience). Wiley.

Weissberger, A. & Perry, E. S. Techniques of Chemistry: Vol. 13 Laboratory Engineering & Manipulations. 3rd ed. 531p. 1979. 74.95x (ISBN 0-471-03275-1). Wiley.

Weissberger, A., ed. Techniques of Chemistry. Incl. Vol. 1. Physical Methods of Chemistry, 5 pts. Rossiter, B. 1971-72; Pt. 1A. Components of Scientific Instruments. 40.50 o.p. (ISBN 0-471-92724-4); Pt. 2A. Electrochemical Methods. 94.95x (ISBN 0-471-92727-9); Pt. 1B. Automatic Recording & Control, Computers in Chemical Research. 43.00 (ISBN 0-471-92725-2); Pt. 3B. Spectroscopy & Spectometry in Infrared, Visible & Ultraviolet. 73.50 (ISBN 0-471-92731-7); Pt. 3C. Polarimetry. 47.95 o.p. (ISBN 0-471-92732-5); Pt. 3D. X-Ray, Nuclear, Molecular Beam & Radioactivity Methods. 62.95 o.p. (ISBN 0-471-92733-3); Pt. 4. Determination of Mass, Transport & Electrical-Magnetic Properties. 54.50 (ISBN 0-686-70205-0); Pt. 5. o.p. (ISBN 0-471-92734-1); Pt. 6. Supplement & Cumulative Index. LC 75-29544. 256p. 1976. 31.50x (ISBN 0-471-92899-2); Vol. 2. Organic Solvents: Physical Properties & Methods of Purification. 3rd ed. Riddick, John A. & Bunger, William B. LC 72-114919. 1971. Pt. 1. 96.50 (ISBN 0-471-92726-0); Vol. 3. **Photochromism. Brown, G. H. LC 45-8533. 1971. 93.00 (ISBN 0-471-92894-1); Vol. 4. Elucidation of Organic Structures by Physical & Chemical Methods, 3 pts. Bentley, K. W. & Kirby, G. W. 1972-73. Pt. 1. 82.50x (ISBN 0-471-92896-8); Pt. 2. 84.95x (ISBN 0-471-92897-6); Vol. 5. Techniques of Electroorganic Synthesis, 2 pts. Weingerb, N. L., ed. Pt. 1. 98.50 (ISBN 0-686-70206-9); Pt. 2. 86.00 o.s.i. (ISBN 0-471-93272-8); Vol. 6. Investigation of Rates & Mechanisms of Reactions, 2 pts. 3rd ed. Lewis, E. S., ed. LC 73-8850. 1974. Pt. 1. 88.50 o.p. (ISBN 0-471-93095-4); Pt. 2. 83.50x (ISBN 0-471-93127-6); Vol. 7. Membranes in Separations. Hwang, S. T. & Kammermeyer, K. LC 74-2218. 1975. 87.95 (ISBN 0-471-93268-X); Vol. 10. Applications of Biochemical Systems in Organic Chemistry, 2 pts. Jone, Bryan J., et al, eds. 1976. Pt. 1. 65.95 (ISBN 0-471-93267-1); Pt. 2. 65.00 o.s.i. (ISBN 0-471-93270-1). Pub. by Wiley-Interscience). Wiley.**

Weissberger, A. & Rossiter, B. W., eds. Techniques of Chemistry: Optical, Spectroscopic & Radioactivity Methods: Iternferometry, Light Scattering, Microscopy, Microwave & Magnetic Resonance Spectroscopy, Vol. 1, Pt. 3A. 791p. 1972. 60.00 (ISBN 0-471-92729-5). Wiley.

Weissberger, Arnold & Hsu, Hsien-Wen. Separations by Centrifugal Phenomena. (Techniques of Chemistry Ser.: Vol. 16). 400p. 61.50x (ISBN 0-471-05564-6, Pub. by Wiley-Interscience). Wiley.

Weissberger, Arnold, ed. Technique of Organic Chemistry: Vol. 9, Pt. 1, Chemical Applications of Spectroscopy. 486p. 1968. 29.25 (ISBN 0-470-93160-4). Krieger.

Weissberger, Arnold, et al, eds. Technique of Organic Chemistry: Vol. 13, Gas Chromotography. 437p. 1968. 36.50 (ISBN 0-470-93263-5). Krieger.

--Technique of Organic Chemistry: Vol. 9, Pt. 2, Microwave Molecular Spectra. LC 45-8533. 747p. 1970. 67.50 (ISBN 0-471-93161-6). Krieger.

--Techniques of Chemistry: Vol. 1, Pt. 2B. (Electrochemical Methods). 425p. 1971. 49.50 o.p. (ISBN 0-471-92728-7). Krieger.

Weissbort, Daniel. Modern Poetry in Translation. 214p. 1983. text ed. 14.75x (ISBN 0-85635-481-3, Pub. by Carcanet New Pr England). Humanities.
--Soundings. 1979. 6.95 o.p. (ISBN 0-85635-217-9, Pub. by Carcanet New Pr England). Humanities.
Weissbort, Daniel, ed. Modern Poetry in Translation 1983. (Persea Series of Poetry in Translation). (Orig.). 1983. pap. 9.95 (ISBN 0-89255-075-9). Persea Bks.
Weissbort, Daniel, ed. & tr. see Gorbanevskaya, Natalya.
Weissbort, Daniel, tr. see Dore, Gustave.
Weissbort, Daniel, tr. see Simon, Claude.
Weissbort, Daniel, tr. see Vinokurov, Evgeny.
Weisselberg, R. C. & Cowley, J. M. Executive Strategist: An Armchair Guide to Scientific Decision Making. 1969. 4.95 o.p. (ISBN 0-07-069095-2, P&RB). McGraw.
Weissenborn, Juergen & Klein, Wolfgang, eds. Here & There: Crosslinguistic Studies on Deixis & Demonstration. (Pragmatics & Beyond Ser.: III: 2-3). 296p. (Orig.). 1982. pap. 32.00 (ISBN 90-272-2519-2). Benjamins North Am.
Weissenborn, Jurgen & Klein, Wolfgang, eds. Here & There: Cross-linguistic Studies on Deixis & Demonstration. 1982. 28.00 o.p. (ISBN 90-272251-9-2). Benjamins North Am.
Weisser, Albert. The Modern Renaissance of Jewish Music. (Music Reprint Ser.). 175p. 1983. Repr. of 1954 ed. lib. bdg. 19.50 (ISBN 0-306-76207-2). Da Capo.
Weisskopf, K., tr. see Lederer, Zdenek.
Weisskopf, Victor F. Knowledge & Wonder: The Natural World As Man Knows It. 2nd ed. (Illus.). 1979. text ed. 16.50x (ISBN 0-262-23098-4); pap. 6.95 (ISBN 0-262-73052-9). MIT Pr.
Weisskopf, Victor F., ed. Nuclear Physics. (Italian Physical Society: Course 23). 1963. 56.50 (ISBN 0-12-368823-X). Acad Pr.
Weissler, Arlene & Weissler, Paul. A Woman's Guide to Fixing the Car. (Illus.). 128p. 1973. 6.95 o.s.i. (ISBN 0-8027-0416-6); pap. 3.95 o.s.i. (ISBN 0-8027-7091-6). Walker & Co.
Weissler, Paul. Automotive Air Conditioning. (Illus.). 1981. text ed. 19.95 (ISBN 0-8359-0261-7); pap. 16.95 (ISBN 0-8359-0260-9). Reston.
--Rabbit-Dasher-Scirocco-Jetta, Guide to the New VW's. LC 76-50369. 1977. pap. 6.95 (ISBN 0-8306-9693-8, 2125). Tab Bks.
--Small Gas Engines: How to Repair & Maintain Them. LC 75-13334. (A Popular Science Bk). (Illus.). 288p. 1975. 13.41i (ISBN 0-06-014564-1, HarpT). Har-Row.
--Weekend Mechanic's Handbook: Complete Auto Repairs You Can Make. rev. ed. LC 82-3992. (Illus.). 480p. 1982. 19.95 (ISBN 0-668-05379-8); pap. 11.95 (ISBN 0-668-05384-4). Arco.
--Weekend Mechanic's Handbook: Complete Auto Repairs You Can Make. LC 79-14179. (Illus.). 1979. lib. bdg. 12.95 (ISBN 0-668-04763-1); pap. 8.95 o.p. (ISBN 0-668-04770-4). Arco.
Weissler, Paul, jt. auth. see Weissler, Arlene.
Weissman, Clark. LISP One-Point-Five Primer. (Orig.). 1967. pap. 20.25x (ISBN 0-8221-1050-4). Dickenson.
Weissman, Dick. Music Making in America. LC 81-70114. (Illus.). 200p. 1982. 12.95 (ISBN 0-8044-5977-0). Ungar.
Weissman, Frances. Helen & All. (Orig.). 1980. pap. 3.95 o.p. (ISBN 0-89260-192-2). Hwong Pub.
--In These Times. (Orig.). 1980. pap. 2.95 o.p. (ISBN 0-89260-148-5). Hwong Pub.
Weissman, G. Cell Biology of Inflammation. (Handbook of Inflammation: Vol. 2). 1980. 133.25 (ISBN 0-444-80141-3). Elsevier.
Weissman, Harold H. Integrating Services for Troubled Families: Dilemmas of Program Design & Implementation. LC 78-62563. (Social & Behavioral Science Ser.). (Illus.). 1978. text ed. 19.95x (ISBN 0-87589-385-6). Jossey-Bass.
--Overcoming Mismanagement in the Human Service Professions: A Casebook of Staff Initiatives. LC 73-10944. (Social & Behavioral Science Ser.). 192p. 1973. 17.95x (ISBN 0-87589-212-4). Jossey-Bass.
Weissman, Heidi S., jt. ed. see Freeman, Leonard M.
Weissman, Irving, et al. Essential Concepts in Immunology. LC 78-57262. 1978. 14.95 (ISBN 0-8053-4406-3). Benjamin-Cummings.
Weissman, Judith R., jt. auth. see Bishop, Robert.
Weissman, Michaele, jt. auth. see Hymowitz, Carol.
Weissman, Myrna, jt. auth. see Klerman, Gerald.
Weissman, Steve, ed. Big Brother & the Holding Company: The World Behind Watergate. LC 78-90631. 349p. 1974. 14.00 (ISBN 0-87867-050-5). Ramparts.
Weissmann, Gerald, ed. Advances in Inflammation Research, Vol. 2. 228p. 1981. 27.00 (ISBN 0-89004-582-8). Raven.
--Advances in Inflammation Research, Vol. 4. 208p. 1982. text ed. 23.00 (ISBN 0-89004-669-7). Raven.
Weissmann, Heidi see Freeman, Leonard.
Weissmann, Heidi S., jt. ed. see Freeman, Leonard M.
Weisstub, David N. & Gostin, Larry O. International Casebook on Law & Psychiatry. (Law & Psychiatry Ser.). 1982. write for info. (ISBN 0-08-023158-6). Pergamon.
Weisstub, David N., ed. Law & Psychiatry III: Selected Papers Presented at the Fourth International Congress on Law & Psychiatry, Pembroke College, Oxford England, 19-22 July 1979. 100p. 1981. pap. 15.00 (ISBN 0-08-026113-2). Pergamon.
Weist, Tom. A History of the Cheyenne People. (Indian Culture Ser.). (Illus.). 1977. write for info. (ISBN 0-89992-506-5); pap. 7.95 (ISBN 0-89992-507-3). Mt Coun Indian.
Weist, Tom, jt. auth. see Henry Tall Bull.
Weist, William B., tr. see Masaryk, Thomas G.
Weisweiller, R. L. Introduction to Foreign Exchange. 172p. (Orig.). 1983. 17.50 (ISBN 0-85941-220-2); pap. 9.95 (ISBN 0-85941-234-2). Woodhead.
Weisz, Frank B. An Estate Planner's Guide to Business Agreements & Estate Documents. LC 81-66934. 223p. 1981. comb bdg. 12.95 o.p. (ISBN 0-87863-065-1). FS&G.
Weisz, Frank B. & Gladstone, Eugene A. Super-Loan: The Book on Interest-Free Loans. 1982. text ed. 16.95 (ISBN 0-87863-146-1). Farnswth Pub.
Weisz, George. The Emergence of Modern Universities in France, 1863-1914. LC 82-13307. 376p. 1983. 35.00 (ISBN 0-691-05375-8). Princeton U Pr.
Weisz, George, jt. ed. see Fox, Robert.
Weisz, Michael & Crane, Richard. Defenses to Civil Rights Actions Against Correctional Employees. 35p. (Orig.). 1980. pap. 2.00 (ISBN 0-942974-14-X). Am Correctional.
Weisz, Paul B. Elements of Biology. 3rd ed. 1969. text ed. 25.95 (ISBN 0-07-069130-4, C). study guide 10.00 (ISBN 0-07-007638-3). McGraw.
--Science of Biology. 4th ed. 1971. text ed. 26.95 (ISBN 0-07-069132-0, C); instr's manual 23.00 (ISBN 0-07-069133-9); study guide by Brenner 13.95 (ISBN 0-07-007640-5). McGraw.
--Science of Zoology. 2nd ed. LC 72-4172. (Illus.). 1972. text ed. 29.95 (ISBN 0-07-069135-5, C); instructors' manual 3.00 (ISBN 0-07-069136-3). McGraw.
Weisz, Paul B. & Keogh, R. N. Science of Biology. 5th ed. 1982. 27.50x (ISBN 0-07-069145-2). lab. manual 14.00x (ISBN 0-07-069146-0); study guide 8.95x (ISBN 0-07-069148-7); instr's. manual 10.00 (ISBN 0-07-069147-9). McGraw.
Weisz, Paul B. & Keogh, Richard N. Elements of Biology. 4th ed. 1977. text ed. 27.50 (ISBN 0-07-069137-1, C); instr's manual 13.95 (ISBN 0-07-069139-8); study guide 13.95 (ISBN 0-07-069138-X). McGraw.
Weiten, Wayne. Psychology Applied to Modern Life: Adjustment in the 80's. LC 82-4438. (Psychology Ser.). 550p. 1982. text ed. 22.95 (ISBN 0-534-01205-1). Brooks-Cole.
Weitenkampf, Frank. American Graphic Art. LC 74-6198. 1974. Repr. of 1912 ed. 37.00x (ISBN 0-8103-4020-8). Gale.
Weitenkampf, Frank, ed. Political Caricature in the United States in Separately Published Cartoons. LC 79-137698. (Illus.). 1971. Repr. of 1953 ed. 15.00 o.p. (ISBN 0-87104-506-0, Co-Pub. by Arno). NY Pub Lib.
Weitenkampf, Frank, ed. see New York Public Library.
Weithas, Arthur, ed. Society of Illustrators: The Twenty Fourth Annual of American Illustration. 400p. 1983. text ed. price not set (ISBN 0-942604-00-8). Madison Square.
Weitz, Barbara. Speak English, Wkbk 1. (Speak Eng. Ser.). (Illus.). 64p. (Orig.). 1980. wkbk. 4.95 (ISBN 0-88499-651-4). Inst Mod Lang.
Weitz, C. Introduction to Physical Anthropology & Archaeology. 1979. pap. 16.95 (ISBN 0-13-492637-4); pap. 8.95 study guide & wkbk. (ISBN 0-13-492645-5). P-H.
Weitz, C., jt. auth. see Miller, E.
Weitz, John. Friends in High Places. 384p. 1982. 15.75 (ISBN 0-02-625920-6). Macmillan.
Weitz, Morris. Problems in Aesthetics: An Introductory Book of Readings. 2nd ed. (Illus.). 1970. text ed. 23.95x (ISBN 0-02-425290-5). Macmillan.
Weitz, Shirley. Nonverbal Communication: Readings with Commentary. 2nd ed. (Illus.). 1978. text ed. 13.95x (ISBN 0-19-502447-8); pap. text ed. 13.95x o.p. (ISBN 0-19-502448-6). Oxford U Pr.
--Sex Roles: Biological, Psychological, & Social Foundations. 1977. text ed. 18.95x (ISBN 0-19-502188-6); pap. text ed. 8.95x (ISBN 0-19-502187-8). Oxford U Pr.
Weitzel, Eugene J. Contemporary Pastoral Counseling. 1969. 12.50 o.p. (ISBN 0-685-07624-5, 80741). Glencoe.
Weitzman, Arthur J., ed. see Marana, Giovanni P.
Weitzman, Cay. Minicomputer Systems: Structure, Implementation, & Application. (Illus.). 384p. 1974. 29.95 (ISBN 0-13-584227-1). P-H.
Weitzman, David. My Backyard History Book. (A Brown Paper School Book). (Illus.). 128p. (gr. 4 up). 1975. 9.95 (ISBN 0-316-92901-8); pap. 5.95 (ISBN 0-316-92902-6). Little.
Weitzman, Eliott, jt. ed. see Chase, Michael.
Weitzman, Kurt. Byzantine Book Illumination & Ivories. 326p. 1981. 200.00x (ISBN 0-686-97578-2, Pub. by Variorum). State Mutual Bk.
Weitzman, Leonore. The Marriage Contract. LC 80-69645. 536p. 1982. pap. 8.95 (ISBN 0-02-934610-X). Free Pr.
Weitzmann, Kurt. Classical Heritage in Byzantine & Near Eastern Art. 326p. 1981. 200.00x (ISBN 0-686-97569-3, Pub. by Variorum). State Mutual Bk.
Weitzmann, Kurt & Alibegasvili, Gaiane. Icons. 422p. 1982. 175.00x (ISBN 0-237-45645-1, Pub. by Evans Bros). State Mutual Bk.
Weixlmann, Joe. American Short-Fiction Criticism & Scholarship, 1959-1977: A Checklist. LC 82-75273. xii, 625p. 1982. lib. bdg. 40.00x (ISBN 0-8040-0381-5). Swallow.
Weizman Institute of Science, Rehovot, Israel, Feb. 1980 & Littauer, U. Z. Neurotransmitters & Their Receptors Organization: Proceedings. LC 80-41130. 570p. 1981. 42.00x o.p. (ISBN 0-471-27893-9, Pub. by Wiley-Interscience). Wiley.
Wejman, Jacqueline & St. Peter, Charles. Jams & Jellies. LC 74-4727. (Illus.). 168p. 1975. pap. 4.95 o.p. (ISBN 0-912238-59-3). One Hund One Prods.
Wejman, Jacqueline & St. Peter, Genevieve. The Art of Preserving. rev. ed. 192p. 1983. pap. 7.95 (ISBN 0-89286-212-2). One Hund One Prods.
Wekerle, Gerda R., et al, eds. New Space for Women. (Westview Special Studies in Women in Contemporary Society). 352p. 1980. lib. bdg. 32.00 (ISBN 0-89158-775-6); pap. 15.00 (ISBN 0-86531-339-3). Westview.
Wel, Robert. Small Appliance Repair: Heater Types. (Audel Mini-Guide Ser.). 96p. 1975. pap. 0.99 o.p. (ISBN 0-672-23801-2, 23801). Audel.
Welander, David, jt. auth. see Verey, David.
Welanetz, Diana von see Von Welanetz, Diana & Von Welanetz, Paul.
Welanetz, Paul von see Von Welanetz, Diana & Von Welanetz, Paul.
Welbon, Guy & Yocum, Glenn, eds. Festivals in South India & Sri Lanka. 1982. 25.00X (ISBN 0-8364-0900-0, Pub.by Manohar India). South Asia Bks.
Welborn, David M. Governance of Federal Regulatory Agencies. LC 77-8012. 1977. 12.50x (ISBN 0-87049-216-0). U of Tenn Pr.
Welborn, Don. On the Subject of Tongues: From the New Testament. 56p. pap. 0.50 (ISBN 0-937396-48-6). Walterick Pubs.
Welborn, Jean C., compiled by. This Is the Day the Lord Hath Made. (Illus.). 1980. 3.95 (ISBN 0-8378-2019-7). Gibson.
Welburn, Andrew, tr. see Steiner, Rudolf & Steiner-von Sivers, Marie.
Welburn, Tyler. Structured COBOL: Fundamentals & Style. LC 80-84013. (Illus.). 536p. 1981. pap. text ed. 20.95 (ISBN 0-87484-543-2); instructor's manual avail. Mayfield Pub.
Welby, Lady Victoria. Significs & Language. (Foundation of Semiotics: 5). 140p. 1983. 16.00 (ISBN 90-272-3275-X). Benjamins North Am.
--What Is Meaning? Studies in the Development of Significance. (Foundations of Semiotics Ser.: 2). xx, 321p. 1983. Repr. of 1903 ed. 28.00 (ISBN 90-272-3272-5). Benjamins North Am.
Welch, Adam C. Visions of the End: A Study in Daniel & Revelation. 260p. 1958. Repr. of 1922 ed. 9.95 (ISBN 0-227-67631-9). Attic Pr.
Welch, Alford, ed. Studies in Qur'an & Tafsir. (Thematic Studies). 8.95 (ISBN 0-686-96213-3, 01-24-74). Scholars Pr CA.
Welch, Alford T., ed. see Gatje, Helmut.
Welch, Anthony. Shah 'Abbas & the Arts of Isfahan. LC 73-76938. (Illus.). 152p. 1973. 19.95 o.p. (ISBN 0-87848-041-2). Asia Soc.
Welch, Anthony & Welch, Stuart C. The Arts of the Islamic Book: The Collection of Prince Sadruddin Aga Khan. LC 82-71587. (Illus.). 1982. 49.50x (ISBN 0-8014-1548-9); pap. 24.95 (ISBN 0-8014-9882-1). Cornell U Pr.
Welch, Chris. Hendrix: A Biography. LC 73-83767. (Illus.). 1972. pap. 5.95 (ISBN 0-8256-3901-8, 030901, Quick Fox). Putnam Pub Group.
Welch, Claude E., Jr. Anatomy of Rebellion. LC 80-19094. 356p. 1980. lib. bdg. 44.50x (ISBN 0-87395-441-6); pap. text ed. 14.95x (ISBN 0-87395-457-2). State U NY Pr.
Welch, Claude E., Jr., ed. Civilian Control of the Military: Theory & Cases From Developing Countries. LC 76-40278. 1976. 39.50x (ISBN 0-87395-348-7). State U NY Pr.
Welch, David. Propaganda & the German Cinema, 1933-1945. (Illus.). 420p. 1983. 34.00 (ISBN 0-19-822598-9). Oxford U Pr.
Welch, E. B. Ecological Effects of Waste Water. LC 78-11371. 1980. 42.50 (ISBN 0-521-22495-0); pap. 14.95 (ISBN 0-521-29525-4). Cambridge U Pr.
Welch, E. Parl. Edmund Husserl's Phenomenology. 1939. pap. 24.50x (ISBN 0-686-51375-4). Elliots Bks.
Welch, Edwin, ed. Two Calvinistic Methodist Chapels 1743-1811: The London Tabernacle & Spa Fields Chapel. 1975. 50.00x (ISBN 0-686-96610-4, Pub by London Rec Soc England). State Mutual Bk.
Welch, Harry, ed. see Transamerica Delaval Inc.
Welch, Holmes H. Buddhist Revival in China. LC 68-15645. (East Asian Ser: No. 33). (Illus.). 1968. 20.00x o.p. (ISBN 0-674-08570-1). Harvard U Pr.
Welch, James. The Death of Jim Loney. LC 79-1713. 1979. 10.53i (ISBN 0-06-014588-9, HarpT). Har-Row.
Welch, Jeffrey, jt. auth. see Olmsted, John C.
Welch, Jennifer. Promoting the Necessity to Read. 1980. write for info. (ISBN 0-89992-504-9); pap. 2.86 (ISBN 0-89992-505-7). MT Coun Indian.
Welch, John. Spiritual Pilgrims: Carl Jung & Teresa of Avila. LC 82-80164. 208p. 1982. 7.95 (ISBN 0-8091-2454-8). Paulist Pr.
Welch, Joseph N., et al. The Constitution: The Story of the Constitution & the Men Who Made It. new ed. LC 56-10288. (Illus.). 114p. 1976. 9.95 (ISBN 0-910220-73-5). Berg.
Welch, Julia C. Gold Town to Ghost Town: The Story of Silver City, Idaho. LC 82-60053. (Illus.). 1982. 7.95 (ISBN 0-89301-087-1). U Pr of Idaho.
Welch, June R. Historic Sites of Texas. LC 72-90435. (Vignettes of Texas Ser.). 1972. 17.95 (ISBN 0-912854-03-0). GLA Pr.
--Riding Fence. (Illus.). 270p. 1982. 18.95 (ISBN 0-912854-12-X). GLA Pr.
Welch, K. R. Herpetology of Europe & Southwest Asia: A Checklist & Bibliography of the Orders Amphisbaenia, Sauria & Serpentes. LC 82-12645. 1983. lib. bdg. write for info. (ISBN 0-89874-533-0). Krieger.
Welch, Louise. Orage With Gurdjieff in America. 200p. (Orig.). pap. 9.95 (ISBN 0-7100-9016-1). Routledge & Kegan.
Welch, Martha M. Pudding & Pie. (Illus.). (gr. k-3). 1968. PLB 3.64 o.p. (ISBN 0-698-30287-7, Coward). Putnam Pub Group.
--Saucy. (Illus.). (gr. k-3). 1968. PLB 3.69 o.p. (ISBN 0-698-30302-4, Coward). Putnam Pub Group.
--Will That Wake Mother? LC 82-45377. (Illus.). 32p. (ps-1). 1982. PLB 8.95 (ISBN 0-396-08090-1). Dodd.
Welch, Martin H., jt. ed. see Guenter, Clarence A.
Welch, Mary. Nous Valons Plus...Passereaux. Date not set. 1.75 (ISBN 0-8297-0843-X). Life Pubs Intl.
Welch, Mel. Basketball. LC 81-52247. (Intersport Ser.). 13.00 (ISBN 0-382-06513-1). Silver.
Welch, Michael J., ed. Radiopharmaceuticals & Other Compounds Labelled with Short-Lived Radionuclides. LC 76-26764. 1977. pap. text ed. 40.00 (ISBN 0-08-021344-8). Pergamon.
Welch, Paul S. Limnological Methods. (Illus.). 1948. text ed. 24.50 o.p. (ISBN 0-07-069175-4, C). McGraw.
Welch, Paula D. & Lerch, Harold A. History of American Physical Education & Sport. (Illus.). 400p. 1981. 18.75x (ISBN 0-398-04447-3). C C Thomas.
Welch, Raquel. Raquel Welch's Health & Beauty Book. (Illus.). Date not set. pap. price not set. NAL.
Welch, Reuben. Beacon Bible Expositions: Vol. 3, Luke. Greathouse, William M. & Taylor, Willard H., eds. 1974. 6.95 (ISBN 0-8341-0314-1). Beacon Hill.
--To Timothy & All Other Disciples. 104p. 1979. pap. 2.95 (ISBN 0-8341-0590-X). Beacon Hill.
--We Really Do Need Each Other. 112p. 1982. pap. 5.95 (ISBN 0-310-70221-6). Zondervan.
Welch, Richard, jt. auth. see Donsbach, Kurt.
Welch, Richard E., Jr., ed. Imperialists vs Anti-Imperialists: The Debate Over Expansionism in the 1890's. LC 79-174162. (AHM Primary Sources in American History Ser.). 1972. text ed. 12.95x (ISBN 0-88295-792-9); pap. text ed. 6.95x (ISBN 0-88295-793-7). Harlan Davidson.
Welch, Robert. New Americanism. LC 66-26864. 1966. pap. 4.95 (ISBN 0-88279-211-3). Western Islands.
Welch, Robert B. Perceptual Modification: Adapting to Altered Sensory Environments. (Academic Press Series in Cognition & Perception). 1978. 34.50 (ISBN 0-12-741850-4). Acad Pr.
Welch Rugby Union Coaching Staff, ed. The Principles of Rugby Football: A Manual for Coaches & Referees. (Illus.). 208p. 1983. 18.50 (ISBN 0-04-796067-1). Allen Unwin.
Welch, Stuart C. King's Book of Kings: The Shah-nameh of Shah Tahmasp. LC 78-188400. (Illus.). 1972. 35.00 (ISBN 0-87099-028-4). Metro Mus Art.
Welch, Stuart C., jt. auth. see Welch, Anthony.
Welch, Susan & Comer, John, eds. Public Opinion: Its Formation, Measurement, & Impact. LC 74-33580. 541p. 1975. pap. text ed. 13.95 (ISBN 0-87484-295-6). Mayfield Pub.
Welch, W. & Duffield, C. G. Caesar: Invasion of Britain. (Illus.). 97p. pap. text ed. 6.50x (ISBN 0-86516-008-2). Bolchazy-Carducci.
Welch, William W. Strategies for Put & Call Option Trading. (Orig.). 1982. pap. text ed. 13.95 (ISBN 0-316-92922-0). Little.
Welcher, Jeanne K. John Evelyn. (English Authors Ser.). lib. bdg. 14.95 (ISBN 0-8057-1184-8, Twayne). G K Hall.
Welcome, John. Irish Horse-Racing. 1983. 18.95 (ISBN 0-686-38872-0, Pub. by Salem Hse Ltd). Merrimack Bk Serv.
--Irish Horse-Racing: An Illustrated History. 1982. 60.00x (ISBN 0-7171-1046-X, Pub. by Gill & Macmillan Ireland). State Mutual Bk.
--The Sporting World of R. S. Surtees. (Illus.). 1982. 22.50x (ISBN 0-19-211766-1). Oxford U Pr.
Weld, Eloise R. Ring of Gold. LC 78-3543. 1978. 10.00 o.p. (ISBN 0-399-12137-4). Putnam Pub Group.
Weld, John S. Meaning in Comedy: Studies in Elizabethan Romantic Comedy. LC 74-30168. 1975. 39.50x (ISBN 0-87395-278-2). State U NY Pr.

Weld, Wayne. World Directory of Theological Education by Extension. LC 73-8894. (Illus.). 416p. (Orig.). 1973. 5.95x o.p. (ISBN 0-87808-134-8); Supplement, 1976. pap. 1.95x o.p. (ISBN 0-87808-907-1). William Carey Lib.

Welden, Terry A. & Ellingsworth, Huber W. Effective Speech-Communication: Theory in Action. 1970. pap. 8.95x o.p. (ISBN 0-673-05026-2). Scott F.

Welder, G. Chemisorption: An Experimental Approach. Klemperer, D., tr. 1977. text ed. 24.95 o.p. (ISBN 0-408-10611-5). Butterworth.

Weldon and Company. Victorian Crochet. LC 72-81611. Orig. Title: Weldon's Practical Crochet. (Illus.). 224p. 1974. pap. 6.95 (ISBN 0-486-22890-8). Dover.

Weldon, Fay. President's Child. 264p. 1983. 14.95 (ISBN 0-385-18450-6). Doubleday.

Weldon, John. Nineteen Eighties, Decade of Shock. LC 80-81458. 1980. pap. 3.95 (ISBN 0-89051-063-6, Pub. by Master Bks). CLP Pubs.

Weldon, John & Levitt, Zola. Psychic Healing. 1982. pap. 5.95 (ISBN 0-8024-6446-7). Moody.

Weldon, John & Wilson, Clifford. Occult Shock & Psychic Forces. LC 80-81458. 496p. 1980. pap. 8.95 (ISBN 0-89051-065-2, Pub. by Master Bks). CLP Pubs.

Weldy, Norma J. Body Fluids & Electrolytes: A Programmed Presentation. 3rd ed. (Illus.). 132p. 1980. pap. 10.95 (ISBN 0-8016-5383-5). Mosby.

Welfare, Simon & Fairley, John. Mysterious World. (Illus.). 224p. 1980. 17.95 o.s.i. (ISBN 0-89479-075-7); pap. 9.95 o.s.i. (ISBN 0-89104-268-7). A & W Pubs.

Welford, A. T. Skilled Performance: Perceptual & Motor Skills. 1976. pap. 8.95x (ISBN 0-673-07709-8). Scott F.

Welford, A. T., ed. Man Under Stress. LC 74-649301. (Illus.). 140p. 1974. 18.50x (ISBN 0-85066-073-4). Intl Pubns serv.

Welford, A. T. & Houssiadas, L., eds. Contemporary Problems in Perception. 188p. 1975. write for info. (ISBN 0-85066-039-4, Pub. by Taylor & Francis). Intl Pubns Serv.

Welford, W. T. & Winston, Roland. The Optics of Nonimaging Concentrators: Light & Solar Energy. 1978. 38.50 (ISBN 0-12-745350-4). Acad Pr.

Welge, Albert, ed. see Derby, Harry L.

Welk, L. & McGeehan, B. This I Believe. 1979. 8.95 o.p. (ISBN 0-13-919092-9). P-H.

Welk, Martin H. Standard Dictionary of Computers & Information Processing. 2nd, rev. ed. 390p. 1977. 23.95 (ISBN 0-686-98126-X). Telecom Lib.

Welke, H. J. Data Processing in Japan. (Information Research & Resource Reports: Vol. 1). 1982. 42.75 (ISBN 0-444-86379-6). Elsevier.

Welker, Lauren. Fashions to Fit Ginny & Jill. 32p. 1982. pap. 4.95 (ISBN 0-87588-183-1). Hobby Hse.

Welkowitz, Joan, et al. Introductory Statistics for the Behavioral Sciences. 316p. 1976. 15.95 o.p. (ISBN 0-12-743260-4); wkbk. 6.95 o.p. (ISBN 0-12-743267-1); ans. key 3.00 o.p. (ISBN 0-12-743268-X). Acad Pr.

Welkowitz, Walter & Deutsch, Sid. Biomedical Instrument: Theory & Design. 1976. 30.00 (ISBN 0-12-744150-6). Acad Pr.

Wellach, Donald F. Proteins of Animal Cell Plasma Membranes, Vol. 1. 1978. 19.20 (ISBN 0-88831-011-0). Eden Pr.

Welland, Dennis, ed. The United States: A Companion to American Studies. (Illus.). 1979. pap. 19.95x (ISBN 0-416-84120-1). Methuen Inc.

Welland, R. Pocket Guide to... COBOL. 64p. 1982. spiral bdg. 6.95 (ISBN 0-201-07750-7). A-W.

Wellborn, Charles. Twentieth Century Pilgrimage: Walter Lippmann & the Public Philosophy. LC 69-17624. 1969. 15.00x (ISBN 0-8071-0303-9). La State U Pr.

Wellek, Rene. The Attack on Literature & Other Essays. LC 81-21889. x, 200p. 1982. 18.00x (ISBN 0-8078-1512-8); pap. 8.95x (ISBN 0-8078-4090-4). U of NC Pr.

Wellek, Rene, ed. The Divine Legation of Moses, 4 vols. 2nd ed. LC 75-11264. (British Philosophers & Theologians of the 17th & 18th Centuries Ser.: Vol. 62). 1978. Set. lib. bdg. 168.00 o.s.i. (ISBN 0-8240-1813-3); lib. bdg. 42.00 ea. o.s.i. Garland Pub.

Wellek, Rene & Ribeiro, Alvaro, eds. Evidence in Literary Scholarship: Essays in Memory of James Marshall Osborn. (Illus.). 1979. 39.00x (ISBN 0-19-812612-3). Oxford U Pr.

Wellek, Rene, ed. see Collier, Arthur.

Wellek, Rene, ed. see Culverwel, Nathanael.

Wellek, Rene, ed. see Digby, Sir Kenelm.

Wellek, Rene, ed. see Glanville, Joseph.

Wellek, Rene, ed. see Norris, John.

Wellek, Rene, ed. see Sherlock, Thomas.

Wellek, Rene, ed. see Smith, John.

Wellek, Rene, ed. see Stanley, Thomas.

Wellek, Rene, ed. see Toland, John.

Wellek, Rene, ed. see Tucker, Abraham.

Wellek, Rene, ed. see Watson, Richard.

Wellek, Rene, ed. see Woolston, Thomas.

Wellens, Hein J. & Kulbertus, Henri E., eds. What's New in Electrocardiography. 1981. lib. bdg. 57.50 (ISBN 90-247-2450-3); pap. text ed. 38.00 (ISBN 0-686-37016-3). Kluwer Boston.

Weller, B. Helping Sick Children Play. 1982. 25.00x (ISBN 0-7020-0792-7, Pub. by Cassell England). State Mutual Bk.

Weller, Charles & Boylan, Brian R. How to Live with Hypoglycemia. 1977. pap. 2.75 (ISBN 0-515-07089-0). Jove Pubns.

Weller, George. Story of Submarines. (gr. 5-8). 1962. PLB 5.99 o.p. (ISBN 0-394-90402-8). Random.

Weller, J. W. Thermal Energy Conservation: Building & Services Design. 1981. 47.25 (ISBN 0-85334-938-X, Pub. by Applied Sci England). Elsevier.

Weller, John, jt. ed. see Ranger, T. O.

Weller, Leonard. Sociology in Israel. LC 72-849. (Contributions in Sociology: No. 11). 1974. lib. bdg. 29.95x (ISBN 0-8371-6417-6, WES/). Greenwood.

Weller, M. Protein Phosphorylation. (Advanced Biochemistry Ser.). 557p. 1979. 64.00x (ISBN 0-85086-062-8, Pub. by Pion England). Methuen Inc.

Weller, Michael. Five Plays. 240p. 1982. pap. 8.95 (ISBN 0-452-25335-7, Z5335, Plume). NAL.

Weller, R. O. & Navarro, J. Cervos. Pathology of Peripheral Nerves: A Practical Approach. (Postgraduate Pathology Ser.). 1977. 39.95 o.p. (ISBN 0-407-00073-9). Butterworth.

Weller, R. O., et al. Clinical Neuropathology. (Illus.). 350p. 1982. 45.00 (ISBN 0-686-82305-2). Springer-Verlag.

Weller, Richard, ed. Humanistic Education. LC 77-71196. 1977. 24.25x (ISBN 0-8211-2256-8); text ed. 22.00x (ISBN 0-686-82937-9). McCutchan.

Weller, Richard H. Verbal Communication in Instructional Supervision. LC 70-161300. (Illus.). 1971. text ed. 12.95x (ISBN 0-8077-2322-3). Tchrs Coll.

Weller, Robert P. & Guggenheim, Scott E., eds. Power & Protest in the Countryside: Studies of Rural Unrest in Asia, Europe & Latin America. (Duke Press Policy Studies). 220p. 1983. 32.75x (ISBN 0-8223-0483-X). Duke.

Weller, Tom. Minims. 1982. twelve copy pack 35.40 (ISBN 0-395-32939-6); pap. text ed. 2.95. HM.

Weller, Walter J. Assembly Level Programming for Small Computers. LC 75-13436. (Illus.). 304p. 1975. 21.95x (ISBN 0-669-00049-3). Lexington Bks.

Welles, Marcia L., jt. ed. see Servodidio, Mirella.

Welles, Philip. Meet the Southwest Deserts. LC 64-8863. (Illus., Orig.). 1964. 5.95 (ISBN 0-912762-15-2). King.

Welles, Rosalind. Entwined Destinies. (Orig.). 1980. pap. 1.25 o.s.i. (ISBN 0-440-12339-9). Dell.

Welles, Sigourney. The Best Bed & Breakfast in the World. LC 82-83265. 348p. 1983. pap. 9.95 (ISBN 0-914788-65-5). East Woods.

Wellesz, Egon see Abraham, Gerald.

Wellesz, Egon see Abraham, Gerald, et al.

Wellhausen, Julius. The Religio-Political Factions in Early Islam. Ostle, R. C. & Walzer, S. M., trs. 1975. pap. 24.50 (ISBN 0-444-10872-6, North Holland). Elsevier.

Welling, Manfred S. German-English Glossary of Plastics Machinery Terms. 280p. 1981. text ed. 14.00x (ISBN 0-02-949800-7, Pub. by Hanser International). Macmillan.

Welling, Richard. Drawing with Markers. (Illus.). 160p. 1974. 18.50 (ISBN 0-8230-1462-2). Watson-Guptill.

Welling, William. Photography in America: The Formative Years, 1839-1900. LC 77-1983. (Illus.). 1978. 29.95i (ISBN 0-690-01421-X, TYC-T). T Y Crowell.

Wellings, Nick, jt. ed. see Boehm, Klaus.

Wellington, Arthur W. Despatches, Correspondence & Memoranda, 8 vols. LC 5-959. Repr. of 1880 ed. Set. 580.00 (ISBN 0-527-95400-4). Kraus Repr.

--Supplementary Despatches & Memoranda, 15 vols. LC 5-958. Repr. of 1872 ed. Set. 891.00 (ISBN 0-527-95401-2). Kraus Repr.

Wellington, Dorothy G., et al. Cancer Mortality: Environmental & Ethnic Factor. LC 79-10560. 1979. 22.00 (ISBN 0-12-745850-6). Acad Pr.

Wellington, Gladys. Three Pieces of Silver. LC 81-81939. 64p. 1983. 6.95 (ISBN 0-86666-036-4). GWP.

Wellington, Harry H. & Winter, Ralph K. Unions & the Cities. LC 79-179327. (Studies of Unionism in Government). 1972. 18.95 (ISBN 0-8157-9294-8); pap. 7.95 (ISBN 0-8157-9293-X). Brookings.

Wellington, Jean S., ed. Dictionary of Bibliographic Abbreviations Found in the Scholarship of Classical Studies & Related Disciplines. LC 82-21068. 416p. 1983. lib. bdg. 45.00 (ISBN 0-313-23523-6, WLC/). Greenwood.

Wellisch, Hans. Universal Decimal Classification: A Programmed Instruction Course. LC 78-63221. 1970. pap. 3.50 o.p. (ISBN 0-911808-06-X). U of Md Lib Serv.

Wellisch, Hans H. The Conversion of Scripts: Its Nature, History, & Utilization. LC 77-2205. 1978. 49.95x (ISBN 0-471-01620-9, Pub. by Wiley-Interscience). Wiley.

Wellisch, J. B., et al, eds. The Public Library & Federal Policy. LC 73-20302. 1974. lib. bdg. 25.00x (ISBN 0-8371-7334-5, PLF/). Greenwood.

Welliver, Dotsey. I Need You Now, God, While the Grape Juice Is Running All Over the Floor. 1975. 3.95 (ISBN 0-89367-032-4). Light & Life.

--Lord, Why Do They Always Want Hot Dogs? 1976. pap. 3.95 (ISBN 0-89367-004-9). Light & Life.

--Smudgkin Elves & Other Lame Excuses. 81p. 1981. pap. 3.95 (ISBN 0-89367-058-8). Light & Life.

Welliver, Neil, illus. Neil Welliver: Paintings, 1966-1980. LC 81-51612. (Illus.). 96p. (Orig.). 1981. pap. 17.50 (ISBN 0-87451-207-7). U Pr of New Eng.

Wellman, Alice. Africa's Animals: Creatures of a Struggling Land. (Illus.). 192p. (gr. 6 up). 1974. PLB 5.49 o.p. (ISBN 0-399-60838-9). Putnam Pub Group.

--The Baby Elephant's Day. (Illus.). 48p. (gr. 3-6). 1973. PLB 4.97 o.p. (ISBN 0-399-60784-6). Putnam Pub Group.

--Tatu & the Honeybird. (Illus.). (gr. k-3). 1972. PLB 4.89 o.p. (ISBN 0-399-60756-0). Putnam Pub Group.

--The White Sorceress. LC 75-37597. 160p. (gr. 6 up). 1976. 6.95 o.p. (ISBN 0-399-20505-5). Putnam Pub Group.

Wellman, B. Leighton. Technical Descriptive Geometry. 2nd ed. 1957. text ed. 27.95 (ISBN 0-07-069234-3, C); problem layouts 18.50 (ISBN 0-07-069237-8); solns. manual 25.00 (ISBN 0-07-069233-5). McGraw.

Wellman, Carl. Morals & Ethics. 328p. 1975. pap. 10.95x (ISBN 0-673-05013-0). Scott F.

Wellman, D. T., ed. Portraits of White Racism. LC 76-47187. 1977. 34.50 (ISBN 0-521-21514-5); pap. 10.95 (ISBN 0-521-29179-8). Cambridge U Pr.

Wellman, Francis L. Success in Court. xviii, 404p. 1982. Repr. of 1941 ed. lib. bdg. 35.00x (ISBN 0-8377-1326-9). Rothman.

Wellman, John D., jt. auth. see Marans, Robert W.

Wellman, Manley W. After Dark. LC 80-650. (Double D Science Ficion Ser.). 192p. 1980. 10.95 o.p. (ISBN 0-385-15604-9). Doubleday.

Wellman, Manly W. Lonely Vigils. (Illus.). 392p. 1981. 15.00 o.p. (ISBN 0-913796-03-4). Carcosa.

--The Old Gods Waken. (Science Fiction Ser.). 1979. 7.95 o.p. (ISBN 0-385-14807-0). Doubleday.

--Rebel Boast: First at Bethel, Last at Appomattox. LC 73-19298. 317p. 1974. Repr. of 1956 ed. lib. bdg. 21.00x (ISBN 0-8371-7316-7, WERB). Greenwood.

Wellmuth, John. Nature & Origins of Scientism. (Aquinas Lecture). 1944. 7.95 (ISBN 0-87462-108-9). Marquette.

Wellner, Cathryn J. Witness to War: A Thematic Guide to Young Adult Literature on World War II, 1965-1981. LC 82-5600. 287p. 1982. 17.00 (ISBN 0-8108-1552-4). Scarecrow.

Wells, A. Building Stereo Speakers. (McGraw-Hill VTX Ser.). 224p. 1983. 9.95 (ISBN 0-07-069251-3, GB). McGraw.

Wells, A., jt. auth. see Northedge, F. S.

Wells, A. F. Models in Structural Inorganic Chemistry. 1970. text ed. 12.95x (ISBN 0-19-501278-X); pap. 7.95x o.p. (ISBN 0-19-501279-8). Oxford U Pr.

--Three-Dimensional Nets & Polyhedra. LC 76-49089. 1977. 63.00x (ISBN 0-471-02151-2, Pub. by Wiley-Interscience). Wiley.

Wells, Alan. Contemporary Sociological Theories: Text-Reader. LC 77-16597. 1978. pap. text ed. 11.95x o.p. (ISBN 0-673-16296-6). Scott F.

Wells, Andy J. Audio Servicing: Theory & Practice. 1st ed. (Illus.). 240p. (Orig.). 1980. pap. text ed. 13.50 (ISBN 0-07-069246-7, G); lab manual 7.95 (ISBN 0-07-069247-5); instr's. manual 2.00 (ISBN 0-07-069248-3). McGraw.

Wells, Anna M. Miss Marks & Miss Wooley. 1978. 10.95 o.p. (ISBN 0-395-25724-7). HM.

Wells, Bob. Five-Yard Fuller's Mighty Model T. (Putnam Sports Shelf). (Illus.). (gr. 5-7). 1970. 5.95 o.p. (ISBN 0-399-20079-7). Putnam Pub Group.

Wells, C. Cleft Palate & Its Associated Speech Disorders. (Speech Ser.). 1971. text ed. 29.95 (ISBN 0-07-069243-2, C). McGraw.

Wells, C. H. Introduction to Molecular Photochemistry. 1972. pap. 13.95x (ISBN 0-412-11250-7, Pub. by Chapman & Hall). Methuen Inc.

Wells, Carolyn. Carolyn Wells' Book of American Limericks. LC 77-174140. (Tower Bks). (Illus.). viii, 91p. 1972. Repr. of 1925 ed. 34.00x (ISBN 0-8103-3929-3). Gale.

--Parody Anthology. LC 67-14060. 1968. Repr. of 1904 ed. 30.00x (ISBN 0-8103-3224-8). Gale.

--The Seven Ages of Childhood. (Illus.). 12p. (Orig.). 1982. pap. 2.50 (ISBN 0-914676-98-9, Pub. by Envelope Bks). Green Tiger Pr.

--Whimsey Anthology. 1906. pap. 2.00 o.p. (ISBN 0-486-20195-3). Dover.

--A Whimsey Anthology. LC 73-5528. xiv, 221p. 1976. Repr. of 1963 ed. 30.00x (ISBN 0-8103-4115-8). Gale.

Wells, Charles, et al, eds. Scientific Foundations of Surgery. 2nd ed. LC 73-93018. (Illus.). 820p. 1974. text ed. 42.50 o.p. (ISBN 0-7216-9208-7). Saunders.

Wells, Charles E. Dementa. 2nd ed. LC 77-7103. (Contemporary Neurology Ser.: No. 15). (Illus.). 1977. text ed. 27.50x o.p. (ISBN 0-8036-9221-8). Davis Co.

Wells, Dare A. Lagrangian Dynamics. (Schaum's Outline Ser). (Orig.). 1967. pap. 8.95 (ISBN 0-07-069258-0, SP). McGraw.

Wells, David. Can You Solve These? 80p. 1983. pap. 3.95 (ISBN 0-13-114074-4). P-H.

Wells, David A., ed. see Timbs, John.

Wells, David F. The Search for Salvation. Marshall, I. Howard, ed. LC 78-13799. (Issues in Contemporary Theology Ser.). 1978. pap. 3.95 o.p. (ISBN 0-87784-706-1). Inter-Varsity.

Wells, Dean W., ed. The Great American Politicians' Cookbook. (Illus.). 264p. 1982. pap. 11.95 (ISBN 0-916242-18-8). Yoknapatawpha.

Wells, Elaine F. Run, Ellen, Run. (YA) 1978. 6.95 (ISBN 0-685-87348-X, Avalon). Bouregy.

Wells, Ellen B., ed. Horsemanship: A Guide to Information Sources. LC 79-16046. (Sports, Games, & Pastimes Information Guide Ser.: Vol. 4). 1979. 42.00x (ISBN 0-8103-1444-4). Gale.

Wells, George. Taurus. 1982. pap. 2.50 (ISBN 0-451-11553-8, AE1553, Sig). NAL.

Wells, Gordon, et al. Learning Through Interaction: The Study of Language Development. LC 80-41113. (Language at Home & at School Ser.). (Illus.). 200p. 1981. text ed. 44.50 (ISBN 0-521-23774-2); pap. text ed. 12.95 (ISBN 0-521-28219-5). Cambridge U Pr.

Wells, H. G. The Complete Short Stories. LC 79-145813. 1971. 14.95 o.p. (ISBN 0-312-15855-6, C4000). St Martin.

--Early Writings in Science & Science Fiction. Philmus, Robert M. & Hughes, David, eds. LC 73-91673. 1975. 28.50x (ISBN 0-520-02679-9). U of Cal Pr.

--The Island of Dr. Moreau. (Special Movie Edition). (RL 8). 1977. pap. 1.25 o.p. (ISBN 0-451-07495-5, Y7495, Sig). NAL.

--Selected Short Stories. 1979. pap. 3.95 (ISBN 0-14-001310-5). Penguin.

--Seven Science Fiction Novels. (gr. 9 up). 15.00 (ISBN 0-486-20264-X). Dover.

--Things to Come. 184p. 1975. Repr. of 1935 ed. lib. bdg. 12.50 (ISBN 0-8398-2318-5, Gregg). G K Hall.

--The Time Machine. (Orig.). (gr. 7-12). 1982. pap. 1.95 (ISBN 0-553-21078-5). Bantam.

--Time Machine. 1975. pap. 2.50x (ISBN 0-460-01915-5, Evman). Biblio Dist.

--The War of the Worlds. (gr. 3 up). Date not set. price not set (ISBN 0-448-41106-7, G&D). Putnam Pub Group.

--War of the Worlds & the Invisible Man. 1983. pap. price not set. WSP.

--The War of the Worlds & the Time Machine. pap. 1.95 o.p. (ISBN 0-385-08274-6, Dolp). Doubleday.

Wells, Helen. Cherry Ames: The Case of the Dangerous Remedy. (gr. 6 up). 1978. pap. 1.25 o.p. (ISBN 0-448-14851-X, G&D). Putnam Pub Group.

--Cherry Ames: The Case of the Forgetful Patient. (gr. 6 up). 1978. pap. 1.25 o.p. (ISBN 0-448-14850-1, G&D). Putnam Pub Group.

--Cherry Ames: The Mystery of Rogue's Cave. (gr. 6 up). 1978. pap. 1.25 o.p. (ISBN 0-448-14852-8, G&D). Putnam Pub Group.

Wells, Helen & Tatham, Julie. Cherry Ames: Army Nurse. (Cherry Ames Ser.: Vol. 3). (gr. 4-8). 1944. 2.95 o.p. (ISBN 0-448-09703-6, G&D). Putnam Pub Group.

--Cherry Ames at Hilton Hospital. (Cherry Ames Ser.: Vol. 20). (Illus.). (gr. 4-8). 1959. 2.95 o.p. (ISBN 0-448-09720-6, G&D). Putnam Pub Group.

--Cherry Ames at Spencer. (Cherry Ames Ser.: Vol. 10). (gr. 4-8). 1949. 2.95 o.p. (ISBN 0-448-09710-9, G&D). Putnam Pub Group.

--Cherry Ames: Boarding School Nurse. (Cherry Ames Ser.: Vol. 17). (gr. 4-8). 1956. 2.95 o.p. (ISBN 0-448-09717-6, G&D). Putnam Pub Group.

--Cherry Ames: Island Nurse. (Cherry Ames Ser.: Vol. 21). (Illus.). (gr. 4-8). 1960. 2.95 o.p. (ISBN 0-448-09721-4, G&D). Putnam Pub Group.

--Cherry Ames: Mountaineer Nurse. (Cherry Ames Ser.: Vol. 12). (gr. 4-8). 1951. 2.95 o.p. (ISBN 0-448-09712-5, G&D). Putnam Pub Group.

--Cherry Ames: Night Supervisor. (Cherry Ames Ser.: Vol. 11). (gr. 4-8). 1950. 2.95 o.p. (ISBN 0-448-09711-7, G&D). Putnam Pub Group.

--Cherry Ames: Private Duty Nurse. (Cherry Ames Ser.: Vol. 7). (gr. 4-8). 1946. 2.95 o.p. (ISBN 0-448-09707-9, G&D). Putnam Pub Group.

--Cherry Ames: Rural Nurse. (Cherry Ames Ser.: Vol. 22). (gr. 4-8). 1961. 2.95 o.p. (ISBN 0-448-09722-2, G&D). Putnam Pub Group.

--Cherry Ames: Staff Nurse. (Cherry Ames Ser.: Vol. 23). (gr. 4-8). 2.95 o.p. (ISBN 0-448-09723-0, G&D). Putnam Pub Group.

--Cherry Ames: Veterans' Nurse. (Cherry Ames Ser.: Vol. 6). (gr. 4-8). 1946. 2.95 o.p. (ISBN 0-448-09706-0, G&D). Putnam Pub Group.

Wells, Helen F., jt. ed. see Clewlow, C. William, Jr.

Wells, Henry & Gowda, H. H. Style & Structure in Shakespeare. 1979. text ed. 14.75x (ISBN 0-7069-0711-6). Humanities.

Wells, Henry W. Elizabethan & Jacobean Playwrights. LC 74-12953. 327p. 1975. Repr. of 1939 ed. lib. bdg. 20.25x (ISBN 0-8371-7777-4, WEJP). Greenwood.

--Introduction to Wallace Stevens. LC 75-45395. 218p. 1976. Repr. of 1964 ed. lib. bdg. 20.75x (ISBN 0-8371-8736-2, WEWS). Greenwood.

Wells, Henry W., tr. Ancient Poetry from China, Japan, & India. LC 68-9365. viii, 464p. 1968. 19.95x o.s.i. (ISBN 0-87249-132-3). U of SC Pr.

Wells, Herbert G. The World of William Clissold: A Novel at a New Angle, 2 vols. LC 72-601. 1926. Repr. lib. bdg. 25.00x o.p. (ISBN 0-8371-6338-2, WEWC). Greenwood.

Wells, J. I. An Essay on War. LC 70-137560. (The Peace Movement in America Ser). 52p. 1972. Repr. of 1808 ed. lib. bdg. 9.95x (ISBN 0-89198-091-1). Ozer.

Wells, Jesse. A History of Prostitution in Western Europe. (Illus.). 104p. 1982. pap. write for info. (ISBN 0-915288-48-6). Shameless Hussy.

Wells, Joan. Downwind from Nobody. LC 78-14882. 1978. 9.95 o.p. (ISBN 0-88266-144-2). Garden Way Pub.

Wells, Karen M. Building Solar: How the Professional Builder is Making Solar Construction Work. (Illus.). 275p. 1983. text ed. 29.95 (ISBN 0-8436-0139-6). CBI Pub.

Wells, Ken & Weston, Paul. Criminal Law. LC 77-17489. (Illus.). 1978. text ed. 21.95x o.p. (ISBN 0-673-16300-8). Scott F.

Wells, Kenneth, jt. auth. see Weston, Paul B.

Wells, Kenneth M. & Weston, Paul B. Criminal Evidence for Police. 2nd ed. (Criminal Justice Ser.). (Illus.). 352p. 1976. 21.95 (ISBN 0-13-193391-4). P-H.

--Criminal Procedure & Trial Practice. LC 76-16101. (Illus.). 1977. 21.95 (ISBN 0-13-193342-6). P-H.

Wells, Kenneth M., jt. auth. see Weston, Paul B.

Wells, Lawrence, ed. see Cook, Ben.

Wells, Lee. Destiny's Star. 1982. pap. 2.50 (ISBN 0-451-11414-0, AE1414, Sig). NAL.

--Starbriar. (Orig.). 1980. pap. 2.25 o.p. (ISBN 0-451-09202-3, E9202, Sig). NAL.

Wells, Leigh. Leigh Wells' Ballet Body Book. LC 82-9202. 1982. 14.95 (ISBN 0-672-52701-4). Bobbs.

Wells, Leon W. The Death Brigade. LC 77-89068. 1978. pap. 4.95 (ISBN 0-8052-5000-X, Pub by Holocaust Library). Schocken.

--The Death Brigade. 320p. pap. 5.95 (ISBN 0-686-95059-3). ADL.

Wells, Leslie, ed. see Hospital, Janette.

Wells, Lloyd A. Psychiatric Nursing Handbook. (Allied Health Professions Handbks.). 1983. 14.50 (ISBN 0-87527-295-9). Green.

Wells, Louis T. & Vernon, Raymond. Manager in the International Economy. 4th ed. (Illus.). 1981. text ed. 24.95 (ISBN 0-13-549550-4). P-H.

Wells, Louis T., Jr. Third World Multinationals: The Rise of Foreign Investment from Developing Countries. 272p. 1983. 25.00 (ISBN 0-262-23113-1). MIT Pr.

Wells, Louis T., Jr., jt. auth. see Smith, David N.

Wells, M. Gentle Architecture. 192p. 1982. pap. 8.95 (ISBN 0-07-069244-0, P&RB). McGraw.

Wells, M. C., jt. ed. see Dean, G. W.

Wells, M. J. Octopus: Physiology & Behaviour of an Advanced Invertebrate. 1978. 58.00x (ISBN 0-412-13260-5, Pub. by Chapman & Hall). Methuen Inc.

Wells, Madeline & Williamson, Jane. So You Want to See A Solar Building? A Tour Guide for Northern New Mexico. (Illus.). 128p. 1982. pap. 6.95 (ISBN 0-942372-04-2). NMSEA.

Wells, Malcolm. Gentle Architecture. (Illus.). 192p. 1981. 24.95 (ISBN 0-07-069245-9, P&RB). McGraw.

Wells, Malcolm, jt. auth. see Anderson, Bruce.

Wells, Malcolm, jt. auth. see Spetgang, Tilly.

Wells, Malcolm, compiled by. Notes from the Energy Underground. 128p. 1980. 10.95 o.p. (ISBN 0-442-25697-3). Van Nos Reinhold.

Wells, Marjorie. Micronesian Handicraft Book of the Trust Territory of the Pacific Islands. (Illus.). 1982. 7.00 (ISBN 0-8062-1781-2). Carlton.

Wells, Norman. Metaphysical Disputation, XXXI, De Ento Finito, on Finite Being. Date not set. price not set o.p. Marquette.

Wells, Norman J., tr. Francis Suarez: On the Essence of Finite Being as Such, on the Existence of the Essence & Their Distinction. LC 82-81397. (Mediaeval Philosophical Texts in Translation). 312p. Date not set. pap. 24.95 (ISBN 0-87462-224-7). Marquette.

Wells, Oliver, et al. Physical Electron Microscope, Vol. 1. Date not set. price not set (ISBN 0-442-29267-8). Van Nos Reinhold.

Wells, Oliver G. Scanning Electron Microscopy. (Illus.). 480p. 1974. 39.50 o.p. (ISBN 0-07-069253-X, P&RB). McGraw.

Wells, P. N. & Woodcock, J. P. Computers in Ultrasonic Diagnostics. 94p. 1980. pap. 37.95x (ISBN 0-471-27889-0, Pub. by Wiley-Interscience). Wiley.

Wells, P. S. Culture Contact & Culture Change. LC 80-40212. (New Studies in Archaeology). (Illus.). 195p. 1981. 27.95 (ISBN 0-521-22808-5). Cambridge U Pr.

Wells, Peter. The American War of Independence. (Illus.). 1978. pap. text ed. 9.50x (ISBN 0-8419-6208-1). Holmes & Meier.

Wells, Peter S. Rural Economy in the Early Iron Age: Excavations at Hascherkeller, 1978-1981. (American School of Prehistoric Research Bulletin: No. 36). (Illus.). 115p. 1983. pap. text ed. 20.00x (ISBN 0-87365-539-7). Peabody Harvard.

Wells, R. Solid State Power Rectifiers. 186p. 1982. text ed. 24.50 (ISBN 0-246-11751-6, Pub. by Granada England). Renouf.

Wells, R. A. Geophysics of Mars. (Developments in Solar System & Space Science Ser.: Vol. 4). 1979. 93.75 (ISBN 0-444-41802-4). Elsevier.

Wells, R. G., jt. auth. see Fredericks, Lee.

Wells, Reuben F. With Caesar's Legions. LC 60-16709. (Illus.). (gr. 7-11). 1951. 8.00x (ISBN 0-8196-0110-1). Biblo.

Wells, Richard L., jt. auth. see Doss, Helen.

Wells, Richard S., jt. auth. see Grossman, Joel B.

Wells, Robert. Science-Hobby Book of Bird Watching. rev. ed. LC 62-11632. (Science Hobby Bks). (Illus.). (gr. 5-10). 1968. PLB 4.95g (ISBN 0-8225-0553-3). Lerner Pubns.

--Science-Hobby Book of Weather Forecasting. rev. ed. LC 62-11631. (Science Hobby Bks). (Illus.). (gr. 5-10). 1968. PLB 4.95g (ISBN 0-8225-0559-2). Lerner Pubns.

--The Winter's Task. 63p. (Orig.). 1979. pap. 7.95x (ISBN 0-85635-210-1, Pub. by Carcanet New England Pr). Humanities.

Wells, Robert, ed. see Virgil.

Wells, Robin H. Spenser's Faerie Queene & the Cult of Elizabeth. LC 82-11568. 208p. 1982. text ed. 27.50x (ISBN 0-389-20324-6). B&N Imports.

Wells, Roe, ed. The Microcirculation in Medicine. 1973. 61.00 (ISBN 0-12-743750-9). Acad Pr.

Wells, Roger. Insurrection: The British Experience, 1795-1803. 256p. 1982. text ed. 30.00x (ISBN 0-86299-019-X, 40155, Pub. by Sutton England). Humanities.

Wells, Roger, Jr., compiled by. English-Eskimo & Eskimo-English Vocabularies. Kelly, John W., tr. LC 82-51153. 72p. 1982. pap. 6.95 (ISBN 0-8048-1403-1). C E Tuttle.

Wells, Ronald V. Spiritual Disciplines for Everyday Living. (Orig.). 1982. text ed. 13.95 (ISBN 0-915744-32-5); pap. 8.95 (ISBN 0-915744-31-7). Character Res.

Wells, Rosemary. None of the Above. (gr. 7 up). 1975. pap. 1.75 o.p. (ISBN 0-380-00554-9, 52613). Avon.

Wells, Rufus M. Invertebrate Respiration. (Studies in Biology: No. 127). 72p. 1980. pap. text ed. 8.95 (ISBN 0-7131-2806-2). E Arnold.

Wells, S., ed. see Muir, Kenneth.

Wells, S. E., jt. auth. see Spencer, T. J.

Wells, Sara J., et al. Manual of Cardiovascular Assessment. 1982. pap. text ed. 16.95 (ISBN 0-8359-4233-3). Reston.

Wells, Stanley. Literature & Drama: With Special Reference to Shakespeare & His Contemporaries. (Concepts of Literature Ser.). 1970. 14.95x (ISBN 0-7100-6909-X); pap. 7.95 (ISBN 0-7100-6910-3). Routledge & Kegan.

--Shakespeare: An Illustrated Dictionary. (Illus.). 1978. 17.95x (ISBN 0-19-520054-3). Oxford U Pr.

Wells, Stanley, ed. Shakespeare in the Nineteenth Century. LC 49-1639. (Shakespeare Survey Ser.: No. 35). (Illus.). 206p. 1982. 39.50 (ISBN 0-521-24752-7). Cambridge U Pr.

Wells, Stanley, jt. ed. see Muir, Kenneth.

Wells, Stepen G., ed. Origin & Evolution of North American Deserts. (Publications of the Committee on Desert & Arid Zones Ser.). (Illus.). 128p. 19.95x (ISBN 0-8263-0605-5, O-11); pap. 9.95x (ISBN 0-8263-0606-3, O-12). U of NM Pr.

Wells, Stuart. Instructional Technology in Developing Countries: Decision Making Processes in Education. LC 76-24371. (Illus.). 1976. 27.95 o.p. (ISBN 0-275-23750-8). Praeger.

Wells, Susan. Mend Your Own China & Glass. (Illus.). 80p. 1976. 11.50 (ISBN 0-7135-1875-8); pap. 8.95 o. p. (ISBN 0-7135-1883-9). Transatlantic.

Wells, Thelma. Aging & Health Promotion. LC 81-12734. 232p. 1981. text ed. 26.95 (ISBN 0-89443-398-9). Aspen Systems.

Wells, Theodora. Keeping Your Cool Under Fire: Communicating Non-Defensively. Manley, Robert G., ed. (Illus.). 1979. 19.95 (ISBN 0-07-069250-5). McGraw.

Wells, Walter. Communications in Business. 3rd ed. (Business Ser.). 553p. 1981. text ed. 21.95x (ISBN 0-534-00943-3). Kent Pub Co.

Wells, Warner, ed. & tr. see Hachiya, Michihiko.

Wells, Warre B., tr. see Vercel, Roger.

Wells, William D., jt. auth. see Reynolds, Fred D.

Wells, William W. & Eisenberg, Frank, Jr., eds. Cyclitols & Phosphoinositides. (National Institute of Arthritis, Metabolism, & Digestive Diseases). 1978. 51.00 (ISBN 0-12-741750-8). Acad Pr.

Wellsfry, Norval L., jt. auth. see Ames, Michael D.

Wellstead, Graham. Ferrets & Ferreting. (Illus.). 192p. 1981. 12.95 (ISBN 0-87666-938-0, PS-792). TFH Pubns.

Wellstone, Paul D. How the Rural Poor Got Power: Narrative of a Grass-Roots Organizer. LC 77-22109. 240p. 1978. 14.00x (ISBN 0-87023-249-5); pap. text ed. 7.00x (ISBN 0-87023-139-1). U of Mass Pr.

Wellstone, Paul D., jt. auth. see Casper, Barry M.

Wellwarth, George E. Spanish Underground Drama. LC 76-39288. (Illus.). 188p. 1972. 18.95x (ISBN 0-271-01154-8). Pa St U Pr.

Wellwarth, George E., jt. ed. see Benedikt, Michael.

Wellwarth, George E., jt. ed. & tr. see Benedikt, Michael & Wellwarth, George E.

Welmers, William E. Grammar of Vai. (Publ. in Linguistics Ser: Vol. 84). 1977. pap. 15.50x (ISBN 0-520-09555-3). U of Cal Pr.

Wels, Byron. Personal Computers: What They Are & How to Use Them. (Illus.). 1978. 12.95 o.p. (ISBN 0-13-657874-8, Spec); pap. 5.95 o.p. (ISBN 0-13-657866-7). P-H.

Wels, Byron G. Here Is Your Hobby: Amateur Radio. (Here Is Your Hobby Ser.). (Illus.). (gr. 5-11). 1968. PLB 5.29 o.p. (ISBN 0-399-60241-0). Putnam Pub Group.

--Here Is Your Hobby: Candlemaking. (Here Is Your Hobby Ser.). (Illus.). (gr. 6-8). 1977. PLB 4.69 o.p. (ISBN 0-399-61059-6). Putnam Pub Group.

--Here Is Your Hobby: Magic. (Here Is Your Hobby Ser.). (Illus.). (gr. 5-9). 1967. PLB 5.29 o.p. (ISBN 0-399-60250-X). Putnam Pub Group.

--Newer & Better Dog Obedience Training. (Illus.). (gr. 5-8). 1974. 5.95 o.p. (ISBN 0-399-20401-6). Putnam Pub Group.

Welsby, Derek A., jt. auth. see Martland, Richard E.

Welsch, Glenn A. Cases in Profit Planning & Control. 1970. pap. text ed. 12.95 (ISBN 0-13-118471-7). P-H.

Welsch, Glenn A. & Zlatkovich, Charles T. Intermediate Accounting. 6th ed. (Illus.). 1982. 29.95x (ISBN 0-256-02598-3); pap. 7.50x working papers vol. 1 (ISBN 0-256-02601-7); pap. 7.50x (ISBN 0-256-02602-5); pap. 7.50x (ISBN 0-256-02599-1); pap. 6.95x (ISBN 0-256-02600-9); 6.95. Irwin.

Welsch, Roger L. Omaha Tribal Myths & Tricksters Tales. LC 82-75752. x, 285p. 1981. 21.95x (ISBN 0-8040-0700-4, SB). Swallow.

Welsch, Ulrike. World I Love to See. 1977. pap. 6.95 o.p. (ISBN 0-395-25400-0). HM.

Welsh, David. Jan Kochanowski. (World Authors Ser.). 15.95 (ISBN 0-8057-2490-7, Twayne). G K Hall.

Welsh, David, jt. auth. see Van Zyl Slabbert, F.

Welsh, David, ed. see Van Der Merwe, H. W.

Welsh, David, tr. see Dygat, Stanislaw.

Welsh, J. & McKeag, R. M. Structured Systems Programming. (Ser. in Computer Science). (Illus.). 1980. text ed. 28.95 (ISBN 0-13-854562-6). P-H.

Welsh, James M. Abel Gance. (Filmmakers Ser.). 1978. lib. bdg. 12.95 (ISBN 0-8057-9254-6, Twayne). G K Hall.

Welsh, James R. Fundamentals of Plant Genetics & Breeding. LC 80-14638. 304p. 1981. text ed. 27.95 (ISBN 0-471-02862-2). Wiley.

Welsh, John & White, Jerry. The Entrepreneur's Master Planning Guide: How to Launch A Successful New Business. (Illus.). 408p. 1983. 24.95 (ISBN 0-13-282814-6); pap. 11.95 (ISBN 0-13-282806-5). P-H.

Welsh, Joseph P., jt. auth. see Koerner, Robert M.

Welsh, Marion E. Tales from a Human Warehouse. LC 77-88592. 1982. pap. 5.95 (ISBN 0-8283-1714-3). Branden.

Welt, Bernard. Serenade. Elmslie, Kenward, ed. (Orig.). 1980. pap. 5.00 (ISBN 0-915990-15-6). Z Pr.

Welt, Suzanne F. Covered Bridges of Oregon. (Illus.). 48p. 1982. 20.00 (ISBN 0-88014-044-5). Mosaic Pr OH.

Welten, Max, ed. Vebreitungsatlas der Farn- und Blutenpflanzen der Schweiz, 2 Vols. 1982. Vol. 1, 704pp. text ed. 48.00; Vol. 2, 752pp. text ed. 98.95 (ISBN 3-7643-1308-0). Birkhauser.

Welter, Barbara. Dimity Convictions: The American Woman in the Nineteenth Century. LC 76-8305. 230p. 1976. 14.95x (ISBN 0-8214-0352-4); pap. 6.95x (ISBN 0-8214-0358-3, 82-82444). Ohio U Pr.

Welter, Mildred P. My Mama Needs Me. LC 82-12654. (Illus.). 32p. (ps-1). 1983. 9.00 (ISBN 0-688-01670-7); PLB 8.59 (ISBN 0-688-01671-5). Lothrop.

Welti, David. Infrared Vapour Spectra. 1970. 83.00x (ISBN 0-471-26080-0, Pub. by Wiley Heyden). Wiley.

Welton, David A. & Mallan, John T. Children & Their World: Strategies for Teaching Social Studies. 2nd ed. 1981. 20.25 (ISBN 0-395-30769-4); Instr's. manual 1.25 (ISBN 0-395-30770-8). HM.

Welton, Pat, jt. auth. see Jones, Ken.

Welty, Don A. & Welty, Dorothy R. The Teacher Aide in the Instructional Team. (Illus.). 1976. pap. text ed. 12.95 (ISBN 0-07-069263-7, G). McGraw.

Welty, Dorothy R., jt. auth. see Welty, Don A.

Welty, Edwin C., Jr., jt. auth. see Axelrod, Herbert R.

Welty, Eudora. The Golden Apples. LC 49-10054. pap. 4.95 (ISBN 0-15-636090-X, Harv). HarBraceJ.

--The Optimist's Daughter. 208p. Date not set. pap. 3.95 (ISBN 0-394-72667-7, Vin). Random.

--Selected Stories. 6.95 (ISBN 0-394-60445-8). Modern Lib.

--Stories of Elizabeth Spencer. 1983. pap. 7.95 (ISBN 0-14-006436-2). Penguin.

Welty, James R. Engineering Heat Transfer, SI Version. LC 78-5179. 1978. text ed. 44.95 (ISBN 0-471-02860-6). Wiley.

Welty, James R., et al. Fundamentals of Momentum, Heat & Mass Transfer. 2nd ed. LC 76-16813. 897p. 1976. text ed. 42.95 (ISBN 0-471-93354-6). Wiley.

Welzenbach, Lanora F. Contracting for Services. 1982. pap. 25.00 (ISBN 0-915164-15-9). Natl Assn Coll.

Wemper, G. Mechanics of Solids with Applications to Thin Bodies. 1982. lib. bdg. 79.00 (ISBN 90-286-0880-X, Pub. by Martinus Nijhoff Netherlands). Kluwer Boston.

Wen, C. Y. & Lee, E. Stanley, eds. Coal Conversion Technology. LC 79-12975. (Energy Science & Technology: No. 2). (Illus.). 1979. text ed. 38.50 (ISBN 0-201-08300-0). A-W.

Wenburg, John R., jt. auth. see Wilmot, William W.

Wenck, Dorothy. Supermarket Nutrition. (Illus.). 336p. 1981. text ed. 16.95 (ISBN 0-8359-7321-2); pap. 10.95 (ISBN 0-8359-7320-4). Reston.

Wende, John R., jt. auth. see Sandberg, Karl C.

Wende, S., et al. Cerebral Magnification Angiography: Physical Basis & Clinical Results. LC 73-22648. (Illus.). 160p. 1974. 88.60 (ISBN 0-387-06651-9). Springer-Verlag.

Wendel, Hermann. Danton: Dictator of the French Revolution. 1935. text ed. 49.50x (ISBN 0-686-83522-0). Elliots Bks.

Wendel, Robert L., jt. auth. see Saucier, Weems A.

Wendel, T. M. & Williams, W. H. Introduction to Data Processing & COBOL. LC 68-31668. (Illus.). 1969. text ed. 16.95 o.p. (ISBN 0-07-069273-4, G); instructor's guide 2.95 o.p. (ISBN 0-07-069274-2). McGraw.

Wendelgard, Von Staden see Staden, Wendelgard von.

Wendell, B. Literary History of America. LC 68-24945. (American History & Americana Ser., No. 47). 1969. Repr. of 1901 ed. lib. bdg. 34.95x (ISBN 0-8383-0257-2). Haskell.

Wendell, Barrett. English Composition. LC 63-12917. 11.00 o.p. (ISBN 0-8044-0831-9). Ungar.

--Literary History of America. LC 68-30589. 1968. Repr. of 1900 ed. 45.00x (ISBN 0-8103-3226-4). Gale.

--Literary History of America. Repr. of 1900 ed. lib. bdg. 15.50x (ISBN 0-8371-0745-8, WELH). Greenwood.

Wendell, Charles. The Evolution of the Egyptian National Image: From Its Origins to Ahmad Lufti al-Sayyid. 1973. 46.50x (ISBN 0-520-02111-8). U of Cal Pr.

Wendell, Hasan & Al-Banna, Hasan. Five Tracts of Hasan Al-Banna: A Selection from the Majmu'at Rasa'il Al-'imam Al-Shahid Hasan Al-Banna. LC 77-83119. (Publications in Near Eastern Studies: Vol. 20). 1978. pap. 15.00x o.s.i. (ISBN 0-520-09584-7). U of Cal Pr.

Wendell, Paul J., ed. Corporate Controller's Manual. LC 80-54167. 1981. 54.00 (ISBN 0-686-76213-4). Warren.

Wendell, Susan, jt. ed. see Copp, David.

Wender, Dorothea, tr. Hesiod & Theognis. (Classics Ser.). 1976. pap. 3.95 (ISBN 0-14-044283-9). Penguin.

Wender, Herbert. The Rise & Fall of Ancient Worlds. LC 75-39330. 300p. 1976. 8.75 o.p. (ISBN 0-8022-2178-5). Philos Lib.

Wender, Irving & Pino, Piero, eds. Organic Syntheses Via Metal Carbonyls, Vol. II. LC 67-13965. 1977. 57.50 o.p. (ISBN 0-471-93367-8, Pub. by Wiley-Interscience). Wiley.

Wender, Paul H. Minimal Brain Dysfunction in Children. LC 77-142142. (Personality Processes Ser). 1971. 35.00x (ISBN 0-471-93362-7). Wiley.

Wender, Paul H. & Klein, Donald F. Mind, Mood, & Medicine: A Guide to the New Biopsychiatry. 1982. pap. 7.95 (ISBN 0-452-00601-5, Mer). NAL.

Wendland, E. H., ed. Sermon Studies on the Gospels. (Series C). 1982. 8.95 (ISBN 0-8100-0149-7, 15NO378). Northwest Pub.

Wendland, W. L. Elliptic Systems in the Plane. (Monographs & Studies Ser.: No. 3). 404p. 1979. text ed. 71.50 (ISBN 0-273-01013-1). Pitman Pub MA.

Wendlandt, W. W. & Collins, L. W., eds. Thermal Analysis. (Benchmark Papers in Analytical Chemistry: Vol. 2). 1976. 56.00 (ISBN 0-12-787750-9). Acad Pr.

Wendlandt, Wesley W. Thermal Methods of Analysis. 2nd ed. LC 73-18444. (Chemical Analysis Ser.: Vol. 19). 528p. 1974. 62.00x (ISBN 0-471-93366-X, Pub. by Wiley-Interscience). Wiley.

Wendlandt, Wesley W., et al. Chemistry: An Audio-Tutorial Approach. 352p. 1975. pap. text ed. 12.95 o.p. (ISBN 0-675-08704-X); media: audiocassettes o.s.i. 160.00 o.p. (ISBN 0-675-08686-8). Merrill.

Wendlinger, Robert M., jt. auth. see Reid, James M.

Wendon, G. W. Aluminium & Bronze Flake Powders. 1982. 159.00x (ISBN 0-686-81701-X, Pub. by Electrochemical Scotland). State Mutual Bk.

Wendorf, Fred & Close, Angela E., eds. Advances in World Archaeology, Vol. I. (Serial Publication Ser.). 1982. 37.50 (ISBN 0-12-039901-6). Acad Pr.

Wendorf, Richard, ed. see Collins, William.

Wendrich, Kenneth A. Essays on Music in American Education & Society. LC 82-45213. (Illus.). 160p. (Orig.). 1982. lib. bdg. 20.25 (ISBN 0-8191-2385-4); pap. text ed. 9.50 (ISBN 0-8191-2386-2). U Pr of Amer.

Wendt, Albert. Pouliuli. LC 80-15158. (Pacific Classics Ser.: No. 8). 147p. 1980. pap. 4.95 (ISBN 0-8248-0728-6). UH Pr.

--Sons for the Return Home. LC 74-191754. 218p. 1974. 11.50x (ISBN 0-582-71718-3). Intl Pubns Serv.

Wendt, F. W., et al, eds. Mechanics of Composite Materials: International Conference on the Mechanics & Chemistry & Solid Propellants. 1970. write for info. o.p (ISBN 0-08-006421-3). Pergamon.

Wendt, Frantz, tr. see Allardt, Erik & Andre, Nils.

Wendt, H. & Frosch, P. J. Clinico-Pharmacological Models for the Assay of Tropical Corticoids. (Illus.). 62p. (Japanese.). 1982. pap. 24.00 (ISBN 3-8055-3686-0). S Karger.

--Klinisch-farmakologische modellen voor het testen van Diflucortolonvalerianaat. (Illus.). 64p. (Dutch.). 1982. pap. 24.00 (ISBN 3-8055-3684-4). S Karger.

--Modelli sperimentali clinico-farmacologici per la valutazione di preparati topici corticosteroidei. (Illus.). 64p. (Ital.). 1982. pap. 24.00 (ISBN 3-8055-3685-2). S Karger.

Wendt, Herbert. In Search of Adam. Cleugh, James, tr. LC 72-14091. (Illus.). 540p. 1973. Repr. of 1956 ed. lib. bdg. 39.75x (ISBN 0-8371-6755-8, WEIS). Greenwood.

Wendt, Jo Ann. Beyond the Dawn. 480p. (Orig.). 1983. pap. 3.50 (ISBN 0-446-30566-9). Warner Bks.

Wendt, Larry, jt. auth. see Robson, Ernest.

Wendt, Lloyd. The Wall Street Journal: The Story of Dow Jones & the Nation's Business Newspaper. (Illus.). 448p. 1982. 16.95 (ISBN 0-528-81116-9). Rand.

Wendt, Lloyd & Kogan, Herman. Give the Lady What She Wants: The Story of Marshall Fields & Company. LC 52-7501. (Illus.). 1979. pap. 5.95 (ISBN 0-89708-020-3). And Bks.

Wendt, N. & Walker, E. N. Real Estate Investment Analysis & Taxation. (Illus.). 1979. 22.95 (ISBN 0-07-069281-5, P&RB). McGraw.

Wendt, Paul F. Housing Policy-the Search for Solutions: A Comparison of the United Kingdom, Sweden, West Germany & the United States since World War II. LC 82-20942. (Publications of the Institute of Business & Economic Research, University of California). xii, 283p. 1983. Repr. of 1962 ed. lib. bdg. 35.00x (ISBN 0-313-23695-X, WEHO). Greenwood.

Wendzel, Robert L. International Politics: Policymakers & Policymaking. LC 80-36681. 476p. 1981. text ed. 20.50 (ISBN 0-471-05046-6). Wiley.

--International Relations: A Policymaker Focus. 2nd ed. LC 79-1215. 1979. text ed. 12.95 (ISBN 0-471-05261-2). Wiley.

Weneser, J. & Lederman, L., eds. Nuclear & Particle Physics, Vol. 1. 220p. 1969. 64.00x (ISBN 0-677-12780-4). Gordon.

--Vienna Conference Fourteen: High Energy Physics, Nineteen Sixty-Eight Supplement to Comments on Nuclear & Particle Physics. 46p. 1969. 18.00 (ISBN 0-677-13860-1). Gordon.

Wen Fong, jt. tr. see Rorex, Robert A.

Weng, Will. The New York Times Crossword Puzzles Omnibus, Vol. 2. 1982. pap. 8.95 (ISBN 0-8129-1018-4). Times Bks.

Wenger, Dennis R., jt. auth. see Bucholz, Robert W.

Wenger, Edna K. Stories I Like to Read. (Illus.). Date not set. 5.65 o.p. (ISBN 0-87813-913-3). Christian Light. Postponed.

Wenger, Eliezer. Brochos Study Guide, Bk. 2. rev. ed. 1980. pap. 1.35 o.p. (ISBN 0-89655-129-6). BRuach HaTorah.

--Chagaynu, Vols. 2-3. 3rd ed. (Illus.). 112p. 1982. text ed. cancelled (ISBN 0-89655-109-1); pap. text ed. 3.50 (ISBN 0-89655-106-7). BRuach HaTorah.

--Chagaynu, Vol. 4. 3rd ed. (Illus.). 96p. (gr. 5 up). 1983. text ed. write for info. (ISBN 0-89655-115-6); pap. text ed. 3.00 (ISBN 0-89655-113-X). Bruach HaTorah.

--Chagaynu: Textbook on the Laws of Rosh HaShonah, Yom Kippur, Sukkos, Vol. 1. rev. 3rd. ed. (Illus.). 96p. (gr. 4 up). 1981. pap. 3.25 (ISBN 0-89655-103-2). Bruach HaTorah.

--Jewish Book of Lists & Summaries, Vol. 2. (gr. 5 up). 1979. pap. 1.25 (ISBN 0-89655-141-5). BRuach HaTorah.

Wenger, J. C. A Lay Guide to Romans. LC 82-15789. 160p. (Orig.). 1983. pap. 8.95 (ISBN 0-8361-3316-1). Herald Pr.

--Separated Unto God. 1955. pap. 8.95 (ISBN 0-8361-1426-4). Herald Pr.

Wenger, John C. Compendio De Historia y Doctrina Menonitas. Suarez, Ernesto, tr. Orig. Title: Glimpses of Mennonite History & Doctrine. (Span). 1960. pap. 2.50x (ISBN 0-8361-1148-6); 3.95x (ISBN 0-8361-1147-8). Herald Pr.

--God's Word Written. LC 66-24292. (Conrad Grebel Lecture Ser.). (Illus., Essays on the nature of biblical revelation, inspiration, & authority). 1966. pap. 5.95 o.p. (ISBN 0-8361-1900-2); pap. 5.95 o.p. (ISBN 0-8361-1900-2). Herald Pr.

Wenger, Nanette K. & Hellerstein, H. K. Rehabilitation of the Coronary Patient. LC 78-12531. 1978. 38.95x (ISBN 0-471-93369-4, Pub. by Wiley Medical). Wiley.

Wenger, Nanette K., et al. Cardiology for Nurses. McIntyre, Mildred C., ed. 1980. text ed. 37.50 (ISBN 0-07-069290-4, C). McGraw.

Wenham, Brian, ed. The Third Age of Broadcasting. 256p. (Orig.). 1983. pap. 5.95 (ISBN 0-571-11981-6). Faber & Faber.

Wenham, Clare, ed. see Stibbs, Alan.

Wenham, David, jt. ed. see France, R. T.

Wenham, David, ed. see Stibbs, Alan.

Wenham, J. W. Christ & the Bible. LC 72-97950. 187p. 1973. pap. 3.95 o.p. (ISBN 0-87784-760-6). Inter-Varsity.

Wenham, John W. Elements of New Testament Greek. 1966. text ed. 7.95x (ISBN 0-521-09842-4); key 3.50 (ISBN 0-521-06769-3). Cambridge U Pr.

Wen-Jei Yang, jt. ed. see Mizushina, Tokuro.

Wenk, Arthur B. Claude Debussy & the Poets. LC 74-82854. 1976. 47.50x (ISBN 0-520-02827-9). U of Cal Pr.

--Claude Debussy & Twentieth Century Music. (Music Ser.). 184p. 1983. lib. bdg. 21.95 (ISBN 0-8057-9454-9, Twayne). G K Hall.

Wenk, Ernst & Harlow, Nora, eds. School Crime & Disruption. LC 78-51102. (Dialogue Bks). 1978. pap. 9.75 (ISBN 0-931364-04-3). Intl Dialogue Pr.

Wenkam, Robert. Hawaii: Kauai, Oahu, Maui, Molokai, Lanai, & Hawaii. LC 72-4186. (Illus.). 160p. 1972. pap. 8.95 (ISBN 0-528-88160-4). Rand.

Wenke, Robert J. Patterns in Prehistory: Mankind's First Three Million Years. (Illus.). 1980. 35.00x (ISBN 0-19-502556-3); pap. text ed. 16.95x (ISBN 0-19-502557-1). Oxford U Pr.

Wen Lang Li. Vocational Education & Social Inequality in the United States. LC 80-6259. (Illus.). 146p. (Orig.). 1982. lib. bdg. 19.99 (ISBN 0-8191-1857-5); pap. text ed. 8.25 (ISBN 0-8191-1858-3). U Pr of Amer.

Wenley, Robert M. Stoicism & Its Influence. LC 63-10288. (Our Debt to Greece & Rome Ser). Repr. of 1930 ed. 15.00x o.p. (ISBN 0-8154-0245-7). Cooper Sq.

Wenner, Manfred W. North Yemen. (Nations of the Contemporary Middle East Ser.). 128p. 1983. lib. bdg. 16.50x (ISBN 0-89158-774-8). Westview.

Wenner, S. Albert. Promotion & Marketing for Shopping Centers. 1980. 35.00 (ISBN 0-913598-13-5). Intl Coun Shop.

Wennerstrom, Mary H. Anthology of Musical Structure & Style. 550p. 1982. pap. 22.95 (ISBN 0-13-038372-4). P-H.

--Anthology of Twentieth Century Music. 1969. pap. 21.95 (ISBN 0-13-038489-5). P-H.

Wennerstrom, Steve, jt. auth. see Chisam, Scott C.

Wenninger, Magnus J. Polyhedron Models. LC 69-10200. (Illus.). 1971. 32.50 (ISBN 0-521-06917-3); pap. 13.95 (ISBN 0-521-09859-9). Cambridge U Pr.

--Spherical Models. LC 78-58806. 1979. 29.95 (ISBN 0-521-22279-6); pap. 11.95 (ISBN 0-521-29432-0). Cambridge U Pr.

Wennrich, Peter. Anglo-American & German Abbreviations in Environmental Protection. 624p. 1979. 60.00x (ISBN 0-89664-096-5, Pub. by K G Saur). Gale.

Wenrich, Ralph C. & Wenrich, William J. Leadership in Administration of Vocational & Technical Education. LC 73-86161. 1974. text ed. 22.95 (ISBN 0-675-08878-X). Merrill.

Wenrich, William J., jt. auth. see Wenrich, Ralph C.

Wensel, Louise. Acupuncture in Medical Practice. (Illus.). 320p. 1980. text ed. 18.95 (ISBN 0-8359-0128-9). Reston.

Wensell, Ulises. Come to Our House: Meet Our Family. LC 78-57836. (ps-2). 1978. 5.95 o.p. (ISBN 0-528-82442-2). Rand.

Wentworth, Anna, jt. auth. see Tucker, James C.

Wentworth, Donald R., jt. auth. see Brue, Stanley L.

Wentworth, Felix & Christopher, Martin, eds. Managing International Distribution. 296p. 1979. text ed. 37.00x (ISBN 0-566-02108-0). Gower Pub Ltd.

Wentworth, Harold & Flexner, Stuart B. Dictionary of American Slang. 2nd ed. LC 75-8644. 766p. 1975. 15.34i (ISBN 0-690-00670-5). T Y Crowell.

Wentworth, Harold, jt. ed. see Chadsey, Charles P.

Wentworth Institute. Laboratory Manual for Microwave Measurements. (Illus.). 1971. pap. text ed. 11.95 (ISBN 0-13-521211-1). P-H.

Wentworth, Josie A. Migraine Prevention Cookbook. LC 82-45277. (Illus.). 216p. 1983. 13.95 (ISBN 0-385-18052-7). Doubleday.

Wentworth, Michael J. James Tissot: Catalogue Raisonne of His Prints. LC 78-59696. (Illus.). 1978. 20.00 (ISBN 0-912964-20-7). Minneapolis Inst Arts.

Wentworth, Patricia. Through the Wall. 1982. pap. 2.25 (ISBN 0-553-22837-4). Bantam.

Wentworth, Sally. Flying High. (Harlequin Presents Ser.). 192p. 1983. pap. 1.95 (ISBN 0-373-10581-9). Harlequin Bks.

Wentworth, Wayne E., jt. auth. see Becker, Ralph S.

Wentworth-Rohr, Ivan. Symptom Reduction Through Clinical Biofeedback. 256p. 1983. text ed. 26.95x (ISBN 0-89885-135-1). Human Sci Pr.

Wentz, Frank M. Principles & Practice of Periodontics: With an Atlas of Treatment. (Illus.). 320p. 1978. photocopy ed. spiral 42.75x (ISBN 0-398-03672-1). C C Thomas.

Wentz, Pat J. & Yarling, James R., eds. Student Teaching Survival Kit. (Illus.). 209p. (Orig.). 1982. pap. text ed. 8.50 incl. wkbk. (ISBN 0-686-37630-7). Gulf Coast Ed.

Wentz, Richard E. The Saga of the American Soul. LC 80-5598. 163p. 1980. pap. text ed. 8.25 (ISBN 0-8191-1150-3). U Pr of Amer.

Wentz, W. Y. The Fairy-Faith in Celtic Countries. LC 77-12812. 1973. text ed. 22.50x o. p. (ISBN 0-87696-057-3); pap. text ed. 12.00x (ISBN 0-391-00773-4). Humanities.

Wentz, Walter B. Marketing. (Illus.). 1979. text ed. 22.95 (ISBN 0-8299-0227-9); study guide 8.95 (ISBN 0-8299-0263-5); instr.' manual avail. (ISBN 0-8299-0581-2). West Pub.

--Marketing Research: Management, Methods, & Cases. 2nd ed. 1979. text ed. 24.95 o.p. (ISBN 0-06-047006-2, CW); instr's manual avail. o.p. (ISBN 0-06-367032-1). B&N Imports.

Wentzell, A. Theorie Zufaelliger Prozesse. (Mathematische Reihe: No. 65). 264p. (Ger.). 1979. 48.40 (ISBN 3-7643-1021-9). Birkhauser.

Wentzell, A. D. A Course in the Theory of Stochastic Processes. 1981. 39.95 (ISBN 0-07-069305-6). McGraw.

Wenzel, Bernice M. & Zeigler, H. Philip, eds. Tonic Functions of Sensory Systems, Vol. 290. (Annals of the New York Academy of Sciences). 435p. 1977. 37.00x (ISBN 0-89072-036-3). NY Acad Sci.

Wenzl, Herman J. Chemical Technology of Wood. 1970. 97.50 (ISBN 0-12-743450-X). Acad Pr.

Wepsiec, Jan. Sociology: An/International Bibliography of Serial Literature 1880-1980. 176p. 1982. 37.00 (ISBN 0-7201-1652-X, Pub. by Mansell England). Wilson.

Werbel, Leslie M., jt. auth. see Thompson, Paul E.

Werblowsky, R. J., jt. ed. see Mving, E.

Werblowsky, Zui. Beyond Tradition & Modernity: Changing Religions in a Changing World. (Jordan Lectures in Comparative Religion, 11th Ser.). 146p. 1976. text ed. 21.00x (ISBN 0-485-17411-1, Athlone Pr). Humanities.

Werchik, Jack. California Preparation & Trial. 3rd ed. LC 74-76804. 693p. 1981. 48.00 (ISBN 0-911110-11-9). Parker & Son.

Were, G. S. & Wilson, D. A. East Africa Through a Thousand Years: A History of the Years A. D. 1000 to the Present Day. LC 78-137451. (gr. 11-12). 1970. text ed. 22.50x (ISBN 0-8419-0062-0, Africana); pap. text ed. 15.50x (ISBN 0-8419-0065-5, Africana). Holmes & Meier.

Were, Gideon. A History of South Africa. LC 73-89025. (Illus.). 188p. 1974. text ed. 19.50x (ISBN 0-8419-0140-6, Africana); pap. text ed. 14.75x (ISBN 0-8419-0141-4). Holmes & Meier.

Werf, Tjeerd van der see Van der Werf, Tjeerd.

Werff, Fred Vander see Wilson, Doug & Vander Werff, Fred.

Werff Der, Van see Van Der Werff, A. & Huls, H.

Werge, Thomas, jt. auth. see Gallagher, Edward J.

Werger, M. J., jt. auth. see Holzner, W.

Werhane, Patricia H., jt. auth. see Donaldson, Thomas.

Werhare, P., jt. auth. see Donaldson, T.

Werkman, Sidney. Bringing up Children Overseas: A Guide for Families. LC 76-43490. 1977. 11.95 o.p. (ISBN 0-465-00759-7). Basic.

Werkmeister, Lucyle. Jemmie Boswell & the London Daily Press, 1785-1795. LC 63-15049. (Orig.). 1963. pap. 4.00 o.p. (ISBN 0-87104-100-6). NY Pub Lib.

Werkmeister, W. H. Kant: The Architectonic & Development of His Philosophy. 267p. 1980. 18.50x (ISBN 0-87548-345-3). Open Court.

Werler, John E., jt. auth. see Tennant, Alan.

Werlich, R., tr. see Andolenko, S.

Werlin, Herbert. Governing an African City: A Study of Nairobi. LC 73-84989. 275p. 1974. text ed. 35.00x (ISBN 0-8419-0139-2, Africana). Holmes & Meier.

Werlin, Mark & Werlin, Marvin. The Savior. 480p. 1981. pap. 2.95 o.s.i. (ISBN 0-440-17748-0). Dell.

Werlin, Mark, jt. auth. see Werlin, Marvin.

Werlin, Marvin & Werlin, Mark. The St. Clair Summer. 1981. pap. 3.50 (ISBN 0-451-11201-6, AE1201, Sig). NAL.

Werlin, Marvin, jt. auth. see Werlin, Mark.

Wermuth, Bendicht, jt. ed. see Weiner, Henry.

Wermuth, Paul G. Bayard Taylor. (United States Authors Ser.). 1973. lib. bdg. 14.95 (ISBN 0-8057-0718-2, Twayne). G K Hall.

Werneck, Tom. Solving the Magic Pyramid: A Guide to the World's Newest Mind Boggler. (Illus.). 114p. 1982. pap. 2.95 (ISBN 0-399-50647-0, Perige); pap. 53.10 (ISBN 0-399-50648-9). Putnam Pub Group.

Wernecke, Herbert H. Celebrating Christmas Around the World. LC 62-13232. 1980. pap. 5.95 (ISBN 0-664-24318-5). Westminster.

--Christmas Customs Around the World. LC 82-13602. 1983. pap. 9.95 (ISBN 0-664-24258-8, CHAC25). Westminster.

Werner, jt. auth. see Mayros.

Werner, jt. auth. see Wilson.

Werner, A. M., jt. auth. see Manaser, J. C.

Werner, Ben, Jr. Dig It, Man. (Illus.). 144p. (gr. 8up). 1972. 4.95 (ISBN 0-912954-07-8). Edmond Pub Co.

Werner, Carol, jt. auth. see Werner, Mike.

Werner, Chalmers, ed. see Ball, J. Dyer.

Werner, Charles. Reading to Learn: A Unit Approach. LC 74-30264. 400p. 1975. pap. 13.95 (ISBN 0-87909-701-9); instructor's manual o.p. avail. Reston.

Werner, Charles, jt. auth. see Gottlieb, Bertram.

Werner, D. M., jt. auth. see Mayros, Van.

Werner, David. Donde No Hay Doctor. LC 77-12027. (Illus.). 414p. 1977. pap. 9.00 o.p. (ISBN 0-942364-03-1). Hesperian Found.

--Where There Is No Doctor. LC 77-12027. (Illus.). 420p. 1980. pap. 9.00 o.p. (ISBN 0-942364-00-7). Hesperian Found.

--Where There Is No Doctor: A Village Health Care Book. 6th, rev. ed. LC 77-12027. Orig. Title: Donde No Hay Doctor. (Illus.). 414p. 1977. pap. 9.00 (ISBN 0-942364-03-1). Hesperian Found.

Werner, Dietrich, ed. The Biology of Diatoms. LC 76-55574. (Botanical Monographs: Vol. 13). 1977. 67.50x (ISBN 0-520-03400-7). U of Cal Pr.

Werner, Emmy E. Cross Cultural View of Alternate Care Givers. (Illus.). 1983. pap. price not set (ISBN 0-8391-1805-8, 17892). Univ Park.

Werner, Emmy E. & Smith, Ruth S. Kauai's Children Come of Age. LC 76-56352. (Illus.). 1977. text ed. 14.00x (ISBN 0-8248-0475-9). UH Pr.

--Vulnerable but Invincible: A Study of Resilient Children & Youth. 1982. 19.95 (ISBN 0-07-069445-1). McGraw.

Werner, Floyd G. Common Names of Insects & Related Organisms. 1982. pap. 4.00 o.p. (ISBN 0-938522-18-3). Entomol Soc.

Werner, Forman, jt. auth. see Bancroft-Hunt, Norman.

Werner, G. A., jt. auth. see O'Neal, James.

Werner, Gary. Burning Wood. (Illus.). 1983. softcover 6.00 (ISBN 0-686-64446-8); lib. bdg. 10.00 (ISBN 0-915262-53-3). S J Durst.

Werner, H., jt. auth. see Fisher, Ernest C.

Werner, Hazeldell. Golden Harvest. 1980. pap. 2.75 o.p. (ISBN 0-451-09452-2, E9452, Sig). NAL.

Werner, Helmut, ed. see Spengler, Oswald.

Werner, Jayne S. Peasant Politics & Religious Sectarianism: Peasant & Priest in the Cao Dai in Viet Nam. LC 81-52078. (Yale University Southeast Asian Ser.: Monograph No. 23). 123p. (Orig.). 1981. 10.50x (ISBN 0-686-35745-0). Yale U SE Asia.

Werner, Joan K. Neuroscience: A Clinical Perspective. LC 79-64779. (Illus.). 225p. 1980. text ed. 16.50x o.p. (ISBN 0-7216-9116-1). Saunders.

Werner, Karel. Yoga & Indian Philosophy. 1977. 11.00 (ISBN 0-685-62253-3, Pub. by Motilal Banarsidass India). Orient Bk Dist.

Werner, Mario, ed. Microtechniques for the Clinical Laboratory: Concepts & Applications. LC 75-34373. 1976. 51.50 o.p. (ISBN 0-471-93370-8, Pub. by Wiley Medical). Wiley.

Werner, Mario, jt. ed. see Goldberg, David M.

Werner, Mike & Werner, Carol. How to Create & Sell Photo Products. (Illus.). 368p. 1983. 19.95 (ISBN 0-89879-088-3); pap. 14.95 (ISBN 0-89879-098-0). Writers Digest.

Werner, Peter H. & Burton, Elsie. Learning Through Movement: Teaching Cognitive Content Through Physical Activities. LC 78-11895. (Illus.). 320p. 1979. pap. text ed. 14.50 (ISBN 0-8016-5415-7). Mosby.

Werner, Peter H. & Rini, Lisa. Perceptual Motor Development Equipment: Inexpensive Ideas & Activities. LC 75-43744. 160p. 1976. text ed. 18.95x o.s.i. (ISBN 0-471-93371-6). Wiley.

Werner, R., jt. ed. see Scott, W. A.

Werner, Raymond J., jt. auth. see Kratovil, Robert.

Werner, Rita, jt. auth. see Spangler, Mary.

Werner, Rudolf. Biochemistry: A Comprehensive Review for Medical Students. 500p. 1983. text ed. 19.50 (ISBN 0-86720-014-6). Sci Bks Intl.

Werner, Ruth M. Public Financing of Voluntary Agency Foster Care. LC 76-54383. (Orig.). 1976. pap. 4.50 (ISBN 0-87868-163-9, AM-29). Child Welfare.

Werner, S. O., jt. auth. see Wilson, J. Douglas.

Werner, Sarah, et al. Atlas of Neonatal Electroencephalography. LC 77-83692. 224p. 1977. 89.00 (ISBN 0-89004-080-X). Raven.

Werner, William E., jt. auth. see Benton, Allen H.

Werner, William, Jr., jt. auth. see Benton, Allen H.

Werner-Beland, Jean A. Grief Response for the Critically Ill. (Illus.). 1980. text ed. 14.95 o.p. (ISBN 0-8359-2591-9); pap. text ed. 13.95 (ISBN 0-8359-2590-0). Reston.

Wernham, R. B. The Making of Elizabethan Foreign Policy, 1558-1603. (Illus.). 120p. 1981. 16.50x (ISBN 0-520-03966-1); pap. 5.75x (ISBN 0-520-03974-2, CAMPUS 244). U of Cal Pr.

Wernick, J. A., jt. auth. see Nesbitt, E. A.

Wernick, Robert. Blitzkreig. LC 76-25750. (World War II). (Illus.). (gr. 6 up). 1976. PLB 19.92 (ISBN 0-8094-2455-X, Pub by Time-Life). Silver.

--The Vikings. LC 78-24119. (The Seafarers Ser.). (Illus.). 1979. lib. bdg. 19.92 (ISBN 0-8094-2708-7). Silver.

Wernick, Robert, jt. auth. see Creff, Albert.

Wernicke-Rothmayer, Johanna. Armin T. Wegner. 435p. (Ger.). 1982. write for info. (ISBN 3-8204-5789-5). P Lang Pubs.

Werning, Waldo J. Christian Stewards: Confronted & Committed. 1983. pap. 8.95 (ISBN 0-570-03879-0). Concordia.

Wernstedt, Frederick L., jt. auth. see Simkins, Paul D.

Werry, John S., jt. auth. see Quay, Herbert C.

Werry, John S. & Burrows, Graham D., eds. Advances in Human Psychopharmacology, Vol. 1. (Orig.). 1980. 45.00 (ISBN 0-89232-142-3). Jai Pr.

Werry, John S., jt. ed. see Burrows, Graham D.

Wersba, Barbara. The Carnival in My Mind. LC 81-48640. (Charlotte Zolotow Bk.). 224p. (YA) (gr. 7 up). 1982. 10.10i (ISBN 0-06-026409-8, HarpJ); PLB 10.89g (ISBN 0-06-026410-1). Har-Row.

Wershoven, Carol. The Female Intruder in the Novels of Edith Wharton. LC 81-68349. 300p. 1982. 24.50 (ISBN 0-8386-3126-6). Fairleigh Dickinson.

Werstein, Irving. Cruise of the Essex: An Incident from the War of 1812. (gr. 7 up). 1969. 6.25 (ISBN 0-8255-9201-1). Macrae.

--Proud People: Black Americans. (Illus.). (gr. 7 up). 1970. 4.95 o.p. (ISBN 0-87131-084-8). M Evans.

--Supremo: The Story of Lord Louis Mountbatten. (Illus.). (gr. 7up). 1971. 6.25 (ISBN 0-8255-9203-8). Macrae.

Wert, Charles A. & Thomson, Robb W. Physics of Solids. 2nd ed. LC 77-98055. (Materials Science & Engineering Ser.). 1970. text ed. 43.50 (ISBN 0-07-069435-4, C). McGraw.

Wert, William F. Van see Van Wert, William F.

Wertenbaker, Lael. To Mend the Heart: The Dramatic Story of Cardiac Surgery & Its Pioneers. (Illus.). 1980. 14.95 o.p. (ISBN 0-670-47092-9). Viking Pr.

--World of Picasso. LC 67-30587. (Library of Art Ser.). (Illus.). (gr. 6 up). 1967. 19.92 (ISBN 0-8094-0271-8, Pub. by Time-Life). Silver.

Wertenbaker, Thomas J. Bacon's Rebellion, Sixteen Seventy-Six. 60p. 1980. pap. 2.95 (ISBN 0-8139-0132-4). U Pr of Va.

--The Golden Age of Colonial Culture. LC 79-20891. 1980. Repr. of 1949 ed. lib. bdg. 18.25x (ISBN 0-313-22144-8, WEGA). Greenwood.

Wertenschlag, Eva, ed. see Birkhauser, Kaspar.

Werth, Alexander. Russia under Krushchev. LC 75-2704. 352p. 1975. Repr. of 1962 ed. lib. bdg. 20.25x (ISBN 0-8371-8028-7, WERK). Greenwood.

Werth, Ronald N., jt. ed. see Baldi, Philip.

Wertham, Frederic. Show of Violence. Repr. of 1949 ed. lib. bdg. 15.50x (ISBN 0-8371-1040-8, WESV); pap. 5.95x (ISBN 0-8371-8945-4, WES). Greenwood.

Wertham, Frederick. German Euthanasia: A Sign for Cain. 1977. 1.25 (ISBN 0-910728-09-7). Hayes

Wertheim, Alexander H. & Wagennar, Willem A., eds. Tutorials on Motion Perception. LC 82-16554. (NATO Conference Ser. III, Human Factors: Vol. 20). 280p. 1982. 39.50 (ISBN 0-306-41126-1, Plenum Pr). Plenum Pub.

Wertheim, Arthur, ed. American Popular Culture in Historical Perpective: An Annotated Bibliography. (Clio Bibliography Ser.: No. 14). 254p. 1983. lib. bdg. 55.00 (ISBN 0-87436-049-8). ABC-Clio.

Wertheim, Arthur F. Radio Comedy. LC 78-10679. (Illus.). 1979. 25.00x (ISBN 0-19-502481-8). Oxford U Pr.

Wertheimer, Barbara M. Exploring the Arts: A Handbook for Trade Union Program Planners. LC 68-66648. 64p. 1969. pap. 1.00 (ISBN 0-87546-019-4). ILR Pr.

Wertheimer, Barbara M. & Nelson, Ann H. Trade Union Women: A Study of Their Participation in New York City Locals. LC 74-32398. (Special Studies). (Illus.). 202p. 1975. 28.95 o.p. (ISBN 0-275-05850-6). Praeger.

Wertheimer, Barbara M., ed. Labor Education for Women Workers. 304p. 1980. 29.95 (ISBN 0-87722-193-6). Temple U Pr.

Wertheimer, Barbara M. & Nelson, Anne H., eds. Women As Third-Party Neutrals: Gaining Acceptability. LC 78-620003. 64p. 1978. pap. 2.75 (ISBN 0-87546-066-6). ILR Pr.

Wertheimer, Leonard. Books in Other Languages. 4th ed. 1979. pap. 48.00x (ISBN 0-89664-147-3, Pub. by K G Saur). Gale.

Wertheimer, Max. Productive Thinking: Enlarged Edition. LC 82-10913. (Phoenix Ser.). 328p. 1982. pap. 8.95 (ISBN 0-226-89376-6). U of Chicago Pr.

Wertheimer, Michael & Rappoport, Leon. Psychology & the Problems of Today. 1978. pap. 12.50x (ISBN 0-673-07890-6). Scott F.

Wertheimer, Michael, jt. auth. see Johnson, Margo.

Wertheimer, Michael, jt. auth. see Scott, William A.

Wertheimer, Stephen, jt. ed. see Dermer, Joseph.

Werther, William & Davis, Keith. Personnel Management. (Management Ser.). (Illus.). 528p. (Orig.). 1981. text ed. 25.95x (ISBN 0-07-069436-2); instructor's manual & test bank 20.95 (ISBN 0-07-069437-0). McGraw.

Werther, William B., jt. ed. see Lockhart, Carol A.

Wertmuller, Lina. The Head of Alvise. LC 82-3528. 288p. 1982. 12.50 (ISBN 0-688-01124-1). Morrow.

Wertsch, James V., tr. from Rus. The Concept of Activity in Soviet Psychology. LC 80-5453. 1981. 32.50 (ISBN 0-87332-158-8). M E Sharpe.

Wertsman, Vladimir. The Armenians in America 1618-1976: A Chronology & Fact Book. LC 77-20704. (Ethnics Chronology Ser.). 138p. 1978. lib. bdg. 8.50 (ISBN 0-379-00529-8). Oceana.

--The Romanians in America Seventeen Forty-Eight to Nineteen Seventy-Four: A Chronology & Fact Book. LC 75-11506. (Ethnic Chronology Ser.: No. 19). 118p. 1975. text ed. 8.50 (ISBN 0-379-00518-2). Oceana.

--The Russians in America Seventeen Twenty-Seven to Nineteen Seventy: A Chronology & Fact Book. LC 76-7416. (Ethnic Chronology Ser: No. 24). 140p. 1977. lib. bdg. 8.50x (ISBN 0-379-00522-0). Oceana.

--The Ukrainians in America 1608-1975: A Chronology & Fact Book. LC 76-6679. (Ethnic Chronology Ser.: No. 25). 140p. 1976. lib. bdg. 8.50 (ISBN 0-379-00523-9). Oceana.

Wertsman, Vladimir, ed. The Romanians in America & Canada: A Guide to Information Sources. LC 80-191. (Gale Information Guide Library, Ethnic Information Guide Ser.: Vol. 5). 175p. 1980. 42.00x (ISBN 0-8103-1417-7). Gale.

Wertsman, Vladimir, jt. ed. see Sokolyszyn, Aleksander.

Wertz, Dorothy C., jt. auth. see Wertz, Richard W.

Wertz, J. E., jt. auth. see Henderson, B.

Wertz, John E. & Bolton, James R. Electron Spin Resonance, Elementary Theory & Practical Applications. (Advanced Chemistry Ser.). 496p. 1972. text ed. 49.95 (ISBN 0-07-069454-0, C). McGraw.

Wertz, Richard W. & Wertz, Dorothy C. Lying-In: A History of Childbirth in America. LC 78-26045. 1979. pap. 5.95 (ISBN 0-8052-0615-9). Schocken.

Wertz, Richard W., ed. Readings on Ethical & Social Issues in Biomedicine. 320p. 1973. pap. 15.95 ref. ed. (ISBN 0-13-755884-8). P-H.

Wesberry, James P. Bread in a Barren Land. LC 81-8668. 1982. pap. 4.95 (ISBN 0-8054-5103-X). Broadman.

Wesbrook, Stephen D., jt. auth. see Janowitz, Morris.

Weschcke, Carl, ed. see Denning & Phillips.

Weschcke, Carl L., ed. see Denning, Melita & Phillips, Osborne.

Weschcke, Carl L., ed. see Devine, Mary.

Weschcke, Carl L., et al, eds. see Cunningham, Scott.

Weschler, Judith, ed. On Aesthetics in Science. LC 77-26175. 1978. 17.50x (ISBN 0-262-23088-7); pap. 5.95 (ISBN 0-262-73056-1). MIT Pr.

Weschler, Lawrence. Seeing is Forgetting the Name of the Thing One Sees: A Life of Contemporary Artist Robert Irwin. (Illus.). 226p. 1983. pap. 5.95 (ISBN 0-520-04920-9, CAL 617). U of Cal Pr.

Wescott, Roger W., ed. Language Origins. Hewes, Gordon W. & Stokoe, William C. LC 74-25443. 1974. pap. 6.50x o.p. (ISBN 0-932130-04-6). Linstok Pr.

Wescott, W. W. Numbers, Their Occult Power & Mystic Virtue. 127p. 5.00 (ISBN 0-686-38230-7). Sun Bks.

Wesenberg-Lund, C. Biologie der Suesswasserinsekten. (Illus.). 682p. 1980. Repr. of 1943 ed. lib. bdg. 80.00x (ISBN 3-7682-1281-5). Lubrecht & Cramer.

--Biologie der Suesswassertiere: Wirbellose Tiere. (Illus.). 1967. 64.00 (ISBN 3-7682-0426-X). Lubrecht & Cramer.

Wesley, Edgar B. Guarding the Frontier: A Study of Frontier Defense from 1815 to 1825. LC 70-110883. (Illus.). xi, 217p. Repr. of 1935 ed. lib. bdg. 15.00 o.p. (ISBN 0-8371-4567-8, WEGF). Greenwood.

Wesley, George. Spare the Rod. LC 78-57982. 1978. pap. text ed. 9.75 (ISBN 0-8191-0660-7). U Pr of Amer.

Wesley, George R. A History of Hysteria. LC 79-51464. 1979. pap. text ed. 9.75 (ISBN 0-8191-0751-4). U Pr of Amer.

Wesley, James. Canyon Showdown. (YA) 1981. 6.95 (ISBN 0-686-73957-4, Avalon). Bouregy.

--Dead Man's Trail. (YA) 1979. 6.95 (ISBN 0-686-52550-7, Avalon). Bouregy.

--Diamond Range. 192p. (YA) 1975. 6.95 (ISBN 0-685-52911-8, Avalon). Bouregy.

--The Guns of Redemption. (YA) 1978. 6.95 (ISBN 0-685-19057-9, Avalon). Bouregy.

--Showdown at Eureka. (YA) 1978. 6.95 (ISBN 0-685-85782-4, Avalon). Bouregy.

--Showdown at the MB Ranch. 192p. (YA) 1976. 6.95 (ISBN 0-685-66575-5, Avalon). Bouregy.

--Trail to Boot Hill. 1981. pap. 6.95 (ISBN 0-686-84694-X, Avalon). Bouregy.

--Trouble at the Lazy-K. (YA) 1978. 6.95 (ISBN 0-685-87352-8, Avalon). Bouregy.

Wesley, John. The Appeals to Men of Reason & Religion. Gragg, Gerald R., ed. (The Works of John Wesley: Vol. XI). (Illus.). 1976. 39.95x (ISBN 0-19-812498-8). Oxford U Pr.

--John Wesley in Wales, 1739-1790. Williams, A. H., ed. 141p. 1971. text ed. 12.00x (ISBN 0-900768-90-8). Verry.

--The Journal of John Wesley. new ed. Parker, Percy L., ed. 419p. 1974. pap. 8.95 (ISBN 0-8024-4390-7). Moody.

Wesley, Mary. Speaking Terms. LC 71-137018. (Illus.). (gr. 3-7). 1971. 6.95 (ISBN 0-87645-041-9). Gambit.

Wesleyan Bible Commentary. Job-Song of Solomon. (Wesleyan Bible Commentary). 21.95 (ISBN 0-8010-2409-9). Baker Bk.

Wesley-Smith, P. The Unequal Treaty Eighteen Ninety-Seven to Nineteen Ninety-Seven. (East Asian Historical Monographs). (Illus.). 26.00x (ISBN 0-19-580436-8). Oxford U Pr.

Wesling, Donald. The Chances of Rhyme: Device & Modernity. 1980. 18.95x (ISBN 0-520-03861-4). U of Cal Pr.

Wesling, Donald see Engberg, Robert.

Wesner, Marlene & Wesner, Miles E. A Fresh Look at the Gospel. (Orig.). 1983. pap. 5.95 (ISBN 0-8054-1955-1). Broadman.

Wesner, Miles E., jt. auth. see Wesner, Marlene.

Wesner, Terry H. & Nustad, Harry L. Elementary Algebra with Applications. 400p. 1983. text ed. write for info. (ISBN 0-697-08550-3); instr's. manual avail. (ISBN 0-697-08554-6); test bank manual avail. (ISBN 0-697-08555-4). Wm C Brown.

Wesner, Terry H., jt. auth. see Nustad, Harry L.

Wesolowski, Wayne E. Model Railroad Scratchbuilding. LC 80-28367. 232p. 1981. 16.95 o.p. (ISBN 0-8306-9657-1); pap. 9.95 o.p. (ISBN 0-8306-1217-3, 1217). TAB Bks.

Wesolowsky, George O. Multiple Regression & Analysis of Variance: An Introduction for Computer Users in Management & Economics. LC 76-5884. 1976. 45.95x (ISBN 0-471-93373-2, Pub. by Wiley-Interscience). Wiley.

Wess, Julius & Bagger, Jonathan. Supersummetry & Supergravity. (Princeton Series in Physics). 192p. 1983. 40.00 (ISBN 0-691-08327-4); pap. 12.50 (ISBN 0-691-08326-6). Princeton U Pr.

Wessel, Andrew E. Computer-Aided Information Retrieval. 176p. 1975. 23.50 o.p. (ISBN 0-686-74202-8). Krieger.

--Computer-Aided Information Retrieval. LC 74-32146. (Information Sciences Ser). 208p. 1975. text ed. 23.95 o.p. (ISBN 0-471-93376-7, Pub. by Wiley-Interscience). Wiley.

--Implementation of Complex Information Systems. LC 79-9892. (Information Sciences Ser.). 1979. 32.50x (ISBN 0-471-02661-1, Pub. by Wiley-Interscience). Wiley.

--The Social Use of Information: Ownership & Access. LC 76-18211. (Information Sciences Ser.). 1976. 29.95x (ISBN 0-471-93377-5, Pub. by Wiley-Interscience). Wiley.

Wessel, Milton R., jt. auth. see Gilchrist, Bruce.

Wessell, Leonard P. Karl Marx, Romantic Irony & the Proletariat: Studies in the Mythopoetic Origins of Marxism. LC 79-12386. 1979. text ed. 25.00x (ISBN 0-8071-0587-2). La State U Pr.

Wessell, Nils H., jt. auth. see Gowa, Joanne.

Wessells, Norman K. Tissue Interactions & Development. LC 76-42696. 1977. pap. text ed. 14.95 (ISBN 0-8053-9620-9). Benjamin-Cummings.

Wessells, Virginia G., jt. ed. see Nicholls, Marion E.

Wessels, Norman K., ed. see Symposium of the Society for Developmental Biology.

Wessels, Walter J. Minimum Wages, Fringe Benefits & Working Conditions. 1981. pap. 4.25 (ISBN 0-8447-3413-6). Am Enterprise.

Wessing, Robert. Cosmology & Social Behavior in a West Javanese Settlement: Papers in International Studies. LC 77-620054. (No. 47). 1978. pap. 12.00 (ISBN 0-89680-072-5, Ohio U Ctr Intl). Ohio U Pr.

Wessler, Richard L., jt. auth. see Wessler, Ruth A.

Wessler, Ruth A. & Wessler, Richard L. The Principles & Practice of Rational-Emotive Therapy. LC 80-8319. (Social & Behavioral Science Ser.). 1980. text ed. 21.95x (ISBN 0-87589-473-9). Jossey-Bass.

--The Principles & Practice of Rational-Emotive Therapy. 15.95 (ISBN 0-686-36787-1). Inst Rat Liv.

Wessman, James W. Anthropology & Marxism. LC 80-14042. 385p. 1980. 18.95x (ISBN 0-87073-708-2); pap. text ed. 9.95x (ISBN 0-87073-709-0). Schenkman.

Wesson, Donald R. & Adams, Kenneth, eds. Polydrug Abuse: The Results of a National Collaborative Study. 1978. 40.50 (ISBN 0-12-745250-8). Acad Pr.

Wesson, Laurence G., Jr. Physiology of the Human Kidney. LC 68-29036. (Illus.). 736p. 1969. 99.50 o.p. (ISBN 0-8089-0524-4). Grune.

Wesson, R. Modern Governments: Three Worlds of Politics. 1981. 22.95 (ISBN 0-13-594945-9). P-H.

Wesson, Robert. The Aging of Communism. 180p. 1980. 23.95 (ISBN 0-03-057053-0); pap. 8.95 (ISBN 0-03-060302-1). Praeger.

--Democracy in Latin America: Promise & Problems. (Political Science Ser.). 220p. 1982. 26.95 (ISBN 0-03-061641-7). Praeger.

--Soviet Union: Looking to the Nineteen Eighties. LC 79-24546. 1980. lib. bdg. 35.00 (ISBN 0-527-95452-7). Kraus Intl.

Wesson, Robert, ed. see Alexander, Robert J.

Wesson, Robert, ed. see Needler, Martin C.

Wesson, Robert G. Communism & Communist Systems. 1978. pap. 12.95 ref. (ISBN 0-13-153437-8). P-H.

--Foreign Policy for a New Age. LC 76-13999. (Illus.). 1977. pap. text ed. 23.50 (ISBN 0-395-24652-0). HM.

West, A. & Janson, P., eds. Local Networks for Computer Communications. 1982. 59.75 (ISBN 0-444-86287-0). Elsevier.

West, A. S. Piling Practice. (Illus.). 122p. 1975. 17.50 o.p. (ISBN 0-408-70288-5). Transatlantic.

West, Alick. The Mountain in the Sunlight: Studies in Conflict & Unity. LC 79-16755. 1980. Repr. of 1958 ed. lib. bdg. 20.00x (ISBN 0-313-22013-1, WEMO). Greenwood.

West, Amanda W. Glenrose Calling. 1979. pap. 2.50 o.s.i. (ISBN 0-515-05081-4). Jove Pubns.

West, Anthony. John Piper. 1979. 37.50 (ISBN 0-436-56590-0, Pub. by Secker & Warburg). David & Charles.

West, Anthony J. The American Family Christian Philosophy of Life. (Illus.). 1979. 37.75 o.p. (ISBN 0-89266-203-4). Am Classical Coll Pr.

West, B. B., et al. Food Service in Institutions. 5th ed. 839p. 1977. 35.95 (ISBN 0-471-93393-7). Wiley.

--Food for Fifty. 6th ed. LC 78-21921. 1979. text ed. 29.95 (ISBN 0-471-02688-3). Wiley.

West, Betty M. Diabetic Menus, Meals & Recipes. rev. ed. LC 76-53412. 1978. 12.95 (ISBN 0-385-04651-0). Doubleday.

--Diabetic Menus, Meals, & Recipes. 1979. lib. bdg. 12.95 o.p. (ISBN 0-8161-6689-7, Large Print Bks). G K Hall.

West, Bill. Junior Arms Library 1849-1970, 5 vols. Set. 96.00x o.p. (ISBN 0-685-91572-7). Vol. 1 (ISBN 0-911614-01-X). Vol. 2 (ISBN 0-911614-02-8). Vol. 3 (ISBN 0-911614-03-6). Vol. 4 (ISBN 0-911614-04-4). Vol. 5 (ISBN 0-911614-06-0). B West.

--U.S.A. Arms Manufacters Catalogues, 1877-1900, 3 vols. Set. 34.00 o.p. (ISBN 0-685-91573-5). Vol. 1 (ISBN 0-911614-14-1). Vol. 2 (ISBN 0-911614-09-5). B West.

--West Arms Library of Big-5, U. S. Arms Manufacturers, 6 vols. (Illus.). 1981. Set. 174.00x o.p. (ISBN 0-685-27896-4). Vol. 1 (ISBN 0-911614-12-5). Vol. 2 (ISBN 0-911614-07-9). Vol. 3 (ISBN 0-911614-08-7). Vol. 4 (ISBN 0-911614-10-9). Vol. 5 (ISBN 0-911614-05-2). B West.

--Winchester-Complete: All Wins & Forerunners, 1849-Date. LC 74-84313. (Illus.). 1975. 35.00x o.p. (ISBN 0-911614-05-2). B West.

West, Bill W., jt. auth. see Mietus, Norbert J.

West, Celeste & Wheat, Valerie. The Passionate Perils of Publishing. LC 77-94898. (Illus.). 1978. pap. 7.00x (ISBN 0-685-87759-0). Booklegger Pr.

West, Celeste, ed. Words in Our Pockets: The Feminist Writers' Guild Handbook on How to Get Published & Get Paid. LC 81-2106. (Illus.). 350p. 1982. 15.00x (ISBN 0-686-61673-1); pap. 7.00x (ISBN 0-686-61674-X). Booklegger Pr.

West, Christopher J. Inflation: A Management Guide to Company Survival. 155p. 1976. 33.95x o.s.i. (ISBN 0-470-15087-4). Halsted Pr.

West, Colin D. Liquid Piston Stirling Engine. 144p. 1982. text ed. 18.95 (ISBN 0-442-29237-6). Van Nos Reinhold.

West, Cornel. Prophesy Deliverance! An Afro-American Revolutionary Christianity. LC 82-13483. 186p. 1982. pap. 11.95 (ISBN 0-664-24447-5). Westminster.

West, D., jt. ed. see Woodman, A. J.

West, D. R. Ternary Equilibrium Diagrams. 2nd ed. (Illus.). 1982. 18.00x (ISBN 0-686-92715-X, Pub. by Chapman & Hall); pap. 8.95x (ISBN 0-412-22820-3). Methuen Inc.

West, Don. A Don West Reader. 250p. 1982. pap. 5.00 (ISBN 0-931122-26-0). West End.

West, E. G. Copper & Its Alloys. (Ellis Harwood Series in Industrial Metals). 241p. 1982. 64.95X (ISBN 0-470-27533-2). Halsted Pr.

West, Earle H. The Black American & Education. LC 72-76947. 1972. pap. text ed. 6.95x o.p. (ISBN 0-675-09082-2). Merrill.

West, Edwin G. & Miller, Roger L. Canadian Economics Today, Vol. 1: The Macro View. 1978. pap. text ed. 15.95 scp (ISBN 0-06-385472-4, HarpC); tchr's. ed. o.p. avail.; scp study guide 9.95 (ISBN 0-06-385474-0); inst. manual avail. (ISBN 0-06-377980-3); test bk. avail. (ISBN 0-06-377981-1). Har-Row.

West, Elisabeth, tr. see Pataky-Brestyanszky, Ilona.

West, Elizabeth, tr. see Bernath, Maria.

West, Elmer H. How to Sell a Dealership. 64p. (Orig.). 1980. pap. 7.95 o.p. (ISBN 0-682-49645-6). Exposition.

West, Elsie L., ed. see Irving, Washington.

West, Emmy & Govan, Christine. Danger Downriver. (Illus.). 160p. (gr. 4-6). 1972. PLB 5.50 o.p. (ISBN 0-670-25575-0). Viking Pr.

West, F. J. Justiciarship in England 1066-1232. (Studies in Medieval Life & Thought: No. 12). 1966. 47.50 (ISBN 0-521-06772-3). Cambridge U Pr.

West, F. W., ed. Pahlavi Texts. (Vols. 5, 18, 24, 37, 47). 5 vols. 55.00 (ISBN 0-686-97478-6); 11.00 ea. Lancaster-Miller.

West, G. B., jt. auth. see Ellis, G. P.

West, G. B., jt. ed. see Ellis, G. P.

West, G. F., jt. auth. see Grant, F. S.

West, Geoffrey, ed. Black's Veterinary Dictionary. 13th ed. (Illus.). 906p. 1979. 27.50x o.p. (ISBN 0-389-20125-1). B&N Imports.

--Black's Veterinary Dictionary. rev., 14th ed. LC 83-22783. (Illus.). 912p. 1983. text ed. 28.50x (ISBN 0-389-20330-0). B&N Imports.

West, H. H. Analysis of Structures: An Intergration of Classical & Modern Methods. 689p. 1980. text ed. 36.95 (ISBN 0-471-02036-2). Wiley.

West, Harvey, intro. by. The Washington Year: A Contemporary View, 1980-1981. LC 81-20237. (Illus.). 200p. (Orig.). 1982. pap. 14.95 (ISBN 0-935558-07-1). Henry Art.

West, Helen L., jt. auth. see Ernst, Nora S.

West, Henry W. Land Policy in Buganda. LC 73-152635. (African Studies: No. 3). 1972. 34.50 (ISBN 0-521-08116-5). Cambridge U Pr.

West, James. Introduction to the Old Testament. 2nd ed. 1981. text ed. 21.95x (ISBN 0-02-425920-9). Macmillan.

West, James L., jt. ed. see Hoge, James O.

West, James L., III. The Making of "This Side of Paradise". LC 82-40487. (Illus.). 136p. 1983. 16.50x (ISBN 0-8122-7867-4). U of Pa Pr.

--William Styron: A Descriptive Bibliography. 1977. lib. bdg. 35.00 (ISBN 0-8161-7968-9, Hall Reference). G K Hall.

West, James L., III, jt. ed. see Casclato, Arthur D.

West, James L. W., jt. ed. see Hoge, James O., III.

West, Jane. A Gossip's Story, & a Legendary Tale, 2 vols. Luria, Gina, ed. LC 73-22192. (The Feminist Controversy in England, 1788-1810 Ser.). 1974. lib. bdg. 50.00 ea. o.s.i. (ISBN 0-8240-0884-7). Garland Pub.

West, Jenny. The Windmills of Kent. 128p. 1982. 29.00x (ISBN 0-7050-0065-6, Pub. by C Skilton Scotland). State Mutual Bk.

West, Jerry. Happy Hollisters. LC 79-88129. (Happy Hollister Ser.: No. 1). (Illus.). (gr. 2-6). 1979. Repr. 2.95 (ISBN 0-448-16870-7, G&D). Putnam Pub Group.

--The Happy Hollisters & the Ice Carnival Mystery. LC 78-88132. (Happy Hollisters Ser.: No. 4). (Illus.). (gr. 1-5). 1979. Repr. 2.95 (ISBN 0-448-16873-1, G&D). Putnam Pub Group.

--The Happy Hollisters at Sea Gull Beach. LC 79-88131. (Happy Hollisters Ser.: No. 3). (Illus.). (gr. 1-5). 1979. Repr. 2.95 (ISBN 0-448-16872-3, G&D). Putnam Pub Group.

--Happy Hollisters on a River Trip. LC 79-88130. (Happy Hollisters Ser.: No. 2). (Illus.). (gr. 1-5). 1979. Repr. 2.95 (ISBN 0-448-16871-5, G&D). Putnam Pub Group.

West, John. The Medieval Forest. Reeves, Marjorie, ed. (Then & There Ser.). (Illus.). 96p. (Orig.). (gr. 7-12). 1978. pap. text ed. 3.10 (ISBN 0-582-21726-1). Longman.

West, John A. & Toonder, Jan G. The Case for Astrology. 1970. 6.95 o.p. (ISBN 0-698-10045-X, Coward). Putnam Pub Group.

West, John B. Pulmonary Pathophysiology: The Essentials. 2nd ed. 232p. 1981. pap. 14.50 (ISBN 0-683-08935-8). Williams & Wilkins.

West, John B., ed. High Altitude Physiology. LC 81-6575. (Benchmark Papers in Human Physiology: Vol. 15). 480p. 1981. 55.00 (ISBN 0-87933-388-X). Hutchinson Ross.

West, John D. & Kirby, Jonell, eds. Troubled Family Interaction & Group Intervention. 1982. 3.00 (ISBN 0-686-36359-0, 70766). Am Personnel.

West, John F. Appalachian Dawn. LC 73-77500. 1973. 9.95 (ISBN 0-87716-041-4, Pub. by Moore Pub Co). F Apple.

--The Ballad of Tom Dula. 212p. 9.95 (ISBN 0-87716-019-8, Pub. by Moore Pub Co); pap. 4.50 (ISBN 0-686-66593-7). F Apple.

West, Julius. History of the Chartist Movement. LC 68-9763. Repr. of 1920 ed. 25.00x (ISBN 0-678-00406-4). Kelley.

West, Kathleene. The Armadillo on the Rug. 20p. 1978. 3.00 (ISBN 0-686-38175-0). Seal Pr WA.

--No Warning. 1977. 3.00 (ISBN 0-918116-11-2). Jawbone Pr.

West, Keith. How to Draw Plants: The Art of Botanical Illustrations. (Illus.). 152p. 1983. 22.50 (ISBN 0-8230-2355-9). Watson-Guptill.

West, Kirsten, jt. auth. see Perryman, Penelope.

West, Kitty. Guide to Retouching Negatives & Prints. (Illus.). 1972. pap. 2.95 o.p. (ISBN 0-8174-0271-3, Amphoto). Watson-Guptill.

--Hand Coloring Your Photographs with Oils & Dyes. (Illus.). 1961. pap. 2.95 (ISBN 0-8174-0234-9, Amphoto). Watson-Guptill.

--Modern Retouching Manual. 2nd ed. (Illus.). 160p. 1973. 10.95 o.p. (ISBN 0-8174-0508-9, Amphoto). Watson-Guptill.

West, L. J., jt. ed. see Siegel, R. K.

West, Leonard J. Acquisition of Typewriting Skills. 2nd ed. 448p. 1983. text ed. 24.95 (ISBN 0-672-98444-X). Bobbs.

West Linn Unified School District. FORE Secondary. Rev. ed. Bagai, Eric & Bagai, Judith, eds. (System FORE Ser.: Vol. 5). (Illus.). 243p. 1977. 14.00x (ISBN 0-943292-05-0). Foreworks.

West, Louis J. & Stein, Marvin. Critical Issues in Behavioral Medicine. (Illus.). 272p. 1982. pap. text ed. 25.00 (ISBN 0-397-50528-0, Lippincott Medical). Lippincott.

West, Luther S. & Peters, Oneita B. Annotated Bibliography of Musca Domestica Linnaeus. 1973. 38.95 (ISBN 0-7129-0536-7, Co-Pub. with Dawsons of Pall Mall, England). Northern Mich.

West, M. A., jt. ed. see Harriman, A.

West, M. A., jt. ed. see Miller, J. N.

West, M. L. Greek Metre. (Illus.). 1982. 35.00 (ISBN 0-19-814018-5). Oxford U Pr.

West, M. L., ed. Delectus ex Iambis et Elegis Graecis. (Classical Texts Ser.). 306p. 1980. text ed. 24.00x (ISBN 0-19-814589-6). Oxford U Pr.

West, Michael, ed. A General Service List of English Words. 1953. text ed. 23.95x (ISBN 0-582-52526-8). Longman.

West, Morris. Daughter of Silence. 256p. 1982. pap. 2.95 (ISBN 0-553-20694-X). Bantam.

--Harlequin. 1983. pap. 3.50 (ISBN 0-553-22913-3). Bantam.

--The Shoes of the Fisherman. 1982. pap. 3.50 (ISBN 0-553-20902-7). Bantam.

--The World is Made of Glass. 356p. 1983. 15.95 (ISBN 0-688-02031-3). Morrow.

West, N. E., ed. Temperate Deserts & Semi-Deserts. (Ecosystems of the World Ser.: Vol. 5). 522p. 1982. 170.25 (ISBN 0-444-41931-4). Elsevier.

West, N. E. & Skujins, J., eds. Nitrogen in Desert Ecosystems. LC 78-17672. (US-IBP Synthesis Ser.: Vol. 9). 307p. 1978. 31.50 (ISBN 0-87933-333-2). Hutchinson Ross.

West, Nathanael. The Dream Life of Balso Snell & A Cool Million. Bd. with Cool Million. 179p. 1963. pap. 5.95 (ISBN 0-374-50292-7, N244). FS&G.

West, Nick. Alfred Hitchcock & the Three Investigators in the Mystery of the Nervous Lion. Hitchcock, Alfred, ed. (Three Investigators Ser: No. 16). (Illus.). (gr. 4-7). 1971. 2.95 o.p. (ISBN 0-394-82308-7, BYR); PLB 5.39 (ISBN 0-394-92308-1). Random.

--Alfred Hitchcock & the Three Investigators in the Mystery of the Coughing Dragon. LC 74-117549. (Three Investigator's Ser: No. 14). (Illus.). (gr. 4-7). 1970. 2.95 o.p. (ISBN 0-394-81411-8, BYR); PLB 5.39 (ISBN 0-394-91411-2). Random.

West, Nicola. Lucifer's Brand. (Harlequin Presents Ser.). 192p. 1983. pap. 1.95 (ISBN 0-373-10589-4). Harlequin Bks.

West, Nigel. The Circus: MI5 Operations, 1945-1972. LC 82-42928. 384p. 1983. 16.95 (ISBN 0-686-42920-6). Stein & Day.

West, Ouida. The Magic of Massage: Your Health is in your Hands. (Illus.). 192p. (Orig.). 1983. pap. 12.95 (ISBN 0-933328-60-5). Delilah Bks.

West, Owen. The Pit. 1982. pap. 2.95 (ISBN 0-515-05696-0). Jove Pubns.

West, Patricia E. The Aquarian Book of Change. LC 81-90541. (Illus.). 178p. (gr. 8-12). 1982. pap. 4.50 o.p. (ISBN 0-942384-00-8). Red Dragon.

--Astrology Handbook for Therapists & Holistic Health Practitioners. (Orig.). 1983. pap. 5.50 (ISBN 0-942384-02-4). Red Dragon.

West, Paul. Out Of My Depths: A Swimmer in the Universe. LC 82-9722. (Illus.). 168p. 1983. 12.95 (ISBN 0-385-18083-7, Anchor Pr). Doubleday.

West, Peggy J., ed. Growing with Television: A Study of Biblical Values & the Television Experience - Adult Leader's Guide. 32p. 1980. pap. 2.95 (ISBN 0-8164-2272-9); pap. 2.45 student leaflet (ISBN 0-8164-2618-X). Seabury.

West Publishing Company. Everyone's Law Encyclopedia: A Guide to American Law. (Illus.). 3000p. 1983. text ed. 660.00 (set) (ISBN 0-314-73224-1). West Pub.

West, R. Henry James. LC 73-21774. (Studies in Henry James, No. 17). 1974. lib. bdg. 39.95x (ISBN 0-8383-1833-9). Haskell.

West, R. G. The Pre-Glacial Pleistocene of the Norfolk & Suffolk Coasts. LC 77-90191. (Illus.). 1980. 110.00 (ISBN 0-521-21962-0). Cambridge U Pr.

West, R. G., jt. auth. see Sparks, B. W.

West, R. G., jt. ed. see Walker, D.

West, R. N. Position Studies of Condensed Matter. 132p. 1974. pap. write for info (ISBN 0-85066-070-X, Pub. by Taylor & Francis). Intl Pubns Serv.

West, Raymond O., ed. Public Health & Community Medicine. 7th ed. (Medical Examination Review Book Ser.: Vol .6). 1981. pap. 11.95 (ISBN 0-87488-106-4). Med Exam.

West, Rebecca. Black Lamb & Grey Falcon. 1982. pap. 10.95 (ISBN 0-14-006355-2). Penguin.

--Saint Augustine. (A Thomas More Book to Live). 173p. 1983. 10.95 (ISBN 0-88347-148-5). Thomas More.

West, Richard. An English Journey. 224p. 1982. 18.95 (ISBN 0-7011-2584-5, Pub. by Chatto-Bodley-Jonathan). Merrimack Bk Serv.

West, Richard R., jt. auth. see Tinic, Seha M.

West, Richard S. Admirals of American Empire: The Combined Story of George Dewey, Alfred Thayer Mahan, Winfield Scott Schley & William Thomas Sampson. LC 73-156216. 354p. 1948. Repr. lib. bdg. 15.00 o.p. (ISBN 0-8371-6167-3, WEAE). Greenwood.

West, Robert. The Oxocarbons. LC 80-515. (Organic Chemistry Ser.). 1980. 34.50 (ISBN 0-12-744580-3). Acad Pr.

West, Robert, jt. auth. see Stone, F. G.

West, Robert, jt. ed. see Stone, F. G.

West, Robert C. Andean Reflections: Letters From Carl O. Sauer While on a South American Trip Under a Grant From the Rockefeller Foundation, 1942. (Dellplain Latin American Studies Ser.: Vol. 11). 160p. 1982. lib. bdg. 15.00 (ISBN 0-86531-436-5). Westview.

West, Robert C., jt. auth. see Augelli, John P.

West, Robert C., et al. The Tabasco Lowlands of Southeastern Mexico. LC 70-631545. (University Studies, Coastal Studies Ser.: No. 27). (Illus.). xvi, 194p. 1969. pap. 4.00x o.p. (ISBN 0-8071-0035-8). La State U Pr.

West, Robert E., ed. Rutland in Retrospect. LC 78-56622. (Illus.). 176p. 1978. 20.00 o.p. (ISBN 0-914960-14-8); pap. 17.00 (ISBN 0-914960-11-3). Academy Bks.

West, Robin. The Greatest Show On Earth: How to Create Your Own Circus. LC 83-23580. (Illus.). 64p. (gr. k-3). 1983. PLB 8.95 (ISBN 0-87614-212-9). Carolrhoda Bks.

West, Ronald R., jt. ed. see Scott, Robert W.

West, Stephen, ed. see Barron, Stephanie, et al.

West, Stephen G. & Wicklund, Robert A. A Primer of Social Psychological Theories. LC 80-16292. 320p. 1980. text ed. 21.95 (ISBN 0-8185-0395-5). Brooks-Cole.

West, Thomas, jt. auth. see Mullins, Carolyn.

West, W, ed. Chemical Applications of Spectroscopy. LC 45-8533. (Technique of Organic Chemistry Ser.: Vol.9, Pt.1). 486p. Repr. of 1968 ed. text ed. 29.25 (ISBN 0-686-84519-6). Krieger.

West, Wallace. Everlasting Exiles. (YA) 6.95 (ISBN 0-685-07431-5, Avalon). Bouregy.

West, William A. & Etter, Don D. Curtis Park: A Denver Neighborhood. 1980. 9.95 (ISBN 0-87081-077-4). Hist Denver.

West, William R. & Stremnel, Stephen H. Exploring, Visualizing, Communicating: A Composition Text. (Ser. in English Composition). 1979. pap. text ed. 10.95 (ISBN 0-13-297556-4). P-H.

Westall, Robert. Break of Dark. (gr. 7 up). 1982. 9.50 (ISBN 0-688-00875-5). Morrow.

--Devil on the Road. LC 79-10427. 256p. (gr. 6 up). 1979. 9.95 (ISBN 0-688-80227-3); lib. bdg. 9.36 (ISBN 0-688-84227-5). Greenwillow.

Westberg, Granger. Ante la Perdida de un Ser Querido. Rodriguez, Jorge A., tr. 1980. Repr. of 1978 ed. 1.20 (ISBN 0-311-46081-X). Casa Bautista.

Westberg, Sigurd F. Deep Tracks in Africa. 1976. 6.95 o.p. (ISBN 0-910452-28-8); pap. 5.45 o.p. (ISBN 0-910452-41-5). Covenant.

Westbrook, James H. Aim for a Job in Restaurants & Food Service. LC 70-114136. (Career Guidance Ser). 1971. pap. 4.50 (ISBN 0-668-02229-9). Arco.

Westbrook, Max. Walter Van Tilburg Clark. (United States Authors Ser.). 1970. lib. bdg. 12.95 (ISBN 0-8057-0148-6, Twayne). G K Hall.

Westbrook, Max, jt. auth. see Handy, William J.

Westbrook, Perry D. John Burroughs. (United States Authors Ser.). 1974. lib. bdg. 13.95 (ISBN 0-8057-0117-6, Twayne). G K Hall.

--Mary Wilkins Freeman. (Unoited States Authors Ser.). 12.95 (ISBN 0-8057-0288-1, Twayne). G K Hall.

--The New England Town in Fact & Fiction. LC 80-67077. 288p. 1982. 30.00 (ISBN 0-8386-3011-1). Fairleigh Dickinson.

--William Bradford. (United States Authors Ser.). 1978. lib. bdg. 12.95 (ISBN 0-8057-7243-X, Twayne). G K Hall.

Westburg, Granger E. Good Grief. 1.75 o.p. (ISBN 0-686-92329-4, 6395). Hazelden.

Westburg, John, jt. ed. see Beck, Elmer A.

Westburg, John E., ed. Down to Earth Poems by the Mentor Circle of Poets: Eleven Years of Award Winning Poems, 1964-1975. 100p. 1976. pap. 8.00 (ISBN 0-87423-016-0). Westburg.

Westburg, John E., ed. see Jowers, Lawrence V.

Westby, Barbara M., ed. Sears List of Subject Headings. 11th ed. 654p. 1977. 18.00 o.p. (ISBN 0-8242-0610-X). Wilson.

Westby, George, jt. auth. see Apter, Michael J.

Westcott, A. & Symons, C. Whispering River. LC 78-108727. (Illus.). (gr. 3-5). 1970. PLB 6.75x (ISBN 0-87783-049-5); pap. 2.95x deluxe ed (ISBN 0-87783-116-5). Oddo.

Westcott, Alvin. Billy Lump's Adventure. LC 68-56817. (Illus.). (gr. 2-4). PLB 6.75x (ISBN 0-87783-002-9). Oddo.

--Rockets & Crackers. LC 75-108729. (Illus.). (gr. 4 up). 1970. PLB 6.75x (ISBN 0-87783-033-9); pap. 2.95x deluxe ed. (ISBN 0-87783-105-X). Oddo.

--Word Bending with Aunt Sarah. LC 68-56821. (Illus.). (gr. 2-3). 1968. PLB 6.75x (ISBN 0-87783-052-5); pap. 2.95x deluxe ed (ISBN 0-87783-118-1). Oddo.

Westcott, Alvin & Schluep, J. Fun with Timothy Triangle. LC 66-11445. (Illus.). (gr. 4 up). 1970. pap. 2.95x deluxe ed. (ISBN 0-87783-014-2); answer key 0.29x (ISBN 0-87783-164-5). Oddo.

Westcott, Alvin, jt. auth. see Symons.

Westcott, Brooke F. Commentary on the Epistles of Saint John. (Gr). 8.95 (ISBN 0-8028-3290-3). Eerdmans.

Westcott, Frederick B. Colossians: A Letter to Asia. 1981. lib. bdg. 7.50 (ISBN 0-86524-070-1, 5102). Klock & Klock.

Westcott, Jan. Queen's Grace. 1977. Repr. of 1959 ed. lib. bdg. 19.95x (ISBN 0-89244-062-7). Queens Hse.

--A Woman of Quality. LC 78-17236. 1978. 10.00 (ISBN 0-399-12223-0). Putnam Pub Group.

Westcott, Linn. HO Primer Model Railroading for All. 2nd ed. (Illus.). 80p. 1964. pap. 5.50 (ISBN 0-89024-503-7). Kalmbach.

--Track Plans for Sectional Track. 2nd ed. (Illus.). 40p. 1961. pap. 3.95 (ISBN 0-89024-510-X). Kalmbach.

Westcott, Richard, jt. auth. see Bilovsky, Frank.

Westcott, William D. How to Raise & Train a Keeshond. (Orig.). pap. 2.95 (ISBN 0-87666-326-9, DS1091). TFH Pubns.

Westcott, William W. Study of Kabala. 4.95x (ISBN 0-685-22119-9). Wehman.

Westdal, S. J. Identification of Roman Coin Inscriptions. 4th ed. 1982. softcover 10.00 (ISBN 0-915262-72-X). S J Durst.

Westenholz, Aage. Old Sumerian and Old Akkadian Texts in Philadelphia, Chiefly from Nippur, Part 1. LC 74-21135. (Bibliotheca Mesopotamica Ser.: Vol. 1). (Illus.). xii, 213p. 1975. 24.50x (ISBN 0-89003-009-X); pap. 17.00x (ISBN 0-686-68506-7). Undena Pubns.

Westenholz, C. Von see Von Westenholz, C.

Westerberg, A. W., et al. Process Flowsheeting. LC 78-51682. (Illus.). 1979. 34.50 (ISBN 0-521-22043-2). Cambridge U Pr.

Westerberg, Kermit B., tr. see Ljungmark, Lars.

Westerby, Herbert. Liszt, Composer, & His Piano Works. LC 73-97337. (Illus.). xxii, 336p. Repr. of 1936 ed. lib. bdg. 12.50x (ISBN 0-8371-4365-9, WELI). Greenwood.

Westergaard, John, et al, eds. Modern British Society: A Bibliography. LC 76-51508. 1978. 25.00 (ISBN 0-312-53775-1). St Martin.

Westergaard, Marjorie. Directory of Handwriting Analysts. 5th ed. LC 82-640893. 88p. 1983. pap. text ed. 8.95 (ISBN 0-9609578-5-5). M Westergaard.

Westergaard, Waldemar, ed. see Lindenov, Christopher.

Westerhoff, John H., jt. auth. see Holmes, Urban T.

Westerhoff, John H., III. Building God's People in a Materialistic Society. 144p. 1983. pap. 8.95 (ISBN 0-8164-2466-7). Seabury.

--Will Our Children Have Faith? 144p. 1983. pap. 6.95 (ISBN 0-8164-2435-7). Seabury.

Westerhoff, John H., III, jt. auth. see Neville, Gwen K.

Westerhoff, John H., III, ed. Who Are We? The Quest for a Religious Education. LC 78-12392. 382p. 1978. pap. 10.95 (ISBN 0-89135-014-4). Religious Educ.

Westerhoff, John H., III, jt. auth. see Holmes, Urban T.

Westerhuis, J. H. Parturient Hypocalcaemia Prevention in Parurient Cows Prone to Milk Fever by Dietary Measures. new ed. (Agricultural Research Reports). 78p. 1974. pap. 14.00 (ISBN 90-220-0506-2, PDC63, Pub. by PUDOC). Unipub.

Westerlund, Stuart R. Humane Education & Realms of Humaneness: Readings. LC 82-15936. (Illus.). 286p. 1983. lib. bdg. 23.00 (ISBN 0-8191-2724-8); pap. text ed. 11.50 (ISBN 0-8191-2725-6). U Pr of Amer.

Westerman, Maxine. Elementary Fashion Design & Trade Sketching. 2nd ed. (Illus.). 1983. text ed. 13.50 (ISBN 0-87005-438-4). Fairchild.

Westermann, Claus. Genesis One-Eleven. Scullion, John J., tr. LC 82-72655. 692p. cloth 29.95 (ISBN 0-8066-1962-7, 10-2543). Augsburg.

--Isaiah Forty to Sixty Six: A Commentary. Stalker, David M., tr. LC 69-18647. (Old Testament Library). 1969. 15.95 (ISBN 0-664-20851-7). Westminster.

--A Thousand Years & a Day. LC 62-8544. 292p. 1982. pap. 7.95 (ISBN 0-8006-1913-7, 1-1913). Fortress.

Westermann, Claus & Mays, James L., eds. Essays on Old Testament Hermeneutics. LC 63-10637. 1979. pap. 8.50 (ISBN 0-8042-0107-2). John Knox.

Westermark, Victoria, jt. auth. see Corey, Mary.

Westermeyer, Joseph. Poppies, Pipes, & People: Opium & Its Use In Laos. (Illus.). 360p. 1982. 28.50 (ISBN 0-520-04622-6). U of Cal Pr.

Western Central Atlantic Fisheries Commission. Report of the First Session of the Working Party on Fishery Statistics. (FAO Fishery Reports: No. 212). 1979. pap. 7.50 (ISBN 92-5-100698-9, F1575, FAO). Unipub.

Western Heritage Conservation Inc. The Outstanding Wonder: Zion Canyon's Cable Mountain Draw Works. (Illus.). 66p. 1980. pap. 1.95 (ISBN 0-686-84052-6). Zion.

Western, J. S. & Hughes, Colin A. The Mass Media in Australia: Second Edition. 2nd ed. LC 82-2685. (Illus.). 209p. 1983. text ed. 22.50x (ISBN 0-7022-1682-8); pap. text ed. 12.50x (ISBN 0-7022-1692-5). U of Queensland Pr.

Western Publishing Co. Editors, ed. New Grosset Road Atlas of the United States, Canada, & Mexico. (Illus., Orig.). 1981. pap. 4.95 o.p. (ISBN 0-448-16283-0, G&D). Putnam Pub Group.

Western Resources Conference - 1968. Public Land Policy: Proceedings. Foss, Phillip O., ed. LC 70-109923. 1969. pap. 9.50 o.p. (ISBN 0-87081-001-4). Colo Assoc.

Western Resources Conference, 3rd, Colorado State University, 1961. Land & Water: Planning for Economic Growth: Proceedings. Amoss, Harold L. & McNickle, Roma K., eds. LC 76-44432. (Illus.). 1976. Repr. of 1962 ed. lib. bdg. 18.00x (ISBN 0-8371-9037-1, AMLW). Greenwood.

Western Writers of America. The Women Who Made the West. LC 79-8442. (Illus.). 1980. 11.95 (ISBN 0-385-15801-7). Doubleday.

Westernhagen, C. Von see Von Westernhagen, Curt.

Westernhagen, Curt Von see Von Westernhagen, Curt.

Westfall, Gloria, jt. auth. see Kohler, Carolyn.

Westfall, Jane A., ed. Visual Cells in Evolution. 174p. 1982. text ed. 26.50 (ISBN 0-89004-760-X). Raven.

Westfall, Minter J., Jr., jt. auth. see Needham, James G.

Westfall, R. S. The Construction of Modern Science. LC 77-84001. (History of Science Ser.). (Illus.). 1978. 29.95 (ISBN 0-521-21863-2); pap. 8.95 (ISBN 0-521-29295-6). Cambridge U Pr.

--Never at Rest: A Biography of Isaac Newton. LC 77-84001. (Illus.). 850p. 1981. 55.00 (ISBN 0-521-23143-4). Cambridge U Pr.

Westgate, et al. An Introduction to Word Processing Four Plus. 276p. 1982. text ed. 32.95x (ISBN 0-7715-0460-8). Forkner.

Westgate, Douglas G. Office Procedures 2000. 512p. 1977. text ed. 17.25x (ISBN 0-7715-0897-2); tchr's. manual 39.95x (ISBN 0-7715-0898-0). Forkner.

Westheimer, David. Von Ryan's Return. LC 79-24078. 1980. 10.95 (ISBN 0-698-11003-X, Coward). Putnam Pub Group.

Westheimer, David, jt. auth. see Sherlock, John.

Westheimer, Ruth. Dr. Ruth's Guide to Good Sex. 256p. 1983. 14.50 (ISBN 0-446-51260-5). Warner Bks.

Westhoff, Dennis, jt. auth. see Frazier, William C.

Westhues, K. First Sociology. 1982. text ed. 21.00x (ISBN 0-07-069466-4); pap. text ed. 16.50 (ISBN 0-07-069463-X); test manual 6.95 (ISBN 0-07-069464-8). McGraw.

Westin, Alan F. Anatomy of a Constitutional Law Case. (Orig.). 1958. pap. text ed. 7.95x (ISBN 0-02-426540-3). Macmillan.

Westin, Alan F., ed. Whistle-Blowing! Loyalty & Dissent in the Corporation. LC 80-15800. 192p. 1980. 15.95 (ISBN 0-07-069483-4, P&RB). McGraw.

Westin, Av. Newswatch. 1982. 15.95 (ISBN 0-671-42179-4). S&S.

Westlake, Donald. Kahawa. LC 81-51887. (Illus.). 280p. 1982. 15.95 (ISBN 0-670-41132-9). Viking Pr.

--Why Me? 204p. 1983. 13.50 (ISBN 0-670-76569-4). Viking Pr.

Westlake, Donald E. & Garfield, Brian. Gangway. 1973. 5.95 o.p. (ISBN 0-87131-116-X). M Evans.

Westlake, H. D. Timoleon & His Relations with Tyrants. 1952. 12.00 (ISBN 0-7190-1217-1). Manchester.

Westlake, John. Chapters on the Principles of International Law. xix, 275p. 1982. Repr. of 1894 ed. lib. bdg. 27.50x (ISBN 0-8377-1328-5). Rothman.

Westlake, Robert J., ed. Shaping the Future of Mental Health Care. LC 76-3437. 1976. prof ref 17.50x (ISBN 0-88410-133-9). Ballinger Pub.

Westland, Cor & Knight, Jane. Playing, Living, Learning: A Worldwide Perspective on Children's Opportunities to Play. LC 81-69902. (Illus.). 211p. (Orig.). 1982. pap. 13.95x (ISBN 0-910251-02-9). Venture Pub PA.

Westland, Lynn. Iron Trail to Stirrup. 192p. (YA) 1975. 6.95 (ISBN 0-685-55330-2, Avalon). Bouregy.

Westley, Bruce. News Editing. 3rd ed. LC 79-88796. (Illus.). 1980. text ed. 21.50 (ISBN 0-395-27993-3). HM.

Westley, Bruce H., jt. auth. see Stempel, Guido H., III.

Westley, Glen D. Planning the Location of Urban-Suburban Rail Lines: An Application of Cost-Benefit & Optimal Path Analysis. LC 78-6476. 1978. prof ref 18.50x (ISBN 0-88410-668-3). Ballinger Pub.

Westley, Richard, jt. auth. see May, William.

Westley, William A. Violence & the Police: A Sociological Study of Law, Custom, & Morality. 1970. pap. 4.95 o.p. (ISBN 0-262-73027-8, 187). MIT Pr.

Westly. Polyether Antibiotics: Vol. 2, Naturally Occuring Acid, Ionophores. 392p. 1983. 65.00 (ISBN 0-8247-1888-7). Dekker.

Westman, Jack C. Individual Differences in Children. LC 72-10131. 362p. 1973. 21.00 o.p. (ISBN 0-471-93690-1). Krieger.

Westman, Jack C., ed. Individual Differences in Children. LC 72-10131. (Personality Processes Ser.). 368p. 1973. 31.00 o.p. (ISBN 0-471-93690-1, Pub. by Wiley-Interscience). Wiley.

Westman, Paul. Alan Shepard: First American in Space. LC 79-19866. (Taking Part Ser.). (Illus.). (gr. 3 up). 1979. PLB 7.95 o.p. (ISBN 0-87518-184-8). Dillon.

--Andrew Young: Champion of the Poor. Schneider, Tom, ed. (Taking Part Ser.). (Illus.). 48p. (gr. 3 up). 1983. PLB 7.95 (ISBN 0-87518-239-9). Dillon Pr.

--Jesse Jackson: I Am Somebody. LC 80-20521. (Taking Part Ser.). 48p. (gr. 3 up). 1980. PLB 7.95 (ISBN 0-87518-203-8). Dillon.

--Ray Kroc: Mayor of McDonaldland. LC 79-19913. (Taking Part Ser.). (Illus.). (gr. 3 up). 1980. PLB 7.95 (ISBN 0-87518-185-6). Dillon.

Westman, Robert S., ed. The Copernican Achievement. 1976. 37.50x (ISBN 0-520-02877-5). U of Cal Pr.

Westmeyer, Nancy. Parish Life: Formation for Mission & Ministry. 1983. pap. 8.95t (ISBN 0-8091-2489-0). Paulist Pr.

Westmore, Michael G. The Art of Theatricial Makeup for Stage & Screen. (Illus.). 1972. pap. text ed. 17.95 (ISBN 0-07-069485-0, G). McGraw.

Westmorland, Mildmay F. Otia Sacra. LC 75-31684. 200p. 1975. Repr. of 1648 ed. lib. bdg. 30.00x (ISBN 0-8201-1162-7). Schol Facsimiles.

Westoff, Leslie A. Breaking Out of the Middle-Age Trap. 1980. 11.95 o.p. (ISBN 0-453-00378-8, H378). NAL.

Weston & Brigham. Essentials of Managerial Finance. 6th ed. LC 78-56194. 736p. 1982. text ed. 26.95 (ISBN 0-03-059548-7). Dryden Pr.

Weston, A., jt. auth. see Kleindienst, V. K.

Weston, Anthony. The Chinese Revolution. Yapp, Malcolm, et al, eds. (World History Ser.). (Illus.). 32p. (gr. 10). 1980. Repr. of 1977 ed. lib. bdg. 6.95 (ISBN 0-89908-139-8); pap. text ed. 2.25 (ISBN 0-89908-114-2). Greenhaven.

Weston, Burns H., jt. ed. see Lillich, Richard B.

Weston, Corinne & Greenberg, Janelle R. Subjects & Sovereigns: The Grand Controversy Over Legal Sovereignty in Stuart England. LC 80-40588. 400p. 1981. 44.50 (ISBN 0-521-23272-4). Cambridge U Pr.

Weston, Curtis, jt. auth. see Shinn, Glen C.

Weston, Edward G., jt. auth. see Griffith, John L.

Weston, G. F. & Bittleston, R. Alphanumeric Displays: Devices, Drive Circuits & Applications. 208p. 1983. 32.50i (ISBN 0-07-069468-0, P&RB). McGraw.

Weston, G. J., jt. auth. see Sherwin, E.

Weston, Glen E., jt. ed. see Oppenheim, S. Chesterfield.

Weston, Harold. Freedom in the Wilds: A Saga of the Adirondacks. LC 79-160118. (Illus.). 232p. 1972. 9.95 (ISBN 0-9600450-0-7); pap. 4.50 (ISBN 0-685-25194-2). Adirondack Trail.

Weston, J. Fred & Sorge, Bart W. Guide to International Financial Management. 1977. 19.95 (ISBN 0-07-069488-5, C); text ed. 14.95 (ISBN 0-07-069487-7). McGraw.

Weston, J. Fred, jt. auth. see Copeland, Thomas E.

Weston, J. Fred & Goudzwaard, Maurice B., eds. The Treasurer's Handbook. LC 75-39474. 1976. 45.00 (ISBN 0-87094-118-6). Dow Jones-Irwin.

Weston, J. Fred, ed. see UCLA Extension.

Weston, P. & Fraley, P. Police Personnel Management. 1980. 19.95 (ISBN 0-13-683631-3). P-H.

Weston, Paul, jt. auth. see Wells, Ken.

Weston, Paul B. & Wells, Kenneth. Criminal Justice Introduction & Guidelines: A Revision of Law Enforcement & Criminal Justice. LC 74-19946. 1976. text ed. 22.95x (ISBN 0-673-16035-1); instructor's manual free o.p. (ISBN 0-87620-167-2). Scott F.

Weston, Paul B. & Wells, Kenneth M. The Administration of Justice. 4th ed. (Illus.). 240p. 1981. text ed. 18.95 (ISBN 0-13-006395-9). P-H.

--Criminal Investigation: Basic Perspectives. 3rd ed. (Criminal Justice Ser.). (Illus.). 1980. text ed. 23.95 (ISBN 0-13-193201-2). P-H.

Weston, Paul B., jt. auth. see Wells, Kenneth M.

Weston, Peter. Andromeda. LC 78-21400. 1979. 8.95 o.p. (ISBN 0-312-03649-3). St Martin.

Weston, Ralph & Schwarz, Harold. Chemical Kinetics. (Fundamental Topics in Physical Chemistry Ser). (Illus.). 1972. ref. ed. 25.95 (ISBN 0-13-128660-9). P-H.

Weston, Reiko. Cooking the Japanese Way. LC 81-12656. (Easy Menu Ethnic Cookbooks Ser.). (Illus.). 48p. (gr. 5 up). 1983. PLB 7.95g (ISBN 0-8225-0905-9). Lerner Pubns.

Weston, Trevor. A Doctor's Guide to Home Medical Care. (Illus.). 224p. 1983. pap. 6.95 (ISBN 0-8092-5970-2). Contemp Bks.

Weston-Smith, M., jt. ed. see Duncan, R.

Westphal, Clarence. Mooney, the Pet Lion. (Nature & Science Bk.). (Illus.). (gr. k-6). PLB 5.95 o.p. (ISBN 0-513-00379-7). Denison.

Westphal, E. Pulses in Ethopia, Their Taxonomy & Agricultural Significance. 263p. 1974. 40.00 o.p. (ISBN 90-220-0502-X, PDC193, Pub. by PUDOC). Unipub.

Westphal, Ethel. Nicolai Rimsky-Korsakov, Composer of Russian Romantic Music. Rahmas, Sigurd C., ed. (Outstanding Personalities Ser.: No. 94). 32p. (gr. 9-12). 1982. 2.95 (ISBN 0-87157-594-9); pap. text ed. 1.95 (ISBN 0-87157-094-7). SamHar Pr.

Westphal, F. Art of Philosophy: An Introductory Reader. LC 78-38042. (Illus.). 352p. 1972. pap. text ed. 14.95 (ISBN 0-13-048025-8). P-H.

Westphal, Fred A. Activity of Philosophy: A Concise Introduction. (Philosophy Ser). 1969. pap. text ed. 13.95 (ISBN 0-13-003608-0). P-H.

Westphal, Frederick W. Beginning Woodwind Class Method. 4th ed. 230p. 1983. pap. text ed. write for info. (ISBN 0-697-03565-4). Wm C Brown.

Westphal, Larry E. & Rhee, Yung W. Korean Industrial Competence: Where It Came From. (Working Paper: No. 469). 76p. 1981. 5.00 (ISBN 0-686-36176-8, WP-0469). World Bank.

Westphal, Patricia, jt. ed. see Joiner, Elizabeth.

Westphal, Ruth. Plein Air Painters of California: The Southland. LC 82-90314. (Illus.). 228p. 1982. 75.00 (ISBN 0-9610520-0-7). Westphal Pub.

Westphall, Victor. Public Domain in New Mexico, 1854-1891. LC 64-17807. (Illus.). 212p. 1965. 7.50x o.p. (ISBN 0-8263-0104-5). U of NM Pr.

--Thomas Benton Catron & His Era. LC 73-75304. 1973. 12.50 o.s.i. (ISBN 0-8165-0341-9); pap. 6.95 (ISBN 0-8165-0454-7). U of Ariz Pr.

Westreich, Budd, ed. Third International Directory of Private Presses (Letterpress) (Illus.). 160p. 1982. 25.00 (ISBN 0-936300-04-3); pap. 15.00 (ISBN 0-936300-03-5). Pr Arden Park.

Westrup, J. A. see Abraham, Gerald.

Westrup, Jack. Introduction to Musical History. (Repr. of 1955 ed). 1963. text ed. 8.50x o. p. (ISBN 0-09-031591-X, Hutchinson U Lib); pap. text ed. 9.25x (ISBN 0-09-031592-8, Hutchinson U Lib). Humanities.

Westwater, James, photos by. Ohio. McCutchen, Richard S. LC 81-86040. (Illus.). 128p. 1982. 29.50 (ISBN 0-912856-77-7). Graphic Arts Ctr.

Westwood, Gordon see Schofield, M., pseud.

Westwood, J. N. Russia since Nineteen Seventeen. LC 79-27598. 1980. 22.50 (ISBN 0-312-69607-8). St Martin.

--Soviet Locomotive Technology During Industrilization 1928-1952. 1982. 80.00 (ISBN 0-686-42925-7, Pub. by Macmillan England). State Mutual Bk.

Westwood, Jennifer. Stories of Charlemagne. LC 74-12435. (gr. 6 up). 1976. 10.95 (ISBN 0-87599-213-7). S G Phillips.

Westwood, W. & Cooper, B. S. Analytical Methods in Use in Non-Ferrous Mining & Metallurgy: A Selective Review. 54p. (Orig.). 1973. 14.50 (ISBN 0-900488-17-4). IMM North Am.

Wetanson, Burt & Hoobler, Thomas. The Treasure Hunters. LC 82-60692. 240p. 1983. pap. 2.95 (ISBN 0-86721-235-7). Playboy Pbks.

Wetenhall, John, jt. auth. see Cass, David B.

Wetering, Janwillen Van De see Van de Wetering, Janwillen.

Wetherall, Charles F. Diet. Galbraith, Judy, ed. (Illus.). 208p. (Orig.). 1981. pap. 1.95 (ISBN 0-936750-01-4). Wetherall.

--Kicking the Coffee Habit. Galbraith, Judy, ed. 190p. (Orig.). 1981. pap. 4.95 (ISBN 0-936750-02-2). Wetherall.

--Quit. (Illus.). 208p. (Orig.). 1980. pap. 2.50 (ISBN 0-936750-00-6). Wetherall.

--Single Man's Survival Guide. (Illus.). 160p. 1983. pap. 4.95 (ISBN 0-936750-06-5). Wetherall.

Wetherall, June. Isle of Rapture. 1979. pap. 2.25 o.p. (ISBN 0-523-40341-0). Pinnacle Bks.

Wetherall, P. J., jt. auth. see Chatterjee, P. K.

Wetherbe, J., jt. auth. see Dickson, G. W.

Wetherbe, James C. Cases in Systems Design. (Data Processing & Information Systems Ser.). 1979. pap. text ed. 10.50 (ISBN 0-8299-0229-5). West Pub.

--Systems Analysis for Computer-Based Informtion Systems. 1979. text ed. 18.50 (ISBN 0-8299-0228-7). West Pub.

Wetherbee, Martha. Martha Wetherbee's Handbook of New Shaker Baskets. (Illus.). 50p. 1982. pap. 3.50 (ISBN 0-9609384-0-0). Taylor Home.

Wetherby, Terry. Conversations: Working Women Talk about Doing a Man's Job. LC 76-53343. 1977. pap. 6.95 o.p. (ISBN 0-89087-922-2). Les Femmes Pub.

Wethered, Audrey. Movement & Drama in Therapy. 1973. 10.95 (ISBN 0-8238-0148-9). Plays.

Wetherell, C. Etudes for Programmers. LC 77-13961. (Illus.). 1978. pap. 16.95 ref. (ISBN 0-13-291807-2). P-H.

Wetherell, June. A Time for Desire. 1977. pap. 1.95 o.p. (ISBN 0-523-40091-8). Pinnacle Bks.

Wetherill, G. B., jt. auth. see Hine, J.

Wetherill, G. Barrie. Sampling Inspection & Quality Control. 2nd ed. 1977. pap. 10.50x (ISBN 0-412-14960-5, Pub. by Chapman & Hall). Methuen Inc.

--Sequential Methods in Statistics. 2nd ed. (Monographs in Applied Probability & Statistics). 1975. pap. 14.95x (ISBN 0-412-21810-0, Pub. by Chapman & Hall). Methuen Inc.

Wetherill, G. W., et al, eds. Annual Review of Earth & Planetary Sciences, Vol. 11. LC 72-82137. (Illus.). 500p. 1983. text ed. 44.00 (ISBN 0-8243-2011-5). Andrews & McMeel.

Wetherill, P. M. The Literary Text: An Examination of Critical Methods. 1974. 30.00x (ISBN 0-520-02709-4). U of Cal Pr.

Wetherill, P. M., ed. Flaubert: La Dimension du Texte. 288p. (Fr.). 1982. pap. 12.50 (ISBN 0-7190-0842-5). Manchester.

Wethern, George & Colnett, Vincent. A Wayward Angel. LC 78-1989. 1978. 8.95 o.p. (ISBN 0-399-90006-3, Marek). Putnam Pub Group.

Wetlesen, Jon, jt. ed. see Gullvag, Ingemund.

Wetmore, C. M., jt. auth. see Weber, W. A.

Wetmore, Marge C. Sugar: The Clumsy Colt. 1983. 5.75 (ISBN 0-8062-2132-1). Carlton.

Wetmore, Monroe N. Index Verborum Catullianus. 1912. 49.50x (ISBN 0-685-89758-3). Elliots Bks.

Wets, R. J., jt. auth. see Sorenson, C. D.

Wets, R. J., jt. auth. see Sorenson, D.

Wets, R. J., ed. Stochastic Systems: Modeling, Indentification Optimization II. (Mathematical Programming Studies: Vol. 6). 1977. pap. 27.75 (ISBN 0-7204-0570-X, North-Holland). Elsevier.

Wets, Roger J., ed. Stochastic Systems: Modeling, Identification, & Optimization I. Benes, Vaclav E. LC 76-50621. (Mathematical Programming Studies: Vol. 5). pap. 20.50 (ISBN 0-7204-0569-6, North-Holland). Elsevier.

Wetsel, David. L' Ecriture et le Reste: The "Pensees" of Pascal in the Exegetical Tradition of Port-Royal. LC 81-9610. (Illus.). 256p. 1981. 22.50x (ISBN 0-8142-0324-8). Ohio St U Pr.

Wettengel, G. A. Vollstandiges Theoretisch-Praktisches Lehrbuch der Anfertigung und Reparatur: Italischer und Deutscher Geigen. 72.50 o.s.i. (ISBN 90-6027-367-2, Pub. by Frits Knuf Netherlands). Pendragon NY.

Wetter, J. Gillis. International Arbitral Process: Public & Private, Vols. 1-5. LC 79-479. 1979. lib. bdg. 50.00 ea. (ISBN 0-379-20379-0). Oceana.

Wetterau, Bruce. Complete Word-Finder Crossword Dictionary. (Orig.). 1981. pap. 3.95 (ISBN 0-451-09910-9, E9910, Sig). NAL.

--The Macmillan Concise Dictionary of World History. 672p. 1983. 39.95 (ISBN 0-02-626110-3). Macmillan.

Wetterberg, Walt. Hutch Meets Ada. LC 79-18999. 128p. (Orig.). 1979. pap. 3.95x (ISBN 0-89795-006-2). Farm Journal.

Wetterer, Margaret K. The Giant's Apprentice. LC 81-10810. (Illus.). 48p. (gr. 1-4). 1982. PLB 8.95 (ISBN 0-689-50229-X, McElderry Bk). Atheneum.

Wettern, Desmond. The Decline of British Sea Power. (Illus.). 224p. 1982. 29.95 (ISBN 0-86720-627-6). Sci Bks Intl.

Wettig, Gerhard. Broadcasting & Detente. LC 77-72285. 1977. 18.95x (ISBN 0-312-10588-6). St Martin.

--Community & Conflict in the Socialist Camp 1965-1972: The Soviet Union, the GDR, & the German Problem. LC 75-6048. 174p. 1975. 26.00 (ISBN 0-312-15295-7). St Martin.

Wettstone, Eugene, ed. Gymnastics Safety Manual: The Official Manual of the United States Gymnastics Safety Association. 2nd ed. LC 79-65860. (Illus.). 1979. lib. bdg. 12.95x (ISBN 0-271-00242-5); pap. text ed. 7.95x (ISBN 0-271-00244-1). Pa St U Pr.

Wetzel, Elizabeth. A Is for Aggravation: Alphabet Book. LC 82-83566. 224p. 1983. 12.95 (ISBN 0-689-11382-X). Atheneum.

Wetzel, Guy F. Automotive Diagnosis & Tune-up. new ed. (gr. 9-12). 1974. text ed. 19.96 (ISBN 0-87345-100-7). McKnight.

Wetzel, Joseph, tr. see Sigwart.

Wetzel, Richard D. Frontier Musicians on the Connoquenessing, Wabash & Ohio: A History of the Music & Musicians of George Rapp's Harmony Society (1805-1906) LC 74-80809. (Illus.). 293p. 1976. 16.00x (ISBN 0-8214-0208-0, 82-82436). Ohio U Pr.

Wetzel, Robert G., jt. auth. see Franko, David A.

Wetzsteon, Ross. The Obie Winners: The Best of Off-Broadway. LC 79-6096. (Illus.). 816p. 1980. 15.95 o.p. (ISBN 0-385-17005-X). Doubleday.

Weulersee, G., jt. auth. see Renard, G.

Wevill, David. Casual Ties. Weisman, Dale & Taylor, R. D., eds. 110p. (Orig.). 1983. 9.95 (ISBN 0-931604-14-1); pap. 4.95 (ISBN 0-686-84099-2). Curbstone Pub NY TX.

Wexler, David A. & Rice, Laura N. Innovations in Client-Centered Therapy. LC 74-10538. (Personality Processes Ser.). 1974. 49.95x (ISBN 0-471-93715-0, Pub. by Wiley-Interscience). Wiley.

Wexler, Elizabeth, jt. auth. see Levine, Erwin L.

Wexler, H., jt. auth. see Scorer, R. S.

Wexler, Jerome. Secrets of the Venus's Fly Trap. LC 80-2775. (Illus.). 64p. (gr. 2-5). 1981. PLB 7.95 (ISBN 0-396-07941-5). Dodd.

Wexler, Jerome, jt. auth. see Selsam, Millicent E.

Wexler, Joyce P. Laura Riding's Pursuit of Truth. LC 76-51688. xii, 169p. 1979. 14.00x (ISBN 0-8214-0364-8, 80-82550). Ohio U Pr.

Wexler, Kenneth & Culicover, Peter W. Formal Principles of Language Acquisition. 1980. 37.00x (ISBN 0-262-23099-2). MIT Pr.

Wexler, P., ed. Information Resources in Toxicology. 1982. 50.00 (ISBN 0-444-00616-8). Elsevier.

Wexler, Philip. Critical Social Psychology. (Critical Social Thought Ser.). 176p. 1983. 17.50 (ISBN 0-7100-9194-X). Routledge & Kegan.

Wexley, Kenneth & Latham, Gary. Developing & Training Human Resources in Organizations. 1982. pap. text ed. 12.50x (ISBN 0-673-16001-7). Scott F.

Wexman, Virginia W. & Bisplinghoff, Gretchen. Roman Polanski: A Guide to References & Resources. 1979. lib. bdg. 17.50 (ISBN 0-8161-7906-9, Hall Reference). G K Hall.

Wexo, John B., ed. see Wildlife Education, Ltd.

Weyand, Carolyn A., jt. auth. see O'Farrell, Timothy J.

Weyand, Clint. Thank You for Being. LC 78-101834. (Illus.). 1977. pap. 5.95 (ISBN 0-9601922-0-4). Weyand-Shaw.

Weyandt, Dorothy. I Was a Guide for Three U.S. Presidents. LC 75-25219. 1976. pap. 10.00 (ISBN 0-917424-02-6). Weyandt.

Weydenthal, Jan B. de see De Weydenthal, Jan B.

Weygand & Hilgetag, G. Preparative Organic Chemistry. LC 72-6800. 1973. 86.00 o.p. (ISBN 0-471-93749-5, Pub. by Wiley-Interscience). Wiley.

Weygandt, Jerry J., jt. auth. see Kieso, Donald E.

Weyl, A. Jules Fon Roberts Collections of Coins of Asia, Africa & Australia. (Illus.). 1983. Repr. of 1878 ed. lib. bdg. 40.00 (ISBN 0-915262-78-9). S J Durst.

Weyl, Hermann. Open World: Three Lectures on the Metaphysical Implications of Science. 1932. text ed. 24.50x (ISBN 0-686-83658-8). Elliots Bks.

--Symmetrie. 2nd ed. (Science & Society Ser.: No. 11). 158p. (Ger.). 1981. text ed. 15.00x (ISBN 3-7643-1280-7). Birkhauser.

Weyl, Hermann, et al. Das Kontinuum und Andere Monographien, 4 vols. in 1. Incl. Kantinuum; Mathematische Analyse Des Raumproblems; Neuere Funktionentheorie. Landau; Hypothesen. Reimann. LC 72-81808. 16.95 (ISBN 0-8284-0134-9). Chelsea Pub.

Weyl, Nathaniel. Karl Marx: Racist. 1979. 11.95 o.p. (ISBN 0-87000-448-4, Arlington Hse). Crown.

Weyl, Peter K. Oceanography: An Introduction to the Marine Environment. 1970. 27.95x (ISBN 0-471-93744-4). Wiley.

Weyl, Richard. Geology of Central America. 2nd ed. (Beitraege Zur Regionalen Geologie der Erde: Vol. 15). (Illus.). 371p. 1980. lib. bdg. 69.60 (ISBN 3-443-11015-0). Lubrecht & Cramer.

Weyland, Jack. Peppertide. LC 82-25171. 181p. 1983. 7.95 (ISBN 0-87747-967-4). Deseret Bk.

Weyler, Rex. Blood of the Land. LC 82-2349. (Illus.). 304p. 1982. 16.95 (ISBN 0-89696-134-6, An Everest House Book). Dodd.

Weyman, Darrell & Weyman, Valerie. Landscape Processes: An Introduction to Geomorphology. (Processes in Physical Geography Ser). (Illus.). 1977. pap. text ed. 7.95x (ISBN 0-04-551026-1). Allen Unwin.

Weyman, Valerie, jt. auth. see Weyman, Darrell.

Weymuller, Fred, jt. auth. see Faulkner, Ed.

Weyr, Thomas, tr. see Friedlander, Saul.

Weyr, Tom, tr. see Vandenberg, Philipp.

Weyrauch, Walter O. & Katz, Sanford N. American Family Law in Transition. 650p. 1983. text ed. 35.00 (ISBN 0-87179-390-3). BNA.

Weyrick, Robert C. Fundamentals of Automatic Control. (Illus.). 480p. 1975. text ed. 23.95 (ISBN 0-07-069493-1, G); solutions manual 3.00 (ISBN 0-07-069494-X). McGraw.

Wezel, Antonius L. van see Mizrahi, Avshalom & Van Wezel, Antonius L.

Wezel, Ru van. Video Handbook. (Illus.). 403p. 1982. 55.00 (ISBN 0-408-00490-8). Focal Pr.

Wha-Duk Ahn. A Theory of Earth Management. 1979. 8.95 o.p. (ISBN 0-533-04244-5). Vantage.

Whale, A. Barrett. Joint Stock Banking in Germany. 369p. 1968. 34.00x (ISBN 0-7146-1259-6, F Cass Co). Biblio Dist.

Whale, John. Politics of the Media. LC 77-88395. (Political Issues of Modern Britain). 1977. text ed. 13.00x o.p. (ISBN 0-391-00550-2). Humanities.

Whale, John & Hebblethwaite, Peter. The Man Who Leads the Church: An Assessment of Pope John Paul II. LC 80-7745. 256p. 1980. 10.95i o.p. (ISBN 0-06-069345-2, HarpR). Har-Row.

Whalen, A. D. Detection of Signals in Noise. (Electrical Science Ser). 1971. 52.00 (ISBN 0-12-744850-0). Acad Pr.

Whalen, Carol K. & Henker, Barbara, eds. Hyperactive Children: The Social Ecology of Identification & Treatment. LC 80-324. 1980. 27.50 (ISBN 0-12-745950-2). Acad Pr.

Whalen, Donald J., ed. Handbook for Development Officers at Independent Schools. 2nd ed. 350p. 1982. 30.00 (ISBN 0-89964-194-6). CASE.

Whalen, Doris H. Handbook for Business Writers. 1978. pap. text ed. 9.95 o.p. (ISBN 0-15-530800-9, HC); instructor's manual avail. o.p. (ISBN 0-15-530801-7). HarBraceJ.

--Handbook of Business English. 264p. 1980. pap. text ed. 9.95 o.p. (ISBN 0-686-64977-X, HC); instructor's manual avail. o.p. HarBraceJ.

Whalen, G., jt. auth. see Graf, R.

Whalen, Richard E., jt. ed. see Gorski, Roger A.

Whalen, Richard E., et al, eds. Neural Control of Behavior. 1970. 49.50 (ISBN 0-12-745050-5). Acad Pr.

Whalen, William J. Minority Religions in America. LC 79-38979. 312p. (Orig.). 1972. pap. 2.95 o.p. (ISBN 0-8189-0239-6). Alba.

Whaler, J. Counterpoint & Symbol. LC 76-117997. (Studies in Blake, No. 3). 1970. Repr. of 1956 ed. lib. bdg. 32.95x (ISBN 0-8383-1052-4). Haskell.

Whaley. Problems & Materials on Negotiable Instruments. 1981. text ed. 18.95 (ISBN 0-316-93214-0). Little.

Whaley, Barton. Codeword BARBAROSSA. (Illus.). 1973. pap. 4.95x (ISBN 0-262-73038-3). MIT Pr.

Whaley, Donald, jt. auth. see Malott, Richard W.

Whaley, Douglas. Problems & Materials on Secured Transactions. LC 81-86024. 1982. text ed. 18.00 (ISBN 0-316-93216-7). Little.

Whaley, Lucille & Wong, Donna L. Essentials of Pediatric Nursing. LC 81-14042. 943p. 1982. text ed. 32.95 (ISBN 0-8016-5422-X). Mosby.

Whaley, Lucille F. & Wong, Donna L. Nursing Care of Infants & Children. 2nd ed. (Illus.). 1694p. 1983. text ed. 38.95 (ISBN 0-8016-5419-X). Mosby.

Whaley, Stephen & Cook, Stanley. Man Unwept: Visions from the Inner Eye. (Illus.). 384p. 1974. pap. text ed. 11.00 o.p. (ISBN 0-07-069481-8, C). McGraw.

Whall, Ann, jt. auth. see Fitzpatrick, Joyce.

Whalley, B. H. Production Management Handbook. 512p. 1980. text ed. 49.25x (ISBN 0-566-02133-1). Gower Pub Ltd.

Whalley, George. Poetic Process. LC 73-5274. 256p. 1973. Repr. of 1953 ed. lib. bdg. 20.25x (ISBN 0-8371-6878-3, WHPP). Greenwood.

Whalley, Irene, ed. The Beatrix Potter Collection, Vol. 1. 320p. 1982. 80.00x (ISBN 0-85692-070-3, Pub. by J M Dent). State Mutual Bk.

Whalley, Joyce I. The Pen's Excellence. LC 80-51966. (Illus.). 408p. 1982. pap. 20.00 (ISBN 0-8008-6282-1, Pentalic). Taplinger.

Whalley, L., jt. auth. see Burlace, C. J.

Whalon, Marion K., ed. Performing Arts Research: A Guide to Information Sources. LC 75-13828. (Performing Arts Information Guide Ser.: Vol. 1). 240p. 1976. 42.00x (ISBN 0-8103-1364-2). Gale.

Wharton, A. J. Diesel Engines: Questions & Answers. (Marine Engineering Ser.). 1975. pap. 9.95x (ISBN 0-540-07342-3). Sheridan.

Wharton, Anne H. Through Colonial Doorways. LC 70-141040. 1970. Repr. of 1893 ed. 30.00x (ISBN 0-8103-3588-3). Gale.

Wharton, C. B., jt. auth. see Heald, M. A.

Wharton, Christopher W. Molecular Enzymology. (Tertiary Level Biology Ser.). 335p. 1981. 46.95x o.p. (ISBN 0-470-27152-3). Halsted Pr.

Wharton, Donald P., ed. In the Trough of the Sea: Selected American Sea-Deliverance Narratives, 1610-1766. LC 78-22721. (Contributions in American Studies: No. 44). (Illus.). 1979. lib. bdg. 29.95x (ISBN 0-313-20870-0, WTR/). Greenwood.

Wharton, Edith. The Age of Innocence. 384p. 1983. pap. 3.95 (ISBN 0-686-83694-4, ScribT). Scribner.

--Fighting France, from Dunkerque to Belfort. LC 74-12840. (Illus.). 238p. 1975. Repr. of 1915 ed. lib. bdg. 18.50x (ISBN 0-8371-7759-6, WHFF). Greenwood.

Wharton, H. T., tr. see Sappho.

Wharton, James. Bounty of the Chesapeake: Fishing in Colonial Virginia. (Illus.). 78p. (Orig.). 1957. pap. 2.95 (ISBN 0-8139-0137-5). U Pr of Va.

Wharton, John. Jobs in Japan: Complete Guide to Living & Working in Japan. (Illus.). 220p. 1983. pap. 9.95 (ISBN 0-911285-00-8). Global Pr Co.

Wharton, Robert. Review of the Nearctic Alysiini (Hymenoptera, Braconidae) (U. C. Publications in Entomology Ser.: Vol. 88). 122p. 1980. 16.00x (ISBN 0-520-09611-8). U of Cal Pr.

Wharton School of Finance & Commerce, University of Pennsylvania. A Study of Mutual Funds: Report of the Committee on Interstate & Foreign Commerce-(87th Congress, 2nd Session, House Report No. 2274) LC 62-62400. xxxiii, 595p. 1982. Repr. of 1962 ed. lib. bdg. 38.50 (ISBN 0-89941-181-9). W. S. Hein.

Whately, Richard. Elements of Logic. LC 75-17581. 360p. 1975. lib. bdg. 42.00x (ISBN 0-8201-1157-0). Schol Facsimiles.

Whatever Pub. Inc. Life & Love. 184p. (Orig.). 1982. pap. 4.95 (ISBN 0-9609856-0-3). R Garfield.

Whatley, Arthur & Kelley, Lane. Personnel Management in Action: Skill Building Experiences. (Management Ser). (Illus.). 1977. pap. text ed. 11.95 o.s.i. (ISBN 0-8299-0123-X); instrs.' manual avail. o.s.i. (ISBN 0-8299-0582-0). West Pub.

Whatley, Arthur A., jt. auth. see Kelley, Nelson L.

Whatley, F. R. & Whatley, J. M. Light & Plant Life. (Studies in Biology: No. 124). 96p. 1980. pap. text ed. 8.95 (ISBN 0-7131-2785-6). E Arnold.

Whatley, J. M., jt. auth. see Whatley, F. R.

Whatley, Robert L. Honestly, I Love You, Douglas County. (Illus.). 256p. 1983. 12.50 (ISBN 0-932298-33-8). Copple Hse.

Whatmore, George B. & Kohli, Daniel R. The Physiopathology & Treatment of Functional Disorders. LC 74-17154. (Illus.). 258p. 1974. 39.50 o.s.i. (ISBN 0-8089-0851-0). Grune.

Whatmore, John. The CTC Book of Cycling: The Cyclists' Touring Club of Britain. (Illus.). 256p. 1983. 24.95 (ISBN 0-7153-8370-1). David & Charles.

Whattam, jt. auth. see Martin.

Wheare, Kenneth C. The Constitutional Structure of the Commonwealth. LC 82-11866. 201p. 1982. Repr. of 1960 ed. lib. bdg. 27.50x (ISBN 0-313-23624-0, WHCO). Greenwood.

Wheat, Doug. Floater's Guide to Colorado. (Illus.). 256p. 1983. 8.95 (ISBN 0-934318-16-6). Falcon Pr MT.

Wheat, Ed. Amor que no se apaga. Date not set. 2.50 (ISBN 0-88113-010-9). Edit Betania.

Wheat, Ed & De Wheat, Gaye. El Placer Sexual Ordenado por Dios. 224p. Date not set. 3.25 (ISBN 0-88113-320-5). Edit Betania.

Wheat, Ed & Wheat, Gaye. Intended for Pleasure. rev. ed. (Illus.). 256p. 1981. 10.95 (ISBN 0-8007-1253-6). Revell.

Wheat, Gaye, jt. auth. see Wheat, Ed.

Wheat, Gaye de see Wheat, Ed & De Wheat, Gaye.

Wheat, Margaret M. Survival Arts of the Primitive Paiutes. LC 67-30392. (Illus.). xiii, 119p. 1967. pap. 7.50 (ISBN 0-87417-048-6). U of Nev Pr.

Wheat, Myron W., Jr., jt. auth. see Goldberger, Emanuel.

Wheat, Valerie, jt. auth. see West, Celeste.

Wheatcroft, Andrew. Arabia & The Gulf in Original Photographs Eighteen Eighty to Nineteen-Fifty. 200p. 1983. 38.95 (ISBN 0-7103-0016-6). Routledge & Kegan.

--The Tennyson Album: A Biography in Original Photographs. (Illus.). 200p. 1980. 14.95 (ISBN 0-7100-0494-X). Routledge & Kegan.

--The World Atlas of Revolution. 1983. write for info. (ISBN 0-671-46286-5). S&S.

Wheatcroft, Andrew, compiled by see Dolin, Anton.

Wheatcroft, Andrew, ed. see Hubmann, Franz.

Wheatcroft, John. Catherine, Her Book. LC 81-66295. 14.95 (ISBN 0-686-43055-7). Cornwall Bks.

Wheatley. Modern Marketing: Study Guide. 1978. pap. 6.95x (ISBN 0-673-15128-X). Scott F.

Wheatley, D. N. The Centriole: A Central Enigma of Cell Biology. 232p. 1982. 81.00 (ISBN 0-444-80359-9). Elsevier.

Wheatley, David, ed. Psychopharmacology of Old Age. (British Association for Psychopharmacology Monographs). (Illus.). 1982. 29.50 (ISBN 0-19-261373-1). Oxford U Pr.

--Psychopharmacology of Sleep. 256p. 1981. text ed. 32.00 (ISBN 0-89004-593-3). Raven.

--Stress & the Heart. 2nd ed. 430p. 1981. softcover 27.50 (ISBN 0-89004-520-8). Raven.

Wheatley, Denys N. Cell Growth & Division. (Studies in Biology: No. 148). 64p. 1982. pap. text ed. 8.95 (ISBN 0-7131-2859-3). E Arnold.

Wheatley, Edward W., jt. auth. see Fox, Edward J.

Wheatley, George. Schooling a Young Horse. LC 68-29868. (Illus.). 1968. 4.95 o.p. (ISBN 0-668-02816-5). Arco.

--The Young Rider's Companion. LC 81-27509. (Adult & Young Adult Bks.). (Illus.). 120p. (gr. 4 up). 1981. PLB 14.95g (ISBN 0-8225-0767-6, AACR1). Lerner Pubns.

Wheatley, Henry B. Dedication of Books to Patron & Friend. LC 68-30615. 1968. Repr. of 1887 ed. 30.00x (ISBN 0-8103-3316-3). Gale.

--Literary Blunders. LC 68-30616. 1969. Repr. of 1893 ed. 34.00x (ISBN 0-8103-3317-1). Gale.

--London, Past & Present: A Dictionary of Its History Associations & Traditions, 3 Vols. LC 68-17956. 1968. Repr. of 1891 ed. Set. 113.00x (ISBN 0-8103-3499-2). Gale.

Wheatley, James M. Patterns in Thackeray's Fiction. 1969. pap. 2.95 o.p. (ISBN 0-262-73023-5). MIT Pr.

Wheatley, Melvin. Christmas Is for Celebrating. 1977. pap. 3.95 (ISBN 0-8358-0366-X). Upper Room.

Wheaton, Barbara K. Savoring the Past: The French Kitchen & Table from 1300 to 1789. LC 82-40486. (Illus.). 448p. (Orig.). 1983. 35.00x (ISBN 0-8122-7865-8); pap. 17.95x (ISBN 0-8122-1146-4). U of Pa Pr.

Wheaton, Bruce R. & Heilbron, J. L., eds. An Inventory of Published Letters to & from Physicists 1900-1950. LC 80-51581. (Berkeley Papers in History of Science: No. 6). 1983. pap. 20.00x (ISBN 0-918102-06-5). U Cal Hist Sci Tech.

Wheaton, Chistopher S. Primary Cinema Resources: An Index of Screen Plays, Interviews & Special Collections at the University of Southern California. 1975. lib. bdg. 26.00 (ISBN 0-8161-1198-7, Hall Reference). G K Hall.

Wheaton, F. W. Aquacultural Engineering. LC 77-22876. (Ocean Engineering Ser.). 1977. 61.95 (ISBN 0-471-93755-X, Pub by Wiley-Interscience). Wiley.

Wheaton, Henry. History of the Law of Nations in Europe & America. LC 5-29665. xiv, 797p. 1982. Repr. of 1845 ed. lib. bdg. 35.00 (ISBN 0-89941-161-4). W S Hein.

Wheaton, Philip. Razzmatazz. LC 80-12978. 346p. 1980. 12.95 (ISBN 0-89696-097-8, An Everest House Book). Dodd.

Wheaton, Philip, jt. ed. see Mays, Jeb.

Whedon, Julia. Good Sport. LC 79-7670. 216p. 1981. 10.95 o.p. (ISBN 0-385-15528-X). Doubleday.

Wheelen, Thomas L. & Hunger, J. David. Strategic Management & Business Policy. LC 82-13886. 944p. 1983. text ed. 23.95 (ISBN 0-201-09011-2); instrs' manual 400 pg. avail. (ISBN 0-201-09012-0). A-W.

Wheeler, Allen, jt. auth. see Long, Harold.

Wheeler, Arthur L. Catullus & the Traditions of Ancient Poetry. (Sather Classical Lectures: Vol. 9). 1974. 30.00x (ISBN 0-520-02640-3). U of Cal Pr.

Wheeler, B. E. Diseases in Crops. (Studies in Biology: No. 64). 64p. 1978. pap. text ed. 8.95 (ISBN 0-7131-2553-5). E Arnold.

--Introduction to Plant Diseases. LC 70-94877. 1969. 19.25 o.p. (ISBN 0-471-93751-7, Pub. by Wiley-Interscience). Wiley.

Wheeler, Bobby G. The Rebel Cowboy. (YA) 1979. 6.95 (ISBN 0-685-90727-9, Avalon). Bouregy.

Wheeler, Bonnie. Challenged Parenting: A Practical Handbook for Parents of Children with Handicaps. 210p. 1983. pap. 6.95 (ISBN 0-8307-0835-9, 5316502). Regal.

Wheeler, Brandon W., jt. auth. see Crowdis, David G.

Wheeler, Carol A. & Dalton, Marie. Word Processing Simulations for Electronic Typewriters & Text Editors. LC 81-11630. (Word Processing Ser.). 224p. 1982. pap. 12.95 (ISBN 0-471-08158-2). Wiley.

Wheeler, Carol J. The Dapper Zapper Creative Microwave Cooking: Microwaving Atlanta-Style. LC 82-670072. 192p. (Orig.). 1981. pap. 9.95 (ISBN 0-9608448-0-5). C J Wheeler.

Wheeler, Charles E. Gold Hill Showdown. (YA) 1980. 6.95 (ISBN 0-686-73929-9, Avalon). Bouregy.

--The Secret of the Flying T. (YA) 1979. 6.95 (ISBN 0-685-65275-0, Avalon). Bouregy.

Wheeler, Cindy. A Good Day, a Good Night. LC 79-3017. (Illus.). (ps-2). 1980. 8.61i o.p. (ISBN 0-397-31900-2, HarpJ); PLB 9.89 (ISBN 0-397-31901-0). Har-Row.

--Marmalade's Nap. LC 81-20868. (Illus.). 24p. (ps-1). 1983. 4.95 (ISBN 0-394-85022-X); lib. bdg. 8.99 (ISBN 0-394-95022-4). Knopf.

--Marmalade's Picnic. LC 81-20792. (Illus.). 24p. (ps-1). 1983. 4.95 (ISBN 0-394-85023-8); lib. bdg. 8.99 (ISBN 0-394-95023-2). Knopf.

Wheeler, Cork. First Book of Animals: First Nature Book. (gr. 2-5). 1982. 10.95 (ISBN 0-86020-632-7, Usbore-Hayes). EDC.

Wheeler, Daniel, ed. see Massie, Robert & Sweezey, Marilyn P.

Wheeler, David. Human Resource Development & Economic Growth in Developing Countries: A Simultaneous Model. (Working Paper: No. 407). 130p. 1980. 5.00 (ISBN 0-686-36087-7, WP-0407). World Bank.

Wheeler, David Russell. Three-D-Light: A Handbook Laboratory in the Rendering of the Universal Mesh. LC 76-21441. (Illus.). 1976. pap. 12.95 (ISBN 0-918562-01-5). Biohydrant.

Wheeler, Douglas L. Republican Portugal: A Political History, 1910-1926. LC 77-15059. (Illus.). 352p. 1978. 32.50 (ISBN 0-299-07450-1). U of Wis Pr.

Wheeler, Douglas L., jt. ed. see Graham, Lawrence S.

Wheeler, E. R., jt. auth. see Wheeler, R. E.

Wheeler, E. Todd. Hospital Design & Function. 1964. 51.50 (ISBN 0-07-069505-9, P&RB). McGraw.

--Hospital Modernization & Expansion. 1971. 49.50 (ISBN 0-07-069520-2, P&RB). McGraw.

Wheeler, Elmer. Sizzlemanship. 312p. 1983. 12.95 (ISBN 0-13-811513-3, Reward); pap. 6.95 (ISBN 0-13-811505-2). P-H.

--Tested Sentences that Sell. 228p. Date not set. 10.95 (ISBN 0-686-84599-4, Reward); pap. 5.95 (ISBN 0-13-909101-7). P-H.

Wheeler, Esther & Lasker, Anabel C. Flowers & Plants for Interior Decoration. 1969. 10.00 (ISBN 0-8208-0065-1). Hearthside.

Wheeler, Eugene D., jt. auth. see Gughemetti, Joseph M.

Wheeler, Eva F. A History of Wyoming Writers. (Illus.). 92p. 1982. pap. 7.00 (ISBN 0-686-38836-4). E F Wheeler.

Wheeler, George M., ed. Wheeler's Photographic Survey of the American West, 1871-1873: With Fifty Landscape Photographs by Timothy O'Sullivan & William Bell. (Illus.). 64p. 1983. pap. 5.00 (ISBN 0-486-24466-0). Dover.

Wheeler, Gerald & Kirkpatrick, Larry. Physics: Building a World View. (Illus.). 576p. 1983. prof. ref. 20.95 (ISBN 0-13-672204-0). P-H.

Wheeler, Gerald E. Prelude to Pearl Harbor: The United States Navy & the Far East, 1921-1931. LC 63-9468. 224p. 1963. 13.00x (ISBN 0-8262-0020-6); pap. 8.00x (ISBN 0-8262-0186-5). U of Mo Pr.

Wheeler, Gershon. Introduction to Microwaves. (Illus.). 1963. ref. ed. 21.95 (ISBN 0-13-487843-4). P-H.

Wheeler, Gershon J., jt. auth. see Barker, Forrest L.

Wheeler, Harvey, jt. auth. see Burdick, Eugene.

Wheeler, J. M., jt. ed. see Foote, G. W.

Wheeler, James O., jt. auth. see Brunn, Stanley D.

Wheeler, Jimmy W., jt. ed. see Leveson, Irving.

Wheeler, Jon D. Tax Desk Book for Farming & Ranching. 2nd ed. LC 78-55900. 1978. 39.50 o.p. (ISBN 0-87624-556-4). Inst Busn Plan.

Wheeler, K. The Railroaders. LC 73-84316. (Old West Ser). (Illus.). (gr. 5 up). 1973. 17.28 (ISBN 0-8094-1467-8, Pub. by Time-Life). Silver.

Wheeler, Karen & Arnell, Peter, eds. Michael Graves: Buildings & Projects 1966-1981. LC 81-51400. (Illus.). 304p. 1982. 45.00 (ISBN 0-8478-0431-3); pap. 29.95 (ISBN 0-8478-0405-4). Rizzoli Intl.

Wheeler, Keith. The Alaskans. LC 77-79673. (Old West Ser.). (Illus.). (gr. 5 up). 1977. 17.28 (ISBN 0-8094-1506-2, Pub. by Time-Life). Silver.

--Bombers Over Japan. LC 82-5627. (World War II Ser.). lib. bdg. 19.92 (ISBN 0-8094-3428-8, Pub. by Time-Life). Silver.

--The Chroniclers. LC 75-34961. (The Old West). (Illus.). (gr. 5 up). 1976. 17.28 (ISBN 0-8094-1531-3, Pub. by Time-Life). Silver.

--The Fall of Japan. (World War II Ser.). 1983. lib. bdg. 19.92 (ISBN 0-8094-3408-3, Pub. by Time-Life). Silver.

--The Road to Tokyo. LC 79-810. (World War II Ser.). PLB 19.92 (ISBN 0-8094-2539-4). Silver.

--The Scouts. LC 78-1364. (The Old West Ser.). (Illus.). 1978. 17.28 (ISBN 0-8094-2306-5). Silver.

--Townsmen. LC 74-2180. (Old West Ser.). (Illus.). 240p. (gr. 5 up). 1975. lib. bdg. 17.28 (ISBN 0-8094-1490-2). Silver.

--War Under the Pacific. LC 80-13222. (World War II Ser.). 19.92 (ISBN 0-8094-3376-1). Silver.

Wheeler, Kenneth W. & Lussier, Virginia L., eds. Women, the Arts, & the Nineteen Twenties in Paris & New York. LC 81-7510. 170p. 1982. 24.95 (ISBN 0-87855-908-6). Transaction Bks.

Wheeler, Ladd, ed. Review of Personality & Social Psychology, No. 3. 3rd ed. (Illus.). 320p. 1982. 25.00 (ISBN 0-8039-1854-2); pap. 12.50 (ISBN 0-8039-1855-0). Sage.

Wheeler, Lora J., ed. International Business & Foreign Trade. LC 67-31263. (Management Information Guide Ser.: No. 14). 1968. 42.00x (ISBN 0-8103-0814-2). Gale.

Wheeler, M. J. First Came the Indians. LC 82-13916. (Illus.). 32p. (gr. 1-5). 1983. 9.95 (ISBN 0-689-50258-3, McElderry Bk). Atheneum.

Wheeler, Michael, jt. auth. see Mayer, Andre.

Wheeler, Mortimer. Indus Civilization. 3rd ed. LC 22-11272. (Illus.). 1968. 34.50 (ISBN 0-521-06958-0); pap. 9.95 (ISBN 0-521-09538-7). Cambridge U Pr.

Wheeler, Otis B. Literary Career of Maurice Thompson. LC 64-23151. (University Studies, Humanities Ser.: No. 14). 1965. 12.50x (ISBN 0-8071-0826-X). La State U Pr.

Wheeler, R. & Whitcomb, H. Judicial Administration: Text & Readings. 1977. text ed. 20.95 (ISBN 0-13-511675-9). P-H.

Wheeler, R. E. & Wheeler, E. R. Mathematics: An Everyday Language. LC 78-13072. 1979. text ed. 25.95 (ISBN 0-471-03423-1); student supplement 7.50 (ISBN 0-471-04924-7); tchrs. manual o.p. 6.00 (ISBN 0-471-05409-7). Wiley.

Wheeler, Raymond. Sonnets from a Breaking Dawn. LC 72-92733. 120p. 1973. 5.00 (ISBN 0-911838-26-0). Windy Row.

Wheeler, Raymond H., jt. auth. see Ross, Jack C.

Wheeler, Richard. IWO. (Illus.). 256p. 1980. 14.37i (ISBN 0-690-01878-9). Har-Row.

--We Knew Stonewall Jackson. LC 76-58009. (Illus.). 1977. 11.49i (ISBN 0-690-01218-7). T Y Crowell.

Wheeler, Richard P. Shakespeare's Development & Problem Comedies: Turn & Counter-Turn. 275p. 1981. 22.00x (ISBN 0-520-03902-5). U of Cal Pr.

Wheeler, Robert G., et al, eds. Intrauterine Devices: Development, Evaluation, & Program Implementation. 1974. 40.00 (ISBN 0-12-745550-7). Acad Pr.

Wheeler, Robinetta T., jt. ed. see Bower, Fay L.

Wheeler, Ruric. Modern Mathematics: An Elementary Approach, Alternative Edition. 585p. 1981. text ed. 21.95 (ISBN 0-8185-0413-7). Brooks-Cole.

Wheeler, Ruric E. Modern Mathematics: An Elementary Approach. 5th ed. 625p. 1981. text ed. 23.95 (ISBN 0-8185-0430-7). Brooks-Cole.

Wheeler, Ruric E. & Peeples, W. D., Jr. Finite Mathematics: With Applications to Business & the Social Sciences. LC 80-13916. 550p. 1980. text ed. 24.95 (ISBN 0-8185-0418-8). Brooks-Cole.

--Modern Mathematics with Applications to Business & the Social Sciences. 3rd ed. LC 79-18636. 1980. text ed. 25.95 (ISBN 0-8185-0366-1). Brooks-Cole.

Wheeler, Russell C. Dental Anatomy, Physiology & Occlusion. 5th ed. LC 72-95834. (Illus.). 520p. 1974. text ed. 24.50 (ISBN 0-7216-9262-1). Saunders.

--Pulp Cavities of the Permanent Teeth: An Anatomical Guide to Manipulative Endodontics. (Illus.). 225p. 1976. text ed. 17.50x o.p. (ISBN 0-7216-9280-X). Saunders.

Wheeler, Russell R. see Levin, A. Leo.

Wheeler, S., jt. auth. see Brim, Q. G.

Wheeler, Stanton, ed. On Record: Files & Dossiers in American Life. LC 73-98421. 450p. 1970. 14.95x (ISBN 0-87154-919-0). Russell Sage.

Wheeler, Thomas G. All Men Tall. LC 70-77313. (gr. 8 up). 1969. 10.95 (ISBN 0-87599-157-2). S G Phillips.

--Fanfare for the Stalwart. LC 67-22813. (gr. 8 up). 1967. 10.95 (ISBN 0-87599-139-4). S G Phillips.

--Loose Chippings. LC 69-11990. (Illus.). (YA) 1969. 10.95 (ISBN 0-87599-152-1). S G Phillips.

--Lost Threshold. LC 68-16349. (Illus.). (gr. 7 up). 1968. 10.95 (ISBN 0-87599-140-8). S G Phillips.

Wheeler, Tom. American Guitars: An Illustrated History. LC 81-48050. (Illus.). 384p. 1983. 29.76i (ISBN 0-06-014996-5, HarpT). Har-Row.

--The Guitar Book: A Handbook for Electric & Acoustic Guitarists. rev. ed. LC 77-11791. 1978. 23.99 (ISBN 0-06-014579-X, HarpT). Har-Row.

Wheeler, Tony. Australia, Travel Survival Kit. (Illus.). 1982. pap. 7.95 o.p. (ISBN 0-908086-04-0). Hippocrene Bks.

--New Zealand: A Travel Survival Kit. (Illus.). 112p. 1983. pap. 5.95 o.s.i. (ISBN 0-9598080-9-4, Pub by Lonely Planet Australia). Hippocrene Bks.

--Papua, New Guinea. 2nd ed. (Travel Paperbacks Ser.). (Illus.). 224p. 1981. pap. 7.95 o.p. (Pub. by Lonely Australia). Hippocrene Bks.

--Sri Lanka, (Updated Supplement) (Travel Paperbacks Ser.). (Illus.). 176p. 1981. pap. 5.95 (ISBN 0-908086-32-6, Pub. by Lonely Planet Australia). Hippocrene Bks.

Wheeler,. W., jt. auth. see Crowdis, David G.

Wheeler, W. H. Wet Fire. LC 77-82063. (Pacesetter Ser.). (Illus.). 64p. (gr. 4 up). 1978. PLB 8.65 (ISBN 0-516-02174-5). Childrens.

Wheeler, W. M. Social Life Among the Insects: Being a Series of Lectures Delivered at the Lowell Institute in Boston in March, 1922. LC 23-12888. Repr. of 1923 ed. 34.00 (ISBN 0-384-67870-X). Johnson Repr.

Wheeler, Walston, tr. see Brusewitz, Gunnar.

Wheeler, Walter C., ed. see Hohfeld, Wesley N.

Wheeler, William & Hayward, Charles H. Wood Carving. rev. ed. (Illus.). 1979. pap. 6.95 (ISBN 0-8069-8790-1). Sterling.

Wheeler, William A. Explanatory & Pronouncing Dictionary of the Noted Names of Fictions. LC 66-25811. 1966. Repr. of 1889 ed. 34.00x (ISBN 0-8103-0165-2). Gale.

--Familiar Allusions: A Hand-Book of Miscellaneous Information. LC 66-24371. 1966. Repr. of 1882 ed. 45.00x (ISBN 0-8103-0166-0). Gale.

--Who Wrote It. LC 68-30667. 1968. Repr. of 1881 ed. 30.00x (ISBN 0-8103-3228-0). Gale.

Wheeler-Bennett, John. Friends, Enemies & Sovereigns. LC 76-23198. 1977. 8.95 o.p. (ISBN 0-312-30555-9). St Martin.

--Special Relationships: America in Peace & War. LC 75-29974. 1976. 12.95 o.p. (ISBN 0-312-75145-1). St Martin.

Wheelis, Allen. On Not Knowing How to Live. 1976. pap. 2.25i o.p. (ISBN 0-06-090535-2, CN535, CN). Har-Row.

--On Not Knowing How to Live. LC 75-4294. 128p. (YA) 1975. 5.95i (ISBN 0-06-014562-5, HarpT). Har-Row.

Wheelis, Mark, jt. auth. see Gonick, Larry.

Wheelock, Arthur K., Jr. Jan Vermeer. LC 81-1754. (Library of Great Painters). (Illus.). 160p. Date not set. 40.00 (ISBN 0-8109-1730-0). Abrams.

Wheelock, Frederic M. Latin: An Introductory Course Based on Ancient Authors, Including Readings. 3rd ed. LC 63-8289. 1963. 14.95x (ISBN 0-06-480944-7). B&N Imports.

--Latin: An Introductory Course Based on Ancient Authors, Including Readings. pap. 5.50 (ISBN 0-06-460104-8, CO 104, COS); wkbk. by Paul T. Comeau 4.95 (ISBN 0-06-460192-7, CO 192). B&N NY.

--Latin Literature: A Book of Readings. (COS Ser.). 331p. (Latin.). (gr. 10-12). 1967. pap. 3.95 (ISBN 0-06-460080-7, 80). B&N NY.

Wheelock, John H., ed. Editor to Author: The Letters of Maxwell E. Perkins. new ed. LC 50-6473. 1977. Repr. of 1950 ed. lib. bdg. 14.95 (ISBN 0-910220-81-6). Berg.

Wheelock, Keith. Nasser's New Egypt. LC 75-14708. (Foreign Policy Research Institute Ser: No. 8). (Illus.). 326p. 1975. Repr. of 1960 ed. lib. bdg. 18.25x (ISBN 0-8371-8233-6, WHNE). Greenwood.

Wheelwright, Edith G. Medicinal Plants & Their History. (Illus.). 9.00 (ISBN 0-8446-5258-X). Peter Smith.

Wheelwright, Jane. The Death of a Woman. 288p. 1981. 12.95 o.p. (ISBN 0-312-18744-0). St Martin.

Wheelwright, John. Collected Poems. Rosenfeld, Alvin H., ed. LC 79-175817. 304p. 1983. 12.50 (ISBN 0-8112-0426-X); pap. 10.00 (ISBN 0-8112-0849-4, NDP544). New Directions.

Wheelwright, Philip & Fuss, Peter, eds. Five Philosophers. LC 63-14019. 1963. pap. 2.95 (ISBN 0-672-63035-4). Odyssey Pr.

Wheelwright, Richard, jt. ed. see Shaffer, W. D.

Wheelwright, Steven C., jt. auth. see Makridakis, Spyros.

Wheelwright, Steven C., jt. ed. see Makridakis, Spyros.

Wheelwright, Thea. Along the Maine Coast. 128p. 1981. 9.98 (ISBN 0-517-14160-4). Crown.

--Travels in New England, Volumes I & II. (Illus.). 1977. 15.95 o.p. (ISBN 0-685-76359-5, C N Potter Bks). Crown.

Wheelwright, Thea, ed. see Chadbourne, Ava H.

Wheildon, William M., Jr., jt. auth. see King, Alan G.

Whelan, A. Developments in Rubber Technology, Vols. 1 & 2. Lee, K. S., ed. 1979-81. Vol. 1. 53.50 (ISBN 0-85334-862-6, Pub. by Applied Sci England); 49.25 (ISBN 0-85334-949-5). Elsevier.

--Injection Moulding Materials. 1982. 65.75 (ISBN 0-85334-993-2, Pub. by Applied Sci England). Elsevier.

Whelan, A. & Brydson, J. A., eds. Developments with Thermosetting Plastics. LC 74-34013. 198p. 1975. 39.95x o.s.i. (ISBN 0-470-93772-6). Halsted Pr.

Whelan, A. & Craft, J. L., eds. Developments in Injection Molding, Vols. 1 & 2. Vol. 1, 1978. 53.50 (ISBN 0-85334-798-0, Pub. by Applied Sci England); Vol. 2, 1980. 80.00 (ISBN 0-85334-968-1). Elsevier.

--Developments in Injection Moulding No. 2: Improving Efficiency. (Illus.). 345p. 1982. 80.00 (ISBN 0-85334-968-1, Pub. by Applied Sci England). Elsevier.

--Developments in PVC Production & Processing. (Illus.). 1977. 35.00x (ISBN 0-85334-741-7, Pub. by Applied Sci England). Elsevier.

Whelan, A. & Dunning, D., eds. Developments in Plastics Technology, Vol. 1. (Illus.). 285p. 1983. 57.50 (ISBN 0-85334-155-9, Pub. by Applied Sci England). Elsevier.

Whelan, A. & Lee, K. S., eds. Developments in Rubber Technology, Vol. 3. (Illus.). 240p. 1982. 61.50 (ISBN 0-85334-135-4, Pub. by Applied Sci England). Elsevier.

Whelan, Dan, jt. auth. see Levin, Bella.

Whelan, Elizabeth & Whelan, Stephen. Making Sense Out of Sex: A New Look at Being a Man. (Illus.). 192p. (gr. 9-12). 1975. 6.95 o.p. (ISBN 0-07-069527-X, GB); PLB 6.84 o.p. (ISBN 0-07-069528-8). McGraw.

Whelan, Elizabeth M. A Baby?...Maybe: A Guide to Making the Most Fateful Decision of Your Life. rev. ed. LC 79-55437. 256p. 1980. 11.95 o.p. (ISBN 0-672-52628-X); pap. 8.95 (ISBN 0-672-52629-8). Bobbs.

--Sex & Sensibility: A New Look at Being a Woman. 160p. (gr. 9-12). 1974. 6.95 o.p. (ISBN 0-07-069523-7, GB); PLB 6.84 o.p. (ISBN 0-07-069524-5). McGraw.

Whelan, Elizabeth M. & Stare, Fredrick J. The One Hundred Percent Natural, Purely Organic, Cholesterol-Free, Megavitamin, Low-Carbohydrate Nutrition Hoax. LC 82-71260. 256p. 1983. 14.95 (ISBN 0-689-11335-8). Atheneum.

Whelan, Gloria. A Clearing in the Forest. LC 78-3608. (gr. 6-8). 1978. 7.95 o.p. (ISBN 0-399-20639-6). Putnam Pub Group.

--A Time to Keep Silent. LC 79-11608. (gr. 7-12). 1979. 7.95 (ISBN 0-399-20693-0). Putnam Pub Group.

Whelan, H., jt. ed. see Silvestone, T.

Whelan, James. Allende: Death of a Marxist Dream. 200p. 1981. 14.95 o.p. (ISBN 0-87000-503-0, Arlington Hse). Crown.

Whelan, John, ed. Oman: A Middle East Economic Digest Guide. (MEED Practical Guide Ser.). (Illus.). 198p. (Orig.). 1982. pap. 15.00 (ISBN 0-7103-0013-1, Kegan Paul). Routledge & Kegan.

Whelan, Joseph G. Soviet Diplomacy & Negotiating Behavior: The Emerging New Context for U. S. Diplomacy. (Replica Edition Ser.). 573p. 1982. softcover 29.50x (ISBN 0-86531-946-4). Westview.

Whelan, Michael. Wonderworks: Science Fiction & Fantasy Art. Freas, Polly & Freas, Kelly, eds. LC 79-12575. (Illus.). 1979. 13.95 o.p. (ISBN 0-915442-75-2, Starblaze); pap. 9.95 (ISBN 0-915442-74-4, Starblaze); collector's edition 30.00 (ISBN 0-915442-83-3). Donning Co.

Whelan, P. E., ed. Medical Device Register, 1983. LC 81-645923. 1400p. 1983. 75.00x (ISBN 0-942036-03-4). Directory Systems Inc.

Whelan, Richard. Double Take: How Great Photographers Have Seen & Photographed the Same Subjects. 192p. 1981. 19.95 (ISBN 0-517-54382-6, C N Potter Bks); pap. 10.95 (ISBN 0-517-54569-1, C N Potter Bks). Crown.

Whelan, Stanley. Art of Erotic Massage. 1979. pap. 1.75 o.p. (ISBN 0-451-08824-7, E8824, Sig). NAL.

Whelan, Stephen, jt. auth. see Whelan, Elizabeth.

Whelan, W. J. From Genetic Experimentation to Biotechnology the Critical Transition. LC 81-19838. 266p. 1982. 39.95x (ISBN 0-471-10148-6, Pub. by Wiley-Interscience). Wiley.

Whelan, W. J., jt. ed. see Schultz, J.

Whelan, Wayne L. Academic Litigation as Educational Consumerism. 32p. 1979. 3.50 (ISBN 0-686-38136-X, 23-1791). Natl League Nurse.

Wheldon, Keith. Renoir & His Art. (The Artist & His Art Ser.). (Illus.). 128p. 1981. 9.98 o.p. (ISBN 0-89196-091-0, Bk Value Intl). Quality Bks IL.

Whelpton, Barbara, tr. see Alazard, Jean.

Whelpton, P. K., jt. auth. see Thompson, W. S.

Whelpton, Robin, jt. auth. see Curry, Stephen H.

Wherrett, B. S., ed. Laser Advances & Applications Proceedings: Proceedings of the National Quantum Electronics Conference, 4th, Heriot-Watt University, Edinburgh, 1979. LC 80-40119. 278p. 1980. 53.95 (ISBN 0-471-27792-4). Wiley.

Whetham, Edith H., ed. Agrarian History of England & Wales, 1914-1939, Vol. 8. LC 66-19763. (Agrarian History of England & Wales Ser.). 1978. 49.50 (ISBN 0-521-21780-6). Cambridge U Pr.

Whetmore, Edward J. Mediamerica: Form, Content & Consequence of Mass Communication. 1979. pap. text ed. 13.95x o.p. (ISBN 0-534-00604-3). Wadsworth Pub.

--Mediamerica: Form, Content, & Consequence of Mass Communication. 2nd ed. 384p. 1982. pap. text ed. 15.95x (ISBN 0-534-01037-7). Wadsworth Pub.

Whetten, David A., jt. ed. see Cameron, Kim S.

Whetten, David A., jt. auth. see Rodgers, David L.

Whetten, L. L. The Canal War: Four-Power Conflict in the Middle East. 1974. 27.50x (ISBN 0-262-23069-0). MIT Pr.

Whetten, Lawrence L. New International Communism: The Foreign & Defense Policies of the Latin European Communist Parties. LC 81-47963. 288p. 1982. 27.95x (ISBN 0-669-05146-2). Lexington Bks.

Whetten, Lawrence L., ed. The Present State of Communist Internationalism. 1983. price not set (ISBN 0-669-05582-4). Lexington Bks.

Whetton, Douglass. McElroy, Ace of the Forty Squadron, R.F.C - R.A.F. (Illus.). 1979. cancelled (ISBN 0-315-32853-3). AJAY Ent.

--Mannock, Patrol Leader Supreme. LC 77-371981. (Illus.). 1977. softcover 4.95 o.p. (ISBN 0-939440-00-8). AJAY Ent.

Whichcote, Benjamin. Select Sermons of Benjamin Whichcote. LC 77-16025. 1977. Repr. of 1742 ed. 41.00x (ISBN 0-8201-1306-9). Schol Facsimiles.

Whicher, George F., ed. William Jennings Bryan & the Campaign of 1896. (Problems in American Civilization Ser.). 1953. pap. text ed. 5.50 o.p. (ISBN 0-669-24000-1). Heath.

Whicher, Olive, jt. auth. see Adams, George.

Whichler, Stephen E., jt. ed. see Konvitz, Milton R.

Whicker, Alan. Within Whicker's World. (Illus.). 384p. 1983. 22.50 (ISBN 0-241-10747-4, Pub. by Hamish Hamilton England). David & Charles.

Whiddon, N. & Hall, Linda. Teaching Softball. LC 79-91259. 1980. pap. text ed. 6.95x (ISBN 0-8087-3704-X). Burgess.

Whiddon, N. Susan & Reynolds, Howard. Teaching Basketball. (Sport Teaching Ser.). (Orig.). 1983. pap. 7.95x (ISBN 0-8087-3714-7). Burgess.

Whiffen, D. H., ed. Expression of Results in Quantum Chemistry. new ed. 1978. write for info. (ISBN 0-08-022367-2). Pergamon.

Whiffen, Marcus. American Architecture Since 1780: A Guide to the Styles. 1969. 22.50x (ISBN 0-262-23034-8); pap. 7.95 (ISBN 0-262-73057-X). MIT Pr.

Whiffen, Marcus & Koeper, Frederick. American Architecture: Sixteen Seven to Nineteen Seventy-Six. 500p. 1981. 30.00 (ISBN 0-262-23105-0). MIT Pr.

Whigham, Peter. Do's & Don'ts of Translation. 16p. 1982. text ed. 7.00 (ISBN 0-918824-34-6). Turkey Pr.

Whigham, Peter, tr. & intro. by see Catullus.

Whigham, Peter, tr. see Meleager.

Whimbey, Arthur. Intelligence Can Be Taught. 1980. pap. 5.95 o.p. (ISBN 0-525-93128-7). Dutton.

Whimbey, Arthur & Barbarena, Celia. A Cognitive-Skills Approach to the Disciplines: Intelligence Beyond Arthur Jensen. Woditsch, Gary, ed. LC 77-87114. (CUE Project Technical Paper Ser.: No. 2). 1977. pap. 3.50 (ISBN 0-89372-004-6). General Stud Res.

Whimbey, Arthur & Lochhead, Jack. Developing Mathematical Skills. (Illus.). 480p. 1981. pap. text ed. 16.50 (ISBN 0-07-069517-2, C); instr's. manual 14.95 (ISBN 0-07-069518-0). McGraw.

Whimbey, Arthur & Lockhead, Jack. Problem Solving & Comprehension: A Short Course in Analytical Reasoning. 2nd ed. LC 79-67418. (Illus.). 1980. pap. 9.50 o.p. (ISBN 0-89168-026-8). Franklin Inst Pr.

Whincup, Gregory, tr. see Anhui Medical School Hospital.

Whinney, Margaret. Sculpture in Britain: 1530-1830. (Pelican History of Art Ser: No. 23). (Illus.). 1964. 50.00 o.p. (ISBN 0-670-62436-5). Viking Pr.

Whinnom, Keith. Diego de San Pedro. (World Authors Ser.: Spain: No. 310). 1974. lib. bdg. 8.95 o.p. (ISBN 0-8057-2788-4, Twayne). G K Hall.

Whipkey, K. L. & Whipkey, Mary N. The Power of Calculus. 3rd ed. LC 78-24067. 1979. 25.95 (ISBN 0-471-03140-2); tchrs. manual 2.00 (ISBN 0-471-05500-X). Wiley.

Whipkey, Kenneth L., et al. The Power of Mathematics: Applications to the Management & the Social Sciences. 2nd ed. LC 80-19576. 622p. 1981. text ed. 25.95 (ISBN 0-471-07709-7). Wiley.

Whipkey, Mary N., jt. auth. see Whipkey, K. L.

Whipp, jt. auth. see Cerretilli.

Whipple, A. B. Storm. (Planet Earth Ser.). 1982. lib. bdg. 19.92 (ISBN 0-8094-4313-9, Pub. by Time-Life). Silver.

--Yankee Whalers in the South Seas. LC 72-77517. (Illus.). 1972. pap. 5.75 (ISBN 0-8048-1057-5). C E Tuttle.

Whipple, Barbara, jt. auth. see Quiller, Stephen.

Whipple, Cal. The Clipper Ships. LC 79-24764. (Seafarers Ser.). PLB 19.92 (ISBN 0-8094-2678-1). Silver.

--Fighting Sail. LC 78-52043. (The Seafarers Ser.). (Illus.). 1978. PLB 19.92 (ISBN 0-8094-2655-2). Silver.

--The Mediterranean. LC 80-29149. (World War II Ser.). PLB 19.92 (ISBN 0-8094-3384-2). Silver.

--The Whalers. LC 78-31228. (The Seafarers Ser.). (Illus.). 1979. lib. bdg. 19.92 (ISBN 0-8094-2671-4). Silver.

Whipple, Chandler. Indian & the White Man in Connecticut. LC 73-92510. (First Encounter Ser). (Illus.). 95p. (Orig.). 1972. pap. 3.50 (ISBN 0-912944-17-X). Berkshire Traveller.

--The Indian & the White Man in New England. LC 73-93961. (First Encounter Ser.). (Illus., Orig.). 1976. 12.00 (ISBN 0-912944-41-2); pap. 8.00 (ISBN 0-912944-38-2). Berkshire Traveller.

--The Indian & the Whiteman in Massachusetts & Rhode Island. LC 73-93961. (First Encounter Ser). (Illus.). 156p. 1973. pap. 3.50 o.p. (ISBN 0-912944-12-9). Berkshire Traveller.

Whipple, Colvin, jt. auth. see Beecher, Addison.

Whipple, Dorothy V. Dynamics of Development: Euthenic Pediatrics. 648p. 1966. 20.50 o.p. (ISBN 0-07-069525-3, C). McGraw.

Whipple, Edwin P. The Literature of the Age of Elizabeth. 364p. 1982. Repr. of 1869 ed. lib. bdg. 50.00 (ISBN 0-8495-5841-7). Arden Lib.

--Outlooks on Society, Literature & Politics. 345p. 1982. Repr. of 1888 ed. lib. bdg. 50.00 (ISBN 0-89987-890-3). Darby Bks.

--Recollections of Eminent Men with Other Papers. 397p. 1982. Repr. of 1886 ed. lib. bdg. 45.00 (ISBN 0-8495-5840-9). Arden Lib.

Whipple, Jane, ed. see Bothwell, Jean.

Whipple, Lee. Whole Again. 232p. 1980. 9.95 o.p. (ISBN 0-89803-023-4). Caroline Hse.

Whipple, Leland, jt. auth. see Villard, Kenneth L.

Whipple, M. A., jt. ed. see Heizer, Robert F.

Whipple, Maurine. Giant Joshua. Repr. 12.50 (ISBN 0-914740-17-2). Western Epics.

Whipple, Thomas W., jt. auth. see Courtney, Alice E.

Whisenand, P. The Effective Police Manager. 1981. 21.95 (ISBN 0-13-244509-3). P-H.

Whisenand, P. M. Police Supervision: Theory & Practice. 2nd ed. (Illus.). 576p. 1976. 20.95 (ISBN 0-13-686311-6). P-H.

Whisenand, Paul M. & Ferguson, R. Fred. The Managing of Police Organizations. 2nd ed. (Illus.). 1978. text ed. 23.95 (ISBN 0-13-550731-6). P-H.

Whisenhunt, Donald W. Depression in Texas. Rosenbaum, Robert J., ed. (Texas History Ser.). (Illus.). 43p. 1982. pap. text ed. 1.95x (ISBN 0-89641-105-2). American Pr.

Whishaw, Francis. Railways of Great Britain & Ireland. LC 68-56390. (Illus.). Repr. of 1842 ed. 30.00x (ISBN 0-678-05629-3). Kelley.

Whisker, James B. The Citizen Soldier & United States Military Policy. 7.50 o.p. (ISBN 0-88427-035-1); pap. 4.50 o.p. (ISBN 0-88427-036-X). Green Hill.

--The Citizen Soldier & U. S. Military Policy. LC 78-27029. 1979. 10.00 (ISBN 0-88427-035-1); pap. 4.50o.p. (ISBN 0-88427-036-X, Dist.B by Caroline Hse). North River.

--Dictionary of Concepts on American Politics. LC 80-15591. 285p. 1980. pap. 11.95 (ISBN 0-471-07716-X). Wiley.

--The Right to Hunt. LC 81-1524. 192p. 1981. 11.95 (ISBN 0-88427-042-4). North River.

--The Social, Political & Religious Thought of Alfred Rosenberg: An Interpretive Essay. LC 81-40652. 150p. (Orig.). 1982. lib. bdg. 20.25 (ISBN 0-8191-2023-5); pap. text ed. 8.75 (ISBN 0-8191-2024-3). U Pr of Amer.

Whisnant, David E. James Boyd. (United States Authors Ser.). lib. bdg. 13.95 (ISBN 0-8057-0080-3, Twayne). G K Hall.

--Modernizing the Mountainer. LC 81-15911. 1980. pap. 8.95 (ISBN 0-686-37450-9). Appalach Consortium.

Whisnant, J. P., jt. ed. see Siekert, Robert.

Whistler, R. L. & BeMiller, J. N., eds. Industrial Gums: Polysaccharides & Their Derivatives. 2nd ed. 1973. 84.50 (ISBN 0-12-746252-X). Acad Pr.

Whistler, Roy L. & Paschall, Eugene F., eds. Starch: Chemistry & Technology, 2 vols. Incl. Vol. 1. Fundamental Aspects. 1965. 67.50 (ISBN 0-12-746261-9); Vol. 2. Industrial Aspects. 1967. 82.50 (ISBN 0-12-746262-7). Acad Pr.

Whistler, Roy L. & Wolfrom, Melville L., eds. Methods in Carbohydrate Chemistry, 8 vols. Incl. Vol. 1. Analysis & Preparation of Sugars. 1962. 67.50 (ISBN 0-12-746201-5); Vol. 2. Reactions of Carbohydrates. 1963. 67.50 (ISBN 0-12-746202-3); Vol. 3. Cellulose. 1963. 67.50 (ISBN 0-12-746203-1); Vol. 4. Starch. 1964. 64.00 (ISBN 0-12-746204-X); Vol. 5. General Polysaccharides. 1965. 64.00 (ISBN 0-12-746205-8); Vol. 6. 1971. 67.50 (ISBN 0-12-746206-6); Vol. 7. 57.00 (ISBN 0-12-746207-4); Vol. 8. 1980. 42.00 (ISBN 0-12-746208-2). Acad Pr.

Whiston, Lionel A. For Those in Love: Making Your Marriage Last a Lifetime. 128p. 1983. 9.95 (ISBN 0-687-13285-1). Abingdon.

Whitacre, Rodney A. Johannine Polemic: The Role of Tradition & Theology. LC 82-5457. (SBL Dissertation Ser.). 292p. 1982. pap. 13.00 (ISBN 0-89130-579-3, 06-01-67). Scholars Pr CA.

Whitaker. Agricultural Buildings & Structures. (Illus.). 1979. text ed. 20.95 (ISBN 0-8359-0176-9); instrs'. manual avail. (ISBN 0-8359-0177-7). Reston.

Whitaker & Napier. The Family Crucible. LC 74-1872. 1978. 15.34i (ISBN 0-06-014568-4, HarpT). Har-Row.

Whitaker & Sons Ltd., ed. British Books in Print, 1982, 2 vol. set. 6000p. 1982. 150.00 (ISBN 0-85021-134-4). Bowker.

Whitaker, Ben, ed. The Fourth World: Victims of Group Oppression. LC 72-93008. 1973. 10.00x o.p. (ISBN 0-8052-3482-9). Schocken.

--Radical Future. 7.95 o.p. (ISBN 0-224-61204-2). Transatlantic.

Whitaker, Emily, jt. auth. see Whitaker, Irwin.

Whitaker, George O. & Meyers, Joan. Dinosaur Hunt. LC 65-12614. (Illus.). (gr. 5-8). 1965. 5.95 o.p. (ISBN 0-15-223501-9, HJ). HarBraceJ.

Whitaker, Haiganoosh & Whitaker, Harry A., eds. Studies in Neurolinguistics, 2 vols. LC 75-13100. (Perspectives in Neurolinguistics & Psycholinguistics). 1976-79. Vol. 1. subscription 38.50 43.50 (ISBN 0-12-746301-1); Vol. 2. subscription 38.50 43.50 (ISBN 0-12-746302-X); Vol. 3. subscription 31.00 36.50 (ISBN 0-12-746303-8); Vol. 4. by subscription 32.00 37.50 (ISBN 0-12-746304-6). Acad Pr.

Whitaker, Harry A., jt. ed. see Whitaker, Haiganoosh.

Whitaker, Irwin & Whitaker, Emily. A Potter's Mexico. LC 77-29047. (Illus.). 1978. 17.50 o.p. (ISBN 0-8263-0472-9). U of NM Pr.

Whitaker, J. H., ed. Submarine Canyons & Deep-Sea Fans. LC 75-5540. (Benchmark Papers in Geology Ser: Vol. 24). 449p. 1976. 59.00 (ISBN 0-12-787754-1). Acad Pr.

Whitaker, John O., Jr. The Audubon Field Guide to North American Mammals. LC 79-3525. (Illus.). 752p. 1980. 12.50 (ISBN 0-394-50762-2). Knopf.

Whitaker, John R see Zweig, Gunter.

Whitaker, Linton A. & Randall, Peter, eds. Symposium on Reconstruction of Jaw Deformity. LC 78-4867. (Symposia of the Educational Foundaion of the American Society of Plastic & Reconstructive Surgeons, Inc. Ser.). 308p. 1978. text ed. 64.00 o.p. (ISBN 0-8016-5610-9). Mosby.

Whitaker, Norman. Process Instrumentation Primer. 117p. 1980. 37.95x (ISBN 0-87814-128-6). Pennwell Pub.

Whitaker, Robert, et al. Concepts of General, Organic, & Biological Chemistry. LC 80-82738. (Illus.). 704p. 1981. text ed. 29.95 (ISBN 0-395-29273-5); study guide 8.50 (ISBN 0-395-29275-1); manual 1.00instr's (ISBN 0-395-29274-3); lab manual 12.50 (ISBN 0-395-29276-X); instr's manual to lab excercises 1.50. (ISBN 0-395-30518-7). HM.

Whitaker, Robert C. Hang in There. 1974. 1.25 (ISBN 0-88270-106-1). Bridge Pub.

Whitaker, Romulus. Common Indian Snakes: A Field Guide. (Illus.). 154p. (Orig.). 1979. pap. text ed. 4.00x o.s.i. (ISBN 0-333-90198-3). R Curtis Bks.

Whitaker, S. Elementary Heat Transfer Analysis (in SI-Metric Units) LC 74-3246. 1976. text ed. 16.50 (ISBN 0-08-018959-8). Pergamon.

--Fundamental Principles of Heat Transfer. 1977. 38.50 o.p. (ISBN 0-08-017866-9). Pergamon.

Whitaker, Stephen. Fundamental Principles of Heat Transfer. LC 82-13031. 574p. 1983. Repr. of 1977 ed. PLB 32.50 (ISBN 0-89874-543-8). Krieger.

Whitaker, Thomas R. William Carlos Williams. (U. S. Authors Ser.: No. 143). 1968. lib. bdg. 11.95 o.p. (ISBN 0-8057-0816-2, Twayne). G K Hall.

Whitbeck, Philip H., jt. ed. see Shafritz, Jay M.

Whitbread, Jane. Stop Hurting! Start Living! 210p. 1981. 13.95 o.s.i. (ISBN 0-440-08377-X). Delacorte.

Whitburn, Joel. The Billboard Book of Top Forty Hits: 1955-1982. (Illus.). 512p. 1983. pap. 15.00 (ISBN 0-8230-7511-7, Billboard Pub). Watson-Guptill.

Whitburn, Joel, compiled by. Pop Annual 1955-1977. 623p. 1978. 50.00x (ISBN 0-686-80393-0). Gale.

--Top Country & Western Records Nineteen Forty-Nine to Nineteen Seventy-One. LC 72-6752. 184p. 1972. soft bdg. 25.00x (ISBN 0-686-81470-3, Pub. by Record Research). Gale.

--Top Easy Listening Records Nineteen Sixty-One to Nineteen Seventy-Four. LC 75-10541. (Illus.). 152p. 1975. soft bdg. 25.00x (ISBN 0-686-81471-1, Pub. by Record Research). Gale.

--Top LP's Nineteen Forty-Five to Nineteen Seventy-Two. LC 74-75179. 224p. 1973. soft bdg. 32.00x (ISBN 0-686-81472-X, Pub. by Record Research). Gale.

--Top Pop Artists & Singles Nineteen Fifty-Five to Nineteen Seventy-Eight. LC 79-67484. (Illus.). 664p. 1979. 64.00x (ISBN 0-686-81473-8, Pub. by Record Research). Gale.

--Top Rhythm & Blues Records Nineteen Forty-Nine to Nineteen Seventy-One. LC 73-78333. (Illus.). 184p. 1973. soft bdg. 25.00x (ISBN 0-686-81474-6, Pub. by Record Research). Gale.

--Top Singles Nineteen Forty to Nineteen Fifty-Five. LC 73-76719. (Illus.). 88p. 1979. soft bdg. 20.00x (ISBN 0-686-81475-4, Pub. by Record Research). Gale.

Whitby, M. C., et al. Rural Resource Development. 2nd ed. (Illus.). 240p. 1978. 29.95x (ISBN 0-416-70730-0); pap. 12.95x (ISBN 0-416-70720-3). Methuen Inc.

Whitby, Martin, jt. auth. see Hodge, Ian.

Whitby, Thomas & Lorkovic, Tanja. Introduction to Soviet National Bibliography. LC 79-4112. Orig. Title: Gosudarstvennaia Bibliografiia SSSR. 229p. 1979. lib. bdg. 25.00x o.p. (ISBN 0-87287-128-2). Libs Unl.

Whitby, W. M. & Anderson, R. R., eds. Fianza Satisfecha: Attributed to Lope De Vega. 1971. 44.50 (ISBN 0-521-07912-8). Cambridge U Pr.

Whitby-Strevens, C., jt. auth. see Richards, M.

Whitcomb, Donald D. & Johnson, Janet H. Quseir al-Qadim, 1980: Preliminary Report. LC 81-72088. (American Research Center in Egypt, Reports Ser.: Vol. 7). (Illus.). 418p. (Orig.). 1982. 27.50x (ISBN 0-89003-113-4); pap. 22.50x (ISBN 0-89003-112-6). Undena Pubns.

Whitcomb, Donald S. & Johnson, Janet H. Quseir Al-Qadim 1978 Preliminary Report. (American Research in Egypt, Reports Ser.: Vol. 1). (Illus.). 352p. 1981. pap. 15.50 (ISBN 0-936770-01-5, Pub. by Am Res Ctr Egypt). Undena Pubns.

Whitcomb, H., jt. auth. see Wheeler, R.

Whitcomb, Helen & Cochran, L. Charm for Miss Teen. 1969. text ed. 8.60 (ISBN 0-07-069647-0, G); tchr's manual & key 6.00 (ISBN 0-07-069648-9). McGraw.

--The Modern Ms. 2nd ed. 1975. text ed. 8.92 (ISBN 0-07-069663-2, G); tchr's manual & key 7.00 (ISBN 0-07-069664-0). McGraw.

Whitcomb, Helen & Lang, R. Charm: The Career Girls Guide to Business & Personal Success. 2nd ed. text ed. 14.05 (ISBN 0-07-069655-1, G); instructor's manual & key 7.65 (ISBN 0-07-069657-8). McGraw.

Whitcomb, Helen & Lang, Rosalind. Today's Woman. 3rd ed. 1976. 15.10 (ISBN 0-07-069670-5, G); instructor's manual & key 7.50 (ISBN 0-07-069672-1). McGraw.

Whitcomb, John C. The Early Earth. pap. 4.50 (ISBN 0-88469-060-1). BMH Bks.

--Esther, the Triumph of God's Sovereignty. 128p. (Orig.). 1979. pap. 4.95 (ISBN 0-88469-081-4). BMH Bks.

--Esther: Triumph of God's Sovereignty. (Every Man's Bible Commentary Ser.). 1979. pap. 4.50 (ISBN 0-8024-2016-8). Moody.

--Solomon to the Exile: Studies in Kings & Chronicles. (Old Testament Studies Ser.). 1971. pap. 3.95 o.p. (ISBN 0-8010-9516-6). Baker Bk.

--The World That Perished. pap. 4.50 (ISBN 0-88469-059-8). BMH Bks.

Whitcomb, John C. & DeYoung, Donald B. The Moon: Its Creation, Form & Significance. 7.95 o.p. (ISBN 0-8010-9619-7). Baker Bk.

Whitcomb, Joyce S. Prairie Poet: This Land Called South Dakota & Other Poems. 1978. 4.00 o.p. (ISBN 0-682-49235-3). Exposition.

Whitcomb, Norma & Randall, Frances. Food & Thought Desserts. pap. 3.95 (ISBN 0-88469-065-2). BMH Bks.

Whitcomb, Norma A. & Randall, Frances. Food & Thought: Salads & Sandwiches. pap. 3.95 (ISBN 0-88469-066-0). BMH Bks.

Whitcomb, Selden L. Chronological Outlines of American Literature. LC 68-30590. 1968. Repr. of 1894 ed. 34.00x (ISBN 0-8103-3227-2). Gale.

Whitcraft, John E., jt. auth. see Rosenberg, R. Robert.

Whitcut, Janet. Learning with LDOCE. (Illus.). 1979. pap. text ed. 3.25x (ISBN 0-582-55607-4); cassette 8.50x (ISBN 0-582-55629-5). Longman.

White & Richardson. Microstructural Science, Vol. 10. 1982. 75.00 (ISBN 0-444-00707-5). Elsevier.

White, jt. auth. see Grubbs, Robert.

White, A. T. Graphs, Groups & Surfaces. LC 73-86088. (Mathematical Studies Ser.: Vol. 8). 156p. 1974. pap. 34.00 (ISBN 0-444-10570-0, North-Holland). Elsevier.

White, A. T., jt. auth. see Biggs, N. L.

White, A. W. The Violin: How to Construct from Beginning to Completion Eighteen Ninety-Three. (Illus.). 44p. pap. 12.50. Saifer.

White, Abraham, et al. Principles of Biochemistry. 6th ed. 1978. 39.95 (ISBN 0-07-069759-0, C). McGraw.

White, Alan. Absolute Knowledge: Hegel & the Problem of Metaphysics. 190p. 1983. text ed. 22.95x (ISBN 0-8214-0717-1, 82-84861); pap. 11.95 (ISBN 0-8214-0718-X, 82-84879). Ohio U Pr.

--Schelling: An Introduction to the System of Freedom. LC 82-16034. 224p. 1983. text ed. 20.00x (ISBN 0-300-02896-2). Yale U Pr.

White, Alan R. G. E. Moore: A Critical Exposition. LC 78-26069. 1979. Repr. of 1969 ed. lib. bdg. 20.75x (ISBN 0-313-20805-0, WHGM). Greenwood.

White, Alan R., ed. Philosophy of Action. (Oxford Readings in Philosophy Ser). 1968. pap. text ed. 8.95x (ISBN 0-19-875006-4). Oxford U Pr.

White, Allen S., ed. Directory of American College Theatre. 1976. pap. 7.00x o.p. (ISBN 0-940528-06-1). Am Theatre Assoc.

White, Anne. Healing Adventure: Understanding Divine Healing. 168p. 1972. pap. 4.95 (ISBN 0-912106-35-2, Pub. by Logos). Bridge Pub.

White, Anne, jt. auth. see White, Nelson.

White, Anne T. The St. Lawrence: Seaway of North America. LC 61-11147. (Rivers of the World Ser.). (Illus.). (gr. 4-7). 1961. PLB 3.98 (ISBN 0-8116-6352-3). Garrard.

White, Anne T. & Lietz, Gerald S. Windows on the World. LC 65-21427. (Wonder of Wonders - Man Ser). (gr. 4-7). 1965. PLB 7.12 (ISBN 0-8116-6801-0). Garrard.

White, Anthony G. Basic Texts in Public Administration: A Selected Bibliography. 8p. 1978. pap. 1.50 (ISBN 0-686-37410-X). Vance Biblios.

White, Antonia. The Hound & the Falcon. 172p. 1983. pap. 5.95 (ISBN 0-86068-172-6, Virago Pr). Merrimack Bk Serv.

White, Antonia, tr. see Colette.

White, Arthur H. Back School & Other Conservative Approaches to Low Back Pain. (Illus.). 198p. 1983. text ed. 32.50 (ISBN 0-8016-5423-8). Mosby.

White, Arthur H., jt. auth. see Mulry, Ray C.

White, Arthur O., jt. ed. see Goodenow, Ronald K.

White, B. Kirke, compiled by. Pittsylvania County Inventory: Circuit Court Clerk. 50p. (Orig.). 1977. pap. 2.00 (ISBN 0-686-98188-X). VA State Lib.

White, B. T. Tanks & Other A. F. V. 's of the Blitzkrieg Era, 1939-1941. (Illus.). 161p. 1982. 9.95 (ISBN 0-7137-0704-6, Pub. by Blandford Pr England). Sterling.

--Tanks & Other Armoured Fighting Vehicles, 1942-1945. (Illus.). 172p. 1983. 9.95 (ISBN 0-7137-0705-4, Pub. by Blandford Pr England). Sterling.

White, Benjamin. Silver: Its History & Romance. LC 71-174144. (Illus.). xxviii, 325p. 1972. Repr. of 1920 ed. 42.00x (ISBN 0-8103-3930-7). Gale.

White, Benjamin V. & White, Helen. The Excitement of Change: A Book of Personal Growth. 190p. 1975. 1.00 (ISBN 0-8164-1206-5). Seabury.

White, Bertha R. Index to American International Law Cases. 1982. write for info. (ISBN 0-379-20097-X). Oceana.

--Law of Buying & Selling. 2nd ed. LC 68-54012. (Legal Almanac Ser: No. 41). (Illus.). 113p. 1979. 5.95 (ISBN 0-379-11112-8, LA). Oceana.

White, Betty. Dancing Made Easy. 1976. pap. 4.95 o.p. (ISBN 0-380-00613-8, 41962). Avon.

White, Brenda. The Literature & Study of Urban & Regional Planning. (Student Literature Guides). 1974. 16.95x (ISBN 0-7100-7991-5); pap. 7.95 (ISBN 0-7100-7992-3). Routledge & Kegan.

White, Brian, jt. auth. see Brady, John.

White, Burton L., et al. The Origins of Human Competence: The Final Report of the Harvard Preschool Project. LC 77-81793. 464p. 1979. 21.95x o.p. (ISBN 0-669-01943-7). Lexington Bks.

White, C. A., jt. auth. see Kennedy, J. F.

White, C. Langdon, et al. Regional Geography of Anglo-America. 5th ed. (Illus.). 1979. text ed. 28.95 (ISBN 0-13-770883-1). P-H.

White, C. W. & Peercy, P. S., eds. Laser & Electron Beam Processing of Materials. 1980. 46.00 (ISBN 0-12-746850-1). Acad Pr.

White, Carl M., et al. Sources of Information in the Social Sciences. 2nd ed. LC 73-9825. 1500p. 1973. text ed. 30.00 (ISBN 0-8389-0134-4). ALA.

White, Carol. They Do It All with Mirrors. LC 77-20113. 1978. 8.95 o.p. (ISBN 0-698-10873-6, Coward). Putnam Pub Group.

White, Carol H. Holding Hands: The Complete Guide to Palmistry. (Illus.). (gr. 6-8). 1980. 8.95 o.p. (ISBN 0-399-20659-0). Putnam Pub Group.

White, Caroline. Patrons & Partisans: A Study of Politics in Two Southern Italian Comuni. LC 79-53406. (Cambridge Studies in Social Anthropology: No. 31). (Illus.). 1980. 22.00 (ISBN 0-521-22872-7). Cambridge U Pr.

White, Charles S., ed. The Caurasi Pad of Sri Hit Harivams: Introduction, Translation, Notes, & Edited Hindi Text. LC 76-54207. (Asian Studies at Hawaii Ser: No. 16). 1977. pap. text ed. 10.50x (ISBN 0-8248-0359-0). UH Pr.

White, Chelsea C., jt. auth. see Sage, Andrew P.

White, D. How to Find Out About Iron & Steel. 1970. 17.25 o.s.i. (ISBN 0-08-015790-4); pap. 9.50 (ISBN 0-08-015789-0). Pergamon.

White, D. Fedotoff. The Growth of the Red Army. 486p. 1982. Repr. of 1944 ed. lib. bdg. 50.00 (ISBN 0-89987-892-X). Darby Bks.

White, D. J. Decision Methodology. LC 74-1754. 1975. 34.95 o.p. (ISBN 0-471-94045-3, Pub. by Wiley-Interscience). Wiley.

--Finite Dynamic Programming: An Approach to Finite Markov Decision Processes. LC 77-26333. 1978. 59.95x (ISBN 0-471-99629-7, Pub. by Wiley-Interscience). Wiley.

--Optimality & Efficiency. 232p. 1982. 49.95x (ISBN 0-471-10223-7, Pub. by Wiley-Interscience). Wiley.

White, D. J., ed. Cyclosporin A: Proceedings of the International Symposium, Cambridge, U. K., September 1981. 350p. 1982. 36.75 (ISBN 0-444-80410-2, Biomedical Bks). Elsevier.

White, D. M. Predicacion Expositiva. Estrello, Francisco E., tr. Orig. Title: The Excellence of Exposition. 1980. 4.75 (ISBN 0-311-42061-3). Casa Bautista.

--Zaccaria Seriman. 1961. 18.50 (ISBN 0-7190-1218-X). Manchester.

White, D. N. Recent Advances in Perinatal Pathology & Physiology. LC 80-41367. (Ultra Sound in Biomedicine Research Ser.: Vol. 4). 245p. 1982. 61.95x (ISBN 0-471-27925-0, Pub. by Res Stud Pr). Wiley.

White, D. O., jt. auth. see Burnet, F. Macfarlane.

White, Dale. Is Something up There: The Story of Flying Saucers. LC 68-17801. (gr. 3-7). 1968. PLB 7.95 o.p. (ISBN 0-385-02314-6). Doubleday.

White, Dan, jt. auth. see Muse, Bill.

White, David A. The Grand Continuum: Reflections on Joyce & Metaphysics. LC 82-4740. (Critical Essays in Modern Literature). 208p. 1983. text ed. 19.95x (ISBN 0-8229-3803-0). U of Pittsburgh Pr.

White, David C. An Atlas of Radiation Histopathology. LC 75-17867. (AEC Technical Information Center Ser.). 236p. 1975. pap. 14.00 (TID-26676); microfiche 4.50 (ISBN 0-87079-235-0, TID-26676). DOE.

White, David H. Vicente Folch, Governor in Spanish Florida, Seventeen Eighty-Seven to Eighteen Eleven. LC 80-5792. 120p. (Orig.). 1981. text ed. 18.50 (ISBN 0-8191-1598-3); pap. text ed. 8.00 (ISBN 0-8191-1599-1). U Pr of Amer.

White, David O; see Weaver, Glenn.

White Deer of Autumn. Ceremony-In the Circle of Life. (Illus.). 32p. (Orig.). (gr. 2-6). 1982. 11.95 (ISBN 0-940742-02-0); pap. 4.75 (ISBN 0-940742-05-5). Carnival Pr.

White, DeVere. The Minister for Justice. 1971. p.n.s. 0.00 (ISBN 0-87645-045-1). Gambit.

White, Don. The Perfect Secretary. (Illus.). 96p. 1982. pap. 4.50 (ISBN 0-89387-069-2). Curtis Pub Co.

White, Donald, et al. Questions & Answers on Maryland Real Estate. 208p. 1980. pap. text ed. 12.95 (ISBN 0-8359-6139-7). Reston.

White, Donald R., ed. see Girdlestone, Robert B.

White, Donnamaie E., jt. auth. see Svoboda, Antonin.

White, Dorothy, tr. see Pope John XXIII.

White, Dorothy, et al. Fundamentals: The Foundations of Nursing. 324p. 1972. 19.95 o.p. (ISBN 0-13-331991-1). P-H.

White, Dorothy S. Black Africa & De Gaulle: from the French Empire to Independence. LC 79-1733. (Illus.). 1979. 19.75x (ISBN 0-271-00214-X). Pa St U Pr.

White, Doug. Agitation & Addition. (Mud Pump Manual Ser.: No. 9). 1982. pap. 10.75x (ISBN 0-87201-621-8). Gulf Pub.

White, Douglas, jt. auth. see Weaver, Thomas.

White, E. B. Charlotte's Web. LC 52-9760. (Illus.). (ps-3). 1952. 7.64i (ISBN 0-06-026385-7, HarpJ); large type ed. 10.00 (ISBN 0-06-026387-3); PLB 8.89 (ISBN 0-06-026386-5). Har-Row.

--Essays of E. B. White. LC 77-7717. 1977. 14.37i (ISBN 0-06-014576-5, HarpT). Har-Row.

--One Man's Meat. 1978. pap. 1.95i o.p. (ISBN 0-06-080420-3, P 420, PL). Har-Row.

--One Man's Meat. 336p. 1982. 14.37i (ISBN 0-06-015060-2, HarpT). Har-Row.

--Poems & Sketches of E. B. White. LC 81-47240. 232p. 1983. pap. 5.72i (ISBN 0-06-090969-2, CN 969, CN). Har-Row.

--Stuart Little. LC 45-9585. (Illus.). (ps-4). 1945. 7.64i (ISBN 0-06-026395-4, HarpJ); PLB 8.89 (ISBN 0-06-026396-2). Har-Row.

White, e. B., jt. auth. see Strunk, William, Jr.

White, E. N. Maintenance Planning, Control & Documentation. 1979. text ed. 37.25x (ISBN 0-566-02144-7). Gower Pub Ltd.

White, Earl. Nourishing the Seeds of Self Esteem: A Handbook of Group Activities for Nurturing Esteem in Self & Others. LC 79-56144. (Illus.). 220p. (Orig.). 1980. perfect bdg. 12.00 (ISBN 0-9603656-0-5). Whitenwife Pubns.

White, Edmund. A Boy's Own Story. Whitehead, Bill, ed. 202p. 1982. 13.95 (ISBN 0-525-24128-0, 01354-410). Dutton.

White, Edward. Patterns of American Legal Thought. 1978. 20.00 (ISBN 0-672-83417-0, Bobbs-Merrill Law). Michie-Bobbs.

White, Edwin A. & Dykman, Jackson A. Annotated Constitution & Canons for the Government of the Episcopal Church, Vols. I & II. rev. ed. 1982. 110.00 set (ISBN 0-8164-0541-7). Seabury.

White, Elizabeth, pseud. The Sun Girl. LC 79-666054. (Illus.). 1978. Repr. of 1941 ed. 4.75 (ISBN 0-89734-046-9). Mus Northern Ariz.

White, Ellen E. Friends for Life. 176p. 1983. pap. 2.25 (ISBN 0-380-82578-3, Flare). Avon.

White, Ellen G. Day of Benediction. (Newsprint Ser.). 172p. 1982. pap. 0.25 (ISBN 0-8163-0493-9). Pacific Pr Pub Assn.

--The Desire of Ages. 1940. 5.95 o.p. (ISBN 0-8163-0029-1, 04259-8); pap. 0.95 newsprint ed. o.p. (ISBN 0-8163-0030-5, 04261-4); pap. 3.50 o.p. (ISBN 0-8163-0031-3, 04254-9); deluxe ed. 9.50 o.p. (ISBN 0-8163-0032-1, 04257-2). Pacific Pr Pub Assn.

--The Desire of Ages. (Red Gift Edition Ser.). 863p. 1982. 6.95 (ISBN 0-8163-0524-2). Pacific Pr Pub Assn.

--The Great Controversy. (Newsprint Ser.). 420p. 1982. pap. 1.25 (ISBN 0-8163-0511-0). Pacific Pr Pub Assn.

--Mind, Character, & Personality: Guidelines to Mental & Spiritual Health, 2 vols. (Christian Home Library). 1978. 5.95 ea. o.p. Vol. 1 (ISBN 0-8127-0148-8). Vol. 2 (ISBN 0-8127-0149-6). Review & Herald.

White, Ellen G., ed. Great Controversy. (Red Gift Edition Ser.). 719p. 1982. 6.95 (ISBN 0-8163-0525-0). Pacific Pr Pub Assn.

White, Elliott, ed. Sociobiology & Human Politics. LC 79-3016. 304p. 1981. 25.95x (ISBN 0-669-03602-1). Lexington Bks.

White, Eric W. Benjamin Britten: His Life & Operas. rev. ed. Evans, John, ed. LC 82-10882. (Illus.). 320p. 1983. text ed. 30.00x (ISBN 0-520-04893-8); pap. text ed. 12.95x (ISBN 0-520-04894-6). U of Cal Pr.

--Stravinsky, a Critical Survey. LC 79-9863. 1979. Repr. of 1948 ed. lib. bdg. 20.25x (ISBN 0-313-21463-8, WHST). Greenwood.

White, Ernest. Saint Paul: The Man & His Mind. 1958. 2.95 o.p. (ISBN 0-87508-567-9). Chr Lit.

White, Etson. Revelation of God. 1983. 8.95 (ISBN 0-533-05567-9). Vantage.

White, Eugene N. The Regulation & Reform of the America Banking System, 1900-1929. LC 82-61395. 256p. 1983. 25.00x (ISBN 0-691-04232-2). Princeton U Pr.

White, F. Clifton & Gill, William J. Why Reagan Won: A Narrative History of the Conservative Movement 1964-1981. LC 81-52142. 276p. 1982. 14.95 (ISBN 0-89526-668-7). Regnery-Gateway.

White, Florence, ed. Voltaire's Essay on Epic Poetry: A Study & Edition. LC 74-90363. 1970. Repr. of 1915 ed. 8.50x (ISBN 0-87753-044-0). Phaeton.

White, Florence M. Cesar Chavez: Man of Courage. LC 72-6803. (Americans All Ser.). (Illus.). 96p. (gr. 3-6). 1973. PLB 7.12 (ISBN 0-8116-4579-7). Garrard.

--Escape: The Life of Harry Houdini. LC 78-26248. (Illus.). 112p. (gr. 4-6). 1979. PLB 7.79 o.p. (ISBN 0-671-32937-5). Messner.

--Malcolm X: Black & Proud. LC 74-16264. (Americans All Ser). (Illus.). 96p. (gr. 3-6). 1975. PLB 7.12 (ISBN 0-8116-4582-7). Garrard.

White, Frank M. Elementary Fluid Mechanics. (Illus.). 1979. text ed. 32.95 (ISBN 0-07-069667-5, C); solution manual 25.00 (ISBN 0-07-069668-3). McGraw.

--Viscous Fluid Flow. (Illus.). 640p. 1974. text ed. 38.50 (ISBN 0-07-069710-8, C). McGraw.

White, Fred. One Hundred & One Apple Computer Programming Tips & Tricks. new ed. 128p. (Orig.). 1982. pap. 8.95 (ISBN 0-86668-015-2). ARCsoft.

--Thirty-Three New Apple Computer Programs for Home, School & Office. new ed. (Illus.). 96p. (Orig.). 1982. pap. 8.95 (ISBN 0-86668-016-0). ARCsoft.

White, Fred, jt. auth. see Collins, Bobby.

White, Fred C., jt. auth. see Kundell, James E.

White, Freda. West of the Rhone. (Illus.). 240p. 1980. 6.95 (ISBN 0-571-05804-3). Faber & Faber.

White, Frederick A. Our Acoustic Environment. LC 75-8888. 501p. 1975. 37.50 o.p. (ISBN 0-471-93920-X, Pub. by Wiley-Interscience). Wiley.

White, G. Edward. The American Judicial Tradition. LC 75-32356. 1976. 25.00x (ISBN 0-19-502017-0). Oxford U Pr.

--The American Judicial Tradition: Profiles of Leading American Judges. LC 75-32356. 1978. pap. 10.95 (ISBN 0-19-502361-7, GB534, GB). Oxford U Pr.

--Tort Law in America: An Intellectual History. 1980. text ed. 25.00x (ISBN 0-19-502586-5). Oxford U Pr.

White, Gail. Fishing for Leviathan. 1983. pap. 2.95 (ISBN 0-939736-39-X). Wings ME.

White, Gay B. The World's First Airline: The St. Peterburg-Tampa Airboat Line, 1914. 1982. pap. 3.95 (ISBN 0-912522-72-0). Aero-Medical.

White, Gene. The New Orleans Guide. 2nd ed. (Illus.). 84p. 1982. pap. 3.95x (ISBN 0-9607056-0-0). Monticello Pr.

White, George R. Concrete Technology. 3rd ed. LC 76-5304. 1977. pap. text ed. 9.80 (ISBN 0-8273-1095-1); instructor's guide 3.25 (ISBN 0-8273-1092-7). Delmar.

White, Gifford. Eighteen Thirty Citizens of Texas. 1982. 24.95 (ISBN 0-686-83118-7). Eakin Pubns.

White, Gilbert. The Portrait of a Tortoise. 64p. 1982. pap. 2.50 (ISBN 0-380-58123-X, 58123, Discus). Avon.

White, Gilbert F. & Haas, J. Eugene. Assessment of Research on Natural Hazards. LC 75-2058. (Environmental Studies Ser.). (Illus.). 487p. 1975. 30.00x (ISBN 0-262-23071-2). MIT Pr.

White, Gilbert F., jt. ed. see Holdgate, Martin W.

White, Gordon. Party & Professionals: The Political Role of Teachers in Contemporary China. LC 81-5256. 350p. 1981. 30.00 (ISBN 0-87332-188-X). M E Sharpe.

--Video Techniques. 288p. 1982. pap. 30.95 (ISBN 0-408-00506-8). Focal Pr.

White, Gordon, jt. auth. see Blecher, Marc J.

White, Gordon & Murray, Robin, eds. Revolutionary Socialist Development in the Third World. LC 82-23705. 272p. 1983. 26.00x (ISBN 0-8131-1485-3). U Pr of Ky.

White, Gordon E., jt. auth. see Hafer, W. Keith.

White, Gordon E., jt. auth. see Jugenheimer, Donald W.

White, Graham J. FDR & the Press. LC 78-11423. 1979. 13.95x (ISBN 0-226-89512-2). U of Chicago Pr.

White, Gregory J. Emergency Childbirth: A Manual. (Illus.). 62p. wire-bound 4.95 (ISBN 0-686-37623-4). Police Train.

White, H. C., jt. auth. see Kirschner, H. E.

White, H. P. The Continuing Conurbation: Change & Development in Greater Manchester. 207p. 1980. text ed. 30.75x (ISBN 0-566-00248-5). Gower Pub Ltd.

White, H. P. see Thomas, David J.

White, H. V., jt. auth. see Coates, W. H.

White, Harold. Luton Past & Present. 152p. 1982. 35.00x (ISBN 0-900804-20-3, Pub. by White Crescent England). State Mutual Bk.

White, Harvey M., jt. ed. see Berenson, Gerald.

White, Helen. Jesse Hill Ford: An Annotated Checklist of His Published Works & of His Papers. (Mississippi Valley Collection Bulletin, No. 7). (Illus.). 55p. 1974. pap. 5.95x o.p. (ISBN 0-87870-083-8). Memphis St Univ.

White, Helen & Sugg, Redding S, Jr. Shelby Foote. (United States Authors Ser.). 1982. lib. bdg. 15.95 (ISBN 0-8057-7366-5, Twayne). G K Hall.

White, Helen, jt. auth. see White, Benjamin V.

White, Helen A. & Williams, Maxcine, eds. The Alaska-Yukon Wild Flowers Guide. LC 74-79085. (Illus.). 218p. 1974. pap. 12.95 (ISBN 0-88240-032-0). Alaska Northwest.

White, Helen C., et al. Seventeenth-Century Verse & Prose: 1600-1660. 2nd ed. 1971. Vol. 1. 22.95x (ISBN 0-02-427110-1). Macmillan.

White, Henry E., Jr. Making Marriage Successful. 420p. 1983. text ed. 18.95x (ISBN 0-8290-1261-3). Irvington.

White, Herbert. Copyright Dilemma. 1978. pap. text ed. 10.00 (ISBN 0-8389-0262-6). ALA.

White, Herbert S., jt. auth. see Fry, Bernard M.

White, Howard A. Freedmen's Bureau in Louisiana. LC 70-103131. 1970. 19.50 (ISBN 0-8071-0919-3). La State U Pr.

White, Iain, tr. see Schwob, Marcel.

White, J. B. Wastewater Engineering. 330p. 1978. text ed. 49.50 (ISBN 0-686-43047-6). E Arnold.

White, J. E. Applied Seismic Methods. (Methods in Geochemistry & Geophysics: Vol. 18). Date not set. price not set (ISBN 0-444-42139-4). Elsevier.

White, J. E. Manchip. Ancient Egypt: Its Culture & History. (Illus.). 9.50 (ISBN 0-8446-0336-8). Peter Smith.

White, J. Enrico. Method of Itegrated Tangents with Applications in Local Riemannian Geometry. (Monographs & Studies: No. 13). 256p. 1982. text ed. 43.95 (ISBN 0-273-08515-8). Pitman Pub MA.

White, J. F. The Cambridge Movement. LC 79-50916. (Illus.). 1979. 39.50 (ISBN 0-521-06781-2). Cambridge U Pr.

White, J. H., jt. auth. see Long, M. J.

White, J. L. Fiber Structure & Properties: Proceedings. 264p. 1979. pap. 21.50x (ISBN 0-471-05697-9, Pub. by Wiley-Interscience). Wiley.

White, J. M. & Barnes, R. P. Manual for Hands on Biology: An Audio Tutorial Approach. 1974. 21.95x (ISBN 0-471-94016-X). Wiley.

White, J. P. Towards a Compulsory Curriculum. (Students Library of Education). 1977. 9.95x (ISBN 0-7100-8720-9); pap. 4.95 (ISBN 0-686-67931-8). Routledge & Kegan.

White, J. P. & O'Connell, J. F., eds. A Prehistory of Australia, New Guinea & Sahul: International Edition. LC 81-71781. Date not set. 29.50 (ISBN 0-12-746730-0). Acad Pr.

White, J. Perry. Twentieth Century Choral Music: An Annotated Bibliography of Music Suitable for Use by High School Choirs. LC 82-10239. x, 153p. 1982. 17.50 (ISBN 0-8108-1568-0). Scarecrow.

White, J. R. Successful Supervision. 1976. 27.50 (ISBN 0-07-084458-5, P&RB). McGraw.

White, Jack. The Last Eleven. (Abbey Theater Ser.). pap. 2.50x (ISBN 0-912262-46-X). Proscenium.

White, James. The Escape Orbit. pap. 2.50 (ISBN 0-441-21590-4, Pub. by Ace Science Fiction). Ace Bks.

--Sector General. 208p. (Orig.). 1983. pap. 2.75 (ISBN 0-345-30851-4, Del Rey). Ballantine.

White, James A. The Founding of Cliff Haven: Early Years of the Catholic Summer School of America. LC 53-1915. (Monograph Ser.: No. 24). 1950. 7.50x (ISBN 0-930060-06-7). US Cath Hist.

White, James B. The Legal Imagination: Studies in the Nature of Legal Thought & Expression. 1973. 26.00 (ISBN 0-316-93602-2). Little.

White, James F. Sacraments as God's Self Giving. 160p. (Orig.). 1983. pap. 8.95 (ISBN 0-687-36707-7). Abingdon.

--Worldliness of Worship. 1967. 12.95x (ISBN 0-19-501214-3). Oxford U Pr.

White, James L., jt. auth. see Grubbs, Robert L.

White, James P., jt. auth. see Rooth, Anne R.

White, James S. The Spells of Lamazee. LC 82-14578. 1982. limited signed 60.00 (ISBN 0-932576-13-3); pap. 8.95 (ISBN 0-932576-12-5). Breitenbush Pubns.

White, James W. Migration in Metropolitan Japan: Social Change & Political Behavior. (Japan Research Monographs: No. 2). 364p. (Orig.). 1982. pap. 12.00x (ISBN 0-912966-53-X). IEAS.

White, Jan. Designing... for Magazines. LC 76-3692. (Illus.). 176p. 1976. 19.25 o.p. (ISBN 0-8352-0900-8). Bowker.

White, Jan V. Editing by Design: Word-&-Picture Communication for Editors & Designers. LC 73-18167. (Illus.). 230p. 1974. 19.25 o.p. (ISBN 0-8352-0692-0). Bowker.

White, Jeffrey R., ed. Products Liability, 2 vols. 1200p. 1983. Vol. 1. 125.00 set (ISBN 0-941916-07-3); Vol. 2. 0.00 (ISBN 0-941916-08-1). Assn Trial Ed.

--The Trial Lawyer & the Federal Rules of Evidence. 630p. 1980. 15.00 (ISBN 0-941916-03-0). Assn Trial Ed.

White, Jerry. The Uneasy Marriage. (Critical Concern Ser.). 1983. write for info. (ISBN 0-88070-018-1). Multnomah.

White, Jerry & White, Mary. Friends & Friendship: The Secrets of Drawing Closer. LC 82-81758. 196p. 1982. pap. 4.95 (ISBN 0-89109-500-4). NavPress.

White, Jerry, jt. auth. see Welsh, John.

White, Jerry E. & White, Mary E. Your Job: Survival or Satisfaction. 1976. 5.95 (ISBN 0-310-34321-6). Zondervan.

White, John. Flirting with the World: A Challenge to Loyalty. LC 81-21491. 156p. 1982. pap. 5.95 (ISBN 0-87788-156-1). Shaw Pubs.

--Rejection. 192p. 1982. pap. 5.95 (ISBN 0-201-08310-8). A-W.

White, John A. The Politics of Foreign Aid. LC 74-77769. 320p. 1974. 26.00 (ISBN 0-312-62685-1). St Martin.

--Siberian Intervention. Repr. of 1950 ed. lib. bdg. 19.25x (ISBN 0-8371-1976-6, WHIS). Greenwood.

White, John A., et al. Principles of Engineering Economic Analysis. LC 77-4663. 1977. text ed. 30.95 (ISBN 0-471-01773-6); tchrs. manual o.p. 5.00 (ISBN 0-471-03689-7). Wiley.

White, John H., Jr. Early American Locomotives. LC 79-188951. (Illus.). 142p. (Orig.). 1972. pap. 6.00 (ISBN 0-486-22772-3). Dover.

White, John H., Jr., ed. Horsecars, Cable Cars & Omnibuses Ca. 1880. LC 73-80949. (Illus., Orig.). 1974. pap. 6.50 (ISBN 0-486-23009-0). Dover.

White, John K. The Fractured Electorate: Political Parties & Social Change in Southern New England. LC 82-40471. (Illus.). 196p. 1983. 16.00 (ISBN 0-87451-258-1); pap. 8.00 (ISBN 0-87451-260-3). U Pr of New Eng.

White, John L., ed. Semeia Twenty-Two: Studies in Ancient Letter Writing. (Semeia Ser.). 9.95 (ISBN 0-686-96286-9, 06 20 22). Scholars Pr CA.

White, John M. Physical Chemistry Laboratory Experiments. (Illus.). 576p. 1975. ref. ed. 23.95 (ISBN 0-13-665927-6). P-H.

White, John S., ed. see Plutarch.

White, John T. A Countryman's Guide to the South East. (Illus.). 1978. 14.95 (ISBN 0-7100-8838-8). Routledge & Kegan.

White, John W., ed. Frontiers of Consciousness. 1975. pap. 2.95 o.p. (ISBN 0-380-00393-7, 48850). Avon.

White, Jon. E., selected by see Frith, Francis.

White, Jon M. Everyday Life in Ancient Egypt. (Everyday Life Ser.). (Illus.). (gr. 7-9). 1964. 6.75 o.p. (ISBN 0-399-20050-9). Putnam Pub Group.

White, Joseph L. The Limits of Trade Union Militancy: The Lancashire Textile Workers, 1910-1914. LC 77-87965. (Contributions in Labor History: No. 5). (Illus.). 1978. lib. bdg. 19.95x (ISBN 0-313-20029-7, WLT/). Greenwood.

White, K. D. Farm Equipment of the Roman World. LC 73-82450. (Illus.). 248p. 1975. 65.00 (ISBN 0-521-20333-3). Cambridge U Pr.

White, K. J., jt. ed. see Payne, C. J.

White, Karol. The Corporate Mentor. LC 82-40010. 272p. 1983. 18.95 o.p. (ISBN 0-8128-2875-5). Stein & Day.

White, Kathleen M. & Speisman, Joseph C. Adolescence. LC 76-26158. (Life-Span Human Development Ser.). 1976. pap. 8.95 (ISBN 0-8185-0205-3). Brooks-Cole.

White, Kay. The Boxer. 1977. pap. 2.50 (ISBN 0-7028-1035-5). Palmetto Pub.

White, Kay & Joshua, Joan. Practical Guide to the Dogs. 1976. 11.95 o.p. (ISBN 0-600-37046-1). Transatlantic.

White, Kay, tr. see Sarkany, Pal & Ocsag, Imre.

White, Kenneth, ed. Alogical Modern Drama. (Faux Titre Band Ser.: No. 10). 68p. 1982. pap. text ed. 9.25x (ISBN 90-6203-784-4, Pub. by Rodopi Holland). Humanities.

White, Kenneth S. Einstein & Modern French Drama: An Analogy. LC 82-21789. 132p. (Orig.). 1983. lib. bdg. 17.75 (ISBN 0-8191-2942-9); pap. text ed. 7.75 (ISBN 0-8191-2943-7). U Pr of Amer.

--Man's New Shapes: French Avant-Garde Drama's Metamorphoses. LC 79-62911. 1979. pap. text ed. 7.00 (ISBN 0-8191-0717-4). U Pr of Amer.

--Savage Comedy since King Ubu: A Tangent to "The Absurd". 1977. pap. text ed. 7.00 (ISBN 0-8191-0152-4). U Pr of Amer.

White, Kent. Prairie Fire. 200p. (Orig.). 1983. pap. 4.95 (ISBN 0-938936-07-7). Daring Pr.

--Prairie Fire. 200p. 1983. lib. bdg. 14.95 (ISBN 0-938936-12-3); pap. 4.95. Daring Pr.

White, Kerr L. & Henderson, Maureen M. Epidemiology as a Fundamental Science: Its Uses in Health Services Planning, Administration & Evaluation. (Illus.). 1976. pap. text ed. 12.95x (ISBN 0-19-502081-2). Oxford U Pr.

White, Kerr L., jt. ed. see Kohn, Robert.

White, Kinnard, jt. auth. see Coop, Richard H.

White, L. P. & Plaskett, L. G. Biomass as Fuel. LC 81-66689. 211p. 1982. 29.50 (ISBN 0-686-81667-6). Acad Pr.

White, L. W., jt. auth. see Ward, W. F.

White, Laura C., tr. Who is Padre Pio? (Illus.). 44p. 1955. pap. 0.75 (ISBN 0-686-81642-0). TAN Bks Pubs.

White, Lawrence B., Jr. & Broekel, Ray. The Trick Book. LC 77-11249. (gr. 3-7). 1979. PLB 6.95a o.p. (ISBN 0-385-13581-5). Doubleday.

White, Lawrence J. Corporate Governance in the 1980s: New Roles & Images for Directors & Executives. (Seven Springs Studies). 1981. pap. 3.00 (ISBN 0-943006-04-X). Seven Springs.

--The Public Library in the Nineteen Eighties: The Problems of Choice. LC 82-48604. (Lexington Books Special Series in Libraries & Librarianship). 244p. 1983. 22.95x (ISBN 0-669-06342-8). Lexington Bks.

--Regulation of Air Pollution Emissions from Motor Vehicles. 1982. 13.95 (ISBN 0-8447-3492-6); pap. 4.95 (ISBN 0-8447-3487-X). Am Enterprise.

White, Lawrence J., jt. auth. see Goldberg, Lawrence G.

White, Lawrence J., jt. ed. see Keenan, Michael.

White, Leon S. Patriot for Liberty. LC 74-30451. (gr. 7 up). 1975. 7.95 o.p. (ISBN 0-397-31619-4, HarpJ). Har-Row.

White, Leonard & Tarsky, Bernard, eds. Clinical Biofeedback: Efficacy & Mechanisms. LC 81-1048. 468p. 1982. 39.50x (ISBN 0-89862-619-6). Guilford Pr.

White, Leonard D. City Manager. LC 68-57647. (Illus.). 1969. Repr. of 1927 ed. lib. bdg. 19.75x (ISBN 0-8371-0750-4, WHCM). Greenwood.

White, Leonard D., jt. auth. see Smith, Thomas V.

White, Leslie A. Pueblo of San Felipe. LC 32-30651, 1932. pap. 12.00 (ISBN 0-527-00537-1). Kraus Repr.

--Pueblo of Santa Ana, New Mexico. LC 43-10004. 1942. pap. 34.00 (ISBN 0-527-00559-2). Kraus Repr.

--Pueblo of Santo Domingo, New Mexico. LC 35-17202. 1935. pap. 23.00 (ISBN 0-527-00542-8). Kraus Repr.

White, Lonnie J., ed. see Morison, James.

White, Loring. Frontier Patrol: The Army & the Indians in Northeastern California, 1861. (ANCRR Research Paper: No. 2). 28p. 1974. 4.00 (ISBN 0-686-38943-3). Assn NC Records.

White, Louise G. & Clark, Robert P. Political Analysis: Technique & Practice. LC 82-22827. (Political Science Ser.). 300p. 1983. pap. text ed. 14.95 (ISBN 0-534-01284-1). Brooks-Cole.

White, Louise G., jt. auth. see Bryant, Coralie.

White, Lucia, jt. auth. see White, Morton.

White, Lyman C. International Non-Governmental Organizations: Their Purposes, Methods, & Accomplishments. LC 68-8340. (Illus.). 1968. Repr. of 1951 ed. lib. bdg. 18.00x (ISBN 0-8371-0266-9, WHIN). Greenwood.

White, Lynn, Jr. Dynamo & Virgin Reconsidered: Machina Ex Deo. 1971. pap. 3.95x (ISBN 0-262-73024-3). MIT Pr.

--Medieval Religion & Technology: Collected Essays. LC 77-83113. (Center for Medieval & Renaissance Studies, UCLA: No. 13). 1978. 38.50x (ISBN 0-520-03566-6). U of Cal Pr.

--Medieval Technology & Social Change. 1966. pap. 5.95 (ISBN 0-19-500266-0, GB). Oxford U Pr.

--The Transformation of the Roman World: Gibbon's Problem After Two Centuries. (UCLA Center for Medieval & Renaissance Studies). 1966. 11.00 o.p. (ISBN 0-520-01334-4); pap. 5.95x o.p. (ISBN 0-520-02491-5). U of Cal Pr.

White, Lynn T., 3rd. Careers in Shanghai: The Social Guidance of Personal Energies in a Developing Chinese City, 1949-1966. 1978. 30.00x (ISBN 0-520-03361-2). U of Cal Pr.

White, M. J. Animal Cytology & Evolution. 3rd ed. LC 79-190418. (Illus.). 1000p. 1973. 105.00 o.p. (ISBN 0-521-07071-6); pap. 32.50 (ISBN 0-521-29227-1). Cambridge U Pr.

--The Chromosomes. 6th ed. 1973. pap. 9.95x o.p. (ISBN 0-412-11930-7, Pub. by Chapman & Hall). Methuen Inc.

White, Margaret E., ed. see Harding, Chester A.

White, Marguerite B. Curriculum Development from a Nursing Model: The Crisis Theory Framework. (Springer Series on the Teaching of Nursing: Vol. 8). 1983. pap. text ed. price not set (ISBN 0-8261-3281-2). Springer Pub.

White, Marian E., et al, eds. High Interest - Easy Reading: For Junior & Senior High School Students. rev. ed. 1979. pap. 3.85 (ISBN 0-8141-2094-6); pap. 2.75 members (ISBN 0-686-86420-4). NCTE.

White, Marianne & Nahrung, Loma. Something in Common. 180p. 1982. pap. 10.95 (ISBN 0-85564-204-1, Pub. by U of W Austral Pr). Intl Schol Bk Serv.

White, Marjorie L. The Birmingham District: An Industrial History & Guide. LC 81-70145. (Illus.). 324p. 1981. 19.95 (ISBN 0-686-36923-8); pap. 14.95 (ISBN 0-686-36924-6). Birmingham Hist Soc.

--Downtown Birmingham-Architectural & Historical Walking Tour Guide. 2nd ed. Plosser, George G. & Sprague, Richard W., eds. LC 77-608282. (Illus.). 144p. 1980. 12.00 (ISBN 0-686-36925-4); pap. 7.00 (ISBN 0-686-36926-2). Birmingham Hist Soc.

White, Marsh W. & Manning, Kenneth V. Experimental College Physics. 3rd ed. (Illus.). 1954. text ed. 23.50 (ISBN 0-07-069749-3, C). McGraw.

White, Martin S. Profit from Information: A Guide to the Establishment, Operation & Use of an Information Consultancy. 132p. 1981. 22.50 (ISBN 0-233-97336-2, 05830-0, Pub. by Gower Pub Co England). Lexington Bks.

White, Mary. How to Do Bead Work. (Illus.). 8.00 (ISBN 0-8446-0291-4). Peter Smith.

--How to Do Beadwork. (Illus.). 160p. 1972. pap. 3.50 (ISBN 0-486-20697-1). Dover.

--How to Make Baskets. LC 72-162523. Repr. of 1902 ed. 30.00x (ISBN 0-8103-3064-4). Gale.

--More Baskets & How to Make Them. LC 76-162524. Repr. of 1912 ed. 31.00 o.p. (ISBN 0-8103-3065-2). Gale.

White, Mary, jt. auth. see White, Jerry.

White, Mary E., jt. auth. see White, Jerry E.

White, Mary Lou. Adventuring with Books. LC 81-11179. 482p. 1981. pap. text ed. 9.00 (ISBN 0-8389-3271-1). ALA.

White, Maureen, jt. auth. see Tsoukalis, Loukas.

White, Mel. Mike Douglas: When the Going Gets Tough. 1982. 9.95 (ISBN 0-8499-0318-1). Word Pub.

White, Melvin R. & Whiting, Frank M. Playreader's Repertory: Drama or Stage. 1970. pap. 12.50x (ISBN 0-673-05699-6). Scott F.

White, Melvin R., jt. auth. see Coger, Leslie I.

White, Michael. Payment Systems in Britain. 148p. 1981. text ed. 39.75x (ISBN 0-566-02294-X). Gower Pub Ltd.

White, Michael, jt. auth. see Golembiewski, Robert T.

White, Michelle J. Nonprofit Firms in a Three Sector Economy. LC 81-52791. (Coupe Ser.: No. 6). (Illus.). 181p. (Orig.). 1981. pap. 10.00 (ISBN 0-87766-312-2, URI 32700). Urban Inst.

White, Mike, jt. auth. see Ralston, John.

White, Minor. Mirrors-Messages-Manifestations. limited ed. (Illus.). 242p. 1982. Repr. of 1969 ed. 60.00 (ISBN 0-89381-102-5); original print 900.00 (ISBN 0-89381-105-X). Aperture.

White, Morris, jt. auth. see Epstein, Abraham.

White, Morton. The Philosophy of the American Revolution. LC 77-18081. (American Social Thought Ser.). 1978. 19.95x (ISBN 0-19-502381-1, GB 625); pap. 7.95 (ISBN 0-19-502891-0). Oxford U Pr.

--Science & Sentiment in America: Philosophical Thought from Jonathan Edwards to John Dewey. 1972. 19.95x (ISBN 0-19-501519-3). Oxford U Pr.

--Social Thought in America: The Revolt Against Formalism. 335p. 1976. pap. 6.95 (ISBN 0-19-519837-9, 459, GB). Oxford U Pr.

White, Morton & White, Lucia. The Intellectual Versus the City: From Thomas Jefferson to Frank Lloyd Wright. LC 62-17229. 1977. pap. 7.95 (ISBN 0-19-519969-3, GB519, GB). Oxford U Pr.

White, Morton, ed. Age of Analysis: Twentieth Century Philosophers. (Orig.). pap. 2.95 (ISBN 0-451-62150-6, ME2150, Ment). NAL.

--Documents in the History of American Philosophy: From Jonathan Edward to John Dewey. 1972. text ed. 22.50x (ISBN 0-19-501556-8); pap. text ed. 12.95x (ISBN 0-19-501555-X). Oxford U Pr.

White, Mosazelle N., ed. see Gear, Bonnie.

White, Mosezelle, ed. see Morant, Mack B.

White, Mosezelle, ed. see Roberts, Bobby, III.

White, Mosezelle, ed. see Williams, Hobie L.

White, Nancy & Esten, John. Style in Motion: Munkacsi Photographs of the Twenties, Thirties, Forties & Fifties. (Illus.). 1979. 25.00 o.p. (ISBN 0-517-53858-X, C N Potter Bks). Crown.

White, Nathan. U.S. Policy Toward Korea: Analysis, Alternatives, & Recommendations. (Westview Replica Edition). 1979. softcover 25.00 o.p. (ISBN 0-89158-490-0). Westview.

White, Ned. Inside Television: A Guide to Critical Viewing. 205p. 1981. 12.00 (ISBN 0-686-82346-X); 78 pgs. with worksheets 10.00 (ISBN 0-686-82347-8). Sci & Behavior.

White, Nelson & White, Anne. Collected Rituals from the T. O. T. & Other Sources. LC 82-50719. 100p. (Orig.). 1982. pap. 20.00 (ISBN 0-939856-28-X). Tech Group.

--Secret Magic Revealed. 2nd ed ed. LC 82-50720. (Illus.). 120p. (Orig.). 1982. pap. 25.00 (ISBN 0-939856-29-8). Tech Group.

White, Nelson H. Magick & the Law: Vol. 5, or How to Set-Up & Operate Your Own Occult Shop. LC 80-50273. (Illus.). 75p. (Orig.). 1982. pap. 10.00 (ISBN 0-939856-31-X). Tech Group.

White, Nelson H. see Zarathustra, Frater, pseud.

White, Newman I. & Jackson, Walter C. An Anthology of Verse by American Negroes. 1968. 10.95 (ISBN 0-87716-002-3, Pub. by Moore Pub Co). F Apple.

White, Nicholas P. Plato on Knowledge & Reality. LC 76-10993. 400p. 1976. 25.00 (ISBN 0-915144-21-2); pap. 15.00 (ISBN 0-915144-22-0). Hackett Pub.

White, O. R., et al, eds. The Solar Output & Its Variation. LC 76-15773. (Illus.). 1977. 18.50x (ISBN 0-87081-071-5). Colo Assoc.

White, Opal T. General American Speech for the Bilingual Spanish Speaking Student. 1979. pap. text ed. 10.95 (ISBN 0-8403-1967-3, 40196701). Kendall-Hunt.

White, Osmar. The Super-Roo of Mungalongaloo. (Illus.). 1975. 2.95 o.p. (ISBN 0-85885-112-1). David & Charles.

White, Owen R. & Haring, Norris G. Exceptional Teaching: Individually Planned Educations. 2nd ed. (Special Education Ser.). 368p. 1980. text ed. 21.95 (ISBN 0-675-08156-4). Additional supplements may be obtained from publisher. Merrill.

White, P. Thy Kingdom Come. 4.75 o.p. (ISBN 0-8062-1061-3). Carlton.

White, Patrick. The Eye of the Storm. 1975. pap. 2.50 o.s.i. (ISBN 0-380-00214-0, 40634). Avon.

--Flaws in the Glass. 1983. pap. 5.95 (ISBN 0-14-006293-9). Penguin.

--A Fringe of Leaves. 1977. pap. 1.95 o.s.i. (ISBN 0-380-01826-8, 36160). Avon.

--A Fringe of Leaves. LC 76-18961. 1977. 13.95 (ISBN 0-670-33073-6). Viking Pr.

--The Solid Mandala. 1983. pap. price not set (ISBN 0-14-002975-3). Penguin.

White, Paul. Alias Jungle Doctor: An Autobiography. (Illus.). 236p. 1977. pap. 6.95 (ISBN 0-85364-205-2). Attic Pr.

--Fabulas de la Selva. Orig. Title: Jungle Doctor's Fables. 80p. Date not set. pap. price not set (ISBN 0-311-39000-5). Casa Bautista.

--Get Moving! 128p. 1976. pap. 2.95 (ISBN 0-85364-202-8). Attic Pr.

--What's Happened to Auntie Jean? (Illus.). 30p. (gr. 1-3). 1976. 2.75 o.p. (ISBN 0-8307-0436-1, 57-009-06). Regal.

--What's Happening to Mother? (Illus.). 30p. (gr. 1-3). 1976. 2.75 o.p. (ISBN 0-8307-0438-8, 57-010-07). Regal.

White, Paul D. My Life and Medicine. LC 70-137020. (Illus.). 1973. 12.95 (ISBN 0-87645-039-7). Gambit.

White, Peter, ed. Benjamin Tompson, Colonial Bard: A Critical Edition. LC 79-21367. (Illus.). 230p. 1980. text ed. 18.95x (ISBN 0-271-00250-6). Pa St U Pr.

White, Peter, tr. see Von Lang, Jochen & Sibyll, Claus.

White, R. Respiratory Infections & Tumors. (Topics in Respiratory Disease Ser.). 104p. 1982. 17.95 (ISBN 0-85200-425-7, Pub. by MTP Pr England). Kluwer Boston.

White, R. E. The Answer Is the Spirit. LC 79-23825. 1980. pap. 6.50 (ISBN 0-664-24311-8). Westminster.

--Christian Ethics: The Historical Development. LC 80-39765. 335p. 1981. pap. 10.95 (ISBN 0-8042-0791-7). John Knox.

White, R. G., et al. Noise & Vibration. 866p. 1982. 122.95x (ISBN 0-470-27553-7). Halsted Pr.

White, R. L. Basic Quantum Mechanics. 1966. text ed. 34.95 o.p. (ISBN 0-07-069660-8, C). McGraw.

White, R. W. & Watt, N. F. The Abnormal Personality. 5th ed. LC 80-22055. 793p. 1981. text ed. 26.95 (ISBN 0-471-04599-3). Wiley.

White, Ralph D. Aspects of Male Infertility. (International Perspectives in Urology Ser.). (Illus.). 296p. 1982. lib. bdg. 38.00 (ISBN 0-683-02451-5). Williams & Wilkins.

White, Ralph K. Autocracy & Democracy: An Experimental Inquiry. LC 71-138137. (Illus.). 330p. 1972. Repr. of 1960 ed. lib. bdg. 19.25x (ISBN 0-8371-5710-2, WHAD). Greenwood.

White, Ray L. Gore Vidal. (U. S. Authors Ser.: No. 135). 1968. lib. bdg. 11.95 (ISBN 0-8057-0760-3, Twayne). G K Hall.

--Sherwood Anderson: A Reference Guide. 1977. lib. bdg. 31.00 (ISBN 0-8161-7818-6, Hall Reference). G K Hall.

White, Ray L., ed. see Anderson, Sherwood.

White, Reginald E. Beneath the Cross of Jesus. (Pivot Family Reader Ser). 236p. 1975. pap. 2.25 o.p. (ISBN 0-87983-109-X). Keats.

--Stranger of Galilee. LC 60-10096. (Pivot Family Reader Ser). 240p. 1975. pap. 2.25 o.p. (ISBN 0-87983-108-1). Keats.

White, Reginald J. Life in Regency England. (English Life Ser.). (Illus.). (gr. 7-9). 1964. 6.75 o.p. (ISBN 0-399-20136-X). Putnam Pub Group.

--Short History of England. (Illus.). 1967. 44.50 (ISBN 0-521-06784-7); pap. 12.95 (ISBN 0-521-09439-9). Cambridge U Pr.

White, Richard. The Roots of Dependency: Subsistence, Environment, & Social Change among the Choctaws, Pawnees, & Navajos. LC 82-11146. (Illus.). 500p. 1983. 26.50x (ISBN 0-8032-4722-2). U of Nebr Pr.

--Sword of the North. 13.95 (ISBN 0-89803-147-8). Caroline Hse.

White, Richard M., jt. auth. see Hu, Chenming.

White, Richard N., et al. Structural Engineering, Vol. 3: Behavior of Members & Systems. LC 75-174772. 544p. 1974. text ed. 39.50x (ISBN 0-471-94072-0). Wiley.

--Structural Engineering, Combined Edition, 2 vols. in 1. LC 76-202. 570p. 1976. text ed. 39.50x (ISBN 0-471-94067-4). Wiley.

--Structural Engineering, Vol. 1: Introduction to Design Concepts & Analysis. 2nd ed. LC 75-174772. 288p. 1976. text ed. 30.95x o.p. (ISBN 0-471-94066-6). Wiley.

White, Robb. Deathwatch. 1973. pap. 2.25 (ISBN 0-440-91740-9, LFL). Dell.

--Fire Storm. (gr. 5-9). 1979. 6.95a o.p. (ISBN 0-385-14630-2); PLB 6.95a (ISBN 0-385-14631-0). Doubleday.

--The Frogmen. LC 72-76220. 240p. (gr. 9-12). 1973. PLB 5.95 o.p. (ISBN 0-385-00139-8). Doubleday.

White, Robert, ed. The Duck Book: Investment for Survival in the 1980's. LC 82-80608. 1982. 15.00 (ISBN 0-688-01229-9); pap. 6.50 (ISBN 0-688-01190-X). Morrow.

White, Robert B., Jr., ed. English Literary Journal to Nineteen Hundred: A Guide to Information Sources. LC 73-16998. (American Literature English Literature & World Literatures in English Information Guide Ser.: Vol. 8). 250p. 1977. 42.00x (ISBN 0-8103-1228-X). Gale.

White, Robert C. Sewell's Dog's Medical Dictionary. 1976. cased 16.95 (ISBN 0-7100-8365-3); pap. 6.95 (ISBN 0-7100-8366-1). Routledge & Kegan.

White, Robert L. John Peale Bishop. (United States Authors Ser.: No. 99). 12.50 o.p. (ISBN 0-8057-0068-4, Twayne). G K Hall.

White, Robert R., ed. Atlas of Pediatric Surgery. LC 82-222. 640p. 1982. Repr. of 1965 ed. write for info. o.p. (ISBN 0-89874-476-8). Krieger.

White, Roger. Another Song, Another Season: Poems & Portrayals. 1979. 8.50 o.p. (ISBN 0-85398-087-X, 332-036-10, Pub. by G Ronald England); pap. 2.00 (ISBN 0-85398-088-8, 332-037, Pub. by G Ronald England). Baha'i.

--Wordstar with Style. 1983. text ed. 17.95 (ISBN 0-8359-8794-9); pap. text ed. 12.95 (ISBN 0-8359-8793-0). Reston.

White, Roger & Brockington, Dave. Tales Out of School. (Routledge Education Bks.). 148p. 1983. write for info. (ISBN 0-7100-9448-5); pap. 7.95 (ISBN 0-7100-9445-0). Routledge & Kegan.

White, Ronald C., Jr. The Social Gospel: Religion & Reform in Changing America. Hopkins, C. Howard, ed. LC 75-34745. (Illus.). 326p. 1975. 29.95 (ISBN 0-87722-083-2); pap. 9.95x (ISBN 0-87722-084-0). Temple U Pr.

White, Ruthe. Touch Me Again, Lord. 144p. (Orig.). 1983. pap. 5.95 (ISBN 0-89840-038-4). Heres Life.

White, Sandra, jt. ed. see Otto, Wayne.

White, Sharon. The Man Who Talked With Angels. 226p. (Orig.). 1982. pap. 5.95 (ISBN 0-89221-088-5, Pub. by SonLife). New Leaf.

White, Sheila J., jt. ed. see Teller, Virginia.

White, Sidney H. Sidney Howard. (United States Authors Ser.). 1977. lib. bdg. 13.95 (ISBN 0-8057-7191-3, Twayne). G K Hall.

White, Simon. The English Captain. LC 77-3191. 1977. 7.95 o.p. (ISBN 0-312-25357-5). St Martin.

White, Stephen. Political Culture & Soviet Politics. 1979. 26.00 (ISBN 0-312-62249-X). St Martin.

White, Stephen & Gardner, John. Communist Political Systems: An Introduction. LC 82-6021. 304p. 1982. 20.00x (ISBN 0-686-81984-5). St Martin.

White, Stephen, jt. ed. see Nelson, Daniel.

White, Steve. S-COM, No. 6: Sierra Death Dealers. (Men of Action Ser.). 192p. (Orig.). 1982. pap. 1.95 (ISBN 0-446-30142-6). Warner Bks.

White, Steven F., ed. Poets of Nicaragua: A Bilingual Anthology 1918-1979. 1982. 20.00 (ISBN 0-686-91915-7); pap. 9.00 (ISBN 0-87775-133-1). Unicorn Pr.

White, Stewart E. Forty-Niners. 1918. text ed. 8.50x (ISBN 0-686-83552-2). Elliots Bks.

--Unobstructed Universe. 1959. pap. 5.95 (ISBN 0-525-47042-5, 0578-170). Dutton.

White, Stuart C., jt. auth. see Goaz, Paul W.

White, T. H. Darkness at Pemberley. LC 77-20549. 1978. pap. 4.00 (ISBN 0-486-23613-7). Dover.

--England Have My Bones. (Illus.). 306p. 1982. 13.95 (ISBN 0-399-12725-9). Putnam Pub Group.

--A Joy Proposed. LC 82-10945. 88p. 1983. text ed. 8.95 (ISBN 0-8203-0637-1). U of Ga Pr.

--The Maharajah & Other Stories. 228p. 1981. 12.95 (ISBN 0-399-12650-3). Putnam Pub Group.

--The Maharajah & Other Stories. 224p. 1983. pap. 2.95 (ISBN 0-425-05862-X). Berkley Pub.

--Mistress Masham's Repose. 1980. PLB 9.95 (ISBN 0-8398-2615-X, Gregg). G K Hall.

White, T. H. & Potts, L. J. Letters to a Friend: The Correspondence Between T. H. White & L. J. Potts. Gallix, Francois, ed. LC 81-15749. 288p. 1982. 14.95 (ISBN 0-399-12693-7). Putnam Pub Group.

White, T. Kenneth. The Technical Connection: The How To's of Time Management for the Technical Manager. LC 81-11476. 203p. 1981. 26.95 (ISBN 0-471-94034-8). Ronald Pr.

White, Ted. Jewels of Elsewhen. LC 81-5435. (Illus., Orig.). 1981. pap. 5.95 o.p. (ISBN 0-686-78997-0, Starblaze). Donning Co.

--Phoenix Prime. Stine, Hank, ed. LC 82-12872. (Quest of the Wolf Trilogy Ser.: Vol. 1). (Illus.). 168p. 1983. pap. 5.95 (ISBN 0-89865-251-0, Starblaze). Donning Co.

--The Sorceress of Qar. Stine, Hank, ed. (Illus.). 176p. pap. 5.95 (ISBN 0-89865-288-X). Donning Co.

White, Ted, et al. Broadcast News Writing, Reporting & Production. 384p. 1983. text ed. 17.95 (ISBN 0-02-427010-5). Macmillan.

White, Terence H. The Once & Future King. 1958. 12.95 (ISBN 0-399-10597-2). Putnam Pub Group.

--The Sword in the Stone. (Illus.). 1939. 11.95 (ISBN 0-399-10783-5). Putnam Pub Group.

White, Theodore H. America in Search of Itself: The Making of the President, 1956-1980. 480p. Date not set. pap. 8.95 (ISBN 0-686-43171-5). Warner Bks.

White, Timothy. Catch a Fire. (Illus.). 320p. Date not set. 16.95 (ISBN 0-03-063531-4); pap. 9.95 (ISBN 0-03-062109-7). HR&W.

White, Tony, tr. see Broue, Pierre & Temime, Emile.

White, Trentwell M. The Thing in the Road. 1.50 o.p. (ISBN 0-8338-0066-3). M Jones.

White, Trentwell M. & Elhmann, Paul W. Writers of Colonial New England. LC 70-16525. 176p. 1971. Repr. of 1929 ed. 34.00x (ISBN 0-8103-3742-8). Gale.

White, Vernon S., ed. see Sawmill Clinic, 3rd, Portland, Oregon, Feb.1974.

White, Victor. God & the Unconscious. LC 82-19153. (Jungian Classics Ser.). 274p. 1982. pap. 13.50 (ISBN 0-88214-503-7). Spring Pubns.

White, Virginia, ed. Grant Proposals That Succeeded. (Nonprofit Management & Finance). 230p. 1982. 22.50x (ISBN 0-306-40873-2, Plenum Pr). Plenum Pub.

White, Wallace. One Dark Night. (Triumph Ser.). (Illus.). (gr. 7 up). 1979. PLB 8.90 s&l (ISBN 0-531-02896-8). Watts.

White, Warren, ed. Plumes & Visibility: Measurements & Model Components-Supplement, Vol. 15 No. 12. (Illus.). 230p. 1982. pap. 30.00 (ISBN 0-08-028741-7). Pergamon.

White, Warren T., et al. Machine Tools & Machining Practices, 2 vols. LC 76-27863. 1977. Vol. 1. text ed. 29.95 (ISBN 0-471-94035-6); Vol. 2. text ed. 29.95 (ISBN 0-471-94036-4). Wiley.

White, Will W., III. The Sunfish Book. 250p. 1983. 14.95 o.p. (ISBN 0-914814-31-1). Sail Bks.

White, William. Directory & Gazetteer of Leeds & Clothing Districts of Yorkshire. LC 71-83368. Repr. of 1853 ed. 37.50x (ISBN 0-678-05503-3). Kelley.

--Photomacrography. 1983. 49.95x (ISBN 0-240-51189-1). Focal Pr.

White, William, jt. auth. see Cody, William J., Jr.

White, William, jt. auth. see Glessing, Robert.

White, William A. A Certain Rich Man. LC 79-104763. (Novel As American Social History Ser.). 446p. 1970. 18.00x (ISBN 0-8131-1206-0); pap. 8.00x (ISBN 0-8131-0127-1). U Pr of Ky.

--Crimes & Criminals. (Historical Foundations of Forensic Psychiatry & Psychology Ser.). viii, 276p. 1983. lib. bdg. 29.50 (ISBN 0-306-76179-3). Da Capo.

--Masks in a Pageant. LC 73-110884. (Illus.). 1971. Repr. of 1928 ed. lib. bdg. 18.75x o.p. (ISBN 0-8371-4568-6, WHMP). Greenwood.

White, William C., jt. auth. see Boskind-White, Marlene.

White, William D. Public Health & Private Gain. 137p. 1979. 19.95x (ISBN 0-416-60081-6). Methuen Inc.

--Public Health & Private Gain: The Economics of Licensing Clinical Laboratory Personnel. LC 78-55998. (Illus.). 1979. text ed. 14.95 (ISBN 0-88425-014-8). Maaroufa Pr.

--U. S. Tactical Air Power: Missions, Forces, & Costs. (Studies in Defense Policy). 121p. 1974. pap. 4.95 (ISBN 0-8157-9371-5). Brookings.

White, William F. Psychosocial Principles Applied to Classroom Teaching. LC 69-13228. (Illus.). 1969. text ed. 21.95 (ISBN 0-07-069760-4, C). McGraw.

White, William G., jt. auth. see Cummins, D. Duane.

White, William G., jt. auth. see Cummins, Duane D.

White, William J. Airships for the Future. rev. ed. LC 76-19768. (Illus.). (YA) 1978. 12.95 o.p. (ISBN 0-8069-0090-3); PLB 11.69 o.p. (ISBN 0-8069-0091-1). Sterling.

White, William, Jr. The American Chameleon. LC 76-51162. (Nature Ser.). (Illus.). (gr. 7 up). 1977. 7.95 o.p. (ISBN 0-8069-3532-4); PLB 7.49 o.p. (ISBN 0-8069-3533-2). Sterling.

--The Guppy: Its Life Cycle. LC 73-83441. (Colorful Nature Ser.). 64p. (gr. 5 up). 1974. 10.95 (ISBN 0-8069-3476-X); PLB 13.29 (ISBN 0-8069-3477-8). Sterling.

--A Mosquito Is Born. LC 77-93319. (Sterling Nature Series). (Illus.). (gr. 5 up). 1978. 7.95 o.p. (ISBN 0-8069-3534-0); PLB 7.49 o.p. (ISBN 0-8069-3535-9). Sterling.

White, William L. Lost Boundaries. LC 48-6112. (YA) (gr. 7-12). 1967. pap. 0.50 o.p. (ISBN 0-15-653610-2, Harv). HarBraceJ.

White, Willie. Fifty-Two Winning Sermons. 117p. (Orig.). 1973. spiral 2.95 (ISBN 0-686-84103-4). College Pr Pub.

White, Willie see Boatman, Don E.

White, Willmon L., ed. see Bailey, David H. & Gottlieb, Louise.

White, Winston. Beyond Conformity. LC 60-13780. 1961. 9.95 (ISBN 0-02-935080-8). Free Pr.

Whitebread, Charles. Standards Relating to Transfer Between Courts. LC 76-17798. (IJA-ABA Juvenile Justice Standards Project Ser.). 80p. 1980. prof ref 14.00x (ISBN 0-88410-230-0); pap. 7.00x (ISBN 0-88410-818-X). Ballinger Pub.

Whitebread, Charles H. Criminal Procedure: An Analysis of Constitutional Cases & Concepts, 1982 Supplement. 88p. 1982. pap. text ed. write for info. (ISBN 0-88277-087-X). Foundation Pr.

Whited, Charles. Destiny. (Spirit of America Ser.: Vol. 2). 448p. 1982. 3.50 (ISBN 0-553-22615-0). Bantam.

--Spirit of America, Vol. 1: Challenge. 1982. pap. 3.50 (ISBN 0-553-20181-6). Bantam.

Whited, David. Hollow Fox. 24p. (Orig.). 1979. pap. text ed. 2.00 (ISBN 0-686-35894-5). Skydog OR.

Whited, N. W. Automotive Oscilloscope. LC 76-3937. (Illus.). 99p. (gr. 10-12). 1977. pap. 7.00 (ISBN 0-8273-1033-1). Delmar.

Whitefield, Edwin. Hudson River Houses: Edwin Whitefield's the Hudson River & Rail Road Illustrated. LC 80-22371. (Illus.). 96p. 1981. 15.00 (ISBN 0-88427-043-2). North River.

Whitefield, George. George Whitefield's Journals. 1978. 15.95 (ISBN 0-85151-147-3). Banner of Truth.

--Journals of George Whitefield, 1737-1741. LC 73-81363. (Illus.). 1969. Repr. of 1905 ed. 57.00x (ISBN 0-8201-1069-8). Schol Facsimiles.

Whitefield, Goerge. George Whitefield's Letters: Seventeen Thirty-Four to Seventeen Forty-Two. 1976. 15.95 (ISBN 0-85151-239-9). Banner of Truth.

Whiteford, Mike. How to Talk Baseball. LC 82-19920. (Illus.). 144p. (Orig.). 1983. pap. 6.95 (ISBN 0-934878-21-8). Dembner Bks.

Whitehead. In the Service of Old Age. 9.95 (ISBN 0-471-26083-5, Pub. by Wiley Heyden). Wiley.

Whitehead, Albert C. Standard Bearer: A Story of Army Life in the Time of Caesar. (Illus.). (gr. 7-11). 1943. 8.00x (ISBN 0-8196-0116-0). Biblo.

Whitehead, Alfred N. Essays in Science & Philosophy. LC 68-21332. (Illus.). 1968. Repr. of 1947 ed. lib. bdg. 30.00x (ISBN 0-8371-0268-5, WHES). Greenwood.

--Process & Reality: Corrected Edition. LC 77-90011. 1979. pap. text ed. 8.95 (ISBN 0-02-934570-7). Free Pr.

--Whitehead's American Essays in Social Philosophy. Johnson, A. H., ed. LC 74-11997. 206p. 1975. Repr. of 1959 ed. lib. bdg. 15.50x (ISBN 0-8371-7716-2, WHAE). Greenwood.

Whitehead, Alfred N. & Russell, Bertrand. Principia Mathematica, 3 Vols. Set. 325.00 (ISBN 0-521-06791-X). Cambridge U Pr.

--Principia Mathematica to Fifty-Six. 2nd ed. 1925-27. pap. 27.95 (ISBN 0-521-09187-X). Cambridge U Pr.

Whitehead, Bill, ed. see Barthelme, Donald.

Whitehead, Bill, ed. see O'Doherty, Brian.

Whitehead, Bill, ed. see White, Edmund.

Whitehead, Carleton. Creative Meditation. 128p. 1975. 6.95 o.p. (ISBN 0-396-07139-2). Dodd.

Whitehead, Christine, tr. see Lora, G.

Whitehead, David. Yesterday's Town: Hereford. 1981. 39.50x o.p. (ISBN 0-86023-119-4, Pub. by Barracuda England). State Mutual Bk.

Whitehead, David, jt. ed. see Crawford, Michael.

Whitehead, Douglas E., ed. Current Operative Urology. 1975. text ed. 97.00x o.p. (ISBN 0-06-142683-0, Harper Medical). Lippincott.

Whitehead, E. Douglas & Leiter, Elliot, eds. Current Operative Urology, 2 vols. 2nd ed. (Illus.). 1500p. 1983. text ed. write for info (ISBN 0-06-142684-9, Harper Medical). Lippincott Medical.

Whitehead, Eric. The Patricks: Hockey's Royal Family. LC 79-6879. (Illus.). 288p. 1980. 11.95 o.p. (ISBN 0-385-15662-6). Doubleday.

Whitehead, Evelyn E. The Parish in Community & Ministry. LC 78-58960. 128p. 1978. pap. 3.95 o.p. (ISBN 0-8091-2133-6). Paulist Pr.

Whitehead, Evelyn E., jt. auth. see Whitehead, James D.

Whitehead, G. Kenneth. Hunting & Stalking Deer Throughout the World. LC 81-211471. (Illus.). 300p. 1982. 19.95 (ISBN 0-312-40156-6). St Martin.

Whitehead, George. Growing for Showing. (Illus.). 176p. 1978. 13.95 (ISBN 0-571-11206-4); pap. 7.95 (ISBN 0-571-11706-6). Faber & Faber.

Whitehead, Harold. Administration of Marketing & Selling. 22.75x (ISBN 0-392-07566-0, SpS). Sportshelf.

Whitehead, Harriet, jt. ed. see Ortner, Sherry.

Whitehead, Harry. An A-Z of Offshore Oil & Gas. text ed. 39.95x (ISBN 0-87201-052-X). Gulf Pub.

Whitehead, Hector F. The Yorkshire Terrier. LC 76-10824. (Illus.). 1976. bds. 2.25 o.p. (ISBN 0-668-03979-5). Arco.

Whitehead, James. Local Men. LC 79-10660. 1979. 10.00 (ISBN 0-252-00763-8); pap. 3.95 o.p. (ISBN 0-252-00764-6). U of Ill Pr.

Whitehead, James D. & Whitehead, Evelyn E. Method in Ministry: Theological Reflection & Christian Ministry. 240p. 1980. 12.95 o.p. (ISBN 0-8164-0455-0); pap. 7.95 (ISBN 0-8164-2363-6). Seabury.

Whitehead, John. Design & Analysis of Sequential Clinical Trials. (Mathematics & Its Applications). 315p. 1983. 69.95x (ISBN 0-470-27355-0). Halsted Pr.

Whitehead, John W. Second American Revolution. 1982. pap. 10.95 (ISBN 0-89191-572-9). Cook.

Whitehead, L., ed. see Lora, G.

Whitehead, Lawrence, jt. ed. see Thorp, Rosemary.

Whitehead, Lloyd A. Autumn Leaves. 1979. 5.95 o.s.i. (ISBN 0-932970-09-5). Prinit Pr.

Whitehead, R. J., jt. auth. see Bamman, Henry A.

Whitehead, Richard. Muscosal Biopsy of the Gastrointestinal Tract. 2nd ed. LC 78-57918. (Major Problems in Pathology Ser.: Vol. 3). (Illus.). 200p. 1979. text ed. 26.00x o.p. (ISBN 0-7216-9304-0); slides 42.50 o.p. (ISBN 0-7216-9862-X). Saunders.

Whitehead, Robert. Children's Literature: Strategies of Teaching. (Orig.). 1968. pap. text ed. 16.95 (ISBN 0-13-132589-2). P-H.

Whitehead, Robert L., jt. auth. see Sims, Donald G.

Whitehead, T. P. Quality Control in Clinical Chemistry. LC 76-44522. (Quality Control Methods in the Clinical Laboratory Ser). 1977. text ed. 37.50 (ISBN 0-471-94075-5, Pub. by Wiley Medical). Wiley.

Whitehead, Tony. Mental Illness & the Law. 190p. 1982. 19.95x (ISBN 0-631-12721-6, Pub. by Basil Blackwell England); pap. 8.95x (ISBN 0-631-12615-5, Pub. by Basil Blackwell England). Biblio Dist.

Whitehead, William & Macartney-Filgate, Terence. Dieppe Nineteen Forty-Two. 1980. 12.95 o.p. (ISBN 0-312-20989-4). St Martin.

Whitehill, Robert, tr. see Megged, Aharon.

Whitehill, Walter, jt. auth. see King, Ernest.

Whitehill, Walter M. Boston: Portrait of a City. (Illus.). 112p. 1964. 6.95 (ISBN 0-517-51725-6). Crown.

Whitehill, Walter M. & Nichols, Frederic D. Palladio in America. LC 77-95342. (Illus.). 1976. pap. 7.95 (ISBN 0-8478-0169-1). Rizzoli Intl.

Whitehill, Walter M., intro. by. Paul Revere's Boston 1735-1818. LC 74-21766. (Illus.). 300p. 1975. 29.95 (ISBN 0-87846-088-8, 694622). NYGS.

Whitehorne, John & Jones, Brian. Register of Oxyrhnchites 30 BC - AD 96. LC 81-18494. (BASP Supplements). 1982. 33.50 (ISBN 0-89130-529-7, 31-00-25). Scholars Pr CA.

Whitehouse, G. Gynaecological Radiology. (Illus.). 224p. 1981. text ed. 57.00 (ISBN 0-632-00726-5, B 5424-6). Mosby.

Whitehouse, Gary, et al. IIE Microsoftware: Economic Analysis. 1981. 140.00, 175.00 non-members (ISBN 0-89806-013-3). Am Inst Indus Eng.

--IIE Microsoftware: Production Control. 1981. 140.00, 175.00 non-members (ISBN 0-89806-012-5). Am Inst Indus Eng.

--IIE Microsoftware: Project Management. 1981. 140.00, 175.00 non-members (ISBN 0-89806-030-3). Am Inst Indus Eng.

--IIE Microsoftware: Work Measurement. 1982. 140.00, 175.00 non-members (ISBN 0-89806-035-4). Am Inst Indus Eng.

Whitehouse, Gary E. Systems Analysis & Design Using Network Techniques. (Industrial & Systems Engineering Ser). (Illus.). 464p. (Reference ed.). 1973. 31.95 (ISBN 0-13-881474-0). P-H.

Whitehouse, Gary E. & Wechsler, Ben L. Applied Operations Research: A Survey. LC 76-16545. 1976. 36.95x (ISBN 0-471-94077-1); solutions manual 5.00x (ISBN 0-471-02552-6). Wiley.

Whitehouse, Geoffrey T. Everywoman's Guide to Natural Health. 1978. pap. 4.95 o.p. (ISBN 0-7225-0277-X). Newcastle Pub.

Whitehouse, H. L. Towards an Understanding of the Mechanism of Heredity. 3rd ed. LC 73-82629. 513p. 1973. 26.00 (ISBN 0-312-81130-6); pap. 16.95 (ISBN 0-312-81095-4). St Martin.

Whitehouse, Harold L. Genetic Recombination. LC 81-21981. 415p. 1982. 54.95 (ISBN 0-471-10205-9, Pub. by Wiley-Interscience). Wiley.

Whitehouse, J. C., tr. see Durkheim, Emile.

Whitehouse, Jack E. How & Where to Find the Facts: Researching Criminology. LC 82-61338. 125p. (Orig.). 1983. pap. 6.95 (ISBN 0-88247-695-5). R & E Res Assoc.

--How & Where to Find the Facts: Researching Corrections Including Probation & Parole. LC 82-61337. 125p. (Orig.). 1983. pap. 6.95 (ISBN 0-88247-694-7). R & E Res Assoc.

--How & Where to Find the Facts: Researching Illegal Drugs. LC 82-61339. 125p. (Orig.). 1983. pap. 6.95 (ISBN 0-88247-696-3). R & E Res Assoc.

--How & Where to Find the Facts: Researching Police Science. LC 82-50374. 125p. (Orig.). 1983. pap. 6.95 (ISBN 0-88247-691-2). R & E Res Assoc.

--A Police Bibliography. LC 77-15909. (AMS Studies in Criminal Justice: No. 3). 1980. Set. 75.00 (ISBN 0-404-16040-9). AMS Pr.

--A Research Guide for Law Enforcement & the Criminal Justice System. LC 81-86247. 150p. 1983. 19.95 (ISBN 0-88247-666-1). R & E Res Assoc.

Whitehouse, M. W., tr. see Rainsford, K. D. & Brune, K.

Whitehouse, Michael W., jt. ed. see Scherrer, Robert A.

Whitehouse, R. H., jt. ed. see Tanner, J. M.

Whitehouse, Roger. A London Album Eighteen-Forty to Nineteen-Fifteen. (Illus.). 192p. 1982. pap. 14.95 (ISBN 0-436-57091-2, Pub. by Secker & Warburg). David & Charles.

Whitehouse, Wilfrid & Yanagisawa, Eizo, trs. Lady Nijo's Own Story: The Candid Diary of a 13th Century Japanese Imperial Court Concubine. LC 73-93503. 1974. pap. 9.50 o.p. (ISBN 0-8048-1117-2). C E Tuttle.

Whitehurst, Bert W. How To Find Trademarks. (Illus.). 60p. 1982. lib. bdg. 15.00x (ISBN 0-686-97766-1); pap. text ed. 12.00x (ISBN 0-686-97767-X). Galleon-Whitehurst.

Whitehurst, Carol A. Women in America: The Oppressed Majority. 1977. pap. text ed. 10.95x o.p. (ISBN 0-673-16331-8). Scott F.

Whitehurst, D. D., et al. Coal Liquefaction: The Chemistry & Technology of Thermal Process. 1980. 22.50 (ISBN 0-12-747080-8). Acad Pr.

Whitehurst, Grover J. & Vasta, Ross F. Child Behavior. LC 76-14009. (Illus.). 1977. text ed. 25.50 (ISBN 0-395-24446-3); test item manual 1.10 (ISBN 0-395-24447-1); wkbk. 9.50 (ISBN 0-395-25794-8). HM.

Whitehurst, Grover J. & Zimmerman, Barry J., eds. The Functions of Language & Cognition. LC 78-20004. (Developmental Psychology Ser.). 1979. 26.00 (ISBN 0-12-747050-6). Acad Pr.

Whitehurst, Robert N., jt. auth. see Libby, Roger W.

Whitelaw, Denny. Slightly Sexy, Comedy from Europe. (Illus.). 120p. 1982. pap. 15.00 (ISBN 0-940178-14-1). Sitare Inc.

Whitelaw, R. R. Marketing & Economics. 1969. 25.00 o.p. (ISBN 0-08-006583-X); pap. 11.25 (ISBN 0-08-006582-1). Pergamon.

Whitelegg, E. & Arnot, Madeleine, eds. The Changing Experience of Women. 416p. 1982. text ed. 30.00x (ISBN 0-85520-517-2, Pub. by Martin Robertson England); pap. text ed. 9.95x (ISBN 0-85520-518-0). Biblio Dist.

Whiteley, D. E. Thessalonians. (New Clarendon Bible Ser). (Illus.). 1969. 8.95x (ISBN 0-19-836906-9). Oxford U Pr.

Whiteley, John, jt. auth. see Ellis, Albert.

Whiteley, John M. Character Development in College Students: The Freshman Year, Vol. I. 1982. text ed. 13.95 (ISBN 0-915744-30-9); pap. 10.95 (ISBN 0-915744-22-8). Character Res.

Whiteley, John M., jt. auth. see Ellis, Albert.

Whiteley, John M., jt. auth. see Erickson, V. Lois.

Whiteley, Joseph L., ed. see Livy.

Whitelocke, Lester T. An Analytical Concordance of the Books of the Apocrypha. LC 78-61389. 1978. pap. text ed. 18.75 ea.; Vol. 1. (ISBN 0-8191-0603-8); Vol. 2. (ISBN 0-8191-0604-6). U Pr of Amer.

Whitely, P. R. Biscuit Manufacture. 1971. 48.00 (ISBN 0-444-20072-X). Elsevier.

Whitely, Roger. Assess the IRS. 1978. 6.50 o.p. (ISBN 0-533-02946-5). Vantage.

Whitely, Wilfred H. To Plan is to Choose. LC 72-97699. (Hans Wolff Memorial Lecture Ser.). 50p. 1973. pap. text ed. 3.00 (ISBN 0-941934-04-7). Ind U Afro-Amer Arts.

Whiteman, Arthur. Nigeria: Its Petroleum Geology, Resources & Potential, Vol.1. 176p. 1983. 59.00x (ISBN 0-8448-1426-1). Crane-Russak.

--Nigeria: Its Petroleum Geology, Resources & Potential, Vol. 2. 238p. 1982. 110.00x (ISBN 0-86010-265-3, Pub. by Graham & Trotman England). State Mutual Bk.

Whiteman, Charles H. Linear Rational Expaectations Models: A User's Guide. 130p. 1983. 19.50 (ISBN 0-8166-1181-5); pap. 9.95 (ISBN 0-8166-1179-3). U of Minn Pr.

Whiteman, Harold B., Jr. Neutrality, 1941. 1941. text ed. 29.50x (ISBN 0-686-83645-6). Elliots Bks.

Whiteman, J., jt. auth. see Freeman, N. T.

Whiteman, J. R., ed. The Mathematics of Finite Elements & Application IV: Proceedings. 1982. 54.50 (ISBN 0-12-747254-1). Acad Pr.

Whiteman, Peter C. Tropical Pasture Science. (Illus.). 1981. 58.00x (ISBN 0-19-859471-2); pap. 24.50x (ISBN 0-686-96830-1). Oxford U Pr.

Whiter, Robert. The Bicycle Manual on Maintenance & Repairs. (Illus.). 1980. pap. 6.95 (ISBN 0-8092-7135-4). Contemp Bks.

Whitern, Wilfred H., jt. auth. see Axelrod, Herbert R.

Whitern, Wilfred L. Livebearers. (Illus.). 93p. 1979. 4.95 (ISBN 0-87666-518-0, KW-049). TFH Pubns.

Whitern, Wilfred L. & Gordon, Myron. Guppies. (Illus.). 96p. 1980. 4.95 (ISBN 0-87666-523-7, KW058). TFH Pubns.

Whiteside, Andrew G. The Socialism of Fools: Georg Ritter Von Schonerer & Austrian Pan-Germanism. 512p. 1975. 42.50x (ISBN 0-520-02434-6). U of Cal Pr.

Whiteside, Conon D. EDP Systems for Credit Management. LC 74-156330. 1971. 29.95x o.p. (ISBN 0-471-94080-1, Pub. by Wiley-Interscience). Wiley.

Whiteside, Elena. The Way Living in Love. LC 72-89132. 282p. 1972. 5.95 o.p. (ISBN 0-910068-06-2). Am Christian.

Whiteside, I. W. Sharon's UFO Code for Outer Space. 64p. (Orig.). 1983. pap. 4.00 (ISBN 0-682-49969-2). Exposition.

Whiteside, Thomas. An Agent in Place: The Wennerstrom Affair. 160p. 1983. pap. 2.50 (ISBN 0-345-30326-1). Ballantine.

--The Blockbuster Complex. 207p. 1981. 12.95 (ISBN 0-8195-5057-4). Wesleyan U Pr.

--Computer Capers. 1979. pap. 2.95 (ISBN 0-451-62173-5, ME2173, Ment). NAL.

--Pendulum & the Toxic Cloud: The Dioxin Threat from Vietnam to Seveso. 1979. 20.00x o.p. (ISBN 0-300-02274-3); pap. 6.95x (ISBN 0-300-02283-2). Yale U Pr.

--Selling Death: Cigarette Smoking & Advertising. LC 75-162434. 1971. 5.95 o.p. (ISBN 0-87140-541-5). Liveright.

Whiteside, Tom. Sociology of Educational Innovation. 1978. pap. 5.95x (ISBN 0-416-55830-5). Methuen Inc.

Whiteway, Catherine E., jt. auth. see Elward, Margaret.

Whitfield, Allyson. SPWAO Market Guide. 20p. 2.00 o.p. (ISBN 0-916176-14-2). Sproing.

Whitfield, Francis J., ed. see Hjelmslev, Louis.

Whitfield, Francis J., ed. see Mirsky, Dimitry S.

Whitfield, J. H. A Short History of Italian Literature. 1980. pap. 6.50 (ISBN 0-7190-0782-8). Manchester.

Whitfield, J. H., ed. see Guarini, Battista.

Whitfield, Jane S. Whitfield's University Rhyming Dictionary. Stillman, Frances, ed. (Apollo Eds.). pap. 3.95i (ISBN 0-8152-0080-3, A80). T Y Crowell.

Whitfield, Jane S., jt. auth. see Stillman, Frances.

Whitfield, Joseph. The Treasure of el Dorado. 3rd ed. LC 77-89125. (Illus.). 1981. 10.95 (ISBN 0-911050-49-3). Occidental.

Whitfield, M. & Jagner, D. Marine Electrochemistry: A Practical Introduction. LC 80-42023. 529p. 1981. 71.95x (ISBN 0-471-27976-5, Pub. by Wiley-Interscience). Wiley.

Whitfield, Raoul. Green Ice. 1980. lib. bdg. 13.95 (ISBN 0-8398-2720-2, Gregg). G K Hall.

Whitfield, Roderick. The Art of Paintings from Dunhuang: The Art of Central Asia, the Stein Collection in the British Museum, Vol. II. LC 81-80657. (Illus.). 340p. 1983. through April 30, 1983 375.00 (ISBN 0-87011-555-3); after April 30, 1983 425.00 (ISBN 0-686-81735-4). Kodansha.

Whitfield, Stephen J. Into the Dark: Hannah Arendt & Totalitarianism. 338p. 1980. 29.95 (ISBN 0-87722-188-X). Temple U Pr.

Whitfield, Susan, jt. auth. see Davis, Bertha.

Whitfield, Vallie J. Real Estate Operation Education Designation: Business License Real Estate. LC 77-7338. 37p. 7.95 (ISBN 0-930920-05-8); pap. 3.00 (ISBN 0-930920-06-6). Whitfield.

Whitford, Frank. Egon Schiele. (The World of Art Ser.). (Illus.). 1981. 19.95x (ISBN 0-19-520245-7); pap. 9.95 (ISBN 0-19-520246-5). Oxford U Pr.

--Grosz. (Oresko-Jupiter Art Bks). (Illus.). 96p. 1981. cancelled o.p. (ISBN 0-933516-88-6, Pub. by Oresko-Jupiter England). Hippocrene Bks.

Whitford, Margaret. Merleau-Ponty's Critique of Sartre's Philosophy. LC 81-68140. (French Forum Monographs: No. 33). 180p. (Orig.). 1982. pap. 15.00x (ISBN 0-917058-32-1). French Forum.

Whitford, Mary M. Price Guide to Furniture Made in America: 1875-1905. 16p. 1982. pap. text ed. 5.00 (ISBN 0-916838-70-6). Schiffer.

Whitham, G. B. Linear & Nonlinear Waves. LC 74-2070. (Pure & Applied Mathematics Ser.). 560p. 1974. 39.95x (ISBN 0-471-94090-9, Pub. by Wiley-Interscience). Wiley.

Whitin, T. M., jt. auth. see Hadley, George.

Whiting. The Home Front: Germany. LC 81-21406. (World War II Ser.). PLB 19.92 (ISBN 0-8094-3420-2, 0-8094-257-6). Silver.

Whiting, Allen S. China Crosses the Yalu: The Decision to Enter the Korean War. LC 68-13744. 1960. 12.50x (ISBN 0-8047-0627-1); pap. 6.95 (ISBN 0-8047-0629-8, SX86). Stanford U Pr.

Whiting, Allen S. & Dernberger, Robert F. China's Future: Foreign Policy & Economic Development in the Post-Mao Era. 1977. 13.95 (ISBN 0-07-069958-5, P&RB); pap. 5.95 (ISBN 0-07-069959-3). McGraw.

Whiting, Charles. Hitler's Werewolves. (War Bks.). 240p. 1983. pap. 2.95 (ISBN 0-86721-197-0). Jove Pubns.

Whiting, Charles G. Valery: Jeune Poete. (Yale Romantic Studies). 1960. pap. 37.50x (ISBN 0-685-69883-1). Elliots Bks.

Whiting, D. P. International Trade & Payments. 160p. 1978. 30.00x (ISBN 0-7121-0952-8, Pub. by Macdonald & Evans). State Mutual Bk.

Whiting, Frank M., jt. auth. see White, Melvin R.

Whiting, Gerald. Department Store. LC 79-67166. (Careers Ser.). PLB 12.68 (ISBN 0-382-06356-2). Silver.

Whiting, Gertrude. Old-Time Tools & Toys of Needlework. (Illus.). 10.00 (ISBN 0-8446-0292-2). Peter Smith.

Whiting, H. T. Teaching the Peristent Non-Swimmer. 12.50x o.p. (ISBN 0-7135-1562-7, SpS). Sportshelf.

Whiting, J. R. A Handful of History. 112p. 1982. pap. text ed. 9.00x (ISBN 0-86299-000-9, 61269, Pub. by Sutton England). Humanities.

Whiting, John & Bottomley, Tom. Chapman's Log & Owner's Manual. 192p. 1980. 14.95 (ISBN 0-87851-801-0); deluxe ed. o.p. 75.00 (ISBN 0-686-96737-2). Hearst Bks.

Whiting, Karen L., jt. auth. see Spadaccini, Victor M.

Whiting, Larry & Rogers, David, eds. Rural Policy Research Alternatives. (Illus.). 1978. pap. text ed. 8.50x (ISBN 0-8138-1875-3). Iowa St U Pr.

Whiting, Larry, jt. ed. see Heady, Earl O.

Whiting, Larry, ed. see North Central Regional Center for Rural Development.

Whiting, Percy H. Five Great Problems of Salesmen & How to Solve Them. 1964. 14.95 (ISBN 0-07-069960-7, GB). McGraw.

Whiting, Robert. The Chrysanthemum & the Bat: Baseball Samurai Style. 256p. 1983. pap. 3.95 (ISBN 0-380-63115-6, Discus). Avon.

Whitley, David S., jt. ed. see Clewlow, C. William, Jr.

Whitley, Dianna. Burt Reynolds: Portrait of a Superstar. (Illus.). 1979. pap. 5.95 (ISBN 0-448-15479-X, G&D). Putnam Pub Group.

Whitley, Kathleen, jt. auth. see Clayton, Barbara.

Whitley, M. Stanley. Generative Phonology Workbook. LC 77-91063. 126p. 1978. pap. 6.50 (ISBN 0-299-07544-3). U of Wis Pr.

Whitley, Richard, ed. Social Processes of Scientific Development. 1974. 24.50x (ISBN 0-7100-7705-X). Routledge & Kegan.

Whitley, Richard, et al. Masters of Business. (Illus.). 1982. 28.00x (ISBN 0-422-76500-7, Pub. by Tavistock). Methuen Inc.

Whitley, W. T. Art in England: Eighteen Hundred to Eighteen Thirty-Seven. LC 79-169854. (Illus.). 718p. 1973. Repr. of 1928 ed. lib. bdg. 50.00 o.s.i. (ISBN 0-87817-109-6). Hacker.

Whitlock, Baird W. John Hoskyns, Serjeant-at-Law. LC 81-40426. (Illus.). 750p. (Orig.). 1981. lib. bdg. 39.25 (ISBN 0-8191-2147-9); pap. text ed. 26.00 (ISBN 0-8191-2148-7). U Pr of Amer.

Whitlock, Brand. Forty Years of It. LC 69-10171. 1969. Repr. of 1914 ed. lib. bdg. 20.75x (ISBN 0-8371-0752-0, WHFY). Greenwood.

--J. Hardin & Son. Miller, Paul W., ed. LC 82-2240. xlii, 465p. 1982. lib. bdg. 18.95 (ISBN 0-8214-0640-X, 82-84135); pap. 8.95 (ISBN 0-8214-0641-8, 82-84143). Ohio U Pr.

--On the Enforcement of Law in Cities. LC 69-14952. (Criminology, Law Enforcement, & Social Problems Ser.: No. 74). 1969. Repr. of 1913 ed. 6.50x (ISBN 0-87585-074-X). Patterson Smith.

Whitlock, Dave & Boyle, Robert, eds. Fly-Tyer's Almanac. (Sportsmen's Classics Ser.). 220p. (YA) 1975. 12.95 o.p. (ISBN 0-517-52372-8). Crown.

Whitlock, Dorothy & Brett, Martin. Council & Synods with Other Documents Relating to the English Church, Vol. 1, A.D. 871-1204, 2 Vols. 1981. text ed. 139.00x (ISBN 0-19-822394-3). Oxford U Pr.

Whitlock, F. A. Psychophysiological Aspects of Skin Disease, Vol. 8. LC 76-20942. (Illus.). 1976. 10.00 (ISBN 0-7216-9301-6). Saunders.

--Symptomatic Affective Disorders. (Personality & Psychopathology Ser.). 24.50 (ISBN 0-12-747580-X). Acad Pr.

Whitlock, Flint, jt. auth. see Watson, Mary A.

Whitlock, Marlene. Basic Skills Citizenship Workbook. (Basic Skills Workbooks). 32p. (gr. 3-6). 1983. 0.99 (ISBN 0-8209-0539-9, SSW-3). ESP.

--Basic Skills Listening Skills Workbook. (Basic Skills Workbooks). 32p. (gr. 2-3). 1983. 0.99 (ISBN 0-8209-0589-5, EEW-12). ESP.

--Developing Citizenship. (Social Studies). 24p. (gr. 3-6). 1979. wkbk. 5.00 (ISBN 0-8209-0254-3, SS-21). ESP.

--Listening Skills. (Early Education Ser.). 24p. (gr. 1-3). 1977. wkbk. 5.00 (ISBN 0-8209-0209-8, K-11). ESP.

Whitlock, Quentin, jt. auth. see Dean, Chris.

Whitlock, Ralph. Bulls Through the Ages. (Illus.). 176p. 1983. 15.95 (ISBN 0-7188-2330-3, Pub by Salem Hse Ltd). Merrimack Bk Serv.

--The Folklore of Devon. (Folklore of the British Isles Ser.). (Illus.). 224p. 1977. 13.50x o.p. (ISBN 0-87471-954-2). Rowman.

--The Folklore of Wiltshire. (Folklore of the British Isles Ser.). (Illus.). 205p. 1976. 14.50x o.p. (ISBN 0-87471-772-8). Rowman.

--Warrior Kings of Saxon England. 1977. text ed. 10.75x o.p. (ISBN 0-391-00719-X). Humanities.

--Water Divining & Other Dowsing: A Practical Guide. (Illus.). 144p. 1982. 14.95 (ISBN 0-7153-8220-9). David & Charles.

Whitlock, Reid E., jt. auth. see Rhode, Grant F.

Whitlock, Ruth. Choral Insights. (Orig.). 1982. pap. text ed. 1.45 student bk., 15 p. (ISBN 0-8497-4154-8, V71S); tchr's ed., 31 p. 3.45 (ISBN 0-8497-4153-X, V71T). Kjos.

--Choral Insights: Renaissance Edition. Anderson, Linda A., ed. (Orig.). 1982. pap. text ed. 1.45 student ed., 16 p. (ISBN 0-8497-4155-6, V72S); tchr's ed., 31 p. 3.45 (ISBN 0-8497-4156-4, V72T). Kjos.

Whitlow. Geotechnics Four Checkbook. 1983. text ed. price not set (ISBN 0-408-00676-5); pap. text ed. price not set (ISBN 0-408-00631-5). Butterworth.

Whitlow, David, jt. auth. see Peck, David.

Whitman, Alfred. Print-Collector's Handbook. LC 72-177279. (Tower Bks). (Illus.). xii, 152p. 1972. Repr. of 1901 ed. 42.00x (ISBN 0-8103-3938-2). Gale.

Whitman, Cedric H. The Heroic Pardox: Essays on Homer, Sophocles, & Aristophanes. Segal, Charles, ed. LC 82-5155. 176p. 1982. 18.50x (ISBN 0-8014-1453-9). Cornell U Pr.

Whitman, David def., jt. auth. see Lynn, Laurence E., Jr.

Whitman, John. The Psychic Power of Plants. 192p. (Orig.). 1974. pap. 1.50 o.p. (ISBN 0-451-06253-1, W6253, Sig). NAL.

--Starting from Scratch: A Guide to Indoor Gardening. (Illus.). 1978. pap. 1.95 o.p. (ISBN 0-451-08024-6, J8024, Sig). NAL.

Whitman, Malcolm D. Tennis Origins & Mysteries. LC 68-58970. 1968. Repr. of 1932 ed. 34.00x (ISBN 0-8103-3542-5). Gale.

Whitman, Marina V. International Trade & Investment: Two Perspectives. LC 81-6326. (Essays in International Finance Ser.: No. 143). 1981. pap. text ed. 2.50x (ISBN 0-88165-050-1). Princeton U Int Finan Econ.

Whitman, Mark. The Films of Clint Eastwood. (Illus.). 96p. 1982. pap. 3.95 (ISBN 0-8253-0109-2); pap. 94.80 Prepack of 24 titles write for additional title info. (ISBN 0-686-83062-8). Beaufort Bks NY.

Whitman, Nancy C. & Braun, Frederick G. The Metric System: A Laboratory Approach for Teachers. LC 77-22793. 1978. pap. text ed. 17.95 (ISBN 0-471-02763-4). Wiley.

Whitman, Richard F. & Boase, Paul H. Speech Communication: Principles & Contexts. 480p. 1983. text ed. 15.95 (ISBN 0-02-427370-8). Macmillan.

Whitman, Roback C. The Mysteries of Astrology & the Wonders of Magic. (Library of the Occult Bks.). (Illus.). 121p. 1981. 59.85 (ISBN 0-89920-028-1). Am Inst Psych.

Whitman, Robert F., ed. see Shaw, George B.

Whitman, Robert V., jt. auth. see Lambe, T. William.

Whitman, Roger C. More First Aid for the Ailing House: Money-Saving Ways to Improve Your House & Property. 1976. 16.95 (ISBN 0-07-069985-2, P&RB). McGraw.

Whitman, Ruth. Becoming a Poet. LC 82-4855. 1982. pap. 8.95 (ISBN 0-87116-131-1). Writer.

Whitman, Thomas L. & Scibak, John W., eds. Behavior Modification with the Severely & Profoundly Retarded: Research & Application. LC 82-22720. (Monograph). Date not set. write for info. (ISBN 0-12-747280-0). Acad Pr.

Whitman, Walt. An American Primer. pap. 3.00 o.s.i. (ISBN 0-87286-052-3). City Lights.

--A Choice of Whitman's Verse. Hall, Donald, ed. 176p. 1968. pap. 5.95 (ISBN 0-571-08613-6). Faber & Faber.

--I Hear America Singing. LC 72-1446. (Illus.). 32p. (ps-3). 1975. 4.95 o.s.i. (ISBN 0-440-04144-9, Sey Lawr); PLB 4.58 o.s.i. (ISBN 0-440-04143-0, Sey Lawr). Delacorte.

--Illustrated Leaves of Grass. Chapnick, Howard, ed. LC 74-123465. (Illus.). 1971. 7.95 o.p. (ISBN 0-448-02074-2, G&D). Putnam Pub Group.

--Leaves of Grass. 1971. pap. 2.25 (ISBN 0-451-51702-4, CE1702, Sig Classics). NAL.

--Leaves of Grass. Bradley, Sculley & Blodgett, Harold W., eds. (Critical Editions Ser.). 500p. 1973. pap. text ed. 13.95x (ISBN 0-393-09388-3). Norton.

--Leaves of Grass. Cowley, Malcolm, ed. (Poets Ser). 1976. pap. 2.50 (ISBN 0-14-042199-8). Penguin.

--Leaves of Grass. 6.95 (ISBN 0-394-60410-5). Modern Lib.

--Leaves of Grass & Selected Prose. Buell, Lawrence, ed. 1981. pap. 4.95x (ISBN 0-394-30940-5, T40, Mod LibC). Modern Lib.

--Leaves of Grass: Selections. Miller, Edwin H., ed. LC 74-91458. (Crofts Classics Ser.). 1970. pap. text ed. 3.50x (ISBN 0-88295-102-5). Harlan Davidson.

--Overhead the Sun: Lines from Walt Whitman. LC 69-20284. (Illus.). 40p. (ps up). 1969. 6.95 (ISBN 0-374-35676-9). FS&G.

--Specimen Days. Kazin, Alfred, ed. LC 76-104907. (Illus.). 1971. 50.00 (ISBN 0-87923-033-9); ltd. ed. 75.00 (ISBN 0-87923-032-0). Godine.

--Walt Whitman's Blue Book: The 1860-61 Leaves of Grass Containing His Manuscript Additions & Revisions, 2 vols. Incl. Vol. 1. Facsimile of the Unique Copy in the Oscar Lion Collection; Vol. 2. Textual Analysis. Golden, Arthur. LC 68-1489. 1968. boxed 60.00 set (ISBN 0-87104-214-2). NY Pub Lib.

Whitmont, Edward C. Psyche & Substance: Essays on Homoeopathy in the Light of Jungian Psychology. 222p. 1983. pap. 9.95 (ISBN 0-913028-66-5). North Atlantic.

Whitmore, Cilla. Manner of a Lady. 1979. pap. 1.50 o.s.i. (ISBN 0-440-15378-6). Dell.

--Mansion for a Lady. (Orig.). 1980. pap. 1.50 o.s.i. (ISBN 0-440-16097-9). Dell.

Whitmore, G. A. & Findlay, M. C., eds. Stochastic Dominance. LC 76-55111. (Illus.). 416p. 1978. 23.95x o.p. (ISBN 0-669-01310-2). Lexington Bks.

Whitmore, John K., jt. ed. see Hall, Kenneth R.

Whitmore, Ken. Jump! (Illus.). 144p. (gr. 3-7). 1983. bds. 6.95 (ISBN 0-19-271461-9, Pub. by Oxford U Pr Childrens). Merrimack Bk Serv.

Whitmore, Sandra J., illus. Scenes from Longfellow's Poems: A Coloring Book. (gr. 1-4). 1978. pap. 1.95 o.p. (ISBN 0-915592-31-2). Maine Hist.

Whitnah, Dorothy & Winnett, Thomas. Outdoor Guide to the San Francisco Bay Area. (Illus.). 416p. 1983. pap. 9.95 (ISBN 0-89997-026-5). Wilderness Pr.

Whitnah, Dorothy L. Guide to the Golden Gate National Recreation Area. Winnett, Thomas, ed. LC 76-57009. (Illus.). 160p. (Orig.). 1978. pap. 6.95 (ISBN 0-911824-54-5). Wilderness.

Whitnell, Barbara. The Ring of Bells. 1982. 15.95 (ISBN 0-698-11149-4, Coward). Putnam Pub Group.

Whitney. Inflation Since Nineteen Forty-Five. 368p. 1982. 32.95 (ISBN 0-03-061352-3). Praeger.

Whitney, Blair. John G. Neihardt. (United States Authors Ser.). lib. bdg. 13.95 (ISBN 0-8057-7170-0, Twayne). G K Hall.

Whitney, David C. The American Presidents: Biographies of the Chief Executives from Washington Through Carter. rev. ed. LC 78-19340. 1979. 10.95 o.p. (ISBN 0-385-14737-6). Doubleday.

Whitney, E. L. Government of the Colony of South Carolina. LC 77-95455. (Studies in Black History & Culture, No. 54). 1970. Repr. of 1895 ed. lib. bdg. 44.95x (ISBN 0-8383-1211-X). Haskell.

Whitney, Edson L. The American Peace Society: A Centennial History. LC 77-137562. (Peace Movement in America Ser). 360p. 1972. Repr. of 1928 ed. lib. bdg. 19.95x (ISBN 0-89198-092-X). Ozer.

Whitney, Eleanor N. & Cataldo, Corrine. Understanding Normal & Clinical Nutrition. (Illus.). 1000p. 1983. text ed. 26.95 (ISBN 0-314-69685-7); tchrs.' manual avail. (ISBN 0-314-71137-6). West Pub.

Whitney, Eleanor N. & Hamilton, Eva M. Understanding Nutrition. (Illus.). 1977. text ed. 18.50 o.s.i. (ISBN 0-8299-0052-7); instrs.' manual avail. o.s.i. (ISBN 0-8299-0583-9). West Pub.

--Understanding Nutrition. 2nd ed. (Illus.). 793p. 1981. text ed. 23.95 (ISBN 0-8299-0419-0). West Pub.

Whitney, Eleanor N., jt. auth. see Hamilton, Eva M.

Whitney, Elinor, jt. auth. see Mahoney, Bertha.

Whitney, Frederick C. Mass Media & Mass Communications in Society. 488p. 1975. pap. text ed. write for info. o.p. (ISBN 0-697-04302-9); instr's manual avail. o.p. Wm C Brown.

Whitney, Frederick C., jt. auth. see Black, Jay.

Whitney, George & Hughes, Donna. Individualized Instruction: Together, Not Alone. LC 73-81098. (Illus.). 117p. (Orig.). 1973. pap. 5.50x o.p. (ISBN 0-87562-046-9). Spec Child.

Whitney, George D. This Is the Beagle. (Illus.). 12.95 (ISBN 0-87666-243-2, PS609). TFH Pubns.

Whitney, George G. Born to Survive, 1936-1946. (Illus.). 200p. Date not set. pap. 12.95 (ISBN 0-686-84299-5). Banyan Bks.

Whitney, Gleaves. Colorado Front Range: A Landscape Divided. (Illus.). 120p. (Orig.). 1983. pap. price not set (ISBN 0-933472-71-4). Johnson Bks.

Whitney, Janet. Abigail Adams. Repr. of 1947 ed. lib. bdg. 20.75x (ISBN 0-8371-3435-8, WHAA). Greenwood.

Whitney, John R. & Howe, Susan W. Religious Literature of the West. LC 70-158996. (Orig.). 1971. 8.95 o.p. (ISBN 0-8066-1118-9, 10-5467). Augsburg.

Whitney, Leon F. All About Guppies. (Orig.). pap. 7.95 (ISBN 0-87666-083-9, PS603). TFH Pubns.

--Breed Your Dog. (Orig.). 1962. pap. 2.95 (ISBN 0-87666-255-6, DS1021). TFH Pubns.

--Complete Book of Dog Care. rev. ed. LC 80-631. (Illus.). 280p. 1982. 15.95 (ISBN 0-385-15547-6). Doubleday.

--Groom Your Dog. (Orig.). 1962. pap. 2.50 o.p. (ISBN 0-87666-313-7, DS1023). TFH Pubns.

--Keep Your Pigeons Flying. 2nd ed. Osman, Colin, ed. LC 61-11434. (Illus.). 256p. 1983. pap. 9.95 (ISBN 0-8397-4402-1). Eriksson.

--This Is the Cocker Spaniel. (Illus.). 13.95 (ISBN 0-87666-271-8, PS612). TFH Pubns.

Whitney, Mary, jt. auth. see Philp, R.

Whitney, Maurice. Backgrounds in Music Theory. 1954. pap. 7.95 (ISBN 0-02-872870-X). Schirmer Bks.

Whitney Museum of American Art. Thirty-Two Color Postcards of Twentieth-Century American Art. 1978. pap. 3.50 (ISBN 0-486-23629-3). Dover.

Whitney Museum of American Art, jt. auth. see Armstrong, Tom.

Whitney, Phyllis. Fire & the Gold. (YA) (RL 7). 1974. pap. 1.50 o.p. (ISBN 0-451-07320-7, W7320, Sig). NAL.

--The Highest Dream. (YA) (RL 7). 1975. pap. 1.75 (ISBN 0-451-11218-0, AE1218, Sig). NAL.

--Nobody Likes Trina. (RL 6). 1976. pap. 1.75 (ISBN 0-451-11532-5, AE1532, Sig). NAL.

--Secret of the Haunted Mesa. (RL 8). 1977. pap. 1.25 o.p. (ISBN 0-451-07913-2, Y7913, Sig). NAL.

Whitney, Phyllis A. Domino. (General Ser.). 1979. lib. bdg. 14.95 (ISBN 0-8161-3016-7, Large Print Bks). G K Hall.

--The Golden Unicorn. 1976. Repr. lib. bdg. 13.95 o.p. (ISBN 0-8161-6409-6, Large Print Bks). G K Hall.

--Mystery of the Angry Idol. (RL 5). 1974. pap. 1.50 (ISBN 0-451-09617-7, W9617, Sig). NAL.

--The Mystery of the Black Diamonds. 176p. (RL 4). 1974. pap. 1.75 (ISBN 0-451-11487-6, AE1487, Sig). NAL.

--Mystery of the Green Cat. LC 57-5435. (Illus.). 1957. 6.95 (ISBN 0-664-32160-7). Westminster.

--Mystery of the Scowling Boy. (RL 5). 1975. pap. 1.25 o.p. (ISBN 0-451-07530-7, Y7530, Sig). NAL.

--Mystery of the Strange Traveler. 176p. (RL 4). 1974. pap. 1.75 (ISBN 0-451-09847-1, E9847, Sig). NAL.

--The Secret of the Emerald Star. (RL 5). 1979. pap. 1.50 o.p. (ISBN 0-451-08524-8, W8524, Sig). NAL.

--Secret of the Samurai Sword. (Young Adult Mystery Ser.). (RL 5). 1974. pap. 1.50 o.p. (ISBN 0-451-09155-8, W9155, Sig). NAL.

--Secret of the Spotted Shell. (Young Adult Mystery). 192p. (RL 6). 1974. pap. 1.25 o.p. (ISBN 0-451-07468-8, Y7468, Sig). NAL.

--Secret of the Stone Face. LC 77-1261. (gr. 5-9). 1977. 8.95 (ISBN 0-664-32612-9). Westminster.

--Secret of the Tiger's Eye. (RL 7). 1978. pap. 1.50 o.p. (ISBN 0-451-08298-2, W8298, Sig). NAL.

--Song of the Shaggy Canary. (RL 6). 1976. pap. 1.50 (ISBN 0-451-09793-9, W9793, Sig). NAL.

--Step to the Music. 208p. (RL 7). 1974. pap. 1.50 o.p. (ISBN 0-451-07531-5, W7531, Sig). NAL.

--Vermilion. 320p. 1982. pap. 3.50 (ISBN 0-449-24555-1, Crest). Fawcett.

Whitney, R. W. The Kent State Massacre. new ed. Rahmas, D. Steve, ed. (Events of Our Times Ser.). 32p. 1975. lib. bdg. 2.95 incl. catalog cards (ISBN 0-686-11233-4); pap. 1.95 vinyl laminated covers (ISBN 0-686-11234-2). SamHar Pr.

Whitney, Roy P. The Story of Paper. (TAPPI PRESS Reports). (Illus.). 28p. 1980. pap. 4.95 (ISBN 0-89852-385-0, 01-01-R085). TAPPI.

Whitney, Simon N. Antitrust Policies, 2 vols. LC 58-9954. 1958. Vol. 1. 26.00 (ISBN 0-527-02801-0); Vol. 2. 30.00 (ISBN 0-527-02848-7). Kraus Repr.

Whitney, Stephen. A Field Guide to the Grand Canyon. (Illus.). 320p. 1982. 22.50 (ISBN 0-688-01328-7); pap. 12.50 (ISBN 0-686-83108-X). Morrow.

--Singled Out. LC 78-4183. 1978. 8.95 o.p. (ISBN 0-688-03290-7). Morrow.

Whitney, Stephen, jt. auth. see Niels, Lauersen.

Whitney, Steven, jt. auth. see Lauersen, Niels.

Whitney, Thomas P., tr. see Solzhenitsyn, Aleksandr I.

Whitney, Thomas R. A Defence of the American Policy As Opposed to the Encroachments of Foreign Influence, & Especially to the Interference of the Papacy in the Political Interests & Affairs of the United States. LC 75-145496. (The American Immigration Library). 372p. 1971. Repr. of 1856 ed. lib. bdg. 20.95x (ISBN 0-89198-029-6). Ozer.

Whitney, William D. Selected Writings of William Dwight Whitney. Silverstein, Michael, ed. 1971. 22.50x (ISBN 0-262-19087-7). MIT Pr.

Whitney, William J. Electrical Wiring: Residential. LC 78-12869. 1979. pap. text ed. 16.95 (ISBN 0-471-05643-X); solutions manual 4.00 (ISBN 0-471-05357-0). Wiley.

Whiton, Sherrill. Interior Design & Decoration. 4th ed. (Illus.). 1974. text ed. 42.95 scp (ISBN 0-397-47315-X, HarpC); pap. text ed. 39.95 scp (ISBN 0-397-47302-8, HarpC). Har-Row.
Whitridge, Jackie, jt. auth. see Adams, Joan.
Whitrow, M., ed. ISIS Cumulative Bibliography, 1913-1965, 2 vols. LC 72-186272. 1966. Vol. 3, Subjects 772pg. 64.00 (ISBN 0-7201-0296-0, Pub. by Mansell England); Vols. 1-2, Personalities & Institutions, 1971 1527 pg. 112.00 (ISBN 0-7201-0183-2). Wilson.
Whitrow, Magda. Isis Cumulative Bibliography, 1913-1965: Volumes 4 & 5, Civilizations & Periods. 1100p. 1982. 160.00 (ISBN 0-7201-0549-8). Mansell.
Whitsitt, Robert E., II. TI Extended BASIC: Normally Sold with Command Module. Quiram, Jacquelyn F., ed. LC 80-54899. 224p. (Orig.). 1981. pap. text ed. 12.95 o.p. (ISBN 0-89512-045-3). Tex Instr Inc.
Whitson, Betty J. & McFarlane, Judith. The Pediatric Nursing Skills Manual. 304p. 1980. pap. 10.50 (ISBN 0-471-04511-X, Pub. by Wiley Med). Wiley.
Whitson, Denton. For the Glory of Venice. LC 74-99298. 1970. 10.95 (ISBN 0-87716-027-9, Pub. by Moore Pub Co). F Apple.
Whitson, Dick. How to Control Your Shyness & Become More Successful with Women. 1976. pap. 6.95 (ISBN 0-917194-01-2). Prog Studies.
Whitson, Dick, ed. see Amann, Dick & Smith, Dick.
Whitson, Gary, ed. Nuclear-Cytoplasmic Interactions in the Cell Cycle. (Cell Biology Ser.). 1980. 44.50 (ISBN 0-12-747750-0). Acad Pr.
Whitson, M. E. & Elston, C. A. Basic Agricultural Mathematics. rev. ed. 61p. 1966. spiral 7.95 (ISBN 0-87484-043-0). Mayfield Pub.
Whitson, William, tr. see Josephus, Flavius.
Whitson, William W. Foreign Policy & U. S. National Security: Major Postelection Issues. LC 76-2070. (Praeger Special Studies). 384p. 1976. 36.95 o.p. (ISBN 0-275-56540-8); pap. text ed. 15.95 o.p. (ISBN 0-275-85700-X). Praeger.
Whitt, Frank R. & Wilson, David G. Bicycling Science: Ergonomics & Mechanics. 2nd ed. (Illus.). 320p. 1982. 19.95x (ISBN 0-262-23111-5); pap. 9.95 (ISBN 0-262-73060-X). MIT Pr.
--Bicycling Science: Ergonomics & Mechanics. 1975. pap. 6.95 o.p. (ISBN 0-262-73046-4). MIT Pr.
Whittaker, Arabelle & Warkentin, Viola. Chol Texts on the Supernatural. (Publications in Linguistics & Related Fields Ser.: No. 13). 171p. 1965. pap. 2.25 (ISBN 0-88312-013-5); 2.25. Summer Inst Ling.
Whittaker, C. R., jt. ed. see Garnsey, P. D.
Whittaker, David M., jt. auth. see Elias, Thomas S.
Whittaker, Edmund T. & Watson, George N. A Course of Modern Analysis. 4th ed. 1927. 92.50 (ISBN 0-521-06794-4); pap. text ed. 27.95 (ISBN 0-521-09189-6). Cambridge U Pr.
Whittaker, Elwyn T., jt. auth. see Startup, Richard.
Whittaker, Lou, jt. ed. see Press, Larry.
Whittaker, Molly. New Testament Greek Grammar: An Introduction. (Student Christian Movement Press Ser.). 1980. pap. 7.50x (ISBN 0-19-520343-7); key to exercise 3.95x (ISBN 0-19-520344-5). Oxford U Pr.
Whittaker, Molly, ed. Tatian: Oratorio ad Graecos & Fragments. (Early Christian Texts). 1982. 27.50x (ISBN 0-19-826809-2). Oxford U Pr.
Whittaker, Peter. Chloroplasts & Mitochondria. 2nd ed. (Studies in Biology: No. 31). 88p. 1982. pap. text ed. 8.95 (ISBN 0-7131-2828-3). E Arnold.
Whittaker, Robert H. Communities & Ecosystems. 2nd ed. (Illus.). 352p. 1975. pap. text ed. 14.95x (ISBN 0-02-427390-2). Macmillan.
--Ordination of Plant Communities. 1982. 29.50 (ISBN 90-6193-565-2, Pub. by Junk Pubs Netherlands). Kluwer Boston.
Whittaker, Robert H. & Levin, Simon A., eds. Niche: Theory & Application. LC 74-23328. (Benchmark Papers in Ecology Ser.: No. 3). 1975. 53.50 (ISBN 0-12-787757-6). Acad Pr.
Whittaker, Roger, jt. auth. see Sanders, Irwin.
Whittaker, Ruty. The Faith & Fiction of Muriel Spark. LC 81-21296. 180p. 1982. 19.95x (ISBN 0-312-27963-9). St Martin.
Whittaker, Thomas. Reason: A Philosophical Essay with Historical Illustrations. LC 68-19298. (Illus.). 1968. Repr. of 1934 ed. lib. bdg. 16.00x (ISBN 0-8371-0269-3, WHR). Greenwood.
Whittal, Arnold. Music Since the First World War. LC 77-1650. 1977. 20.00x (ISBN 0-312-55492-3). St Martin.
Whittal, Yvonne. Chains of Gold. (Harlequin Presents Ser.). 192p. 1983. pap. 1.95 (ISBN 0-373-10590-8). Harlequin Bks.
--House of Mirrors. (Harlequin Romances Ser.). 192p. 1983. pap. 1.75 (ISBN 0-373-02538-6). Harlequin Bks.
--Late Harvest. (Harlequin Presents Ser.). 192p. 1983. pap. 1.75 (ISBN 0-373-10574-6). Harlequin Bks.
--The Silver Falcon. (Harlequin Presents Ser.). 192p. 1983. pap. 1.95 (ISBN 0-373-10598-3). Harlequin Bks.
--Web of Silk. (Harlequin Presents Ser.). 192p. 1983. pap. 1.95 (ISBN 0-373-10582-7). Harlequin Bks.
Whittall, Arnold, tr. see Von Westernhagen, Curt.
Whittall, Mary, tr. see Dahlhaus, Carl.
Whittall, Mary, tr. see Schuh, Willi.
Whittall, Mary, tr. see Von Westernhagen, Curt.

Whittemore, A. S., jt. ed. see Breslow, N. E.
Whittemore, Alice, ed. see SIAM Institute for Mathematics & Society Conference, Alta, Utah, July 5-9, 1976.
Whittemore, Carroll E., ed. Symbols of the Church. 64p. 1983. pap. 1.95 (ISBN 0-687-40786-9). Abingdon.
Whittemore, Edward. Nile Shadows. LC 82-2915. 448p. 1983. 17.50 (ISBN 0-03-018531-9). HR&W.
--Sinai Tapestry. 1978. pap. 1.95 o.p. (ISBN 0-380-37853-1, 37853). Avon.
Whittemore, Hank. Find the Magician! LC 80-5510. 276p. 1980. 11.95 o.p. (ISBN 0-670-31738-1). Viking Pr.
Whittemore, Lewis B. The Church & Secular Education. LC 78-17152. 1978. Repr. of 1960 ed. lib. bdg. 18.25x (ISBN 0-313-20540-X, WHCS). Greenwood.
Whittemore, Reed. The Feel of Rock: Poems of Three Decades. LC 82-70052. 124p. (Orig.). 1982. 10.00 (ISBN 0-931848-44-X); pap. 5.50 (ISBN 0-931848-45-8). Dryad Pr.
--The Poet As Journalist: Life at the New Republic. LC 76-14897. 220p. 1976. 8.95 (ISBN 0-915220-16-4). New Republic.
Whittemore-Barclay, Suzanne. Expressions of My Impressions. 1978. 4.95 o.p. (ISBN 0-533-03760-3). Vantage.
Whitten, C. A., et al, eds. Recent Crustal Movement, 1977. (Developments in Geotectonics: Vol. 13). 1979. 83.00 (ISBN 0-444-41783-4). Elsevier.
Whitten, Les. A Killing Pace. LC 82-73008. 288p. 1983. 13.95 (ISBN 0-689-11369-2). Atheneum.
Whitten, Philip, jt. auth. see Wickman, Peter.
Whitten, Phillip M., jt. auth. see Hunter, David E.
Whitten, R. C., jt. auth. see Ripley, J. A., Jr.
Whitten, Ralph U., jt. auth. see Bridwell, Randall.
Whittenburg, Gerald E. West's Federal Taxation: Practice Sets, 1983 Edition. 288p. 1982. pap. text ed. 7.95 (ISBN 0-314-68799-8). West Pub.
Whittenburg, Gerald E. & Whittington, Ray. Income Tax Fundamentals. 550p. 1982. pap. text ed. 19.95 (ISBN 0-314-63312-X). West Pub.
Whitteridge, G. William Harvey & the Circulation of the Blood. 1971. 19.50 (ISBN 0-444-19663-3). Elsevier.
Whittick, Arnold. Symbols for Designers. LC 71-175760. (Illus.). xvi, 168p. 1972. Repr. of 1935 ed. 45.00x (ISBN 0-8103-3119-5). Gale.
--Woman into Citizen. LC 79-26516. (Illus.). 327p. 1979. 9.95 (ISBN 0-87436-269-5). ABC-Clio.
Whittier, Charles. Dear Dad, Our Life in the Theater Around the Turn of the Century. LC 72-83013. (Illus.). 200p. 1972. pap. 3.95 (ISBN 0-87027-125-3). Cumberland Pr.
Whitting, G. C. see Von Wiesner, J. & Von Regel, C.
Whittingham, C. P. The Mechanism of Photosynthesis. 136p. 1974. pap. text ed. 13.95 (ISBN 0-7131-2434-2). E Arnold.
Whittingham, Richard. The Chicago Bears: An Illustrated History. rev. ed. LC 79-8734. (Illus.). 1980. 14.95 o.p. (ISBN 0-528-81825-2). Rand.
--The Los Angeles Dodgers: An Illustrated History. LC 81-48051. (Illus.). 256p. 1982. 21.10i (ISBN 0-06-014997-3, HarpT). Har-Row.
--The White Sox: A Pictorial History. (Illus.). 1983. 15.95 (ISBN 0-8092-5769-6); pap. 7.95 (ISBN 0-8092-5768-8). Contemp Bks.
Whittington, G. & Whyte, I. D. An Historical Geography of Scotland. write for info. (ISBN 0-12-747360-2); pap. write for info. (ISBN 0-12-747362-9). Acad Pr.
Whittington, Geoffrey. Inflation Accounting: An Introduction to the Debate. LC 82-9657. (Management & Industrial Relations Ser.: No. 3). 256p. Date not set. price not set (ISBN 0-521-24903-1); pap. price not set (ISBN 0-521-27055-3). Cambridge U Pr.
Whittington, Jennifer, ed. Literary Recordings: A Checklist of the Archive of Recorded Poetry & Literature in the Library of Congress. LC 79-607981. vi, 299p. 1981. pap. 8.50 (ISBN 0-8444-0317-2). Lib Congress.
Whittington, Ray, jt. auth. see Whittenburg, Gerald E.
Whittle, A. W., jt. ed. see Case, H. J.
Whittle, Agnes L. A Bridge to Nowhere. 80p. 1983. 7.95 (ISBN 0-8059-2866-9). Dorrance.
Whittle, P. Optimisation Over Time: Dynamic Programming & Stochastic Control, Vol. 1. (Probability & Mathematical Statistics-Applied Probability & Statistics Section Ser.). 317p. 1982. text ed. 46.95x (ISBN 0-471-10120-6, Pub. by Wiley-Interscience). Wiley.
--Probability. LC 76-863. 1976. pap. 19.95x (ISBN 0-471-01657-8, Pub. by Wiley-Interscience). Wiley.
Whittle, Peter. Optimization Under Constraint: Theory & Applications of Nonlinear Programming. LC 75-149574. (Ser. on Probability & Mathematical Statistics: Applied Section). 241p. 1971. 49.95x (ISBN 0-471-94130-1, Pub. by Wiley-Interscience). Wiley.
--Prediction & Regulation by Linear Least-Square Methods. 2nd, rev. ed. 224p. 1983. 29.50x (ISBN 0-8166-1147-5); pap. 12.95x (ISBN 0-8166-1148-3). U of Minn Pr.
Whittle, Robin. Reinforcement Detailing Manual. (Viewpoint Ser.). (Illus.). 120p. 1981. spiral bdg. 47.50x (ISBN 0-7210-1223-X, Pub. by Viewpoint). Scholium Intl.

Whittle, Tyler. Victoria & Albert at Home. 208p. 1980. 12.95 (ISBN 0-7100-0541-5). Routledge & Kegan.
Whittlesey, Marietta. Freelance Forever: Successful Self-Employment. 416p. 1982. 7.95 (ISBN 0-380-81398-X, 81398). Avon.
--Killer Salt. 1978. pap. 2.95 o.s.i. (ISBN 0-380-39297-6, 62141X). Avon.
Whittock, Trevor. Reading of the Canterbury Tales. (Orig.). 1969. 49.50 (ISBN 0-521-06795-2); pap. 12.95 (ISBN 0-521-09557-3). Cambridge U Pr.
Whitton, B. A., jt. auth. see Carr, N. G.
Whitton, B. A., jt. ed. see Carr, N. G.
Whitton, John B. & Larson, Arthur. Propaganda Towards Disarmament in the War of Words. LC 63-19593. 305p. 1964. 15.00 (ISBN 0-379-00110-1). Oceana.
Whitty, G., jt. ed. see Young, Michael.
Whitty, Geoff, jt. auth. see Gleeson, Denis.
Whitwell, David & Ostling, Acton, Jr., eds. The College & University Band: An Anthology of Papers from the Conferences of the College Band Directors National Association, 1941-1975. 315p. 1977. 4.00 (ISBN 0-940796-00-7, 1004). Music Ed.
Whitwell, J. C. & Toner, Richard. Conservation of Mass & Energy. (Chemical Engineering Ser). 512p. 1973. text ed. 38.50 (ISBN 0-07-070080-X, C); solns. manual 18.50 (ISBN 0-07-070081-8). McGraw.
Whitwell, W. L. & Winborne, Lee W. The Architectural Heritage of the Roanoke Valley. LC 81-12987. (Illus.). 217p. 1982. 14.95x (ISBN 0-8139-0905-8). U Pr of Va.
Whitworth, J. A., jt. ed. see Kincaid-Smith, P. S.
Whitworth, John R. & Sutton, Dorothy L. Stanford Binet: Form L-M, Compilation. 256p. 1982. pap. 22.50 (ISBN 0-87879-324-0). Acad Therapy.
WHO Expert Committee. Geneva, 1973, 20th. WHO Expert Committee on Drug Dependence: Report. (Technical Report Ser.: No. 551). (Also avail. in French & Spanish). 1974. pap. 2.80 (ISBN 92-4-120551-2). World Health.
WHO Expert Committee on Pesticide Residues, jt. auth. see FAO Working Party on Pesticide Residues.
WHO-WMO Symposium on Urban Climates & Building Climatology, Brussels, 1968. Proceedings. (Technical Notes Ser.: No. 108). 390p. (Fr. ed. also avail.). 1970. pap. 50.00 (ISBN 0-686-93905-0, WMO). Unipub.
Wholeben, Brent E. The Design, Implementation & Evaluation of Mathematical Modeling Procedures for Decisioning Among Educational Alternatives. LC 80-5437. 474p. 1980. lib. bdg. 27.50 (ISBN 0-8191-1093-0); pap. text ed. 17.00 (ISBN 0-8191-1094-9). U Pr of Amer.
Wholey, Joseph S. Zero-Base Budgeting & Program Evaluation. LC 77-4610. 176p. 1978. 17.95 (ISBN 0-669-01730-2). Lexington Bks.
Whordley, Derek & Doster, Rebecca. Humanics National Orientation Preschool Assessment. rev. ed. 200p. 1982. pap. 14.95 (ISBN 0-89334-031-6). Humanics Ltd.
Whordley, Derek & Doster, Rebecca J. Humanics National Orientation to Preschool Assessment. 200p. (Orig.). 1983. pap. 14.95 (ISBN 0-89334-031-6). Humanics Ltd.
Whordley, Derek, jt. auth. see Caballero, Jane A.
Whyatt, Frances, jt. ed. see Seidman, Hugh.
Whybow, Solene. The Life of Animals with Shells. LC 78-56609. (Easy Reading Edition of Introduction to Nature Ser.). (Illus.). 1979. PLB 12.68 (ISBN 0-382-06189-6). Silver.
Whybray, R. N. Thanksgiving for a Liberated Prophet: An Interpretation of Isaiah Chapter Fifty-Three. (JSOT Supplement Ser.: No. 4). 184p. 1978. text ed. 29.95x o.p. (ISBN 0-905774-09-4, Pub. by JSOT Pr England); pap. text ed. 16.95x (ISBN 0-905774-04-3, Pub. by JSOT Pr England). Eisenbrauns.
Whymper, Edward. Scrambles Amongst the Alps in the Years Eighteen Sixty to Eighteen Sixty-Nine. LC 81-50250. (Illus.). 176p. 1981. 12.95 (ISBN 0-89815-055-8); pap. 5.95 (ISBN 0-89815-043-4). Ten Speed Pr.
Whynes, David K. & Bowles, Roger A. The Economic Theory of the State. 1981. 29.00x (ISBN 0-312-23662-X). St Martin.
Whysler, R. O. Get Going! Tips on Managing Your Time & Increasing Your Effectiveness. (Illus.). 75p. (Orig.). 1982. pap. 13.00x looseleaf (ISBN 0-935402-11-X); lib. bdg. 12.00x (ISBN 0-935402-12-8). Intl Comm Serv.
Whyte, A., jt. ed. see Ockleford, C.
Whyte, A. F., tr. see De Callieres.
Whyte, Alexander & Turnbull, Ralph G., eds. Best of Alexander Whyte. (Best Ser.). 1979. pap. 3.95 o.p. (ISBN 0-8010-9628-6). Baker Bk.
Whyte, Ann V. & Burton, Ian. Environmental Risk Assessment: Scope 15. LC 79-42903. (Scope (the Scientific Committee on Problems of the Environment)). 157p. 1980. 29.95x (ISBN 0-471-27701-0, Pub. by Wiley-Interscience). Wiley.
Whyte, I. D., jt. auth. see Whittington, G.
Whyte, Iain B. Bruno Taut & the Architecture of Activism. LC 81-12301. (Urban & Architectural Studies: No. 6). (Illus.). 320p. 1982. 59.50 (ISBN 0-521-23655-X). Cambridge U Pr.

Whyte, Jean-Luc. Godard: Three Films. LC 75-4352. (Masterworks Film Ser.). (Illus.). 1975. pap. 4.95i o.p. (ISBN 0-06-430065-X, IN-65, HarpT). Har-Row.
Whyte, Kay. Design in Embroidery. (Illus.). 240p. 1969. 14.75 o.p. (ISBN 0-8231-4008-3). Branford.
Whyte, L. L. The Unconscious Before Freud. (Classics in Psychology Ser.). 1979. 27.50x (ISBN 0-312-82870-5). St Martin.
--The Unconscious Before Freud. Koestler, Arthur, ed. (Classics in Psychology & Psychiatry Ser.). 256p. 1983. Repr. write for info. (ISBN 0-904014-41-X). F Pinter Pubs.
Whyte, Malcolm & Koski, Vernon. Beasties. (Illus.). 32p. 1970. pap. 3.95 (ISBN 0-912300-11-6). Troubador Pr.
Whyte, Martin K. Small Groups & Political Ritual in China. 288p. 1983. pap. text ed. 8.95x (ISBN 0-520-04941-1, CAMPUS 157). U of Cal Pr.
--Small Groups & Political Rituals in China. 1974. 30.00x (ISBN 0-520-02499-0). U of Cal Pr.
Whyte, Martin K., jt. auth. see Parish, William L.
Whyte, R. O. & Noir, T. R. Grasses in Agriculture. (Agricultural Studies Ser.: No. 42). 418p. 1959. pap. 26.25 (ISBN 0-686-92868-7, F212, FAO). Unipub.
Whyte, Robert O. Rural Nutrition in Monsoon Asia. (Oxford in Asia College Texts Ser). 1974. pap. 29.50x o.p. (ISBN 0-19-580250-0). Oxford U Pr.
Whyte, W. & Alberti, G. Power, Politics, & Progress: Social Change in Rural Peru. 1976. 22.95 (ISBN 0-444-99028-3). Elsevier.
Whyte, W. S. Revision Notes on Plane Surveying. 1971. text ed. 4.95 o.p. (ISBN 0-408-00067-8). Butterworth.
Whyte, William F. & Hammer, Tove H. Worker Participation & Ownership: Cooperative Strategies for Strengthening Local Economies. LC 82-23413. (ILR Paperback Ser.). 168p. (Orig.). 1983. pap. price not set (ISBN 0-87546-097-6). ILR Pr.
Whyte, William F. & Williams, Lawrence K. Toward an Integrated Theory of Development: Economic & Noneconomic Variables in Rural Development. LC 68-20192. (Paperback Ser.: No. 5). 96p. 1968. pap. 3.00 (ISBN 0-87546-030-5) (ISBN 0-87546-271-5). ILR Pr.
Whyte, William H., Jr. Organization Man. 1957. 14.95 o.p. (ISBN 0-671-54330-X). S&S.
--The Organization Man. 1956. pap. 7.95 (ISBN 0-671-21235-4, Touchstone Bks). S&S.
Wiarda, Howard & Kline, Harvey F. Latin American Politics & Development. LC 78-56434. (Illus.). 1979. text ed. 19.95 (ISBN 0-395-27056-1). HM.
Wiarda, Howard J. Corporatism & National Development in Latin America. (Replica Edition Ser.). 325p. 1981. lib. bdg. 33.00 (ISBN 0-86531-031-9). Westview.
--Critical Elections & Critical Coups: State, Society & the Military in the Processes of Latin American Development. LC 79-4433. (Papers in International Studies: Latin America: No. 5). 1979. pap. 7.00 (ISBN 0-89680-082-2, Ohio U Ctr Intl). Ohio U Pr.
Wiarda, Howard J., ed. The Continuing Struggle for Democracy in Latin America. LC 79-13551. (Westview Special Studies on Latin America). lib. bdg. 28.50 (ISBN 0-89158-663-6); text ed. 11.50. Westview.
Wiart, C., jt. ed. see Volmat, R.
Wiaschin, Ken. The Illustrated Encyclopedia of the World's Greatest Movie Stars & Their Films. (Illus.). 1979. 24.95 o.p. (ISBN 0-517-53714-1, Dist. by Crown); pap. 9.95 o.p. (ISBN 0-517-53715-X). Crown.
Wiatr, Jerzy J., ed. State of Sociology in Eastern Europe Today. LC 70-93888. (Perspectives in Sociology Ser.). 298p. 1971. 9.95x o.p. (ISBN 0-8093-0424-4). S Ill U Pr.
Wiatrowski, Claude A. & House, Charles H. Logic Circuits & Microcomputer Systems. Cerra, Frank J., ed. (McGraw-Hill Series in Electrical Engineering: Computer Engineering & Switching Theory-Electronics & Electronic Circuits). (Illus.). 512p. 1980. text ed. 33.95 (ISBN 0-07-070090-7); solns. manual 15.00 (ISBN 0-07-070091-5). McGraw.
Wibberley, Leonard. Little League Family. LC 77-12887. (gr. 3-5). 1978. 6.95 (ISBN 0-385-12873-8); PLB o.p. (ISBN 0-385-12874-6). Doubleday.
Wibberly, Leonard. Voyage by Bus. 1971. 5.95 o.p. (ISBN 0-688-02716-4). Morrow.
Wibe, Soren, jt. ed. see Puu, Tonn.
Wiberg, Donald M. State Space & Linear Systems. (Schaum Outline Ser). 1971. pap. 8.95 (ISBN 0-07-070096-6, SP). McGraw.
Wiberg, E. & Amberger, E. Hydrides of the Elements of Main Groups, 1-4. 1971. 141.50 (ISBN 0-444-40807-X). Elsevier.
Wicander, E. Reed, jt. auth. see Dietrich, R. V.
Wichern, Dean W., jt. auth. see Johnson, Richard A.
Wichman, Juliet R., jt. auth. see Cole, Dora J.
Wichmann, Rudolf, tr. see Luxemburg, Rosa & Bukharin, Nikolai.
Wichterle, I., et al. Vapor-Liquid Equilibrium Data Bibliography: Supplement II, 1979. LC 79-109407. 286p. 1979. 95.75 (ISBN 0-444-41822-9). Elsevier.
Wichterle, I., et al, eds. Vapor Liquid Equilibrum Data Bibliography. 1973. 95.75 (ISBN 0-444-41161-5). Elsevier.

Wichterlie, I., et al. Vapor-Liquid Equilibrium Data Bibliography: Supplement 1. 1982. 100.00 (ISBN 0-444-41464-9). Elsevier.

Wick, Alexander, jt. auth. see Dolphin, David.

Wick, Wendy C. George Washington, an American Icon: The Eighteenth-Century Graphic Portraits. LC 81-607889. (Illus.). 186p. 1982. 17.50x (ISBN 0-86528-015-0); pap. 9.95x (ISBN 0-86528-014-2). U Pr of Va.

Wicka, Donna K. & Falk, Mervyn L. Advice to Parents of a Cleft Palate Child. 2nd ed. 80p. 1982. 10.75x (ISBN 0-398-04704-9). C C Thomas.

Wickelgren, Wayne A. Cognitive Psychology. (Illus.). 1979. ref. ed. 23.95 (ISBN 0-13-139543-2). P-H.

--Learning & Memory. (Experimental Psychology Ser.). 1977. 23.95 (ISBN 0-13-527663-2). P-H.

Wickens. Beginners Guide to Spinning. 1982. text ed. 9.95 (ISBN 0-408-00573-4). Butterworth.

Wickens, Elaine, jt. auth. see Cannon, Calvin.

Wickens, G. M. Arabic Grammar. LC 77-82523. 180p. 1980. 32.50 (ISBN 0-521-21885-3); pap. 13.95 (ISBN 0-521-29301-4). Cambridge U Pr.

Wickens, M. R., jt. auth. see Phillips, P. C. B.

Wickens, Paul A. Christ Denied. 49p. 1982. pap. 1.25 (ISBN 0-686-81637-4). TAN Bks Pubs.

Wicker, Allan W. An Introduction to Ecological Psychology. 300p. 1983. pap. text ed. 12.95x (ISBN 0-8290-1291-5). Irvington.

Wickersham Commission - National Commission On Law Observance And Enforcement. Wickersham Commission, National Commission on Law Observance & Enforcement: Complete Reports, Including the Mooney-Billings Report, 14 Vols. LC 68-55277. (Criminology, Law Enforcement, & Social Problems Ser.: No. 6). (Illus.). 1968. Repr. of 1931 ed. 250.00x (ISBN 0-87585-006-5). Patterson Smith.

Wickersham, Cornelius W. & Montague, Gilbert H., eds. Olive Branch: Petition of the American Congress to George Third, 1775, & the Letters of the American Envoys, August-September, 1775. 1954. 10.00 o.p. (ISBN 0-87104-139-1); pap. 5.00 o.p. (ISBN 0-87104-138-3). NY Pub Lib.

Wickert, Maria. Studies in John Gower. Meindl, Robert J., tr. LC 81-40128. 264p. (Orig., Ger.). 1982. lib. bdg. 21.25 (ISBN 0-8191-1992-X); pap. text ed. 10.25 (ISBN 0-8191-1993-8). U Pr of Amer.

Wickes, George. The Amazon of Letters: The Life & Loves of Natalie Barney. LC 76-17302. (Illus.). 1976. 10.00 o.p. (ISBN 0-399-11864-0). Putnam Pub Group.

Wickett, Ann, jt. auth. see Humphry, Derek.

Wickey, J. W. Matropolitan Transportation Planning. 2nd ed. 1983. write for info. (ISBN 0-07-016816-4); solns. manual avail. (ISBN 0-07-016817-2). McGraw.

Wickham, Cnythia. Common Plants As Natural Remedies. (Illus.). 144p. 1983. pap. 9.95 (ISBN 0-584-11030-8, Pub by Salem Hse Ltd). Merrimack Bk Serv.

Wickham, Cynthia. The Indoor Garden: The House Plant Lover's Complete Companion. LC 77-62. (Illus.). 256p. 1977. 17.50 o.s.i. (ISBN 0-89104-073-0). A & W Pubs.

Wickham, E. C., ed. see Horace.

Wickham, Glynne. The Medieval Theatre. LC 74-82174. 1974. 18.95 o.p. (ISBN 0-312-52815-9). St Martin.

Wickham, Hilary & Wickham, K. J. Motor Boating: A Practical Handbook. (Illus.). 224p. 1976. 14.00 o.s.i. (ISBN 0-370-10347-5); pap. 10.50 o.s.i. (ISBN 0-370-10348-3). Transatlantic.

Wickham, K. J., jt. auth. see Wickham, Hilary.

Wickins, P. L. The Industrial & Commercial Workers' Union of Africa. (Illus.). 1978. 18.95x o.p. (ISBN 0-19-570124-0). Oxford U Pr.

Wicklein, John. Electronic Nightmare. 282p. 1981. 14.95 (ISBN 0-686-98118-9). Telecom Lib.

Wickler, Wolfgang. The Marine Aquarium. Vevers, Gwynne, tr. from Ger. (Illus.). 178p. (Orig.). 1973. pap. 9.95 (ISBN 0-87666-784-1, PS-695). TFH Pubns.

--Mimicry in Plants & Animals. (Illus., Orig.). 1968. pap. text ed. 3.95 (ISBN 0-07-070100-8, SP). McGraw.

Wicklund, Millie M. Hallmark Piece or, The Suicide Book. 48p. (Orig.). 1983. 8.00 (ISBN 0-930012-27-5). Mudborn.

Wicklund, R. A. & Brehm, J. W. Perspectives on Cognitive Dissonance. LC 75-43699. 1976. 16.50x o.s.i. (ISBN 0-470-15008-4). Halsted Pr.

Wicklund, R. A. & Gollwitzer, P. M. Symbolic Self Completion. 256p. 1982. text ed. 24.95 (ISBN 0-89859-213-5). L Erlbaum Assocs.

Wicklund, Robert A. Freedom & Reactance. LC 74-4004. 205p. 1974. text ed. 24.95 (ISBN 0-89859-295-X). L Erlbaum Assocs.

Wicklund, Robert A., jt. auth. see West, Stephen G.

Wickman, Peter & Whitten, Philip. Readings in Criminology. 1978. pap. text ed. 13.95 (ISBN 0-669-01534-2). Heath.

Wickman, Peter M. & Dailey, Timothy E. White-Collar & Economic Crime: Multidisciplinary & Cross-National Perspectives. LC 81-47561. 304p. 1981. 25.95x (ISBN 0-669-04665-5). Lexington Bks.

Wickramasinghe, C., jt. auth. see Hoyle, Fred.

Wickramasinghe, Chandra, jt. auth. see Hoyle, Fred.

Wickramasinghe, Priya. Spicy & Delicious: Exotic & Tasty Recipes from India & Sri Lanka. 166p. 1979. 12.00x o.p. (ISBN 0-460-04390-0, Pub. by J. M. Dent England). Biblio Dist.

Wickremaratne, L. A. Genesis of an Orientalist. 1983. 17.50x (ISBN 0-8364-0867-5). South Asia Bks.

Wicks, Keith. Stars & Planets. (gr. 2-4). 1980. PLB 6.90 o.p. (ISBN 0-531-03247-7). Watts.

Wicks, Laurel A. Brusbuns & Other High Altitude Delights. (Illus.). 120p. 1981. write for info. Wicks L A.

Wicks, Malcolm. Old & Cold: Hypothermia & Social Policy. LC 78-321889. (Studies in Social Policy & Welfare). 1978. text ed. 20.00x (ISBN 0-435-82939-4). Heinemann Ed.

Wicks, R. J., jt. auth. see Edelstein, C. D.

Wicks, Robert G. & Keough, Lawrence. Society, Systems & Man: Selections for Reading & Composition. LC 75-161496. 1972. text ed. 14.50x (ISBN 0-673-15730-X). Scott F.

Wicks, Robert J. Applied Psychology for Law Enforcement & Correction Officers. 192p. 1973. pap. text ed. 17.95 (ISBN 0-07-070103-2, G). McGraw.

--Christian Introspection: Self-Ministry Through Self-Understanding. 128p. 1983. pap. 7.95 (ISBN 0-8245-0583-2). Crossroad NY.

--Counseling Strategies & Intervention Techniques for the Human Services. LC 76-55408. 1977. pap. text ed. 8.95 scp o.p. (ISBN 0-397-47365-6, HarpC). Har-Row.

--Helping Others: Ways of Listening, Sharing & Counseling. 1982. 14.95 (ISBN 0-89876-040-2). Gardner Pr.

Wicks, Robert J. & Josephs, Ernest H., Jr. Practical Psychology of Leadership for Criminal Justice Officers: A Basic Programmed Text. 128p. 1973. spiral 8.75x (ISBN 0-398-02783-8). C C Thomas.

Wicks, Robert J. & Cooper, H. H. C., eds. International Corrections. LC 77-8721. 208p. 1979. 22.95x (ISBN 0-669-01638-1). Lexington Bks.

Wickstead, John H. Marine Zooplankton. (Studies in Biology: No. 62). 64p. 1976. pap. text ed. 8.95 (ISBN 0-7131-2549-7). E Arnold.

Wicksteed, Phillip H., tr. see Reville, Albert.

Wickstrom, Lois, ed. see Joseph, Alaine, et al.

Wickstrom, Lois, ed. see Kidwell, Connie, et al.

Wickstrom, Ralph L. Fundamental Motor Patterns. 3rd ed. LC 82-21659. (Illus.). 250p. 1983. text ed. price not set (ISBN 0-8121-0879-5). Lea & Febiger.

Wickwar, J. W. Witchcraft & the Black Art: A Book Dealing with the Psychology & Folklore of the Witches. LC 71-151817. 1971. Repr. of 1925 ed. 42.00x (ISBN 0-8103-3692-8). Gale.

Widdemer, Mabel C. Washington Irving: Boy of Old New York. LC 62-16619. (Childhood of Famous Americans Ser.). (Illus.). (gr. 3-7). 1946. 3.95 o.p. (ISBN 0-672-50183-X). Bobbs.

Widder, D. V. The Heat Equation. (Pure & Applied Mathematics Ser.). 1975. 46.50 (ISBN 0-12-748540-6). Acad Pr.

--Transform Theory. (Pure & Applied Mathematics Ser.: Vol. 42). 1971. 51.00 (ISBN 0-12-748550-3). Acad Pr.

Widdows, Richard E. General Biology Laboratory Manual. 2nd ed. 1978. pap. text ed. 12.95 (ISBN 0-8403-1803-0). Kendall-Hunt.

Widdowson, Gregory C. An Outline of Lay Sanctity. LC 79-84532. 1979. pap. 2.95 o.p. (ISBN 0-87973-737-9). Our Sunday Visitor.

Widdowson, H. G. Discovering Discourse. (Orig.). 1979. pap. text ed. 8.95x (ISBN 0-19-451355-6); tchr's ed. 11.50x (ISBN 0-19-451356-4). Oxford U Pr.

--Explorations in Applied Linguistics. 1979. pap. text ed. 11.95x (ISBN 0-19-437080-1). Oxford U Pr.

--Teaching Language As Communication. 1978. pap. text ed. 11.00x (ISBN 0-19-437077-1). Oxford U Pr.

Widdowson, H. G., jt. auth. see Allen, J. P.

Widdowson, H. G., ed. Exploring Funcions. (Reading & Thinking in English Ser.). 1979. pap. text ed. 8.95x (ISBN 0-19-451353-X); tchr's. ed. 11.50x (ISBN 0-19-451354-8). Oxford U Pr.

--Reading & Thinking in English: Concepts in Use. (Reading & Thinking in English Ser.). (Illus.). 89p. 1980. pap. text ed. 8.95x (ISBN 0-19-451351-3); tchr's ed. 11.50x (ISBN 0-19-451352-1). Oxford U Pr.

--Reading & Thinking in English: Discourse in Action. (Reading & Thinking in English Ser.). (Illus.). 128p. 1980. pap. 8.95x (ISBN 0-19-451357-2); 11.50x (ISBN 0-19-451358-0). Oxford U Pr.

Widdowson, P. E. M. Forster's Howards End: Fiction as History. 15.00x (ISBN 0-686-96999-5, Pub. by Scottish Academic Pr Scotland). State Mutual Bk.

Widdowson, Peter. E. M. Forster's Howards End: Fiction As History. (Text & Context Ser.). 1977. pap. text ed. 8.75x (ISBN 0-85621-068-4); pap. text ed. 4.50x o. p. (ISBN 0-85621-067-6). Humanities.

Widdowson, Peter, ed. Re-Reading English. 1982. 16.95x (ISBN 0-416-74700-0); pap. 8.95x (ISBN 0-416-31150-4). Methuen Inc.

Widdowson, Rosalind. Joy of Yoga. LC 82-45874. (Illus.). 96p. 1983. pap. 9.95 (ISBN 0-385-19006-9, Dolp). Doubleday.

Wideman, Charles J. & Gehlen, Sr. Raphaelis. The Biological World. 3.00 o.p. (ISBN 0-8294-0216-0). Loyola.

Wideman, John E. Sent for You Yesterday. 208p. pap. 3.50 (ISBN 0-380-82644-5, Bard). Avon.

Widenor, William C. Henry Cabot Lodge & the Search for an American Foreign Policy. 1980. 24.50x (ISBN 0-520-03778-2). U of Cal Pr.

--Henry Cabot Lodge & the Search for an American Foreign Policy. (Illus.). 402p. 1983. pap. 8.95 (ISBN 0-520-04962-4, CAL 631). U of Cal Pr.

Widera, G. E. O., ed. Pressure Vessel Design. (PVP: Vol. 57). 217p. 1982. 44.00 (H00214). ASME.

Widick, B. J., jt. auth. see Howe, I.

Widiss, Alan I., ed. Arbitration: Commercial Disputes, Insurance, & Tort Claims. LC 79-89068. 1979. text ed. 25.00 (ISBN 0-686-58546-1, A1-1271). PLI.

Widiss, Alan I., et al. No-Fault Automobile Insurance in Action. 1977. 24.00 (ISBN 0-379-00391-0). Oceana.

Widler, Robert L. Reflections of Leisure: A Tribute. 96p. 1980. 4.95 (ISBN 0-686-84026-7); autographed ed. 15.00 (ISBN 0-686-84027-5). U OR Ctr Leisure.

Widman, Lisle. The Making of International Monetary Policy. 272p. 1982. 30.00 (ISBN 0-935328-14-9). Intl Law Inst.

Widmann, Frances K. Clinical Interpretation of Laboratory Tests. 9th ed. LC 82-14927. (Illus.). 605p. 1983. pap. text ed. 18.95 (ISBN 0-8036-9323-0). Davis Co.

Widmann, Frances K., ed. Technical Manual. 8th ed. 442p. 1981. 26.00 (ISBN 0-397-57113-5). Am Assn Blood.

Widmer, Kingsley. Henry Miller. (United States Authors Ser.). 1963. lib. bdg. 12.95 (ISBN 0-8057-0504-X, Twayne). G K Hall.

--Nathaniel West. (United States Author Ser.). 1982. lib. bdg. 11.95 (ISBN 0-8057-7356-8, Twayne). G K Hall.

--Paul Goodman. (United States Author Ser.). 1980. lib. bdg. 12.95 (ISBN 0-8057-7292-8, Twayne). G K Hall.

Widmer, Patricia P. Pat Widmer's Dog Training Book. 1980. pap. 2.95 (ISBN 0-451-12102-3, AE2102, Sig). NAL.

Widom, B., jt. auth. see Rowlinson, J. S.

Widutis, Florence. The Person & the Planet: A Problems Course (a Curriculum & Teaching Manual) 48p. (gr. 11-12). Date not set. pap. cancelled o.s.i. (ISBN 0-8283-1747-X). Branden.

Wiebe, Ronald W. & Rowlison, Bruce A. Let's Talk About Church Staff Relationships. 64p. 1983. pap. 3.95 (ISBN 0-938462-12-1). Green Leaf CA.

Wiebenson, Dora, ed. Architectural Theory & Practice from Alberti to Ledoux. 140p. 1982. 25.00 (ISBN 0-686-97825-0, 89573-4). U of Chicago Pr.

Wiebers, Jacob & Rogers, Wallace. Essential Human Anatomy & Physiology: Study Guide. 2nd ed. 1980. pap. text ed. 9.95x (ISBN 0-673-15323-1). Scott F.

Wiecek, William M., jt. auth. see Hyman, Harold M.

Wiechers, G., jt. ed. see Jackson, H. L.

Wiechmann, Ulrich E. Marketing Management in Multinational Firms: The Consumer Packaged Goods Industry. LC 75-19831. (Special Studies). 1976. text ed. 26.95 o.p. (ISBN 0-275-55850-9). Praeger.

Wieck, Fred, tr. see Volker, Klaus.

Wieck, Lynn, jt. auth. see King, Eunice M.

Wieckert, Jeanne E. & Bell, Irene W. Media-Classroom Skills: Games for the Middle School, Vol. 1. LC 81-2304. (Illus.). 250p. 1981. lib. bdg. 18.50 (ISBN 0-87287-227-0). Libs Unl.

--Media-Classroom Skills: Games for the Middle School, Vol. 2. LC 81-2304. (Illus.). 286p. 1981. lib. bdg. 18.50 (ISBN 0-87287-236-X). Libs Unl.

Wieczorek & Natapoff. A Conceptual Approach to the Nursing of Children: Health Care from Birth Through Adolescence. text ed. 32.50 (ISBN 0-686-97973-7, Lippincott Nursing). Lippincott.

Wieczynski, Joseph L. Modern Encyclopedia of Russian & Soviet History: Mersh, Vols. 6 & 7. 1978. 32.00 ea. (ISBN 0-87569-064-5). Academic Intl.

--Modern Encyclopedia of Russian & Soviet History. (MERSH: Vol. 2, 23, 24, 25, 26, 27, 28, 29, 30). 32.00 ea. Academic Intl.

Wieczynski, Joseph L., ed. The Modern Encyclopedia of Russian & Soviet History: Mersh. Incl. Vol. 1, 4 (ISBN 0-87569-064-5); Vol. 3 (ISBN 0-87569-064-5); Vol. 5. 1977; Vol. 19. 1980. 32.00 (ISBN 0-87569-064-5); Weber, Harry B., ed. 1980. 32.00 (ISBN 0-87569-038-6). 31.50 ea. Academic Intl.

--Modern Encyclopedia of Russian & Soviet History: Mersh, Vol. 8. 1978. 32.00 ea. Academic Intl.

--Modern Encyclopedia of Russian & Soviet History: Mersh, 50 vols, Vols. 9, 10 & 11. 1979. 32.00 ea. Academic Intl.

--Modern Encyclopedia of Russian & Soviet History: Mersh, Vols. 12-13. 1979. 32.00 ea. Academic Intl.

--Modern Encyclopedia of Russian & Soviet History: Mersh, Vols. 14, 32.00 ea.; Vols. 15,16,17,18. 1980 32.00 ea. Academic Intl.

--Modern Encyclopedia of Russian & Soviet History: Mersh, Vols. 19, 20, 21, & 22. 32.00 ea. Academic Intl.

Wied, George. Introduction to Quantitative Cytochemistry. 1966. 75.00 (ISBN 0-12-748850-2). Acad Pr.

Wied, George & Bahr, Gunter F. Introduction to Quantitative Cytochemistry, 2. 1970. 72.00 (ISBN 0-12-748852-9). Acad Pr.

Wiedel, Janine. Looking at Iran. LC 78-6038. (Looking at Other Countries Ser.). (Illus.). (gr. 4-7). 1979. 10.53i (ISBN 0-397-31797-2, HarpJ). Har-Row.

Wiedeman, Varley E., jt. auth. see Graham, Julia B.

Wiedemann, Hans G. Thermal Analysis. Vol. I: Theory Instrumentation-Applied Sciences Industrial-Applications. 628p. 1980. 95.00x (ISBN 3-7643-1085-5). Birkhauser.

Wiedemer, John. Handbook for Real Estate Investors. 1982. text ed. cancelled (ISBN 0-8359-2758-X). Reston.

--Real Estate Investment. (Illus.). 1979. text ed. 19.95 o.p. (ISBN 0-87909-718-3); instrs'. manual avail. o.p. (ISBN 0-8359-7184-8). Reston.

Wiedemer, John P. Real Estate Finance. 3rd ed. (Illus.). 384p. 1980. text ed. 19.95 (ISBN 0-8359-6522-8); instrs' package incl. (ISBN 0-8359-6523-6). Reston.

Wiedenbach, Ernestine. Family-Centered Maternity Nursing. 2nd ed. (Illus.). 1967. 7.95 o.p. (ISBN 0-399-40011-7). Putnam Pub Group.

Wiedenhofer, Maggie. A History of Port Arthur. (Illus.). 1982. 32.50x (ISBN 0-686-98393-9). Oxford U Pr.

Wieder, Charles. Fear & Force Versus Education. LC 77-11235. 1978. pap. 4.95 o.s.i. (ISBN 0-8283-1706-2). Branden.

Wieder, H. H. Laboratory Notes on Electrical & Galvano-Magnetic Measurements. (Materials Science Monographs: Vol. 2). 1979. 53.25 (ISBN 0-444-41763-X). Elsevier.

Wieder, Laurance. Man's Best Friend. (Illus.). 64p. 1982. pap. 12.95 (ISBN 0-8109-2266-5). Abrams.

Wieder, Laurence. The Coronet of Tours. 74p. 1972. 2.95 o.p. (ISBN 0-87886-018-5). Ithaca Hse.

Wieder, Sol. The Foundations of Quantum Theory. 1973. text ed. 27.00 o.s.i. (ISBN 0-12-749050-7). Acad Pr.

--An Introduction to Solar Energy for Scientists & Engineers. LC 81-13014. 301p. 1982. text ed. 25.95x (ISBN 0-471-06048-8). Wiley.

Wiederanders, Rex E. & Addeo, Edmond G. Biotonics: Stamina Through Six-Second Exercises That Really Work. LC 77-8208. (Funk & W Bk.). (Illus.). 1977. 7.95i o.p. (ISBN 0-308-10332-7). T Y Crowell.

Wiederhold, Gio. Database Design. 2nd ed. Munson, Eric, ed. (Computer Science Ser.). (Illus.). 784p. 1983. text ed. 32.00 (ISBN 0-07-070132-6, C). McGraw.

Wiederholt, J. Lee & Hammill, Donald D. The Resource Teacher: A Guide to Effective Practices. 2nd ed. (Illus.). 400p. 1983. pap. text ed. price not set (ISBN 0-936104-33-3, 0085). Pro Ed.

Wiederholt, Wigbert C. Therapy for Neurologic Disorders. LC 81-14768. 437p. 1982. 45.00 (ISBN 0-471-09508-7, Pub. by Wiley Med). Wiley.

Wiederholt, Wigbert C., ed. Neurology for Non-Neurologists. LC 82-3995. 1982. 37.50 (ISBN 0-12-788925-6). Acad Pr.

Wiederman, Mary P., ed. Microcirculation. LC 73-22327. (Benchmark Papers in Human Physiology Ser.). 448p. 1974. 55.50 (ISBN 0-12-787760-6). Acad Pr.

Wiefels, H., ed. Analysis, Design, & Evaluation of Man-Machine Systems: Proceedings of the IFAC-IFIP-IEA-IFORS Symposium, Baden-Baden, FR Germany, 27-29 September 1982. (IFAC Proceedings Ser.). 550p. 1983. 137.00 (ISBN 0-08-029348-4). Pergamon.

Wiegand, G. Carl, ed. The Menace of Inflation: Its Causes & Consequences. 1976. pap. 8.95 (ISBN 0-8159-6215-0). Devin.

Wiegel, R. L., ed. Directional Wave Spectra Applications. LC 82-70873. 512p. 1982. pap. text ed. 36.00 (ISBN 0-87262-303-3). Am Soc Civil Eng.

Wiegel, Robert L. Oceanographical Engineering. 1964. ref. ed. 41.95 (ISBN 0-13-629600-9). P-H.

Wiegel, Robert L., et al. Earthquake Engineering. (Civil Engineering Ser). 1969. ref. ed. 41.95 (ISBN 0-13-222646-4). P-H.

Wiegele, Thomas C., ed. Biology & the Social Sciences: An Emerging Revolution. 300p. (Orig.). 1981. lib. bdg. 32.50 (ISBN 0-86531-201-X); pap. 15.00 (ISBN 0-86531-202-8). Westview.

Wieger, L. Chinese Characters, Their Origin, Etymology, History, Classification & Signification. 2nd ed. Davrout, L., tr. 1927. pap. 12.50 (ISBN 0-486-21321-8). Dover.

Wiegert, Richard G., ed. Ecological Energetics. LC 75-30762. (Benchmark Papers in Ecology: Vol. 4). 448p. 1976. 52.50 (ISBN 0-12-787763-0). Acad Pr.

Wiegner, Kathleen. Encounters. 1972. pap. 3.00 (ISBN 0-87924-019-9). Membrane Pr.

Wiehler, G. Magnetic Peripheral Data Storage: Programmed Introduction. 29.95 (ISBN 0-471-26084-3, Wiley Heyden). Wiley.

Wieland, Heinrich. On the Mechanism of Oxidation. 1932. text ed. 42.50x (ISBN 0-686-83656-1). Elliots Bks.

Wielert, Marna S. Amour: Poems. 1979. 4.95 o.p. (ISBN 0-533-03816-2). Vantage.

Wielgus, Chuck, Jr. & Wolff, Alex. The In-Your-Face Basketball Book. LC 79-92194. (Illus.). 1980. 11.95 (ISBN 0-89696-067-6, An Everest House Book); pap. 7.95 (ISBN 0-89696-081-1). Dodd.

Wieman, Henry N. Religious Experience & Scientific Method. Repr. of 1926 ed. lib. bdg. 18.50x (ISBN 0-8371-4368-3, WIRE). Greenwood.

--Source of Human Good. LC 63-2226. 318p. 1964. lib. bdg. 10.95x o.p. (ISBN 0-8093-0116-4). S Ill U Pr.

Wiemann, John M. & Harrison, Randall P., eds. Nonverbal Interaction. (Sage Annual Reviews of Communication Research: Vol. 11). (Illus.). 320p. 1983. 25.00 (ISBN 0-8039-1930-1); pap. 12.50 (ISBN 0-8039-1931-X). Sage.

Wieme. Agar Gel Electophoresis. 1960. 22.10 (ISBN 0-444-40638-7). Elsevier.

Wien, Carol A. The Great American Log Cabin Quilt Book. (Illus.). 128p. 1973. 23.75 (ISBN 0-525-93205-4, 02306-690); pap. 13.50 (ISBN 0-525-47673-3, 01311-390). Dutton.

Wienbeck, Martin, ed. Motility of the Digestive Tract. 636p. 1982. text ed. 75.50 (ISBN 0-89004-806-1). Raven.

Wiener & Bazerman. Writing Skills Handbook. 1982. pap. text ed. 7.95 (ISBN 0-686-84586-2). HM.

Wiener, Frederick B. Briefing & Arguing Federal Appeals. rev. ed. LC 61-10553. 544p. 1967. 20.00 (ISBN 0-87179-096-3). BNA.

Wiener, Harvey & Bazerman, Charles. Reading Skills Handbook. 2nd ed. 11.50 (ISBN 0-395-31710-X); 1.00 (ISBN 0-395-31711-8). HM.

Wiener, Harvey S. Creating Compositions. 3rd ed. Butcher, Phillip A., ed. (Illus.). 448p. 1981. pap. text ed. 13.95x (ISBN 0-07-070160-1, C); instr's. manual 10.00x (ISBN 0-07-070161-X). McGraw.

Wiener, Harvey S. & Bazerman, Charles. English Skills Handbook: Reading & Writing. LC 76-14015. (Illus.). 1977. pap. text ed. 11.50 o.p. (ISBN 0-395-20595-6); manual 1.00instr's. o.p. (ISBN 0-395-20669-3). HM.

--Writing Skills Handbook. LC 82-83202. 144p. 1982. pap. text ed. 5.95 (ISBN 0-395-32588-9). HM.

Wiener, Harvey S., jt. auth. see Muller, Gilbert H.

Wiener, Joel H. Radicalism & Freethought in Nineteenth-Century Britain: The Life of Richard Carlile. LC 82-6168. (Contributions in Labor History Ser.: No. 13). 288p. 1983. lib. bdg. 29.95 (ISBN 0-313-23532-5, WRD/). Greenwood.

Wiener, M., et al. Clinical Pharmacology & Therapeutics in Nursing. 1979. text ed. 32.50 (ISBN 0-07-070138-5, HP); instructor's manual 9.95 (ISBN 0-07-070139-3). McGraw.

Wiener, Martin. English Culture & the Decline of the Industrial Spirit, 1850-1980. LC 80-22684. (Illus.). 256p. 1981. 18.95 (ISBN 0-521-23418-2); pap. 7.95 (ISBN 0-521-27034-0). Cambridge U Pr.

Wiener, Matthew B., jt. auth. see Romano, Joseph A.

Wiener, Norbert. Cybernetics, or Control & Communication in the Animal & the Machine. 2nd ed. (Illus., Orig.). 1961. 20.00x (ISBN 0-262-23007-0); pap. 6.95 (ISBN 0-262-73009-X). MIT Pr.

--God & Golem, Inc. A Comment on Certain Points Where Cybernetics Impinges on Religion. 1964. 11.00x o.p. (ISBN 0-262-23009-7); pap. 4.95 (ISBN 0-262-73011-1). MIT Pr.

--I Am a Mathematician. 1964. 12.00x o.p. (ISBN 0-262-23075-5); pap. 6.95 (ISBN 0-262-73007-3). MIT Pr.

--Norbert Wiener: Collected Works: Vol. 3: The Hopf-Wiener Integral Equation; Prediction & Filtering; Quantum Mechanics & Relativity; Miscellaneous Mathematical Papers. Masani, P., ed. (Mathematicians of Our Time Ser.). (Illus.). 800p. 1982. 50.00x (ISBN 0-262-23107-7). MIT Pr.

--Time Series. 1964. pap. 8.95x (ISBN 0-262-73005-7). MIT Pr.

Wiener, Norbert & Schade, J. P. Progress in Biocybernetics, 3 vols. Incl. Vol. 1. 20.75 (ISBN 0-444-40639-5); Vol. 2. 19.25 (ISBN 0-444-40640-9); Vol. 3. 22.00 (ISBN 0-444-40641-7). 1964-66. Elsevier.

Wiener, Philip P. Evolution & the Founders of Pragmatism. 9.00 (ISBN 0-8446-0964-1). Peter Smith.

Wiener, Philip P. & Fisher, John, eds. Violence & Aggression in the History of Ideas. 288p. 1974. pap. 22.50x (ISBN 0-8135-0772-3). Rutgers U Pr.

Wiener, Philip P., ed. see Nakamura, Hajime.

Wiener, R. & Christian, R. Insolvency Accounting. new ed. 1977. 29.95 (ISBN 0-07-070135-0, P&RB). McGraw.

Wiener, Solomon. Questions & Answers on American Citizenship. (gr. 9-12). 1982. pap. text ed. 3.95 (ISBN 0-88345-485-8, 21244). Regents Pub.

Wiener, Solomon, et al. Marketing & Advertising Careers. (Career Concise Guides Ser). (Illus.). (gr. 7 up). 1977. PLB 8.90 (ISBN 0-531-01307-3). Watts.

Wiengartner, Ronald, ed. see Kinsman, Barbara.

Wieniewa, Celina, tr. see Milosz, Czeslaw.

Wieniewska, Celina, tr. see Szczypiorski, Andrzej.

Wier, Delight B. I Married a Farmer. 1974. pap. 3.00 o.p. (ISBN 0-87069-266-6). Wallace-Homestead.

Wier, John S. The Tyranny of Fear. LC 79-63153. 1979. 6.95 o.p. (ISBN 0-533-04247-X). Vantage.

Wiernik, Peter H. Controversies in Oncology. LC 81-11420. 415p. 1982. 40.00 (ISBN 0-471-05925-0, Pub. by Wiley Med). Wiley.

--Supportive Care of the Cancer Patient. LC 82-71817. (Illus.). 320p. 1982. 37.50 (ISBN 0-87993-182-5). Futura Pub.

Wiersbe, David & Wiersbe, Warren. Making Sense of the Ministry. 128p. (Orig.). 1983. pap. 5.95 (ISBN 0-686-82021-5). Moody.

Wiersbe, W. Best of A.W. Tozer. 249p. 1979. 8.25 (ISBN 0-87509-180-6); pap. 3.50 (ISBN 0-87509-182-2). Chr Pubns.

Wiersbe, Warren. The Annotated Pilgrim's Progress. LC 80-427. 1980. 8.95 (ISBN 0-8024-0229-1). Moody.

--Be Challenged! rev. ed. LC 82-12404. Orig. Title: Be a Real Teen. 1982. pap. 3.95 (ISBN 0-8024-1080-4). Moody.

--Be Complete. 160p. 1981. pap. 4.50 (ISBN 0-88207-257-9). Victor Bks.

--Five Secrets of Living. 1978. pap. 2.50 (ISBN 0-8423-0870-9). Tyndale.

--Live Like a King. 1976. 4.95 (ISBN 0-8024-4908-5); pap. 5.95 (ISBN 0-8024-4907-7). Moody.

--Meet Your King. 1980. pap. 5.95 (ISBN 0-88207-799-6). Victor Bks.

--The Strategy of Satan. 1979. 2.95 (ISBN 0-8423-6665-2). Tyndale.

--Thoughts for Men on the Move. 1970. pap. 2.95 (ISBN 0-8024-0132-5). Moody.

Wiersbe, Warren, jt. auth. see Wiersbe, David.

Wiersbe, Warren W. Be a Real Teen. 128p. (Orig.). (YA) 1971. pap. 2.50 o.p. (ISBN 0-8024-6047-X). Moody.

--Be Confident. 176p. 1982. pap. 4.50 (ISBN 0-88207-269-2). Victor Bks.

--Be Faithful. 1981. pap. 4.50 (ISBN 0-88207-268-4). Victor Bks.

--Be Free. 160p. 1975. pap. 4.50 (ISBN 0-88207-716-3). Victor Bks.

--Be Joyful. LC 74-76328. 1974. pap. 4.50 (ISBN 0-88207-705-8). Victor Bks.

--Be Mature. 1978. pap. 4.50 (ISBN 0-88207-771-6). Victor Bks.

--Be Ready. 1979. pap. 4.50 (ISBN 0-88207-782-1). Victor Bks.

--Be Real. LC 72-77014. 190p. 1972. pap. 4.50 (ISBN 0-88207-046-0). Victor Bks.

--Be Rich. 176p. 1976. pap. 4.50 (ISBN 0-88207-730-9). Victor Bks.

--Be Right. 1977. pap. 4.50 (ISBN 0-88207-729-5). Victor Bks.

--Listen! Jesus Is Praying. 1982. pap. 4.95 (ISBN 0-8423-2167-5). Tyndale.

--Live Like a King: Living the Beatitudes Today. 1977. pap. 3.25 o.p. (ISBN 0-8024-4907-7). Moody.

--Meet Yourself in the Parables. 1979. pap. 4.50 (ISBN 0-88207-790-2). Victor Bks.

--Meet Yourself in the Psalms. 192p. 1983. pap. 4.50 (ISBN 0-88207-740-6). Victor Bks.

Wiersbe, Warren W., jt. auth. see Sugden, Howard F.

Wiershe, Warren. Live Like a King. study ed 7.95 (ISBN 0-8024-4915-8). Moody.

Wiersma, William. Research Methods in Education: An Introduction. 3rd ed. LC 79-91099. 354p. 1980. text ed. 18.95 (ISBN 0-87581-250-3). Peacock Pubs.

Wiersma, William, jt. auth. see Lemke, Elmer.

Wiersma, William, jt. auth. see Hinkle, Dennis E.

Wierwille, Victor P. Christians Should Be Prosperous. pap. 0.50 (ISBN 0-686-76945-7). Am Christian.

--God's Magnified Word. LC 77-87405. (Studies in Abundant Living: Vol. 4). 1977. 4.95 (ISBN 0-910068-14-3). Am Christian.

--The New Dynamic Church. (Studies in Abundant Living: Vol. 2). 242p. 1971. 4.95 (ISBN 0-910068-03-8). Am Christian.

--Power for Abundant Living. 6.95 o.p. (ISBN 0-910068-01-1). Am Christian.

Wiesbecker, Henry, jt. auth. see Cooper, William.

Wieschoff, Heinrich A. Anthropological Bibliography of Negro Africa. 1948. 48.00 (ISBN 0-527-02697-2). Kraus Repr.

Wiese, B. Von see Von Wiese, B.

Wiese, Michael. Film & Video Budgets. 1983. pap. 14.95 (ISBN 0-941188-02-7). M Wiese Film Prod.

Wiesel, Elie. The Accident. 96p. (Orig.). 1982. pap. 2.50 (ISBN 0-553-22688-6). Bantam.

--Dawn. 1973. pap. 2.25 o.p. (ISBN 0-380-01132-8, 52779, Bard). Avon.

--Dawn. 112p. 1982. pap. 2.95 (ISBN 0-553-22536-7). Bantam.

--Five Biblical Portraits. LC 81-40458. vii, 157p. 1983. pap. 4.95 (ISBN 0-268-00962-7, 85-09622). U of Notre Dame Pr.

--A Jew Today. Weisel, Marion, tr. from Fr. LC 79-11251. 1979. pap. 3.95 (ISBN 0-394-74057-2, Vin). Random.

--Legends of Our Time. LC 82-3225. 198p. 1982. pap. 6.95 (ISBN 0-8052-0714-7). Schocken.

--Night. 128p. 1972. pap. 2.25 o.p. (ISBN 0-380-00995-1, 46797, Discus). Avon.

--The Oath. 1974. pap. 2.50 o.p. (ISBN 0-380-00115-2, 36632). Avon.

--One Generation After. LC 82-3226. 198p. 1982. pap. 6.95 (ISBN 0-8052-0713-9). Schocken.

--Somewhere a Master: Further Tales of the Hasidic Masters. 336p. 1982. 15.50 (ISBN 0-671-44170-1). Summit Bks.

--Souls on Fire. 320p. (Orig.). 1982. 17.50 (ISBN 0-671-45210-X); pap. 7.95 (ISBN 0-671-44171-X). Summit Bks.

--Splinters: Words of Anger & Faith. LC 81-85303. 288p. 1982. 12.95 o.p. (ISBN 0-8052-5038-7). Holocaust Lib.

Wiesel, Elie, pref. by. Selected & Annotated Resource List of Materials on the Holocaust. 65p. 5.00 (ISBN 0-686-74934-0). ADL.

Wieselberg, Helen. The Lords of Dair. LC 77-17313. 1978. 8.95 o.p. (ISBN 0-399-12117-X). Putnam Pub Group.

Wiesen, Jeremy L., jt. auth. see Kempin, Frederick G., Jr.

Wiesenfeld, S. L., jt. auth. see Hamrick, Becky.

Wiesenthal, Simon. The Sunflower: With a Symposium. LC 75-35446. 1977. 7.50 (ISBN 0-8052-3612-0); pap. 5.95 (ISBN 0-8052-0578-0). Schocken.

Wieser, Friedrich Von see Von Wieser, Friedrich.

Wieser, J., tr. see Walter, H.

Wiesner, E. & Willer, S. Lexikon der Genetik der Hundekrankheiten. (Illus.). 480p. 1983. 29.50 (ISBN 3-8055-3616-X). S. Karger.

Wiesner, J. Von see Von Wiesner, J. & Von Regel, C.

Wiesner, Jerome B., jt. ed. see Dahl, Norman C.

Wiess, Christine & Hardwick, Ann B. The Complete Calorie-Slim Cookbook. (Illus.). 246p. 1982. pap. 12.00 (ISBN 0-910347-01-8). Chatham Comm Inc.

Wiessman, Ginny & Sanders, Coyne S. The Dick Van Dyke Show. (Illus.). 160p. 1983. 22.50 (ISBN 0-312-19976-7); pap. 9.95 (ISBN 0-312-19977-5). St Martin.

Wiessner, John, Jr. Space Bugs: Earth Invasion. 176p. (gr. 5-8). Date not set. 6.95 (ISBN 0-8059-2856-1). Dorrance.

Wiest, Jerome D. & Levy, Ferdinand K. A Management Guide to PERT-CPM: With Gert-PDM, DCPM & Other Networks. 2nd ed. (Illus.). 1977. ref. ed. 21.00x (ISBN 0-13-549113-4); pap. text ed. 15.95 (ISBN 0-13-549105-3). P-H.

Wiest, Roger J. M. De see Davis, Stanley N. & De Wiest, Roger J. M.

Wigan, Bernard, ed. Liturgy in English. 2nd ed. 1964. 8.95x o.p. (ISBN 0-19-213410-8). Oxford U Pr.

Wigander, K. & Svenson, A. Structured Analysis & Design of Information Systems. 288p. 1983. 29.95 (ISBN 0-07-015061-3, P&RB). McGraw.

Wigderson, Mim. My Four-Legged Kids. 174p. (Orig.). 1982. pap. 7.75 (ISBN 0-937816-20-5). Tech Data.

Wigdor, David. Roscoe Pound. LC 72-852. (Contributions in American History: No. 33). 356p. 1974. lib. bdg. 29.95x (ISBN 0-8371-6419-2, WIP/). Greenwood.

Wigge, B. F. & Wood, M. Payroll Systems & Procedures. 1970. 6.08 (ISBN 0-07-070152-0, G); key 4.25 (ISBN 0-07-070153-9). McGraw.

Wiggert, James M., jt. auth. see Morris, Henry M.

Wiggin, Frances T. Maine Composers & Their Music. 1976. pap. 4.00 o.p. (ISBN 0-915592-26-6). Maine Hist.

Wiggin, Kate D. Birds' Christmas Carol. (Illus.). (gr. 4-6). 8.95 (ISBN 0-395-07205-0); memorial ed. 9.95 (ISBN 0-395-07204-2). HM.

--Rebecca of Sunnybrook Farm. (Thrushwood Bks.). (gr. 7-9). 3.95 o.p. (ISBN 0-448-02527-2, G&D). Putnam Pub Group.

--Rebecca of Sunnybrook Farm. LC 75-32202. (Classics of Children's Literature, 1621-1932: Vol. 63). (Illus.). 1976. Repr. of 1902 ed. PLB 38.00 o.s.i. (ISBN 0-8240-2312-9). Garland Pub.

--Rebecca of Sunnybrook Farm. (Deluxe Illustrated Classics Ser.). 1977. 4.50 (ISBN 0-307-12212-3, Golden Pr). Western Pub.

Wiggin, Maurice. Fly Fishing. (Teach Yourself Ser.). 1974. pap. 4.95 o.s.i. (ISBN 0-679-10430-5). McKay.

--Troubled Waters. 14.50x (ISBN 0-392-06465-0, SpS). Sportshelf.

Wiggins, Arthur W. Physical Science with Environmental Applications. 384p. 1974. text ed. 22.50 (ISBN 0-395-17072-9); instr's manual 1.00 (ISBN 0-395-17852-5); study guide 7.50 (ISBN 0-395-17071-0); Set. 20-35 mm slides 15.95 (ISBN 0-395-18187-9). HM.

Wiggins, James D. & English, Dori. Affective Education: A Methods & Techniques Manual for Growth. 1977. pap. text ed. 8.50 (ISBN 0-8191-0217-2). U Pr of Amer.

Wiggins, Lee M. Panel Analysis: Latent Probability Models for Attitudes & Behavior Processes. Boudon, Raymond & McFarland, David D., eds. LC 72-97441. (Progress in Mathematical Social Sciences Ser.: Vol. 1). 1973. 19.95 (ISBN 0-444-41112-7). Elsevier.

Wiggins, Marianne. Went South. 1980. 9.95 o.s.i. (ISBN 0-440-09420-8). Delacorte.

Wiggins, Norman A., jt. auth. see Stephenson, Gilbert T.

Wiggins, Peter Desa, tr. Satires of Ludovico Ariosto: A Renaissance Autobiography. LC 74-80810. xiv, 187p. 1976. 12.95x (ISBN 0-8214-0171-8, 82-81701). Ohio U Pr.

Wiggins, Ronald L. The Arbitration of Industrial Engineering Disputes. LC 77-106490. 368p. 1970. 17.50 o.p. (ISBN 0-87179-106-4). BNA.

Wigginton, Dave, ed. see Glubetich, Dave.

Wigginton, Eliot, ed. Foxfire Four, Foxfire Five, Foxfire Six. (Illus.). 1520p. 1980. Set. pap. 20.85 boxed set (ISBN 0-385-17215-X, Anch). Doubleday.

Wigginton, Eliot, jt. ed. see Page, Linda.

Wigginton, Eliott. Foxfire Books, Bks. 1-3. (Illus.). 1312p. 1975. Set. pap. 23.85 (ISBN 0-385-11253-X, Anch). Doubleday.

Wigginton, F. P. The Complete Guide to Profitable Real Estate Listings. 141p. 1983. pap. 6.95 (ISBN 0-87094-413-4). Dow Jones-Irwin.

Wigglesworth, V. B. Insect Hormones. rev. ed. Head, J. J., ed. LC 76-62977. (Carolina Biology Readers Ser.). (Illus.). 32p. (gr. 11 up). 1983. pap. 2.00 (ISBN 0-89278-270-6, 45-9670). Carolina Biological.

Wigglesworth, Vincent B. Insect Physiology. 7th ed. 1974. 13.95x (ISBN 0-686-92724-9, Pub. by Chapman & Hall); pap. 11.50x (ISBN 0-686-98600-8). Methuen Inc.

--Principles of Insect Physiology. 7th ed. (Illus.). 1972. 49.95x o.p. (ISBN 0-412-11400-3, Pub. by Chapman & Hall). Methuen Inc.

Wight, D. G. An Atlas of Liver Pathology. (Current Histopathology Ser.: Vol. 3). (Illus.). 199p. 1982. text ed. 55.00 (ISBN 0-85200-205-X, Lippiincott Medical). Lippincott.

Wight, H. & Williamson, D. Preparation for General Chemistry. 1974. 22.00 (ISBN 0-07-070165-2, C). McGraw.

Wight, Martin. The Gold Coast Legislative Council. Perham, Margery, ed. LC 74-14030. (Studies in Colonial Legislatures: Vol. 2). (Illus.). 285p. 1974. Repr. of 1947 ed. lib. bdg. 18.25x (ISBN 0-8371-7783-9, WIGC). Greenwood.

Wight, O. W., ed. & tr. see De Chateaubriand, Francois R.

Wight, O. W., tr. see De Stael.

Wight, R. Icones Planatarum Indiae Orientalis, 6vols. in 3. 1936. 216.00 (ISBN 3-7682-0153-8). Lubrecht & Cramer.

Wightman, A. S. & Sharp, D. H., eds. Local Currents & Their Applications. LC 73-77075. 160p. 1975. pap. 15.00 (ISBN 0-444-10521-2, North-Holland). Elsevier.

Wightman, David. Toward Economic Cooperation in Asia. 1963. 49.50x (ISBN 0-685-69884-X). Elliots Bks.

Wightman, W. P. Science in a Renaissance Society. 1972. text ed. 12.50x (ISBN 0-09-111650-3, Hutchinson U Lib); pap. text ed. 6.50x (ISBN 0-09-111651-1). Humanities.

Wightman, W. R. Forever on the Fringe: Six Studies in the Development of Manitoulin Island. 320p. 1982. 35.00x (ISBN 0-8020-5545-1). U of Toronto Pr.

Wighton, John L. An Experimentation Approach to the Fluids Laboratory: A Lab Manual. LC 78-23968. (Illus.). 224p. 1979. pap. 12.95x (ISBN 0-910554-26-9). Eng Pr.

Wiginton, John C., jt. auth. see Neave, Edwin H.

Wigley, Philip G. Canada and the Transition to Commonwealth: British-Canadian Relations, 1917-1926. LC 76-11095. (Cambridge Commonwealth Ser.). 1977. 44.50 (ISBN 0-521-21157-3). Cambridge U Pr.

Wigley, Richard & Cook, James. Community Health: Concepts & Issues. 1975. pap. text ed. 9.95 (ISBN 0-442-21633-5). Van Nos Reinhold.

Wigmore, Ann. Be Your Own Doctor. 1982. 3.95x o.p. (ISBN 0-89529-193-2). Cancer Control Soc.

--Be Your Own Doctor: A Positive Guide to Natural Living. 2nd ed. 194p. 1983. pap. 3.95 (ISBN 0-686-43188-X). Avery Pub.

--Naturama Living Textbook. (Illus.). 398p. 12.95 (ISBN 0-940312-02-6). Hippocrates.

Wigmore, John H., ed. see Illinois Association For Criminal Justice.

Wignall, H. Hosiery Technology. 12.50x (ISBN 0-87245-382-0). Textile Bk.

Wigner, E. P., jt. ed. see Salam, A.

Wigner, E. P., ed. see Symposia in Applied Mathematics-New York-1959.

Wigner, Eugene P. Symmetries & Reflections. LC 79-89843. 1979. pap. text ed. 10.00 (ISBN 0-918024-16-1). Ox Bow.

Wigner, Eugene P., ed. Dispersion Relations & Their Connection with Causality. (Italian Physical Society Ser.: Course 29). 1964. 56.50 (ISBN 0-12-368829-9). Acad Pr.

Wignjowijoto, Hortojo, jt. auth. see Lindholm, Richard W.

Wihlborg, Clas G., jt. ed. see Levich, Richard M.

Wiig, Elisabeth H. & Semel, Eleanor M. Language Assessment & Intervention for the Learning Disabled. (Special Education Ser.). 464p. 1980. text ed. 22.95 (ISBN 0-675-08180-7). Merrill.

Wiig, Elisabeth H., jt. auth. see Shames, George H.

Wiig, Karl M., jt. auth. see Mansvelt-Beck, Frederick W.

Wiio, Osmo. Information & Communication Systems: An Introduction to the Concepts of Information, Communication, & Communication Research. (Communication & Information Science Ser.). 1983. 21.50x (ISBN 0-89391-070-8). Ablex Pub.

Wiita, Betty S. Dried Flowers for All Seasons. LC 82-2801. 1982. 18.95 (ISBN 0-442-24559-9). Van Nos Reinhold.

Wijesinha, Rajiva. The Androgynous Trollope: Attitudes to Women Amongst Early Victorian Novelists. LC 81-40260. 360p. 1982. lib. bdg. 24.25 (ISBN 0-8191-2060-X); pap. text ed. 13.50 (ISBN 0-8191-2061-8). U Pr of Amer.

Wijnbergen, S. Van. Short-Run Macro-Economic Adjustment Policies in South Korea: A Quantitative Analysis. LC 82-8408. (World Bank Staff Working Papers: No. 510). (Orig.). 1982. pap. 5.00 (ISBN 0-8213-0000-8). World Bank.

Wijngaard, E. H., jt. ed. see De Moor, W.

Wijngaards, John. Handbook to the Gospels: A Guide to the Gospel Writings & the Life & Times of Jesus. (Illus.). 1983. pap. 8.95 (ISBN 0-89283-118-9). Servant.

Wikan, Unni. Life Among the Poor in Cairo. 1980. 25.00x (ISBN 0-422-76970-3, Pub. by Tavistock); pap. 11.95x (ISBN 0-422-76980-0). Methuen Inc.

Wikborg, Eleanor. Carson McCullers' The Member of the Wedding: Aspects of Structure & Style. (Gothenburg Studies in English: No. 31). 200p. 1975. pap. text ed. 18.50x (ISBN 91-7346-005-2). Humanities.

Wike, Victoria S. Kant's Antinomies of Reason: Their Origin & Their Resolution. LC 81-43867. 186p. (Orig.). 1982. lib. bdg. 22.00 (ISBN 0-8191-2345-5); pap. text ed. 10.00 (ISBN 0-8191-2346-3). U Pr of Amer.

Wikesr, Kathleen, ed. Lafile. 2000p. 1983. 34.95 (ISBN 0-911241-03-5). Am Soc Landscape.

Wikler, Lynn, et al. Behavior Modification Parent Group: A Training Manual for Professionals. LC 76-14587. 1976. pap. 9.00x o.p. (ISBN 0-913590-31-2). Slack Inc.

Wikler, Madeline, jt. auth. see Goldstein, Andrew.

Wikler, Madeline, jt. auth. see Saypol, Judyth.

Wikler, Madeline, jt. auth. see Saypol, Judyth R.

Wikoff, Jack. Adirondack Portfolio. (Orig.). 1983. pap. 7.95 (ISBN 0-940170-09-4). Open Bk Pubns.

--Adirondack Portfolio, 2 vols. in 1. Bd. with Penelope. 472p. 1983. 20.00 (ISBN 0-940170-11-6). Open Bk Pubns.

--Adirondack Portfolio. Bd. with Penelope. 232p. 1983. 20.00 (ISBN 0-940170-11-6). Station Hill Pr.

--Adirondack Portfolio. 232p. 1983. pap. 7.95 (ISBN 0-940170-09-4). Station Hill Pr.

--Penelope. 240p. (Orig.). 1983. pap. 7.95 (ISBN 0-940170-10-8). Open Bk Pubns.

--Penelope. 1983. pap. 7.95 (ISBN 0-940170-10-8). Station Hill Pr.

Wikse, John R. About Possession: The Self As Private Property. LC 76-43207. 1977. 16.95x (ISBN 0-271-00502-5). Pa St U Pr.

Wikstrom, Gunnar, Jr. & Wikstrom, Nelson, eds. Municipal Government, Politics, & Policy: A Reader. LC 80-5599. (Illus.). 480p. (Orig.). 1982. lib. bdg. 36.00 (ISBN 0-8191-2195-9); pap. text ed. 20.50 (ISBN 0-8191-2196-7). U Pr of Amer.

Wikstrom, Nelson, jt. ed. see Wikstrom, Gunnar, Jr.

Wiktor. Constitutions of Canada-Federal & Provincial. LC 78-62326. (Binders 1 & 2 avail.). 1978. 225.00 (ISBN 0-379-20303-0). Oceana.

Wiktor, Christian. Unperfected Treaties of the United States of America 1776-1976, 5 vols. LC 76-2647. 1976-80. lib. bdg. 48.00 (ISBN 0-379-00560-3). Oceana.

Wiktor, Christian L., ed. Canadian Bibliography of International Law. 750p. 1983. 75.00x (ISBN 0-8020-5615-6). U of Toronto Pr.

Wilansky, Albert. Modern Methods in Topological Vector Spaces. 1978. text ed. 39.95 (ISBN 0-07-070180-6, C). McGraw.

--Topology for Analysis. LC 81-1616. 1983. Repr. of 1970 ed. write for info. (ISBN 0-89874-343-5). Krieger.

Wilber, C. K. & Jameson, K. P., eds. Socialist Models of Development. 240p. 1982. 40.00 (ISBN 0-08-027921-X). Pergamon.

Wilber, Charles. Political Economy of Development & Underdevelopment. 2nd ed. 1978. pap. text ed. 11.00 (ISBN 0-394-32230-4). Random.

Wilber, Charles G. Turbidity in the Aquatic Environment: An Environmental Factor in Fresh & Oceanic Waters. (Illus.). 136p. 1983. 18.75x (ISBN 0-398-04726-X). C C Thomas.

Wilber, Charles K. & Jameson, Kenneth P. Confronting Reality: America's Economic Crisis & Beyond. 304p. 1983. text ed. 21.95x (ISBN 0-268-00742-X); pap. text ed. 8.95x (ISBN 0-268-00743-8). U of Notre Dame Pr.

Wilber, Charles K., jt. ed. see Jameson, Kenneth P.

Wilber, Donald N. Annotated Bibliography of Afghanistan. 3rd rev. ed. LC 68-22209. (Bibliographies Ser.). 262p. 1968. pap. 15.00x o.p. (ISBN 0-87536-226-5). HRAFP.

Wilber, Ken. The Spectrum of Consciousness. LC 76-39690. (Illus.). 1977. 12.00 (ISBN 0-8356-0495-0, Quest); pap. 6.95 (ISBN 0-8356-0493-4). Theos Pub Hse.

--Up from Eden: A Transpersonal View of Human Evolution. LC 82-42678. (Illus.). 384p. 1983. pap. 8.95 (ISBN 0-394-71424-5). Shambhala Pubns.

Wilberforce, William. Real Christianity: Contrasted with the Prevailing Religious System. Houston, James M., ed. LC 82-8061. (Classics of Faith & Devotion Ser.). 1982. Casebound 9.95 (ISBN 0-930014-90-1). Multnomah.

Wilbert, Johannes, ed. Folk Literature of the Yamana Indians: Martin Gusinde's Collection of Yamana Narratives. LC 76-20026. 1977. 30.00x (ISBN 0-520-03299-3). U of Cal Pr.

Wilbert, Johannes & Simoneau, Karin, eds. Folk Literature of the Toba Indians. LC 82-620030. (Latin American Studies: No. 54). 1983. text ed. write for info. (ISBN 0-87903-054-2). UCLA Lat Am Ctr.

Wilbourn, Carole. Cats Prefer It This Way. LC 76-49. (Illus.). 224p. 1976. 8.95 o.p. (ISBN 0-698-10744-6, Coward). Putnam Pub Group.

Wilbraham, Antony C., jt. auth. see Matta, Michael S.

Wilbur, C. Keith, jt. auth. see Wilbur, Ruth E.

Wilbur, Charles E., tr. see Hugo, Victor.

Wilbur, Charles K., jt. ed. see Jameson, Kenneth P.

Wilbur, Henry W. President Lincoln's Attitude Toward Slavery & Emancipation. 1914. 10.00x (ISBN 0-8196-0267-1). Biblo.

Wilbur, James B., ed. see Conference On Value Inquiry - 1st & 2nd.

Wilbur, James B., ed. see Conference On Value Inquiry - 3rd.

Wilbur, Karl M., ed. The Mollusca: Metabolic Biochem & Molecular Biomechanics, Vol. 1. Incl. The Mollusca: Biochemistry of Mollusca Environmental Biochemistry. price not set (ISBN 0-12-751402-3). Date not set. price not set (ISBN 0-12-751401-5). Acad Pr.

--The Mollusca: Vol. 3: Development. Date not set. write for info. (ISBN 0-12-751403-1). Acad Pr.

Wilbur, Karl M. & Yonge, C. M., eds. Physiology of Mollusca, Vol. 2. 1966. Vol. 1. 67.50 (ISBN 0-12-751302-7). Acad Pr.

Wilbur, Ken. Eye to Eye: The Quest for the New Paradigm. LC 81-43732. (Illus.). 336p. 1983. pap. 9.95 (ISBN 0-385-18036-5, Anch). Doubleday.

Wilbur, L. Perry. On Your Way to the Top in Selling. 192p. 1983. 14.95 (ISBN 0-13-634352-X); pap. 6.95 (ISBN 0-13-634345-7). P-H.

Wilbur, Leslie, et al. Improving College English Skills. rev. ed. 1972. pap. 12.50x (ISBN 0-673-07655-5). Scott F.

Wilbur, M. D., jt. auth. see Keith, C.

Wilbur, R. American Sign Language & Sign Systems. 328p. 1979. text ed. 19.95 (ISBN 0-8391-0994-6). Univ Park.

Wilbur, Richard. The Mind-Reader. LC 75-42312. 1977. pap. 3.25 (ISBN 0-15-659805-1, Harv). HarBraceJ.

--Opposites: Poems & Drawings. LC 78-71154. (Illus.). 1979. pap. 1.75 (ISBN 0-15-670087-5, VoyB). HarBraceJ.

--Responses: Prose Pieces, 1948-1976. LC 76-24903. 1976. 13.95 (ISBN 0-15-176930-3). HarBraceJ.

Wilbur, Richard, ed. see Poe, Edgar A.

Wilbur, Richard, tr. Andromache by Racine. LC 82-47658. 114p. 1982. 10.95 (ISBN 0-15-107052-0). HarBraceJ.

--Moliere: Four Comedies. (Illus.). 640p. 1982. 19.95 (ISBN 0-15-161781-3). HarBraceJ.

Wilbur, Richard, tr. see Moliere, Jean Baptiste.

Wilbur, Ruth E. & Wilbur, C. Keith. Bid Us God Speed: The History of the Edwards Church, Northhampton, Massachusetts 1833-1983. LC 82-22347. (Illus.). 120p. 1983. 12.95 (ISBN 0-914016-93-8). Phoenix Pub.

Wilbur, Terence H. Prolegomena to a Grammar of Basque. (Current Issues in Linguistic Theory Ser.). x, 188p. 1979. 23.00 (ISBN 90-272-0909-X, 8). Benjamins North Am.

Wilburn, James R., ed. Freedom, Order & the University. LC 82-5274. 1982. 12.95 (ISBN 0-932612-12-1). Pepperdine U Pr.

--Productivity: A National Priority. 79p. (Orig.). 1982. pap. 7.95 (ISBN 0-932612-13-X). Pepperdine U Pr.

Wilby. Concrete for Structural Engineers. 1977. 29.95 o.p. (ISBN 0-408-00256-5). Butterworth.

Wilby, C. B. Design Graphs for Concrete Shell Roofs. 1981. 39.00 (ISBN 0-85334-899-5, Pub. by Applied Sci England). Elsevier.

Wilce, J. H. The Section Complanata of the Genus Lycopodium. (Illus.). 1965. pap. 24.00 (ISBN 3-7682-5419-4). Lubrecht & Cramer.

Wilcher, Marshall E. Environmental Cooperation in the North Atlantic Area. LC 79-3423. 1980. pap. text ed. 9.50 (ISBN 0-8191-0890-1). U Pr of Amer.

Wilcke, Harold L., et al, eds. Soy Protein & Human Nutrition. LC 78-25585. 1979. 34.50 (ISBN 0-12-751450-3). Acad Pr.

Wilcock, D. F., jt. ed. see Pinkus, O.

Wilcock, G. K. & Gray, J. A. Geriatric Problems in General Practice. (General Practice Ser.). 1982. 26.95x (ISBN 0-19-261313-8). Oxford U Pr.

Wilcock, John, jt. auth. see Pepper, Elizabeth.

Wilcock, W. L. see Marton, L.

Wilcox, Barbara & Bellamy, G. Thomas. Design of High School Programs for Severely Handicapped Students. LC 82-1216. (Illus.). 280p. (Orig.). 1982. pap. text ed. 15.95 (ISBN 0-933716-18-4). P H Brookes.

Wilcox, Collin. Hiding Place. pap. 1.75 (ISBN 0-515-05193-4). Jove Pubns.

--Long Way Down. 1979. pap. 1.75 o.s.i. (ISBN 0-515-05195-0). Jove Pubns.

--Stalking Horse: A Mystery. 1982. 10.50 (ISBN 0-394-51173-5). Random.

Wilcox, Collin, jt. auth. see Pronzini, Bill.

Wilcox, David R., ed. see Wine Advisory Board.

Wilcox, Diane L., tr. see Azaad, Meyer.

Wilcox, Donald J. In Search of God & Self: Renaissance & Reformation Thought. 1975. pap. text ed. 12.50 (ISBN 0-395-17178-4). HM.

Wilcox, Fred, ed. The Grass Roots: An Anti-Nuke Sourcebook. LC 80-11762. (Illus.). 192p. 1980. 17.95 (ISBN 0-89594-032-9); pap. 8.95 (ISBN 0-89594-031-0). Crossing Pr.

Wilcox, Fred A. Waiting for an Army to Die: The Tragedy of Agent Orange. LC 82-42791. 256p. 1983. pap. 7.95 (ISBN 0-394-71518-7, Vin). Random.

Wilcox, G. M. With Kinglake in the Holy Land. (Illus.). (gr. 7 up). 12.75x (ISBN 0-392-01895-0, LTB). Sportshelf.

Wilcox, Gary, et al, eds. see ICN-UCLA Symposia on Molecular & Cellular Biology.

Wilcox, Jarrod W. A Method for Measuring Decision Assumptions. 256p. 1972. 20.00x (ISBN 0-262-23055-0). MIT Pr.

Wilcox, John, jt. ed. see Fajardo, Salvador J.

Wilcox, John A. Leaf Beetle Host Plants in Northeastern North America: Coleoptera: Chrysomelidae. 32p. 1979. pap. 4.95x (ISBN 0-916846-09-1). Flora & Fauna.

Wilcox, John R. Taking Time Seriously: James Luther Adams. LC 78-61391. 1978. pap. text ed. 10.50 (ISBN 0-8191-0600-3). U Pr of Amer.

Wilcox, John T. Truth & Value In Nietzsche: A Study of His Metaethics & Epistemology. LC 82-45066. 250p. 1982. pap. text ed. 11.00 (ISBN 0-8191-2354-4). U Pr of Amer.

Wilcox, Laird. Directory of the American Left: Supplement. 1983. pap. 5.95 (ISBN 0-933592-28-0). Edit Res Serv.

Wilcox, Laird M. Directory of the American Right: Supplement, 1983. 1983. pap. 5.95 (ISBN 0-933592-27-2). Edit Res Serv.

--Directory of the Occult & Paranormal: Supplement, 1983. 1983. pap. 5.95 (ISBN 0-933592-29-9). Edit Res Serv.

Wilcox, Lyle, jt. ed. see McMains, Harvey.

Wilcox, M. Basic Algebra. new ed. (gr. 9-10). 1977. 14.64 (ISBN 0-201-08573-9, Sch Div); tchr's ed. 18.60 (ISBN 0-201-08574-7). A-W.

Wilcox, Roger. Communication at Work: Writing & Speaking. LC 76-14651. (Illus.). 1977. pap. text ed. 17.95 (ISBN 0-395-24372-6). HM.

Wilcox, Roger P. Oral Reporting in Business & Industry. 1967. text ed. 22.95 (ISBN 0-13-639302-0). P-H.

Wilcox, Shirley, ed. Eighteen Twenty-eight Tax Records of Prince George's County MD. 1983. price not set. Prince Georges County Gen Soc.

Wilcox, Walter W., et al. Economics of American Agriculture. 3rd ed. (Illus.). 512p. 1974. ref. ed. 24.95 (ISBN 0-13-229666-7). P-H.

Wilcox, Wayne. Protagonist Powers & the Third World. Lambert, Richard D., ed. LC 76-102760. (The Annals of the American Academy of Political & Social Science: Vol. 386). 1969. 15.00 (ISBN 0-87761-122-X); pap. 7.95 (ISBN 0-87761-121-1). Am Acad Pol Soc Sci.

Wilcoxon, George D. Athens Ascendant. (Illus.). 1979. text ed. 16.75 o.p. (ISBN 0-8138-1935-0); pap. text ed. 10.95x o.p. (ISBN 0-8138-1130-9). Iowa St U Pr.

Wilczak, Paul F., ed. Toward the Extended Christian Family. LC 80-69137. (Marriage & Family Living in Depth Bk.). (Illus.). 80p. 1980. pap. 2.45 (ISBN 0-87029-170-X, 20247-3). Abbey.

Wilczynski, E. J. Projective Differential Geometry. LC 61-17959. 9.95 o.p. (ISBN 0-8284-0155-1). Chelsea Pub.

Wild, jt. auth. see Crawford.

Wild, A. E., jt. ed. see Balls, M.

Wild, Anne, jt. auth. see Jenkins, Gerald.

Wild, Gillian M., jt. auth. see Heslop, R. B.

Wild, J. P. Textile Manufacture in the Northern Roman Provinces. LC 74-77294. (Cambridge Classical Studies). (Illus.). 1970. 27.50 (ISBN 0-521-07491-6). Cambridge U Pr.

Wild, Jocelyn, jt. auth. see Wild, Robin.

Wild, Peter. Peligros. 65p. 1971. 2.95 (ISBN 0-87886-008-8). Ithaca Hse.

Wild, Peter & Graziano, Frank, eds. New Poetry of the American West. (Illus.). 96p. (Orig.). 1982. 14.00 (ISBN 0-937406-20-1); Ltd. ed. 28.00 (ISBN 0-937406-21-X); pap. 5.50 (ISBN 0-686-98138-3). Logbridge-Rhodes.

Wild, R. Concepts for Operations Management. 185p. 1978. 59.95x (ISBN 0-471-99539-8, Pub. by Wiley-Interscience). Wiley.

--Mass Production Management: The Design & Operation of Production Flow-Line Systems. LC 72-611. 256p. 1973. 34.95 (ISBN 0-471-94405-X, Pub. by Wiley-Interscience). Wiley.

--Work Organization: A Study of Manual Labor & Mass Production. LC 74-13085. 222p. 1975. 39.95x (ISBN 0-471-94406-8, Pub. by Wiley-Interscience). Wiley.

Wild, R. A. Australian Community Studies & Beyond. (Studies in Society: No. 7). 241p. 1982. text ed. 27.50x (ISBN 0-86861-219-7). Allen Unwin.

Wild, Robert. Enthusiasm in the Spirit. LC 75-14742. 176p. 1975. pap. 2.45 o.p. (ISBN 0-87793-102-X). Ave Maria.

Wild, Robin & Wild, Jocelyn. Dunmousie Monsters. LC 72-94143. (Illus.). 32p. (gr. k-2). 1975. 5.95 o.p. (ISBN 0-698-20264-3, Coward). Putnam Pub Group.

Wild, Ronald. Heathcote: A Study of Local Government & Resident Action in a small Australian Town. 160p. 1983. text ed. 28.50x (ISBN 0-86861-093-3). Allen Unwin.

Wild, Victor. The Complete Book of How to Succeed with Women. (Illus.). 208p. (Orig.). 1981. pap. 11.95 (ISBN 0-938444-01-8). Wildfire Pub.

--The Science of Revolution: Fundamentals of Marxism-Leninism, Mao Tse Tung Thought & the Line of the Revolutionary Communist Party, U. S. A. (Orig.). 1980. pap. 1.50 (ISBN 0-89851-036-8). RCP Pubns.

--Your Fortune in the Microcomputer Business: Getting Started, Vol. I. (Illus.). 304p. 1982. pap. 15.95 (ISBN 0-938444-04-2). Wildfire Pub.

--Your Fortune in the Microcomputer Business: Growth, Survival, Success, Vol. II. (Illus.). 256p. 1982. pap. 15.95 (ISBN 0-938444-05-0). Wildfire Pub.

Wildavsky, Aaron, jt. auth. see Caiden, Naomi.

Wildavsky, Aaron, jt. auth. see Heclo, Hugh.

Wildavsky, Aaron, ed. The Policy Organization. (Managing Information Ser.: Vol. 5). (Illus.). 224p. 1983. 25.00 (ISBN 0-8039-1912-3); pap. 12.50 (ISBN 0-8039-1913-1). Sage.

Wildavsky, Aaron, jt. ed. see Boskin, Michael J.

Wilde, Carroll O., ed. Functional Analysis: Proceedings. 1970. 34.50 (ISBN 0-12-751750-2). Acad Pr.

Wilde, Daniel U. An Introduction to Computing: Problem-Solving Algorithms & Data Structures. LC 72-5754. (Illus.). 448p. 1973. ref. ed. 24.95 (ISBN 0-13-479519-9). P-H.

Wilde, Jane F. Ancient Cures, Charms & Usages of Ireland. LC 74-137347. 1970. Repr. of 1890 ed. 37.00x (ISBN 0-8103-3599-9). Gale.

Wilde, Jennifer. Dare to Love. 560p. (Orig.). 1983. pap. 3.95 (ISBN 0-446-30590-1). Warner Bks.

--Love Me, Marietta. 560p. (Orig.). 1983. pap. 3.95 (ISBN 0-446-30723-8). Warner Bks.

--Love's Tender Fury. 560p. (Orig.). 1983. pap. 3.95 (ISBN 0-446-30528-6). Warner Bks.

--Once More, Miranda. 576p. (Orig.). 1983. pap. 3.95 (ISBN 0-345-30694-5). Ballantine.

Wilde, Johannes. Venetian Art from Bellini to Titian. (Oxford Studies in the History of Art & Architecture Ser). (Illus.). 1974. pap. text ed. 15.95x (ISBN 0-19-817331-8). Oxford U Pr.

Wilde, Larry. The Complete Book of Ethnic Humor. (Illus.). 1979. pap. 5.95 (ISBN 0-523-41320-3). Pinnacle Bks.

--The Last Official Italian Joke Book. 1978. pap. 2.25 (ISBN 0-523-41970-8). Pinnacle Bks.

--The Last Official Polish Joke Book. (Illus.). 1977. pap. 2.25 (ISBN 0-523-41971-6). Pinnacle Bks.

--More of the Official Polish Italian Joke Book. 224p. (Orig.). 1975. pap. 2.25 (ISBN 0-523-41988-0). Pinnacle Bks.

--More Smart Kids-Dumb Parents Joke Book. (Orig.). 1979. pap. 2.25 (ISBN 0-523-41910-4). Pinnacle Bks.

--The New Official Cat Lovers Joke Book. 192p. (Orig.). 1983. pap. 1.95 (ISBN 0-523-42004-8). Pinnacle Bks.

--The Official Bedroom-Bathroom Joke Book. 224p. (Orig.). 1980. pap. 2.25 (ISBN 0-523-41793-4). Pinnacle Bks.

--The Official Cat Lovers & Dog Lovers Joke Book. 1978. pap. 2.25 (ISBN 0-523-41792-6). Pinnacle Bks.

--The Official Dirty Joke Book. (Illus.). 1978. pap. 2.25 (ISBN 0-523-41780-2). Pinnacle Bks.

--The Official Golfers Joke Book. 1977. pap. 2.25 (ISBN 0-523-41727-6). Pinnacle Bks.

--The Official Jewish Irish Jokebook. (Orig.). 1974. pap. 2.25 (ISBN 0-523-41582-6). Pinnacle Bks.

--The Official Polish Joke Book. rev. ed. 160p. 1981. pap. 1.95 (ISBN 0-523-41885-X). Pinnacle Bks.

--The Official Religious - Not So Religious Joke Book. (Orig.). 1976. pap. 1.95 (ISBN 0-523-41628-8). Pinnacle Bks.

--The Official Sick Joke Book. (Larry Wilde Bestselling Humor Ser.). 1979. pap. 2.25 (ISBN 0-523-41972-4). Pinnacle Bks.

--The Official Smart Kids-Dumb Parents Joke Book. (Illus., Orig.). 1977. pap. 2.25 (ISBN 0-523-41911-2). Pinnacle Bks.

--The Official Virgins-Sex Maniacs Jokebook. 224p. (Orig.). 1975. pap. 2.25 (ISBN 0-523-41781-0). Pinnacle Bks.

Wilde, Mary P. & Davis, Gevevieve. How to Tell if He's Cheating: And What to Do About It. 112p. (Orig.). 1983. pap. 3.95 (ISBN 0-936750-05-7). Wetherall.

Wilde, Oscar. The Artist as Critic: Critical Writings of Oscar Wilde. Ellman, Richard, ed. (Phoenix). 474p. 1983. pap. 10.95 (ISBN 0-226-89764-8). U of Chicago Pr.

--The Ballad of Reading Gaol. (Illus.). 64p. 1981. pap. 4.50 (ISBN 0-904526-26-7, Pub. by Journeyman England). Lawrence Hill.

--The Birthday of the Infanta. LC 79-14329. (Illus.). (gr. 7 up). 1979. 7.95 o.p. (ISBN 0-670-16974-9). Viking Pr.

--The Birthday of the Infanta & Other Stories by Oscar Wilde. LC 81-1402. (Illus.). 80p. 1982. 14.95 (ISBN 0-689-30850-7). Atheneum.
--The Canterville Ghost: The Star Child. Seshamani, Geeta, ed. (Illus.). 72p. 1982. pap. text ed. 3.95x (ISBN 0-86131-295-3, Pub. by Orient Longman Ltd India). Apt Bks.
--The Complete Shorter Fiction of Oscar Wilde. Murray, Isobel M., ed. 1980. 17.95x (ISBN 0-19-251001-0). Oxford U Pr.
--Essays & Lectures. Stansky, Peter & Shewan, Rodney, eds. LC 76-17753. (Aesthetic Movement & the Arts & Crafts Movement Ser.). 1978. Repr. of 1908 ed. lib. bdg. 44.00x o.s.i. (ISBN 0-8240-2455-9). Garland Pub.
--The Happy Prince. LC 77-78348. (Illus.). (gr. 3 up). 1977. 9.95 (ISBN 0-458-92910-7). Methuen Inc.
--The Happy Prince. (Illus.). (gr. 2-5). 1981. 14.95 (ISBN 0-19-279750-6). Oxford U Pr.
--Happy Prince & Other Stories. (gr. 4-7). 1962. pap. 2.25 (ISBN 0-14-030164-X, Puffin). Penguin.
--The Happy Prince & Other Tales. Lurie, Alison & Schiller, Justin G., eds. Incl. A House of Pomergranates. LC 75-32193. (Classics of Children's Literature 1621-1932 Ser.). PLB 38.00 o.s.i. (ISBN 0-8240-2304-8). Garland Pub.
--Importance of Being Earnest. 1980. pap. 5.95 (ISBN 0-413-31000-0). Methuen Inc.
--The Importance of Being Earnest. Jackson, Russell, ed. (New Mermaids Ser.). 1980. pap. 6.95x (ISBN 0-393-90045-2). Norton.
--Lady Windermere's Fan. 72p. 1966. pap. 5.95 (ISBN 0-413-30960-6). Methuen Inc.
--The Nightingale & the Rose. (Illus.). (gr. 4 up). 1981. 11.95 (ISBN 0-19-520231-7). Oxford U Pr.
--Picture of Dorian Gray. 1977. Repr. of 1891 ed. lib. bdg. 15.95x (ISBN 0-89244-064-3). Queens Hse.
--The Picture of Dorian Gray & Other Writings. Ellmann, Richard, ed. (Bantam Classics Ser.). 512p. (YA) (gr. 9-12). 1983. pap. 2.95 (ISBN 0-553-21096-3). Bantam.
--Picture of Dorian Gray & Selected Stories. 1962. pap. 1.95 (ISBN 0-451-51654-0, CJ1654, Sig Classics). NAL.
--The Plays of Oscar Wilde. 6.95 (ISBN 0-394-60490-3). Modern Lib.
--Selected Letters of Oscar Wilde. Hart-Davis, Rupert, ed. 1979. 25.00x (ISBN 0-19-212205-3). Oxford U Pr.
--The Selfish Giant. LC 78-31878. (gr. k-3). 1979. 9.95 (ISBN 0-07-070215-2). McGraw.

Wilde, Oscar see Swan, D. K.

Wilde, William H. Henry Kendall. LC 75-41479. (World Authors Ser.). 1976. lib. bdg. 15.95 (ISBN 0-8057-6229-9, Twayne). G K Hall.

Wilde, William H., jt. ed. see Andrews, Barry G.

Wildemann, E. De. Prodrome De la Flore Algologique Des Indes Neerlandaises et Partie Des Territoires De Borneo Etc. 193p. 1978. lib. bdg. 44.00x (ISBN 3-87429-145-6). Lubrecht & Cramer.

Wildenberg, D., ed. Computer Simulation in University Teaching. 1981. 42.75 (ISBN 0-444-86142-4). Elsevier.

Wildenthal, K. Degradative Processes in Heart & Skeletal Muscle. (Research Monographs in Cell & Tissue Physiology: Vol. 3). 1980. 110.25 (ISBN 0-444-80235-5). Elsevier.

Wilder, Aldridge D., Jr., jt. auth. see Strickland, William D.

Wilder, Alec. American Popular Song: The Great Innovators, 1900-1950. (Illus.). 1972. 25.00x (ISBN 0-19-501445-6). Oxford U Pr.
--American Popular Song: The Great Innovators, 1900-1950. Maher, James T., ed. LC 70-159643. 1975. pap. 10.95 (ISBN 0-19-501925-3, GB439, GB). Oxford U Pr.

Wilder, B. Joseph & Bruni, Joseph. Seizure Disorders: A Pharmacological Approach to Treatment. 256p. 1981. text ed. 27.00 (ISBN 0-89004-539-9). Raven.

Wilder, Carolyn. Making Paper & Fabric Flowers. LC 68-8520. (Illus.). 1969. 4.95 (ISBN 0-8208-0317-0). Hearthside.

Wilder, Don, jt. auth. see Rechin, Bill.

Wilder, Laura I. Little House on the Prairie. (YA) 1975. pap. 2.50i (ISBN 0-06-080357-6, P357, PL). Har-Row.

Wilder, Lilyan. The Lilyan Wilder Speak for Success Program. 288p. 1983. 13.95 (ISBN 0-02-628530-4). Macmillan.

Wilder, Marshall P., ed. The Wit & Humor of America, 10 Vols. 1982. Repr. of 1908 ed. Set. lib. bdg. 175.00 (ISBN 0-89987-891-1). Darby Bks.

Wilder, Robert E. Gridiron Glory Days: Football at Mercer, 1892-1942. LC 82-6366. (Illus.). 213p. 1982. 15.95 (ISBN 0-86554-052-7). Mercer Univ Pr.

Wilder, Rosilyn. A Space Where Anything Can Happen: Creative Drama in a Middle School. LC 77-82855. (Illus.). 184p. 1977. 12.95 (ISBN 0-932720-69-2); pap. text ed. 6.95 (ISBN 0-932720-70-6). New Plays Bks.

Wilder, Thornton. American Characteristics & Other Essays. Gallup, Donald, ed. LC 79-1692. 1979. 16.30i (ISBN 0-06-014639-7, HarpT). Har-Row.
--Bridge of San Luis Rey. LC 67-22516. 1967. 12.45i (ISBN 0-06-014631-1, HarpT). Har-Row.
--Our Town. 1975. pap. 2.25 (ISBN 0-380-00557-3, 61978-4, Bard). Avon.
--Three Plays by Thornton Wilder. 1976. pap. 2.50 (ISBN 0-380-00527-1, 57257, Bard). Avon.

Wilder, Thornton see Moon, Samuel.

Wilder, Warren F., jt. auth. see Giese, Frank S.

Wilder, William. Communication, Social Structure & Development in Rural Malaysia. (London School of Economics Monographs on Social Anthropology: No. 56). 224p. 1982. text ed. 34.25x (ISBN 0-485-19556-9, Athlone Pr). Humanities.

Wilder-Smith, A. E. Creation of Life. LC 78-133984. 269p. 1981. pap. 7.95 (ISBN 0-89051-070-9, Pub by Master Bks). CLP Pubs.
--He Who Thinks Has to Believe. LC 81-65988. 1981. pap. 2.95 (ISBN 0-89051-073-3, Pub by Master Bks). CLP Pubs.
--Natural Sciences Know Nothing of Evolution. LC 80-67425. 1980. pap. 5.95 (ISBN 0-89051-062-8, Pub. by Master Bks). CLP Pubs.
--Why Does God Allow It? LC 80-80283. 1980. pap. 2.95 (ISBN 0-89051-060-1, Pub. by Master Bks). CLP Pubs.

Wilder-Smith, Beate. The Day Nazi Germany Died. LC 82-71148. 1982. pap. 2.95 (ISBN 0-89051-083-0, Pub. by Master Bks). CLP Pubs.

Wildgen, Wolfgang. Catastrophe Theoretical Semantics: An Elaboration & Application of Rene Thom's Theory. (Pragmatics & Beyond: III-5). 120p. (Orig.). 1982. pap. 16.00 (ISBN 90-272-2525-7). Benjamins North Am.

Wildhorn, Sorrell, et al. How to Save Gasoline: Public Policy Alternatives for the Automobile. LC 75-26641. (Rand Corporation Research Studies). 228p. 1976. prof ref 25.00x (ISBN 0-88410-453-2). Ballinger Pub.

Wildi, Theodore. Electric Power Technology. LC 80-39799. (Electronic Technology Ser.). 686p. 1981. 26.95 (ISBN 0-471-07764-X); solution manual 6.00x (ISBN 0-471-09239-8). Wiley.

Wilding, Michael. The Wilding Way: The Story of My Life. (Illus.). 240p. 1982. 10.95 (ISBN 0-312-87954-7). St Martin.

Wilding, Michael, ed. see Miller, John.

Wilding, Suzanne & Savitt, Sam. Ups & Downs: A Basic Guide to Riding & Horsemanship. (Illus.). 160p. 1973. 9.95 (ISBN 0-312-83405-5). St Martin.

Wilding-White, Ted. All About UFO's. LC 77-17599. (World of the Unknown Ser). (Illus.). (gr. 4-5). 1978. PLB 7.95 (ISBN 0-88436-468-2). EMC.

Wildlife Education, Ltd. Giraffes. Wexo, John B., ed. (Zoobooks). (Illus.). 20p. (Orig.). 1982. pap. 1.50 (ISBN 0-937934-09-7). Wildlife Educ.

Wildlife Society, Inc. A Manual of Wildlife Conservation. Teague, Richard D., ed. LC 72-143895. (Illus.). 206p. (Orig.). 1971. pap. text ed. 4.25 o.p. (ISBN 0-933564-01-5). Wildlife Soc.

Wildman, Eugene. Montezuma's Ball. LC 82-71447. 183p. 1970. 8.95x (ISBN 0-8040-0211-8); pap. 4.95 (ISBN 0-8040-0212-6). Swallow.
--Nuclear Love. LC 82-73005. 85p. 1972. 7.95 (ISBN 0-8040-0568-0); pap. 4.95 (ISBN 0-8040-0569-9). Swallow.

Wildman, Eugene, ed. Anthology of Concretism. 2nd enl. ed. LC 82-70118. 165p. 1969. 10.00x (ISBN 0-8040-0012-3); pap. 4.95x (ISBN 0-8040-0013-1). Swallow.
--Experiments in Prose. LC 82-70621. (Illus.). 351p. 1969. 15.95x (ISBN 0-8040-0103-0); pap. 7.95x (ISBN 0-8040-0104-9). Swallow.

Wildman, Faye. A Race for Love. 192p. (Orig.). 1980. pap. 1.50 (ISBN 0-671-57048-X, Pub. by Silouette Bks). S&S.
--Rain Lady. 192p. (Orig.). 1980. pap. 1.50 (ISBN 0-671-57029-3, Pub. by Silhouette Bks). S&S.

Wildman, Manfred, ed. see Gross, William & Matsch, Lee A.

Wildman, Murray S. Money Inflation in the United States: A Study in Social Pathology. Repr. lib. bdg. 16.00x (ISBN 0-8371-1408-X, WIMI). Greenwood.

Wildman, Richard. Bygone Bedford. 96p. 1982. 25.00x (ISBN 0-900804-09-2, Pub. by White Crescent England). State Mutual Bk.

Wildman, Terry M., jt. auth. see Sherman, Thomas M.

Wildon, Lester N., ed. Helping Special Student Groups. LC 80-84261. 1982. 7.95x (ISBN 0-87589-879-3, CLA-7). Jossey-Bass.

Wildorf, Barry L., jt. auth. see Gruber, Edward C.

Wildridge, Thomas T. Grotesque in Church Art. LC 68-30633. 1969. Repr. of 1899 ed. 30.00x (ISBN 0-8103-3077-6). Gale.

Wilds, Claudia. Finding Birds in the National Capital Area. (Illus.). 216p. 1983. pap. 12.50 (ISBN 0-87474-959-X). Smithsonian.

Wilds, John. Afternoon Story: History of the New Orleans Statesitem. LC 76-27188. (Illus.). 1976. 20.00x (ISBN 0-8071-0192-3). La State U Pr.

Wildsmith, Brian. Animal Games. (Illus.). (ps-3). 1981. 7.95 (ISBN 0-19-279731-X). Oxford U Pr.
--Animal Homes. (Illus.). (ps-3). 1981. 7.95 (ISBN 0-19-279732-8). Oxford U Pr.
--Animal Shapes. (Illus.). (ps-3). 1981. 7.95 (ISBN 0-19-279733-6). Oxford U Pr.
--Animal Tricks. (Illus.). (ps-3). 1981. 7.95 (ISBN 0-19-279743-3). Oxford U Pr.
--Birds by Brian Wildsmith. (Illus.). (gr. k-4). 1980. pap. 6.95 (ISBN 0-19-272117-8). Oxford U Pr.
--Cat on the Mat. (Illus.). 16p. (ps). 1983. pap. 1.95 (ISBN 0-19-272123-2, Pub by Oxford U Pr Childrens). Merrimack Bk Serv.
--The Circus. (Illus.). (ps-3). 1980. pap. 4.95x (ISBN 0-19-272102-X). Oxford U Pr.
--Pelican. LC 82-12431. (Illus.). 64p. (ps-2). 1983. 8.95 (ISBN 0-394-85668-6); PLB 9.99 (ISBN 0-394-95668-0). Pantheon.
--The Rich Man & the Shoe-Maker. (Illus.). (ps-3). 1980. pap. 5.95 (ISBN 0-19-272104-6). Oxford U Pr.
--Seasons. (Illus.). (ps-3). 1981. 6.95 (ISBN 0-19-279730-1). Oxford U Pr.
--The Trunk. (Illus.). 16p. (ps). 1983. pap. 1.95 (ISBN 0-19-272124-0, Pub by Oxford U Pr Childrens). Merrimack Bk Serv.
--Wild Animals. (Illus.). (ps). 1979. pap. 4.95 (ISBN 0-19-272103-8). Oxford U Pr.

Wildsmith, Brian, adapted by. & illus. The Miller, The Boy & The Donkey. (Illus.). (ps-1). 1981. pap. 6.95 (ISBN 0-19-272114-3). Oxford U Pr.

Wildung, Raymond E. see Drucker, Harvey.

Wile, Annadel, ed. Declassified Documents Reference System Annual Collection Nineteen Seventy Five. 1976. 425.00 (ISBN 0-8408-0161-0). Res Pubns Conn.
--Declassified Documents Reference System Annual Collection. 1976. 1977. 425.00 (ISBN 0-8408-0162-9). Res Pubns Conn.

Wile, Daniel B. Couples Therapy: A Nontraditional Approach. LC 81-4958. 229p. 1981. 25.95x (ISBN 0-471-07811-5, Pub. by Wiley Interscience). Wiley.

Wile, Edith B. One Way Weekend. LC 80-22892. 1983. 14.95 (ISBN 0-87949-196-5). Ashley Bks.

Wileman, J. P. Brazilian Exchange: The Study of an Inconvertible Currency. Repr. of 1896 ed. lib. bdg. 18.50x (ISBN 0-8371-1082-3, WIBE). Greenwood.

Wilen, Joan & Wilen, Lydia. Name Me, I'm Yours. (Illus.). 144p. (Orig.). 1982. pap. 3.95 (ISBN 0-941298-04-3). Mary Ellen Ent.

Wilen, Joan, jt. auth. see Wilen, Lydia.

Wilen, Lydia & Wilen, Joan. Name Me, I'm Yours! Date not set. pap. 3.95 (ISBN 0-449-90079-7, Columbine). Fawcett.

Wilen, Lydia, jt. auth. see Wilen, Joan.

Wilensky, Harold L. & Lebeaux, Charles N. Industrial Society & Social Welfare. 1965. pap. text ed. 11.95 (ISBN 0-02-935150-2). Free Pr.

Wilensky, Julius M. Cape Cod: Where to Go, What to Do, How to Do It. 2nd. rev. ed. LC 70-83970. (Illus.). 1976. 12.95 o.p. (ISBN 0-918752-00-0). Wescott Cove.

Wiles, Cheryl & Ryan, William. Communication for Dental Auxiliaries. 1982. text ed. 15.95 (ISBN 0-8359-0897-6); pap. text ed. 12.95 (ISBN 0-8359-0896-8). Reston.

Wiles, David K. Energy, Winter, & Schools: Crisis & Decision Theory. (Politics of Education Ser.). (Illus.). 176p. 1979. 21.95x (ISBN 0-669-02544-5). Lexington Bks.

Wiles, Domini. Death Flight. LC 76-57735. 1977. 8.95 o.p. (ISBN 0-698-10802-7, Coward). Putnam Pub Group.

Wiles, G. P. Paul's Intercessory Prayers. (Society for New Testament Studies Monographs: No. 24). 360p. 1974. 54.50 (ISBN 0-521-20274-4). Cambridge U Pr.

Wiles, Jon. Planning Guidelines for Middle School Education. LC 76-19245. 1976. pap. text ed. 5.95 (ISBN 0-8403-1531-7). Kendall-Hunt.

Wiles, Jon & Bondi, Joseph. Curriculum Development: A Guide to Practice Elementary Education. 1979. text ed. 21.95 (ISBN 0-675-08315-X). Merrill.
--Principles of School Administration. 448p. Date not set. text ed. 22.95 (ISBN 0-675-20054-7). Merrill.

Wiles, Jon W. & Bondi, Joseph, Jr. The Essential Middle School. (Illus.). 432p. 1981. text ed. 21.95 (ISBN 0-675-08086-X). Merrill.

Wiles, Kimball & Lovell, John T. Supervision for Better Schools. 4th ed. (Illus.). 336p. 1975. ref. ed. 23.95 (ISBN 0-13-876102-7). P-H.

Wiles, M. A., tr. see Halley.

Wiles, Maurice & Santer, M., eds. Documents in Early Christian Thought. LC 74-31807. 304p. 1976. 39.50 (ISBN 0-521-20669-3); pap. 9.95 (ISBN 0-521-09915-3). Cambridge U Pr.

Wiles, Maurice, ed. see Lyons, J. A.

Wiles, Maurice F. Making of Christian Doctrine. 1967. 29.95 (ISBN 0-521-06803-7); pap. 9.95 (ISBN 0-521-09962-5). Cambridge U Pr.

Wiles, P., ed. Prediction of Communist Economic Performance. LC 75-123677. (Soviet & East European Studies). (Illus.). 1971. 39.50 (ISBN 0-521-07885-7). Cambridge U Pr.

Wiles, Peter. Economic Institutions Compared. LC 76-6175. 608p. 1977. 43.95x o.p. (ISBN 0-470-15083-1). Halsted Pr.

Wiles, Peter, tr. see Vailland, Roger.

Wiley, Bell I. Confederate Women. LC 74-5995. (Contributions in American History Ser.: No. 38). (Illus.). xiv, 204p. 1975. lib. bdg. 25.00x (ISBN 0-8371-7534-8, WCW/); pap. text ed. 5.95 (ISBN 0-8371-8357-X, WCW). Greenwood.

Wiley, Bell I., ed. see Pember, Phoebe Y.

Wiley, Bell T., ed. see National Historical Society.

Wiley, Constance & Wiley, Wilson. Boxers. Foyle, Christina, ed. (Foyle's Handbks). (Illus.). 1973. 3.95 (ISBN 0-685-55794-4). Palmetto Pub.

Wiley, Edward O. Phylogenetics: Theory & Practice of Phylogenetic Systematics. LC 81-5080. 552p. 1981. 42.50x (ISBN 0-471-05975-7, Pub. by Wiley-Interscience). Wiley.

Wiley, Farida, ed. John Burroughs' America. (American Naturalists Ser.). (Illus.). 304p. 10.50 (ISBN 0-8159-5109-4); pap. 5.25 (ISBN 0-8159-5114-0). Devin.

Wiley, Farida A. Ferns of Northeastern United States. (Illus.). 7.50 (ISBN 0-8446-4840-X). Peter Smith.

Wiley, Farida A., ed. Ernest Thompson Seton's America. (American Naturalists Ser.). (Illus.). 1975. pap. 9.95 (ISBN 0-85699-121-X). Devin.

Wiley, Jack. The Tumbling Book. (Illus.). (gr. 7 up). 1977. 8.95 o.p. (ISBN 0-679-20418-0). McKay.

Wiley, James W., jt. auth. see Snyder, Noel F.

Wiley, John. Structural Steel Design. 2nd ed. Tall, Lambert, ed. 892p. text ed. 49.50 (ISBN 0-89874-602-7). Krieger.

Wiley, M., ed. Estuarine Processes, 2 vols. Vol. 1. 1976. 40.00 (ISBN 0-12-751801-0); Vol. 2. 1977. 39.50 (ISBN 0-12-751802-9). Acad Pr.

Wiley, Margaret L. Creative Sceptics. 1966. text ed. 9.75x o.p. (ISBN 0-04-211001-7). Humanities.
--Subtle Knot: Creative Scepticism in Seventeenth-Century England. LC 68-54994. (Illus.). 1968. Repr. of 1952 ed. lib. bdg. 15.75x (ISBN 0-8371-0753-9, WISK). Greenwood.

Wiley, Martin L., ed. Estuarine Interactions. 1978. 49.50 (ISBN 0-12-751850-9). Acad Pr.

Wiley, Mason, jt. auth. see Wallace, Carol McD.

Wiley, Paul F., jt. auth. see Neunhoeffer, Hans.

Wiley, Peter & Gottlieb, Robert. Empires in the Sun: The Rise of the American West. LC 81-13857. 352p. 1982. 15.95 (ISBN 0-399-12635-X). Putnam Pub Group.

Wiley, R. J. Real Estate Investment: Analysis & Strategy. 400p. 1976. 23.95 (ISBN 0-471-06582-X, Pub. by Wiley-Interscience). Wiley.

Wiley, Richard G. Electronic Intelligence: An Analysis of Radar Signals. (Artech House Radar Library). (Illus.). 234p. 1982. 40.00 (ISBN 0-89006-124-6). Artech Hse.

Wiley, Robert J. Real Estate Accounting & Mathematics Handbook. LC 80-12990. (Real Estate for Professional Practitioners Ser.). 310p. 1980. 35.95x (ISBN 0-471-04812-7, Pub by Ronald Pr). Wiley.
--Real Estate Investment: Analysis & Strategy. LC 75-14950. 1976. 23.95 o.p. (ISBN 0-471-06582-X). Ronald Pr.

Wiley, William L. Gentleman of Renaissance France. LC 75-152622. (Illus.). 1971. Repr. of 1954 ed. lib. bdg. 17.75x (ISBN 0-8371-6169-X, WIGR). Greenwood.

Wiley, Wilson, jt. auth. see Wiley, Constance.

Wilf, H. S., jt. ed. see Ralston, Anthony.

Wilford, D. Sykes. Monetary Policy & the Open Economy: Mexico's Experience. LC 77-14386. (Praeger Special Studies). 1977. 26.95 o.p. (ISBN 0-03-028156-3). Praeger.

Wilford, Jane, jt. auth. see Ladley, Barbara.

Wilford, John N. The Mapmakers: The Story of the Great Pioneer on Cartography from Antiquity to the Space Age. LC 81-52868. (Illus.). 448p. 1982. pap. 8.95 (ISBN 0-394-75303-8, Vin). Random.

Wilgen, John K., jt. auth. see Feld, Werner J.

Wilgus, D. K. & Sommer, Carol, eds. Folklore International: Essays in Traditional Literature, Belief, & Custom in Honor of Wayland Debs Hand. LC 67-16249. (Illus.). xiv, 259p. Repr. of 1967 ed. 37.00x (ISBN 0-8103-5023-8). Gale.

Wilhelm, Carl & Amkreutz, Johann, eds. Dictionary of Data Processing, 2 Vols. 2nd ed. 1349p. 1981. Set. 105.00 (ISBN 3-921899-25-7). Intl Pubns Serv.

Wilhelm, Donald F., ed. Understanding Presses & Press Operations. LC 81-51805. (Manufacturing Update Ser.). 250p. 1981. 32.00 (ISBN 0-87263-069-2). SME.

Wilhelm, Friedrich & Schlegel, Karl F. Surgery of the Spine. Hackenbroch, M. & Witt, A. N., eds. Stiasny, G., tr. LC 76-19607. (Atlas of Orthopaedic Operations: Vol. 1). (Illus.). 262p. 1980. text ed. 72.50 o.p. (ISBN 0-7216-4445-7). Saunders.

Wilhelm, Glenda & Wilhelm, Tim. Bicycling Basics. (Illus.). 48p. (gr. 3-7). 1982. 8.95 (ISBN 0-13-077958-X). P-H.

Wilhelm, Hans. The Trapp Family Book. (Illus.). 88p. (gr. 2-4). 1983. 14.95 (ISBN 0-434-97248-7, Pub. by Heinemann England). David & Charles.

Wilhelm, Hubert G. Organized German Settlement & Its Effects on the Frontier of South-Central Texas. Cordasco, Francesco, ed. LC 80-905. (American Ethnic Groups Ser.). (Illus.). 1981. lib. bdg. 25.00x (ISBN 0-405-13464-9). Ayer Co.

Wilhelm, Irma J., jt. ed. see Dulcy, Faye.

Wilhelm, James. Il Miglior Fabbro: The Cult of the Difficult in Daniel, Dante & Pound. (Illus.). 132p. (Orig.). 1982. 12.95 (ISBN 0-915032-03-1); pap. 8.95 (ISBN 0-915032-56-2). Natl Poet Foun.

Wilhelm, James J., ed. & tr. The Poetry of Arnaut Daniel. LC 80-8955. 200p. 1981. lib. bdg. 25.00 o.s.i. (ISBN 0-8240-9446-8). Garland Pub.

Wilhelm, John. John Wilhelm's Guide to Mexico. 5th ed. 1978. 12.50 o.p. (ISBN 0-07-070289-6, GB). McGraw.

Wilhelm, Kate. The Infinity Box: A Collection of Speculative Fiction. LC 74-15894. 318p. (YA) 1975. 8.95i (ISBN 0-06-014653-2, HarpT). Har-Row.
--Juniper Time. LC 78-22447. 1979. 12.45i (ISBN 0-06-014657-5, HarpT). Har-Row.
--The Mile-Long Spaceship. 13.00 (ISBN 0-8398-2600-1, Gregg). G K Hall.
Wilhelm, Lewis W. Sir George Calvert, Baron of Baltimore. 172p. 1884. 9.50 (ISBN 0-686-36847-9). Md Hist.
Wilhelm, R. B., et al. Mammals of Lacreek National Wildlife Refuge, South Dakota. (Special Publications Ser.: No. 17). (Illus.). 39p. (Orig.). 1981. pap. 4.00 (ISBN 0-89672-091-8). Tex Tech Pr.
Wilhelm, Richard, tr. Chinese Folktales. 215p. 1974. 8.50 o.p. (ISBN 0-7135-1813-8). Transatlantic.
Wilhelm, Sidney M. Blacks in a White America. 192p. 1983. 18.95 (ISBN 0-87073-492-X); pap. 9.95 (ISBN 0-87073-493-8). Schenkman.
Wilhelm, Tim, jt. auth. see Wilhelm, Glenda.
Wilhelm, Wilbert E. Manufacturing Engineering Models for Design & Analysis of Production Systems. (Orig.). 1978. pap. text ed. 18.00 (ISBN 0-89806-000-1, 126); pap. text ed. 9.00 members. Inst Indus Eng.
Wilhelms, F., et al. Consumer Economics. 3rd ed. 1966. text ed. 11.72 o.p. (ISBN 0-07-070283-7, G). McGraw.
Wilhelmsen, Frederick D. The Paradoxical Structure of Existence. 1970. pap. 3.95x (ISBN 0-918306-00-0). U of Dallas Pr.
Wilhelmsen, Inga, jt. auth. see Allwood, Martin S.
Wilhelmsson, Lars. Making Forever Friends. (Religion-Devotional Ser.). 150p. (Orig.). 1982. pap. write for info. (ISBN 0-941018-04-0). Martin Pr.
--Vital Christianity. (Religion Ser.). 250p. 1982. 9.95 (ISBN 0-941018-03-2). Martin Pr.
Wilhite, Bob & Lemke, Bob. Standard Guide to U. S. Coin & Paper Money Valuations. 9th ed. LC 79-67100. (Illus.). 1982. pap. 2.25 (ISBN 0-87341-025-4). Krause Pubns.
Wilhite, Robert & Mishler, Clifford. Standard Guide to U.S. Coin & Paper Money Valuations. 5th ed. LC 78-60747. (Illus.). 1978. pap. 1.50 o.s.i. (ISBN 0-87341-021-1). Krause Pubns.
Wilhoit, J. C., Jr. Elementary Partial Differential Equations for Engineers & Scientists. LC 78-62181. 1978. pap. text ed. 11.50 (ISBN 0-8191-0501-5). U Pr of Amer.
Wiliams, Guy. Instructions to Young Collectors. 14.50x (ISBN 0-392-07941-0, SpS). Sportshelf.
Wilimovsky, Norman J., ed. Environment of the Cape Thompson Region, Alaska, 2 vols. LC 66-60018. (AEC Technical Information Center Ser.). 1250p. 1966. pap. 39.25 (ISBN 0-87079-196-6, PNE-481); microfiche 4.50 (ISBN 0-87079-232-6, PNE-481). DOE.
Wilk, Janet. Holiday Cooking for Kids. (Illus.). 64p. 1982. pap. 3.25. Ideals.
Wilke, Arthur see Mohan, Raj.
Wilke, Arthur S. The Hidden Professoriate: Credentialism, Professionalism, & the Tenure Crisis. LC 77-84774. (Contributions in Sociology Ser.: No. 29). (Illus.). 1979. lib. bdg. 29.95x (ISBN 0-8371-9886-0, WHP/). Greenwood.
Wilke, John T. A Neuropsychological Model of Knowing. LC 81-40175. 88p. (Orig.). 1981. lib. bdg. 17.75 (ISBN 0-8191-1768-4); pap. text ed. 7.00 (ISBN 0-8191-1769-2). U Pr of Amer.
Wilke, Mrs., jt. auth. see Willke, J. C.
Wilken, Robert L. The Myth of Christian Beginnings. LC 80-11884. 218p. 1980. 14.95 (ISBN 0-268-01347-0); pap. text ed. 4.95 (ISBN 0-268-01348-9). U of Notre Dame Pr.
Wilken, Robert L., jt. auth. see Meeks, Wayne A.
Wilkens, Emily. More Secrets from the Super Spas. LC 82-19918. (Illus.). 1983. 17.50 (ISBN 0-934878-24-2); pap. 9.95 (ISBN 0-934878-25-0). Dembner Bks.
Wilkens, Herbert. The Two German Economies. 180p. 1981. text ed. 44.50x (ISBN 0-566-00304-X). Gower Pub Ltd.
Wilkens, Leslie Von see Von Wilkens, Leonie.
Wilkens, Lewis L., tr. see Pannenberg, Wolfhart.
Wilkerson, Albert E., ed. The Rights of Children: Emergent Concepts in Law & Society. LC 73-79230. 323p. 1974. 24.95 (ISBN 0-87722-052-2). Temple U Pr.
Wilkerson, B. All About Children's Church. LC 80-70732. 150p. (Orig.). 1981. pap. 5.95 (ISBN 0-87509-295-0); Leader's guide. 2.95 (ISBN 0-87509-310-8). Chr Pubns.
Wilkerson, Barbara. Childhood: The Positive Years. LC 82-71493. (Illus.). 125p. 1982. pap. 3.50 (ISBN 0-87509-322-1); Leader's guide. 6.95 (ISBN 0-87509-321-3). Chr Pubns.
Wilkerson, Cynthia. Sweeter Than Candy. 272p. 1982. pap. 3.25 o.p. (ISBN 0-505-51856-2). Tower Bks.
Wilkerson, David. Beyond the Cross & the Switchblade. (Orig.). pap. 1.75 o.s.i. (ISBN 0-89129-151-2). Jove Pubns.
--Cross & the Switchblade. 1976. pap. 2.50 (ISBN 0-515-06493-9). Jove Pubns.
--Hey, Preach, You're Comin' Through. 1975. pap. 1.25 o.s.i. (ISBN 0-89129-064-8, PV064). Jove Pubns.
--Jesus Person: Pocket Promise Book. LC 72-86208. 96p. 1979. pap. 1.95 (ISBN 0-8307-0191-5). Regal.
--Suicide. 1978. pap. 1.95 (ISBN 0-8007-8331-X, Spire Bks). Revell.
Wilkerson, Don. Marijuana: Revised & Updated. 160p. 1983. pap. 4.95 (ISBN 0-8007-5107-8, Power Bks.). Revell.
Wilkerson, Frederick. British & American Flintlocks. (Country Life Collectors Guides Ser). 1972. 4.95 o.p. (ISBN 0-600-43590-3). Transatlantic.
Wilkerson, Geroge J., jt. auth. see Polnac, Lennis R.
Wilkerson, Gwen & Schinauer, Betty. In His Strength. Rev. ed. LC 77-92619. 144p. 1982. pap. 4.95 (ISBN 0-8307-0825-1). Regal.
Wilkerson, Rich. Hold Me While You Let Me Go. LC 82-83838. 196p. (Orig.). 1983. pap. 4.95 (ISBN 0-89081-370-1). Harvest Hse.
Wilkerson, Sylvia. Sprint Cars. LC 81-6165. (World of Racing Ser.). (Illus.). 48p. (gr. 4 up). 1981. PLB 10.60 (ISBN 0-516-04717-5); pap. 3.95 (ISBN 0-516-44717-3). Childrens.
Wilkerson, Thomas. Boaz, Vol. One. LC 82-73553. (Illus.). 50p. (Orig.). 1982. pap. 5.00 (ISBN 0-934996-19-9). Am Stud Pr.
Wilkes & Zeff. First Book of Numbers. (First Book of Numbers). (gr. k-3). 1982. 9.95 (ISBN 0-86020-665-3, Usborne-Hayes). EDC.
Wilkes, Alan, jt. ed. see Kennedy, R. A.
Wilkes, Charles. United States Exploring Expedition During the Years 1838-42 Under the Command of Charles Wilkes: Botanical Section, Vols. 15-17. Incl. Vol. 15. Phanoregamia. Gray, A. 192.00 (ISBN 3-7682-0714-5); Vol. 16. Cryptogamia, Filices, Lycopodiaceae & Hydropterides. Brackenridge, W. D. (Illus.). 72.00 (ISBN 3-7682-0715-3); Vol. 17. Cryptogamia Musci, Lichenes, Algae, Fungi Phanerogamia of Pacific North America. Sullivent, W. B., et al. (Illus.). 80.00 (ISBN 3-7682-0716-1). 1968. Repr. of 1854 ed. Set. 316.00 (ISBN 3-7682-0709-9). Lubrecht & Cramer.
Wilkes, Defoe. Book of Children's Classic. (Children's Classic Ser.). (gr. 3-6). 1982. 10.95 (ISBN 0-686-83167-5, Usborne-Hayes). EDC.
Wilkes, Eric. Long-Term Prescribing: Drug Management of Chronic Disease & Other Problems. 256p. 1982. 34.50 (ISBN 0-571-11898-4); pap. 22.95 (ISBN 0-571-11899-2). Faber & Faber.
Wilkes, F. M. Capital Budgeting Techniques. LC 76-18280. 1977. 63.95x o.s.i. (ISBN 0-471-99416-2, Pub. by Wiley-Interscience). Wiley.
Wilkes, G. A. The Complete Plays of Ben Jonson, Vol. 4. 1982. 99.00x (ISBN 0-19-812603-4). Oxford U Pr.
Wilkes, G. A. & Reid, J. C. Literatures of Australia & New Zealand. McLeod, A. L., ed. LC 71-121856. 1971. 18.95x (ISBN 0-685-01602-1). Pa St U Pr.
Wilkes, Glenn. Basketball. 4th ed. (P. E. Activities Ser.). 112p. 1982. pap. text ed. write for info. o.p. (ISBN 0-697-07191-X). Wm C Brown.
Wilkes, James O., jt. auth. see Carnahan, Brice.
Wilkes, John. Hernan Cortes: Conquistador in Mexico. LC 76-22436. (Cambridge Topic Bks). (Illus.). (gr. 5-10). 1977. PLB 6.95g (ISBN 0-8225-1205-X). Lerner Pubns.
Wilkes, John, jt. ed. see Aldred, Jennifer.
Wilkes, Lambert H., jt. auth. see Smith, Harris P.
Wilkes, M. V. Short Introduction to Numerical Analysis. (Illus., Orig.). pap. 7.95 (ISBN 0-521-09412-7, 412). Cambridge U Pr.
Wilkes, Mary & Crosswait, C. Bruce. Professional Development: The Dynamics of Success. 406p. 1981. text ed. 14.95 (ISBN 0-15-572001-5, HC). HarBraceJ.
Wilkes, Maurice, et al. The Preparation of Programs for An Electronic Digital Computer. (The Charles Babbage Institute Reprint Series for the History of Computing: Vol. 1). (Illus.). 1982. write for info. limited edition (ISBN 0-938228-03-X). Tomash Pubs.
Wilkes, P. Solid State Theory in Metallurgy. LC 72-180020. (Illus.). 480p. (Orig.). 1973. 68.50 (ISBN 0-521-08454-7); pap. 21.95 (ISBN 0-521-09699-5). Cambridge U Pr.
Wilkes, Peter. An Illustrated History of Farming. (Illus.). 1978. 12.50 o.s.i. (ISBN 0-904978-84-2). Transatlantic.
Wilkes, Ruth. Social Work with Undervalued Groups. (Tavistock Library of Social Work Practice). 149p. 1981. 19.95x (ISBN 0-422-77100-7, Pub. by Tavistock England); pap. 9.25x (ISBN 0-422-77110-4, Pub. by Tavistock England). Methuen Inc.
Wilkes, Stanley W., Jr., jt. auth. see Tees, David W.
Wilkie, Bernard. Creating Special Effects for TV & Film. (Media Manual Ser.). 1977. media manual 10.95 (ISBN 0-240-50947-1). Focal Pr.
Wilkie, James W. The Mexican Revolution: Federal Expenditure & Social Change Since 1910. 2nd rev ed. LC 74-103072. 1970. 33.50x (ISBN 0-520-01919-9); pap. 7.50x (ISBN 0-520-01869-9, CAMPUS36). U of Cal Pr.
Wilkie, James W., ed. Statistical Abstract of Latin America. LC 56-63569. (Statistical Abstract of Latin America Ser.: Vol. 20). 1980. lib. bdg. 47.50x o.p. (ISBN 0-87903-238-3); pap. text ed. 32.50x o.p. (ISBN 0-87903-237-5). UCLA Lat Am Ctr.
--Statistical Abstract of Latin America, 1978. LC 56-63569. (Statistical Abstract of Latin America Ser.: Vol. 19). 1979. text ed. 35.50x (ISBN 0-87903-236-7); pap. 32.50x (ISBN 0-87903-235-9). UCLA Lat Am Ctr.
--Statistical Abstract of Latin America, 1981, Vol. 21. LC 56-63569. 1981. lib. bdg. 50.00x (ISBN 0-87903-239-1). UCLA Lat Am Ctr.
Wilkie, James W. & Haber, Stephen, eds. Statistical Abstract of Latin America, Vol. 22. LC 56-63569. (Statistical Abstract of Latin America Ser.). 1983. lib. bdg. 75.00x (ISBN 0-87903-241-3). UCLA Lat Am Ctr.
Wilkie, James W. & Turovsky, Paul, eds. Statistical Abstract of Latin America, 1976. LC 56-63569. (Statistical Abstracts of Latin America Ser.: Vol. 17). (Illus.). 500p. 1976. pap. text ed. 35.00x (ISBN 0-87903-230-8). UCLA Lat Am Ctr.
Wilkie, Jane. Confessions of an Ex-Fan Magazine Writer. LC 80-780. (Illus.). 288p. 1981. 12.95 o.p. (ISBN 0-385-15921-8). Doubleday.
--The Divorced Woman's Handbook: An Outline for Starting the First Year Alone. (Illus.). 1980. pap. 4.95 (ISBN 0-688-08607-1). Quill NY.
Wilkie, Katharine & Moseley, Elizabeth. Atlantis. LC 79-473. (Illus.). 192p. (gr. 7 up). 1979. PLB 7.79 o.p. (ISBN 0-671-32910-3). Messner.
Wilkie, Katharine E. Clyde Beatty: Boy Animal Trainer. LC 68-55145. (Childhood of Famous Americans Ser.). (Illus.). (gr. 3-7). 1968. 3.95 o.p. (ISBN 0-672-50032-9). Bobbs.
--Daniel Boone: Taming the Wilds. LC 60-6468. (Discovery Books). (Illus.). (gr. 2-5). 1960. PLB 6.69 (ISBN 0-8116-6251-9). Garrard.
--Pocahontas: Indian Princess. LC 69-10375. (Indian Books Ser). (Illus.). (gr. 2-5). 1969. PLB 6.69 (ISBN 0-8116-6605-0). Garrard.
--Simon Kenton: Young Trail Blazer. LC 60-8882. (Childhood of Famous Americans Ser.). (Illus.). (gr. 3-7). 1960. 3.95 o.p. (ISBN 0-672-50166-X). Bobbs.
--Will Clark: Boy in Buckskins. LC 62-16614. (Childhood of Famous Americans Ser.). (Illus.). (gr. 3-7). 1953. 3.95 o.p. (ISBN 0-672-50186-4). Bobbs.
Wilkie, Katherine. Helen Keller. new ed. (Childhood of Famous Americans Ser.). (Illus.). 204p. (Orig.). (gr. 2 up). 1983. pap. 3.95 (ISBN 0-672-52749-9). Bobbs.
Wilkie, W. E. The Cardinal Protectors of England: Rome & the Tudors Before the Reformation. LC 73-82462. 224p. 1974. 44.50 (ISBN 0-521-20332-5). Cambridge U Pr.
Wilkin, Eloise, illus. Baby's First Christmas. LC 80-80710. (Board Bks). (Illus.). 14p. (ps). 1980. 3.50 (ISBN 0-394-84575-7). Random.
--Baby's Mother Goose. 24p. (ps). 1975. 2.95 (ISBN 0-307-10411-7, Golden Pr). Western Pub.
--Eloise Wilkin Four Baby's First Golden Books, 4 bks. (Illus.). (ps). 1981. boxed set 5.95 (ISBN 0-307-13650-7, Golden Pr); 1.50 ea. Western Pub.
--How Big Is Baby? (Baby's First Golden Bks.). (Illus.). 8p. (ps). 1980. 1.50 (ISBN 0-307-10756-6, Golden Pr). Western Pub.
--The Little Book. (Baby's First Golden Bks.). (Illus.). 8p. (ps). 1981. 1.50 (ISBN 0-307-10755-8, Golden Pr). Western Pub.
--Nursery Rhymes. LC 78-64606. (Board Bks). (Illus.). (ps). 1979. bds. 3.50 (ISBN 0-394-84129-8, BYR). Random.
Wilkin, Leon O., Jr., jt. auth. see Lewis, Benjamin.
Wilkins, Cletus, Jr., jt. ed. see Feit, Eugene D.
Wilkins, D. A. Notional Syllabuses. 1977. pap. text ed. 7.95x (ISBN 0-19-437071-2). Oxford U Pr.
Wilkins, David. Second-Language Learning & Teaching. 96p. 1972. pap. text ed. 9.95 (ISBN 0-7131-5759-3). E Arnold.
Wilkins, E. J., jt. auth. see Hansen, T. L.
Wilkins, Earle W., et al. MGH Textbook of Emergency Medicine: Emergency Care As Practiced at the Massachusetts General Hospital. (Illus.). 840p. 1978. 56.00 (ISBN 0-683-09083-6). Williams & Wilkins.
Wilkins, Earle W., Jr. MGH Textbook of Emergency Medicine. 2nd ed. (Illus.). 1056p. 1983. text ed. price not set (ISBN 0-683-09084-4). Williams & Wilkins.
Wilkins, Eliza G. Know Thyself in Greek & Latin Literature. Taran, Leonardo, ed. LC 78-66584. (Ancient Philosophy Ser.: Vol. 28). 111p. 1979. lib. bdg. 13.00 o.s.i. (ISBN 0-8240-9572-3). Garland Pub.
Wilkins, Ernest J. Impacto Hispanico: Lectures Contemporaneas. LC 78-14336. 1979. pap. text ed. 11.50 (ISBN 0-471-03537-8). Wiley.
Wilkins, Ernest J., jt. auth. see Hansen, Terrence L.
Wilkins, Esther M. Clinical Practice of the Dental Hygienist: The True Role of the Dental Hygienist As Dental Health Educator & Clinical Operator for Specific Preventive Techniques. 5th ed. LC 82-8966. (Illus.). 913p. 1983. 37.50 (ISBN 0-8121-0844-2). Lea & Febiger.
Wilkins, Frances. Growing up in the Age of Chivalry. LC 77-84931. (Illus.). (gr. 6-8). 1978. 6.95 o.p. (ISBN 0-399-20634-5). Putnam Pub Group.
Wilkins, Francis. Growing Up Between the Wars. (Illus.). 72p. (gr. 7-12). 1980. 14.95 (ISBN 0-7134-0775-1, Pub by Batsford England). David & Charles.
Wilkins, Gloria & Miller, Susanne. Strategies for Success: An Effective Guide for Teachers of Secondary Level Slow Learners. 364p. 1982. pap. text ed. 24.95x (ISBN 0-8077-2701-6). Tchrs Coll.
Wilkins, Gregory L. African Influence in the United Nations, 1967-1975: The Politics & Techniques of Gaining Compliance to U. N. Principles & Resolutions. LC 80-5735. 263p. (Orig.). 1981. lib. bdg. 22.25 (ISBN 0-8191-1424-3); pap. text ed. 11.50 (ISBN 0-8191-1425-1). U Pr of Amer.
Wilkins, Joan A. Breaking the T.V. Habit. 160p. 1982. 9.95 (ISBN 0-684-17788-9, ScribT). Scribner.
Wilkins, John. The Discovery of a World in the Moone, Nineteen Thirty-Eight. LC 73-14920. 1973. lib. bdg. 27.00x (ISBN 0-8201-1123-6). Schol Facsimiles.
--Essay Towards a Real Character & a Philosophical Language. (Linguistics 13th-18th Centuries Ser.). 612p. (Fr.). 1974. Repr. of 1668 ed. lib. bdg. 148.50x o.p. (ISBN 0-8287-0884-3, 71-5018). Clearwater Pub.
--Mercury: Or the Secret & Swift Messenger: Showing How a Man with Privacy & Speed Communicate his Thoughts to a Friend at any Distance (1707) (Foundations of Semiotics: 6). xxv, 122p. 1983. 14.00 (ISBN 90-272-3276-8). Benjamins North Am.
Wilkins, Kay S., ed. Women's Education in the United States: A Guide to Information Sources. LC 79-54691. (Education Information Guide Ser.: Vol. 4). 1979. 42.00z (ISBN 0-8103-1410-X). Gale.
Wilkins, Leslie T., jt. ed. see Carter, Robert M.
Wilkins, Lewis L., tr. see Pannenberg, Wolfhart.
Wilkins, R. A. & Viamonte, M. Interventional Radiology. (Illus.). 512p. 1982. text ed. 59.95 (ISBN 0-632-00769-9, B 5256-1). Mosby.
Wilkins, Ronald J. Achieving Social Justice: A Christian Perspective. (To Live Is Christ Ser.). 1981. pap. text ed. 4.60 (ISBN 0-697-01775-3); tchr's manual, pap. 3.75 (ISBN 0-697-01776-1); spirit masters 10.95 (ISBN 0-697-01777-X). Wm C Brown.
--Challenge! rev. ed. (To Live Is Christ Ser). 1983. pap. 4.60 (ISBN 0-697-01850-4); tchr's manual, pap. 3.75 (ISBN 0-697-01851-2); tests 12.95. Wm C Brown.
--Christian Faith: The Challenge of the Call. 72p. 1978. pap. 3.25 (ISBN 0-697-01684-6); tchrs.' manual 3.75 (ISBN 0-697-01688-9); spirit masters 10.95 (ISBN 0-697-01690-0); tests 9.95. Wm C Brown.
--Christian Living: The Challenge of Response. 72p. 1978. pap. 3.25 (ISBN 0-697-01686-2); tchrs. manual 3.75 (ISBN 0-697-01689-7); tests 9.95 (ISBN 0-686-84110-7). Wm C Brown.
--The Emerging Church. rev. ed. (To Live Is Christ Ser). 1981. pap. 4.75 (ISBN 0-697-01760-5); tchr.' manual 4.75 (ISBN 0-697-01761-3); activity kit 34.00 (ISBN 0-697-01650-1). Wm C Brown.
--Focus on Faith in Jesus. (To Live in Christ Ser.). 1980. pap. 3.25 (ISBN 0-697-01719-2); parish ed. 3.75 (ISBN 0-697-01720-6); spirit masters 10.95; tests 10.25. Wm C Brown.
--Focus on Faith in Jesus: Extended Study. (To Live Is Christ Ser.). 206p. 1980. pap. 3.80 (ISBN 0-697-01717-6); tchr's manual 3.85 (ISBN 0-697-01718-4); spirit masters 10.95; tests 10.25. Wm C Brown.
--Focus on Growth in the Church. (To Live in Christ Ser.). 1980. pap. 3.25 (ISBN 0-697-01723-0); parish ed., tchr's manual 3.75; spirit masters 10.95; tests 10.25. Wm C Brown.
--Focus on Growth in the Church: Extended Study. (To Live Is Christ Ser.). 216p. 1980. pap. 3.80 (ISBN 0-697-01721-4); tchr's manual 3.85 (ISBN 0-697-01722-2); spirit masters 10.95; tests 10.25. Wm C Brown.
--Focus on Life. rev. ed. (To Live Is Christ Ser). 1975. pap. write for info. o.p. (ISBN 0-697-01615-3); tchr's manual 3.75 o.p. (ISBN 0-697-01645-5). Wm C Brown.
--The JESUS Book. (To Live Is Christ Ser.). 208p. 1979. pap. 4.50x (ISBN 0-697-01639-0); tchrs. manual 3.40x (ISBN 0-697-01649-8); spirit master 10.95 (ISBN 0-697-01692-7). Wm C Brown.
--The Jesus Book: Short Ed. (To Live Is Christ Ser.). 112p. 1979. pap. 3.25 (ISBN 0-697-01695-1); tchr's manual 3.75 (ISBN 0-697-01714-1); spirit masters 10.95 (ISBN 0-697-01692-7). Wm C Brown.
--Man & Woman. Rev. ed. (To Live Is Christ Ser.). 1980. pap. 4.60x (ISBN 0-697-01750-8); tchr's manual 4.75x (ISBN 0-697-01751-6); spirit masters 10.95 (ISBN 0-697-01752-4). Wm C Brown.
--Reading the New Testament. (To Live Is Christ Ser). 160p. 1983. pap. 4.00 extended study (ISBN 0-697-01810-5); tchr's manual 3.00 (ISBN 0-697-01811-3); spirit masters 12.95; tchr's manual 3.75 (ISBN 0-697-01680-3). Wm C Brown.
--Religion in North America. (To Live Is Christ Ser.). 208p. 1979. pap. 4.50 (ISBN 0-697-01701-X); tchr's manual 3.00 (ISBN 0-686-77606-2); spirit masters 10.95 (ISBN 0-697-01735-4). Wm C Brown.
--The Religions of the World. rev. ed. (To Live Is Christ Ser.). 240p. 1979. pap. 4.60 (ISBN 0-697-01715-X); tchr's manual 3.00 (ISBN 0-697-01728-1); spirit masters 10.95 (ISBN 0-697-01730-3). Wm C Brown.

--Understanding Christian Morality. (To Live Is Christ Ser.). 256p. 1982. pap. 4.60; tchr's manual 3.75 (ISBN 0-697-01800-8); spirit masters 10.95 (ISBN 0-697-01801-6). Wm C Brown.

--Understanding Christian Morality: Short Edition. (To Live Is Christ Ser.). 112p. 1977. pap. 3.85 (ISBN 0-697-01661-7); tchr's manual 4.25 (ISBN 0-697-01667-6). Wm C Brown.

--Understanding Christian Worship: School Edition. (To Live Is Christ Ser.). 216p. 1982. pap. 4.65 (ISBN 0-697-01802-4); tchr's manual 3.75 (ISBN 0-697-01800-8). Wm C Brown.

--Understanding Christian Worship: Short Edition. (To Live Is Christ Ser.). 80p. 1977. pap. 3.60 (ISBN 0-697-01663-3); tchrs.' ed. 4.25 (ISBN 0-697-01669-2). Wm C Brown.

--Understanding the Bible: School Edition. rev. ed. (To Live Is Christ Ser.). 212p. 1982. pap. 4.60 (ISBN 0-697-01786-9); tchr's manual 3.75 (ISBN 0-697-01787-7); spirit masters 12.95. Wm C Brown.

--Understanding the Bible: Short Edition. (To Live Is Christ Ser.). 1977. pap. 3.60 (ISBN 0-697-01659-5); tchr's manual 4.25 (ISBN 0-697-01665-X); spirit masters 12.95. Wm C Brown.

Wilkins, Ronnie D., jt. auth. see DeLoach, Charlene P.

Wilkins, Roy & Mathews, Tom. Standing Fast: The Autobiography of Roy Wilkins. LC 81-70185. (Illus.). 384p. 1982. 16.95 (ISBN 0-670-14229-8). Viking Pr.

Wilkins, Tony & Grace, Ron. Beginner's Guide to Do-It-Yourself. (Illus.). 159p. 1974. 8.95 o.p. (ISBN 0-7207-0657-2). Transatlantic.

Wilkins, William J. The Sword & the Gavel. (Illus.). 328p. 1981. text ed. 14.95 o.p. (ISBN 0-916076-46-6). Writing.

Wilkinson. Hepatorenal Disorders. (Kidney Diseases Ser.: Vol. 3). 192p. 1982. 32.75 (ISBN 0-8247-1833-X). Dekker.

--Placental Transfer. 228p. 1979. text ed. 49.50 o.p. (ISBN 0-272-79531-3). Univ Park.

Wilkinson, jt. auth. see Mitchell.

Wilkinson, jt. auth. see Tweedie.

Wilkinson, et al. Clinical Anesthesia: Case Selections from the University of California, San Francisco. LC 79-23938. (Illus.). 324p. 1980. 49.50 (ISBN 0-8016-3423-7). Mosby.

Wilkinson, A. & Dawson, P. R. The Use of Fluxes in Reducing Metal Losses as Fume & or Dross in Secondary Brass Production, 1977. 1981. 40.00x (ISBN 0-686-97159-0, Pub. by W Spring England). State Mutual Bk.

Wilkinson, A., jt. auth. see Dawson, P. R.

Wilkinson, Alex C., ed. Classroom Computers & Cognitive Science. (Educational Technology Ser.). Date not set. write for info. (ISBN 0-12-752070-8). Acad Pr.

Wilkinson, Andrew. Language & Education. (Oxford Studies in Education Ser.). 1977. pap. text ed. 6.50x o.p. (ISBN 0-19-911101-4). Oxford U Pr.

Wilkinson, B. The High Middle Ages in England, 1154-1377. LC 77-8490. (Conference on British Studies Bibliographical Handbooks). 1978. 19.95 (ISBN 0-521-21732-6). Cambridge U Pr.

Wilkinson, Barry & Horrocks, David. Computer Peripherals. LC 81-3218. 310p. 1981. pap. 19.75x o.s.i. (ISBN 0-8448-1388-5). Crane-Russak Co.

Wilkinson, Bruce & Boa, Kenneth. Talk Thru the Bible. 469p. 1983. Repr. of 1981 ed. 14.95 (ISBN 0-8407-5286-5). Nelson.

Wilkinson, Bud. Sports Illustrated Football Defense. 1973. 5.95i (ISBN 0-397-00833-3); pap. 2.95i (ISBN 0-397-00993-3, LP-086). Har-Row.

--Sports Illustrated Football Quarterback. LC 75-17678. (Sports Illustrated Ser). (Illus.). 1976. 5.95 o.p. (ISBN 0-397-01097-4); pap. 2.95i (ISBN 0-397-01105-9). Har-Row.

Wilkinson, Bud & Sports Illustrated Editors. Sports Illustrated Football Offense. LC 72-2924. (Illus.). 1972. 5.95i (ISBN 0-397-00834-1); pap. 2.95i (ISBN 0-397-00910-0, LP-69). Har-Row.

Wilkinson, Charles F., jt. ed. see Strickland, Bernard F.

Wilkinson, D., jt. ed. see Rho, M.

Wilkinson, D. S. Nursing & Management of Skin Diseases: A Guide to Practical Dermatology for Doctors & Nurses. 4th ed. 403p. 1977. 16.95 (ISBN 0-571-04875-7); pap. 11.95 (ISBN 0-571-04876-5). Faber & Faber.

Wilkinson, David. Cohesion & Conflict: Lessons from the Study of Three-Party Interaction. LC 76-5951. 250p. 1976. text ed. 27.50 (ISBN 0-312-14665-5). St Martin.

--Deadly Quarrels: Lewis F. Richardson & the Statistical Study of War. 1980. 25.75x (ISBN 0-520-03829-0). U of Cal Pr.

Wilkinson, E. M., tr. see LaTouche, Robert.

Wilkinson, Elizabeth M., ed. see Bullough, Edward.

Wilkinson, Elizabeth M., ed. see Schiller, J. Friedrich.

Wilkinson, Frank. Bygones. 540p. 1981. 14.95 (ISBN 0-399-12572-8). Putnam Pub Group.

Wilkinson, Frederick. Famous Battles. LC 80-50959. (New Reference Library Ser.). PLB 11.96 (ISBN 0-382-06395-3). Silver.

Wilkinson, Frederick, ed. The Book of Shooting for Sport & Skill. (Illus.). 352p. 1980. 19.95 o.p. (ISBN 0-517-54177-7, Michelman Bks). Crown.

Wilkinson, Geoffrey, jt. auth. see Cotton, Albert F.

Wilkinson, Geoffrey, jt. auth. see Cotton, F. Albert.

Wilkinson, Geoffrey & Stone, F. G., eds. Comprehensive Organometallic Chemistry: The Synthesis, Reactions & Structures of Organometallic Compounds. LC 82-7595. 9000p. 1982. 2150.00 (ISBN 0-08-025269-9). Pergamon.

Wilkinson, Henry R., jt. auth. see Monkhouse, Francis.

Wilkinson, J., jt. auth. see Goudie, A.

Wilkinson, J. B. & Moore, R. J. Harry's Cosmeticology. 7th ed. (Illus.). 1982. 95.00 (ISBN 0-8206-0295-7). Chem Pub.

Wilkinson, J. B. & Moore, R. J., eds. Harry's Cosmeticology. 1982. 160.00x (ISBN 0-7114-5679-8, Pub. by Macdonald & Evans). State Mutual Bk.

Wilkinson, J. Harvie. From Brown to Bakke: The Supreme Court & School Integration 1954-1978. 1979. 25.00x (ISBN 0-19-502567-9). Oxford U Pr.

Wilkinson, James H. Algebraic Eigenvalue Problem. (Monographs on Numerical Analysis Ser). 1965. 77.00x (ISBN 0-19-853403-5). Oxford U Pr.

Wilkinson, Jean. Work with us in a Hospital. LC 80-83295. (Illus.). (gr. 1-5). 1982. PLB 9.25g (ISBN 0-516-02421-3). Childrens.

--Work with us in a Hotel. LC 80-83295. (Illus.). (gr. 1-5). 1982. PLB 9.25g (ISBN 0-516-02422-1). Childrens.

--Work with us in a Printing Company. LC 80-83295. (Illus.). (gr. 1-5). 1982. PLB 9.25g (ISBN 0-516-02424-8). Childrens.

--Work with us in an Oil Company. LC 80-83295. (Illus.). (gr. 1-5). 1982. PLB 9.25g (ISBN 0-516-02423-X). Childrens.

--Work with us in Telephone Company. LC 80-83295. (Illus.). (gr. 1-5). 1982. PLB 9.25g (ISBN 0-516-02425-6). Childrens.

Wilkinson, Jean, jt. auth. see Reese, Lyn.

Wilkinson, Jill & Canter, Sandra. Social Skills Training Manual: Assessment, Programme Design & Management. LC 81-12957. 148p. 1982. 33.95x (ISBN 0-471-10056-0, Pub. by Wiley-Interscience); pap. 13.95x (ISBN 0-471-10067-6). Wiley.

Wilkinson, John. Narrative of a Blockade Runner. (Collector's Library of the Civil War). 1983. 26.60 (ISBN 0-8094-4254-X). Silver.

Wilkinson, John, jt. auth. see Chichester, Michael.

Wilkinson, John P. D., jt. auth. see Levy, Samuel.

Wilkinson, Joseph W. Accounting & Information Systems. LC 81-13153. (Wiley Series in Accounting & Information Systems). 845p. 1982. text ed. 31.95 (ISBN 0-471-04986-7); tchr's manual avail. (ISBN 0-471-04987-5). Wiley.

Wilkinson, Judith. The Overhead Projector. (Illus.). 79p. (Orig.). 1979. pap. 7.50x (ISBN 0-900229-95-0). Intl Pubns Serv.

Wilkinson, Karl. Rewinding Small Motors. (Illus.). (YA) (gr. 10 up). 1965. pap. 7.50x o.s.i. (ISBN 0-408-00308-1). Transatlantic.

Wilkinson, L., jt. auth. see Waterson, A. P.

Wilkinson, L. P. The Roman Experience. LC 81-40779. 234p. 1981. pap. text ed. 8.75 (ISBN 0-8191-1809-5). U Pr of Amer.

Wilkinson, L. P., tr. see Virgil.

Wilkinson, Louise, ed. Communicating in the Classroom. (Language, Thought and Culture Ser.). 1982. 32.00 (ISBN 0-12-752060-0). Acad Pr.

Wilkinson, M., jt. auth. see Russell, R. R.

Wilkinson, Marcia. Cervical Spondylosis: Its Early Diagnosis & Treatment. 2nd ed. (Illus.). 1971. 11.25 o.p. (ISBN 0-7216-9355-5). Saunders.

Wilkinson, Martin. Children & Divorce. (Practice of Social Work Ser.: No. 6). 208p. 1981. 19.95x (ISBN 0-631-12514-0, Pub. by Basil Blackwell England); pap. 12.00x (ISBN 0-631-12524-8). Biblio Dist.

Wilkinson, Pamela F. Ridin' the Rainbow. LC 81-67744. (Illus.). 40p. 1983. 10.95 (ISBN 0-931722-10-1); pap. 5.95 (ISBN 0-931722-09-8); signed ltd. ed. 32.50x (ISBN 0-931722-08-X); PLB 9.45 (ISBN 0-931722-11-X). Corona Pub.

Wilkinson, Paul. In Celebration of Play: An Integrated Approach to Play & Child Development. LC 79-3841. 320p. 1980. 25.00 (ISBN 0-312-41078-6). St Martin.

Wilkinson, Philip, jt. auth. see Grace, Clive.

Wilkinson, Sylvia. Automobiles. LC 82-4441. (New True Bks.). (Illus.). (gr. k-4). 1982. PLB 9.25g (ISBN 0-516-01608-3). Childrens.

--Bone of My Bones. 252p. 1982. 13.95 (ISBN 0-399-12628-7). Putnam Pub Group.

--Can-Am. LC 80-27530. (World of Racing Ser.). (Illus.). 48p. (gr. 4 up). 1981. PLB 10.60 (ISBN 0-516-04710-8); pap. 3.95 (ISBN 0-516-44710-6). Childrens.

--Champ Cars. LC 81-7687. (World of Racing Ser.). (Illus.). (gr. 4 up). 1982. PLB 10.60g (ISBN 0-686-83169-1); pap. 3.95 (ISBN 0-516-44711-4). Childrens.

--Formula Atlantic. LC 81-7644. (World of Racing Ser.). (Illus.). 48p. (gr. 4 up). 1981. PLB 10.60 (ISBN 0-516-04713-2); pap. 3.95 (ISBN 0-516-44713-0). Childrens.

--Formula One. LC 81-7670. (World of Racing Ser.). (Illus.). 48p. (gr. 4 up). 1981. PLB 10.60 (ISBN 0-516-04716-7); pap. 3.95 (ISBN 0-516-44716-5). Childrens.

--Shadow of the Mountain. 1977. 8.95 o.s.i. (ISBN 0-395-25170-2). HM.

Wilkinson, Sylvia & Campbell, Ed, eds. Change: A Handbook for the Teaching of English & Social Studies. 225p. 1971. 3.00 (ISBN 0-686-15542-4). Learning Inst NC.

Wilkinson, William R. Executive Musical Chairs. 176p. 1983. 15.00 (ISBN 0-911735-00-3). Warrington.

Wilkinson-Latham, Christopher. The Royal Green Jackets. (Men-at-Arms Ser.). (Illus.). 40p. 1976. pap. 7.95 o.p. (ISBN 0-85045-249-X). Hippocrene Bks.

Wilkinson-Latham, Robert. Swords & Other Edged Weapons. LC 77-13385. (Arco Color Ser.). (Illus.). 1978. lib. bdg. 8.95 (ISBN 0-668-04475-6); pap. 6.95 (ISBN 0-668-04486-1). Arco.

--Uniforms & Weapons of the Crimean War. LC 77-82072. (Illus.). 1978. 11.95 o.p. (ISBN 0-88254-451-9). Hippocrene Bks.

Wilkon, Jozef & Bauman, Kurt. The Contest of the Birds. Bell, Anthea, tr. 32p. 1981. 15.95x (ISBN 0-686-97124-8, Pub. by Andersen-Hutchinson England). State Mutual Bk.

Wilkowski, Jean M. Conference Diplomacy II A Case Study: The UN Conference on Science & Technology for Development, Vienna, 1979. LC 82-12103. 56p. 1982. 4.00 (ISBN 0-934742-20-0, Inst Study Diplomacy). Geo U Sch For Serv.

Wilks, Ed, jt. auth. see Lipman, David.

Wilks, Ivor. Asante in the Nineteenth Century. LC 74-77834. (African Studies: No. 13). (Illus.). 872p. 1975. 74.50 (ISBN 0-521-20463-1). Cambridge U Pr.

Wilks, Michael, jt. ed. see Baker, Derek.

Wilks, Y., jt. auth. see Charniak, E.

Will & Nicolas. Chaga. LC 55-7615. (Illus.). (gr. k-3). 1955. 4.95 (ISBN 0-15-215894-4, HJ). HarBraceJ.

Will, Charles A. Life Company Underwriting. LC 74-78029. 1974. pap. text ed. 11.00 (ISBN 0-915322-07-2). LOMA.

Will, Connie A. & Eighmy, Judith B. Being a Long-Term Care Nursing Assistant. (Illus.). 1983. pap. text ed. 10.95 (ISBN 0-89303-232-8). R J Brady.

Will, Frederic. Archilochos. (World Authors Ser.: Greece: No. 59). 1969. lib. bdg. 7.95 o.p. (ISBN 0-8057-2060-X, Twayne). G K Hall.

--Herondas. (World Authors Ser.). lib. bdg. 15.95 (ISBN 0-8057-2420-6, Twayne). G K Hall.

Will, George F. The Pursuit of Happiness & Other Sobering Thoughts. LC 77-25956. 1979. pap. 6.95i (ISBN 0-06-090738-X, CN 738, CN). Har-Row.

--The Pursuit of Virture & Other Tory Notions. 1983. pap. 6.75 (ISBN 0-671-45712-8, Touchstone Bks). S&S.

--Statecraft As Soulcraft. 1983. 14.50 (ISBN 0-671-42733-4). S&S.

Will, George F. & Hyde, George E. Corn among the Indians of the Upper Missouri. LC 64-63592. 323p. 1964. 21.50x (ISBN 0-8032-0892-8); pap. 3.95x (ISBN 0-8032-5846-1, BB 195, Bison). U of Nebr Pr.

Will, Mimi, jt. auth. see Porat, Freida.

Will, Paul J., et al. Public Education Religion Studies: An Overview. Taylor, Mark, ed. LC 80-12237. (Aids for the Study of Religion Ser.). Date not set. 17.50 (ISBN 0-89130-401-0, 01-03-07); pap. 12.00 (ISBN 0-89130-402-9). Scholars Pr CA.

Will, R. Ted & Hasty, Ronald W. Retailing. 2nd ed. 1977. text ed. 22.95 scp o.p. (ISBN 0-06-389403-3, HarpC); instrs. manual avail. o.p. (ISBN 0-06-378009-7). Har-Row.

Will, Thomas E. Telecommunications Structure & Management in the Executive Branch of Government: 1900-1970. 1978. lib. bdg. 25.50 o.p. (ISBN 0-89158-286-X). Westview.

Willa Cather Pre-Centennial Conference, 1972. Five Essays on Willa Cather: The Merrimack Symposium. Murphy, John J., ed. LC 74-78413. pap. 2.50 (ISBN 0-686-09909-5). Cather Bk.

Willadeene. Denim, Lace, & Bandanas. 1976. pap. 3.95 (ISBN 0-682-48595-0). Exposition.

Willadeene & Joan. Sounds of My Soul. (Illus.). 64p. 1981. pap. 4.00 (ISBN 0-682-49811-4). Exposition.

Willams, Mary C., jt. ed. see Owen, Guy.

Willan. Great Cooks & Their Recipes: From Taillevent to Escoffier. Date not set. 7.98 o.p. (ISBN 0-517-29245-9). Crown.

Willan, Ann. La Varenne Cooking Course. LC 82-3473. (Illus.). 500p. 1982. 34.95 (ISBN 0-688-00539-X). Morrow.

Willan, T. S. Elizabethan Manchester. 1980. 19.00 (ISBN 0-7190-1336-4). Manchester.

Willard, Beatrice E., jt. auth. see Zwinger, Ann H.

Willard, Beatrice L. Plant Sociology of Alpine Tundra, Trail Ridge, Rocky Mountain National Park, Colorado. Raese, Jon W., ed. LC 79-26590. (CSM Quarterly Ser.: Vol. 74, No. 4). (Illus.). 119p. 1979. pap. 10.00 (ISBN 0-686-63162-5). Colo Sch Mines.

Willard, Berton C. Russell W. Porter, Arctic Explorer, Artist, Telescope Maker. LC 76-8090. (Illus.). 1976. 12.50 (ISBN 0-87027-168-7). Cumberland Pr.

Willard, Charles A. Argumentation & the Social Grounds of Knowledge. LC 81-16199. 322p. 1983. text ed. 20.00 (ISBN 0-8173-0096-1). U of Ala Pr.

Willard, Frances E. & Livermore, Mary A. American Women: Fifteen Hundred Biographies with over Fourteen Hundred Portraits, 2 vols. LC 73-7985. Orig. Title: Woman of the Century. 824p. 1974. Repr. of 1897 ed. Set. 99.00x (ISBN 0-8103-3225-6). Gale.

Willard, Helen D., intro. by. William Blake Water-Color Drawings from the Museum of Fine Arts, Boston. (Illus.). 64p. 1954. pap. 1.25 (ISBN 0-686-83417-8). Mus Fine Arts Boston.

Willard, Hobarth, et al. Instrumental Methods of Analysis. 6th ed. Date not set. text ed. price not set o.s.i. (ISBN 0-442-24502-5). Van Nos Reinhold.

--Instrumental Methods of Analysis. 5th ed. 850p. 1974. text ed. 18.95x (ISBN 0-442-29479-4); solutions manual 2.50x (ISBN 0-442-29483-2). Van Nos Reinhold.

Willard, John W. Simon Willard & His Clocks. Orig. Title: History of Simon Willard, Inventor & Clockmaker. (Illus.). 1968. pap. 4.00 o.p. (ISBN 0-486-21943-7). Dover.

Willard, Josiah Flynt. Tramping with Tramps: Studies & Sketches of Vagabond Life. LC 72-129317. (Criminology, Law Enforcement, & Social Problems Ser.: No. 140). (Illus.). 414p. (With index added). 1972. Repr. of 1907 ed. lib. bdg. 12.50x (ISBN 0-87585-140-1). Patterson Smith.

Willard, Ken. Big Fun with Little Engines. Angle, Burr, ed. (Illus., Orig.). 1984. pap. price not set (ISBN 0-89024-055-8). Kalmbach.

Willard, Mervyn. Nutritional Management for the Practicing Physician. 1982. 26.95 (ISBN 0-201-08320-5, 08320, Med-Nurse). A-W.

Willard, Mildred W. The Ice Cream Cone. (Beginning to Read Ser). (Illus.). 32p. (gr. 1-3). 1973. 2.50 o.s.i. (ISBN 0-695-80418-9); PLB 3.39 o.s.i. (ISBN 0-695-40418-0). Follett.

Willard, Nancy. All on a May Morning. (Illus.). 32p. (gr. k-2). 1975. 5.95 o.p. (ISBN 0-399-20477-6). Putnam Pub Group.

--Household Tales of Moon & Water. LC 82-4804. 96p. 1982. 9.95 (ISBN 0-15-142184-6). HarBraceJ.

--The Merry History of a Christmas Pie: With a Delicious Description of a Christmas Soup. LC 74-79675. (Illus.). 48p. (gr. k-4). 1974. 4.95 o.p. (ISBN 0-399-20421-0). Putnam Pub Group.

--Shoes Without Leather. LC 75-45512. (Illus.). 32p. (gr. k-2). 1976. 6.95 o.p. (ISBN 0-399-20499-7). Putnam Pub Group.

--Simple Pictures Are Best. LC 78-6424. (Illus.). (ps-3). 1978. pap. 2.95 (ISBN 0-15-682625-9, VoyB). HarBraceJ.

--Snow Rabbit. (Illus.). 1975. 5.95 o.p. (ISBN 0-399-20474-1). Putnam Pub Group.

--Uncle Terrible: More Adventures of Anatole. (Illus.). 120p. 1982. 9.95 (ISBN 0-15-292793-X). HarBraceJ.

Willardson, R. K. & Beer, A. C., eds. Semiconductors & Semimetals. Incl. Vol. 1. Physics of III-V Compounds. 1967. 69.00 (ISBN 0-12-752101-1); Vol. 2. Physics of III-V Compounds. 1966. 69.00 (ISBN 0-12-752102-X); Vol. 3. Optical Properties of III-V Compounds. 1967. 69.00 (ISBN 0-12-752103-8); Vol. 4. Physics of III-V Compounds. 1968. 69.00 (ISBN 0-12-752104-6); Vol. 5. Infrared Detectors. 1970. 69.00 (ISBN 0-12-752105-4); Vol. 6. Injection Phenomena. 1970. 69.00 (ISBN 0-12-752106-2); Vol. 7A. Semiconductor Applications & Devices. 1971. 69.00 (ISBN 0-12-752107-0); Vol. 7B. Applications & Devices. 1971. 69.00 (ISBN 0-12-752147-X); Vol. 8. Techniques for Studying Semiconducting Materials. 1971. 69.00 (ISBN 0-12-752108-9); Vol. 9. Modulation Techniques. 1972. 69.00 (ISBN 0-12-752109-7); Vol. 10. 1975. 69.00 (ISBN 0-12-752110-0); Vol. 11. 1976. 25.00 (ISBN 0-12-752111-9); Vol. 12. 1977. 65.00 (ISBN 0-12-752112-7). Acad Pr.

Willardson, R. K., et al, eds. Semiconductors & Semimetals: Cadmium Telluride. 1978. Vol. 13. 35.00 (ISBN 0-12-752113-5); Vol. 14. 1979. 44.00 (ISBN 0-12-752114-3). Acad Pr.

Willardson, Robert & Beer, A., eds. Semiconductors & Semimetals, Vol. 16: Defects, HgCd, Se, HgCdO & Te. 1981. 37.50 (ISBN 0-12-752116-X). Acad Pr.

Willardson, Robert & Beer, A. C., eds. Semiconductors & Semimetals: Contacts, Junctions, Emitters, Vol. 15. 1981. 48.00 (ISBN 0-12-752115-1). Acad Pr.

Willbanks, Ray. Randolph Stow. (World Authors Ser.). 1978. lib. bdg. 15.95 (ISBN 0-8057-6313-9, Twayne). G K Hall.

Willcock, M. M. Commentary on Homer's Iliad Books 1-6. LC 74-108403. 1970. pap. text ed. 8.95 o.p. (ISBN 0-312-15225-6). St Martin.

Willcock, M. M., ed. see Plautus.

Willcocks, David, jt. auth. see Jacques, Reginald.

Willcocks, David & Ruttner, John, eds. Fifty Carols for Christmas & Advent. (Carols for Choirs, Book 2). 1970. 12.00 (ISBN 0-19-353566-1); pap. 7.00 (ISBN 0-19-353565-3). Oxford U Pr.

Willcocks, John, jt. ed. see Galton, Maurice.

Willcox, Alfred B., et al. Introduction to Calculus One & Two. 1971. text ed. 31.95 (ISBN 0-395-05543-1). HM.

Willcox, Kathleen M. Your Guide to Israel. LC 66-70968. (Your Guide Ser.). 1966. 5.25x o.p. (ISBN 0-8002-0781-5). Intl Pubns Serv.

Willcox, L. C., tr. see Giraudoux, Jean.
Willcox, Sheila. The Event Horse. LC 73-5923. (Illus.). 160p. 1973. 11.49i (ISBN 0-397-01000-1). Har-Row.
Willcox, W. F. International Migrations: Statistics. (Demographic Monographs Ser.). 1969. Vol. 1, 1112p. 145.00x (ISBN 0-677-02210-7); Vol. 2, 716p. 94.00x (ISBN 0-677-02380-4); Set. 213.00 (ISBN 0-677-02910-1). Gordon.
Willcox, William B. & Arnstein, Walter L. A History of England Vol. III: The Age of Aristocracy 1688 to 1830. 4th ed. Smith, Lacey B., ed. 304p. 1983. pap. text ed. 10.95 (ISBN 0-669-04379-6). Heath.
Willcox, William B., ed. see Franklin, Benjamin.
Willcoxen, Harriett. First Lady of India: The Story of Indira Ghandi. LC 69-10999. (gr. 7-8). 1969. 7.95 o.p. (ISBN 0-385-08954-6). Doubleday.
Wille, N. Die Schizophyceen der Plankton-Expedition der Humboldt-Stiftung. (Illus.). 1968. Repr. of 1904 ed. 16.80 (ISBN 3-7682-0808-7). Lubrecht & Cramer.
Wille, Wayne, pref. by. The World Book Year Book. LC 62-4818. (Illus.). 608p. (gr. 6-12). 1980. PLB write for info. o.p. (ISBN 0-7166-0481-7). World Bk.
Wille, Wayne, jt. ed. see World Book Inc.
Willeford, George, Jr. Medical Word Finder. 3rd ed. 464p. 1983. 19.95 (ISBN 0-13-573527-0, Busn). P-H.
Willeke, Bernard H. Imperial Government & Catholic Missions in China During the Years 1784-1785. (Missiology Ser). 1948. 3.00 (ISBN 0-686-11584-8). Franciscan Inst.
Willeke, Klaus, ed. Generation of Aerosols & Facilities for Exposure Experiments. LC 79-53420. (Illus.). 1980. 49.95 (ISBN 0-250-40293-9). Ann Arbor Science.
Willem, J. U. S. Trade Dollar. (Illus.). 1983. Repr. of 1961 ed. softcover supplement included 15.00 (ISBN 0-915262-98-3). S J Durst.
Willemain, Thomas R. Statistical Methods for Planners. (Illus.). 352p. 1980. 19.95x (ISBN 0-262-23101-8). MIT Pr.
Willemain, Thomas R. & Larson, Richard C., eds. Innovative Resouce Planning in Urban Public Safety Systems Vol. IV: Emergency Medical Systems Analysis: Papers on the Planning & Evaluation of Services. LC 77-80341. (Illus.). 224p. 1977. 23.95x (ISBN 0-669-01483-4). Lexington Bks.
Willems, Arnold & Hendrickson, Gordon. Living Wyoming's Past. (Illus.). (gr. 4). 1983. 12.95 (ISBN 0-87108-251-9); tchr's. guide 4.95 (ISBN 0-87108-250-0); ac tivity tablet 3.95 (ISBN 0-87108-252-7); activit y cards 9.95 (ISBN 0-87108-253-5). Pruett.
Willems, J. L., ed. see IFPtC4 Working Conference, Amsterdam, 1976.
Willems, Nicholas & Lucas, William M., Jr. Structural Analysis for Engineers. (Illus.). 1977. text ed. 36.50 (ISBN 0-07-070295-0, C); solns. manual 14.50 (ISBN 0-07-070296-9). McGraw.
Willems, Nicholas, et al. Strength of Materials. (Illus.). 576p. 1981. text ed. 31.95 (ISBN 0-07-070297-7, C); solns. manual 15.50 (ISBN 0-07-070298-5). McGraw.
Willenbrock, J. H., ed. Construction of Power Generation Facilities. LC 82-70491. 624p. 1982. pap. text ed. 44.00 (ISBN 0-87262-306-8). Am Soc Civil Eng.
Willenbrock, Jack H. & Thomas, H. Randolph, eds. Planning, Engineering & Construction of Electric Power Generation Facilities. LC 79-21427. (Construction Management & Engineering Ser.). 1980. 67.95x (ISBN 0-471-03808-3, Pub. by Wiley-Interscience). Wiley.
Willene, Lilly. The Petroleum Secretary's Handbook. 173p. 1982. 25.95x (ISBN 0-87814-195-2). Pennwell Books Division.
Willer, Earl C. Treasury of Inspirational Illustrations. (Preaching Helps Ser). 1974. pap. 2.95 o.p. (ISBN 0-8010-9557-3). Baker Bk.
Willer, S., jt. auth. see Wiesner, E.
Willer, Thomas F., compiled by. Southeast Asian References in the British Parliamentary Papers, 1801-1972-73: An Index. LC 77-620034. (Papers in International Studies: Southeast Asia: No. 48). 1977. pap. 8.50 (ISBN 0-89680-033-4, Ohio U Ctr Intl). Ohio U Pr.
Willerding, Margaret F. College Algebra & Trigonometry. 2nd ed. LC 74-22391. 613p. 1975. text ed. 26.95x (ISBN 0-471-94671-0). Wiley.
Willert, Albrecht. Religiose Existenz und Literarische Produktion. 377p. (Ger.). 1982. write for info. (ISBN 3-8204-5994-4). P Lang Pubs.
Willert, Arthur. Aspects of British Foreign Policyy. 1928. text ed. 29.50x (ISBN 0-686-83482-8). Elliots Bks.
Willerton, Chris. Teaching the Adult Bible Class. 2.95 (ISBN 0-89137-609-7). Quality Pubns.
Willet, Frank & Eyo, Ekpo. Treasures of Ancient Nigeria. LC 79-3497. (Illus.). 1980. 20.00 (ISBN 0-394-50975-7); pap. 16.95 (ISBN 0-394-73858-6). Knopf.
Willet, Shelagh M. & Ambrose, David R. Lesotho. (World Bibliographical Ser.: No. 3). 496p. 1980. 54.25 (ISBN 0-903450-11-9). ABC-Clio.
Willett, John. The Theatre of Erwin Piscator: Half a Century of Politics in the Theatre. LC 79-11941. (Illus.). 1979. text ed. 26.50x (ISBN 0-8419-0501-0). Holmes & Meier.
Willett, Joseph W. The World Food Situation: Problems & Prospects to 1985, 2 vols, Vols.1 & 2. LC 75-37594. 1976. 37.50 ea. (ISBN 0-685-66659-X). Vol. 1 (ISBN 0-379-00572-7). Vol. 2 (ISBN 0-379-00573-5). Oceana.
Willett, Peter. The Classic Racehorse. LC 82-11072. (Illus.). 272p. 1982. Repr. of 1981 ed. 23.00 (ISBN 0-8131-1477-2). U Pr of Ky.
Willett, Thomas D., jt. auth. see Stubblebine, Craig W.
Willetts, Duncan, jt. auth. see Amin, Mohamed.
Willetts, Harry, tr. see Solzhenitsyn, Aleksandr I.
Willetts, Peter, ed. Pressure Groups in the Global System. (Global Politics Ser.). 256p. 1982. pap. 14.00 (ISBN 0-86187-224-X). F Pinter Pubs.
Willetts, R. F. The Civilization of Ancient Crete. 1978. 42.50x (ISBN 0-520-03406-6). U of Cal Pr.
--Everyday Life in Ancient Crete. (Everyday Life Ser.). (Illus.). (gr. 9 up). 1969. 6.75 o.p. (ISBN 0-399-20049-5). Putnam Pub Group.
Willetts, William. Chinese Calligraphy: Its History & Aesthetic Motivation. (Illus.). 276p. 1981. 49.00x (ISBN 0-19-580478-3). Oxford U Pr.
Willey, Ann M. & Carter, Thomas P., eds. Clinical Genetics: Problems in Diagnosis & Counseling. 1982. 22.00 (ISBN 0-12-751860-6). Acad Pr.
Willey, Basil. More Nineteenth-Century Studies: A Group of Honest Doubters. LC 80-40635. 304p. 1981. pap. 10.95 (ISBN 0-521-28067-2). Cambridge U Pr.
--Nineteenth-Century Studies; Coleridge to Matthew Arnold. LC 80-40634. 288p. 1981. pap. 11.95 (ISBN 0-521-28066-4). Cambridge U Pr.
Willey, Gordon R. Introduction to American Archaeology, Vol. 1: North & Middle America. 1966. text ed. 30.95 (ISBN 0-13-477836-7). P-H.
Willey, Gordon R., ed. Archaeological Researches in Retrospect. LC 81-43603. (Illus.). 316p. 1982. pap. text ed. 13.50 (ISBN 0-8191-2239-4). U Pr of Amer.
Willey, Keith & Smith, Robin. Red Centre: The Landscape & People of Outback Australia. (Illus.). 106p. 1976. 12.00 o.p. (ISBN 0-584-97049-8). Transatlantic.
Willgoose, Carol. The Curriculum in Physical Education. 3rd ed. (Illus.). 1979. ref. ed. 22.95 (ISBN 0-13-196303-1). P-H.
Willi, Jurg. Couples in Collusion. LC 78-70619. 265p. 1982. 25.00 (ISBN 0-87668-489-4). Aronson.
William, Anlyan G., ed. see Duke University.
William Fox Mining Journal Books Ltd. Tin: The Working of a Commodity Agreement. 418p. 1980. 35.00x (ISBN 0-900117-05-2, Pub. by Mining Journal England). State Mutual Bk.
William H. Wise & Co. Editors, ed. The New Wise Cookbook. LC 78-73410. 208p. (Orig.). 1981. pap. 12.95 spiral bdg. (ISBN 0-448-15464-1, G&D). Putnam Pub Group.
William, Lindsey & Wilson, Clifford. Energy Non-Crisis. 2nd, rev., enl. ed. 240p. pap. 3.95 (ISBN 0-89051-068-7). CLP Pubs.
William, Meiden, jt. auth. see Hendrix, William.
William, Raymond. Keywords: A Vocabulary of Culture & Society. 1976. pap. 8.95 (ISBN 0-19-519855-7, GB). Oxford U Pr.
William T. Pecora Memorial Symposium, 2nd. Annual. Proceedings. McEwen, Robert B., ed. LC 77-83705. (Illus., Eng.). 1976. pap. text ed. 8.00 (ISBN 0-937294-08-X). ASP.
William-Ellis, Annabel. Fairy Tales from East & West. (Illus., Orig.). 1978. pap. 2.95 o.p. (ISBN 0-8467-0535-4, Pub. by Two Continents). Hippocrene Bks.
William Of Ockham. Predestination, God's Foreknowledge & Future Contingents. Kretzmann, Norman & Adams, Marilyn M., trs. LC 69-19995. 15.00 (ISBN 0-915144-14-X); pap. text ed. 4.95x (ISBN 0-915144-13-1). Hackett Pub.
William of St. Thierry, jt. auth. see Bernard of Clairvaux.
William-Olsson, Inger, jt. auth. see Berfenstam, Ragnar.
Williams. Advances in Free Radical Chemistry, Vol. 6. 1980. 83.00x (ISBN 0-471-26087-8, Pub. by Wiley Heyden). Wiley.
--Current Endocrine Concepts. 252p. 1982. 37.50 (ISBN 0-03-062119-4). Praeger.
--A Field Guide to the National Parks of East Africa. 29.95 (ISBN 0-686-42781-5, Collins Pub England). Greene.
--Pneumatic & Hydraulic Conveying of Solids. (Chemical Industries Ser.). 392p. 1983. price not set (ISBN 0-8247-1855-0). Dekker.
--Predictive Value of Short Term Screening Tests in Carcinogenicity Evaluation. (Applied Methods in Oncology Ser.: Vol. 3). 1980. 56.25 (ISBN 0-444-80281-9). ELsevier.
Williams & Arlott. A Field Guide to the Birds of East Africa. 29.95 (ISBN 0-686-42756-4, Collins Pub England). Greene.
--A Field Guide to the Orchids of Britain & Europe. 29.95 (ISBN 0-686-42774-2, Collins Pub England). Greene.
Williams & Head. Principles of Risk Management & Insurance, 2 vols. 2nd ed. 1981. 18.00 ea. o.p. IIA.
Williams & Long. Toward A Self-Managed Life Style. 3rd ed. 1982. 12.95 (ISBN 0-686-84653-2); supplementary materials avail. Hm.
Williams, jt. auth. see Capron.
Williams see International Seminar, Imperial College of Science & Technology, UK.
Williams, jt. auth. see Marshall.
Williams, jt. auth. see Needles.
Williams, ed. see King, Helen H.
Williams, A. E., jt. auth. see Beynon, J. H.
Williams, A. F. & Lom, W. L. Liquified Petroleum Gases: A Guide to Properties, Applications & Usage of Propane & Butane. LC 73-15141. (Illus.). 403p. 1973. 89.95 o.p. (ISBN 0-470-94850-7). Halsted Pr.
Williams, A. F., jt. auth. see Lom, W. L.
Williams, A. H., ed. see Wesley, John.
Williams, A. O. International Trade & Investment: A Managerial Approach. 461p. 1982. text ed. 29.95x (ISBN 0-471-03293-X). Ronald Pr.
Williams, A. O., jt. auth. see Chater, Hara H.
Williams, Alan. The Kid's & Grown-Ups' Toy-Making Book. LC 79-66602. (Illus.). 1979. 14.95 o.p. (ISBN 0-688-03507-8); pap. 7.95 o.p. (ISBN 0-688-08507-5). Morrow.
--The Police of Paris. LC 78-24189. 1979. 30.00x (ISBN 0-8071-0491-4). La State U Pr.
--Shah-Mak. LC 76-26087. 1976. 8.95 o.p. (ISBN 0-698-10773-X, Coward). Putnam Pub Group.
Williams, Alan L., jt. auth. see Haughton, Victor M.
Williams, Alan L., jt. auth. see Williams, Geoffrey L.
Williams, Alexander. Ali Baba & the Forty Thieves. LC 78-72132. (Illus.). (gr. 3-5). 1979. 6.75 (ISBN 0-89799-085-4); pap. 3.50 (ISBN 0-89799-056-0). Dandelion Pr.
Williams, Alfred. Folksongs of the Upper Thames. LC 68-31150. 1968. Repr. of 1923 ed. 34.00x (ISBN 0-8103-3421-6). Gale.
--Life in a Railway Factory. LC 79-56941. 1980. lib. bdg. 28.00 o.s.i. (ISBN 0-8240-0126-5). Garland Pub.
--Round about Middle Thames: Glimpses of Rural Victorian Life. 192p. 1982. text ed. 8.50x (ISBN 0-86299-032-7, Pub. by Sutton England). Humanities.
Williams, Alice C. Thru' the Turnstile: Tales of My Two Centuries. LC 76-15977. 1976. 6.95 o.p. (ISBN 0-395-24404-8). HM.
Williams, Allan M., jt. auth. see Phillips, David R.
Williams, Alma see Allen, W. S.
Williams, Andrew E., jt. auth. see Williams, John G.
Williams, Ann. The Crusades. Reeves, Marjorie, ed. (Then & There Ser.). (Illus.). 95p. (gr. 7-12). 1975. pap. text ed. 3.10 (ISBN 0-582-20441-0). Longman.
Williams, Arthur. Broadcasting & Democracy in West Germany. LC 77-90539. (International & Comparative Broadcasting Ser.). 218p. 1978. 24.95 (ISBN 0-87722-111-1). Temple U Pr.
Williams, Arthur B. Designer's Handbook of Integrated Circuits. 944p. 1983. 59.50 (ISBN 0-686-82175-0, C). McGraw.
--Handbook of Electronic Filter Design. 1980. 37.50 (ISBN 0-07-070430-9). McGraw.
Williams, Arthur L., et al. Introduction to Chemistry. 3rd ed. (Chemistry Ser.). (Illus.). 896p. 1981. text ed. 25.95 (ISBN 0-201-08726-X); study guide 8.95 (ISBN 0-201-08727-8). A-W.
--Introduction to Laboratory Chemistry: General. 2nd ed. LC 77-79451. (Chemistry Ser.). 1978. pap. text ed. 10.95 (ISBN 0-201-08458-9). A-W.
--Introduction to Laboratory Chemistry: Organic & Biochemistry. 2nd ed. LC 77-81204. (Chemistry Ser.). 1978. pap. text ed. 10.95 (ISBN 0-201-08459-7). A-W.
Williams, B. L. & Wilson, K., eds. A Biologist's Guide to the Principle Techniques of Practical Biochemistry. (Illus.). 336p. 1981. pap. text ed. write for info (ISBN 0-7131-2829-1). E Arnold.
Williams, B. S. & Williams, H. Orchid Growers Manual. 7th ed. 1973. Repr. of 1894 ed. 60.00 (ISBN 3-7682-0043-4). Lubrecht & Cramer.
Williams, B. W. The Joke of Christianizing China. pap. 1.00 (ISBN 0-686-95350-9). Am Atheist.
Williams, Barbara. Albert's Toothache. LC 74-4040. (Illus.). 32p. (ps-1). 1974. 9.95 (ISBN 0-525-25368-8); pap. 3.95 (ISBN 0-525-45037-8). Dutton.
--The Horrible, Impossible, Bad Witch Child. (Illus.). 1982. pap. 1.95 (ISBN 0-380-80283-X, 80283, Camelot). Avon.
--I Know a Fireman. (Community Helper Bks.). (Illus.). (gr. 1-3). 1967. PLB 4.29 o.p. (ISBN 0-399-60280-1). Putnam Pub Group.
--I Know a Garageman. (Community Helpers Bks.). (Illus.). (gr. 1-3). 1968. PLB 4.29 o.p. (ISBN 0-399-60281-X). Putnam Pub Group.
--I Know a Mayor. (Community Helper Bks.). (Illus.). (gr. 1-3). 1967. PLB 4.29 o.p. (ISBN 0-399-60285-2). Putnam Pub Group.
--I Know a Policeman. (Community Helper Bks.). (Illus.). (gr. 1-3). 1967. PLB 4.29 o.p. (ISBN 0-399-60288-7). Putnam Pub Group.
--I Know a Salesperson. LC 78-8385. (Community Helper Books). (Illus.). 1978. PLB 4.29 o.p. (ISBN 0-399-61118-5). Putnam Pub Group.
--Kevin's Grandma. (ps-1). 1975. 9.25 (ISBN 0-525-33115-8, 0898-270); pap. 3.95 (ISBN 0-525-45039-4, 0383-120). Dutton.
--Let's Go to an Indian Cliff Dwelling. (Let's Go Ser.). (Illus.). (gr. 4-6). 1965. PLB 4.29 o.p. (ISBN 0-399-60376-X). Putnam Pub Group.
--Tell the Truth, Marly Lee. 128p. (gr. 4-6). 1982. 9.95 (ISBN 0-525-44020-8, 0966-290). Dutton.
--Twelve Steps to Better Exposition. 2nd ed. 1978. pap. text ed. 8.95 (ISBN 0-675-08441-5). Merrill.
--Whatever Happened to Beverly Bigler's Birthday. LC 78-20575. (Let Me Read Ser). (Illus.). (gr. 1-5). 1979. pap. 1.95 (ISBN 0-15-696083-4, VoyB). HarBraceJ.
Williams, Bea, jt. auth. see Lund, Morten.
Williams, Ben A. Leave Her to Heaven. 429p. 1981. Repr. PLB 16.95 (ISBN 0-89966-257-9). Buccaneer Bks.
Williams, Ben J. & Foreyt, John P., eds. Pediatric Behavioral Medicine. 288p. 1981. 29.95 (ISBN 0-03-059599-1). Praeger.
Williams, Benjamin, ed. Remodelers Handbook. LC 76-53565. (Illus.). 1976. pap. 16.75 (ISBN 0-910460-21-3). Craftsman.
Williams, Bernard. Moral Luck: Philosophical Essays 1973-80. LC 81-10152. 240p. 1982. 34.50 (ISBN 0-521-24372-6); pap. 10.95 (ISBN 0-521-28691-3). Cambridge U Pr.
--Morality: An Introduction to Ethics. LC 70-172503. 1972. pap. 3.95xi (ISBN 0-06-131632-6, TB1632, Torch). Har-Row.
--Problems of the Self: Philosophical Papers, 1956-1972. 240p. 1973. 37.50 (ISBN 0-521-20225-6); pap. 11.95 (ISBN 0-521-29060-0). Cambridge U Pr.
Williams, Bernard, et al. Obscenity & Film Censorship. LC 81-10247. 192p. 1982. 24.95 (ISBN 0-521-24267-3); pap. 9.95 (ISBN 0-521-28565-8). Cambridge U Pr.
Williams, Bob. Excelsior. (Illus.). 232p. (Orig.). 1982. 11.95 (ISBN 0-911506-15-2). Thueson.
--Hoosier Hysteria! Indiana High School Basketball. (Illus.). 350p. 1982. 14.95 (ISBN 0-89651-300-9); pap. 9.95 (ISBN 0-89651-301-7). Icarus.
Williams, Brenda. The Thorn & the Rose: A Three-Act Play. LC 82-62676. 112p. (Orig.). 1983. pap. 6.50 (ISBN 0-935834-11-7). Rainbow-Betty.
Williams, Brett. John Henry: A Bio-Bibliography. LC 82-12056. (Popular Culture Bio-Bibliographies Ser.). 192p. 1983. lib. bdg. 29.95 (ISBN 0-313-22250-9, WJH/). Greenwood.
Williams, Brian. Aircraft. LC 76-13645. (Modern Knowledge Library). (Illus.). 48p. (gr. 5 up). 1976. 3.95 o.p. (ISBN 0-531-02440-7); PLB 3.95 o.p. (ISBN 0-531-01195-X). Watts.
--Come to Russia. LC 78-68589. (Come to Ser.). (Illus.). (gr. 4-6). 1979. PLB 9.40 s&l (ISBN 0-531-09157-0, Warwick Press). Watts.
--Exploring Under the Sea. LC 78-67839. (Explorer Books). (Illus.). (gr. 3-5). 1979. 2.95 (ISBN 0-531-09133-3, Warwick Press); PLB 7.90 s&l (ISBN 0-531-09118-X). Watts.
--Exploring War & Weapons. LC 78-6738. (Explorer Books). (Illus.). (gr. 3-5). 1979. 2.95 (ISBN 0-531-09132-5, Warwick Press); PLB 7.90 s&l (ISBN 0-531-09117-1). Watts.
Williams, Brian G. Compton Scattering: A Tool for the Investigation of Electron Momentum Distribution. LC 76-42261. (Illus.). 1977. text ed. 57.50x (ISBN 0-07-070360-4, C). McGraw.
Williams, Bruce, jt. auth. see Gray, Virginia.
Williams, Bryan L. & Wilson, Keith, eds. Principles & Techniques of Practical Biochemistry. 2nd ed. (Illus.). 328p. 1982. pap. text ed. 24.50 (ISBN 0-8391-1732-9, 18287). Univ Park.
Williams, C. A., Jr. Risk Management & Insurance. 3rd ed. 1976. text ed. 18.95 (ISBN 0-07-070558-5, C). McGraw.
Williams, C. Abdy. Story of Notation. LC 69-16797. 1968. Repr. of 1903 ed. 34.00x (ISBN 0-8103-3557-3). Gale.
--Story of Organ Music. LC 69-16789. 1968. Repr. of 1905 ed. 30.00x (ISBN 0-8103-3558-1). Gale.
Williams, C. Arthur, Jr. & Head, George L. Principles of Risk Management & Insurance, 2 Vols. 2nd ed. LC 81-66112. 685p. 1981. Vol. 1. text ed. 18.00 (ISBN 0-89463-022-9); Vol. 2. text ed. 18.00. Am Inst Property.
Williams, C. Arthur, Jr. & Heins, Richard M. Risk Management & Insurance. 4th ed. (Insurance Ser.). (Illus.). 672p. 1980. text ed. 26.95 (ISBN 0-07-070564-X, C); instr's. manual 10.95 (ISBN 0-07-070565-8). McGraw.
Williams, C. Arthur, Jr., et al. Principles of Risk Management & Insurance, 2 vols. 1978. write for info. o.p. (CPCU 1). IIA.
Williams, C. F. The Story of the Organ. LC 78-90250. (Illus.). 328p. 1972. Repr. of 1903 ed. 34.00x (ISBN 0-8103-3067-9). Gale.
Williams, C. K. The Lark, The Thrush, The Starling. (Burning Deck Poetry Ser.). (Illus.). 1983. pap. 3.00 (ISBN 0-930901-15-0); signed ed. 20.00 (ISBN 0-930901-14-2). Burning Deck.
Williams, C. S. Aristotle's De Generatione Et Corruptione. (Clarendon Aristotle Ser.). 1982. 29.95x (ISBN 0-19-872062-9); pap. 13.50x (ISBN 0-19-872063-7). Oxford U Pr.
Williams, Caleb. Observations on the Criminal Responsibility of the Insane. (Historical Foundations of Forensic Psychiatry & Psychology Ser.). 148p. 1983. Repr. of 1856 ed. lib. bdg. 19.50 (ISBN 0-306-76178-5). Da Capo.

Williams, Calvin O. The Blob. 1978. 4.95 o.p. (ISBN 0-533-03393-4). Vantage.

Williams, Carl E. & Crosby, John F. Choice-Challenge: Contemporary Readings in Marriage. 2nd ed. 240p. 1979. pap. text ed. write for info. (ISBN 0-697-07556-7); instrs.' manual avail. (ISBN 0-697-07596-6). Wm C Brown.

Williams, Carlton, ed. see Colburn, Robert E.

Williams, Carol. The Switzers. LC 81-3131. (Orig.). 1981. 9.95 o.p. (ISBN 0-89865-170-0); pap. 6.95 (ISBN 0-89865-139-5). Donning Co.

Williams, Carrie. Springtime Crafts for Everyone. (Illus.). (gr. 3-6). 1979. pap. 0.95 (ISBN 0-448-15922-8, G&D). Putnam Pub Group.

Williams, Catherine, jt. auth. see Chapman, E. N.

Williams, Cecil B. Henry Wadsworth Longfellow. (United States Authors Ser.). 1964. lib. bdg. 11.95 (ISBN 0-8057-0456-6, Twayne). G K Hall.

Williams, Cecil J. see Clark, Barbara R.

Williams, Charles. Charles Williams Novels, 7 vols. Set. pap. 32.95 (ISBN 0-686-81706-0). Eerdmans.

--Dead Calm. LC 82-48820. 192p. 1983. pap. 2.84i (ISBN 0-06-080655-9, P 655, PL). Har-Row.

--Novels. Incl. War in Heaven. pap. 3.95 (ISBN 0-8028-1219-8); Many Dimensions. pap. 4.95 (ISBN 0-8028-1221-X); The Place of the Lion. pap. 3.95 (ISBN 0-8028-1222-8); Shadows of Ecstacy. pap. 3.95 (ISBN 0-8028-1223-6); Descent into Hell. pap. 3.95 (ISBN 0-8028-1220-1). 1965. pap. 32.95 boxed set (ISBN 0-8028-1215-5). Eerdmans.

--The Sailcloth Shroud. LC 82-48819. 192p. 1983. pap. 2.84i (ISBN 0-06-080654-0, P 654, PL). Har-Row.

Williams, Charles F. The Complete Guide to Hong Kong. (The Complete Guide to Asia Ser.). (Illus.). 112p. 1981. pap. 6.95 (ISBN 962-7031-02-X, Pub. by CFW Pubns Hong Kong). C E Tuttle.

Williams, Charles G. Madame de Sevigne. (World Authors Ser.). 13.95 (ISBN 0-8057-6438-0, Twayne). G K Hall.

Williams, Charles S. & Becklund, Orville A. Optics: A Short Course for Engineers & Scientists. LC 73-39046. (Pure & Applied Optics Ser). 440p. 1972. 44.95x o.s.i. (ISBN 0-471-94830-6). Wiley.

--Optics: A Short Course for Engineers & Scientists. 414p. 1983. text ed. write for info. (ISBN 0-89874-617-5). Krieger.

Williams, Chester. Gable. (Signet Film Ser). 1975. pap. 1.25 o.p. (ISBN 0-451-06304-X, Y6304, Sig). NAL.

Williams, Christie. Brunch. LC 80-85004. (Illus.). 177p. (Orig.). 1981. pap. 5.95 (ISBN 0-911954-59-7). Nitty Gritty.

Williams, Christine L. Pediatric Risk Factors for Major Chronic Disease. 250p. 1983. 18.50 (ISBN 0-87527-237-1). Green.

Williams, Cicely D. & Jelliffe, Derrick B. Mother & Child Health: Delivering the Servicea. 1972. pap. 21.95x (ISBN 0-19-264153-0). Oxford U Pr.

Williams, Clarence O., jt. auth. see Myers, Alonzo F.

Williams, Claudette. Lady Magic. 192p. (Orig.). 1983. pap. 2.25 (ISBN 0-449-20093-0, Crest). Fawcett.

Williams, Clifford. Free Will & Determinism: A Dialogue. LC 79-24164. 1980. lib. bdg. 12.50 (ISBN 0-915144-78-6); pap. text ed. 2.95 (ISBN 0-915144-77-8). Hackett Pub.

Williams, Colbert V. The Methodist Contribution to Education in the Bahamas. 256p. 1982. text ed. 34.00x (ISBN 0-86299-027-0, Pub. by Sutton England). Humanities.

Williams, Colin W. John Wesley's Theology Today. LC 60-5238. 256p. 1983. pap. 8.95 (ISBN 0-687-20531-X). Abingdon.

Williams, Cortez. A Grantsmanship & Proposal Writing Manual. 380p. 1981. pap. 15.00 (ISBN 0-9609114-0-5). Develop Res.

--Women in Business: A Manual for the New Entrepreneur. 179p. 1982. pap. 15.00 (ISBN 0-9609114-1-3). Develop Res.

Williams, Cortez H. The Complete Grants Reference Book: Writing the Proposal, Getting the Money, & Managing the Project. 300p. Date not set. 24.95 (ISBN 0-13-159780-9); pap. 14.95 (ISBN 0-13-159772-8). P-H. Postponed.

Williams, Curtis A. & Chase, Merrill W., eds. Methods in Immunology & Immunochemistry, 5 vols. Vol. 1. 1968. subscription 55.50 64.50 (ISBN 0-12-754401-1); Vol. 2. 1968. subscription 55.50 64.50 (ISBN 0-12-754402-X); Vol. 3. 1971. by subscription 55.50 64.50 (ISBN 0-12-754403-8); Vol. 4 1977. subscription 55.50 64.50 (ISBN 0-12-754404-6); Vol. 5 1976. subscription 55.50 64.50 (ISBN 0-12-754405-4). Acad Pr.

Williams, D. Modern Trends in Neurology, Vol. 6. 1975. 19.95 o.p. (ISBN 0-407-00016-X). Butterworth.

Williams, D. A. & Jones, G. Liquid Fuels. 1963. pap. 9.75 o.p. (ISBN 0-08-010385-5). Pergamon.

Williams, D. Alan & Tate, Thad W. Colonial Virginia-A History. (A History of the American Colonies Ser.). (Orig.). 1983. lib. bdg. write for info. (ISBN 0-527-18722-4). Kraus Intl.

Williams, D. B. Agriculture in the Australian Economy. 422p. 1982. pap. text ed. 45.00 (ISBN 0-424-00092-X, Pub. by Sydney U Pr). Intl Schol Bk Serv.

Williams, D. F. & Cunningham, J. Materials in Clinical Dentistry. (Illus.). 1980. pap. text ed. 21.95x (ISBN 0-19-267006-9). Oxford U Pr.

Williams, D. H. & Fleming, I. Spectroscopic Methods in Organic Chemistry. 3rd ed. (Illus.). 1980. pap. text ed. 22.50 (ISBN 0-07-084108-X). McGraw.

Williams, D. I. Pediatric Urology. (Illus.). 1968. 34.95 o.p. (ISBN 0-407-35150-7). Butterworth.

--Urology. (Operative Surgery Ser.). 1977. 140.00 (ISBN 0-407-00612-5). Butterworth.

Williams, D. L., jt. auth. see Ridley, A.

Williams, D. O., jt. ed. see Stock, J. P.

Williams, Dakin & Mead, Shepherd. Tennessee Williams: An Intimate Unauthorized Biography. 300p. 1983. 16.95 (ISBN 0-87795-488-7). Arbor Hse.

Williams, Daniel D. The Spirit & the Forms of Love. LC 81-40368. 316p. 1981. lib. bdg. 22.00 (ISBN 0-8191-1691-2); pap. text ed. 12.25 (ISBN 0-8191-1692-0). U Pr of Amer.

--What Present-Day Theologians Are Thinking. rev. ed. LC 78-16410. 1978. Repr. of 1959 ed. lib. bdg. 20.75x (ISBN 0-313-20587-6, WIWP). Greenwood.

Williams, Darnell L. A Guide to Stocks & Bonds for the Beginner. 1979. 7.95 o.p. (ISBN 0-533-03821-9). Vantage.

Williams, David. Diffusions, Markov Processes & Martingales: Volume 1: Foundation. LC 78-16634. (Probability & Mathematical Statistics Ser.: Applied Section). 1979. 58.95x (ISBN 0-471-99705-6, Pub. by Wiley-Interscience). Wiley.

--Murder for Treasure. 224p. 1981. 9.95 o.p. (ISBN 0-312-55296-3). St Martin.

--The River Horsemen. (Anansi Fiction Ser.: No. 43). 224p. (Orig.). 1981. pap. 9.95 (ISBN 0-88784-086-8, Pub. by Hse Anansi Pr Canada). U of Toronto Pr.

--A World of His Own: The Double Life of George Borrow. (Illus.). 188p. 1982. 17.95x (ISBN 0-19-211762-9). Oxford U Pr.

Williams, David J. Polymer Science & Engineering. (Physical & Chemical Engineering Sciences Ser.). (Illus.). 1971. ref. ed. 35.95 (ISBN 0-13-685636-5). P-H.

Williams, Diane. Demons & Beasts in Art. LC 75-84407. (Fine Art Books). (Illus.). (gr. 5-11). 1970. PLB 4.95g (ISBN 0-8225-0165-1). Lerner Pubns.

Williams, Don & Gerrity, Bill. Philemon: Inductive Bible Study. LC 79-64290. 1979. pap. 2.75 o.p. (ISBN 0-8307-0703-4, 5412706). Regal.

--Philippians: Inductive Bible Study. LC 79-64292. (Inductive Bible Study Ser.). 176p. 1979. pap. 3.95 o.p. (ISBN 0-8307-0704-2, 5412803). Regal.

Williams, Don, jt. auth. see Verbsky, Ray.

Williams, Donald J., ed. see International Symposium on Solar Terrestrial Physics.

Williams, Dorian. Book of Horses. LC 70-164017. (Illus.). 1971. 10.53i (ISBN 0-397-00888-0). Har-Row.

--Great Moments in Sports: Show Jumping. (Illus.). 128p. 1974. 10.95 o.p. (ISBN 0-7207-0680-7). Transatlantic.

--The Horseman's Companion. 574p. 1980. 15.00 o.p. (ISBN 0-312-39217-6). St Martin.

Williams, Dorothy, jt. auth. see Cocteau, Jean.

Williams, Doyle Z., jt. auth. see Needles, Belverd E.

Williams, Doyle Z., jt. auth. see Needles, Belverd E., Jr.

Williams, Doyle Z., jt. ed. see Needles, Belverd E., Jr.

Williams, Dudley & Spangler, John. General Physics. Date not set. text ed. price not set o.s.i. (ISBN 0-442-26155-1). Van Nos Reinhold.

Williams, Dudley, ed. Molecular Physics, 2 pts. 2nd ed. (Methods in Experimental Physics). Pt.a, 1974. 63.50 (ISBN 0-12-476003-1); Pt.b,1974. 67.00 (ISBN 0-12-476043-0). Acad Pr.

Williams, E. D. & Siebenmann, R. E. Histological Typing of Endocrine Tumours. (World Health Organization: No. 23). 33.50 (ISBN 0-686-95504-8, 70-1-023-00); 118.50 (ISBN 0-686-99516-3). Am Soc Clinical.

Williams, E. J. Studies in Probability & Statistics. 1976. 34.00 (ISBN 0-7204-0434-7, North-Holland). Elsevier.

Williams, E. N. Eighteenth-Century Constitution: Documents & Commentary. (English Constitutional History Ser). 47.95 o.p. (ISBN 0-521-06810-X); pap. 19.95 (ISBN 0-521-09123-3). Cambridge U Pr.

Williams, E. W., ed. see Williams, R. H.

Williams, Earl J., jt. auth. see Tanner, C. Kenneth.

Williams, Ederyn, jt. auth. see Short, John.

Williams, Sir Edgar, ed. Dictionary of National Biography: 8th Supplement 1961-1970. 1981. 74.00x (ISBN 0-19-865207-0). Oxford U Pr.

Williams, Edward. The Jazz Traditions. rev. ed. 256p. 1983. 18.95 (ISBN 0-19-503290-X). Oxford U Pr.

Williams, Edward, jt. auth. see Burns, Arthur.

Williams, Edward A. The Siting of Major Facilities. (Illus.). 288p. 1982. 42.50 (ISBN 0-07-070420-1, P&RB). McGraw.

Williams, Edward H., jt. auth. see Hoag, Ernest B.

Williams, Edward J. The Rebirth of the Mexican Petroleum Industry: Developmental Directions & Policy Implications. LC 79-1546. 240p. 1979. 23.95x (ISBN 0-669-02908-4). Lexington Bks.

Williams, Edward R., jt. auth. see House, Peter W.

Williams, Effie M. A Hive of Busy Bees. 1976. Repr. of 1939 ed. 3.00 (ISBN 0-686-15479-7). Rod & Staff.

Williams, Emmett, tr. see Spoerri, Daniel.

Williams, Eric. From Columbus to Castro: The History of the Carribean, 1492-1969. LC 82-49083. (Illus.). 608p. 1983. pap. 8.95 (ISBN 0-394-71502-0, Vin). Random.

Williams, Eric E. Capitalism & Slavery. LC 61-13088. 1961. Repr. of 1944 ed. 19.00x o.p. (ISBN 0-8462-0301-4). Russell.

Williams, Esther A. & Gottman, John M. A User's Guide to the "Gottman-Williams Time Series Analysis Computer Programs for Social Scientists". 86p. 1982. pap. 9.95 (ISBN 0-521-28059-1). Cambridge U Pr.

Williams, Ethel L. Biographical Directory of Negro Ministers. 3rd ed. 578p. 1975. lib. bdg. 28.00 o.p. (ISBN 0-8161-1183-9, Hall Reference). G K Hall.

Williams, Eugene. Increase Your Employment Opportunities With the Audiovisual Portfolio. 1980. 12.95 (ISBN 0-686-37448-7). Competent Assocs.

Williams, Eunice. Drawings by Fragonard in North American Collections. LC 78-22017. (Illus.). pap. 5.00 (ISBN 0-89468-036-6). Natl Gallery Art.

Williams, F. & Wood, N. Developmental Art Therapy. 210p. 1977. pap. text ed. 17.95 (ISBN 0-8391-1140-1). Univ Park.

Williams, F., jt. auth. see Hartman, W.

Williams, F. Dale. Emergency Communications: An Organizational & Operational Handbook. LC 82-90229. (Illus.). 180p. 1983. Vol. I. pap. 9.95 (ISBN 0-9608354-0-7); Vol. II. pap. write for info (ISBN 0-664-24467-X). FDW Arts.

--Modern CW-RTTY & the Z80 Timex-Sinclair Computers. (Illus., Orig.). Date not set. pap. price not set (ISBN 0-9608354-1-5). FDW Arts.

Williams, F. P., jt. auth. see Gooriah, B. D.

Williams, Francis E. Orokaiva Society. LC 82-25129. (Illus.). xxiii, 355p. 1983. Repr. of 1930 ed. lib. bdg. 59.50x (ISBN 0-313-23846-4, WI0R). Greenwood.

--The Vailala Madness & Other Essays. Schwimmer, Erik, ed. LC 76-41133. 1977. text ed. 17.50x (ISBN 0-8248-0519-4). UH Pr.

Williams, Frank J., jt. auth. see Freund, John E.

Williams, Frederick. Executive Communication Power: Basic Skills for Management Success. 192p. 1983. 12.95 (ISBN 0-13-294157-0); pap. 6.95 (ISBN 0-13-294116-3). P-H.

--Explorations of the Linguistic Attitudes of Teachers. LC 76-1890. (Ser. in Sociolinguistics). 1976. pap. text ed. 9.95 o.p. (ISBN 0-88377-052-0). Newbury Hse.

Williams, Frederick D. & Brown, Harry J., eds. The Diary of James A. Garfield, Vol. III: 1875-1877. 599p. 22.50x (ISBN 0-87013-169-9). Mich St U Pr.

Williams, Frederick D., jt. ed. see Brown, Harry J.

Williams, Frederick G., ed. see De Sena, Jorge.

Williams, Fry & Lancaster-Smith. Problems in Practice Index. (Problems in Practice Ser.: Vol. 12). 1983. write for info. (ISBN 0-8036-3868-X). Davis Co.

Williams, G. A., et al. Challenges to Science: Physical Science. 1973. text ed. 13.84 (ISBN 0-07-070410-4, W); tchr's. ed. 24.00 (ISBN 0-07-070411-2); work-study guide 5.36 (ISBN 0-07-003754-X); tests 48.20 (ISBN 0-07-070412-0). McGraw.

Williams, G. E., ed. Megacycles: Long-Term Episodity in Earth & Planetary History. LC 79-19908. (Benchmark Papers in Geology: Vol. 57). 448p. 1981. 49.00 (ISBN 0-87933-366-9). Hutchinson Ross.

Williams, G. H. Dictionary of Weeds of Western Europe: Their Common Names & Importance. 1982. 74.50 (ISBN 0-444-41978-0). Elsevier.

Williams, G. H., ed. Advances in Free Radical Chemistry, 4 vols. 1967-75. Vol. 2. 64.50 (ISBN 0-12-017002-7); Vol. 3. 64.50 (ISBN 0-12-017003-5); Vol. 4. 64.50 (ISBN 0-12-017004-3); Vol. 5. 64.50 (ISBN 0-12-017005-1). Acad Pr.

Williams, G. M. Cytochemical Markers in Rodent Hepatocarcinogenesis. (Lectures in Toxicology: No. 17). (Illus.). 1983. 60.00 (ISBN 0-08-029786-2). Pergamon.

Williams, G. Walton. The Best Friend. LC 72-6056. (Illus.). (gr. 4-6). 1969. pap. 1.50 (ISBN 0-910220-29-8). Berg.

--The Winter Folk. (Illus.). pap. 3.95 (ISBN 0-932298-11-7). Copple Hse.

Williams, Garnett P. see Rhodes, Dallas D.

Williams, Garth. Baby Farm Animals. (Big Picture Bk.). 24p. (gr. 1-3). 1953. 2.95 (ISBN 0-307-10545-8, Golden Pr); PLB 7.62 (ISBN 0-307-60545-0). Western Pub.

--Big Golden Animal ABC. (gr. k-2). 1957. 2.95 (ISBN 0-307-10457-5, Golden Pr); PLB 7.62 o.p. (ISBN 0-307-60457-8). Western Pub.

--The Chicken Book: A Traditional Rhyme. LC 69-12504. (Illus.). (ps-3). 1970. 5.95 o.s.i. (ISBN 0-440-01202-3); PLB 5.47 o.s.i. (ISBN 0-440-01203-1). Delacorte.

Williams, Gary A., ed. PAT System of Learning: Automobile Mechanics Refresher Course, 5 bks. Incl. Bk. 1. Tune-up--Ignition & Fuel Induction Systems. LC 73-87937 (ISBN 0-913040-32-0); Bk. 2. Engines, Lubricating & Cooling Systems. LC 73-87938 (ISBN 0-913040-33-9); Bk. 3. Electrical Systems, Heating & Air Conditioning. LC 73-87939 (ISBN 0-913040-34-7); Bk. 4. Brakes, Steering, Front Suspension, Wheels & Tires. LC 73-87940 (ISBN 0-913040-35-5); Bk. 5. Automatic & Manual Transmissions & Drive Trains. LC 73-87941. (Rev. ed. of Bk. 5 august, 1974) (ISBN 0-913040-36-3). (Illus., Orig.). 1973. pap. 6.25 ea. o.p. H M Gousha.

Williams, Gary M., jt. ed. see Borek, Carmia.

Williams, Gavin, ed. Nigeria: Economy & Society. 226p. 1976. 17.50x o.p. (ISBN 0-8476-1429-8). Rowman.

Williams, Gavin, jt. ed. see Allen, Chris.

Williams, Geoffrey L. & Williams, Alan L. Crisis in European Defense. LC 74-81480. 356p. 1974. 26.00 (ISBN 0-312-17325-3). St Martin.

Williams, George A. Elementary Physics: Atoms, Waves, Particles. 2nd ed. (Illus.). 448p. 1976. text ed. 33.50 (ISBN 0-07-070402-3, C); instr's. manual 14.95 (ISBN 0-07-070403-1). McGraw.

Williams, George A. & Barnes, Richard. Physical Science. Siegelman, Irwin, ed. (Challenges to Science). (YA) (gr. 9-12). 1978. text ed. 18.96 (ISBN 0-07-070415-5, W); tchr's ed. 23.20 (ISBN 0-07-070416-3); tests 46.64 (ISBN 0-07-017325-7). McGraw.

Williams, George H. The Polish Brethren, 2 vols. (Harvard Theological Studies: No. 30). pap. 12.00 ea. (ISBN 0-89130-201-8, 02-00-30). Scholars Pr CA.

--Radical Reformation. LC 62-7066. 1962. 24.95 (ISBN 0-664-20372-8). Westminster.

Williams, George M. Improving Parish Management: Working Smarter, Not Harder. 112p. pap. 9.95 (ISBN 0-89622-176-8). Twenty-Third.

Williams, George S. Greenhouse Flowers & Bedding Plants for Agribusiness Studies. LC 74-24772. xiv, 282p. 1975. 10.65 (ISBN 0-8134-1671-X, 1671); text ed. 8.00x. Interstate.

--Nursery Crops & Landscape Designs for Agri-Business Studies. LC 75-10482. 1975. 10.65 (ISBN 0-8134-1717-1); text ed. 8.00x. Interstate.

Williams, George Walton, ed. The Complete Poetry of Richard Crashaw. LC 68-14177. (Illus.). 707p. 1972. 25.00x o.p. (ISBN 0-8147-9154-9). NYU Pr.

Williams, Gerald, jt. auth. see Hand, William P.

Williams, Gerald E. Digital Technology. 2nd ed. 512p. 1981. text ed. 21.95 (ISBN 0-574-21555-7, 13-4555); instr. guide avail. (ISBN 0-574-21556-5, 13-4556); lab manual 11.95 (ISBN 0-574-21557-3, 13-4557). SRA.

--Electronics for Everyone. 1979. text ed. 19.95 (ISBN 0-574-21525-5, 13-4525); instr's. guide 2.50 (ISBN 0-574-21526-3, 13-4526). SRA.

--Practical Transistor Circuit Design & Analysis. (Illus.). 420p. 1973. text ed. 24.95 (ISBN 0-07-070398-1, G); instr's guide 2.95 (ISBN 0-07-070400-7); exercises 13.95 (ISBN 0-07-070399-X). McGraw.

Williams, Gerald R. Legal Negotiation & Settlement. LC 82-19975. 207p. 1983. pap. text ed. write for info. (ISBN 0-314-68093-4); tchrs.' manual avail. (ISBN 0-314-73521-6). West Pub.

Williams, Gerwyn. Tackle Rugger. rev. ed. (Tackle Ser). (Illus.). 96p. 1976. pap. text ed. 6.95x o.p. (ISBN 0-09-125371-3, SpS). Sportshelf.

Williams, Glyndur, intro. by see Anson, George.

Williams, Gordon. Change & Decline: Roman Literature in the Early Empire. LC 76-24598. (Sather Classical Lectures: No. 45). 1978. 27.50x (ISBN 0-520-03333-7). U of Cal Pr.

--Technique & Ideas in the Aeneid. LC 82-7008. 312p. 1983. text ed. 27.50x (ISBN 0-300-02852-0). Yale U Pr.

--Tradition & Originality in Roman Poetry. 1968. 59.00x o.p. (ISBN 0-19-814347-8). Oxford U Pr.

Williams, Gordon, jt. auth. see Saxton, Martha.

Williams, Gordon L. Financial Survival in the Age of New Money. 1981. 14.95 o.s.i. (ISBN 0-671-25474-X). S&S.

Williams, Greer. Western Reserve's Experiment in Medical Education & Its Outcome. 1980. 35.00x (ISBN 0-19-502679-9). Oxford U Pr.

Williams, Gurney. Ghosts & Poltergeists. (Illus.). (gr. 4-6). 1979. PLB 6.90 s&l (ISBN 0-531-02214-5). Watts.

Williams, Gurney, III, jt. auth. see Glazer, Joan.

Williams, Guy. Instructions for Home Handyman. (Illus.). 14.50x (ISBN 0-392-03419-0, SpS). Sportshelf.

--Let's Look at London. (Illus.). 14.50x (ISBN 0-392-03730-0, LTB). Sportshelf.

Williams, Guy R. The World of Model Aircraft. (Illus.). 224p. 1973. 14.95 o.p. (ISBN 0-399-11087-9). Putnam Pub Group.

--The World of Model Cars. LC 75-29665. (Illus.). 1976. 14.95 o.p. (ISBN 0-399-11694-X). Putnam Pub Group.

--The World of Model Ships & Boats. (Illus.). 1971. 14.95 o.p. (ISBN 0-399-10880-7). Putnam Pub Group.

--The World of Model Trains. (Illus.). 1970. 14.95 o.p. (ISBN 0-399-10882-3). Putnam Pub Group.

Williams, Gwyn, compiled by. The Burning Tree: Poems from the First Thousand Years of Welsh Verse. LC 78-11853. 1979. Repr. of 1956 ed. lib. bdg. 20.00x (ISBN 0-313-21185-X, WIBT). Greenwood.

Williams, Gwyn, ed. & tr. Welsh Poems: Sixth Century to 1600. 1974. 16.95x (ISBN 0-520-02603-9). U of Cal Pr.

Williams, Gwyn A. The Welsh in Their History. (Illus.). 218p. 1982. text ed. 26.00x (ISBN 0-7099-2711-8, Pub. by Croom Helm Ltd England). Biblio Dist.

Williams, H., jt. auth. see Williams, B. S.

Williams, H. B., jt. auth. see Andrew, William G.

Williams, H. Bruce. Vascular Malformations & Melanotic Lesions: Symposium, Vol. 22. LC 82-6422. (Illus.). 421p. 1983. text ed. 79.50 (ISBN 0-8016-5602-8). Mosby.

Williams, H. H. & Jones, A. Marine Helminths & Human Health. 47p. 1977. 41.00X (ISBN 0-85198-382-0, CAB Bks). State Mutual Bk.

Williams, H. James. The Love Garden. 32p. Date not set. 5.95 (ISBN 0-8059-2860-X). Dorrance.

Williams, H. L., jt. auth. see Wall, W. D.

Williams, H. P. Model Building in Mathematical Programming. LC 77-7380. 1978. 67.95 (ISBN 0-471-99526-6); pap. 29.95x (ISBN 0-471-99541-X, Pub. by Wiley-Interscience). Wiley.

Williams, Hank, Jr. Living Proof. 1983. pap. 3.50 (ISBN 0-440-05213-0). Dell.

Williams, Hank, Jr. & Bane, Michael. Living Proof: An Autobiography. LC 79-11741. (Illus.). 1979. 10.95 (ISBN 0-399-12369-5). Putnam Pub Group.

Williams, Harold A. Baltimore Afire. (Illus.). 95p. 1979. 9.95 (ISBN 0-686-36500-3). Md Hist.

--Bodine: A Legend in His Time. (Illus.). 12.50 o.p. (ISBN 0-910254-00-1). Bodine.

Williams, Harold H. Book Clubs & Printing Societies of Great Britain & Ireland. LC 68-26622. 1971. Repr. of 1929 ed. 40.00x (ISBN 0-8103-3749-5). Gale.

Williams, Harriet. Perceptual & Motor Development. (Illus.). 1983. 20.95 (ISBN 0-13-656892-0). P-H.

Williams, Harry. With Mungo Park in West Africa. 12.75x (ISBN 0-392-08653-0, SpS). Sportshelf.

Williams, Harry A. True Resurrection. 192p. 1983. pap. 7.95 (ISBN 0-87243-115-0). Templegate.

Williams, Harry F., jt. ed. see Hesse, Everett W.

Williams, Hector. The Lamps, Pt. V. (Kenchreai Estern Port of Corinth Ser.). (Illus.). xvi, 104p. 1981. write for info. (ISBN 90-04-06198-3). E J Brill.

Williams, Helen M. Letters from France, 8 vols. in 2. LC 75-22224. 2048p. 1975. 200.00x set (ISBN 0-8201-1158-9). Schol Facsimiles.

Williams, Henry T., ed. Window Gardening. (Illus.). 1976. pap. 3.95 o.s.i. (ISBN 0-8027-7104-1). Walker & Co.

Williams, Hiram. Hiram Williams: A One-Man Retrospective Exhibition. (Illus.). 36p. (Orig.). 1983. pap. 7.50 (ISBN 0-8130-0763-1). U Presses Fla.

Williams, Hobie L. The American Artists Today in Black, Vol. II. White, Mosezelle & Roberts, Bobby, II, eds. 103p. (Orig.). 1982. pap. text ed. 7.95 (ISBN 0-936026-12-X). R&M Pub Co.

Williams, Horatio. The Politics of National Integration in Liberia. 1983. 11.50 (ISBN 0-533-05140-1). Vantage.

Williams, Howard. The Diary of a Rowing Tour from Oxford to London in 1875. (Illus.). 168p. 1982. text ed. 16.75x (ISBN 0-904387-69-0, Pub. by Sutton England); pap. text ed. 8.25x (ISBN 0-904387-70-4, 61182). Humanities.

Williams, Howel & McBirney, Alexander R. Volcanology. LC 79-50180. (Illus.). 1982. Repr. of 1979 ed. text ed. 33.50x (ISBN 0-87735-321-2). Freeman C.

Williams, Howell & Curtis, G. H. The Sutter Buttes of California: A Study of Plio-Pleistocene Volcanism. (Library Reprint Ser.: No. 97). 1979. Repr. of 1977 ed. 15.95x (ISBN 0-520-03808-8). U of Cal Pr.

Williams, Hugh J. Introduction to Organic Chemistry. 200p. 1982. 22.95x (ISBN 0-471-10206-7, Pub. by Wiley-Interscience); pap. write for info. (ISBN 0-471-10207-5). Wiley.

Williams, I. P. The Origin of the Planets. (Monographs on Astronomical Subjects). 108p. 1977. 18.50x o.s.i. (ISBN 0-8448-1061-4). Crane-Russak Co.

Williams, Irene, jt. auth. see Simmons, Vickie.

Williams, J. Introduction to Marine Pollution Control. 173p. 1979. 39.95x (ISBN 0-471-01904-6, Pub. by Wiley-Interscience). Wiley.

Williams, J. see Niles, J. J.

Williams, J. B. The Lives of Philip & Matthew Henry. 1974. 15.95 (ISBN 0-85151-178-3). Banner of Truth.

Williams, J. D. Public Administration: The People's Business. (Illus.). 585p. 1980. text ed. 18.95 (ISBN 0-316-94235-9); instructor's manual free (ISBN 0-316-94236-7). Little.

Williams, J. David. Questions That Count: British Literature to 1750. LC 82-15893. 98p. (Orig.). 1983. lib. bdg. 18.50 (ISBN 0-8191-2742-6); pap. text ed. 4.25 (ISBN 0-8191-2743-4). U Pr of Amer.

Williams, J. E. Superconductivity & Its Applications. 1970. 22.00x (ISBN 0-85086-010-5, Pub. by Pion England); pap. 10.95x o.p. (ISBN 0-85086-016-4). Methuen Inc.

Williams, J. E., jt. ed. see Price, D.

Williams, J. G., jt. auth. see Edginton, C. R.

Williams, J. L. Victor Paul Wierwielle & the Way International. LC 79-22007. 1979. pap. 3.95 (ISBN 0-8024-9233-9). Moody.

Williams, J. Mark & Shapiro, Gary. A Search for the Eighteenth Century Village at Michilimackinac: A Soil Resistivity Survey. (Archaeological Completion Report Ser.: No. 4). (Illus.). 79p. (Orig.). 1982. pap. 7.00 (ISBN 0-911872-43-4). Mackinac Island.

Williams, J. R., et al. Ethanol, Methanol, & Gasohol. (Illus.). 200p. cancelled (ISBN 0-250-40382-X). Ann Arbor Science.

Williams, J. Richard. Design & Installation of Solar Heating & Hot Water System. LC 82-72856. (Illus.). 427p. 1982. 39.95 (ISBN 0-250-40593-8). Ann Arbor Science.

--Passive Solar Heating. LC 82-72857. (Illus.). 300p. 1982. 24.50 (ISBN 0-250-40601-2). Ann Arbor Science.

--Solar Energy: Technology & Applications. rev. ed. LC 77-73635. (Illus.). 1977. 6.95 o.p. (ISBN 0-250-40167-3); pap. 6.95 (ISBN 0-250-40194-0). Ann Arbor Science.

Williams, J. W. Ultracentrifugation of Macromolecules: Modern Topics. 1973. 24.00 (ISBN 0-12-755160-3). Acad Pr.

Williams, Jack & Yung Teng Chia-Yee. Readings in Chinese Geography: Vol. 1, Chinese Text, Vol. 2, Vocabulary, Notes & Translations. Set. pap. text ed. 12.00x (ISBN 0-87022-862-5). UH Pr.

Williams, Jack, jt. auth. see Brunn, Stanley.

Williams, Jacqueline B. & Silverman, Goldie. No Salt No Sugar No Fat Cookbook. LC 81-83793. (Illus.). 150p. (Orig.). 1982. pap. 5.95 (ISBN 0-911954-65-1). Nitty Gritty.

Williams, James D., jt. auth. see Ono, Dane R.

Williams, James G. Women Recounted: Narrative Thinking & the God of Israel. (Bible & Literature Ser.: No. 6). 128p. 1982. text ed. 21.95 (ISBN 0-907459-18-8, Pub. by Almond Pr England); pap. 10.95 (ISBN 0-907459-19-6). Eisenbrauns.

Williams, Jay. Leonardo Da Vinci. LC 65-20599. (Horizon Caravel Bks.). 154p. (YA) (gr. 7 up). 1965. 12.45 (ISBN 0-06-026535-3, HarpJ); PLB 14.89 o.p. (ISBN 0-06-026536-1). Har-Row.

--World of Titian. LC 68-28257. (Library of Art Ser.). (Illus.). (gr. 6 up). 1968. 19.92 (ISBN 0-8094-0274-2, Pub. by Time-Life). Silver.

Williams, Jay & Abrashkin, R. Danny Dunn & the Swamp Monster. (Illus.). (gr. 5 up). 1971. PLB 8.95 o.p. (ISBN 0-07-070539-9, GB). McGraw.

Williams, Jay & Abrashkin, Raymond. Danny Dunn & the Anti-Gravity Paint. (Danny Dunn Ser.: No. 7). (Illus.). (gr. 4-6). 1979. pap. 1.95 (ISBN 0-671-43678-3). Archway.

--Danny Dunn & the Anti-Gravity Paint. (Illus.). (gr. 4-7). 1964. PLB 8.95 (ISBN 0-07-070531-3, GB). McGraw.

--Danny Dunn & the Fossil Cave. (Danny Dunn Ser.: No. 11). (Illus.). (gr. 4-6). 1979. pap. 1.95 (ISBN 0-671-43290-7). Archway.

--Danny Dunn & the Fossil Cave. (gr. 4-7). 1964. PLB 6.95 o.p. (ISBN 0-07-070526-7, GB). McGraw.

--Danny Dunn & the Heat Ray. (Danny Dunn Ser.: No. 14). (Illus.). (gr. 4-6). 1979. pap. 1.95 (ISBN 0-671-44381-X). Archway.

--Danny Dunn & the Homework Machine. (Danny Dunn Ser.: No. 5). (Illus.). (gr. 4-6). 1979. pap. 1.95 (ISBN 0-671-44340-2). Archway.

--Danny Dunn & the Homework Machine. (gr. 4-7). 1958. 7.95 o.p. (ISBN 0-07-070519-4, GB). McGraw.

--Danny Dunn & the Smallifying Machine. (Danny Dunn Ser.: No. 1). (Illus.). (gr. 4-6). 1971. pap. 1.95 (ISBN 0-671-44383-6). Archway.

--Danny Dunn & the Smallifying Machine. (Illus.). (gr. 3-7). 1969. PLB 8.95 o.p. (ISBN 0-07-070537-2, GB). McGraw.

--Danny Dunn & the Universal Glue. (Danny Dunn Ser.: No. 4). (Illus.). (gr. 4-6). 1979. pap. 1.95 (ISBN 0-671-43877-8). Archway.

--Danny Dunn & the Universal Glue. LC 77-78764. (Illus.). (gr. 4-6). 1977. 8.95 (ISBN 0-07-070550-X, GB). McGraw.

--Danny Dunn & the Voice from Space. (Danny Dunn Ser.: No. 12). (Illus.). (gr. 4-6). 1979. pap. 2.25 (ISBN 0-671-42684-2). Archway.

--Danny Dunn & the Voice from Space. (gr. 4-6). 1967. PLB 8.95 (ISBN 0-07-070535-6, GB). McGraw.

--Danny Dunn & the Weather Machine. (Danny Dunn Ser.: No. 10). (Illus.). (gr. 4-6). 1979. pap. 1.95 (ISBN 0-671-43681-3). Archway.

--Danny Dunn & the Weather Machine. (gr. 4-7). 1959. 8.95 (ISBN 0-07-070521-6, GB); PLB 6.95 o.p. (ISBN 0-07-070522-4). McGraw.

--Danny Dunn Invisible Boy. (Danny Dunn Ser.: No. 2). (Illus.). (gr. 4-6). 1975. pap. 1.95 (ISBN 0-671-45068-9). Archway.

--Danny Dunn, Invisible Boy. (Illus.). 144p. (gr. 3-7). 1974. 7.95 (ISBN 0-07-070546-1, GB); PLB 6.95-op (ISBN 0-07-070547-X). McGraw.

--Danny Dunn on the Ocean Floor. (Danny Dunn Ser.: No. 9). (Illus.). (gr. 4-6). 1979. pap. 1.95 (ISBN 0-686-85644-9). Archway.

--Danny Dunn, Scientific Detective. (Danny Dunn Ser.: No. 3). (Illus.). (gr. 4-6). 1977. pap. 1.95 (ISBN 0-671-44382-8). Archway.

--Danny Dunn, Time Traveler. (gr. 4-7). 1964. PLB 8.95 o.p. (ISBN 0-07-070530-5, GB). McGraw.

Williams, Jay & Abrashkin, William. Danny Dunn, Scientific Detective. 1975. 5.95 o.p. (ISBN 0-07-070548-8, GB); PLB 6.95 o.p. (ISBN 0-07-070549-6). McGraw.

Williams, Jeanne. Freedom Trail. 160p. (gr. 6 up). 1973. 5.95 o.p. (ISBN 0-399-20336-2). Putnam Pub Group.

--Trails of Tears: American Indians Driven from Their Lands. (Illus.). (gr. 5-9). 1972. PLB 5.29 (ISBN 0-399-60757-9). Putnam Pub Group.

--Winter Wheat. LC 74-21080. 162p. (gr. 6-8). 1975. 6.95 o.p. (ISBN 0-399-20445-8). Putnam Pub Group.

--A Woman Clothed in Sun. LC 77-5652. 1977. 8.95 o.p. (ISBN 0-698-10838-8, Coward). Putnam Pub Group.

Williams, Jelly K. A Dutch Reader. 112p. 1981. 32.00x (ISBN 0-85950-349-6, Pub. by Thornes England). State Mutual Bk.

Williams, Jennifer, ed. see Peters, Ellis.

Williams, Jerome. Oceanographic Instrumentation. LC 72-92657. (Illus.). 160p. 1973. 15.00x o.p. (ISBN 0-87021-503-5). Naval Inst Pr.

Williams, Jerome & Williams, Lelia. Science Puzzles. (Illus.). (gr. 4-6). 1979. PLB 7.90 s&l (ISBN 0-531-02876-3). Watts.

Williams, Jerome, et al. Sea & Air: The Marine Environment. 2nd ed. LC 72-93196. 338p. 1973. 15.95x (ISBN 0-87021-596-5). Naval Inst Pr.

Williams, Jerry. And-Yet They Came: Portuguese Migration From the Azores to the United States (1820-1978) 1982. text ed. 14.95x (ISBN 0-913256-57-9, Dist. by Ozer); pap. text ed. 9.95x (ISBN 0-913256-60-9, Dist. by Ozer). Ctr Migration.

Williams, Jerry T., ed. Southern Literature 1968-1975: A Checklist of Scholarship. lib. bdg. 40.00 o.p. (ISBN 0-8161-8051-2, Hall Reference). G K Hall.

Williams, Joan. Pariah & Other Stories. 192p. 1983. 13.45i (ISBN 0-316-94233-2). Little.

--The Wintering. LC 78-134571. 1971. 7.50 o.p. (ISBN 0-15-125225-4). HarBraceJ.

Williams, Joan, jt. auth. see Williams, Joe B.

Williams, Joanna G., ed. Kaladarsana: American Studies in the Art of India. (Studies in South Asian Culture: Vol. 9). (Illus.). xvi, 183p. 1981. write for info. (ISBN 90-04-06498-2). E J Brill.

Williams, Joe B. & Williams, Joan. U. S. Statistical Rankings. 138p. 1981. pap. 25.00 (ISBN 0-939644-02-9). Media Prods & Mktg.

Williams, John. Butcher's Crossing. 1978. lib. bdg. 9.95 (ISBN 0-8398-2451-3, Gregg). G K Hall.

--Living Churches: A Reconsideration of Their Basis of Life & Leadership. 144p. 1975. pap. 3.95 (ISBN 0-85364-122-6). Attic Pr.

Williams, John, jt. auth. see Woods, Gerald.

Williams, John A., ed. Islam. LC 61-15500. (Great Religions of Modern Man Ser). 1961. 8.95 o.s.i. (ISBN 0-8076-0165-9). Braziller.

Williams, John C. & Monroe, Howard C. Natural History of Northern California. LC 75-6200. (Illus.). 1976. perfect bdg. 13.95 (ISBN 0-8403-1140-0). Kendall-Hunt.

Williams, John D. Compleat Strategyst. rev. ed. 1965. 22.50 (ISBN 0-07-070396-5, P&RB). McGraw.

Williams, John E. & Best, Deborah L. Measuring Sex Stereotypes: A Thirty-Nation Study. (Cross-Cultural Research & Methodology: Vol. 6). (Illus.). 384p. 1982. 27.50 (ISBN 0-8039-1837-2). Sage.

Williams, John e., jt. auth. see Dowling, Ann.

Williams, John G. & Williams, Andrew E. Field Guide to Orchids of North America. (Illus.). 144p. 1983. flexi-cover 10.95 (ISBN 0-87663-415-3). Universe.

Williams, John H. Argentine International Trade Under Incontrovertible Paper Money 1880-1900. Repr. of 1920 ed. lib. bdg. 16.25x (ISBN 0-8371-1050-5, WIAT). Greenwood.

Williams, John R., ed. Physionomie du Theatre de l'Odeon. 3.95 (ISBN 0-917786-27-0). French Lit.

Williams, John S. Consecrated Ingenuity: The Shakers & Their Inventions. (Illus.). 1957. 1.00 o.p. (ISBN 0-937942-01-4). Shaker Mus.

Williams, John T. Costumes & Settings for Shakespeare's Plays. LC 82-11426. (Illus.). 120p. 1982. text ed. 16.50x (ISBN 0-389-20322-X). B&N Imports.

Williams, John W. & Ostrow, Patricia C. Health Accounting for Quality Assurance: A Manual for Assessing & Improving Outcomes of Care. rev. ed. 116p. 1982. pap. text ed. 25.00 (ISBN 0-910317-08-9). Am Occup Therapy.

Williams, John W., ed. Ultracentrifugal Analysis in Theory & Experiment: Proceedings. 1963. 55.00 (ISBN 0-12-755150-6). Acad Pr.

Williams, Jonathan, ed. see Meatyard, Ralph E.

Williams, Joseph J. Hebrewisms of West Africa: From Nile to Niger with the Jews. LC 67-19534. (Illus.). 1930. 17.00x (ISBN 0-8196-0194-2). Biblo.

Williams, Joseph M. Style: Ten Lessons in Clarity & Grace. 1981. text ed. 10.95x (ISBN 0-673-15393-2). Scott F.

Williams, Joy. Taking Care. LC 81-11969. 246p. 1982. 12.50 (ISBN 0-394-52157-9). Random.

Williams, Joyce W. & Smith, Marjorie. Middle Childhood: Behavior & Development. 2nd ed. 1980. text ed. 22.95 (ISBN 0-02-427900-5). Macmillan.

Williams, Juanita H., ed. Psychology of Women: Selected Readings. 1979. pap. text ed. 12.95x (ISBN 0-393-09068-X). Norton.

Williams, K., ed. see Glasspool, Michael G.

Williams, K., ed. see Ratnesar, Padnam.

Williams, K., ed. see Tatford, E. Patrick.

Williams, Kathleen. Spenser's World of Glass: A Reading of The Faerie Queen. (California Library Reprint Series: No. 34). 1973. 28.50x (ISBN 0-520-02369-2). U of Cal Pr.

Williams, Keith C. Behavioral Aspects of Marketing. 1981. pap. 17.50 (ISBN 0-434-92300-1, Pub. by Heinemann). David & Charles.

Williams, Kenneth & Donnelly, Paul. Medical Care Quality & the Public Trust. LC 81-84918. 375p. 1982. 34.95 (ISBN 0-931028-22-1). Pluribus Pr.

Williams, Kenneth G. Problems in Peripheral Vascular Disease. (Problems in Practice Ser.: Vol. 10). (Illus.). 175p. 1983. 16.50 (ISBN 0-8036-9332-X). Davis Co.

Williams, Kenneth G. & Lancaster-Smith, Michael J. Problems in Gastroenterology. Fry, J., ed. LC 81-68108. (Problems in Practice Ser.: Vol. 7). 218p. 1982. text ed. 16.50 (ISBN 0-8036-9335-4). Davis Co.

Williams, Kenny J. & Duffey, Bernard, eds. Chicago's Public Wits: A Chapter in the American Comic Spirit. (Illus.). xiv, 328p. 1983. 22.50 (ISBN 0-8071-1043-4). La State U Pr.

Williams, Kit. Masquerade. LC 80-14127. (Illus.). 32p. 1980. 10.95 (ISBN 0-8052-3747-X). Schocken.

--Masquerade: The Answers & Clues Explained. LC 82-40502. 48p. 1983. pap. 3.95 (ISBN 0-89480-369-7). Workman Pub.

Williams, L. A. Industrial Marketing Management & Controls. 1968. 28.95 (ISBN 0-444-19790-7). Elsevier.

Williams, L. B., jt. auth. see Falusi, A. O.

Williams, L. H., jt. auth. see Hara, H.

Williams, L. Pearce. The Origins of Field Theory. LC 80-5710. 160p. 1980. lib. bdg. 17.75 (ISBN 0-8191-1175-9); pap. text ed. 8.25 (ISBN 0-8191-1176-7). U Pr of Amer.

Williams, L. Pearce & Steffens, Henry J. The History of Science in Western Civilization: Modern Science 1700-1900, Vol. III. LC 77-18484. 1978. pap. text ed. 14.75 (ISBN 0-8191-0333-0). U Pr of Amer.

Williams, Larry, jt. auth. see Humbert, Jack.

Williams, Larry R. Secrets of Commodity Trading. cancelled 14.95 (ISBN 0-89526-650-4). Regnery-Gateway.

--Secrets of Stock Trading. cancelled 14.95 (ISBN 0-89526-649-0). Regnery-Gateway.

Williams, Lawrence & Barker, Eric J. Europe from the Air. 1974. pap. text ed. 5.95x o.p. (ISBN 0-435-34040-9). Heinemann Ed.

Williams, Lawrence K., jt. auth. see Whyte, William F.

Williams, Lelia, jt. auth. see Williams, Jerome.

Williams, Lewis T. & Lefkowitz, Robert J. Receptor Binding Studies in Adrenergic Pharmacology. LC 78-3011. 167p. 1978. 21.50 (ISBN 0-89004-164-4). Raven.

Williams, Lloyd H. Pirates of Colonial Virginia. LC 73-78670. (Illus.). 1972. Repr. of 1937 ed. 30.00x (ISBN 0-8103-3817-3). Gale.

Williams, Lois, jt. auth. see Wink, Richard L.

Williams, Luella K. A Place For Her. 250p. 1983. 14.95 (ISBN 0-8180-2304-X). Horizon.

Williams, M. Dickens Concordance. LC 73-129194. (Studies in Fiction, No. 34). 1970. Repr. of 1907 ed. lib. bdg. 48.95x (ISBN 0-8383-1160-1). Haskell.

--Essentials of Pulmonary Medicine. LC 81-50836. (Illus.). 190p. 1982. pap. 14.95 (ISBN 0-7216-9394-6). Saunders.

Williams, M., jt. ed. see Powell, J. M.

Williams, M. A. Autoradiography & Immunocytochemistry. 1978. pap. 27.75 (ISBN 0-7204-0637-4, North Holland). Elsevier.

Williams, M. B., ed. Pathways to the Information Society: Proceedings of the Sixth International Conference on Computer Communication, London, 1982. 1018p. 1982. 55.00 (ISBN 0-444-86464-4, North Holland). Elsevier.

Williams, M. R. Decision-Making in Forest Management. (Forestry Research Press Ser.). 143p. 1981. 39.95x (ISBN 0-471-10097-8, Pub. by Res Stud Pr). Wiley.

Williams, Majorie L. Japanese Prints: Realities of the "Floating World". LC 82-45941. (Themes in Art Ser.). (Illus.). 72p. (Orig.). 1983. pap. 7.95x (ISBN 0-910386-71-4, Pub. by Cleveland Mus Art). Ind U Pr.

Williams, Margery. The Velveteen Rabbit. (Illus.). 48p. (gr. 3-10). 1983. 10.95 (ISBN 0-87923-444-X). Godine.

--Velveteen Rabbit. Klimo, Kate, ed. (Illus.). 48p. 1983. 6.95 (ISBN 0-671-44498-0, Little). S&S.

--The Velveteen Rabbit. LC 82-15606. (Illus.). 48p. (gr. k-4). 1983. 11.95 (ISBN 0-03-063517-9); ltd. ed. 100.00 (ISBN 0-03-063612-4). HR&W.

Williams, Marilyn, jt. auth. see Shevky, Eshref.

Williams, Marjorie L. Chinese Painting: An Escape from the "Dusty" World. LC 81-65665. (Themes in Art Ser.). (Illus.). 74p. 1981. pap. 6.95 o.p. (ISBN 0-910386-63-3, Pub. by Cleveland Mus Art). Ind U Pr.

Williams, Mark. Deep Sea Treasure. (Illus.). 24.95 (ISBN 0-434-86660-1, Pub. by Heinemann). David & Charles.

Williams, Mark B., tr. see Yagi, Koji.

Williams, Martha E., ed. Annual Review of Information Science & Technology, Vol. 11. LC 66-25096. 1976. 35.00 (ISBN 0-87715-212-8). Am Soc Info Sci.

--The Annual Review of Information Science & Technology, Vol. 11, 1976. LC 66-25096. (Illus.). 1976. text ed. 42.50 (ISBN 0-87715-212-8). Knowledge Indus.

--Annual Review of Information Science & Technology, Vol. 13. LC 66-25096. 1978. text ed. 42.50 (ISBN 0-914236-21-0). Knowledge Indus.

--The Annual Review of Information Science & Technology, Vol. 18. LC 66-25096. 400p. 1983. 45.00 (ISBN 0-86729-050-1). Knowledge Indus.

--Annual Review of Information Science & Technology (ARIST) 1980, Vol. 15. LC 66-25096. 400p. 1980. text ed. 42.50 (ISBN 0-914236-65-2). Knowledge Indus.

--Annual Review of Information Science & Technology, 1981, Vol. 16. LC 66-25096. 422p. 1981. text ed. 42.50x (ISBN 0-914236-90-3). Knowledge Indus.

--Annual Review of Information Science & Technology, 1982, Vol. 17. LC 66-25096. 367p. 1982. text ed. 45.00x (ISBN 0-86729-032-3). Knowledge Indus.

--Computer-Readable Data Bases: A Directory & Data Sourcebook. LC 66-46249. 1979. text ed. 95.00 softcover (ISBN 0-914236-45-8). Knowledge Indus.

Williams, Martha E. & Rouse, Sandra H., eds. Computer-Readable Bibliographic Data Bases: A Directory & Data Sourcebook. LC 76-46249. 1976. 68.00 (ISBN 0-87715-114-8). Am Soc Info Sci.

Williams, Martin. Jazz Masters in Transition, 1957-1969. (Quality Paperbacks Ser.). (Illus.). 288p. 1983. pap. 7.95 (ISBN 0-306-80175-2). Da Capo.

--TV: The Casual Art. 1982. 17.95x (ISBN 0-19-502992-5). Oxford U Pr.

--Where's the Melody? A Listener's Introduction to Jazz. (Quality Paperbacks Ser.). 224p. 1983. pap. 7.95 (ISBN 0-306-80183-3). Da Capo.

Williams, Martin, ed. The Art of Jazz: Essays on the Development & Nature of Jazz. LC 79-10083. (Roots of Jazz Ser.). 248p. 1979. Repr. of 1959 ed. lib. bdg. 25.00 (ISBN 0-306-79556-6). Da Capo.

Williams, Martin, jt. ed. see Blackbeard, Bill.

Williams, Martin T. Jazz Tradition. LC 71-83058. 1970. 18.95x (ISBN 0-19-500664-X). Oxford U Pr.

Williams, Maxcine, jt. ed. see White, Helen A.

Williams, Maxville B. First for Freedom. LC 76-25333. 1976. 9.95 (ISBN 0-87716-067-8, Pub. by Moore Pub Co). F Apple.

Williams, Melvin, ed. Ergogenic Aids in Sports. 1983. text ed. price not set (ISBN 0-931250-39-0). Human Kinetics.

Williams, Merrill. His Spirit in You. 1982. 2.95 (ISBN 0-8341-0783-X). Beacon Hill.

Williams, Michael. American Catholics in the War: National Catholic War Council, 1917-1921. LC 74-75244. (The United States in World War 1 Ser.). x, 467p. 1974. Repr. of 1921 ed. lib. bdg. 23.95x (ISBN 0-89198-110-1). Ozer.

--British Population. 2nd ed. (Studies in the British Economy Ser.). 1975. pap. text ed. 6.50x o.p. (ISBN 0-435-33960-5). Heinemann Ed.

--Draining of the Somerset Levels. LC 73-75830. (Illus.). 1970. 64.50 (ISBN 0-521-07486-X). Cambridge U Pr.

--Groundless Belief: An Essay on the Possibilities of Epistemology. LC 76-52338. 1977. 17.50x o.p. (ISBN 0-300-02128-3). Yale U Pr.

--Show Jumping in Britain. 6.50x (ISBN 0-392-09530-0, SpS). Sportshelf.

Williams, Michael, ed. Geography & the Integrated Curriculum. 1976. text ed. 21.95x o. p. (ISBN 0-435-35730-1); pap. text ed. 12.95x (ISBN 0-435-35731-X). Heinemann Ed.

Williams, Michael A., ed. Charisma & Sacred Biography. (JAAR Thematic Studies). 1982. 19.50 (ISBN 0-686-87063-8, 01-24-83). Scholars Pr CA.

Williams, Michael Z., jt. auth. see Filippone, Samuel R.

Williams, Miller. Distractions. LC 80-39502. 1981. 11.95 (ISBN 0-8071-0796-4); pap. 4.95x (ISBN 0-8071-0797-2). La State U Pr.

Williams, Miller, jt. auth. see Ciardi, John.

Williams, Miller, ed. A Roman Collection: Stories, Poems & Other Good Pieces by the Writing Residents of the American Academy in Rome. LC 79-5507. 368p. 1980. text ed. 12.50x (ISBN 0-8262-0293-4). U of Mo Pr.

Williams, Miller, ed. & tr. see Parra, Nicanor.

Williams, Mona. The Messenger. 1978. pap. 2.75 (ISBN 0-451-11621-6, AE1621, Sig). NAL.

--This House Is Burning. 1979. pap. 2.50 o.p. (ISBN 0-451-11622-4, AE1622, Sig). NAL.

--This House is Burning. 1982. pap. 2.50 (ISBN 0-451-11622-4, AE1622, Sig). NAL.

Williams, Monier, ed. Sanskirt-English Dictionary: Etymologically & Philologically Arranged with Special Reference to Cognate Indo-European Languages. LC 73-495007. 1333p. 1981. Repr. of 1899 ed. 50.00x (ISBN 0-8002-0204-X). Intl Pubns serv.

Williams, Monier, et al. Sanskrit-English Dictionary. 1367p. 1981. Repr. 45.00 (ISBN 0-89581-173-1). Lancaster-Miller.

Williams, Morag. Comprehensive Guide to Deep Freezing. 1972. pap. 2.50 o.p. (ISBN 0-600-31799-4). Transatlantic.

Williams, Moris. Comportamento Do Crente. Balthazar, Vera & Caruso, Luis, eds. Caruso, Luis, tr. (Portuguese Bks.). 218p. 1980. pap. 2.60 (ISBN 0-8297-0650-X). Life Pubs Intl.

Williams, Moyra. Brain Damage, Behaviour, & the Mind. LC 78-16370. 1979. 34.95x (ISBN 0-471-99704-8, Pub. by Wiley-Interscience). Wiley.

Williams, N. G., jt. auth. see Harriss, E. G.

Williams, N. H. Combinatorial Set Theory. (Studies in Logic: Vol. 91). 1977. 38.50 (ISBN 0-7204-0722-2, North-Holland). Elsevier.

Williams, Neva. Patrick Des Jarlait: The Story of an American Indian Artist. LC 74-33523. (Voices of the American Indian). (Illus.). 56p. (gr. 5 up). 1975. PLB 5.95g (ISBN 0-8225-0642-4). Lerner Pubns.

Williams, Norman, Jr., ed. American Land Planning Law: Cases & Materials. 1978. text ed. 35.00 (ISBN 0-88285-041-5). Ctr Urban Pol Res.

Williams, Norman L. Sir Walter Raleigh. 295p. 1982. Repr. of 1962 ed. lib. bdg. 40.00 (ISBN 0-8495-5821-2). Arden Lib.

Williams, Numan A., jt. auth. see Gaunt, Larry D.

Williams, O. W. Pioneer Surveyor - Frontier Lawyer. Myres, S. D., ed. (Illus.). 1968. 10.00 o.p. (ISBN 0-87404-011-6). Tex Western.

Williams, Oscar, ed. The Mentor Book of Major British Poets. pap. 3.95 (ISBN 0-451-62070-4, ME2070, Ment). NAL.

Williams, Oscar & Honig, eds. The Mentor Book of Major American Poets. pap. 3.95 (ISBN 0-451-62076-3, ME2076, Ment). NAL.

Williams, P. F. Camping Complete. 1972. 10.00 o.p. (ISBN 0-7207-0477-4). Transatlantic.

--Canoeing Skills & Canoe Expedition Technique. (Illus.). 1977. 16.25x o.p. (ISBN 0-7207-0036-1, SpS). Sportshelf.

Williams, P. H., jt. ed. see Ingram, D. S.

Williams, Pat & Jenkins, Jerry. The Power Within You. LC 82-24825. 196p. 1983. price not set (ISBN 0-664-27008-5, Bridgebooks Publciations). Westminster.

Williams, Pat, jt. auth. see Hill, Douglas.

Williams, Pat E., jt. auth. see Peterson, Carol J.

Williams, Patrick & Pearce, Joan T. The Vital Network: A Theory of Communication & Society. LC 77-94757. (Contributions in Librarianship & Information Science: No 25). 1978. lib. bdg. 25.00x (ISBN 0-313-20324-5, WCS/). Greenwood.

Williams, Paul. Dylan: What Happened? (Illus.). 128p. (Orig.). 1980. pap. 4.95 (ISBN 0-89708-021-1, Co-Pub. by Entwhistle Bks). And Bks.

--Das Energi. LC 73-80135. 156p. 1980. ltd. ed., signed 25.00 (ISBN 0-934558-11-6); pap. 4.95 (ISBN 0-934558-00-0). Entwhistle Bks.

--Das Energi. 1976. pap. 2.95 (ISBN 0-446-30649-5). Warner Bks.

Williams, Paul H. Antenna Theory & Design. 22.75x (ISBN 0-392-07549-0, SpS). Sportshelf.

Williams, Paul L. The Moral Philosophy of Peter Abelard. LC 80-5604. 191p. 1980. lib. bdg. 20.00 (ISBN 0-8191-1137-6); pap. text ed. 9.75 (ISBN 0-8191-1138-4). U Pr of Amer.

Williams, Paul L. & Moore, Jerry R., eds. Criterion-Referenced Testing for the Social Studies, No. 64. LC 80-84889. (Bulletin Ser.). 92p. 1980. pap. 6.25 (ISBN 0-87986-034-0). Coun Soc Studies.

Williams, Paul L., ed. see Fellowship of Catholic Scholars.

Williams, Paul N. Investigative Reporting & Editing. LC 77-4855. (Illus.). 1978. 16.95 (ISBN 0-13-504662-9). P-H.

Williams, Penelope. Paper Dolls of the Middle East. LC 78-8507. (Unicef Storycraft Bks). (Illus.). (ps-3). 1978. pap. 3.50 o.p. (ISBN 0-529-05433-7, Philomel). Putnam Pub Group.

Williams, Peter. The Organ Music of J. S. Bach, 2 vols. LC 77-71431. (Illus.). Vol. 1, Jan. 1981. 79.50 (ISBN 0-521-21723-7); Vol. 2. 64.50 (ISBN 0-521-21517-X). Cambridge U Pr.

Williams, Peter, ed. Social Process & the City: Urban Studies Yearbook, 1. 242p. 1983. text ed. 27.50x (ISBN 0-86861-237-5). Allen Unwin.

Williams, Peter J. The Surface of the Earth: An Introduction to Geotechnical Science. LC 81-3683. (Illus.). 228p. (Orig.). 1982. pap. text ed. 19.95x (ISBN 0-582-30043-6). Longman.

Williams, Peter L. & Warwick, Roger. Functional Neuroanatomy of Man. LC 74-10038. (Illus.). 460p. 1975. text ed. 10.00x o.p. (ISBN 0-7216-9450-0). Saunders.

Williams, Peter L., jt. ed. see Warwick, Roger.

Williams, Peter W. Popular Religions in America. (P-H Studies on Religions Ser.). 1980. pap. text ed. 13.95 (ISBN 0-13-686113-X). P-H.

Williams, Philip. French Politicians & Elections, Nineteen Fifty-One to Nineteen Sixty-Eight. (Illus.). 1970. 41.50 o.p. (ISBN 0-521-07709-5); pap. 12.95x (ISBN 0-521-09608-1). Cambridge U Pr.

Williams, Philip, jt. ed. see Varma, Ved P.

Williams, Philip L. The Emergence of the Theory of the Firm: From Adam Smith to Alfred Marshall. 1979. 26.00 (ISBN 0-312-24387-1). St Martin.

Williams, Phillip G. How to Form Your Own Illinois Corporation Before the Inc. Dries: A Step-by-Step Guide, with Forms. 136p. (Orig.). 1983. lib. bdg. 9.95 (ISBN 0-936284-25-0); pap. 9.95 (ISBN 0-936284-26-9). P Gaines Co.

Williams, Phyliss S., jt. auth. see Kenda, Margaret E.

Williams, Phyllis S. Nourishing Your Unborn Child. 1975. pap. 4.95 (ISBN 0-380-00472-0, 60657-7). Avon.

Williams, Preston P. & Joseph, Marilyn S. Differential Diagnosis: Obstetrics. LC 78-1662. (Arco Diagnosis Ser.). (Illus.). 1978. pap. text ed. 100.00x (ISBN 0-668-04161-7). Arco.

Williams, R., jt. ed. see Axton, Marie.

Williams, R. F. The Shoot Apex & Leaf Growth. (Illus.). 280p. 1975. 42.50 (ISBN 0-521-20453-4). Cambridge U Pr.

Williams, R. H. With the Border Ruffians: Memories of the Far West, 1852-1868. Williams, E. W., ed. LC 82-8400. (Illus.). xxii, 490p. 1982. 27.50x (ISBN 0-8032-4721-4, BB 799, Bison); pap. 9.950x (ISBN 0-8032-9704-1). U of Nebr Pr.

Williams, R. Hal. Years of Decision: American Politics in the 1890's. LC 78-6407. (Critical Episodes in American Politics Ser). 1978. pap. text ed. 11.50 (ISBN 0-471-94878-0). Wiley.

Williams, R. L. & Karacan, I. Sleep Disorders: Diagnosis & Treatment. LC 78-18896. 1978. 64.00 (ISBN 0-471-94682-6, Pub. by Wiley-Medical). Wiley.

Williams, R. L., ed. The Commune of Paris, Eighteen Seventy-One. (Major Issues in History Ser.). text ed. 9.50x (ISBN 0-471-94851-9, Pub. by Wiley); pap. text ed. 5.50 (ISBN 0-471-94852-7, Pub. by Wiley). Krieger.

Williams, R. Leroy. Blue Skies Calling Wild Wings. new ed. (Illus.). 1978. pap. 3.00 (ISBN 0-932044-09-3). M O Pub Co.

--The Life Machine. new ed. (Illus.). 1978. pap. 3.00 (ISBN 0-932044-10-7). M O Pub Co.

--Nostalgic & Fun Poems. (Illus.). 1978. pap. 3.00 (ISBN 0-932044-15-8). M O Pub Co.

Williams, R. M. Evaluation of Field & Laboratory Methods for Testing Termite Resistance of Timber & Building Materials in Ghana, with Relevant Biological Studies. 1973. 35.00x (ISBN 0-85135-065-8, Pub. by Centre Overseas Research). State Mutual Bk.

Williams, R. T., jt. auth. see Morrison, John S.

Williams, Raburn M., jt. auth. see Miller, Roger L.

Williams, Ralph C., Jr., ed. Lymphocytes & Their Interactions. 240p. 1975. text ed. 20.00 (ISBN 0-89004-052-4). Raven.

Williams, Ralph Vaughan & Holst, Gustav. Heirs & Rebels: Letters Between Ralph Vaughn Williams & Gustav Holst. Williams, Ursala V. & Holst, Gustav, eds. LC 73-86441. (Illus.). xii, 111p. 1974. Repr. of 1959 ed. lib. bdg. 12.50x (ISBN 0-8154-0487-5). Cooper Sq.

Williams, Raymond. The Country & the City. LC 72-98128. 1975. pap. 7.95 (ISBN 0-19-519810-7, GB423, GB). Oxford U Pr.

--The English Novel from Dickens to Lawrence. 196p. 1983. pap. text ed. 7.95x (ISBN 0-391-02815-4). Humanities.

--Politics & Letters: Interviews with New Left Review. 1979. 27.50 (ISBN 0-8052-7063-9, Pub. by NLB); pap. 9.50 (ISBN 0-8052-7102-3). Schocken.

--Problems in Materialism & Culture: Selected Essays. 288p. 1981. 19.50x o.p. (ISBN 0-8052-7093-0, Pub. by Verso); pap. 8.75 (ISBN 0-8052-7092-2). Schocken.

--Television: Technology & Cultural Form. LC 75-10714. 160p. 1975. 7.50x (ISBN 0-8052-3597-3); pap. 4.95 (ISBN 0-8052-0501-2). Schocken.

Williams, Raymond W. Techniques & Components of Analogue Computation. 1962. 37.50 (ISBN 0-12-756250-8). Acad Pr.

Williams, Redford B., jt. auth. see Gentry, W. Doyle.

Williams, Redford B. & Gentry, W. Doyle, eds. Behavioral Approaches to Medical Treatment. LC 76-30327. 288p. 1977. prof ref 22.50x (ISBN 0-88410-136-3). Ballinger Pub.

Williams, Redford B., Jr., jt. ed. see Surwit, Richard S.

Williams, Reese. A Pair of Eyes. 80p. (Orig.). 1983. 12.95 (ISBN 0-934378-31-2); pap. 5.95 (ISBN 0-934378-32-0). Tanam Pr.

Williams, Richard. The Loggers. LC 75-24792. (The Old West). (Illus.). (gr. 5 up). 1976. 17.28 (ISBN 0-8094-1527-5, Pub. by Time-Life). Silver.

--The Northwest Coast. LC 73-87559. (American Wilderness Ser). (Illus.). (gr. 6 up). 1973. lib. bdg. 15.96 (ISBN 0-8094-1193-8, Pub. by Time-Life). Silver.

Williams, Richard L. The Cascades. LC 74-13323. (American Wilderness). (Illus.). (gr. 6 up). 1974. PLB 15.96 (ISBN 0-8094-1246-2, Pub. by Time-Life). Silver.

Williams, Robert. The Lowbrow Art of Robert Williams. Shelton, Gilbert, ed. (Illus.). 96p. (Orig.). 1981. pap. 10.95 (ISBN 0-89620-087-6). Rip off.

--The Power of Multiplan. 168p. 1982. pap. 14.95 (ISBN 0-13-687343-X). P-H.

Williams, Robert, ed. The Energy Conservation Papers. LC 74-32304. (Ford Foundation Energy Pology Project Ser.). 416p. 1975. prof ref 22.50 (ISBN 0-88410-335-8). Ballinger Pub.

Williams, Robert A., jt. auth. see Rockwell, Robert E.

Williams, Robert B. John Dewey: Recollections. LC 81-40841. 208p. (Orig.). 1982. lib. bdg. 22.25 (ISBN 0-8191-2312-9); pap. text ed. 10.75 (ISBN 0-8191-2313-7). U Pr of Amer.

Williams, Robert C., jt. auth. see Cantelon, Philip L.

Williams, Robert H. Textbook of Endocrinology. 6th ed. (Illus.). 1270p. 1981. 70.00 (ISBN 0-7216-9398-9). Saunders.

Williams, Robert H., jt. auth. see Ross, Marc H.

Williams, Robert H., ed. Textbook of Endocrinology. 5th ed. LC 73-76190. (Illus.). 1138p. 1974. text ed. 35.00 o.p. (ISBN 0-7216-9397-0). Saunders.

--Toward a Solar Civilization. (Illus.). 264p. 1978. 17.50x (ISBN 0-262-23089-5); pap. 6.95x (ISBN 0-262-73054-5). MIT Pr.

Williams, Robert L. & Long, James D. Toward a Self-Managed Life Style. 2nd ed. LC 78-56435. (Illus.). 1979. text ed. 12.95 (ISBN 0-395-26760-9); instr's. manual 1.00 (ISBN 0-395-26759-5). HM.

--Toward a Self-Managed Life Style. 3rd ed. LC 82-81112. 288p. 1982. pap. text ed. 12.95 (ISBN 0-395-32590-0); write for info. instr's manual (ISBN 0-395-32591-9). HM.

Williams, Robert L., jt. auth. see Long, James D.

Williams, Robert L. & Williams, Willie S., eds. Testing. members 2.50 (ISBN 0-686-36424-4, 70664); non-members 3.00 (ISBN 0-686-37314-6). Am Personnel.

Williams, Robert L., et al. Electroencephalography (EEG) of Human Sleep: Clinical Applications. LC 73-20032. 192p. 1974. 50.00 o.p. (ISBN 0-471-94686-9, Pub. by Wiley Medical). Wiley.

Williams, Robert M., ed. UCLA Business Forecast for the Nation & California in 1982. (Illus.). 110p. 50.00 o.s.i. (ISBN 0-686-97260-0). U of Cal Pr.

--UCLA Business Forecast for the Nation & California in 1983: Proceedings of an Annual Conference, December 15, 1982. 1983. 60.00x. UCLA Busn Forecasting.

--The World Economic Outlook for 1976. (Orig.). 1976. pap. 30.00 o.p. (ISBN 0-913404-01-2). UCLA Busn Forecasting.

Williams, Robin M., Jr. Reduction of Intergroup Tensions. LC 47-6441. 1947. pap. 6.00 (ISBN 0-527-03285-9). Kraus Repr.

Williams, Roger. Key into the Language of America. 5th ed. LC 70-157500. Repr. of 1643 ed. 43.00x (ISBN 0-8103-3723-1). Gale.

Williams, Roger, jt. auth. see Bunis, Al.

Williams, Roger, jt. auth. see Hahn, Albert.

Williams, Roger B. see Baynton-Williams, Roger.

Williams, Roger J. Nutrition in a Nutshell. LC 62-15322. 1963. pap. 2.50 (ISBN 0-385-03031-2, Dolp). Doubleday.

Williams, Rosa M., ed. Restoration: Our Philosophy Through Inspired Poems. LC 79-66586. 1980. write for info. (ISBN 0-9602366-1-9); pap. 4.50x. Sooty-Face.

Williams, Rowan. The Truce of God. 128p. (Orig.). 1983. pap. 3.95 (ISBN 0-8298-0660-1). Pilgrim NY.

Williams, Roy, ed. Machining Hard Materials. LC 82-50538. (Manufacturing Update Ser.). 240p. 1982. 32.00 (ISBN 0-87263-083-8). SME.

Williams, Ruby R. My Master's Will: Inspirational & Spiritual Verses. 1978. 4.50 o.p. (ISBN 0-533-03664-X). Vantage.

Williams, S. J. & Torrens, P. R. Introduction to Health Services. 397p. 1980. 24.50 (ISBN 0-471-04612-4, Pub. by Wiley Med). Wiley.

Williams, S. J., ed. see Meurig, H. & Thomas, W. O.

Williams, Sam P. Guide to the Research Collections of the New York Public Library. LC 75-15878. 368p. 1975. text ed. 35.00 o.p. (ISBN 0-8389-0125-5). ALA.

Williams, Sam P., ed. Law Books in Review: 1974-1981. 1981. Set. 180.00 (ISBN 0-686-74113-7); Each Year. 35.00 (ISBN 0-686-74114-5). Glanville.

Williams, Samuel C. History of the Lost State of Franklin. rev. ed. LC 73-19813. (Perspectives in American History Ser.: No. 23). (Illus.). 378p. Repr. of 1933 ed. lib. bdg. 22.50x (ISBN 0-87991-348-7). Porcupine Pr.

Williams, Sarkey V., jt. auth. see Eisenberg, John M.

Williams, Sharon A. International & National Protection of Cultural Property: A Comparative Study. LC 78-2409. 302p. 1978. 44.00 (ISBN 0-379-20294-8). Oceana.

Williams, Solomon. The Lily White Marina. 1983. 6.95 (ISBN 0-533-04952-0). Vantage.

Williams, Stanley T. American Spirit in Letters. 1926. text ed. 22.50x (ISBN 0-686-83468-2). Elliots Bks.

Williams, Stephen. Caddoan Indians One. Horr, David A., ed. (American Indian Ethnohistory Ser.). 1978. lib. bdg. 42.00 o.s.i. (ISBN 0-8240-0763-8). Garland Pub.

Williams, Stephen & Brain, Jeffrey P. Excavations at the Lake George Site: Yazoo County, Mississippi, 1958-1960. (Peabody Museum Papers: Vol. 74). (Illus.). 600p. 1983. pap. text ed. 45.00x (ISBN 0-87365-200-2). Peabody Harvard.

Williams, Stephen J. How to Get Into & Finance Graduate & Professional Schools: A Step-by-Step Guide for Current & Returning Students. 192p. 1983. pap. 5.95 (ISBN 0-02-015940-4). Macmillan.

Williams, Sue R. Essentials of Nutrition & Diet Therapy. 3rd ed. LC 81-14195. (Illus.). 390p. 1982. pap. text ed. 16.95 (ISBN 0-8016-5575-7). Mosby.

--Mowry's Basic Nutrition & Diet Therapy. 6th ed. LC 79-26165. (Illus.). 216p. 1980. pap. text ed. 12.95 (ISBN 0-8016-5556-0). Mosby.

--Nutrition & Diet Therapy. 4th ed. LC 80-27219. (Illus.). 840p. 1981. text ed. 24.95 o.p. (ISBN 0-8016-5554-4). Mosby.

--Self-Study Guide for Nutrition & Diet Therapy. 2nd ed. LC 77-18113. 208p. 1978. pap. text ed. 8.50 o.p. (ISBN 0-8016-5573-0). Mosby.

Williams, Sunnie. The Nomie Book: Growing up from Shy. (Illus.). 104p. (Orig.). (gr. 3-6). 1981. pap. 2.75 (ISBN 0-9605444-0-2). Wee Smile.

Williams, Susan, ed. Expressionism. (Illus.). 36p. 1974. 8.95 o.p. (ISBN 0-312-27790-3). St Martin.

Williams, T. Harry. The Selected Essays of T. Harry Williams. LC 82-18646. 288p. 1983. 19.95 (ISBN 0-8071-1095-7). La State U Pr.

--The Union Restored, 1861-1876. LC 63-8572. (Life History of the United States). (Illus.). (gr. 5 up). 1974. PLB 10.60 (ISBN 0-8094-0555-5, Pub. by Time-Life). Silver.

--The Union Sundered, 1849-1865. LC 63-8572. (Life History of the United States). (Illus.). (gr. 5 up). 1974. PLB 10.60 (ISBN 0-8094-0554-7, Pub. by Time-Life). Silver.

Williams, T. Harry, intro. by. Military Analysis of the Civil War: An Anthology by the Editors of Military Affairs. LC 76-41550. 1977. 25.00 (ISBN 0-527-63575-8). Kraus Intl.

Williams, Ted. Rogues of Bataan. 1980. 6.75 o.p. (ISBN 0-8062-1322-1). Carlton.

--The Science of Hitting. (Illus.). (gr. 7 up). 1971. 9.95 o.p. (ISBN 0-671-20892-6). S&S.

Williams, Ted & Underwood, John. My Turn at Bat: The Story of My Life. (gr. 5 up). 1969. 7.95 o.p. (ISBN 0-671-20228-6). S&S.

Williams, Ted, jt. auth. see Underwood, John.

Williams, Tennessee. The Bag People. Date not set. 19.95 (ISBN 0-396-08106-1). Dodd.

--Cat on a Hot Tin Roof. pap. 1.95 (ISBN 0-451-09689-4, J9689, Sig). NAL.

--Clothes for a Summer Hotel. 96p. 1983. 12.00 (ISBN 0-8112-0870-2, NDP556); pap. 4.75 (ISBN 0-8112-0871-0). New Directions.

--Four Plays by Tennessee Williams. Incl. Summer & Smoke; Orpheus Descending; Suddenly Last Summer; Period of Adjustment. 1976. pap. 3.50 (ISBN 0-451-51672-9, CE1672, Sig Classics). NAL.

--Small Craft Warnings. LC 72-80978. 1972. 4.95 (ISBN 0-8112-0461-8, NDP348). New Directions.

--A Streetcar Named Desire. 1973. pap. 2.50 (ISBN 0-451-12180-5, AE2180, Sig). NAL.

--Tennessee Williams' Letters to Donald Windham. Windham, Donald, ed. 1980. pap. 4.95 o.p. (ISBN 0-14-005728-5). Penguin.

--The Theatre of Tennessee Williams, Vol. 5. Incl. The Milk Train Doesn't Stop Here Anymore; Kingdom of Earth. rev. ed; Small Craft Warnings; The Two-Character Play. rev. ed. LC 78-159743. 384p. 1976. 19.95 (ISBN 0-8112-0593-2). New Directions.

--Three by Tennessee Williams. Incl. Bird of Youth; The Rose Tattoo; Night of the Iguana. 1976. pap. 2.95 (ISBN 0-451-51569-2, CE1569, Sig Classics). NAL.

Williams, Tennessee see Laurel Editions Editors.

Williams, Tennessee see Moon, Samuel.

Williams, Tennessee see Strasberg, Lee.

Williams, Terrell G. Consumer Behavior: Concepts & Strategies. 590p. 1981. pap. text ed. 23.95 (ISBN 0-8299-0420-4). West Pub.

Williams, Terry. Crossing the Thin Line. 0.95 (ISBN 0-89486-077-1). Hazelden.

Williams, Theodore M., ed. see Chrysostomos, Archimandrite.

Williams, Thomas. The Followed Man. LC 78-16629. 1978. 10.95 (ISBN 0-399-90025-X, Marek). Putnam Pub Group.

--The Night of Trees. LC 78-23832. 1978. 9.95 o.p. (ISBN 0-399-90026-8, Marek). Putnam Pub Group.

--Town Burning. 1970. 8.95 (ISBN 0-394-44918-5). Random.

Williams, Thomas A. & Johnson, James H. Mental Health in the Twenty-First Century. LC 78-20270. 208p. 1979. 23.95x (ISBN 0-669-02718-9). Lexington Bks.

Williams, Thomas A., jt. auth. see Freund, John E.

Williams, Thomas A., jt. auth. see Anderson Sweeney, David R.

Williams, Thomas E. Silverstreet. 224p. 1983. 15.00 (ISBN 0-682-49929-3). Exposition.

Williams, Tom, jt. auth. see Meyer, Dan.

Williams, Trevor A. Learning to Manage Our Futures: The Participative Redesign of Societies in Turbulent Transition. LC 81-16019. 211p. 1982. 23.95 (ISBN 0-471-08135-3, Pub. by Wiley-Interscience). Wiley.

Williams, Trevor I. A Short History of Twentieth-Century Technology, 1900-1950. (Illus.). 1982. 25.00 (ISBN 0-19-858159-9). Oxford U Pr.

Williams, Trevor I., jt. auth. see Derry, Thomas K.

Williams, Trevor I., ed. Industrial Research in the United Kingdom: A Reference Guide to Organizations & Establishments. 872p. 1980. 165.00x (ISBN 0-686-75639-8, Pub. by Longman). Gale.

Williams, Ursala V., ed. see Williams, Ralph Vaughan & Holst, Gustav.

Williams, V. D. Riding. 8.50 (ISBN 0-392-09544-0, SpS). Sportshelf.

Williams, Vera B. Something Special for Me. LC 82-11884. (Illus.). 32p. (gr. k-3). 1983. 10.00 (ISBN 0-688-01806-8); PLB 9.55 (ISBN 0-688-01807-6). Greenwillow.

Williams, Vergil L. Dictionary of American Penology: An Introductory Guide. LC 77-94751. 1979. lib. bdg. 45.00x (ISBN 0-313-20327-X, WAP/). Greenwood.

Williams, Vergil L. & Fish, Mary. Convicts, Codes & Contraband: The Prison Life of Men & Women. LC 73-16233. 192p. 1974. prof ref 16.50 (ISBN 0-88410-204-1). Ballinger Pub.

Williams, W. Hematology: PreTest Self-Assessment & Review. 240p. Date not set. 31.95 (ISBN 0-07-051930-7). McGraw-Pretest.

Williams, W. E. Allen Lane: A Personal Portrait. (Illus.). 96p. 1973. 6.95 o.p. (ISBN 0-370-10474-9). Transatlantic.

--The State Against Blacks. (New Press Ser.). 208p. 1982. 14.95 (ISBN 0-07-070378-7). McGraw.

Williams, W. H. H. L. Mencken. (United States Authors Ser.: No. 297). 1977. lib. bdg. 13.95 (ISBN 0-8057-7200-6, Twayne). G K Hall.

Williams, W. H., jt. auth. see Wendel, T. M.

Williams, W. T. Pattern Analysis in Agricultural Science. 1977. 53.25 (ISBN 0-444-99844-6). Elsevier.

Williams, Walter. Government by Agency: Lessons from the Grants in Aid Experience. LC 80-527. (Quantitive Studies in Social Relations Ser.). 1980. 26.00 (ISBN 0-12-755950-7). Acad Pr.

--The Implementation Perspective: A Guide for Managing Social Service Delivery Programs. 1980. 17.95x (ISBN 0-520-04054-6); pap. 3.95 (ISBN 0-520-04063-5). U of Cal Pr.

--Mr. Bill in Space. 40p. 1982. pap. 6.95 (ISBN 0-02-040890-0); pap. 83.40 prepack of 12 (ISBN 0-02-040880-3). Macmillan.

Williams, Walter & Elmore, Richard F., eds. Social Program Implementation. (Quantitative Studies in Social Relations Ser.). 1976. 29.50 (ISBN 0-12-756850-6). Acad Pr.

Williams, Walter, Jr. Intergovernmental Military Forces & World Public Order. LC 75-167280. 703p. 1971. lib. bdg. 32.50x (ISBN 0-379-00063-6). Oceana.

Williams, Wayland W. Seafarers (Poetry) 1924. text ed. 19.50x (ISBN 0-686-83730-4). Elliots Bks.

Williams, Wayne. Dr. Zarkov Number Fun. (Flash Gordon Puzzles Ser.). (Illus.). (gr. 3-6). 1979. pap. 0.95 (ISBN 0-448-15949-X, G&D). Putnam Pub Group.

Williams, Wiley J., jt. auth. see Cheney, Frances N.

Williams, William A. Empire As a Way of Life: An Essay on the Causes & Character of America's Present Predicament Along with a Few Thoughts About an Alternative. 1982. pap. 7.95 (ISBN 0-19-503045-1, GB 669, GB). Oxford U Pr.

--Empire As a Way of Life: An Essay on the Causes & Character of America's Present Predicament, Along with a Few Thoughts About an Alternative. 1980. 17.95x (ISBN 0-19-502766-3). Oxford U Pr.

Williams, William C. Pictures from Brueghel: Collected Poems 1950-1962. LC 62-10410. 1967. pap. 5.95 (ISBN 0-8112-0234-8, NDP118). New Directions.

--White Mule. LC 37-11249. (Stecher Trilogy: Vol. 1). 1967. pap. 8.00 (ISBN 0-8112-0238-0, NDP226). New Directions.

--Yes, Mrs. Williams: A Personal Record of My Mother. 2nd ed. LC 59-9887. 160p. (Orig.). 1982. pap. 5.95 (ISBN 0-8112-0832-X, NDP534). New Directions.

Williams, William C., tr. see Soupault, Philippe.

Williams, William H., jt. ed. see Miller, Harlan B.

Williams, William J., et al. Hematology. 2nd ed. (Illus.). 1977. text ed. 75.00 (ISBN 0-07-070376-0, HP). McGraw.

Williams, William P. Jeremy Taylor, Seventeen Hundred to Nineteen Seventy-Six: An Annotated Checklist. LC 78-68302. (Garland Reference Library of the Humanities: No. 177). 1979. lib. bdg. 12.00 o.s.i. (ISBN 0-8240-9756-4). Garland Pub.

Williams, William W. Coastal Changes. LC 75-3873. (Illus.). 220p. 1975. Repr. of 1960 ed. lib. bdg. 16.00x (ISBN 0-8371-8088-0, WICOC). Greenwood.

Williams, Willie S., jt. ed. see Williams, Robert L.

Williams-Ellis, Annabel. Fairy Tales from Here & There. (Illus., Orig.). 1978. pap. 2.95 o.p. (ISBN 0-8467-0536-2, Pub. by Two Continents). Hippocrene Bks.

--Fairy Tales from Near & Far. (Illus., Orig.). 1978. pap. 2.95 o.p. (ISBN 0-8467-0534-6, Pub. by Two Continents). Hippocrene Bks.

Williamsen, Vern G. The Minor Dramatists of Seventeenth-Century Spain. (World Authors Ser.). 1982. lib. bdg. 17.95 (ISBN 0-8057-6496-8, Twayne). G K Hall.

Williams-Gardner, A. Industrial Drying. 328p. 1977. 29.95x (ISBN 0-87201-197-6). Gulf Pub.

Williams-Mitchell, Christobel. Dressed for the Job: The Story of Occupational Costume. (Illus.). 144p. 1983. 16.95 (ISBN 0-7137-1020-9, Pub. by Blandford Pr England). Sterling.

Williamson. First Picture Atlas. LC 80-52176. 1981. 12.90 (ISBN 0-531-09182-1). Watts.

Williamson, Alan. Presence. LC 82-47964. (Poetry Ser.: No. 9). 75p. 1983. 11.95 (ISBN 0-394-52850-6); pap. 6.95 (ISBN 0-394-71259-5). Knopf.

Williamson, Ann P. How to Read a Newspaper, 3 bks. (Illus.). 1976. wkbk. 4.00x ea. o.p. Bk. A, 38p (ISBN 0-89061-275-7). Bk. B, 43p (ISBN 0-89061-276-5). Bk. C, 40p (ISBN 0-89061-277-3). Jamestown Pubs.

Williamson, Arthur, jt. auth. see Darby, John.

Williamson, Audrey. The Mystery of the Princes: An Investigation into a Supposed Murder. 216p. 1981. pap. text ed. 8.25x (ISBN 0-904387-58-5, Pub. by Sutton England). Humanities.

Williamson, Cecile & Limouze, Cary, eds. Shakespeare & the Arts: A Collection of Essays from the Ohio Shakespeare Conference, Wright State University, Dayton, Ohio, 1981. LC 82-17486. (Illus.). 256p. (Orig.). 1983. lib. bdg. 23.50 (ISBN 0-8191-2819-8); pap. text ed. 11.50 (ISBN 0-8191-2820-1). U Pr of Amer.

Williamson, Chilton, Jr. Roughnecking It: Or, Life in the Overthrust. 1982. 14.95 (ISBN 0-671-43966-9). S&S.

Williamson, Craig. The Old English Riddles of the "Exeter Book". LC 76-46278. (Illus.). xx, 484p. 1977. 33.00x (ISBN 0-8078-1272-2). U of NC Pr.

Williamson, D., jt. auth. see Wight, H.

Williamson, D., et al. Gallium Arsinide Solar Cells in House Fabrication Project: Progress in Solar Energy Supplements. 50p. 1982. pap. text ed. 7.50x (ISBN 0-89553-077-5). Am Solar Energy.

Williamson, Darcey. Old Confectioner's Handbook. 212p. (Orig.). 1982. pap. 7.95 (ISBN 0-89288-078-3). Maverick.

Williamson, Edmund G. & Biggs, Donald A. Student Personnel Work: A Program of Development Relationships. LC 74-28492. 384p. 1975. text ed. 34.95x (ISBN 0-471-94880-2). Wiley.

Williamson, Edward G. American Political Writers, Eighteen Hundred One to Nineteen-Seventy Three. (United States Author Ser.). 1981. lib. bdg. 13.95 (ISBN 0-8057-7326-6, Twayne). G K Hall.

Williamson, George C. The Book of Famille Rose. LC 72-104208. (Illus.). 231p. 1970. 72.50 (ISBN 0-8048-0880-5). C E Tuttle.

--The Talent of T. S. Eliot. lib. bdg. 34.50 (ISBN 0-686-81914-4). Porter.

Williamson, George H. Secret Places of the Lion. 230p. 1983. pap. 7.95 (ISBN 0-89281-039-4). Destiny Bks.

Williamson, H. D., jt. auth. see Douglas, S. W.

Williamson, H. G. Israel in the Book of Chronicles. LC 76-11096. 1977. 37.50 (ISBN 0-521-21305-3). Cambridge U Pr.

Williamson, Hugh R. Historical Enigmas. 1974. 8.95 o.p. (ISBN 0-312-37380-5). St Martin.

--Th Poetry of T. S. Eliot. 1982. lib. bdg. 34.50 (ISBN 0-686-81915-2). Porter.

Williamson, J., jt. auth. see Dolan, D.

Williamson, J. A. Short History of British Expansion, 2 vols. Incl. Vol. 1. Old Colonial Empire. 3rd ed. 470p. 1969. o.p. (ISBN 0-312-71785-7); Vol. 2. Modern Empire & Commonwealth. 6th ed. 408p. 1967 (ISBN 0-312-71820-9). (Illus.). 22.50 (ISBN 0-685-23147-X). St Martin.

Williamson, J. G. Late Nineteenth Century American Growth. LC 74-76946. (Illus.). 290p. 1975. 44.50 (ISBN 0-521-20469-0). Cambridge U Pr.

Williamson, J. N. Death Doctor. (Death Ser.). 1982. pap. 2.95 (ISBN 0-8217-1108-3). Zebra.

--Premonition. 288p. 1981. pap. 2.25 (ISBN 0-8439-0959-5, Leisure Bks). Nordon Pubns.

--The Ritual. 320p. 1982. pap. 3.25 o.s.i. (ISBN 0-8439-1168-9, Leisure Bks). Nordon Pubns.

Williamson, J. P. English-Dakota Dictionary. Repr. 15.00 (ISBN 0-87018-061-4). Ross.

Williamson, J. Peter. Foundation Investment Strategies: New Possibilities in the 1981 Tax Law. (Seven Springs Studies). 1981. pap. 3.00 (ISBN 0-943006-05-8). Seven Springs.

Williamson, Jack. Brother to Demons, Brother to Gods. LC 78-11210. 1979. 10.00 o.p. (ISBN 0-672-52140-7). Bobbs.

--Darker Than You Think. Del Rey, Lester, ed. LC 75-440. (Library of Science Fiction). 1975. lib. bdg. 17.50 o.s.i. (ISBN 0-8240-1442-1). Garland Pub.

--The Humanoids. (Science Fiction Ser.). 1980. lib. bdg. 13.50 o.p. (ISBN 0-8398-2549-8, Gregg). G K Hall.

--The Legion of Space. Del Ray, Lester, ed. LC 75-441. (Library of Science Fiction). 1975. lib. bdg. 17.50 o.s.i. (ISBN 0-8240-1443-X). Garland Pub.

--The Queen of the Legion. 304p. 1983. pap. 2.95 (ISBN 0-686-82611-6, Timescape). PB.

--Seetee. 1979. pap. 1.95 o.s.i. (ISBN 0-515-05150-0). Jove Pubns.

Williamson, Jack, jt. auth. see Pohl, Frederick.

Williamson, James. Mosby's Randers. LC 82-668. (Collector's Library of the Civil War). 26.60 (ISBN 0-8094-4225-6). Silver.

Williamson, James A. The Ocean in English History: Being the Ford Lectures. LC 78-12510. 1979. Repr. of 1941 ed. lib. bdg. 20.50x (ISBN 0-313-21157-4, WIOE). Greenwood.

Williamson, Jane, jt. auth. see Wells, Madeline.

Williamson, Jane, et al, eds. see Women's Action Alliance.

Williamson, Janet A. Current Perspectives in Nursing Education, Vol. 2. LC 75-32544. (Current Perspectives Ser.). (Illus.). 1978. 12.50 o.p. (ISBN 0-8016-5578-1); pap. 9.50 o.p. (ISBN 0-8016-5579-X). Mosby.

Williamson, John. The Exchange Rate System. (Policy Analyses in International Economics Ser.: No. 7). 1983. 6.00 (ISBN 0-88132-012-9). Inst Intl Eco.

--The Lending Policies of the International Monetary Fund. (Policy Analyses in International Economics Ser.: No. 1). 80p. (Orig.). 1982. pap. 6.00x (ISBN 0-88132-000-5). Inst Intl Eco.

--The Open Economy & the World Economy: A Textbook in International Economics. 1983. text ed. 23.95x (ISBN 0-465-05287-8). Basic.

Williamson, John, jt. auth. see Bergsten, C. Fred.

Williamson, John, jt. auth. see Ostrow, Patricia C.

Williamson, John, ed. IMF Conditionality. (Series: No. 5). 700p. 1983. 30.00 (ISBN 0-88132-006-4). Inst Intl Eco.

Williamson, John McKim. Software Sayings of Jack Mack: Wit & Humor with Word Processing. 2nd ed. LC 82-60964. (Jack Mack Paperbacks). 134p. 1982. pap. 8.95 (ISBN 0-910391-00-9). J Mack.

Williamson, John W. Assessing & Improving Health Care Outcomes: The Health Accounting Approach to Assessment & Improvement. LC 78-2367. 1978. prof ref 25.00x (ISBN 0-88410-706-X). Ballinger Pub.

--Improving Medical Practice & Health Care: A Bibliographic Guide to Information Management in Quality Assurance & Continuing Education. LC 77-24711. 1048p. 1977. prof ref 50.00x (ISBN 0-88410-702-7). Ballinger Pub.

Williamson, John W., et al. Principles of Quality Assurance & Cost Containment in Health Care: A Guide for Medical Students, Residents, & Other Health Professionals. LC 82-48072. (Higher Education Ser.). 1982. text ed. 14.95x (ISBN 0-87589-531-X). Jossey Bass.

--Teaching Quality Assurance & Cost Containment in Health Care: A Faculty Guide. LC 82-48071. (Higher Education Ser.). 1982. text ed. 19.95x (ISBN 0-87589-530-1). Jossey Bass.

Williamson, Joseph. The History of the City of Belfast, Maine. Belfast Free Library, ed. LC 82-60448. (Illus.). 956p. 1982. Repr. of 1877 ed. 50.00 (ISBN 0-89725-035-4). NE History.

Williamson, Kenneth L., jt. auth. see Fieser, Louis F.

Williamson, Lamar, Jr. Mark Interpretation: A Bible Commentary for Teaching & Preaching. Mays, James L. & Achtemeier, Paul J., eds. LC 82-17161. 289p. 1983. 17.95 (ISBN 0-8042-3121-4). John Knox.

Williamson, Lamar, Jr., jt. auth. see Beck, Madeline H.

Williamson, Liz, ed. see Fischer-Munstermann, Uta.

Williamson, Mark. Island Populations. (Illus.). 298p. 1983. pap. 19.95 (ISBN 0-19-854139-2). Oxford U Pr.

Williamson, Mitch. Safe Riding: Staying Alive on Your Motorcycle. LC 80-11435. 256p. 1980. pap. 7.95 (ISBN 0-89696-101-X, An Everest House Book); 11.95 (ISBN 0-89696-098-6). Dodd.

Williamson, Nancy. Handy Helpful Household Hints. 1979. pap. 3.95 (ISBN 0-89728-066-0). Omega Pubns Or.

Williamson, Oliver E. Antitrust Law & Economics, Vol. 1. LC 80-66819. (Illus.). 341p. (Orig.). 1980. text ed. 28.95x (ISBN 0-931920-19-1). Dame Pubns.

--Markets & Hierarchies: A Study in the Internal Organizations. 320p. 1983. pap. text ed. 11.95 (ISBN 0-02-934780-7). Free Pr.

Williamson, Paul. Introduction to Medieval Ivory Carvings. (The Victoria & Albert Museum Introductions to the Decorative Arts Ser.). (Illus.). 48p. 1982. 9.95 (ISBN 0-88045-006-1). Stemmer Hse.

Williamson, Porter B. Patton's Principles: A Handbook for Managers Who Mean It! (Illus.). 1982. pap. 4.95 (ISBN 0-671-45973-2, Touchstone Bks). S&S.

Williamson, R. Fluoresent Brightening Agents. (Textile Science & Technology Ser.: Vol. 4). 1980. 40.50 (ISBN 0-444-41914-4). Elsevier.

Williamson, R., ed. Genetic Engineering, Vol. 3. (Serial Publication). 192p. 1982. 22.00 (ISBN 0-12-270303-0). Acad Pr.

Williamson, R., jt. ed. see Malt, R. A.

Williamson, R. W., jt. auth. see Lynch, R. M.

Williamson, Ray A., ed. Archaeoastronomy in the Americas. LC 81-19147. (Anthropological Papers: No. 22). (Illus.). 405p. (Orig.). 1981. pap. 19.95 (ISBN 0-87919-094-9). Ballena Pr.

Williamson, Richard & Trotter, Hale. Multivariable Mathematics: Linear Algebra, Calculus, Differential Equations. 2nd ed. (Illus.). 1979. ref. 31.95 (ISBN 0-13-604850-1). P-H.

Williamson, Richard, et al. Calculus of Vector Functions. 3rd ed. LC 75-167788. (Illus.). 576p. 1972. ref. ed. 31.95 (ISBN 0-13-112367-X). P-H.

Williamson, Robert. Business Organization. 1981. pap. 9.95 (ISBN 0-434-92262-5, Pub. by Heinemann). David & Charles.

Williamson, Robert, jt. auth. see Lynch, Richard.

Williamson, Robert C., et al. Social Psychology. LC 80-52451. 698p. 1981. text ed. 18.95 (ISBN 0-87581-264-3). Peacock Pubs.

Williamson, Stan. No-Bark Dog. (Beginning-to-Read Ser.). (Illus.). (gr. 1-3). 1962. lib. bdg. 4.39 (ISBN 0-695-46340-3, Dist. by Caroline Hse); pap. 1.95 (ISBN 0-695-36340-9). Follett.

Williamson, Tony. Technicians of Death. LC 78-55426. 1978. 8.95 o.p. (ISBN 0-689-10920-2). Atheneum.

Williamson, Wayne B. Growth & Decline in the Episcopal Church. LC 79-12303. (Illus.). 1979. pap. 4.95 o.p. (ISBN 0-87808-328-6). William Carey Lib.

Williamson, William B. Decisions in Philosophy of Religion. (Philosophy Ser.). 1976. text ed. 15.95 (ISBN 0-675-08629-9). Merrill.

--Ian Ramsey, Makers of the Modern Theological Mind. Patterson, Bob E., ed. 1982. 6.95 (ISBN 0-8499-2947-4). Word Pub.

Williamson, Yvonne M. Research Methodology & Its Application to Nursing. LC 80-22919. 325p. 1981. 18.00 (ISBN 0-471-03313-8, Pub. by Wiley Med). Wiley.

Williams-Wood, Cyril. English Transfer-Printed Pottery & Porcelain: A History of Over-Glaze Printing. (Illus.). 256p. 1981. 65.00 (ISBN 0-571-11694-9). Faber & Faber.

Willians, Judy, jt. auth. see Lent, James.

Willie, Charles V. Family Life of Black People. LC 79-127082. 1970. pap. text ed. 6.95x (ISBN 0-675-09297-3). Merrill.

--The Ivory & Ebony Towers: Race Relations & Higher Education. LC 80-8946. 192p. 1981. 20.95x (ISBN 0-669-04479-2). Lexington Bks.

--The Sociology of Urban Education: Desegregation & Integration. LC 78-4403. (Illus.). 208p. 1978. 21.95x (ISBN 0-669-02348-5). Lexington Bks.

Willie, Charles V. & Edmonds, Ronald R., eds. Black Colleges in America. LC 78-17147. 1978. pap. text ed. 9.95x (ISBN 0-8077-2528-5). Tchrs Coll.

Willig, P. L., jt. auth. see Russell, C. V.

Willig, Rosette F., tr. from Japanese. & intro. by. The Changelings: A Classical Japanese Court Tale. LC 81-50789. 264p. 1983. 19.50x (ISBN 0-8047-1124-0). Stanford U Pr.

Willig, S. Nurse's Guide to the Law. 1970. 13.95 o.p. (ISBN 0-07-070580-1, HP). McGraw.

Willig, Sharon, jt. auth. see Striffler, Nancy.

Willigan, Dennis J. & Lynch, K. Sources & Methods of Historical Demography. (Studies in Social Discontinuity Ser.). 1982. 39.50 (ISBN 0-12-757022-5); pap. 18.00. Acad Pr.

Williman, Daniel. The Black Death: The Impact of the Fourteenth-Century Plague. 160p. 1983. 13.50 (ISBN 0-86698-050-4). Medieval & Renaissance NY.

Williman, Joseph P., ed. see Andereggen, Anton.

Willimon, William H. The Service of God. 240p. 1983. 10.95 (ISBN 0-687-38094-4). Abingdon.

Willimon, William H. & Cabell, Harriet W. Family, Friends & Other Funny People: Memories of Growing up Southern. LC 80-80511. (Illus.). 94p. (Orig.). 1980. pap. 5.95 (ISBN 0-87716-115-1, Pub. by Moore Pub Co). F Apple.

Willing, Jean S., jt. auth. see Siedel, George J.

Willing, Jules Z. The Reality of Retirement: The Inner Experience of Becoming a Retired Person. 1981. pap. 6.95 (ISBN 0-688-00394-X). Quill NY.

Willing, Martha. Beyond Conception: Our Children's Children. LC 76-160416. (Illus.). 241p. 1971. 6.95 (ISBN 0-87645-044-3); pap. 3.95 (ISBN 0-87645-086-9). Gambit.

Willinger, Kurt & Gurney, Gene. The American Jeep. 1983. 17.95 (ISBN 0-517-54734-1); pap. 8.95 (ISBN 0-517-54735-X). Crown.

Willingham. Auditing Concepts & Methods. 1983. write for info. (ISBN 0-07-070610-7). McGraw.

Willingham, John & Carmichael, D. R. Auditing Concepts & Methods. 2nd ed. (Illus.). 512p. 1975. text ed. 17.95 o.p. (ISBN 0-07-070601-8, C); instructors' manual 6.50 o.p. (ISBN 0-07-070605-0). McGraw.

Willingham, John J. & Carmichael, D. R. Auditing Concepts & Methods. 3rd ed. 1979. text ed. 25.95 (ISBN 0-07-070606-9, C); instr's. manual 19.95 (ISBN 0-07-070607-7). McGraw.

Willingham, John J., jt. auth. see Carmichael, D. R.

Willingham, John J., jt. auth. see Elliott, Robert K.

Willingham, Warren W. College Placement & Exemption. LC 74-24718. 1974. 6.95 o.p. (ISBN 0-87447-018-8, 292720); pap. 6.95 (ISBN 0-686-96690-2, 292721). College Bd.

Willingham, Warren W., et al. The Source Book for Higher Education: A Critical Guide to Literature & Information. LC 72-97458. 1973. 5.95 o.p. (ISBN 0-87447-084-6, 209010). College Bd.

Willingham, William F; see Weaver, Glenn.

Willis, A., jt. ed. see De Lorre, C.

Willis, A. J. Story of Africa. LC 72-86247. 1973. 17.75x (ISBN 0-8419-0128-7, Africana). Holmes & Meier.

Willis, A. T., jt. auth. see Willis, R. A.

Willis, A. T., et al. Management of Anaerobic Infections: Prevention & Treatment. LC 80-42345. (Antimicrobial Chemotherapy Research Studies Ser.). 112p. 1981. 27.95x (ISBN 0-471-28037-2, Pub. by Res Stud Pr). Wiley.

Willis, C. A. & Handloser, J. S. Health Physics Operational Monitering, 3 vols. Incl. Vol. 1. 820p. 1972. 126.00 (ISBN 0-677-12320-5); Vol. 2. 504p. 1972. 74.00 (ISBN 0-677-12330-2); Vol. 3. 556p. 1972. 87.00 (ISBN 0-677-12340-X). Set. 262.00 (ISBN 0-677-13670-6). Gordon.

Willis, Charles D. Blueprint Reading for Commercial Construction. LC 77-87887. 1979. pap. 13.80 (ISBN 0-8273-1654-2); instructor's guide 4.25 (ISBN 0-8273-1655-0). Delmar.

Willis, Christopher. Problem-Solving in General Chemistry. LC 76-14004. (Illus.). 1977. pap. text ed. 13.50 (ISBN 0-395-24532-X). HM.

Willis, Cleve E., jt. ed. see Field, Barry C.

Willis, David. Klass: Status & Privilege in the Soviet Union. LC 82-70941. 352p. 1983. 13.95 (ISBN 0-88015-003-3). Empire Bks.

Willis, David L., jt. auth. see Wang, Chih H.

Willis, Dean, jt. ed. see Naib, Zuther M.

Willis, Diane J., jt. auth. see Swanson, B. Marion.

Willis, Donald C. Horror & Science Fiction Films: A Checklist. LC 72-3682. 1972. 23.00 o.p. (ISBN 0-8108-0508-1). Scarecrow.

Willis, E. H., jt. ed. see Millhone, J. P.

Willis, Edwin O. Behavior of Spotted Antbirds. 162p. 1972. 9.00 (ISBN 0-943610-10-9). Am Ornithologists.

Willis, Elbert. Being Fully Persuaded. 1977. 1.25 (ISBN 0-89858-017-X). Fill the Gap.

--Keys to Prosperity. 1978. 1.25 (ISBN 0-89858-016-1). Fill the Gap.

--Producing Faith. 1976. cancelled (ISBN 0-89858-003-X). Fill the Gap.

--Victorious Faith. 1976. cancelled (ISBN 0-89858-004-8). Fill the Gap.

Willis, Eugene, jt. auth. see Hoffman, William H., Jr.

Willis, Eugene, jt. auth. see Hoffman, William H.

Willis, F. Roy. The French Paradox: Understanding Contemporary France. (Publication Ser.: 264). 151p. 1982. pap. 9.95x (ISBN 0-8179-7642-6). Hoover Inst Pr.

--Italy Chooses Europe. 1971 (ISBN 0-19-501383-2). pap. 6.95x o.p. (ISBN 0-19-501384-0). Oxford U Pr.

--Western Civilization: An Urban Perspective, 2 vols. 3rd ed. (Vol. 1, 688 pp.:vol. 2, 560 pp.). 1981. Vol. 1. pap. text ed. 16.95 (ISBN 0-669-03364-2); Vol. 2. pap. text ed. 14.95 (ISBN 0-669-03365-0); instr's guide 1.95 (ISBN 0-669-03366-9). Heath.

--World Civilizations, 2 vols. 1982. Vol. 1. pap. 16.95, 800pp. (ISBN 0-669-04687-6); Vol. 2. pap. 16.95, 720pp. (ISBN 0-669-04688-4); instr's guide 1.95 (ISBN 0-669-04686-8). Heath.

Willis, George, ed. Qualitative Evaluation Concepts & Cases in Curriculum Criticism. LC 77-23647. (Education Ser.). 1978. 26.00 (ISBN 0-8211-2257-6); text ed. 23.50 ten copies (ISBN 0-685-04974-4). McCutchan.

Willis, Henry P. History of the Latin Monetary Union: A Study of International Monetary Action. LC 68-54443. (Illus.). 1968. Repr. of 1901 ed. lib. bdg. 20.00x (ISBN 0-8371-0271-5, WILM). Greenwood.

Willis, Hulon. A Brief Handbook of English. 2nd ed. 292p. 1981. pap. text ed. 8.95 (ISBN 0-15-505556-9, HC); instr's. key avail. (ISBN 0-15-505558-5); exercise bk. avail. (ISBN 0-15-505557-7). HarBraceJ.

Willis, Irene, jt. auth. see Richards, Arlene K.

Willis, Irene C. Brontes. (Great Lives Ser.). (YA) 1968. pap. 3.95 o.p. (ISBN 0-7156-0042-7). Dufour.

--The Brontes. 1982. lib. bdg. 34.50 (ISBN 0-686-81916-0). Porter.

Willis, J. C. A Dictionary of the Flowering Plants & Ferns Vol. 1: Generic & Family Names. 8th ed. LC 72-83581. 1300p. 1973. 99.00 (ISBN 0-521-08699-X). Cambridge U Pr.

Willis, James, tr. see Petit, Paul.

Willis, Jane. Teaching English Through English. (Handbooks for Language Teachers). (Illus.). 192p. 1981. pap. text ed. 9.50 (ISBN 0-582-74608-6). Longman.

Willis, Janice D. The Diamond Light of the Eastern Dawn. 1972. 6.95 o.p. (ISBN 0-671-21166-8, Touchstone Bks); pap. 2.45 o.p. (ISBN 0-671-21526-4). S&S.

Willis, Janice D., compiled by. The Diamond Light: An Introduction to Tibetan Buddhist Meditations. 1973. pap. 2.45 o.p. (ISBN 0-671-21526-4, Touchstone Bks). S&S.

Willis, Jeanne. The Tale of Fearsome Fritz. (Illus.). 24p. (gr. k-3). 1983. 11.95 (ISBN 0-03-063519-5). HR&W.

Willis, Jerry. Computers, Teachers & Learning. Moursund, David, ed. 225p. 1983. pap. 9.95 (ISBN 0-88056-065-7). Dilithium Pr.

Willis, Jerry & Miller, Merl. Computers for Everybody. LC 80-70784. 145p. 1979. pap. 5.95 (ISBN 0-918398-49-5). Dilithium Pr.

--Computers for Everybody. 2nd ed. 186p. 1982. pap. 7.95 (ISBN 0-88056-094-0). Dilithium Pr.

--The Preppy Computer Handbook. 172p. Date not set. pap. cancelled (ISBN 0-88056-093-2). Dilithium Pr.

Willis, Jerry, ed. see Knecht, Ken.

Willis, Jerry, ed. see Maddux, Cleborne D.

Willis, Jerry, jt. auth. see Smithy-Willis, Debra.

Willis, John. Dance World, 1974, Vol. 9. (Illus.). 224p. 1974. 15.00 o.p. (ISBN 0-517-51650-0). Crown.

--Dance World, 1975, Vol. 10. (Illus.). 224p. 1975. 15.00 o.p. (ISBN 0-517-52320-5). Crown.

--Dance World, 1976, Vol. 11. (Illus.). 224p. 1976. 15.95 o.p. (ISBN 0-517-52659-X). Crown.

--Screen World: 1973, Vol. 24. 1973. 8.95 o.p. (ISBN 0-517-50415-4). Crown.

--Screen World: 1975, Vol. 26. (Illus.). 256p. 1975. 9.95 o.p. (ISBN 0-517-52102-4). Crown.

--Screen World: 1977, Vol. 28. 1977. 12.95 o.p. (ISBN 0-517-52970-X). Crown.

--Screen World 1978, Vol. 29. (Illus.). 1978. 12.95 o.p. (ISBN 0-517-53451-7). Crown.

--Screen World: 1979, Vol. 30. (Illus.). 1979. 15.95 o.p. (ISBN 0-517-53835-0). Crown.

--Screen World: 25th Anniversary Edition, Vol. 25. (Illus.). 256p. 1974. 9.95 o.p. (ISBN 0-517-51532-6). Crown.

--Theatre World: 1981-82, Vol. 38. 1983. 25.00 (ISBN 0-517-54945-X). Crown.

Willis, John R. God's Frontiersmen: The Yale Band in Illinois. LC 79-65011. 1979. pap. text ed. 11.00 (ISBN 0-8191-0781-6). U Pr of Amer.

--A History of Christian Thought, Vol. II. 400p. 1983. 18.00 (ISBN 0-682-49973-0). Exposition.

Willis, M. B., jt. auth. see Preston, T. R.

Willis, M. R., jt. auth. see Gill, G. B.

Willis, Malcolm B. Canine Genetics: A Definitive Study. LC 80-10188. (Illus.). 464p. Date not set. price not set cancelled (ISBN 0-668-04935-9, 4935-9). Arco. Postponed.

Willis, Martha R., jt. auth. see Friedman, Myles I.

Willis, Paul E. Profane Culture. 1978. 19.50x (ISBN 0-7100-8789-6). Routledge & Kegan.

Willis, R. A. Spread of Tumors in the Human Body. 3rd ed. 1973. 49.95 o.p. (ISBN 0-407-39901-1). Butterworth.

Willis, R. A. & Willis, A. T. Principles of Pathology & Bacteriology. 3rd ed. (Illus.). 1972. 54.95 o.p. (ISBN 0-407-62751-0). Butterworth.

Willis, R. E. The Black Woman. 1978. 7.95 o.p. (ISBN 0-533-03807-3). Vantage.

Willis, Roy, tr. see Heusch, Luc de.

Willis, Thomas. Two Discourses Concerning the Soul of Brutes, Which Is That of the Sensations of Man. Pordage, S., tr. from Lat. LC 72-161936. (History of Psychology Ser). 1971. 32.00x (ISBN 0-8201-1096-5). Schol Facsimiles.

Willis, Wendell, jt. auth. see Weed, Mike.

Willis, William D. & Grossman, Robert G. Medical Neurobiology: Neuroanatomical & Neurophysiological Principles Basic to Clinical Neuroscience. 2nd ed. LC 76-41192. (Illus.). 1977. 29.50 o.p. (ISBN 0-8016-5583-8). Mosby.

Willis, William D., Jr., jt. ed. see Pinsker, Harold.

Willison, G. O. The Bearded Collie. (Foyle's Handbks). 1971. 3.95 (ISBN 0-685-55805-3). Palmetto Pub.

Willison, George F. Saints & Strangers. 520p. 1983. pap. price not set (ISBN 0-940160-19-6). Parnassus Imprints.

Willison, I. see Watson, George.

Willison, M. Replica Shadowing & Freeze-Etching Techniques. rev. ed. (Practical Methods in Electron Microscopy: Vol. 8). 1980. 24.00 (ISBN 0-444-80165-0). Elsevier.

Williston, Ed M., ed. Small Log Sawmills: Profitable Product Selection, Process Design & Operation. LC 80-84893. (A Forest Industries Bk.). (Illus.). 367p. 1981. 52.50 o.p. (ISBN 0-686-86359-3); pap. 42.50 (ISBN 0-87930-091-4). Miller Freeman.

Williston, Glenn R. Drawing a Conclusion: Middle Level. (Comprehension Skills Ser.). (Illus.). 64p. (gr. 6-8). 1976. pap. text ed. 3.20x (ISBN 0-89061-067-3, CB-4M). Jamestown Pubs.

--Making a Judgment: Middle Level. (Comprehension Skills Ser.). (Illus.). 64p. (gr. 6-8). 1976. pap. text ed. 3.20x (ISBN 0-89061-065-7, CB-2M). Jamestown Pubs.

--Recognizing Tone: Middle Level. (Comprehension Skill Ser.). (Illus.). 64p. (gr. 6-8). 1976. pap. text ed. 3.20x (ISBN 0-89061-069-X, CB-6M). Jamestown Pubs.

--Retaining Concepts & Organizing Facts: Middle Level. (Comprehension Skills Ser.). (Illus.). 64p. (gr. 6-8). 1976. pap. text ed. 3.20x (ISBN 0-89061-071-1, CB-8M). Jamestown Pubs.

--Understanding Characters: Middle Level. (Comprehension Skills Ser.). (Illus.). 64p. (gr. 6-8). 1976. pap. text ed. 3.20x (ISBN 0-89061-066-5, CB-3M). Jamestown Pubs.

--Understanding the Main Idea: Middle Level. (Comprehension Skills Ser.). (Illus.). 64p. (gr. 6-8). 1976. pap. text ed. 3.20x (ISBN 0-89061-064-9, CB-1M). Jamestown Pubs.

Williston, Glenn R., jt. auth. see Giroux, James A.

Willius, Fredrick A., jt. ed. see Keys, Thomas E.

Willke, J. C. Handbook on Abortion. rev. ed. 1979. 5.00 (ISBN 0-910728-14-3); pap. 2.25 (ISBN 0-910728-12-7). Hayes

Willke, J. C. & Wilke, Mrs. Marriage. 1979. pap. 2.95 (ISBN 0-910728-13-5). Hayes Bk Co.

Willke, J. C. & Willke, Mrs. How to Teach the Pro-Life Story. 1973. pap. 3.50 o.p. (ISBN 0-910728-06-2). Hayes

--Sex & Love. 1979. pap. 2.95 (ISBN 0-910728-10-0). Hayes

--Sex Education in the Classroom. 1977. 4.95 (ISBN 0-910728-11-9). Hayes

--Wonder of Sex, How to Teach Children. 1964. pap. 1.50 (ISBN 0-910728-00-3). Hayes

Willke, Mrs., jt. auth. see Willke, J. C.

Willman, Paul. Fairness, Collective Bargaining, & Income Policy. (Illus.). 208p. 1982. 34.95x (ISBN 0-19-827252-9). Oxford U Pr.

Willmer, John E. The National Political Boundary. (CISE Learning Package Ser.: No.15). 56p. (Orig.). 1975. pap. text ed. 3.00x (ISBN 0-936876-28-X). Learn Res Intl Stud.

Willmington, H. L. The King Is Coming. 2nd ed. 1981. pap. 5.95 (ISBN 0-8423-2086-5). Tyndale.

Willmore, A. P. & Willmore, S. R., eds. Aerospace Research Index: A Guide to World Research in Aeronautics, Meteorology, Astronomy, & Space Science. 597p. 1981. 155.00x (ISBN 0-686-75634-7, Pub. by Longman). Gale.

Willmore, S. R., jt. ed. see Willmore, A. P.

Willmore, T. J. Total Curvature in Riemannian Geometry. (Mathematics & Its Applications Ser.). 168p. 1982. 39.95x (ISBN 0-470-27354-2). Halsted Pr.

Willmott, A. John, jt. auth. see Schmidt, Frank W.

Willmott, G. Data Processing in Computer Studies. 144p. 1982. pap. text ed. write for info (ISBN 0-7131-0746-4). E Arnold.

Willmott, H. P. Empires in Balance: Japanese & Allied Pacific Strategies to April 1942. LC 82-6475. (Illus.). 520p. 1982. 24.95 (ISBN 0-87021-535-3). Naval Inst Pr.

--Sea Warfare: Weapons, Tactics & Strategy. (Illus.). 165p. 1981. 22.50 (ISBN 0-917319-02-8). Sheridan.

Willmott, J. C. Atomic Physics. 357p. 1975. pap. 24.95x (ISBN 0-471-94931-0, Pub. by Wiley-Interscience). Wiley.

Willner, Ann R. Public Protest in Indonesia. LC 75-631234. 1968. pap. 1.75x o.s.i. (ISBN 0-89680-001-6, Ohio U Ctr Intl). Ohio U Pr.

Willock, Colin. Africa's Rift Valley. (The World's Wild Places Ser.). (Illus.). 1974. lib. bdg. 15.96 (ISBN 0-8094-2011-2). Silver.

Willock, Colin, ed. ABC of Fishing. (Illus.). 1971. deluxe ed. 15.00 o.p. (ISBN 0-233-95921-1). Transatlantic.

Willott, James F. The Auditory Psychobiology of the Mouse. (Illus.). 504p. 1983. 56.50x (ISBN 0-398-04712-X). C C Thomas.

Willoughby, A. F, jt. ed. see Landsberg, P. T.

Willoughby, Bebe, jt. auth. see Litowinsky, Olga.

Willoughby, D. A. & Giroud, J. P., eds. Inflamation: Mechanisms & Treatment. 1018p. 1981. text ed. 69.95 (ISBN 0-8391-1649-7). Univ Park.

Willoughby, Elaine. No, No, No, & Yes. LC 72-5282. (Venture Ser). (Illus.). 40p. (gr. 1). 1973. PLB 6.69 (ISBN 0-8116-6721-9). Garrard.

Willoughby, Geoff. Ferrari 308 & Mondial. (AutoHistory Ser.). (Illus.). 136p. 1982. 14.95 (ISBN 0-85045-454-9, Pub. by Osprey England). Motorbooks Intl.

Willoughby, L. A., ed. see Schiller, J. Friedrich.

Willoughby, Larry. Austin: A Pictorial History. Friedman, Donna R., ed. LC 80-22807. (Illus.). 208p. 1981. pap. 16.95 (ISBN 0-89865-078-X). Donning Co.

Willoughby, Lee D. The Baja People. (Making of America Ser.: No. 32). 320p. 1983. pap. 3.25 (ISBN 0-440-00374-1, Bryans). Dell.

--The Barbary Coasters. (The Making of America Ser.: No. 36). (Orig.). 1983. pap. 3.25 (ISBN 0-440-00457-8). Dell.

--The Canadians. (Making of America Ser.: No. 38). (Orig.). 1983. pap. 3.25 (ISBN 0-440-00978-2, Emerald). Dell.

--The Carribbeans. (The Making of America Ser.: No. 40). (Orig.). 1983. pap. 3.25 (ISBN 0-440-01081-0). Dell.

--The Prophet's People. (The Making of America Ser.: No. 39). (Orig.). 1983. pap. 3.25 (ISBN 0-440-06858-4). Dell.

--The Smugglers. (The Making of America Ser.: No. 34). 320p. 1983. pap. 3.25 (ISBN 0-440-08014-2, Bryans). Dell.

--The Voyageurs. (Making of America Ser.: No. 35). (Orig.). 1983. pap. 3.25 (ISBN 0-440-09245-0). Dell.

--The Whalers. (The Making of America Ser.: No. 37). (Orig.). 1983. pap. 3.25 (ISBN 0-440-09769-X). Dell.

--The Yukon Breed. (The Making of America Ser.: No. 33). (Orig.). 1983. pap. 3.25 (ISBN 0-440-09899-8, Bryans). Dell.

Willoughby, M. L. N. Hematology & Oncology: BIMR Pediatrics Ser. (Vol. I). 320p. 1982. text ed. 39.95 (ISBN 0-407-02308-9). Butterworth.

Willoughby, R. A., jt. auth. see Cullum, J. K.

Willoughby, Robert H., jt. auth. see Sheppard, William C.

Willoughby, Robert J., jt. auth. see Loken, Newton C.

Willoughby, Stephen S., ed. Guidelines for the Preparation of Teachers of Mathematics. 2nd ed. LC 73-10607. 1979. pap. text ed. 4.00 (ISBN 0-87353-177-9). NCTM.

Willoughby, William E. & Jacobs, Nancy F. The ABC's of the IBM. 100p. 1983. pap. 5.95 (ISBN 0-89588-102-0). Sybex.

Willoughby, William F. Government Organization in War Time & After. LC 74-75246. (The United States in World War 1 Ser). xix, 370p. 1974. Repr. of 1919 ed. lib. bdg. 19.95x (ISBN 0-89198-111-X). Ozer.

Willox, Lorena I. Shadows in the Sunshine. 1982. 14.95 (ISBN 0-916620-61-1). Portals Pr.

Willrich, Mason. Non-Proliferation Treaty: Framework for Nuclear Arms Control. 1969. 17.50 (ISBN 0-87215-060-7). Michie-Bobbs.

Willrich, Mason & Taylor, Theodore B. Nuclear Theft: Risks & Safeguards. LC 73-19861. (Ford Foundation Energy Policy Ser). (Illus.). 1974. pap. 14.95 (ISBN 0-88410-207-6). Ballinger Pub.

Willrich, Mason, et al. Administration of Energy Shortages: Natural Gas and Petroleum. LC 75-46542. 312p. 1976. text ed. 22.50x prof ref (ISBN 0-88410-606-3). Ballinger Pub.

Wills, Ann M. Tempest & Tenderness. (Superromance Ser.). 295p. 1983. pap. 2.95 (ISBN 0-373-70062-8). Harlequin Bks.

Wills, Christopher. Genetic Variability. (Illus.). 1981. text ed. 49.50x (ISBN 0-19-857570-X). Oxford U Pr.

Wills, David W. & Newman, Richard, eds. Black Apostles at Home & Abroad: Afro-Americans & the Christian Mission from the Revolution to Reconstruction. 420p. 1982. lib. bdg. 40.00 (ISBN 0-8161-8482-8, Hall Reference). G K Hall.

Wills, Garry. Explaining America: The Federalist. LC 79-6542. 336p. 1980. 14.95 (ISBN 0-385-14689-2). Doubleday.

--Inventing America: Jefferson's Declaration of Independence. LC 78-11212. 1979. pap. 6.95 (ISBN 0-394-72735-5, Vin). Random.

--The Kennedy Imprisonment. 1983. pap. 3.95 (ISBN 0-686-43232-0). PB.

--Lead Time: A Journalist's Education. LC 82-45372. 408p. 1983. 18.95 (ISBN 0-385-17695-3). Doubleday.

--Nixon Agonistes. LC 72-80426. 1978. 14.95 (ISBN 0-910220-88-3). Berg.

--Nixon Agonistes: The Crisis of the Self Made Man. rev. ed. 1979. pap. 4.95 (ISBN 0-451-62148-4, ME2148, Ment). NAL.

Wills, Geoffrey. English Glass Bottles for the Collector. 82p. 1981. 25.00x (ISBN 0-686-97677-0, Pub. by Bartholomew & Son England). State Mutual Bk.

--A Friend for Frances. (Illus.). 40p. (ps-3). 1983. 4.99 (ISBN 0-910313-04-0). Parker Bro.

--Victorian Glass. (Illus.). 1977. 24.00 o.s.i. (ISBN 0-7135-1949-5). Transatlantic.

Wills, I. H., jt. auth. see Banas, Norma.

Wills, Irene, jt. auth. see Richards, Arlene.

Wills, John. Theatre World, 1975-1976, Vol. 32. (Illus.). 1976. 14.95 o.p. (ISBN 0-517-52665-4). Crown.

Wills, Lois B. Wait for Me. LC 76-4264. 1976. 6.95 o.p. (ISBN 0-8158-0336-2). Chris Mass.

Wills, Maury & Freeman, Don. How to Steal a Pennant. LC 75-34442. (Illus.). 1976. 8.95 o.p. (ISBN 0-399-11699-0). Putnam Pub Group.

Wills, Michael R. The Metabolic Consequences of Chronic Renal Failure. 2nd ed. LC 77-19215. 224p. 1978. text ed. 34.50 (ISBN 0-8391-1232-7). Univ Park.

Wills, Russell, jt. auth. see Hendricks, C. G.

Wills, Sheryle L. & Tremblay, Sharyn F. Critical Care Review for Nurses. LC 82-42829. 475p. (Orig.). 1983. pap. write for info. (ISBN 0-940122-06-5). Multi Media CO.

Wills, Sheryle L. & Tremblay, Sharyn F., eds. Critical Care Review for Nurses. (Illus.). 495p. 1983. pap. write for info. (ISBN 0-940122-06-5). Mosby.

Wills, Thomas. Basic Processes in Helping Relationship. 1982. 39.50 (ISBN 0-12-757680-0). Acad Pr.

Wills, Walter J. Introduction to Agricultural Sales. 1982. text ed. 17.95 (ISBN 0-8359-3139-0); instrs'. manual avail. (ISBN 0-8359-3140-4). Reston.

--Introduction to Grain Marketing. LC 74-155289. 155p. 1972. 12.35 (ISBN 0-8134-1299-4, 1299); text ed. 9.25x. Interstate.

Willsky, Alan S. Digital Signal Processing & Control & Estimation Theory: Points of Tangency, Areas of Intersection, & Parallel Directions. 1979. 27.50x (ISBN 0-262-23091-7). MIT Pr.

Willson, A. Leslie, tr. see Grass, Gunter.

Willson, Alan N., Jr., ed. Nonlinear Networks: Theory & Analysis. LC 74-19558. 1975. 15.95 (ISBN 0-87942-046-4). Inst Electrical.

Willson, Denis. A European Experiment: The Launching of the Jet Project. 178p. 1981. 23.00 (ISBN 0-9960021-8-9, Pub. by A Hilger England); pap. 15.50 (ISBN 0-9960022-1-9). Heyden.

Willson, J. Robert & Carrington, Elsie R. Obstetrics & Gynecology. 7th ed. (Illus.). 800p. 1983. text ed. 39.95 (ISBN 0-8016-5597-8). Mosby.

Willson, James D. & Campbell, John B. Controllership: The Work of the Managerial Accountant. 3rd ed. LC 80-39552. 889p. 1981. 65.00 (ISBN 0-471-05711-8). Ronald Pr.

Willson, Jeanne, jt. ed. see Leslie, A.

Willson, John. Mosaic & Tessellated Patterns: How to Create Them, with 32 Plates to Color. (Illus.). 64p. (Orig.). 1983. pap. 2.95 (ISBN 0-486-24379-6). Dover.

Willson, Mary F. Plant Reproductive Ecology. 300p. 1983. 40.00 (ISBN 0-471-08362-3, Pub. by Wiley-Interscience). Wiley.

Willson, Meredith. And There I Stood with My Piccolo. LC 75-26870. 255p. 1976. Repr. of 1949 ed. lib. bdg. 16.25x (ISBN 0-8371-8486-X, WIMP). Greenwood.

Willson, Nicholas, ed. Infections of the Nervous System. LC 77-720159. (Neuropathology: An Illustrated Course). 18p. 1979. 100.00x (ISBN 0-8036-2913-3); slide & cassette incl. Davis Co.

Willson, Peggy & Cichetti, Barbara. Hikes in the Baltimore Area. (Illus.). 60p. 1981. pap. 2.95 (ISBN 0-9609610-0-3). Rainbow Ent.

Willson, Robert F., Jr. Writing: Analysis & Application. 1980. pap. text ed. 13.95 (ISBN 0-02-428120-4). Macmillan.

Willson, Robert F., Jr., jt. ed. see Reaske, Christopher R.

Willson, Victor L., ed. see Glass, Gene V., et al.

Willums, Jan-Olaf, ed. New Concepts in Air Pollution Research. LC 73-19210. 184p. 1974. pap. 24.95x o.s.i. (ISBN 0-470-94956-2). Halsted Pr.

Willumsen, Dorrit. If It Really Were a Film. Rasmussen, Anne M., tr. Orig. Title: Hvis Det Virkelig Var en Film. 126p. (Orig.). 1982. pap. 6.00 (ISBN 0-915306-35-2). Curbstone.

Wilm, Emil C. Immanuel Kant: Seventeen Twenty-Four to Nineteen Twenty-Four. 1925. text ed. 18.50x (ISBN 0-686-83577-8). Elliots Bks.

--Theories of Instinct. 1925. text ed. 39.50x (ISBN 0-686-83818-1). Elliots Bks.

Wilmanns, W. & Hartenstein, R., eds. Aktuelle Probleme der Haematologie und Onkologie. (Beitraege Zur Onkologie; Contributions to Oncology: Vol. 13). (Illus.). xii, 388p. 1982. pap. 57.00 (ISBN 3-8055-3506-6). S Karger.

Wilmer, Clive. Devotions. 63p. 1982. pap. text ed. 7.00x (ISBN 0-85635-359-0, 60773, Pub. by Carcanet New Pr England). Humanities.

--The Dwelling Place. 59p. 1977. text ed. 8.50x (ISBN 0-85635-232-2, Pub. by Carcanet New Pr England). Humanities.

Wilmer, Clive, tr. see Radnoti, Miklos.

Wilmer, Lambert A; see Poe, Edgar Allan.

Wilmerding, John. American Art. (Pelican History of Art Ser.). (Illus.). 522p. 1982. pap. 16.95x (ISBN 0-14-056199-4, Pelican). Penguin.

--An American Perspective: JoAnn & Julian Ganz. 1981. pap. 9.95 (ISBN 0-89468-002-1). Natl Gallery Art.

--Important Information Inside: The Art of John F. Peto & the Idea of Still Life Painting in Nineteenth Century America. write for info. Natl Gallery Art.

--Important Information Inside: The Art of John F. Peto & the Idea of Still-Life Painting in 19th Century America. LC 82-48489. (Icon Editions). (Illus.). 1983. 33.65i (ISBN 0-06-438941-3, HarpT). Har-Row.

--Still Life Paintings of John F. Peto. (Illus.). 1982. pap. write for info. (ISBN 0-89468-059-5). Natl Gallery Art.

Wilmerding, John, et al. An American Perspective: Nineteenth Century Art from the Collection of Jo Ann & Julian Ganz, Jr. LC 81-11092. (Illus.). 180p. 1981. 35.00x (ISBN 0-87451-221-2); pap. 9.95. U Pr of New Eng.

Wilmeth, Don B., ed. American & English Popular Entertainment: A Guide to Information Sources. LC 79-22869. (Performing Arts Information Guide Ser.: Vol. 7). 1980. 42.00x (ISBN 0-8103-1454-1). Gale.

--American Stage to World War I: A Guide to Information Sources. LC 78-53488. (Performing Arts Information Guide Ser.: Vol. 4). 1978. 42.00x (ISBN 0-8103-1392-8). Gale.

Wilmington, Martin W. Middle East Supply Centre. Evans, Laurence, ed. LC 70-136278. 1971. 34.50x (ISBN 0-87395-081-X). State U NY Pr.

Wilmington, Michael, jt. auth. see McBride, Joseph.

Wilmink, J. & Sami, M., eds. Microprocessing & Microprogramming: Second Symposium, Venice, 1976. 1977. 64.00 (ISBN 0-7204-0557-2, North-Holland). Elsevier.

Wilmink, J., jt. ed. see Nicoud, J. D.

Wilmore, Gayraud S. Black & Presbyterian: The Heritage & the Hope. LC 82-23907. 132p. (Orig.). 1983. pap. price not set (ISBN 0-664-24440-8, Geneva Press Pub). Westminster.

Wilmore, Jack H., jt. auth. see Behnke, Albert R., Jr.

Wilmore, Jack H., ed. Exercise & Sport Sciences Review, 3 vols. 1973. Vol. 1. 1973. 48.00 (ISBN 0-12-227401-6); Vol. 2. 1974. 49.50 (ISBN 0-12-227402-4); Vol. 3. 1975. 66.50 (ISBN 0-12-227403-2). Acad Pr.

Wilmore, Sylvia B. Crows, Jays, Ravens (& Their Relatives) (Illus.). 1979. pap. 9.95 (ISBN 0-87666-878-3, PS-779). TFH Pubns.

Wilmot, John. The Debt to Pleasure. Adlard, John, ed. (Fyfield Ser.). 141p. 1979. pap. 3.95 o.p. (ISBN 0-85635-092-3, Pub. by Carcanet New Pr England). Humanities.

Wilmot, Philip D. & Slingerland, Aart. Technology Assessment & the Oceans. LC 77-73026. 1977. lib. bdg. 46.50 o.p. (ISBN 0-89158-725-X). Westview.

Wilmot, William W. Dyadic Communication. 2nd ed. (Human Communication Ser.). (Illus.). 1979. pap. text ed. 9.95 (ISBN 0-201-08489-9). A-W.

Wilmot, William W. & Wenburg, John R. Communication Involvement: Personal Perspectives. LC 80-16247. 452p. 1981. Repr. of 1974 ed. lib. bdg. cancelled o.p. (ISBN 0-89874-185-8). Krieger.

Wilmot-Buxton, E. M. Alcuin. 223p. 1982. Repr. of 1922 ed. lib. bdg. 40.00 (ISBN 0-89760-941-7). Telegraph Bks.

Wilmott, A. J., tr. see Hausen, Helmuth.

Wilner, Daniel. Radiologic Diagnosis of Tumors of Bones & Allied Disorders, 4 vols. (Illus.). 4248p. 1982. Set. text ed. 395.00 o.p. (ISBN 0-7216-9459-4); Vol. 1, 1180p. 115.00 o.p. (ISBN 0-7216-9476-4); Vol. 2, 711p. 95.00 o.p. (ISBN 0-7216-9477-2); Vol. 3, 1115p. 115.00 o.p. (ISBN 0-7216-9478-0); Vol. 4, 1175p. 115.00x o.p. (ISBN 0-7216-9479-9). Saunders.

--Radiology of Bone Tumors & Allied Disorders. (Illus.). 4248p. 1982. 450.00 set (ISBN 0-7216-9459-4); Vol. 1 125.00 (ISBN 0-7216-9476-4); Vol. 2 115.00 (ISBN 0-7216-9477-2); Vol. 3 125.00 (ISBN 0-7216-9478-0); Vol. 4 125.00 (ISBN 0-7216-9479-9). Saunders.

Wilner, Daniel M., et al. Introduction to Public Health. 7th ed. (Illus.). 470p. 1978. 28.95 (ISBN 0-02-428190-5, 42819). Macmillan.

Wilpert, Bernhard, ed. see Heller, Frank A.

Wilshaw, T. R., jt. auth. see Lawn, B. R.

Wilshire, H. G., jt. ed. see Webb, R. H.

Wilsing, N., jt. auth. see Kupka, I.

Wilson. Educational Administration. 1966. text ed. 19.95x (ISBN 0-675-09849-1). Merrill.

--Fur Trade in Canada. (Focus on Canadian History). (YA) (gr. 6-10). 1981. PLB 8.40 o.p. (ISBN 0-531-02180-7). Watts.

Wilson & Werner. Simplified Stair Layout. 2nd ed. LC 70-188808. 64p. 1973. pap. 7.00 (ISBN 0-8273-0103-0). Delmar.

Wilson, jt. auth. see Clarke.

Wilson, jt. auth. see Memory.

Wilson, jt. auth. see Minard.

Wilson, et al. Human Sexuality: A Text with Readings. 2nd ed. 1980. pap. text ed. 16.95 (ISBN 0-8299-0328-3); study guide 7.50 (ISBN 0-8299-0322-4); instrs.' manual avail. (ISBN 0-8299-0584-7). West Pub.

Wilson, A. Marketing of Professional Services. 1972. 29.95 (ISBN 0-07-094239-0, P&RB). McGraw.

Wilson, A., jt. auth. see Wilson, S.

Wilson, A. D. & Crisp, S. Organolithic Macromolecular Materials. (Illus.). 1977. 39.00 (ISBN 0-85334-699-2, Pub. by Applied Sci England). Elsevier.

Wilson, A. D. & Prosser, H. J. Developments in Ionic Polymers, Vol. 1. (Illus.). 335p. 1983. 69.75 (ISBN 0-85334-159-1, Pub. by Applied Sci England). Elsevier.

Wilson, A. G. Entropy in Urban & Regional Modeling. (Monographs in Spatial & Environmental Systems Analysis). 166p. 1971. 15.50x (ISBN 0-85086-021-0, Pub. by Pion England); pap. 11.00x (ISBN 0-85086-022-9). Methuen Inc.

--Geography & the Environment: Systems Analytical Methods. LC 80-41696. 304p. 1981. 38.95x (ISBN 0-471-27956-0, Pub. by Wiley-Interscience); pap. 18.95x (ISBN 0-471-27957-9, Pub. by Wiley-Interscience). Wiley.

--Patterns & Processes in Urban & Regional Systems. (London Papers in Regional Science). 324p. 1973. pap. 14.00x (ISBN 0-85086-035-0, Pub. by Pion England). Methuen Inc.

Wilson, A. G., et al. Optimisation in Locational & Transport Analysis. 1981. 46.95x (ISBN 0-471-28005-4, Pub. by Wiley-Interscience). Wiley.

Wilson, A. G., et al, eds. Models of Cities & Regions. LC 77-5338. 64.95x (ISBN 0-471-99540-1, Pub. by Wiley-Interscience). Wiley.

Wilson, A. J. Electoral Politics in an Emergent State. LC 74-79136. (Perspectives on Development Ser.: No. 3). (Illus.). 269p. 1975. 32.50 (ISBN 0-521-20429-1). Cambridge U Pr.

Wilson, A. Jeyaratnam. Politics in Sri Lanka: Nineteen Forty-Five to Nineteen Seventy-Three. LC 73-90319. 350p. 1974. 26.00 (ISBN 0-312-62860-9). St Martin.

Wilson, A. N. The Life of John Milton. 320p. 1983. 19.95 (ISBN 0-19-211776-9). Oxford U Pr.

--Who Was Oswald Fish? 256p. 1983. 16.95 (ISBN 0-436-57606-6, Pub. by Secker & Warburg). David & Charles.

Wilson, Adrian. The Design of Books. LC 67-14162. (Illus.). 160p. 1974. pap. 10.95 (ISBN 0-87905-019-5). Peregrine Smith.

Wilson, Alan. Clergy Reserves of Upper Canada: A Canadian Mortmain. LC 72-353178. (Illus.). 1968. 17.50x o.p. (ISBN 0-8020-3216-8). U of Toronto Pr.

Wilson, Allan N. Casino Gambler's Guide. rev & enl. ed. LC 71-127841. (Illus.). 1970. 14.37i (ISBN 0-06-014674-5, HarpT). Har-Row.

Wilson, Amrit. Finding A Voice: Asian Women in Britain. 180p. 1983. pap. 6.95 (ISBN 0-86068-012-6, Virago Pr). Merrimack Bk Serv.

Wilson, Amy A., ed. see Greenblat, Sidney L.

Wilson, Angus. The Wild Garden or Speaking of Writing. 1963. 17.95x (ISBN 0-520-01346-8); pap. 1.25 (ISBN 0-520-01347-6, CAL112). U of Cal Pr.

Wilson, Angus, ed. East Anglia in Verse. 112p. 1983. 13.95 (ISBN 0-436-57607-4, Pub. by Secker & Warburg). David & Charles.

--The Portable Charles Dickens. 1983. pap. 18.75 (ISBN 0-670-27231-0). Viking Pr.

Wilson, Angus, ed. see Dickens, Charles.

Wilson, Arthur M. Diderot. 1972. 39.95x (ISBN 0-19-501506-1). Oxford U Pr.

--French Foreign Policy During the Administration of Cardinal Fleury: 1726-1743; a Study in Diplomacy & Commercial Development. LC 70-138193. 433p. 1972. Repr. of 1936 ed. lib. bdg. 20.25x (ISBN 0-8371-5333-6, WIFP). Greenwood.

Wilson, Arthur N. Diamonds: From Birth to Eternity. Ross, Michael & Eash, Dianne, eds. 1982. 43.95 (ISBN 0-87311-010-2). Gemological.

Wilson, B. M.G.S. 1793-1814: Canadian Recipients. 1976. lib. bdg. 24.00 o.p. (ISBN 0-685-51516-8, Pub. by Spink & Son England). S J Durst.

Wilson, Barbara. The Geography Lesson. (Illus.). 34p. 1977. 3.00 (ISBN 0-686-38179-3). Seal Pr WA.

--Thin Ice & Other Stories. LC 81-4713. 128p. (Orig.). 1981. pap. 4.95 (ISBN 0-931188-09-1). Seal Pr WA.

--Walking on the Moon. 150p. 1983. price not set (ISBN 0-931188-18-0). Seal Pr WA.

Wilson, Barbara & Da Silva, eds. Backbone Four: Humor by Northwest Women. 120p. (Orig.). 1982. 4.95 (ISBN 0-931188-14-8). Seal Pr WA.

--Backbone Three: Essays, Interviews & Photographs by Northwest Women. 90p. (Orig.). 1981. 4.95 (ISBN 0-686-38168-8). Seal Pr WA.

--Backbone Two: New Fiction by Northwest Women. 160p. (Orig.). 1980. 4.95 (ISBN 0-686-38164-5). Seal Pr WA.

Wilson, Barrie A. The Anatomy of Argument. LC 80-5606. 452p. 1980. pap. text ed. 13.50 (ISBN 0-8191-1211-9). U Pr of Amer.

Wilson, Bernard E. The Newberry Library Catalog of Early American Printed Sheet Music. 1983. lib. bdg. 330.00 (ISBN 0-8161-0389-5, Hall Library). G K Hall.

Wilson, Beth P. The Great Minu. (Picture Bk.). (Illus.). 32p. (gr. k-3). 1974. 4.95 (ISBN 0-695-80409-X); PLB 4.98 (ISBN 0-695-40409-1). Follett.

--Martin Luther King, Jr. (See & Read Biographies). (Illus.). (gr. k-3). 1971. PLB 5.99 o.p. (ISBN 0-399-60452-9). Putnam Pub Group.

--Muhammad Ali. (See & Read Biographies). (Illus.). 64p. (gr. 2-4). 1974. PLB 4.49 o.p. (ISBN 0-399-60888-5). Putnam Pub Group.

--Stevie Wonder. LC 78-6054. (See & Read Biography Ser.). (Illus.). (gr. 1-4). 1979. PLB 5.99 (ISBN 0-399-61106-1). Putnam Pub Group.

Wilson, Betty L., jt. ed. see Wilson, William K.

Wilson, Bob. The Art of Goalkeeping. (Illus.). 176p. 1983. 9.95 (ISBN 0-7207-1278-5, Pub by Michael Joseph). Merrimack Bk Serv.

--The Good that Lives After Them. Kings, John, ed. (Illus.). 170p. 1982. 14.50 (ISBN 0-9608192-0-7). B Wilson.

--Soccer. (Pelham Pictorial Sports Instructors Ser.). 1977. 8.95 o.p. (ISBN 0-7207-0793-5). Transatlantic.

Wilson, Bradford & Edington, George. First Child, Second Child: Your Birth Order Profile. 1983. pap. 3.50 (ISBN 0-8217-1144-X). Zebra.

Wilson, Bryan. The Noble Savages: An Essay on Charisma-the Rehabilitation of a Concept. LC 74-81444. (Quantum Bk Ser.). 1975. 17.95x (ISBN 0-520-02815-5). U of Cal Pr.

--Religion in Sociological Perspective. 1982. 13.95x (ISBN 0-19-826663-4); pap. 5.95x (ISBN 0-19-826664-2). Oxford U Pr.

Wilson, C. Applied Statistics for Engineers. 1972. 24.75 (ISBN 0-85334-529-5, Pub. by Applied Sci England). Elsevier.

--Comprehensive Analytical Chemistry, Vol. 3: Elemental Analysis. Svehla, G., ed. LC 58-10158. 399p. 1975. 93.75 (ISBN 0-444-41162-3). Elsevier.

--Comprehensive Analytical Chemistry, Vol. 4: Instrumentation for Spectroscopy. Svehla, G., ed. LC 58-10158. 374p. 1975. 93.75 (ISBN 0-444-41163-1). Elsevier.

--Comprehensive Analytical Chemistry, Vol. 5: Emission Spectroscopy, Vol. 5. Svehla, G., ed. LC 58-10158. 383p. 1975. 93.75 (ISBN 0-444-41164-X). Elsevier.

Wilson, C., jt. auth. see Alexis, Marcus.

Wilson, C., jt. auth. see Svehla, G.

Wilson, C., jt. ed. see Svehla, G.

Wilson, C., et al see Svehla, G.

Wilson, C. B., jt. ed. see Coppock, J. T.

Wilson, C. B., jt. ed. see Rosenblum, M. L.

Wilson, C. L. & Wilson, D. W., eds. Comprehensive Analytical Chemistry, Vols. 1 & 2. Incl. Vol 1: Classical Analysis, 3 Pts. 1959-62. Pt. A. 93.750 (ISBN 0-444-40647-6); Pt. B. 106.50 (ISBN 0-444-40648-4); Pt. C. 106.50 (ISBN 0-444-40649-2); Vol. 2: Electrical Methods & Physical Separation Methods, 4 pts. 1964-71. Pt. A. 68.00 (ISBN 0-444-40650-6); Pt. B. 93.75 (ISBN 0-444-40651-4); Pt. C. 93.75; Pt. D: Coulometric Methods. 1975. 110.75 (ISBN 0-444-41044-9). Elsevier.

Wilson, C. Philip. The Fear of Being Fat: The Treatment of Anorexia Nervosa & Bulimia. LC 82-11338. 544p. 1983. write for info. (ISBN 0-87668-480-0). Aronson.

Wilson, C. Vincent. The Westminster Concise Handbook for the Bible. LC 79-15498. 1979. pap. 4.50 (ISBN 0-664-24272-3). Westminster.

Wilson, C. W., ed. World Nuclear Directory: A Guide to Organizations & Research Activities in Atomic Energy. 6th ed. 850p. 1981. 195.00x (ISBN 0-686-76212-6, Pub. by Longman). Gale.

Wilson, Carol D., jt. auth. see Burke, John G.

Wilson, Carolyn F. Violence Against Women: An Annotated Bibliography. 1981. lib. bdg. 20.00 (ISBN 0-8161-8497-6, Hall Reference). G K Hall.

Wilson, Carroll L., ed. Coal-Bridge to the Future. (World Coal Study: Vol. 1). 276p. 1980. prof ref 20.00x (ISBN 0-88410-099-5). Ballinger Pub.

--Future Coal Prospects: Country & Regional Assessments. (World Coal Study: Vol. II). 1980. prof ref 50.00x (ISBN 0-88410-098-7). Ballinger Pub.

Wilson, Carter. Treasures on Earth. 256p. 1983. pap. 3.95 (ISBN 0-380-63305-1, Bard). Avon.

Wilson, Cathy R., jt. auth. see Wilson, Holton J.

Wilson, Charles. Queen Elizabeth & the Revolt of the Netherlands. LC 76-119009. 1970. 28.50x (ISBN 0-520-01744-7). U of Cal Pr.

--The Transformation of Europe, 1558-1648. LC 75-17283. 1976. 42.50x (ISBN 0-520-03075-3). U of Cal Pr.

Wilson, Charles C. & Wilson, Elizabeth A. Health & Fun. (Health for Young America Ser.). (gr. 3). 1968. text ed. 2.88 o.p. (ISBN 0-672-70822-1); tchrs' ed. 2.88 o.p. (ISBN 0-685-07150-2); tchrs' manual 1.20 o.p. (ISBN 0-685-07151-0). Bobbs.

--Health & Growth. (Health for Young America Ser.). (gr. 4). text ed. 3.12 o.p. (ISBN 0-672-70826-4); tchrs' ed. 3.12 o.p. (ISBN 0-685-07152-9); tchrs' manual 1.20 o.p. (ISBN 0-685-07153-7). Bobbs.

--Health & Happiness. (Health for Young America Ser.). (Illus.). (gr. 6). text ed. 3.52 o.p. (ISBN 0-672-70834-5); tchrs' ed. 3.52 o.p. (ISBN 0-685-07154-5); tchrs' manual 1.20 o.p. (ISBN 0-685-07155-3). Bobbs.

--Health & Living. (Health for Young America Ser.). (gr. 5). text ed. 3.16 o.p. (ISBN 0-672-70830-2); tchrs' ed. 3.16 o.p. (ISBN 0-685-07156-1); tchrs' manual 1.20 o.p. (ISBN 0-685-07157-X). Bobbs.

--Health at School. (Health for Young America Ser.). (gr. 1). text ed. 2.60 o.p. (ISBN 0-672-70814-0); tchrs' ed. 2.60 o.p. (ISBN 0-685-07158-8); tchrs' manual 1.20 o.p. (ISBN 0-685-07159-6). Bobbs.

--Health Day by Day. (Health for Young America Ser.). (gr. 2). text ed. 2.76 o.p. (ISBN 0-672-70818-3); tchrs' ed. 2.76 o.p. (ISBN 0-685-07160-X); tchrs' manual 1.20 o.p. (ISBN 0-685-07161-8). Bobbs.

--Men, Science & Health. (Health for Young America Ser). (gr. 7). text ed. 3.80 o.p. (ISBN 0-672-70838-8); tchrs' ed. 3.80 o.p. (ISBN 0-685-07172-3); 1.20 o.p. (ISBN 0-685-07173-1). Bobbs.

Wilson, Charles E., et al. Kinematics & Dynamics of Machinery. 752p. 1983. text ed. 33.50 scp (ISBN 0-06-044437-1, HarpC); solutions manual avail. (ISBN 0-06-364577-7). Har-Row.

Wilson, Charles M. Green Treasures: Adventures in the Discovery of Edible Plants. (Illus.). 176p. (gr. 7 up). 1974. 6.25 (ISBN 0-8255-9104-X). Macrae.

--Let's Try Barter. 1976. pap. 6.95 (ISBN 0-8159-6115-4). Devin.

Wilson, Charles M., ed. New Crops for the New World. LC 73-138140. (Illus.). 1971. Repr. of 1945 ed. lib. bdg. 20.00x (ISBN 0-8371-5713-7, WINC). Greenwood.

Wilson, Christopher & Hall, Deborah. Preventing Burnout in Education: A Self-Help Approach to Managing Stress. (Illus.). 154p. (Orig.). 1981. pap. text ed. 9.95 (ISBN 0-940156-02-4). Wright Group.

Wilson, Clifford, jt. auth. see Gish, Duane T.

Wilson, Clifford, jt. auth. see Weldon, John.

Wilson, Clifford, jt. auth. see William, Lindsey.

Wilson, Clifford A. That Incredible Book the Bible. 1973. pap. 1.75 o.p. (ISBN 0-8024-8680-0). Moody.

Wilson, Colin. Anti-Sartre: With an Essay on Camus. LC 80-24098. (Milford Series: Popular Writers of Today: Vol. 34). 64p. (Orig.). 1981. lib. bdg. 9.95x (ISBN 0-89370-149-1); pap. text ed. 3.95x (ISBN 0-89370-249-8); signed ed. 19.95x (ISBN 0-89370-006-1). Borgo Pr.

--Frankenstein's Castle: The Right Brain-Door to Wisdom. 128p. 1982. 11.95 (ISBN 0-906798-11-6, Pub. by Salem Hse Ltd.); pap. 6.95 (ISBN 0-906798-12-4). Merrimack Bk Serv.

--The Haunted Man: The Strange Genius of David Lindsay. LC 79-194. (The Milford Ser: Popular Writers of Today Vol. 20). 1979. lib. bdg. 9.95x (ISBN 0-89370-128-9); pap. 3.95x (ISBN 0-89370-228-5). Borgo Pr.

--Mysteries. 1980. pap. 8.95 (ISBN 0-399-50461-3). Putnam Pub Group.

--Mysteries. LC 78-20286. 1978. 15.00 o.p. (ISBN 0-399-12246-X). Putnam Pub Group.

--The New Existentialism. 188p. 1983. pap. 8.95 (ISBN 0-7045-0415-4, Pub by Salem Hse Ltd). Merrimack Bk Serv.

--The Outsider. LC 79-84901. 308p. 1982. pap. 7.95 (ISBN 0-87477-206-0). J P Tarcher.

--Poetry & Mysticism. LC 70-88225. pap. 3.00 o.s.i. (ISBN 0-87286-054-X). City Lights.

--Poltergeist: A Study in Destructive Haunting. 384p. 1982. 13.95 (ISBN 0-399-12716-X). Putnam Pub Group.

--The Quest for Wilhelm Reich. LC 78-22774. 1981. 12.95 (ISBN 0-385-01845-2). Doubleday.

--Religion & the Rebel. LC 74-9134. 338p. 1974. Repr. of 1957 ed. lib. bdg. 27.50x (ISBN 0-8371-7596-8, WIRA). Greenwood.

--Starseekers. LC 80-1273. 256p. 1981. 17.95 o.p. (ISBN 0-385-17253-2). Doubleday.

--Stature of Man. Repr. of 1959 ed. lib. bdg. 19.25x (ISBN 0-8371-0273-1, WISM). Greenwood.

--The War Against Sleep: The Philosophy of Gurdjieff. 95p. 1981. pap. 6.95 (ISBN 0-85030-198-X). Newcastle Pub.

Wilson, Colin, ed. Dark Dimensions: A Celebration of the Occult. LC 78-56249. 1978. 7.95 o.p. (ISBN 0-89696-001-3, An Everest House Book). Dodd.

Wilson, Constance P., jt. ed. see Kim, Paul K.

Wilson, Craig M. YHWH...Is Not a Radio Station in Minneapolis: And Other Things Everyone Should Know. LC 82-48405. (Illus.). 96p. (Orig.). 1983. pap. 4.76 (ISBN 0-06-069432-7, HarpR). Har-Row.

Wilson, D., jt. auth. see Swift, William.

Wilson, D. A., jt. auth. see Were, G. S.

Wilson, D. G., et al, eds. Moving Boundary Problems. 1978. 27.00 (ISBN 0-12-757350-X). Acad Pr.

Wilson, D. L., jt. auth. see Lester, J. C.

Wilson, D. W., jt. ed. see Wilson, C. L.

Wilson, Dan. An Opening Way. LC 61-11637. (Orig.). 1961. pap. 1.50 o.p. (ISBN 0-87574-113-4). Pendle Hill.

Wilson, Daniel J., jt. ed. see Paskoff, Paul F.

Wilson, Dave & Wilson, Jeanne. Mr. Terwillger's Secret. LC 80-21835. (Easy-Read Story Bks.). (gr. k-3). 1979. 8.60 (ISBN 0-531-04191-3); pap. 7.90 (ISBN 0-531-02472-5). Watts.

Wilson, David. Air Photo Interpretation For Archaeologists. LC 82-10679. (Illus.). 224p. 1982. 29.95x (ISBN 0-312-01527-5). St Martin.

Wilson, David, ed. Projecting Britain: Ealing Studios Film Posters. (Illus.). 96p. 1982. 19.95 (ISBN 0-85170-122-1). NY Zoetrope.

--Sight & Sound: A Fiftieth Anniversary Selection. (Illus.). 352p. 1982. 19.95 (ISBN 0-571-11943-3). Faber & Faber.

Wilson, David A. Bits & Pieces. 40p. 1969. pap. 1.50 o.p. (ISBN 0-934852-02-2). Lorien Hse.

--The Dance of the Rites. 150p. 1983. pap. 7.00 (ISBN 0-934852-27-8). Lorien Hse.

--The Finer Art of Painting. 40p. (Orig.). 1983. pap. 3.00 (ISBN 0-934852-26-X). Lorien Hse.

--IBM PC DiskGuide. (DiskGuides Ser.). 32p. (Orig.). 1983. pap. text ed. 8.95 (ISBN 0-931988-94-2). Osborne-McGraw.

--Politics in Thailand. LC 82-11829. 307p. 1982. Repr. of 1962 ed. lib. bdg. 35.00x (ISBN 0-313-23552-X, WIPO). Greenwood.

--VisiCalc DiskGuide. (DiskGuides Ser.). 32p. (Orig.). 1983. pap. 6.95 (ISBN 0-931988-98-5). Osborne-McGraw.

Wilson, David B., ed. Did the Devil Make Darwin Do It? Modern Perspectives on the Creation-Evolution Controversy. 280p. 1983. text ed. 24.00 (ISBN 0-8138-0433-7); pap. 10.95 (ISBN 0-8138-0434-5). Iowa St U Pr.

Wilson, David G., jt. auth. see Whitt, Frank R.

Wilson, David H. & Hall, Malcolm H. Casualty Officer's Handbook. 4th ed. (Illus.). 1979. text ed. 29.95 o.p. (ISBN 0-407-00140-9). Butterworth.

Wilson, David H., ed. see Casualty Surgeons Association of Great Britain.

Wilson, David M. The Archaeology of Anglo-Saxon England. (Illus.). 532p. 1981. pap. 21.95 (ISBN 0-521-28390-6). Cambridge U Pr.

--The Vikings & Their Origins. LC 79-56390. (Illus.). 96p. 1980. pap. 7.95 o.s.i. (ISBN 0-89104-184-2, A & W Visual Library). A & W Pubs.

Wilson, David M., ed. The Northern World: The History & Heritage of Northern Europe, A. D. 400-1100. (Illus.). 248p. 1980. 40.00 o.p. (ISBN 0-686-62715-6, 1365-8). Abrams.

Wilson, David T., jt. ed. see Spekman, Robert E.

Wilson, Derek. History of South & Central Africa. 1975. pap. text ed. 9.95x (ISBN 0-521-20559-X). Cambridge U Pr.

--A Short History of Suffolk. 1977. 17.95 o.p. (ISBN 0-7134-0574-0, Pub. by Batsford England). David & Charles.

Wilson, Derek, jt. auth. see Shaman, Margaret.

Wilson, Dick. The People's Emperor: A Biography of Mao-Tse-Tung. LC 77-15176. (Illus.). 552p. 1980. 17.50 o.p. (ISBN 0-385-11645-4). Doubleday.

Wilson, Dick, ed. Mao Tse-Tung in the Scales of History. LC 76-57100. (Contemporary China Institute Publications Ser.). 1977. 42.50 (ISBN 0-521-21583-8); pap. 10.95 (ISBN 0-521-29190-9). Cambridge U Pr.

Wilson, Donald L. Total Mind Power: How to Use the Other 90 Percent of Your Mind. LC 76-25543. (Illus.). 9.95 o.s.i. (ISBN 0-913290-14-9). Camaro Pub.

Wilson, Donald R. Words for School Administrators: Example of Commondations & Constructive Suggestions for Through Teacher Evalvation. LC 80-71091. 170p. 1981. 11.95 (ISBN 0-939136-00-7). Civic Educ Assn.

Wilson, Doris B. & Wilson, Wilfred J. Human Anatomy. 2nd ed. (Illus.). 1983. 29.95x (ISBN 0-19-503108-3). Oxford U Pr.

Wilson, Dorothy. Welfare State in Sweden. Pinker, R. A., ed. LC 80-469661. (Studies in Social Policy & Welfare). 1980. text ed. 20.00x (ISBN 0-435-82960-2). Heinemann Ed.

Wilson, Dorothy C. The Big Little World of Doc Pritham. 1982. pap. 7.95 (ISBN 0-686-37113-5). Juniper Maine.

--Handicap Race: The Inspiring Story of Roger Arnett. 1967. 7.95 o.p. (ISBN 0-07-070749-9, GB). McGraw.

--Ten Fingers for God. 288p. 1982. pap. 5.95 (ISBN 0-8407-5834-0). Nelson.

--Twelve Who Cared. LC 77-81398. 1977. 6.95 o.p. (ISBN 0-915684-22-5). Christian Herald.

Wilson, Dorothy J., jt. auth. see Wilson, Thomas.

Wilson, Doug & Vander Werff, Fred. New Techniques for Catching Bottom Fish. LC 77-17923. (Illus.). 160p. 1977. pap. 5.95 (ISBN 0-916076-16-4). Writing.

Wilson, Duncan. Leonard Woolf: A Political Biography. LC 78-16778. 1978. 25.00x (ISBN 0-312-48001-6). St Martin.

Wilson, Sir Duncan. Tito's Yugoslavia. LC 79-11009. 1980. 32.50 (ISBN 0-521-22655-4). Cambridge U Pr.

Wilson, Dunning S., jt. auth. see Gallager, Nancy E.

Wilson, Dwight. Armageddon Now! The Premillenarian Response to Russia & Israel Since 1917. 1977. pap. 5.95 o.p. (ISBN 0-8010-9512-3). Baker Bk.

Wilson, E., jt. auth. see Akhmanova, O. S.

Wilson, E. A. The Modern Russian Dictionary for English Speakers: English-Russian. LC 81-12141. 1200p. 1982. 39.50 (ISBN 0-08-020554-2). Pergamon.

Wilson, E. B., Jr., jt. auth. see Pauling, Linus.

Wilson, E. N., jt. auth. see Michalos, James.

Wilson, Earl. Earl Wilson's New York. (Illus.). 1964. pap. 4.95 o.p. (ISBN 0-671-20032-1). S&S.

--You Try Being a Teenager: A Challenge to Parents to Understand. LC 82-8314. 250p. 1982. pap. 5.95 (ISBN 0-930014-97-9). Multnomah.

Wilson, Edgar B. Introduction to Scientific Research. 1952. pap. 5.95 (ISBN 0-07-070846-0, SP). McGraw.

Wilson, Edmund. Dead Sea Scrolls 1947-1969. 1969. 18.95x (ISBN 0-19-500665-8). Oxford U Pr.

--The Devils & Canon Barham: Essays on Poets, Novelists & Monsters. LC 72-93789. 232p. 1973. 7.95 (ISBN 0-374-13843-5). FS&G.

--The Fourties. Edel, Leon, ed. & intro. by. (Illus.). 1983. 22.50 o.p. (ISBN 0-374-15762-6). FS&G.

--Patriotic Gore: Studies in the Literature of the American Civil War. 1962. 27.00x (ISBN 0-19-500666-6). Oxford U Pr.

--The Portable Edmund Wilson. Dabney, Lewis M., ed. 1983. pap. 6.95 (ISBN 0-14-015098-6). Penguin.

--To the Finland Station. 608p. (Definitive ed.). 1972. 15.00 o.p. (ISBN 0-374-27833-4); pap. 8.95 (ISBN 0-374-51045-8). FS&G.

--Upstate. (Illus.). 384p. 1971. 10.95 (ISBN 0-374-28189-0); pap. 4.95 o.p. (ISBN 0-374-51165-9). FS&G.

Wilson, Edmund, jt. auth. see Thomas, Norman.

Wilson, Edward. Russia & Black Africa Before World War Two. LC 73-84939. 300p. 1974. text ed. 42.50x (ISBN 0-8419-0109-0). Holmes & Meier.

Wilson, Edward A. Joseph Conrad. 1982. lib. bdg. 34.50 (ISBN 0-686-81917-9). Porter.

Wilson, Edward M. Spanish & English Literature of the Sixteenth & Seventeenth Centuries. Cruickshank, Don, ed. LC 79-53063. (Illus.). 352p. 1980. 37.50 (ISBN 0-521-22844-1). Cambridge U Pr.

Wilson, Edward O., jt. auth. see Lumsden, Charles J.

Wilson, Edwin. The Theater Experience. 2nd ed. (Illus.). 1980. text ed. 26.95 (ISBN 0-07-070667-0); pap. text ed. 17.95 (ISBN 0-07-070668-9); instr's. manual 15.00 (ISBN 0-07-070669-7). McGraw.

--The Theater Experience. (Illus.). 416p. 1975. text ed. 13.95-op o.p. (ISBN 0-07-070661-1, C); pap. text ed. 11.50 o.p. (ISBN 0-07-070662-X). McGraw.

Wilson, Edwin & Goldfarb, Alvin. Living Theater: An Introduction to Theater History. (Illus.). 512p. 1982. text ed. 22.95 (ISBN 0-07-070732-4, C); pap. text ed. 17.95 (ISBN 0-07-070730-8); write for info. instr's manual. McGraw.

Wilson, Edwin, intro. by. Theatre Facts, 1981. (Illus.). 20p. 1982. pap. text ed. 1.95 (ISBN 0-930452-22-4). Theatre Comm.

Wilson, Elizabeth. Mirror Writing: An Autobiography. 162p. 1983. pap. 6.95 (ISBN 0-86068-241-2, Virago Pr). Merrimack Bk Serv.

--Only Halfway to Paradise: Women in Post-War Britain 1945-1968. 1980. 22.00x (ISBN 0-422-76870-7, Pub by Tavistock England); pap. 8.95 (ISBN 0-422-76880-4). Methuen Inc.

--Women & the Welfare State. (Tavistock Women's Studies). 1977. 25.00x (ISBN 0-422-76050-1, Pub. by Tavistock England); pap. 9.95x (ISBN 0-422-76060-9). Methuen Inc.

Wilson, Elizabeth A., jt. auth. see Wilson, Charles C.

Wilson, Ellen. Ernie Pyle: Boy from Back Home. LC 61-12697. (Childhood of Famous Americans Ser.). (Illus.). (gr. 3-7). 1955. 3.95 o.p. (ISBN 0-672-50051-5). Bobbs.

Wilson, Ellen Axson, jt. auth. see Wilson, Woodrow.

Wilson, Ellen G. The Loyal Blacks. LC 75-45762. (Illus.). 1976. 10.95 o.p. (ISBN 0-399-11683-4). Putnam Pub Group.

Wilson, Emily H. Hope & Dignity: Older Black Women of the South. 1983. write for info. (ISBN 0-87722-302-5). Temple U Pr.

Wilson, Erica. Erica Wilson's Christmas World. (Illus.). 160p. 1982. pap. 11.95 (ISBN 0-684-17651-3, ScribT). Scribner.

Wilson, Ernest T. Angola Beloved. LC 67-31008. 1967. pap. 2.50 (ISBN 0-87213-961-1). Loizeaux.

Wilson, Eunice & Gile, Joanne. Fashion Bags. 1979. 12.95 o.p. (ISBN 0-7134-1073-6, Pub. by Batsford England). David & Charles.

Wilson, F. Basic Resuscitation & Primary Care. 352p. 1980. text ed. 27.50 (ISBN 0-85200-316-1). Univ Park.

--French Political Parties under the Fifth Republic. 256p. 1982. 26.95 (ISBN 0-03-062046-5). Praeger.

--A Review of the Biological Control of Insects and Weeds in Australia and Australian New Guinea. 104p. 1960. 30.00X (ISBN 0-85198-065-1, CAB Bks). State Mutual Bk.

Wilson, F., jt. auth. see Barnes, D.

Wilson, F. P. The Elizabethan Theatre. 1982. lib. bdg. 34.50 (ISBN 0-686-81918-7). Porter.

Wilson, F. Paul. An Enemy of the State. LC 79-7883. (Science Fiction Ser.). 1980. 11.95 o.p. (ISBN 0-385-15422-4). Doubleday.

Wilson, Florence & Neuhauser, Duncan. Health Services in the U. S. rev. ed. 1982. text ed. 15.50x (ISBN 0-88410-700-0). Ballinger Pub.

Wilson, Florence A. & Neuhauser, Duncan. Health Services in the United States. 2nd ed. 368p. 1982. text ed. 17.50x (ISBN 0-88410-713-2). Ballinger Pub.

Wilson, Forrest. Post-Modern Malpractice. (Illus.). 1983. pap. 6.00. Arts & Arch.

Wilson, Frances E. Until Summer. 1981. pap. 6.95 (ISBN 0-686-84685-0, Avalon). Bouregy.

Wilson, Francis. Labour in the South African Gold Mines 1936-1969. LC 77-161290. (African Studies: No. 6). 1972. 44.50 (ISBN 0-521-08303-6). Cambridge U Pr.

--The Larousse Guide to Weather Forecasting. LC 82-81529. (Larousse Nature Guides Ser.). (Illus.). 1982. 17.95 (ISBN 0-88332-288-9, 8219); pap. 8.95 (ISBN 0-88332-280-3, 8218). Larousse.

Wilson, Francis G. A Theory of Public Opinion. LC 74-33748. 308p. 1975. Repr. of 1962 ed. lib. bdg. 19.25x (ISBN 0-8371-7980-7, WITP). Greenwood.

Wilson, Frank C. The Musculoskeletal System. LC 75-22187. (Illus.). 288p. 1975. text ed. 20.75 o.p. (ISBN 0-397-52071-9, Lippincott Medical). Lippincott.

Wilson, Frank C., ed. The Musculoskeletal System: Basic Processes & Disorders. 2nd ed. (Illus.). 292p. 1982. text ed. 32.50 (ISBN 0-397-52096-4, Lippincott Medical). Lippincott.

Wilson, Frank L., jt. auth. see Roth, David.

Wilson, Frank W., ed. Machining the Space-Age Metals. LC 65-13378. (Manufacturing Data Ser). 1965. pap. 6.10x o.p. (ISBN 0-87263-005-6). SME.

Wilson, Frank W., ed. see American Society Of Tool And Manufacturing Engineers.

Wilson, Frank W., ed. see American Society Of Tool & Manufacturing Engineers.

Wilson, Franklin D. Residential Consumption, Economic Opportunity & Race. LC 79-51705. (Studies in Population). 1979. 22.50 (ISBN 0-12-757980-X). Acad Pr.

Wilson, Fred, ed. Lesser Known Chess Masterpieces: 1906-1915. LC 74-80134. 384p. 1976. pap. 4.00 o.p. (ISBN 0-486-23146-1). Dover.

Wilson, Frieberger, jt. auth. see Wilson, Saul.

Wilson, G., jt. ed. see Svehla, G.

Wilson, G. M. Alexander MacDonald: Leader of the Miners. 244p. 27.00 (ISBN 0-686-95415-7). Pergamon.

Wilson, G. T., jt. auth. see Rachman, S. J.

Wilson, G. Terence & O'Leary, K. Daniel. Principles of Behavior Therapy. (Ser. in Social Learning Theory). (Illus.). 1980. text ed. 23.95 (ISBN 0-13-701102-4). P-H.

Wilson, G. Terence & Franks, Cyril M., eds. Contemporary Behavior Therapy. LC 82-949. 597p. 1982. 35.00 (ISBN 0-89862-614-5). Guilford Pr.

Wilson, Gabriel H. Current Radiology, Vol. 4. (Current Radiology Ser.). 400p. 1983. 55.00 (ISBN 0-471-09549-4, Pub. by Wiley Med). Wiley.

Wilson, Gabriel H., ed. Current Radiology, Vol. 1. (Illus.). 1978. 55.00 (ISBN 0-471-09498-6, Pub. by Wiley Med). Wiley.

--Current Radiology, Vol. 2. 1979. 55.00 (ISBN 0-471-09499-4, Pub. by Wiley Med). Wiley.

Wilson, Gabriel H. & Hanafee, William N., eds. Current Radiology, Vol. 3. (Current Radiology Ser.: Vol. 3). 472p. 1982. 55.00 (ISBN 0-471-09509-5, Pub. by Wiley Med). Wiley.

Wilson, Gahan. And Then We'll Get Him! LC 78-1312. 1978. 12.95 o.s.i. (ISBN 0-399-90003-9, Marek); pap. 5.95 o.s.i. (ISBN 0-399-90014-4). Putnam Pub Group.

--Nuts. LC 79-4485. 1979. pap. 4.95 o.s.i. (ISBN 0-399-90062-4, Marek). Putnam Pub Group.

Wilson, Gar. Tigers of Justice. (Phoenix Force Ser.). 192p. 1983. pap. 1.95 (ISBN 0-686-37702-8, Pub. by Worldwide). Harlequin Bks.

Wilson, Gar, jt. auth. see Pendleton, Don.

Wilson, Geoffrey. Ephesians. 1978. pap. 3.95 (ISBN 0-85151-263-1). Banner of Truth.

--First & Second Thessalonians. 1975. pap. 3.95 (ISBN 0-85151-339-5). Banner of Truth.

Wilson, George A. Reckoning With Life. 1942. text ed. 34.50x (ISBN 0-686-83723-1). Elliots Bks.

Wilson, George W., et al. The Impact of Highway Investment on Development. LC 77-23153. (Brookings Institution, Transport Reasearch Program Ser.). (Illus.). 1977. Repr. of 1966 ed. lib. bdg. 18.75x (ISBN 0-8371-9453-9, WIIH). Greenwood.

Wilson, Gilbert L., jt. auth. see Pepper, George H.

Wilson, Glenn, jt. auth. see Eysenck, H. J.

Wilson, Godfrey & Wilson, Monica. Analysis of Social Change. 1968. 24.95 o.p. (ISBN 0-521-06820-7); pap. 8.95 (ISBN 0-521-09554-9). Cambridge U Pr.

Wilson, Graham K. Interest Groups in the United States. 1981. 29.95x (ISBN 0-19-827425-4); pap. 9.95x (ISBN 0-19-876095-7). Oxford U Pr.

--Unions in American National Politics. LC 79-15559. 1979. 22.50x (ISBN 0-312-83305-9). St Martin.

Wilson, Graham S. & Miles, A. A., eds. Topley & Wilson's Principles of Bacteriology, Virology & Immunity, 2 vols. 6th ed. (Illus.). 284p. 1975. Set. 225.00 (ISBN 0-683-08378-3). Williams & Wilkins.

Wilson, Greta O., ed. Regents, Reformers, & Revolutionaries: Indonesian Voices of the Colonial Days. LC 77-20686. (Asian Studies at Hawaii: No. 21). 1978. pap. text ed. 10.00x (ISBN 0-8248-0541-0). UH Pr.

Wilson, H. E. Our Nig: Sketches from the Life of a Free Black. Gates, Henry L., ed. LC 82-49197. 192p. 1983. pap. 2.95 (ISBN 0-394-71558-6, Vin). Random.

Wilson, H. H., tr. Rig-Veda Sanhita: A Collection of Ancient Hindu Hymns of the Rig-Veda: The Oldest Authority on the Religious & Social Institutions of the Hindus, 7 vols. 1977. Repr. of 1850 ed. Set. text ed. 128.50x (ISBN 0-391-01102-2). Humanities.

Wilson, Harris W. & Hoeveler, Diane L., eds. English Prose & Criticism in the Nineteenth Century: A Guide to Information Sources. LC 74-11527. (American Literature, English Literature, & World Literature in English Info. Guide Ser.: Vol. 18). 1979. 42.00x (ISBN 0-8103-1235-2). Gale.

Wilson, Helen V. Helen Van Pelt Wilson's African Violet Book. (Illus.). 1970. 11.95 (ISBN 0-8015-3852-1, Hawthorn); pap. 7.25 (ISBN 0-8015-3858-0, 0704-210, Hawthorn). Dutton.

Wilson, Henry. History of the Rise & Fall of the Slave Power in America, 3 Vols. LC 70-77218. 1872-1877. Repr. 70.00x o.p. (ISBN 0-8371-3031-X, Pub. by Negro U Pr). Greenwood.

Wilson, Henry L. Diplomatic Episodes in Mexico, Belgium & Chile. LC 70-123496. 1971. Repr. of 1927 ed. 15.50 o.p. (ISBN 0-8046-1383-4). Kennikat.

Wilson, Holly. Coaches' Guide to Sports Injuries. 1983. pap. text ed. price not set (ISBN 0-931250-37-4). Human Kinetics.

Wilson, Holly S. & Kneisl, Carol R. Psychiatric Nursing. LC 78-7775. 1979. 27.95 o.p. (ISBN 0-201-08340-X, Med-Nurse); wkbk. 8.95 o.p. (ISBN 0-201-08342-6); instr's guide 3.95 o.p. (ISBN 0-201-08341-8). A-W.

--Psychiatric Nursing. 2nd ed. 1983. 26.95 (ISBN 0-201-11702-9, Med-Nurse); activity bk 9.95 (ISBN 0-201-11703-7, Med-Nurse); instr's guide 3.95 (ISBN 0-201-08341-8). A-W.

Wilson, Holton J. & Wilson, Cathy R. Economics in American Society: An Introduction to Economic Issues. 1977. pap. text ed. 7.95x o.p. (ISBN 0-02-479700-6). Glencoe.

Wilson, Ian. The Shroud of Turin: The Burial Cloth of Jesus Christ? LC 77-81551. (Illus.). 1978. 4.95 (ISBN 0-385-12736-7). Doubleday.

Wilson, J. Moral Education & the Curriculum. 1969. inquire for price o.p. (ISBN 0-08-013897-7); pap. 5.25 o.p. (ISBN 0-08-013898-5). Pergamon.

--Octavio Paz. LC 78-18108. 1979. 32.50 (ISBN 0-521-22306-7); pap. 11.95 (ISBN 0-521-29509-2). Cambridge U Pr.

Wilson, J., jt. auth. see Rudden, M. N.

Wilson, J. A. Basic Electronics: Theory & Practice. (Illus.). (gr. 11-12). 1977. pap. text ed. 23.95 (ISBN 0-07-070670-0, G). McGraw.

--Industrial Electronics & Control. LC 78-7424. 528p. 1978. text ed. 23.95 (ISBN 0-574-21515-8, 13-4515). SRA.

Wilson, J. A. & Kaufman, Milton. Learning Electricity & Electronics Through Experiments. (Illus.). 1979. pap. text ed. 7.50 o.p. (ISBN 0-07-070675-1, G). McGraw.

Wilson, J. A., jt. auth. see Kaufman, Milton.

Wilson, J. Christy. Afghanistan: Forbidden Harvest. 1981. pap. 4.95 o.p. (ISBN 0-89191-476-5, 54767). Cook.

Wilson, J. Douglas & Werner, S. O. Simplified Roof Framing. 2nd ed. (gr. 10-12). 1948. text ed. 13.05 (ISBN 0-07-070959-9, W). McGraw.

Wilson, J. Eugene. How to Fight the IRS & Win II. 212p. 1983. pap. 19.95 (ISBN 0-9601416-7-7). J C Print.

Wilson, J. G. Cosmic Rays. 150p. 1976. write for info. (ISBN 0-85109-500-3, Pub. by Taylor & Francis). Intl Pubns Serv.

Wilson, J. R. Emotion & Object. LC 76-179160. 240p. 1972. 24.95 (ISBN 0-521-08450-4). Cambridge U Pr.

Wilson, J. R., et al. Experiments in Physical Chemistry. 2nd ed. 1968. 44.00 o.s.i. (ISBN 0-08-012541-7). Pergamon.

Wilson, J. S., ed. Multinational Enterprises. 1974. 45.00 (ISBN 9-0286-0124-4). Heinman.

Wilson, J. Walter & Plunkett, Orda A. The Fungous Diseases of Man. 1965. 55.00x (ISBN 0-520-01344-1). U of Cal Pr.

Wilson, Jackson, intro. by. Looking Backward: Two Thousand to Eighteen Eighty-Seven. New ed. (YA) 1981. pap. 3.95 (ISBN 0-394-30942-1, T42, Mod LibC). Modern Lib.

Wilson, James A. Principles of Animal Physiology. 2nd ed. 1979. text ed. 25.95 (ISBN 0-02-428360-6). Macmillan.

Wilson, James C. Vietnam in Prose & Film. LC 82-6635. (Illus.). 140p. 1982. lib. bdg. 18.95x (ISBN 0-89950-050-1). McFarland & Co.

Wilson, James G. Environmental & Birth Defects. (Environmental Science: An Interdisciplinary Monograph). 1973. 51.00 (ISBN 0-12-757750-5). Acad Pr.

Wilson, James G. & Newall, A. B. General & Inorganic Chemistry. 2nd ed. (Illus.). 1971. text ed. 21.95x (ISBN 0-521-07073-2). Cambridge U Pr.

Wilson, James G., ed. see Halleck, Fitz-Greene.

Wilson, James H. Under the Old Flag. Repr. of 1912 ed. lib. bdg. 36.75x o.p. (ISBN 0-8371-4663-1, WIUF). Greenwood.

Wilson, James Q. American Government: Institution & Policies. 2nd ed. 720p. 1983. text ed. 22.95 (ISBN 0-669-03757-5); instr's. guide 1.95 (ISBN 0-669-05262-0); test item file 1.95 (ISBN 0-669-05265-5); student handbook 7.95 (ISBN 0-669-05263-9). Heath.

--American Government: Institutions & Policies. 1980. text ed. 20.95 (ISBN 0-669-01621-7); student handbk. 7.95 (ISBN 0-669-02521-6); inst. guide free to adopters (ISBN 0-669-02531-3); test item file free to adopters (ISBN 0-669-02522-4); test item file avail. 0.00expanded (ISBN 0-669-04375-3). Heath.

--Thinking About Crime. 1977. pap. 3.95 (ISBN 0-394-72185-3, Vin). Random.

Wilson, James Q., ed. Crime & Public Policy. 400p. 1983. 22.95 (ISBN 0-917616-52-9); pap. 8.95 (ISBN 0-917616-51-0). ICS Pr.

Wilson, Jane, jt. auth. see Morgan, Robert F.

Wilson, Janet K., ed. Genetics for Blood Bankers. 118p. 1980. 23.00 (ISBN 0-914404-59-8). Am Assn Blood.

Wilson, Janice. Sexpression: Improving Your Sexual Communication. 240p. 1980. 10.95 o.p. (ISBN 0-13-807610-3, Spec); pap. 4.95 o.p. (ISBN 0-13-807602-2). P-H.

Wilson, Jeanne. The Golden Harlot. 1980. 10.00 o.p. (ISBN 0-312-33737-X). St Martin.

Wilson, Jeanne, jt. auth. see Wilson, Dave.

Wilson, Jerome D. & Ricketson, William F. Thomas Paine. (United States Authors Ser). 1978. lib. bdg. 11.95 (ISBN 0-8057-7206-5, Twayne). G K Hall.

Wilson, Jerry & Fuqua, Paul. Terrorism - the Executive's Guide to Survival. (Illus.). 168p. 1978. 16.95 (ISBN 0-87201-821-0). Gulf Pub.

Wilson, Jerry, jt. auth. see Fuqua, Paul.

Wilson, Jerry D. An Environmental Approach to Physical Science. 1974. pap. text ed. 15.95 o.p. (ISBN 0-669-83386-X). Heath.

--Physics: Concepts & Aplications. 2nd ed. (Illus.). 848p. 1981. text ed. 25.95 (ISBN 0-669-03373-1); instr's guide 1.95 (ISBN 0-669-01948-8); student guide 16.95 (ISBN 0-669-03362-6); lab guide 15.95 (ISBN 0-669-01947-X). Heath.

Wilson, Jeyaratnam & Dalton, Dennis, eds. The States of South Asia: Problems of National Integration. 361p. 1983. text ed. 24.00x (ISBN 0-8248-0823-1). UH Pr.

Wilson, Jim. Go Preach the Kingdom Heal the Sick. 127p. 1979. pap. text ed. 4.95 (ISBN 0-227-67659-9). Attic Pr.

--Growth in Prayer. 74p. 1969. pap. 3.95 (ISBN 0-227-67475-8). Attic Pr.

--Healing Through the Power of Christ. 64p. 1969. pap. 3.25 (ISBN 0-227-67478-2). Attic Pr.

--Purpose. 80p. 1974. pap. 3.25 (ISBN 0-227-67707-2). Attic Pr.

Wilson, Joan H. Herbert Hoover: The Forgotten Progressing. (The Library of American Biography). 256p. 1975. pap. text ed. 5.95 (ISBN 0-316-94416-5). Little.

Wilson, Joe F. The United States, Chile & Peru in the Tacna & Arica Plebiscite. LC 78-66124. (Orig.). 1979. pap. text ed. 12.50 (ISBN 0-8191-0685-2). U Pr of Amer.

Wilson, John. Becky. LC 66-10507. (Illus.). (gr. k-3). 1967. 9.89i (ISBN 0-690-12669-7). T y Crowell.

--Chattanooga's Story. (Illus.). 473p. 1980. 20.00 (ISBN 0-686-36855-X). Wilson J.

--Language & the Pursuit of Truth. 1956. 22.95 o.p. (ISBN 0-521-06821-5); pap. 5.50x (ISBN 0-521-09421-6). Cambridge U Pr.

--Philosophy & Religion: The Logic of Religious Belief. LC 78-14000. 1979. Repr. of 1961 ed. lib. bdg. 16.25x (ISBN 0-313-20738-0, WIPH). Greenwood.

--Religion in American Society: The Effective Presence. LC 77-16808. 1978. ref. ed. 22.95 (ISBN 0-13-773259-7). P-H.

--Social Theory. (Illus.). 256p. 1983. pap. text ed. 13.95 (ISBN 0-13-819573-0). P-H.

--Specimens of the British Critics. LC 78-12061. 1979. 40.00x (ISBN 0-8201-1326-3). Schol Facsimiles.

--Thinking with Concepts. 1970. 26.95 (ISBN 0-521-06825-8); pap. 6.95x (ISBN 0-521-09601-4). Cambridge U Pr.

Wilson, John & Cowell, Barbara. Dialogues on Moral Education. 180p. (Orig.). 1983. pap. price not set (ISBN 0-89135-035-7). Religious Educ.

Wilson, John & International Agency for the Prevention of Blindness. World Blindness & Its Prevention. 1980. text ed. 27.50x (ISBN 0-19-261249-2). Oxford U Pr.

Wilson, John, jt. auth. see Oliver, Eric.

Wilson, John A. Culture of Ancient Egypt. LC 56-4923. (Illus.). 1956. pap. 5.95 (ISBN 0-226-90152-1, P11, Phoen). U of Chicago Pr.

Wilson, John A., jt. auth. see Robeck, Mildred C.

Wilson, John A., et al. Psychological Foundations of Learning & Teaching. 2nd ed. (Illus.). 608p. 1974. pap. text ed. 21.95 (ISBN 0-07-070856-8, C); instr's. manual 14.95 (ISBN 0-07-070844-4). McGraw.

Wilson, John D. The Elizabethan Shakespeare. 1982. lib. bdg. 34.50 (ISBN 0-686-81913-6). Porter.

--Fortunes of Falstaff. 1943. 24.95 (ISBN 0-521-06830-4); pap. 7.95 (ISBN 0-521-09246-9). Cambridge U Pr.

--Martin Marprelate & Shakespeares Fluellen. 1982. lib. bdg. 34.50 (ISBN 0-686-81921-7). Porter.

--The Meaning of Tempest. 1982. lib. bdg. 34.50 (ISBN 0-686-81920-9). Porter.

--Six Tragedies of Shakespeare. 1982. lib. bdg. 34.50 (ISBN 0-686-81919-5). Porter.

--Stephen & Arnold as Critics of Wordsworth. 1982. lib. bdg. 34.50 (ISBN 0-686-81922-5). Porter.

--What Happens in Hamlet. 3rd ed. 1951. 49.50 (ISBN 0-521-06835-5); pap. 12.95x (ISBN 0-521-09109-8, 109). Cambridge U Pr.

Wilson, John F. Practice & Theory of Electrochemical Machining. LC 80-15384. 266p. 1982. Repr. of 1971 ed. lib. bdg. 25.50 (ISBN 0-89874-229-3). Krieger.

--Public Religion in American Culture. 240p. 1979. lib. bdg. 22.95 (ISBN 0-87722-159-6). Temple U Pr.

--Pulpit in Parliament: Puritanism During the English Civil Wars, 1640-1648. LC 69-18074. 1969. 26.00x o.p. (ISBN 0-691-07157-8). Princeton U Pr.

--Religion: A Preface. (Illus.). 240p. 1982. pap. text ed. 11.95 (ISBN 0-13-773192-2). P-H.

Wilson, John F. & Mulder, John M. Religion in American History: Interpretive Essays. 448p. 1978. text ed. 18.95 (ISBN 0-13-771998-1); pap. text ed. 15.95 (ISBN 0-13-771980-9). P-H.

Wilson, John F. & Slavens, Thomas P., eds. Research Guide to Religious Studies. (Sources of Information in the Humanities Ser.). 192p. Date not set. text ed. 20.00 (ISBN 0-8389-0330-4). ALA.

Wilson, John L. Business System Options. 1978. 7.95 (ISBN 0-686-98070-0). Telecom Lib.

Wilson, John R. The Mind. rev. ed. LC 80-52250. (Life Science Library). 13.40 (ISBN 0-8094-4103-9). Silver.

Wilson, John R., ed. Shaping the American Character. LC 80-5656. 398p. 1980. lib. bdg. 23.00 (ISBN 0-8191-1165-1); pap. text ed. 13.75 (ISBN 0-8191-1166-X). U Pr of Amer.

Wilson, Jose. American Cooking: The Eastern Heartland. LC 70-150960. (Foods of the World Ser.). (gr. 6 up). 1971. lib. bdg. 17.28 (ISBN 0-8094-0079-0, Pub. by Time-Life). Silver.

Wilson, Joseph T. & Udall, Lee. Folk Festivals: A Handbook for Organization & Management. LC 81-23103. (Illus.). 312p. 1982. 21.50x (ISBN 0-87049-300-0); pap. 9.95x (ISBN 0-87049-336-1). U of Tenn Pr.

Wilson, Josephine M., jt. auth. see Pauk, Walter.

Wilson, Josleen, jt. auth. see Feinman, Max L.

Wilson, Josleen, jt. auth. see Thodes, Sonya.

Wilson, Joyce, jt. auth. see Shen, Peter.

Wilson, Justin & Hadley, Jay. Justin Wilson's Cajun Fables. LC 82-18568. 32p. 1982. 8.95 (ISBN 0-88289-362-9). Pelican.

Wilson, K., jt. auth. see Robinson, H. S.

Wilson, K., jt. ed. see Williams, B. L.

Wilson, K. V. From Associations to Structure: The Course of Cognition. (Advances in Psychology Ser.: Vol. 6). 1980. 36.25 (ISBN 0-444-86043-6). Elsevier.

Wilson, Karen L. Cities of the Delta-Mendes Part II: Preliminary Report on the 1979 & 1980 Seasons. LC 81-52799. (American Research Center in Egypt, Reports: Vol. 5). (Illus.). ix, 95p. 1982. 19.50x (ISBN 0-89003-083-9); pap. 13.50x (ISBN 0-89003-082-0). Undena Pubns.

Wilson, Kax. A History of Textiles. (Illus.). 1979. lib. bdg. 32.00 (ISBN 0-89158-491-9); pap. 18.00 (ISBN 0-686-86882-X). Westview.

Wilson, Keith. Railways in Canada: The Iron Link. (Focus on Canadian History Ser.). (Illus.). 96p. (gr. 6-10). 1982. PLB 8.40 (ISBN 0-531-04573-0). Watts.

Wilson, Keith, jt. ed. see Williams, Bryan L.

Wilson, Kenneth C. Understanding Station Carrier, Vol. VI. 1975. 6.00 (ISBN 0-686-98062-X). Telecom Lib.

Wilson, Kenneth M., jt. auth. see McKearin, Helen.

Wilson, Ker. The Kennedys Abroad: Ann & Peter in London. 10.50 (ISBN 0-392-08636-0, SpS). Sportshelf.

Wilson, L. B., jt. auth. see Page, E. S.

Wilson, Lanford. Angels Fall. 1982. 13.00 (ISBN 0-8090-2648-1); pap. 6.25 (ISBN 0-8090-1245-6). Hill & Wang.

--The Gingham Dog. LC 76-88015. 110p. 1969. 5.25 (ISBN 0-8090-4950-3). Hill & Wang.

--Talley's Folly. 1980. pap. 5.95 (ISBN 0-8090-1242-1, Mermaid); 9.95 (ISBN 0-8090-9128-3). Hill & Wang.

--Thymus Vulgaris: A One-Act Play. Date not set. 1.65 (ISBN 0-686-83804-1). Dramatists Play.

Wilson, LaVisa C. Caregiver Training for Child Care: A Multimedia Program. (Elementary Education Ser.). 1977. pap. text ed. 9.95 (ISBN 0-675-08482-2). Additional supplements may be obtained from publisher. Merrill.

Wilson, LeGrand J. The Confederate Soldier. Silver, James W., ed. LC 72-95936. (Illus.). 213p. 1973. Repr. of 1902 ed. 8.95 o.p. (ISBN 0-87870-016-1). Memphis St Univ.

Wilson, Leigh A. From the Bottom Up. LC 82-15975. 160p. 1983. 12.95 (ISBN 0-8203-0647-9). U of Ga Pr.

Wilson, Leland L., jt. auth. see Poppy, Willard J.

Wilson, Leslie, jt. ed. see Prescott, David.

Wilson, Lionel. Attack of the Killer Grizzly. Bennett, Russell, ed. LC 79-22057. (Quest, Adventure, Survival Ser.). (Illus.). 46p. (gr. 4-9). 1982. pap. 7.93g (ISBN 0-8172-2051-8). Raintree Pubs.

--The First Stunt Stars of Hollywood. LC 78-14465. (Famous Firsts Ser.). (Illus.). 1978. PLB 10.76 (ISBN 0-89547-048-9). Silver.

--The Mystery of Dracula. LC 78-23283. (Unsolved Mysteries of the World Ser.). 11.96 (ISBN 0-89547-065-9). Silver.

--The Mystery of Human Wolves. LC 78-11033. (Unsolved Mysteries of the World Ser.). PLB 11.96 (ISBN 0-89547-067-5). Silver.

Wilson, Lionel, jt. ed. see Fielder, Gilbert.

Wilson, Logan. American Academics: Then & Now. (Illus.). 1979. pap. text ed. 18.95x (ISBN 0-19-502482-6). Oxford U Pr.

--Shaping American Higher Education. 1972. 9.00 (ISBN 0-8268-1379-8). ACE.

Wilson, Loring D. The Handy Sportsman. (Stoeger Bks). 1977. pap. 5.95 o.s.i. (ISBN 0-695-80848-6). Follett.

Wilson, Lorraine, jt. auth. see Price, Sylvia.

Wilson, Louis R. Louis Round Wilson's Historical Sketches. LC 76-25332. 1976. 15.00 (ISBN 0-87716-063-5, Pub. by Moore Pub Co). F Apple.

Wilson, Louis R., et al. The Library in College Instruction. LC 73-7383. 347p. 1973. Repr. of 1951 ed. lib. bdg. 19.75x (ISBN 0-8371-6928-3, WILC). Greenwood.

Wilson, Louise. This Stranger, My Son. pap. 2.50 (ISBN 0-451-11301-2, AE1301, Sig). NAL.

--This Stranger My Son: A Mother's Story. 1968. 6.95 (ISBN 0-399-10797-5). Putnam Pub Group.

Wilson, M. C. & Schuder, D. L. Insects of Ornamental Plants. 2nd ed. LC 85-50792. (Practical Insect Pest Management Ser.). (Illus.). 150p. 1982. pap. text ed. 6.95x (ISBN 0-917974-93-X). Waveland Pr.

Wilson, M. Curtis, et al. Practical Insect Pest Management: Insects of Man's Household & Health, No. 5. LC 77-82251. (Illus.). 1977. 7.95x (ISBN 0-917974-07-7). Waveland Pr.

--Practical Insect Pest Management: Insects of Ornamental Plants, No. 4. LC 77-82602. (Illus.). 1977. 6.95x o.p. (ISBN 0-917974-06-9). Waveland Pr.

--Practical Insect Pest Management. 2nd. ed. LC 79-57132. (Insects of Livestock & Agronomic Crops Ser: No.2). (Illus.). 208p. 1980. pap. text ed. 8.95x (ISBN 0-917974-39-5). Waveland Pr.

--Practical Insect Pest Management: Insects of Vegetables & Fruit, Vol. 3. 2nd ed. LC 81-70506. (Illus.). 144p. 1982. pap. text ed. 6.95x (ISBN 0-917974-65-4). Waveland Pr.

Wilson, M. Emett. Relativity of Survival & Evolution. 1983. 10.00 (ISBN 0-533-05584-9). Vantage.

Wilson, M. Jane, ed. Clinical Aspects of the Positive Direct Antiglobulin Test. 60p. 1980. 11.00 (ISBN 0-914404-57-1). Am Assn Blood.

Wilson, M. T. Managing a Sales Force. LC 75-552155. (Illus.). 184p. 1970. 40.00x (ISBN 0-7161-0048-7). Intl Pubns Serv.

Wilson, McClure. The Anatomic Foundation of Neuroradiology of the Brain. 2nd ed. 1972. 24.50 (ISBN 0-316-94413-0). Little.

Wilson, Major L. Space, Time, & Freedom. LC 74-287. 309p. 1974. lib. bdg. 29.95x (ISBN 0-8371-7373-6, WIT/). Greenwood.

Wilson, Margaret. The Able McLaughlins. LC 23-13896. 262p. 1976. Repr. of 1923 ed. 13.95 (ISBN 0-910220-68-9). Berg.
--Tirso de Molina. (World Authors Ser.). 1977. lib. bdg. 15.95 (ISBN 0-8057-6281-7). G K Hall.
Wilson, Margaret, ed. Essential Descartes. 1969. pap. 3.95 (ISBN 0-451-62151-4, ME2151, Ment). NAL.
Wilson, Margaret, et al. Philosophy: An Introduction. 1972. text ed. 24.95 (ISBN 0-13-664110-5). P-H.
Wilson, Margaret D. Descartes. (The Arguments of the Philosophers Ser.). 1978. 22.50x (ISBN 0-7100-8852-3); pap. 9.95 (ISBN 0-7100-9208-3). Routledge & Kegan.
Wilson, Margaret G. The American Woman in Transition: The Urban Influence, 1870-1920. (Contributions in Women's Studies: No. 6). 1979. lib. bdg. 27.50x (ISBN 0-313-20638-4, WAM/). Greenwood.
Wilson, Margery. Double Your Energy & Live Without Fatigue. 240p. 1983. pap. 5.95 (ISBN 0-13-218917-8, Reward). P-H.
Wilson, Margo, jt. auth. see Daley, Martin.
Wilson, Marion E., et al. Microbiology in Patient Care. 3rd ed. (Illus.). 1979. text ed. 26.95 (ISBN 0-02-428310-X); instrs'. manual avail. Macmillan.
--Laboratory Manual & Workbook in Microbiology: Applications to Patient Care. 2nd ed. 1979. pap. text ed. 12.95x (ISBN 0-02-428370-3). Macmillan.
Wilson, Marjorie K., tr. see Lorenz, Konrad.
Wilson, Mary, jt. auth. see Young, Biloine W.
Wilson, Mary W. Japanese Cooking. (Illus.). 128p. 1983. pap. 6.95 (ISBN 0-915942-20-8). Owlswood Prods.
Wilson, Maurice. Growing on the Job. Herr, Edwin L., ed. (Cooperative Work Experience Education for Careers Program). (Illus.). (gr. 11-12). 1976. pap. text ed. 7.96 (ISBN 0-07-028337-0, G); tchrs manual 3.50 (ISBN 0-07-028338-9). McGraw.
Wilson, Meredith. American Cat Breed Encyclopedia. (Illus.). 1978. 12.95 (ISBN 0-87666-855-4, H-997). TFH Pubns.
--Encyclopedia of American Cat Breeds. (Illus.). 352p. 1978. 9.95 o.p. (ISBN 0-87666-855-4). TFH Pubns.
Wilson, Michael. The English Chamber Organ: History & Development 1650-1850. LC 68-27600. xxii, 190p. 1968. 14.95x o.s.i. (ISBN 0-87249-119-6). U of SC Pr.
--Health Is for People. 134p. 1980. 12.95x o.p. (ISBN 0-232-51326-0, Pub. by Darton-Longman-Todd England). State Mutual Bk.
Wilson, Michael, ed. Jane's Avionics, 1982-1983. (Jane's Yearbooks). (Illus.). 400p. 1982. 110.00 (ISBN 0-86720-611-X). Sci Bks Intl.
Wilson, Michael, intro. by. The National Gallery, London. New ed. (Illus.). 144p. 1982. 19.95 o.p. (ISBN 0-85667-157-6, Pub. by Sotheby Pubns England); pap. 12.50 (ISBN 0-85667-156-8, Pub. by Sotheby Pubns England). Biblio Dist.
Wilson, Michael E., jt. ed. see Kenamore, Jane A.
Wilson, Michael L. Outline of Bible History & Major Christian Movements. 1974. pap. 4.00 (ISBN 0-88027-014-4). Firm Foun Pub.
Wilson, Mitchell. Energy. rev. ed. LC 63-21614. (Life Science Library). (Illus.). (gr. 5 up). 1969. PLB cancelled (ISBN 0-8094-0460-5, Pub. by Time-Life). Silver.
Wilson, Monica. Religion & the Transformation of Society: A Study in Social Change in Africa. LC 73-134622. (Scott Holland Memorial Lecturers of 1969 Ser). (Illus.). 1971. 24.95 (ISBN 0-521-07991-8). Cambridge U Pr.
Wilson, Monica, jt. auth. see Wilson, Godfrey.
Wilson, Monica, ed. see Matthews, Z. K.
Wilson, N. L. Concept of Language. 1971. 12.50x o.p. (ISBN 0-8020-7026-4). U of Toronto Pr.
Wilson, N. Scarlyn. Teach Yourself First French. (Teach Yourself Ser.). 1969. pap. 4.50 (ISBN 0-679-10215-9). McKay.
Wilson, Nancy L. & Wilson, Roger H. Please Pass the Salt: A Manual for Low Salt Eaters. (Illus.). 224p. 1983. 14.95 (ISBN 0-89313-027-3). G F Stickley.
Wilson, Nelly. Bernard-Lazare. LC 77-82524. 1979. 44.50 (ISBN 0-521-21802-0). Cambridge U Pr.
Wilson, O. W. & McLaren, Roy C. Police Administration. 4th ed. 1977. text ed. 24.50 (ISBN 0-07-070726-X, C). McGraw.
Wilson, Ostis B. Courtship & Marriage. 12p. 1976. pap. 0.15 (ISBN 0-686-36260-8). Faith Pub Hse.
Wilson, P. S. Interest & Discipline in Education. (Students Library of Education). 1971. 14.95x (ISBN 0-7100-7049-7); pap. 6.50 (ISBN 0-7100-7908-7). Routledge & Kegan.
Wilson, Pat, intro. by see Lincoln, Warren B., et al.
Wilson, Patricia P. Household Equipment: Selection & Management. LC 75-31023. (Illus.). 384p. 1976. text ed. 24.50 (ISBN 0-395-20596-4); resource manual 5.35 (ISBN 0-395-20597-2). HM.
Wilson, Patrick. Public Knowledge, Private Ignorance: Toward a Library & Information Policy. LC 76-52327. (Contributions in Librarianship & Information Sciences: No. 10). 1977. lib. bdg. 25.00x (ISBN 0-8371-9485-7, WPN/). Greenwood.
--Science in S. Asia, Past & Present. (Occasional Publication Ser.). 112p. 1966. pap. 2.00 o.p. (ISBN 0-89192-142-7). Interbk Inc.
Wilson, Paul. Black Death, White Hands. 160p. 1983. text ed. 19.50x (ISBN 0-86861-300-2). Allen Unwin.
Wilson, Paul H., ed. see Guth, Hans P.
Wilson, Paul H., ed. see Guth, Hans P. & Schuster, Edgar H.
Wilson, Paul R. Public Housing for Australia. (Illus.). 1976. 15.00x (ISBN 0-7022-1363-2); pap. 9.95x (ISBN 0-686-37771-0). U of Queensland Pr.
Wilson, Pauline. Community Elite & the Public Library: Uses of Information in Leadership. LC 76-15336. (Contributions in Librarianship & Information Science: No. 18). 1977. lib. bdg. 25.00x (ISBN 0-8371-9031-2, WCE/). Greenwood.
--Stereotype & Status: Librarians in the U. S. LC 82-6119. (Contributions in Librarianship & Information Science Ser.: No. 41). 240p. 1982. lib. bdg. 27.50 (ISBN 0-313-23516-3, WIL/). Greenwood.
Wilson, Peter. Forty Games for Frivolous People. (Illus.). 1979. pap. 3.95 (ISBN 0-8256-3154-8, Quick Fox). Putnam Pub Group.
Wilson, Peter, jt. auth. see Fry, Eric C.
Wilson, Philip K., et al. Policies & Procedures of a Cardiac Rehabilitation Program: Immediate to Long-term Care. LC 78-5899. (Illus.). 253p. 1978. pap. 12.00 o.p. (ISBN 0-8121-0635-0). Lea & Febiger.
Wilson, R. A., tr. see Ebeling, Gerhard.
Wilson, R. A., tr. see Schlosser, Felix.
Wilson, R. A., tr. see Soggin, J. Alberto.
Wilson, R. J. Piazza Armerina. (Illus.). 96p. 1983. 12.50 (ISBN 0-292-76472-3). U of Tex Pr.
--Sicily Under the Roman Empire. (Illus.). 160p. 1982. text ed. 65.00x (ISBN 0-85668-160-1, 41418, Pub. by Aris & Phillips England). Humanities.
Wilson, R. J., jt. auth. see Fiorini, S.
Wilson, R. J., ed. Graph Theory & Combinatorics. (Research Notes in Mathematics: No. 34). 148p. (Orig.). 1979. pap. text ed. 23.00 (ISBN 0-273-08435-6). Pitman Pub MA.
Wilson, R. Jackson, jt. auth. see Weinstein, Allen.
Wilson, R. Jackson, ed. Reform, Crisis & Confusion: 1900-1929. 1970. pap. text ed. 3.95x (ISBN 0-394-30260-5). Phila Bk Co.
Wilson, R. Jackson, frwd. by see Gilbert, James.
Wilson, R. L. The Colt Heritage: The Official History of Colt Firearms, Eighteen Thirty-Six to Present. 1979. 39.95 o.p. (ISBN 0-671-24827-8); 35.00 o.p. (ISBN 0-686-66215-6). S&S.
Wilson, R. M., jt. auth. see Broer, M. R.
Wilson, R. McL., jt. ed. see Best, E.
Wilson, R. R., ed. Lincoln in Caricature. (Illus.). pap. cancelled o.s.i. (ISBN 0-8180-0825-3). Horizon.
Wilson, R. T. The Camel. (Intermediate Tropical Agriculture Ser.). (Illus.). 192p. 1983. pap. text ed. 14.95x (ISBN 0-582-77501-9). Longman.
Wilson, R. Turner. The Mode in Costume. (Illus.). 480p. 1983. pap. 13.95 (ISBN 0-686-83797-5, ScribT). Scribner.
Wilson, Ralph E. General Catalogue of Stellar Radial Velocities. 2nd ed. 1963. 5.00 (ISBN 0-87279-612-4). Carnegie Inst.
Wilson, Raymond. Ohiyesa: Charles Eastman, Santee Sioux. LC 82-4937. (Illus.). 1983. 15.95 (ISBN 0-252-00978-9). U of Ill Pr.
Wilson, Rex & Loyola, Gloria, eds. Rescue Archeology: Papers from the First New World Conference on Rescue Archeology. 272p. (Orig.). 1982. pap. 14.95 (ISBN 0-89133-102-6). Preservation Pr.
Wilson, Richard & Jones, William. Energy, Ecology & the Environment. 353p. 1974. 16.25 (ISBN 0-12-757550-2). Acad Pr.
Wilson, Richard, jt. auth. see Crouch, Edmond.
Wilson, Richard, ed. see Greenblat, Sidney L.
Wilson, Richard, et al. Health Effects of Fossil Fuel Burning: Assessment & Mitigation. 416p. 1980. prof ref 35.00x (ISBN 0-88410-714-0). Ballinger Pub.
Wilson, Richard E. & Drage, Martha O. Collaboration in Health Care Education. LC 23-1617. 65p. 1976. 4.95 (ISBN 0-686-38245-5). Natl League Nurse.
Wilson, Richard F., ed. Designing Academic Program Reviews. LC 81-48479. 1982. 7.95x (ISBN 0-87589-895-5, HE-37). Jossey-Bass.
Wilson, Robert & Wilson, Robert, eds. The Film Criticism of Otis Ferguson. LC 72-174660. 491p. 1971. 29.95 (ISBN 0-87722-005-0); pap. 14.95 (ISBN 0-87722-033-6). Temple U Pr.
Wilson, Robert, jt. ed. see Robinson, Keith.
Wilson, Robert A. The Earth Will Shake. LC 82-10490. 363p. 1982. 14.95 (ISBN 0-87477-211-7). J P Tarcher.
--Genesis of the Meiji Government in Japan, 1868-1871. LC 78-6546. (University of California Publications in History: Vol. 56). 1978. Repr. of 1957 ed. lib. bdg. 20.50x (ISBN 0-8371-9091-6, WIGM). Greenwood.
--Prometheus Rising. 260p. 1983. pap. 9.95 (ISBN 0-941404-19-6). Falcon Pr Az.
Wilson, Robert A. & Schulz, David A. Urban Sociology. (Series in Sociology). (Illus.). 1978. ref. ed. 22.95 (ISBN 0-13-939520-2). P-H.
Wilson, Robert C. Crooked Tree. LC 79-23321. 1980. 10.95 (ISBN 0-399-12488-8). Putnam Pub Group.
Wilson, Robert E. The Modern School Superintendent: His Principles & Practices. LC 77-2905. (Illus.). 1977. Repr. of 1960 ed. lib. bdg. 20.00x (ISBN 0-8371-9575-6, WIMO). Greenwood.
Wilson, Robert E. see Heat Transfer & Fluid Mechanics Institute.
Wilson, Robert F. Fluids, Electrolytes, & Metabolism. 148p. 1975. spiral 11.50x (ISBN 0-398-02643-2). C C Thomas.
Wilson, Robert F., jt. auth. see Crowell, Benedict.
Wilson, Robert F., jt. ed. see Walt, Alexander J.
Wilson, Robert H. Characterization in Malory. 1982. lib. bdg. 34.50 (ISBN 0-686-81923-3). Porter.
Wilson, Robert M. Diagnostic & Remedial Reading for Classroom & Clinic. 4th ed. (Illus.). 448p. 1981. text ed. 20.95 (ISBN 0-675-08048-7). Additional supplements may be obtained from publisher. Merrill.
--Diagnostic & Remedial Reading for Classroom. 3rd ed. (Elementary Education Ser.). 1977. pap. text ed. 15.95 (ISBN 0-675-08536-5). Additional supplements may be obtained from publisher. Merrill.
Wilson, Robert W., ed. see Fitch, Henry S.
Wilson, Robert W., et al. Innovation, Competition & Government Policy in the Semiconductor Industry. LC 80-8317. 240p. 1980. 23.95x (ISBN 0-669-03995-0). Lexington Bks.
Wilson, Roberta, ed. see Manning, Barbara S.
Wilson, Robley, Jr. Dancing for Men. LC 82-2602. (Drue Heinz Literaure Prize Winner Ser.). vi, 154p. 1982. 12.95 (ISBN 0-8229-3466-3). U of Pittsburgh Pr.
Wilson, Roger B., ed. Sir Daniel Gooch: Memoirs & Diary. (Illus.). 1972. 10.00 o.p. (ISBN 0-7153-5609-7). David & Charles.
Wilson, Roger H., jt. auth. see Wilson, Nancy L.
Wilson, Ron & Lee, Pat. Marshland World. (Illus.). 160p. 1983. 16.95 (ISBN 0-7137-1199-X, Pub. by Blandford Pr England). Sterling.
Wilson, Rowena. Man in a Million. (Candlelight Romance Ser.: No. 664). (Orig.). 1981. pap. 1.50 o.s.i. (ISBN 0-440-15528-2). Dell.
--Well Met by Moonlight. (Candlelight Romance Ser.: No. 683). 192p. (Orig.). 1981. pap. 1.75 o.s.i. (ISBN 0-440-19553-5). Dell.
Wilson, Ruby E. Frank J. North: Pawnee Scout, Commander & Pioneer. (Illus.). Date not set. 18.95 (ISBN 0-8040-0767-5, SB). Swallow. Postponed.
Wilson, Ruth. Our Blood & Tears: Black Freedom Fighters. 224p. (gr. 6 up). 1972. PLB 4.99 o.p. (ISBN 0-399-60717-X). Putnam Pub Group.
Wilson, S. & Wilson, A. The Belly Dance Book: The Serena Technique for Learning Belly Dancing. 224p. 1983. 9.95 (ISBN 0-07-070811-8, GB). McGraw.
Wilson, S. E., et al. Intra-Abdominal Infection. 1982. 50.00x (ISBN 0-07-070815-0). McGraw.
Wilson, S. G. The Gentiles & the Gentile Mission in Luke-Acts. LC 72-90489. (Society for New Testament Studies, Monograph No. 23). 304p. 1973. 44.50 (ISBN 0-521-20134-9). Cambridge U Pr.
Wilson, Sam, et al. Human Sexuality: A Text with Readings. (Illus.). 1977. pap. text ed. 12.95 o.s.i. (ISBN 0-8299-0131-0). West Pub.
Wilson, Samuel & Roe, Richard, eds. Biology Anthology: Readings in the Life Sciences. LC 74-2810. 320p. 1974. pap. text ed. 11.50 (ISBN 0-8299-0019-5). West Pub.
Wilson, Samuel, et al. Readings in Human Sexuality. LC 75-4362. (Illus.). 252p. 1975. pap. text ed. 10.50 (ISBN 0-8299-0050-0). West Pub.
Wilson, Samuel, Jr. & Lemann, Bernard. New Orleans Architecture Vol. 1: The Lower Garden District. Christovich, Mary L. & Toledano, Roulhac, eds. LC 72-172272. (New Orleans Architecture Ser.). (Illus.). 1971. 22.50 (ISBN 0-911116-51-6). Pelican.
Wilson, Samuel, Jr., ed. see Huber, Leonard, et al.
Wilson, Saul & Wilson, Frieberger. Nung Grammar. (SIL Publications in Linguistics Ser.: No. 62). 126p. 1980. pap. 8.50x (ISBN 0-88312-081-X); microfiche 2.25x (ISBN 0-88312-481-5). Summer Inst Ling.
Wilson, Seth. Learning from Jesus. Gardner, Lynn, ed. LC 77-155407. (The Bible Study Textbook Ser.). (Illus.). 1977. 15.90 (ISBN 0-89900-056-8). College Pr Pub.
Wilson, Simon. Surrealist Painting. (Phaidon Color Library). (Illus.). 84p. 1983. 27.50 (ISBN 0-7148-2234-5, Pub. by Salem Hse Ltd); pap. 18.95 (ISBN 0-7148-2244-2). Merrimack Bk Serv.
Wilson, Sloan. The Man in the Gray Flannel Suit II. 1983. 15.95 (ISBN 0-87795-474-7). Arbor Hse.
Wilson, Snoo. Pleasure Principle. 1981. pap. 6.95 (ISBN 0-413-32010-3). Methuen Inc.
Wilson, Stephen R. Informal Groups: An Introduction. (P-H Ser. in Sociology). 1978. ref. ed. 22.95 (ISBN 0-13-464636-3). P-H.
Wilson, Steve. Dealer's Wheels. LC 82-5547. 187p. 1982. 10.95 (ISBN 0-312-18533-2). St Martin.
Wilson, Sylvia E. Huyck Family in America. 736p. 1982. 35.00x (ISBN 0-932334-54-7). Heart of the Lakes.
Wilson, Terence G., jt. auth. see Franks, Cyril M.
Wilson, Terry C. Researcher's Guide to Statistics: Glossary & Decision Map. LC 78-56267. 1978. pap. text ed. 8.25 (ISBN 0-8191-0519-8). U Pr of Amer.
Wilson, Thomas. Arte of Rhetorique Fifteen Hundred & Fifty-Three. LC 62-7014. 1977. Repr. of 1553 ed. 33.00x (ISBN 0-8201-1259-3). Schol Facsimiles.
Wilson, Thomas & Wilson, Dorothy J. The Political Economy of the Welfare State. (Studies in Economics: No. 19). 240p. 1982. text ed. 29.50x (ISBN 0-04-336077-7); pap. text ed. 12.95x (ISBN 0-04-336078-5). Allen Unwin.
Wilson, Thomas B. Ontario Marriage Notices. 435p. 1982. lib. bdg. 21.00 (ISBN 0-912606-07-X). Hunterdon Hse.
Wilson, Thomas C., jt. auth. see Shortt, Joseph.
Wilson, Timothy. All Is My Own Dream. LC 82-8690. 600p. 1982. 14.95 (ISBN 0-8362-6609-9). Andrews & McMeel.
Wilson, Tom. It's a Ziggy World. 1975. pap. 1.75 (ISBN 0-451-11968-1, AE1968, Sig). NAL.
--Life Is Just a Bunch of Ziggys... 1975. pap. 1.75 (ISBN 0-451-11992-4, AE1992, Sig). NAL.
--Never Get Too Personally Involved in Your Own Life. Date not set. pap. 1.75 (ISBN 0-451-11984-3, AE1984, Sig). NAL.
--Pets Are Friends You Like Who Like You Right Back. 1978. pap. 1.50 (ISBN 0-451-11578-3, AW1578, Sig). NAL.
--Plants Are Some of My Favorite People. 1978. pap. 1.75 (ISBN 0-451-12161-9, AE2161, Sig). NAL.
--This Book Is for the Birds. 1980. pap. 1.75 (ISBN 0-451-11960-6, AE1960, Sig). NAL.
--Ziggy Faces Life. 1982. pap. 1.75 (ISBN 0-451-11428-0, AE1428, Sig). NAL.
--Ziggy Faces Life...Again! 1982. pap. 1.95 (ISBN 0-451-11790-5, AJ1790, Sig). NAL.
--Ziggy's Big Little Book. (Illus.). 208p. 1983. pap. 3.95 (ISBN 0-8362-1990-2). Andrews & McMeel.
--Ziggy's Gift. LC 82-72413. 62p. (Orig.). (gr. 1up). 1982. pap. 6.95 (ISBN 0-8362-1938-4). Andrews & McMeel.
--Ziggys of the World, Unite! 1977. pap. 1.50 (ISBN 0-451-11271-7, AW1271, Sig). NAL.
Wilson, Tom & Morehead, Loy. New American Crossword Puzzle Dictionary. 1971. pap. 2.95 (ISBN 0-451-11806-5, AE1806, Sig). NAL.
Wilson, Tom, jt. auth. see Winberg, Ellie.
Wilson, Trevor. Great Chicken Dishes of the World. LC 77-25392. (Illus.). 1979. 10.95 o.p. (ISBN 0-07-070754-5, GB). McGraw.
Wilson, Vincent, Jr. Book of Distinguished American Women. (Illus.). 1983. 4.50 (ISBN 0-910086-05-2). Am Hist Res.
Wilson, Vivian. Bibliography of Published Works by Kenneth E. Boulding. 1982. 10.00x (ISBN 0-87081-140-1). Colo Assoc.
Wilson, Walter. Animal Stories. (Illus.). 128p. (gr. 2-6). 1971. pap. 2.95 (ISBN 0-8024-1070-7). Moody.
Wilson, Wilfred J., jt. auth. see Wilson, Doris B.
Wilson, William. Joyce Treiman: Paintings 1961-1972. (Illus.). 28p. 1972. 3.00x (ISBN 0-686-99823-5). La Jolla Mus Contemp Art.
--Microphysical World. 1954. 3.75 o.p. (ISBN 0-8022-1898-9). Philos Lib.
--With Their Whole Strength. LC 80-2084. 128p. (gr. 6 up). 1981. pap. 2.95 (ISBN 0-385-17435-7, Im). Doubleday.
Wilson, William, jt. auth. see Carlsen, Peter.
Wilson, William B. & Nadol, Joseph B., Jr. Quick Reference to Ear, Nose & Throat Disorders. (Illus.). 352p. 1982. pap. text ed. 22.50 (ISBN 0-397-50519-1, Lippincott Medical). Lippincott.
Wilson, William E. Guillen de Castro. (World Authors Ser.: Spain: No. 253). 1973. pap. 15.95 (ISBN 0-8057-2202-5, Twayne). G K Hall.
Wilson, William E., jt. auth. see Garcia-Prada, Carlos.
Wilson, William J. Say When. LC 77-14812. (Emmaus Book). 128p. 1978. pap. 1.95 o.p. (ISBN 0-8091-2074-7). Paulist Pr.
Wilson, William K. & Wilson, Betty L., eds. Directory of Research Grants, 1981. 6th. ed. 368p. 1981. pap. 52.50x o.p. (ISBN 0-912700-92-0). Oryx Pr.
Wilson, William L. A Borderland Confederate. Summers, Festus P., ed. LC 73-7384. (Illus.). 138p. 1973. Repr. of 1962 ed. lib. bdg. 15.00x o.p. (ISBN 0-8371-6930-5, WIBC). Greenwood.
Wilson, William S., tr. from Japanese. Ideals of the Samurai: Writings of Japanese Warriors. LC 82-60937. (Illus., Orig.). 1982. pap. 5.95 (ISBN 0-89750-081-4, 418). Ohara Pubns.
Wilson, Woodrow. A Crossroads of Freedom: Nineteen Twelve Campaign Speeches of Woodrow Wilson. Davidson, Joan W., ed. 1956. text ed. 65.00x (ISBN 0-686-83518-2). Elliots Bks.
Wilson, Woodrow & Wilson, Ellen Axson. The Priceless Gift. McAdoo, Eleanor Wilson, ed. LC 75-3874. (Illus.). 324p. 1975. Repr. of 1962 ed. lib. bdg. 20.50x o.p. (ISBN 0-8371-8095-3, WIPG). Greenwood.
Wilson, Yates. Family Planning on A Crowded Planet. LC 82-24160. 96p. 1983. Repr. of 1971 ed. lib. bdg. 22.50x (ISBN 0-313-22680-6, YAFP). Greenwood.
Wilson, Yvonne M. Kitten Without A Name. (Illus.). 23p. (gr. 1-2). 1982. pap. 1.25 (ISBN 0-686-97302-X). BMA Pr.
Wilson-Barnett, J. & Fordham, Morva. Recovery from Illness. 150p. 1982. 12.50 (ISBN 0-471-10408-6, Pub. by Wiley Med). Wiley.
Wilson-Fulkerson, Roberta, ed. see Abraham, Samuel V

Wilson-Kastner, Patricia. Coherence in a Fragmented World: Jonathan Edwards' Theology of the Holy Spirit. LC 78-62667. 1978. pap. text ed. 7.25 (ISBN 0-8191-0587-2). U Pr of Amer.
Wilson-Kastner, Patricia, et al. A Lost Tradition: Women Writers of the Early Church. LC 80-6290. 210p. (Orig.). 1981. lib. bdg. 19.75 (ISBN 0-8191-1642-4); pap. text ed. 10.75 (ISBN 0-8191-1643-2). U Pr of Amer.
Wilson-Ludlam, Mae R. A Course in Basic Astrology & Its Phraseology. (Illus.). 84p. (Orig.). 1982. pap. 7.95 (ISBN 0-88053-768-X). Macoy Pub.
Wilss, Wolfram. The Science of Translation: Theoretical & Applicative Aspects. (Tubinger Beitrage zur Linguistik: 180). 290p. (Orig.). 1982. pap. 22.00 (ISBN 3-87808-975-9). Benjamins North Am.
Wilstach, Frank J., ed. Dictionary of Similes. 2nd ed. 578p. 1981. Repr. of 1924 ed. 45.00x (ISBN 0-8103-4370-3). Gale.
Wilt, Joy. Handling Your Disagreements. LC 81-24191. (Ready-Set-Grow Ser.). (Illus.). (gr. 3 up). 1982. PLB 10.60g (ISBN 0-516-02511-2). Childrens.
--A Kid's Guide to Managing Money. LC 81-21768. (Ready-Set-Grow Ser.). (Illus.). (gr. 3 up). 1982. PLB 10.60g (ISBN 0-516-02512-0). Childrens.
--A Kid's T V Guide. LC 81-21787. (Ready-Set-Grow Ser.). (Illus.). (gr. 3 up). 1982. PLB 10.60g (ISBN 0-516-02513-9). Childrens.
--Making Up Your Own Mind. LC 81-24190. (Ready-Set-Grow Ser.). (Illus.). (gr. 3 up). 1982. PLB 10.60g (ISBN 0-516-02514-7). Childrens.
--Mine & Yours. LC 81-21794. (Ready-Set-Grow Ser.). (Illus.). (gr. 3 up). 1982. PLB 10.60g (ISBN 0-516-02515-5). Childrens.
--Saying What You Mean. LC 81-21792. (Ready-Set-Grow Ser.). (Illus.). (gr. 3 up). 1982. PLB 10.60g (ISBN 0-516-02516-3). Childrens.
Wilton, Andrew. Turner Abroad: France, Italy, Germany, Switzerland. 208p. 1982. 80.00x (ISBN 0-7141-8047-5, Pub. by Brit Mus Pubns England). State Mutual Bk.
Wilton, George W. Fingerprints: History, Law & Romance. LC 70-164057. 1971. Repr. of 1938 ed. 37.00x (ISBN 0-8103-3755-X). Gale.
Wilton, W. B. A-Z of Business Mathematics. 192p. 1980. pap. 12.50 (ISBN 0-434-92260-9, Pub. by Heinemann). David & Charles.
Wiltse, Charles M., ed. see Webster, Daniel.
Wiltse, David. The Serpent. 320p. 1983. 14.95 (ISBN 0-440-07590-4). Delacorte.
--The Wedding Guest. 1983. pap. 3.50 (ISBN 0-440-19493-8). Dell.
Wiltshire, Peter. Making Television Programmes. (Cambridge Dinosaur Information Ser.). (Illus.). 26p. (gr. 7-10). 1983. pap. 1.50 (ISBN 0-521-27161-4). Cambridge U Pr.
Wilwerding, Walter J. Animal Drawing & Painting. (Illus.). 1966. pap. 5.00 (ISBN 0-486-21716-7). Dover.
Wiman, B., et al. The Physiological Inhibitors of Blood Coagulation & Fibrinolysis. 1979. 61.00 (ISBN 0-444-80092-1, Biomedical Pr). Elsevier.
Wimberly, Lowry C. Folklore in the English & Scottish Ballads. 1965. pap. 4.00 o.p. (ISBN 0-486-21388-9). Dover.
Wimer, Arthur & Brix, Dale. Workbook for Head Writing & News Editing. 4th ed. 230p. 1978. write for info. wire coil o.p. (ISBN 0-697-04328-2). Wm C Brown.
Wimersma, Greidanus Van see Gispen, W. H. & Van Wimersma, Greidanus.
Wimmer, Roger D. & Dominick, Joseph R. Mass Media Research: An Introduction. 416p. 1982. text ed. 22.95x (ISBN 0-534-01228-0). Wadsworth Pub.
Wimsatt, ed. see Boswell, James.
Wimsatt, James I. Chaucer & the Poems of "CH". (Chaucer Studies: No. IX). (Illus.). 144p. 1982. text ed. 47.50x (ISBN 0-8476-7200-X). Rowman.
Wimsatt, W. K., ed. Literary Criticism, Idea & Act: The English Institute, 1939-1972. 1974. 40.00x (ISBN 0-520-02585-7). U of Cal Pr.
Wimsatt, W. K., jt. ed. see Brady, Frank.
Winans, Robert B. A Descriptive Checklist of Book Catalogues Separately Printed in America, 1693-1800. 1981. 35.00 (ISBN 0-912296-47-X, Dist. by U Pr of Va). Am Antiquarian.
Winans, Samuel R. Xenophon: Symposium. 95p. Date not set. Repr. of 1881 ed. 6.00x (ISBN 0-86516-020-1). Bolchazy-Carducci.
Winant, Fran. Looking at Women. (Illus.). 44p. 1980. pap. 2.00 (ISBN 0-686-96916-2). Violet Pr.
Winant, John G. Letter from Grosvenor Square. Repr. of 1947 ed. lib. bdg. 15.00x o.p. (ISBN 0-8371-2563-4, WIGS). Greenwood.
Winawer, Sidney J., et al, eds. Colorectal Cancer: Prevention, Epidemiology, & Screening. (Progress in Cancer Research & Therapy: Vol. 13). 432p. 1980. 52.50 (ISBN 0-89004-447-3). Raven.
Winberg, Ellie & Wilson, Tom. Single Rooms: Stories of an Urban Subculture. 192p. 1981. text ed. 14.50 o.p. (ISBN 0-87073-495-4); pap. text ed. 7.95 (ISBN 0-87073-496-2). Schenkman.
Winbery, Carlton L., jt. auth. see Brooks, James A.
Winborne, Lee W., jt. auth. see Whitwell, W. L.
Winbury, Martin & Abiko, Yasushi, eds. Ischemic Myocardium & Antianginal Drugs. (Perspectives in Cardiovascular Research Ser.: Vol. 3). 272p. 1979. 27.50 (ISBN 0-89004-380-9). Raven.
Winch, D. Adam Smith's Politics. LC 77-82525. (Cambridge Studies in the History & Theory of Politics Ser.). 1978. 34.50 (ISBN 0-521-21827-6); pap. 11.95 (ISBN 0-521-29288-3). Cambridge U Pr.
Winch, D., jt. auth. see Howson, S.
Winch, Peter, ed. Studies in the Philosophy of Wittgenstein. (International Library of Philosophy & Scientific Method). 1969. text ed. 19.00x (ISBN 0-7100-6393-8). Humanities.
Winch, Terence. Total Strangers. LC 82-19278. (Illus.). 20p. (Orig.). 1982. pap. 7.50 (ISBN 0-915124-77-7). Toothpaste.
Winchell, Carol Ann. The Hyperkinetic Child. LC 74-28527. 178p. 1975. lib. bdg. 27.50 (ISBN 0-8371-7813-4, WMC/). Greenwood.
Winchell, H. Optical Properties of Minerals: A Determinative Table. 1964. 24.00 (ISBN 0-12-759150-8). Acad Pr.
Winchell, Mark R. Joan Didion. (United States Authors Ser.). 1980. lib. bdg. 11.95 (ISBN 0-8057-7308-8, Twayne). G K Hall.
Winchester, A. M. Biology & Its Relation to Mankind. 5th ed. 1975. text ed. 15.95x (ISBN 0-442-29534-0); instructor's manual 2.50x (ISBN 0-442-29533-2). Van Nos Reinhold.
--Genetics: A Survey of the Principles of Heredity. 5th ed. LC 76-14001. (Illus.). 1977. text ed. 25.50 (ISBN 0-395-24557-5); instr's. manual & solutions 1.90 (ISBN 0-395-24559-1); 20 transparencies 15.95 (ISBN 0-395-24560-5). HM.
--Human Genetics. 3rd ed. 1979. pap. text ed. 9.95 (ISBN 0-675-08314-1). Merrill.
Winchester, A. M. & Mertens, Thomas R. Human Genetics. 1982. text ed. 16.95 (ISBN 0-675-20008-3). Merrill.
Winchester, Albert. Heredity, Evolution & Humankind. LC 75-45130. (Illus.). 350p. 1976. text ed. 19.95 (ISBN 0-8299-0106-X). West Pub.
Winchester, Albert M. Heredity: An Introduction to Genetics. pap. 4.95 (ISBN 0-06-460167-6, CO 167, COS). B&N NY.
Winchester, Jack. The Solitary Man. 192p. 1980. 10.95 (ISBN 0-698-11034-X, Coward). Putnam Pub Group.
Winchester, James H. Hurricanes, Storms, Tornadoes. (Science Survey Ser.). (Illus.). (gr. 6 up). 1968. PLB 5.49 o.p. (ISBN 0-399-60272-0). Putnam Pub Group.
Winchester, Kenneth & Dunbar, David. Walking Tours of New England. LC 79-7884. (Illus., Orig.). 1980. pap. 8.95 o.p. (ISBN 0-385-15296-5, Dolp). Doubleday.
Winchester, Linda. Fun Animals. (How to Draw Ser.: No. 2151). (Illus.). 48p. (gr. 2-5). 1983. pap. 0.99 (ISBN 0-307-20151-1). Western Pub.
Winchester, Mark B., ed. The International Essays for Business Decision Makers 1977. 247p. 1977. Vol. 1 1976. pap. 7.95 o.p. (ISBN 0-87201-268-9); Vol. 2 1977. pap. 7.95 (ISBN 0-87201-269-7). Gulf Pub.
Winchester, Otis, jt. auth. see Weathers, Winston.
Winchester, Simon. American Heartbeat: Some Notes from a Midwestern Journey. 202p. 1976. 12.50 o.p. (ISBN 0-571-10878-4). Transatlantic.
--Northern Ireland in Crisis: Reporting the Ulster Troubles. LC 74-84649. 250p. 1975. 22.50x (ISBN 0-8419-0180-5). Holmes & Meier.
--Their Noble Lordships. 1982. 14.50 (ISBN 0-394-52418-7). Random.
Winckel, Fritz. Music, Sound & Sensation: A Modern Exposition. Binkley, Thomas, tr. (Illus.). 1967. pap. text ed. 4.50 (ISBN 0-486-21764-7). Dover.
Winckler, Paul A., ed. History of Books & Printing: A Guide to Information Sources. LC 79-13006. (Books, Publishing & Libraries Information Guide: Vol. 2). 1979. 42.00x (ISBN 0-8103-1408-8). Gale.
Wincor, R. Copyright, Patents & Trademarks. LC 80-17681. (Legal Almanac Ser.: No. 14). 1980. 5.95 (ISBN 0-379-11138-1). Oceana.
Wincor, Richard. Contracts in Plain English. 128p. 1975. 22.95 o.p. (ISBN 0-07-070966-1, P&RB). McGraw.
--Literary Property: A Guide to Business Practices in the Communications Industry. 1967. 5.00 o.p. (ISBN 0-517-50739-0, C N Potter Bks). Crown.
Wind, Betty, jt. auth. see Forell, Betty.
Wind, Betty, jt. auth. see Latourette, Jane.
Wind, Betty, jt. auth. see Warren, Mary P.
Wind, Edgar. The Eloquence of Symbols: Studies in Humanist Art. Anderson, Jaynie, ed. (Illus.). 1982. 39.00x (ISBN 0-19-817341-5). Oxford U Pr.
--Pagan Mysteries in the Renaissance. (Illus.). 1958. text ed. 49.50x (ISBN 0-686-83672-3). Elliots Bks.
Wind, Gary & Rich, Norman. Principles of Surgical Technique: The Art of Surgery. LC 82-17451. (Illus.). 240p. 1982. pap. text ed. 29.50 (ISBN 0-8067-2160-X). Urban & S.
Wind, Herbert W., jt. auth. see Nicklaus, Jack.
Wind, Yoram, et al. New-Product Forecasting: Models & Applications. LC 80-8388. 576p. 1981. 35.95x (ISBN 0-669-04102-5). Lexington Bks.
Wind, Yoram J. Product Policy: Concepts, Methods & Strategies. 1981. text ed. 29.95 (ISBN 0-201-08343-4). A-W.
Windal, Floyd & Corley, Robert. The Accounting Professional: Ethics, Responsibility, & Liability. (Illus.). 1980. text ed. 25.95 (ISBN 0-13-003020-1). P-H.
Windeknecht, Margaret. Creative Overshot. (Shuttlecraft Guild Monograph: Vol. 31). (Illus.). 1978. pap. 8.45 (ISBN 0-916658-34-1). HTH Pubs.
Windeknecht, Margaret B. Creative Monk's Belt. LC 77-57344. (Shuttle Craft Guild Monograph: No. 30). (Illus.). 40p. 1977. pap. 7.95 (ISBN 0-916658-33-3). HTH Pubs.
Windeknect, Thomas G. General Dynamical Processes: A Mathematical Introduction. (Mathematics in Science & Engineering Ser). 1971. 36.50 (ISBN 0-12-759550-3). Acad Pr.
Windeler, Robert. Julie Andrews. (Illus.). 224p. 1983. 10.95 (ISBN 0-312-44848-1). St Martin.
Winden, Hans-Willi. Wie Kam und Wie Kommt Es Zum Osterglauben? 352p. (Ger.). 1982. write for info. (ISBN 3-8204-5820-4). P Lang Pubs.
Windham, Donald. Footnote to a Friendship: A Memoir of Truman Capote & Others. (Illus.). 1983. wrappers, ltd. ed. 25.00x (ISBN 0-917366-06-9). S Campbell.
--Stone in the Hourglass. 1981. wrappers, ltd. ed. 15.00x (ISBN 0-917366-05-0). S Campbell.
--Tanaquil: The Hardest Thing of All. (Illus.). 1972. wrappers, ltd. ed. 75.00x (ISBN 0-917366-02-6). S Campbell.
Windham, Donald, ed. see Williams, Tennessee.
Windham, Douglas & Bidwell, Charles, eds. Issues in Macroanalysis. (Analysis of Educational Productivity Ser.: Vol. 2). 280p. 1980. prof ref 22.50x (ISBN 0-88410-192-4). Ballinger Pub.
Windham, Kathryn T. The Ghost in the Sloss Furnaces. (Illus.). 24p. 1978. pap. 3.00 (ISBN 0-686-36927-0). Birmingham Hist Soc.
Windhorn, Stan & Langley, Wright. Yesterday's Florida Keys. (Seemann's Historic Cities Ser.: No. 12). (Illus.). 128p. 1982. pap. 9.95 (ISBN 0-911607-00-5). Langley Pr.
--Yesterday's Key West: Seemann's Historic Cities Ser. LC 73-80596. (No. 4). (Illus.). 144p. 1983. Repr. of 1973 ed. pap. price not set (ISBN 0-911607-01-3). Langley Pr.
Winding, jt. auth. see Mourier.
Windish, David F. Tax-Advantaged Investments. 416p. 1983. 35.00 (ISBN 0-13-884841-6). NY Inst Finance.
Windle, Joy, ed. see Zinkhon, Robert W.
Windle, William F. Textbook of Histology. 5th ed. 1976. text ed. 18.95 o.p. (ISBN 0-07-070977-7, C). McGraw.
Windley, B. F. & Nagvi, S. M. Archaean Geochemistry. (Proceedings). 1978. 66.00 (ISBN 0-444-41718-4). Elsevier.
Windley, B. F., ed. The Early History of the Earth: Based on the Proceedings of a NATO Advanced Study Institute Held at the University of Leicester 5-11 April 1975. LC 75-26610. 567p. 1976. 129.95x (ISBN 0-471-01488-5, Pub. by Wiley-Interscience). Wiley.
Windley, Brian F. The Evolving Continents. LC 76-56416. 1977. 64.95x (ISBN 0-471-99475-8); pap. 24.95 (ISBN 0-471-99476-6, Pub. by Wiley-Interscience). Wiley.
Windling, Terri & Arnold, Mark A. Elsewhere, Vol. II. 384p. 1982. pap. 2.95 (ISBN 0-441-20404-X, Pub. by Ace Science Fiction). Ace Bks.
Windling, Terry & Arnold, Mark, eds. Elsewhere, Vol. I. 384p. (Orig.). 1982. pap. 2.75 (ISBN 0-441-20403-1, Pub. by Ace Science Fiction). Ace Bks.
Windmueller, Ida, jt. auth. see Horowitz, Inge.
Windmueller, Ida, tr. see Horowitz, Inge & Windmueller, Ida.
Windmuller, John P. & Lambert, Richard D., eds. Industrial Democracy in International Perspective. LC 76-62834. (Annals Ser.: No. 431). 1977. 7.50 o.p. (ISBN 0-87761-214-5); pap. 7.95 (ISBN 0-87761-215-3). Am Acad Pol Soc Sci.
Window, A. L. & Holister, G. S. Strain Gauge Technology. (Illus.). x, 356p. 1982. 78.00 (ISBN 0-85334-118-4, Pub. by Applied Sci England). Elsevier.
Windrow, Martin. Rommel's Desert Army. (Men-at-Arms Ser.). (Illus.). 40p. 1976. pap. 7.95 o.p. (ISBN 0-85045-095-0). Hippocrene Bks.
--Waffen SS. LC 73-83334. (Men-at-Arms Ser). (Illus.). 40p. 1973. pap. 7.95 o.p. (ISBN 0-88254-169-2). Hippocrene Bks.
Windschuttle, Elizabeth. Women, Class & History: Feminist Perspectives on Australia 1788-1978. 604p. 1982. pap. 13.95 (ISBN 0-00-635722-9, Pub. by W Collins Australia). Intl Schol Bk Serv.
Windsor, A. T., ed. Using the ICL Data Dictionary: Proceedings of the User Group. 153p. 1980. pap. write for info (ISBN 0-906812-06-2, Pub. by Shiva Pub England). Imprint Edns.
Windsor, Duane. Fiscal Zoning in Suburban Communities. LC 78-20632. (Illus.). 208p. 1979. 21.95 o.p. (ISBN 0-669-02751-0). Lexington Bks.
Windsor, Patricia. Killing Time. (YA) (gr. 7-12). 1983. pap. 2.25 (ISBN 0-440-94471-6, LFL). Dell.
--Mad Martin. LC 76-3837. (gr. 5 up). 1976. 7.95 o.p. (ISBN 0-06-026517-5, HarpJ); PLB 9.89 (ISBN 0-06-026518-3). Har-Row.
--Something's Waiting for You, Baker D. LC 74-3588. (Story of Suspense Ser). 224p. (gr. 7-12). 1974. PLB 10.89 (ISBN 0-06-026524-8, HarpJ). Har-Row.
Windt, Peter Y. An Introduction to Philosophy: Ideas in Conflict. 644p. 1982. text ed. 18.50 (ISBN 0-8299-0421-2). West Pub.
Windt, Theodore O. & Ingold, Beth. Essays in Presidential Rhetoric. 352p. 1982. pap. text ed. 15.95 (ISBN 0-8403-2865-6). Kendall-Hunt.
Wine Advisory Board. Gourmet Wine Cooking the Easy Way. 3rd ed. Wilcox, David R., ed. (Illus.). 1980. 5.95 (ISBN 0-932664-01-6). Wine Appreciation.
Wine, Martin, ed. Drama of the English Renaissance. (Orig.). 1969. pap. 7.95x (ISBN 0-394-30866-2, T101, Mod LibC). Modern Lib.
Wine, Sherwin T. Humanistic Judaism. LC 77-90496. (Library of Liberal Religion). 123p. 1978. 12.95 o.p. (ISBN 0-87975-102-9). Prometheus Bks.
Winecoff, Larry & Powell, Conrad. Focus: Seven Steps to Educational Problem Solving: a Systematic Planning Guide. rev. ed. 1979. pap. 7.50 (ISBN 0-87812-087-4). Pendell Pub.
Winefield, Helen R. & Peay, Marilyn. Behavioral Science in Medicine. 368p. 1980. pap. text ed. 19.95 (ISBN 0-8391-4108-4). Univ Park.
Winefordner, J. D., ed. Trace Analysis: Spectroscopic Methods for Elements. LC 75-41460. (Chemical Analysis Ser.: Vol. 46). 1976. 62.50x (ISBN 0-471-95401-2, Pub. by Wiley-Interscience). Wiley.
Winegarten, Renee. The Double Life of George Sand: Woman & Writer. LC 78-54501. 1978. 15.00 o.s.i. (ISBN 0-465-01683-9). Basic.
Winegartner, E. C., ed. Coal Fouling & Slagging Parameters. 34p. 1974. 6.50 o.p. (ISBN 0-685-48048-8, H00086). ASME.
Wineinger, Tom, jt. auth. see Rolland, Alvin E.
Winer, B. J. Statistical Principles in Experimental Design. 2nd ed. (Psychology Ser.). text ed. 43.00 (ISBN 0-07-070981-5, C). McGraw.
Winer, Marc S., jt. auth. see Simmons, Seymour.
Wines, Enoch C. State of Prisons & of Child-Saving Institutions in the Civilized World. LC 68-55784. (Criminology, Law Enforcement, & Social Problems Ser.: No. 24). 1968. Repr. of 1880 ed. 20.00x (ISBN 0-87585-024-3). Patterson Smith.
Wines, Frederick H. Punishment & Reformation. (Historical Foundations of Forensic Psychiatry & Psychology Ser.). xii, 481p. 1983. Repr. of 1919 ed. lib. bdg. 45.00 (ISBN 0-306-76184-X). Da Capo.
Wines, W. F. Foods, Fads & Foolishness. rev. ed. 165p. 1982. pap. 5.95 (ISBN 0-911579-00-1). Fleur-Di-Lee.
Winetrout, Kenneth. Arnold J. Toynbee. (World Leaders Ser.: No. 47). 1975. lib. bdg. 10.95 o.p. (ISBN 0-8057-3725-1, Twayne). G K Hall.
Winez, Yvonne. Pocketful of Puppets: Three Plump Fish & Other Short Stories. Keller, Merily H., ed. (Puppetry in Education Ser.). (Illus.). 48p. (Orig.). 1982. pap. 5.50 (ISBN 0-931044-08-1). Renfro Studios.
Wing, A. J., et al. The Renal Unit. 2nd ed. 1981. pap. 15.95 o.p. (ISBN 0-471-08914-1, Pub. by Wiley Med). Wiley.
Wing & Sons New York. The Book of Complete Information about Pianos: 1918 - 1920. (Keyboard Studies: Vol. 6). (Illus.). 140p. 75.00 o.s.i. (ISBN 90-6027-370-2, Pub. by Frits Knuf Netherlands). Pendragon NY.
Wing, Gerri. The Awakening. 1979. 5.50 o.p. (ISBN 0-533-02839-6). Vantage.
Wing, J. H., ed. see International Symposium, Mannheim, 26-29 of July, 1972.
Wing, J. K. Reasoning about Madness. 1978. 13.95x (ISBN 0-19-217662-5). Oxford U Pr.
Wing, J. K. & Brown, G. W. Institutionalism & Schizophrenia. LC 75-118068. (Illus.). 1970. 39.50 (ISBN 0-521-07882-2). Cambridge U Pr.
Wing, J. K. & Morris, Brenda, eds. Handbook of Psychiatric Rehabilitation Practice. 1981. pap. text ed. 15.95x (ISBN 0-19-261276-X). Oxford U Pr.
Wing, J. K. & Olsen, Rolf, eds. Community Care for the Mentally Disabled. (Illus.). 1979. pap. text ed. 16.95x (ISBN 0-19-261146-1). Oxford U Pr.
Wing, J. K. & Wing, Lorna, eds. Psychoses of Uncertain Aetiology. LC 81-17092. (Handbook of Psychiatry: Vol. 3). (Illus.). 1982. 49.50 (ISBN 0-521-24101-4); pap. 19.95 (ISBN 0-521-28438-4). Cambridge U Pr.
Wing, J. K., et al. Measurement & Classification of Psychiatric Symptoms. LC 73-89008. (Illus.). 224p. 1974. 27.95 (ISBN 0-521-20382-1). Cambridge U Pr.
Wing, John, jt. auth. see Leech, John.
Wing, Lorna, jt. ed. see Wing, J. K.
Wing, Marge. How to Paint on Fabrics: Freehand Tracing, Stamping, & Stencil Methods for Beginner & Advanced Craftsman. 1977. 6.95 o.p. (ISBN 0-517-52663-8); pap. 4.95 o.p. (ISBN 0-517-52664-6). Crown.
Wing, Omar. Circuit Theory with Computer Methods. (Illus.). 1978. text ed. 32.95 (ISBN 0-07-070987-4, C). McGraw.
Wingard, Lemual B., Jr., et al. Applied Biochemistry & Bioengineering: Enzyme Technology, Vol. 2. (Serial Publication). 1979. 42.50 (ISBN 0-12-041102-4); lib ed 57.00 (ISBN 0-12-041172-5); microfiche 34.50 (ISBN 0-12-041173-3). Acad Pr.
Wingard, Lemuel B., Jr., ed. Applied Biochemistry & Bioengineering, Vol.1. 1976. 55.00 (ISBN 0-12-041101-6); lib. ed. 74.50 (ISBN 0-12-041170-9); 47.50 (ISBN 0-12-041171-7). Acad Pr.
Wingate, Isabel. Textile Fabrics & Their Selection. 7th ed. 1976. 24.95 (ISBN 0-13-912840-9). P-H.

Wingate, Isabel B., et al. Know Your Merchandise. 3rd ed. 1964. text ed. 14.96 o.p. (ISBN 0-07-070990-4, G). McGraw.
--Know Your Merchandise: For Retailers & Consumers. 4th ed. (Illus.). 544p. 1975. text ed. 20.70 (ISBN 0-07-070985-8, G); tchr's ed. 4.95 (ISBN 0-07-070986-6). McGraw.
Wingate, John. Avalanche. LC 76-54635. 1977. 7.95 o.p. (ISBN 0-312-06247-8). St Martin.
Wingate, John W., et al. Retail Merchandise Management. LC 73-168617. (Illus.). 1972. ref. ed. 23.95 (ISBN 0-13-778753-7). P-H.
--Problems in Retail Merchandising. 6th ed. (Illus.). 336p. 1973. pap. text ed. 14.95 (ISBN 0-13-720680-1). P-H.
Wingate, Martin B. Management for Physicians. 1983. pap. text ed. write for info. (ISBN 0-87488-246-X). Med Exam.
Wingate, P. J. Bandages of Soft Illusion. 98p. pap. 8.75 (ISBN 0-686-36794-4). Md Hist.
--H. L. Mencken's Un-Neglected Anniversary. 73p. 1980. pap. 6.00 (ISBN 0-686-36712-X). Md Hist.
Wingate, Phillip J. H. L. Mencken's Un-Neglected Anniversary. LC 79-91602. 80p. 1980. 6.00 (ISBN 0-935968-07-5). EPM Pubns.
Wingate, Richard. Lost Outpost of Atlantis. LC 78-74584. (Illus.). 1980. 12.95 o.p. (ISBN 0-89696-048-X, An Everest House Book). Dodd.
Wingate, Ronald. Wingate of the Sudan. LC 74-22507. (Illus.). 274p. 1975. Repr. of 1955 ed. lib. bdg. 19.25x (ISBN 0-8371-7862-2, WIWS). Greenwood.
Wingate, William. Crystal. 336p. 1983. 13.95 (ISBN 0-312-17819-0). St Martin.
--Fireplay. 1977. 8.95 o.p. (ISBN 0-698-10846-9, Coward). Putnam Pub Group.
Winger. Mecanografia Gregg Segundo Curso. 98p. 1982. 7.65 (ISBN 0-07-071081-3, G). McGraw.
Winger, F. E. & Weaver, D. H. Gregg Tailored Timings: Electric Typewriter, Edition. 1971. text ed. 6.52 (ISBN 0-07-070999-8, G). McGraw.
--Gregg Tailored Timings: Manual Typewriter Edition. 1971. text ed. 6.52 (ISBN 0-07-070998-X, G). McGraw.
Winger, Fred E., et al. Gregg Typing: Refresher-Advanced Course. (Illus.). 1979. 14.20 (ISBN 0-07-071006-6, G); inst. manual & key 5.95 (ISBN 0-07-071007-4). McGraw.
--Gregg Typing Text-Kit Basic Course. (Illus.). 1979. text ed. 14.20 (ISBN 0-07-071005-8, G); inst. manual & key 5.95 (ISBN 0-07-071007-4). McGraw.
Winger, Virginia, jt. auth. see Camblos, Ruth.
Winget, Lynn W., jt. auth. see Saviano, Eugene.
Winget, Lynn W., ed. see Alfonso X.
Wingfield, Arthur & Byrnes, Dennis L. The Psychology of the Human Memory. 429p. 1981. pap. 15.25 (ISBN 0-12-759650-X). Acad Pr.
Wingfield, Sheila. Admissions: Poems Nineteen Seventy-Four to Nineteen Seventy-Seven. 1977. text ed. 13.00x o.p. (ISBN 0-85105-334-3, Dolmen Pr). Humanities.
--Collected Poems, 1938-1982. 1983. 17.50 (ISBN 0-8090-3535-9); pap. 11.50 (ISBN 0-8090-1500-5). Hill & Wang.
--Her Storms: Selected Poems 1938-1977. 1977. text ed. 19.50x o.p. (ISBN 0-85105-335-1, Dolmen Pr). Humanities.
Wing-hung Lam. Chinese Theology in Construction. LC 81-15483. 320p. 1983. pap. 11.95x (ISBN 0-87808-180-1). William Carey Lib.
Wingler, Hans. Bauhaus: Weimar, Dessau, Berlin, Chicago. (Illus.). 1969. 125.00 (ISBN 0-262-23033-X); pap. 25.00 (ISBN 0-262-73047-2). MIT Pr.
Wingo, Bruce. Georgia in American Society. 1982. 14.95 (ISBN 0-932298-38-9). Copple Hse.
Wingo, G. Max, jt. auth. see Morse, William C.
Wingo, Max G. Philosophies of American Education. 1974. text ed. 18.95 (ISBN 0-669-84400-4). Heath.
Wingrave, Helen & Harrold, Robert. Spanish Dancing. (Illus., Orig.). 1978. pap. 2.95 o.p. (ISBN 0-8467-0449-8, Pub. by Two Continents). Hippocrene Bks.
Wingren, Roy M., jt. auth. see Faires, Virgil M.
Wingrove & Caret. Quimica Organica. (Span.). 1983. pap. text ed. price not set (ISBN 0-06-319450-3, Pub. by HarLA Mexico). Har-Row.
Wingrove, Alan S. & Caret, Robert L. Organic Chemistry. 1334p. 1981. text ed. 37.95scp (ISBN 0-06-163400-X, HarpC); scp study guide & answer bk. 16.50 (ISBN 0-06-163413-1). Har-Row.
Wingrove, C. Ray, jt. auth. see Rooke, M. Leigh.
Wingrove, C. Ray, jt. ed. see Barry, John R.
Wing-tsit, Chan, jt. ed. see Wei-Hsun Fu, Charles.
Wing-Tsit Chan, jt. tr. see Rump, Ariane.
Winick, M. Nutrition & the Killer Diseases. LC 81-3317. (Current Concepts in Nutrition Ser.: Vol. 10). 191p. 1981. 40.95x (ISBN 0-471-09130-8, Pub. by Wiley-Interscience). Wiley.
--Nutrition in Health & Disease. 261p. 1980. text ed. 24.95x (ISBN 0-471-05713-4, Pub. by Wiley-Interscience). Wiley.
Winick, Myron. Adolescent Nutrition. LC 81-19748. (Current Concepts in Nutrition Ser.). 188p. 1982. text ed. 40.00x (ISBN 0-471-86543-5, Pub. by Wiley-Interscience). Wiley.
--Growing up Healthy: A Parent's Guide to Good Nutrition. 256p. 1983. pap. 2.95 (ISBN 0-425-05869-7). Berkley Pub.
--Hunger Disease: Studies by the Jewish Physicians in the Warsaw Ghetto. LC 78-26397. (Current Concepts in Nutrition Ser.: Vol. 7). 1979. 34.50x (ISBN 0-471-05003-2, Pub. by Wiley-Interscience). Wiley.
--Malnutrition & Brain Development. (Illus.). 1976. text ed. 18.95x (ISBN 0-19-501983-0). Oxford U Pr.
--Nutrition & Cancer. LC 77-22650. (Current Concepts in Nutrition: Vol. 6). 1977. 42.95x (ISBN 0-471-03394-4, Pub. by Wiley-Interscience). Wiley.
--Nutrition & Gastroenterology. LC 80-16169. (Current Concepts in Nutrition Ser.: Vol. 9). 221p. 1980. 46.50x (ISBN 0-471-08173-6, Pub. by Wiley Interscience). Wiley.
--Nutritional Disorders of American Women. LC 76-54393. (Current Concepts in Nutrition Ser.: Vol. 5). 1977. 29.95x o.p. (ISBN 0-471-02393-0, Pub. by Wiley-Interscience). Wiley.
Winick, Myron, ed. Nutrition & Aging. LC 75-34225. (Current Concepts in Nutrition: Vol. 4). 192p. 1976. 31.50x o.p. (ISBN 0-471-95432-2, Pub. by Wiley-Interscience). Wiley.
--Nutritional Management of Genetic Disorders, Vol. 8. LC 79-16192. (Current Concepts in Nutrition Ser.). 1979. 45.95x (ISBN 0-471-05781-9, Pub. by Wiley-Interscience). Wiley.
Winickoff, Richard N., jt. auth. see Komaroff, Anthony L.
Winifred, Robins. Gold Country Renaissance. LC 81-21743. (Illus.). 144p. (Orig.). 1983. pap. 6.95 (ISBN 0-87701-175-3). Chronicle Bks.
Winikoff, Beverly, ed. Nutrition & National Policy. (Illus.). 1978. text ed. 30.00x (ISBN 0-262-23087-9). MIT Pr.
Winitz. Articulatory Acquisition & Behavior. 1969. text ed. 24.95 (ISBN 0-13-049320-1). P-H.
Winitz, H. Phonetics: A Manual for Listening. 64p. 1979. pap. text ed. 9.95 (ISBN 0-8391-0822-2). Univ Park.
Winitz, Harris. From Syllable to Conversation. (Illus.). 136p. 1976. pap. 12.95 (ISBN 0-8391-0821-4). Univ Park.
Winitz, Harris, ed. The Learnables, Bk. 5. 48p. (Orig.). 1981. pap. 5.00x (ISBN 0-939990-05-9); used with 5 cassettes in English & German 30.00 (ISBN 0-686-30274-5). Intl Linguistics.
--The Learnables, Bk. 6. 48p. (Orig.). 1981. pap. 5.00x (ISBN 0-939990-06-7); used with 5 cassettes in English & German 30.00 (ISBN 0-686-30275-3). Intl Linguistics.
--The Learnables, Bk. 7. 48p. (Orig.). 1981. pap. 5.00x (ISBN 0-939990-07-5); used with 5 cassettes in English & German 30.00 (ISBN 0-686-30273-7). Intl Linguistics.
--The Learnables, Bk. 8. 48p. (Orig.). 1981. pap. 5.00x (ISBN 0-939990-08-3); used with 5 cassettes in English & German 30.00 (ISBN 0-686-30272-9). Intl Linguistics.
--Treating Articulation Disorders: For Clinicians by Clinicians. 1983. pap. text ed. price not set (ISBN 0-8391-1814-7, 17833). Univ Park.
--Treating Language Disorders: For Clinicians by Clinicians. 1983. pap. text ed. price not set (ISBN 0-8391-1813-9, 19674). Univ Park.
Winitz, M., jt. auth. see Greenstein, Jesus P.
Winjum, James, jt. auth. see Mautz, R. K.
Wink, John. Haunting the Winerunner. (Illus.). 76p. (Orig.). 1982. pap. 5.95 (ISBN 0-941780-14-7). Parkhurst-Little.
Wink, Richard. Fundamentals of Music. LC 76-20867. (Illus.). 1977. text ed. 18.50 (ISBN 0-395-20598-0); cassette 7.00 (ISBN 0-395-25049-8). HM.
Wink, Richard L. & Williams, Lois. Invitation to Listening. 2nd ed. LC 75-31007. (Illus.). 352p. 1976. text ed. 18.50 (ISBN 0-395-18651-X); instr's. manual 1.35 (ISBN 0-395-18778-8); 6 LP records 22.95 (ISBN 0-395-19372-9). HM.
Winkel, ed. Elementary School Library Collection. 12th ed. LC 79-10366. 1979. 38.95 o.p. (ISBN 0-910654-11-2). Bro-Dart Found.
Winkelman, Marian F. Sprigs of Truth. 1983. 6.50 (ISBN 0-533-05372-2). Vantage.
Winkelstein, Alan, jt. auth. see Boggs, Dane R.
Winkfield, Trevor, tr. see Roussel, Raymond.
Winkle, Carl, jt. auth. see Marier, Donald.
Winkle, Gary M., jt. auth. see Cook, John W.
Winkle, Matthew Van see Van Winkle, Matthew.
Winkle, Van see Heyne & Van Winkle.
Winkleman, Gretchen, jt. auth. see Howie, Patricia A.
Winkler, jt. auth. see McCuen.
Winkler, Alice. Let's Bake Bread. LC 72-13341. (Early Craft Bks). (Illus.). 36p. (gr. 1-4). 1973. PLB 3.95g (ISBN 0-8225-0856-7). Lerner Pubns.
Winkler, Anthony & McCuen, Jo Ray. Writing Sentences, Paragraphs, & Essays. 256p. 1980. pap. text ed. 10.95 (ISBN 0-574-22060-7, 13-5060); instr's. guide avail. (ISBN 0-574-22061-5, 13-5061). SRA.
Winkler, Anthony C. Poetry As System. 1971. pap. 7.95x o.p. (ISBN 0-673-07606-7). Scott F.
Winkler, Anthony C. & McCuen, Jo R. Rhetoric Made Plain. 3rd ed. 458p. 1981. text ed. 13.95 (ISBN 0-15-577077-2, HC); 1.95 (ISBN 0-15-577078-0). HarBraceJ.
Winkler, Anthony C., jt. auth. see McCuen, JoRay.
Winkler, Carl A., jt. auth. see Wright, A. Nelson.
Winkler, Connie. The Computer Careers Handbook. LC 82-18460. (Illus.). 176p. 1983. lib. bdg. 12.95 (ISBN 0-668-05528-6); pap. 7.95 (ISBN 0-668-05530-8). Arco.
Winkler, David W., ed. An Ecological Study of Mono Lake, California. (Illus.). 190p. 1977. pap. 7.50 (ISBN 0-939714-00-0). Mono Basin Res.
Winkler, E. M. Stone, Properties, Durability in Man's Environment. LC 72-8059. (Applied Mineralogy Ser.: Vol. 4). (Illus.). 230p. 1973. 53.70 (ISBN 0-387-81313-6). Springer-Verlag.
Winkler, Gabriele. Prayer Attitude in the Eastern Church. 1978. pap. 1.45 (ISBN 0-937032-01-8). Light&Life Pub Co MN.
Winkler, H. G. Petrogenesis of Metamorphic Rocks. 4th ed. LC 76-3443. 1976. pap. 6.80 (ISBN 0-387-90413-1). Springer-Verlag.
Winkler, John. Bargaining for Results. 1981. pap. 22.50 (ISBN 0-434-92350-8, Pub. by Heinemann). David & Charles.
Winkler, John K. Farm Animal Health & Disease Control. 2nd ed. LC 81-18656. (Illus.). 230p. 1982. text ed. 21.00 (ISBN 0-8121-0843-4). Lea & Febiger.
Winkler, Kenneth, ed. & intro. by see Berkeley, George.
Winkler, Kenneth D. Pilgrim of the Clear Light: The Biography of Dr. Walter Y. Evans-Wentz. Lama A., intro. by. LC 81-70193. (Illus.). 140p. (Orig.). 1982. pap. 4.95 (ISBN 0-942058-00-3). Dawnfire.
Winkler, O., ed. Vacuum Metallurgy. Bakish, R. LC 74-118258. (Illus.). 906p. 1971. 170.25 (ISBN 0-444-40857-6). Elsevier.
Winkler, Paul, jt. ed. see Gorman, Michael.
Winkler, Ruthild, jt. auth. see Eigen, Manfred.
Winkles, N. B., Jr. Gambling Times Guide to Craps. (Gambling Times on Gambling Games Ser.). (Illus.). 156p. (Orig.). 1983. pap. text ed. 5.95 (ISBN 0-89746-013-8). Lyle Stuart.
Winkless, Nels. Making the Computer Disappear. 300p. 1983. pap. write for info. (ISBN 0-918398-79-7). Dilithium Pr.
Winks, H. L. & Winks, Robin W. The St. Lawrence. LC 80-50937. (Rivers of the World Ser.). PLB 12.68 (ISBN 0-382-06368-6). Silver.
Winks, Honor L. The Colorado. LC 80-52504. (Rivers of the World Ser.). PLB 12.68 (ISBN 0-382-06372-4). Silver.
Winks, Robin W. An American's Guide to Britain. rev. ed. (Illus.). 464p. 1983. 14.95 (ISBN 0-686-83849-1, ScribT). Scribner.
--Western Civilization: A Brief History. (Illus.). 1979. pap. text ed. 19.95 (ISBN 0-13-951400-7). P-H.
Winks, Robin W., jt. auth. see Winks, H. L.
Winks, Robin W., ed. Historian As Detective: Essays on Evidence. 1970. pap. 7.50xi (ISBN 0-06-131933-3, TB1933, Torch). Har-Row.
--Historiography of the British Empire-Commonwealth. LC 66-15555. 1966. 25.00 o.p. (ISBN 0-8223-0193-8). Duke.
--Other Voices, Other Views: An International Collection of Essays from the Bicentennial. LC 77-84751. (Contributions in American Studies: No. 34). 1978. lib. bdg. 29.95 (ISBN 0-8371-9844-5, WAO/). Greenwood.
Winloch, A. J. Developments in Adhesives, Vol. 2. (Applied Science Ser.). 1981. 74.00 (ISBN 0-85334-958-4). Elsevier.
Winlund, et al. Chart Guide Mexico West. (Illus.). 74p. (Orig.). 1983. pap. 44.00 (ISBN 0-938206-05-2). ChartGuide.
Winlund, Edmond. Chart Guide for Catalina Island 1982-1983. rev. ed. (Illus.). 16p. (Orig.). 1982. pap. 5.00 (ISBN 0-938206-06-0). ChartGuide.
Winn, Charles S. Careers in Focus Program Guide. 1975. 9.95 (ISBN 0-07-071067-8, G). McGraw.
Winn, Charles S. & Baker, M. C. Exploring Occupations in Food Service & Home Economics. (Careers in Focus Ser.). 1975. text ed. 8.96 (ISBN 0-07-071041-4, G); tchr's manual & key 4.00 (ISBN 0-07-071042-2); wksheet bklet 8.96 (ISBN 0-07-071063-5). McGraw.
Winn, Charles S. & Davis, L. M. Exploring Occupations in Science, Fine Arts & Humanities. (Careers in Focus Ser.). 1975. text ed. 8.96 (ISBN 0-07-071045-7, G); tchr's. manual & key 4.00 (ISBN 0-07-071046-5); wkshts. 10.96 (ISBN 0-07-071065-1). McGraw.
Winn, Charles S. & Healy, C. Discovering You. (Careers in Focus Ser.). 1975. text ed. 8.96 (ISBN 0-07-071051-1, G); tchr's. manual & key 4.00 (ISBN 0-07-071052-X); wksheet bklets 17.96 (ISBN 0-07-071066-X). McGraw.
Winn, Charles S. & Heath, L. Exploring Occupations in Electricity & Electronics. (Careers in Focus Ser.). 1975. text ed. 8.96 (ISBN 0-07-071025-2, G); tchr's manual & key 4.00 (ISBN 0-07-071026-0); worksheets 5.96 (ISBN 0-07-071055-4). McGraw.
Winn, Charles S. & Peterson, M. Exploring Business & Office Occupations. (Careers in Focus Ser.). 1976. text ed. 8.96 (ISBN 0-07-071037-6, G); tchr's. manual & key 4.00 (ISBN 0-07-071038-4); pkg. of 10 wksheet bklets 17.96 (ISBN 0-07-071061-9). McGraw.
Winn, Charles S. & Vorndran, B. J. Exploring Occupations in Personal Services, Hospitality & Recreation. (Careers in Focus Ser.). 1975. text ed. 8.96 (ISBN 0-07-071033-3, G); tchr's manual & key 4.00 (ISBN 0-07-071034-1); pkg. of 10 wksheet bklets 17.96 (ISBN 0-07-071059-7). McGraw.
Winn, Charles S. & Walsh, L. A. Exploring Transportation Occupations. (Careers in Focus Ser.). 1976. text ed. 8.96 (ISBN 0-07-071023-6, G); tchr's. manual & key 4.00 (ISBN 0-07-071024-4); wksheet booklet 17.96 (ISBN 0-07-071054-6). McGraw.
Winn, Charles S., et al. Exploring Health Occupations. (Careers in Focus Ser.). 1976. text ed. 8.96 (ISBN 0-07-071027-9, G); tchr's. manual & key 4.00 (ISBN 0-07-071028-7); worksheets 5.96 (ISBN 0-07-071056-2). McGraw.
--Exploring Occupations in Agribusiness & Natural Resources. (Careers in Focus Ser.). 1975. pap. text ed. 8.96 (ISBN 0-07-071043-0, G); tchr's. manual & key 4.00 (ISBN 0-07-071044-9); worksheets 17.96 (ISBN 0-07-071064-3). McGraw.
--Exploring Occupations in Communication & Graphic Arts. (Careers in Focus Ser.). 1976. text ed. 8.96 (ISBN 0-07-071031-7, G); tchr's manual & key 4.00 (ISBN 0-07-071032-5); wksheets 10.96 (ISBN 0-07-071058-9). McGraw.
--Exploring Occupations in Engineering & Manufacturing. (Careers in Focus Ser.). 1976. text ed. 8.96 (ISBN 0-07-071035-X, G); tchr's manual & key 4.00 (ISBN 0-07-071036-8); wksheets 10.96 (ISBN 0-07-071060-0). McGraw.
--Exploring Occupations in Public & Social Services. (Careers in Focus Ser.). 1975. text ed. 8.96 (ISBN 0-07-071029-5, G); tchr's manual & key 4.00 (ISBN 0-07-071030-9); wksheets 8.96 (ISBN 0-07-071057-0). McGraw.
--Exploring Marketing Occupations. (Careers in Focus Ser). (Illus.). 160p. (gr. 6-9). 1975. pap. text ed. 8.96 (ISBN 0-07-071039-2, G); tchr's manual & key 4.00 (ISBN 0-07-071040-6); wkshts. 8.96 (ISBN 0-07-071062-7). McGraw.
--Exploring Construction Occupations. (Careers in Focus Ser.). 1975. text ed. 7.96 (ISBN 0-07-071021-X, G); tchr's. manual & key 4.00 (ISBN 0-07-071022-8). McGraw.
Winn, Chris & Beadle, Jeremy. Rodney Tootle's Grown-Up Grappler & Other Treasures from the Museum of Outlawed Inventions. (Illus.). 32p. (gr. 4-6). 1983. 9.95 (ISBN 0-316-94752-0, Pub. by Atlantic Monthly Pr.). Little.
Winn, David. Gangland. LC 81-18577. 256p. 1982. 12.95 (ISBN 0-394-50396-1). Knopf.
Winn, Edward B. Le see LeWinn, Edward B.
Winn, Howard E., jt. auth. see Winn, Lois K.
Winn, Jane, jt. auth. see Markell, Jane.
Winn, Lois K. & Winn, Howard E. The Journey of the Humpback Whale: Wings in the Sea. Date not set. cancelled (ISBN 0-8289-0484-7). Greene. Postponed.
Winn, Paul R., jt. auth. see Johnson, Ross H.
Winnacker & Wirtz. Nuclear Energy in Germany. LC 79-88088. 1979. 37.00 (ISBN 0-89448-018-9, 690003). Am Nuclear Soc.
Winnacker, Ernest L. & Schone, H. H., eds. Genes & Tumor Genes: Ninth Workshop-Conference Hoechst. 176p. 1982. text ed. 24.00 (ISBN 0-89004-678-6). Raven.
Winneberger, John H. Manual of Grey Water Treatment Practice. LC 76-5236. (Illus.). 1976. 18.75 o.p. (ISBN 0-250-40136-3). Ann Arbor Science.
Winneberger, John T. Nitrogen, Public Health & the Environment: Some Tools for Critical Thought. LC 81-70873. (Illus.). 77p. 1982. text ed. 14.95 (ISBN 0-250-40522-9). Ann Arbor Science.
Winner. Microbiology in Patient Care. 2nd ed. text ed. 6.25 o.p. (ISBN 0-686-97991-5, Lippincott Nursing). Lippincott.
Winner, Anna K. Basic Ideas of Occult Wisdom. LC 75-116528. (Orig.). 1970. pap. 4.50 (ISBN 0-8356-0391-1, Quest). Theos Pub Hse.
Winner, Ellen. Invented Worlds: The Psychology of the Arts. (Illus.). 512p. 1982. text ed. 25.00x (ISBN 0-674-46360-9). Harvard U Pr.
Winner, Irene P., ed. The Dynamics of East European Ethnicity Outside of Eastern Europe: With Special Emphasis on the American Case. 242p. 1983. 22.95 (ISBN 0-87073-234-X); pap. 13.95 (ISBN 0-87073-235-8). Schenkman.
Winner, Irene P., jt. ed. see Winner, Thomas G.
Winner, Langdon. Autonomous Technology: Technics-Out-of-Control As a Theme in Political Thought. LC 76-40100. 1977. 22.00x (ISBN 0-262-23078-X); pap. 7.95 (ISBN 0-262-73049-9). MIT Pr.
Winner, Robert. Flogging the Czar. 96p. 1983. 13.95 (ISBN 0-935296-38-7); pap. 7.95 (ISBN 0-935296-39-5). Sheep Meadow.
--Origins. (Slow Loris Poetry Ser.). 24p. 1982. pap. 4.95 (ISBN 0-918366-24-0). Slow Loris.
Winner, Thomas G. & Winner, Irene P., eds. The Peasant & the City in Eastern Europe: Interpenetrating Structures. 256p. 1983. 22.95 (ISBN 0-87073-275-7). Schenkman.
Winner, Viola H. Henry James & the Visual Arts. LC 73-109223. (Illus.). 202p. 1970. 13.95x (ISBN 0-8139-0285-1). U Pr of Va.

Winner, Walter P. Airman's Information Manual, 1983. 18th ed. (Illus.). 304p. pap. 5.95w (ISBN 0-911721-94-0). Aviation.
Winner, Walter P., ed. see Federal Aviation Administration.
Winnett, Thomas, jt. auth. see Whitnah, Dorothy.
Winnett, Thomas, ed. see Darvill, Fred T., Jr.
Winnett, Thomas, ed. see Green, David.
Winnett, Thomas, ed. see Grodin, Joseph & Grodin, Sharon.
Winnett, Thomas, ed. see Hargrove, Penny & Liebrenz, Noelle.
Winnett, Thomas, ed. see Linkhart, Luther.
Winnett, Thomas, ed. see Pierce, Robert & Pierce, Margaret.
Winnett, Thomas, ed. see Reid, Robert.
Winnett, Thomas, ed. see Schaffer, Jeffrey P.
Winnett, Thomas, ed. see Schaffer, Jeffrey P., et al.
Winnett, Thomas, jt. ed. see Smith, Robert.
Winnett, Thomas, ed. see Smith, Robert.
Winnett, Thomas, ed. see Smith, Roger.
Winnett, Thomas, ed. see Spangle, Francis & Rusmore, Jean.
Winnett, Thomas, ed. see Whitnah, Dorothy L.
Winnicott, D. W. Therapeutic Consultations in Child Psychiatry. LC 70-158448. (Illus.). 1971. text ed. 15.95x (ISBN 0-465-08511-3). Basic.
Winnicott, Donald W. Playing & Reality. 1982. 21.00x (ISBN 0-422-73740-2, Pub. by Tavistock England); pap. 9.95x (ISBN 0-422-78310-2). Methuen Inc.
Winnig. Romerzimmer. (Easy Reader, A). pap. 2.95 (ISBN 0-88436-041-5, 45261). EMC.
Winning, Hasso Von see Von Winning, Hasso.
Winning, R. A Poetry Chapbook. 20p. 1983. write for info. Moons Quilt Pr.
Winnington, Richard. Film Criticism & Caricatures, 1943-1953. (Illus.). 1976. 17.00x o.p. (ISBN 0-06-497766-8). B&N Imports.
Winnington-Ingram, R. P. Sophocles. LC 79-50511. 1980. 59.50 (ISBN 0-521-22672-4); pap. 19.95 (ISBN 0-521-29684-6). Cambridge U Pr.
Winny, J., ed. see Chaucer, Geoffrey.
Winocour, Jack, ed. Story of the Titanic: As Told by Its Survivors. 9.50 (ISBN 0-8446-3194-9). Peter Smith.
Winograd, Garry. Public Relations. LC 77-77288. 1977. pap. 9.95 (ISBN 0-87070-543-1). Museum Mod Art.
Winograd, S. Arithmetic Complexity of Computations. LC 79-93154. (CBMS-NSF Regional Conference Ser.: No. 33). 93p. 1980. pap. text ed. 11.50 (ISBN 0-89871-163-0). Soc Indus-Appl Math.
Winograd, Terry. Language As a Cognitive Process: Vol. 1 syntax. LC 81-14855. (Computer Science Ser.). (Illus.). 608p. 1981. text ed. 29.95 (ISBN 0-201-08571-2). A-W.
--Understanding Natural Language. 1972. 28.50 (ISBN 0-12-759750-6). Acad Pr.
Winokur, Alice, jt. auth. see Gipe, George.
Winokur, George. Depression: The Facts. (The Facts Ser.). 1981. text ed. 12.95x (ISBN 0-19-261315-4). Oxford U Pr.
Winokur, James L. American Property Law: Cases, History, Policy & Practice. (Contemporary Legal Education Ser.). 1296p. 1982. text ed. 29.00 (ISBN 0-87215-405-X). Michie-Bobbs.
Winokur, Melvin, jt. auth. see Kroschwitz, Jacqueline I.
Winokur, Stephen. A Primer of Verbal Behavior: An Operant View. (Prentice Hall Experimental Psychology Ser). (Illus.). 192p. 1976. text ed. 23.95 (ISBN 0-13-700609-8). P-H.
Winold, A. & Rehm, J. Introduction to Music Theory. 2nd ed. 1979. pap. 20.95 (ISBN 0-13-489666-1). P-H.
Winpenny, Thomas R. Industrial Progress & Human Welfare: The Rise of the Factory System in 19th Century Lancaster. 142p. (Orig.). 1982. lib. bdg. 18.75 (ISBN 0-8191-2628-4); pap. 8.00 (ISBN 0-8191-2629-2). U Pr of Amer.
Winquist, Charles E. Homecoming: Interpretation, Transformation & Individuation. LC 78-9565. 1978. pap. 9.95 (ISBN 0-89130-240-9, 01-00-18). Scholars Pr Ca.
--Practical Hermeneutics: A Revised Agenda for the Ministry. LC 79-22848. (Scholars Press General Ser.: No. 1). 12.95 (ISBN 0-89130-363-4, 00-03-01); pap. 8.95 (ISBN 0-89130-364-2). Scholars Pr CA.
Winsberg, Fred. Clinical Ultrasound Reviews. 2nd ed. (Clinical Ultrasound Review Ser.). 474p. 1982. 65.00 (ISBN 0-471-08262-7, Pub. by Wiley Med). Wiley.
Winsberg, Fred, jt. auth. see Hobbins, John C.
Winship, George P., ed. Journey of Coronado Fifteen Forty to Fifteen Forty-Two. Repr. of 1904 ed. lib. bdg. 14.00x o.p. (ISBN 0-8371-2359-3, WIJC). Greenwood.
Winskell, Cyril, jt. auth. see Barnett, Winston.
Winslade, William J. & Ross, Judith W. The Insanity Plea. 256p. 1983. 14.95 (ISBN 0-686-83836-X, ScribT). Scribner.
--The Insanity Plea. 240p. 1983. 14.95 (ISBN 0-684-17897-4). Scribner.
Winslow, Alan. Ruth: A Biography of the Future. LC 76-2298. 1977. 8.95 o.p. (ISBN 0-87949-047-0). Ashley Bks.
Winslow, Anna G. Diary of Anna Green Winslow, a Boston Schoolgirl of 1771. Earle, Allic M., ed. LC 71-124586. (Illus.). 1970. Repr. of 1894 ed. 30.00x (ISBN 0-8103-3586-7). Gale.
Winslow, C. E. A. Evolution & Significance of the Modern Public Health Campaign. 1923. text ed. 29.50x (ISBN 0-686-83541-7). Elliots Bks.
Winslow, Charles-Edward A. The Conquest of Epidemic Disease: A Chapter in the History of Ideas. LC 79-48055. 424p. 1980. 25.00 (ISBN 0-299-08240-7); pap. 9.95 (ISBN 0-299-08244-X). U of Wis Pr.
Winslow, Donald J. Life-Writing: A Glossary of Terms in Biography, Autobiography & Related Forms. (Biography Monographs). 64p. (Orig.). pap. 4.50x (ISBN 0-8248-0748-0). UH Pr.
Winslow, F. H., jt. ed. see Bovey, F. A.
Winslow, Forbes. The Plea of Insanity in Criminal Cases. (Historical Foundations of Forensic Psychiatry & Psychology Ser.). vii, 78p. 1983. Repr. of 1843 ed. lib. bdg. 17.50 (ISBN 0-306-76180-7). Da Capo.
Winslow, George, jt. auth. see Jones, Larry.
Winslow, Ken, ed. The Video Programs Index. 4th ed. 1979. pap. text ed. 6.95 o.p. (ISBN 0-935478-01-9). Natl Video.
Winslow, Octavius. Personal Declension & Revival of Religion in the Soul. 1978. pap. 3.45 (ISBN 0-85151-261-5). Banner of Truth.
Winslow, Ola E. American Broadside Verse from Imprints of the 17th & 18th Centuries. 1930. 65.00x (ISBN 0-686-51344-4). Elliots Bks.
Winslow, Pauline. The Counsellor Heart. 224p. 1980. 8.95 o.p. (ISBN 0-312-17014-9). St Martin.
Winslow, Pauline G. Coppergold. LC 77-15324. 1978. 8.95 o.p. (ISBN 0-312-16966-3). St Martin.
Winslow, Pete. A Daisy in the Memory of a Shark. LC 73-84310. (Pocket Poets Ser.: No. 31). (Orig.). 1973. pap. 2.00 o.p. (ISBN 0-87286-073-6). City Lights.
Winslow, Robert W. & Dallin, Leon. Music Skills for Classroom Teachers. 6th ed. 325p. 1983. write for info. plastic comb. (ISBN 0-697-03566-2). Wm C Brown.
Winslow, Susan. Brother, Can You Spare a Dime? 12.95 o.p. (ISBN 0-87196-325-6). Facts on File.
Winslow, Taylor F. How to Become the Successful Construction Contractor: Estimating, Sales, Management, Vol. 2. LC 75-19189. (Illus.). 1976. pap. 18.50 o.p. (ISBN 0-910460-15-9). Craftsman.
--How to Become the Successful Construction Contractor: Plans, Specifications, Building, Vol. 1. LC 75-19189. (Illus.). 1977. pap. 17.75 o.p. (ISBN 0-910460-14-0). Craftsman.
Winsome, Douglas. Embroidery. 5.50x (ISBN 0-392-08247-0, SpS). Sportshelf.
Winsor, Ernest. Using the Indigent Court Costs Law. Spriggs, Marshall T., ed. (Tools of the Trade for Massachusetts Lawyers Ser.). (Illus.). 25p. (Orig.). 1983. pap. 0.00p.n.s. (ISBN 0-910001-02-2). MA Poverty Law.
Winsor, G. McLeod. Station X. 336p. 1975. Repr. of 1919 ed. lib. bdg. 13.50 (ISBN 0-8398-2319-3, Gregg). G K Hall.
Winsor, Kathleen. Forever Amber. 1971. pap. 3.95 (ISBN 0-451-12164-3, AE2164, Sig). NAL.
Winspear, Violet. The Silver Slave, Dear Puritan & Rapture of the Desert. (Harlequin Romances Series (3-in-1)). 576p. 1983. pap. 3.50 (ISBN 0-373-20069-2). Harlequin Bks.
Winstanley, David. A Schoolmaster's Notebook. Kelly, E. & Kelly, T., eds. 128p. 1957. 19.00 (ISBN 0-7190-1118-3). Manchester.
Winstanley, Gerrard. The Law of Freedom & Other Writings. Hill, Christopher, ed. LC 82-14604. (Past & Present Publications Ser.). 395p. Date not set. price not set (ISBN 0-521-25299-7). Cambridge U Pr.
Winstanley, Lilian. Tolstoy. 1982. lib. bdg. 34.50 (ISBN 0-686-81924-1). Porter.
Winstanley, William. Lives of the Most Famous English Poets. LC 63-7095. 1963. Repr. of 1687 ed. 30.00x (ISBN 0-8201-1051-5). Schol Facsimiles.
Winstead-Fry, Patricia, jt. auth. see Miller, Sally.
Winsted, Wendy. Ferrets. (Illus.). 96p. 1981. 4.95 (ISBN 0-87666-930-5, KW-074). TFH Pubns.
Winstedt, Richard O. A History of Malaya. (Perspectives in Asian History Ser.: No. 11). (Illus.). Repr. of 1935 ed. lib. bdg. 25.00x (ISBN 0-87991-603-6). Porcupine Pr.
Winston, Betty. The Africans. (Orig.). 1983. pap. 3.95 (ISBN 0-440-00076-9). Dell.
Winston, Clara, jt. ed. see Winston, Richard.
Winston, Clara, tr. see Andersen, Hans C.
Winston, Clara, tr. see Arendt, Hannah.
Winston, Clara, tr. see Benary-Isbert, Margot.
Winston, Clara, tr. see George, Uwe.
Winston, Clara, tr. see Kooiker, Leonie.
Winston, Daoma. Emerald Station. 1974. pap. 3.50 (ISBN 0-380-00738-X, 63933-5). Avon.
--The Haversham Legacy. 1974. 9.95 o.p. (ISBN 0-671-21754-2). S&S.
--Moorhaven. 1976. pap. 3.50 o.p. (ISBN 0-380-00236-1, 223929). Avon.
Winston, George P. John Fiske. (United States Author Ser.). lib. bdg. 14.95 (ISBN 0-8057-0256-3, Twayne). G K Hall.
Winston, Gordon C. The Timing of Economic Activities: Firms, Households, & Markets in Time-Specific Analysis. LC 82-1328. 303p. 1982. 29.95 (ISBN 0-521-24720-9). Cambridge U Pr.
Winston, Henry. Class, Race & Black Liberation. LC 77-923. 1977. 8.00 o.p. (ISBN 0-7178-0484-4); pap. 2.75 o.p. (ISBN 0-7178-0491-7). Intl Pub Co.
--Strategy for a Black Agenda: A Critique of New Theories of Liberation in the United States & Africa. LC 73-80570. 1973. 7.50 o.p. (ISBN 0-7178-0403-8); pap. 2.75 o.p. (ISBN 0-7178-0404-6). Intl Pub Co.
Winston, M. B. Getting Publicity. LC 81-16219. 250p. 1982. pap. 8.50x (ISBN 0-471-08225-2). Wiley.
Winston, Michael R., jt. ed. see Logan, Rayford W.
Winston, Patrick H. Artificial Intelligence. LC 76-55648. 1977. 23.95 (ISBN 0-201-08454-6). A-W.
Winston, Patrick H. & Horn, Berthold K. Lisp. (Illus.). 300p. 1981. pap. text ed. 18.95 (ISBN 0-201-08329-9). A-W.
Winston, Patrik H. & Brown, Richard H., eds. Artificial Intelligence: An MIT Perspective. Incl. Vol. 1. Expert Problem Solving, Natural Language Understanding, Intelligent Computer Coaches, Representation & Learning. 27.50x (ISBN 0-262-23096-8); Vol. 2. Understanding Vision, Manipulation, Computer Design, Symbol Manipulation. 27.50x (ISBN 0-262-23097-6). 1979. MIT Pr.
Winston, Richard & Winston, Clara, eds. Thomas Mann Diaries: 1918-1921, 1933-1939. (Illus.). 32p. 1982. 25.00 (ISBN 0-8109-1304-6). Abrams.
Winston, Richard, tr. see Andersen, Hans C.
Winston, Richard, tr. see Arendt, Hannah.
Winston, Richard, tr. see Benary-Isbert, Margot.
Winston, Richard, tr. see George, Uwe.
Winston, Richard, tr. see Kooiker, Leonie.
Winston, Roger B., Jr., jt. ed. see Miller, Theodore K.
Winston, Roland, jt. auth. see Welford, W. T.
Winston, Sandra. The Entrepreneurial Woman. LC 78-55594. 1979. 8.95 o.p. (ISBN 0-88225-259-3). Newsweek.
Winstone, Harold, jt. ed. see Jasper, Ronald.
Winter. State & Local Government in Decentralized Republic. 1981. 22.95 (ISBN 0-02-428740-7). Macmillan.
Winter, Alexander. New York State Reformatory in Elmira. LC 74-172602. (Criminology, Law Enforcement, & Social Problems Ser.: No. 192). 1975. cancelled. Patterson Smith.
Winter, D., ed. Lie Algebras & Related Topics, New Brunswick, New Jersey 1981: Proceedings. (Lecture Notes in Mathematics: Vol. 933). 236p. 1983. pap. 11.00 (ISBN 0-387-11563-3). Springer-Verlag.
Winter, D. G. The Application of the Rotating Disc Electrode to the Determination of Kinetic Parameters in Electrochemical Systems, 1980. 1981. 50.00x (ISBN 0-686-97033-0, Pub. by W Spring England). State Mutual Bk.
Winter, D. G. & Strachan, A. M. The Reclamation of Scrap Hard Metal by Treatment with Moltenzing, 1978. 1981. 39.00X (ISBN 0-686-97146-9, Pub. by W Spring England). State Mutual Bk.
Winter, David. Faith Under Fire. LC 77-92353. (Daystar Devotional Ser.). Orig. Title: One Hundred Days in the Arena. 1981. pap. 2.50 (ISBN 0-87788-252-5). Shaw Pubs.
--Hereafter: What Happens After Death? LC 72-94097. (Illus.). 96p. 1973. pap. 1.75 (ISBN 0-87788-341-6). Shaw Pubs.
--The Search for the Real Jesus. 160p. (Orig.). 1982. pap. 5.95 (ISBN 0-8192-1318-7). Morehouse.
Winter, David J. Abstract Lie Algebras. 1972. 22.00x (ISBN 0-262-23051-8). MIT Pr.
Winter, Denis. The First of the Few: Fighter Pilots of the First World War. 256p. 1982. 30.00x o.p. (ISBN 0-7139-1278-2, Pub. by Penguin Bks). State Mutual Bk.
--The First of the Few: Fighter Pilots of the First World War. LC 82-13478. (Illus.). 224p. 17.50 (ISBN 0-8203-0642-8). U of Ga Pr.
Winter, Douglas B. Stephen King. (Starmont Reader's Guide Ser.: No. 16). 128p. 1982. Repr. lib. bdg. 11.95x (ISBN 0-89370-023-1). Borgo Pr.
Winter, Douglas E. Reader's Guide to Stephen King. Schlobin, Roger C., ed. (Reader's Guides to Contemporary Science Fiction & Fantasy Authors Ser.: Vol. 16). (Illus., Orig.). 1982. 11.95x (ISBN 0-916732-44-4); pap. text ed. 5.95x (ISBN 0-916732-43-6). Starmont Hse.
Winter, Elmer L. Your Future in Your Own Business. LC 79-114130. 188p. 1975. pap. 4.50 (ISBN 0-668-02236-1). Arco.
Winter, Eugene. Towards a Contextual Grammar of English. 224p. 1983. text ed. 29.50x (ISBN 0-04-425027-4); pap. text ed. 9.95x (ISBN 0-04-425028-2). Allen Unwin.
Winter, Francis De see Bereny, Justin A.
Winter, Francis de see Clark, Elizabeth F. & De Winter, Francis.
Winter, Francis de see De Winter, Francis.
Winter, Frank H. Prelude to the Space Age: The Rocket Societies: 1924-1940. (Illus.). 250p. (Orig.). 1983. pap. text ed. 15.00x (ISBN 0-87474-963-8). Smithsonian.
Winter, Frederick W., jt. ed. see Gardner, David M.
Winter, George, et al. Design of Concrete Structures. 8th ed. (Illus.). 640p. 1972. text ed. 26.50 o.p. (ISBN 0-07-071115-1, C). McGraw.
Winter, George D. Evaluation of Biomaterials. LC 79-42730. (Advances in Biomaterials Ser.). 553p. 1980. 151.95x (ISBN 0-471-27658-8, Pub. by Wiley-Interscience). Wiley.
Winter, George D., et al. Biomaterials, Nineteen Eighty, Vol. 3. LC 81-15923. (Advances in Biomaterials Ser.). 829p. 1982. 71.00x (ISBN 0-471-10126-5, Pub. by Wiley-Interscience). Wiley.
Winter, George H. & Nilson, Arthur H. Design of Concrete Structures. 9th ed. (Illus.). 1979. text ed. 33.95 (ISBN 0-07-071116-X, C). McGraw.
Winter, Gordon. Country Camera, Eighteen Forty-Four to Nineteen Fourteen: Rural Life As Depicted in Photographs from the Early Days of Photography to the Outbreak of the First World War. LC 76-148407. (Illus.). 1971. Repr. of 1966 ed. 30.00x (ISBN 0-8103-3399-6). Gale.
--The Country Life Picture Book of Britain. (Illus.). 1983. 19.95 (ISBN 0-393-01735-4, Pub. by Country Life). Norton.
Winter, H. Frank & Shourd, Melvin L. Review of Human Physiology. new ed. LC 77-11355. (Illus.). 1978. pap. text ed. 14.95x o.p. (ISBN 0-7216-9467-5). Saunders.
Winter, Herbert R. & Bellows, Thomas J. People & Politics. 2nd ed. LC 80-20518. 534p. 1981. text ed. 20.95 (ISBN 0-471-08153-1); tchr's. manual 2.00 (ISBN 0-471-08977-X). Wiley.
Winter, J. Alan, et al. Vital Problems for American Society: Meanings & Means. 1968. text ed. 9.50 (ISBN 0-685-55648-4, 30569). Phila Bk Co.
Winter, J. M. Socialism & the Challenge of War: Ideas & Politics in Britain, 1912-1918. 1974. 26.50x (ISBN 0-7100-7839-0). Routledge & Kegan.
Winter, J. M., ed. R. H. Tawney: The American Labour Movement & Other Essays. 1979. 25.00x o.p. (ISBN 0-312-66124-X). St Martin.
--War & Economic Development. LC 74-82219. (Illus.). 320p. 1975. 44.50 (ISBN 0-521-20535-2). Cambridge U Pr.
Winter, J. M., ed. see Tawney, R. H.
Winter, Jay, ed. The Working Class in Modern British History. LC 82-9424. 336p. Date not set. price not set (ISBN 0-521-23444-1). Cambridge U Pr.
Winter, John. String Sculpture. 1972. pap. text ed. 5.85 (ISBN 0-88488-016-8). Creative Pubns.
Winter, Lorenz. Heinrich Mann & His Public: A Socioliterary Study of the Relationship Between an Author & His Public. Gorman, John, tr. LC 72-81616. 1970. 7.95x o.p. (ISBN 0-87024-123-0). U of Miami Pr.
Winter, Marian H. The Pre-Romantic Ballet. LC 73-80010. (Illus.). 306p. 1974. 37.50 o.p. (ISBN 0-87127-050-1). Dance Horiz.
Winter, Mary, jt. auth. see Morris, Earl W.
Winter, Michael M. Saint Peter & the Popes. LC 78-21507. 1979. Repr. of 1960 ed. lib. bdg. 20.75x (ISBN 0-313-21158-2, WISP). Greenwood.
Winter, Ralph D. & Hawthorne, Steven C., eds. Perspectives on the World Christian Movement: A Reader. LC 81-69924. (Illus.). 864p. (Orig.). 1981. 19.95X (ISBN 0-87808-187-9); pap. 14.95x (ISBN 0-87808-189-5). William Carey Lib.
Winter, Ralph K., jt. auth. see Wellington, Harry H.
Winter, Robert B. Congenital Deformities of the Spine. (Illus.). 432p. 1983. 59.00 (ISBN 0-86577-079-4). Thieme-Stratton.
Winter, Rolf. Quantum Physics. 1979. text ed. 29.95x (ISBN 0-534-00697-3). Wadsworth Pub.
Winter, Ruth. Beware of the Food You Eat. rev. ed. Orig. Title: Poisons in Your Food. 247p. (YA) 1971. 6.95 o.p. (ISBN 0-517-50011-6). Crown.
--The Consumer's Dictionary of Cosmetic Ingredients. rev. ed. 1976. 7.95 o.p. (ISBN 0-517-52736-7); pap. 4.95 (ISBN 0-517-52737-5). Crown.
--A Consumer's Dictionary of Food Additives. 1978. 8.95 o.p. (ISBN 0-517-53160-7); pap. 4.95 (ISBN 0-517-53161-5). Crown.
--Scent Talk among Animals. LC 76-52935. 1977. 9.57i (ISBN 0-397-31732-8, HarpJ). Har-Row.
--The Scientific Case Against Smoking. 128p. 1980. 6.95 o.p. (ISBN 0-517-53947-0, Michelman Bks); pap. 4.95 o.p. (ISBN 0-517-54141-6, Michelman Bks). Crown.
Winter, Terry. Evidence: The Truth about Christianity. rev. ed. LC 79-87769. 1979. pap. 1.50 (ISBN 0-89081-067-2, 2039). Harvest Hse.
Winter, Thelma F. Art & Craft of Ceramic Sculpture. LC 73-20150. (Illus.). 269p. 1973. 34.95x o.p. (ISBN 0-470-95475-2). Halsted Pr.
Winter, William. Life & Art of Edwin Booth. LC 68-8939. (Illus.). 1968. Repr. of 1893 ed. lib. bdg. 17.25x (ISBN 0-8371-0275-8, WIEB). Greenwood.
--Life & Art of Richard Mansfield, with Selections from His Letters. Repr. of 1910 ed. lib. bdg. 36.00x o.p. (ISBN 0-8371-4084-6, WIRM). Greenwood.
Winter, William D. Marine Insurance. 3rd ed. (Insurance Ser.). (Illus.). 1952. text ed. 35.00 (ISBN 0-07-071119-4, C). McGraw.
Winter, William H., ed. see Johnson, Overton.
Winter, William J. The World of Model Airplanes. Model Aviation Editors, ed. (Illus.). 1983. 19.95 (ISBN 0-686-83861-0, ScribT). Scribner.
Winterbone, D., ed. see Benson, Rowland S.

Winterborn, Benjamin. Changing Scenes. Thompson, Marie K. & Roth, Beth N., eds. (Illus., Orig.). 1980. 17.95 (ISBN 0-19-213226-1). Oxford U Pr.
Winterbotham, R. Lord of Nardos. (YA) 6.95 (ISBN 0-685-07443-9, Avalon). Bouregy.
Winterfeld, Henry. Detectives in Togas. LC 56-6922. (Illus.). (gr. 4-6). 1966. pap. 2.25 (ISBN 0-15-625315-1, VoyB). HarBraceJ.
--Mystery of the Roman Ransom. McCormick, Edith, tr. from Ger. LC 77-3673. (Illus.). (gr. 5-9). 1977. pap. 1.75 (ISBN 0-15-662340-4, VoyB). HarBraceJ.
Winterich, John T. Early American Books & Printing. LC 74-3022. 1974. Repr. of 1935 ed. 40.00x (ISBN 0-8103-3661-8). Gale.
Wintermans, J. F. & Kuiper, P. J., eds. Biochemistry & Metabolism of Plant Lipids: Proceedings of the International Symposium on the Biochemistry & Metabolism of Plant Lipids, Fifth, Groningen, the Netherlands, June 7-10, 1982. (Developments in Plant Biology Ser.: Vol. 8). 600p. 1982. 85.00 (ISBN 0-444-80457-9, Biomedical Pr). Elsevier.
Winternitz, Emanuel. Leonardo da Vinci as a Musician. LC 81-16475. (Illus.). 288p. 1982. 29.95x (ISBN 0-300-02631-5). Yale U Pr.
Winternitz, Maurice. A History of Indian Literature, 2 vols. 2nd ed. Ketkar, S. & Kohn, H., trs. Incl. Vol. 1. Introduction, Veda, National Epics, Puranas & Tantras; Vol. 2. Buddhist Literature & Jaina Literature. 1977. Repr. of 1972 ed. text ed. 39.25x (ISBN 0-391-01075-1). Humanities.
Winternitz, Milton C. Collected Studies of the Pathology of War Gas Poisoning. (Illus.). 1920. 125.00x (ISBN 0-685-69885-8). Elliots Bks.
Winterowd, W. Ross. The Contemporary Writer: A Practical Rhetoric. 2nd ed. 481p. 1981. text ed. 13.95 (ISBN 0-15-513726-3, HC); instr's. manual avail. (ISBN 0-15-513727-1). HarBraceJ.
Winters, Arthur, jt. auth. see Packard, Sidney.
Winters, Arthur A. & Goodman, Stanley. Fashion Sales Promotion Handbook. 3rd ed. 1967. pap. text ed. 10.95 (ISBN 0-672-96040-0); tchr's manual 6.67 (ISBN 0-672-96041-9). Bobbs.
Winters, Donald L. Farmers Without Farms: Agricultural Tenancy in Nineteenth-Century Iowa. LC 78-4021. (Contributions in American History Ser.: No. 79). (Illus.). 1978. lib. bdg. 25.00 (ISBN 0-313-20408-X, WFL/). Greenwood.
Winters, Francis X. Politics & Ethics. pap. 1.95 o.p. (ISBN 0-8091-1862-9). Paulist Pr.
Winters, Howard D. Riverton Culture. (Reports of Investigations Ser.: No. 13). (Illus.). 164p. 1969. pap. 5.00 (ISBN 0-89792-035-X). Ill St Museum.
Winters, L. Alan. An Econometric Model of the Export Sector. (Cambridge Studies in Applied Econometrics). 192p. 1981. 47.50 (ISBN 0-521-23720-3). Cambridge U Pr.
Winters, Nancy. Daddy. LC 79-20165. 1979. 8.95 o.p. (ISBN 0-399-90055-1, Marek). Putnam Pub Group.
Winters, R. W. & Greene, H. L., eds. Nutritional Support of the Seriously Ill Patient, Vol. 1. LC 82-18426. (Bristol-Myers Nutrition Symposia Ser.). Date not set. price not set (ISBN 0-12-759801-4). Acad Pr.
Winters, Robert W. Principles of Pediatric Fluid Therapy. 2nd ed. 1982. pap. text ed. 16.95 (ISBN 0-316-94738-5). Little.
Winters, Robert W. & Bell, Ralph B. Acid-Base Physiology in Medicine: A Self-Instruction Program. 3rd ed. 1982. text ed. 19.95 (ISBN 0-316-94739-3). Little.
Winters, Stanley A. & Cox, Eunice W. Competency-Based Instruction for Exceptional Children. (Illus.). 160p. 1976. spiral 16.75x (ISBN 0-398-03402-8). C C Thomas.
Winters, Thomas A., jt. auth. see Nelson, Gayle L.
Winters, W. D., et al. A Stereotaxic Brain Atlas for Macaca Nemestrina. LC 69-16743. (Illus.). 1969. 70.00x (ISBN 0-520-01445-6). U of Cal Pr.
Winters, Y. Primitivism & Decadence. LC 70-92994. (Studies in Comparative Literature, No. 35). 1969. Repr. of 1937 ed. lib. bdg. 32.95x (ISBN 0-8383-1213-6). Haskell.
Winters, Yvor. Collected Poems. LC 82-70316. 146p. 1960. pap. 6.95x (ISBN 0-8040-0047-6). Swallow.
--Collected Poems of Yvor Winters. LC 82-74342. 230p. 1978. 15.95 (ISBN 0-8040-0799-3). Swallow.
--Early Poems of Yvor Winters Nineteen-Twenty to Nineteen-Twenty-Eight. LC 82-70472. 148p. 1966. 9.95x (ISBN 0-8040-0072-7). Swallow.
--Forms of Discovery: Critical & Historical Essays on the Forms of the Short Poem in English. LC 82-70746. 378p. 1967. 8.95 o.p. (ISBN 0-8040-0118-9); pap. 8.95x (ISBN 0-8040-0119-7). Swallow.
--Function of Criticism: Problems & Exercises. LC 82-70811. 200p. 1957. pap. 5.95x (ISBN 0-8040-0130-8). Swallow.
--In Defense of Reason: Three Classics of Contemporary Criticism. LC 82-70944. 611p. 1947. pap. 12.95x (ISBN 0-8040-0151-0). Swallow.
Winters, Yvor & Fields, Kenneth, eds. Quest for Reality: An Anthology of the Short Poems in English. 199p. 1969. 10.00x o.p. (ISBN 0-8040-0257-6); pap. 7.95x (ISBN 0-8040-0258-4). Swallow.
Winterschmidt, Roger C. The Six Historical, Political & Inevitable Solutions to the Crisis of Mankind. (Illus.). 142p. 1983. 87.85 (ISBN 0-86722-021-X). Inst Econ Pol.
Winterton, Bert W. The Processes of Heredity. 304p. (Orig.). 1980. pap. 14.95 (ISBN 0-8403-2835-4). Kendall-Hunt.
Winther, Jens E., jt. auth. see Birn, Herluf.
Winther, Oscar O. The Transportation Frontier: Trans-Mississippi West, 1865-1890. LC 64-10639. (Histories of the American Frontier Ser.). (Illus.). 238p. 1974. pap. 9.95x (ISBN 0-8263-0317-X). U of NM Pr.
Winthrop, Elizabeth. Marathon Miranda. LC 78-20615. 160p. (gr. 4-6). 1979. 9.95 (ISBN 0-8234-0349-1). Holiday.
--Miranda in the Middle. 128p. 1982. pap. 1.95 (ISBN 0-553-15158-4, Skylark). Bantam.
--That's Mine. LC 77-73832. (Illus.). (gr. k-2). 1977. PLB 7.95 (ISBN 0-8234-0308-4). Holiday.
Wintle, Justin, ed. Makers of Nineteenth Century Culture, 1800-1914. 709p. 1983. 37.50 (ISBN 0-7100-9295-4). Routledge & Kegan.
Winton, Alison. Proust's Additions, 2 vols. Incl. Vol. 1. (ISBN 0-521-21610-9); Vol. 2. (ISBN 0-521-21611-7). LC 76-58869. 1977. 75.00 set (ISBN 0-521-21612-5). Cambridge U Pr.
Winton, Chester A. Theory & Measurement in Sociology. LC 74-9539. 1974. text ed. 5.95x o.s.i. (ISBN 0-470-95515-5). Halsted Pr.
Winton, Dorothy de. Sunrise Cookbook. 1976. 3.50 (ISBN 0-686-27657-4). Cole-Outreach.
Winton, J. R. Lloyds Bank, Nineteen Eighteen to Nineteen Sixty-Nine. (Illus.). 222p. 1982. 37.50x (ISBN 0-19-920125-0). Oxford U Pr.
Winton, John. Air Power at Sea: Nineteen Thirty-Nine to Nineteen Forty-Five. LC 76-41384. (Illus.). 1977. 12.95i (ISBN 0-690-01222-5, TYC-T). T Y Crowell.
--Sir Walter Raleigh. (Illus.). 1975. 15.00 o.p. (ISBN 0-698-10648-2, Coward). Putnam Pub Group.
Wintrobe, Maxwell M. Blood, Pure & Eloquent. new ed. (Illus.). 1980. text ed. 50.00 (ISBN 0-07-071135-6, HP). McGraw.
Wintrobe, Ronald, jt. auth. see Breton, Albert.
Wintz, Jack, ed. Has Change Shattered Our Faith? A Hopeful Look at the Church Today, Vol. 2. (Catholic Update Seer.). (Illus.). 111p. 1976. pap. 1.95 o.p. (ISBN 0-912228-22-9). St Anthony Mess Pr.
--Living Our Faith After the Changes. (The Catholic Update Ser.: Vol. 3). 1977. pap. 1.95 o.p. (ISBN 0-912228-45-8). St Anthony Mess Pr.
Wintz, Paul, jt. auth. see Gonzalez, Rafael C.
Winwar, Frances. Wingless Victory: A Biography of Gabriele d'Annunzio & Eleonore Duse. LC 74-10363. 374p. 1974. Repr. of 1956 ed. lib. bdg. 20.50x (ISBN 0-8371-7671-9, WIWV). Greenwood.
Winward, Stephen F. Guide to the Prophets. LC 68-55819. 1976. pap. 6.50 (ISBN 0-8042-0131-5). John Knox.
Winward, Walter. The Canaris Fragments. rev. ed. 320p. 1983. 14.95 (ISBN 0-688-01554-9). Morrow.
--Hammerstrike. 1979. 10.95 o.p. (ISBN 0-671-24668-2). S&S.
--The Midas Touch. 288p. 1983. pap. 2.95 (ISBN 0-515-07135-8). Jove Pubns.
--Seven Minutes Past Midnight. 1980. 12.95 o.p. (ISBN 0-671-24932-0). S&S.
--Seven Minutes Past Midnight. 320p. 1983. pap. 3.50 (ISBN 0-515-07136-6). Jove Pubns.
Wionczek, M. S., ed. see International Workshop, World Hydrocarbon Markets.
Wionczek, Miguel S. International Indebtedness & World Economic Stagnation. 135p. 1981. 20.00 (ISBN 0-08-024702-4). Pergamon.
Wiredu, K. Philosophy & an African Culture. LC 79-51230. 1980. 34.50 (ISBN 0-521-22794-1); pap. 10.95 (ISBN 0-521-29647-1). Cambridge U Pr.
Wiren, Gary. Golf. (Sport Ser.). (Illus.). (gr. 10 up). 1971. text ed. 4.95 ref. ed. o.p. (ISBN 0-13-358028-8); pap. 6.95 ref. ed. (ISBN 0-13-358010-5). P-H.
Wires, Richard. Studying Civilization, Vol. II. 8th ed. 1981. pap. text ed. 7.95x (ISBN 0-673-15503-X). Scott F.
--Studying Civilizations Past & Present, Vol. 1. 8th ed. 1981. pap. text ed. 7.95x study guide (ISBN 0-673-15502-1). Scott F.
Wirker, Stewart, jt. auth. see King, Louise T.
Wirsens, Claes, jt. auth. see Ingelman-Sundberg, Axel.
Wirshing, J. R., jt. auth. see Wirshing, R. H.
Wirshing, R. H. & Wirshing, J. R. Civil Engineering Drafting. 1983. pap. 14.95 (ISBN 0-07-071127-5, G). McGraw.
Wirsing, Marie E. Teaching & Philosophy: A Synthesis. LC 79-47998. 238p. 1980. pap. text ed. 10.00 (ISBN 0-8191-0994-0). U Pr of Amer.
Wirsing, Robert G. Socialist Society & Free Enterprise Politics: A Study of Voluntary Associations in Urban India. LC 76-6775. 1977. 12.95 o.p. (ISBN 0-89089-066-8). Carolina Acad Pr.
Wirszubski, Chaim. Libertas As a Political Idea at Rome. (Cambridge Classical Studies). 1950. 19.95 (ISBN 0-521-06848-7). Cambridge U Pr.
Wirt, Frederick & Kirst, Michael. Political & Social Foundations of Education. 2nd ed. LC 75-20297. 1975. 20.50 o.p. (ISBN 0-8211-1016-0); text ed. 18.25x o.p. (ISBN 0-685-57428-8). McCutchan.
--Schools in Conflict: The Politics of Education. Rev. ed. LC 81-83250. (Education Ser.). 336p. 1982. 20.50x (ISBN 0-8211-2261-4); text ed. 18.50x (ISBN 0-686-83035-0). McCutchan.
Wirt, Frederick, jt. ed. see Gove, Samuel.
Wirt, Frederick, et al. On the City's Rim: Politics & Policy in Surburbia. LC 70-185325. 272p. 1971. 17.95x o.p. (ISBN 0-669-81976-X). Heath.
Wirt, Frederick M. Power in the City: Decision Making in San Francisco. LC 73-90662. 1975. 28.50x (ISBN 0-520-02654-3); pap. 6.95 (ISBN 0-520-03640-9). U of Cal Pr.
Wirt, Frederick M., jt. ed. see Gove, Samuel K.
Wirt, Robert D., et al. Multidimensional Description of Child Personality: A Manual for the Personality Inventory for Children. LC 79-57301. 116p. 1977. pap. 10.40 (ISBN 0-87424-152-9). Western Psych.
Wirt, Sherwood. The Confessions of Augustine in Modern English. 1977. pap. 4.95 o.p. (ISBN 0-310-34641-X). Zondervan.
--Go Tell It. 63p. 1979. pap. 1.95 (ISBN 0-8341-0580-2). Beacon Hill.
--Spiritual Disciplines: Devotional Writings from the Great Christians Leaders of the Seventheenth Century. 180p. 1983. pap. 7.95 (ISBN 0-89107-277-2, Crossway Bks). Good News.
Wirt, Sherwood E. Faith's Heroes. LC 78-71943. 1979. pap. 3.95 (ISBN 0-89107-162-8, Crossway Bks). Good News.
--Sed de Dios. Marosi, Esteban, ed. Sipowicz, Eswin, tr. 219p. (Span.). 1982. pap. 2.50 (ISBN 0-8297-1252-6). Life Pubs Intl.
Wirth, Arthur G. Education in the Technological Society: The Vocational-Liberal Studies Controversy in the Early Twentieth Century. LC 81-618. 272p. 1980. lib. bdg. 21.25 (ISBN 0-8191-1222-4); pap. text ed. 11.50 (ISBN 0-8191-1223-2). U Pr of Amer.
--John Dewey As Educator: His Design for Work in Education (1894-1904) LC 78-13365. 1979. Repr. of 1966 ed. lib. bdg. 16.00 (ISBN 0-88275-743-1). Krieger.
Wirth, J. R., jt. ed. see Cohen, D.
Wirth, Jessica R., ed. Assessing Linguistic Arguments. LC 76-25529. 1976. 14.95x o.s.i. (ISBN 0-470-98916-5). Halsted Pr.
Wirth, Michael J., jt. auth. see Walthall, Wylie A.
Wirth, N., jt. auth. see Jensen, K.
Wirth, Niklaus. Systematic Programming: An Introduction. (Illus.). 208p. 1973. 26.00 (ISBN 0-13-880369-2). P-H.
Wirth, Niklavs. Algorithms Plus Data Structures Equals Programs. (Illus.). 400p. 1976. 27.95 (ISBN 0-13-022418-9). P-H.
Wirth, Oswald. Introduction to the Study of the Tarot. LC 82-50753. 64p. (Orig.). pap. 4.95 (ISBN 0-87728-559-4). Weiser.
--Introduction to the Study of the Tarot. (Illus.). 64p. 1981. pap. 4.95 (ISBN 0-85030-263-3). US Games Syst.
Wirth, R. H., jt. auth. see Fritz, N.
Wirth, Richard H. SnoDrift Ice Cream Company In-Basket. (Illus.). 160p. 1983. practice set 6.50 (ISBN 0-07-071145-3, HP); tchr's manual & key 2.50 (ISBN 0-07-071146-1). McGraw.
Wirthlin, T., jt. auth. see Wehrli, F.
Wirtshafter, Robert M., jt. ed. see Feldman, Stephen L.
Wirtz, jt. auth. see Winnacker.
Wirtz, Stefan J. Phanomen: Tourismus. 460p. (Ger.). 1982. write for info. (ISBN 3-8204-5794-1). P Lang Pubs.
Wirtz, Willard. The Boundless Resource: A Prospectus for an Education-Work Policy. LC 75-30556. 1975. 8.95 (ISBN 0-915220-07-5); pap. 3.95 (ISBN 0-915220-10-5). New Republic.
Wiryosujono, S., ed. see CCOP-IOC SEATAR Working Group Meeting, July 1979, Bandung, Indonesia.
Wirz, H. J. & Smolderen, J. J. Numerical Methods in Fluid Dynamics. (McGraw-Hill - Hemisphere Series in Thermal & Fluids Engineering). (Illus.). 1978. text ed. 45.00 o.p. (ISBN 0-07-071120-8, C). McGraw.
Wisbey, R. A. Computer in Literary & Linguistic Research. LC 70-152645. (Publications of the Literary & Linguistic Computing Centre: No. 1). 1971. 54.50 (ISBN 0-521-08146-7). Cambridge U Pr.
Wisch, Nathaniel, ed. Comprehensive. 3rd ed. (Medical Examination Review Books: Vol. 1). 1972. spiral bdg. 15.00 o.p. (ISBN 0-87488-101-3). Med Exam.
Wisch, Nathaniel, et al, eds. Internal Medicine Specialty Board Review. 7th ed. 1981. pap. 28.50 (ISBN 0-87488-303-2). Med Exam.
Wischnitzer, S. Atlas & Laboratory Guide for Vertebrate Embryology. 1975. 15.95 (ISBN 0-07-071137-2, C). McGraw.
--Introduction to Electron Microscopy. 2nd ed. LC 77-93757. 1971. 21.00 (ISBN 0-08-006944-4). Pergamon.
Wischnitzer, Saul. Barron's Guide to Allied Health Science Careers. 1983. pap. text ed. cancelled (ISBN 0-8120-2427-3). Barron.
--Barron's Guide to Medical, Dental & Allied Health Science Careers. rev. ed. LC 76-41772. 286p. (gr. 12). 1982. pap. 6.95 (ISBN 0-8120-2281-5). Barron.
Wisconsin University. Regionalism in America. Jensen, Merrill, ed. LC 75-18407. (Illus.). 425p. 1975. Repr. of 1965 ed. lib. bdg. 22.25x o.p. (ISBN 0-8371-8340-5, WURA). Greenwood.
Wisdom, Aline C. Introduction to Library Services for Library Media Technical Assistants. (Illus.). 416p. 1974. 19.95 (ISBN 0-07-071140-2, G); instructors' manual 3.50 (ISBN 0-07-071141-0). McGraw.
Wisdom, J. C., jt. auth. see Houghton, B.
Wisdom, John. Logical Constructions. 1969. pap. text ed. 3.45 (ISBN 0-685-19743-3). Phila Bk Co.
Wisdom, Linda. Dancer in the Shadows. 192p. (Orig.). 1980. pap. 1.50 (ISBN 0-671-57049-8, Pub. by Silhouette Bks). S&S.
Wisdom's Goldenrod Staff, ed. Astro-Noesis. (Illus.). Date not set. 16.95 (ISBN 0-943914-00-0). Larson Pubns Inc.
Wisdon, J. O. Challengeability in Modern Science. 1982. 80.00x o.p. (ISBN 0-86127-106-8, Pub. by Avebury England). State Mutual Bk.
Wise, A., jt. auth. see Monie, J.
Wise, Alan F. Water, Sanitary & Waste Services for Buildings. (Mitchell's Building Construction Ser.). 156p. 1979. pap. 17.95x o.s.i. (ISBN 0-470-26888-3). Halsted Pr.
Wise, Arthur E. Legislated Learning: The Bureaucratization of the American Classroom. 238p. 1982. 12.95 (ISBN 0-520-03759-6); pap. 6.95 (ISBN 0-520-04792-3). U of Cal Pr.
Wise, Bernice Kemmler. Teaching Materials for the Learning Disabled. LC 80-18114. 70p. 1980. pap. text ed. 5.00 (ISBN 0-8389-0311-8). ALA.
Wise, Charles, jt. ed. see Frederickson, H. George.
Wise, David, jt. auth. see Cummings, Milton C., Jr.
Wise, David A., jt. auth. see Manski, Charles F.
Wise, David B. Wise Encyclopedia of Cookery. rev. ed. (Illus.). 1971. Repr. 9.95 (ISBN 0-448-00639-1, G&D). Putnam Pub Group.
Wise, David B., ed. Complete Illustrated Encyclopedia of the World's Automobiles. LC 78-53134. (Illus.). 320p. 1978. 24.95 o.s.i. (ISBN 0-89479-050-1). A & W Pubs.
Wise, Donald, rev. by see Wuest, Kenneth.
Wise, Francis H. Who's Boss? Training Your Baby or Child in Self-Management. Wise, Joyce M., ed. (Illus.). 235p. (Orig.). 1982. pap. 8.25 (ISBN 0-915766-58-2). Wise Pub.
--Youth & Drugs: Prevention, Detection and Cure. 1971. pap. 4.95 (ISBN 0-695-80996-2). Follett.
Wise, Francis H. & Wise, Joyce M. Dr. Wise Learn to Read Series, Vol. 2. Incl. Vol. 1. Readers 1-5 Phonetic Reader Ser (ISBN 0-915766-42-6); Vol. 2. Readers 6-10 in Phonetic Reader Ser (ISBN 0-915766-43-4). (Illus.). 105p. (gr. k-1). 1979. pap. 7.50 ea. Wise Pub.
--Storybooks. (Storybook Series: Vol. 3). (Illus.). 105p. (gr. k-1). 1979. pap. 7.50 (ISBN 0-915766-44-2). Wise Pub.
Wise, G., et al, eds. Topics in Child Neurology, Vol. 2. (Illus.). 250p. 1983. text ed. 40.00 (ISBN 0-89335-150-4). SP Med & Sci Bks.
Wise, Harold, jt. auth. see Gurney, Gene.
Wise, Herbert, jt. auth. see Weiss, Jeffrey.
Wise, Herbert & Fraser, Phyllis, eds. Great Tales of Terror & the Supernatural. 9.95 (ISBN 0-394-60446-6). Modern Lib.
Wise, Herbert H. Attention to Detail. (Illus.). 160p. 1981. 24.95 (ISBN 0-8256-3174-2, Quick Fox); pap. 11.95 (ISBN 0-8256-3171-8, Quick Fox). Putnam Pub Group.
--Attention to Detail. rev. ed. 160p. 1982. 12.95 (ISBN 0-399-50696-9, Perigee). Putnam Pub Group.
--Kitchen Detail. (Illus.). 160p. 1980. 27.50 (ISBN 0-8256-3204-8, Quick Fox); pap. 12.95 (ISBN 0-8256-3198-X). Putnam Pub Group.
--Rooms with a View. (Illus.). 1978. pap. 6.95 (ISBN 0-8256-3128-9, Quick Fox). Putnam Pub Group.
Wise, Herbert H. & Friedman-Weiss, Jeffrey. Living Places. LC 76-8071. 1976. pap. 6.95 (ISBN 0-8256-3067-3, Quick Fox). Putnam Pub Group.
Wise, Herbert H. & Weiss, Jeffrey. Made with Oak. (Illus.). 96p. 1975. pap. 6.95 (ISBN 0-8256-3052-5, Quick Fox). Putnam Pub Group.
Wise, James H., jt. ed. see Hyman, Irwin A.
Wise, Joyce M., jt. auth. see H, Francis.
Wise, Joyce M., jt. auth. see Wise, Francis H.
Wise, Joyce M., ed. see Wise, Francis H.
Wise, Karen. Confessions of a Totaled Woman. 128p. 1983. pap. 3.95 (ISBN 0-8407-5785-9). Nelson.
Wise, Kelly, ed. The Photographers' Choice. LC 75-5029. (Illus.). 1976. 27.50 o.p. (ISBN 0-89169-001-8). Addison Hse.
--Portrait: Theory. LC 81-80880. (Illus.). 176p. 1982. 35.00 (ISBN 0-912810-34-3); pap. 19.95 (ISBN 0-912810-35-1). Lustrum Pr.
Wise, M. J. & Rawstron, E. M. R. O. Buchanan & Economic Geography. (Advanced Edonoic Geography Ser.). 1973. lib. bdg. 20.00x o.p. (ISBN 0-7135-1766-2). Westview.
Wise, M. J., jt. auth. see Smith, Wilfred.
Wise, Mary R., ed. Vocablos y Expresiones Medicos Mas Usuales En Veinte Idiomas Vernaculos Peruanos. (Peruvian Working Papers Ser.: No. 2). 1973. pap. 3.00x o. p. (ISBN 0-88312-652-4); microfiche 2.25 (ISBN 0-88312-315-0). Summer Inst Ling.
Wise, Pat S., jt. auth. see Tobin, Helen M.
Wise, Philip, jt. auth. see Humphreys, Fisher.

Wise, Robert. The Ghost Town Monster. LC 74-16076. (Seawolf Mysteries Ser). (gr. 3-6). 1974. PLB 6.95 (ISBN 0-88436-142-X); pap. 3.95 (ISBN 0-88436-143-8). EMC.
--Mystery of Tanglefoot Island. LC 74-16077. (Seawolf Mysteries Ser.). (gr. 3-6). 1974. PLB 6.95 (ISBN 0-88436-144-6); pap. 3.50 o.p. (ISBN 0-88436-145-4). EMC.
--Mystery of Totem Pole Inlet. LC 74-16078. (Seawolf Mysteries Ser.). (gr. 3-6). 1974. PLB 6.95 (ISBN 0-88436-138-1); pap. 3.95 (ISBN 0-88436-139-X). EMC.
--Treasure of Raven Hill. LC 74-16079. (Seawolf Mysteries Ser). (gr. 3-6). 1974. PLB 6.95 (ISBN 0-88436-140-3); pap. 3.95 (ISBN 0-88436-141-1). EMC.
Wise, Sue, jt. auth. see Stanley, Liz.
Wise, Susan & Piper, David. European Portraits Sixteen Hundred to Nineteen Hundred in The Art Institute of Chicago. LC 78-57638. (Illus.). 183p. (Orig.). 1978. pap. 10.00 (ISBN 0-86559-029-X). Art Inst Chi.
Wise, Susan, jt. ed. see Keefe, John W.
Wise, T. J. A Bibliography of the Writings in Prose & Verse of Walter Savage Landor. 426p. 1981. 79.00x (ISBN 0-686-97613-4, Pub. by Dawson). State Mutual Bk.
Wise, T. N. & Freyberger, H., eds. Consultation Liaison Throughout the World. (Advances in Psychosomatic Medicine: Vol. 11). (Illus.). xii, 250p. 1983. 112.75 (ISBN 3-8055-3667-4). S Karger.
Wise, Terence. Armies of the Crusades. (Men-at-Arms Ser). 1978. pap. 7.95 o.p. (ISBN 0-85045-125-6). Hippocrene Bks.
--Ten Sixty Six, Year of Destiny. 1980. text ed. 19.50x o.p. (ISBN 0-85045-320-8). Humanities.
Wise, Thomas J. Coleridgeiana. 1982. lib. bdg. 34.50 (ISBN 0-686-81925-X). Porter.
--Introduction to the Ashley Library Catalog 1922-30. 64p. Date not set. pap. 10.00. Saifer.
Wise, Thomas J., ed. see Shelley, Percy B.
Wise, Thomas N. see Hendler, Nelson H.
Wise, William. Animal Rescue: Saving Our Endangered Wildlife. LC 78-1678. (Illus.). (gr. 5 up). 1978. PLB 6.29 o.p. (ISBN 0-399-61121-5). Putnam Pub Group.
--Monster Myths of Ancient Greece. (Illus.). 48p. (gr. 7-11). 1981. PLB 6.99 (ISBN 0-399-61143-6). Putnam Pub Group.
Wise, William A. Aaron Burr. (Lives to Remember Ser.). (gr. 7 up). 1968. PLB 5.49 o.p. (ISBN 0-399-60000-0). Putnam Pub Group.
--Amazing Animals of Australia. (See & Read Science). (Illus.). (gr. 1-3). 1970. PLB 4.49 o.p. (ISBN 0-399-60013-2). Putnam Pub Group.
--Amazing Animals of North America. (See & Read Science). (Illus.). (gr. k-3). 1971. PLB 6.29 o.p. (ISBN 0-399-60015-9). Putnam Pub Group.
--Booker T. Washington. (See & Read Biographies). (Illus.). (gr. 2-4). 1968. PLB 4.49 o.p. (ISBN 0-399-60066-3). Putnam Pub Group.
--Charles A. Lindbergh. LC 79-110324. (American Hero Biographies). (Illus.). (gr. 3-6). 1970. PLB 5.29 o.p. (ISBN 0-399-60087-6). Putnam Pub Group.
--Giant Birds & Monsters of the Air. (See & Read Science). (Illus.). (gr. k-3). 1969. PLB 6.29 o.p. (ISBN 0-399-60196-1). Putnam Pub Group.
--Giant Snakes & Other Amazing Reptiles. (See & Read Science). (Illus.). (gr. k-3). 1970. PLB 4.49 o.p. (ISBN 0-399-60197-X). Putnam Pub Group.
--In the Time of the Dinosaurs. (See & Read Science). (Illus.). (gr. 1-3). 1963. PLB 4.49 o.p. (ISBN 0-399-60635-1). Putnam Pub Group.
--Monsters from Outer Space? LC 77-16504. (See & Read Science). (Illus.). 1978. PLB 6.99 (ISBN 0-399-61089-8). Putnam Pub Group.
--Monsters of North America. LC 75-23109. (See & Read Science). (Illus.). (gr. k-4). 1978. PLB 6.99 (ISBN 0-399-60992-X). Putnam Pub Group.
--Monsters of the Ancient Seas. (See & Read Science). (Illus.). (gr. 1-4). 1968. PLB 4.49 o.p. (ISBN 0-399-60473-1). Putnam Pub Group.
--Monsters of the Deep. LC 72-97316. (See & Read Science). (Illus.). (gr. 1-4). 1975. PLB 6.29 o.p. (ISBN 0-399-60844-3). Putnam Pub Group.
--Monsters of the Middle Ages. (See & Read Storybooks). (Illus.). (gr. k-3). 1971. PLB 6.29 o.p. (ISBN 0-399-60472-3). Putnam Pub Group.
--Monsters of Today & Yesterday. (See & Read Science). (Illus.). (gr. 1-3). 1967. PLB 4.49 o.p. (ISBN 0-399-60474-X). Putnam Pub Group.
Wise, Winifred E. Benjamin Franklin. (World Pioneer Biography Ser.). (Illus.). (gr. 5-9). 1970. PLB 3.86 o.p. (ISBN 0-399-60053-1). Putnam Pub Group.
Wiseberg, Laurie S. & Scoble, Harry M., eds. Human Rights Directory: Latin America, Africa, Asia. 243p. 1980. 12.00 (ISBN 0-939338-00-9). Garrett Pk.
Wisely, Charlotte. Welcome Intruder. (Rapture Romance Ser.: No. 4). 1983. pap. 1.95 (ISBN 0-451-12007-8, AJ2007). NAL.
Wisely, William. A Tool of Power: The Political History of Money. LC 76-57701. 416p. Repr. of 1977 ed. text ed. 33.95 (ISBN 0-471-02235-7). Krieger.
Wiseman, A. J., jt. auth. see Lockhart, J. A.
Wiseman, Alan. Handbook of Enzyme Biotechnology. LC 75-2466. 275p. 1975. 89.95 (ISBN 0-470-95617-8). Halsted Pr.
--Topics in Enzyme & Fermentation Biotechnology, Vol. 1. LC 76-25441. 1977. 54.95 (ISBN 0-470-98896-7). Halsted Pr.
--Topics in Enzyme & Fermentation Biotechnology, Vol. 7. LC 77-511. 345p. 1982. 84.95 (ISBN 0-470-27366-6). Halsted Pr.
Wiseman, Alan, ed. Topics in Enzyme & Fermentation Biotechnology, Vol. 2. LC 76-25441. 1978. 49.95x o.s.i. (ISBN 0-470-99318-9). Vol. 2. Halsted Pr.
Wiseman, Ann. Cuts of Cloth: Quick Classics to Sew & Wear. LC 78-16375. (Illus.). 1978. 6.95 o.p. (ISBN 0-316-94853-5); pap. 3.95 o.p. (ISBN 0-316-94852-7). Little.
--Making Things, Bk. 2. (Illus.). 176p. 1975. 12.95 o.p. (ISBN 0-316-94850-0); pap. 7.95 o.p. (ISBN 0-316-94851-9). Little.
Wiseman, Bernard. Don't Make Fun. (Illus.). (gr. 4-8). 8.95 (ISBN 0-686-43089-1). HM.
--Hooray for Patsy's Oink! LC 79-21625. (Bernard Wiseman Bks.). (Illus.). 32p. (gr. k-2). 1980. PLB 6.69 (ISBN 0-8116-6079-6). Garrard.
--The Lucky Runner. LC 79-14215. (For Real Ser.). (Illus.). (gr. 1-5). 1979. PLB 6.69 (ISBN 0-8116-4313-1). Garrard.
--Morris Has a Birthday Party! LC 82-22860. (Illus.). 44p. (gr. 1-3). 1983. 9.00 (ISBN 0-316-94854-3). Little.
--Morris Is a Cowboy. LC 60-9460. (I Can Read Books). (Illus.). (gr. k-3). 1960. PLB 8.89 o.p. (ISBN 0-06-026556-6, HarpJ). Har-Row.
--Oscar Is a Mama. LC 79-24737. (Bernard Wiseman Bks.). (Illus.). 32p. (gr. k-4). 1980. PLB 6.69 (ISBN 0-8116-6081-8). Garrard.
--Penny's Poodle Puppy, Pickle. LC 79-26403. (Bernard Wiseman Bks.). (Illus.). 32p. (gr. k-4). 1980. PLB 6.69 (ISBN 0-8116-6080-X). Garrard.
--Quick Quackers. LC 79-14216. (Easy Venture Ser.). (Illus.). (gr. k-2). 1979. PLB 6.69 (ISBN 0-8116-6077-X). Garrard.
--Tails Are Not for Painting. LC 79-18373. (Bernard Wiseman Bks.). (Illus.). 32p. (gr. k-4). 1980. PLB 6.69 (ISBN 0-8116-6078-8). Garrard.
Wiseman, D. J. & Millard, A. R., eds. Essays on the Patriarchal Narratives. 1983. text ed. 14.95x (ISBN 0-931464-13-7); pap. 9.95 (ISBN 0-931464-12-9). Eisenbrauns.
Wiseman, D. J., ed. see Kidner, Derek.
Wiseman, H. Victor, ed. Local Government in England 1958-69. 1970. 13.75x o.p. (ISBN 0-7100-6822-0). Routledge & Kegan.
--Political Science: An Outline for the Intending Student. (Outlines Ser). 1967. cased 14.95x (ISBN 0-7100-2997-7). Routledge & Kegan.
Wiseman, Henry, ed. Peacekeeping: Appraisals & Proposals. (International Peace Academy Ser.). 400p. 1983. 40.00 (ISBN 0-08-027554-0). Pergamon.
Wiseman, Ian, jt. auth. see Rubinsky, Yuri.
Wiseman, J. A. & Cashin, J. A. Schaum's Outline of Advanced Accounting. 1982. pap. 8.95 (ISBN 0-07-071138-0). McGraw.
Wiseman, Jack. Beyond Positive Economics? LC 82-16874. 232p. 1982. 25.00x (ISBN 0-312-07780-7). St Martin.
Wiseman, Jacqueline P. Stations of the Lost: The Treatment of Skid Row Alcoholics. LC 79-13632. 1979. pap. 9.95 (ISBN 0-226-90307-9, P853). U of Chicago Pr.
Wiseman, James. The Land of the Ancient Corinthians. (Studies in Mediterranean Archaeology Ser.: No. L). (Illus.). 1978. pap. text ed. 45.00x (ISBN 91-85058-78-5). Humanities.
Wiseman, James & Aleksova, Blaga, eds. Studies in the Antiquities of Stobi, Vol. III. LC 75-641175. (Illus.). 323p. 1983. 62.50x (ISBN 0-691-03563-6). Princeton U Pr.
Wiseman, P. Introduction to Industrial Organic Chemistry. 2nd ed. (Illus.). 1979. 41.00 (ISBN 0-85334-795-6, Pub. by Applied Sci England); pap. 24.75 (ISBN 0-85334-850-2). Elsevier.
Wiseman, Robert F. The Complete Horseshoeing Guide. rev. ed. LC 72-9279. (Illus.). 160p. 1973. 12.95 (ISBN 0-8061-1049-X). U of Okla Pr.
Wiseman, Thomas. Savage Day. 1983. pap. 3.95 (ISBN 0-440-19071-1). Dell.
Wisenthal, J. L., ed. see Shaw, George B.
Wiser, James L. Political Philosophy: A History of the Search for Order. 400p. 1983. prof. ref. 22.95 (ISBN 0-13-684845-1). P-H.
Wish, Harvey. The American Historian: A Social-Intellectual History of the Writing of the American Past. LC 82-21150. viii, 366p. 1983. Repr. of 1960 ed. lib. bdg. 45.00x (ISBN 0-313-23847-2, WHAM). Greenwood.
Wishard, Armin, jt. ed. see Lavroff, Ellen C.
Wishart, Barry J. & Reichman, Louis C. Modern Sociological Issues. 2nd ed. 1979. pap. text ed. 13.95x (ISBN 0-02-428760-1). Macmillan.
Wishik, Cindy. Kids Dish It...Sugar-Free. (Illus.). 160p. 1982. pap. 8.95 (ISBN 0-918146-22-4). Peninsula WA.
Wishny, Judith, jt. auth. see Kaufman, Tanya.
Wishy, Bernard, jt. ed. see Scott, Donald M.
Wishy, Bernard, tr. see Vossler, Otto.
Wiskemann, Elizabeth. Italy Since Nineteen Forty-Five. LC 78-179497. 1972. 22.50 (ISBN 0-312-43925-3). St Martin.
Wisler, Chester O. & Brater, E. F. Hydrology. 2nd ed. LC 59-14981. 1959. 33.95x (ISBN 0-471-95634-1). Wiley.
Wisler, G. Clifton. A Cry of Angry Thunder. LC 79-7885. (Double D Western Ser.). 1980. 10.95 o.p. (ISBN 0-385-15657-X). Doubleday.
Wislicenus, G. F., jt. ed. see Robertson, J. M.
Wismar, Beth L. An Atlas for Histology. (Illus.). 200p. 1983. lib. bdg. 16.95 (ISBN 0-683-09150-6). Williams & Wilkins.
Wismar, Beth L. & Ackerman, G. Adolph. Visual Approach to Histology. (Illus.). 82p. 1970. text ed. 190.00x o.p. (ISBN 0-8036-9480-6); 7 tape cassettes 75.00x o.p. (ISBN 0-8036-9482-2); 5.00x o.p. (ISBN 0-8036-9481-4). Davis Co.
Wismer, D. A. Optimization Methods for Large-Scale Systems with Applications. 1971. 37.50 o.p. (ISBN 0-07-071154-2, P&RB). McGraw.
Wisner, Bill. The Fishermen's Sourcebook. (Illus.). 352p. 1983. 24.95 (ISBN 0-02-630570-4). Macmillan.
--Strange Sea Stories & Legends. (Orig.). 1981. pap. 3.50 (ISBN 0-451-12358-1, AE2358, Sig). NAL.
Wisner, Robert J., ed. see Smart, James R.
Wisner, William L., jt. auth. see Cook, Joseph J.
Wisneski, Henry, tr. see Meneghini, G. B.
Wisniak, J. Phase Diagram: A Literature Source Book, 2 vols. (Physical Sciences Data Ser.: Vol. 10). 1981. 298.00 (ISBN 0-444-41981-0). Elsevier.
Wisniak, J. & Tamir, A. Liquid-Liquid Equilibrium & Extraction: A Literature Source Book. (Vol. 7B). 1982. 191.50 (ISBN 0-444-42023-1). Elsevier.
--Liquid Phase Equilibrium & Extraction. (Physical Sciences Data Ser.: Vol. 7A). 1980. 159.75 (ISBN 0-444-41909-8). Elsevier.
--Mixing & Excess Thermodynamic Properties: A Literature Source Book. (Physical Sciences Data Ser.: Vol. 1). 1978. 149.00 (ISBN 0-444-41687-0). Elsevier.
--Mixing & Excess Thermodynamic Properties: Suppl. 1: A Literature Source Book. (Physical Science Data Ser.: Vol. 11). 1982. 138.50 (ISBN 0-444-42072-X). Elsevier.
Wisniewski, Richard. New Teachers in Urban Schools. 1968. pap. text ed. 2.95x (ISBN 0-685-55644-1, 30674). Phila Bk Co.
Wispe, Lauren G., ed. Altruism, Sympathy & Helping: Psychological & Sociological Principles. LC 78-3350. 1978. 33.50 (ISBN 0-12-760450-2). Acad Pr.
Wispelaere, C. de see De Wispelaere, C.
Wisse, Frederik. The Profile Method for Classifying & Evaluating Manuscript Evidence. 1982. pap. 17.00x (ISBN 0-8028-1918-4). Eerdmans.
Wissemann, Michael. Die Parther In der Augusteischen Dichtung. 186p. (Ger.). 1982. write for info. (ISBN 3-8204-5948-0). P Lang Pubs.
Wisser, jt. auth. see McCarr.
Wissler, Clark. Adventures in the Wilderness. 1925. text ed. 22.50x (ISBN 0-686-83455-0). Elliots Bks.
Wissman, Ruth. Whispers in the Wind. LC 79-8947. 192p. 1980. 8.95 o.p. (ISBN 0-385-15778-9). Doubleday.
Wister, Owen. Virginian. (Illus.). 1925. 15.95 (ISBN 0-02-630580-1); large print ed. 9.95 (ISBN 0-02-489480-X). Macmillan.
--The Virginian. 1979. pap. 2.25 (ISBN 0-451-51489-0, CE1489, Sig Classics). NAL.
Wistrand, Erik. Caesar & Contemporary Roman Society. (Acta Regiae Societatis Scientiarum et Litterarum Goteborg, Humaniora: No. 15). 1979. pap. text ed. 11.25x. Humanities.
--Miscellanea Propertiana. (Studia Graeca et Latina Gothoburgensia: No. 38). 1977. pap. text ed. 13.50x (ISBN 91-7346-041-9). Humanities.
Wistreich, George, jt. auth. see Kane, Rosalyn.
Wistreich, George A. & Lechtman, Max D. Laboratory Exercises in Microbiology. 3rd ed. 1976. lab manual 8.95x o.p. (ISBN 0-02-479210-1). Glencoe.
--Microbiology & Human Disease. 3rd ed. 1981. text ed. 31.95x (ISBN 0-02-470910-7). Macmillan.
Wistrich, Robert. Who's Who In Nazi Germany. 368p. 1982. 17.75 (ISBN 0-02-630600-X). Macmillan.
Wiswall, F. L. Development of Admiralty, Jurisdiction & Practice Since 1800. LC 77-108113. (Illus.). 1971. 44.50 (ISBN 0-521-07751-6). Cambridge U Pr.
Wiswell, Ella L., jt. auth. see Smith, Robert J.
Wiswell, Ella L., tr. see Golovnin, V. N.
Wiswell, Phil. I Hate Charades & Forty-Nine Other New Games. LC 80-54341. (Illus.). 128p. 1981. 7.95 (ISBN 0-8069-4582-6); lib. bdg. 9.99 (ISBN 0-8069-4583-4). Sterling.
Wit, Augusta de see De Wit, Augusta.
Wit, Dorothy de see De Wit, Dorothy.
Wit, Toke De see De Wit, Toke.
Witbeck, Alan R., jt. auth. see Allsen, Philip E.
Witchell, F. C. Roses for Every Garden. (Leisure Plan Bks). 1971. pap. 2.95 o.p. (ISBN 0-600-44178-4). Transatlantic.
Witcofski, Richard L., jt. auth. see Pizzarello, Donald J.
Witcover, Jules. The Main Chance. 1979. 12.95 (ISBN 0-670-45112-6). Viking Pr.
--Marathon: The Pursuit of the Presidency 1972-1976. 1978. pap. 2.95 o.p. (ISBN 0-451-08034-3, E8034, Sig). NAL.
Witek, John. Response Television: Combat Advertising of the 1980's. LC 81-66514. (Illus.). 240p. 1981. text ed. 22.95 (ISBN 0-87251-064-6). Crain Bks.
Witemeyer, Hugh. The Poetry of Ezra Pound: Forms & Renewal, 1908-1920. 1969. 24.50x o.p. (ISBN 0-520-01542-8); pap. 6.95 (ISBN 0-520-04515-7, CAL 526). U of Cal Pr.
Withall, Sabrina. The Baby's Book of Babies. LC 82-48238. (Illus.). 48p. (Orig.). (ps). 1983. pap. 3.80i (ISBN 0-06-091015-1, CN 1015, CN). Har-Row.
Witham, Francis, jt. auth. see Devlin, Robert.
Witham, H., jt. auth. see Vandervell, T.
Witherell, Anne L. Louis Pecour's Seventeen Hundred 'Recueil de Dances.' Buelow, George, ed. LC 82-13496. (Studies in Musicology: No. 60). 1983. 44.95 (ISBN 0-8357-1367-9, Pub. by UMI Res Pr). Univ Microfilms.
Witherick, M. E. & Mason, C. M. Dimensions of Change in a Growth Area. 271p. 1981. text ed. 29.00x (ISBN 0-566-00426-7). Gower Pub Ltd.
Witherow, Lucy. Big Bells, Little Bells. Mahany, Patricia, ed. (Happy Day Bks.). (Illus.). 24p. (ps-2). 1983. pap. 1.29 (ISBN 0-87239-632-0, 3552). Standard Pub.
Witherow, M. The Secretary on the Job. 2nd ed. 1976. text ed. 11.16 (ISBN 0-07-071182-8, G); instructor's manual & key 6.40 (ISBN 0-07-071183-6). McGraw.
--Secretary on the Job. 3rd ed. 1983. text ed. 11.16 (ISBN 0-07-071187-9, G); price not set tchr's manual & key (ISBN 0-07-071188-7). McGraw.
--Secretary on the Job: A Practice Set for Secretarial Students. 1967. text ed. 9.96 o.p. (ISBN 0-07-071180-1, G). McGraw.
Withers, G. A., jt. auth. see Throsby, D. C.
Withers, H. R., jt. ed. see Meyn, Rodney E.
Withers, Robert S. Introduction to Film. (Illus.). 304p. (Orig.). 1983. pap. 5.72i (ISBN 0-686-37885-7, COS CO 202). B&N NY.
Witherspoon, Robert. Codevelopment: City Rebuilding by Business & Government. LC 82-50871. (Development Component Ser.). (Illus.). 48p. 1982. pap. 10.00 (ISBN 0-87420-614-6, D24). Urban Land.
Withey, J. A., jt. auth. see Sein, Kenneth.
Withey, Lynne. Dearest Friend: A Life of Abigail Adams. LC 80-70694. (Illus.). 615p. 1981. 17.95 (ISBN 0-02-934760-2); pap. 9.95 (ISBN 0-02-934770-X). Free Pr.
Withey, Stephen B., jt. auth. see Scott, William A.
Withiam, Jack, Jr., jt. auth. see Neubert, Christopher.
Withim, Gloria. Elegant Eating in Hard Times: Fifty-Nine Vegetarian Main Dishes. LC 82-14916. 96p. 1982. 13.95 (ISBN 0-89594-087-6); pap. 4.95 (ISBN 0-89594-086-8). Crossing Pr.
Withington, Amelia & Grimes, David. Adolescent Sexuality: A Handbook for Counselors, Teachers & Parents. 135p. 1983. 18.50 (ISBN 0-8290-1270-2); pap. 9.95 (ISBN 0-8290-1271-0). Irvington.
Withington, Edward. Medical History from Earliest Times: A Popular History of the Healing Art 1894. 430p. pap. 25.00 (ISBN 0-87556-415-1). Saifer.
Withington, Frederic G. Environment for Systems Programs. LC 77-81204. (IBM Ser.). (Illus.). 1978. text ed. 22.95 (ISBN 0-201-14459-X). A-W.
Withington, W. A. & Fisher, Margaret, eds. Southeast Asia. LC 78-54259. (World Cultures Ser). (Illus.). (gr. 6 up). 1983. text ed. 11.20 1-4 copies; text ed. 8.96 5 or more (ISBN 0-88296-134-9); tchrs' ed 8.96 (ISBN 0-88296-370-8). Fideler.
Withner, C. L. The Orchids: Scientific Survey. (Illus.). 1959. 35.95x (ISBN 0-471-06827-6, Pub. by Wiley-Interscience). Wiley.
Withorn, Ann. The Circle Game: Services for the Poor in Massachusetts, 1966-1978. LC 82-6926. (Illus.). 1983. lib. bdg. 17.50x (ISBN 0-87023-376-9). U of Mass Pr.
Withrington, Donald, ed. Shetland & the Outside World, 1469 to 1969. (Illus.). 248p. 1982. 36.00x (ISBN 0-19-714107-2). Oxford U Pr.
Withrow, Dorothy E., et al. Gateways to Readable Books. 5th ed. 299p. 1975. 14.00 (ISBN 0-8242-0566-9). Wilson.
Withycombe, E. G. The Oxford Dictionary of English Christian Names. 3rd ed. 1977. 15.95x (ISBN 0-19-869124-6). Oxford U Pr.
--The Oxford Dictionary of English Christian Names. 3rd ed. 1977. pap. 9.95 (ISBN 0-19-281213-0, GB511, GB). Oxford U Pr.
Witke, Roxane, jt. auth. see Rinden, Robert.
Witker. Derecho Economico. (Span.). 1983. pap. text ed. write for info. (ISBN 0-06-319370-1, Pub. by HarLA Mexico). Har-Row.
Witkin, Kate & Philp, Richard. To Move, to Learn. LC 76-62864. (Illus.). 180p. 1977. 19.95 (ISBN 0-87722-091-3). Temple U Pr.
Witkin-Lanoil, Georgia. Human Sexuality: A Student's Resource Kit. 192p. 1983. pap. text ed. 11.50 scp (ISBN 0-06-047162-X, HarpC); instr's. manual avail. (ISBN 0-06-367170-0). Har-Row.
Witlig, Monique. Les Guerilleres. 1973. pap. 2.95 o.p. (ISBN 0-380-00817-3, 54957, Bard). Avon.
Witman, Gretchin M., jt. auth. see DeGraaf, Richard M.
Witmer, Edith. Rays Adventures with New Neighbors. 1981. 5.50 (ISBN 0-686-30774-7). Rod & Staff.

Witmer, Enos E. Space-Time & Microphysics: A New Synthesis. LC 79-66152. 1979. pap. text ed. 10.00 (ISBN 0-8191-0794-8). U Pr of Amer.

Witmer, Helen, jt. auth. see Powers, Edwin.

Witmer, T. Richard, tr. see Viete, Francois.

Witmore, Nyla. Homemaking Programs, Talks & Activities. LC 82-5626. (Illus.). 160p. (Orig.). 1982. pap. 4.95 (ISBN 0-87239-565-0, 2973). Standard Pub.

Witney, Dudley, jt. auth. see Gill, Brendan.

Witney, K. P. The Jutish Forest: A Study of the Weald of Kent from 450 to 1380 AD. (Illus.). 1976. text ed. 37.75x o.p. (ISBN 0-485-11165-9, Athlone Pr). Humanities.

Witschi, H. R. Scientific Basis of Toxicity Assessment. (Developments in Toxicology & Environmental Science Ser.: Vol. 6). 1980. 61.00 (ISBN 0-444-80200-2). Elsevier.

Witt, A. N., ed. see Wilhelm, Friedrich & Schlegel, Karl F.

Witt, Elmer N. Help It All Make Sense, Lord! LC 72-85147. 115p. 1972. pap. 3.50 (ISBN 0-570-03138-9, 12-2387). Concordia.

Witt, Harold. The Snow Prince Poems & Collages. (Illus.). 120p. (Orig.). 1982. pap. 8.75 (ISBN 0-9608574-1-9). Blue Unicorn.

Witt, Herbert, jt. auth. see Brink, Victor Z.

Witt, John. William Henry Hunt (Seventeen Ninety to Eighteen Sixty-Four) Life & Work with a Catalogue. (Illus.). 208p. 1982. 75.00 (ISBN 0-8390-0290-4). Allanheld & Schram.

Witt, John see Sunderland, John.

Witt, Mary A., et al. The Humanities: Cultural Roots & Continuities. 1980. Vol. 1. pap. text ed. 14.95 (ISBN 0-669-01450-8); Vol. 2. 0.14.95 (ISBN 0-669-01451-6); 13.95 (ISBN 0-669-02825-8). Heath.

Witt, Peter A., jt. ed. see Goodale, Thomas.

Witt, Reni L. PMS: What Every Woman Should Know About Premenstrual Syndrome. LC 82-42724. 200p. 1983. 14.95 (ISBN 0-8128-2903-4). Stein & Day.

Witt, Robert E. Marketing Doctoral Dissertation Abstracts, 1981. (Bibliography Ser.). 138p. 1982. pap. 11.00 (ISBN 0-686-83902-1). Am Mktg.

Witt, Robt. E., ed. Marketing Doctoral Dissertation Abstracts. 135p. 1982. 11.00 (ISBN 0-686-84358-4). Am Mktg.

Witt, Ronald G. Hercules at the Crossroads: The Life, Works, Thought of Coluccio Salutati. (Duke Monographs in Medieval & Renaissance Studies: No. 6). 1983. 65.00 (ISBN 0-8223-0527-5). Duke.

Witt, Roselyn. W. Norman Cooper: A View of a Holy Man. LC 81-70657. 96p. 1982. 7.50 (ISBN 0-87516-492-7); pap. 4.50 (ISBN 0-87516-471-4). De Vorss.

Witt, Scott. How to be Twice as Smart: Boosting Your Brainpower & Unleashing the Miracles of Your Mind. LC 82-14358. 262p. 1983. pap. 4.95 (ISBN 0-13-402339-0, Reward). P-H.

Witt, Thomas E. De see Steinert, Marlis G.

Witt, U. & Perske, J. SMS: A Program Package for Simulation & Gaming of Stochastic Market Processes & Learning Behavior. (Lecture Notes in Economics & Mathematical Systems Ser.: Vol. 202). (Illus.). 266p. 1983. pap. 18.50 (ISBN 0-387-11551-X). Springer-Verlag.

Wittcoff, Harold & Reuben, Bryan G. Industrial Organic Chemicals in Perspective, Part 2: Technology, Formulation & Use. LC 79-19581. 502p. 1980. 59.95x (ISBN 0-471-05780-0, Pub. by Wiley-Interscience). Wiley.

Wittcoff, Harold A. & Reuben, Bryan G. Industrial Organic Chemicals in Perspective, Part 1: Raw Materials & Manufacture. LC 79-19581. 1980. 36.50x (ISBN 0-471-03811-3, Pub. by Wiley-Interscience). Wiley.

Witte, Edwin E. Development of the Social Security Act. (Illus.). 238p. 1962. 25.00x o.p. (ISBN 0-299-02540-3); pap. 9.95x (ISBN 0-299-02544-6). U of Wis Pr.

Witte, John, ed. Dialogues with Northwest Writers: Interviews with Nine NW Writers, Including Tom Robbins, Mary Barnard & Richard Hugo. LC 82-19063. (Illus.). 280p. (Orig.). 1982. pap. 8.00 (ISBN 0-918402-06-9). NW Review Bks.

Witte, John F. Democracy, Authority, & Alienation in Work: Worker's Participation in an American Corporation. LC 80-16241. 216p. 1982. pap. 5.95 (ISBN 0-226-90421-0). U of Chicago Pr.

Witte, Kaaren. Angels in Faded Jeans. LC 79-84795. (Illus., Orig.). 1979. pap. 2.75 (ISBN 0-686-58510-0). Jeremy Bks.

Witte, Mike, jt. auth. see McGraw, Tug.

Witte, Randy, tr. see Camarillo, Leo.

Witte, Ulrich. Die Bezeichnungen Fur Den Bottcher Im Niederdeutschen Sprachbereich. xii, 489p. (Ger.). 1982. write for info. (ISBN 3-8204-6288-0). P Lang Pubs.

Witte, Willard E., jt. auth. see Lombra, Raymond.

Wittels, Harriet & Greisman, Joan. The Clear & Simple Thesaurus Dictionary. (Dictionaries). (Illus.). pap. 5.95 (ISBN 0-448-12198-0, G&D). Putnam Pub Group.

Wittels, Harriet, jt. auth. see Greisman, Joan.

Wittemann, Betsy & Webster, Nancy. Daytripping & Dining in Southern New England. 2nd ed. LC 78-57197. (Daytripping & Dining Ser.). (Illus.). 166p. 1978. pap. 5.95 o.p. (ISBN 0-934260-50-8). Imprint CT.

Wittemore, Edward. Quin's Shanghai Circus. 304p. 1982. pap. 3.50 (ISBN 0-380-61200-3, 61200, Bard). Avon.

Witten, David M. Breast. (Atlas of Tumor Radiology Ser.). (Illus.). 1969. 49.50 o.p. (ISBN 0-8151-9343-2). Year Bk Med.

Witten, David M., et al. Emmett's Clinical Urography, 3 vols. 4th ed. LC 76-19614. (Illus.). 1977. Set. 195.00x (ISBN 0-7216-9471-3); Vol. 1. 70.00x (ISBN 0-7216-9472-1); Vol. 2. 70.00x (ISBN 0-7216-9473-X); Vol. 3. 70.00x (ISBN 0-7216-9474-8). Saunders.

Wittenberg, Charles M. Authentic & Original Illustrations in Full Colors Depicting Scenes of the Future Life of Man As Described by Apparitions During a Series of Spiritualistic Seances. (Illus.). 99p. 1982. 192.00 o.p. (ISBN 0-86650-021-9). Gloucester Art.

Wittenberg, Jack, jt. auth. see Ferrucci, Joseph T.

Wittenborn, Dirk. Esme. 1983. 15.95 (ISBN 0-440-02138-3, Sey Lawr). Delacorte.

Wittenborn, J. R. Response to Meprobamate-A Predictive Analysis. LC 70-107228. 113p. 1970. 15.00 (ISBN 0-911216-11-1). Raven.

Wittenborn, J. R., et al, eds. Psychopharmacology & the Individual Patient. LC 71-116996. 256p. 1970. 21.00 (ISBN 0-911216-13-8). Raven.

Witter, Evelyn. Claw Foot. LC 74-33524. (Voices of the American Indian). (Illus.). 68p. (gr. 5 up). 1976. PLB 5.95 o.p. (ISBN 0-8225-0641-6). Lerner Pubns.

--How to Make Sunday School Fun for Everybody. Ronaldson, Dolores, ed. (Illus.). 80p. Date not set. pap. text ed. price not set (ISBN 0-916260-22-4). Meriwether Pub.

Witter, Michael, jt. auth. see Beckford, George.

Witters, Weldon, jt. auth. see Witters-Jones, Patricia.

Witters, Weldon L. & Jones-Witters, Patricia. Human Sexuality: A Biological Perspective. 498p. 1980. pap. text ed. 9.95 (ISBN 0-442-29589-8). Van Nos Reinhold.

Witters-Jones, Patricia & Witters, Weldon. Drugs & Society: A Biological Perspective. LC 82-21738. 400p. 1983. pap. text ed. 14.95 (ISBN 0-534-01412-7). Brooks-Cole.

Wittes, Simon. People & Power: A Study of Crisis in Secondary Schools. LC 70-632404. 106p. 1970. 12.00x (ISBN 0-87944-078-3); pap. 8.00x (ISBN 0-87944-077-5). Inst Soc Res.

Wittfoht, A. M. The Technical Terms in Plastics Engineering. 1976. 64.00 (ISBN 0-444-99846-2). Elsevier.

Wittfoht, A. M., ed. Plastics Technical Dictionary, 3 vols. (Illus.). 1700p. 1983. Set. text ed. 135.00x (ISBN 0-02-949940-2, Pub. by Hanser International). Macmillan.

--Plastics Technical Dictionary: Part 1: English-German. (Illus.). 600p. 1982. text ed. 59.00x (ISBN 0-02-949980-1, Pub. by Hanser International). Macmillan.

--Plastics Technical Dictionary: Part 2: German-English. (Illus.). 600p. 1983. text ed. 59.00x (ISBN 0-02-949960-7, Pub. by Hanser International). Macmillan.

--Plastics Technical Dictionary: Part 3: Reference Volume. (Illus.). 508p. 1982. text ed. 49.00x (ISBN 0-02-949970-4, Pub. by Hanser International). Macmillan.

Wittgen, Rudolf. Die Absatzwege der Baumwollindustrie In Den 80er Jahren. xiv, 308p. (Ger.). 1982. write for info. (ISBN 3-8204-5821-2). P Lang Pubs.

Wittgenstein, Ludwig. Blue & Brown Books. pap. 4.95xi (ISBN 0-06-131211-8, TB1211, Torch). Har-Row.

--Last Writings, Preliminary Studies for Part Two Philosophical Investigations. Luckhardt, C. G. & Aue, Maximilian A. E., trs. LC 82-42549. 256p. 1982. lib. bdg. 28.50x (ISBN 0-226-90445-8). U of Chicago Pr.

--Philosophical Grammar. Kenny, A. J., tr. 1974. 35.75x (ISBN 0-520-02664-0); pap. 9.95 (ISBN 0-520-03725-1). U of Cal Pr.

--Remarks on Colour. Anscombe, G. E., ed. McAlister, Linda L. & Schattle, Margarete, trs. from Ger. 1978. 19.50x (ISBN 0-520-03357-4); pap. 3.45 (ISBN 0-520-03727-8, CAL 406). U of Cal Pr.

--Remarks on Frazer's Golden Bough. Miles, A. C. & Rhees, R., trs. from Ger. LC 79-4038. 1979. Repr. of 1971 ed. text ed. 9.50x (ISBN 0-391-00984-2). Humanities.

--Remarks on the Foundations of Mathematics. 1967. pap. 6.95x o.p. (ISBN 0-262-73017-0, 74). MIT Pr.

--Remarks on the Foundations of Mathematics. rev ed. Von Wright, G. H. & Rhees, R., eds. Anscombe, G. E., tr. from Ger. 1978. text ed. 32.50x (ISBN 0-262-23080-1). MIT Pr.

--Tractatus Logico-Philosophicus. Pears, D. F. & McGuinness, B. F., trs. from Ger. 114p. 1972. text ed. 16.00x (ISBN 0-391-00359-3); pap. text ed. 4.95x (ISBN 0-7100-7923-0). Humanities.

--Zettel. Anscombe, G. E. M. & Von Wright, G. H., eds. Anscombe, G. E. M., tr. 1967. 27.50x (ISBN 0-520-01355-7); pap. 4.95 (ISBN 0-520-01635-1, CAL189). U of Cal Pr.

Wittich, Walter A., jt. ed. see Berger, James L.

Wittig, Arno F. Schaum's Outline of Introduction to Psychology. (Schaum's Outling Ser.). 1977. pap. 5.95 (ISBN 0-07-071194-1, SP). McGraw.

Wittig, J. Alice. U. S. Government Publications for the School Media Center. LC 79-24798. 121p. 1979. lib. bdg. 12.50 (ISBN 0-87287-214-9). Libs Unl.

Wittig, Michele A. & Petersen, Anne C., eds. Sex Related Differences in Cognitive Functioning: Developmental Issues. LC 79-9827. (Cognition & Perception Ser.). 1979. 33.50 (ISBN 0-12-761150-9). Acad Pr.

Wittig, S., et al. Participating Reader. 1978. pap. 11.95 (ISBN 0-13-650200-8). P-H.

Wittig, Susan, tr. see Uspensky, Boris.

Wittke, Carl. German-Americans & the World War. LC 74-75245. (The United States in World War 1 Ser). xi, 223p. 1974. Repr. of 1936 ed. lib. bdg. 13.95x (ISBN 0-89198-112-8). Ozer.

Wittke, Carl F. Refugees of Revolution. Repr. of 1952 ed. lib. bdg. 20.25x (ISBN 0-8371-2988-5, WIRR). Greenwood.

Wittkopf, Eugene R., jt. auth. see Kegley, Charles W., Jr.

Wittkower, R. Art & Architecture in Italy, Sixteen Hundred. 1973. 16.95x (ISBN 0-14-056116-1, Pelican). Penguin.

Wittkower, Rudolf. Architectural Principles in the Age of Humanism. (Illus.). 1971. pap. 6.95 (ISBN 0-393-00599-2). Norton.

Wittles, Harriet & Greisman, Joan. How to Spell It: A Dictionary of Commonly Misspelled Words. (Illus.). 336p. (gr. 1 up). 1982. pap. 6.95 (ISBN 0-448-14756-4, G&D). Putnam Pub Group.

Wittliff, James L. & Dapunt, Otto. Steroid Receptors & Hormone Dependent Neoplasia. LC 80-80877. (Illus.). 320p. 1980. 54.00x (ISBN 0-89352-043-8). Masson Pub.

Wittliff, James L. & Dapunt, Otto, eds. Hormone Cell Interaction in Reproductive Tissue. (Illus.). 320p. 1983. write for info (ISBN 0-89352-172-8). Masson Pub.

Wittliff, William & Clark, Sara. Raggedy Man. 1979. pap. 2.75 (ISBN 0-523-41702-0). Pinnacle Bks.

Wittman, A. & Klos, J. Dictionary of Data Processing. 3rd. rev. ed. 1977. 89.50 (ISBN 0-444-99823-3). Elsevier.

Wittman, F. H., ed. Autoclaved Aerated Concrete: Moisture & Properties. (Developments in Civil Engineering Ser.: No. 6). 380p. 1982. 81.00 (ISBN 0-444-42117-3). Elsevier.

Wittman, George. The Role of American Intelligence Organizations. (Reference Shelf Ser.). 1976. 6.25 (ISBN 0-8242-0599-5). Wilson.

Wittman, Karl S. Basic Sciences for Health Careers. 1976. text ed. 18.95 (ISBN 0-07-071195-X, G); tchr's manual & key 5.00 (ISBN 0-07-071197-6); activities & projects 9.95 (ISBN 0-07-071196-8). McGraw.

Wittman, Sally. The Wonderful Mrs. Trumbly. LC 81-47737. (Illus.). 40p. (gr. k-3). 1982. 9.13i (ISBN 0-06-026511-6, HarpJ); PLB 8.89g (ISBN 0-06-026512-4). Har-Row.

Wittmann, F. H., jt. auth. see Bazant, Z. P.

Wittmers, Lorentz E., Jr., jt. ed. see Pozos, Robert S.

Witton, Dorothy. Teen-Age Mexican Stories. 192p. (gr. 7-12). 1973. PLB 6.19 o.p. (ISBN 0-8313-0106-6). Lantern.

Wittram, Reinhard. Russia & Europe. (Library of European Civilization). (Illus.). 180p. 1974. 8.75 o.s.i. (ISBN 0-500-32028-4). Transatlantic.

Wittreich, Joseph, jt. ed. see Ide, Richard S.

Wittreich, Joseph A., Jr. Milton & the Line of Vision. LC 75-12215. (Illus.). 280p. 1975. 30.00 (ISBN 0-299-06910-9). U of Wis Pr.

Wittreich, Joseph A., Jr., ed. Nineteenth-Century Accounts of William Blake by Benjamin Heath Malkin, Henry Crabb Robinson, John Thomas Smith, Allan Cunningham, Frederick Tatham, & William Butler Yeats. LC 78-133330. 1970. 35.00x (ISBN 0-8201-1085-X). Schol Facsimiles.

Wittreich, Joseph A., Jr., ed. see Meadowcourt, Richard.

Wittreich, Joseph A., Jr., jt. ed. see Rothstein, Eric.

Wittrock, Merlin C., ed. Learning & Instruction. LC 76-18038. (Readings in Educational Research Ser.). 1977. 30.75 (ISBN 0-8211-2255-X); text ed. 28.00 ten or more copies (ISBN 0-685-52960-6). McCutchan.

Wittrup, Robert C. Human Anatomy & Physiology Laboratory Manual with Cat Dissections. (Orig.). 1981. pap. text ed. 14.95x (ISBN 0-8087-2384-7). Burgess.

Witty, Doreen, jt. auth. see Costello, Jeanne.

Witty, Helen & Colchie, Elizabeth S. Better Than Store-Bought. LC 78-20195. 1979. 14.37i (ISBN 0-06-014693-1, HarpT). Har-Row.

Witty, Paul. How to Become a Better Reader. 1962. text ed. 10.07 o.s.i. (ISBN 0-574-30086-4, 3-0086); 0.87 o.s.i. (ISBN 0-574-30089-9, 3-0089). SRA.

Witwer, Daniel B., jt. auth. see Pacifico, Carl R.

Witzenmann, Herbert. Beppe Assenza. (Illus.). 160p. 1979. 29.95 (ISBN 0-85440-340-X, Pub. by Steinerbooks). Anthroposophic.

Witzke, P. T., jt. auth. see McHale, T. J.

Witzke, Paul T., jt. auth. see McHale, Thomas J.

Witzmann, Reingard, jt. auth. see Wechsberg, Joseph.

Wixted, John T., tr. from Chines see Chuang, Wei.

Wizenberg, Larry, jt. ed. see Bobrow, Edwin E.

Wiznitzer, Martine R. Basic Mathematic Skills. 1979. pap. 5.95 (ISBN 0-07-055226-6, Trafalgar Hse Pub). McGraw.

Wlecke, Albert O. Wordsworth & the Sublime: An Essay on Romantic Self-Consciousness. (Perspectives in Criticism: No. 23). 1973. 26.50x (ISBN 0-520-02233-5). U of Cal Pr.

Wlodarski, Robert J. A Bibliography of Catalina Island Investigations & Excavations (1850-1980) (Occasional Papers: No. 9). (Illus.). 30p. 1982. pap. 3.00 (ISBN 0-917956-33-8). UCLA Arch.

WMO-CHy Working Group on Representative & Experimental Basins. Some Recommendations for the Operation of Representative & Experimental Basins & the Analysis of Data. (WMO-IHD Report Ser.: No. 15). 34p. (Fr. ed. also avail.). 1971. pap. write for info. o.p. (WMO). Unipub.

Wmo-Ecafe Regional Conference, Bangkok, 14-21 August 1973. The Role of Meteorological Services in the Economic Development of Asia & the South-West Pacific: Proceedings, No. 422. (Illus.). 172p. 1976. pap. 26.00 (ISBN 92-63-10422-0, W186, WMO). Unipub.

WMO Executive Committee, 26th Session. Drought: Lectures. (Special Environmental Report Ser: No. 5). (Illus.). 113p. 1975. pap. 18.00 (ISBN 92-63-00403-X, W251, WMO). Unipub.

WMO-IAMAP Symposium. Long-Term Climatic Fluctuations: Proceedings, No. 421. (Illus.). 503p. 1975. pap. 22.50 o.p. (ISBN 92-63-10421-2, WMO). Unipub.

WMO-IAMAP Symposium on Long-Term Climatic Fluctuations, Norwich, 1975. Proceedings. (WMO Pubns. Ser.: No. 421). 503p. 1975. pap. 42.00 (ISBN 0-686-93908-5, WMO). Unipub.

WMO-IUGG Symposium on Numerical Weather Prediction, Tokyo, 1968. Proceedings. pap. 52.00 (ISBN 0-686-93903-4, W342, WMO). Unipub.

WMO-IUGG Symposium on Research & Development Aspects of Long-Range Forecasting, Boulder, Colo., 1964. Proceedings. (Technical Notes Ser.). (Illus.). 339p. 1965. pap. 40.00 (ISBN 0-686-93910-7, WMO). Unipub.

WMO Scientific Conference on Weather Modification, 2nd, Boulder, Colo., 1976. Papers. (WMO Pubns. Ser.: No. 443). 592p. 1976. pap. 50.00 (ISBN 0-686-93895-X, W201, WMO). Unipub.

WMO Sixth Session, September 8-18, 1975, Colombo. Regional Association Two, Asia: Abridged Final Report of the Sixth Session. (WMO: No. 420). 1976. pap. 25.00 (ISBN 92-63-10430-1, W486, WMO). Unipub.

WMO Symposium on the Interpretation of Broad-Scale NWP Products for Local Forecasting Purposes. Papers. (WMO Ser.: No. 450). (Illus.). 1976. pap. 30.00 (ISBN 92-63-10450-6, W206, WMO). Unipub.

WMO Technical Conference on Instruments & Methods of Observation (TECIMO), Hamburg, 1977. Papers. (WMO Pubns Ser.: No. 480). 264p. (Fr. ed. also avail.). 1977. pap. 40.00 (ISBN 0-686-93894-1, 220, WMO). Unipub.

Wobschall, Darold. Circuit Design for Electronic Instrumentation: Analog & Digital Devices from Sensor to Display. LC 79-9084. (Illus.). 1979. 35.00 (ISBN 0-07-071230-1). McGraw.

Wodarski, John S. Rural Community Mental Health Practice. 288p. 1983. pap. text ed. 24.50 (ISBN 0-8391-1785-X, 19402). Univ Park.

Wode, Henning & Felix, Sascha W., eds. Language Development at the Crossroads. (Language & Development Ser.: 5). 250p. 1983. pap. 25.00 (ISBN 3-87808-571-0). Benjamins North Am.

Wodehouse, Lawrence, ed. American Architects from the Civil War to the First World War: A Guide to Information Sources. LC 73-17525. (Art & Architecture Information Guide Ser.: Vol. 3). 380p. 1976. 42.00x (ISBN 0-8103-1269-7). Gale.

--American Architects from the First World War to the Present: A Guide to Information Sources. LC 74-10259. (Art & Architecture Information Guide Ser.: Vol. 4). 380p. 1977. 42.00x (ISBN 0-8103-1270-0). Gale.

--British Architects, Eighteen Forty-Nineteen Seventy-Six: A Guide to Information Sources. LC 78-54116. (Art & Architecture Information Guide Ser.: Vol. 8). 1978. 42.00x (ISBN 0-8103-1393-6). Gale.

--Indigenous Architecture Worldwide: A Guide to Information Sources. LC 79-26580. (Art & Architecture Information Guide Ser.: Vol. 12). 1980. 42.00x (ISBN 0-8103-1450-9). Gale.

Wodehouse, P. G. The Code of the Woosters. 1975. pap. 3.95 (ISBN 0-394-72028-8, Vin). Random.

--La Granda Predika Handikapo. Baur, Arthur, tr. (Wodehouse in Translation Ser.: No. 4). (Illus.). 48p. 1982. pap. text ed. 14.50 (ISBN 0-87008-203-5). Heineman.

--The Great Sermon Handicap. (Wodehouse in Translation Ser.: No. 1). 48p. (Orig.). 1982. pap. 14.50 (ISBN 0-87008-200-0). Heineman.

--Das Grosse Predigt-Handikap. Foerster, Iris & Foerster, Rolf, trs. from Eng. (Wodehouse in Translation Ser.: No. 3). (Illus.). 48p. (Orig.). 1982. pap. 14.50 (ISBN 0-87008-202-7). Heineman.

--Magnum Praedicantum Certamen. Hewison, William, tr. from Eng. (Wodehouse in Translation Ser.: No. 2). (Illus.). 48p. (Orig.). 1982. pap. 14.50 (ISBN 0-87008-201-9). Heineman.

--The Mating Season. LC 82-48822. 256p. 1983. pap. 3.37 (ISBN 0-06-080659-1, P 659, PL). Har-Row.

--Most of P. G. Wodehouse. 1960. 12.95 o.p. (ISBN 0-671-49325-6). S&S.

--P. G. Wodehouse Pack. 1981. pap. 12.35 gift box (ISBN 0-14-095195-4). Penguin.

--Thank You, Jeeves. LC 82-48821. 192p. 1983. pap. 3.37i (ISBN 0-06-080657-5, P 651, PL). Har-Row.

--Uncle Fred in the Springtime. 1976. pap. 3.50 (ISBN 0-14-000971-X). Penguin.

--Very Good, Jeeves. 256p. 1975. pap. 3.50 (ISBN 0-14-001173-0). Penguin.

--The World of Mr. Mulliner. 1979. pap. 5.95 o.p. (ISBN 0-380-43141-6, 43141). Avon.

Woditsch, Gary. Developing Generic Skills: A Model for Competency-Based General Education. LC 77-72186. (CUE Project Occasional Paper Ser.: No. 3). 1977. pap. 3.25 (ISBN 0-89372-003-8). General Stud Res.

Woditsch, Gary, ed. see Cappuzzello, Paul & Schlesinger, Mark.

Woditsch, Gary, ed. see Ewens, Thomas.

Woditsch, Gary, ed. see Schlesinger, Mark.

Woditsch, Gary, ed. see Whimbey, Arthur & Barbarena, Celia.

Woehr, Richard, et al. Pasaporte, First Year Spanish. LC 79-26709. 1980. text ed. 21.95x (ISBN 0-471-02758-8); o.p. tchr's ed. (ISBN 0-471-04193-9); 9.50 o.p. wkbk (ISBN 0-471-02759-6); 3.00 o.p.tapes (ISBN 0-471-05837-8). Wiley.

Woelfel, Charles J. Accounting: An Introduction. 2nd ed. LC 76-54513. (Illus.). 1977. text ed. 26.50x (ISBN 0-673-16067-X); o.p. solutions manual (ISBN 0-685-75087-6); o.p. study guide & practice sets (ISBN 0-685-75088-4). Scott F.

Woelfflin, Heinrich. Sense of Form in Art. LC 57-12877. (Illus., Orig.). pap. 6.50 (ISBN 0-8284-0153-5). Chelsea Pub.

Woelfle, R. M. A Guide for Better Technical Presentations. (IEEE Press Selected Reprint Ser.). 229p. 1975. 20.95 o.p. (ISBN 0-471-01471-0, Pub. by Wiley-Interscience); pap. 13.50 o.p. (ISBN 0-471-01470-2). Wiley.

Woelfle, Robert M., ed. A Guide for Better Technical Presentations. LC 74-19559. 1975. 22.95 (ISBN 0-87942-055-3). Inst Electrical.

Woelful, Charles J. Accounting: An Introduction, Working Papers, Pt. II. 2nd ed. 1977. pap. text ed. 6.95x (ISBN 0-673-16070-X). Scott F.

--Accounting: An Introduction, Working Papers, Pt. I. 1977. pap. text ed. 10.50x (ISBN 0-673-16069-6). Scott F.

Woerdeman, M. W., jt. auth. see Langman, Jan.

Woerdman, M. W., jt. auth. see Langman, Jan.

Woerkom, Dorothy Van. Try Again, Mendellsohn! LC 78-5765. (Illus.). (gr. k-3). 1980. reinforced lib. bdg. 6.95 o.p. (ISBN 0-517-53228-X). Crown.

Woerkom, Dorothy Van see Van Woerkom, Dorothy.

Woerth, Sheila T., et al, eds. Your Child's Birth: A Comprehensive Guide for Pregnancy, Birth, & Postpartum. (Avery's Childbirth Education Ser.). (Illus.). 96p. (Orig.). 1982. pap. 5.95 (ISBN 0-89529-182-7). Avery Pub.

Woessner, H., jt. auth. see Bauer, F. L.

Woessner, Warren. Landing. 53p. 1973. 4.95 (ISBN 0-87886-035-5); pap. 2.95 (ISBN 0-87886-036-3). Ithaca Hse.

Woestehoff, Ellsworth S. Students with Reading Disabilities & Guidance. (Guidance Monograph). pap. 2.40 o.p. (ISBN 0-395-09948-X, 9-78848). HM.

Wofford, Azile. Book Selection for School Libraries. 318p. 1962. 10.00 (ISBN 0-8242-0005-5). Wilson.

--School Library at Work. (Illus.). 256p. 1959. 8.00 (ISBN 0-8242-0045-4). Wilson.

Wofford, J. C. Organizational Behavior: Foundation for Organizational Effectiveness. 480p. 1982. 22.95x (ISBN 0-534-01106-3). Kent Pub Co.

Wofford, Jerry C., et al. Organizational Communication. (Management Ser.). (Illus.). 1977. text ed. 29.00 (ISBN 0-07-070230-6, C); instr's. manual 18.95 (ISBN 0-07-070231-4). McGraw.

Wofford, Joan W., jt. auth. see Jentz, Barry C.

Wofford, Louise. Boy Cat & the Light Mystery. 1983. pap. 5.95 (ISBN 0-932298-20-6). Copple Hse.

Wogaman, J. Philip. A Christian Method of Moral Judgment. LC 76-40108. 1977. 12.50 o.s.i. (ISBN 0-664-20763-4); pap. 8.95 (ISBN 0-664-24134-4). Westminster.

--The Great Economic Debate: An Ethical Analysis. LC 77-3870. 1977. 10.95 (ISBN 0-664-20780-4); pap. 8.95 (ISBN 0-664-24141-7). Westminster.

Wogan, Gerald N., jt. ed. see Mateles, Richard I.

Woggon, Guillermo. Alla En El Pesebre. Cranberry, Nola, tr. from Eng. (Libros Para Colorear). (Illus.). 16p. (Span.). 1982. pap. 1.20 (ISBN 0-311-38562-1). Casa Bautista.

--Animales Que Dios Creo. Cranberry, Nola, tr. from Eng. (Libros Para Colorear). (Illus.). 16p. (Span.). 1982. pap. 1.20 (ISBN 0-311-38560-5). Casa Bautista.

--Cultivemos Una Huerta. Cranberry, Nola, tr. (Libros Para Colorear). (Illus.). 16p. (Span.). 1982. pap. 1.20 (ISBN 0-311-38564-8). Casa Bautista.

--Versiculos "Llave". Cranberry, Nola, tr. (Libros Para Colorear). (Illus.). 16p. (Span.). 1982. pap. 1.20 (ISBN 0-311-38565-6). Casa Bautista.

Wohl, A. Victorian Family. LC 77-9234. 1978. 25.00x (ISBN 0-312-84276-7). St Martin.

Wohl, A., jt. auth. see Wohl, H.

Wohl, Anthony S., ed. see Mearns, Andrew, et al.

Wohl, Burton. Soldier in Paradise. LC 77-8852. 1977. 9.95 o.p. (ISBN 0-399-11865-9). Putnam Pub Group.

Wohl, G., jt. auth. see Edwards, A.

Wohl, Gary S., jt. auth. see Burton, D.

Wohl, Gerald. Structured COBOL: A Direct Approach. 1979. pap. text ed. 17.95 (ISBN 0-574-21230-2, 13-4230); instr's guide avail. (ISBN 0-574-21231-0, 13-4231); student manual 7.50 (ISBN 0-574-21232-9, 13-4232); solutions manual 3.25 (ISBN 0-574-21233-7, 13-4233). SRA.

Wohl, Gerald & Murach, Mike. BASIC: A Direct Approach. LC 77-2851. 1977. pap. text ed. 5.95 (ISBN 0-574-21125-X, 13-4125). SRA.

Wohl, H. & Wohl, A. Portugal. 29.95 (ISBN 0-935748-48-2). ScalaBooks.

Wohl, James P. The Blind Trust Kills. LC 78-55654. 1978. 8.95 o.p. (ISBN 0-672-52525-9). Bobbs.

Wohl, Martin & Martin, Brian V. Traffic System Analysis for Engineers & Planners. (Transportation Ser.). 1967. text ed. 46.50 (ISBN 0-07-071274-3, C). McGraw.

Wohl, Milton. Preparation for Writing: Grammar. LC 78-647. 1978. pap. text ed. 9.95 (ISBN 0-88377-106-3). Newbury Hse.

--Techniques for Writing: Composition. LC 78-646. 1978. pap. text ed. 9.95 (ISBN 0-88377-107-1). Newbury Hse.

Wohl, Paul. Gun Trader's Guide. 8th ed. (Stoeger Bks). (Illus.). 1977. pap. 7.95 o.s.i. (ISBN 0-695-80843-5). Follett.

Wohlenberg, Ernest H., jt. auth. see Morrill, Richard L.

Wohlers, Ronald W. Lumped & Distributed Passive Networks: A Generalized & Advanced Viewpoint. (Electrical Science Monographs). 1969. 17.50 (ISBN 0-12-761450-8). Acad Pr.

Wohlfarth, E. P. Ferromagnetic Materials: A Handbook on the Properties of Magnetically Ordered Substances, Vol. 3. 836p. Date not set. 159.50 (ISBN 0-444-86378-8). Elsevier.

--Handbook of Ferromagnetic Materials, Vols. 1 & 2. Date not set. Set. 200.00 (ISBN 0-444-85313-8); Vol. 1. 116.50 (ISBN 0-444-85311-1); Vol. 2. 116.50 (ISBN 0-444-85312-X). Elsevier.

Wohlforth, E. P., ed. see Weiss, R. J.

Wohlmuth, Ed. The Overnight Guide to Public Speaking: The Ed Wohlmuth Method. 128p. 1983. 7.95 (ISBN 0-89471-200-4); lib. bdg. 15.90 (ISBN 0-89471-199-7). Running Pr.

Wohlrabe, Raymond A. Fundamental Physical Forces. LC 78-82400. (Introducing Modern Science Ser.). (Illus.). (gr. 7 up). 1969. 5.95 o.p. (ISBN 0-397-31074-9, HarpJ). Har-Row.

--Metals. LC 64-19046. (Introducing Modern Science Books Ser). (Illus.). (gr. 7-9). 1964. 8.95 o.p. (ISBN 0-397-30764-0, HarpJ). Har-Row.

Wohlrabe, Raymond A., jt. auth. see Barnouw, Adriaan J.

Wohlstetter, Albert & Gilinsky, Victor. Nuclear Policies: Fuel Without the Bomb. LC 78-13724. 128p. 1978. prof ref 20.00x (ISBN 0-88410-084-7). Ballinger Pub.

Wohlstetter, Roberta. Pearl Harbor: Warning & Decision. 1962. 25.00x (ISBN 0-8047-0597-6); pap. 8.95 (ISBN 0-8047-0598-4, SP14). Stanford U Pr.

Wohmann, Gabriele. Return Indefinite. Hawkes, James, tr. 192p. 1983. 11.95 (ISBN 0-941324-05-2). Van Vactor & Goodheart.

Wohrer, Anne, jt. auth. see Pop, Iggy.

Woikinson, Frederick. World War I Weapons & Uniforms. (Illus.). 14.95x o.p. (ISBN 0-8464-0981-X). Beekman Pubs.

Woinowsky-Krieger, S., jt. auth. see Timoshenko, Stephen P.

Woititz, Janet G. Marriage on the Rocks: How to Live with an Alcoholic. 1979. 7.95 o.s.i. (ISBN 0-440-05918-6). Delacorte.

Woiwode, Larry. Poppa John. 204p. 1983. pap. 6.95 (ISBN 0-89107-280-2, Crossway Bks). Good News.

Wojciechowska, Maja. Don't Play Dead Before You Have To. 1971. pap. 1.50 o.p. (ISBN 0-440-92105-8, LFL). Dell.

Wojciechowski, Andrzej, tr. see Barron, Stephanie, et al.

Wojciechowski, B. W. Chemical Kinetics for Chemical Engineers. LC 75-23119. 333p. (Orig.). 1975. pap. text ed. 11.95 o.p. (ISBN 0-88408-069-2). Sterling Swift.

Wojciechowski, Bohdan W. Chemical Kinetics for Chemical Engineers. 2nd ed. (Illus.). 333p. 1982. pap. text ed. 11.95 o.p. (ISBN 0-88408-130-3). Sterling Swift.

Wojciechowski, Jercy A., ed. Conceptual Basis of the Classification of Knowledge: Proceedings of the Ottawa Conference. 503p. 1978. text ed. 58.00x (ISBN 0-89664-016-7, Pub. by K G Saur). Gale.

Wojciechowski, William V. & Neff, Paula E. Comprehensive Review of Respiratory Therapy. LC 81-1947. 549p. 1981. 19.95 (ISBN 0-471-08408-5, Pub. by Wiley Med). Wiley.

Wojcio & Gustason. Music in Motion: 22 Songs in Signing Exact English, for Children. (Illus.). 106p. (ps up). Date not set. price not set (ISBN 0-916708-07-1). Modern Signs.

Wojna, Ryszard, tr. Poland: The Country & Its People. LC 80-451948. 208p. (Orig.). 1979. pap. 6.00x o.p. (ISBN 0-8002-2278-4). Intl Pubns Serv.

Wojowasito, Soewojo. A Kawi Lexicon. Mills, Roger F., ed. LC 78-57221. (Michigan Papers on South & Southeast Asia: No. 17). xv, 629p. (Orig.). 1980. pap. 16.00x (ISBN 0-89148-017-X). Ctr S&SE Asian.

Wojslaw, Charles F. Electronic Concepts: Principles & Circuits. (Illus.). 416p. 1980. text ed. 20.95 (ISBN 0-8359-1660-X); instrs.' manual avail. (ISBN 0-8359-1661-8). Reston.

Wojtczak, L., jt. auth. see Kocinski, J.

Wojtyla, Karol. Collected Poems. 191p. 1982. 10.95 (ISBN 0-394-52810-7). Random.

Wolanin, Mary O. & Phillips, Linda R. Confusion: Prevention & Care. LC 80-18508. (Illus.). 415p. 1981. pap. text ed. 24.95 (ISBN 0-8016-5629-X). Mosby.

Wolanin, Ron, jt. auth. see Grossman, Irwin.

Wolansky, William D., et al. Fundamentals of Fluid Power. LC 76-13963. (Illus.). 1977. text ed. 28.50 (ISBN 0-395-18956-X); write for info. instr's. manual o.s. (ISBN 0-395-18955-1). HM.

Wolberg, Barbara J. Zooming in: Photographic Discoveries Under the Microscope. LC 73-18631. 64p. (gr. 5-8). 1974. 7.75 o.p. (ISBN 0-15-299970-1, HJ). HarBraceJ.

Wolberg, J. Application of Computers to Engineering Analysis. 1971. 27.50 o.p. (ISBN 0-07-071300-6, P&RB). McGraw.

Wolchik, jt. auth. see Sodaro.

Wolchonok, Louis. Art of Three Dimensional Design: How to Create Space Figures. LC 34-9269. 1969. pap. 5.95 (ISBN 0-486-22201-2). Dover.

Wolck, I. D., ed. Subject Catalogue-Africa, 3 vols. Incl. Vol. 2. Politics. 85.00x (ISBN 0-686-77395-0); Vol. 3. Literature. 85.00 (ISBN 0-686-77396-9); Vol. 4. Social & Cultural Anthropology. 140.00x (ISBN 0-686-77397-7); Vol. 5. Geography & Social Sciences. 150.00x (ISBN 3-598-20925-8). 1979 (Pub. by K G Saur). Gale.

Wolcott, Imogene. The Yankee Cook Book. 384p. (Orig.). (YA) 1981. pap. 10.95 (ISBN 0-8289-0456-1). Greene.

Wolcott, Laura. Gray Dream, & Other Stories of New England Life, 2 vols. in 1. 1918. text ed. 14.50x (ISBN 0-686-83563-8). Elliots Bks.

Wolcott, Leon O., jt. auth. see Gaus, John M.

Wolcott, Mark W., ed. Ambulatory Surgery & the Basics of Emergency Surgical Care. (Illus.). 699p. 1981. pap. text ed. 45.00 flexible bdg. o.p. (ISBN 0-397-50480-2, Lippincott Medical). Lippincott.

Wolcott, Reed. Rose Hill. LC 76-7951. (Illus.). 1976. 9.95 o.p. (ISBN 0-399-11622-2). Putnam Pub Group.

Wolcott, Roger, ed. see Prescott, W. H.

Wolcotts-Legal Forms. California Notary's Journal. 202p. 1982. 11.95 (ISBN 0-910531-00-5); pap. 7.95 (ISBN 0-910531-01-3). Wolcotts.

Wold, H., jt. auth. see Joreskog, K. G.

Wold, Milo & Cykler, Edmund. An Introduction to Music & Art in the Western World. 6th ed. 380p. 1980. pap. text ed. write for info. o.p. (ISBN 0-697-03119-5); instrs.' man. avail. o.p. (ISBN 0-697-03120-9). Wm C Brown.

Wold, Milo A. & Cykler, Edmund. An Introduction to Music & Art in the Western World. 7th ed. 410p. 1982. pap. text ed. write for info. (ISBN 0-697-03124-1); instr's. manual avail. (ISBN 0-697-03125-X). Wm C Brown.

Wold, Richard J. & Hinz, William J., eds. Geology & Tectonics of the Lake Superior Basin. LC 82-15425. (Memoir Ser.: No. 156). (Illus.). 1982. 38.50x (ISBN 0-8137-1156-8). Geol Soc.

Wold, Robert M., ed. Visual & Perceptual Aspects for the Achieving & Underachieving Child. LC 69-20314. (Illus., Orig.). 1969. pap. 10.00x o.p. (ISBN 0-87562-016-7). Spec Child.

Wolde, Gunilla. Betsy & Peter Are Different. LC 78-66265. (Betsy Bks.). (Illus.). (ps). 1982. 1.95 (BYR); PLB 4.99 (ISBN 0-394-95423-8). Random.

--Betsy & the Chicken Pox. LC 76-9323. (Illus.). (ps-k). Date not set. 1.95 (ISBN 0-394-85425-X, BYR); PLB 4.99 (ISBN 0-394-95425-4). Random.

--Betsy & the Doctor. LC 78-50057. (Betsy Bks.). (Illus.). (ps). 1978. 1.75 (ISBN 0-394-85382-2, BYR); PLB 4.99 (ISBN 0-394-95382-7). Random.

--Betsy & the Vacuum Cleaner. LC 78-66266. (Betsy Bks.). (Illus.). (ps). 1982. 1.95 (ISBN 0-394-85426-8, BYR); PLB 4.99 (ISBN 0-394-95426-2). Random.

--Betsy's First Day at Nursery School. LC 76-9322. (Betsy Bks.). (Illus.). (ps-k). 1976. 1.75 (ISBN 0-394-85381-4, BYR); PLB 4.99 (ISBN 0-394-95381-9). Random.

--Betsy's Fixing Day. LC 78-50056. (Illus.). (ps). Date not set. 1.75 (ISBN 0-394-85424-1, BYR); PLB 4.99 (ISBN 0-394-95424-6). Random.

--Tommy Cleans His Room. LC 77-157099. (Illus.). (ps-1). 1971. 1.25 o.p. (ISBN 0-395-12602-9). HM.

--Tommy Takes a Bath. LC 73-157098. (Illus.). (ps-1). 1971. 1.25 o.p. (ISBN 0-395-12604-5). HM.

Woldin, Beth W. Benjamin's Perfect Solution. LC 78-12245. (Illus.). (ps-2). 1979. PLB 6.95 o.p. (ISBN 0-7232-6160-1). Warne.

Woldman, Albert A. Lincoln & the Russians. LC 78-110297. ix, 311p. Repr. of 1952 ed. lib. bdg. 14.00x o.p. (ISBN 0-8371-4503-1, WOLR). Greenwood.

Wolenik, Robert. Buying & Selling Currency for Profit. rev. ed. (Illus.). 1980. pap. 5.95 o.p. (ISBN 0-8092-7452-3). Contemp Bks.

Wolenik, Robert, jt. auth. see Van Trees, James.

Wolensky, Robert P. & Miller, Edward J. The Small City & Regional Community: Proceedings of the 1982 Conference, Vol. V. LC 79-644450. viii, 450p. 1982. pap. text ed. 14.50 (ISBN 0-932310-04-4). UWSP Found Pr.

Wolf. Journey in Faith. pap. 3.00 (ISBN 0-8164-5646-1); leader's guide 0.95 (ISBN 0-8164-5645-3). Seabury.

Wolf, Aline D. Look at the Child. LC 78-58153. (Illus.). 1978. 9.95x (ISBN 0-9601016-2-4); pap. 5.95 (ISBN 0-686-96844-1). Parent-Child Pr.

--A Parents' Guide to the Montessori Classroom. (Illus.). 1980. pap. 4.00x (ISBN 0-9601016-0-8). Parent-Child Pr.

Wolf, Alison, jt. auth. see Wallace, Ruth A.

Wolf, Allan C., jt. auth. see Hornbrook, John F.

Wolf, Barbara & Wolf, Frederick B. Exploring Faith & Life: A Journey in Faith for Junior High - Manual for Clergy & Leaders. 64p. (Orig.). 1983. pap. 3.95 (ISBN 0-8164-2437-3). Seabury.

--Exploring Faith & Life: A Journey in Faith for Junior High - Manual for Sponsors. 32p. (Orig.). 1983. pap. 2.95 (ISBN 0-8164-2436-5). Seabury.

Wolf, Barbara B., jt. auth. see Wolf, Frederick B.

Wolf, Bernard. Anna's Silent World. LC 76-52943. 1977. 12.45 (ISBN 0-397-31739-5, HarpJ). Har-Row.

--Connie's New Eyes. LC 76-17014. (gr. 6-12). 1976. 12.45 (ISBN 0-397-31697-6, HarpJ). Har-Row.

--Don't Feel Sorry for Paul. LC 74-9925. (Illus.). 96p. (gr. 3-6). 1974. 12.45 (ISBN 0-397-31588-0, HarpJ). Har-Row.

--In This Proud Land: The Story of a Mexican American Family. LC 78-9680. (Illus.). (gr. 3-6). 1979. 12.45 (ISBN 0-397-31815-4, HarpJ). Har-Row.

Wolf, Beverly, jt. auth. see Barry, Ruth.

Wolf, Bryan J. Romantic Re-Vision: Culture & Consciousness in Nineteenth-Century American Painting & Literature. LC 82-2741. (Illus.). 320p. 1983. lib. bdg. 27.50x (ISBN 0-226-90501-2). U of Chicago Pr.

Wolf, Burton, jt. auth. see Rice, William.

Wolf, Charles, Jr. The Indonesian Story. LC 73-5212. 201p. 1973. Repr. of 1948 ed. lib. bdg. 16.75x (ISBN 0-8371-6866-X, WOIS). Greenwood.

Wolf, Charles P., jt. ed. see Finsterbusch, Kurt.

Wolf, Charlotte. Garrison Community: A Study of an Overseas American Military Colony. LC 70-81523. (Contributions in Sociology Ser.: No. 2). 1969. lib. bdg. 29.95 (ISBN 0-8371-1853-0, WOG/). Greenwood.

Wolf, Christa. Der Geteilte Himmel. (Easy Readers B Ser.). 80p. (Ger.). 1980. pap. text ed. 3.95 (ISBN 0-88436-883-1, 45263). EMC.

--No Place on Earth. Van Heurck, Jan, tr. from Ger. 124p. 1982. 11.95 (ISBN 0-374-22298-3). FS&G.

--The Quest for Christa T. Middleton, Christopher, tr. from German. 185p. 1970. pap. 4.95 (ISBN 0-374-51534-4). FS&G.

Wolf, Clarence, Jr. Seven Letters: The Securities Market & You. LC 81-66095. 64p. Date not set. pap. 1.95 (ISBN 0-686-84242-1). Banyan Bks.

Wolf, Daniel. The American Space: Meaning in Nineteenth-Century Landscape Photography. 1983. 49.95 (ISBN 0-8195-5071-X). Wesleyan U Pr.

Wolf, Deborah G. The Lesbian Community. LC 77-93478. 1979. 14.95x (ISBN 0-520-03657-3); pap. 4.95 (ISBN 0-520-04248-4, CAL 484). U of Cal Pr.

Wolf, Donald & Wolf, Margot L., eds. The Human Body. LC 82-80879. (Matter-of-Fact Bks.). (Illus.). 64p. (gr. 3-8). 1982. pap. 3.95 (ISBN 0-448-04086-7, G&D). Putnam Pub Group.

Wolf, Donald D. & Wolf, Margot L. Dinosaurs. (Matter of Fact Books Ser.). (Illus.). 64p. 1982. pap. 3.95 (ISBN 0-448-04084-0, G&D). Putnam Pub Group.

--Stars, Moons & Planets. LC 82-80878. (Matter-of-Fact Bks.). (Illus.). 64p. (gr. 3-8). 1982. pap. 3.95 (ISBN 0-448-04089-1, G&D). Putnam Pub Group.

Wolf, Donald D. & Wolf, Margot L., eds. Flowering Plants. LC 82-80883. (Matter-of-Fact Bks.). (Illus.). 64p. (gr. 3-8). 1982. 3.95 (ISBN 0-448-04085-9, G&D). Putnam Pub Group.

--Insects. LC 82-80882. (Matter-of Fact Bks.). (Illus.). 64p. (gr. 3-8). 1982. pap. 3.95 (ISBN 0-448-04087-5, G&D). Putnam Pub Group.

--Rocks & Minerals. LC 82-80880. (Matter-of-Fact Bks.). (Illus.). 64p. (gr. 3-8). 1982. pap. 3.95 (ISBN 0-448-04088-3, G&D). Putnam Pub Group.

Wolf, E., ed. Progress in Optics, Vol. 18. 1980. 64.00 (ISBN 0-444-85445-2, North-Holland). Elsevier.

--Progress in Optics, Vol. 19. 1982. 57.50 (ISBN 0-444-85444-4, North Holland). Elsevier.

Wolf, E. J. Separation Methods in Organic Chemistry & Biochemistry. 1969. 41.00 (ISBN 0-12-761650-0). Acad Pr.

Wolf, Earl C. One, Two & Three John: Everybody Ought to Know. (Beacon Small-group Bible Studies). 80p. 1982. pap. 2.25 (ISBN 0-8341-0791-0). Beacon Hill.

Wolf, Edwin, 2nd, jt. ed. see Keynes, Geoffrey L.

Wolf, Elliott, ed. Seattle Epicure. (Epicure Ser.). 1983. pap. 5.95 (ISBN 0-89716-115-7). Peanut Butter.

--Sun Valley Epicure. (Epicure Ser.). 1982. pap. 2.95 (ISBN 0-89716-118-1). Peanut Butter.

--Vail Epicure. (Epicure Ser.). 1982. pap. 2.95 (ISBN 0-89716-117-3). Peanut Butter.

Wolf, Enid G. Beginning Mathematics Concepts. pap. 2.75x (ISBN 0-88323-116-6, 143); tchr's manual 1.00 (ISBN 0-88323-117-4, 144). Richards Pub.
--More Mathematics Concepts. 1975. pap. 2.75x (ISBN 0-88323-126-3, 214). Richards Pub.
Wolf, Eric R. Europe & the People without History. LC 81-24031. (Illus.). 440p. 1982. 29.95 (ISBN 0-520-04459-2); pap. 8.95 (ISBN 0-520-04898-9). U of Cal Pr.
--Peasants. (Illus., Orig.). 1966. pap. 9.95 ref. ed. (ISBN 0-13-655456-3). P-H.
Wolf, Eric R. & Hansen, Edward C. The Human Condition in Latin America. (Illus.). 1972. 17.50 o.p. (ISBN 0-19-501570-3); pap. 7.95x (ISBN 0-19-501569-X). Oxford U Pr.
Wolf, Frank L. Elements of Probability & Statistics. 2nd ed. (McGraw-Hill Ser. in Probability & Statistics). (Illus.). 416p. 1974. 17.95 o.p. (ISBN 0-07-071341-3, C); instructor's manual 2.95 o.p. (ISBN 0-07-071342-1). McGraw.
Wolf, Frederick B. & Wolf, Barbara B. Exploring Faith & Life: A Journey in Faith for Junior High Student's Reader. 128p. 1983. pap. 5.95 o.p. (ISBN 0-8164-2431-4). Seabury.
Wolf, Frederick B., jt. auth. see Wolf, Barbara.
Wolf, G. A. Collecting Data from Patients. (Illus.). 286p. 1977. pap. text ed. 17.95 (ISBN 0-8391-0983-0). Univ Park.
Wolf, George D. William Warren Scranton: Pennsylvania Statesman. LC 80-21736. (Keystone Bks.). (Illus.). 220p. 1981. 16.95x (ISBN 0-271-00278-6). Pa St U Pr.
Wolf, Gordon D., jt. auth. see Cheeks, James E.
Wolf, H., ed. The Fix-Point Approach to Interdependent Systems. (Contributions to Economic Analysis Ser.: Vol. 132). 1982. 53.25 (ISBN 0-444-85451-7). Elsevier.
Wolf, H. F. Silicon Semiconductor Data. 1969. inquire for price (ISBN 0-08-013019-4); write for info. xerox copyflo avail. Pergamon.
Wolf, H. K. & MacFarlane, P., eds. Optimization of Computer ECG Processing. 1980. 42.75 (ISBN 0-444-85413-4). Elsevier.
Wolf, H. K., ed. see World Conference on Medical Informatics, 2nd.
Wolf, Harvey J. & Frangia, George W. Behavioral Applications in Public Management: A Reader. LC 79-63852. (Illus.). 1979. pap. text ed. 8.50 (ISBN 0-8191-0744-1). U Pr of Amer.
Wolf, Helmut. Heat Transfer. 512p. 1983. text ed. 32.50 scp (ISBN 0-06-047181-6, HarpC); sol. manual avail. (ISBN 0-06-367180-8). Har-Row.
Wolf, Herbert. Haggai & Malachi. (Everyman's Bible Commentary Ser.). 128p. (Orig.). 1976. pap. 4.50 (ISBN 0-8024-2037-0). Moody.
Wolf, Howard. Forgive the Father: A Memoir of Changing Generations. LC 78-14396. 1978. 8.95 (ISBN 0-915220-44-X). New Republic.
Wolf, Hugo. The Complete Morike Songs. (Music Ser.). 208p. 1983. pap. 8.95 (ISBN 0-486-24380-X). Dover.
Wolf, Isabel, ed. The Practical Guide to Nutrition. 192p. (Orig.). Date not set. cancelled (ISBN 0-915658-62-3); pap. cancelled (ISBN 0-915658-61-5). Meadowbrook Pr.
Wolf, J. A., Jr., jt. auth. see Kamal, M. H.
Wolf, J. J. Studies in Stock Speculation, 2 vols. 1966. Repr. of 1924 ed. Vol. 1. flexible cover 6.00 (ISBN 0-87034-017-4); Vol. 2. flexible cover 6.00 (ISBN 0-87034-018-2). Fraser Pub Co.
Wolf, James. Men of Chesley. 1982. 9.95 (ISBN 0-8062-1920-3). Carlton.
Wolf, James R. Guide to the Continental Divide Trail: Northern Colorado, Vol. 4. LC 76-17632. (Orig.). 1982. pap. 9.95 (ISBN 0-934326-04-5). Continent Divide.
Wolf, Janet. Her Book. LC 81-48651. (Illus.). 40p. (ps-2). 1982. 9.13i (ISBN 0-06-026581-7, HarpJ); PLB 9.89g (ISBN 0-06-026582-5). Har-Row.
Wolf, Jess. Public Relations-Publicity: Fundamentals for Shopping Center Professionals. 14.00 (ISBN 0-686-84001-1). Intl Coun Shop.
Wolf, Joan. The American Duchess. 1982. pap. 2.25 (ISBN 0-451-11918-5, AE1918, Sig). NAL.
--The Counterfeit Marriage. (Orig.). 1980. pap. 1.75 o.p. (ISBN 0-451-09064-0, E9064, Sig). NAL.
--His Lordship's Mistress. 1982. pap. 2.25 (ISBN 0-451-11459-0, AE1459, Sig). NAL.
--A London Season. (Orig.). 1981. pap. 1.95 o.p. (ISBN 0-451-09570-7, J9570, Sig). NAL.
--Margarita. 1982. pap. 2.25 (ISBN 0-451-11556-2, AE1556, Sig). NAL.
--The Scottish Lord. 1982. pap. 2.25 (ISBN 0-451-11273-3, AE1273, Sig). NAL.
Wolf, Joan, tr. see Lasker-Schuler, Else.
Wolf, Joan S. & Stephens, Thomas M. Effective Skills in Parent & Teacher Conferencing the Parent's Perspective. pap. 4.95 (ISBN 0-936882-81-6). NCEMMH.
Wolf, John. The Minolta Guide. (Modern Camera Guide Ser.). (Illus.). 1979. 11.95 o.p. (ISBN 0-8174-2453-9, Amphoto); pap. 7.95 (ISBN 0-8174-2128-9). Watson-Guptill.
Wolf, John C. Minolta Reflex Photography. LC 76-16460. (Illus.). 1977. 11.95 o.p. (ISBN 0-8174-2409-1, Amphoto). Watson-Guptill.
--Minolta SR-T-102-101-100 Guide. (Illus.). 128p. 1975. 4.95 o.p. (ISBN 0-8174-0169-5, Amphoto). Watson-Guptill.
--The Nikon Guide. (Modern Camera Guide Ser.). (Illus.). 1977. 11.95 (ISBN 0-8174-2432-6, Amphoto); pap. 6.95 (ISBN 0-8174-2110-6). Watson-Guptill.
--Nikon Guide. rev ed. (Modern Camera Guide Ser.). (Illus.). 1981. pap. 7.95 (ISBN 0-8174-5045-9, Amphoto). Watson-Guptill.
Wolf, John Q. Life in the Leatherwoods. rev. ed. Wolf, John Q., Jr., ed. (Illus.). 172p. 1980. pap. 4.95 o.p. (ISBN 0-87870-200-8). Memphis St Univ.
Wolf, Joseph J. Security in the Eastern Mediterranean: Re-Thinking American Policy. 19p. pap. 1.00 (ISBN 0-87855-739-3). Transaction Bks.
Wolf, Joseph J. & Cleveland, Harlan. The Growing Dimensions of Security. 86p. pap. 5.00x (ISBN 0-87855-740-7). Transaction Bks.
Wolf, K., jt. auth. see Chilingarian, G. V.
Wolf, K. H., ed. Handbook of Strata-Bound & Stratiform Ore Deposits, 3 Pts. in 10 Vols. Incl. Vol. 1: Classifications & Historical Studies. 1976. 70.25 (ISBN 0-444-41401-0); Vol. 2: Geochemical Studies. 1976. 70.25 (ISBN 0-444-41402-9); Vol. 3: Supergene & Surficial Ore Deposits: Textures & Fabrics. 1976. 70.25 (ISBN 0-444-41403-7); Vol. 4: Tectonics & Metamorphism. 1976. 70.25 (ISBN 0-444-41404-5); Regional Studies: Vol. 5: Regional Studies. 1976. 70.25 (ISBN 0-444-41405-3); Vol. 6: Copper, Zinc Lead & Silver Deposits. 1976. 113.00 (ISBN 0-444-41406-1); Vol. 7: Gold, Uranium, Iron, Manhannese, Mercury, Selenium, Tungsten & Phosphorus Deposits. 1976. 113.00 (ISBN 0-444-41407-X); General Studies: Vol. 8: General Studies. 1981. 113.00 (ISBN 0-444-41823-7); Vol. 9. 1981. 113.00 (ISBN 0-444-41824-5); Vol. 10: Bibliography & Ore Occurrence Data & Indexes for Vols. 8-10. 72.25 (ISBN 0-444-41825-3). (Pt. 1, Vols. 1-4: Pt. 2, Vol. 5-7: Pt. 3, Vols. 8-10). Vols. 1-7. 459.79 (ISBN 0-444-41274-3); **Vols. 1-4. 244.75 (ISBN 0-685-74759-X); Vols. 8-10. 236.73 (ISBN 0-686-85927-8). Elsevier.**
Wolf, Larry L. Species Relationships in the Avian Genus Aimophila. 220p. 1977. 12.00 (ISBN 0-943610-23-0). Am Ornithologists.
Wolf, Larry L., jt. auth. see Stiles, F. Gary.
Wolf, Leonard. Bluebeard: The Life & Crimes of Gilles de Rais. (Illus.). 288p. 1980. 12.95 o.p. (ISBN 0-517-54061-4). Crown.
--False Messiah. 1982. 13.95 (ISBN 0-395-32528-5). HM.
--Wolf's Complete Book of Terror. 1979. 16.95 (ISBN 0-517-53634-X, C N Potter); pap. 8.95 o.p. (ISBN 0-517-53635-8, C N Potter Bks). Crown.
Wolf, Louis, jt. auth. see Agee, Philip.
Wolf, Margaret S. & Duffy, Mary E. Simulations-Games: A Teaching Strategy for Nursing Education. 39p. 1978. 3.95 (ISBN 0-686-38276-5, 23-1756). Natl League Nurse.
Wolf, Margery. House of Lim: Study of a Chinese Farm Family. 1960. pap. text ed. 10.95 (ISBN 0-13-394973-7). P-H.
Wolf, Margot L., jt. auth. see Wolf, Donald D.
Wolf, Margot L., jt. ed. see Wolf, Donald.
Wolf, Margot L., jt. ed. see Wolf, Donald D.
Wolf, Martin, jt. auth. see Havrylyshyn, Oil.
Wolf, Michael, jt. auth. see Dunphy, Pat.
Wolf, Miriam, ed. How to Feed a Starving Artist. 320p. (Orig.). 1983. 15.95 (ISBN 0-87842-157-2); pap. 10.95 (ISBN 0-87842-151-3). Mountain Pr.
Wolf, Myron. Blue Book Illustrated Price Guide to Collectable Cameras, 1839-1981: 2nd Silver Issue. 2nd ed. (Illus.). 224p. 1980. pap. 14.95 o.p. (ISBN 0-9604352-0-4). Photo Memorabilia.
Wolf, P., ed. Tumor Associated Markers: The Importance of Identification in Clinical Medicine. LC 79-87540. (Illus.). 208p. 1979. 28.50x (ISBN 0-89352-065-9). Masson Pub.
Wolf, Paul L. Interpretation of Biochemical Multitest Profiles: An Analysis of 100 Important Conditions. LC 76-54053. (Illus.). 296p. 1977. 29.00x (ISBN 0-89352-002-0). Masson Pub.
--Interpretation of Electrophoretic Patterns of Proteins & Isoenzymes: A Clinical Pathologic Guide. 1982. 25.75 (ISBN 0-89352-035-7). Masson Pub.
Wolf, Paul L., et al. Practical Clinical Enzymology: Techniques & Interpretations & Biochemical Profiling. LC 80-12468. 592p. 1981. Repr. of 1973 ed. lib. bdg. 33.50 (ISBN 0-89874-162-9). Krieger.
Wolf, Paul R. Elements of Photogrammetry. (Illus.). 1974. text ed. 32.50 (ISBN 0-07-071337-5, C); solutions manual 8.00 (ISBN 0-07-071338-3). McGraw.
Wolf, Ray. Insulating Window Shade. 86p. 1982. pap. 14.95 (ISBN 0-87857-311-9, 15-889-0). Rodale Pr Inc.
--Solar Air Heater. (Illus.). 64p. 1982. pap. 14.95 (ISBN 0-87857-359-3, 15-001-0). Rodale Pr Inc.
Wolf, Ray, ed. Home Soyfood Equipment. (Illus.). 80p. 1982. pap. 14.95 (ISBN 0-87857-361-5, 15-002-0). Rodale Pr Inc.
--Solar Growing Frame. 80p. 1982. pap. 14.95 spiral bdg. (ISBN 0-87857-305-4, 15-885-0). Rodale Pr Inc.
Wolf, Richard C., ed. see Brauer, Jerald C.
Wolf, Richard C., ed. see Carter, Paul A.
Wolf, Richard C., ed. see Clebsch, William A.
Wolf, Richard C., ed. see Handy, Robert T.
Wolf, Richard C., ed. see Loetscher, Lefferts A.
Wolf, Richard C., ed. see Loewenberg, Bert J.
Wolf, Richard C., ed. see McAvoy, Thomas T.
Wolf, Richard C., ed. see Schlesinger, Arthur M., Sr.
Wolf, Richard M., jt. auth. see Tyler, Ralph W.
Wolf, Robert C. Fossils of Iowa: Field Guide to Paleozois Deposits. (Illus.). 203p. 1983. pap. 10.50 (ISBN 0-8138-1334-4). Iowa St U Pr.
Wolf, Robert E., tr. see Franzke, Andreas.
Wolf, Robert E., tr. see Vogt, Paul.
Wolf, Stanley. Chicken Cookbook. Reynolds, Maureen, ed. LC 80-81190. (Illus.). 192p. 1980. pap. 4.95 o.p. (ISBN 0-911954-56-2). Nitty Gritty.
--Guide to Electronic Measurements & Laboratory Practice. 2nd ed. (Illus.). 480p. 1983. text ed. 26.95 (ISBN 0-13-369652-9). P-H.
--New Ways to Enjoy Chicken. (Illus.). 216p. 1983. pap. 6.95 (ISBN 0-911954-76-7). Nitty Gritty.
Wolf, Stewart, jt. ed. see Epstein, Henry F.
Wolf, Susan, jt. auth. see Isenberg, Barbara.
Wolf, Walter, jt. auth. see Tubis, Manuel.
Wolf, William B. The Basic Barnard: An Introduction to Chester I. Barnard & His Theories of Organization & Management. LC 73-620199. (ILR Paperback Ser.: No. 14). 152p. 1974. pap. 10.00 (ISBN 0-87546-054-2); pap. 10.50 special hard bdg. o.s.i. (ISBN 0-87546-284-7). ILR Pr.
--Conversations with Chester I. Barnard. LC 72-619666. (ILR Paperback Ser.: No. 12). 68p. 1973. pap. 6.25 special bdg. (ISBN 0-87546-280-4); pap. 3.25 (ISBN 0-87546-047-X). ILR Pr.
--Management & Consulting: An Introduction to James O. McKinsey. LC 78-11840. (ILR Paperback Ser.: No. 17). 120p. 1979. pap. 8.95 (ISBN 0-87546-071-2). ILR Pr.
Wolf, William B., ed. Top Management of the Personnel Function: Current Issues & Practices. LC 79-27383. (Frank W. Pierce Memorial Lectureship & Conference Ser.: No. 6). 88p. 1980. 8.95 (ISBN 0-87546-076-3); pap. 5.95 (ISBN 0-87546-077-1). ILR Pr.
Wolfbein, Seymour L. Employment, Unemployment & Public Policy. 1965. pap. text ed. 3.45x (ISBN 0-685-47635-9). Phila Bk Co.
--Occupational Information: A Career Guidance View. 1968. pap. text ed. 3.45x (ISBN 0-685-41967-3). Phila Bk Co.
Wolfe, Alan. America's Impasse. 1982. pap. 8.00 (ISBN 0-89608-158-3). South End Pr.
Wolfe, Barnard. The Daily Life of a Chinese Courtesan Climbing up a Tricky Ladder: With a Chinese Courtesan's Dictionary. 436p. 1980. pap. 18.00 (ISBN 0-686-38450-4). Oriental Bk Store.
Wolfe, Bertram D. Fabulous Life of Diego Rivera. LC 63-20061. 1969. pap. 8.95 (ISBN 0-8128-1259-X). Stein & Day.
Wolfe, Betty. The Banner Book. LC 74-80378. (Illus.). 96p. 1974. 7.95 (ISBN 0-8192-1173-7). Morehouse.
Wolfe, Bob & Wolfe, Diane. Emergency Room. LC 82-19878. (Illus.). 40p. (gr. 1-4). 1983. PLB 7.95g (ISBN 0-87614-206-4). Carolrhoda Bks.
Wolfe, Burton H. Hitler & the Nazis. (gr. 7 up). 1970. PLB 5.49 o.p. (ISBN 0-399-60261-5). Putnam Pub Group.
Wolfe, C. B., Jr. Austroboletuc & Tylopilus Subgenus Porphyrellus, with Special Emphasis on North American Tax. (Bibliotheca Mycologica: No. 69). (Illus.). 1980. lib. bdg. 16.00x (ISBN 3-7682-1251-3). Lubrecht & Cramer.
Wolfe, D. L. Curso Basico De Espanol. 1970. text ed. 20.95x (ISBN 0-02-429280-X); wkbk. 5.95 (ISBN 0-02-429290-7). Macmillan.
--Curso Intermedio de Espanol. 1972. text ed. 20.95x (ISBN 0-02-429150-1). Macmillan.
Wolfe, David E., jt. auth. see Christensen, Clay B.
Wolfe, Diane, jt. auth. see Wolfe, Bob.
Wolfe, Don M. see Milton, John.
Wolfe, Douglas A., jt. auth. see Randles, Ronald H.
Wolfe, Fred H. The Divine Pattern. 1983. pap. 5.95 (ISBN 0-8054-5244-3). Broadman.
Wolfe, G. R. New York: A Guide to the Metropolis. 448p. 1982. pap. 12.95 (ISBN 0-07-071396-0). McGraw.
Wolfe, Gary, ed. Science Fiction Dialogues, Vol. I. LC 82-16352. (Orig.). 1983. pap. 8.95 (ISBN 0-89733-067-6). Academy Chi Ltd.
Wolfe, Gary K. David Lindsay. LC 81-21679. (Starmont Reader's Guide Ser.: No. 10). 64p. 1982. Repr. lib. bdg. 10.95x (ISBN 0-89370-041-X). Borgo Pr.
--Reader's Guide to David Lindsay. Schlobin, Roger C., ed. LC 82-5563. (Reader's Guides to Contemporary Science Fiction & Fantasy Authors Ser.: Vol. 9). (Illus., Orig.). 1982. 10.95x (ISBN 0-916732-29-0); pap. text ed. 4.95x (ISBN 0-916732-26-6). Starmont Hse.
Wolfe, Gene. Castle of the Otter. LC 82-70013. 1982. 16.95 (ISBN 0-917488-10-5); limited ed. o.p. 26.95 (ISBN 0-917488-11-3). Ziesing Bros.
--The Citadel of the Autarch. (The Book of the New Sun Ser.: Vol. 4). 1983. 14.95 (ISBN 0-671-45251-7, Timescape). PB.
--The Devil in a Forest. LC 76-5318. 224p. (gr. 7 up). 1976. 6.95 o.s.i. (ISBN 0-695-80667-X); PLB 6.99 o.s.i. (ISBN 0-695-40667-1). Follett.
--Gene Wolfe's Book of Days. LC 80-1074. (Science Fiction Ser.). 192p. 1981. 10.95 o.p. (ISBN 0-385-15991-9). Doubleday.
--The Shadow of the Torturer. (The Book of the New Sun Ser.: Vol. 1). 272p. 1981. pap. 2.75 (ISBN 0-671-45070-0, Timescape). PB.
--The Shadow of the Torturer, Vol. 1. (First in 4 vol. ser.). 1980. 11.95 o.p. (ISBN 0-686-60923-9, 25325). S&S.
--The Sword of the Lictor. (The Book of the New Sun: Vol. 3). 1982. 14.95 (ISBN 0-671-43595-7, Timescape); pap. 2.95 (ISBN 0-671-45450-1). PB.
Wolfe, Herbert J. Printing & Litho Inks. (Illus.). 537p. 24.95 o.p. (ISBN 0-913720-13-5, Sandstone). Beil F C.
Wolfe, Humbert. George Moore. 1982. lib. bdg. 34.50 (ISBN 0-686-81926-8). Porter.
--The Poems from the Irish. 1982. lib. bdg. 34.50 (ISBN 0-686-81928-4). Porter.
--Tennyson. 1982. lib. bdg. 34.50 (ISBN 0-686-81929-2). Porter.
--W. B. Yeats. 1982. lib. bdg. 34.50 (ISBN 0-686-81930-6). Porter.
Wolfe, Ithmer, jt. auth. see Gould, Geraldine.
Wolfe, James, jt. auth. see Couloumbis, Ted.
Wolfe, James H. & Couloumbis, Theo. A. Introduction to International Relations: Power & Justice. (Illus.). 1978. text ed. 22.95 (ISBN 0-13-485300-8). P-H.
Wolfe, Janet L., jt. auth. see Ellis, Albert.
Wolfe, John H. & Phelps, E. R. Mechanics' Vest Pocket Reference Book. 1945. 6.95 o.p. (ISBN 0-13-572024-9). P-H.
--Practical Shop Mathematics, Vol. 1: Elementary. 4th ed. 1958. 16.80 (ISBN 0-07-071358-8, W); ans. key 2.80 (ISBN 0-07-071393-6). McGraw.
Wolfe, John N. Xeroradiography of the Breast. 2nd ed. (Illus.). 720p. 1983. 109.50x (ISBN 0-398-04703-0). C C Thomas.
Wolfe, Joseph, ed. see Watson, J. B.
Wolfe, Judith. Coping Successfully with Teenagers. LC 82-84009. 288p. 1983. 12.95 (ISBN 0-932966-30-6). Permanent Pr.
Wolfe, Linda. Cooking of the Caribbean Islands. LC 75-108615. (Foods of the World Ser.). (Illus.). (gr. 6 up). 1970. PLB 17.28 (ISBN 0-8094-0071-5, Pub. by Time-Life). Silver.
--Cosmo Report. 368p. 1982. pap. 3.95 (ISBN 0-553-22685-1). Bantam.
Wolfe, Linda D. Physical Anthropology: A Laboratory Text. (Illus.). 180p. 1983. pap. text ed. 10.95 (ISBN 0-89892-049-3). Contemp Pub Co of Raleigh.
Wolfe, Linnie M. John of the Mountains: The Unpublished Journals of John Muir. LC 79-83859. 496p. 1979. 22.50 (ISBN 0-299-07880-9); pap. 8.95 (ISBN 0-299-07884-1). U of Wis Pr.
--Son of the Wilderness: The Life of John Muir. LC 78-53294. (Illus.). 398p. 1978. 20.00 (ISBN 0-299-07730-6); pap. 8.95 (ISBN 0-299-07734-9). U of Wis Pr.
Wolfe, Louis. Aquaculture: Farming in Water. (Illus.). 108p. (gr. 7-11). 1972. PLB 4.29 o.p. (ISBN 0-399-60718-8). Putnam Pub Group.
--Disease Detectives. LC 78-10464. (Illus.). (gr. 4-6). 1979. PLB 6.90 s&l (ISBN 0-531-02921-2). Watts.
--Let's Go to a Planetarium. (Lets Go Ser.). (Illus.). (gr. 3-6). 1958. PLB 4.29 o.p. (ISBN 0-399-60390-5). Putnam Pub Group.
--Ships That Explore the Deep. LC 75-125324. (Illus.). (gr. 6-9). 1971. PLB 3.86 o.p. (ISBN 0-399-60580-0). Putnam Pub Group.
Wolfe, Mary Gorgen. Clear-Cut Pattern Making (by the Flat Pattern Method) LC 81-16511. 221p. 1982. text ed. 18.95x (ISBN 0-471-09937-6); avail. tapes (ISBN 0-471-08655-X). Wiley.
Wolfe, Michael & Peterson, James A. Executive Fitness: The Nautilus Way. LC 82-81801. Date not set. 14.95 (ISBN 0-88011-073-2). Leisure Pr.
Wolfe, Morris, jt. auth. see McNeil, Bill.
Wolfe, Peter. Jean Rhys. (English Authors Ser.). 1980. 13.95 (ISBN 0-8057-6698-7, Twayne). G K Hall.
Wolfe, Philip M., et al. A Practical Guide to Selecting Small Business Computers. 1982. pap. text ed. 16.00 (ISBN 0-89806-033-8); pap. text ed. 8.00 members. Inst Indus Eng.
Wolfe, R. & Kreissman, C. J., eds. Applied Solid State Science: Advances in Materials & Device Research, 3 vols. Vol.1. 1969. 63.50 (ISBN 0-12-002901-4); Vol.2. 1971. 63.50 (ISBN 0-12-002902-2); Vol. 3. 1972. 63.50 (ISBN 0-12-002903-0). Acad Pr.
Wolfe, Ralph, et al. Low-Cost Pole Building Construction. rev. ed. LC 80-10232. (Illus.). 176p. 1980. pap. 10.95 (ISBN 0-88266-170-1). Garden Way Pub.
Wolfe, Ralph D., jt. auth. see Clegg, Peter D.
Wolfe, Randy P., jt. auth. see Sulton, Cynthia G.
Wolfe, Raymond, ed. Applied Solid State Science: Advances in Materials & Device Research. Incl. Vol. 4. 1974. 63.50 (ISBN 0-12-002904-9); Vol. 5. 1975. 69.00 (ISBN 0-12-002905-7); 88.50 (ISBN 0-12-002974-X); 50.00 (ISBN 0-12-002975-8); Vol. 6. 1976. 58.50 (ISBN 0-12-002906-5); 74.00 (ISBN 0-12-002976-6); 42.00 (ISBN 0-12-002977-4). (Serial Publication). Acad Pr.
Wolfe, Richard J., jt. ed. see Lancour, Harold.
Wolfe, Robert, ed. Captured German & Related Records: A National Archives Conference. LC 74-82495. (National Archives Conferences Ser.: Vol. 3). (Illus.). xix, 279p. 1974. 17.00x (ISBN 0-8214-0172-6, 82-81719). Ohio U Pr.
Wolfe, Robert L. The Truck Book. LC 80-15683. (Illus.). 32p. (ps-3). 1981. PLB 7.95g (ISBN 0-87614-125-4). Carolrhoda Bks.

Wolfe, Rolland E. The Twelve Religions of the Bible. LC 82-20401. (Studies in the Bible & Early Christianity: Vol. 2). (Illus.). 440p. 1983. 44.95x (ISBN 0-686-84104-2). E Mellen.

Wolfe, S. Anthony, tr. see Tessier, Paul A.

Wolfe, Sidney M. & Coley, Christopher M. Pills That Don't Work: A Consumer's & Doctor's Guide to Prescription Drugs that Lack Evidence of Effectiveness. 221p. 1982. 6.95 (ISBN 0-686-96250-8). Pub Citizen Health.

Wolfe, Sidney M., jt. auth. see Warner, Rebecca.

Wolfe, Sidney M., jt. auth. see Bargmann, Eve.

Wolfe, Stephen. Biology: The Foundations. 1977. 24.95x (ISBN 0-534-00490-3). Wadsworth Pub.

Wolfe, Stephen L. Biology of the Cell. 2nd ed. 560p. 1981. text ed. 29.95x (ISBN 0-534-00900-X). Wadsworth Pub.

--Biology: The Foundations. 2nd ed. 608p. 1982. pap. text ed. 24.95x (ISBN 0-534-01169-1). Wadsworth Pub.

Wolfe, Stephen L. & Wysack, Roy L. Handbook for Space Pioneers. LC 78-5523. (Illus.). 1978. 14.95 o.p. (ISBN 0-448-16178-8, G&D); pap. 7.95 o.p. (ISBN 0-448-16185-0). Putnam Pub Group.

Wolfe, Suzanne, jt. auth. see Mullins, June.

Wolfe, Thomas. The Autobiography of an American Novelist. Field, Leslie, ed. (Illus.). 128p. 1983. text ed. 15.00x (ISBN 0-674-05316-8); pap. text ed. 5.95x (ISBN 0-674-05317-6). Harvard U Pr.

--Hills Beyond. pap. 1.50 o.p. (ISBN 0-451-50925-0, CW925, Sig Classics). NAL.

--Look Homeward Angel. 359p. 1981. Repr. lib. bdg. 16.95 (ISBN 0-89966-293-5). Buccaneer Bks.

--Web & the Rock. 640p. 1973. pap. 3.95i (ISBN 0-06-080313-4, P313, PL). Har-Row.

--Welcome to Our City: A Play in Ten Scenes. Kennedy, Richard S., ed. LC 82-20838. (Southern Literary Ser.). 160p. 1983. 12.95 (ISBN 0-8071-1085-X). La State U Pr.

--You Can't Go Home Again. LC 40-27633. 1940. 15.34i (ISBN 0-06-014710-5, HarpT). Har-Row.

--You Can't Go Home Again. 576p. 1973. pap. 3.95i (ISBN 0-06-080314-2, P314, PL). Har-Row.

Wolfe, Thomas E., jt. auth. see Allen, Robert D.

Wolfe, Thomas W. The Salt Experience. LC 78-26779. (The Rand Corporation). 432p. 1979. prof ref 25.00x (ISBN 0-88410-079-0). Ballinger Pub.

Wolfe, Thomas W., jt. auth. see Hosmer, Steven T.

Wolfe, Tom. From Bauhaus to Our House. 1982. pap. 2.95 (ISBN 0-671-45449-8). PB.

Wolfe, W. L., jt. ed. see Moss, T. S.

Wolfe, W. L., ed. see U. S. Specialty Group on Infrared Detectors.

Wolfe Howe, De M. see Howe, Mark A.

Wolfendale, A. W., ed. Progress in Cosmology. 1982. 54.50 (ISBN 90-277-1441-X, Pub. by Reidel Holland). Kluwer Boston.

Wolfenden, E. P. Hiligaynon Reference Grammar. McKaughan, Howard P., ed. LC 79-152473. (PALI Language Texts: Philippines). (Orig.). 1971. pap. text ed. 6.00x o.p. (ISBN 0-87022-867-6). UH Pr.

Wolfenden, Elmer. A Description of Hiligaynon Syntax. (Linguistics & Related Fields Ser: No. 46). 1975. 8.00x (ISBN 0-88312-056-9); microfiche 2.25x (ISBN 0-88312-456-4). Summer Inst Ling.

Wolfenden, Elmer, Jr. & Alejandro, Rufino, eds. Intensive Tagalog Conversation Course. 175p. 1966. pap. 3.50 o.p. (ISBN 0-88312-774-1); microfiche 2.25 o.p. (ISBN 0-88312-394-0). Summer Inst Ling.

Wolfenden, Joan. Recipes to Relish: Good Cooking & Entertaining at Home. (Illus.). 175p. 1982. 12.95 (ISBN 0-7207-1303-X, Pub. by Michael Joseph). Merrimack Bk Serv.

Wolfenstine, Manfred R. The Manual of Brands & Marks. Adams, Ramon F., ed. LC 68-31379. (Illus.). 355p. 1981. 24.95 (ISBN 0-8061-0867-3); pap. 14.50 (ISBN 0-8061-1762-1). U of Okla Pr.

Wolfers, Arnold & Martin, Laurence W., eds. The Anglo-American Tradition in Foreign Affairs: Readings from Thomas More to Woodrow Wilson. 1956. text ed. 37.50x (ISBN 0-686-51345-2). Elliots Bks.

Wolfers, E. P., ed. Looking North to South-East Asia: The View from Australia. LC 76-50495. 1977. text ed. 12.00x (ISBN 0-8248-0531-3). UH Pr.

Wolfers, Michael. Black Man's Burden Revisited. LC 74-82176. 192p. 1975. 18.95 o.p. (ISBN 0-312-08330-0). St Martin.

--Politics in the Organization of African Unity. (Studies in African History). (Illus.). 1976. text ed. 14.95x o.p. (ISBN 0-416-76960-8); pap. text ed. 10.95x (ISBN 0-416-76970-5). Methuen Inc.

Wolfert, Helen. Landlady & Tenant. LC 79-90842. 94p. 1980. 9.95 (ISBN 0-935296-06-9); pap. 4.95 (ISBN 0-935296-07-7). Sheep Meadow.

Wolfert, Paula. Couscous & Other Good Food from Morocco. LC 72-9165. (Illus.). 368p. 1973. 16.30i (ISBN 0-06-014721-0, HarpT). Har-Row.

Wolff, Alex, jt. auth. see Wielgus, Chuck, Jr.

Wolff, Bertram L., tr. see Dibelius, Martin.

Wolff, Charles E. & John, Mar. What Now, U. S. A. A Political Science Manual for the Eighties. 1982. 5.75 (ISBN 0-8062-1880-0). Carlton.

Wolff, Christian. Preliminary Discourse on Philosophy in General. Blackwell, Richard, tr. LC 63-20239. (Orig.). 1963. pap. 2.95 o.p. (ISBN 0-672-60395-0, LA167). Bobbs.

Wolff, Craig T. Wayne Gretzky: Portrait of a Hockey Player. 64p. (gr. 3-7). 1983. pap. 1.95 (ISBN 0-380-82420-5, 82420-5, Camelot). Avon.

Wolff, Cynthia G. A Feast of Words. LC 76-40736. 1977. 22.50x (ISBN 0-19-502117-7). Oxford U Pr.

Wolff, E. Relationship Between Experimental Embryology & Molecular Biology. 170p. 1967. 39.00x (ISBN 0-677-12800-2). Gordon.

Wolff, E. G. Grundlagen Einer Autonomen Musikasthetik, 2 vols. (Illus.). 150p. 65.00 o.s.i. (ISBN 90-6027-371-0, Pub. by Frits Knuf Netherlands). Pendragon NY.

Wolff, Geoffrey. Black Sun: The Brief Transit & Violent Eclipse of Harry Crosby. LC 77-5019. (Illus.). 1977. pap. 12.95 (ISBN 0-394-47450-3, Vin). Random.

Wolff, George. Theodore Roethke. (United States Authors Ser.). 1981. lib. bdg. 10.95 (ISBN 0-8057-7323-1, Twayne). G K Hall.

Wolff, H., ed. see Calvino, Italo.

Wolff, Hans W. Amos the Prophet: The Man & His Background. Reumann, John, ed. McCurley, Foster, tr. from Ger. LC 72-87062. 110p. 1973. pap. 2.95 o.p. (ISBN 0-8006-0012-6, 1-12). Fortress.

--Confrontations with Prophets. LC 82-48585. 80p. 1983. pap. 3.95 (ISBN 0-8006-1702-9). Fortress.

--Hosea. Hanson, Paul D., ed. Stansell, Gary, tr. from Ger. LC 70-179634. (Hermeneia: a Critical & Historical Commentary on the Bible). Orig. Title: Dodekapropheton-Hosea. 292p. 1973. 22.95 (ISBN 0-8006-6004-8, 20-6004). Fortress.

Wolff, Hans W., jt. auth. see Brueggemann, Walter.

Wolff, Harold G. Headache & Other Head Pain. 4th ed. Dalessio, Donald J., ed. (Illus.). 1980. text ed. 39.50x (ISBN 0-19-502624-1). Oxford U Pr.

Wolff, Herbert, jt. auth. see Robbins, Carol T.

Wolff, Janet. Aesthetics & the Sociology of Art. (Controversies in Sociology Ser.: No. 14). 128p. 1983. text ed. 22.50x (ISBN 0-04-301152-7); pap. text ed. 8.95x (ISBN 0-04-301153-5). Allen Unwin.

--The Social Production of Art. 208p. 1981. 25.00x (ISBN 0-312-73467-0). St Martin.

Wolff, John U. & Poedjosoedarmo, Soepomo. Communicative Codes in Central Java. (Linguistics Ser.: VIII). 207p. 1982. 7.50 (ISBN 0-87727-116-X). Cornell SE Asia.

Wolff, Joseph L. Readings in Educational Psychology. 1969. pap. text ed. 14.95x (ISBN 0-8290-1311-3). Irvington.

Wolff, Jurgen M. & Lipe, Dewey. Help for the Overweight Child: A Parent's Guide to Helping Children Lose Weight. 1980. pap. 2.95 o.p. (ISBN 0-14-005318-2). Penguin.

Wolff, Konrad. Schnabel's Interpretation of Piano Music. 1979. 15.00 o.p. (ISBN 0-393-01217-4); pap. 4.95 (ISBN 0-393-00929-7). Norton.

Wolff, Kurt H., ed. see Mannheim, Karl.

Wolff, Manfred E. Burger's Medicinal Chemistry: The Basis of Medicinal Chemistry, 3 pts. 4th ed. LC 78-10791. 1980. Pt. 1. 54.00x (ISBN 0-471-01570-9, Pub. by Wiley-Interscience); Pt. 2. 150.00 (ISBN 0-471-01571-7); Pt. 3. 134.00 (ISBN 0-471-01572-5). Wiley.

Wolff, Margaret A. Finger Painting. (Pitman Art Ser.: Vol. 60). pap. 1.95 o.p. (ISBN 0-448-00569-7, G&D). Putnam Pub Group.

Wolff, Marianne, jt. ed. see Fenoglio, Cecilia M.

Wolff, Martha, ed. Anonymous Masters of the Fifteenth Century. (Illus.). 1983. 120.00 (ISBN 0-89835-023-9). Abaris Bks.

Wolff, Michael, et al, eds. The Waterloo Directory of Victorian Periodicals. 1203p. 1981. 215.00 (ISBN 0-08-026079-9). Pergamon.

Wolff, Nancy. Tempo: An Office-Procedures Simulation. 1983. write for info. client co. manual (ISBN 0-574-20708-2, 13-3708); write for info. employee handbook (ISBN 0-574-20705-8, 13-3705); write for info. working papers (ISBN 0-574-20707-4, 13-3707); write for info. model answers (ISBN 0-574-20674-4, 13-3674); write for info. office manager handbook (ISBN 0-574-20706-6, 13-3706). SRA.

Wolff, P. A., jt. auth. see Platzman, P. M.

Wolff, Philippe. Western Languages. Partridge, F., tr. from Fr. LC 78-104744. (Illus., Orig.). 1971. pap. 2.45 o.p. (ISBN 0-07-071534-3, SP). McGraw.

Wolff, Reinhold, jt. auth. see Krauss, Henning.

Wolff, Robert. Philosophy: A Modern Encounter. LC 76-25427. 1976. text ed. 17.95 o.p. (ISBN 0-13-663385-4); pap. text ed. 18.95 (ISBN 0-13-663377-3). P-H.

Wolff, Robert L. The Golden Key: A Study of the Fiction of George MacDonald. 1961. 34.50x o.p. (ISBN 0-686-51395-9). Elliots Bks.

--William Carleton, Irish Peasant Novelist: A Preface to His Fiction. LC 79-4399. 200p. 1980. lib. bdg. 18.00 o.s.i. (ISBN 0-8240-3527-5). Garland Pub.

Wolff, Robert L., ed. see Conybeare, William J.

Wolff, Robert L., ed. see Craigie, Pearl M.

Wolff, Robert L., ed. see Froude, James A.

Wolff, Robert L., ed. see Gissing, George.

Wolff, Robert L., ed. see Gould, Frederick J.

Wolff, Robert L., ed. see Guyton, Emma J. W.

Wolff, Robert L., ed. see Ingelow, Jean.

Wolff, Robert L., ed. see Jewsbury, Geraldine E.

Wolff, Robert L., ed. see Linton, Eliza L.

Wolff, Robert L., ed. see Maxwell, William H.

Wolff, Robert L., ed. see Newman, John H.

Wolff, Robert L., ed. see Oliphant, Margaret O.

Wolff, Robert L., ed. see Robinson, Frederick W.

Wolff, Robert L., ed. see Smith, Sarah.

Wolff, Robert L., ed. see Trollope, Anthony.

Wolff, Robert L., ed. see Trollope, Frances M.

Wolff, Robert L., ed. see Yonge, Charlotte.

Wolff, Robert L., ed. see Yonge, Charlotte M.

Wolff, Robert P. About Philosophy. 2nd ed. (Illus.). 448p. 1981. text ed. 20.95 (ISBN 0-13-000695-5). P-H.

--Ideal of the University. 1970. pap. 5.95x (ISBN 0-8070-3189-5, BP371). Beacon Pr.

--In Defense of Anarchism. 1970. pap. 3.95xi (ISBN 0-06-131541-9, TB 1541, Torch). Har-Row.

--Ten Great Works of Philosophy. 480p. 1973. pap. 3.50 (ISBN 0-451-62004-6, ME2004, Ment). NAL.

Wolff, Robert P., ed. Introductory Philosophy. 1979. text ed. 22.95 (ISBN 0-13-500876-X). P-H.

--Rule of Law. LC 72-139669. 1971. pap. 3.95 o.p. (ISBN 0-671-20891-8, Touchstone Bks). S&S.

--Styles of Political Action in America. LC 81-40796. 256p. 1981. pap. text ed. 8.25 (ISBN 0-8191-1802-8). U Pr of Amer.

Wolff, Robert P., et al. Critique of Pure Tolerance. LC 65-20788. 1969. pap. 3.95x (ISBN 0-8070-1559-8, BP328). Beacon Pr.

Wolff, Sheldon. Sister Chromatid Exchange. LC 81-13102. 306p. 1982. 70.00x (ISBN 0-471-05987-0, Pub. by Wiley-Interscience). Wiley.

Wolff, Tobias, ed. Matters of Life & Death: New American Stories. 256p. 1983. 12.95 (ISBN 0-931694-14-0); pap. 12.95 (ISBN 0-931694-17-5). Wampeter Pr.

--New American Short Stories. 176p. 1982. pap. 7.95 (ISBN 0-931694-17-5). Wampeter Pr.

Wolff, U., jt. auth. see Von Heimendahl, Manfred.

Wolff, Victoria. Fabulous City. 1980. pap. 2.50 o.p. (ISBN 0-523-40676-2). Pinnacle Bks.

--Spell of Egypt. 288p. 1980. pap. 2.50 o.p. (ISBN 0-523-41033-6). Pinnacle Bks.

Wolffheim, Nelly. Psychology in the Nursery School. Hannam, Charles L., tr. LC 77-162630. 143p. 1972. Repr. of 1953 ed. lib. bdg. 17.75x (ISBN 0-8371-6197-5, WONS). Greenwood.

Wolfflin, Heinrich. Renaissance & Baroque. Simon, Kathrin, tr. (Illus.). 197p. 1967. pap. 5.95x (ISBN 0-8014-9046-4, CP46). Cornell U Pr.

Wolfgang, Aaron, ed. Nonverbal Behavior: Applications & Cultural Implications. 1979. 16.50 (ISBN 0-12-761350-1). Acad Pr.

Wolfgang, Charles F. Helping Active and Passive Preschoolers Through Play. (Elementary Education Ser.). 1977. pap. text ed. 9.95 (ISBN 0-675-08550-0). Merrill.

Wolfgang, Harriet. Shorthaired Cats. 1963. 12.95 (ISBN 0-87666-180-0, H920). TFH Pubns.

Wolfgang, Martin E., ed. Prisons: Present & Possible. LC 77-3860. 256p. 1979. 21.95 (ISBN 0-669-01674-8). Lexington Bks.

Wolfgang, Marvin. Patterns in Criminal Homicide. LC 74-34157. (Criminology, Law Enforcement, & Social Problems Ser.: No. 211). 413p. 1975. 20.00x (ISBN 0-87585-211-4). Patterson Smith.

Wolfgang, Marvin E., jt. auth. see Ferracuti, Franco.

Wolfgang, Marvin E., jt. auth. see Sellin, Thorsten.

Wolfgang, Marvin E., ed. International Terrorism. (The Annals of the American Academy of Political & Social Science: Vol. 463). 208p. 1982. 15.00 (ISBN 0-8039-1860-7); pap. 10.00 (ISBN 0-8039-1861-5). Sage.

Wolfgang, Marvin E. & Lambert, Richard D., eds. Africa in Transition. new ed. LC 77-183. (Annals Ser.: No. 432). 1977. pap. 7.95 (ISBN 0-87761-217-X). Am Acad Pol Soc Sci.

--Bicentennial Conference on the Constitution: A Report to the Academy. LC 76-5778. (Annals Ser.: No. 426). 1976. 15.00 (ISBN 0-87761-202-1); pap. 7.95 (ISBN 0-87761-203-X). Am Acad Pol Soc Sci.

--The Future Society: Aspects of America in the Year 2000. LC 73-78958. (The Annals of the American Academy of Political & Social Science: 408). 300p. (Orig.). 1973. 15.00 (ISBN 0-87761-166-1); pap. 7.95 (ISBN 0-87761-165-3). Am Acad Pol Soc Sci.

--Social Effects of Inflation. (The Annals of the American Academy of Political & Social Science: No. 456). 250p. 1981. 15.00 (ISBN 0-87761-264-1); pap. 7.95 (ISBN 0-87761-265-X). Am Acad Pol Soc Sci.

Wolfgang, Marvin E. & Short, James F., Jr., eds. Collective Violence. LC 77-130998. (Annals of the American Academy of Political & Social Science: No. 391). 1970. pap. 7.95 (ISBN 0-87761-129-7). Am Acad Pol Soc Sci.

Wolfgang, Marvin E., ed. see American Academy of Political & Social Science, Annual Meeting, 83rd.

Wolfgang, Marvin E., ed. see American Academy of Political & Social Science Annual Meeting, 82nd.

Wolfgang, Marvin E., ed. see American Academy of Political & Social Science, 78th.

Wolfgang, Marvin E., ed. see American Academy of Political & Social Science, 79th.

Wolfgang, Marvin E., jt. ed. see Radzinowicz, Sir Leon.

Wolfgang, Marvin E., jt. ed. see Sellin, Thorsten.

Wolfgang, Marvin E., et al. Criminology Index: Research & Theory in Criminology in the United States, 1945-1972, 2 vols. LC 75-4571. 2432p. 1975. Set. 79.95 o.p. (ISBN 0-444-99002-X). Elsevier.

Wolfgang, Rudolf. Harbor & Town: A Maritime Cultural History. (Illus.). 233p. 1982. 22.50 (ISBN 0-88254-720-8, Pub.by Edition Leipiz Germany). Hippocrene Bks.

Wolfgang Von Goethe, Rudolf see Von Goethe, Johann W. & Steiner, Rudolf.

Wolfhard, H. G., jt. auth. see Gaydon, A. G.

Wolfheim, Jaclyn H. Primates of the World: Distribution, Abundance & Conservation. LC 82-13464. (Illus.). 854p. 1983. 57.50 (ISBN 0-295-95899-5). U of Wash Pr.

Wolfinger, R. Politics of Progress. 1974. pap. text ed. 15.95 (ISBN 0-13-685024-3). P-H.

Wolfinger, Raymond, et al. Dynamics of American Politics. 2nd ed. (Illus.). 1980. text ed. 22.95 (ISBN 0-13-221143-2); study guide & wkbk. 7.95 (ISBN 0-13-221127-0). P-H.

Wolfinger, Raymond E. & Rosenstone, Steven J. Who Votes? LC 79-48068. 160p. 1980. 20.00x (ISBN 0-300-02541-6); pap. 5.95x (ISBN 0-300-02552-1). Yale U Pr.

Wolfman, Bernard. Federal Income Taxation of Business Enterprise. 2nd, abr. ed. LC 81-8173. 1544p. 1982. text ed. 32.50 (ISBN 0-316-95115-3). Little.

--Federal Income Taxation of Business Enterprise. 1095p. 1971. 24.50 o.p. (ISBN 0-316-95113-7); pap. 1979 suppl. o.p. (ISBN 0-316-95114-5). Little.

Wolfman, Bernard & Holden, James P. Ethical Problems in Federal Tax Practice. (Contemporary Legal Education Ser.). 343p. 1981. pap. text ed. 18.00 (ISBN 0-87215-399-1). Michie-Bobbs.

Wolford, Chester L. The Anger of Stephen Crane: Fiction & the Epic Tradition. LC 82-8491. (Illus.). xviii, 169p. 1983. 15.95x (ISBN 0-8032-4717-6). U of Nebr Pr.

Wolford, Larry M., jt. auth. see Epker, Bruce N.

Wolfowitz, J. Selected Papers. 642p. 1980. 38.00 (ISBN 0-387-90463-8). Springer-Verlag.

Wolfowitz, Jacob. Coding Theorems of Information Theory. 2nd ed. (Ergebnisse der Mathematik und Ihrer Grenzgebiete: Vol. 31). 1964. 28.30 (ISBN 0-387-08548-3). Springer-Verlag.

Wolfram, J. C. Anleitung Zur Kenntnisz, Beurtheilung und Erhaltung der Orgeln. (Bibliotheca Organologica Ser.: Vol. 3). Repr. of 1972 ed. wrappers 25.00 o.s.i. (ISBN 90-6027-159-9, Pub. by Frits Knuf Netherlands). Pendragon NY.

Wolfram, Walt & Christian, Donna, eds. Dialects & Educational Equity. 104p. 13.50 (ISBN 0-686-95332-0); members 11.00 (ISBN 0-686-99497-3). NCTE.

Wolfrom, Melville L., jt. ed. see Whistler, Roy L.

Wolfskill, George. Revolt of the Conservatives. LC 73-17626. (Illus.). 303p. 1974. Repr. of 1962 ed. lib. bdg. 18.50x (ISBN 0-8371-7251-9, WORC). Greenwood.

Wolfson, Edward. Four-Handed Dentistry for Dentists & Assistants. LC 73-11100. (Illus.). 180p. 1974. 14.95 o.p. (ISBN 0-8016-5612-5). Mosby.

Wolfson, Evelyn, jt. auth. see Robinson, Barbara.

Wolfson, Gary, ed. Young American Photography. LC 74-13172. (Illus.). 108p. 1976. pap. 9.95 (ISBN 0-912810-17-3). Lustrum Pr.

Wolfson, Harry A. The Philosophy of Spinoza: Unfolding the Latent Processes of His Reasoning. 872p. 1983. pap. text ed. 15.00x (ISBN 0-674-66595-3). Harvard U Pr.

Wolfson, Marty. Great Events In American History. (Illus.). 1969. pap. 1.60 (ISBN 0-916114-00-7). Wolfson.

--How to Watch Sports on TV & Enjoy It. (Illus.). 1972. pap. 2.50 (ISBN 0-916114-02-3). Wolfson.

Wolfson, Marty, jt. auth. see Bartlett, Ronald.

Wolfson, Marty, jt. auth. see Schlesinger, Reuben.

Wolfson, Murray. Marx: Economist, Philosopher, Jew. 1982. 26.00x (ISBN 0-312-51788-2). St Martin.

Wolfson, Nessa. CHP: The Conversational Historical Present in American English Narrative. 130p. 1982. 29.50x (ISBN 90-70176-61-0); pap. 19.50x (ISBN 90-70176-60-2). Foris Pubns.

Wolfson, Rita P., jt. auth. see Weiss, Elizabeth.

Wolfson, Susan, jt. auth. see Bach, Ira J.

Wolfson, Warren, jt. auth. see Mauet, Thomas.

Wolin, Simon & Slusser, Robert M., eds. The Soviet Secret Police. LC 74-20280. 408p. 1975. Repr. of 1957 ed. lib. bdg. 39.75x (ISBN 0-8371-7852-5, WOSS). Greenwood.

Wolins, Martin & Wozner, Yochanan. Revitalizing Residental Settings: Problems & Potential in Education, Health, Rehabilitation, & Social Service. LC 81-20804. (Social & Behavioral Science Ser.). 1982. text ed. 25.95x (ISBN 0-87589-517-4). Jossey-Bass.

Wolitz, Seth L. The Proustian Community. LC 73-171349. 1971. 17.50x o.p. (ISBN 0-8147-9153-0). NYU Pr.

Wolitzer, Hilma. In the Palomar Arms. 1983. 13.95 (ISBN 0-374-17656-6). FS&G.

Wolitzer, Meg. Sleepwalking. 1982. 12.50 (ISBN 0-394-52155-2). Random.

Wolk, Allan. The Naming of America: How Continents, Countries, States, Counties, Cities, Towns, Villages, Hamlets, & Post Offices Came by Their Names. LC 77-31833. (gr. 7 up). 1978. 9.95 o.p. (ISBN 0-525-66562-5). Lodestar Bks.

Wolke, Robert L. Chemistry Explained. (Illus.). 1980. text ed. 24.95 (ISBN 0-13-129163-7). P-H.

Wolkenstein, V. S. Problems in General Physics. 349p. 1975. 9.45 (ISBN 0-8285-1957-9, Pub. by Mir Pubs USSR). Imported Pubns.

Wolkin, Rachel, jt. auth. see Barcus, F. Earle.

Wolkoff, Judie. Happily Ever After... Almost. LC 81-18028. 224p. (gr. 6-9). 1982. 10.95 (ISBN 0-02-793340-7). Bradbury Pr.

--Wally. LC 77-75364. 204p. (gr. 3-6). 1977. 8.95 (ISBN 0-02-793350-4). Bradbury Pr.

--Where the Elf King Sings. LC 80-15298. 176p. (gr. 5-7). 1980. 8.95 (ISBN 0-02-793360-1). Bradbury Pr.

Wolkstein, Diane & Kramer, Samuel N. Inanna: Queen of Heaven & Earth. LC 80-8690. (Illus.). 192p. 11.49i (ISBN 0-06-014713-X, HarpT); pap. 4.76i (ISBN 0-06-090854-8). Har-Row.

Woll, Allen L. The Hollywood Musical Goes to War. 208p. 1983. text ed. 19.95x (ISBN 0-88229-704-X); pap. text ed. 9.95x (ISBN 0-88229-811-9). Nelson-Hall.

--The Latin Image in American Film. LC 77-620044. (Latin American Studies Ser: Vol. 39). 1978. pap. text ed. 6.95 (ISBN 0-87903-039-9). UCLA Lat Am Ctr.

Woll, Bencie, jt. ed. see Kyle, Jim.

Woll, Josephine & Treml, Vladimir. Soviet Dissident Literature: A Critical Guide. 1983. lib. bdg. 25.00 (ISBN 0-8161-8626-X, Hall Reference). G K Hall.

Woll, Peter. Administrative Law: The Formal Process. (California Library Reprint Ser: No. 58). 1974. 30.00x (ISBN 0-520-02802-3). U of Cal Pr.

--American Government: Readings & Cases. 7th ed. 608p. 1981. pap. text ed. 10.95 o.p. (ISBN 0-316-95143-9); tchr's manual avail. o.p. Little.

--Constitutional Law: Cases & Comments. 800p. 1981. text ed. 27.95 (ISBN 0-13-167957-0). P-H.

--Public Policy. LC 81-40886. 272p. 1982. lib. bdg. 23.00 (ISBN 0-8191-2097-9); pap. text ed. 11.50 (ISBN 0-8191-2098-7). U Pr of Amer.

Wollam, Gary L. & Hall, W. Dallas, eds. Hypertension Management. 350p. 1983. text ed. write for info. (ISBN 0-86792-009-2). Wright-PSG.

Wollard, Joy J. Nutritional Management of the Cancer Patient. LC 78-68523. 216p. 1979. text ed. 19.50 (ISBN 0-89004-357-4); pap. text ed. 13.00 (ISBN 0-685-94934-6). Raven.

Wollaston, A. N. English Persian Dictionary. 462p. 1978. Repr. of 1842 ed. 22.00 o.p. (ISBN 0-89684-156-1, Pub. by Cosmo Pubns India). Orient Bk Dist.

--An English-Persian Dictionary Compiled from Original Sources. 2nd ed. 1904. text ed. 21.00x (ISBN 0-391-01068-9). Humanities.

Wollaston, William. The Religion of Nature Delineated, 1724 & Related Commentaries. LC 74-1469. 1974. 38.00x (ISBN 0-8201-1127-9). Schol Facsimiles.

Wolle, Muriel S. The Bonanza Trail: Ghost Towns & Mining Camps of the West. LC 82-73898. (Illus.). 510p. 1953. Repr. pap. 17.95 (ISBN 0-8040-0685-7). Swallow.

--Montana Pay Dirt: A Guide to the Mining Camps of the Treasure State. LC 63-14650. (Illus.). 436p. 1983. Repr. of 1963 ed. 29.95 (ISBN 0-8040-0210-X, 82-71421). Ohio U Pr.

--Stampede to Timberline: The Ghost Towns & Mining Camps of Colorado. 2nd, rev. ed. LC 82-73708. 583p. 1974. 24.95 (ISBN 0-8040-0672-5). Swallow.

--Timberline Tailings: Tales of Colorado's Ghost Town & Mining Camps. LC 82-74086. (Illus.). 337p. 1977. 19.95 (ISBN 0-8040-0739-X). Swallow.

Wollheim, Donald A. Wollheim's World Best Science Fiction, No. 6. 1982. pap. 2.50 (ISBN 0-87997-788-4, UE1788). DAW Bks.

Wollheim, Donald A., ed. The Annual World's Best SF, Vol. 18, 1982. 1982. pap. 2.95 (ISBN 0-87997-728-0, UE1728). Daw Bks.

--The Best from the Rest of the World. (Science Fiction Ser). 1977. pap. 1.75 o.p. (ISBN 0-87997-343-9, UE1343). DAW Bks.

--Wollheim's World's Best Science Fiction: Series Four. (Science Fiction Ser.). Date not set. pap. 2.25 (ISBN 0-686-73798-9, UE 1585). DAW Bks.

Wollheim, R. & Hopkins, J. Philosophical Essays on Freud. LC 82-1123. 250p. 1983. 44.50 (ISBN 0-521-24076-X); pap. 12.95 (ISBN 0-521-28425-2). Cambridge U Pr.

Wollheim, Richard. Art & Its Objects. 2nd ed. LC 79-20790. 1980. 29.95 (ISBN 0-521-22898-0); pap. 9.95 (ISBN 0-521-29706-0). Cambridge U Pr.

--Sigmund Freud. 316p. 1981. pap. 8.95 (ISBN 0-521-28385-X). Cambridge U Pr.

Wollitz, Kenneth. The Recorder Book. 1982. 17.50 (ISBN 0-394-47973-4); pap. 8.95 (ISBN 0-394-74999-5). Knopf.

Wollman, Leo, et al. Eating Your Way to a Better Sex Life. 245p. (Orig.). (YA) 1982. pap. 3.50 (ISBN 0-523-41851-5). Pinnacle Bks.

Wollman-Tsamir, Pinchas. The Graphic History of the Jewish Heritage. 224p. 1982. 22.50. Shengold.

Wollrab, James E. Rotational Spectra & Molecular Structure. (Physical Chemistry Ser.: Vol. 13). 1967. 62.00 (ISBN 0-12-762150-4). Acad Pr.

Wollstonecraft, Mary. An Historical & Moral View of the Origin & Progress of the French Revolution & the Effect It Has Produced in Europe. LC 74-28416. 530p. 1975. Repr. of 1794 ed. lib. bdg. 60.00x (ISBN 0-8201-1149-X). Schol Facsimiles.

--Vindication of the Rights of Woman. Hagelman, Charles W., Jr., ed. 1967. pap. 3.95 o.p. (ISBN 0-393-00373-6, Norton Lib). Norton.

--Vindication of the Rights of Woman. Kramnick, Miriam, ed. (English Library). 1978. pap. 3.95 (ISBN 0-14-043199-3). Penguin.

Wollstonecraft, Mary & Mill, John S. The Rights of Women. Incl. The Subjugation of Women. 1955. Repr. of 1929 ed. 5.00x (ISBN 0-460-00825-0, Evman). Biblio Dist.

--A Vindication of the Rights of Woman & the Subjection of Women. 300p. 1983. pap. text ed. 5.95x (ISBN 0-460-01825-6, Pub. by Evman England). Biblio Dist.

Wollstonecraft, Mary see Day, Thomas.

Wollstonecraft, Mary, ed. Female Reader. LC 79-27565. 1980. 55.00x (ISBN 0-8201-1347-6). Schol Facsimiles.

Wollzenmuller, Franz. How to Succeed at Cycling. (Illus.). 128p. 1982. 12.95 (ISBN 0-8069-4158-8); lib. bdg. 15.69 (ISBN 0-8069-4159-6); pap. 6.95 (ISBN 0-8069-4152-9). Sterling.

Wolman, jt. auth. see Klein.

Wolman, Arnold. The Complete Poetry of Arnold Wolman. (Illus.). 96p. (Orig.). lib. bdg. 15.00 (ISBN 0-686-97659-2); pap. 9.95 (ISBN 0-686-97660-6); tchrs.' ed. 15.00 (ISBN 0-686-97661-4); wkbk. 7.50 (ISBN 0-686-97662-2). Peradam Pub Hse.

--Ho Ho Ho. (Billy, the Bear Ser.). (Illus.). 36p. (Orig.). pap. 7.50 (ISBN 0-686-97657-6). Peradam Pub Hse.

--Tickle, the Pickle, Meets God. rev., 2nd ed. (Tickle, the Pickle Trilogy Ser.). (Illus.). 16p. (Orig.). 1975. pap. 2.50 (ISBN 0-686-97654-1). Peradam Pub Hse.

--Tickle, the Pickle, Meets Marsha, the Mushroom. Duval, Arnaud, tr. from Eng. (Tickle, the Pickle Trilogy Ser.). (Illus.). 24p. (Fr.). 1975. pap. 5.00 (ISBN 0-686-97653-3). Peradam Pub Hse.

Wolman, Arnold, ed. see Magorian, James.

Wolman, Benjamin. Children's Fears. 1979. pap. 2.25 o.p. (ISBN 0-451-08885-9, E8885, Sig). NAL.

Wolman, Benjamin B. Children's Fears. 1978. 8.95 o.p. (ISBN 0-448-14564-2, G&D). Putnam Pub Group.

--Handbook of Parapsychology. 1070p. 1981. pap. text ed. 17.95 o.p. (ISBN 0-442-26479-8). Van Nos Reinhold.

Wolman, Benjamin B., ed. Handbook of Treatment of Mental Disorders in Childhood & Adolescence. LC 77-7928. (Illus.). 1978. ref. ed. 59.95 (ISBN 0-13-382234-6). P-H.

--Manual of Child Psychopathology. (Illus.). 1392p. 1971. text ed. 125.00 (ISBN 0-07-071545-9, C). McGraw.

--Progress: Vol. 1 of the International Encyclppedia of Psychiatry, Psychology, Psychoanalysis & Neurology. 1983. 89.00 (ISBN 0-918228-28-X). Aesculapius Pubs.

--The Therapist's Handbook: Treatment Methods of Mental Disorders. 2nd ed. 480p. 1982. text ed. 32.50 (ISBN 0-442-25616-7). Van Nos Reinhold.

Wolman, Benjamon B. & Money, John. Handbook of Human Sexuality. (Illus.). 1980. text ed. 45.00 (ISBN 0-13-378422-3). P-H.

Wolman, Judith. I Can Bake Cookies. LC 78-72108. (Illus.). (gr. k-5). 1979. 6.75 (ISBN 0-89799-112-5); pap. 3.50 (ISBN 0-89799-027-7). Dandelion Pr.

--Lizzie & the Tooth Fairy. LC 78-72115. (Illus.). (ps). 1979. 6.75 (ISBN 0-89799-123-0); pap. 3.50 (ISBN 0-89799-015-3). Dandelion Pr.

Wolman, Moshe, ed. Pigments in Pathology. 1969. 77.00 (ISBN 0-12-762450-3). Acad Pr.

Wolman, Y. Peptides Nineteen Seventy-Four: Proceedings of the Thirteenth European Peptide Symposium, Israel, April, 1974. LC 75-8603. 1975. 62.95x o.p. (ISBN 0-470-95957-6). Halsted Pr.

Wolman, Yecheskel. Chemical Information: A Practical Guide to Utilization. 250p. 1983. avail. (ISBN 0-471-10319-5, Pub. by Wiley-Interscience). Wiley.

Woloch, G. Michael, ed. see Grimal, Pierre.

Woloshin, David, tr. see Jaspers, Karl.

Wolowelsky, Joel B., ed. Jewish Education: A Special Issue of Tradition, Vol. 19. LC 81-84305. 76p. 1981. pap. 8.95 (ISBN 0-89885-124-6). Human Sci Pr.

Wolpa, Mark E. The Sports Medicine Guide: Teaching & Preventing Common Athletic Injuries. 2nd ed. (Illus.). 160p. (Orig.). 1983. pap. 6.95 (ISBN 0-88011-099-6). Leisure Pr.

Wolpe, Joseph. The Practice of Behavior Therapy. 3rd ed. (Illus.). 425p. 1982. 39.50 (ISBN 0-08-027165-0, J115); pap. 13.95 (ISBN 0-08-027164-2). Pergamon.

--Theme & Variations: A Behavior Therapy Casebook. 200p. 1976. text ed. 23.00 (ISBN 0-08-020422-8); pap. text ed. 13.75 (ISBN 0-08-020421-X). Pergamon.

Wolpert, Edward M. Understanding Research in Education: An Introductory Guide to Critical Reading. 256p. 1981. pap. text ed. 15.50 (ISBN 0-8403-2448-0). Kendall-Hunt.

Wolpert, Robert C. & Genet, Russell M. Advances in Photoelectric Photometry. LC 82-84767. 200p. (Orig.). 1983. pap. 18.95 (ISBN 0-911351-01-9). Fairborn Observ.

Wolpert, Robert C., jt. ed. see Genet, Russell M.

Wolpert, Stanley. A New History of India. 2nd ed. LC 81-38. (Illus.). 1982. 25.00x (ISBN 0-19-502949-6); pap. text ed. 9.95x (ISBN 0-19-502950-X). Oxford U Pr.

Wolpert, Stanley A. Tilak & Gokhale: Revolution & Reform in the Making of Modern India. (California Library Reprint Ser.). 1977. 36.50x (ISBN 0-520-03339-6). U of Cal Pr.

Wolpoff, Milford H. Introduction to Paleoanthopology. 1980. text ed. 24.00x (ISBN 0-394-32197-9). Random.

--Paleoanthropology. 416p. 1980. text ed. 24.00 (ISBN 0-394-32197-9). Knopf.

Wolsch, Lois A., jt. auth. see Wolsch, Robert A.

Wolsch, Robert A. & Wolsch, Lois A. From Speaking to Writing to Reading: Relating the Arts of Communication. 2nd ed. LC 82-3228. 1982. pap. text ed. 17.95x (ISBN 0-8077-2607-9). Tchrs Coll.

Wolseley, Charles. The Reasonableness of Scripture-Belief. LC 73-2618. 488p. 1973. Repr. of 1672 ed. lib. bdg. 53.00x (ISBN 0-8201-1113-9). Schol Facsimiles.

Wolseley, Garnet. South African Diaries of Sir Garnet Wolseley, 1875. Preston, Adrian, ed. 293p. 1971. 45.00x (ISBN 0-8002-3100-7). Intl Pubns Serv.

Wolseley, Gerald. South African Journal of Sir Garnet Wolseley, 1879-1880. Preston, Adrian, ed. 359p. 1973. 45.00x (ISBN 0-86961-040-6). Intl Pubns Serv.

Wolseley, Roland E. The Changing Magazine: Trends in Readership & Management. (Illus.). 160p. 1973. 8.95 o.s.i. (ISBN 0-8038-1179-9). Hastings.

Wolsky, Alexander. Tielherd in Chardin's Biological Ideas. (Tielherd Studies). 1981. 2.00 (ISBN 0-89012-024-2). Anima Pubns.

Wolt, Irene, jt. auth. see Gottlieb, Robert.

Wolter, Allan. John Duns Scotus & the Treatise on God as First Principle. 1983. 10.00 (ISBN 0-8199-0860-6). Franciscan Herald.

Wolter, Ulf, ed. Rudolf Bahro: Critical Responses. Vale, Michel, tr. from Ger., Fr., Ital. LC 80-5453. 1980. 27.50 (ISBN 0-87332-159-6). M E Sharpe.

Woltering, Denise M., ed. see Miller, Boulton B.

Wolters, Richard. The World of Silent Flight. LC 78-15822. (Illus.). 1979. 15.95 o.p. (ISBN 0-07-071561-0, GB). McGraw.

Wolters, Richard A. Family Dog. rev. ed. 1975. 12.50 (ISBN 0-87690-173-9, 01214-360). Dutton.

--The Kid's Dog: A Training Book. LC 76-23803. (Illus.). (gr. 6-9). 1978. 7.95a (ISBN 0-385-11550-4); PLB (ISBN 0-385-11551-2). Doubleday.

--Water Dog. 1964. 12.50 (ISBN 0-525-23021-1, 01214-360). Dutton.

Woltz, P. & Arlen, R. College Accounting: A Comprehensive Approach. 864p. 1983. 20.95x (ISBN 0-07-071481-9, C); write for info study guide (ISBN 0-07-071482-7). McGraw.

Woltz, Phebe M. & Arlen, Richard T. College Accounting: An Introduction. 1979. text ed. 19.95 (ISBN 0-07-071551-3, C); tests 25.00 (ISBN 0-07-071555-6); exams 12.95 (ISBN 0-07-071567-X); practice sets 1 6.95 (ISBN 0-07-071553-X); practice set 2 8.00 (ISBN 0-07-071554-8); transparencies, 225.00 (ISBN 0-07-074795-4); study guide 9.95 (ISBN 0-07-071552-1); working papers & solutions guide 16.50 (ISBN 0-07-071556-4). McGraw.

--College Accounting: An Introduction. 2nd ed. Mason, Donald G., ed. 494p. 1983. text ed. 15.95 (ISBN 0-07-071599-8, C); study guide 10.00 (ISBN 0-07-071605-6). McGraw.

Wolverton, Mike. And Now...the News. 136p, 1977. 13.95 (ISBN 0-87201-041-4). Gulf Pub.

Wolverton, Mike, jt. auth. see Wolverton, Ruth.

Wolverton, Ruth & Wolverton, Mike. How to Convert Ordinary Garages into Exciting Family Rooms. (Illus.). 406p. 1981. 18.95 o.p. (ISBN 0-8306-9682-2, 1210); pap. 10.95 (ISBN 0-8306-1210-6). TAB Bks.

--New Media. LC 80-25697. (First Bks). (gr. 4 up). 1981. PLB 8.90 (ISBN 0-531-04194-8). Watts.

--Trucks & Trucking. LC 82-6967. (First Bks.). (Illus.). 72p. 1982. PLB 8.90 (ISBN 0-531-04468-8). Watts.

Wolvin, Andrew D., jt. auth. see Berko, Roy M.

Womach, Merril & Womach, Virginia. Probado por Fuego. (Span.). Date not set. 1.75 o.p. (ISBN 0-686-76337-8). Life Pubs Intl.

Womach, Virginia, jt. auth. see Womach, Merril.

Womack, Brantly. The Foundations of Mao Zedong's Political Thought, 1917-1935. LC 81-16317. 256p. 1982. text ed. 17.50x (ISBN 0-8248-0752-9). UH Pr.

Womack, David A. The Pyramid Principle. LC 76-46312. 1977. pap. 4.95 o.p. (ISBN 0-87123-462-9, 210462). Bethany Hse.

Womack Educational Publications Editors. Fluid Power Data Booklet. 48p. pap. 0.00 write for info. o.p. Womack Educ Pubns.

Womack, R. C., jt. auth. see Hedges, Charles S.

Woman's Day, ed. The Best of Woman's Day Crochet. 1976. 9.95 o.p. (ISBN 0-671-22225-2). S&S.

Woman's Day Editors. Woman's Day Book of Best Loved Toys & Dolls. 1982. 18.95 (ISBN 0-686-86951-6). Van Nos Reinhold.

--The Woman's Day Book of Weekend Crafts: More Than 100 Quick-to-Finish Projects. LC 77-15496. 1978. 11.95 o.s.i. (ISBN 0-395-26284-4). HM.

--Woman's Day Creative Stitchery From Scraps. 1982. 15.95 (ISBN 0-442-29393-3). Van Nos Reinhold.

Woman's Day Editors, ed. see Lane, Rose W.

Women Against Racism, jt. auth. see Stone, Merlin.

Women of Christ Church Cathedral. Cathedral Cooking School Cookbook. Core, Lucy & Lyman, Clara, eds. (Illus.). 192p. (Orig.). 1974. spiral bdg. 7.95 (ISBN 0-88289-033-6). Pelican.

Women's Action Alliance. Women's Action Almanac: A Complete Resource Guide. Williamson, Jane, et al, eds. LC 79-16326. (Illus.). 1979. 12.95 o.p. (ISBN 0-688-03525-6, Quill); pap. 7.95 o.p. (ISBN 0-688-08525-3). Morrow.

Women's Aglow Editors. Reflections. 216p. 1979. pap. 6.95 o.p. (ISBN 0-930756-48-7, 4230-AD1). Women's Aglow.

Women's Club of Havana. Flowering Plants from Cuban Gardens. (Illus.). 1958. 17.95 (ISBN 0-87599-131-9). S G Phillips.

Women's Co-Operative Guild. Maternity: Letters from Working-Women, Collected by the Women's Co-Operative Guild with a Preface by the Right Hon. Herbert Samuel, M.P., London 1915. LC 79-56940. (The English Working Class Ser.). 1980. lib. bdg. 20.00 o.s.i. (ISBN 0-8240-0127-3). Garland Pub.

Women's Service League of West Feliciana Parish. Plantation Country. 325p. 1981. 9.95 (ISBN 0-9609422-0-3). Womens Serv.

Womer, Frank B. Basic Concepts in Testing. (Guidance Monograph). 1968. pap. 2.40 o.p. (ISBN 0-395-09925-0, 9-78824). HM.

Womersley, J. R., jt. auth. see Peirce, F. T.

Wonacott, A. J., jt. auth. see Arndt, U. W.

Wonder, John P., jt. auth. see Espinosa, Aurelio M.

Wonders, William C., ed. The North. (Studies in Canadian Geography). (Illus.). 1972. 12.50x o.p. (ISBN 0-8020-1923-4); pap. 6.00x o.p. (ISBN 0-8020-6164-8). U of Toronto Pr.

Wong, Benita M. The Culinary Art of Modern Taiwan. (East Asian Folklore & Social Life Monographs: Vol. 104). 24p. 1980. 11.50 (ISBN 0-89986-335-3). Oriental Bk Store.

Wong, Bruce M. TSFR: The Taoist Way to Total Sexual Fitness, For Men. 80p. 1982. pap. 9.95 (ISBN 0-910295-00-X). Golden Dragon Pub.

Wong, Cynthia B. & Swazey, Judith P. Dilemmas of Dying: Policies & Procedures for Decisions Not to Treat. 1981. lib. bdg. 18.50 (ISBN 0-8161-2179-6, Hall Medical). G K Hall.

Wong, Diane Yen-Mei. Dear Diane: Letters from Our Daughters. Kim, Elaine, intro. by. (Illus.). 90p. (Eng. & Korean.). 1983. pap. 4.95 (ISBN 0-936434-08-2). SF Stud Ctr.

--Dear Diane: Letters from Our Daughters. Kim, Elaine, intro. by. 80p. (Orig., Eng. & Chinese.). 1983. pap. 4.95 (ISBN 0-936434-07-4). SF Stud Ctr.

--Dear Diane: Questions & Answers for Asian American Women. Kim, Elaine, intro. by. (Illus.). 96p. (Orig.). 1983. pap. 4.95 (ISBN 0-936434-09-0). SF Stud Ctr.

Wong, Donna L., jt. auth. see Whaley, Lucille.

Wong, Donna L., jt. auth. see Whaley, Lucille F.

Wong, Douglas L. The Deceptive Hands of Wing Chu. LC 76-55613. (Illus.). 112p. 1977. pap. 5.95 (ISBN 0-86568-002-7). Unique Pubns.

--Kung-Fu: The Way of Life. LC 76-55617. (Illus.). 112p. 1975. pap. 5.50 (ISBN 0-86568-003-5). Unique Pubns.

--Shaolin Fighting. LC 76-55613. (Illus.). 1975. pap. 5.50 (ISBN 0-86568-006-X). Unique Pubns.

Wong, E. Introduction to Random Processes: A Dowden & Culver Book. (Springer Texts in Electrical Engineering). 175p. 1983. pap. 17.95 (ISBN 0-387-90757-2). Springer-Verlag.

Wong, H. & Bernstein. Ideas & Investigations in Science: Earth Science. Incl. Foundations & the Solar System. pap. text ed. 4.72 (ISBN 0-13-450015-6); Physical Science. pap. text ed. 4.72 (ISBN 0-13-450023-7); Meteorology & Oceaography. pap. text ed. 4.72 (ISBN 0-13-450031-8); Geodynamics. pap. text ed. 4.72 (ISBN 0-13-450049-0). 1977. 17.20 o.p. (ISBN 0-685-85628-3); tchr's guide o.p. 8.97 (ISBN 0-13-450007-5); lab data bk. 5.28 (ISBN 0-686-96833-6). P-H.

Wong, Hon Sun. How I Overcame Inoperable Cancer. 6.00x o.p. (ISBN 0-682-48284-6). Cancer Control Soc.

Wong, Irene. Great Asia Steam Book. LC 77-89302. 1978. pap. 5.95 (ISBN 0-394-73563-3, Dist. by Random). Taylor & Ng.

Wong, J. Y. Theory of Ground Vehicles. 330p. 1978. 39.95x (ISBN 0-471-03470-3, Pub. by Wiley-Interscience). Wiley.

--Yeh Ming-Ch'en. LC 75-18119. (Studies in Chinese History Literature and Institutions Ser.). (Illus.). 268p. 1976. 54.50 (ISBN 0-521-21023-2). Cambridge U Pr.

Wong, John Y. Anglo-Chinese Relations, 1838-1860: A Calendar of Documents in British Foreign Office Records. (British Academy Oriental Documents Ser.). 400p. 1983. 36.00 (ISBN 0-19-726014-4). Oxford U Pr.

Wong, Kau-Fui V., jt. ed. see Sengupta, Subrata.

Wong, Mary G. Nun: A Memoir. LC 82-47656. 420p. 1983. 16.95 (ISBN 0-15-167739-5). HarBraceJ.

Wong, Ming, jt. auth. see Huard, Pierre.

Wong, Richard W. Prayers from an Island. LC 68-25014. 1980. pap. 2.49 (ISBN 0-8042-2499-4). John Knox.

Wong, S. T. & Schulman, Sylvia. Madame Wong's Long-Life Chinese Cookbook. (Illus.). 1977. 12.95 o.p. (ISBN 0-8092-7926-6); pap. 7.95 (ISBN 0-8092-8030-2). Contemp Bks.

Wong, Seok P., jt. ed. see Irwin, John V.

Wong, Shirleen S. Kung Tzu-Chen. (World Authors Ser.). 1975. lib. bdg. 15.95 (ISBN 0-8057-6184-5, Twayne). G K Hall.

Wong, Stanford. Stanford Wong's Blackjack Newsletter, Vol. 1. (Stanford Wong's Blackjack Newsletter Ser.). (Illus.). 85p. (Orig.). 1979. pap. 10.00 (ISBN 0-935926-04-6). Pi Yee Pr.

--Stanford Wong's Blackjack Newsletters, Vol. 4: 1982. (Illus.). 214p. (Orig.). 1982. pap. 35.00 (ISBN 0-935926-07-0). Pi Yee Pr.

--Stanford Wong's Blackjack Newsletters, 1980, Vol. 2. (Stanford Wong's Blackjack Newsletters Ser.). (Illus.). 222p. 1980. pap. 20.00 (ISBN 0-935926-05-4). Pi Yee Pr.

Wong, Thomas K., jt. ed. see Kolber, Alan R.

Wong, Timothy C. Wu Ching-tzu. (World Authors Ser.). 1978. lib. bdg. 15.95 (ISBN 0-8057-6336-8, Twayne). G K Hall.

Wong, Ting & Schulman, Sylvia. More Long-Life Chinese Cooking from Madame Wong. (Illus.). 320p. 1983. pap. 7.95 (ISBN 0-8092-5609-6). Contemp Bks.

Wong, Warren J., ed. see Brauer, Richard.

Wong-Fraser, Agatha S. Symmetry & Selectivity in the U. S. Defense Policy: A Grand Design or a Major Mistake? LC 80-5610. 172p. 1980. lib. bdg. 20.50 (ISBN 0-8191-1182-1); pap. text ed. 9.75 (ISBN 0-8191-1183-X). U Pr of Amer.

Wong-Fraser, Agatha S. Y. The Political Utility of Nuclear Weapons: Expectations & Experience. LC 80-5609. 357p. 1980. lib. bdg. 22.50 (ISBN 0-8191-1234-8); pap. text ed. 13.25 (ISBN 0-8191-1235-6). U Pr of Amer.

Wongmo, Karma C., ed. see Rinpoche, Namgyal.

Wonham, W. M. Linear Multivariable Control: A Geometric Approach. (Lecture Notes in Economics & Mathematical Systems: Vol. 101). x, 344p. 1974. pap. 34.00 (ISBN 0-387-90354-2). Springer-Verlag.

Wonnacott, P. & Wonnacott, R. Economics. 2nd ed. 1982. 25.95x (ISBN 0-07-071595-5); study guide 9.95 (ISBN 0-07-071596-3). McGraw.

--Introduction to Macroeconomics. 2nd ed. 1982. 15.95x (ISBN 0-07-071582-3). McGraw.

--Introduction to Microeconomics. 2nd ed. 1982. 15.95x (ISBN 0-07-071583-1). McGraw.

Wonnacott, Paul. U. S. Intervention in the Exchange Market for DM, 1977-80. (Princeton Studies in International Finance: No. 51). 1982. pap. text ed. 4.50x (ISBN 0-88165-222-9). Princeton U Int Finan Econ.

Wonnacott, Paul & Wonnacott, Ron. Economics. (Illus.). 1979. text ed. 24.95 (ISBN 0-07-071571-8, C); instr's. manual 20.95 (ISBN 0-07-071572-6); study guide 9.95 (ISBN 0-07-071573-4). McGraw.

Wonnacott, R., jt. auth. see Wonnacott, P.

Wonnacott, Ron, jt. auth. see Wonnacott, Paul.

Wonnacott, Ronald J. & Wonnacott, Thomas H. Econometrics. 2nd ed. LC 78-31257. (Probability & Mathematical Statistics Ser.). 1979. text ed. 35.95 (ISBN 0-471-95981-2); solutions manual 9.95 (ISBN 0-471-07837-9). Wiley.

Wonnacott, Ronald J., jt. auth. see Wonnacott, Thomas H.

Wonnacott, Ronald J., jt. auth. see Wonnacott, Thomas J.

Wonnacott, Thomas H. & Wonnacott, Ronald J. Introductory Statistics. 3rd ed. (Wiley Ser. in Probability & Mathematical Statistics). 1977. text ed. 31.50 (ISBN 0-471-95982-0). Wiley.

--Introductory Statistics for Business & Economics. 2nd ed. LC 76-55773. (Probability & Mathematical Statistics Ser.). 1977. text ed. 31.95 (ISBN 0-471-95980-4, Pub. by Wiley-Hamilton). Wiley.

--Regression: A Second Course in Statistics. (Probability & Mathematical Statistics: Applied & Probability & Statistics). 556p. 1981. 34.95 (ISBN 0-471-95974-X). Wiley.

Wonnacott, Thomas H., jt. auth. see Wonnacott, Ronald J.

Wonnacott, Thomas J. & Wonnacott, Ronald J. Statistics: Discovering Its Power. LC 80-26507. (Probability & Mathematical Statistics Ser.). 378p. 1981. text ed. 22.95 (ISBN 0-471-01412-5). Wiley.

Woo, Juliana J, jt. auth. see Szilard, Paula.

Wood. Two Hundred One Persian Verbs - Arabic Script. 1984. 9.95 (ISBN 0-8120-2562-8). Barron.

--Two Hundred One Persian Verbs - Romanization. 1984. 9.95 (ISBN 0-8120-2563-6). Barron.

Wood, jt. auth. see Johnson.

Wood, A. A Theory of Pay. LC 78-1038. 1978. 32.50 (ISBN 0-521-22073-4). Cambridge U Pr.

Wood, A. L. Beachcombing for Japanese Glass Floats. LC 66-28020. (Illus.). 228p. 1975. pap. 6.50 o.p. (ISBN 0-8323-0215-5). Binford.

Wood, Alan, ed. see McGinnis, Terri.

Wood, Alastair J., jt. auth. see Wood, Margaret.

Wood, Audrey. Balloonia. (Illus.). 32p. 1981. 5.50 (ISBN 0-85953-122-8, Pub. by Child's Play England). Playspaces.

--Moonflute. pap. 8.95 (ISBN 0-914676-44-X). Green Tiger Pr.

--Princess & the Dragon. 32p. 1981. 5.50 (ISBN 0-85953-150-3, Pub. by Child's Play England). Playspaces.

--Quick As a Cricket. (Illus.). 32p. 1982. 8.00 (ISBN 0-85953-151-1, Pub. by Child's Play England). Playspaces.

Wood, B. A. Human Evolution. (Outline Studies in Biology). 1978. pap. 6.50x (ISBN 0-412-15600-8, Pub. by Chapman & Hall). Methuen Inc.

Wood, B. D. Applications of Thermodynamics. 2nd ed. 1982. 31.95 (ISBN 0-201-08741-3); solutions manual 2.00 (ISBN 0-201-08789-8). A-W.

Wood, Barbara. Domina. LC 82-45279. (Illus.). 504p. 1983. 15.95 (ISBN 0-385-17653-8). Doubleday.

--Yesterday's Child. 272p. 1981. pap. 2.50 o.p. (ISBN 0-380-50765-X, 50765). Avon.

Wood, Barbara, ed. see Vero, Radu.

Wood, Barbara S. Children & Communication: Verbal & Nonverbal Language Development. 2nd ed. (Illus.). 320p. 1981. text ed. 19.95 (ISBN 0-13-131920-5). P-H.

Wood, Bari. The Killing Gift. LC 75-18630. 320p. 1975. 8.95 (ISBN 0-399-11562-5). Putnam Pub Group.

--The Tribe. 1981. 12.95 (ISBN 0-453-00393-1, H393). NAL.

--The Tribe. 1981. pap. 3.95 (ISBN 0-451-12428-6, AE2428, Sig). NAL.

Wood, Barry. Questions Non-Christians Ask. 160p. 1980. pap. 4.95 (ISBN 0-8007-5047-0, Power Bks). Revell.

--Questions Teenagers Ask About Dating & Sex. 160p. (Orig.). 1981. pap. 5.95 (ISBN 0-8007-5058-6, Power Bks). Revell.

--Show Windows: Seventy Five Years of the Art of Display. (Illus.). 176p. 1982. 40.00 (ISBN 0-312-92767-3). Congdon & Weed.

Wood, Basil C. The What, When, & Where Guide to Northern California. LC 75-2858. (Illus.). 144p. 1977. pap. 4.95 (ISBN 0-385-05052-6). Doubleday.

--The What, When & Where Guide to Southern California. rev. ed. LC 78-3264. (Illus.). 1979. pap. 4.95 (ISBN 0-385-14043-6). Doubleday.

Wood, Beth, jt. auth. see Barry, Tom.

Wood, C. Intrauterine Devices. (Illus.). 1971. 6.95 o.p. (ISBN 0-407-21700-2). Butterworth.

Wood, C. M. & Lee, N. Geography of Pollution. 150p. 1974. pap. 10.50 (ISBN 0-7190-0564-7). Manchester.

Wood, Carroll E., jt. auth. see Githens, Thomas S.

Wood, Charles D., jt. auth. see Swindler, Daris R.

Wood, Charles T. The Quest for Eternity: Medieval Manners & Morals. LC 82-40476. (Illus.). 176p. 1983. pap. 8.95 (ISBN 0-87451-259-X). U Pr of New Eng.

Wood, Chauncey. The Elements of Chaucer's Troilus. 275p. Date not set. 35.00 (ISBN 0-8223-0498-8). Duke.

Wood, Chris, jt. auth. see Moore, George.

Wood, Christopher. A Dove Against Death. 224p. 1982. 15.75 (ISBN 0-670-28066-6). Viking Pr.

--Victorian Panorama: Paintings of Victorian Life. 256p. 1977. 41.00 o.p. (ISBN 0-571-10780-X). Faber & Faber.

Wood, Christopher, ed. Dictionary of Victorian Painters. 2nd ed. (Illus.). 764p. 1978. 135.00x (ISBN 0-902028-72-3, Pub. by Antique Collectors Club England). Gale.

Wood, Clement, ed. Complete Rhyming Dictionary. 1936. 10.95 (ISBN 0-385-00046-4). Doubleday.

Wood, Corinne S. Human Sickness & Health: A Biocultural View. LC 78-71608. 376p. 1979. pap. 13.95 (ISBN 0-87484-418-5). Mayfield Pub.

Wood, D. N. Use of Earth Sciences Literature. 1973. 24.95 o.p. (ISBN 0-408-70448-9). Butterworth.

Wood, Dave. Wisconsin Life Trip. 1982. 4.95 (ISBN 0-934860-21-1). Adventure Pubns.

Wood, David, et al, eds. Control of Insect Behavior by Natural Products: Proceedings. LC 69-13486. 1970. 42.50 (ISBN 0-12-762650-6). Acad Pr.

Wood, David M. Power & Policy in Western European Democracies. 2nd ed. LC 81-19841. 177p. 1982. pap. text ed. 11.50 (ISBN 0-471-09006-9). Wiley.

Wood, Dena L., jt. auth. see Memmler, Ruth L.

Wood, Dennis. Principles of Animal Physiology. 350p. 1982. pap. text ed. 19.95x (ISBN 0-7131-2861-5). E Arnold.

Wood, Derek. Jane's World Aircraft Recognition Handbook: Second Edition. 2nd ed. (Illus.). 512p. 1982. 19.95 (ISBN 0-86720-637-3); pap. 9.95 (ISBN 0-86720-636-5). Sci Bks IntL.

Wood, Derrick. Paradigms & a Programming Methodology: An Introduction. 1983. text ed. p.n.s. (ISBN 0-914894-45-5). Computer Sci.

Wood, Donald F. & Johnson, James C. Contemporary Transportation. 641p. 1980. 23.95 (ISBN 0-87814-112-X). Pennwell Books Division.

--Readings in Contemporary Transportation. 256p. 1980. 13.95 (ISBN 0-87814-126-X). Pennwell Pub.

Wood, Donald N. & Leps, A. Arvo. Mass Media & the Individual. (Illus.). 550p. 1983. text ed. 15.95 (ISBN 0-314-69687-3); instrs.' manual avail. (ISBN 0-314-71139-2). West Pub.

Wood, Donna, ed. New Trade Names 1982 & 1983 Supplements to Trade Names Directory. 200p. 1982. pap. 160.00x supplement to 3rd ed. (ISBN 0-8103-0693-X). Gale.

--Trade Names Dictionary: Company Index. 3rd ed. 1000p. 1982. 200.00x (ISBN 0-8103-0697-2). Gale.

Wood, Douglas K. Men Against Time: Nicolas Berdyaev, T. S. Eliot, Aldous Huxley, & C. G. Jung. LC 82-526. x, 254p. 1982. text ed. 22.50x (ISBN 0-7006-0222-4). Univ Pr KS.

Wood, E. F. The Living Ocean. LC 75-15138. (Biology & Environment Ser.). 200p. 1975. 18.95 o.p. (ISBN 0-312-49000-3). St Martin.

Wood, E. J. Inshore Dinghy Fishing. (Leisure Plan Bks). pap. 2.95 o.p. (ISBN 0-600-40083-2). Transatlantic.

Wood, E. J., ed. Strycture & Function of Invertebrate Respiratory Proteins. (Life Chemistry Reports: Supplement). 350p. 1982. 85.00 (ISBN 3-7186-0136-2). Harwood Academic.

Wood, Edward J. Curiosities of Clocks & Watches from the Earliest Times. LC 70-174149. (Illus.). x, 443p. 1974. Repr. of 1866 ed. 37.00x (ISBN 0-8103-3984-6). Gale.

Wood, Elizabeth A. Crystals & Light: An Introduction to Optical Crystallography. LC 76-27458. (Illus.). 156p. 1977. pap. text ed. 3.50 (ISBN 0-486-23431-2). Dover.

Wood, Elizabeth C. Beard's Massage: Principles & Techniques. 2nd ed. LC 73-86389. (Illus.). 190p. 1974. text ed. 15.95x o.p. (ISBN 0-7216-9591-4). Saunders.

Wood, Elizabeth C., jt. auth. see Becker, Paul.

Wood, Ellen. Mind & Politics: An Approach to the Meaning of Liberal & Socialist Individualism. LC 74-153556. 224p. 1972. 30.00x (ISBN 0-520-02029-4). U of Cal Pr.

Wood, Esther. Country Fare: Reminiscences & Recipes from a Maine Childhood. LC 76-11305. 1976. 15.00x (ISBN 0-912274-59-X); pap. 5.95 o.p. (ISBN 0-912274-66-2). NH Pub Co.

Wood, Fiona. Use & Perception of an Academic Library. (ANUP Library: Occassional Paper No. 3). 80p. (Orig.). 1982. pap. text ed. 13.95 (ISBN 0-7081-1958-1, 1151, Pub. by ANUP Australia). Bks Australia.

Wood, Forrest G. Black Scare: The Racist Response to Emancipation & Reconstruction. 1968. 30.00x (ISBN 0-520-01361-1); pap. 2.45 (ISBN 0-520-01664-5, CAL190). U of Cal Pr.

Wood, Fred S., jt. auth. see Daniel, Cuthbert.

Wood, G. V., jt. auth. see Thomas, A. D.

Wood, Geoffrey E. see Griffiths, Brian.

Wood, Geoffrey E., jt. ed. see Batchelor, Roy A.

Wood, Gerald L. Guinness Book of Animal Facts & Feats. 3rd ed. (Illus.). 1983. 19.95 (ISBN 0-85112-235-3, Pub. by Guinness Superlatives England). Sterling.

Wood, Geraldine. Saudi Arabia. (First Bks). (Illus.). (gr. 4-6). 1978. PLB 8.90 s&l (ISBN 0-531-02234-X). Watts.

Wood, Glenn L. & Lilly, Claude C. III. Personal Risk Management & Insurance, 2 Vols. 2nd ed. LC 80-69852. 935p. 1980. text ed. 18.00 ea. vol. Am Inst Property.

Wood, Glenn L., et al. Personal Risk Management & Insurance, 2 vols. 2nd ed. 1980. write for info. o.p. (CPCU 2). IIA.

Wood, Gordon. Cognitive Psychology: A Skills Approach. LC 82-12799. (Psychology Ser.). 400p. 1982. text ed. 22.95 (ISBN 0-534-01262-0). Brooks-Cole.

Wood, Gordon S. The Confederation & the Constitution: The Critical Issues. LC 79-66423. 1979. pap. text ed. 9.25 (ISBN 0-8191-0821-9). U Pr of Amer.

--The Creation of the American Republic, 1776-1787. 672p. 1972. pap. 8.95x (ISBN 0-393-00644-1, Norton Lib). Norton.

--Creation of the American Republic, 1776-1787. (Institute of Early American History & Culture Ser.). xiv, 653p. (Orig.). 1969. 25.00x (ISBN 0-8078-1104-1). U of NC Pr.

Wood, H., jt. auth. see Swettenham, John.

Wood, Herbert, jt. auth. see Swettenham, John.

Wood, Houston, jt. auth. see Mehan, Hugh.

Wood, Ira, jt. auth. see Piercy, Marge.

Wood, J., tr. see Barth, A.

Wood, J. A. Meteorites & the Origin of Planets. (International Ser. in the Earth & Planetary Sciences). 1968. text ed. 10.00 o.p. (ISBN 0-07-071581-5, C); pap. text ed. 8.00 o.p. (ISBN 0-07-071580-7). McGraw.

Wood, J. B. Troubleshooting Your Handgun. 1978. pap. 5.95 o.s.i. (ISBN 0-695-80944-X). Follett.

--Troubleshooting Your Rifle & Shotgun. (Illus.). 1978. pap. 5.95 o.s.i. (ISBN 0-695-81198-3). Follett.

Wood, J. H. Commercial Bank Loan & Investment Behavior. Walters, A. A., ed. LC 75-1192. (Monographs in Applied Econometrics Ser). 153p. 1975. 38.95x (ISBN 0-471-95998-7, Pub. by Wiley-Interscience). Wiley.

Wood, J. M. & Evans, M. S. Natal Plants: 1898-1912, 6 vols. in 2. (Illus.). 1970. 160.00 (ISBN 3-7682-0671-8). Lubrecht & Cramer.

Wood, James. A Black Horse Running. LC 74-30874. 1977. 7.95 o.s.i. (ISBN 0-8149-0757-1). Vanguard.

Wood, James E., Jr., ed. Jewish-Christian Relations in Today's World. 164p. pap. 1.95 (ISBN 0-686-95175-1). ADL.

Wood, James H., ed. Neurobiology of Cerebrospinal Fluid 2. 850p. 1983. 89.50x (ISBN 0-306-40969-0, Plenum Pr). Plenum Pub.

Wood, James N., jt. auth. see Naef, Weston J.

Wood, James P. Colonial Massachusetts. LC 71-82917. (Colonial History Ser.). (Illus.). (gr. 5 up). 1969. 6.75 o.p. (ISBN 0-525-67101-3). Lodestar Bks.

--Colonial New Hampshire. LC 73-10270. (Colonial History Ser.). (Illus.). 160p. (gr. 5 up). 1973. 7.95 o.p. (ISBN 0-525-66316-9). Lodestar Bks.

--New England Academy, Wilbraham to Wilbraham & Monson. LC 77-172619. (Illus.). 152p. (Orig.). 1971. pap. 2.95 (ISBN 0-912668-00-8). Dothard.

--Of Lasting Interest. LC 75-17465. (Illus.). 264p. 1975. Repr. of 1958 ed. lib. bdg. 19.00x (ISBN 0-8371-8309-X, WOLI). Greenwood.

Wood, Jean & Armstrong, Nancy M. In Our Hogan: Adventure Stories of Navajo Children. (Indian Culture Ser.). (gr. 4-8). 1976. 1.95 o.p. (ISBN 0-89992-058-6). MT Coun Indian.

Wood, Jerline. Kamra's Christmas Story. (Illus.). 48p. (gr. k-5). 1982. pap. 2.95 (ISBN 0-910071-00-4). Gneiss Bks.

Wood, JoAnne. My Little Doll House. Wood, JoAnne, ed. (Put & Play Ser.). (ps). 1981. 4.50 (ISBN 0-307-05102-1, Golden Pr). Western Pub.

--My Little Farm. Wood, JoAnne, ed. (Put & Play Ser.). (ps). 1981. 4.50 (ISBN 0-307-05103-X, Golden Pr). Western Pub.

Wood, John. Description of Bath, 1765. 16.00x o.p. (ISBN 0-87556-416-X). Saifer.

--The Solar System. 1979. 11.95 o.p. (ISBN 0-13-822007-7); pap. 11.95 (ISBN 0-13-822015-8). P-H.

Wood, John B., tr. see Erhard, Ludwig.

Wood, John C., ed. John Maynard Keynes: Critical Assessments. (Assessments of Leading Economists Ser.). 2096p. 1983. Set of 4 vols. text ed. 495.00x (ISBN 0-7099-2729-0, Pub. by Croom Helm Ltd England). Biblio Dist.

Wood, John E. Sun, Moon, & Standing Stones. (Illus.). 1978. 19.95x (ISBN 0-19-211443-3). Oxford U Pr.

Wood, John J. & Vannette, Walter M. Sheep Is Life: An Assessment of Livestock Reduction in the Former Navajo-Hopi Joint Use Area. rev. ed. (Northern Arizona University Anthropological Papers: No. 1). (Illus.). xxiii, 182p. 1982. pap. 13.50 (ISBN 0-910953-00-7). N Arizona U.

Wood, John T. What Are You Afraid of? A Guide to Dealing with Your Fears. 192p. 1975 (ISBN 0-13-951889-4, Spec). pap. 2.95 o.p. (ISBN 0-13-951871-1). P-H.

Wood, John V. Railroads Through the Coeur D'Alenes. LC 82-4168. (Illus.). 230p. (Orig.). 1983. 17.95 (ISBN 0-87004-297-1); pap. 12.95 (ISBN 0-87004-291-2). Caxton.

Wood, Joyce. Grandmother Lucy in Her Garden. LC 74-15362. (Illus.). 32p. (ps-3). 1975. 4.91 o.p. (ISBN 0-529-05239-3, A4642W, Philomel). Putnam Pub Group.

Wood, Judson P., tr. see Miranda, Francisco De.

Wood, June. Introductory Algebra. 3rd ed. (Mathematics Ser.). 1977. text ed. 22.95 (ISBN 0-675-08511-X). Additional supplements may be obtained from publisher. Merrill.

Wood, June & Outcalt, David. Elementary Algebra for College Students: A Revision of a First Course in Algebra. (Mathematics Ser.). 1977. text ed. 18.95 (ISBN 0-675-08510-1). Additional supplements may be obtained from publisher. Merrill.

Wood, June P. Introductory & Intermediate Algebra. 4th ed. 1983. text ed. 22.95 (ISBN 0-675-20001-6); student guide 9.50 (ISBN 0-675-20039-3). Additional supplements may be obtained from publisher. Merrill.

Wood, Katherine D., jt. auth. see Palmer, Gladys L.

Wood, L. J., jt. auth. see Diamond.

Wood, Leslie B. The Restoration of the Tidal Thames. 250p. 1982. 69.00x o.p. (ISBN 0-85274-447-1, Pub. by A Hilger). State Mutual Bk.

Wood, Linda see O'Toole, James, et al.

Wood, Lorraine. I Am Jeremiah. Pena, Lilian M., ed. 290p. 1982. pap. 3.95 (ISBN 0-942128-00-1). Desert Light.

Wood, Louisa F. Behind Those Garden Garden Walls in Historic Savannah. (Illus.). 80p. 1982. text ed. 15.00 (ISBN 0-9610106-0-6); pap. text ed. 9.95 (ISBN 0-686-38453-9). Historic Sav.

Wood, Lucile A., jt. auth. see Rambo, Beverly J.

Wood, Lucile A. & Rambo, Beverly J., eds. Nursing Skills for Allied Health Services. 2nd ed. (Illus.). 1977. Vol. 1. pap. text ed. 9.50 o.p. (ISBN 0-7216-9603-1); Vol. 2. 9.50 o.p. (ISBN 0-7216-9604-X); single vol. 14.00 o.p. (ISBN 0-7216-9606-6). Saunders.

Wood, Lucille, jt. auth. see McLaughlin, Roberta.

Wood, M. Basic Business Math. 592p. 1982. text ed. 15.12x (ISBN 0-07-071601-3, G); learning guide 6.12x (ISBN 0-07-071604-8). McGraw.

Wood, M. & Cohen, S. Payroll Records & Procedures. 272p. 1983. 9.95 (ISBN 0-07-071627-7, Gregg). McGraw.

Wood, M., jt. auth. see Wigge, B. F.

Wood, M., tr. see Nicod, Jean.

Wood, M. M., ed. Developmental Therapy: A Textbook for Teachers As Therapists for Emotionally Disturbed Young Children. (Illus.). 308p. 1975. pap. text ed. 17.95 (ISBN 0-8391-0761-7). Univ Park.

Wood, M. W. The History of Alameda County, California. facsimile ed. (Illus.). 1000p. Repr. of 1883 ed. simulated lea. 27.50 (ISBN 0-910740-09-7). Holmes.

Wood, Marcia D., jt. auth. see Thompson, Ann M.
Wood, Margaret & Wood, Alastair J. Drugs & Anesthesia: Pharmacology for Anesthesiologists. (Illus.). 736p. 1982. lib. bdg. 57.00 (ISBN 0-683-09251-0). Williams & Wilkins.
Wood, Marilynn T., jt. auth. see Brink, Pamela J.
Wood, Marion M., jt. auth. see Larwood, Laurie.
Wood, Marion N. Coping with the Gluten-Free Diet. (Illus.). 164p. 1982. pap. 14.95x spiral (ISBN 0-398-04718-9). C C Thomas.
--Delicious & Easy Rice Flour Recipes: Gluten-Free: a Sequel to Gourmet Food on a Wheat-Free Diet. 160p. 1972. spiral 14.95x (ISBN 0-398-02441-3). C C Thomas.
Wood, Mary A. & Gee, E. Gordon. Fair Employment Practice & Standards, Cases & Materials. (Contemporary Legal Education Ser.). 896p. 1982. text ed. 32.50 (ISBN 0-87215-498-X); 6.00 (ISBN 0-87215-553-6). Michie-Bobbs.
Wood, Mary L. Language Disorders in School-Age Children. 208p. 1982. 21.95 (ISBN 0-13-522946-4). P-H.
Wood, Mary M. The Developmental Therapy Objectives. 210p. 1978. pap. text ed. 7.95 (ISBN 0-8391-1378-1). Univ Park.
--Developmental Therapy Sourcebook, Vol. 1. 208p. (Orig.). 1981. pap. text ed. 15.95 (ISBN 0-8391-1600-4). Univ Park.
--Developmental Therapy Sourcebook, Vol. 2. 256p. (Orig.). 1981. pap. text ed. 15.95 (ISBN 0-8391-1601-2). Univ Park.
Wood, Merle. The Davis Family: A Personal Recordkeeping Practice Set. 2nd ed. (Illus.). (gr. 10-12). 1981. 7.68 (ISBN 0-07-071623-4, G); tchr's manual & key 3.00 (ISBN 0-07-071624-2). McGraw.
Wood, Merle & Sanders, Margaret M. General Office Procedures. (Office Procedures Ser.). (Illus.). 352p. 1981. pap. text ed. 15.75 (ISBN 0-07-071593-9, G); instr's. manual & key 7.35 (ISBN 0-07-071594-7). McGraw.
Wood, Merle W. Data Processing in Marketing. (Occupational Manuals & Projects in Marketing). 1971. 5.96 o.p. (ISBN 0-07-071630-7, G); tchr's manual 3.00 o.p. (ISBN 0-07-071631-5). McGraw.
Wood, Merle W. & McKenna, M. Receptionist: A Practical Course in Office Reception Techniques. 1966. text ed. 15.80 (ISBN 0-07-071590-4, G); tchr's manual & key 7.40 (ISBN 0-07-071591-2). McGraw.
Wood, Michael. America in the Movies. 1976. pap. 5.95 o.s.i. (ISBN 0-440-50289-6, Delta). Dell.
Wood, Morrison. Cooking with Wine. pap. 1.50 o.p. (ISBN 0-686-67765-X, W7950, Sig). NAL.
--With a Jug of Wine. 1983. pap. 9.25 (ISBN 0-374-51773-8). FS&G.
Wood, N., jt. auth. see Williams, F.
Wood, Norma S., jt. auth. see Stroup, Herbert W., Jr.
Wood, Norman. The Complete Book of Dental Care. (Illus.). 320p. (Orig.). 1978. pap. 6.95 o.s.i. (ISBN 0-89104-227-X, A & W Visual Library). A & W Pubs.
Wood, Norman K. & Goaz, Paul W. Differential Diagnosis of Oral Lesions. 2nd ed. LC 80-18691. (Illus.). 662p. text ed. 42.95 (ISBN 0-8016-5617-6). Mosby.
Wood, Oliver G., Jr. Commercial Banking. LC 78-420. 376p. 1978. text ed. 21.95x (ISBN 0-442-29535-9). Kent Pub Co.
--Introduction to Money & Banking. 420p. 1980. text ed. 16.95 (ISBN 0-442-25787-2). Van Nos Reinhold.
--Introduction to Money & Banking. LC 79-65818. 420p. 1980. text ed. 22.95x (ISBN 0-442-25787-2). Kent Pub Co.
Wood, Orrin G., Jr. Your Hidden Assets: The Key to Getting Executive Jobs. LC 81-67116. 300p. 1981. 17.95 (ISBN 0-87094-266-2). Dow Jones-Irwin.
Wood, P., jt. auth. see Jackson, D. D.
Wood, Pamela. The Salt Book. LC 76-53419. 480p. 1977. pap. 8.95 (ISBN 0-385-11423-0, Anchor Pr); pap. 5.95 o.p. (ISBN 0-686-96705-4, Anch). Doubleday.
Wood, Paul W. Stained Glass Crafting. rev. ed. LC 67-27750. (Illus.). (gr. 10 up). 1971. 9.95 (ISBN 0-8069-5094-3); PLB 12.49 (ISBN 0-8069-5095-1). Sterling.
--Stained Glass Crafting. LC 67-27750. (Illus.). 104p. 1983. pap. 7.95 (ISBN 0-8069-7724-8). Sterling.
--Working with Stained Glass. LC 80-54350. (Illus.). 104p. 1981. 10.95 (ISBN 0-8069-5440-X); lib. bdg. 13.29 (ISBN 0-8069-5441-8); pap. 6.95 (ISBN 0-8069-8966-1). Sterling.
Wood, Peter. The California Diet & Exercise Program. 280p. 1983. 13.95 (ISBN 0-89037-257-8). Anderson World.
--Caribbean Isles. LC 74-24663. (American Wilderness Ser.). (Illus.). 184p. (gr. 6 up). 1975. PLB 15.96 (ISBN 0-8094-1214-4). Silver.
Wood, Peter H. Black Majority: Negroes in Colonial South Carolina from 1670 Through the Stono Rebellion. 384p. 1975. pap. 7.95 (ISBN 0-393-00777-4, Norton Lib). Norton.
Wood, Peter H., jt. auth. see Fenn, Elizabeth A.
Wood, Phyllis A. A Five Color Buick & a Blue Eyed Cat. (RL 6). 1977. pap. 1.50 (ISBN 0-451-11375-6, AW1375, Sig). NAL.
--A Five-Color Buick & a Blue-Eyed Cat. LC 74-19156. (A Hiway Book). (gr. 7 up). 1975. 7.95 (ISBN 0-664-32562-9). Westminster.
--Get a Little Lost, Tia. 1979. pap. 1.75 (ISBN 0-451-09872-2, E9872, Sig). NAL.
--Get a Little Lost, Tia. LC 78-17762. (A Hiway Book). (gr. 7-10). 1978. 8.95 (ISBN 0-664-32636-6). Westminster.
--I Think This Is Where We Came in. (RL 6). 1977. pap. 1.50 (ISBN 0-451-11482-5, AW1482, Sig). NAL.
--I Think This Is Where We Came in. LC 75-33093. (A Hiway Bk). 1976. 7.95 (ISBN 0-664-32582-3). Westminster.
--I've Missed a Sunset or Three. (Young Adult Ser.). (RL 6). 1975. pap. 1.25 o.p. (ISBN 0-451-07944-2, Y7944, Sig). NAL.
--Win Me & You Lose. LC 76-44299. (A Hiway Book). (gr. 7 up). 1977. 8.95 (ISBN 0-664-32605-6). Westminster.
Wood, R. D. & Imahori, K. A Monograph & Iconograph of the Characeae, 2 vols. 1965. 120.00 (ISBN 3-7682-0245-3). Lubrecht & Cramer.
Wood, R. G. Computers in Radiotherapy: Physical Aspects. (Computers in Medicine Ser.). 1974. 9.95 o.p. (ISBN 0-407-50002-2). Butterworth.
Wood, R. S. The Two Ounce Backpacker. A Problem Solving Manual for Use in the Wilds. LC 82-80236. 128p. 1982. pap. 2.95 (ISBN 0-89815-070-1). Ten Speed Pr.
Wood, R. S., jt. auth. see Savage, N. E.
Wood, Ralph C. & Weiser, Frederick S. The Four Gospels in the Pennsylvania German Dialect: Bd. with Daniel Schumacher's Baptismal Register, Vol. I. 1968. 20.00 (ISBN 0-911122-24-9). Penn German Soc.
Wood, Ralph L. Modern Handbook of Humor. 1967. 34.95 (ISBN 0-07-071737-0, P&RB). McGraw.
Wood, Raymond & Northern, Jerry. Manual of Otolaryngology: A Symptom-Oriented Text. 256p. 1979. pap. 17.95 (ISBN 0-683-09252-9). Williams & Wilkins.
Wood, Raymond G. Computers in Radio Therapy Planning. (Medical Computing Ser.). 171p. 1981. 47.95x (ISBN 0-471-09994-5, Pub. by Res Stud Pr). Wiley.
Wood, Richard H. A Cyclopedic Dictionary of Ecclesiastical Terms According to the Use of the Episcopal Church. 1983. 10.95 (ISBN 0-8062-2141-0). Carlton.
Wood, Robert. A Thirty-Day Experiment in Prayer. LC 78-65160. 1978. pap. 3.75 (ISBN 0-8358-0380-5). Upper Room.
--Thirty Days Are Not Enough: More Images for Meditative Journaling. 112p. (Orig.). 1983. pap. 3.75 (ISBN 0-8358-0445-3). Upper Room.
--What's Next? (ps-2). 1982. PLB 8.95 (ISBN 0-395-31611-1); 8.70. HM.
Wood, Robert E., jt. auth. see Mandell, Muriel.
Wood, Robert S. Desolation Wilderness. 2nd rev. ed. LC 75-4122. (Illus.). 256p. 1977. pap. 4.95 (ISBN 0-89815-044-2). Ten Speed Pr.
Wood, Robert S., ed. The Process of International Organization. 1971. pap. text ed. 7.50 (ISBN 0-685-55645-X, 31301). Phila Bk Co.
Wood, Robert W. How to Tell the Birds from the Flowers. (Illus.). (gr. 4 up). 1959. pap. 1.95 (ISBN 0-486-20523-1). Dover.
Wood, Robert W., jt. ed. see Cooper, Raymond D.
Wood, S. R. & Nichols, H. E. Midwest Railroader Remembers: C&O & Steam. Carlson, R. W. & Lorenz, R., eds. (Illus.). 106p. 1982. pap. 12.95 (ISBN 0-942322-01-0). Midwest Railroader.
Wood, Samellyn, et al. Parenting: Four Patterns in Child Rearing. 334p. (Orig.). 1978. pap. 6.95 o.s.i. (ISBN 0-89104-178-8, A & W Visual Library). A & W Pubs.
Wood, Samuel see Newbery, F.
Wood, Sidney. The Vikings Workguides. (Exploring History Ser.). (Illus.). 7p. (Orig.). 1977. duplicating masters 12.50 (ISBN 0-05-003134-1). Longman.
Wood, Susan, ed. see Le Guin, Ursula K.
Wood, Susan, intro. by see Leguin, Ursula K.
Wood, Thomas D. & Sweet, Franklin H. Modern Accounting Principles & Practices: A Professional Handbook. (Illus.). 1978. 34.95 o.p. (ISBN 0-13-586214-0, Busn). P-H.
Wood, V., jt. auth. see Pilch, Michael.
Wood, W. B., et al. Biochemistry: A Problems Approach. 2nd ed. 1981. 16.95 (ISBN 0-8053-9840-6); solutions manual 3.95 (ISBN 0-8053-9841-4). Benjamin-Cummings.
Wood, W. Raymond & McMillan, R. Bruce, eds. Prehistoric Man & His Environment: A Case Study in the Ozark Highland. (Studies in Archaeology Ser.). 1976. 40.00 (ISBN 0-12-762950-5). Acad Pr.
Wood, W. S., jt. auth. see Fawcett, H. H.
Wood, W. S., jt. ed. see Fawcett, Howard H.
Wood, Wallis W., jt. auth. see Richardson, H. L.
Wood, William. Captains of the Civil War. 1921. text ed. 8.50x (ISBN 0-686-83501-8). Elliots Bks.
--Elizabethan Sea-Dogs. 1918. text ed. 8.50x (ISBN 0-686-83535-2). Elliots Bks.
--In Defense of Liberty. 1928. text ed. 22.50x (ISBN 0-686-83580-8). Elliots Bks.
--Winnings of Freedom. 1927. text ed. 22.50x (ISBN 0-686-83858-0). Elliots Bks.
Wood, William, ed. Cultural-Ecological Perspectives on Southeast Asia: A Symposium. LC 76-620062. (Papers in International Studies: Southeast Asia: No. 41). 1977. pap. 11.00 (ISBN 0-89680-027-X, Ohio U Ctr Intl). Ohio U Pr.
Wood, Willis, jt. ed. see Colowick, Sidney.
Woodall, Corbett. Disjointed Life. 1980. pap. 9.95 (ISBN 0-434-87796-4, Pub. by Heinemann). David & Charles.
Woodall, Irene R. Leadership, Management & Role Delineation: Issues for the Dental Team. LC 77-8533. (Illus.). 316p. 1977. pap. 13.95 o.p. (ISBN 0-8016-5621-4). Mosby.
--Legal, Ethical & Management Aspects of the Dental Care System. 2nd ed. LC 82-8198. (Illus.). 285p. 1983. pap. text ed. 14.50 (ISBN 0-8016-5683-4). Mosby.
Woodall, Jean. The Socialist Corporation & Technocratic Power: The Polish United Workers' Party, Industrial Organization & Workforce Control, 1958-1980. (Soviet & East European Studies). (Illus.). 270p. 1982. 39.50 (ISBN 0-521-24269-X). Cambridge U Pr.
Woodall, Jean, ed. Policy & Politics in Contemporary Poland: Reform, Failure & Crisis. 256p. 1982. pap. 14.00 (ISBN 0-86187-222-3). F Pinter Pubs.
Woodall Publishing Co. Woodall's 1978 RV Buyer's Guide. (Illus.). 1978. pap. 5.95 o.p. (ISBN 0-448-14656-8, G&D). Putnam Pub Group.
Woodard, Bob, ed. Petroleum Technology for Exploration Support Personnel. 1982. 48.00 (ISBN 0-686-84040-2). Inst Energy.
Woodard, Daphne, tr. see Simenon, Georges.
Woodard, Jean. Brandy's Awakening. 1982. 6.95 (ISBN 0-686-84179-4, Avalon). Bouregy.
Woodard, Robert. Basic Land Management. 1982. 50.00 (ISBN 0-89419-211-6). Inst Energy.
Woodberry, George. Ralph Waldo Emerson. LC 68-24947. (American Biography Ser., No. 32). 1969. Repr. of 1907 ed. lib. bdg. 49.95x (ISBN 0-8383-0262-9). Haskell.
--Virgil. LC 72-3495. (Studies in European Literature, No. 56). 1972. Repr. lib. bdg. 40.95x (ISBN 0-8383-1564-X). Haskell.
Woodberry, George E. History of Wood-Engraving. LC 69-17490. 1969. Repr. of 1883 ed. 30.00x (ISBN 0-8103-3890-4). Gale.
Woodberry, George E., ed. see Poe, Edgar Allan.
Woodbine, G. E., ed. see Bracton, Henry De.
Woodbine, George E., ed. Four Thirteenth Century Law Tracts. 1910. 32.50x (ISBN 0-685-69888-2). Elliots Bks.
Woodbridge, F. J. The Son of Apollo: Themes of Plato. 272p. (gr. 7 up). 1972. Repr. of 1929 ed. 10.00x (ISBN 0-8196-0278-7). Biblo.
Woodbridge, George, jt. auth. see DeBartolo, Dick.
Woodbridge, Hensley C. Spanish & Spanish-American Literature: An Annotated Guide to Selected Bibliographies. (Selected Bibliographies in Language & Literature: 4). 74p. 1983. 10.50x (ISBN 0-87352-954-5); pap. 5.75x (ISBN 0-87352-955-3). Modern Lang.
Woodbridge, Homer E. G. B. Shaw: Creative Artist. LC 63-14294. (Arcturus Books Paperbacks). 193p. 1965. pap. 1.65 o.p. (ISBN 0-8093-0159-8). S Ill U Pr.
Woodbridge, John & Woodbridge, Sally. Architecture, San Francisco: The Guide. LC 82-14291. (Illus.). 208p. 1982. pap. 10.95 (ISBN 0-89286-204-1). One Hund One Prods.
Woodbridge, John D. Biblical Authority: A Critique of the Rogers-McKim Proposal. 256p. (Orig.). 1982. pap. 8.95 (ISBN 0-310-44751-8). Zondervan.
Woodbridge, Mark E., compiled by. American Federation of Labor & Congress of Industrial Organizations Pamphlets,1889-1955: A Bibliography & Subject Index to the Pamphlets Held in the AFL-CIO Library. LC 77-4564. 1977. lib. bdg. 25.00x (ISBN 0-8371-9686-8, WAF/). Greenwood.
Woodbridge, Sally, jt. auth. see Woodbridge, John.
Woodbridge, Sally, et al. Bay Area Houses. LC 76-9261. (Illus.). 1976. 39.95x (ISBN 0-19-502084-7). Oxford U Pr.
Woodburn, John H. Know Your Skin. (Science Survey Ser.). (Illus.). (gr. 6 up). 1967. PLB 4.89 (ISBN 0-399-60342-5). Putnam Pub Group.
--The Whole Earth Energy Crisis: Our Dwindling Sources of Energy. (Illus.). 192p. (gr. 6 up). 1973. PLB 5.69 o.p. (ISBN 0-399-60855-9). Putnam Pub Group.
Woodburne, Russell T. Essentials of Human Anatomy. 7th ed. (Illus.). 635p. 1983. text ed. 34.50x (ISBN 0-19-503171-7). Oxford U Pr.
--A Guide to Dissection in Gross Anatomy. 4th ed. (Illus.). 1980. pap. text ed. 8.95x spiral bdg. (ISBN 0-19-502670-5). Oxford U Pr.
Woodbury, D., et al, eds. Antiepleptic Drugs. 1972. 35.25 (ISBN 0-7204-4121-8, North Holland). Elsevier.
Woodbury, D. M., et al, eds. Antiepileptic Drugs. LC 70-181310. (Illus.). 560p. 1972. 34.50 (ISBN 0-911216-29-4). Raven.
Woodbury, John & Schwartz, Elroy. Silent Sin. (Orig.). 1971. pap. 1.75 o.p. (ISBN 0-451-07927-2, E7927, Sig). NAL.
Woodbury, Marda. A Guide to Sources of Educational Information. 2nd ed. LC 82-80549. xiii, 430p. 1982. text ed. 37.50 (ISBN 0-87815-041-2). Info Resources.
--Selecting Materials for Instruction: Issues & Policies. LC 79-18400. (Illus.). 1979. lib. bdg. 23.50 (ISBN 0-87287-197-5); lib. bdg. 56.40 set (ISBN 0-87287-285-8). Libs Unl.
--Selecting Materials for Instruction: Media & the Curriculum. LC 79-18400. (Illus.). 1980. lib. bdg. 23.50 (ISBN 0-87287-212-2); lib. bdg. 56.40 set (ISBN 0-87287-285-8). Libs Unl.
--Selecting Materials for Instruction: Subject Areas & Implementation. LC 79-18400. (Illus.). 1980. lib. bdg. 56.40 (ISBN 0-87287-213-0); lib. bdg. 54.00 set (ISBN 0-87287-285-8). Libs Unl.
Woodbury, Robert A., et al. Pharmacology Review. 4th ed. 1981. pap. 11.95 (ISBN 0-87488-205-2). Med Exam.
Woodbury, Robert S. Studies in the History of Machine Tools. (History of Science & Technology Ser). 625p. 1973. pap. 9.95 (ISBN 0-262-73033-2). MIT Pr.
Woodbury, T. C., jt. auth. see Grange, W. J.
Woodcock. Birds of the Indian Sub-Continent. 21.95 (ISBN 0-686-42724-6, Collins Pub England). Greene.
--Mathematics for the National Certificate in Engineering. 1970. 10.95 o.p. (ISBN 0-408-58075-5). Butterworth.
Woodcock & Heinzel. The Birds of Britian & Europe. pap. 8.95 (ISBN 0-686-42721-1, Collins Pub England). Greene.
Woodcock, jt. auth. see King.
Woodcock, Alexander & Davis, Monte. Catastrophe Theory. 1979. pap. 2.75 (ISBN 0-380-48397-1, 48397). Avon.
--Catastrophe Theory: The Landscapes of Change. (Illus.). 1978. 9.95 o.p. (ISBN 0-525-07812-6). Dutton.
Woodcock, C. L., jt. auth. see Bell, P. R.
Woodcock, C. L., ed. Progress in Acetabularia Research. 1977. 34.50 (ISBN 0-12-763750-8). Acad Pr.
Woodcock, David, jt. auth. see Martin, Hubert.
Woodcock, George. Thomas Merton-Monk & Poet: A Critical Study. 1978. 7.95 (ISBN 0-374-51485-2); pap. 3.95 (ISBN 0-374-51487-9). FS&G.
--To the City of the Dead: An Account of Travels in Mexico. LC 74-31872. (Illus.). 271p. 1975. Repr. of 1957 ed. lib. bdg. 19.00x (ISBN 0-8371-7946-7, WOCI). Greenwood.
Woodcock, J. P. Theory & Practice of Blood Flow Measurement. 1975. 23.95 o.p. (ISBN 0-407-41280-8). Butterworth.
Woodcock, J. P., jt. auth. see Wells, P. N.
Woodcock, J. T., jt. auth. see Jones, M. H.
Woodcock, John. Clinical Blood Flow Measurement. 192p. 1976. 45.00x (ISBN 0-686-97987-7, Pub. by Pitman Bks England). State Mutual Bk.
Woodcock, Leonard. China-United States Relations in Transition. LC 82-12135. 25p. 1982. 1.25 (ISBN 0-934742-21-9, Inst Study Diplomacy). Geo U Sch For Serv.
Woodcock, P. G., ed. Short Dictionary of Mythology. 19.95 (ISBN 0-8022-1927-6). Philos Lib.
Woodcock, Roy. Weather. LC 80-50958. (New Reference Library Ser.). PLB 11.96 (ISBN 0-382-06394-5). Silver.
Woodcock, Sarah, jt. auth. see Walker, Katherine S.
Woodcock, Susan R., jt. auth. see Pritchett, Morgan H.
Wooden, Howard E. Edward Laning: American Realist (1906-1981) - A Retrospective Exhibition. LC 82-61463. (Illus.). 56p. 1982. pap. 6.00 (ISBN 0-939324-05-9). Wichita Art Mus.
--Lily Harmon, Fifty Years of Painting: A Retrospective Exhibition. LC 82-62680. 56p. 1982. pap. 6.00 (ISBN 0-939324-07-5). Wichita Art Mus.
--The Neglected Generation of American Realist Painters: 1930-1948. LC 81-51507. (Illus.). 64p. 1981. pap. 5.00 (ISBN 0-939324-02-4). Wichita Art Mus.
Wooden, John R. Practical Modern Basketball. 2nd ed. LC 79-13731. 452p. 1980. text ed. 22.95x (ISBN 0-471-05865-3). Wiley.
Wooden, Kenneth. Weeping in the Playtime of Others: The Plight of Incarcerated Children. 1976. 9.95 (ISBN 0-07-071642-0, GB); pap. 6.95 (ISBN 0-07-071643-9). McGraw.
Wooden, Warren W. John Foxe. (English Authors Ser.). 176p. 1983. lib. bdg. 17.95 (ISBN 0-8057-6830-0, Twayne). G K Hall.
Wooden, Wayne S. What Price Paradise? Changing Social Patterns in Hawaii. LC 80-6240. 157p. 1981. lib. bdg. 19.25 (ISBN 0-8191-1520-7); pap. text ed. 9.25 (ISBN 0-8191-1521-5). U Pr of Amer.
Wooden, Wayne S. & Parker, Jay. Men Behind Bars: Sexual Exploitation in Prison. 250p. 1982. 15.95x (ISBN 0-306-41074-5, Plenum Pr). Plenum Pub.
Woodenboat Magazine Editors. Wooden Boat: An Appreciation of the Craft. (Illus.). 288p. 1982. 25.00 (ISBN 0-201-09280-8). A-W.
Woodford, F. P., jt. auth. see Richens, A.
Woodford, F. P., jt. ed. see Kiernan, C. C.

Woodford, P. & Kernan, D. Bridges to English, 6 bks. Rebrisz, J., ed. Incl. Bk. 1 (ISBN 0-07-034481-7). tchr's manual (ISBN 0-07-034482-5); wkbk. (ISBN 0-07-034483-3); Bk. 2 (ISBN 0-07-034487-6). tchr's manual (ISBN 0-07-034488-4); wkbk. (ISBN 0-07-034489-2); Bk. 3 (ISBN 0-07-034493-0). tchr's manual (ISBN 0-07-034494-9); wkbk. (ISBN 0-07-034495-7); Bk. 4 (ISBN 0-07-034499-X). tchr's manual (ISBN 0-07-034500-7); wkbk. (ISBN 0-07-034501-5); Bk. 5 (ISBN 0-07-034505-8). tchr's manual (ISBN 0-07-034506-6); wkbk. (ISBN 0-07-034507-4); Bk. 6 (ISBN 0-07-034511-2). tchr's manual (ISBN 0-07-034512-0); wkbk. (ISBN 0-07-034513-9). (Illus.). 1981. pap. text ed. 4.00 ea.; tchr's manual 2.00 ea.; wkbk. 3.52 ea.; tests 30.00 ea.; cassettes & cue cards avail. McGraw.

Woodford, P. E., et al. El Espanol: Sentirlo. 3rd ed. (Learning Spanish the Modern Way II). (Illus.). (gr. 10). 1971. text ed. 19.80 (ISBN 0-07-071645-5, W); tchr's. ed. 22.56 (ISBN 0-07-071646-3); wkbk. 5.92 (ISBN 0-07-071647-1); test pkg. replacements 59.36 (ISBN 0-07-071649-8). McGraw.

--Espanol: A Sentirlo. 5th ed. 1981. text ed. 18.44 (ISBN 0-07-071691-9); tchrs. edition 20.72 (ISBN 0-07-071692-7); cassettes 372.00 (ISBN 0-07-098721-1); filmstrips 146.32 (ISBN 0-07-098722-X). wkbk. 5.64 (ISBN 0-07-071693-5); tests 106.56 (ISBN 0-07-071694-3); test replacements 54.64 (ISBN 0-07-071695-1); tapes 368.00 (ISBN 0-07-098720-3). McGraw.

Woodford, Peggy. Mozart: His Life & Times. expanded ed. (Life & Times Ser.). (Illus.). 192p. 1981. Repr. of 1977 ed. 12.95 (ISBN 0-87666-643-8, Z-42). Paganiniana Pubns.

--Schubert, His Life & Times. expanded ed. (Illus.). 192p. Repr. of 1978 ed. 12.95 (ISBN 0-87666-640-3, Z-39). Paganiniana Pubns.

Woodford, Protase E. Spanish Language, Hispanic Culture. 1974. text ed. 26.50 (ISBN 0-07-071680-3); wkbk. 14.95 (ISBN 0-07-071681-1); instr's. manual 10.95 (ISBN 0-07-071685-4); tapes 450.00 (ISBN 0-07-071682-X). McGraw.

Woodford, Protase E., et al. Espanol: A Sentirlo. 4th ed. (YA) (gr. 10 up). 1977. text ed. 19.12 (ISBN 0-07-071656-0, W); tchr's. ed. 21.32 (ISBN 0-07-071657-9); wkbk. 5.84 (ISBN 0-07-071658-7); test pkg. replacements 56.68 (ISBN 0-07-071660-9). McGraw.

Woodford, Susan. Looking at Pictures. LC 82-14613. (Cambridge Introduction to the History of Art 6 Ser.). (Illus.). 128p. Date not set. 14.95 (ISBN 0-521-24371-8); pap. 1.25 (ISBN 0-521-28647-6). Cambridge U Pr.

Woodforde, C. Stained Glass in Somerset. 20.00x o.p. (ISBN 0-87556-418-6). Saifer.

Woodforde, John. Farm Buildings in England & Wales. (Illus.). 176p. 1983. 15.95 (ISBN 0-7100-9275-X). Routledge & Kegan.

--The Strange Story of False Teeth. 152p. 1983. pap. 8.95 (ISBN 0-7100-9307-1). Routledge & Kegan.

Woodgate, Ralph W. The Handbook of Machine Soldering: A Guide for the Soldering of Electronic Printed Wiring Assemblies. 240p. 1983. 25.50 (ISBN 0-471-87540-6, Pub. by Wiley Interscience). Wiley.

Woodger, J. H., tr. see Tarski, Alfred.

Woodhall, M. Educacion, Trabajo y Emples: Resena Sumaria. 40p. 1981. pap. 5.00 (ISBN 0-88936-271-8, IDRC-TS30S, IDRC). Unipub.

Woodham, Leonora. Stanza My Stone: Wallace Stevens & the Hermetic Traditions. LC 82-81679. 212p. 1983. 14.50 (ISBN 0-911198-68-7). Purdue.

Woodhams, Wilbur, ed. see Bayne, Stephen.

Woodham-Smith, Cecil. The Reason Why. LC 81-70067. 1982. pap. 8.95 (ISBN 0-689-70622-7). Atheneum.

--Reason Why. 1960. pap. 5.50 (ISBN 0-525-47053-0, 0534-160). Dutton.

Woodhead, Daniel & Beene, Wayne, eds. A Dictionary of Iraqi Arabic: Arabic-English. (Richard Slade Harrell Arabic Ser). 509p. 1967. pap. 9.50 (ISBN 0-87840-003-6). Georgetown U Pr.

Woodhead, R. W., jt. auth. see Anderson, S. D.

Woodhead, R. W., jt. auth. see Halpin, D. W.

Woodhead, Ronald, jt. auth. see Antill, James M.

Woodhead, Ronald W., jt. auth. see Antill, James M.

Woodhead, Ronald W., jt. auth. see Halpin, Daniel W.

Woodhead-Galloway, John. Collagen: The Anatomy of Protein. (Studies in Biology: No. 117). 64p. 1979. pap. text ed. 8.95 (ISBN 0-7131-2783-X). E Arnold.

Woodhill, Joan M., jt. auth. see Nobile, Sylvia.

Woodhouse, A. S. Milton: The Poet. 1982. lib. bdg. 34.50 (ISBN 0-686-81933-0). Porter.

Woodhouse, Adrian. Angus McBean. 1983. 40.00 (ISBN 0-686-38873-9, Pub. by Quartet Bks). Merrimack Bk Serv.

Woodhouse, C. M. Capodistria: The Founder of Greek Independence. new ed. (Illus.). 1973. 32.00x o.p. (ISBN 0-19-211196-5). Oxford U Pr.

--Karamanlis: The Restorer of Greek Democracy. (Illus.). 1982. 44.00x (ISBN 0-19-822584-9). Oxford U Pr.

Woodhouse, Florence, et al. Fundamental Reading Skills. 1979. pap. text ed. 7.95 (ISBN 0-8403-1955-X, 40195501). Kendall-Hunt.

Woodhouse, Martin. Moonhill. LC 74-79679. 1976. 7.95 o.p. (ISBN 0-698-10601-6, Coward). Putnam.

Woodhouse, Robert. History of the Calculus of Variations in the Eighteenth Century. LC 64-20969. 11.50 (ISBN 0-8284-0177-2). Chelsea Pub.

Woodhouse, S. C., ed. Latin-English & English-Latin Dictionary. (Routledge Pocket Dictionaries Ser.). 496p. (Orig.). 1982. pap. 8.95 (ISBN 0-7100-9267-9). Routledge & Kegan.

Woodhull, Marianna. Epic of Paradise Lost: Twelve Essays. LC 68-57833. 1968. Repr. of 1907 ed. 9.00x (ISBN 0-87752-124-7). Gordian.

Woodin, J. C. & Hayes, Louis. Home & Building Maintenance. 18.64 (ISBN 0-87345-466-9). McKnight.

Wooding, Charles J. Evolving Culture: A Cross-Cultural Study of Surinam, West Africa & the Caribbean. LC 80-5612. 343p. 1981. lib. bdg. 24.25 (ISBN 0-8191-1377-8); pap. text ed. 13.50 (ISBN 0-8191-1378-6). U Pr of Amer.

Woodington, Cynthia C. & Perry, Leslie A. Teaching the Reading Teachers. (Illus.). 144p. 1983. spiral 14.75x (ISBN 0-398-04762-6). C C Thomas.

Woodiwiss, Anthony. Corporate Liberalism: The Ideology of American Monopoly Capital. LC 77-91346. 1979. 18.95x o.p. (ISBN 0-312-16998-1). St Martin.

Woodiwiss, Kathleen E. The Flame & the Flower. 1972. pap. 3.95 (ISBN 0-380-00525-5, 82750-6). Avon.

--A Rose in Winter. 640p. 1982. pap. 6.95 (ISBN 0-380-81679-2, 81679). Avon.

--Shanna. 1977. pap. 3.95 (ISBN 0-380-38588-0, 81869-8). Avon.

--The Wolf & the Dove. 1977. pap. 3.95 (ISBN 0-380-00778-9, 81919-8). Avon.

Woodland, A. D. International Trade & Resource Allocation. (Advanced Textbooks in Economics Ser.: Vol. 19). 512p. 1982. 64.00 (ISBN 0-444-86370-2, North Holland). Elsevier.

Woodland, A. W., ed. Petroleum & the Continental Shelf of North-West Europe, Vol. 1: Geology. LC 75-14329. 501p. 1975. 79.95 o.p. (ISBN 0-470-95993-2). Halsted Pr.

Woodland, Margaret, jt. auth. see Morley, David C.

Woodley, Richard. The Bad News Bears Go to Japan. 1978. pap. 1.50 o.s.i. (ISBN 0-440-90427-7). Dell.

--The Bad News Bears in Breaking Training. pap. 1.50 o.s.i. (ISBN 0-440-90417-X). Dell.

--Deadly Encounter. 192p. (Orig.). 1980. pap. 1.95 o.s.i. (ISBN 0-515-04844-5). Jove Pubns.

--One Last Season. (Orig.). 1981. pap. 2.95 o.s.i. (ISBN 0-440-16698-5). Dell.

Woodman, A. J. & West, D., eds. Quality & Pleasure in Latin Poetry. 184p. 1975. 29.95 (ISBN 0-521-20532-8). Cambridge U Pr.

Woodman, Harold D., jt. auth. see Davis, Allen F.

Woodman, Natalie J. & Lenna, Harry R. Counseling with Gay Men & Women: A Guide for Facilitating Positive Life-Styles. LC 80-8002. (Social & Behavioral Science Ser.). 1980. text ed. 16.95x (ISBN 0-87589-468-2). Jossey-Bass.

Wood-Martin, W. G. Traces of the Elder Faiths of Ireland, 2 Vols. LC 70-102631. (Irish Culture & History Ser). 1970. Repr. of 1902 ed. Set. 40.00x o.p. (ISBN 0-8046-0807-5). Kennikat.

Woodress, James. Critical Essays on Walt Whitman. (Critical Essays in American Literature Ser.). 342p. 1983. lib. bdg. 35.00 (ISBN 0-8161-8632-4). G K Hall.

--Willa Cather: Her Life & Art. Landmark, ed. LC 82-7041. (Landmark Edition Ser.). 288p. 1982. Repr. of 1970 ed. 21.95x (ISBN 0-8032-4719-2). U of Nebr Pr.

Woodress, James, ed. American Fiction, Nineteen Hundred to Nineteen-Fifty: A Guide to Information Sources. LC 73-17501. (American Literature, English Literature, & World Literatures in English Information Guide Ser.: Vol. 1). 246p. 1974. 42.00x (ISBN 0-8103-1201-8). Gale.

--American Literary Scholarship, 1981. annual LC 65-19450. (American Literary Scholarship Ser.). 600p. 1983. 40.00 (ISBN 0-8223-0552-6). Duke.

Woodress, James, jt. ed. see Morris, Richard B.

Woodress, James L. Booth Tarkington, Gentleman from Indiana. LC 69-14155. 1969. Repr. of 1955 ed. lib. bdg. 20.25x (ISBN 0-8371-0757-1, WOBT). Greenwood.

--Yankee's Odyssey: Life of Joel Barlow. LC 69-14157. 1969. Repr. of 1958 ed. lib. bdg. 18.00x (ISBN 0-8371-0758-X, WOYO). Greenwood.

Woodright. Snap Crackle Plots Ready to Read Serials Books. (gr. 3-6). 1982. 4.50 (ISBN 0-686-82485-7). Creative Pubns.

Woodroofe, M. Nonlinear Renewal Theory in Sequential Analysis. LC 81-84856. (CBMS-NSF Regional Conference Ser.: No. 39). v, 119p. 1982. 14.50 (ISBN 0-89871-180-0). Soc Indus Appl Math.

Woodroofe, Michael. Probability with Application. new ed. (Illus.). 372p. 1974. text ed. 34.95 (ISBN 0-07-071718-4, C). McGraw.

Woodrow, Ralph. Amazing Discoveries Within the Book of Books. (Illus.). 1979. pap. 3.95 (ISBN 0-916938-04-2). R Woodrow.

--Divorce & Remarriage: What Does the Bible Really Say? LC 82-99960. (Illus.). 1982. pap. 3.95 (ISBN 0-916938-06-9). R Woodrow.

--His Truth Is Marching On! Advanced Studies on Prophecy in the Light of History. (Illus.). 1977. pap. 3.95 (ISBN 0-916938-03-4). R Woodrow.

Woodruff, A. Bond. Directed Readings: Introduction to Psychology. 2nd ed. 144p. 1980. pap. text ed. 6.95 (ISBN 0-8403-2243-7). Kendall-Hunt.

Woodruff, A. W. see Lincicome, David R.

Woodruff, Archibald, Jr. Farm Mortgage Loans of Life Insurance Companies. 1937. text ed. 39.50x (ISBN 0-686-83543-3). Elliots Bks.

Woodruff, D. P. The Solid-Liquid Interface. LC 72-91362. (Cambridge Solid State Science Ser.). (Illus.). 150p. 1973. 32.50 (ISBN 0-521-20123-3). Cambridge U Pr.

--The Solid-Liquid Interface. LC 72-91362. (Cambridge Solid State Science Ser.). (Illus.). 182p. 1980. pap. 12.95 (ISBN 0-521-29971-3). Cambridge U Pr.

Woodruff, D. P., jt. auth. see King, D. A.

Woodruff, David S., jt. ed. see Atchley, W. R.

Woodruff, Diana. Can You Live to Be One Hundred? 1979. pap. 2.25 o.p. (ISBN 0-451-08468-3, E8468, Sig). NAL.

Woodruff, Diana S. & Birren, James E. Aging: Scientific Perspectives & Social Issues. 421p. 1975. text ed. 13.95x (ISBN 0-442-20800-6). Van Nos Reinhold.

--Aging: Scientific Perspectives & Social Issues. 2nd ed. LC 82-19768. (Psychology Ser.). 448p. 1983. text ed. 24.95 (ISBN 0-534-01253-1). Brooks-Cole.

Woodruff, Evelyn L., jt. auth. see Peterson-Hunt, William S.

Woodruff, Everett B. & Lammers, Herbert B. Steam-Plant Operation. 4th ed. 1976. 29.50 (ISBN 0-07-071731-1, P&RB). McGraw.

Woodruff, Grace. Your Joy May Be Full. (Orig.). pap. 2.00 (ISBN 0-685-08708-5). Creative Pr.

Woodruff, Lorande L., ed. Development of the Sciences: Second Series. 1941. text ed. 39.50x (ISBN 0-686-83526-3). Elliots Bks.

Woodruff, Marian. It Must Be Music. (Sweet Dreams Ser.: No. 26). 176p. 1982. pap. 1.95 (ISBN 0-553-22692-4). Bantam.

Woodruff, Sue. Meditations with TM Mechtild of Magdeburg. LC 82-73366. (Meditations with TM Ser.). (Illus.). 128p. (Orig.). 1982. pap. 6.95 (ISBN 0-939680-06-8). Bear & Co.

Woodruff, Una. Amarant. 128p. 1981. 20.00 (ISBN 0-399-12625-2). Putnam Pub Group.

Woodruff, William. The Impact of Western Man: A Study of Europe's Role in the World Economy 1750-1960. LC 81-40861. (Illus.). 448p. 1982. lib. bdg. 25.50 (ISBN 0-8191-2485-0); pap. text ed. 14.25 (ISBN 0-8191-2486-9). U Pr of Amer.

Woods & Woods. Horn of Africa. 1981. 8.90 (ISBN 0-531-04275-8). Watts.

Woods, Alice. George Meredith's Poems. 1982. lib. bdg. 34.50 (ISBN 0-686-81934-9). Porter.

Woods, Archie L., jt. auth. see Quanbeck, Alton H.

Woods, Arthur. Dangerous Drugs. 1931. text ed. 29.50x (ISBN 0-686-83520-4). Elliots Bks.

--Policeman & Public. LC 71-172604. (Criminology, Law, Enforcement & Social Problems Ser.). (Illus.). 1975. Repr. of 1912 ed. 7.50x (ISBN 0-87585-194-0). Patterson Smith.

Woods, Audrey. Magic Shoelaces. 32p. 1981. 5.50 (ISBN 0-85953-109-0, Pub. by Child's Play England). Playspaces.

--Orlando's Littlewhile Friends. (Illus.). 1981. 6.00 (ISBN 0-85953-111-2, Pub. by Child's Play England); pap. 5.50 (ISBN 0-85953-106-6). Playspaces.

--Scaredy Cats. 32p. 1981. 5.50 (ISBN 0-85953-110-4, Pub. by Child's Play England). Playspaces.

--Twenty-Four Robbers. (Illus.). 32p. 1981. 5.50 (ISBN 0-85953-100-7, Pub. by Child's Play England). Playspaces.

Woods, Betty. Ghost Towns & How to Get Them. Smith, James C., ed. LC 77-78518. 1978. pap. 2.95 (ISBN 0-913270-30-X). Sunstone Pr.

Woods, Bill, jt. auth. see Woods, Erin.

Woods, C. Stacey. Some Ways of God. LC 74-3184. 144p. (Orig.). 1975. pap. 2.95 o.p. (ISBN 0-87784-715-0). Inter-Varsity.

Woods, Donald. Asking for Trouble: The Education of a White African. LC 82-70568. 374p. 1982. pap. 9.13 (ISBN 0-8070-0241-0, BP644). Beacon Pr.

Woods, Eleanor. A Gentle Whisper. (Candlelight Ecstasy Ser.). (Orig.). 1983. pap. 1.95 (ISBN 0-440-12997-4). Dell.

--Loving Exile. (Candlelight Ecstasy Ser.: No. 141). (Orig.). 1983. pap. 1.95 (ISBN 0-440-14650-X). Dell.

Woods, Erin & Woods, Bill. Bicycling the Backroads of Northwest Washington. LC 76-19258. (Illus.). 216p. (Orig.). 1976. pap. 7.95 o.p. (ISBN 0-916890-44-9). Mountaineers.

Woods, G. Flexible Polyurethane Foams: Chemistry & Technology. (Illus.). xii, 334p. 1982. 65.00x (ISBN 0-85334-981-9). Intl Ideas.

--Flexible Polyurethane Foams: Chemistry & Technology. 1982. 57.50 (ISBN 0-85334-981-9). Elsevier.

Woods, George. Reclassification of the Perceval Romances. (Studies in Comparative Literature, No. 35). 1970. pap. 9.95x (ISBN 0-8383-0083-9). Haskell.

Woods, George B., jt. auth. see Buckley, Jerome H.

Woods, Gerald & Williams, John. Creative Techniques in Landscape Photography. LC 80-8396. (Illus.). 200p. 1981. 18.95i o.p. (ISBN 0-06-014835-7, HarpT). Har-Row.

Woods, Geraldine. Drug Use & Drug Abuse. LC 79-11739. (First Bks.). (Illus.). (gr. 4 up). 1979. 8.90 (ISBN 0-531-02941-7). Watts.

Woods, Geraldine & Woods, Harold. Is James Bond Dead? LC 80-13633. (Monsters & Mysteries Ser.). (gr. 4-10). 1980. pap. 2.25 (ISBN 0-88436-763-0). EMC.

--Is There Life on Other Planets? LC 80-12900. (Monsters & Mysteries Ser.). (gr. 4-10). 1980. pap. 2.25 (ISBN 0-88436-762-2). EMC.

--Magical Beasts & Unbelievable Monsters. LC 80-20627. (Monsters & Mysteries Ser.). (gr. 4-10). 1980. pap. 2.25 (ISBN 0-88436-765-7). EMC.

--Real Scary Sea Monsters. LC 80-13374. (Monsters & Mysteries Ser.). (gr. 4-10). 1980. pap. 2.25 (ISBN 0-88436-760-6). EMC.

Woods, Geraldine, jt. auth. see Woods, Harold.

Woods, Grace E. Care of the Mentally Handicapped: Past & Future. 1983. text ed. write for info. (ISBN 0-7236-0674-9). Wright-PSG.

--Handicapped Children in the Community. 1983. text ed. write for info. (ISBN 0-7236-0675-7). Wright-PSG.

Woods, Guy N see Gospel Advocate.

Woods, Harold & Woods, Geraldine. Bill Cosby: Making America Laugh & Learn. Schneider, Thomas, ed. (Taking Part Ser.). (Illus.). 48p. (gr. 3 up). 1983. PLB 7.95 (ISBN 0-87518-240-2). Dillon Pr.

Woods, Harold, jt. auth. see Woods, Geraldine.

Woods, John. The Valley of Minor Animals. LC 82-71647. 88p. 1982. 14.00 (ISBN 0-937872-08-3); pap. 6.00 (ISBN 0-937872-09-1). Dragon Gate.

Woods, John B., et al. Student Teaching: The Entrance to Professional Physical Education. 1973. pap. text ed. 9.50 o.s.i. (ISBN 0-12-763050-3). Acad Pr.

Woods, John E., tr. see Penzoldt, Ernst.

Woods, Katherine, tr. see Saint-Exupery, Antoine De.

Woods, Katherine, tr. see Saint-Exupery, Antoine de.

Woods, Katherine W., tr. see Vallentin, Antonina.

Woods, L. C. The Thermodynamics of Fluid Systems. (Oxford Engineering Science Ser). (Illus.). 1975. 65.00x (ISBN 0-19-856125-3). Oxford U Pr.

Woods, Lawrence A. & Pope, Nolan F. The Librarian's Guide to Microcomputer Technology & Applications. 150p. 1983. 34.50 (ISBN 0-86729-045-5); pap. 27.50 (ISBN 0-86729-044-7). Knowledge Indus.

Woods, Loren. Fishes. (Beginning Science Bks). (gr. 2-4). 2.50 o.s.i. (ISBN 0-695-82890-8). Follett.

Woods, Loren P. Tropical Fish. LC 74-118956. (Beginning-to-Read Bks). (Illus.). (gr. 2-4). 1971. PLB 2.97 o.s.i. (ISBN 0-695-40175-0); pap. 1.50 o.s.i. (ISBN 0-695-30175-6). Follett.

Woods, M. E., jt. auth. see Hollis, F.

Woods, Marjorie B. Your Wedding: How to Plan & Enjoy It. 208p. 1983. pap. 2.95 (ISBN 0-515-05843-2). Jove Pubns.

Woods, Michael. Mounting & Framing Pictures. LC 82-82919. (Illus.). 96p. 1983. pap. 6.95 (ISBN 0-668-05714-9, 5714). Arco.

Woods, Nancy F. Human Sexuality in Health & Illness. 2nd ed. LC 78-11511. (Illus.). 400p. 1979. pap. 14.95 (ISBN 0-8016-5619-2). Mosby.

Woods, Patricia D. French-Indian Relations on the Southern Frontier, 1699-1762. Berkhofer, Robert, ed. LC 80-17788. (Studies in American History & Culture: No. 18). 281p. 1980. 39.95 (ISBN 0-8357-1100-5, Pub. by UMI Res Pr). Univ Microfilms.

Woods, Paul, ed. Career Opportunities for Psychologists: Expanding & Emerging Areas. LC 76-15351. 1976. pap. 6.00x o.p. (ISBN 0-912704-03-9). Am Psychol.

Woods, Paul J. The Psychology Major: Employment & Training Strategies. LC 79-19256. (Orig.). 1979. pap. 18.00x (ISBN 0-912704-10-1). Am Psychol.

Woods, Peter & Hammersley, Martyn, eds. School Experience. LC 76-44644. 1977. 26.00x (ISBN 0-312-70140-3). St Martin.

Woods, R. A. Biochemical Genetics. 2nd ed. LC 79-41695. (Outline Studies in Biology). 80p. 1980. pap. 6.50x (ISBN 0-412-22400-3, Pub. by Chapman & Hall England). Methuen Inc.

Woods, R. G. & Barrow, R. St. Introduction to Philosophy of Education. 2nd ed. 200p. 1982. 18.95x (ISBN 0-416-30330-7); pap. 7.95x (ISBN 0-416-30340-4). Methuen Inc.

Woods, R. J., jt. ed. see Spinks, J. W.

Woods, Ralph. Pocketful of Prayers. 1976. pap. 1.50 o.s.i. (ISBN 0-89129-217-9). Jove Pubns.

Woods, Ralph F., jt. ed. see Cavanagh, Denis.

Woods, Ralph L., compiled by. Friendship. LC 69-16102. (Illus.). 1969. boxed 5.50 (ISBN 0-8378-1715-3). Gibson.

Woods, Ralph L., ed. The Golden Treasury of the Familiar. 992p. 1980. 29.95 (ISBN 0-02-631510-6). Macmillan.

Woods, Richard. Mysterion: An Approach to Mystical Spirituality. 372p. 1981. 15.95 (ISBN 0-88347-127-2). Thomas More.

--Symbion. LC 82-73365. 264p. (Orig.). 1982. pap. 8.95 (ISBN 0-939680-08-4). Bear & Co.

Woods, Richard D. & Alvarez-Altman, Grace, eds. Spanish Surnames in the Southwestern United States: A Dictionary. 1978. lib. bdg. 18.00 o.p. (ISBN 0-8161-8145-4, Hall Reference). G K Hall.

Woods, Richard G., ed. Future Dimensions of World Food & Populations. (Winrock Ser.). 425p. 1981. lib. bdg. 25.00 (ISBN 0-86531-160-9). Westview.

Woods, Richard S., ed. Audit Decisions in Accounting Practice. 350p. 1973. 16.50 o.p. (ISBN 0-471-06554-4, 98631, Pub. by Wiley-Hamilton). Wiley.

Woods, Robert A. & Kennedy, Albert J. Zone of Emergence: Observations of Lower, Middle & Upper Working Class Communities of Boston, 1905-1914. 2nd ed. 1969. 20.00x (ISBN 0-262-23040-2). MIT Pr.

Woods, Robin W. Birds of the Falkland Islands. (Illus.). 1975. 27.50 (ISBN 0-904614-00-X, Pub. by Anthony Nelson Ltd, England). Buteo.

--Falkland Island Birds. (Illus.). 1982. 15.00 (ISBN 0-904614-07-7). Buteo.

Woods, Ruth. Little Quack. (Beginning-to-Read Ser.). (Illus.). (gr. 1-3). 1961. PLB 4.39 (ISBN 0-695-45253-3, Dist. by Caroline Hse); pap. 1.95 (ISBN 0-695-35253-9). Follett.

Woods, Samuel H., Jr. Oliver Goldsmith: A Reference Guide. 1982. lib. bdg. 28.00 (ISBN 0-8161-8339-2, Hall Reference). G K Hall.

Woods, Sara. Call Back Yesterday. 224p. 1983. 10.95 (ISBN 0-312-11424-9). St Martin.

--Exit Murderer. LC 77-17767. 1978. 7.95 o.p. (ISBN 0-312-27587-0). St Martin.

--The Law's Delay. LC 76-28070. 1977. 7.95 o.p. (ISBN 0-312-47565-9). St Martin.

--Proceed to Judgment. 1979. 8.95 o.p. (ISBN 0-312-64776-X). St Martin.

Woods, Stockton. The Man Who Heard Too Much. 224p. (Orig.). 1983. pap. 2.50 (ISBN 0-449-12390-1, GM). Fawcett.

Woods, Stuart. Run Before the Wind: A Novel. LC 82-14266. 1983. 16.50 (ISBN 0-393-01651-X). Norton.

Woods, Susan L., jt. auth. see Underhill, Sandra L.

Woods, Sylvia. Drover's Dog. LC 82-24205. (Illus.). 112p. (gr. 3-6). 1983. 9.95 (ISBN 0-571-11993-X). Faber & Faber.

--The Harp of Brandiswhiere: A Suite for Celtic Harp. Snyder, Don, ed. (Illus.). 64p. 1982. pap. 9.95 (ISBN 0-9602990-2-5). Woods Bks.

Woods, W. A., ed. see Bradshaw, P.

Woods, Walter A. Consumer Behavior: Adapting & Experiencing. LC 80-23769. (Illus.). 485p. 1980. 27.50 (ISBN 0-444-00430-0, North Holland). Elsevier.

Woods, William. A History of the Devil. (Illus.). 256p. 1974. 6.95 o.p. (ISBN 0-399-11327-4). Putnam Pub Group.

Woodside, Alexander & Wyatt, David K., eds. Moral Order & the Question of Change: Essays on Southeast Asian Thought. LC 82-51022. (Yale University Southeast Asia Studies Monograph: No. 24). 413p. 1982. pap. 16.00x (ISBN 0-938692-02-X). Yale U SE Asia.

Woodside, Alexander B. Community & Revolution in Modern Vietnam. LC 75-18429. (Illus.). 418p. 1976. pap. text ed. 19.95 (ISBN 0-395-20367-8). HM.

Woodside, Arch G., jt. auth. see DeLozier, M. Wayne.

Woodson, H. H. Electromechanical Dynamics: Discrete Systems, Pt. 1. 394p. 1968. text ed. 37.95x (ISBN 0-471-95985-5). Wiley.

Woodson, Linda. From Cases to Composition. 1982. pap. text ed. 12.50x (ISBN 0-673-15448-3). Scott F.

Woodson, Robert. A Summons to Life: Mediating Structures & the Prevention of Youth Crime. 176p. 1981. prof ref 19.00x (ISBN 0-88410-826-0). Ballinger Pub.

Woodson, Robert L., ed. Black Perspectives on Crime & the Criminal Justice System. 1977. lib. bdg. 17.00 (ISBN 0-8161-8039-3, Hall Reference). G K Hall.

Woodson, T. T. Introduction to Engineering Design. 1966. text ed. 28.95 o.p. (ISBN 0-07-071760-5, C); instructor's manual 7.95 o.p. (ISBN 0-07-071761-3). McGraw.

Woodson, Wesley E. Human Factors Design Handbook: Information & Guidelines for the Design of Systems, Facilities, Equipment, & Products for Human Use. LC 80-13299. (Illus.). 1049p. 1981. 82.50 (ISBN 0-07-071765-6). McGraw.

Woodson, Wesley E. & Conover, Donald W. Human Engineering Guide for Equipment Designers. 2nd rev ed. (Illus.). 1965. 44.00x (ISBN 0-520-01363-8). U of Cal Pr.

Woodstock, George, ed. see Meredith, George.

Woodward. The Problematic Science. 410p. 1982. 35.00 (ISBN 0-03-059363-8). Praeger.

Woodward & Bernstein. Final Days. 1976. pap. 3.95 (ISBN 0-380-00844-0, 62497-4). Avon.

Woodward, A. Smith, ed. see Von Zittel, K. A.

Woodward, Arthur. The Denominators of the Fur Trade. (Illus.). 1979. 13.00 (ISBN 0-87026-041-3). Westernlore.

Woodward, Bob & Armstrong, Scott. The Brethren. 1980. 13.95 o.p. (ISBN 0-671-24110-9). S&S.

Woodward, Bob & Bernstein, Carl. The Final Days. 1976. 13.95 o.p. (ISBN 0-671-22298-8). S&S.

Woodward, Bob, jt. auth. see Bernstein, Carl.

Woodward, C. V. & Chestnut, Mary B., eds. Mary Chestnut's Civil War. LC 80-36661. 886p. 1981. 35.00 (ISBN 0-300-02459-2); pap. 14.95 (ISBN 0-300-02979-9, Y-450). Yale U Pr.

Woodward, C. Vann. American Counterpoint: Slavery & Racism in the North-South Dialogue. 320p. 1983. pap. 7.95 (ISBN 0-19-503269-1, GB 727, GB). Oxford U Pr.

--The Strange Career of Jim Crow. 3rd rev. ed. 1974. pap. 5.95 (ISBN 0-19-501805-2, GB). Oxford U Pr.

--Tom Watson: Agrarian Rebel. 1963. pap. 9.95 (ISBN 0-19-500707-7, GB). Oxford U Pr.

Woodward, C. Vann, ed. Mary Chestnut's Civil War. pap. 14.95 (ISBN 0-686-42824-2, Y-450). Yale U Pr.

Woodward, D., tr. see Bablet, Denis.

Woodward, Dan & Biondo, Norma. Living Around the Now Child. LC 72-75052. text ed. 6.95x o.p. (ISBN 0-675-09109-8); pap. text ed. 7.95 (ISBN 0-675-09108-X). Merrill.

Woodward, David. Armies of the World: 1854-1914. LC 78-60254. 1979. 12.95 o.p. (ISBN 0-399-12252-4). Putnam Pub Group.

--Detour from Tibet. 1975. pap. 2.95 o.p. (ISBN 0-8024-1775-2). Moody.

Woodward, Delores M. The Learning Disabled Adolescent. 200p. 1983. price not set (ISBN 0-89443-875-1). Aspen Systems.

Woodward, Dolores M. Mainstreaming the Learning Disabled Adolescent: A Manual of Strategies & Materials. LC 80-19566. 249p. 1981. text ed. 27.95 (ISBN 0-89443-299-0). Aspen Systems.

Woodward, Dow O. & Woodward, Val. Concepts of Molecular Genetics. (Illus.). 1976. text ed. 29.95 (ISBN 0-07-071780-X, C). McGraw.

Woodward, E. G., jt. auth. see Ruben, M.

Woodward, F. Managing the Transport Services Function. 336p. 1978. text ed. 30.25x (ISBN 0-566-02032-7). Gower Pub Ltd.

Woodward, George, ed. Radio Amateur's Handbook. 1983 rev. ed. LC 41-3345. Date not set. price not set (ISBN 0-87259-060-7). Am Radio.

Woodward, Grace S. Cherokees. (Civilization of the American Indian Ser.: No. 65). (Illus.). 1979. 17.95 (ISBN 0-8061-0554-2); pap. 10.95 (ISBN 0-8061-1815-6). U of Okla Pr.

Woodward, Herbert N. Capitalism Can Survive in a No-Growth Economy. LC 76-12887. 1976. 9.95 (ISBN 0-912650-05-2). Brookdale Pr.

--Human Survival in a Crowded World. LC 82-23921. 158p. 1983. pap. 9.95x (ISBN 0-89950-068-4). McFarland & Co.

Woodward, James B. The Symbolic Art of Gogol: Essays on His Short Fiction. 131p. 1982. 11.95 (ISBN 0-89357-093-1). Slavica.

Woodward, Jean. The Eyes of Love. 1982. pap. 6.95 (ISBN 0-686-84748-2, Avalon). Bouregy.

--Smile of Love. 1981. pap. 6.95 (ISBN 0-686-84706-7, Avalon). Bouregy.

--The Summer at Whispering Hope. (YA) 1979. 6.95 (ISBN 0-685-95878-7, Avalon). Bouregy.

--Valley of Romance. 192p. (YA) 1976. 6.95 (ISBN 0-685-66572-0, Avalon). Bouregy.

Woodward, Joan. Industrial Organization: Theory & Practice. 2nd ed. (Illus.). 1980. 42.00x (ISBN 0-19-874123-5); pap. 20.00x (ISBN 0-19-874122-7). Oxford U Pr.

Woodward, John. The Ancient Painted Images of the Columbia Gorge. (Illus.). 100p. (Orig.). 1982. pap. 39.95 (ISBN 0-916552-28-4). Acoma Bks.

--To Do the Sick No Harm: A Study of the British Voluntary Hospital System to 1875. (International Library of Social Policy). 1974. 21.50x (ISBN 0-7100-7970-2). Routledge & Kegan.

Woodward, John B. Low Speed Marine Diesel Engines. LC 80-39635. (Ocean Engineering: a Wiley Ser.). 271p. 1981. 44.95 (ISBN 0-471-06335-5, Pub. by Wiley-Interscience). Wiley.

--Marine Gas Turbines. LC 74-31383. (Ocean Engineering Ser). 390p. 1975. 49.95x (ISBN 0-471-95962-6, Pub. by Wiley-Interscience). Wiley.

Woodward, Kathleen. At Last, the Real Distinguished Thing: The Late Poems of Eliot, Pound, Stevens & Williams. LC 80-23126. 193p. 1980. 14.50 (ISBN 0-8142-0306-X). Ohio St U Pr.

Woodward, Laura, ed. Women's Sports Foundation's Cookbook. LC 82-81816. (Illus.). 224p. (Orig.). 1982. pap. 9.95 (ISBN 0-88011-083-X). Leisure Pr.

Woodward, Nancy H. If Your Child Is Drinking... What You Can Do to Fight Alcohol Abuse at Home, at School, & in the Community. 360p. 1981. 12.95 (ISBN 0-399-12457-8). Putnam Pub Group.

--Teas of the World. (Illus.). 128p. 1980. pap. 7.95 o.p. (ISBN 0-02-082870-5, Collier). Macmillan.

Woodward, Otway. Divided Island. (Studies in 20th Century History). 48p. 1977. pap. text ed. 4.50x o.p. (ISBN 0-435-31761-X). Heinemann Ed.

Woodward, P. E., jt. auth. see Lado, Robert.

Woodward, R. B. & Hoffmann, R. The Conservation of Orbital Symmetry. LC 79-103636. (Illus.). 184p. 1970. pap. 14.95x (ISBN 0-89573-109-6). Verlag Chemie.

Woodward, Ralph L., Jr., ed. Positivism in Latin America, 1850-1960. LC 72-152809. (Problems in Latin American Civilization Ser.). 1971. pap. text ed. 4.95 o.p. (ISBN 0-669-52431-X). Heath.

Woodward, Richard J., et al. Drilled Pier Foundations. LC 81-18633. 1983. Repr. of 1972 ed. cancelled o.p. (ISBN 0-89874-435-0). Krieger.

Woodward, Robert. The Technique Book for Cross-Country Skiing. LC 82-83918. (Illus.). 176p. (Orig.). 1983. pap. 6.95 (ISBN 0-88011-123-2). Leisure Pr.

Woodward, Robert G., ed. Advanced Land Management. 1982. 20.00 (ISBN 0-89419-243-4). Inst Energy.

Woodward, Sandra K. Norfolk Cookery Book: The Culinary Heritage of a Southern Seaport. Friedman, Donna R., ed. LC 81-15302. (Regional Cookbook Ser.). (Illus.). 224p. (Orig.). 1981. pap. 6.95 (ISBN 0-89865-164-6, AACR2). Donning Co.

Woodward, Stanley. The Sea. (Illus.). 7.50 o.p. (ISBN 0-87482-006-5). Wake-Brook.

Woodward, Stephen, jt. auth. see Osborne, Grant R.

Woodward, Stephen B., jt. auth. see Osborne, Grant R.

Woodward, Thomas B. To Celebrate. 144p. (Orig.). 1973. pap. 3.95 (ISBN 0-8164-5705-0). Seabury.

Woodward, Val, jt. auth. see Woodward, Dow O.

Woodward, W. E. George Washington: The Image & the Man. LC 70-184103. 1926. cloth 1972 7.95 (ISBN 0-87140-806-6); pap. 3.95 paper 1972 (ISBN 0-686-86290-2). Liveright.

Woodward, William. Tom Paine. LC 72-7512. 359p. 1973. Repr. of 1945 ed. lib. bdg. 19.75x (ISBN 0-8371-6520-2, WOTB). Greenwood.

Woodward, William H. Vittorino Da Feltre & Other Humanist Educators. LC 63-22510. (Orig.). 1964. text ed. 11.00 (ISBN 0-8077-2359-2); pap. text ed. 6.00x (ISBN 0-8077-2356-8). Tchrs Coll.

Woodward, William H., ed. Desiderius Erasmus Concerning the Aim & Method of Education. LC 64-18613. (Orig.). 1964. text ed. 10.50 (ISBN 0-8077-2350-9); pap. text ed. 4.25x o.p. (ISBN 0-8077-2347-9). Tchrs Coll.

--Studies in Education During the Age of the Renaissance 1400 to 1600. LC 67-17748. (Orig.). 1967. pap. text ed. 7.00x (ISBN 0-8077-2353-3). Tchrs Coll.

Woodwell, Donald R. Automating Your Financial Portfolio: An Investor's Guide to Personal Computers. LC 82-73637. 220p. 1983. 17.50 (ISBN 0-87094-399-5). Dow Jones-Irwin.

Woodwell, George M. & Pecan, Erene, eds. Carbon & the Biosphere: Proceedings. LC 73-600092. (AEC Symposium Ser.). 399p. 1973. pap. 18.00 (ISBN 0-87079-006-4, CONF-720510); microfiche 4.50 (ISBN 0-87079-156-7, CONF-720510). DOE.

Woodworth, David, ed. Directory of Overseas Summer Jobs, Nineteen Eighty-Three. 176p. 1983. pap. 7.95 (ISBN 0-907638-11-2, Pub. by Vacation-Work England). Writers Digest.

Woodworth, G. Walter. Money Market & Monetary Management. 2nd ed. 1972. text ed. 35.95 scp o.p. (ISBN 0-06-047216-2, HarpC). Har-Row.

Woodworth, Ralph. Light in a Dark Place. (Illus.). 1978. pap. 3.50 o.p. (ISBN 0-89367-022-7). Light & Life.

Woodworth, Robert S. Heredity & Environment: A Critical Survey of Recently Published Material on Twins & Foster Children. LC 41-23998. 1941. pap. 4.00 (ISBN 0-527-03279-4). Kraus Repr.

Woodworth, Robert T. & Peterson, Richard B. Collective Negotiation for Public & Professional Employees. 1969. pap. 9.95x o.p. (ISBN 0-673-05137-4). Scott F.

Woodworth, Robert T., jt. auth. see Knudson, Harry R.

Woodwright. Snap Crackle Plots Ready-to-Read Serials Books. Incl. Who is Nova; Dan April's Casebook (ISBN 0-88488-241-1); Pike's Adventures (ISBN 0-88488-242-X); The Crisp Family Circus (ISBN 0-88488-243-8). (gr. 3-6). 1982. 4.50 ea. Creative Pubns.

Woody, Bette. Managing Crisis Cities: The New Black Leadership & the Politics of Resource Allocation. LC 82-941. (Contributions in Political Science Ser.: No. 82). 256p. 1982. lib. bdg. 27.50 (ISBN 0-313-23095-1, WGW/). Greenwood.

Woody, Charles D. Memory, Learning, & Higher Function: A Cellular View. (Illus.). 512p. 1982. 65.00 (ISBN 0-387-90525-1). Springer-Verlag.

Woody, Elsbeth S. Handbuilding Ceramic Forms. LC 78-9017. (Illus.). 238p. 1978. 20.00 o.p. (ISBN 0-374-16773-7); pap. 13.95 (ISBN 0-374-51449-6). FS&G.

--Pottery on the Wheel. (Illus.). 224p. 1975. 17.95 (ISBN 0-374-23656-9); pap. 12.95 (ISBN 0-374-51234-5). FS&G.

Woody, Robert H., jt. auth. see Godbold, E. Stanley.

Woodyard, George W., jt. ed. see Lyday, Leon F.

Wooff, Terence. Developments in Art Teaching. (Changing Classroom). (Illus.). 1976. text ed. 9.75x o.p. (ISBN 0-7291-0039-1); pap. text ed. 4.75x o.p. (ISBN 0-7291-0034-0). Humanities.

Woog, Henri. The Tableau Economique of Francois Quesnay: An Essay in the Explanation of its Mechanism & a Critical Review of the Interpretations of Marx, Bilimovic & Oncken. (Illus.). 100p. Repr. of 1950 ed. lib. bdg. 15.00x (ISBN 0-87991-831-4). Porcupine Pr.

Woo Jung Ju. The Rise & Fall of the Djakarta-Peking Axis, & the Origins of Johnson's War. 301p. 1977. pap. text ed. 11.00 (ISBN 0-8191-0055-2). U Pr of Amer.

Wool, I. G. see Harris, Robert S., et al.

Wool, John D. The Bank Book. 1973. pap. 3.25x (ISBN 0-88323-111-5, 199). Richards Pub.

--Getting Ready to Drive. (Illus.). 1967. pap. text ed. 2.75x (ISBN 0-88323-031-3, 129). Richards Pub.

--How to Write Yourself Up. rev. ed. 1983. pap. 2.75x (ISBN 0-88323-133-6, 225). Richards Pub.

--Preparing for a Job Interview. 1977. pap. 2.75x (ISBN 0-88323-136-0, 226). Richards Pub.

--Useful Arithmetic, Vol. 2. rev. ed. 1981. pap. 2.75x (ISBN 0-88323-165-4, 169); tchr's. key 1.00x (ISBN 0-88323-168-9, 254). Richards Pub.

--Using Money Series, 4 bks. rev. ed. Incl. Bk. 1. Counting My Money (ISBN 0-88323-074-7, 171); Bk. 2. Making My Money Count (ISBN 0-88323-075-5, 172); Bk. 3. Buying Power (ISBN 0-88323-076-3, 173); Bk. 4. Earning, Spending & Saving (ISBN 0-88323-077-1, 174). 1982. pap. 2.75x ea.; tchr's answer key 1.00x (ISBN 0-88323-137-9, 224). Richards Pub.

Wool, John D. & Bohn, Raymond J. Learning About Handwriting (Manuscript) 1969. pap. 2.75x (ISBN 0-88323-050-X, 149). Richards Pub.

--Learning About Measurement. 1969. pap. 2.75x (ISBN 0-88323-052-6, 151). Richards Pub.

--Learning About Time. 1969. pap. 2.75x (ISBN 0-88323-053-4, 152). Richards Pub.

--Learning About Writing (Cursive) 1969. pap. 2.75x (ISBN 0-88323-051-8, 150). Richards Pub.

Wool, John D., jt. auth. see Bohn, Raymond J.

Wool, Robert, jt. auth. see Cook, John A.

Woolcock, J. B. Bacterial Infection & Immunity in Domestic Animals. (Developments in Animal & Veterinary Science Ser.: Vol. 3). 1979. 64.00 (ISBN 0-444-41768-0). Elsevier.

Woolcock, Stephen. Western Policies on East-West Trade. (Chatham House Papers Ser.: No. 15). 96p. (Orig.). 1982. pap. 10.00 (ISBN 0-7100-9314-4). Routledge & Kegan.

Woolcott, T. W. Liquified Petroleum Gas Tanker Practice. (Illus.). 1977. 32.50 (ISBN 0-85174-295-5). Heinman.

--Liquified Petroleum Gas Tanker Practice. 1981. 60.00x (ISBN 0-85174-295-5, Pub. by Brown, Son & Ferguson). State Mutual Bk.

Wooldridge, H. E. Polyphonic Period, 2 pts. LC 72-97072. (Oxford History of Music Ser.). (330-1400 pt. 1, 1400-1600 pt. 2). 1973. Repr. of 1929 ed. Pt. 1. 25.00x (ISBN 0-8154-0470-0); Pt. 2. 25.00x (ISBN 0-8154-0520-0). Cooper Sq.

Wooldridge, K. R. Progress in Pharmaceutical Research. (Illus.). 186p. 1982. pap. text ed. 21.95 (ISBN 0-632-00787-7, B 5613-3). Mosby.

Wooldridge, Powhatan & Leonard, Robert C. Behavioral Science & Nursing Theory. 240p. 1983. pap. text ed. 14.95 (ISBN 0-8016-5623-0). Mosby.

Wooldridge, Rhoda. And Oh How Proudly. LC 72-4576. (Illus.). (gr. 5-8). 1972. 6.00 o.p. (ISBN 0-8309-0071-3). Ind Pr MO.

--Chouteau & the Founding of St. Louis. LC 75-9750. (Illus.). 215p. (gr. 6-8). 1975. 8.00 o.p. (ISBN 0-8309-0146-9). Ind Pr MO.

--Hannah's House. LC 71-182432. (Illus.). (gr. 4-6). 1972. 7.00 o.p. (ISBN 0-8309-0073-X). Ind Pr MO.

Wooldridge, Sidney W. Geographer As Scientist: Essays on the Scope & Nature of Geography. LC 69-14158. 1969. Repr. of 1956 ed. lib. bdg. 16.00x (ISBN 0-8371-0763-6, WOGS). Greenwood.

Wooldridge, Susanna. Travelling Alone: A Practical Guide for Business Women. (Illus.). 1979. 10.00 o.p. (ISBN 0-671-18442-3). S&S.

Wooldridge, W. J. Woodturning Techniques. LC 81-86412. (Illus.). 168p. 1982. 16.95 (ISBN 0-8069-5468-X); lib. bdg. 14.99 (ISBN 0-686-82976-X); pap. 10.95 (ISBN 0-8069-7068-5). Sterling.

Woolery, Arlo. The Art of Valuation. LC 78-5471. 160p. 1978. 16.95x o.p. (ISBN 0-669-02340-X). Lexington Bks.

Woolery, George W. Children's Television: The First Thirty-five Years, 1946-1981: Animated Cartoon Series, Pt. I. LC 82-5841. 404p. 1983. 27.50 (ISBN 0-8108-1557-5). Scarecrow.

Woolery, John C., jt. auth. see Gerwick, Ben C.

Wooley, A. E. Photographic Lighting. 3rd ed. (Illus.). 1975. 11.95 (ISBN 0-8174-0356-6, Amphoto). Watson-Guptill.

--Topcon-Auto One Hundred-Unirex Manual. (Illus.). 1972. 7.95 o.p. (ISBN 0-8174-0522-4, Amphoto). Watson-Guptill.

Wooley, Al E. Creative Thirty-Five Millimeter Techniques. 2nd ed. 1970. 11.95 o.p. (ISBN 0-8174-0385-X, Amphoto). Watson-Guptill.

Woolf, Cecil & Sewell, Brocard, eds. New Quests for Corvo: A Collection of Essays. 1961. 6.95 (ISBN 0-685-09185-6); pap. 3.00 (ISBN 0-685-09186-4). Dufour.

Woolf, Daniel J., tr. see Beringer, Johann B.

Woolf, Douglas, jt. ed. see Braman, Sandra.

Woolf, Eugene T. Theodore Winthrop: Portrait of an American Author. LC 81-40124. 280p. (Orig.). 1982. lib. bdg. 22.25 (ISBN 0-8191-1772-2); pap. text ed. 11.75 (ISBN 0-8191-1773-0). U Pr of Amer.

Woolf, James D. Sir Edmond Gosse. (English Authors Ser.: No. 117). 12.50 o.p. (ISBN 0-8057-1232-1, Twayne). G K Hall.

Woolf, Leonard, et al. Human Dimensions: In Nonfiction & Poetry. 1979. pap. text ed. 11.95 (ISBN 0-13-444935-5). P-H.

Woolf, S. J., ed. Fascism in Europe. 416p. 1981. 24.00x (ISBN 0-416-30230-0); pap. 8.95x (ISBN 0-416-30240-8). Methuen Inc.

Woolf, Stuart. A History of Italy Seventeen Hundred to Eighteen Sixty: The Social Constraints of Political Change. 1979. 55.00x (ISBN 0-416-80880-8). Methuen Inc.

Woolf, Stuart, ed. see Venturi, Franco.

Woolf, Virginia. Between the Acts. LC 41-51933. 1970. pap. 3.95 (ISBN 0-15-611870-X, Harv). HarBraceJ.

--Contemporary Writers. LC 76-15984. 1976. pap. 2.45 (ISBN 0-15-621450-4, Harv). HarBraceJ.

--Diary of Virginia Woolf, Vol. 4: 1931-1935. Bell, Ann O., ed. LC 77-73111. 416p. 1982. 19.95 (ISBN 0-15-125602-0). HarBraceJ.

--Letter to a Young Poet. 1982. lib. bdg. 34.50 (ISBN 0-686-81936-5). Porter.

--The Letters of Virginia Woolf, Vol. V. LC 75-25538. 1979. 14.95 o.p. (ISBN 0-15-150928-X). HarBraceJ.

--The Letters of Virginia Woolf: Nineteen Thirty-Six to Nineteen Forty-One, Vol. VI. Nicholson, Nigel & Trautmann, Joanne, eds. LC 75-25538. 576p. 1980. 19.95 o.p. (ISBN 0-15-150929-8). HarBraceJ.

--The Letters of Virginia Woolf, 1929-1931, Vol. 4. 1979. 14.95 o.p. (ISBN 0-15-150927-1). HarBraceJ.

--The London Scene. 1982. 10.00 (ISBN 0-394-52866-2). Random.

--Mrs. Dalloway. LC 25-9749. 1949. 11.95 (ISBN 0-15-162862-9). HarBraceJ.

--Night & Day. LC 73-5730. 508p. 1973. pap. 7.95 (ISBN 0-15-665600-0, HB263, Harv). HarBraceJ.

--Pointz Hall: The Earlier & Later Transcripts of "Between the Acts". Leaska, Mitchell A., ed. LC 81-3684. 576p. 1983. lib. bdg. 35.00x (ISBN 0-911463-00-3). Univ Pubs NY.

--Roger Fry: A Biography. LC 75-34023. (Illus.). 307p. 1976. pap. 5.95 (ISBN 0-15-678520-X, Harv). HarBraceJ.

--A Room of One's Own. LC 29-27524. 1963. pap. 2.95 (ISBN 0-15-678732-6, Harv). HarBraceJ.

--Three Guineas. LC 38-27681. 1963. pap. 2.95 (ISBN 0-15-690177-3, Harv). HarBraceJ.

--To the Lighthouse. LC 37-28677. (Modern Classic Ser.). 1949. 6.95 o.p. (ISBN 0-15-190737-4). HarBraceJ.

--The Waves. LC 77-92142. 297p. 1978. pap. 4.95 (ISBN 0-15-694960-1, Harv). HarBraceJ.

--Women & Writing. Barrett, Michele, intro. by. LC 79-3371. 208p. 1980. 8.95o.p. (ISBN 0-15-693658-5, Harv); pap. 3.95 (ISBN 0-15-693658-5, Harv). HarBraceJ.

Woolfe. Videotex: Television - Telephone Information Services. 1980. 29.95 (ISBN 0-471-26089-4, Wiley Heyden). Wiley.

Woolfe, Raymond D., Jr. Steeplechasing. (Illus.). 256p. 1983. 50.00 (ISBN 0-670-32356-X, Studio). Viking Pr.

Woolfenden, Glen E., jt. auth. see Bancroft, G. Thomas.

Woolfolk, Anita & Nicolich, Lorraine. Educational Psychology for Teachers. (Illus.). 1980. text ed. 22.95 (ISBN 0-13-240598-9); pap. 10.95 study guide & wkbk. (ISBN 0-13-240556-3). P-H.

Woolfolk, Joanna. Honeymoon for Life: How to Live Happily Ever After. LC 77-15966. 252p. 1982. pap. 8.95 (ISBN 0-8128-6102-7). Stein & Day.

Woolfolk, Margaret. Cooking with Berries. 1979. 10.00 o.p. (ISBN 0-517-53429-0, C N Potter Bks). Crown.

Woolfolk, Robert I. & Richardson, Frank C. Stress, Sanity & Survival. 1979. pap. 2.75 (ISBN 0-451-12096-5, AE2096, Sig). NAL.

Woolfolk, William. Beautiful Couple. 1969. pap. 1.25 o.p. (ISBN 0-451-06027-X, Y6027, Sig). NAL.

Woolfolk, William & Cross, Donna W. Daddy's Little Girl: The Unspoken Bargain Between Fathers & Their Daughters. 220p. 1983. pap. 5.95 (ISBN 0-13-196279-5). P-H.

Woolford, Ellen & Washabaugh, William, eds. The Social Context of Creolization. 149p. 1982. 15.50 (ISBN 0-89720-045-4); pap. 12.50 (ISBN 0-89720-046-2). Karoma.

Woolfson, M. M. Introduction to X-Ray Crystallography. LC 69-16289. (Illus.). 1970. 62.50 (ISBN 0-521-07440-1); pap. 18.95x (ISBN 0-521-29343-X). Cambridge U Pr.

Woolhouse, H. W., ed. Advances in Botanical Research, 2 vols. (Serial Publication). 1981. Vol. 8. 59.50 (ISBN 0-12-005908-8); Vol. 9. 49.50 (ISBN 0-12-005909-6). Acad Pr.

Woollacott, Robert M. & Zimmer, Russell L., eds. The Biology of Bryozoans. 1977. 59.50 (ISBN 0-12-763150-X). Acad Pr.

Woollaston, Toss. Sage Tea. 268p. 1982. 17.95 (ISBN 0-00-216982-7, Pub. by W Collins Australia). Intl Schol Bk Serv.

Woollcott, Alexander. The Letters of Alexander Woollcott. Kaufman, B. & Hennessey, J., eds. LC 74-163542. (Illus.). 410p. 1972. Repr. of 1944 ed. lib. bdg. 18.50x o.p. (ISBN 0-8371-6199-1, WOLW). Greenwood.

Woollerton, Henry & McLean, Colleen J. Acupuncture Energy in Health & Disease: A Practical Guide for Advanced Students. (Illus.). 128p. (Orig.). 1983. pap. 6.95 (ISBN 0-7225-0482-9, Pub. by Thorsons Pubs England). Sterling.

Woollett, Mick. Racing Bikes. (Illus.). 64p. 1983. pap. 4.95 (ISBN 0-7134-1294-1, Pub. by Batsford England). David & Charles.

Woolley, A. E. Photography: A Practical & Creative Introduction. (Illus.). 336p. 1973. text ed. 26.50 (ISBN 0-07-071860-1, C). McGraw.

--Topcon Unirex - Auto 100 Manual. (Illus.). 160p. 1972. 7.95 o.p. (ISBN 0-8174-0522-4, Amphoto). Watson-Guptill.

Woolley, Alan R., jt. auth. see Croucher, Ronald.

Woolley, Bryan. November Twenty-Second. 304p. 1983. pap. 2.95 (ISBN 0-425-05748-8). Berkley Pub.

Woolley, Catherine. Ginnie & Geneva Cookbook. LC 74-20669. (Illus.). 96p. (gr. 3-7). 1975. PLB 7.92 o.p. (ISBN 0-688-31324-8). Morrow.

--Libby Shadows a Lady. LC 74-2029. (Illus.). 192p. (gr. 3-7). 1974. lib. bdg. 9.55 (ISBN 0-688-31787-1). Morrow.

--Libby's Uninvited Guest. LC 70-108722. (Illus.). (gr. 3-7). 1970. 9.95 (ISBN 0-688-21809-1). Morrow.

--Look Alive, Libby. (Illus.). (gr. 3-7). 1962. 9.95 (ISBN 0-688-21754-0). Morrow.

--A Room for Cathy. (Illus.). (gr. 3-7). 1956. PLB 9.55 (ISBN 0-688-31687-5). Morrow.

Woolley, Charles L. Digging up the Past. 2nd ed. LC 77-13325. (Illus.). 1977. Repr. of 1954 ed. lib. bdg. 19.75x (ISBN 0-8371-9853-4, WODU). Greenwood.

Woolley, David E. & Evanson, John M. Collagenase in Normal & Pathological Connective Tissues, LC 79-19557. 1980. 59.95x (ISBN 0-471-27668-5, Pub. by Wiley-Interscience). Wiley.

Woolley, Davis C., ed. Encyclopedia of Southern Baptists, Vol. III. LC 58-5417. (Illus.). 1971. 19.95 (ISBN 0-8054-6511-1). Broadman.

Woolley, Diana. Advertising Law Handbook. 2nd ed. 106p. 1976. text ed. 21.00x o.p. (ISBN 0-220-66306-8, Pub. by Busn Bks England). Renouf.

Woolley, Leonard. Ur of the Chaldees. 272p. 1982. 75.00x (ISBN 0-906969-21-2, Pub. by Benn Pubns). State Mutual Bk.

Woolley, Sir Leonard. The Buildings of the Third Dynasty. (Ur Excavations: Archaeology, No. 6). 1974. 30.00x (ISBN 0-686-17772-X). Univ Mus of U PA.

Woolman, M. & Valentine, C. G. From Electrons to Power: AC & DC. 1968. text ed. 11.95x o.p. (ISBN 0-02-479180-6, 47918). Glencoe.

Woolmer, J. Howard. Malcolm Lowry, A Bibliography. LC 82-50810. (Illus.). 162p. 1983. 30.00 (ISBN 0-913506-12-5). Woolmer-Brotherson.

Woolner, Frank & Lyman, Hal. Striped Bass Fishing. 192p. 1983. 15.95 (ISBN 0-8329-0279-9); pap. 9.95 (ISBN 0-8329-0281-0). Winchester Pr.

Woolrey, Sharon, jt. auth. see Cullen, Matthew.

Woolrich, Cornell. Angels of Darkness. LC 77-20720. 1978. 10.00 (ISBN 0-89296-037-X); ltd. ed., o.p. 25.00 (ISBN 0-89296-038-8). Mysterious Pr.

--Deadline at Dawn. 1983. pap. 2.25 (ISBN 0-345-30653-8). Ballantine.

--Manhattan Love Song. 1980. lib. bdg. 10.95 (ISBN 0-8398-2659-1, Gregg). G K Hall.

--Night Has a Thousand Eyes. 304p. 1983. pap. 2.50 (ISBN 0-345-30667-8). Ballantine.

--Phantom Lady. 256p. 1982. pap. 2.50 (ISBN 0-345-30652-X). Ballantine.

--Rendezvous in Black. 1979. lib. bdg. 9.95 (ISBN 0-8398-2537-4, Gregg). G K Hall.

Woolsey, Clinton N., ed. Cortical Sensory Organization: Multiple Somatic Areas, Vol. 1. LC 81-81433. (Illus.). 264p. 1981. 34.50 (ISBN 0-89603-030-X). Humana.

--Cortical Sensory Organization: Multiple Visual Areas, Vol. 2. LC 81-81433. (Illus.). 240p. 1981. 34.50 (ISBN 0-89603-031-8). Humana.

Woolsey, G. A., jt. ed. see Emelus, K. G.

Woolsey, Gene, jt. auth. see Hesse, Rick.

Woolsey, James, ed. Nuclear Arms: Ethics, Strategy, Politics. 350p. 1983. 22.95 (ISBN 0-917616-55-3); pap. 8.95 (ISBN 0-917616-56-1). ICS Pr.

Woolsey, Janette, jt. auth. see Sechrist, Elizabeth H.

Woolston, Bill. Harvest: Wheat Ranching in the Palouse. (Illus.). 128p. 1982. 24.95 (ISBN 0-915664-02-X). Thorn Creek Pr.

Woolston, Howard B. Prostitution in the United States. LC 69-14953. (Criminology, Law Enforcement, & Social Problems Ser.: No. 29). (Illus.). 1969. Repr. of 1921 ed. 18.00x (ISBN 0-87585-029-4). Patterson Smith.

Woolston, Thomas. Discours sur les Miracles de Jesus-Christ, 2 vols. (Holbach & His Friends Ser.). 510p. (Fr.). 1974. Repr. of 1769 ed. lib. bdg. 139.50x o.p. (ISBN 0-8287-0885-1, 1538-9). Clearwater Pub.

--Discourses on the Miracles of Our Savior. Wellek, Rene, ed. LC 75-11268. (British Philosophers & Theologians of the 17th & 18th Centuries Ser.: Vol. 67). 565p. 1979. lib. bdg. 42.00 o.s.i. (ISBN 0-8240-1778-1); lib. bdg. 2700.00 set of 101 vols. o.s.i. (ISBN 0-686-60102-5). Garland Pub.

Woolvet, G. A. Transducers in Digital Systems. rev. ed. (IEE Control Engineering Ser.: No. 3). (Illus.). 201p. 1979. pap. 23.00 (ISBN 0-906048-13-3). Inst Elect Eng.

Woodley, A. & McIntosh, N. A. The Door Stood Open. 261p. 1980. write for info (ISBN 0-905273-14-1, Pub. by Taylor & Francis). Intl Pubns Serv.

Woosnam, Phil & Gardner, Paul. Sports Illustrated Soccer. LC 72-5629. (Illus.). 96p. 1972. 5.95i (ISBN 0-397-00908-9); pap. 2.95i (ISBN 0-397-00909-7, LP-70). Har-Row.

Wooster, Ralph A. People in Power: Courthouse & Statehouse in the Lower South, 1850-1860. LC 69-20116. 1969. 14.50x (ISBN 0-87049-090-7). U of Tenn Pr.

--Politicians, Planters, & Plain Folk: Courthouse & Statehouse in the Upper South, 1850-1860. LC 75-32339. 204p. 1975. 14.50x (ISBN 0-87049-166-0). U of Tenn Pr.

--The Secession Conventions of the South. LC 75-27659. (Illus.). 294p. 1976. Repr. of 1962 ed. lib. bdg. 18.50x (ISBN 0-8371-8436-3, WOSC). Greenwood.

Wooten, Bill, jt. ed. see Spillmann, Lothar.

Wooten, David C., jt. auth. see Rau, John G.

Wooten, Edna L., jt. auth. see Barham, Jerry N.

Wooten, Frederick. Optical Properties of Solids. 1972. 52.50 (ISBN 0-12-763450-9). Acad Pr.

Wooton, Barbara. Freedom under Planning. LC 78-9994. 1979. Repr. of 1945 ed. lib. bdg. 16.00x (ISBN 0-313-21099-3, WOFU). Greenwood.

Wooton, E. O. & Standley, P. C. Flora of New Mexico. 1971. Repr. of 1915 ed. 32.00 (ISBN 3-7682-0745-5). Lubrecht & Cramer.

Wooton, Graham. Politics of Influence: British Ex-Servicemen, Cabinet Decisions & Cultural Change, 1917-1957. LC 63-5612. (Illus.). 1963. 17.50x (ISBN 0-674-68900-3). Harvard U Pr.

Wooton, Margaret, ed. New Directions in Drama Teaching. 224p. (Orig.). 1982. pap. text ed. 15.00x (ISBN 0-435-18927-1). Heinemann Ed.

Wooton, William, jt. auth. see Drooyan, Irving.

Wooton, William, et al. Modern Trigonometry. rev. ed. 1979. text ed. 17.60 (ISBN 0-395-21687-7); instr's. guide & solutions 8.32 (ISBN 0-395-21688-5). HM.

Wootters, John. The Complete Book of Practical Handloading. (Stoeger Bks). 1977. pap. 5.95 o.s.i. (ISBN 0-695-80844-3). Follett.

Wootton, Anthony. The Amazing Fact Book of Spiders, Vol. 11. LC 80-80669. (Illus.). 32p. (gr. 4 up). 1980. 5.95 (ISBN 0-86550-020-7); PLB 8.95 (ISBN 0-686-96985-5); pap. 2.95 (ISBN 0-86550-021-5). A & P Bks.

Wootton, D. B., jt. ed. see Wake, W. C.

Wootton, Graham. Pressure Politics in Contemporary Britain. LC 77-26372. 272p. 1978. 23.95x (ISBN 0-669-02167-9). Lexington Bks.

Wootton, Lutian R. & Reynolds, John C., Jr. Trends & Issues Affecting Curiculum. 1977. pap. text ed. 7.50x o.p. (ISBN 0-8191-0112-5). U Pr of Amer.

Wootton, Lutian R., et al, eds. Trends & Issues Affecting Curriculum: Programs and Practices. LC 80-5784. 281p. 1980. lib. bdg. 21.25 (ISBN 0-8191-1224-0); pap. text ed. 11.50 (ISBN 0-8191-1225-9). U Pr of Amer.

Wootton, Richard. Honky Tonkin' A Travel Guide to American Music. LC 80-503. (Illus.). 192p. 1980. pap. 7.95 (ISBN 0-914788-26-4). East Woods.

Woozley, A. O., ed. see Locke, John.

Woram, John M. The Recording Studio Handbook. 2nd ed. LC 76-62250. (Illus.). 550p. 1976. 39.50 (ISBN 0-914130-01-3). Elar Pub Co.

--The Recording Studio Handbook. 2nd ed. LC 76-62250. (Illus.). 550p. 1983. 39.50 (ISBN 0-686-83422-4). Elar Pub Co.

Worcel, M., et al, eds. New Trends in Arterial Hypertension. (INSERM Symposium Ser.: No. 17). 1982. 65.00 (ISBN 0-444-80324-6). Elsevier.

Worcester, Dean K., Jr. Life & Times of Thomas Turner of East Hoathly. 1948. text ed. 29.50x (ISBN 0-686-83607-3). Elliots Bks.

Worcester, Donald, ed. see Boyd, Maurice.

Worcester, Donald E. The Apaches: Eagles of the Southwest. LC 78-21377. (Civilization of the American Indian Ser.: No. 149). (Illus.). 1979. 19.95 (ISBN 0-8061-1495-9). U of Okla Pr.

Worcester, Donald E. & Schaeffer, Wendell G. Growth & Culture of Latin America. 1971. Set. 2 vols. in one ed. 25.00x o.p. (ISBN 0-19-501421-9). Oxford U Pr.

--Growth & Culture of Latin America Vol. 1: From Conquest to Independence. 2nd ed. 1970. pap. 11.95x (ISBN 0-19-501104-X). Oxford U Pr.

--Growth & Culture of Latin America Vol. 2: The Continuing Struggle for Independence. 2nd ed. 1971. pap. 11.95x (ISBN 0-19-501105-8). Oxford U Pr.

Worcester, Donald E., ed. see Cadenhead, Ivie E., Jr.

Worcester, G. R. Junks & Sampans of the Yangtze. LC 68-54115. (Illus.). 626p. 1971. 58.95 (ISBN 0-87021-335-0). Naval Inst Pr.

Worcester, Noah. A Solemn Review of the Custom of War: Showing That War Is the Effect of Popular Delusion & Proposing a Remedy. LC 73-137561. (Peace Movement in America Ser). 1972. Repr. of 1833 ed. lib. bdg. 9.95x (ISBN 0-89198-093-8). Ozer.

Worcester, Robert M. & Harrop, Martin, eds. Political Communications: The General Election Campaign of 1979. (Illus.). 208p. 1982. text ed. 37.50x (ISBN 0-04-324007-0). Allen Unwin.

Worcester, Thomas K. & Pamplin, Robert B., Jr. A Portrait of Colorado. (Illus.). 1976. 9.95 o.p. (ISBN 0-911518-43-6, Pub. by OMSI). Touchstone Pr Ore.

Worchel, S. & Goethals, G. Adjustment & Human Relations. 592p. 1981. text ed. 20.00 (ISBN 0-394-32226-6); wkbk. 5.95 (ISBN 0-394-32737-3). Knopf.

Worchel, Stephen. Psychology: Principles & Applications. (Illus.). 672p. 1983. text ed. 22.95 (ISBN 0-13-732453-7). P-H.

Worchester Art Museum. The Cook Book. (Illus.). 206p. 1976. pap. 9.95 (ISBN 0-686-36748-0). Md Hist.

Worchester, Thomas, ed. Goodbye Goose. (Illus.). 88p. 1981. 27.00 (ISBN 0-9607286-0-0). F Sherman.

Worden, B. The Rump Parliament, 1648-1653. LC 73-77264. 500p. 1974. 49.50 (ISBN 0-521-20205-1); pap. 19.95 (ISBN 0-521-29213-1). Cambridge U Pr.

Worden, Diane, compiled by. Workshop on the Role of Earthworms in the Stabilization of Organic Residues: Volume 2, Bibliography. 490p. (Orig.). 1981. pap. 50.00 (ISBN 0-939294-08-7). Beech Leaf.

Worden, Diane D., jt. ed. see Black, Charles T.

Worden, Frederic G., jt. ed. see Schmitt, Francis O.

Worden, William J. Grief Counseling & Grief Therapy: A Handbook for the Mental Health Practitioner. 1982. text ed. 14.95 (ISBN 0-8261-4161-7). Springer Pub.

Worden, William L. Cargoes: Matson's First Century in the Pacific. LC 80-21666. 208p. 1981. 12.95 (ISBN 0-8248-0708-1). UH Pr.

Wordie, Ross. Estate Management in Eighteenth-Century England. (Royal Historical Society-Studies in History: No. 30). 303p. 1982. text ed. 42.00x (ISBN 0-901050-85-7, Pub. by Swiftbks England). Humanities.

Wordsell, W. C., jt. auth. see Stapf, O.

Wordsworth, Christopher, ed. Movie Maker's Handbook. 320p. 1979. 25.00 (Amphoto). Watson-Guptill.

Wordsworth, Dorothy, jt. auth. see Wordsworth, William.

Wordsworth, Jane. Women of the North. (Illus.). 224p. 1981. 19.95 (ISBN 0-686-84828-4, Pub. by W Collins Australia). Intl Schol Bk Serv.

Wordsworth, Jonathan. William Wordsworth: The Borders of Vision. 1982. 34.95x (ISBN 0-19-812097-4). Oxford U Pr.

Wordsworth, Morris A., jt. auth. see Munford, Kerry.

Wordsworth, William. Poetical Works, 5 vols. De Selincourt, Ernest & Darbishire, Helen, eds. Incl. Vol. 1. 1940. o.p. (ISBN 0-19-811827-9); Vol. 2. 2nd ed. 1952. o.p. (ISBN 0-19-811828-7); Vol. 3. 2nd ed. 1954. o.p. (ISBN 0-19-811829-5); Vol. 4. 1947. 52.50x (ISBN 0-19-811830-9); Vol. 5. 1949. 52.50 (ISBN 0-19-811831-7). (Oxford English Texts Ser.). Oxford U Pr.

--Poetical Works with Introd. & Notes. new rev ed. Hutchinson, Thomas & De Selincourt, Ernest, eds. (Oxford Standard Authors Ser.). 1950. pap. 39.95x (ISBN 0-19-254152-8); pap. 11.50x (ISBN 0-19-281052-9, OPB). Oxford U Pr.

--Preface to Lyrical Ballads. Owen, W. J., ed. LC 78-12680. (Angelista Ser.: Vol. IX). 1979. Repr. of 1957 ed. lib. bdg. 18.00x (ISBN 0-313-21177-9, WOPL). Greenwood.

--Selected Poems. 14.95x (ISBN 0-19-250189-5, WC 189). Oxford U Pr.

Wordsworth, William & Wordsworth, Dorothy. The Letters of William & Dorothy Wordsworth. De Selincourt, Ernest, ed. Incl. Vol. I. The Early Years 1787-1805. 2nd ed. Shaver, Chester L., ed. 1967. 58.00x (ISBN 0-19-811464-8); Vol. II. The Middle Years, Pt. 1: 1806-1811. 2nd ed. Moorman, Mary, rev. by. 1969. 63.00x (ISBN 0-19-811491-5); Vol. II. The Middle Years, Pt. 2: 1812-1820. 2nd ed. Moorman, Mary & Hill, Alan G., eds. 1969. 59.00x (ISBN 0-19-812403-1). Oxford U Pr.

Worell, Judith, ed. Psychological Development in the Elementary Years. (Educational Psychology Ser.). 504p. 39.50 (ISBN 0-12-764050-9). Acad Pr.

Worell, Judith, et al. Psychology for Teachers & Students. (Illus., Orig.). 1980. pap. text ed. 22.50 (ISBN 0-07-071870-9, C); tchr's manual 11.00 (ISBN 0-07-071871-7). McGraw.

Worf, Douglas L., ed. Biological Monitoring for Environmental Effects. LC 79-2977. 240p. 1980. 25.95x (ISBN 0-669-03306-5). Lexington Bks.

Worf, P. R. Elements of Photogrammetry. 2nd ed. 597p. 1983. text ed. 37.50x (ISBN 0-07-071345-6, C). McGraw.

Worick, W. & Schaller, W. Alcohol, Tobacco & Drugs: Their Use & Abuse. 1977. pap. 11.95 (ISBN 0-13-021436-1). P-H.

Worick, W. Wayne. Safety Education: Man, His Machines & His Environment. (Illus.). 320p. 1975. 17.95 (ISBN 0-13-785683-0). P-H.

Work. Laboratory Techniques in Biochemistry, Vol. 6, Pt. 2. 2nd ed. Date not set. 72.50 (ISBN 0-444-80420-X). Elsevier.

Work, C. R., ed. see Fellows, E. Barrett Prettyman.

Work, E., jt. auth. see Work, T.

Work, E., jt. ed. see Work, T. S.

Work in America Institute, Inc. The Future of Older Workers in America: New Options for an Extended Work Life. LC 80-52063. (Work in America Institute Studies in Productivity). 144p. (Orig.). 1982. pap. 9.95 (ISBN 0-08-029542-8). Pergamon.

Work in America Institute Inc. Job Strategies for Urban Youth: Sixteen Pilot Programs for Action. LC 79-64686. (Work in America Institute Studies in Productivity). (Orig.). 1982. pap. 7.95 (ISBN 0-08-029540-1); pap. 3.95 summary (ISBN 0-08-029541-X). Pergamon.

Work in America Institute, Inc. Productivity Through Work Innovations. 168p. 1982. 15.00 (ISBN 0-08-029545-2, L120); pap. 6.50 (ISBN 0-08-029546-0). Pergamon.

Work, T. & Burdon. Laboratory Techniques in Biochemistry & Molecular Biology, Vol. 1, Pt. 2. rev. ed. 1980. 57.50 (ISBN 0-444-80191-X). Elsevier.

Work, T. & Work, E. Laboratory Techniques in Biochemistry & Molecular Biology, Vol. 8: Cell Culture for Biochemists. 1980. 65.75 (ISBN 0-444-80248-7). Elsevier.

Work, T. S. & Pardon, P. H., eds. Laboratory Techniques in Biochemistry & Molecular Biology: Vol. 9, Sequencing of Proteins & Peptides. 1981. 76.25 (ISBN 0-444-80275-4). Elsevier.

Work, T. S. & Work, E., eds. Laboratory Techniques in Biochemistry & Molecular Biology, Vols. 1-7. (Illus.). 1969-1979. Vol. 1. 70.75 (ISBN 0-444-10036-9); Vol. 2. 63.00 (ISBN 0-444-10055-5); Vol. 3. 89.00 (ISBN 0-444-10386-4); Vol. 4. 98.25 (ISBN 0-444-10985-4); Vol. 5. 107.75 (ISBN 0-444-11216-2); Vol. 6. 84.25 (ISBN 0-7204-4221-4); Vol. 7. 84.25 (ISBN 0-7204-4224-9). Elsevier.

--Laboratory Techniques in Biochemistry & Molecular Biology: Vol. 1, Pt. 3, Immunochemical Techniques for the Indentification & Estimation of Macromolecules. 2nd. rev. ed. 1982. 83.00 (ISBN 0-444-80245-2). Elsevier.

Work, Virginia. Jodi: The Curse of the Broken Feather. LC 11-154. 128p. 1981. pap. 2.95 (ISBN 0-8024-4418-0). Moody.

--Jodi: The Mystery of the Missing Message. LC 11-987. 128p. (gr. 5-8). 1980. pap. 2.95 (ISBN 0-8024-4416-4). Moody.

Workbasket Magazine Staff, ed. Aunt Ellen's Embroidery Handbook: A Treasury of Techniques & Designs. LC 82-60950. (Illus.). 64p. (Orig.). 1983. pap. 2.95 (ISBN 0-86675-331-1, 3311). Mod Handcraft.

Workbench Magazine staff. The Workbench Treasury of Occasional & End Table Projects. LC 82-18769. (Illus.). 56p. (Orig.). 1983. pap. 3.95 (ISBN 0-86675-006-1, 61). Mod Handcraft.

Working Party on Agriculture & Environment, 4th Session, Manila, 1978. Report. (FAO Fisheries Reports: No. 215). 8p. 1979. pap. 7.50 (ISBN 0-686-94002-4, F1830, FAO). Unipub.

Working Party on Crop & Livestock Insurance, Bankok, 1956. Report. 44p. 1957. pap. 4.50 (ISBN 0-686-93273-0, F389, FAO). Unipub.

Working Party on Tuna & Billfish Tagging in the Atlantic & Adjacent Seas. Final Report. (FAO Fisheries Reports: No. 118, Suppl. 1). 40p. 1971. pap. 6.00 (ISBN 0-686-92814-8, F1702, FAO). Unipub.

Workman, Bernard A., et al, eds. New Caxton Encyclopedia, 20 vols. (Illus.). (gr. 9-12). 1977. Set. lib. bdg. 399.33 set (ISBN 0-8393-6183-1). Purnell Ref Bks.

Workman, Brooke. Writing Seminars in the Content Area: In Search of Hemingway, Salinger, & Steinbeck. 1983. pap. 13.75 (ISBN 0-8141-5886-2). NCTE.

Workman, E. L., jt. auth. see Sanchez, Irene.

Workman, Herbert. Persecution in the Early Church. 1980. pap. 6.95x (ISBN 0-19-283025-2). Oxford U Pr.

Workman, Lewis C. Mathematical Foundations of Life Insurance: Instructor's Manual. (FLMI Insurance Education Program Ser.). 314p. 1982. pap. 13.00 tchrs ed. (ISBN 0-915322-54-4). LOMA.

--Mathematical Foundations of Life Insurance: Student Guide. (FLMI Insurance Education Program Ser.). 257p. 1982. pap. 7.00 workbook (ISBN 0-915322-53-6). LOMA.

--Mathematical Foundations of Life Insurance. LC 82-80669. (Insurance Education Program Ser.). 467p. 1982. text ed. 12.50 (ISBN 0-915322-52-8). LOMA.

--Teaching Part 6: Fundamental Mathematics of Life Insurance. 1975. 8.00 o.p. (ISBN 0-915322-08-0). LOMA.

--Workbook for Fundamental Mathematics of Life Insurance. 1970. 6.50 o.p. (ISBN 0-915322-00-5). LOMA.

Workman, Richard W. Growing Native: Native Plants for Landscape Use in Coastal South Florida. (Illus.). 64p. pap. 9.95 (ISBN 0-686-84239-1). Banyan Bks.

Workshop Conference Hoechst Schloss Reisenburg, 11th, October 11-15, 1981 & Bartmann, W. Structure of Complexes Between Biopolymers & Low Molecular Weight Molecules: Proceeding. 1982. 42.95x (ISBN 0-471-26144-0, Pub. by Wiley Heyden). Wiley.

Workshop on Controlled Reproduction of Cultivated Fishes. Reports & Relevant Papers. (FAO-EIFAC Technical Papers: No. 25). 180p. 1975. pap. 11.75 (ISBN 0-686-93008-8, F766, FAO). Unipub.

Workshop on the Genetic Conservation of Rice. Proceedings. (Illus.). 54p. 1978. pap. 5.00 (ISBN 0-686-93116-5, RQ43, IRRI). Unipub.

Workshop on the Phenomenon Known as "El Nino", Ecuador, 1974. Report. (FAO Fisheries Reports: No. 163). 24p. 1975. pap. 7.50 (ISBN 0-686-93985-9, F806, FAO). Unipub.

Worland, Peter B. Introduction to Basic Programming: A Structured Approach. LC 78-56436. (Illus.). 1979. pap. text ed. 15.95 (ISBN 0-395-26775-7); solutions manual 1.00 (ISBN 0-395-26776-5). HM.

World Almanac, ed. The World Almanac Book of the Strange. (Illus., Orig.). 1977. pap. 3.50 (ISBN 0-451-11890-1, AE1890, Sig). NAL.

World Almanac Editors. The World Almanac & Book of Facts for 1982. 976p. (Orig.). 1981. 8.95 o.p. (ISBN 0-911818-23-5); pap. 4.50 o.p. (ISBN 0-911818-22-7). World Almanac.

--The World Almanac Book of Buffs, Masters, Mavens & Uncommon Experts. LC 80-8179. 1980. 12.50 o.p. (ISBN 0-13-967836-0). P-H.

--The World Almanac Book of the Strange, No. 2. 1982. pap. 3.50 (ISBN 0-451-11890-1, AE1890, Sig). NAL.

--The World Almanac Book of Who. LC 80-81180. 1980. 12.50 o.p. (ISBN 0-13-967844-1). P-H.

World Almanac Publications Editors. The World Almanac Book of Who. LC 79-67561. (Orig.). 1980. pap. 5.95 o.p. (ISBN 0-448-16544-9, G&D). Putnam Pub Group.

World Association of Girl Guides & Girl Scouts. Basics of the World Association of Girl Guides & Girl Scouts. 1976. pap. text ed. 1.00 (ISBN 0-900827-28-9, 23-961). GS.

--Trefoil Round the World. (Illus.). (gr. 4-12). 1967. Repr. of 1978 ed. 5.00 (ISBN 0-900827-29-7, 23-962). GS.

World Association Of World Federalists - Youth And Student Division - 6th Intl. Study Conference. World Peace Through World Economy. 1968. pap. text ed. 5.75x o.p. (ISBN 0-391-02070-6). Humanities.

World Bank. IDA in Retrospect: The First Two Decades of the International Development Association. (Illus.). 142p. 1982. 17.95 (ISBN 0-19-520407-7); pap. 6.00 (ISBN 0-19-520408-5). Oxford U Pr.

--World Development Report, 1982. (Illus.). 182p. (Orig.). 1982. 20.00x (ISBN 0-19-503224-1); pap. 8.00 (ISBN 0-19-503225-X). Oxford U Pr.

World Bank Staff. World Tables: 1980. LC 79-3649. (World Bank Occasional Paper Ser.). (Illus.). 1980. text ed. 40.00x (ISBN 0-8018-2389-7); pap. text ed. 20.00x (ISBN 0-8018-2390-0). Johns Hopkins.

World Book-Childcraft International Inc. Staff. Childcraft - the How & Why Library, 15 vols. LC 79-88042. (Illus.). (gr. k-6). 1980. PLB write for info. o.p. (ISBN 0-7166-0180-X). World Bk.

World Book-Childcraft International Inc., ed. Childcraft-the How & Why Library, 15 vols. Incl. Vol. 1. Poems & Rhymes; Vol. 2. Stories & Fables; Vol. 3. Children Everywhere; Vol. 4. World & Space; Vol. 5. About Animals; Vol. 6. The Green Kingdom; Vol. 7. How Things Work; Vol. 8. About Us; Vol. 9. Holidays & Birthdays; Vol. 10. Places to Know; Vol. 11. Make & Do; Vol. 12. Look & Learn; Vol. 13. Mathemagic; Vol. 14. About Me; Vol. 15. Guide for Parents. (Illus.). (gr. k-6). 1981. PLB write for info. (ISBN 0-7166-0181-8). World Bk.

World Book Editorial Staff. The World Book of Test Taming. LC 81-69689. (Illus.). 736p. (gr. 4-12). 1982. write for info. (ISBN 0-7166-3151-2). World Bk.

World Book Editorial Staff, ed. The World Book Student Handbook: Information Finder, Vol. 2. rev. ed. LC 81-51365. (Illus.). 432p. (gr. 7-12). 1981. PLB write for info. (ISBN 0-7166-3122-9). World Bk.

--The World Book Student Handbook: Student Guide, Vol. I. rev. ed. LC 81-51365. (Illus.). 304p. (gr. 7-12). 1981. PLB write for info. (ISBN 0-7166-3121-0). World Bk.

World Book Editors, ed. Science Year: The World Book Science Annual. LC 65-21776. (Illus.). 400p. (gr. 7-12). 1981. lib. bdg. write for info. (ISBN 0-7166-0582-1); lib. bdg. 10.95 Aristocrat ed. o.p. (ISBN 0-686-72114-4). World Bk.

World Book Encyclopedia Inc Staff. Today 1979. (World Book Today Yearly Diaries Ser.). 1978. 8.95 o.p. (ISBN 0-7166-2028-6). World Bk.

World Book Inc. Best-Loved Bible Stories: Old Testament & New Testament, 2 vols. LC 79-55309. (Illus.). 90p. (gr. 4-8). 1980. write for info. (ISBN 0-7166-2059-6). World Bk.

--Christmas in the Netherlands. LC 80-54076. (Round the World Christmas Program Ser.). (Illus.). 80p. (ps-9). 1981. write for info. (ISBN 0-7166-3112-1). World Bk.

World Book, Inc. The World Book Encyclopedia, 22 vols. rev. ed. LC 79-84167. (Illus.). (gr. 4-12). 1980. Set. PLB write for info. o.p. (ISBN 0-7166-0080-3). World Bk.

World Book Inc. & Tressler, Arthur G., eds. Medical Update 1983: The World Book Family Health Annual. (Illus.). 272p. 1982. lib. bdg. write for info. (ISBN 0-7166-1183-X). World Bk.

World Book Inc. & Wille, Wayne, eds. The World Book Year Book. LC 62-4818. (Illus.). 608p. (gr. 6-12). 1983. PLB write for info. (ISBN 0-7166-0483-3). World Bk.

World Book, Inc. Editorial Staff, ed. Today, Nineteen Eighty Two: A Personal Record & Reference Book. LC 76-27228. (World Book Today Yearly Diaries Ser.). (Illus.). 1981. write for info. (ISBN 0-7166-2033-2). World Bk.

World Book Inc. Staff. Childcraft Annual - About Dogs. LC 65-25105. (Childcraft - the How & Why Library). (Illus.). (gr. k-6). 1977. PLB write for info (ISBN 0-7166-0677-1). World Bk.

--Childcraft Annual-Mathemagic. LC 65-25105. (Childcraft--the How & Why Library). (Illus.). (gr. k-6). 1978. PLB write for price info (ISBN 0-7166-0678-X). World Bk.

--Childcraft Annual-Prehistoric Animals. LC 65-25105. (Childcraft-the How & Why Library). (Illus.). 304p. (gr. k-6). 1976. write for info (ISBN 0-7166-0676-3). World Bk.

--Childcraft Annual: Story of the Sea. LC 65-25105. (Childcraft-the How & Why Library). (Illus.). (gr. k-6). 1979. write for info. (ISBN 0-7166-0679-8). World Bk.

--Childcraft Annual: The Magic of Words. LC 65-25105. (Childcraft How & Why Library). (Illus.). 304p. (gr. k-6). 1975. write for price info. (ISBN 0-7166-0675-5). World Bk.

World Book, Inc Staff. Christmas in France. LC 80-50994. (Round the World Christmas Program Ser.). (Illus.). 80p. (ps-9). 1980. write for info. (ISBN 0-7166-3106-7). World Bk.

World Book, Inc. Staff. Cyclo-Teacher Learning Aid. (gr. 1-12). write for price info. (ISBN 0-685-36760-6). World Bk.

--The Puzzle Book (Childcraft Annual) LC 65-25105. (Illus.). 304p. (ps-6). 1982. PLB write for info. (ISBN 0-7166-0682-8). World Bk.

--Today Nineteen Eighty. LC 76-27228. (World Book Today Yearly Diaries Ser.). 1979. 8.95 o.p. (ISBN 0-7166-2031-6). World Bk.

--The World Book Encyclopedia, 22 vols. LC 80-50324. (Illus.). 13000p. (gr. 4-12). 1981. lib. bdg. write for info. o.p. (ISBN 0-7166-0081-1). World Bk.

--The World Book Encyclopedia, 22 vols. LC 81-51201. (Illus.). (gr. 4-12). 1982. Set. PLB write for info. (ISBN 0-7166-0082-X). World Bk.

--The World Book Illustrated Home Medical Encyclopedia, 4 vols. LC 79-56907. (Illus.). 1038p. 1980. write for info. (ISBN 0-7166-2060-X). World Bk.

World Book, Inc. Staff & Garbarino, Merwyn. The Indian Book. LC 65-25105. (Childcraft Annual Ser.). (Illus.). 304p. (gr. k-6). 1980. PLB write for info. (ISBN 0-7166-0680-1). World Bk.

World Book Inc., Staff, ed. Childcraft: The How & Why Library. LC 81-70893. (Illus.). 5000p. (gr. k-6). 1982. lib. bdg. write for info. (ISBN 0-7166-0182-6). World Bk.

World Book, Inc. Staff, ed. Medical Update: The World Book Family Health Annual. (Illus.). 264p. 1981. lib. bdg. write for info. (ISBN 0-7166-1182-1). World Bk.

World Book Inc., Staff, ed. Science Year: The World Book Science Annual. LC 65-21776. (Illus.). 400p. (gr. 7-12). 1982. PLB write for info. (ISBN 0-7166-0583-X). World Bk.

World Book, Inc. Staff, ed. The World Book Atlas of the United States & Canada. LC 80-54104. (Illus.). 446p. (gr. 4-12). 1981. PLB write for info. (ISBN 0-7166-3114-8). World Bk.

--The World Book Complete Word Power Library, 2 vols, Vol. 1 & 2. LC 80-53648. (gr. 7-12). 1981. Vol. 1, 404pgs. write for info. (ISBN 0-7166-3110-5); Vol. 2, 437 Pgs. write for info. (ISBN 0-7166-3111-3). World Bk.

--The World Book of America's Presidents, 2 vols. LC 81-69687. (Illus.). 448p. 1982. Set. PLB write for info. (ISBN 0-7166-3148-2). World Bk.

World Book Inc, Staff, ed. The World Book Year Book. LC 62-4818. (Illus.). 608p. (gr. 6-12). 1982. PLB write for info. (ISBN 0-7166-0482-5). World Bk.

World Book Staff. The Bug Book. LC 65-25105. (Illus.). 304p. (gr. k-6). 1981. write for price info. (ISBN 0-7166-0681-X). World Bk.

--Christmas in Austria. LC 82-70813. (Round the World Christmas Program Ser.). (Illus.). 80p. 1982. write for info. (ISBN 0-7166-0883-9). World Bk.

World Book Year Book, ed. Sacred Land: Interleaving Color Maps of the Holy Land. (Illus., Orig.). pap. 1.25 o.p. (ISBN 0-87981-088-2). Holman.

World Climate Conference of Experts on Climate & Mankind, Geneva, 1979. Proceedings. (WMO Pubns. Ser.: No. 537). 79p. 1979. pap. 40.00 o.p. (ISBN 0-686-93911-5, WMO). Unipub.

World Coal Study. Coal: A Bridge to the Future. LC 81-47090. (Illus.). 280p. Date not set. pap. 5.95i (ISBN 0-06-090883-1, CN 883, CN). Har-Row. Postponed.

World Conference on Agarian Reform & Rural Development, Rome, 1979. Report. (FAO Development Documents: No. 62). 67p. 1979. pap. 7.50 (ISBN 0-686-92900-4, F1846, FAO). Unipub.

World Conference on First Medical Informatics, Aug. 5-10, 1974. Medinfo 1974: Proceedings, 2 Vols. Anderson, J. & Forsythe, J. M., eds. LC 74-83267. 1192p. 1975. Set. 127.75 (ISBN 0-444-10771-1, North-Holland). Elsevier.

World Conference on Medical Informatics, 2nd. Medinfo 1977: Proceedings. Shires, D. B. & Wolf, H. K., eds. (IFIP Ser.). 1977. 127.75 (ISBN 0-7204-0754-0, North-Holland). Elsevier.

World Congress of Psychiatry 5th, Mexico, D. F. Nov. 25 - Dec. 4, 1971. Psychiatry: Proceedings, 2 vols. De La Fuente, R., ed. LC 73-77080. (International Congress Ser.: No. 274). 1650p. 1974. pap. text ed. 267.50 o.p. (ISBN 0-444-15033-1). Elsevier.

World Congress of Rehabilitation International. Participation of People with Disabilities: International Perspectives. 1981. 4.50 (ISBN 0-686-94877-7). Rehab Intl.

World Congress on Pain, 1st, Florence, 1975. Advances in Pain Research & Therapy: Proceedings, Vol. 1. Bonica, John J. & Albe-Fessard, Denise, eds. LC 75-32095. 1056p. 1976. 96.50 (ISBN 0-89004-090-7). Raven.

World Congress on Pain, 2nd, Montreal, Aug. 1978. Proceedings. Bonica, John J., et al, eds. LC 79-87468. (Advances in Pain Research & Therapy Ser.: Vol. 3). 984p. 1979. text ed. 92.50 (ISBN 0-89004-270-5). Raven.

World Council of Churches, Geneva, Switzerland. Classified Catalog of the Ecumenical Movement, 2 vols. 1972. lib. bdg. 190.00 (ISBN 0-8161-0925-7, Hall Library). G K Hall.

World Energy Conference, ed. Energy Terminology: A Multi-Lingual Glossary. 275p. 1983. 100.00 (ISBN 0-08-029314-X, B110); pap. 35.00 (ISBN 0-08-029315-8). Pergamon.

World Food Conference, Ames, Iowa June, 1976. Proceedings. Schaller, Frank, ed. 1977. text ed. 9.50x (ISBN 0-8138-1825-7). Iowa St U Pr.

World Food Congress, 1st, Washington, D. C., 1963. Report, Vol. 1. (Orig.). 1963. pap. 4.00 o.p. (ISBN 0-685-02465-2, FAO). Unipub.

World Health Organization. Schizophrenia: An International Follow-Up Study. LC 78-17808. 1979. 67.95x (ISBN 0-471-99623-8, Pub. by Wiley-Interscience). Wiley.

World Hydrogen Energy Conference, Fourth. Hydrogen Energy Process IV: Proceedings of the World Hydrogen Energy Conference, Fourth, Pasadena, CA 13-17 June, 1982. Veziroglu, T. N. & Van Vorst, W. D., eds. Kelley, J. H. (Advances in Hydrogen Energy Ser.: No. 3). 2000p. 1982. 350.00 (ISBN 0-08-028699-2). Pergamon.

World Meteorological Organization. Collection, Storage & Retrieval of Meteorological Data. (World Weather Watch Planning Report Ser.: No. 28). 1969. pap. 8.00 (ISBN 0-685-22296-9, W240, WMO). Unipub.

--Influence of Weather Conditions on the Occurrence of Apple Scab. (Technical Note Ser.: No. 55). 1963. pap. 5.00 (ISBN 0-685-22309-4, W26, WMO). Unipub.

--International Cloud Atlas. abr. ed. (Illus.). 1969. pap. 36.00 (ISBN 0-685-22311-6, W329, WMO). Unipub.

--Introduction to GARP. (GARP Publications Ser.: No. 1). 1969. pap. 5.00 (ISBN 0-685-22314-0, W293, WMO). Unipub.

--Manual for Depth-Area-Duration Analysis of Storm Precipitation. 1969. pap. 20.00 o.p. (ISBN 0-685-22315-9, WMO). Unipub.

--Marine Cloud Album. (Illus.). pap. 5.00 (ISBN 0-685-57279-X, W378, WMO). Unipub.

--Note on Climatological Normals. (Technical Note Ser.). 1967. pap. 5.00 (ISBN 0-685-22328-0, W52, WMO). Unipub.

--Planning of the Global Telecommunication System. (World Weather Watch Planning Report Ser.: No. 16). 1966. pap. 6.00 (ISBN 0-685-22330-2, W232, WMO). Unipub.

--Protection Against Frost Damage. (Technical Note Ser.). 1968. pap. 11.00 (ISBN 0-685-22333-7, W23, WMO). Unipub.

--Reduction & Use of Data Obtained by TIROS Meteorological Satellites. (Technical Note Ser.). 1963. pap. 6.00 (ISBN 0-685-22335-3, W22, WMO). Unipub.

--Role of Meteorological Satellites in the World Weather Watch. (World Weather Watch Planning Report Ser.: No. 18). 1967. pap. 14.00 o.p. (ISBN 0-685-22336-1, WMO). Unipub.

--Scope of the Nineteen Seventy-Two to Nineteen Seventy-Five Plan. (World Weather Watch Planning Report Ser.: No. 30). 1969. pap. 12.00 (ISBN 0-685-22337-X, W242, WMO). Unipub.

--Short-Period Averages for 1951-1960 & Provisional Average for CLIMAT TEMP SHIP Stations. (Eng. & Fr.). pap. 36.00 (ISBN 0-685-22339-6, W37, WMO). Unipub.

--Sites for Wind-Power Installations. (Technical Note Ser.). 1964. pap. 5.00 (ISBN 0-685-22340-X, W30, WMO). Unipub.

--Statistical Analysis & Prognosis in Meteorology. (Technical Note Ser.). 1966. pap. 41.00 (ISBN 0-685-22343-4, W41, WMO). Unipub.

--Weather & Food. 1962. pap. 2.00 (ISBN 0-685-22347-7, W17, WMO). Unipub.

--Weather & Water. 1966. pap. 2.00 (ISBN 0-685-22348-5, W51, WMO). Unipub.

World Meteorological Organization Congress, 6th, Geneva, 1971. Abridged Report with Resolutions. 229p. (Orig.). 1972. pap. 35.00 o.p. (ISBN 0-685-24968-9, 292, WMO). Unipub.

World Meteorological Organization Executive Committee. Abridged Report with Resolutions of the Twenty-Eighth Session of the WMO Executive Committee, Geneva, 1976. (WMO Publications Ser.: No. 445). 449p. 1977. pap. 25.00 o.p. (ISBN 92-63-10445-X, WMO). Unipub.

World Meteorological Organization, Executive Committee, 23rd Session, 1971. Report. pap. 20.00 (ISBN 0-686-94461-5, W101, WMO). Unipub.

World Meteorological Organization, Executive Committee, 25th Session, 1973. Report. pap. 25.00 (ISBN 0-686-94462-3, W140, WMO). Unipub.

World Meteorological Organization, Executive Committee, 26th Session, 1974. Report. pap. 25.00 (ISBN 0-686-94463-1, W158, WMO). Unipub.

World Meteorological Organization, Executive Committee, 29th Session, 1977. Report. pap. 25.00 (ISBN 0-686-94464-X, W361, WMO). Unipub.

World Meteorological Organization (WMO) Congress, 6th Session. Abridged Report with Resolutions. (Publications Ser.: No. 292). pap. 35.00 (ISBN 0-686-94228-0, W100, WMO). Unipub.

World Meteorological Organization (WMO) Annual Report, 1970. (Publications Ser.: No. 287). pap. 20.00 (ISBN 0-686-94235-3, W97, WMO). Unipub.

World Meterological Organization, 3rd Congress. Abridged Report with Resolutions. (WMO Pubns. Ser.: No. 88). 249p. (Fr.). 1959. pap. write for info. o.p. (WMO). Unipub.

World Organization of National College Physicians (WONCA) International Classification of Health Problems in Primary Care. 2nd ed. 1979. text ed. 16.95x o.p. (ISBN 0-19-261195-X); pap. text ed. 9.95x (ISBN 0-19-261186-0). Oxford U Pr.

World Petroleum Congress, ed. Proceedings of the Tenth World Petroleum Congress, 6 vols. Incl. Vol. 1. General. 1980. 99.95 (ISBN 0-471-26090-8); Vol. 2. Exploration: Supply & Demand. 444p. 1980. 233.00 (ISBN 0-471-26091-6); Vol. 3. 424p. 1980. 285.00 (ISBN 0-471-26092-4); Vol. 4. Storage, Transportation & Processing & Training. 486p. 1980. 285.00 (ISBN 0-471-26093-2); Vol. 5. Conservation, Environment, Safety & Training. 372p. 1980. 233.00 (ISBN 0-471-26094-0); Vol. 6. Index. 1980. 99.95 (ISBN 0-471-26095-9). Set. 998.00 (ISBN 0-686-86042-X, Wiley Heyden). Wiley.

World Petroleum Congress, 9th, Japan, 1975. Proceedings. Applied Science Publishers Ltd., ed. Incl. Vol. 1. Introduction; Vol. 2. Geology; Vol. 3. Exploration & Transportation; Vol. 4. Drilling & Production; Vol. 5. Processing & Storage; Vol. 6. Conservation & Safety; Vol. 7. Index. (Illus.). 1975. 615.00 set (ISBN 0-85334-670-4, Pub. by Applied Sci England). Elsevier.

World Scientific Conference on the Biology & Culture of Shrimps & Prawns, Mexico City, 1967. Proceedings, Vol. 1. (FAO Fisheries Reports: No. 57). 75p. 1968. pap. 7.50 (ISBN 0-686-92989-6, F1672, FAO). Unipub.

World Scientific Meeting on the Biology of Tunas & Related Species. Proceedings. (FAO Fisheries Reports: No. 6, Vol. 4). 426p. 1964. pap. 25.50 (ISBN 0-686-93000-2, F1650, FAO). Unipub.

World Tennis Magazine Editors, jt. auth. see Lumiere, Cornel.

World Tourism Organization, ed. Economic Review of World Tourism, 1982. (Illus.). 73p. (Orig.). 1982. pap. 40.00x (ISBN 0-8002-3030-2). Intl Pubns Serv.

World Trade Conference, Rome, 5-16 Nov. 1974. Report. pap. 5.00 (ISBN 0-686-94397-X, UN75/2A3, UN). Unipub.

World Without War Council, jt. ed. see Mackey, Janet.

Worley, Eloise. Pharmacology & Medications. 3rd ed. LC 75-45151. (Illus.). 175p. 1976. pap. text ed. 7.50x o.p. (ISBN 0-8036-9592-6). Davis Co.

Worley, Jo-Lynne, et al, eds. see Berson, Ginny.

Worley, Robert C. A Gathering of Strangers: Understanding the Life of Your Church. LC 76-21091. 1976. pap. 6.95 (ISBN 0-664-24124-7). Westminster.

Wormald, Francis. The Winchester Psalter. (Illus.). 128p. 1973. 49.00x (ISBN 0-19-921004-7). Oxford U Pr.

Wormbrand, Richard & Wurmbrand, Richard. My Answer to the Moscow Atheists. 1977. 7.95 o.p. (ISBN 0-87000-372-0, Arlington Hse). Crown.

Wormeley, Katherine P., tr. see Sainte-Beuve, C. A.

Wormell, Deborah. Sir John Seeley & the Uses of History. LC 79-51832. 303p. 1980. 42.50 (ISBN 0-521-22720-8). Cambridge U Pr.

Wormer, Joe Van see Van Wormer, Joe.

Wormer, Joe van see Van Wormer, Joe.

Wormhoudt, Arthur, tr. from Classical Arabic. Dhikra 'Abd Rabbihi & al Sulami & Others. (Arab Translation Ser.: No. 61). 160p. (Orig.). 1982. pap. 6.50x (ISBN 0-916358-12-7). Wormhoudt.

Wormhoudt, Arthur, tr. from Arabic. Dhikra al Mutanabbi from the Yatimat al Dahr of Al Tha'alibi. (Arab Translation Ser.: No. 49). 175p. 1980. pap. 6.50x o.p. (ISBN 0-916358-99-2). Wormhoudt.

--Dhikra al Sahib ibn Abbad. (Arab Translation Ser.: No. 56). 150p. 1981. pap. 6.50x o.p. (ISBN 0-916358-06-2). Wormhoudt.

Wormhoudt, Arthur, tr. Dhikra Saif Al Daula & Abu Firas. LC 75-32687. (Arab Translation Ser.: No. 17). 1975. pap. 6.50x o.p. (ISBN 0-916358-67-4). Wormhoudt.

Wormhoudt, Arthur, tr. from Classical Arabic. Diwan Dhu'l Rumma. (Arab Translation Ser.: No. 62). (Illus.). 160p. 1982. pap. 6.50x (ISBN 0-916358-15-1). Wormhoudt.

--Diwan Jamil Buthaina. (Arab Translation Ser.: No. 64). (Illus.). 160p. (Orig.). 1982. pap. 6.50x (ISBN 0-916358-16-X). Wormhoudt.

Wormhoudt, Arthur, tr. Diwan Jarwal ibn Aws Called al Hutaia. (Arab Translations Ser.: No. 46). 1980. pap. 6.50x (ISBN 0-916358-96-8). Wormhoudt.

Wormhoudt, Arthur, tr. from Arabic. Diwan Jarwal Ibn Malik Ibn Makhzum Al 'absi Called Al Hutaia. (Arab Translation Ser.: No. 46). 175p. pap. 6.50x o.p. (ISBN 0-916358-96-8). Wormhoudt.

Wormhoudt, Arthur, tr. Diwan Labid. (Arab Translation Ser.: No. 25). 1976. pap. 6.50x (ISBN 0-916358-75-5). Wormhoudt.

Wormhoudt, Arthur, tr. from Classical Arabic. The Diwan of Muslim ibn al Walid. (Arab Translation Ser.: No. 54). 175p. 1980. pap. 6.50x (ISBN 0-916358-02-X). Wormhoudt.

Wormhoudt, Arthur, tr. The Naqaid (Satires) of Jarir & al Farazdaq. (Arab Translation Ser.: No. 7). 175p. 1974. pap. 6.50 o.p. (ISBN 0-916358-57-7). Wormhoudt.

Wormhoudt, Arthur, tr. see Al Tha'alibi.

Wormhoudt, Sarah M. Angels, Words & Wayward Beasts. (Orig.). 1982. pap. 5.50x (ISBN 0-916358-17-8). Wormhoudt.

Wormley, David N., jt. auth. see De Silva, Clarence W.

Wormser, Baron. The White Words. 1983. 12.95 (ISBN 0-686-42961-3); pap. 6.95 (ISBN 0-686-42962-1). HM.

Wormser, Rene A. The Story of the Law. 1972. pap. 6.95 o.p. (ISBN 0-671-21333-4, Touchstone Bks). S&S.

Wormser, Richard. The Black Mustanger. (Illus.). (gr. 5-9). 1971. 8.95 (ISBN 0-688-21104-6); PLB 6.96 o.s.i. (ISBN 0-688-31104-0). Morrow.

Wormsley, K. G. Duodenal Ulcer, Vol. 1. 1977. 14.40 (ISBN 0-904406-53-9). Eden Pr.

--Duodenal Ulcer, Vol. 2. Horrobin, D. F., ed. (Annual Research Reviews). 1979. 28.00 (ISBN 0-88831-058-7). Eden Pr.

Wormuth, Diana, tr. see Lundkvist, Artur.

Worner, Karl H. Stockhausen: Life & Work. Hopkins, Bill, ed. & tr. LC 76-174460. (Illus.). 1973. 26.50x (ISBN 0-520-02143-6); pap. 3.95 (ISBN 0-520-03272-1). U of Cal Pr.

Woronoff, Jon. Japan: The Coming Economic Crisis. 300p. 1980. 11.95 (ISBN 0-914778-44-7, Pub. by Lotus Japan); pap. 6.95. Phoenix Bks.

--Japan's Wasted Workers. (Illus.). 296p. 1983. 19.95x (ISBN 0-86598-123-X); pap. text ed. 10.95 (ISBN 0-86598-100-0). Allanheld.

Woronzoff, Alexander. Andrej Belyj's "Petersburg," James Joyce's "Ulysses" & the Symbolist Movement. x, 215p. 1982. write for info. (ISBN 3-261-05016-0). P Lang Pubs.

Worrall, A. & Worrall, O. The Gift of Healing. LC 65-26006. 1976. pap. 6.95i (ISBN 0-06-069687-7, RD 154, HarpR). Har-Row.

Worrall, Ambrose A. & Worrall, Olga N. Explore Your Psychic World. LC 79-85062. 1970. pap. 5.95i (ISBN 0-06-069686-9, HarpR); pap. 3.95 (ISBN 0-686-96729-1, RD 156). Har-Row.

Worrall, J., ed. see Lakatos, Imre.

Worrall, John D., ed. Safety & the Work Force: Incentives & Disincentives in Worker's Compensation. 1983. price not set (ISBN 0-87546-101-8). ILR Pr.

Worrall, Nick. Nikolai Gogol & Ivan Turgenev. (Grove Press Modern Dramatists Ser.). (Illus.). 196p. 1982. pap. 9.95 (ISBN 0-394-62431-9, Ever). Grove.

Worrall, O., jt. auth. see Worrall, A.

Worrall, Olga N., jt. auth. see Worrall, Ambrose A.

Worrall, W. E. Clays & Ceramic Raw Materials. LC 75-12684. 203p. 1975. 36.95x o.p. (ISBN 0-470-96085-X). Halsted Pr.

Worrell, A. C. Principles of Forest Policy. 1970. text ed. 33.50 (ISBN 0-07-071891-1, C). McGraw.

Worrell, Albert C., jt. auth. see Sinden, J. A.

Worrell, W. L., jt. ed. see Rosenblatt, G. M.

Worsham, Fabian. The Green Kangaroo. pap. 3.00 o.s.i. (ISBN 0-686-81812-1). Anhinga Pr.

Worsham, Genevieve. Cotton Carta. LC 77-83627. (Illus.). (gr. 2-4). 1978. PLB 6.75x (ISBN 0-87783-144-0); pap. 2.95x deluxe ed. (ISBN 0-87783-149-1). Oddo.

Worsham, John P. Checklist of Major Federal Actions Significantly Affecting the National Environment: An Information Resource Survey of Environmental Impact Statements, 1970-77. (Public Administration Ser.: No. P 133). 1978. pap. 5.50 o.p. (ISBN 0-88066-009-0). Vance Biblios.

Worsley, J. R. Talking about Acupuncture. 1982. 25.00x (ISBN 0-906540-24-0, Pub. by Element Bks). State Mutual Bk.

Worsley, J. R., jt. auth. see Points & Meridians.

Worsley, Peter. Marx & Marxism. (Key Sociologists Ser.). 1982. pap. 3.95x (ISBN 0-85312-375-6). Methuen Inc.

Worst, Edward. Foot Treadle Loom Weaving. rev ed. (Illus.). 1975. pap. 4.95 o.p. (ISBN 0-88930-011-9, Pub. by Cloudburst Canada). Madrona Pubs.

Worster, Donald. Dust Bowl: The Southern Plains in the 1930's. (Illus.). 1979. 19.95x (ISBN 0-19-502550-4). Oxford U Pr.

Worsthorne, Simon T. Venetian Opera in the Seventeenth Century. 1954. 36.00x o.p. (ISBN 0-19-816116-6). Oxford U Pr.

Worstman, Gail L. Gail Worstman's Goodtime Hardtimes Cookbook. LC 82-81587. 165p. 1982. pap. 8.95 (ISBN 0-933686-01-3). Gray Beard.

Worswick, Clark, ed. Imperial China: Photography, Eighteen Fifty to Nineteen Twelve. 1978. pap. 12.95 o.p. (ISBN 0-517-53538-6). Crown.

Worswick, G. David, ed. The Concept & Measurement of Involuntary Unemployment. LC 75-42385. 1976. 42.00 o.p. (ISBN 0-89158-527-3). Westview.

Worth. Labor & Delivery. 1983. write for info. (ISBN 0-07-071818-0); pap. write for info. McGraw.

Worth, C. Breastfeeding Basics. 128p. 1983. 14.95 (ISBN 0-07-071816-4); pap. 6.95 (ISBN 0-07-071815-6). McGraw.

--Labor & Birth: A Coaching Guide for Fathers & Friends. (Having a Baby Ser.). 160p. 1983. 14.95 (ISBN 0-07-071818-0, GB); pap. 6.95. McGraw.

Worth, Cliff L., ed. Loss or Damage Claims Against Carriers-Guide to Traffic Procedures for Printers & Converters: L. 2nd ed. 31p. 1982. 14.95 (ISBN 0-89852-398-2, 01 01 R098). TAPPI.

Worth, Fred L. The Complete Unabridged Super Trivia Encyclopedia, Vol. II. 624p. 1981. pap. 3.95 (ISBN 0-446-90493-7). Warner Bks.

Worth, Fred L., jt. auth. see McCombs, Don.

Worth, George J. William H. Ainsworth. (English Authors Ser.). 14.95 (ISBN 0-8057-1008-6, Twayne). G K Hall.

Worth, H. G. & Curnow, D. H. Metabolic Pathways in Medicine. 192p. 1980. text ed. 29.50 (ISBN 0-7131-4336-3). E Arnold.

Worth, Maureen R., jt. auth. see Van Hoose, William H.

Worth, Maureen R., jt. auth. see VanHoose, William H.

Worth, Melvin H. Principles & Practice of Trauma Care. (Illus.). 438p. 1982. lib. bdg. 39.95 (ISBN 0-683-09295-2). Williams & Wilkins.

Worth, Richard. Israel & the Arab States. (Impact Ser.). 96p. (gr. 7 up). 1983. PLB 8.90 (ISBN 0-531-04545-5). Watts.

--Poland: The Treat to National Renewal. (Impact Bks). (Illus.). 96p. (gr. 7 up). 1982. PLB 8.90 (ISBN 0-531-04424-6). Watts.

Worth, Robert M. & Shah, Narayan K. Nepal Health Survey, 1965-1966. LC 72-76764. (Illus., Orig.). 1969. pap. text ed. 8.00x (ISBN 0-87022-870-6). UH Pr.

Worth, Thomas. Basic for Everyone. (Illus.). 368p. 1976. 16.95 (ISBN 0-13-061481-5); pap. write for info. P-H.

--Cobol for Beginners. (Illus.). 1977. pap. text ed. 17.95 (ISBN 0-13-139378-2). P-H.

Worth, Veryl M. Willow Pattern China: With Separate Price Guide. 2nd ed. (Illus.). 1981. pap. 9.95 (ISBN 0-939248-01-8); write for info. price guide (ISBN 0-939248-02-6). H S Worth.

Wortham, Thomas, et al, eds. Selected Letters of W. D. Howells, Vol. 4: 1892-1901. (Critical Editions Program). 1981. lib. bdg. 30.00 (ISBN 0-8057-8530-2, Twayne). G K Hall.

Worthame, Jim. Notes to Help Me Hang in There. LC 79-91345. 1980. 12.50 (ISBN 0-89002-128-7); pap. 5.00 (ISBN 0-89002-127-9). Northwoods Pr.

Worthing, Charles R., ed. The Pesticide Manual. 6th ed. 655p. 1979. 59.95x (ISBN 0-901436-44-5, Pub. by British Crop Protection England). Intl Schol Bk Serv.

Worthing, Michelle G. Elements of Music: A Programmed Approach. 2nd ed. 272p. 1983. write for info. wire coil bndg. (ISBN 0-697-03564-6). Wm C Brown.

Worthington, Avis. Bitter Honey. (Orig.). 1980. pap. 2.25 o.p. (ISBN 0-523-40573-1). Pinnacle Bks.

--Love's Willing Servant. 384p. (Orig.). 1980. pap. 2.50 o.p. (ISBN 0-523-41017-4). Pinnacle Bks.

Worthington, Bonnie & Taylor, Lynda. A Doctor Discusses Nutrition During Pregnancy & Breast Feeding. (Illus.). 1981. pap. 2.50 (ISBN 0-686-70167-4). Budlong.

Worthington, E. B., ed. The Evolution of IBP, Vol. 1. LC 75-2722. (International Biological Programme Ser.). (Illus.). 276p. 1975. 55.00 (ISBN 0-521-20736-3). Cambridge U Pr.

Worthington, E. Barton, ed. Arid Land Irrigation in Developing Countries: Environmental Problems & Effects. 1977. text ed. 115.00 (ISBN 0-08-021588-2). Pergamon.

Worthington, Frank see Swan, D. K.

Worthington, George E. & Topping, Ruth. Specialized Courts Dealing with Sex Delinquency, a Study of the Procedure in Chicago, Boston, Philadelphia, & New York. LC 69-14954. (Criminology, Law Enforcement, & Social Problems Ser.: No. 50). 1969. Repr. of 1925 ed. 18.00x (ISBN 0-87585-050-2). Patterson Smith.

Worthington, Joan, jt. auth. see Worthington, Phoebe.

Worthington, Lowell. Forty-Five & Satisfied. write for info. (ISBN 0-89137-313-6). Quality Pubns.

Worthington, Phoebe & Worthington, Joan. Teddy Bear Gardener. (Illus.). 16p. (ps). 1983. 6.95 (ISBN 0-7232-2969-4). Warne.

Worthington, Vivian. A History of Yoga. 176p. 1982. pap. 8.95 (ISBN 0-7100-9258-X). Routledge & Kegan.

Worthington-Williams, Mike, ed. Vintage Car Annual. (Illus.). 1979. 16.50x o.p. (ISBN 0-906116-08-2). Intl Pubns Serv.

Worthley, Jean R. The Complete Family Nature Guide. (Illus.). 1977. pap. 2.25 o.p. (ISBN 0-380-01651-6, 33092). Avon.

Wortis, Joseph, ed. Mental Retardation & Developmental Disabilities: An Annual Review. Incl. Vol. 5. 1973. o.p. (ISBN 0-87630-068-9); Vol. 6. 1974. (ISBN 0-87630-087-5); Vol. 7. 1975 (ISBN 0-685-57357-5); Vol. 8. 1976 (ISBN 0-87630-123-5); Vol. 9. 1977 (ISBN 0-87630-138-3); Vol. 10. 1978 (ISBN 0-87630-170-7); Vol. 11. LC 73-647002. 1979 (ISBN 0-87630-214-2). Vols. 6, 8, 11. 25.00 ea. Brunner-Mazel.

Wortley, Ben A. Jurisprudence. LC 66-29259. 473p. 1967. 19.00 (ISBN 0-379-00323-6). Oceana.

Wortley, Ben A., ed. Introduction to the Law of the European Economic Community. LC 72-39410. (Melland Schill Lecture Ser.: No. 12). 134p. 1972. lib. bdg. 11.00 (ISBN 0-379-11912-9). Oceana.

--Law of the Common Market. LC 74-6695. 248p. 1974. 17.50 (ISBN 0-379-11914-5). Oceana.

Wortley, Rothesay S. Letters from a Flying Officer. (Illus.). 192p. 1982. pap. text ed. 8.25x (ISBN 0-86299-017-3, Pub. by Sutton England). Humanities.

Wortman, Camille, jt. auth. see Loftus, Elizabeth.

Wortman, Doris N., ed. Double-Crostics Omnibus, No. 7. 1972. 3.95 o.p. (ISBN 0-671-21415-2, Fireside). S&S.

Wortman, Elmo. Almost Too Late. LC 81-40242. 288p. 1981. 13.50 (ISBN 0-394-50935-8). Random.

Wortman, Julie A. & Johnson, David P. Legacies: Kansas' Older County Courthouses. LC 81-84055. (Illus.). 64p. pap. 3.00 (ISBN 0-87726-025-7). Kansas St Hist.

Wortman, Leon. Business Problem Solving Using the IBM Pc. 416p. 1983. 27.95 (ISBN 0-89303-281-6); pap. 21.95 (ISBN 0-89303-282-4). R J Brady.

Wortman, Leon A. Effective Management for Engineers & Scientists. LC 80-19665. 275p. 1981. 24.95x (ISBN 0-471-05523-9, Ronald Pr). Wiley.

--Sales Manager's Problem-Solver. 272p. 1983. 19.95 (ISBN 0-471-09775-6). Ronald Pr.

Wortman, Marlene S., et al, eds. Women in American Law, Sixteen Fifty to Nineteen Eighty: A Documentary Perspective in Legal & Social History. 250p. 1983. text ed. 45.00x (ISBN 0-8419-0752-8); pap. text ed. 19.75x (ISBN 0-8419-0753-6). Holmes & Meier.

Wortman, Max S., jt. auth. see Hodgetts, Richard M.

Wortmann, J. C., jt. auth. see Bertrand, J. W.

Wortmen, Max S., Jr. & Luthans, Fred. Emerging Concepts in Management. 2nd ed. (Illus.). 480p. 1975. pap. text ed. 9.95 (ISBN 0-02-430040-3). Macmillan.

Worton, Scott M., jt. auth. see Hayes, Paul W.

Wortz, Melinda. UC Irvine. (Illus.). 96p. 1975. 7.00X (ISBN 0-686-99815-4). La Jolla Mus Contemp Art.

Worzbyt, John C., jt. auth. see Quirk, John P.

Woshinsky, Oliver H., jt. auth. see Coogan, William H.

Wosmek, Frances. The ABC of Ecology. LC 82-70224. (Illus.). 60p. (Orig., Eng. & Span.). (ps-3). 1982. pap. 2.50 (ISBN 0-943864-00-3). Davenport.

Wotkyns, Roger S., jt. auth. see Eiseman, Ben.

Wotruba, Thomas. Sales Management. 1980. text ed. 24.50x (ISBN 0-673-16142-0). Scott F.

Wotzkow, Helm. Art of Hand-Lettering: Its Mastery & Practice. (Illus.). (YA) (gr. 9-12). pap. 4.95 (ISBN 0-486-21797-3). Dover.

Wouk, A. A Course of Applied Functional Analysis. (Pure & Applied Mathematics Ser.). 443p. 1979. text ed. 41.50x (ISBN 0-471-96238-4, Pub. by Wiley-Interscience). Wiley.

Wouk, Herman. Aurora Dawn. 1983. pap. 2.95 (ISBN 0-686-84926-4). PB.

--The Caine Mutiny. 1983. pap. 4.95 (ISBN 0-671-83356-1). PB.

--Don't Stop the Carnival. 1983. pap. 3.95 (ISBN 0-686-84927-2). PB.

--Winds of War: T. V. tie-in edition. LC 77-70195. 1983. pap. 4.95 (ISBN 0-671-83312-X). PB.

Wowk, Kathleen. Playing Cards of the World. 160p. 1982. 60.00x (ISBN 0-7188-2408-3, Pub. by Lutterworth Pr England). State Mutual Bk.

--Playing Cards of the World. (Illus.). 160p. 1982. 25.00 (ISBN 0-7188-2408-3). US Games Syst.

Woy, James B., ed. Business Trends & Forecasting Information Sources. LC 65-28351. (Management Information Guide Ser.: No. 9). 1965. 42.00x (ISBN 0-8103-0809-6). Gale.

--Investment Information: A Detailed Guide to Selected Sources. LC 79-118791. (Management Information Guides Ser.: No. 19). 1970. 42.00x (ISBN 0-8103-0819-3). Gale.

Woy, Jean, ed. see Alexander, Herbert.

Woy, Jean, ed. see Baum, Lawrence.

Woy, Jean, ed. see Palley, Marion & Hale, George.

Woyczynski, W. A., jt. ed. see Chao, J. A.

Woytek, S. J., jt. auth. see Weiland, R. G.

Wozencraft, John M. & Jacobs, I. M. Principles of Communication Engineering. LC 65-16429. 1965. 48.95x (ISBN 0-471-96240-6). Wiley.

Wozner, Yochanan, jt. auth. see Wolins, Martin.

Wozniak, John M. English Composition in Eastern Colleges 1850-1940. LC 78-59125. (Illus.). 1978. pap. text ed. 12.75 (ISBN 0-8191-0549-X). U Pr of Amer.

Wozniak, John S. Contact, Negotiation, & Conflict: An Ethnohistory of the Eastern Dakota, 1819-1839. LC 78-62248. 1978. pap. text ed. 9.50 (ISBN 0-8191-0569-4). U Pr of Amer.

Wozniak, Robert H., jt. auth. see Osier, Donald V.

Wozniakowski, H., jt. auth. see Traub, J. F.

Woznicki, Andrew N. Journey to the Unknown: Catholic Doctrine on Ethnicity & Migration. 105p. (Orig.). 1982. pap. 3.95 (ISBN 0-910727-01-5). Golden Phoenix.

WPA Writer's Project. Negro in Virginia. LC 69-18577. (American Negro: His History & Literature Ser., No. 2). 1969. Repr. of 1940 ed. 14.00 (ISBN 0-405-01910-6). Ayer Co.

Wragg, David W. Publicity & Customer Relations in Transport Management. 144p. 1982. text ed. 33.00x (ISBN 0-566-00442-9). Gower Pub Ltd.

Wraith, R. E. & Hutchesson, P. G. Administrative Tribunals. (Royal Institute of Public Administration). 1973. text ed. 49.95x o.p. (ISBN 0-04-347002-5). Allen Unwin.

Wraith, Ronald. Local Administration in West Africa. rev. ed. LC 72-76471. 235p. 1972. text ed. 24.50x (ISBN 0-8419-0123-6, Africana). Holmes & Meier.

Wrangham, Elizabeth. The Communications Revolution. Yapp, Malcolm, et al, eds. (World History Ser.). (Illus.). 32p. (gr. 10). 1980. Repr. of 1977 ed. lib. bdg. 6.95 (ISBN 0-89908-134-7); pap. text ed. 2.25 (ISBN 0-89908-109-6). Greenhaven.

Wrangham, Elizabeth, et al. The Family. Yapp, Malcolm, et al, eds. (World History Ser.). (Illus.). 32p. (gr. 10). 1980. lib. bdg. 6.95 (ISBN 0-89908-148-7); pap. text ed. 2.25 (ISBN 0-89908-123-1). Greenhaven.

Wrasman, Marilyn W. & Haag, Diana B. Speak for Yourself. Ring, Constance, tr. (Illus.). 106p. 1976. pap. text ed. 4.95 o.p. (ISBN 0-914296-57-4). Activity Rec.

Wratten, Stephen D., jt. auth. see Edwards, Peter.

Wray, Evelyn. Horror at Henning House. (YA) 1980. 6.95 (ISBN 0-686-73933-7, Avalon). Bouregy.

Wray, G. R. Modern Yarn Production from Man-Made Fibres. 9.00 o.p. (ISBN 0-87245-404-5). Textile Bk.

Wray, Gordon R., jt. auth. see Duxbury, Victor.

Wray, Harry & Conroy, Hilary, eds. Japan Examined: Perspectives on Modern Japanese History. LC 82-15926. 421p. 1983. lib. bdg. 22.50x (ISBN 0-8248-0806-1); pap. text ed. 12.95x (ISBN 0-8248-0839-8). UH Pr.

Wray, J. Harry, jt. auth. see Holsworth, Robert D.

Wray, Lynn & Meyer, Leo. National Standards for Total System Balance: Air Distribution-Hydronic Systems-Sound. 1982. 45.00 (ISBN 0-910289-00-X). Assoc Air Balance.

Wray, M. & Hill, S. Employer Involvement in Schemes of Unified Vocational Preparation. (NFER Research Publications). 152p. 1982. pap. text ed. 16.75x (ISBN 0-7005-0492-3, NFER). Humanities.

Wray, Ralph. Advertising Services. Lynch, Richard, ed. (Career Competencies in Marketing). (Illus.). 1979. pap. text ed. 7.32 (ISBN 0-07-071900-4, G); tchr's manual & key 4.50 (ISBN 0-07-071901-2). McGraw.

Wrede, Patricia C. Daughter of Witches. 2.50 (ISBN 0-686-83918-8, Pub. by Ace Science Fiction). Ace Bks.

Wrede, Robert C. Introduction to Vector & Tensor Analysis. 418p. 1972. pap. text ed. 7.50 (ISBN 0-486-61879-X). Dover.

Wrede, Stuart. The Architecture of Erik Gunnar Asplund. (Illus.). 1980. 30.00x (ISBN 0-262-23095-X). MIT Pr.

Wrede, William. Messianic Secret. Greig, J. C., tr. 314p. 1972. 19.95 (ISBN 0-227-67717-X). Attic Pr.

Wreen, Michael see Beardsley, Monroe C.

Wren, A., ed. Computer Scheduling of Public Transportation: Urban Passenger Vehicle & Crew Scheduling. 1981. 51.00 (ISBN 0-444-86170-X). Elsevier.

Wren, Brian. Education for Justice: Pedagogical Principles. LC 77-8696. 160p. (Orig.). 1982. pap. 7.95x (ISBN 0-88344-110-1). Orbis Bks.

Wren, Carol T., et al, eds. Language Learning Disabilities: Diagnosis & Remediation. 1983. price not set (ISBN 0-89443-935-9). Aspen Systems.

Wren, Daniel A. Evolution of Management Thought. 2nd ed. LC 78-10959. (Management & Administration Ser.). 1979. text ed. 31.95 (ISBN 0-471-04695-7). Wiley.

Wren, Daniel A. & Voich, Dan, Jr. Principles of Management: Process & Behavior. 2nd ed. LC 75-43472. 1976. 30.50 (ISBN 0-471-06628-1, Pub. by Wiley-Hamilton). Wiley.

Wren, F. L., jt. auth. see Butler, D. H.

Wren, Melvin C. The Course of Russian History. 4th ed. (Illus.). 1979. text ed. 25.95 (ISBN 0-02-430130-2). Macmillan.

Wren, Percival C. The Disappearance of General Jason. 438p. 1973. Repr. of 1940 ed. 15.00 (ISBN 0-686-53001-2). Ultramarine Pub.

Wrench, David. Readings in Psychology: Foundations & Applications. 1971. 9.95 o.p. (ISBN 0-07-071921-7, C). McGraw.

Wrench, G. T. The Wheel of Health: The Sources of Long Life & Health Among the Hunza. LC 72-80274. 147p. 1972. pap. 1.75 o.p. (ISBN 0-8052-0355-9). Schocken.

Wrenn, C. Gilbert. The World of the Contemporary Counselor. LC 72-4800. 368p. (Orig.). 1973. pap. text ed. 14.95 (ISBN 0-395-13901-5). HM.

Wrenn, C. Gilbert, jt. auth. see Schwarzrock, Shirley.

Wrenn, C. L. The English Language. 1977. pap. 9.95x (ISBN 0-416-85810-4). Methuen Inc.

--W. B. Yeats. 1982. lib. bdg. 34.50 (ISBN 0-686-81935-7). Porter.

Wrenn, C. L., jt. auth. see Quirk, Randolph.

Wrenn, Catherine B., jt. auth. see Kreith, Frank.

Wrenn, Harold H., jt. auth. see Boas, George.

Wrenn, John H. John Dos Passos. (United States Author Ser.). 1961. lib. bdg. 11.95 (ISBN 0-8057-0208-3, Twayne). G K Hall.

Wrenn, Lawrence G. Annulments. 3rd ed. 150p. (Orig.). 1978. pap. 4.00x (ISBN 0-943616-01-8). Canon Law Soc.

--Decisions. 182p. (Orig.). 1980. pap. 4.50x (ISBN 0-943616-02-6). Canon Law Soc.

Wreto, Tore. Johan Ludvig Runeberg. (World Author Ser.). 1980. lib. bdg. 15.95 (ISBN 0-8057-6344-9, Twayne). G K Hall.

Wriggins, W. Howard & Adler-Karlsson, Gunnar. Reducing Global Inequities. (Nineteen Eighties Project (Council on Foreign Relations)). 1978. text ed. 10.95 o.p. (ISBN 0-07-071925-X, P&RB); pap. text ed. 5.95 (ISBN 0-07-071926-8). McGraw.

Wrigglesworth, Hazel J., tr. An Anthology of Ilianen Manobo Folktales. (San Carlos Humanities Ser.: No. 11). 299p. 1982. 15.75 (ISBN 0-686-37561-0, Pub. by San Carlos Philippines); pap. 12.00 (ISBN 0-686-37562-9). Cellar.

Wright. Extractive Metallurgy of Tin Process Metallurgy. 1982. 76.75 (ISBN 0-444-42113-0). Elsevier.

--Lettering. (Grosset Art Introduction Ser.: Vol. 21). pap. 2.95 (ISBN 0-448-00530-1, G&D). Putnam Pub Group.

Wright, jt. auth. see Sell.

Wright, A. & Newberry, P. G. Electric Fuses. (IEE Power Ser.: No. 2). 208p. 1982. pap. 36.00 (ISBN 0-906048-78-8). Inst Elect Eng.

Wright, A., jt. auth. see Byrne, D.

Wright, A. D. Counter Reformation. LC 82-3210. 344p. 1982. 25.00x (ISBN 0-312-17021-1). St Martin.

Wright, A. E. & Moseley, F. Ice Ages: Ancient & Modern; Geological Journal Special Issue, No. 6. (Liverpool Geological Society & the Manchester Geological Association). 320p. 1980. 67.95 (ISBN 0-471-27753-3, Pub. by Wiley-Interscience). Wiley.

Wright, A. Nelson & Winkler, Carl A. Active Nitrogen. (Physical Chemistry Ser.: Vol. 14). 1968. 78.00 (ISBN 0-12-765150-0). Acad Pr.

Wright, Andrew. Anthony Trollope: Dream & Art. LC 82-13365. 192p. 1983. lib. bdg. 20.00x (ISBN 0-226-90806-2). U of Chicago Pr.

--A Reader's Guide to English & American Literature. 1970. pap. 7.97x (ISBN 0-673-05697-X). Scott F.

--Visual Materials for the Language Teacher. (Longman Handbooks for Language Teachers). (Illus.). 192p. 1975. pap. text ed. 8.95x (ISBN 0-582-52267-6). Longman.

Wright, Andrew see Allen, W. S.

Wright, Andrew, jt. auth. see Altick, Richard D.

Wright, Ann, jt. auth. see Wright, James.

Wright, Anne, ed. see Wright, James.

Wright, Annie M. Grandma Mae Cooks with Love: A Superior Selection of Southern & Other Favorities. LC 81-90429. 37p. 1982. 6.95 (ISBN 0-533-05183-5). Vantage.

Wright, B. D. & Mayers, P. L. Interactive Statistics for Education. Date not set. price not set (ISBN 0-07-072081-9). McGraw.

Wright, Barbara, tr. see Queneau, Raymond.

Wright, Beatrice A. Physical Disability: A Psychological Approach. 512p. Date not set. text ed. 20.50 scp (ISBN 0-06-047241-3, HarpC). Har-Row. Postponed.

Wright, Becky A. Collection of Employer Contributions: Institute Proceedings, May 10-13, 1982, Las Vegas. 103p. (Orig.). 1982. pap. 10.00 (ISBN 0-89154-196-9). Intl Found Employ.

Wright, Becky A., ed. Benefit Plan Professionals Institute: Proceedings, June 20-23, 1982, Lake Tahoe, Nev. 82p. (Orig.). 1982. pap. 10.00 (ISBN 0-89154-199-3). Intl Found Employ.

--EDP Institute Proceedings, Dec. 13-16, 1981. 111p. (Orig.). 1982. pap. 10.00 (ISBN 0-89154-178-0). Intl Found Employ.

--Food Industry Institute Proceedings April 18-21, 1982. 99p. (Orig.). 1982. pap. 10.00 (ISBN 0-89154-197-7). Intl Found Employ.

Wright, Benjamin C. Banking in California 1849-1910. Bruchey, Stuart, ed. LC 80-1173. (The Rise of Commercial Banking Ser.). (Illus.). 1981. Repr. of 1910 ed. lib. bdg. 18.00x (ISBN 0-405-13686-2). Ayer Co.

Wright, Benjamin D. & Masters, Geofferey N. Rating Scale Analysis. LC 81-84992. (Illus.). 1982. 24.00 (ISBN 0-941938-01-8). Mesa Pr IL.

Wright, Benjamin F., ed. see Hamilton, Alexander, et al.

Wright, Betty, ed. see Glades County Commissioners & Bass, Billy O.

Wright, Beverly W. God Made Everything. Mahany, Patricia, ed. LC 82-80029. (Happy Day Bks.). (Illus.). 24p. (Orig.). (ps-3). 1982. pap. 1.29 (ISBN 0-87239-537-5, 3583). Standard Pub.

Wright, Brian. Canal Children. (Orig.). (RL 5). 1979. pap. 1.50 o.p. (ISBN 0-451-08668-6, W8668, Sig). NAL.

Wright, Bruce. Black Robes White Justice. 216p. Date not set. cancelled (ISBN 0-13-077636-X). P-H. Postponed.

Wright, C. Frege's Conception of Numbers As Objects. 150p. 1983. pap. 16.50 (ISBN 0-08-025726-7). Pergamon.

Wright, C. D. Translations of the Gospel Back into Tongues. (SUNY Poetry Ser.). 84p. 1982. 19.50x (ISBN 0-87395-652-4); pap. 6.95 (ISBN 0-87395-685-0). State U NY Pr.

Wright, C. D., ed. see Forch, Carolyn.

Wright, Carol. Hotels. LC 78-61229. (Careers Ser.). PLB 12.68 (ISBN 0-382-06197-7). Silver.

--The Travel Survival Guide. 192p. 1983. 17.50 (ISBN 0-7153-8310-8). David & Charles.

Wright, Carol von Presseltin. New York. (Blue Guides Ser.). 1983. 22.00x (ISBN 0-393-01559-9); pap. 12.70x (ISBN 0-393-30011-0). Norton.

Wright, Carroll. The Industrial Evolution of the United States. (History of American Economy Ser). Repr. 15.00 (ISBN 0-384-69425-X). Johnson Repr.

Wright, Charles. Country Music: Selected Early Poems. LC 82-8626. 161p. 1982. 15.00 (ISBN 0-8195-5066-3); pap. 8.95 (ISBN 0-8195-6075-8). Wesleyan U Pr.

--The Southern Cross: Poems. 1981. 10.50 (ISBN 0-394-52148-X); pap. 5.95 (ISBN 0-394-74888-3). Random.

Wright, Charles & Neil, Charles, eds. The Protestant Dictionary: Containing Articles on the History, Doctrines, & Practices of the Christian Church. LC 73-155436. 1971. Repr. of 1933 ed. 56.00x (ISBN 0-8103-3388-0). Gale.

Wright, Charles A. Handbook of the Law of Federal Courts. 4th ed. (Hornbook Ser.). 773p. 1983. text ed. write for info. (ISBN 0-314-71354-9). West Pub.

--Handbook on the Law of Federal Courts. 4th ed. (Hornbook Ser.). 900p. 1983. write for info (ISBN 0-314-74293-X). West Pub.

Wright, Charles D. Clearing Away. 1980. pap. 4.00 o.p. (ISBN 0-917652-22-3). Confluence Pr.

Wright, Charles H. Zechariah & His Prophecies. 1980. 24.95 (ISBN 0-86524-020-5, 3801). Klock & Klock.

Wright, Charlotte. A Fish Feast. 132p. (Orig.). 1982. pap. 6.95 (ISBN 0-87418-73-8). Pacific Search.

Wright, Christopher. Rembrandt & His Art. (The Artist & His Art Ser.). (Illus.). 128p. 1981. 9.98 o.p. (ISBN 0-89196-089-9, Bk Value Intl). Quality Bks IL.

--Rembrandt Self-Portraits. LC 82-70176. (Illus.). 144p. 1982. 25.00 (ISBN 0-670-59356-7, Studio). Viking Pr.

Wright, Christopher, ed. see Bunyan, John.

Wright, Christopher, ed. see Walton, Mrs. O. F.

Wright, Conrad. Religion in American Life. LC 72-180481. (Life in America Ser). (Illus.). 182p. (gr. 7-12). 1972. pap. text ed. 7.68 (ISBN 0-395-03145-1). HM.

Wright, Creighton B. Vascular Grafting: Clinical Applications & Techniques. (Illus.). 384p. 1983. text ed. write for info. (ISBN 0-7236-7023-4). Wright-PSG.

Wright, Cynthia. Alphabet Soup. 60p. (Orig.). 1981. pap. text ed. 8.95 (ISBN 0-8497-5900-5). Kjos.

--Spring Fires. 432p. (Orig.). 1983. pap. 3.50 (ISBN 0-345-27514-4). Ballantine.

Wright, D. Frankin. Arithmetic for College Students. 3rd ed. 1979. text ed. 18.95 (ISBN 0-669-01050-2); instr's manual 1.95 (ISBN 0-669-01049-9); study guide 6.95x (ISBN 0-669-01706-X). Heath.

Wright, D. Franklin. Arithmetic for College Students. 4th ed. 432p. 1983. text ed. 19.95 (ISBN 0-669-04857-7). Heath.

Wright, D. G. Revolution & Terror in France 1789-95. (Seminar Studies in History). 146p. 1974. pap. text ed. 5.95x (ISBN 0-582-35209-6). Longman.

Wright, David. Metrical Observations. 41p. 1980. pap. text ed. write for info. (ISBN 0-85635-309-4, Pub. by Carcanet New Pr England). Humanities.

--To the Gods the Shades. (Poetry Ser.). 1979. 9.95 o.p. (ISBN 0-85635-181-4, Pub. by Carcanet New Pr England). Humanities.

Wright, David & Andrejko, Dennis A. Passive Solar Architecture: Logic & Beauty. 256p. 1982. 24.95 (ISBN 0-442-23860-6); pap. 16.95 (ISBN 0-686-83194-2). Van Nos Reinhold.

Wright, David F., ed. Essays in Evangelical Social Ethics. 192p. pap. text ed. 8.95 (ISBN 0-85364-290-7). Attic Pr.

Wright, David M. Keynesian System. LC 62-15667. (Millar Lecture Ser: No. 4). 1962. 7.50 o.p. (ISBN 0-8232-0455-3). Fordham.

Wright, David W., jt. auth. see Cragan, John F.

Wright, Dermot. Marine Engines & Boating Mechanics. 1977. 19.95 o.p. (ISBN 0-7153-5988-6). David & Charles.

Wright, Donald R. The Early History of Niumi: Settlement & Foundation of Mandinka State on the Gambia River. LC 77-620032. (Papers in International Studies: Africa: No. 32). (Illus.). 1977. pap. 8.00x (ISBN 0-89680-064-4, Ohio U Ctr Intl). Ohio U Pr.

--Oral Traditions from the Gambia: Mandinka Griots, Vol. 1. LC 79-14855. (Papers in International Studies: Africa Ser.: No. 37). 1979. pap. text ed. 12.00 (ISBN 0-89680-083-0, Ohio U Ctr Intl). Ohio U Pr.

Wright, Donald R., ed. Oral Tradition from the Gambia: Vol. II: Family Elders. LC 79-14855. (Papers in International Studies: Africa: No. 38). 1980. pap. 15.00 (ISBN 0-89680-084-9, Ohio U Ctr Intl). Ohio U Pr.

Wright, Dudley. The Book of Vampires. 1973. Repr. of 1924 ed. 30.00x (ISBN 0-685-32597-0). Gale.

Wright, E. N. & Inglis, I. Bird Problems in Agriculture. 210p. 1980. 60.00x (ISBN 0-901436-48-8, CAB Bks). State Mutual Bk.

Wright, Edmund H., et al, eds. Scott Specialized Catalogue of Canadian Stamps & Covers 1983. (Illus.). 160p. 1982. pap. 3.50 (ISBN 0-89487-050-5). Scott Pub Co.

Wright, Elizabeth M. Rustic Speech & Folklore. LC 68-18011. 1968. Repr. of 1913 ed. 34.00x (ISBN 0-8103-3294-9). Gale.

Wright, Ellen, ed. see Wright, Richard.

Wright, Elliott. Holy Company: Christian Heros & Heroines. 1980. 12.95 (ISBN 0-02-631590-4). Macmillan.

Wright, Elliott, jt. auth. see Butt, Howard.

Wright, Erik O. Class, Crisis & the State. (Illus.). 1978. 19.50x (ISBN 0-902308-93-9, Pub by NLB); pap. 7.95 (ISBN 0-8052-7003-5). Schocken.

Wright, Ernest, jt. auth. see Boling, Robert G.

Wright, Eugene P. Thomas Deloney. (English Authors Ser.). 1981. lib. bdg. 13.95 (ISBN 0-8057-6761-4, Twayne). G K Hall.

Wright, Ezekiel & Inesse, Daniel. God Is Gay: An Evolutionary Spiritual Work. 1981. pap. 3.95 (ISBN 0-934350-00-0). Tayu Pr.

--God Is Gay: An Evolutionary Spiritual Work. 2nd, rev. ed. 1982. pap. 4.95 (ISBN 0-934350-01-9). Tayu Pr.

Wright, F. A., ed. Lempriere's Classical Dictionary. new rev. ed. 1969. Repr. of 1788 ed. 22.00 (ISBN 0-7100-1734-0). Routledge & Kegan.

Wright, F. F., jt. auth. see Council on Education in the Geological Sciences.

Wright, F. W. The Radiological Diagnosis of Lung & Mediastinal Tumours. Trapnell, David H., ed. (Radiology in Clinical Diagnosis Ser.: Vol. 6). (Illus.). 1973. 55.95 o.p. (ISBN 0-407-38385-9). Butterworth.

Wright, Fay. Out of Season. 1981. pap. 3.50 (ISBN 0-917652-26-6). Confluence Pr.

Wright, Frank L. Drawings & Plans of Frank Lloyd Wright: The Early Period (1893-1909) 2nd ed. Orig. Title: Ausgefuhrte Bauten Und Entwurfe Von Frank Lloyd Wright. (Illus.). 112p. 1983. pap. 9.95 (ISBN 0-486-24457-1). Dover.

--The Early Work of Frank Lloyd Wright. (Architecture Ser.). (Illus.). 160p. 1983. pap. 7.50 (ISBN 0-486-24381-8). Dover.

--Future of Architecture. 4.95 (ISBN 0-452-00521-3, F521, Mer). NAL.

Wright, Franz, tr. see Char, Rene.

Wright, Fred, et al, eds. Forensic Psychology & Psychiatry. LC 80-17982. (Annuals of the New York Academy of Sciences: Vol. 347). 364p. 1980. 60.00x (ISBN 0-89766-084-6); pap. 60.00x (ISBN 0-89766-085-4). NY Acad Sci.

Wright, Fred B., ed. see Symposium On Ergodic Theory - New Orleans - 1961.

Wright, G., jt. auth. see Moskowitz, H.

Wright, G. Ernest. Biblical Archaeology. rev. ed. LC 57-5020. (Illus.). 1963. 27.50 (ISBN 0-664-20420-1). Westminster.

--Isaiah. LC 59-10454. (Layman's Bible Commentary, Vol. 11). 1964. pap. 3.95 (ISBN 0-8042-3071-4). John Knox.

Wright, G. Ernest & Filson, F. V., eds. Westminster Historical Maps of Bible Lands. pap. 2.50 (ISBN 0-664-29077-9). Westminster.

Wright, G. Ernest & Freedman, David N., eds. The Biblical Archaeologist Reader, Vol. 1. LC 75-9592. 342p. 1975. text ed. 9.00x (ISBN 0-686-32090-5, Am Sch Orient Res); pap. text ed. 6.00x (ISBN 0-686-32091-3). Eisenbrauns.

Wright, G. H. The Libraries in Colleges of Commerce & Technology: A Guide to the Use of a Library as an Instrument of Education. 176p. 1966. 10.50 (ISBN 0-233-95837-1, 05831-9, Pub. by Gower Pub Co England). Lexington Bks.

Wright, G. H. von. Wittgenstein. 232p. 1983. 29.50x (ISBN 0-8166-1210-2); pap. 13.95x (ISBN 0-8166-1215-3). U of Minn Pr.

Wright, G. N. Bridges of Britain. 96p. 1981. 30.00x (ISBN 0-686-97139-6, Pub. by D B Barton England). State Mutual Bk.

Wright, G. R. & Marlo, J. Police Officer & Criminal Justice. 1970. text ed. 12.90 o.p. (ISBN 0-07-072097-5, G). McGraw.

Wright, Gene. The Science Fiction Image. 320p. 1983. 19.95x (ISBN 0-87196-527-5). Facts on File.

Wright, Genny, jt. auth. see Davis, Bruce.

Wright, Georg H. Von see Malcolm, Norman & Von Wright, Georg H.

Wright, George B., jt. auth. see Feldman, Edwin B.

Wright, George T. The Poet in the Poem. LC 74-2404. 167p. 1974. Repr. of 1960 ed. 9.00x (ISBN 0-87752-169-7). Gordian.

--W. H. Auden. rev. ed. (United States Authors Ser.). 1981. lib. bdg. 11.95 (ISBN 0-8057-7346-0, Twayne). G K Hall.

--W. H. Auden. LC 68-24302. (U. S. Authors Ser.: No. 144). 1969. lib. bdg. 10.95 o.p. (ISBN 0-8057-0028-5, Twayne). G K Hall.

Wright, Gertrude & Luedke, Ralph D., eds. Tempting Treasures Cookbook. 1978. pap. 3.25 o.p. (ISBN 0-89542-606-4). Ideals.

Wright, Glen. Gold of the Gods. LC 81-12864. (Fascinating Tales of the Pacific Ser.). (Illus.). (gr. 4 up). 1982. PLB 8.65g (ISBN 0-516-02471-X). Childrens.

--Land Divers of Pentecost. LC 81-81012737. (Fascinating Tales of the Pacific Ser.). (Illus.). (gr. 4 up). 1982. PLB 8.65g (ISBN 0-516-02472-8). Childrens.

--A Mountain Blows its Top. LC 81-12897. (Fascinating Tales of the Pacific Ser.). (Illus.). (gr. 4 up). 1982. PLB 8.65g (ISBN 0-516-02473-6). Childrens.

--The Pigeon with Nine Heads. LC 81-12879. (Fascinating Tales of the Pacific Ser.). (Illus.). (gr. 4 up). 1982. PLB 8.65g (ISBN 0-516-02474-4). Childrens.

--Snatched by a Killer Wave. LC 81-12877. (Fascinating Tales of the Pacific Ser.). (Illus.). (gr. 4 up). 1982. PLB 8.65g (ISBN 0-516-02475-2). Childrens.

--Unfriendly Natives of the Pacific. LC 81-12776. (Fascinating Tales of the Pacific Ser.). (Illus.). (gr. 4 up). 1982. PLB 8.65g (ISBN 0-516-02476-0). Childrens.

Wright, Glover. The Torch. 312p. 1980. 11.95 (ISBN 0-399-12479-9). Putnam Pub Group.

Wright, Gordon. Between the Guillotine & Liberty: Two Centuries of the Crime Problem in France. (Illus.). 288p. 1983. 19.95 (ISBN 0-19-503243-8). Oxford U Pr.

--Learning to Ride, Hunt & Show. rev. ed. LC 66-17404. (Illus.). 1966. 14.95 (ISBN 0-385-05182-4). Doubleday.

--Ordeal of Total War, 1939-1945. (Rise of Modern Europe Ser). pap. 5.95xi (ISBN 0-06-131408-0, TB1408, Torch). Har-Row.

Wright, Gordon P. & Olson, David G. Designing Water Pollution Detection Systems: Environmental Law Enforcement on the U.S. Coastal Waters & the Great Lakes. LC 74-7343. 416p. 1974. prof ref 20.00 (ISBN 0-88410-304-8). Ballinger Pub.

Wright, H. Beric. Executive Ease & Dis-Ease. LC 75-1072. 1975. 24.95x o.p. (ISBN 0-470-96450-2). Halsted Pr.

Wright, H. M., tr. see Coedes, G.

Wright, H. Norman. The Living Marriage. (Illus.). 128p. 1975. 11.95 (ISBN 0-8007-0722-2). Revell.

--Premarital Counseling. rev. ed. LC 77-2355. 1981. 12.95 (ISBN 0-8024-6812-8). Moody.

Wright, Harold, tr. see Tanikawa, Shuntaro.

Wright, Harold B. Shepherd of the Hills. 1958. 3.95 (ISBN 0-448-01056-9, G&D). Putnam Pub Group.

Wright, Harrison M., ed. New Imperialism: Analysis of Late Nineteenth Century Expansion. 2nd ed. (Problems in European Civilization Ser.). 1976. pap. text ed. 5.50 (ISBN 0-669-96008-X). Heath.

Wright, Hastings K. & Tilson, M. David. Postoperative Disorders of the Gastrointestinal Tract. (Illus.). 224p. 1973. 39.50 (ISBN 0-8089-0813-8). Grune.

Wright, Helen, intro. by. Factory Life As It Is. 1982. pap. 2.50 (ISBN 0-943730-00-7). Lowell Pub.

Wright, Helen, et al, eds. Legacy of George Ellery Hale. 1972. 40.00x (ISBN 0-262-23049-6). MIT Pr.

Wright, Henry A. & Bailey, Arthur W. Fire Ecology: United States & Southern Canada. LC 81-14770. 501p. 1982. 44.95x (ISBN 0-471-09033-6, Pub. by Wiley-Interscience). Wiley.

Wright, Henry B. The Campaign of Plataea: Campaign of Plataea: September, Four Hundred & Seventy-Nine B.C. 1904. pap. 29.50x (ISBN 0-685-89737-0). Elliots Bks.

Wright, Herbert E., Jr., ed. Late Quaternary Environments of the United States, Volume 2: The Holocene. (Illus.). 384p. 1983. 45.00x (ISBN 0-8166-1171-8). U of Minn Pr.

Wright, Howard C. Port Hudson: Its History from an Interior Point of View. (Illus.). 1978. pap. 4.50 o.p. (ISBN 0-686-04883-0). Eagle Pr.

Wright, Ione S. & Nekhom, Lisa M. Historical Dictionary of Argentina. LC 78-7918. (Latin American Historical Dictionaries Ser.: No. 17). 1978. 39.50 o.p. (ISBN 0-8108-1144-8). Scarecrow.

Wright, J. Eugene, Jr. Erikson: Identity & Religion. 240p. (Orig.). 1982. pap. 11.95 (ISBN 0-8164-2362-8). Seabury.

Wright, J. M., jt. auth. see Shaw, M. E.

Wright, J. Patrick. On a Clear Day You Can See General Motors. 304p. 1980. pap. 3.95 (ISBN 0-380-51722-1, 62992-5). Avon.

Wright, J. S., et al. Advertising. 5th ed. (Marketing Ser.). 1982. 24.95x (ISBN 0-07-072069-X); instr's. manual 20.95x (ISBN 0-07-072070-3). McGraw.

Wright, Jack & Lewis, Peter. Modern Criminal Justice. 1977. text ed. 25.50 (ISBN 0-07-072075-4, C). McGraw.

Wright, Jackson, jt. auth. see Farr, James A.

Wright, James. Collected Prose. Wright, Anne, ed. (Poets on Poetry Ser.). 352p. 1982. pap. 8.95 (ISBN 0-472-06344-8). U of Mich Pr.

--The History & Antiquities of the County of Rutland. (Classical County Histories Ser.). (Illus.). 229p. 1973. Repr. of 1790 ed. 27.50x o.p. (ISBN 0-87471-391-9). Rowman.

--Leave It to the Sunlight. 20p. (Orig.). 1981. pap. 2.50 o.p. (ISBN 0-937406-17-1). Logbridge-Rhodes.

--Moments of the Italian Summer. LC 76-40994. 1976. 15.00 (ISBN 0-931848-06-7); pap. 5.75 (ISBN 0-931848-07-5). Dryad Pr.

--A Reply to Matthew Arnold. 20p. (Orig.). 1981. pap. 2.50 o.p. (ISBN 0-937406-18-X). Logbridge-Rhodes.

--Saint Judas. LC 59-12481. 56p. pap. 6.95 (ISBN 0-8195-1110-2). Wesleyan U Pr.

--The Temple in Nimes. (Metacom Limited Edition Ser.: No. 5). 28p. 1982. ltd. 25.00x (ISBN 0-911381-04-X). Metacom Pr.

--This Journey. 91p. 1982. 10.00 (ISBN 0-394-52365-2). Random.

Wright, James & Wright, Ann. The Summers of James & Annie Wright. 100p. (Orig.). 1980. pap. 4.95 (ISBN 0-935296-18-2). Sheep Meadow.

Wright, James, tr. see Hesse, Hermann.

Wright, James, et al. Unmuzzled Ox Anthology, No. 13. Andre, Michael, ed. 1980. pap. 4.95 (ISBN 0-934450-06-4). Unmuzzled Ox.

Wright, Jean. Learning to Learn in Higher Education. (New Patterns of Learning Ser.). (Illus.). 214p. 1982. text ed. 28.00x (ISBN 0-7099-2744-4, Pub. by Croom Helm Ltd England). Biblio Dist.

Wright, Jeff, ed. see Codrescu, Andrei & Notley, Alice.

Wright, Jim. Bobby Clarke: Pride of the Team. (Putnam Sports Shelf). (Illus.). (gr. 6-8). 1977. PLB 6.29 o.p. (ISBN 0-399-61067-7). Putnam Pub Group.

--Mike Schmidt: Baseball's Young Lion. LC 78-12671. (Sports Shelf Biography Ser.). (Illus.). (gr. 5 up). 1979. PLB 6.99 o.p. (ISBN 0-399-61132-0). Putnam Pub Group.

Wright, John. Genius of Wordsworth. 1982. lib. bdg. 34.50 (ISBN 0-686-81937-3). Porter.

--Ground & Air Survey for Field Scientists. (Monographs on Soil & Resources Survey). (Illus.). 1982. 34.95x (ISBN 0-19-857560-2). Oxford U Pr.

--Military Collections at the Essex Institute. (E. I. Museum Booklet Ser.). (Illus.). 64p. Date not set. pap. text ed. 4.95 (ISBN 0-88389-104-2). Essex Inst. Postponed.

--Plautus: Curculio. Hornsby, Roger, ed. LC 81-846. (American Philological Association Textbook Ser.). 1981. pap. text ed. 6.95 (ISBN 0-89130-469-X, 40-03-06). Scholars Pr CA.

Wright, John, tr. see Bertrand, Louis A.

Wright, John G., et al, trs. see Trotsky, Leon.

Wright, John K. Aids to Geographical Research: Bibliographies, Periodicals, Atlases, Gazeteers & Other Reference Books. rev. ed. LC 73-106702. 1971. Repr. of 1947 ed. lib. bdg. 16.25x (ISBN 0-8371-3384-X, WRGR). Greenwood.

Wright, John P. The Sceptical Realism of David Hume. ix, 256p. 1983. 29.50x (ISBN 0-8166-1223-4); pap. 13.95x (ISBN 0-8166-1224-2). U of Minn Pr.

Wright, John S. & Mertes, John. Advertising's Role in Society. LC 74-1325. 350p. 1974. pap. text ed. 14.50 (ISBN 0-8299-0007-1). West Pub.

Wright, John S., et al. Advertising. 4th ed. (Illus.). 1977. text ed. 24.95 o.p. (ISBN 0-07-072067-3, C); instr's manual 11.50 o.p. (ISBN 0-07-072068-1). McGraw.

Wright, John W. The Commercial Connection. 1979. pap. 5.95 o.s.i. (ISBN 0-440-55286-9, Delta). Dell.

Wright, Jonathan R. Above Parties: The Political Attitudes of the German Protestant Church Leadership 1918-1933. (Oxford Historical Monographs Ser.). 1974. 22.50x o.p. (ISBN 0-19-821856-7). Oxford U Pr.

Wright, Judith. The Double Tree: Selected Poems 1942-1976. (New Poetry Ser.). 1978. 9.95 o.p. (ISBN 0-395-26480-4); pap. 5.95 o.p. (ISBN 0-395-26466-9). HM.

Wright, Judith, ed. New Land, New Language: An Anthology of Australian Verse. 1958. pap. 5.95x o.p. (ISBN 0-19-550298-1). Oxford U Pr.

Wright, Kathryn. Historic Homes of Billings. (Illus.). 112p. (Orig.). 1981. 12.95 (ISBN 0-934318-05-0); pap. 7.95 (ISBN 0-686-98518-4). Falcon Pr MT.

Wright, Keith, ed. see Codrescu, Andrei & Notley, Alice.

Wright, Kevin N. An Organizational Approach to Correctional Effectiveness. 83p. 1979. softcover 7.95 (ISBN 0-932930-10-7). Pilgrimage Inc.

Wright, L. L. Man & His Seven Principles: An Ancient Basis for a New Psychology. Small, Emmett & Todd, Helen, eds. (Theosophical Manual: No. 4). 1975. pap. 2.00 (ISBN 0-913004-21-9). Point Loma Pub.

Wright, Lance, jt. ed. see Boyne, D. A.

Wright, Larry. Teleological Explanations: An Etiological Analysis of Goals & Functions. LC 75-17284. 1976. 23.50x (ISBN 0-520-03086-9). U of Cal Pr.

Wright, Lawrence. Deep Fresh: The Fascinating History of the Bathroom & the Water Closet. 224p. (Orig.). 1980. pap. 7.95 (ISBN 0-7100-0647-0). Routledge & Kegan.

--Perspectives in Perspective. (Illus.). 300p. 1983. write for info. (ISBN 0-7100-0791-4). Routledge & Kegan.

Wright, Leigh R. & Allen, J. Dev. A Collection of Agreements & Other Documents Affecting the States of Malayasia, 1761-1763, 2 vols. LC 80-24804. 1981. 85.00 set (ISBN 0-379-00781-9). Oceana.

Wright, Leoline L. After Death, What? rev. ed. Small, W. Emmett & Todd, Helen, eds. (Theosophical Manual: No. 5). 96p. 1974. pap. 2.50 (ISBN 0-913004-15-4). Point Loma Pub.

Wright, Leoline L., et al. Reincarnation: A Lost Chord in Modern Thought. Small, Emmett & Todd, Helen, eds. (Theosophical Manual). 122p. 1975. pap. 3.25 (ISBN 0-8356-0453-5). Point Loma Pub.

Wright, Leonard M., Jr. Fly-Fishing Heresies: A New Gospel for American Anglers. (Illus.). 1978. pap. 5.95 o.s.i. (ISBN 0-695-80923-7). Follett.

Wright, Linda R. The Success Helper. 1980. 1.25 (ISBN 0-8423-6687-3). Tyndale.

Wright, Logan & Schaefer, Arlene B. Encyclopedia of Pediatric Psychology. 958p. 1979. text ed. 27.95 (ISBN 0-8391-1353-6). Univ Park.

Wright, Louis B. Everyday Life in Colonial America. (Everyday Life in America Ser.). (Illus.). (gr. 7-10). 1966. 6.75 o.p. (ISBN 0-399-20057-6). Putnam Pub Group.

--Tradition & the Founding Fathers. LC 74-23551. 1975. 9.95x (ISBN 0-8139-0621-0). U Pr of Va.

Wright, Louis B. & Fowler, Elaine. Everyday Life in the New Nation: 1787-1860. (Everday Life in America Ser.). (Illus.). 256p. (gr. 6 up). 1972. 6.75 o.p. (ISBN 0-399-20251-X). Putnam Pub Group.

Wright, Louis B. & Macleod, Julia H. First Americans in North Africa. Repr. of 1945 ed. lib. bdg. 15.00x o.p. (ISBN 0-8371-1861-1, WRFA). Greenwood.

Wright, Louis B., ed. Cultural Life of the American Colonies. (New American Nation Ser.). pap. 5.95xi o.p. (ISBN 0-06-133005-1, TB3005, Torch). Har-Row.

Wright, Louis B. & Fowler, Elaine W., eds. English Colonization in North America. LC 68-29505. (Documents of Modern History Ser). (Orig.). 1969. 18.95 (ISBN 0-312-25410-5). St Martin.

Wright, Louis B., ed. see Dodds, John W.

Wright, Louis B., ed. see Shakespeare, William.

Wright, Louis B., ed. see Strachey, William & Jourdain, Sylvester.

Wright, M. Use of Criminology Literature. 1974. 17.95 o.p. (ISBN 0-408-70548-5). Butterworth.

Wright, M. G. Discounted Cash Flow. 2nd ed. 1973. 24.95 (ISBN 0-07-084425-9, P&RB). McGraw.

Wright, M. I. Pathology of Deafness. 188p. 1971. 17.00 (ISBN 0-7190-0418-7). Manchester.

Wright, Margaret. Practical Optimization. LC 81-66366. 1981. 22.00 (ISBN 0-12-283952-8). Acad Pr.

Wright, Marion A. & Shankman, Arnold. Human Rights Odyssey. LC 78-50870. 1978. 12.95 (ISBN 0-87716-087-2, Pub. by Moore Pub Co). F Apple.

Wright, Marion I. & Sullivan, Robert J. The Rhode Island Atlas. (Illus.). 225p. (Orig., Contains considerable text). 1983. pap. 12.95 (ISBN 0-917012-19-4). RI Pubns Soc.

Wright, Mary. Cornish Guernsey & Knit-Frocks. 72p. 1980. 10.00x o.p. (ISBN 0-906720-05-2, Pub. by Hodge England). State Mutual Bk.

Wright, Mary C. The Last Stand of Chinese Conservatism: The T'ung-Chih Restoration, 1862-1874. xii, 426p. 1957. 25.00x (ISBN 0-8047-0475-9); pap. 8.95 (ISBN 0-8047-0476-7, SX128). Stanford U Pr.

Wright, Maurice, ed. Public Spending Decisions: Growth & Restraint in the 1970's. (Illus.). 1980. text ed. 30.00x (ISBN 0-04-350056-0). Allen Unwin.

Wright, Maurice, jt. ed. see Hood, Christopher.

Wright, Michael, ed. The Complete Book of Gardening. 1979. 20.00i (ISBN 0-397-01292-6). Har-Row.

--Complete Book of Gardening. (Illus.). 416p. 1980. pap. 14.95 (ISBN 0-446-37641-8). Warner Bks.

Wright, Michael & Brown, Dennis, eds. Complete Indoor Gardner. (Pan Bk Ser). (Illus.). 1975. 15.00 o.p. (ISBN 0-394-49594-2); pap. 7.95 o.p. (ISBN 0-394-73045-3). Random.

Wright, Mildred S. Jasper County, Texas Cemeteries. LC 76-44116. (Illus.). 1979. pap. 22.75 o.s.i. (ISBN 0-917016-05-X). M S Wright.

--St. Clair County, Alabama Genealogical Notes. LC 74-82803. (Illus.). pap. 10.00 (ISBN 0-917016-01-7). M S Wright.

--St. Clair County, Alabama Genealogical Notes, Vol. 2. LC 74-82803. (Illus.). viii, 67p. 1982. 17.50 (ISBN 0-917016-24-6); pap. 12.50 (ISBN 0-917016-25-4). M S Wright.

Wright, Mildred S. & Quick, William D. United States Spanish-American War Fortifications at the Sabine Pass, Texas. LC 82-99801. (Illus.). x, 50p. (Orig.). 1982. 20.00 (ISBN 0-917016-22-X); pap. 12.00 (ISBN 0-917016-23-8). M S Wright.

Wright, Mildred W. Henri Goes to the Mardi Gras. LC 78-136813. (Illus.). (gr. k-3). 1971. PLB 3.97 o.p. (ISBN 0-399-60233-X). Putnam Pub Group.

Wright, Nancy D. & Allen, Gene P., eds. National Directory of State Agencies, 1982-1983. LC 74-18864. v, 793p. 1982. text ed. 67.50 (ISBN 0-87815-042-0). Info Resources.

Wright, Nancy M. Down the Strings. 192p. (gr. 7 up). 1982. 10.95 (ISBN 0-525-66769-5, 01063-320). Lodestar Bks.

Wright, Nathalia, ed. The Complete Works of Washington Irving, Journals & Notebooks, Vol. 1: 1803-1806. (Critical Editions Program). 1969. lib. bdg. 32.00 (ISBN 0-8057-8500-0, Twayne). G K Hall.

Wright, Nicholas. The Red Baron. (Illus.). (gr. 6-8). 1977. PLB 7.95 (ISBN 0-07-072040-1, GB). McGraw.

Wright, Norm. Celebration of Marriage. LC 82-83835. (Illus.). 160p. (Orig.). 1983. pap. 4.95 (ISBN 0-89081-327-2). Harvest Hse.

Wright, Norman. Answer to Anger & Frustration. LC 76-51531. (Answer Ser.). 1977. pap. 1.95 (ISBN 0-89081-030-3, 0303). Harvest Hse.

--Answer to Depression. LC 76-21111. (Answer Ser.). 1976. pap. 1.95 (ISBN 0-89081-059-1, 0591). Harvest Hse.

--Answer to Discipline. LC 76-21113. (Answer Ser.). 1976. pap. 1.95 (ISBN 0-89081-061-3, 0613). Harvest Hse.

--Answer to Divorce. LC 76-52831. (Answer Ser.). 1977. pap. 1.95 (ISBN 0-89081-033-8, 0338). Harvest Hse.

--Answer to Family Communication. LC 76-52832. (Answer Ser.). 1977. pap. 1.95 (ISBN 0-89081-031-1, 0311). Harvest Hse.

--An Answer to Loneliness. (Orig.). pap. 1.95 (ISBN 0-89081-077-X). Harvest Hse.

--An Answer to Parent-Teen Relationships. (Orig.). pap. 1.95 (ISBN 0-89081-075-3). Harvest Hse.

--An Answer to Submission & Decision Making. pap. 1.95 (ISBN 0-89081-078-8). Harvest Hse.

--Answer to Worry & Anxiety. LC 76-21110. (Answer Ser.). 1976. pap. 1.95 (ISBN 0-89081-058-3, 0583). Harvest Hse.

--Fulfilled Marriage. LC 76-21981. (Answer Ser.). 1976. pap. 1.95 (ISBN 0-89081-060-5, 0605). Harvest Hse.

--Improving Your Self-Image. LC 76-51532. (Answer Ser.). 1977. pap. 1.95 (ISBN 0-89081-032-X, 032X). Harvest Hse.

Wright, Norman & Inmon, Marvin. Preparing Youth for Dating, Courtship & Marriage-Teacher's Guide. LC 78-56879. (Orig.). 1978. pap. 14.95 (ISBN 0-89081-147-4, 1474); transparencies & repro masters incl. Harvest Hse.

Wright, Norman P. A Mexican Medley for the Curious. 1961. 35.00 (ISBN 0-911268-30-8). Rogers Bk.

Wright, O., jt. auth. see Plossl, G.

Wright, P. & Cumming, A. P. Solid Polyurethane Elastomers. 338p. 1969. 64.00x (ISBN 0-677-61690-2). Gordon.

Wright, P. H. & Poquette, Radnor J. Highway Engineering. 4th ed. LC 78-13643. 1979. text ed. 39.95 (ISBN 0-471-07260-5); solutions manual avail. (ISBN 0-471-05981-1). Wiley.

Wright, P. Poyntz. The Parish Church Towers of Somerset: Their Construction, Craftsmanship & Chronology, 1350-1550. 1981. 100.00x o.p. (ISBN 0-686-75434-4, Pub. by Avebury Pub England). State Mutual Bk.

Wright, P. Wayne. Positive Power. 1983. 7.95 (ISBN 0-533-05596-2). Vantage.

Wright, Patricia. Heart of the Storm. LC 78-22775. 1980. 10.00 o.p. (ISBN 0-385-14232-3). Doubleday.

--The Storms of Fate. 512p. 1983. pap. 3.50 (ISBN 0-449-20176-7, Crest). Fawcett.

Wright, Patrick. Walkies. (Illus.). 64p. 1983. pap. 4.95 (ISBN 0-686-81851-2); pap. 49.50 prepack of 10. St Martin.

Wright, Paul H., jt. auth. see Ashford, Norman.

Wright, Philip L., jt. ed. see Nesbitt, W. H.

Wright, Quincy. Contemporary International Law: A Balance Sheet. rev. ed. (Orig.). 1961. pap. text ed. 2.45x (ISBN 0-685-19716-6). Phila Bk Co.

Wright, R. Glenn, jt. auth. see Harris, Mark.

Wright, R. Glenn, jt. auth. see Newman, Richard.

Wright, R. L. D. Understanding Statistics: An Informal Introduction for the Behavioral Sciences. (Illus.). 500p. 1976. text ed. 20.95 (ISBN 0-15-592877-5, HC); Using Statistics, a study guide to accompany Understanding Statistics, by Peter Johnson & R. L. Wright 6.95 (ISBN 0-15-592879-1). HarBraceJ.

Wright, Richard. American Hunger. LC 76-47248. 1977. 12.45i (ISBN 0-06-014768-7, HarpT). Har-Row.

--American Hunger. LC 76-47248. 1979. pap. 1.95i o.p. (ISBN 0-06-080464-5, P 464, PL). Har-Row.

--American Hunger. LC 76-47248. 160p. 1983. pap. 4.76i (ISBN 0-06-090991-9, CN 991, CN). Har-Row.

--Black Boy: A Record of Childhood & Youth. LC 79-83628. 1969. Repr. of 1945 ed. 15.34i (ISBN 0-06-014761-X, HarpT). Har-Row.

--Outsider. 1965. pap. 2.84i (ISBN 0-06-080022-4, P22, PL). Har-Row.

--Richard Wright Reader. Wright, Ellen & Fabre, Michel, eds. LC 77-76690. (Illus.). 1978. 15.95 o.p. (ISBN 0-06-014737-7, HarpT); pap. 7.95i (ISBN 0-06-014736-9, TD-292, HarpT). Har-Row.

--Uncle Tom's Children. 1965. pap. 2.95i (ISBN 0-06-080055-0, P55, PL). Har-Row.

--White Man, Listen! LC 78-17905. 1978. Repr. of 1957 ed. lib. bdg. 19.75x (ISBN 0-313-20533-7, WRWM). Greenwood.

Wright, Richard & Wright, Rochelle. Cross-Country Ski Routes: British Columbia. rev. ed. (Illus., Orig.). 1979. pap. 6.95 (ISBN 0-913140-35-X). Signpost Bk Pub.

Wright, Richard A. African Philosophy: An Introduction. 2nd ed. LC 78-65457. 1978. pap. 11.00 (ISBN 0-8191-0505-8). U Pr of Amer.

Wright, Richard E., commentary by. Rugs & Flatweaves of the Transcaucasus. LC 80-80962. 1980. 24.00 (ISBN 0-9604210-0-9). Wright R E.

Wright, Richard O., ed. Whose FBI? new ed. LC 74-60. 405p. 1974. 24.50x (ISBN 0-87548-148-5). Open Court.

Wright, Richard R., ed. see Fisher, B. A.

Wright, Richardson. The Gardener's Bed Book. Repr. of 1929 ed. 20.00 o.p. (ISBN 0-686-20654-1). Lib Serv Inc.

Wright, Rita J., ed. Texas Trade & Professional Associations, 1983. LC 79-54294. 100p. pap. text ed. 7.50 (ISBN 0-686-83436-4). U. of Tex Busn Res.

Wright, Rita J., jt. auth. see Pluta, Joseph E.

Wright, Robert, jt. auth. see Rawnsley, C. F.

Wright, Robert C. Frederick Manfred. (United States Authors Ser.). 1979. lib. bdg. 13.95 (ISBN 0-8057-7247-2, Twayne). G K Hall.

Wright, Robert E., jt. auth. see Manera, Elizabeth S.

Wright, Robert G., jt. auth. see Gore, George J.

Wright, Robert L., jt. ed. see Wright, Rochelle.

Wright, Robin, ed. Poems of Protest. (Pocket Poet Ser.). 1966. pap. 1.25 (ISBN 0-8023-9052-8). Dufour.

Wright, Robin M., jt. ed. see Barreiro, Jose.

Wright, Rochelle, jt. auth. see Wright, Richard.

Wright, Rochelle & Wright, Robert L., eds. Danish Emigrant Ballads & Songs. 1983. price not set (ISBN 0-8093-1064-3). S Ill U Pr.

Wright, Roosevelt, jt. auth. see Watts, Thomas D., Jr.

Wright, Roosevelt, Jr., jt. auth. see McNeil, John S.

Wright, Roy D., jt. auth. see Gist, Noel P.

Wright, Rusty. The Other Side of Life. LC 78-78167. 1979. pap. 2.25 o.p. (ISBN 0-89840-000-7). Heres Life.

Wright, Ruth, jt. auth. see Davis, J. William.

Wright, Samson. Samson Wright's Applied Physiology. rev. 13th ed. Neil, Eric & Keele, Cyril A., eds. (Illus.). 1982. pap. text ed. 65.00x (ISBN 0-19-263211-6); pap. text ed. 39.50x (ISBN 0-19-263210-8). Oxford U Pr.

Wright, Sandra L., ed. Quilts from Happy Hands. 192p. 1981. 9.95 (ISBN 0-941468-01-1). Happy Hands.

Wright, Sarah E. This Child's Gonna Live. 1971. pap. 2.45 o.s.i. (ISBN 0-440-58790-5, Delta). Dell.

Wright, Sewall. Systems of Mating & Other Papers. facsimile ed. 1958. pap. 9.15x o.p. (ISBN 0-8138-2315-3). Iowa St U Pr.

Wright, Shannon & Keeley, Steve. The Women's Book of Racquetball. (Illus.). 1980. 14.95 o.p. (ISBN 0-8092-7066-8); pap. 7.95 o.p. (ISBN 0-8092-7064-1). Contemp Bks.

Wright, Stephen. American Racer: Nineteen Hundred to Nineteen Forty. LC 79-91735. (American Racer Ser.). (Illus.). 265p. 1980. 22.95x (ISBN 0-9603676-0-8). Megden Pub.

Wright, T. M. Strange Seed: A Contemporary Novel of Unutterable Terror. LC 78-57400. 1978. 7.95 o.p. (ISBN 0-89696-021-8, An Everest House Book). Dodd.

Wright, Tappan. Islandia. pap. 9.95 (ISBN 0-452-25210-5, Z5210, Plume). NAL.

Wright, Theodore P., Jr. American Support of Free Elections Abroad. LC 80-15872. 184p. 1980. Repr. of 1964 ed. lib. bdg. 20.25x (ISBN 0-313-22507-9, WRAM). Greenwood.

Wright, Thomas. Biographia Britannica Literaria, 2 vols. LC 68-22061. 1968. Repr. of 1842 ed. Set. 66.00x (ISBN 0-8103-3154-3). Gale.

--Homes of Other Days: A History of Domestic Manners & Sentiments in England During the Middle Ages. LC 67-23902. (Social History References Ser.). (Illus.). 1968. Repr. of 1871 ed. 30.00x (ISBN 0-8103-3263-9). Gale.

--Narratives of Sorcery & Magic, from the Most Authentic Sources. LC 73-177421. 1974. Repr. of 1851 ed. 47.00x (ISBN 0-8103-3821-1). Gale.

--The Romance of the Lace Pillow. Date not set. 21.95 (ISBN 0-903585-12-X). Robin & Russ.

--Romance of the Shoe. LC 68-26624. 1968. Repr. of 1922 ed. 34.00 o.p. (ISBN 0-8103-3543-3). Gale.

Wright, Tom. Large Gardens & Parks: Maintenance, Management & Design. 194p. (Orig.). 1982. text ed. 35.50x (ISBN 0-246-11402-9, Pub by Granada England). Renouf.

Wright, Tom, tr. see Uchiyama, Kosho.

Wright, V., jt. auth. see Bird, H. A.

Wright, Vincent. The Government & Politics of France. LC 78-9274. 1978. text ed. 21.45x (ISBN 0-8419-0409-X); pap. text ed. 11.50x (ISBN 0-8419-0410-3). Holmes & Meier.

Wright, Vincent, jt. ed. see Lagroye, Jacques.

Wright, W. D. Historians & Slavery. 1978. pap. text ed. 11.00 o.p. (ISBN 0-8191-0612-7). U Pr of Amer.

Wright, Walter F. Art & Substance in George Meredith: A Study in Narrative. LC 80-14417. vii, 211p. 1980. Repr. of 1953 ed. lib. bdg. 21.00x (ISBN 0-313-22514-1, WRAS). Greenwood.

Wright, Walter L., Jr., tr. see Mehmed, Pasha.

Wright, Will. Sixguns & Society. 1975. pap. 7.95 (ISBN 0-520-03491-0). U of Cal Pr.

--The Social Logic of Health. 215p. 1982. 14.95 (ISBN 0-8135-0948-3). Rutgers U Pr.

Wright, William. The Brontes in Ireland. LC 76-29146. (Illus.). 1983. Repr. of 1894 ed. 10.00 (ISBN 0-916620-12-3). Portals Pr.

--Grammar of the Arabic Language, 2 Vols. 3rd ed. 1933-1967. Vol. 1. 42.00 (ISBN 0-521-06875-4); Vol. 2. pap. text ed. 32.50 (ISBN 0-521-09455-0); Vols. 1 & 2. pap. 34.50 (ISBN 0-521-09455-0). Cambridge U Pr.

--Heiress: The Rich Life of Marjorie Merriweather Post. LC 77-26168. (Illus.). 1978. 12.50 (ISBN 0-915220-36-9). New Republic.

--Rich Relations. 256p. 1981. 12.95 (ISBN 0-399-12462-4). Putnam Pub Group.

--The Von Bulow Affair. 384p. 1983. 16.95 (ISBN 0-440-09166-7). Delacorte.

Wright, William H. The Grizzly Bear: The Narrative of a Hunter-Naturalist. LC 77-1772. (Illus.). xii, 290p. 1977. 18.95x (ISBN 0-8032-0927-4); pap. 5.95 (ISBN 0-8032-5865-8, BB 646, Bison). U of Nebr Pr.

Wright, Wilmer. Management Accounting Simplified. (Illus.). 1979. 21.00 (ISBN 0-07-072080-0). McGraw.

Wrightman, Dwayne, jt. auth. see Robinson, Roland.

Wrights, John I. Plant Propogation for the Amateur Gardener. (Illus.). 1983. 16.95 (ISBN 0-7137-1155-8, Pub. by Blandford Pr England). Sterling.

Wrightsman, Dwayne. An Introduction to Monetary Theory & Policy. 3rd, rev. ed. LC 82-48746. 384p. 1982. 14.95 (ISBN 0-02-935910-4); pap. text ed. 9.95 (ISBN 0-02-935920-1). Free Pr.

Wrightsman, Lawrence & Deaux, Kay. Social Psychology in the Eighties. 3rd ed. LC 80-23440. 760p. 1980. 22.95 (ISBN 0-8185-0415-3). Brooks-Cole.

Wrightsman, Lawrence S., et al. Psychology: A Scientific Study of Human Behavior. 5th ed. LC 78-59674. (Illus.). 1979. text ed. 23.95 (ISBN 0-8185-0280-0). Brooks-Cole.

Wrightson, G., jt. ed. see Siekmann, J.

Wrightson, Keith & Levine, David. Poverty & Piety in an English Village: Terling, 1525-1700. LC 78-1102. (Studies in Social Discontinuity Ser.). 1979. 19.50 (ISBN 0-12-765950-1). Acad Pr.

Wrigley, C. J., ed. A History of British Industrial Relations, 1875-1914. LC 82-6993. (Illus.). 288p. 1982. lib. bdg. 22.50x (ISBN 0-87023-377-7). U of Mass Pr.

Wrigley, Chris, ed. A. J. P. Taylor: A Complete Annotated Bibliography & Guide to His Historical & Other Writings. 608p. 1980. text ed. 75.00x (ISBN 0-391-02097-8). Humanities.

Wrigley, E. A., ed. The Study of Nineteenth Century Society. LC 71-174258. (Illus.). 512p. 1972. 49.50 (ISBN 0-521-08412-1). Cambridge U Pr.

Wrigley, E. A., jt. ed. see Abrams, P.

Wrigley, Elizabeth S., jt. ed. see Davies, David W.

Wrigley, N. Statistical Applications in the Spatial Sciences. 310p. 1980. 32.00x (ISBN 0-85086-075-X, Pub. by Pion England). Methuen Inc.

Wrinch, Dorothy. Fourier Transforms & Structure Factors. pap. 3.00 (ISBN 0-686-60368-0). Polycrystal Bk Serv.

Wringe, Colin. Developments in Modern Language Teaching. (Changing Classroom Ser.). 1976. text ed. 9.75x o.p. (ISBN 0-7291-0095-2); pap. text ed. 4.00x o.p. (ISBN 0-7291-0090-1). Humanities.

Wrisley, Betsy, jt. auth. see Orr, Carolyn.

Wriston, Henry M. Policy Perspectives. LC 64-17776. 188p. 1964. text ed. 10.00x (ISBN 0-87057-081-1, Pub by Brown U Pr.). U Pr of New Eng.

Writers' Group of the Dearborn Branch of the American Association of University Women. Mingled Threads. Reith, Alma C., et al, eds. LC 82-50876. 1982. 7.00 (ISBN 0-9609430-0-5). Writers' Group.

Writers' Program of the Work Projects Administration of the City of New York. Writers' Program, New York: The Film Index: A Bibliography Vol. 2, The Film as Industry, Vol. 3, The Film in Society, 2 Vols. in One. 480p. lib. bdg. 75.00 (ISBN 0-527-29334-2). Kraus Intl.

Writer's Service, Inc., ed. see Stubblefield, Al.

Wrobleski, Henry M. & Hess, Karen M. Introduction to Law Enforcement & Criminal Justice. (Criminal Justice Ser.). (Illus.). 1979. text ed. 21.95 (ISBN 0-8299-0250-3); instrs.' manual avail. (ISBN 0-8299-0602-9). West Pub.

Wrobleski, Henry M., ed. see Hess, Karen M.

Wrone, David R. see Guth, DeLloyd J.

Wrong, Dennis H. & Gracey, H. L. Readings for Introductory Sociology. 3rd ed. 1977. pap. text ed. 13.95x (ISBN 0-02-430700-9). Macmillan.

Wrong, George M. Conquest of New France. 1918. text ed. 8.50x (ISBN 0-686-83510-7). Elliots Bks.

--Washington & His Comrades in Arms. 1921. text ed. 8.50x (ISBN 0-686-83852-1). Elliots Bks.

Wronski, Wojcech & Davies, Kenneth J. Photo Interpretation for Planners. (Illus.). 36p. 1972. pap. text ed. 3.00 (ISBN 0-87985-040-X, M-81). Eastman Kodak.

Wroth, Lawrence C. Colonial Printer. (Illus.). 1964. pap. 3.95 o.p. (ISBN 0-8139-0250-9). U Pr of Va.

--Tobacco or Codfish: Lord Baltimore Makes His Choice. (Illus.). 1954. pap. 3.00 o.p. (ISBN 0-87104-210-X). NY Pub Lib.

Wroth, Mary. The Poems of Lady Mary Wroth. LC 82-20843. 3004p. 1983. text ed. 30.00 (ISBN 0-8071-1074-4). La State U Pr.

Wroth, William. Christian Images in Hispanic New Mexico: The Taylor Museum Collection of Santos. LC 82-4404. (Illus.). 250p. 1982. 35.00 (ISBN 0-295-95934-7); pap. 20.00 (ISBN 0-295-95933-9). Taylor Museum.

Wrottesley, John. The Great Northern Railway: Expansion & Competition, Vol. 2. 1979. 31.50 (ISBN 0-7134-1592-4, Pub. by Batsford England). David & Charles.

Wrright, Peter H. Rome, England, the United States & the Forces for the Decline & the Death of the Empires. 155p. 1983. 69.55 (ISBN 0-86722-042-2). Inst Econ Pol.

Wruble, Lawrence D. & Lewis, Myron. Medical Examination Review: Gastroenterology, Vol. 22. 4th ed. 1982. pap. text ed. 24.50 (ISBN 0-87488-141-2). Med Exam.

Wruble, Lawrence D., et al, eds. Gastroenterology. 4th ed. Lewis, Myron & Levinson, Michael. (Medical Examination Review Book: Vol.22). 24.50 (ISBN 0-87488-141-2). Med Exam.

Wruck, Charlotte. Jewels for Their Ears: Why Earrings Are As Popular Today As They Were 10,000 Years Ago. 1979. 8.95 o.p. (ISBN 0-533-03935-5). Vantage.

Wu. Prostaglandins in Clinical Medicine. 1982. 59.95 (ISBN 0-8151-9609-1). Year Bk Med.

Wu, Chien-Shiung, jt. ed. see Yuan, Luke C.

Wu, Eleanor B. Morris see Morris Wu, Eleanor B.

Wu, Frederick H. Accounting Information Systems: Theory & Practice. (Illus.). 608p. 1983. text ed. 23.00 (ISBN 0-07-072121-1, C). Supplementary materials available from publisher. write for info. instr's manual (ISBN 0-07-072122-X). McGraw.

Wu, Jack A., jt. auth. see Wu, Nesa L.

Wu, Kent K. Diagnosis & Treatment of Polyostotic Spinal Tumors. (Illus.). 310p. 1982. 49.75x (ISBN 0-398-04671-9). C C Thomas.

Wu, Margaret S. Introduction to Computer Data Processing. 2nd ed. 521p. 1979. text ed. 22.95 (ISBN 0-15-541635-9, HC); avail. instructor's manual 2.50 (ISBN 0-15-541636-7); study guide 8.95 (ISBN 0-15-541637-5). HarBraceJ.

--Introduction to Computer Data Processing with BASIC. 468p. 1980. text ed. 18.95 (ISBN 0-15-541638-3, HC). HarBraceJ.

Wu, Nesa & Coppins, Richard. Linear Programming & Extensions. (Industrial Engineering & Management Science Ser.). (Illus.). 480p. 1981. 29.95 (ISBN 0-07-072117-3, C); solutions manual 8.95 (ISBN 0-07-072118-1). McGraw.

Wu, Nesa L. ANSI FORTRAN IV & FORTRAN 77: Programming with Business Applications. 3rd ed. 336p. 1982. pap. text ed. write for info. (ISBN 0-697-08153-2); solutions manual avail. (ISBN 0-697-08156-7). Wm C Brown.

Wu, Nesa L. & Wu, Jack A. Introduction to Management Science. 1980. 25.95 (ISBN 0-395-30774-0); Solutions Manual 2.15 (ISBN 0-395-30775-9). HM.

Wu, T. H. Soil Mechanics. 2nd ed. LC 75-26633. 440p. 1982. Repr. of 1979 ed. text ed. 24.00x (ISBN 0-918498-02-3). T H Wu.

Wu, T. K. & Mitchell, J. Polymer Analysis: Journal of Applied Polymer Science: Applied Polymer Symposium 34. 176p. 1979. pap. text ed. 29.95x (ISBN 0-471-05695-2). Wiley.

Wu, Theodore Y. & Hutchinson, John W., eds. Advances in Applied Mechanics: Serial Publication, Vol. 23. Date not set. price not set (ISBN 0-12-002023-8); price not set Lib. ed. (ISBN 0-12-002057-2); price not set Microfiche (ISBN 0-12-002058-0). Acad Pr.

Wu, Tien-Wei. Lin Biao & the Gang of Four: Contra-Confucianism in Historical & Intellectual Perspectives. 1983. 30.00x (ISBN 0-8093-1022-8). S Ill U Pr.

Wu, Tsong-Shien. The Value of Children: a Cross National Study: Taiwan, Vol. 5. 1977. pap. text ed. 3.00x (ISBN 0-8248-0386-8, Eastwest Ctr). UH Pr.

Wu, William W. Elements of Digital Satellite Communication. 1983. text ed. p.n.s. (ISBN 0-914894-39-0). Computer Sci.

Wubneh, Mulatu. A Spatial Analysis of Urban-Industrial Development in Ethiopia. (Foreign & Comparative Studies Program, African Ser.: No. 39). (Orig.). 1982. pap. text ed. 16.00x (ISBN 0-915984-62-8). Syracuse U Foreign Comp.

Wu Cheng Yih & H. Y. Hou, eds. The Vegetation of China, Vol. 1. 1983. 82.50 (ISBN 0-677-31080-3). Gordon.

Wucherpfennig, Wolf, jt. ed. see Harris, Edward P.

Wu-Chi, Liu. Su Man-Shu. (World Authors Ser.). lib. bdg. 15.95 (ISBN 0-8057-2870-8, Twayne). G K Hall.

Wu-chi Liu & Yucheng Lo, Irving, eds. Sunflower Splendor. (Anchor Literary Library). 1983. pap. 6.95 (ISBN 0-686-42702-5, Anch). Doubleday.

Wuebben, Paul, et al. The Experiment As a Social Occassion. 330p. 1974. 12.00x o.p. (ISBN 0-87709-720-8); pap. cancelled o.p. (ISBN 0-87709-220-6). Boyd & Fraser.

Wuehrmann, Arthur H. & Manson-Hing, Lincoln R. Dental Radiology. 5th ed. LC 81-2040. (Illus.). 508p. 1981. text ed. 37.95 (ISBN 0-8016-5643-5). Mosby.

Wuenn, Vera. Black Bread. 1978. 6.90 o.p. (ISBN 0-533-03541-4). Vantage.

Wuertz-Schaefer, Karin. Hiking Virginia's National Forests. LC 77-70414. (Illus.). 204p. 1977. pap. 7.95 (ISBN 0-914788-05-1). East Woods.

Wuest, Kenneth. Practical Use of the Greek New Testament. Wise, Donald, rev. by. 160p. 1982. text ed. 9.95 (ISBN 0-8024-6737-7). Moody.

Wuest, Kenneth S. Word Studies in the Greek New Testament, for the English Reader, 16 bks. Incl. Bk. 1. Golden Nuggets. pap. 3.95 (ISBN 0-8028-1242-2); Bk. 2. Bypaths. pap. 2.95 (ISBN 0-8028-1318-6); Bk. 3. Treasures. pap. 2.95 (ISBN 0-8028-1243-0); Bk. 4. Untranslatable Riches. pap. 2.95 (ISBN 0-8028-1241-4); Bk. 5. Studies in Vocabulary. pap. 2.95 (ISBN 0-8028-1240-6); Bk. 6. Great Truths to Live by. pap. 3.95 (ISBN 0-8028-1246-5); Bk. 7. Mark. pap. 4.95 (ISBN 0-8028-1230-9); Bk. 8. Romans. pap. 4.95 (ISBN 0-8028-1231-7); Bk. 9. Galatians. pap. 3.95 (ISBN 0-8028-1232-5); Bk. 10. Ephesians & Colossians. pap. 4.95 (ISBN 0-8028-1233-3); Bk. 11. Philippians. pap. 3.95 (ISBN 0-8028-1234-1); Bk. 12. The Pastoral Epistles. pap. 3.95 (ISBN 0-8028-1236-8); Bk. 13. Hebrews. pap. 3.95 (ISBN 0-8028-1235-X); Bk. 14. First Peter. pap. 3.95 (ISBN 0-8028-1237-6); Bk. 15. In These Last Days. pap. 4.95 (ISBN 0-8028-1238-4); Bk. 16. Prophetic Light in the Present Darkness. pap. 2.95 (ISBN 0-8028-1239-2). **Set. 61.20 (ISBN 0-8028-1248-1); current 4 vols. 62.50 (ISBN 0-8028-2280-0). Eerdmans.**

Wu Han. Chu Yuan-Chang. Mammitzsch, Ulrich, tr. Date not set. price not set o.p. West Wash Univ.

Wujek, E. D. & Rupp, R. F. Diatoms of the Tittabawassee River, Michigan. (Bibliotheca Phycologica: No. 50). (Illus.). 160p. 1981. pap. text ed. 20.00x (ISBN 3-7682-1271-8). Lubrecht & Cramer.

Wu Jingrong, ed. see Beijing Foreign Institute.

Wulf, Helen H. Aphasia, My World Alone. rev. ed. 144p. 1979. 9.50x. Wayne St U Pr.

--Aphasia, My World Alone: A Personal Record. LC 79-11334. 128p. 1974. 9.50 (ISBN 0-8143-1516-X). Wayne St U Pr.

Wulf, Kathleen M. Sometimes I'm Afraid. LC 79-63910. (Illus.). 1979. pap. 5.95 (ISBN 0-87716-102-X, Pub. by Moore Pub Co). F Apple.

Wulf, Lucienne De see De Wulf, Lucienne.

Wulf, W. A., et al. HYDRA-C.mmp: An Experimental Computer System. (Advanced Computer Science Ser.). (Illus.). 351p. 1981. 38.95x (ISBN 0-07-072120-3). McGraw.

Wulf, William, et al. Fundamental Structures of Computer Science. LC 79-12374. 1981. text ed. 25.95 (ISBN 0-201-08725-1); instr's manual (ISBN 0-201-08728-6). A-W.

Wulff, Hans E. Traditional Crafts of Persia. (Illus.). 1967. pap. 8.95 o.p. (ISBN 0-262-73028-6). MIT Pr.

Wulff, J., ed. Structure & Properties of Materials, 4 vols. Incl. Vol. 1. Structures. Moffatt, G. W., et al. 236p. pap. 17.50x o.p. (ISBN 0-471-61265-0); Vol. 3. Mechanical Behavior. Hayden, H. W., et al. 247p. pap. 18.50 o.p. (ISBN 0-471-36469-X); Vol. 4. Electronic Properties. Rose, R. M., et al. 306p. pap. 16.50 o.p. (ISBN 0-471-73548-5). 1964-66. Set. pap. 36.95 o.p. (ISBN 0-471-96495-6). Wiley.

Wulff, Keith M., ed. Regulation of Scientific Inquiry: Societal Concerns with Research. (AAAS Selected Symposium: No. 37). 1979. softcover 21.50 (ISBN 0-89158-492-7). Westview.

Wulff, Lee. The Atlantic Salmon. (Illus.). 288p. 1983. 24.95 (ISBN 0-8329-0267-5). Winchester Pr.

Wulfinghoff, M., tr. see ACHEMA Symposium, 1970, Frankfurt.

Wulfmeyer, K. Tim. Broadcast Newswriting: A Workbook. 118p. 1983. pap. text ed. 8.95 (ISBN 0-8138-0226-1). Iowa St U Pr.

Wulverhorst, A. H. Verster Van, jt. auth. see Schlegel, H.

Wunder, John R. Inferior Courts, Superior Justice: A History of the Justices of the Peace on the Northwest Frontier, 1853-1889. LC 78-66720. (Contributions in Legal Studies: No. 7). 1979. lib. bdg. 27.50 (ISBN 0-313-20620-1, WIC/). Greenwood.

Wunderli, Peter & Muller, Wulf. Romania Historica et Romania Hodierna. xi, 431p. (Ger.). 1982. write for info. (ISBN 3-8204-5791-7). P Lang Pubs.

Wunderlich, Berhard. Macromolecular Physics: Crystals, Structure, Morphology & Defects, 2 vols. 1973. Vol. 1, 1973. 60.50 (ISBN 0-12-765601-4); Vol. 2, 1976. 72.00 (ISBN 0-12-765602-2). Acad Pr.

Wunderlich, Bernhard. Macromolecular Physics: Vol. 3, Crystal Melting. LC 72-82632. 1980. 45.00 (ISBN 0-12-765603-0). Acad Pr.

Wunderlich, Christof. The Mongoloid Child: Recognition & Care. Tinsley, Royal L., Jr., et al, trs. from Ger. LC 76-15755. 1977. 12.50x___o.s.i. (ISBN 0-8165-0610-8); pap. 5.95x (ISBN 0-8165-0519-5). U of Ariz Pr.

Wunderlich, D. Foundations of Linguistics. Lass, R., tr. from Ger. LC 77-82526. (Cambridge Studies in Linguistics Monographs: No. 22). 1979. 64.50 (ISBN 0-521-22007-6); pap. 18.95x (ISBN 0-521-29334-0). Cambridge U Pr.

Wunderlich, J. G., jt. auth. see Hugot, A.

Wunderlich, Ray C. Sugar & Your Health. LC 78-50566. (Illus.). 507p. 1982. write for info. (ISBN 0-910812-21-7); pap. 12.75 (ISBN 0-910812-22-5). Johnny Reads.

Wunderlin, Richard. Guide to the Vascular Plants of Central Florida. Date not set. 26.00 (ISBN 0-8130-0748-8). U Presses Fla.

Wunderlin, Richard P., jt. auth. see Lakela, Olga.

Wundram, Manfred. Art of the Renaissance. LC 73-175861. (History of Art Ser.). (Illus.). 196p. 1972. 8.95x o.p. (ISBN 0-87663-170-7). Universe.

Wunsch, A. David. Complex Variables with Applications. LC 82-16288. (Illus.). 416p. 1983. text ed. 20.95 (ISBN 0-201-08885-1). A-W.

Wunsch, Carl, jt. ed. see Warren, Bruce A.

Wunsch, E., jt. ed. see Voelter, W.

Wurden, F. H. What are the Prospects in Washington State? (Reprint Ser.: No. 5). (Illus.). 9p. 1959. 0.25 (ISBN 0-686-36915-7). Geologic Pubns.

Wurgaft, Lewis. The Imperial Imagination: Magic & Myth in Kipling's India. (Illus.). 352p. 1983. 22.95 (ISBN 0-8195-5082-5). Wesleyan U Pr.

Wurm, Stephen A. Papuan Languages of Oceania. 330p. pap. 41.00 o.p. (ISBN 3-87808-357-2). Benjamins North Am.

Wurm, Ted & Demoro, Harre W. The Silver Short Line: History of the Virginia & Truckee Railroad. LC 81-20185. (Illus.). 216p. Date not set. 25.00 (ISBN 0-8310-7152-4). Howell North. Postponed.

Wurman, Richard S., ed. Football-Access. (Access Sports Ser.). (Illus.). 1982. pap. 4.95 (ISBN 0-9604858-1-3). Access Pr.

--Hawaii-Access. (Access Guidebook Ser.). (Illus.). 1982. pap. 9.95 (ISBN 0-9604858-4-8). Access Pr.

--Los Angles-Access. rev. ed. (Access Guidebook Ser.). (Illus.). 1982. pap. 9.95 (ISBN 0-9604858-2-1). Access Pr.

--San Francisco-Access. (Access Guidebook Ser.). (Illus.). 1982. pap. 8.95 (ISBN 0-9604858-3-X). Access Pr.

--Yellow Pages of Learning Resources. 70p. 1972. 7.95x (ISBN 0-262-23061-5); pap. 2.95x (ISBN 0-262-73032-4). MIT Pr.

Wurman, Richard S., ed. see Kahn, Louis I.

Wurmbrand, Richard. In God's Underground. Orig. Title: Christ in the Communist Prisons. 1973. pap. text ed. 2.75 (ISBN 0-88264-003-8). Diane Bks.

--Reaching Toward the Heights. 1979. pap. 6.95x (ISBN 0-88264-142-5). Diane Bks.

Wurmbrand, Richard, jt. auth. see Wormbrand, Richard.

Wurtman, Judith J. The American Eater: Some Nutritional Problems & Some Solutions. (Vital Issues, Vol. XXIX 1979-80: No. 2). 0.60 (ISBN 0-686-81607-2). Ctr Info Am.

--The Carbohydrate Craver's Diet. 214p. 1983. 12.95 (ISBN 0-395-33160-9). HM.

--Eating Your Way Through Life. LC 77-84121. 231p. 1979. text ed. 16.00 o.p. (ISBN 0-89004-280-2); pap. text ed. 10.50 (ISBN 0-685-99040-0). Raven.

Wurtman, Judith J., jt. ed. see Wurtman, Richard J.

Wurtman, Richard J. & Wurtman, Judith J., eds. Control of Feeding Behavior, & Biology of the Brain in Protein-Calorie Malnutrition. LC 75-14593. (Nutrition & the Brain Ser: Vol. 2). 323p. 1977. 34.50 (ISBN 0-89004-046-X). Raven.

--Determinants of the Availability of Nutrients to the Brain. LC 75-14593. (Nutrition & the Brain Ser.: Vol. 1). 336p. 1977. 34.50 (ISBN 0-89004-045-1). Raven.

--Nutrition & the Brain: Disorders of Eating & Nutrients in Treatment of Brain Diseases. (Nutrition & the Brain Ser.: Vol. 3). 314p. 1979. text ed. 35.00 (ISBN 0-89004-245-4). Raven.

--Nutrition & the Brain: Toxic Effects of Food Constituents on the Brain. LC 79-2073. (Nutrition & the Brain Ser.: Vol. 4). 232p. 1979. text ed. 27.50 (ISBN 0-89004-246-2). Raven.

Wurtman, Richard J., et al. Pineal. LC 68-26632. 1969. 40.50 (ISBN 0-12-765850-5). Acad Pr.

Wurts, Janny. Sorcerer's Legacy. 256p. 1982. pap. 2.50 (ISBN 0-441-77540-3, Pub. by Ace Science Fiction). Ace Bks.

Wurts, Richard. The New York World's Fair 1939-1940 in 155 Photographs. Appelbaum, S., ed. 11.50 (ISBN 0-8446-5622-4). Peter Smith.

Wurtzebach, Charles H. & Harvey, Robert O. Texas Guide to Real Estate Licensing Examinations for Salespersons & Brokers. 352p. 1982. text ed. 23.95 (ISBN 0-471-87757-3). Wiley.

Wurtzebach, Charles H., jt. auth. see Arnold, Alvin L.

Wurtzel, Alan. Television Production. (Illus.). 1979. text ed. 25.95 (ISBN 0-07-072130-0, C). McGraw.

--Television Production. 2nd ed. Provenzano, Marian D., ed. (Illus.). 656p. 1983. text ed. 26.95 (ISBN 0-07-072131-9, C). McGraw.

Wurzer, Karl. One Hundred Styles of French Cooking. LC 81-47704. (Illus.). 464p. 1981. 17.95 (ISBN 0-448-16387-X, G&D). Putnam Pub Group.

Wust, Klaus. Record of Hawksbill Church 1788-1850, Page County, Virginia. 1979. pap. 5.25 (ISBN 0-917968-06-9). Shenandoah Hist.

--Virginia Fraktur: Penmanship As Folk Art. LC 79-189313. (Illus.). 1972. pap. 4.75 o.p. (ISBN 0-917968-03-4). Shenandoah Hist.

Wuster, Eugene, ed. Road to Inforterm. (Vol.1 of Inforterm Series (International Information Centers for Terminology) Ser.: Vol. 1). 144p. 1974. pap. 25.00x (ISBN 0-686-80394-9). Gale.

Wustrack, Michael K. Die Mechelner Alabaster-Manufaktur Des 16. Und Fruhen 17. Jahrhunderts. 422p. (Ger.). 1982. write for info. (ISBN 3-8204-5713-5). P Lang Pubs.

Wuthenau, Alexander Von see Von Wuthenau, Alexander.

Wuthnow, Robert. The Consciousness Reformation. 1976. 28.50x (ISBN 0-520-03138-5). U of Cal Pr.

Wuthnow, Robert, ed. The Religious Dimension: New Directions in Quantitative Research. LC 79-6948. 1979. 27.50 (ISBN 0-12-766050-X). Acad Pr.

Wu Wei-P'Ing. Chinese Acupuncture. Chancellor, Philip, tr. from Fr. 184p. 1962. text ed. 12.95x o.p. (ISBN 0-8464-0999-2). Beekman Pubs.

Wyand, Roy & Graham, John, eds. The International Software Directory: Microcomputers. 1982. 59.95 (ISBN 0-907352-03-0). Imprint Edns.

Wyant. Of Principals & Projects. 1980. 5.00 (ISBN 0-686-38075-4). Assn Tchr Ed.

Wyant, Frank R. The United States, OPEC & Multinational Oil. LC 77-217. 240p. 1977. 22.95x o.p. (ISBN 0-669-01433-8). Lexington Bks.

Wyatt, A. J. Old English Riddles. 1982. lib. bdg. 34.50 (ISBN 0-686-81939-X). Porter.

Wyatt, Alfred J. & Chambers, R. W., eds. Beowulf, with the Finnsburg Fragment. 1914. text ed. 43.50 (ISBN 0-521-06882-7). Cambridge U Pr.

Wyatt, Clair L. Radiometric Calibration: Theory & Methods. 1978. 35.00 (ISBN 0-12-766150-6). Acad Pr.

Wyatt, David K., ed. Iron Man of Laos: Prince Phetsarath Ratanavongsa. Murdoch, John B., tr. 1978. 5.00 o.p. (ISBN 0-87727-110-0, DP 110). Cornell SE Asia.

Wyatt, David K., jt. ed. see Woodside, Alexander.

Wyatt, E. M. Puzzles in Wood. LC 79-67740. (Illus.). 64p. 1981. pap. 4.50 (ISBN 0-918036-09-7). Woodcraft Supply.

Wyatt, Edwin M. Modern Drafting. (Illus., Orig.). 1962. pap. 3.00 o.p. (ISBN 0-02-829760-1). Glencoe.

Wyatt, Isabel. Book of Fairy Princes. LC 78-31605. (Illus.). (gr. 2 up). 1979. 9.95 o.p. (ISBN 0-89742-005-5, Dawne-Leigh); pap. 6.95 o.p. (ISBN 0-89742-006-3). Celestial Arts.

--King Beetle-Tamer & Other Lighthearted Wonder Tales. LC 79-21245. (Illus.). 160p. (gr. 3-12). 1980. 9.95 o.p. (ISBN 0-89742-029-2, Dawne-Leigh); pap. 6.95 o.p. (ISBN 0-89742-028-4). Celestial Arts.

--A Man, A Maiden, & A Tree: A Christmas Mystery Play. (Illus.). 64p. (Orig.). pap. 2.95 (ISBN 0-88010-056-7, Pub. by Michael Pr. England). Anthroposophic.

Wyatt, John W. & Wyatt, Madie B. Business Law: Principles & Cases. 6th ed. (Illus.). 1979. text ed. 26.95x (ISBN 0-07-072162-9, C); instr's manual 16.95x (ISBN 0-07-072164-5); study guide 10.00 (ISBN 0-07-072163-7); test & comments 18.95 (ISBN 0-07-072165-3). McGraw.

Wyatt, L. M. Materials of Construction for Steam Power Plant. (Illus.). 1976. 53.50 (ISBN 0-85334-661-5, Pub. by Applied Sci England). Elsevier.

Wyatt, M. Colby, ed. The Performance of Paper Made with Thermomechanical Pulp: A Workshop on Thermomechanical Pulp. (TAPPI PRESS Reports). 11p. 1978. pap. 4.95 (ISBN 0-89852-374-5, 01-01-R074). TAPPI.

Wyatt, Madie B., jt. auth. see Wyatt, John W.

Wyatt, Molly. Kim's Winter. 1982. pap. 1.75 (ISBN 0-451-11435-3, Sig Vista). NAL.

Wyatt, Olive M. Teach Yourself Lip-Reading. (Illus.). 172p. 1974. 8.75x (ISBN 0-398-02128-7). C C Thomas.

Wyatt, Oliver H. & Dew-Hughes, D. Metals, Ceramics & Polymers. LC 70-178286. (Illus.). 500p. 1974. 94.50 (ISBN 0-521-08238-2); pap. 29.95 (ISBN 0-521-09834-3). Cambridge U Pr.

Wyatt, P. A. Energy & Entropy in Chemistry. (Topics in Physics & Chemistry Ser.). 1967. 25.00x (ISBN 0-312-25130-0). St Martin.

Wyatt, Richard J., jt. auth. see Jeste, Dilip.

Wyatt, Roy. Cuttings from a Country Garden. 1983. 11.95 (ISBN 0-932298-35-4). Copple Hse.

Wyatt, Will. The Secret of the Sierra Madre: The Man Who Was B. Traven. LC 79-8570. (Illus.). 384p. 1980. 14.95 o.p. (ISBN 0-385-15600-6). Doubleday.

Wyatt, William E. General Architectural Drafting. (gr. 10-12). 1976. text ed. 20.80 (ISBN 0-87002-072-2); student guide 5.28 (ISBN 0-87002-166-4); drafting masters 15.96 (ISBN 0-87002-189-3). Bennett IL.

Wyatt-Brown, Bertram. Southern Honor: Ethics & Behavior in the Old South. 1982. 29.95x (ISBN 0-19-503119-9). Oxford U Pr.

--Southern Honor: Ethics & Behavior in the Old South. 622p. 1983. pap. 9.95 (ISBN 0-19-503310-8, GB 737, GB). Oxford U Pr.

Wybar, Taylor. Pediatric Opthalmology. 632p. 1983. 75.00 (ISBN 0-8247-1841-0). Dekker.

Wybourne, Brian G. Classical Groups for Physicists. LC 73-17363. 416p. 1974. 49.95x o.p. (ISBN 0-471-96505-7, Pub. by Wiley-Interscience). Wiley.

Wyckoff, Alexander, et al. Early American Dress. LC 65-20869. (Illus.). Repr. of 1965 ed. 35.00 (ISBN 0-685-06984-2). Amaryllis Pr.

Wyckoff, D. Daryl. Railroad Management. LC 75-5237. 224p. 1976. 20.95x (ISBN 0-669-99770-6). Lexington Bks.

--Truck Drivers in America. LC 78-24793. (Illus.). 176p. 1979. 18.95x (ISBN 0-669-02818-5). Lexington Bks.

Wyckoff, D. Daryl & Maister, David H. The Domestic Airline Industry. LC 76-54612. (Lexington Casebook Series in Industry Analysis). 288p. 1977. 21.95x (ISBN 0-669-01307-2); instructors manual free (ISBN 0-669-01843-0). Lexington Bks.

--Owner-Operators: Independent Trucker. LC 74-23978. (Illus.). 192p. 1975. 17.95x (ISBN 0-669-96800-5). Lexington Bks.

--The U. S. Motor-Carrier Industry. (Lexington Casebook Series in Industry Analysis). (Illus.). 272p. 1977. 21.95x (ISBN 0-669-01113-4); instructors manual free (ISBN 0-669-01454-0). Lexington Bks.

Wyckoff, D. Daryl & Sasser, W. Earl. The Chain-Restaurant Industry. LC 77-2048. (Lexington Casebook Series in Industry Analysis). 1978. 22.95x (ISBN 0-669-01440-0); instructors manual free (ISBN 0-669-03248-4). Lexington Bks.

--The U. S. Lodging Industry. LC 78-24716. (The Lexington Industry Analysis Casebook). 336p. 1981. 27.95x (ISBN 0-669-02819-3). Lexington Bks.

Wyckoff, Edith H. The Fabled Past: Tales of Long Island. (Empire State Historical Publications Ser.). (Illus.). 1977. 15.00 o.p. (ISBN 0-8046-9146-0). Kennikat.

Wyckoff, Elizabeth see Euripides.

Wyckoff, James. Sharkey. LC 77-76273. (Double D Western Ser.). 1980. 10.95 o.p. (ISBN 0-385-11564-4). Doubleday.

--Who Really Invented the Submarine? (Who Really Invented Ser). (Illus.). (gr. 5 up). 1965. PLB 4.29 o.p. (ISBN 0-399-60667-X). Putnam Pub Group.

Wyckoff, Jerome. The Adirondack Landscape. LC 67-28445. (Illus.). 1979. pap. 2.25 (ISBN 0-935272-08-9). ADK Mtn Club.

Wyckoff, Ralph W. Crystal Structures, Vol. 3. LC 78-23589. 989p. 1981. Repr. of 1951 ed. lib. bdg. 54.50 (ISBN 0-88275-800-4). Krieger.

--Crystal Structures: Vol. 2. (Inorganic Compounds Rxn, Rnmx2, Rnmx3 - Crystal Structures) LC 78-23589. 596p. 1983. Repr. lib. bdg. write for info. (ISBN 0-89874-388-5). Krieger.

Wyckoff, Richard. Jesse Livermore's Methods of Trading in Stocks. 64p. 1972. pap. 3.00 o.p. (ISBN 0-685-25837-8). Windsor.

Wyckoff, Richard D. Forecasting Price Movements & Turning Points in the Course of the Stock Market. (The Recondite Sources of Stock Market Action Library). (Illus.). 127p. 1983. 55.85 (ISBN 0-86654-054-7). Inst Econ Finan.

--How Fortunes are Made in Wall Street by Exploiting the Price Declines of Stock Market Panics. (A New Stock Market Library Bk.). (Illus.). 131p. 1983. 59.85 (ISBN 0-86654-058-X). Inst Econ Finan.

--The Making of a Wall Street Flunger. (A New Stock Library Book). (Illus.). 127p. 1983. 66.65 (ISBN 0-86654-047-4). Inst Econ Finan.

--Wall Street Ventures & Adventures Through Forty Years. LC 68-28651. (Illus.). Repr. of 1930 ed. lib. bdg. 20.75x (ISBN 0-8371-0767-9, WYWS). Greenwood.

Wyden, Peter. Bay of Pigs. 1980. 8.95 (ISBN 0-671-25413-8, Touchstone). S&S.

Wydick, Richard C. Plain English for Lawyers. LC 79-53956. 91p. 1979. lib. bdg. 9.95 (ISBN 0-89089-175-3); pap. text ed. 3.95 (ISBN 0-89089-176-1). Carolina Acad Pr.

Wye, Deborah. Louise Bourgeois. LC 82-60847. (Illus.). 116p. 1982. pap. 12.50 (ISBN 0-87070-257-2). Museum Mod Art.

Wyer, R. S. Cognitive Organization & Change: An Information Processing Approach. LC 74-12312. 502p. 1975. 23.00 (ISBN 0-470-96899-0). Krieger.

Wyeth, Betsy J. & Wyeth, Jamie. The Stray. (Illus.). 200p. 1979. 12.95 (ISBN 0-374-37280-2); pap. 7.25 (ISBN 0-374-51746-0). FS&G.

Wyeth, Betsy J., ed. Wyeths by N. C. Wyeth. LC 73-137021. (Illus.). 1971. 12.95 o.s.i. (ISBN 0-87645-046-X). Gambit.

Wyeth, Jamie, jt. auth. see Wyeth, Betsy J.

Wyeth, John A. The Life of Nathan Bedford Forrest. 1975. 30.00 (ISBN 0-89029-023-7). Pr of Morningside.

Wyke, Barry, ed. Vetilatory & Phonatory Control Systems: An International Symposium. (Illus.). 1974. text ed. 49.00x (ISBN 0-19-264158-1). Oxford U Pr.

Wyker, Arthur & Gillenwater, Jay Y. Method of Urology. LC 75-8588. 380p. 1975. 22.50 (ISBN 0-683-09300-2). Krieger.

Wykes, C. M., jt. auth. see Jones, R.

Wykoff, Gerald L. Beyond the Glitter. LC 81-69981. (Illus.). 216p. 1982. text ed. 17.95 (ISBN 0-9607892-1-9). Adamas Pub.

Wyk Smith, A. Van see Van Wyk Smith, M.

Wyland, Francie. Motherhood, Lesbianism & Child Custody. 36p. 1977. pap. 1.95 (ISBN 0-905046-05-6). Falling Wall.

Wyland, Johanna L. Housewives' Guide in Laundering. new ed. 25p. 1977. pap. 3.50 (ISBN 0-932044-01-8). M O Pub Co.

Wyld, Henry C. Historical Study of the Mother Tongue. Repr. of 1906 ed. lib. bdg. 17.50x (ISBN 0-8371-1873-5, WYMT). Greenwood.

Wyld, Henry C., ed. The Universal Dictionary of the English Langauge. rev. ed. 1447p. 1978. 45.00 (ISBN 0-7100-2333-2). Routledge & Kegan.

Wyld, Lionel D. Walter D. Edmonds, Storyteller. LC 82-10443. (York State Bks.). (Illus.). 168p. 1982. text ed. 20.00x (ISBN 0-8156-0180-8). Syracuse U Pr.

Wylder, Delbert E. Emerson Hough. (United States Authors Ser.). 13.95 (ISBN 0-8057-7328-2, Twayne). G K Hall.

Wylder, Robert C., jt. auth. see Roloff-Stoddard, Joan.

Wylen, G. J. Van see Sonntag, R. E. & Van Wylen, G. J.

Wylen, Gordon J. An see Van Wylen, Gordon J. & Sonntag, Richard E.

Wylen, Gordon J. Van see Sonntag, Richard E. & Van Wylen, Gordon J.

Wylen, Gordon J. Van see Van Wylen, Gordon J. & Sonntag, Richard E.

Wyler, Rose, jt. auth. see Ames, Gerald.

Wyler, Rose, jt. auth. see Baird, Eva-Lee.

Wyler, Rose, jt. auth. see Elting, Mary.

Wylie, Andrew. Yellow Flowers. 1972. pap. 4.95 (ISBN 0-934450-04-8). Unmuzzled Ox.

Wylie, C. Ray. Differential Equations. (Illus.). 1979. text ed. 28.50 (ISBN 0-07-072197-1, C); ans. manual 17.95 (ISBN 0-07-072198-X). McGraw.

Wylie, C. Ray & Barrett, Louis C. Advanced Engineering Mathematics. 5th ed. (Illus.). 1120p. 1982. 35.95x (ISBN 0-07-072188-2); solns. manual 20.00 (ISBN 0-07-072189-0). McGraw.

Wylie, Clarence R., Jr. Advanced Engineering Mathematics. 4th ed. (Illus.). 864p. 1975. text ed. 27.95 (ISBN 0-07-072180-7, C); solns. manual 19.95 (ISBN 0-07-072183-1). McGraw.

--Foundations of Geometry. (Illus.). 1982. text ed. 29.95 (ISBN 0-07-072191-2, C). McGraw.

Wylie, E. Benjamin & Streeter, Victor L. Fluid Transients. (Illus.). 1978. text ed. 48.00x o.p. (ISBN 0-07-072187-4, C). McGraw.

Wylie, E. Benjamin, jt. auth. see Streeter, Victor L.

Wylie, Edwin, jt. auth. see Balmer, Philip.

Wylie, Edwin J. & Ehrenfeld, William K. Extracranial Occlusive Cerebrovascular Disease. LC 70-118596. (Illus.). 1970. 13.00 o.p. (ISBN 0-7216-9612-0). Saunders.

Wylie, Elinor. Last Poems of Elinor Wylie. 1982. cancelled (ISBN 0-89733-012-9); pap. 5.00 (ISBN 0-89733-011-0). Academy Chi Ltd.

Wylie, F. J. The Use of Radar at Sea. 5th ed. LC 76-12012. 1978. 19.95x (ISBN 0-87021-965-0). Naval Inst Pr.

Wylie, Hal & Julien, Eileen, eds. Contemporary African Literature. (Annual Selected Papers of the ALA). 130p. 1983. 22.00X (ISBN 0-686-82391-5); pap. 14.00X (ISBN 0-89410-370-9). Three Continents.

Wylie, J. C. Irish Land Law: Including 1980. 99.00x (ISBN 0-903486-07-5, Pub. by Prof Bks England). State Mutual Bk.

Wylie, James. The Homestead Grays. LC 77-3641. 1977. 9.95 o.p. (ISBN 0-399-12003-3). Putnam Pub Group.

Wylie, Joanne. The Creative Guide for Preschool Teachers. 1966. pap. 12.50 (ISBN 0-672-75074-0). Bobbs.

Wylie, Joseph C. Military Strategy: A General Theory of Power Control. LC 80-36885. vii, 111p. 1980. Repr. of 1967 ed. lib. bdg. 19.25x (ISBN 0-313-22679-2, WYMS). Greenwood.

Wylie, Kenneth. The Political Kingdoms of the Temne: Temne Government in Sierra Leone, 1825-1900. LC 77-1067. 300p. 1977. text ed. 39.50x (ISBN 0-8419-0149-X, Africana). Holmes & Meier.

Wylie, Philip. Gladiator. LC 73-13270. (Classics of Science Fiction Ser.). 353p. 1974. 12.50 (ISBN 0-88355-124-1); pap. 3.95 o.p. (ISBN 0-88355-153-5). Hyperion Conn.

Wylie, Philip & Balmer, Edwin. After Worlds Collide. 192p. 1963. pap. 2.75 o.p. (ISBN 0-446-30383-6). Warner Bks.

Wylie, Shaun, jt. auth. see Hilton, Peter J.

Wyllie, Diana E. Elizabeth Bishop & Howard Nemerov: A Reference Guide. 1983. lib. bdg. 33.00 (ISBN 0-8161-8527-1, Hall Reference). G K Hall.

Wyllie, Ethel K. Today's Custom Tailoring. 1979. text ed. 19.96 (ISBN 0-87002-245-8); tchr's guide 4.64 (ISBN 0-87002-210-5). Bennett IL.

Wyllie, M. R. Fundamentals of Well Log Interpretation. 3rd ed. 1963. 39.50 (ISBN 0-12-767253-2). Acad Pr.

Wyllie, Peter J. Dynamic Earth: Textbook in Geosciences. LC 73-155909. (Illus.). 1971. 39.95x o.p. (ISBN 0-471-96889-7, Pub. by Wiley-Interscience). Wiley.

--The Dynamic Earth: Textbook in Geosciences. LC 82-21239. 432p. 1983. Repr. of 1971 ed. lib. bdg. write for info. (ISBN 0-89874-584-5). Krieger.

--The Way the Earth Works: An Introduction to the New Global Geology & Its Revolutionary Development. LC 75-23197. 296p. 1976. pap. text ed. 15.95x (ISBN 0-471-96896-X). Wiley.

Wyllie, Robert W. Spiritism in Ghana: A Study of New Religious Movements. Cherry, Conrad, ed. LC 79-20486. (Studies in Religion: No. 21). 139p. 14.00 (ISBN 0-89130-355-3, 01-00-14); pap. 9.95 (ISBN 0-89130-356-1). Scholars Pr CA.

Wylson, Anthony. Design for Leisure Entertainment. Mills, Edward D., ed. (Illus.). 1980. 49.95 (ISBN 0-408-00343-X). Butterworth.

Wyman, Harold E. & Ketz, J. Edward. Managing Corporate Energy Needs: The Role of Management Accounting. 116p. pap. 12.95 (ISBN 0-86641-029-5, 82136). Natl Assn Accts.

Wyman, L. C. & Kluckhohn, Clyde. Navaho Classification of Their Song Ceremonials. LC 38-23008. 1938. pap. 8.00 (ISBN 0-527-00549-5). Kraus Repr.

Wyman, L. C., jt. auth. see Kluckhohn, Clyde.

Wyman, Leland C. The Sacred Mountains of the Navajo. (No. 4). (Illus.). 1967. pap. 2.50 (ISBN 0-89734-012-4). Mus Northern Ariz.

Wyman, Thomas B. The Genealogies & Estates of Charlestown, Massachusetts, 1629-1818. Dearborn, David C., frwd. by. LC 82-60408. 1060p. 1982. Repr. of 1879 ed. 65.00x (ISBN 0-89725-031-1). NE History.

Wymer, John. Lower Palaeolithic Archaeology in Britain: As Represented by the Thames Valley. LC 67-30791. (Illus.). 1969. text ed. 25.50x o.p. (ISBN 0-212-35964-9). Humanities.

Wymer, John, jt. auth. see Singer, Ronald.

Wymer, N see Allen, W. S.

Wymer, Norman. Inventors. LC 82-50398. (History Eye Witness Ser.). PLB 15.96 (ISBN 0-382-06666-9). Silver.

--With Mackenzie in Canada. (Illus.). (gr. 7 up). 12.75x (ISBN 0-392-01928-0, LTB). Sportshelf.

Wymer, Ray G., ed. Thorium Fuel Cycle: Proceedings. LC 67-62083. (AEC Symposium Ser.). 847p. 1968. pap. 29.95 (ISBN 0-87079-228-8, CONF-660524); microfiche 4.50 (ISBN 0-87079-229-6, CONF-660524). DOE.

Wymore, A. Wayne. Mathematical Theory of Systems Engineering: The Elements. LC 76-16814. 368p. 1977. Repr. of 1967 ed. text ed. 21.00 (ISBN 0-88275-434-3). Krieger.

Wynar, Bohdan S. Economic Thought in Kievan Rus. 128p. (Ukrainian.). 1975. pap. 7.50x (ISBN 0-87287-162-2). Ukrainian Acad.

Wynar, Bohdan S., ed. American Reference Books Annual 1983, Vol. 14. 900p. 1983. lib. bdg. 47.50 (ISBN 0-87287-383-8). Libs Unl.

--Recommended Reference Books for Small & Medium-Sized Libraries & Media Centers 1981. LC 81-15638. 263p. 1981. lib. bdg. 19.50 o.p. (ISBN 0-87287-271-8). Libs Unl.

Wynar, Bohdan S. & Depp, Roberta J., eds. Colorado Bibliography. LC 82-15325. 1980. lib. bdg. 60.00 (ISBN 0-87287-211-4). Libs Unl.

Wynar, Bohdan S., jt. ed. see Holte, Susan.

Wynar, Bohdan S., et al. Introduction to Cataloging & Classification. 6th ed. LC 80-16462. (Library Science Text Ser.). 1980. lib. bdg. 36.00 (ISBN 0-87287-220-3); pap. text ed. 22.00 (ISBN 0-87287-221-1). Libs Unl.

Wynar, Bohdan S., et al, eds. American Reference Books Annual 1981, Vol. 12. LC 75-120328. 821p. 1981. lib. bdg. 45.00 (ISBN 0-87287-250-5). Libs Unl.

--American Reference Books Annual 1982, Vol. 13. LC 75-120328. 800p. 1982. lib. bdg. 47.50 (ISBN 0-87287-287-4). Libs Unl.

Wynar, Lubomyr R. & Buttlar, Lois. Ethnic Film & Filmstrip Guide for Libraries & Media Centers: A Selective Filmography. LC 80-18056. 277p. 1980. lib. bdg. 25.00 (ISBN 0-87287-233-5). Libs Unl.

Wynder, Ernest L. & Hoffman, Dietrich, eds. Tobacco & Tobacco Smoke. 1967. 77.50 (ISBN 0-12-767450-0). Acad Pr.

Wyndham, Francis & King, David. Trotsky: A Documentary. (Illus.). 1973. pap. 7.95 (ISBN 0-14-003522-2). Penguin.

Wyndham, Lee. Holidays in Scandinavia. LC 74-13043. (Around the World Holiday Ser). (Illus.). 96p. (gr. 4-7). 1975. PLB 7.12 (ISBN 0-8116-4955-5). Garrard.

--Tales the People Tell in Russia. LC 76-123164. (Illus.). 96p. (gr. 3-5). 1970. PLB 4.64 o.p. (ISBN 0-671-32326-1). Messner.

--Thanksgiving. LC 63-13890. (Holiday Books Ser). (Illus.). (gr. 2-5). 1963. PLB 7.56 (ISBN 0-8116-6551-8). Garrard.

Wyndham, Robert. Chinese Mother Goose Rhymes. (Illus.). 48p. 1982. pap. 4.95 (ISBN 0-399-20866-6, Philomel). Putnam Pub Group.

--Tales the People Tell in China. LC 74-154971. (Illus.). 96p. (gr. 3 up). 1971. PLB 7.29 o.p. (ISBN 0-671-32428-4). Messner.

Wyne, Marvin D. & O'Connor, Peter D. Exceptional Children: A Developmental View. 1979. pap. text ed. 19.95 (ISBN 0-669-95786-0); instr's manual 1.95 (ISBN 0-669-02422-8). Heath.

Wynen Thomas, Ann Van see Van Wynen Thomas, Ann & Thomas, A. J., Jr.

Wynette, Tammy. Stand by Your Man. 1979. 11.95 o.p. (ISBN 0-671-22884-6). S&S.

Wyngaarden, James B., jt. ed. see Smith, Lloyd H., Jr.

Wynia, G. W. The Politics of Latin American Development. LC 77-87395. (Illus.). 1978. 37.50 (ISBN 0-521-21922-1); pap. 11.95x (ISBN 0-521-29310-3). Cambridge U Pr.

Wynkoop, Mildred B. The Occult & the Supernatural. 1976. pap. 1.50 o.p. (ISBN 0-8341-0420-2). Beacon Hill.

--The Theology of Love. 1972. 8.95 (ISBN 0-8341-0102-5). Beacon Hill.

Wynkoop, Shari H., jt. auth. see Kime, Helen R.

Wynn. Short Story: Twenty-Five Masterpieces. LC 78-71722. 1979. pap. text ed. 5.95 (ISBN 0-312-72218-4). St Martin.

Wynn, Bobby C., ed. Crime & Juvenile Delinquency 1980. 40p. 1982. reference bk. 25.00 (ISBN 0-667-00647-8). Microfilming Corp.

--Utopian Literature: Pre-1900 Imprints. 33p. 1982. 25.00 (ISBN 0-667-00628-1). Microfilming Corp.

Wynn, C. H. Structure & Function of Enzymes. 2nd ed. (Studies in Biology: Nol 42). 72p. 1980. pap. text ed. 8.95 (ISBN 0-7131-2767-8). E Arnold.

Wynn, Neil A. From Progressivism to Prosperity: World War I & American Society. 200p. 1983. 29.50x (ISBN 0-8419-0767-6). Holmes & Meier.

Wynn, Ralpf M. Obstetrics & Gynecology. 3rd ed. LC 82-20879. (Illus.). 310p. 1982. text ed. write for info. (ISBN 0-8121-0875-2). Lea & Febiger.

Wynn, Richard, et al. American Education. 8th ed. (Illus.). 1976. text ed. 23.50 (ISBN 0-07-072208-0, C); instrs. manual 4.50 (ISBN 0-07-072209-9). McGraw.

Wynne, Barry. Behind the Mask of Tutankhamen. (Illus.). 1977. pap. 1.95 o.p. (ISBN 0-685-79803-8, 40-1094). Pinnacle Bks.

Wynne, Canon R. C. English-Mbukushu Dictionary. 1980. 125.00x o.p. (ISBN 0-86127-203-X, Pub. by Avebury Pub England). State Mutual Bk.

Wynne, Edward. The Politics of School Accountibility. LC 74-190055. 300p. 1972. 21.75x (ISBN 0-8211-2250-9); text ed. 19.50x (ISBN 0-685-24960-3). McCutchan.

--Social Security: A Reciprocity System Under Pressure. (Westview Special Studies in Contemporary Social Issues). 220p. 1980. softcoveer 21.50 (ISBN 0-89158-930-9). Westview.

Wynne, Edward A. Looking at Schools: Good, Bad, & Indifferent. LC 79-2798. 272p. 1980. 25.95x (ISBN 0-669-03292-1). Lexington Bks.

Wynne, Edward J., Jr. & Thompson, Henry O., eds. Prayer for Today's People: Sermons on Prayer by Carl Michalson (1915-1965) LC 82-17583. 88p. (Orig.). 1983. lib. bdg. 18.50 (ISBN 0-8191-2771-X); pap. text ed. 7.50 (ISBN 0-8191-2772-8). U Pr of Amer.

Wynne, Frances H. & Stevens, Cheryl J. Genealogy to Enrich the Curricula. LC 82-82074. (Illus.). 96p. (Orig.). 1982. pap. 10.50 (ISBN 0-88127-007-5). Oracle Pr LA.

Wynne, George G. Cutback Management. (Learning from Abroad Ser.: Vol. 6). 84p. 1983. pap. text ed. 5.95x (ISBN 0-87855-930-2). Transaction Bks.

--Traffic Restraints in Residential Areas, Vol. II. (Learning from Abroad Ser.). 48p. 1980. pap. 5.95 (ISBN 0-87855-845-4). Transaction Bks.

--Winning Designs: Vol. 4, The Competitions Renaissance. (Learning from Abroad Ser.). 60p. 1981. pap. text ed. 3.95x (ISBN 0-87855-893-4). Transaction Bks.

Wynne, George W., jt. auth. see Roth, Gabriel.

Wynne, James D. Learning Statistics: A Common-Sense Approach. 1982. text ed. 23.95x (ISBN 0-02-430680-0). Macmillan.

Wynne, John P. Philosophies of Education from the Standpoint of the Philosophy of Experimentalism. Repr. of 1947 ed. lib. bdg. 17.75x (ISBN 0-8371-2793-9, WYPE). Greenwood.

Wynne, Michael. Hoofmarks. LC 80-51730. 220p. 1982. pap. 7.95 (ISBN 0-89526-673-3). Regnery-Gateway.

Wynne, Michael J., jt. auth. see Bold, Harold C.

Wynne, Pamela. Love In a Mist, No. 38. Cartland, Barbara, ed. 160p. 1982. pap. 2.50 (ISBN 0-553-20500-5). Bantam.

Wynne, Patricia, illus. The Animal ABC. LC 77-74470. (Illus.). (ps-k). 1977. bds. 3.50 (ISBN 0-394-83589-1, BYR). Random.

Wynne, Richard H. Lizards in Captivity. (Illus.). 192p. 1981. 7.95 (ISBN 0-87666-921-6, PS-769). TFH Pubns.

Wynn-Parry, C. B. Rehabilitation of the Hand. 4th rev. ed. LC 80-41761. (Illus.). 1981. text ed. 79.95 (ISBN 0-407-38502-9). Butterworth.

Wynn-Parry, C. E. Rehabilitation of the Hand. 3rd ed. 1973. Repr. of 1977 ed. 49.95 o.p. (ISBN 0-407-38501-0). Butterworth.

Wynorski, James. They Came from Outer Space. LC 80-2249. 336p. 1981. 11.95 o.p. (ISBN 0-385-18502-2). Doubleday.

Wynter, Andrew. Curiosities of Civilization. LC 67-23949. (Social History Reference Ser.: No. 11). 1968. Repr. of 1860 ed. 30.00x (ISBN 0-8103-3264-7). Gale.

--Our Social Bees. LC 67-23950. (Social History Reference Ser.). (Illus.). 1969. Repr. of 1861 ed. 30.00x (ISBN 0-8103-3265-5). Gale.

--Subtle Brains & Lissom Fingers. 3rd ed. LC 67-27868. (Social History Reference Ser.). (Illus.). 1968. Repr. of 1863 ed. 30.00x (ISBN 0-8103-3267-1). Gale.

Wyon, Olive, tr. see Brunner, Emil.

Wypyski, Eugene M., jt. auth. see Newman, Edwin S.

Wyrick-Spirduso, Waneen, jt. auth. see Locke, Lawrence F.

Wysack, Roy L., jt. auth. see Wolfe, Stephen L.

Wyschogrod, Michael. The Body of Faith: The Corporeal Election of Israel. 320p. (Orig.). 1983. pap. price not set (ISBN 0-8164-2479-9). Seabury.

Wyse, Lois. Blonde, Beautiful Blonde: How to Look, Live, Work & Think Blonde. LC 80-10551. (Illus.). 192p. 1980. 12.95 (ISBN 0-87131-311-1). M Evans.

--I Love You Better Now. LC 72-115802. 1970. 7.64i (ISBN 0-690-00350-1). T Y Crowell.

Wyse, Marion. The Prophet & the Prostitute. 1979. pap. 4.95 (ISBN 0-8423-4910-3). Tyndale.

Wysinger, Voss E. The Celestial Democracy. LC 66-24014. 149p. 1966. lib. bdg. 12.00 (ISBN 0-914002-01-5); text ed. 12.00 (ISBN 0-914002-02-3); pap. text ed. 9.00 (ISBN 0-686-36904-1). V E Wysinger.

Wysor, Bettie. Echoes. 288p. 1983. pap. 2.95 (ISBN 0-515-06122-0). Jove Pubns.

Wysotsky, Michael Z. Wide Screen Cinema & Stereophonic Sound. (Library of Image & Sound Technology). 1970. 16.50 o.p. (ISBN 0-8038-8044-8). Focal Pr.

--Wide-Screen Cinema & Sterophonic Sound. (Library of Image & Sound Technology). 1974. 17.95 o.p. (ISBN 0-8038-8044-8). Hastings.

Wyss, J. R see Swan, D. K.

Wyss, Johann. Swiss Family Robinson. (Illus.). (gr. 4-6). il. jr. lib. 5.95 (ISBN 0-448-05822-7, G&D); Companion Lib. Ed. 2.95 (ISBN 0-448-05468-X); deluxe ed. 8.95 (ISBN 0-448-06022-1). Putnam Pub Group.

Wyss, Orville & Eklund, C. E. Microorganisms & Man. LC 70-146674. 1971. text ed. 25.50 o.p. (ISBN 0-471-96900-1). Wiley.

Wyss, Thelma H. Show Me Your Rocky Mountains! LC 82-9471. 133p. (gr. 3-8). 1982. 5.95 (ISBN 0-87747-920-8). Deseret Bk.

Wyszecki, Gunter & Stiles, W. S. Color Science: Concepts & Methods Quantitative Data & Formulae. 2nd ed. (Pure & Applied Optics Ser.). 1200p. 1982. 75.50x (ISBN 0-471-02106-7, Pub. by Wiley-Interscience). Wiley.

--Color Science: Concepts, Methods & Quantitative Data & Formulae. LC 66-26763. 1967. 59.95x o.p. (ISBN 0-471-96920-6, Pub. by Wiley-Interscience). Wiley.

Wythe, George. Brazil, an Expanding Economy. LC 68-8076. (Illus.). 1968. Repr. of 1949 ed. lib. bdg. 20.75x (ISBN 0-8371-0277-4, WYBE). Greenwood.

Wyzanski, Charles E. Whereas... a Judge's Premises: Essays in Judgement, Ethics, & the Law. LC 76-43310. 1976. Repr. of 1965 ed. lib. bdg. 20.00x (ISBN 0-8371-9298-6, WYWH). Greenwood.

Wyzewa, T. De see De Wyzewa, T. & De Saint-Foix, G.

X

Xanthakos, Petros P. Slurry Walls. LC 79-10095. 704p. 44.50 (ISBN 0-07-072215-3). McGraw.

Xanthos, Paul, jt. auth. see Johnson, Joan D.

Xavier University Library, New Orleans. Manuscripts on Slavery: Guide to the Xavier University Library-Heartman Manuscript Collection. 238p. 1982. lib. bdg. 35.00 (ISBN 0-8161-0375-5, Hall Library). G K Hall.

Xenakis, Iannis. Arts, Sciences: Alloys. Kanach, Sharon, tr. from Fre. (Pendragon Monographs in Musicology Ser.). 150p. 1983. lib. bdg. 32.00 (ISBN 0-918728-22-3). Pendragon NY.

Xenophon. March up Country: A Modern Translation of the Anabasis. Rouse, W. H., tr. 1958. pap. 5.95 (ISBN 0-472-06095-3, 95, AA). U of Mich Pr.

--Opera Omnia, 4 vols. Marchant, E. C., ed. Incl. Vol. 1. Historia Graeca, Bks. 1-7. 2nd ed. 1909. 18.95x (ISBN 0-19-814552-7); Vol. 2. Commentarii, Oeconomicus, Convivium, Apologia Socratis. 2nd ed. 1921. 18.95x (ISBN 0-19-814553-5); Vol. 3. Expedito Cyri. 1904. 17.50x (ISBN 0-19-814554-3); Vol. 4. Institutio Cyri. 1919. o.p. (ISBN 0-19-814555-1); Vol. 5. Opuscula. 1920. o.p. (ISBN 0-19-814556-X). (Oxford Classical Texts Ser). Oxford U Pr.

--Recollections of Socrates. Benjamin, Anna, tr. Bd. with Socrates' Defense Before the Jury. LC 64-66080. 1965. pap. 5.95 (ISBN 0-672-60449-3, LLA205). Bobbs.

--The Respublica Lacedaemoniorum Ascribed to Xenophon. Chrimes, K. M., ed. 1948. pap. 8.50 (ISBN 0-7190-1207-4). Manchester.

Xerox Educational Services. Easy to Make Holiday Fun Things. (Elephant Bks.). (gr. 1-6). 1977. pap. 1.25 o.s.i. (ISBN 0-448-14449-2, G&D). Putnam Pub Group.

--Math Games & Puzzles. (Elephant Bks). (gr. 1-6). 1977. pap. 1.25 o.s.i. (ISBN 0-448-14453-0, G&D). Putnam Pub Group.

--My Activity Book About Nature. (Elephant Bks). (gr. 1-6). 1977. pap. 1.25 o.s.i. (ISBN 0-448-14451-4, G&D). Putnam Pub Group.

--Singing Games & Singing Fun. (Elephant Bks). (gr. 1-6). 1977. pap. 1.25 o.s.i. (ISBN 0-448-14448-4, G&D). Putnam Pub Group.

Xerox Rank (UK) Ltd, Uxbridge, UK, ed. Brave New World? Living with Information Technology. 188p. 1983. 15.90 (ISBN 0-08-025847-6). Pergamon.

Xia Dao-Xing. Measure & Integration Theory on Infinite-Dimensional Spaces: Abstract Harmonic Analysis. (Pure & Applied Mathematics Ser.). 1972. 69.00 (ISBN 0-12-767650-3). Acad Pr.

Xiankun, Meng, tr. see Jiasan, Yang.

Xianshi, Fu. Mount Taishan. Nianpei, Li, tr. from Chinese. (Illus.). 37p. (Orig.). 1982. pap. 0.95 (ISBN 0-8351-1040-0). China Bks.

Xianyi, Yang, tr. see Qing, Ai.

Xing, Wang, ed. China Remembers Edgar Snow. (Illus.). 79p. (Orig.). 1982. pap. 1.95 (ISBN 0-8351-1025-7). China Bks.

Xinhua Publishing House. The China Directory of Industry & Commerce & Economic Annual: 1982-1983. (Illus.). 1960p. 1982. 495.00 (ISBN 0-86720-500-8). Sci Bks Intl.

Xinwu, Liu & Meng, Wang. Prize-Winning Stories from China (1978-1979) (Illus.). 535p. 1981. pap. 9.95 (ISBN 0-8351-1032-X). China Bks.

Xuequin, Cao see Cao Xuequin.

Xuequin, Cao see Cao Xuequin & Gao E.

Xuewu, Li, tr. see Jiasan, Yang.

Xyzyx Information Corporation. Home Emergency Repair Book. 1978. pap. 6.95 o.p. (ISBN 0-07-072229-3, SP). McGraw.

Y

Yaacov Ro'I. The Limits to Power: Soviet Policy in the Middle East. 1979. 30.00x (ISBN 0-312-48695-2). St Martin.

Yabes, Leopoldo Y., ed. Philippine Short Stories, 1941-1955. 1982. Set, 2 vols. text ed. 48.00x; Combined ed.: 2 vols. in one. pap. text ed. 40.00x (ISBN 0-8248-0767-7). UH Pr.

Yablonsky, Lewis. Father's & Sons. 1982. 14.50 (ISBN 0-671-25461-8). S&S.

--The Violet Gang. 250p. 1983. 24.50x (ISBN 0-8290-1317-2); pap. text ed. 9.95x (ISBN 0-8290-1318-0). Irvington.

Yablonsky, Lewis, jt. auth. see Haskell, Martin R.

Yacenko, Miquel. Antologia Poetica de Miguel Yacenko. 1979. pap. 2.25 (ISBN 0-311-08756-6). Casa Bautista.

Yachnin, Rissa & Stam, David, eds. Turgenev in English: A Check List of Works by & About Him. LC 61-11067. (Orig.). 1962. pap. 5.00 o.p. (ISBN 0-87104-211-8). NY Pub Lib.

Yacone, Linda A. Cardiovascular Problems. Van Meter, Margaret, ed. (RN Nursing Assessment Ser.). 160p. 1983. 10.95 (ISBN 0-87489-289-9). Med Economics.

Yaconelli, Mike, jt. auth. see Rice, Wayne.

Yadav, C. S. Land Use in Big Cities: A Study of Delhi. 1979. text ed. 22.25x (ISBN 0-391-01840-X). Humanities.

Yadav, K. C., ed. see Saraswati, Dayanand.

Yadava, Ganga P. Dhanapala & His Times: A Socio-Cultural Study Based Upon His Works. 276p. 1982. text ed. 16.00x (ISBN 0-391-02785-9, 40902, Pub. by Concept India). Humanities.

Yadava, J. S. & Vinayshil, Gautam, eds. The Communication of Ideas. 256p. 1980. text ed. 16.50x (ISBN 0-391-02128-1). Humanities.

Yadegari, Mohammad. Ideological Revolution in the Muslim World. Quinlan, Hamid, ed. LC 82-74123. (Illus.). 95p. 1983. pap. 3.50 (ISBN 0-89259-040-8). Am Trust Pubns.

Yadin, Yigael. Message of the Scrolls. 1969. pap. 3.95 o.p. (ISBN 0-671-20420-3, Touchstone Bks). S&S.

Yaeger, Randolf. Renaissance New Testament, Vol. 14. 660p. 1983. 22.50 (ISBN 0-88289-859-0). Pelican.

Yaffe, Byron & Goldblatt, Howard. Factfinding in Public Employment Disputes in New York State: More Promise Than Illusion. LC 76-635611. (ILR Paperback Ser.: No. 10). 140p. 1971. pap. 3.50 (ISBN 0-87546-044-5); pap. 6.50 special hard bdg. (ISBN 0-87546-278-2). ILR Pr.

Yaffe, L., ed. Nuclear Chemistry, Vols. 1-2. 1968. 63.00 o.p. (ISBN 0-686-76855-8). Vol. 1 (ISBN 0-12-767901-4). Vol. 2 (ISBN 0-12-767902-2). Acad Pr.

Yaffe, Maurice & Nelson, Edward. The Influence of Pornography on Behaviour. 26.00 (ISBN 0-12-767850-6). Acad Pr.

Yagawa, Sumiko. The Crane Wife. Paterson, Katherine, tr. from Japanese. LC 80-29278. (Junior Bks.). Orig. Title: Tsuru-Nyobo. (Illus.). 32p. 1981. 9.95 (ISBN 0-688-00496-2). Morrow.

Yager, J., jt. auth. see Segal, S.

Yager, Joseph A. International Cooperation in Nuclear Energy. LC 81-1414. 226p. 1981. 22.95 (ISBN 0-8157-9676-5); pap. 8.95 (ISBN 0-8157-9675-7). Brookings.

Yager, Joseph A. & Steinberg, Eleanor B. Energy & U. S. Foreign Policy. LC 74-19193. (Ford Foundation Energy Policy Project Ser.). (Illus.). 462p. 1974. prof ref 25.00 (ISBN 0-88410-027-8); pap. text ed. 15.00 (ISBN 0-88410-028-6). Ballinger Pub.

Yager, Joseph A., jt. auth. see Steinberg, Eleanor B.

Yager, Joseph A., ed. Nonproliferation & U. S. Foreign Policy. LC 80-20483. 464p. 1980. 24.95 (ISBN 0-8157-9674-9); pap. 9.95 (ISBN 0-8157-9673-0). Brookings.

Yaggy, Duncan & Anylan, William G, eds. Health Care for the Poor & Elderly: Meeting the Challenge. (Duke Press Policy Studies). 240p. Date not set. text ed. 25.00. Duke.

Yaggy, Duncan, ed. see Duke University.

Yagi, K., ed. Reactivity of Flavins. (Illus.). 220p. 1975. 19.50 o.p. (ISBN 0-8391-0831-1). Univ Park.

Yagi, Koji. A Japanese Touch for Your Home. Williams, Mark B., tr. from Japanese. LC 82-80646. (Illus.). 84p. 1982. 15.95 (ISBN 0-87011-526-X). Kodansha.

Yagi, Kunio, ed. Biochemical Aspects of Nutrition. 248p. 1979. text ed. 64.50 o.p. (ISBN 0-8391-1444-3). Univ Park.

--Lipid Peroxides in Biology & Medicine: Symposium. LC 82-16430. 1982. 29.50 (ISBN 0-12-768050-0). Acad Pr.

Yagiela, John A., jt. auth. see Jastak, J. Theodore.

Yaglom, A. M., jt. auth. see Monin, A. S.

Yaglom, I. M. Geometric Transformations, Vol. 2. LC 67-20607. (New Mathematical Library: No. 21). 1968. pap. 8.75 (ISBN 0-88385-621-2). Math Assn.

--Geometric Transformations, Vol. 3. Shenitzer, Abe, tr. LC 72-5702. (New Mathematical Library: No. 24). 1975. pap. 8.75 (ISBN 0-88385-624-7). Math Assn.

--Mathematical Structures & Mathematical Modeling. 296p. 1983. write for info. (ISBN 0-677-06110-2). Gordon.

Yahm, J. J. Lesson Plans for Hair Structure & Chemistry. 1973. 37.50 (ISBN 0-87350-052-0); wkbk. 12.45 (ISBN 0-87350-053-9). Milady.

Yahn, Linda C., jt. auth. see Stefansson, Evelyn.

Yahr, Melvin D., ed. The Basal Ganglia. LC 75-25114. (Association for Research in Nervous & Mental Disease Research Publications: Vol. 55). 496p. 1976. 53.00 (ISBN 0-89004-099-0). Raven.

--The Treatment of Parkinsonism: The Role of Dopa & Decarboxylase Inhibitors. (Advances in Neurology Ser.: Vol. 2). 317p. 1973. text ed. 27.50 (ISBN 0-911216-04-9). Raven.

Yahr, Melvin D. & Purpura, Dominick P., eds. Neurophysiological Basis of Normal & Abnormal Motor Activities. LC 67-28247. 512p. 1967. 41.50 (ISBN 0-911216-04-9). Raven.

Yahr, Robert B. Are There GA (A) PS in Financial Reporting for the Life Insurance Industry? Dufey, Gunter, ed. LC 80-39883. (Research for Business Decisions: No. 29). 182p. 1981. 39.95 (ISBN 0-8357-1146-3, Pub. by UMI Res Pr). Univ Microfilms.

Yahraes, Herbert, jt. auth. see Segal, Julius.

Yahuda, Michael B. China's Role in World Affairs. LC 78-19218. 1978. 25.00 (ISBN 0-312-13358-8). St Martin.

Yahya, Dahiru. Morocco in the Sixteenth Century: Problems & Patterns in African Foreign Policy. (Ibadan History Ser.). 224p. 1981. text ed. 36.75x (ISBN 0-391-01787-X). Humanities.

Yahya, S. M. Fundamentals of Compressible Flow. LC 81-13390. 310p. 1982. 18.95x o.p. (ISBN 0-470-27282-1). Halsted Pr.

Yajima, S. Concept of the Semi-Homogeneous Reactor & Present Status of Research in Japan. (Review Ser.: No. 19). (Illus.). 32p. 1961. pap. write for info. o.p. (ISBN 92-0-157261-1, STI/PUB/15/19, IAEA). Unipub.

Yakhontoff, Victor A. The Chinese Soviets. LC 78-138195. 296p. 1972. Repr. of 1934 ed. lib. bdg. 16.00x (ISBN 0-8371-5290-9, YACS). Greenwood.

Yakovlev, Nikolai N., jt. auth. see Sivachev, Nikolai V.

Yakowitz, Sidney J. Computational Probability & Simulation. LC 77-3002. (Applied Mathematics & Computation Ser.: No. 12). 1977. text ed. 24.50 (ISBN 0-201-08892-4, Adv Bk Prog); pap. text ed. 17.50 (ISBN 0-201-08893-2). A-W.

--Mathematics of Adaptive Control Processes. (Modern Analytic & Computational Methods in Science & Mathematics: Vol. 14). 1969. 26.95 (ISBN 0-444-00048-8, North Holland). Elsevier.

Yakubovich, V. A. & Starzhinskii, V. M. Linear Differential Equations with Periodic Coefficients, 2 vols. 775p. Repr. of 1975 ed. text ed. 56.75 (ISBN 0-470-96953-9). Krieger.

Yakushova, A., jt. auth. see Gorshkov, G.

Yaldiz, Marianne, jt. auth. see Hartel, Herbert.

Yale Daily News. The Insider's Guide to the Colleges, Nineteen Eighty-One to Eighty-Two. 404p. 1981. 11.95 (ISBN 0-399-12553-1, Perige); pap. 5.95 (ISBN 0-399-50502-4). Putnam Pub Group.

Yale Daily News Staff, ed. The Insider's Guide to the Colleges. 9th ed. 502p. 1983. pap. 9.95 (ISBN 0-312-92330-9). Congdon & Weed.

Yale Daily News, Staff of. The Insider's Guide to the Colleges. (Paragon). 1979. 7.95 o.s.i. (ISBN 0-399-12387-3); pap. 5.95 o.s.i. (ISBN 0-399-50403-6). Putnam Pub Group.

Yale, David R. The Publicity Handbook. 320p. 1982. pap. 3.50 (ISBN 0-553-20832-2). Bantam.

Yale, Diane. Dark Terror. 1981. pap. 6.95 (ISBN 0-686-84692-3, Avalon). Bouregy.

--Deadly Manor. 1982. 6.95 (ISBN 0-686-84159-X, Avalon). Bouregy.

Yale French Studies. The Language of Difference: Writing in Quebec(ois, No. 65. Sarkonak, Ralph, ed. (Yale French Studies). 1983. pap. text ed. 10.95x (ISBN 0-300-03025-8). Yale U Pr.

--Montaigne: Essays in Reading. Defaux, Gerard, ed. (French Studies: No. 64). 288p. (Orig.). 1983. pap. 10.95x (ISBN 0-300-02977-2). Yale U Pr.

--Montaigne: Essays in Reading, No. 64. Defaux, Gerard, ed. (Yale French Studies). 264p. (Orig.). 1983. pap. text ed. 10.95x (ISBN 0-300-02977-2). Yale U Pr.

Yale Univ. Library. List of Newspapers in Library of Yale. (Yale Historical Pubs., Miscellany Ser.: No. II). 1916. 57.50x (ISBN 0-685-69889-0). Elliots Bks.

Yale University. The Record of the Celebration of the Two Hundredth Anniversary of the Founding of Yale College, Held at Yale University in New Haven, Connecticut, October 20-23, 1901 A.D. 1902. deluxe ed. 65.00x (ISBN 0-686-50032-6). Elliots Bks.

Yale University Division of Student Mental Hygiene Staff. Psychosocial Problems of College Men. Wedge, Bryant M., ed. 1958. text ed. 13.50x (ISBN 0-686-83715-0). Elliots Bks.

Yallop, David A. Deliver Us from Evil. (Illus.). 336p. 1982. 15.95 (ISBN 0-698-11113-3, Coward). Putnam Pub Group.

Yalman, Nur. Under the Bo Tree: Studies in Caste, Kinship & Marriage in the Interior of Ceylon. 1967. 32.50x (ISBN 0-520-01368-9); pap. 7.45x (ISBN 0-520-02054-5, CAMPUS62). U of Cal Pr.

Yalom, Irvin D. Inpatient Group Psychotherapy. 1983. text ed. 16.95x (ISBN 0-465-03298-2). Basic.

Yalom, Irvin D. & Elkin, Ginny. Every Day Gets a Little Closer. LC 74-78308. 1974. 14.95x (ISBN 0-465-02119-0). Basic.

Yalom, Irvin D., et al. Encounter Groups: First Facts. LC 72-89174. 1973. 16.95x (ISBN 0-465-01968-4). Basic.

Yalon, Reuven. B'yad Halashon, Bk. 1. rev. ed. (Heb). 1967. pap. text ed. 6.95 (ISBN 0-912022-00-0, HBW-1900); pap. 6.95, teachers' guide (ISBN 0-912022-01-9, HB-1900). EMC.

--B'yad Halashon, Bk. 2. (Heb). 1968. text ed. 6.95 (ISBN 0-912022-02-7); teachers' guide 6.95 (ISBN 0-912022-03-5). student test bklet. 0.80 (ISBN 0-912022-25-6). EMC.

--Package, a Package; Halot & Candles for the Sabbath. (Illus.). 1972. pap. 0.60 o.p. (ISBN 0-912022-18-3). EMC.

Yalow, R. S., jt. ed. see Berson, S. A.

Yamada, Kenneth M. Cell Interactions & Development: Molecular Mechanisms. LC 82-11050. 287p. 1983. 39.95x (ISBN 0-471-07987-1, Pub. by Wiley-Interscience). Wiley.

Yamada, Sadami. Animal Sumi-E in Three Weeks. LC 65-27100. (Illus.). 32p. pap. 3.50 o.p. (ISBN 0-87040-006-1). Japan Pubns.

--Complete Sumi-E Techniques. LC 66-24010. 1966. pap. 11.95 (ISBN 0-87040-361-3). Japan Pubns.

Yamada, Y. & Roche, R. L., eds. An International Dialogue of Experiences In Elevated Temperature Design: Benchmark Problem Studies & Piping System At Elevated Temperatures. (PVP Ser.: Vol. 66). 204p. 1982. 30.00 (H00223). ASME.

Yamada, Y & Roche, R. L., eds. An International Dialogue of Experiences In Elevated Temperature Design: Material Behavior at Elevated Temperatures & Components Analysis. (PVP Ser.: Vol. 60). 178p. 1982. 34.00 (H00217). ASME.

Yamaguchi. Recent Advances on the Lacrimal System. 1981. 54.75x (ISBN 0-89352-140-X). Masson Pub.

Yamaguchi, N. & Fujisawa, K., eds. Recent Advances in EEG & EMG Data Processing. 1982. 68.00 (ISBN 0-444-80356-4). Elsevier.

Yamaguchi, Susumu. The Mahayana Way to Buddhahood. Buddhist Books International, tr. from Japanese. LC 82-4416. 1982. 9.95x (ISBN 0-914910-11-6). Buddhist Bks.

Yamaguti, Satyu. Monogenetic Trematodes of Hawaiian Fishes. (Illus.). 1968. text ed. 20.00x (ISBN 0-87022-891-9). UH Pr.

Yamakawa, Reiko, tr. see O'Hara, Betsy.

Yamakov, Y. I., et al. Catalysis by Supported Complexes. (Studies in Surface Science & Catalysis Ser.: Vol. 8). 1981. 89.50 (ISBN 0-444-42014-2). Elsevier.

Yamamori, Tetsunao & Taber, Charles R., eds. Christopaganism or Indigenous Christianity? LC 75-6616. (Applied Cultural Anthropology Ser.). 256p. 1975. pap. 5.95 o.p. (ISBN 0-87808-423-1). William Carey Lib.

Yamamoto, J. Isamu. The Moon Doctrine. 48p. (Orig.). pap. 0.50 o.p. (ISBN 0-87784-158-6). Inter-Varsity.

Yamamoto, Kaoru, ed. Child & His Image: Self Concept in the Early Years. LC 72-163283. (Illus., Orig.). 1972. pap. text ed. 14.95 (ISBN 0-395-12571-5). HM.

--Children in Time & Space. LC 79-91. 1979. pap. text ed. 10.50 (ISBN 0-8077-2553-6). Tchrs Coll.

Yamamoto, Mitsu. Bridges to Fear. (Readers Ser.: Stage 3). 1977. pap. text ed. 2.95 (ISBN 0-88377-088-1). Newbury Hse.

Yamamoto, Mitsu, adapted by. Call of the Wild. LC 78-26979. (Readers Ser.: Stage 3). 1979. pap. text ed. 2.95 (ISBN 0-88377-156-X). Newbury Hse.

Yamamoto, Shizuko. Barefoot Shiatsu: Whole-Body Approach to Health. 1979. pap. 11.50 (ISBN 0-87040-439-3). Japan Pubns.

Yamamoto, Shozo, jt. ed. see Nozaki, Mitsuhiro.

Yamamura, H. D., jt. ed. see Enna, S. J.

Yamamura, Henry I., jt. auth. see Yoshida, Hiroshi.

Yamamura, Henry I., et al, eds. Neurotransmitter Receptor Binding. LC 78-3010. 205p. 1978. 23.00 (ISBN 0-89004-231-4). Raven.

Yamamura, Kozo. Economic Policy in Postwar Japan: Growth Versus Economic Democracy. (Center for Japanese & Korean Studies, UC Berkeley). 1967. 30.00x o.s.i. (ISBN 0-520-01369-7). U of Cal Pr.

Yamamura, Kozo, ed. Policy & Trade Issues of Japan: American & Japanese Perspectives. LC 82-15918. (Publications of the School of International Studies on Asia: No. 36). 480p. 1982. 25.00 (ISBN 0-295-95900-2). U of Wash Pr.

Yamamura, Sakae. Theory of Linear Induction Motors. 2nd ed. LC 78-21550. 1979. 39.95x o.s.i. (ISBN 0-470-26583-3). Halsted Pr.

Yamamura, Y., ed. Allergology. (Proceedings). 1974. 125.75 (ISBN 0-444-15073-0). Elsevier.

Yamamura, Yuichi. Immunomodulation by Microbial Products & Related Synthetic Compounds. (International Congress Ser.: Vol. 563). 1982. 106.50 (ISBN 0-444-90234-1). Elsevier.

Yamane, Taro. Mathematics for Economists: An Elementary Survey. 2nd ed. 1968. text ed. 29.95 (ISBN 0-13-562496-7). P-H.

Yamasaki, Toyoko. Bonchi: A Novel. Summersgill, Harue & Summersgill, Travis, trs. LC 81-23071. (Japanese.). 1982. 14.95 (ISBN 0-8248-0794-4). UH Pr.

Yamashiro, Stanley M., jt. auth. see Grodins, Fred S.

Yamashita, Yasumasa, et al. An Atlas of Representative Stellar Spectra. LC 78-535. 1978. 79.95 o.s.i. (ISBN 0-470-26315-6). Halsted Pr.

Yamauchi, Edwin. Foes from the Northern Frontiers. (Baker Studies in Biblical Archaeology). 128p. (Orig.). 1982. pap. 6.95 (ISBN 0-8010-9918-8). Baker Bk.

Yamauchi, Edwin M. Las Excavaciones Y las Escrituras. 1978. 4.50 (ISBN 0-311-03658-9). Casa Bautista.

Yamazaki, T., jt. auth. see Morinaga, H.

Yamey, B. S. & Edey, H. C. Accounting in England & Scotland: 1543-1800. LC 82-48374. (Accountancy in Transition Ser.). 244p. 1982. lib. bdg. 25.00 (ISBN 0-8240-5332-X). Garland Pub.

Yamey, Basil S. Further Essays on the History of Accounting. LC 82-82491. (Accountancy in Transition Ser.). 244p. 1982. lib. bdg. 30.00 (ISBN 0-8240-5339-7). Garland Pub.

Yamori, Yukio, et al. Prophylactic Approach to Hypertensive Disease: Symposium. (Perspectives in Cardiovascular Research Ser.: Vol. 4). 624p. 1979. 64.50 (ISBN 0-89004-339-6). Raven.

Yan, M. J., ed. Dynamic & Seismic Analysis of Systems & Components. (PVP Ser.: Vol. 65). 192p. 1982. 44.00 (H00222). ASME.

Yan, Martin. Joy of Wokking. LC 82-45516. (Illus.). 1982. 14.95 (ISBN 0-385-18341-0); pap. 8.95 (ISBN 0-385-18342-9). Doubleday.

--The Yan Can Cook Book. LC 80-2987. (Illus.). 355p. 1982. 14.95 (ISBN 0-385-17903-0); pap. 8.95 (ISBN 0-385-17606-6). Doubleday.

Yanagisawa, Eizo, jt. tr. see Whitehouse, Wilfrid.

Yancey, Philip. Open Windows. 204p. 1982. 9.95 (ISBN 0-89107-256-X, Crossway Bks). Good News.

--Where Is God When It Hurts. 1977. pap. 4.95 (ISBN 0-310-35411-0). Zondervan.

Yancey, Philip & Lawhead, Steve. Welcome to the Family. 160p. 1982. pap. 4.95 (ISBN 0-310-35491-9). Zondervan.

Yancey, William L., jt. auth. see Rainwater, Lee.

Yandell, Keith E. God, Man & Religion: Readings in Philosophy of Religion. Bossard, Samuel B., ed. 512p. 1972. pap. text ed. 17.50 (ISBN 0-07-072247-1, C). McGraw.

Yandian, Bob. The Holy Spirit: Oil & Wine. 32p. (Orig.). 1982. pap. 1.50x (ISBN 0-943436-00-1). Grace Fellow.

Yandle, Bruce, Jr., jt. auth. see Macauley, Hugh, Jr.

Yanella, Donald. Ralph Waldo Emerson. (United States Authors Ser.). 1982. lib. bdg. 10.95 (ISBN 0-8057-7344-4, Twayne). G K Hall.

Yaney, Joseph P. Personnel Management: Reaching Organizational & Human Goals. new ed. (Business Ser). 448p. 1975. text ed. 17.95 (ISBN 0-675-08760-0). Additional supplements may be obtained from publisher. Merrill.

Yang, C. K. Chinese Communist Society: The Family & the Village. 1965. pap. 4.95 o.p. (ISBN 0-262-74001-X). MIT Pr.

--Religion in Chinese Society: A Study of Contemporary Social Functions of Religion & Some of Their Historical Factors. 1961. pap. 8.95x o.p. (ISBN 0-520-01371-9). U of Cal Pr.

Yang, Edward S. Fundamentals of Semiconductor Devices. Orig. Title: Semiconductor Electronic Devices. (Illus.). 1978. text ed. 36.50 (ISBN 0-07-072236-6, C); solutions manual 7.95 (ISBN 0-07-072237-4). McGraw.

Yang, Gladys, intro. by. Seven Contemporary Chinese Women Writers. 282p. 1982. pap. 4.95 (ISBN 0-295-96017-5, Pub. by Chinese Lit Beijing). U of Wash Pr.

Yang, Gladys, tr. see Chang Tien-Yi.

Yang, Gladys, tr. see Congwen, Shen.

Yang, Gladys, tr. see Guangtian, Li.

Yang, Gladys, tr. see Li, Sun.

Yang, Gladys, tr. see Lu Hsun.

Yang, Gladys, tr. see Shoushen, Jin.

Yang, Martin M. Socio-Economic Results of Land Reform in Taiwan. 1970. 20.00x (ISBN 0-8248-0091-5, Eastwest Ctr). UH Pr.

Yang, Nai C. Design of Functional Pavements. LC 72-5486. (Modern Sculpture Ser.). (Illus.). 480p. 1972. 51.50 (ISBN 0-07-072243-9, P&RB). McGraw.

Yang, Richard & Lazzerini, Edward J. The Chinese World. LC 77-81184. (World of Asia Ser.). (Illus., Orig.). 1978. pap. 4.95x (ISBN 0-88273-504-7). Forum Pr IL.

Yang, S. J. Low-Noise Electrical Motors. (Monographs in Electrical & Electronic Engineering). (Illus.). 112p. 1981. 34.50x (ISBN 0-19-859332-5). Oxford U Pr.

Yang, W. J., jt. ed. see Ghista, D. N.

Yang, Winston L. & Li, Peter, eds. Classical Chinese Fiction. A Guide to Its Study & Appreciation: Essays & Bibliographies. 1978. lib. bdg. 35.00 (ISBN 0-8161-7808-9, Hall Reference). G K Hall.

Yang, Winston L. & Mao, Nathan K., eds. Modern Chinese Fiction A Guide to Its Study & Appreciation: Essays & Bibliographies. 320p. 1981. lib. bdg. 45.00 (ISBN 0-8161-8113-6, Hall Reference). G K Hall.

Yang Hsien-Yi, tr. see Lu Hsun.

Yang Ming-shih. T'ai-Chi Ch'uan. (Quick & Easy Ser.). (Illus.). 60p. (Orig.). 1974. pap. 3.95 (ISBN 0-8048-1400-7, Pub. by Shufunmato Co Ltd Japan). C E Tuttle.

Yankee, H. W. Machine Drafting & Related Technology. 2nd ed. 1981. 19.95 (ISBN 0-07-072252-8). McGraw.

Yankelovich, Daniel. The New Morality: A Profile of American Youth in the Seventies. 176p. (Orig.). 1974. pap. 2.95 o.p. (ISBN 0-686-76803-5, P&RB). McGraw.

Yanker, Gary D. The Complete Book of Exercise Walking. (Illus.). 288p. (Orig.). 1983. pap. 8.95 (ISBN 0-8092-5535-9). Contemp Bks.

Yann, Richard, jt. auth. see Keddie, Nikki R.

Yannatos, James. Explorations in Musical Materials: A Working Approach to Making Music. (Illus.). 1978. pap. text ed. 17.95 (ISBN 0-13-295956-9). P-H.

Yannela, Donald & Roch, John, trs. American Prose to Eighteen Twenty: A Guide to Information Sources. LC 79-63741. (American Literature, English Literature, & World Literatures in English Information Guide Ser.: Vol. 21). 600p. 1979. 42.00x (ISBN 0-8103-1361-8). Gale.

Yannis, Alex. Total Soccer. (Illus.). 1980. 23.95 (ISBN 0-07-072244-7). McGraw.

Yannopoulos, G., jt. ed. see Shlaim, A.

Yannopoulos, G. N., jt. auth. see Shlaim, A.

Yannuzzi, Laurence A., et al. The Macula: A Comprehensive Text & Atlas. (Illus.). 424p. 1978. 79.95 (ISBN 0-683-09322-3). Williams & Wilkins.

Yano, K. & Bochner, S. Curvature & Betti Numbers. 1953. pap. 15.00 (ISBN 0-527-02748-0). Kraus Repr.

Yano, Shigeko & Kawakami, Yukiko. One Spring Day. 1979. 7.95 (ISBN 0-8170-0821-7). Judson.

Yanoff, Morris. Where Is Joey? Lost Among the Hare Krishnas. LC 82-75596. x, 260p. 1982. 15.95 (ISBN 0-8040-0414-5). Swallow.

Yanouzas, John N., jt. auth. see Veiga, John F.

Yanov, Alexander. The Russian New Right: Right-Wing Ideologies in the Contemporary U. S. S. R. Dunn, Stephen P., tr. from Rus. LC 78-620020. (Research Ser: No. 35). 1978. pap. 5.95x (ISBN 0-87725-135-5). U of Cal Intl St.

Yanovsky, M. Anatomy of Social Accounting Systems. 1969. pap. 5.95x o.p. (ISBN 0-412-20690-0, Pub. by Chapman & Hall). Methuen Inc.

Yanowitch, Murray. Social & Economic Inequality in the Soviet Union: Six Studies. LC 77-71634. 1977. 15.00 o.p. (ISBN 0-87332-105-7); pap. 7.95 (ISBN 0-87332-148-0). M E Sharpe.

Yanowitch, Murray, ed. Contemporary Soviet Economics: A Collection of Readings from Soviet Sources. LC 68-14426. 1969. Set. 20.00 o.p. (ISBN 0-87332-011-5); 17.50 o.p. Vol. 1 (ISBN 0-87332-030-1). Vol.2. 17.50 (ISBN 0-87332-031-X). M E Sharpe.

--Soviet Work Attitudes: The Issue of Participation in Management. Vale, Michel, tr. LC 79-4871. 1979. 22.50 (ISBN 0-87332-147-2). M E Sharpe.

Yanowitch, Murray & Fisher, Wesley A., eds. Social Stratification & Mobility in the USSR. LC 72-77202. (Illus.). 375p. 1973. text ed. 25.00 (ISBN 0-87332-008-5). M E Sharpe.

Yanowitch, Murray, tr. see Rutkevich, M. N.

Yansane, Aguibou Y., ed. Decolonization & Dependency: Problems of Development of African Societies. LC 79-7189. (Contributions in Afro-American & African Studies: No. 48). (Illus.). 1980. lib. bdg. 35.00 (ISBN 0-313-20873-5, YDE/). Greenwood.

Yanz, Linda, ed. see Randall, Magaret.

Yao, jt. auth. see Kempczinski.

Yao, Alice C. & Lind, John. Placental Transfusion: A Clinical & Physiological Study. 188p. 1982. 19.75x (ISBN 0-398-04437-6). C C Thomas.

Yao, Fun-Sun F. & Artusio, Joseph F., eds. Anesthesiology. 480p. 1983. text ed. 32.50 (ISBN 0-397-50509-4, Lippincott Medical). Lippincott.

Yao, James S., jt. ed. see Bergan, John J.

Yao, L. S., jt. ed. see Beck, J. V.

Yao, S. C., jt. ed. see Pfund, P. A.

Yap, Elsa P. & Bunye, Maria V. Cebuano-Visayan Dictionary. McKaughan, Howard P., ed. LC 74-152461. (PALI Language Texts: Philippines). (Orig.). 1971. pap. text ed. 10.00x (ISBN 0-87022-093-4). UH Pr.

Yap, Elsa P., jt. auth. see Bunye, Maria V.

Yap, Lorene, jt. auth. see Weicher, John C.

Yapp, Brunsdon. Birds in Medieval Manuscripts. 208p. 1981. 50.00x o.p. (ISBN 0-904654-54-0, Pub. by Brit Lib England). State Mutual Bk.

--Birds in Medieval Manuscripts. LC 82-5520. (Illus.). 192p. 1982. 35.00 (ISBN 0-8052-3818-2). Schocken.

Yapp, Malcolm. The Ancient Near East. Killingray, Margaret, et al, eds. (World History Ser.). (Illus.). 32p. (gr. 10). 1980. Repr. of 1977 ed. lib. bdg. 6.95 (ISBN 0-89908-025-1); pap. text ed. 2.25 (ISBN 0-89908-000-6). Greenhaven.

--British Raj & Indian Nationalism. Killingray, Margaret & O'Connor, Edmund, eds. (World History Ser.). (Illus.). 32p. (gr. 10). 1980. Repr. of 1977 ed. lib. bdg. 6.95 (ISBN 0-89908-228-9); pap. text ed. 2.25 (ISBN 0-89908-203-3). Greenhaven.

--Chingis Khan & the Mongol Empire. Killingray, Margaret & O'Connor, Edmund, eds. (World History Ser.). (Illus.). 32p. (gr. 10). 1980. Repr. of 1977 ed. lib. bdg. 6.95 (ISBN 0-89908-030-8); pap. text ed. 2.25 (ISBN 0-89908-005-7). Greenhaven.

--Gandhi. Killingray, Margaret & O'Connor, Edmund, eds. (World History Ser.). (Illus.). 32p. (gr. 10). 1980. Repr. of 1977 ed. lib. bdg. 6.95 (ISBN 0-89908-128-2); pap. text ed. 2.25 (ISBN 0-89908-103-7). Greenhaven.

--The Growth of the State. Killingray, Margaret & O'Connor, Edmund, eds. (Greenhaven World History Ser.). (Illus.). 32p. (gr. 10). 1980. Repr. of 1977 ed. lib. bdg. 6.95 (ISBN 0-89908-229-7); pap. text ed. 2.25 (ISBN 0-89908-204-1). Greenhaven.

--Ibn Sina & the Muslim World. Killingray, Margaret & O'Connor, Edmund, eds. (World History Ser.). (Illus.). 1980. lib. bdg. 6.95 (ISBN 0-89908-037-5); pap. text ed. 2.25 (ISBN 0-89908-012-X). Greenhaven.

--Nationalism. Killingray, Margaret & O'Connor, Edmund, eds. (World History Ser.). (Illus.). 32p. (gr. 10). 1980. Repr. of 1977 ed. lib. bdg. 6.95 (ISBN 0-89908-227-0); pap. text ed. 2.25 (ISBN 0-89908-202-5). Greenhaven.

Yapp, Malcolm, ed. see Addison, John, et al.

Yapp, Malcolm, ed. see Duckworth, John, et al.

Yapp, Malcolm, ed. see Harrison, John, et al.

Yapp, Malcolm, ed. see Heater, Derek & Owen, Gwyneth.

Yapp, Malcolm, ed. see Killingray, David.

Yapp, Malcolm, ed. see Killingray, Margaret.

Yapp, Malcolm, ed. see O'Connor, Edmund.

Yapp, Malcolm, ed. see Painter, Desmond.

Yapp, Malcolm, ed. see Painter, Desmond & Shepard, John.

Yapp, Malcolm, ed. see Pearson, Eileen.

Yapp, Malcolm, ed. see Tames, Richard.

Yapp, Malcolm, jt. auth. see Read, James.

Yapp, Malcolm, et al, eds. see Addison, John, et al.

Yapp, Malcolm, et al, eds. see Amey, Peter.

Yapp, Malcolm, et al, eds. see Amey, Peter, et al.

Yapp, Malcolm, et al, eds. see Amey, Peter.

Yapp, Malcolm, et al, eds. see Byres, Terence.

Yapp, Malcolm, et al, eds. see Clifford, Alan.

Yapp, Malcolm, et al, eds. see Cripwell, Kenneth.

Yapp, Malcolm, et al, eds. see Garrett, Sean.

Yapp, Malcolm, et al, eds. see Guyatt, John.

Yapp, Malcolm, et al, eds. see Kanitkar, Helen & Kanitkar, Hemant.

Yapp, Malcolm, et al, eds. see Killingray, David.

Yapp, Malcolm, et al, eds. see Killingray, David, et al.

Yapp, Malcolm, et al, eds. see Killingray, David.

Yapp, Malcolm, et al, eds. see Killingray, Margaret.

Yapp, Malcolm, et al, eds. see Knox, D. M.

Yapp, Malcolm, et al, eds. see Knox, Diana.

Yapp, Malcolm, et al, eds. see Nicholson, Alasdair.

Yapp, Malcolm, et al, eds. see O'Connor, Edmund.

Yapp, Malcolm, et al, eds. see Painter, Desmond.

Yapp, Malcolm, et al, eds. see Tames, Richard.

Yapp, Malcolm, et al, eds. see Townson, Duncan.

Yapp, Malcolm, et al, eds. see Weston, Anthony.

Yapp, Malcolm, et al, eds. see Wrangham, Elizabeth.

Yapp, Malcolm, et al, eds. see Wrangham, Elizabeth, et al.

Yapp, Martin, ed. see Booth, Martin, et al.

Yapp, Peter, ed. The Travellers' Dictionary of Quotation: Who Said What, about Where. 200p. 1983. price not set (ISBN 0-7100-0992-5). Routledge & Kegan.

Yaqub, Adil. Elementary Functions. 368p. 1975. text ed. 21.95 o.p. (ISBN 0-395-17093-1); write for info. instr's. manual o.p. (ISBN 0-395-17871-1). HM.

Yaqub, Adil, jt. auth. see Thompson, Robert C.

Yarber, Robert, jt. ed. see Hurtik, Emil.

Yarber, Robert E. Reviewing Basic Grammar. 1982. pap. text ed. 9.95x (ISBN 0-673-16043-2). Scott F.

Yarber, Robert E., jt. auth. see Hogins, James B.

Yarber, Robert E., et al. The Reader & the Writer: Essays for College Writing. 1982. pap. text ed. 10.95x (ISBN 0-673-16042-4). Scott F.

Yarbo, Chelsea Q. Hyacinths. LC 80-720. (Science Fiction Ser.). 192p. 1983. 11.95 (ISBN 0-385-15453-4). Doubleday.

Yarbo, Peggy. Reference Materials. (Language Arts Ser.). 24p. (gr. 5-9). 1980. wkbk. 5.00 (ISBN 0-8209-0314-0, RM-1). ESP.

Yarbra, Chelsea Q. Tempting Fate. 1982. pap. 3.95 (ISBN 0-451-11865-0, AE1865, Sig). NAL.

Yarbro, Charles Q. Sins of Omission. 1980. pap. 2.25 o.p. (ISBN 0-451-09165-5, E9165, Sig). NAL.

Yarbro, Chelsea Q. Blood Games. 1980. pap. 2.50 o.p. (ISBN 0-451-09405-0, E9405, Sig). NAL.

--The Godforsaken. 400p. (Orig.). 1983. pap. 3.95 (ISBN 0-446-30102-7). Warner Bks.

--Hotel Transylvania. 1979. pap. 1.95 o.p. (ISBN 0-451-08461-6, J8461, Sig). NAL.

--Music When Sweet Voices Die. LC 78-13324. 1979. 9.95 o.p. (ISBN 0-399-12004-1). Putnam Pub Group.

--Path of the Eclipse. 1982. pap. 2.95 o.p. (ISBN 0-451-11340-3, AE1340, Sig). NAL.

--Path of the Eclipse. 518p. 1981. 13.95 o.p. (ISBN 0-312-59802-5). St Martin.

Yarbro, Peggy. Basic Skills Reference Materials Workbook. (Basic Skills Workbooks). 32p. (gr. 4-7). 1983. 0.99 (ISBN 0-8209-0579-8, RMW-1). ESP.

Yarbrough, Camille. Cornrows. LC 78-24010. (Illus.). (gr. 2-6). 1979. 7.95 (ISBN 0-698-20462-X, Coward). Putnam Pub Group.

--Cornrows. (Illus.). 48p. (Orig.). (gr. k-3). 1981. pap. 2.95 (ISBN 0-698-20529-4, Coward). Putnam Pub Group.

Yarbrough, Cornelia & Madsen, Clifford K. Competency-Based Music Education. (Illus.). 1980. text ed. 15.95 (ISBN 0-13-154963-4); pap. text ed. 7.95 (ISBN 0-13-154955-3). P-H.

Yarbrough, James D., jt. ed. see Chambers, Janice E.

Yardley, D. C., jt. auth. see Stevens, I. N.

Yardley, James T. Introduction to Molecular Energy Transfer. LC 80-10898. 1980. 36.00 (ISBN 0-12-768550-2). Acad Pr.

Yardley, Paul T. Millstones & Milestones: The Career of B. F. Dillingham. LC 81-11506. (Illus.). 256p. 1982. 17.50 (ISBN 0-8248-0761-8). UH Pr.

Yaremko, Robert M., et al. Reference Handbook of Research & Statistical Methods in Psychology: For Students & Professionals. 335p. 1982. pap. text ed. 11.50 scp (ISBN 0-06-047332-0, HarpC). Har-Row.

Yarger, Susan R., compiled by. State Constitutional Conventions, 1959-1975: A Bibliography. 88p. 1976. lib. bdg. 19.95 (ISBN 0-8371-8683-8, YSC/). Greenwood.

Yarington, David J. The Great American Reading Machine. LC 77-18186. 1978. 6.00 (ISBN 0-8104-5999-X); pap. 6.00 o.p. (ISBN 0-8104-5998-1). Boynton Cook Pubs.

Yariv, Amnon. An Introduction to Theory & Applications of Quantum Mechanics. LC 81-16007. 300p. 1982. text ed. 26.95x (ISBN 0-471-06053-4). Wiley.

--Quantum Electronics. 2nd ed. LC 75-1392. 544p. 1975. text ed. 42.95x (ISBN 0-471-97176-6). Wiley.

Yariv, Fran. Sharon of Glencoe. (Orig.). 1980. write for info. (ISBN 0-515-05192-6). Jove Pubns.

Yariv, Fran P. Last Exit. 256p. (Orig.). 1981. pap. 2.50 o.s.i. (ISBN 0-515-05416-X). Jove Pubns.

Yarling, James R., jt. ed. see Wentz, Pat J.

Yarmish, Joshua, jt. auth. see Yarmish, Rina.

Yarmish, Rina & Yarmish, Joshua. Assembly Language Fundamentals, 360-370. LC 79-64125. 1979. text ed. 22.95 (ISBN 0-201-08798-7). A-W.

Yarmolinsky, Adam & Foster, Gregory D. Paradoxes of Power: The Military Establishment in the Eighties. LC 82-48523. 160p. 1983. 15.00x (ISBN 0-253-34291-0). Ind U Pr.

Yarmolinsky, Adam & Lambert, Richard D., eds. The Military & American Society. LC 72-93251. (The Annals of the American Academy of Political & Social Science: No. 406). 300p. 1973. 15.00 (ISBN 0-87761-161-0). Am Acad Pol Soc Sci.

Yarmolinsky, Avraham, ed. see Dostoyevsky, Fyodor.

Yarmolinsky, Avrahm, ed. Soviet Short Stories. LC 75-17467. 301p. 1976. Repr. of 1960 ed. lib. bdg. 19.25x (ISBN 0-8371-8310-3, YASS). Greenwood.

Yarmolinsky, Avrahm, ed. see Chekhov, Anton.

Yarmolinsky, Avrahm, ed. see Dostoyevsky, Fyodor.

Yarmolinsky, Avrahm, ed. see Pushkin, Alexander.

Yarn, David H. The Four Gospels as One. 281p. 1982. 8.95 (ISBN 0-87747-948-8). Deseret Bk.

Yarnell, Allen. Democrats & Progressives: The 1948 Presidential Election As a Test of Postwar Liberalism. 1974. 26.50x (ISBN 0-520-02539-3). U of Cal Pr.

Yaron, D. & Tapiero, C., eds. Operations Research in Agriculture & Water Resources. 1980. 74.50 (ISBN 0-444-86044-4). Elsevier.

Yarrington, Roger. Community Relations Handbook. (Public Communication Ser.). (Illus.). 224p. 1983. text ed. 24.95x (ISBN 0-582-28088-5); pap. text ed. 12.95x (ISBN 0-582-28087-7). Longman.

Yarrow, Leon J., jt. auth. see Shereshefsky, Pauline M.

Yarrow, P. J., jt. ed. see Suddaby, Elizabeth.

Yarshater, Ehsan & Bishop, Dale, eds. Biruni Symposium: Iran Center, Columbia University. LC 81-21748. 72p. 1983. pap. 10.00x (ISBN 0-88206-502-5). Caravan Bks.

Yarshater, Ehsan, jt. ed. see Ettinghausen, Richard.

Yar-Shater, Esham, ed. Encyclopedia Iranica, 3 vols. (Orig.). 1982. Fasicle 1. pap. 20.00 (ISBN 0-7100-9090-0); Fasicle 2. pap. 37.50 (ISBN 0-7100-9091-9); Fasicle 3. pap. 37.50 (ISBN 0-7100-9092-7). Routledge & Kegan.

Yarwood, Doreen. Five Hundred Years of Technology in the Home. (Illus.). 168p. 1983. 31.50 (ISBN 0-7134-3506-2, Pub. by Batsford England). David & Charles.

--Outline of English Costume. 1972. 17.95 o.p. (ISBN 0-7134-0852-9, Pub. by Batsford England). David & Charles.

Yarwood, Edmund. Vsevolod Garshin. (World Authors Ser.). 15.95 (ISBN 0-8057-6469-0, Twayne). G K Hall.

Yarwood, Guy. Sinatra in His Own Words. (Illus.). 128p. (Orig.). 1983. pap. 6.95 (ISBN 0-399-41012-0). Delilah Bks.

Yarwood, J., ed. Vacuum & Thin Film Technology. 1978. text ed. 27.00 (ISBN 0-08-022112-2). Pergamon.

Yasaka, T., ed. Progress in Health Monitoring (AMHTS) (International Congress Ser.: No. 539). 1982. 98.75 (ISBN 0-444-90198-1). Elsevier.

YASD Committee, ed. Look, Listen, Explain. 28p. 1975. pap. text ed. 4.00 (ISBN 0-8389-3171-5). ALA.

Yashima, Taro. Crow Boy. (Picture Puffin Ser). (Illus.). (gr. k-3). 1976. pap. 3.95 (ISBN 0-14-050172-X, Puffin). Penguin.

--Seashore Story. (Illus.). (gr. k-3). 1967. 4.95 o.p. (ISBN 0-670-62710-0). Viking Pr.

--Umbrella. (Illus.). (ps-1). 1958. PLB 10.95 (ISBN 0-670-73858-1). Viking Pr.

Yasko, Joyce. Care of the Client Receiving External Radiation Therapy. 1982. text ed. 16.95 (ISBN 0-8359-0689-2); pap. text ed. 13.95 (ISBN 0-8359-0688-4). Reston.

--Guidelines for Cancer Care: Symptom Management. 1983. text ed. 15.00 (ISBN 0-8359-2647-8); pap. text ed. 12.95 (ISBN 0-8359-2646-X). Reston.

Yasko, Joyce & Lauffer, Barbara. Care of the Client Receiving Chemotherapy. 1982. text ed. 16.95 (ISBN 0-8359-0687-6); pap. text ed. 13.95 (ISBN 0-8359-0686-8). Reston.

Yaslow, Samuel. Elements of Mechanical Drafting. LC 78-67463. (Drafting Ser.). 375p. 1979. pap. text ed. 18.00 (ISBN 0-8273-1837-5); instructor's guide 4.75 (ISBN 0-8273-1838-3). Delmar.

Yasny-Starkman, Shulamit, jt. tr. see Everwine, Peter.

Yasuda, Chizuko, illus. Children Praise Jesus. (Baby's First Fabric Bks.). (Illus.). (ps). 1983. fabric 1.95 (ISBN 0-8307-0878-2). Regal.

--Jesus & the Children. (Baby's First Fabric Bks.). (Illus.). 6p. (ps). 1983. fabric 1.95 (ISBN 0-8307-0877-4). Regal.

--Jesus Loves You. (Baby's First Fabric Bks.). (Illus.). 6p. (ps). 1983. fabric 1.95 (ISBN 0-686-82454-7). Regal.

--Jesus Tells About the Kind Shepherd. (Baby's First Fabric Bks.). (Illus.). 6p. (ps). 1983. 1.95 (ISBN 0-8307-0875-8). Regal.

Yasugi, Y., jt. auth. see Billerbeck, K.

Yasuhara, Ann. Recursive Function Theory & Logic. (Computer Science & Applied Mathematics Ser.). 1971. 49.50 (ISBN 0-12-768950-8). Acad Pr.

Yasuhara, Diana, jt. auth. see Yasuhara, Mark.

Yasuhara, Mark & Yasuhara, Diana. Aloha... Forever!! LC 75-21285. 1977. pap. 1.95 (ISBN 0-89221-007-9). New Leaf.

Yates, Alfred G., Jr. The Pocket Estate & Gift Tax Calculator. 110p. (Orig.). 1983. pap. 5.65 (ISBN 0-87218-420-X). Natl Underwriter.

--The Pocket Income Tax Calculator. rev. ed. LC 81-85617. 80p. 1983. pap. 5.65 (ISBN 0-87218-411-0). Natl Underwriter.

Yates, Anthony P., jt. auth. see Goldfarb, I. William.

Yates, Aubrey J. Behavior Therapy. LC 71-88910. (Psychology Ser). 1970. 35.50x (ISBN 0-471-97243-6). Wiley.

Yates, B. How to Find Out About the United Kingdom Cotton Industry. 1967. 14.75 o.s.i. (ISBN 0-08-012360-0); pap. 6.25 o.p. (ISBN 0-08-012361-9). Pergamon.

Yates, Brian T. Doing the Dissertation: The Nuts & Bolts of Psychological Research. (Illus.). 232p. 1982. spiral 14.75x (ISBN 0-398-04650-6). C C Thomas.

Yates, Brock. The Decline & Fall of the American Automobile Industry. LC 82-70939. 352p. 1983. 13.95 (ISBN 0-88015-004-1). Empire Bks.

--Racers & Drivers. LC 68-9303. (gr. 4 up). 1976. 6.95 o.p. (ISBN 0-672-51836-8). Bobbs.

Yates, Brock W. Indianapolis Five Hundred. rev. ed. LC 61-10844. (Illus.). (gr. 7 up). 1961. PLB 8.89 (ISBN 0-06-026641-4, HarpJ). Har-Row.

Yates, D. A., et al. Tres Cuentistas Hispanoamericanos. 1969. pap. text ed. 8.95x (ISBN 0-02-430840-4). Macmillan.

Yates, Donald A., jt. auth. see Lewald, H. Ernest.

Yates, Douglas. The Ungovernable City: The Politics of Urban Problems & Policy Making. 1977. text ed. 19.95x (ISBN 0-262-24020-3); pap. 5.95x (ISBN 0-262-74013-3). MIT Pr.

Yates, Douglas T., jt. auth. see Nelson, Richard R.

Yates, Elizabeth. Amos Fortune, Free Man. (gr. 7 up). 1967. 11.50 (ISBN 0-525-25570-2, 01117-330). Dutton.

--A Book of Hours. 1976. 5.95 (ISBN 0-8164-0901-3); pap. 2.95 (ISBN 0-8164-0900-5). Seabury.

--Mountain Born. (Illus.). (gr. 4-7). 1943. 5.95 o.p. (ISBN 0-698-20095-0, Coward). Putnam Pub Group.

--My Widening World: The Continuing Diary of Elizabeth Yates. LC 82-23713. (Illus.). 120p. (gr. 7 up). 1983. price not set (ISBN 0-664-32702-8). Westminster.

--Prudence Crandall: Woman of Courage. (Illus.). (gr. 7 up). 1955. 8.50 o.p. (ISBN 0-525-37883-9). Dutton.

--Skeezer: Dog with a Mission. 1974. pap. 1.50 o.p. (ISBN 0-380-00105-5, 48223). Avon.

Yates, Elizabeth, ed. see MacDonald, George.

Yates, Frances A. The Rosicrucian Enlightenment. LC 77-90875. (Illus.). 1978. pap. 9.95 (ISBN 0-394-73568-4). Shambhala Pubns.

--Shakespeare's Last Plays. 1975. 16.00 (ISBN 0-7100-8100-6). Routledge & Kegan.

Yates, George R., jt. auth. see Bock, R. Darrell.

Yates, George T., 3rd & Young, John H., eds. Limits to National Jurisdiction Over the Sea. LC 74-3036. (Virginia Legal Studies). (Illus.). 1974. 15.00x (ISBN 0-8139-0572-9). U Pr of Va.

Yates, H. David, jt. auth. see Rhone, L. C.

Yates, J. Frank see Boykin, A. Wade, et al.

Yates, K. M. Los Profetas Del Antiguo Testamento. Corona, Simon, tr. from Eng. Orig. Title: Preaching from the Prophets. 336p. (Span.). 1982. pap. 4.95 (ISBN 0-311-04026-8). Casa Bautista.

Yates, Kyle M. & Owens, J. J. Nociones Esenciales Del Hebreo Biblico. Daglio, S. Daniel, tr. 308p. 1980. Repr. of 1978 ed. 6.50 (ISBN 0-311-42056-7). Casa Bautista.

Yates, Marguerite W., jt. auth. see Yates, Raymond F.

Yates, Maria S. see Knorre, Marty, et al.

Yates, Miles & Charles, John. Believing in God. 1982. pap. 1.70 (ISBN 0-88028-021-2). Forward Movement.

Yates, Norris W. American Humorist: Conscience of the Twentieth Century. facsimile ed. 1964. pap. 14.50x o.p. (ISBN 0-8138-2205-X). Iowa St U Pr.

--Robert Benchley. LC 68-24296. (U. S. Authors Ser.: No. 138). 1968. lib. bdg. 10.95 o.p. (ISBN 0-8057-0048-X, Twayne). G K Hall.

Yates, Raymond F. & Yates, Marguerite W. Early American Crafts & Hobbies. LC 82-48834. (Illus.). 224p. 1983. pap. 5.72i (ISBN 0-06-463575-9, EH 575). B&N NY.

Yates, Richard. Disturbing the Peace. 288p. 1975. 7.95 o.s.i. (ISBN 0-440-03390-X, Sey Lawr). Delacorte.

--The Easter Parade. 1977. 7.95 o.s.i. (ISBN 0-440-02197-9). Delacorte.

--Eleven Kinds of Loneliness: Short Stories. LC 72-603. 230p. 1962. Repr. lib. bdg. 19.75x o.p. (ISBN 0-8371-5727-7, YALO). Greenwood.

--Liars in Love. 1981. 14.95 o.s.i. (ISBN 0-686-34359-X, Sey Lawr). Delacorte.

--Revolutionary Road. 1983. pap. 7.95 (ISBN 0-440-57428-5, Delta). Dell.

Yates, Robert & Gordon, Mildred. Male Reproductive System: Fine Structure Analysis by Scanning & Transmission Electron Microscopy. LC 77-71435. (Illus.). 214p. 1977. 55.25x (ISBN 0-89352-004-7). Masson Pub.

Yates, Virginia. Listening & Note Taking. (McGraw-Hill Basic Skills System). (Illus.). 1979. pap. text ed. 13.50 (ISBN 0-07-044413-7, C); cassettes & transcripts 150.00 (ISBN 0-07-044414-5). McGraw.

Yates, W. E., jt. auth. see Akesson, N. B.

Yates, W. E., ed. see Grillparzer, F.

Yau, John. Corpse & Mirror. LC 82-15544. (National Poetry Ser.). 96p. 1983. pap. 7.95 (ISBN 0-03-063041-X). HR&W.

Yau, W. W., et al. Modern Size-Exclusion Liquid Chromatography: Practice of Gel Permeation & Gel Filtration Chromatography. LC 79-12739. 1979. 45.00x (ISBN 0-471-03387-1, Pub. by Wiley-Interscience). Wiley.

Yavemer, Symond, jt. auth. see Stanislawczyk, Irene E.

Yaverbaum, L. Fluidized Bed Combustion of Coal & Waste Materials. LC 77-89628. (Pollution Technology Review No. 35, Energy Technology Review Ser.: No. 15). (Illus.). 1978. 39.00 o.p. (ISBN 0-8155-0671-6). Noyes.

Yavetz, Zwi. Julius Caesar & His Public Image. 320p. 1982. 19.95x (ISBN 0-8014-1462-8). Cornell U Pr.

Yavitz, Boris & Newman, William H. Strategy in Action: The Execution, Politics & Payoff of Business Planning. LC 81-71956. 1982. 19.95 (ISBN 0-02-935970-8). Free Pr.

Yaw, John. Grand National Championship Races. LC 77-92293. (Superwheels & Thrill Sports Bks.). (Illus.). (gr. 4-9). 1978. PLB 7.95g (ISBN 0-8225-0424-3). Lerner Pubns.

Yawkey, Thomas & Jones, Kenneth. Caring. (Illus.). 211p. 1982. 16.95 (ISBN 0-13-114835-4); pap. 8.95 (ISBN 0-13-114827-3). P-H.

Yawkey, Thomas D. Child Care in Early Development & Education. LC 82-81416. 300p. 1983. pap. text ed. 13.50 (ISBN 0-87581-282-1). Peacock Pubs.

Yawkey, Thomas D. & Aronin, Eugene L. Activities for Career Development in Early Childhood Curriculum. new ed. (Career Programs Ser.). 208p. 1976. pap. text ed. 9.95 (ISBN 0-675-08652-3). Merrill.

Yawkey, Thomas D., jt. auth. see Pelligrini, Anthony D.

Yawkey, Thomas D., et al. Language Arts & the Young Child. LC 80-52447. 259p. 1981. pap. text ed. 9.95 (ISBN 0-87581-263-5). Peacock Pubs.

Yayashi, Masato, jt. auth. see Dachslager, Howard.

Yazaki, Takeo. Social Change & the City in Japan: From Earliest Times Through the Industrial Revolution. Swain, David L., tr. LC 67-28969. (Illus.). 1968. 20.50 o.p. (ISBN 0-87040-117-3). Japan Pubns.

--Socioeconomic Structure of the Tokyo Metropolitan Complex. Matsuda, Mitsugu, tr. (Social Science & Linguistics Institute Special Publications). (Illus.). 401p. 1970. pap. 10.00x (ISBN 0-8248-0240-3). UH Pr.

Yazijian, H. & Blumenthal, S. Government by Gunplay: Assasination Conspiracy Theories from Dallas to Today. 1976. pap. 1.50 o.p. (ISBN 0-451-06935-8, Y6935, Sig). NAL.

Yazijian, Harvey, jt. auth. see Louis, J. C.

Ycas, M. The Biological Code. Neuberger, A. & Tatum, E. L., eds. (Frontiers of Biology Ser.: Vol. 12). 1969. 46.50 (ISBN 0-444-10325-2, North-Holland). Elsevier.

Ydit, Meir M. The Song of Songs: A Drama Based on the Original Text of the Scriptures. 1982. 6.95 (ISBN 0-533-05460-5). Vantage.

Ydur, Rudy. How Not to Write. LC 80-83032. 96p. 1983. pap. 5.95 (ISBN 0-930592-06-9). Lumeli Pr.

Yeadon, David. Backroad Journeys of the West Coast States. LC 78-69500. (Illus.). 1979. pap. 6.95i o.p. (ISBN 0-06-090672-3, CN 672, CN). Har-Row.

Yeager, Bunny. Art of Glamour Photography. (Illus.). 1962. pap. 2.95 o.p. (ISBN 0-8174-0203-9, Amphoto). Watson-Guptill.

Yeager, D. & Gourley, R. Introduction to Electron & Electromechanical Devices. 1976. 20.95 o.p. (ISBN 0-13-481408-8). P-H.

Yeager, David C. Decimal Story Problems. (gr. 4-9). 1982. 5.50 (ISBN 0-88488-238-1). Creative Pubns.

--Fraction Story Problems. (gr. 4-9). 1982. 5.50 (ISBN 0-88488-237-3). Creative Pubns.

--Percent Story Problems. (gr. 4-9). 1982. 5.50 (ISBN 0-88488-239-X). Creative Pubns.

--Think Reader Reading Comprehension Skills Ser, 4 bks. (gr. 1-6). 1981. 4.75 ea. Bk. 1 (ISBN 0-88488-224-1). Bk. 2 (ISBN 0-88488-225-X). Bk. 3 (ISBN 0-88488-226-8). Bk. 4 (ISBN 0-88488-227-6). Creative Pubns.

--The Writing Discovery Book: New Ways to Improve Writing Skills, Grade 4-8. 1982. pap. text ed. 8.95 (ISBN 0-673-15647-8). Scott F.

Yeager, Ernest & Salkind, Alvin J., eds. Techniques of Electrochemistry. LC 73-37940. (Techniques of Electrochemistry Ser.). 464p. Vol. 1, 1972 - 581 Pgs. 64.00 (ISBN 0-471-97700-4, Pub. by Wiley-Interscience); Vol. 2, 1973 - 458 Pgs. 54.95 (ISBN 0-471-97701-2); Vol. 3, 1978 - 495 Pgs. 59.50 (ISBN 0-471-02919-X). Wiley.

Yeager, Frederick, jt. auth. see Seitz, Neil.

Yeager, Howard L., jt. ed. see Eisenberg, Adi.

Yeager, Leland B., jt. auth. see Rabin, Alan A.

Yeager, Mary. Competition & Regulation: The Development of Oligopoly in the Meat Packing Industry, Vol. 2. Porter, Glenn, ed. LC 76-52011. (Industrial Development & the Social Fabric). 250p. 1981. 40.00 (ISBN 0-89232-058-3). Jai Pr.

Yeager, Peter C., jt. auth. see Clinard, Marshall B.

Yeager, Randolf. Renaissance New Testament, Vol. 12. 660p. 1983. 22.50 (ISBN 0-88289-458-7). Pelican.

--Renaissance New Testament, Vol. 13. 660p. 1983. 22.50 (ISBN 0-88289-958-9). Pelican.

Yeager, Randolph O. The Renaissance New Testament, Vol. 10. LC 79-28652. 660p. 1982. 22.50 (ISBN 0-88289-258-4). Pelican.

--The Renaissance New Testament, Vol. 11. 660p. 22.50 (ISBN 0-88289-758-6). Pelican.

Yeandle, P. T. Mathematics: Questions & Answers. (Marine Engineering Ser.). 144p. 1979. pap. 9.95x (ISBN 0-540-07337-7). Sheridan.

Yearley, Clifton K. Money Machines: The Breakdown & Reform of Governmental & Party Finance in the North, 1860-1920. LC 74-112605. 1970. 40.50x (ISBN 0-87395-072-0); pap. 14.95x (ISBN 0-87395-221-9). State U NY Pr.

Yearley, Clifton K., Jr. Britons in American Labor. LC 73-13822. (Studies in Historical & Political Science Ser. 75: Ser. 75, No. 1). 332p. 1974. Repr. of 1957 ed. lib. bdg. 17.75x (ISBN 0-8371-7120-2, YEBA). Greenwood.

Yearley, Lee H. The Ideas of Newman: Christianity & Human Religiosity. LC 77-13894. 1978. 16.95x (ISBN 0-271-00526-2). Pa St U Pr.

Yearling, Robert A. Machine Trades Blueprint Reading. (Illus.). 320p. 1983. text ed. 18.95 (ISBN 0-13-542001-6). P-H.

Yearns, W. B., jt. auth. see Warner, Ezra J.

Yearsley, Macleod. Folklore of Fairy-Tale. LC 68-31517. 1968. Repr. of 1924 ed. 34.00x (ISBN 0-8103-3457-7). Gale.

Yearwood, Lennox S., ed. Black Organizations: Issues on Survival Techniques. LC 79-5500. 286p. 1980. pap. 10.25 (ISBN 0-8191-0898-7); 20.75 (ISBN 0-8191-0897-9). U Pr of Amer.

Yeater, M. L., ed. Neutron Physics: Proceedings. (Nuclear Science & Technology: Vol. 2). 1962. 53.50 (ISBN 0-12-769050-6). Acad Pr.

Yeates, Don, jt. auth. see Daniels, Alan.

Yeates, Donald, jt. ed. see Daniels, Alan.

Yeates, M. N., jt. auth. see Maccuaig, R. D.

Yeates, Maurice. An Introduction to Quantitative Analysis in Human Geography. (Illus.). 288p. 1973. pap. text ed. 19.50 o.p. (ISBN 0-07-072251-X, C). McGraw.

--North American Urban Patterns. LC 80-17708. (Scripta Series in Geography). 168p. 1980. 34.95x (ISBN 0-470-27017-9, Pub. by Halsted Pr). Wiley.

Yeates, Maurice H., jt. auth. see Conkling, Edgar C.

Yeates, Maurice Y. Introduction to Quantitative Analysis in Economic Geography. 1968. pap. 6.95 o.p. (ISBN 0-07-072259-5, C). McGraw.

Yeatman, Linda. Treasury of Animal Stories. Klimo, Kate, ed. (Illus.). 160p. (gr. k-4). 1982. 6.95 (ISBN 0-671-45632-6, Little Simon). S&S.

Yeatman, Robert J., jt. auth. see Sellar, Walter C.

Yeats, Alexander J. Trade & Development Policies: Leading Issues for the 1980's. 220p. 1981. 30.00 (ISBN 0-312-81203-5). St Martin.

--Trade Barriers Facing Developing Countries. LC 78-10537. 1979. 36.00x (ISBN 0-312-81207-8). St Martin.

Yeats, J. B. Letters from Bedford Park: A Selection from the Correspondence of John Butler Yeats, 1890-1901. Murphy, William M., ed. 77p. (Hand printed limited ed). 1972. text ed. 13.00x o.p. (ISBN 0-391-01593-1). Humanities.

Yeats, Jack B. The Charmed Life. 1974. 17.95 (ISBN 0-7100-7667-3). Routledge & Kegan.

Yeats, W. B. The Secret Rose: A Variorum Edition. Marcus, Pillip L., ed. 312p. 28.50x o.p. (ISBN 0-8014-1194-7). Cornell U Pr.

Yeats, W. B., ed. see Blake, William.

Yeats, W. B., tr. see Patanjali, Swami S.

Yeats, William B. Eleven Plays of William Butler Yeats. Jeffares, A. Norman, ed. Incl. On Baile's Strand; Deidre; Player Queen; Resurrection; Words Upon the Window Pane; Full Moon in March; Herne's Egg; Cathleen Ni Houlihan; Only Jealousy of Emer; Purgatory; Death of Cuchulain. 1967. pap. 4.95 (ISBN 0-02-012970-X, Collier). Macmillan.

--Literatim Transcription of the Manuscripts of William Butler Yeats's The Speckled Bird. O'Donnell, William H., ed. LC 76-6047. 486p. 1976. lib. bdg. 60.00x (ISBN 0-8201-1171-6). Schol Facsimiles.

Yeats, William B; see Moon, Samuel.

Yeats, William B; see Schaff, Harrison H.

Yeats, William B., ed. Oxford Book of Modern Verse, 1892-1935. 1936. 19.95 (ISBN 0-19-812120-2). Oxford U Pr.

Yeatts, Harry W., jt. auth. see Craig, Robert J.

Yeazell, Ruth B., ed. The Death & Letters of Alice James: Selected Correspondence. (Illus.). 224p. 1983. pap. 6.95 (ISBN 0-520-04963-2, CAL 632). U of Cal Pr.

Yeck, Fred. Building Your Own Home. rev. ed. LC 78-3419. (Illus.). 1979. pap. 4.95 o.p. (ISBN 0-668-04637-6, 4637). Arco.

Yeck, John D. & Maguire, John T. Planning & Creating Better Direct Mail. 1961. 19.95 o.p. (ISBN 0-07-072264-1, P&RB). McGraw.

Yedidiah, S. Centrifugal Pump Problems. 229p. 1980. 44.95x (ISBN 0-87814-131-6). Pennwell Books Division.

Yedlin, T., ed. Women in Eastern Europe & the Soviet Union. 320p. 1980. 29.95 (ISBN 0-03-055311-3). Praeger.

Yee, Dennis K. Chinese Romanization Self-Study Guide. DeFrancis, John, ed. LC 74-189616. (PALI Language Texts: Chinese). 1975. pap. text ed. 1.95x (ISBN 0-8248-0227-6). UH Pr.

Yee, Janice C. This Gift I Present: Of Poetry from Hawaii. (gr. 7 up). 1974. 5.95 o.p. (ISBN 0-931420-01-6); pap. text ed. 4.00 o.p. (ISBN 0-685-88630-1). Pi Pr.

Yee, Lee, ed. The New Realism: Writings from China after the Cultural Revolution. 280p. 1983. 22.50 (ISBN 0-88254-794-1); pap. 14.95 (ISBN 0-88254-810-7). Hippocrene Bks.

Yee, Rhoda. Chinese Village Cookbook. LC 75-18964. (Illus.). 1976. pap. 5.95 (ISBN 0-394-73152-2, Dist. by Random). Taylor & Ng.

--Dim Sum. LC 77-89297. (Illus.). 1977. pap. 5.95 (ISBN 0-394-73463-7, Dist. by Random). Taylor & Ng.

--Szechwan & Northern Cooking: From Hot to Cold Food. (Orig.). pap. 5.95 (ISBN 0-912738-14-6). Taylor & Ng.

Yefimov, Igor. Arkhivy Strashnogo Suda. 302p. (Rus.). 1982. pap. 10.50 (ISBN 0-938920-25-1). Hermitage MI.

Yefimov, N. V. Quadratic Forms & Matrices: An Introductory Approach. (Eng.). 1964. pap. 14.00 (ISBN 0-12-769956-2). Acad Pr.

Yefung, Sun. Social Needs Versus Economic Efficiency in China: Sun Yefang's Critique of Socialist Economics. Fung, K. K., tr. LC 82-10265. 220p. 1982. 35.00 (ISBN 0-87332-209-6). M E Sharpe.

Yeh, K. C. & Liv, C. H. Theory of Ionospheric Waves. (International Geophysics Ser., Vol. 17). 1972. 68.50 (ISBN 0-12-770450-7). Acad Pr.

Yeh, R., ed. Current Trends in Programming Methodology: Program Validation, Vol. 2. 1978. 24.95x (ISBN 0-13-195719-8). P-H.

Yeh, Raymond T., jt. auth. see Preparata, Franco P.

Yeh, Raymond T., ed. Current Trends in Programming Methodology: Software Specification & Design, Vol. 1. (Illus.). 1977. 24.95 (ISBN 0-13-195701-5). P-H.

Yeh, Raymond T., jt. ed. see Chandy, K.

Yehl, Joan K. & Bandlow, Richard F. P. O. W. E. R. The Reading - Writing Connection. (Illus.). 320p. 1981. pap. text ed. 12.95 (ISBN 0-675-08064-9). Additional supplements may be obtained from publisher. Merrill.

Yehoshua, A. B. Between Right & Right. LC 80-721. 224p. 1981. 11.95 o.p. (ISBN 0-385-17035-1). Doubleday.

Yelaha, Shankar A., ed. Canadian Social Policy. 321p. 1978. pap. text ed. 10.75x (ISBN 0-88920-050-5, Pub. by Wilfrid Laurier U Pr Canada). Humanities.

Yelon, Stephen L. & Weinstein, Grace. A Teacher's World. (Illus.). 1977. pap. text ed. 23.50 (ISBN 0-07-072267-6, C); instr's. manual 10.95 (ISBN 0-07-072273-0). McGraw.

Yen, T. F. & Chilingarian, G. V. Oil Shale. (Developments in Petroleum Science: Vol. 5). 1976. 61.75 (ISBN 0-444-41408-8). Elsevier.

Yen, T. F., ed. Recycling & Disposal of Solid Wastes. LC 72-96910. (Illus.). 372p. 1980. Repr. of 1974 ed. 39.95 (ISBN 0-250-40015-4). Ann Arbor Science.

--The Role of Trace Metals in Petroleum. LC 74-77404. (Illus.). 221p. 1982. 39.95 (ISBN 0-250-40061-8). Ann Arbor Science.

--Science & Technology of Oil Shale. LC 75-10415. (Illus.). 1976. 32.50 o.p. (ISBN 0-250-40092-8); pap. 29.95 (ISBN 0-250-40242-4). Ann Arbor Science.

Yen, T. F. & Kawahara, F. K., eds. Chemical & Geochemical Aspects of Fossil Energy Extraction. LC 82-72858. (Illus.). 266p. 1983. 37.50 (ISBN 0-250-40462-1). Ann Arbor Science.

Yen, T. F., jt. ed. see Chilingarian, G. V.

Yen, Wendy M., jt. auth. see Allen, Mary J.

Yenal, Edith. Christine De Pisan: A Bibliography of Writings By Her & About Her. LC 82-10386. 192p. 1982. 13.00 (ISBN 0-8108-1574-5). Scarecrow.

Yenal, Engin. The Ottoman City in Comparative Perspective, Istanbul, 1453-1923: A Selected Bibliography of Urban History. (Architecture Ser.: A 14). 1978. pap. 6.00 o.p. (ISBN 0-88066-006-6). Vance Biblios.

Yen Ching Hwang. The Overseas Chinese & the 1911 Revolution. (East Asian Historical Monographs). 1977. 27.50x o.p. (ISBN 0-19-580311-6). Oxford U Pr.

Yendo, K. A Monograph of the Genus Alaria. (Illus.). 1919. 24.00 (ISBN 3-7682-1066-9). Lubrecht & Cramer.

Yener, Yaman, jt. auth. see Kakac, Sadik.

Yengoyan, Aram, jt. ed. see Becker, A. L.

Yeni-Komshian, Grace H., et al, eds. Child Phonology: Vol. I Production. LC 80-981. (Perspectives in Neurolinguistics Psycholinguistics Ser.). 1980. 31.00 (ISBN 0-12-770601-1). Acad Pr.

Yenser, Stephen. Circle to Circle: The Poetry of Robert Lowell. LC 74-79778. 400p. 1976. 34.50x (ISBN 0-520-02790-6). U of Cal Pr.

Yeo, C. A., jt. auth. see Heichelheim, Fritz M.

Yeo Kim Wah. The Politics of Decentralization: Colonial Controversy in Malaya, 1920-1929. 395p. 1982. 34.95 (ISBN 0-19-582524-1). Oxford U Pr.

Yeoman, Lynn, jt. ed. see Busch, Harris.

Yeoman, M. M., ed. Differentiation "In Vitro". Proceedings of the British Society for Cell Biology Symposium, 4, University of Edinburgh, Sept. 24-26, 1980. Truman, D. E. LC 81-6094. (British Society for Cell Biology Symposium Ser.: No. 4). (Illus.). 300p. 1982. 59.50 (ISBN 0-521-23926-5). Cambridge U Pr.

Yeoman, R. S. A Guide Book of United States Coins. 236p. 1982. 5.95 (ISBN 0-307-19831-6, 9051, Golden Pr). Western Pub.

--Handbook of United States Coins. 1979. 4.95 (ISBN 0-307-09050-7, Golden Pr). Western Pub.

--Handbook of United States Coins. 40th, rev. ed. Bressett, Kenneth E., ed. (Illus.). 224p. 1982. 3.50 (ISBN 0-307-01983-7, Pub. by Whitman Coin Products). Western Pub.

--Moneys of the Bible. (Illus.). 1982. Repr. of 1961 ed. softcover 7.00 (ISBN 0-915262-77-0). S J Durst.

--Red Guidebook of U. S. Coins. 1983p. 5.95x (ISBN 0-685-22090-7). Wehman.

Yeomans, K. A., jt. auth. see Davis, E. W.

Yeomans, Patricia Henry, jt. auth. see Henry, William.

Yeomans, William N. Jobs Eighty & Eighty-One. LC 77-357858. 1979. 10.95 (ISBN 0-399-12418-7); pap. 4.95 (ISBN 0-399-50389-7, Perigee). Putnam Pub Group.

--Jobs '82-'83. 320p. 1982. 13.95 (ISBN 0-399-12671-6, Perige); pap. 6.95 o.p. (ISBN 0-399-50583-0). Putnam Pub Group.

Yeon, Ha Cheong. Primary Health Care in Korea: An Approach to Evaluation. 214p. 1981. text ed. 12.00x (ISBN 0-8248-0763-4, Korea Devel Inst). UH Pr.

Yep, Laurence. Child of the Owl. (YA) 1978. pap. 1.75 o.p. (ISBN 0-440-91230-X, LFL). Dell.

--Dragon of the Lost Sea. LC 81-48644. 224p. (YA) (gr. 7 up). 1982. 10.10i (ISBN 0-06-026746-1, HarpJ); PLB 10.89g (ISBN 0-06-026747-X). Har-Row.

--Sweetwater. (Illus.). (gr. 3-5). 1975. pap. 1.25 o.p. (ISBN 0-380-00193-4, 21907, Camelot). Avon.

--Sweetwater. LC 72-9867. (A Trophy Bk.). (Illus.). 224p. (gr. 5 up). 1983. pap. 3.13i (ISBN 0-06-440135-9, Trophy). Har-Row.

Yepsen, Roger, ed. see Organic Gardening & Farming Editors.

Yergin, Daniel & Hillenbrand, Martin, eds. Global Insecurity: A World Plan for Energy & Econonic Upheaval. 420p. 1982. 15.95 o.p. (ISBN 0-395-30517-9). HM.

Yergin, Daniel H. Shattered Peace: Origins of the Cold War & the National Security State. 1977. o.s. 15.00 (ISBN 0-395-24670-9); pap. text ed. 12.95 (ISBN 0-395-27267-X). HM.

Yeric, Jerry L. & Todd, John. Public Opinion: The Visible Politics. LC 82-81415. 260p. 1983. pap. text ed. 8.95 (ISBN 0-87581-281-3). Peacock Pubs.

Yerkes, James. The Christology of Hegel. (SUNY Hegalian Studies). 240p. 1982. 39.50x (ISBN 0-87395-648-6); pap. 12.95x (ISBN 0-87395-649-4). State U NY Pr.

--The Christology of Hegel. LC 78-6563. 1978. pap. 9.95 (ISBN 0-89130-233-6, 01-01-23). Scholars Pr Ca.

Yerkey, A. Neil, jt. auth. see Bernier, Charles L.

Yerkow, Charles. Automobiles: How They Work. (How It Works Ser.). (Illus.). (gr. 5-9). 1965. PLB 4.89 o.p. (ISBN 0-399-60034-5). Putnam Pub Group.

--Fun & Safety on Two Wheels: Bicycles, Mopeds, Scooters, Motorcycles. LC 78-32137. (Illus.). (gr. 5 up). 1980. 8.95 (ISBN 0-399-20687-6). Putnam Pub Group.

--Here Is Your Hobby: Motorcycling. (Here Is Your Hobby Ser.). (Illus.). 128p. (gr. 7-12). 1973. PLB 5.29 o.p. (ISBN 0-399-60820-6). Putnam Pub Group.

--Motorcycles: How They Work. (How It Works Ser.). (Illus.). (gr. 6-8). 1971. PLB 4.49 o.p. (ISBN 0-399-60477-4). Putnam Pub Group.

Yermakov, Nicholas. Epiphany. 1982. pap. 2.50 (ISBN 0-451-11884-7, AE1884, Sig). NAL.

Yerofeyev, Viktor, jt. ed. see Aksyonov, Vasily.

Yerushalmi, Yosef H. Zakhor: Jewish History & Jewish Memory. LC 82-15989. (Samuel & Althea Stroum Lectures in Jewish Studies). 192p. 1982. 17.50 (ISBN 0-295-95939-8). U of Wash Pr.

Yescombe, E. R. Plastics & Rubbers: World Sources of Information. 1976. 57.50 (ISBN 0-85334-675-5, Pub. by Applied Sci England). Elsevier.

Yessner, Seymour, et al, eds. Twenty-Five Minnesota Poets Two. (Illus.). 1977. pap. 4.00 (ISBN 0-685-79565-9). Nodin Pr.

Yetiv, Jack & Bianchine, Joseph R. Recent Advances in Clinical Therapeutics: Psychopharmacology, Neuropharmacology, Gastrointestinal Therapeutics. (Vol. 2). write for info (ISBN 0-8089-1542-8). Grune.

Yette, Samuel F. The Choice: The Issue of Black Survival in America. LC 82-83686. 320p. (Orig.). 1982. 13.95 (ISBN 0-911253-00-9); pap. 7.95 (ISBN 0-911253-01-7). Cottage Bks.

Yevangulova, O., intro. by. Leningrad in Works of Graphic Art & Painting. (Illus.). 257p. 1980. 27.50 (ISBN 0-89893-009-X). CDP.

Yevtushenko, Yevgeny. A Dove in Santiago. Thomas, D. M., tr. from Rus. 64p. 1983. 13.50 (ISBN 0-670-28070-4). Viking Pr.

--The Face Behind the Face. LC 78-17749. 1979. 10.00 o.p. (ISBN 0-399-90027-6, Marek); pap. 4.95 (ISBN 0-399-90028-4). Putnam Pub Group.

--Ivan the Terrible & Ivan the Fool. LC 79-21282. 1980. 9.95 (ISBN 0-399-90064-0, Marek). Putnam Pub Group.

Yewey, Theodore L. The First Five Hundred Days. 1977. pap. 3.75 (ISBN 0-89536-074-8). CSS Pub.

Yezierska, Anzia. The Open Cage: Collection. Harris, Alice K., ed. LC 78-61060. 1979. o. p. 12.95 (ISBN 0-89255-035-X); pap. 5.95 (ISBN 0-89255-036-8). Persea Bks.

Yglesias, Helen. Sweetsir. 1981. 13.95 o.s.i. (ISBN 0-671-25092-2). S&S.

Yiannopoulos, Athanassios N. Negligence Clauses in Ocean Bills of Lading: Conflict of Laws & the Brussels Convention of 1924, a Comparative Study. LC 62-10479. 1962. 17.50x o.p. (ISBN 0-8071-0840-5). La State U Pr.

Yih, C. S., ed. Advances in Applied Mechanics, Vol. 20. (Serial Publication Ser.). 1980. 36.00 (ISBN 0-12-002020-3); lib. ed. 48.00 (ISBN 0-12-002051-3); 25.50 (ISBN 0-12-002052-1). Acad Pr.

Yih, Chia-Shun, ed. Advances in Applied Mechanics, Vol. 14. (Serial Publication). 1974. 65.00 (ISBN 0-12-002014-9). Acad Pr.

--Advances in Applied Mechanics, Vol. 15. (Serial Publication Ser.). 1975. 63.00 (ISBN 0-12-002015-7); lib. ed. 80.50 (ISBN 0-12-002041-6); microfiche 46.00 (ISBN 0-12-002042-4). Acad Pr.

Yih, Chia-Shun see Von Mises, Richard & Von Karman, Theodore.

Yi Hun-Gu. Land Utilization & Rural Economy in Korea. LC 68-57650. (Illus.). 1968. Repr. of 1936 ed. lib. bdg. 19.25x (ISBN 0-8371-0975-2, YILU). Greenwood.

Yi-Jing Shu, ed. The Cytopathology of Esophageal Carcinoma. (Masson Monographs in Diagnostic Cytopathology: Vol. 3). (Illus.). 120p. 1983. lib. bdg. write for info. (ISBN 0-89352-171-X). Masson Pub.

Yi Kyu-Tae. Modern Transformation of Korea. (Illus.). 1970. 12.50x o.p. (ISBN 0-8188-0221-9). Paragon.

Yin, Robert I., ed. Paper Coating Additives: Description of Functional Properties & List of Available Products. 4th ed. 72p. 1982. pap. 34.95 (ISBN 0-89852-401-6, 01 01 R101). TAPPI.

Yin, Robert K., et al. Changing Urban Bureaucracies: How New Practices Get Routinized. LC 78-20378. 416p. 1979. 26.95 (ISBN 0-669-02749-9). Lexington Bks.

Yin-Fei Lo, Eileen. The Dim Sum Book: Art of the Chinese Teahouse. (Illus.). 224p. 1982. 14.95 (ISBN 0-517-54581-0). Crown.

Ying, Mei. Zhen Zhen's Dream. (Illus.). 45p. (Orig.). (ps-4). 1982. pap. 2.95 (ISBN 0-686-81669-2). China Bks.

Yinger, J. M. Middle Start. LC 76-47186. (ASA Rose Monographs). (Illus.). 1977. 21.95 (ISBN 0-521-21604-4); pap. 8.95 (ISBN 0-521-29207-7). Cambridge U Pr.

Yinger, J. Milton. Scientific Study of Religion. (Illus.). 1970. text ed. 20.95x (ISBN 0-02-430900-1). Macmillan.

Yinger, John M. Minority Group in American Society. 1965. text ed. 21.50 o.p. (ISBN 0-07-072271-4, C); pap. text ed. 15.95 o.p. (ISBN 0-07-072270-6). McGraw.

--Toward a Field Theory of Behavior: Personality & Social Structure. 1965. text ed. 15.95 o.p. (ISBN 0-07-072269-2, C). McGraw.

Ying-Fai Lam, H. Analog & Digital Filters: Design & Realization. (P-H Series in Electrical & Computer Engineering). 1979. 39.95 (ISBN 0-13-032755-7). P-H.

Yip, George S. Barriers to Entry. LC 81-47993. 240p. 1982. 24.95x (ISBN 0-669-05225-6). Lexington Bks.

Yip, Sidney, jt. auth. see Boon, Jean P.

Yip, Sidney, jt. auth. see Boutin, Henri.

Yip, Wai-Lim. Chinese Poetry: Major Modes & Genres. LC 74-76394. 1976. 34.00x (ISBN 0-520-02727-2). U of Cal Pr.

Yiu-Chiu, Victoria S. & Chiu, Lee C. Atlas of Obstetrical Ultrasonography. (Illus.). 312p. 1982. 49.50 (ISBN 0-8391-1765-5, 18074). Univ Park.

Yizze, James P., jt. auth. see Munem, Mustafa.

Ylinen, R., jt. ed. see Bloomberg, Hans.

Ylla. Polar Bear Brothers. LC 60-5793. (Illus.). (gr. k-3). 1960. PLB 10.89 o.p. (ISBN 0-06-026791-7, HarpJ). Har-Row.

--Two Little Bears. LC 54-8963. (Illus.). (ps-1). 1954. PLB 12.89 (ISBN 0-06-026811-5, HarpJ). Har-Row.

YMCA of the USA. YMCA Camping Centennial, No. 2 Program. (YMCA Centennial Ser.). (Illus.). 48p. 1983. pap. write for info. (ISBN 0-88035-007-5). YMCA USA.

YMCA of USA. The New Y-Indian Guide Program, 7 Bks. (Illus.). 1982. pap. 10.00 (ISBN 0-88035-005-9). YMCA USA.

--YMCA Day Camp Manual, 7 pts. (Illus.). 172p. 1982. pap. 19.95 (ISBN 0-88035-004-0). YMCA USA.

--YMCA School Age Child Care. 165p. 1982. pap. 50.00 (ISBN 0-686-83762-2, 0-88350067). YMCA USA.

Yntema, Hessel E., ed. American Journal of Comparative Law Reader. LC 66-11925. 493p. (Orig.). 1966. 12.50 (ISBN 0-379-11702-9); pap. 6.00 (ISBN 0-379-11702-9). Oceana.

Yoakum, James D. & Spalinger, Donald E., eds. American Pronghorn Antelope. LC 79-89207. (Illus.). 244p. (Orig.). 1979. pap. 4.50 (ISBN 0-933564-05-8). Wildlife Soc.

Yob, Parry C. YOB System: Exposure Control from Camera to Image. (Illus.). 1979. 15.95 o.p. (ISBN 0-8174-2513-6, Amphoto); pap. 9.95 o.p. (ISBN 0-8174-2175-0). Watson-Guptill.

Yockey, Ross, jt. auth. see Bookspan, Martin.

Yockstick, Elizabeth, jt. auth. see Gish, Noel J.

Yockstick, Elizabeth, ed. see Fisher, J. & Dryer, R.

Yockstick, Elizabeth, ed. see Irvin, Judith L. & Downey, Joan M.

Yockstick, M. L. Arizona Studies Program. (gr. 4). 49.00 o.p. (ISBN 0-943068-18-5). Graphic Learning.

--Arizona Studies Program. Olivares, Angelina S., tr. (Spanish.). (gr. 4). 49.00 o.p. (ISBN 0-943068-19-3). Graphic Learning.

Yockstick, M. L., ed. see Fisher, J. & Dryer, R.

Yocum, Glenn, jt. ed. see Welbon, Guy.

Yoder, Claude H., et al. Chemistry. 2nd ed. 876p. 1980. text ed. 26.95 (ISBN 0-686-65003-4, HC); instr's manual avail. HarBraceJ.

Yoder, D. Personnel Management & Industrial Relations. 6th ed. 1970. 22.95 o.p. (ISBN 0-13-659201-5). P-H.

Yoder, D., et al. Handbook of Personnel Management & Labor Relations. 1958. 18.50 (ISBN 0-07-072275-7, P&RB). McGraw.

Yoder, D. E., jt. ed. see McLean, J. E.

Yoder, Dale. Demands for Labor: Opportunities for Research. LC 49-7101. 1948. pap. 2.00 (ISBN 0-527-03297-2). Kraus Repr.

Yoder, Dale & Heneman, Herbert G., Jr. ASPA Handbook of Personnel & Industrial Relations. 1698p. 1979. 52.00 (ISBN 0-87179-307-5). BNA.

Yoder, Dale & Staudohar, Paul D. Personnel Management & Industrial Relations. 7th ed. (Illus.). 512p. 1982. text ed. 24.95 (ISBN 0-13-659193-0). P-H.

Yoder, Dale & Heneman, Herbert G., eds. Administration & Organization, Vol. 6. LC 74-80467. (ASPA Handbook of Personnel & Industrial Relations,). 142p. 1977. pap. 10.00 (ISBN 0-87179-205-2). BNA.

Yoder, Dale & Heneman, Herbert G., Jr., eds. Employee & Labor Relations. LC 74-80467. (Handbook of Personnel & Industrial Relations Ser: Vol. 3). 232p. 1976. pap. 10.00 (ISBN 0-87179-305-9). BNA.

--Motivation & Commitment: Wage & Salary Administration. rev. ed. LC 74-24765. (ASPA Handbook of Personnel & Industrial Relations Ser.: Vol. 2). 266p. 1975. pap. 10.00 (ISBN 0-87179-354-7). BNA.

--PAIR Policy & Program Management, Vol.7. LC 74-80467. (ASPA Handbook of Personal & Industrial Relations). 182p. 1978. pap. 10.00 (ISBN 0-87179-206-0). BNA.

--Planning & Auditing PAIR, Vol. 4. LC 74-80467. (ASPA Handbook of Personnel & Industrial Relations). 200p. 1979. pap. 10.00 (ISBN 0-87179-203-6). BNA.

--Professional PAIR, Vol. VIII. (ASPA Handbook of Personnel & Industrial Relations). 268p. 1979. pap. 10.00 (ISBN 0-87179-207-9). BNA.

--Staffing Policies & Strategies: ASPA Handbook of Personnel & Industrial Relations, Vol. 1. 2nd, rev. ed. (Illus.). 306p. pap. text ed. 10.00 (ISBN 0-87179-318-0). BNA.

--Training & Development, Vol.5. LC 74-80467. (ASPA Handbook of Personnel & Industrial Relations). 160p. 1977. pap. 10.00 (ISBN 0-87179-204-4). BNA.

Yoder, Dale, Jr. & Heneman, Herbert G., Jr., eds. ASPA Handbook of Personnel & Industrial Relations: Employee & Labor Relations, Vol. 3. 2nd, rev. ed. LC 79-15194. (Illus.). 232p. 1979. pap. text ed. 10.00 (ISBN 0-87179-305-9). BNA.

Yoder, Don, jt. auth. see Moll, Lloyd.

Yoder, Elmina & Miller, Lula. Praises We Sing. 1980. 4.95 (ISBN 0-87813-515-4). Christian Light.

Yoder, John H. Christian Witness to the State. 1977. pap. 3.95 (ISBN 0-87303-165-2). Faith & Life.

--The Original Revolution. LC 76-181577. (Christian Peace Shelf Ser.). 208p. 1972. pap. 5.95 (ISBN 0-8361-1812-X). Herald Pr.

Yoder, Jon A. Upton Sinclair. LC 74-78450. (Literature & Life Ser.). 160p. 1975. 11.95 (ISBN 0-8044-2989-8). Ungar.

Yoder, R. A. Emerson & the Orphic Poet in America. LC 76-24599. 1978. 25.75x (ISBN 0-520-03317-5). U of Cal Pr.

Yodfat, Aryeh & Arnon-Ohanna, Yuval. P. L. O. Strategy & Tactics. 1981. 25.00 (ISBN 0-312-61761-5). St Martin.

Yodfat, Aryeh Y. The Soviet Union & the Arabian Peninsula: Soviet Policy Towards the Persian Gulf & Arabia. LC 82-42717. 208p. 1982. 25.00x (ISBN 0-312-74907-4). St Martin.

Yoeli, M., jt. auth. see Brzozowski, J. A.

Yoels, William C., jt. auth. see Karp, David A.

Yogananda, Paramahansa. Autobiography of a Yogi. LC 78-151319. (Illus.). 1971. 7.50 o.p. (ISBN 0-87612-075-3); Bengali ed. 4.00 o.p. (ISBN 0-87612-071-0); Dutch ed. 18.50 o.p. (ISBN 90-202-4016-1); German ed. 16.50 o.p. (ISBN 3-87041-015-9); Gujarati ed. 4.00 o.p. (ISBN 0-87612-072-9); Japanese ed. 9.00 o.p. (ISBN 0-87612-073-7); pap. 2.50 o.p. (ISBN 0-87612-079-6). Self Realization.

--Autobiography of a Yogi. (Illus.). 1971. pap. 7.50 British ed. (ISBN 0-09-021051-4); pap. 14.50 Danish ed. (ISBN 87-418-7082-4); pap. 15.00 French ed. (ISBN 0-87612-066-4); pap. 17.00 Greek ed. (ISBN 0-87612-069-9); pap. 12.50 Italian ed. (ISBN 0-87612-067-2); pap. 16.50 Spanish ed. (ISBN 0-87612-068-0); pap. 4.00 Hindi ed. (ISBN 0-87612-077-X); pap. 13.50 Portuguese ed. (ISBN 0-87612-081-8). Self Realization.

--Autobiography of a Yogi. rev., 12th ed. LC 80-52927. (Illus.). 520p. 1981. 10.95 (ISBN 0-87612-080-X); pap. 2.50 (ISBN 0-87612-079-6). Self Realization.

--Law of Success. 1980. pap. 0.95 (ISBN 0-87612-150-4); pap. 1.25 Span. ed. (ISBN 0-87612-151-2); pap. 2.00 French ed. (ISBN 0-87612-152-0). Self Realization.

--Man's Eternal Quest. LC 75-17183. (Illus.). 484p. 1975. 9.95 (ISBN 0-87612-233-0); Italian ed. 15.50 (ISBN 0-686-86739-4); pap. 5.50 (ISBN 0-87612-232-2). Self Realization.

--Science of Religion. LC 81-528923. 1982. 6.00 (ISBN 0-87612-004-4); Span. ed. 2.50 (ISBN 0-87612-001-X); pap. 10.50 german ed. (ISBN 3-87041-225-9); pap. 3.50 (ISBN 0-87612-005-2). Self Realization.

--Scientific Healing Affirmations. 11th ed. LC 81-53040. (Illus.). 1962. pap. 1.95.(ISBN 0-87612-140-7); pap. 1.95 Span. ed. (ISBN 0-87612-141-5); pap. 8.50 German ed. (ISBN 3-87041-241-0); pap. 4.50 Italian ed. (ISBN 0-87612-143-1). Self Realization.

--Whispers from Eternity. 8th ed. LC 52-43234. (Illus.). 1959. 3.95 (ISBN 0-87612-100-8); pap. 3.75 span. ed. (ISBN 0-87612-101-6). Self Realization.

--Whispers from Eternity, First Vision. 1949. 6.95 (ISBN 0-87612-102-4). Self Realization.

Yogananda, Paramhansa. The Second Coming of Christ, Vol. I. LC 79-50352. 1980. pap. 10.95 (ISBN 0-937134-00-7). Amrita Found.

--Sermon on the Mount as Spiritually Interpretted by Paramhansa Yogananda. LC 79-91531. 1980. pap. 6.95 (ISBN 0-937134-01-5). Amrita Found.

--Songs of the Soul. LC 80-69786. 1980. pap. 6.95 (ISBN 0-937134-02-3). Amrita Found.

--Whispers from Eternity. 1978. pap. 8.95 (ISBN 0-937134-03-1). Amrita Found.

Yogeshananda, Swami, compiled by. The Visions of Sri Ramakrishna. 150p. 1974. 2.75 (ISBN 0-87481-451-0). Vedanta Pr.

Yogesvara dasa & Jyotirmayi-devi dasa. Gopal the Invincible. (Childhood Pastimes of Krishna Ser.). (Illus.). 16p. (gr. 1-4). 1983. PLB 6.95 (ISBN 0-89647-017-2). Bala Bks.

Yogi, Maharishi Mahesh, tr. from Sanskrit. & commentary by. Maharishi Mahesh Yogi on the Bhagavad-Gita, Pts. 1-6. lib. bdg. 13.50x (ISBN 0-88307-290-4). Gannon.

Yogis, John. Law Dictionary: The Canadian Edition. (Barron's Educational Ser.). (Orig.). 1983. pap. text ed. 5.95 (ISBN 0-8120-2116-9). Barron.

Yogi Vithaldas. Yoga System of Health. 1981. pap. 3.95 (ISBN 0-686-82888-7). Cornerstone.

Yohan, E., jt. auth. see Tanin, O.

Yohn, Rick. Discover Your Spiritual Gift & Use It. 1975. pap. 4.95 (ISBN 0-8423-0668-4). Tyndale.

--Getting Control of Your Life. 168p. (How to Overcome Temptation.). 1983. pap. 3.95 (ISBN 0-8407-5836-7). Nelson.

--God's Answer to Life's Problems: A Study Manual. LC 76-17438. 1976. 3.95 (ISBN 0-89081-050-8). Harvest Hse.

--God's Answers to Financial Problems: A Study Manual. LC 77-94132. 1978. pap. 3.95 (ISBN 0-89081-129-6, 1296). Harvest Hse.

--God's Holy Spirit for Christian Living: A Study Manual. LC 77-71215. 1977. pap. 3.95 (ISBN 0-89081-042-7, 0427). Harvest Hse.

--Now That I'm a Disciple: A Study Manual. LC 76-20397. 1976. 2.95 o.p. (ISBN 0-89081-055-9). Harvest Hse.

--What Every Christian Should Know about Bible Prophecy. LC 81-85895. 82p. (Orig.). 1982. pap. 3.95 (ISBN 0-89081-311-6, 3116). Harvest Hse.

Yoke, Carl B. Reader's Guide to Roger Zelazny. rev. ed. Schlobin, Roger C., ed. LC 79-17107. (Reader's Guides to Contemporary Science Fiction & Fantasy Authors Ser.: Vol. 2). (Illus., Orig.). 1983. 11.95x (ISBN 0-916732-42-8); pap. text ed. 5.95x (ISBN 0-916732-41-X). Starmont Hse.

Yokell, Michael D. Environmental Benefits & Costs of Solar Energy. LC 79-3688. 160p. 1980. 18.95x (ISBN 0-669-03468-1). Lexington Bks.

Yoken, Melvin B. Claude Tillier. (World Author Ser.). 1976. lib. bdg. 15.95 (ISBN 0-8057-6222-1, Twayne). G K Hall.

Yoken, Melvin B., tr. see Bosquet, Alain.

Yokley, E. C. Municipal Corporations, 4 vols. 3rd ed. 1956. Set. with 1980 cum. suppl. 200.00 (ISBN 0-87215-063-1); 1980 cum suppl seperately 90.00 (ISBN 0-87215-340-1). Michie-Bobbs.

Yokoyama. Physiology of the Mammary Gland. 398p. 1978. text ed. 49.95 o.p. (ISBN 0-8391-1303-X). Univ Park.

Yolen, Jane. The Acorn Quest. LC 80-2755. (Illus.). 64p. (gr. 3-6). 1981. 9.13i (ISBN 0-690-04106-3, TYC-J); PLB 9.89 (ISBN 0-690-04107-1). Har-Row.

--Brothers of the Wind. (Illus.). 1981. 10.95x (ISBN 0-399-20787-2, Philomel). Putnam Pub Group.

--Commander Toad & the Planet of the Grapes. (Break-of-day Ser.). (Illus.). 64p. 1982. lib. bdg. 6.99 (ISBN 0-698-30724-0, Coward); pap. 3.95 (ISBN 0-698-20540-5). Putnam.

--Commander Toad in Space. (Break-of-Day Bk.). (Illus.). 64p. (gr. 3-5). 1980. PLB 6.99 (ISBN 0-698-30724-0, Coward); pap. 3.95 (ISBN 0-698-20522-7). Putnam Pub Group.

--The Dream Weaver. (Illus.). (gr. 6 up). 1979. 10.95 (ISBN 0-529-05517-1, Philomel). Putnam Pub Group.

--Greyling. LC 68-28481. (Illus.). (gr. k-3). 1968. 7.99 o.p. (ISBN 0-529-00543-3, Philomel). Putnam Pub Group.

--How Beastly! A Menagerie of Nonsense Poems. LC 79-22416. (Illus.). 48p. (gr. 4-6). 1980. 8.95 (ISBN 0-529-05421-3, Philomel). Putnam Pub Group.

--The Magic Three of Solatia. LC 74-5010. (Illus.). 256p. (gr. 4-10). 1974. 8.61i (ISBN 0-690-00532-6, TYC-J). Har-Row.

--Mermaid's Three Wisdoms. LC 77-18325. (Illus.). (gr. 4 up). 1981. 8.95 o.p. (ISBN 0-399-20845-3, Philomel). Putnam Pub Group.

--Neptune Rising: Songs & Tales of the Undersea Folk. (Illus.). 160p. 1982. 10.95 (ISBN 0-399-20918-2, Philomel). Putnam Pub Group.

--The Robot & Rebecca: The Mystery of the Code-Carrying Kids. LC 79-27391. (Capers Ser.). (Illus.). 96p. (gr. 3-6). 1980. PLB 4.99 (ISBN 0-394-94488-7); pap. 1.95 o.p. (ISBN 0-394-84488-2). Knopf.

--Shirlick Holmes & the Case of the Wandering Wardrobe. (Illus.). 80p. (gr. 9-12). 1981. 8.95 (ISBN 0-698-20498-0, Coward). Putnam Pub Group.

--Sleeping Ugly. (Break-of-Day Ser.). (gr. 1-4). 1981. 6.99 (ISBN 0-698-30721-6, Coward). Putnam Pub Group.

--Spider Jane. LC 77-17193. (Break-of-Day Bk.). (Illus.). (gr. k-4). 1978. PLB 6.99 (ISBN 0-698-30696-1, Coward). Putnam Pub Group.

--Spider Jane on the Move: Break-of-Day Bk. (Illus.). (gr. 6-9). 1980. PLB 6.99 (ISBN 0-698-30714-3, Coward). Putnam Pub Group.

--Touch Magic: Fantasy, Faerie & Folklore in the Literature of Childhood. 128p. (gr. 6 up). 1981. 12.95 (ISBN 0-399-20830-5, Philomel). Putnam Pub Group.

--The Transfigured Hart. LC 75-2377. (Illus.). (gr. 4 up). 1975. 9.57i (ISBN 0-690-00736-1, TYC-J). Har-Row.

--World on a String: The Story of Kites. (Illus.). (gr. 5 up). 1975 (Philomel). PLB 5.99 o.s.i. (ISBN 0-529-00394-5). Putnam Pub Group.

--Writing Books for Children. Rev. ed. 1983. pap. 8.95 (ISBN 0-87116-133-8). Writer.

Yolles, Stanley, ed. see South Oaks Foundation Conference, April 8-9 1976.

Yolles, Stanley F., et al. The Aging Employee. 1983. 19.95 (ISBN 0-89885-106-8). Human Sci Pr.

Yolton, John W. John Locke & Education. 1971. pap. text ed. 2.95x (ISBN 0-685-04758-X). Phila Bk Co.

--Thinking & Perceiving. LC 61-11288. 175p. 1962. pap. 5.00x (ISBN 0-87548-067-5, P 89). Open Court.

Yolton, John W., ed. The Locke Reader. LC 76-9181. 1977. 37.50 (ISBN 0-521-21282-0); pap. 11.95 (ISBN 0-521-29084-8). Cambridge U Pr.

Yon, Andre, jt. auth. see LeSage, Laurent.

Yon, Jeannine, jt. auth. see Ghelis, Charis.

Yoneyama, Kyoko. The Collection of Stuffed Dolls from a Fancy World. (Illus.). 1977. 11.50 o.p. (ISBN 0-87040-401-6). Japan Pubns.

Yong, R. N. & Selig, E. T., eds. Application of Plasticity & Generalized Stress-Strain in Geotechnical Engineering. LC 81-71796. 360p. 1982. pap. text ed. 27.25 (ISBN 0-87262-294-0). Am Soc Civil Eng.

Yonge, jt. auth. see Barrett.

Yonge, C. M., jt. ed. see Wilbur, Karl M.

Yonge, Charlotte. The Daisy Chain. LC 75-32169. (Classics of Children's Literature, 1621-1932: Vol. 33). (Illus.). 1977. Repr. of 1868 ed. PLB 38.00 o.s.i. (ISBN 0-8240-2282-3). Garland Pub.

--The Heir of Redclyffe. Wolff, Robert L., ed. LC 75-476. (Victorian Fiction Ser.). 1975. Repr. of 1853 ed. lib. bdg. 66.00 o.s.i. (ISBN 0-8240-1554-1). Garland Pub.

Yonge, Charlotte M. Abbeychurch; or, Self-Control & Self-Conceit, 1844. Wolff, Robert L., ed. Bd. with The Castle-Builders; or, the Deferred Confirmation, 1854. LC 75-470. (Victorian Fiction Ser.). 1975. lib. bdg. 66.00 o.s.i. (ISBN 0-8240-1548-7). Garland Pub.

--The Clever Woman of the Family, 1865. Wolff, Robert L., ed. LC 75-1523. (Victorian Fiction Ser.). 1975. lib. bdg. 66.00 o.s.i. (ISBN 0-8240-1595-9). Garland Pub.

--History of Christian Names. 1966. Repr. of 1884 ed. 40.00x (ISBN 0-8103-3139-X). Gale.

--Magnum Bonum; or, Mother Carey's Brood, 1879. Wolff, Robert L., ed. (Victorian Fiction Ser). 1975. lib. bdg. 66.00 o.s.i. (ISBN 0-8240-1598-3). Garland Pub.

Yonge, Maurice see Russell, F. S.

Yonisuke, Ikeda. JFCC Catalogue of Cultures. 3rd ed. 320p. 1980. 35.00x (ISBN 0-89955-221-8, Pub. by Japan Sci Soc Japan). Intl Schol Bk Serv.

Yonker, Tom. But Teach, You Ain't Listenin', or How to Cope with Violence in a Public School Classroom. LC 82-60524. 125p. (Orig.). 1983. pap. 9.95 (ISBN 0-88247-678-5). R & E Res Assoc.

Yoon, Won Z. Japan's Scheme for the Liberation of Burma: The Role of the Minami Kikan & the "Thirty Comrades". LC 73-620093. (Papers in International Studies: Southeast Asia: No. 27). (Illus.). 1973. pap. 4.50x o.p. (ISBN 0-89680-015-6, Ohio U Ctr Intl). Ohio U Pr.

Yoors, Jan. Gypsies. 1969. pap. 3.95 o.s.i. (ISBN 0-671-20342-8, Touchstone Bks). S&S.

Yorburg, Betty. Introduction to Sociology. 486p. 1982. text ed. 18.50 scp (ISBN 0-06-047333-9, HarpC); instr's. manual avail. (ISBN 0-06-367332-0). Har-Row.

Yordon, Judy E. Roles in Interpretation. 352p. 1982. pap. text ed. write for info. (ISBN 0-697-04199-9); instructor's manual avail. (ISBN 0-697-04212-X). Wm C Brown.

Yorgason, Blaine M. The Windwalker. 112p. 1979. 5.95 (ISBN 0-88494-362-3). Bookcraft Inc.

Yorgason, Blaine M. & Yorgason, Brenton G. Seeker of the Gentle Heart. 156p. 1982. 6.95 (ISBN 0-88494-456-5). Bookcraft Inc.

Yorgason, Brenton G., jt. auth. see Yorgason, Blaine M.

Yorinks, Arthur. It Happened in Pinsk. (Illus.). 32p. (ps up). 1983. 11.95 (ISBN 0-374-33651-2). FS&G.

Yorio, Carlos A. & Morse, L. A. Who Done Did It? A Crime Reader for Students of English. 192p. 1981. pap. text ed. 10.95 (ISBN 0-13-958207-X). P-H.

York, Alexander. Back to Basics Natural Beauty Handbook. 1978. pap. text ed. 1.95 o.s.i. (ISBN 0-515-04536-5). Jove Pubns.

York, Andrew. The Combination. LC 82-45615. (Crime Club Ser.). 192p. 1983. 11.95 (ISBN 0-385-18434-4). Doubleday.

York, Carol B. The Midnight Ghost. (Break-of-Day Bk.). (Illus.). 64p. (gr. 1-3). 1974. PLB 6.59 o.p. (ISBN 0-698-30513-2, Coward). Putnam Pub Group.

--The Tree House Mystery. 96p. (gr. 2-5). 1973. PLB 4.69 o.p. (ISBN 0-698-30488-8, Coward). Putnam Pub Group.

York, Christopher C. The Ram & the Black Sheep. (Daring Relations Involving Families & Their Black Sheep). (Illus.). 175p. 1983. 49.95x (ISBN 0-8187-0050-5). C C York.

York, Courtney & York, Gerlene. Jones-Watson-Hale Families (S.C. Tenn-Ark) 70p. (Orig.). 1969. pap. 6.50 (ISBN 0-916660-15-X). Hse of York.

York, D. Planet Earth. 1975. 14.95 (ISBN 0-07-072290-0, C). McGraw.

York, Gerlene, jt. auth. see York, Courtney.

York, Mary, jt. auth. see Schickedanz, Judith.

York, Richard L., jt. auth. see Brown, John P.

York, Rosemary, compiled by. Prince Charles in His Own Words. (Illus.). 128p. 1981. pap. 5.95 (ISBN 0-8256-3954-9, Quick Fox). Putnam Pub Group.

Yorke, Margaret. Cast for Death. 1983. pap. 2.25 (ISBN 0-686-43163-4). Bantam.

--Devil's Work. 224p. 1982. 10.95 (ISBN 0-312-19867-1). St Martin.

--The Scent of Fear. 224p. 1981. 9.95 o.p. (ISBN 0-312-70048-2). St Martin.

Yorkey, Richard. Checklists for Vocabulary Study. (English As a Second Language Bk.). (Illus.). 1981. pap. text ed. 4.65x (ISBN 0-582-79767-5). Longman.

--Intercom, Vol. 3. Rev. ed. Segal, Margaret, ed. 160p. (gr. 10 up). 1982. pap. text ed. write for info. (ISBN 0-88018-824-3); write for info. (ISBN 0-88018-830-8); write for info. (ISBN 0-88018-836-7); set cassette avail. (ISBN 0-88018-848-0). Atlantis Pub.

Yorkey, Richard, et al. Intercom, Vol. 4. Pavlik, Cheryl, ed. 160p. (gr. 10 up). 1983. pap. text ed. write for info; write for info. (ISBN 0-88018-832-4); write for info (ISBN 0-88018-838-3); write for info cassette (ISBN 0-88018-850-2). Atlantis Pub.

--Intercom, Vol 4. Rev. ed. Pavlik, Cheryl, ed. 160p. (gr. 10 up). 1983. pap. text ed. write for info (ISBN 0-88018-827-8); write for info (ISBN 0-88018-833-2); deluxe ed. write for info (ISBN 0-88018-839-1); write for info (ISBN 0-88018-851-0). Atlantis Pub.

Yoseloff, M. L., jt. auth. see Weiss, N. A.

Yoseloff, Thomas, ed. & intro. by see Cather, Thomas.

Yoshfda, Z. I, ed. New Synthetic Methodology & Biologically Active Substances. (Studies in Organic Chemistry Ser.: Vol. 6). 1982. 68.00 (ISBN 0-444-99742-3). Elsevier.

Yoshida, H., et al, eds. CNS Pharmacology Neuropeptides: Proceedings of the Eighth International Congress of Pharmacology, Tokyo, Japan,19-24 July, 1981. (Advances in Pharmacology & Therapeutics II: Vol. 1). (Illus.). 300p. 1982. 70.00 (ISBN 0-08-028021-8). Pergamon.

Yoshida, Hiroshi & Yamamura, Henry I. Pharmacological & Biochemical Aspects of Neurotransmitter Receptors. LC 82-11066. 302p. 1983. 45.00 (ISBN 0-471-86754-3, Pub. by Wiley Med). Wiley.

Yoshida, Shigeru. The Yoshida Memoirs: The Story of Japan in Crisis. LC 72-12336. 305p. 1973. Repr. of 1962 ed. lib. bdg. 17.75x (ISBN 0-8371-6733-7, YOYM). Greenwood.

Yoshihara, Kunio. Japanese Investment in Southeast Asia. LC 77-18017. (Center for Southeast Asian Studies, Kyoto University Monograph Ser). 1978. text ed. 15.00x o.p. (ISBN 0-8248-0603-4); pap. text ed. 10.00x (ISBN 0-8248-0604-2). UH Pr.

Yoshikawa, Thomas T., et al, eds. Infectious Diseases: Diagnosis & Management. (Illus.). 864p. 1980. 42.00 (ISBN 0-471-09500-1, Pub. by Wiley Med). Wiley.

Yoshino, M. Y. Japanese Marketing System: Adaptations & Innovations. 1971. 22.50x (ISBN 0-262-24012-2). MIT Pr.

--Japan's Managerial System: Tradition & Innovation. 1969. pap. 7.95x (ISBN 0-262-74006-0, 192). MIT Pr.

Yoshino, Masatoshi M., ed. Water Balance of Monsoon Asia: A Climatological Approach. (Illus.). 1971. text ed. 22.50x (ISBN 0-87022-895-1). UH Pr.

Yoshinori, Takeuchi. The Heart of Buddhism: In Search of the Timeless Spirit of Primitive Buddhism. 192p. (Orig.). 1983. 19.95 (ISBN 0-8245-0577-8). Crossroad NY.

Yosida, K. Functional Analysis. 5th ed. (Grundlehren der Mathematischen Wissenschaften: Vol. 123). 1978. 39.00 (ISBN 0-387-10210-8). Springer-Verlag.

Yost, Charles W., jt. auth. see Bloomfield, Lincoln P.

Yost, Edna. Frank & Lillian Gilbreth: 1949. (Hive Management History Ser.: No. 88). (Illus.). 384p. 1983. lib. bdg. 22.50 (ISBN 0-87960-119-1); pap. 12.50 (ISBN 0-87960-121-3). Hive Pub.

Yost, Edward, jt. auth. see Herbert, Theodore T.

Yost, Lynn. Like New: Cleaning Every Spot, Spill & Stain in Your Home. (Illus.). 160p. 1981. pap. 4.95 (ISBN 0-8256-3252-8, Quick Fox). Putnam Pub Group.

Yost, Nellie S. Buffalo Bill: His Family, Friends, Fame, Failures, & Fortunes. LC 82-75802. (Illus.). 500p. 1979. 18.50 (ISBN 0-8040-0766-7). Swallow.

--Call of the Range. LC 82-70183. 437p. 1966. 17.95 (ISBN 0-8040-0028-X, SB). Swallow.

--Medicine Lodge: The Story of a Kansas Frontier Town. LC 82-71322. (Illus.). 237p. 1970. 8.95 o.p. (ISBN 0-8040-0198-7); pap. 5.95 (ISBN 0-8040-0199-5). Swallow.

Yost, Nellie S., ed. see Young, Paul E.

Yotey, H. L., jt. auth. see Phillips, Uad.

Yott, Donald H. Conjunctions: An in Depth Delineation, 2 vols. 1981. pap. 4.95 ea. Vol. 1 (ISBN 0-87728-524-1). Vol. 2 o.p (ISBN 0-87728-534-9). Weiser.

Youdim, M. B. Aromatic Amino Acid Hydroxylases & Mental Disease. LC 79-40642. 1980. 99.95x (ISBN 0-471-27606-5, Pub. by Wiley-Interscience). Wiley.

Youdim, M. B. & Lovenberg, W., eds. Essays in Neurochemistry & Neuropharmacology, Vol. 5. Sharman, D. F. & Lagnado, J. R., trs. LC 80-40964. 152p. 1981. 49.95x (ISBN 0-471-27879-3, Pub. by Wiley-Interscience). Wiley.

Youdim, M. B., et al, eds. Essays in Neurochemistry & Neuropharmacology, 4 vols. LC 76-21043. 1977-80. Vol. 1. 49.95x (ISBN 0-471-99424-3, Pub. by Wiley-Interscience); Vol. 2. 41.95x (ISBN 0-471-99516-9); Vol. 3. 44.95x (ISBN 0-471-99613-0, Pub. by Wiley-Interscience); Vol. 4. 79.95x (ISBN 0-471-27645-6). Wiley.

Youdim, M. B. H. Monoamine Oxidase Inhibitors: The State of the Art. Paykel, E. S., ed. LC 80-41258. 214p. 1981. 43.95x (ISBN 0-471-27880-7, Pub. by Wiley-Interscience). Wiley.

Youkeles, Merrill, et al. Helping People: Preparing to Enter a Mental Health Career. 176p. 1981. 14.95 o.p. (ISBN 0-13-386185-6); pap. 6.95 o.p. (ISBN 0-13-386177-5). P-H.

Youldon, Gillian. Alphabet. LC 77-20858. (All A-Board Bks). 16p. (ps-2). 1981. 5.90 (ISBN 0-531-02468-7); 2.95 (ISBN 0-531-02538-1); 1.95 (ISBN 0-531-05163-3). Watts.

--Colors. (Picture Play Ser.). (Illus.). (ps-2). 1979. PLB 5.90 s&l (ISBN 0-531-00439-2); 1.95 (ISBN 0-531-05168-4). Watts.

Youmans, Guy P., et al. The Biologic & Clinical Basis of Infectious Diseases. 2nd ed. LC 78-65974. (Illus.). 849p. 1980. pap. text ed. 24.50 (ISBN 0-7216-9647-3). Saunders.

Youmans, Julian R. Neurological Surgery, 6 vols. 2nd ed. LC 77-84693. (Illus.). 5152p. 1982. Vol. 1. text ed. 80.00x (ISBN 0-7216-9662-7); Vol. 2. text ed. 80.00x (ISBN 0-7216-9663-5); Vol. 3. text ed. 80.00x (ISBN 0-7216-9664-3); Vol. 4. text ed. 80.00x (ISBN 0-7216-9665-1); Vol. 5. text ed. 80.00x (ISBN 0-7216-9666-X); Vol. 6. text ed. 80.00x (ISBN 0-7216-9667-8); text ed. 450.00 Set (ISBN 0-7216-9658-9). Saunders.

Young. Dictionary of American Artists, Sculptors, & Engravers. 1968. 60.00 (ISBN 0-686-43150-2). Apollo.

--The Golden Eye. 29.95 (ISBN 0-935748-52-0). ScalaBooks.

--How to Read Faster & Remember More. 3.95 (ISBN 0-448-14683-5, G&D). Putnam Pub Group.

--Placental Transfer Methods. 264p. 1982. 56.50 (ISBN 0-03-063034-7). Praeger.

--St. Peter. pap. 9.95write for info. (ISBN 0-935748-15-6). ScalaBooks.

Young, jt. auth. see Obert.

Young, tr. see Chekhov, Anton.

Young, et al. Five Finger Music. 64p. (gr. 1-6). 1962. pap. text ed. 7.95 (ISBN 0-87487-633-8). Summy.

Young, A. Tropical Soils & Soil Survey. LC 75-19573. (Cambridge Geographical Studies: No. 9). 1976. 69.50 (ISBN 0-521-21054-2). Cambridge U Pr.

--Tropical Soils & Soil Survey. LC 75-19573. (Cambridge Geographical Studies: No. 9). 468p. 1980. pap. 17.95 (ISBN 0-521-29768-0). Cambridge U Pr.

Young, A. Morgan. Japan in Recent Times, 1912-1926. LC 76-136554. 347p. 1973. Repr. of 1929 ed. lib. bdg. 18.75x (ISBN 0-8371-5480-4, YOJR). Greenwood.

Young, A. P. & Cresswell, R. W. The Urban Transport Future. LC 81-19560. (Illus.). 224p. 1982. pap. text ed. 45.00x (ISBN 0-86095-703-9). Longman.

Young Adult Services Division. Sex Education for Adolescents. 1980. pap. text ed. 3.00 (ISBN 0-8389-3248-7). ALA.

Young, Al. Ask Me Now. 1980. 11.95 o.p. (ISBN 0-07-072360-5). McGraw.

Young, Alan. Dada & After. 247p. 1981. text ed. 36.75x (ISBN 0-391-02359-4, Pub. by Manchester England). Humanities.

Young, Alan, ed. see Rickword, Edgell.

Young, Alan R. Henry Peacham. (English Authors Ser.). 1979. lib. bdg. 9.95 (ISBN 0-8057-6732-0, Twayne). G K Hall.

Young, Alex. Goals at Goodison. 15.00x (ISBN 0-392-15084-0, SpS). Sportshelf.

Young, Alexander. The Sogo Shosha: Japanese Multi-National Trading Companies. LC 78-18935. (Westview Special Studies in International Economics). 1979. lib. bdg. 30.00 (ISBN 0-89158-425-0). Westview.

Young, Alfred, jt. auth. see Grace, John A.

Young, Allen, jt. auth. see Jay, Karla.

Young, Alvin L., jt. auth. see Bovey, Rodney W.

Young, Ann E. Wife Number Nineteen: The Story of a Life in Bondage, Being a Complete Expose of Mormonism, & Revealing the Sorrows, Sacrifices & Sufferings of Women in Polygamy. LC 72-2634. (American Women Ser: Images & Realities). (Illus.). 632p. 1972. Repr. of 1875 ed. 27.00 (ISBN 0-405-04488-7). Ayer Co.

Young, Anthony & Dent, David. Soil Survey & Land Evaluation. (Illus.). 304p. 1981. text ed. 35.00x (ISBN 0-04-631013-4); pap. text ed. 17.95x (ISBN 0-04-631014-2). Allen Unwin.

Young, Anthony, jt. auth. see Riley, Denis R.

Young, Art, jt. ed. see Fulwiler, Toby.

Young, Arthur. The Surgeon's Knot. 288p. 1982. 14.95 (ISBN 0-312-77693-4). St Martin.

Young, Arthur C., ed. The Letters of George Gissing to Eduard Bertz. 377p. 1982. Repr. of 1961 ed. lib. bdg. 30.00 (ISBN 0-686-98145-6). Darby Bks.

Young, Arthur M. The Bell Notes: Journey from Physics to Metaphysics. 1979. 10.00 o.s.i. (ISBN 0-440-00550-7, Sey Lawr); pap. 5.95 o.s.i. (ISBN 0-440-00551-5). Delacorte.

--The Geometry of Meaning. 1976. 10.95 o.s.i. (ISBN 0-440-04991-1, Sey Lawr); pap. 4.95 o.s.i. (ISBN 0-440-04987-3). Delacorte.

--The Reflexive Universe: Evolution of Consciousness. 1976. 15.95 o.s.i. (ISBN 0-440-05925-9, Sey Lawr); pap. 9.95 o.s.i. (ISBN 0-440-05924-0). Delacorte.

Young, Betty. Silky Terrier. (Illus.). 1970. pap. 2.95 (ISBN 0-87666-393-5, DS1044). TFH Pubns.

Young, Billie, ed. see Brooks, Marie E.

Young, Billie, ed. see Chagall, David.

Young, Billie, ed. see DeLauer, Marjel Jean.

Young, Billie, ed. see Mahan, William.

Young, Billie, ed. see Thurber, Carol C.

Young, Biloine W. & Wilson, Mary. How Carla Saw the Shalako God. (Illus.). 28p. (gr. 1-4). 1972. 1.50 o.p. (ISBN 0-8309-0088-8). Ind Pr MO.

--Jenny Redbird Finds Her Friends. (Illus.). 28p. (gr. 1-4). 1972. 1.50 o.p. (ISBN 0-8309-0087-X). Ind Pr MO.

--Medicine Man Who Went to School. (Illus.). 28p. (gr. 1-4). 1972. 1.50 o.p. (ISBN 0-8309-0086-1). Ind Pr MO.

Young, Bob, jt. ed. see Levidow, Les.

Young, Bonnie. All About Me. 1977. 12.95 ea. Blue (ISBN 0-8024-0204-6). Pink (ISBN 0-8024-0205-4). Yellow (ISBN 0-8024-0206-2). Moody.

Young, C. & Symonik. Practical English: An Introduction to Composition. 2nd ed. (gr. 9-12). 1971. 11.70 o.p. (ISBN 0-07-072641-8, G); instructors' manual 2.70 o.p. (ISBN 0-07-072642-6). McGraw.

Young, C. C., jt. auth. see Mills, Gayley C.

Young, C. W., jt. auth. see Muggia, F. M.

Young, Carl W. International Relations of Manchuria: A Digest & Analysis of Treaties, Agreements, & Negotiations Concerning the Three Eastern Provinces of China. LC 30-3997. (Illus.). 1969. Repr. of 1929 ed. lib. bdg. 15.25x (ISBN 0-8371-0771-7, YOMA). Greenwood.

Young, Carlton R., et al, eds. Ecumenical Praise. 1977. 14.95x (ISBN 0-916642-07-0). Hope Pub.

Young, Carol M. & Dupoizat, Marie-France, eds. Vietnamese Ceramics. (Illus.). 192p. 1982. 80.00. Oxford U Pr.

Young, Carter T. Red Grass. large print ed. LC 81-5340. 302p. 1981. Repr. of 1976 ed. 8.95x o.p. (ISBN 0-89621-275-0). Thorndike Pr.

--Winter Drift. LC 79-7886. (Double D Western Ser.). 192p. 1980. 10.95 o.p. (ISBN 0-385-12327-2). Doubleday.

--Winter Drift. large print ed. LC 82-839. 275p. 1982. Repr. of 1980 ed. 9.95x (ISBN 0-89621-352-8). Thorndike Pr.

Young, Catherine M. To See Our World. LC 79-65448. (Illus.). 1979. 29.95 o.p. (ISBN 0-688-03540-X). Morrow.

Young, Christopher R., jt. auth. see Wattenmaker, Richard J.

Young, Clara M. The Herald Wind: Translations of Sung Dynasty Poems, Lyrics & Songs. LC 81-2621. 113p. 1981. Repr. of 1955 ed. lib. bdg. 19.25x (ISBN 0-313-23079-X, YOHW). Greenwood.

Young, Colin L., jt. auth. see Conder, John R.

Young, Crawford. Politics of Cultural Pluralism. (Illus.). 574p. 1979. pap. 9.95 (ISBN 0-299-06744-0). U of Wis Pr.

Young, D., ed. Developmental Neurobiology of Arthropods. (Illus.). 200p. 1973. 49.50 (ISBN 0-521-20229-9). Cambridge U Pr.

Young, D. H., jt. auth. see Timoshenko, Stephen P.

Young, Dale. Marmac Guide to Houston. Nicholson, Diana M., ed. (Guidebook Ser.). 296p. (Orig.). 1983. pap. 6.95 (ISBN 0-939944-03-0). Marmac Pub.

Young, Darroch, jt. auth. see Carter, Juanita E.

Young, Darroch F., jt. auth. see Carter, Juanita E.

Young, David, jt. auth. see Friebert, Stuart.

Young, David B., ed. Gastrointestinal Physiology IV. (International Review of Physiology Ser.). (Illus.). 1983. text ed. 34.50 (ISBN 0-8391-1725-6, 14192). Univ Park.

Young, David J. The Structure of English Clauses. 1980. 30.00 (ISBN 0-312-76759-5). St Martin.

Young, Davis A. Creation & the Flood: An Alternative to Flood Geology & Thestic Evolution. 1977. 6.95 o.p. (ISBN 0-8010-9912-9). Baker Bk.

Young, Dennis R. If Not for Profit, for What? A Behavioral Theory of the Nonprofit Sector Based on Entrepreneurship. Simon, John, frwd. by. LC 82-48482. 192p. 1983. 20.95x (ISBN 0-669-06154-9). Lexington Bks.

Young, Diony, ed. Obstetrical Intervention & Technology in the 1980s. LC 82-21301. (Women & Health Ser.: Vol. 7, Nos. 3 & 4). 200p. 1983. text ed. 24.95 (ISBN 0-86656-143-9, B143). Haworth Pr.

Young, Don, jt. auth. see Francis, Dave.

Young, Donald, jt. ed. see Sellin, Thorsten.

Young, Donald F. Introduction to Applied Mechanics: An Integrated Treatment for Students in Engineering, Life Science & Interdisciplinary Programs. LC 74-153162. (Illus.). 1972. 10.50x (ISBN 0-8138-1075-2). Iowa St U Pr.

Young, Donald F., et al. Essentials of Mechanics. (Illus.). 576p. 1974. text ed. 12.50x (ISBN 0-8138-1110-4). Iowa St U Pr.

Young, Donald R. Motion Pictures: A Study in Social Legislation. LC 79-160248. (Moving Pictures Ser). vi, 109p. 1971. Repr. of 1922 ed. lib. bdg. 10.95x (ISBN 0-89198-049-0). Ozer.

Young, Donald R. & Moore, Wilbert E. Trusteeship & the Management of Foundations. LC 75-87819. 158p. 1969. 6.00x (ISBN 0-87154-970-0). Russell Sage.

Young, Douglas. Between Sundays. Hunting, Constance, ed. 1978. pap. text ed. 5.95 (ISBN 0-913006-14-9). Puckerbrush.

--The Rocking Horse: Children's Stories. Hunting, Constance, ed. (Illus.). 88p. (Orig.). 1982. pap. 5.95 (ISBN 0-913006-26-2). Puckerbrush.

Young, Dudley. Out of Ireland: The Poetry of WB Yeats. 1975. text ed. 14.75x (ISBN 0-85635-119-9, Pub. by Carcanet New Pr England). Humanities.

Young, E., et al. Conor Cruise O'Brien: An Appraisal. (Chapbooks Ser.). pap. 2.50x (ISBN 0-912262-33-8). Proscenium.

Young, E. A. & Fisk, E. K., eds. Town Populations. LC 82-73139. (Aboriginal Component in the Australian Economy Ser.: No. 2). 171p. (Orig.). 1982. pap. text ed. 16.95 (ISBN 0-909150-77-X, 1221). Bks Australia.

Young, Ed. High on a Hill: A Book of Chinese Riddles. LC 79-24070. (Illus.). 64p. (gr. 3-5). 1980. 8.95 o.s.i. (ISBN 0-529-05553-8, Philomel); PLB 8.99 o.s.i. (ISBN 0-529-05554-6). Putnam Pub Group.

--The Rooster's Horns: A Chinese Puppet Play to Make & Perform. LC 78-9283. (Unicef Storycraft Bks). (ps-3). 1978. 6.95 (ISBN 0-529-05446-9); PLB 6.99 (ISBN 0-529-05447-7). Putnam Pub Group.

--The Terrible Nung Gwama: A Chinese Folktale. LC 78-18766. (Unicef Storycraft Bks.). (Illus.). (ps-3). 1978. 6.95 o.s.i. (ISBN 0-529-05444-2, Philomel); PLB 6.99 o.s.i. (ISBN 0-529-05445-0). Putnam Pub Group.

--Up a Tree. LC 82-47733. (Illus.). 32p. (ps-3). 8.61i (ISBN 0-06-026813-1, HarpJ); PLB 8.89g (ISBN 0-06-026814-X). Har-Row.

Young, Edith. Inside Out: An Autobiography. (Illus.). 1971. 10.00 o.p. (ISBN 0-7100-6997-9). Routledge & Kegan.

Young, Edna C. & Perachio, Joseph J. The Patterned Elicitation Syntax Screening Test: PESST. 45p. 1981. pap. text ed. 15.95 (ISBN 0-88450-746-7, 2082-B). Communication Skill.

Young, Edward. Edward Young: Selected Poems. Hepworth, Brian, ed. (Fyfield). 1979. 7.95x (ISBN 0-85635-140-7, Pub. by Carcanet New Pr England); pap. 5.25x (ISBN 0-85635-141-5, Pub. by Carcanet New Pr England). Humanities.

--Poetical Works, 2 vols. Set. lib. bdg. 25.25x o.p. (ISBN 0-8371-2921-4, YOPW). Greenwood.

Young, Edwin, jt. ed. see Derber, Milton.

Young, Edwin H., jt. auth. see Brownell, Lloyd E.

Young, Eric. Francisco Goya. LC 77-95304. (Art for All Ser.). (Illus.). 1978. pap. 5.95 o.p. (ISBN 0-312-30319-X). St Martin.

Young, Erika, tr. see Matthaei, Renate.

Young, Ezra. Lands of the Unexpected: Memoirs of the Middle East. new ed. Smith, James C., Jr., ed. LC 78-75083. (Illus.). 1979. pap. 7.95 (ISBN 0-913270-77-6). Sunstone Pr.

Young, F. A. & McCann, W. P. Samuel Wilderspin & the Infant School Movement. 228p. 1983. text ed. 34.50x (ISBN 0-7099-2903-X, Pub. by Croom Helm Ltd England). Biblio Dist.

Young, Frank. Automobile: From Prototype to Scrapyard. LC 82-81165. (Inside Story Ser.). (Illus.). 40p. (gr. 4 up). 1982. PLB 9.90 (ISBN 0-531-03460-7). Watts.

Young, Fred J. How to Get Rich & Stay Rich. rev. ed. LC 82-83771. 175p. 1983. 12.95 (ISBN 0-8119-0491-1). Fell.

Young, G. Douglas, jt. auth. see Roll, Richard J.

Young, G. M. Portrait of an Age: Victorian England. 1977. 49.00x o.p. (ISBN 0-19-212961-9). Oxford U Pr.

Young, G. M., ed. see Macaulay, Thomas B.

Young, Gary. In the Durable World. 1983. pap. price not set (ISBN 0-931460-21-2). Bieler.

Young, Gavin. Halfway Around the World. LC 81-40223. (Illus.). 480p. 1981. 16.50 (ISBN 0-394-52114-5). Random.

Young, George. English Prosody on Inductive Lines. LC 69-10176. 1969. Repr. of 1928 ed. lib. bdg. 17.50x (ISBN 0-8371-0772-5, YOIL). Greenwood.

--A History of Whitby, Vol. 2. 1981. 30.00x (ISBN 0-686-98240-1, Pub. by Caedmon of Whitby). State Mutual Bk.

--Pendulum of Progress: Essays in Political Science & Scientific Politics. 1931. text ed. 24.50x (ISBN 0-686-83692-8). Elliots Bks.

Young, George M. Age of Tennyson. 1982. lib. bdg. 34.50 (ISBN 0-686-81938-1). Porter.

--Victorian England: Portrait of an Age. 2nd ed. 1964. pap. 8.95 (ISBN 0-19-500259-8, GB). Oxford U Pr.

Young, Gerald L. Human Ecology As an Interdisciplinary Domain: An Epistemological Bibliography. (Public Administration Ser.: P 72). 1978. pap. 7.00 o.p. (ISBN 0-88066-007-4). Vance Biblios.

Young, Grace C. & Young, William H. Beginner's Book of Geometry. LC 76-114211. Orig. Title: First Book of Geometry. (gr. 1-5). 1970. Repr. of 1905 ed. text ed. 12.00 (ISBN 0-8284-0231-0). Chelsea Pub.

Young, Grace C., jt. auth. see Young, William H.

Young, H. Edwin. A Winning Walk. LC 82-70048. 1982. pap. 4.95 (ISBN 0-8054-5191-9). Broadman.

Young, Harben B. & Ferguson, Lucy R. Puberty to Manhood in Italy & America. (Development Psychology Ser.). 294p. 1981. 28.50 (ISBN 0-12-773150-4). Acad Pr.

Young, Harold C. Planning, Programming, Budgeting Systems in Academic Libraries: An Exploratory Study of PPBS in University Libraries Having Membership in the Association of Research Libraries. LC 76-10667. 180p. 1976. 38.00x (ISBN 0-8103-0264-0). Gale.

Young, Harold C., jt. ed. see Young, Margaret L.

Young, Hartsell. ALA Glossary of Library & Information Science. 1983. text ed. price not set (ISBN 0-8389-0371-1). ALA.

Young, Howard. Rational Counseling Primer. pap. 1.95 (ISBN 0-686-36791-X). Inst Rat Liv.

Young, Howard, jt. auth. see Coles, Clarence.

Young, Howard S. A Rational Counseling Primer. 1.95 o.p. (ISBN 0-686-92210-7, 4325). Hazelden.

Young, Hugh D. Fundamentals of Mechanics & Heat. 2nd ed. (Fundamentals of Physics Ser.). (Illus.). 736p. 1973. text ed. 35.00 (ISBN 0-07-072628-8, C); instr's. manual 10.00 (ISBN 0-07-072639-6). McGraw.

--Fundamentals of Waves, Optics & Modern Physics. 2nd ed. 1975. 33.50 (ISBN 0-07-072521-7, C). McGraw.

--Statistical Treatment of Experimental Data. 1962. pap. 5.95 (ISBN 0-07-072646-9, SP). McGraw.

Young, Hy & Silberman, Mary. Black Badges Are Bad Business-& Other Short Stories, Vol. 1. (American Short Story Ser.). 84p. 1979. pap. 3.50 (ISBN 0-934040-01-X). Quality Ohio.

Young, I. H. Directed Homework in Gregg Shorthand. (Diamond Jubilee Ser.). 1965. text ed. 9.28 (ISBN 0-07-072335-4, G). McGraw.

Young, Ian. Double Exposure: Gay Poems. 44p. 1978. 3.50 (ISBN 0-912278-16-1). Crossing Pr.

Young, Ian, ed. On the Line: New Gay Fiction. LC 81-640. 224p. 1981. 15.95 (ISBN 0-89594-048-5); pap. 6.95 (ISBN 0-89594-049-3). Crossing Pr.

Young, Irwin, ed. Practica musicae of Franchinus Gafurius. (Illus.). 312p. 1969. 25.00 o.p. (ISBN 0-299-05180-3). U of Wis Pr.

Young, J. Francis, jt. auth. see Mindess, Sidney.

Young, J. H. & Young, S. H. Terracotta Figurines from Kourion in Cyprus. (Museum Monographs). (Illus.). 260p. 1955. bound 11.00xsoft (ISBN 0-934718-03-2). Univ Mus of U PA.

Young, J. Terry. The Spirit Within You. LC 76-47762. 1977. 4.95 o.p. (ISBN 0-8054-1945-4). Broadman.

Young, J. W. Projective Geometry. (Carus Monograph: No. 4). 185p. 1930. 16.50 (ISBN 0-88385-004-4). Math Assn.

Young, James J. Divorce Ministry & the Marriage Tribunal. LC 82-60851. 1982. pap. 5.95 (ISBN 0-8091-2477-7). Paulist Pr.

Young, James S. Washington Community: 1800-1828. LC 66-14080. (Illus.). 1968. pap. 4.95 (ISBN 0-15-694825-7, Harv). HarBraceJ.

Young, James S., ed. Problems & Prospects of Presidential Leadership in the Nineteen-Eighties, Vol. 1. LC 82-19981. (Problems & Prospects of the Presidency). (Illus.). 136p. (Orig.). 1982. lib. bdg. 17.25 (ISBN 0-8191-2837-6); pap. text ed. 6.75 (ISBN 0-8191-2838-4). U Pr of Amer.

Young, Jay, jt. auth. see Ledbetter, Elaine.

Young, Jean & Young, Jim. Great Trash: New Trends in Antiquing, Auctions, Bargaining, Bartering, Buying for Resale, Collectibles, Garage Sales, Flea Markets, House Sales, Folk Art & Fine Art, Careers in Collecting, & Raising Cash. LC 78-24700. (Illus.). 1979. pap. 4.95i o.p. (ISBN 0-06-090681-2, CN681, CN). Har-Row.

Young, Jeffrey T. Classical Theories of Value: From Smith to Sraffa. 1978. lib. bdg. 18.00 o.p. (ISBN 0-89158-287-8). Westview.

Young, Jim, jt. auth. see Young, Jean.

Young, John. Great Northern Suburban. 1977. 9.95 o.p. (ISBN 0-7153-7477-X). David & Charles.

Young, John & Nakajima, Kimiko. Learn Japanese: College Text, 4 Vols. 1967-69. Vol. 1. pap. text ed. 8.50x (ISBN 0-8248-0061-3, Eastwest Ctr); Vol. 2. pap. 9.50x (ISBN 0-8248-0069-9); Vol. 3. pap. 10.00x (ISBN 0-8248-0073-7); Vol. 4. pap. 10.00x (ISBN 0-8248-0074-5). UH Pr.

Young, John & Newton, Jan. Capitalism & Human Obsolescence: Corporate Control vs. Individual Survival in Rural America. LC 78-71099. (LandMark Study). 272p. 1980. text ed. 21.50 (ISBN 0-916672-22-0); pap. text ed. 9.50 (ISBN 0-686-82848-8). Allanheld.

Young, John, jt. auth. see Bush, Grace.

Young, John B. Privacy. LC 77-12583. 1978. 51.95x (ISBN 0-471-99590-8, Pub. by Wiley-Interscience). Wiley.

Young, John E. & Bush, Grace A. Geometry for Elementary Teachers. LC 77-155559. 300p. 1971. text ed. 22.50x (ISBN 0-8162-9984-6); instr's manual 6.00 (ISBN 0-686-76946-5, 0-8162-9994). Holden-Day.

Young, John H., jt. ed. see Yates, George T., 3rd.

Young, John R. The Schooling of the Horse. rev. ed. LC 81-11539. (Illus.). 400p. 1982. 22.50 (ISBN 0-8061-1787-7). U of Okla Pr.

Young, John S. The Weather Tomorrow. LC 81-40227. 196p. 1981. 11.50 (ISBN 0-394-52149-8). Random.

Young, John Z. Programs of the Brain. (Illus.). 1978. 22.50x (ISBN 0-19-857545-9). Oxford U Pr.

--Programs of the Brain. (Illus.). 1981. pap. 7.95 (ISBN 0-19-286019-4, GB 641, GB). Oxford U Pr.

Young, Jordan M. Brazil: Emerging World Power. LC 82-15185. (Orig.). 1982. pap. 5.95 (ISBN 0-89874-262-5). Krieger.

Young, Jordan R. How to Become a Successful Freelance Writer. 28p. (Orig.). 1981. pap. 4.95 (ISBN 0-940410-02-8). Moonstone.

--A Night in the Hard Rock Cafe & Other Poems. 25p. 1980. pap. 3.95 (ISBN 0-940410-01-X). Moonstone.

Young, Jordon R. How to Become a Successful Freelance Writer: A Practical Guide to Getting Published. 3rd ed. LC 81-90476. 160p. 1983. pap. 7.95 (ISBN 0-940410-05-2). Moonstone.

Young, Joyce. Fundraising for Non-Profit Groups: How to Get Money from Corporations, Foundations & Government. 2nd ed. 102p. 1981. pap. 4.95 (ISBN 0-88908-077-1). Self Counsel Pr.

Young, K., et al, eds. The MRCGP Study Book. 150p. 1980. 37.00 (ISBN 0-906141-13-3, Pub. by Update Pubns England); pap. 31.50 (ISBN 0-686-33355-1). Kluwer Boston.

Young, K. P., jt. auth. see Garner, L. E.

Young, Keith. Geology: The Paradox of Earth & Man. 416p. 1975. text ed. 27.95 (ISBN 0-395-05561-X); instr's. manual 1.50 (ISBN 0-395-18267-0); slides (set of 20 35mm) 15.95 (ISBN 0-395-18188-7). HM.

Young, Kenneth. Churchill & Beaverbrook: A Study in Friendship & Politics. (Illus.). 1967. 6.50 o.p. (ISBN 0-685-11952-1). Heineman.

--Rhodesia & Independence. 1967. 7.25 o.p. (ISBN 0-685-11979-3). Heineman.

Young, L. C. Mathematics & Their Times. (Mathematics Studies: Vol. 48). 1981. 38.50 (ISBN 0-444-86135-1). Elsevier.

Young, Laurence C. Lectures on the Calculus of Variations & Optimal Control Theory. 2nd ed. LC 79-57387. 1980. 16.95 (ISBN 0-8284-0304-X). Chelsea Pub.

Young, Leo, ed. Advances in Microwaves. Incl. Vol. 1. 1966. 68.50 (ISBN 0-12-027901-0); Vol. 2. 1967. 68.50 (ISBN 0-12-027902-9); Vol. 3. 1968. 68.50 (ISBN 0-12-027903-7); Vol. 4. 1969. 68.50 (ISBN 0-12-027904-5); Vol. 5. 1970. 68.50 (ISBN 0-12-027905-3); Vol. 6. 1971. 68.50 (ISBN 0-12-027906-1); Vol. 7. 1971. 68.50 (ISBN 0-12-027907-X); Suppl. 1. Theory & Design of Microwave Filters & Circuits. Matsumoto, A. 1970. 53.50 (ISBN 0-12-027964-4). Acad Pr.

Young, Leontine. The Fractured Family. LC 73-2738. 168p. 1973. 8.95 o.p. (ISBN 0-07-072376-1, GB); pap. 3.95 (ISBN 0-07-072377-X). McGraw.

--Life Among the Giants. 1966. 4.95 o.p. (ISBN 0-07-072375-3, GB); pap. 4.95 (ISBN 0-07-072374-5). McGraw.

--Out of Wedlock: A Study of the Problems of the Unmarried Mother & Her Child. 1964. pap. 2.95 o.p. (ISBN 0-07-072556-X, SP). McGraw.

--Wednesday's Children: A Study of Child Neglect & Abuse. LC 78-12941. 1979. Repr. of 1964 ed. lib. bdg. 18.75x (ISBN 0-313-20637-6, YOWC). Greenwood.

Young, Lisa, jt. ed. see Christiano, David.

Young, Lloyd Y., jt. ed. see Katcher, Brian S.

Young, Louise B. & Trainor, William T., eds. Science & Public Policy. LC 70-83742. (Illus.). 626p. 1971. lib. bdg. 22.50 (ISBN 0-379-00332-5). Oceana.

Young, Loy, jt. auth. see Young, Robert.

Young, Lynne & Fitzgerald, Brigid. Listening & Learning: Lectures, Modules I-V. 176p. 1982. pap. text ed. 5.95. Module I. Module II. Module III (ISBN 0-88377-723-1). Module IV. Module V. tchrs manual 3.95. Newbury Hse.

Young, M. E., ed. International Directory of Conchologists, 1982-83. LC 73-91404. 1982-83. 5.00 (ISBN 0-913792-06-3). Shell Cab.

Young, Madilyn, ed. see Brewer, J. E.

Young, Margaret L. & Young, Harold C., eds. Subject Directory of Special Libraries & Information Centers, 5 vols. 6th rev. ed. Incl. Vol. 1. Business & Law Libraries (ISBN 0-8103-0306-X); Vol. 2. Education & Information Science Libraries, Including Audiovisual, Picture, Publishing, Rare Book, & Recreational Libraries (ISBN 0-8103-0307-8); Vol. 3. Health Sciences Libraries, Including All Aspects of Basic & Applied Medical Sciences (ISBN 0-8103-0308-6); Vol. 4. Social Sciences & Humanities Libraries, Including Aera-Ethnic, Art, Geography-Map, History, Music Religion-Theology, Theatre, & Urban-Regional Planning Libraries (ISBN 0-8103-0309-4); Vol. 5. Science & Technology Libraries Including Agriculture, Energy, Environment-Conservation, & Food Sciences Libraries (ISBN 0-8103-0310-8). LC 79-21711. 163p. 1981. Set. 410.00 set o.p. (ISBN 0-8103-0305-1); 86.00 ea. o.p. Gale.

Young, Margaret W. Cities of the World: Supplement. 1983. pap. 65.00x (ISBN 0-8103-1110-0). Gale.

Young, Margaret W. & Stetler, Susan T., eds. Cities of the World: A Compilation of Current Information on Cultural, Geographical & Political Conditions in the Countries & Cities of Six Continents, Based on the Department of State's "Post Reports", 4 Vols. LC 81-20177. (Illus.). 1431p. 1982. Set. 160.00x (ISBN 0-8103-1111-9). Vol. 1: Africa. Vol. 2: The Western Hemisphere. Vol. 4: Asia, the Pacific & the Asiatic Middle East. Gale.

Young, Marilyn B., jt. auth. see Rosenberg, William G.

Young, Marjabelle & Buchwald, Ann. Stand up, Shake Hands, "Say How Do You Do?". LC 77-80159. (Illus.). 1977. 9.95 (ISBN 0-88331-100-3). Luce.

--White Gloves & Party Manners. LC 65-25830. (Illus.). (gr. 1-7). 1965. 9.95 (ISBN 0-88331-054-6). Luce.

Young, Mary de see De Young, Mary.

Young, Michael. The Imaginary Friend. LC 77-9925. (Moods & Emotions Ser.). (Illus.). (gr. k-3). 1977. PLB 12.85 o.p. (ISBN 0-8172-0960-3). Raintree Pubs.

Young, Michael & Whitty, G., eds. Society, State & Schooling. 283p. 1980. write for info. (ISBN 0-905273-02-8, Pub. by Taylor & Francis); pap. write for info. (ISBN 0-905273-01-X). Intl Pubns Serv.

Young, Michael W. Fighting with Food: Leadership, Values & Social Control in a Massin Society. (Illus.). 1972. 29.95 (ISBN 0-521-08223-4). Cambridge U Pr.

Young, Miriam. Peas in a Pod. (Illus.). (gr. k-3). 1971. PLB 3.86 o.p. (ISBN 0-399-60507-X). Putnam Pub Group.

--Something Small. (Illus.). (gr. 3-6). 1970. PLB 4.29 o.p. (ISBN 0-399-60589-4). Putnam Pub Group.

Young, N., jt. auth. see Evans, F. C.

Young, Nancy A., ed. see Levin, Paul.

Young, Nancy F. The Chinese in Hawaii: An Annotated Bibliography. (Social Science & Linguistics Institute Special Publications). 1973. pap. 6.00x (ISBN 0-8248-0265-9). UH Pr.

Young Nations Conference, Sydney, 1976. Paradise Postponed: Essays on Research & Development in the South Pacific: Proceedings. Mamak, Alexander & McCall, Grant, eds. 1979. text ed. 31.00 (ISBN 0-08-023005-9); pap. text ed. 15.50 (ISBN 0-08-023004-0). Pergamon.

Young, Nigel. An Infantile Disorder? The Crisis & Decline of the New Left. LC 76-30272. 1978. lib. bdg. 32.50 (ISBN 0-89158-549-4). Westview.

Young, Noela. Keep Out. LC 76-43587. (Illus.). (ps-3). 1977. 5.95 (ISBN 0-529-05334-9, Philomel). Putnam Pub Group.

Young, Oran R. Resource Regimes: Natural Resources & Social Institutions. Krasner, Stephen, ed. LC 81-21979. (Studies in the International Political Economy Ser.). 284p. 1982. 25.00x (ISBN 0-520-04573-4). U of Cal Pr.

Young, Otis E., Jr. Western Mining: An Informal Account of Precious-Metals Prospecting, Placering, Lode Mining, & Milling on the American Frontier from Spanish Times to 1893. LC 76-108800. (Illus.). 1970. 19.95 (ISBN 0-8061-0909-2); pap. 9.95 (ISBN 0-8061-1352-9). U of Okla Pr.

Young, Otis E., Jr. & Lenon, Robert. Black Powder & Hand Steel: Miners & Machines on the Old Western Frontier. LC 75-4634. (Illus.). 200p. 1976. pap. 12.95 (ISBN 0-8061-1269-7). U of Okla Pr.

Young, P., jt. auth. see Kemp, J. F.

Young, Pam & Jones, Peggy. Sidetracked Home Executives. (Orig.). 1983. pap. 6.95 (ISBN 0-446-37765-1). Warner Bks.

--The Sidetracked Sisters Catch Up on the Kitchen. 224p. 1983. pap. 6.95 (ISBN 0-446-37526-8). Warner Bks.

Young, Parker, jt. ed. see Bickel, Robert D.

Young, Paul. Datsun Tune-up for Everybody. LC 80-5102. (Illus.). 120p. 1980. pap. 7.95 (ISBN 0-89815-026-4). Ten Speed Pr.

--Honda Tune-up for Everybody. LC 81-50156. (Illus.). 144p. (Orig.). 1981. pap. 7.95 (ISBN 0-89815-031-0). Ten Speed Pr.

Young, Paul B. Toyota Tune-up for Everybody. LC 79-63720. (Illus.). 149p. 1979. pap. 7.95 (ISBN 0-913668-89-3). Ten Speed Pr.

Young, Paul E. Back Trail of an Old Cowboy. Yost, Nellie S., ed. LC 82-7096. vi, 229p. 1983. 14.95 (ISBN 0-8032-4901-2). U of Nebr Pr.

Young, Paul T. Emotion in Man & Animal. 2nd ed. LC 72-83380. 496p. 1973. Repr. of 1943 ed. 23.50 (ISBN 0-88275-084-4). Krieger.

Young, Pauline V. Social Treatment in Probation & Delinquency. 2nd ed. LC 69-14955. (Criminology, Law Enforcement, & Social Problems Ser.: No. 47). 1969. Repr. of 1952 ed. 24.00x (ISBN 0-87585-047-2). Patterson Smith.

Young, Percy M. A Future for English Music: Lectures by Sir Edward Elgar. 312p. 1981. 40.00x (ISBN 0-686-97030-6, Pub. by Dobson Bks England). State Mutual bk.

--The Oratorios of Handel. 244p. 1981. 40.00x (ISBN 0-686-97050-0, Pub. by Dobson Bks England). State Mutual Bk.

Young, Peter. Edgehill, Sixteen Forty-Two. 344p. 1980. 24.00x (ISBN 0-900093-26-9, Pub. by Peter Dix). State Mutual Bk.

--Great Battles of the World on Land, Sea & Air. (Illus.). 320p. 1981. 14.98 o.p. (ISBN 0-89196-100-3, Bk Value Intl). Quality Bks IL.

--Marston Moor, Sixteen Forty-Four. 1980. 24.00x (ISBN 0-900093-07-2, Pub. by Peter Dix). State Mutual Bk.

--Naseby, Sixteen Forty-Five: The Campaign & Battle. 1980. 36.00x o.p. (ISBN 0-906418-02-X, Pub. by Peter Dix). State Mutual Bk.

--Power of Speech: A History of Standard Telephones & Cables 1883-1983. 224p. 1983. text ed. 18.95x (ISBN 0-04-382039-5). Allen Unwin.

Young, Peter & Adair, John. From Hastings to Culloden. 1980. 36.00x o.p. (ISBN 0-906418-03-8, Pub. by Peter Dix). State Mutual Bk.

Young, Peter, jt. auth. see Toynbee, Margaret.

Young, Philip. Ernest Hemingway: A Reconsideration. 2nd ed. LC 65-26101. 1966. 16.95x (ISBN 0-271-73060-9). Pa St U Pr.

Young, Phillip T. Twenty-Five Hundred Historical Woodwind Instruments: An Inventory of the Major Collections. (Illus.). 1982. lib. bdg. 5.00 (ISBN 0-918728-17-7). Pendragon NY.

Young, R. A. Introduction to Forest Science. 554p. 1982. text ed. 26.50 (ISBN 0-471-06438-6). Wiley.

Young, R. B. Criminal Law: Codes & Cases. 1972. text ed. 12.92 o.p. (ISBN 0-07-072340-0, G). McGraw.

Young, R. E. Control in Hazardous Environments. (IEE Control Engineering Ser.: No. 17). 128p. 1982. pap. 30.00 (ISBN 0-906048-69-9). Inst Elect Eng.

--Supervisory Remote Control Systems. (IEE Control Engineering Ser.: No. 4). (Illus.). 192p. 1977. casebound 35.75 (ISBN 0-901223-94-8). Inst Elect Eng.

Young, Richard A. & Cross, Frank L., eds. Operation & Maintenance for Air Particulate Control Equipment. LC 80-65506. (Illus.). 166p. 1980. 29.95 (ISBN 0-250-40367-6). Ann Arbor Science.

Young, Robert & Young, Loy. Reincarnation: Your Denied Birthright. (Illus.). 1978. pap. text ed. 7.95 (ISBN 0-932872-01-8). Awareness.

Young, Robert, ed. Untying the Text: A Post-Structuralist Anthology. 320p. 1981. text ed. 19.95 (ISBN 0-7100-0804-X); pap. 9.95 (ISBN 0-7100-0805-8). Routledge & Kegan.

Young, Robert D. Be Brief About It. LC 80-16436. 1980. pap. 8.95 (ISBN 0-664-24321-5). Westminster.

Young, Robert E., jt. auth. see Pritzker, Alan B.

Young, Robert F. & Greyser, Stephen A. Managing Cooperative Advertising: A Strategic Approach. LC 82-48572. 1983. write for info. (ISBN 0-669-06301-0). Lexington Bks.

Young, Robert J. French Foreign Policy, Nineteen Eighteen to Nineteen Forty-Five: A Guide to Research & Research Materials. Kimmich, Christoph M., ed. LC 80-53892. 242p. 1981. lib. bdg. 17.50 (ISBN 0-8420-2178-7). Scholarly Res Inc.

--Introduction to Polymers. LC 80-42133. 350p. 1981. 42.00x (ISBN 0-412-22170-5, Pub by Chapman & Hall England); pap. 19.95x (ISBN 0-412-22180-2). Methuen Inc.
Young, Robert, Jr. Movie Memo. (Illus.). 64p. 1982. 24.00 (ISBN 0-88014-058-5). Mosaic Pr OH.
Young, Robert L., jt. auth. see Obert, Edward F.
Young, Roger. Modern Cooking Equipment & Its Applications. (Illus.). 1979. 22.50x (ISBN 0-7198-2684-5). Intl Ideas.
Young, Roz. Queen of the North Parlor. 198p. 1976. pap. 4.95 (ISBN 0-913428-23-X). Landfall Pr.
Young, S. Electronics in the Life Sciences. LC 73-8083. 198p. 1973. 21.95x o.s.i. (ISBN 0-470-97943-7). Halsted Pr.
Young, S. H., jt. auth. see Young, J. H.
Young, S. J. An Introduction to ADA. (Computers & Their Applications Ser.). 320p. 1983. 69.95x (ISBN 0-470-27551-0); pap. 29.95x (ISBN 0-470-27350-X). Halsted Pr.
Young, S. S., jt. auth. see Turner, H. Newton.
Young, Samuel. Beacon Bible Expositions, Vol. 4: John. Greathouse, William M. & Taylor, Willard H., eds. 196p. 1979. 5.95 (ISBN 0-8341-0315-X). Beacon Hill.
Young, Scott. Face-off in Moscow. LC 73-4356. (Face-off Ser). (Illus.). 40p. (gr. 6-12). 1973. 4.95 o.p. (ISBN 0-912022-56-6); pap. 3.95 (ISBN 0-912022-54-X). EMC.
--Learning to Be Captain. LC 73-4354. (Face-off Ser). (Illus.). 36p. (gr. 6-12). 1973. PLB 4.95 o.p. (ISBN 0-912022-58-2); pap. 3.95 (ISBN 0-912022-53-1). EMC.
--The Moscow Challengers. LC 73-4355. (Face-off Ser). (Illus.). 40p. (gr. 6-12). 1973. 4.95 o.p. (ISBN 0-912022-57-4); pap. 3.95 (ISBN 0-912022-55-8). EMC.
--The Silent One Speaks up. LC 73-4353. (Face-off Ser). (Illus.). 36p. (gr. 6-12). 1973. 4.95 o.p. (ISBN 0-912022-59-0); pap. 3.95 (ISBN 0-912022-52-3). EMC.
Young, Sheila. Betty Bonnet Paper Dolls in Full Color. (Toy Bks., Paper Dolls). (Illus.). 32p. (Orig.). (gr. 3 up). 1982. pap. 3.50 (ISBN 0-486-24415-6). Dover.
Young, Simon, tr. see Matthaei, Renate.
Young, Stark, tr. see Chekhov, Anton.
Young, T., jt. auth. see Ellory, J. C.
Young, T. Cuyler, Jr., jt. ed. see Levine, Louis D.
Young, T. D., et al. The Literature of the South. rev. ed. 1968. text ed. 20.95x (ISBN 0-673-05660-0). Scott F.
Young, T. W., jt. auth. see Pegler, D. N.
Young, Thomas. Linear Integrated Circuits. LC 80-22791. (Electronic Technology Ser.). 495p. 1981. text ed. 27.95x (ISBN 0-471-97941-4). Wiley.
Young, Thomas D. John Crowe Ranson: An Annotated Bibliography. Cain, William, ed. LC 82-48279. (Modern Critics & Critical Schools Ser.). 250p. 1982. lib. bdg. 30.00 (ISBN 0-8240-9249-X). Garland Pub.
Young, Thomas D. & Inge, M. Thomas. Donald Davidson. (United States Authors Ser.). lib. bdg. 13.95 (ISBN 0-8057-0188-5, Twayne). G K Hall.
Young, Thomas D., ed. The New Criticism & After. LC 76-6165. 90p. 1976. 7.50x (ISBN 0-8139-0672-5). U Pr of Va.
Young, Viola M. Pseudomonas Aeruginosa: Ecological Aspects & Patient Colonization. LC 76-56919. 155p. 1977. 14.00 (ISBN 0-89004-149-0). Raven.
Young, Virginia. Trustee of a Small Public Library. (Small Public Library Ser.). 12p. 1978. pap. text ed. 1.00 o.p. (ISBN 0-8389-5514-2). ALA.
Young, W. Ogg & Ray's Essentials of American National Government. 10th ed. 1969. pap. 14.95 (ISBN 0-13-633651-5). P-H.
Young, W. J., tr. see De Guibert, Joseph.
Young, Warren. The Helicopters. (Epic of Flight Ser.). 1982. lib. bdg. 19.96 (ISBN 0-8094-3351-6, Pub. by Time-Life). Silver.
Young, Warren C. Christian Approach to Philosophy. (Twin Brook Ser.). 1973. pap. 6.95 (ISBN 0-8010-9904-8). Baker Bk.
Young, Warren C., jt. auth. see Roark, Raymond J.
Young, Wayne D., jt. auth. see Brunell, Lillian F.
Young, Wesley O. & Striffler, David F. Dentist, His Practice & His Community. 2nd ed. LC 69-17807. (Illus.). 1969. 15.95x o.p. (ISBN 0-7216-9651-1). Saunders.
Young, Whitney M., Jr. Beyond Racism: Building an Open Society. 1971. pap. 2.95 o.p. (ISBN 0-07-072373-7, SP). McGraw.
Young, William, jt. auth. see Mitchell, Charlie.
Young, William H. & Young, Grace C. Theory of Sets of Points. 2nd ed. LC 75-184793. 330p. 1972. text ed. 17.95 (ISBN 0-8284-0259-0). Chelsea Pub.
Young, William H., jt. auth. see Young, Grace C.
Young, William J. Organization of Instrumentation Guidelines. 110p. 1982. 29.95x (ISBN 0-87814-187-1). Pennwell Books Division.
Young, William L. Teach Yourself English: Self Preparation for English Proficiency Examinations. rev. ed. LC 68-8682. (Orig.). (gr. 8-12). 1977. pap. 4.25 (ISBN 0-8120-0373-X). Barron.
Youngberg, Norma R. Creative Techniques for Christian Writers. LC 68-21888. 262p. 1968. 4.75 o.p. (ISBN 0-8163-0025-9, 03629-3). Pacific Pr Pub Assn.
Youngberg, Ruth T. Dorothy L. Sayers: A Reference Guide. 178p. 1982. lib. bdg. 27.50 (ISBN 0-8161-8198-5, Hall Reference). G K Hall.
Youngbirg, Norma. Heart of Darkness Notes. Bd. with Secret Sharer Notes. (Orig.). pap. 2.95 (ISBN 0-8220-0587-5). Cliffs.
Youngblood, Joan E. Sunset to Sunrise. new ed. (Illus.). 20p. 1978. pap. 2.00 (ISBN 0-932044-11-5). M O Pub Co.
Youngblood, Ronald & Inch, Morris, eds. The Living & Active Word of God: Studies in Honor of Samuel J. Schultz. 1983. 17.50x (ISBN 0-931464-11-0). Eisenbrauns.
Youngblood, Ronald F. Exodus. (Everyman's Bible Commentary Ser.). (Orig.). 1983. pap. 3.95 (ISBN 0-8024-2002-8). Moody.
Young-Bruehl, Elisabeth. Vigil: A Novel. LC 82-17160. 184p. 1983. 12.95 (ISBN 0-8071-1075-2). La State U Pr.
Younger, Erin, jt. ed. see Masayesva, Victor.
Younger, Ronald M. Australia & the Australians. 1970. text ed. 18.25x o.p. (ISBN 0-391-00013-6). Humanities.
Younggulst, Walter. Investing in Natural Resources. 269p. 1983. pap. 8.95 (ISBN 0-87094-415-0). Dow Jones-Irwin.
Youngjohns, B. A. Co-operative Organisation: An Introduction. 34p. (Orig.). 1977. pap. 2.75x (ISBN 0-903031-43-4, Pub. by Intermediate Tech England). Intermediate Tech.
Youngman, M. B., et al. Analysing Jobs. 168p. 1978. text ed. 31.50x (ISBN 0-566-02089-0). Gower Pub Ltd.
Youngren, William. Semantics, Linguistics & Criticism. 1971. pap. text ed. 3.95x (ISBN 0-685-47631-6). Phila Bk Co.
Youngs, F. A. The Proclamations of the Tudor Queens. LC 75-30442. 304p. 1976. 49.50 (ISBN 0-521-21044-5). Cambridge U Pr.
Youngs, J. William. American Realties, 2 vols. (Orig.). 1981. Vol. 1. pap. text ed. 9.95 ea. (ISBN 0-316-97727-6). Vol. 2 (ISBN 0-316-97729-2). tchr's manual avail. (ISBN 0-316-97728-4). Little.
Youngs, R., jt. auth. see Rowell, R. M.
Youngson, A. J. Hong Kong: Economic Growth & Development. 1982. 16.95x (ISBN 0-19-581381-2). Oxford U Pr.
Youngson, A. J., ed. Economic Development in the Long Run. LC 72-79503. 1973. text ed. 26.00 (ISBN 0-312-22890-2). St Martin.
Yount, David & Dobson, Peter N., eds. Proceedings of the Fourth Topical Conference in Particle Physics (1971) 550p. 1972. pap. text ed. 15.00x (ISBN 0-8248-0210-1). UH Pr.
Yount, John. Hardcastle. 1980. 10.95 (ISBN 0-399-90061-6, Marek). Putnam Pub Group.
--The Trapper's Last Shot. LC 72-11433. 1973. 7.95 o.p. (ISBN 0-394-46378-1). Random.
Yourcenar, Marguerite. A Coin in Nine Hands. Katz, Dori, tr. from Fr. 116p. 1982. 11.95 (ISBN 0-374-12522-8). FS&G.
--Fires. Katz, Dori, tr. from Fr. 1981. 12.95 (ISBN 0-374-15500-3); pap. 8.25 (ISBN 0-374-51748-7). FS&G.
Yourdan, Edward. Techniques of Program Structure & Design. (Illus.). 384p. 1976. 29.95 (ISBN 0-13-901702-X). P-H.
Yourdon, E., ed. Structured Walkthroughs. 2nd ed. 1980. 15.95 (ISBN 0-13-855221-5). P-H.
Yourdon, Edward. Design of On-Line Computer Systems. (Illus.). 576p. 1972. ref. ed. 32.95 (ISBN 0-13-201301-0). P-H.
--Managing the System Life Cycle: A Software Development Methodology Overview. LC 81-72107. (Illus.). 160p. (Orig.). 1982. pap. 27.00 (ISBN 0-917072-26-X). Yourdon.
Yourdon, Edward & Constantine, Larry L. Structured Design: Fundamentals of a Discipline of Computer Program & System Design. 1979. text ed. 32.95 (ISBN 0-13-854471-9). P-H.
Yourdon, Edward, et al. Learning to Program in Structured COBOL, Pts. 1 & 2. (Software Ser.). 1979. text ed. 20.95 (ISBN 0-13-527713-2). P-H.
Yourgrau, Wolfgang & Mandelstam, Stanley. Variational Principles in Dynamics & Quantum Theory. 3rd ed. LC 78-73521. 1979. pap. text ed. 4.50 (ISBN 0-486-63773-5). Dover.
Yourgrau, Wolfgang, et al. Treatise on Irreversible & Statistical Thermophysics: An Introduction to Nonclassical Thermodynamics. (Illus.). xx, 268p. 1982. pap. 6.50 (ISBN 0-486-64313-1). Dover.
Yousef. Animal Production in the Tropics. 394p. 1982. 38.95 (ISBN 0-03-060482-6). Praeger.
Yousef, Fathi S., jt. auth. see Condon, John C.
Youssef, Nadia H. Women & Work in Developing Societies. LC 76-4537. 1976. Repr. lib. bdg. 21.50x (ISBN 0-8371-8836-9, YOWW). Greenwood.
--Women & Work in Developing Societies. (Population Monograph Ser.: No. 15). x, 137p. 1976. pap. 5.95 (ISBN 0-8371-9407-5, YOW:). Greenwood.
Yousuf Ali, A. Al-Quran-Al-Karim. pap. 14.95 soft cover (ISBN 0-686-83568-9). Kazi Pubns.
Youtsey, John W. & Rarey, Kaneut P. Respiratory Patient Care. (Illus.). 432p. 1981. text ed. 24.95 (ISBN 0-13-774604-0). P-H.
Yovits, Marshall, ed. Advances in Computers, Vol. 20. (Serial Publications Ser.). 1981. 36.50 (ISBN 0-12-012120-4); lib. ed. 42.00 (ISBN 0-12-012188-3); microfiche 22.50 (ISBN 0-12-012189-1). Acad Pr.
--Advances in Computers, Vol. 22. (Serial Publication). Date not set. price not set (ISBN 0-12-012122-0); price not set lib. ed. (ISBN 0-12-012192-1); price not set microfiche (ISBN 0-12-012193-X). Acad Pr.
Yovits, Marshall C. Advances in Computers, Vol. 18. LC 59-15761. (Serial Publication). 1979. 44.50 (ISBN 0-12-012118-2); lib. ed. 57.00 (ISBN 0-12-012184-0); microfiche 32.00 (ISBN 0-12-012185-9). Acad Pr.
Yoxall, W. H. Dynamic Models in Earth-Science Instruction. LC 82-4385. (Illus.). 200p. Date not set. price not set (ISBN 0-521-24262-2). Cambridge U Pr.
Ysseldyke, James E., jt. auth. see Salvia, John.
Ysselyke, James E. & Algozzine, Robert. Critical Issues in Special & Remedial Education. 1982. pap. 12.95 (ISBN 0-395-31712-6). HM.
Yu, Anthony, ed. Journey to the West, Vol. 4-Final Volume. LC 75-27896. 544p. 1983. lib. bdg. 35.00x (ISBN 0-226-97148-1). U of CHICAGO PR.
Yu, Anthony C., ed. The Journey to the West, Vol. I. LC 75-27896. 1977. lib. bdg. 35.00x (ISBN 0-226-97145-7). U of Chicago Pr.
--The Journey to the West, Vol. 2. LC 75-27896. 1978. lib. bdg. 35.00x (ISBN 0-226-97146-5, Phoen); pap. 9.95 (ISBN 0-226-97151-1). U of Chicago Pr.
--Journey to the West, Vol. 3. LC 75-27896. 1980. lib. bdg. 35.00x (ISBN 0-226-97147-3). U of Chicago Pr.
Yu, Beongcheon, tr. see Soseki, Natsume.
Yu, Chai-Shin. Early Buddhism & Christianity. 1981. 20.00x (ISBN 0-8364-0797-0, Pub. by Motilal Banarsidass). South Asia Bks.
Yu, Francis T. Optical Information Processing. 562p. 1983. 52.50x (ISBN 0-471-09780-2, Pub. by Wiley-Interscience). Wiley.
Yu, Frederick T., ed. Behavioral Sciences & the Mass Media. LC 68-25421. 270p. 1968. 9.95x (ISBN 0-87154-983-2). Russell Sage.
Yu, George T., ed. Intra-Asian International Relations. LC 77-24382. (Westview Special Studies on China & East Asia-South & Southeast Asia). 1978. lib. bdg. 22.00 (ISBN 0-89158-125-1). Westview.
Yu, Huai. Feast of Mist & Flowers. Levy, Howard S., tr. 1969. pap. 15.00 (ISBN 0-686-00723-9, Pub. by Langstaff-Levy). Oriental Bk Store.
Yu, Leslie Tseng-Tseng & Tuchman, Gail S. Chinese Painting in Four Seasons. 195p. 1981. 22.95 (ISBN 0-13-133025-X); pap. text ed. 10.95 (ISBN 0-13-133017-9). P-H.
Yu, Li. Jou Pu Tuan. 1967. pap. 1.95 o.s.i. (ISBN 0-394-17104-7, B106, BC). Grove.
Yu, Paul N. & Goodwin, John F., eds. Progress in Cardiology, Vol. 2. LC 77-157474. (Illus.). 300p. 1973. text ed. 15.00 (ISBN 0-8121-0409-9). Lea & Febiger.
Yu, Paul N., et al, eds. Progress in Cardiology, Vol. 10. LC 77-157474. (Illus.). 409p. 1981. text ed. 38.50 (ISBN 0-8121-0815-9). Lea & Febiger.
Yu, T. S., jt. auth. see Fu, K. S.
Yuan, Luke C. & Wu, Chien-Shiung, eds. Elementary Particles: Science, Technology & Society. 1971. 61.00 (ISBN 0-12-774850-4). Acad Pr.
Yuan, S. W., ed. Energy, Resources & Environment: Proceedings of the First U. S.-China Conference. (Illus.). 560p. 1982. pap. 85.00 (ISBN 0-08-029396-4); pap. 68.00 (ISBN 0-08-029397-2). Pergamon.
Yuan, Shao. Foundations of Fluid Mechanics. 1967. text ed. 32.95 (ISBN 0-13-329813-2). P-H.
Yuan-Cheng Fung, see Fung, Yuan-Cheng.
Yuan Chi-Wang. Essentials of Chinese Calligraphy. (Pitman Art Ser.: Vol. 75). (Illus.). 32p. 1975. pap. 1.95 o.p. (ISBN 0-448-00588-3, G&D). Putnam Pub Group.
--Oriental Brushwork. (Pitman Art Ser.: Vol. 51). pap. 1.95 o.p. (ISBN 0-448-00560-3, G&D). Putnam Pub Group.
Yuan Kao, ed. see Heckner, Fritz.
Yuasa, Nobuyuki, tr. see Basho.
Yuceoglu, U., jt. ed. see Laurenson, R. M.
Yucheng Lo, Irving, jt. ed. see Wu-chi Liu.
Yuchtman-Yaar, Ephraim, jt. ed. see Spiro, Shimon E.
Yudelman, David. The Emergence of Modern South Africa: State, Capital, & the Incorporation of Organized Labor on the South African Gold Fields, 1902-1939. LC 82-9375. (Contributions in Comparative Colonial Studies: No. 13). (Illus.). 288p. 1983. lib. bdg. 35.00 (ISBN 0-313-23170-2, YMS/). Greenwood.
Yudin, N. P., jt. auth. see Shirokov, Y. M.
Yudkin, John. This Nutrition Business. LC 77-10150. 1978. 10.00 o.p. (ISBN 0-312-80055-X). St Martin.
Yudkin, John, ed. Diet of Man: Needs & Wants. (Illus.). 1978. text ed. 49.25 (ISBN 0-85334-750-6, Pub. by Applied Sci England). Elsevier.
Yudkin, Leon I. Jewish Writing & Identity in the Twentieth Century. LC 82-827. 180p. 1982. 22.50x (ISBN 0-312-44234-3). St Martin.
Yudkin, Michael & Offord, Robin. Biochemistry. 1975. text ed. 29.95 (ISBN 0-395-17199-7); instr's. manual 1.10 (ISBN 0-395-18266-2); slides (set of 20 35mm) 15.50 (ISBN 0-395-18189-5). HM.
--A Guidebook to Biochemistry. rev. 4th ed. LC 79-41606. (Illus.). 200p. 1980. 53.50 (ISBN 0-521-23084-5); pap. 16.95 (ISBN 0-521-29794-X). Cambridge U Pr.
Yudof, Mark G. When Government Speaks: Law, Politics, & Government Expression in America. LC 81-1965. 326p. 1983. 32.50 (ISBN 0-520-04254-9). U of Cal Pr.
Yudof, Mark G., jt. auth. see Kirp, David L.
Yudovich, M., jt. auth. see Kotov, A.
Yue, Roger, jt. auth. see Hsia, Linda.
Yuen, C. K. & Fraser, D. Digital Spectral Analysis. (Applicable Mathematics Ser.). 168p. 1979. pap. text ed. 23.00 (ISBN 0-273-08439-9). Pitman Pub MA.
Yuen, C. K., jt. auth. see Beauchamp, K. G.
Yuen, Ko, pseud. Khing Kang King: The Classic of Purity - Being Liber XXI. LC 73-11427. 1973. 8.75x o.p. (ISBN 0-913576-07-7). Thelema Pubns.
--Liber XXI, Khing Kang King - The Classic of Purity. LC 73-11427. (Illus.). 1976. 14.95x (ISBN 0-913576-16-6). Thelema Pubns.
Yuhas, John M., et al, eds. Biology of Radiation Carcinogenesis. LC 74-14486. 371p. 1976. 38.00 (ISBN 0-89004-010-9). Raven.
Yui, Tsunehiko, jt. auth. see Hirschmeier, Johannes.
Yuill, Douglas, et al. Regional Policy in the European Community. 1980. 27.50 (ISBN 0-312-66931-3). St Martin.
Yuill, G. M. Treatment of Renal Failure. 1975. pap. 5.00 (ISBN 0-7190-0628-7). Manchester.
Yuill, Phyllis J. Little Black Sambo: A Closer Look. (Illus.). 52p. (Orig.). 1976. pap. 3.50 (ISBN 0-930040-23-6). CIBC.
Yuille, John C., ed. Imagery, Memory & Cognition: Essays in Honor of Allan Paivio. (Illus.). 352p. 1982. text ed. 39.95 (ISBN 0-89859-215-1). L Erlbaum Assocs.
Yuji, Gomi. Guide to Japanese Taxes, 1982-83. LC 66-50788. (Illus.). 282p. (Orig.). 1982. pap. 27.50 (ISBN 0-686-84552-8). Intl Pubns Serv.
Yuji, Guo. Children's Sports in China. LC 80-54763. PLB 8.56 (ISBN 0-382-06588-3). Silver.
Yuker, Harold E. & Block, J. Richard. Challenging Barriers to Change: Attitudes Towards the Disabled. LC 79-84738. 68p. 1979. 4.75 (ISBN 0-686-42976-1). Human res Ctr.
Yukl, Gary. Leadership in Organizations. (Illus.). 336p. 1981. text ed. 23.95 (ISBN 0-13-527176-2) P-H.
Yules, Richard B. Atlas for Surgical Repair of Cleft Lip, Cleft Palate, & Noncleft Velopharyngeal Incompetence. (Illus.). 212p. 1971. photocopy ed. spiral 30.50x (ISBN 0-398-02136-8). C C Thomas.
Yulish, Stephen M. The Search for a Civic Religion: A History of the Character Education Movement in America, Eighteen Ninety to Nineteen Thirty-Five. LC 80-5619. 318p. 1980. lib. bdg. 22.00 (ISBN 0-8191-1173-2); pap. text ed. 12.25 (ISBN 0-8191-1174-0). U Pr of Amer.
Yulsman, Jerry. The Canon Guide. (Modern Camera Guides Ser.). (Illus.). cancelled (ISBN 0-8174-2433-4, Amphoto); pap. cancelled (ISBN 0-8174-0179-2). Watson-Guptill.
--Color Photography Simplified. (Modern Photo Guide Ser.). (Illus.). 1977. 10.95 o.p. (ISBN 0-8174-2425-3, Amphoto); pap. 5.95 o.p. (ISBN 0-8174-0176-8). Watson-Guptill.
--The Complete Book of Eight mm Movie Making. Date not set. cancelled o.p. (ISBN 0-698-10953-8, Coward). Putnam Pub Group.
--The Complete Book of Eight mm (Super-8, Single-8, Standard-8) Movie Making. 224p. 1972. 6.95 o.p. (ISBN 0-698-10461-7, Coward). Putnam Pub Group.
--Complete Book of Thirty-Five MM Photography. LC 75-45425. (Illus.). 224p. (YA) 1976. 8.95 o.p. (ISBN 0-698-10734-9, Coward). Putnam Pub Group.
Yund, Gloria S., jt. auth. see Sanchez, Irene B.
Yung, O. L. Commercial, Business & Trade Laws of Hong Kong. 1982. loose-leaf 125.00 (ISBN 0-379-22005-9). Oceana.
Yung, Teng C. The Bookworm. DeFrancis, John, ed. LC 73-189613. (Pali Language Texts-Chinese). (Illus.). 60p. (Orig.). 1975. pap. text ed. 1.95x (ISBN 0-8248-0223-3). UH Pr.
--The Heartless Husband. DeFrancis, John, ed. LC 70-189612. (Pali Language Texts - Chinese). (Illus.). 40p. 1975. pap. text ed. 1.95x (ISBN 0-8248-0222-5). UH Pr.
--The Herd Boy & the Weaving Maid. DeFrancis, John, ed. LC 76-189611. (Pali Language Texts - Chinese). (Illus.). 38p. (Orig.). 1975. pap. text ed. 1.95x (ISBN 0-8248-0221-7). UH Pr.
--The Poet Li Po. DeFrancis, John, ed. LC 77-189614. (Pali Language Texts - Chinese). (Illus.). 80p. (Orig.). 1975. pap. text ed. 1.95x (ISBN 0-8248-0224-1). UH Pr.
Yungmei, Tang, photos by. China, Here We Come! (Illus.). 64p. (gr. 5-10). 1981. 9.95 (ISBN 0-399-20826-7). Putnam Pub Group.
Yung-Ping Chen, jt. ed. see Scholen, Kenneth.
Yung Teng Chia-Yee, jt. auth. see Williams, Jack.
Yu-Ning, Li, ed. Shang Yang's Reforms & State Control in China. LC 76-4301. (The China Book Project Ser.). 275p. 1977. 27.50 (ISBN 0-87332-080-8). M E Sharpe.
Yunis, Edmond J., et al. Tissue Typing & Organ Transplantation. 1973. 48.00 (ISBN 0-12-775160-2). Acad Pr.
Yunis, G. J. New Chromosomal Syndromes. 1977. 53.50 (ISBN 0-12-775165-3). Acad Pr.

Yunis, Jorge, ed. Molecular Structure of Human Chromosomes. 1977. 45.00 (ISBN 0-12-775168-8). Acad Pr.

Yunis, Jorge J., ed. Human Chromosome Methodology. 2nd ed. 1974. 40.50 (ISBN 0-12-775155-6). Acad Pr.

Yunus, Noor A. Preparing & Using Aids for English Language Teaching. (Illus.). 120p. (Orig.). 1981. pap. text ed. 7.95 (ISBN 0-19-581809-1). Oxford U Pr.

Yura, Helen & Friesner, Arlyne. Curriculum Process for Developing or Revising Baccalaureate Nursing Programs. 65p. 1978. 4.95 (ISBN 0-686-38257-9, 15-1700). Natl League Nurse.

Yura, Helen & Torres, Gertrude J. The Process of Curriculum Development. (Faculty-Curriculum Development Ser.: Pt. I). 102p. 1974. 5.50 (ISBN 0-686-38265-X, 15-1521). Natl League Nurse.

Yura, Helen, jt. auth. see Torres, Gertrude.

Yurchenco, Henrietta. Fiesta of Folk Songs of Spain & Latin America. (Illus.). (gr. 2 up). 1967. PLB 5.97 o.p. (ISBN 0-399-60165-1). Putnam Pub Group.

Yurdhuck, Ruth. C. G. F. N. S. Examination Review. 1983. pap. text ed. price not set. (ISBN 0-87488-512-4). Med Exam.

Yurick, Sol. Richard A. 480p. pap. 3.50 (ISBN 0-380-62430-3). Avon.

Yurieff, Zoya. Joseph Wittlin. (World Authors Ser.: No. 224). 15.95 o.p. (ISBN 0-8057-2988-7, Twayne). G K Hall.

Yurka, Blanche. Bohemian Girl: Blanche Yurka's Theatrical Life. LC 79-81449. xii, 306p. 1970. 11.95 (ISBN 0-8214-0071-1, 82-80778). Ohio U Pr.

Yurko, John. Video Basics. (Illus.). 48p. (ps-7). 1983. 8.95 (ISBN 0-13-941781-8). P-H.

Yusuf, Abdulqawi. Legal Aspects of Trade Preferences for Developing States. 1982. lib. bdg. 43.50 (ISBN 90-247-2583-6, Pub. by Martinus Nijhoff Netherlands). Kluwer Boston.

Yutang, Lin, ed. Wisdom of China & India. 1955. 5.95 (ISBN 0-394-60476-8). Modern Lib.

Yutang, Lin, ed. see Confucius.

Z

Zaanen, jt. auth. see Luxemburg.

Zaba, Joseph & Doherty, W. T. Practical Petroleum Engineers' Handbook. 5th ed. LC 58-12306. 960p. 1970. 47.95x (ISBN 0-87201-744-3). Gulf Pub.

Zabalaoui, Judith. How to Use Your Business or Profession as a Tax Shelter. 1983. text ed. 18.00 (ISBN 0-8359-2985-X). Reston.

Zabeeh, Farhang. Understanding Human: A New Synthesis. LC 78-65843. 1979. pap. 11.50 (ISBN 0-8191-0670-4). U Pr of Amer.

Zabih, Sepehr. The Communist Movement in Iran. 1966. 33.00x (ISBN 0-520-01377-8). U of Cal Pr.

Zabik, Roger, jt. auth. see Niemeyer, Roy K.

Zabin, J. B., jt. auth. see Hampton, R. E.

Zabinski, Michael P., jt. auth. see Harms, Edward.

Zable, Jeffrey. Ashes Bear Witness of the Burning. 16p. 1982. 1.00 o.p. (ISBN 0-686-32646-6). Ptolemy-Brown.

Zablocki, Benjamin. The Joyful Community: An Account of the Bruderhof, a Communal Movement Now in Its Third Generation. 1980. pap. 5.95 (ISBN 0-226-97749-8, P885, Phoen). U of Chicago Pr.

Zaborsky, Oskar. Immobilized Enzymes. 190p. 1984. text ed. write for info. (ISBN 0-89874-611-6). Krieger.

Zaborsky, Oskar R. & Mitsui, Akira, eds. CRC Handbook of Biosolar Resources: Vol. I Basic Principles, 2 Pts. 1982. Pt. 1, 704 pgs. 99.50 (ISBN 0-8493-3471-3); Pt. 2, 608 pgs. 99.50 (ISBN 0-8493-3472-1). CRC Pr.

Zabriskie, George A., jt. auth. see Zabriskie, Sherry L.

Zabriskie, John. Clinical Immunology of the Heart. LC 80-17927. (Perspectives in Clinical Immunology Ser.). 238p. 1981. 46.50 (ISBN 0-471-02676-X, Pub. by Wiley Med). Wiley.

Zabriskie, John B., jt. ed. see Read, Stanley E.

Zabriskie, John B., et al. Clinical Immunology of the Kidney. LC 82-4876. (Wiley Ser. in Clinical Immunology). 453p. 1982. 59.50x (ISBN 0-471-02675-1, Pub. by Wiley Med). Wiley.

Zabriskie, Sherry L. & Zabriskie, George A. Empanadas: with Calzones, Pasties, Pierogis, Piroshkis, Samones, & other International Turnovers. 1983. pap. 5.95 (ISBN 0-517-54756-2, C N Potter Bks). Crown.

Zabrodsky, S. S. Hydrodynamics & Heat Transfer in Fluidized Beds. 1966. 35.00x (ISBN 0-262-24007-6). MIT Pr.

Zabronski, Ann, jt. auth. see Peebles Press International.

Zaccaria, Joseph. Theories of Occupational Choice & Vocational Development. (Guidance Monograph). 1970. pap. 2.40 o.p. (ISBN 0-395-09934-X, 9-78834). HM.

Zaccaria, Joseph & Bopp, Steven. Approaches to Guidance in Contemporary Education. 2nd ed. 320p. 1980. 22.50 (ISBN 0-910328-31-5); pap. 15.50 (ISBN 0-910328-32-3). Carroll Pr.

Zaccaria, Joseph S. & Moses, Harold. Bibliotherapy in Rehabilitation, Educational & Mental Health Settings. 1978. pap. text ed. 8.80x (ISBN 0-87563-149-5). Stipes.

Zacchello, Joseph. Secrets of Romanism. 232p. 1981. pap. 4.25 (ISBN 0-87213-981-6). Loizeaux.

Zach, Paul. Florida, Insight Travel Guide. 1982. 17.50 (ISBN 0-686-93907-7). Hippocrene Bks.

Zach, Paul, ed. Hippocrene. (Insight Guides Ser.). (Illus.). 453p. 1982. 25.00 (ISBN 0-686-98374-2); pap. 17.50 (ISBN 0-686-98375-0). Hippocrene Bks.

Zachar, D. Soil Erosion. (Developments in Soil Science: Vol. 10). 1982. 93.75 (ISBN 0-444-99725-3). Elsevier.

Zacharia, Don. The Match Trick. 1982. 13.50 (ISBN 0-671-44017-9, Linden). S&S.

Zachariades, Porter. The Strength & Stiffness of Polymers. (Plastics Engineering Ser.). 368p. 1983. price not set (ISBN 0-8247-1846-1). Dekker.

Zachariah, K. C. Demographic Aspects of Migration, Vol. 2. (Working Paper: No. 415). vi, 385p. 1980. 5.00 (ISBN 0-686-36194-6, WP-0415). World Bank.

--Demographic Aspects of Migration in West Africa, Vol. 1. (Working Paper: No. 414). vi, 363p. 1980. 5.00 (ISBN 0-686-36193-8, WP-0414). World Bank.

--Historical Study of Internal Migration in the Indian Sub-Continent. 15.00 o.p. (ISBN 0-210-31248-3). Asia.

Zacharis, John C. & Bender, Coleman C. Speech Communication: A Rational Approach. LC 75-45057. 260p. 1976. text ed. 17.95x (ISBN 0-673-15731-8); o.p. instructor's manual (ISBN 0-471-01462-1). Scott F.

Zachary, Hugh. Top Level Death. (Raven House Mysteries Ser.). 224p. 1982. pap. cancelled (ISBN 0-373-63044-1, Pub. by Worldwide). Harlequin Bks.

Zacher, Hans F., jt. auth. see Kohler, Peter A.

Zacher, Mark W., jt. auth. see M'Gonigle, R. Michael.

Zachert, Ursula, compiled by. Wolfenbuttel: Herzog August Bibliothek, Verzeichnis medizinischer und naturwissenschaftlicher 1472 to 1830, 15 volumes in 4 parts. 1976. lib. bdg. 280.00 Reihe A Alphabetischer Index 4 vols. (ISBN 0-527-97704-7); Reihe B. Chronologischer Index, 3 Vols. 264.00; Reihe C. Ortsindex, 3 Vols. 264.00 (ISBN 3-262-00084-1). Kraus Intl.

Zack, Arnold, jt. auth. see Bloch, Richard I.

Zack, Jinny. Sugar Isn't Always Sweet. Tanner, Don, ed. (Illus.). 204p. (Orig.). 1983. pap. 5.95 (ISBN 0-88005-002-0). Uplift Bks.

Zackel, Fred. Cinderella After Midnight. LC 79-9445. 1980. 11.95 (ISBN 0-698-10990-2, Coward). Putnam Pub Group.

--Cocaine & Blue Eyes. LC 78-5379. 1978. 8.95 o.p. (ISBN 0-698-10934-1, Coward). Putnam Pub Group.

--Cocaine & Blue Eyes. 320p. 1983. pap. 2.95 (ISBN 0-425-06241-4). Berkley Pub.

Zacur, Susan R. Health Care Labor Relations: The Nursing Perspective. Kalisch, Philip & Kalisch, Beatrice, eds. LC 82-13525. (Studies in Nursing Management: No. 5). 166p. 1982. 34.95 (ISBN 0-8357-1371-7, Pub. by UMI Res Pr). Univ Microfilms.

Zadeh & Fu, King-Sun, eds. Fuzzy Sets & Their Applications to Cognitive & Decision Processes. 1975. 40.00 (ISBN 0-12-775260-9). Acad Pr.

Zadeh, L. A. & Desoer, C. A. Linear System Theory. LC 78-26008. 650p. 1979. Repr. of 1963 ed. lib. bdg. 31.50 (ISBN 0-88275-809-8). Krieger.

Zadeh, L. A., et al, eds. Computing Methods in Optimization Problems Two. 1969. 54.00 (ISBN 0-12-775250-1). Acad Pr.

Zadig, E. The Complete Illustrated Book of Boating. 1972. 12.95 o.p. (ISBN 0-13-160143-1). P-H.

Zadoks, Jan C. & Schein, Richard D. Epidemiology & Plant Disease Management. (Illus.). 1979. text ed. 24.95x (ISBN 0-19-502451-6); pap. text ed. 12.95x (ISBN 0-19-502452-4). Oxford U Pr.

Zaehner, R. C., ed. & tr. Hindu Scriptures. 1978. 9.95x (ISBN 0-460-10944-8, Evman); pap. 2.75x (ISBN 0-460-11944-3, Evman). Biblio Dist.

Zaehner, Robert C. At Sundry Times: An Essay in the Comparison of Religions. LC 76-49621. 1977. Repr. of 1958 ed. lib. bdg. 19.00x (ISBN 0-8371-9354-0, ZAST). Greenwood.

--Hindu & Muslim Mysticism. LC 74-83675. 1969. pap. 4.50 o.p. (ISBN 0-8052-0237-4). Schocken.

--Mysticism: Sacred & Profane. 1961. pap. 5.95x (ISBN 0-19-500229-6, GB56). Oxford U Pr.

--The Teachings of the Magi. 1976. pap. 5.95 (ISBN 0-19-519857-3, 470, GB). Oxford U Pr.

--Zurvan: A Zoroastrian Dilemma. 1973. Repr. of 1955 ed. 19.00x (ISBN 0-8196-0280-9). Biblo.

Zaehner, Robert C., ed. Bhagavad-Gita. 1969. 45.00x (ISBN 0-19-826522-0). Oxford U Pr.

--The Bhagavad-Gita. 1969. pap. 10.95 (ISBN 0-19-501666-1, GB389, GB). Oxford U Pr.

Zaetz, Jay L. Organization of Sheltered Workshop Programs for the Mentally Retarded Adult. (Illus.). 248p. 1971. photocopy ed. spiral 24.75x (ISBN 0-398-02158-9). C C Thomas.

Zaffo, George. Airplanes & Trucks & Trains, Fire Engines, Boats & Ships, & Building & Wrecking Machines. (Illus.). (gr. k-3). 1968. 6.95 (ISBN 0-448-01887-X, G&D). Putnam Pub Group.

--Big Book of Real Boats & Ships. (Grow-up Books Ser.). (gr. 2-7). 1972. 1.95 o.p. (ISBN 0-448-02254-0, 2254-0; G&D). Putnam Pub Group.

--Giant Book of Things in Space. LC 73-78682. (gr. k-3). 1969. PLB 12.95a (ISBN 0-385-02150-X). Doubleday.

Zaffrann, Ronald T., jt. auth. see Colangelo, Nicholas.

Zafran, Eric & Ackerman, Gerald M. French Salon Paintings from Southern Collections. Morris, Kelly, ed. LC 82-82944. (Illus.). 176p. (Orig.). 1983. pap. 10.00 (ISBN 0-939802-15-5). High Mus Art.

Zagat, Helen. Faith & Works. 1955. 6.95 (ISBN 0-686-24360-9). Divine Sci Fed.

Zagel, James. Confessions & Interrogations After Miranda: A Comprehensive Guideline of the Law. 6th ed. 1982. 4.00 (ISBN 0-686-36763-4). Natl Dist Atty.

Zager, Melody. Growing up At Gold Creek. 1982. pap. 2.50 (ISBN 0-448-16925-8, Pub. by Tempo). Ace Bks.

--Growing up at Gold Creek, Vol. 1: The Gonna People. (Illus.). (gr. 5 up). 1979. 9.00 o.p. (ISBN 0-8309-0218-X). Ind Pr MO.

Zager, Robert, jt. auth. see Rosow, Jerome M.

Zager, Robert, ed. The Innovative Organization: Productivity Programs in Action. Rosow, Michael P. 300p. 27.50 (ISBN 0-686-84779-2). Work in Amer.

Zager, Robert & Rosow, Michael P., eds. The Innovative Organization: Productivity Programs in Action. (Pergamon Press Work in America Institute Ser.). (Illus.). 384p. 1982. 27.50 (ISBN 0-08-029547-9, L120, J127). Pergamon.

Zagon, Eileen, jt. auth. see Salinger, Florence.

Zagoren, Adelaide M., compiled by. Involving Alumni in Career Assistance Programs. 111p. 1982. 14.50 (ISBN 0-89964-192-X). CASE.

Zagoren, Ruby. Chaim Weizmann: First President of Israel. LC 74-177893. (Century Biographies Ser.). (Illus.). (gr. 4-8). 1972. PLB 3.98 (ISBN 0-8116-4755-2). Garrard.

Zagoria, Janet D., ed. see Nicolaevsky, Boris I.

Zagorin, P. Rebels & Rulers, 1500-1660, 2 vols. Incl. Vol. 1. Society, States, & Early Modern Revolution: Agrarian & Urban Rebellions (ISBN 0-521-24472-2). pap. (ISBN 0-521-28711-1); Vol. 2. Provincial Rebellion: Revolutionary Civil Wars, 1560-1660 (ISBN 0-521-24473-0). pap. (ISBN 0-521-28712-X). LC 81-17039. 304p. 1982. 37.50 ea.; pap. 9.95 ea. Cambridge U Pr.

Zagorin, Perez, ed. Culture & Politics: From Puritanism to Enlightenment. 1980. 21.50x (ISBN 0-520-03863-0). U of Cal Pr.

Zahan, Dominique. The Religion, Spirituality, & Thought of Traditional Africa. Ezra, Kate & Martin, Lawrence M., trs. vi, 180p. 1979. pap. 5.95 (ISBN 0-226-97778-1). U of Chicago Pr.

Zahareas, Anthony & Mujica, Barbara, eds. Readings in Spanish Literature. 1975. pap. text ed. 7.50x o.p. (ISBN 0-19-501845-1). Oxford U Pr.

Zahareas, Anthony N., ed. see Ruiz, Juan.

Zahl, Paul. Who Will Deliver Us? 96p. (Orig.). 1983. pap. price not set (ISBN 0-8164-2468-3). Seabury.

Zahlan, A. B. Science & Science Policy in the Arab World. LC 79-3380. 1980. 26.00x (ISBN 0-312-70232-9). St Martin.

Zahlan, A. B., ed. see United Nations Economic Commission for Western Asia, Natural Resources, Science & Technology Division.

Zahlan, Rosemarie S. The Origins of the United Arab Emirates: A Political & Social History of the Trucial States. LC 78-6964. 1978. 26.00x (ISBN 0-312-58882-8). St Martin.

Zahn, Douglas A., jt. auth. see Boen, James R.

Zahn, Frank. Macroeconomic Theory & Policy. (Illus.). 320p. 1975. 19.95 (ISBN 0-13-542555-7). P-H.

Zahn, Frank, jt. auth. see Hosek, William R.

Zahn, Gordon C., intro. by see Merton, Thomas.

Zahn, Hans E. Glossairies of Financial & Economic Terms: English-German. 530p. 1977. 100.00 (ISBN 0-7121-5492-2, Pub. by Macdonald & Evans). State Mutual Bk.

Zahn, Markus. Electromagnetic Field Theory: A Problem Solving Approach. 723p. 1979. text ed. 40.95 (ISBN 0-471-02198-9); tchr's manual 12.00x (ISBN 0-471-05415-1). Wiley.

Zahn, Sara L. The Beckoning Ghost. (YA) 1979. 6.95 (ISBN 0-686-52548-5, Avalon). Bouregy.

Zahn, Theodor. Introduction to the New Testament, 3 vols. 1977. 48.00 (ISBN 0-86524-119-8, 8003). Klock & Klock.

Zahorski, Witold W., ed. Coal Workers' Pneumoconiosis: A Critical Review. LC 73-92706. (National Library of Medicine). (Illus.). 120p. 1974. text ed. 15.00x (ISBN 0-87451-097-X). U Pr of New Eng.

Zahradnik, Milos. The Production & Application of Fluorescent Brightening Agents. 400p. 1983. 29.95x (ISBN 0-471-10125-7, Pub. by Wiley-Interscience). Wiley.

Zahradnik, R., jt. auth. see Hobza, P.

Zahuaranec, Bernard J., ed. Shark Repellents from the Sea: New Perspectives. (AAAS Selected Symposium 83). 225p. 1983. price not set (ISBN 0-86531-593-0). Westview.

Zaichkowsky, Leonard D., et al. Growth & Development: The Child & Physical Activity. LC 79-23443. 228p. 1980. pap. text ed. 13.95 (ISBN 0-8016-5663-X). Mosby.

Zaidenberg, Arthur. Anyone Can Sculpt. rev. ed. LC 76-138776. (Illus.). 208p. 1972. 14.95i (ISBN 0-06-014800-4, HarpT). Har-Row.

--Drawing All Animals. (Funk & W Bk.). (Illus.). 176p. 1974. pap. 7.95i (ISBN 0-308-10108-1, F99). T Y Crowell.

Zaidi, S. Rural India & Malnutrition: Implications, Problems & Prospects. 294p. 1982. text ed. 19.50x (ISBN 0-391-02720-4, Pub. by Concept). Humanities.

Zaidi, S. Hafeez. Village Culture in Transition: A Study of East Pakistan Rural Society. 1970. text ed. 10.00x (ISBN 0-8248-0086-9, Eastwest Ctr). UH Pr.

Zaidman, Samuel D. Abstract Differential Equations. LC 79-9061. (Research Notes in Mathematics Ser.: No. 36). 130p. (Orig.). 1979. pap. text ed. 18.95 (ISBN 0-686-31216-3). Pitman Pub MA.

Zaika, V. E. Specific Production of Aquatic Invertebrates. Gollek, B., ed. Mercado, A., tr. from Rus. LC 73-12320. 154p. 1973. 49.95 o.p. (ISBN 0-470-98111-3). Halsted Pr.

Zainal, A. S. Micro-Morphological Studies of Soft Rot Fungi in Wood. (Bibliotheca Mycologica: No. 70). (Illus.). 1980. lib. bdg. 24.00 (ISBN 3-7682-1252-1). Lubrecht & Cramer.

Zais, James P., et al. Housing Assistance for Older Americans: The Reagan Prescription. LC 82-50957. (Changing Domestic Priorities Ser.). 125p. (Orig.). 1982. pap. text ed. 9.95 (ISBN 0-87766-317-3, 34300). Urban Inst.

Zaitzevsky, Cynthia. Frederick Law Olmsted & the Boston Park System. (Illus.). 288p. 1982. text ed. 30.00x (ISBN 0-674-31830-7, Belknap Pr). Harvard U Pr.

Zajac, A., jt. auth. see Hecht, E.

Zajac, E. E. Fairness of Efficiency: An Introduction to Public Utility Pricing. LC 78-26076. 144p. 1979. pap. 9.95x (ISBN 0-88410-681-0). Ballinger Pub.

Zajic, J., jt. auth. see Hobst, L.

Zajic, J. E. Microbial Biogeochemistry. 1969. 42.50 (ISBN 0-12-775350-8). Acad Pr.

Zajic, Josef, jt. auth. see Hobst, Leos.

Zak, Michele, jt. ed. see Moots, Patricia A.

Zak, Therese A., ed. see Corwin, Sheila.

Zak, Therese A., ed. see Hemsoth, et al.

Zak, Therese A., ed. see Learning Achievement Corp.

Zak, Therese A., ed. see Learning Achievement Corporation.

Zak, Therese A., ed. see Lehman, Scott C.

Zak, Therese A., ed. see Pickens, L.

Zakharyev, L. N., et al. Radiation from Apertures in Convex Bodies: Flush-Mounted Antennas. Beckmann, Petr, tr. from Rus. LC 76-114987. (Electromagnetics Ser.: Vol. 4). 1970. 25.00x (ISBN 0-911762-06-X). Golem.

Zakhoder, Boris. The Crocodile's Toothbrush. Rudolph, Marguerita, tr. LC 72-6958. (Illus.). 48p. (gr. k-3). 1973. PLB 8.95 (ISBN 0-07-072719-8, GB). McGraw.

Zaks, Rodnay. From Chips to Systems: An Introduction to Microprocessors. 4th ed. LC 81-51126. (Illus.). 420p. 1981. pap. 16.95x (ISBN 0-89588-063-6, C201A). Sybex.

--A Microprogrammed APL Implementation. LC 78-58355. 1978. pap. text ed. 38.00 (ISBN 0-89588-005-9, Z-10). Sybex.

--Your First BASIC Program. 200p. 1983. pap. text ed. 9.95 (ISBN 0-89588-092-X). Sybex.

Zakus, Sharron. Clinical Skills & Assisting Techniques for the Medical Assistant. LC 80-27135. (Illus.). 351p. 1981. pap. text ed. 19.95 (ISBN 0-8016-5672-9). Mosby.

Zakutinsky, R., ed. see Goldberg, Yaffa G.

Zakutinsky, Ruth. Case of the Missing Baseball Cards. 84p. (gr. 3-6). 1982. pap. 3.95 (ISBN 0-911643-01-X). Aura Pub.

--Judah & Yoni. (Illus.). 32p. (ps-4). 1975. write for info. (ISBN 0-911643-04-4). Aura Pub.

--We're Really Going Home. (Illus.). 32p. (ps-4). 1979. write for info. (ISBN 0-911643-02-8). Aura Pub.

Zaky, A. A. & Hawley, R. Dielectric Solids. (Solid-State Physics Ser.). 1970. pap. 5.00 o.p. (ISBN 0-7100-6604-X). Routledge & Kegan.

Zalaznick, Charles. Real Estate Development & Construction Financing 1982: Course Handbook. (Real Estate Law & Practice Course Handgook Ser.). 763p. 1982. pap. text ed. 30.00 (ISBN 0-686-68829-5, N4-4349). PLI.

Zalben, Jane. Penny & the Captain. LC 76-54826. (Illus.). (gr. 1-4). 1978. 5.95 o.s.i. (ISBN 0-529-05424-8, Philomel); PLB 5.99 o.s.i. (ISBN 0-529-05425-6). Putnam Pub Group.

Zalben, Jane B. Norton's Nighttime. LC 78-12144. (Illus.). 32p. (ps-3). 1979. 6.95 o.s.i. (ISBN 0-529-05430-2, 05430, Philomel); PLB 6.99 o.s.i. (ISBN 0-529-05431-0). Putnam Pub Group.

--A Perfect Nose for Ralph. LC 79-23260. (Illus.). 32p. (ps-1). 1980. 6.95 (ISBN 0-399-20744-9, Philomel); PLB 6.99 (ISBN 0-399-61154-1). Putnam Pub Group.

--Porcupine's Christmas Blues. (Illus.). 32p. 1982. 9.95 (ISBN 0-399-20893-3, Philomel). Putnam Pub Group.

Zalburg, Sanford. A Spark Is Struck! Jack Hall & the ILWU in Hawaii. LC 79-91284. (Illus.). 1980. pap. 5.95 (ISBN 0-8248-0672-7). UH Pr.

Zald, Mayer N. & McCarthy, John D. The Dynamic of Social Movements: Resource Mobilization, Social Control, & Tactics. 1979. text ed. 17.95 (ISBN 0-316-98473-6). Little.

Zaldivar, Gladys. Fabulacion De Enea-the Keeper of the Flame. Rivers, Elias L., tr. from Eng. & Span. (Coleccion Vortex). 67p. pap. write for info. o.p. Ediciones.

--Zejeles Para el Clavel. LC 80-70836. (Coleccion Vortex). 55p. (Orig., Span.). 1980. pap. write for info. o.p. Ediciones.

Zales, Michael R. Eating, Sleeping & Sexuality: Recent Advances in Basic Life Functions. LC 81-17015. 320p. 1981. 25.00 (ISBN 0-87630-233-9). Brunner-Mazel.

Zales, Michael R., ed. Affective & Schizophrenic Disorders: New Approaches to Diagnosis & Treatment. 304p. 1983. 25.00 (ISBN 0-87630-324-6). Brunner-Mazel.

Zaleski, Jean & Honig, Edwin. Cow-Lines. (Illus.). 1982. pap. 14.95 (ISBN 0-914278-37-1). Copper Beech.

Zaleski, Marek B., et al. Immunogenetics. 512p. 1983. text ed. 34.95 (ISBN 0-273-01925-2). Pitman Pub MA.

Zaleznik, Abraham & Moment, D. Dynamics of Interpersonal Behavior. LC 64-23867. 1964. 30.95x (ISBN 0-471-98120-6, Pub. by Wiley-Hamilton). Wiley.

Zalk, Sue R., jt. auth. see Bitman, Sam.

Zalla, T. & Diamond, R. B. Economic & Technical Aspects of Fertilizer Production & Use in West Africa. (IFDC MSU Working Papers Ser.: No. 22). (IFDC Miscellaneous Publication A-1). 1977. 4.00 (ISBN 0-686-95956-6). Intl Fertilizer.

Zallen, Harold. Ideas Plus Dollars: Research Methodology & Funding. 2nd ed. LC 79-55737. (Illus.). 1980. 12.95 (ISBN 0-915582-03-1). Academic World.

Zaller, R., jt. ed. see Greaves, R.

Zaller, Robert, jt. ed. see Greaves, Richard.

Zallinger, Peter. Prehistoric Animals. (Pictureback Ser.). (Illus.). 32p. (ps-3). 1981. PLB 4.99 (ISBN 0-394-93737-6); pap. 1.50 (ISBN 0-394-83737-1). Random.

Zalta, Edward N. Abstract Objects. 1983. lib. bdg. 39.50 (ISBN 90-277-1474-6, Pub. by Reidel Holland). Kluwer Boston.

Zaltman, G. & Wallendorf, M. Consumer Behavior: Basic Findings & Management Implications. LC 78-23335. 1979. text ed. 30.95 (ISBN 0-471-98126-5); tchrs. manual 6.00 (ISBN 0-471-04862-3). Wiley.

Zaltman, Gerald & LeMasters, Karen. Theory Construction in Marketing: Some Thoughts on Thinking. (Marketing Ser.). 209p. 1982. text ed. 29.95 (ISBN 0-471-98127-3). Wiley.

Zaltman, Gerald, jt. auth. see Bonoma, Thomas V.

Zaltman, Gerald, jt. auth. see Wallendorf, Melanie.

Zaltman, Gerald, et al. Innovations & Organizations. LC 73-5873. 224p. 1973. 25.95x (ISBN 0-471-98129-X, Pub. by Wiley-Interscience). Wiley.

Zalucki, H. Dictionary of Russian Technical & Scientific Abbreviations. (Rus. & Ger.). 1968. 70.25 (ISBN 0-444-40657-3). Elsevier.

Zaluzec, N. J., jt. ed. see Johari, Om.

Zaman, V. Handbook of Medical Parasitology. 200p. 1982. pap. text ed. 27.50 (ISBN 0-86792-000-9, Pub by Adis Pr Australia). Wright-PSG.

Zambrano, E. & Vasquez, E. Paleogeographic & Petroleum Synthesis of Western Venezuela. 70p. 1972. 60.00x (ISBN 2-7108-0194-9, Pub. by Graham & Trotman England). State Mutual Bk.

Zamenhof, L. L. Fundamenta Krestomatio. 17th ed. (Esperanto.). 1969. 9.25x (ISBN 0-685-71609-0, 1189). Esperanto League North Am.

Zamiatin, Eugene. We. Zilboorg, Gregory, tr. 1959. pap. 4.25 (ISBN 0-525-47039-5, 0413-120). Dutton.

--We. (Science Fiction Ser). 276p. 1975. Repr. of 1934 ed. lib. bdg. 15.00 o.p. (ISBN 0-8398-2320-7, Gregg). G K Hall.

Zamm, Alfred. Why Your House May Endanger Your Health. 1980. 10.95 o.s.i. (ISBN 0-671-24128-1). S&S.

Zammattio, Carlo, et al. Leonardo the Scientist. LC 80-18436. (Illus.). 192p. 1980. 9.95 o.p. (ISBN 0-07-007933-1). McGraw.

Zammuto, A. P. & Mufich, C. J. Drafting Experiences in Metrics. 80p. pap. 5.60 (ISBN 0-87006-241-7). Goodheart.

Zammuto, Raymond F. Assessing Organizational Effectiveness: Systems Change, Adaptation & Strategy. LC 81-9130. (Administrative Systems Ser.). 1982. 44.50x (ISBN 0-87395-552-8); pap. 14.95x (ISBN 0-87395-553-6). State U NY Pr.

Zamora, Lois P., ed. The Apocalyptic Vision in America: Interdisciplinary Essays on Myth & Culture. LC 81-85524. 272p. 1982. 19.95 (ISBN 0-686-82270-6). Bowling Green Univ.

Zamora, Ramon, et al. Pet Basic: Training Your Pet. (Illus.). 320p. 1981. 19.95 (ISBN 0-8359-5525-7); pap. 14.95 (ISBN 0-8359-5524-9). Reston.

Zamoyski, Adam. Paderewski. LC 81-69136. (Illus.). 1982. 19.95 (ISBN 0-689-11248-3). Atheneum.

Zamparelli, Thomas L. John Strevens: The Man & His Works. (Illus.). 50p. 1983. 12.00. K E Schon.

Zampetti, Pietro. A Dictionary of Venetian Painters: Vol. 3, 17th Century. (Illus.). 1971. 36.00x o.p. (ISBN 0-85317-181-5, Pub. by A & C Black England). Humanities.

Zamrik, S. Y. & Dietrich, D., eds. Pressure Vessels & Piping: Design Technology, 1982-A Decade of Progress. 647p. 1982. 85.00 (G00213). ASME.

Zamzow, Dennis, jt. auth. see Feigel, William.

Zanca, Kenneth. The Judas Within. (Orig.). 1978. pap. 2.50 (ISBN 0-914544-25-X). Living Flame Pr.

--Reasons for Rejoicing: Readings in Christian Hope. (Orig.). 1976. pap. 2.50 (ISBN 0-914544-12-8). Living Flame Pr.

Zanca, Kenneth J. Mourning: The Healing Journey 1980. (Orig.). 2.95 (ISBN 0-914544-30-6). Living Flame Pr.

Zanchetti, A. Advances in Beta-Blocker Therapy II. 1982. 66.00 (ISBN 0-444-90276-7). Elsevier.

Zand, Dale. Information-Organization-Power: Management in a Knowledge Society. Newton, William R., ed. (Illus.). 224p. 1981. 14.95 (ISBN 0-07-072743-0). McGraw.

Zand, P., jt. auth. see Shepherd, W.

Zanden, James Vander see Vander Zanden, James.

Zanden, James W. Human Development. 2nd ed. 665p. 1981. text ed. 21.00 (ISBN 0-394-32370-X); wkbk. 8.00 (ISBN 0-394-32371-8). Knopf.

Zanden, James W. Vander see Vander Zanden, James W.

Zander, Alvin. Groups at Work: Unresolved Issues in the Study of Organizations. LC 77-82918. (Social & Behavioral Science Ser). 1977. text ed. 15.95x (ISBN 0-87589-347-3). Jossey-Bass.

--Motives & Goals in Groups. (Social Psychology Ser). 1971. 35.00 (ISBN 0-12-775550-0). Acad Pr.

Zander, Horst. Shakespeare Bearbeitet. (Tubinger Beitrage zur Anglistik: 3). 350p. 1983. pap. 21.00 (ISBN 3-87808-963-5). Benjamins North Am.

Zander, Karen S. Primary Nursing: Development & Management. LC 79-28837. 384p. 1980. text ed. 31.75 (ISBN 0-89443-170-6). Aspen Systems.

Zander, Karen S. & Bower, Kathleen A., eds. Practical Manual for Patient-Teaching. LC 78-7039. 394p. 1978. pap. text ed. 15.95 o.p. (ISBN 0-8016-5678-8). Mosby.

Zander, Mary, et al. Toward Income Adequacy for the Elderly: Implications of the SSI Programs for New York City Recipients. 243p. 1982. pap. 5.00 (ISBN 0-88156-004-9). Comm Serv Soc NY.

Zander, Maximilian. Phosphorimetry: The Application of Phosphoresence to the Analysis of Organic Compounds. Goodwin, Thomas H., tr. LC 68-18686. 1968. 46.00 (ISBN 0-12-775650-7). Acad Pr.

Zanderbergen, Geo. Laugh It up. LC 76-24209. (Spotlight Ser.). (Illus.). (gr. 4). 1976. PLB 6.95 (ISBN 0-913940-52-6). Crestwood Hse.

--Made for Music. LC 76-24208. (Spotlight Ser.). (Illus.). (gr. 4). 1976. PLB 6.95 (ISBN 0-913940-51-8). Crestwood Hse.

--Nashville Music. LC 76-24207. (Spotlight Ser.). (Illus.). (gr. 4). 1976. PLB 6.95 (ISBN 0-913940-50-X). Crestwood Hse.

--Stay Tuned. LC 76-24210. (Spotlight Ser.). (Illus.). (gr. 4). 1976. PLB 6.95 (ISBN 0-913940-53-4). Crestwood Hse.

Zandvoort, R. W. Wartime English. LC 74-5556. 254p. 1974. Repr. of 1957 ed. lib. bdg. 17.00x (ISBN 0-8371-7509-7, ZAWE). Greenwood.

Zane, Christie, jt. auth. see Zane, Frank.

Zane, Frank & Zane, Christie. The Zane Way to a Beautiful Body Through Weight Training for Men & Women. (Illus.). 1979. 14.95 (ISBN 0-671-24367-5). S&S.

Zaner, Richard M. The Context of Self: A Phenomenological Inquiry Using Medicine As a Clue. LC 80-18500. (Continental Thought Ser.: Vol. 1). (Illus.). xiv, 282p. 1981. 18.95x (ISBN 0-8214-0443-1, 82-83327); pap. 9.95x (ISBN 0-8214-0600-0, 82-83335). Ohio U Pr.

Zaner, Richard M., ed. see Schutz, Alfred.

Zanetti, Adriano. The World of Insects. Atthill, Catherine, tr. LC 79-1424. (Abbeville Press Encyclopedia of Natural Science). (Illus.). 256p. 1979. 13.95 (ISBN 0-89659-036-4); pap. 7.95 o. p. (ISBN 0-89659-030-5). Abbeville Pr.

Zaneveld, J. S. Iconography of Antartic & Sub-Antarctic Benthie Marine Algae: Chlorophycophyto & Chrysophycophyta, Part 1. 1969. pap. 16.00 (ISBN 3-7682-0631-9). Lubrecht & Cramer.

Zaneveld, L. J. & Chatterton, Robert T. Biochemistry of Mammalian Reproduction. LC 82-1914. 561p. 1982. 65.00 (ISBN 0-471-05731-2, Pub. by Wiley-Interscience). Wiley.

Zang, Kerry. Traumatic Ankle Conditions. LC 75-42990. 153p. 1976. 19.25 (ISBN 0-87993-077-2). Futura Pub.

Zangrando, Robert L. The NAACP Crusade Against Lynching, 1909 to 1950. 320p. 1980. 29.95 (ISBN 0-87722-174-X). Temple U Pr.

Zangwill, Israel. Children of the Ghetto. (Victorian Library Ser). (Illus.). 448p. 1977. Repr. of 1893 ed. text ed. 15.75x o.p. (ISBN 0-7185-5028-5, Leicester). Humanities.

Zangwill, O. L., jt. ed. see Shepherd, Michael.

Zangwill, Willard I., jt. auth. see Garcia, C. B.

Zani & Kitsao, eds. Mafarkano Na Michezo Mingine. (Swahili Literature Ser.). (Orig., Swahili.). 1978. pap. text ed. 3.95x o.p. (ISBN 0-686-74450-0, 00614). Heinemann Ed.

Zanishi, M., jt. ed. see Motta, M.

Zankov, L. V., et al. Teaching & Development: A Soviet Investigation. Szekely, Beatrice B., ed. Schultz, Arlo, tr. LC 77-82338. (Illus., Orig., Russian.). 1977. 27.50 (ISBN 0-87332-109-X). M E Sharpe.

Zann, Leon P. Living Together in the Sea. (Illus.). 416p. 1980. 29.95 (ISBN 0-87666-500-8, H-990). TFH Pubns.

Zanna, M. P. & Higgins, E. T., eds. Consistency in Social Behavior: The Ontario Symposium, Vol. 2. 336p. 1982. text ed. 29.95 (ISBN 0-89859-221-6). L Erlbaum Assocs.

Zannetos, Zenon S. Theory of Oil Tankship Rates: An Economic Analysis of Tankship Operations. (Economics Monograph: No. 4). 1966. 25.00x (ISBN 0-262-24006-8). MIT Pr.

Zant, James H., jt. auth. see Keller, Marion.

Zant, Nancy P. Van see Van Zant, Nancy P.

Zanten, Ann V., jt. auth. see Chappell, Sally K.

Zanten, Ann van see Chappell, Sally & Van Zanten, Ann.

Zanten, David Van see Van Zanten, David.

Zanzig, Thomas. Jesus is Lord! (Illus.). 208p. pap. 7.95 (ISBN 0-88489-149-6). St Marys.

--Jesus of History, Christ of Faith. LC 81-86361. (Illus.). 192p. (Orig.). (gr. 9-10). 1981. pap. text ed. 6.00 (ISBN 0-88489-145-3); tchr's. manual 9.00 (ISBN 0-88489-146-1). St Mary's.

Zapantis, Andrew L. Greek-Soviet Relations, 1917-1941. (East European Monographs: No. 96). 640p. 1982. 35.00x (ISBN 0-88033-004-X). East Eur Quarterly.

Zapata, Luis. Adonis Garcia: A Picaresque Novel. Lacey, E. A., tr. from Span. 208p. (Orig.). 1981. 20.00 (ISBN 0-917342-79-8, Gay Sunshine); pap. 7.95 (ISBN 0-686-36892-4). Bookpeople.

Zapel, Arthur L., ed. see Gladman, Donna.

Zapel, Arthur L., ed. see Hatton, Thomas J.

Zapel, Arthur L., ed. see Hines, Rosemary W.

Zapel, Arthur L., ed. see Hon, David C.

Zapel, Arthur L., ed. see Kehret, Peg.

Zapel, Arthur L., ed. see Litherland, Janet.

Zapel, Arthur L., ed. see Maschke, Ruby.

Zapel, Arthur L., ed. see Matthews, Arthur C.

Zapel, Arthur L., ed. see Meili, Janet & Meili, Philip.

Zapel, Arthur L., ed. see Miller, James H.

Zapel, Arthur L., ed. see Schmid, Vernon L.

Zapel, Arthur L., ed. see Shute, Stephanie.

Zapel, Arthur L., ed. see Smith, Judy G.

Zapfe, Helmuth see Hurzeler, Johannes.

Zappa, C. R., ed. see Dittman, Richard & Schmieg, Glenn.

Zappa, C. Robert, ed. see Sorenson, Anton M., Jr.

Zappa, Frank, jt. ed. see Zappa, Moon.

Zappa, Moon & Zappa, Frank, eds. The Official Valley Girl Coloring Book. 32p. 1982. pap. 2.95 (ISBN 0-8431-0622-0). Price Stern.

Zappler, Georg, ed. see Benowicz, Robert J.

Zappler, Georg, tr. see Durin, Bernard.

Zappler, Lisbeth. The Natural History of the Nose. LC 73-9051. (gr. 3-5). 1976. 4.95 o.p. (ISBN 0-385-00708-6). Doubleday.

Zappulla, Elio. Evaluating Administrative Performance: Current Trends & Techniques. 400p. 1983. 0.29.95 (ISBN 0-89863-059-2). Star Pub CA.

Zar, Jerrold H. Biostatistical Analysis. (Illus.). 608p. 1974. ref. ed. 30.95 (ISBN 0-13-076984-3). P-H.

Zar, Jerrold H., jt. auth. see Brower, James E.

Zar, Zachariah, jt. auth. see Timms, Moira.

Zarambouka, Sofia. Lysistrata & the Birds. Loftin, Tee, tr. from Greek. (Aristophanes for Children Ser.). (Illus.). 70p. (gr. k-3). 1982. pap. cancelled (ISBN 0-934812-02-0). Tee Loftin.

Zaranka, William, ed. The Brand-X Anthology of Fiction: A Parody Anthology. (Illus.). 350p. 1983. 17.95 (ISBN 0-918222-41-9); prepub. 11.95 (ISBN 0-918222-42-7). Apple Wood.

Zarathustra, Frater, pseud. The What & Why of Magick. LC 82-91047. 48p. 1982. pap. 4.00 (ISBN 0-939856-30-1). Tech Group.

Zarb, Frank G., jt. auth. see Fabozzi, Frank J.

Zarb, George A., jt. auth. see Hickey, Judson C.

Zarchy, Harry. Stamp Collector's Guide. (Illus.). (gr. 7-11). 1956. PLB 6.99 o.p. (ISBN 0-394-91672-7). Knopf.

Zarefsky, David, jt. auth. see Patterson, J. W.

Zaremba, Joseph, ed. Mathematical Economics & Operations Research: A Guide to Information Sources. LC 73-17586. (Economics Information Guide Ser.: Vol. 10). 1978. 42.00x (ISBN 0-8103-1298-0). Gale.

--Statistics & Econometrics: A Guide to Information Sources. (Economics Information Guide Ser.: Vol. 15). 650p. 1980. 42.00x (ISBN 0-8103-1466-5). Gale.

Zaremba, S. K., ed. see Symposium at the Centre for Research in Mathematics, University of Montreal, Sept., 1971.

Zarembka, Paul, ed. Frontiers in Econometrics. (Economic Theory & Mathematical Economics Ser.). 1973. 41.50 (ISBN 0-12-776150-0). Acad Pr.

--Research in Political Economy, Vol. 1. (Orig.). 1978. lib. bdg. 40.00 (ISBN 0-89232-020-6). Jai Pr.

--Research in Political Economy, Vol. 2. 289p. 1979. 40.00 (ISBN 0-89232-120-2). Jai Pr.

--Research in Political Economy, Vol. 3. 329p. 1980. lib. bdg. 40.00 (ISBN 0-89232-156-3). Jai Pr.

--Research in Political Economy, Vol. 4. 300p. 1981. 40.00 (ISBN 0-89232-205-5). Jai Pr.

Zaretsky, Eli. Capitalism, the Family & Personal Life. 1976. pap. 4.95xi (ISBN 0-06-131972-4, TB1972, Torch). Har-Row.

Zaric, Z. Structure of Turbulence in Heat & Mass Transfer. 1982. 90.00 (ISBN 0-07-072731-7). McGraw.

Zaring, Jane. Sharkes in the North Woods. (gr. 5-8). 1982. 9.95 (ISBN 0-395-32271-5). HM.

--Sharkes in the North Woods. 9.95 (ISBN 0-686-43090-5). HM.

Zaring, W. M., jt. auth. see Takeuti, G.

Zariski, Oscar. Oscar Zariski: Collected Papers. Incl. Vol. 1. Foundations of Algebric Geometry & Resolution of Singularities. Hironaka, H. & Mumford, D., eds. 1972. 35.00x (ISBN 0-262-08049-4); Vol. 2. Holomorphic Functions & Linear Systems. Artin, M. & Mumford, D., eds. 1973. 35.00x (ISBN 0-262-01038-0); Vol. 3. Topology of Curves & Surfaces, & Special Topics in the Theory of Algebraic Varieties. Artin, M. & Mazur, B., eds. LC 73-171558. 1978. 45.00x (ISBN 0-262-24021-1); Vol. 4. Equisingularity on Algebraic Varieties. Lipman, J. & Teissier, B., eds. 1979. 55.00x (ISBN 0-262-24022-X). (Mathematicians of Our Times Ser.). MIT Pr.

Zaritsky, Howard M. & Bremer, James. Capital Gains Desk Book. 438p. 1982. 42.50 (ISBN 0-686-97524-3). P-H.

Zarkovich, S. S. Quality of Statistical Data. 365p. 1966. pap. 24.50 (ISBN 0-686-92787-7, F353, FAO). Unipub.

Zarlino, Gioseffo. The Art of Counterpoint. Marco, Guy A. & Palisca, Claude V., trs. from Ital. (Music Reprint Ser.). (Illus.). xxvi, 294p. 1983. Repr. of 1976 ed. lib. bdg. 29.50 (ISBN 0-306-76206-4). Da Capo.

Zarnecki, G. Art of the Medieval World: Architecture, Sculpture, Painting, the Sacred Arts. 1976. 26.95 (ISBN 0-13-047514-9). P-H.

Zaro, Joan S. A Guide for Beginning Psychotherapists. LC 77-76080. 1977. 37.50 (ISBN 0-521-21687-7); pap. 9.95 (ISBN 0-521-29230-1). Cambridge U Pr.

Zaroulis, Nancy L. The Poe Papers: A Tale of Passion. 1977. 7.95 o.p. (ISBN 0-399-11939-6). Putnam Pub Group.

Zarr, Melvyn. Bill of Rights & the Police. 2nd ed. Sloan, Irving J., ed. LC 73-104113. (Legal Alamanac Ser.: No. 40). 123p. 1980. 5.95 (ISBN 0-379-11130-6). Oceana.

Zarrella, John. Designing with the 8088 Microprocessor. 180p. (Orig.). 1983. pap. write for info. (ISBN 0-935230-07-6). Microcomputer Appns.

--Language Translators. LC 82-48049. (Microprocessor Software Engineering Concepts Ser.). 200p. (Orig.). 1982. pap. 12.95 (ISBN 0-935230-06-8). Microcomputer Appns.

Zarrella, John, ed. Microprocessor Operating Systems, Vol. 2. LC 81-80864. 158p. (Orig.). 1982. pap. 12.95 (ISBN 0-935230-04-1); Set. pap. write for info. (ISBN 0-935230-05-X). Microcomputer Appns.

Zarren, H. S. The Respiratory System: Disease, Diagnosis, Treatment. (Clinical Monographs Ser.). (Illus.). 1973. pap. 7.95 o.p. (ISBN 0-87618-056-X). R J Brady.

Zarren, Harvey. Health, Infection & Diseases. (Clinical Monograph Ser.). (Illus.). 1975. pap. 7.95 o.p. (ISBN 0-87618-064-0). R J Brady.

Zarrilli, Phillip B., ed. Martial Arts in Actor Training. LC 81-9697. (Illus.). 1983. 17.95x (ISBN 0-89676-052-9); pap. 12.95x (ISBN 0-89676-053-7). Drama Bk.

Zarrop, M. B., jt. ed. see Holly, Sean.

Zartman, I. William. The Fifty-Percent Solution: How to Bargain Successfully with Hijackers, Strikers, Bosses, Oil Magnates, Arabs, Russians, & Other Worthy Opponents in This Modern World. LC 75-14851. 550p. 1983. 9.95x (ISBN 0-300-03033-9); text ed. 22.00 (ISBN 0-300-03012-6, Y-460). Yale U Pr.

Zartman, I. William, ed. The Political Economy of Nigeria. 304p. 1983. 30.95 (ISBN 0-03-061476-7); pap. 13.95 (ISBN 0-03-061827-4). Praeger.

Zartman, William I. Government & Politics in Northern Africa. LC 75-32656. (Illus.). 1977. Repr. of 1963 ed. lib. bdg. 19.00x (ISBN 0-8371-8554-8, ZAGP). Greenwood.

Zaruba, Q. Landslides & Their Control. 2nd ed. (Developments in Geotechnical Engineering Ser.: Vol. 31). 1982. 64.00 (ISBN 0-444-99700-8). Elsevier.

Zaruba, Q. & Mencl, V. Engineering Geology. (Developments in Geotechnical Engineering: Vol. 10). 1976. text ed. 47.00 (ISBN 0-444-99877-2). Elsevier.

Zaruba, Robert J. Questions & Answers on the Rules of the Road. 4th ed. LC 82-72002. (Illus.). 112p. 1982. pap. text ed. 10.00x (ISBN 0-87033-290-2). Cornell Maritime.

Zaslavsky, Claudia. Africa Counts. LC 72-91248. (Illus.). 1979. pap. 9.95 (ISBN 0-88208-104-7). Lawrence Hill.

Zaslavsky, Robert. Platonic Myth & Platonic Writing. LC 80-5563. 306p. 1981. lib. bdg. 23.00 (ISBN 0-8191-1382-4); pap. text ed. 12.50 (ISBN 0-8191-1381-6). U Pr of Amer.

Zaslavsky, Victor. The Neo-Stalinist State: Class Ethnicity & Consensus in Soviet Society. LC 82-5800. 208p. 1982. 25.00 (ISBN 0-87332-229-0). M E Sharpe.

Zasloff, Joseph J. & Brown, MacAlister. Communist Indochina & U. S. Foreign Policy: Forging New Relations. LC 77-28462. 1978. lib. bdg. 27.50 (ISBN 0-89158-150-2). Westview.

Zaslow, David. Pint-Sized Poetry. (ps-4). 1982. 5.95 (ISBN 0-86653-095-9, GA 435). Good Apple.

--Thoughts Like Clouds... (gr. 3-7). 1982. 6.95 (ISBN 0-86653-094-0, GA 434). Good Apple.

Zaslow, Ira M. Veterinary Trauma & Critical Care. (Illus.). 400p. 1983. write for info. (ISBN 0-8121-0868-X). Lea & Febiger.

Zassenhaus, Hans. Number Theory & Algebra: Collected Papers Dedicated to Henry B. Mann, Arnold E. Ross & Olga Taussky-Todd. 1977. 64.50 (ISBN 0-12-776350-3). Acad Pr.

Zassenhaus, Hans J. Theory of Groups. 2nd ed. LC 56-13058. 16.95 (ISBN 0-8284-0053-9). Chelsea Pub.

Zassenhaus, Hiltgunt. Walls: Resisting the Third Reich - One Woman's Story. LC 73-16443. 256p. 1974. 10.10 (ISBN 0-8070-6388-6); pap. 4.95 (ISBN 0-8070-6389-4, BP534); pap. 2.95 (ISBN 0-8070-6375-4, BP557). Beacon Pr.

Zatlin, Linda G. Nineteenth Century Anglo-Jewish Novel. (English Authors Ser.). 14.95 (ISBN 0-8057-6787-8, Twayne). G K Hall.

Zatlin-Boring, Phyllis. Jaime Salom. (World Author Ser.). 1982. lib. bdg. 15.95 (ISBN 0-8057-6430-5, Twayne). G K Hall.

Zatuchni, Gerald I., et al, eds. Pregnancy Termination. (Illus.). 1979. text ed. 22.50x o.p. (ISBN 0-06-142900-7, Harper Medical). Lippincott.

Zatz, Asa, tr. see Ibarguengoitia, Jorge.

Zatz, Joel L. Pharmaceutical Calculations. 2nd ed. LC 80-23382. 388p. 1981. 24.95x (ISBN 0-471-07757-7, Pub. by Wiley-Interscience). Wiley.

Zauderer, Erich. Partial Differential Equations of Applied Mathematics. (Pure & Applied Mathematics Ser.). 600p. 1983. 42.50x (ISBN 0-471-87517-1, Pub. by Wiley-Interscience). Wiley.

Zauner, Lou, jt. auth. see Zauner, Phyllis.

Zauner, Phyllis & Zauner, Lou. California Gold. 1980. pap. 3.75 (ISBN 0-936914-11-4). Zanel Pubns.

--Sacramento. 1979. 3.75 (ISBN 0-936914-12-2). Zanel Pubns.

Zavala, Iris M. & Rodriquez, Raphael, eds. The Intellectual Roots of Independence: An Anthology of Puerto Rican Political Essays. LC 79-3021. 1980. text ed. 16.50 (ISBN 0-85345-520-1, CL5201); Pb521x. pap. 8.50 (ISBN 0-85345-521-X, PB 521X). Monthly Rev.

Zavalloni, Marisa, jt. auth. see Rubin, Vera.

Zavarin, Valentina, tr. see Uspensky, Boris.

Zavattero, Janette. The Sylmar Tunnel Disaster. LC 78-57409. 1978. 10.95 o.p. (ISBN 0-89696-006-4, An Everest House Book). Dodd.

Zavitkovski, J., ed. The Enterprise, Wisconsin, Radiation Forest: Radioecological Studies, Pt. 2. LC 76-30437. (ERDA Technical Information Center Ser.). 220p. 1977. pap. 13.50 (ISBN 0-87079-102-8, TID-26113-PT. 2); microfiche 4.50 (ISBN 0-87079-194-X, TID-26113-PT. 2). DOE.

Zavos, Spiro. Faith of Our Fathers. LC 82-2060. 155p. 1983. text ed. 14.50 (ISBN 0-7022-1751-4); pap. 8.95 (ISBN 0-7022-1761-1). U of Queensland Pr.

Zawacki, Robert, jt. auth. see Warrick, Donald.

Zawacki, Robert A., jt. auth. see Couger, Daniel.

Zawawi, Sharifa M. Say It in Swahili. (Say It Language Ser.). 205p. (Orig.). 1972. pap. 2.75 (ISBN 0-486-22792-8). Dover.

Zax, Melvin & Spector, Gerald A. An Introduction to Community Psychology. LC 73-20190. (Illus.). 496p. 1974. text ed. 29.50x (ISBN 0-471-98135-4). Wiley.

Zayas, Zoila de see De Zayas, Zoila.

Zayas-Bazan, Eduardo & Fernandez, Gaston J. Que me Cuenta: Temas de hoy de Siempre. 272p. 1983. pap. text ed. 9.95 (ISBN 0-669-05965-X). Heath.

Zayas-Bazan, Eduardo, tr. see Montaner, Carlos A.

Zayed, Ismail. Zionism: The Myth & the Reality. Date not set. price not set (ISBN 0-89259-013-0). Am Trust Pubns.

Zbar, Paul. Basic Electricity: A Text-Lab Manual. 4th ed. (Illus.). 384p. 1974. pap. text ed. 13.50 (ISBN 0-07-072787-2, G). McGraw.

Zbar, Paul & Orne, Peter. Basic Television: Theory & Servicing - a Text Lab Manual. (Illus.). 1978. pap. text ed. 14.50 (ISBN 0-07-072752-X, G); instructor's guide 2.00 (ISBN 0-07-072753-8). McGraw.

Zbar, Paul B. Basic Electricity: A Text-Lab Manual. 5th ed. LC 82-17155. 384p. 1982. text ed. 13.50x (ISBN 0-07-072801-1, C); instr's. guide 3.00 (ISBN 0-07-072802-X). McGraw.

--Basic Electronics: A Text-Lab Manual. 4th ed. 1976. text ed. 13.50 (ISBN 0-07-072761-9, G); inst. guide 3.00 (ISBN 0-07-072762-7). McGraw.

--Basic Radio: Theory & Servicing, a Text-Lab Manual. 3rd ed. 1969. text ed. 11.50 (ISBN 0-07-072764-3, G). McGraw.

Zbar, Paul B. & Electronic Industries Association. Electricity-Electronics Fundamentals: A Text-Lab Manual. 2nd ed. (Illus.). 1977. pap. 13.50x (ISBN 0-07-072748-1, G); instr's. guide 1.50 (ISBN 0-07-072749-X). McGraw.

Zbar, Paul B. & Malvino, Albert P. Basic Electronics: A Text-Lab Manual. 5th ed. (EIA Basic Electricity-Electronics Ser.). (Illus.). 352p. 1983. pap. text ed. 13.50 (ISBN 0-07-072803-8, G); write for info. instr's guide (ISBN 0-07-072804-6). McGraw.

Zbar, Paul B. & Orne, R. Electronics Instruments & Measurement. (Illus.). 1965. text ed. 14.50 (ISBN 0-07-072754-6, G); instructors' guide free (ISBN 0-07-072755-4). McGraw.

Zbar, Paul B., jt. auth. see Electronic Industries Association.

Zborowski, Mark & Herzog, Elizabeth. Life Is with People: The Culture of the Shtetl. LC 62-13141. 1962. pap. 7.95 (ISBN 0-8052-0020-7). Schocken.

Zbozny, Frank, ed. Annuale Mediaevale, Vol. 19. 97p. 1979. pap. text ed. 13.50x. Humanities.

Zdansky, Erick. Roentgen Diagnosis of the Heart & Great Vessels. 2nd ed. Boyd, Linn J., tr. LC 63-22433. (Illus.). 423p. 1965. 99.50 o.p. (ISBN 0-8089-0552-X). Grune.

Zdanys, Jonas. Voice on an Anthill. 1981. pap. 4.00 (ISBN 0-87141-063-X). Manyland.

Zderad, Loretta T., jt. auth. see Paterson, Josephine G.

Zea, Leopoldo. Latin-American Mind. Abbott, James H. & Dunham, Lowell, trs. (Illus.). 1970. 14.95x o.p. (ISBN 0-8061-0563-1); pap. 8.95x (ISBN 0-8061-1278-6). U of Okla Pr.

Zebel, S. H. Balfour: A Political Biography. 1973. 37.50 (ISBN 0-521-08536-5). Cambridge U Pr.

Zebroff, Kareen. Yoga & Nutrition. LC 78-13437. (Illus.). 1979. pap. 3.95 o.p. (ISBN 0-668-04711-9). Arco.

Zebrowski, Ernest, Jr. Physics for the Technician. 1974. text ed. 21.50 (ISBN 0-07-072780-5, G); ans. key 4.50 (ISBN 0-07-072786-4). McGraw.

--Practical Physics. (Illus.). 1980. pap. 17.50 (ISBN 0-07-072788-0); instructor's manual 4.00 (ISBN 0-07-072789-9). McGraw.

Zebrowski, George. Macrolife. LC 76-26283. (Illus.). 1979. 14.37i (ISBN 0-06-014792-X, HarpT). Har-Row.

Zebrowski, George, jt. auth. see Dann, Jack.

Zebrowski, George, et al. Journey to Another Star & Other Stories. Elwood, Roger, ed. LC 73-21478. (Science Fiction Bks). (Illus.). 48p. (gr. 4-8). 1974. PLB 3.95g (ISBN 0-8225-0957-1). Lerner Pubns.

Zebrowski, Mark. Deccani Paintings. (Illus.). 256p. 1983. text ed. 100.00x (ISBN 0-85667-153-3, Pub. by Sotheby Pubns England). Biblio Dist.

--Deccani Paintings. LC 82-45907. (Illus.). 256p. 1983. 85.00 (ISBN 0-520-04878-4). U of Cal Pr.

Zec, Donald. Marvin. (Illus.). 272p. 1980. 10.95 o.p. (ISBN 0-312-51780-7). St Martin.

Zecher, J. Richard, jt. auth. see Phillips, Susan M.

Zechman, Roberta, jt. auth. see Radeloff, Deanna J.

Zechmann. Barbecuing. 1983. cancelled 3.95 (ISBN 0-8120-5399-0). Barron.

Zechmeister, Eugene B. & Nyberg, Stanley E. Human Memory: An Introduction to Research & Theory. LC 81-7640. 384p. (Orig.). 1981. pap. text ed. 13.95 (ISBN 0-8185-0458-7). Brooks-Cole.

Zechner, L. see Von Wiesner, J. & Von Regel, C.

Zeck, Gerry. I Love to Dance! LC 82-4232. (Illus.). 64p. (gr. 1-5). 1982. lib. bdg. 8.95g (ISBN 0-87614-198-X). Carolrhoda Bks.

Zeck, Gerry, jt. auth. see Zeck, Pam.

Zeck, Pam & Zeck, Gerry. Mississippi Sternwheelers. LC 81-15553. (Illus.). 32p. (gr. 2-5). 1982. PLB 7.95g (ISBN 0-87614-180-7). Carolrhoda Bks.

Zeckhauser, Richard F. & Leebaert, Derek, eds. What Role for Government? Lessons from Policy Research. (Duke Press Policy Studies). 350p. 1983. 32.75 (ISBN 0-8223-0481-3). Duke.

Zeckhauser, Richard J., jt. auth. see McClelland, Peter D.

Zedler, Beatrice H. How Philosophy Begins. (Aquinas Lecture Ser.). 55p. 1983. 7.95 (ISBN 0-87462-151-8). Marquette.

Zedler, Beatrice H., ed. Saint Thomas Aquinas: On the Unity of the Intellect Against the Averroists. (Medieval Philosophical Texts in Translation: No. 19). 1968. pap. 7.95 (ISBN 0-87462-219-0). Marquette.

Zee, David S., jt. auth. see Leigh, R. John.

Zeeman, E. C. Catastrophe Theory: Selected Papers (1972-1977) LC 77-21459. 1977. text ed. 38.50 (ISBN 0-201-09014-7, Adv Bk Prog); pap. text ed. 24.50 (ISBN 0-201-09015-5). A-W.

Zeevaert, Leonardo. Foundation Engineering for Difficult Subsoil Conditions. LC 79-17288. 670p. 1979. Repr. of 1973 ed. lib. bdg. 30.50 o.p. (ISBN 0-89874-010-X). Krieger.

Zeevy, Rechavam, jt. auth. see Har-El, Menashe.

Zeevy, Rechavam, jt. auth. see Oliphant, Laurence.

Zeff, jt. auth. see Wilkes.

Zeff, S. A., jt. auth. see Keller, T. F.

Zeff, Stephen A. The Accounting Postulates & Principles Controversy of the 1960s. LC 82-82493. (Accountancy in Transition Ser.). 574p. 1982. lib. bdg. 75.00 (ISBN 0-8240-5341-9). Garland Pub.

--Accounting Principles Through the Years: The Views of Professional & Academic Leaders, 1938-1954. LC 82-82492. (Accountancy in Transition Ser.). 475p. 1982. lib. bdg. 60.00 (ISBN 0-8240-5340-0). Garland Pub.

Zeff, Stephen A. & Keller, Thomas F. Financial Accounting Theory One: Issues & Controversies. 2nd ed. (Illus.). 640p. 1973. text ed. 24.95 (ISBN 0-07-072779-1, C); pap. text ed. 19.95 (ISBN 0-07-072778-3). McGraw.

Zefirov, N. S., jt. auth. see Drozd, V. N.

Zegeer, D. A., jt. ed. see Crickmer, D. F.

Zegger, Hrisey D. May Sinclair. (English Authors Ser). 1976. lib. bdg. 14.95 (ISBN 0-8057-6666-9, Twayne). G K Hall.

Zeggeren, F. Van see Van Zeggeren, F. & Storey, S. H.

Zegveld, Walter, jt. auth. see Rothwell, Roy.

Zehna, Peter W., jt. auth. see Barr, Donald R.

Zehner, Robert B. Access, Travel, & Transportation in New Communities. LC 76-28228. (New Communities Research Ser.). 256p. 1977. prof ref 19.50x (ISBN 0-88410-462-1). Ballinger Pub.

--Indicators of the Quality of Life in New Communities. LC 77-3353. (New Communities Research Ser.). 272p. 1977. prof ref 19.50x (ISBN 0-88410-461-3). Ballinger Pub.

Zehr, Douglas R. Assessment of Variation in Scampania Nemorosa & Selected Related Species (Hepatophyta) (Bryophytorum Bibliotheca: No. 15). (Illus.). 140p. 1980. pap. 16.00x (ISBN 3-7682-1282-3). Lubrecht & Cramer.

Zehring, John W. Careers In State & Local Government. 236p. 1980. 10.95 (ISBN 0-912048-15-8). Impact VA.

--Preparing for Work. 1980. pap. 3.95 (ISBN 0-88207-582-9). Victor Bks.

Zeidner, Lisa. Alexandra Freed. LC 82-48735. 1983. 13.95 (ISBN 0-394-52750-X). Knopf.

Zeiger, Arthur. Encyclopedia of English. LC 59-8821. (Orig.). 1957. pap. 3.95 (ISBN 0-686-85657-0). Arco.

Zeiger, Arthur, jt. auth. see Waldhorn, Arthur.

Zeiger, Helane. Fifteen-Love. 192p. (gr. 6 up). 1982. pap. 1.95 (ISBN 0-686-81831-8, Pub. by Tempo). Ace Bks.

Zeigler, B. P., et al, eds. see Symposium on Modelling & Simulation Methodology, Israel, August 1978.

Zeigler, E. Physical Education & Sport Philosophy. 1977. text ed. 16.95 (ISBN 0-13-668731-8). P-H.

Zeigler, Earle F. Decision Making in Physical Education & Athletics Administration: A Case Method Approach. 181p. 1982. pap. text ed. 10.00x (ISBN 0-87563-221-1). Stipes.

--Physical Education & Sport: An Introduction. LC 81-8287. (Illus.). 303p. 1982. text ed. 19.50 (ISBN 0-8121-0795-0). Lea & Febiger.

Zeigler, Earle F. & Bowie, Gary W. Management Competency Development in Sport & Physical Education. LC 82-13066. 280p. 1983. text ed. write for info. (ISBN 0-8121-0830-2). Lea & Febiger.

Zeigler, Earle F., ed. History of Physical Education & Sport. LC 78-9066. (P-H Foundations of Physical Education & Sport Ser.). (Illus.). 1979. ref. ed. 22.95 (ISBN 0-13-391656-1). P-H.

Zeigler, Earle F. & Spaeth, Marcia J., eds. Administrative Theory & Practice in Physical Education & Athletics. (Illus.). 496p. 1975. 21.95 o.p. (ISBN 0-13-008581-2). P-H.

Zeigler, H. Philip, jt. ed. see Wenzel, Bernice M.

Zeigler, L., jt. auth. see Van Dallen, H.

Zeigler, L. Harmon, jt. auth. see Dye, Thomas R.

Zeil, W. The Andes: A Geological Review. (Beitraege zur regionalen Geologie der Erde: Vol. 13). (Illus.). lib. bdg. 60.20 (ISBN 3-443-11013-4). Lubrecht & Cramer.

Zeiler, Michael D. & Harzem, Peter. Advances in Analysis of Behaviour: Reinforcement & the Organisation of Behaviour, Vol. 1. LC 78-31697. (Wiley Series on Advances in Analysis of Behaviour). 1980. 67.95x (ISBN 0-471-27573-5, Pub. by Wiley-Interscience). Wiley.

Zeiler, Michael D., jt. ed. see Harzem, Peter.

Zeilik, Michael & Gaustad, John E. Astronomy: The Cosmic Perspective. 880p. 1983. text ed. 32.95 scp (ISBN 0-06-047387-8, HarpC); instr's. manual avail. (ISBN 0-06-367370-3). Har-Row.

Zeines, B. Principles of Applied Electronics. LC 63-7559. 425p. (Orig.). 1963. 16.00 (ISBN 0-471-98157-5). Krieger.

Zeini, Hanny El see Sety, Omm & El Zeini, Hanny.

Zeisel, Hans. The Limits of Law Enforcement. LC 82-8644. (Illus.). 180p. 1983. lib. bdg. 20.00x (ISBN 0-226-97901-6). U Of Chicago Pr.

--Say It with Figures. rev., 5th ed. LC 67-22535. 1968. 13.41xi (ISBN 0-06-037201-X, HarpT). Har-Row.

Zeisel, William, jt. ed. see Lightman, Marjorie.

Zeisel, William, jt. ed. see Rosof, Patricia J.

Zeisel, William, jt. auth. see Rosof, Patricia J.

Zeit, Calvin, jt. auth. see Drescher, Henrik.

Zeitak, ed. Directory of International & National Medical Societies. 350p. 1982. pap. 70.00 (ISBN 0-08-027991-0). Pergamon.

Zeitler, E., ed. Percutaneous Vascular Recanalization: Technique - Application - Clinical Results. (Illus.). 1978. pap. 33.50 o.p. (ISBN 0-387-08875-X). Springer-Verlag.

Zeitlin, Irving M. Ideology & the Development of Sociological Theory. 2nd ed. (Series in Sociology). (Illus.). 336p. 1981. text ed. 22.95 (ISBN 0-13-449769-4). P-H.

Zeitlin, Jacob & Rinaker, Clarissa, eds. Types of Poetry, 2 vols. LC 78-57868. (Granger Poetry Library). 1979. Repr. of 1926 ed. Set. 76.50x o.p. (ISBN 0-89609-105-8). Granger Bk.

Zeitlin, Jacob, ed. see Sherman, Stuart P.

Zeitlin, Maurica. American Society, Inc. 2nd ed. 1977. 13.95 o.p. (ISBN 0-395-30776-7). HM.

Zeitlin, Maurice. Classes, Class Conflict, & the State: Empirical Studies in Class Analysis. 1980. text ed. 17.95 (ISBN 0-316-98541-4). Little.

--Political Power & Social Theory, Vol. 2. 375p. (Orig.). 1981. 42.50 (ISBN 0-89232-143-1). Jai Pr.

Zeitlin, Maurice, ed. Political Power & Social Theory, Vol. 1. 1980. lib. bdg. 42.50 (ISBN 0-89232-115-6). Jai Pr.

--Political Power & Social Theory, Vol. 3. 375p. 1981. 42.50 (ISBN 0-89232-204-7). Jai Pr.

Zeitlin, Richard H. Germans in Wisconsin. (Illus.). 1977. pap. 1.25 o.s.i. (ISBN 0-87020-173-5). State Hist Soc Wis.

Zeitz. Private Urban Renewal: A Different Residential Trend. LC 78-19568. (Illus.). 160p. 1979. 16.95x o.p. (ISBN 0-669-02627-1). Lexington Bks.

Zeitz, James V. Spirituality & Analogia Entis According to Erich Przywara, S. J. Metaphysics & Religious Experience, the Ignation Exercises, the Balance in 'Similarity' & 'Greater Dissimilarity' According to Lateran IV. LC 82-17588. 358p. (Orig.). 1983. lib. bdg. 26.25 (ISBN 0-8191-2783-3); pap. text ed. 14.00 (ISBN 0-8191-2784-1). U Pr of Amer.

Zejdlik, Cynthia M. Spinal Cord Injury. LC 82-23904. (Nursing Ser.). 700p. 1983. text ed. 35.00 (ISBN 0-534-01339-2). Brooks-Cole.

Zekowski, Arlene. Histories & Dynasties. LC 81-85002. (Illus.). 192p. 1982. 17.95 (ISBN 0-686-82852-6); pap. 7.95 (ISBN 0-686-82853-4). Am Canadian.

--Seasons of the Mind. LC 69-20441. (Archives of Post-Modern Literature). (Illus.). 1969. pap. 7.00 (ISBN 0-913844-06-3). Am Canadian.

Zelan, Karen, jt. auth. see Bettelheim, Bruno.

Zelayeta, Elena. Elena's Fiesta Recipes. pap. 4.95 o.p. (ISBN 0-517-53758-3, Pub. by Ward Ritchie). Crown.

--Elena's Secrets of Mexican Cooking. 1968. pap. 6.50 (ISBN 0-385-00197-5, Dolp). Doubleday.

Zelazko, W. Banach Algebras. 1973. 57.50 (ISBN 0-444-40991-2). Elsevier.

Zelazny, Jack. Jack of Shadows. pap. 1.75 o.p. (ISBN 0-451-09370-4, E9370, Sig). NAL.

Zelazny, Roger. Bridge of Ashes. 1979. 10.00 (ISBN 0-8398-2466-1, Gregg). G K Hall.

--The Courts of Chaos. 1979. pap. 2.25 (ISBN 0-380-47175-2, 62232-7). Avon.

--Damnation Alley. 1979. lib. bdg. 10.00 (ISBN 0-8398-2505-6, Gregg). G K Hall.

--The Doors of His Face, the Lamps of His Mouth & Other Stories. 1974. pap. 1.50 o.s.i. (ISBN 0-380-01146-8, 38182). Avon.

--Doorways in the Sand. LC 74-20423. 224p. (YA) 1976. 12.45i (ISBN 0-06-014789-X, HarpT). Har-Row.

--The Dream Master. 1976. Repr. of 1966 ed. lib. bdg. 10.00 (ISBN 0-8398-2345-2, Gregg). G K Hall.

--Eye of Cat. 1982. 13.95 (ISBN 0-671-25519-3, Timescapape). PB.

--Four Roger Zelazny Novels. 1979. 48.00 (ISBN 0-444-47120-0, Gregg). G K Hall.

--Isle of the Dead. 208p. 1976. Repr. of 1969 ed. lib. bdg. 11.00 (ISBN 0-8398-2346-0, Gregg). G K Hall.

--Lord of Light. 1976. pap. 2.95 (ISBN 0-380-01403-3, 63214-4). Avon.

--Lord of Light. 1979. lib. bdg. 14.00 (ISBN 0-8398-2499-8, Gregg). G K Hall.

--Nine Princes in Amber. 1979. lib. bdg. 15.00 (ISBN 0-8398-2427-0, Gregg). G K Hall.

--Sign of the Unicorn. 1976. pap. 2.50 (ISBN 0-380-00831-9, 62562-8). Avon.

--Today We Choose Faces. 1978. lib. bdg. 10.00 (ISBN 0-8398-2407-6, Gregg). G K Hall.

Zelazny, Roger & Saberhagen, Fred. Coils. LC 82-1993. (Illus.). 250p. 1982. pap. 7.95 (ISBN 0-671-44915-X, Wallaby). S&S.

Zeldin, Theodore. The French. (Illus.). 512p. 1983. 22.50 (ISBN 0-394-52947-2). Pantheon.

Zeldis, Chayym. The Brothel. LC 78-13456. 1979. 12.50 (ISBN 0-399-12296-6). Putnam Pub Group.

--The Marriage Bed. LC 77-92376. 1978. 8.95 o.p. (ISBN 0-399-12138-2). Putnam Pub Group.

Zel'Dovich, Ya. B. & Novikov, I. D. Relativistic Astrophysics: Vol. 2, The Structure & Evolution of the Universe. Steigman, Gary, ed. Fishbone, Leslie, tr. LC 77-128549. (Illus.). 768p. 1983. Repr. lib. bdg. 65.00x (ISBN 0-226-97957-1); Vol. 1. 40.00x (ISBN 0-226-97955-5). U of Chicago Pr.

Zel'Dovich, Ya B., et al. Physics of Shock Waves & High Temperature Hydrodynamic Phenomena, 2 Vols. Vol. 1 1966. 63.50 (ISBN 0-12-778701-1); Vol. 2 1967. 63.50 (ISBN 0-12-778702-X); Set. 91.00 (ISBN 0-686-96641-4). Acad Pr.

Zeleny, Jindrich. The Logic of Marx. Carver, Terrell, ed. & tr. LC 80-11434. 251p. 1980. 27.50x (ISBN 0-8476-6767-7). Rowman.

Zeleny, Lawrence. The Bluebird: How You Can Help its Fight for Survivial. pap. 6.95X (ISBN 0-253-20212-4). Nature Bks Pubs.

Zeleny, M. Linear Multiobjective Programming. LC 73-22577. (Lecture Notes in Economics & Mathematical Systems: Vol. 95). (Illus.). x, 220p. 1974. pap. 12.00 o.p. (ISBN 0-387-06639-X). Springer-Verlag.

Zeleny, Milan. Multiple Criteria Decision Making. 1981. 31.95x (ISBN 0-07-072795-3); instr's. manual 19.95 (ISBN 0-07-072796-1). McGraw.

Zeleny, Milan, ed. Autopoiesis, Dissipative Structures & Spontaneous Social Orders. (AAAS Selected Symposium Ser.: No. 55). 150p. 1980. lib. bdg. 20.00 (ISBN 0-86531-033-5). Westview.

Zeleznak, Shirley. Backpacking. Schroeder, Howard, ed. LC 79-27800. (Back to Nature). (Illus.). (gr. 3-5). 1980. lib. bdg. 7.95 (ISBN 0-89686-069-8). Crestwood Hse.

--Camping. Schroeder, Howard, ed. LC 80-425. (Back to Nature Sports Ser.). (Illus.). 1980. lib. bdg. 7.95 (ISBN 0-89686-071-X). Crestwood Hse.

--Jogging. Schroeder, Howard, ed. LC 79-27770. (Back to Nature Ser.). (Illus.). (gr. 3-5). 1979. lib. bdg. 7.95 (ISBN 0-89686-068-X). Crestwood Hse.

Zeligs, Dorothy F. Psychoanalysis & the Bible: A Study in Depth of Seven Leaders. LC 73-85071. 1973. 15.00x (ISBN 0-8197-0360-5). Bloch.

Zelinsky, D., ed. see Evanston Conference, Oct. 11-15, 1975.

Zelinsky, Daniel. First Course in Linear Algebra. 2nd ed. 1973. text ed. 24.00 (ISBN 0-12-779060-8). Acad Pr.

Zelinsky, Wilbur. A Bibliographic Guide to Population Geography. LC 75-36518. (Geography Ser.: Research Paper, No. 80). 257p. 1976. Repr. of 1962 ed. lib. bdg. 19.00x (ISBN 0-8371-8645-5, ZEPG). Greenwood.

--The Cultural Geography of the United States. LC 72-4503. (Illus.). 176p. 1973. pap. 13.95 ref. ed. (ISBN 0-13-195495-4). P-H.

Zelis, Robert F., jt. ed. see Flaim, Stephen.

Zelizer, Viviana A. Morals & Markets: The Development of Life Insurance in the United States. 210p. 1983. pap. text ed. 12.95x (ISBN 0-87855-929-9). Transaction Bks.

Zelkowitz, Marvin V., et al. Principles of Software Engineering & Design. LC 78-27315. (Illus.). 1979. text ed. 28.95 (ISBN 0-13-710202-X). P-H.

Zell, Hans & Silver, Helene. Reader's Guide to African Literature. LC 76-83165. 1971. text ed. 16.00x o.p. (ISBN 0-8419-0018-3, Africana); pap. text ed. 9.50x (ISBN 0-8419-0019-1, Africana). Holmes & Meier.

Zell, Hans, ed. Reader's Guide to Contemporary African Literature. 2nd, rev ed. 300p. 1983. text ed. 20.00x (ISBN 0-686-69153-9, Africana); pap. text ed. 10.00x. Holmes & Meier.

Zell, Hans & Bundy, Carol, eds. A New Reader's Guide to African Literature. 2nd rev. ed. 600p. (Orig.). 1983. text ed. 37.00x (ISBN 0-8419-0639-4, Africana); pap. text ed. 20.00x. Holmes & Meier.

Zell, Hans M. African Books in Print, Part 1: English Language & African Languages. LC 74-9951. 496p. 1975. 37.50 o.p. (ISBN 0-7201-0535-8, Pub. by Mansell England). Wilson.

Zell, Hans M., ed. A New Reader's Guide to African Literature. (Illus.). 300p. 1983. text ed. 16.00x (ISBN 0-8419-0639-4); pap. text ed. 9.50x (ISBN 0-8419-0640-8). Africana Pub.

Zellan, Audrey P. Happy Apple Told Me. LC 74-84766. (Illus.). 54p. (gr. 1-4). 1975. 7.50 o.p. (ISBN 0-8309-0133-7). Ind Pr MO.

Zelle, Raeone & Coyner, Athleen B. Care of Developmentally Disabled Infants & Children. (Illus.). 500p. 1983. pap. 27.50 (ISBN 0-8036-9775-9). Davis Co.

Zeller, Eduard. Outlines of the History of Greek Philosophy. 1980. Repr. of 1931 ed. text ed. 6.00 (ISBN 0-486-23920-9). Dover.

Zeller, Hubert van see Van Zeller, Hubert.

Zeller, Karl, jt. ed. see Schempp, Walter.

Zeller, R. A. & Carmines, E. G. Measurement in Social Science. LC 79-51231. (Illus.). 1980. 29.95 (ISBN 0-521-22243-5); pap. 9.95 (ISBN 0-521-29941-1). Cambridge U Pr.

Zeller, Richard A. & Carmines, Edward G. Statistical Analysis of Social Data. 1978. 23.50 (ISBN 0-395-30777-5); Tchrs Manual 1.00 (ISBN 0-395-30779-1); Lab Manual 9.50 (ISBN 0-395-30778-3). HM.

Zeller, Susan B. Your Career in Radio & Television Broadcasting. LC 81-22861. (Arco's Career Guidance Ser.). 192p. 1982. lib. bdg. 7.95 (ISBN 0-668-05329-1); pap. 4.50 (ISBN 0-668-05331-3). Arco.

Zeller-Cambon, M., tr. see Muschg, Adolf.

Zellers, Margaret. Bahamas: The Inn Way. (The Inn Way Ser.). (Illus.). 166p. 1982. pap. cancelled (ISBN 0-937334-02-2, Pub. by Geomedia). Berkshire Traveller.

--Fielding's Caribbean 1983. 880p. (Orig.). 1982. 12.95 (ISBN 0-688-01343-0). Morrow.

--Fielding's Caribbean 1983. rev. ed. 875p. 1982. 12.00 (ISBN 0-688-01343-0). Fielding.

--Fielding's Sightseeing Guide to Europe Exploring Off the Beaten Path. 495p. pap. 9.95 (ISBN 0-686-38813-5). Fielding.

--The Inn Way...Caribbean. LC 77-20748. (Illus.). 1978. pap. 4.95 o.p. (ISBN 0-912944-44-7, Pub. by Geomedia). Berkshire Traveller.

--The Inn Way...Switzerland. LC 77-80067. (Illus.). 1977. pap. 3.95 o.p. (ISBN 0-912944-43-9, Pub. by Geomedia). Berkshire Traveller.

--Switzerland... the Inn Way. rev. ed. 1980. pap. 4.95 (ISBN 0-912944-61-7, Pub. by Geomedia). Berkshire Traveller.

Zellick, G. The Prisoner & the Law: Essays on Prisoner's Rights. 1982. 70.00x o.p. (ISBN 0-86127-403-2, Pub. by Avebury Pub England). State Mutual Bk.

Zellner, A., ed. Bayesian Analysis in Econometrics & Statistics. (Studies in Bayesian Econometrics Ser.). 465p. 1979. 76.75 (ISBN 0-444-85270-0, North Holland). Elsevier.

Zellner, A., jt. ed. see Fienberg, S. E.

Zellweger, Hans, jt. auth. see Ionasescu, Victor.

Zelnik, Martin, jt. auth. see Panero, Julius.

Zelonky, Joy. I Can't Always Hear You. LC 79-23891. (Life & Living from a Child's Point of View Ser.). (Illus.). (gr. k-5). 1980. PLB 13.30 (ISBN 0-8172-1355-4). Raintree Pubs.

--My Best Friend Moved Away. LC 79-24111. (Life & Living from a Child's Point of View Ser.). (Illus.). (gr. k-5). 1980. PLB 13.30 (ISBN 0-8172-1353-8). Raintree Pubs.

Zelter, M. Exploring Shorthand. 96p. 1980. text ed. 5.15x (ISBN 0-7715-0735-6). Forkner.

Zelvin, Elizabeth. I Am the Daughter. (Illus.). 88p. 1981. pap. 3.00 (ISBN 0-89823-025-X). New Rivers Pr.

Zeman, W., ed. The Dissection of a Degenerative Disease. Rider, J. A. 394p. 1975. 97.75 o.p. (ISBN 0-444-16715-3). Elsevier.

Zeman, Z. A. Nazi Propaganda. 2nd ed. (Illus.). 265p. 1973. pap. 6.95 (ISBN 0-19-285060-1, GB394, GB). Oxford U Pr.

Zeman, Zavis P. & Hoffman, David, eds. The Dynamics of the Technological Leadership of the World. 58p. 1980. pap. text ed. 3.00x (ISBN 0-920380-44-1, Inst Res Pub Canada). Renouf.

Zemanian, A. H. Realizability Theory for Continuous Linear Systems. (Mathematics in Science & Engineering Ser.: Vol. 97). 1972. 46.00 (ISBN 0-12-779550-2). Acad Pr.

Zemans, Fredrick H., ed. Perspectives on Legal Aid: An International Survey. LC 79-833. 1979. lib. bdg. 29.95 (ISBN 0-313-20986-3, ZLA/). Greenwood.

Zemansky, Mark & Dittman, Richard. Heat & Thermodynamics. 6th ed. (Illus.). 560p. 1981. text ed. 27.50 (ISBN 0-07-072808-9, C). McGraw.

Zemansky, Mark W., et al. Basic Engineering Thermodynamics. 2nd ed. (Illus.). 512p. 1975. text ed. 32.50 (ISBN 0-07-072815-1, C). McGraw.

Zembaty, Jane, jt. auth. see Mappes, Thomas.

Zembaty, Jane S., jt. auth. see Mappes, Thomas A.

Zemel, Carol M. The Formation of a Legend: van Gogh Criticism, 1890-1920. Kuspit, Donald, ed. LC 80-22706. (Studies in Fine Arts: Criticism: No. 10). 254p. 1980. 39.95 (ISBN 0-8357-1094-7, Pub. by UMI Res Pr). Univ Microfilms.

Zemel, J., jt. ed. see Siddall, G.

Zemelman, Steven. Making Sense of It: Patterns in English Grammar. 1980. pap. text ed. 10.95 (ISBN 0-13-547570-8). P-H.

Zemke, Lorna & Daniel, Katinka S. Kodaly Thirty-Five Lesson Plans & Folk Song Supplement. 2nd ed. LC 76-39689. 1976. pap. text ed. 9.95 (ISBN 0-916656-04-7). Mark Foster Mus.

Zemke, Sr. Lorna. Kodaly Concept: Its History, Philosophy, Development. 2nd ed. LC 77-78027. (Orig.). 1977. pap. text ed. 10.95 (ISBN 0-916656-08-X). Mark Foster Mus.

Zemke, Ron & Kramlinger, Thomas. Figuring Things Out: A Trainer's Guide to Needs & Tasks Analysis. LC 81-12805. (Illus.). 352p. Date not set. text ed. 27.50 (ISBN 0-201-09098-8). A-w.

Zemke, Ron, jt. auth. see Stern, Frances M.

Zemlin, W. R. Speech & Hearing Science: Anatomy & Physiology. 2nd ed. (Illus.). 704p. 1981. text ed. 27.95 (ISBN 0-13-827378-2). P-H.

Zemlin, Willard R. Speech & Hearing Science: Anatomy & Physiology. 1968. ref. ed. 31.95 (ISBN 0-13-827386-3). P-H.

Zempel, Edward, jt. auth. see Verkler, Linda.

Zemsky, Robert. Merchants, Farmers & River Gods: An Essay on Eighteenth-Century American Politics. LC 70-116559. 1971. 12.95 (ISBN 0-87645-035-4). Gambit.

Zenanko, Tom. Walleye Fishing Today. Zenanko, Tom, ed. (Illus.). 212p. (Orig.). 1982. pap. 9.95 (ISBN 0-9610296-0-9). Zenanko Outdoors.

Zender, Karl & Morris, Linda. Persuasive Writing: A College Reader. 316p. 1981. pap. text ed. 10.95 (ISBN 0-15-598300-8, HC); instructors manual 1.95, (ISBN 0-15-598301-6). HarBraceJ.

Zener, Robert V. Guide to Federal Environmental Law. LC 81-8087. 457p. 1981. text ed. 45.00 o.p. (ISBN 0-686-73151-4, C1-1169). PLI.

Zener, Robert V. & Herzog, Richard B. Guide to Federal Environmental Law. 457p. 1981. text ed. 45.00 (ISBN 0-686-96094-7, C1-1169). PLI.

Zenger, Donald & Mazzullo, Sal, eds. Dolomitization. (Benchmark Papers in Geology Ser.: Vol. 65). 1982. cancelled (ISBN 0-686-82843-7). Acad Pr.

Zenger, Sharon K. & Zenger, Weldon. Curriculum Planning: A Ten Step Process. LC 82-60521. 150p. (Orig.). 1983. pap. 12.95 (ISBN 0-88247-675-0). R & E Res Assoc.

Zenger, Weldon, jt. auth. see Zenger, Sharon K.

Zenk, Gordon K. Project SEARCH: The Struggle for Control of Criminal Information in America. LC 78-67654. (Contributions in Political Science: No. 23). (Illus.). 1979. lib. bdg. 25.00 (ISBN 0-313-20639-2, ZEP/). Greenwood.

Zenker, W. Juxtaoral Organ: Morphology & Clinical Aspects. LC 81-23069. (Illus.). 117p. 1982. text ed. 22.50 (ISBN 0-8067-2221-5). Urban & S.

Zenkovsky, Betty J., jt. ed. see Zenkovsky, Serge A.

Zenkovsky, Serge. Medieval Russia's Epics, Chronicles, & Tales. rev. ed. 1974. pap. 10.50 (ISBN 0-525-47363-7, 01019-310). Dutton.

Zenkovsky, Serge A. & Zenkovsky, Betty J., eds. The Nikonian Chronicle, Vol. 1. 400p. 1983. 35.00 (ISBN 0-940670-00-3). Kingston Pr.

Zenkovsky, Serge A., ed. see Cizevskij, Dmitrij.

Zenner, Walter P., jt. auth. see Deshen, Shlomo.

Zeno-Gandia, Manuel. La Charca (The Pond) Wagenheim, Kal, tr. from Span. 250p. 1983. 18.95 (ISBN 0-943862-03-5); pap. 10.00 (ISBN 0-943862-04-3). Waterfront NJ.

Zenon, Renee. Le Traitement des Mythes dans le Theatre de Jean Giraudoux. LC 80-5815. 148p. (Orig.). 1981. lib. bdg. 19.00 (ISBN 0-8191-1576-2); pap. text ed. 8.25 (ISBN 0-8191-1577-0). U Pr of Amer.

Zenz, Gary L. Purchasing & the Management of Materials in Motion. 5th ed. LC 80-21649. (Marketing Ser.). 514p. 1981. text ed. 29.95x (ISBN 0-471-06091-7); 6.50 o.p. tchrs.' ed. (ISBN 0-471-08935-4). Wiley.

Zenzinger, B. W., tr. see Krautkraemer, J. & Krautkraemer, H.

Zeoli, Billy & Hartley, Alan. Tom Landry & the Dallas Cowboys. (Illus.). 32p. (gr. 1 up). 1973. 0.79 (ISBN 0-8007-8504-5, Spire Comics). Revell.

Zepeda, Ofelia. A Papago Grammar. 175p. 1983. pap. text ed. 8.95x (ISBN 0-8165-0792-9). U of Ariz Pr.

Zepeda, Ofelia, ed. When it Rains: Papago & Pima Poetry. (Sun Tracks Ser.). 90p. 1982. 8.95 o.s.i. (ISBN 0-8165-0780-5); pap. 4.50 (ISBN 0-8165-0785-6). U of Ariz Pr.

Zepke, Brent E. Law for Non-Lawyers. (Littlefield, Adams Quality Paperbacks: No. 355). 224p. (Orig.). 1983. pap. text ed. 6.95 (ISBN 0-8226-0355-1). Littlefield.

Zerafa, Judy. Go For It! LC 82-60065. 156p. 3.95 (ISBN 0-89480-213-5). Workman Pub.

Zerbe, F. Bryan Money. 1983. pap. 10.00 soft cover (ISBN 0-942666-00-3). S J Durst.

Zerbe, Jerome & Connolly, Cyril. Les Pavillons of the Eighteenth Century. (Illus.). 1980. 14.98 (ISBN 0-393-01279-4). Norton.

Zerbe, Richard, Jr., ed. Research in Law & Economics: Annual, Vol. 2. (Orig.). 1980. lib. bdg. 40.00 (ISBN 0-89232-131-8). Jai Pr.

Zerbe, Richard O., ed. Research in Law & Economics, Vol. 1. (Orig.). 1979. lib. bdg. 40.00 (ISBN 0-89232-028-1). Jai Pr.

--Research in Law & Economics, Vol. 3. 275p. 1981. 40.00 (ISBN 0-89232-231-4). Jai Pr.

Zerbst, Robert H. Principles of Real Estate Valuation with Energy Applications. LC 81-70321. (Development Component Ser.). (Illus.). 23p. 1981. pap. 10.00 (ISBN 0-87420-603-0, D19). Urban Land.

Zerin, Edward. What Catholics Should Know About Jews: And Other Christians. 1980. pap. 3.25 (ISBN 0-697-01739-7). Wm C Brown.

Zerker, Sally F. The Rise & Fall of the Toronto Typographical Union, 1832-1972: A Case Study in Foreign Domination. 416p. 1982. 40.00x (ISBN 0-8020-5547-8); pap. 14.95 (ISBN 0-8020-6431-0). U of Toronto Pr.

Zernich, T., jt. auth. see Hardiman, G.

Zernova, Ruth. Zhenskie Rasskazy: Women's Stories. 160p. (Rus.). 1981. pap. 7.50 (ISBN 0-938920-04-9). Hermitage MI.

Zerowin, Jeffrey, jt. auth. see Corras, James.

Zerwick, Max. A Grammatical Analysis of Greek New Testament. (Scripta Pontificii Instituti Biblici: Vol. 1). 1974. pap. 20.00 (ISBN 0-8294-0316-7). Loyola.

Zesch, Lindy & Bartow, Arthur, eds. Toward Expanding Horizons & Exploring Our Art. (The TCG National Conference Report Ser.). (Illus.). 96p. (Orig.). 1980. pap. text ed. 6.00 o.p. (ISBN 0-930452-14-3). Theatre Comm.

Zesmer, David M. Guide to Shakespeare. LC 73-34590. pap. 5.95 (ISBN 0-06-460164-1, CO 164, COS). B&N NY.

Zetler, Robert L. & Crouch, W. G. Successful Communication in Science & Industry Writing, Reading & Speaking. 1961. text ed. 12.00 o.p. (ISBN 0-07-072812-7, G). McGraw.

Zetterberg, Hans L. Sociology in the United States of America. LC 72-10703. 156p. 1973. Repr. of 1956 ed. lib. bdg. 15.50x (ISBN 0-8371-6623-3, ZESO). Greenwood.

Zetterberg, J. Peter. Evolution Versus Creationism: The Public Education Controversy. 1983. lib. bdg. 22.50 (ISBN 0-89774-061-0). Oryx Pr.

Zettl, Herbert. Sight, Sound, Motion: Applied Media Aesthetics. 1973. text ed. 28.95x (ISBN 0-534-00238-2). Wadsworth Pub.

--Television Production Handbook. 3rd ed. 1976. 24.95x (ISBN 0-534-00414-8); 8.95x (ISBN 0-534-00530-6). Wadsworth Pub.

Zettler, Howard E., ed. Ologies & Isms: A Thematic Dictionary. new ed. LC 78-8328. 1978. 70.00x (ISBN 0-8103-1014-7). Gale.

Zetzel, Elizabeth & Meissner, W. W. Basic Concepts of Psychoanalytic Psychiatry. LC 72-76916. 1973. text ed. 15.00x o.p. (ISBN 0-465-00571-3). Basic.

Zevin, Jack, jt. auth. see Massialas, Byron G.

Zevit, Ziony. Matres Lectionis in Ancient Hebrew Epigraphs. LC 80-19652. (American Schools of Oriental Research, Monograph: Vol. 2). 43p. 1980. text ed. 12.00x (ISBN 0-89757-402-8, Am Sch Orient Res); pap. text ed. 8.00x (ISBN 0-89757-400-1). Eisenbrauns.

Zeydel, Edwin H., et al, eds. see Tieck, Johann L.

Zey-Ferrell, Mary. Dimensions of Organizations. 2 bks. LC 78-10271. (Illus.). 1979. Text. pap. 20.95x o.p. (ISBN 0-673-16303-2); Readings. pap. 13.95x o.p. (ISBN 0-673-16304-0). Scott F.

Zey-Ferrell, Mary & Aiken, Michael. Complex Organizations: Critical Perspectives. 1981. pap. text ed. 12.95x o.p. (ISBN 0-673-15269-3). Scott F.

Zgusta, Ladislav, ed. Theory & Method in Lexicography. 1980. pap. text ed. 5.75 (ISBN 0-917496-14-0). Hornbeam Pr.

Zhabin, V. F., jt. ed. see Bogomolov, Yu. G.

Zhabotinskii, Vladimir. The Jewish War Front. LC 79-97309. 255p. 1975. Repr. of 1940 ed. lib. bdg. 15.75x (ISBN 0-8371-2638-X, ZHJW). Greenwood.

Zhadova, Larissa A. Malevich: Suprematism & Revolution in Russian Art, 1910-1930. LC 82-80246. (Illus.). 1982. 45.00 (ISBN 0-500-09147-1). Thames Hudson.

Zhang Yihuan, ed. History & Development of Ancient Chinese Architecture. 1030p. 1982. 1500.00 (ISBN 0-677-31030-7). Gordon.

Zhdanov, Andrei. Speech on the Journals Leningrad & Zvezda: The Central Committee Resolution on the Journals. Ashbee, F. & Tidmarsh, I., trs. from Russ. 1978. 12.50x (ISBN 0-931554-02-0); pap. 4.00x o. p. (ISBN 0-931554-03-9). Strathcona.

Zhdanov, G. S. Crystal Physics. 1966. 63.00 (ISBN 0-12-779650-9). Acad Pr.

Zheng Shifeng, et al. China. LC 80-23641. (Illus.). 230p. 1980. 60.00 o.p. (ISBN 0-07-056830-8). McGraw.

Zhenhua, Wang. The Tail Competition. 14p. (Orig.). (gr. 3). 1982. pap. 1.00 (ISBN 0-8351-1041-9). China Bks.

Zhevlakov, K. A., et al. Rings That are Nearly Associative. (Pure and Applied Mathematics Ser.). 1982. 56.00 (ISBN 0-12-779850-1). Acad Pr.

Zhikov, V. V., jt. auth. see Levitan, B. M.

Zhito, Lee, ed. see Shemel, Sidney & Krislovsky, M. William.

Zhitomirsky, V., tr. see Bykhovsky, Isidor I.

Zhivkov, T. Todor Zhivkov: Statesman & Builder of New Bulgaria. (Leaders of the World Ser.: Vol. 5). (Illus.). 438p. 1982. 20.00 (ISBN 0-08-028205-9). Pergamon.

Zhivkova, L., ed. Ludmila Zhivkova: Her Many Worlds - New Culture & Beauty - Concepts & Action. 300p. 1982. 15.00 (ISBN 0-08-028171-0). Pergamon.

Zhi-Yong Sheng, ed. see International Burn Seminar Shanghai, June 1981.

Zhou Erfu. Doctor Norman Bethune. Bailey, Alison, tr. from Chinese. (Illus.). 1982. pap. write for info. (ISBN 0-8351-0997-6). China Bks.

Zhou Guo, ed. China & the World, No. 2. (China & the World Ser.). 123p. 1982. pap. 1.95 (ISBN 0-8351-1115-6). China Bks.

Zhou Long Ru. English-Chinese Dictionary of Abbreviation & Acronyms. 1290p. 1980. 9.95 (ISBN 0-8351-1106-7). China Bks.

Ziabicki, A. Fundamentals of Fibre Formation: The Science of Fibre Spinning & Drawing. 488p. 1976. 107.95x (ISBN 0-471-98220-2, Pub. by Wiley-Interscience). Wiley.

Ziadeh, Nicola A. Urban Life in Syria Under the Early Mamluks. Repr. of 1953 ed. lib. bdg. 15.75x (ISBN 0-8371-3162-6, ZILS). Greenwood.

Ziai, Mohsen. Bedside Pediatrics: Diagnostic Evaluation of the Child. 1983. write for info. (ISBN 0-316-98752-2). Little.

Ziatkis, A. & Poole, C. F., eds. Electron Capture: Theory & Practice in Chromatography. (Journal of Chromatography Library: Vol. 20). 1982. 76.75 (ISBN 0-444-41954-3). Elsevier.

Zibell, Wilfried, jt. auth. see Webster, Donald H.

Zich, A. The Rising Sun. LC 76-52547. (World War II Ser.). (Illus.). (gr. 6 up). 1977. PLB 19.92 (ISBN 0-8094-2463-0, Pub. by Time-Life). Silver.

Zichella, L. & Pancheri, P., eds. Psychoneuroendocrinology in Reproduction. (Developments in Endocrinology Ser.: Vol. 5). 602p. 1979. 75.75 (ISBN 0-444-80172-3, North Holland). Elsevier.

Zichichi, A., ed. Elementary Processes at High Energy, Pts. a-B, Pts. A-b. 1972. 67.00 ea. (ISBN 0-12-780586-9) (ISBN 0-12-780587-7). Acad Pr.

--Hadrons & Their Interactions: Current - Field Algebra, Soft Pions, Supermultiplets, & Related Topics. 1968. 81.00 (ISBN 0-12-780540-0). Acad Pr.
--Strong & Weak Interactions. 1967. 81.00 (ISBN 0-12-780545-1). Acad Pr.
--Symmetries in Elementary Particle Physics. 1965. pap. 32.50 (ISBN 0-12-780556-7). Acad Pr.
--Theory & Phenomenology in Particle Physics, 2 pts. 1969. Pt. A. 64.00 (ISBN 0-12-780571-0); Pt. B. 73.00 (ISBN 0-12-780572-9); Set. 92.00 (ISBN 0-686-76858-2). Acad Pr.
Zichlichi, A., ed. Recent Developments in Particle Symmetries. 1966. 53.50 (ISBN 0-12-780562-1). Acad Pr.
Zicree, Marc S. The Twilight Zone Companion. 512p. 1982. pap. 9.95 (ISBN 0-553-01416-1). Bantam.
Zide, Donna C. Above the Wind & Fire. 512p. (Orig.). 1983. pap. 3.75 (ISBN 0-446-30296-1). Warner Bks.
--Lost Splendor. 464p. (Orig.). 1980. pap. 2.50 o.p. (ISBN 0-446-91274-3). Warner Bks.
Zidonis, Frank, jt. auth. see Bateman, Donald.
Ziebe, Jurgen. Der Erwerb Eigener Aktien und Eigener GmbH-Geschaftsanteile In Den Staaten der Europaischen Gemeinschaft. 179p. (Ger.). 1982. write for info. (ISBN 3-8204-7112-X). P Lang Pubs.
Zieber, Eugene. Heraldry in America. LC 68-31267. (Reference Ser., No. 44). 1969. lib. bdg. 49.95x o.p. (ISBN 0-8383-0322-6). Haskell.
Ziebold, Thomas O. & Mongeon, John E., eds. Alcoholism & Homosexuality. LC 82-9217. (Research on Homosexuality Ser.: No. 5). 117p. 1982. text ed. 20.00 (ISBN 0-917724-93-3, B93). Haworth Pr.
Ziebur, Allen D., jt. auth. see Fisher, Robert C.
Zief, Morris & Mitchell, James W. Contamination Control in Trace Element Analysis. LC 76-16837. (Chemical Analysis Ser.: Vol. 47). 336p. 1976. 53.00x (ISBN 0-471-61169-7, Pub. by Wiley-Interscience). Wiley.
Zieg, Kermit C., Jr. & Nix, William E. The Commodity Options Market: Dynamic Trading Strategies for Speculation & Commercial Hedging. LC 78-449. 1978. 35.00 o.p. (ISBN 0-87094-161-5). Dow Jones-Irwin.
Ziegel, Erna & Cranley, Mecca. Obstetric Nursing. 7th ed. (Illus.). 1979. text ed. 28.95x (ISBN 0-02-431560-5). Macmillan.
Ziegelmueller, George W. & Dause, Charles A. Argumentation: Inquiry & Advocacy. LC 74-7358. (Speech Communications Ser.). (Illus.). 336p. 1975. 21.95 (ISBN 0-13-046029-X). P-H.
Ziegenfuss, J. Patients Rights in Professional Practice. 1983. price not set (ISBN 0-442-29434-4). Van Nos Reinhold.
Ziegenfuss, James T., Jr. Patients' Rights & Organizational Models: Sociotechnical Systems Research on Mental Health Programs. LC 82-21786. (Illus.). 364p. (Orig.). 1983. lib. bdg. 25.75 (ISBN 0-8191-2950-X); pap. text ed. 14.00 (ISBN 0-8191-2951-8). U Pr of Amer.
Ziegenfuss, Mary Lou. Christmas in Those Days. Feeling, Durbin, tr. (Illus.). 21p. (Eng. & Cherokee.). 1981. pap. 5.00x (ISBN 0-940392-01-1). Indian U Pr.
Zieger, Robert H. Madison's Battery Workers, 1934-1952: A History of Federal Labor Union 19587. LC 77-1530. (ILR Paperback Ser.: No. 16). 140p. 1977. pap. 4.50 (ISBN 0-87546-062-3); pap. 7.50 special hard bdg. o.s.i. (ISBN 0-87546-289-8). ILR Pr.
Ziegler. An Introduction to Thermomechanics. (Series in Applied Mathematics & Mechanics: Vol. 21). Date not set. 68.00 (ISBN 0-444-86503-9, North Holland). Elsevier.
--War, Peace & International Politics. 2nd ed. 1981. pap. text ed. 11.95 (ISBN 0-316-98493-0); test bank avail. (ISBN 0-316-98494-9). Little.
Ziegler, Alfred J. Archetypal Medicine. Hartman, Gary V., tr. from Ger. Orig. Title: Morbismus: von der Besten aller Gesundheiten. 175p. (Orig.). 1983. pap. 13.50 (ISBN 0-88214-322-0). Spring Pubns.
Ziegler, Ann & Bazen, Frances. Student Solutions Manual for A. J. Washington's Basic Technical Mathematics. 3rd ed. 1981. pap. 9.95 (ISBN 0-8053-9534-2). Benjamin-Cummings.
Ziegler, Arthur P. & Kidney, Walter C. Historic Preservation in Small Towns. LC 79-19422. (Illus.). 146p. (Orig.). 1980. pap. text ed. 10.95 (ISBN 0-910050-43-0). AASLH.
Ziegler, Avis. Doctors' Administrative Program, 8 vols. Incl. Dap 1. Patient Contact & Public Relations (ISBN 0-87489-150-7); Dap 2. Bookkeeping & Tax Reports (ISBN 0-87489-151-5); Dap 3. Insurance & Third-Party-Payable Claims (ISBN 0-87489-152-3); Dap 4. Correspondence (ISBN 0-87489-153-1); Dap 5. Billing & Collections; Dap 6. Patient Records Control (ISBN 0-87489-155-8); Dap 7. Clinical Assisting (ISBN 0-87489-156-6); Dap 8. Supplies & Office Maintenance (ISBN 0-87489-157-4). 1979-82. Set. write for info. (ISBN 0-87489-158-2); Ea. Vol. write for info. Med Economics.
Ziegler, B. Introduction to Palaeobiology: General Paleontology. (Ellis Horwood Series in Geology). 256p. 1982. 84.95X o.p. (ISBN 0-470-27552-9). Halsted Pr.
Ziegler, B., jt. auth. see Jochim, H.
Ziegler, Bill. On the Move. (Paint by Number: No. 1483). (Illus.). 32p. (gr. 1 up). 1983. pap. 1.99 (ISBN 0-307-21483-4). Western Pub.
Ziegler, D. J., jt. auth. see Hjelle, L. A.
Ziegler, Daniel J., jt. auth. see Hjelle, Larry A.
Ziegler, E. K. Simple Living. 1975. pap. 1.25 o.s.i. (ISBN 0-89129-078-8, PV078). Jove Pubns.
Ziegler, Edward, jt. ed. see Pfafflin, James.
Ziegler, Gloria, compiled by. A Josef Marx Anthology. 1983. 9.00 (ISBN 0-941084-09-4). McGinnis & Marx.
Ziegler, H. An Introduction to Thermomechanics. (North-Holland Ser. in Applied Mathematics & Mechanics: Vol. 21). 1977. 53.25 (ISBN 0-7204-0432-0, North-Holland). Elsevier.
--An Introduction to Thermomechanics. 2nd rev. ed. (North-Holland Ser. in Applied Mathematics & Mechanics: Vol. 21). 340p. 1983. 53.25 (ISBN 0-444-86503-9, North Holland). Elsevier.
--Vector Valued Nevanlinna Theory. (Research Notes in Mathematics Ser.: No. 73). 256p. 1982. pap. text ed. 19.95 (ISBN 0-273-08530-1). Pitman Pub MA.
Ziegler, J. F., jt. auth. see Littmark, U.
Ziegler, James F., ed. Helium: Stopping Powers & Ranges in All Elemental Matter. LC 77-13219. 1978. text ed. 43.00 (ISBN 0-08-021606-4). Pergamon.
Ziegler, Johann, jt. auth. see Janscha, Laurens.
Ziegler, Maria, jt. ed. see Laumer, Helmut.
Ziegler, Michael, jt. auth. see King, Michael.
Ziegler, P. A. Geological Atlas of Western & Central Europe, 2 pts. (Illus.). 170p. 1982. 68.00 (ISBN 0-444-42084-3). Elsevier.
Ziegler, Phil. Sentinels of Time. (Illus.). 1983. pap. 8.95t (ISBN 0-89272-160-X). Down East.
Ziegler, Philip. Diana Cooper. LC 81-48129. (Illus.). 1982. 16.95 (ISBN 0-394-50026-1). Knopf.
--Melbourne. LC 81-70066. 1982. pap. 10.95 (ISBN 0-689-70623-5, 274). Atheneum.
Ziegler, Richard, jt. auth. see Flaherty, Patrick F.
Ziegler, Richard, jt. auth. see Kell, Walter.
Ziegler, Ronald, ed. Wilderness Waterways: A Guide to Information Sources. LC 78-10410. (Sports, Games, & Pastimes Information Guide Ser.: Vol. 1). 1979. 42.00x (ISBN 0-8103-1434-7). Gale.
Ziegler, Ronald M. German Literature: A Guide to Basic Reference Sources. LC 82-81592. 104p. (Orig.). Date not set. pap. 5.95 (ISBN 0-937232-02-5). Outside Ent. Postponed.
Ziegler, Sandra. At the Dentist - What Did Christopher See? LC 76-18960. (Going Places Ser.). (Illus.). (ps-3). 1976. 5.95 (ISBN 0-913778-63-X). Childs World.
--At the Hospital - a Surprise for Krissy. LC 76-16592. (Going Places Ser.). (Illus.). (ps-3). 1976. 5.95 (ISBN 0-913778-62-1). Childs World.
--Our Christmas Handbook. LC 80-14587. (Illus.). 112p. pap. 5.95 (ISBN 0-89565-180-7, 3041). Standard Pub.
Ziegler, Thomas W. Transport in High Resistance Epithelia, Vol. 1. Horrobin, D., ed. 1978. 21.60 (ISBN 0-88831-012-9). Eden Pr.
Ziegler, William L., jt. auth. see Luick, John F.
Ziel, Aldert Van Der see Van Der Ziel, Aldert.
Ziel, Ron & Eagleson, Mike. The Twilight of World Steam. LC 72-92373. 304p. 1973. Repr. 2.95 (ISBN 0-448-02432-2, G&D). Putnam Pub Group.
Zielinski, J., jt. auth. see Kaserand, Michael.
Zielke, W. How to Put Method into Your Thinking. LC 73-77706. 296p. 9.00x (ISBN 0-900537-20-5). Leviathan Hse.
Ziemann, Hugo & Gillette, F. L. The Original White House Cookbook. 619p. 1983. 16.95 (ISBN 0-8159-6413-7). Devin.
Ziemba, W. T. Stochastic Optimization Models in Finance. 1975. 54.50 (ISBN 0-12-780850-7). Acad Pr.
Ziemer, Rodger E. & Tranter, William. Principles of Communciations: Systems Modulation & Noise. LC 75-25015. (Illus.). 736p. 1976. text ed. 36.95 (ISBN 0-395-20603-0); solutions manual 8.50 (ISBN 0-395-20604-9). HM.
Ziemian, Joseph. The Cigarette Sellers of Three Crosses Square. new ed. David, Janina, tr. from Polish. LC 74-11900. (Books for Adults & Young Adults Ser.). (Illus.). 180p. (gr. 6 up). 1975. 6.95g (ISBN 0-8225-0757-9). Lerner Pubns.
Ziemianek, Maria Swiecicka see Swiecicka-Ziemianek, Maria.
Ziemke, Earl. The Soviet Juggernaut. LC 80-23634. (World War II Ser.). PLB 19.92 (ISBN 0-8094-3388-5). Silver.
Zienkiewicz, O. C. The Finite Element Method. 3rd ed. (Illus.). 1978. text ed. 45.00 (ISBN 0-07-084072-5, C). McGraw.
--Finite Elements & Approximations. 300p. 1982. 34.95x (ISBN 0-471-98240-7, Pub. by Wiley-Interscience). Wiley.
Zienkiewicz, O. C., jt. auth. see Pande, G. N.
Zienkiewicz, O. C., jt. auth. see Stagg, K. G.
Zienkiewicz, O. C., ed. see Lewis, R. W. & Morgan, K.
Zienkiewicz, O. C., et al, eds. Numerical Methods in Offshore Engineering. LC 77-12565. (Numerical Methods in Engineering Ser.). 1978. 100.00x (ISBN 0-471-99591-6, Pub. by Wiley-Interscience). Wiley.
Zierep, Juergen & Oertel, Herbert, Jr., eds. Convective Transport & Instability Phenomena. (Illus.). 577p. 1982. text ed. 65.00 (ISBN 3-7650-1114-2). Sheridan.
Zieve, Philip D. & Levin, Jack. Disorders of Hemostasis. LC 76-1252. (Major Problems in Internal Medicine Ser.: Vol. 10). 1976. text ed. 14.50 o.p. (ISBN 0-7216-9685-6). Saunders.
Ziewacz, Lawrence, jt. auth. see Rubenstein, Bruce.
Zif, J., jt. auth. see Izraeli, D.
Ziff, Gil. Tibet: Being the Recollections & Adventures of the Hermit Yungdrung, Called Small Ears. 348p. 1981. pap. 4.95 o.p. (ISBN 0-517-54436-9); 18-copy prepack 89.10 o.p. (ISBN 0-517-54440-7). Crown.
Ziff, Larzer. The American Eighteen Nineties: Life & Times of a Lost Generation. LC 79-14754. viii, 376p. 1979. 21.50x o.p. (ISBN 0-8032-4900-4); pap. 5.95x (ISBN 0-8032-9900-1, BB 711, Bison). U of Nebr Pr.
Ziff, Morris, et al, eds. Rheumatoid Arthritis. (Advances in Inflammation Research Ser.: Vol. 3). 365p. 1982. text ed. 48.50 (ISBN 0-89004-657-3). Raven.
Zifferblatt, Steven M. Improving Study & Homework Behaviors. (Illus.). 96p. (Orig.). 1970. pap. 5.95 o.p. (ISBN 0-87822-012-7, 0127). Res Press.
Ziffren, Mickey. A Political Affair. 1980. pap. 2.50 o.s.i. (ISBN 0-440-17228-4). Dell.
Zifing, Lawrence & Kim, C. I. An Introduction to Asian Politics. (Illus.). 1977. text ed. 22.95 (ISBN 0-13-478081-7). P-H.
Zigal, Thomas, jt. ed. see Oliphant, Dave.
Zigel, Feodor F. Lectures on Slavonic Law. LC 72-97042. (Central & East European Ser.: No. 4). 1974. Repr. of 1902 ed. 15.00 (ISBN 0-87569-055-6). Academic Intl.
Ziglar, Zig. Confessions of a Happy Christian. 199p. 1982. pap. 5.95 (ISBN 0-88289-400-5). Pelican.
--Confessions of a Happy Christian. 192p. 1982. pap. 2.75 (ISBN 0-553-22739-4). Bantam.
--Nos Veremos en la Cumbre. Rev ed. Fernandez, Sergio, tr. from Eng. Orig. Title: See You at the Top. 352p. (Span.). 1982. pap. 8.50 (ISBN 0-311-46100-X). Casa Bautista.
--See You at the Top. LC 77-670008. Orig. Title: Biscuits, Fleas, & Pump Handles. 1982. Repr. of 1974 ed. 12.95 (ISBN 0-88289-126-X). Pelican.
Zigler, E. & Balla, D. Mental Retardation: The Developmental-Difference Controversy. (Illus.). 352p. 1982. text ed. 36.00 (ISBN 0-89859-170-8). L Erlbaum Assocs.
Zigmond, Naomi & Vallecorsa, Ada. Assessment for Instructional Planning: A Guide for Teachers of Children & Adolescents. (Illus.). 400p. 1983. 23.95 (ISBN 0-13-049643-X). P-H.
Zikmund, Barbara B. & Mulder, John C. Discovering the Church. LC 82-23870. (Library of Living Faith). 120p. 1983. pap. price not set (ISBN 0-664-24441-6). Westminster.
Zikmund, Joseph & Dennis, Deborah E., eds. Suburbia: A Guide to Information Sources. LC 78-10523. (Urban Studies Information Guide Ser: Vol. 9). 1979. 42.00x (ISBN 0-8103-1435-5). Gale.
Zikmund, William & Lindstrom, William J. A Collection of Outstanding Cases in Marketing Management. (Illus.). 1979. pap. text ed. 15.95 (ISBN 0-8299-0234-1); instrs.' manual avail. (ISBN 0-8299-0585-5). West Pub.
Zikorus, Frederick J. Mechanical Estimating of Water & Waste Treatment Plants. LC 80-65512. (Illus.). 300p. Date not set. cancelled (ISBN 0-250-40370-6). Ann Arbor Science.
Zilbergeld, Bernie. The Shrinking of America: Myths of Psychological Change. 1983. 16.50i (ISBN 0-316-98794-8); 16.50. Little.
Zilboorg, Gregory, tr. see Korolenko, Vladimir.
Zilboorg, Gregory, tr. see Zamiatin, Eugene.
Zile, Judy van see Van Zile, Judy.
Zill, Dennis, et al. College Mathematics for Students of Business, Life Science & Social Science. 2nd ed. 624p. 1981. text ed. 25.95x (ISBN 0-534-00886-0). Wadsworth Pub.
Zillman, Donald N. & Lattman, Laurence H. Energy Law. LC 82-20933. (University Casebook Ser.). 852p. 1982. text ed. write for info. (ISBN 0-88277-076-4). Foundation Pr.
Zilly, R. G., jt. auth. see O'Brien, James J.
Zils, Michael. World Guide to Scientific Associations & Learned Societies, Vol 13. (Handbook of International Documentation & Information). 619p. 1981. 150.00x (ISBN 0-686-98306-8, K G Saur). Gale.
Zils, Michael, ed. Directory of North & South American Universities. 1978. 58.00x (ISBN 0-89664-001-9, Pub. by K G Saur). Gale.
--International Directory of Booksellers. 1978. 120.00x (ISBN 0-89664-014-0, Pub. by K G Saur). Gale.
Zim, Herbert S. Alligators & Crocodiles. rev. ed. LC 78-6615. (gr. 4-6). 1978. PLB 7.44 o.p. (ISBN 0-688-32170-4). Morrow.
--The Big Cats. LC 76-819. (Illus.). 64p. (gr. 3-7). 1976. PLB 7.20 o.p. (ISBN 0-688-32072-4). Morrow.
--Blood. (Illus.). (gr. 3-7). 1968. PLB 8.16 (ISBN 0-688-31109-1). Morrow.
--Bones. (Illus.). (gr. 3-7). 1969. PLB 8.16 (ISBN 0-688-31115-6). Morrow.
--Codes & Secret Writing. (Illus.). (gr. 5-9). 1948. PLB 8.16 (ISBN 0-688-31178-4). Morrow.
--Comets. (Illus.). (gr. 3-7). 1957. PLB 8.16 (ISBN 0-688-31180-6). Morrow.
--Corals. (Illus.). (gr. 3-7). 1966. PLB 8.16 (ISBN 0-688-31186-5). Morrow.
--Diamonds. (Illus.). (gr. 3-7). 1959. PLB 8.16 (ISBN 0-688-31236-5). Morrow.
--Dinosaurs. (Illus.). (gr. 3-7). 1954. PLB 8.16 (ISBN 0-688-31239-X). Morrow.
--Frogs & Toads. (Illus.). (gr. 3-7). 1950. PLB 8.16 (ISBN 0-688-31316-7). Morrow.
--Golden Hamsters. (Illus.). (gr. 3-7). 1951. 8.16 (ISBN 0-688-31353-1). Morrow.
--Goldfish. (Illus.). (gr. 3-7). 1947. PLB 8.16 (ISBN 0-688-31340-X). Morrow.
--Homing Pigeons. (Illus.). (gr. 3-7). 1949. PLB 8.16 (ISBN 0-688-31398-1). Morrow.
--Little Cats. LC 77-20257. (Illus.). (gr. 3-7). 1978. 8.75 (ISBN 0-688-22149-1); PLB 8.40 (ISBN 0-688-32149-6). Morrow.
--Medicine. LC 74-4299. (Illus.). 64p. (gr. 3-7). 1974. 7.20 (ISBN 0-688-21786-9); PLB 8.16 (ISBN 0-688-31786-3). Morrow.
--Monkeys. (Illus.). (gr. 3-7). 1955. PLB 7.20 o.p. (ISBN 0-688-31517-8). Morrow.
--The New Moon. LC 79-21896. (Illus.). 64p. (gr. 4-6). 1980. 8.25 (ISBN 0-688-22219-6); PLB 7.92 (ISBN 0-688-32219-0). Morrow.
--Ostriches. (Illus.). (gr. 3-7). 1958. PLB 7.63 (ISBN 0-688-21542-4). Morrow.
--Owls. rev. ed. (Illus.). (gr. 3-7). 1977. PLB 8.16 (ISBN 0-688-32109-7). Morrow.
--Parakeets. (Illus.). (gr. 5 up). 1953. PLB 7.63 (ISBN 0-688-31544-5). Morrow.
--Rabbits. (Illus.). (gr. 3-7). 1948. PLB 8.16 (ISBN 0-688-31566-6). Morrow.
--Sharks. (Illus.). (gr. 4-6). 1966. PLB 7.63 (ISBN 0-688-26810-2). Morrow.
--Snakes. (Illus.). (gr. 3-7). 1949. PLB 8.16 (ISBN 0-688-31549-6). Morrow.
--The Sun. rev. ed. LC 74-34461. (Illus.). 64p. (gr. 3-7). 1975. PLB 8.16 (ISBN 0-688-32033-3). Morrow.
--The Universe. rev. ed. (Illus.). 64p. (gr. 3-7). 1973. PLB 7.20 o.p. (ISBN 0-688-31976-9); pap. 1.25 o.p. (ISBN 0-688-25096-3). Morrow.
--Waves. (Illus.). (gr. 3-7). 1967. PLB 8.16 (ISBN 0-688-31479-1). Morrow.
--What's Inside of Animals. (Illus.). (gr. 11 up). 1953. PLB 8.59 (ISBN 0-688-26518-9). Morrow.
--What's Inside of Me. (Illus.). (ps-3). 1952. PLB 8.59 (ISBN 0-688-31551-8). Morrow.
--Your Brain & How It Works. LC 78-168479. (Illus.). 64p. (gr. 3-7). 1972. PLB 8.16 (ISBN 0-688-31922-X). Morrow.
--Your Heart & How It Works. (Illus.). (gr. 3-7). 1959. PLB 8.16 (ISBN 0-688-31552-6). Morrow.
--Your Skin. LC 78-10878. (Illus.). (gr. 4-6). 1979. 8.75 (ISBN 0-688-22178-5); PLB 8.40 (ISBN 0-688-32178-X). Morrow.
--Your Stomach & Digestive Tract. LC 72-6734. (Illus.). 64p. (gr. 3-7). 1973. 6.00 o.p. (ISBN 0-688-21838-5); PLB 8.16 (ISBN 0-688-31838-X). Morrow.
Zim, Herbert S. & Gabrielson, Ira N. Birds. (Golden Guide Ser). (Illus.). 1956. PLB 11.54 (ISBN 0-307-63505-8, Golden Pr); pap. 2.95 (ISBN 0-307-24490-3). Western Pub.
Zim, Herbert S. & Krantz, Lucretia. Commercial Fishing. LC 73-4931. (Illus.). 64p. (gr. 3-7). 1973. 8.50 (ISBN 0-688-20091-5); PLB 8.16 (ISBN 0-688-30091-X); pap. 1.25 (ISBN 0-688-05267-3). Morrow.
--Crabs. LC 73-16328. (Illus.). 64p. (gr. 3-7). 1974. 6.25 o.p. (ISBN 0-688-20114-8); PLB 8.16 (ISBN 0-688-30114-2). Morrow.
--Sea Stars & Their Kin. LC 75-17633. (Illus.). 64p. (gr. 3-7). 1976. PLB 7.63 (ISBN 0-688-32053-8); 7.95 (ISBN 0-688-22053-3). Morrow.
--Snails. LC 74-16262. (Illus.). 64p. (gr. 3-7). 1975. 8.00 (ISBN 0-688-22012-6); PLB 8.16 (ISBN 0-688-32012-0). Morrow.
Zim, Herbert S. & Martin, Alexander C. Flowers. (Golden Guide Ser). (Illus.). (gr. 6 up). 1950. PLB 10.38 (ISBN 0-307-63511-2, Golden Pr); pap. 2.95 (ISBN 0-307-24491-1). Western Pub.
Zim, Herbert S. & Shoemaker, Hurst H. Fishes. (Golden Guide Ser). PLB 10.38 (ISBN 0-307-63508-2, Golden Pr); pap. 2.95 (ISBN 0-307-24498-9). Western Pub.
Zim, Herbert S. & Skelly, James R. Cargo Ships. (How Things Work Ser). (Illus.). (gr. 3-7). 1970. PLB 7.44 (ISBN 0-688-31143-1). Morrow.
--Hoists, Cranes, & Derricks. LC 74-79098. (How Things Work Ser). (Illus.). (gr. 3-7). 1974. PLB 8.16 (ISBN 0-688-31395-7); pap. 1.25 (ISBN 0-688-26395-X). Morrow.
--Metric Measure. LC 74-702. (Illus.). 64p. (gr. 3-7). 1974. PLB 8.16 (ISBN 0-688-30118-5). Morrow.
--Pipes & Plumbing Systems. LC 73-14589. (Illus.). 64p. (gr. 3-7). 1974. 8.50 (ISBN 0-688-20101-6); PLB 8.16 (ISBN 0-688-30101-0); pap. 1.25 (ISBN 0-688-25101-3). Morrow.
--Tractors. LC 78-189893. (Illus.). 64p. (gr. 3-7). 1974. PLB 8.16 (ISBN 0-688-31782-0); pap. 1.25 (ISBN 0-686-76940-6). Morrow.
--Trucks. LC 75-107973. (Illus.). (gr. 3-7). 1974. PLB 8.16 (ISBN 0-688-31565-8); pap. 1.25 (ISBN 0-688-26565-0). Morrow.

Zim, Herbert S. & Smith, Hobart M. Reptiles & Amphibians. (Golden Guide Ser). (Illus.). (gr. 6 up). 1953. PLB 11.54 (ISBN 0-307-63506-6, Golden Pr); pap. 2.95 (ISBN 0-307-24495-4). Western Pub.

Zim, Herbert S., jt. auth. see Mitchell, Robert.

Zim, Herbert S. & Skelly, James R., eds. Telephone Systems. LC 74-151937. (How Things Work Ser). (Illus.). (gr. 3-7). 1974. 5.75 o.p. (ISBN 0-688-21781-8); PLB 6.48 o.p. (ISBN 0-688-31781-2); pap. 1.25 (ISBN 0-688-26781-5). Morrow.

Zim, Herbert S., ed. see Reid, George K.

Zima, Joseph P. Interviewing: Key to Effective Management. 352p. 1983. pap. text ed. write for info. (ISBN 0-574-22720-2, 13-5720); write for info. instr's. guide (ISBN 0-574-22721-0, 13-5721). SRA.

Ziman, John M. Elements of Advanced Quantum Theory. LC 69-16290. (Illus.). 1969. 37.50 (ISBN 0-521-07458-4); pap. 16.95 (ISBN 0-521-09949-8). Cambridge U Pr.

--The Force of Knowledge. LC 75-23529. (Illus.). 368p. 1976. 44.50 (ISBN 0-521-20649-9); pap. 17.95 (ISBN 0-521-09917-X). Cambridge U Pr.

--Models of Disorder. LC 77-82527. (Illus.). 1979. 77.50 (ISBN 0-521-21784-9); pap. 27.95 (ISBN 0-521-29280-8). Cambridge U Pr.

--Principles of the Theory of Solids. 2nd ed. (Illus.). 456p. 1972. text ed. 44.50 (ISBN 0-521-08382-6); pap. 19.95 (ISBN 0-521-29733-8). Cambridge U Pr.

--Public Knowledge: An Essay Concerning the Social Dimension of Science. 1968. 24.95 (ISBN 0-521-06894-0); pap. 10.95 (ISBN 0-521-09519-0). Cambridge U Pr.

--Reliable Knowledge. LC 78-3792. (Illus.). 1979. 24.95 (ISBN 0-521-22087-4). Cambridge U Pr.

--Teaching & Learning About Science & Society. LC 80-40326. (Illus.). 148p. 1980. 23.95 (ISBN 0-521-23221-X). Cambridge U Pr.

Zimansky, Curt A., ed. see Rymer, Thomas.

Zimbalist, Andrew, ed. Case Studies on the Labor Process. LC 79-22728. 314p. 1981. 16.50 (ISBN 0-85345-518-X, CL 518X); pap. 7.50 (ISBN 0-85345-519-8). Monthly Rev.

Zimbardo, Philip. The Cognitive Control of Motivation: The Consequences of Choice & Dissonance. 1969. text ed. 15.50x (ISBN 0-673-05447-0). Scott F.

--Shyness. 1978. pap. 2.95 (ISBN 0-515-06714-8). Jove Pubns.

Zimbardo, Philip & Maslach, Christina. Psychology for Our Times: Readings. 2nd ed. 1977. pap. 10.95x (ISBN 0-673-15052-6). Scott F.

Zimbardo, Philip G. Essentials of Psychology & Life. 10th ed. 1980. text ed. 21.95x (ISBN 0-673-15184-0). Scott F.

--Psychology & Life. 10th ed. 1979. text ed. 24.50x (ISBN 0-673-15183-2). Scott F.

Zimbardo, Philip G. & Radl, Shirley. Shy Child. LC 82-45079. (Illus.). 240p. 1982. pap. 6.95 (ISBN 0-385-18175-2, Dolp). Doubleday.

Zimbardo, Philip G. & Radl, Shirley L. The Shyness Workbook. 208p. 1983. pap. 6.95 (ISBN 0-89104-141-9, A & W Visual Library). A & W Pubs.

Zimbardo, Philip G., jt. auth. see Dempsey, David.

Zimbardo, Philip G., et al. Influencing Attitudes & Changing Behavior: An Introduction to Method, Theory & Applications of Social Control & Personal Power. (Topics in Social Psychology). 1977. pap. text ed. 9.95 (ISBN 0-201-08796-0). A W.

Zimberg, Sheldon, ed. The Clinical Management of Alcoholism. LC 82-9457. 256p. 1982. 30.00 (ISBN 0-87630-307-6). Brunner-Mazel.

Zimelman, Nathan. How to Fly Like a Bird Even if You're Only A Boy. pap. 8.95 (ISBN 0-914676-92-X). Green Tiger Pr.

--If I Were Strong Enough. LC 81-19076. (Illus.). 32p. (gr. k-3). 1982. 9.95 (ISBN 0-687-18670-6). Abingdon.

--Mean Chickens & Wild Cucumbers. LC 82-17221. 32p. (gr. k-3). 1983. 9.95 (ISBN 0-02-793730-5). Macmillan.

Ziment, I. Practical Pulmonary Disease. (Family Practice Today: A Comprehensive Post Graduate Library). 226p. 1982. text ed. 14.85 (ISBN 0-471-09560-5, Pub. by Wiley Med.). Wiley.

Zimering, Stanley, jt. auth. see Saltman, Jules.

Zimiles, Martha & Zimiles, Murray. Early American Mills. (Illus.). 352p. 1973. 15.00 o.p. (ISBN 0-517-50060-4). Crown.

Zimiles, Murray, jt. auth. see Zimiles, Martha.

Zimmer, Dirk. The Trick-or-Treat Trap. LC 81-47113. (Illus.). 32p. (gr. k-3). 1982. 9.13i (ISBN 0-06-026860-3, HarpJ); PLB 8.89g (ISBN 0-06-026861-1). Har-Row.

Zimmer, Hans, ed. Annual Reports in Inorganic & General Syntheses, Vol. 5. 42.00 (ISBN 0-12-040705-1). Acad Pr.

Zimmer, Hans, jt. ed. see Niedenzu, Kurt.

Zimmer, Joseph. The History of the Forty-Third Infantry Division. (Divisional Ser.: No. 23). (Illus.). 96p. 1982. Repr. of 1946 ed. 22.50x (ISBN 0-89839-068-0). Battery Pr.

Zimmer, K. Combined Intermediate-Advanced Typewriting for the College Student. 1974. pap. 12.95x o.p. (ISBN 0-02-479880-0, 47988). Glencoe.

Zimmer, K., jt. auth. see Stewart, M. M.

Zimmer, Karl E., tr. see Steiner, Rudolf.

Zimmer, Kenneth. Advanced Typewriting for the College Student. LC 72-93634. 256p. 1973. pap. text ed. 7.95x o.p. (ISBN 0-02-479850-9); wkbk 4.95x o.p. (ISBN 0-02-479860-6, 47986). Glencoe.

--High School Typewriting. LC 74-9198. 320p. 1977. text ed. 11.52 (ISBN 0-02-479730-8); tchr's manual 10.50 (ISBN 0-686-61288-4); text ed. 11.52 vocational course (ISBN 0-686-96723-2); Set 1. working papers 4.20 (ISBN 0-02-479750-2); Set 2. working papers 4.20 (ISBN 0-686-61289-2); Set 3. working papers 4.20 (ISBN 0-686-61290-6). Glencoe.

Zimmer, Kenneth & Jones, Vauncille. Basic Typewriting for the College Student. 1972. pap. text ed. 7.95x o.p. (ISBN 0-02-479800-2, 47980); wkbk. 4.95x o.p. (ISBN 0-02-479810-X, 47981). Glencoe.

--Intermediate Typewriting for the College Student. 1972. pap. text ed. 6.95x o.p. (ISBN 0-02-479820-7, 47982); wkbk 4.95x o.p. (ISBN 0-02-479830-4, 47983). Glencoe.

Zimmer, Louis, jt. auth. see LaCarrubba, Joseph.

Zimmer, Lowell J. Music Handbook for the Child in Special Education. 1976. pap. 4.25 (ISBN 0-913574-99-6, 01260). Eur-Am Music.

Zimmer, Michael, ed. Cogeneration Handbook II. 310p. 1982. Wkbk. 48.00 (ISBN 0-86587-103-5). Gov Insts.

Zimmer, Norma. Norma. 189p. 1983. pap. 2.95 (ISBN 0-8423-4714-3). Tyndale.

Zimmer, Rudolf A. Applications in Technology of Right Triangular Trigonometry: Unit 5. 64p. 1980. pap. text ed. 5.95 (ISBN 0-8403-2278-X). Kendall-Hunt.

Zimmer, Rudolph A. Basic Trigonometry with Applications in Technology. LC 80-82834. 256p. 1980. pap. text ed. 11.95 (ISBN 0-8403-2273-9). Kendall-Hunt.

--Primary Trigonometric Ratios: Unit 3. 48p. 1980. pap. text ed. 5.50 (ISBN 0-8403-2276-3). Kendall-Hunt.

--Secondary (Reciprocal) Trigonometric Ratios: Unit 4. 48p. 1980. pap. text ed. 5.50 (ISBN 0-8403-2277-1). Kendall-Hunt.

Zimmer, Russell L., jt. ed. see Woollacott, Robert M.

Zimmer, Ruth K. James Shirley: A Reference Guide. 1980. lib. bdg. 22.00 (ISBN 0-8161-7974-3, Hall Reference). G K Hall.

Zimmerer, Thomas W. & Preston, Paul. Management for Supervisors: Readings & Cases. (Illus.). 1978. pap. text ed. 12.95 (ISBN 0-13-548792-7). P-H.

Zimmerli, Walther. I Am Yahweh. Brueggemann, Walter, ed. Scott, Doug, tr. from German. LC 81-85326. 160p. Date not set. 15.95 (ISBN 0-8042-0519-1). John Knox.

Zimmerman, jt. auth. see Kaufman, Herbert E.

Zimmerman, A. M., et al, eds. Drugs & the Cell Cycle. (Cell Biology Ser.). 1973. 50.00 (ISBN 0-12-781260-1). Acad Pr.

Zimmerman, Ada M. The Playhouse. 32p. 1980. 2.55 (ISBN 0-686-30763-1). Rod & Staff.

Zimmerman, Arnold W., jt. ed. see Meade, Frank H.

Zimmerman, Arthur F. Francisco De Toledo, Fifth Viceroy of Peru, 1569-1581. LC 69-10177. (Illus.). 1968. Repr. of 1938 ed. lib. bdg. 17.00x (ISBN 0-8371-0425-4, ZIFT). Greenwood.

Zimmerman, Barry J., jt. ed. see Whitehurst, Grover J.

Zimmerman, Benedict, tr. see John Of The Cross.

Zimmerman, Bill. Airlift to Wounded Knee. LC 82-73815. (Illus.). 348p. 1976. 14.95 (ISBN 0-8040-0691-1). Swallow.

Zimmerman, Caroline. How to Break into the Media Professions. LC 80-24397. 216p. 1981. 11.95 (ISBN 0-385-15933-1). Doubleday.

--How to Break into the Media Professions. LC 79-6665. 1981. pap. 6.95 (ISBN 0-385-15934-X, Dolp). Doubleday.

Zimmerman, David R. The Essential Guide to Nonprescription Drugs. LC 82-48139. (Illus.). 704p. 1983. pap. 10.53i (ISBN 0-06-091023-2, CN 1023, CN). Har-Row.

--The Essential Guide to Nonprescription Drugs. (Illus.). 704p. 1983. 27.50 (ISBN 0-06-014915-9, HarpT). Har-Row.

Zimmerman, E., et al. Drug Effects on Neuroendocrine Regulation. LC 73-77069. (Progress in Brain Research Ser.: Vol. 39). 500p. 1973. 128.50 (ISBN 0-444-41129-1). Elsevier.

Zimmerman, Elwood C. & Hardy, D. Elmo. Insects of Hawaii, 13 vols. Incl. Vol. 1. Introduction. o.p. (ISBN 0-685-22570-4); Vol. 2. Apterygota to Thysanoptera. 486p. 1948. 12.00x (ISBN 0-87022-902-8); Vol. 3. Heteroptera. 266p. 1948. 9.00x (ISBN 0-87022-903-6); Vol. 4. Homoptera: Auchenorhyncha. 278p. 1948. 9.00x (ISBN 0-87022-904-4); Vol. 5. Homoptera: Sternorhyncha. 474p. 1948. 12.00x (ISBN 0-87022-905-2); Vol. 6. Ephemeroptera-Neuroptera-Trichoptera. 218p. (Supplement to Vols. 1-5 included). 1957. 9.00x (ISBN 0-87022-906-0); Vol. 7. Macrolepidoptera. 556p. 1958. 15.00x (ISBN 0-87022-907-9); Vol. 8. Lepidoptera, Pyraloidea. 468p. 1958. 12.00x (ISBN 0-87022-908-7); Vol. 10. Diptera: Nematocera-Brachycera 1. 380p. 1960. 11.00x (ISBN 0-87022-910-9); Vol. 11. Diptera: Brachycera 2-Cyclorrhapha 1. 468p. 1964. 12.00x (ISBN 0-87022-911-7); Diptera: Dolichopodidae & Appendix (Phoridae) Tenorio, Jo Ann. 80p. (Supplement to Vol. 11). 1969. 7.00x (ISBN 0-87022-921-4); Vol. 12. Diptera: Cyclorrhapha 2. 824p. 1965. 25.00x **(ISBN 0-87022-912-5); Vol. 9. Microlepidoptera, 2 parts. 1978. 60.00x set (ISBN 0-8248-0487-2). (Illus.). UH Pr.**

Zimmerman, Enid, jt. auth. see Hubbard, Guy.

Zimmerman, Eric. Carving Horses in Wood. LC 83-414. (Illus.). 128p. (Orig.). 1983. pap. 6.95 (ISBN 0-8069-7706-X). Sterling.

Zimmerman, Everett. Defoe & the Novel. LC 73-91682. 1975. 21.50x (ISBN 0-520-02688-8). U of Cal Pr.

Zimmerman, Franklin B. Henry Purcell (Sixteen Fifty-Nine to Sixteen Ninety-Five): His Life & Times. 2nd rev. ed. LC 82-40485. 464p. 1983. 37.50 (ISBN 0-8122-7869-0); pap. 19.95 (ISBN 0-8122-1136-7). U of Pa Pr.

Zimmerman, Fred W. Exploring Woodworking. LC 81-6923. 208p. 1981. 12.00 (ISBN 0-87006-398-7); wkbk.. 3.80 (ISBN 0-87006-281-6). Goodheart.

--Leathercraft. LC 77-8007. (Illus.). 120p. 1977. text ed. 5.80 (ISBN 0-87006-387-1). Goodheart.

Zimmerman, Gary. Managing Your Own Money: A Self-Teaching Guide. LC 80-12294. (Wiley Self-Teaching Guide Ser.). 224p. 1980. pap. text ed. 9.50 (ISBN 0-471-05226-4). Wiley.

Zimmerman, Gordon, et al. Speech Communication: A Contemporary Introduction. 2nd ed. (Illus.). 1980. pap. 16.50 (ISBN 0-8299-0326-7). West Pub.

Zimmerman, Gordon I. Public Speaking Today. (Illus.). 1979. pap. text ed. 14.50 (ISBN 0-8299-0259-7); instrs.' manual avail. (ISBN 0-8299-0586-3). West Pub.

Zimmerman, Harry, ed. Progress in Neuropathology, Vol. IV. 424p. 1979. 45.00 (ISBN 0-89004-388-4). Raven.

Zimmerman, Harry M. Progress in Neuropathology, Vol. V. 400p. 1982. text ed. write for info. (ISBN 0-89004-728-6). Raven.

Zimmerman, Helmut. Tropical Frogs. (Illus.). 1979. 4.95 (ISBN 0-87666-926-7, KW-028). TFH Pubns.

Zimmerman, Henry & Zimmerman, Isaac. Elements of Organic Chemistry. 1977. text ed. 15.95 o.p. (ISBN 0-02-479910-6). Glencoe.

Zimmerman, Isaac, jt. auth. see Zimmerman, Henry.

Zimmerman, Jan. The Technological Woman: Interfacing with Tomorrow. 304p. 1983. 24.95 (ISBN 0-03-062829-6). Praeger.

Zimmerman, Joan & Rector, Alan. Computers for the Physician's Office. 1978. 58.95 (ISBN 0-471-27888-2). Res Stud Pr.

Zimmerman, John E. Dictionary of Classical Mythology. (YA) 1964. 17.26i (ISBN 0-06-007740-9, HarpT). Har-Row.

Zimmerman, John H. They Counted Not the Cost: A History of the Memorial Union Corporation, 1919-1929. Anderson, Larry E., ed. (Illus.). 48p. 1982. pap. 5.00 (ISBN 0-934068-01-1). Memorial Union.

Zimmerman, John W., jt. auth. see Tregoe, Benjamin B.

Zimmerman, Joseph F. The Federated City: Community in Large Cities. 128p. 1972. text ed. 16.95 o.p. (ISBN 0-312-28595-7); pap. text ed. 7.95 (ISBN 0-312-28560-4). St Martin.

Zimmerman, Joseph F., jt. auth. see Prescott, Frank W.

Zimmerman, L. E. & Sobin, L. H. Histological Typing of Tumours of the Eye & its Adnexa. (Illus.). 82p. 31.50 (ISBN 0-686-95509-9, 70-1-024-20); text ed. 111.50 incl. slides (70-1-024-00). Am Soc Clinical.

Zimmerman, L. Z., jt. auth. see Crowley, J. S.

Zimmerman, Lance, jt. auth. see Campbell, J. L.

Zimmerman, Louis J. Poor Lands, Rich Lands: The Widening Gap. (Orig.). pap. text ed. 3.95x (ISBN 0-685-19752-2). Phila Bk Co.

Zimmerman, M. G. Tales of a Teller: An Informal Guide to a Fine Art. Johnson, Dave, ed. (Illus.). 167p. 1975. pap. text ed. 14.95 (ISBN 0-9608944-0-3, 7039104). G Zimmerman.

Zimmerman, Marilyn P. Musical Characteristics of Children. LC 73-176274. (From Research to the Music Classroom Ser). 32p. (Orig.). 1971. pap. 2.00x (ISBN 0-940796-10-4, 1032). Music Ed.

Zimmerman, Marjorie. Treasure on Squaw Mountain. LC 75-36696. (gr. 5-9). 1976. pap. 2.25 (ISBN 0-912692-85-5). Cook.

Zimmerman, Martha. Should I Keep My Baby? 112p. (Orig.). 1983. pap. 3.95 (ISBN 0-87123-578-1). Bethany Hse.

Zimmerman, Martin B. The U. S. Coal Industry: The Economics of Policy Choice. 256p. 1981. text ed. 27.50x (ISBN 0-262-24023-8). MIT Pr.

Zimmerman, Martin H., jt. auth. see Lamb, I. Mackenzie.

Zimmerman, Mary F., jt. auth. see McConnell, Edwina A.

Zimmerman, Michael. Eclipse of the Self: The Development of Heidegger's Concept of Authenticity. LC 80-19042. xxx, 331p. 1981. 19.95x (ISBN 0-8214-0570-5, 82-83616); pap. 11.95x (ISBN 0-8214-0601-9, 82-83624). Ohio U Pr.

Zimmerman, Mildred K., jt. auth. see Zimmerman, O. T.

Zimmerman, Morris, et al, eds. Percursor Processing in the Biosynthesis of Proteins. LC 80-16863. (Annals of the New Yok Academy of Sciences: Vol. 343). 449p. 1980. 81.00x (ISBN 0-89766-072-2); pap. 81.00x (ISBN 0-686-77789-1). NY Acad Sci.

Zimmerman, Nan, jt. auth. see Ullman, Montague.

Zimmerman, O. T. & Lavine, Irvin. Chemical Engineering Costs. 1950. 19.50 o.p. (ISBN 0-940770-00-8). Indus Res Serv.

--Chemical Engineering Laboratory Equipment. 2nd ed. 1955. 17.50 o.s.i. (ISBN 0-940770-02-4). Indus Res Serv.

--Conversion Factors & Tables. 3rd ed. 1961. 16.00x (ISBN 0-940770-03-2). Indus Res Serv.

--Handbook of Material Trade Names, with Supplements 1, 2, 3, & 4, 5 bks. 1953-65. Set. 177.60x (ISBN 0-940770-01-6); 45.35x; Supplement 1. 29.40x; Supplement 2. 30.40x; Supplement 3. 32.60x; Supplement 4. 43.10x. Indus Res Serv.

--Psychrometric Tables & Charts. 2nd ed. 1964. 30.00x (ISBN 0-940770-04-0). Indus Res Serv.

Zimmerman, O. T. & Zimmerman, Mildred K. College Placement Directory. 4th ed. 1965. 20.40x (ISBN 0-940770-05-9). Indus Res Serv.

Zimmerman, Paul A., ed. Creation, Evolution & God's Word. LC 70-182220. 176p. 1972. pap. 3.50 (ISBN 0-570-03122-2, 12-2358). Concordia.

Zimmerman, R. Floral Forms in Design. (Illus.). 22.50 o.p. (ISBN 0-87245-409-6). Textile Bk.

Zimmerman, Ruth. Abyssinians. (Illus.). 96p. 1980. 4.95 (ISBN 0-87666-861-9, KW-O63). TFH Pubns.

Zimmerman, Ruth, jt. auth. see Hinman, Dorothy.

Zimmerman, Stephen W., jt. auth. see Harrington, Avery R.

Zimmerman, Steven & Conrad, Leo. Business Applications for the IBM Personal Computer. (Illus.). 224p. 1983. 16.95 (ISBN 0-89303-243-3). R J Brady.

--Osborne User's Guide: Applications & Programming. (Illus.). 264p. 1982. text ed. 19.95 (ISBN 0-89303-207-7); pap. 14.95 (ISBN 0-89303-206-9). R J Brady.

--Pocket Computer Users Guide for the TRS-80TM, PC-1, & Sharp 1211. (Microcomputer Power Ser.). 192p. 1983. pap. write for info. (ISBN 0-697-09980-6). Wm C Brown.

--Practical Programs for Your Pocket Computer: For the TRS-80TM, Pc-1, and Sharp 1211. (Microcomputer Power Ser.). 224p. 1983. pap. write for info. (ISBN 0-697-09975-X). Wm C Brown.

Zimmerman, Thomas J. Focus on Life Student Project Book. rev ed. (To Live Is Christ Ser.). 40p. 1976. write for info. wkbk. o.p. (ISBN 0-697-01655-2). Wm C Brown.

Zimmerman, William. A Book of Questions: To Keep Thoughts & Feelings. 270p. 1983. write for info. (ISBN 0-935966-02-1); pap. write for info. (ISBN 0-935966-01-3). Guarionex Pr.

--How to Tape Instant Oral Biographies. (Illus.). 108p. 1982. pap. 4.95 (ISBN 0-448-12330-4, G&D). Putnam Pub Group.

--Soviet Perspectives on International Relations, 1956-1967. LC 68-56326. (Studies of the Russian Inst. Columbia Univ). 1969. 26.00 o.p. (ISBN 0-691-07525-5); pap. 7.95x (ISBN 0-691-02168-6). Princeton U Pr.

Zimmermann, Charles F. Uranium Resources on Federal Lands. LC 78-20738. (Illus.). 352p. 1979. 29.95x o.p. (ISBN 0-669-02847-9). Lexington Bks.

Zimmermann, E. & George, R., eds. Narcotics & the Hypothalamus. LC 74-83453. 286p. 1974. 30.00 (ISBN 0-911216-87-1). Raven.

Zimmermann, Ekkart. Political Violence, Crises & Revolutions: Theories & Research. 1983. lib. bdg. 45.00 (ISBN 0-8161-9027-5, Univ Bks). G K Hall.

Zimmermann, Erich W. Conservation in the Production of Petroleum. 1957. text ed. 29.50x (ISBN 0-686-83511-5). Elliots Bks.

Zimmermann, George. Ohio: Off the Beaten Path. (Illus.). 160p. 1983. pap. 5.95 (ISBN 0-914788-67-1). East Woods.

Zimmermann, Georges D. Songs of Irish Rebellion: Political Street Ballads & Rebel Songs, 1780-1900. LC 67-21410. 342p. Repr. of 1967 ed. 30.00x (ISBN 0-8103-5025-4). Gale.

Zimmermann, Gunter. Die Antwort Der Reformatoren Auf Die Zehntenfrage. 175p. 1982. write for info. (ISBN 3-8204-5745-3). P Lang Pubs.

Zimmermann, Jon, et al. Contemporary German Life. new ed. (Illus.). 384p. 1982. text ed. 26.95 (ISBN 0-07-072835-6, C); instr's. manual 26.00 (ISBN 0-07-072836-4). McGraw.

Zimmermann, M. H., jt. ed. see Tomlinson, P. B.

Zimmermann, U. Linear & Combinatorial Optimization in Ordered Algebraic Structures. (Annals of Discreet Mathematics Ser.: Vol. 10). 1981. 72.50 (ISBN 0-444-86153-X). Elsevier.

Zimmern, Alfred E. The Third British Empire. 3rd ed. LC 79-4333. 1979. Repr. of 1934 ed. lib. bdg. 20.75x (ISBN 0-313-20990-1, ZITB). Greenwood.

Zimmernman, Fred W. Upholstering Methods. LC 80-25308. (Illus.). 196p. 1981. text ed. 13.20 (ISBN 0-87006-313-8). Goodheart.

Zimmerrian, Donald, jt. auth. see Golden, Lawrence G.

Zimolzak, Chester & Stansfield, Charles. The Human Landscape: Geography & Culture. 1979. text ed. 23.95 (ISBN 0-675-08290-0). Additional supplements may be obtained from publisher. Merrill.

Zimolzak, Chester E. & Stansfield, Charles A. The Human Landscape. 2nd ed. 448p. 1983. text ed. 25.95 (ISBN 0-675-20043-1). Additional supplements may be obtained from publisher. Merrill.

Zimpfer, David G. Paraprofessionals in Counseling, Guidance & Personnel Services. (APGA Reprint Ser.: No. 5). 280p. 1974. pap. 9.75 nonmembers (ISBN 0-686-11456-6, 72097); pap. 6.75 (ISBN 0-686-34300-X). Am Personnel.

Zimring. The Changing Legal World of Adolescents. (Illus.). 245p. 1982. text ed. 14.95 (ISBN 0-02-935960-0). Free Pr.

Zimring, Franklin E. & Frase, Richard S. The Criminal Justice System. 1038p. 1980. text ed. 26.00 (ISBN 0-316-98795-6). Little.

Zinberg, Norman E., ed. Alternate States of Consciousness. LC 76-46722. 1977. 14.95 (ISBN 0-02-935770-5); pap. text ed. 7.95 (ISBN 0-02-935930-9). Free Pr.

Zincone, Louis, et al. Principles of Economics: Study Guide. 2nd ed. 1981. pap. text ed. 7.95x o.p. (ISBN 0-673-15494-7). Scott F.

--Principles of Macroeconomics: Study Guide. 2nd ed. 1981. pap. text ed. 4.95x o.p. (ISBN 0-673-15496-3). Scott F.

Zindel, Paul. The Girl Who Wanted A Say. 1982. pap. 2.25 (ISBN 0-553-22540-5). Bantam.

--My Darling, My Hamburger. LC 70-85025. (gr. 8 up). 1969. 10.53i (ISBN 0-06-026823-9, HarpJ); PLB 10.89 (ISBN 0-06-026824-7). Har-Row.

--The Pigman. LC 68-10784. (gr. 7 up). 1968. 9.57i (ISBN 0-06-026827-1, HarpJ); PLB 9.79 (ISBN 0-06-026828-X). Har-Row.

Ziner, Feenie & Galdone, Paul. Counting Carnival. (Illus.). (gr. k-2). 1962. PLB 4.69 o.p. (ISBN 0-698-30057-2, Coward). Putnam Pub Group.

Zines, Leslie, jt. auth. see Cowen, Zelman.

Zingale, Nancy, jt. auth. see Flanigan, William.

Zingale, Nancy H., jt. auth. see Flanigan, William H.

Zingg, Ernst J., jt. auth. see Mayor, Georges.

Zink, David. The Stones of Atlantis. LC 77-28714. (Illus.). 1978. 9.95 o.p. (ISBN 0-13-846923-7). P-H.

Zink, David D. Leslie Stephen. (English Authors Ser.). lib. bdg. 14.95 (ISBN 0-8057-1512-6, Twayne). G K Hall.

Zink, J. Champions on the School Bus: A Positive Approach to Discipline for School Bus Drivers. 28p. 1982. softcover 3.95 (ISBN 0-686-94911-0). J Zink.

Zink, R. A., jt. ed. see Brendel, W.

Zink, Sidney. Concepts of Ethics. 1962. 17.95 (ISBN 0-312-16100-X). St Martin.

Zink, Steven D. U. S. Government Publications Catalogs. LC 81-18352. (SLA Bibliography Ser.: No. 8). 112p. 1981. pap. 11.75 (ISBN 0-87111-285-X). SLA.

Zinkhon, Robert W. No Pressure Steam Cooking. Windle, Joy, ed. LC 77-89308. (Illus.). 1978. pap. 5.95 (ISBN 0-394-73564-1). Taylor & Ng.

Zinkin, Maurice. Development for Free Asia. LC 75-20982. 243p. 1975. lib. bdg. 17.00x (ISBN 0-8371-8343-X, ZIFA). Greenwood.

Zinkus, Dan, ed. see Morton, Ruth.

Zinman, David. Fifty Classic Motion Pictures. 1970. 9.95 o.p. (ISBN 0-517-50477-4). Crown.

--Fifty from the Fifties. LC 78-14988. (Illus.). 1979. 25.00 o.p. (ISBN 0-87000-318-6, Arlington Hse). Crown.

Zinman, Leonard, jt. auth. see Libertino, John A.

Zinn, Howard. La Guardia in Congress. LC 72-4007. 288p. 1972. Repr. of 1959 ed. lib. bdg. 17.00x (ISBN 0-8371-6434-6, ZILG). Greenwood.

--Postwar America: 1945-1971. LC 72-88273. (History of American Society Ser). 260p. (Orig.). 1973. pap. 6.95 (ISBN 0-672-60936-3). Bobbs.

Zinn, W., ed. Magnetic Semiconductors: 1975 Discussion Meeting at Julich, Germany. 1976. 42.75 (ISBN 0-7204-0420-7, North-Holland). Elsevier.

Zinner, K. A. Supercharging of Internal Combustion Engines. (Illus.). 290p. 1981. pap. 32.40 (ISBN 0-387-08544-0). Springer-Verlag.

Zinner, Paul E. Communist Strategy & Tactics in Czechoslovakia, 1918-48. LC 75-32464. 264p. 1976. Repr. of 1963 ed. lib. bdg. 17.50x (ISBN 0-8371-8550-5, ZICS). Greenwood.

Zinnes, Dina A. Contemporary Research in International Relations: A Perspective & a Critical Assessment. LC 75-11290. (Illus.). 1976. 30.00 (ISBN 0-02-935730-6). Free Pr.

Zinnes, Dina A. & Gillespie, John V., eds. Mathematical Models in International Relations. LC 75-25000. (Special Studies). (Illus.). 1976. 47.95 o.p. (ISBN 0-275-55870-3). Praeger.

Zinnes, Dina A., jt. ed. see Gillespie, Judith A.

Zinnes, Dina A., jt. ed. see Gillispie, John V.

Zinngrabe. Sheet Metal Blueprint Reading: For the Building Trades. LC 79-2748. 138p. 1980. 13.80 (ISBN 0-8273-1352-7); instr.'s guide 4.25 (ISBN 0-8273-1353-5). Delmar.

Zinngrabe, C. J. & Schumacher, F. W. Practical Layout for Sheet Metal Shop. LC 75-6063. 1975. pap. text ed. 9.80 (ISBN 0-8273-0224-X); instructor's guide 3.75 (ISBN 0-8273-0225-8). Delmar.

--Safety for Sheet Metal Workers. LC 76-49325. (gr. 9-12). 1977. pap. 7.00 (ISBN 0-8273-1614-3); tchr's. guide 2.00 (ISBN 0-8273-1615-1). Delmar.

--Sheet Metal Hand Processes. LC 73-2159. 1974. 10.80 (ISBN 0-8273-0220-7); instr.'s guide 2.00 (ISBN 0-8273-0221-5). Delmar.

--Sheet Metal Machine Processes. LC 73-2160. 1975. pap. text ed. 10.80 (ISBN 0-8273-0222-3); instr.'s guide 2.75 (ISBN 0-8273-0223-1). Delmar.

Zinsser, William. Writing With a Word Processor. LC 82-48140. (Illus.). 128p. 1983. 9.57i (ISBN 0-06-015055-6, HarpT). Har-Row.

Zintak, Dennis, ed. Improving Production with Coolants & Lubricants. LC 82-80849. (Manfacturing Update Ser.). 260p. 1982. 32.00 (ISBN 0-87263-081-1). SME.

Zintz, Walter. Nova Venturion's Bootstrap Venture Manual. 1981. softcover 16.50 (ISBN 0-915254-08-5). Nova Venturion.

--Nova Venturion's Handbook for Non-Salesmen. Date not set. cancelled (ISBN 0-915254-09-3). Nova Venturion.

--The Teaching Job Hunt. LC 73-88726. 27p. 1973. pap. 3.00 (ISBN 0-915254-05-0, 05-0). Nova Venturion.

Zinzella, Harry M. Guidance Without a Face: Exercises in Meditative Comprehension. 1983. 6.95 (ISBN 0-686-81909-8). Vantage.

Zion, Gene. All Falling Down. LC 51-12571. 32p. (ps-1). 1951. 8.61i (ISBN 0-06-026830-1, HarpJ); PLB 10.89 (ISBN 0-06-026831-X). Har-Row.

--Dear Garbage Man. LC 57-5355. (Illus.). (gr. k-3). 1957. PLB 10.89 (ISBN 0-06-026841-7, HarpJ). Har-Row.

--Harry by the Sea. LC 65-21302. (Illus.). (gr. k-3). 1965. 10.89 (ISBN 0-06-026856-5, HarpJ). Har-Row.

--The Meanest Squirrel I Ever Met. LC 62-19851. (Illus.). 1982. pap. 2.95 (ISBN 0-689-70756-8, A-132, Aladdin). Atheneum.

--No Roses for Harry. LC 58-7752. (Illus.). (gr. k-3). 1958. 9.57i (ISBN 0-06-026890-5, HarpJ); PLB 10.89 (ISBN 0-06-026891-3). Har-Row.

--The Plant Sitter. LC 59-5329. (Illus.). (gr. k-3). 1959. PLB 10.89 (ISBN 0-06-026901-4, HarpJ). Har-Row.

--The Summer Snowman. LC 55-9178. (Illus.). (ps-1). 1955. PLB 10.89 (ISBN 0-06-026910-3, HarpJ). Har-Row.

Zion, Sidney. Read All About It! The Collected Adventures of a Maverick Reporter. 368p. 1982. 16.50 (ISBN 0-671-43458-6). Summit Bks.

Zipes, Jack. The Trials & Tribulations of Little Red Riding Hood: Versions of the Tale in Socio-Cultural Context. (Illus.). 320p. 1983. text ed. 29.95x (ISBN 0-89789-023-X). J F Bergin.

Zippin, Leo, jt. auth. see Montgomery, Deanne.

Zipse, Philip, jt. auth. see Parzynski, William.

Zirato, Bruno, jt. auth. see Key, Pierre V.

Zireau, Lillee. Beekeeping. LC 77-185674. (Handicraft Ser.: Bk. 6). (Illus.). 32p. (Orig.). (gr. 7-12). 1971. lib. bdg. 2.45 incl. catalog cards o.p. (ISBN 0-87157-906-5); pap. 1.25 vinyl laminated covers o.p. (ISBN 0-87157-406-3). SamHar Pr.

Ziring, Lawrence. Pakistan: The Enigma of Political Development. (Illus.). 256p. 1981. lib. bdg. 29.75x o.p. (ISBN 0-89158-982-1, Pub. by Dawson Pub). Westview.

--The Subcontinent in World Politics: India, Its Neighbors & the Great Powers. rev. 2nd ed. 268p. 1982. 29.95 (ISBN 0-03-060287-4); pap. 13.95 (ISBN 0-03-060288-2). Praeger.

Zirkel, G. & Rosenfeld. Beginning Statistics. 1975. 26.00 (ISBN 0-07-072840-2, C); instr's manual 5.00 (ISBN 0-07-072841-0). McGraw.

Zirker, Jack B., ed. Coronal Holes & High Speed Wind Streams. LC 77-84528. (Illus.). 1977. text ed. 15.00x (ISBN 0-87081-109-6). Colo Assoc.

Zirkle, Raymond E., ed. Biological Effects of External X & Gamma Radiation, Part 2. (National Nuclear Energy Ser.: Vol. 22C). 487p. 1956. pap. 35.50 (ISBN 0-87079-146-X, TID-5220); microfilm 4.50 (ISBN 0-87079-147-8, TID-5220). DOE.

Zirkoff, Boris de see Blavatsky, H. P.

Zirkoff, Boris De see Blavatsky, Helena P.

Zirkoff, Boris de see De Zirkoff, Boris.

Zisenwine, David & Rossel, Seymour, eds. Anti-Semitism in Europe: Sources of the Holocaust. new ed. LC 76-47452. (The Jewish Concepts & Issues Ser.). 128p. (gr. 7-9). 1976. pap. text ed. 2.45x avail discussion guide included o.p. (ISBN 0-87441-228-5). Behrman.

Ziskind, Sylvia. Telling Stories to Children. 157p. 1976. 12.00 (ISBN 0-8242-0588-X). Wilson.

Zissos, ed. System Design with Microprocessors. 2nd ed. Date not set. price not set; pap. price not set (ISBN 0-12-781740-9). Acad Pr.

Zistel, Era. The Dangerous Year. (gr. 3-7). 1967. PLB 4.99 o.p. (ISBN 0-394-91897-5). Random.

--Good Companions. 1981. pap. 1.95 o.p. (ISBN 0-451-09813-7, J9813, Sig). NAL.

Ziswiler, V. Extinct & Vanishing Animals: A Biology of Extinction & Survival. Bunnell, F. & Bunnell, P., trs. (Heidelberg Science Library: Vol. 2). 1967. pap. 6.50 o.p. (ISBN 0-387-90003-9). Springer-Verlag.

Zitko, Howard J. Tantra Yoga: The Sexual Gateway to Spiritual Fulfillment. pap. 7.95 (ISBN 0-686-43276-2). World Univ AZ.

--World University Insights: With Your Future in Mind. Orig. Title: New Age Perspectives in Questions & Answers. 208p. 1980. pap. 6.20 (ISBN 0-941902-01-3). World Univ AZ.

Zitlow, David R., jt. auth. see Stewart, James W.

Zitner, Rosalind & Hayden, Shelby M. Our Youngest Parents: A Study of the Use of Support Services by Adolescent Mothers. (Orig.). 1980. pap. text ed. 5.50 (ISBN 0-87868-179-5, YF-2). Child Welfare.

Zitner, Sheldon P., et al. Preface to Literary Analysis. 1964. pap. 9.95x (ISBN 0-673-05216-8). Scott F.

Zito, Mario. How to Avoid Pitfalls & Pratfalls in English. LC 79-3810. 1980. pap. text ed. 12.25 (ISBN 0-8191-0930-4). U Pr of Amer.

Zittel, K. A. Von see Von Zittel, K. A.

Zivin, Gail. The Development of Self-Regulation Through Private Speech. LC 78-27615. (Origins of Behavior Ser.). 1980. 36.95x (ISBN 0-471-98380-2, Pub by Wiley-Interscience). Wiley.

Zivojinovic, Dragan. The United States & Vatican Policies, 1914-1918. LC 78-52438. 1978. 17.50x (ISBN 0-87081-112-6). Colo Assoc.

Zlatkis, A., jt. auth. see Ettre, L. S.

Zlatkis, A., ed. Advances in Chromatography, 1974. (Proceedings). 1975. 85.00 (ISBN 0-444-41267-0). Elsevier.

--Advances in Chromatography, 1975. (Proceedings). 1976. 85.00 (ISBN 0-444-41382-0). Elsevier.

Zlatkis, Albert, et al. A Concise Introduction to Organic Chemistry. 624p. 1973. text ed. 29.95 (ISBN 0-07-072850-X, C). McGraw.

Zlatkovich, Charles T., jt. auth. see Welsch, Glenn A.

Zlobin, Vladimir. A Difficult Soul: Zinaida Gippius. Karlinsky, Simon, ed. (Documentary Studies in Modern Russian Poetry). 200p. 1980. 17.95x (ISBN 0-520-03867-3). U of Cal Pr.

Zlot, William, et al. Arithmetic. (Sourcebook of Fundamental Mathematics Ser.). 198p. 1973. 6.50 o.p. (ISBN 0-685-91065-2). Krieger.

Zlotin, R. I. & Khodashova, K. S., eds. The Role of Animals in Biological Cycling of Forest-Steppe Ecosystems. Lewus, William & Grant, W. E., trs. from Russian. LC 80-12228. 240p. 1980. 22.50 (ISBN 0-87933-377-4). Hutchinson Ross.

Zlotowitz, Bernard M., ed. see Segal, Abraham.

Zlutnik, Steven, jt. ed. see Katz, Roger C.

Zmud, Robert W. Information Systems In Organizations. 1983. text ed. 25.95x (ISBN 0-673-15438-6). Scott F.

Zmuda, Joseph. Analyze Handwriting Immediately. (Illus.). 108p. 1982. 28.00 (ISBN 0-941572-01-3). Z Graphic Pubns.

Znamensky, V. A., jt. ed. see Ferguson, H. L.

Znamerovskay, Tatyana. Titian. (Illus.). 1977. pap. 3.95 o.p. (ISBN 0-8109-2084-0). Abrams.

Znaniecki, Florian. Cultural Reality. (Sociological Classics Ser.). 404p. 1983. text ed. 14.95 (ISBN 0-88105-009-1); pap. text ed. 9.95 (ISBN 0-88105-010-5). Cap & Gown.

--Modern Nationalities. LC 72-7875. 196p. 1973. Repr. of 1952 ed. lib. bdg. 17.50x (ISBN 0-8371-6549-0, ZNMN). Greenwood.

Znosko-Borovsky, Eugene. Art of Chess Combination: A Guide for All Players of the Game. Sergeant, Philip W., tr. (Illus.). 1936. pap. 4.00 (ISBN 0-486-20583-5). Dover.

--How to Play the Chess Openings. 1971. pap. 2.25 (ISBN 0-486-22795-2). Dover.

Zobel, Hiller B. Boston Massacre. (Illus.). 1970. 8.50 o.s.i. (ISBN 0-393-05376-8); pap. 6.95 (ISBN 0-393-00606-9). Norton.

Zocchi, Giuseppe & Dee, Elaine E. Views of Florence & Tuscany 11. rev. ed. LC 68-59110. (Illus.). 1971. pap. 7.00 (ISBN 0-88397-070-8, Pub. by Intl Exhibit Foun). C E Tuttle.

Zoch, Barbara, ed. Harris Pennsylvania Marketers Industrial Directory 1982-1983. Segulin, Fran. (Illus.). 782p. 1982. 79.50 (ISBN 0-916512-44-4). Harris Pub.

Zodhiates, Joan, ed. see Miller, J. R.

Zodhiates, Joan, ed. see Morrison, George H.

Zodhiates, Spiros. Christianity: Not Just a Religion. (Illus.). 1977. pap. 3.95 (ISBN 0-89957-523-4). AMG Pubs.

--Conquering the Fear of Death. (I Corinthians). (Illus.). 1970. 12.95 o.s.i. (ISBN 0-89957-500-5). AMG Pubs.

--Conquering the Fear of Death. 2nd ed. 869p. 1982. pap. 12.95 (ISBN 0-89957-500-5). AMG Pubs.

--Conscience. LC 82-71843. 1982. pap. 4.95 (ISBN 0-89957-555-2). AMG Pubs.

--Did Jesus Teach Capitalism? LC 82-71267. (Illus.). 1982. pap. 3.50 (ISBN 0-89957-548-X). AMG Pubs.

--Formula for Happiness. LC 80-67974. 256p. (Orig.). 1980. pap. 6.25 (ISBN 0-89957-046-1). AMG Pubs.

--Jesus & the Demon World. LC 82-71842. 1982. pap. 4.95 (ISBN 0-89957-556-0). AMG Pubs.

--Life After Death!? Zodhiates, Spiros, tr. from Greek. Orig. Title: What Happens After Death? (Illus.). 1977. pap. 3.95 (ISBN 0-89957-525-0). AMG Pubs.

--The Perfect Gift. (Illus.). 1973. pap. 3.95 (ISBN 0-89957-511-0). AMG Pubs.

--The Pursuit of Happiness. 2nd ed. 665p. 1982. pap. 9.95 (ISBN 0-89957-508-0). AMG Pubs.

--The Song of the Virgin. LC 82-71643. (Illus.). 1974. pap. 2.25 (ISBN 0-89957-510-2). AMG Pubs.

--Trilogy. Vol. 1 The Patience of Hope. 5.95 ea.; Vol. 2 The Work of Faith. 5.95 ea.; Vol. 3 The Labor of Love. 5.95 ea.; Set. 14.95 (ISBN 0-89957-558-7). AMG Pubs.

--Why God Permits Accidents. LC 79-51340. 1982. pap. 2.25 (ISBN 0-89957-537-4). AMG Pubs.

--Why Pray? LC 82-71266. 1982. pap. 4.95 (ISBN 0-89957-554-4). AMG Pubs.

--You Can Be a Winner. LC 79-51339. 216p. 1982. pap. 5.95 (ISBN 0-89957-048-8). AMG Pubs.

Zodhiates, Spiros, ed. Learn or Review New Testament Greek: The Answer Book. 1977. pap. 3.95 (ISBN 0-89957-519-6). AMG Pubs.

Zoeller, Donald J. Using Technical & Economic Experts in Litigation: A Course Handbook. 302p. 1981. pap. 30.00 (ISBN 0-686-96161-7, H4-4860). PLI.

Zoerb, Alice A. My Life Memories. 1978. 12.95 (ISBN 0-9602888-0-5). Heritage Rec.

--Personal Records. (Orig.). 1979. pap. text ed. 4.95 (ISBN 0-9602888-1-3). Heritage Rec.

Zoete, Beryl De see Moravia, Alberto.

Zoeteman, B. C., jt. auth. see Van Lelyveld, H.

Zogner, Lothar. Bibliogaphia Cartographica, Vol. 4. 206p. 1977. pap. 20.00 (ISBN 3-7940-3474-0, Pub. by K G Saur). Shoe String.

--Bibliographia Cartographica, Vol. 1. pap. 20.00 (ISBN 3-7940-3471-6, Pub. by K G Saur). Shoe String.

--Bibliographia Cartographica, Vol. 2. 195p. 1975. pap. 20.00 (ISBN 3-7940-3472-4, Pub. by K G Saur). Shoe String.

--Bibliographia Cartographica, Vol. 3. 209p. 1976. pap. 20.00 (ISBN 3-7940-3473-2, Pub. by K G Saur). Shoe String.

--Bibliographia Cartographica, Vol. 5. xx, 212p. 1978. pap. 20.00 (ISBN 3-598-20619-4, Pub. by K G Saur). Shoe String.

--Bibliographia Cartographica, Vol. 6. xii, 255p. 1979. pap. 27.00 (ISBN 3-598-20620-8, Pub. by K G Saur). Shoe String.

--Bibliographia Cartographica, Vol. 7. 244p. 1980. pap. 27.00 (ISBN 3-598-20622-4, Pub. by K G Saur). Shoe String.

Zogner, Redaktion L., ed. Bibliographia Cartographica, Vol. 8. xii, 223p. 1983. 28.00 (ISBN 3-598-20624-0, Pub. by K G Saur). Shoe String.

Zograph, G. A. Languages of South Asia: A Descriptive Grammar. (The Languages of Asia & Africa Ser.: Vol. 3). (Illus.). 160p. (Orig.). 1982. pap. 20.00 (ISBN 0-7100-0914-3). Routledge & Kegan.

Zohar, Danah. Israel. LC 77-88352. (Countries Ser.). (Illus.). 1978. PLB 12.68 (ISBN 0-686-51152-2). Silver.

Zohary, Michael. Plants of the Bible. LC 82-4535. (Illus.). 224p. 1982. 16.95 (ISBN 0-521-24926-0). Cambridge U Pr.

Zohn, H., ed. Der Farbenvolle Untergang: Osterreichisches Lesebuck. 1971. pap. 9.50 o.p. (ISBN 0-13-199000-4). P-H.

Zohn, Harry, ed. & tr. see Weber, Marianne.

Zohn, Harry, ed. see Zweig, Friderike.

Zohn, Harry, tr. see Raeithel, Gert.

Zohn, Harry, tr. see Rattner, Joseph.

Zokeisha. Farm House. Klimo, Kate, ed. (Chubby Shape Bks.). (Illus.). 16p. 1983. 2.95 (ISBN 0-671-46130-3, Little). S&S.

--Firehouse. Klimo, Kate, ed. (Chubby Shape Bks.). (Illus.). 16p. (ps-k). 1983. 2.95 (ISBN 0-671-46128-1, Little). S&S.

--A Little Book of Baby Animals. Klimo, Kate, ed. (Chubby Board Bks). (Illus.). 16p. 1982. bds. 2.95 (ISBN 0-671-44840-4, Little Simon). S&S.

--A Little Book of Colors. Klimo, Kate, ed. (Chubby Board Bks.). (Illus.). 16p. 1982. bds. 2.95 (ISBN 0-671-45570-2, Little Simon). S&S.

--Mother Goose. Klimo, Kate, ed. (Chubby Shape Bks.). (Illus.). 16p. (ps-k). 1983. 2.95 (ISBN 0-671-46127-3, Little): S&S.

--Mousehouse. Klimo, Kate, ed. (Chubby Shape Bks.). (Illus.). 16p. 1983. 2.95 (ISBN 0-671-46129-X, Little). S&S.

Zola, Emile. Claude's Confession. Cox, George D., tr. from Fr. 1979. Repr. of 1882 ed. 19.50x (ISBN 0-86527-030-9). Fertig.

--Germinal. 1970. pap. 2.95 (ISBN 0-451-51577-3, CE1577, Sig Classics). NAL.

--Therese Raquin: T. V. Tie-in. 1981. pap. 3.50 (ISBN 0-14-005775-7). Penguin.

--Three Faces of Love. Gant, R., tr. LC 67-29442. 7.95 o.s.i. (ISBN 0-8149-0247-2). Vanguard.

--Zola. Bernard, Marc, ed. Leblon, Jean M., tr. (Illus.). 1977. Repr. of 1960 ed. lib. bdg. 19.75x (ISBN 0-8371-9820-8, BEZO). Greenwood.

Zola, Irving K. Missing Pieces: A Chronicle of Living with a Disability. 246p. 1982. pap. 14.95 (ISBN 0-87722-232-0); pap. write for info. (ISBN 0-87722-311-4). Temple U Pr.

--Socio-Medical Inquiries: Recollections, Reflections & Reconsiderations. 1983. write for info. (ISBN 0-87722-303-3). Temple U Pr.

Zola, Irving K., jt. auth. see Crewe, Nancy M.

Zola, Meguido. Gretzky! Gretzky! Gretzky! (Picture Life Ser.). (Illus.). 48p. (gr. k-3). 1983. PLB 7.90 (ISBN 0-531-04597-8). Watts.

--Karen Kain. (Picture Life Ser.). 48p. (gr. k-3). 1983. PLB 7.90 (ISBN 0-531-04598-6). Watts.

Zolar. Everything You Want to Know About Black Magic, Metaphysical Astrology, Mediumship, Crystal Gazing, Revelations by Zolar. LC 72-3136. (Zolar's Everything You Want to Know About Ser). 224p. 1972. pap. 1.50 o.p. (ISBN 0-668-02658-8). Arco.

Zolar, F., ed. The Encyclopedia of Ancient & Forbidden Knowledge. pap. 3.50 (ISBN 0-445-08449-9). Popular Lib.

Zolbrod, Leon M. Haiku Painting. LC 82-48792. (Great Japanese Art Ser.). (Illus.). 48p. 1983. 18.95 (ISBN 0-87011-560-X). Kodansha.

Zolbrod, Paul G., jt. ed. see Tobias, Richard C.

Zolina, R., tr. see Budyko, M. I.

Zoll, Max A. A Flamingo Is Born. LC 77-13761. (Illus.). (gr. k-3). 1978. 5.95 (ISBN 0-399-20632-9). Putnam Pub Group.

Zoller, Bob. Night of Fire, Days of Rain. LC 82-7491. (gr. 4-8). 1982. pap. 3.50 (ISBN 0-8307-0844-8, 5900008). Regal.

Zollers, Frances E. & Foreman, Gail H. Business Law: A Practical Approach. LC 76-44036. 1978. pap. text ed. 15.00 (ISBN 0-8273-1431-0); instructor's guide 4.25 (ISBN 0-8273-1432-9). Delmar.

Zollinger & Zollinger. Atlas of Surgical Operations. 1983. 78.00 (ISBN 0-02-431970-8). Macmillan.

Zollinger, H., jt. auth. see Rys, P.

Zollschan, G. K. & Hirsch, W. Social Change: Explorations, Diagnosis, & Conjectures. LC 75-8736. 1976. text ed. 22.50x o.s.i. (ISBN 0-470-98408-2); pap. text ed. 10.50 o.s.i. (ISBN 0-470-98409-0). Halsted Pr.

Zolna, Ed & Conklin, Mike. Mastering Softball. (Mastering Ser.). (Illus.). 1981. 12.95 (ISBN 0-8092-7184-2); pap. 6.95 (ISBN 0-8092-7183-4). Contemp Bks.

Zolo, Don. Legion of Roots. 180p. 1982. pap. 3.95 (ISBN 0-9608852-0-X). General Means.

Zolondek, Leon, ed. & tr. see Di'Bil b. 'Ali.

Zolotow, Charlotte. The Bunny Who Found Easter. (Illus.). 32p. (gr. k-3). 1983. pap. 3.95 (ISBN 0-395-34068-3). HM.

--Flocks of Birds. LC 81-43029. (Illus.). 32p. (ps-3). 1981. 7.64i (ISBN 0-690-04112-8, TYC-J); PLB 7.89g (ISBN 0-690-04113-6). Har-Row.

--If You Listen. LC 79-2688. (An Ursula Nordstrom Bk.). (Illus.). 32p. (ps-3). 1980. 8.95i (ISBN 0-06-027049-7, HarpJ); PLB 10.89 (ISBN 0-06-027050-0). Har-Row.

--Janey. LC 72-9861. (Illus.). 24p. (ps-3). 1973. 7.95 o.p. (ISBN 0-06-026927-8, HarpJ); PLB 9.89 (ISBN 0-06-026928-6). Har-Row.

--May I Visit? LC 75-25305. (Illus.). 32p. (ps-3). 1976. 8.61i (ISBN 0-06-026932-4, HarpJ); PLB 8.89 o.p. (ISBN 0-06-026933-2). Har-Row.

--One Step, Two... rev. ed. LC 80-11749. (Illus.). 32p. (gr. k-1). 1981. 8.95; PLB 8.59 (ISBN 0-686-82933-6). Lothrop.

--The Quarreling Book. LC 63-14445. (Illus.). (gr. k-3). 1963. 7.64i (ISBN 0-06-026975-8, HarpJ); PLB 7.89 (ISBN 0-06-026976-6). Har-Row.

--The Song. (ps-3). 1982. 9.50 (ISBN 0-688-00618-3); PLB 8.59 (ISBN 0-688-00817-8). Greenwillow.

--Summer Is... LC 82-45185. (Illus.). 32p. (gr. k-4). 1983. 9.57i (ISBN 0-690-04303-1, TYC-J); PLB 9.89g (ISBN 0-690-04304-X). Har-Row.

--Three Funny Friends. LC 61-5779. (Illus.). (ps-1). 1961. PLB 8.89 (ISBN 0-06-027040-3, HarpJ). Har-Row.

--When I Have a Little Girl. LC 65-24656. (Illus.). (gr. k-3). 1965. 5.72i (ISBN 0-06-027045-4, HarpJ); PLB 7.89 (ISBN 0-06-027046-2). Har-Row.

--When I Have a Son. LC 67-14072. (Illus.). (gr. k-3). 1967. PLB 9.89 (ISBN 0-06-027044-6, HarpJ). Har-Row.

--When the Wind Stops. LC 75-2635. (Illus.). 32p. (ps-3). 1975. 9.57i o.p. (ISBN 0-06-026971-5, HarpJ); PLB 9.89 o.p. (ISBN 0-06-026972-3). Har-Row.

Zolotow, Maurice. Billy Wilder in Hollywood. LC 77-75684. (Illus.). 1977. 10.00 o.p. (ISBN 0-399-11789-X). Putnam Pub Group.

--Confessions of a Racetrack Fiend: Or, How to Pick the Six, & My Other Secrets for the Weekend Horseplayer. 180p. 1983. 10.95 (ISBN 0-312-16220-0). St Martin.

Zoltan, J. Cicatrix Optima. 232p. 1977. text ed. 59.50 (ISBN 0-8391-0815-X). Univ Park.

Zoltners, A. A. Marketing Planning Models. (TIMS Studies in the Management Sciences: Vol. 18). 1982. 55.50 (ISBN 0-444-86369-9, North Holland). Elsevier.

Zombeck, Martin V. Handbook of Space Astronomy & Astrophysics. LC 82-12944. (Illus.). 341p. 1983. 24.95 (ISBN 0-521-24194-4). Cambridge U Pr.

Zondag-Hamaker, Karen. Astro-Psychology. 1980. pap. 8.95 o.p. (ISBN 0-87728-465-2). Weiser.

Zondergeld, Rein, jt. auth. see Krichbaum, Jorg.

Zong, In-sob. A Guide to Korean Literature. LC 82-84416. 296p. 1983. 20.00 (ISBN 0-930878-29-9). Hollym Intl.

Zong, In Sob, ed. Folk Tales from Korea. 3rd. ed. LC 82-82600. 257p. 1979. Repr. 16.80 (ISBN 0-930878-26-4). Hollym Intl.

Zong In-Sob, et al. The Beast-Tales Told in Northeastern Asia. (Asian Folklore & Social Life Monographs: Vol. 103). 1981. 14.00 (ISBN 0-89986-334-5). Oriental Bk Store.

Zonneveld, Wim. A Formal Theory of Exceptions in Generative Phonology. (Illus.). 1978. pap. text ed. 23.00x o.p. (ISBN 0-686-86091-8). Humanities.

Zook, Ardith. Captain Gaius Sees a Miracle. 1980. pap. 0.89 (ISBN 0-570-06133-4, 59-1251, Arch Bk). Concordia.

Zook, Elvin G., ed. The Primary Care of Facial Injuries. LC 79-16117. (Illus.). 184p. 1980. text ed. 25.50 (ISBN 0-88416-205-2). Wright-PSG.

Zook, Mary. Leider in der Nacht. (Ger.). pap. 3.15 (ISBN 0-686-32327-0). Rod & Staff.

Zook, Mary R. The Choice Is Yours. 1976. 6.30 (ISBN 0-686-18181-6). Rod & Staff.

--The Fisherman's Daughter. 1977. 4.40 (ISBN 0-686-20046-2). Rod & Staff.

--Little Missionaries. 184p. 1979. 6.15 (ISBN 0-686-30764-X). Rod & Staff.

--Price of Peace & Other Stories. 1975. 7.15 (ISBN 0-686-11148-6). Rod & Staff.

Zook, Wayne H. Constructing & Manufacturing Wood Products. (Illus.). 434p. (gr. 9-12). 1974. 19.96 (ISBN 0-87345-048-5). McKnight.

Zoological Society of London - 29th Symposium. Conservation & Productivity of Natural Waters. Edwards, R. W. & Garrod, D. J., eds. 1972. 51.50 (ISBN 0-12-613329-8). Acad Pr.

Zopf, Paul E., Jr. Cultural Accumulation in Latin America. LC 79-48091. 393p. 1980. text ed. 23.00 (ISBN 0-8191-1012-4); pap. text ed. 14.75 (ISBN 0-8191-1013-2). U Pr of Amer.

Zorab, P. A. Scoliosis & Muscle. (Clinics in Developmental Medicine Ser., Research Monographs: Vol. 4A). 220p. 1974. 26.00 o.p. (ISBN 0-685-59047-X). Lippincott.

Zorback, W. Werner & Tipson, R. Stuart, eds. Synthetic Procedures in Nucleic Acid Chemistry: Vol. 1. 570p. (Orig.). 1968. 31.00 (ISBN 0-470-98415-5). Krieger.

Zorkoczy, Peter. Information Technology: An Introduction. LC 82-10115. (Illus.). 137p. 1983. 29.95 (ISBN 0-86729-037-4). Knowledge Indus.

Zorn, Fritz. Mars. 1981. 12.95 (ISBN 0-394-51755-5). Knopf.

Zornig, Harold F., jt. auth. see Anderson, L. O.

Zornow, William F. Lincoln & the Party Divided. LC 73-152619. 264p. 1972. Repr. of 1954 ed. lib. bdg. 18.75x (ISBN 0-8371-6054-5, ZOLP). Greenwood.

Zorski, H. Trends in Appplications of Pure Mathematics to Mechanics, Vol. 2. (Monographs & Studies: No. 5). 341p. 1979. text ed. 65.95 (ISBN 0-273-08421-6). Pitman Pub MA.

Zorski, H., ed. Trends in Applications of Pure Mathematics to Mechanics, Vol. II. new ed. (Monographs & Studies in Mathematics: No. 5). (Illus.). 1979. cancelled o.p. (ISBN 0-8224-8421-8). Pitman Pub MA.

Zorzoli, Ruben O., tr. see Narramore, Clyde M.

Zoschenko, Mikhail. Lyudi. Blair, H. & Greene, M., eds. (Rus.). text ed. 13.95 (ISBN 0-521-06895-9). Cambridge U Pr.

Zoshchenko, Mikhail. Rasskazy Nazara Il'icha, Gospodina Sinebriukhova. 89p. (Russian.). 1982. pap. 3.50 (ISBN 0-933884-33-8). Berkeley Slavic.

--Scenes from the Bathhouse: And Other Stories of Communist Russia. Monas, Sidney, tr. 1961. pap. 5.95 (ISBN 0-472-06070-8, 70, AA). U of Mich Pr.

Zoshchenko, Mikhail M. Rasskazy Nazara Il'icha, Gospodina Sinebriukhova. (Rus.). 1978. pap. 3.00 o.p. (ISBN 0-933884-02-8). Berkeley Slavic.

Zoss, Leslie M. Applied Instrumentation in Process Industries: Control Systems: Theory, Troubleshooting & Design, Vol. 4. 174p. 1979. 43.95x (ISBN 0-87201-391-X). Gulf Pub.

Zotos, John. Mathematical Models of the Chemical, Physical & Mathematical Properties of Engineering Alloys. LC 76-22228. 448p. 1977. 29.95 o.p. (ISBN 0-669-00884-2). Lexington Bks.

Zotter, Josefa, ed. Cortina-Grosset Basic German Dictionary. 1977. pap. 2.95 (ISBN 0-448-14029-2, G&D). Putnam Pub Group.

Zotterman, Yngve, ed. Olfaction & Taste. (Vol. 1). 1963. text ed. inquire for price o.p. (ISBN 0-08-009814-2). Pergamon.

Zottoli, Robert, jt. auth. see McConnaughey, Bayard H.

Zottoli, Robert A. Introduction to Marine Environments. 2nd ed. LC 78-6938. 252p. 1978. pap. text ed. 12.50 (ISBN 0-8016-5694-X). Mosby.

Zoubek, C., jt. auth. see Leslie, L. Et Al.

Zoubek, C. E., jt. auth. see Leslie, L. A.

Zoubek, Charles E. Gregg Expert Speed Building. (Diamond Jubilee Ser.). 1968. text ed. 22.00 (ISBN 0-07-073050-4, G); instructor's handbk. 5.75 (ISBN 0-07-073053-9); student transcript 7.50 (ISBN 0-07-073051-2). McGraw.

--Progressive Dictation with Previews. 1956. text ed. 18.00 (ISBN 0-07-073032-6, G). McGraw.

--Short Business Letters for Dictation & Transcription. (Diamond Jubilee Ser.). 1970. text ed. 16.00 (ISBN 0-07-073075-X, G). McGraw.

--Speed Dictation with Previews in Gregg Shorthand. (Diamond Jubilee Ser.). 1963. text ed. 17.60 (ISBN 0-07-073041-5, G). McGraw.

Zoubek, Charles E. & Rifkin, Morris W. Gregg Reporting Shortcuts. 2nd ed. 1959. 25.00 (ISBN 0-07-073040-7, G). McGraw.

Zoubek, Charles E., jt. auth. see Leslie, Louis A.

Zoutendijk, G. Mathematical Programming Methods. 1976. 64.50 (ISBN 0-7204-0421-5, North-Holland). Elsevier.

Zouwen, J. van der, jt. ed. see Geyer, R. F.

Zozayang. Diamond Mountain, 2 vols. (Emille Museum Folk Art Ser.). (Illus.). 1975. Vol. 1. pap. 20.00 set (ISBN 0-89581-225-8). Vol. 2. Lancaster-Miller.

Zozzora, Frank. Engineering Drawing Problems. 2nd ed. 1958. text ed. 11.95 o.p. (ISBN 0-07-073407-0, C). McGraw.

Zrenner, E. Neurophysiological Aspects of Color Vision in Primates. (Studies of Brain Function: Vol. 9). (Illus.). 218p. 1983. 37.00 (ISBN 0-387-11653-2). Springer-Verlag.

Zsilka, Janos. System of the Hungarian Sentence Patterns. (Uralic & Altaic Ser: Vol. 67). 1967. pap. text ed. 7.00x o.p. (ISBN 0-87750-023-1). Res Ctr Lang Semiotic.

Zuanich, Margaret A., jt. auth. see Lipscomb, Susan D.

Zubay, Geoffrey. Biochemistry. (Chemistry Ser.). (Illus.). 1100p. 1983. text ed. 40.00 (ISBN 0-201-09091-0); Solutions Guide avail.; Overhead Transparencies avail. (ISBN 0-201-09093-7). A-W.

Zubieta, Jon, jt. ed. see Karlin, Kenneth D.

Zubini, Fabio, jt. auth. see Arnould, Michel.

Zubiri, Xavier. Nature, History, God. Fowler, Thomas B., Jr., tr. from Span. LC 80-1355. 441p. 1981. lib. bdg. 26.25 (ISBN 0-8191-1530-4); pap. text ed. 15.50 (ISBN 0-8191-1531-2). U Pr of Amer.

Zubrzycki, Stefan. Lectures in Probability Theory & Mathematical Statistics. 1973. 22.95 (ISBN 0-444-00120-4, North Holland). Elsevier.

Zucchero. Rental Homes: The Tax Shelter that Works & Grows for You. 1983. text ed. 13.95 (ISBN 0-8359-6644-5). Reston.

Zucconi, Paul J. Generally Accepted Accounting Principles for Life Insurance Companies. Crane, John R., ed. (FLMI Insurance Education Program Ser.). 28p. 1982. pap. text ed. 3.00 (ISBN 0-915322-51-X). LOMA.

Zuck, Lowell H., ed. Christianity & Revolution: Radical Christian Testimonies, 1520-1650. LC 74-25355. (Documents in Free Church History Ser.: No. 2). 324p. 1975. 29.95 (ISBN 0-87722-040-9); pap. 12.95 (ISBN 0-87722-044-1). Temple U Pr.

Zuck, Roy. Job. (Everyman's Bible Commentary Ser.). 1978. pap. 4.50 (ISBN 0-8024-2017-6). Moody.

Zuck, Roy B. & Clark, Robert. Childhood Education in the Church. LC 74-15350. (Illus.). 500p. 1975. 13.95 (ISBN 0-8024-1249-1). Moody.

Zuck, Roy B., jt. auth. see Walvoord, John F.

Zuck, Roy B. & Benson, Warren, eds. Youth Education in the Church. 1978. text ed. 17.95 (ISBN 0-8024-9841-8). Moody.

Zucker, C., jt. auth. see Kushner, M.

Zucker, Ernest. Standard Gold & Silver: The Way Out of the Crisis. 1958. pap. 5.00 (ISBN 0-527-99980-6). Kraus Repr.

Zucker, F. J., jt. auth. see Collin, Robert E.

Zucker, Jeff & Hummel, Kay. Oregon Indians: Culture, History & Current Affairs; an Atlas & Introduction. (Illus.). 192p. (Orig.). 1983. write for info. (ISBN 0-87595-094-9, Western Imprints); pap. write for info. (ISBN 0-87595-109-0, Western Imprints). Oreg Hist Soc.

Zucker, Judi & Zucker, Shari. How to Eat Without Meat: Naturally. LC 81-11424. (Illus.). 128p. (Orig.). 1981. pap. 4.95 (ISBN 0-912800-97-6). Woodbridge Pr.

Zucker, Judi, jt. auth. see Zucker, Shari.

Zucker, M., jt. auth. see Belfield, W. O.

Zucker, Martin, jt. auth. see Belfield, Wendel.

Zucker, Martin, jt. auth. see Belfield, Wendel Q.

Zucker, Norman L. The Coming Crisis in Israel: Private Faith & Public Policy. 1973. 20.00x (ISBN 0-262-24018-1); pap. 5.95 (ISBN 0-262-74012-5). MIT Pr.

Zucker, Shari & Zucker, Judi. How to Survive Snack Attacks--Naturally. LC 79-12781. (Illus., Orig.). 1979. pap. 4.95 (ISBN 0-912800-63-1). Woodbridge Pr.

Zucker, Shari, jt. auth. see Zucker, Judi.

Zucker, Stanley. Ludwig Bamberger: German Liberal Politician & Social Critic,1823-1899. LC 74-17839. 1975. 16.95 o.p. (ISBN 0-8229-3298-9). U of Pittsburgh Pr.

Zuckerman, et al. A New System of Anatomy: Being a Dissector's Guide & Atlas. 2nd ed. (Illus.). 1981. 65.00x (ISBN 0-19-263137-3); pap. 37.50x (ISBN 0-19-263136-5). Oxford U Pr.

Zuckerman, A. Decade of Viral Hepatitis. 1980. 50.75 (ISBN 0-444-80190-1). Elsevier.

--Dynamic Aspects of Host-Parasite Relationships, Vol. 2. LC 70-189940. 225p. 1975. 35.00 (ISBN 0-470-98430-9). Krieger.

Zuckerman, A., ed. Dynamic Aspects of Host-Parasite Relationships, Vol. 2. LC 70-189940. 225p. 1976. 49.95 o.s.i. (ISBN 0-470-98430-9). Halsted Pr.

Zuckerman, A. J. Virus Diseases of the Liver. 1970. 15.95 o.p. (ISBN 0-407-43700-2). Butterworth.

Zuckerman, Anita Stiefel. Just Like In the Movies. 380p. 1983. 14.95 (ISBN 0-937858-22-6). Newmarket.

Zuckerman, B. M., et al, eds. Plant Parasitic Nematodes: Morphology, Anatomy, Taxonomy, & Ecology, Vols. 1 & 2. 1971. Vol. 1. 58.00 (ISBN 0-12-782201-1); Vol. 2. 54.50 (ISBN 0-12-782202-X); Set. 94.00 (ISBN 0-686-96642-2). Acad Pr.

Zuckerman, Bert M. & Rohde, Richard A. Plant Parasitic Nematodes, Vol. 3. LC 78-127710. 1981. 65.00 o.p. (ISBN 0-12-782403-0). Acad Pr.

Zuckerman, Herbert S., jt. auth. see Niven, Ivan.

Zuckerman, Lord, ed. see Publications Department Staff.

Zuckerman, M. M. Algebra & Trigonometry: A Straightforward Approach. 595p. 1981. text ed. 24.95 (ISBN 0-471-09392-0). Wiley.

--Intermediate Algebra: A Straightforward Approach for College Students. 666p. 1981. text ed. 20.95x o.p. (ISBN 0-471-09388-2). Wiley.

--Intermediate Algebra: A Straightforward Approach for College Students. alternate ed. 398p. 1981. text ed. 24.95 (ISBN 0-471-09385-8). Wiley.

--Intermediate Algebra: A Straightforward Approach. 2nd ed. 493p. 1982. text ed. 22.95 (ISBN 0-471-09731-4); sampler 6.50 (ISBN 0-471-87676-3). Wiley.

--Workbook to Accompany Intermediate Algebra: A Straightforward Approach for College Students. 369p. 1981. pap. text ed. 9.95 wkbk o.p. (ISBN 0-471-09386-6). Wiley.

Zuckerman, Marvin, ed. Biological Bases for Sensation Seeking, Impulsivity & Anxiety. 320p. 1983. text ed. write for info. (ISBN 0-89859-255-0). L Erlbaum Assocs.

Zuckerman, Marvin S. Words, Words, Words: An English Vocabulary Builder & Anthology. LC 73-7372. (Illus.). 384p. 1974. pap. text ed. 7.95x o.p. (ISBN 0-02-479980-7). Glencoe.

Zuckerman, Michael. Peaceable Kingdoms: New England Towns in the Eighteenth Century. LC 82-18365. ix, 329p. 1983. Repr. of 1970 ed. lib. bdg. 39.75x (ISBN 0-313-22634-2, ZUPK). Greenwood.

Zuckerman, Michael, ed. Friends & Neighbors: Group Life in America's First Plural Society. 255p. 1982. 29.95 (ISBN 0-87722-253-3). Temple U Pr.

Zuckerman, Solly. Nuclear Illusion & Reality. LC 82-40419. 160p. 1983. pap. 2.95 (ISBN 0-394-71363-X, Vin). Random.

Zuckerman, Solly, ed. Ovary. 2nd ed. Incl. Vol. 1. General Aspects. 1977. 61.00 (ISBN 0-12-782601-7); Vol. 2. Physiology. 1977. 65.00 (ISBN 0-12-782602-5); Vol. 3. Regulation of Oogenesis & Sleriodogenesis. 1978. 51.00, subscription 168.50 (ISBN 0-12-782603-3). 1977. Acad Pr.

Zuckman, Harvey L. & Gaynes, Martin J. Mass Communications in a Nutshell. 2nd ed. LC 82-20029. 473p. 1982. pap. text ed. 6.95 (ISBN 0-314-69869-8). West Pub.

Zuckmayer, Carl, jt. auth. see Barth, Karl.

Zucrow, Maurice J. & Hoffman, Joe D. Gas Dynamics, 2 vols. LC 76-6855. 768p. Vol. 1. text ed. 59.95 (ISBN 0-471-98440-X); Vol. 2. text ed. 53.50x (ISBN 0-471-01806-6). Wiley.

Zuelzer, Wolf. The Nicolai Case: A Biography. LC 82-1990. (Illus.). 473p. 1982. 30.00X (ISBN 0-8143-1701-4). Wayne St U Pr.

Zuesse, Eric, ed. Bargain Finder: The Encyclopedic Money Saving Guide to New York City, for Residents & Tourists. 352p. 1983. pap. 4.95 (ISBN 0-9608950-0-0). Consumers All.

Zuesse, Evan M. Ritual Cosmos: The Sanctification of Life in African Religions. LC 79-13454. x, 256p. 1980. 19.95x (ISBN 0-8214-0398-2, 82-82907). Ohio U Pr.

Zuev, V. E. & Naats, I. E. Inverse Problems of Lidar Sensing of the Atmosphere. (Springer Ser. in Optical Sciences: Vol. 29). (Illus.). 260p. 1983. 41.00 (ISBN 0-387-10913-7). Springer-Verlag.

Zuev, V. E., jt. ed. see Fymat, A. L.

Zug, John, jt. auth. see Liffring-Zug, Joan.

Zuidema, G. D. & Skinner, D. B., eds. Current Topics in Surgical Research. Incl. Vol. 1. 1969 (ISBN 0-12-153601-7); Vol. 2. 1970 (ISBN 0-12-153602-5); Vol. 3. Skinner, D. B. & Ebert, Paul A., eds. 1971. 58.50 (ISBN 0-12-153603-3). 63.00 ea. Acad Pr.

Zuidema, George D., jt. auth. see Shackelford, Richard T.

Zuidema, George D., jt. auth. see Shackleford, Richard T.

Zuidema, George D., jt. ed. see Judge, Richard D.

Zuidema, George D., jt. auth. see Judge, Richard D.

Zuk, Gerald H. & Boszormenyi-Nagy, Ivan, eds. Family Therapy & Disturbed Families. LC 66-28684. (Orig.). 1967. pap. 6.95x o.p. (ISBN 0-8314-0012-9). Sci & Behavior.

Zukas, Jonas A., et al. Impact Dynamics. LC 81-11683. 452p. 1982. 47.50x (ISBN 0-471-08677-0, Pub. by Wiley-Interscience). Wiley.

Zukav, Gary. The Dancing Wu Li Masters: An Overview of the New Physics. LC 78-25827. (Illus.). 1979. 14.95 (ISBN 0-688-03402-0); pap. 6.95 (ISBN 0-688-08402-8). Morrow.

Zuker, Joel S. Arthur Penn: A Guide to Reference & Resources. 1979. lib. bdg. 24.00 (ISBN 0-8161-8116-0, Hall Reference). G K Hall.

Zuker, R. Fred & Hegener, Karen C. Peterson's Guide to College Admissions: Getting into the College of Your Choice. 3rd. Ed. ed. 310p. 1983. pap. 9.95 (ISBN 0-87866-224-3, 2243). Peterson's Guides.

Zukerman, Erva. Child Welfare. 224p. 1982. text ed. 17.95 (ISBN 0-02-935900-7). Free Pr.

Zukerman, Eugenia. Deceptive Cadence. LC 80-15021. 276p. 1980. 11.95 (ISBN 0-670-26236-6). Viking Pr.

Zukin, Jane. Milk-Free Diet Cookbook: Cooking for the Lactose Intolerant. LC 81-8569. 155p. 1982. 12.95 (ISBN 0-8069-5566-X); lib. bdg. 15.69 (ISBN 0-8069-5567-8); pap. 6.95 (ISBN 0-8069-7544-X). Sterling.

Zukin, S. Beyond Marx & Tito. LC 74-12978. (Illus.). 272p. 1975. 37.50 (ISBN 0-521-20630-8). Cambridge U Pr.

Zukofsky, Louis. Prepositions: The Collected Critical Essays of Louis Zukofsky. 200p. 1981. 19.95x (ISBN 0-520-03224-1); pap. 5.95 (ISBN 0-520-04361-8, CAL 500). U of Cal Pr.

--A Test of Poetry. 1981. 12.95 (ISBN 0-393-01446-0, Pub. C Z Pubns); pap. 6.95 (ISBN 0-393-00050-8). Norton.

Zukowsky, John. The Plan of Chicago: 1909-1979. LC 79-55997. (Illus.). 52p. (Orig.). 1979. pap. 4.95 (ISBN 0-86559-039-7). Art Inst Chi.

Zukowsky, John & Draper, Joan E. Edward H. Bennett: Architect & City Planner, 1874-1954. LC 82-71084. (Illus.). 64p. (Orig.). 1982. pap. 10.95 (ISBN 0-86559-048-6). Art Inst Chi.

Zukowsky, John, et al. Chicago Architects Design: A Century of Architectural Drawings from the Art Institute of Chicago. LC 82-60339. (Illus.). 192p. 1982. pap. 25.00 (ISBN 0-8478-0466-6). Rizzoli Intl.

Zulch, K. J. Histological Typing of Tumors of the Central Nervous System. (World Health Organization International Histological Classification Tumors Ser.). (Illus.). 66p. 1979. text ed. 34.00 (ISBN 0-89189-131-5, 70-1-021-20, Pub. by World Health Switzerland); incl. slides 143.50 (ISBN 92-4-176021-4, 70-1-021-00, Pub. by World Health Switzerland). Am Soc Clinical.

Zulker, Judi & Zulker, Shari. How to Eat Without Meat. 1981. 3.95x (ISBN 0-912800-96-8). Cancer Control Soc.

Zulker, Shari, jt. auth. see Zulker, Judi.

Zullig, Monika, jt. auth. see Brang, Peter.

Zuman, P. Elucidation of Organic Electrode Processes. (Current Chemical Concepts Ser.). 1969. 36.50 (ISBN 0-12-782750-1). Acad Pr.

Zuman, Petr, jt. auth. see Meites, Louis.

Zumberge, James H. & Nelson, Clemens A. Elements of Physical Geology. LC 75-26843. 432p. 1976. text ed. 25.95x (ISBN 0-471-98674-7). Wiley.

Zumberge, James H. & Rutford, Robert H. Laboratory Manual for Physical Geology. 6th ed. 185p. 1983. write for info. wire coil (ISBN 0-697-05043-2); instrs.' manual avail. (ISBN 0-697-05045-9). Wm C Brown.

Zumbuhl, H. J. The Fluctuations of the Grindenwald Glaciers in the Written & Illustrated Sources of the 12th to 19th Centuries. 278p. 1980. text ed. 67.10x (ISBN 3-7643-1199-1). Birkhauser.

Zumchak, Eugene. Microcomputer Design & Troubleshooting. Date not set. pap. 17.95 (ISBN 0-672-21819-4). Sams.

Zum-Gahr, K. H., jt. ed. see Hornbogen, E.

Zumwalt, Eva. Love's Sweet Charity. LC 81-43537. (Starlight Romance Ser.). 192p. 1982. 11.95 (ISBN 0-385-17866-2). Doubleday.

Zumwatt, L. R., jt. ed. see Simnad, M. T.

Zunde, Pranas, ed. see ASIS Annual Meeting, 37th.

Zundell, George. Hydration & Intermolecular Interaction: Infrared Investigations with Polyelectrolyte Membranes. 1970. 59.50. Acad Pr.

Zunder, William. The Poetry of John Donne: Literature & Culture in the Elizabethan & Jacobean Period. LC 82-8764. 132p. 1982. text ed. 24.50x (ISBN 0-389-20292-4). B&N Imports.

Zuniga-Martinez, Maria, jt. auth. see Lum, Doman.

Zunkel, Charles & Zunkel, Cleda. Turn Again to Life. new ed. LC 74-11107. 144p. 1974. 4.95 o.p. (ISBN 0-87178-881-0). Brethren.

Zunkel, Cleda, jt. auth. see Zunkel, Charles.

Zunker, Vernon G. Career Counseling. LC 80-23030. 357p. 1980. text ed. 19.95 (ISBN 0-8185-0428-5). Brooks-Cole.

Zunz, Olivier. The Changing Face of Inequality: Urbanization, Industrial Development, & Immigrants in Detroit, 1880 to 1920. LC 82-6986. (Illus.). 496p. 1983. lib. bdg. 43.00x (ISBN 0-226-99457-0). U of Chicago Pr.

Zupan, J. Clustering of Large Data Sets. (Chemometrics Research Studies). 122p. 1982. text ed. 31.95x (ISBN 0-471-10455-8, Pub. by Res Stud Pr). Wiley.

Zupan, Jeffrey M, jt. auth. see Pushkarev, Boris S.

Zuper, Bernie, jt. auth. see Andrews, Bart.

Zupnich. Pieter Brugel. (Color Slide Program of the Great Masters). 1970. 17.95 (ISBN 0-07-073587-5, P&RB). McGraw.

Zuraw, Robert A., jt. auth. see Lewanski, Robert T.

Zurbuchen, Mary S. Introduction to Old Javanese Language and Literature: A Kawi Prose Anthology. LC 76-16235. (Michigan Papers in South & Southeast Asian Languages & Linguistics: No. 3). xii, 150p. 1976. pap. 7.00x (ISBN 0-89148-053-6). Ctr S&SE Asian.

Zurcher, Arnold. Constitutions & Constitutional Trends Since World War Two. 2nd ed. LC 75-23266. 357p. 1975. Repr. of 1955 ed. lib. bdg. 20.75x (ISBN 0-8371-8351-0, ZUCT). Greenwood.

Zurcher, Arnold J. The Struggle to Unite Europe: 1940-1958. LC 75-23454. 254p. 1975. Repr. of 1958 ed. lib. bdg. 17.50x (ISBN 0-8371-8322-7, ZUSU). Greenwood.

Zurcher, Arnold J. & Dustan, Jane. The Foundation Administrator: A Study of Those Who Manage America's Foundations. LC 73-188395. 172p. 1972. 10.75x (ISBN 0-87154-996-4). Russell Sage.

Zurcher, Arnold J., jt. auth. see Sloan, Harold S.

Zurcher, Arnold J., jt. auth. see Smith, Edward C.

Zuredjian, George Z., ed. see Boyce, Jefferson C.

Zureik, E., jt. auth. see Nakhleh, K.

Zurflieh, Thomas. Basic Technical Mathematics Explained. (Illus.). 640p. 1974. text ed. 23.95 (ISBN 0-07-073595-6, G); inst. guide & answer key 4.00 (ISBN 0-07-073599-9). McGraw.

Zurier, Rebecca. The American Firehouse: An Architectural & Social History. LC 82-73304. (Illus.). 288p. 1982. 29.95 (ISBN 0-89659-314-2). Abbeville Pr.

Zur Linden, Wilhelm see Linden, Wilhelm Zur.

Zusi, Richard L. Structural Adaptations of the Head & Neck in the Black Skimmer Rynchops Nigra Linnaeus. (Illus.). 101p. 1962. 5.00 (ISBN 0-686-35789-2). Nuttall Ornithological.

Zusne, Leonard. Names in the History of Psychology: A Biographical Sourcebook. LC 74-26643. 1975. 17.95x o.s.i. (ISBN 0-470-98676-X). Halsted Pr.

Zuspan, jt. auth. see Symonds.

Zuspan, Frederick P. & Quilligan, Edward J. Practical Manual of Obstetric Care: A Pocket Reference for Those Who Treat the Pregnant Patient. LC 81-14050. (Illus.). 414p. 1982. pap. text ed. 13.95 (ISBN 0-8016-4064-4). Mosby.

Zusy, Mary J., jt. auth. see Raffensperger, Ellen.

Zuurdeeg, Atie D. Narrative Techniques & Their Effects in la Morte le Roi Artu. 12.00 (ISBN 0-917786-19-X). French Lit.

Zuvekas, Clarence, Jr., jt. auth. see Luzuriaga, Carlos.

Zuwaylif, Fadil H. Applied Business Statistics. 1974. text ed. 23.95 (ISBN 0-201-08906-8). A-W.

--General Applied Statistics. 3rd ed. LC 78-67937. 1979. text ed. 20.95 (ISBN 0-201-08994-7); solutions manual 14.95. A-W.

Zuwaylif, Fadil H., et al. Management Science: An Introduction. LC 78-5827. (Management & Administration Ser.). 1979. text ed. 34.95 (ISBN 0-471-98675-5); 6.00x o.p. sol. manual (ISBN 0-471-03222-0). Wiley.

Zuylan, Guirne Van see Van Zuylan, Guirne.

Zuylen, Guirne Van see Van Zuylen, Guirne.

Zverev, Anatol I. Handbook of Filter Synthesis. 1967. 64.95x (ISBN 0-471-98680-1, Pub. by Wiley-Interscience). Wiley.

Zverev, Anatol I., jt. auth. see Blinchikoff, Herman J.

Zvesper, J. Political Philosophy & Rhetoric. LC 76-11097. (Cambridge Studies in the History & Theory of Politics Ser.). 1977. 32.50 (ISBN 0-521-21323-1). Cambridge U Pr.

Zvi Hashin, Tel-Aviv University, Tel-Aviv, Israel & Carl T. Herakovich, Virginia Polytechnic Institute & State University, Blacksburg, Virginia USA, ed. Mechanics of Composite Materials: Recent Advances. Proceedings of the International Union of Theoretical & Applied Mechanics Symposium, August 16-19, 1982, Blacksburg, Virginia, USA. (Illus.). 450p. 1983. 75.01 (ISBN 0-08-029384-0, A145). Pergamon.

Zvorykin. The Firebird & Other Russian Fairy Tales. (Illus.). 1978. 16.95 (ISBN 0-670-31544-3, Studio). Viking Pr.

Zvorykin, A. A., et al. Cultural Policy in the Union of Soviet Socialist Republics. (Studies & Documents on Social Policies). 68p. 1970. pap. 5.00 (ISBN 92-3-100849-8, U751, UNESCO). Unipub.

Zwaga, Harm, jt. auth. see Easterby, Ronald.

Zwanenberg, R. M. van & King, Anne. An Economic History of Kenya & Uganda 1800-1970. new ed. (Illus.). 256p. 1975. text ed. 25.00x o.p. (ISBN 0-391-00400-X). Humanities.

Zwar, Desmond. New Frontiers of Medical Research: The Drama of Discovering Tomorrow's Cures. LC 80-6168. 300p. 1983. 19.95 (ISBN 0-8128-2807-0). Stein & Day.

Zwass, Adam. Monetary Cooperation Between East & West. LC 73-92368. 248p. 1975. 22.50 (ISBN 0-87332-057-3). M E Sharpe.

Zwass, Vladimir. Introduction to Computer Sciences. (Illus.). 256p. (Orig.). 1980. pap. 5.50 (ISBN 0-06-460193-5, CO 193, COS). B&N NY.

--Programming in FORTRAN. 224p. 1980. pap. 5.29i (ISBN 0-06-460194-3, CO 194, COS). B&N NY.

Zweck, Dina Von see VonZweck, Dina.

Zweibach, B. Civility & Disobedience. LC 74-12977. 256p. 1975. 27.95 (ISBN 0-521-20711-8). Cambridge U Pr.

Zweibel, Joel B. Creditors: Rights Handbook. 1982. pap. 27.50 (ISBN 0-87632-317-4). Boardman.

Zweifach, Benjamin W., et al, eds. The Inflammatory Process. Vol. 1. 2nd ed. 1974. 83.50 (ISBN 0-12-783401-X); Vol. 2. 64.00 (ISBN 0-12-783402-8); Vol. 3. 67.00 (ISBN 0-12-783403-6); Set. 152.50 (ISBN 0-685-48732-6). Acad Pr.

Zweifel, Frances W. Handbook of Biological Illustration. LC 61-19734. (Orig.). 1961. pap. 5.50x (ISBN 0-226-99699-9, Phoen). U of Chicago Pr.

Zweig. Novellen. (Easy Reader, C). pap. 3.95 (ISBN 0-88436-042-3, 45273). EMC.

Zweig, Ferdynand. The Student in the Age of Anxiety. LC 77-1136. 1977. Repr. of 1964 ed. lib. bdg. 20.50x (ISBN 0-8371-9519-5, ZWST). Greenwood.

Zweig, Friderike. Greatness Revisited. Zohn, Harry, ed. (Illus.). 152p. 1982. pap. 7.95. Branden.

Zweig, Gunter, ed. Analytical Methods for Pesticides, Plant Growth Regulators & Food Additives, 10 vols. Incl. Vol. 1. Principles, Methods & General Applications. 1963. 72.00 (ISBN 0-12-784301-9); Vol. 2. Insecticides. 1964. 72.00 o.s.i. (ISBN 0-12-784302-7); Vol. 3. Fungicides, Nematocides & Soil Fumigants, Rodenticides, & Food & Feed Additives. 1964. 42.00 (ISBN 0-12-784303-5); Vol. 4. Herbicides (Plant Growth Regulators) 1964. 42.00 (ISBN 0-12-784304-3); Vol. 5. 1967. 68.50 (ISBN 0-12-784305-1); Vol. 6. 78.50 (ISBN 0-12-784306-X); Vol. 7. Thin-Layer & Liquid Chromatography & Analysis of Pesticides of International Importance. 1974. 78.50 (ISBN 0-12-784307-8); Vol. 8. Government Regulations, Pheromone Analyses, Additional Pesticides. Zweig, Gunter & Sharma, Joseph, eds. 1976. 72.00 (ISBN 0-12-784308-6); Vol. 10. Newer & Updated Methods. Zweig, Gunter & Sharma, Joseph, eds. 1978. 61.00 (ISBN 0-12-784310-8); Vol. 11. 1980. 52.00 (ISBN 0-12-784311-6). Set. 581.00. Acad Pr.

--Paper Chromatography & Electrophoresis, 2 vols. Incl. Vol. 1. Electrophoresis & Stabilizing Media. Whitaker, John R, ed. 1967. 56.00 (ISBN 0-12-784330-2); Vol. 2. Paper Chromatography. Sherma, Joseph, ed. 1970. 76.00 (ISBN 0-12-784331-0). Acad Pr.

Zweig, Gunter & Sherma, Joseph, eds. Polymers Vol. I. (CRC Handbook of Chromatography Ser.). 200p. 1982. 56.00 (ISBN 0-8493-3073-4). CRC Pr.

Zweig, Stefan. Beware of Pity. 1983. 14.95 (ISBN 0-517-54673-6, Harmony Bks). Crown.

Zweigenhaft. Jews in Protestant Establishment. 144p. 1982. 23.95 (ISBN 0-03-062607-2); pap. 10.95 (ISBN 0-03-062606-4). Praeger.

Zweng, M., ed. see International Congress on Mathematical Education Staff, Fourth.

Zwerdling, Ella. The ABC's of Casework with Children: A Social Work Teacher's Notebook. LC 73-93887. (Orig.). 1974. pap. 2.95 (ISBN 0-87868-120-5, CW-30). Child Welfare.

Zwerling, Isreal, jt. auth. see Lager, Eric.

Zwerman, William L. New Perspectives on Organization Theory: An Empirical Reconsideration of the Marxian & Classical Analyses. LC 71-90791. (Contributions in Sociology Ser.: No. 1). (Illus.). 1971. lib. bdg. 25.00 (ISBN 0-8371-1851-4, ZWN/); pap. 4.95 (ISBN 0-8371-5973-3). Greenwood.

Zwerski, Abraham J. It Happens to Doctors, Too. 9.95 (ISBN 0-89486-158-1). Hazelden.

Zwick, Earl J., jt. auth. see Rector, Robert E.

Zwick, Edward, ed. Literature & Liberalism: An Anthology of Sixty Years of the New Republic. LC 76-2448. 1976. 15.00 (ISBN 0-915220-06-7, 23097); pap. 5.95 (ISBN 0-915220-31-8). New Republic.

Zwick, Peter. National Communism. 270p. 1982. lib. bdg. 28.50 (ISBN 0-86531-427-6); pap. text ed. 12.00 (ISBN 0-86531-428-4). Westview.

Zwiebel, William J., ed. Introduction to Vascular Ultrasonography. Date not set. price not set (ISBN 0-8089-1531-2). Grune.

Zwienen, John Van see Van Zwienen, John.

Zwier, Robert. Born-Again Politics: The New Christian Right in America. (Illus.). 132p. 1982. pap. 4.95 (ISBN 0-87784-828-9). Inter-Varsity.

Zwinger, Ann. Wind in the Rock: A Naturalist Explores the Canyon Country of the Southwest. LC 78-2176. (Illus.). 1978. 16.30i (ISBN 0-06-014209-X, HarpT). Har-Row.

Zwinger, Ann, jt. auth. see Teale, Edwin W.

Zwinger, Ann H. & Willard, Beatrice E. Land Above the Trees: A Guide to American Alpine Tundra. LC 72-79702. (Illus.). 448p. 1972. 19.18i (ISBN 0-06-014823-3, HarpT). Har-Row.

Zwirn, Jerrold. Congressional Publications: A Research Guide to Legislation, Budgets & Treaties. 200p. 1983. lib. bdg. 22.50 (ISBN 0-87287-358-7). Libs Unl.

Zwirz, Bob. The Digest Book of Fishing. (Sports & Leisure Library). (Illus.). 1979. pap. 2.95 o.s.i. (ISBN 0-695-81283-1). Follett.

Zwitman, Daniel, jt. auth. see Sonderman, Judith.

Zwitman, Daniel H. The Disfluent Child: A Management Program. 80p. 1978. text ed. 15.00 (ISBN 0-8391-1277-7, 7500-B). Communication Skill.

Zycha, H. & Siepmann, R. Mucorales. (Illus.). 40.00 (ISBN 3-7682-0145-7). Lubrecht & Cramer.

Zygmund, A. Trigonometric Series. LC 77-82528. 1977. 99.50 (ISBN 0-521-07477-0). Cambridge U Pr.

Zygmund, A., jt. auth. see Saks, S.

Zylka, T. Geological Dictionary. 1493p. 1980. 90.00x o.p. (ISBN 0-569-07698-6, Pub. by Collet's). State Mutual Bk.

Zyl Slabbert, F. Van see Van Zyl Slabbert, F. & Welsh, David.

Zysman, John. Political Strategies for Industrial Order: State, Market, & Industry in France. 1977. 30.00x (ISBN 0-520-02889-9). U of Cal Pr.

SUBJECT INDEX

A

A-C CARRIER CONTROL SYSTEMS
see Carrier Control Systems
A-THIRTY-SIX (FIGHTER-BOMBER PLANES)
see Mustang (Fighter Planes)
ABANDONED CHILDREN
see Child Welfare
ABANDONMENT (MARINE INSURANCE)
see Insurance, Marine
ABATEMENT OF TAXES
see Tax Remission
ABBEYS
see also Cathedrals
also names of specific abbeys, e.g. Lindisfarne Abbey
Crossley, Frederick H. The English Abbey: Its Life & Work in the Middle Ages. LC 82-25127. (Illus.). xiv, 114p. 1983. Repr. of 1935 ed. lib. bdg. 45.00x (ISBN 0-313-23849-9, CRFE). Greenwood.
ABBREVIATIONS
see also Acronyms; Ciphers; Shorthand; Signs and Symbols
also subdivision Abbreviations under subjects, e.g. Law-Abbreviations
Acronyms & Abbreviations Covering the United Nations System & Other International Organizations. 26.00 (ISBN 0-686-84918-3, A/C/E/F/R/S.81.I.26). UN.
ABBREVIATIONS, MEDICAL
see Medicine-Abbreviations
ABDOMEN
see also Intestines; Kidneys; Liver; Stomach
Dunphy, Pat & Wolf, Michael. The Sexy Stomach: How to Get it & How to Keep it. LC 82-83928. (Illus.). 64p. (Orig.). 1983. pap. 4.95 (ISBN 0-88011-096-1). Leisure Pr.
Shepherd, John A. Management of the Acute Abdomen. (Illus.). 1982. 42.50x (ISBN 0-19-261322-7). Oxford U Pr.
ABDOMEN-RADIOGRAPHY
Goldberg, Barry B. Abdominal Gray Scale Ultrasonography. LC 77-5889. (Diagnostic & Therapuetic Radiology Ser.). 372p. 1977. 55.00x (ISBN 0-471-01510-5, Pub. by Wiley Med). Wiley.
ABDOMEN-SURGERY
see also Intestines-Surgery
Logan-Edwards, R. Manual of Laparoscopy & Culdoscopy. new ed. 160p. 1983. text ed. write for info. (ISBN 0-407-00195-6). Butterworth.
ABDOMINAL DELIVERY
see Cesarean Section
ABERRATION, CHROMATIC AND SPHERICAL
see Lenses; Mirrors; Optical Instruments
ABILITY-TESTING
see also Employees, Rating Of; Intelligence Tests; Mathematical Ability-Testing; Motor Ability-Testing; Musical Ability-Testing; Scholastic Aptitude Test; Teachers, Rating Of
also names of specific tests, e.g. Rorschach Test
Cognative Abilities Test. write for info. (RivEd). HM.
College English Placement Test. write for info. (RivEd). HM.
Iowa Test of Basic Skills. write for info. (RivEd). HM.
Paget, Kathleen & Brackett, Bruce, eds. The Psychoeducational Assessment of Pre-School Children. Date not set. price not set (ISBN 0-8089-1475-8). Grune.
Test of Academic Progress. write for info. (RivEd). HM.
The Three-R's Test. write for info. (RivEd). HM.
ABILITY, EXECUTIVE
see Executive Ability
ABILITY TESTS
see Ability-Testing
ABIOGENESIS
see Life-Origin
ABNAKI INDIANS
see Indians of North America-Canada
ABNORMAL CHILDREN
see Exceptional Children; Handicapped Children
ABNORMAL PSYCHOLOGY
see Psychology, Pathological
ABNORMALITIES, HUMAN
see also Monsters
Briggs, Gerald G. Teratogenic Drugs in Clinical Practice. 400p. 1983. price not set (ISBN 0-683-01057-3). Williams & Wilkins.
Damjanov, Ivan & Knowles, Barbara, eds. The Human Teratomas. (Contemporary Biomedicine Ser.). 416p. 1983. 49.50 (ISBN 0-89603-040-7). Humana.
Goodman, Richard M. & Gorlin, Robert J. Malformations in Infants & Children: An Illustrated Guide. (Illus.). 450p. 1983. text ed. 35.00x (ISBN 0-19-503254-3); pap. text ed. 19.50x (ISBN 0-19-503255-1). Oxford U Pr.
Johnson, E. M. & Kochhar, D. M., eds. Teratogenesis & Reproductive Toxicology. (Handbook of Experimental Pharmacology Ser.: Vol. 65). (Illus.). 400p. 1983. 116.00 (ISBN 0-387-11906-X). Springer-Verlag.
Marshall. Cryptorchidism & Related Anomalies. 128p. 1982. 19.50 (ISBN 0-03-059282-8). Praeger.
Nyhan, William L. & Jones, Kenneth L., eds. Dysmorphology: Pt. B of Annual Review of Birth Defects, 1981. LC 82-10006. (Birth Defects; Original Article Ser.: Vol. 18, No. 3B). 328p. 1982. 56.00 (ISBN 0-8451-1048-9). A R Liss.
--Prenatal Dianosis & Mechanisms of Teratogenesis: Pt. A of Annual Review of Birth Defects, 1981. LC 82-9992. (Birth Defects; Original Article Ser.: Vol. 18, No. 3A). 232p. 1982. 36.00 (ISBN 0-8451-1047-0). A R Liss.
Winter, Robert B. Congenital Deformities of the Spine. (Illus.). 432p. 1983. 59.00 (ISBN 0-86577-079-4). Thieme-Stratton.
ABOLITION OF SLAVERY
see Abolitionists; Slavery
ABOLITIONISTS
Blackett, R. J. Building an Antislavery Wall: Black Americans in the Atlantic Abolitionist Movement, 1830 to 1860. LC 82-21724. 264p. 1983. text ed. 25.00x (ISBN 0-8071-1082-5). La State U Pr.
Santrey, Laurence. Young Frederick Douglass: Fight for Freedom. LC 82-15993. (Illus.). 48p. (gr. 4-6). 1983. PLB 6.89 (ISBN 0-89375-857-4); pap. text ed. 1.95 (ISBN 0-89375-858-2). Troll Assocs.
ABORIGINES
see Ethnology; Native Races
ABORTION
Banks, Bill & Banks, Sue. Ministering to Abortion's Aftermath. 144p. (Orig.). 1982. pap. 3.95 (ISBN 0-89228-057-3). Impact Bks MO.
Corsaro, Maria & Korzenlowsky, Carole. A Woman's Guide to a Safe Abortion. LC 82-15652. (Illus.). 120p. 1983. 12.95 (ISBN 0-03-060603-9); pap. 9.95 (ISBN 0-03-060602-0). HR&W.
Grady, John L. Abortion: Yes or No? 32p. 1968. pap. 1.00 (ISBN 0-686-81634-X). TAN Bks Pubs.
Gregory, Hamilton, ed. The Religious Case for Abortion. LC 82-61786. 96p. (Orig.). 1983. pap. 9.95 (ISBN 0-910915-00-8). Madison Polk.
Hensley, Jeffrey. The Zero People. 310p. 1983. pap. 7.95 (ISBN 0-89283-126-X). Servant.
Mall, David. In Good Conscience: Abortion & Moral Necessity. xii, 212p. 1982. 18.50 (ISBN 0-9608410-1-6); pap. 8.50 (ISBN 0-9608410-0-8). Kairos Bks.
Odell, Catherine M. & Odell, William. The First Human Right: A Pro-Life Primer. LC 82-61466. 1983. pap. 4.95 (ISBN 0-87973-620-8, 620). Our Sunday Visitor.
Quay, Effie A. And Now Infanticide. 2nd ed. 1980. pap. 1.00 (ISBN 0-937930-01-6). Sun Life.
Scientists for Life. The Position of Modern Science on the Beginning of Human Life. 47p. (Orig.). 1975. pap. 1.00 (ISBN 0-937930-02-4). Sun Life.
Steiner, Gilbert Y., ed. The Abortion Dispute & the American System. LC 82-45978. 100p. 1983. pap. 6.95 (ISBN 0-8157-8125-3). Brookings.
ABORTION-PUBLIC OPINION
Lippis, John. The Challenge to Be Pro Life. 2nd, rev. ed. (Illus.). 28p. (gr. 8-12). 1982. pap. write for info. (ISBN 0-9609902-0-8). Santa Barb Pro.
Paige, Connie. The Right-to-Lifers: Who They Are, What They Are, & Where They Get Their Money. 256p. 1983. 13.95. Summit Bks.
ABSENT TREATMENT
see Mental Healing
ABSENTEE VOTING
see Voting
ABSOLUTE RIGHTS
see Natural Law
ABSOLUTISM
see Despotism
ABSORPTION
Institute of Petroleum. Chemisorption & Catalysis. 1970. 47.95x (ISBN 0-471-26164-5, Pub. by Wiley Heyden). Wiley.
ABSORPTION, ATMOSPHERIC
see Solar Radiation
ABSTINENCE
see Fasting; Temperance
ABSTRACT ALGEBRA
see Algebra, Abstract
ABSTRACT AUTOMATA
see Machine Theory
ABSTRACT MACHINES
see Machine Theory
ABSTRACTING
see also Indexing
Rowley, Jennifer E. Abstracting & Indexing. 155p. 1982. 15.00 (ISBN 0-85157-336-3, Pub. by Bingley England). Shoe String.
ABSTRACTING AND INDEXING SERVICES
see also Information Storage and Retrieval Systems
Brewer, Annie M. Indexes, Abstracts & Digests. 801p. 1982. 150.00x (ISBN 0-8103-1686-2). Gale.
ABSTRACTION
Zalta, Edward N. Abstraci Objects. 1983. lib. bdg. 39.50 (ISBN 90-277-1474-6, Pub. by Reidel Holland). Kluwer Boston.
ABUSE
see Invective
ABUSE OF POWER
see Despotism
ACADEMIC ACHIEVEMENT
O'Day, Danton. How to Succeed at University. 1982. pap. 2.95 (ISBN 0-7723-0074-7, YE74). NAL.
ACADEMIC ADJUSTMENT
see Student Adjustment
ACADEMIC DEGREES
see Degrees, Academic
ACADEMIC DISSERTATIONS
see Dissertations, Academic
ACADEMIES (LEARNED SOCIETIES)
see Learned Institutions and Societies; Societies
ACARI
see Mites
ACCELERATED READING
see Rapid Reading
ACCELERATORS, ELECTRON
see Particle Accelerators
ACCESSORIES (DRESS)
see Dress Accessories
ACCIDENT LAW
see also Employers' Liability; Negligence; Personal Injuries; Torts; Traffic Violations; Workmen's Compensation
Coleman, Jules. Justice & the Costs of Accidents: A Philosophic Analysis. (Philosophy & Society Ser.). 250p. 1983. text ed. 25.00x (ISBN 0-8476-7183-6). Rowman.
Hare, Francis H., Jr. & Ricci, Edward M., eds. The Anatomy of a Personal Injury Lawsuit. 2nd ed. LC 81-70743. (Illus.). 508p. 1981. pap. 35.00 (ISBN 0-941916-00-6). Assn Trial Ed.
ACCIDENTS
see also Ambulances; Burns and Scalds; Disasters; Employers' Liability; Explosions; Fires; First Aid in Illness and Injury; Industrial Accidents; Medical Emergencies; Physically Handicapped; Shipwrecks; Shock; Traffic Accidents; Traumatism
also subdivision Wounds and Injuries under names of regions and organs of the body
Jones-Lee, M. W., ed. The Value of Life & Safety: Proceedings of a Conference Held by the Geneva Association. 310p. 1982. 55.50 (ISBN 0-444-86439-3, North Holland). Elsevier.

Possible Death on the Highway: Attempted Murder or An Accident, Example of a Logical Map. (Analysis Ser.: No. 11). 1983. pap. 10.00 (ISBN 0-686-42847-1, 0686428463). Inst Analysis.

S. D. Myers, Inc. Accident Prevention Bulletin, No. 17.01. (Illus.). 97p. 1977. 15.00 (ISBN 0-939320-04-5). Myers Inc.

ACCIDENTS–LAW AND LEGISLATION

see Accident Law

ACCIDENTS–PREVENTION

see also Industrial Safety; Safety Education; also subdivisions Safety Appliances or Safety Measures under subjects, e.g. Railroads–Safety Appliances, Automobiles–Safety Measures

American Health Research Institute, Ltd. Accident Prevention & Injury Control: A Medical & Behavioral Subject Analysis & Research Index with Bibliography. Bartone, John C., ed. 120p. 1983. 29.95 (ISBN 0-88164-030-1); pap. 21.95 (ISBN 0-88164-031-X). ABBE Pubs Assn.

--Accidents in Occupations & Industry: A Medical Subject Analysis & Research Index with Bibliography. Bartone, John C., ed. 120p. 1983. 29.95 (ISBN 0-88164-012-3); pap. 21.95 (ISBN 0-88164-013-1). ABBE Pubs Assn.

ACCIDENTS, INDUSTRIAL

see Industrial Accidents

ACCIDENTS, SPACECRAFT

see Astronautics–Accidents

ACCIDENTS, TRAFFIC

see Traffic Accidents

ACCLIMATIZATION (PLANTS)

see Botany–Ecology

ACCOMMODATION (PSYCHOLOGY)

see Adjustment (Psychology)

ACCOUNTABILITY

see Criminal Liability; Liability (Law)

ACCOUNTANTS

see also Accounting–Law; Accounting–Vocational Guidance; Tax Consultants

Dickerson, R. W. Accountants & the Law of Negligence. LC 82-48361. (Accountancy in Transition Ser.). 668p. 1982. lib. bdg. 65.00 (ISBN 0-8240-5312-5). Garland Pub.

Keats, Charles. Magnificent Masquerade. LC 82-48369. (Accountancy in Transition Ser.). 292p. 1982. lib. bdg. 30.00 (ISBN 0-8240-5322-2). Garland Pub.

The National Directory of Certified Public Accountants. LC 82-62277. xvii, 1002p. 1982. 75.00x (ISBN 0-312-55945-3). St Martin.

Tinsley, James A. Texas Society of Certified Public Accountants. rev. ed. (Illus.). 216p. 1983. Repr. of 1962 ed. 24.95x (ISBN 0-89096-152-2). Tex A&M Univ Pr.

ACCOUNTING

see also Auditing; Bookkeeping; Business Mathematics; Cost Accounting; Financial Statements; Liquidation; Managerial Accounting; Productivity Accounting; Tax Accounting also subdivision Accounting under names of industries, professions, trades, etc., e.g. Printing–Accounting

Accounting in Action. 1982. pap. 7.50 (ISBN 0-686-84205-7). Am Inst CPA.

American Institute of Accountants. Fiftieth Anniversary Celebration. LC 82-48350. (Accountancy in Transition Ser.). 568p. 1982. lib. bdg. 60.00 (ISBN 0-8240-5302-8). Garland Pub.

American Institute of Certified Public Accountants. Audit & Accounting Guide: Audits of Employee Benefit Plans. 1983. write for info. Am Inst CPA.

--MAP Handbook: 1983. write for info. Am Inst CPA.

Arnett, Harold E. Proposed Funds Statements for Managers & Investors. 137p. pap. 12.95 (ISBN 0-86641-019-8, 79114). Natl Assn Accts.

Arpan, Jeffrey S. & Radebaugh, Lee H. International Accounting & Multinational Enterprises. LC 80-26070. 400p. 1982. text ed. 27.95 (ISBN 0-471-87746-8); tchr's manual avail. (ISBN 0-471-89512-1). Wiley.

Audit Problems Encountered in Small Business Engagements. 9.00 (ISBN 0-686-42705-X). Am Inst CPA.

Baker, Richard & Hayes, Rick S. Accounting for Small Manufacturers. LC 80-12001. (Small Business Management Ser.). 197p. 1980. 31.95x (ISBN 0-471-05704-5). Wiley.

Bedford, Norton M., et al. Advanced Accounting: An Organizational Approach. 4th ed. LC 78-6961. (Accounting & Information Systems Ser.). 892p. 1979. text ed. 32.95 (ISBN 0-471-02927-0). Wiley.

Beyer, Robert & Trawicki, Donald. Profitability Accounting: For Planning & Control. 2d ed. LC 72-91123. 414p. Repr. of 1972 ed. text ed. 28.50 (ISBN 0-471-06523-4). Krieger.

Blensly, Douglas L. & Plank, Tom M. Accounting Desk Book. 7th ed. LC 82-6231. 472p. 1982. text ed. 54.50 (ISBN 0-87624-010-4). Inst Busn Plan.

Bray, Sewell F. Four Essays in Accounting Theory bound with Some Accounting Terms & Concepts. LC 82-48352. (Accountancy in Transition Ser.). 160p. 1982. lib. bdg. 20.00 (ISBN 0-8240-5305-2). Garland Pub.

Brenner, Vincent C. & Davies, Jonathan. West's Intermediate Accounting. (Illus.). 1100p. 1983. text ed. 24.95 (ISBN 0-314-63307-3); instrs.' manual avail. (ISBN 0-314-63310-3); Working Papers, Pt. I avail. (ISBN 0-314-72286-6); Working Papers, Pt. II avail. (ISBN 0-314-72287-4); student guide avail. (ISBN 0-314-63308-1); solutions manual avail. (ISBN 0-314-63309-X). West Pub.

Broed, Paul. Accounting the Easy Way. (Easy Way Ser.). 320p. 1983. pap. 5.95 (ISBN 0-8120-2623-3). Barron.

Buckley, J. W., et al. SEC Accounting. 484p. 1980. text ed. 27.95 (ISBN 0-471-01861-9); avail. tchrs. manual (ISBN 0-471-07778-X). Wiley.

Caplan, Edwin H. & Champoux, Joseph E. Cases in Management Accounting: Context & Behavior. 88p. pap. 12.95 (ISBN 0-686-37886-5, 78101). Natl Assn Accts.

Cavert, C. Edward & Metcalf, Richard M. Accounting. 467p. 1982. text ed. 17.95x student guide (ISBN 0-931920-43-4). Dame Pubns.

Chambers, R. J. Accounting is Disarray: A Case for the Reform of Company Accounts. LC 82-48354. (Accountancy in Transition Ser.). 258p. 1982. lib. bdg. 25.00 (ISBN 0-8240-5307-9). Garland pub.

Chilton, Carl S., Jr. The Successful Professional Client Accounting Practice. LC 82-15143. 217p. 1983. 39.95 (ISBN 0-13-868208-9, Busn). P-H.

Clarke, F. L. The Tangled Web of Price Variation Accounting: The Development of Ideas Underlying Professional Prescriptions in Six Counties. LC 82-82485. (Accountancy in Transition Ser.). 466p. 1982. lib. bdg. 55.00 (ISBN 0-8240-5300-1). Garland Pub.

Cutforth, A. E. Methods of Amalgamation. LC 82-48358. (Accountancy in Transition Ser.). 354p. 1982. lib. bdg. 35.00 (ISBN 0-8240-5310-9). Garland Pub.

Dascher, Paul E. & Janell, Paul A. Accounting: A Book of Readings. LC 80-70470. 539p. 1983. pap. text ed. 11.95x (ISBN 0-931920-30-2). Dame Pubns.

Dean, G. W. & Wells, M. C., eds. Forerunners of Realizable Values Accounting in Financial Reporting. LC 82-82486. (Accountancy in Transition Ser.). 342p. 1982. lib. bdg. 45.00 (ISBN 0-8240-5334-6). Garland Pub.

Disclosure Checklists. 1982. pap. 5.00 (ISBN 0-686-84281-2). Am Inst CPA.

Doyle, Dennis M. Efficient Accounting & Record Keeping. Brownstone, David, ed. LC 78-2474. (The Small Business Profit Program Ser.). 116p. 1977. pap. text ed. 5.95 (ISBN 0-471-05044-X). Wiley.

Drebin, Allan R. & Chan, James L. Objectives of Accounting & Financial Reporting by Governmental Units: A Research Study, 2 vols. Incl. Vol. I. (Illus.). 128p. pap. no charge; Vol. II. (Illus.). 200p. pap. 7.50 (ISBN 0-686-84260-X). 1981. Municipal.

Edey, Harold C. Accounting Queries. LC 82-82487. (Accountancy in Transition Ser.). 296p. 1982. lib. bdg. 40.00 (ISBN 0-8240-5335-4). Garland Pub.

EDP Engagements. 1982. pap. 3.50 (ISBN 0-686-84282-0). Am Inst CPA.

Edwards, Donald E. & Kettering, Ronald C. Computer Assisted Practice Set in Financial Accounting: Cook's Solar Energy Systems. LC 82-83660. 96p. 1983. pap. 9.95 (ISBN 0-395-33492-6); write for info. instr's. manual (ISBN 0-395-33493-4). HM.

Edwards, James D. & Hermanson, Roger H. How Accounting Works: A Guide for the Perplexed. LC 82-73625. 190p. 1983. 14.95 (ISBN 0-87094-394-4). Dow Jones-Irwin.

Fabricant, Solomon. Studies in Social & Private Accounting. LC 82-82488. (Accountancy in Transition Ser.). 300p. 1982. lib. bdg. 40.00 (ISBN 0-8240-5337-0). Garland Pub.

Financial Accounting Standards Board. Accounting Standards: Vol. 1: Original Pronouncements as of June 1, 1982. 1800p. 22.50 (ISBN 0-07-020821-2). McGraw.

--Accounting Standards: Vol. 2: Current Text As of June 1, 1982. 1800p. 1982. 24.50 (ISBN 0-07-020822-0). McGraw.

--Financial Accounting Standards Board Current Text 1982-1984. 1800p. 1982. loose leaf ed.-domestic 210.00 (ISBN 0-07-020901-4). McGraw.

--Financial Accounting Standards Board Current Text 1982-1984: International. 1800p. 1982. loose leaf ed.-international 300.00 (ISBN 0-07-020902-2). McGraw.

Francia, Arthur J. & Strawser, Robert H. Accounting for Managers. LC 82-71152. 1982. text ed. 24.95x (ISBN 0-931920-38-8). Dame Pubns.

Gaffikin, Michael & Aitken, Michael, eds. The Development of Accounting Theory: Significant Contributors to Accounting Thought in the 20th Century. LC 82-82489. (Accountancy in Transition Ser.). 284p. 1982. lib. bdg. 40.00 (ISBN 0-8240-5336-2). Garland Pub.

Galutier, M. W. & Underdown, B. Basic Accounting Practice. 2nd ed. 448p. 1980. 42.00x (ISBN 0-273-01597-4, Pub. by Pitman.Bks England). State Mutual Bk.

Garnsey, Gilbert. Holding Companies & Their Published Accounts Bound with Limitations of A Balance Sheet. LC 82-48364. (Accountancy in Transition Ser.). 232p. 1982. lib. bdg. 25.00 (ISBN 0-8240-5315-X). Garland Pub.

Garvy, George. Debits & Clearing Statistics & Their Use. LC 82-15572. ix, 144p. 1982. Repr. of 1959 ed. lib. bdg. 22.50x (ISBN 0-313-23660-7, GADE). Greenwood.

Gittes, David L. A Practical Guide to Fund Accounting & Auditing. LC 81-20907. 270p. 1982. text ed. 89.50 (ISBN 0-87624-433-9). Inst Busn Plan.

Glautier, M. W. & Underdown, B. Accounting Theory & Practice. 2nd ed. 688p. 1982. 50.00x (ISBN 0-273-01541-9, Pub. by Pitman Bks England). State Mutual Bk.

Goldschmidt, Y. & Admon, K. Profit Measurement During Inflation: Accounting, Economic & Financial Aspects. LC 77-4500. (Operations Managment Ser.). 1977. 39.95x (ISBN 0-471-01983-6, Pub. by Wiley-Interscience). Wiley.

Gorton, Richard K. Practical Accounting: Ways to Increase Office Efficiency & Improve Career Skills. 85p. (Orig.). 1982. pap. 19.95 (ISBN 0-686-37985-3). Advance Pr.

Granof, Michael H. Accounting for Managers & Investors. 768p. 1983. 27.95 (ISBN 0-13-002725-1). P-H.

Hamilton, Robert. An Introduction to Merchandise, Parts IV & V: Italian Bookkeeping & Practical Bookkeeping, with a Note by B. S. Yamey. LC 82-48366. (Accountancy in Transition Ser.). 247p. 1982. lib. bdg. 25.00 (ISBN 0-8240-5317-6). Garland Pub.

Helmkamp, John G. & Imdieke, Leroy F. Principles of Accounting. LC 82-20124. 1150p. 1983. text ed. 26.95 instrs. manual (ISBN 0-471-08510-3). Wiley.

IFAC Ethics Guidelines, Nos. 1 & 2. 1982. pap. 3.50 ea. (ISBN 0-686-84289-8). Am Inst CPA.

Illustrations of Accounting for Innovative Financing Arrangements. (Financial Report Survey Ser.: No. 25). 1982p. pap. 9.50 (ISBN 0-686-84291-X). Am Inst CPA.

Industry Accounting Manuals: 1980-1981 Edition. 44p. pap. 4.95 (ISBN 0-86641-058-9, 8097). Natl Assn Accts.

International Congress on Accounting 1929. LC 82-48378. (Accountancy in Transition Ser.). 1400p. 1982. lib. bdg. 112.00 (ISBN 0-8240-5320-6). Garland Pub.

International Congress on Accounting, 4th, 1933. LC 82-48369. (Accountancy in Transition Ser.). 818p. 1982. lib. bdg. 80.00 (ISBN 0-8240-5321-4). Garland Pub.

Kettle, Russell, compiled by. Deloitte & Co., 1845-1956: Bound with Fifty Seven Years in an Accountants Office. LC 82-48359. (Accountancy in Transition Ser.). 206p. 1982. lib. bdg. 25.00 (ISBN 0-8240-5311-7). Garland Pub.

Korn, S. Winton & Boyd, Thomas. Accounting for Decision Makers. 2nd ed. (Professional Development Programs). 320p. 1983. text ed. 55.95x (ISBN 0-471-87246-6). Wiley.

Langer, Steven, ed. Accounting-Financial Report. 3rd ed. 1982. pap. 85.00 ea. Pt. I: Public Accounting Firms (ISBN 0-916506-71-1). Pt. II: Industry, Government, & Education, Non-Profit (ISBN 0-916506-72-X). Abbott Langer Assocs.

Lee, Chauncey. The American Accompant. LC 82-48375. (Accountancy in Transition Ser.). 318p. 1982. lib. bdg. 30.00 (ISBN 0-8240-5324-9). Garland Pub.

Lewis, R. & Pendrill, D. Advanced Financial Accounting. 528p. 1981. 50.00x (ISBN 0-273-01640-7, Pub. by Pitman Bks England). State Mutual Bk.

Liad, Woody M. & Boockholdt, James L. Cost Accounting: Managerial Planning, Decision Making, & Control. LC 81-69691. 606p. 1983. text ed. 27.95x (ISBN 0-931920-34-5). Dame Pubns.

Lynch, R. M. & Williamson, R. W. Accounting for Management. 3rd ed. 560p. 1983. 25.00x (ISBN 0-07-039221-8, C); Supplementary materials avail. solutions manual 15.00 (ISBN 0-07-039222-6). McGraw.

McGee, Robert W. Fundamentals of Accounting & Finance: A Handbook for Business & Professional People. (Illus.). 216p. 1983. 14.95 (ISBN 0-13-332437-0); pap. 6.95 (ISBN 0-13-332429-X). P-H.

Meigs, Walter B. & Meigs, Robert F. Financial Accounting. 4th ed. (Illus.). 735p. 1983. text ed. 24.95x (ISBN 0-07-041534-X, C); instr's manual 25.00 (ISBN 0-07-041535-8); study guide 9.95 (ISBN 0-07-041536-6). Supplementary material avail. McGraw.

Montgomery, A. Thompson. Introduction to Accounting. LC 80-69850. Orig. Title: Financial Accounting Information. 286p. 1982. Repr. of 1978 ed. text ed. 14.00 (ISBN 0-89463-031-8). Am Inst Property.

Mosich, A. N. & Larsen, E. J. Modern Advanced Accounting. 3rd ed. 768p. 1983. 29.95x (ISBN 0-07-040127-6, C); study guide 10.50x (ISBN 0-07-040129-2). McGraw.

Municipal Finance Officers Association. An Accounting Handbook for Small Cities & Other Governmental Units. LC 78-71711. 153p. 1978. 15.00 (ISBN 0-686-84267-7). Municipal.

Needles. Financial Accounting. 1983. text ed. 24.95 (ISBN 0-686-84524-2); write for info. supplementary materials. HM.

Newcomb, V. N. Practical Accounting for Business Studies. 200p. 1983. price not set (ISBN 0-471-90007-9, Pub. by Wiley-Interscience). Wiley.

Piven, Peter. Compensation Management: A Guidelenes for Small Firms. (Illus.). 32p. 1982. 15.00x (ISBN 0-913962-47-3). Am Inst Arch.

Predecessor-Successor Accountants. (Statements on Standards for Accounting & Review Services Ser.: No. 4). 1982. pap. 1.60 (ISBN 0-686-84309-6). Am Inst CPA.

Rachlin, Norman S. & Cerwinske, Laura. Eleven Steps to Building a Profitable Accounting Practice. LC 82-10106. (Illus.). 320p. 1983. 29.95 (ISBN 0-07-051103-9). McGraw.

Ratcliffe, THomas A. Introduction to Accounting. 1982. 17.00 (ISBN 0-89419-197-7). Inst Energy.

Riddle, G. W. Accounting Level III. 272p. 1982. pap. text ed. 17.50 (ISBN 0-7121-0175-6). Intl Ideas.

Rorem, C. Rufus. Accounting Method. LC 82-48382. (Accountancy in Transition Ser.). 613p. 1982. lib. bdg. 60.00 (ISBN 0-8240-5327-3). Garland Pub.

Singer, H. W. Standardized Accountancy in Germany with A New Appendix. LC 82-48372. (Accountancy in Transition Ser.). 94p. 1982. lib. bdg. 18.00 (ISBN 0-8240-5329-X). Garland Pub.

Smith, Jack L. & Keith, Robert M. Accounting Principles. 1152p. 1983. 25.00 (ISBN 0-07-059060-5, C); study guide, 320p 9.95x (ISBN 0-07-059062-1). Supplementary materials avail. McGraw.

Statments on Standards MAS, 3 Vols. 1982 ed. pap. 4.80 (ISBN 0-686-84315-0). Am Inst CPA.

Sterling, Robert R. & Lemke, Kenneth W., eds. Maintenance of Capital: Financial vs Physical. LC 82-16847. 323p. 1982. 15.00 (ISBN 0-914348-32-9). Scholars Bk.

Stern, Stanley. Understanding Accounting. LC 82-18434. 160p. 1983. lib. bdg. 10.95 (ISBN 0-668-05726-2). Arco.

Suggested Guidelines for CPA Participation in the ABA Preferred Group Bonding Plan. 1980. pap. 2.50 (ISBN 0-686-84318-5). Am Inst CPA.

Triple-Entry Bookkeeping & Income Momentum, Vol. 18. (Studies in Accounting Research). 53p. 1982. 6.00 (ISBN 0-86539-041-X). Am Accounting.

Weaver, D. H. Transparencies for Accounting: Systems & Procedures. 4th ed. Date not set. 110.00 (ISBN 0-07-086512-4). McGraw.

Weaver, D. H., et al. Accounting: Systems & Procedures. 4th ed. 1982. evaluation manual 1.32 (ISBN 0-07-069340-4). McGraw.

Whittington, Geoffrey. Inflation Accounting: An Introduction to the Debate. LC 82-9657. (Management & Industrial Relations Ser.: No. 3). 256p. Date not set. price not set (ISBN 0-521-24903-1); pap. price not set (ISBN 0-521-27055-3). Cambridge U Pr.

Woltz, P. & Arlen, R. College Accounting: A Comprehensive Approach. 864p. 1983. 20.95x (ISBN 0-07-071481-9, C); write for info study guide (ISBN 0-07-071482-7). McGraw.

Woltz, Phebe M. & Arlen, Richard T. College Accounting: An Introduction. 2nd ed. Mason, Donald G., ed. 494p. 1983. text ed. 15.95 (ISBN 0-07-071599-8, C); study guide 10.00 (ISBN 0-07-071605-6). McGraw.

Wu, Frederick H. Accounting Information Systems: Theory & Practice. (Illus.). 608p. 1983. text ed. 23.00 (ISBN 0-07-072121-1, C). Supplementary materials available from publisher. write for info. instr's manual (ISBN 0-07-072122-X). McGraw.

ACCOUNTING–BIBLIOGRAPHY

American Institute of Accountants. Library Catalogue. LC 82-48337. (Accountancy in Transition Ser.). 242p. 1982. lib. bdg. 25.00 (ISBN 0-8240-5303-6). Garland Pub.

ACCOUNTING–DATA PROCESSING

Accounting & Information Systems: Answers to Questions on Subject Matter for the Learning Guide, CEBS Course 6. 1982. pap. text ed. 15.00 (ISBN 0-89154-186-1). Intl Found Employ.

Accounting & Information Systems: Learning Guide, CEBS Course 6. 1982. spiral binding 18.00 (ISBN 0-89154-185-3). Intl Found Employ.

Ashton, Robert H. Human Information Processing in Accounting, Vol. 17. (Studies in Accounting Research). 215p. 1982. 6.00 (ISBN 0-86539-038-X). Am Accounting.

Hamilton, S. S. Accounting Applications for the Microcomputer. Date not set. 6.95 (ISBN 0-07-025736-1). McGraw.

Leitch, Robert A. & Davis, K. Roscoe. Accounting Information Systems. (Illus.). 720p. 1983. 29.95 (ISBN 0-13-002949-1). P-H.

Needleman, Theodore. Microcomputers for Accountants. (Illus.). 186p. 1983. 24.95 (ISBN 0-13-580696-8); pap. 14.95 (ISBN 0-13-580688-7). P-H.

Proceedings from the National Automation Conference on Increasing the Productivity of the Financial Manager Through Effective Use of Computer Technology. 291p. pap. 24.95 (ISBN 0-86641-053-8, 81133). Natl Assn Accts.

ACCOUNTING–DICTIONARIES

Abdeen, Adnan. English-Arabic Dictionary for Accounting & Finance. LC 79-41213. 1981. 23.95x (ISBN 0-471-27673-1, Pub. by Wiley-Interscience). Wiley.

ACCOUNTING–EXAMINATIONS, QUESTIONS, ETC.

Here are entered collections of questions actually set in examinations. Problems for classroom use or private study are entered under Accounting–Problems, Exercises, etc.

American Institute of Certified Public Accountants. Uniform CPA Examination: Questions & Unofficial Answers: Nov. 1982 supplement. 1983. write for info. Am Inst CPA.

Examiner (Intermittent) (Career Examination Ser.: C-2622). (Cloth bdg. avail. on request). pap. 8.00 (ISBN 0-8373-2622-2). Natl Learning.

Ficek, Edmund. Comprehensive CPA Business Law Review. 1st ed. (Illus.). 640p. 1983. text ed. 26.95 (ISBN 0-07-020671-6, C); instr's. manual 10.95 (ISBN 0-07-020672-4). McGraw.

McQuaig, Douglas J. College Accounting Fundamentals. 2nd ed. 1983. 29 chaps. 21.50 (ISBN 0-395-29408-8); supplementary materials avail.; computer assisted practice set, denton appliance, with workbook & solutions manual 9.95; medical practice set, CW Hale with workbook & solutions manual 9.95; legal practice set, Mt. Chandler with workbook & solutions manual 9.95. HM.

Rudman, Jack. Junior Account Clerk. (Career Examination Ser.: C-515). (Cloth bdg. avail. on request). pap. 10.00 (ISBN 0-8373-0515-2). Natl Learning.

ACCOUNTING–FORMS, BLANKS, ETC.

see Business–Forms, Blanks, etc.

ACCOUNTING–HISTORY

Hatton, Edward. The Merchants Magazine or Trades-Man's Treasury. LC 82-48367. (Accountancy in Transition Ser.). 200p. 1982. lib. bdg. 22.00 (ISBN 0-8240-5318-4). Garland Pub.

Yamey, B. S. & Edey, H. C. Accounting in England & Scotland: 1543-1800. LC 82-48374. (Accountancy in Transition Ser.). 244p. 1982. lib. bdg. 25.00 (ISBN 0-8240-5332-X). Garland Pub.

Yamey, Basil S. Further Essays on the History of Accounting. LC 82-82491. (Accountancy in Transition Ser.). 244p. 1982. lib. bdg. 30.00 (ISBN 0-8240-5339-7). Garland Pub.

Zeff, Stephen A. The Accounting Postulates & Principles Controversy of the 1969s. LC 82-82493. (Accountancy in Transition Ser.). 574p. 1982. lib. bdg. 75.00 (ISBN 0-8240-5341-9). Garland Pub.

--Accounting Principles Through the Years: The Views of Professional & Academic Leaders, 1938-1954. LC 82-82492. (Accountancy in Transition Ser.). 475p. 1982. lib. bdg. 60.00 (ISBN 0-8240-5340-0). Garland Pub.

History of the Accounting Profession: Years Trial 1969-1980. 1982. 20.00 (ISBN 0-686-84285-5). Am Inst CPA.

ACCOUNTING–LAW

see also Tax Accounting

Digest of State Accountancy Laws & State Board Regulations. 1982. pap. 17.50 (ISBN 0-686-84279-0). Am Inst CPA.

Federal Conflict of Interest Laws as Applied to Government Service by Parteners & Employees of Accounting Firms. 1981. pap. 8.00 (ISBN 0-686-84283-9). Am Inst CPA.

Ficek, Edmund. Comprehensive CPA Business Law Review. 1st ed. (Illus.). 640p. 1983. text ed. 26.95 (ISBN 0-07-020671-6, C); instr's. manual 10.95 (ISBN 0-07-020672-4). McGraw.

Hills, George S. The Law of Accounting & Financial Statements. LC 82-48368. (Accountancy in Transitions Ser.). 354p. 1982. lib. bdg. 35.00 (ISBN 0-8240-5319-2). Garland Pub.

Merz, C. Mike & Groebner, David E. Toward a Code of Ethics for Management Accountants. 160p. pap. 14.95 (ISBN 0-86641-009-0, 81129). Natl Assn Accts.

United States of America Before the Securities & Exchange Commission in the Matter of McKesson & Robbins, Inc. Testimony of Expert Witnesses. LC 82-48376. (Accountancy in Transition Ser.). 652p. 1982. lib. bdg. 65.00 (ISBN 0-8240-5331-1). Garland Pub.

United States of America Before the Securities & Exchange Commission in the Matter of McKesson & Robbins, Inc. Report on Investigation. LC 82-48373. (Accountancy in Transition Ser.). 501p. 1982. lib. bdg. 50.00 (ISBN 0-8240-5330-3). Garland Pub.

ACCOUNTING–PROBLEMS, EXERCISES, ETC.

Jennings, A. R. Financial Accounting: An Instructional Manual. 580p. (Orig.). 1982. pap. text ed. 13.00 (ISBN 0-905435-23-0). Verry.

Lucey, T. Quantitative Techniques: An Instructional Manual. 589p. 1982. pap. text ed. 12.00x (ISBN 0-905435-27-3). Verry.

McDonough, Michael. Assistant Accountant. 3rd ed. LC 82-18439. 160p. 1983. pap. text ed. 8.00 (ISBN 0-668-05613-4, 5613). Arco.

ACCOUNTING–STUDY AND TEACHING

Sheldahl, Terry K. Beta Alpha Psi, from Alpha to Omega: Pursuing a Vision of Professional Education for Accountants, 1919-1945. LC 82-48386. (Accountancy in Transition Ser.). 800p. 1982. lib. bdg. 60.00 (ISBN 0-8240-5301-X). Garland Pub.

ACCOUNTING–VOCATIONAL GUIDANCE

Felix, James V. Accounting Career Strategies: The Comprehensive Career Planning Guide for Accounting & Financial Professionals. LC 82-73146. (Illus.). 225p. 1982. 19.95 (ISBN 0-910595-00-3). Career Plan.

ACCOUNTS, COLLECTING OF

see Collecting of Accounts

ACCUMULATORS

see Storage Batteries

ACHIEVEMENT, ACADEMIC

see Academic Achievement

ACHIEVEMENT MOTIVATION

Shinn, George. The Miracle of Motivation. 246p. 1983. 9.95 (ISBN 0-8423-4353-9); pap. 6.95 (ISBN 0-8423-4354-7). Tyndale.

ACID PRECIPITATION (METEOROLOGY)

see Acid Rain

ACID RAIN

Boyle, Robert H. & Boyle, R. Alexander. Acid Rain. LC 82-21410. 128p. (Orig.). 1983. 14.95 (ISBN 0-8052-3854-9); pap. 8.95 (ISBN 0-8052-0746-5). Schocken.

Carroll, John E. Acid Rain: An Issue in Canadian-American Relations. LC 82-82205. (Canadian-American Committee). 98p. (Orig.). 1982. pap. 6.00 (ISBN 0-89068-064-7). Natl Planning.

ACIDS

see also names of acids, Sulphuric Acid

Perrin, D. D., ed. Ionisation Constants of Inorganic Acids & Bases in Aqueous Solution, No.29. 2nd ed. (Chemical Data Ser.). 194p. 1982. 50.00 (ISBN 0-08-029214-3). Pergamon.

ACNE

Fulton, James E. & Black, Elizabeth. Dr. Fulton's Step-By-Step Program for Clearing Acne. LC 82-47522. (Illus.). 256p. 1983. 12.45i (ISBN 0-06-038020-9, HarpT). Har-Row.

ACOLYTES

see Altar Boys

ACOUSTIC ENGINEERING

see Acoustical Engineering

ACOUSTIC NERVE

Glattke, Theodore J. Auditory Evoked Potentials. 1983. pap. 16.95 (ISBN 0-686-82638-8, 14710). Univ Park.

ACOUSTIC TUMORS

see Acoustic Nerve

ACOUSTICAL ENGINEERING

see also Architectural Acoustics; Noise; Noise Control; Telecommunication; Underwater Acoustics

Auld, B. Acoustic Fields & Waves in Solids, 2 vols. LC 72-8926. 1973. Set. 96.00x (ISBN 0-471-03702-8); 52.00x ea. Vol. 1 (ISBN 0-471-03700-1). Vol. 2 (ISBN 0-471-03701-X, Pub. by Wiley-Interscience). Wiley.

Ristic, Velimir M. Principles of Acoustic Devices. 325p. 1983. 37.50 (ISBN 0-471-09153-7, Pub. by Wiley-Interscience). Wiley.

White, R. G., et al. Noise & Vibration. 866p. 1982. 122.95x (ISBN 0-470-27553-7). Halsted Pr.

ACOUSTICS

see Architectural Acoustics; Hearing; Sound; Underwater Acoustics

ACQUISITION OF LANGUAGE

see Children–Language

ACQUISITIONS (LIBRARIES)

see also Searching, Bibliographical

Illustrated Catalog of Acquisitions. (Illus.). 1983. pap. 13.50 (ISBN 0-8120-2656-X). Barron.

Riggs, John B. Guide to Manuscripts in the Eleutharian Mills Historical Library, Supplement Containing Acessions for Years 1966 through 1975. 293p. 1978. cloth 15.00x (ISBN 0-914650-15-7). Eleutharian Mills-Hagley.

ACROGENS

see Ferns

ACRONYMS

Acronyms & Abbreviations Covering the United Nations System & Other International Organizations. 26.00 (ISBN 0-686-84918-3, A/C/E/F/R/S.81.I.26). UN.

ACTING

see also Acting for Television; Actors and Actresses; College and School Drama; Drama; Drama in Education; Theater

Crawford, Jerry L. Acting: In Person & In Style. 3rd ed. 480p. 1983. pap. text ed. write for info. (ISBN 0-697-04234-0). Wm C Brown.

Lewis, M. K. & Lewis, Rosemary. Your Film Acting Career: How to Break into the Movies & TV & Survive in Hollywood. (Illus.). 1983. 10.95 (ISBN 0-517-54911-5); pap. 6.95 (ISBN 0-517-54912-3). Crown.

Palmore, Paul. An Actor's Handbook: A Guide for the Beginning & Intermediate Actor. (Silliman University Humanities Ser.: No. 4). (Illus.). 114p. 1982. pap. 5.75x (ISBN 0-686-37574-2, Pub. by New Day Philippines). Cellar.

Shore, Michael. Act Now. 183p. (Orig.). 1982. pap. 6.95 (ISBN 0-910243-00-X). M Shore Assocs.

ACTING–COSTUME

see Costume

ACTING–MAKE-UP

see Make-Up, Theatrical

ACTING AS A PROFESSION

Brill, Chip, ed. N. Y. C. Casting Survival Guide & Datebook 1983. 3rd ed. 300p. 10.00 (ISBN 0-87314-038-9). Peter Glenn.

ACTING FOR TELEVISION

Lewis, M. K. & Lewis, Rosemary. Your Film Acting Career: How to Break into the Movies & TV & Survive in Hollywood. (Illus.). 1983. 10.95 (ISBN 0-517-54911-5); pap. 6.95 (ISBN 0-517-54912-3). Crown.

ACTINIDE ELEMENTS

see also names of specific elements, e.g. Uranium

Hellwege, K. H., ed. Magnetic & Other Properties of Xides & Related Compounds: Hexagonal Ferrites. Special Lanthanide & Actinide Compounds. (Landolt-Boernstein Ser.: Group III, Vol. 12, Pt. C). (Illus.). 650p. 1983. 408.00 (ISBN 0-387-10137-3). Springer-Verlag.

ACTIONS AND DEFENSES

see also Civil Procedure; Evidence (Law); Forms (Law); Pleading; Torts

Newberg on Class Action, 6 vols. (incl. 1980 suppl.). 1977. Set. 325.00 (ISBN 0-07-046335-2). McGraw.

ACTIVATION ANALYSIS

see Radioactivation Analysis

ACTIVE TRANSPORT

see Biological Transport

ACTIVITIES, STUDENT

see Student Activities

ACTORS, AFRO-AMERICAN

see Afro-American Actors

ACTORS AND ACTRESSES

see also Acting; Comedians; Make-Up, Theatrical; Moving-Picture Actors and Actresses; Moving-Pictures–Biography; Theater

Anobile, Richard. The Book of Fame. Date not set. pap. 7.95 (ISBN 0-449-90044-4, Columbine). Fawcett.

McClelland, Doug. Hollywood on Ronald Reagan: Friends & Enemies Discuss Our President, the Actor. (Illus.). 125p. (Orig.). 1983. pap. 11.95 (ISBN 0-571-12522-0). Faber & Faber.

Moger, Art. Hello, My Real Name Is.... (Illus.). 160p. 1983. pap. 6.95 (ISBN 0-8065-0802-7). Citadel Pr.

Rosenberg, Harold. The Act & the Actor: Making the Self. 238p. pap. 7.95 (ISBN 0-226-72675-4). U of Chicago Pr.

Seldin, Scott. Yes, Boss. LC 82-72103. (Illus.). 128p. 1982. 10.95 (ISBN 0-943778-01-8); pap. 5.95 (ISBN 0-943778-02-6). Blythe-Pennington.

ACTORS AND ACTRESSES–CORRESPONDENCE, REMINISCENCES, ETC.

Broun, Heywood H. A Studied Madness. LC 79-84436. 298p. 1983. pap. 4.95 (ISBN 0-933256-40-X). Second Chance.

Higham, Charles & Moseley, Roy. Princess Merle: The Romantic Life of Merle Oberon. LC 82-18201. (Illus.). 304p. 1983. 14.95 (ISBN 0-698-11231-8, Coward). Putnam Pub Group.

Howard, Leslie. Trivial Fond Records. Howard, Ronald, ed. 1982. 39.00x (ISBN 0-686-82340-0, Pub. by W Kimber). State Mutual Bk.

Newton, Margaret. Shad: A Biography of Lloyd "Shad" Heller. Jenkins, Michael, ed. LC 82-60547. (Illus.). 294p. (Orig.). 1982. pap. 7.95 (ISBN 0-910157-00-6). Pin Oak Pub Co.

Palmer, Lilli. Night Music. LC 82-48148. 320p. 1983. 14.95 (ISBN 0-06-015105-6, HarpT). Har-Row.

Schuller, Robert. The Inside Story. 8.95 (ISBN 0-686-82099-1). Word Pub.

ACTORS AND ACTRESSES–PORTRAITS

Hamm, Margherita A. Eminent Actors in Their Homes. 336p. 1982. Repr. of 1902 ed. lib. bdg. 40.00 (ISBN 0-89984-915-6). Century Bookbindery.

Jacobi, Lotte. Theatre & Dance Photographs. 46p. (Orig.). 1982. pap. 10.95 (ISBN 0-914378-93-7). Countryman.

Lacy, Madison S. & Morgan, Don. Hollywood Cheesecake. 288p. 1983. pap. 9.95 (ISBN 0-686-82477-6). Citadel Pr.

ACTORS AND ACTRESSES–FRANCE

Swindell, Larry. Charles Boyer: The Reluctant Lover. LC 81-43419. (Illus.). 288p. 1983. 15.95 (ISBN 0-385-17052-1). Doubleday.

ACTORS AND ACTRESSES–GREAT BRITAIN

Dithmar, Edward A. John Drew. 137p. 1982. Repr. of 1900 ed. lib. bdg. 35.00 (ISBN 0-89760-143-2). Telegraph Bks.

Howard, Leslie. Trivial Fond Records. Howard, Ronald, ed. 1982. 39.00x (ISBN 0-686-82340-0, Pub. by W Kimber). State Mutual Bk.

Lanchester, Elsa. Elsa Lanchester, Herself. (Illus.). 416p. 1983. 17.95 (ISBN 0-312-24376-6). St Martin.

ACTORS AND ACTRESSES–UNITED STATES

Hagen, Uta. Sources: A Memoir. LC 82-62095. 1982. 19.95 (ISBN 0-933826-54-0); pap. 7.95 (ISBN 0-933826-55-9). Performing Arts.

Parish, James R. & Terrace, Vincent. Actors' Television Credits, Supplement II: 1977-1981. LC 82-5961. 337p. 1982. 22.50 (ISBN 0-8108-1559-1). Scarecrow.

ACTRESSES

see Actors and Actresses

ACTUARIAL SCIENCE

see Insurance, Life; Insurance, Life–Mathematics

ACULEATA

see Ants; Bees

ACUPUNCTURE

Cooperative Group of Shandong Medical College & Shandong College of Traditional Chinese Medicine, Jinan, China. Anatomical Atlas of Chinese Acupuncture Points. 265p. 1983. 32.00 (ISBN 0-08-029784-6). Pergamon.

Jiasan, Yang, ed. The Way to Locate Acu-Points. Xiankun, Meng & Xuewu, Li, trs. from Chinese. (Illus.). 72p. (Orig.). 1982. pap. 12.95 (ISBN 0-8351-1028-1). China Bks.

Points & Meridians & Worsley, J. R. Traditional Chinese Acupuncture, Vol. 1. 1982. 195.00x (ISBN 0-906540-03-8, Pub. by Element Bks). State Mutual Bk.

Ulett, George A. Principles & Practice of Physiologic Acupuncture. 240p. 1982. 42.50 (ISBN 0-87527-309-2). Green.

Woollerton, Henry & McLean, Colleen J. Acupuncture Energy in Health & Disease: A Practical Guide for Advanced Students. (Illus.). 128p. (Orig.). 1983. pap. 6.95 (ISBN 0-7225-0482-9, Pub. by Thorsons Pubs England). Sterling.

Worsley, J. R. Talking about Acupuncture. 1982. 25.00x (ISBN 0-906540-24-0, Pub. by Element Bks). State Mutual Bk.

ACUTE CATARRHAL JAUNDICE

see Hepatitis, Infectious

ADAGES

see Proverbs

ADAM (BIBLICAL CHARACTER)

Flynn, Leslie B. What Is Man? 132p. 1983. pap. 4.50 (ISBN 0-88207-104-1). Victor Bks.

Myra, H. L. Escape from the Twisted Planet. 1983. pap. 5.95 (ISBN 0-8499-2949-0). Word Pub.

ADAMS, HENRY, 1838-1918

Adams, Henry. The Education of Henry Adams. 8.95 (ISBN 0-395-08352-4, SenEd). HM.

ADAPTATION (BIOLOGY)

see also Genetics; Man–Influence of Environment; Origin of Species; Stress (Physiology)

Hooke, J. M. Historical Change In Physical Environment. 256p. 1982. text ed. 49.95 (ISBN 0-686-37995-0). Butterworth.

Jamison, P. L. & Seguras, S. L., eds. The Eskimo of Northwestern Alaska: A Biological Perspective. LC 77-18941. (US-IBP Synthesis Ser.: Vol. 8). 319p. 1978. 46.00 (ISBN 0-87933-319-7). Hutchinson Ross.

Ortner, Donald J., ed. How Humans Adapt: A Biocultural Odyssey. (Illus.). 500p. 1983. text ed. 17.50x (ISBN 0-87474-726-0); pap. text ed. 9.95x (ISBN 0-87474-725-2). Smithsonian.

Turner, N. C. & Kramer, P. J. Adaptation of Plants to Water & High Temperature Stress. 482p. 1980. text ed. 49.95x (ISBN 0-471-05372-4, Pub. by Wiley-Interscience). Wiley.

ADAPTATION (PHYSIOLOGY)

Dyson-Hudson, Rada & Little, Michael A. Rethinking Human Adaptation. (Special Study). 200p. 1982. lib. bdg. 20.00 (ISBN 0-86531-511-6). Westview.

ADAPTATION (PSYCHOLOGY)

see Adjustment (Psychology)

ADAPTATIONS, FILM

see Film Adaptations

ADAPTIVE CONTROL SYSTEMS

see also Feedback Control Systems

Harris, C. J. & Billings, S. A. Self Tuning & Adaptive Control: Theory & Applications. (IEE Control Engineering Ser.: No. 15). 352p. 1981. casebound 44.00 (ISBN 0-906048-62-1). Inst Elect Eng.

ADAPTIVE CONTROL SYSTEMS–MATHEMATICAL MODELS

Ioannou, P. A. & Kokotovic, P. V. Adaptive Systems with Reduced Models. (Lecture Notes in Control & Information Sciences Ser.: Vol. 47). 162p. 1983. pap. 10.00 (ISBN 0-387-12150-1). Springer-Verlag.

ADC

see Child Welfare

ADDING MACHINES

see Calculating-Machines

ADDITION

Burkes, Joyce M. The Math Machine Book for Addition. LC 81-90590. (The Word Machine & Math Machine Books). (Illus.). 48p. (gr. 1-5). 1983. pap. write for info. (ISBN 0-931218-13-6). Joybug.

Frank Schaffer Publications. Addition. (Help Your Child Learn Ser.). (Illus.). 24p. (gr. 1-3). 1978. workbook 1.29 (ISBN 0-86734-007-X, FS 3008). Schaffer Pubns.

Hawkins, Colin. Adding Animals. (Illus.). 12p. 1982. 9.95 (ISBN 0-399-20940-9). Putnam Pub Group.

Mock, Valerie E. Addition & Subtraction Riddles. (Learning Workbooks Mathematics). (gr. 3-5). pap. 1.50 (ISBN 0-8224-4189-6). Pitman.

--Addition Drill. (Learning Workbooks Mathematics). 1981. pap. 1.50 (ISBN 0-8224-4184-5). Pitman.

ADDRESSES

see Speeches, Addresses, etc.

ADEN

Lapidoth, R. The Red Sea & the Gulf of Aden. 1982. lib. bdg. 65.00 (ISBN 90-247-2501-1, Pub. by Martinus Nijhoff Netherlands). Kluwer Boston.

ADENOSINETRIPHOSPHATE

Bridger, William A. & Hendessen, J. Frank. Cell ATP. (Transport in Life Science Ser.). 200p. 1983. 39.50 (ISBN 0-471-08507-3, Pub. by Wiley-Interscience). Wiley.

ADHESION

Allen, K. W., ed. Adhesion, Vols. 1-5. 1977-81. Vol. 1. 45.00 (ISBN 0-85334-735-2, Pub. by Applied Sci England); Vol. 2. 41.00 (ISBN 0-85334-743-3); Vol. 3. 41.00 (ISBN 0-85334-808-1); Vol. 4. 43.00 (ISBN 0-85334-861-8); Vol. 5. 65.75 (ISBN 0-85334-929-0). Elsevier.

Bikales, Norbert M., ed. Adhesion & Bonding. LC 78-172950. 220p. Repr. of 1971 ed. pap. text ed. 16.00 (ISBN 0-471-07230-3). Krieger.

Wake, W. C. Adhesion & the Formation of Adhesives. 2nd ed. (Illus.). 326p. 1982. 49.25 (ISBN 0-85334-134-6, Pub. by Applied Sci England). Elsevier.

ADHESIVES

see also Cement

Gutcho, Marcia, ed. Adhesives Technology: Developments Since 1979. LC 82-19096. (Chemical Technology Review: No. 215). (Illus.). 452p. 1983. 48.00 (ISBN 0-8155-0921-9). Noyes.

Jones, Peter. Fasteners, Joints & Adhesives: A Guide to Engineering Solid Constructions. 416p. 1983. 24.95 (ISBN 0-13-307694-6); pap. 14.95 (ISBN 0-13-307686-5). P-H.

Wake, W. C. Developments in Adhesives, Vol. 1. 1977. 57.50 (ISBN 0-85334-749-2, Pub. by Applied Sci England). Elsevier.

Winloch, A. J. Developments in Adhesives, Vol. 2. (Applied Science Ser.). 1981. 74.00 (ISBN 0-85334-958-4). Elsevier.

ADIPOSITY

see Obesity

ADIRONDACK MOUNTAINS

De Soamo, Maitland C. Joe Call: The Lewis Giant. LC 81-3334. (Illus.). 1891. 12.50 (ISBN 0-686-83970-6). Adirondack Yes.

--Summers on the Saranacs. LC 80-81853. (Illus.). 1980. 22.50 (ISBN 0-9601158-6-2). Adirondack Yes.

Headley, Joel T. The Adirondack, or, Life in the Woods: Facsim of 1849 ed., with added chapters. LC 82-15610. (Illus.). 512p. 24.95 (ISBN 0-916346-47-1). Harbor Hill Bks.

Jamieson, Paul, ed. The Adirondack Reader. 2nd ed. 544p. 1983. 29.50 (ISBN 0-935272-21-6); pap. 18.50 (ISBN 0-935272-22-4). ADK Mtn Club.

ADJECTIVE LAW

see Procedure (Law)

ADJUDICATION, ADMINISTRATIVE

see Administrative Procedure

ADJUSTMENT (PSYCHOLOGY)

see also Conflict (Psychology); Student Adjustment

Atwater, Eastwood. Psychology of Adjustment: Personal Growth in a Changing World. 2nd ed. (Illus.). 448p. 1983. pap. 19.95 (ISBN 0-13-734855-X). P-H.

Bruno, Frank J. Human Adjustment & Personal Growth: Seven Pathways. LC 76-54654. 499p. 1977. text ed. 21.95 (ISBN 0-471-11435-9). Wiley.

Ikels, Charlotte. Adaptation & Aging: Chinese in Hong Kong & the United States. 1983. 27.50 (ISBN 0-208-01999-5, Archon). Shoe String.

Warga, Richard G. Personal Awareness: A Psychology of Adjustment. 3rd ed. LC 82-81113. 528p. 1982. text ed. 21.95 (ISBN 0-395-32586-2). HM.

ADJUSTMENT (STUDENTS)

see Student Adjustment

ADJUVANT ARTHRITIS

see Rheumatoid Arthritis

ADLER, ALFRED, 1870-1937

Adler, Alfred. Souvenirs Fresh & Rancid. 224p. 1982. 14.95 (ISBN 0-394-53218-X). Grove.

--Souvenirs Fresh & Rancid. 224p. 1982. pap. 5.95 (ISBN 0-394-62467-X, Ever). Grove.

Rattner, Joseph. Alfred Adler. Zohn, Harry, tr. from Ger. LC 82-40251. (Literature & Life Ser.). 190p. 1983. 11.95 (ISBN 0-8044-5988-6). Ungar.

ADMINISTRATION

see Administrative Law; Civil Service; Management; Political Science; State, The

also subdivision Politics and Government under names of countries, states, cities, etc.

ADMINISTRATION, AGRICULTURAL

see Agricultural Administration

ADMINISTRATION, BUSINESS

see Business

ADMINISTRATION, NURSING SERVICE

see Nursing Service Administration

ADMINISTRATION, PUBLIC

see Public Administration

ADMINISTRATION OF CRIMINAL JUSTICE

see Criminal Justice, Administration Of

ADMINISTRATION OF JUSTICE

see Justice, Administration Of

ADMINISTRATIVE ABILITY

see Executive Ability

ADMINISTRATIVE ADJUDICATION

see Administrative Procedure

ADMINISTRATIVE AGENCIES

see also Independent Regulatory Commissions

Cooper, Frank E. Administrative Agencies & the Courts. LC 51-62547. (Michigan Legal Studies). xxv, 470p. 1982. Repr. of 1951 ed. lib. bdg. 35.00 (ISBN 0-89941-171-1). W S Hein.

ADMINISTRATIVE COMMUNICATION

see Communication in Management

ADMINISTRATIVE LAW

see also Administrative Agencies; Administrative Procedure; Civil Service; Colonies–Administration; Constitutional Law; Independent Regulatory Commissions; Local Government; Police Power; Public Administration; Public Contracts

Administrative Law Treatise, Vol. 4. 2nd ed. Date not set. price not set. K C Davis.

Bracey, Lucius H. & Rogers, Walter R. Wills: A Virginia Law Practice System. 305p. 1982. looseleaf with forms 75.00 (ISBN 0-686-84233-2). Michie-Bobbs.

Burrus, Bernie R. Administrative Law & Local Government. LC 63-63661. (Michigan Legal Publications Ser.). 139p. 1982. Repr. of 1963 ed. lib. bdg. 30.00 (ISBN 0-89941-170-3). W S Hein.

Gellhorn, Walter & Byse, Clark. Administrative Law Problems, 1983: For Use in Conjunction with Administrative Law, Cases & Comments, Seventh Edition. (University Casebook Ser.). 129p. 1982. pap. text ed. write for info. (ISBN 0-88277-113-2); write for info. tchr's manual (ISBN 0-88277-126-4). Foundation Pr.

Marshaw, Jerry L. Bureaucratic Justice: Administrative Law from an Internal Perspective. LC 82-17506. 240p. 1983. text ed. 25.00x (ISBN 0-300-02808-3). Yale U Pr.

Nathan, Richard P. The Administrative Presidency. 200p. 1983. pap. 9.95 (ISBN 0-471-86871-X). Wiley.

Neely, Alfred S. Administrative Law in West Virginia. 850p. 1982. 35.00 (ISBN 0-686-84232-4). Michie-Bobbs.

Rendleman, Doug, ed. Enforcement of Judgements & Liens in Virginia. 433p. 1982. 35.00 (ISBN 0-87215-419-X). Michie-Bobbs.

Rothschild, Donald P. & Koch, Charles H. Fundamentals of Administrative Practice & Procedure. (Contemporary Legal Education Ser.). 954p. 1981. text ed. 27.00 (ISBN 0-87215-412-2). Michie-Bobbs.

Smith, George P. & Gallo, Barbara G. Virginia Forms, Vol. II. 368p. 1982. 65.00 (ISBN 0-87215-527-7). Michie-Bobbs.

Tomain, Joseph P. & Hollis, Shelia S. Energy Decision Making: The Interaction Law & Policy. LC 81-47747. 224p. 1983. 24.95x (ISBN 0-669-04800-3). Lexington Bks.

ADMINISTRATIVE LAW–GREAT BRITAIN

Wade, H. W. Administrative Law. 5th ed. 1982. 55.00 (ISBN 0-19-876138-4); pap. 29.95 (ISBN 0-19-876139-2). Oxford U Pr.

ADMINISTRATIVE PROCEDURE

see also Licenses

Report on the ILO-NORWAY African Regional Training Course for Senior Social Security Managers & Administrative Officials: Nairobi, 24 November-12 December 1980. 290p. 1982. 19.95 (ISBN 92-2-102857-7). Intl Labour Office.

Robinson, Glen O., et al. The Administrative Process: Supplement. 2nd ed. (American Casebook Ser.). 182p. 1983. pap. text ed. write for info. (ISBN 0-314-72079-0). West Pub.

Tomain, Joseph P. & Hollis, Shelia S. Energy Decision Making: The Interaction Law & Policy. LC 81-47747. 224p. 1983. 24.95x (ISBN 0-669-04800-3). Lexington Bks.

ADMISSION TO COLLEGE

see Universities and Colleges–Admission

ADOLESCENCE

see also Adolescent Psychiatry; Youth

also headings beginning with the word Adolescent

Bayard, Robert T. & Bayard, Jean. How to Deal with Your Acting-Up Teenager: Pratical Help for Desperate Parents. 228p. 1983. 11.95 (ISBN 0-87131-407-X). M Evans.

Clarke-Stewart, Alison & Koch, Joanne. Children: Development Through Adolescence. 625p. 1983. text ed. 23.95 (ISBN 0-471-03069-4); tchrs. manual avail. (ISBN 0-471-87302-0); solutions avail. (ISBN 0-471-87197-4). Wiley.

Forisha, Barbara. Experience of Adolescence: Development in Context. 1983. text ed. 21.95x (ISBN 0-673-15353-3). Scott F.

Lux, J. Scott. How to Help Your Teenagers Become Themselves. 140p. 1982. pap. 7.95 (ISBN 0-9609324-0-2). Family Friends.

Withington, Amelia & Grimes, David. Adolescent Sexuality: A Handbook for Counselors, Teachers & Parents. 135p. 1983. 18.50 (ISBN 0-8290-1270-2); pap. 9.95 (ISBN 0-8290-1271-0). Irvington.

ADOLESCENCE–HEALTH AND HYGIENE

see Youth–Health and Hygiene

ADOLESCENCE–PHOTOGRAPHY

see Photography of Children and Youth

ADOLESCENCE–PSYCHOLOGY

see Adolescent Psychology

ADOLESCENT GIRLS

see also Pregnant Schoolgirls

Bongiovanni, Alfred M., ed. Adolescent Gynecology: A Guide for Clinicians. 275p. 1983. 32.50x (ISBN 0-306-41203-9, Plenum Pr). Plenum Pub.

Cottle, Thomas J. Golden Girl: The Story of an Adolescent Suicide. 304p. 14.95 (ISBN 0-399-12639-2). Putnam Pub Group.

McGuire, Paula. It Won't Happen to Me: Teenagers Talk about Pregnancy. 1983. pap. 6.95 (ISBN 0-440-53845-9, Delta). Dell.

Stewart, Marjabella Y. The Teen Girls Guide to Social Success. 1982. pap. 2.50 (ISBN 0-451-11886-3, Sig Vista). NAL.

ADOLESCENT PARENTS

Frank, Daniel B. Deep Blue Funk & Other Stories: Portraits of Teenage Parents. 1983. pap. 3.95 (ISBN 0-686-83916-1, 25994-3). U of Chicago Pr.

Sugar, Max, ed. Adolescent Parenthood. 256p. 1983. text ed. 25.00 (ISBN 0-89335-185-7). SP Med & Sci Bks.

ADOLESCENT PSYCHIATRY

Arnold, L. E. & Cinningham, Lavern L., eds. Preventing Adolescent Alienation: An Interprofessional Approach. LC 82-48532. 160p. 1983. 19.95 (ISBN 0-669-06269-3). Lexington Bks.

Friedrich, M. H. Adoleszentenpsychosen. (Bibliotheca Psychiatrica: No. 163). (Illus.). vi, 140p. 1983. pap. 41.50 (ISBN 3-8055-3640-2). S Karger.

Gossett, John T. & Lewis, Jerry M. To Find a Way: The Outcome of Hospital Treatment of Disturbed Adolescents. LC 82-17900. 200p. 1983. 20.00 (ISBN 0-87630-326-2). Brunner-Mazel.

Steinberg, Derek. The Clinical Psychiatry of Adolescence: An Approach to Diagnosis, Treatment, & the Organisation of Work. (Studies in Child Psychiatry). 350p. 1983. price not set (ISBN 0-471-10314-4, Pub. by Wiley Interscience). Wiley.

ADOLESCENT PSYCHOLOGY

Adams, Gerald R. & Gullotta, Thomas. Adolescent Life Experiences. LC 82-20748. (Psychology Ser.). 600p. 1983. text ed. 20.95 (ISBN 0-534-01242-6). Brooks-Cole.

Boyce, Nancy L. & Larson, Vicki L. Adolescents' Communication: Development & Disorders. 250p. 1983. three-ring binder 15.95 (ISBN 0-9610370-0-8). Thinking Ink Pr.

Chilman, Catherine S. Adolescent Sexuality in a Changing American Society: Social & Psychological Perspectives for the Human Service Professions. (Personality Processes Ser.). 320p. 1983. price not set (ISBN 0-471-09162-6, Pub. by Wiley-Interscience). Wiley.

Cullinhan, Douglas & Epstein, Michael. Behavior Disorders of Children & Adolescents. (Illus.). 384p. 1983. 23.95 (ISBN 0-13-072041-0). P-H.

Giffin, Mary & Felsenthal, Carol. A Cry for Help. LC 82-45395. 336p. 1983. 16.95 (ISBN 0-385-15599-9). Doubleday.

Heilling, Roma J. Adolescent Suicidal Behavior: A Family Systems Model. Nathan, Peter E., ed. (Research in Clinical Psychology Ser.: No. 7). 1983. 39.95 (ISBN 0-8357-1390-3). Univ Microfilms.

Ketterman, Grace H. You & Your Child's Problems: How to Understand & Solve Them. 352p. 1983. 14.95 (ISBN 0-8007-1355-9). Revell.

Sprinthall, Norman A. & Collins, W. Andrews. Adolescent Psychology: A Developmental View. (Illus.). 608p. Date not set. text ed. price not set (ISBN 0-201-16301-2). A-W.

Tallman, Irving & Marotz-Braden, Ramon, eds. Adolescent Socialization in Cross-Cultural Perspective. (Monograph). Date not set. price not set (ISBN 0-12-683180-7). Acad Pr.

ADOPTION

see also Foster Home Care

Curto, Josephine. How to Become a Single Parent: A Guide for Single People Considering Adoption or Natural Parenthood Alone. 252p. 1983. 14.95 (ISBN 0-13-396192-3); pap. 6.95 (ISBN 0-13-396184-2). P-H.

Fitzgerald, John & Murcer, Bill. Building New Families: Through Adoption & Fostering. (The Practice of Social Work Ser.: No. 10). 44p. 1982. text ed. 25.00x (ISBN 0-631-13148-5, Pub. by Basil Blackwell England); pap. text ed. 9.95x (ISBN 0-631-13193-0, Pub. by Basil Blackwell England). Biblio Dist.

Heim, Alice. Thicker Than Water? Adoption. 208p. 1983. 21.50 (ISBN 0-436-19155-5, Pub. by Secker & Warburg); pap. 12.50 (ISBN 0-436-19156-3, Pub. by Secker & Warburg). David & Charles.

Hoopes, Janet L. New Publication on Adoption Offered by the Child Welfare League Prediction in Child Development: A Longitudinal Study of Adoptive & Nonadoptive Families--the Delaware Family Study. 104p. 1982. 9.50 (ISBN 0-87868-170-1). Child Welfare.

Joe, Barbara. Public Policies Toward Adoption. 84p. 1979. pap. text ed. 5.00 (ISBN 0-87766-253-3). Urban Inst.

Silber, Kathleen & Speedlin, Phylis. Dear Birthmother. Myers, Gail E., ed. 214p. (Orig.). 1983. 16.00 (ISBN 0-931722-20-9); pap. 7.95 (ISBN 0-931722-19-5). Corona Pub.

Souaid, Robert, et al. Adoption: A Guide for Those Who Want to Adopt. 25p. (Orig.). 1982. pap. 1.00 (ISBN 0-686-37425-8). Coun NY Law.

Zimmerman, Martha. Should I Keep My Baby? 112p. (Orig.). 1983. pap. 3.95 (ISBN 0-87123-578-1). Bethany Hse.

ADOPTION–JUVENILE LITERATURE

Lapsley, Susan. I Am Adopted. (Illus.). 28p. (ps-2). 1983. bds. 3.95 (ISBN 0-370-02032-4, Pub by The Bodley Head). Merrimack Bk Serv.

ADRENAL CORTEX HORMONES

see Adrenocortical Hormones

ADRENAL STEROIDS

see Adrenocortical Hormones; Steroids

ADRENERGIC MECHANISMS

Von Euler. Release & Uptake Functions in Adrenergic Nerve Granules. 110p. 1982. 50.00x (ISBN 0-85323-084-6, Pub. by Liverpool Univ England). State Mutual Bk.

ADRENOCORTICAL HORMONES

Suzuki, T. Physiology of Adrenocortical Secretion. (Frontiers of Hormone Research: Vol. 11). (Illus.). viii, 200p. 1983. 78.00 (ISBN 3-8055-3644-5). S Karger.

Wendt, H. & Frosch, P. J. Clinico-Pharmacological Models for the Assay of Tropical Corticoids. (Illus.). 62p. (Japanese.). 1982. pap. 24.00 (ISBN 3-8055-3686-0). S Karger.

--Modelli sperimentali clinico-farmacologici per la valutazione di preparati topici corticosteroidei. (Illus.). 64p. (Ital.). 1982. pap. 24.00 (ISBN 3-8055-3685-2). S Karger.

ADSORPTION

see also Adhesion; Ion Exchange

Ottewill, R. H., ed. Adsorption from Solution. write for info. (ISBN 0-12-530980-5). Acad Pr.

ADULT EDUCATION

see also Education of the Aged; Non-Formal Education

Andrews & Houston. Adult Learners: A Research Study. 1981. 5.00 (ISBN 0-686-38071-1). Assn Tchr Ed.

Berkley, Sandra & Moore, Gary W. Delta's Oral Placement Test. 62p. (Orig.). 1982. pap. text ed. 18.95 (ISBN 0-937354-05-8). Delta Systems.

Birge, Lynn. Serving Adult Learners. (ALA Ser. in Librarianship). 230p. 1981. pap. text ed. 18.00 (ISBN 0-8389-0346-0). ALA.

Carrol, Frieda. Continuing Education Alternatives Workbook. 50p. 1983. 8.95. Biblio Pr GA.

Heinrich, June S. & Heinrich, June S. Educating Older People: Another View of Mainstreaming. LC 82-60801. (Fastback Ser.: No. 181). 50p. 1982. pap. 0.75 (ISBN 0-87367-181-3). Phi Delta Kappa.

Kidd, J. R. How Adults Learn. 324p. 1972. 16.95 (ISBN 0-695-81171-1). Follett.

Lovell, R. Bernard. Adult Learning. (New Patterns of Learning Ser.). 170p. 1982. 14.95 (ISBN 0-470-27368-2). Halsted Pr.

Prospects for Adult Education & Development in Asia & the Pacific. 69p. 1981. pap. 7.00 (ISBN 0-686-81856-3, UB98, UNESCO). Unipub.

Thorndike, Eard L. & Bergman, Elsie O. Adult Learning. 335p. Repr. of 1928 ed. lib. bdg. 50.00 (ISBN 0-89987-821-0). Darby Bks.

Update Publicare Research Staff. Continuing Education Alternatives Update: Notebook of Back Issues. 35p. 1983. pap. text ed. 8.00 (ISBN 0-686-38892-5). Update Pub Co.

ADULT EDUCATION–GREAT BRITAIN

Blyth, John A. English University Adult Education 1908-1958. 384p. 1982. 20.00 (ISBN 0-7190-0903-0). Manchester.

Cotterell, A. B. & Heley, E. W., eds. Tertiary-A Radical Approach to Post-Compulsory Education. 160p. 1980. 39.00x (ISBN 0-85950-402-6, Pub. by Thornes England). State Mutual Bk.

Devereux, William. Adult Education in Inner London 1870-1980. 352p. 1982. 50.00x (ISBN 0-85683-059-3, Pub. by Shepeard-Walwyn England). State Mutual Bk.

ADULTERY

Petersen, J. Allen. The Myth of the Greener Grass. 1983. 8.95 (ISBN 0-8423-4656-2). Tyndale.

ADULTHOOD

see also Aged

Atwater, Eastwood. Psychology of Adjustment: Personal Growth in a Changing World. 2nd ed. (Illus.). 448p. 1983. pap. 19.95 (ISBN 0-13-734855-X). P-H.

O'Kane, Monica L. Living with Adult Children: A Helpful Guide for Parents & Grown Children Sharing the Same Roof. (Illus.). 190p. 1982. 9.95 (ISBN 0-9609198-1-3); pap. 4.95 (ISBN 0-9609198-0-5). Diction Bks.

ADVENT

see also Second Advent

Davidson, Robert, ed. Creative Ideas for Advent. 114p. (Orig.). 1980. pap. 9.95 (ISBN 0-940754-06-1). Ed Ministries.

Lawrence, Emeric. Jesus Present & Coming: Daily Meditations on the Advent & Christmas Masses. LC 82-20380. 128p. 1982. pap. 7.95 (ISBN 0-8146-1284-9). Liturgical Pr.

ADVENTURE AND ADVENTURERS

see also Discoveries (In Geography); Explorers; Frontier and Pioneer Life; Heroes; Sea Stories; Seafaring Life; Shipwrecks; Underwater Exploration; Voyages and Travels

Attenborough, David. Journeys to the Past. 1983. 21.95 (ISBN 0-686-38869-0, Pub. by Salem Hse Ltd). Merrimack Bk Serv.

--Zoo Quest Expeditions. 1983. 21.95 (ISBN 0-686-38870-4, Pub. by Salem Hse Ltd). Merrimack Bk Serv.

Bonington, Chris. Quest for Adventure. (Illus.). 448p. Date not set. 30.00 (ISBN 0-686-82352-4). Crown.

Burns, Wayne. Journey Through the Dark Woods. LC 82-15822. 230p. (Orig.). 1982. pap. 6.95 (ISBN 0-686-42801-3). Howe St Pr.

Fiennes, Ranulph. To the Ends of the Earth: The Transglobe Expedition, the First Polo-to Pole Circumnavigation of the Globe. (Illus.). 1983. 15.95 (ISBN 0-87795-490-9). Arbor Hse.

Skinner, Constance L. Adventures of Oregon. 1920. text ed. 8.50x (ISBN 0-686-83454-2). Elliots Bks.

ADVERTISEMENT WRITING

see Advertising Copy

ADVERTISING

see also Catalogs, Commercial; Commercial Art; Display of Merchandise; Market Surveys; Marketing; Packaging; Propaganda; Public Relations; Publicity; Radio Advertising; Sales Promotion; Salesmen and Salesmanship; Television Advertising

also subdivided by topic, e.g. Advertising–Banks and Banking

Baker, S. Systematic Approach to Advertising Creativity. 288p. 1983. pap. 10.95 (ISBN 0-07-003353-6, GB). McGraw.

Bolen, William H. Advertising. LC 80-18915. (Marketing Ser.). 504p. 1981. text ed. 25.95 (ISBN 0-471-03486-X); avail. tchrs. manual (ISBN 0-471-08937-0). Wiley.

Burke, J. D. Advertising in the Marketplace. 1980. text ed. 17.60 (ISBN 0-07-009035-1); instr's manual & key 4.55 (ISBN 0-07-009036-X). McGraw.

Courtney, Alice E. & Whipple, Thomas W. Sex Stereotyping in Advertising. 1983. price not set (ISBN 0-669-03955-1). Lexington Bks.

Faison, Edmund W. Advertising: A Behavioral Approach for Managers. LC 79-21379. (Marketing Ser.). 783p. 1980. text ed. 28.95 (ISBN 0-471-04956-5); avail. tchrs. manual (ISBN 0-471-07768-2). Wiley.

Fletcher, Alan D. & Bowers, Thomas A. Fundamentals of Advertising Research. 2nd ed. LC 82-24217. (Grid Series in Advertising & Journalism). 334p. 1983. price not set. Grid Pub.

Frey, Albert W. & Halterman, Jean C. Advertising. 4th ed. 594p. 1970. 30.95x (ISBN 0-471-06597-8, 33291). Wiley.

Kornfeld, Lewis. To Catch a Mouse, Make a Noise Like a Cheese. LC 82-13320. 1982. 15.00 (ISBN 0-13-922930-2, Busn). P-H.

Lowe, E. Successful Retailing through Advertising. 192p. 1983. 7.95 (ISBN 0-07-084588-3, P&RB). McGraw.

Nicholl, David S. Advertising. 240p. 1978. 30.00x (ISBN 0-7121-0166-7, Pub. by Macdonald & Evans). State Mutual Bk.

OECD Staff. Advertising Directed At Children: Endorsements in Advertising. 64p. (Orig.). 1982. pap. 6.00x (ISBN 92-64-12276-1). OECD.

PROMODATA (Promotion, Marketing & Advertising Data), 1982. 2nd ed. 336p. 1982. 87.50x (ISBN 0-8002-3071-X). Intl Pubns Serv.

Reuijl, Jan C. On the Determination of Advertising Effectiveness: An Empirical Study of the German Cigarette Market. 1982. lib. bdg. 30.00 (ISBN 0-89838-125-8). Kluwer-Nijhoff.

Rodriguez, Raymond L. Promoters: Structure & Function. Chamberlin, Michael J., ed. 540p. 1982. 41.50 (ISBN 0-03-059919-9). Praeger.

Stansfield, Richard H. Advertising Manager's Handbook. 1982. 57.50 (ISBN 0-85013-128-6). Dartnell Corp.

Wheeler, Elmer. Tested Sentences that Sell. 228p. Date not set. 10.95 (ISBN 0-686-84599-4, Reward); pap. 5.95 (ISBN 0-13-909101-7). P-H.

Young, Robert F. & Greyser, Stephen A. Managing Cooperative Advertising: A Strategic Approach. LC 82-48572. 1983. write for info. (ISBN 0-669-06301-0). Lexington Bks.

ADVERTISING–AGENTS

see Advertising Agencies

ADVERTISING–CIGARETTES

Reuijl, Jan C. On the Determination of Advertising Effectiveness: An Empirical Study of the German Cigarette Market. 1982. lib. bdg. 30.00 (ISBN 0-89838-125-8). Kluwer-Nijhoff.

ADVERTISING–DIRECT-MAIL

see also Catalogs, Commercial; Mail-Order Business

Holtz, H. Mail Order Magic: Sure-Fire Techniques to Expand Any Business by Direct Mail. 256p. 1983. 15.95 (ISBN 0-07-029628-6); pap. 7.95 (ISBN 0-07-029631-6). McGraw.

ADVERTISING–DIRECTORIES

Danish Association of Advertising Agencies, ed. Media Scandinavia, 1982. 31st ed. LC 72-623099. 618p. (Eng. & Danish.). 1982. 75.00x (ISBN 87-87827-13-1). Intl Pubns Serv.

Marks, Stanley J. & Marks, Ethel M. The Blue Book of the U. S. Consumer Market, 1983. 1983. pap. 50.00 (ISBN 0-686-38795-3). Bur Intl Aff.

ADVERTISING–HISTORY

Pope, Daniel. The Making of Modern Advertising. 275p. 1983. 18.95 (ISBN 0-465-04325-9). Basic.

ADVERTISING–HOTELS, TAVERNS, ETC.

Gottlieb, Leon. Foodservice-Hospitality Advertising & Promotion. 363p. 1982. text ed. 18.50 (ISBN 0-672-97868-7); Tchr's Ed. 3.33 (ISBN 0-672-97869-5). Bobbs.

ADVERTISING–LAW

see Advertising Laws

ADVERTISING–MATHEMATICAL MODELS

Gensch, D. Advertising Planning: Mathematical Models in Advertising Media Planning. 1973. 12.95 (ISBN 0-444-41074-0). Elsevier.

ADVERTISING–PSYCHOLOGICAL ASPECTS

Fletcher, Alan. Advertising & Society. 256p. 1983. text ed. write for info. (ISBN 0-87251-082-4). Crain Bks.

ADVERTISING–REAL ESTATE BUSINESS

Danks, Lawrence J. Real Estate Advertising. 260p. 1982. 24.95 (ISBN 0-88462-420-X). Real Estate Ed Co.

ADVERTISING–RETAIL TRADE

see Advertising

ADVERTISING–YEARBOOKS

Advertising Age Yearbook, 1983. LC 81-641487. 340p. 1983. price not set (ISBN 0-87251-081-6). Crain Bks.

Danish Association of Advertising Agencies, ed. Media Scandinavia, 1982. 31st ed. LC 72-623099. 618p. (Eng. & Danish.). 1982. 75.00x (ISBN 87-87827-13-1). Intl Pubns Serv.

ADVERTISING, ART IN

see Commercial Art

ADVERTISING, CONSUMER

see Advertising

ADVERTISING, DIRECT

see Advertising–Direct-Mail

ADVERTISING, MAGAZINE

Potter, William G. & Faber, Arlene. Serials Automation for Acquisition & Inventory Control. 192p. 1982. pap. text ed. 15.00 (ISBN 0-8389-3267-3). ALA.

ADVERTISING, MAGAZINE–DIRECTORIES

see Advertising–Directories

ADVERTISING, MAIL

see Advertising–Direct-Mail

ADVERTISING, NEWSPAPER

Notman, Larry. Ad Kit Four. 5.00 (ISBN 0-686-84765-2). Newspaper Serv.

--Ad Kit Three. 5.00 (ISBN 0-686-84769-5). Newspaper Serv.

--Ad Kit Two. 5.00 (ISBN 0-686-84768-7). Newspaper Serv.

--Front Office Worker. 5.00 (ISBN 0-686-84771-7). Newspaper Serv.

--Getting Started. 5.00 (ISBN 0-686-84764-4). Newspaper Serv.

--Management: Starting Out. 10.00 (ISBN 0-686-84770-9). Newspaper Serv.

--Professional Ad Sales. 5.00 (ISBN 0-686-84766-0). Newspaper Serv.

--Promotions & Sections. (Illus.). 40p. (Orig.). 1983. pap. 5.00x (ISBN 0-918488-11-7). Newspaper Serv.

--Working Ad Kit. 5.00 (ISBN 0-686-84767-9). Newspaper Serv.

ADVERTISING, NEWSPAPER–DIRECTORIES

see Advertising–Directories

ADVERTISING, PICTORIAL

see Posters

ADVERTISING, RADIO

see Radio Advertising

ADVERTISING, RETAIL

see Advertising

ADVERTISING, TELEVISION

see Television Advertising

ADVERTISING AGENCIES

Weilbacher, William M. Choosing an Ad Agency. 192p. 1983. pap. price not set (ISBN 0-87251-083-2). Crain Bks.

ADVERTISING AGENCIES–EUROPE

European Handbook of Advertising Agencies-Europa Handbuch, 1982-83. 21st ed. LC 76-18691. 746p. (Ger., Eng. & Fr.). 1982. pap. 60.00x (ISBN 0-8002-3102-3). Intl Pubns Serv.

ADVERTISING ART

see Commercial Art

ADVERTISING BUSINESS

see Advertising Agencies

ADVERTISING COPY

Jefkins, Frank. Advertisement Writing. 256p. 1976. 25.00x (ISBN 0-7121-0138-1, Pub. by Macdonald & Evans). State Mutual Bk.

Latman, Alan & Lightstone, James F., eds. Kaminstein Legislative History Project: A Compendium & Analytical Index of Materials Leading to the Copyright Act of 1976, Vol. II; Sections 109-114. LC 81-5953. xxxviii, 490p. 1982. text ed. 95.00x (ISBN 0-8377-0732-3). Rothman.

ADVERTISING LAWS

Lawson, R. G. Advertising Law. 400p. 1978. 60.00x (ISBN 0-7121-1239-1, Pub. by Macdonald & Evans). State Mutual Bk.

ADVERTISING LAYOUT AND TYPOGRAPHY

Borgman, Harry. Advertising Layout: A Step-by-Step Guide for Print & T.V. (Illus.). 160p. 1983. 22.50 (ISBN 0-8230-0154-7). Watson-Guptill.

ADVERTISING RESEARCH

see also Market Surveys

Harris, Richard J., ed. Information Processing Research in Advertising. 1983. text ed. write for info. (ISBN 0-89859-204-6). L Erlbaum Assocs.

ADVERTISING TYPOGRAPHY

see Advertising Layout and Typography

ADVISORY OPINIONS

Hignite, Haskel. Sound Advice for Everyone. LC 82-60526. 125p. 1983. pap. 4.95 (ISBN 0-88247-681-5). R & E Res Assoc.

ADVOCATES

see Lawyers

AERIAL LAW

see Aeronautics–Laws and Regulations

AERIAL NAVIGATION

see Navigation (Aeronautics)

AERIAL PHOTOGRAPHY

see Photography, Aerial

AERIAL ROCKETS

see Rockets (Ordnance)

AERIAL WARFARE

see Air Warfare

AEROBIOLOGY

see Air–Microbiology

AERODROMES

see Airports

AERODYNAMICS

see also Aeronautics; Boundary Layer; Turbulence; Wind Tunnels

Aynsley, R. M. Architectural Aerodynamics. 1977. 41.00 (ISBN 0-85334-698-4, Pub. by Applied Sci England). Elsevier.

Bridge Aerodynamics. 140p. 1981. 90.00x (ISBN 0-7277-0135-5, Pub. by Tech Pr). State Mutual Bk.

Cebeci, T., ed. Numerical & Physical Aspects of Aerodynamic Flows, California State University 1981: Proceedings. (Illus.). 636p. 1983. 78.00 (ISBN 0-387-11044-5). Springer-Verlag.

Etkin, Bernard. Dynamics of Atmospheric Flight. LC 73-165946. (Illus.). 579p. 1972. text ed. 39.95x (ISBN 0-471-24620-4). Wiley.

Houghton, E. I. & Carruthers, N. B. Aerodynamics for Engineering Students. 704p. 1982. pap. text ed. 39.50 (ISBN 0-7131-3433-X). E Arnold.

Krasnov. Aerodynamics of Bodies of Revolution: A Rand Corporation Research Study. 1970. 17.50 (ISBN 0-444-00076-3). Elsevier.

AERODYNAMICS, SUBSONIC

see Aerodynamics

AEROLITES

see Meteorites

AERONAUTICAL INSTRUMENTS

U. S. Department of Transportation Federal Aviation Administration. Instrument Flying Handbook. (Illus.). 268p. (Orig.). 1982. pap. 8.50 (ISBN 0-941272-20-6). Astro Pubs.

AERONAUTICAL NAVIGATION

see Navigation (Aeronautics)

AERONAUTICAL RESEARCH

see also Astronautical Research

Culick, F. E., ed. Guggenheim Aeronautical Laboratory at the California Institute of Technology: The First Fifty Years. LC 82-50314. (Illus.). 1983. pap. 7.50 (ISBN 0-911302-46-8). San Francisco Pr.

Roe, P. L. Numerical Methods in Aeronautical Fluid Dynamics. (IMA Conference Ser.). Date not set. 55.50 (ISBN 0-12-592520-4). Acad Pr.

AERONAUTICAL SPORTS

see Airplane Racing; Airplanes–Models

AERONAUTICS

see also Aerodynamics; Air Lines; Air Pilots; Air-Ships; Airplanes; Airports; Astronautics; Electronics in Aeronautics; Flight; Flying-Machines; Flying Saucers; Helicopters; Interplanetary Voyages; Kites; Navigation (Aeronautics); Stability of Airplanes

Bent, R. D. & McKinley, J. L. Aircraft Basic Science. 5th ed. 1980. 20.05 (ISBN 0-07-004791-X); instr's. manual 4.00 (ISBN 0-07-002447-2); study guide & test bk. avail. McGraw.

Carlson, Glenn. Airplane Talk. 276p. 1982. pap. 16.95 (ISBN 0-686-43398-X, Pub. by Watosh Pub). Aviation.

Fowler, Ron. Pre-Flight Planning. (Illus.). 320p. 1983. 17.95 (ISBN 0-02-540300-1). Macmillan.

Scott, Catherine D., et al, eds. Directory of Aerospace Resources: A Guide to Special Collections in College, University, Historical Societies, & the National, State, & Local Archives of the United States. (Smithsonian Institution Libraries Research Guides). 112p. 1982. pap. 9.95x (ISBN 0-87474-851-8). Smithsonian.

University Aviation Association. Collegiate Aviation Directory: A Guide to College Level Aviation-Aerospace Study. Schukert, Michael A., ed. 128p. 1982. pap. text ed. 2.55 (ISBN 0-8403-2876-1). Kendall-Hunt.

AERONAUTICS–BIOGRAPHY

see also Air Pilots

Desmond, Kevin. Richard Shuttleworth. (Illus.). 192p. 1982. 19.95 (ISBN 0-86720-629-2). Sci Bks Intl.

Renstrom, Arthur G. Wilbur & Orville Wright: Pictorial Materials. LC 82-600194. (Illus.). xxi, 201p. 1982. 6.00 (ISBN 0-8444-0399-7). Lib Congress.

Who's Who in Aviation & Aerospace. 1982. 60.00 (ISBN 0-686-84717-2). Warren.

AERONAUTICS–DICTIONARIES

Gunston, Bill. Jane's Aerospace Dictionary. 492p. 1980. 34.95 (ISBN 0-86720-573-3). Sci Bks Intl.

AERONAUTICS–FLIGHTS

see also Space Flight

Chichester, Francis. Solo to Sydney. 224p. 1982. 30.00x (ISBN 0-85177-254-4, Pub. by Conway Maritime England). State Mutual Bk.

AERONAUTICS–HANDBOOKS, MANUALS, ETC.

Airlife Publishing Ltd., ed. Pooley's Flight Guide: United Kingdom & Ireland. 400p. 1982. 59.00x (ISBN 0-902037-07-2, Pub. by Airlife England). State Mutual Bk.

Drisdale, Tommy & Hanes, Steven. The Ultralight Aviator's Handbook. (Illus.). 336p. (Orig.). 1982. pap. 16.95 (ISBN 0-912185-00-7). Skyflight Intl.

Winner, Walter P. Airman's Information Manual, 1983. 18th ed. (Illus.). 304p. pap. 5.95w (ISBN 0-911721-94-0). Aviation.

AERONAUTICS–HISTORY

Compton, Joy B. A Decade of Glory. (Illus.). 64p. 1983. 10.50 (ISBN 0-89962-322-0). Todd & Honeywell.

The Explorers. (Epic of Flight Ser.). 1983. lib. bdg. 19.96 (ISBN 0-686-42792-0, Pub. by Time-Life). Silver.

Gillispie, Charles C. The Montgolfier Brothers & the Invention of Aviation, 1783-1784: With a Word on the Importance of Ballooning for the Science of Heat & for the Art of Building Railroads. LC 82-61363. (Illus.). 272p. 1983. 35.00 (ISBN 0-691-08321-5). Princeton U Pr.

Jablonski, E. America in the Air War. LC 82-5539. (Epic of Flight Ser.). lib. bdg. 19.96 (ISBN 0-8094-3342-7, Pub. by Time-Life). Silver.

Jackson, Donald D. Flying the Mail. LC 82-2020. (Epic of Flight Ser.). lib. bdg. 19.96 (ISBN 0-8094-3330-3, Pub. by Time-Life). Silver.

Miller, Ronald E. & Sawer, David. The Technical Development of Modern Aviation. (Airlines History Project Ser.). Date not set. price not set (ISBN 0-404-19328-5). AMS Pr.

Mudge, Robert W. Adventures of a Yellowbird. (Airlines History Project Ser.). Date not set. price not set (ISBN 0-404-19329-3). AMS Pr.

Ogilvy, David. The Shuttleworth Collection. 1982. 45.00x (ISBN 0-906393-18-3, Pub. by Airlife England). State Mutual Bk.

Rowe, Basil. Under My Wings. (Airlines History Project Ser.). Date not set. price not set (ISBN 0-404-19333-1). AMS Pr.

Seagrave, Sterling. The Bush Pilots. (Epic of Flight Ser.). 1983. lib. bdg. 19.96 (ISBN 0-8094-3309-5, Pub. by Time-Life). Silver.

Smith, Henry L. Airways Abroad: The Story of American World Air Routes. (Airlines History Project Ser.). Date not set. price not set (ISBN 0-404-19336-6). AMS Pr.

Taylor, Michael. Fantastic Flying Machines. (Illus.). 144p. 1982. 12.95 (ISBN 0-86720-552-0). Sci Bks Intl.

Taylor, Michael & Mondey, David. Giants in the Sky. (Illus.). 216p. 1982. 17.95 (ISBN 0-86720-626-8). Sci Bks Intl.

AERONAUTICS–JUVENILE LITERATURE

see also Airplanes–Juvenile Literature

Sabin, Louis. Wilbur & Orville Wright: The Flight to Adventure. LC 82-15879. (Illus.). 48p. (gr. 4-6). 1983. PLB 6.89 (ISBN 0-89375-851-5); pap. text ed. 1.95 (ISBN 0-89375-852-3). Troll Assocs.

AERONAUTICS–LAWS AND REGULATIONS

Federal Administration, Dept. of Transportation. Pilot's Federal Aviation Regulations: (Composite Edition) 1983. 252p. 1982. pap. 5.95 (ISBN 0-686-81816-4). Astro Pubs.

Federal Aviation Administration. Federal Aviation Regulations fo Pilots, 1982. 7th ed. Winner, Walter P., ed. 160p. 1983. pap. 4.00w (ISBN 0-911721-95-9). Aviation.

Federal Aviation Administration. Department of Transportation. Pilot's Federal Aviation Regulations: 1983 Composite Edition. 256p. 1983. pap. text ed. 6.00 (ISBN 0-686-82514-4). Astro Pubs.

Kean, A. Essays in Air Law. 1982. lib. bdg. 74.00 (ISBN 90-247-2543-7, Pub. by Martinus Nijhoff Netherlands). Kluwer Boston.

Macavoy, Paul W. & Snow, John W., eds. Regulation of Passenger Fares & Competition Among Airlines. 1977. pap. 7.25 (ISBN 0-8447-3256-7). Am Enterprise.

Pahl, Walther. Die Luftwege der Erde: Politische Geographie des Weltluftverkehrs. (Airlines History Project Ser.). (Illus.). Date not set. price not set (ISBN 0-404-19330-7). AMS Pr.

AERONAUTICS–MEDICAL ASPECTS

see Aviation Medicine

AERONAUTICS–NAVIGATION

see Navigation (Aeronautics)

AERONAUTICS–PICTORIAL WORKS

Seo, Hiroshi. Civil Aircraft of the World. (Illus.). 96p. 1982. 12.95 (ISBN 0-86720-559-8). Sci Bks Intl.

Taylor, Michael & Mondey, David. Giants in the Sky. (Illus.). 216p. 1982. 17.95 (ISBN 0-86720-626-8). Sci Bks Intl.

AERONAUTICS–RESEARCH

see Aeronautical Research

AERONAUTICS–VOCATIONAL GUIDANCE

Bell, Rivian & Koenig, Teresa. Careers in an Airplane Factory. LC 82-17136. (Early Career Bks.). (Illus.). 36p. (gr. 2-5). 1983. PLB 5.95g (ISBN 0-8225-0349-2). Lerner Pubns.

AERONAUTICS–YEARBOOKS

Jane's Airport Equipment 1982-1983. (Jane's Yearbooks). (Illus.). 400p. 120.00 (ISBN 0-86720-610-1). Sci Bks Intl.

Jane's All the World's Aircraft 1982-1983. (Jane's Yearbooks). (Illus.). 840p. 140.00 (ISBN 0-86720-621-7). Sci Bks Intl.

Mondey, David & Taylor, Michael. Jane's 1982-83 Aviation Annual. (Illus.). 158p. 1982. 15.95 (ISBN 0-86720-632-2). Sci Bks Intl.

Wilson, Michael, ed. Jane's Avionics, 1982-1983. (Jane's Yearbooks). (Illus.). 400p. 1982. 110.00 (ISBN 0-86720-611-X). Sci Bks Intl.

AERONAUTICS–GREAT BRITAIN

Airlife Publishing Ltd., ed. Pooley's Flight Guide: United Kingdom & Ireland. 400p. 1982. 59.00x (ISBN 0-902037-07-2, Pub. by Airlife England). State Mutual Bk.

Sharp, Martin. The History of De-Havillands. 1982. 70.00x (ISBN 0-906393-20-5, Pub. by Airlife England). State Mutual Bk.

AERONAUTICS, COMMERCIAL

see also Air Lines; Air Mail Service; Transport Planes

Kean, A. Essays in Air Law. 1982. lib. bdg. 74.00 (ISBN 90-247-2543-7, Pub. by Martinus Nijhoff Netherlands). Kluwer Boston.

Lissitzyn, Oliver J. International Air Transport & National Policy. (Airlines History Project Ser.). Date not set. write for info. (ISBN 0-404-19327-7). AMS Pr.

Macavoy, Paul W. & Snow, John W., eds. Regulation of Passenger Fares & Competition Among Airlines. 1977. pap. 7.25 (ISBN 0-8447-3256-7). Am Enterprise.

Munson, Ken. U. S. Commercial Aircraft. (Illus.). 192p. 1982. 19.95 (ISBN 0-86720-628-4). Sci Bks Intl.

Reeves, Earl. Aviation's Place in Tomorrow's Business. (Airlines History Project Ser.). Date not set. price not set (ISBN 0-404-19331-5). AMS Pr.

Smith, Henry L. Airways: The History of Commercial Aviation in the United States. (Airlines History Project Ser.). (Illus.). Date not set. price not set (ISBN 0-404-19335-8). AMS Pr.

Stevenson, Arthur J. The New York-Newark Air Freight System. LC 82-160111. (Research Papers: Nos. 199-200). (Illus.). 440p. 1982. pap. 16.00x (ISBN 0-89065-106-X). U Chicago Dept Geog.

Stroud, John. Annals of British & Commonwealth Air Transport, 1919-1960. (Airlines History Project Ser.). Date not set. price not set (ISBN 0-404-19337-4). AMS Pr.

AERONAUTICS, ELECTRONICS IN

see Electronics in Aeronautics

AERONAUTICS AND STATE–GREAT BRITAIN

Hayward, Keith. Government & British Civil Aerospace: A Case Study in Post-War Technology Policy. 224p. 1983. write for info. (ISBN 0-7190-0877-8). Manchester.

AEROPLANES

see Airplanes

AEROSOLS

see also Fume Control

Friedlander, S. K. Smoke, Dust & Haze: Fundamentals of Aerosol Behavior. LC 76-26928. 317p. 1977. 35.50 (ISBN 0-471-01468-0, Pub. by Wiley Interscience). Wiley.

Marple, V. A. & Liu, B. Y. H., eds. Aerosol In the Mining & Industrial Work Environments: Fundamentals & Status, 3 vol. set, Vol. 1. LC 82-70701. (Illus.). 360p. 1983. 37.50 (ISBN 0-250-40531-8); Set. 93.75 (ISBN 0-250-40533-4). Ann Arbor Science.

--Aerosols In the Mining & Industrial Work Environments: Characterization, 3 vol. set, Vol. 2. LC 82-70701. (Illus.). 283p. 1983. 18.75 (ISBN 0-250-40532-6); Set. 93.75 (ISBN 0-250-40533-4). Ann Arbor Science.

--Aerosols In the Mining & Industrial Work Environment: Instrumentation, 3 Vols, Vol. 3. LC 82-70701. (Illus.). 500p. 1983. 37.50 (ISBN 0-250-40597-0). Ann Arbor Science.

Ruhnke, L. H. & Deepak, A. Hygroscopic Aerosols in the Planetary Boundary Layer. (Illus.). Date not set. price not set (ISBN 0-937194-02-6). Spectrum Pr.

AEROSPACE INDUSTRIES

see also Aircraft Industry

Laurenson, R. M. & Yuceoglu, U., eds. Advances In Aerospace Structures & Materials, 1982. (AD-03). 1982. 30.00 (H00240). ASME.

Who's Who in Aviation & Aerospace. 1982. 60.00 (ISBN 0-686-84717-2). Warren.

AEROSPACE LAW

see Aeronautics–Laws and Regulations

AESCHYLUS

Rosenmeyer, Thomas G. The Art of Aeschylus. (Illus.). 393p. 1983. pap. 12.95 (ISBN 0-520-04608-0, CAL 541). U of Cal Pr.

Spatz, Lois. Aeschylus. (World Authors Ser.). 1982. lib. bdg. 15.95 (ISBN 0-8057-6522-0, Twayne). G K Hall.

AESTHETICS

see Esthetics

AFFECTION

see Friendship; Love

AFFIRMATIVE ACTION PROGRAMS

see also Minorities–Employment

Cannon, Joan B. & Smith, Ed. Resources for Affirmative Action: An Annotated Directory of Books, Periodicals, Films, Training Aids, & Consultants on Equal Opportunity. LC 82-83304. 190p. (Orig.). 1982. pap. 12.95 (ISBN 0-912048-32-8). Garrett Pk.

Harvey, John F. & Dickinson, Elizabeth M., eds. Librarians' Affirmative Action Handbook. LC 82-10644. 316p. 1983. 18.50 (ISBN 0-8108-1581-8). Scarecrow.

Rudman, Jack. Affirmative Action Officer. (Career Examination Ser.: C-2647). (Cloth bdg. avail. on request). pap. 10.00 (ISBN 0-8373-2647-8). Natl Learning.

--Principal Affirmative Action Officer. (Career Examination Ser.: C-2689). (Cloth bdg. avail. on request). pap. 12.00 (ISBN 0-8373-2689-3). Natl Learning.

AFFLICTION

see Suffering

AFFREIGHTMENT

see Freight and Freightage

AFGHANISTAN–POLITICS AND GOVERNMENT

Arnold, Anthony. Afghanistan's Two-Party Communism: Parcham & Khalq. (Publication Ser.: No. 279). 260p. 1983. pap. 10.95 (ISBN 0-8179-7792-9). Hoover Inst Pr.

AFLATOXINS

Heathcote, J. G. & Hibbert, J. R. Aflatoxins: Chemical & Biological Aspects. (Developments in Food Science Ser.: Vol. 1). 1978. 51.00 (ISBN 0-444-41686-2). Elsevier.

AFRICA

see also names of countries or regions of Africa, e.g. Egypt, Congo, Ghana, Sahara, etc. geographic subdivisions of Africa e.g. Africa, East; Africa, Sub-Saharan

Carim, Enver, ed. Africa Guide: 1983. (World of Information Ser.). pap. 24.95 (ISBN 0-911818-31-6). World Almanac.

Carrington, John F. Talking Drums of Africa. (Illus.). 96p. 1949. 14.00. G Vanderstoel.

Gailey, Harry A. Africa: Troubled Continent-A Problem Approach. 160p. (Orig.). 1983. pap. 6.50 (ISBN 0-89874-342-7). Krieger.

Geoffrion, Charles A., ed. Africa: A Study Guide to Better Understanding. (African Humanities Ser.). (Orig.). 1970. pap. text ed. 2.00 (ISBN 0-941934-03-9). Ind U Afro-Amer Arts.

Legum, Colin, ed. Africa Contemporary Record 1981-82, Vol. 14. 1200p. 1983. text ed. 159.50x (ISBN 0-8419-0551-7). Holmes & Meier.

Nicol, D. Africa: A Subjective View 1964. pap. text ed. 4.95x (ISBN 0-686-84195-6). Humanities.

Rainier, Peter. My Vanished Africa. 1940. text ed. 29.50x (ISBN 0-686-83628-6). Elliots Bks.

AFRICA–BIBLIOGRAPHY

Beck, Roger B. A Bibliography of Africana in the Institute for Sex Research, Indiana University. (Afican Humanities Ser.). 134p. (Orig.). 1979. pap. text ed. 5.00 (ISBN 0-941934-29-2). Ind U Afro-Amer Arts.

Sweetland, James H. A Bibliography of Africana in the Lilly Library. Gosebrink, Jean E., ed. (African Humanities Ser.). 76p. (Orig.). 1977. pap. text ed. 4.00 (ISBN 0-941934-26-8). Ind U Afro-Amer Arts.

AFRICA–BIOGRAPHY

Alexander, Curtis. Doc Ben Speaks Out. (Monograph: No. 1). 52p. 1982. pap. 2.95 (ISBN 0-938818-04-X, Pub by Alkebulan Hist Res Soc). ECA Assoc.

Blouin, Andree & MacKellar, Jean. My Country, Africa: The Autobiography of the Black Passionaria. 302p. 1983. 19.95 (ISBN 0-03-062759-1). Praeger.

AFRICA–CIVILIZATION

Ahmed, Said B. The Swahili Chronicle of Ngazija. Harries, Lyndon, ed. (African Humanities Ser.). (Illus.). 136p. (Orig.). 1977. pap. text ed. 5.00 (ISBN 0-941934-20-9). Ind U Afro-Amer Arts.

Merriam, Alan P. The Arts & Humanities in African Studies. (African Humanities Ser.). 17p. (Orig.). 1972. pap. text ed. 2.00 (ISBN 0-941934-34-9). Ind U Afro-Amer Arts.

--Culture History of the Basongye. (African Humanities Ser.). (Illus.). 76p. (Orig.). 1975. pap. text ed. 4.00 (ISBN 0-941934-13-6). Ind U Afro-Amer Arts.

Reynolds, B. The Material Culture of the Peoples of the Gwembe Valley. (Kariba Studies: Vol. 3). 276p. 1968. 22.50 (ISBN 0-7190-1241-4). Manchester.

Sembene, Ousmane. Man is Culture. (Hans Wolff Memorial Lecture Ser.). 24p. (Orig., Eng. & Fr.). 1979. pap. text ed. 2.50 (ISBN 0-941934-14-4). Ind U Afro-Amer Arts.

AFRICA–CLIMATE

Proceedings of the Technical Conference on Climate-Africa. 535p. 1982. pap. 35.00 (ISBN 92-63-00596-6, W 535, WMO). Unipub.

AFRICA–COLONIZATION

McCulloch, Jock. Black Soul White Artifact: Fanon's Clinical Psychology & Social Theory. LC 82-14605. 240p. Date not set. price not set (ISBN 0-521-24700-4). Cambridge U Pr.

Offiong, Daniel O. Imperialism & Dependency: Obstacles in African Development. 304p. 1983. 12.95 (ISBN 0-88258-126-0); pap. 6.95 (ISBN 0-88258-127-9). Howard U Pr.

AFRICA–COMMERCE

Da Mota, A. Teixeira. Some Aspects of Portugese Colonisation & Sea Trade in West Africa in the 15th & 16th Centuries. (Hans Wolff Memorial Lecture Ser.). 29p. (Orig.). 1978. pap. text ed. 2.50 (ISBN 0-941934-22-5). Ind U Afro-Amer Arts.

Foreign Trade Statistics for Africa. (Ser. "B", Trade by Commodity: No. 31). 4.00 (ISBN 0-686-84898-5, E/F.78.II.U.3). UN.

Page, John, Jr. Shadow Prices for Trade Strategy & Investment Planning in Egypt. LC 82-8594. (World Bank Staff Working Papers: No. 521). (Orig.). 1982. pap. 5.00 (ISBN 0-8213-0009-1). World Bank.

AFRICA–DESCRIPTION AND TRAVEL

Best, Alan C. & Blij, Harm J. An African Survey. LC 76-44520. 626p. 1977. text ed. 32.95 (ISBN 0-471-20063-8). Wiley.

Uwechue, Ralph. Know Africa, 3 Vols. Incl. Vol. 1. Africa Today; Vol. 3. Makers of Modern Africa; Vol. 3. Africa Who's Who. 3290p. 1981. 250.00 set (ISBN 0-686-42731-9, Pub. by Africa Journal Limited). Gale.

AFRICA–ECONOMIC CONDITIONS

Inikori, J. E., ed. Forced Migration: The Impact of the Export Slave Trade on African Societies. 352p. 1983. text ed. 22.00x (ISBN 0-8419-0795-1); pap. text ed. 13.50x (ISBN 0-8419-0799-4). Holmes & Meier.

AFRICA–FOREIGN RELATIONS

DeLancey, Mark W., ed. Aspects of International Relations in Africa. (African Humanities Ser.). 253p. (Orig.). 1980. pap. 9.00 (ISBN 0-941934-28-4). Ind U Afro-Amer Arts.

The Middle East & North Africa 1982-83. 1013p. 1983. 105.00 (ISBN 0-905118-75-8, EUR 35). Europa.

Rubin, Arnold. Black Nanban: Africans in Japan During the Sixteenth Century. (African Humanities Ser.). (Illus., Orig.). 1974. pap. text ed. 2.00 (ISBN 0-941934-11-X). Ind U Afro-Amer Arts.

AFRICA–HISTORY

Brooks, George E., Jr. Themes in African & World History: A Schema for Integrating Africa into World History; Tropical Africa: The Colonial Heritage; The African Heritage & the Slave Trade. (African Humanities Ser.). 45p. (Orig.). 1973. pap. text ed. 2.00 (ISBN 0-941934-06-3). Ind U Afro-Amer Arts.

Clark, Leon E. Through African Eyes: Coming of Age in Africa, Vol. 1. 120p. 1982. pap. 5.95 (ISBN 0-938960-07-5). CITE.

--Through African Eyes: From Tribe to Town - Problems of Adjustment, Vol. 2. (Illus.). 125p. 1981. pap. 5.95 (ISBN 0-938960-08-3). CITE.

--Through African Eyes: Nation-Building - Tanzania & the World. (Vol. 6). (Illus.). 160p. 1981. pap. 5.95 (ISBN 0-938960-12-1). CITE.

--Through African Eyes: The African Past & the Coming of the European. (Vol. 3). (Illus.). 144p. 1981. pap. 5.95 (ISBN 0-938960-09-1). CITE.

--Through African Eyes: The Colonial Experience - An Inside View, Vol. 4. 135p. 1981. pap. 5.95 (ISBN 0-938960-10-5). CITE.

--Through African Eyes: The Rise of Nationalism - Freedom Regained, Vol. 5. 141p. 1981. pap. 5.95 (ISBN 0-938960-11-3). CITE.

Da Mota, A. Teixeira. Some Aspects of Portugese Colonisation & Sea Trade in West Africa in the 15th & 16th Centuries. (Hans Wolff Memorial Lecture Ser.). 29p. (Orig.). 1978. pap. text ed. 2.50 (ISBN 0-941934-22-5). Ind U Afro-Amer Arts.

Harris, Joseph E., ed. Global Dimensions of the African Diaspora. 1983. 19.95 (ISBN 0-88258-022-1). Howard U Pr.

Mattiessen, Peter. The Tree Where Man Was Born. 353p. 1983. pap. 7.95 (ISBN 0-525-48032-3, 0772-230, Obelisk). Dutton.

Stevenson, Catherine B. Victorian Women Travel Writers in Africa. (English Authors Ser.). 184p. 1982. lib. bdg. 17.95 (ISBN 0-8057-6835-1, Twayne). G K Hall.

AFRICA–KINGS AND RULERS

The African Kings. (Treasures of the World Ser.). 1983. lib. bdg. 26.60 (ISBN 0-686-42743-2, Pub. by Stonehenge). Silver.

AFRICA–LANGUAGES

Corum, Claudia W. An Introduction to the Swazi (Siswati) Language. (African Language Texts Ser.). (Orig.). pap. text ed. 5.00 (ISBN 0-941934-01-2). Ind U Afro-Amer Arts.

Demuth, Katherine & Sekhesa, Tholoana. Basic SeSotho: An Oral Approach. (African Language Texts Ser.). (Orig.). 1978. pap. text ed. 5.00 (ISBN 0-941934-24-1). Ind U Afro-Amer Arts.

Whitely, Wilfred H. To Plan is to Choose. LC 72-97699. (Hans Wolff Memorial Lecture Ser.). 50p. 1973. pap. text ed. 3.00 (ISBN 0-941934-04-7). Ind U Afro-Amer Arts.

AFRICA–NATIVE RACES

see also names of specific African peoples, tribes, etc., e.g. Bantus; also various geographic subdivisions pertaining to Africa under the main heading Ethnology

Launay, Robert. Traders Without Trade: Responses to Change in Two Dyula Communities. LC 82-4500. (Cambridge Studies in Social Anthropology: No. 42). 196p. 1983. 34.50 (ISBN 0-521-24179-0). Cambridge U Pr.

Mattiessen, Peter. The Tree Where Man Was Born. 353p. 1983. pap. 7.95 (ISBN 0-525-48032-3, 0772-230, Obelisk). Dutton.

AFRICA–POLITICS AND GOVERNMENT

see also Afro-Asian Politics; Pan-Africanism

Arlinghaus, Bruce, ed. Africa Security Issues: Sovereignty, Stability, & Solidarity. 200p. Date not set. price not set. Westview.

Arlinghaus, Bruce E., ed. Arms for Africa: Military Assistance & Foreign Policy in the Developing World. LC 81-48668. 256p. 1982. 26.95x (ISBN 0-669-05527-1). Lexington Bks.

Best, Alan C. & Blij, Harm J. An African Survey. LC 76-44520. 626p. 1977. text ed. 32.95 (ISBN 0-471-20063-8). Wiley.

Chabal, Patrick. Amilcar Cabral; Revolutionary Leadership & People's War. LC 82-14632. (African Studies: No. 37). (Illus.). 280p. Date not set. price not set (ISBN 0-521-24944-9); pap. price not set (ISBN 0-521-27113-4). Cambridge U Pr.

Chaliand, Gerard. The Struggle for Africa: Politics of the Great Powers. LC 82-5967. 1982. 18.50 (ISBN 0-312-76868-0). St Martin.

Jinadu, L. Adele. Structure & Choice in African Politics. (Hans Wolff Memorial Lecture Ser.). 52p. (Orig.). 1979. pap. text ed. 3.00 (ISBN 0-941934-23-3). Ind U Afro-Amer Arts.

Marshall, H. H. From Dependence to Statehood in Commonwealth Africa: Selected Documents, World War I to Independence, 2 vols. Incl. Vol. 1. Southern Africa (ISBN 0-379-20348-0); Vol. 2. Central Africa. LC 80-10407. 1982. lib. bdg. 75.00 ea. Oceana.

Rothchild, Donald & Olorunsola, Victor A., eds. State vs Ethnic Claims: African Policy Dilemmas. (Special Studies on Africa). 1982. lib. bdg. 25.00 (ISBN 0-86531-503-5); pap. text ed. 11.95 (ISBN 0-86531-504-3). Westview.

AFRICA–RELATIONS (GENERAL) WITH FOREIGN COUNTRIES

Moss, Joanna. The Lome Conventions & Their Implications for the United States. Replica ed. 225p. 1982. softcover 19.50 (ISBN 0-86531-935-9). Westview.

Offiong, Daniel O. Imperialism & Dependency: Obstacles in African Development. 304p. 1983. 12.95 (ISBN 0-88258-126-0); pap. 6.95 (ISBN 0-88258-127-9). Howard U Pr.

AFRICA–RELIGION

MacGaffey, Wyatt. Modern Kongo Prophets: Religion in a Plural Society. (African Systems of Thought Ser.). (Illus.). 304p. 1983. 22.50x (ISBN 0-253-33865-4). Ind U Pr.

--Modern Kongo Prophets: Religion in a Plural Society. (Midland Bks.). (Illus.). 304p. (Orig.). 1983. pap. 15.00x (ISBN 0-253-20307-4). Ind U Pr.

Zahan, Dominique. The Religion, Spirituality, & Thought of Traditional Africa. Ezra, Kate & Martin, Lawrence M., trs. vi, 180p. 1979. pap. 5.95 (ISBN 0-226-97778-1). U of Chicago Pr.

AFRICA–SOCIAL CONDITIONS

Inikori, J. E., ed. Forced Migration: The Impact of the Export Slave Trade on African Societies. 352p. 1983. text ed. 22.00x (ISBN 0-8419-0795-1); pap. text ed. 13.50x (ISBN 0-8419-0799-4). Holmes & Meier.

Robinson, Pearl T. & Skinner, Elliot P., eds. Transformation & Resiliency in Africa. 336p. 1983. 14.95 (ISBN 0-88258-054-X). Howard U Pr.

AFRICA, CENTRAL–DESCRIPTION AND TRAVEL

Megill, Esther. Joining the Journey: A Guide to the People & Pilgrimage of Central Africa. (Orig.). 1983. pap. write for info. (ISBN 0-377-00127-9). Friend Pr.

AFRICA, EAST–ECONOMIC CONDITIONS

Maliyamkono, T. L. & Ishumi, A. G. Training & Productivity in Eastern Africa. (Eastern African Universities Research Project Ser.). 400p. 1982. text ed. 60.00x (ISBN 0-435-89582-6). Heinemann Ed.

AFRICA, EAST–HISTORY

Bennett, Norman R. Arab Versus European: Diplomacy & War in Nineteenth-Century East Central Africa. 550p. 1983. 45.00 (ISBN 0-8419-0861-3). Holmes & Meier.

Moorehead, Alan. The Blue Nile. LC 82-48895. (Illus.). 304p. 1983. pap. 12.95 (ISBN 0-394-71449-0, Vin). Random.

AFRICA, GERMAN SOUTHWEST

see Namibia

AFRICA, NORTH

Here are entered works dealing collectively with Morocco, Algeria, Tunisia, and Libya.

Gopal, Rishane & Gopal, Kokila K. West Asia & North Africa: A Documentary Study of Major Crises, 1974-78. 434p. 1981. 37.50x (ISBN 0-86590-012-4). Apt Bks.

AFRICA, NORTH–POLITICS

Damis, John. Conflict in Northwest Africa: The Western Sahara Dispute. (Publication Ser.: 278). (Illus.). 196p. 1983. 19.95 (ISBN 0-8179-7781-3). Hoover Inst Pr.

AFRICA, SOUTH

see South Africa

AFRICA, SOUTHERN

Here are entered works on the area south of Zaire and Tanzania. Works on the Republic of South Africa are entered under South Africa.

Cape Times Directory of Southern Africa, 1982, 2 vols. LC 34-38958. 2200p. 1982. Set. 72.50x (ISBN 0-8002-3069-8). Intl Pubns Serv.

Hill, Christopher & Barber, James. The West & South Africa. (Chatham House Papers on Foreign Policy Ser.). (Orig.). 1983. pap. 10.00 (ISBN 0-7100-9232-6). Routledge & Kegan.

AFRICA, SOUTHERN–ECONOMIC CONDITIONS

International Labour Office. Labour Relations in Southern Africa: Proceedings of & Documents Submitted to a Seminar, Gaborone, 2-4 December 1981. (Labour-Management Relations Ser.: No. 61). 58p. (Orig.). 1982. pap. 7.15 (ISBN 92-2-103005-9). Intl Labour Office.

Nattrass, Jill. The South African Economy: Its Growth & Change. (Illus.). 348p. 1981. text ed. 24.95x (ISBN 0-19-570194-1). Oxford U Pr.

AFRICA, SOUTHERN–POLITICS AND GOVERNMENT

Jaster, Robert S. Southern Africa in Conflict. 1982. pap. 4.75 (ISBN 0-8447-1098-9). Am Enterprise.

Shamuyarira, Nathan. Liberation Movements in Southern Africa. (Hans Wolff Memorial Lecture Ser.). 38p. (Orig.). 1978. pap. text ed. 3.00 (ISBN 0-941934-21-7). Ind U Afro-Amer Arts.

AFRICA, SOUTHWEST

see Namibia

AFRICA, SUB-SAHARAN

Africa South of the Sahara 1982-83. 1982. 120.00 (ISBN 0-905118-74-X, EUR 34). Europa.

AFRICA, SUB-SAHARAN–DESCRIPTION AND TRAVEL

Udo, Reuden K. The Human Geography of Tropical Africa. 256p. 1982. pap. 39.00x (ISBN 0-435-95919-0, Pub. by Heinemann England). State Mutual Bk.

AFRICA, SUB-SAHARAN–ECONOMIC CONDITIONS

Udo, Reuden K. The Human Geography of Tropical Africa. 256p. 1982. pap. 39.00x (ISBN 0-435-95919-0, Pub. by Heinemann England). State Mutual Bk.

AFRICA, SUB-SAHARAN–HISTORY

Lamb, David. The Africans. LC 81-48271. (Illus.). 384p. 1983. 17.95 (ISBN 0-394-51887-X). Random.

AFRICA, SUB-SAHARAN–POLITICS AND GOVERNMENT

Mawhood, Philip. Local Government for Development: The Experience of Tropical Africa. (Public Administration in Developing Countries Ser.). 250p. 1983. price not set (ISBN 0-471-10510-4, Pub. by Wiley-Interscience). Wiley.

AFRICA, WEST

Hill, Christopher & Barber, James. The West & South Africa. (Chatham House Papers on Foreign Policy Ser.). (Orig.). 1983. pap. 10.00 (ISBN 0-7100-9232-6). Routledge & Kegan.

AFRICA, WEST–ECONOMIC CONDITIONS

Francophone West Africa: Business Opportunities in the 1980s. 385p. 450.00X (ISBN 0-686-99848-0, Pub. by Metra England). State Mutual Bk.

AFRICA, WEST–NATIVE RACES

Pern, S. Masked Dancers of West Africa: The Dogon. (Peoples of the Wild Ser.). 1982. 15.96 (ISBN 0-7054-0706-3, Pub. by Time-Life). Silver.

AFRICA, WEST–POLITICS AND GOVERNMENT

Ekoko, A. E. British Defence Strategy in Western Africa 1880-1914. 200p. 1983. text ed. 30.00x (ISBN 0-7146-3219-8, F Cass Co). Biblio Dist.

AFRICA, WEST–SOCIAL LIFE AND CUSTOMS

Oppong, C., ed. Female & Male in West Africa. 280p. 1983. text ed. 35.00x (ISBN 0-04-301158-6); pap. text ed. 12.50x (ISBN 0-04-301159-4). Allen Unwin.

AFRICAN AMERICANS

see Afro-Americans

AFRICAN ART

see Art, African

AFRICAN-ASIAN POLITICS

see Afro-Asian Politics

AFRICAN DRAMA–HISTORY AND CRITICISM

Etherton, Michael. The Development of African Drama. (Orig.). 1983. text ed. write for info. (ISBN 0-8419-0812-5); pap. text ed. write for info. (ISBN 0-8419-0813-3). Holmes & Meier.

AFRICAN FICTION

see Short Stories, African

AFRICAN FOLK-LORE

see Folk-Lore, African

AFRICAN LITERATURE

Soumaoro, Bourama & Bird, Charles S. Seyidu Kamara Ka Donkiliw. (Occasional Papers in Mande Studies). 101p. (Orig.). 1976. pap. text ed. 5.00 (ISBN 0-941934-18-7). Ind U Afro-Amer Arts.

AFRICAN LITERATURE–BIBLIOGRAPHY

State Library, Pretoria, ed. South African National Bibliography, 1981. LC 50-57958. 822p. 1981. 66.50x (ISBN 0-7989-0070-9). Intl Pubns Serv.

Wylie, Hal & Julien, Eileen, eds. Contemporary African Literature. (Annual Selected Papers of the ALA). 130p. 1983. 22.00X (ISBN 0-686-82391-5); pap. 14.00X (ISBN 0-89410-370-9). Three Continents.

AFRICAN LITERATURE–HISTORY AND CRITICISM

Chinweizu, Onwuchekwa J. & Madubuike, Ihechukwu. Toward the Decolonization of African Literature, Vol. I. 320p. 1983. 12.95 (ISBN 0-88258-122-8); pap. 6.95 (ISBN 0-88258-123-6). Howard U Pr.

Dorsey, David F., et al, eds. Design & Intent in African Literature. 137p. 1982. 22.00 (ISBN 0-89410-354-7); pap. 14.00 (ISBN 0-89410-355-5). Three Continents.

Johnson & Lemuel, A., eds. Toward Defining the African Aesthetic. Cailler, Bernadette, et al. (Annual Selected Papers of the ALA). 140p. 1983. 22.00X (ISBN 0-89410-356-3); pap. 14.00X (ISBN 0-89410-357-1). Three Continents.

Madubuike, Ihechukwu. The Senegalese Novel: A Sociological Study of the Impact of the Politics of Assimilation. LC 81-51650. (Illus.). 182p. 1983. 18.00 (ISBN 0-89410-000-9); pap. 7.00 (ISBN 0-89410-001-7). Three Continents.

Ngara, Emmanuel. Stylistic Criticism & the African Novel. 160p. 1982. 30.00x (ISBN 0-686-82316-8, Pub. by Heinemann England). State Mutual Bk.

Zell, Hans & Bundy, Carol, eds. A New Reader's Guide to African Literature. 2nd rev. ed. 600p. (Orig.). 1983. text ed. 37.00x (ISBN 0-8419-0639-4, Africana); pap. text ed. 20.00x. Holmes & Meier.

AFRICAN LITERATURE–TRANSLATIONS INTO ENGLISH

Bird, Charles & Koita, Mamadou. The Songs of Seydou Camara: Volume 1-Kambili. (Occasional Papers in Mande Studies). 120p. (Orig.). 1974. pap. text ed. 5.00 (ISBN 0-941934-12-8). Ind U Afro-Amer Arts.

AFRICAN LITERATURE (FRENCH)

Erickson, John D. Nommo: African Fiction in French. (Francophone Studies: Black Africa). 17.00 (ISBN 0-917786-08-4). French Lit.

AFRICAN MUSIC

see Music, African

AFRICAN PHILOSOPHY

see Philosophy, African

AFRICAN POETRY (COLLECTIONS)

Awooner, Kofi, et al. There Is a Song, We Shall Sing It. (African Poetry Ser.). write for info. Greenfld Rev Pr.

AFRICAN POETRY–HISTORY AND CRITICISM

Goodwin, Ken. Understanding African Poetry: A Study of Ten Poets. 256p. 1982. text ed. 25.00x (ISBN 0-435-91325-5); pap. text ed. 12.50x (ISBN 0-435-91326-3). Heinemann Ed.

AFRICAN RELATIONS

see Pan-Africanism

AFRICAN STUDIES

Dolezal, Ivan. Asian & African Studies, Vol. 18. 323p. 1982. text ed. 13.75x (ISBN 0-7007-0156-7, 41190, Pub. by Curzon Pr England). Humanities.

Kpomassie, Tete-Michel. An African in Greenland. Kirkup, James, tr. (Illus.). 224p. 14.95 (ISBN 0-15-105589-0). HarBraceJ.

Ohrn, Steven G. Cataloguing in Context: The African Studies Program Slide Archives. (Occasional Papers on Visual Communication). 49p. (Orig.). 1975. pap. text ed. 3.00 (ISBN 0-941934-16-0). Ind U Afro-Amer Arts.

AFRICAN TALES

see Tales, African

AFRO-AMERICAN ACTORS

This heading used beginning January 1976. See Negro Actors and Actresses for earlier works.

Hyatt, Marshall, ed. The Afro-American Cinematic Experience: An Annotated Bibliography & Filmography. LC 82-22974. 280p. 1983. lib. bdg. 24.95 (ISBN 0-8420-2213-9). Scholarly Res Inc.

AFRO-AMERICAN ART

This heading used beginning January 1976. See Negro Art for earlier works.

Ferris, William. Afro-American Folk Art & Crafts. (Illus.). 444p. 1983. lib. bdg. 39.95 (ISBN 0-8161-9045-3, Univ Bks). G K Hall.

AFRO-AMERICAN ATHLETES

This heading used beginning January 1976. See Negro Athletes for earlier works.

Rogosin, Donn. Invisible Men: Life in Baseball's Negro Leagues. LC 82-73026. (Illus.). 320p. 1983. 14.95 (ISBN 0-689-11363-3). Atheneum.

AFRO-AMERICAN AUTHORS

This heading used beginning January 1976. See Negro Authors for earlier works.

see also American Literature–Afro-American Authors

Campbell, Dorothy W. Index to Black American Authors in Collective Biographies. 162p. 1983. lib. bdg. 27.50 (ISBN 0-87287-349-8). Libs Unl.

Nunes, Maria L. The Craft of an Absolute Winner: Characterization & Narratology in the Novels of Machado de Assis. LC 82-11717. (Contributions in Afro-American & African Studies: No. 71). 208p. 1983. lib. bdg. 27.95 (ISBN 0-313-23631-3, NCW/). Greenwood.

AFRO-AMERICAN BUSINESS PEOPLE

see Afro-Americans in Business

AFRO-AMERICAN CHILDREN

This heading used beginning January 1976. See Negro Children for earlier works.

Wilmore, Gayraud S. Black & Presbyterian: The Heritage & the Hope. LC 82-23907. 132p. (Orig.). 1983. pap. price not set (ISBN 0-664-24440-8, Geneva Press Pub). Westminster.

AFRO-AMERICAN COLLEGES

see Afro-American Universities and Colleges

AFRO-AMERICAN DIALECT

see Black English

AFRO-AMERICAN ENGLISH

see Black English

AFRO-AMERICAN FOLK-LORE

This heading used beginning January 1976. See Folk-Lore, Negro for earlier works.

Bell, Michael J. The World from Brown's Lounge: An Ethnography of Black Middle-Class Play. LC 82-4732. 208p. 1983. 14.95 (ISBN 0-252-00956-8). U of Ill Pr.

AFRO-AMERICAN LITERATURE (ENGLISH)

see American Literature–Afro-American Authors

AFRO-AMERICAN MUSIC

This heading used beginning January 1976. See Negro Music for earlier works.

see also Jazz Music; Rock Music; Spirituals (Songs)

Floyd, Samuel A., Jr. & Reisser, Marsha J. Black Music in the United States: An Annotated Bibliography of Selected Reference & Research Materials. LC 82-49044. 420p. 1983. lib. bdg. 30.00 (ISBN 0-527-30164-7). Kraus Intl.

Gargan, William & Sharma, Sue. Find that Tune: An Index to Rock, Folk-Rock, Disco & Soul in Collections. 400p. 1983. lib. bdg. 39.95 (ISBN 0-918212-70-7). Neal-Schuman.

Roach, Hildred. Black American Music: Past & Present. 208p. 1983. Repr. of 1973 ed. text ed. price not set (ISBN 0-89874-610-8). Krieger.

Southern, Eileen. Music of Black Americans. 2nd ed. 600p. 1983. text ed. write for info. (ISBN 0-393-95270-3). Norton.

AFRO-AMERICAN ORATORS

This heading used beginning January 1976. See Negro Orators for earlier works.

Jones, Edward L. Black Orator's Workbook. 1982. pap. 12.95 (ISBN 0-9602458-4-7). Ed-Lynne Jones.

AFRO-AMERICAN SPIRITUALS

see Spirituals (Songs)

AFRO-AMERICAN STUDIES

Bibliotheca Press Research Project. The Directory of Special Black Libraries, Museums, Halls of Fames, Colleges, Art Galleries, Etc. 300p. 1983. text ed. 39.95 (ISBN 0-939476-90-8). Biblio Pr GA.

Murray, Albert. The Omni-Americans: Black Experience & American Culture. LC 82-48899. 240p. 1983. pap. 6.95 (Vin). Random.

Research Libraries of the New York Public Library & Library of Congress. Bibliographic Guide to Black Stuides: 1982. 1983. lib. bdg. 85.00 (ISBN 0-8161-6968-3, Biblio Guides). G K Hall.

AFRO-AMERICAN SUFFRAGE

see Afro-Americans–Politics and Suffrage

AFRO-AMERICAN UNIVERSITIES AND COLLEGES

This heading used beginning January 1976. See Negro Universities and Colleges for earlier works.

Newby, James E. Teaching Faculty in Black Colleges & Universities: A Survey of Selected Social Science Disciplines, 1977-1978. LC 82-17620. (Illus.). 112p. (Orig.). 1983. lib. bdg. 18.50 (ISBN 0-8191-2787-6); pap. text ed. 8.25 (ISBN 0-8191-2788-4). U Pr of Amer.

AFRO-AMERICAN WOMEN

This heading used beginning January 1976. See Women, Negro for earlier works.

Black Women in Sport. 75p. 8.95 (ISBN 0-88314-036-5). AAHPERD.

Mebane, Mary. Mary, Wayfarer. 252p. 1983. 16.75 (ISBN 0-686-84092-5). Viking Pr.

Wilson, Emily H. Hope & Dignity: Older Black Women of the South. 1983. write for info. (ISBN 0-87722-302-5). Temple U Pr.

AFRO-AMERICAN YOUTH

Green, Mildred D. Black Women Composers: A Genesis. (Music Ser.). 174p. 1983. lib. bdg. 18.95 (ISBN 0-8057-9450-6, Twayne). G K Hall.

AFRO-AMERICANS

This heading used beginning January 1976. See Negroes for earlier works. Here are entered works on the Black people of the United States. Works on Black people outside of the United States are entered under the heading Blacks. Theoretical works discussing the Black race from an anthropological point of view are entered under the heading Black Race.

see also Slavery in the United States; United States–History–Civil War, 1861-1865–Afro-Americans

also subdivision Afro-Americans under names of wars, e.g. World War, 1939-1945–Afro-Americans; and headings beginning with Afro-American

Brignano, Russell. Black Americans in Autobiography: An Annotated Bibliography of Autobiographies & Autobiographical Books Written Since the Civil War. 180p. Date not set. text ed. 25.00x (ISBN 0-8223-0559-3). Duke.

Franklin, John H. & Meier, August, eds. Black Leaders of the Twentieth Century. 1983. pap. 7.95 (ISBN 0-252-00939-8). U of Ill Pr.

Gibson, Walter. Black Americans: Biological Facts & Fancies. 1983. 7.95 (ISBN 0-533-05522-9). Vantage.

Hancock, Sibyl. Famous Firsts of Black Americans. (gr. 3-9). 1983. 9.95 (ISBN 0-88289-240-1). Pelican.

Harris, Jacqueline. Martin Luther King, Jr. (Impact Biography Ser.). (Illus.). 128p. (gr. 7 up). 1983. PLB 8.90 (ISBN 0-531-04588-9). Watts.

Miner, Jane C. The Tough Guy: Black in a White World. Schroeder, Howard, ed. LC 82-1408. (Crisis Ser.). (Illus.). 64p. (gr. 4-5). 1982. lib. bdg. 7.95 (ISBN 0-89686-169-4). Crestwood Hse.

Ploski, Harry. The Negro Almanac: A Reference Work on the Afro-American. 4th ed. 1250p. 1983. 67.95 (ISBN 0-471-87710-7, Pub. by Wiley-Interscience). Wiley.

Santrey, Laurence. Young Frederick Douglass: Fight for Freedom. LC 82-15993. (Illus.). 48p. (gr. 4-6). 1983. PLB 6.89 (ISBN 0-89375-857-4); pap. text ed. 1.95 (ISBN 0-89375-858-2). Troll Assocs.

AFRO-AMERICANS–CHILDREN

see Afro-American Children

AFRO-AMERICANS–CIVIL RIGHTS

This heading used beginning January 1976. See Negroes–Civil Rights for earlier works.

see also Afro-Americans–Politics and Suffrage

Brown, Oscar C., Sr. By a Thread. 1982. 8.95 (ISBN 0-533-05464-8). Vantage.

Weisbrot, Robert. Father Divine & the Struggle for Racial Equality. Meier, August, ed. LC 82-2644. (Blacks in the New World Ser.). 272p. 1983. 17.50 (ISBN 0-686-84862-4). U of Ill Pr.

AFRO-AMERICANS–ECONOMIC CONDITIONS

This heading used beginning January 1976. See Negroes–Economic Conditions for earlier works.

see also Afro-Americans–Employment; Afro-Americans in Business

Marable, Manning. How Capitalism Underdeveloped Black America. 285p. 1982. 20.00 (ISBN 0-89608-166-4); pap. 7.50 (ISBN 0-89608-165-6). South End Pr.

AFRO-AMERICANS–EMPLOYMENT

This heading used beginning January 1976. See Negroes–Employment for earlier works.

see also Afro-Americans in Business

Foner, Philip S. & Lewis, Ronald L., eds. The Black Worker: A Documentary History from Colonial Times to the Present: The Era from World War II to the AFL-CIO Merger, 1937-1954, Vol. VII. 1983. 29.95 (ISBN 0-87722-197-9). Temple U Pr.

AFRO-AMERICANS–FOLK-LORE

see Afro-American Folk-Lore

AFRO-AMERICANS–HEALTH AND HYGIENE

Johnson, Audreye E., ed. The Black Experience: Considerations for Health & Human Services. LC 82-84461. (Dialogue Bks.). 160p. 1983. 9.75 (ISBN 0-89881-014-0). Intl Dialogue Pr.

McFalls, Joseph A. & Tolnay, Stewart E. Black Fertility in the U. S. A Social Demographic History. 400p. Date not set. text ed. 40.00 (ISBN 0-8223-0560-7). Duke.

AFRO-AMERICANS–HISTORY

This heading used beginning January 1976. See Negroes–History for earlier works.

Aptheker, Herbert, ed. Writings in Periodicals Edited by W. E. B. Du Bois: Selections from "The Crisis". (The Completed Published Works of W. E. B. Du Bois). (Orig.). 1983. lib. bdg. 125.00 (ISBN 0-527-25351-0). Kraus Intl.

Faulkner, Janette & Henderson, Robbin. Ethnic Notions: Black Images in the White Mind. (Illus.). 80p. (Orig.). pap. 11.00x (ISBN 0-686-42913-3). Berkeley Art.

Foner, Philip S. & Lewis, Ronald L., eds. The Black Worker: A Documentary History from Colonial Times to the Present: The Era from World War II to the AFL-CIO Merger, 1937-1954, Vol. VII. 1983. 29.95 (ISBN 0-87722-197-9). Temple U Pr.

Foner, Phillip S. History of Black Americans: From the Emergence of the Cotton Kingdom to the Eve of the Compromise of 1850, Vol II. LC 74-5987. (Contributions in American History Ser.: No. 102). 600p. 1983. lib. bdg. 45.00 (ISBN 0-8371-7966-1, FBA/2). Greenwood.

Price, Clement A. Freedom Not Far Distant: A Documentary History of Afro-Americans in New Jersey, Vol. 16. (Illus.). 334p. 1980. 17.95 (ISBN 0-911020-01-2). NJ Hist Soc.

Woodward, C. Vann. American Counterpoint: Slavery & Racism in the North-South Dialogue. 320p. 1983. pap. 7.95 (ISBN 0-19-503269-1, GB 727, GB). Oxford U Pr.

Yette, Samuel F. The Choice: The Issue of Black Survival in America. LC 82-83686. 320p. (Orig.). 1982. 13.95 (ISBN 0-911253-00-9); pap. 7.95 (ISBN 0-911253-01-7). Cottage Bks.

AFRO-AMERICANS–HISTORY–TO 1863

This heading used beginning January 1976. See Negroes–History for earlier works.

Davis, Allison. Leadership, Love & Aggression. 256p. 15.95 (ISBN 0-15-149348-0). HarBraceJ.

Foner, Philip S. & Lewis, Ronald L., eds. The Black Worker: A Documentary History from Colonial Times to the Present: The Era from World War II to the AFL-CIO Merger, 1937-1954, Vol. VII. 1983. 29.95 (ISBN 0-87722-197-9). Temple U Pr.

Foner, Phillip S. History of Black Americans: From the Compromise of 1850 to the End of the Civil War, Vol. III. LC 82-11702. (Contributions in American History Ser.: No. 103). 528p. 1983. lib. bdg. 39.95 (ISBN 0-8371-7967-X, E449). Greenwood.

Rose, Willie L. Slavery & Freedom. expanded ed. Freehling, William W., ed. 272p. 1983. pap. 7.95 (ISBN 0-19-503266-7, GB 723, GB). Oxford U Pr.

AFRO-AMERICANS–OCCUPATIONS

see Afro-Americans–Employment

AFRO-AMERICANS–POLITICS AND SUFFRAGE

This heading used beginning January 1976. See Negroes–Politics and Suffrage for earlier works.

see also Afro-Americans–Civil Rights

Brown, Ed. Race & Class in Southern Politics & a History of Voter Education Project. 1979. 2.00 (ISBN 0-686-38003-7). Voter Ed Proj.

Executive Director's Presentation to the Congressional Black Caucus on September 25, 1981. 1981. 1.00 (ISBN 0-686-38017-7). Voter Ed Proj.

Farouk, Brimah K. Profile of Missisippi Black Voting Strength & Political Representation. 1982. 1.00 (ISBN 0-686-38028-2). Voter Ed Proj.

Harding, Vincent. There Is a River: The Black Struggle for Freedom in American. LC 82-40024. 480p. 1983. pap. 6.95 (ISBN 0-394-71148-3, Vin). Random.

Hudlin, Richard A. Black Population & Representation in Selected Alabama Counties & Places. 1982. 1.00 (ISBN 0-686-38022-3). Voter Ed Proj.
--Black Population, Voting Age Population, & Registrants for Counties in Georgia: 1980. 1982. 1.00 (ISBN 0-686-38024-X). Voter Ed Proj.
--Profile of Georgia Black Voting Strength & Political Representation. 1982. 1.00 (ISBN 0-686-38027-4). Voter Ed Proj.
--Survey of Black School Board Members in the South. Lewis, Shelby & Kenneth, Ellis, eds. 1981. 1.00 (ISBN 0-686-38021-5). Voter Ed Proj.
Hudlin, Richard A. & Farouk, Brimah K. Profile of Alabama Black Voting Strength & Political Representation. 1982. 1.00 (ISBN 0-686-38026-6). Voter Ed Proj.
--Profile of Georgia's Black Voting Strength & Political Representation. 1981. 1.00 (ISBN 0-686-38015-0). Voter Ed Proj.
--Profile of Mississippi's Black Voting Strength & Political Representation. 1981. 1.00 (ISBN 0-686-38016-9). Voter Ed Proj.
--Roster of Blacks in the U.S. House & Senate: 1869 to 1981. 1981. 1.00 (ISBN 0-686-38014-2). Voter Ed Proj.
--Voting Rights Act: Questions & Answers. 1981. 1.00 (ISBN 0-686-38020-7). Voter Ed Proj.
Langley, Michael. Protection of Minority Political Participation Abadoned in Supreme Court's Ruling on Mobile Elections. 1980. 1.00 (ISBN 0-686-38004-5). Voter Ed Proj.
Towe, William H. Barriers to Black Political Participation in North Carolina. 1972. 3.00 (ISBN 0-686-37999-3). Voter Ed Proj.
Weisbrot, Robert. Father Divine & the Struggle for Racial Equality. Meier, August, ed. LC 82-2644. (Blacks in the New World Ser.). (Illus.). 272p. 1983. 17.50 (ISBN 0-686-84862-4). U of Ill Pr.

AFRO-AMERICANS–RELIGION

This heading used beginning January 1976. See Negroes–Religion for earlier works.

West, Cornel. Prophesy Deliverance! An Afro-American Revolutionary Christianity. LC 82-13483. 186p. 1982. pap. 11.95 (ISBN 0-664-24447-5). Westminster.
Wilmore, Gayraud S. Black & Presbyterian: The Heritage & the Hope. LC 82-23907. 132p. (Orig.). 1983. pap. price not set (ISBN 0-664-24440-8, Geneva Press Pub). Westminster.

AFRO-AMERICANS–SOCIAL CONDITIONS

This heading used beginning January 1976. See Negroes–Social Conditions for earlier works.

Banerjee, S. Deferred Hopes: Blacks in Contemporary America. 425p. 1983. text ed. 30.00x (ISBN 0-391-02800-6, Pub. by Radiant Pub India). Humanities.
Johnson, Audreye E., ed. The Black Experience: Considerations for Health & Human Services. LC 82-84461. (Dialogue Bks.). 160p. 1983. 9.75 (ISBN 0-89881-004-0). Intl Dialogue Pr.
McFalls, Joseph A. & Tolnay, Stewart E. Black Fertility in the U. S. A Social Demographic History. 400p. Date not set. text ed. 40.00 (ISBN 0-8223-0560-7). Duke.

AFRO-AMERICANS–SOCIAL LIFE AND CUSTOMS

This heading used beginning January 1976. See Negroes–Social Life and Customs for earlier works.

Bell, Michael J. The World from Brown's Lounge: An Ethnography of Black Middle-Class Play. LC 82-4732. 208p. 1983. 14.95 (ISBN 0-252-00956-8). U of Ill Pr.
Stewart, Jeffery C., ed. Essays from the Harlem Renaissance: The Critical Temper of Alain Locke. LC 80-9046. 435p. 1982. lib. bdg. 52.00 (ISBN 0-8240-9318-6). Garland Pub.

AFRO-AMERICANS–STUDY AND TEACHING

see Afro-American Studies

AFRO-AMERICANS–SUFFRAGE

see Afro-Americans–Politics and Suffrage

AFRO-AMERICANS–YOUTH

see Afro-American Youth

AFRO-AMERICANS–ALABAMA

Hudlin, Richard A. Black Population & Representation in Selected Alabama Counties & Places. 1982. 1.00 (ISBN 0-686-38022-3). Voter Ed Proj.
Hudlin, Richard A. & Farouk, Brimah K. Profile of Alabama Black Voting Strength & Political Representation. 1982. 1.00 (ISBN 0-686-38026-6). Voter Ed Proj.

AFRO-AMERICANS–GEORGIA

Hudlin, Richard A. Black Population, Voting Age Population, & Registrants for Counties in Georgia: 1980. 1982. 1.00 (ISBN 0-686-38024-X). Voter Ed Proj.
--Profile of Georgia Black Voting Strength & Political Representation. 1982. 1.00 (ISBN 0-686-38027-4). Voter Ed Proj.
Hudlin, Richard A. & Farouk, Brimah K. Profile of Georgia's Black Voting Strength & Political Representation. 1981. 1.00 (ISBN 0-686-38015-0). Voter Ed Proj.

AFRO-AMERICANS–MISSISSIPPI

Farouk, Brimah K. Profile of Missisippi Black Voting Strength & Political Representation. 1982. 1.00 (ISBN 0-686-38028-2). Voter Ed Proj.
Hudlin, Richard A. & Farouk, Brimah K. Profile of Mississippi's Black Voting Strength & Political Representation. 1981. 1.00 (ISBN 0-686-38016-9). Voter Ed Proj.

AFRO-AMERICANS–NEW YORK (CITY)

Naison, Mark. Communists in Harlem During the Depression. Meier, August, ed. LC 82-10848. (Blacks in the New World Ser.). 360p. 19.95 (ISBN 0-252-00644-5). U of Ill Pr.

AFRO-AMERICANS–SOUTHERN STATES

Farouk, Brimah K. & Hudlin, Richard A. Population Trends in Majority Black Counties in Eleven Southern States: 1900 to 1980. 1981. 1.00 (ISBN 0-686-38018-5). Voter Ed Proj.
Howard, Victor B. Black Liberation in Kentucky: Emancipation & Freedom, 1861-1884. LC 82-40461. 240p. 1983. 23.00x (ISBN 0-8131-1433-0). U Pr of Ky.
Hudlin, Richard A. Black Population Concentrations in Southern Counties. 1982. 1.00 (ISBN 0-686-38023-1). Voter Ed Proj.
--Voter Regristation in Eleven Southern States, by Race: 1960-1980, in U.S. Bureau of the Census: Statistical Abstract of the United States: 1981. 1981. 0.10 ea. Voter Ed Proj.

AFRO-AMERICANS–TEXAS

Barr, Alwyn & Calvert, Robert A. Black Leaders: Texans for their Times. 11.95 (ISBN 0-87611-055-3); pap. 8.95 (ISBN 0-87611-056-1). Tex St Hist Assn.

AFRO-AMERICANS–VIRGINIA

Breen, T. H. & Innes, Stephen. Myne Owne Ground: Race & Freedom on Virginia's Eastern Shore, 1640-1676. 152p. 1982. pap. 5.95x (ISBN 0-19-503206-3). Oxford U Pr.

AFRO-AMERICANS IN BUSINESS

This heading used beginning January 1976. See Negro Businessmen for earlier works.

Reed, William. Who's Who in Black Corporate America. Doggett, Edna, ed. (Illus.). 268p. 1982. 65.00 (ISBN 0-686-43317-3). Whos Who Corp.

AFRO-AMERICANS IN MOTION PICTURES

Here are entered works discussing the portrayal of Afro-Americans in motion pictures. Works discussing all aspects of Afro-American involvement in motion pictures are entered under Afro-Americans in the Motion Picture Industry. Works discussing specific aspects of Afro-American involvement are entered under the particular subject, e.g. Afro-American Motion Picture Actors and Actresses. This heading used beginning January 1976. See Negroes In Moving-Pictures for earlier works.

Hyatt, Marshall, ed. The Afro-American Cinematic Experience: An Annotated Bibliography & Filmography. LC 82-22974. 280p. 1983. lib. bdg. 24.95 (ISBN 0-8420-2213-9). Scholarly Res Inc.

AFRO-AMERICANS IN THE MOTION PICTURE INDUSTRY

Here are entered works discussing all aspects of Afro-American involvement in motion pictures. Works discussing the portrayal of Afro-Americans in motion pictures are entered under Afro-Americans in Motion Pictures. Works discussing specific aspects of Afro-American involvement are entered under the particular subject, e.g. Afro-American Motion Picture Actors and Actresses. This heading used beginning January 1976. See Negroes In The Moving-Picture Industry for earlier works.

see also Afro-Americans in Motion Pictures

Hyatt, Marshall, ed. The Afro-American Cinematic Experience: An Annotated Bibliography & Filmography. LC 82-22974. 280p. 1983. lib. bdg. 24.95 (ISBN 0-8420-2213-9). Scholarly Res Inc.

AFRO-ASIAN POLITICS

Jha, L. K. North South Debate. 153p. 1982. text ed. 10.75x (ISBN 0-391-02769-7, 41257). Humanities.

AFTER-DINNER SPEECHES

see Public Speaking

AGATHA (INSECTS)

see May-Flies

AGE

see Age Groups; Longevity; Middle Age; Youth

AGE (LAW)

Goodman, Eugene B. All the Justice I Could Afford. 320p. 16.95 (ISBN 0-15-104778-2). HarBraceJ.

AGE AND EMPLOYMENT

see also Youth–Employment

Doering, Mildred & Rhodes, Susan R. The Aging Worker: Research & Recommendations. 352p. 1983. 29.95 (ISBN 0-8039-1949-2). Sage.
Nusberg, Charlotte, ed. Mandatory Retirement: Blessing or Curse? 27p. (Orig.). 1978. pap. text ed. 3.50 (ISBN 0-910473-06-4). Intl Fed Ageing.
Rosow, Jerome M. & Zager, Robert. The Future of Older Workers in America: New Options for an Extended Working Life. 135p. softcover 9.95 (ISBN 0-686-84776-8). Work in Amer.

AGE GROUPS

Francis, Leslie J. Experience of Adulthood: A Profile of 26-39 Year Olds. 221p. 1982. text ed. 32.00x (ISBN 0-566-00562-X). Gower Pub Ltd.
--Youth in Transit: A Profile of 16-25 year olds. 189p. 1982. text ed. 32.00x (ISBN 0-566-00530-1). Gower Pub Ltd.
Herzog, A. Reguls & Rodgers, Willard L. Subjective Well-Being among Different Age Groups. 124p. 1982. pap. 14.00x (ISBN 0-87944-283-2). Inst Soc Res.

AGE OF ROCKS

see Geological Time; Geology, Stratigraphic

AGED

see also Aging; Education of the Aged; Retirement; Retirement Income; Social Work with the Aged

Barasch, Marc & Aguilera-Hellweg, Max, eds. Breaking One Hundred: Americans Who Have Lives Over a Century. (Illus.). 64p. (Orig.). 1983. 9.95 (ISBN 0-688-01925-0). Morrow.
Begus, Sarah & Goodman, Allen C. An Annotated Bibliography of Recent Research on the Elderly. (Public Administration Ser.: Bibliography P 1083). 63p. 1982. pap. 9.75 (ISBN 0-88066-273-5). Vance Biblios.
Berdes, Celia. Social Services for the Aged Dying & Bereaved in International Perspective. 82p. (Orig.). 1978. pap. text ed. 5.00 (ISBN 0-910473-04-8). Intl Fed Ageing.
Browne, William P. & Olson, Laura K., eds. Aging & Public Policy: The Politics of Growing Old in America. LC 82-6138. (Contributions in Political Science Ser.: No. 83). (Illus.). 304p. 1983. lib. bdg. 35.00 (ISBN 0-313-22855-8, BAG/). Greenwood.
Groseclose, Kel. Three-Speed Dad in a Ten-Speed World. 160p. (Orig.). 1983. pap. 4.95 (ISBN 0-87123-585-4). Bethany Hse.
Haber, Carole. Beyond Sixty-Five: The Dilemma of Old Age in America's Past. LC 82-12786. 175p. Date not set. price not set (ISBN 0-521-25096-X). Cambridge U Pr.
Hudson, Kenneth. Help the Aged: Twenty-One Years of Experiment & Achievement. 208p. 1983. 15.95 (ISBN 0-370-30463-2, Pub. by The Bodley Head). Merrimack Bk Serv.
John, Martha T. Teaching & Loving the Elderly. 274p. 1983. pap. text ed. 19.75 (ISBN 0-398-04812-6). C C Thomas.
Kosberg, Jordan I. Attitudes Toward the Elderly: Do We Honor & Respect Our Senior Citizens? (Vital Issues, Vol. XXIX 1979-80). 0.50 (ISBN 0-686-81611-0). Ctr Info Am.
Krauskopf, Joan M. Advocacy for the Aging. LC 82-23729. (Handbook Ser.). 603p. 1983. text ed. write for info. (ISBN 0-314-72235-1). West Pub.
Matthews, Joseph. Sourcebook for Older Americans. (Orig.). 1983. pap. 10.95 (ISBN 0-917316-55-X). Nolo Pr.
Michaels, Joseph. Prime of Your Life: A Practical Guide to Your Mature Years. 1983. pap. 9.70 (ISBN 0-316-56945-3). Little.
Nusberg, Charlotte, ed. Self-Determination by the Elderly. (Orig.). 1981. pap. text ed. 2.50 (ISBN 0-910473-11-0). Intl Fed Ageing.
--The Voluntary Agency as an Instrument of Social Change: Effective Advocacy on Behalf of the Aging. (Orig.). 1976. pap. text ed. 2.00 (ISBN 0-910473-01-3). Intl Fed Ageing.
Nusberg, Charlotte & Osako, Masako M., eds. The Situation of the Asian-Pacific Elderly. 116p. (Orig.). 1981. pap. text ed. 5.00 (ISBN 0-910473-10-2). Intl Fed Ageing.
Peace, Sheila. An International Perspective on the Status of Older Women. 100p. (Orig.). 1981. pap. text ed. 5.00 (ISBN 0-910473-08-0). Intl Fed Ageing.
Pulvino, Charles J. & Colangelo, Nicholas. Exercises in Counseling the Elderly: A Manual to Accompany Counseling for the Growing Years-65 & Over. LC 81-71403. 120p. (Orig.). 1982. pap. 40.95 (ISBN 0-932796-11-7). Ed Media Corp.
Robey, Harriet. There's a Dance in the Old Dame Yet. (General Ser.). 1982. lib. bdg. 14.95 (ISBN 0-8161-3478-2, Large Print Bks). G K Hall.
Rudzitis, Gundars. Residential Location Determinants of the Older Population. LC 82-10966. (Research Papers Ser.: No. 202). (Illus.). 117p. 1982. pap. text ed. 8.00 (ISBN 0-89065-107-8). U Chicago Dept Geog.
Shanes, Ethel. National Survey of the Aged 1975. LC 82-80683. 1982. write for info. (ISBN 0-89138-938-5). ICPSR.
Smith, Robert J. Crime Against the Elderly: Implications for Policy-Makers & Practitioners. 61p. 1979. pap. text ed. 5.00 (ISBN 0-910473-07-2). Intl Fed Ageing.

AGED–BIBLIOGRAPHY

Lacayo, Carmela G. National Study to Assess the Service Needs of the Hispanic Elderly. Smith, Margaret, ed. 502p. Date not set. 45.00; pap. text ed. price not set. Assn Personas Mayores.
--A Research, Bibliographic, & Resource Guide on the Hispanic Elderly. Lacayo, Carmela G., ed. 421p. 1981. 20.00; pap. text ed. write for info. Assn Personas Mayores.

AGED–CARE AND HYGIENE

see also Geriatric Nursing; Geriatrics; Nursing Homes

Ball, Avis J. What Shall I Do with a Hundred Years? 130p. (Orig.). 1982. pap. 6.95 (ISBN 0-932910-44-0). Potentials Development.
Cox, Michael A. Oxycal vs. Arthritis. 171p. (Orig.). 1982. pap. 5.95 (ISBN 0-686-43305-X). R Tanner Assocs Inc.
Fahey, Charles J. The Infirm Elderly: Their Care is an Agenda Item for All Segments of Society. (Vital Issues Ser.: Vol. XXXI, No. 10). 0.80 (ISBN 0-686-84151-4). Ctr Info Am.
Health, Physical Education, Recreation & Dance for the Older Adult: A Modular Approach. 264p. 1980. 8.95 (ISBN 0-88314-101-9). AAHPERD.
Lacayo, Carmela G. Serving the Hispanic Elderly of the United States: A National Community Service Directory. 234p. 1982. write for info. Assn Personas Mayores.
Moirashine. Long Term Care of the Aging. LC 82-62399. 176p. 1982. pap. 14.50 (ISBN 0-943432-00-6). Slack Inc.
Morris, Woodrow W. & Bader, Iva M. Hoffman's Daily Needs & Interests of Older People. 2nd ed. (Illus.). 400p. 1983. text ed. 36.50x (ISBN 0-398-04782-0). C C Thomas.
Nusberg, Charlotte, ed. Home Help Services for the Aging Around the World. (Orig.). 1975. pap. text ed. 4.50 (ISBN 0-910473-00-5). Intl Fed Ageing.
Pagliaro, Louis A. & Pagliaro, Ann M., eds. Pharmacologic Aspects of Aging. (Illus.). 480p. 1983. text ed. 24.95 (ISBN 0-8016-3748-1). Mosby.
Seidl, Frederick & Applebaum, Robert. Delivering In-Home Services to the Aged & Disabled: The Wisconsin Experiment. LC 81-48068. (Illus.). 1983. write for info. (ISBN 0-669-05243-4). Lexington Bks.

AGED–DWELLINGS

Boldy & Heuman. Housing For the Elderly: Planning & Policy Formation in Western Europe & North America. LC 82-10684. 224p. 1982. 25.00x (ISBN 0-312-39349-0). St Martin.
Parker, Rosetta E. Housing for the Elderly: The Handbook for Managers. Moore, Betty T., ed. (Institute of Real Estate Management Monographs: Series on Specific Property Types). (Illus.). 150p. (Orig.). 1983. pap. 19.95 (ISBN 0-912104-68-6). Inst Real Estate.
Zais, James P., et al. Housing Assistance for Older Americans: The Reagan Prescription. LC 82-50957. (Changing Domestic Priorities Ser.). 125p. (Orig.). 1982. pap. text ed. 9.95 (ISBN 0-87766-317-3, 34300). Urban Inst.

AGED–ECONOMIC CONDITIONS

see also Age and Employment; Old Age Pensions; Retirement Income

Garbacz, Christopher. Economic Resources for the Elderly: Prospects for the Future. (Replica Edition Ser.). 235p. 1983. softcover 20.00x (ISBN 0-86531-947-2). Westview.
Maves, Paul B. A Place to Live in Later Years. LC 82-72650. 112p. 1982. pap. 4.95 (ISBN 0-8066-1957-0, 10-4987). Augsburg.
Phillipson, Chris. Capitalism & the Construction of Old Age. (Critical Texts in Social Work & the Welfare State). 192p. 1982. text ed. 26.25x (ISBN 0-333-28642-1, Pub. by Macmillan England); pap. text ed. 10.50x (ISBN 0-333-28644-8). Humanities.
Zander, Mary, et al. Toward Income Adequacy for the Elderly: Implications of the SSI Programs for New York City Recipients. 243p. 1982. pap. 5.00 (ISBN 0-88156-004-9). Comm Serv Soc NY.

AGED–EDUCATION

see Education of the Aged

AGED–EMPLOYMENT

see Age and Employment

AGED–LEGAL STATUS, LAWS, ETC.

Dunham, Arthur & Nusberg, Charlotte. Toward Planning for the Aging in Local Communities: An International Perspective. 49p. (Orig.). 1978. pap. text ed. 4.00 (ISBN 0-910473-05-6). Intl Fed Ageing.
Lammers, William. Public Policy & the Aging. 250p. 1983. pap. 7.95 (ISBN 0-87187-246-3). Congr Quarterly.
Nusberg, Charlotte & Fast, Franziska, eds. The U. N. World Assembly on the Elderly: The Aging as a Resource; The Aging as a Corcern & the Situation of the Elderly in Austria. 52p. (Orig.). 1981. pap. text ed. 3.50. Intl Fed Ageing.
Warren, Tully E. Senior Citizens & Political Power: What's the Situation? (Vital Issues, Vol. XXVIII 1978-79: No. 1). 0.50 (ISBN 0-686-81616-1). Ctr Info Am.

AGED–MEDICAL CARE

Aronson, Miriam K. & Bennett, Ruth, eds. The Acting-Out Elderly: Issues for Helping Professionals. Gurland, Barry. LC 82-23430. (Advanced Models & Practice in Aged Care: No. 1). 92p. 1983. text ed. 20.00 (ISBN 0-917724-76-3). Haworth Pr.
Kleiman, M. B., ed. Social Gerontology: Interdisciplinary Topics in Gerontology, Vol. 17. (Illus.). viii, 200p. 1983. pap. 78.00 (ISBN 3-8055-3649-6). S Karger.

AGED–NUTRITION

Feldman. Nutrition in the Middle & Later Years. (Illus.). 352p. 1982. text ed. 29.50 (ISBN 0-7236-7046-3). Wright-PSG.
Somogyi, J. C. & Fidanza, F., eds. Nutritional Problems of the Elderly. (Bibliotecha Nutritio et Dieta Ser.: No. 33). (Illus.). viii, 190p. 1983. pap. 78.00 (ISBN 3-8055-3700-X). S Karger.
Watkin, Donald M. Handbook of Nutrition, Health, & Aging. LC 82-14450. 290p. 1983. 32.00 (ISBN 0-8155-0929-4). Noyes.

AGED–PERSONALITY

see Aged–Psychology

AGED–PRAYER-BOOKS AND DEVOTIONS

Mooney, Patrick. A Gift of Love: Remembering the Old Anew. 48p. (Orig.). 1983. pap. 1.50 (ISBN 0-89622-168-7). Twenty-Third.

AGED-PSYCHOLOGY
Aronson, Miriam K. & Bennett, Ruth, eds. The Acting-Out Elderly: Issues for Helping Professionals. Gurland, Barry. LC 82-23430. (Advanced Models & Practice in Aged Care: No. 1). 92p. 1983. text ed. 20.00 (ISBN 0-917724-76-3). Haworth Pr.
Butler, Robert N. & Lewis, Myrna I. Aging & Mental Health. (Medical Library). (Illus.). 400p. 1983. pap. price not set (ISBN 0-452-25405-1, 1002-8). Mosby.
Hareven, Tamara K. & Adams, Kathleen J., eds. Aging & Life Course Transitions: An Interdisciplinary Perspective. LC 82-989. (Adult Development & Aging Ser.). 281p. 1982. text ed. 24.50 (ISBN 0-89862-125-9). Guilford Pr.
Kelly, Phil. The Elderly: A Guide for Counselors. 1.25 (ISBN 0-89486-122-0). Hazelden.
Lieberman, Morton & Tobin, Sheldon. The Experience of Old Age: Stress, Coping, & Survival. 400p. 1983. 25.00 (ISBN 0-686-82532-2). Basic.
Lockett, Betty A. Aging, Politics & Research: Setting the Federal Agenda for Research on Aging. 1983. text ed. price not set (ISBN 0-8261-4430-6). Springer Pub.
Patterson, Roger L. Overcoming Deficits of Aging: A Behavioral Approach. (Applied Clinical Psychology Ser.). 306p. 1982. 35.00x (ISBN 0-306-40947-X, Plenum Pr). Plenum Pub.

AGED-RECREATION
Fe, Lu. God Bless Our HUD Home: Downtowner Congregate Housing. 1983. 7.95 (ISBN 0-533-05597-0). Vantage.
Fifty Positive Vigor Exercises for Senior Citizens. 14p. 1979. 2.25 (ISBN 0-686-38065-7). AAHPERD.
Health, Physical Education, Recreation & Dance for the Older Adult: A Modular Approach. 264p. 1980. 8.95 (ISBN 0-88314-101-9). AAHPERD.
Munsterberg, Hugo. The Crown of Life: Artisitc Creativity in Old Age. (Illus.). 256p. pap. 12.95 (ISBN 0-15-623202-2, Harv). HarBraceJ.
Rudman, Jack. Senior Citizens' Activities Specialist. (Career Examination Ser.: C-900). (Cloth bdg. avail. on request). pap. 12.00 (ISBN 0-8373-0900-X). Natl Learning.
--Supervising Senior Citizens Club Leader. (Career Examination Ser.: C-2829). (Cloth bdg. avail. on request). pap. 12.00 (ISBN 0-8373-2829-2). Natl Learning.
Service-Learning: Programs for the Aging. 50p. 1980. 4.25 (ISBN 0-88314-170-1). AAHPERD.

AGED-SEXUAL BEHAVIOR
Sex After Forty. (Blank Books Ser.). 128p. 1982. cancelled (ISBN 0-939944-07-3). Marmac Pub.
Weg, Ruth B., ed. Sexuality in the Later Years: Roles & Behavior. LC 82-11395. write for info. (ISBN 0-12-741320-0). Acad Pr.

AGED-SOCIAL CONDITIONS
Barrow, Georgia M. & Smith, Patricia A. Aging: The Individual & Society. 2nd ed. (Illus.). 400p. 1983. pap. text ed. 15.95 (ISBN 0-314-69635-0). West Pub.
Beaver, Marion L. Human Service Practice with the Elderly. (Illus.). 256p. 1983. 19.95 (ISBN 0-686-38827-5). P H.
Cox, Frances M. Aging in a Changing Village Society: A Kenyan Experience. (Orig.). 1977. pap. text ed. 3.00 (ISBN 0-910473-03-X). Intl Fed Ageing.
Edwards, Dan W. & Letman, Sloan T. Aging in the Urban Community. 120p. 1983. pap. text ed. 12.50 (ISBN 0-934872-05-8). Carlinshar.
Kleiman, M. B., ed. Social Gerontology: Interdisciplinary Topics in Gerontology, Vol. 17. (Illus.). viii, 200p. 1983. pap. 78.00 (ISBN 3-8055-3649-6). S Karger.
Kraft, John & Osterbind, Carter C., eds. Older People in Florida, Nineteen Eighty to Nineteen Eighty-One: A Statistical Abstract. 264p. (Orig.). 1981. pap. 11.50 (ISBN 0-8130-0703-8). U Presses Fla.
Maves, Paul B. A Place to Live in Later Years. LC 82-72650. 112p. 1982. pap. 4.95 (ISBN 0-8066-1957-0, 10-4987). Augsburg.
Neugarten, Bernice I. Age or Need? Public Policies for Older People. (Sage Focus Editions). (Illus.). 288p. 1982. 25.00 (ISBN 0-8039-1908-5); pap. 12.50 (ISBN 0-8039-1909-3). Sage.
Riley, Matilda W., et al, eds. Aging in Society. 288p. 1982. text ed. write for info. (ISBN 0-89859-267-4). L Erlbaum Assocs.
Torres-Gil, Fernando M. Politics of Aging Among Elder Hispanics. LC 82-16067. 230p. (Orig.). 1983. lib. bdg. 23.00 (ISBN 0-8191-2756-6); pap. text ed. 10.75 (ISBN 0-8191-2757-4). U Pr of Amer.
Unruh, David. Invisible Lives: Social Worlds of the Aged. (Sociological Observations Ser.: Vol. 14). (Illus.). 200p. 1982. 22.00 (ISBN 0-8039-1954-9); pap. 10.95 (ISBN 0-8039-1955-7). Sage.

AGED-TRANSPORTATION
Ashford, Norman & Bell, W. G., eds. Mobility & Transport for Elderly & Handicapped Persons: International Conference Held in Cambridge, England, July, 1981. (Transportation Studies: Vol. 2). Date not set. price not set (ISBN 0-677-16380-0). Gordon.

AGED WORKERS
see Age and Employment

AGENCIES, EMPLOYMENT
see Employment Agencies

AGENCIES, THEATRICAL
see Theatrical Agencies

AGFANS
see Pushtuns

AGGLUTINANTS
see Adhesives

AGGREGATES
see Set Theory

AGGRESSIVENESS (PSYCHOLOGY)
see also Assertiveness (Psychology)
American Health Research Institute, Ltd. Aggression: A Psychological, Behavioral & Medical Subject Analysis with Research Index & Bibliography. Bartone, John C., ed. 120p. 1983. 29.95 (ISBN 0-88164-028-X); pap. 21.95 (ISBN 0-88164-029-8). ABBE Pubs Assn.
Averill, James R. Anger & Aggression: An Essay on Emotion. (Springer Series in Social Psychology). (Illus.). 402p. 1983. 29.90 (ISBN 0-387-90719-X). Springer-Verlag.
Bach, George R. & Torbet, Laura. The Inner Enemy: How to Fight Fair with Yourself. LC 82-14397. 224p. 1983. 11.95 (ISBN 0-688-01557-3). Morrow.
Blanchard, Robert J. & Blanchard, Caroline, eds. Advances in the Study of Aggression, Vol. 1. (Serial Publication). 238p. 1983. price not set (ISBN 0-12-037701-2). Acad Pr.
Geen, Russell & Donnerstein, Edward, eds. Aggression: Theoretical & Methodologic Issues. LC 82-24348. Date not set. Vol. 1: Theoretical Issues. price not set (ISBN 0-12-278801-X); Vol. 2: Issues in Research. price not set (ISBN 0-12-278802-8). Acad Pr.
Lauer, Hans E. Aggression & Repression in the Individual & Society. Castelliz, K. & Davies, Saunders, trs. from Ger. 111p. 1981. pap. 7.95 (ISBN 0-85440-359-0, Pub. by Steinerbooks). Anthroposophic.
Simmel, Edward C. & Hahn, Martin E., eds. Aggressive Behavior: Genetic & Neural Approaches. 1983. text ed. write for info. (ISBN 0-89859-253-4). L Erlbaum Assocs.

AGILITY
see Motor Ability

AGING
see also Immortalism
Alter, Joseph D. Life After Fifty. (Illus.). 144p. 1983. 12.50 (ISBN 0-89313-060-5). G F Stickley.
Barash, David P. Aging: An Exploration. 232p. 1983. 14.95 (ISBN 0-295-95993-2). U of Wash Pr.
Beall, C. M., ed. Cross-Cultural Studies of Biological Aging. 100p. 1982. 19.50 (ISBN 0-08-028946-0). Pergamon.
Bergener, Manfred. Aging in the Eighties & Beyond. 1983. text ed. price not set (ISBN 0-8261-3690-7). Springer Pub.
Boskey, James B. & Hughes, Susan C. Teaching about Aging: Religious & Advocacy Perspectives. LC 82-17589. 184p. (Orig.). 1983. lib. bdg. 20.75 (ISBN 0-8191-2802-3); pap. text ed. 10.00 (ISBN 0-8191-2803-1). U Pr of Amer.
Codrescu, Andrei & Notley, Alice. Three Zero, Turning Thirty. Wright, Keith & Wright, Jeff, eds. (Illus.). 54p. (Orig.). 1982. pap. 5.00 (ISBN 0-938878-14-X). Hard Pr.
Frolkis, V. V. Aging & Life-Prolonging Processes. (Illus.). 380p. 1983. 39.20 (ISBN 0-387-81685-2). Springer-Verlag.
Hareven, Tamara K. & Adams, Kathleen J., eds. Aging & Life Course Transitions: An Interdisciplinary Perspective. LC 82-989. (Adult Development & Aging Ser.). 281p. 1982. text ed. 24.50 (ISBN 0-89862-125-9). Guilford Pr.
Ikels, Charlotte. Adaptation & Aging: Chinese in Hong Kong & the United States. 1983. 27.50 (ISBN 0-208-01999-5, Archon). Shoe String.
Korenman. Endocrine Aspects of Aging. (Current Endocrinology Ser.: Vol. 6). 1982. 39.95 (ISBN 0-444-00681-8). Elsevier.
Kroc Foundation Conference, Oct. 12-16, 1981. Alzheimer's Disease, Down's Syndrome, & Aging: Proceedings, Vol. 396. Sinex, F. Marott & Merril, Carl R., eds. 199p. 1982. 35.00 (ISBN 0-89766-182-6); pap. write for info. (ISBN 0-89766-183-4). NY Acad Sci.
Leisure & Aging. (Leisure Today Ser.). 32p. 1.50 (ISBN 0-88314-119-1). AAHPERD.
Lesnoff-Caravaglia, Gari, ed. Perspectives on Aging. 141p. 1977. pap. text ed. 7.95x (ISBN 0-686-84084-4). Irvington.
Magan, Geralyn G., ed. Aging, Race & Culture: Issues in Long Term Care. LC 82-72776. 150p. 1983. pap. 6.50 (ISBN 0-943774-11-X). AAHA.
Melamed, Elissa. Mirror, Mirror: The Terror of Not Being Young. 1983. price not set (ISBN 0-671-43429-2, Linden). S&S.
Mortimer, James & Pirozzolo, Francis J., eds. The Aging Motor System, Vol. 3. 270p. 1982. 29.95 (ISBN 0-03-059283-6). Praeger.
Myers, Phyllis. Aging in Place. LC 82-8296. 106p. (Orig.). 1982. pap. 7.50 (ISBN 0-89164-075-4). Conservation Foun.
Oberleder, Muriel. Avoid the Aging Trap. Date not set. 11.95 (ISBN 0-686-82383-4). Acropolis.
Pearson, Durk & Shaw, Sandy. Life Extension. 896p. 1983. pap. 12.95 (ISBN 0-446-87990-8). Warner Bks.
Reggie the Retiree, pseud. Laughs & Limericks on Aging. large print ed. (Illus.). 96p. 1982. pap. 4.95 (ISBN 0-9609960-0-1). Reggie the Retiree.
Report of the World Assembly on Aging. 101p. 1983. pap. 9.00 (ISBN 0-686-43286-X, UN 82/1/16, UN). Unipub.
Saul, S. Aging: An Album of People Growing Old. 2nd ed. 200p. 1983. text ed. 12.50 (ISBN 0-471-87331-4). Wiley.
Secrets of Staying Young & Living Longer. 1981. 4.95 (ISBN 0-686-42901-X). Harian.

AGING-PSYCHOLOGICAL ASPECTS
see Aged-Psychology; Genetic Psychology

AGING-RESEARCH
Lockett, Betty A. Aging, Politics & Research: Setting the Federal Agenda for Research on Aging. 1983. text ed. price not set (ISBN 0-8261-4430-6). Springer Pub.
Reed, Robert D. How & Where to Research & Find Information on Aging in America. LC 82-60572. 80p. (Orig.). 1983. pap. 4.50 (ISBN 0-686-81658-7). R & E Res Assoc.
Stanford, E. P. & Lockery, Shirley, eds. Trends & Status of Minority Aging, Vol. 8. (Proceedings of the Institute on Minority Aging). 150p. (Orig.). 1982. pap. 10.00 (ISBN 0-916304-57-4). Campanile.

AGNOSTICISM
see also Atheism; Belief and Doubt; Positivism; Rationalism; Skepticism
Ingersall, Robert G. Faith or Agnosticism. 24p. Date not set. pap. 3.00 (ISBN 0-686-83985-4). Am Atheist.

AGORAPHOBIA
Metzger, Judith. Escape from Fear: Can Agoraphobia be Cured. LC 82-81597. Date not set. pap. price not set (ISBN 0-941712-02-8). Intl Pub Corp OH.
Seidenberg, Robert & DeCrow, Karen. Women Who Marry Houses: Panic & Protest in Agoraphobia. LC 82-14934. 204p. 1983. 15.95 (ISBN 0-07-016284-0, GB); pap. 7.95 (ISBN 0-07-016283-2). McGraw.
Thorpe, Geoffrey L. & Burns, Laurence E. The Agoraphobic Syndrome: Behavioral Approaches to Evaluation & Treatment. 200p. 1983. 34.95x (ISBN 0-471-10495-7, Pub. by Wiley-Interscience). Wiley.

AGRARIAN QUESTION
see Agriculture-Economic Aspects; Agriculture and State

AGRARIAN REFORM
see Land Reform

AGREEMENTS
see Contracts

AGREEMENTS, INTERSTATE
see Interstate Agreements

AGRIBUSINESS
see Agriculture-Economic Aspects

AGRICULTURAL ADMINISTRATION
Dalton, G. E. Managing Agricultural Systems. xii, 163p. Date not set. 24.75 (ISBN 0-85334-165-6, Pub. by Applied Sci England). Elsevier.

AGRICULTURAL BANKS
see Agricultural Credit; Banks and Banking

AGRICULTURAL CHEMICALS
see also Fertilizers and Manures; Fungicides; Growth Promoting Substances; Herbicides; Insecticides; Pesticides; Trace Elements
Crop Response to the Supply of Macronutrients. 46p. 1982. pap. 6.75 (ISBN 90-220-0807-X, PDC247, Pudoc). Unipub.
McLaren. Chemical Manipulation of Crop Growth. 1982. text ed. 89.95 (ISBN 0-408-10767-7). Butterworth.
Wagner, Sheldon L. Clinical Toxicology of Agricultural Chemicals. LC 82-14421. (Illus.). 306p. 1983. 28.00 (ISBN 0-8155-0930-8). Noyes.

AGRICULTURAL CHEMISTRY
see also Agricultural Chemicals; Dairy Products-Analysis and Examination; Fertilizers and Manures; Soil Chemistry; Soils
Unsworth. Effects of Gaseous Air Pollution in Agriculture & Horticulture. 1982. text ed. 89.95 (ISBN 0-686-37584-X). Butterworth.

AGRICULTURAL CLIMATOLOGY
see Crops and Climate

AGRICULTURAL COOPERATION
see Agriculture, Cooperative

AGRICULTURAL CREDIT
see also Mortgage Loans
Woodruff, Archibald, Jr. Farm Mortgage Loans of Life Insurance Companies. 1937. text ed. 39.50x (ISBN 0-686-83543-3). Elliots Bks.

AGRICULTURAL ECONOMICS
see Agriculture-Economic Aspects

AGRICULTURAL ENGINEERING
see also Agricultural Machinery; Drainage; Farm Buildings; Irrigation
Dole, D. J., intro. by. Agricultural Engineering, 1980: Agricultural Conferences. 290p. (Orig.). 1980. pap. text ed. 45.00x (ISBN 0-85825-138-8, Pub. by Inst Engineering Australia). Renouf.
O'Shea, J. A., intro. by. Survey of Research & Investigations in Agricultural Engineering, 1978. 129p. (Orig.). 1978. pap. text ed. 20.25x (ISBN 0-85825-098-5, Pub. by Inst Engineering Australia). Renouf.
--Survey of Research & Investigations in Agricultural Engineering, 1982. 110p. (Orig.). 1982. pap. text ed. 18.00x (ISBN 0-85825-180-9, Pub. by Inst Engineering Australia). Renouf.
O'Shea, John A., intro. by. Agricultural Engineering: 1978. 325p. (Orig.). 1978. pap. text ed. 54.00x (ISBN 0-85825-097-7, Pub. by Inst Engineering Australia). Renouf.
Perrens, S. J., intro. by. Agricultural Engineering, 1982. (Agricultural Conferences Ser.). 225p. (Orig.). 1982. pap. text ed. 42.00x (ISBN 0-85825-176-0, Pub. Inst Engineering Australia). Renouf.

AGRICULTURAL ESTIMATING AND REPORTING
see also Crop Yields
Li, P. H. & Sakai, A., eds. Plant Cold Hardiness & Freezing Stress: Vol. 2: Mechanisms & Crop Implications. LC 78-7038. (Symposium). 1982. 39.50 (ISBN 0-12-447602-3). Acad Pr.

AGRICULTURAL EXHIBITIONS
see Fairs

AGRICULTURAL IMPLEMENTS
see also names of particular implements
Hurt, R. Douglas. American Farm Tools: From Hand Power to Steam Power. 1982. 20.00x (ISBN 0-89745-027-2); pap. 9.95x (ISBN 0-89745-026-4). Sunflower U Pr.
Spedding, C. R. An Introduction to Agricultural Systems. 1979. 20.50 (ISBN 0-85334-823-5, Pub. by Applied Sci England). Elsevier.

AGRICULTURAL INNOVATIONS
Improvement of Oil-Seed & Industrial Crops by Induced Mutations. 353p. 1982. pap. 42.00 (ISBN 92-0-011082-7, ISP 608, IAEA). Unipub.

AGRICULTURAL LABORERS
see also Migration, Internal; Peasantry
International Labour Organisation, 5th Conference of American States Members,Petropolis. Application & Supervision of Labour Legislation in Agriculture: Report I. 56p. 1952. 3.40 (ISBN 0-686-84712-1, CRA 1952/5/I). Intl Labour Office.

AGRICULTURAL LAWS AND LEGISLATION
see also Land Tenure-Law
Agrarian Reform & Employment. vii, 186p. 1971. 5.70 (ISBN 92-2-100083-4). Intl Labour Office.

AGRICULTURAL MACHINERY
see also Agricultural Engineering; Agricultural Implements; Machinery
Chek-Chart. Tractor & Farm Implement Lubrication Guide, 1983. 384p. 1983. pap. 34.00x (ISBN 0-88098-023-0). H. M. Gousha.

AGRICULTURAL MACHINERY-JUVENILE LITERATURE
Althea. Machines on a Farm. (Cambridge Dinosaur Information Ser.). (Illus.). 26p. (gr. 7-10). 1983. pap. 1.50 (ISBN 0-521-27156-8). Cambridge U Pr.

AGRICULTURAL MARKETING
see Farm Produce-Marketing

AGRICULTURAL MECHANICS
see Agricultural Engineering

AGRICULTURAL PESTS
see also Garden Pests; Insects, Injurious and Beneficial; Pest Control; Plant Diseases; Weeds also subdivision Diseases and Pests under names of crops, etc., Fruit-Diseases and Pests
Judenko, E. Analytical Method for Assessing Yield Losses Caused by Pests on Cereal Crops with & Without Pesticides. 1973. 35.00x (ISBN 0-85135-061-5, Pub. by Centre Overseas Research). State Mutual Bk.
King, W. J. Cotton in the Gambia: Report on the Cotton Development Project 1975 to 1978. 1980. 35.00x (ISBN 0-85135-109-3, Pub. by Centre Overseas Research). State Mutual Bk.
Locust & Grasshopper Agricultural Manual. 1982. 195.00 (ISBN 0-85135-120-4, Pub. by Centre Overseas Research). State Mutual BK.
Service, M. W. Methods for Sampling Adult Simulidae, with Special Reference to the Simulium Damnosum Complex. 1977. 35.00x (ISBN 0-85135-087-9, Pub. by Centre Overseas Research). State Mutual Bk.
Tunstall, J. P. & King, W. J. The Gumbia Cotton Handbook. 1979. 40.00x (ISBN 0-85135-100-X, Pub. by Centre Overseas Research). State Mutual Bk.
Wright, E. N. & Inglis, I. Bird Problems in Agriculture. 210p. 1980. 60.00x (ISBN 0-901436-48-8, CAB Bks). State Mutual Bk.

AGRICULTURAL POLICY
see Agriculture and State

AGRICULTURAL PRICES
see also Farm Produce-Marketing; Food Prices
Prices of Agricultural Products & Selected Inputs in Europe & North America, 1980-81. 122p. 1982. pap. 15.00 (ISBN 0-686-82548-9, UN 82/2E6, UN). Unipub.

AGRICULTURAL PRODUCTION FUNCTIONS
see Agriculture-Economic Aspects-Mathematical Models

AGRICULTURAL PROGRAMS
see Agricultural Administration

AGRICULTURAL RESEARCH
see also Plant-Breeding
Andrew, Chris O. & Hildebrand, Peter E. Planning & Conducting Applied Agricultural Research. 96p. 1982. lib. bdg. 12.00 (ISBN 0-86531-461-6); pap. text ed. 7.95 (ISBN 0-86531-460-8). Westview.
Report of an Exploratory Workshop on the Role of Anthropologists & Other Social Scientists in Interdisciplinary Teams Developing Improved Food Production Technology. 101p. 1983. pap. 13.50 (ISBN 0-686-42855-2, R179, IRRI). Unipub.

Research on Algae, Blue-Green Algae, & Phototrophic Nitrogen Fixation at the International Rice Research Institute (1963-81) Summarization, Problems & Prospects. (IRRI Research Paper Ser.: No. 78). 21p. 1983. pap. 5.00 (ISBN 0-686-42858-7, R182, IRRI). Unipub.
Shaner, W. W. & Philipp, P. F., eds. Readings in Farming Systems Research & Development. (Special Studies in Agriculture-Aquaculture Science & Policy). 166p. 1982. lib. bdg. 19.00 (ISBN 0-86531-502-7). Westview.

AGRICULTURAL TOOLS
see Agricultural Implements
AGRICULTURAL WARRANTS
see Agricultural Credit
AGRICULTURAL WORKERS
see Agricultural Laborers
AGRICULTURE
see also Animal Industry; Aquaculture; Cattle; Crop Yields; Dairying; Domestic Animals; Drainage; Farm Buildings; Farm Life; Farm Management; Farmers; Farms; Fertilizers and Manures; Field Crops; Food Industry and Trade; Forage Plants; Forests and Forestry; Fruit; Gardening; Grain; Grasses; Horticulture; Insects, Injurious and Beneficial; Irrigation; Livestock; Plant-Breeding; Reclamation of Land; Seeds; Soil Science; Soil Surveys; Soils; Trees; Vegetable Gardening; Vegetables
also headings beginning with the word Agricultural, and names of agricultural products
Brady, N. C., ed. Advances in Agronomy, Vol. 35. (Serial Publication). 1982. 35.00 (ISBN 0-12-000735-5); 45.50 (ISBN 0-12-000790-8); 24.50 (ISBN 0-12-000791-6). Acad Pr.
Charles-Edwards, D., ed. Physiological Determinants of Crop Growth. Date not set. 26.00 (ISBN 0-12-169360-0). Acad Pr.
Foth, Henry D. Fundamentals of Soil Science. 6th ed. LC 77-86509. 436p. 1978. 28.95 (ISBN 0-471-26792-9). Wiley.
Furuseth, Owen J. & Pierce, John T. Agricultural Land in an Urban Society. Knight, C. Gregory, ed. (Resource Publications in Geography Ser.). (Orig.). 1982. pap. 5.00 (ISBN 0-89291-149-2). Assn Am Geographers.
Harrell, Pauline C. & Chase, Charlotte. Arrowhead Farm: 300 Years of New England Husbandry & Cooking. (Illus.). 240p. 1983. 16.95 (ISBN 0-914378-98-8); pap. 10.95. Countryman.
Improvement of Nutritional Quality of Food Crops. (FAO Plant Production & Protection Paper: No. 34). 92p. 1981. pap. 7.50 (ISBN 92-5-101166-4, F2298, FAO). Unipub.
Intercropping: Proceedings of the Second Symposium on Intercropping in Semi-Arid Areas, held at Morogoro, Tanzania 4-7 August 1980. 168p. 1983. pap. 12.00 (ISBN 0-88936-318-8, IDRC). Unipub.
International Seminar on Energy Conservation & Use of Renewable Energies in the Bio-Industries, Trinity College, Oxford, UK, 2nd 6-10 Sept. 1982. Energy Conservation & Use of Renewable Energies in the Bio-Industries: Proceedings. Vogt, F., ed. (Illus.). 750p. 1982. 100.00 (ISBN 0-08-029781-1). Pergamon.
Pearce, S. C. The Agricultural Field Experiment: A Statistical Examination of Theory & Practice. 400p. 1983. write for info. (ISBN 0-471-10511-2, Pub. by Wiley-Interscience). Wiley.
Pond, Wilson G. & Mumpton, Frederick A., eds. Zeo-Agriculture: The Use of Natural Zeolites in Agriculture & Aquaculture. 450p. 1983. lib. bdg. 50.00x (ISBN 0-86531-602-3). Westview.
Seeds Semences Semillas. (FAO Plant Production & Protection Paper: No. 39). 569p. 1983. pap. 41.75 (ISBN 92-5-001226-8, F2361, FAO). Unipub.
Simulation of Plant Growth & Crop Production. 308p. 1982. pap. 33.75 (ISBN 90-220-0809-6, PDC250, Pudoc). Unipub.
Sonka, S. T. Computers in Farming: Selection & Use. 356p. 1983. 19.95 (ISBN 0-07-059653-0). McGraw.
The State of Food & Agriculture 1981. 177p. 1983. pap. 32.50 (ISBN 92-5-101201-6, F2266, FAO). Unipub.
Subba. Advances in Agriculture Microbiology. 1982. text ed. 89.95 (ISBN 0-408-10848-7). Butterworth.
Timmer, W. J. The Human Side of Agriculture: Theory & Practice of Agricultural Extension. LC 80-53419. 223p. 1982. 10.00 (ISBN 0-533-04849-4). Vantage.

AGRICULTURE–ACCOUNTING
Warren, Martyn. Financial Management for Farmers: The Basic Techniques of Money-Farming. 288p. 1982. 55.00X (ISBN 0-09-148930-X, Pub. by Hutchinson); pap. 40.00x (ISBN 0-09-148931-8). State Mutual Bk.

AGRICULTURE–ADMINISTRATION
see Agricultural Administration
AGRICULTURE–ECONOMIC ASPECTS
see also Agricultural Credit; Agricultural Prices; Farm Management; Farm Produce–Marketing; Rent
Buck, Solon J. Agrarian Crusade. 1920. text ed. 8.50x (ISBN 0-686-83457-7). Elliots Bks.
Cayre, Henri. Agricultural Plenty: A Monograph. 176p. 1982. 40.00x (ISBN 0-85614-070-8, Pub. by Gentry England). State Mutual Bk.
Courtney, P. P. Plantation Agriculture. (Advanced Economic Geographies Ser.). 296p. 1982. 35.00x (ISBN 0-7135-1256-3, Pub. by Bell & Hyman England). State Mutual Bk.
The Energy Problem & the Agro-Food Sector. (Orig.). 1982. pap. 7.50x (ISBN 92-64-12343-1). OECD.
Frederick, Kenneth D. Water for Western Agriculture. LC 82-47985. (A Resources for the Future Research Paper). (Illus.). 256p. (Orig.). 1982. pap. text ed. 15.00x (ISBN 0-8018-2832-5). Resources Future.
Gittinger, J. Price. Economic Analysis of Agricultural Projects. 2nd ed. LC 82-15262. (World Bank Ser.). 512p. 1982. text ed. 37.50x (ISBN 0-8018-2912-7); pap. text ed. 13.50x (ISBN 0-8018-2913-5). Johns Hopkins.
OECD. Problems of Agricultural Trade. 178p. 1982. pap. 18.00x (ISBN 92-64-12368-7). OECD.
Ritson, Christopher. Agricultural Economics: Principles & Policy. 409p. 1982. pap. text ed. 14.95x (ISBN 0-86531-453-5). Westview.

AGRICULTURE–ECONOMIC ASPECTS–MATHEMATICAL MODELS
Hanf, C. H. & Schiefer, G. W. Planning & Decision in Agribusiness-Principles & Experiences: A Case Study Approach to the Use of Models in Decision Making. (Developments in Agricultural Economics Ser.: No. 1). 374p. 1982. 83.00 (ISBN 0-444-42134-3). Elsevier.

AGRICULTURE–ECONOMIC ASPECTS–AFRICA
Ghai, Dharam & Radwan, Samir, eds. Agrarian Policies & Rural Poverty in Africa. (World Employment Programme Study Ser.). ix, 311p. (Orig.). 1983. 21.40 (ISBN 92-2-103109-8); pap. 15.70 (ISBN 92-2-103100-4). Intl Labour Office.
La-Anyane, Seth. Economics of Agricultural Development in Tropical Africa. 150p. 1983. write for info. (ISBN 0-471-90034-6, Pub. by Wiley-Interscience). Wiley.

AGRICULTURE–ECONOMIC ASPECTS–CHINA
Institute of Economics, Academia Sinica. Agricultural Development in China, Japan, & Korea. 1036p. 1983. 40.00 (ISBN 0-295-95997-5, Pub. by Inst Econ Acad Sinica Taiwan). U of Wash Pr.

AGRICULTURE–ECONOMIC ASPECTS–EUROPE
Marsh, John S. European Agriculture in an Uncertain World. (The Atlantic Papers: No. 75/1). 72p. (Orig.). 1975. pap. text ed. 4.75x (ISBN 0-686-83633-2). Allanheld.
OECD. Prospects for Agricultural Production & Trade in Eastern Europe: Bulgaria, Czechoslavakia, Romania, Vol. 2. 216p. (Orig.). 1982. pap. 26.00x (ISBN 92-64-12369-5). OECD.

AGRICULTURE–ECONOMIC ASPECTS–INDIA
Swaminathan, C. Science & Integrated Rural Development, Vol. 1. 370p. 1982. text ed. 21.50x (ISBN 0-391-02752-2, Pub. by Concept India). Humanities.

AGRICULTURE–ECONOMIC ASPECTS–JAPAN
Institute of Economics, Academia Sinica. Agricultural Development in China, Japan, & Korea. 1036p. 1983. 40.00 (ISBN 0-295-95997-5, Pub. by Inst Econ Acad Sinica Taiwan). U of Wash Pr.

AGRICULTURE–ECONOMIC ASPECTS–KOREA
Institute of Economics, Academia Sinica. Agricultural Development in China, Japan, & Korea. 1036p. 1983. 40.00 (ISBN 0-295-95997-5, Pub. by Inst Econ Acad Sinica Taiwan). U of Wash Pr.

AGRICULTURE–ECONOMIC ASPECTS–RUSSIA
Brown, Lester. U. S. & Soviet Agriculture: The Shifting Balance of Power. LC 82-61876. (Worldwatch Papers). 1982. pap. 2.00 (ISBN 0-916468-51-8). Worldwatch Inst.
Johnson, D. Gale & Brooks, Karen M. Prospects for Soviet Agriculture in the 1980's. LC 82-48625. (Publication Series on the Soviet Union in the 1980's). 224p. 1983. 15.00 (ISBN 0-253-34619-3). Ind U Pr.

AGRICULTURE–HANDBOOKS, MANUALS, ETC.
Bishop, Douglas & Carter, Lark P. Activity Guide for Crop Science & Food Production. 1983. 5.12 (ISBN 0-07-005432-0, G). McGraw.
Moore, Julie & Ferguson, Sara K., eds. The Updata Index to U.S. Department of Agriculture Agricultural Handbooks Numbers 1-540. LC 81-71639. 1982. 49.50x (ISBN 0-9607840-0-4); lib. bdg. 49.50x (ISBN 0-9607840-0-4). Updata Pubns.
Thear, Katie. The Family Smallholding. (Illus.). 168p. 1983. 22.50 (ISBN 0-7134-1935-0, Pub. by Batsford England); pap. 14.95 (ISBN 0-7134-1936-9, Pub. by Batsford England). David & Charles.

AGRICULTURE–HISTORY
Halley. Agricultural Note. 17th ed. 1982. text ed. 39.95 (ISBN 0-408-10701-4). Butterworth.

AGRICULTURE–LAWS AND LEGISLATION
see Agricultural Laws and Legislation
AGRICULTURE–PRICES
see Agricultural Prices
AGRICULTURE–RESEARCH
see Agricultural Research
AGRICULTURE–STUDY AND TEACHING
Clip Art: Agricultural Communicators in Education, Bk. 5. 192p. 1982. pap. text ed. 14.95x (ISBN 0-8134-2253-1). Interstate.
Marsteller, Phyllis, ed. Peterson's Guides to Graduate Study: Biological, Agricultural, & Health Sciences, 1983. 1800p. 1982. pap. 21.95 (ISBN 0-87866-187-5). Petersons Guides.

AGRICULTURE–AFRICA
Liebenow, J. Gus. Agriculture, Education, & Rural Transformation: With Particular Reference to East Africa. (African Humanities Ser.). 31p. (Orig.). 1969. pap. text ed. 2.00 (ISBN 0-941934-00-4). Ind U Afro-Amer Arts.
Mondot-Bernard, J. & Labonne, M. Satisfaction of Food Requirements in Mali to 2000 A. D. 214p. (Orig.). 1982. pap. 15.00x (ISBN 92-64-12300-8). OECD.

AGRICULTURE–ASIA
Grain Legumes Production in Asia. 550p. 1983. pap. 14.75 (ISBN 92-833-1480-8, APO 129, APO). Unipub.

AGRICULTURE–AUSTRALIA AND NEW ZEALAND
Gillison, A. N. & Anderson, D. J., eds. Vegetation Classification in Australia. 229p. 1983. text ed. 18.95 (ISBN 0-7081-1309-5, Pub. by CSIRO Australia). Intl Schol Bk Serv.
Scott, Peter. Australian Agriculture: Resource Development & Spatial Organization. (Geography of World Agriculture Ser.: Vol.9). (Illus.). 150p. 1981. 15.00x (ISBN 963-05-2445-7). Intl Pubns Serv.

AGRICULTURE–CANADA
Troughton, M. J. Canadian Agriculture. (Geography of World Agriculture Ser.: Vol. 10). (Illus.). 355p. 1982. 42.50x (ISBN 963-05-2653-0). Intl Pubns Serv.

AGRICULTURE–EUROPE
Foxall, Gordon R. Co-Operative Marketing in European Agriculture. 116p. 1982. text ed. 29.50x (ISBN 0-566-00512-3). Gower Pub Ltd.
Marsh, John S. European Agriculture in an Uncertain World. (The Atlantic Papers: No. 75/1). 72p. (Orig.). 1975. pap. text ed. 4.75x (ISBN 0-686-83633-2). Allanheld.
Thran, P. & Brockhuizen, S., eds. Agro-Climatic Atlas of Europe. (Agro-Ecological Atlas Ser.: Vol. 1). 1965. 202.25 (ISBN 0-444-40569-0). Elsevier.

AGRICULTURE–FRANCE
Auge-Laribe, Michel & Pinot, Pierre. Agriculture & Food Supply in France During the War. (Economic & Social History of the World War Ser.). 1927. text ed. 75.00x (ISBN 0-686-83458-5). Elliots Bks.
Clout, Hugh. The Land of France, 1815-1914. (London Research Series in Geography: No. 1). 176p. 1983. text ed. 24.95x (ISBN 0-04-911003-9). Allen Unwin.

AGRICULTURE–GREAT BRITAIN
Lockhart, J. A. & Wiseman, A. J. Introduction to Crop Husbandry. 5th ed. (Illus.). 300p. 1983. 40.00 (ISBN 0-08-029793-5); pap. 16.00 (ISBN 0-08-029792-7). Pergamon.

AGRICULTURE–INDIA
Das, Arvind N. Agrarian Movements in India: Studies on 20th Century Bihar. (Illus.). 200p. 1982. text ed. 29.50x (ISBN 0-7146-3216-3, F Cass Co). Biblio Dist.
Husain, M. Crop Combinations in India. 200p. 1982. text ed. 19.50x (ISBN 0-391-02754-9, Pub. by Concept India). Humanities.

AGRICULTURE–NEAR EAST
Regional Study on Rainfed Agriculture & Agro-Climatic Inventory of Eleven Countries in the Near East Region. 160p. 1982. pap. 7.50 (ISBN 92-5-101222-9, F2336, FAO). Unipub.

AGRICULTURE–PAPUA–NEW GUINEA (TERRITORY)
Sillitoe, Paul. Roots of the Earth: Crops in the Highlands of Papua New Guinea. 320p. 1983. 35.00 (ISBN 0-686-82458-X). Manchester.

AGRICULTURE–RUSSIA
Michael, Louis Guy. More Corn for Bessarabia: The Russian Experience, 1910-1917. 228p. 1983. 17.95. Wayne St U Pr.

AGRICULTURE–UNITED STATES
Here are entered works on agriculture in the United States as a whole, as well as specific areas of the United States.
Liebman, Ellen. California Farmland: A History of Large Agricultural Landholdings. LC 82-20759. 280p. 1983. text ed. 25.95x (ISBN 0-86598-107-8). Allanheld.

AGRICULTURE, COOPERATIVE
Foxall, Gordon R. Co-Operative Marketing in European Agriculture. 116p. 1982. text ed. 29.50x (ISBN 0-566-00512-3). Gower Pub Ltd.

AGRICULTURE, SOILLESS
see Hydroponics
AGRICULTURE AND STATE
see also Agricultural Administration; Agricultural Laws and Legislation; Land Reform
Baum, Kenneth H & Schertz, Lyle P. Modeling Farm Decisions for Policy Analysis. 500p. 1983. lib. bdg. 20.00x (ISBN 0-86531-589-2). Westview.
Knutson, Ronald & Penn, J. B. Agricultural & Food Policy. (Illus.). 384p. 1983. text ed. 25.95 (ISBN 0-13-018911-1). P-H.
Ort, Walter & Hammann, Hermann. Konsistenzprobleme der Investitionsforderung In der Regionalpolitik und Agrarstrukturpolitik. 118p. (Ger.). 1982. write for info. (ISBN 3-8204-5741-0). P Lang Pubs.

AGRICULTURE AND STATE–GREAT BRITAIN
Pearce, Joan. The Common Agricultural Policy: Prospects for Change. (Chatham House Papers: No. 13). 122p. 1982. pap. 10.00 (ISBN 0-7100-9069-2). Routledge & Kegan.

AGRICULTURE AND STATE–INDIA
Agricultural Policy in India: Growth & Equity. 94p. 1983. pap. 8.00 (ISBN 0-88936-347-1, IDRC 201, IDRC). Unipub.

AGRONOMY
see Agriculture
AGROSTOLOGY
see Grasses
AID TO DEPENDENT CHILDREN
see Child Welfare
AID TO DEVELOPING COUNTRIES
see Economic Assistance
AID TO UNDERDEVELOPED AREAS
see Technical Assistance
AIKEN, CONRAD POTTER, 1889-1973
Lorenz, Clarissa M. Lorelei Two: My Life with Conrad Aiken. LC 82-17347. (Illus.). 248p. 1983. 19.95 (ISBN 0-8203-0661-4). U of Ga Pr.

AIKIDO
Stevens, John. Aikido: The Way of Harmony. LC 82-42680. (Illus.). 256p. (Orig.). 1983. pap. 14.95 (ISBN 0-394-71426-1). Shambhala Pubns.
Tourda, Wayne F. & Dye, David A. Intermediate Aikido. 97p. (Orig.). 1982. pap. 15.00 (ISBN 0-686-38101-7). Aikido Fed.

AIR–BACTERIOLOGY
see Air-Microbiology
AIR–JUVENILE LITERATURE
Jefferies, Lawrence. Air, Air, Air. LC 82-15808. (Question & Answer Bks.). (Illus.). 32p. (gr. 3-6). 1983. PLB 8.59 (ISBN 0-89375-880-9); pap. text ed. 1.95 (ISBN 0-89375-881-7). Troll Assocs.
Lloyd, David. Air. LC 82-9440. (Illus.). 32p. (ps-4). 1983. 9.95 (ISBN 0-8037-0141-1). Dial Bks Young.
Smith, Henry. Amazing Air. LC 82-80991. (Science Club Ser.). (Illus.). 48p. (gr. 3-6). 1983. PLB 8.16 (ISBN 0-688-00973-5); pap. 5.25 (ISBN 0-688-00977-8). Lothrop.

AIR–MICROBIOLOGY
see also Communicable Diseases
Nilsson, S. T., ed. Atlas of Airborne Fungal Spores in Europe. (Illus.). 145p. 1983. 50.00 (ISBN 0-387-11900-0). Springer-Verlag.

AIR–POLLUTION
see also Acid Rain; Air Quality; Automobiles–Motors–Exhaust Gas; Dust; Fume Control; Motor Vehicles–Pollution Control Devices; Smog
Chemical Engineering Magazine. Industrial Air Pollution Engineering. 1980. 30.25 (ISBN 0-07-010693-2). McGraw.
De Wispelaere, C., ed. Air Pollution Modeling & Its Application: Part 2. (NATO-Challenges of Modern Society: Vol. 3). 855p. 1983. 95.00x (ISBN 0-306-41115-6, Plenum Pr). Plenum Pub.
Georgii, H. & Pankrath, J. Deposition of Atmospheric Pollutants. 1982. 37.00 (ISBN 90-277-1438-X, Pub. by Reidel Holland). Kluwer Boston.
Hay, Alastair. The Chemical Scythe: The Lessons of 2, 4, 5-T & Dioxin. LC 82-12249. (Disaster Research in Practice Ser.). 250p. 1982. 27.50x (ISBN 0-306-40973-9, Plenum Pr). Plenum Pub.
Manning, W. J. & Feder, W. A. Biomonitoring Air Pollutants with Plants. 1980. 26.75 (ISBN 0-85334-916-9, Pub. by Applied Sci England). Elsevier.
Nieuwstadt, F. & Van Dop, H., eds. Atmospheric Turbulence & Air Pollution. 1982. lib. bdg. 43.50 (ISBN 90-277-1365-0, Pub. by Reidel Holland). Kluwer Boston.
Schneider, T. & Grant, L., eds. Air Pollution by Nitrogen Oxides: Proceedings of the US-Dutch International Symposium, Maastricht, May 24-28, 1982. (Studies in Environmental Science: No. 21). 1118p. 1982. 159.75 (ISBN 0-444-42127-0). Elsevier.

AIR–POLLUTION–LAWS AND LEGISLATION
Crandall, Robert W. Controlling Industrial Pollution: The Economics & Politics of Clean Air. LC 82-45982. 220p. 1983. 24.95 (ISBN 0-8157-1604-4); pap. 9.95 (ISBN 0-8157-1603-6). Brookings.
White, Lawrence J. Regulation of Air Pollution Emissions from Motor Vehicles. 1982. 13.95 (ISBN 0-8447-3492-6); pap. 4.95 (ISBN 0-8447-3487-X). Am Enterprise.

AIR BRUSH ART
see Airbrush Art
AIR CARGO
see Aeronautics, Commercial
AIR CARRIERS
see Air Lines
AIR CONDITIONING
see also Refrigeration and Refrigerating Machinery; Ventilation
also specific subject with or without subdivision air-conditioning, e.g. Dwellings–Air conditioning
Conde, D. F. & Harris, N. Modern Air Conditioning Practice. 3rd ed. 464p. 1983. 26.50x (ISBN 0-07-026833-9, G); write for info. solutions manual (ISBN 0-07-026834-7). McGraw.
El Khashab, A. G. Heating Ventilating & Air-Conditioning Systems Estimating Manual. 2nd ed. 320p. 1983. 37.50 (ISBN 0-07-034536-8, P&RB). McGraw.

Gosling, C. T. Applied Air Conditioning & Refrigeration. 2nd ed. 1980. 45.00 (ISBN 0-85334-877-4, Pub. by Applied Sci England). Elsevier.
Gupta, Vinod. Natural Cooling of Buildings. 31p. 1981. pap. 4.75x (ISBN 0-910661-00-6). Innovative Inform.
Heating, Air Conditioning & Refrigeration Equipment. 1981. 695.00 (ISBN 0-686-38426-1, 203). Busn Trend.
Sherrat, A. F. Air Conditioning System Design for Buildings. 256p. 1983. 30.00 (ISBN 0-07-084591-3). McGraw.
Watts, John R. Evaporated Air Conditioning. 2nd ed. (Illus.). 300p. 1983. 26.95 (ISBN 0-8311-1151-8). Indus Pr.

AIR FREIGHT
see Aeronautics, Commercial

AIR LAW
see Aeronautics-Laws and Regulations

AIR LINES
see also Air Pilots
also names of specific air lines
Airlines (Industry Audit Guides) 1981. pap. 8.50 (ISBN 0-686-84207-3). Am Inst CPA.
Davies, R. E. Airlines of the United States Since 1914. (Illus.). 746p. 1983. Repr. of 1972 ed. text ed. 35.00x (ISBN 0-87474-356-7). Smithsonian.
--A History of the World's Airlines. (Airlines History Project Ser.). (Illus.). Date not set. 39.50 (ISBN 0-404-19325-0). AMS Pr.
Macavoy, Paul W. & Snow, John W., eds. Regulation of Passenger Fares & Competition Among Airlines. 1977. pap. 7.25 (ISBN 0-8447-3256-7). Am Enterprise.
Pahl, Walther. Die Luftwege der Erde: Politische Geographie des Weltluftverkehrs. (Airlines History Project Ser.). (Illus.). Date not set. price not set (ISBN 0-404-19330-7). AMS Pr.
Rickenbacker, Edward V. Rickenbacker. (Airlines History Project Ser.). (Illus.). Date not set. price not set (ISBN 0-404-19332-3). AMS Pr.
Serling, Robert J. The Only Way to Fly: The Story of Western Airlines, America's Senior Air Carrier. (Airlines History Project Ser.). (Illus.). Date not set. price not set (ISBN 0-404-19334-X). AMS Pr.

AIR LINES-LAWS AND REGULATIONS
see Aeronautics-Laws and Regulations

AIR MAIL SERVICE
Jackson, Donald D. Flying the Mail. LC 82-2020. (Epic of Flight Ser.). lib. bdg. 19.96 (ISBN 0-8094-3330-3, Pub. by Time-Life). Silver.

AIR NAVIGATION
see Aeronautics; Navigation (Aeronautics)

AIR PILOTS
see also Astronauts
also subdivision Piloting under special types of aircraft, e.g. Airplanes-Piloting
BALPA Medical Study Group. Fit to Fly: A Medical Handbook for Pilots. 80p. 1980. pap. text ed. 5.25x (ISBN 0-246-11401-0, Pub. by Granada England). Renouf.
Federal Aviation Administration, Dept. of Transportation. Airman's Information Manual & ATC Procedures. (Illus.). 260p. (Orig.). 1983. pap. text ed. 8.00 (ISBN 0-686-81817-2). Astro Pubs.
Keith, Ronald. Bush Pilot with a Briefcase: The Happy-go-lucky Story of Grant McConachie. (Airlines History Project Ser.). (Illus.). Date not set. price not set (ISBN 0-404-19326-9). AMS PR.
Seagrave, Sterling. The Bush Pilots. (Epic of Flight Ser.). 1983. lib. bdg. 19.96 (ISBN 0-8094-3309-5, Pub. by Time-Life). Silver.
Smith, Frank K. Weekend Wings: The Complete Adventures of the Original Weekend Pilot. 1982. 13.95 (ISBN 0-394-52527-2). Random.

AIR PILOTS-CORRESPONDENCE, REMINISCENCES, ETC.
Rhode, Bill. The Flying Devils: A True Story of Aerial Barnstorming. 1983. 10.95 (ISBN 0-533-05554-7). Vantage.
Smith, Elinor. Aviatrix. large type ed. LC 82-5849. 466p. 1982. Repr. of 1981 ed. 12.95 (ISBN 0-89621-368-4). Thorndike Pr.

AIR POLLUTION
see Air-Pollution

AIR PORTS
see Airports

AIR POWER
see also Air Warfare
Armitage, M. M. & Mason, R. A. Air Power in the Nuclear Age. LC 82-17551. (Illus.). 264p. 1983. 24.95 (ISBN 0-252-01030-2). U of Ill Pr.

AIR QUALITY
see also Air-Pollution
Fronza, G., ed. Mathematical Models for Planning & Controlling Air Quality: Proceedings, Vol. 17. 255p. 1982. 50.00 (ISBN 0-08-029950-4). Pergamon.
Rowe, Robert D & Chestnut, Lauraline G., eds. Managing Air Quality & Scenic Resources at National Parks & Wilderness Areas. (Replica Edition). 310p. 1982. softcover 20.00x (ISBN 0-86531-941-3). Westview.

AIR-SHIPS
see also Aeronautics
Percefull, Aaron W. Balloons, Zeppelins & Dirigibles. (First Bks.). (Illus.). 72p. (gr. 4 up). 1983. PLB 8.90 (ISBN 0-531-04535-8). Watts.
Ventry, Lord & Kolesnik, Eugene M. Airship Saga. 192p. 1983. 16.95 (ISBN 0-7137-1001-2, Pub. by Blandford Pr England). Sterling.

AIR STRATEGY
see Air Warfare

AIR TERMINALS
see Airports

AIR TRAFFIC CONTROL
see also Airplanes-Dispatching; Electronics in Aeronautics
Borins, Sandford F. The Language of the Skies: The Bilingual Air Traffic Control Conflict in Canada. (Canadian Public Administration Series: IPAC). 352p. 1983. 30.00x (ISBN 0-7735-0402-8); pap. 12.95 (ISBN 0-7735-0403-6). McGill-Queens U Pr.
Jane's Airport Equipment 1982-1983. (Jane's Yearbooks). (Illus.). 400p. 120.00 (ISBN 0-86720-610-1). Sci Bks Intl.

AIR TRANSPORT
see Aeronautics, Commercial

AIR TRANSPORT MANAGEMENT
see Air Lines

AIR WARFARE
see also Air Power; Airplanes, Military; Atomic Warfare
also subdivision Aerial Operations under names of wars, e.g. World War, 1939-1945-Aerial Operations
Beaman, John. BF One-Zero-Nine in Action, Part 2. (Illus.). 58p. 1983. 4.95 (ISBN 0-89747-138-5). Squad Sig Pubns.
Davis, Larry. P-Fifty-One Mustang in Color. (Fighting Colors Ser.). (Illus.). 32p. 1982. softcover 5.95 (ISBN 0-89747-135-0, 6505). Squad Sig Pubns.
Davis, Larry & Greer, Don. Air War over Korea. (Aircraft Special Ser.). (Illus.). 96p. 1982. 8.95 (ISBN 0-89747-137-7, 6035). Squad Sig Pubns.
Drendel, Lou. Air War over Southeast Asia, Vol. I. (Illus.). 80p. 1982. softcover 8.95 (ISBN 0-89747-134-2, 6034). Squad Sig Pubns.
--Air War Over Southeast Asia, Vol. II. (Vietnam Studies Group Ser.). (Illus.). 80p. 1983. 8.95 (ISBN 0-89747-141-5). Squad Sig Pubns.
--F-Sixteeen Falcon in Action. (Aircraft in Action Ser.). (Illus.). 50p. 1982. saddlestitch 4.95 (ISBN 0-89747-133-4). Squad Sig Pubns.
Jablonski, E. America in the Air War. LC 82-5539. (Epic of Flight Ser.). lib. bdg. 19.96 (ISBN 0-8094-3342-7, Pub. by Time-Life). Silver.
Stahl, P. W., ed. KG Two Hundred. (Illus.). 224p. 1981. 19.95 (ISBN 0-86720-564-4). Sci Bks IntL.
Stern, Rob. SB2C Helldiver in Action. (Aircraft in Action Ser.). (Illus.). 50p. 1982. saddlestitch 4.95 (ISBN 0-89747-128-8, 1054). Squad Sig Pubns.

AIRBRUSH ART
Dember, Sol & Dember, Steven. Complete Airbush Techniques. 2nd ed. 1980. pap. write for info. (ISBN 0-672-21783-X). Sams.
Perry, Dave. Little Fox's Airbrush Stencil Techniques. (Illus.). 125p. 1982. pap. 14.95 (ISBN 0-9603530-8-9). Southwest Screen Print.
--Little Fox's Airbrush Stencil Techniques. (Illus.). 125p. (Orig.). 1982. pap. text ed. 14.95 (ISBN 0-9603530-8-9). Southwest Screen Print.
Vero, Radu. Airbrush: The Complete Studio Handbook. Wood, Barbara, ed. (Illus.). 192p. 1983. 24.95 (ISBN 0-8230-0166-0). Watson-Guptill.

AIRCRAFT, FIXED WING
see Airplanes

AIRCRAFT CARRIERS
Messimer, Dwight R. Pawns of War: The Loss of the U. S. S. Langley & the U. S. S. Pecos. (Illus.). 1983. 18.95 (ISBN 0-87021-515-9). Naval Inst Pr.

AIRCRAFT IDENTIFICATION
see Airplanes-Recognition

AIRCRAFT INDUSTRY
see also Airplanes; Used Aircraft
Hayward, Keith. Government & British Civil Aerospace: A Case Study in Post-War Technology Policy. 224p. 1983. write for info. (ISBN 0-7190-0877-8). Manchester.
Mondey, David. Planemakers: 2 Westland. (Planemakers Ser.). (Illus.). 160p. 1982. 15.95 (ISBN 0-86720-555-5). Sci Bks Intl.
Postma, Thijs. Fokker Aircraft. (Illus.). 160p. 1980. 19.95 (ISBN 0-86720-578-4). Sci Bks Intl.
Sharp, Martin. The History of De-Havillands. 1982. 70.00x (ISBN 0-906393-20-5, Pub. by Airlife England). State Mutual Bk.

AIRCRAFT INSTRUMENTS
see Aeronautical Instruments

AIRCRAFT PRODUCTION
see Aerospace Industries

AIRCRAFT RECOGNITION
see Airplanes-Recognition

AIRDROMES
see Airports

AIRLINERS
see Transport Planes

AIRLINES
see Air Lines

PAINTERS-SCANDINAVIA
Selz, J. Edvard Munch. (Q.A.P. Art Ser.). (Illus.). pap. 4.95 (ISBN 0-517-51837-6). Crown.

AIRPLANE CARRIERS
see Aircraft Carriers

AIRPLANE INDUSTRY
see Aircraft Industry

AIRPLANE RACING
Davisson, Bud. The World of Sport Aviation. LC 82-1054. (Illus.). 242p. 1982. 24.00 (ISBN 0-87851-151-2). Hearst Bks.

AIRPLANE RECOGNITION
see Airplanes-Recognition

AIRPLANES
see also Air Mail Service; Air-Ships; Aircraft Industry; Autogiros; Bombers; Fighter Planes; Flying-Machines; Guided Missiles; Helicopters; Jet Planes; Used Aircraft also specific makes of airplanes, e.g. Boeing bombers; Lockheed airplanes; and headings beginning with the word Airplane
Adkins, Hal. The Directory of Homebuilt Ultra Light Aircraft. (Illus.). 106p. (Orig.). 1982. pap. 10.00 (ISBN 0-910907-00-5). Haljan Pubns.
Jane's All the World's Aircraft 1982-1983. (Jane's Yearbooks). (Illus.). 840p. 140.00 (ISBN 0-86720-621-7). Sci Bks Intl.
Munson, Ken. U. S. Commercial Aircraft. (Illus.). 192p. 1982. 19.95 (ISBN 0-86720-628-4). Sci Bks Intl.
Spenser, Jay P. Bellanca C. F. The Emergence of the Cabin Monoplane in the United States. LC 81-607557. (Famous Aircraft of the National Air & Space Museum Ser.: Vol. 6). (Illus.). 96p. 1982. pap. 7.95 (ISBN 0-87474-881-X). Smithsonian.

AIRPLANES-AERODYNAMICS
see Aerodynamics

AIRPLANES-CARRIERS
see Aircraft Carriers

AIRPLANES-DESIGN AND CONSTRUCTION
Stinton. Anatomy of the Aeroplane. 1966. 12.50 (ISBN 0-444-19815-6). Elsevier.

AIRPLANES-DISPATCHING
Rudman, Jack. Dispatcher. (Career Examination Ser.: C-213). (Cloth bdg. avail. on request). pap. 12.00 (ISBN 0-8373-0213-7). Natl Learning.

AIRPLANES-FREIGHT
see Aeronautics, Commercial

AIRPLANES-HISTORY
see also Aeronautics-Flights
Miller, Jay. The X Planes: From the X-1 to the X-29. (Illus.). 192p. 1983. 29.95 (ISBN 0-686-84079-8). Specialty Pr.
Postma, Thijs. Fokker Aircraft. (Illus.). 160p. 1980. 19.95 (ISBN 0-86720-578-4). Sci Bks Intl.
Roberts, Kenneth D. Wooden Planes in Nineteenth Century America. 2nd ed. (Illus.). 324p. Repr. of 1978 ed. 30.00x (ISBN 0-913602-53-1). K Roberts.
Seo, Hiroshi. Civil Aircraft of the World. (Illus.). 96p. 1982. 12.95 (ISBN 0-86720-559-8). Sci Bks Intl.

AIRPLANES-INSTRUMENTS
see Aeronautical Instruments

AIRPLANES-JUVENILE LITERATURE
see also Aeronautics-Juvenile Literature; Airplanes, Military-Juvenile Literature
Althea. Man Flies On. (Cambridge Dinosaur Wingate Ser.). (Illus.). 32p. (gr. 10-12). 1983. pap. 1.95 (ISBN 0-521-27173-8). Cambridge U Pr.
--Man in the Sky. (Cambridge Dinosaur Wingate Ser.). (Illus.). 32p. (gr. 10-12). 1983. pap. 1.95 (ISBN 0-521-27172-X). Cambridge U Pr.

AIRPLANES-MODELS
Winter, William J. The World of Model Airplanes. Model Aviation Editors, ed. (Illus.). 1983. 19.95 (ISBN 0-686-83861-0, ScribT). Scribner.

AIRPLANES-PILOTS
see Air Pilots

AIRPLANES-RACING
see Airplane Racing

AIRPLANES-RECOGNITION
Wood, Derek. Jane's World Aircraft Recognition Handbook: Second Edition. 2nd ed. (Illus.). 512p. 1982. 19.95 (ISBN 0-86720-637-3); pap. 9.95 (ISBN 0-86720-636-5). Sci Bks IntL.

AIRPLANES-STABILITY
see Stability of Airplanes

AIRPLANES, JET PROPELLED
see Jet Planes

AIRPLANES, MILITARY
see also Bombers; Fighter Planes
Brown, Eric. Wings of the Navy. Green, William, ed. (Illus.). 192p. 1980. 19.95 (ISBN 0-86720-579-2). Sci Bks Intl.
Drendel, Lou. SR-Seventy-One Blackbird in Action. (Illus.). 50p. 1982. 4.95 (ISBN 0-89747-136-9, 1055). Squad Sig Pubns.
Ellis, Paul. Aircraft of the Royal Navy. (Illus.). 192p. 1982. 17.95 (ISBN 0-86720-556-3). Sci Bks Intl.
--Aircraft of the USAF. (Illus.). 192p. 1980. 19.95 (ISBN 0-86720-576-8); pap. 12.95 (ISBN 0-86720-577-6). Sci Bks Intl.
Green, William & Swanborough, Gordon. The Observer's Directory of Military Aircraft. LC 82-71835. (Illus.). 256p. 1983. 16.95 (ISBN 0-668-05649-5, 5649). Arco.
Linn, Don. Harrier in Action. (Illus.). 50p. 1982. 4.95 (ISBN 0-89747-139-3). Squad Sig Pubns.
Mondey, David. The Hamlyn Concise Guide to Axis Aircraft of World War II. (Hamlyn Concise Guides Ser.). (Illus.). 224p. 1983. 9.95 (ISBN 0-686-84614-1, Pub. by Hamlyn Pub England). Presidio Pr.
--The Hamyln Concise Guide to Axis Aircraft of World War II. (Hamlyn Concise Guides). (Illus.). 224p. 1983. 9.95 (ISBN 0-686-83851-3, Hamlyn Pub England). Presidio Pr.
Seo, Hiroshi. Military Aircraft of the World. (Illus.). 96p. 1982. 12.95. Sci Bks Intl.

AIRPLANES, MILITARY-JUVENILE LITERATURE
Cave, Ron & Cave, Joyce. What About... Fighters. (What About Ser.). (Illus.). 32p. (gr. k-3). 1983. PLB 7.90 (ISBN 0-531-03468-2). Watts.

AIRPLANES, MILITARY-RECOGNITION
see Airplanes-Recognition

AIRPLANES, PILOTLESS
see Guided Missiles

AIRPLANES, USED
see Used Aircraft

AIRPORTS
Crampton Associates, ed. Airport Transit Guide. (Illus.). 64p. (Orig.). 1982. pap. write for info. (ISBN 0-9610142-0-2). Crampton Assoc.
Horonjeff, R. & McKelvey, F. X. Planning & Design of Airports. 3rd ed. 640p. 1983. 49.95 (ISBN 0-07-030367-3). McGraw.
Jane's Airport Equipment 1982-1983. (Jane's Yearbooks). (Illus.). 400p. 120.00 (ISBN 0-86720-610-1). Sci Bks Intl.
Miller, Jeffrey. Stapleton International Airport: The First Fifty Years. (Illus.). 1983. price not set (ISBN 0-87108-614-X). Pruett.
Reese, Richard G. Pilot's Guide to Southwestern Airports. (Illus.). 1983. 3 ring binder 28.95b (ISBN 0-686-43374-2, Pub. by RGR Pubns.). Aviation.
Rudman, Jack. Airport Attendant. (Career Examination Ser.: C-306). (Cloth bdg. avail. on request). pap. 10.00 (ISBN 0-8373-0306-0). Natl Learning.
--Airport Security Guard. (Career Examination Ser.: C-456). (Cloth bdg. avail. on request). pap. 10.00 (ISBN 0-8373-0456-3). Natl Learning.
--Senior Airport Attendant. (Career Examination Ser.: C-307). (Cloth bdg. avail. on request). pap. 12.00 (ISBN 0-8373-0307-9). Natl Learning.
--Senior Airport Security Guard. (Career Examination Ser.: C-457). (Cloth bdg. avail. on request). pap. 12.00 (ISBN 0-8373-0457-1). Natl Learning.

AIRSHIPS
see Air-Ships

AKSAKOV, IVAN SERGEEVICH, 1823-1886
Durkin, Andrew R. Sergei Aksakov & Russian Pastoral. 421p. Date not set. 30.00x (ISBN 0-686-82101-7). Rutgers U Pr.

AKU LANGUAGE
see Yoruba Language

AKUAPEM LANGUAGE
see Twi Language

AKWAPIM LANGUAGE
see Twi Language

ALABAMA
see also names of cities, countries, etc. in Alabama, e.g. Montgomery
Sather, Julia D. Alabama. (Illus.). 128p. 1982. 29.50 (ISBN 0-912856-82-3). Graphic Arts Ctr.

ALABAMA-DESCRIPTION AND TRAVEL
Strode Publishers. Rivers of Alabama. Klein, E. L., ed. (Illus.). 211p. (gr. 7 up). 1968. 6.95 (ISBN 0-87397-003-9). Strode.

ALABAMA-ECONOMIC CONDITIONS
Center for Business & Economic Research. Economic Abstract of Alabama, 1982. Sawyer, Carolyn, ed. (Illus.). 405p. 1982. 10.00 (ISBN 0-943394-01-5). U of Ala Ctr Bus.

ALABAMA-GENEALOGY
Wright, Mildred S. St. Clair County, Alabama Genealogical Notes, Vol. 2. LC 74-82803. (Illus.). viii, 67p. 1982. 17.50 (ISBN 0-917016-24-6); pap. 12.50 (ISBN 0-917016-25-4). M S Wright.

ALABAMA-HISTORY
Coker, William S. & Coker, Hazel P. The Siege of Mobile, Seventeen Eighty in Maps: With Data on Troop Strength, Military Units, Ships, Casualties, & Prisoners of War. LC 82-675288. (Spanish Borderlands Ser.: Vol. 9). (Illus.). 131p. (Orig.). 1982. pap. text ed. 12.95x (ISBN 0-933776-11-X). Perdido Bay.
Gosse, Philip H. Letters from Alabama (U. S.) Chiefly Relating to Natural History. annotated facsimile ed. LC 82-61822. (Illus.). 352p. 1983. pap. 12.95 (ISBN 0-910773-00-9). Overbrook Hse.
Porter, Benjamin F. Reminiscences of Men & Things in Alabama. Walls, Sara, ed. (Illus.). 1983. 19.50 (ISBN 0-916620-56-5). Portals Pr.

ALABAMA-POLITICS AND GOVERNMENT
Langley, Michael. Protection of Minority Political Participation Abadoned in Supreme Court's Ruling on Mobile Elections. 1980. 1.00 (ISBN 0-686-38004-5). Voter Ed Proj.

ALABAMA-SOCIAL LIFE AND CUSTOMS
Liddell, Viola G. With a Southern Accent. LC 82-10893. 272p. 1982. pap. 8.95 (ISBN 0-8173-0130-5). U of Ala Pr.

ALASKA
see also names of cities, regions, etc. in Alaska, e.g. Aleutian Islands
Alaska Magazine, ed. The Alaska Almanac: Facts about Alaska. 7th ed. (Illus.). 186p. 1983. pap. 4.95 (ISBN 0-88240-240-4). Alaska Northwest.
Ulibarri, George. Documenting Alaska: A Guide to National Archives Relating to Alaska. (Illus.). 300p. 25.00 (ISBN 0-686-83926-9). U of Alaska Pr.

ALASKA-DESCRIPTION AND TRAVEL
Alaska Geographic Staff, ed. Island of the Seals: The Pribilofs. (Alaska Geographic Ser.: Vol. 9 No. 3). (Illus., Orig.). 1982. pap. 9.95 (ISBN 0-88240-169-6). Alaska Northwest.

Alaska Magazine Staff & Alaska Geographic, eds. Introduction to Alaska. (Illus.). 64p. 1983. pap. 4.95 (ISBN 0-88240-230-7). Alaska Northwest.
Cahn, Robert. The Fight to Save Wild Alaska. (Illus.). 34p. 1982. pap. write for info. (ISBN 0-930698-14-2). Natl Audubon.
Kent, Rockwell. Wilderness: A Journal of Quiet Adventure in Alaska. (Illus.). 260p. 1983. pap. 8.95 (ISBN 0-918172-12-8). Leetes Isl.

ALASKA–DESCRIPTION AND TRAVEL–GUIDEBOOKS

Eppenbach, Sarah & Easter, Deb. Alaska's Southeast: Touring the Inside Passage. (Illus.). 223p. (Orig.). 1983. pap. 9.95 (ISBN 0-914718-79-7). Pacific Search.
Fodor's Alaska: 1983. 192p. 1983. traveltex 6.95 (ISBN 0-679-00894-2). McKay.
Mosby, Jack & Dapkus, Dave. Alaska Paddling Guide. (Illus.). 120p. (Orig.). 1982. pap. 7.95 (ISBN 0-9608550-0-9). J & R Enter.
Searby, Ellen. The Inside Passage Traveler. 6th ed. (Illus.). 144p. 1983. pap. 5.95 (ISBN 0-9605526-3-4). Windham Bay.

ALASKA–ECONOMIC CONDITIONS

Kruse, John A. Subsistence & the North Slope Imprint: The Effects of Energy Development. (ISER Report Ser.: No. 56). 45p. 1982. pap. 6.50 (ISBN 0-88353-034-1). U Alaska Inst Res.
Morehouse, Thomas A., ed. Alaskan Resources Development: Issues of the 1980's. 350p. 1983. lib. bdg. 25.00x (ISBN 0-86531-512-4). Westview.

ALASKA–HISTORY

Alaska Magazine, ed. Bits & Pieces of Alaskan History: Vol. II: 1960-1974. (Illus.). pap. 14.95 (ISBN 0-88240-228-5). Alaska Northwest.
Holbo, Paul S. Tarnished Expansion: The Alaska Scandal, the Press, & Congress, 1867-1871. LC 82-17513. (Illus.). 170p. 1983. text ed. 12.95x (ISBN 0-87049-380-9). U of Tenn Pr.

ALASKA–JUVENILE LITERATURE

Stefansson, Evelyn & Yahn, Linda C. Here is Alaska. 4th ed. (Illus.). 192p. (gr. 5 up). 1983. 12.95 (ISBN 0-684-17865-6, ScribJ). Scribner.

ALBANIA

Schnytzer, Adi. Stalinist Economic Strategy in Practice: The Case of Albania. (Economies of the World Ser.). (Illus.). 180p. 1983. 34.95 (ISBN 0-686-84829-2). Oxford U Pr.
Ward, Philip. Albania: A Travel Guide. (Oleander Travel Bks.: Vol. 10). (Illus.). 160p. 1983. 26.50 (ISBN 0-906672-41-4); pap. 16.00 (ISBN 0-906672-42-2). Oleander Pr.

ALBANY–HISTORY

Dumbleton, Susanne. In & Around Albany Calendar & Chronicle of Past Events. (Illus.). 28p. (Orig.). 1982. pap. 8.95 (ISBN 0-9605460-2-2). Wash Park.

ALBEE, EDWARD, 1928-

Amacher, Richard E. Edward Albee. Rev. ed. (United States Author Ser.). 1982. lib. bdg. 12.95 (ISBN 0-8057-7349-5, Twayne). G K Hall.
Wasserman, Julian N. & Linsley, Joy L., eds. Edward Albee: An Interview & Essays. 184p. 1983. text ed. 18.00 (ISBN 0-8156-8106-2); pap. text ed. 10.00 (ISBN 0-8156-8107-0). U of St Thomas.

ALCALOIDS

see Alkaloids

ALCHEMY

see also Magic; Medicine, Magic, Mystic, and Spagiric
Fenner, Edward T. Rasayana Siddhi: Medicine & Alchemy in the Buddhist Tantras. (Traditional Healing Ser.). 300p. 1983. 39.95 (ISBN 0-932426-28-X). Trado-Medic.
Lindsay, Jack. Ancient Egyptian Alchemy. O'Quinn, John, ed. 44p. 1981. pap. text ed. 5.95 (ISBN 0-9609802-4-5). Life Science.
Sandbauch, John. Astrology, Alchemy & Tarot. 307p. 1982. pap. 4.95 (ISBN 0-930706-08-0). Seek-It Pubns.
Waite, A. E. Secret Tradition in Alchemy. 128p. 1982. pap. 24.50 (ISBN 0-7224-0129-9). Robinson & Watkins.

ALCHEMY–BIBLIOGRAPHY

Ferguson, John. Biblioteca Chimica; Catalog of the Alchemical & Pharmaceutical Books in the Library of James Young, 2 vols. 1100p. 150.00 (ISBN 0-87556-493-3). Saifer.

ALCOHOL

see also Alcoholic Beverages; Alcoholism; Temperance also names of alcoholic liquors
Lender, Mark E. & Martin, James K. Drinking in America: A History. (Illus.). 256p. 1982. 19.95 (ISBN 0-02-918530-0). Free Pr.

ALCOHOL AND YOUTH

Jeanneret, O., ed. Alcohol & Youth. (Child Health & Development Ser.: Vol. 2). (Illus.). x, 200p. 1982. 78.00 (ISBN 3-8055-3655-0). S Karger.
Krupski, AnnMarie. Inside the Adolescent Alcoholic. 4.95 (ISBN 0-89486-159-X). Hazelden.

ALCOHOL AS FUEL

Chem Systems, Inc. Parametric Analysis Support for Alcohol Fuels Process Development. (Progress in Solar Energy Ser.: Suppl.). 150p. 1983. pap. text ed. 13.50 (ISBN 0-89553-136-4). Am Solar Energy.
--Process Design & Economic for Ethanol from Corn Stover Via Dilute Acid. (Progress in Solar Energy Ser.: Suppl.). 150p. 1983. pap. text ed. 13.50 (ISBN 0-89553-137-2). Am Solar Energy.
Rothman, Harry & Greenshields, Roderick. Energy from Alcohol: The Brazilian Experience. LC 82-21956. 200p. 1983. 20.00x (ISBN 0-8131-1479-9). U Pr of Ky.

ALCOHOL INTOXICATION

see Alcoholism

ALCOHOLIC BEVERAGE INDUSTRY

see Wine and Wine Making

ALCOHOLIC BEVERAGES

see also Cocktails; Temperance; Wine and Wine Making
American Health Research Institute, Ltd. Alcohol Drinking: A Medical Subject Analysis & Research Index with Bibliography. Bartone, John C., ed. 120p. 1983. 29.95 (ISBN 0-88164-010-7); pap. 21.95 (ISBN 0-88164-011-5). ABBE Pubs Assn.
Cooper, Rosalind. Spirits & Liqueurs. (Illus.). 112p. 1982. pap. 5.95 (ISBN 0-89586-194-1). H P Bks.
Lipske, Michael & Center for Science in the Public Interest Staff. Chemical Additives in Booze. Jacobson, Michael, ed. 133p. (Orig.). 1983. pap. 4.95 (ISBN 0-89329-098-X). Ctr Sci Public.

ALCOHOLICS

see also Church Work with Alcoholics
Forum Favorites, 2 Vols. 1970. Set. write for info.; Vol. 1. write for info.; Vol. 2. write for info. Al Anon.
Kinney, Jean & Leaton, Gwen. Understanding Alcohol. LC 81-22557. (Medical Library). (Illus.). 268p. 1982. pap. 8.95 (ISBN 0-452-25338-1, 2706-0). Mosby.
Orford, Jim & Harwin, Judith, eds. Alcohol & the Family. LC 82-50090. 304p. 1982. 29.95 (ISBN 0-312-01706-5). St Martin.

ALCOHOLICS–PERSONAL NARRATIVES

DeJong, Alexander D. Help & Hope for the Alcoholic. 128p. 1982. pap. 3.95 (ISBN 0-8423-1408-3). Tyndale.
The Drunkard's Children. 1983. 5.95 (ISBN 0-686-37693-5). Rod & Staff.
Tamasi, Barbara. I'll Stop Tomorrow. 1982. 5.95 (ISBN 0-941478-03-3). Paraclete Pr.

ALCOHOLISM

see also Alcohol and Youth; Alcoholics
Barnes, Grace M., compiled by. Alcohol & Youth: A Comprehensive Bibliography. LC 82-15397. 464p. 1982. lib. bdg. 45.00 (ISBN 0-313-23136-2, BAY/). Greenwood.
Begleiter, Henry & Kissin, Benjamin, eds. The Pathogenesis of Alcoholism: Biological Factors. (The Biology of Alcoholism Ser.: Vol. 7). 666p. 1983. 62.50x (ISBN 0-686-84491-2, Plenum Pr). Plenum Pub.
Begleiterr, Henry & Kissin, Benjamin, eds. The Pathogenesis of Alcoholism: Psychosocial Factors. (The Biology of Alcoholism Ser.: Vol. 6). 724p. 1983. 69.50x (ISBN 0-306-41053-2, Plenum Pr). Plenum Pub.
Burgin, James. Guide Book for the Family with Alcohol Problems. 3.95 (ISBN 0-89486-155-7). Hazelden.
Chafetz, Morris E. The Alcoholic Patient: Diagnosis & Management. 300p. 1983. 22.50 (ISBN 0-87489-276-7). Med Economics.
Cohen, Sidney. The Alcoholism Problem: Selected Issues. 192p. 1983. text ed. 19.95 (ISBN 0-86656-209-5, B209); pap. text ed. 10.95 (ISBN 0-86656-179-X). Haworth Pr.
Costales, Claire & Berry, Jo. Staying Dry: A Practical Solution to Alcohol Abuse. rev. ed. 1983. pap. 4.95 (ISBN 0-8307-0885-5). Regal.
Forrest, Gary G. How to Cope with a Teenage Drinker: New Alternatives & Hope for Parents & Families. LC 82-73023. 128p. 1983. 9.95 (ISBN 0-689-11346-3). Atheneum.
Golding, P., ed. Alcoholism: A Modern Perspective. (Illus.). 539p. 1982. 44.00 (ISBN 0-942068-00-9). Bogden & Son.
Green, Bill. Alcoholism. Rahmas, Sigurd C., ed. (Topics of Our Times Ser.: No. 19). 32p. (Orig.). 1982. 2.95x (ISBN 0-87157-820-4); pap. text ed. 1.95 (ISBN 0-87157-320-2). SamHar Pr.
Hafen, Brent Q. & Brog, Molly J. Alcohol. 2nd ed. (Illus.). 250p. 1983. pap. text ed. 9.95 (ISBN 0-314-69652-0). West Pub.
Jellinek, E. M. Alcohol Addiction & Chronic Alcoholism. 1942. text ed. 29.50x (ISBN 0-686-83459-3). Elliots Bks.
Kinney, Jean & Leaton, Gwen. Understanding Alcohol. LC 81-22557. (Medical Library). (Illus.). 268p. 1982. pap. 8.95 (ISBN 0-452-25338-1, 2706-0). Mosby.
Lawson, Gary & Peterson, James. Alcoholism & the Family: A Guide to Treatment & Prevention. 300p. 1983. write for info. (ISBN 0-89443-674-0). Aspen Systems.
Luks, Allan. Will America Sober Up? LC 82-73964. 192p. 1983. 13.41 (ISBN 0-8070-2154-7). Beacon Pr.
Schultz, Cathy, ed. Alcoholism: Triad to Recovery. 160p. 1983. 12.95 (ISBN 0-89769-075-3); pap. 6.95 (ISBN 0-89769-047-8). Pine Mntn.
Sherouse, Deborah L. Professional's Handbook on Geriatric Alcoholism. (Illus.). 288p. 1983. text ed. price not set (ISBN 0-398-04828-2). C C Thomas.
Smith, Christopher J. & Hanham, Robert Q. Alcohol Abuse: Geographical Perspectives. Knight, C. Gregory, ed. LC 82-25529. (Resource Publications in Geography Ser.). 85p. (Orig.). 1983. pap. 5.00 (ISBN 0-89291-166-2). Assn Am Geographers.
Stimmel, Barry, ed. Current Controversies in Alcoholism. (Advances in Alcohol & Substance Abuse, Vol 2, No. 3). 128p. 1983. text ed. 19.95 (ISBN 0-86656-225-7, B225). Haworth Pr.
Vaillant, George E. The Natural History of Alcoholism. (Illus.). 384p. 1983. text ed. 25.00x (ISBN 0-674-60375-3). Harvard U Pr.

ALCOHOLISM–TREATMENT

Hay, William H. & Nathan, Peter E., eds. Clinical Case Studies in the Behavioral Treatment of Alcoholism. 324p. 1982. 27.50x (ISBN 0-306-40940-2, Plenum Pr). Plenum Pub.

ALCOHOLS

see also Alcohol
Gmehling, J. & Onken, U. Vapor-Liquid Equilibrium Data Collection: Volume I, Part 2C-Organic Hydroxy Compounds: Alcohols (Supplement 1) (Dechema Chemistry Data Ser.). (Illus.). 698p. 1982. lib. bdg. 110.00x (ISBN 3-921-56729-7). Scholium Intl.

ALCORAN

see Koran

ALCOTT, LOUISA MAY, 1832-1888

Meigs, Cornelia. The Story of Louisa Alcott. 223p. 1982. Repr. of 1935 ed. lib. bdg. 40.00 (ISBN 0-89987-591-2). Darby Bks.
The Promise of Destiny: Children & Women in the Stories of Louisa May Alcott. Marsella, Joy A. LC 82-15573. (Contributions to the Study of Childhood & Youth Ser.: No. 2). 208p. 1983. lib. bdg. 27.95 (ISBN 0-313-23603-8, MLO/). Greenwood.

ALCUIN, 735-804

Wilmot-Buxton, E. M. Alcuin. 223p. 1982. Repr. of 1922 ed. lib. bdg. 40.00 (ISBN 0-89760-941-7). Telegraph Bks.

ALE-HOUSES

see Hotels, Taverns, etc.

ALEUTS

Green, Rayna. Native American Women: A Contextual Bibliography. LC 82-48571. 160p. 1983. 19.50x (ISBN 0-253-33976-6). Ind U Pr.

ALEXANDER THE GREAT, 356-323 B.C.

Bercovici, Konrad. Alexander, a Romantic Biography. 335p. 1982. Repr. of 1928 ed. lib. bdg. 30.00 (ISBN 0-686-81681-1). Century Bookbindery.

ALFA-ROMEO (AUTOMOBILE)

see Automobiles, Foreign-Types-Alfa-Romeo

ALGAE

Fryxell, Greta A., ed. Survival Strategies of the Algae. LC 82-12865. (Illus.). 176p. Date not set. price not set (ISBN 0-521-25067-6). Cambridge U Pr.
Gupta, J. S. Textbook of Algae. 348p. 1981. 60.00x (ISBN 0-686-84468-8, Pub. by Oxford & I B H India). State Mutual Bk.
Kavaler, Lucy E. Green Magic: Algae Rediscovered. LC 81-43872. (Illus.). 128p. (gr. 5 up). 1983. 10.53i (ISBN 0-690-04221-3, TYC-J); PLB 10.89g (ISBN 0-690-04222-1). Har-Row.
Nakamura, Hiroshi. Spirulina: Food for a Hungry World; A Pioneer's Story in Aquaculture. Hills, Christopher, ed. Wargo, Robert, tr. from Japanese. (Illus.). 224p. (Orig.). 1982. pap. 10.95 (ISBN 0-916438-47-3). Univ of Trees.
Prescott, Gerald W. Algae of the Western Great Lakes Area: With Illustrated Key to the Genera of Desmids on Freshwater Diatoms. (Illus.). 977p. 1983. lib. bdg. 60.80X (ISBN 3-87429-206-1, Pub. by Koeltz Germany); pap. text ed. 28.00X (ISBN 3-87429-205-3). Lubrecht & Cramer.
Research on Algae, Blue-Green Algae, & Phototrophic Nitrogen Fixation at the International Rice Research Institute (1963-81) Summarization, Problems & Prospects. (IRRI Research Paper Ser.: No. 78). 21p. 1983. pap. 5.00 (ISBN 0-686-42858-7, R182, IRRI). Unipub.

ALGEBRA

see also Algorithms; Combinatorial Analysis; Equations; Groups, Theory Of; Mathematical Analysis; Modules (Algebra); Numbers, Theory Of; Probabilities; Sequences (Mathematics)
Aufmann, Richard N. & Barker, Vernon C. Introductory Algebra: An Applied Approach. LC 82-82886. 512p. 1983. pap. text ed. 19.95 (ISBN 0-395-32593-5); write for info. supplementary materials. HM.
Auslander, M. & Lluis, E., eds. Representations of Algebras, Workshopnotes, Puebla, Mexico 1980. (Lecture Notes in Mathematics: Vol. 944). 258p. 1982. pap. 14.00 (ISBN 0-387-11577-3). Springer-Verlag.
Barz, P. Le & Hervier, Y., eds. Enumerative Geometry & Classical Algebra. (Progress in Mathematics Ser.: Vol. 24). 246p. 1982. text ed. 20.00 (ISBN 3-7643-3106-2). Birkhauser.
Basilevsky. Applied Matrix Algebra in the Statistical Sciences. Date not set. price not set (ISBN 0-444-00756-3). Elsevier.
Calmet, J., ed. Computer Algebra: EUROCAM 82, Marseille, France 1982. (Lecture Notes in Computer Science: Vol. 144). 301p. 1983. pap. 14.00 (ISBN 0-387-11607-9). Springer-Verlag.
Chaudhuri, N. P. Abstract Algebra. 288p. 8.00x (ISBN 0-07-451563-2). McGraw.
Conte, A., ed. Algebraic Threefolds, Varenna, Italy 1981, Second Session: Proceedings. (Lecture Notes in Mathematics: Vol. 947). 315p. 1982. pap. 16.50 (ISBN 0-387-11587-0). Springer-Verlag.
Drooyan, Irving & Wooton, William. Elementary Algebra for College Students. 5th ed. LC 78-31666. 375p. 1980. text ed. 20.95 (ISBN 0-471-03607-2); solutions manual 8.95 (ISBN 0-471-05868-8). Wiley.
Easton, Richard J. & Graham, George P. Intermediate Algebra. LC 72-4744. (Illus.). 258p. 1973. text ed. 22.95x (ISBN 0-471-22939-3); student wkbk. 12.95x (ISBN 0-471-22943-1). Wiley.
Engelsohn, Harold S. & Feit, J. Basic Mathematics: Algebra with Arithmetic. LC 79-21287. 532p. 1980. text ed. 23.95 (ISBN 0-471-24145-8). Wiley.
Eulenburg, Milton D., et al. Introductory Algebra. 3rd ed. LC 74-24338. 360p. 1975. text ed. 21.95x (ISBN 0-471-24686-7); avail. answers (ISBN 0-471-24687-5). Wiley.
Gonis, Antonios & Panagoulias, Panagiotis. Mastering Skills in College Algebra & Trigonometry. (Illus.). 720p. Date not set. price not set. A-W.
Hackworth, Robert D. & Howland, Joseph W. College Algebra & Trigonometry As Socrates Might Have Taught Them. rev. ed. (Illus.). 295p. 1981. pap. text ed. 14.95x (ISBN 0-943202-01-9). H & H Pub.
Kadison, Richard V. & Ringrose, John R., eds. Fundamentals of the Theory of Operator Algebras, Vol. 1. LC 82-13768. Date not set. price not set (ISBN 0-12-393301-3). Acad Pr.
Keedy, M. L. Algebra: An Intermediate Course. 512p. 1983. text ed. 18.95 (ISBN 0-201-14799-8). A-W.
--Algebra: An Introductory Course. (Illus.). 512p. 1983. text ed. 18.95 (ISBN 0-201-14798-X). A-W.
Keedy, Mervin L. Introductory Algebra. 4th ed. LC 82-13771. (Illus.). 566p. pap. text ed. 18.95 (ISBN 0-686-82170-X). A-W.
Kolman, Bernard & Shapiro, Arnold, eds. Test Bank for College Algebra. 1982. 2.50 (ISBN 0-12-417888-X); Test Bank for College Alegebra & Trigonometry. 2.50 (ISBN 0-12-417846-4). Acad Pr.
Kunz, E. Introduction to Commutative Algebra & Algebraic Geometry. Date not set. text ed. price not set (ISBN 3-7643-3065-1). Birkhauser.
Lefort, G. Algebra & Analysis. 1966. 44.00 (ISBN 0-7204-2016-4). Elsevier.
Lial, Margaret L. & Miller, Charles D. Algebra & Trigonometry. 3rd ed. 1983. text ed. 20.95x (ISBN 0-673-15794-6). Scott F.
McKeague, Charles P. Intermediate Algebra: A Text-Workbook. 1981. 16.00 (ISBN 0-12-484763-3); instr's Manual 3.50 (ISBN 0-12-484761-7). Acad Pr.
Mitchell, Robert. Number Power Three: Algebra. (Number Power Ser.). 176p. (Orig.). 1983. pap. 4.95 (ISBN 0-8092-5518-9). Contemp Bks.
Novak, David. Introductory Algebra. 586p. 1983. pap. 20.95 (ISBN 0-669-03804-0). Heath.
Pierce, Richard S. Associative Algebras. (Graduate Texts in Mathematics: Vol. 88). 416p. 1982. 39.00 (ISBN 0-387-90693-2). Springer-Verlag.
Rolland, Alvin E. & Wineinger, Tom. Elementary Algebra. 320p. 1982. text ed. 20.95X (ISBN 0-534-01142-X). Wadsworth Pub.
Sharp, R. Y., ed. Commutative Algebra: Durham, 1981. LC 82-12781. (London Mathematical Society Lecture Note Ser.: No. 72). 200p. Date not set. pap. 24.95 (ISBN 0-521-27125-8). Cambridge U Pr.
Sobel, Max A. & Lerner, Norbert. College Algebra. (Illus.). 576p. 1983. text ed. 21.95 (ISBN 0-13-141796-7). P-H.
Wesner, Terry H. & Nustad, Harry L. Elementary Algebra with Applications. 400p. 1983. text ed. write for info. (ISBN 0-697-08550-3); instr's. manual avail. (ISBN 0-697-08554-6); test bank manual avail. (ISBN 0-697-08555-4). Wm C Brown.
Wood, June P. Introductory & Intermediate Algebra. 4th ed. 1983. text ed. 22.95 (ISBN 0-675-20001-6); student guide 9.50 (ISBN 0-675-20039-3). Additional supplements may be obtained from publisher. Merrill.
Zuckerman, M. M. Intermediate Algebra: A Straightforward Approach. 2nd ed. 493p. 1982. text ed. 22.95 (ISBN 0-471-09731-4); sampler 6.50 (ISBN 0-471-87676-3). Wiley.

ALGEBRA–PROGRAMMED INSTRUCTION

Saxon, John H. Algebra One & Half: An Incremental Development. 1983. text ed. 15.94 (ISBN 0-939798-03-4). Grassdale.
Saxon, John H., Jr. Algebra Half: An Incremental Development. 1983. text ed. 13.18 (ISBN 0-939798-05-0); tchr's ed. 13.18 (ISBN 0-939798-06-9). Grassdale.
--Algebra I: An Incremental Development. 462p. 1982. tchr's. ed 14.51 (ISBN 0-939798-02-6). Grassdale.

ALGEBRA–STUDY AND TEACHING

Drooyan, Irving & Wooton, William. Elementary Algebra with Geometry. LC 75-35736. 334p. 1976. text ed. 22.95x (ISBN 0-471-22245-3). Wiley.
Vaughn, Jim. Jumbo Algebra Yearbook. (Jumbo Math Ser.). 96p. (gr. 9). 1981. wkbk. 14.00 (ISBN 0-8209-0038-9, JMY-9). ESP.

ALGEBRA, ABSTRACT

see also Algebra, Boolean; Groups, Theory Of; Lattice Theory; Lie Algebras; Logic, Symbolic and Mathematical; Matrices

Durbin, John R. Modern Algebra: An Introduction. LC 78-15778. 329p. 1979. text ed. 24.50 (ISBN 0-471-02158-X); tchrs. manual 6.00 (ISBN 0-471-03753-2); solutions avail. (ISBN 0-471-86456-0). Wiley.

Gilbert, William J. Modern Algebra with Applications. LC 76-22756. 348p. 1976. 32.95x (ISBN 0-471-29891-3, Pub by Wiley-Interscience). Wiley.

Hillman, Abraham P. & Alexanderson, Gerald L. A First Undergraduate Course in Abstract Algebra. 3rd ed. 512p. 1982. text ed. 30.95x (ISBN 0-534-01195-0). Wadsworth Pub.

ALGEBRA, BOOLEAN

see also Lattice Theory

Johnstone, Peter. Stone Spaces. LC 82-4506. (Cambridge Studies in Advanced Mathematics: No. 3). 300p. Date not set. price not set (ISBN 0-521-23893-5). Cambridge U Pr.

ALGEBRA OF LOGIC

see Logic, Symbolic and Mathematical

ALGEBRAIC CURVES

see Curves, Algebraic

ALGEBRAIC FUNCTIONS

see Functions, Algebraic

ALGEBRAIC GEOMETRY

see Geometry, Algebraic

ALGEBRAIC NUMBER THEORY

Froehlich, A. Gelois Module Structure of Algebraic Integers. (Ergebnisse der Mathematik und Ihrer Grenzgebiete Ser. 3. Folge.: Vol. 1). 280p. 1983. 32.00 (ISBN 0-387-11920-5). Springer-Verlag.

ALGEBRAIC RINGS

see Rings (Algebra)

ALGEBRAIC SPACES

Johnstone, Peter. Stone Spaces. LC 82-4506. (Cambridge Studies in Advanced Mathematics: No. 3). 300p. Date not set. price not set (ISBN 0-521-23893-5). Cambridge U Pr.

ALGEBRAIC SURFACES

see Surfaces, Algebraic

ALGEBRAIC TOPOLOGY

see also Homology Theory; K-Theory; Measure Theory

Gitter, Samuel, ed. Symposium on Algebraic Topology in Honor of Jose Adem. LC 82-13812. (Contemporary Mathematics Ser.: Vol. 12). 23.00 (ISBN 0-8218-5010-5). Am Math.

Selick, et al, eds. Current Trends in Algebraic Topology. (Canadian Mathematical Ser.: Vol.2). Pt.1. 26.00 (ISBN 0-686-84832-2, CMS2.1); Pt.2. 24.00 (ISBN 0-8218-6002-X, CMS2.2); Set (Vols. 1 & 2) 42.00 (ISBN 0-8218-6003-8). Am Math.

ALGEBRAS, LIE

see Lie Algebras

ALGEBRAS, LINEAR

see also Complexes; Lie Algebras; Topology; Vector Spaces

Agnew, Jeanne & Knapp, Robert C. Linear Algebra with Applications. 2nd ed. LC 82-20752. (Mathematics Ser.). 400p. text ed. 22.95 (ISBN 0-534-01364-3). Brooks-Cole.

Apostol, T. M. Calculus: One-Variable Calculus with an Introduction to Linear Algebra, Vol. 1. 2nd ed. LC 73-20899. 666p. 1967. text ed. 30.95x (ISBN 0-471-00005-1). Wiley.

Bugrov, Y. S. & Nikolsky, S. M. Fundamentals of Linear Algebra & Analytical Geometry. 189p. 1982. pap. 3.45 (ISBN 0-8285-2445-9, Pub. by Mir Pubs USSR). Imported Pubns.

Robinson, Enders A. Least Squares Regression Analysis in Terms of Linear Algebra. LC 81-82322. (Illus.). 520p. 1981. 25.00 (ISBN 0-910835-01-2). Goose Pond Pr.

Weil, A. Adeles & Algebraic Groups. (Progress in Mathematics Ser.: Vol. 23). 126p. 1982. text ed. 10.00x (ISBN 3-7643-3092-9). Birkhauser.

ALGEBRAS, TOPOLOGICAL

see Topological Algebras

ALGEBRAS, W

see C Algebras

ALGERIA-POLITICS AND GOVERNMENT

Sullivan, Antony. Robert Thomas Bugeaud, France & Algeria 1784-1849: Politics, Power & the Good Society. 1983. 24.50 (ISBN 0-208-01969-3, Archon Bks). Shoe String.

ALGONQUIAN INDIANS

see Indians of North America-Canada

ALGORITHMS

see also Machine Theory; Numerical Analysis; Programming (Electronic Computers); Programming (Mathematics); Programming Languages (Electronic Computers); Transformations (Mathematics)

Booth, Taylor L. & Chien, Yi-Tzuu. Computing: Fundamentals & Applications. LC 73-20157. 497p. 1974. 29.95x (ISBN 0-471-08847-1). Wiley.

Conte, S. D. & De Boor, C. Elementary Numerical Analysis: An Algorithmic Approach. 3rd ed. 1980. 26.95 (ISBN 0-07-012447-7). McGraw.

Ghedini, Silvano. Software for Photometric Astronomy. LC 82-8574. (Illus.). 1982. pap. text ed. 26.95 (ISBN 0-943396-00-X). Willman-Bell.

Greene, D. & Knuth, D., eds. Mathematics for the Analysis of Algorithms. 2nd ed. (Progress in Computer Science: Vol. 1). 123p. text ed. 10.00x (ISBN 3-7643-3102-X). Birkhauser.

Moffat, David V. Common Algorithms in Pascal with Programs for Reading. (Software Ser.). 192p. 1983. pap. 8.95 (ISBN 0-13-152637-5). P-H.

Newman, Morris. Algorithmic Matrix Theory. 1983. text ed. p.n.s. (ISBN 0-914894-47-1). Computer Sci.

ALIBAMU INDIANS

see Indians of North America-Eastern States

ALIEN LABOR, EUROPEAN

Immigrant Workers in Europe: Their Legal Status. 245p. 1982. pap. 18.75 (ISBN 92-3-101867-1, U1221, UNESCO). Unipub.

ALIENATION (PHILOSOPHY)

Shoham, S. G. & Grahame, A., eds. Alientation & Anomie Revisited. 280p. 1982. pap. text ed. 23.50x (ISBN 0-391-02817-0, Pub. by Ramot Pub Co Israel). Humanities.

Shoham, S. Giora, ed. Alienation & Anomie Revisited. Grahame, Anthony. 280p. (Orig.). 1982. pap. text ed. 23.50x (ISBN 0-911378-44-8). Sheridan.

ALIENATION (SOCIAL PSYCHOLOGY)

see also Social Isolation

Shoham, S. G. & Grahame, A., eds. Alientation & Anomie Revisited. 280p. 1982. pap. text ed. 23.50x (ISBN 0-391-02817-0, Pub. by Ramot Pub Co Israel). Humanities.

Shoman, S. Giora. The Violence of Silence: The Impossibility of Dialogue. 300p. 1982. 27.00 (ISBN 0-905927-06-0). Transaction Bks.

Thom, Gary B. The Human Nature of Social Maladies: Alienation, Anomie, Ambivalence. 200p. 1983. text ed. 23.95x (ISBN 0-86598-105-1). Allanheld.

--The Human Nature of Social Maladies: Alienation, Anomie, Ambivalence. 200p. 1983. text ed. 23.95x (ISBN 0-86598-105-1). Rowman.

ALIENISTS

see Psychiatrists

ALIENS

see also Citizenship; Self-Determination, National
also Chinese in the United States; Americans in Foreign Countries, and similar headings

Conner, Roger. Breaking Down the Barriers: The Changing Relationship Between Illegal Immigration & Welfare. 1982. pap. text ed. 2.50 (ISBN 0-935776-03-6). F A I R.

Lillich, Richard B. International Law of State Responsibility for Injuries to Aliens. LC 82-13697. (Virginia Legal Studies). 1982. write for info. (ISBN 0-8139-0961-9). U Pr of Va.

ALIMENTARY CANAL

Latimer, Paul R. A Behavioral Medicine Approach: Functional Gastrointestinal Disorders. 176p. 1983. text ed. 23.95 (ISBN 0-8261-4310-5). Springer Pub.

Nolan, Daniel J. Radiological Atlas of Gastrointestinal Disease. 256p. 1982. write for info. (ISBN 0-471-25917-9, Pub. by Wiley Med). Wiley.

Young, David B., ed. Gastrointestinal Physiology IV. (International Review of Physiology Ser.). (Illus.). 1983. text ed. 34.50 (ISBN 0-8391-1725-6, 14192). Univ Park.

ALIMENTATION

see Nutrition

ALIPHATIC COMPOUNDS

see also Polyamines

Gunstone, F. D. Aliphatic & Related Natural Product Chemistry, Vol. 2. 278p. 1982. 110.00x (ISBN 0-85186-652-2, Pub. by Royal Soc Chem England). State Mutual Bk.

ALKALOIDS

see also names of Alkaloids

The Alkaloids, Vol. 1. 1969. 100.00x (ISBN 0-85186-257-8, Pub. by Royal Soc Chem England). State Mutual Bk.

Brossi, Arnold, ed. The Alkaloids: Chemistry & Pharmacology, Vol. 21. Date not set. price not set (ISBN 0-12-469521-3). Acad Pr.

Glasby, John S. Encyclopedia of the Alkaloids, Vol. 4. 370p. 1983. 65.00x (ISBN 0-306-41217-9, Plenum Pr). Plenum Pub.

Manske, R. & Rodrigo, R., eds. The Alkaloids: Chemistry & Pharmacology, Vol. 20. 1982. 59.50 (ISBN 0-12-469520-5). Acad Pr.

Saxton, J. Edwin. Monoterpenoid Indole Alkaloids, Part 4. (Chemistry of Heterocyclic Compounds Monographs). 1000p. 1983. 200.00 (ISBN 0-471-89748-5). Ronald Pr.

ALKORAN

see Koran

ALKYLATION

Topchiev, A., et al. Alkylation with Olefins. 1964. 18.30 (ISBN 0-444-40579-8). Elsevier.

ALL HALLOWS' EVE

see Halloween

ALL-VOLUNTEER FORCES

see Military Service, Voluntary

ALLERGY

see also Cookery for Allergics

Asthma & Allergy Foundation of America & Norback, Craig T., eds. The Allergy Encyclopedia. (Medical Library). 256p. 1982. pap. 7.95 (ISBN 0-452-25345-4, 3717-1). Mosby.

Beall, Gildon N. Allergy & Clinical Immunology. (UCLA Internal Medicine Today Ser.). 352p. 1983. 29.50 (ISBN 0-471-09568-0, Pub. by Wiley Med). Wiley.

Frazier, Claude A. Bi-Annual Review of Allergy, 1983. 1983. write for info. (ISBN 0-87488-294-X). Med Exam.

Golos, Natalie & Golbitz, Frances G. If This Is Tuesday It Must Be Chicken or How to Rotate Your Food for Better Health. Martin, Joan, ed. LC 81-13509. 109p. (Orig.). 1981. pap. 6.95 (ISBN 0-941962-00-8). Human Eco Res.

International Congress of Allergology. Abstracts: Eighth Conference, Tokyo, 1973. Munro-Ashman, D. & Pugh, D., eds. (International Congress Ser.: No. 300). 1974. pap. 14.25 (ISBN 0-444-15066-8). Elsevier.

Klaustermeyer, William B. Practical Allergy & Immunology: Family Practice Today-A Comprehensive Postgraduate Library. 216p. 1983. 14.95 (ISBN 0-471-09564-8, Pub. by Wiley Med). Wiley.

Lessof, M. H. Clinical Reations to Food. 1983. 17.50 (ISBN 0-471-10436-1, Pub. by Wiley Med). Wiley.

Randolph, Theron G. & Moss, Ralph W. An Alternative Approach to Allergies. 320p. 1982. pap. 3.95 (ISBN 0-553-20830-6). Bantam.

Ricci, M. & Marone, G., eds. Progress in Clinical Immunology. (Monographs in Allergy: Vol. 18). (Illus.). viii, 222p. 1983. 90.00 (ISBN 3-8055-3697-6). S Karger.

Speer, Frederic. Food Allergy. 2nd ed. 1983. text ed. write for info. (ISBN 0-7236-7016-1). Wright-PSG.

Yamamura, Y., ed. Allergology. (Proceedings). 1974. 125.75 (ISBN 0-444-15073-0). Elsevier.

ALLIED HEALTH PERSONNEL

see also Medical Secretaries; Medical Technologists

Dyche, June. Educational Program Development for Employees in Health Care Agencies. 384p. (Orig.). 1982. pap. text ed. 23.50 (ISBN 0-9609732-0-6). Tri-Oak.

Jensen, Steven A. Paramedic Handbook. LC 82-42830. 176p. (Orig.). 1983. pap. 7.95 (ISBN 0-940122-05-7). Multi Media CO.

ALLIGATOR PEAR

see Avocado

ALLIGATORS

Here are entered works on the American species of crocodiles. General works are entered under the heading Crocodiles.

Toops, Connie M. The Alligator-Monarch of the Everglades. LC 79-51891. 64p. Date not set. pap. 1.95 (ISBN 0-686-84286-3). Banyan Bks.

ALLORHYTHMIA

see Arrhythmia

ALLOYS

see also Metallurgy; Pewter
also aluminum Alloys, Steel Alloys and similar headings

Caglioti, G. & Milone, A. F., eds. Mechanical & Thermal Behaviour of Metallic Materials: Proceedings of the International School of Physics, "Enrico Fermi," Course LXXXII, Varenna, Italy, 30 June-10 July, 1981. (Enrico Fermi International Summer School of Physics Ser.: Vol. 82). 500p. 1982. 99.75 (ISBN 0-444-86500-4, North Holland). Elsevier.

Herman, Herbert, ed. Treatise on Materials Science & Technology: Embrittlement of Engineering Alloys, Vol. 25. (Serial Publication). Date not set. price not set (ISBN 0-12-341825-9). Acad Pr.

Khachaturyan, A. G. Theory of Phase Transformations in Alloys. 620p. 1983. 59.95x (ISBN 0-471-07873-5, Pub. by Wiley-Interscience). Wiley.

Prince, A. Alloy Phase Equilibria. 1970. pap. 31.75 (ISBN 0-444-40462-7). Elsevier.

ALMANACS

see also Calendars; Music-Yearbooks; Nautical Almanacs; Yearbooks

Bacheller, Martin A., ed. The Hammond Almanac of a Million Facts & Records 1983. (Illus.). 1040p. 1982. 7.95 (ISBN 0-8437-4032-9). Hammond Inc.

Guinness Book of World Records. 1983. 3.95 (ISBN 0-686-43004-2). Bantam.

Hammond Almanac: The One Volume Encyclopedia of a Million Facts & Records, 1983. 1983. pap. 4.95 (ISBN 0-451-82075-4, XE2075, Sig). NAL.

Newspaper Enterprises Associates, Inc. World Almanac Book of Facts 1983. 976p. 1982. 10.95 (ISBN 0-385-18348-8). Doubleday.

Wallace, Irving, et al. The People's Almanac Presents the Book of Lists, No. 2. 560p. 1982. pap. 3.50 (ISBN 0-553-13101-X). Bantam.

ALMOST PERIODIC FUNCTIONS

Levitan, B. M. & Zhikov, V. V. Almost Periodic Functions & Differential Equations. Longdon, L. V., tr. LC 82-4352. 150p. 1983. 34.50 (ISBN 0-521-24407-2). Cambridge U Pr.

ALMS AND ALMS-GIVING

see Charities; Charity

ALOES

Fit Magazine Editors. Aloe Vera: The Miracle Plant. 64p. 1983. pap. 3.95 (ISBN 0-89037-261-6). Anderson World.

ALOPECIA

see Baldness

ALPHABET

see also Alphabets; Writing
also subdivision Alphabet, or Writing under groups of languages, or under particular languages, e.g. Greek Languages-Alphabet, Chinese Language-Writing

Hayes, Marilyn. Basic Skills Alphabet Workbook. (Basic Skills Workbooks). 32p. (gr. k-1). 1983. 0.99 (ISBN 0-8209-0551-8, EEW-2). ESP.

King, Tony. The Moving Alphabet Book. (Illus.). 14p. 1982. 9.95 (ISBN 0-399-20923-9). Putnam Pub Group.

ALPHABETS

see also Lettering

Copley, Frank S. A Set of Alphabets in Modern Use with Examples of Each Style; Letters, Cyphers, Figures, Monograms, Borders, Compasses & Flourishes. 200p. pap. 15.00 (ISBN 0-87556-490-9). Saifer.

Spielman, Patrick. Alphabets & Designs For Wood Signs. (Illus.). 132p. 1983. 13.95 (ISBN 0-8069-5482-5); pap. 6.95 (ISBN 0-8069-7702-7). Sterling.

ALPINE GARDENS

Heath, Royton. Collectors Alpines. (Illus.). 144p. 1982. 39.95 (ISBN 0-600-36784-3). Timber.

ALSACE-DESCRIPTION AND TRAVEL

Michelin Green Guide: Elsass Vogesen. (Green Guide Ser.). (Ger.). 1983. pap. write for info. (ISBN 2-06-023740-8). Michelin.

ALTAR BOYS

Peace, Philip C. More Than Candlelighting: A Guide for Training Acolytes. LC 82-18973. (Illus.). 64p. (Orig.). 1983. pap. 4.95 (ISBN 0-8298-0642-3). Pilgrim NY.

ALTERNATING CURRENTS

see Electric Currents, Alternating

ALTERNATIVE EDUCATION

see Non-Formal Education

ALTRUISM

see also Self-Interest

Smithson, M. & Amato, P. R. Dimensions of Helping Behaviour. (The International Series in Experimental Social Psychology). 165p. 1983. 22.50 (ISBN 0-08-027412-9). Pergamon.

ALUCONIDAE

see Owls

ALUMNI

see Universities and Colleges-Alumni

AMALGAMATION OF CORPORATIONS

see Consolidation and Merger of Corporations

AMANA (IOWA) COLONIES

Liffring-Zug, Joan. Seven Amana Villages: Recipes, Crafts, Folk Arts. 36p. pap. 2.75 (ISBN 0-9603858-7-8). Penfield.

Liffring-Zug, Joan & Zug, John. The Amana Colonies. 48p. pap. 4.75 (ISBN 0-9603858-9-4). Penfield.

Liffring-Zug, Joan, compiled by. The Amanas Yesterday: A Religious Communal Society. 48p. pap. 4.85 (ISBN 0-9603858-8-6). Penfield.

AMATEUR JOURNALISM

see College and School Journalism; Journalism

AMATEUR RADIO STATIONS

Rayer. Beginners Guide to Amateur Radio. 1982. text ed. write for info (ISBN 0-408-01132-7). Butterworth.

AMAUROSIS

see Blindness

AMAZON RIVER AND VALLEY

France, Ghollean T. & France, Anne E. Amazon Forest & River. (Illus.). Date not set. pap. cancelled (ISBN 0-8120-5330-3). Barron.

Hanbury-Tenison, R. Aborigines of the Amazon Rain Forest. (Peoples of the Wild Ser.). 1983. 15.96 (ISBN 0-7054-0707-1, Pub. by Time-Life). Silver.

Phair, Anthony. Amazon II: Amazing Secret Discoveries by an Expedition to the Far Amazon. (Illus.). 267p. 17.95 (ISBN 0-9608114-0-0). USA Intl Pub.

Weinstein, Barbara. The Amazon Rubber Boom, 1850-1920. LC 82-80926. (Illus.). 376p. 1983. 29.50x (ISBN 0-8047-1168-2). Stanford U Pr.

AMAZONS

Hames, Raymond B. & Vickers, William T., eds. Adaptive Response of Native Amazonians: Studies in Anthropology Ser. LC 82-18399. Date not set. price not set (ISBN 0-12-321250-2). Acad Pr.

AMBASSADORS

Asencio, Diego & Asencio, Nancy. Our Man Is Inside. 288p. 1983. 17.00i (ISBN 0-316-05294-9, Pub. by Atlantic Monthly Pr). Little.

AMBULANCES

Rudman, Jack. Ambulance Corpsman. (Career Examination Ser.: C-2650). (Cloth bdg. avail. upon request). pap. 10.00 (ISBN 0-8373-2650-8). Natl Learning.

AMBULATORY CARE

see Ambulatory Medical Care

AMBULATORY MEDICAL CARE

Aiding Ambulatory Patients. LC 82-21253. (Nursing Photobook Ser.). (Illus.). 160p. 13.95 (ISBN 0-916730-49-2). Intermed Comm.

Balkam, Jean & Moran, Cathleen. Pediatric Ambulatory Care Guidelines. 384p. 1983. pap. text ed. 17.95 (ISBN 0-89303-263-8). R J Brady.

Cypress, Beulah K. Medication Therapy in Office Visits for Selected Diagnoses: National Ambulatory Medical Care Survey, United States, 1980. Cox, Klaudia, ed. (Ser. 13: No. 71). 65p. 1982. pap. text ed. 1.85 (ISBN 0-8406-0266-9). Natl Ctr Health Stats.

Gardocki, Gloria J. Utilization of Outpatient Care Resources. Cox, Klaudia, ed. (Special Report Ser.). 60p. 1983. pap. text ed. 1.75 (ISBN 0-8406-0271-5). Natl Ctr Health Stats.

Koch, Hugh. Drug Utilization in Office-Based Practice: A Summary of Findings National Ambulatory Medical Care United States, 1980, Ser.13-72. Shipp, Audrey, ed. 55p. 1982. pap. text ed. 1.95 (ISBN 0-8406-0270-7). Natl Ctr Health Stats.

AMERICA

see also specific American areas e.g. Caribbean area; North America; also names of countries e.g. Argentine Republic; United States

Levy, Charles K. A Guide to Dangerous Animals of North America: Including Central America. (Illus.). 192p. 1983. pap. 9.95 (ISBN 0-8289-0503-7). Greene.

Oates. Portrait of America, 2 Vols. 3rd ed. 1983. 12.95 ea. HM.

Oates, Stephen. Portrait of America, Vol. 1 & 2. 3rd ed. LC 82-81984. 480p. 1982. Vol. 1. pap. text ed. 12.95 (ISBN 0-395-32778-4); Vol. 2. pap. text ed. 12.95 (ISBN 0-395-32779-2); write for info. instr's manual (ISBN 0-395-32780-6). HM.

Shuster, Bud. Believing in America. 288p. 1983. 13.95 (ISBN 0-688-01834-3). Morrow.

Tyler. Image of America. 1981. 13.95 (ISBN 0-686-84618-4, Nonpareil Bks). Godine.

Weigle, Luther A. American Idealism. 1928. text ed. 22.50x (ISBN 0-686-83462-3). Elliots Bks.

AMERICA-ANTIQUITIES

see also Paleo-Indians

Phillips, Philip & Brown, James A. Pre-Columbian Shell Engravings from the Craig Mound at Spiro, Oklahoma: Paperback Edition, Pt. 2. (Illus.). 600p. 1983. pap. text ed. 35.00x (ISBN 0-87365-802-7). Peabody Harvard.

Shutler, Richard, Jr., ed. Early Man in the New World. (Illus.). 200p. 1983. 29.95 (ISBN 0-8039-1958-1); pap. 14.95 (ISBN 0-8039-1959-X). Sage.

Wells, Peter S. Rural Economy in the Early Iron Age: Excavations at Hascherkeller, 1978-1981. (American School of Prehistoric Research Bulletin: No. 36). (Illus.). 115p. 1983. pap. text ed. 20.00x (ISBN 0-87365-539-7). Peabody Harvard.

AMERICA-BIOGRAPHY

Crosby, Gary & Firestone, Ross. Going My Own Way. LC 82-45196. (Illus.). 312p. 1983. 15.95 (ISBN 0-385-17055-6). Doubleday.

Who's Who in America Index, 1982-1983: By Professional Area & Geographic Location. LC 4-16934. 514p. 1982. 50.00 (ISBN 0-8379-1502-3). Marquis.

AMERICA-CIVILIZATION

Ostrander, Gilman M. American Enlightenment. 1970. pap. text ed. 1.95x (ISBN 0-88273-222-6). Forum Pr IL.

AMERICA-DESCRIPTION AND TRAVEL

Buryn, Ed. Vagabonding in the U. S. A. A Guide to Independent Travel. LC 82-83637. (Illus.). 432p. 1982. pap. 10.95 (ISBN 0-916804-02-X). ExPress CA.

Dinnerstein, Leonard & Jackson, Kenneth T., eds. American Vistas: Eighteen Seventy-Seven to the Present. 4th ed. 448p. 1982. pap. 8.95 (ISBN 0-19-503166-0). Oxford U Pr.

--American Vistas: Sixteen Hundred Seven to Eighteen Seventy-Seven. 4th ed. 320p. 1982. pap. 7.95 (ISBN 0-19-503164-4). Oxford U Pr.

AMERICA-DISCOVERY AND EXPLORATION

see also United States-Exploring Expeditions

Brown, Vinson. Peoples of the Sea Wind. 250p. 1983. price not set. Naturegraph.

Ericson, Carolyn & Ingmire, Frances, eds. First Settlers of the Louisiana Territory, 2 vols, Vol. 1. LC 82-84532. 235p. (Orig.). pap. 19.50 (ISBN 0-911317-09-0). Ericson Bks.

--First Settlers of the Mississippi Territory, 2 vols. LC 82-83848. 110p. (Orig.). pap. 19.50 (ISBN 0-911317-07-4). Ericson Bks.

Fearon, Henry B. Sketches of America. (The Americas Collection Ser.). (Illus.). 454p. 1982. pap. 24.95 (ISBN 0-936332-16-6). Falcon Hill Pr.

Horgan, Paul. Conquistadors in North American History. 320p. 1982. 20.00 (ISBN 0-87404-071-X); pap. 10.00 (ISBN 0-87404-072-8). Tex Western.

Quinn, David B. & Quinn, Alison M. The First Colonists: Documents on the Planting of the First English Settlements in North America, 1584-1590. 199p. 1982. pap. 5.00 (ISBN 0-86526-195-4). NC Archives.

Sage, Rufus B. Rocky Mountain Life: Or, Startling Scenes & Perilous Adventures in the Far West During an Expedition of Three Years. LC 82-20165. (Illus.). 351p. 1983. 23.50x (ISBN 0-8032-4142-9); pap. 7.50 (ISBN 0-8032-9137-X, BB 835, Bison). U of Nebr Pr.

Willoughby, Lee D. The Voyageurs. (Making of America Ser.: No. 35). (Orig.). 1983. pap. 3.25 (ISBN 0-440-09245-0). Dell.

AMERICA-ECONOMIC CONDITIONS

Lebergott, Stanley G. The Americans: An Economic Record. 1983. pap. text ed. write for info (ISBN 0-393-95311-4). Norton.

AMERICA-HISTORY

Armour, R. It All Started With Columbus. rev. ed. 1971. pap. 2.95 (ISBN 0-07-002298-4). McGraw.

Ericson, Carolyn & Ingmire, Frances, eds. First Settlers of the Louisiana Territory, 2 Vols, Vols. I & II. Incl. Vol. II. 243p. pap. 19.50 (ISBN 0-911317-13-9). LC 82-84532. 1983. Set. pap. 30.00 (ISBN 0-911317-14-7). Ericson Bks.

--First Settlers of the Missouri Territory, Vol. I. Incl. Vol. II. 185p. pap. 15.00 (ISBN 0-911317-11-2); Vols. I & II, 2 Vols. Set. pap. 25.00 (ISBN 0-911317-12-0). LC 82-84533. 182p. 1983. pap. 15.00 (ISBN 0-911317-10-4). Ericson Bks.

Feinberg, Barry. Bertrand Russell's America: 1945-1970. 1982. 20.00 (ISBN 0-89608-157-5); pap. 8.00 (ISBN 0-89608-156-7). South End Pr.

Lancelot-Harrington, Katherine. America--Past & Present: Challenge. (America--Past & Present Ser.: Vol II). 160p. 1982. pap. text ed. 9.95 (ISBN 0-88377-255-8). Newbury Hse.

Trachenberg, Alan. The Incorporation of America: Culture & Society in the Guilded Age. 1982. 12.95 (ISBN 0-8090-5827-8); pap. 6.95 (ISBN 0-8090-0145-4). Hill & Wang.

Wheeler, George M., ed. Wheeler's Photographic Survey of the American West, 1871-1873: With Fifty Landscape Photographs by Timothy O'Sullivan & William Bell. (Illus.). 64p. 1983. pap. 5.00 (ISBN 0-486-24466-0). Dover.

Wolfe, Alan. America's Impasse. 1982. pap. 8.00 (ISBN 0-89608-158-3). South End Pr.

AMERICAN ABORIGINES

see Indians; Indians of North America; Indians of South America, and similar headings

AMERICAN ART

see Art, American

AMERICAN AUTHORS

see Authors, American

AMERICAN CIVIL WAR

see United States-History-Civil War, 1861-1865

AMERICAN COCKER SPANIEL

see Dogs-Breeds-Cocker Spaniel

AMERICAN COMPOSERS

see Composers, American

AMERICAN DIARIES

Arksey, Laura & Pries, Nancy, eds. American Diaries: An Annotated Bibliography of Published American Diaries & Journals to 1980, 2 Vols. Incl. Vol. 1. Diaries Written from 1492 to 1844 (ISBN 0-8103-1800-8); Diaries Written from 1845 to 1980 (ISBN 0-8103-1801-6). 600p. 1983. 60.00x ea. Gale.

AMERICAN DRAMA (COLLECTIONS)

Carroll, Dennis, ed. Kumu Kahua Plays. LC 82-23724. (Orig.). 1983. pap. text ed. 10.95x (ISBN 0-8248-0805-3). UH Pr.

Wordplays Two: New American Drama. 1982. 16.95 (ISBN 0-933826-42-7); pap. 6.95 (ISBN 0-933826-43-5). Performing Arts.

AMERICAN DRAMA (COLLECTIONS)-20TH CENTURY

Foster, Rick, ed. West Coast Plays Ten: Hotel Universe & Ghosts, the Day Roosevelt Died, An Evening in Our Century, & Inching Through the Everglaglades. (Illus.). 186p. (Orig.). 1981. pap. 6.00 (ISBN 0-934782-09-1). Cal Theatre.

Gassner, John, intro. by. Best American Plays. (Third Series, 1945-1951). (Illus.). 736p. 15.95 (ISBN 0-517-50950-4). Crown.

Halline, Allan G., ed. & intro. by. Six Great American Plays. 7.95 (ISBN 0-394-60457-1). Modern Lib.

AMERICAN DRAMA-AFRO-AMERICAN AUTHORS-HISTORY AND CRITICISM

King, Woodie, Jr. Black Theatre Present Condition. LC 81-14141. (Illus.). 102p. (Orig.). pap. 7.95 (ISBN 0-89062-133-0, Pub by National Black Theatre Touring Circuit). Pub Ctr Cult Res.

AMERICAN DRAMA-BIBLIOGRAPHY

Coven, Brenda. American Women Dramatists of the Twentieth Century: A Bibliography. LC 82-5942. 244p. 1982. 15.00 (ISBN 0-8108-1562-1). Scarecrow.

AMERICAN DRAMA-HISTORY AND CRITICISM

Cohen, Sarah B., ed. From Hester Street to Hollywood: The Jewish-American Stage & Screen. LC 82-47924. (Jewish Literature & Culture Ser.). 288p. 1983. 22.50x (ISBN 0-253-32500-5). Ind U Pr.

Skinner, Dana R. Our Changing Theatre. 327p. 1982. Repr. of 1931 ed. lib. bdg. 35.00 (ISBN 0-8495-4967-1). Arden Lib.

AMERICAN DRAMA-HISTORY AND CRITICISM-20TH CENTURY

Auerbach, Doris. Sam Shepard, Arthur Kopit, & the Off-Broadway Theater. (United States Authors Ser.). 1982. lib. bdg. 13.95 (ISBN 0-8057-7371-1, Twayne). G K Hall.

Koon, Helene W., ed. Death of a Salesman: A Collection of Critical Essays. 115p. 1983. 10.95 (ISBN 0-13-198135-8); pap. 4.95 (ISBN 0-13-198127-7). P-H.

AMERICAN DRAWINGS

see Drawings, American

AMERICAN EAGLE

see Bald Eagle

AMERICAN ESSAYS

Emerson, Ralph W. Essays: Second Series. Ferguson, Alfred R. & Carr, Jean F., eds. (Collected Works of Ralph Waldo Emerson Ser.: Vol. III). (Illus.). 320p. 1983. text ed. 25.00x (ISBN 0-674-13990-9, Belknap Pr). Harvard U Pr.

AMERICAN ESSAYS-20TH CENTURY

Trillin, Calvin. Uncivil Liberties. LC 82-48713. 228p. 1983. pap. 7.95 (ISBN 0-385-18764-5, Anch). Doubleday.

AMERICAN FICTION (COLLECTIONS)

see also Short Stories, American; Western Stories

Messerli, Douglas, ed. The Contemporary American Fiction. Abish, Walter, et al. 370p. (Orig.). 1983. 14.95 (ISBN 0-940650-22-3); pap. 9.95 (ISBN 0-940650-23-1). Sun & Moon MD.

Wilson, Barbara & Da Silva, eds. Backbone Two: New Fiction by Northwest Women. 160p. (Orig.). 1980. 4.95 (ISBN 0-686-38164-5). Seal Pr WA.

AMERICAN FICTION-HISTORY AND CRITICISM

Huf, L. M. Portrait of the Artist as a Young Woman. LC 82-40263. (Literature & Life Ser.). 200p. 1983. 13.50 (ISBN 0-8044-2406-3). Ungar.

Messenger, Christian. Sport & the Spirit of Play in American Fiction. 352p. 1983. pap. write for info. Columbia U Pr.

AMERICAN FICTION-HISTORY AND CRITICISM-19TH CENTURY

Duban, James. Melville's Major Fiction: Politics, Theology, & Imagination. (Illus.). 250p. 1982. 22.00 (ISBN 0-87580-086-6). N Ill U Pr.

Moore, Susan R. The Drama of Discrimination in Henry James. LC 82-11111. (Scholars' Library). 127p. 1983. text ed. 32.50 (ISBN 0-7022-1668-2). U of Queensland Pr.

AMERICAN FICTION-HISTORY AND CRITICISM-20TH CENTURY

Aldridge, John W. The American Novel & the Way We Live Now. 192p. 1983. 16.95 (ISBN 0-19-503198-9). Oxford U Pr.

Alsen, Eberhard. Salinger's Glass Stories As A Composite Novel. LC 82-50411. 300p. 1983. 22.50X (ISBN 0-87875-243-9). Whitston Pub.

Harwell, Richard, ed. Gone With the Wind as Book & Film. (Illus.). 300p. 1983. 19.95 (ISBN 0-686-82616-7). U of SC Pr.

Hotchner, A. E. Papa Hemingway: The Ecstasy & Sorrow. (Illus.). 352p. 1983. Repr. 16.95 (ISBN 0-688-02041-0). Morrow.

Hussman, Lawrence E. Dreiser & His Fiction: A Twentieth-Century Quest. LC 82-40493. 224p. 1983. 22.50x (ISBN 0-8122-7875-5). U of Pa Pr.

Reep, Diana. The Rescue & Romances: Popular Novels Before World War 1. LC 82-61169. 144p. 1982. 12.95 (ISBN 0-87972-211-8); pap. 6.95 (ISBN 0-87972-212-6). Bowling Green Univ.

Svoboda, Frederic J. Hemingway & the Sun Also Rises: The Crafting of a Style. LC 82-20026. (Illus.). 216p. 1983. text ed. 19.95x (ISBN 0-7006-0228-3). Univ Pr KS.

Watson, Charles N., Jr. The Novels of Jack London: A Reappraisal. LC 82-70548. 324p. 1983. 19.95 (ISBN 0-299-09300-X). U of Wis Pr.

AMERICAN FOLK-LORE

see Folk-Lore, American

AMERICAN FOLK SONGS

see Folk-Songs, American

AMERICAN INDIANS

see Indians; Indians of North America; Indians of South America, and similar headings

AMERICAN LEGENDS

see Legends, American

AMERICAN LETTERS

Aderman, Ralph M. & Kleinfield, Herbert L., eds. Letters of Washington Irving: Vol. III, 1839-1846. (Critical Editions Program). 1982. lib. bdg. 50.00 (ISBN 0-8057-8524-8, Twayne). G K Hall.

--Letters of Washington Irving: Vol. IV, 1847-1859. (Critical Editions Program). 1982. lib. bdg. 45.00 (ISBN 0-8057-8525-6, Twayne). G K Hall.

McElvaine, Robert S., ed. Down & Out in the Great Depression: Letters from the "Forgotten Man". LC 82-7022. (Illus.). xvii, 251p. 1983. 23.00x (ISBN 0-8078-1534-9); pap. 8.95 (ISBN 0-8078-4099-8). U of NC Pr.

Puritan Personal Writings: Autobiographies & Other Writings, Vol. 8. LC 78-270. (American Puritan Writings Ser.). 240p. 1982. 57.50 (ISBN 0-404-60808-6). AMS Pr.

Puritan Personal Writings: Diaries, Vol. 7. LC 78-269. (American Puritan Writings Ser.). 1982. 57.50 (ISBN 0-404-60807-8). AMS Pr.

AMERICAN LIBRARY ASSOCIATION

Wedgeworth, Robert, ed. ALA Yearbook, 1982. 432p. 1982. lib. bdg. 60.00 (ISBN 0-8389-0350-9). ALA.

AMERICAN LITERATURE (COLLECTIONS)

Here are entered only collections from several authors. For collections of a particular period, see appropriate subdivision below, e.g. American Literature-Colonial and Revolutionary periods.

see also College Readers; Spanish-American Literature

Baraka, Amiri & Baraka, Amina, eds. Confirmation: An Anthology of African-American Women. 416p. 1983. 17.95 (ISBN 0-688-01580-8). Morrow.

Hogan, Ed, et al, eds. The Aspect Anthology: A Ten-Year Retrospective. LC 81-52957. (Illus.). 272p. 1981. pap. 4.95 (ISBN 0-939010-01-1). Zephyr Pr.

Schlueter, Paul. Names & American Literature. (International Library of Names). 250p. 1983. text ed. 24.50x (ISBN 0-8290-1284-2). Irvington.

Van Swearingen, Phyllis. Bits of Americana: Whirly Girlys to Country Gossip. (Illus.). 80p. 1982. 5.50 (ISBN 0-682-49939-0). Exposition.

AMERICAN LITERATURE (COLLECTIONS)-20TH CENTURY

Emblidge, David, ed. The Third Berkshire Anthology. (Illus.). 208p. (Orig.). 1982. pap. 7.50 (ISBN 0-9609540-0-7). Berkshire Writ.

AMERICAN LITERATURE-AFRO-AMERICAN AUTHORS

see also Afro-American Authors

Bakara, Amiri & Baraka, Amina, eds. Confirmation: An Anthology of African-American Women. 416p. 1983. pap. 9.95 (ISBN 0-688-01582-4). Quill NY.

Luffe, Heinz C. Zur Textkonstitution Afro-Amerikanischer Initiationsliteratur. 194p. (Ger.). 1982. write for info. (ISBN 3-8204-5956-1). P Lang Pubs.

Sims, Rudine. Shadow & Substance. 112p. 1982. pap. text ed. 9.00 (ISBN 0-8389-3278-9). ALA.

AMERICAN LITERATURE-AFRO-AMERICAN AUTHORS-HISTORY AND CRITICISM

Bruck, P. & Karrer, W., eds. The Afro-American Novel Since Nineteen Sixty. 325p. 1982. pap. text ed. 27.75x (ISBN 90-6032-219-3, Pub. by B R Gruner Netherlands). Humanities.

AMERICAN LITERATURE-BIBLIOGRAPHY

Perry, Thomas A. A Bibliography of American Literature Translated into Romanian. 1983. 35.00 (ISBN 0-8022-2414-8). Philos Lib.

AMERICAN LITERATURE-HISTORY AND CRITICISM

Allen, Mary. Animals in American Literature. LC 82-17369. (Illus.). 218p. 1983. 14.95 (ISBN 0-252-00975-4). U of Ill Pr.

Armour, R. American Lit Relit. 1970. pap. 2.95 (ISBN 0-07-002283-6). McGraw.

Blei, Norbert. Adventures in an American's Literature. 224p. (Orig.). 1982. pap. 5.95 (ISBN 0-933180-41-1). Ellis Pr.

Butcher, Philip, ed. The Ethnic Image of Modern American Literature: 1900-1950, Vols. 1 & 2. 1983. 14.95 ea.; Set. 27.50 (ISBN 0-88258-110-4). Vol. 1 (ISBN 0-88258-119-8). Vol. 2 (ISBN 0-88258-120-1). Howard U Pr.

Lewis, Mumford. The Golden Day: A Study in American Literature & Culture. LC 82-24199. xxx, 144p. 1983. Repr. of 1957 ed. lib. bdg. 22.50x (ISBN 0-313-23845-6, MUG0). Greenwood.

Lynn, Kenneth S. The Air-Line to Seattle: Studies in Literary & Historical Writing about America. 240p. 1983. lib. bdg. 17.50x (ISBN 0-226-49832-8). U of Chicago Pr.

Perry, Bliss. American Spirit in Literature. 1918. text ed. 8.50x (ISBN 0-686-83469-0). Elliots Bks.

Pilkington, William T. Imagining Texas: The Literature of the Lone Star State. Rosenbaum, Robert J., ed. (Texas History Ser.). (Illus.). 37p. 1981. pap. text ed. 1.95x (ISBN 0-89641-095-1). American Pr.

Spitzer, Leo. Essays on English & American Literature. Hatcher, Anna, ed. 307p. 1983. Repr. of 1968 ed. 15.00 (ISBN 0-87752-227-8). Gordian.

Stoddard, Ellwyn R., et al, eds. Borderlands Sourcebook: A Guide to the Literature on Northern Mexico & the American Southwest. LC 82-40331. (Illus.). 500p. 1983. 48.50x (ISBN 0-8061-1718-4). U of Okla Pr.

Valmai, Fenster. Guide to American Literature. 250p. 1983. lib. bdg. 23.50 (ISBN 0-87287-373-0). Libs Unl.

Wheeler, Eva F. A History of Wyoming Writers. (Illus.). 92p. 1982. pap. 7.00 (ISBN 0-686-38836-4). E F Wheeler.

Woodress, James, ed. American Literary Scholarship, 1981. annual LC 65-19450. (American Literary Scholarship Ser.). 600p. 1983. 40.00 (ISBN 0-8223-0552-6). Duke.

AMERICAN LITERATURE-HISTORY AND CRITICISM-BIBLIOGRAPHY

Duke, Maurice & Bryer, Jackson R., eds. American Women Writers: Bibliographical Essays. LC 82-6156. 464p. 1983. lib. bdg. 29.95 (ISBN 0-313-22116-2, DAW/). Greenwood.

AMERICAN LITERATURE-HISTORY AND CRITICISM-19TH CENTURY

Donavan, Josephine. New England Local Color Literature: A Women's Tradition. LC 82-40252. 250p. 1982. 12.95 (ISBN 0-8044-2138-2). Ungar.

Liljegren, S. B. Revolt Against Romanticism in American Literature as Evidenced in the Work of S. L. Clemens. 59p. pap. 12.50 (ISBN 0-87556-576-X). Saifer.

Montegemery, Marion. Why Poe Drank Liquor: Vol. II in the Trilogy, The Prophetic Poet & the Spirit of the Age. 442p. 1982. 19.95 (ISBN 0-89385-026-8). Sugden.

Montgomery, Marion. Why Hawthorne Was Melancholy: Vol. III, of the Trilogy, the Prophetic Poet & the Spirit of the Age. 486p. 1983. 19.95 (ISBN 0-89385-027-6). Sugden.

Myerson, Joel, ed. Studies in the American Renaissance 1982. (Studies in American Renaissance). 1982. lib. bdg. 45.00 (ISBN 0-8057-9015-2, Twayne). G K Hall.

AMERICAN LITERATURE-HISTORY AND CRITICISM-20TH CENTURY

Berg, Stephen, ed. In Praise of What Persists. LC 81-47651. (Illus.). 320p. 1983. 14.95 (ISBN 0-06-014921-3, HarpT). Har-Row.

Bradford, M. E. Generations of the Faithful Heart: On the Literature of the South. 216p. (Orig.). 1982. text ed. 14.95 (ISBN 0-89385-024-1); pap. 5.95 (ISBN 0-89385-023-3). Sugden.

Butcher, Philip, ed. The Ethnic Image of Modern American Literature: 1900-1950, Vols. 1 & 2. 1983. 14.95 ea.; Set. 27.50 (ISBN 0-88258-110-4). Vol. 1 (ISBN 0-88258-119-8). Vol. 2 (ISBN 0-88258-120-1). Howard U Pr.

Kiernan, Robert F. American Writing since Nineteen Forty-Five: A Critical Survey. 200p. 1983. 14.95 (ISBN 0-8044-2458-6); pap. 7.95 (ISBN 0-8044-6359-X). Ungar.

Thomas, F. Richard. Literary Admirers of Alfred Stieglitz. LC 82-10543. 116p. 1983. price not set (ISBN 0-8093-1097-X). S Ill U Pr.

AMERICAN LITERATURE-MEXICAN-AMERICAN AUTHORS

Tatum, Charles M. Chicano Literature. (United States Authors Ser.). 1982. lib. bdg. 14.95 (ISBN 0-8057-7373-8, Twayne). G K Hall.

AMERICAN MUSIC

see Music, American

AMERICAN NEWSPAPERS-HISTORY

Brendon, Piers. The Life & Death of the Press Barons. LC 82-73017. 288p. 1983. 14.95 (ISBN 0-689-11341-2). Atheneum.

AMERICAN PAINTING

see Painting, American

AMERICAN PAINTINGS

see Paintings, American

AMERICAN PERIODICALS

Canan, Craig T. Southern Progressive Periodicals Directory. LC 80-644934. 1982. 4.00 (ISBN 0-935396-01-2). Prog Educ.

--U. S. Progressive Periodicals Directory. LC 81-85888. 1982. 8.00 (ISBN 0-935396-02-0). Prog Educ.

AMERICAN POETRY (COLLECTIONS)

Bell, Rebecca S. & Severin, C. S., eds. The Whisper of Dreams: A Collection of Poetry. (CSS Collection of National Poetry Ser.). (Illus.). 232p. 1982. pap. 9.95 (ISBN 0-942170-04-0). CSS Pubns.

Dow, Philip, ed. Golden Gate Watershed: Nineteen American Poets. (Illus.). 400p. cloth 24.95 (ISBN 0-15-136418-4). HarBraceJ.

Dow, Phillip, ed. Golden Gate Watershed: Nineteen American Poets. 400p. pap. 10.95 (ISBN 0-15-636101-9, Harv). HarBraceJ.

Herringshaw, Thomas W., ed. Local & National Poets of America: With Interesting Biographical Sketches & Choice Selections From Over One Thousand Living American Poets. 1036p. 1982. Repr. of 1890 ed. lib. bdg. 150.00 (ISBN 0-89760-021-5). Telegraph Bks.

Mikkelson, Shirley J., ed. Wild Prairie Roses: A Collection of Verse by North Dakotans. 104p. 1980. pap. 6.95 (ISBN 0-943536-00-6). Quill Bks.

AMERICAN POETRY (COLLECTIONS)-20TH CENTURY

Editorial Board, Grange Book Co., ed. The World's Best Poetry: Supplement One: Twentieth Century English & American Verse, 1900-1929. (The Granger Anthology Ser.: No. 1). 400p. 1983. 39.50 (ISBN 0-89609-236-4). Granger Bk.

Editorial Board, Granger Book Co., ed. American Poetry Index, Vol. 1. 1983. price not set (ISBN 0-89609-238-0). Granger Bk.

Erb, Gary E. & Severance, Tom. People on Peace: What We All Can Do Rather Than Have a Nuclear War. LC 82-83102. (Illus.). 68p. (Orig.). 1982. pap. 2.50 (ISBN 0-939634-01-5). Laughing Waters.

Rotella, Guy. Three Contemporary Poets of New England. (United States Authors Ser.). 200p. 1983. lib. bdg. 16.95 (ISBN 0-8057-7377-0, Twayne). G K Hall.

AMERICAN POETRY-HISTORY AND CRITICISM

Donahue, Moraima. Figuras y Contrafuguras en la obra Poetica de Fernando Alegria. Miller, Yvette E., ed. 141p. 1980. pap. 7.95 (ISBN 0-935480-05-6). Lat Am Lit Rev Pr.

Rodway, Allan. The Craft of Criticism. LC 82-4499. 192p. 1982. 32.50 (ISBN 0-521-23320-8); pap. 9.95 (ISBN 0-521-29909-8). Cambridge U Pr.

Van Dyne, Susan, ed. Woman's Voices in American Poetry: The Beauty of Inflections or the Beauty of Innuendoes. 54p. 1981. pap. 3.50 (ISBN 0-87391-024-9). Smith Coll.

AMERICAN POETRY-HISTORY AND CRITICISM-19TH CENTURY

Hollis, C. Carroll. Language & Style in Leaves of Grass. LC 82-20881. 320p. 1983. text ed. 27.50X (ISBN 0-8071-1096-5). La State U Pr.

Kennedy, Sloane W. John Greenleaf Whittier, His Life, Genius & Writings. 373p. 1982. Repr. of 1903 ed. lib. bdg. 25.00 (ISBN 0-8495-3139-X). Arden Lib.

AMERICAN POETRY-HISTORY AND CRITICISM-20TH CENTURY

Brodsky, Louis D. Mississippi Vistas. LC 82-20065. (Center for the Study of Southern Culture Ser.). 80p. 1983. 10.00 (ISBN 0-87805-173-2). U Pr of Miss.

Diggory, Terrence. Yeats & American Poetry: The Traditional of the Self. LC 82-15070. 280p. 1983. 25.00x (ISBN 0-691-06558-6). Princeton U Pr.

Tomlinson, Charles. Poetry & Metamorphosis. LC 82-19893. 112p. Date not set. 19.95 (ISBN 0-521-24848-5). Cambridge U Pr.

Wald, Alan M. The Revolutionary Imagination: The Poetry & Politics of John Wheelwright & Sherry Mangan. LC 82-8498. 370p. 1983. 28.00x (ISBN 0-8078-1535-7). U of NC Pr.

AMERICAN PORTRAITS

see Portraits

AMERICAN POTTERY

see Pottery, American

AMERICAN PROSE LITERATURE (COLLECTIONS)

see also American Essays; American Fiction (Collections); Short Stories, American

Reed, Ishmael, ed. Quilt Three. 164p. (Orig.). 1982. pap. 4.95 (ISBN 0-931676-07-X). Reed & Youngs Quilt.

AMERICAN REPUBLICS

see America

AMERICAN REVOLUTION

see United States-History-Revolution, 1775-1783

AMERICAN SAMOA

see Samoan Islands

AMERICAN SCULPTURE

see Sculpture-United States

AMERICAN SONGS

see Songs, American

AMERICAN STUDIES

Sharlin, Harold I., ed. Business & Its Environment: Essays for Thomas C. Cochran. LC 82-6143. (Contributions in American Studies: No. 63). (Illus.). 264p. 1983. lib. bdg. 35.00 (ISBN 0-313-21438-7, SHB/). Greenwood.

AMERICAN TALES

see Tales, American

AMERICAN TELEPHONE AND TELEGRAPH COMPANY

Federal Communications Commission. Competitive Impact Statement on the AT&T Anti-Trust Case. 1982. 50.00 (ISBN 0-686-37962-4). Info Gatekeepers.

AMERICAN THOROUGHBRED HORSE

see Thoroughbred Horse

AMERICAN WIT AND HUMOR

Aderton, Mimi & Liss, Douglas. The Book of Gross. (Illus.). 96p. (Orig.). 1983. pap. 3.95 (ISBN 0-8065-0838-8). Citadel Pr.

Allen, Woody. Without Feathers. 224p. 1983. pap. 2.95 (ISBN 0-345-30128-5). Ballantine.

Berg, Dave. Mad's Dave Berg Looks at Modern Thinking. (Illus.). 192p. (Orig.). 1976. pap. 1.95 (ISBN 0-446-30434-4). Warner Bks.

Breathed, Berke. Bloom County: American Tails. (Illus.). 160p. (Orig.). 1983. pap. 6.70i (ISBN 0-316-10710-7). Little.

Buysse, James L. The Definitive Guide on How Not to Quit Smoking. (Illus.). 63p. (Orig.). 1982. pap. 3.95 (ISBN 0-911435-00-X). King Freedom.

Cassidy, John. The Hacky Sack Book. 80p. 1982. pap. 8.95 (ISBN 0-932592-05-8). Klutz Pr.

Castleman, Harry & Podrazik, Walter J. Five Hundred Five Television Questions Your Friends Can't Answer. (Five Hundred Five Quiz Ser.). (Orig.). 1983. 10.95 (ISBN 0-8027-0731-9); pap. 6.95 (ISBN 0-8027-7210-2). Walker & Co.

Drescher, Henrik & Zeit, Calvin. True Paranoid Facts. LC 82-61411. (Illus.). 64p. (Orig.). 1982. pap. 3.95 (ISBN 0-688-01854-8). Quill NY.

Flunk this Thirty-two Question Test & You Destroy Western Society. (Analysis Ser.: No. 7). 1982. pap. 10.00 (ISBN 0-686-42842-0). Inst Analysis.

Freedman, Matt & Hoffman, Paul. What WASP Do Instead. pap. 3.95 (ISBN 0-312-86581-3). ST Martin.

Ianelli, Richard. The Devil's New Dictionary. 320p. 1983. 14.95 (ISBN 0-8065-0791-8). Citadel Pr.

J, Mr. Still More of the World's Best Dirty Jokes. (Illus.). 120p. 1983. pap. 3.95 (ISBN 0-8065-0834-5). Citadel Pr.

Jaffee, Al. Mad's Vastly Overrated Al Jaffee. 160p. 1983. pap. 5.95 (ISBN 0-446-37584-5). Warner Bks.

Kelley, David W. How to Talk Your Way Out of a Traffic Ticket. (Illus.). 80p. (Orig.). 1982. pap. 5.00 (ISBN 0-9609982-0-9). Mark III Prods.

Leininger, Steve. The Official Country & Western Joke Book. 1983. pap. 1.95 (ISBN 0-523-41913-9). Pinnacle Bks.

Lerner, Laurence. A.R.T.H.U.R. & M.A.R.T.H.A. Loves of the Computer. 1980. pap. 7.50 (ISBN 0-436-24440-3, Pub by Secker & Warburg). David & Charles.

Marquis, Don. Archy & Mehitabel. (Anchor Literary Library). 1982. pap. 4.50 (ISBN 0-686-42701-7, Anch). Doubleday.

Mecutcheon, Randall J. Get Off My Brain. (Illus.). 84p. 1982. pap. 4.95 (ISBN 0-934904-18-9). J & L Lee.

Posserello, Jodie A. The Totally Awesome Val Guide. Black, Sue, as told to. (Illus.). 96p. pap. 2.95 (ISBN 0-8431-0621-2). Price Stern.

Rogers, Will. How to Be Funny & Other Writings of Will Rogers. Gragert, Steven K., ed. LC 82-80505. (The Writings of Will Rogers Ser.: No. 5). (Illus.). 185p. 1982. Vol. 3. 10.95 (ISBN 0-914956-23-X). Okla State Univ Pr.

--Radio Broadcasts of Will Rogers. Gragert, Steven K., ed. LC 82-61001. (The Writings of Will Rogers Ser.: VI, Vol. I). (Illus.). 200p. 1983. price not set (ISBN 0-914956-24-8). Okla State Univ Pr.

--Will Roger's Weekly Articles: The Hoover Years 1931-1933. Gragert, Steven K., ed. LC 79-57650. (Writings of Will Rogers Ser.: No. 4). (Illus.). 280p. 1982. 17.95 (ISBN 0-914956-19-1). Okla State Univ Pr.

Rubin, Alan. Gopher Broke: And 59 other Sight Gags. (Illus.). 64p. 1983. pap. 2.95 (ISBN 0-517-54778-3). Crown.

Simpson, Jack B. Hay...But Not in the Barn. 138p. (Orig.). 1982. pap. 3.95 (ISBN 0-686-84394-0). J B Simpson.

Stevenson, James. The Bruckner Octagon. (Illus.). 112p. 1983. 15.75 (ISBN 0-670-19264-3). Viking Pr.

Thurber, James. Credos & Curios. LC 82-48236. 192p. 1983. pap. 4.76i (ISBN 0-06-091018-6, CN 1018, CN). Har-Row.

--Fables for Our Time. LC 82-48237. (Illus.). 128p. 1983. pap. 3.80i (ISBN 0-06-090999-4, CN 999, CN). Har-Row.

Wilder, Marshall P., ed. The Wit & Humor of America, 10 Vols. 1982. Repr. of 1908 ed. Set. lib. bdg. 175.00 (ISBN 0-89987-891-1). Darby Bks.

Williamson, John McKim. Software Sayings of Jack Mack: Wit & Humor with Word Processing. 2nd ed. LC 82-60964. (Jack Mack Paperbacks). 134p. 1982. pap. 8.95 (ISBN 0-910391-00-9). J Mack.

AMERICAN WIT AND HUMOR-ANIMALS

Bond, Simon. Bizarre Sights & Odd Visions. 1983. pap. 2.95 (ISBN 0-517-54605-1, C N Potter Bks). Crown.

Coker, Paul. The Mad Book of Pet Care, Etiquette & Advice. 192p. (Orig.). 1983. pap. 1.95 (ISBN 0-446-30065-9). Warner Bks.

Davis, Jim. Garfield Eats His Heart Out. (Illus.). 128p. (Orig.). 1983. pap. 4.95 (ISBN 0-345-30912-X). Ballantine.

--Here Comes Garfield. 1982. pap. 4.95 (ISBN 0-686-82437-7). Ballantine.

Loring, Murray & Glasofer, Seymour. Animal Laffs. LC 82-9985. (Illus.). 96p. 1982. pap. 3.95 (ISBN 0-8246-0287-0). Jonathan David.

Rosado, Puig. Animal Life. (Illus.). 64p. 1982. pap. 8.95 (ISBN 0-312-03781-3). St Martin.

Schneider, Rex. Ain't We Got Fun? (Illus.). 68p. (Orig.). 1982. pap. 3.95 (ISBN 0-9609640-0-2). Blue Mouse.

Thomas, Dawn C. I Love My Cat. (Illus.). 1982. pap. write for info (ISBN 0-9610186-0-7). Boojum Pr.

Waddington, Margaret. Reading Between the Lions. LC 82-72480. (Illus.). 64p. (Orig.). 1982. pap. 4.95 (ISBN 0-914960-39-3). Academy Bks.

AMERICAN WIT AND HUMOR-ARTS AND LETTERS

Van Swearingen, Phyllis. Bits of Americana: Whirly Girlys to Country Gossip. (Illus.). 80p. 1982. 5.50 (ISBN 0-682-49939-0). Exposition.

AMERICAN WIT AND HUMOR-ARTS AND SCIENCE

Gardner, Gerald. The I Hate Hollywood Joke Book. 128p. (Orig.). 1982. pap. 1.95 (ISBN 0-345-29630-3). Ballantine.

Lawless, Ken. Real Extraterrestrials Don't Phone. (Illus.). 96p. 1982. pap. 3.95 (ISBN 0-943392-11-X). Tribeca Comm.

McBurney, Bill. Star People. (Illus.). 64p. 1983. pap. 2.95 (ISBN 0-943392-08-X). Tribeca Comm.

AMERICAN WIT AND HUMOR-BUSINESS, PROFESSIONS, ETC.

Fisk, Jim & Barron, Robert. Buzzwords: The Official MBA Dictionary. 1983. pap. 5.95 (ISBN 0-671-47006-X, Wallaby). S&S.

AMERICAN WIT AND HUMOR-CHURCH AND CLERGY

Anderheggen, George C. A Wish for Your Christmas. (Illus.). 13p. (Orig.). 1982. write for info. Bookling Pub.

Hendra, Tony & Kelly, Sean. Not the Bible. 96p. (Orig.). 1983. pap. 4.95 (ISBN 0-345-30249-4). Ballantine.

AMERICAN WIT AND HUMOR-EDUCATION

Morales, Gil. Wake Me When the Semester's Over. 96p. (Orig.). 1983. pap. 3.95 (ISBN 0-345-30714-3). Ballantine.

Reardon, Eugene F. & Jeakle, William T. How to College: A Humorous Guide to the Four Years. LC 82-99932. (Illus.). 208p. 1982. pap. 4.95x (ISBN 0-910617-00-7). Primer Pr CA.

AMERICAN WIT AND HUMOR-HISTORY AND CRITICISM

Sloane, David E. The Literary Humor of the Urban Northeast, 1830 to 1890. LC 82-12688. (Illus.). 319p. 1983. text ed. 22.50X (ISBN 0-8071-1055-8). La State U Pr.

AMERICAN WIT AND HUMOR-MARRIAGE AND FAMILY LIFE

Keane, Bil. Love: The Family Circus. 104p. 1983. pap. 3.95 (ISBN 0-8362-2007-2). Andrews & McMeel.

AMERICAN WIT AND HUMOR-MEDICINE

McKinley, Robert L. The Neurotic's Handbook. 131p. 1977. pap. 5.00 (ISBN 0-9609644-0-1). Candle Bks.

AMERICAN WIT AND HUMOR-POLITICS, GOVERNMENT, ARMED SERVICES

Borgman, Jim. Smorgasborgman. Borgman, Lynn G., ed. (Illus.). 160p. (Orig.). 1982. pap. 6.95 (ISBN 0-9609632-0-0). Armadillo Pr.

Buchwald, Art. Laid Back in Washington. 384p. 1983. pap. 3.25 (ISBN 0-425-05779-8). Berkley Pub.

Crane, Bonnie L. Blanche Ames: Artist & Activist. (Illus.). 40p. (Orig.). 1982. pap. 4.95 (ISBN 0-934358-10-9). Brockton Art.

Danziger, Jeff. The Complete Reagan Diet. LC 82-61449. (Illus.). 96p. (Orig.). 1982. pap. 3.20 (ISBN 0-688-01908-0). Quill NY.

Lurie, Ranan. Lurie's Almanac. 160p. 1983. 12.95 (ISBN 0-8362-1252-5); pap. 6.95 (ISBN 0-8362-1253-3). Andrews & McMeel.

Mauldin, Bill. Bill Mauldin's Army. 384p. 1983. pap. 12.95 (ISBN 0-89141-159-3). Presidio Pr.

Sytsma, Curt. The Rhyme & Reason of Curt Sytsma. LC 81-67557. (Illus.). 224p. 1982. 14.95 (ISBN 0-942170-05-9). CSS Pubns.

AMERICAN WIT AND HUMOR-SCIENCE

Gonick, Larry & Hosler, Jay. Cartoon Guide to Computer Science. (Illus.). 224p. (Orig.). (gr. 11-12). 1983. pap. 4.76i (ISBN 0-06-460417-9, COS CO 417). B&N NY.

Gonick, Larry & Wheelis, Mark. Cartoon Guide to Genetics. (Illus.). 224p. (Orig.). 1983. pap. 4.76i (ISBN 0-06-460416-0, COS CO 416). B&N NY.

AMERICAN WIT AND HUMOR-SOCIAL LIFE AND CUSTOMS

Bachrach, Judy & DeMonte, Claudia. The Height Report: A Tall Woman's Handbook. 72p. 1983. pap. 5.95 (ISBN 0-8362-6406-1). Andrews & McMeel.

Berenstain, Stan & Berenstain, Jan. The Berenstains' Baby Book. (Illus.). 1983. 14.95 (ISBN 0-87795-509-3). Arbor Hse.

Bloomingdale, Teresa. Up a Family Tree. 1983. pap. 2.95 (ISBN 0-686-43063-8). Bantam.

Chambers, Lisa. Real Women Never Pump Iron. (Illus.). 96p. 1982. pap. 3.95 (ISBN 0-943392-10-1). Tribeca Comm.

Cooper, Jeffrey. How to Make Love to an Extraterrestrial. LC 82-62491. 96p. (Orig.). 1983. pap. 3.50 (ISBN 0-688-01888-2). Quill NY.

Cucumber Group. Why Cucumbers Are Better Than Men. (Illus.). 32p. 1983. pap. 2.95 (ISBN 0-87131-399-5). M Evans.

Debartolo, Dick & North, Harry. The Mad Book of Sex & Violence & Home Cooking. 192p. (Orig.). 1983. pap. 1.95 (ISBN 0-446-30033-0). Warner Bks.

Feeley, Mrs. Falk. A Swarm of Wasps: A Guide to the Manners (Lovely), Mores (Traditional), Morals (Well...), & Way of Life of the Fortunate Few Who Have Always Had Money. (Illus.). 132p. 1983. pap. 4.95 (ISBN 0-688-02048-8). Quill NY.

Glass, Lillian & Liebmann-Smith, Richard. How to Deprogram Your Valley Girl. LC 82-21964. (Illus.). 64p. 1983. 2.95 (ISBN 0-89480-239-9). Workman Pub.

Guisewite, Cathy. Cathy's Valentine Day Survival Kit. 24p. 1983. pap. 2.95 (ISBN 0-8362-1204-5). Andrews & McMeel.

Lebowitz, Fran. Social Studies. 1982. pap. 3.25 (ISBN 0-671-45047-6). PB.

Prombles, E. S. Flatulence Denied: Stalking the Fartological Imperative. (Orig.). 1983. pap. price not set (ISBN 0-941086-02-X). Melodious Pubns.

Reggie the Retiree, pseud. Laughs & Limericks on Aging. large print ed. (Illus.). 96p. 1982. pap. 4.95 (ISBN 0-9609960-0-1). Reggie the Retiree.

Sequoia, Anna. The Official J. A. P. Handbook: The Complete Guide to Jewish American Princesses & Princes. (Illus.). 1982. pap. 5.95 (ISBN 0-452-25359-4, Plume). NAL.

Shapiro, Raymond, ed. Lonely in Baltimore: Personal Columns. (Illus., Orig.). 1983. pap. 4.95 (ISBN 0-394-71465-2, Vin). Random.

Stewart, Arlene & Van Raalte, Joan. No Bad Babies: An Owner's Manual. (Illus.). 96p. (Orig.). 1983. pap. 3.95 (ISBN 0-688-02129-8). Quill NY.

Trillin, Calvin. Third Helpings. LC 82-19517. 192p. 1983. 12.95 (ISBN 0-89919-173-8). Ticknor & Fields.

AMERICAN WIT AND HUMOR-SPORTS AND GAMES

Crouser, R. L. It's Unlucky to be Behind at the End of the Game: And Other Great Sports Retorts. (Illus.). 160p. 1983. 10.95 (ISBN 0-688-01968-4). Morrow.

--It's Unlucky to be Behind at the End of the Game and Other Great Sports Retorts. (Illus.). 160p. (Orig.). 1983. pap. 3.95 (ISBN 0-688-01970-6). Quill NY.

Jacobs, Frank & Davis, Jack. The Mad Jock Book. (Illus.). 192p. 1983. pap. 1.95 (ISBN 0-446-30079-9). Warner Bks.

McDougal, Stan. World's Greatest Golf Jokes. 1983. pap. 4.95 (ISBN 0-8065-0831-0). Citadel Pr.

Schlossberg, Dan. Baseballaffs. LC 82-10020. (Illus.). 96p. 1982. pap. 3.95 (ISBN 0-8246-0288-9). Jonathan David.

AMERICAN WIT AND HUMOR, PICTORIAL

see also Comic Books, Strips, Etc.

Mauldin, Bill. Bill Mauldin's Army. 384p. 1983. pap. 12.95 (ISBN 0-89141-159-3). Presidio Pr.

Schultz, Thom, compiled by. Pew Peeves. LC 82-50731. (Illus.). 80p. (Orig.). 1982. pap. 3.95 (ISBN 0-936664-07-X). T Schultz Pubns.

Smith, Bruce. The World According to Warbucks: Capitalist Quotations from the Richest Man in the World. (Illus.). 96p. 1982. 6.95 (ISBN 0-8329-0266-7). New Century.

AMERICANS IN FOREIGN COUNTRIES

Lane, Rose W. & Boylston, Helen D. Travels with Zenobia: Paris to Albania by Model T Ford. Holtz, William, ed. LC 82-13554. 128p. 1983. text ed. 13.00x (ISBN 0-8262-0390-6). U of Mo Pr.

Morris, Wright. Solo. LC 82-48674. (An American Dreamer in Europe: 1933-34 Ser.). 192p. 1983. 13.41i (ISBN 0-06-015165-X, HarpT). Har-Row.

Torbiorn, I. Living Abroad: Personal Adjustment & Personnel Policy in the Overseas Setting. 200p. 1982. text ed. 32.00x (ISBN 0-471-10094-3, Pub. by Wiley-Interscience). Wiley.

AMERICANS IN FOREIGN COUNTRIES–EMPLOYMENT
Torbiorn, I. Living Abroad: Personal Adjustment & Personnel Policy in the Overseas Setting. 200p. 1982. text ed. 32.00x (ISBN 0-471-10094-3, Pub. by Wiley-Interscience). Wiley.
AMILLENNIALISM
see Millennium
AMINES
see also Polyamines
Ochiai, E. Aromatic Amine Oxides. 1967. 61.00 (ISBN 0-444-40429-5). Elsevier.
AMINO ACIDS
Devenyi, T. & Gergely, J. Amino Acid Peptides & Proteins. 1974. 56.00 (ISBN 0-444-41127-5). Elsevier.
Holden, J. T., ed. Amino Acid Pools: Distribution, Formation & Function of Free Amino Acids. 1962. 58.75 (ISBN 0-444-40288-8). Elsevier.
Underhill, Frank P. Physiology of the Amino Acids. 1915. text ed. 32.50x. Elliots Bks.
AMISH
Hostetler, John A. Amish Life. 2nd ed. LC 82-83964. (Illus.). 48p. (Orig.). 1983. pap. 4.95 (ISBN 0-8361-3326-9). Herald Pr.
The Kalona Heritage. (Illus.). 48p. pap. 4.75 (ISBN 0-941016-01-3). Penfield.
Miller, Levi. Our People: The Amish & Mennonites of Ohio. (Illus.). 56p. (Orig.). 1982. pap. 2.50 (ISBN 0-8361-3331-5). Herald Pr.
AMISH COOKERY
see Cookery, American
AMMIANUS, MARCELLINUS, 330-395
Elliott, Thomas G. Ammianus Marcellinus & Fourth Century History. 277p. 1983. 35.00x (ISBN 0-686-84471-8). Samuel Stevens.
AMMON'S HORN
see Hippocampus (Brain)
AMMUNITION
Hoyem, George A. The History & Development of Small Arms Ammunition: Cartridge Value Guide to Vols. One & Two. LC 80-67532. (Illus.). 16p. 1982. pap. 4.00x (ISBN 0-9604982-1-4). Armory Pubns.
AMMUNITION–LAW AND LEGISLATION
see Firearms–Laws and Regulations
AMORTIZATION TABLES
see Interest and Usury–Tables, Etc.
AMPHIBIANS
see also Frogs
Arnold & Burton. A Field Guide to Reptiles & Amphibians of Britain & Europe. 29.95 (ISBN 0-686-42777-7, Collins Pub England). Greene.
Ballinger, Royce E. & Lynch, John D. How to Know the Amphibians & Reptiles. (Pictured Key Nature Ser.). 300p. 1983. write for info. wire coil (ISBN 0-697-04786-5). Wm C Brown.
Epple, Anne O. Amphibians of New England. LC 82-73602. (Illus.). 1983. pap. 8.95t (ISBN 0-89272-159-6). Down East.
Nussbaum, Ronald A. & Brodie, Edmund D., Jr. Amphibians & Reptiles of the Pacific Northwest. LC 82-60055. (Illus.). 1983. 19.95 (ISBN 0-89301-086-3). U Pr of Idaho.
Palmer, Jean. Reptiles & Amphibians. (Blandford Pet Handbooks Ser.). 96p. 1983. 7.50 (ISBN 0-686-43144-8, Pub. by Blandford Pr England). Sterling.
Tata, J. R. Metamorphosis. Head, J. J., ed. (Carolina Biology Readers Ser.). (Illus.). 16p. 1983. pap. text ed. 1.60 (ISBN 0-89278-246-3). Carolina Biological.
AMPHIMIXIS
see Reproduction
AMPLIFIERS (ELECTRONICS)
Clayton, G. B. Operational Amplifier Experimental Manual. new ed. 112p. 1983. text ed. price not set (ISBN 0-408-01106-8); pap. price not set (ISBN 0-408-01239-0). Butterworth.
AMSTERDAM–DESCRIPTION
Baedeker's City Guide: Amsterdam. 192p. 1983. pap. 9.95 (ISBN 0-86145-119-8, Pub. by Auto Assn-British Tourist Authority England). Merrimack Bk Serv.
AMUSEMENT PARKS
Beard, Richard R. Walt Disney's EPCOT: Creating the New World of Tomorrow. (Illus.). 240p. 1982. 35.00 (ISBN 0-8109-0819-0). Abrams.
Birnbaum, Stephen. Walt Disney World 1983. rev. ed. 1982. 4.95 (ISBN 0-395-32952-3). HM.
Bush, Lee O. & Chukayne, Edward C. Euclid Beach Park: A Second Look. (Illus.). 229p. 1979. 12.95 (ISBN 0-935408-01-0). Amusement Pk Bks.
--Euclid Beach Park is Closed for the Season. (Illus.). 331p. 1977. 19.95 (ISBN 0-913228-22-2); pap. 12.95 (ISBN 0-686-43325-4). Amusement Pk Bks.
Munch, Richard W. Harry G. Travers Legends of Terror, Vol. 1. Hershey, Richard & Bush, Lee, eds. (Roller Coaster Designers Ser.). (Illus.). 175p. 1982. pap. 14.95 (ISBN 0-935408-02-9). Amusement Pk Bks.
Van Steenwyk, Elizabeth. Behind the Scenes at the Amusement Park. Tucker, Kathleen, ed. (Behind the Scenes Ser.). (Illus.). 48p. (gr. 2-7). 1983. PLB 9.25 (ISBN 0-8075-0605-2). A Whitman.
AMUSEMENTS
see also Aquatic Sports; Cards; Charades; Children's Parties; Circus; Conjuring; Creative Activities and Seatwork; Dancing; Entertaining; Family Recreation; Games; Hobbies; Indoor Games; Mathematical Recreations; Moving-Pictures; Performing Arts; Play; Puzzles; Recreation; Riddles; School Sports; Sports; Theater; Toys; Ventriloquism
Bell, Sally C. & Langdon, Dolly. Romper Room's Miss Sally Presents Two Hundred Fun Things to Do with Little Kids. LC 80-1807. (Illus.). 1983. pap. 7.95 (ISBN 0-385-15735-5, Dolp). Doubleday.
Birnbaum, Stephen. Disneyland 1983. 1982. 4.95 (ISBN 0-395-32924-8). HM.
Home Entertainment in the 1980s. (Reports Ser.: No. 511). 206p. 1982. 985.00 (ISBN 0-686-38952-2). Intl Res Dev.
Home Entertainment Products. 1982. 695.00 (ISBN 0-686-38436-9, 555). Busn Trend.
Melsom, Andrew. House Party Games & Amusements for the Upper Class & Other Folks. Orig. Title: Are You There, Moriarty? (Illus.). 114p. 1983. pap. 4.76i (ISBN 0-06-463577-5, EH 577). B&N NY.
Morris, Scot. Omni Games. (Illus.). 192p. 1983. pap. 9.95 (ISBN 0-03-060297-1). HR&W.
Robinson, Jeri. Activities for Anyone, Anytime, Anywhere. LC 82-15353. 96p. 1983. 13.51 (ISBN 0-316-75144-8); pap. 5.25 (ISBN 0-316-75145-6). Little.
Rockwell, Robert E. & Williams, Robert A. Hug a Tree & Other Things to Do Outdoors with Young Children. 112p. 1983. pap. 7.95 (ISBN 0-87659-105-5). Gryphon Hse.
Rouard, Marguerite & Simon, Jacques. Children's Play Spaces: From Sandbox to Adventure Playground. (Illus.). 160p. 1983. 37.95 (ISBN 0-87951-056-0); pap. 13.95 (ISBN 0-87951-166-4). Overlook Pr.
ANA
see Aphorisms and Apothegms; Proverbs; Quotations
ANABOLISM
see Metabolism
ANAESTHESIA
see Anesthesia
ANALOGY (LAW)
see Law–Interpretation and Construction
ANALOGY (RELIGION)
Zeitz, James V. Spirituality & Analogia Entis According to Erich Przywara, S. J. Metaphysics & Religious Experience, the Ignation Exercises, the Balance in 'Similarity' & 'Greater Dissimilarity' According to Lateran IV. LC 82-17588. 358p. (Orig.). 1983. lib. bdg. 26.25 (ISBN 0-8191-2783-3); pap. text ed. 14.00 (ISBN 0-8191-2784-1). U Pr of Amer.
ANALYSIS (CHEMISTRY)
see Chemistry, Analytic
also and names of substances analyzed
ANALYSIS (MATHEMATICS)
see Calculus; Functions; Harmonic Analysis; Mathematical Analysis
ANALYSIS (PHILOSOPHY)
Gold, Michael E. Dialogue on Comparable Worth. (Orig.). 1983. pap. price not set (ISBN 0-87546-099-2). ILR Pr.
Viete, Francois. The Analytic Art. Witmer, T. Richard, tr. from Fr. & Lat. LC 82-21381. (Illus.). 300p. 1983. 45.00X (ISBN 0-87338-282-X). Kent St U Pr.
ANALYSIS, CHROMATOGRAPHIC
see Chromatographic Analysis
ANALYSIS, ELECTROCHEMICAL
see Electrochemical Analysis
ANALYSIS, FACTORIAL
see Factor Analysis
ANALYSIS, FOURIER
see Fourier Analysis
ANALYSIS, INTERACTION (EDUCATION)
see Interaction Analysis in Education
ANALYSIS, JOB
see Job Analysis
ANALYSIS, MICROSCOPIC
see Metallography; Microscope and Microscopy
ANALYSIS, SPECTRUM
see Spectrum Analysis
ANALYSIS, STOCHASTIC
see Stochastic Analysis
ANALYSIS, VOLUMETRIC
see Volumetric Analysis
ANALYSIS OF BLOOD
see Blood–Analysis and Chemistry
ANALYSIS OF FOOD
see Food–Analysis; Food Adulteration and Inspection
ANALYSIS OF TIME SERIES
see Time-Series Analysis
ANALYSIS OF VARIANCE
see also Experimental Design; Multivariate Analysis; Sampling (Statistics)
Li, Ching Chun. Analysis of Unbalanced Data: A Pre-Program Introduction. LC 82-4253. (Illus.). 160p. 1983. 19.95 (ISBN 0-521-24749-7). Cambridge U Pr.
Morrison, Donald F. Applied Linear Statistical Methods. 544p. 1983. 30.95 (ISBN 0-13-041020-9). P-H.
ANALYSIS SITUS
see Topology
ANALYTICAL CHEMISTRY
see Chemistry, Analytic
ANALYTICAL GEOMETRY
see Geometry, Analytic
ANALYTICAL MECHANICS
see Mechanics, Analytic
ANALYTICAL PHILOSOPHY
see Analysis (Philosophy)
ANARCHISM AND ANARCHISTS
see also Anomy; Liberty; Socialism; Terrorism
Institut Francais d'Histoire Sociale, Paris. L' Anarchisme (Anarchism) 1982. 27.00 (ISBN 3-598-10442-1, Pub. by K G Saur). Shoe String.
Porter, David, ed. Vision on Fire: Emma Goldman on the Spanish Revolution. LC 82-74015. (Illus.). 400p. (Orig.). 1983. pap. 7.50t (ISBN 0-9610348-2-3). Commonground Pr.
Saltman, Richard B. The Social & Political Thought of Michael Bakunin. LC 82-9348. (Contributions in Political Science Ser.: No. 88). 256p. 1983. lib. bdg. 35.00 (ISBN 0-313-23378-0, SPB/). Greenwood.
Ward, Colin. Anarchy in Action. 152p. pap. 3.50 (ISBN 0-900384-20-4). Left Bank.
ANATOMY
see also Dissection; Histology; Nervous System; Physiology; Veterinary Anatomy
also specific subjects, with or without the subdivision Anatomy
Anderson, James E. Grant's Atlas of Anatomy. 8th ed. (Illus.). 640p. 1983. 35.00 (ISBN 0-683-00211-2). Williams & Wilkins.
Arnould-Taylor, W. E. A Textbook of Anatomy & Physiology. 112p. 1978. 30.00x (ISBN 0-85950-044-6, Pub. by Thornes England). State Mutual Bk.
Holtzmeier, Dawn K. Applied Anatomy & Physiology: A Laboratory Manual & Workbook for Health Careers. 304p. 1983. pap. text ed. 18.50 (ISBN 0-8403-2915-6). Kendall-Hunt.
Kapit, Wynn & Elson, Lawrence. The Anatomy Coloring Book. 1981. pap. text ed. 8.95 scp (ISBN 0-06-453914-8, HarpC). Har-Row.
McGrath, Philomena & Mills, P. Atlas of Sectional Anatomy. (Illus.). viii, 232p. 1983. bound 82.25 (ISBN 3-8055-3624-0). S Karger.
Weinreb, Eva L. Anatomy & Physiology. 896p. 1982. text ed. write for info. (ISBN 0-201-08852-5). A-W.
ANATOMY–DICTIONARIES
Nomina Anatomica. 5th ed. 168p. 1983. text ed. price not set (ISBN 0-683-06550-5). Williams & Wilkins.
ANATOMY–LABORATORY MANUALS
Benson, Harold J., et al. Anatomy & Physiology Laboratory Textbook: Short & Complete Version, 2 vols. 3rd ed. 350p. 1983. pap. text ed. write for info. wire coil short version (ISBN 0-697-04739-3); instrs' manual avail. (ISBN 0-697-04740-7); pap. text ed. write for info. complete version, 570p. (ISBN 0-697-04737-7); instrs' manual avail. (ISBN 0-697-04738-5). Wm C Brown.
ANATOMY, ARTISTIC
see also Medicine and Art
Da Vinci, Leonardo. Leonardo on the Human Body. O'Malley, Charles D. & Saunders, J. B., trs. (Fine Art Ser.). (Illus.). 506p. 1983. pap. 10.00 (ISBN 0-486-24483-0). Dover.
Warren, Henry. Artistic Anatomy of the Human Figure. (A Human Development Library Bk.). (Illus.). 131p. 1983. 47.85 (ISBN 0-86650-053-7). Gloucester Art.
ANATOMY, COMPARATIVE–ATLASES
Eddy, S., et al. Atlas of Drawings for Vertebrate Anatomy. 3rd ed. 176p. 1964. text ed. 14.95x (ISBN 0-471-23168-1). Wiley.
ANATOMY, DENTAL
see Teeth
ANATOMY, HUMAN
see also Body, Human; Extremities (Anatomy)
also names of organs and regions of the body, e.g. Heart, Pelvis, Skull
Ashley, Ruth. Human Anatomy. LC 76-65. (Self-Teaching Guides). 274p. 1976. pap. text ed. 7.95 (ISBN 0-471-03508-4). Wiley.
Camp, Diana Van. Basic Skills Human Body Workbook: Grade 5. (Basic Skills Workbooks). 32p. 1982. tchrs' ed. 0.99 (ISBN 0-8209-0420-1, HBW-F). ESP.
--Basic Skills Human Body Workbook: Grade 8. (Basic Skills Workbook). 32p. 1982. tchrs' ed. 0.99 (ISBN 0-8209-0423-6, HBW-I). ESP.
--Basic Skills Human Workbook: Grade 7. (Basic Skills Workbook). 32p. 1982. tchrs' ed. 0.99 (ISBN 0-8209-0422-8, HBW-H). ESP.
--Basic Skills Human Workbooks: Grade 6. (Basic Skills Workbooks). 32p. 1982. tchrs' ed. 0.99 (ISBN 0-8209-0421-X, HBW-G). ESP.
McClintic, J. Robert. Human Anatomy. (Illus.). 544p. 1983. pap. text ed. 28.95 (ISBN 0-8016-3225-0). Mosby.
Neal, Kenneth G. & Kalbus, Barbara H. Anatomy & Physiology: A Laboratory Manual & Study Guide. 4th ed. 448p. 1983. pap. text ed. write for info. (ISBN 0-8087-1449-X). Burgess.
Patty, Catherine. The Human Body. (Sound Filmstrip Kits Ser.). (gr. 3-6). 1980. tchrs ed. 24.00 (ISBN 0-8209-0428-7, FCW-5). ESP.
ANATOMY, HUMAN–JUVENILE LITERATURE
Berger, Melvin. Why I Cough, Sneeze, Shiver, Hiccup, & Yawn. LC 82-45587. (A Let's-Read-&-Find-Out Science Bk.). (Illus.). 40p. (gr. k-3). 1983. 9.57i (ISBN 0-690-04253-1, TYC-J); PLB 9.89g (ISBN 0-690-04254-X). Har-Row.
ANATOMY, MICROSCOPIC
see Histology
ANATOMY, REGIONAL
see Anatomy, Surgical and Topographical
ANATOMY, SURGICAL AND TOPOGRAPHICAL
see also names of organs and regions of the body
Basmajian, John V. Surface Anatomy: An Instruction Manual. 2nd ed. LC 77-3831. (Illus.). 78p. 1983. pap. 5.95 (ISBN 0-683-00359-3). Williams & Wilkins.
Joseph, J. Textbook of Regional Anatomy. 624p. 1982. 70.00x (ISBN 0-333-28911-0, Pub. by Macmillan England). State Mutual Bk.
ANATOMY, VEGETABLE
see Botany–Anatomy
ANATOMY, VETERINARY
see Veterinary Anatomy
ANATOMY OF PLANTS
see Botany–Anatomy
ANCESTRY
see Genealogy; Heredity
ANCIENT ART
see Art, Ancient
ANCIENT HISTORY
see History, Ancient
ANCIENT POTTERY
see Pottery, Ancient
ANDE LANGUAGE
see Campa Language
ANDERSEN, HANS CHRISTIAN, 1805-1875
McConnell, Josephine. The Fairy Tale Writer: Hans Christian Andersen. 42p. (Orig.). 1982. pap. 3.95 (ISBN 0-931494-35-4). Brunswick Pub.
ANDO, HIROSHIGE
see Hiroshige, 1797-1858
ANDREWS, JULIE
Windeler, Robert. Julie Andrews. (Illus.). 224p. 1983. 10.95 (ISBN 0-312-44848-1). St Martin.
ANDROIDS
CES Industries, Inc. Staff. Robot Operation & Programming. (Ed-Lab Experiment Manual Ser.). (Illus.). (gr. 9-12). 1982. write for info. lab manual (ISBN 0-86711-032-5). CES Industries.
International Conference, 1st Stratford-upon-Avon, UK April 1-3, 1981. Robot Vision & Sensory Controls: Proceedings. 348p. 1981. pap. text ed. 90.00x (ISBN 0-903608-15-4). Scholium Intl.
Susnjara, Ken. A Manager's Guide to Industrial Robots. LC 81-86624. (Illus.). 181p. 1982. 24.95 (ISBN 0-86551-018-0). Corinthian.
ANECDOTES
Morley, Robert. Pardon Me, But You're Eating My Doily: & Other Embarrassing Moments of Famous People. 160p. 1983. 8.95 (ISBN 0-312-59656-1). St Martin.
Nicholas, Cornelius J. Auld Tayles. LC 81-81936. 64p. 1983. 6.95 (ISBN 0-86666-046-1). GWP.
ANEMIA, DREPANOCYTIC
see Sickle Cell Anemia
ANESTHESIA
see also Anesthesiology; Hypnotism–Therapeutic Use
Atkinson, R. S. & Rushman, G. B. A Synopsis of Anaesthesia. 9th ed. (Illus.). 976p. 1982. pap. text ed. 33.50 (ISBN 0-7236-0621-8). Wright-PSG.
Chung, David. Anesthesia in Patients with Ischemic Heart Disease. (Current Topics in Anesthesia Ser.: No. 6). 192p. 1982. text ed. 32.50 (ISBN 0-7131-4407-6). E Arnold.
Lebowitz, Philip W. & Newberg, Leslie A. Clinical Anesthesia Procedures of the Massachusetts General Hospital. 2nd ed. 1982. pap. text ed. 14.95 (ISBN 0-316-51867-0). Little.
Mannino, Mary J., ed. The Nurse Anesthetist & the Law. Date not set. price not set (ISBN 0-8089-1496-0). Grune.
Miller, Ronald D., ed. Year Book of Anesthesia 1983. 1983. 35.00 (ISBN 0-8151-5929-3). Year Bk Med.
Peter, K. & Jesch, F. Inhalation Anaesthesia: Today & Tomorrow. (Anaesthesiology & Intensive Care Medicine Ser.: Vol. 150). (Illus.). 259p. 1983. 31.70 (ISBN 0-387-11757-1). Springer-Verlag.
Snow, John C. Manual of Anesthesia. (Spiral Manual Ser.). 1982. spiralbound 15.95 (ISBN 0-316-80222-0). Little.
Sutcliffe. Handbook of Emergency Anesthesia. 1983. text ed. price not set (ISBN 0-408-00395-2). Butterworth.
ANESTHESIA–HISTORY
Smith, W. D. Under the Influence: A History of Nitrous Oxide & Oxygen Anaesthesia. 208p. 1982. 40.00 (ISBN 0-333-31681-9, Pub. by Macmillan England). State Mutual Bk.
ANESTHESIOLOGY
see also Anesthesia
Anaesthesiology. (International Congress Ser.: No. 452). (Abstracts). 1978. pap. 63.50 (ISBN 0-444-90046-2). Elsevier.
Hulsz Suarez, E., et al. Anaesthesiology. (International Congress Ser.: No. 399). (Proceedings). 1977. 136.50 (ISBN 0-444-15237-7). Elsevier.
Knapp, Richard B. The Gift of Surgery to Mankind: A History of Modern Anesthesiology. (Illus.). 144p. 1983. text ed. price not set (ISBN 0-398-04817-7). C C Thomas.

Miyazaki, M. E., et al, eds. Anaesthesiology. (International Congress Ser.: No. 292). (Proceedings). 1974. 78.00 (ISBN 0-444-15043-9). Elsevier.

Samayoa, ed. Anaesthesiology. (International Congress Ser.: No. 490). (Abstracts). 1979. 30.75 (ISBN 0-444-90100-0). Elsevier.

Slack, Steven J. & DeKornfeld, Thomas J. Anesthesiology: Continuing Education Review. 2nd ed. 1983. pap. text ed. price not set (ISBN 0-87488-353-9). Med Exam.

Vasconcelos, G., ed. Anaesthesiology. (International Congress Ser.: No. 387). (Abstracts). 1976. pap. 28.50 (ISBN 0-444-15220-2). Elsevier.

ANEURYSMS

Ito, Zentaro. Microsurgery of Cerebral Aneurysms. (Illus.). 350p. 1982. 279.00 (ISBN 0-444-90267-8, Excerpta Medica). Elsevier.

ANGELOLOGY

see Angels

ANGELS

MacDonald, Hope. When Angels Appear. 128p. (Orig.). 1982. pap. 4.95 (ISBN 0-310-28531-3). Zondervan.

ANGER

Averill, James R. Anger & Aggression: An Essay on Emotion. (Springer Series in Social Psychology). (Illus.). 402p. 1983. 29.90 (ISBN 0-387-90719-X). Springer-Verlag.

LaHaye, Tim & Phillips, Bob. Anger Is a Choice. 160p. (Orig.). 1982. pap. 5.95 (ISBN 0-310-27071-5). Zondervan.

Lester, Andrew D. Coping with Your Anger: A Christian Guide. LC 82-24730. 120p. 1983. pap. 5.95 (ISBN 0-664-24471-8). Westminster.

Warren, Neil C. Make Anger Your Ally: Harnessing Our Most Baffling Emotion. LC 82-45933. 216p. 1983. 13.95 (ISBN 0-385-18788-2). Doubleday.

ANGINA PECTORIS

Purcell, Julia Ann & Johnston, Barbara. Angina de Pecho. Hull, Nancy R., ed. Gonzalez, Olimpia, tr. (Illus.). 24p. 1982. 3.50 (ISBN 0-686-83978-1). Pritchett & Hull.

ANGIOGRAPHY

Abrams, Herbert L. Abrams Angiography: Vascular & Interventional Radiology, 3 vols. 2nd ed. 1983. Vol. 1. text ed. (ISBN 0-316-00466-9); Vol. 2. text ed. (ISBN 0-316-00467-7); Vol. 3. text ed. (ISBN 0-316-00468-5); text ed. 275.00 set. Little.

Bradac, G. B. & Oberson, R. Angiography & Computed Tomography in Cerebroarterial Occlusive Diseases. (Illus.). 290p. 1982. 68.00 (ISBN 0-387-11453-X). Springer-Verlag.

Krayenbuehl, H. Cerebral Angiography in Clinic & Practice. (Illus.). 603p. 1982. 85.00 (ISBN 0-86577-067-0). Thieme-Stratton.

Lasjaunias, Pierre. Craniofacial & Upper Cervical Arteries: Collateral Circulation & Angiographic Protocols. 300p. 1983. lib. bdg. write for info. (ISBN 0-683-04898-8). Williams & Wilkins.

Veiga-Pires, J. A. & Grainger, Ronald G., eds. Pioneers in Angiography: The Portugese School of Angiography. (Illus.). 131p. 1981. text ed. 24.95 (ISBN 0-85200-448-6, Pub. by MTP Pr England). Kluwer Boston.

ANGIOLOGY

see Blood-Vessels; Blood-Vessels–Diseases

ANGIOSPERMS

see also Dicotyledons; Monocotyledons

Heywood, V. H., ed. Flowering Plants of the World. (Illus.). 1978. 13.50x (ISBN 0-19-217674-9). Oxford U Pr.

ANGLICAN CHURCH

see Church of England

ANGLING

see Fishing

ANGLO-AMERICAN CATALOGING RULES

Ala-Cla-La. AACR2 Revisions. LC 82-13719. 24p. 1982. pap. text ed. 2.50 (ISBN 0-686-37952-7). ALA.

Cook, Donald. AACR2 Decisions & Rule Interpretations. 480p. 1982. text ed. 50.00 (ISBN 0-8389-3281-9). ALA.

Olson, Nancy B. A Manual of AACR2 Examples for Microcomputer Software & Video Games. Swanson, Edward, ed. 75p. 1983. pap. text ed. 7.00 (ISBN 0-936996-14-5). Soldier Creek.

Swanson, Edward. A Manual of AACR2 Examples for Technical Reports. 1983. pap. text ed. 7.00 (ISBN 0-936996-15-3). Soldier Creek.

ANGLO-AMERICAN LAW

see Law–Great Britain; Law–United States

ANGLO-SAXON LANGUAGE

Bean, Marian C. The Development of Word Order Patterns in Old English. (Illus.). 150p. 1983. text ed. 25.75x (ISBN 0-389-20356-4). B&N Imports.

Toon, Thomas E. The Politics of Early Old English Sound Change. (Quantitative Analyses of Linguistic Structure Ser.). Date not set. price not set (ISBN 0-12-694980-8). Acad Pr.

ANGLO-SAXON LANGUAGE–DIALECTS

Toon, Thomas E. The Politics of Early Old English Sound Change. (Quantitative Analyses of Linguistic Structure Ser.). Date not set. price not set (ISBN 0-12-694980-8). Acad Pr.

ANGLO-SAXON LANGUAGE–GLOSSARIES, VOCABULARIES, ETC.

Cameron, Angus & Kingsmill, Allison, eds. Old English Word Studies: A Preliminary Word & Author List. (Old English Ser.). 208p. 1983. 60.00x (ISBN 0-8020-5526-5); fiche incl. U of Toronto Pr.

ANGLO-SAXON LITERATURE

Dumville, David & Lapidge, Michael, eds. The Anglo-Saxon Chronicle Seventeen: The Annals of St. Neots. 108p. 1983. text ed. 30.00x (ISBN 0-85991-117-9, Pub. by Boydell & Brewer). Biblio Dist.

ANGLO-SAXON LITERATURE–HISTORY AND CRITICISM

Crossley-Holland, Kevin, ed. The Anglo-Saxon World. LC 82-24331. 200p. 1983. text ed. 22.50x (ISBN 0-389-20367-X). B&N Imports.

ANGLO-SAXONS

Toon, Thomas E. The Politics of Early Old English Sound Change. (Quantitative Analyses of Linguistic Structure Ser.). Date not set. price not set (ISBN 0-12-694980-8). Acad Pr.

ANGORA RABBITS

see Rabbits

ANIMAL BABIES

see Animals, Infancy of

ANIMAL BEHAVIOR

see Animals, Habits and Behavior Of

ANIMAL COMMUNICATION

Crail, Ted. Apetalk & Whalespeak: The Quest for Interspecies Communication. 320p. 1983. pap. 7.95 (ISBN 0-8092-5527-8). Contemp Bks.

Smith, Penelope. Animal Talk: A Guide to Communicating with & Understanding Animals. (Illus.). 76p. 1982. pap. 5.00 (ISBN 0-936552-02-6). Pegasus Pubns.

ANIMAL DISEASES

see Veterinary Medicine

ANIMAL DRAWING

see Animal Painting and Illustration

ANIMAL ECOLOGY

see also Adaptation (Biology); Animal Populations

Huey, Raymond B. & Pianka, Eric R., eds. Lizard Ecology: Studies of a Model Organism. (Illus.). 720p. 1983. text ed. 35.00x (ISBN 0-674-53673-8). Harvard U Pr.

Kunz, Thomas H., ed. Ecology of Bats. 450p. 1982. 49.50x (ISBN 0-306-40950-X, Plenum Pr). Plenum Pub.

McCall, P. L. & Tevesz, M. J. S., eds. Animal-Sediment Relations, Vol. 2. LC 82-16523. (Topics in GeoBiology). 352p. 1982. 42.50x (ISBN 0-306-41078-8, Plenum Pr). Plenum Pub.

Montgomery, G. Gene, ed. The Evolution & Ecology of Armadillos, Sloths, & Vermilinguas. (Illus.). 400p. (Orig.). 1983. pap. text ed. 35.00x (ISBN 0-87474-649-3). Smithsonian.

ANIMAL ELECTRICITY

see Electrophysiology

ANIMAL HOMES

see Animals, Habitations Of

ANIMAL HUSBANDRY

see Domestic Animals; Livestock

ANIMAL INDUSTRY

see also Cattle Trade; Dairying; Domestic Animals; Livestock; Poultry Industry

Acker, Duane. Animal Science & Industry. (Illus.). 720p. 1983. 27.95 (ISBN 0-13-037416-4). P-H.

FAO Production Yearbook 1981, Vol. 35. (FAO Statistics Ser.: No. 40). 306p. 1982. 30.50 (ISBN 92-5-001198-9, F2241, FAO). Unipub.

Yousef. Animal Production in the Tropics. 394p. 1982. 38.95 (ISBN 0-03-060482-6). Praeger.

ANIMAL INSTINCT

see Instinct

ANIMAL KINGDOM

see Zoology

ANIMAL LANGUAGE

see Animal Communication

ANIMAL MIGRATION–JUVENILE LITERATURE

McClung, Robert M. Mysteries of Migration. LC 82-15740. (Illus.). 64p. (gr. 4-6). 1983. PLB write for info. (ISBN 0-8116-2950-3). Garrard.

ANIMAL NAVIGATION

Purves, P. E. & Pilleri, G., eds. Echolocation in Whales & Dolphins. write for info. (ISBN 0-12-567960-2). Acad Pr.

ANIMAL NUTRITION

see also Feeds;

also subdivision Feeding and Feeds under names of animals and groups of animals, e.g. Poultry–Feeding and Feeds

Edney, A. T., ed. Dog & Cat Nutrition: A Handbook for Students, Veterinarians, Breeders & Owners. (Illus.). 124p. 1982. 24.00 (ISBN 0-08-028891-X); pap. 12.00 (ISBN 0-08-028890-1). Pergamon.

Hintz, Harold F. Horse Nutrition: A Practical Guide. LC 82-16294. (Illus.). 256p. 1983. 15.95 (ISBN 0-668-05416-6). Arco.

Robbins, Charles T., ed. Wildlife Feeding & Nutrition. LC 82-13720. Date not set. price not set (ISBN 0-12-589380-9). Acad Pr.

ANIMAL OILS

see Oils and Fats

ANIMAL PAINTING AND ILLUSTRATION

Kuhn, Bob. The Animal Art of Bob Kuhn: A Lifetime of Drawing & Painting. 1982. pap. 15.95 (ISBN 0-89134-050-5). North Light Pub.

ANIMAL PICTURES

Rowland-Entwistle, Theodore. Illustrated Facts & Records Book of Animals. LC 82-18406. (Illus.). 236p. 1983. 9.95 (ISBN 0-668-05730-0, 5730). Arco.

ANIMAL POETRY

see Animals–Poetry

ANIMAL POPULATIONS

see also Population Genetics

Williamson, Mark. Island Populations. (Illus.). 298p. 1983. pap. 19.95 (ISBN 0-19-854139-2). Oxford U Pr.

ANIMAL PRODUCTS

see also Dairy Products; Meat; Raw Materials; also names of particular products, e.g. Ivory, Wool, etc.

Animal Blood Processing & Utilization. (FAO Agricultural Services Bulletin Ser.: No. 32). 101p. 1982. pap. 7.75 (ISBN 92-5-100491-9, F2315, FAO). Unipub.

Camels & Camel Milk. (FAO Animal Production & Health Papers: No. 26). 69p. 1982. pap. 7.50 (ISBN 92-5-101169-9, F2310, FAO). Unipub.

ANIMAL PSYCHOLOGY

see Psychology, Comparative

ANIMAL SIGNS

see Animal Tracks

ANIMAL SOCIETIES

Here are entered works on groups of animals which are characterized by specific social patterns due to their proximity, interrelationships and-or similarities.

Kohl, Judith & Kohl, Herbert. Pack, Band & Colony: The World of Social Animals. (Illus.). 132p. (gr. 6 up). 1983. 10.95 (ISBN 0-686-81645-5). FS&G.

ANIMAL STORIES

see Animals, Legends and Stories Of

ANIMAL TRACKS

Bang & Dahlstrom. Collins Guide to Animal Tracks & Signs. 29.95 (ISBN 0-686-42775-0, Collins Pub England). Greene.

Headstrom, Richard. Identifying Animal Tracks: Mammals, Birds & Other Animals of the Eastern United States. (Illus.). 128p. 1983. pap. 2.50 (ISBN 0-486-24442-3). Dover.

ANIMALS

see also Animals and Civilization; Invertebrates; Mammals; Vertebrates; Zoo Animals; Zoology also names of kinds of animals, e.g. Bears, cats, deer, etc.

Alexander, R. McNeill. Optima for Animals. 120p. 1982. pap. text ed. 13.95 (ISBN 0-7131-2843-7). E Arnold.

Cooper, Diana. Animal Hotel. 224p. 1983. 12.95 (ISBN 0-312-03782-1). St Martin.

Foy, Sally & Oxford Scientific Films. The Grand Design: Form & Color in Animals. (Illus.). 192p. 1983. 24.95 (ISBN 0-13-362574-5). P-H.

Freshney, Ian R., ed. Culture of Animal Cells: A Manual of Basic Technique. LC 82-24960. 280p. 1983. write for info. (ISBN 0-8451-0223-0). A R Liss.

Gentry, Christine. When Dogs Run Wild: The Sociology of Feral Animals & Wildlife. (Illus.). 220p. 1983. lib. bdg. 16.95X (ISBN 0-89950-062-5). McFarland & Co.

Goto, H. E. Animal Toxonomy. (No. 143). 64p. 1982. pap. text ed. 8.95 (ISBN 0-7131-2847-X). E Arnold.

Justus, Fred. Animals: Males, Females & Babies. (Early Education Ser.). 24p. (ps-1). 1981. wkbk. 5.00 (ISBN 0-8209-0226-8, K-28). ESP.

Levy, Charles K. A Guide to Dangerous Animals of North America: Including Central America. (Illus.). 192p. 1983. pap. 9.95 (ISBN 0-8289-0503-7). Greene.

McFerron, Martha. Animals & Babies. (Science Ser.). 24p. (gr. 2-3). 1980. wkbk. 5.00 (ISBN 0-8209-0160-1, S-22). ESP.

Ovenden & Corbet. The Wild Animals of Britain & Europe. pap. 8.95 (ISBN 0-686-42743-2, Collins Pub England). Greene.

Proceedings of the Seventieth Convention: International Association of Fish & Wildlife Agencies. 1981. 13.00 (ISBN 0-932108-05-9). IAFWA.

Reader's Digest Editors. Our Magnificent Wildlife: How to Enjoy & Preserve It. LC 74-30861. (Illus.). 352p. 1975. 16.98 (ISBN 0-89577-022-9). RD Assn.

Wood, Dennis. Principles of Animal Physiology. 350p. 1982. pap. text ed. 19.95x (ISBN 0-7131-2861-5). E Arnold.

Wood, Gerald L. Guinness Book of Animal Facts & Feats. 3rd ed. (Illus.). 1983. 19.95 (ISBN 0-85112-235-3, Pub. by Guinness Superlatives England). Sterling.

ANIMALS–FOOD

see Animals, Food Habits of

ANIMALS–JUVENILE LITERATURE

see also Animal Pictures; Animals, Habits and Behavior of–Juvenile Literature

also Juvenile works, indentified by grade key, may be found in other subdivision or in headings beginning with the word Animal

DeBruin, Jerry. Young Scientists Explore Animals, Bk. 2. (gr. 4-7). 1982. 3.95 (ISBN 0-86653-073-8, GA 406). Good Apple.

Jefferies, Lawrence. Amazing World of Animals. LC 82-20061. (Question & Answer Bks.). (Illus.). 32p. (gr. 3-6). 1983. PLB 8.59 (ISBN 0-89375-898-1); pap. text ed. 1.95 (ISBN 0-89375-899-X). Troll Assocs.

Klimo, Kate, ed. Meet Baby Animals with E.T. (Illus.). 14p. 1982. 3.50 (ISBN 0-671-46434-5, Little). S&S.

Paige, Rae. The Sesame Street Question & Answer Book about Animals. LC 81-84709. (Illus.). 48p. (ps-3). 1983. 6.95 (ISBN 0-307-15816-0, Golden Pr); PLB price not set (ISBN 0-307-65816-3). Western Pub.

Peters, Sharon. Animals at Night. LC 82-19226. (Now I Know Ser.). (Illus.). 32p. (gr. k-2). 1982. lib. bdg. 8.89 (ISBN 0-89375-903-1). Troll Assocs.

Stewart, K. K. God Made Me Special. Mahany, Patricia, ed. (Happy Day Bks.). (Illus.). 24p. (ps-2). 1983. 1.29 (ISBN 0-87239-635-5, 3555). Standard Pub.

Taylor, Ron. Fifty Facts About Animals. (Fifty Facts About Ser.). (Illus.). 32p. (gr. 4-6). 1983. PLB 8.90 (ISBN 0-531-09208-9). Watts.

ANIMALS–LEGENDS AND STORIES

see Animals, Legends and Stories of

Bilai, V. I. Antibiotic Producing Microscopic Fungi. 1963. 19.50 (ISBN 0-444-40054-0). Elsevier.

ANIMALS–POETRY

Fuller, Roy, ed. Fellow Mortals: An Anthology of Animal Verse. 304p. 1981. 45.00x (ISBN 0-7121-0635-9, Pub. by Macdonald & Evans). State Mutual Bk.

Lear, Edward. The Owl & the Pussycat. LC 82-12092. (Illus.). 32p. (ps-3). 1983. reinforced binding 12.95 (ISBN 0-8234-0474-9). Holiday.

ANIMALS, AQUATIC

see Fresh-Water Biology; Marine Fauna

ANIMALS, CRUELTY TO

see Animals, Treatment Of

ANIMALS, DISEASES OF

see Veterinary Medicine

ANIMALS, DOMESTIC

see Domestic Animals

ANIMALS, EXTINCT

see Extinct Animals

ANIMALS, FOOD HABITS OF

Robbins, Charles T., ed. Wildlife Feeding & Nutrition. LC 82-13720. Date not set. price not set (ISBN 0-12-589380-9). Acad Pr.

ANIMALS, FOSSIL

see Paleontology

ANIMALS, HABITATIONS OF

Sweton, Ernest T. Wild Animals at Home. 126p. 1982. Repr. of 1913 ed. lib. bdg. 30.00 (ISBN 0-89760-852-6). Telegraph Bks.

ANIMALS, HABITS AND BEHAVIOR OF

see also Animals, Food Habits of; Animals, Infancy of; Animals, Legends and Stories of; Birds–Behavior; Instinct; Nature Study; Psychology, Comparative also names of particular animals

Clark, Stephen R. The Nature of the Beast: Are Animals Moral? 136p. 1982. text ed. 14.95 (ISBN 0-19-219130-6). Oxford U Pr.

Discovering Animal Behavior. (Discovering Science Ser.). 1983. lib. bdg. 15.96 (ISBN 0-86706-105-7, Pub. by Stonehenge). Silver.

Sparks, John. The Discovery of Animal Behavior. 1982. 24.95 (ISBN 0-316-80492-4). Little.

Sweton, Ernest T. Wild Animals at Home. 126p. 1982. Repr. of 1913 ed. lib. bdg. 30.00 (ISBN 0-89760-852-6). Telegraph Bks.

Tinbergen, N. Social Behavior in Animals. 1965. pap. 8.95x (ISBN 0-412-20000-7, Pub. by Chapman & Hall England). Methuen Inc.

ANIMALS, HABITS AND BEHAVIOR OF–JUVENILE LITERATURE

see also Animals–Juvenile Literature

Fisher, Aileen. Ways of Animals, 10 bks. Incl. Animal Disguises (ISBN 0-8372-0860-2); Animal Houses (ISBN 0-8372-0859-9); Animal Jackets (ISBN 0-8372-0861-0); Filling the Bill (ISBN 0-8372-0864-5); Going Places (ISBN 0-8372-0865-3); No Accounting for Taste (ISBN 0-8372-0868-8); Now That Days Are Colder (ISBN 0-8372-0862-9); Sleepy Heads (ISBN 0-8372-0866-1); Tail Twisters (ISBN 0-8372-0863-7); You Don't Look Like Your Mother, Said the Robin to the Fawn (ISBN 0-8372-0867-X). (Nature Ser.). (ps-6). 1973. 7.98 ea.; Set. 79.80 (ISBN 0-8372-0880-7); resource guide 3.21 (ISBN 0-8372-0869-6); filmstrips, cassettes, & records avail. Bowmar-Noble.

Hopf, A. Strange Sex Lives in the Animal Kingdom. 1981. 8.95 (ISBN 0-07-030319-3). McGraw.

Podendorf, Illa. Animal Homes. LC 82-4466. (New True Bks.). (Illus.). 48p. (gr. k-4). 1982. PLB 9.25 (ISBN 0-516-01666-0). Childrens.

ANIMALS, INFANCY OF

Plooij, Frans X. The Behavioral Development of Free-Living Chimpanzee Babies & Infants. Lipsitt, Lewis P., ed. (Monographs on Infancy). (Illus.). 208p. (Orig.). 1983. text ed. 18.50 (ISBN 0-89391-114-3). Ablex Pub.

ANIMALS, LEGENDS AND STORIES OF

see also Animals, Habits and Behavior of; Animals in Literature; Fables; Nature Study also subdivision Legends and Stories under names of animals; Cats (In religion, Folk-Lore, etc.; Goldfinch (In Religion, Folk-Lore, etc.); and similar headings

Whalley, Irene, ed. The Beatrix Potter Collection, Vol. 1. 320p. 1982. 80.00x (ISBN 0-85692-070-3, Pub. by J M Dent). State Mutual Bk.

ANIMALS, ORIENTATION OF

see Orientation

ANIMALS, PREHISTORIC

see Extinct Animals; Paleontology

ANIMALS, PROTECTION OF

see Animals, Treatment Of; Wildlife Conservation

ANIMALS, RARE

see Rare Animals

ANIMALS, RESPIRATION OF

see Respiration

ANIMALS, RESTRAINT OF

see Animals, Treatment of

ANIMALS, SEA

see Marine Fauna

ANIMALS, TREATMENT OF

see also Vivisection

Bryant, Alan. Second Chance: The Story of the New Quay Hospital. (Illus.). 208p. 1982. 11.95 (ISBN 0-312-70828-9). St Martin.

Carlson, Delbert G. & Giffin, James M. Cat Owner's Home Veterinary Handbook. LC 82-23383. (Illus.). 392p. 1983. 17.95 (ISBN 0-87605-814-4). Howell Bk.

Dodds, W. Jean & Orlans, F. Barbara, eds. Scientific Perspectives in Animal Welfare: Symposium. LC 82-24375. Date not set. 17.50 (ISBN 0-12-219140-4). Acad Pr.

Favre, David S. & Loring, Murray, eds. Animal Law. LC 82-23130. 296p. 1983. lib. bdg. 35.00 (ISBN 0-89930-021-9, LAL/, Quorum). Greenwood.

Miller, Harlan B. & Williams, William H., eds. Ethics & Animals. (Contemporary Issues in Biomedicine, Ethics, & Society Ser.). 416p. 1983. 39.50 (ISBN 0-89603-036-9). Humana.

ANIMALS AND CIVILIZATION

Ventura, Piero. Man & the Horse. (Illus.). 80p. 1982. 11.95 (ISBN 0-399-20842-9). Putnam Pub Group.

ANIMALS AS CARRIERS OF DISEASE

Thrash, Agatha M. & Thrash, Calvin L., Jr. The Animal Connection: Cancer & Other Diseases from Animals & Foods of Animal Origin. 262p. (Orig.). 1983. pap. write for info. (ISBN 0-942658-04-3). Yuchi Pines.

ANIMALS IN LITERATURE

see also Animals, Legends and Stories Of

also Birds in Literature, Horses in Literature and similar headings

Allen, Mary. Animals in American Literature. LC 82-17369. (Illus.). 218p. 1983. 14.95 (ISBN 0-252-00975-4). U of Ill Pr.

ANIMATED CARTOONS

see Moving-Picture Cartoons

ANIONS

Morton, Maurice, ed. Anionic Polymerization. LC 82-11627. 268p. 1983. 39.00 (ISBN 0-12-508080-8). Acad Pr.

Smirnov, B. M. Negative Ions. 1982. 58.50 (ISBN 0-07-058447-8). McGraw.

ANNALS

see History

ANNIHILATION, POSITRON

see Positron Annihilation

ANNIVERSARIES

see also Days; Festivals; Holidays

also subdivision Anniversaries, etc. under names of individuals, e.g. Lincoln, Abraham, Pres. U. S. Anniversaries, etc.

Gregory, Ruth W. Anniversaries & Holidays. 4th ed. 1983. pap. text ed. price not set (ISBN 0-8389-0389-4). ALA.

Pichaske, David R. The Jubilee Diary: April 10, 1980-April 19, 1981. (Illus.). 240p. (Orig.). 1982. pap. 5.95 (ISBN 0-686-81707-9). Ellis Pr.

ANNUALS

see Almanacs; Calendars; Yearbooks

ANNUITIES

see also Interest and Usury-Tables, Etc.; Pensions; also subdivisions Pensions and Salaries, Pensions, etc. under appropriate subjects, e.g. Teachers-Salaries, Pensions, etc.

Donald, D. W. Compound Interest & Annuities--Certain. 1975. 21.50 (ISBN 0-434-90366-3, Pub. by Heinemann). David & Charles.

ANOMALIES, CONGENITAL

see Abnormalities, Human

ANOMY

Shoham, S. Giora, ed. Alienation & Anomie Revisited. Grahame, Anthony. 280p. (Orig.). 1982. pap. text ed. 23.50x (ISBN 0-911378-44-8). Sheridan.

Thom, Gary B. The Human Nature of Social Maladies: Alienation, Anomie, Ambivalence. 200p. 1983. text ed. 23.95x (ISBN 0-86598-105-1). Allanheld.

--The Human Nature of Social Maladies: Alienation, Anomie, Ambivalence. 200p. 1983. text ed. 23.95x (ISBN 0-86598-105-1). Rowman.

ANONYMS AND PSEUDONYMS

Marble, Annie R. Pen Names & Personalities. 256p. 1983. Repr. of 1930 ed. lib. bdg. 40.00 (ISBN 0-89984-824-9). Century Bookbindery.

ANOREXIA

see Appetite

ANOREXIA NERVOSA

Landau, Elaine. Why Are They Starving Themselves? Understanding Anorexia Nervosa & Bulimia. 128p. (gr. 9-12). 1983. PLB 9.29 (ISBN 0-671-45582-6). Messner.

Levenkron, Stephen. Treating & Overcoming Anorexia Nervosa. 224p. 1983. pap. 3.50 (ISBN 0-446-90982-3). Warner Bks.

Wilson, C. Philip. The Fear of Being Fat: The Treatment of Anorexia Nervosa & Bulimia. LC 82-11338. 544p. 1983. write for info. (ISBN 0-87668-480-0). Aronson.

ANOREXIGENIC AGENTS

see Weight Reducing Preparations

ANOXEMIA

Sutton, John R. & Houston, Charles S., eds. Hypoxia: Man at Altitude. LC 81-84773. (Illus., Orig.). 1982. pap. text ed. 24.95 (ISBN 0-86577-048-4). Thieme-Stratton.

ANSELM, SAINT, ARCHBISHOP OF CANTERBURY, 1033-1109

Anselm Studies: An Occasional Journal. (Orig.). 1983. lib. bdg. 30.00 (ISBN 0-527-03662-5). Kraus Intl.

Evans, Gillian, ed. St. Anselm, Archbishop of Canterbury: A Concordance to the Works of St. Anselm, 4 vols. LC 82-48973. (Orig.). 1983. Set. lib. bdg. 325.00 (ISBN 0-527-03661-7). Kraus Intl.

ANSWERS TO QUESTIONS

see Questions and Answers

ANT

see Ants

ANTARCTIC REGIONS

see also Scientific Expeditions

also names of exploring expeditions, and names of explorers

Adams, Richard & Lockley, Ronald. Voyage Through the Antarctic. LC 82-48484. (Illus.). 160p. 1982. 13.95 (ISBN 0-394-52858-1). Knopf.

Barnes, James N. Let's Save Antarctica! (Illus.). 112p. 1983. pap. 6.95 (ISBN 0-87663-581-8). Universe.

ANTEDILUVIAN ANIMALS

see Paleontology

ANTENNAS (ELECTRONICS)

Brown, R. G., et al. Lines, Waves & Antennas: The Transmission of Electric Energy. 2nd ed. (Illus.). 471p. 1973. text ed. 22.50 (ISBN 0-8260-1431-3). Wiley.

Jasik, Henry & Johnson, Richard C. Antenna Engineering Handbook. 1408p. 1984. 96.00 (ISBN 0-07-032291-0). McGraw.

Noll, Edward M. Dipole & Longwire Antennas. 1969. pap. 7.50 (ISBN 0-672-24006-8). Sams.

ANTHEMS, NATIONAL

see National Songs

ANTHOLOGIES

see also Readers

Foreman, Dave & Koehler, Bart, eds. Don't Fence Me in: A Wilderness Campfire Anthology. Spurs, Jackson. (A Ned Ludd Book). (Illus.). 400p. (Orig.). Date not set. pap. price not set (ISBN 0-942688-03-1). Dream Garden.

Laughlin, J. & Glassgold, Peter, eds. New Directions Forty-Six. LC 37-1751. 192p. 1983. 17.25 (ISBN 0-8112-0865-6); pap. 8.75 (ISBN 0-8112-0866-4, NDP553). New Directions.

Santerre, Richard, ed. Anthologie, 9 Vols. (Litterature Franco-Americaine de la Nouvelle-Angle Terre Ser.). (Fr.). (gr. 10 up). 1981. pap. text ed. 49.50x (ISBN 0-911409-24-6). Natl Mat Dev.

Taft, Michael. Blues Lyric Poetry: An Anthology. LC 82-48266. 500p. 1983. lib. bdg. 75.00 (ISBN 0-686-42832-3). Garland Pub.

Vinz, Mark & Ray, Grayce, eds. Dakota Territory: A Ten Year Anthology. 147p. 1982. pap. 9.75 (ISBN 0-911042-26-1). N Dak Inst.

ANTHRACITE COAL

see Coal

ANTHROPO-GEOGRAPHY

see also Geography, Political; Geopolitics; Human Ecology; Man-Influence of Environment; Regionalism

Aikens, C. Melvin. Fremont-Promontory-Plains Relationships in Northern Utah. (University of Utah Anthropological Papers: No. 82). 112p. 1966. pap. 10.00x (ISBN 0-87480-213-X). U of Utah Pr.

FLowerdew, Robin, ed. Institutions & Geographical Patterns. LC 82-42541. 352p. 1982. 27.50x (ISBN 0-312-41886-8). St Martin.

Man, Location & Behavior: An Introduction to Human Geography. LC 72-4790. 414p. Repr. of 1972 ed. text ed. 18.95 (ISBN 0-471-18150-1). Krieger.

Rubenstein, James. The Cultural Landscape: An Introduction to Human Geography. (Illus.). 500p. 1983. text ed. 19.95 (ISBN 0-314-69674-1); instrs.' manual avail. (ISBN 0-314-71118-X). West Pub.

ANTHROPOGEOGRAPHY-AFRICA

Udo, Reuden K. The Human Geography of Tropical Africa. 256p. 1982. pap. 39.00x (ISBN 0-435-95919-0, Pub. by Heinemann England). State Mutual Bk.

ANTHROPOLOGY

see also Age Groups; Anthropo-Geography; Archaeology; Color of Man; Educational Anthropology; Ethnology; Ethnopsychology; Language and Languages; Man; Medical Anthropology; Nomads; Physical Anthropology; Social Change; Women also names of races, tribes etc., and subdivision Race Question under names of countries, e.g. United States-Race Question

Alland, Alexander, Jr. To Be Human: An Introduction to Anthropology. LC 79-19497. 657p. 1980. text ed. 20.95 (ISBN 0-471-01747-7); tchrs' ed 7.00 (ISBN 0-471-06054-2). Wiley.

American Museum of Natural History, New York. The New Catalog of the American Museum of Natural History. 1983. lib. bdg. 1300.00 (ISBN 0-8161-0274-0, Hall Library). G K Hall.

Beddoe, John. The Anthropological History Europe. 1982. 20.00 (ISBN 0-941694-07-0). Inst Study Man.

Bloch, Maurice. Marxism & Anthropology. (Illus.). 1982. 18.95x (ISBN 0-19-876091-4). Oxford U Pr.

Buck, Peter H. Anthropology & Religion. 1939. text ed. 11.50x (ISBN 0-686-83471-2). Elliots Bks.

Ferris, William. Afro-American Folk Art & Crafts. (Illus.). 444p. 1983. lib. bdg. 39.95 (ISBN 0-8161-9045-3, Univ Bks). G K Hall.

Field, Henrey. The Track of Man, Adventures of an Anthropologist: Volume 2: The White House Years, 1941-1945. 134p. 10.95 (ISBN 0-686-84234-0). Banyan Bks.

Fleure, H. J. & Peake, Harold. Hunters & Artists. (Corridors of Time Ser.: No. 2). 1927. text ed. 24.50x (ISBN 0-686-83573-5). Elliots Bks.

--Merchant Ventures in Bronze. (Corridors of Time Ser.: No. 7). 1931. text ed. 24.50x (ISBN 0-686-83625-1). Elliots Bks.

--Peasants & Potters. (Corridors of Time Ser.: No. 3). 1927. text ed. 24.50x (ISBN 0-686-83689-8). Elliots Bks.

--Steppe & the Sown. (Corridors of Time Ser.: No.5). 1928. text ed. 24.50x (ISBN 0-686-83785-1). Elliots Bks.

--Way of the Sea. (Corridors of Time Ser.: No. 6). 1929. text ed. 24.50x (ISBN 0-686-83850-5). Elliots Bks.

Freeman, Derek. Margaret Mead & Samoa: The Making & Unmaking of an Anthropological Byth. (Illus.). 416p. 1983. 25.00 (ISBN 0-674-54830-2). Harvard U Pr.

Hodder, Ian. The Present Past: An Introduction to Anthropology for Archaeologists. LC 82-17437. (Illus.). 240p. 1983. text ed. 22.50x (ISBN 0-87663-736-5). Universe.

Holz, Harald. Anthropodizee: Zur Inkarnation von Vernunft in Geschichte. 555p. Date not set. price not set (ISBN 3-8204-5823-9). P Lang Pubs.

International Committee for Social Science Information & Documentation (UNESCO), ed. International Bibliography of Social & Cultural Anthropology - Bibliographie Internationale D'Anthropologie Sociale et Culturelie, Vol. 24. LC 58-4366. (International Bibliogaraphy of the Social Sciences - Bibliographie Internationale des Sciences Sociales). 393p. 1981. 90.00x (ISBN 0-422-80930-6). Intl Pubns Serv.

Kearney, Michael. World View. Langness, L. L. & Edgerton, Robert B., eds. (Publications in Anthropology & Related Fields Ser.). (Illus.). 256p. (Orig.). 1983. pap. text ed. 7.95x (ISBN 0-88316-551-1). Chandler & Sharp.

Launay, Robert. Traders Without Trade: Responses to Change in Two Dyula Communities. LC 82-4500. (Cambridge Studies in Social Anthropology: No. 42). 196p. 1983. 34.50 (ISBN 0-521-24179-0). Cambridge U Pr.

Levi-Strauss, Claude. Structural Anthropology, Vol. 2. Layton, Monique, tr. LC 82-16115. xvi, 384p. 1976. pap. 10.95 (ISBN 0-226-47491-7). U of Chicago Pr.

Parkin, David, ed. Semantic Anthropology. Date not set. 30.00 (ISBN 0-12-545180-6). Acad Pr.

Peake, Harold & Fleure, H. J. Apes & Men. 1927. text ed. 24.50x (ISBN 0-686-83473-9). Elliots Bks.

Shackley, Myra. Still Living. (Illus.). 1983. 16.95 (ISBN 0-500-01298-9). Thames Hudson.

Skorupski, John. Symbol & Theory: A Philosophical Study of Theories of Religion in Social Anthropology. LC 76-3037. 280p. Date not set. pap. 10.95 (ISBN 0-521-27252-1). Cambridge U Pr.

Waters, Donald J. Strange Ways & Sweet Dreams: Afro-American Folklore from the Hampton Institute. 466p. 1983. lib. bdg. 49.95 (ISBN 0-8161-9022-4, Univ Bks). G K Hall.

ANTHROPOLOGY, BIBLICAL

see Man (Theology)

ANTHROPOLOGY, PHILOSOPHIC

see Philosophical Anthropology

ANTHROPOLOGY, PHILOSOPHICAL

see Philosophical Anthropology

ANTHROPOLOGY, PHYSICAL

see Physical Anthropology

ANTHROPOLOGY, THEOLOGICAL

see Man (Theology)

ANTHROPOLOGY, URBAN

see Urban Anthropology

ANTHROPONOMY

see Names, Personal

ANTHROPOPHAGY

see Cannibalism

ANTHROPOSOPHY

see also Karma; Reincarnation; Theosophy

Edmunds, L. Francis. Anthroposophy, a Way of Life. 1982. 35.00x (ISBN 0-903580-65-9, Pub. by Element Bks). State Mutual Bk.

--Anthroposophy as a Healing Force. 14p. Date not set. pap. 2.25 (ISBN 0-88010-037-0, Pub.by Steinerbooks). Anthroposophic.

Emmichoven, F. W. The Anthroposophical Understanding of the Soul. Schwarzkopf, Friedemann, tr. from Ger. 170p. (Orig.). 1983. pap. 8.95 (ISBN 0-88010-019-2). Anthroposophic.

Raab, Rex & Klingborg, Arne. Eloquent Concrete: How Rudolf Steiner Employed Reinforced Concrete. (Illus.). 141p. 1979. pap. 19.95 (ISBN 0-85440-354-X, Pub. by Steinerbooks). Anthroposophic.

Social Understanding Through Spiritual Scientific Knowledge. 20p. 1982. pap. 1.95 (ISBN 0-88010-075-3). Anthroposohic.

Steiner, Rudolf. The Being of Man & His Future Evolution. Wehrle, Pauline, tr. from Ger. 148p. 1981. 18.00 (ISBN 0-85440-402-3, Pub. by Steinerbooks); pap. 11.95 (ISBN 0-85440-405-8). Anthroposophic.

--The Constitution of the School of Spiritual Science. 2nd ed. Adams, George & Rudel, Joan, trs. from Ger. 78p. 1980. pap. 5.00 (ISBN 0-88010-039-7, Pub. by Anthroposophical Society London). Anthroposophic.

--The Dead Are with Us. Osmond, D. S., tr. from Ger. 32p. 1973. pap. 2.50 (ISBN 0-85440-274-8, Pub. by Steinerbooks). Anthroposophic.

--The Etherisation of the Blood: The Entry of the Etheric Christ into the Evolution of the Earth. 4th ed. Freeman, Arnold & Osmond, D. S., trs. from Ger. 42p. 1980. pap. 2.95 (ISBN 0-85440-248-9, Pub. by Steinerbooks). Anthroposophic.

--The Festival & Their Meaning. 399p. 1981. 21.00 (ISBN 0-85440-370-1, Pub. by Steinerbooks); pap. 15.00 (ISBN 0-85440-380-9). Anthroposophic.

--The Foundation Stone. 72p. 1979. pap. 5.50 (ISBN 0-85440-346-9, Pub. by Steinerbooks). Anthroposophic.

--The Inner Aspect of the Social Question. Davy, Charles, tr. from Ger. 72p. 1974. pap. 3.95 (ISBN 0-85440-050-8, Pub. by Steinerbooks). Anthroposophic.

--Jesus & Christ. Bledsoe, John, tr. from Ger. 23p. 1976. pap. 1.50 (ISBN 0-88010-042-7). Anthroposophic.

Unger, Carl. Life Forces from Anthroposophy. 1982. pap. 1.95 (ISBN 0-916786-63-3). St George Bk Serv.

Witzenmann, Herbert. Beppe Assenza. (Illus.). 160p. 1979. 29.95 (ISBN 0-85440-340-X, Pub. by Steinerbooks). Anthroposophic.

ANTI-COLONIALISM

see Colonies

ANTI-CORROSIVE PAINT

see Corrosion and Anti-Corrosives

ANTI-DISCRIMINATION LAWS

see Race Discrimination

ANTI-INFECTIVE AGENTS

see also Antibiotics; Chemotherapy

Kuemmerle. Antimicrobial Chemotherapy. 1983. price not set (ISBN 0-86577-082-4). Thieme-Stratton.

ANTI LANGUAGE

see Campa Language

ANTI-OBESITY DRUGS

see Weight Reducing Preparations

ANTI-POVERTY PROGRAMS

see Economic Assistance, Domestic

ANTI-REFORMATION

see Counter-Reformation

ANTIBACTERIAL AGENTS

see Anti-Infective Agents

ANTIBIOTICS

Berdy, Janos. Antibiotics from Higher Forms of Life: Higher Plants, Vol. VIII. (CRC Handbook of Antibiotic Compounds Ser.). 248p. 1982. 64.00 (ISBN 0-8493-3460-8). CRC Pr.

Berdy, Janos, ed. Antibiotics from Higher Forms of Life: Lichens, Algae, & Animal Organisms, Vol. IX. (CRC Handbook of Antibiotic Compounds Ser.). 248p. 1982. 44.00 (ISBN 0-8493-3461-6). CRC Pr.

Bilai, V. I. Antibiotic Producing Microscopic Fungi. 1963. 19.50 (ISBN 0-444-40054-0). Elsevier.

Eickenberg, H. U., ed. The Influence of Antibiotics on the Host-Parasite Relationship. (Illus.). 270p. 1982. pap. 25.00 (ISBN 0-387-11680-X). Springer-Verlag.

Emmerson, A. M. The Microbiology & Treatment of Life-Threatening Infections. (Antimicrobial Chemotherapy Ser.). 175p. 1982. 31.95 (ISBN 0-471-90049-4, Pub. by Res Stud Pr). Wiley.

Gause, G. F. Search for New Antibiotics: Problems & Perspectives. 1960. text ed. 29.50x (ISBN 0-686-83732-0). Elliots Bks.

Glasby, John S. Encyclopedia of Antibiotics. 2nd ed. LC 78-13356. 467p. 1979. 92.00x (ISBN 0-471-99722-6, Pub. by Wiley-Interscience). Wiley.

Greenwood, David. Antibiotics of the Beta-Lactam Group. (Antimicrobial Chemotherapy Research Studies). 84p. 1982. 19.95 (ISBN 0-471-10473-6, Pub by Res Stud Pr). Wiley.

Gregory, G. I. Recent Advances in the Chemistry of B-Lactam Antibiotics. 388p. 1982. 69.00x (ISBN 0-85186-815-0, Pub. by Royal Soc Chem England). State Mutual Bk.

Russell, A. D. & Quesnel, Louis B., eds. Antibiotics: Assessment of Antimicrobial Activity & Resistance. (Society for Applied Bacteriology Tech. Ser.: No. 18). Date not set. price not set (ISBN 0-12-604480-5). Acad Pr.

Sabath, L. D. Action of Antibiotics in Patients. (Illus.). 250p. (Orig.). 1982. pap. text ed. 25.50 (ISBN 3-456-81228-0, Pub by Hans Huber Switzerland). J K Burgess.
Umezawa, H. & Hooper, I. R., eds. Aminoglycoside Antibiotics. (Handbook of Experimental Pharmacology Ser.: Vol. 62). (Illus.). 400p. 1982. 125.00 (ISBN 0-387-11532-3). Springer-Verlag.
Van Furth, R. Developments in Antibiotic Treatment of Respiratory Infections. 1982. 39.50 (ISBN 90-247-2493-7, Pub by Martinus Nijhoff Netherlands). Kluwer Boston.

ANTIBIOTICS RESISTANCE IN MICRO-ORGANISMS
see Drug Resistance in Micro-Organisms

ANTIBODIES
see Immunoglobulins

ANTICHRIST
Soloviev, Vladimir. The Antichrist. 1982. pap. 5.50 (ISBN 0-86315-501-4). St George Bk Serv.

ANTIETAM, BATTLE OF, 1862
Sears, Stephen. Landscape Turned Red: The Battle of Antietam. LC 82-19519. (Illus.). 416p. 1983. 17.95 (ISBN 0-89919-172-X). Ticknor & Fields.

ANTIGENS
see also Immunoglobulins
Wachtel, Stephen, ed. H-Y Antigen & the Biology of Sex Determination. Date not set. price not set (ISBN 0-8089-1514-2). Grune.

ANTIMICROBIAL AGENTS
see Anti-Infective Agents

ANTIMILITARISM
see Militarism

ANTINEOPLASTIC AGENTS
Bardos, T. J. & Kalman, T. I., eds. New Approaches to the Design of Antineoplastic Agents. 344p. Date not set. p.n.s. (ISBN 0-444-00724-5, Biomedical Pr). Elsevier.
Colowich, Sidney P. & Kaplan, Nathan O., eds. Methods in Enzymology: Vol. 93, Pt. F: Immunochemical Techniques, Conventional Antibodies, FC Receptors & Cytotoxicity. 393p. 1983. price not set (ISBN 0-12-181993-0). Acad Pr.
Laszlo, John. Antiemetics & Cancer Chemotherapy. (Illus.). 200p. 1982. pap. 19.95 (ISBN 0-683-04899-6). Williams & Wilkins.

ANTIOCH
Brown, Raymond & Meier, John. Antioch & Rome. 256p. 1983. 8.95 (ISBN 0-8091-0339-7); pap. 4.95 (ISBN 0-8091-2532-3). Paulist Pr.

ANTIQUE COLLECTING
see Antiques

ANTIQUES
Here are entered works on old decorative or utilitarian objects having aesthetic, historic and financial value. Works on decorative art objects are entered under Art Objects.
see also Art Objects;
also particular kinds of antique objects, especially the subdivisions Catalogs, Collectors and Collecting or Exhibitions when they occur under such objects, e.g. Kitchen Utensils; Firearms–Catalogs; Glassware–Collectors and Collecting; Furniture–Exhibitions
Barlow, Ronald S. How to be Successful in the Antique Business. (Illus.). 256p. 1982. pap. 6.95 (ISBN 0-686-83705-3, ScribT). Scribner.
Boram, Clifford. How to Get Parts Cast for Your Antique Stove. 5.00 (ISBN 0-686-38103-3). Autonomy Hse.
Curtis, Tony, ed. Lyle Official Antiques Review, 1983. (Illus.). 1983. 24.95. Apollo.
Emmerling, Mary & Trask, Richard. Collecting American Country: A Style & Source Book. (Illus.). 1983. 35.00 (ISBN 0-517-54957-3, C N Potter Bks). Crown.
Ferguson & King. Guide to Antique Shops in Britain 1983. (Illus.). 1983. 16.00. Apollo.
Grotz, George. Grotz's Decorative Collectibles Price Guide. LC 82-45288. (Illus.). 256p. 1983. pap. 14.95 (ISBN 0-385-17870-0, Dolp). Doubleday.
Luckey, Carl F. Collecting Antique American Bird Decoys: Identification & Value Guide. (Illus.). 208p. 1983. pap. 14.95 (ISBN 0-89689-043-0). Bks Americana.
McKeown, James M. & McKeown, Joan C. Price Guide to Antique & Classic Still Cameras, 1983-1984. (Illus., Orig.). 1983. pap. 15.95 (ISBN 0-931838-05-3). Centennial Photo Serv.
Miller's Antique Price Guide. 1982. 22.50 (ISBN 0-686-43136-7). Apollo.
The Official Antiques Encyclopedia. 1st ed. LC 82-82659. 544p. 1983. 9.95 (ISBN 0-87637-365-1). Hse of Collectibles.
The Official Guide to Buying & Selling Antiques. 1st ed. LC 82-84643. 544p. 1983. 9.95 (ISBN 0-87637-369-4). Hse of Collectibles.
The Official 1984 Price Guide to Antiques & Other Collectibles. 4th ed. LC 80-84705. 768p. 1983. 9.95 (ISBN 0-87637-374-0). Hse of Collectibles.
Rinker, Harry L., ed. Warman's Antiques & Their Prices. 17th ed. LC 79-4331. (Illus.). 712p. 1983. pap. 10.95 (ISBN 0-911594-03-5). Warman.
Schroeder's Antiques Price Guide. 608p. Date not set. 9.95 (ISBN 0-89145-213-3). Collector Bks.
Vonk. Art & Antique World Wide. 1981. 35.00 (ISBN 90-7041-371-X). Apollo.
Voss, Thomas M. Antique American Country Furniture. LC 82-48009. (Illus.). 384p. 1983. pap. 7.95 (ISBN 0-06-464061-2, BN 4061). B&N NY.

ANTIQUES–COLLECTORS AND COLLECTING
see Antiques

ANTIQUITIES, BIBLICAL
see Bible–Antiquities

ANTIQUITIES, GRECIAN
see Greece–Antiquities

ANTIQUITIES, INDUSTRIAL
see Industrial Archaeology

ANTIQUITIES, PREHISTORIC
see Man, Prehistoric

ANTIQUITIES, ROMAN
see Rome–Antiquities; Rome (City)–Antiquities

ANTIQUITY OF MAN
see Man–Origin

ANTISEMITISM
Grosser, Paul E. & Halperin, Edwin G. The Causes & Effects of Anti-Semitism. 1983. 15.00 (ISBN 0-8022-2418-0). Philos Lib.
Martire. Antisemitism in the U. S. A. Study of Prejudice in the 1980's. 188p. 1982. 23.95 (ISBN 0-03-061907-6). Praeger.
Poliakov, Leon. The History of Anti-Semitism, Vol.IV: Suicidal Europe, Eighteen-Seventy-Nineteen Thirty-Three. (Anti-Semitism Ser.). 528p. 1983. 17.50 (ISBN 0-8149-0863-2). Vanguard.

ANTISLAVERY
see Slavery

ANTITANK WARFARE
see Tank Warfare

ANTITOXINS
see Toxins and Antitoxins

ANTITRUST LAW
see also Corporation Law
Breit, William & Elzinga, Kenneth G. The Antitrust Casebook. 400p. 1982. text ed. 16.95 (ISBN 0-03-060147-9). Dryden Pr.
Hawk, Barry E. United States Antitrust Laws & Multinational Business. (Seven Springs Studies). 1982. pap. 3.00 (ISBN 0-943006-06-6). Seven Springs.
Mueller, Rudolf & Schneider, Hannes. The German Antitrust Law. 296p. 1981. 77.00x (ISBN 0-7121-5481-7, Pub. by Macdonald & Evans). State Mutual Bk.
Oppenheim, S. Chesterfield & Shields, Carrington. Newspapers & the Antitrust Laws. 531p. 1982. 35.00 (ISBN 0-87215-476-9). Michie-Bobbs.
Seplaki, Les. Antitrust & the Economics of the Market Text, Readings, Cases. 640p. (Orig.). 1982. pap. text ed. 15.95 (ISBN 0-686-83984-6). HarBraceJ.
Shepard. Antitrust & American Business Abroad. 2nd ed. 1981. 120.00 (ISBN 0-07-002435-9). McGraw.
Siena, James V., ed. Antitrust & Local Government. LC 82-16825. 224p. 1982. text ed. 32.95 (ISBN 0-932020-16-X); pap. text ed. 19.95 (ISBN 0-932020-17-8). Seven Locks Pr.
Stigler, George. The Organization of Industry. LC 82-20013. viii, 328p. 1968. pap. 10.95 (ISBN 0-226-77432-5). U of Chicago Pr.

ANTIVIVISECTION
see Vivisection

ANTLIATA
see Diptera

ANTS
Buckley, R. Ant-Plant Interactions in Australia. 1982. text ed. 54.50 (ISBN 90-6193-684-5, Pub. by Junk Pubs Netherlands). Kluwer Boston.
Moody, J. V. & Francke, O. F. The Ants (Hymenoptera, Formicidae) of Western Texas: Part I - Subfamily Myrmicinae. (Graduate Studies Ser.: No. 27). 80p. (Orig.). 1982. pap. 12.00 (ISBN 0-89672-107-8). Tex Tech Pr.

ANUS PRETERNATURAL
see Colostomy

ANXIETY
see also Fear; Obsessive-Compulsive Neuroses
Clarke, J. Christopher & Jackson, Arthur. Hypnosis & Behavior Therapy: The Treatment of Anxiety & Phobias. 1983. text ed. price not set (ISBN 0-8261-3450-5). Springer Pub.
Demaray, Donald E. Watch Out For Burnout: Its Signs, Prevention, & Cure. 112p. (Orig.). 1983. pap. 4.95. Baker Bk.
Drews, Toby R. Get Rid of Anxiety & Stress. 1982. pap. 4.95 (ISBN 0-88270-537-7). Bridge Pub.
Guide to Cope System. 50p. 1982. pap. 2.00 (ISBN 0-686-37415-0). Ideals PA.
Krohne, H. W. Achievement, Stress & Anxiety. 1981. 34.50 (ISBN 0-07-035521-5). McGraw.
Ottens, Allen J. Coping with Academic Anxiety. (Personal Adjustment Ser.). 140p. 1983. lib. bdg. 7.97 (ISBN 0-8239-0607-8). Rosen Pr.
Rogers, Michael. How to Overcome Nervousness. 22p. 1973. pap. 1.95 (ISBN 0-88010-051-6, Pub. by New Knowledge Bks England). Anthroposophic.
Schwarzwer, R., et al. Advances in Test Anxiety Research, Vol. 1. xii, 176p. 1982. pap. text ed. 19.95 (ISBN 0-89859-256-9). L Erlbaum Assocs.
Spielberger, C. D., et al. Stress & Anxiety, Vol. 8. 1981. 34.95 (ISBN 0-07-060239-5). McGraw.
Zuckerman, Marvin, ed. Biological Bases for Sensation Seeking, Impulsivity & Anxiety. 320p. 1983. text ed. write for info. (ISBN 0-89859-255-0). L Erlbaum Assocs.

AORTIC REGURGITATION
see Heart–Diseases

APACHE INDIANS
see Indians of North America–Southwest, New

APARTHEID
see Segregation; South Africa–Race Question

APARTMENT HOUSES
see also Condominium (Housing); Landlord and Tenant; Real Estate Management
Coughlan, Bill & Franke, Monte. Going CO-OP: The Complete Guide to Buying & Owning Your Own Apartment. LC 82-72501. 224p. 1983. 14.42 (ISBN 0-8070-0868-0); pap. 7.21 (ISBN 0-8070-0869-9). Beacon Pr.

APHASIA
Schuell, Hildred. Aphasia Theory & Therapy: Selected Lectures & Papers of Hildred Schuell. 2nd ed. Sies, Luther F., ed. LC 82-20228. (Illus.). 344p. 1983. pap. text ed. 12.25 (ISBN 0-8191-2768-X). U Pr of Amer.

APHORISMS AND APOTHEGMS
see also Proverbs; Quotations
Gross, John, compiled by. The Oxford Book of Aphorisms. 320p. 1983. 15.95 (ISBN 0-19-214111-2). Oxford U Pr.
Hubbard, L. Ron. When in Doubt, Communicate... Minshull, Ruth & Lefson, Edward, eds. 150p. (Orig.). 1982. pap. cancelled (ISBN 0-937922-08-0). SAA Pub.

APHRODISIACS
Hill, Eric. The Aphrodisiac Gourmet. (Illus.). 136p. 1983. pap. 3.95 (ISBN 0-931290-74-0). Aries Pub.

APICULTURE
see Bee Culture

APOCALYPTIC LITERATURE
Beskow, Per. Strange Tales About Jesus: A Survey of Unfamiliar Gospels. LC 82-16001. 144p. 1983. pap. 6.95 (ISBN 0-8006-1686-3, 1-1686). Fortress.

APOLOGETICS
see also Analogy (Religion); Bible–Evidences, Authority, etc.; Faith and Reason; Religion and Science; Theodicy; Witness Bearing (Christianity) also subdivision Doctrinal and Controversial works under names of particuliar denominations, and also subdivision Apologetic Works under religious denominations, e.g. Catholic Church–Apologetic Works
Dyrness, William A. Christian Apologetics in a World Community. LC 82-21383. 180p. 1983. pap. 5.95 (ISBN 0-87784-399-6). Inter-Varsity.
Geffre, Claude & Jossua, Jean-pierre, eds. True & False Universality of Christianity. (Concilium Ser.: Vol. 135). 128p. (Orig.). 1980. pap. 5.95 (ISBN 0-8164-2277-X). Seabury.

APOLOGETICS, JEWISH
see Judaism

APOSTLES
Cross, L. S. Paul's Letters Made Easy for Devotions. 120p. (Orig.). 1982. pap. 4.95 (ISBN 0-89221-090-7, Pub by SonLife). New Leaf.
McIntyre, William. Christ's Cabinet. Rev. ed. 143p. 1982. Repr. of 1937 ed. 2.95 (ISBN 0-86544-017-4). Salvation Army.
Quadflieg, Josef. The Twelve Apostles. O'Connell, Matthew J., tr. from Ger. (Illus.). 156p. (Orig.). (gr. 5-6). 1982. 8.95 (ISBN 0-916134-49-0). Pueblo Pub CO.
Vale, Eugene. The Thirteenth Apostle. 352p. 1983. pap. 7.95 (ISBN 0-9609674-0-0). Jubilee Pr.

APOSTLES–ART
Ness, Gladys M. Jesus & the Twelve in 30 A. D. 64p. 1983. 6.95 (ISBN 0-8059-2863-4). Dorrance.

APOSTLES' CREED
Packer, J. I. The Apostle's Creed. 1983. pap. 3.95 (ISBN 0-8423-0051-1); Leader's Guide 2.95 (ISBN 0-8423-0052-X). Tyndale.

APOTHEGMS
see Aphorisms and Apothegms

APPALACHIAN DULCIMER
see Dulcimer

APPALACHIAN MOUNTAINS
An Appalachian Studies Teacher's Manual. 283p. 1981. pap. 10.00 (ISBN 0-9606832-1-6). Children's Mus.
Batteau, Allen, ed. Applachia & America: Autonomy & Regional Dependence. LC 82-40462. (Illus.). 296p. 1983. 26.00x (ISBN 0-8131-1480-2). U Pr of Ky.
Farr, Sidney S. More than Moonshine: Appalachian Recipes & Recollections. LC 82-13524. 176p. 1983. 11.95 (ISBN 0-8229-3475-2); pap. 4.95 (ISBN 0-8229-5347-1). U of Pittsburgh Pr.
Kelly, James C. & Baker, William C. The Sword of the Lord & Gideon. LC 80-15899. 1980. pap. 2.95 (ISBN 0-686-37452-5). Appalach Consortium.
Manning, Robert E., ed. Mountain Passages: An Appalachia Anthology. (Illus.). 320p. (Orig.). 1983. pap. 9.95 (ISBN 0-910146-43-8). Appalach Mtn.
Murray, Kenneth. Down to Earth: People of Appalachia. 2nd ed. LC 74-6233. 1974. pap. 5.95 (ISBN 0-686-37451-7). Appalach Consortium.
Raitz, Karl B. & Ulack, Richard. Land, People, & Development in Appalachia. 375p. 1983. lib. bdg. 30.00x (ISBN 0-86531-075-0). Westview.
Whisnant, David E. Modernizing the Mountainer. LC 81-15911. 1980. pap. 8.95 (ISBN 0-686-37450-9). Appalach Consortium.

APPARATUS, ELECTRICAL
see Electric Apparatus and Appliances

APPARATUS, MEDICAL
see Medical Instruments and Apparatus

APPARATUS, PHYSIOLOGICAL
see Physiological Apparatus

APPARATUS, SCIENTIFIC
see Scientific Apparatus and Instruments

APPARITIONS
see also Demonology; Ghosts; Miracles; Poltergeists; Spiritualism; Visions
MacKenzie, Andrew. Hauntings & Apparitions. 12p. 1982. 40.00x (ISBN 0-434-44051-5, Pub. by Heinemann England). State Mutual Bk.

APPEAL
see Appellate Procedure

APPEL, KAREL, 1921-
Leavitt, Thomas. Karel Appel, West Coast Exhibition 1961-1962. (Illus.). 23p. 1962. 3.00x (ISBN 0-686-99844-8). La Jolla Mus Contemp Art.

APPELLATE PROCEDURE
see also Appellate Procedure; Civil Procedure; Pleading; Trial Practice
MacCrate, Robert & Hopkins, James D. Appelate Justice in New York. LC 82-72701. (Orig.). 1982. pap. 6.95 (ISBN 0-938870-27-0, 8571). Am Judicature.

APPETITE
see also Anorexia Nervosa; Diet; Hunger
Rahamimoff, P. & Harell, Moshe. Appetite & Lack of Appetite in Infancy & Early Childhood. 179p. 1979. 15.00x (ISBN 0-87397-146-9). Strode.

APPETIZERS
see Cookery (Appetizers); Cookery (Relishes)

APPLIANCES, ELECTRIC
see Electric Apparatus and Appliances

APPLICATIONS FOR POSITIONS
see also Employment Interviewing; Resumes (Employment)
Croft, Barbara L. The Checklist Kit for Resume Writing & Job Application Letters. 16p. 1982. 3.50 (ISBN 0-9609580-0-2). Different Drum.
Price, Jonathan. How to Find Work. 267p. 1983. pap. 3.50 (ISBN 0-451-12070-1, Sig). NAL.

APPLIED ART
see Art Industries and Trade

APPLIED MECHANICS
see Mechanics, Applied

APPLIED PSYCHOLOGY
see Psychology, Applied

APPLIED SCIENCE
see Technology

APPLIQUE
Patera, Charlotte. Cutwork Applique: Making Ornamental Fabric Designs. (Illus.). 168p. 1983. pap. 12.95 (ISBN 0-8329-0271-3). New Century.

APPORTIONMENT (ELECTION LAW)
see also Election Districts
Jewell, Malcolm E., ed. The Politics of Reapportionment. LC 82-18695. (The Atherton Press Political Science Ser.). xii, 334p. 1982. Repr. of 1962 ed. lib. bdg. 39.75x (ISBN 0-313-23317-9, JERA). Greenwood.

APPRAISAL
see Assessment; Valuation

APPRAISAL OF BOOKS
see Bibliography–Best Books; Books and Reading; Criticism; Literature–History and Criticism

APPRECIATION OF ART
see Art Appreciation

APPRECIATION OF MUSIC
see Music–Analysis, Appreciation

APPREHENSION
see Perception

APPRENTICES
see also Employees, Training of
Gray, Lois S. & Beamesderfer, Alice O. Apprenticeship Training: Where Does It Stand Today? (Vital Issues, Vol. XXIX 1979-80: No. 5). 0.60 (ISBN 0-686-81610-2). Ctr Info Am.
Shanahan, William F. Arco's Guide to Apprenticeship Programs. (Arco Occupational Guides Ser.). 216p. 1983. lib. bdg. 12.95 (ISBN 0-668-05454-9); pap. 6.95 (ISBN 0-668-05461-1). Arco.

APPROXIMATE COMPUTATION
see also Perturbation (Mathematics)
Vichnevetsky, R. & Bowles, J. B. Fourier Analysis of Numerical Approximations of Hyperbolic Equations. LC 81-85699. (SIAM Studies in Applied Mathematics: No. 5). xii, 140p. 1982. 21.50 (ISBN 0-89871-181-9). Soc Indus Appl Math.

APPROXIMATION THEORY
see also Numerical Analysis; Perturbation (Mathematics)
Barroso, J. A., ed. Functional Analysis, Holomorphy & Approximation Theory: Proceedings of the Seminario de Analise Funcional, Holomorfia e Teoria da Approximacao, Universidade Federal do Rio de Janeiro, Aug. 4-8, 1980. (North Holland Mathematics Studies: Vol. 71). 486p. 1982. 63.75 (ISBN 0-444-86527-6, North Holland). Elsevier.
Prolla, J. B. Approximation Theory & Functional Analysis. (Proceedings). 1979. 64.00 (ISBN 0-444-85264-6). Elsevier.

APRAXIA
Perkins, William. Dysarthria & Apraxia: Current Therapy of Communication Disorders, Vol. 2. (Illus.). 128p. 1983. write for info. (ISBN 0-86577-086-7). Thieme-Stratton.

APTITUDE TESTS
see Ability–Testing

APULEIUS MADAURENSIS
Haight, Elizabeth H. Apuleius & His Influence. 190p. 1983. Repr. of 1927 ed. lib. bdg. 12.50 (ISBN 0-89760-369-9). Telegraph Bks.

AQUACULTURE
see also Fish-Culture

Fishelson, Lev. Tilapia in Aquaculture. (Illus.). 600p. pap. 69.00 (ISBN 0-86689-018-1). Balaban Intl Sci Serv.

Hambly, Barbara. The Walls of Air. 320p. (Orig.). 1983. pap. 2.95 (ISBN 0-345-29670-2, Del Rey). Ballantine.

Muir, James F. & Roberts, Ronald J., eds. Recent Advances in Aquaculture. 450p. 1982. lib. bdg. 49.7506679195x (ISBN 0-86531-464-0). Westview.

Pond, Wilson G. & Mumpton, Frederick A., eds. Zeo-Agriculture: The Use of Natural Zeolites in Agriculture & Aquaculture. 450p. 1983. lib. bdg. 50.00x (ISBN 0-86531-602-3). Westview.

AQUARIUM PLANTS

Schoitz & Dahlstrom. Collins Guide to Aquarium Fishes & Plants. 29.95 (ISBN 0-686-42787-4, Collins Pub England). Greene.

AQUARIUMS

see also Fish-Culture; Goldfish; Tropical Fish

Sterba, Gunther & Mills, Dick. The Aquarium Encyclopedia: Freshwater & Saltwater Fish & Plants. (Illus.). 608p. 1983. 35.00 (ISBN 0-262-19207-1). MIT Pr.

Videla, E., illus. Your First Aquarium. (Illus.). 32p. 1982. 3.95 (ISBN 0-87666-548-2, ST001). TFH Pubns.

AQUATIC BIRDS

see Water-Birds

AQUATIC CHEMISTRY

see Water Chemistry

AQUATIC ECOLOGY

see also Fresh-Water Ecology; Marine Ecology

Hynes. The Ecology of Running Waters. 580p. 1982. 60.00x (ISBN 0-85323-100-1, Pub. by Liverpool Univ England). State Mutual Bk.

Langford, T. E. Electricity Generation & the Ecology of Natural Waters. 376p. 1982. 90.00x (ISBN 0-85323-334-9, Pub. by Liverpool Univ England). State Mutual Bk.

Manual of Methods in Aquatic Environment Research: Toxicity Tests, Pt. 6. (FAO Fisheries Technical Papers: No. 185). 23p. 1982. pap. 7.50 (ISBN 92-5-101178-8, F2312, FAO). Unipub.

AQUATIC RESOURCES

see also Algae; Fisheries; Fishery Products; Marine Resources

Adams, V. Dean, ed. Aquatic Resources Management of the Colorado River Ecosystem. Lamarra, Vincent A. LC 82-72349. 400p. 1983. 29.95 (ISBN 0-686-84637-0). Ann Arbor Science.

AQUATIC SPORTS

see also Boats and Boating; Canoes and Canoeing; Fishing; Rowing; Sailing; Swimming; Yachts and Yachting

Action in Aquatics. 238p. 9.50 (ISBN 0-88314-005-5). AAHPERD.

David, Andrew. River Thrill Sports. LC 82-24966. (Superwheels & Thrill Sports Bks.). (Illus.). 48p. (gr. 4up). 1983. PLB 7.95g (ISBN 0-8225-0506-1). Lerner Pubns.

New Horizons in Aquatics. 112p. 9.95 (ISBN 0-686-38063-0). AAHPERD.

Shank, Carolyn. A Child's Way to Water Play. LC 82-82119. (Illus.). 176p. (Orig.). 1983. pap. 6.95 (ISBN 0-88011-053-8). Leisure Pr.

AQUICULTURE

see Aquaculture

ARAB ARCHITECTURE

see Architecture, Islamic

ARAB ART

see Art, Islamic

ARAB COUNTRIES

Shaw, R. Paul. Mobilising Human Resources in the Arab World. (Arab World Ser.). 288p. 1983. price not set (ISBN 0-7103-0040-9, Kegan Paul). Routledge & Kegan.

ARAB COUNTRIES–ECONOMIC CONDITIONS

Atkinson, Gerald M. Arab Banks & the Financial Leadership of the World. (The Great Currents of History Library Bk.). (Illus.). 137p. 1983. 97.85 (ISBN 0-86722-029-5). Inst Econ Pol.

Basic Needs in the Arab Region: Environmental Aspects, Technologies & Policies. (UNEP Reports & Proceedings Ser.: No. 5). 216p. 1983. pap. 11.00 (ISBN 92-807-1030-3, UNEP 070, UNEP). Unipub.

Changing Patterns in World Economy & the Transition to a New International Economic Order with Special Reference to the Arab World. 16p. 1982. pap. 5.00 (ISBN 92-808-0315-8, TUNU 202, UNU). Unipub.

Guecioueur, Adda, ed. The Problems of Arab Economic Development & Integration. (Special Studies on the Middle East). 275p. 1983. price not set (ISBN 0-86531-595-7). Westview.

Urban, JoDeen A. Regional Instability & Expatriate Labor in the Persian Gulf. 1983. 9.50 (ISBN 0-8315-0186-3). Speller.

ARAB COUNTRIES–FOREIGN RELATIONS

Levins, Hoag. Arab Reach: The Secret War Against Israel. LC 82-45255. 336p. 1983. 17.95 (ISBN 0-385-18057-8). Doubleday.

ARAB COUNTRIES–HISTORY

Freeman-Grenville, G. S. P., ed. Memoirs of An Arabian Princess. (Illus.). 308p. 1982. 17.95 (ISBN 0-85692-062-2, Pub. by Salem Hse Ltd.). Merrimack Bk Serv.

O'Fahey, R. S. & Abu, Salim M. Land in Dar Fur: Charters & Related Documents from the Dar Fur Sultanate. LC 82-4186. (Fontes Historiae Africanae Series Arabica: No. 3). (Illus.). 176p. Date not set. price not set (ISBN 0-521-24643-1). Cambridge U Pr.

ARAB COUNTRIES–POLITICS AND GOVERNMENT

Basic Needs in the Arab Region: Environmental Aspects, Technologies & Policies. (UNEP Reports & Proceedings Ser.: No. 5). 216p. 1983. pap. 11.00 (ISBN 92-807-1030-3, UNEP 070, UNEP). Unipub.

Farah, Tawfic E., ed. Political Behavior in the Arab States. 240p. 1983. lib. bdg. 20.00 (ISBN 0-86531-524-8); pap. text ed. 9.95 (ISBN 0-86531-525-6). Westview.

ARAB-ISRAEL BORDER CONFLICTS, 1949-

see Israel-Arab Border Conflicts, 1949-

ARAB-ISRAEL WAR, 1967

see Israel-Arab War, 1967

ARAB-JEWISH RELATIONS

see Jewish-Arab Relations

ARAB PHILOSOPHY

see Philosophy, Arab

ARAB SCIENCE

see Science, Arab

ARABIA–DESCRIPTION AND TRAVEL

Rihani, Ameen. Around the Coasts of Arabia. LC 82-4462. 1983. 45.00x (ISBN 0-88206-056-2). Caravan Bks.

Wheatcroft, Andrew. Arabia & The Gulf in Original Photographs Eighteen Eighty to Nineteen-Fifty. 200p. 1983. 38.95 (ISBN 0-7103-0016-6). Routledge & Kegan.

ARABIA–HISTORY

Leatherdale, Clive. Britain & Saudi Arabia 1925-1939: An Imperial Oasis. 200p. 1983. text ed. 37.50x (ISBN 0-7146-3220-1, F Cass Co). Biblio Dist.

Rihani, Ameen. Arabian Peak & Desert. LC 82-4457. 1983. 40.00x (ISBN 0-88206-055-4). Caravan Bks.

--Ibn Sa'oud of Arabia. LC 82-4573. 1983. 45.00x (ISBN 0-88206-057-0). Caravan Bks.

ARABIC LANGUAGE

Ali, S. Teach Yourself Arabic. 7.00 (ISBN 0-686-83575-1). Kazi Pubns.

Berlitz Arabic for Your Trip. 192p. 1982. 8.95 (ISBN 0-02-965150-6, Berlitz). Macmillan.

Berlitz Editors. Arabic for Travel Cassettepack. 1983. 14.95 (ISBN 0-02-962780-X, Berlitz); cassette incl. Macmillan.

--English for Arabic Phrasebook. 1982. pap. 4.95 (ISBN 0-02-965540-4, Berlitz). Macmillan.

Catalog of the Arabic Collection, Harvard University. 1983. lib. bdg. 1450.00 (ISBN 0-8161-0398-4, Hall Library). G K Hall.

Foreign Service Institute. Modern Written Arabic, Vol. 2. 385p. Date not set. with 8 cassettes 125.00x (ISBN 0-88432-088-X, A320). J Norton Pubs.

Qureshi, Z. H. Arabic for Beginners. pap. 2.00 (ISBN 0-686-83564-6). Kazi Pubns.

--Arabic Writing for Beginners: Part Two. pap. 2.00 (ISBN 0-686-83572-7). Kazi Pubns.

ARABIC LANGUAGE–DIALECTS

Al-Tajir, Mahdi A. Baharnah Dialect of Arabic: A Study in Language & Linguistic Origin. (Library of Arab Linguistics). 188p. 1983. 50.00 (ISBN 0-7103-0024-7). Routledge & Kegan.

Karam, Emil. Spoken Arabic: The Language of Lebanon. LC 82-5513. 1982. pap. 8.95 (ISBN 0-932506-18-6); pap. 16.50 with cassette (90 min.). St Bedes Pubns.

ARABIC LANGUAGE–DICTIONARIES

Abdallah. Abdallah Dictionary of International Relations & Conference Terminology in English-Arabic. 1982. 40.00x (ISBN 0-86685-289-1). Intl Bk Ctr.

Barakat, Gamal. English-Arabic Dictionary of Diplomacy & Related Terminology. 1982. 25.00x (ISBN 0-86685-290-5). Intl Bk Ctr.

Dagher, Yusuf. Arabic Dictionary of Pseudonyms. (Arabic.). 1982. 16.00x (ISBN 0-86685-300-6). Intl Bk Ctr.

Dahdah. Dictionary of Arabic Grammar, in Charts & Tables. (Illus., Arabic-Arabic.). 1982. 30.00x (ISBN 0-86685-292-1). Intl Bk Ctr.

Elias, Elias. Elias' English-Arabic Dictionary. 1979. 30.00x (ISBN 0-86685-288-3). Intl Bk Ctr.

ARABIC LITERATURE–HISTORY AND CRITICISM

Moosa, Matti. The Origins of Modern Arabic Fiction. LC 82-51657. 238p. 1983. 18.00x (ISBN 0-89410-166-8); pap. 8.00 (ISBN 0-89410-167-6). Three Continents.

ARABIC MEDICINE

see Medicine, Arabic

ARABIC PHILOSOPHY

see Philosophy, Arab; Philosophy, Islamic

ARABIC POETRY (COLLECTIONS)

Bread, Hashish & Moon: Four Modern Arab Poets. (Keepsake Ser.: Vol. 9). 72p. 1982. 12.00 (ISBN 0-87775-134-X); pap. 6.00 (ISBN 0-87775-135-8). Unicorn Pr.

ARABS

see also Bedouins; Palestinian Arabs

Patai, Raphael. The Arab Mind. rev. ed. 448p. 1983. 19.95 (ISBN 0-686-83811-4, ScribT); pap. 10.95 (ISBN 0-686-83812-2). Scribner.

ARABS IN PALESTINE

see Palestinian Arabs

ARAN ISLANDS

Shaw, Ruth W. J. M. Synge's Guide to Aran Islands. 1983. pap. 5.95 (ISBN 0-8159-6835-3). Devin.

ARANEIDA

see Spiders

ARAPAHO INDIANS

see Indians of North America–The West

ARBITRATION, INDUSTRIAL

see also Collective Bargaining; Grievance Procedures; Strikes and Lockouts

Palmer, John R. The Use of Accounting Information in Labor Negotiations. 69p. pap. 7.95 (ISBN 0-86641-051-1, 7791). Natl Assn Accts.

ARBITRATION, INTERNATIONAL

see also Diplomatic Negotiations in International Disputes; Disarmament; Jurisdiction (International Law)

Amos, Sheldon. Political & Legal Remedies for War. 254p. 1982. Repr. of 1880 ed. lib. bdg. 24.00x (ISBN 0-8377-0213-5). Rothman.

Hodlering, Michael F., et al, eds. Arbitration & the Law, 1982. (Arbitration & the Law Ser.). 472p. (Orig.). 1983. text ed. 75.00 (ISBN 0-686-37920-9). Am Arbitration.

Niezing, Johan. Strategy & Structure: Studies in Peace Research II. LC 78-319637. (Publications of the Polemological Centre of the Free University of Brussels: Vol. 8). (Illus.). 68p. 1978. pap. 11.50x (ISBN 90-265-0274-5). Intl Pubns Serv.

Shea, Gordon F. Creative Negotiating: Productive Tools & Techniques for Solving Problems, Resolving Conflicts & Settling Differences. 1983. 17.95 (ISBN 0-8436-0885-4). CBI Pub.

ARBITRATION AND AWARD

see also Compromise (Law)

Butler, William E., ed. International Commercial Arbitration: Soviet Commercial & Maritime Arbitration. LC 80-10606. 1980. 75.00 (ISBN 0-686-84383-5). Oceana.

Forry, John I. A Practical Guide to Foreign Investment in the United States, Suppl. 2nd ed. 350p. 1983. text ed. 80.00 (ISBN 0-906524-05-9); pap. text ed. 30.00 (ISBN 0-906524-06-7). BNA.

Reports of International Arbitral Awards, Vol. 18. 532p. 1983. 33.00 (ISBN 0-686-84907-8, UN80/5/7, UN). Unipub.

ARBORICULTURE

see Forests and Forestry; Trees

ARC WELDING

see Electric Welding

ARCHAEOLOGISTS

Clarke, Michael & Penny, Nicholas, eds. The Arrogant Connoisseur: Richard Payne Knight 1751-1824. 208p. 1982. 45.00 (ISBN 0-7190-0871-9). Manchester.

ARCHAEOLOGY

see also Architecture, Ancient; Christian Art and Symbolism; Ethnology; Excavations (Archaeology); Funeral Rites and Ceremonies; Gems; Heraldry; Historic Sites; Industrial Archaeology; Man, Prehistoric; Mummies; Mythology; Numismatics; Pottery; Pyramids; Temples; Tombs; Underwater Archaeology

also subdivision Antiquities under names of countries, regions, cities, etc., e.g. Crete–Antiquities

Binford, Lewis R. In Pursuit of the Past: Decoding the Archaeological Record. (Illus.). 1983. 18.50 (ISBN 0-500-05042-2). Thames Hudson.

Branigan, Keith, ed. The Atlas of Archaeology. (Illus.). 240p. 1982. 25.00 (ISBN 0-312-05957-4). St Martin.

Clay, Albert T. Neo-Babylonian Letters From Erech. 1920. text ed. 26.50x (ISBN 0-686-83634-0). Elliots Bks.

Discovering Archaeology. LC 81-51992. (Discovering Science Ser.). lib. bdg. 15.96 (ISBN 0-86706-055-7, Pub. by Stonehenge). Silver.

Fleure, H. J. & Peake, Harold. Hunters & Artists. (Corridors of Time Ser.: No. 2). 1927. text ed. 24.50x (ISBN 0-686-83573-5). Elliots Bks.

--Merchant Ventures in Bronze. (Corridors of Time Ser.: No. 7). 1931. text ed. 24.50x (ISBN 0-686-83625-1). Elliots Bks.

--Peasants & Potters. (Corridors of Time Ser.: No. 3). 1927. text ed. 24.50x (ISBN 0-686-83689-8). Elliots Bks.

--Steppe & the Sown. (Corridors of Time Ser.: No.5). 1928. text ed. 24.50x (ISBN 0-686-83785-1). Elliots Bks.

--Way of the Sea. (Corridors of Time Ser.: No. 6). 1929. text ed. 24.50x (ISBN 0-686-83850-5). Elliots Bks.

Goetze, Albrecht. Old Babylonian Omen Texts. 1947. text ed. 29.50x (ISBN 0-686-83651-0). Elliots Bks.

Greene, Kevin. Archaeology: An Introduction. (Illus.). 168p. 1983. text ed. 25.00x (ISBN 0-389-20362-9). B&N Imports.

Hackman, George G., ed. Temple Documents of the Third Dynasty of Ur From Umma. 1937. text ed. 27.50x (ISBN 0-686-83806-8). Elliots Bks.

Kenward, Harry & Hall, Allan, eds. Environmental Archaeology in the Urban Context. (CBA Research Report: No. 43). 140p. 1982. pap. text ed. 32.95x (ISBN 0-906780-12-8, Pub. by Coun Brit Archaeology England). Humanities.

Krupp, E. C., ed. Archaeoastronomy & the Roots of Science. (AAAS Selected Symposium Ser.: No. 71). 400p. 1983. price not set (ISBN 0-86531-406-3). Westview.

Lister, Robert H. & Lister, Florence C. Those Who Came Before: Southwestern Archeology in the National Park System. Houk, Rose & Priehs, T. J., eds. 1983. pap. price not set (ISBN 0-911408-62-2). SW Pks Mnmts.

Moorehead, Warren K. Archaeology of the Arkansas River Valley. 1931. text ed. 100.00x (ISBN 0-686-83475-5). Elliots Bks.

Peake, Harold & Fleure, H. J. Apes & Men. 1927. text ed. 24.50x (ISBN 0-686-83473-9). Elliots Bks.

Powell. Barclodiad y Gawres. 94p. 1982. 50.00x (ISBN 0-85323-400-0, Pub. by Liverpool Univ England). State Mutual Bk.

Tremayne, Archibald. Records From Erech, Time of Cyrus & Cambyses. 1926. text ed. 29.50x (ISBN 0-686-83726-6). Elliots Bks.

Woolley, Leonard. Ur of the Chaldees. 272p. 1982. 75.00x (ISBN 0-906969-21-2, Pub. by Benn Pubns). State Mutual Bk.

ARCHAEOLOGY–ADDRESSES, ESSAYS, LECTURES

Binford, Lewis R., ed. Working at Archaeology. (Studies in Archaeology). Date not set. price not set Lib. ed. (ISBN 0-12-100060-5). Acad Pr.

ARCHAEOLOGY–BIBLIOGRAPHY

Moeller, Roger W., ed. Archaelogical Bibliograph for Eastern North America. 198p. 1977. pap. 7.00 (ISBN 0-936322-03-9). Am Indian Arch.

ARCHAEOLOGY–HISTORY

Deagan, Kathleen, ed. Spanish St. Augustine: The Archaelogy of a Colonial Creole Community (Monographs) (Studies in Historical Archaeology). Date not set. price not set (ISBN 0-12-207880-2). Acad Pr.

King, Philip J. American Archaeology in the Mideast: A History of the American Schools of Oriental Research. (Illus.). 310p. 1983. text ed. 15.00x (ISBN 0-89757-508-3, Pub. by Am Sch Orient Res). Eisenbrauns.

Szekely, Edmond B. Archeosophy: A New Science. (Illus.). 32p. 1973. pap. 4.80 (ISBN 0-89564-057-0). IBS Intl.

ARCHAEOLOGY–JUVENILE LITERATURE

Snyder, Thomas F. Archeology Search Book. O'Neill, Martha, ed. (Search Ser.). (Illus.). 32p. (gr. 4-12). 1982. 32.46 (ISBN 0-07-059467-8, W). McGraw.

Tantillo, Joe. Amazing Ancient Treasures. LC 82-8287. (Illus.). 64p. (gr. 1 up). 1983. pap. 2.95 (ISBN 0-394-85489-6). Pantheon.

ARCHAEOLOGY–METHODOLOGY

see also Photography in Archaeology

Barker, Philip. Techniques of Archaeological Excavation. 2nd, rev., & extended ed. LC 82-23792. (Illus.). 288p. 1983. text ed. 25.00x (ISBN 0-87663-399-8); pap. text ed. 12.50x (ISBN 0-87663-587-7). Universe.

Dillon, Brian D., ed. Practical Archaeology: Field & Laboratory Techniques & Archaeological Logistics. (Archaeological Research Tools Ser.: Vol. 2). 1982. pap. 8.50 (ISBN 0-917956-42-7). UCLA Arch.

--The Student's Guide to Archaelogical Illustrating. rev. ed. (Archaeological Research Tools Ser.: Vol. 1). (Illus.). 154p. 1983. pap. 8.50 (ISBN 0-917956-38-9). UCLA Arch.

Major-Poetzl, Pamela. Michel Foucault's Archaeology of Western Culture: Toward a New Science of History. LC 81-19689. xiii, 276p. 1982. 24.00x (ISBN 0-8078-1517-9). U of NC Pr.

Moore, James A. & Keene, Arthur S., eds. Archaeological Hammers & Theories. LC 82-11669. write for info. (ISBN 0-12-505980-9). Acad Pr.

Schiffer, Michael B., ed. Advances in Archaeological Method & Theory, Vol. 6. Date not set. price not set (ISBN 0-12-003106-X). Acad Pr.

--Advances in Archaeological Method & Theory: Selections for Students, Vols. 1-4. LC 82-13810. (Serial Publication). 712p. 1982. text ed. 19.95 (ISBN 0-12-624180-5). Acad Pr.

ARCHAEOLOGY, BIBLICAL

see Bible–Antiquities

ARCHAEOLOGY, INDUSTRIAL

see Industrial Archaeology

ARCHAEOLOGY, SUBMARINE

see Underwater Archaeology

ARCHITECTS

Landau, Sarah B. P. B. Wight: Architect, Contractor, & Critic, 1838-1925. (Illus.). 108p. 1981. pap. 14.95 (ISBN 0-86559-051-6). Art Inst Chi.

Murvin, H. L. The Architect's Responsibilities in the Project Delivery Process. 2nd ed. (Illus.). 200p. 1982. pap. 19.95 (ISBN 0-9608498-0-7). H L Murvin.

Oliver, Richard & Architectural History Foundation. Bertram Grosvenor Goodhue. (American Monograph Ser.). (Illus.). 192p. 1982. 30.00x (ISBN 0-262-15024-7). MIT Pr.

Rudman, Jack. Senior Architect. (Career Examination Ser.: C-1326). (Cloth bdg. avail. on request). pap. 12.00 (ISBN 0-8373-1326-0). Natl Learning.

ARCHITECTS–CORRESPONDENCE, REMINISCENCES, ETC.

Blake, Peter. Harry Seidler: Australian Embassy, Paris. (Illus.). 56p. 1983. pap. 15.00 (ISBN 0-8390-0306-4). Allanheld & Schram.

ARCHITECTS–LEGAL STATUS, LAWS, ETC.

see also Building Laws; Engineering Law

Murvin, H. L. The Architect's Responsibilities in the Project Delivery Process. 2nd ed. (Illus.). 200p. 1982. pap. 19.95 (ISBN 0-9608498-0-7). H L Murvin.

ARCHITECTURAL ACOUSTICS

Cremer, L. & Muller, H. Principles & Applications of Room Acoustics, Vols. 1 & 2. Shultz, T. J., tr. (Illus.). 1982. Geometrical, Statistical & Psychological Room Acoustics. 94.50 (ISBN 0-85334-114-1, Pub. by Applied Sci England); Wave Theoretical Room Acoustics. 69.75 (ISBN 0-85334-113-3). Elsevier.

Lawrence, A. Architectural Acoustics. 1970. 35.00 (ISBN 0-444-20059-2). Elsevier.

Mackenzie, R. Auditorium Acoustics. 1975. 47.25 (ISBN 0-85334-646-1). Elsevier.

ARCHITECTURAL DESIGN

see Architecture–Details; Decoration and Ornament, Architectural; Architecture–Designs and Plans

ARCHITECTURAL DETAILS

see Architecture–Details

ARCHITECTURAL DRAWING

see also Architecture–Designs and Plans; Architecture–Details

Bies, John D. Architectural Drafting: Structure & Environment. (Illus.). 352p. 1983. pap. text ed. 15.95 (ISBN 0-686-82303-6). Bobbs.

Duncan, Robert I. Architectural Graphics & Communication Problems. 144p. 1982. pap. text ed. 11.95 (ISBN 0-8403-2764-1). Kendall-Hunt.

Levinson, E. D. Architectural Rendering. 256p. 1983. 18.95x (ISBN 0-07-037413-9). McGraw.

Liebing, Ralph W. & Paul, Mimi F. Architectural Working Drawings. 2nd ed. 352p. 1982. 25.00 (ISBN 0-471-86649-0, Pub. by Wiley-Interscience). Wiley.

Powell, Helen & Leatherbarrow, David, eds. Masterpieces of Architectural Drawing. (Illus.). 192p. 1983. 45.00 (ISBN 0-89659-326-6). Abbeville Pr.

Ratensky, Alexander. Drawing & Modelmaking: A Primer for Students of Architecture & Design. (Illus.). 144p. 1983. 17.50 (ISBN 0-8230-7369-6, Whitney Lib). Watson-Guptill.

Wright, Frank L. Drawings & Plans of Frank Lloyd Wright: The Early Period (1893-1909) 2nd ed. Orig. Title: Ausgefuhrte Bauten Und Entwurfe Von Frank Lloyd Wright. (Illus.). 112p. 1983. pap. 9.95 (ISBN 0-486-24457-1). Dover.

ARCHITECTURAL ENGINEERING

see Building; Building, Iron and Steel; Strains and Stresses; Strength of Materials; Structures, Theory Of

ARCHITECTURAL IRONWORK

Badger, Carl B. Badger's Illustrated Catalogue of Cast-Iron Architecture. 1982. pap. 8.95 (ISBN 0-486-24223-4). Dover.

ARCHITECTURAL LAW AND LEGISLATION

see Architects–Legal Status, Laws, etc.; Building Laws; Engineering Law

ARCHITECTURAL LIBRARIES

Vance, Mary. New Publications for Architecture Libraries. (Architecture Ser.: Bibliography A-816). 1982. pap. 7.50 (ISBN 0-88066-201-8). Vance Biblios.

ARCHITECTURAL LIGHTING

see Lighting, Architectural and Decorative

ARCHITECTURAL MODELS

Ratensky, Alexander. Drawing & Modelmaking: A Primer for Students of Architecture & Design. (Illus.). 144p. 1983. 17.50 (ISBN 0-8230-7369-6, Whitney Lib). Watson-Guptill.

ARCHITECTURAL PERSPECTIVE

see Perspective

ARCHITECTURAL PHOTOGRAPHY

see Photography, Architectural

ARCHITECTURE

see also Abbeys; Building; Buildings; Castles; Cathedrals; Church Architecture; Concrete Construction; Decoration and Ornament, Architectural; Environmental Engineering (Buildings); Factories; Farm Buildings; Historic Buildings; Hospitals–Design and Construction; Lighting; Lighting, Architectural and Decorative; Moving-Picture Theaters; Naval Architecture; School Buildings; Sepulchral Monuments; Strains and Stresses; Strength of Materials; Structural Engineering; Theaters–Construction; Tombs

also headings beginning with the word Architectural

Architectural Record Magazine Staff. Building for the Arts. 1978. 42.50 (ISBN 0-07-002325-5). McGraw.

Atkin, William W. Architectural Presentation Techniques. 196p. 1982. pap. 10.95 (ISBN 0-442-21074-4). Van Nos Reinhold.

Fjeld, Per-Olaf. Sverere Fehn: On the Thought of Construction. LC 82-42845. (Illus.). 168p. 1983. pap. 25.00 (ISBN 0-8478-0471-2). Rizzoli Intl.

Gordon, Barclay F. Olympic Architecture: Building for the Summer Games. 160p. 1983. 16.00 (ISBN 0-471-06069-0, Pub. by Wiley-Interscience). Wiley.

Kahlili, Nader. Racing Alone: Houses Made with Earth & Fire. LC 82-48419. 224p. 1983. 14.37 (ISBN 0-686-82602-7, HarpR). Har-Row.

McClung, William A. The Architecture of Paradise: Survivals of Eden & Jerusalem. LC 81-24071. (Illus.). 172p. 1983. text ed. 22.50x (ISBN 0-520-04587-4). U of Cal Pr.

MacFarlane, A. A. Architectural Supervision on Site. 1973. 30.75 (ISBN 0-85334-574-0, Pub. by Applied Sci England). Elsevier.

Precis IV. (Illus.). 128p. 1983. pap. 15.00 (ISBN 0-8478-5373-X). Rizzoli Intl.

Richardson, Margaret. The Craft Architects. (Illus.). 160p. 1983. 25.00 (ISBN 0-8478-0483-6); pap. 15.00 (ISBN 0-686-84064-X). Rizzoli Intl.

Sculley, Dean, ed. Cooper Union School of Architecture: Solitary Travelers, Vols. 1 & 2. (Illus.). 149p. 1983. pap. 35.00 (ISBN 0-8390-0310-2). Allanheld & Schram.

Taylor, Jennifer & Andrews, John. Architecture: A Performing Art. 176p. 69.00x (ISBN 0-7188-2532-2, Pub. by Lutterworth Pr England). State Mutual Bk.

Venturi, Rauch & Scott Brown. Venturi, Rauch & Scott Brown. (Architecture Ser.: Bibliography A 840). 63p. 1982. pap. 9.75 (ISBN 0-88066-250-6). Vance Biblios.

Wilson, Forrest. Post-Modern Malpractice. (Illus.). 1983. pap. 6.00. Arts & Arch.

ARCHITECTURE–BIBLIOGRAPHY

Fowler, Laurence H. & Baer, Elizabeth, eds. The Fowler Architectural Collection of the Johns Hopkins University. 1982. 15.20. Res Pubns Conn.

Research Libraries of the New York Public Library & Library of Congress. Bibliographic Guide to Art & Architecture: 1982. 1983. lib. bdg. 125.00 (ISBN 0-8161-6967-5, Biblio Guides). G K Hall.

Vance Bibliographics. Index to Architecture: Bibliography A 637-A 876 (January 1982-December 1982) 1983. pap. 10.50 (ISBN 0-88066-327-8, A 877). Vance Biblios.

ARCHITECTURE–CONSERVATION AND RESTORATION

see also Buildings–Repair and Reconstruction

Hutchins, Nigel. Restoring Old Houses. 240p. 1982. pap. 19.95 (ISBN 0-7706-0021-2). Van Nos Reinhold.

Maddex, Diane, ed. Whole Preservation Catalog. (Illus.). 400p. 1983. 29.95 (ISBN 0-89133-107-7); pap. 19.95 (ISBN 0-89133-108-5). Preservation Pr.

Maddex, Diane & Marsh, Ellen, eds. The Little Brown Book: A Desk Reference for the Preservationist. 144p. 1983. pap. 9.95 (ISBN 0-89133-106-9). Preservation Pr.

Nylander, Jane C. Fabrics for Historic Buildings. 3rd ed. (Illus.). 96p. 1983. pap. 9.95 (ISBN 0-89133-109-3). Preservation Pr.

Nylander, Richard. Wallpapers for Historic Buildings. (Illus.). 96p. (Orig.). 1983. pap. 9.95 (ISBN 0-89133-110-7). Preservation Pr.

ARCHITECTURE–DATA PROCESSING

Evans, Nigel. The Architect & the Computer, a Guide Through the Jungle. (Illus.). 40p. 1982. pap. 6.00 (ISBN 0-900630-77-9, Pub. by RIBA). Intl Schol Bk Serv.

ARCHITECTURE–DECORATION AND ORNAMENT

see Decoration and Ornament, Architectural

ARCHITECTURE–DESIGNS AND PLANS

see also Architecture, Domestic–Designs and Plans; Hospitals–Design and Construction; Theaters–Construction

Ambrose, James & Vergun, Dimitry. Simplified Building Design for Wind & Earthquake Forces. LC 79-26660. 142p. 1980. 26.95x (ISBN 0-471-05013-X, Pub. by Wiley-Interscience). Wiley.

Broadbent, Geoffrey. Design in Architecture: Architecture & the Human Sciences. LC 71-39233. 504p. 1978. pap. 23.95x (ISBN 0-471-99527-4). Wiley.

De Vido, Alfredo. Designing Your Client's House: The Architect's Guide for Meeting Design Goals & Budgets. (Illus.). 176p. 1983. 25.00 (ISBN 0-8230-7142-1, Whitney Lib). Watson-Guptill.

Grant, Donald P. Design by Objectives: Multiple Objective Design Analysis & Evaluation in Architectural, Environmental & Product Design. LC 82-73290. 50p. (Orig.). 1982. pap. text ed. 4.00 (ISBN 0-910821-00-3). Design Meth.

Jensen, Robert & Conway, Patricia. Ornamentalism: The New Decorativeness in Architecture & Design. (Illus.). 312p. 1982. 40.00 (ISBN 0-517-54383-4, C N Potter Bks). Crown.

Lever, Jill & Richardson, Margaret. Great Drawings from the Royal Institute of British Architects. (Illus.). 124p. 1983. pap. 15.00 (ISBN 0-8478-0481-X). Rizzoli Intl.

Llewellyn, Robert, photos by. The Academic Village: Thomas Jefferson University. (Illus.). 80p. 1982. 22.50 (ISBN 0-934738-03-3). Thomasson-Grant.

Radford, William A. Old House Measured & Scaled Drawings for Builders & Carpenters: An Early 20th Century Pictorial Sourcebook, with 183 Detailed Plates. 2nd ed. (Illus.). 200p. 1983. pap. 7.95 (ISBN 0-486-24438-5). Dover.

Risebero, Bill. Modern Architecture & Design. 256p. 1982. 50.00x (ISBN 0-906969-18-2, Pub. by Benn Pubns). State Mutual Bk.

Robertson, J. C. The Basic Principles of Architectural Design. (Illus.). 127p. 1983. 47.25 (ISBN 0-86650-058-8). Gloucester Art.

Russell, Beverly. Designers' Workplaces: Thirty-Three Offices by Designers for Designers. (Illus.). 144p. 1983. 27.50 (ISBN 0-8230-7492-7, Whitney Lib). Watson-Guptill.

Schild, Erich, et al. Environmental Physics in Construction: Its Application in Architectural Design. 211p. 1982. text ed. 65.00 (ISBN 0-246-11224-7). Renouf.

--Environmental Physics in Construction: Its Applications in Architectural Design. 220p. 1982. 95.00x (ISBN 0-246-11224-7, Pub. by Granada England). State Mutual Bk.

The Chicago Architects Design. LC 82-60339. (Illus.). 174p. Date not set. pap. 25.00 (ISBN 0-8478-0466-6). Art Inst Chi.

Ungers, O. M. Architecture as Theme. LC 82-60199. (Illus.). 128p. 1982. pap. 25.00 (ISBN 0-8478-5363-2). Rizzoli Intl.

ARCHITECTURE–DETAILS

see also Ceilings; Foundations; Windows; Woodwork

Ashihara, Yoshinobu & Riggs, Lynne E. The Aesthetic Townscape. (Illus.). 196p. 1983. 20.00 (ISBN 0-262-01069-0). MIT Pr.

One Hundred & Six Home Designs. 96p. Date not set. 1.50 (ISBN 0-918894-20-4). Home Planners.

Robertson, J. C. The Basic Principles of Architectural Design. (Illus.). 127p. 1983. 47.25 (ISBN 0-86650-058-8). Gloucester Art.

ARCHITECTURE–DICTIONARIES

Barry, W. R., ed. Architectural, Construction, Manufacturing & Engineering Glossary of Terms. 519p. 1979. pap. 40.00 (ISBN 0-930284-05-4). Am Assn Cost Engineers.

Stierlin, Henri. Encyclopedia of World Architecture. 416p. 1982. pap. 16.95 (ISBN 0-442-27957-4). Van Nos Reinhold.

ARCHITECTURE–HANDBOOKS, MANUALS, ETC.

Alder, Jim. Guide to Service Selection & Integration in Low Rise Buildings. (Illus.). 160p. 1983. pap. 24.95 (ISBN 0-89397-153-7). Nichols Pub.

Proulx, E. Annie. Plan & Make Your Own Fences & Gates, Walkways, Walls & Drives. Halpin, Anne, ed. (Illus.). 224p. 1983. 16.95 (ISBN 0-87857-452-2, 14-048-0); pap. 11.95 (ISBN 0-87857-453-0, 14-048-1). Rodale Pr Inc.

Rosengarten, A. A Handbook of Architectural Styles. Smith, Roger T., ed. 532p. 1983. pap. 12.50 (ISBN 0-88072-011-5). Tanager Bks.

ARCHITECTURE–HISTORY

Biesantz, Hagen & Klingborg, Arne. The Goetheanum: Rudolf Steiner's Architectural Impulse. Schmid, Jean, tr. from Ger. (Illus.). 131p. 1979. pap. 14.95 (ISBN 0-85440-355-8, Pub. by Steinerbooks). Anthroposophic.

Bush-Brown, Albert. Skidmore, Owings & Merrill: Architecture & Urbanism, 1974-1982. (Illus.). 400p. 1983. 49.95 (ISBN 0-8038-0401-6). Architectural.

Farmer, W. D. Homes for Pleasant Living. 39th ed. (Orig.). 1982. pap. 4.50 (ISBN 0-931518-16-4). W D Farmer.

--Homes for Pleasant Living: Country & Victorian Style Homes. (Illus.). 113p. (Orig.). 1982. pap. 5.00 (ISBN 0-931518-15-6). W D Farmer.

Jencks, Charles & Chaitkin, William. Architecture Today. LC 80-27124. (Illus.). 359p. 1982. 65.00 (ISBN 0-8109-0669-4). Abrams.

Lampugnani, Vittorio M. Architecture of the Twentieth Century in Drawings. LC 82-42534. (Illus.). 192p. 1982. 35.00 (ISBN 0-8478-0464-X). Rizzoli Intl.

Lynes, Russell. The Tastemakers. LC 82-25116. (Illus.). xiv, 362p. 1983. Repr. of 1955 ed. lib. bdg. 45.00x (ISBN 0-313-23843-X, LYTA). Greenwood.

Mignot, Claude. Nineteenth Century Architecture. LC 82-42844. (Illus.). 304p. 1983. cancelled (ISBN 0-8478-0477-1). Rizzoli Intl.

Philbrick, John & Philbrick, Helen. Gardening for Health & Nutrition: An Introduction to the Method of Bio-Dynamic Gardening Inaugurated by Rudolf Steiner. (Illus.). 93p. 1971. pap. 4.40 (ISBN 0-8334-1715-0, Pub. by Steinerbooks NY). Anthroposophic.

Saint, Andrew. The Image of the Architect. LC 82-48909. (Illus.). 192p. 1983. 19.95 (ISBN 0-300-03013-4). Yale Univ Pr.

Sky, Alison & Stone, Michelle. Unbuilt America: Forgotten Architecture in the United States from Thomas Jefferson to the Space Age. (Illus.). 308p. 1983. Repr. of 1976 ed. 24.95 (ISBN 0-89659-341-X). Abbeville Pr.

ARCHITECTURE–LAW AND LEGISLATION

see Architects–Legal Status, Laws, etc.; Building Laws; Engineering Law

ARCHITECTURE–PERIODICALS

Bloomfield, Julia, ed. Oppositions, Vol. 27-28: Double Issue. (Illus.). 288p. 1983. pap. 30.00 (ISBN 0-686-83765-7). Rizzoli Intl.

ARCHITECTURE–PICTORIAL WORKS

Orkin, Ruth. More Pictures from My Window. LC 82-42846. (Illus.). 144p. 1983. pap. 17.50 (ISBN 0-8478-0476-3). Rizzoli Intl.

Smith, Albert G., Jr. The American House Styles of Architecture Coloring Book. (Illus.). 48p. (Orig.). (gr. 3 up). 1983. pap. 2.25 (ISBN 0-486-24472-5). Dover.

ARCHITECTURE–RESTORATION

see Architecture–Conservation and Restoration

ARCHITECTURE–ASIA

Rosengarten, Andrew. The Illustrated Book of Indian, Egyptian & West Asiatic Architecture. (The Masterpieces of World Architecture Library). (Illus.). 120p. 1983. Repr. of 1878 ed. 97.85 (ISBN 0-89901-082-2). Found Class Reprints.

ARCHITECTURE–AUSTRALIA

Blake, Peter. Harry Seidler: Australian Embassy, Paris. (Illus.). 56p. 1983. pap. 15.00 (ISBN 0-8390-0306-4). Allanheld & Schram.

Drew, Philip. Two Towers: Australia Square MLC Centre by Harry Seidler. (Illus.). 56p. 1983. pap. 15.00 (ISBN 0-8390-0307-2). Allanheld & Schram.

ARCHITECTURE–CANADA

Bernstein, William & Cawker, Ruth. Contemporary Canadian Architecture. (Illus.). 192p. 1983. 25.00 (ISBN 0-8038-1281-7). Architectural.

Kalman, Harold & Roaf, John. Exploring Ottawa: An Architectural Guide to the Nation's Capital. (Illus.). 208p. (Orig.). 1983. pap. 10.95 (ISBN 0-8020-6395-0). U of Toronto Pr.

ARCHITECTURE–CHINA

Zhang Yihuan, ed. History & Development of Ancient Chinese Architecture. 1030p. 1982. 1500.00 (ISBN 0-677-31030-7). Gordon.

ARCHITECTURE–EGYPT

Phillips, James. Ancient Egyptian Architecture. (Architecture Ser.: Bibliography A-784). 73p. 1982. pap. 11.25 (ISBN 0-88066-203-4). Vance Biblios.

Rosengarten, Andrew. The Illustrated Book of Indian, Egyptian & West Asiatic Architecture. (The Masterpieces of World Architecture Library). (Illus.). 120p. 1983. Repr. of 1878 ed. 97.85 (ISBN 0-89901-082-2). Found Class Reprints.

Smith, W. S. & Simpson, W. Art & Architect of Ancient Egypt. (Pelican History of Art Ser.: No. 14). 1981. pap. 35.00 (ISBN 0-670-13378-7). Viking Pr.

ARCHITECTURE–EUROPE

see also Architecture, Domestic–Europe

Vandonne, Maurice. The Fully Illustrated Book of Old & Romantic Europe. (The Masterpieces of World Architecture Library). (Illus.). 89p. 1983. 91.75 (ISBN 0-89901-095-4). Found Class Reprints.

ARCHITECTURE–GERMANY

Fergusson, James. An Historical & Illustrated Vision of German Architecture. (Illus.). 127p. 1983. Repr. of 1885 ed. 89.75 (ISBN 0-89901-105-5). Found Class Reprints.

Schulte Strathaus, Ulrike J. Das Zuercher Kunsthaus-ein Museumsbau Von Moser. (Institut fuer Geschichte und Theorie der Architecture Ser.: Vol. 22). 158p. Date not set. pap. text ed. 18.95 (ISBN 3-7643-1242-4). Birkhauser.

ARCHITECTURE–GREAT BRITAIN

see also Architecture, Domestic–Great Britain

Architectural Design Special Issue. British Architecture. (Illus.). 240p. 1983. pap. 29.95 (ISBN 0-312-10035-3). St Martin.

Brighton, Trevor. Buildings of Britain, 1550-1750: North Midlands. 160p. 1982. 50.00x (ISBN 0-86190-059-6, Pub. by Moorland). State Mutual Bk.

McIntyre, Anthony. British Buildings. (Illus.). 352p. 1983. 31.50 (ISBN 0-7153-8122-9). David & Charles.

Tite, Graham. Buildings of Britain, 1550-1750: South East England. 160p. 1982. 50.00x (ISBN 0-86190-064-2, Pub. by Moorland). State Mutual Bk.

Tyack, Geoffrey. Buildings of Britain, 1550-1750: South Midlands. 160p. 1982. 50.00x (ISBN 0-86190-063-4, Pub. by Moorland). State Mutual Bk.

ARCHITECTURE–HUNGARY

Feuer-Toth, Rozsa. Renaissance Architecture in Hungary. Feherdy, Imre, tr. from Hungarian. (Illus.). 243p. 1981. 27.50x (ISBN 963-207-592-7). Intl Pubns Serv.

ARCHITECTURE–INDIA

Pereira, Jose. Elements of Indian Architecture. 1983. 34.00x (ISBN 0-8364-0868-3). South Asia Bks.

Rajan, K. V. Invitation to Indian Architecture. (Heritage India Ser.). (Illus.). 100p. 1982. text ed. 27.00x (ISBN 0-391-02735-2). Humanities.

Rosengarten, Andrew. The Illustrated Book of Indian, Egyptian & West Asiatic Architecture. (The Masterpieces of World Architecture Library). (Illus.). 120p. 1983. Repr. of 1878 ed. 97.85 (ISBN 0-89901-082-2). Found Class Reprints.

ARCHITECTURE–IRELAND

Kearns, Kevin C. Georgian Dublin: Ireland's Imperilled Architectural Heritage. (Illus.). 224p. 1983. 31.50 (ISBN 0-7153-8440-6). David & Charles.

ARCHITECTURE–ITALY

see also Architecture, Roman

Blake, Jeremy. La Falsa Prospettiva in Italian Renaissance Architecture. (Illus.). 1982. 250.00 (ISBN 0-85362-192-6). Routledge & Kegan.

Tobriner, Stephen. The Genesis of Noto: An Eighteenth-Century Sicilian City. 296p. 1981. 150.00x (ISBN 0-302-00543-9, Pub. by Zwemmer England). State Mutual Bk.

ARCHITECTURE–JAPAN

see also Architecture, Domestic–Japan

Rose, Alan. Build Your Own Japanese Pagoda. 40p. 1982. pap. 8.95 (ISBN 0-399-50679-9, Perige). Putnam Pub Group.

ARCHITECTURE–NEAR EAST

Phillips, James. Early Christian & Early Byzantine Architecture in Palestine (Including Jordan) Vol. II, the Sites. (Architecture Ser.: Bibliography A 854). 54p. 1982. pap. 8.25 (ISBN 0-88066-264-6). Vance Biblios.

ARCHITECTURE–ROME

see Architecture–Italy; Architecture, Roman

ARCHITECTURE–RUSSIA
Hamilton, George H. Art & Architecture of Russia. 1983. pap. 16.95 (ISBN 0-14-056106-4, Pelican). Penguin.
Johnson, D. Gale & Brooks, Karen M. Prospects for Soviet Agriculture in the 1980's. LC 82-48625. (Midland Bks.: No. 300). 224p. 1983. pap. 7.95 (ISBN 0-253-20300-7). Ind U Pr.
ARCHITECTURE–SPAIN
Feduchi, L. Spanish Folk Architecture, Vol. 1. (Illus.). 389p. 1982. 59.95 (ISBN 84-7031-017-8, Pub. by Editorial Blume Spain). Intl Schol Bk Serv.
ARCHITECTURE–UNITED STATES
see also Architecture, Domestic–United States
Arnell, Peter & Bickford, Ted, eds. Southwest Center: The Houston Competition. (Illus.). 120p. 1983. pap. 12.50 (ISBN 0-8478-0488-7). Rizzoli Intl.
Buck, Peter. Arts & Crafts of Hawaii: Houses, Sec. II. (Special Publication Ser.: No. 45). (Illus.). 52p. 1957. pap. 3.00 (ISBN 0-910240-35-3). Bishop Mus.
Cummings, Kathleen R. Architectural Records in Chicago. (Illus.). 92p. 1981. pap. 12.95 (ISBN 0-86559-052-4). Art Inst Chi.
Hamlin, Talbot F. American Spirit in Architecture. 1926. text ed. 22.50x (ISBN 0-686-83465-8). Elliots Bks.
Lancaster, Clay. The American Bungalow: 1880 to 1920's. (Illus.). 224p. 1983. 29.95 (ISBN 0-89659-340-1). Abbeville Pr.
Maycock, Susan E. An Architectural History of Carbondale, Illinois. (Illus., Orig.). 1983. price not set (ISBN 0-8093-1128-3); pap. price not set (ISBN 0-8093-1120-8). S Ill U Pr.
Sky, Alison & Stone, Michelle. Unbuilt America: Forgotten Architecture in the United States from Thomas Jefferson to the Space Age. (Illus.). 308p. 1983. Repr. of 1976 ed. 24.95 (ISBN 0-89659-341-X). Abbeville Pr.
Southern Oregon Chapter-AIA. Architectural Guidebook to Lane Country. (Illus.). 156p. (Orig.). 1983. pap. price not set (ISBN 0-87595-085-X, Western Imprints). Oreg Hist Soc.
The. Chicago Architects Design. LC 82-60339. (Illus.). 174p. Date not set. pap. 25.00 (ISBN 0-8478-0466-6). Art Inst Chi.
Wolfe, Tom. From Bauhaus to Our House. 1982. pap. 2.95 (ISBN 0-671-45449-8). PB.
ARCHITECTURE, ANCIENT
see also Pyramids; Temples
also Architecture–Egypt; Architecture, greek and similar headings
Smith, W. S. & Simpson, W. Art & Architect of Ancient Egypt. (Pelican History of Art Ser.: No. 14). 1981. pap. 35.00 (ISBN 0-670-13378-7). Viking Pr.
ARCHITECTURE, ARAB
see Architecture, Islamic
ARCHITECTURE, BAROQUE
Norberg-Schulz, Christian. Late Baroque & Rococo Architecture. (History of World Architecture Ser.). (Illus.). 220p. 1983. pap. 17.50. Rizzoli Intl.
ARCHITECTURE, CHURCH
see Church Architecture
ARCHITECTURE, COMPUTER
see Computer Architecture
ARCHITECTURE, DOMESTIC
see also Apartment Houses; Bathrooms; Country Homes; Farm Buildings; House Construction; Solar Houses
Adams, Charles C. Middletown Upper Houses. 900p. 1983. 60.00 (ISBN 0-914016-95-4). Phoenix Pub.
Helick, R. Martin. Little Boxes. 1982. spiral 17.50 (ISBN 0-912710-10-1). Regent Graphic Serv.
--Varieties of Human Habitation. LC 73-19343. 1970. spiral 17.50x (ISBN 0-912710-02-0). Regent Graphic Serv.
Olwell, Carol & Waldhorn, Judith. A Gift to the Street. (Illus.). 220p. 1982. pap. 17.95 (ISBN 0-312-32713-7). St Martin.
Ribalta, Marta. Habitat: Areas of Communication, No. 3. (Illus.). 264p. 1982. pap. 9.95 (ISBN 84-7031-447-5, Pub. by Editorial Blume Spain). Intl Schol Bk Serv.
--Habitat: The Living Room, No. 1. (Illus.). 86p. 1982. pap. 9.95 (ISBN 84-7031-229-4, Pub. by Editorial Blume Spain). Intl Schol Bk Serv.
Ribalta, Marta, ed. Habitat, No. 2. (Illus.). 176p. 1982. pap. 9.95 (ISBN 84-7031-437-8, Pub. by Editorial Blume Spain). Intl Schol Bk Serv.
Shurcliff, William. Super Solar Houses: Saunder's Low-Cost, One Hundred Percent Solar Designs. (Illus.). 196p. 1983. 16.95 (ISBN 0-931790-48-4); pap. 11.95 (ISBN 0-931790-47-6). Brick Hse Pub.
Snell, Wilma S. How to Build an Heirloom Miniature House from a Kit. Stern, Marcia & Hayden, Bob, eds. (Illus., Orig.). 1985. pap. price not set (ISBN 0-89024-062-0). Kalmbach.
ARCHITECTURE, DOMESTIC–DESIGNS AND PLANS
Four Hundred Home Plans. 320p. 5.95 (ISBN 0-918894-26-3). Home Planners.
Metz, Don, ed. The Compact House Book: Thirty-two Award Winning Designs. (Illus.). 192p. (Orig.). 1982. pap. 10.95 (ISBN 0-88266-323-2). Garden Way Pub.
ARCHITECTURE, DOMESTIC–EUROPE
Buttner, Horst & Meissner, Gunter. Town Houses of Europe. (Illus.). 351p. 1982. 45.00 (ISBN 0-312-81157-8). St Martin.
ARCHITECTURE, DOMESTIC–FRANCE
Meirion-Jones, Gwyn. The Vernacular Architecture of Brittany. 420p. 1982. text ed. 57.00x (ISBN 0-85976-060-X, Pub. by Donald England). Humanities.
ARCHITECTURE, DOMESTIC–GREAT BRITAIN
Clemenson, Heather. English Country Houses & Landed Estates. LC 82-3298. (Illus.). 256p. 1982. 30.00x (ISBN 0-312-25414-8). St Martin.
Evans, Tony & Green, Candide L. English Cottages. (Illus.). 160p. 1983. 25.00 (ISBN 0-670-29670-8, Studio). Viking Pr.
Smith, Roge T. Gothic Architecture in England with an Illustrated Glossary of Technical Terms. (Illus.). 164p. 1983. 91.85 (ISBN 0-86650-059-6). Gloucester Art.
ARCHITECTURE, DOMESTIC–IRELAND
Craig, Maurice. Architecture in Ireland. (Aspects of Ireland Ser.). (Illus.). 57p. (Orig.). 1978. pap. 5.95 (ISBN 0-906404-01-0, Pub. by Dept Foreign Ireland). Irish Bks Media.
Dunraven, Geraldine. Irish Houses Castles & Gardens: Open to the Public. (Illus.). 34p. 1982. pap. 3.95 (ISBN 0-900346-34-5, Pub. by Salem Hse Ltd.). Merrimack Bk Serv.
ARCHITECTURE, DOMESTIC–JAPAN
Fujioka, Michio. Japanese Residences & Gardens: A Tradition of Integration. Horton, H. Mack, tr. LC 82-48793. (Great Japanese Art Ser.). (Illus.). 48p. 1983. 18.95 (ISBN 0-87011-561-8). Kodansha.
Itoh, Teiji & Futagawa, Yukio. Traditional Japanese Houses. (Illus.). 360p. 1983. 75.00 (ISBN 0-8478-0479-8). Rizzoli Intl.
ARCHITECTURE, DOMESTIC–UNITED STATES
see also Architecture–United States
Duprey, Kenneth. Old Houses on Nantucket. (Illus.). 256p. 1983. 16.95 (ISBN 0-8038-5399-8). Hastings.
Harland, Marion. Romantic Colonial Homesteads & Their Stories of Strange Intrigue. (An American Culture Library Bk.). (Illus.). 128p. 1983. Repr. of 1897 ed. 78.45 (ISBN 0-89901-096-2). Found Class Reprints.
Langworthy, J. Lamont & McNeil, Katherine. Hillside Homes. LC 82-82433. (Illus.). 128p. (Orig.). 1983. pap. 10.00 (ISBN 0-9609334-0-9). IO.
McArdle, Alma deC. & McArdle, Deirdred B. Carpenter Gothic: Nineteenth Century Ornamented Houses of New England. (Illus.). 160p. 1983. pap. 14.95 (ISBN 0-8230-7101-4, Whitney Lib). Watson-Guptill.
ARCHITECTURE, ECCLESIASTICAL
see Church Architecture
ARCHITECTURE, GOTHIC
see also Cathedrals; Church Architecture
Grodecki, Louis. Gothic Architecture. (History of World Architecture Ser.). (Illus.). 220p. 1983. pap. 17.50 (ISBN 0-8478-0473-9). Rizzoli Intl.
Smith, Roge T. Gothic Architecture in England with an Illustrated Glossary of Technical Terms. (Illus.). 164p. 1983. 91.85 (ISBN 0-86650-059-6). Gloucester Art.
ARCHITECTURE, ISLAMIC
Beazley, E. & Haverson, M. Living with the Desert: Working Buildings of the Iranian Plateau. (Illus.). 140p. 1983. text ed. 44.00x (ISBN 0-85668-192-X, 60245, Pub. by Aris & Phillips England). Humanities.
ARCHITECTURE, LIBRARY
see Library Architecture
ARCHITECTURE, MEDIEVAL
see also Castles; Cathedrals
Nickel, Heinrich L. Medieval Architecture in Eastern Europe. LC 82-6254. (Illus.). 210p. 1982. text ed. 35.00x (ISBN 0-8419-0811-7). Holmes & Meier.
ARCHITECTURE, MODERN–20TH CENTURY
Bernstein, William & Cawker, Ruth. Contemporary Canadian Architecture. (Illus.). 192p. 1983. 25.00 (ISBN 0-8038-1281-7). Architectural.
Chappell, Sally K. & Zanten, Ann V. Barry Byrne & John Lloyd Wright: Architecture & Design. LC 82-71372. (Illus.). 72p. 1982. pap. 9.95 (ISBN 0-913820-11-3). Chicago Hist.
Collymore, Peter. The Architecture of Ralph Erskine. 180p. 1982. 90.00x (ISBN 0-246-11250-6, Pub. by Granada England). State Mutual Bk.
Curtis, William. Modern Architecture Since Nineteen Hundred. 400p. 1983. text ed. 39.95 (ISBN 0-13-586667-7); pap. text ed. 21.95 (ISBN 0-13-586666-9). P-H.
Dean, David. Architecture of the 1930's. (Illus.). 160p. 1983. 25.00 (ISBN 0-8478-0485-2); pap. 15.00 (ISBN 0-8478-0484-4). Rizzoli Intl.
Oppenheimer, Andrea. Bruno Zevi on Modernism. (Illus.). 240p. 1983. pap. 15.95 (ISBN 0-8478-0487-9). Rizzoli Intl.
Portoghesi, Paolo. Postmodern: The Architecture of the Post-Industrial Society. (Illus.). 160p. 1983. 25.00 (ISBN 0-8478-0472-0). Rizzoli Intl.
Risebero, Bill. Modern Architecture & Design. 256p. 1982. 50.00x (ISBN 0-906969-18-2, Pub. by Benn Pubns). State Mutual Bk.
ARCHITECTURE, MOORISH
see Architecture, Islamic
ARCHITECTURE, MUSLIM
see Architecture, Islamic
ARCHITECTURE, NAVAL
see Naval Architecture; Ship-Building
ARCHITECTURE, PRIMITIVE
Wallis, Frank A. The History of Pagan Architecture. (An Essential Knowledge Library Bk.). (Illus.). 117p. 1983. Repr. of 1908 ed. 78.45 (ISBN 0-89901-097-0). Found Class Reprints.
ARCHITECTURE, RENAISSANCE
Murray, Peter. Renaissance Architecture. (History of World Architecture Ser.). (Illus.). 200p. 1983. pap. 17.50 (ISBN 0-8478-0474-7). Rizzoli Intl.
ARCHITECTURE, ROCOCO
Harries, Karsten. The Bavarian Rococo Church: Between Faith & Aestheticism. LC 82-1116. (Illus.). 304p. 1983. text ed. 37.00x (ISBN 0-300-02720-6). Yale U Pr.
ARCHITECTURE, ROMAN
see also Architecture–Italy; Temples
Letarouilly, Paul M. Edifices de Rome Moderne. (Illus.). 368p. 1982. Repr. of 1840 ed. 55.00 (ISBN 0-910413-00-2). Princeton Arch.
Ward-Perkins, J. B. Roman Imperial Architecture. (Pelican History of Art Ser.: No. 45). 1981. 35.00 (ISBN 0-670-60349-X). Viking Pr.
ARCHITECTURE, RURAL
see Architecture, Domestic; Country Homes; Farm Buildings
ARCHITECTURE, SARACENIC
see Architecture, Islamic
ARCHITECTURE AND ENERGY CONSERVATION
Berkeley Planning Associates Inc. & Energyworks Inc. Energy Cost Control Guide for Multifamily Properties. Kirk, Nancye J., ed. (Illus.). 100p. (Orig.). 1982. pap. 19.95 (ISBN 0-912104-67-8). Inst Real Estate.
ARCHITECTURE AND SPACE
see Space (Architecture)
ARCHITECTURE AND THE PHYSICALLY HANDICAPPED
Moore, Gary T. & Cohen, U. Designing Environments for Handicapped Children: A Design Guide & Case Study. LC 79-89670. 1979. write for info. U of Wis Ctr Arch-Urban.
ARCHIVES
see also Business Records; Libraries; Manuscripts; Public Records
Bilyeu, Richard. The Tanelorn Archives: A Primary & Secondary Bibliography of the Works of Michael Moorcock,1949-1979. 160p. 1982. lib. bdg. 15.95x (ISBN 0-686-84015-1); pap. text ed. 7.95x (ISBN 0-686-84016-X). Borgo Pr.
Cunha, George M. & Cunha, Dorothy G. Library & Archives Conservation: 1980's & Beyond, 2 Vols. LC 82-10806. 1983. Vol. I. write for info. (ISBN 0-8108-1587-7); Vol. II Bibliography. write for info. (ISBN 0-8108-1604-0). Scarecrow.
Dougherty, Raymond P. Archives From Erech. (Goucher College Cuneiform Inscription Ser.: Vol. 3). 1933. text ed. 27.50x (ISBN 0-686-83476-3). Elliots Bks.
Fennelly, Lawrence J. Museum, Archive, & Library Security. new ed. 866p. 1982. text ed. 55.00 (ISBN 0-409-95058-0). Butterworth.
Peterson, Trudy H. Basic Archival Workshop Exercises. 86p. 1982. pap. text ed. 11.00 (ISBN 0-931828-54-6). Soc Am Archivists.
Sandifer, Kevin W. A Layman's Look at Starting a Religious Archives. Hall, Renee, et al, eds. 48p. (Orig.). 1982. pap. text ed. 7.50 (ISBN 0-910653-00-3). K W Sandifer.
Task Force on Institutional Evaluation. Evaluation of Archival Institutions: Services, Principles, & Guide to Self-Study. 48p. 1982. pap. text ed. 5.00 (ISBN 0-931828-55-4). Soc Am Archivists.
ARCHIVES–BIBLIOGRAPHY
Moussavi, Fakhreddin, compiled by. Guide to the Hanna Collection & Related Archival Materials at the Hoover Institution on War, Revolution & Peace on the Role of Education in Twentieth-Century Society. (Bibliographical Ser.: No. 64). 250p. 1982. lib. bdg. 19.95 (ISBN 0-8179-2641-0). Hoover Inst Pr.
ARCHIVES–GREAT BRITAIN
Booker, John M. The Wiston Archives. 541p. 1975. 65.00x (ISBN 0-900801-35-2). State Mutual Bk.
Osborne, Noel H. The Lytton Manuscripts. 79p. 1967. 30.00x (ISBN 0-900801-10-7). State Mutual Bk.
Steer, Francis W. The Mitford Archives, Vol. 1. 83p. 1961. 29.00x (ISBN 0-900801-23-9). State Mutual Bk.
--The Mitford Archives, Vol. 2. 67p. 1970. 39.00x (ISBN 0-900801-02-6). State Mutual Bk.
Steer, Francis W., ed. The Lavington Estate Archives. 128p. 1964. 30.00x (ISBN 0-900801-12-3). State Mutual Bk.
ARCTIC EXPEDITIONS
see Arctic Regions
ARCTIC REGIONS
see also Scientific Expeditions
also names of expeditions and names of explorers
Dyer, Irra & Chyssostomidis, C., eds. Arctic Policy & Technology. (Illus.). 400p. 1983. text ed. 69.95 (ISBN 0-89116-361-1). Hemisphere Pub.
Freuchen, Peter. Arctic Adventure: My Life in the Frozen North. 467p. 1982. Repr. of 1935 ed. lib. bdg. 35.00 (ISBN 0-89987-269-7). Darby Bks.
ARDENNES, BATTLE OF THE, 1944-1945
Phillips, Robert F. To Save Bastogne. LC 82-42721. 272p. 1983. 18.95 (ISBN 0-8128-2907-7). Stein & Day.
AREA MEASUREMENT
Breed, C. B. Surveying. 3rd ed. 495p. 1971. 31.95x (ISBN 0-471-10070-6). Wiley.
AREOLAR TISSUE
see Connective Tissues
ARGENTINE NATIONAL CHARACTERISTICS
see National Characteristics, Argentine
ARGENTINE REPUBLIC–DESCRIPTION AND TRAVEL
Guedalla, Philip. Argentine Tango. 254p. 1982. Repr. of 1933 ed. lib. bdg. 30.00 (ISBN 0-89987-313-8). Darby Bks.
ARGENTINE REPUBLIC–POLITICS AND GOVERNMENT
Ditella, Guido. Argentina under Peron, 1973-76: The Nation's Experience with a Labor-Based Government. LC 81-23281. 256p. 1982. 25.00x (ISBN 0-312-04871-8). St Martin.
Gillespie, Richard. Soldiers of Peron: Argentina's Montoneros. 328p. 1982. 29.95 (ISBN 0-19-821131-7). Oxford U Pr.
ARGOT
see Slang
ARGUMENTATION
see Debates and Debating; Logic; Oratory; Reasoning
ARGUMENTS, LEGAL
see Forensic Orations
ARHYTHMIA
see Arrhythmia
ARIAS
see Songs
ARID REGIONS
see also Deserts
Hagin, Josef & Tucker, Billy. Fertilization of Dryland & Irrigated Soils. (Advanced Series in Agricultural Sciences: Vol. 12). (Illus.). 210p. 1982. 39.50 (ISBN 0-387-11121-2). Springer-Verlag.
Lopez, Enrique Campos & Anderson, Robert J., eds. Natural Resources & Development in Arid & Semi-Arid Regions. 350p. 1982. lib. bdg. 25.00 (ISBN 0-86531-418-7). Westview.
ARISTIDES, AELIUS
Plutarch. Plutarch's Themistocles & Aristides. Perrin, Bernadotte, ed. 1901. text ed. 65.00x (ISBN 0-686-83702-9). Elliots Bks.
ARISTOTLE
Barnes, Johnathan. Aristotle. Thomas, Keith, ed. (Past Masters Ser.). 96p. 1983. pap. 3.95 (ISBN 0-19-287581-7, GB). Oxford U Pr.
Barnes, Jonathan. Aristotle. (Past Masters Ser.). 96p. 1982. 13.95 (ISBN 0-19-287582-5). Oxford U Pr.
Misra, K. S. Modern Tragedies & Aristotle's Theory. 252p. 1982. text ed. 18.75x (ISBN 0-7069-1425-2, Pub. by Vikas India). Humanities.
Schmitt, Charles. John Case & Aristotelianism in Renaissance England. (McGill-Queen's Studies in the History of Ideas). 368p. 1983. 37.50x (ISBN 0-7735-1005-2). McGill-Queens U Pr.
Schmitt, Charles B. Aristotle & the Renaissance. (Martin Classical Lectures: No. XXVII). (Illus.). 208p. 1983. text ed. 18.50x (ISBN 0-674-04525-4). Harvard U Pr.
ARITHMETIC
see also Accounting; Addition; Division; Fractions; Metric System; Multiplication; Numeration; Subtraction
Engelsohn, Harold S. & Feit, J. Basic Mathematics: Algebra with Arithmetic. LC 79-21287. 532p. 1980. text ed. 23.95 (ISBN 0-471-24145-8). Wiley.
Frank, Alan R. & McFarland, Thomas. Coin Skills Curriculum. (Illus.). 100p. (Orig.). 1983. pap. text ed. write for info. (ISBN 0-936104-28-7, 0360). Pro Ed.
Novak, David. Arithmetic. 514p. 1983. pap. 20.95 (ISBN 0-669-04397-4). Heath.
Wright, D. Franklin. Arithmetic for College Students. 4th ed. 432p. 1983. text ed. 19.95 (ISBN 0-669-04857-7). Heath.
ARITHMETIC–JUVENILE LITERATURE
Amir-Moez, Ali R. & Menzel, Donald H. Fun with Numbers: Lines & Angles. (Handbooks Ser.). (gr. 3-6). 1981. pap. 1.95 (ISBN 0-87534-179-9). Highlights.
Johnson, Vivienne. What Makes Arith-Me-Tick? (gr. 3-6). 1982. 6.95 (ISBN 0-86653-086-X, GA 437). Good Apple.
ARITHMETIC–PROGRAMMED INSTRUCTION
Hackworth, Robert D. & Howland, Joseph W. Programmed Arithmetic. (Illus.). 446p. (Orig.). 1979. pap. text ed. 13.95x (ISBN 0-943202-00-0). H & H Pub.
ARITHMETIC–STUDY AND TEACHING
Ginsburg, Herbert. Children's Arithmetic: How They Learn It & How You Teach It. (Illus.). 208p. 1983. pap. text ed. 15.00 (ISBN 0-936104-29-5, 0377). Pro Ed.
Husserl, E. Studien zur Arithmetik und Geometrie. 1983. 91.50 (ISBN 90-247-2497-X, Pub. by Martinus Nijhoff Netherlands). Kluwer Boston.
ARITHMETIC–1961-
Keedy, Mervin L. Arithmetic. 4th ed. (Illus.). 560p. 1983. pap. text ed. 18.95 (ISBN 0-201-14780-7). A-W.
ARITHMETIC, COMMERCIAL
see Business Mathematics
ARITHMETIC, MECHANICAL
see Calculating-Machines

ARIZONA–ANTIQUITIES
Andrews, Peter P. & Layhe, Robert, eds. Excavations on Black Mesa, Nineteen Eighty: A Descriptive Report. LC 82-72189. (Research Paper Ser.: No. 24). Date not set. price not set (ISBN 0-88104-003-7). S Ill U Pr.

ARIZONA–DESCRIPTION AND TRAVEL
All about Arizona. 1981. 5.95 (ISBN 0-686-42886-2). Harian.
Chronic, Halka. Roadside Geology of Arizona. 320p. 1983. pap. 9.95 (ISBN 0-87842-147-5). Mountain Pr.

ARIZONA–DESCRIPTION AND TRAVEL–GUIDE-BOOKS
Bowman, Eldon. A Guide to the General Crook Trail. (Illus.). 1978. pap. 2.00 (ISBN 0-89734-045-0). Mus Northern Ariz.
Lockard, Peggy Hamilton. This Is Tucson: Guidebook to the Old Pueblo. (Illus.). 260p. 1982. pap. 8.00 (ISBN 0-914468-08-1). Pepper Pub.

ARIZONA–HISTORY
Altshuler, Constance W. Starting with Defiance: Nineteenth Century Arizona Military Posts. (Historical Monograph: No. 7). (Illus.). 88p. 1982. 10.00 (ISBN 0-910037-19-1); pap. 6.00 (ISBN 0-910037-20-5). AZ Hist Soc.
Weiner, Melissa R. & Ruffner, Budge. Arizona Territorial Cookbook: The Food & Lifestyles of a Frontier. Browder, Robyn, ed. LC 82-2489. (Regional Cookbook Ser.). (Illus.). 232p. Date not set. pap. 8.95 (ISBN 0-89865-312-6, AACR2). Donning Co.

ARMADA, 1588
Usherwood, Stephen. The Great Enterprise: The History of the Spanish Armada. 192p. 1982. 39.00x (ISBN 0-7135-1309-8, Pub. by Bell & Hyman England). State Mutual Bk.

ARMADILLOS
Montgomery, G. Gene, ed. The Evolution & Ecology of Armadillos, Sloths, & Vermilinguas. (Illus.). 400p. (Orig.). 1983. pap. text ed. 35.00x (ISBN 0-87474-649-3). Smithsonian.

ARMAMENTS
see also Ammunition; Armed Forces; Armies; Disarmament; Industrial Mobilization; Munitions; Navies
also Armies and navies of individual countries, e.g. United States–Army; Defenses under names of countries
Tucker, Gardiner. Toward Rationalizing Allied Weapons Production. (The Atlantic Papers: No. 76/1). 54p. (Orig.). 1976. pap. text ed. 4.75 (ISBN 0-686-83681-2). Allanheld.

ARMED FORCES
see also Armies; Military Service, Voluntary; Navies; Sociology, Military; Soldiers; United States–Armed Forces
also specific branches of the Armed Forces under names of countries, e.g. France–Army; or subdivision Armed Forces under countries, e.g. United States–Armed Forces
Harries-Jenkins, Gwyn. Armed Forces & the Welfare Societies: Challenges in the 1980's. LC 82-10500. 256p. 1982. 27.50x (ISBN 0-312-04926-9). St Martin.
Marrs, Texe. You & the Armed Forces: Career & Educational Oportunities fo a Secure Future. LC 82-16386. 176p. 1983. lib. bdg. 12.95 (ISBN 0-668-05685-1); pap. 7.95 (ISBN 0-668-05693-2). Arco.
Puleston, W. D. Armed Forces of the Pacific. 1941. text ed. 39.50x (ISBN 0-686-83478-X). Elliots Bks.

ARMED FORCES IN FOREIGN COUNTRIES
Olson, David V. Badges & Distinctive Insignia of the Kingdom of Saudi Arabia, Vol. I. (Illus.). 192p. (Orig.). Date not set. pap. 10.00 (ISBN 0-9609690-0-4). Olson QMD.

ARMENIAN CHURCH
Garsoian, Nina & Mathews, Thomas, eds. East of Byzantium: Syria & Armenia in the Formative Period. LC 82-9665. (Dumbarton Oaks Symposium). (Illus.). 266p. 1982. 35.00x (ISBN 0-88402-104-1). Dumbarton Oaks.

ARMENIAN LANGUAGE
Nercessian, Y. T. Attribution & Dating of Armenian Bilingual Trams. (Illus.). 52p. (Orig.). 1983. write for info. (ISBN 0-9606842-1-2). ANS.

ARMENIAN LITERATURE (COLLECTIONS)
Surmelian, Leon. Apples of Immortality: Folktales of Armenia. LC 82-24260. (Unesco Collection of Representative Works, Series of Translations from the Literature of the Union of Soviet Socialist Republics). (Illus.). 319p. 1983. Repr. of 1968 ed. lib. bdg. 39.75x (ISBN 0-313-23417-5, SUAP). Greenwood.

ARMENIAN TALES
see Tales, Armenian

ARMIES
see also Disarmament; Militarism; Military Art and Science; Military Service, Compulsory; Navies; Sociology, Military; Soldiers
also Armies of individual countries, e.g. Great Britain–Army
Kishlansky, Mark A. The Rise of the New Model Army. LC 79-4285. (Cambridge Paperback Library). 337p. Date not set. pap. 14.95 (ISBN 0-521-27377-3). Cambridge U Pr.

ARMIES–MUSIC
see Military Music

ARMIES–STAFFS
The History of Army Command & General Staff. write for info. Sunflower U Pr.

ARMIES–SUPPLIES
see Military Supplies

ARMOR
see Arms and Armor

ARMORED CARS (TANKS)
see Tanks (Military Science)

ARMORED MILITARY VEHICLES
see Armored Vehicles, Military

ARMORED VEHICLES, MILITARY
see also Tanks (Military Science)
Hogg, Ian V. Armour in Conflict. (Illus.). 288p. 1980. 16.95 (ISBN 0-86720-587-3). Sci Bks Intl.
White, B. T. Tanks & Other Armoured Fighting Vehicles, 1942-1945. (Illus.). 172p. 1983. 9.95 (ISBN 0-7137-0705-4, Pub. by Blandford Pr England). Sterling.

ARMORED VESSELS
see Warships

ARMS, COATS OF
see Heraldry

ARMS, PROFESSION OF
see Military Service As a Profession

ARMS AND ARMOR
see also Firearms; Rifles; Swords; Tournaments
Ancient Armour & Weapons of Japan & Their Ten Complements. 2800p. Date not set. pap. price not set Boxed Set (ISBN 0-87556-476-3). Saifer.
Buck, Peter. Arts & Crafts of Hawaii: War & Weapons, Sec. X. (Special Publication Ser.: No. 45). (Illus.). 57p. 1957. pap. 3.00 (ISBN 0-910240-43-4). Bishop Mus.
Dunnigan, James F. How to Make War: A Comprehensive Guide to Modern Warfare. rev., upd. ed. (Illus.). 444p. 1983. pap. 7.95 (ISBN 0-688-01975-7). Quill NY.
Jane's Infantry Weapons, 1982-1983. (Jane's Yearbooks). (Illus.). 710p. 140.00 (ISBN 0-86720-598-9). Sci Bks Intl.
Kemp, Anthony & Haythornthwaite, Philip. Weapons & Equipment Series, 3 vols. (Illus.). 525p. 1982. boxed set 50.00 (ISBN 0-7137-1296-1, Pub. by Blandford Pr England). Sterling.
Mallory, Franklin B. Serial Numbers of U. S. Martial Arms. 96p. 1983. 10.00 (ISBN 0-9603306-1-5). Springfield Res Serv.
Perrett, Bryan. Weapons of the Falklands Conflict. (Illus.). 1983. 9.95 (ISBN 0-7137-1315-1, Pub. by Blandford Pr England). Sterling.
Siegel, Mark A & Jacobs, Nancy R., eds. Arms Sales: A Reflection of Foreign Policy? 80p. 1982. pap. 11.95 (ISBN 0-936474-26-2). Instruct Aides TX.
Suenaga, M. Pictorial History of Ancient Japanese Weapons, Armour, & Artifacts. (Illus.). 100p. Date not set. pap. 12.50 (ISBN 0-87556-582-4). Saifer.

ARMS AND ARMOR–JUVENILE LITERATURE
Cormack, Sandy. Small Arms: A Concise History of Their Development. (Illus.). 154p. 1983. 16.95 (ISBN 0-686-43006-9, Profile Pr England). Hippocrene Bks.
Watts, Edith. A Young Person's Guide to European Arms & Armor in the Metropolitan Museum of Art. Wasserman, Rosanne, ed. (Illus.). 40p. (Orig.). (gr. 7-8). 1982. pap. 1.95 (ISBN 0-87099-282-1). Metro Mus Art.

ARMS CONTROL
see Disarmament

ARMY
see Armies; Military Art and Science;
also France–Army; United States–Army, and similar headings

ARMY SCHOOLS
see Military Education

ARMY SUPPLIES
see Military Supplies

ARMY WAGONS
see Vehicles, Military

ARNOLD, MATTHEW, 1822-1888
Honan, Park. Matthew Arnold: A Life. 512p. 1983. pap. text ed. 9.95x (ISBN 0-674-55465-5). Harvard U Pr.

AROMATIC COMPOUNDS
Maarse, H. & Belz, R. Isolation, Separation & Identification of Volatile Compounds in Aroma Research. 1982. lib. bdg. 54.50 (ISBN 90-277-1432-0, Pub. by Reidel Holland). Kluwer Boston.

ARRHYTHMIA
Gould, Lawrence, ed. Drug Treatment of Cardiac Arrhythmias. LC 82-83705. 448p. 1983. monograph 49.50 (ISBN 0-87993-190-6). Futura Pub.
Parratt, J. R., ed. Early Post-Infarction Arrthythmias. 366p. 1982. 79.00x (ISBN 0-333-32672-5, Pub. by Macmillan England). State Mutual Bk.
Parratt, James R. Early Arrhythmias Resulting from Myocardial Ischaemia: Mechanisms & Prevention by Drugs. 1982. 55.00 (ISBN 0-19-520401-8). Oxford U Pr.

ARSENIC
Lederer, William H. & Fensterheim, Robert J., eds. Arsenic: Industrial, Biomedical, Enviornmental Perspectives. 464p. 1982. text ed. 42.00 (ISBN 0-442-21496-0). Van Nos Reinhold.

ARSON
Barracato, John S. Arson: How Can it be Curbed? (Vital Issues Ser.: Vol. XXXI, No. 1). 0.80 (ISBN 0-686-84133-6). Ctr Info Am.

ART
see also Anatomy, Artistic; Animal Painting and Illustration; Antiques; Archaeology; Architecture; Art Nouveau; Art Objects; Artists; Bronzes; Caricature; Carving (Art Industries); Christian Art and Symbolism; Collage; Collectors and Collecting; Commercial Art; Costume; Costume in Art; Creation (Literary, Artistic, etc.); Decoration and Ornament; Design, Decorative; Drawing; Esthetics; Expressionism (Art); Folk Art; Forgery of Works of Art; Gems; Glass Painting and Staining; Graphic Arts; Illumination of Books and Manuscripts; Illustration of Books; Impressionism (Art); Interior Decoration; Jewelry; Lithography; Medicine and Art; Mosaics; Mural Painting and Decoration; Painting; Performing Arts; Photography, Artistic; Photography of Art; Pictures; Portraits; Posters; Pottery; Preraphaelitism; Sculpture; Women in Art
also subdivision Art under special headings, e.g., jesus christ–art; also Animals in Art; Birds in Art; Nude in Art; Sea in Art, and similar headings
Bova, Ben. Vision of the Future: The Art of Robert McCall. LC 81-20542. (Illus.). 192p. 1982. 25.00 (ISBN 0-686-83927-7). Abrams.
Eddington, Thomas. Contemporary Artistic & the Metaphysics of the Art Expression. (An Essential Knowledge Library Bk.). (Illus.). 137p. 1983. 43.55 (ISBN 0-86650-051-0). Gloucester Art.
Hofmekler, Ori. Hofmekler's People. LC 82-83651. (Illus.). 128p. 1983. pap. 9.95 (ISBN 0-03-063371-0). HR&W.
Ozick, Cynthia. Art & Ardor. 256p. 1983. 16.95 (ISBN 0-394-53082-9). Knopf.
Pedoe, Dan. Geometry & the Visual Arts. (Illus.). 353p. 1983. pap. 6.00 (ISBN 0-486-24458-X). Dover.
Roberts, David. Yesterday the Holy Land. Van der Mass, Ed, tr. from Dutch. (Illus.). 144p. (Eng.). 1982. 16.95 (ISBN 0-310-45620-7). Zondervan.
Smagula, Howard J. Currents: Contemporary Directions in the Visual Arts. 384p. 1983. text ed. 16.95 (ISBN 0-13-195743-0). P-H.
Vonk. Art & Antique World Wide. 1981. 35.00 (ISBN 90-7041-371-X). Apollo.

ART–ADDRESSES, ESSAYS, LECTURES
Lee, Sherman E. Past, Present, East & West. Saissenlin, Remy & Goodman, Nelson, eds. (Illus.). 1983. 25.00 (ISBN 0-8076-1064-X). Braziller.
Lippard, Lucy R. Get the Message? Activist Essays on Art & Politics. (Illus.). 288p. 1983. pap. 10.95 (ISBN 0-525-48037-4, 01064-310). Dutton.

ART–ANALYSIS, INTERPRETATION, APPRECIATION
see Art–Philosophy; Art–Study and Teaching; Art Criticism; Esthetics; Painting; Pictures

ART–BIBLIOGRAPHY
Research Libraries of the New York Public Library & Library of Congress. Bibliographic Guide to Art & Architecture: 1982. 1983. lib. bdg. 125.00 (ISBN 0-8161-6967-5, Biblio Guides). G K Hall.

ART–CATALOGS
see also Art–Exhibitions
Coopersmith, Georgia. Twentieth Anniversary Exhibition of the Vogels Collection. (Illus.). 94p. Date not set. pap. 12.50. Brainerd.
Curators at the Musei Vaticani & the Metropolitan Museum of Art. The Vatican Collections: The Papacy & Art. Shultz, Ellen & Horbar, Amy, eds. (Illus.). 256p. 1982. 24.50 (ISBN 0-87099-321-6); pap. 14.95 (ISBN 0-87099-320-8). Metro Mus Art.
Dearborn, Elwyn. The Down East Printmaker: Carroll Thayer Berry. (Illus.). Date not set. write for info. (ISBN 0-89272-170-7); write for info. ltd. ed. (ISBN 0-89272-169-3). Down East.
Riordan, John C. The Art Collection at Potsdam. (Illus.). 118p. (Orig.). 1982. pap. 10.00 (ISBN 0-942746-04-X). Brainerd.

ART–COLLECTORS AND COLLECTING
see also Art As an Investment
David, Carl. Collecting & Care of Fine Art. (Illus.). 160p. 1981. 10.00 (ISBN 0-517-54287-0). Crown.
Howarth, Shirley R., ed. Directory of Corporate Art Collections. 200p. 1983. pap. 35.00 (ISBN 0-943488-01-X). Intl Art Alliance.
Krause, Martin F., Jr. Master Drawings & Watercolors From the Collection of the Indianapolis Museum of Art. LC 82-84037. (Centennial Catalogue Ser.). (Illus.). 256p. (Orig.). 1983. 30.00x (ISBN 0-936260-06-8); pap. 20.00x (ISBN 0-936260-07-6). Ind Mus Art.
Mucsi, Andras. Catalogue of the Old Masters Gallery at the Christian Museum in Esztergom. Halapy, Lili, tr. from Hungarian. (Illus.). 136p. 1975. pap. 7.50x (ISBN 963-13-4290-5). Intl Pubns Serv.
Nash, Alice. Collector's Handbook. (Illus.). 40p. (Orig.). 1982. 3.95 (ISBN 0-911431-00-4). Harmon-Meek Gal.
Smithsonian Institution, Washington D.C. Descriptive Catalog of Painting & Sculpture in the National Museum of American Art. 1983. lib. bdg. 125.00 (ISBN 0-8161-0408-5, Hall Library). G K Hall.
Wilmerding, John. An American Perspective: JoAnn & Julian Ganz. 1981. pap. 9.95 (ISBN 0-89468-002-1). Natl Gallery Art.

ART–CRITICISM
see Art Criticism

ART–DICTIONARIES, INDEXES, ETC.
Fielding, Mantle. Dictionary of American Painters, Sculptors & Engravers. 1974. 30.00 (ISBN 0-913274-03-8). Apollo.
Gowing, Lawrence, ed. The Encyclopedia of Visual Arts, 2 vols. 1983. 100.00 set (ISBN 0-13-276543-8). P-H.
Grund. Benezit Dictionary of Artists, 10 Vols. Date not set. 500.00 (ISBN 0-686-43137-5). Apollo.
Jackson. The Concise Dictionary of Artist's Signatures. 1981. 50.00 (ISBN 0-933516-39-8). Apollo.
MacDonald. Dictionary of Canadian Artists, 6 Vols. 1977. 100.00 (ISBN 0-686-43129-4). Apollo.
Wallace, Grocet. The New York Historical Society's Dictionary of Artists in America, 1564-1860. 1979. 65.00 (ISBN 0-686-43145-6). Apollo.
Young. Dictionary of American Artists, Sculptors, & Engravers. 1968. 60.00 (ISBN 0-686-43150-2). Apollo.

ART–ECONOMIC ASPECTS
Chamberlain, Betty. The Artist's Guide to the Art Market. 4th ed. 263p. 1983. 12.95 (ISBN 0-8230-0328-0). Watson-Guptill.
Parsons, James. The Art Fever: Passages Through the Western Art Trade. Fox, Steve & Schlede, Nancy, eds. (Illus.). 111p. 1981. 29.95 (ISBN 0-686-37628-5). Gallery West.
Weil, Stephen E. Beauty & the Beasts: On Museums, Art, the Law, & the Market. 304p. 1983. text ed. 17.50x (ISBN 0-87474-958-1); pap. text ed. 9.95x (ISBN 0-87474-957-3). Smithsonian.

ART–EDUCATION
see Art–Study and Teaching

ART–EXHIBITIONS
Auping, Michael. John Chamberlain: Wall Reliefs 1960-1983. LC 82-83513. (Illus.). 85p. (Orig.). 1983. pap. 15.00 (ISBN 0-916758-10-9). Ringling Mus Art.
Brewer, Donald J. Louis & Charlotte Bergman Collection. (Illus.). 60p. 1967. 5.00x (ISBN 0-686-99837-5). La Jolla Mus Contemp Art.
Brewer, Donald J. & Kirby, Sheldon. A Survey 1957-1968 Sheldon Kirby. 24p. 1968. 1.00x (ISBN 0-686-99835-9). La Jolla Mus Contemp Art.
Brice Marden, Marbles, Paintings & Drawings Text. (Illus.). 30p. (Orig.). 1982. pap. text ed. 10.50 (ISBN 0-938608-09-6). Pace Gallery Pubns.
Carmean, E. R. David Smith. 1982. pap. 17.50 (ISBN 0-89468-061-7). Natl Gallery Art.
Joseph, John & Pierce, Enneking. The Boston Anthenaeum Art Exhibition Index, 1827-1874. 1980. 75.00 (ISBN 0-686-43152-9). Apollo.
McDonald, Robert. The Carolyn & Jack Farris Collection: Selected Contemporary Works. LC 82-81520. (Illus.). 68p. 1982. 13.50 (ISBN 0-934418-13-6). La Jolla Mus Contemp Art.
Marlor. History of the Brooklyn Art Association with an Index of Exhibitions. 1970. 45.00 (ISBN 0-686-43147-2). Apollo.
Messer, Thomas M. Sixty Works: The Peggy Guggenheim Collection. (Illus.). 68p. 1982. pap. write for info. (ISBN 0-89207-037-4). S R Guggenheim.
National Academy of Design Exhibition Record, 1861-1900, 2 Vols. 1973. 75.00 (ISBN 0-686-43146-4). Apollo.
Pisano, Ronald G. An American Place. (Illus.). 44p. (Orig.). 1981. write for info. catalogue. Parrish Art.

ART–FORGERIES
see Forgery of Works of Art

ART–GALLERIES AND MUSEUMS
see Art Museums

ART–HISTORIOGRAPHY
Kleinbauer, W. E. & Slavens, Thomas P. Research Guide to the History of Western Art. 240p. 1982. text ed. 20.00 (ISBN 0-8389-0329-0). ALA.

ART–HISTORY
Here are entered general works on art history. For works on the history of art of specific nationalities or countries see Art, Chinese; Art, French; Art, Jewish; etc., with or without the subdivision History.
Armour, R. It All Started with Nudes: An Artful History of Art. 1977. pap. 7.95 (ISBN 0-07-002271-2). McGraw.
Barnes, Carl F., Jr. Villard de Honnecourt-The Artist & His Drawings: A Critical Bibliography. 1982. lib. bdg. 28.95 (ISBN 0-8161-8481-X, Hall Reference). G K Hall.
Carpenter, James M. Visual Art: A Critical Introduction. 289p. 1982. pap. text ed. 19.95 (ISBN 0-15-594935-7, HC). HarBraceJ.
Cohen, Kathleen & Croix, Horst de la. Study Guide to Art through the Ages. 7th ed. 309p. study guide 7.95 (ISBN 0-15-503761-7). HarBraceJ.
Cornell, Sara. Art: A History of Changing Style. 456p. 1983. 29.95 (ISBN 0-686-84550-1); pap. text ed. 19.95 (ISBN 0-686-84551-X). P-H.
Emmerich, Andre. Art Before Columbus. (Illus.). 1983. pap. price not set (ISBN 0-671-47073-6, Touchstone Bks). S&S.
Gombrich, E. H. The Story of Art. 13th ed. 506p. 1983. 25.00 (ISBN 0-686-84548-X); pap. text ed. 14.95 (ISBN 0-686-84549-8). P-H.
Lynes, Russell. The Tastemakers. LC 82-25116. (Illus.). xiv, 362p. 1983. Repr. of 1955 ed. lib. bdg. 45.00x (ISBN 0-313-23843-X, LYTA). Greenwood.
The Popes. (Treasures of the World Ser.). 1982. lib. bdg. 26.60 (ISBN 0-86706-047-6, Pub. by Stonehenge). Silver.
Sweet, Waldo. Artes Latinae, Level II. 203p. 1982. pap. text ed. 5.75x reference notebook (ISBN 0-686-84390-8). Bolchazy-Carducci.

--Artes Latinae, Bk.1 Level 1. 295p. 1982. pap. text ed. 9.95x (ISBN 0-686-84389-4). Bolchazy-Carducci.
--Artes Latinae: Guide to Filmstrip Series. 48p. 1982. pap. text ed. 2.00x (ISBN 0-686-84391-6). Bolchazy-Carducci.
Tibbs, Thomas S. Root. (Illus.). 12p. 1969. 2.00x (ISBN 0-686-99830-8). La Jolla Mus Contemp Art.

ART–HISTORY–20TH CENTURY
see Art, Modern–20th Century

ART–JUVENILE LITERATURE
Striker, Susan. Build a Better Mousetrap. (Illus.). 64p. 1983. pap. 4.95 (ISBN 0-03-057876-0). HR&W.

ART–MARKETING
Rissover, F. & Birch, D. Mass Media & the Popular Arts. 3rd ed. 496p. 1983. 15.95x (ISBN 0-07-052956-6, C). McGraw.
Weil, Stephen E. Beauty & the Beasts: On Museums, Art, the Law, & the Market. 304p. 1983. text ed. 17.50x (ISBN 0-87474-958-1); pap. text ed. 9.95x (ISBN 0-87474-957-3). Smithsonian.

ART–MUSEUMS
see Art Museums

ART–PERIODICALS
The Frick Art Reference Library Index to Art Periodicals. 1983. lib. bdg. 1500.00 (ISBN 0-8161-0387-9, Hall Library). G K Hall.
Look Magazine & the American Federation of the Arts. Look at America. (Illus.). 14p. 1957. 1.00x (ISBN 0-686-99845-6). La Jolla Mus Comtemp Art.

ART–PHILOSOPHY
Anand, Mulk R., ed. The Kama Sutra of Vatsyayana. 1982. 175.00x (ISBN 0-85692-093-2, Pub. by J M Dent). State Mutual Bk.
Cikovsky, Nicolai, Jr., intro. by. & Lectures on the Affinity of Painting with the Other Fine Arts by Samuel F. B. Morse. LC 82-13551. (Illus.). 144p. 1983. text ed. 20.00x (ISBN 0-8262-0389-2). U of Mo Pr.
Danto, Arthur C. The Transfiguration of the Commonplace: A Philosophy of Art. 288p. 1983. pap. text ed. 6.95x (ISBN 0-674-90346-3). Harvard U Pr.
Dutton, Denis. The Forger's Art: Forgery & the Philosophy of Art. LC 82-11029. (Illus.). 250p. 1983. 22.50 (ISBN 0-520-04341-3). U of Cal Pr.
Rosenberg, Harold. The De-Definition of Art. LC 83-1101. (Illus.). 256p. 1983. pap. 8.95 (ISBN 0-226-72673-8). U of Chicago Pr.
Tibbs, Thomas S. Affect-Effect. (Illus.). 13p. 1969. 3.00x (ISBN 0-686-99832-4). La Jolla Mus Contemp Art.
Urrutia, Lawrence. Projections: Antimaterialism. (Illus.). 20p. 1970. 5.00x (ISBN 0-686-99828-6). La Jolla Mus Contemp Art.

ART–PRICES
see also Art–Catalogs; Art As an Investment
also Paintings–Prices, and similar headings
Ayers, Tim, ed. Art at Auction: The Year at Sotheby's 1981-82; Two Hundred Forty Eighth Season. 392p. 1982. text ed. 45.00 (ISBN 0-85667-165-7, Pub. by Sotheby Pubns England). Biblio Dist.

ART–PRIVATE COLLECTIONS
Hood, Graham, ed. An Inventory of the Contents of the Governor's Palace Taken After the Death of Lord Botetourt. 19p. (Orig.). pap. 0.50 (ISBN 0-87935-063-6). Williamsburg.
Messer, Thomas M. Sixty Works: The Peggy Guggenheim Collection. (Illus.). 68p. 1982. pap. write for info. (ISBN 0-89207-037-4). S R Guggenheim.
The Princes of the Renaissance. (Treasures of the World Ser.). 1983. lib. bdg. 26.60 (ISBN 0-86706-084-0, Pub. by Stonehenge). Silver.
The Rulers of Britain. (Treasures of the World Ser.). lib. bdg. 26.60 (ISBN 0-86706-068-9, Pub. by Stonehenge). Silver.
The Rulers of Russia. (Treasures of the World Ser.). 1983. lib. bdg. 26.60 (ISBN 0-86706-076-X, Pub. by Stonehenge). Silver.
Rumford, Beatrix T., ed. The Abby Aldrich Rockefeller Art Collection. LC 75-36926. (Illus.). 31p. (Orig.). 1975. pap. 2.00 (ISBN 0-87935-033-4). Williamsburg.

ART–STUDY AND TEACHING
Hubbard, Guy & Zimmerman, Enid. Artstrands: A Program of Individualized Art Instruction. (Illus.). 223p. 1982. pap. text ed. 12.95 (ISBN 0-917974-88-3). Waveland Pr.
Hyska, June E. & Vanasse, Debra L. Changes. (Illus.). 200p. (Orig.). 1982. tchr's. ed 13.80 (ISBN 0-934696-03-9); 14.20 (ISBN 0-934696-04-7). Mosaic Pr.

ART–STUDY AND TEACHING (ELEMENTARY)
Dittmar, Mark. Jumbo Art Yearbook: Grade 3 & 4. (Jumbo Art Ser.). 96p. (gr. 3-4). 1981. wkbk. 14.00 (ISBN 0-8209-0046-X, JAY-34). ESP.
--Jumbo Art Yearbook: Grade 5 & 6. (Jumbo Art Ser.). 96p. (gr. 5-6). 1981. wkbk. 14.00 (ISBN 0-8209-0047-8, JAY-56). ESP.
--Jumbo Art Yearbook: Grade 7 & 8. (Jumbo Art Ser.). 96p. (gr. 7-8). 1982. wkbk. 14.00 (ISBN 0-8209-0048-6, JAY-78). ESP.

ART–SUBJECTS
see Art–Themes, Motives, Etc.

ART–THEMES, MOTIVES, ETC.
Beckman, Ericka & Casebere, Jim. Cave Canem. (Illus.). 1982. 25.00x (ISBN 0-9607244-1-9); pap. 6.50x (ISBN 0-9607244-2-7). Cave Canem Bks.
Neuberstaat, Karl. The Plant World as an Inspiration for the Creation of Artistic Forms. (Illus.). 121p. 1983. 83.45 (ISBN 0-86650-063-4). Gloucester Art.

ART–THERAPEUTIC USE
see Art Therapy

ART–TRADE
see Art Industries and Trade

ART–VOCATIONAL GUIDANCE
see Art As a Profession

ART, AFRICAN
Adams, Monni. Designs for Living: Symbolic Communication in African Art. (Illus.). 150p. 1982. pap. text ed. 12.00x (ISBN 0-674-19969-3). Carpenter Ctr.
The African Kings. (Treasures of the World Ser.). 1983. lib. bdg. 26.60 (ISBN 0-686-42743-2, Pub. by Stonehenge). Silver.
Celenko, Theodore. A Treasury of African Art From the Harrison Eiteljorg Collection. LC 82-47954. (Illus.). 240p. 1983. 57.50x (ISBN 0-253-11057-2). Ind U Pr.
McClusky, Pamela. African Masks & Muses: Selections of African Art in the Seattle Art Museum. LC 77-93881. (Illus.). 50p. (Orig.). 1983. pap. 8.95 (ISBN 0-295-96000-0, Pub. by Seattle Art Museum). U of Wash Pr.
Seck, Assane, intro. by. Contemporary Art of Senegal. (Illus.). 54p. 1980. pap. 5.00 (ISBN 0-686-83420-8). Mus Fine Arts Boston.

ART, AFRO-AMERICAN
see Afro-American Art

ART, AMERICAN
see also Afro-American Art
Art in America: Annual Guide to Galleries, Museums, Artists 1982. (Illus.). 186p. 1982. 19.95 (ISBN 0-918212-67-7). Neal-Schuman.
Casebere, James. In the Second Half of the Twentieth Century. (Illus.). 16p. (Orig.). 1982. pap. 4.00 (ISBN 0-939784-01-7). CEPA Gall.
Charlesworth, Sarah. In-Photography. (Illus.). 16p. (Orig.). 1982. pap. 4.00 (ISBN 0-939784-03-3). CEPA Gall.
Crane, Bonnie L. Blanche Ames: Artist & Activist. (Illus.). 40p. (Orig.). 1982. pap. 4.95 (ISBN 0-934358-10-9). Brockton Art.
Full of Facts & Sentiment: The Art of Frank H. Shapleigh. LC 82-14355. (Illus.). 64p. 1982. pap. text ed. 10.00X (ISBN 0-686-84660-5). NH Hist Soc.
Hislop, R. Auction Prices American Artists, 70-78. 65.00. Apollo.
--Auction Prices American Artists, 80-82. 46.00. Apollo.
Kruger, Barbara. No Progress in Pleasure. (Illus.). 16p. (Orig.). 1982. pap. 4.00 (ISBN 0-939784-02-5). CEPA Gall.
Mather, Frank T., Jr. American Spirit in Art. 1927. text ed. 22.50x (ISBN 0-686-83466-6). Elliots Bks.
A New Major California Art Reference Book: California Artists, 1935-1956. 1981. 50.00 (ISBN 0-686-43140-5). Apollo.
Smith. A Biographical Index of America Artists. Date not set. 30.00 (ISBN 0-686-43139-1). Apollo.
Stavitsky, Gail. Henry Koerner: From Vienna to Pittsburgh. (Illus.). 85p. (Orig.). 1983. pap. 12.95 (ISBN 0-88039-005-0). Mus Art Carnegie.
Tolf, Robert. Discover Fort Lauderdale's Top Twelve Attractions. (Florida Keepsake Ser.: No. 1). (Illus.). 28p. Date not set. 3.00 (ISBN 0-686-84227-8). Banyan Bks.

ART, AMERICAN–BIBLIOGRAPHY
Representative Art & Artist of New Mexico School of America Research. 1976. 15.00 (ISBN 0-686-43122-7). Apollo.

ART, ANCIENT
Buchthal, Hugo. Art of the Mediterranean World: 100-1400 A. D. Folda, Jaroslav, et al, eds. (Art History Ser.: No. V.). (Illus.). 207p. 1983. 75.00 (ISBN 0-916276-11-2). Decatur Hse.
Smith, W. S. & Simpson, W. Art & Architect of Ancient Egypt. (Pelican History of Art Ser.: No. 14). 1981. pap. 35.00 (ISBN 0-670-13378-7). Viking Pr.

ART, APPLIED
see Art Industries and Trade

ART, ARAB
see Art, Islamic

ART, ASIAN
Department of Asiatic Art, Museum of Fine Arts. Asiatic Art in the Museum of Fine Arts, Boston. LC 82-61853. (Illus.). 216p. 1982. pap. 18.50 (ISBN 0-87846-226-0). Mus Fine Arts Boston.
Hartel, Herbert, intro. by. Along the Ancient Silk Routes: Central Asian Art from the West Berlin State Museums. (Illus.). 224p. 1982. 45.00 (ISBN 0-8109-1800-5). Abrams.
Robinson, James & Mino, Yutaka. A Collector's Choices: Asian Art from the Collection of Dr. Walter Compton. LC 82-84073. (Illus.). 64p. (Orig.). 1983. pap. text ed. price not set. Ind Mus Art.
Trunber, Henry & Rathbun, William. Treasures of Asian Art from the Idemitsu Collection. LC 81-52557. (Illus.). 204p. 1981. pap. 13.95 (ISBN 0-932216-06-4). Seattle Art.

ART, AUSTRALIAN
Choate, R., ed. A Guide to Sources of Information on the Arts in Australia. (Guides to Australian Information Sources Ser.). 120p. 1983. pap. 10.50 (ISBN 0-08-029835-4). Pergamon.
Kean, Roslyn. Australian Art Guide. 1981. 5.95 (ISBN 0-9507160-3-0, Pub. by Art Guide England). Morgan.
Mollison, James & Murray, Laura. The Australian National Gallery: An Introduction. (Illus.). 1983. 49.95 (ISBN 0-500-99300-9). Thames Hudson.

ART, BALINESE
Rhodius, Hans & Darling, John. Walter Spies & Balinese Art. Stowell, John, ed. (Illus.). 96p. 1980. 25.00 (ISBN 0-686-43012-3, Tropical Mus Amsterdam Netherlands). Heinman.

ART, BAROQUE
Buffum, Imbrie. Studies in the Baroque From Montaigne to Rotrov. 1957. text ed. 47.50x (ISBN 0-686-83793-2). Elliots Bks.

ART, BRITISH
Waddell, Heather. London Art Guide. 1981. 5.95 (ISBN 0-9507160-4-9, Pub. by Art Guide England). Morgan.

ART, BRITISH–HISTORY
Darcy, C. P. The Encouragement of the Fine Arts in Lancashire, 1760-1860. 1977. 22.00 (ISBN 0-7190-1330-5). Manchester.
Hamilton, Richard. Collected Words Nineteen Fifty-Three to Eighty-One. (Illus.). 1983. 24.95 (ISBN 0-500-01293-8). Thames Hudson.

ART, BUDDHIST
Genoud, C. & Inoue, T. Buddhist Wall-Painting of Ladakh. (Illus.). 116p. 1981. text ed. 67.95x (ISBN 2-88086-001-6, Pub. by Editions Olizane Switzerland). Humanities.
Klimburg-Salter, Deborah E. Buddist Art & Culture of the Hindu Kush. (Illus.). 256p. 1983. 35.00 (ISBN 0-87773-765-7). Great Eastern.

ART, BYZANTINE
Vikan, Gary. Byzantine Pilgrimage Art. (Byzantine Collection Publications Ser.: No. 5). (Illus.). 52p. 1982. pap. 4.50x (ISBN 0-88402-113-0). Dumbarton Oaks.

ART, CANADIAN
MacDonald. Dictionary of Canadian Artists, 6 Vols. 1977. 100.00 (ISBN 0-686-43129-4). Apollo.

ART, CELTIC
Sibbett, Ed, Jr. Celtic Design Coloring Book. 48p. 1979. pap. 2.00 (ISBN 0-486-23796-6). Dover.

ART, CHINESE
see also Art, Oriental
Anderson, Martha G. & Arnoldi, Mary Jo. Art in Achebe's: Things Fall Apart & Arrow of God. (Graduate Student Paper Competition Ser.: No. 1). (Illus., Orig.). 1978. pap. text ed. 2.00 (ISBN 0-941934-25-X). Ind U Afro-Amer Arts.
Chinese Rubbings. (Illus.). 176p. (Engl. & Chinese.). 1982. pap. 6.95 (ISBN 0-8351-1112-1). China Bks.
Chinese Wood-Block Prints. (Illus.). 122p. 1982. pap. 6.95 (ISBN 0-8351-1111-3). China Bks.
Cleary, Thomas. The Flower Ornament Scripture: A Translation of the Avatamsaka Sutra Vol. I. Orig. Title: Avatamsaka Sutra (Sanskrit) Hua-yen (Chinese) 500p. (Chinese.). 1983. 25.00 (ISBN 0-87773-767-3). Great Eastern.
The Emperors of China. LC 81-51333. (Treasures of the World Ser.). lib. bdg. 26.60 (ISBN 0-86706-056-5, Pub. by Stonehenge). Silver.
Jones, Owen. Chinese Design & Pattern in Full Color. 48p. 1981. pap. 6.95 (ISBN 0-486-24204-8). Dover.
Lai, T. C. Chinese Decorated Letter Papers. (Illus.). 138p. 12.95 (ISBN 0-86519-098-4). Lee Pubs Group.
--Treasures of a Chinese Studio. (Illus.). 152p. 12.95 (ISBN 0-86519-095-X). Lee Pubs Group.
Lawton, Thomas. Chinese Art of the Warring States Period: Change & Continuity, 480-222 B.C. LC 82-600184. (Illus.). 204p. (Orig.). 1983. 35.00x (ISBN 0-934686-39-4); pap. 20.00x (ISBN 0-934686-50-5). Freer.
Meilin, Han. One Hundred Chickens. (Illus.). 100p. 1980. 35.00 (ISBN 0-8351-1046-X). China Bks.
--Still in the Land of the Living. (Illus.). 200p. 1980. 29.95 (ISBN 0-8351-1047-8). China Bks.
Rubel, Mary. Double Happiness: Getting More from Chinese Popular Art. (Illus.). 172p. (Orig.). 1981. pap. 6.98 (ISBN 0-9609154-0-0). Magaru Enterprises.
Wan-go Weng & Boda, Yang. The Palace Museum, Peking: Treasures of the Forbidden City. (Illus.). 320p. 1982. 65.00 (ISBN 0-8109-1477-8). Abrams.
Williamson, George C. The Book of Famille Rose. LC 72-104208. (Illus.). 231p. 1970. 72.50 (ISBN 0-8048-0880-5). C E Tuttle.

ART, CHRISTIAN
see Christian Art and Symbolism

ART, COMMERCIAL
see Commercial Art

ART, DECORATIVE
see also Bronzes; Decoration and Ornament; Design, Decorative; Embroidery; Enamel and Enameling; Furniture; Illustration of Books; Mosaics; Mural Painting and Decoration; Needlework; Pottery; Textile Design
also Art, African; Art, Byzantine, and similar headings
Minter-Dowd, Christine. Finders' Guide to Decorative Arts in the Smithsonian Institution. (Finders' Guides to the Collections in the Smithsonian Institution Ser.: Vol. 2). (Illus.). 212p. 1983. text ed. 19.95x (ISBN 0-87474-636-1); pap. text ed. 9.95x (ISBN 0-87474-637-X). Smithsonian.
Shaw, Jackie. Tole Technique & Decorative Arts, 4 Vols. (Orig.). 1974. Vol. 1. pap. 3.95 (ISBN 0-941284-01-8); Vol. 2. pap. 3.95 (ISBN 0-941284-02-6); Vol. 3. pap. 3.95 (ISBN 0-941284-03-4); Vol. 4. pap. 3.95 (ISBN 0-941284-04-2). Deco Design Studio.
Smith, Lawrence & Harris, Victor. Japanese Decorative Arts. 128p. 1982. 40.00x (ISBN 0-7141-1421-9, Pub. by Brit Mus Pubns England). State Mutual Bk.
Sussman, Varda. Decorated Jewish Oil Lamps. (Illus.). 144p. 1982. text ed. 50.00x (ISBN 0-85668-164-4, 40455, Pub. by Aris & Phillips England). Humanities.

ART, DUTCH
Alpers, Svetlana. The Art of Describing Dutch Art in the Seventeenth Century. LC 82-13468. (Illus.). 1983. 37.50 (ISBN 0-226-01512-2). U of Chicago Pr.

ART, EARLY CHRISTIAN
see Christian Art and Symbolism

ART, ECCLESIASTICAL
see Christian Art and Symbolism

ART, EFFECT OF
see Art Therapy

ART, EGYPTIAN
Kendall, Timothy. Kush: Lost Kingdom of the Nile: A Loan Exhibition from the Museum of Fine Arts Boston. LC 82-73157. (Illus.). 64p. (Orig.). 1982. pap. 7.00 (ISBN 0-934358-11-7). Brockton Art.
Smith, W. S. & Simpson, W. Art & Architect of Ancient Egypt. (Pelican History of Art Ser.: No. 14). 1981. pap. 35.00 (ISBN 0-670-13378-7). Viking Pr.
Tomory, Edith. A History of Fine Arts in India & the West. (Illus.). 532p. 1982. text ed. 45.00x (ISBN 0-686-42713-0, Pub. by Orient Longman Ltd India). Apt Bks.

ART, ENGLISH
see Art, British

ART, EUROPEAN
The Barbarian Kings. (Treasures of the World Ser.). 1982. lib. bdg. 22.60 (ISBN 0-86706-071-9, Pub. by Stonehenge). Silver.
Tomory, Edith. A History of Fine Arts in India & the West. (Illus.). 532p. 1982. text ed. 45.00x (ISBN 0-686-42713-0, Pub. by Orient Longman Ltd India). Apt Bks.

ART, FOLK
see Folk Art

ART, FRENCH
De Honnecourt, Villard. The Sketchbook of Villard de Honnecourt. Bowie, Theodore, ed. LC 82-15540. (Illus.). 144p. 1982. lib. bdg. 35.00x (ISBN 0-313-23747-6, VISK). Greenwood.
Feeny, Maura. A La Mode: Womens Fashion in French Art, 1850-1900. 44p. 1982. pap. 4.00 (ISBN 0-686-37427-4). S & F Clark.
The French Kings. (Treasures of the World Ser.). 1982. lib. bdg. 26.60 (ISBN 0-686-42796-3, Pub. by Stonehenge). Silver.
Lucie-Smith, Edward, intro. by. Masterpieces from the Pompidou Center. (Orig.). 1983. pap. 14.95 (ISBN 0-500-27282-4). Thames Hudson.
Paulson, Ronald. Representations of Revolution, 1789-1820. LC 82-13458. (Illus.). 416p. 1983. text ed. 29.95x (ISBN 0-300-02864-4). Yale U Pr.

ART, GERMAN
Roters, Eberhard. Berlin Nineteen Ten to Nineteen Thirty-Three. LC 82-50423. (Illus.). 268p. 1982. 60.00 (ISBN 0-8478-0439-9). Rizzoli Intl.

ART, GRAPHIC
see Graphic Arts

ART, GREEK
The Greek Conquerors. LC 81-52542. (Treasures of the World Ser.). lib. bdg. 26.60 (ISBN 0-86706-066-2, Pub. by Stonehenge). Silver.
Kurtz, Donna & Sparkes, Brian, eds. The Eye of Greece: Studies in the Art of Athens. LC 81-21672. (Illus.). 256p. 1982. 59.50 (ISBN 0-521-23726-2). Cambridge U Pr.

ART, IMMORAL
see Erotic Art

ART, INDIAN
see Indians of Central America–Art; Indians of Mexico–Art; Indians of North America–Art

ART, INDIC
Bernier, Ronald M. Temple Arts of Kerala. (Illus.). 258p. 1982. 99.00x (ISBN 0-940500-79-5, Pub by S Chand India). Asia Bk Corp.
Champakalakshmi, A. Vaisnava Iconography in the Tamil Country. 135p. 1981. text ed. 50.00 (ISBN 0-86131-216-3, Pub. by Orient Longman Ltd India). Apt Bks.
Tomory, Edith. A History of Fine Arts in India & the West. (Illus.). 532p. 1982. text ed. 45.00x (ISBN 0-686-42713-0, Pub. by Orient Longman Ltd India). Apt Bks.
Wacziarg, Francis & Nath, Aman. Rajasthan: The Painted Walls of Shekhavati. (Illus.). 120p. 1983. 35.00 (ISBN 0-8390-0309-9). Allanheld & Schram.

Williams, Joanna G., ed. Kaladarsana: American Studies in the Art of India. (Studies in South Asian Culture: Vol. 9). (Illus.). xvi, 183p. 1981. write for info. (ISBN 90-04-06498-2). E J Brill.

ART, IRANIAN
see Art, Persian

ART, IRISH
see also Art, Celtic

Crookshank, Anne O. Irish Art from Sixteen Hundred. (Aspects of Ireland Ser.: Vol. 4). (Illus.). 80p. Date not set. pap. 5.95 (ISBN 0-906404-04-5, Pub. by Dept Foreign Ireland). Irish Bks Media.

De Paor, Maire. Early Irish Art. (Aspects of Ireland Ser.: Vol. 3). (Illus.). 57p. 1979. pap. 5.95 (ISBN 0-906404-03-7, Pub. by Dept Foreign Ireland). Irish Bks Media.

Potterton, Homan & Keaveney, Raymond. National Gallery of Ireland: Fifty Pictures. (Illus.). 50p. pap. 9.95 (ISBN 0-903162-05-9, Pub. by Salem Hse Ltd.). Merrimack Bk Serv.

ART, ISLAMIC

Edwards, Holly. Patterns & Precision: The Arts & Sciences of Islam. (Illus.). 56p. pap. 6.50 (ISBN 0-87474-399-0). Smithsonian.

Jenkins, Marilyn, ed. Islamic Art in the Kuwait National Museum. (Illus.). 200p. 1983. text ed. 39.95x (ISBN 0-85667-174-6, Pub. by Sotheby Pubns England). Biblio Dist.

Sharif, Zeenat. Muslim Womans Home Companion. Quinlan, Hamid, ed. LC 82-70459. (Illus.). 180p. 1983. text ed. 6.50 (ISBN 0-89259-042-4); pap. 4.50 (ISBN 0-686-42956-7). Am Trust Pubns.

ART, ITALIAN

Bellini, Paolo, ed. Italian Masters of the Seventeenth Century, Vols. 46,47. (Illus.). 1982. 120.00 (ISBN 0-89835-046-8). Abaris Bks.

Cirker, Haywood, ed. Italian Master Drawings from the Uffizi. (Fine Art Ser.). (Illus.). 96p. (Orig.). 1983. pap. 5.00 (ISBN 0-486-24467-9). Dover.

Hall, R. J. The History of Ideas & Images in Italian Art. LC 82-48154. (Icon Editions). (Illus.). 320p. 1983. 24.01i (ISBN 0-06-433317-5, HarpT). Har-Row.

Leach, Mark, ed. Italian Masters of the Seventeenth Century, Vols. 44,45. (Illus.). 1982. 120.00 (ISBN 0-89835-041-7). Abaris Bks.

Licht, Fred. Canova. LC 82-16309. (Illus.). 280p. 1983. 85.00 (ISBN 0-89659-327-4). Abbeville Pr.

ART, JAPANESE
see also Art, Oriental

Condon, Camy & Nagasawa, Kimiko. Kites, Crackers & Craftsmen. Narita, Kikue, ed. (Illus.). 144p. (Orig.). 1974. pap. 7.50 (ISBN 0-8048-1402-3, Pub. by Shufunotomo Co Ltd Japan). C E Tuttle.

Grafton, Carol B., ed. Treasury of Japanese Designs & Motifs for Artists & Craftsmen. (Illus.). 96p. (Orig.). 1982. pap. 4.00 (ISBN 0-486-24435-0). Dover.

Hillier, J. Japanese Color Prints. (Phaidon Color Library). (Illus.). 84p. 1983. 25.00 (ISBN 0-7148-2167-5, Pub. by Salem Hse Ltd); pap. 17.95 (ISBN 0-7148-2165-9). Merrimack Bk Serv.

Index of Japenese Painters Society of Friends of Eastern Art. 1982. 10.00 (ISBN 0-686-43130-8). Apollo.

Lancaster, Clay. The Japanese Influence in America. LC 82-22650. (Illus.). 314p. 1983. Repr. of 1963 ed. 39.95 (ISBN 0-89659-342-8). Abbeville Pr.

Lee, Sherman E. & Cunningham, Michael R. Reflections of Reality in Japanese Art. LC 82-45940. (Illus.). 350p. 1983. price not set (ISBN 0-910386-70-6, Pub. by Cleveland Mus Art). Ind U Pr.

Munsterberg, Hugo. The Ceramic Art of Japan: A Handbook for Collectors. LC 63-20586. (Illus.). 272p. 1964. 37.50 (ISBN 0-8048-0083-9). C E Tuttle.

Smith, Lawrence & Harris, Victor. Japanese Decorative Arts. 128p. 1982. 40.00x (ISBN 0-7141-1421-9, Pub. by Brit Mus Pubns England). State Mutual Bk.

Sussman, Varda. Decorated Jewish Oil Lamps. (Illus.). 144p. 1982. text ed. 50.00x (ISBN 0-85668-164-4, 40455, Pub. by Aris & Phillips England). Humanities.

Tohei, Koichi. Kiatsu. (Illus.). 180p. 1983. pap. text ed. 11.95 (ISBN 0-87040-511-X). Japan Pubns.

Vergez, Robert. Okumura Masanobu: Early Ukiyo-e Master. LC 82-48780. (Great Japanese Art Ser.). (Illus.). 48p. 1983. 18.95 (ISBN 0-87011-564-2). Kodansha.

Williams, Majorie L. Japanese Prints: Realities of the "Floating World". LC 82-45941. (Themes in Art Ser.). (Illus.). 72p. (Orig.). 1983. pap. 7.95x (ISBN 0-910386-71-4, Pub. by Cleveland Mus Art). Ind U Pr.

ART, JEWISH

Costanza, Mary S. The Living Witness: Art in the Concentration Camps & Ghettos. 1982. 19.95 (ISBN 0-02-906660-3). Free Pr.

Moore, Clare. The Visual Dimension: Aspects of Jewish Art. (Publications of the Oxford Centre for Postgraduate Hebrew Study: Vol. 5). 320p. 1983. text ed. 35.00x (ISBN 0-86598-081-0). Allanheld.

ART, KINETIC
see Kinetic Art

ART, LATIN-AMERICAN

Brewer, Donald J. Twentieth Century Latin American Naive Art. (Illus.). 24p. 1964. 0.50x (ISBN 0-686-99842-1). La Jolla Mus Contemp Art.

The Kings of El Dorado. (Treasures of the World Ser.). 1983. lib. bdg. 26.60 (ISBN 0-86706-081-6, Pub. by Stonehenge). Silver.

ART, MEDIEVAL
see also Art, Byzantine; Illumination of Books and Manuscripts

Buchthal, Hugo. Art of the Mediterranean World: 100-1400 A. D. Folda, Jaroslav, et al, eds. (Art History Ser.: No. V.). (Illus.). 207p. 1983. 75.00 (ISBN 0-916276-11-2). Decatur Hse.

ART, MEXICAN

Espejel, Carlos. Mexican Folk Crafts. (Illus.). 237p. 1982. 35.00 (ISBN 84-7031-058-5, Pub. by Editorial Blume Spain). Intl Schol Bk Serv.

ART, MODERN

Frascina, Francis & Harrison, Charles. Modern Art & Modernism: An Anthology of Critical Texts from Manet to Pollock. LC 82-48153. (Icon Editions). (Illus.). 352p. 1983. 19.23i (ISBN 0-06-433215-2, HarpT). Har-Row.

ART, MODERN-19TH CENTURY

Clement & Hutton. Artists of the 19th Century. 1969. 50.00 (ISBN 0-686-43125-1). Apollo.

Hislop, R. Auction Prices of 19th Century Artists, 2 Vols. 1980. 176.00 (ISBN 0-903872-13-7). Apollo.

Post-Impressionism: Cross-Currents in European & American Painting, 1880-1906. LC 80-13795. (Illus.). pap. 2.00 (ISBN 0-89468-046-3). Natl Gallery Art.

ART, MODERN-20TH CENTURY
see also Dadaism; Expressionism (Art); Kinetic Art; Letter Pictures; Surrealism

Belting, Hans. Studies in the History of Art 1982, Vol. 12. (Illus.). pap. write for info. (ISBN 0-89468-063-3). Natl Gallery Art.

Borza, Eugene, et al. Studies in the History of Art 1982, Vol. 10. LC 72-600309. (Illus.). pap. 18.95 (ISBN 0-89468-005-6). Natl Gallery Art.

Brown, Jonathan, et al. Studies in the History of Art 1982, Vol. 11. (Illus.). pap. 8.95 (ISBN 0-89468-058-7). Natl Gallery Art.

Fraser, Gordon. Bill Brandt: Nudes 1945-1980. 132p. 1982. 55.00x (ISBN 0-86092-064-X, Pub. by Fraser Bks). State Mutual Bk.

Henderson, Linda D. The Fourth Dimension & Non-Euclidean Geometry in Modern Art. LC 82-15076. (Illus.). 496p. 1983. 55.00x (ISBN 0-686-43212-6); pap. 16.50 (ISBN 0-691-10142-6). Princeton U Pr.

Hislop, R. Auction Prices of Impressionist & 20th Century Artists 1970-1980, 2 Vols. 160.00 (ISBN 0-903872-12-9). Apollo.

Kahn, Wolf. Pastel Light. LC 82-19152. (Contemporary Artists Ser.: No. 1). (Illus.). 50p. (Orig.). 1983. 10.95 (ISBN 0-930794-80-X). Station Hill Pr.

Kass, Ray. Morris Graves: Vision of the Inner Eye. (Illus.). 176p. (Orig.). 1983. 35.00 (ISBN 0-8076-1068-2); pap. 15.00 (ISBN 0-8076-1069-0). Braziller.

Lambert, Yvon & Barthes, Roland. Cy Twombly: A Catologue Raisome. (Illus.). 222p. 1983. 95.00 (ISBN 0-8390-0305-6). Allanheld & Schram.

Olson, Roberta J., et al. Studies in the History of Art 1978, Vol. 8. (Illus.). pap. 9.95 (ISBN 0-89468-050-1). Natl Gallery Art.

Pace Gallery Publications, ed. Chuck Close, Recent Work. (Illus.). 40p. 1983. pap. write for info. (ISBN 0-938608-11-8). Pace Gallery Pubns.

Peppiatt, Michael & Bellony-Rewald, Alice. Imagination's Chamber. 232p. 1982. 45.00 (ISBN 0-686-42857-9). NYGS.

Post-Impressionism: Cross-Currents in European & American Painting, 1880-1906. LC 80-13795. (Illus.). pap. 2.00 (ISBN 0-89468-046-3). Natl Gallery Art.

Ross, Alan. Bill Brandt: Portraits. 120p. 1982. 80.00x (ISBN 0-86092-062-3, Pub. by Fraser Bks). State Mutual Bk.

Ruda, Jeffrey, et al. Studies in the History of Art 1975, Vol. 7. (Illus.). pap. 9.95 (ISBN 0-89468-049-8). Natl Gallery Art.

Schulz, Anne M., et al. Studies in the History of Art 1979, Vol. 9. (Illus.). pap. 11.95 (ISBN 0-89468-051-X). Natl Gallery Art.

ART, MODERN-20TH CENTURY-EXHIBITIONS

Anderson, Troels & Atkins, Guy. Asger Jorn. LC 82-60792. (Illus.). 98p. 1982. pap. 9.00 (ISBN 0-89207-034-X). S R Guggenheim.

Baier, Lesley K. & Shestack, Alan. The Katherine Ordway Collection, Yale University Art Gallery. (Illus.). 128p. 1983. pap. write for info. (ISBN 0-89467-025-5). Yale Art Gallery.

Carmean, E. A., Jr. & Clark, Trinkett. The Morton G. Neumann Family Collection: Selected Works, Vol. 2. LC 80-20844. (Illus.). pap. 5.00 (ISBN 0-89468-045-5). Natl Gallery Art.

Carmean, E. A., Jr. & Hunter, Sam. The Morton G. Neumann Family Collection: Selected Works, Vol. 1. LC 80-20844. (Illus.). pap. 2.00 (ISBN 0-89468-044-7). Natl Gallery Art.

Hulten, Pontus & Granath, Olle. Oyvind Fahlstrom. LC 82-60794. (Illus.). 120p. 1982. pap. 9.00 (ISBN 0-89207-035-8). S R Guggenheim.

Hulten, Pontus & Hjort, Oystein. Sleeping Beauty-Art Now. LC 82-60793. (Illus.). 136p. 1982. pap. 9.00 (ISBN 0-89207-036-6). S R Guggenheim.

Lucie-Smith, Edward, intro. by. Masterpieces from the Pompidou Center. (Orig.). 1983. pap. 14.95 (ISBN 0-500-27282-4). Thames Hudson.

Robbins, Daniel. Edward Koren: Prints & Drawings, 1959-1981. Littlefield, Thomson, ed. (Illus.). 56p. (Orig.). 1982. pap. 10.00x (ISBN 0-910763-00-3). SUNY Albany U Art.

Speyer, A. James & Rorimer, Anne. Seventy-fourth American Exhibition. (Illus.). 64p. Date not set. pap. 8.95 (ISBN 0-86559-050-8). Art Inst Chi.

Williams, Hiram. Hiram Williams: A One-Man Retrospective Exhibition. (Illus.). 36p. (Orig.). 1983. pap. 7.50 (ISBN 0-8130-0763-1). U Presses Fla.

ART, MODERN-20TH CENTURY-HISTORY

Batterberry, M. Twentieth Century Art. 1969. 9.95 (ISBN 0-07-004080-X). McGraw.

Johnson, Brooks & Styron, Thomas. Still Modern After All These Years. LC 82-83632. (Illus.). 48p. (Orig.). 1982. pap. 6.00 (ISBN 0-940744-40-6). Chrysler Museum.

Lynton, Norbert. The Story of Modern Art. 382p. 1983. 30.00 (ISBN 0-686-84546-3); pap. text ed. 14.95 (ISBN 0-686-84547-1). P-H.

ART, MOORISH
see Art, Islamic

ART, MUSLIM
see Art, Islamic

ART, OCCIDENTAL
see Art

ART, ORIENTAL
see also Art, Asian; Art, Chinese; Art, Japanese

Emerson, James C., ed. The Life of Christ in the Conception & Expression of Chinese & Oriental Artists. (The Great Art Masters of the World Ser.). (Illus.). 117p. 1983. 61.75 (ISBN 0-86650-054-5). Gloucester Art.

The Official 1984 Price Guide to Oriental Collectibles. 1st ed. LC 82-84651. 544p. 1983. 9.95 (ISBN 0-87637-375-9). Hse of Collectibles.

Saotome, Mitsugi. Aikido & the Harmony of Nature. (Illus.). 330p. (Orig.). 1983. 25.75 (ISBN 0-8038-0487-3); pap. 17.95 (ISBN 0-8038-0403-2). Hastings.

ART, PERSIAN

Ettinghausen, Richard & Yarshater, Ehsan, eds. Highlights of Persian Art. LC 79-4746. (Persian Art Ser.). 1983. 75.00x (ISBN 0-89158-295-9). Caravan Bks.

ART, POLYNESIAN

Cape, Peter. Please Touch: A Srvey of the Three-Dimensional Arts in New Zealand. (Illus.). 160p. 1980. 29.95 (ISBN 0-00-216957-6, Pub. by W Collins Australia). Intl Schol Bk Serv.

ART, POPULAR
see Art Industries and Trade; Folk Art

ART, PREHISTORIC

Pfeiffer, John E. The Creative Explosion: An Inquiry into the Origins of Art & Religion. LC 82-47531. (Illus.). 320p. 1982. 28.80i (ISBN 0-06-013345-7, HarpT). Har-Row.

ART, RENAISSANCE

Ames-Lewis, Francis. Drawing in Early Renaissance Italy. pap. 14.95 (ISBN 0-686-42818-8, Y-447). Yale U Pr.

Cole, Bruce. The Renaissance Artist at Work: From Pisano to Titian. LC 82-48102. (Icon Editions). (Illus.). 208p. 1983. 19.23i (ISBN 0-06-430902-9, HarpT). Har-Row.

Hislop, R. Auction Prices of Old Masters. 1980. 156.00 (ISBN 0-903872-14-5). Apollo.

ART, RUSSIAN

Hamilton, George H. Art & Architecture of Russia. 1983. pap. 16.95 (ISBN 0-14-056106-4, Pelican). Penguin.

ART, SARACENIC
see Art, Islamic

ART, SCANDINAVIAN

Anderson, Troels & Atkins, Guy. Asger Jorn. LC 82-60792. (Illus.). 98p. 1982. pap. 9.00 (ISBN 0-89207-034-X). S R Guggenheim.

Hulten, Pontus & Granath, Olle. Oyvind Fahlstrom. LC 82-60794. (Illus.). 120p. 1982. pap. 9.00 (ISBN 0-89207-035-8). S R Guggenheim.

Hulten, Pontus & Hjort, Oystein. Sleeping Beauty-Art Now. LC 82-60793. (Illus.). 136p. 1982. pap. 9.00 (ISBN 0-89207-036-6). S R Guggenheim.

Varnedor, Kirk, illus. Northern Light: Realism & Symbolism in Scandinavian Painting, 1880-1910. 240p. 1982. pap. 17.95 (ISBN 0-686-82279-X). Bklyn Mus.

ART, SPANISH

Hogan, Steven, ed. Spanish Art: The Masterpieces of Spanish Art in the Great Museums of Spain. (Illus.). 93p. 1983. 87.55 (ISBN 0-86650-060-X). Gloucester Art.

The Kings of Spain. (Treasures of the World Ser.). 1982. lib. bdg. 26.60 (Pub. by Stonehenge). Silver.

Pelauzy, M. A. & Roca, F. Catala. Spanish Folk Crafts. (Illus.). 240p. 1982. 35.00 (ISBN 84-7031-060-7, Pub. by Editorial Blume Spain). Intl Schol Bk Serv.

ART AND HISTORY
see also History in Art

Chatelain, Alfred V. Ancient Europe in the Vision of the Rarest Available Steel Engravings. (Illus.). 99p. Repr. of 1887 ed. 227.75 (ISBN 0-89901-112-8). Found Class Reprints.

ART AND LAW
see Law and Art

ART AND MEDICINE
see Medicine and Art

ART AND MYTHOLOGY

Waters, Clara E. A Handbook of Legendary & Mythological Art. 520p. 1983. pap. 9.50 (ISBN 0-88072-013-1). Tanager Bks.

ART AND PHOTOGRAPHY

Davis, Douglas, intro. by. Photography As Fine Art. (Illus.). 224p. 1983. 50.00 (ISBN 0-525-24184-1, 038-83). Dutton.

ART AND RELIGION
see also Art and Mythology; Christian Art and Symbolism; Idols and Images

Chantre, Jean-Claude. Les Considerations Religieuses et Esthetiques D'un "Sturmer und Dranger". 650p. (Fr.). 1982. write for info. (ISBN 3-261-04989-8). P Lang Pubs.

Pfeiffer, John E. The Creative Explosion: An Inquiry into the Origins of Art & Religion. LC 82-47531. (Illus.). 320p. 1982. 28.80i (ISBN 0-06-013345-7, HarpT). Har-Row.

ART AND SOCIETY
see also Art and Religion; Art and State; Art Industries and Trade; Folk Art

Keil, Charles. The TIV Song: The Sociology of Art in a Classless Society. LC 78-3178. (Illus.). xiv, 302p. 1983. pap. 9.95 (ISBN 0-226-42963-6). U of Chicago Pr.

ART AND STATE
see also Federal Aid to the Arts; State Encouragement of Science, Literature, and Art

Redstone, L. G. Public Art: New Directions. 1981. 37.95 (ISBN 0-07-051345-7). McGraw.

ART AND THEATER
see Actors and Actresses-Portraits; Theaters-Stage-Setting and Scenery

ART APPRECIATION

Chasse, Paul. Les Arts et La Litterature Ches la Franco-Americains de la nouvelle-angleterre. (Fr.). (gr. 9-10). 1975. pap. text ed. 1.25 (ISBN 0-911409-10-6). Natl Mat Dev.

Woodford, Susan. Looking at Pictures. LC 82-14613. (Cambridge Introduction to the History of Art 6 Ser.). (Illus.). 128p. Date not set. 14.95 (ISBN 0-521-24371-8); pap. 1.25 (ISBN 0-521-28647-6). Cambridge U Pr.

ART AS A PROFESSION
see also Commercial Art As a Profession

Holden, Donald. Art Career Guide. 4th, rev., enl. ed. 320p. 1983. 14.95 (ISBN 0-8230-0252-7). Watson-Guptill.

Riemer, Jeffrey W. & Brooks, Nancy A. Framing the Artist: A Social Portrait of Mid-American Artists. LC 82-13514. 98p. 1982. 18.25 (ISBN 0-8191-2675-6); pap. text ed. 7.00 (ISBN 0-8191-2676-4). U Pr of Amer.

ART AS AN INVESTMENT

Walker, John. Experts' Choice: One Hundred Years of the Art Trade. LC 92-19596. (Illus.). 208p. 1983. text ed. 35.00 (ISBN 0-941434-31-1, 0031). Stewart Tabori & Chang.

ART COLLECTORS
see Art-Collectors and Collecting

ART CRITICISM
see also Art Appreciation

D'Agostino, Peter & Muntadas, Antonio, eds. The Un-Necessary Image. LC 82-51275. (Illus.). 104p. (Orig.). 1982. pap. 8.95 (ISBN 0-934378-30-4). Tanam Pr.

Heyl, Bernard C. New Bearings in Esthetics & Art Criticism: A Study in Semantics & Evaluation. 1943. text ed. 13.50x (ISBN 0-686-83646-4). Elliots Bks.

Lukach, Joan. Hilla Rebay: In Search of the Spirit in Art. (Illus.). 1983. 30.00 (ISBN 0-8076-1067-4). Braziller.

Rodin. Rodin on Art & Artists: With Sixty Illustrations of His Work. 2nd ed. (Fine Art Ser.). (Illus.). 160p. 1983. pap. 6.95 (ISBN 0-486-24487-3). Dover.

ART DECO

Stone, Susanah H. The Oakland Paramount. (Art Ser.). (Illus.). 96p. 1983. 11.95 (ISBN 0-89581-607-5). Lancaster-Miller.

ART EDUCATION
see Art-Study and Teaching

ART FORGERIES
see Forgery of Works of Art

ART GALLERIES
see Art Museums

ART IN ADVERTISING
see Commercial Art

ART IN MOTION
see Kinetic Art

ART INDUSTRIES AND TRADE
see also Antiques; Arms and Armor; Art, Decorative; Folk Art; Jewelry
also particular industries, trades, etc., e.g. Glass Painting and Staining; Leather work; Mosaics

Bator, Paul M. The International Trade in Art. LC 82-17405. vii, 128p. 1982. pap. 6.95 (ISBN 0-226-03910-2). U of Chicago Pr.

Chamberlain, Betty. The Artist's Guide to the Art Market. 4th ed. 263p. 1983. 12.95 (ISBN 0-8230-0328-0). Watson-Guptill.

Garvan, Beatrice B. & Hummel, Charles F. The Pennsylvania Germans: A Celebration of Their Arts 1683-1850. LC 82-61416. (Illus.). 200p. 1982. pap. 18.95 (ISBN 0-87633-048-0). Phila Mus Art.

ART MUSEUMS

Annual Report. LC 70-173826. (Illus.). 1975. pap. 1.00 (ISBN 0-89468-031-5). Natl Gallery Art.

Annual Report, 1977. LC 70-173826. (Illus.). pap. 1.00 (ISBN 0-89468-032-3). Natl Gallery Art.
Annual Report, 1978. LC 70-173826. (Illus.). pap. 1.00 (ISBN 0-89468-052-8). Natl Gallery Art.
Annual Report, 1979. LC 70-173826. (Illus.). pap. 1.00 (ISBN 0-89468-033-1). Natl Gallery Art.
Annual Report, 1980. LC 70-173826. (Illus.). pap. 1.00 (ISBN 0-89468-034-X). Natl Gallery Art.
Annual Report, 1981. LC 70-173826. (Illus.). pap. 2.00 (ISBN 0-89468-035-8). Natl Gallery Art.
Bowron, Edgar P., ed. The North Carolina Museum of Art: Introduction to the Collection. LC 82-21982. (Illus.). 320p. 1983. pap. 19.95 (ISBN 0-8078-4097-1). U of NC Pr.
Jullian, Philippe & O'Neill, John P. La Belle Epoque. (Illus.). 48p. 1982. pap. 6.95 (ISBN 0-87099-329-1). Metro Mus Art.
Krantz, Les. The Texas Art Review. 1982. 35.00 (ISBN 0-87201-018-X). Gulf Pub.
Krause, Martin F., Jr. Master Drawings & Watercolors From the Collection of the Indianapolis Museum of Art. LC 82-84037. (Centennial Catalogue Ser.). (Illus.). 256p. (Orig.). 1983. 30.00x (ISBN 0-936260-06-8); pap. 20.00x (ISBN 0-936260-07-6). Ind Mus Art.
Kuznetsov, Yury & Linnik, Irene. Dutch Painting in Soviet Museums. LC 80-66702. (Illus.). 523p. 1982. 45.00 (ISBN 0-8109-0803-4). Abrams.
McLanathan, Richard. East Building: A Profile. LC 78-606059. (Illus.). pap. 4.00 (ISBN 0-89468-037-4). Natl Gallery Art.
--World Art in American Museums: A Personal Guide. 384p. 1983. 15.95 (ISBN 0-385-18515-4, Anchor Pr). Doubleday.
Mollison, James & Murray, Laura. The Australian National Gallery: An Introduction. (Illus.). 1983. 49.95 (ISBN 0-500-99300-9). Thames Hudson.
Morton, Sean. Exhibit Boston: Gallery Approach Guide for Artists. LC 81-72013. 60p. 1982. pap. 5.00 (ISBN 0-9607908-0-2). Exhibit Pr.
Mucsi, Andras. Catalogue of the Old Masters Gallery at the Christian Museum in Esztergom. Halapy, Lili, tr. from Hungarian. (Illus.). 136p. 1975. pap. 7.50x (ISBN 963-13-4290-5). Intl Pubns Serv.
Museums & Art Galleries in Great Britain & Ireland, 1982. LC 58-46943. (Illus.). 102p. 1982. pap. 4.50x (ISBN 0-900486-32-5). Intl Pubns Serv.
Searing, Helen. New American Art Museums. Date not set. text ed. 24.95 (ISBN 0-520-04895-4); pap. text ed. write for info. (ISBN 0-520-04896-2). U of Cal Pr.
Weil, Stephen E. Beauty & the Beasts: On Museums, Art, the Law, & the Market. 304p. 1983. text ed. 17.50x (ISBN 0-87474-958-1); pap. text ed. 9.95x (ISBN 0-87474-957-3). Smithsonian.

ART NOUVEAU

Mckillip, Rebecca. Art Nouveau Abstract Designs. (The International Design Library). (Illus.). 48p. (Orig.). 1983. pap. 2.95 (ISBN 0-88045-023-1). Stemmer Hse.
Piche, Thomas. Art Nouveau Glass & Pottery. Meyer, Faith, ed. (Illus.). 16p. (Orig.). 1982. pap. text ed. 4.00 (ISBN 0-932660-06-1). U of NI Dept Art.

ART OBJECTS

Here are entered works on decorative art objects. Works on old decorative or utilitarian objects having aesthetic, historic and financial value are entered under Antiques.
see also Antiques
also classes of art objects and names of particular objects, e.g. Bronzes, Glassware, Jewelry, Metal-work, Plate, Pottery
Lawton, Thomas. Chinese Art of the Warring States Period: Change & Continuity, 480-222 B.C. LC 82-600184. (Illus.). 204p. (Orig.). 1983. 35.00x (ISBN 0-934686-39-4); pap. 20.00x (ISBN 0-934686-50-5). Freer.

ART OBJECTS–PRICES

Gordon's Print Price Annual, 1982. 1982. 260.00 (ISBN 0-686-43133-2). Apollo.

ART OBJECTS, FORGERY OF

see Forgery of Works of Art

ART PATRONAGE

Here are entered works dealing with the patronage of art by individuals and corporations. Works on government sponsorship of art are entered under Art and State; State Encouragement of Science, Literature, and Art.
see also Art and State
Hedin, Thomas. The Sculpture of Gaspard & Balthazard Marsy: Art & Patronage in the Early Reign of Louis XIV. LC 82-17415. (Illus.). 288p. 1983. text ed. 49.00x (ISBN 0-8262-0395-7). U of Mo Pr.
Kean, Beverly W. All the Empty Palaces: The Great Merchant Patrons of Modern Art in Pre-Revolutionary Russia. LC 82-8536. (Illus.). 336p. 1983. 29.50 (ISBN 0-87663-412-9). Universe.
Lightbown, Ronald W. Donatello & Michelozzo: An Artistic Partnership & Its Patrons in the Early Renaissance, 2 vols. (Illus.). 460p. 1980. 74.00x (ISBN 0-19-921024-1). Oxford U Pr.
Maharaja Ranjit Singh as Patron of the Arts. 1982. 29.00x (ISBN 0-8364-0865-9, Pub. by Marg). South Asia Bks.

ART PHOTOGRAPHY

see Photography of Art

ART THERAPY

Furrer, P. J. Art Therapy Activities & Lesson Plans for Individual & Groups: A Practical Guide for Teachers, Therapists, Parents & those Interested in Promoting Personal Growth in Themselves & Others. (Illus.). 144p. 1982. pap. 12.75x spiral (ISBN 0-398-04799-5). C C Thomas.
Jungels, Georgiana. To Be Remembered: Art & the Older Adult in Therapeutic Settings. (Illus.). Date not set. pap. 4.95 (ISBN 0-932910-43-2). Potentials Development.
Keyes, Margaret F. Inward Journey: Art as Therapy. rev. ed. (Reality of the Psyche Ser.). (Illus.). 144p. (Orig.). 1983. pap. 8.95 (ISBN 0-87548-368-2). Open Court.

ARTERIES

see also Blood-Vessels; Coronary Arteries
Sprung, Charles L. The Pulmonary Artery Catheter: Methodology & Clinical Applications. 1983. pap. 16.95 (ISBN 0-8391-1808-2, 15520). Univ Park.

ARTERIES–RADIOGRAPHY

Abrams, Herbert L. Coronary Arteriography. 1982. text ed. write for info. (ISBN 0-316-00469-3). Little.

ARTERIOGRAPHY

see Arteries–Radiography

ARTERIOSCLEROSIS

Bond, M. G., et al, eds. Clinical Diagnosis of Atherosclerosis: Quantitative Methods of Evaluation. (Illus.). 544p. 1983. 19.50 (ISBN 0-387-90780-7). Springer-Verlag.
Kritchevsky, David & Gibney, Michael J., eds. Animal & Vegetable Proteins in Lipid Metabolism & Atherosclerosis. LC 82-23961. (Current Topics in Nutrition & Disease Ser.: Vol. 8). 200p. 1983. write for info. (ISBN 0-8451-1607-X). A R Liss.
Rietsma, W. D. Atherosclerosis. (Jonxis Lectures Ser.: Vol. 2). 1979. 34.50 (ISBN 0-444-90075-6). Elsevier.
Schettler, F. G., et al, eds. Atherosclerosis VI: Proceedings. (Illus.). 982p. 1983. 44.00 (ISBN 0-387-11450-5). Springer-Verlag.

ARTHRITIS

see also Rheumatoid Arthritis
Bombelli, R. Osteoarthritis of the Hip: Classification & Pathogenesis-The Role of Osteotomy as Consequent Therapy. 2nd, rev. & enl ed. (Illus.). 386p. 1983. 165.00 (ISBN 0-387-11422-X). Springer-Verlag.
Carr, Rachel. Arthritis: Relief Beyond Drugs. (Illus.). 160p. 1983. pap. 6.68i (ISBN 0-06-464054-X, BN 4054). B&N NY.
Cox, Michael A. Oxycal vs. Arthritis. 171p. (Orig.). 1982. pap. 5.95 (ISBN 0-686-43305-X). R Tanner Assocs Inc.
Kahn, Ada P. Arthritis. (Help Yourself to Health Ser.). 96p. (Orig.). 1983. pap. 3.95 (ISBN 0-8092-5598-7). Contemp Bks.
Keough, Carol & Prevention Magazine Editors. Natural Relief for Arthritis. (Illus.). 320p. 1983. 15.95 (ISBN 0-87857-456-5, 05-901-0). Rodale Pr Inc.
Mandell, Marshall. Dr. Mandell's Lifetime Arthritis Relief System. 252p. 1983. 13.95 (ISBN 0-698-11176-1, Coward). Putnam Pub Group.
Tobe, John. How to Conquor Arthritis. 1976. 11.95x (ISBN 0-686-37944-6). Cancer Control Soc.
Weber, Charles. Arthritis As a Chronic Potassium Deficiency. Rev. ed. 63p. 1981. pap. 8.00 (ISBN 0-9610114-0-8). Kalium.

ARTHRITIS DEFORMAS

see Rheumatoid Arthritis

ARTHROPODA

see also Crustacea; Insects
Clarke. Biology of the Arthropoda. 1975. 22.50 (ISBN 0-444-19559-9). Elsevier.

ARTHROSIS DEFORMANS

see Rheumatoid Arthritis

ARTHUR, KING (ROMANCES, ETC.)

Barber, Richard, ed. Arthurian Literature II. (Illus.). 224p. 1983. text ed. 42.50x (ISBN 0-8476-7196-8). Rowman.
Karr, Phyllis A. The King Arthur Companion. (Illus.). 192p. 1983. 15.95 (ISBN 0-686-84044-5). Reston.
Krishna, Valerie. The Alliterative Morte Arthure: A New Verse Translation. LC 82-24838. 144p. (Orig.). 1983. lib. bdg. 19.75 (ISBN 0-8191-3035-4); pap. text ed. 8.25 (ISBN 0-8191-3036-2). U Pr of Amer.
Schultz, James A. The Shape of the Round Table: Structures of Middle High German Arthurian Romance. 240p. 1983. 25.00x (ISBN 0-8020-2466-1). U of Toronto Pr.

ARTICULATION (EDUCATION)

Ausberger, Carolyn & Mullica, Karyn. Group Games Galore: Wkbk. (Worksheets Unlimited Ser.). 120p. (gr. k-7). wkbk. 27.00 (ISBN 0-686-84661-3). Communication Skill.
--My Own Notebook: Wkbk. (Worksheets Unlimited Ser.). 120p. (gr. k-8). 1982. wkbk. 27.00 (ISBN 0-88450-840-4). Communication Skill.
Formaad, William. Articulation Therapy Through Play. 1974. pap. 6.95 (ISBN 0-914420-51-8). Exceptional Pr Inc.

ARTICULATIONS

see Joints

ARTIFICIAL ANUS

see Colostomy

ARTIFICIAL CONSCIOUSNESS

see Conscious Automata

ARTIFICIAL FIBERS

see Textile Fibers, Synthetic

ARTIFICIAL FUELS

see Synthetic Fuels

ARTIFICIAL INSEMINATION, HUMAN

Hafez, E. S. Instrumental Insemination. 1982. 79.00 (ISBN 90-247-2530-5, Pub. by Martinus Nijhoff Netherlands). Kluwer Boston.

ARTIFICIAL INTELLIGENCE

see also Adaptive Control Systems; Error-Correcting Codes (Information Theory)
American Association for Artifical Intelligence. National Conference on Artificial Intelligence: Proceedings. 456p. (Orig.). 1982. pap. text ed. 25.00x (ISBN 0-86576-043-8). W Kaufmann.
Elithorn, A. & Jones, D., eds. Artificial & Human Thinking. 1973. 12.50 (ISBN 0-444-41023-6). Elsevier.
Findler, N. & Meltzer. Artificial Intelligence & Heuristic Programming. 1971. 23.50 (ISBN 0-444-19597-1). Elsevier.
Krutch, John. Experiments in Artificial Intelligence for Small Computers. 1981. pap. 8.95 (ISBN 0-672-21785-6). Sams.
Michalski, Ryszard S. & Carbonell, Jaime G., eds. Machine Learning: An Artificial Intelligence Approach. LC 82-10654. (Illus.). 600p. 1983. 39.50x (ISBN 0-935382-05-4). Tioga Pub Co.
Rich, E. Artificial Intelligence. 480p. 1982. 24.95x (ISBN 0-07-052261-8). McGraw.
Siekmann, J. & Wrightson, G., eds. The Automation of Reasoning I: Classical Papers on Computational Logic 1957-1966. (Symbolic Computation Ser.). 516p. 1983. 35.00 (ISBN 0-387-12043-2). Springer-Verlag.
--The Automation of Reasoning II: Classical Papers on Computational Logic 1967-1970. (Symbolic Computation Ser.). 640p. 1983. 39.00 (ISBN 0-387-12044-0). Springer-Verlag.
Wahlster, W., ed. Artificial Intelligence, Bad Honnef, FRG 1982: Proceedings. (Informatik Fachberichte Ser.: Vol. 58). 246p. 1983. pap. 14.00 (ISBN 0-387-11960-4). Springer-Verlag.

ARTIFICIAL ISLANDS

see Offshore Structures

ARTIFICIAL LAKES

see Reservoirs

ARTIFICIAL LIMBS

Morecki, A. & Ekiel, J. Cybernetic Systems of Limb Movements in Man, Animals & Robots. LC 82-15717. 250p. 1983. 79.95x (ISBN 0-470-27374-7). Halsted Pr.

ARTIFICIAL ORGANS

see also Prosthesis
Federlin, Konrad & Pfeifeer, Ernst F. Islet Pancreas Transplantation & Artificial Pancreas. 315p. 39.95 (ISBN 0-86577-062-X). Thieme-Stratton.
International Society for Artificial Organs. International Society for Artificial Organs, 3rd, Paris, July 8-10, 1981: Proceeding, Supplement to Vol. 5. Funck, J. L. & Bretano, eds. LC 78-640817. (Illus.). 864p. 1982. text ed. 90.00 (ISBN 0-936022-06-X); pap. text ed. 115.00 (ISBN 0-936022-05-1). Intl Soc Artificial Organs.

ARTIFICIAL PACEMAKER (HEART)

see Pacemaker, Artificial (Heart)

ARTIFICIAL SATELLITES IN TELECOMMUNICATION

see also Radiotelephone; Television
ARINC Research Corporation. Thirty Twenty GHz Communications Satellite Trunking Network Study. 1981. 100.00 (ISBN 0-686-37982-9). Info Gatekeepers.
Beach, Phil R. The Satellite Services Sourcebook. 336p. (Orig.). 1982. pap. 75.00 (ISBN 0-910339-00-7). Beach Assocs.
Crowe, Steve. Satellite Television & Your Backyard Dish. Krieger, Robin, ed. LC 81-90593. (Illus.). 200p. (Orig.). 1982. 20.00 (ISBN 0-910419-00-0); pap. 15.00 (ISBN 0-910419-01-9); trade special 15.00 (ISBN 0-910419-02-7). Satellite.
Direct Broadcast Satellite Systems. (Reports Ser.: No. 514). 187p. 1982. 985.00 (ISBN 0-686-38955-7). Intl Res Dev.
Long, Mark & Keating, Jeffrey. The World of Satellite Television. McClure, Matthew, ed. (Illus.). 224p. 1983. 15.95 (ISBN 0-913990-46-9); pap. 8.95 (ISBN 0-913990-45-0). Book Pub Co.
Wu, William W. Elements of Digital Satellite Communication. 1983. text ed. p.n.s. (ISBN 0-914894-39-0). Computer Sci.

ARTIFICIAL SUNLIGHT THERAPY

see Ultra-Violet Rays–Therapeutic Use

ARTIFICIAL TEETH

see Prosthodontics

ARTIFICIAL THINKING

see Artificial Intelligence

ARTILLERY

Jane's Armour & Artillery, 1982-1983. (Jane's Yearbooks). (Illus.). 700p. 140.00 (ISBN 0-86720-620-9). Sci Bks Intl.
Richardson, Doug. Naval Armament. (Illus.). 160p. 1982. 19.95 (ISBN 0-86720-553-9). Sci Bks Intl.

ARTISANS

see also Apprentices; Cottage Industries; Home Labor; Service Industries
also particular classes of artisans, e.g. Barbers; Cabinet-workers
Barrett, Janice R. & Schuller, Linda J. Illinois Artisans & Craftsmen: A Guide, Resource, & Reference. (Illinois Artisans & Craftsmen Ser.: No. 1). (Illus.). 200p. 1982. 35.00 (ISBN 0-943902-00-2); pap. 14.95 (ISBN 0-943902-01-0). Insearch Pr.
Blamires, D. David Jones: Artist & Writer. 1978. pap. 8.50 (ISBN 0-7190-0730-5). Manchester.
Cardwell, D. S., ed. Artisan to Graduate. 1974. 23.50 (ISBN 0-7190-1272-4). Manchester.

ARTISTIC ANATOMY

see Anatomy, Artistic

ARTISTIC PHOTOGRAPHY

see Photography, Artistic

ARTISTS

see also Actors and Actresses; Architects; Art As a Profession; Authors; Engravers; Illustrators; Musicians; Potters; Printmakers; Sculptors
also names of artists, e.g. Leonardo Da Vinci
Ashbery, John & Moffett, Kenworth. Fairfield Porter. (Illus.). 108p. 1983. pap. 25.00 (ISBN 0-87846-231-7). Mus Fine Arts Boston.
Beaupre, Normand R. L' Enclume et le Couteau: The Life & Work of Adelard Cote Folk Artist. (Illus.). 98p. (Eng. & Fr.). 1982. pap. 9.00 (ISBN 0-911409-13-0). Natl Mat Dev.
Berger, Margaret L. Aline Meyer Liebman: Pioneer Collector & Artist. (Illus.). 148p. 1982. 30.00 (ISBN 0-9605914-0-0). M L Berger.
Carmean, E. A., Jr. & Clark, Trinkett. The Morton G. Neumann Family Collection: Selected Works, Vol. 2. LC 80-20844. (Illus.). pap. 5.00 (ISBN 0-89468-045-5). Natl Gallery Art.
Carmean, E. A., Jr. & Hunter, Sam. The Morton G. Neumann Family Collection: Selected Works, Vol. 1. LC 80-20844. (Illus.). pap. 2.00 (ISBN 0-89468-044-7). Natl Gallery Art.
Cloud, Carey C. Cloud Nine: The Dreamer & the Realist. (Illus.). 140p. 1983. 16.95 (ISBN 0-686-38768-6). Cloudcrest.
Foskett, Daphne. Samuel Cooper (Sixteen Nine to Sixteen Seventy-Two) (Illus.). 151p. 1974. 17.95. Faber & Faber.
Haulice. Index of Artistic Biography, 2 Vols. 1973. 50.00 (ISBN 0-686-43143-X). Apollo.
--Index to Artistic Biography. Suppl. ed. Date not set. 60.00 (ISBN 0-686-43141-3). Apollo.
Kuhn, Bob. The Animal Art of Bob Kuhn: A Lifetime of Drawing & Painting. 1982. pap. 15.95 (ISBN 0-89134-050-5). North Light Pub.
Munsterberg, Hugo. The Crown of Life: Artistic Creativity in Old Age. (Illus.). 256p. cloth 24.95 (ISBN 0-15-123156-7); pap. 12.95 (ISBN 0-15-623202-2). HarBraceJ.
Olivier, Julien. Pas De Gene: Omer Marcoux Violoneux et Sculpteur. (Oral History Ser.). (Illus.). 94p. (Fr.). (gr. 9-10). 1981. pap. 2.50x (ISBN 0-911409-06-8). Natl Mat Dev.
Olsen, Tillie. Silences. 1983. pap. 4.50 (ISBN 0-440-38337-4, LE). Dell.
Reichardt, Jasia & Abakanowicz, Magdalena. Magdalena Abakanowicz. LC 82-11511. (Illus.). 192p. (Orig.). 1983. pap. 24.95 (ISBN 0-89659-323-1). Abbeville Pr.
Rosenberg, Harold. Art on the Edge: Creators & Situations. LC 82-24807. (Illus.). xiv, 304p. 1983. pap. 8.95 (ISBN 0-226-72674-6). U of Chicago Pr.
Smith. Mallett's Index of Artists, 2 Vols. Date not set. 50.00 (ISBN 0-686-43138-3). Apollo.
Tuckerman. Book of the Artists. Date not set. 25.00 (ISBN 0-686-43151-0). Apollo.
Wolf, Miriam, ed. How to Feed a Starving Artist. 320p. (Orig.). 1983. 15.95 (ISBN 0-87842-157-2); pap. 10.95 (ISBN 0-87842-151-3). Mountain Pr.
Wortz, Melinda. UC Irvine. (Illus.). 96p. 1975. 7.00X (ISBN 0-686-99815-4). La Jolla Mus Contemp Art.

ARTISTS–CORRESPONDENCE, REMINISCENCES, ETC.

Cloud, Carey C. Cloud Nine: The Dreamer & the Realist. (Illus.). 140p. 1983. 16.95 (ISBN 0-686-38768-6). Cloudcrest.
Gorokhoff, Galina, ed. Anna Lea Merritt: Memoirs. (Illus.). 325p. Date not set. price not set (ISBN 0-87846-227-9). Mus Fine Arts Boston.
Haulice. Index of Artistic Biography, 2 Vols. 1973. 50.00 (ISBN 0-686-43143-X). Apollo.
--Index to Artistic Biography. Suppl. ed. Date not set. 60.00 (ISBN 0-686-43141-3). Apollo.
Olivier, Julien. Pas De Gene: Omer Marcoux Violoneux et Sculpteur. (Oral History Ser.). (Illus.). 94p. (Fr.). (gr. 9-10). 1981. pap. 2.50x (ISBN 0-911409-06-8). Natl Mat Dev.
Rose, Elizabeth A. The Lizzie's Own Journal La Vie Heureuse. Carson, Robert R., ed. 1983. 10.00 (ISBN 0-686-84439-4). Vantage.

ARTISTS–PSYCHOLOGY

Getzels, Jacob W. & Csikszentmihalyi, Mihaly. The Creative Vision: A Longitudinal Study of Problem Finding in Art. LC 76-16862. 304p. 1976. 31.95x (ISBN 0-471-01486-9, Pub. by Wiley-Interscience). Wiley.

ARTISTS–CANADA

Goldstein, M. & Waldman, S., eds. The Creative Black Book North America 1983: Vol. I. (Illus.). 400p. 1983. 30.00 (ISBN 0-916098-08-7). Friendly Pubns.

Wagg, Susan. Percy Erskine Nobbs: Architect, Artist Craftsman-Architecte, Artiste, Atrisan. (Illus.). 114p. 1982. pap. 12.95 (ISBN 0-7735-0395-1). McGill-Queens U Pr.

ARTISTS–EUROPE

Fifield, William. In Search of Genius. LC 82-8193. 1982. 13.95 (ISBN 0-688-03717-8). Morrow.

ARTISTS–FRANCE

Boyle-Turner, Caroline. Paul Serusier. Foster, Stephen, ed. LC 82-21783. (Studies in Fine Arts: The Avant-Garde: No. 37). 1983. write for info. (ISBN 0-8357-1388-1). Univ Microfilms.

ARTISTS–GERMANY

Heilbut, Anthony. Exiled in Paradise: German Refugee Artists & Intellectuals in America, from the 1930's to the Present. 480p. 1983. 23.50 (ISBN 0-670-51661-9). Viking Pr.

ARTISTS–GREAT BRITAIN

Cuppleditch, David. Phil May: The Artist & His Wit. 128p. 1982. 50.00x (ISBN 0-284-98592-9, Pub. by C Skilton Scotland). State Mutual Bk.

Jarrett, Patricia. Roland Batchelor: A Twentieth-Century View of the Human Comedy. 88p. 1982. 50.00x (ISBN 0-284-98613-5, Pub. by C Skilton Scotland). State Mutual Bk.

ARTISTS–ITALY

Buffa, Sebastian, ed. Italian Artists of the Sixteenth Century, Vols. 34-38. (Illus.). Date not set. 120.00 (ISBN 0-89835-034-4). Abaris Bks.

ARTISTS–MEXICO

Garcia, Rupert. Frida Kahlo. (Chicano Studies Library Publication: No. 7). (Orig.). 1983. pap. text ed. price not set (ISBN 0-918520-05-3). UC Chicano.

ARTISTS–UNITED STATES

Armstrong, Richard. Kim MacConnel: Collection Applied Design. 1976. 3.00x (ISBN 0-686-99808-1). La Jolla Mus Contemp Art.

--Richard Anuszkiewicz. (Illus.). 28p. 1976. 2.00x (ISBN 0-686-99811-1). La Jolla Mus Contemp Art.

Belloli, Jay. Ron Cooper. (Illus.). 38p. 1973. 6.00x (ISBN 0-686-99822-7). La Jolla Mus Contemp Art.

Brewer, Donald J. & Reich, Sheldon. Marsden Hartley-John Marin. (Illus.). 48p. 1966. 3.00x (ISBN 0-686-99839-1). La Jolla Mus Contemp Art.

Celant, Germano. Marcia Hafif. (Illus.). 14p. 1975. 2.00x (ISBN 0-686-99816-2). La Jolla Mus Contemp Art.

--Stephan Rosenthal. (Illus.). 14p. 1975. 3.50x (ISBN 0-686-99814-6). La Jolla Mus Contemp Art.

David Herschler & Melvin Schuler. (Illus.). 1971. 1.00x (ISBN 0-686-99826-X). La Jolla Mus Contemp Art.

Ferrato, Philip. The Porter Family. (Illus.). 23p. 1980. catalogue 1.00. Parrish Art.

Gibson, Arrell M. The Santa Fe & Taos Colonies: Age of the Muses, Nineteen Hundred to Nineteen Forty-Two. LC 82-40452. (Illus.). 328p. 1983. 24.95 (ISBN 0-8061-1835-0). U of Okla Pr.

Goldstein, M. & Waldman, S., eds. The Creative Black Book North America 1983: Vol. I. (Illus.). 400p. 1983. 30.00 (ISBN 0-916098-08-7). Friendly Pubns.

Griffith, J. Neal. Linton Park: American Primitive. 125p. (Orig.). 1982. pap. 5.00 (ISBN 0-935648-11-9). Halldin Pub.

Kord, Catherine. Richard Artschwager, Chuck Close, Joe Zucker. (Illus.). 28p. 1976. 2.00x (ISBN 0-686-99810-3). La Jolla Mus Contemp Art.

Kramer, William. Hans Burkhardt: Artist & Patron of the Arts. (Santa Susana Pr California Masters Ser.: No. 6). (Illus.). 1983. 150.00 (ISBN 0-937048-34-8). CSUN.

Lafferty, Sarah R. Selections: Six in Ohio. (Illus.). 1982. write for info. (ISBN 0-917562-24-0). Contemp Arts.

Marck, Jan V. D. Arman Selected Works. (Illus.). 48p. 1974. 8.00x (ISBN 0-686-99820-0). La Jolla Mus Contemp Art.

Pisano, Ronald. William Merritt Chase in the Company of Friends. (Illus.). 70p. 1979. catalogue 1.00 (ISBN 0-943526-06-X). Parrish Art.

Pisano, Ronald G. The Long Island Landscape, Eighteen Sixty-Five through Nineteen Fourteen: The Halcyon Years. (Illus.). 44p. (Orig.). 1981. write for info. catalogue (ISBN 0-943526-03-5). Parrish Art.

Plagens, Peter. DeWain Valentine. 24p. 1975. 6.50x (ISBN 0-686-99813-8). La Jolla Mus Contemp Art.

Preisman, F. Robin Bright, Faiya Fredman, Reesey Shaw. (Illus.). 8p. 1974. 1.50x (ISBN 0-686-99818-9). La Jolla Mus Contemp Art.

Seldis, Henry J. Helen Lundeberg: A Retrospective Exhibition. (Illus.). 32p. 1971. 5.00x (ISBN 0-686-99825-1). La Jolla Mus Contemp Art.

Selz, Peter. Fletcher Benton-Recent Work. (Illus.). 4p. 1972. 0.50x (ISBN 0-686-99824-3). La Jolla Mus Contemp Art.

Trenton, Patricia & Hassrick, Peter H. The Rocky Mountains: A Vision for Artists in the Nineteenth Century. LC 82-21879. (Illus.). 440p. 1983. 65.00 (ISBN 0-8061-1808-3). U of Okla Pr.

Weschler, Lawrence. Seeing is Forgetting the Name of the Thing One Sees: A Life of Contemporary Artist Robert Irwin. (Illus.). 226p. 1983. pap. 5.95 (ISBN 0-520-04920-9, CAL 617). U of Cal Pr.

Zamparelli, Thomas L. John Strevens: The Man & His Works. (Illus.). 50p. 1983. 12.00. K E Schon.

ARTISTS, WOMEN

see Women Artists

ARTISTS' MARKS

Cuplan. Classified Directory of Artists's Signatures, Symbols, & Monograms. Date not set. 185.00. Apollo.

Jackson. The Concise Dictionaty of Artist's Signatures. 1981. 50.00 (ISBN 0-933516-39-8). Apollo.

ARTISTS' MATERIALS

Kay, Reed. Painter's Guide to Studio Methods & Materials. (Illus.). 352p. 1982. 19.95 (ISBN 0-13-647958-8); pap. 12.95 (ISBN 0-13-647941-3). P-H.

ARTS, THE

see also Artists

Abbs, Peter. English Within the Arts. 148p. (Orig.). 1983. pap. 8.50 (ISBN 0-89874-599-3). Krieger.

Art Address Verlag. International Directory of the Arts, 1983-1984. 2000p. 1983. 110.00 (ISBN 3-921529-03-4). Bowker.

Fifield, William. In Search of Genius. LC 82-8193. 1982. 13.95 (ISBN 0-688-03717-8). Morrow.

Martin, F. David & Jacobus, Lee A. The Humanities Through the Arts. 3rd ed. (Illus.). 520p. 1983. pap. text ed. 19.95 (ISBN 0-07-040639-1, C). McGraw.

Pollock, M., ed. Common Denominators in Art & Science. 220p. 1983. 27.00 (ISBN 0-08-028457-4). Pergamon.

Zhivkova, L., ed. Ludmila Zhivkova: Her Many Worlds - New Culture & Beauty - Concepts & Action. 300p. 1982. 15.00 (ISBN 0-08-028171-0). Pergamon.

ARTS, THE–CRITICISM

see Art Criticism

ARTS, THE–HISTORY

see also Art Criticism

Nichols, Stephen G., Jr. Romanesque Signs: Early Medieval Narrative & Iconography. LC 82-7028. (Illus.). 264p. 1983. text ed. 23.50x (ISBN 0-300-02833-4). Yale U Pr.

ARTS, THE–MANAGEMENT

Jeffri, Joan. Arts Money: Raising It, Saving It, & Earning It. 250p. 1983. pap. 17.95 (ISBN 0-918212-68-5). Neal-Schuman.

Porter, Robert, ed. United Arts Fundraising, 1982. 64p. 1983. pap. 15.00 (ISBN 0-915400-42-1). Am Council Arts.

ARTS, THE–PHILOSOPHY

Bell, Charles. The Anatomy & Philosophy of Expression as Connected with the Fine Arts. 265p. 1982. Repr. of 1846 ed. lib. bdg. 100.00 (ISBN 0-89760-096-7). Telegraph Bks.

Gosson, Stephen. Schoole of Abuse Fifteen Seventy-Nine & A Short Apologie of the Schoole of Abuse Eighteen Sixty-Eight. 80p. pap. 12.50 (ISBN 0-87556-104-7). Saifer.

ARTS, THE–PSYCHOLOGY

Gardner, Howard. The Arts & Human Development. LC 72-13404. (Illus.). 395p. 1973. 35.95x (ISBN 0-471-29145-5, Pub. by Wiley-Interscience). Wiley.

ARTS, THE–STUDY AND TEACHING

Arts & Aesthetics: An Agenda for the Future. 430p. 14.95 (ISBN 0-686-84058-5). AAHPERD.

Coming to Our Senses: The Significance of Arts for American Education. 334p. 9.95 (ISBN 0-686-84059-3). AAHPERD.

ARTS, THE, SPANISH

Weigle, Marta & Larcombe, Claudia, eds. Hispanic Arts & Ethohistory in the Southwest: New Papers Inspired by the Work of E. Boyd. LC 82-74221. (A Spanish Colonial Arts Society Book). (Illus.). 350p. 1983. 35.00 (ISBN 0-941270-14-9); pap. 20.00 (ISBN 0-941270-13-0). Ancient City Pr.

ARTS, DECORATIVE

see Art, Decorative; Art Industries and Trade; Decoration and Ornament; Design, Decorative; Handicraft; Interior Decoration

also subjects referred to under these headings

ARTS, FINE

see Art; Arts, the

ARTS, GRAPHIC

see Graphic Arts

ARTS, USEFUL

see Industrial Arts; Technology

ARTS IN THE CHURCH

see Art and Religion; Christian Art and Symbolism

ARYAN LANGUAGES

see Indo-European Languages

ASANTE LANGUAGE

see Twi Language

ASBESTOS

American Health Research Institute, Ltd. Asbestos & Asbestosis: A Medical Subject Analysis & Research Index with Bibliography. Bartone, John C., ed. 120p. 1983. 29.95 (ISBN 0-941864-84-7); pap. 21.95 (ISBN 0-941864-85-5). ABBE Pubs Assn.

Riordon, P. H. & Hollister, V. F., eds. Geology of Asbestos Deposits. LC 80-52898. (Illus.). 118p. (Orig.). 1981. pap. 32.00x (ISBN 0-89520-277-8, 277-8). Soc Mining Eng.

ASCETICAL THEOLOGY

see Asceticism

ASCETICISM

see also Christian Life; Fasting; Hedonism; Meditation; Monasticism and Religious Orders; Mysticism; Prayer; Retreats; Spiritual Direction; Spiritual Life

Constable, Giles. Attitudes Toward Self-Inflicted Suffering in the Middle Ages. (Stephen J. Brademas Lectures Ser.). 28p. (Orig.). Date not set. pap. text ed. 2.50 (ISBN 0-916586-87-1). Hellenic Coll Pr.

ASCOMYCETES

Sivanesan, A. The Bitunicate Ascomycetes & their Anamorphs. (Illus.). 500p. 1983. lib. bdg. 56.00X (ISBN 3-7682-1329-3). Lubrecht & Cramer.

ASCORBIC ACID

see Vitamins

ASDIC

see Sonar

ASHANTI LANGUAGE

see Twi Language

ASIA

see also names of regions, countries, cities, etc. in Asia

Asia Yearbook, 1983. 1983. pap. write for info. (ISBN 0-8120-2697-7). Barron.

Carim, Enver, ed. Asia & Pacific: 1983. (World of Information Ser.). 328p. 1983. pap. 24.95 (ISBN 0-911818-34-0). World Almanac.

ASIA–BIBLIOGRAPHY

Lee, Don Y. An Annotated Bibliography on Inner Asia. 1983. 25.50x (ISBN 0-939758-04-0). Eastern Pr.

ASIA–CIVILIZATION

Khosla, Sarla. Gupta Civilization. 1982. 38.00x (ISBN 0-686-81734-6, Pub. by Intellectual India). South Asia Bks.

ASIA–DESCRIPTION AND TRAVEL–GUIDEBOOKS

Far Eastern Economic Review Staff, ed. All Asia Guide. new ed. (Illus.). 688p. 1982. pap. 9.95 (ISBN 0-8048-1363-9, Pub. by Far Eastern Economic Review Hong Kong). C E Tuttle.

George, Terry, ed. The On-Your-Own Guide to Asia. rev.& 6th ed. LC 77-90889. (Illus.). 416p. (Orig.). 1983. pap. 6.95 (ISBN 0-8048-1406-6, Co-Pub by Volunteers in Asia). C E Tuttle.

Singapore Travel Guide. (Berlitz Travel Guides). (Illus.). 1982. pap. 4.95 (ISBN 0-02-969800-6, Berlitz). Macmillan.

ASIA–ECONOMIC CONDITIONS

Economic & Social Survey of Asia & the Pacific, 1979. 33rd ed. LC 76-643956. (Illus.). 161p. (Orig.). 1982. pap. 14.00x (ISBN 0-8002-3009-4). Intl Pubns Serv.

Economic & Social Survey of Asia & the Pacific 1980. 143p. 1983. pap. 11.00 (ISBN 0-686-43279-7, UN 81/2F1, UN). Unipub.

Economic Bulletin for Asia & the Pacific, Vol. XXXI, No. 2. 113p. 1983. pap. 10.00 (ISBN 0-686-43278-9, UN 81/2F17, UN). Unipub.

Law & Public Enterprise in Asia: Colloquim Report & Papers. 421p. 1976. 15.00 (ISBN 0-275-23000-7). Intl Ctr Law.

United Nations. Economic & Social Survey of Asia & the Pacific. new ed. 1980. pap. 11.00 (ISBN 0-686-84897-7, E.81.II.F.1). UN.

United Nations, ed. Statistical Yearbook for Asia & the Pacific 1980: Annuaire Statistique Pour L'Asie et le Pacifique. 13th ed. LC 76-641968. 526p. (Orig.). 1981. pap. 33.00x (ISBN 0-8002-3008-6). Intl Pubns Serv.

ASIA–POLITICS AND GOVERNMENT

see also Afro-Asian Politics

Jones, Gavin W. Review of the Integration of Population & Development Policies & Programs in Asia. (Development Studies Centre Occaisional Papers: No. 30). 53p. (Orig.). 1982. pap. text ed. 4.95 (ISBN 0-909150-83-4, 1231). Bks Australia.

Law & Public Enterprise in Asia: Colloquim Report & Papers. 421p. 1976. 15.00 (ISBN 0-275-23000-7). Intl Ctr Law.

ASIA–SOCIAL CONDITIONS

Economic & Social Survey of Asia & the Pacific 1980. 143p. 1983. pap. 11.00 (ISBN 0-686-43279-7, UN 81/2F1, UN). Unipub.

Gunatilleke, Godfrey & Tiruchelvan, Nellan, eds. Ethical Dilemmas of Development in Asia. LC 81-47964. 1983. write for info. (ISBN 0-669-05147-0). Lexington Bks.

ASIA–STATISTICS

Quarterly Bulletin of Statistics for Asia & the Pacific, Vol. XI, No. 4, 1981. 83p. 1983. pap. 8.00 (ISBN 0-686-43284-3, UN 82/2F4, UN). Unipub.

ASIA, SOUTH–FOREIGN RELATIONS

Ziring, Lawrence. The Subcontinent in World Politics: India, Its Neighbors & the Great Powers. rev. 2nd ed. 268p. 1982. 29.95 (ISBN 0-03-060287-4); pap. 13.95 (ISBN 0-03-060288-2). Praeger.

ASIA, SOUTH–POLITICS

Wilson, Jeyaratnam & Dalton, Dennis, eds. The States of South Asia: Problems of National Integration. 361p. 1983. text ed. 24.00x (ISBN 0-8248-0823-1). UH Pr.

Ziring, Lawrence. The Subcontinent in World Politics: India, Its Neighbors & the Great Powers. rev. 2nd ed. 268p. 1982. 29.95 (ISBN 0-03-060287-4); pap. 13.95 (ISBN 0-03-060288-2). Praeger.

ASIA, SOUTHEASTERN

see also names of individual states in Southeast Asia, e.g. Indonesia; names of regions, cities, etc.

Dutt, Ashok K. Southeast Asia: Realm of Contrasts. 3rd rev. ed. 275p. 1983. lib. bdg. 28.50x (ISBN 0-86531-561-2); pap. text ed. 15.00x (ISBN 0-86531-562-0). Westview.

Gesick, Lorraine, et al, eds. The Classical States of Southeast Asia. Date not set. pap. price not set. Yale U SE Asia.

Osborne, Milton. South East Asia. rev. ed. 208p. (Orig.). 1983. pap. text ed. 8.95 (ISBN 0-86861-269-3). Allen Unwin.

ASIA, SOUTHEASTERN–DEFENSES

Scalapino, Robert A. & Wanandi, Jusuf, eds. Economic, Political & Security Issues in Southeast Asia in the 1980s. (Research Papers & Policy Studies: No. 7). 240p. (Orig.). 1982. pap. 10.00x (ISBN 0-912966-52-1). IEAS.

ASIA, SOUTHEASTERN–DESCRIPTION AND TRAVEL

Chia, L. S. & MacAndrews, C. Southeast Asian Seas: Frontiers for Development. 1982. 36.50x (ISBN 0-07-099247-9). McGraw.

Loose, S. & Ramb, R. Southeast Asia Handbook: Singapore, Burma, Brunei, Borneo, Malaysia, Thailand. (Illus.). 550p. 1983. pap. 13.95 (ISBN 3-922025-07-2). Bradt Ent.

ASIA, SOUTHEASTERN–ECONOMIC CONDITIONS

ASEAN Today-Your Partner of Tomorrow. 295p. 1981. pap. 18.00 (ISBN 0-89192-348-9). Transbooks.

Jorgensen-Dahl, Arnfinn. Regional Organisation & Order in South-East Asia. 200p. 1982. 60.00x (ISBN 0-333-30663-5, Pub. by Macmillan England). State Mutual Bk.

Lee, S. Y. Financial Structures & Monetary Policy. 300p. 1982. 49.00x (ISBN 0-333-28617-0, Pub. by Macmillan England). State Mutual Bk.

Scalapino, Robert A. & Wanandi, Jusuf, eds. Economic, Political & Security Issues in Southeast Asia in the 1980s. (Research Papers & Policy Studies: No. 7). 240p. (Orig.). 1982. pap. 10.00x (ISBN 0-912966-52-1). IEAS.

Wawn, Brian. The Economics of ASEAN Countries. LC 82-5958. 1983. 27.50x (ISBN 0-312-23673-5). St Martin.

ASIA, SOUTHEASTERN–FOREIGN RELATIONS

Pye, Lucian W. Redefining American Policy in Southeast Asia. 1982. pap. 3.75 (ISBN 0-8447-1095-4). Am Enterprise.

ASIA, SOUTHEASTERN–HISTORY

McCoy, Alfred W., et al, eds. Southeast Asia Under Japanese Occupation. (Illus.). v, 302p. 1980. pap. 12.00 (ISBN 0-686-38044-4). Yale U SE Asia.

ASIA, SOUTHEASTERN–POLITICS

Institute of Southeast Asia Studies. Southeast Asia Affairs 1982. x, 396p. 1982. text ed. 40.00x (ISBN 0-686-83754-1, 00155). Heinemann Ed.

Scalapino, Robert A. & Wanandi, Jusuf, eds. Economic, Political & Security Issues in Southeast Asia in the 1980s. (Research Papers & Policy Studies: No. 7). 240p. (Orig.). 1982. pap. 10.00x (ISBN 0-912966-52-1). IEAS.

ASIA, SOUTHEASTERN–SOCIAL CONDITIONS

Jones, G. W. & Richter, H. V. Population Resettlement Programs in Southeast Asia. LC 82-73138. (Development Studies Centre Monograph: No. 30). 189p. (Orig.). 1982. pap. text ed. 17.95 (ISBN 0-909150-73-7, 1230). Bks Australia.

ASIA, WESTERN

Gopal, Rishane & Gopal, Kokila K. West Asia & North Africa: A Documentary Study of Major Crises, 1974-78. 434p. 1981. 37.50x (ISBN 0-86590-012-4). Apt Bks.

ASIAN-AFRICAN POLITICS

see Afro-Asian Politics

ASIAN AMERICANS

Kim, Bok-Lim C. Asian Americans: Changing Patterns, Changing Needs. xxiii, 271p. 1978. 12.00 (ISBN 0-932014-03-8). AKCS.

Kim, Elaine. With Silk Wings: Asian American Women at Work. (Illus.). 150p. 1983. pap. 10.95 (ISBN 0-936434-06-6). SF Stud Ctr.

Wong, Diane Yen-Mei. Dear Diane: Letters from Our Daughters. Kim, Elaine, intro. by. (Illus.). 90p. (Eng. & Korean.). 1983. pap. 4.95 (ISBN 0-936434-08-2). SF Stud Ctr.

--Dear Diane: Letters from Our Daughters. Kim, Elaine, intro. by. 80p. (Orig., Eng. & Chinese.). 1983. pap. 4.95 (ISBN 0-936434-07-4). SF Stud Ctr.

--Dear Diane: Questions & Answers for Asian American Women. Kim, Elaine, intro. by. (Illus.). 96p. (Orig.). 1983. pap. 4.95 (ISBN 0-936434-09-0). SF Stud Ctr.

ASIAN ARCHITECTURE

see Architecture–Asia

ASIAN ART

see Art, Asian

ASIAN FOLK-LORE

see Folk-Lore, Asian

ASIAN STUDIES

see Oriental Studies

ASIAN TALES

see Tales, Asian

ASIANS

see also names of individual races e.g. East Indians, Mongols.

Mehta, Asoka. Perception of Asian Personality. 264p. 1978. 15.95x (ISBN 0-940500-63-9). Asia Bk Corp.

ASQUITH, HERBERT HENRY

see Oxford and Asquith, Herbert Henry Asquith, 1st Earl Of, 1852-1928

ASSAMESE LITERATURE–HISTORY AND CRITICISM
Bhattacharyya, B. K. Humour & Satire in Assame Literature. 263p. 1982. 39.95x (ISBN 0-940500-46-9, Pub. by Sterling India). Asia Bk Corp.

ASSASSINATION
see also Murder; Terrorism
Finke, Blythe F. Assassination: Case Studies. Rahmas, Sigurd C., ed. (Topics of Our Times Ser.: No. 17). 32p. (Orig.). 1982. 2.95x (ISBN 0-87157-318-0); pap. text ed. 1.95 (ISBN 0-87157-818-2). SamHar Pr.

ASSAULT, CRIMINAL
see Rape

ASSEMBLER LANGUAGE (COMPUTER PROGRAM LANGUAGE)
Howe, Hubert S., Jr. TRS-Eighty Model III Assembly Language Tutor. 192p. 1983. 29.95 (ISBN 0-13-931279-X); pap. 16.95 (ISBN 0-13-931261-7); software 29.95 (ISBN 0-13-931287-0). P-H.
Inman, Don & Inman, Kurt. Assembly Language Graphics for the TRS-80 Color Computer. 1982. text ed. 19.95 (ISBN 0-8359-0318-4); pap. text ed. 14.95 (ISBN 0-8359-0317-6). Reston.
McCaul, Earles. TRS-80 Assembly Language Made Simple. 1981. pap. 12.95 (ISBN 0-672-21851-8). Sams.

ASSEMBLY, SCHOOL
see Schools–Exercises and Recreations

ASSEMBLY LANGUAGE (COMPUTER PROGRAM LANGUAGE)
see Assembler Language (Computer Program Language)
Howe, Hubert. TRS-80 MOD III Assembly Language. 1983. price not set. P-H.

ASSEMBLY-LINE METHODS
see also Automation
Assembly Automation: Proceedings of the 3rd International Conference, Stuttgart, Germany 25-27 May 1982. (Illus.). 626p. 1982. pap. text ed. 90.00x (ISBN 0-903608-25-1, Pub. by IFSPUBS). Scholium Intl.

ASSERTIVENESS (PSYCHOLOGY)
Cawood, Diana. Assertiveness for Managers. 200p. (Orig.). 1983. pap. price not set (ISBN 0-88908-562-5). Self Counsel Pr.
Chenevert, Melodie. STAT: Special Techiques in Assertiveness Training for Women in the Health Professions. (Illus.). 144p. 1983. text ed. 10.95 (ISBN 0-8016-1135-0). Mosby.

ASSESSMENT
Here are entered works on tax assessment. Works on the technique of property valuation for other than taxation purposes are entered under specific headings with subdivision Valuation, e.g. Real Property–Valuation. Works on assessment in a particular field of taxation are entered under the heading covering taxation in that field, e.g. Real Property Tax.
see also Real Property–Valuation; Taxation, Exemption From; Valuation
Rudman, Jack. Administrative Assessor. (Career Examination Ser.: C-2596). (Cloth bdg. avail. on request). pap. 12.00 (ISBN 0-8373-2596-X). Natl Learning.
--Appraisal Investigator. (Career Examination Ser.: C-452). (Cloth bdg. avail. on request). pap. 12.00 (ISBN 0-8373-0452-0). Natl Learning.

ASSESSMENT OF PERSONALITY
see Personality Assessment

ASSETS, LIQUID
Asset Management: Learning Guide, CEBS Course 7. 1982. spiral binding 18.00 (ISBN 0-89154-193-4). Intl Found Employ.

ASSINIBOIN INDIANS
see Indians of North America–The West

ASSISTANCE TO UNDERDEVELOPED AREAS
see Technical Assistance

ASSOCIATION
see Social Groups

ASSOCIATION FOOTBALL
see Soccer

ASSOCIATIONS (LAW)
see Corporations, Nonprofit

ASSOCIATIONS, INSTITUTIONS, ETC.
see also Community Life; Cooperation; Meetings; Social Group Work; Societies
also names of specific types of associations, institutions, etc. e.g., Corporations; Public Institutions; Trade and Professional Associations; subdivision Societies under appropriate subjects
Alliband, Terry. Voluntary Agencies in Rural Community Development. (Library of Management for Development). 128p. 1983. pap. write for info. (ISBN 0-931816-28-9). Kumarian Pr.
Nordhoff, Nancy S. & Larsen, Jo. Fundamental Practices for Success with Volunteer Boards of Non-Profit Organizations, 4 vols, Vol. I. LC 82-83808. (Fundamental Practices Ser.). 140p. 1982. pap. 11.95 (ISBN 0-9609972-0-2). Fun Prax.
O'Connell, Brian. Effective Leadership in Voluntary Organizations. 224p. 1976. 8.95 (ISBN 0-695-81119-3). Follett.
Vineyard, Sue. Beyond Banquets, Plaques & Pins: Creative Ways to Recognize Volunteers & Staff. 2nd ed. (Illus.). 24p. 1981. pap. text ed. 3.50 (ISBN 0-911029-01-X). Heritage Arts.
Voluntary Organizations: An NCVO Directory 1982-83. 192p. 1982. pap. text ed. 12.25x (ISBN 0-7199-1061-7, Pub. by Bedford England). Renouf.

ASSOCIATIONS, INSTITUTIONS, ETC.–DIRECTORIES
Center for Self Sufficiency Research Division Staff. Index to Self-Sufficiency Related Institutes, Associations, Organizations, Schools, & Others. 200p. 1983. pap. text ed. 19.95 (ISBN 0-910811-19-9). Center Self.
Nusberg, Charlotte, ed. The Voluntary Agency as an Instrument of Social Change: Effective Advocacy on Behalf of the Aging. (Orig.). 1976. pap. text ed. 2.00 (ISBN 0-910473-01-3). Intl Fed Ageing.
Oeckl, Albert, ed. Taschenbuch des Oeffentlichen Lebens (Handbook of Public & Private Institutions), 1982-83. 32nd ed. 1189p. (Ger.). 1982. 57.50x (ISBN 0-8002-3074-4). Intl Pubns Serv.

ASSOCIATIONS, INTERNATIONAL
see International Agencies

ASSOCIATIVE RINGS
Amitsur, S. A & Saltman, D. J., eds. Algebraists' Homage: Papers in Ring Theory & Related Topics. LC 82-18934. (Contemporary Mathematics Ser.: vol. 13). 30.00 (ISBN 0-8218-5013-X, CONM/13). Am Math.

ASSURANCE (INSURANCE)
see Insurance

ASSYRO-BABYLONIAN INSCRIPTIONS
see Cuneiform Inscriptions

ASTRAL PROJECTION
Blackmore, Susan J. Beyond the Body: An Investigation of Out-of-the-Body Experiences. 288p. 1982. 40.00x (ISBN 0-434-07470-5, Pub. by Heinemann England). State Mutual Bk.
Rogo, D. Scott. Leaving the Body: A Practical Guide to Astral Projection. (Illus.). 190p. 1983. 14.95 (ISBN 0-13-528034-6); pap. 5.95 (ISBN 0-13-528026-5). P-H.

ASTROBIOLOGY
see Life on Other Planets

ASTROGATION
see Navigation (Astronautics)

ASTROLABES
Mills, H. R. The Versatile Astrolabe & Planisphere. 1981. 30.00x (ISBN 0-85950-332-1, Pub. by Thornes England). State Mutual Bk.

ASTROLOGY
see also Horoscopes; Occult Sciences
Delson, Paula. Chinese Astrology. (Illus.). 248p. 1982. Repr. 11.95 (ISBN 0-88254-700-3). Hippocrene Bks.
Eysenck, H. J. & Nias, D. K. Astrology: Science or Superstition. 1982. 45.00x (ISBN 0-85117-214-8, Pub. by M Temple Smith). State Mutual Bk.
Foxe, Sonja & Miles, Barbara. Essential Chicago: An Astrological Portrait of the Windy City. (Illus.). 1982. pap. 3.80 (ISBN 0-933646-21-6). Aries Pr.
Freeman, Martin. Forecasting by Astrology. 160p. 1983. pap. 7.95 (ISBN 0-85030-297-8). Newcastle Pub.
Hall, Manly P. Blessed Angels. pap. 2.95 (ISBN 0-89314-807-5). Philos Res.
--Collected Writings, No. 3. pap. 10.00 (ISBN 0-89314-507-6). Philos Res.
KeGan, Frank R. Intro to the Xray I, Links the Objective Patterns of Astrology & the Process Symbolism of the I Ching. (Illus.). 1982. pap. 5.00 (ISBN 0-933646-20-8). Aries Pr.
--Stars & Dice: Pythagorean Astrology. (Illus.). 1983. pap. 5.00t (ISBN 0-933646-22-4). Aries Pr.
Khma, Andres T. Wisdom of Sidereal Astrology. (Illus.). 503p. 1983. pap. 18.00 (ISBN 0-89540-127-4). Sun Pub.
Kingsford, Anna & Maitland, Edward. Clothed With the Sun. 248p. 11.50 (ISBN 0-686-38213-7). Sun Bks.
Linares, Enrique. A Scientific Approach to the Metaphysics of Astrology. Robertson, Arlene, ed. 170p. (Orig.). 1982. pap. 7.95 (ISBN 0-930706-10-2). Seek-It Pubns.
Lind, Ingrid. Astrologically Speaking. 276p. 1982. 34.00x (ISBN 0-686-82394-X, Pub. by L N Fowler). State Mutual Bk.
Lofthus, Myrna. A Spiritual Approach to Astrology: A Complete Textbook of Astrology. LC 78-62936. (Illus.). 428p. 1983. 12.50 (ISBN 0-916360-10-5). CRCS Pubns NV.
MacNaughton, Robin. How to Transform Your Life Through Astrology. 224p. 1983. pap. 3.50 (ISBN 0-553-23203-7). Bantam.
Merriman, Raymond. The Gold Book: Geocosmic Correlations to Gold Price Cycles. Robertson, Arlene, ed. 320p. (Orig.). 1982. pap. 50.00 (ISBN 0-930706-13-7). Seek-It Pubns.
Morbidoni, Barbara. Zodiantics: An Astrology Handbook. Rev. ed. LC 77-2070. (Illus.). 1982. pap. 5.00 (ISBN 0-933646-18-6). Aries Pr.
Parker, Samanthe. Star Vision. (Illus.). 64p. (Orig.). 1982. pap. 4.95 (ISBN 0-910241-00-7). Shaunter Ent.
Raphael. Raphael's Key to Astrology. 118p. 6.50 (ISBN 0-686-38233-1). Sun Bks.
Rice, Paul & Rice, Valeta. Aquarius: Through the Numbers. 48p. 1983. pap. 2.50 (ISBN 0-87728-575-6). Weiser.
--Aries: Through the Numbers. 48p. 1983. pap. 2.50 (ISBN 0-87728-565-9). Weiser.
--Cancer: Through the Numbers. 48p. 1983. pap. 2.50 (ISBN 0-87728-568-3). Weiser.
--Capricorn: Through the Numbers. 48p. 1983. pap. 2.50 (ISBN 0-87728-574-8). Weiser.
--Gemini: Through the Numbers. 48p. 1983. pap. 2.50 (ISBN 0-87728-567-5). Weiser.
--Leo: Through the Numbers. 48p. 1983. pap. 2.50 (ISBN 0-87728-569-1). Weiser.
--Libra: Through the Numbers. 48p. 1983. pap. 2.50 (ISBN 0-87728-571-3). Weiser.
--Pisces: Through the Numbers. 48p. 1983. pap. 2.50 (ISBN 0-87728-576-4). Weiser.
--Sagittarius: Through the Numbers. 48p. 1983. pap. 2.50 (ISBN 0-87728-573-X). Weiser.
--Scorpio: Through the Numbers. 48p. 1983. pap. 2.50 (ISBN 0-87728-572-1). Weiser.
--Taurus: Through the Numbers. 48p. 1983. pap. 2.50 (ISBN 0-87728-566-7). Weiser.
--Virgo: Through the Numbers. 48p. 1983. pap. 2.50 (ISBN 0-87728-570-5). Weiser.
Robson, Vivian E. A Beginners Guide to Practical Astrology. 184p. 9.00 (ISBN 0-686-38212-9). Sun Bks.
Rose, Christina. Astrological Counseling. 128p. 1983. pap. 7.95 (ISBN 0-85030-301-X). Newcastle Pub.
Sandbauch, John. Astrology, Alchemy & Tarot. 307p. 1982. pap. 4.95 (ISBN 0-930706-08-0). Seek-It Pubns.
Schulman, Martin. Karmic Astrology: The Moon's Nodes & Reincarnation. (Vol. 1). 1975. 4.95 (ISBN 0-87728-288-9). Weiser.
Starck, Marcia. Astrology: Key to Holistic Health. Robertson, Arlene, ed. 220p. (Orig.). 1982. pap. 9.95 (ISBN 0-930706-11-0). Seek-It Pubns.
Takra, Andres. The Wisdom of Siderial Astrology. 520p. 18.00 (ISBN 0-686-38239-0). Sun Bks.
Thornton, Penny. Synastry: A Comprehensive Guide to the Astrology of Relationships. 160p. 1983. pap. 8.95 (ISBN 0-85030-276-5). Newcastle Pub.
Turner, Gwyn. The Complete Home Astrologer. 110p. (Orig.). 1979. pap. 8.95 (ISBN 0-7100-0130-4). Routledge & Kegan.
Tyl, Noel. Guide to the Principles & Practices of Astrology. 1979. 17.95 (ISBN 0-686-43166-9). Llewellyn Pubns.
Van Nostrand, Frederic. Mars Through the Signs. 64p. 1982. pap. 4.95 (ISBN 0-940058-05-7). Clancy Pubns.
West, Patricia E. Astrology Handbook for Therapists & Holistic Health Practitioners. (Orig.). 1983. pap. 5.50 (ISBN 0-942384-02-4). Red Dragon.
Wilson-Ludlam, Mae R. A Course in Basic Astrology & Its Phraseology. (Illus.). 84p. (Orig.). 1982. pap. 7.95 (ISBN 0-88053-768-X). Macoy Pub.

ASTRONAUTICAL ACCIDENTS
see Astronautics–Accidents

ASTRONAUTICAL INSTRUMENTS
Shapley, Harlow. Inner Metagalaxy. 1957. text ed. 39.50x (ISBN 0-686-83589-1). Elliots Bks.

ASTRONAUTICAL RESEARCH
Napolitano, L. Astronautical Research, 1970. (Proceedings). 1971. 97.75 (ISBN 0-444-10101-2). Elsevier.

ASTRONAUTICS
see also Astronauts; Navigation (Astronautics); Outer Space; Outer Space–Exploration; Space Flight; Space Sciences
Estes, John E. & Senger, Leslie W. Remote Sensing: Techniques for Environmental Analysis. LC 73-8601. 340p. 1974. 24.95x (ISBN 0-471-24595-X). Wiley.
Soward, A. M. Stellar & Planetary Magnetism. (The Fluid Mechanics of Astrophysics & Geophysics Ser.: Vol. 2). 1982. write for info. (ISBN 0-677-16430-0). Gordon.

ASTRONAUTICS–ACCIDENTS
Forkosch, Morris D. Outer Space & Legal Liability. 1982. lib. bdg. 43.50 (ISBN 90-247-2582-8, Pub. by Martinus Nijhoff Netherlands). Kluwer Boston.

ASTRONAUTICS–RESEARCH
see Astronautical Research

ASTRONAUTICS AND STATE
Gray, Colin S. U. S. Military Space Policy to the Year 2000. 1983. text ed. 28.00 (ISBN 0-89011-591-5). Abt Bks.

ASTRONAUTS
Greene, Vaughn M. Astronauts of Ancient Japan. LC 78-78289. (Illus.). 200p. (Orig.). 1978. 8.95 (ISBN 0-8048-1311-6, Dist. by C E Tuttle). Merlin Engine Wks.

ASTRONAVIGATION
see Navigation (Astronautics)

ASTRONOMERS
Webb, George E. Tree Rings & Telescopes: The Scientific Career of A. E. Douglass. 250p. 1983. 19.50x (ISBN 0-8165-0798-8). U of Ariz Pr.

ASTRONOMICAL INSTRUMENTS
see also Astrolabes; Telescope
Eccles, M. J. & Sim, M. E. Low Light Level Detectors in Astronomy. LC 82-12881. (Cambridge Astrophysics Ser.: No. 3). (Illus.). 200p. Date not set. price not set (ISBN 0-521-24088-3). Cambridge U Pr.

ASTRONOMICAL PHOTOMETRY
see Photometry, Astronomical

ASTRONOMICAL PHYSICS
see Astrophysics

ASTRONOMY
see also Almanacs; Astrology; Astrophysics; Comets; Constellations; Cosmogony; Earth; Geodesy; Life on Other Planets; Mechanics, Celestial; Meteorites; Moon; Nautical Almanacs; Nautical Astronomy; Nebulae; Outer Space; Satellites; Solar System; Space Environment; Space Sciences; Spectrum Analysis; Stars; Statistical Astronomy; Sun; Tides; Zodiac
Beckman, J. E. & Phillips, J. P. Submillimetre Wave Astronomy. LC 82-4487. (Illus.). 370p. 1982. 47.50 (ISBN 0-521-24733-0). Cambridge U Pr.
Berendzen. Man Discovers the Galaxies. 1976. 15.95 (ISBN 0-07-004845-2). McGraw.
British Astronomical Association. Observing the Moon. (Illus.). 64p. 1983. pap. text ed. 10.95 (ISBN 0-89490-085-4). Enslow Pubs.
Burgess, Eric. Celestial Basic: Astronomy on Your Computer. LC 82-60187. (Illus.). 300p. 1982. pap. text ed. 13.95 (ISBN 0-89588-087-3). Sybex.
Chartrand, Mark R. Skyguide Gift Box. (Illus.). 280p. 1982. 12.95 (ISBN 0-307-47011-3). Western Pub.
Cherrington, Ernest H. Exploring the Moon Through Binoculars & Small Telescopes. (Illus.). 224p. 1983. pap. 10.00 (ISBN 0-486-24491-1). Dover.
Discovering Astronomy. (Discovering Science Ser.). 1982. lib. bdg. 15.96 (ISBN 0-86706-063-8, Pub. by Stonehenge). Silver.
Ferris, Timothy. The Red Limit: The Search for the Edge of the Universe. rev. ed. (Illus.). 288p. 1983. pap. 14.95 (ISBN 0-688-01836-X). Quill NY.
Fricke, W. & Teleki, G., eds. Sun & Planetary System. 1982. 65.00 (ISBN 90-277-1429-0, Pub. by Reidel Holland). Kluwer Boston.
Friedjung, M. & Viotti, R., eds. The Nature of Symbiotic Stars. 1982. 43.50 (ISBN 0-686-37436-3, Pub. by Reidel Holland). Kluwer Boston.
Genet, Russell M. & Wolpert, Robert C., eds. Microcomputers in Astronomy. LC 82-84769. 200p. (Orig.). 1983. pap. 18.95 (ISBN 0-911351-03-5). Fairborn Observ.
Hodge, P. W. Concepts of Contemporary Astronomy. 2nd ed. 1979. 23.95 (ISBN 0-07-029147-0). McGraw.
Humphries, C. M., ed. Instrumentation for Astronomy with Large Optical Telescopes. 1982. 48.00 (ISBN 90-277-1388-X, Pub. by Reidel Holland). Kluwer Boston.
Jacobs, Francine. Cosmic Countdown: What Astronomers Have Learned About the Life of the Universe. (Illus.). 192p. 1983. 9.95 (ISBN 0-87131-404-5). M Evans.
Jaschek, C. & Heintz, W., eds. Automated Data Retrieval in Astronomy. 1982. 48.00 (ISBN 90-277-1435-5, Pub. by Reidel Holland). Kluwer Boston.
Justus, Fred. Our Solar System. (Science Ser.). 24p. (gr. 7). 1979. wkbk. 5.00 (ISBN 0-8209-0145-8, S-7). ESP.
Kopal, Z. & Rahe, J. Binary & Multiple Stars as Tracers of Stellar Evolution. 1982. 67.50 (ISBN 90-277-1436-3, Pub. by Reidel Holland). Kluwer Boston.
Krupp, E. C., ed. Archaeoastronomy & the Roots of Science. (AAAS Selected Symposium Ser.: No. 71). 400p. 1983. price not set (ISBN 0-86531-406-3). Westview.
Lovell, B. Astronomy. 1970. 71.75 (ISBN 0-444-20102-5). Elsevier.
McGraw-Hill Publishing Co. Encyclopedia of Astronomy. 464p. 1983. 44.50 (ISBN 0-07-045251-2, P&RB). McGraw.
Mariolopoulos, E. Compendium in Astronomy. 1982. 49.50 (ISBN 90-277-1373-1, Pub. by Reidel Holland). Kluwer Boston.
Mills, H. R. Positional Astronomy & Astro-Navigation Made Easy: A New Approach Using the Pocket Calculator. 284p. 1978. 65.00x (ISBN 0-85950-062-4, Pub. by Thornes England). State Mutual Bk.
Rees, M. & Stoneham, R. Supernovae: A Survey of Current Research. 1982. 69.00 (ISBN 90-277-1442-8, Pub. by Reidel Holland). Kluwer Boston.
Roelofs. Astronomy & Land Surveying. 1950. 11.50 (ISBN 0-444-40771-5). Elsevier.
Schaifers, K. & Voigt, H. H., eds. Astronomy & Astrophysics: Interstellar Matter, Galaxy, Universe. (Landolt-Boernstein, New Series. Group VI: Vol. 2, Subvol. C). (Illus.). 490p. 1983. 780.00 (ISBN 0-387-10977-3). Springer-Verlag.
Smith, Debbi K. Secrets from a Stargazer's Notebook. 512p. 1982. pap. 3.50 (ISBN 0-553-22587-1). Bantam.
Snow, Theodore P., Jr. The Dynamic Universe: An Introduction to Astronomy. 500p. 1983. text ed. 19.95 (ISBN 0-314-69681-4); instrs.' manual avail. (ISBN 0-314-71129-5); study guide avail. (ISBN 0-314-71130-9). West Pub.
Tattersfield, D. Projects & Demonstrations in Astronomy. 352p. 1979. 75.00x (ISBN 0-85950-087-X, Pub. by Thornes England). State Mutual Bk.
Wayman, P. Reports on Astronomy. 1982. 67.50 (ISBN 90-277-1423-1, Pub. by Reidel Holland). Kluwer Boston.
Zombeck, Martin V. Handbook of Space Astronomy & Astrophysics. LC 82-12944. (Illus.). 341p. 1983. 24.95 (ISBN 0-521-24194-4). Cambridge U Pr.

ASTRONOMY–ADDRESSES, ESSAYS, LECTURES
Boehme, S., et al. Astronomy & Astrophysics Abstracts, Vol. 31: Literature 1982, Pt. 1. 776p. 1983. 66.00 (ISBN 0-387-12072-6). Springer-Verlag.
ASTRONOMY–ATLASES
see Stars–Atlases
ASTRONOMY–CHARTS, DIAGRAMS, ETC.
see also Stars–Atlases
Mills, H. R. The Versatile Astrolabe & Planisphere. 1981. 30.00x (ISBN 0-85950-332-1, Pub. by Thornes England). State Mutual Bk.
ASTRONOMY–CURIOSA AND MISCELLANEA
Moore, Patrick. Guinness Book of Astronomy Facts & Feats. 2nd ed. (Illus.). 304p. 1983. 19.95 (ISBN 0-85112-258-2, Pub. by Guinness Superlatives England); pap. 12.95 (ISBN 0-85112-291-4, Pub. by Guinness Superlatives England). Sterling.
ASTRONOMY–EPHEMERIDES
see Nautical Almanacs
ASTRONOMY–HISTORY
Learner, Richard. Astronomy through the Telescope: The 500-year Story of the Instruments, the Inventors & their Discoveries. 224p. 1982. 59.00x (ISBN 0-686-81700-1, Pub. by Evans Bros). State Mutual Bk.
ASTRONOMY–JUVENILE LITERATURE
Branley, Franklyn M. The Planets in Our Solar System. LC 79-7894. (A Trophy Let's-Read-and-Find-out Science Bk.). (Illus.). 40p. (gr. k-3). 1983. pap. 3.80i (ISBN 0-06-445001-5, Trophy). Har-Row.
--Secret Three. LC 81-43037. (A Trophy Let's Read-&-Find-Out Science Bk.). (Illus.). 40p. (gr. k-3). 1983. pap. 3.80i (ISBN 0-06-445002-3, Trophy). Har-Row.
Herbst, Judith. Sky Above & Worlds Beyond. LC 82-13749. (Illus.). 224p. (gr. 5 up). 1983. 13.95 (ISBN 0-689-30974-0). Atheneum.
ASTRONOMY–OBSERVATIONS
see also Errors, Theory Of
Hall, Douglas S. & Genet, Russell M. Photoelectric Photometry of Variable Stars: A Practical Guide for the Smaller Observatory. (Illus.). 282p. (Orig.). 1982. pap. 17.95 (ISBN 0-911351-00-0). Fairborn Observ.
Learner, Richard. Astronomy through the Telescope: The 500-year Story of the Instruments, the Inventors & their Discoveries. 224p. 1982. 59.00x (ISBN 0-686-81700-1, Pub. by Evans Bros). State Mutual Bk.
ASTRONOMY–OBSERVERS' MANUALS
Barker, Edmund S. Webb Society Deep-Sky Observer's Handbook: Vol. 4, Galaxies. Glyn-Jones, Kenneth, ed. 250p. 1982. 40.00x (ISBN 0-7188-2527-6, Pub. by Lutterworth Pr England). State Mutual Bk.
ASTRONOMY–PROBLEMS, EXERCISES, ETC.
Meeus, Jean. Astronomical Formulae for Calculators. LC 82-8495. 1982. pap. text ed. 14.95 (ISBN 0-943396-01-8). Willman-Bell.
ASTRONOMY–STUDY AND TEACHING
Justus, Fred. Beyond Our Solar System. (Science Ser.). 24p. (gr. 8). 1976. wkbk. 5.00 (ISBN 0-8209-0146-6, S-8). ESP.
ASTRONOMY–TABLES, ETC.
Moore, Patrick, ed. Yearbook of Astronomy, 1983. (Illus.). 1983. 15.95 (ISBN 0-393-01700-1). Norton.
ASTRONOMY, NAUTICAL
see Nautical Astronomy
ASTRONOMY, STATISTICAL
see Statistical Astronomy
ASTROPHYSICS
see also Mechanics, Celestial; Spectrum Analysis
Boehme, S., et al. Astronomy & Astrophysics Abstracts, Vol. 31: Literature 1982, Pt. 1. 776p. 1983. 66.00 (ISBN 0-387-12072-6). Springer-Verlag.
Burke, P. G. & Eissner, W. B., eds. Atoms in Astrophysics. (Physics of Atoms & Molecules Ser.). 350p. 1983. 49.50x (ISBN 0-306-41097-4, Plenum Pr). Plenum Pub.
Kippenhahn, Rudolf. One Hundred Billion Suns: The Birth, Life, & Death of the Stars. (Illus.). 256p. 1983. 25.00 (ISBN 0-465-05263-0). Basic.
Schaifers, K. & Voigt, H. H., eds. Astronomy & Astrophysics: Interstellar Matter, Galaxy, Universe. (Landolt-Boernstein, New Series. Group VI: Vol. 2, Subvol. C). (Illus.). 490p. 1983. 780.00 (ISBN 0-387-10977-3). Springer-Verlag.
Texas Symposium on Relativistic Astrophysics, Tenth: Proceedings, Vol. 375. 467p. 1981. 102.00 (ISBN 0-89766-139-7, Ramaty & Jones); pap. write for info. (ISBN 0-89766-140-0). NY Acad Sci.
Van Allen, James A. Origins of Magnetospheric Physics. 128p. 1983. text ed. 19.95x (ISBN 0-87474-940-9). Smithsonian.
Zombeck, Martin V. Handbook of Space Astronomy & Astrophysics. LC 82-12944. (Illus.). 341p. 1983. 24.95 (ISBN 0-521-24194-4). Cambridge U Pr.
ASYMPTOTIC EXPANSIONS
Basawa, I. V. & Scott, D. J. Asymptotic Optimal Inference for Non-Ergodic Models. (Lecture Notes in Mathematics Ser.: Vol. 17). 170p. 1983. pap. 15.00 (ISBN 0-387-90810-2). Springer-Verlag.

ATATURK, KAMAL, PRES. TURKEY, d. 1938
Richie, Claude G. Kemal Ataturk, Father of the Turkish Republic. Rahmas, Sigurd C., ed. (Outstanding Personalities Ser.: No. 92). 32p. (gr. 9-12). 1982. 2.95 (ISBN 0-87157-592-2); pap. text ed. 1.95 (ISBN 0-87157-092-0). SamHar Pr.
ATCHISON, TOPEKA AND SANTA FE RAILWAY COMPANY
Ducker, James H. Men of the Steel Rails: Workers on the Atchison, Topeka, & Santa Fe Railroad, 1869-1900. LC 82-17541. (Illus.). 232p. 1983. 17.95 (ISBN 0-8032-1662-9). U of Nebr Pr.
ATELIERS
see Workshops
ATGET, EUGENE
Szarkowski, John & Hambourg, Maria M. The Work of Atget: The Art of Old Paris, Vol. II. 1982. 40.00 (ISBN 0-87070-212-2, Pub. by Museum Mod Art). NYGS.
ATHEISM
see also Agnosticism; Rationalism; Skepticism
Bard, Martin. The Peril of Faith. 166p. (Orig.). 1982. pap. 5.00 (ISBN 0-910309-05-1). Am Atheist.
Berry, Newton & Drew, Christopher. The Best of Dial-an-Atheist, Vol. 1. 124p. (Orig.). 1982. pap. 4.00 (ISBN 0-910309-06-X). Am Atheist.
Diehl, Helmut. Atheismus Im Religionsunterricht. 622p. (Ger.). 1982. write for info. (ISBN 3-8204-6280-5). P Lang Pubs.
Ingersoll, Robert G. The Trail of C. B. Reynolds. 31p. pap. 3.00 (ISBN 0-686-83988-9). Am Atheist.
Neusch, Marcel. The Sources of Modern Atheism: One Hundred Years of Debate Over God. LC 82-60596. 1983. pap. 9.95 (ISBN 0-8091-2488-2). Paulist Pr.
O'Hair, Madalyn M. Nobody Has a Prayer. 105p. (Orig.). 1982. pap. 3.00 (ISBN 0-910309-07-8). Am Atheist.
O'Hair, Madalyn Murray & Murray, Jon. All the Questions You Ever Wanted to Ask American Atheists With all the Answers, 2 Vols. 344p. (Orig.). 1982. pap. 10.00 (ISBN 0-910309-04-3). Am Atheist.
ATHENS–DESCRIPTION
Athens Travel Guide. (Berlitz Travel Guides). 1982. pap. 4.95 (ISBN 0-02-969020-X, Berlitz). Macmillan.
Baedeker's City Guide: Athens. 160p. 1983. pap. 9.95 (ISBN 0-86145-114-7, Pub. by Auto Assn-British Tourist Authority England). Merrimack Bk Serv.
ATHENS–SOCIAL LIFE AND CUSTOMS
Royal National Foundation. Athens Civilization: The Past & the Future. 1968. 6.50 (ISBN 0-444-40747-2). Elsevier.
ATHEROSCLEROSIS
see Arteriosclerosis
ATHLETES
see also Athletic Ability
Geffen, Roger J. Going Pro: The Athlete's Market Guide. (Illus.). 256p. (Orig.). 1983. pap. 9.95 (ISBN 0-8092-5562-6). Contemp Bks.
ATHLETES–BIOGRAPHY
Richards, Renee & Ames, John. Second Serve: The Renee Richards Story. LC 82-48510. (Illus.). 420p. 1983. 16.95 (ISBN 0-8128-2897-6). Stein & Day.
ATHLETES–RELIGIOUS LIFE
Black, William T. Mormon Athletes, Bk. 2. LC 82-14648. (Illus.). 285p. 1982. 7.95 (ISBN 0-87747-929-1). Deseret Bk.
ATHLETES, AFRO-AMERICAN
see Afro-American Athletes
ATHLETES, WOMEN
Black Women in Sport. 75p. 8.95 (ISBN 0-88314-036-5). AAHPERD.
ATHLETIC ABILITY
Cockerill, Ian M. & Macgillivary, William W., eds. Vision & Sport. 224p. 1981. 40.00x (ISBN 0-85950-463-8, Pub. by Thornes England). State Mutual Bk.
ATHLETIC MEDICINE
see Sports Medicine
ATHLETICS
see also Boxing; Coaching (Athletics); Fencing; Gymnastics; Jiu-Jitsu; Jumping; Olympic Games; Physical Education and Training; Rowing; Skating; Sports; Swimming; Track-Athletics; Walking; Weight Lifting
also names of specific sports names of schools, colleges, etc.
Alberger, Particia L., ed. Winning Techniques for Athletic Fund Raising. 97p. 1981. 14.50 (ISBN 0-89964-188-1). CASE.
Greenspan, Emily. Little Winners: The World of the Child Sports Superstar. (Illus.). 320p. 1983. 14.45i (ISBN 0-316-32667-4). Little.
Ruxin, Robert H. An Athlete's Guide to Agents. LC 82-47781. (Midland Bks.: No. 290). 176p. 1983. 18.75x (ISBN 0-253-10400-9); pap. 6.95 (ISBN 0-253-20290-6). Ind U Pr.
ATHLETICS–HISTORY
Onigman, Marc. Day-by-Day in Athletics History. (Illus.). 300p. (Orig.). 1983. pap. 9.95 (ISBN 0-88011-033-3). Leisure Pr.
ATHLETICS–MEDICAL ASPECTS
see Sports Medicine
ATHOS (MONASTERIES)
Mount Athos: An Illustrated Guide to the Monasteries & their Histories. (Illus.). 200p. pap. 20.00 (ISBN 0-89241-369-7). Caratzas Bros.

ATLANTA
Alexander, Stan & Broussard, Sharon. An Analysis of the 1973 Atlanta Elections. 1973. 3.00 (ISBN 0-686-38001-0). Voter Ed Proj.
Bryant, James C. Charlie Brown Remembers Atlanta: Memoirs of a Public Man. LC 82-71963. 370p. 1982. 12.95 (ISBN 0-934870-07-1). R L Bryan.
Gwin, Yolande. Yolande's Atlanta. 1983. 9.95 (ISBN 0-931948-44-4). Peachtree Pubs.
Maister, Philippa. The Insider's Atlanta. (Illus.). 252p. (Orig.). 1982. pap. 7.95 (ISBN 0-9608596-0-8). Good Hope GA.
Rooks, Charles S. The Atlanta Elections of Nineteen Sixty-nine. 1970. 4.00 (ISBN 0-686-37998-5). Voter Ed Proj.
Shavin, Norman & Galphin, Bruce. Atlanta: Triumph of a People. (Illus.). 456p. 1982. 29.95 (ISBN 0-910719-00-4). Capricorn Corp.
ATLANTIC, BATTLE OF THE, 1939-1945
see World War, 1939-1945–Atlantic Ocean
ATLANTIC ALLIANCE
see North Atlantic Treaty Organization
ATLANTIC CITY, NEW JERSEY
Funnell, Charles E. By the Beautiful Sea: The Rise & High Times of That Great American Resort, Atlantic City. 1983. 7.95 (ISBN 0-8135-0986-6). Rutgers U Pr.
ATLANTIC COAST
Reiger, George. Wanderer on My Native Shore. 1983. price not set (ISBN 0-671-25423-5). S&S.
ATLANTIC MONTHLY (MAGAZINE)
Monteiro, George & Eppard, Philip. A Guide to the Atlantic Monthly Contributors' Club. 1983. lib. bdg. 35.00 (ISBN 0-8161-8492-5, Hall Reference). G K Hall.
ATLANTIC OCEAN
Blumberg, Rhoda. The First Travel Guide to the Bottom of the Sea. LC 82-17938. (Illus.). 96p. (gr. 4 up). 1983. 9.00 (ISBN 0-688-01692-8). Lothrop.
ATLASES
see also Automobile Touring–Road Guides
also subdivision Maps under names of countries, cities, etc., e.g. United States–Maps; London–Maps; also subdivision Atlases under subjects, e.g. Anatomy, Human–Atlases
Graphic Atlas of the World. (Illus.). 112p. 1978. 10.00x (ISBN 0-7028-0267-0). Intl Pubns Serv.
Raintree, George P. The Prentice-Hall Great International Atlas. 416p. 1981. 69.95 (ISBN 0-13-695833-8). P-H.
Research Libraries of the New York Public Library & Library of Congress. Bibliographic Guide to Maps & Atlases: 1982. 1983. lib. bdg. 150.00 (ISBN 0-8161-6976-4, Biblio Guides). G K Hall.
ATLASES, AMERICAN
see Atlases
ATLASES, ASTRONOMICAL
see Stars–Atlases
ATMOSPHERE
see also Meteorology
also headings beginning with the word Atmospheric
Allen, Oliver. Atmosphere. (Planet Earth Ser.). 1983. lib. bdg. 19.92 (ISBN 0-8094-4337-6, Pub. by Time-Life). Silver.
Eagleson, P. S. Land Surface Processes in Atmospheric General Circulation Models. LC 82-9740. 572p. 59.50 (ISBN 0-521-25222-9). Cambridge U Pr.
Gedzelman, Stanley D. The Science & Wonders of the Atmosphere. LC 79-23835. 1980. text ed. 28.95x (ISBN 0-471-02972-6); Avail. Tchr's Manual (ISBN 0-471-08013-6). Wiley.
Goldberg, E. D., ed. Atmospheric Chemistry, Berlin, 1982. (Dahlem Workshop Reports, Physical & Chemical: Vol. 4). (Illus.). 400p. 1983. 20.00 (ISBN 0-387-11651-6). Springer-Verlag.
Hoskins, Brian & Pearce, Robert, eds. Large-Scale Dynamical Processes in the Atmosphere. Date not set. price not set (ISBN 0-12-356680-0). Acad Pr.
Zuev, V. E. & Naats, I. E. Inverse Problems of Lidar Sensing of the Atmosphere. (Springer Ser. in Optical Sciences: Vol. 29). (Illus.). 260p. 1983. 41.00 (ISBN 0-387-10913-7). Springer-Verlag.
ATMOSPHERE, UPPER
Georgii, H. W. & Jaeschke, W., eds. Chemistry of the Unpolluted & Polluted Troposphere. 1982. 63.00 (ISBN 90-277-1487-8, Pub. by Reidel Holland). Kluwer Boston.
ATMOSPHERIC ABSORPTION OF SOLAR RADIATION
see Solar Radiation
ATOLLS
see Coral Reefs and Islands
ATOMIC BOMB–MORAL AND RELIGIOUS ASPECTS
see Atomic Warfare–Moral and Religious Aspects
ATOMIC BOMB–SAFETY MEASURES
Smeathers, Bryan K. Prepare for & Survive a Nuclear Attack! LC 82-73105. (Illus.). 120p. (Orig.). 1983. pap. write for info. (ISBN 0-910629-00-5). Audubon Pub Co.
ATOMIC BOMB AND DISARMAMENT
see Atomic Weapons and Disarmament
ATOMIC ENERGY
see also Atomic Power; Atomic Power Industry; Nuclear Engineering; Nuclear Reactors
Bashkin, S. & Stoner, J. O., Jr. Atomic Energy-Level & Grotrian Diagrams, Vol. 4: Manganese I-XXV. 354p. 1983. 72.50 (ISBN 0-444-86463-6, North Holland). Elsevier.

Pringle, Peter & Spigelman, James. The Nuclear Barons. 592p. 1983. pap. 4.95 (ISBN 0-380-62364-1, 62364-1, Discus). Avon.
Snow, Donald M. The Nuclear Future: Toward a Strategy of Uncertainty. LC 82-7110. 224p. 1983. text ed. 25.00 (ISBN 0-8173-0117-8); pap. text ed. 12.95 (ISBN 0-8173-0118-6). U of Ala Pr.
ATOMIC ENERGY–DICTIONARIES
Hilgartner, Stephen, et al. Nukespeak: The Selling of Nuclear Technology in America. (Illus.). 1983. pap. 6.95 (ISBN 0-14-006684-5). Penguin.
ATOMIC ENERGY–INTERNATIONAL CONTROL
see Atomic Power–International Control
ATOMIC ENERGY–JUVENILE LITERATURE
Krogman, Dane & Holelson, Doug. Skeleton Boy: The Nuclear Hero. (Illus.). 80p. 1982. 8.95 (ISBN 0-910519-00-5). Daneco Pubns.
ATOMIC ENERGY–LAW AND LEGISLATION
see Atomic Power–Law and Legislation
ATOMIC ENERGY–PHYSIOLOGICAL EFFECT
Raynaud, C., ed. Nuclear Medicine & Biology Advances: Proceedings of the Third World Congress on Nuclear Medicine & Biology, August 29 - September 2, 1982, Paris, France, 7 Vols. 3685p. 1982. Set. 300.00 (ISBN 0-08-029814-1). Pergamon.
ATOMIC ENERGY INDUSTRIES
see also Nuclear Engineering
Walker, William & Lonnroth, Mans. Nuclear Power Struggles: Industrial Competition & Proliferation Control. (Illus.). 192p. 1983. text ed. 24.00x (ISBN 0-04-338104-9). Allen Unwin.
ATOMIC ENERGY INDUSTRIES–SAFETY REGULATIONS
see Atomic Power–Law and Legislation
ATOMIC FUEL
see Nuclear Fuels
ATOMIC MEDICINE
see Nuclear Medicine
ATOMIC NUCLEI
see Nuclear Physics
ATOMIC PILES
see Nuclear Reactors
ATOMIC POWER
see also Atomic Energy; Atomic Power Plants; Controlled Fusion
Argentesi, F. & Avenhaus, R., eds. Mathematical & Statistical Methods in Nuclear Safeguards. (Ispra Courses on Nuclear Engineering & Technology Ser.). 440p. 1982. 87.50 (ISBN 3-7186-0124-9). Harwood Academic.
Berger, John. Nuclear Power: The Unviable Option. 384p. 1976. 4.50 (ISBN 0-686-43096-4). Ramparts.
Cameron, I. R. Nuclear Fission Reactors. 410p. 1982. 42.50x (ISBN 0-306-41073-7, Plenum Pr). PLenum Pub.
CINDA Eighty-Two: 1977-1982. 633p. 1982. pap. 49.00 (ISBN 92-0-039082-X, ICIN82, IAEA). Unipub.
Guidebook on the Introduction of Nuclear Power. 349p. 1982. pap. 42.00 (ISBN 92-0-155082-0, IDC 217, IAEA). Unipub.
Hart, David. Nuclear Power in India: A Comparative Analysis. 192p. 1983. text ed. 24.00x (ISBN 0-04-338101-4). Allen Unwin.
Hellman, Caroline J. C. & Hellman, Richard. The Competitive Economics of Nuclear & Coal Power. LC 82-47500. 208p. 1982. 23.95x (ISBN 0-669-05533-6). Lexington Bks.
Marwah, Onkar & Schulz, Ann, eds. Nuclear Proliferation & the Near-Nuclear Countries. 1975. 22.50x (ISBN 0-88410-605-5). Ballinger Pub.
Nuclear Power & the Environment. 195p. 1982. pap. 14.00 (ISBN 92-0-129082-9, ISP635, IAEA). Unipub.
OECD Staff. Nuclear Energy & Its Fuel Cycle: Prospects to 2025. 262p. 1982. pap. 24.00 (ISBN 92-64-12306-7). OECD.
--Nuclear Energy Prospects to 2000. 130p. (Orig.). 1982. pap. 14.00x (ISBN 92-64-02326-7). OECD.
Price, Jerome B. The Antinuclear Movement. (Social Movements: Past & Present). 1982. lib. bdg. 15.95 (ISBN 0-8057-9705-X, Twayne). G K Hall.
Shaw, E. N. Europe's Nuclear Power Experiment: History of the OECD Dragon Project. (Illus.). 300p. 1982. 25.00 (ISBN 0-08-029324-7). Pergamon.
ATOMIC POWER–INTERNATIONAL CONTROL
Beres Rene, Louis. Mimicking Sisyphus: America's Countervailing Nuclear Strategy. LC 82-48437. 160p. 1982. 19.95x (ISBN 0-669-06419-X); pap. 11.95 (ISBN 0-669-06137-9). Lexington Bks.
Boardman, Robert & Keeley, James. Nuclear Exports & World Politics. LC 82-10779. 272p. 1982. 26.00x (ISBN 0-312-57976-4). St Martin.
ATOMIC POWER–LAW AND LEGISLATION
Stason, Edwin B. & Estep, Samuel D. Atoms & the Law, 2 bks. (Michigan Legal Publications Ser.). xxvii, 1512p. 1982. Repr. of 1959 ed. lib. bdg. 55.00 (ISBN 0-89941-176-2). W. S. Hein.
ATOMIC POWER ENGINEERING
see Nuclear Engineering
ATOMIC POWER INDUSTRY
Boardman, Robert & Keeley, James. Nuclear Exports & World Politics. LC 82-10779. 272p. 1982. 26.00x (ISBN 0-312-57976-4). St Martin.

ATOMIC POWER PLANTS

Commission of European Communities, ed. Plutonium Recycling Scenario in Light Water Reactors: Assessment of the Environmental Impact of the European Community. 240p. 1982. write for info. (ISBN 3-7186-0118-4). Harwood Academic.

Operating Experience with Nuclear Power Stations in Member States in 1980. 619p. 1983. pap. 70.00 (ISBN 92-0-159082-2, ISP 617, IAEA). Unipub.

ATOMIC SPECTRA

Ramirez-Munoz, J. Atomic Absorption Spectroscopy. 1968. 63.50 (ISBN 0-444-40468-6). Elsevier.

Stebbings, R. F. & Dunning, F. B., eds. Rydberg States of Atoms & Molecules. LC 82-1181. (Illus.). 500p. Date not set. price not set (ISBN 0-521-24823-X). Cambridge U Pr.

ATOMIC WARFARE

see also Air Warfare; Atomic Weapons

Breuer, Reinhard & Lechleitner, Hans. The EMP Factor: The Twenty-Minute War. Orig. Title: Der Lautlose Schlag. (Illus.). 150p. (Orig.). 1983. pap. 6.95 (ISBN 0-914842-99-4). Madrona Pubs.

Brown, Gordon & McGraw, Marsha, eds. The Role of the Academy in Addressing the Issues of Nuclear War. 138p. 1982. pap. text ed. write for info. (ISBN 0-910969-00-0). Hobart & Wm Smith.

Feldman, Shai. Israeli Nuclear Deterrence: A Strategy for the 1980's. LC 82-9679. 314p. 1983. 25.00x (ISBN 0-231-05546-3); pap. 9.95 (ISBN 0-231-05547-1). Columbia U Pr.

Frei, Daniel & Catrina, Christian. Risks of Unintentional Nuclear War. LC 82-16333. 255p. 1983. pap. text ed. 10.95 (ISBN 0-86598-106-X). Allanheld.

Greene, Owne & Rubin, Barry. London After the Bomb: What a Nuclear Attack Really Means. (Ser. K). (Illus.). 152p. 1983. pap. 4.95 (ISBN 0-19-285123-3). Oxford U Pr.

Herken, Gregg. Accidental Nuclear War: On the Brink of a Holocaust? (Vital Issues Ser.: Vol. XXXI, No. 8). 0.80 (ISBN 0-686-84147-6). Ctr Info Am.

Pogodeinski, Michael. How to Survive Nuclear War. (Illus.). 224p. (Orig.). 1982. pap. 7.95 (ISBN 0-89621-072-3). Thorndike Pr.

Risks of Unintentional Nuclear War. 255p. 1983. pap. 19.00 (UN 82/0/1, UN). Unipub.

Risks of Unintentional Nuclear War. 19.00 (ISBN 0-686-84919-1, E.82.O.1). UN.

Woolsey, James, ed. Nuclear Arms: Ethics, Strategy, Politics. 350p. 1983. 22.95 (ISBN 0-917616-55-3); pap. 8.95 (ISBN 0-917616-56-1). ICS Pr.

ATOMIC WARFARE–MORAL AND RELIGIOUS ASPECTS

Cohen, Sam. The Truth About the Neutron Bomb: The Inventor of the Bomb Speaks Out. LC 82-14239. 260p. 1983. 12.50 (ISBN 0-688-01646-4). Morrow.

Federation of American Scientists. Seeds of Promise: The First Real Hearing on Nuclear Freeze. 192p. 1983. pap. 9.95 (ISBN 0-686-84755-5). Brick Hse Pub.

Freund, Ronald. What One Christian Can Do to Help Prevent Nuclear War. LC 82-15584. xiv, 185p. (Orig.). 1982. pap. 7.95 (ISBN 0-8190-0650-5, FC 144). Fides Claretian.

Lefever, Ernest W. & Hunt, E. Stephen, eds. The Apocalyptic Premise: Nuclear Arms Debated. LC 82-18315. 429p. (Orig.). 1982. 14.00 (ISBN 0-89633-062-1); pap. 9.00 (ISBN 0-89633-063-X). Ethics & Public Policy.

Sider, Ronald J. & Taylor, Richard K. Nuclear Holocaust & Christian Hope: A Book for Christian Peacemakers. 360p. 1983. pap. 6.95 (ISBN 0-8091-2512-9). Paulist Pr.

ATOMIC WARFARE–PSYCHOLOGICAL ASPECTS

see also Psychological Warfare

American Psychiatric Association. Psychosocial Aspects of Nuclear Developments, Task Force Report, Twenty. LC 82-71902. (Monographs). 96p. 1982. 12.00x (ISBN 0-89042-220-6, 42-220-6). Am Psychiatric.

ATOMIC WEAPONS

see also Atomic Weapons and Disarmament; Ballistic Missiles

Bertram & Kincade. Nuclear Proliferation in the 1980's. LC 82-42602. 290p. 1983. 27.50x (ISBN 0-312-57975-6). St Martin.

Cunningham, Ann Marie & Fitzpatrick, Mariana. Future Fire: Weapons for the Apocalypse. 256p. 1983. pap. 8.95 (ISBN 0-446-37031-2). Warner Bks.

Fish, Hamilton. Masters of Terrorism. 1982. 14.95 (ISBN 0-686-81786-9). Devin.

Freedman, Lawrence. The Evolution of Nuclear Strategy. 473p. 1982. pap. 10.95 (ISBN 0-312-27270-7). St Martin.

Kaplan, Fred. The Wizards of Armageddon: Strategists of the Nuclear Age. 1983. price not set (ISBN 0-671-42444-0). S&S.

Nieman, Thomas. Better Read Than Dead. (Illus.). 193p. 1982. pap. 14.95 (ISBN 0-87364-254-6). Paladin Ent.

Nuclear Weapons: Report of the Secretary General. 233p. 1982. 7.95 (ISBN 0-686-84616-8, UNNOCODE 101, UN). Unipub.

ATOMIC WEAPONS–TESTING

McGonnagle, Warren J., ed. International Advances in Nondestructive Testing, Vol. 9. 400p. 1982. write for info. (ISBN 0-677-16440-8). Gordon.

ATOMIC WEAPONS AND DISARMAMENT

Albert, Michael & Dellinger, Dave, eds. Mobilizing for Survival. 300p. 1983. 20.00 (ISBN 0-89608-176-1); pap. 7.50 (ISBN 0-89608-175-3). South End Pr.

Barnaby, Frank & Thomas, Geoffrey, eds. The Nuclear Arms Race: Control or Catastrophe. LC 81-21282. 265p. 1982. 25.00x (ISBN 0-312-57974-8). St Martin.

Buteaux, Paul. Strategy, Doctrine, & the Politcs of Alliance: Theatre Nuclear Force Modernization in NATO. Replica ed. 150p. 1982. softcover 17.00 (ISBN 0-86531-940-5). Westview.

Drinan, Robert F. Beyond the Nuclear Freeze. 176p. (Orig.). 1983. pap. 7.95 (ISBN 0-8164-2406-3). Seabury.

Kennan, George F. The Nuclear Delusion: Soviet-American Relations in the Atomic Age. 1982. 13.95 (ISBN 0-394-52946-4). Pantheon.

Scientists, the Arms Race & Disarmament. 323p. 1982. 24.95 (ISBN 92-3-102021-8, U1231, UNESCO). Unipub.

Seaborg, Glenn T. & Loeb, Benjamin S. Kennedy, Khrushchev, & the Test Ban. (Illus.). 336p. 1983. pap. 7.95 (ISBN 0-520-04961-6, CAL 629). U of Cal Pr.

Seeds of Promise: The First Real Hearings on the Nuclear Freeze. 224p. 1983. pap. 9.95 (ISBN 0-931790-54-9). Brick Hse Pub.

The United Nations Disarmament Yearbook: 1981, Vol. 6. 458p. 1982. pap. 35.00 (ISBN 0-686-82550-0, UN 82/9/6, UN). Unipub.

Zuckerman, Solly. Nuclear Illusion & Reality. LC 82-40419. 160p. 1983. pap. 2.95 (ISBN 0-394-71363-X, Vin). Random.

ATOMS

see also Electrons; Magnetic Resonance; Neutrons; Nuclear Physics; Particle Accelerators; Protons

Burke, P. G. & Eissner, W. B., eds. Atoms in Astrophysics. (Physics of Atoms & Molecules Ser.). 350p. 1983. 49.50x (ISBN 0-306-41097-4, Plenum Pr). Plenum Pub.

Mittleman, Marvin H. Introduction to the Theory of Laser-Atom Interactions. (Physics of Atoms & Molecules Ser.). 195p. 1982. 35.00x (ISBN 0-306-41049-4, Plenum Pr). Plenum Pub.

Palmer, D., et al. Atomic Collision Phenomena in Solids. 1970. 68.00 (ISBN 0-444-10021-0). Elsevier.

ATOMS–SPACE ARRANGEMENT

see Stereochemistry

ATOMS–SPECTRA

see Atomic Spectra

ATOMS, NUCLEI OF

see Nuclear Physics

ATONEMENT

Lidgett, John S. The Biblical Doctrine of the Atonement. 522p. 1983. 19.50 (ISBN 0-86524-145-7). Klock & Klock.

ATTACK AND DEFENSE (MILITARY SCIENCE)

see also Civil Defense; Deterrence (Strategy)

Bellany, Ian & Blacker, Coit D., eds. Antiballistic Missile Defence in the 1980s. 200p. 1983. text ed. 30.00 (ISBN 0-7146-3207-4, F Cass Co). Biblio Dist.

Freeman, Charles. Defence. (Today's World Ser.). (Illus.). 72p. (gr. 7-12). 1983. 14.95 (ISBN 0-7134-0969-X, Pub. by Batsford England). David & Charles.

ATTITUDE (PSYCHOLOGY)

see also Conformity; Job Satisfaction; Stereotype (Psychology)

American Health Research Institute, Ltd. Attitude & Attitudes: A Psychological & Medical Subject Analysis with Research Index & Bibliography. Bartone, John C., ed. 120p. 1983. 29.95 (ISBN 0-88164-026-3); pap. 21.95 (ISBN 0-88164-027-1). ABBE Pubs Assn.

Chapman, Elwood N. Your Attitude is Showing. 4th ed. 96p. 1982. text ed. 8.95 (ISBN 0-574-20680-9, 13-3680); write for info leader's guide (ISBN 0-574-20681-7, 13-3681); self-paced exercise guide 4.95 (ISBN 0-574-20682-5, 13-3682). SRA.

Siebold. Attitudes & Behavior. 256p. 1983. 22.95 (ISBN 0-03-060293-9). Praeger.

ATTORNEYS

see Lawyers

ATTRIBUTES OF GOD

see God–Attributes

ATTRITION

see Penance

ATYPICAL CHILDREN

see Exceptional Children

AUBIGNE, THEODORE AGRIPPA D', 1552-1630

Cameron, Keith. A Concordance of Agrippa d'Aubigne's "Les Traigques". 400p. 1982. 95.00x (ISBN 0-85989-143-7, Pub. by Exeter Univ England). State Mutual Bk.

AUCTIONS

see also Sales

Hislop, R. Auction Prices of Impressionist & 20th Century Artists 1970-1980, 2 Vols. 160.00 (ISBN 0-903872-12-9). Apollo.

--Auction Prices of Old Masters. 1980. 156.00 (ISBN 0-903872-14-5). Apollo.

--Auction Prices of 19th Century Artists, 2 Vols. 1980. 176.00 (ISBN 0-903872-13-7). Apollo.

International Auction Records Mayer. 1982. 158.00 (ISBN 0-686-43123-5). Apollo.

Theran. Leonard's Annual Index of Art Auctions. Date not set. 175.00 (ISBN 0-686-43126-X). Apollo.

AUDEN, WYSTAN HUGH, 1907-1973

Callan, Edward. Auden: A Carnival of Intellect. 320p. 1983. 25.00 (ISBN 0-19-503168-7). Oxford U Pr.

Levy, Alan. W. H. Auden: In the Autumn of the Age of Anxiety. LC 82-84008. (Illus.). 128p. 1983. pap. 9.95 (ISBN 0-932966-31-4). Permanent Pr.

Mendelson, Edward. Early Auden. 432p. 1983. pap. text ed. 8.95x (ISBN 0-686-82625-6). Harvard U Pr.

Miller, Charles H. Auden: An American Friendship. (Illus.). 208p. 1983. 13.95 (ISBN 0-684-17845-1, ScribT). Scribner.

AUDI (AUTOMOBILE)

see Automobiles, Foreign–Types–Audi

AUDIENCES

see Television Audiences; Theater Audiences

AUDIENCES, TELEVISION

see Television Audiences

AUDIO EQUIPMENT

see Sound–Apparatus

AUDIO TAPES

see Phonotapes

AUDIO-VISUAL AIDS

see Audio-Visual Materials

AUDIO-VISUAL EDUCATION

see also Audio-Visual Materials; Visual Education also subdivision Audio-Visual Aids, or Study and Teaching under subjects, e.g. Music–Audio-Visual aids

Brown, James W. & Lewis, Richard B. AV Instructional Technology Manual for Independent Study. 5th ed. (Illus.). 208p. 1982. pap. text ed. 15.00 (ISBN 0-07-008170-0, C). McGraw.

Carroll, Walter J., ed. The Education Media Handbook, 1983. 1983. 26.00 (ISBN 0-88367-475-0). Olympic Media.

--Media Profiles: The Audiovisual Marketing Newsletter, 1983, Vol. 1. 1983. 48.00x (ISBN 0-88367-450-5). Olympic Media.

--Media Profiles: The Career Development Edition, 1983, Vol. 15. 1983. 185.00 (ISBN 0-88367-350-9). Olympic Media.

--Media Profiles: The Health Science Edition, 1983, Vol. 10. 1983. 87.50 (ISBN 0-88367-210-3). Olympic Media.

--Media Profiles: The Whole Earth Edition, 1983, Vol. 1. 1983. 18.00x. Olympic Media.

--The Salestrainer's Media Handbook. 1983. 24.00 (ISBN 0-88367-375-4). Olympic Media.

Clor, Harry M. The Mass Media & Democracy. 1974. pap. 10.50 (ISBN 0-395-30789-9). HM.

Creating Slide-Tape Programs, 1980. LC 80-730423. 1982. 29.95 (ISBN 0-686-84114-X); members 20.95 (ISBN 0-686-84115-8). Assn Ed Comm Tech.

The Economics of New Educational Media: Volume 3: Cost & Effectiveness Overview & Synthesis. 150p. 1982. pap. 13.25 (ISBN 92-3-101997-X, UNESCO). Unipub.

Evaluate Checklist: Am Instrument for Self-Evaluating an Educational Media Program in Colleges & Universities. 20p. 1982. 5.95 (ISBN 0-89240-031-5); members 4.95 (ISBN 0-686-84119-0). Assn Ed Comm Tech.

Evaluating Instructional Materials: Filmstrip. 1982. 25.95 (ISBN 0-686-84117-4); members 20.95 (ISBN 0-686-84118-2). Assn Ed Comm Tech.

Freedom to Learn: A Handbook. LC 79-730811. 1982. 24.95 (ISBN 0-686-84120-4); 20.95 (ISBN 0-686-84121-2). Assn Ed Comm Tech.

Minor, E. O. & Fyre, H. R. Techniques for Producing Visual Instructional Media. 1977. 28.95 (ISBN 0-07-042406-3). McGraw.

Rudman, Jack. Audio-Visual Aide. (Career Examination Ser.: C-2903). (Cloth bdg. avail. on request). pap. 12.00 (ISBN 0-8373-2903-5). Natl Learning.

Tell Me What You See. LC 77-730595. 1982. 18.95 (ISBN 0-686-84124-7); members 12.95 (ISBN 0-686-84125-5). Assn Ed Comm Tech.

AUDIO-VISUAL MATERIALS

see also Moving-Pictures; Phonorecords also subdivision Audio-visual aids, or study and teaching under subjects, e.g. Music

Allen, S. Manager's Guide to Audiovisuals. 1972. pap. 4.50 (ISBN 0-07-001093-5). McGraw.

Dictionary of Audio Visual Terms. 1983. text ed. write for info. Butterworth.

Merrill-Oldham, Jan. Conservation & Preservation of Library Materials. LC 82-1875. 1982. pap. text ed. 10.00 (ISBN 0-917590-07-4). Univ Conn Lib.

Morse, Carmel L. Audio Visual Primer. (Illus.). 60p. (Orig.). pap. 3.95 (ISBN 0-686-38776-7). Backwoods Pubns.

R. R. Bowker Staff. Audiovisual Market Place, 1983. new ed. 470p. pap. 39.95 (ISBN 0-8352-1577-6). Bowker.

AUDIO-VISUAL MATERIALS CENTERS

see Instructional Materials Centers

AUDIOLOGY

see also Deafness

Jerger, Susan & Jerger, James. Audiologic Tests of Central Auditory Function. 1983. pap. text ed. 13.95 (ISBN 0-8391-1801-5, 15644). Univ Park.

AUDIOMETER

see Audiometry

AUDIOMETRY

Beagley, H. A. & Barnard, S. A. Manual of Audiometric Techniques. (Illus.). 96p. 1983. pap. 12.95 (ISBN 0-19-261372-3). Oxford U Pr.

Jerger, Susan & Jerger, James. Audiologic Tests of Central Auditory Function. 1983. pap. text ed. 13.95 (ISBN 0-8391-1801-5, 15644). Univ Park.

AUDIT, MANAGEMENT

see Management Audit

AUDITING

see also Accounting; Financial Statements also subdivision Accounting under names of industries, trades, etc.

American Institute of Certified Public Accountants. Audit & Accounting Guide: Audits of Employee Benefit Plans. 1983. write for info. Am Inst CPA.

--Auditing & EDP. 1983. write for info. Am Inst CPA.

Audit & Control Considerations in A Minicomputer Environment. 1981. pap. 9.00 (ISBN 0-686-84213-8). Am Inst CPA.

Audit Approaches for a Computerized Inventory System. 1980. pap. 9.00 (ISBN 0-686-84211-1). Am Inst CPA.

Audit Problems Encountered in Small Business Engagements. 9.00 (ISBN 0-686-42705-X). Am Inst CPA.

Brink, V. Z., et al. Modern Internal Auditing: An Operational Approach. 3rd ed. 795p. 1973. 49.95 (ISBN 0-471-06524-2). Wiley.

Casler, Darwin J. & Crockett, James R. Operational Auditing: An Introduction. Holman, Richard, ed. (Illus.). 80p. pap. text ed. 27.00 (ISBN 0-89413-097-8). Inst Inter Aud.

Cutforth, Arthur E. Audits. LC 82-48357. (Accountancy in Transition Ser.). 164p. 1982. lib. bdg. 20.00 (ISBN 0-8240-5309-5). Garland Pub.

Hubbard, Thomas D. & Johnson, Johnny R. Auditing: Concepts, Standards, Procedures. LC 82-72439. 925p. 1983. text ed. 28.95x (ISBN 0-931920-44-2). Dame Pubns.

Market for Compilation, Review & Audit Services. (Auditing Research Monographs: No. 4). 1981. pap. 9.00 (ISBN 0-686-84303-7). Am Inst CPA.

Operational Audit Engagements. 1982. pap. 4.50 (ISBN 0-686-84305-3). Am Inst CPA.

Planning Considerations for an Audit of a Federally Assisted Program. 1981. pap. 1.75 (ISBN 0-686-84306-1). Am Inst CPA.

Rudman, Jack. Administrative Auditor of Accounts. (Career Examination Ser.: C-2598). pap. 12.00 (ISBN 0-8373-2598-6); avail. Natl Learning.

--Supervising Audit Clerk. (Career Examination Ser.: C-887). (Cloth bdg. avail. on request). pap. 10.00 (ISBN 0-8373-0887-9). Natl Learning.

--Supervising Auditor. (Career Examination Ser.: C-2681). (Cloth bdg. avail. on request). pap. 12.00 (ISBN 0-8373-2681-8). Natl Learning.

Santocki, J. Case Studies in Auditing. 288p. 1978. 30.00x (ISBN 0-7121-0373-2, Pub. by Macdonald & Evans). State Mutual Bk.

Study & Evaluation of Internal Control in EDP Systems. (Industry Audit Guide Ser.). 1981. pap. 6.00 (ISBN 0-686-84317-7). Am Inst CPA.

Taylor, D. H. & Glezen, G. W. Auditing: Integrated Concepts & Procedures. 2nd ed. 931p. 1982. text ed. 29.95 (ISBN 0-471-08166-3); write for info. tchr's. manual (ISBN 0-471-86343-2); write for info. test (ISBN 0-471-87680-1). Wiley.

Users' Guide to Understanding Audits & Auditors' Reports. 1982. 1.00 (ISBN 0-686-84322-3). Am Inst CPA.

Willingham. Auditing Concepts & Methods. 1983. write for info. (ISBN 0-07-070610-7). McGraw.

AUDITING–LAW

see Accounting–Law

AUDITING–PROBLEMS, EXERCISES, ETC.

ILA's Board of Regents. Certified Internal Auditor Examination: May 1982–Questions & Suggested Solutions, No. 9. 51p. 1982. pap. text ed. 4.00 (ISBN 0-89413-096-X). Inst Inter Aud.

AUDITORY NERVE

see Acoustic Nerve

AUDITORY PATHWAYS

see also Acoustic Nerve; Cerebral Cortex; Ear; Hearing

Romand, R., ed. Development of Auditory & Vestibular Systems. Date not set. price not set (ISBN 0-12-594450-0). Acad Pr.

AUGUSTINE, SAINT, ABP. OF CANTERBURY, d. 604

West, Rebecca. Saint Augustine. (A Thomas More Book to Live). 173p. 1983. 10.95 (ISBN 0-88347-148-5). Thomas More.

AUGUSTINIANS

St. Augustine. The City of God. 7.95 (ISBN 0-394-60397-4). Modern Lib.

AUGUSTINUS, AURELIUS, SAINT, BP. OF HIPPO, 354-430

Pusey, E. B., tr. The Confessions of St Augustine. 379p. 1982. Repr. of 1982 ed. lib. bdg. 20.00 (ISBN 0-8495-0081-8). Arden Lib.

Ulanov, Barry, tr. from Lat. Prayers of St. Augustine. 160p. 1983. pap. price not set (ISBN 0-8164-2454-3). Seabury.

AUSCHWITZ (CONCENTRATION CAMP)

see Oswiecim (Concentration Camp)

AUSTEN, JANE, 1775-1817

DeRose, Peter & McGuire, S. W. A Concordance to the Works of Jane Austen, 3 Vols. LC 82-48281. 1647p. 1982. lib. bdg. 250.00 (ISBN 0-8240-9245-7). Garland Pub.

Gilson, David, ed. A Bibliography of Jane Austen. (Soho Bibliographies Ser.). (Illus.). 900p. 1982. 110.00x (ISBN 0-19-818173-6). Oxford U Pr.

Todd, Janet, ed. Jane Austen. (Women & Literature Ser.: No. 3). (Orig.). 1983. text ed. price not set (ISBN 0-8419-0863-X); pap. text ed. price not set (ISBN 0-8419-0864-8). Holmes & Meier.

AUSTIN, MARY (HUNTER), 1868-1934

Fink, Augusta. I-Mary: A Biography of Mary Austin. 320p. 1983. 17.50 (ISBN 0-8165-0789-9). U of Ariz Pr.

AUSTIN, TEXAS

Crowell, Lynda & Mariotti, Maryanne. The Parent's Guide to Austin, 1982-83. (Illus.). 208p. 1982. pap. 5.95 (ISBN 0-938934-02-3). C&M Pubns.

AUSTIN FRIARS

see Augustinians

AUSTRALASIA

Rees, Henry. Australasia. 464p. 1975. 35.00x (ISBN 0-7121-0134-9, Pub. by MacDonald & Evans). State Mutual Bk.

AUSTRALIA

see also names of cities, regions, etc. in Australia, e.g. Melbourne

Australia, 1980. 375.00 (ISBN 0-686-99855-3, Pub. by Metra England). State Mutual Bk.

A Day in the Life of Australia. (Illus.). 288p. 1982. 35.00 (ISBN 0-8109-1801-3). Abrams.

Forge, Suzanne. Victorian Splendour: Australian Interior Decoration, 1837-1901. (Illus.). 162p. 1981. 65.00x (ISBN 0-19-554299-1). Oxford U Pr.

Menghetti, D. & Birtles, T. G. North Australia Research Bulletin. new ed. (North Australia Research Bulletin: No. 8). 101p. (Orig.). 1982. pap. text ed. 12.95 (ISBN 0-86784-154-0, 1256, Pub. by ANUP Austr alia). Bks Australia.

AUSTRALIA–ANTIQUITIES

Bowdler, Sandra, ed. Coastal Archaeology in Eastern Australia. 151p. (Orig.). 1982. pap. text ed. 17.95 (ISBN 0-86784-015-3, 1185, Pub. by ANUP Australia). Bks Australia.

White, J. P. & O'Connell, J. F., eds. A Prehistory of Australia, New Guinea & Sahul: International Edition. LC 81-71781. Date not set. 29.50 (ISBN 0-12-746730-0). Acad Pr.

AUSTRALIA–BIOGRAPHY

Braithwaite, Errol. Companion Guide to Westland. (Illus.). 1982. pap. 12.95 (ISBN 0-00-216967-3, Pub. by W Collins Australia). Intl Schol Bk Serv.

Business Who's Who of Australia. 16th ed. LC 64-56752. 821p. 1982. write for info. (ISBN 0-8002-3042-6). Intl Pubns Serv.

Jones, Henry L. Sixty Years in Australia. 1983. 7.95 (ISBN 0-533-05580-6). Vantage.

Mathams, R. J. Sub Rosa: Memoirs of an Australian Intelligence Analyst. 200p. 1983. text ed. 19.95x (ISBN 0-86861-380-0). Allen Unwin.

Waterson, D. B. & Arnold, John. Biographical Register of the Queensland Parliament 1930-1980. new ed. 144p. (Orig.). 1982. pap. text ed. 13.95 (ISBN 0-7081-1957-3, 1243, Pub. by ANUP Australia). Bks Australia.

AUSTRALIA–COMMERCE

Austrian Export Directory: Export-Adressbuch von Osterreich 1982/83. 1982/83 ed. LC 52-24185. 501p. (Orig., Eng., Fr., & Span.). 1982. pap. 45.00x (ISBN 0-8002-3043-4). Intl Pubns Serv.

AUSTRALIA–DESCRIPTION AND TRAVEL

Daniell, Jo, illus. Thorn Bird Country. (Illus.). 128p. 1983. pap. 12.95 (ISBN 0-446-37573-X). Warner Bks.

Loveday, P., ed. Service Delivery to Outstations. new ed. (North Ausralia Research Unit Monograph: No. 2). 97p. (Orig.). 1982. pap. text ed. 9.95 (ISBN 0-86784-160-5, 1257, Pub. by ANUP Australia). Bks Australia.

AUSTRALIA–DESCRIPTION AND TRAVEL–GUIDEBOOKS

McDermott, John W. How to Get Lost & Found in Australia. 1980. 9.95 (ISBN 0-686-37615-3). Orafa Pub Co.

AUSTRALIA–DISCOVERY AND EXPLORATION

Dampier, William. Voyage to New Holland. 256p. 1982. text ed. 22.50x (ISBN 0-904387-75-5, Pub. by Alan Sutton England); pap. text ed. 10.50x (ISBN 0-86299-006-8). Humanities.

Perry, T. M. The Discovery of Australia: The Charts & Maps of the Navigators & Explorers. (Illus.). 160p. 1983. 100.00 (ISBN 0-241-10863-2, Pub. by Hamish Hamilton England). David & Charles.

AUSTRALIA–ECONOMIC CONDITIONS

Australia Bureau of Statistics. Yearbook Australia 1981. 65th ed. LC 9-6317. (Illus.). 843p. (Orig.). 1981. pap. 30.00x (ISBN 0-8002-3012-4). Intl Pubns Serv.

Gruen, F. H., ed. Surveys of Australian Economics, Vol. III. 272p. 1983. text ed. 35.00x (ISBN 0-86861-396-7). Allen Unwin.

Hagger, A. J., ed. Guide to Australian Economic & Social Statistics. (Guides to Australian Information Ser.). 120p. 1983. pap. 10.50 (ISBN 0-08-029833-8). Pergamon.

Head, Brian. State & Economy in Australia. 248p. 1982. 18.50x (ISBN 0-19-554261-4). Oxford U Pr.

Perkins, J. O. The Australian Financial System after the Campbell Report. 152p. 1982. pap. 14.00 (ISBN 0-522-84253-4, Pub. by Melbourne U Pr Australia). Intl Schol Bk Serv.

Sheenan, J. A Guide to Sources of Information on Australian Business. (Guides to Australian Information Sources Ser.). 120p. 1983. pap. 10.50 (ISBN 0-08-029831-1). Pergamon.

AUSTRALIA–FOREIGN RELATIONS

Carroll, John. Intruders in the Bush: The Australian Quest for Identity. 1982. pap. 11.95 (ISBN 0-19-554308-4). Oxford U Pr.

AUSTRALIA–HISTORY

Barwick, Diane & Urry, James, eds. Aboriginal History, Vol. 5. 178p. (Orig.). 1982. pap. text ed. 14.95 (ISBN 0-86784-37604-8, 1188, Pub. by ANUP Australia). Bks Australia.

Bolton, Geoffrey. Spoils & Spoilers: Australians Make their Environment 1788-1980. (Australian Experience Ser.: No. 3). (Illus.). 200p. 1982. pap. text ed. 12.50 (ISBN 0-86861-226-X). Allen Unwin.

Carroll, John. Intruders in the Bush: The Australian Quest for Identity. 1982. pap. 11.95 (ISBN 0-19-554308-4). Oxford U Pr.

Dutton, Tom. The Hiri in History. new ed. (Pacific Research Monograph: No. 8). 159p. (Orig.). 1982. pap. text ed. 14.95 (ISBN 0-909150-63-X, 1258, Pub. by ANUP Australia). Bks Australia.

Griffin, Graeme M. & Tobin, Des. In the Midst of Life: The Australian Response to Death. (Illus.). 191p. 1983. pap. 9.95 (ISBN 0-522-84248-8, Pub. by Melbourne U Pr). Intl Schol Bk Serv.

Murphy, B. Dictionary of Australian History. 340p. 1982. 19.00 (ISBN 0-07-072946-8). McGraw.

Powell, Alan. Far Country: A Short History of the Northern Territory. (Illus.). 301p. 1982. pap. text ed. 19.95 (ISBN 0-522-84226-7, Pub. by Melbourne U Pr Australia). Intl Schol Bk Serv.

Warhurst, John. Jobs or Dogma: The Industrial Assistance Commission & Australian Politics. LC 82-8653. (Policy, Politics, & Administration Ser.). (Illus.). 255p. 1983. text ed. 19.50x (ISBN 0-7022-1850-2); pap. text ed. 8.50x (ISBN 0-7022-1982-7). U of Queensland Pr.

AUSTRALIA–INDUSTRIES

Business Who's Who of Australia. 16th ed. LC 64-56752. 821p. 1982. write for info. (ISBN 0-8002-3042-6). Intl Pubns Serv.

Control Engineering, 1982 Conference: Merging of Technology & Theory to Solve Industrial Automation Problems. 247p. (Orig.). 1982. pap. text ed. 42.00x (ISBN 0-85825-168-X, Pub. by Inst Engineering Australia). Renouf.

Ebeling, Doug. Industrial Innovation in Australia. 45p. (Orig.). 1981. pap. text ed. 18.75x (ISBN 0-85825-161-2, Pub. by Inst Engineering Australia). Renouf.

Energy Australia. 160p. (Orig.). 1979. pap. text ed. 18.00x (ISBN 0-85825-121-3, Pub. by Inst Engineering Australia). Renouf.

The Engineering Conference, 1982. 261p. (Orig.). 1982. pap. text ed. 37.50x (Pub. by Inst Engineering Australia). Renouf.

The Future of the Electronics & Telecommunications Industries in Australia. 93p. (Orig.). 1978. pap. text ed. 18.00x (ISBN 0-85825-099-3, Pub. by Inst Engineering Australia). Renouf.

Hobart: Changing Society: A Challenge for Engineering. 261p. (Orig.). 1982. pap. text ed. 37.50x (Pub. by Inst Engineering Australia). Renouf.

Manufacturing in Australia, 2 vols. 263p. (Orig.). 1980. pap. text ed. 12.00x (ISBN 0-85825-131-0, Pub. by Inst Engineering Australia). Renouf.

Technology for Development: First International Conference. 367p. (Orig.). 1980. pap. text ed. 60.00x (ISBN 0-85825-140-X, Pub. by Inst Engineering Australia). Renouf.

Thiele, Steven. Yugul: An Arnhem Land & Gattle Station. 73p. (Orig.). 1982. pap. text ed. 9.95 (ISBN 0-86784-007-2, 1189, Pub. by ANUP Australia). Bks Australia.

AUSTRALIA–MAPS

Perry, T. M. The Discovery of Australia: The Charts & Maps of the Navigators & Explorers. (Illus.). 160p. 1983. 100.00 (ISBN 0-241-10863-2, Pub. by Hamish Hamilton England). David & Charles.

AUSTRALIA–NATIVE RACES

Howard, Michael C. Aboriginal Politics in Southwestern Australia. (Illus.). 181p. 1982. pap. text ed. 23.00 (ISBN 0-686-83950-1, Pub. by U of W Austral Pr). Intl Schol Bk Serv.

Jueneke, Klaus. Huts of the High Country. LC 82-71656. 251p. 1982. pap. text ed. 34.95 (ISBN 0-7081-1389-3, 1233). Bks Australia.

AUSTRALIA–POLITICS AND GOVERNMENT

Howard, Michael C. Aboriginal Politics in Southwestern Australia. (Illus.). 181p. 1982. pap. text ed. 23.00 (ISBN 0-686-83950-1, Pub. by U of W Austral Pr). Intl Schol Bk Serv.

Jaensch, Dean. The Australian Party System. 234p. 1983. text ed. 28.50x (ISBN 0-86861-077-1). Allen Unwin.

Loveday, P. & Jaensch, D. NAC Election in the Northern Territory 1981. (North Australia Research Unit Monograph). 67p. (Orig.). 1982. pap. text ed. 9.95 (ISBN 0-86784-120-6, 1232). Bks Australia.

Phillips, Dennis. Cold War 2 & Australia. 144p. 1983. text ed. 18.50x (ISBN 0-86861-125-5). Allen Unwin.

Warhurst, John. Jobs or Dogma: The Industrial Assistance Commission & Australian Politics. LC 82-8653. (Policy, Politics, & Administration Ser.). (Illus.). 255p. 1983. text ed. 19.50x (ISBN 0-7022-1850-2); pap. text ed. 8.50x (ISBN 0-7022-1982-7). U of Queensland Pr.

Wild, Ronald. Heathcote: A Study of Local Government & Resident Action in a small Australian Town. 160p. 1983. text ed. 28.50x (ISBN 0-86861-093-3). Allen Unwin.

AUSTRALIA–RELATIONS (GENERAL)

King, Peter, ed. Australia's Vietnam: Australia in the Second Indo-China War. 288p. 1983. text ed. 28.50x (ISBN 0-86861-037-2). Allen Unwin.

AUSTRALIA–SOCIAL CONDITIONS

Cheok, Cheong Kee & Lean, Lim Lin. Demographic Impact on Socio-Economic Development. LC 81-71612. (Development Studies Centre Monograph: No. 29). 129p. (Orig.). 1982. pap. text ed. 14.95 (ISBN 0-909150-69-9, 1224). Bks Australia.

Hagger, A. J., ed. Guide to Australian Economic & Social Statistics. (Guides to Australian Information Ser.). 120p. 1983. pap. 10.50 (ISBN 0-08-029833-8). Pergamon.

Metzner, Joachim K. Agriculture & Population Pressure in Sikka, Isle of Flores. LC 81-71133. (Development Studies Centre Monograph: No. 28). 355p. (Orig.). 1982. pap. text ed. 24.95 (ISBN 0-909150-59-1, 1227). Bks Australia.

Young, E. A. & Fisk, E. K., eds. Town Populations. LC 82-73139. (Aboriginal Component in the Australian Economy Ser.: No. 2). 171p. (Orig.). 1982. pap. text ed. 16.95 (ISBN 0-909150-77-X, 1221). Bks Australia.

AUSTRALIA–STATISTICS

Australia Bureau of Statistics. Yearbook Australia, 1982. 66th ed. LC 9-6317. (Illus.). 843p. (Orig.). 1982. pap. 35.00x (ISBN 0-8002-3026-4). Intl Pubns Serv.

Hagger, A. J., ed. Guide to Australian Economic & Social Statistics. (Guides to Australian Information Ser.). 120p. 1983. pap. 10.50 (ISBN 0-08-029833-8). Pergamon.

Statisches Zantralamt. Statistisches Handbuch fur Die Republik Osterreich, 1982. 33rd ed. (Illus.). 662p. (Orig., Ger.). pap. 57.50 (ISBN 0-8002-3048-5). Intl Pubns Serv.

AUSTRALIAN ABORIGINES–GOVERNMENT RELATIONS

see Australia–Native Races

AUSTRALIAN ARCHITECTURE

see Architecture–Australia

AUSTRALIAN ART

see Art, Australian

AUSTRALIAN LITERATURE (COLLECTIONS)

Coleman, Peter & Shrubb, Lee, eds. Quadrant: Twenty-Five Years. LC 82-19998. 568p. 1983. 22.50 (ISBN 0-7022-1820-0). U of Queensland Pr.

AUSTRALIAN LITERATURE–BIBLIOGRAPHY

National Library of Australia. Australian National Bibliography 1981. 21st ed. LC 63-33739. 1231p. 1982. 67.50x (ISBN 0-8002-3014-0). Intl Pubns Serv.

AUSTRALIAN LITERATURE–HISTORY AND CRITICISM

Krauth, Nigel. New Guinea Images in Australian Literature. LC 82-2812. (Portable Australian Authors Ser.). 279p. 1982. text ed. 22.50 (ISBN 0-7022-1960-6, AACR2); pap. 10.95 (ISBN 0-7022-1970-3). U of Queensland Pr.

AUSTRALIAN LOVEBIRD

see Budgerigars

AUSTRALIAN MUSIC

see Music, Australian

AUSTRALIAN NATIONAL CHARACTERISTICS

see National Characteristics, Australian

AUSTRALIAN PAINTERS

see Painters–Australia

AUSTRALOPITHECINES

Reichs, Kathleen J., ed. Hominid Origins: Inquiries Past & Present. LC 82-20161. (Illus.). 278p. (Orig.). 1983. lib. bdg. 22.50 (ISBN 0-8191-2864-3); pap. text ed. 11.75 (ISBN 0-8191-2865-1). U Pr of Amer.

AUSTRIA

see also names of cities, regions, etc. in Austria, e.g. Vienna

Statistisches Zentralamt, Austria, ed. Statistisches Handbuch fur die Republik Osterreich, 1981. 32nd ed. (Illus.). 668p. (Ger.). pap. 57.50x (ISBN 0-8002-3067-1). Intl Pubns Serv.

AUSTRIA–CIVILIZATION

Johnston, William M. The Austrian Mind: An Intellectual & Social History. (Illus.). 531p. 1983. pap. 10.95 (ISBN 0-520-04955-1, CAL 624). U of Cal Pr.

AUSTRIA–DESCRIPTION AND TRAVEL–GUIDEBOOKS

Baedeker's Austria. (Illus.). 250p. 1983. pap. 12.95 (ISBN 0-13-056127-4). P-H.

Harrison, Shirley & Harrison, John. Austria & Switzerland. LC 82-61195. (Pocket Guide Ser.). (Illus.). 1983. pap. 4.95 (ISBN 0-528-84892-5). Rand.

Michelin Green Guide: Osterreich. (Green Guide Ser.). (Ger.). 1983. pap. write for info. (ISBN 2-06-025150-8). Michelin.

AUSTRIA–ECONOMIC CONDITIONS

Arndt, Sven W., ed. Political Economy of Austria. 1982. 16.95 (ISBN 0-8447-2241-3); pap. 8.95 (ISBN 0-8447-2240-5). Am Enterprise.

AUSTRIA–HISTORY

see also Hungary–History

Rabinbach, Anson. The Crisis of Austrian Socialism: From Red Vienna to Civil War, Nineteen Twenty Seven-Nineteen Thirty Four. LC 82-10919. (Illus.). 312p. 1983. lib. bdg. 22.00 (ISBN 0-226-70121-2). U of Chicago Pr.

Sully, Melanie A. Continuity & Change in Austrian Socialism: The Eternal Quest for the Third Way. (East European Monographs: No. 114). 320p. 1982. 25.00x (ISBN 0-88033-008-2). East Eur Quarterly.

AUSTRIA–POLITICS AND GOVERNMENT

Arndt, Sven W., ed. Political Economy of Austria. 1982. 16.95 (ISBN 0-8447-2241-3); pap. 8.95 (ISBN 0-8447-2240-5). Am Enterprise.

Sully, Melanie A. Continuity & Change in Austrian Socialism: The Eternal Quest for the Third Way. (East European Monographs: No. 114). 320p. 1982. 25.00x (ISBN 0-88033-008-2). East Eur Quarterly.

AUTHOR AND PUBLISHER

see Authors and Publishers

AUTHORITY

see also Despotism

Das Gupta, Jyotirindra. Authority, Priority, & Human Development. (Illus.). 126p. 9.95x (ISBN 0-19-561391-0). Oxford U Pr.

Watt, E. D. Authority. LC 82-42542. 140p. 1982. 19.95x (ISBN 0-312-06121-8). St Martin.

AUTHORITY (RELIGION)

see also Bible–Evidences, Authority, Etc.; Catholic Church–Infallibility; Experience (Religion); Popes–Infallibility

Shaw, Graham. The Cost of Authority: Manipulation & Freedom in the New Testament. LC 82-48545. 320p. 1983. pap. 16.95 (ISBN 0-8006-1707-X). Fortress.

AUTHORS

see also Anonyms and Pseudonyms; Women Authors also particular classes of writers, e.g. Dramatists, Historians, Poets; also names of authors, e.g. Shakespeare, William

Bruccoli, Mary, ed. Dictionary of Literary Biography Documentary Series: An Illustrated Chronicle, Vol. 3. 450p. 1983. 74.00x (ISBN 0-8103-1115-1, Pub. by K G Saur). Gale.

Carlisle, E. Fred. Loren Eiseley: The Development of a Writer. LC 82-8459. 216p. 1983. 18.95 (ISBN 0-252-00987-8). U of Ill Pr.

Cogell, Elizabeth C. Ursula K. Leguin: A Primary & Secondary Bibliography. 1983. lib. bdg. 39.95 (ISBN 0-8161-8155-1, Hall Reference). G K Hall.

Connolly, Julian W. Ivan Bunin. (World Authors Ser.). 1982. lib. bdg. 18.95 (ISBN 0-8057-6513-1, Twayne). G K Hall.

Davidson, Arnold E. Mordecai Richler. LC 82-40282. (Literature & Life Ser.). 190p. 1983. 11.95 (ISBN 0-8044-2140-4). Ungar.

Dedner, Burghard. Carl Sternheim. (Twayne's World Authors Ser.). 1982. lib. bdg. 18.95 (ISBN 0-8057-6518-2, Twayne). G K Hall.

Directory of the American Society of Journalists & Authors, 1981-82. 1982. 40.00 (ISBN 0-686-82230-7). Educ Indus.

Evory, Ann, ed. Contemporary Authors New Revision Series, Vol. 8. 600p. 1983. 74.00x (ISBN 0-8103-1937-3). Gale.

Fortune, Richard. Alexander Sukhovo-Kobylin. (World Authors Ser.). 1982. lib. bdg. 18.95 (ISBN 0-8057-6515-8, Twayne). G K Hall.

Gerber, Leslie E. & McFadden, Margaret. Loren Eiseley. LC 82-40294. (Literature & Life). 200p. 1983. 11.95 (ISBN 0-8044-5424-8). Ungar.

Kessler, Carol F. Elizabeth Stuart Phelps. (United States Authors Ser.). 1982. lib. bdg. 14.95 (ISBN 0-8057-7374-6, Twayne). G K Hall.

Land, Myrick. The Fine Art of Literary Mayhem: A Lively Account of Famous Writers & Their Feuds. 2nd, Rev. ed. 272p. Date not set. pap. 8.95 (ISBN 0-938530-11-9, 11-9). Lexikos.

Maes-Jelinek, Hena. Wilson Harris. (World Authors Ser.). 1982. lib. bdg. 17.95 (ISBN 0-8057-6506-9, Twayne). G K Hall.

Marquis Who's Who Publications Index to All Books, 1981-1982. LC 74-17540. 750p. 1982. 24.50 (ISBN 0-8379-1412-4). Marquis.

May, Hal, ed. Contemporary Authors, Vol. 107. 600p. 1983. 74.00x (ISBN 0-8103-1907-1). Gale.

Thompson, Raymond H. Gordon R. Dickson: A Primary & Secondary Bibliography. 1983. lib. bdg. 27.50 (ISBN 0-8161-8363-5, Hall Reference). G K Hall.

Vinson, James & Kirkpatrick, D. L., eds. Twentieth-Century Western Writers. 1000p. 1983. 75.00x (ISBN 0-8103-0227-6, Pub. by Macmillan England). Gale.

Woolf, Virginia. Letter to a Young Poet. 1982. lib. bdg. 34.50 (ISBN 0-686-81936-5). Porter.

AUTHORS–CORRESPONDENCE, REMINISCENCES, ETC.

Baumann, Winfried. Erinnerung und Erinnertes In Gor'kijs "Kindheit". 196p. (Ger.). 1982. write for info. (ISBN 3-8204-5760-7). P Lang Pubs.

Dembo, L. S., ed. Interviews with Contemporary Writers. LC 82-51092. 384p. 1983. 25.00 (ISBN 0-299-09330-1); pap. 8.95 (ISBN 0-299-09334-4). U of Wis Pr.
Jones, John G., ed. Mississippi Writers Talking, Vol. 2. LC 81-23057. (Illus.). 228p. 1983. 15.00 (ISBN 0-87805-174-0); pap. 8.95 (ISBN 0-87805-175-9). U Pr of Miss.
Loos, Anita. Gentlemen Prefer Blondes But Gentlemen Marry Brunettes. LC 82-48893. 256p. 1983. pap. 3.95 (ISBN 0-686-43024-7, Vin). Random.
Rothschild, Loren R., ed. The Letters of William Somerset Maugham to Lady Juliet Duff. (Illus.). 112p. write for info. limited ed. 300 copies. Rassela Pr.
Trenner, Richard, ed. E. L. Doctorow: Essays & Conversations. 286p. 1983. 14.95 (ISBN 0-86538-023-6); pap. 8.95 (ISBN 0-86538-024-4). Ontario Rev NJ.

AUTHORS–JUVENILE LITERATURE

Yates, Elizabeth. My Widening World: The Continuing Diary of Elizabeth Yates. LC 82-23713. (Illus.). 120p. (gr. 7 up). 1983. price not set (ISBN 0-664-32702-8). Westminster.

AUTHORS, AFRO-AMERICAN

see Afro-American Authors

AUTHORS, AMERICAN

Angyal, Andrew J. Loren Eiseley. (United States Authors Ser.). 182p. 1983. lib. bdg. 15.95 (ISBN 0-8057-7381-9, Twayne). G K Hall.
Armour, Richard. Drug Store Days: My Youth Among the Pills & Potions. rev. ed. LC 82-23762. (Illus.). 192p. 1983. pap. 5.95 (ISBN 0-88007-125-7). Woodbridge Pr.
Bannister, Henry S. Donn Byrne: A Descriptive Bibliography, 1912-1935. LC 80-8485. 350p. 1982. lib. bdg. 50.00 (ISBN 0-8240-9502-2). Garland Pub.
Berg, Stephen, ed. In Praise of What Persists. LC 81-47651. (Illus.). 320p. 1983. 14.95 (ISBN 0-06-014921-3, HarpT). Har-Row.
Bowden, J. H. Peter De Vries. (United States Authors Ser.). 177p. 1983. lib. bdg. 15.95 (ISBN 0-8057-7388-6, Twayne). G K Hall.
Connelly, Stephen E. Allan Seager. (United States Authors Ser.). 144p. 1983. lib. bdg. 16.95 (ISBN 0-8057-7386-X, Twayne). G K Hall.
Faulkner, Florence. A Challenge for Two. 1982. 6.95 (ISBN 0-686-84158-1, Avalon). Bouregy.
Faust, Langdon L., ed. American Women Writers: A Critical Reference Guide from Colonial Times to the Present, Vol. 1, A-L. Abr. ed. LC 82-40286. 445p. 1983. pap. 14.95 (ISBN 0-8044-6164-3). Ungar.
--American Women Writers: A Critical Reference Guide from Colonial Times to the Present, Vol. 2, M-Z. Abr. ed. LC 82-40286. 445p. 1983. pap. 14.95 (ISBN 0-8044-6165-1). Ungar.
Fogdall, Alberta B. Royal Family of the Columbia: Dr. John McLoughlin & His Family. LC 78-17170. (Illus.). 1982. 16.95 (ISBN 0-8323-0413-1). Binford.
Foster, Edward H. Richard Brautigan. (United States Authors Ser.). 176p. 1983. lib. bdg. 14.95 (ISBN 0-8057-7378-9, Twayne). G K Hall.
Fowler, Douglas. S. J. Perelman. (United States Authors Ser.). 192p. 1983. lib. bdg. 12.95 (ISBN 0-8057-7376-2, Twayne). G K Hall.
Giles, James R. Irwin Shaw. (United States Authors Ser.). 220p. 1983. lib. bdg. 13.95 (ISBN 0-8057-7382-7, Twayne). G K Hall.
Hassler, Donald M. Hal Clement. (Starmont Reader's Guide Ser.: No. 11). 64p. 1982. Repr. lib. bdg. 10.95x (ISBN 0-89370-042-8). Borgo Pr.
Hotchner, A. E. Papa Hemingway: The Ecstasy & Sorrow. (Illus.). 352p. 1982. pap. 8.95 (ISBN 0-688-02042-9). Quill NY.
Johnson, Joyce. Minor Characters. 262p. 1983. 13.95 (ISBN 0-395-32513-7). HM.
Johnston, Jill. Mother Bound. LC 82-48592. 200p. 1983. 12.95 (ISBN 0-394-52757-7). Knopf.
Jones, John G., ed. Mississippi Writers Talking, Vol. 2. LC 81-23057. (Illus.). 228p. 1983. 15.00 (ISBN 0-87805-174-0); pap. 8.95 (ISBN 0-87805-175-9). U Pr of Miss.
Jones, Samuel A. Thoreau Amongst Friends & Philistines & Other Thoreauviana. Hendrick, George, ed. & LC 82-6444. xxvi, 241p. 1983. 23.95 (ISBN 0-8214-0675-2, 82-84432). Ohio U Pr.
Kert, Bernice. The Hemingway Women. (Illus.). 1983. 20.00 (ISBN 0-393-01720-6). Norton.
Lainoff, Seymour. Ludwig Lewisohn. (United States Authors Ser.). 1982. lib. bdg. 15.95 (ISBN 0-8057-7375-4, Twayne). G K Hall.
LeClair, Thomas & McCaffery, Larry, eds. Anything Can Happen: Interviews with Contemporary American Novelists. LC 82-2867. (Illus.). 320p. 1983. 15.95 (ISBN 0-252-00970-3). U of Ill Pr.
Prokosch, Frederic. Voices: A Memoir. 1982. 18.50 (ISBN 0-374-28509-8). FS&G.
Sarton, May. Plant Dreaming Deep. 192p. 1983. pap. 3.95 (ISBN 0-393-30108-7). Norton.
Straight, Michael. After Long Silence. (Illus.). 1983. 17.50 (ISBN 0-393-01729-X). Norton.
Vrana, Stan A. Interviews & Conversations with Twentieth Century Authors Writing in English: An Index. LC 82-3275. 259p. 1982. 16.00 (ISBN 0-8108-1542-7). Scarecrow.
Waldrop, Ruth W. Alabama Authors. 151p. (Orig.). 1980. pap. 7.95 (ISBN 0-87397-182-5). Strode.
Windham, Donald. Footnote to a Friendship: A Memoir of Truman Capote & Others. (Illus.). 1983. wrappers, ltd. ed. 25.00x (ISBN 0-917366-06-9). S Campbell.
Witte, John, ed. Dialogues with Northwest Writers: Interviews with Nine NW Writers, Including Tom Robbins, Mary Barnard & Richard Hugo. LC 82-19063. (Illus.). 280p. (Orig.). 1982. pap. 8.00 (ISBN 0-918402-06-9). NW Review Bks.
Wolfe, Thomas. The Autobiography of an American Novelist. Field, Leslie, ed. (Illus.). 128p. 1983. text ed. 15.00x (ISBN 0-674-05316-8); pap. text ed. 5.95x (ISBN 0-674-05317-6). Harvard U Pr.
Wyld, Lionel D. Walter D. Edmonds, Storyteller. LC 82-10443. (York State Bks.). (Illus.). 168p. 1982. text ed. 20.00x (ISBN 0-8156-0180-8). Syracuse U Pr.

AUTHORS, AMERICAN–BIBLIOGRAPHY

Waldrop, Ruth W. Alabama Authors. 151p. (Orig.). 1980. pap. 7.95 (ISBN 0-87397-182-5). Strode.
Wheeler, Eva F. A History of Wyoming Writers. (Illus.). 92p. 1982. pap. 7.00 (ISBN 0-686-38836-4). E F Wheeler.

AUTHORS, ARGENTINE

Mallea, Eduardo. History of an Argentine Passion. Miller, Yvette E., ed. Litchblau, Myron, tr. 184p. 1982. pap. 10.95 (ISBN 0-935480-10-2). Lat Am Lit Rev Pr.

AUTHORS, AUSTRIAN

Pfanner, Helmut F. Exile in New York: German & Austrian Writers After 1933. (Illus.). 272p. 1983. 18.95x (ISBN 0-8143-1727-8). Wayne St U Pr.

AUTHORS, CANADIAN

Lecker, Robert & David, Jack. The Annotated Bibliography to Canada's Major Authors: Vol. 4-A. J. M. Smith, Earle Birney, Dorothy Livesay & F. R. Scott. 1983. lib. bdg. 42.50 (ISBN 0-8161-8638-3, Hall Reference). G K Hall.
Russell, Delbert W. Anne Herbert. (World Authors Ser.). 170p. 1983. lib. bdg. 18.95 (ISBN 0-8057-6531-X, Twayne). G K Hall.

AUTHORS, CATHOLIC

see Catholic Authors

AUTHORS, CHINESE

Yang, Gladys, intro. by. Seven Contemporary Chinese Women Writers. 282p. 1982. pap. 4.95 (ISBN 0-295-96017-5, Pub. by Chinese Lit Beijing). U of Wash Pr.

AUTHORS, ENGLISH

Batchelor, Roy. Edwardian Novelists. 1982. 25.00 (ISBN 0-312-23907-6). St Martin.
Bedell, Meredith. Stella Benson. (English Authors Ser.). 172p. 1983. lib. bdg. 18.95 (ISBN 0-8057-6845-9, Twayne). G K Hall.
Edwards, A. S. Stephen Hawes. (English Authors Ser.: No. 354). 152p. 1983. lib. bdg. 18.95 (ISBN 0-8057-6840-8, Twayne). G K Hall.
Helgerson, Richard. Self-Crowned Laureates: Spenser, Jonson, Milton, & the Literary System. LC 82-8496. 330p. 1983. text ed. 22.00x (ISBN 0-520-04808-3). U of Cal Pr.
Kelly, Richard. George DuMaurier. (English Authors Ser.). 200p. 1983. lib. bdg. 16.95 (ISBN 0-8057-6841-6, Twayne). G K Hall.
Levine, Richard A. The Victorian Experience: The Novelists. LC 75-15338. 272p. 1983. pap. 10.95 (ISBN 0-8214-0747-3, 82-85165). Ohio U Pr.
Mallon, Thomas. Edmund Blunden. (English Authors Ser.). 158p. 1983. lib. bdg. 17.95 (ISBN 0-8057-6829-7, Twayne). G K Hall.
Miller, George E. Edward Hyde, Earl of Clarendon. (English Authors Ser.: No. 337). 192p. 1983. lib. bdg. 18.95 (ISBN 0-8057-6823-8, Twayne). G K Hall.
Selig, Robert L. George Gissing. (English Authors Ser.). 192p. 1983. lib. bdg. 15.95 (ISBN 0-8057-6831-9, Twayne). G K Hall.
Sullivan, Harry R. Frederic Harrison. (English Authors Ser.: No. 341). 232p. 1983. lib. bdg. 18.95 (ISBN 0-8057-6827-0, Twayne). G K Hall.
Vannatta, Dennis. H. E. Bates. (English Authors Ser.). 177p. 1983. lib. bdg. 17.95 (ISBN 0-8057-6844-0, Twayne). G K Hall.
Vrana, Stan A. Interviews & Conversations with Twentieth Century Authors Writing in English: An Index. LC 82-3275. 259p. 1982. 16.00 (ISBN 0-8108-1542-7). Scarecrow.
Watts, Cedric. R. B. Cunninghae Graham. (English Authors Ser.). 155p. 1983. lib. bdg. 18.95 (ISBN 0-8057-6843-2, Twayne). G K Hall.
Wooden, Warren W. John Foxe. (English Authors Ser.). 176p. 1983. lib. bdg. 17.95 (ISBN 0-8057-6830-0, Twayne). G K Hall.

AUTHORS, FRENCH

Bond, David. The Fiction of Andre Pieyre de Mandiargues. LC 82-5894. 176p. 1982. text ed. 22.00x (ISBN 0-8156-2265-1); pap. text ed. 12.95x (ISBN 0-8156-2283-X). Syracuse U Pr.
Leki, Ilona. Alain Robbe-Grillet. (World Authors Ser.). 200p. 1983. lib. bdg. 16.95 (ISBN 0-8057-6529-8, Twayne). G K Hall.
Russell, Delbert W. Anne Herbert. (World Authors Ser.). 170p. 1983. lib. bdg. 18.95 (ISBN 0-8057-6531-X, Twayne). G K Hall.
Stewart, Joan Hinde. Colette. (World Authors Ser.). 198p. 1983. lib. bdg. 13.95 (ISBN 0-8057-6527-1, Twayne). G K Hall.
Yenal, Edith. Christine De Pisan: A Bibliography of Writings By Her & About Her. LC 82-10386. 192p. 1982. 13.00 (ISBN 0-8108-1574-5). Scarecrow.

AUTHORS, GERMAN

Genton, Elisabeth. Goethe Zeit: La Vie et les Opinions de Heinrich Leopold Wagner (1747-1779) 516p. 1980. write for info. (ISBN 3-8204-6541-3). P Lang Pubs.
Hardin, James. John Beer. (World Authors Ser.). 128p. 1983. lib. bdg. 18.95 (ISBN 0-8057-6536-0, Twayne). G K Hall.
Pfanner, Helmut F. Exile in New York: German & Austrian Writers After 1933. (Illus.). 272p. 1983. 18.95x (ISBN 0-8143-1727-8). Wayne St U Pr.
Rowland, Herbert. Matthias Claudius. (World Author Ser.). 146p. 1983. lib. bdg. 18.95 (ISBN 0-8057-6538-7, Twayne). G K Hall.

AUTHORS, IRISH

Kenner, Hugh. A Colder Eye: The Modern Irish Writers. LC 82-48723. 1983. 16.95. Knopf.

AUTHORS, ITALIAN

Lajolo, Davide. An Absurd Vice: A Biography of Cesare Pavese. Pietralunga, Mario, tr. Pietralunga, Mark. LC 82-14482. 288p. (Ital.). 1983. 18.50 (ISBN 0-8112-0850-8); pap. 9.25 (ISBN 0-8112-0851-6, NDP545). New Directions.

AUTHORS, JAPANESE

Powell, Irena. Writers & Society in Modern Japan. LC 82-48432. 230p. 1983. 24.95 (ISBN 0-87011-558-8). Kodansha.

AUTHORS, RUSSIAN

Berberova, Nina. Kursiv Moi, 2 vols. (Illus.). 720p. (Orig., Rus.). 1982. Set. pap. 34.00 (ISBN 0-89830-065-7). Vol. 1 (ISBN 0-89830-066-5). Vol.2 (ISBN 0-89830-067-3). Russica Pubs.

AUTHORS, SCANDINAVIAN

Thompson, Laurie. Stig Dagerman. (World Authors Ser.: No. 676). 166p. 1983. lib. bdg. 19.95 (ISBN 0-8057-6523-9, Twayne). G K Hall.

AUTHORS, SCOTTISH

Nickerson, Roy. Robert Louis Stevenson in California. LC 82-9643. (Illus.). 128p. (Orig.). 1982. pap. 5.95 (ISBN 0-87701-246-6). Chronicle Bks.

AUTHORS, SPANISH

Cabrera, Vicente. Juan Benet. (World Authors Ser.). 176p. 1983. lib. bdg. 17.95 (ISBN 0-8057-6532-8, Twayne). G K Hall.
Herzberger, David K. Jesus Fernandez Santos. (World Authors Ser.). 168p. 1983. lib. bdg. 18.95 (ISBN 0-8057-6534-4, Twayne). G K Hall.

AUTHORS, WOMEN

see Women Authors

AUTHORS AND PRINTERS

see Authorship–Handbooks, Manuals, etc.; Printing–Style Manuals

AUTHORS AND PUBLISHERS

see also Copyright; Literary Agents

Curtis, Richard. How to Be Your Own Literary Agent. 1983. 12.95 (ISBN 0-395-33123-4). HM.

AUTHORSHIP

Here are entered guides to authorship in general. Guides in individual fields are entered under appropriate terms if in common usage, e.g. Playwriting, Technical Writing, Television Authorship; otherwise under the name of the genre or subject with subdivision Authorship, e.g. Poetry–Authorship. The subdivision Authorship is also used under names of individual authors or works in cases of dubious or disputed authorship, e.g. Shakespeare, William, 1564-1616–Authorship.

see also Advertising Copy; Authors; Authors and Publishers; Autobiography; Biography (As a Literary Form); Characters and Characteristics in Literature; Children'S Literature–Technique; Copyright; Creative Writing; Drama–Technique; Fiction–Authorship; Fiction–Technique; Historiography; Journalism; Moving-Picture Authorship; Plots (Drama, Novel, Etc.); Report Writing; Rhetoric; Short Story; Television Authorship; Versification; Women Authors

Author Aid-Research Associates International. Freelancers of North America: Editors, Ghost-Writers-Collaborators, Copywriters, Speechwriters, Business-Technical-Medical Writers 1983-84. 350p. Date not set. pap. price not set (ISBN 0-911085-01-7). Author Aid.
Beaugrande, Robert de. Text Production. Freedle, Roy O., ed. (Advances in Discourse Processes Ser.: Vol. 11). 400p. 1983. text ed. 37.50 (ISBN 0-89391-158-5); pap. text ed. 18.50 (ISBN 0-89391-159-3). Ablex Pub.
Bell & Klammer. The Practicing Writer. 1983. pap. text ed. 11.95 (ISBN 0-686-84570-6, RM89); instr's. manual avail. (RM90). HM.
Cassel, Dana K., ed. Directory of Florida Markets For Writers, 1983. 1983. 12.95. Cassell Commun Inc.
Falk, Kathryn. How to Write a Romance & Get it Published: With Intimate Advice form the World's Most Popular Romance Writers. 1983. 14.95 (ISBN 0-517-54944-1). Crown.
Flesch, Rudolf & Lass, A. H. A New Guide to Better Writing. 1982. pap. 2.50 (ISBN 0-446-31091-3). Warner Bks.
Gale, Steven H. Readings for Todays Writers. LC 79-21312. 1980. pap. text ed. 13.50x (ISBN 0-673-15672-9); tchrs' manual 1.40 (ISBN 0-471-07846-8). Scott F.
Gardner, John. Becoming a Novelist. LC 82-48662. (Becoming a... Ser.). 144p. 1983. 13.41i (ISBN 0-06-014956-6, HarpT). Har-Row.
Heyrick, Benjamin A. Short Studies in Composition. 104p. 1982. Repr. of 1905 ed. lib. bdg. 30.00 (ISBN 0-89760-366-4). Telegraph Bks.
Manera, Elizabeth S. & Wright, Robert E. Annotated Writer's Guide to Professional Educational Journals. 188p. 1982. pap. 9.95 (ISBN 0-9609782-0-8). Bobets.
Marks, Percy. The Craft of Writing. 231p. 1982. Repr. of 1932 ed. lib. bdg. 30.00 (ISBN 0-89760-581-0). Telegraph Bks.
O'Gara, Elaine. Travel Writer's Markets. 58p. (Orig.). 1982. pap. 6.00 (ISBN 0-9609172-0-9). R B Shapiro.
Quirk, Leslie W. How to Write a Short Story. 77p. 1982. Repr. of 1911 ed. lib. bdg. 25.00 (ISBN 0-89987-675-7). Darby Bks.
Skurnick, Blanch J. The Heath Basic Writer. 448p. 1982. pap. text ed. 11.95 (ISBN 0-669-05172-1). Heath.
Tattan, L. A. Publish Yourself without Killing Yourself. 191p. (Orig.). 1981. pap. 9.95 (ISBN 0-937362-01-8). InPrint.
Young, Jordon R. How to Become a Successful Freelance Writer: A Practical Guide to Getting Published. 3rd ed. LC 81-90476. 160p. 1983. pap. 7.95 (ISBN 0-940410-05-2). Moonstone.

AUTHORSHIP–HANDBOOKS, MANUALS, ETC.

see also Printing–Style Manuals; Technical Writing

Barnwell. Writing for a Reason. 1983. pap. text ed. 12.95 (ISBN 0-686-84569-2, RM86); instr's manual avail. (RM87). HM.
Barnwell, William. Writing for a Reason. LC 82-83174. 432p. 1983. pap. text ed. 12.95 (ISBN 0-395-32597-8); write for info. instr's. manual (ISBN 0-395-32598-6). HM.
Bell, Arthur & Klammer, Thomas. The Practicing Writer. LC 82-83411. 224p. 1983. pap. text ed. 12.95 (ISBN 0-395-32564-1); write for info. instr's. manual (ISBN 0-395-32565-X). HM.
Clark, Bernadine, ed. The Writer's Resource Guide. 2nd ed. 504p. 1983. 16.95 (ISBN 0-89879-102-2). Writers Digest.
Emerson, Connie. How to Make Money Writing Fillers. 252p. 1983. 12.95 (ISBN 0-89879-104-9). Writers Digest.
Fawcett, Susan & Sandberg, Alvin. Grassroots: The Writer's Handbook. 2d ed. 288p. 1982. pap. text ed. 11.95 (ISBN 0-395-32572-2); instr's. annotated ed. 12.95 (ISBN 0-395-32573-0). HM.
Fredette, Jean. Fiction Writer's Market 1983-84. 2nd ed. 672p. 1983. 17.95 (ISBN 0-89879-108-1). Writers Digest.
Heffernan, James A. W. & Lincoln, John R. Writing: A College Workbook. 1982. pap. text ed. 6.95x (ISBN 0-393-95177-4); instr's. manual avail.; diagnostic tests avail. Norton.
Knott, Leonard L. Writing for the Joy. 204p. 1983. 11.95 (ISBN 0-89879-106-5). Writers Digest.
Morrison, Leger & Birt, Robert F. Illustrated Guide for Term Papers, Reports, Theses, & Dissertations: With Index & Rules for Punctuation & for Expression of Numbers. (Illus.). ix, 102p. 1971. pap. text ed. 3.85 (ISBN 0-686-38130-0). Morrison Pub Co.
Morrison, Leger R. & Birt, Robert F. End-of-Line Division Manual. xx, 342p. (Orig.). pap. text ed. 7.95 (ISBN 0-686-38128-9). Morrison Pub Co.
--Guide to Confused Words. xxvi, 272p. (Orig.). 1972. pap. 6.55 (ISBN 0-686-38127-0). Morrison Pub Co.
Peterson, Franklynn & Kesselman-Turkel, Judi. The Magazine Writer's Handbook. 263p. 1983. 17.95 (ISBN 0-13-543751-2); pap. 8.95 (ISBN 0-13-543744-X). P-H.
Polking, Kirk, ed. The Writer's Encyclopedia. 480p. 1983. 19.95 (ISBN 0-89879-103-0). Writers Digest.
Vizetelly, Frank H. The Preparation of Manuscripts for the Printer. 148p. 1982. Repr. of 1905 ed. lib. bdg. 25.00 (ISBN 0-8495-5531-0). Arden Lib.
Wiener, Harvey S. & Bazerman, Charles. Writing Skills Handbook. LC 82-83202. 144p. 1982. pap. text ed. 5.95 (ISBN 0-395-32588-9). HM.

AUTHORSHIP–STUDY AND TEACHING

Myers, Miles & Gray, James, eds. Theory & Practice in the Teaching of Composition: Processing, Distancing, & Modeling. 1983. pap. write for info. (ISBN 0-8141-5399-2). NCTE.
Workman, Brooke. Writing Seminars in the Content Area: In Search of Hemingway, Salinger, & Steinbeck. 1983. pap. 13.75 (ISBN 0-8141-5886-2). NCTE.

AUTISM

see also Fantasy

Mesibov, Gary & Schopler, Eric, eds. Autism in Adolescents & Adults. (Current Issues in Autism Ser.). 435p. 1983. 35.00x (ISBN 0-306-41057-5, Plenum Pr). Plenum Pub.
Tinbergen, Niko & Tinbergen, Elisabeth A. Autistic Children: New Hope for Cure. (Illus.). 380p. 1983. text ed. 39.50x (ISBN 0-04-157010-3). Allen Unwin.

AUTO MECHANICS

see Automobile Mechanics

AUTOBIOGRAPHIES

see also Diaries;

also classes of persons, e.g. Actors; also subdivision Biography under particular subjects, countries, etc., e.g. United States–Biography

Chiang, Monlin. Tides From the West: A Chinese Autobiography. 1947. text ed. 23.50x (ISBN 0-686-83825-4). Elliots Bks.

Dietze, Charles E. The Henderson Crusade. (Illus.). 164p. (Orig.). 1983. pap. 4.95 (ISBN 0-9610198-0-8). G G L Pub Co.

AUTOBIOGRAPHY

see also Biography (As a Literary Form)

Fleishman, Avrom. Figures of Autobiography: The Language of Self-Writing in Victorian & Modern England. LC 81-23163. 512p. 1983. text ed. 29.50x (ISBN 0-520-04666-8). U of Cal Pr.

Phillion, Numa. Numa: A Life Reading. 224p. 1983. 12.50 (ISBN 0-89962-303-4). Todd & Honeywell.

AUTOBIOGRAPHY–BIBLIOGRAPHY

Briscoe, Mary L., et al. A Bibliography of American Autobiography, 1945-1980. LC 82-70547. 384p. 1982. text ed. 30.00 (ISBN 0-299-09090-6). U of Wis Pr.

AUTOBIOGRAPHY–HISTORY

Dietze, Charles E. The Henderson Crusade. (Illus.). 164p. (Orig.). 1983. pap. 4.95 (ISBN 0-9610198-0-8). G G L Pub Co.

AUTOBIOGRAPHY–TECHNIQUE

see Autobiography

AUTOCODES

see Programming Languages (Electronic Computers)

AUTOGENIC TRAINING

Donald, Kathleen & Holloway, Elizabeth. A Guide to Group Self Hypnosis for Participants & Leaders. 300p. (Orig.). 1983. pap. text ed. write for info. (ISBN 0-915202-37-9). Accel Devel.

Duke, Robert E. How to Lose Weight & Stop Smoking Through Self-Hypnosis (includes audio cassette) 140p. 1983. text ed. 18.95x (ISBN 0-8290-1276-1). Irvington.

Petrie, Sidney & Stone, Robert B. Helping Yourself with Autogenics. LC 82-14488. 205p. 1983. 14.95 (ISBN 0-13-387407-9, Parker); pap. 4.95 (ISBN 0-13-387399-4). P-H.

AUTOGENOUS WELDING

see Welding

AUTOGIROS

Crowe, Alf. A Guide to Autogyros. 2nd ed. (Illus.). 64p. 1982. pap. 8.00 (ISBN 0-933078-08-0). M Arman.

AUTOGRAPH LETTERS

see Autographs

AUTOGRAPHS

see also Manuscripts

Casoni, Jennifer. Sincerely, Lyndon: The Handwriting of Lyndon Baines Johnson. 100p. (Orig.). 1983. pap. 14.95 (ISBN 0-9608816-1-1). Univ Autograph.

AUTOGRAPHS–CATALOGS

see Autographs–Collections

AUTOGRAPHS–COLLECTIONS

Reese, Michael, II. Autographs of the Confederacy. LC 81-68377. 250p. 47.95 (ISBN 0-940746-00-X); deluxe ed. 89.95 (ISBN 0-686-42866-8). Cohasco.

AUTOIMMUNE DISEASES

Pinchera, A. & Vanhaelst, L., eds. Autoimmunity & Endocrine Diseases. (Jounal: Hormone Research: Vol. 16, No. 5). (Illus.). 84p. 1982. pap. 24.75 (ISBN 3-8055-3658-5). S Karger.

AUTOMATA

see also Conscious Automata; Machine Theory

Industrial Robots: A Delphi Forecast of Markets & Technology. LC 82-50754. 232p. 1982. 65.00 (ISBN 0-87263-087-0). SME.

Maurice, Klaus & Mayr, Otto. The Clockwork Universe: German Clocks & Automata 1550-1650. LC 80-16780. (Illus.). 331p. 1980. 19.95 (ISBN 0-87474-628-0). Smithsonian.

Miller, Richard K. Robots in Industry: General Applications. (Illus.). 203p. pap. 65.00 (ISBN 0-89671-043-2). Southeast Acoustics.

Nielsen, M. & Schmidt, E. M., eds. Automata, Languages, & Programming: Aarhus, Denmark 1982. (Lecture Notes in Computer Science: Vol. 140). 614p. 1982. pap. 27.60 (ISBN 0-387-11576-5). Springer-Verlag.

Robotics Today Nineteen Eighty Two. LC 79-643432. 388p. 1982. 42.00 (ISBN 0-87263-084-6). SME.

AUTOMATA–JUVENILE LITERATURE

Ryder, Joanne. C-3PO's Book About Robots. LC 82-20424. (Illus.). 32p. (gr. 3-8). 1983. pap. 1.25 saddle-stitched (ISBN 0-394-85690-2). Random.

AUTOMATIC COMPUTERS

see Computers

AUTOMATIC CONTROL

see also Automation; Carrier Control Systems; Cybernetics; Electric Controllers; Error-Correcting Codes (Information Theory); Feedback Control Systems; Pneumatic Control; Process Control

Fleming, W. H. & Gorostiza, L. G., eds. Advances in Filtering & Optimal Stochastic Control: Proceedings; Cocoyoc, Mexico 1982. (Lecture Notes in Control & Information Science: Vol. 42). 392p. 1983. pap. 17.50 (ISBN 0-387-11936-1). Springer-Verlag.

Frederick, Dean K. & Carlson, A. Bruce. Linear Systems in Communication & Control. LC 71-155118. 575p. 1971. 36.95x (ISBN 0-471-27721-5). Wiley.

Gupta, Someshwar C. & Hasdorff, Lawrence. Fundamentals of Automatic Control. LC 82-20338. 602p. 1983. Repr. of 1970 ed. lib. bdg. write for info. (ISBN 0-89874-578-0). Krieger.

International Conference, 1st, Stratford-upon-Avon, UK June 2-4, 1981. Automated Guided Vehicle Systems: Proceedings. 231p. 1981. pap. text ed. 88.00x (ISBN 0-903608-18-9). Scholium Intl.

International Conference, 1st Stratford-upon-Avon, UK April 1-3, 1981. Robot Vision & Sensory Controls: Proceedings. 348p. 1981. pap. text ed. 90.00x (ISBN 0-903608-15-4). Scholium Intl.

Moroney, Paul. Issues in the Implementation of Digital Feedback Compensators. (Signal Processing, Optimization, & Control Ser.). (Illus.). 224p. 1983. 30.00x (ISBN 0-262-13185-4). MIT Pr.

Morris, N. M. Control Engineering. 3rd ed. 256p. 1983. write for info. (ISBN 0-07-084666-9). McGraw.

Palm, William J. Modeling, Analysis & Control of Dynamic Systems. 800p. 1983. text ed. 36.95 (ISBN 0-471-05800-9); solutions manual avail. (ISBN 0-471-89887-2). Wiley.

Schmitt, N. M. & Farwell, R. F. Understanding Electronic Control of Automation Systems. LC 81-85603. (Understanding Ser.). (Illus.). 280p. 1983. pap. 6.95 (ISBN 0-89512-052-6). Tex Instr Inc.

Tzafestas, S. G., ed. Distributed Parameter Control Systems: Theory & Application. (International Series on Systems & Control: Vol. 6). 525p. 1982. 60.00 (ISBN 0-08-027624-5). Pergamon.

AUTOMATIC COUNTING DEVICES

see Digital Counters

AUTOMATIC DATA PROCESSING

see Electronic Data Processing

AUTOMATIC DATA PROCESSORS

see Computers

AUTOMATIC DATA STORAGE

see Information Storage and Retrieval Systems

AUTOMATIC DIGITAL COMPUTERS

see Electronic Digital Computers

AUTOMATIC DRAFTING

see Computer Graphics

AUTOMATIC FACTORIES

see Automation

AUTOMATIC MACHINE-TOOLS

see Machine-Tools

AUTOMATIC PRODUCTION

see Automation

AUTOMATIC PROGRAMMING LANGUAGES

see Programming Languages (Electronic Computers)

AUTOMATIC SPEECH RECOGNITION

Flanagan, J. L. & Rabiner, L. R., eds. Speech Synthesis. LC 73-9728. (Benchmark Papers in Acoustics: Vol. 3). 511p. 1973. text ed. 55.00 (ISBN 0-87933-044-9). Hutchinson Ross.

Haton, Jean-Paul, ed. Automatic Speech Analysis & Recognition. 1982. lib. bdg. 48.00 (ISBN 90-277-1443-6, Pub. by Reidel Holland). Kluwer Boston.

Wayne, Lea A. Computer Recognition of Speech. (Speech Technology Ser.). (Illus.). 450p. 1982. 79.00 (ISBN 0-686-37642-0); student ed. 54.00 (ISBN 0-686-37643-9). Speech Science.

AUTOMATION

see also Assembly-Line Methods; Automatic Control; Electronic Control; Feedback Control Systems; Man-Machine Systems; Systems Engineering

Assembly Automation: Proceedings of the 3rd International Conference, Stuttgart, Germany 25-27 May 1982. (Illus.). 626p. 1982. pap. text ed. 90.00x (ISBN 0-903608-25-1, Pub. by IFSPUBS). Scholium Intl.

Aune, A. B. & Vlietstra, J. Automation for Safety in Shipping & Offshore Petroleum Operations. 1980. 89.50 (ISBN 0-444-85498-3). Elsevier.

Autofact Four: Conference Proceedings. LC 82-61490. 688p. 1982. 60.00 (ISBN 0-87263-093-5). SME.

Control Engineering, 1982 Conference: Merging of Technology & Theory to Solve Industrial Automation Problems. 247p. (Orig.). 1982. pap. text ed. 42.00x (ISBN 0-85825-168-X, Pub. by Inst Engineering Australia). Renouf.

Csiro, R. W. & Tavast, R. R., eds. Distributed Computer Control Systems 1982: Proceedings of the 4th IFAC Workshop, DCCS-82, Tallinn, USSR, 24-26 May 1982. (IFAC Proceedings Ser.). 175p. 1983. 43.00 (ISBN 0-08-028675-5). Pergamon.

Fraade, David J., ed. Automation of Pharmaceutical Operations. 400p. 1983. 57.50 (ISBN 0-943330-02-5). Pharm Tech.

Hunt, Daniel V. Industrial Robotics Handbook. (Illus.). 300p. 1983. 32.50 (ISBN 0-8311-1148-8). Indus Pr.

Industrial Robots Industry in Japan. (Japanese Industry Studies: No. J76). 228p. 1980. 310.00 (ISBN 0-686-38962-X). Intl Res Dev.

Miller, Richard K. Robots in Industry: General Applications. (Illus.). 203p. pap. 65.00 (ISBN 0-89671-043-2). Southeast Acoustics.

Ouellette, Robert P. & Thomas, L. W. Automation Impacts on Industry. LC 82-48646. (Illus.). 200p. 1983. 27.50 (ISBN 0-250-40609-8). Ann Arbor Science.

Schmitt, N. M. & Farwell, R. F. Understanding Electronic Control of Automation Systems. LC 81-85603. (Understanding Ser.). (Illus.). 280p. 1983. pap. 6.95 (ISBN 0-89512-052-6). Tex Instr Inc.

Tuer, David F. & Bolz, Roger W. Robotics Sourcebook & Dictionary. 304p. 1983. 29.95 (ISBN 0-8311-1152-6). Indus Pr.

AUTOMATION–JUVENILE LITERATURE

Cress, Mary. Automation. (Science Ser.). 24p. (gr. 6 up). 1977. wkbk. 5.00 (ISBN 0-8209-0153-9, S-15). ESP.

Hellman, Hal. Computer Basics. (Illus.). 48p. (gr. 3-7). 1983. pap. 8.95 (ISBN 0-13-164574-9). P-H.

AUTOMOBILE ACCIDENTS

see Traffic Accidents

AUTOMOBILE BRAKES

see Automobiles–Brakes

AUTOMOBILE BODIES

see Automobiles–Bodies

AUTOMOBILE BUYING

see Automobile Purchasing

AUTOMOBILE DRIVERS

see also Automobile Drivers' Tests; Automobile Driving

Colverd, Edward C. & Less, Menahem. Teaching Driver Education To The Physically Disabled: A Sample Course. 40p. 1978. 4.25 (ISBN 0-686-38805-4). Human Res Ctr.

Less, Menaham & Colverd, Edward C. Hand Controls & Assistive Devices For The Physically Disabled Driver. (Illus.). 60p. 1977. 5.00 (ISBN 0-686-38804-6). Human Res Ctr.

Less, Menahem & Colverd, Edward C. Evaluating Driving Potential of Persons With Physical Disabilities. LC 78-62052. (Illus.). 36p. 1978. 4.25 (ISBN 0-686-38803-8). Human Res Ctr.

AUTOMOBILE DRIVERS' LICENSES

see Automobile Drivers' Tests

AUTOMOBILE DRIVERS' TESTS

Drivers License Guide Co. Drivers License Guide, 1983. (Illus.). 96p. 1983. pap. 12.95 (ISBN 0-938964-04-6). Drivers License.

Drivers License Guide Co. Staff. U. S. Identification Manual. (Illus.). 700p. 1983. text ed. 100.00 (ISBN 0-686-38068-1). Drivers License.

AUTOMOBILE DRIVING

Royal Automobile Club, ed. RAC Continental Motoring Guide. (Illus.). 207p. (Orig.). 1982. pap. 7.50x (ISBN 0-86211-031-9). Intl Pubns Serv.

AUTOMOBILE DRIVING–SAFETY MEASURES

see Traffic Safety

AUTOMOBILE ENGINEERING

Coster, Jean. Dictionary for Automotive Engineering. 298p. 1983. 38.00 (ISBN 3-598-10430-8, Pub. by K G Saur). Shoe String.

AUTOMOBILE EXHAUST GAS

see Automobiles–Motors–Exhaust Gas

AUTOMOBILE FUEL SYSTEMS

see Automobiles–Fuel Systems

AUTOMOBILE INDUSTRY AND TRADE

see also Automobiles–Prices; Used Car Trade

American Welding Society. Recommended Practices for Automotive Welding Design: D8.4. 1961. 8.00 (ISBN 0-686-43362-9). Am Welding.

How to Buy & Sell a Used Car in Europe. 3.50 (ISBN 0-686-83755-X). Yara Pr.

Hunker, Jeffrey A., ed. Structural Change in the U. S. Automobile Industry. LC 82-48529. 1983. write for info. (ISBN 0-669-06267-7). Lexington Bks.

AUTOMOBILE INSURANCE

see Insurance, Automobile

AUTOMOBILE MAINTENANCE

see Automobiles–Maintenance and Repair

AUTOMOBILE MECHANICS

Martin, Philip R. Auto Mechanics for the Complete Dummy. 2nd ed. LC 82-62322. (Illus.). 192p. 1983. pap. 4.95 (ISBN 0-930968-02-6). Motormatics.

AUTOMOBILE OPERATION

see Automobile Driving

AUTOMOBILE OWNERSHIP

see also Automobile Purchasing

Mueller-Triol, Ingrid & Hunt-Triol, Gene. How to Import-Covert-Legalize Your Investment Automobile. 47p. 1982. write for info. HIT Pubns.

AUTOMOBILE PARKING

Olsson, Marie. Parking Discounts & Car Pool Formation in Seattle. 115p. (Orig.). 1980. pap. text ed. 3.50 (ISBN 0-87766-226-6). Urban Inst.

Urban Land Institute. Parking Requirements for Shopping Centers. Incl. Summary Recommendations. 23p. pap. 17.50 (ISBN 0-87420-604-9, P32); Summary Recommendations & Research Study Report. LC 81-70789. 136p. pap. 30.00 (ISBN 0-87420-605-7, P33). (Illus.). 1982. pap. Urban Land.

AUTOMOBILE-PARKING METERS

see Parking Meters

AUTOMOBILE PRICES

see Automobiles–Prices

AUTOMOBILE PURCHASING

see also Automobile Ownership

Bohr, Peter. The Money-Wise Guide to Sports Cars. LC 82-47678. (Illus.). 240p. 1982. 19.95 (ISBN 0-15-162052-0); pap. 9.95 (ISBN 0-15-661956-3, Harv). HarBraceJ.

Cars. (What's It Worth Ser.). Date not set. pap. 2.95 (ISBN 0-686-82598-5). Dell.

Edmund's New Car Prices, 1983. (Illus.). 1983. pap. 2.50 (ISBN 0-440-02238-X). Dell.

AUTOMOBILE RACING

see also Model Car Racing

Jenkinson, Dennis. The Automobile Year Book of Sports Car Racing 1953-1972. (Illus.). 1983. 39.50 (ISBN 0-686-43390-4, Pub. by Edita Switerland). Norton.

Quattlebaum, Julian K. The Great Savannah Races. (Brown Thrasher Ser.). (Illus.). 144p. 1983. 19.95 (ISBN 0-8203-0665-7). U of Ga Pr.

AUTOMOBILE REPAIR

see Automobiles–Maintenance and Repair

AUTOMOBILE TOURING–ROAD GUIDES

see also Atlases

Rand McNally Motor Carriers' Road Atlas. 1983. pap. 12.95 (ISBN 0-528-89440-4). Rand.

Rand McNally Road Atlas & Travel Planner, 1983. 1983. 35.00 (ISBN 0-528-89460-9). Rand.

Rand McNally Road Atlas & Vacation Guide, 1983. 1983. pap. 12.95 (ISBN 0-528-89450-1). Rand.

Staff, Hammond, ed. Glove Compartment Road Atlas 1983. Rev. ed. (Illus.). 48p. 1983. pap. 1.95 (ISBN 0-8437-2634-2). Hammond Inc.

AUTOMOBILE TRUCKS

see Motor-Trucks

AUTOMOBILE WORKERS

see Automobile Mechanics

AUTOMOBILES

see also Motor Buses; Motorcycles; Motor-Trucks also names of automobiles under Automobiles–Types; Automobiles, Foreign–Types, e.g. Automobiles–Types–Ford; Automobiles, Foreign–Types–Volkswagen; also headings beginning with the word automobile

Chek-Chart. Automotive Preview, 1983. 16p. 1982. pap. text ed. 2.00x (ISBN 0-88098-019-2). H M Gousha.

Gillis, Jack. The Car Book: 1983 Models. (Illus.). 104p. 1983. pap. 6.95 (ISBN 0-525-48049-8, 0675-200). Dutton.

Harding, Anthony. Guinness Book of Car Facts & Feats. (Illus.). 288p. 1983. 19.95 (ISBN 0-85112-207-8, Pub. by Guinness Superlatives England). Sterling.

Hollander Publishing Co., Inc. Domestic Car Inventory Index, 1972-1982. 910p. 1982. 189.00 (ISBN 0-943032-25-3). Hollander Co.

Hudson-Evans, Richard. Custom Cars & Vans. (Illus.). 64p. 1983. pap. 4.95 (Pub. by Batsford England). David & Charles.

Shilton, Neale. A Million Miles Ago. (Illus.). 140p. 1982. 19.95 (ISBN 0-85429-313-2). Haynes Pubns.

AUTOMOBILES–ACCIDENTS

see Traffic Accidents

AUTOMOBILES–AIR-CONDITIONING

Dwiggins, Boyce. Automotive Air Conditioning. 5th ed. 416p. 1983. pap. text ed. 16.80 (ISBN 0-8273-1940-1); write for info. instr's guide (ISBN 0-8273-1942-8). Delmar.

AUTOMOBILES–BODIES

Fournier, Ron. Metal Fabricator's Handbook: Race & Custom Car. 176p. 1982. pap. 9.95 (ISBN 0-89586-171-2). H P Bks.

Rhone, L. C. & Yates, H. David. Total Auto Body Repair. 2nd ed. 464p. 1982. text ed. 23.95t (ISBN 0-672-97967-5); instr's. guide 3.33 (ISBN 0-672-97969-1); wkbk. 9.95t (ISBN 0-672-97968-3). Bobbs.

Toboldt, Bill. Auto Body Repairing & Repainting. rev. ed. LC 82-14320. (Illus.). 256p. 1982. text ed. 12.00 (ISBN 0-87006-423-1). Goodheart.

AUTOMOBILES–BRAKES

Crouse, W. H. & Anglin, D. L. Automotive Brakes, Suspension & Steering. 6th ed. 1983. 19.95 (ISBN 0-07-014828-7). McGraw.

AUTOMOBILES–COLLECTORS AND COLLECTING

see also Automobiles–History

The Official 1983 Price Guide to Collector Cars. 4th ed. LC 81-81805. 544p. 1983. 9.95 (ISBN 0-87637-357-0). Hse of Collectibles.

Olson, John R. Secrets of Buying & Selling Collector Cars. LC 82-61130. (Illus.). 93p. 1982. pap. 6.95 (ISBN 0-933424-40-X, 1849A). Motorbooks Intl.

Viemeister, Peter. Microcars. (Illus.). 136p. (Orig.). (gr. 4 up). 1982. pap. 8.95 (ISBN 0-9608598-0-2). Hamiltons.

AUTOMOBILES–DIESEL MOTORS

see Automobiles–Motors

AUTOMOBILES–DRIVING

see Automobile Driving

AUTOMOBILES–ENGINES

see Automobiles–Motors

AUTOMOBILES–EXHAUST GAS

see Automobiles–Motors–Exhaust Gas

AUTOMOBILES–FUEL SYSTEMS

Automobile Fuel Consumption in Actual Traffic Conditions. 118p. 1982. pap. 8.50 (ISBN 92-64-12304-0). OECD.

AUTOMOBILES–GEARING

see Automobiles–Steering Gear

AUTOMOBILES–HANDBOOKS, MANUALS, ETC.

see also subdivision–Types–specific type, e.g. Automobiles–Types–Ford, etc.

Car Ownership & Use. (Road Research Ser.). 107p. (Orig.). 1982. pap. 7.50x (ISBN 92-64-12348-2). OECD.

Consumer Guide: 1983 Cars. 1983. pap. 3.95 (ISBN 0-451-12089-2, AE2089, Sig). NAL.

AUTOMOBILES–HISTORY

see also Automobiles–Collectors and Collecting

Barrett, Paul. The Automobile & Urban Transit: The Formation of Public Policy in Chicago. 1983. write for info. (ISBN 0-87722-294-0). Temple U Pr.

Clarke, R. M. American Motors Muscle Cars 1966-1970. (Illus.). 100p. 1982. pap. 11.95 (ISBN 0-907073-58-1, Pub. by Brooklands Bks England). Motorbooks Intl.

De Angelis, George & Francis, Edward P. The Ford Model "A"-As Henry Built It. 3rd ed. (Illus.). 234p. 1983. 16.95 (ISBN 0-911383-02-6). Motor Cities.

Gunnel, John, ed. The Standard Catalog of American Cars, 1946-1975. (Illus.). 704p. 1982. pap. 19.95 (ISBN 0-87341-027-0). Krause Pubns.

OECD Staff. The Future of the Use of the Car. (ECMT Round Tables Ser.). 232p. (Orig.). 1982. pap. 15.50x (ISBN 92-821-1075-3). OECD.

AUTOMOBILES–INSURANCE

see Insurance, Automobile

AUTOMOBILES–JUVENILE LITERATURE

Cole, Joanna. Cars & How They Go. LC 82-45575. (Illus.). 32p. (gr. 2-6). 1983. 9.57i (ISBN 0-690-04261-2, TYC-J); PLB 9.89g (ISBN 0-690-04262-0). Har-Row.

Knudson, Richard L. Racing Yesterday's Cars. (Superwheels & Thrill Sports Bks.). (Illus.). 48p. (gr. 4up). 1983. PLB 7.95g (ISBN 0-8225-0512-6). Lerner Pubns.

--Restoring Yesterday's Cars. LC 82-24966. (Superwheels & Thrill Sports Bks.). (Illus.). 48p. (gr. 4up). 1983. PLB 7.95g (ISBN 0-8225-0440-5). Lerner Pubns.

Lord, Harvey G. Car Care for Kids...& Former Kids. LC 82-13778. (Illus.). 160p. (gr. 4 up). 1983. 11.95 (ISBN 0-689-30975-9); pap. 7.95 (ISBN 0-689-70648-0). Atheneum.

Massucci, Edoardo. Cars for Kids. LC 82-42764. (Illus.). 128p. (gr. 3up). 1983. 27.50 (ISBN 0-8478-0469-0). Rizzoli Intl.

Scarry, Richard. Richard Scarry's Lowly Worm Car & Truck Book. LC 82-61012. (Illus.). 16p. (ps-2). 1983. pap. 2.95 (ISBN 0-394-85760-7). Random.

Sheffer, H. R. Great Cars. Schroeder, Howard, ed. (Movin' On Ser.). (Illus.). 48p. (Orig.). (gr. 5-6). 1983. lib. bdg. 7.95 (ISBN 0-89686-192-9). Crestwood Hse.

AUTOMOBILES–LUBRICATION

Chek-Chart. Lubrications Recommendations Wall Chart, 1983. 12p. (gr. 12). 1983. pap. 4.10 (ISBN 0-88098-018-4). H M Gousha.

--Master Lubrication Handbook, 1983. 792p. 1983. 80.60x (ISBN 0-88098-020-6); Supplement 64.25 (ISBN 0-88098-021-4). H M Gousha.

AUTOMOBILES–MAINTENANCE AND REPAIR

Ballweber, Duane. Practical Applications in Basic Autobody Repair. (Illus.). 288p. 1983. text ed. 15.95 (ISBN 0-13-689216-7). P-H.

Chek-Chart. Car & Light Truck Diesel Engine Service Manual. (Automotive Service Ser.). 128p. (gr. 12). 1983. pap. text ed. 9.95x (ISBN 0-88098-016-8); 3.50x (ISBN 0-686-84028-3). H M Gousha.

--Car Care Guide, 1983. 320p. (gr. 12). 1983. pap. text ed. 39.75 (ISBN 0-88098-022-2, 0162-3443). H M Gousha.

--Complete Automotive Service Library. (Automotive Service Ser.). (Illus.). 665p. (gr. 12). 1983. pap. text ed. 50.85 (ISBN 0-88098-044-3). H M Gousha.

--Nineteen-Eighty Three Lubrication Recommendations & Capacities Booklet. 36p. (gr. 12). 1983. pap. text ed. 4.75 (ISBN 0-88098-017-6). H M Gousha.

--Truck Lubrication Guide, 1983. 80p. 1983. pap. text ed. 31.80x (ISBN 0-88098-024-9). H M Gousha.

Chek-Chart, ed. Service Bulletin, 1983. (Automotive Service Ser.). (Illus.). 96p. 1983. pap. 12.80x (ISBN 0-88098-048-6, 0731-471X). H M Gousha.

Chilton's Auto Repair Manual 1983. LC 76-648878. (Illus.). 1296p. 1982. 18.95 (ISBN 0-8019-7200-0). Chilton.

Crouse, W. H. & Anglin, D. L. Automotive Tune-Up. 1983. text ed. 17.95 (ISBN 0-07-014836-8); wkbk. 8.95 (ISBN 0-07-014837-6). McGraw.

Eighty Five Tests Eighty Five. LC 82-70658. (Illus.). 288p. 1982. pap. 7.95. Chilton.

Ellinger, Herb. Automechanics. 3rd ed. (Illus.). 592p. 1983. text ed. 19.95 (ISBN 0-13-054767-0); wkbk. 8.95 (ISBN 0-13-054775-1). P-H.

Mintzer, Richard I. The Auto Owner's Diary. 112p. (Orig.). 1982. pap. 4.95 (ISBN 0-911275-00-2). Recro Products.

Petersen Publishing Co. How to Tune Your Car. 7th ed. (Petersen's Basic Auto Repair Ser.). (Illus.). 1000p. 1983. pap. 7.95 (ISBN 0-8227-5049-X). Petersen Pub.

Porter, Lindsay. MGB-Guide to Purchase & D.I.Y Restoration. (Illus.). 200p. 1982. write for info. (ISBN 0-85429-303-5). Haynes Pubns.

Rhone, L. C. & Yates, H. David. Total Auto Body Repair. 2nd ed. 464p. 1982. text ed. 23.95t (ISBN 0-672-97967-5); instr's. guide 3.33 (ISBN 0-672-97969-1); wkbk. 9.95t (ISBN 0-672-97968-3). Bobbs.

Robert Bentley, Inc. Toyota Celica Service Manual: 1978-1983. (Illus.). 576p. (Orig.). 1983. pap. 21.95 (ISBN 0-8376-0255-6). Bentley.

Royal Automobile Club (Great Britain), ed. RAC Continental Handbook. 42nd ed. (Illus.). 624p. 1981. 15.00x (ISBN 0-86211-022-X). Intl Pubns Serv.

--RAC Guide & Handbook 1982. 78th ed. (Illus.). 623p. 1982. 15.00x (ISBN 0-86211-032-7). Intl Pubns Serv.

Rudman, Jack. Assistant Automotive Shop Supervisor. (Career Examination Ser.: C-529). (Cloth bdg. avail. on request). pap. 12.00 (ISBN 0-8373-0529-2). Natl Learning.

Sikorsky, R. Drive it Forever: Your Key to Long Automobile Life. 144p. 1983. 12.95 (ISBN 0-07-057294-1, GB). McGraw.

Walkov, Samuel. Understanding your Car. 1979. pap. 9.95 (ISBN 0-672-21623-X). Sams.

AUTOMOBILES–MAINTENANCE AND REPAIR–RATES

Conroy, Larry & O'Connell, Paul. The Consumer Cost Guide to Car Repair. (Illus.). 144p. 1983. text ed. 12.95 (ISBN 0-13-168872-3); pap. 5.95 (ISBN 0-13-168864-2). P-H.

Stansbie, Ken. How to Save Fifty Percent or More on Gas & Car Repairs. 96p. 1983. pap. 4.95 (ISBN 0-86666-035-6). GWP.

AUTOMOBILES–MODELS

see also Model Car Racing

The Automobile Year Book of Models, No.2. (Illus.). 1983. 39.50 (ISBN 2-88001-139-6, Pub. by Edita Switzerland). Norton.

Viemeister, Peter. Microcars. (Illus.). 136p. (Orig.). (gr. 4 up). 1982. pap. 8.95 (ISBN 0-9608598-0-2). Hamiltons.

AUTOMOBILES–MOTORS

Nunnery. Engine Technology. 2nd ed. 1983. text ed. 19.95 (ISBN 0-408-00516-5). Butterworth.

AUTOMOBILES–MOTORS–EXHAUST GAS

see also Motor Vehicles–Pollution Control Devices

White, Lawrence J. Regulation of Air Pollution Emissions from Motor Vehicles. 1982. 13.95 (ISBN 0-8447-3492-6); pap. 4.95 (ISBN 0-8447-3487-X). Am Enterprise.

AUTOMOBILES–OWNERSHIP

see Automobile Ownership

AUTOMOBILES–PARKING

see Automobile Parking

AUTOMOBILES–PRICES

Edmund's Used Car Prices. (Orig.). 1983. pap. 2.50 (ISBN 0-440-02392-0). Dell.

AUTOMOBILES–PURCHASING

see Automobile Purchasing

AUTOMOBILES–REPAIRING

see Automobiles–Maintenance and Repair

AUTOMOBILES–ROAD GUIDES

see Automobile Touring–Road Guides

AUTOMOBILES–SERVICING

see Automobiles–Maintenance and Repair

AUTOMOBILES–SPRINGS AND SUSPENSION

Crouse, W. H. & Anglin, D. L. Automotive Brakes, Suspension & Steering. 6th ed. 1983. 19.95 (ISBN 0-07-014828-7). McGraw.

AUTOMOBILES–STEERING GEAR

Crouse, W. H. & Anglin, D. L. Automotive Brakes, Suspension & Steering. 6th ed. 1983. 19.95 (ISBN 0-07-014828-7). McGraw.

AUTOMOBILES–TYPES–BUICK

Warson, Sydnie A., ed. GMC J Cars: Buick Skylark, Cadillac Cimarron, Chevrolet Cavalier, Oldsmobile Firenza, Pontiac J-2000. (Orig.). pap. 11.95 (ISBN 0-89287-362-0). Clymer Pubns.

AUTOMOBILES–TYPES–CADILLAC

Warson, Sydnie A., ed. GMC J Cars: Buick Skylark, Cadillac Cimarron, Chevrolet Cavalier, Oldsmobile Firenza, Pontiac J-2000. (Orig.). pap. 11.95 (ISBN 0-89287-362-0). Clymer Pubns.

AUTOMOBILES–TYPES–CAMARO

Clarke, R. M. Camaro Muscle Cars 1966-1972. (Illus.). 100p. 1982. pap. 11.95 (ISBN 0-907073-65-4, Pub. by Brooklands Bks England). Motorbooks Intl.

AUTOMOBILES–TYPES–CHEVROLET

see also Automobiles–Types–Corvette

Clarke, R. M. Chevrolet Muscle Cars 1966-1971. (Illus.). 100p. 1982. pap. 11.95 (ISBN 0-907073-61-1, Pub. by Brooklands Bks England). Motorbooks Intl.

Warson, Sydnie A., ed. GMC J Cars: Buick Skylark, Cadillac Cimarron, Chevrolet Cavalier, Oldsmobile Firenza, Pontiac J-2000. (Orig.). pap. 11.95 (ISBN 0-89287-362-0). Clymer Pubns.

AUTOMOBILES–TYPES–COBRA

Christy, John & Friedman, David. Racing Cobras: A Definitive Illustrated History. (Illus.). 208p. 1982. 24.95 (ISBN 0-85045-457-3, Pub. by Osprey England). Motorbooks Intl.

AUTOMOBILES–TYPES–CORVETTE

Given, H. Kyle, III. Corvette! Thirty Years of Great Advertising. Clark, William D., ed. LC 82-73577. (Collector Car Literature Ser.). (Illus.). 176p. 1983. 21.95 (ISBN 0-915038-38-2). Auto Quarterly.

AUTOMOBILES–TYPES–DODGE

Dodge Cost Information Systems. Dodge Construction Systems Costs, 1983. 300p. 1982. 49.95 (ISBN 0-07-017406-7, P&RB). McGraw.

--Dodge Guide to Public Works & Heavy Construction, 1983. 300p. 1982. 49.95 (ISBN 0-07-017408-3, P&RB). McGraw.

--Dodge Manual for Building, Construction, Pricing & Scheduling. 300p. 1982. 39.50 (ISBN 0-07-017407-5, P&RB). McGraw.

Warson, Sydnie A., ed. Dodge Aries & Plymouth Reliant: 1981-1982. (Orig.). pap. 11.95 (ISBN 0-89287-360-4). Clymer Pubns.

AUTOMOBILES–TYPES–FORD

see also Automobiles–Types–Cobra; Automobiles–Types–Pinto

Miller, Ray. Falcon! The New Size Ford. LC 82-90194. (Ford Road Ser.: Vol. 7). (Illus.). 320p. 1982. 29.95 (ISBN 0-913056-11-1). Evergreen Pr.

Sorenson, Lorin. The Classy Ford V8. (Illus.). 240p. 1982. 35.00 (ISBN 0-686-82139-4, F705). Motorbooks Intl.

AUTOMOBILES–TYPES–JEEP

Warson, Sydnie A., ed. AMC Jeep CJ-5, CJ-6, CJ-7: 1968-1981. (Orig.). pap. 11.95 (ISBN 0-89287-364-7). Clymer Pubns.

AUTOMOBILES–TYPES–MERCURY

Jorgenson, Eric, ed. Ford Pinto & Mercury Bobcat: 1971-1980. pap. 11.95 (ISBN 0-89287-211-X). Clymer Pubns.

AUTOMOBILES–TYPES–OLDSMOBILE

Warson, Sydnie A., ed. GMC J Cars: Buick Skylark, Cadillac Cimarron, Chevrolet Cavalier, Oldsmobile Firenza, Pontiac J-2000. (Orig.). pap. 11.95 (ISBN 0-89287-362-0). Clymer Pubns.

AUTOMOBILES–TYPES–PINTO

Jorgenson, Eric, ed. Ford Pinto & Mercury Bobcat: 1971-1980. pap. 11.95 (ISBN 0-89287-211-X). Clymer Pubns.

AUTOMOBILES–TYPES–PLYMOUTH

Warson, Sydnie A., ed. Dodge Aries & Plymouth Reliant: 1981-1982. (Orig.). pap. 11.95 (ISBN 0-89287-360-4). Clymer Pubns.

AUTOMOBILES–TYPES–PONTIAC

Warson, Sydnie A., ed. GMC J Cars: Buick Skylark, Cadillac Cimarron, Chevrolet Cavalier, Oldsmobile Firenza, Pontiac J-2000. (Orig.). pap. 11.95 (ISBN 0-89287-362-0). Clymer Pubns.

AUTOMOBILES–YEARBOOKS

The Automobile Year, No. 30. (Illus.). 1983. 39.95 (ISBN 2-88001-141-8, Pub. by Edita Switzerland). Norton.

The Automobile Year Book of Models, No.2. (Illus.). 1983. 39.50 (ISBN 2-88001-139-6, Pub. by Edita Switzerland). Norton.

Jenkinson, Dennis. The Automobile Year Book of Sports Car Racing 1953-1972. (Illus.). 1983. 39.50 (ISBN 0-686-43390-4, Pub. by Edita Switerland). Norton.

Stark, Harry A., ed. Ward's Nineteen Eighty-Three Automotive Yearbook. 45th ed. LC 40-33639. (Illus.). 400p. 1983. 85.00 (ISBN 0-910589-00-3). Wards Comm.

AUTOMOBILES, DIESEL

see Automobiles–Motors

AUTOMOBILES, FOREIGN

Chilton's Import Car Manual 1983. LC 78-20243. (Illus.). 1488p. 1982. 19.95 (ISBN 0-8019-7240-X). Chilton.

Edmund's Foreign Car Prices 1983. (Orig.). 1983. pap. 2.50 (ISBN 0-440-02368-8). Dell.

McLellan, John. AC & Cobra. (Illus.). 176p. 1982. 29.95 (ISBN 0-901564-57-5, Pub. by Dalton England). Motorbooks Intl.

AUTOMOBILES, FOREIGN–MAINTENANCE AND REPAIR

see Automobiles–Maintenance and Repair

AUTOMOBILES, FOREIGN–TYPES–ALFA-ROMEO

Clarke, R. M. Alfa Romeo Spider 1966-1981. (Illus.). 100p. 1982. pap. 11.95 (ISBN 0-907073-56-5, Pub. by Brooklands Bks England). Motorbooks Intl.

Owen, David. Alfa Romeo Spiders. (AutoHistory Ser.). (Illus.). 136p. 1982. 14.95 (ISBN 0-85045-462-X, Pub. by Osprey England). Motorbooks Intl.

AUTOMOBILES, FOREIGN–TYPES–AUDI

Volkswagen of America, Inc. Audi Five Thousand Official Factory Service Manual, 1977-1983, including Diesel. (Illus.). 1000p. (Orig.). 1983. pap. 34.95 (ISBN 0-8376-0352-8). Bentley.

--Audi Four Thousand-Coupe Service Manual 1980 to 1982. (Illus.). 800p. (Orig.). 1982. pap. 34.95 (ISBN 0-8376-0350-1). Bentley.

AUTOMOBILES, FOREIGN–TYPES–DATSUN

Ahlstrand, Alan & Wauson, Sydnie A. Datsun 280ZX 1979-1981 Includes Turbo Shop Manual. (Illus.). 314p. 1982. pap. 11.95 (ISBN 0-89287-346-9). Clymer Pubns.

AUTOMOBILES, FOREIGN–TYPES–FERRARI

Thompson, Jonathan. Ferrari Turbo. (Illus.). 1982. 24.95 (ISBN 0-85045-465-4, Pub. by Osprey England). Motorbooks Intl.

Thompson, Jonathan, ed. Ferrari Album, No. 2. 96p. 1981. pap. 16.95 (ISBN 0-940014-02-5). Color Market.

--Ferrari Album, No. 3. (Illus.). 96p. 1982. pap. 16.95 (ISBN 0-940014-03-3). Color Market.

Wallace, Wyss. The Complete Guide to the Ferrari 308 Series. (Illus.). 96p. 1982. 14.95 (ISBN 0-901564-58-3, Pub. by Dalton England). Motorbooks Intl.

Willoughby, Geoff. Ferrari 308 & Mondial. (AutoHistory Ser.). (Illus.). 136p. 1982. 14.95 (ISBN 0-85045-454-9, Pub. by Osprey England). Motorbooks Intl.

AUTOMOBILES, FOREIGN–TYPES–FIAT

Walton, Jeremy. Fiat X1-9. (AutoHistory Ser.). (Illus.). 136p. 1982. 14.95 (ISBN 0-85045-456-5, Pub. by Osprey England). Motorbooks Intl.

AUTOMOBILES, FOREIGN–TYPES–LAMBORGHINI

Clarke, R. M. Lamborghini Countach Collection, No. 1. (Illus.). 70p. 1982. pap. 8.95 (ISBN 0-907073-64-6, Pub. by Brooklands Bks England). Motorbooks Intl.

Coltrin, Peter & Marchet, Jean-Francois. Lamborghini Miura. (Illus.). 160p. 1982. 24.95 (ISBN 0-85045-469-7, Pub. by Osprey England). Motorbooks Intl.

AUTOMOBILES, FOREIGN–TYPES–LOTUS

Armour, Graham. Super Profile: Lotus Elan. 56p. Date not set. 9.95 (ISBN 0-85429-330-2). Haynes Pubns.

Walton, Jeremy. Lotus Esprit: Mid-Engined S1, S2, S2.2, S3 & Turbo. (AutoHistory Ser.). (Illus.). 136p. 1982. 14.95 (ISBN 0-85045-460-3, Pub. by Osprey England). Motorbooks Intl.

AUTOMOBILES, FOREIGN–TYPES–M. G.

McComb, F. Wilson. MGB: MGB Roadster & GT, MGC, MGB V8. (AutoHistory Ser.). (Illus.). 136p. 1982. 14.95 (ISBN 0-85045-455-7, Pub. by Osprey England). Motorbooks Intl.

AUTOMOBILES, FOREIGN–TYPES–MASERATI

Norbye, Jan P. Maserati Bora & Merak. (AutoHistory Ser.). (Illus.). 136p. 1982. 14.95 (ISBN 0-85045-471-9, Pub. by Osprey England). Motorbooks Intl.

AUTOMOBILES, FOREIGN–TYPES–MORRIS

Newell, Ray. Super Profile: Morris Minor 21000. 56p. Date not set. 9.95 (ISBN 0-85429-331-0). Haynes Pubns.

AUTOMOBILES, FOREIGN–TYPES–OPEL

Clarke, R. M. Opel GT 1968-1973. (Illus.). 100p. 1982. pap. 11.95 (ISBN 0-907073-63-8, Pub. by Brooklands Bks England). Motorbooks Intl.

AUTOMOBILES, FOREIGN–TYPES–PORSCHE

Harvey, Chris. Super Profile: Porsche 911 Carrera. 56p. Date not set. 9.95 (ISBN 0-85429-311-6). Haynes Pubns.

AUTOMOBILES, FOREIGN–TYPES–RABBIT

Robert Bentley, Inc. Volkswagen Rabbit-Jetta Diesel Service Manual: 1977-83 Including Pickup Truck & Turbo-Diesel. 4th, rev. ed. LC 82-74510. (Illus.). 600p. (Orig.). 1983. pap. 21.95 (ISBN 0-8376-0109-6). Bentley.

--Volkswagen Rabbit-Scirocco-Jetta Service Manual: 1980-83 Gasoline Models Including Pickup Truck & Convertible. 4th, rev. ed. LC 82-74511. (Illus.). 600p. (Orig.). 1983. pap. 21.95 (ISBN 0-8376-0113-4). Bentley.

AUTOMOBILES, FOREIGN–TYPES–TOYOTA

Robert Bentley, Inc. Toyota Celica Service Manual: 1978-1983. (Illus.). 576p. (Orig.). 1983. pap. 21.95 (ISBN 0-8376-0255-6). Bentley.

--Toyota Corolla Tercel Service Manual 1980-1983. 3rd, rev. ed. (Illus.). 485p. (Orig.). 1983. pap. 21.95 (ISBN 0-8376-0348-X). Bentley.

AUTOMOBILES, FOREIGN–TYPES–VOLKSWAGEN

see also Automobiles, Foreign–Types–Rabbit

Hibbard, Jeff. Baja Bugs & Buggies. 106p. 1982. pap. 9.95 (ISBN 0-89586-186-0). H P Bks.

Marcantonio, Alfredo, intro. by. Is the Bug Dead? LC 82-19202. (Illus.). 144p. 1983. pap. 9.95 (ISBN 0-941434-24-9). Stewart Tabori & Chang.

Robert Bentley, Inc. Volkswagen Rabbit-Jetta Diesel Service Manual: 1977-83 Including Pickup Truck & Turbo-Diesel. 4th, rev. ed. LC 82-74510. (Illus.). 600p. (Orig.). 1983. pap. 21.95 (ISBN 0-8376-0109-6). Bentley.

--Volkswagen Rabbit-Scirocco-Jetta Service Manual: 1980-83 Gasoline Models Including Pickup Truck & Convertible. 4th, rev. ed. LC 82-74511. (Illus.). 600p. (Orig.). 1983. pap. 21.95 (ISBN 0-8376-0113-4). Bentley.

Volkswagen of America, Inc. Volkswagen Vanagon Factory Repair Manual 1980-1982. (Illus.). 512p. (Orig.). 1982. pap. 34.95 (ISBN 0-8376-0351-X). Bentley.

AUTOMOTIVE FUEL SYSTEMS

see Automobiles–Fuel Systems

AUTOMOTIVE TRANSPORT WORKERS

see Highway Transport Workers

AUTOMOTIVE VEHICLES

see Motor Vehicles

AUTONOMIC NERVOUS SYSTEM

see Nervous System, Autonomic

AUTOSUGGESTION

see Hypnotism; Mental Suggestion

AVESTA

see also Zoroastrianism

Szekely, Edmond B. The Zend Avesta of Zarathustra. (Illus.). 100p. 1973. pap. 4.80 (ISBN 0-89564-058-9). IBS Intl.

AVIATION

see Aeronautics

AVIATION INDUSTRY

see Air Lines; Aircraft Industry

AVIATION LAW

see Aeronautics–Laws and Regulations

AVIATION MEDICINE

see also Anoxemia; Flight–Physiological Aspects

McNeil, E. L. Airborne Care of the Ill & Injured. (Illus.). 208p. 1983. pap. 14.95 (ISBN 0-387-90754-8). Springer-Verlag.

AVIATION REGULATIONS

see Aeronautics–Laws and Regulations

AVIATORS

see Air Pilots

AVIGATION

see Navigation (Aeronautics)

AVIONICS
see Electronics in Aeronautics
AVOCADO
Doeser, Linda & Richardson, Rosamond. The Little Green Avocado Book. (Illus.). 64p. 1983. 5.95 (ISBN 0-312-48862-9). St Martin.
Koch, Frank D. Avocado Grower's Handbook. Thomson, Paul H., ed. LC 82-83667. 440p. 1983. pap. 25.00 (ISBN 0-9602066-2-0). Bonsall Pub.
AVOCATIONS
see Hobbies
AWARDS
see Arbitration and Award; Rewards (Prizes, etc.)
AXIAL FLOW COMPRESSORS
see Compressors
AXIOLOGY
see Values
AXIOMS
Barth, E. M. & Krabbe, E. C., eds. From Axiom to Dialogue: Foundations of Communication Ser. xi, 337p. 1982. 69.00x (ISBN 3-11-008489-9). De Gruyter.
AZTEC LANGUAGE
Karttunen, Frances. An Analytical Dictionary of Nahuatl. (Texas Linguistics Ser.). 385p. 1983. text ed. 35.00x (ISBN 0-292-70365-1). U of Tex Pr.
Snapp, Allen & Anderson, John. Studies in Uto-Aztecan Grammar Vol. 3: Uto-Azetican Grammatical Sketches, 4 vols. LC 82-86. (Publications in Linguistics: No. 56). 393p. 1982. pap. text ed. 14.00 Set (ISBN 0-88312-086-0, 51800); Five microfiche. 4.50. Summer Inst Ling.
Tuggy, David H. & Brockway, Earl. Studies in Uto-Aztecan Grammar Vol. 2: Modern Aztec Grammatical Sketches, 4 vols. Langacker, Ronald W., ed. LC 78-56488. (Publications in Linguistics: No. 56). 380p. 1979. pap. text ed. 13.50 Set (ISBN 0-88312-072-0); microfiche 3.75. Summer Inst Ling.
AZTECS–JUVENILE LITERATURE
Beck, Barbara L. The Aztecs. rev. ed. (First Bks.). (Illus.). 72p. (gr. 4 up). 1983. PLB 8.90 (ISBN 0-531-04522-6). Watts.
AZTECS–LEGENDS
Szekely, Edmond B. The New Fire. (Illus.). 140p. 1973. pap. 4.80 (ISBN 0-89564-028-7). IBS Intl.
AZUELA, MARIANO, 1873-1952
Martinez, Eliud. The Art of Mariano Azuela: Modernism in la Malhora, el Desquite, la Luciernaga. Miller, Yvette E., ed. 101p. 1980. pap. 5.95 (ISBN 0-935480-02-1). Lat Am Lit Rev Pr.

B

B-FIFTY-TWO BOMBER
Boyne, Walter. Boeing B-52: A Documentary History. (Illus.). 160p. 1982. 19.95 (ISBN 0-86720-550-4). Sci Bks Intl.
BABEL, TOWER OF
Oakeshott, Michael. On History & Other Essays. LC 82-22617. 224p. 1983. text ed. 25.75x (ISBN 0-389-20355-6). B&N Imports.
BABIES
see Infants
BABIES, TEST TUBE
see Fertilization in Vitro, Human
BABISM
see also Bahaism
Momen, Moojan, ed. Studies in Babi & Baha'i History, Vol. 1. (Illus.). 1983. text ed. 25.00 (ISBN 0-933770-16-2). Kalimat.
BABY ANIMALS
see Animals, Infancy of
BABY FOODS
see Infants–Nutrition
BABY SITTERS
Middleton, Susan, ed. Blueprints: Building Educational Programs for People Who Care for Children. (Illus.). 238p. pap. 19.95 (ISBN 0-934140-16-2). Toys N Things.
Mijares, Sharon G. The Babysitter's Manual. (Illus.). 60p. (gr. 6-9). 1983. spiral bdg. 4.98 (ISBN 0-911925-00-7). Grace Pubns.
BABYLONIAN INSCRIPTIONS
see Cuneiform Inscriptions
BABYSITTERS
see Baby Sitters
BACCARAT
Stuart, Lyle. Ultimate Book of Baccarat. (Illus.). 224p. 15.00 (ISBN 0-8184-0339-X). Lyle Stuart.
BACH, JOHANN SEBASTIAN, 1685-1750
Heinrich, Adel. Bach's Die Kunst Der Fuge: A Living Compendium of Fugal Procedures with a Motivic Analysis of All the Fugues. LC 82-20095. (Illus.). 370p. (Orig.). 1983. text ed. 24.75 (ISBN 0-8191-2866-X); pap. text ed. 13.75 (ISBN 0-8191-2867-8). U Pr of Amer.
BACHELORS
Cauhape, Elizabeth. Fresh Starts: Men & Women after Divorce. 227p. 1983. 16.50 (ISBN 0-465-02553-6). Basic.
Dutton, Beth & DeMeo, Victoria. The Little Black Book: A Guide to the One Hundred Most Eligible Bachelors in Washington D.C. 200p. 1983. pap. 5.95 (ISBN 0-312-48821-1). St Martin.
--The Little Black Book: A Guide to the One Hundred Most Eligible Bachelors in Beverly Hills. 200p. 1983. pap. 5.95 (ISBN 0-312-48818-1). St Martin.
Nathan, Norma. Boston's Most Eligible Bachelors. (Illus.). 176p. 1982. pap. 5.95 (ISBN 0-86616-022-1). Lewis Pub Co.
--Norma Nathan's Book of Boston's Most Eligible Bachelors. 1983. pap. 5.95 (ISBN 0-86616-022-1). Greene.
Wetherall, Charles F. Single Man's Survival Guide. (Illus.). 160p. 1983. pap. 4.95 (ISBN 0-936750-06-5). Wetherall.
BACK PACKING
see Backpacking
BACKACHE
Burton, Charles & Nida, Gail. Revised Gravity Lumbar Reduction Therapy Program. 48p. 1982. 6.25 (ISBN 0-88440-026-3). Sis Kenny Inst.
Howorth, Beckett. Cure Your Own Backache. LC 82-17468. (Illus.). 128p. 1983. 9.95 (ISBN 0-87805-172-4). U Pr of Miss.
Kurland, Howard D. Back Pains: Quick Relief Without Drugs. (Illus.). 192p. 1983. pap. 7.95 (ISBN 0-671-41380-5, Fireside). S&S.
O'Donnell, Asta & Lipton, June. Keeping Fit with Asta O'Donnell: An Exercise Program for Problem Backs. (Illus.). 103p. (Orig.). 1983. pap. 12.50 (ISBN 0-9610564-0-1). J L Prods.
Stearn, Jess & Thompson, Alec. How to Cure Your Own Aching Back. Friedman, Robert, ed. (Illus.). 208p. (Orig.). 1983. pap. 6.95 (ISBN 0-89865-178-6). Donning Co.
Wayne, Jerry. The Bad Back Book. LC 82-62473. 1983. pap. 6.95 (ISBN 0-918024-25-0). Ox Bow.
White, Arthur H. Back School & Other Conservative Approaches to Low Back Pain. (Illus.). 198p. 1983. text ed. 32.50 (ISBN 0-8016-5423-8). Mosby.
BACKGAMMON
Barr, Ted. Gambling Times Guide to Backgammon. (Illus., Orig.). 1983. pap. text ed. 5.95 (ISBN 0-89746-006-5). Gambling Times.
BACKPACKING
Doan, Daniel. Fifty More Hikes in New Hampshire: Day Hikes & Backpacking Trips from the Coast to Coos County. rev. ed. (Fifty Hikes Ser.). (Illus.). 224p. 1983. pap. 8.95 (ISBN 0-942440-06-4). Backcountry Pubns.
Hargrove, Penny & Liebrenz, Noelle. Backpackers' Sourcebook. Winnett, Thomas, ed. LC 82-50739. 128p. 1983. pap. 2.95 (ISBN 0-89997-025-7). Wilderness Pr.
Linkhart, Luther. The Trinity Alps: A Hiking & Backpacking Guide. Winnett, Thomas, ed. (Illus.). 192p. 1983. pap. 9.95 (ISBN 0-89997-024-9). Wilderness Pr.
Scott, Herschel L., Jr. Dehydrator Gourmet. LC 82-61641. (Western Backpacking Ser.). (Illus.). 65p. (Orig.). 1983. pap. 3.95 (ISBN 0-88083-003-4). Poverty Hill Pr.
Simer, Peter & Sullivan, John. The National Outdoor Leadership School's Official Wilderness Guide. (Illus.). 1983. price not set (ISBN 0-671-24996-7); pap. price not set (ISBN 0-671-24997-5). S&S.
Walsh, Ken. The Backpacker's Guide to Europe. (Illus.). 288p. (Orig.). 1982. pap. 4.95 (ISBN 0-8329-0270-5). New Century.
BACKWARD AREAS
see Underdeveloped Areas
BACKWARD CHILDREN
see Mentally Handicapped Children
BACON, FRANCIS, VISCOUNT ST. ALBANS, 1561-1626
Fuller, Jean O. Sir Francis Bacon: A Biography. 384p. 1982. 20.00 (ISBN 0-85692-069-X, Pub. by Salem Hse Ltd.). Merrimack Bk Serv.
The Philosophy of Francis Bacon. 140p. 1982. 39.00x (ISBN 0-85323-310-1, Pub. by Liverpool Univ England). State Mutual Bk.
BACTERIA
see also Endotoxin; Spores (Bacteria); Viruses
also names of specific bacteria, e.g. staphyloccoccus
Aly, Raza & Shinefield, Henry R. Bacterial Interference. 192p. 1982. 60.00 (ISBN 0-8493-6285-7). CRC Pr.
Jeljackzewicz, Janusz, et al, eds. Bacteria & Cancer. Date not set. 39.50 (ISBN 0-12-383820-7). Acad Pr.
Mitsuhashi, S. Drug Resistance in Bacteria. 380p. 35.00 (ISBN 0-86577-085-9). Thieme-Stratton.
Woolcock, J. B. Bacterial Infection & Immunity in Domestic Animals. (Developments in Animal & Veterinary Science Ser.: Vol. 3). 1979. 64.00 (ISBN 0-444-41768-0). Elsevier.
BACTERIA–CULTURES AND CULTURE MEDIA
see Microbiology–Cultures and Culture Media
BACTERIA, PATHOGENIC
see also Biological Warfare
also names of specific bacteria e.g. Streptococcus and headings beginning with the word Bacillus, e.g. Bacillus Tuberculosis
Evans, Alfred S. & Feldman, Harry A., eds. Bacterial Infections of Humans Epidemiology & Control. 744p. 1982. 59.50x (ISBN 0-306-40967-4, Plenum Pr). Plenum Pub.
BACTERIAL CULTURES
see Microbiology–Cultures and Culture Media
BACTERIAL RESISTANCE TO ANTIBIOTICS
see Drug Resistance in Micro-Organisms
BACTERIAL SPORES
see Spores (Bacteria)
BACTERIAL WARFARE
see Biological Warfare
BACTERIOCIDAL AGENTS
see Anti-Infective Agents
BACTERIOLOGICAL WARFARE
see Biological Warfare
BACTERIOLOGY
see also Bacteria; Disinfection and Disinfectants; Immunity; Medicine, Preventive; Sewage–Purification; Sewage Disposal
also subdivision Bacteriology under particular subjects, e.g. Milk–Bacteriology
Ingraham, John L. & Maaloe, Ole. Growth of the Bacterial Cell. (Illus.). 375p. 1983. text ed. write for info. (ISBN 0-87893-352-2). Sinauer Assoc.
Kurmann, J. & Rasic, J. Bifidobacteria & Their Use. (Experientia Supplementum: Vol. 39). 304p. Date not set. text ed. price not set (ISBN 3-7643-1214-9). Birkhauser.
Lichstein, Herman C., ed. Bacterial Nutrition. LC 82-11720. (Benchmark Papers in Microbiology: Vol. 19). 400p. 1982. 47.00 (ISBN 0-87933-439-8). Hutchinson Ross.
BACTERIOSTATIC AGENTS
see Anti-Infective Agents
BADGES OF HONOR
see Decorations of Honor; Medals
BADMINTON (GAME)
Badminton-Squash-Racquetball 1982-84. (NAGWS Sports Guides Ser.). 3.75 (ISBN 0-88314-079-9). AAHPERD.
Johnson, M. L. & Johnson, Dewayne J. Badminton. (Illus.). 67p. 1981. pap. text ed. 2.95x (ISBN 0-89641-061-7). American Pr.
BAGDAD
LeStrange, Guy. Baghdad during the Abbasid Caliphate: From Contemporary Arabic & Persian Sources. LC 82-25143. xxxi, 381p. 1983. Repr. of 1942 ed. lib. bdg. 65.00x (ISBN 0-313-23198-2, LEBC). Greenwood.
BAHA'I FAITH
see Bahaism
BAHAISM
see also Babism
Arjmand, Mihdi. Gulshan-i Haqayiq. 320p. (Persian.). 1982. Repr. 12.95 (ISBN 0-933770-15-4). Kalimat.
Momen, Moojan, ed. Studies in Babi & Baha'i History, Vol. 1. (Illus.). 1983. text ed. 25.00 (ISBN 0-933770-16-2). Kalimat.
Thompson, Juliet. Diary of Juliet Thompson. 1983. 14.95 (ISBN 0-933770-27-8). Kalimat.
BAHAMAS–DESCRIPTION AND TRAVEL
Bahamas Travel Guide. (Berlitz Travel Guides). (Illus.). 1982. pap. 4.95 (ISBN 0-02-969760-3, Berlitz). Macmillan.
Birnbaum, Stephen. The Caribbean, Bermuda & the Bahamas. (Get 'em & Go Travel Guide Ser.). 1982. 11.95 (ISBN 0-686-84795-4). HM.
BAIT
see also Fishing Lures
Sternberg, Dick. Fishing with Live Bait. 160p. 1983. 16.95 (ISBN 0-307-46635-3, Golden Pr). Western Pr.
BAJA CALIFORNIA
Gotshall, Daniel W. Marine Animals of Baja California. LC 82-50492. (Illus.). 112p. 1982. ltd. ed. 29.95 (ISBN 0-930118-08-1, Dist. by Western Marine Enterprises); pap. 17.95 (ISBN 0-930030-24-9). Sea Chall.
BAKED PRODUCTS
see also specific baked products, e.g. Bread, Cake, Cookies
Daniel, A. R. Bakery Materials & Methods. 4th ed. 1978. Repr. 20.50 (Pub. by Applied Sci England). Elsevier.
--Bakery Questions Answered. 1972. 18.50 (ISBN 0-85334-540-6, Pub. by Applied Sci England). Elsevier.
BAKERY PRODUCTS
see Baked Products
BAKING
see also Baked Products; Bread; Cake; Cookies; Pastry; Souffles
Jarvey, Paulette S. Let's Dough It Again. (Illus.). 80p. (Orig.). 1982. pap. 6.95 (ISBN 0-9605904-1-2). Hot Off Pr.
Mayo, Patricia T. The Sugarless Baking Book: The Natural Way to Prepare America's Favorite Breads, Pies, Cakes, Puddings & Desserts. LC 82-42757. (Illus.). 116p. (Orig.). 1983. pap. 4.95 (ISBN 0-394-71429-6). Shambhala Pubns.
Powers, Margaret. Gluten Free & Good. (Orig.). Date not set. pap. 7.95 (ISBN 0-9610140-0-8). Old Town Pr.
The Southern Heritage Breads Cookbook. (Illus.). 144p. 1983. 9.95 (ISBN 0-8487-0602-1). Oxmoor Hse.
BAKUNIN, MIKHAIL ALEKSANDROVITCH, 1814-1876
Saltman, Richard B. The Social & Political Thought of Michael Bakunin. LC 82-9348. (Contributions in Political Science Ser.: No. 88). 256p. 1983. lib. bdg. 35.00 (ISBN 0-313-23378-0, SPB/). Greenwood.
BALAENOPTERA
see Whales
BALANCE OF NATURE
see Ecology
BALANCE OF PAYMENTS
see also Balance of Trade
Bigman, David, ed. Floating Exchange Rates & the State of World Trade & Payments. Taya, Teizo. Date not set. price not set professional ref. (ISBN 0-88410-398-6). Ballinger Pub.
Rabin, Alan A. & Yeager, Leland B. Monetary Approaches to the Balance of Payments & Exchange Rates. LC 82-15587. (Essays in International Finance Ser.: No. 148). 1982. pap. text ed. 2.50x (ISBN 0-88165-055-2). Princeton U Int Finan Econ.
BALANCE OF POWER
The Logical Consistency & Soundness of the Balance of Power Theory. (Monograph Series in World Affairs: Vol. 19 Bk. 3). 1983. pap. 5.00 (ISBN 0-87940-070-6). U of Denver Intl.
BALANCE OF TRADE
see also Balance of Payments
Bigman, David, ed. Floating Exchange Rates & the State of World Trade & Payments. Taya, Teizo. Date not set. price not set professional ref. (ISBN 0-88410-398-6). Ballinger Pub.
BALANCE SHEETS
see Financial Statements
BALANCHINE GEORGE, 1904-
Simmonds, Harvey, ed. Choreography by George Balanchine. LC 82-83072. 75.00 (ISBN 0-87130-050-8). Eakins.
BALD EAGLE
McConoughey, Jana. Bald Eagle. Schroeder, Howard, ed. (Wildlife Habits & Habitat Ser.). (Illus.). 48p. (gr. 4-5). 1983. lib. bdg. 8.95 (ISBN 0-89686-218-6). Crestwood Hse.
BALDNESS
Mayhew, John. Hair Techniques & Alternatives to Baldness. (Illus.). 250p. 1983. 29.95 (ISBN 0-932426-25-5). Trado-Medic.
BALI (ISLAND)
Insight Guides. Bali. (Illus.). 280p. 1983. pap. 14.95 (ISBN 0-13-056200-9). P-H.
BALINESE ART
see Art, Balinese
BALKAN PENINSULA–HISTORY
Fine, John V. The Early Medieval Balkans: A Critical Survey from the Sixth to the Late Twelfth Century. LC 82-8452. (Illus.). 368p. 1983. text ed. 29.95x (ISBN 0-472-10025-4). U of Mich Pr.
BALL-BEARINGS
Houghton, P. S. Ball & Roller Bearings. 1976. 98.50 (ISBN 0-85334-598-8, Pub. by Applied Sci England). Elsevier.
BALLADS, ENGLISH–HISTORY AND CRITICISM
Keen, Maurice. The Outlaws of Medieval Legend. (Studies in Social History). 235p. 1977. 25.00 (ISBN 0-7100-8682-2). Routledge & Kegan.
BALLET
Here are entered works on the ballet. Ballet scores are entered under the heading Ballets.
see also Choreography
Barnes, Clive. Inside American Ballet Theatre. (Quality Paperbacks Ser.). (Illus.). 192p. 1983. pap. 11.95 (ISBN 0-306-80192-2). Da Capo.
Gordon, Suzanne. Off Balance: The Real World of Ballet. LC 82-18806. 256p. 1983. 14.95 (ISBN 0-686-38838-0). Pantheon.
Pask, Edward H. The Ballet in Australia: The Second Act 1940-1980. (Illus.). 318p. 1981. 69.00x (ISBN 0-19-554294-0). Oxford U Pr.
Walker, Katherine S. De Basil's Ballets Russes. LC 82-16339. 317p. 1983. 19.95 (ISBN 0-689-11365-X). Atheneum.
BALLET–HISTORY
Buckle, Richard. In the Wake of Diaghilev. LC 82-12096. (Illus.). 400p. 1983. 19.95 (ISBN 0-03-062493-2). HR&W.
Flett, Una. Falling From Grace: My Early Years in Ballet. 194p. 1982. 12.95 (ISBN 0-86241-011-8, Pub. by Salem Hse Ltd.). Merrimack Bk Serv.
BALLET–JUVENILE LITERATURE
Goodale, Katherine D. Pas de Trois, Fun with Ballet Words. (Illus.). 25p. (Orig.). (gr. k-7). 1982. pap. 5.95 (ISBN 0-9609662-0-X). Goodale Pub.
BALLET, WATER
see Synchronized Swimming
BALLET DANCERS
see Dancers
BALLET DANCING–JUVENILE LITERATURE
Oxenbury, Helen. The Dancing Class. (Illus.). 24p. (ps-5). 1983. 5.95 (ISBN 0-8037-1651-6). Dial Bks Young.
BALLISTIC MISSILES
Adams, B. Ballistic Missile Defense. 1971. 25.00 (ISBN 0-444-00111-5). Elsevier.
BALLISTICS
Farrar, C. L. & Leeming, D. W. Military Ballistics: A Basic Manual. 225p. 1983. 26.00 (ISBN 0-08-028342-X); pap. 13.00 (ISBN 0-08-028343-8). Pergamon.
BALLOONS, DIRIGIBLE
see Air-Ships
BALTHUS
see Klossowski, Balthasar, 1910-
BALTIC SEA
Alexandersson, G. The Baltic Straits. 1982. lib. bdg. 32.50 (ISBN 90-247-2595-X, Pub. by Martinus Nijhoff Netherlands). Kluwer Boston.

BALTIMORE COUNTY, MARYLAND–HISTORY
Weaver, Betsy & Frederick, Gary E. Hands, Horses & Engines: A Centennial History of the Baltimore County Fire Service. Campbell, Colin A., ed. (Illus.). 160p. 1982. 16.95 (ISBN 0-9608952-0-5). Baltimore CFSCC.
BALTO-SLAVIC LANGUAGES
see Slavic Languages
BALTO-SLAVIC PHILOLOGY
see Slavic Philology
BALZAC, HONORE DE, 1799-1850
Brumm, Barbara. Marxismus und Realismus Am Beispiel Balzac. 153p. (Ger.). 1982. write for info. (ISBN 3-8204-5784-4). P Lang Pubs.
Ludwig, Emil. Genius & Character: Shakespeare, Voltaire, Goethe, Balzac. 330p. 1982. Repr. of 1927 ed. lib. bdg. 35.00 (ISBN 0-8495-3267-1). Arden Lib.
McCarthy, Mary S. Balzac & His Reader: A Study of the Creation of Meaning in La Comedie Humaine. LC 82-2667. 176p. 1983. 18.00 (ISBN 0-8262-0378-7). U of MO Pr.
Stone, William W. Balzac, James & the Realistic Novel. LC 82-61388. 224p. 1983. 19.50x (ISBN 0-691-06567-5). Princeton U Pr.
BANACH SPACES
see also Hilbert Space
Chao, J. A. & Woyczynski, W. A., eds. Martingale Theory in Harmonic Analysis & Banach Spaces, Cleveland, Ohio 1981: Proceedings. (Lecture Notes in Mathematics: Vol. 939). 225p. 1982. pap. 12.00 (ISBN 0-387-11569-2). Springer-Verlag.
Krein, S. G. Linear Equations in Banach Spaces. 128p. Date not set. text ed. 14.95x (ISBN 3-7643-3101-1). Birkhauser.
Nachbin, Leopoldo. Introduction to Functional Analysis: Banach Spaces & Different Calculus. (Pure & Applied Mathematics: Monographs & Textbooks: Vol. 60). (Illus.). 184p. 1981. 19.75 (ISBN 0-8247-6984-8). Dekker.
BANANA
Simmonds, N. W. Bananas. 2nd ed. LC 82-116. (Tropical Agriculture Ser.). (Illus.). 568p. 1982. pap. text ed. 29.95x (ISBN 0-582-46355-6). Longman.
BAND MUSIC
see also Military Music
Bierley, Paul E. The Music of Henry Fillmore & Will Huff. LC 82-81491. (Music Catalog Ser.). 1982. pap. 5.95 (ISBN 0-918048-02-8). Integrity.
BANDAGES AND BANDAGING
Nussdorf, Maggie & Nussdorf, Stephen. Dress for Health. 1980. 14.95x (ISBN 0-8117-0524-2). Cancer Control Soc.
BANDMASTERS
see Conductors (Music)
BANGKOK, THAILAND–DESCRIPTION
Sinclair, John. Bangkok by Night. (Asia by Night Ser.). (Illus.). 64p. (Orig.). 1981. pap. 4.95 (ISBN 962-7031-10-0, Pub. by CFW Pubns Hong Kong). C E Tuttle.
BANGLADESH
Bhuiyan, Abdul W. Emergence of Bangladesh & the Role of the Awami League. 275p. 1982. text ed. 32.50x (ISBN 0-7069-1773-1, Pub. by Vikas India). Advent NY.
Franda, Marcus. Bangladesh: The First Decade. 1982. 22.00x (ISBN 0-8364-0891-8). South Asia Bks.
BANGLADESH–POLITICS AND GOVERNMENT
Khan, Zillur. Leadership in the Least Developed Nation: Bangladesh. (Foreign & Comparative Studies Program, South Asian Ser., No. 8). (Orig.). 1983. pap. write for info (ISBN 0-915984-85-7). Syracuse U Foreign Comp.
Maniruzzaman, Talukder. Group Interests & Political Changes: Studies of Pakistan & Bangladesh. 1982. 24.00x (ISBN 0-8364-0892-6). South Asia Bks.
BANJO
Perlman, Ken. Clawhammer Style Banjo: A Complete Guide for Beginning & Advanced Banjo Players. (Illus.). 194p. 1983. 19.95 (ISBN 0-13-136374-3); pap. 10.95 (ISBN 0-13-136366-2). P-H.
BANK CLERKS
see Bank Employees
BANK EMPLOYEES
Jannott, Paul F. Teller World. LC 82-18497. 122p. 1983. 19.95 (ISBN 0-87267-040-6). Bankers.
Looper, C. Eugene. Banker's Guide to Personnel Administration. LC 82-24400. 360p. 1983. 39.00 (ISBN 0-87267-041-4). Bankers.
BANK LOANS
see Loans
BANK MANAGEMENT
Fair, D. E. & De Juvigny, F. Leonard. Bank Management in a Changing Domestic & International Environment. 1982. lib. bdg. 57.00 (ISBN 90-247-2606-9, Pub. by Martinus Nijhoff Netherlands). Kluwer Boston.
Sunderland, Neil V. Bank Planning Models. 160p. 1977. 75.00x (ISBN 0-7121-5621-6, Pub. by Macdonald & Evans). State Mutual Bk.
BANK STATEMENTS
see Banks and Banking–Accounting
BANKED BLOOD
see Blood Banks
BANKERS
Banker's Almanac & Year Book 1983. 138th ed. LC 20-372. 2596p. 1983. 160.00x (ISBN 0-611-00658-8). Intl Pubns Serv.
BANKING
see Banks and Banking
BANKING LAW
see also Negotiable Instruments
also topics in the field of banking, e.g. Trust Companies
Boston University Center for Banking Law Studies, ed. Annual Review of Banking Law. 1982. 42.00 (ISBN 0-88262-818-6). Warren.
Gheerbrant, Philip A. Cases in Banking Law. 144p. 1980. 29.00x (ISBN 0-7121-0383-X, Pub. by Macdonald & Evans). State Mutual Bk.
Kim, Seung H. & Miller, Stephen W. Competitive Structure of the International Banking Industry. Miossi, Alfred F., ed. LC 81-47970. 256p. 1983. 25.95x (ISBN 0-669-05189-6). Lexington Bks.
White, Eugene N. The Regulation & Reform of the America Banking System, 1900-1929. LC 82-61395. 256p. 1983. 25.00x (ISBN 0-691-04232-2). Princeton U Pr.
BANKRUPTCY
see also Liquidation
Altman, Edward I. Corporate Financial Distress: A Complete Guide to Predicting, Avoiding & Dealing with Bankruptcy. (Professional Banking & Finance Ser.). 285p. 1982. 29.95 (ISBN 0-471-08707-6, Pub. by Wiley-Interscience). Wiley.
Anosike, Benji O. How to File For "Chapter II" Bankruptcy Relief from Your Business Debts, with or without A Lawyer. 140p. 1983. pap. text ed. 11.95 (ISBN 0-932704-14-X). Do-It-Yourself Pubns.
Chatterton, William A. Consumer & Small Business Bankruptcy: A Complete Working Guide. LC 82-12040. 256p. 1982. text ed. 89.50 (ISBN 0-87624-101-1). Inst Busn Plan.
Cohen, Arnold B. Bankruptcy: Secured Transactions & Other Debtor-Creditor Matters. 646p. 1981. 55.00 (ISBN 0-87215-398-3). Michie-Bobbs.
Pettigrew, Grady L., Jr. Federal Bankruptcy Code: Theory Into Practice. 295p. 1982. wkbk 60.00 (ISBN 0-87179-376-8). BNA.
SCott, W. Stephen. Bankruptcy: A Virginia Law Practice System. 417p. 1982. looseleaf with forms 75.00 (ISBN 0-87215-507-2). Michie-Bobbs.
Shepard. Creditor's Rights in Bankruptcy. 1980. 70.00 (ISBN 0-07-044060-3); annual suppl. 25.00 (ISBN 0-07-044064-6). McGraw.
BANKS, CENTRAL
see Banks and Banking, Central
BANKS AND BANKING
see also Agricultural Credit; Bank Employees; Bankers; Banks and Banking, Central; Consumer Credit; Credit; Foreign Exchange; Interest and Usury; Investment Banking; Money; Negotiable Instruments
Auernheimer, Leonardo & Ekelund, Robert B. The Essential of Money & Banking. LC 81-11466. 445p. 1982. 23.95 (ISBN 0-471-02103-2); avail. instrs' manual (ISBN 0-471-87633-X). Wiley.
Cochran, John A. Money, Banking, & the Economy. 528p. 1983. text ed. 23.95 (ISBN 0-02-323050-9). Macmillan.
Cohen, Kalman J. & Gibson, Stephen E. Management Science in Banking. LC 78-60934. 549p. 1982. text ed. 19.95 (ISBN 0-471-87748-4). Wiley.
Cook, John A. & Wool, Robert. All You Need to Know About Banks. 202p. 1983. 13.95 (ISBN 0-553-05025-7). Bantam.
Eccles, George S. The Politics of Banking. Hyman, Sidney, ed. 320p. 1982. 20.00 (ISBN 0-87480-208-3); pap. 13.00 (ISBN 0-87480-209-1). U of Utah Pr.
Harrell, Rhett D. & Cole, Lisa A. Banking Relations: A Guide for Local Governments. (Illus.). 100p. 1982. pap. 14.00 Nonmember (ISBN 0-686-84372-X); pap. 12.00 Member (ISBN 0-686-84373-8). Municipal.
Harrison, Michael A. Electronic Banking: The Revolution in Financial Services. (Illus.). 200p. 1983. 32.95 (ISBN 0-86729-060-9). Knowledge Indus.
Kruppa, Thomas. Die Bankenhaftung Bei der Sanierung Einter Kapitalgesellschaft Im Insolvenzfall. lxiii, 310p. (Ger.). 1982. write for info. (ISBN 3-8204-7115-4). P Lang Pubs.
Mason, John M. Financial Management of Commercial Banks. LC 78-24809. 442p. 1982. text ed. 25.50 (ISBN 0-471-87745-X); tchrs.' ed avail. (ISBN 0-471-89511-3). Wiley.
Merk, Gerard, ed. Acta Monetaria. 128p. 1980. 59.00x (ISBN 0-686-81993-4, Pub. by Macdonald & Evans). State Mutual Bk.
U. S. Electronic Banking. 1982. 995.00 (E73). Predicasts.
BANKS AND BANKING–ACCOUNTING
American Institute of Certified Public Accountants. Industry Audit Guide: Audits of Banks. write for info. Am Inst CPA.
BANKS AND BANKING–AUTOMATION
U. S. Electronic Banking. 1982. 995.00 (E73). Predicasts.
BANKS AND BANKING–BIBLIOGRAPHY
Banker's Almanac & Year Book 1983. 138th ed. LC 20-372. 2596p. 1983. 160.00x (ISBN 0-611-00658-8). Intl Pubns Serv.
BANKS AND BANKING–DATA PROCESSING
Consumer Electronic Banking. (Reports Ser.: No. 520). 167p. 1982. 985.00 (ISBN 0-686-38960-3). Intl Res Dev.
BANKS AND BANKING–DICTIONARIES
Perry, F. E. A Dictionary of Banking. 304p. 1979. 35.00x (ISBN 0-7121-0428-3, Pub. by Macdonald & Evans). State Mutual Bk.
BANKS AND BANKING–DIRECTORIES
Financial Times Business Publishing Ltd., ed. British Banking Directory. 1982. 125.00x (ISBN 0-902998-42-0, Pub. by Finan Times England). State Mutual Bk.
BANKS AND BANKING–EMPLOYEES
see Bank Employees
BANKS AND BANKING–HISTORY
Slaven, A. & Aldcroft, D., eds. Business, Banking & Urban History: Essays in Honour of S. G. Checkland. 235p. 1982. text ed. 31.50x (ISBN 0-85976-083-9, 40292, Pub. by Donald Scotland). Humanities.
White, Eugene N. The Regulation & Reform of the America Banking System, 1900-1929. LC 82-61395. 256p. 1983. 25.00x (ISBN 0-691-04232-2). Princeton U Pr.
BANKS AND BANKING–LAWS AND LEGISLATION
see Banking Law
BANKS AND BANKING–AFRICA
Dublin, Jack & Dublin, Selma M. Credit Unions in a Changing World: The Tanzania-Kenya Experience. 1983. 18.95 (ISBN 0-8143-1742-1); pap. 9.95 (ISBN 0-8143-1743-X). Wayne St U Pr.
Onoh, J. K. Money & Banking in Africa. LC 82-15266. (Illus.). 256p. 1983. text ed. 35.00 (ISBN 0-582-64439-9). Longman.
BANKS AND BANKING–AUSTRALIA
Hill, John. From Subservience to Strike: Industrial Relations in the Banking Industry. LC 82-2684. (Illus.). 296p. 1983. text ed. 32.50x (ISBN 0-7022-1830-8). U of Queensland Pr.
BANKS AND BANKING–CHINA
Byrd, William. China's Financial System: The Changing Role of Banks. (Replica Edition Ser.). 150p. 1982. softcover 17.00x (ISBN 0-86531-943-X). Westview.
BANKS AND BANKING–EUROPE
Tritten, Kurt. European Banks 1981. 328p. 1981. 110.00x (ISBN 0-7121-5613-5, Pub. by Macdonald & Evans). State Mutual Bk.
BANKS AND BANKING–GREAT BRITAIN
Financial Times Business Publishing Ltd., ed. British Banking Directory. 1982. 125.00x (ISBN 0-902998-42-0, Pub. by Finan Times England). State Mutual Bk.
Gheerbrant, Philip A. Cases in Banking Law. 144p. 1980. 29.00x (ISBN 0-7121-0383-X, Pub. by Macdonald & Evans). State Mutual Bk.
Kelley, Janet. Bankers & Borders: The Case of American Banks in Britain. 1976. 35.00x (ISBN 0-88410-459-1). Ballinger Pub.
BANKS AND BANKING–INDIA
Seshadri, R. K. A Swadeshi Bank from South India: A History of the Indian Bank 1907-1982. (Illus.). 249p. 1982. text ed. 22.50x (ISBN 0-86131-341-0, Pub. by Orient Longman Ltd India). Apt Bks.
BANKS AND BANKING–JAPAN
Financial Times Business Publishing Ltd., ed. Japanese Banking & Capital Markets. 1982. 150.00x (ISBN 0-686-82306-0, Pub. by Finan Times England). State Mutual Bk.
BANKS AND BANKING–MEXICO
Greenow, Linda. Credit & Socioeconomic Change in Colonial Mexico: Loans & Mortgages in Guadalajara, 1720-1820. (Dellplain Latin American Studies: No. 12). 200p. 1982. softcover 16.50x (ISBN 0-86531-467-5). Westview.
BANKS AND BANKING–SWITZERLAND
Ikle, Max. Switzerland: An International Banking & Financial Center. Schiff, Eric, tr. from Ger. LC 72-76544. 156p. 1972. text ed. 34.50 (ISBN 0-87933-002-3). Hutchinson Ross.
Kinsman, Robert. Your New Swiss Bank Book. rev. ed. 285p. 1983. pap. 8.95 (ISBN 0-87094-416-9). Dow Jones-Irwin.
BANKS AND BANKING, CENTRAL
see also Monetary Policy;
also names of individual central banks and central banking systems e.g. Bank of England, Federal Reserve Banks
O'Driscoll, Gerald P. Inflation or Deflation? Prospects for Capital Formation, Employment, & Economic Recovery. (Pacific Institute). 1983. write for info. (ISBN 0-88410-930-5). Ballinger Pub.
Sayers, Richard S. Central Banking after Bagehot. LC 82-18693. 149p. 1982. Repr. of 1957 ed. lib. bdg. 29.75x (ISBN 0-313-23743-3, SACB). Greenwood.
BANKS AND BANKING, COOPERATIVE
Dublin, Jack & Dublin, Selma M. Credit Unions in a Changing World: The Tanzania-Kenya Experience. 1983. 18.95 (ISBN 0-8143-1742-1); pap. 9.95 (ISBN 0-8143-1743-X). Wayne St U Pr.
BANKS AND BANKING, INTERNATIONAL
Ayres, Robert L. Banking on the Poor: The World Bank & World Poverty. 296p. 1983. 17.50x (ISBN 0-262-01070-4). MIT Pr.
Born, Karl B. International Banking in the 19th & 20th Centuries. Berghahn, Volker R., tr. LC 82-42715. 360p. 1983. 30.00x (ISBN 0-312-41975-9). St Martin.
Johns, Richard A. Tax Havens & Offshore Finance: A Study of Transnational Economic Development. LC 82-10755. 270p. 1983. 32.50x (ISBN 0-312-78641-7). St Martin.
Kim, Seung H. & Miller, Stephen W. Competitive Structure of the International Banking Industry. Miossi, Alfred F., ed. LC 81-47970. 256p. 1983. 25.95x (ISBN 0-669-05189-6). Lexington Bks.
Mongia, J. N. Banking Around the World. 583p. 1982. 49.95x (ISBN 0-940500-69-8, Pub by Allied Pubs India). Asia Bk Corp.
Roussakis, Emmanuel N. International Banking: Principles & Practices. 556p. 1983. 39.95 (ISBN 0-03-062387-1). Praeger.
Sampson, Anthony. The Money Lenders: The People & Politics of International Banking. 336p. 1983. pap. 6.95 (ISBN 0-14-006485-0). Penguin.
Schneider, Jerome. Using an Offshore Bank for Profit, Privacy & Tax Protection. Benavidez, Max & Vozoff, Kate, eds. (Illus.). 259p. 1982. 15.00 (ISBN 0-933560-03-6). WFI Pub Co.
BANKS AND BANKING, INVESTMENT
see Investment Banking
BANQUETS
see Dinners and Dining
BAPTISM
Gibbs, A. P. Christian Baptism. 1982. pap. 4.50 (ISBN 0-937396-62-1). Walteick Pubs.
Jeschke, Marlin. Believers Baptism for Children of the Church. 160p. (Orig.). 1983. pap. 7.95 (ISBN 0-8361-3318-8). Herald Pr.
Voorehoeve, H. C. & Bennett, Gordon H. El Bautismo. 2nd ed. Bautista, Sara, tr. from Eng. (La Serie Diamante). 36p. (Span.). 1982. pap. 0.85 (ISBN 0-942504-06-2). Overcomer Pr.
BAPTISM–BIBLICAL TEACHING
Egan, John P. & Colford, Paul D. Baptism of Resistance - Blood & Celebration: A Road to Wholeness in the Nuclear Age. 1983. pap. 5.95 (ISBN 0-89622-164-4). Twenty-Third Pubns.
BAPTISMAL RECORDS
see Registers of Births, Deaths, Marriages, Etc.
BAPTISTS–HISTORY
Lumpkin, William L. A Chronicle of Christian Heritage: Dover Baptist Association, 1783-1983. 145p. (Orig.). 1983. pap. text ed. 7.95 (ISBN 0-931804-11-6). Skipworth Pr.
McBeth, Leon H. History of Baptists. 1983. 17.95 (ISBN 0-8054-6569-3). Broadman.
Pater, Calvin A. Karlstadt as the Father of the Baptist Movements. 324p. 1983. 35.00x (ISBN 0-8020-5555-9). U of Toronto Pr.
Patterson, Morgan W. Baptist History Sourcebook. Date not set. 15.95 (ISBN 0-8054-6568-5). Broadman.
BAPTISTS–MISSIONS
Hughey, J. D. Baptists Partnership in Europe. LC 81-66559. 1982. pap. 4.95 (ISBN 0-8054-6326-7). Broadman.
BAR
see Lawyers
BAR ASSOCIATIONS
Maine Bar Directory 1983. 350p. 1983. write for info. Tower Pub Co.
Maru, Olavi, ed. Supplement to the Digest of Bar Association Ethics Opinions, 1980: Including 1970 & 1975 Supplements & Index. ix, 835p. Date not set. 50.00 (ISBN 0-910059-01-2). Am Bar Foun.
BAR MITZVAH
Jeiven, Helene. Checklist for a Perfect Bar Mitzvah (& a Bat Mitzvah) LC 82-45929. (Illus.). 220p. 1983. pap. 3.95 (ISBN 0-385-18134-5, Dolp). Doubleday.
BARBARY CORSAIRS
see Pirates
BARBECUE COOKERY
see Cookery, Barbecue
BARGAINING
see Collective Bargaining; Negotiation
BARGELLO
see Canvas Embroidery
BARMAIDS
see Bartenders
BAROQUE ARCHITECTURE
see Architecture, Baroque
BAROQUE ART
see Art, Baroque
BARREN FIG TREE (PARABLE)
see Jesus Christ–Parables
BARRISTERS
see Lawyers
BARS (DRINKING ESTABLISHMENTS)
see Hotels, Taverns, Etc.
BARTENDERS
Buller, Jon. Buller's Professional Course in Bartending for Home Study. (Illus.). 128p. 1983. 11.95 (ISBN 0-916782-34-4); pap. 6.95 comb. binding (ISBN 0-916782-33-6). Harvard Common Pr.
Katsigris, Costas & Porter, Mary. The Bar & Beverage Book: Basics of Profitable Management. (Service Management Ser.). 480p. 1983. pap. text ed. 23.95x (ISBN 0-471-08264-3). Wiley.
BARTER
Ansley, Margene. Barter Update Directory. 100p. 1983. pap. text ed. 9.95 (ISBN 0-939476-53-3). Biblio Pr GA.
Barter Publishing Staff. Barter Alert. 60p. 1983. pap. text ed. 9.95 (ISBN 0-686-37637-4). Barter Pub.
--Barter Referral Directory. 300p. Date not set. pap. text ed. 29.95 (ISBN 0-686-37635-8). Barter Pub.
--Business Bartering: A Bibliography. 15p. 1983. pap. text ed. 4.95 (ISBN 0-686-37639-0). Barter Pub.
--The Piggy Back Concept: Reference Pages. 25p. 1983. pap. text ed. 3.00 (ISBN 0-686-37638-2). Barter Pub.

Barter Publishing Staff, ed. Directory of Barter Associations & Organizations Based in Arizona. 50p. 1983. pap. 9.95 (ISBN 0-911617-05-1). Barter Pub.
--Directory of Barter Associations & Organizations Based in California. 25p. 1983. pap. 9.95 (ISBN 0-911617-07-8). Barter Pub.
--Directory of Barter Associations & Organizations Based in Colorado. 50p. 1983. pap. 9.95 (ISBN 0-911617-08-6). Barter Pub.
--Directory of Barter Associations & Organizations Based in Florida. 50p. 1983. pap. 9.95 (ISBN 0-911617-12-4). Barter Pub.
--Directory of Barter Associations & Organizations Based in Maryland. 30p. 1983. pap. 9.95 (ISBN 0-911617-21-3). Barter Pub.
--Directory of Barter Associations & Organizations Based in Massachusetts. 35p. 1983. pap. 9.95 (ISBN 0-911617-22-1). Barter Pub.
--Directory of Barter Associations & Organizations Based in Ohio. 35p. Date not set. pap. 9.95 (ISBN 0-911617-38-8). Barter Pub.
--Directory of Barter Associations & Organizations Based in Pennsylvania. 50p. 1983. pap. 9.95 (ISBN 0-911617-40-X). Barter Pub.
--Directory of Barter Associations & Organizations Based in Washington. 50p. Date not set. pap. 9.95 (ISBN 0-911617-49-3). Barter Pub.
--Directory of Barter Associations Organizations Based in New York. 60p. 1983. pap. 9.95 (ISBN 0-911617-35-3). Barter Pub.
Carrol, Frieda. Creative Uses for the Barter Card. 16p. 1983. pap. 4.95 (ISBN 0-911617-56-6). Barter Pub.
Carrol, Frieda, compiled by. Directory of Barter Directories. 100p. 1983. pap. 19.95 (ISBN 0-911617-55-8). Barter Pub.
--International Directory of Barter Associations & Organizations. 200p. 1983. pap. 19.95 (ISBN 0-911617-54-X). Barter Pub.
Center for Self-Sufficiency Research Division, ed. The Barter Index. 60p. Date not set. pap. text ed. 9.95 (ISBN 0-910811-09-1). Center Self.
Thompson, Robert W. How to Barter for Fun & Profit. 1983. 6.95 (ISBN 0-533-05642-X). Vantage.
Update Publicare Research Staff. Barter Update: Notebook of Back Issues. 35p. 1983. pap. text ed. 8.00 (ISBN 0-686-38888-7). Update Pub Co.

BARTHES, ROLAND

Champagne, Roland A. Literary History in the Wake of Roland Barthes: Re-Defining the Myths of Reading. 15.00 (ISBN 0-917786-36-X). French Lit.
Culler, Jonathan. Roland Barthes. 128p. 1983. 19.95 (ISBN 0-19-520420-4). Oxford U Pr.
--Roland Barthes. 128p. 1983. pap. 4.95 (ISBN 0-19-520421-2, GB738, GB). Oxford U Pr.

BARTHIANISM

see Dialectical Theology

BARTOK, BELA, 1881-1945

Walsh, Stephen. Bartok Chamber Music. LC 81-71299. (BBC Music Guides Ser.). (Illus.). 88p. (Orig.). 1983. pap. 5.95 (ISBN 0-295-95922-3). U of Wash Pr.

BASE-EXCHANGE

see Ion Exchange

BASEBALL

see also Softball; World Series (Baseball)

Angell, Roger. Late Innings. 448p. 1983. pap. 3.95 (ISBN 0-345-30936-7). Ballantine.
Baseball Dope Book 1983. 1983. 7.95 (ISBN 0-89204-112-9). Sporting News.
Baseball Guide 1983. 1983. 9.95 (ISBN 0-89204-111-0). Sporting News.
Baseball Record Book 1983. 1983. 7.95 (ISBN 0-89204-113-7). Sporting News.
Baseball Register 1983. 1983. 9.95 (ISBN 0-89204-110-2). Sporting News.
Baseball Rub Book, 1983. 1983. 2.50 (ISBN 0-89204-115-3). Sporting News.
Baseball Schedule Book, 1983. 1983. 1.95 (ISBN 0-89204-114-5). Sporting News.
Borst, Bill. Baseball Through a Knothole. (Orig.). 1980. pap. 5.95 (ISBN 0-940056-05-4). Chapter & Cask.
Cassady, Howard Hop-a-Long. Conditioning for Baseball: The New York Yankee's Way. LC 82-83935. (Illus.). 176p. (Orig.). 1983. pap. 7.95 (ISBN 0-88011-103-8). Leisure Pr.
Chieger, Bob. Voices of Baseball: Quotations of the Summer Game. LC 82-73027. 288p. (Orig.). 1983. pap. 7.95 (ISBN 0-689-70646-4). Atheneum.
Coleman, Ken & Valenti, Dan. Ken Coleman's Red Sox Quiz Book. 96p. 1983. pap. 4.95 (ISBN 0-943514-04-5). Literations.
Davids, L. Robert. Baseball Research Journal 1982. (Illus.). 183p. (Orig.). 1982. pap. 5.00 (ISBN 0-910137-01-3). Soc Am Baseball Res.
Davids, L. Robert, ed. Baseball Research Journal. (Illus.). 160p. (Orig.). 1983. pap. 5.00 (ISBN 0-910137-06-4). Soc Am Baseball Res.
Davids, Robert L, ed. Insider's Baseball. (Illus.). 288p. 1983. 13.95 (ISBN 0-686-83657-X, ScribT). Scribner.
Einstein, C. The Baseball Reader: Favorites from the Fireside Book of Baseball. 384p. 1983. pap. 8.95 (ISBN 0-07-019531-5, GB). McGraw.
Forker, Dom. Ultimate Yankee Baseball Quiz Book. 1982. pap. 2.50 (ISBN 0-451-11429-9, AE1429, Sig). NAL.
Frommer, Harvey. Baseball's Greatest Records, Streaks & Feats. LC 82-45939. 208p. 1983. 13.95 (ISBN 0-689-11385-4). Atheneum.
Hollander, Zander. The Complete Book of Baseball: 1983 Edition. 1982. pap. 3.95 (ISBN 0-451-12153-8, AE2153, Sig). NAL.
Ibach, Bob & Colletti, Ned. Cub Fan Mania. LC 82-83941. (Illus.). 128p. (Orig.). pap. 5.95 (ISBN 0-88011-109-7). Leisure Pr.
James, Bill. The Bill James Baseball Abstract 1983. 224p. (Orig.). 1983. pap. 6.95 (ISBN 0-345-30367-9). Ballantine.
McBee, Robert & Burgess, Tom, eds. Coaches' Guide to Championship Baseball Drills & Fundamentals. LC 82-45643. 250p. 1982. pap. write for info. (ISBN 0-9609500-0-1). McBee Sports.
Martz, Jim. Hurricane Strikes: University of Miami Baseball. 200p. 1983. 10.95 (ISBN 0-87397-248-1). Strode.
Montgomery, David. The Triathlon Handbook. (Illus.). 192p. (Orig.). 1983. pap. 7.95 (ISBN 0-88011-110-0). Leisure Pr.
Mungo, Raymond. Confessions from Left Field: Baseball Pilgrimage. 192p. 1983. 12.95 (ISBN 0-525-24168-X, 01258-370). Dutton.
The Official 1984 Price Guide to Baseball Cards. 3rd ed. LC 81-862223. 288p. 1983. pap. 2.95 (ISBN 0-87637-376-7). Hse of Collectibles.
Raveling, George. A Rebounder's Workshop: A Drill Manual for Rebounding. LC 82-83922. (Illus.). 112p. (Orig.). 1983. pap. 5.95 (ISBN 0-88011-063-5). Leisure Pr.
--War on the Boards: A Rebounding Manual. LC 82-83921. (Illus.). 112p. (Orig.). 1983. pap. 5.95 (ISBN 0-88011-062-7). Leisure Pr.
Sperling, Dan. A Spectator's Guide to Baseball. 96p. (Orig.). 1983. pap. 2.50 (ISBN 0-380-82628-3). Avon.
Stern, Robert. They Were Number One. LC 82-83920. (Illus.). 400p. 1983. 19.95 (ISBN 0-88011-122-4). Leisure Pr.
Sugar, Bert R., ed. American & National League Baseball Card Classics. 1982. pap. 2.95 ea. (ISBN 0-486-24308-7). Dover.
Sullivan, George E. The Complete Book of Baseball Collectibles. LC 82-16357. (Illus.). 268p. 1983. 14.95 (ISBN 0-668-05529-4); pap. 8.95 (ISBN 0-686-43039-5). Arco.
Torres, Angel. The Baseball Bible. LC 81-81949. (Illus.). 480p. 1983. pap. 14.95 (ISBN 0-86666-080-1). GWP.
Whiteford, Mike. How to Talk Baseball. LC 82-19920. (Illus.). 144p. (Orig.). 1983. pap. 6.95 (ISBN 0-934878-21-8). Dembner Bks.
Whiting, Robert. The Chrysanthemum & the Bat: Baseball Samurai Style. 256p. 1983. pap. 3.95 (ISBN 0-380-63115-6, Discus). Avon.
World Series Record Book, 1982. 1982. 7.95 (ISBN 0-89204-091-2). Sporting News.

BASEBALL-BIOGRAPHY

see also names of baseball players, e.g. Ruth, George Herman

Bartlett, Roland W. The Fans Vote! One Hundred Baseball Superstars. LC 82-5118. (Illus.). 256p. 1983. 17.95 (ISBN 0-88280-088-4); pap. 9.95 (ISBN 0-88280-089-2). ETC Pubns.
Bouton, Bobbie & Marshall, Nancy. Home Games: Two Baseball Wives Speak Out. 1983. 12.95 (ISBN 0-312-38846-2, Pub. by Marek). St Martin.
Burchard, S. H. Sports Star: The Book of Baseball Greats. LC 82-48763. 64p. (gr. 6-10). pap. 4.95 (ISBN 0-15-278061-0, VoyB). HarBraceJ.
Getz, Mike. Baseball's Three Thousand-Hit Men. 1982. 7.95 (ISBN 0-9608076-0-8). Gemmeg Pr.
Minoso, Minnie. Extra Innings. (Illus.). 1982. 10.95. Regnery-Gateway.
Schaap, Dick. Steinbrenner! 320p. 1983. pap. 3.50 (ISBN 0-380-62752-3). Avon.
Smith, Robert & John, Tommy. The Sally & Tommy John Story: Our Life in Baseball. (Illus.). 288p. 1983. 13.95 (ISBN 0-02-559260-2). Macmillan.
Weaver, Earl & Stainback, Berry. It's What You Learn After You Know It All That Counts. Rev. ed. 1983. pap. 8.95 (ISBN 0-671-47239-9, Fireside). S&S.

BASEBALL-HISTORY

Bilovsky, Frank & Westcott, Richard. The Phillies Encyclopedia. LC 82-83945. (Illus.). 500p. 1983. 29.95 (ISBN 0-88011-121-6). Leisure Pr.
Conner, Floyd & Snyder, John. Day-by-Day in Cincinnati Reds History. LC 82-83938. (Illus.). 300p. (Orig.). 1983. pap. 9.95 (ISBN 0-88011-106-2). Leisure Pr.
Davids, L. Robert. This Date in Baseball History. rev. ed. (Illus.). 56p. (Orig.). 1982. pap. 2.50 (ISBN 0-910137-00-5). Soc Am Baseball Res.
Eckhouse, Moe. Day-by-Day in Cleveland Indians History. LC 82-83939. (Illus.). 300p. (Orig.). 1983. pap. 9.95 (ISBN 0-88011-107-0). Leisure Pr.
Gallagher, Mark. Day-by-Day in New York Yankee History. LC 82-83934. (Illus.). 300p. (Orig.). 1983. pap. 9.95 (ISBN 0-88011-102-X). Leisure Pr.
Getz, Mike. Baseball's Three Thousand-Hit Men. 1982. 7.95 (ISBN 0-9608076-0-8). Gemmeg Pr.
Gewecke, Cliff. Day-by-Day in Dodgers History. LC 82-83940. (Illus.). 300p. (Orig.). 1983. pap. 9.95 (ISBN 0-88011-108-9). Leisure Pr.
Leichtman, Robert R. & Japikse, Carl. Active Meditation: The Western Tradition. LC 82-72785. 512p. 1983. 24.50 (ISBN 0-89804-040-X). Ariel OH.
Peterson, James A. & Penny, William J. A Pictorial History of the Chicago Cubs. LC 82-83951. (Illus.). 350p. 1983. 29.95 (ISBN 0-88011-116-X). Leisure Pr.
Rogosin, Donn. Invisible Men: Life in Baseball's Negro Leagues. LC 82-73026. (Illus.). 320p. 1983. 14.95 (ISBN 0-689-11363-3). Atheneum.
Uecker, Bob & Herskowitz, Mickey. Catcher in the Wry: Outrageous But True Stories of Baseball. 240p. 1983. pap. 3.50 (ISBN 0-515-07254-0). Jove Pubns.

BASEBALL-JUVENILE LITERATURE

Aaseng, Nate. Baseball: You Are the Manager. LC 82-268. (You Are the Coach Ser.). (Illus.). 104p. (gr. 4up). 1983. PLB 8.95g (ISBN 0-8225-1552-0). Lerner Pubns.
--Baseball's Hottest Hitters. (Sports Heroes Library). (Illus.). 80p. (gr. 4up). 1983. PLB 7.95g (ISBN 0-8225-1331-5). Lerner Pubns.
--Baseball's Power Hitters. (Sports Heroes Library). (Illus.). 80p. (gr. 4up). 1983. PLB 7.95g (ISBN 0-8225-1332-3). Lerner Pubns.
Cebulash, Mel. Ruth Marini: Dodger Ace. LC 82-20383. (Ruth Marini on the Mound Ser.). 160p. (gr. 4up). 1983. PLB 8.95g (ISBN 0-8225-0726-9). Lerner Pubns.
Hoffman, Phyllis. Play Ball with the New York Yankees. LC 82-20783. (Illus.). 48p. (Orig.). (gr. 4-7). 1983. pap. 2.95 (ISBN 0-689-70759-2, A-135, Aladdin). Atheneum.
Neuman, Jeffrey. Play Ball with the Los Angeles Dodgers. LC 82-20782. (Illus.). 48p. (Orig.). (gr. 4-7). 1983. pap. 2.95 (ISBN 0-689-70760-6, A-136, Aladdin). Atheneum.

BASEBALL CLUBS

see also names of individual clubs, e.g. New York Baseball Club (American League)

Borst, Bill. A Fan's Memoir: The Brooklyn Dodgers 1953-1957. 106p. (Orig.). 1982. pap. 5.95 (ISBN 0-940056-09-7). Chapter & Cask.
Foster, Mark. The Denver Bears: From Sandlots to Sellouts. (Illus.). 1983. price not set (ISBN 0-87108-643-3). Pruett.

BASEBALL STORIES

see also American Wit and Humor-Sports and Games

Plimpton, George. Out of My League. (Penguin Sports Library). 1983. pap. 4.95 (ISBN 0-14-006429-X). Penguin.

BASES, CHEMISTRY

Perrin, D. D., ed. Ionisation Constants of Inorganic Acids & Bases in Aqueous Solution, No.29. 2nd ed. (Chemical Data Ser.). 194p. 1982. 50.00 (ISBN 0-08-029214-3). Pergamon.

BASHFULNESS

Zimbardo, Philip G. & Radl, Shirley L. The Shyness Workbook. 208p. 1983. pap. 6.95 (ISBN 0-89104-141-9, A & W Visual Library). A & W Pubs.

BASHO, MATSUO, 1644-1694

Ueda, Makoto. Matsuo Basho. LC 82-48165. 202p. 1983. pap. 4.95 (ISBN 0-87011-553-7). Kodansha.

BASIC (COMPUTER PROGRAM LANGUAGE)

Albrecht, Bob L., et al. Atari Basic. LC 79-12513. (Self-Teaching Guides). 333p. 1979. pap. text ed. 8.95 (ISBN 0-471-06496-3). Wiley.
Albrecht, R. L., et al. Basic for Home Computers. LC 78-9010. (Self-Teaching Guides). 336p. 1978. 9.50x (ISBN 0-471-03204-2). Wiley.
Albrecht, Robert L., et al. Basic. 2nd ed. LC 77-14998. (Self-Teaching Guide Ser.). 325p. 1978. pap. text ed. 9.95 (ISBN 0-471-03500-9). Wiley.
BASIC for the IBM Personal Computer: A Quick Reference Guide. 1982. of 10 29.50 set (ISBN 0-471-87045-5). Wiley.
Berenson, Howard. Mostly BASIC Applications for Apple II, Bk. 2. Date not set. pap. 12.95 (ISBN 0-672-21864-X). Sams.
--Mostly BASIC Applications for your TRS-80, Bk.2. Date not set. pap. 12.95 (ISBN 0-672-21865-8). Sams.
Boillot, Michel & Horn, L. Wayne. BASIC. 3rd ed. (Illus.). 375p. 1983. pap. text ed. 13.95 (ISBN 0-314-69636-9). West Pub.
Brown, Jerald R. & Finkel, LeRoy. BASIC for the Apple II. LC 82-10962. (Self-Teaching Guide). 410p. 1982. pap. 12.95 (ISBN 0-471-86596-6). Wiley.
Burgess, Eric. Celestial Basic: Astronomy on Your Computer. LC 82-60187. (Illus.). 300p. 1982. pap. text ed. 13.95 (ISBN 0-89588-087-3). Sybex.
CES Industries, Inc. Staff. Basic Language. (Ed-Lab Experiment Manual Ser.). (Illus.). (gr. 9-12). 1982. write for info. lab manual (ISBN 0-86711-061-9). CES Industries.
Coan. Basic Apple BASIC. Date not set. 10.95 (ISBN 0-686-82001-0, 5626). Hayden.
Cranmer, John L. Basic Drilling Engineering Manual. 168p. 1982. 49.95x (ISBN 0-87814-199-5). Pennwell Pub.
Cranmer, John L., Jr. BASIC Reservoir Engineering Manual. 240p. 1982. 49.95x (ISBN 0-87814-196-0). Pennwell Pub.
Eisenbacher, Mario. Programming Your Timex-Sinclair 1000 in BASIC. (Illus.). 160p. 1983. 17.95 (ISBN 0-13-729871-4); pap. 9.95 (ISBN 0-13-729863-3). P-H.
Finkel, Leroy & Brown, Jerald R. Data File Programming in BASIC. LC 80-39790. (Self-Teaching Guide Ser.). 338p. 1981. pap. text ed. 12.95 (ISBN 0-471-08333-X). Wiley.
Forsythe, Alexander I., et al. Computer Science: Programming in BASIC. 148p. 1976. pap. 11.95x (ISBN 0-471-26684-1). Wiley.
Fox, Annie & Fox, David. Armchair BASIC: An Absolute Beginner's Guide to Programming in BASIC. 272p. (Orig.). 1982. pap. 11.95 (ISBN 0-931988-92-6). Osborne-McGraw.
Funkhouser, Robert. IBM BASIC for Business & Home. 1982. text ed. 19.95 (ISBN 0-8359-3019-X); pap. text ed. 14.95 (ISBN 0-8359-3018-1). Reston.
Galanter, Eugene. Kids & Computers: The Parent's Microcomputer Handbook; How to Write & Run Your Own BASIC Programs. LC 82-82310. 192p. 1983. pap. 7.95 (ISBN 0-399-50749-3, Perigee). Putnam Pub Group.
Ghedini, Silvano. Software for Photometric Astronomy. LC 82-8574. (Illus.). 1982. pap. text ed. 26.95 (ISBN 0-943396-00-X). Willman-Bell.
Haskell, Richard. Atari BASIC. (Illus.). 224p. 1983. 19.95 (ISBN 0-13-049809-2); pap. 13.95 (ISBN 0-13-049791-6). P-H.
--TRS-Eighty Extended Color BASIC. (Illus.). 192p. 1983. 19.95 (ISBN 0-13-931253-6); pap. 12.95 (ISBN 0-13-931246-3). P-H.
Held, Gilbert. Apple II BASIC: A Quick Reference Guide. 1982. of 10 29.50 set (ISBN 0-471-87043-9). Wiley.
--IBM PC Basic: Quick Reference Guide. (Illus.). 1982. pap. text ed. 2.95 (ISBN 0-471-87042-0). Wiley.
Helms, Harry. The BASIC Book: A Cross-Referencence Guide to the BASIC Language. (Illus.). 96p. 1983. pap. 6.95 (ISBN 0-07-027959-4, P&RB). McGraw.
Herman, William P. A Look into BASIC Using CP-6. 64p. 1982. pap. text ed. 3.95 (ISBN 0-8403-2761-7). Kendall-Hunt.
Holmes, B. J. Basic Programming: An Instructional Manual. 528p. 1982. pap. text ed. 11.00x (ISBN 0-905435-25-7). Verry.
Kitchen, Andrew. BASIC by Design: Structured Computer Programming in BASIC. (Software Ser.). (Illus.). 528p. pap. text ed. 18.95 (ISBN 0-13-060269-8). P-H.
Kressen, David C. Teach Your Computer to Think in BASIC. Jacobs, Russell, ed. (Illus.). 88p. (YA) (gr. 5-12). 1983. pap. text ed. 7.50 (ISBN 0-918272-10-6). Jacobs.
Lamoitier, J. P. BASIC Exercises for the Atari. 250p. 1983. pap. 12.95 (ISBN 0-89588-101-2); pap. text ed. 12.95. Sybex.
--Basic Exercises for the IBM Personal Computer. LC 82-60234. (Illus.). 252p. (Orig.). 1982. pap. text ed. 13.95 (ISBN 0-89588-088-1). Sybex.
Lien, David A. Learning IBM BASIC for the Personal Computer: CompuSoft Learning Ser. LC 82-73471. (Illus.). 448p. (Orig.). 1982. pap. 19.95 (ISBN 0-932760-13-9). CompuSoft.
--Learning Timex Sinclair BASIC for the Timex Sinclair 1000 & the ZX81. LC 82-73469. (CompuSoft Learning Ser.). (Illus.). 350p. (Orig.). 1983. pap. 14.95 (ISBN 0-932760-15-5). CompuSoft.
Mandell, Steven L. Computers & Data Processing Today with BASIC. (Illus.). 510p. pap. text ed. 8.95 (ISBN 0-314-70646-1). West Pub.
Marcus, Marvin. Discrete Mathematics: A Computational Approach Using BASIC. 1983. price not set (ISBN 0-914894-38-2). Computer Sci.
Mau. Create Word Puzzles with Your Microcomputer. 14.95 (ISBN 0-686-82004-5, 6251). Hayden.
Monro, Don. Start with BASIC on the TRS-80 Color Computer. 1982. text ed. 17.95 (ISBN 0-8359-7073-6); pap. text ed. 12.95 (ISBN 0-8359-7072-8). Reston.
Necessary, James R. The Necessary Steps to Basic: A Modular Approach. 168p. 1982. pap. text ed. 5.95x (ISBN 0-917974-90-5). Waveland Pr.
Norman, Robin. ZX-81 BASIC Book. Date not set. pap. 12.95 (ISBN 0-672-21957-3). Sams.
Payne, Donald. IBM BASIC. 200p. 1983. 22.95 (ISBN 0-13-448696-X); pap. 15.95 (ISBN 0-13-448688-9). P-H.
Peckham, H. Hands On BASIC: For the Apple II Plus Computer. 1982. pap. 19.95 (ISBN 0-07-049179-8). McGraw.
--Hands-On BASIC for the IBM Personal Computer. Adhesive bd. ed. 352p. 1982. 7.98 (ISBN 0-07-049184-4). McGraw.
Shelly, Gary B. & Cashman, Thomas J. Introduction to BASIC Programming. 1982. pap. text ed. 14.95x (ISBN 0-88236-118-X). Anaheim Pub Co.
Siragusa, Chris R. Introduction to Programming BASIC. 2nd ed. 340p. 1983. pap. text ed. write for info. (ISBN 0-87150-386-7, 8020). Prindle.
Society of Manufacturing Engineers. BASIC Programming Solutions for Manufacturing. 300p. 1982. 43.00 (ISBN 0-13-066332-8). P-H.
Spencer, Donald D. BASIC Programming. LC 82-17689. 1983. 14.95 (ISBN 0-89218-062-5). Camelot Pub.
--BASIC Quiz Book. 1983. 5.95x (ISBN 0-89218-076-5). Camelot Pub.
--BASIC Workbook for Microcomputers. 1983. 7.95x (ISBN 0-89218-040-4). Camelot Pub.

--Visual Masters for BASIC Programming. 2d ed. 1982. 9.95x (ISBN 0-89218-049-8). Camelot Pub.

SPSS Inc. SPSS-X Basics. 160p. 1983. 12.95x (ISBN 0-07-060524-6, C). McGraw.

Stephenson. Beginners Guide to BASIC Programming. 1982. text ed. 9.95. Butterworth.

Stern, R. A. & Stern, N. Concepts of Information Processing with Basic. 216p. 1982. pap. text ed. 13.95 (ISBN 0-471-87617-8). Wiley.

Thomas, D. Learn BASIC: A Guide to Programming the Texas Instruments Professional Compact Computer 40 (Texas Instruments Edition) 256p. 1983. write for info. (ISBN 0-07-064258-3, GB). McGraw.

Turner, Lawrence E. & Howson, Rosemary J. Basic BASIC for Basic Beginners. x, 293p. 1982. pap. text ed. 8.95 (ISBN 0-943872-82-0). Andrews Univ Pr.

Vickers, Ralph. Beyond Beginning BASIC. 300p. 1983. pap. 12.95 (ISBN 0-88056-126-2). Dilithium Pr.

Weber, Jeffrey R. & Chen, Daniel. BASIC Programs You Can Use: CP-M Edition. (WSI's How to Use Your Microcomputer Ser.). 250p. 1983. pap. 13.95 (ISBN 0-938862-25-1). Weber Systems.

--BASIC Programs You Can Use: IBM PC Edition. (WSI's How to Use Your Microcomputer Ser.). 250p. 1983. pap. 13.95 (ISBN 0-938862-24-3). Weber Systems.

--BASIC Programs You Can Use: Sinclair ZX81 Edit. (WSI's How to Use Your Microcomputer Ser.). 250p. 1983. pap. 13.95 (ISBN 0-938862-26-X). Weber Systems.

Zaks, Rodnay. Your First BASIC Program. 200p. 1983. pap. text ed. 9.95 (ISBN 0-89588-092-X). Sybex.

BASIC ENGLISH

Keltner, Autumn & Howard, Leann. Basic English for Adult Competency. 112p. 1983. pap. text ed. 4.95 (ISBN 0-13-060418-6). P-H.

BASKET-BALL

see Basketball

BASKET MAKING

Buck, Peter. Arts & Crafts of Hawaii: Twined Baskets, Sec. IV. (Special Publication Ser.: No. 45). (Illus.). 33p. 1957. pap. 3.00 (ISBN 0-910240-37-X). Bishop Mus.

La Plantz, Shereen. Plaited Basketry: The Woven Form. LC 82-90066. 1982. pap. 17.95 (ISBN 0-942002-00-8). Press Plantz.

BASKETBALL

Basketball. (Scorebooks Ser.). 2.95 (ISBN 0-88314-166-3). AAHPERD.

Basketball Schedule 1982-83. 1982. 1.95 (ISBN 0-89204-100-5). Sporting News.

Embry, Mike. Basketball in the Blue Grass State: The Championship Teams. LC 82-83924. (Illus.). 192p. (Orig.). 1983. pap. 7.95 (ISBN 0-88011-120-8). Leisure Pr.

Forker, Dom. The Ultimate Pro-Basketball Quiz Book. 1982. pap. 2.95 (ISBN 0-451-11842-1, AE1842, Sig). NAL.

Hammel, Bob, ed. The Champs 1981: Indiana Basketball. LC 81-47625. (Illus.). 128p. 1981. pap. 6.95x (ISBN 0-253-22700-3). Ind U Pr.

Hollander, Zander. The Complete Handbook of Pro-Basketball: 1983 Edition. 1982. pap. 3.95 (ISBN 0-451-11846-4, AE1846, Sig). NAL.

BASKETBALL-BIOGRAPHY

Johnson, Earvin & Levin, Richard. Magic. (Illus.). 256p. 1983. 13.50 (ISBN 0-670-44804-4). Viking Pr.

BASKETBALL-JUVENILE LITERATURE

Aaseng, Nate. Basketball: You Are the Coach. LC 82-17261. (You Are the Coach Ser.). (Illus.). 104p. (gr. 4up). 1983. PLB 8.95g (ISBN 0-8225-1553-9). Lerner Pubns.

--Basketball's Playmakers. (Sports Heroes Library). (Illus.). 80p. (gr. 4up). 1983. PLB 7.95g (ISBN 0-8225-1330-7). Lerner Pubns.

--Basketball's Sharpshooters. (Sports Heroes Library). (Illus.). 80p. (gr. 4up). 1983. PLB 7.95g (ISBN 0-8225-1329-3). Lerner Pubns.

Lerner, Mark. Careers in Basketball. LC 82-17265. (Early Career Bks.). (Illus.). 36p. (gr. 2-5). 1983. PLB 5.95g (ISBN 0-8225-0311-5). Lerner Pubns.

Liss, Howard. Strange but True Basketball Stories. LC 82-13138. (Random House Sports Library). (Illus.). 144p. (gr. 5-10). 1983. pap. 1.95 (ISBN 0-394-85631-7). Random.

BASKETBALL STORIES

see also American Wit and Humor-Sports and Games

Jones, Larry. Practice to Win. Date not set. pap. 3.95 (ISBN 0-8423-4887-5). Tyndale.

BASKETS

Wetherbee, Martha. Martha Wetherbee's Handbook of New Shaker Baskets. (Illus.). 50p. 1982. pap. 3.50 (ISBN 0-9609384-0-0). Taylor Home.

BASQUES

Paquette, Mary G. Basques to Bakersfield. (Illus.). 138p. 1982. 15.00 (ISBN 0-943500-00-1). Kern Historical.

BASS, ELECTRIC

see Guitar

BASS DRUM

see Drum

BASS FISHING

see also specific varieties of bass, e.g. Striped Bass

Olvington, Ray. Tactics on Bass: How to Fish the 23 Most Common Bass "Hotspots". (Illus.). 320p. 1983. 19.95 (ISBN 0-686-83864-5, ScribT). Scribner.

BASTOGNE, BATTLE OF, 1944-1945

see Ardennes, Battle of the, 1944-1945

BAT

see Bats

BATES, HERBERT ERNEST, 1905-

Vannatta, Dennis. H. E. Bates. (English Authors Ser.). 177p. 1983. lib. bdg. 17.95 (ISBN 0-8057-6844-0, Twayne). G K Hall.

BATHROOMS

Muir, Frank. An Irreverent & Almost Complete Social History of the Bathroom. LC 82-42838. 160p. 1983. 14.95 (ISBN 0-8128-2912-3); pap. 6.95 (ISBN 0-8128-6186-8). Stein & Day.

BATHS

see also Hydrotherapy

Sinnes, A. Cort. Spas & Hot Tubs: How to Plan, Install & Enjoy. 160p. 1982. pap. 7.95 (ISBN 0-89586-161-5). H P Bks.

BATON TWIRLING

Baton Twirling Handbook, 1979. Date not set. 3.50 (ISBN 0-686-43032-8). AAU Pubns.

BATRACHIA

see Amphibians

BATS

Fenton, N. Brock. Just Bats. (Illus.). 176p. 1983. 25.00x (ISBN 0-8020-2452-1); pap. 10.00 (ISBN 0-8020-6464-7). U of Toronto Pr.

Kunz, Thomas H., ed. Ecology of Bats. 450p. 1982. 49.50x (ISBN 0-306-40950-X, Plenum Pr). Plenum Pub.

BATTERIES

see also Artillery

Gabano, J. B., ed. Lithium Batteries. Date not set. price not set (ISBN 0-12-271180-7). Acad Pr.

U. S. Batteries & Electrical Vehicles. 1982. 995.00 (280). Predicasts.

BATTERIES, ELECTRIC

see Electric Batteries; Storage Batteries

BATTLE OF THE ATLANTIC, 1939-1945

see World War, 1939-1945-Atlantic Ocean

BATTLES-JUVENILE LITERATURE

Isaaman. Battlegames. 1983. pap. 4.95 (ISBN 0-86020-685-8, 24052). EDC.

BATTLESHIPS

see Warships

BAUDELAIRE, CHARLES PIERRE, 1821-1867

Feuillerat, Albert. Baudelaire et la Belle aux Cheveux D'or. 1941. text ed. 32.50x (ISBN 0-686-83483-6). Elliots Bks.

BAVARIA-HISTORY

Kershaw, Ian. Popular Opinion & Political Dissent in the Third Reich: Bavaria 1933-1945. 450p. 1983. 49.50 (ISBN 0-19-821922-9). Oxford U Pr.

BAYER, HERBERT

Hebhard, David. Herbert Bayer: Paintings, Architecture, Graphics. (Illus.). 8p. 1962. 0.75x (ISBN 0-686-99843-X). La Jolla Mus Contemp Art.

BAYES SOLUTION

see Bayesian Statistical Decision Theory

BAYESIAN STATISTICAL DECISION THEORY

Jeffrey, Richard C. The Logic of Decision. 2nd ed. LC 82-13465. 1983. lib. bdg. 19.00x (ISBN 0-226-39581-2). U of Chicago Pr.

BEACH, SYLVIA, 1887-1962

Fitch, Noel R. Sylvia Beach & the Lost Generation: A History of Literary Paris in the Twenties & Thirties. (Illus.). 1983. 25.00 (ISBN 0-393-01713-3). Norton.

BEACHES

see also Seashore

Rudman, Jack. Bay Constable II. (Career Examination Ser.: C-885). (Cloth bdg. avail. on request). pap. 12.00 (ISBN 0-8373-0885-2). Natl Learning.

--Beach Supervisor. (Career Examination Ser.: C-836). (Cloth bdg. avail. on request). pap. 10.00 (ISBN 0-8373-0836-4). Natl Learning.

BEACONSFIELD, BENJAMIN DISRAELI, 1ST EARL OF, 1804-1881

Bradford, Sarah. Disraeli. LC 82-48107. (Illus.). 128p. 1983. 19.95 (ISBN 0-8128-2899-2). Stein & Day.

Memorials of Lord Beaconsfield. 248p. 1983. Repr. of 1881 ed. lib. bdg. 50.00 (ISBN 0-89760-099-1). Telegraph Bks.

BEADWORK

Nathanson, Virginia. Making Bead Flowers & Bouquets. (Illus.). 192p. 1983. pap. 4.95 (ISBN 0-486-24464-4). Dover.

BEAGLES (DOGS)

see Dogs-Breeds-Beagles

BEAMS

see Girders

BEARDSLEY, AUBREY VINCENT, 1872-1898

Holdridge, Barbara. Aubrey Beardsley Designs from the Age of Chivalry. (The International Design Libary). (Illus.). 48p. (Orig.). 1983. pap. 2.95 (ISBN 0-88045-022-3). Stemmer Hse.

BEARINGS (MACHINERY)

Here are entered all works relating to the supports used in engineering, more particularly in machinery, especially for the moving parts.

see also Ball-Bearings; Friction; Lubrication and Lubricants

The Ball & Roller Bearing Industry. 1981. 395.00 (ISBN 0-686-38429-6, 326). Busn Trend.

Chang, C. M. & Kennedy, F. E. Advances in Computer-Aided Bearing Design. 156p. 1982. 30.00 (G00222). ASME.

BEASTS

see Bestiaries; Domestic Animals; Zoology

BEAT GENERATION

see Bohemianism

BEATITUDES

The Beautitudes. 20p. 1983. pap. 7.55 (ISBN 0-88479-037-1). Arena Lettres.

Drew, George. The Beatitudes: Attitudes for a Better Future. 63p. (Orig.). 1980. pap. 6.95 (ISBN 0-940754-03-7). Ed Ministries.

BEATLES

Bacon, David & Maslov, Norman. The Beatles' England: There Are Places I'll Remember. LC 81-82555. (Illus.). 144p. 1982. 20.00 (ISBN 0-9606736-0-1); pap. 12.95 (ISBN 0-9606736-1-X). Nine Hundred-Ten Pr.

Marchbank, Pearce, ed. With the Beatles: The Historic Photographs of Dezo Hoffmann. (Illus.). 96p. (Orig.). 1983. pap. 12.95 (ISBN 0-399-41009-0). Delilah Bks.

O'Grady, Terence. The Beatles: A Musical Revolution. (Music Ser.). 206p. 1983. lib. bdg. 15.95 (ISBN 0-8057-9453-0, Twayne). G K Hall.

Vollmer, Jurgen. Rock 'n' Roll Times: The Style & Spirit of the Early Beatles & Their First Fans. LC 82-22240. (Illus.). 108p. (Orig.). 1983. 16.95 (ISBN 0-87951-173-7); pap. 6.95 (ISBN 0-87951-182-6). Overlook Pr.

Wallgren, Mark. The Beatles on Record. LC 82-10305. (Illus.). 336p. Date not set. pap. 9.95 (ISBN 0-671-45682-2, Fireside). S&S.

BEATNIKS

see Bohemianism

BEATON, SIR CECIL

Buckland, Gail. Cecil Beaton War Photographs Nineteen Thirty-Nine to Nineteen Forty-Five. (Illus.). 192p. 1982. 24.95. Sci Bks Intl.

BEAUTIFUL, THE

see Art-Philosophy; Esthetics

BEAUTY

see Art-Philosophy; Beauty, Personal; Esthetics

BEAUTY, PERSONAL

see also Beauty Culture; Beauty Shops; Clothing and Dress; Cosmetics; Costume; Hair; Hairdressing; Skin; Teeth

Alexander, Jerome & Elins, Roberta. Be Your Own Makeup Artist: Jerome Alexander's Complete Makeup Workshop. LC 82-48171. 128p. 1983. 14.95 (ISBN 0-06-015088-2, HarpT). Har-Row.

Banner, Lois W. American Beauty. LC 82-4738. 352p. 1983. 17.95 (ISBN 0-394-51923-X). Knopf.

Brinkley, Christie. Beauty & the Beach. 1983. price not set (ISBN 0-671-46190-7). S&S.

Budd, Mavis. So Beautiful: My Grandmother's Natural Beauty Creams, Lotions, & Remedies. (Illus.). 64p. 1982. 7.95 (ISBN 0-7188-2511-X, Pub. by Salem Hse Ltd.). Merrimack Bk Serv.

Gallant, Ann. Principles & Techniques for the Beauty Specialist. 400p. 1980. 50.00x (ISBN 0-85950-444-1, Pub. by Thornes England). State Mutual Bk.

Harper, Ann & Lewis, Glenn. The Big Beauty Book: Glamour for the Fuller-Figure Woman. (Illus.). 256p. 1983. 17.50 (ISBN 0-03-060561-X). HR&W.

Imber, Gerald & Kurtin, Stephen B. Face Care: The Plan for Looking Younger Longer. 228p. 1983. 14.95 (ISBN 0-89479-127-3). A & W Pubs.

Mastroberti, Raun R. & Mastroberti, Angela. You: The Complete Guide to Beauty for Today & Tomorrow. (Illus.). 95p. 1980. 10.95 (ISBN 0-686-37959-4). Bracale & Assoc.

Rounce, John F. Science for Beauty Therapists. 272p. 1982. 33.00x (ISBN 0-85950-331-3, Pub. by Thornes England). State Mutual Bk.

Saunders, Rubie. The Beauty Book. Barish, Wendy, ed. (Just for Teens). 160p. (gr. 10 up). 1983. pap. 3.50 (ISBN 0-671-46271-7). Wanderer Bks.

--The Beauty Book. (Teen Survival Library). (Illus.). 160p. (gr. 9-12). 1983. PLB 9.79 (ISBN 0-671-46743-3). Messner.

Sommers, Susan. Beauty after Forty: How to put Time on your Side. (Illus.). 288p. 1983. 19.95 (ISBN 0-385-27229-4). Dial.

Stasi, Linda. Simply Beautiful: Quick Tips & Pro Tricks for Looking Great in No Time Flat. (Illus.). 128p. 1983. pap. 4.95 (ISBN 0-312-72591-4); pap. 49.50 ppk of 10 (ISBN 0-312-72592-2). St Martin.

Sternberg, James & Sternberg, Thomas. Great Skin at any Age: How to Keep Your Skin Looking Young without Plastic Surgery. 160p. 1983. 12.95 (ISBN 0-312-34674-3). St Martin.

Szekely, Edmond B. Creative Exercises for Health & Beauty. (Illus.). 48p. 1976. pap. 3.50 (ISBN 0-89564-048-1). IBS Intl.

Tiegs, Cheryl. The Way to Natural Beauty. (Illus.). 288p. 1983. pap. 8.95 (ISBN 0-671-47245-3, Fireside). S&S.

BEAUTY CULTURE

see also Beauty, Personal; Cosmetics; Hairdressing

Hagman, Ann & Arnould-Taylor, W. E. The Aestheticienne: Simple Theory & Practice. 196p. 1981. 30.00x (ISBN 0-85950-308-9, Pub. by Thornes England). State Mutual Bk.

Wilkinson, J. B. & Moore, R. J. Harry's Cosmeticology. 7th ed. (Illus.). 1982. 95.00 (ISBN 0-8206-0295-7). Chem Pub.

Wilkinson, J. B. & Moore, R. J., eds. Harry's Cosmeticology. 1982. 160.00x (ISBN 0-7114-5679-8, Pub. by Macdonald & Evans). State Mutual Bk.

BEAUTY SHOPS

see also Beauty Culture; Beauty, Personal; Cosmetics

Jeremiah, Rosemary W. How You Can Make Money in the Hairdressing Business. 112p. 1982. 29.00x (ISBN 0-85950-330-5, Pub. by Thornes England). State Mutual Bk.

BEAVERS

Lane, Margaret. The Beaver. (Illus.). 32p. 1983. pap. 3.50 (ISBN 0-8037-0637-5, 0340-100). Dial Bks Young.

Nentl, Jerolyn. Beaver. Schroeder, Howard, ed. (Wildlife Habits & Habitat Ser.). (Illus.). 48p. (gr. 4-5). 1983. lib. bdg. 8.95 (ISBN 0-89686-219-4). Crestwood Hse.

BEBOP MUSIC

see Jazz Music

BECKETT, SAMUEL BARCLAY, 1906-

Lyons, Charles. Samuel Beckett. (Grove Press Modern Dramatists Ser.). (Illus.). 196p. 1983. pap. 11.95 (ISBN 0-394-62411-4, Ever). Grove.

Morrison, Kristin. Cantors & Chronicles: The Use of Narrative in the Plays of Samuel Beckett & Harold Pinter. LC 82-16086. 240p. 1983. lib. bdg. 20.00x (ISBN 0-226-54130-4). U of Chicago Pr.

Schultz, Dieter. Fluchtpunkte der Negativitat Spiegelungen der Dramatik Samuel Becketts In Der Marxistischen Literaturkritik. 231p. (Ger.). 1982. write for info. (ISBN 3-8204-7113-8). P Lang Pubs.

BED RUGS

see Coverlets

BED-SORES

Barvenel, J. C. & Forbes, C. D., eds. Pressure Sores. 270p. 1981. 85.00x (ISBN 0-333-31889-7, Pub. by Macmillan England). State Mutual Bk.

BEDDING (HORTICULTURE)

see Gardening

BEDFORDSHIRE, ENGLAND

Dony, John G. & Dyer, James. The Story of Luton. 160p. 1982. 35.00x (ISBN 0-900804-11-4, Pub. by White Crescent England). State Mutual Bk.

Godber, Joyce. The Story of Bedford. 160p. 1982. 35.00x (ISBN 0-900804-24-6, Pub. by White Crescent England). State Mutual Bk.

Houfe, Simon. Old Bedfordshire. 88p. 1982. 25.00x (ISBN 0-900804-15-7, Pub. by White Crescent England). State Mutual Bk.

Meadows, Eric G. & Larkman, Simon. Pictorial Guide to Bedfordshire. 1982. 25.00x (ISBN 0-900804-10-6, Pub. by White Crescent England). State Mutual Bk.

Twaddle, W. Old Dunstable. 64p. 1982. 25.00x (ISBN 0-900804-08-4, Pub. by White Crescent England). State Mutual Bk.

White, Harold. Luton Past & Present. 152p. 1982. 35.00x (ISBN 0-900804-20-3, Pub. by White Crescent England). State Mutual Bk.

Wildman, Richard. Bygone Bedford. 96p. 1982. 25.00x (ISBN 0-900804-09-2, Pub. by White Crescent England). State Mutual Bk.

BEDOUINS

Ross, Heather C. The Art of Bedouin Jewellery. 1982. 59.00x (ISBN 0-907513-01-8, Pub. by Cave Pubns England). State Mutual Bk.

BEDROOM FURNITURE

Boeschen, John. The Build-a-Bed Book. (Illus.). 160p. 1982. 19.95 (ISBN 0-312-10766-8); pap. 10.95 (ISBN 0-312-10767-6). St Martin.

BEDSPREADS

see Coverlets

BEDUINS

see Bedouins

BEE

see Bees

BEE CULTURE

see also Bees; Honey

Morse, Roger. A Year in the Beeyard. (Illus.). 192p. 1983. 14.95 (ISBN 0-686-83827-0, ScribT). Scribner.

BEEF CATTLE

see also names of specific breeds of beef cattle

Baker, Frank H., ed. Beef Cattle Science Handbook: International Stockmen's School Handbooks, Vol. 19. 800p. 1982. 45.00 (ISBN 0-86531-509-4, Pub. in Cooperation with Winrock International). Westview.

BEEKEEPING

see Bee Culture

BEES

see also Bee Culture; Honey

Morse, Roger. A Year in the Beeyard. (Illus.). 192p. 1983. 14.95 (ISBN 0-686-83827-0, ScribT). Scribner.

BEETHOVEN, LUDWIG VAN, 1770-1827

Abraham, Gerald, ed. The New Oxford History of Music, Vol. VIII: The Age of Beethoven, 1790-1830. (Illus.). 778p. 1983. 49.95 (ISBN 0-19-316308-X). Oxford U Pr.

Mellers, Wilfrid. Beethoven & the Voice of God. LC 82-60014. (Illus.). 447p. 1983. 49.95 (ISBN 0-19-520402-6). Oxford U Pr.

Szekely, Edmond B. Ludwig Van Beethoven: Prometheus of the Modern World. (Illus.). 24p. 1973. pap. 2.95 (ISBN 0-89564-060-0). IBS Intl.

BEGIN, MENACHEM
Freedman. Israel in the Begin Era. 288p. 1982. 29.95 (ISBN 0-03-059376-X). Praeger.
Friedlander, Melvin A. Sadat & Begin: The Domestic Politics of Peacemaking. 350p. 1983. softcover 23.50x (ISBN 0-86531-949-9). Westview.
BEHAVIOR
see Conduct of Life
BEHAVIOR (PSYCHOLOGY)
see Animals, Habits and Behavior Of; Human Behavior
BEHAVIOR, COMPARATIVE
see Psychology, Comparative
BEHAVIOR IN ORGANIZATIONS
see Organizational Behavior
BEHAVIOR MODIFICATION
see also Behavior Therapy
Hersen, Michel & Eisler, Richard M., eds. Progress in Behavior Modification, Vol. 14. (Serial Publication). Date not set. price not set (ISBN 0-12-535614-5); price not set lib ed; price not set microfiche (ISBN 0-12-535700-1). Acad Pr.
Laborde, Genie S. Influencing with Integrity. 1983. 19.95 (ISBN 0-686-43050-6). Sci & Behavior.
Showalter, Carol. Three D: The Story of the New Christian Group Diet Program that is Sweeping the Country. 4.95 (ISBN 0-941478-05-X). Paraclete Pr.
Swanson, Lee H. Behavior Modification & Special Education: Perspectives & Trends. 288p. 1978. 29.50 (ISBN 0-8422-5300-9). Irvington.
Whitman, Thomas L. & Scibak, John W., eds. Behavior Modification with the Severely & Profoundly Retarded: Research & Application. LC 82-22720. (Monograph). Date not set. write for info. (ISBN 0-12-747280-0). Acad Pr.
BEHAVIOR OF CHILDREN
see Children–Management
BEHAVIOR THERAPY
Clarke, J. Christopher & Jackson, Arthur. Hypnosis & Behavior Therapy: The Treatment of Anxiety & Phobias. 1983. text ed. price not set (ISBN 0-8261-3450-5). Springer Pub.
Fensterheim, Herbert & Glazer, Howard I., eds. Behavioral Psychotherapy: Basic Principles & Case Studies in an Integrative Clinical Model. 220p. 1983. 20.00 (ISBN 0-87630-325-4). Brunner-Mazel.
Foa, Edna B. & Emmelkamp, Paul M. Failures in Behavior Therapy. (Personality Processes Ser.). 450p. 1983. 39.95 (ISBN 0-471-09238-X, Pub. by Wiley-Interscience). Wiley.
Franks, Cyril M. & Wilson, Terence G. Annual Review of Behavior Therapy, Vol. 8. LC 76-126864. 417p. 1982. text ed. 27.50 (ISBN 0-89862-612-9). Guilford Pr.
Garfield, Sol L. & Bergin, Allen E. Handbook of Psychotherapy & Behavior Change: An Empirical Analysis. 2nd ed. LC 78-8526. 1978. text ed. 60.95x (ISBN 0-471-29178-1). Wiley.
Goldstein, Alan & Foa, Edna B. Handbook of Behavioral Interventions. LC 79-16950. (Personality Processes Ser.). 1980. 38.50x (ISBN 0-471-01789-2, Pub. by Wiley-Interscience). Wiley.
Hall, R. Vance & Houten, Ron V. Managing Behavior: The Measurement of Behavior, Pt. 1. 1983. 4.50 (ISBN 0-89079-072-8). H & H Ent.
Latimer, Paul R. A Behavioral Medicine Approach: Functional Gastrointestinal Disorders. 176p. 1983. text ed. 23.95 (ISBN 0-8261-4310-5). Springer Pub.
Surwit, Richard S. & Williams, Redford B., Jr., eds. Behavioral Treatment of Disease, Vol. 19. (NATO Conference Ser. III: Human Factors). 482p. 1982. 42.50x (ISBN 0-686-83971-4, Plenum Pr). Plenum Pub.
BEHAVIORAL PHARMACOLOGY
see Psychopharmacology
BEHAVIORISM (PSYCHOLOGY)
see also Conditioned Response
Cosgrove, Mark P. B. F. Skinner's Behaviorism: An Analysis. 128p. (Orig.). 1982. pap. 5.95 (ISBN 0-310-44491-8). Zondervan.
Cullinhan, Douglas & Epstein, Michael. Behavior Disorders of Children & Adolescents. (Illus.). 384p. 1983. 23.95 (ISBN 0-13-072041-0). P-H.
Fensterheim, Herbert & Glazer, Howard I., eds. Behavioral Psychotherapy: Basic Principles & Case Studies in an Integrative Clinical Model. 220p. 1983. 20.00 (ISBN 0-87630-325-4). Brunner-Mazel.
Glaros & Coleman, James C. Contemporary Psychology & Effective Behavior. 5th ed. 1983. text ed. 22.95x (ISBN 0-673-15640-0). Scott F.
Mendlewicz, J. Biological Rhythms & Behavior. (Advances in Biological Psychiatry: Vol. 11). (Illus.). iv, 150p. 1983. pap. 54.00 (ISBN 3-8055-3672-0). S Karger.
Rapoport, Anatol. Mathematical Models in the Social Behavioral Sciences. 450p. 1983. 37.50 (ISBN 0-471-86449-8, Pub. by Wiley-Interscience). Wiley.
Tomb, David A. Child Psychiatry & Behavioral Pediatrics Case Studies. (Case Studies Ser.). 1982. pap. text ed. 22.50 (ISBN 0-87488-100-5). Med Exam.
Watson, J. B. Psychology from the Standpoint of a Behaviourist. Wolfe, Joseph, ed. (Classics of Psychology & Psychiatry Ser.). 464p. 1983. Repr. of 1919 ed. write for info. (ISBN 0-904014-44-4). F Pinter Pubs.

BEHISTUN INSCRIPTIONS
see Cuneiform Inscriptions
BEHRHORST, CARROLL, 1922-
Steltzer, Ulli. Health in the Highlands: The Chimaltenango Development Program of Guatemala. LC 82-48872. (Illus.). 128p. 1983. 30.00 (ISBN 0-295-95994-0); pap. 0.00 (ISBN 0-295-96024-8). U of Wash Pr.
BEING
see Ontology
BELGIAN LITERATURE–HISTORY AND CRITICISM
Maeterlinck, M. Maurice Maeterlinck: A Biographical Study with Two Essays. Allinson, Alfred, tr. from French. 142p. 1982. lib. bdg. 30.00 (ISBN 0-89760-579-9). Telegraph Bks.
BELGIUM–DESCRIPTION AND TRAVEL–GUIDEBOOKS
Fodor's Belgium & Luxembourg: 1983. 336p. 1983. traveltex 12.95 (ISBN 0-679-00898-5). McKay.
Michelin Green Guide: Beilgie-Luxemburg. (Green Guide Ser.). (Dutch.). 1983. pap. write for info. (ISBN 2-06-055131-5). Michelin.
Tomes, John. Belgium & Luxembourg. 6th ed. (Blue Guides Ser.). (Illus.). 1983. 25.50 (ISBN 0-393-01656-0); pap. 14.95 (ISBN 0-393-30063-3). Norton.
BELGIUM–HISTORY
Pierard, Louis. Belgian Problems Since the War. 1929. text ed. 29.50x (ISBN 0-686-83484-4). Elliots Bks.
BELGIUM–POLITICS AND GOVERNMENT
Crabb, John H., tr. from Fr. Constitution of Belgium & the Belgian Civil Code as Amended to September 1, 1982 in the Moniteur Belge. LC 82-18059. ix, 428p. 1982. text ed. 65.00x (ISBN 0-8377-0425-1). Rothman.
BELIEF AND DOUBT
Here are entered works treating the subject from the philosophical standpoint. Works on religious belief are entered under the heading Faith.
see also Agnosticism; Faith; Rationalism; Skepticism; Truth
Gutting, Gary. Religious Belief & Religious Skepticism. LC 82-50287. xi, 192p. 1983. pap. text ed. 9.95x (ISBN 0-268-01618-6, 85-16189). U of Notre Dame Pr.
BELIZE
Glassman, Paul. Belize Guide. 128p. (Orig.). 1983. pap. 9.95 (ISBN 0-930016-03-3). Passport Pr.
Turner, B. L., II & Harrison, Peter D., eds. Pulltrouser Swamp: Ancient Maya Habitat, Agriculture, & Settlement in Northern Belize. (Texas Pan American Ser.). (Illus.). 296p. text ed. 22.50x (ISBN 0-292-75067-6). U of Tex Pr.
BELLOC, HILAIRE, 1870-1953
Markel, Michael N. Hilaire Belloc. (English Authors Ser.). 1982. lib. bdg. 15.95 (ISBN 0-8057-6833-5, Twayne). G K Hall.
BELLOWS, GEORGE WESLEY, 1882-1925
Carmean, E. A. Bellows: The Boxing Pictures. (Illus.). 1982. pap. 9.50 (ISBN 0-89468-028-5). Natl Gallery Art.
BELLY DANCE
Wilson, S. & Wilson, A. The Belly Dance Book: The Serena Technique for Learning Belly Dancing. 224p. 1983. 9.95 (ISBN 0-07-070811-8, GB). McGraw.
BELT CONVEYORS
see Conveying Machinery
BEN-GURION, DAVID, 1887-
Kurzman, Dan. Ben-Gurion: Prophet of Fire. 1983. price not set (ISBN 0-671-23094-8). S&S.
BENEDICT, RUTH (FULTON), 1887-1948
Modell, Judith. Ruth Benedict: Patterns of a Life. LC 82-21989. (Illus.). 400p. 1983. 30.00x (ISBN 0-8122-7874-7). U of Pa Pr.
BENEDICTINES
Heufelder, Emmanuel. The Way to God According to the Rule of Saint Benedict. Eberle, Luke, tr. from Ger. (Cistercian Studies: No. 49). 1983. price not set (ISBN 0-87907-849-9). Cistercian Pubns.
BENEFIT SOCIETIES
see Friendly Societies
BENEVOLENT INSTITUTIONS
see Charities; Children–Institutional Care; Hospitals
BENGAL–SOCIAL CONDITIONS
Greenough, Paul R. Prosperity & Misery in Modern Bengal: The Famine of 1943-1944. (Illus.). 362p. 1982. 37.00x (ISBN 0-19-503082-6). Oxford U Pr.
BENNETT, ARNOLD, 1867-1931
Darton, Harvey F. Arnold Bennett. 127p. 1982. lib. bdg. 17.50 (ISBN 0-8495-1139-9). Arden Lib.
BENTHAM, JEREMY, 1748-1832
Harr, Herbert L. Essays on Bentham: Jurisprudence & Political Theory. (Illus.). 250p. 1982. text ed. 29.95x (ISBN 0-19-825348-6); pap. text ed. 12.95x (ISBN 0-19-825468-7). Oxford U Pr.
BENTON, THOMAS HART, 1889-1975
Benton, Thomas H. An Artist in America. 4th rev. ed. LC 82-20279. (Illus.). 480p. 1983. text ed. 25.00 (ISBN 0-8262-0394-9); pap. 12.95 (ISBN 0-8262-0399-X). U of Mo Pr.
BERDIAEV, NIKOLAI ALEKSANDROVICH, 1874-1948
Wood, Douglas K. Men Against Time: Nicolas Berdyaev, T. S. Eliot, Aldous Huxley, & C. G. Jung. LC 82-526. x, 254p. 1982. text ed. 22.50x (ISBN 0-7006-0222-4). Univ Pr KS.

BEREAVEMENT–PSYCHOLOGICAL ASPECTS
Lortz, Richard. Bereavements. LC 80-65001. 215p. 1983. pap. 8.95 (ISBN 0-932966-32-2). Permanent Pr.
Parkes, Colin M. & Weiss, Robert S. Recovery from Bereavement. 1983. 17.95 (ISBN 0-465-06868-5). Basic.
Smith, Carole R. Social Work with the Dying & Bereaved. Campling, Jo, ed. (Practical Social Work Ser.). 160p. 1982. 40.00x (ISBN 0-333-30894-8, Pub. by Macmillan England). State Mutual Bk.
BERG, ALBAN, 1885-1935
Carner, Mosco. Alban Berg. 2nd rev. ed. (Illus.). 255p. 1983. text ed. 35.00x (ISBN 0-8419-0841-9). Holmes & Meier.
Jarman, Douglas. The Music of Alban Berg. (Illus.). 278p. 1983. pap. 11.95 (ISBN 0-520-04954-3, CAL 623). U of Cal Pr.
BERLIN
Erickson, John. The Road To Berlin. (Illus.). 700p. 1983. 30.00 (ISBN 0-89158-795-0). Westview.
BERLIN–HISTORY
Roters, Eberhard. Berlin Nineteen Ten to Nineteen Thirty-Three. LC 82-50423. (Illus.). 268p. 1982. 60.00 (ISBN 0-8478-0439-9). Rizzoli Intl.
BERLIN QUESTION (1945-)
Shlaim, Avi. The United States & the Berlin Blockade, Nineteen Forty-Eight to Nineteen Forty-Nine: A Study in Crisis Decision-Making. LC 81-19363. (International Crisis Behavior Ser.: Vol. 2). 440p. 1983. 38.00x (ISBN 0-520-04385-5). U of Cal Pr.
BERLIOZ, HECTOR, 1803-1869
Macdonald, Hugh. Berlioz. (The Master Musicians Ser.). 272p. 1982. text ed. 17.95x (ISBN 0-460-03156-2, Pub. by J. M. Dent England). Biblio Dist.
BERMUDA ISLANDS
Verrill, Addison E. Bermuda Islands: An Account of Their Scenery, Climate, Productions, Etc. 1903. pap. text ed. 49.50x (ISBN 0-686-83486-0). Elliots Bks.
BERMUDA ISLANDS–DESCRIPTION AND TRAVEL–GUIDEBOOKS
Bermuda Travel Guide. (Berlitz Travel Guides). (Illus.). 1982. pap. 4.95 (ISBN 0-02-969860-X; Berlitz). Macmillan.
Birnbaum, Stephen. The Caribbean, Bermuda & the Bahamas. (Get 'em & Go Travel Guide Ser.). 1982. 11.95 (ISBN 0-686-84795-4). HM.
BERRIES
Alaska Magazine, ed. Alaska Wild Berry Guide & Cookbook. (Illus.). 216p. 1983. pap. 13.95 (ISBN 0-88240-229-3). Alaska Northwest.
Stebbins, Robert L. & Walheim, Lance. Western Fruit, Berries & Nuts: How to Select, Grow & Enjoy. (Illus.). 192p. (Orig.). pap. 7.95 (ISBN 0-89586-078-3). H P Bks.
BERTALANFFY, LUDWIG VON, 1901-1972
Davidson, Mark. Uncommon Sense: The Life & Thought of Ludwig von Bertalanffy (1901-1972), Father of General Systems Theory. LC 82-16900. 256p. 1983. 16.95 (ISBN 0-87477-165-X). HM.
BEST BOOKS
see Bibliography–Best Books
BESTIARIES
Hecht, Arthur & Stevens, Byron. The Business Beastiary. LC 82-42730. 96p. 1983. 14.95 (ISBN 0-8128-2908-5); pap. 7.95 (ISBN 0-8128-6176-0). Stein & Day.
May, John & Marten, Michael. The Book of Beasts. LC 82-40374. (Illus.). 192p. 1983. pap. 12.95 (ISBN 0-670-17915-9). Viking Pr.
BETCHERRYGAH
see Budgerigars
BETON
see Concrete
BETTING
see Gambling
BEVERAGE INDUSTRY
see also Wine and Wine Making
Rudman, Jack. Beverage Control Investigator. (Career Examination Ser.: C-918). (Cloth bdg. avail. on request). pap. 10.00 (ISBN 0-8373-0918-2). Natl Learning.
BEVERAGES
see also Alcoholic Beverages
also names of beverages, e.g. Cocoa, Coffee, Tea
Beverages. (Good Cook Ser.). 1983. lib. bdg. 19.96 (ISBN 0-8094-2946-2, Pub. by Time-Life). Silver.
Brandt, Jane. Grogs, Granites, Slushes & Flings: Drinks Without Liquor. LC 82-40504. (Illus.). 192p. 1983. pap. 4.95 (ISBN 0-89480-358-1). Workman Pub.
Mario, Thomas. Playboy's New Bar Guide. 400p. 1983. pap. 3.95 (ISBN 0-515-07267-2). Jove Pubns.
The U. S. Hot Beverage Market. 1982. 475.00 (ISBN 0-686-38412-1, 126). Busn Trend.
BEYLE, MARIE HENRI
see Stendhal (Marie Henri Beyle), 1783-1842
BHAGAVADGITA
Feuerstein, Georg. Bhagavad Gita: An Introduction. LC 82-42702. 191p. 1983. pap. 6.75 (ISBN 0-8356-0575-2, Quest). Theos Pub Hse.
BHUTAN
Gibbons, Robert & Ashford, Bob. The Kingdoms of the Himalayas: Nepal, Sikkim, & Bhutan. (Illus.). 250p. 1983. 17.50 (ISBN 0-88254-802-6). Hippocrene Bks.
BIBLE–ANIMALS
see Bible–Natural History

BIBLE–ANTHROPOLOGY
see Man (Theology)
BIBLE–ANTIQUITIES
see also Palestine–Antiquities
also subdivision Antiquities under names of Biblical countries and cities
Bowden, John. Archeology & the Bible. 24p. 1982. pap. 3.00 (ISBN 0-910309-00-0). Am Atheist.
Freedman, David N., ed. The Biblical Archaeologist Reader, Vol. 4. 1983. text ed. price not set (ISBN 0-89757-509-1, Pub. by Am Sch Orient Res); pap. text ed. price not set (ISBN 0-89757-506-7). Eisenbrauns.
Szekely, Edmond B. The Great Experiment. (Search for the Ageless Ser.: Vol. 2). (Illus.). 328p. 1977. pap. 8.80 (ISBN 0-89564-023-6). IBS Intl.
--My Unusual Adventures on the Five Continents in Search for the Ageless. (Search for the Ageless Ser.: Vol. 1). (Illus.). 212p. 1977. pap. 7.80 (ISBN 0-89564-022-8). IBS Intl.
BIBLE–APPRECIATION
Pryor, Neale. You Can Trust Your Bible. 3.60 (ISBN 0-89137-524-4). Quality Pubns.
Ulmer, L. The Bible That Wouldn't Burn. 1983. pap. 3.50 (ISBN 0-570-03634-8). Concordia.
BIBLE–ARCHAEOLOGY
see Bible–Antiquities
BIBLE–ATLASES
see Bible–Geography–Maps
BIBLE–BIOGRAPHY
see also Apostles; Children in the Bible; Prophets; Women In the Bible
also names of individuals mentioned in the Bible, e.g. Moses; Mary, Virgin
Alexander, George M. The Handbook of Biblical Personalities. 320p. 1981. pap. 6.95 (ISBN 0-8164-2316-4). Seabury.
Cully, Iris & Cully, Kendig B. From Aaron to Zerubbabel: Profiles of Bible People. 168p. (Orig.). 1976. pap. 1.00 (ISBN 0-8164-1232-4). Seabury.
Estrada, Leobardo. Grandes Hombres de la Biblia. 235p. 1975. pap. 5.25 (ISBN 0-311-04656-8). Casa Bautista.
Wiesel, Elie. Five Biblical Portraits. LC 81-40458. vii, 157p. 1983. pap. 4.95 (ISBN 0-268-00962-7, 85-09622). U of Notre Dame Pr.
BIBLE–BIRDS
see Bible–Natural History
BIBLE–BOTANY
see Bible–Natural History
BIBLE–CANON
MacDonald, Dennis Ronald. The Legend & the Apostle: The Battle for Paul in Story & Canon. LC 82-21953. 144p. (Orig.). 1983. pap. 9.95 (ISBN 0-664-24464-5). Westminster.
BIBLE–CHARACTERS
see Bible–Biography
BIBLE–CHILDREN
see Children in the Bible
BIBLE–CODICES
see Bible–Manuscripts
BIBLE–COMMENTARIES
Here are entered only commentaries on the whole Bible. Commentaries on the New Testament, and portions of the New Testament, precede commentaries on the Old Testament, and portions of the Old testament.
Bowden, John. The Bible Contradicts Itself. 36p. 1982. pap. 3.00 (ISBN 0-686-81732-X). Am Atheist.
Criswell, W. A. Great Doctrines of the Bible, Vol. 2. 192p. 1982. 9.95 (ISBN 0-310-43860-8). Zondervan.
Dean, Robert J. Layman's Bible Book Commentary: Luke, Vol. 17. 1983. 4.75 (ISBN 0-8054-1187-9). Broadman.
Hayes, John H. & Holladay, Carl. Biblical Exegesis. LC 82-17999. 1982. pap. 6.95 (ISBN 0-8042-0030-0). John Knox.
Karris, Robert J., ed. Collegeville Bible Commentary Series, 11 Vols. 1983. Set. pap. 25.00. Liturgical Pr.
McKim, Donald K., ed. The Authoritative Word: Essays on the Nature of Scripture. 288p. 1983. pap. 10.95 (ISBN 0-8028-1948-6). Eerdmans.
McQuilkin, Robertson. Understanding & Applying the Bible. (Orig.). 1983. pap. 9.95 (ISBN 0-8024-0457-X). Moody.
Marshall, Howard I. One & Two Thessalonians. (New Century Bible Commentary Ser.). 256p. 1983. pap. 6.95 (ISBN 0-8028-1946-X). Eerdmans.
Mears, Henrietta C. Panorama du Nouveau Testament. Cosson, Annie, ed. Perru, Philippe Le, tr. from Eng. Orig. Title: What the Bible Is All About. 347p. (Fr.). 1982. pap. 4.75 (ISBN 0-8297-1244-5). Life Pubs Intl.
Pinson, William M. The Word Topical Bible of Issues & Answers. 1983. pap. 7.95 (ISBN 0-8499-2934-2). Word Pub.
Seagren, Daniel R. Love Carved in Stone: Ten Commandments. 1983. pap. text ed. 2.50 (ISBN 0-8307-0840-5). Regal.
Shank, Stanley, ed. Test Your Bible Power: A Good Book Quiz. (Epiphany Bks.). 1983. pap. 1.95 (ISBN 0-345-30663-5). Ballantine.
Thomas Foundation. Keys to Understanding & Teaching Your Bible. (Illus.). 1983. pap. 5.95 (ISBN 0-8407-5826-X). Nelson.

BIBLE–COMMENTARIES–N. T.

Here are entered only Commentaries on the New Testament as a whole.

Collins, Raymond F. Introduction to the New Testament. (Illus.). 480p. 1983. 24.95 (ISBN 0-385-18126-4). Doubleday.

Elliott, John H. & Martin, R. A. Augsburg Commentary on the New Testament. LC 82-70962. 192p. (Orig.). 1982. 7.50 (ISBN 0-8066-1937-6, 10-9042). Augsburg.

Farmer, William R. & Farkasfalvy, Denis. The Formation of the New Testament: An Ecumenical Approach. LC 82-62417. (Theological Inquiries Ser.). 1983. pap. 8.95 (ISBN 0-8091-2495-5). Paulist Pr.

Fehl, Jim, ed. Standard Lesson Commentary, 1983-84. (Illus.). 456p. pap. 6.50 (ISBN 0-87239-616-9). Standard Pub.

Guthrie, Donald. The Epistle to the Hebrews: An Introduction & Commentary. (Tyndale New Testament Commentaries: Vol. 15). 1983. pap. 4.95 (ISBN 0-8028-1427-1). Eerdmans.

Jesus Chist's One Hundred Rule Communication Program: An Axumatyation of the New Testament. (Analysis Ser.: No. 12). 1983. pap. 10.00 (ISBN 0-686-42848-X). Inst Analysis.

BIBLE–COMMENTARIES–N. T. ACTS

Kurz, William S. & Karris, Robert J. The Acts of the Apostles, No. 5. LC 82-20872. (Collegeville Bible Commentary Ser.). (Illus.). 112p. 1983. pap. 2.50 (ISBN 0-8146-1305-5). Liturgical Pr.

Ogilvie, Lloyd J. The Communicator's Commentary-Acts, Vol. 5. (The Communicator's Commentaries Ser.). 1982. 14.95 (ISBN 0-8499-0158-8). Word Pub.

BIBLE–COMMENTARIES–N. T. CATHOLIC EPISTLES

Here are entered commentaries on the Catholic Epistles as a whole, as well as on one or more of the following Epistles: James, John, Jude, Peter.

Cedar, Paul A. The Communicator's Commentary-James 1, 2, Peter, Jude, Vol. 2. Ogilvie, Lloyd J., ed. (The Communicator's Commentaries Ser.). 1983. 14.95. Word Pub.

Hobbs, Herschel H. The Epistles of John. 176p. 1983. 9.95 (ISBN 0-8407-5274-1). Nelson.

BIBLE–COMMENTARIES–N. T. COLOSSIANS

Havener, Ivan & Karris, Robert J. First Thessalonians, Philippians, Philemon, Second Thessalonians, Colossians, Ephesians, No. 8. (Collegeville Bible Commentary Ser.). (Illus.). 112p. 1983. pap. 2.50 (ISBN 0-8146-1308-X). Liturgical Pr.

BIBLE–COMMENTARIES–N. T. CORINTHIANS

Bratcher, R. G. Translator's Guide to Paul's First Letter to the Corinthians. (Helps for Translators Ser.). 1982. pap. 2.55 (ISBN 0-8267-0185-X, 08566). Am Bible.

Chafin, Kenneth L. & Ogilvie, Lloyd J. The Communicator's Commentary: Corinthians 1, 2, Vol. 7. 1983. 14.95 (ISBN 0-8499-0347-5). Word Bks.

Getty, Mary A. & Karris, Robert J. First Corinthians, Second Corinthians, No. 7. (Collegeville Bible Commentary Ser.). 128p. 1983. pap. 2.50 (ISBN 0-8146-1307-1). Liturgical Pr.

Ishee, John A. God's Wisdom-God's Way: Studies in 1 Corinthians. 32p. (Orig.). 1983. pap. 3.50 (ISBN 0-939298-20-1). J M Prods.

BIBLE–COMMENTARIES–N. T. EPHESIANS

Havener, Ivan & Karris, Robert J. First Thessalonians, Philippians, Philemon, Second Thessalonians, Colossians, Ephesians, No. 8. (Collegeville Bible Commentary Ser.). (Illus.). 112p. 1983. pap. 2.50 (ISBN 0-8146-1308-X). Liturgical Pr.

Lloyd-Jones, D. Martyn. Lloyd-Jones Expositions of Ephesians, 8 Vols. 1983. 79.95 (ISBN 0-8010-5623-3). Baker Bk.

BIBLE–COMMENTARIES–N. T. EPISTLES OF JOHN

see Bible–Commentaries–N. T. Catholic Epistles

BIBLE–COMMENTARIES–N. T. EPISTLES OF PAUL

Jeremiah, David. Philippians: Twenty-Six Daily Bible Studies. (Steps to Higher Ground Ser.). 1983. pap. 1.50 (ISBN 0-86508-208-1). BCM Pubns.

Kasemann, Ernst. Perspectives on Paul. LC 79-157540. 184p. 1982. pap. 7.50 (ISBN 0-8006-1730-4, 1-1730). Fortress.

BIBLE–COMMENTARIES–N. T. GALATIANS

Pilch, John J. & Karris, Robert J. Galatians & Romans, No. 6. (Collegeville Bible Commentary Ser.). 80p. 1983. pap. 2.50 (ISBN 0-8146-1306-3). Liturgical Pr.

BIBLE–COMMENTARIES–N. T. GOSPELS

Here are entered commentaries on the Gospels as a whole, as well as on the Individual Gospels, Matthew, Mark, Luke, John.

Bratcher, R. G. Translator's Guide to the Gospel of Luke. (Helps for Translators Ser.). 1982. pap. 3.95 (ISBN 0-8267-0181-7, 08712). Am Bible.

Coniaris, A. M. The Message of the Sunday Gospel Readings, Vol. 1. 1982. pap. 6.95 (ISBN 0-937032-26-3). Light&Life Pub Co MN.

Craddock, Fred B. John. Hayes, John H., ed. LC 82-48095. (Knox Preaching Guides Ser.). 149p. 1982. pap. 4.95 (ISBN 0-8042-3241-5). John Knox.

Holloway, Richard. Signs of Glory. 96p. 1983. pap. 5.95 (ISBN 0-8164-2412-8). Seabury.

Jeremiah, David. John I, II, III: Twenty-Six Daily Bible Studies. (Steps to Higher Ground Ser.). 1983. pap. 1.50 (ISBN 0-86508-206-5). BCM Pubns.

Ludlow, Daniel H. Companion to Your Study of the Four Gospels. 454p. 1982. pap. 9.95 (ISBN 0-87747-945-3). Deseret Bk.

McKenna, David L. The Communicator's Commentary-Mark, Vol. 2. Ogilvie, Lloyd, ed. (The Communicator's Commentaries Ser.). 1982. 14.95 (ISBN 0-8499-0155-3). Word Pub.

Mitchell, John G. An Everlasting Love: A Devotional Commentary on the Gospel of John. LC 82-22285. 1982. 13.95 (ISBN 0-88070-005-X). Multnomah.

Mumford, Thomas M. Horizontal Harmony of the Gospels. 169p. 1982. pap. 5.95 (ISBN 0-87747-942-9). Deseret Bk.

Robertson, Arthur. Matthew. (Everyman's Bible Commentary Ser.). (Orig.). 1983. pap. 4.50 (ISBN 0-8024-0233-X). Moody.

Steiner, Rudolf. The Gospel of St. John & its Relation to the Other Gospels. rev. ed. Easton, Stewart, ed. Lockwood, Samuel & Lockwood, Loni, trs. from Ger. 298p. 1982. 14.00 (ISBN 0-88010-015-X); pap. 8.95 (ISBN 0-88010-014-1). Anthroposophic.

Welch, Reuben. We Really Do Need Each Other. 112p. 1982. pap. 5.95 (ISBN 0-310-70221-6). Zondervan.

BIBLE–COMMENTARIES–N. T. HEBREWS

Hagner, Donald A. Hebrews: A Good News Commentary. LC 82-48410. (Good News Commentary Ser.). 288p. 1983. pap. 8.61 (ISBN 0-06-063555-X, HarpR). Har-Row.

MacRae, George W. Hebrews. Karris, Robert J., ed. (Collegeville Bible Commentary Ser.: No. 10). 64p. 1983. pap. 2.50 (ISBN 0-8146-1310-1). Liturgical Pr.

Peterson, David. Hebrews & Perfection: An Examination of the Concept of Perfection in the Epistle to the Hebrews. LC 82-4188. (Society for New Testament Monograph 47). 260p. 1982. 39.50 (ISBN 0-521-24408-0). Cambridge U Pr.

BIBLE–COMMENTARIES–N. T. JAMES

see Bible–Commentaries–N. T. Catholic Epistles

BIBLE–COMMENTARIES–N. T. JOHN

see Bible–Commentaries–N. T. Gospels

BIBLE–COMMENTARIES–N. T. JUDE

see Bible–Commentaries–N. T. Catholic Epistles

BIBLE–COMMENTARIES–N. T. LUKE

see Bible–Commentaries–N. T. Gospels

BIBLE–COMMENTARIES–N. T. MARK

see Bible–Commentaries–N. T. Gospels

BIBLE–COMMENTARIES–N. T. MATTHEW

see Bible–Commentaries–N. T. Gospels

BIBLE–COMMENTARIES–N. T. PASTORAL EPISTLES

Here are entered commentaries on the Pastoral epistles as a whole as well as those on Titus or Timothy.

Neyrey, Jerome H. First Timothy, Second Timothy, Titus, James, First Peter, Second Peter, Jude, No. 9. Karris, Robert J., ed. (Collegeville Bible Commentary Ser.). 112p. 1983. pap. 2.50 (ISBN 0-8146-1309-8). Liturgical Pr.

BIBLE–COMMENTARIES–N. T. PETER

see Bible–Commentaries–N. T. Catholic Epistles

BIBLE–COMMENTARIES–N. T. PHILIPPIANS

Havener, Ivan & Karris, Robert J. First Thessalonians, Philippians, Philemon, Second Thessalonians, Colossians, Ephesians, No. 8. (Collegeville Bible Commentary Ser.). (Illus.). 112p. 1983. pap. 2.50 (ISBN 0-8146-1308-X). Liturgical Pr.

BIBLE–COMMENTARIES–N. T. REVELATION

Easu & Rodehaver, Gladys K., eds. Book II of Revelations for the Aquarian Age. 1983. pap. 6.95 (ISBN 0-930208-14-5). Mangan Bks.

Freligh, H. M. Studies in Revelation, 4 Vols. Schroeder, E. H., ed. 327p. 1969. pap. text ed. 1.50 ea.; Vol. 1. (ISBN 0-87509-139-3); Vol. 2. (ISBN 0-87509-140-7); Vol. 3. (ISBN 0-87509-141-5); Vol. 4. (ISBN 0-87509-142-3). Chr Pubns.

Perkins, Pheme. The Book of Revelation. Karris, Robert J., ed. (Collegeville Bible Commentary Ser.: No. 11). 96p. 1983. Vol. 11. pap. 2.50 (ISBN 0-8146-1311-X). Liturgical Pr.

BIBLE–COMMENTARIES–N. T. ROMANS

Ishee, John A. Everyman's Gospel: Studies in Romans. 32p. (Orig.). 1983. pap. 3.50 (ISBN 0-939298-19-8). J M Prods.

Kenyon, Don J. Romans, 2 vols. Incl. Vol. 1. Triumph of Truth. pap. text ed. 3.95 (ISBN 0-87509-147-4); leader's guide 2.95 (ISBN 0-87509-265-9); Vol 2. Glory of Grace. pap. text ed. 3.95 (ISBN 0-87509-148-2); leader's guide 2.95 (ISBN 0-87509-266-7). 1978. pap. Chr Pubns.

Landes, Paula F. Augustine on Romans: Propositions From the Epistle to the Romans & Unfinished Commentary on the Epistle to the Romans. LC 82-10259. (Society of Biblical Literature, Texts & Translations Ser.). 124p. 1982. pap. 12.75 (ISBN 0-89130-583-1, 06-02-23). Scholars Pr CA.

Pilch, John J. & Karris, Robert J. Galatians & Romans, No. 6. (Collegeville Bible Commentary Ser.). 80p. 1983. pap. 2.50 (ISBN 0-8146-1306-3). Liturgical Pr.

Resources for Renewal (Romans) Leader's Guide. 48p. (Orig.). 1982. pap. 1.95 (ISBN 0-89367-080-4). Light & Life.

Resources for Renewal (Romans) Student Guide. 64p. 1982. pap. 2.50 (ISBN 0-89367-079-0). Light & Life.

Wenger, J. C. A Lay Guide to Romans. LC 82-15789. 160p. (Orig.). 1983. pap. 8.95 (ISBN 0-8361-3316-1). Herald Pr.

BIBLE–COMMENTARIES–N. T. THESSALONIANS

Havener, Ivan & Karris, Robert J. First Thessalonians, Philippians, Philemon, Second Thessalonians, Colossians, Ephesians, No. 8. (Collegeville Bible Commentary Ser.). (Illus.). 112p. 1983. pap. 2.50 (ISBN 0-8146-1308-X). Liturgical Pr.

Hendrix, John D. To Thessalonians with Love. LC 81-70974. (Orig.). 1983. pap. 6.50 (ISBN 0-8054-1312-X). Broadman.

Palmer, Earl. Thessalonians I & II: A Good News Commentary. LC 82-48409. (Good News Commentary Ser.). 128p. (Orig.). 1983. pap. 6.68 (ISBN 0-06-066455-X, HarpR). Har-Row.

BIBLE–COMMENTARIES–N. T. TIMOTHY

see Bible–Commentaries–N. T. Pastoral Epistles

BIBLE–COMMENTARIES–N. T. TITUS

see Bible–Commentaries–N. T. Pastoral Epistles

BIBLE–COMMENTARIES–O. T.

Here are entered only Commentaries on the Old Testament as a whole.

Charlesworth, James H., ed. Old Testament Pseudepigrapha, Vol. I: Apocalyptic Literature & Testaments. LC 80-2443. 1000p. 1983. 35.00 (ISBN 0-385-09630-5). Doubleday.

Flanders, Henry J., Jr., et al. People of the Covenant: An Introduction to the Old Testament. 2nd ed. (Illus.). 539p. 1973. 22.50 (ISBN 0-471-07011-4). Wiley.

Hecke, Karl-Heinz. Die Alttestamentlichen Perikopen der Reihen III-VI. 203p. (Ger.). 1982. write for info. (ISBN 3-8204-5759-3). P Lang Pubs.

Hightower, James E., Jr. Voices from the Old Testament. LC 81-68611. (Orig.). 1983. pap. 3.95 (ISBN 0-8054-2245-5). Broadman.

L'Heureux, Conrad E. In & Out of Paradise: From Adam & Eve to the Tower of Babel. LC 82-62415. 1983. pap. 4.95 (ISBN 0-8091-2530-7). Paulist Pr.

Miscall, Peter D. The Workings of Old Testament Narrative. LC 82-48570. (Semeia Studies). 160p. 1983. pap. text ed. 8.95 (ISBN 0-8006-1512-3). Fortress.

Suring, Margit L. The Horn-Motif in the Hebrew Bible & Related Ancient Near Eastern Literature & Iconography. (Andrews University Seminary Doctoral Dissertation Ser.). (Illus.). xxvi, 533p. 1982. pap. 9.95 (ISBN 0-943872-36-7). Andrews Univ Pr.

BIBLE–COMMENTARIES–O. T. AMOS

see Bible–Commentaries–O. T. Minor Prophets

BIBLE–COMMENTARIES–O. T. CHRONICLES

see Bible–Commentaries–O. T. Historical Books

BIBLE–COMMENTARIES–O. T. DANIEL

see Bible–Commentaries–O. T. Prophets

BIBLE–COMMENTARIES–O. T. DEUTERONOMY

see Bible–Commentaries–O. T. Pentateuch

BIBLE–COMMENTARIES–O. T. ECCLESIASTES

see Bible–Commentaries–O. T. Poetical Books

BIBLE–COMMENTARIES–O. T. ESTHER

see Bible–Commentaries–O. T. Historical Books

BIBLE–COMMENTARIES–O. T. EXODUS

see Bible–Commentaries–O. T. Pentateuch

BIBLE–COMMENTARIES–O. T. EZEKIEL

see Bible–Commentaries–O. T. Prophets

BIBLE–COMMENTARIES–O. T. EZRA

see Bible–Commentaries–O. T. Historical Books

BIBLE–COMMENTARIES–O. T. GENESIS

see Bible–Commentaries–O. T. Pentateuch

BIBLE–COMMENTARIES–O. T. HABAKKUK

see Bible–Commentaries–O. T. Minor Prophets

BIBLE–COMMENTARIES–O. T. HAGGAI

see Bible–Commentaries–O. T. Minor Prophets

BIBLE–COMMENTARIES–O. T. HISTORICAL BOOKS

Enns, Paul P. Ruth: A Bible Study Commentary. 96p. (Orig.). 1982. pap. 3.95 (ISBN 0-310-44061-0). Zondervan.

Laney, J. Carl. Ezra & Nehemiah. (Everyman's Bible Commentary Ser.). (Orig.). 1982. pap. 4.50 (ISBN 0-8024-2014-1). Moody.

Payne, David F. First & Second Samuel. LC 82-16009. (The Daily Study Bible Ser.). 320p. 1983. 12.95 (ISBN 0-664-21806-7); pap. 6.95 (ISBN 0-664-24573-0). Westminster.

Sailhamer, John. First & Second Chronicles. (Everyman's Bible Commentary Ser.). (Orig.). 1983. pap. 4.50 (ISBN 0-8024-2012-5). Moody.

Thiele, Edwin. The Mysterious Numbers of the Hebrew Kings. 256p. 1982. 12.95 (ISBN 0-310-36010-2). Zondervan.

BIBLE–COMMENTARIES–O. T. HOSEA

see Bible–Commentaries–O. T. Minor Prophets

BIBLE–COMMENTARIES–O. T. ISAIAH

see Bible–Commentaries–O. T. Prophets

BIBLE–COMMENTARIES–O. T. JEREMIAH

see Bible–Commentaries–O. T. Prophets

BIBLE–COMMENTARIES–O. T. JOB

see Bible–Commentaries–O. T. Poetical Books

BIBLE–COMMENTARIES–O. T. JOEL

see Bible–Commentaries–O. T. Minor Prophets

BIBLE–COMMENTARIES–O. T. JONAH

see Bible–Commentaries–O. T. Minor Prophets

BIBLE–COMMENTARIES–O. T. JOSHUA

see Bible–Commentaries–O. T. Historical Books

BIBLE–COMMENTARIES–O. T. JUDGES

see Bible–Commentaries–O. T. Historical Books

BIBLE–COMMENTARIES–O. T. KINGS

see Bible–Commentaries–O. T. Historical Books

BIBLE–COMMENTARIES–O. T. LAMENTATIONS

see Bible–Commentaries–O. T. Prophets

BIBLE–COMMENTARIES–O. T. LEVITICUS

see Bible–Commentaries–O. T. Pentateuch

BIBLE–COMMENTARIES–O. T. MALACHI

see Bible–Commentaries–O. T. Minor Prophets

BIBLE–COMMENTARIES–O. T. MICAH

see Bible–Commentaries–O. T. Minor Prophets

BIBLE–COMMENTARIES–O. T. MINOR PROPHETS

Clark, D. J. & Mundhenk, N. Translator's Handbook on the Books of Obadiah & Micah. (Helps for Translators Ser.). 1982. pap. 3.00 (ISBN 0-8267-0129-9, 08567). Am Bible.

Coffman, James B. Commentary on the Minor Prophets, Vol. 3. (Firm Foundation Commentary Ser.). 322p. 1983. 10.95 (ISBN 0-88027-107-8). Firm Foun Pub.

Jeremiah, David. Malachi: Twenty-Six Daily Bible Studies. (Steps to Higher Ground Ser.). 1983. pap. 1.50 (ISBN 0-86508-207-3). BCM Pubns.

BIBLE–COMMENTARIES–O. T. NAHUM

see Bible–Commentaries–O. T. Minor Prophets

BIBLE–COMMENTARIES–O. T. NEHEMIAH

see Bible–Commentaries–O. T. Historical Books

BIBLE–COMMENTARIES–O. T. NUMBERS

see Bible–Commentaries–O. T. Pentateuch

BIBLE–COMMENTARIES–O. T. OBADIAH

see Bible–Commentaries–O. T. Minor Prophets

BIBLE–COMMENTARIES–O. T. PENTATEUCH

Noordtzij, A. Leviticus. (Bible Student's Commentary Ser.). 288p. 1982. 13.95 (ISBN 0-310-45090-X). Zondervan.

Plaut, W. Gunther. Deuteronomy: A Modern Commentary. (The Torah: A Modern Commentary Ser.). 528p. 1983. 20.00 (ISBN 0-8074-0045-9). UAHC.

Westermann, Claus. Genesis One-Eleven. Scullion, John J., tr. LC 82-72655. 692p. cloth 29.95 (ISBN 0-8066-1962-7, 10-2543). Augsburg.

Youngblood, Ronald F. Exodus. (Everyman's Bible Commentary Ser.). (Orig.). 1983. pap. 3.95 (ISBN 0-8024-2002-8). Moody.

BIBLE–COMMENTARIES–O. T. POETICAL BOOKS

Bush, Barbara. Walking in Wisdom: A Woman's Workshop on Ecclesiastes. (Woman's Workshop Ser.). 128p. (Orig.). 1982. pap. 2.95 (ISBN 0-310-43041-0). Zondervan.

Corfield, Virginia. A Celestial Fix: Reflections in Psalm 119, 89-132. LC 82-90797. (Reflection Ser.: Bk. 3). 121p. 1983. 8.95 (ISBN 0-9603298-3-8). Provident.

Duquoc, Christian & Floristan, Casiano. Job & the Silence of God. (Concilium 1983: Vol. 169). 128p. (Orig.). 1983. pap. 6.95 (ISBN 0-8164-2449-7). Seabury.

Seals, Thomas L. Proverbs: Wisdom for All Ages. 4.95. Quality Pubns.

BIBLE–COMMENTARIES–O. T. PROPHETS

see also Bible–Commentaries–O. T. Minor Prophets

Butler, Trent C. Layman's Bible Book Commentary: Isaiah, Vol. 10. LC 80-68890. 1983. 4.75 (ISBN 0-8054-1180-1). Broadman.

Dalglish, Edward H. Layman's Bible Book Commentary: Jeremiah, Lamentations, Vol. 11. 1983. 4.75 (ISBN 0-8054-1181-X). Broadman.

Greenberg, Moshe. Ezekiel, 1-20: A New Translation with Introduction & Commentary. LC 77-12855. (Anchor Bible Ser.: Vol. 22). (Illus.). 384p. 1983. 16.00 (ISBN 0-385-00954-2, Anchor Pr). Doubleday.

Walton, John H. Jonah: A Bible Study Commentary. 80p. (Orig.). 1982. pap. 3.95 (ISBN 0-310-36303-9). Zondervan.

BIBLE–COMMENTARIES–O. T. PROVERBS

see Bible–Commentaries–O. T. Poetical Books

BIBLE–COMMENTARIES–O. T. PSALMS

see Bible–Commentaries–O. T. Poetical Books

BIBLE–COMMENTARIES–O. T. RUTH

see Bible–Commentaries–O. T. Historical Books

BIBLE–COMMENTARIES–O. T. SAMUEL

see Bible–Commentaries–O. T. Historical Books

BIBLE–COMMENTARIES–O. T. SONG OF SOLOMON

see Bible–Commentaries–O. T. Poetical Books

BIBLE–COMMENTARIES–O. T. ZECHARIAH

see Bible–Commentaries–O. T. Minor Prophets

BIBLE–COMMENTARIES–O. T. ZEPHANIAH

see Bible–Commentaries–O. T. Minor Prophets

BIBLE–CONCORDANCES

Bagster's Keyword Concordance. 96p. 1983. Repr. 5.95 (ISBN 0-8007-1335-4). Revell.

Even-Shoshan, Abraham, ed. The New Biblical Concordance in Three Volumes. (Illus.). 2384p. (Hebrew.). 1982. text ed. 79.00 (ISBN 0-686-42965-6). K Sefer.

--The New Biblical Conmcordance in Two Volumes. (Illus.). 1304p. (Hebrew.). 1981. text ed. 54.00 (ISBN 0-686-42969-9). K Sefer.

Even-Shoshan, Avraham, ed. A New Concordance of the Bible. 1288p. 1982. text ed. 39.00 (ISBN 965-17-0098-X). Ridgefield Pub.

Goodrick, Edward W. & Kohlenberger, John R., III. The NIV Handy Concordance. 384p. (Orig.). 1982. pap. 4.95 (ISBN 0-310-43662-1). Zondervan.

Hatch, Edwin & Redpath, Henry A. A Concordance to the Septuagint & Other Greek Versions of the Old Testament (Including the Apocryphal Books), 3 vols. in 2. 1088p. 1983. Repr. of 1906 ed. Set. 75.00 (ISBN 0-8010-4270-4). Baker Bk.

Morton, A. Q. & Michaelson, S. Critical Concordance to the Pastoral Epistles, I, II Timothy, Titus, Philemon. Baird, Arthur & Freedman, David N., eds. (The Computer Bible Ser.: Vol. XXV). 1982. pap. 35.00 (ISBN 0-935106-20-0). Biblical Res Assocs.

The New Nave's Topical Bible. 1120p. 1983. 19.95 (ISBN 0-310-33710-0). Zondervan.

BIBLE–COVENANTS

see Covenants (Theology)

BIBLE–CRITICISM, HIGHER

see Bible–Criticism, Interpretation, etc.; Bible–Introductions

BIBLE–CRITICISM, INTERPRETATION, ETC.

Here are entered works on the Bible as a whole. Works on the New Testament as a whole and on portions of the New Testament precede works on the Old Testament.

see also Bible As Literature; Sex in the Bible

Alfaro, Juan. Preguntas y Respuestas sobre la Biblia. 64p. (Spanish.). 1982. pap. 1.50 (ISBN 0-89243-162-8). Liguori Pubns.

Barr, James. Holy Scripture: Canon Authority, Criticism. LC 82-20123. 192p. 1983. 18.95 (ISBN 0-664-21395-2); pap. 9.95 (ISBN 0-664-24477-7). Westminster.

Barthel, Manfred. What the Bible Really Says: Casting New Light on the Book of Books. Howson, Mark, tr. from Ger. (Illus.). 416p. 1983. pap. 7.50 (ISBN 0-688-01979-X). Quill NY.

Bogue, Robert H. There Is a Time: The Downbeat of Pristine Christianity. 1983. 11.95 (ISBN 0-533-05592-X). Vantage.

Bowden, Jon G. Bible Absurdities. 20p. 1982. pap. 1.50 (ISBN 0-911826-45-9). Am Atheist.

Braidfoot, Larry. The Bible & America. LC 82-73371. 1983. 3.25 (ISBN 0-8054-5519-1). Broadman.

Brooks, R. T. A Place to Start: The Bible as a Guide for Today. 120p. 1983. pap. 4.95 (ISBN 0-86683-708-6). Winston Pr.

Campbell, R. K. Our Wonderful Bible. 417p. 15.95 (ISBN 0-88172-009-7); pap. 11.95 (ISBN 0-88172-010-0). Believers Bkshelf.

Crawford, C. C. What the Bible Says about Faith. LC 82-72621. (What the Bible Says Ser.). 380p. 1982. 13.50 (ISBN 0-89900-089-4). College Pr Pub.

Cronk, George. The Message of the Bible: An Orthodox Christian Perspective. LC 82-7355. 293p. (Orig.). 1982. pap. 8.95 (ISBN 0-913836-94-X). St Vladimirs.

Daniel, R. P. Let's Play Bible Detective. 36p. pap. 2.00 (ISBN 0-88172-017-8). Believers Bkshelf.

Darby, J. N. Synopsis of the Books of the Bible, 5 vols. Set. 27.50 (ISBN 0-88172-070-4). Believers Bkshelf.

Draper, James T. The Conscience of a Nation. 1983. pap. 7.95 (ISBN 0-8054-1530-0). Broadman.

Fudge, Edward. The Fire that Consumes: A Biblical & History Study of Final Punishment. Date not set. 19.95 (ISBN 0-89890-018-2). Providential Pr.

Gladden, Lee & Gladden, Vivianne C. Heirs of the Gods: A Space Age Interpretation of the Bible. LC 78-53852. (Illus.). 324p. Repr. of 1979 ed. 15.95 (ISBN 0-686-37960-8). Bel-Air.

Gresham, Charles R. What the Bible Says about Resurrection. (What the Bible Says Ser.). 350p. 1983. 13.50 (ISBN 0-89900-090-8). College Pr Pub.

Howard, E. Basic Bible Survey. Gambill, Henrietta, ed. 96p. (Orig.). 1983. pap. 2.95 (ISBN 0-87239-572-3, 3210). Standard Pub.

Ingersoll, Robert G. The Truth about the Holy Bible. 31p. pap. 3.00 (ISBN 0-686-83990-0). Am Atheist.

Kelly, George A. The New Biblical Theorists: Raymond E. Brown & Beyond. 1983. write for info. (ISBN 0-89283-166-9). Servant.

Landy, Francis. Paradoxes & Paradise: Identity & Difference in the Song of Songs. (Bible & Literature Ser.: No. 6). 1983. text ed. 29.95x (ISBN 0-907459-16-1, Pub. by Almond Pr England); pap. text ed. 15.95x (ISBN 0-907459-17-X, Pub. by Almond Pr England). Eisenbrauns.

Macarthur, John, Jr. Why I Trust the Bible. 120p. 1983. pap. 3.95 (ISBN 0-88207-389-3). Victor Bks.

Richards, Kent, ed. Society of Biblical Literature: Seminar Papers 1982. (SBL Ser.). 574p. 1982. pap. text ed. 15.00 (ISBN 0-89130-607-2, 06-09-21). Scholars Pr CA.

Robertson-Nicoll, W., ed. The Expositor's Bible, 6 Vols. 1982. 195.00 (ISBN 0-8010-6685-9). Baker Bk.

Rogerson, John. Beginning Old Testament Study. LC 82-20210. 160p. 1983. pap. price not set (ISBN 0-664-24451-3). Westminster.

Saucy, Robert L. Is the Bible Reliable? 1983. pap. 4.50 (ISBN 0-88207-106-8). Victor Bks.

Saunders, Ernest W. Searching the Scriptures: A History of the Society of Biblical Literature 1880-1980. LC 82-10818. (Society of Biblical Literature - Biblical Scholarship in North America Ser.). pap. 15.00 (ISBN 0-89130-591-2, 06-11-08). Scholars Pr CA.

Senior, Donald & Stuhlmueller, Carroll. The Biblical Foundations for Mission. LC 82-22430. 368p. (Orig.). 1983. 25.00 (ISBN 0-88344-046-6); pap. 14.95 (ISBN 0-88344-047-4). Orbis Bks.

Soncino Books of the Bible, 14 vols. Incl. Chumash. 19.75 (ISBN 0-900689-24-2); Daniel. 10.75 (ISBN 0-900689-36-6); Hoshua & Judges. 10.75 (ISBN 0-900689-25-0); Samuel I-II. 10.75 (ISBN 0-900689-26-9); Chronicles. 10.75 (ISBN 0-900689-37-4); King I-II. 10.75 (ISBN 0-900689-27-7); Isaiah. 10.75 (ISBN 0-900689-28-5); Jeremiah. 10.75 (ISBN 0-900689-29-3); Ezekiel. 10.75 (ISBN 0-900689-30-7); Twelve Prophets. 10.75 (ISBN 0-900689-31-5); Psalms. 10.75 (ISBN 0-900689-32-3); Proverbs. 10.75; Job. 10.75; Five Meeillah. 10.75 (ISBN 0-900689-35-8). Set. 139.75x (ISBN 0-900689-23-4). Bloch.

Stacey, David. Interpreting the Bible. 120p. 1977. pap. 2.00 (ISBN 0-8164-1228-6). Seabury.

Trail, W. The Literary Characteristics & Achievements of the Bible. 335p. 1983. Repr. of 1863 ed. lib. bdg. 85.00 (ISBN 0-89984-471-5). Century Bookbindery.

Tucker, Gene & Knight, Douglas, eds. Humanizing America's Iconic Book. LC 82-836. (SBL Biblical Scholarship in North America Ser.). 188p. 1982. 29.95 (ISBN 0-89130-570-X, 06-11-06); pap. 17.50 (ISBN 0-686-42952-4). Scholars Pr CA.

Warren, Virgil. What the Bible Says about Salvation. LC 82-73345. (What the Bible Says Ser.). 640p. 1982. 13.50 (ISBN 0-89900-088-6). College Pr Pub.

BIBLE–CRITICISM, INTERPRETATION, ETC.–HISTORY

Bird, Phyllis A. The Bible As the Church's Book. Date not set. write for info. Geneva Divinity.

--The Bible As the Church's Book, Vol. 5. LC 82-7049. (Library of Living Faith). 120p. 1982. pap. 5.95 (ISBN 0-664-24427-0). Westminster.

Rollins, Wayne G. Jung & The Bible. LC 82-48091. 156p. 1983. pap. 9.50 (ISBN 0-8042-1117-5). John Knox.

Woodbridge, John D. Biblical Authority: A Critique of the Rogers-McKim Proposal. 256p. (Orig.). 1982. pap. 8.95 (ISBN 0-310-44751-8). Zondervan.

BIBLE–CRITICISM, INTERPRETATION, ETC.–N. T.

Culpepper, R. Alan. Anatomy of the Fourth Gospel: A Study in Literary Design. LC 82-16302. 256p. 1983. 19.95 (ISBN 0-8006-0693-0, 1-693). Fortress.

Duncan, J. & Derrett, M. Studies in the New Testament, Vol. 13: Midrasn, Haggadah, & the Character of the Community. xxi, 261p. 1982. write for info. (ISBN 90-04-06596-2). E J Brill.

Epp, Eldon J. & Gordon, Fee D., eds. New Testament Textual Criticism: Its Significance for Exegesis. (Illus.). 438p. 94.00x (ISBN 0-19-826175-6). Oxford U Pr.

Flanagan, Neal M. The Gospel According to John 7 the Johannine Epistles, No. 4. Karris, Robert J., ed. LC 82-22908. (Collegeville Bible Commentary Ser.). 128p. 1983. pap. 2.50 (ISBN 0-8146-1304-7). Liturgical Pr.

Goldsworthy, Graeme. Gospel & Kingdom: A Chrisian's Guide to the Old Testament. 128p. 1983. pap. 6.95 (ISBN 0-86683-686-1). Winston Pr.

Lawson, LeRoy. The New Testament Church Then & Now Workbook. 48p. 1983. pap. 1.75 (ISBN 0-87239-609-6, 88586). Standard Pub.

Meyer, Marvin W. Who Do People Say That I Am? The Interpretation of Jesus in the New Testament Gospels. 104p. 1983. pap. 5.95 (ISBN 0-8028-1961-3). Eerdmans.

Smitty, William H. Three Hundred Sermon Outlines From the New Testament. LC 81-86666. (Orig.). 1983. pap. 4.50 (ISBN 0-8054-2246-3). Broadman.

Yeager, Randolph O. The Renaissance New Testament, Vol. 10. LC 79-28652. 660p. 1982. 22.50 (ISBN 0-88289-258-4). Pelican.

--The Renaissance New Testament, Vol. 11. 660p. 22.50 (ISBN 0-88289-758-6). Pelican.

BIBLE–CRITICISM, INTERPRETATION, ETC.–N. T. ACTS

Cassidy, Richard J. & Scharper, Philip J., eds. Political Issues in Luke-Acts. LC 82-19060. 192p. (Orig.). 1983. 16.95 (ISBN 0-88344-390-2); pap. 9.95 (ISBN 0-88344-385-6). Orbis Bks.

Criswell, W. A. Acts: An Exposition. 948p. 1983. Repr. 19.95 (ISBN 0-310-44150-1). Zondervan.

Harper, Alfred F. Acts One-Twelve: The Spirit-Filled Church. (Beacon Small-Group Bible Studies). 96p. 1982. pap. 2.25 (ISBN 0-8341-0800-3). Beacon Hill.

Johnson, Luke T. Decision Making in the Church: A Biblical Model. LC 82-17675. 112p. 1983. pap. 5.95 (ISBN 0-8006-1694-4). Fortress.

Kelly, William. The Acts, Catholic Epistles & Revelation. (Introductory Lecture Ser.). 580p. 5.50 (ISBN 0-88172-096-8). Believers Bkshelf.

BIBLE–CRITICISM, INTERPRETATION, ETC.–N. T. APOCRYPHA

Cameron, Ron, ed. The Other Gospels: Non-Canonical Gospel Texts. LC 82-8662. 192p. 1982. pap. 11.95 (ISBN 0-664-24428-9). Westminster.

Neall, Beatrice S. The Concept of Character in the Apocalypse with Implications for Character Education. LC 82-23843. 236p. (Orig.). 1983. lib. bdg. 21.50 (ISBN 0-8191-2983-6); pap. text ed. 10.75 (ISBN 0-8191-2984-4). U Pr of Amer.

BIBLE–CRITICISM, INTERPRETATION, ETC.–N. T. COLOSSIANS

see Bible–Criticism, Interpretation, etc.–N. T. Epistles

BIBLE–CRITICISM, INTERPRETATION, ETC.–N. T. CORINTHIANS

see Bible–Criticism, Interpretation, Etc.–N. T. Epistles

BIBLE–CRITICISM, INTERPRETATION, ETC.–N. T. EPHESIANS

see Bible–Criticism, Interpretation, Etc.–N. T. Epistles

BIBLE–CRITICISM, INTERPRETATION, ETC.–N. T. EPISTLES

Here are entered books on the Epistles as a whole, or on one or more of the following, Colossians, Corinthians, Ephesians, Galatians, Hebrews, James, Epistles of John, Jude, Peter, Philemon, Romans, Thessalonians, Timothy, Titus.

At Ease under Pressure: James-I, II Peter. (New Horizons Bible Study). 64p. 1982. Student's Guide 2.50 (ISBN 0-89367-073-1). Light & Life.

At Ease under Pressure: James I, II Peter. (New Horizons Bible Study). 48p. 1982. pap. 1.95 Leaders' Guide (ISBN 0-89367-072-3). Light & Life.

Barrett, C. K. Essays on Paul. LC 82-2764. 180p. 1982. 18.95 (ISBN 0-664-21390-1). Westminster.

Beacon Hill Staff. One Corinthians, Living as a Responsible Christian. (Beacon Small Group Bible Studies). 60p. 1982. pap. 2.25 (ISBN 0-8341-0755-4). Beacon Hill.

Boice, James M. The Epistles of John. 224p. 1983. pap. 6.95 (ISBN 0-310-21531-5). Zondervan.

Brink, Charles O. Horace on Poetry: Epistles Book II: The Letters to Augustus & Florus, Vol. 3. LC 63-4908. 656p. 1982. 99.50 (ISBN 0-521-20069-5). Cambridge U Pr.

Caudill, Paul R. First Corinthians: A Translation with Notes. 1983. 4.95 (ISBN 0-8054-1391-X). Broadman.

Fairbanks, LeBron. Philippians, Colossians, Experiencing His Peace. (Beacon Small-Group Bible Studies). 72p. 1982. pap. 2.25 (ISBN 0-8341-0778-3). Beacon Hill.

Flanagan, Neal M. The Gospel According to John 7 the Johannine Epistles, No. 4. Karris, Robert J., ed. LC 82-22908. (Collegeville Bible Commentary Ser.). 128p. 1983. pap. 2.50 (ISBN 0-8146-1304-7). Liturgical Pr.

Friskney, Tom. Thirteen Lessons on I & II Thessalonians. LC 82-71253. (Bible Student Study Guide Ser.). 122p. 1982. pap. 2.95 (ISBN 0-89900-172-6). College Pr Pub.

Getz, Gene A. The Measure of a Christian: A Study in James I. (The Measure of...Ser.). 160p. 1983. pap. 4.95 (ISBN 0-8307-0881-2). Regal.

--The Measure of a Christian: A Study in Philippians. (The Measure of...Ser.). 200p. 1983. pap. 4.95 (ISBN 0-8307-0883-9). Regal.

--The Measure of a Christian: A Study in Titus. (A Measure of...Ser.). 200p. 1983. pap. 4.95 (ISBN 0-8307-0882-0). Regal.

Grant, L. M. First & Second Thessalonians. 46p. pap. 2.25 (ISBN 0-88172-079-8). Believers Bkshelf.

Gromacki, Robert G. Stand True to the Charge: An Exposition of I Timothy. 200p. 1982. pap. 7.95 (ISBN 0-8010-3786-7). Baker Bk.

Jewett, Robert. Christian Tolerance: Paul's Message to the Modern Church. LC 82-13480. (Biblical Perspectives on Current Issues Ser.). pap. 9.95 (ISBN 0-664-24444-0). Westminster.

Kelly, William. The Acts, Catholic Epistles & Revelation. (Introductory Lecture Ser.). 580p. 5.50 (ISBN 0-88172-096-8). Believers Bkshelf.

--The Pauline Epistles. (Introductory Lecture Ser.). 551p. 5.50 (ISBN 0-88172-098-4). Believers Bkshelf.

Kenyon, Don J. Romans, 2 vols. Incl. Vol. 1. Triumph of Truth. pap. text ed. 3.95 (ISBN 0-87509-147-4); leader's guide 2.95 (ISBN 0-87509-265-9); Vol 2. Glory of Grace. pap. text ed. 3.95 (ISBN 0-87509-148-2); leader's guide 2.95 (ISBN 0-87509-266-7). 1978. pap. Chr Pubns.

Kuniholm, Whitney. Galatians, Ephesians, Philippians, & Colossians: A Daily Dialogue with God. (Personal Bible Studyguides). 144p. 1983. pap. 4.95 (ISBN 0-87788-292-4). Shaw Pubs.

McDonald, William. Letters to the Thessalonians. rev. ed. 1982. pap. 3.50 (ISBN 0-937396-43-5). Walterick Pubs.

Morgan, G. Campbell. Analyzed Bible, Romans. (G. Campbell Morgan Library). 220p. 1983. pap. 5.95 (ISBN 0-8010-6149-0). Baker Bk.

Morton, A. Q. & Michaelson, S. Critical Concordance to the Pastoral Epistles, I, II Timothy, Titus, Philemon. Baird, Arthur & Freedman, David N., eds. (The Computer Bible Ser.: Vol. XXV). 1982. pap. 35.00 (ISBN 0-935106-20-0). Biblical Res Assocs.

Nielson, Bill. One & Two Thessalonians: The Distinguishing Marks of a Christian. (Beacon Small-Group Bible Studies). 56p. 1982. pap. 2.25 (ISBN 0-8341-0738-4). Beacon Hill.

Olbricht, Thomas H. Message of the New Testament: Ephesians & Colossions. (Way of Life Ser.). 108p. 1983. pap. 3.95 (ISBN 0-89112-170-6). Biblical Research Press.

Phipps, William E. Encounter Through Questioning Paul: A Fresh Approach to the Apostle's Life & Letters. LC 82-17580. (Illus.). 114p. (Orig.). 1983. lib. bdg. 19.00 (ISBN 0-8191-2785-X); pap. text ed. 8.25 (ISBN 0-8191-2786-8). U Pr of Amer.

Sanders, E. P. Paul, the Law & the Jewish People. LC 82-17487. 240p. 1983. 19.95 (ISBN 0-8006-0698-1, 1-698). Fortress.

Shaw, Graham. The Cost of Authority: Manipulation & Freedom in the New Testament. LC 82-48545. 320p. 1983. pap. 16.95 (ISBN 0-8006-1707-X). Fortress.

Swank, J. Grant, Jr. One & Two Peter: A Faith for Testing Times. (Beacon Small-Group Bible Studies). 72p. 1982. pap. 2.25 (ISBN 0-8341-0790-2). Beacon Hill.

Wolf, Earl C. One, Two & Three John: Everybody Ought to Know. (Beacon Small-group Bible Studies). 80p. 1982. pap. 2.25 (ISBN 0-8341-0791-0). Beacon Hill.

BIBLE–CRITICISM, INTERPRETATION, ETC.–N. T. EPISTLES OF JOHN

see Bible–Criticism, Interpretation, Etc.–N. T. Epistles

BIBLE–CRITICISM, INTERPRETATION, ETC.–N. T. GALATIANS

see Bible–Criticism, Interpretation, Etc.–N. T. Epistles

BIBLE–CRITICISM, INTERPRETATION, ETC.–N. T. GOSPELS

Here are entered works on the gospels as a whole, or on one or more of the gospels: John, Luke, Mark, Matthew.

Aland, K., ed. Synopsis of the Four Gospels. 1983. 5.95 (ISBN 0-8267-0500-6, 08564). Am Bible.

Barrett, C. K. Essays on John. LC 82-2759. 180p. 1982. 18.95 (ISBN 0-664-21389-8). Westminster.

Boice, James M. The Gospel of John: Peace in Storm, Vol. IV. 496p. 1983. pap. 9.95 (ISBN 0-310-21461-0). Zondervan.

Cannon, William R. The Gospel of Matthew. 128p. (Orig.). 1983. pap. 4.95 (ISBN 0-8358-0450-X). Upper Room.

Cassidy, Richard J. & Scharper, Philip J., eds. Political Issues in Luke-Acts. LC 82-19060. 192p. (Orig.). 1983. 16.95 (ISBN 0-88344-390-2); pap. 9.95 (ISBN 0-88344-385-6). Orbis Bks.

Coniaris, A. M. The Message of the Sunday Gospels, Vol. 2. 1983. pap. 6.95 (ISBN 0-937032-29-8). Light&Life Pub Co MN.

Davies, Stevan. The Gospel of Thomas & Christian Wisdom. 160p. 1983. pap. 9.95 (ISBN 0-8164-2456-X). Seabury.

Draper, James T., Jr. Faith that Works: Studies in James. 1983. pap. 5.95 (ISBN 0-686-82693-0, 82-0872-5); Leader's Guide 2.95 (ISBN 0-686-82694-9, 82-0873-3). Tyndale.

Fredrikson, Roger L. The Communicator's Commentary-John, Vol. 4. Ogilvie, Lloyd J., ed. (The Communicator's Commentaries Ser.). 1983. 14.95 (ISBN 0-8499-0157-X). Word Pub.

The Gospel of John: The Coming of the Light - John 1-1 - 4-54, Vol. I. 448p. 1983. pap. 9.95 (ISBN 0-310-21421-1). Zondervan.

Gunderson, Vivian. Gospel of Mark. (Illus.). 1982. pap. 1.25 (ISBN 0-8323-0412-3). Binford.

Hailey, Homer. That You May Believe: Studies in the Gospel of John. (Illus.). 1982. 9.95 (ISBN 0-913814-51-2). Nevada Pubns.

Harrington, Daniel J. Access Guide for Scripture Study: Luke. Date not set. 2.95 (ISBN 0-8215-5929-X); 3.95 (ISBN 0-8215-5934-6). Sadlier.

--Access Guide for Scripture Study: Mark. Date not set. 2.95 (ISBN 0-8215-5928-1); 3.95 (ISBN 0-8215-5933-8). Sadlier.

--The Gospel According to Matthew, No. 1. Karris, Robert J., ed. LC 82-20333. (Collegeville Bible Commentary Ser.). (Illus.). 128p. 1983. pap. 2.50 (ISBN 0-8146-1301-2). Liturgical Pr.

Kelber, Werner H. The Oral & the Written Gospel: The Hermeneutics of Speaking & Writing in the Synoptic Tradition, Mark, Paul, & Q. LC 82-7450. 272p. 1983. 22.95 (ISBN 0-8006-0689-2, 1-689). Fortress.

Kelly, William. The Gospels. (Introductory Lecture Ser.). 567p. 5.50 (ISBN 0-88172-097-6). Believers Bkshelf.

Keyes, Sharrel. Luke: Following Jesus. (Fisherman Bible Studyguides Ser.). 80p. 1983. pap. 2.50 (ISBN 0-87788-539-7). Shaw Pubs.

Kodell, Jerome. The Gospel According to Luke, No. 3. Karris, Robert J., ed. LC 82-20350. (Collegeville Bible Commentary Ser.). (Illus.). 128p. 1983. pap. 2.50 (ISBN 0-8146-1303-9). Liturgical Pr.

Larsen, Sandy & Larsen, Dale. Mark: Good News for Today. (Carpenter Studyguides Ser.). 80p. 1983. member's handbook 1.95 (ISBN 0-87788-540-0); saddle-stitched leader's handbook 2.95 (ISBN 0-87788-541-9). Shaw Pubs.

Larson, Bruce. The Communicator's Commentary-Luke, Vol. 3. Ogilvie, Lloyd J., ed. (The Communicator's Commentary Ser.). 1983. 14.95 (ISBN 0-8499-0156-1). Word Pub.

Long, James. Life Letter. 144p. 1982. pap. 4.50 (ISBN 0-88207-590-X). Victor Bks.

Meagher, John C. Five Gospels: An Account of How the Good News Came to Be. 270p. 1983. 17.50 (ISBN 0-86683-731-0); pap. 9.95 (ISBN 0-86683-691-8). Winston Pr.

Meier, John B. Access Guide for Scripture Study: Matthew. Date not set. 2.95 (ISBN 0-8215-5932-X); 3.95 (ISBN 0-8215-5935-4). Sadlier.

O'Quinn, J. Frank, ed. Jesus' Lost Gospels: The Discovery at Nag Hammadi. (Illus.). 48p. 1981. pap. text ed. 6.95 (ISBN 0-9609802-0-2). Life Science.

Schillebeeckx, Edward. God among Us: The Gospel Proclaimed. 278p. 1983. 12.95 (ISBN 0-8245-0575-1). Crossroad NY.

Staton, Knofel. Thirteen Lessons on I, II, III John. LC 80-69722. (Bible Student Study Guide Ser.). 149p. 1980. pap. 2.95 (ISBN 0-89900-169-6). College Pr Pub.

Taylor, Edward. Harmony of the Gospels, 4 Vols. LC 82-5452. 2688p. 1983. Set. 300.00x (ISBN 0-8201-1379-4). Schol Facsimiles.

Theissen, Gerd. The Miracle Stories of the Early Christian Tradition. Riches, John, ed. McDonagh, Francis, tr. LC 82-48546. 416p. 1983. text ed. 27.95 (ISBN 0-8006-0700-7). Fortress.

Van Linden, Philip. The Gospel According to Mark, No. 2. Karris, Robert J., ed. LC 82-20356. (Collegeville Bible Commentary Ser.). (Illus.). 96p. 1983. pap. 2.50 (ISBN 0-8146-1302-0). Liturgical Pr.

Wesner, Marlene & Wesner, Miles E. A Fresh Look at the Gospel. (Orig.). 1983. pap. 5.95 (ISBN 0-8054-1955-1). Broadman.

Whitacre, Rodney A. Johannine Polemic: The Role of Tradition & Theology. LC 82-5457. (SBL Dissertation Ser.). 292p. 1982. pap. 13.00 (ISBN 0-89130-579-3, 06-01-67). Scholars Pr CA.

Wijngaards, John. Handbook to the Gospels: A Guide to the Gospel Writings & the Life & Times of Jesus. (Illus.). 1983. pap. 8.95 (ISBN 0-89283-118-9). Servant.

Williamson, Lamar, Jr. Mark Interpretation: A Bible Commentary for Teaching & Preaching. Mays, James L. & Achtemeier, Paul J., eds. LC 82-17161. 289p. 1983. 17.95 (ISBN 0-8042-3121-4). John Knox.

BIBLE–CRITICISM, INTERPRETATION, ETC.–N. T. HEBREWS

see Bible–Criticism, Interpretation, Etc.–N. T. Epistles

BIBLE–CRITICISM, INTERPRETATION, ETC.–N. T. JAMES

see Bible–Criticism, Interpretation, Etc.–N. T. Epistles

BIBLE–CRITICISM, INTERPRETATION, ETC.–N. T. JOHN

see Bible–Criticism, Interpretation, etc.–N. T. Gospels

BIBLE–CRITICISM, INTERPRETATION, ETC.–N. T. JUDE

see Bible–Criticism, Interpretation, Etc.–N. T. Epistles

BIBLE–CRITICISM, INTERPRETATION, ETC.–N. T. LUKE

see Bible–Criticism, Interpretation, Etc.–N. T. Gospels

BIBLE–CRITICISM, INTERPRETATION, ETC.–N. T. MARK

see Bible–Criticism, Interpretation, Etc.–N. T. Gospels

BIBLE–CRITICISM, INTERPRETATION, ETC.–N. T. MATTHEW

see Bible–Criticism, Interpretation, Etc.–N. T. Gospels

BIBLE–CRITICISM, INTERPRETATION, ETC.–N. T. PETER

see Bible–Criticism, Interpretation, Etc.–N. T. Epistles

BIBLE–CRITICISM, INTERPRETATION, ETC.–N. T. PHILEMON

see Bible–Criticism, Interpretation, Etc.–N. T. Epistles

BIBLE–CRITICISM, INTERPRETATION, ETC.–N. T. REVELATION

Barclay, William. Letters to the Seven Churches. LC 82-2760. 1982. pap. 5.95 (ISBN 0-664-24433-5). Westminster.

Bulter, Paul T. Twenty-Six Lessons on Revelation, Pt. 1. LC 82-71688. (Bible Student Study Guide Ser.). 133p. 1982. pap. 2.95 (ISBN 0-89900-173-4). College Pr Pub.

--Twenty-Six Lessons on Revelations, Pt. 2. LC 82-71688. (Bible Student study Guide Ser.). 284p. 1982. pap. 4.95 (ISBN 0-89900-176-9). College Pr Pub.

Jeske, Richard L. Revelation for Today: Images of Hope. LC 82-16079. 144p. 1983. pap. 6.95 (ISBN 0-8006-1693-6). Fortress.

Kelly, William. The Acts, Catholic Epistles & Revelation. (Introductory Lecture Ser.). 580p. 5.50 (ISBN 0-88172-096-8). Believers Bkshelf.

Lockyer, Herbert, Sr. Apocalipsis: El Drama de los Siglos. Carrodeguas, Andy, ed. Calderon, Wilfredo, tr. from Eng. Orig. Title: Revelation: The Drama of the Ages. 274p. (Span.). 1982. pap. 4.00 (ISBN 0-8297-1292-5). Life Pubs Intl.

Morris, Henry M. The Revelation Record. 1982. 16.95 (ISBN 0-8423-5511-1). Tyndale.

O'Brien, Bonnie B & C, Chester. The Victory of the Lamb. 182p. 1982. pap. 10.95 (ISBN 0-311-72280-6). Casa Bautista.

BIBLE–CRITICISM, INTERPRETATION, ETC.–N. T. ROMANS

see Bible–Criticism, Interpretation, Etc.–N. T. Epistles

BIBLE–CRITICISM, INTERPRETATION, ETC.–N. T. THESSALONIANS

see Bible–Criticism, Interpretation, Etc.–N. T. Epistles

BIBLE–CRITICISM, INTERPRETATION, ETC.–N. T. TIMOTHY

see Bible–Criticism, Interpretation, Etc.–N. T. Epistles

BIBLE–CRITICISM, INTERPRETATION, ETC.–N. T. TITUS

see Bible–Criticism, Interpretation, Etc.–N. T. Epistles

BIBLE–CRITICISM, INTERPRETATION, ETC.–O. T

Armeding, Carl E. The Old Testament & Criticism. 144p. 1983. pap. 6.95 (ISBN 0-8028-1951-6). Eerdmans.

Balentine, Samuel E. The Hidden God: The Hiding of the Face of God in the Old Testament. (Oxford Theological Monographs). 192p. 1983. 29.95 (ISBN 0-19-826719-3). Oxford U Pr.

Clines, D. J. & Gunn, D. M. Art & Meaning: Rhetoric in Biblical Literature. (Journal for the Study of the Old Testament, Supplement Ser.: No. 19). viii, 266p. 1982. text ed. 25.00x (ISBN 0-905774-38-8, Pub. by JSOT Pr England); pap. text ed. 19.95x (ISBN 0-905774-39-6). Eisenbrauns.

Craghan, John F. Love & Thunder: A Sprituality of the Old Testament. 248p. 1983. pap. text ed. 10.95 (ISBN 0-8146-1279-2). Liturgical Pr.

Emerton, J. A. Congress Volume: Vienna, 1980. (Vetus Testamentum Ser.: Vol. 32, Suppl.). (Illus.). xii, 483p. 1981. write for info. (ISBN 90-04-06514-8). E J Brill.

Girdlestone, Robert B. Synonyms of the Old Testament: Numerically Coded to Strong's Exhaustive Concordance. White, Donald R., ed. 400p. 1983. pap. 13.95 (ISBN 0-8010-3789-1). Baker Bk.

Miscall, Peter D. The Workings of Old Testament Narrative. LC 82-48570. (Semeia Studies). 160p. 1983. pap. text ed. 8.95 (ISBN 0-8006-1512-3). Fortress.

--The Workings of Old Testament Narrative. LC 82-5993. (SBL Semeia Studies). 158p. 1983. pap. 8.95 (ISBN 0-89130-584-X, 06-06-12). Scholars Pr CA.

The Old Testament in Syriac: According to the Peshitta Version, Pt. II. xix, 55p. 1982. write for info. (ISBN 90-04-06342-0). E J Brill.

Thompson, Michael E. W. Situation & Theology: Old Testament Interpretations of the Syro-Euphramite War. 1983. text ed. 25.95x (ISBN 0-686-42730-0, Pub. by Almond Pr England); pap. text ed. 12.95x (ISBN 0-907459-15-3, Pub. by Almond Pr England). Eisenbrauns.

Walker, Taiko & Walker, Ashley. Hold the Horse. 1983. 7.95 (ISBN 0-533-05225-4). Vantage.

BIBLE–CRITICISM, INTERPRETATION, ETC.–O. T. AMOS

see Bible–Criticism, Interpretation, Etc.–O. T. Minor Prophets

BIBLE–CRITICISM, INTERPRETATION, ETC.–O. T. CHRONICLES

see Bible–Criticism, Interpretation, Etc.–O. T. Historical Books

BIBLE–CRITICISM, INTERPRETATION, ETC.–O. T. DANIEL

see Bible–Criticism, Interpretation, Etc.–O. T. Prophets

BIBLE–CRITICISM, INTERPRETATION, ETC.–O. T. DEUTERONOMY

see Bible–Criticism, Interpretation, Etc.–O. T. Pentateuch

BIBLE–CRITICISM, INTERPRETATION, ETC.–O. T. ECCLESIASTES

see Bible–Criticism, Interpretation, etc.–O. T. Poetical Books

BIBLE–CRITICISM, INTERPRETATION, ETC.–O. T. ESTHER

see Bible–Criticism, Interpretation, Etc.–O. T. Historical Books

BIBLE–CRITICISM, INTERPRETATION, ETC.–O. T. EXODUS

see Bible–Criticism, Interpretation, Etc.–O. T. Pentateuch

BIBLE–CRITICISM, INTERPRETATION, ETC.–O. T. EZEKIEL

see Bible–Criticism, Interpretation, Etc.–O. T. Prophets

BIBLE–CRITICISM, INTERPRETATION, ETC.–O. T. EZRA

see Bible–Criticism, Interpretation, Etc.–O. T. Historical Books

BIBLE–CRITICISM, INTERPRETATION, ETC.–O. T. GENESIS

see Bible–Criticism, Interpretation, Etc.–O. T. Pentateuch

BIBLE–CRITICISM, INTERPRETATION, ETC.–O. T. HABAKKUK

see Bible–Criticism, Interpretation, Etc.–O. T. Minor Prophets

BIBLE–CRITICISM, INTERPRETATION, ETC.–O. T. HAGGAI

see Bible–Criticism, Interpretation, Etc.–O. T. Minor Prophets

BIBLE–CRITICISM, INTERPRETATION, ETC.–O. T. HISTORICAL BOOKS

Here are entered works on the historical Books as a whole, as well as on one or more of the following: Chronicles, Esther, Ezra, Joshua, Judges, Kings, Nehemiah, Ruth, Samuel.

Couchman, Bob & Couchman, Win. Ruth & Jonah: People in Process. (Carpenter Studyguides Ser.). 64p. 1983. saddle-stiched members' handbk. 1.95 (ISBN 0-87788-736-5); leader's handbook 2.95 (ISBN 0-87788-737-3). Shaw Pubs.

Crises at the Crossroads: Ruth-Esther. (New Horizons Bible Study). 48p. (Orig.). 1982. pap. 1.95 Leader's Guide (ISBN 0-89367-074-X); student guide 2.50 (ISBN 0-89367-075-8). Light & Life.

Rost, Leonhard. The Succession to the Throne of David. (Bible & Literature Ser.: No. 7). Orig. Title: Die Uberlieferung von derThronnachfolge Davids. 160p. 1982. text ed. 25.95x (ISBN 0-686-42728-9, Pub. by Almond Pr England); pap. text ed. 12.95x (ISBN 0-686-42729-7, Pub. by Almond Pr England). Eisenbrauns.

Van Seters, John. In Search of History: Historiography in the Ancient World & the Origins of Biblical History. LC 82-48912. 272p. 1983. text ed. 30.00x (ISBN 0-300-02877-6). Yale U Pr.

BIBLE–CRITICISM, INTERPRETATION, ETC.–O. T. HOSEA

see Bible–Criticism, Interpretation, Etc.–O. T. Minor Prophets

BIBLE–CRITICISM, INTERPRETATION, ETC.–O. T. ISAIAH

see Bible–Criticism, Interpretation, Etc.–O. T. Prophets

BIBLE–CRITICISM, INTERPRETATION, ETC.–O. T. JEREMIAH

see Bible–Criticism, Interpretation, Etc.–O. T. Prophets

BIBLE–CRITICISM, INTERPRETATION, ETC.–O. T. JOB

see Bible–Criticism, Interpretation, Etc.–O. T. Poetical Books

BIBLE–CRITICISM, INTERPRETATION, ETC.–O. T. JOEL

see Bible–Criticism, Interpretation, Etc.–O. T. Minor Prophets

BIBLE–CRITICISM, INTERPRETATION, ETC.–O. T. JONAH

see Bible–Criticism, Interpretation, Etc.–O. T. Minor Prophets

BIBLE–CRITICISM, INTERPRETATION, ETC.–O. T. JOSHUA

see Bible–Criticism, Interpretation, Etc.–O. T. Historical Books

BIBLE–CRITICISM, INTERPRETATION, ETC.–O. T. JUDGES

see Bible–Criticism, Interpretation, Etc.–O. T. Historical Books

BIBLE–CRITICISM, INTERPRETATION, ETC.–O. T. KINGS

see Bible–Criticism, Interpretation, Etc.–O. T. Historical Books

BIBLE–CRITICISM, INTERPRETATION, ETC.–O. T. LAMENTATIONS

see Bible–Criticism, Interpretation, Etc.–O. T. Prophets

BIBLE–CRITICISM, INTERPRETATION, ETC.–O. T. LEVITICUS

see Bible–Criticism, Interpretation, Etc.–O. T. Pentateuch

BIBLE–CRITICISM, INTERPRETATION, ETC.–O. T. MALACHI

see Bible–Criticism, Interpretation, Etc.–O. T. Minor Prophets

BIBLE–CRITICISM, INTERPRETATION, ETC.–O. T. MICAH

see Bible–Criticism, Interpretation, Etc.–O. T. Minor Prophets

BIBLE–CRITICISM, INTERPRETATION, ETC.–O. T. MINOR PROPHETS

Here are entered works on the 12 minor prophets as a whole, as well as books on one or more of the minor prophets.

see also Bible–Criticism, Interpretation, Etc.–O. T. Prophets

Edwards, Richard A. The Sign of Jonah: In the Theology of the Evangelists & Q. (Student Christian Movement Press-Studies in Biblical Theology). 134p. (Orig.). 1971. pap. 6.95x (ISBN 0-19-520375-5). Oxford U Pr.

BIBLE–CRITICISM, INTERPRETATION, ETC.–O. T. NAHUM

see Bible–Criticism, Interpretation, Etc.–O. T. Minor Prophets

BIBLE–CRITICISM, INTERPRETATION, ETC.–O. T. NEHEMIAH

see Bible–Criticism, Interpretation, Etc.–O. T. Historical Books

BIBLE–CRITICISM, INTERPRETATION, ETC.–O. T. NUMBERS

see Bible–Criticism, Interpretation, Etc.–O. T. Pentateuch

BIBLE–CRITICISM, INTERPRETATION, ETC.–O. T. OBADIAH

see Bible–Criticism, Interpretation, Etc.–O. T. Minor Prophets

BIBLE–CRITICISM, INTERPRETATION, ETC.–O. T. PENTATEUCH

Here are entered works on the pentateuch as a whole, as well as books on one or more of the following: Deuteronomy, Exodus, Genesis, Leviticus, Numbers.

Doukhan, Jacques B. The Genesis Creation Story: Its Literary Structure. (Andrews University Seminary Doctoral Dissertation Ser.: Vol. 5). xii, 303p. 1982. pap. 8.95 (ISBN 0-943872-37-5). Andrews Univ Pr.

Fretheim, Terrence. Deuteronomic History. 160p. 1983. pap. 7.00 (ISBN 0-687-10497-1). Abingdon.

Kelly, William. The Pentateuch. (Introductory Lecture Ser.). 524p. 5.50 (ISBN 0-88172-099-2). Believers Bkshelf.

Morgan, G. Campbell. Analyzed Bible, Genesis. (G. Campbell Morgan Library). 280p. 1983. pap. 4.95 (ISBN 0-8010-6148-2). Baker Bk.

Riggans, Walter. Numbers. Gibson, John C., ed. (Daily Study Bible-Old Testament). 300p. (Orig.). 1983. price not set (ISBN 0-664-21393-6); pap. price not set (ISBN 0-664-24474-2). Westminster.

Rodriguez, Angel M. Substitution in the Hebrew Cultus. (Andrews University Seminary Doctoral Dissertation Ser.). xiv, 339p. (Orig.). 1982. pap. 8.95 (ISBN 0-943872-35-9). Andrews Univ Pr.

Taylor, John H., tr. & annotations by. St. Augustine: The Literal Meaning of Genesis, Vol. 1. (Ancient Christian Writers Ser.: Vol. 41). 292p. 1983. 19.95 (ISBN 0-8091-0326-5). Paulist Pr.

--St. Augustine: The Literal Meaning of Genesis, Vol. 2. (Ancient Christian Writers Ser.: Vol. 42). 358p. 1983. 22.95 (ISBN 0-8091-0327-3). Paulist Pr.

Weaver, Horace R. & Laymon, Charles M., eds. The International Lesson Annual, 1983-84. 448p. (Orig.). 1983. pap. 5.95 (ISBN 0-687-19147-5). Abingdon.

BIBLE–CRITICISM, INTERPRETATION, ETC.–O. T. POETICAL BOOKS

Here are entered works on the poetical books as a whole, as well as books on one or more of the following: Job, Ecclesiastes, Psalms, Proverbs, Song of Solomon; For works on Lamentations see Bible–Criticism, Interpretation, Etc–O. T. Prophets.

Deal, William S. New Light on the Shepherd Psalm. 1982. write for info. Crusade Pubs.

Jennings, F. C. Meditations on Ecclesiastes. 143p. 4.75 (ISBN 0-88172-090-9). Believers Bkshelf.

Knight, George A. Psalms: Vol. 1, Psalms 1 to 72. LC 82-20134. (The Daily Study Bible-Old Testament). 350p. 1982. 12.95 (ISBN 0-664-21805-9); pap. 6.95 (ISBN 0-664-24572-2). Westminster.

Murphy, Roland E. Wisdom Literature & Psalms: Interpreting Biblical Texts. Bailey, Lloyd R. & Furnish, Victor P., eds. 160p. (Orig.). 1983. pap. 6.95 (ISBN 0-687-45759-9). Abingdon.

Parker, A. Morgan. Psalms from the Sea. 1982. pap. 1.95 (ISBN 0-8341-0745-7). Beacon Hill.

Rive, Anna. Powers of the Psalms. 128p. (Orig.). 1982. pap. 3.95 (ISBN 0-943832-07-1). Intl Imports.

Tur-Sinai, N. H. The Book of Job. rev. ed. 672p. 1982. Repr. of 1967 ed. text ed. 18.00 (ISBN 965-17-0009-2). Ridgefield Pub.

Wiersbe, Warren W. Meet Yourself in the Psalms. 192p. 1983. pap. 4.50 (ISBN 0-88207-740-6). Victor Bks.

BIBLE–CRITICISM, INTERPRETATION, ETC.–O. T. PROPHETS

Here are entered works on the prophets as a whole as well as those on one or more of the following: Isaiah, Daniel, Lamentations, Ezekiel, Jeremiah.

Ferch, Arthur J. The Son of Man in Daniel Seven. (Andrews University Seminary Doctoral Dissertation Ser.: Vol. 6). x, 237p. 1983. pap. 8.95 (ISBN 0-943872-38-3). Andrews Univ Pr.

Fettke, Steven M. Messages to a Nation in Crisis: An Introduction to the Prophecy of Jeremiah. LC 82-19997. (Illus.). 72p. (Orig.). 1983. pap. text ed. 6.75 (ISBN 0-8191-2839-2). U Pr of Amer.

LaRondelle, Hans K. The Israel of God in Prophecy: Principles of Prophetic Interpretation. LC 82-74358. (Andrews University Monographs, Studies in Religion: Vol.13). 1983. 13.95 (ISBN 0-943872-13-8); pap. 10.95 (ISBN 0-943872-14-6). Andrews Univ Pr.

Wiesel, Elie. Five Biblical Portraits. LC 81-40458. vii, 157p. 1983. pap. 4.95 (ISBN 0-268-00962-7, 85-09622). U of Notre Dame Pr.

Zimmerli, Walther. I Am Yahweh. Brueggemann, Walter, ed. Scott, Doug, tr. from German. LC 81-85326. 160p. Date not set. 15.95 (ISBN 0-8042-0519-1). John Knox.

BIBLE–CRITICISM, INTERPRETATION, ETC.–O. T. PROVERBS

see Bible–Criticism, Interpretation, Etc.–O. T. Poetical Books

BIBLE–CRITICISM, INTERPRETATION, ETC.–O. T. PSALMS

see Bible–Criticism, Interpretation, Etc.–O. T. Poetical Books

BIBLE–CRITICISM, INTERPRETATION, ETC.–O. T. RUTH

see Bible–Criticism, Interpretation, Etc.–O. T. Historical Books

BIBLE–CRITICISM, INTERPRETATION, ETC.–O. T. SAMUEL

see Bible–Criticism, Interpretation, Etc.–O. T. Historical Books

BIBLE–CRITICISM, INTERPRETATION, ETC.–O. T. SONG OF SOLOMON

see Bible–Criticism, Interpretation, Etc.–O. T. Poetical Books

BIBLE–CRITICISM, INTERPRETATION, ETC.–O. T. ZECHARIAH

see Bible–Criticism, Interpretation, Etc.–O. T. Minor Prophets

BIBLE–CRITICISM, INTERPRETATION, ETC. O. T. ZEPHANIAH

see Bible–Criticism, Interpretation, Etc.–O. T. Minor Prophets

BIBLE–CRITICISM, INTERPRETATION, ETC.–THEORY, METHODS, ETC.

see Bible–Hermeneutics

BIBLE–CRITICISM, TEXTUAL–N. T.
Dearing, Vinton A. A Manual of Textual Analysis. LC 82-20947. ix, 108p. 1983. Repr. of 1959 ed. lib. bdg. 27.50x (ISBN 0-313-23734-4, DEMA). Greenwood.
BIBLE–CURIOSA
see Bible–Miscellanea
BIBLE–DEVOTIONAL LITERATURE
see Bible–Meditations
BIBLE–DICTIONARIES
Androgeus, John C., ed. The Lost Gospel of the Ages: Key to Immortality & Companion to the Holy Bible. (Illus.). 979p. 1978. pap. text ed. 95.00 (ISBN 0-9609802-3-7). Life Science.
Davies, Benjamin. Baker's Harmony of the Gospels. (Baker's Paperback Reference Library). 192p. 1983. pap. 6.95 (ISBN 0-8010-2928-7). Baker Bk.
Douglas, J. D., ed. The New Bible Dictionary. 1344p. 1982. 24.95 (ISBN 0-8423-4667-8). Tyndale.
Easton, M. G. Baker's Illustrated Bible Dictionary. (Baker's Paperback Reference Library). 760p. 1983. pap. 15.95 (ISBN 0-8010-3386-1). Baker Bk.
Meredith, J. M. Meredith's Second Book of Bible Lists. 272p. (Orig.). 1983. pap. 5.95 (ISBN 0-87123-319-3). Bethany Hse.
New American Standard Reference Bible: Thinline. 1983. text ed. 15.95 (ISBN 0-8024-6283-9); deluxe ed. 27.95 leather bonded (ISBN 0-8024-6281-2). Moody.
Owings, Timothy. A Cumulative Index of New Testament Greek Grammars. 160p. 1983. pap. 7.95 (ISBN 0-8010-6702-2). Baker Bk.
Peloubet, F. N., ed. The Every Day Bible Dictionary. Orig. Title: Peloubet's Bible Dictionary. 816p. 1983. 14.95 (ISBN 0-310-30850-X); pap. 9.95 (ISBN 0-310-30851-8). Zondervan.
Pocket Bible Dictionary. (Pocketpac Bks.). 1984. pap. 2.95 (ISBN 0-87788-683-0). Shaw Pubs.
Wood, Richard H. A Cyclopedic Dictionary of Ecclesiastical Terms According to the Use of the Episcopal Church. 1983. 10.95 (ISBN 0-8062-2141-0). Carlton.
BIBLE–DRAMA
see Bible As Literature; Mysteries and Miracle-Plays
BIBLE–EVIDENCES, AUTHORITY, ETC.
see also Miracles
Bird, Phyllis A. The Bible As the Church's Book. Date not set. write for info. Geneva Divinity.
--The Bible As the Church's Book, Vol. 5. LC 82-7049. (Library of Living Faith). 120p. 1982. pap. 5.95 (ISBN 0-664-24427-0). Westminster.
Stott, John R. God's Book for God's People. 96p. 1982. pap. 2.95 (ISBN 0-87784-396-1). Inter-Varsity.
BIBLE–EXEGESIS
see Bible–Commentaries; Bible–Hermeneutics
BIBLE–FOLK-LORE
see Folk-Lore, Jewish
BIBLE–GARDENS
see Bible–Natural History
BIBLE–GEOGRAPHY–MAPS
Alexander, Pat. Eerdmans' Atlas of the Bible with A-Z Guide to Places. (Illus.). 68p. 1983. 7.95 (ISBN 0-8028-3583-X). Eerdmans.
Archbishop of York. Palmer's Bible Atlas (Facsimile Edition) 84p. 1982. 14.95 (ISBN 0-686-43010-7, Carta Maps & Guides Pub Isreal). Hippocrene Bks.
Reader's Digest Editors. Atlas of the Bible: An Illustrated Guide to the Holy Land. LC 80-53426. (Illus.). 256p. 1981. 20.50 (ISBN 0-89577-097-0, Pub. by RD Assn). Random.
BIBLE–GLOSSARIES, VOCABULARIES, ETC.
see Bible–Dictionaries
BIBLE–HANDBOOKS, MANUALS, ETC.
Beddow, Virginia, ed. The Year of the Bible Manual. (Orig.). 1983. pap. 1.95 (ISBN 0-87239-646-0, 3036). Standard Pub.
Elwell, Walter, intro. by. Bagster's Bible Handbook. 264p. 1983. Repr. 9.95 (ISBN 0-8007-1334-6). Revell.
Halley. Manual Biblique de Halley. Cosson, Annie, ed. Wiles, M. A., tr. from Eng. Orig. Title: Halley's Bible Handbook. 974p. (Fr.). 1982. pap. 14.00 (ISBN 0-8297-0900-2). Life Pubs Intl.
Hann, Robert R. The Bible. 160p. 1983. pap. 5.95 (ISBN 0-8091-2503-X). Paulist Pr.
Hutchins, John. Hutchins' Guide to Bible Reading. (Illus.). 608p. 1983. 25.00x (ISBN 0-938386-00-X). Button Gwin.
Turner, Nicholas. Handbook for Biblical Studies. LC 82-7111. 156p. 1982. pap. 6.95 (ISBN 0-664-24436-X). Westminster.
BIBLE–HERMENEUTICS
Here are entered works on the principles of Biblical Criticism. Critical works on the Bible are entered under Bible–Criticism, Interpretation, Etc.
Davidson, Richard M. Typology in Scripture: A Study of Hermeneutical Structures. (Andrews University Seminary Doctoral Dissertation Ser.: Vol. 2). (Orig.). 1981. pap. 8.95 (ISBN 0-943872-34-0). Andrews Univ Pr.
Flinn, Frank K., ed. Hermeneutics & Horizons: The Shape of the Future. LC 82-50053. (Conference Ser.: No. 11). xvii, 445p. (Orig.). 1982. pap. text ed. 11.95 (ISBN 0-932894-11-9). Unif Theol Seminary.
Hahn, Ferdinand. Historical Investigation & New Testament Faith. Krentz, Edgar, ed. Maddox, Robert, tr. from Ger. LC 82-48547. 112p. 1983. pap. 6.95 (ISBN 0-8006-1691-X, 1-1691). Fortress.
Kung, Hans & Moltmann, Jurgen, eds. Conflicting Ways of Interpreting the Bible. (Concilium Ser.: Vol. 138). 128p. (Orig.). 1980. pap. 5.95 (ISBN 0-8164-2280-X). Seabury.
BIBLE–HERMENEUTICS–HISTORY
see Bible–Criticism, Interpretation, Etc.–History
BIBLE–HIGHER CRITICISM
see Bible–Criticism, Interpretation, etc.; Bible–Introductions
BIBLE–HISTORY
This head is used for work on the History of Bible texts or versions. For works on historical events see Bible–History of Biblical Events, or Bible–History of Contemporary Events.
MacGregor, Geddes. The Bible in the Making. LC 82-17499. 318p. 1983. pap. 12.75 (ISBN 0-8191-2810-4). U Pr of Amer.
Schmidt, Werner H. The Faith of the Old Testament: A History. Sturdy, John, tr. LC 82-21780. 336p. (Orig.). 1983. price not set (ISBN 0-664-21826-1); pap. price not set (ISBN 0-664-24456-4). Westminster.
BIBLE–HISTORY OF BIBLICAL EVENTS
see also Palestine–History
Cornfeld, Gaalyah & Maier, Paul L., eds. Josephus: The Jewish War. 560p. 1982. 39.95 (ISBN 0-310-39210-1). Zondervan.
Kee, Howard C. Understanding the New Testament. 4th ed. (Illus.). 464p. 1983. text ed. 21.95 (ISBN 0-13-936591-5). P-H.
BIBLE–HISTORY OF BIBLICAL EVENTS–JUVENILE LITERATURE
see Bible Stories
BIBLE–HISTORY OF BIBLICAL EVENTS–SOURCES
see Bible–Evidences, Authority, etc.
BIBLE–HOMILETICAL USE
Craddock, Fred B. John. Hayes, John H., ed. LC 82-48095. (Knox Preaching Guides Ser.). 149p. 1982. pap. 4.95 (ISBN 0-8042-3241-5). John Knox.
Fee, Gordon D. New Testament Exegesis: A Handbook for Students & Pastors. LC 82-24829. (Illus.). 180p. (Orig.). 1983. pap. price not set (ISBN 0-664-24469-6). Westminster.
Wardlaw, Don M., ed. Preaching Biblically. 180p. (Orig.). 1983. pap. price not set (ISBN 0-664-24478-5). Westminster.
BIBLE–ILLUSTRATIONS
see Bible–Pictures, Illustrations, etc.
BIBLE–INSPIRATION
see also Bible–Evidences, Authority, etc.; Inspiration; Revelation
Stott, John R. God's Book for God's People. 96p. 1982. pap. 2.95 (ISBN 0-87784-396-1). Inter-Varsity.
BIBLE–INTERPRETATION
see Bible–Commentaries; Bible–Criticism, Interpretation, etc.; Bible–Hermeneutics
BIBLE–INTRODUCTIONS
Cronk, George. The Message of the Bible: An Orthodox Christian Perspective. LC 82-7355. 293p. (Orig.). 1982. pap. 8.95 (ISBN 0-913836-94-X). St Vladimirs.
Flanders, H. J. & Cresson, B. C. Introduction to the Bible. 558p. 1973. 22.95 (ISBN 0-471-07012-2). Wiley.
Richards, Lawrence O. The Word Bible Handbook. 1982. 10.95 (ISBN 0-8499-0279-7). Word Pub.
BIBLE–INTRODUCTIONS–N. T.
Here are entered Introductions to the New Testament as a whole, or to any part except the Gospels, which are listed separately below.
Kee, Howard C. Understanding the New Testament. 4th ed. (Illus.). 464p. 1983. text ed. 21.95 (ISBN 0-13-936591-5). P-H.
BIBLE–JUVENILE LITERATURE
see also Bible Stories
Beers, V. Gilbert. My Picture Bible to See & to Share. (ps-3). text ed. 11.95 (ISBN 0-88207-818-6). Victor Bks.
Bennett, Marian. Bible Numbers. (Little Happy Day Bks.). (Illus.). 24p. (Orig.). (gr. k-3). 1983. pap. 0.45 (ISBN 0-87239-653-3, 2123). Standard Pub.
Bennett, Marian, ed. Bible Heroes: Grade 4. rev. ed. (Basic Bible Readers Ser.). (Illus.). 128p. (gr. 4). 1983. text ed. 7.95 (ISBN 0-87239-664-9, 2954). Standard Pub.
Bennett, Marian, compiled by. Bible Memory Verses. (Little Happy Day Bks.). (Illus.). 24p. (Orig.). (gr. k-3). 1983. pap. 0.45 (ISBN 0-87239-652-5, 2122). Standard Pub.
Bently, James. Simon & Schuster Children's Bible. (Children's Illustrated Bible Ser.). (Illus.). 240p. (gr. 2-5). 1983. 7.95 (ISBN 0-671-47089-2, Little). S&S.
Falk, Cathy. God's Care. Bennett, Marian, ed. (Bible Activities for Little People Ser.: Bk. 1). 24p. (Orig.). (ps-k). 1983. pap. 1.25 (ISBN 0-87239-676-2, 2451). Standard Pub.
--God's Friends. Bennett, Marian, ed. (Bible Activities for Little People Ser.: BK. 2). 24p. (Orig.). (ps-k). 1983. pap. 1.29 (ISBN 0-87239-677-0, 2452). Standard Pub.
--God's Son. Bennett, Marian, ed. (Bible Activities for Little People Ser.: Bk. 3). 24p. (Orig.). (ps-k). 1983. pap. 1.29 (ISBN 0-87239-678-9, 2453). Standard Pub.
--We Love God. Bennett, Marian, ed. (Bible Lessons for Little People Ser.: Bk. 2). 144p. (Orig.). (ps-k). 1983. pap. 6.95 (ISBN 0-87239-613-4, 3360). Standard Pub.
--We Please God. Bennett, Marian, ed. (Bible Activities Ser.: Bk. 4). 24p. (Orig.). (ps-k). 1983. pap. 1.29 (ISBN 0-87239-679-7, 2454). Standard Pub.
Hayes, Wanda. A Child's First Book of Bible Stories. Gambill, Henrietta, ed. (Illus.). 128p. (ps). 1983. text ed. 6.95 (ISBN 0-87239-659-2, 2949). Standard Pub.
Hutson, Joan. Love Never Ever Ends. Mahany, Patricia, ed. (Happy Day Bks.). (Illus.). 24p. (ps-2). 1983. 1.29 (ISBN 0-87239-641-X, 3561). Standard Pub.
Jessie, Karen. O. T. Books of the Bible. Sparks, Judith A., ed. 48p. (Orig.). (gr. 7 up). 1983. 1.50 (ISBN 0-87239-674-6, 2774). Standard Pub.
McCasland, Dave. The Culture Trap. (gr. 9-12). 1982. pap. 3.95 (ISBN 0-88207-191-2). Victor Bks.
Maschke, Ruby. Bible People Story-N-Puzzle Book. Sparks, Judith Ann, ed. 48p. (Orig.). (gr. 7 up). 1983. pap. 1.50 (ISBN 0-87239-673-8, 2773). Standard Pub.
--Disciples of Christ Story-N-Puzzle Book. 48p. (Orig.). (gr. 7 up). 1983. pap. 1.50 (ISBN 0-87239-675-4, 2775). Standard Pub.
Miller, Marge, ed. I Learn to Read About Jesus: Primer. rev. ed. (Basic Bible Readers). 128p. (gr. 1). 1983. text ed. 7.95 (ISBN 0-87239-660-6, 2950). Standard Pub.
Miller, Marge, compiled by. I Read About God's Care: Grades 1 & 2. rev. ed. (Basic Bible Readers). (Illus.). 128p. (gr. 1). 1983. text ed. 7.95 (ISBN 0-87239-662-2, 2952). Standard Pub.
Ryrie, Charles C. Making the Most of Life. (gr. 9-12). 1983. pap. 3.95 (ISBN 0-88207-587-X). SP Pubns.
Sherlock, Connie. Bible Families. Beegle, Shirley, ed. (Think 'N Check Quizzes Ser.). (Illus.). 16p. (Orig.). (gr. 4-8). 1983. pap. 1.50 (ISBN 0-87239-688-6, 2792). Standard Pub.
Stafford, Linda. Mind Invaders. (YA) (gr. 9-12). 1982. pap. 0.95. Victor Bks.
Stirrup Associates Inc. My Jesus Pocketbook of Li'l Critters. Phillips, Cheryl M., ed. LC 82-63139. (Illus.). 32p. (Orig.). 1983. pap. text ed. 0.49 (ISBN 0-937420-05-0). Stirrup Assoc.
--My Jesus Pocketbook of Manners. Phillips, Cheryl M., ed. LC 82-63141. (Illus.). 32p. 1983. pap. 0.49 (ISBN 0-937420-06-9). Stirrup Assoc.
Stirrup Associates, Inc. My Jesus Pocketbook of the 23rd Psalm. Phillips, Cheryl M., ed. LC 82-63140. (Illus.). 32p. (Orig.). 1983. pap. text ed. 0.49 (ISBN 0-937420-04-2). Stirrup Assoc.
Truitt, Gloria. People of the New Testament: Arch Book Supplement. 1983. pap. 0.89 (ISBN 0-570-06173-3). Concordia.
--People of the Old Testament: Arch Book Supplement. 1983. pap. 0.89 (ISBN 0-570-06172-5). Concordia.
Watson, E. Elaine. I Wish, I Wish. Mahany, Patricia, ed. (Happy Day Bks.). (Illus.). 24p. (ps-2). 1983. 1.29 (ISBN 0-87239-637-1, 3557). Standard Pub.
Wiersbe, Warren. Be Challenged! rev. ed. LC 82-12404. Orig. Title: Be a Real Teen. 1982. pap. 3.95 (ISBN 0-8024-1080-4). Moody.
BIBLE–LAW
see Jewish Law; Law (Theology)
BIBLE–LITERARY CRITICISM
see Bible–Criticism, Interpretation, etc.; Bible–Introductions; Bible As Literature
BIBLE–MANUSCRIPTS
see also Dead Sea Scrolls
MacGregor, Geddes. The Bible in the Making. LC 82-17499. 318p. 1983. pap. 12.75 (ISBN 0-8191-2810-4). U Pr of Amer.
BIBLE–MAPS
see Bible–Geography–Maps
BIBLE–MEDITATIONS
Kolden, Marc. Called by the Gospel. LC 82-72651. 112p. 1983. pap. 4.95 (10-0967). Augsburg.
BIBLE–MEDITATIONS–N. T.
Keating, Thomas. Crisis of Faith. LC 79-13036. 1979. pap. 4.00 (ISBN 0-932506-05-4). St Bedes Pubns.
BIBLE–MEDITATIONS–O. T.
Shaw, Jean. The Better Half of Life: Meditations from Ecclesiastes. 192p. 1983. pap. 5.95 (ISBN 0-310-43551-X). Zondervan.
Shepherd, J. Barrie. Encounters: Poetic Meditations on the Old Testament. LC 82-22422. 176p. (Orig.). 1983. pap. 8.95 (ISBN 0-8298-0637-7). Pilgrim NY.
BIBLE–MIRACLES
see Jesus Christ–Miracles; Miracles
BIBLE–MISCELLANEA
Bostrom, Alice. Search the Word Bible Puzzles. (Illus.). 48p. 1983. pap. 1.50 (ISBN 0-87239-589-8, 2787). Standard Pub.
Gramelsbach, Helen. Seventy-One Creative Bible Story Projects: Patterns for Crafts, Visuals, & Learning Centers. (Illus.). 64p. 1983. pap. 3.95 (ISBN 0-87239-607-X, 2103). Standard Pub.
Houck, Fannie L. Promises of the Bible Puzzle Book. 48p. 1983. pap. 1.50 (ISBN 0-87239-587-1, 2785). Standard Pub.
Johnson, Irene. Prophecy Foretold-Fulfilled: Puzzle Book. (Illus.). 48p. 1983. pap. 1.50 (ISBN 0-87239-590-1, 2788). Standard Pub.
MacKenzie, Joy & Bledsoe, Shirley. A Big Book of Bible Games & Puzzles. 192p. 1982. pap. 6.95 (ISBN 0-310-70271-2). Zondervan.
Sanson, Riley W. Bible Crossword Fun. 48p. 1983. pap. 1.50 (ISBN 0-87239-588-X). Standard Pub.
BIBLE–NATURAL HISTORY
Zohary, Michael. Plants of the Bible. LC 82-4535. (Illus.). 224p. 1982. 16.95 (ISBN 0-521-24926-0). Cambridge U Pr.
BIBLE–OUTLINES, SYLLABI, ETC.
see Bible–Study
BIBLE–PARABLES
see also Jesus Christ–Parables
Drew, George. The Parables in Depth. 55p. (Orig.). 1982. pap. 6.95 (ISBN 0-940754-18-5). Ed Ministries.
BIBLE–PHILOLOGY
see Hebrew Language
BIBLE–PICTURES, ILLUSTRATIONS, ETC.
see also subdivisions Art under names of Bible characters and Biblical subjects, e.g. Jesus Christ–Art
Beers, V. Gilbert. My Picture Bible to See & to Share. (ps-4). 1982. text ed. 11.95 (ISBN 0-88207-818-6, Sonflower Bks). SP Pubns.
Bible Stories Coloring Book. 48p. 1973. pap. 2.00 (ISBN 0-486-20623-8). Dover.
Blake, William. Blake's Job: William Blake's Illustrations of the Book of Job. Damon, S. Foster, ed. LC 66-13155. (Illus.). 76p. 1966. 17.50x (ISBN 0-87057-096-X, Pub. by Brown U Pr). U Pr of New Eng.
Hall, Terry. Bible Panorama. 1983. text ed. 9.95 (ISBN 0-88207-273-0). Victor Bks.
BIBLE–PRINTING
see Bible–History
BIBLE–PROPHECIES
see also Apocalyptic Literature; Prophets
Bennett, Gordon H., ed. El Futuro: En Los Anos de 1980 y adelante One Hundred Forty Preguntas y Respuestas. Flores, Rhode, tr. from Eng. 128p. (Orig., Span.). 1982. pap. write for info. (ISBN 0-942504-14-3). Overcomer Pr.
Christianson, Arne. The Future Is Now. 1983. 8.95 (ISBN 0-533-05552-0). Vantage.
Westermann, Claus. A Thousand Years & a Day. LC 62-8544. 292p. 1982. pap. 7.95 (ISBN 0-8006-1913-7, 1-1913). Fortress.
BIBLE–READERS
see Readers–Bible
BIBLE–READING
Hort, Erasmus. The Bible Book: Resources for Reading the New Testament. 172p. 1983. 14.95 (ISBN 0-8245-0556-5); pap. 7.95 (ISBN 0-8245-0557-3). Crossroad NY.
BIBLE–REVELATION
see Bible–Inspiration
BIBLE–SCIENCE
see Bible and Science
BIBLE–SERMONS
Here are entered works containing sermons which are successively based on at least one whole book of the Bible, virtually forming a commentary in sermon form.
Holbrook, D. L. & Holbrook, Becky T. Give Them God's Way. 3.75 (ISBN 0-89137-417-5). Quality Pubns.
Ramsey, Johnny. Back to Bible Preaching. pap. 4.25 (ISBN 0-89137-007-2). Quality Pubns.
--Search the Scriptures. pap. 5.35 (ISBN 0-89137-008-0). Quality Pubns.
BIBLE–SERMONS–N. T.
Finney, Charles & Parkhurst, L. B. Principles of Liberty. rev. ed. (Finney's Sermons on Romans Ser.). 192p. (Orig.). 1983. pap. 4.95 (ISBN 0-87123-475-0). Bethany Hse.
BIBLE–STORIES
see Bible Stories
BIBLE–STUDY
see also Bible Stories
Bruinsma, Sheryl. Easy-to-Use Object Lessons. (Object Lesson Ser.). 96p. (Orig.). 1983. pap. 3.95 (ISBN 0-8010-0832-8). Baker Bk.
Coleman, Lucien E., Jr. Como Ensenar la Biblia. Diaz, Jorge E., tr. Orig. Title: How to Teach the Bible. 265p. (Span.). 1982. 7.75 (ISBN 0-311-11039-8). Casa Bautista.
Cottrell, Jack. The Bible Says. 128p. (YA) 1983. pap. 2.25 (ISBN 0-87239-480-8). Standard Pub.
DeHaan, M. R. The Chemistry of the Blood. 160p. 1983. pap. 4.95 (ISBN 0-310-23291-0). Zondervan.
Draper, James T., Jr. Discover Joy: Studies in Philippians. 1983. pap. 4.95 (ISBN 0-8423-0606-4); leader's guide 2.95 (ISBN 0-8423-0607-2). Tyndale.
Gerlach, Joel & Bolge, Richard. Preach the Gospel. 1982. 8.95 (ISBN 0-8100-0153-5, 15NO387). Northwest Pub.
Hagin, Kenneth E. Bible Faith Study Course. 1974. pap. 5.00 (ISBN 0-89276-080-X). Hagin Ministry.
--The Bible Way to Receive the Holy Spirit. 1981. pap. 0.50 (ISBN 0-89276-255-1). Hagin Ministry.
Hagins, Kenneth E. Bible Prayer Study Course. 1974. pap. 5.00 (ISBN 0-89276-081-8). Hagin Ministry.
Herr, Ethel. Bible Study for Busy Women. 160p. 1983. pap. 6.95 (ISBN 0-8024-0147-3). Moody.
Hunt, Gladys. Relationships. (Fisherman Bible Studyguides Ser.). 80p. 1983. saddle stitched 2.50 (ISBN 0-87788-721-7). Shaw Pubs.
Jensen, Irving. Irving Jensen's Do-It-Yourself Bible Study: Mark. 120p. (Orig.). 1983. wkbk 3.95 (ISBN 0-89840-035-X). Heres Life.

Klein, Chuck. So You Want to Lead Students. 96p. 1982. pap. 3.95 (ISBN 0-8423-6084-0). Tyndale.
--So You Want to Set the Pace. 96p. 1982. pap. 4.95 (ISBN 0-8423-6083-2). Tyndale.
Maccoby, Hyam. The Sacred Executioner: Human Sacrifice & the Legacy of Guilt. LC 82-80492. (Illus.). 208p. 1983. 19.95 (ISBN 0-500-01281-4). Thames Hudson.
McDowell, Josh. Guide To Understanding Your Bible. 1982. pap. 4.95 (ISBN 0-686-37703-6). Here's Life.
McGee, J. Vernon. Thru the Bible with J. Vernon McGee: Matthew through Romans, Vol. IV. 850p. 1983. 19.95 (ISBN 0-8407-4976-7). Nelson.
Martin, T. E. Beacon Bible Expositions: The Revelation. Greathouse, M., ed. (Beacon Bible Exposition Ser.: Vol. 12). 230p. 1983. 6.95 (ISBN 0-8341-0809-7). Beacon Hill.
Mears, Henrietta C. What the Bible Is All About. rev. ed. 1982. pap. 8.95 (ISBN 0-8307-0862-6). Regal.
Milner, Wanda. Learning to Use the Bible. Mahany, Patricia, ed. (Illus.). 24p. (Orig.). 1983. pap. price not set (ISBN 0-87239-690-8, 3200). Standard Pub.
Mitchell, Phyllis. How to Study the Bible. 95p. (Orig.). 1982. pap. 4.95 (ISBN 0-686-37607-2). Women's Aglow.
Moir, John S. A History of Biblical Studies in Canada: A Sense of Proportion. LC 82-5979. (Society of Biblical Literature: Biblical Scholarship in North America Ser.). 132p. 1982. pap. 17.95 (ISBN 0-89130-581-5, 06 11 07). Scholars Pr CA.
Neighbour, Ralph W., Jr. Sigueme. 68p. 1982. Repr. of 1981 ed. 2.75 (ISBN 0-311-13837-3); 2.65 (ISBN 0-311-13836-5). Casa Bautista.
Osborne, Grant R. & Woodward, Stephen B. Handbook for Bible Study. 188p. 1983. pap. 5.95 (ISBN 0-8010-6701-4). Baker Bk.
Pocketpac Bks. Promises for the Golden Years. 96p. 1983. pap. 1.95 (ISBN 0-87788-320-3). Shaw Pubs.
Ramsey, Johnny. Bible Treasures. pap. 8.50 (ISBN 0-89137-009-9). Quality Pubns.
Scott, W. Bible Handbook, 2 vols. 18.00 (ISBN 0-88172-123-9). Believers Bkshelf.
Stacey, W. David. Groundwork of Biblical Studies. LC 82-70961. 448p. 1982. pap. 12.50 (ISBN 0-8066-1936-8, 10-2893). Augsburg.
Taylor, Willard H. Beacon Bible Expositions. (Beacon Bible Exposition Ser.: Vol. 8). 228p. 1981. 6.95 (ISBN 0-8341-0734-1). Beacon Hill.
That You May Believe (John) Leader's Guide. (New Horizons Bible Study). 48p. 1983. pap. 1.95 (ISBN 0-89367-082-0). Light & Life.
A Through the Bible Reading Program. (Illus.). 112p. (Orig.). 1983. pap. 3.95 (ISBN 0-87239-647-9, 3076). Standard Pub.
Wake Up O' Sleeping World. 48p. 1983. 9.95 (ISBN 0-89962-315-8). Todd & Honeywell.
Walsh, Mary A. & Sickles, Margaret. How to Read the Bible. LC 82-61467. 140p. Date not set. pap. 6.95 (ISBN 0-87973-619-4, 619). Our Sunday Visitor.
Weber, Hans-Ruedi. Experiments with Bible Study. LC 82-13398. 336p. 1983. pap. 12.95 (ISBN 0-664-24461-0). Westminster.
Wendland, E. H., ed. Sermon Studies on the Gospels. (Series C). 1982. 8.95 (ISBN 0-8100-0149-7, 15NO378). Northwest Pub.
Wilkinson, Bruce & Boa, Kenneth. Talk Thru the Bible. 469p. 1983. Repr. of 1981 ed. 14.95 (ISBN 0-8407-5286-5). Nelson.
Willerton, Chris. Teaching the Adult Bible Class. 2.95 (ISBN 0-89137-609-7). Quality Pubns.
Yarn, David H. The Four Gospels as One. 281p. 1982. 8.95 (ISBN 0-87747-948-8). Deseret Bk.

BIBLE-STUDY-OUTLINES, SYLLABI, ETC.
Childress, Harvey. Expanding Outlines of the New Testament Books. 5.95 (ISBN 0-89137-536-8). Quality Pubns.
Ellis, Peter F. & Ellis, Judith M. Access Guide for Scripture Study: John. manuaul 3.95 (ISBN 0-8215-5936-2); guide 2.95 (ISBN 0-8215-5918-4). Sadlier.
Harrington, Daniel J. Access Guide for Scripture Study: Luke. Date not set. 2.95 (ISBN 0-8215-5929-X); 3.95 (ISBN 0-8215-5934-6). Sadlier.
--Access Guide for Scripture Study: Mark. Date not set. 2.95 (ISBN 0-8215-5928-1); 3.95 (ISBN 0-8215-5933-8). Sadlier.
Meier, John B. Access Guide for Scripture Study: Matthew. Date not set. 2.95 (ISBN 0-8215-5932-X); 3.95 (ISBN 0-8215-5935-4). Sadlier.

BIBLE-STUDY-N. T.
Hooker, Morna D. Studying the New Testament. LC 82-70959. 224p. (Orig.). 1982. pap. 7.95 (ISBN 0-8066-1934-1, 10-6140). Augsburg.

BIBLE-STUDY-O. T.
Jeremiah, David. Abraham: Twenty-Six Daily Bible Studies. (Steps to Higher Ground Ser.). 1982. pap. 1.50 (ISBN 0-86508-201-4). BCM Pubns.
Knight, George A. Psalms: Vol. 1, Psalms 1 to 72. LC 82-20134. (The Daily Study Bible-Old Testament). 350p. 1982. 12.95 (ISBN 0-664-21805-9); pap. 6.95 (ISBN 0-664-24572-2). Westminster.
McKeating, Henry. Studying the Old Testament. LC 82-70960. 224p. (Orig.). 1982. pap. 7.95 (ISBN 0-8066-1935-X, 10-6141). Augsburg.
Rogerson, John. Beginning Old Testament Study. LC 82-20210. 160p. 1983. pap. price not set (ISBN 0-664-24451-3). Westminster.

BIBLE-STUDY-TEXT-BOOKS
see also Bible Stories
Shannon, Foster. Green Leaf Bible Series, Vol. II. Rew, Lois J., ed. (Orig.). 1983. pap. 2.50 (ISBN 0-938462-11-3). Green Leaf CA.
Souter, John. What's the Good Word? The All New Super Incredible Bible Study Book for Junior Highs. 64p. 1983. pap. 2.50 (ISBN 0-310-45891-9). Zondervan.

BIBLE-SYMBOLISM
see Symbolism in the Bible

BIBLE-TEACHINGS
see Bible-Theology

BIBLE-THEOLOGY
see also names of specific doctrines, with or without the subdivision Biblical Teaching
Hodges, Zane C. The Gospel Under Siege: A Study on Faith & Works. 125p. (Orig.). 1981. pap. 4.95 (ISBN 0-9607576-0-0). Redencion Viva.

BIBLE-THEOLOGY-O. T.
Schmidt, Werner H. The Faith of the Old Testament: A History. Sturdy, John, tr. LC 82-21780. 336p. (Orig.). 1983. price not set (ISBN 0-664-21826-1); pap. price not set (ISBN 0-664-24456-4). Westminster.

BIBLE-TRANSLATIONS
see Bible-Versions

BIBLE-VERSIONS
Here are entered works on Versions of the Bible in any language except English. For English Version see subdivision Versions, English.
Aland, K., ed. Greek-English New Testament. 26th ed. 1981. 11.50 (ISBN 3-438-05408-6, 56495). Am Bible.
Biblia Hebraica Stuttgartensia. Incl. Vol. 1. Genesis. pap. 3.20 (ISBN 3-438-05201-6, 60980); Vol. 2. Exodus, Leviticus. pap. 3.20 (ISBN 3-438-05202-4, 60981); Vol. 3. Numbers, Deuteronomy. pap. 3.20 (ISBN 3-438-05202-4, 60984); Vol. 4. Joshua, Judges. pap. 3.20 (ISBN 3-438-05204-0, 61301); Vol. 5. 1-2 Samuel. pap. 3.20 (ISBN 3-438-05205-9, 61203); Vol. 6. 1-2 Kings. pap. 3.20 (ISBN 3-438-05206-7, 06987); Vol. 7. Isaiah. pap. 3.20 (ISBN 3-438-05207-5, 61160); Vol. 8. Jeremiah. pap. 3.20 (ISBN 3-438-05208-3, 61201); Vol. 9. Ezekiel. pap. 3.20 (ISBN 3-438-05209-1, 61231); Vol. 10. Twelve Prophets. pap. 3.20 (ISBN 3-438-05210-5, 61261); Vol. 11. Psalms. pap. 3.20 (ISBN 3-438-05211-3, 61300); Vol. 12. Job. Proverbs. pap. 3.20 (ISBN 3-438-05212-1, 61303); Vol. 13. Megilloth. pap. 3.20 (ISBN 3-438-05213-X, 61304); Vol. 14. Daniel, Ezra, Nehemiah. pap. 3.20 (ISBN 3-438-05214-8, 61209); Vol. 15. 1-2 Chronicles. pap. 3.20 (ISBN 3-438-05215-6, 61305). pap. United Bible.
Chupco, Lee & Coachman, Ward. Creek (Muscogee) New Testament Concordance. 167p. 1982. pap. 15.00 spiral bdg. (ISBN 0-940392-10-0). Indian U Pr.
Foster, Lewis & Stedman, Jon. Selecting a Translation of the Bible. Korth, Bob, ed. (Illus.). 128p. (Orig.). 1983. pap. price not set (ISBN 0-87239-645-2). Standard Pub.
Hatch, Edwin & Redpath, Henry A. A Concordance to the Septuagint & Other Greek Versions of the Old Testament (Including the Apocryphal Books, 3 vols. in 2. 1088p. 1983. Repr. of 1906 ed. Set. 75.00 (ISBN 0-8010-4270-4). Baker Bk.
Kubo, Sakae & Specht, Walter. So Many Versions? 320p. 1983. pap. 9.95 (ISBN 0-310-45691-6). Zondervan.
The New King James Version of the Holy Bible. 1982. 29.95 (ISBN 0-686-84640-0); pap. 12.95 (ISBN 0-686-84641-9). Nelson.
Smith, Richard H. A Concise Coptic-English Lexicon. 96p. 1983. 10.95 (ISBN 0-8028-3581-3). Eerdmans.
Strand, Kenneth A. Catholic German Bibles of the Reformation Era: The Versions of Emser, Dietenberger, Eck, & Others. (Illus.). 1982. 25.00 (ISBN 0-89039-300-1). Ann Arbor FL.
Yaeger, Randolf. Renaissance New Testament, Vol. 14. 660p. 1983. 22.50 (ISBN 0-88289-859-0). Pelican.
Yeager, Randolf. Renaissance New Testament, Vol. 12. 660p. 1983. 22.50 (ISBN 0-88289-458-7). Pelican.
--Renaissance New Testament, Vol. 13. 660p. 1983. 22.50 (ISBN 0-88289-958-9). Pelican.

BIBLE-VERSIONS, ENGLISH
Hammond, Gerald. The Making of the English Bible. 256p. 1983. 20.00 (ISBN 0-8022-2419-9). Philos Lib.
MacGregor, Geddes. The Bible in the Making. LC 82-17499. 318p. 1983. pap. 12.75 (ISBN 0-8191-2810-4). U Pr of Amer.

BIBLE-WOMEN
see Women in the Bible

BIBLE-ZOOLOGY
see Bible-Natural History

BIBLE AND SCIENCE
see also Creation
Pun, Pattle P. Evolution: Nature & Scripture in Conflict? 336p. (Orig.). 1982. pap. 9.95 (ISBN 0-310-42561-1). Zondervan.

BIBLE AS LITERATURE
see also Bible-Criticism, Interpretation, etc.; Bible-Parables; Religious Literature
Trail, W. The Literary Characteristics & Achievements of the Bible. 335p. 1983. Repr. of 1863 ed. lib. bdg. 85.00 (ISBN 0-89984-471-5). Century Bookbindery.

BIBLE GAMES AND PUZZLES
Gordon, William C. Bible Word Search. (Quiz & Puzzle Bks.). 112p. 1983. 2.95 (ISBN 0-686-81737-0). Baker Bk.
Marks, Thomas J. More Bible Study Puzzles. (Orig.). 1983. pap. 2.50 (ISBN 0-8054-9108-2). Broadman.
Reynolds, Erma. Bible Sayings Quiz Book. (Quiz & Puzzle Bks.). 96p. (Orig.). 1983. pap. 2.95 (ISBN 0-8010-7720-6). Baker Bk.

BIBLE IN LITERATURE
see also Religion in Literature
Jacobson, Howard. The Exagoge of Ezekiel. LC 82-4410. 240p. 1983. 44.50 (ISBN 0-521-24580-X). Cambridge U Pr.

BIBLE PUZZLES
see Bible Games and Puzzles

BIBLE STORIES
Baby in a Basket. (Palm Tree Bks.). (Illus.). (gr. 1-4). 1982. pap. 0.99 (ISBN 0-570-08501-2). Concordia.
Becky Gets Up. (Palm Tree Bks.). (Illus.). (gr. 1-4). 1982. pap. 0.99 (ISBN 0-570-08507-1). Concordia.
Borsh, Frederick H. Power in Weakness: New Hearing for Gospel Stories of Healing & Discipleship. LC 82-15997. 160p. 1983. pap. 8.95 (ISBN 0-8006-1703-7, 1-1703). Fortress.
Brincat, Matthew De. Salt & Light. 56p. (gr. 6up). 1983. pap. 3.00 (ISBN 0-911423-00-1). Bible-Speak.
Daniel & the Lions. (Palm Tree Bks.). (Illus.). (gr. 1-4). 1982. pap. 0.99 (ISBN 0-570-08504-7). Concordia.
Dede, Vivian. The Stranger at Jacob's Well. (Arch Bk: No. 20). 1983. pap. 0.89 (ISBN 0-570-06164-4). Concordia.
Five Loaves & Two Fish. (Palm Tree Bks.). (Illus.). (gr. 1-4). 1982. pap. 0.99 (ISBN 0-570-08506-3). Concordia.
Gideon the Brave. (Palm Tree Bks.). (Illus.). (gr. 1-4). 1982. pap. 0.99 (ISBN 0-570-08502-0). Concordia.
The Good Samaritan. (Palm Tree Bks.). (Illus.). (gr. 1-4). 1982. pap. 0.99 (ISBN 0-570-08510-1). Concordia.
Jesus Gets Lost. (Palm Tree Bks.). (Illus.). (gr. 1-4). 1982. pap. 0.99 (ISBN 0-570-08505-5). Concordia.
Jonah & the Big Fish. (Palm Tree Bks.). (Illus.). (gr. 1-4). 1982. pap. 0.99 (ISBN 0-570-08503-9). Concordia.
Levi, the Lame Man. new ed. (Palm Tree Bks.). (gr. 1-4). 1982. pap. 0.99 (ISBN 0-570-08508-X). Concordia.
Lops, R. L. H. La Bible de Mace de la Charite Vol. VII: Apocalypse. (Leidse Romanistische Reeks Ser.: Vol. 10). (Illus.). xiii, 263p. 1982. pap. write for info (ISBN 90-04-06758-2). E J Brill.
The Lost Son. (Palm Tree Bks.). (Illus.). (gr. 1-4). 1982. pap. 0.99 (ISBN 0-570-08509-8). Concordia.
Miller, Marge, compiled by. Bible Adventures. rev. ed. (Basic Bible Readers Ser.). (Illus.). 128p. (gr. 3). 1983. text ed. 7.95 (ISBN 0-87239-663-0, 2953). Standard Pub.
Noah's Big Boat. (Palm Tree Bks.). (Illus.). (gr. 1-4). 1982. pap. 0.99 (ISBN 0-570-08500-4). Concordia.
Polyzoides, G. Stories from the New Testament. (Illus.). 112p. 3.20 (ISBN 0-686-83966-8). Divry.
Smeets, J. R. La Bible de Mace de la Charite Vol. V: Cantiques des Catntiques, Maccabees. (Leidse Romanistische Reeks: Vol. 10). (Illus.). vii, 303p. 1982. pap. write for info. (ISBN 90-04-06776-0). E J Brill.
Storr, Catherine & Bennett, Russell, eds. The Prodigal Son. LC 82-23011. (People of the Bible Ser.). (Illus.). 32p. (gr. 1-2). 1983. PLB 11.55 (ISBN 0-8172-1982-X). Raintree Pubs.
Zacchaeus & Jesus. (Illus.). (gr. 1-4). 1982. pap. 0.99 (ISBN 0-570-08511-X). Concordia.

BIBLE STORIES-N. T.
see also Jesus Christ-Biography-Juvenile Literature
Lusk, David T. Within the Halls of Pilate. write for info. (ISBN 0-89137-538-4). Quality Pubns.
Roberts, D. S. Faith, Hope & Love: Learning about I Corinthians 13. (Concept Bks.: Ser. 4). (gr. 1-4). 1983. pap. 3.50 (ISBN 0-570-08526-8). Concordia.
Wellington, Gladys. Three Pieces of Silver. LC 81-81939. 64p. 1983. 6.95 (ISBN 0-86666-036-4). GWP.

BIBLE STORIES-O. T.
Boggs, Sue H. The Secret of Hind's Feet. write for info. (ISBN 0-89137-537-6). Quality Pubns.
Clarke, M. J., et al. Copper, Molybdenum, & Vanadium in Biological Systems. (Structure & Bonding: Vol. 53). (Illus.). 166p. 1983. 37.00 (ISBN 0-387-12042-4). Springer-Verlag.
Limburg, James. Old Testament Stories for a New Time. LC 82-49019. 127p. 1983. pap. 7.95 (ISBN 0-8042-0148-X). John Knox.
Macmaster, Eve. God Gives the Land. (Story Bible Ser.: Vol. 3). (Illus.). 168p. (Orig.). 1982. pap. 5.95 (ISBN 0-8361-3332-3). Herald Pr.
McWhorter, Jane. Meet My Friend David. 4.60 (ISBN 0-89137-420-5). Quality Pubns.
Marjorie, Palmer. God Helps David. (My Bible Story Reader Ser.: Vol. 1). (Illus.). (gr. 2 up). 1983. pap. price not set (ISBN 0-8024-0191-0). Moody.
--God Saves Noah. (My Bible Story Reader Ser.: Vol. 2). (Illus., Orig.). (gr. 2). 1983. pap. price not set (ISBN 0-8024-0192-9). Moody.
Steiner, Rudolf. And The Temple Becomes Man. Osmond, D. S., tr. from Ger. 31p. 1979. pap. 2.50 (ISBN 0-85440-337-X, Pub. by Steinerbooks). Anthroposophic.
Storr, Catherine, retold by. Adam & Eve. LC 82-23060. (People of the Bible Ser.). (Illus.). 32p. (gr. 1-2). 1983. PLB 11.55 (ISBN 0-8172-1981-1). Raintree Pubs.

BIBLE TRANSLATING
see Bible-Versions

BIBLICAL ANTHROPOLOGY
see Man (Theology)

BIBLICAL ARCHAEOLOGY
see Bible-Antiquities

BIBLICAL CHARACTERS
see Bible-Biography

BIBLICAL LAW
see Jewish Law

BIBLICAL RESEARCH
see Bible-Criticism, Interpretation, etc.

BIBLOGRAPHIC SEARCHING, ON-LINE
see on-Line Bibliographic Searching

BIBLIOGRAPHICAL SEARCHING
see on-Line Bibliographic Searching; Searching, Bibliographical

BIBLIOGRAPHY
see also Abstracting and Indexing Services; Anonyms and Pseudonyms; Archives; Book Collecting; Bookbinding; Books; Books and Reading; Cataloging; Classification-Books; Incunabula; Indexes; Indexing; Information Storage and Retrieval Systems; Libraries; Library Science; Manuscripts; Periodicals-Indexes; Printing; Reference Books
also names of literature, e.g. American Literature; also names of persons, places and subjects, with or without the subdivision bibliography
McIlwaine, Ia & McIlwaine, John, eds. Bibliography & Reading: A Festschrift in Honour of Ronald Staveley. LC 82-21489. 180p. 1983. 15.00 (ISBN 0-8108-1601-6). Scarecrow.

BIBLIOGRAPHY-BEST BOOKS
see also Reference Books-Bibliography
The Coffee-Table Book. (Blank Books Ser.). 160p. 1982. cancelled (ISBN 0-939944-20-0). Marmac Pub.
Gingold, Alfred. Items from Our Catalog. 1982. pap. 4.95 (ISBN 0-686-83416-X, 380-81695-4). Avon.
New Year's Resolutions. (Blank Book Ser.). 128p. 1982. cancelled (ISBN 0-939944-21-9). Marmac Pub.
Reader's Digest Editors. Treasury of Great Books. LC 80-50421. (Illus.). 640p. 1980. 14.98 (ISBN 0-89577-084-9). RD Assn.

BIBLIOGRAPHY-BIBLIOGRAPHY
see also Reference Books-Bibliography
Books in Print Supplement, 1982-1983, 2 vol. set. 3500p. 1983. 75.50x (ISBN 0-8352-1664-0). Bowker.
Downs, Robert B., ed. American Library Resources: A Bibliographical Guide Supplement, 1971-1980. 224p. 1981. text ed. 30.00 (ISBN 0-8389-0342-8). ALA.

BIBLIOGRAPHY-EARLY PRINTED BOOKS
see also Bibliography-Rare Books; Printing-History
Joyce, William L. & Hall, David D., eds. Printing & Society in Early America. 1983. text ed. price not set (ISBN 0-912296-55-0, Dist. by U Pr of VA). Am Antiquarian.

BIBLIOGRAPHY-EARLY PRINTED BOOKS-15TH CENTURY
see Incunabula

BIBLIOGRAPHY-PAPERBACK EDITIONS
Paperbound Books in Print: Spring & Fall, 1983, 6 vols. 10000p. 1983. 119.50x (ISBN 0-8352-1584-9). Bowker.
Paperbound Books in Print: Spring, 1983, 3 vol. set. 5000p. 1983. 69.50x (ISBN 0-8352-1585-7). Bowker.
Stephens, Christopher. The Lion Paperback: A Checklist. 32p. 1980. pap. 3.50 (ISBN 0-89366-124-4). Ultramarine Pub.

BIBLIOGRAPHY-RARE BOOKS
see also Bibliography-Early Printed Books; Incunabula; Manuscripts
Carpenter, Kenneth E. Books & Society in History. 300p. 1983. 29.95 (ISBN 0-8352-1675-6). Bowker.

BIBLIOGRAPHY-REFERENCE BOOKS
see Reference Books

BIBLIOGRAPHY-SUBSCRIPTION BOOKS
RSBR Committee, ed. Reference & Subscription Book Reviews, 1980-81. 148p. Date not set. pap. text ed. 20.00 (ISBN 0-8389-3269-X). ALA.

BIBLIOGRAPHY, CRITICAL
see Bibliography-Best Books; Books and Reading; Criticism; Literature-History and Criticism;
also subdivision History and Criticism under names of literatures, e.g. American Literatures-History and Criticism

BIBLIOGRAPHY OF BIBLIOGRAPHIES
see Bibliography-Bibliography

BIBLIOTHERAPY
see also Reading, Psychology of; Therapeutics
Overstad, Beth, ed. Bibliotherapy: Books to Help Young Children. 2nd ed. 80p. 1981. pap. 10.95 (ISBN 0-934140-09-X). Toys N Things.

BICAMERALISM
see Legislative Bodies

BICULTURALISM
Rodriguez, Fred. Education in a Multicultural Society. LC 82-23755. 172p. (Orig.). 1983. lib. bdg. 21.75 (ISBN 0-8191-2977-1); pap. text ed. 10.50 (ISBN 0-8191-2978-X). U Pr of Amer.

BICYCLES AND TRICYCLES
see also Cycling; Mopeds; Motorcycles
Basic Bicycling. 4.50 (ISBN 0-686-84042-9). AAHPERD.
Comprehensive Bicyclists Education Program (CBEP) incl. 7 cassettes, 7 filmstrips & 3 modules 99.50 (ISBN 0-88314-225-2); Module I The Bicycling Environment. 40.00 (ISBN 0-88314-226-0); Module II Haxard Awareness. 40.00 (ISBN 0-88314-227-9); Module III Riding with Trafic. 40.00 (ISBN 0-88314-228-7); Basic Bicycling. 4.50 (ISBN 0-686-38062-2). AAHPERD.
Kane, H. H. The Bicycle as a Factor in Genito Urinary Diseases, Prostratis, Prostatorrhea, or Prostatic Catarrh. 24p. Date not set. pap. 5.00 (ISBN 0-87556-575-1). Saifer.
Murphy, Jim. Two Hundred Years of Bicycles. LC 81-48608. (Illus.). 64p. (gr. 3-6). 1983. 9.57i (ISBN 0-397-32007-8, JBL-J); PLB 9.89g (ISBN 0-397-32008-6). Har-Row.
Sharp, Archibald. Bicycles & Tricycles; Elementary Treatise on Their Design & Construction: 1896. (Illus.). 536p. Date not set. pap. 35.00 (ISBN 0-87556-579-4). Saifer.
Stevenson, Edward. High Tech Bicycle. LC 81-48157. (Illus.). 192p. 1982. 24.04i (ISBN 0-06-014876-4, HarpT). Har-Row.
Velo-news Editors. Ten Years of Championship Bicycle Racing. (Illus.). 128p. (Orig.). 1983. specialty trade 14.95 (ISBN 0-686-42828-5). Velo-News.

BICYCLES AND TRICYCLES–MAINTENANCE AND REPAIR
Andrews, Heber J. How to Prevent Bicycle Theft: Owner's Guide. (Illus.). 32p. 1982. pap. 2.50x (ISBN 0-9609596-0-2). Hands Off.

BIG BEND REGION, TEXAS
Deckert, Frank. Big Bend: Three Steps to the Sky. Pearson, John R., ed. (Illus.). 40p. (Orig.). 1981. pap. 3.95 (ISBN 0-686-38923-9). Big Bend.
Madison, Virginia & Stillwell, Hallie. How Come It's Called That? rev. ed. 130p. 1979. Repr. of 1968 ed. 8.95 (ISBN 0-686-38928-X). Big Bend.
Pearson, John R., ed. Hiker's Guide to Trails of Big Bend National Park. 2nd ed. (Illus.). 32p. (Orig.). 1978. pap. 1.00 (ISBN 0-686-38926-3). Big Bend.
--Road Guide to Backcountry Dirt Roads of Big Bend National Park. (Illus.). 40p. (Orig.). 1980. pap. 1.00 (ISBN 0-686-38927-1). Big Bend.
--Road Guide to Paved & Improved Dirt Roads of Big Bend National Park. (Illus.). 48p. (Orig.). 1980. pap. 1.00 (ISBN 0-686-38925-5). Big Bend.

BIG BUSINESS
see also Competition
Utton, M. A. The Political Economy of Big Business. LC 82-10739. 272p. 1982. 32.50x (ISBN 0-312-62255-4). St Martin.

BIG THICKET, TEXAS
Frary, Michael & Owens, William A. Impressions of the Big Thicket. (Illus.). 112p. 1983. pap. 12.95 (ISBN 0-292-73831-5). U Of Tex Pr.

BIGOTRY
see Toleration

BILE
Hofmann, Alan F. & Huebner, Vicky L. Bile, Bile Acid, Gallstones & Gallstone Dissolution. 340p. 1982. text ed. 39.00 (ISBN 0-85200-497-4, Pub. by MTP Pr England). Kluwer Boston.

BILE ACIDS
Hofmann, Alan F. & Huebner, Vicky L. Bile, Bile Acid, Gallstones & Gallstone Dissolution. 340p. 1982. text ed. 39.00 (ISBN 0-85200-497-4, Pub. by MTP Pr England). Kluwer Boston.

BILIARY CALCULI
see Calculi, Biliary

BILINGUALISM
see also Education, Bilingual
Caso, Adolph. Bilingual Two Language Battery of Tests. 1983. pap. 15.00 (ISBN 0-8283-1857-3). Branden.
Sanchez, Rosaura. Chicano Discourse: Socio-Historic Perspectives. 224p. 1983. pap. text ed. 15.95 (ISBN 0-88377-215-9). Newbury Hse.

BILL OF PARTICULARS
see Bills of Particulars

BILL OF RIGHTS (U. S.)
see United States–Constitution

BILLIARDS
Robin, Eddie. Position Play in Three Cushion Billiards. (Three Cushion Billiards Ser.: Vol. III). (Illus.). 431p. 1983. 36.00. E Robin Pub.

BILLIARDS, POCKET
see also Pool (Game)
Craven, Robert R., compiled by. Billiards, Bowling, Table Tennis, Pinball & Video Games: A Bibliographic Guide. LC 82-21077. 162p. 1983. lib. bdg. 29.95 (ISBN 0-313-23462-0, CBB/). Greenwood.

BILLIES
see Truncheons

BILLS, LEGISLATIVE
Nabors, Eugene. Legislative Reference Checklist: The Key to Legislative Histories from 1789-1903. LC 82-18074. xv, 440p. 1982. text ed. 39.50x (ISBN 0-8377-0908-3). Rothman.

BILLS AND NOTES
see Negotiable Instruments

BILLS OF CREDIT
see Negotiable Instruments

BILLS OF FARE
see Menus

BILLS OF PARTICULARS
Billing Systems for Health Professionals. 7.95 (ISBN 0-910085-05-6). Info Res MI.

BINARY STARS
see Stars, Double

BINDING OF BOOKS
see Bookbinding

BINET-STANFORD TEST
see Stanford-Binet Test

BINOCULAR VISION
Griffin, John R. Binocular Anomalies: Procedures foe Vision Therapy. 2nd ed. LC 82-61252. 1982. 48.00 (ISBN 0-686-43308-4). Prof Press.

BIOACOUSTICS
see also Hearing
Lewis, B., ed. Bioacoustics: A Comparative Approach. (Illus.). Date not set. price not set (ISBN 0-12-446550-1). Acad Pr.

BIOASSAY
see Biological Assay

BIOCHEMICAL ENGINEERING
Chose, T. K., et al, eds. Downstream Processing. (Advances in Biochemical Engineering-Biotechnology: Vol. 26). (Illus.). 225p. 1983. 33.50 (ISBN 0-387-12096-3). Springer-Verlag.
Fiechter, A., ed. Chromatography. (Advances in Biochemical Engineering Ser.: Vol. 25). (Illus.). 145p. 1983. 25.00 (ISBN 0-387-11829-2). Springer-Verlag.

BIOCHEMICAL EVOLUTION
see Chemical Evolution

BIOCHEMISTRY
see Biological Chemistry

BIOCHEMISTRY, QUANTUM
see Quantum Biochemistry

BIOCOMPATIBLE MATERIALS
see Biomedical Materials

BIOCOMPUTERS
see Conscious Automata

BIODYNAMIC GARDENING
see Organic Gardening

BIOELECTRICITY
see Electrophysiology

BIOENERGETICS
Caplan, S. Roy & Essig, Alvin. Bioenergetics & Linear Nonequilibrium Thermodynamics: The Steady State. (Harvard Books in Biophysics: No. 3). (Illus.). 448p. 1983. text ed. 37.50x (ISBN 0-674-07352-5). Harvard U Pr.
Milazzo, G. Topics in Bioelectrochemistry & Bioenergetics, Vol. 5. 350p. 1983. 90.00x (ISBN 0-471-10531-7, Pub. by Wiley-Interscience). Wiley.

BIOENGINEERING
see also Agricultural Engineering; Biological Warfare; Bionics; Biosynthesis; Human Engineering; Sanitary Engineering
Bulgarian Academy of Sciences. International Conference on Chemistry & Biotechnology of Biologically Active Natural Products: First, Varna, Bulgaria, September, 21 to 26, 1981. 1982. pap. 34.50 (ISBN 0-686-37434-7, Pub. by Reidel Holland). Kluwer Boston.
Critser, James R., Jr. Biotechnical Engineering: Equipment & Processes. (Ser.14-82). 1983. 210.00 (ISBN 0-88178-011-1). Lexington Data.
Marks, R. & Payne, P. A. Bioengineering & the Skin. (Illus.). 320p. 1981. text ed. 59.00 (ISBN 0-85200-314-5, Pub. by MTP Pr England). Kluwer Boston.
Reich, Warren T., ed. Encyclopedia of Bioethics, 2 vols. 1982. Set. lib. bdg. 125.00X (ISBN 0-02-925910-X). Macmillan.
Thibault, L., ed. Advances In Bioengineering, 1982. 1982. 40.00 (H00247). ASME.
Walters, LeRoy, ed. Bibliography of Bioethics, Vol. 8. 1982. 60.00 (ISBN 0-686-83896-3). Macmillan.

BIOFEEDBACK TRAINING
Abildness, Abby J. Biofeedback Strategies. (Illus.). 160p. (Orig.). 1982. pap. text ed. 24.00 (ISBN 0-910317-09-7). Am Occup Therapy.
American Psychiatric Association. Biofeedback: Task Force Report Nineteen. LC 80-66989. (Monographs). 119p. 1980. 11.00 (ISBN 0-89042-219-2, 42-219-2). Am Psychiatric.
Basmajian, John V. Biofeedback: Principles & Practice for Clinicians. 330p. Date not set. lib. bdg. price not set (ISBN 0-683-00356-9). Williams & Wilkins.
Wentworth-Rohr, Ivan. Symptom Reduction Through Clinical Biofeedback. 256p. 1983. text ed. 26.95x (ISBN 0-89885-135-1). Human Sci Pr.

BIOGENESIS
see Life–Origin

BIOGEOGRAPHY
see Geographical Distribution of Animals and Plants

BIOGRAPHY
see also Anecdotes; Autobiographies; Autographs; Bibliography; Christian Biography; Genealogy; Heraldry; Portraits
also names of individuals, e.g. Burns, Robert; Einstein, Albert; or classes of persons, e.g. Actors, Authors; and subdivision Biography under particular subjects and under names of countries, cities, etc., e.g. Great Britain–Biography; women–Biography
Clark, Barrett H. Great Short Biographies of Modern Times, the Sevententh, Eighteenth, & Nineteenth Centuries. 1406p. 1982. Repr. of 1928 ed. lib. bdg. 65.00 (ISBN 0-89987-136-4). Darby Bks.
Davis, Allison. Leadership, Love & Aggression. 256p. 15.95 (ISBN 0-15-149348-0). HarBraceJ.
Devlin, Albert J., ed. Eudora Welty's Chronicle: A Story of Mississippi Life. LC 82-19996. 240p. 1983. text ed. 20.00x (ISBN 0-87805-176-7). U Pr of Miss.
White, Timothy. Catch a Fire. (Illus.). 320p. Date not set. 16.95 (ISBN 0-03-063531-4); pap. 9.95 (ISBN 0-03-062109-7). HR&W.
Willison, George F. Saints & Strangers. 520p. 1983. pap. price not set (ISBN 0-940160-19-6). Parnassus Imprints.

BIOGRAPHY–BIBLIOGRAPHY
Biographical Books 1876-1949. 1400p. 1983. 110.00x (ISBN 0-8352-1603-9). Bowker.

BIOGRAPHY–DICTIONARIES, INDEXES, ETC.
Brewer, Annie M. Biography Almanac: Supplement. 181p. 1982. pap. 30.00x (ISBN 0-8103-1141-0). Gale.
Kay, Ernest, ed. Dictionary of International Biography 1982. 17th ed. LC 64-1109. 885p. 1982. 72.50x (ISBN 0-900332-57-3). Intl Pubns Serv.

BIOGRAPHY–HISTORY AND CRITICISM
see Biography (As a Literary Form)

BIOGRAPHY–20TH CENTURY
Mcbride, Davil. Evaders. LC 81-86159. 233p. 1983. pap. 5.95 (ISBN 0-86666-063-1). GWP.

BIOGRAPHY (AS A LITERARY FORM)
see also Autobiography
Runyan, William M. Life Histories & Psychobiography: Explorations in Theory & Method. (Illus.). 304p. 1982. 19.95 (ISBN 0-19-503189-X). Oxford U Pr.
Siebenschuh, William R. Fictional Techniques & Factual Works. LC 82-8373. 200p. 1983. text ed. 18.00x (ISBN 0-8203-0636-3). U of Ga Pr.

BIOLOGICAL ANTHROPOLOGY
see Physical Anthropology

BIOLOGICAL ASSAY
Chenoff, Larry & Chernoff, Neil, eds. Short-Term Bioassays in the Analysis of Complex Environmental Mixtures: Part III. (Environmental Science Reseach: Vol. 27). 511p. 1983. 69.50x (ISBN 0-306-41191-1, Plenum Pr). Plenum Pub.

BIOLOGICAL CHEMISTRY
see also Biochemical Engineering; Bioenergetics; Biosynthesis; Blood–Analysis and Chemistry; Chromatographic Analysis; Cytochemistry; Enzymes; Histochemistry; Immunochemistry; Metabolism; Molecular Biology; Quantum Biochemistry
Adrian, R. H., et al, eds. Reviews of Physiology, Biochemistry & Pharmacology, Vol. 96. (Illus.). 194p. 1983. 39.00 (ISBN 0-387-11849-7). Springer-Verlag.
--Reviews of Physiology, Biochemistry, & Pharmacology, Vol. 97. (Illus.). 180p. 1983. 35.50 (ISBN 0-387-12135-8). Springer-Verlag.
Ahmad, Fazal, et al, eds. Miami Winter Symposium: Vol. 19: From Gene to Protein: Translation into Biotechnology (Symposium) (Serial Publication). 1982. 45.00 (ISBN 0-12-045560-9). Acad Pr.
Armstrong, Frank B. Biochemistry. 2nd ed. (Illus.). 1982. 22.95x (ISBN 0-19-503109-1). Oxford U Pr.
Chemistry of Natural Products: Proceeding of the Sino-American Symposium, October 28-31, 1980. (Chinese Academy of Sciences Joint Symposium Ser.). 1982. 77.00 (ISBN 0-677-31090-0). Gordon.
Clarke, M. J., et al. Copper, Molybdenum, & Vanadium in Biological Systems. (Structure & Bonding: Vol. 53). (Illus.). 166p. 1983. 37.00 (ISBN 0-387-12042-4). Springer-Verlag.
Crandall, G. Douglas. Experiments in Biochemistry. (Illus.). 128p. 1982. pap. 9.95 (ISBN 0-19-503185-7). Oxford U Pr.
Dewar, M. J., et al, eds. Radicals in Biochemistry. (Topics in Current Chemistry Ser.: Vol. 108). (Illus.). 140p. 1983. 28.00 (ISBN 0-686-43338-6). Springer-Verlag.
Dunford, H. B. & Dolphin, D. The Biological Chemistry of Iron. 1982. 59.50 (ISBN 90-277-1444-4, Pub. by Reidel Holland). Kluwer Boston.
Fairweather, D. V. & Eskes, T. K. Amniotic Fluid: Research & Clinical Applications. 2nd ed. 1978. 110.25 (ISBN 90-219-2111-1). Elsevier.
Frederick. Origins & Evolution of Eukaryotic Intracellular Organalles, Vol. 361. 1981. 101.00 (ISBN 0-89766-111-7); pap. write for info. (ISBN 0-89766-112-5). NY Acad Sci.
Goldberg, David M., ed. Annual Review of Clinical Biochemistry, Vol. 1. LC 80-15463. 379p. 1980. 31.95x (ISBN 0-471-04036-3, Pub. by Wiley Med); Vol. 2. 32.95 (ISBN 0-471-08297-X). Wiley.
Hill, H. A. Inorganic Biochemistry, Vol. 2. 362p. 1982. 190.00x (ISBN 0-85186-555-0, Pub. by Royal Soc Chem England). State Mutual Bk.
Holum, J. R. Elements of General & Biological Chemistry: An Introduction to the Molecular Basis of Life. 6th ed. 593p. text ed. 27.95 (ISBN 0-471-09935-X); 11.95 (ISBN 0-471-08236-8); tchr's. manual avail. (ISBN 0-471-89033-2). Wiley.
Hutson, D. H. & Roberts, T. R. Progress in Pesticide Biochemistry, Vol. 3. 500p. 1983. price not set (ISBN 0-471-90053-2, Pub. by Wiley Interscience). Wiley.
Knuttgen, Howard, ed. Biochemistry of Exericise. (International Series on Sport Sciences). 1983. text ed. price not set (ISBN 0-931250-41-2). Human Kinetics.
Rawn, J. David. Biochemistry. 976p. 1983. text ed. 37.95 scp (ISBN 0-06-045335-4, HarpC); scp study guide 11.50 (ISBN 0-06-045334-6). Har-Row.
Roodyn, Donald B., ed. Subcellular Biochemistry, Vol. 9. 425p. 1983. 52.50x (ISBN 0-306-41091-5, Plenum Pr). Plenum Pub.
Russell, N. J. & Powell, G. M. Blood Biochemistry. (Biology in Medicine Ser.). 128p. 1983. text ed. 27.25x (ISBN 0-7099-0003-1, Pub. by Croom Helm Ltd England). Biblio Dist.
Schoffeniels, E., ed. Biochemical Evolution & the Origin of Life. 1971. 30.75 (ISBN 0-444-10081-4). Elsevier.
Scouten, William H. Solid Phase Biochemistry: Analytical & Synthetic Aspects. (Chemical Analysis: Monographs on Analytical Chemistry & its Application). 632p. 1983. 75.00x (ISBN 0-471-08585-5, Pub. by Wiley-Interscience). Wiley.
Smith, Emil L. & Hill, Robert L. Principles of Biochemistry. 7th ed. Incl. General Aspects. 960p. text ed. 36.00x (ISBN 0-07-069762-0); Mammalian Biochemistry. 672p. text ed. 42.00x (ISBN 0-07-069763-9). (Illus.). 1983 (HP). McGraw.
Snell, E. E., et al, eds. Annual Review of Biochemistry, Vol. 52. LC 32-25093. (Illus.). 1175p. 1983. 29.00 (ISBN 0-8243-0852-2). Annual Reviews.
Timbrell, J. A. Principles of Biochemical Toxicology. 240p. 1982. 88.00x (ISBN 0-85066-221-4, Pub. by Taylor & Francis). State Mutual Bk.
Tipson, R. Stuart & Horton, Derek, eds. Advances in Carbohydrate Chemistry & Biochemistry, Vol. 41. (Serial Publication). Date not set. price not set (ISBN 0-12-007241-6); price not set Lib. ed. (ISBN 0-12-007294-7). Acad Pr.
Underhill, Frank P. Physiology of the Amino Acids. 1915. text ed. 32.50x. Elliots Bks.
Usdin, E. Biochemistry of S Adenosylmethionine & Related Compounds. 1982. 195.00x (ISBN 0-686-42937-0, Pub. by Macmillan England). State Mutual Bk.
Werner, Rudolf. Biochemistry: A Comprehensive Review for Medical Students. 500p. 1983. text ed. 19.50 (ISBN 0-86720-014-6). Sci Bks Intl.
Williams, Bryan L. & Wilson, Keith, eds. Principles & Techniques of Practical Biochemistry. 2nd ed. (Illus.). 328p. 1982. pap. text ed. 24.50 (ISBN 0-8391-1732-9, 18287). Univ Park.
Wintermans, J. F. & Kuiper, P. J., eds. Biochemistry & Metabolism of Plant Lipids: Proceedings of the International Symposium on the Biochemistry & Metabolism of Plant Lipids, Fifth, Groningen, the Netherlands, June 7-10, 1982. (Developments in Plant Biology Ser.: Vol. 8). 600p. 1982. 85.00 (ISBN 0-444-80457-9, Biomedical Pr). Elsevier.
Zubay, Geoffrey. Biochemistry. (Chemistry Ser.). (Illus.). 1100p. 1983. text ed. 40.00 (ISBN 0-201-09091-0); Solutions Guide avail.; Overhead Transparencies avail. (ISBN 0-201-09093-7). A-W.

BIOLOGICAL CHEMISTRY–BIBLIOGRAPHY
Fruton, Joseph S. A Bio-Bibliography for the History of the Biochemical Sciences Since 1800. LC 82-72158. 1982. 20.00 (ISBN 0-87169-983-4). Am Philos.

BIOLOGICAL CHEMISTRY–EXAMINATIONS, QUESTIONS, ETC.
Chlapowski, F. Biochemistry: PreTest Self-Assessment & Review. 3rd ed. (PreTest Basic Science Review Bk.). 184p. 1982. 11.95 (ISBN 0-07-051932-3). McGraw.

BIOLOGICAL CHEMISTRY–LABORATORY MANUALS
Work, T. S. & Work, E., eds. Laboratory Techniques in Biochemistry & Molecular Biology, Vols. 1-7. (Illus.). 1969-1979. Vol. 1. 70.75 (ISBN 0-444-10036-9); Vol. 2. 63.00 (ISBN 0-444-10055-5); Vol. 3. 89.00 (ISBN 0-444-10386-4); Vol. 4. 98.25 (ISBN 0-444-10985-4); Vol. 5. 107.75 (ISBN 0-444-11216-2); Vol. 6. 84.25 (ISBN 0-7204-4221-4); Vol. 7. 84.25 (ISBN 0-7204-4224-9). Elsevier.

BIOLOGICAL CLOCKS
see Biological Rhythms

BIOLOGICAL CONTROL OF INSECTS
see Insect Control–Biological Control

BIOLOGICAL CONTROL SYSTEMS
see also Biofeedback Training
Chandebois, Rosine & Faber, J. Automation in Animal Development. (Monographs in Developmental Biology: Vol. 16). (Illus.). iv, 150p. 1983. 69.50 (ISBN 3-8055-3666-6). S Karger.

BIOLOGICAL ENGINEERING
see Bioengineering

BIOLOGICAL FORM
see Morphology

BIOLOGICAL ILLUSTRATION
Farr, Gerald G. Biology Illustrated. (Illus.). 117p. 1979. pap. text ed. 5.95x (ISBN 0-89641-054-4). American Pr.
West, Keith. How to Draw Plants: The Art of Botanical Illustrations. (Illus.). 152p. 1983. 22.50 (ISBN 0-8230-2355-9). Watson-Guptill.

BIOLOGICAL MECHANICS
see Biomechanics
BIOLOGICAL OXIDATION
see Oxidation, Physiological
BIOLOGICAL PEST CONTROL
see Pest Control–Biological Control
BIOLOGICAL PHYSICS
see also Biological Control Systems; Biomechanics; Biomedical Engineering; Bionics; Cells; Fatigue; Medical Electronics; Medical Physics; Molecular Biology; Radiobiology
Anbar, Michael. Textbook of Clinical Biophysics. Gardner, Alvin F., ed. (Allied Health Professions Monographs). 1983. price not set (ISBN 0-87527-316-5). Green.
Morowitz, H. & Quastler, Henry, eds. First National Biophysics Conference, Columbus, Ohio, March 4-6th 1957: Proceedings. 1959. text ed. 75.00x (ISBN 0-686-83712-6). Elliots Bks.
Noble, D. & Blundell, T. L., eds. Progress in Biophysics & Molecular Biology, Vol. 38. (Illus.). 210p. 1982. 77.00 (ISBN 0-08-029683-1). Pergamon.
--Progress in Biophysics & Molecular Biology, Vol. 39. (Illus.). 230p. 1983. 78.00 (ISBN 0-08-030015-4). Pergamon.
Volkenstein, V., ed. General Biophysics, Vol. 1. LC 82-8853. write for info. (ISBN 0-12-723001-7). Acad Pr.
--General Biophysics, Vol. 2. LC 82-8848. Date not set. price not set (ISBN 0-12-723002-5). Acad Pr.
BIOLOGICAL RESEARCH
see also Biology, Experimental
International Symposium on the Brattleboro Rat, Sept. 4-7, 1981. The Brattleboro Rat: Proceedings, Vol. 394. Sokol, Hilda W. & Valtin, Heinz, eds. 828p. 1982. 150.00 (ISBN 0-89766-178-8). NY Acad Sci.
Krushchov, N. Problems of Developmental Biology. 207p. 1981. pap. 6.95 (ISBN 0-8285-2444-0, Pub. by Mir Pubs USSR). Imported Pubns.
BIOLOGICAL RHYTHMS
Beloussov, V. V. Continental Endogenous Regimes. 295p. 1981. 10.00 (ISBN 0-8285-2281-2, Pub. by Mir Pubs USSR). Imported Pubns.
Mendlewicz, J. Biological Rhythms & Behavior. (Advances in Biological Psychiatry: Vol. 11). (Illus.). iv, 150p. 1983. pap. 54.00 (ISBN 3-8055-3672-0). S Karger.
Rifkin, Jeremy. Algeny. 288p. 1983. 14.75 (ISBN 0-670-10885-5). Viking Pr.
BIOLOGICAL STRUCTURE
see Morphology
BIOLOGICAL TRANSPORT
see also Secretion
Civan, Mortimer M. Epithelial Ions & Transport: Application of Biophysical Techniques. (Life Sciences Ser.). 216p. 1983. 59.95 (ISBN 0-471-04869-0, Pub. by Wiley-Interscience). Wiley.
Weiss, D. G. & Gorio, A., eds. Axioplasmic Transport in Physiology & Pathology. (Proceedings in Life Science Ser.). (Illus.). 220p. 1983. 32.00 (ISBN 0-387-11663-X). Springer-Verlag.
BIOLOGICAL WARFARE
Paxton, Jeremy & Harris, Robert. A Higher Form of Killing: The Secret Story of Gas & Germ Warfare. (Illus.). 1983. pap. 7.25 (ISBN 0-8090-1425-4). Hill & Wang.
BIOLOGISTS
Abbott, David, ed. The Biographical Encyclopedias of Sciences: The Biologists. 1982. 30.00x (ISBN 0-584-10853-2, Pub. by Muller Ltd). State Mutual Bk.
BIOLOGY
see also Adaptation (Biology); Anatomy; Bioengineering; Biology, Experimental; Biomathematics; Biometry; Botany; Cells; Cytology; Developmental Biology; Embryology; Evolution; Fresh-Water Biology; Genetics; Heredity; Human Biology; Hybridization; Life (Biology); Marine Biology; Medical Microbiology; Metabolism; Microbiology; Microscope and Microscopy; Morphogenesis; Natural History; Parasitology; Photobiology; Physiology; Protoplasm; Psychobiology; Radiobiology; Reproduction; Seashore Biology; Sex (Biology); Symbiosis; Thermobiology; Variation (Biology); Zoology
Alexander, R. McNeill. Optima for Animals. 120p. 1982. pap. text ed. 13.95 (ISBN 0-7131-2843-7). E Arnold.
Baker, John R. The Biology of Protozoa. (Studies in Biology: No. 138). 64p. 1982. pap. text ed. 8.95 (ISBN 0-7131-2837-2). E Arnold.
Berry, David R. Biology of Yeast. (Studies in Biology: No. 140). 64p. 1982. pap. text ed. 8.95 (ISBN 0-7131-2838-0). E Arnold.
Bongaarts, John & Potter, Robert G., eds. Fertility, Biology & Behavior: An Analysis of the Proximate Determinants (Monograph) (Studies in Population). 216p. 1983. price not set (ISBN 0-12-114380-5). Acad Pr.
Coaker, T. H., ed. Advances in Applied Biology, Vol. 6. LC 76-1065. (Serial Publication). 332p. 1981. 51.50 (ISBN 0-12-040906-2). Acad Pr.
--Advances in Applied Biology, Vol. 7. (Serial Publication). write for info. (ISBN 0-12-040907-0). Acad Pr.
Davis, P. W. & Solomon, E. P. The World of Biology. 2nd ed. 1979. text ed. 24.95 (ISBN 0-07-015552-6); supplementary materials avail. McGraw.
Day, M. J. Plasmids. (Studies in Biology: No. 142). 56p. 1982. pap. text ed. 8.95 (ISBN 0-7131-2846-1). E Arnold.
Essenfeld, Bernice & Kormondy, Edward. Biology. (gr. 10-12). 1983. text ed. price not set (ISBN 0-201-03816-1, School Div); tchrs. ed. avail. (ISBN 0-201-03817-X, Sch Div); lab manual, stud. ed. avail. (ISBN 0-201-03818-8, Sch Div); lab manual, tchr. ed. avail. (ISBN 0-201-03819-6, Sch Div); tests avail. (ISBN 0-201-03823-4, Sch Div). A-W.
Goto, H. E. Animal Toxonomy. (No. 143). 64p. 1982. pap. text ed. 8.95 (ISBN 0-7131-2847-X). E Arnold.
Hefter, R. Yes & No: A Book of Opposites. 1980. 4.50 (ISBN 0-07-027809-1). McGraw.
Jennings, Herbert S. Universe & Life. 1933. text ed. 8.50x (ISBN 0-686-83841-6). Elliots Bks.
Kaplan, Eugene H. Problem Solving in Biology. 3rd ed. 448p. 1983. pap. text ed. 13.95 (ISBN 0-02-362050-1). Macmillan.
Kimball, John W. Biology. 5th ed. LC 82-11636. (Biology Ser.). (Illus.). 875p. 1983. text ed. 24.95 (ISBN 0-201-10245-5); Instrs' Manual avail. (ISBN 0-201-10247-1); Study Guide avail. (ISBN 0-201-10246-3); Transparencies avail. (ISBN 0-201-10249-8); Test Bank avail. (ISBN 0-201-10265-X). A-W.
Levy, Charles K. Elements of Biology. 3rd ed. 204p. 1982. pap. text ed. write for info. Instrs' Manual (ISBN 0-201-04565-6). A-W.
Moscona, Aron A. & Monroy, Alberto, eds. Current Topics in Developmental Biology: Vol. 18: Genome Function, Cell Interactions, & Differentiation. (Serial Publication). Date not set. price not set (ISBN 0-12-153118-X). Acad Pr.
Noland, George B. General Biology. 11th ed. (Illus.). 674p. 1983. text ed. 24.95 (ISBN 0-8016-3704-X). Mosby.
Norstog, Knut J. & Meyerriecks, Andrew J. Biology. 1983. text ed. 26.95 (ISBN 0-675-20000-8); study guide 9.95 (ISBN 0-675-20036-9). Additional supplements may be obtained from publisher. Merrill.
Purves, William & Orians, Gordon. Life. 1000p. 1983. text ed. write for info. (ISBN 0-87150-768-4, 4521). Grant Pr.
Ritchie, Donald D. & Carola, Robert. Biology. 2nd ed. LC 82-11318. (Biology Ser.). (Illus.). 672p. Date not set. text ed. 25.95 (ISBN 0-201-06356-5); Instrs' Manual avail. (ISBN 0-201-06357-3); Study Guide avail. (ISBN 0-201-06358-1); Transparencies avail. (ISBN 0-201-06394-8); Slides avail. (ISBN 0-201-06393-X); Test Bank avail. (ISBN 0-201-06359-X). A-W.
Steen, Edwin B. Dictionary of Biology. 630p. 1971. text ed. 15.00x (ISBN 0-686-83546-8). B&N Imports.
Van Der Merwe, Alwyn, ed. Old & New Questions in Physics, Cosmology, Philosophy, & Theoretical Biology: Essays in Honor of Wolfgang Yourgrau. 905p. 1983. 95.00x (ISBN 0-306-40962-3, Plenum Pr). Plenum Pub.
Watson, D. M. Paleontology & Modern Biology. 1951. text ed. 39.50x (ISBN 0-686-83673-1). Elliots Bks.
Wolfe, Stephen L. Biology: The Foundations. 2nd ed. 608p. 1982. pap. text ed. 24.95x (ISBN 0-534-01169-1). Wadsworth Pub.
BIOLOGY–ADDRESSES, ESSAYS, LECTURES
Haken, H. Evolution of Order & Chaos in Physics, Chemistry, & Biology: Schloss Elmau, FRG, 1982 Proceedings. (Springer Series in Synergetics: Vol. 17). (Illus.). 287p. 1983. 32.00 (ISBN 0-387-11904-3). Springer-Verlag.
BIOLOGY–BIBLIOGRAPHY
Reich, Warren T., ed. Encyclopedia of Bioethics, 2 vols. 1982. Set. lib. bdg. 125.00X (ISBN 0-02-925910-X). Macmillan.
Walters, LeRoy, ed. Bibliography of Bioethics, Vol. 8. 1982. 60.00 (ISBN 0-686-83896-3). Macmillan.
BIOLOGY–DICTIONARIES
Steen. Dictionary of Biology. 1983. pap. text ed. 15.50 (ISBN 0-06-318241-6, Pub. by Har-Row Ltd England). Har-Row.
BIOLOGY–ECOLOGY
see Ecology
BIOLOGY–EXAMINATIONS, QUESTIONS, ETC.
Bancheri, Louis, et al. Biology. (Arco's Regents Review Ser.). 288p. (Orig.). 1983. pap. 3.95 (ISBN 0-668-05697-5, 5697). Arco.
BIOLOGY–FIELD WORK
see also Nature Study
Benton, Allen H. & Werner, William, Jr. Manual of Field Biology & Ecology. 6th ed. 208p. 1982. 14.95x (ISBN 0-8087-4086-5). Burgess.
BIOLOGY–HISTORY
Boylan, Michael. Method & Practice in Aristotle's Biology. LC 82-23708. (Illus.). 300p. (Orig.). 1983. lib. bdg. 22.50 (ISBN 0-8191-2952-6); pap. text ed. 11.75 (ISBN 0-8191-2953-4). U Pr of Amer.
BIOLOGY–LABORATORY MANUALS
Legg, Larry. Biological Science: Lab-Lecture Guide Biology, No. 115. (Illus.). 384p. 19.95x (ISBN 0-88136-000-7). Jostens.
Mason, William H. & Lawrence, Faye B. Laboratory Manual & Study Guide in Animal Biology. 176p. 1982. pap. text ed. 13.95 (ISBN 0-8403-2740-4). Kendall-Hunt.
BIOLOGY–MATHEMATICAL MODELS
Gold, Harvey J. Mathematical Modeling of Biological Systems: An Introductory Guidebook. LC 77-8193. 357p. 1977. 34.95x (ISBN 0-471-02092-3, Pub. by Wiley-Interscience). Wiley.
Miura, Robert M., ed. Some Mathematical Questions in Biology. LC 82-18418. (Lectures on Mathematics in the Life Sciences Ser.: Vol. 15). 19.00 (ISBN 0-8218-1165-7, LLSCI/15). Am Math.
BIOLOGY–METHODOLOGY
Griffith, J. D. Electron Microscopy in Biology, Vol. 2. 349p. 1982. text ed. 85.00x (ISBN 0-471-05526-3, Pub. by Wiley-Interscience). Wiley.
BIOLOGY–PERIODICITY
see Biological Rhythms
BIOLOGY–RESEARCH
see Biological Research
BIOLOGY–SOCIAL ASPECTS
Stanley, Melissa & Andrykovitch, George. Living: An Interpretive Approach to Biology. 204p. Date not set. price not set Instrs' Manual (ISBN 0-201-07174-6); Study Guide 8.95 (ISBN 0-201-07175-4). A-W.
Volpe, E. Peter. Biology & Human Concerns. 3rd ed. 685p. 1983. text ed. write for info. (ISBN 0-697-04734-2); instr's. manual avail. (ISBN 0-697-04748-2); study guide avail. (ISBN 0-697-04747-4); lab manual avail. (ISBN 0-697-04746-6). Wm C Brown.
BIOLOGY–STATISTICAL MODELS
see Biometry
BIOLOGY–STUDY AND TEACHING
Biological Sciences Curriculum Study: Biology Teacher's Handbook. 3rd ed. LC 77-27548. 585p. 1978. text ed. 30.50x (ISBN 0-471-01945-3). Wiley.
Marsteller, Phyllis, ed. Peterson's Guides to Graduate Study: Biological, Agricultural, & Health Sciences, 1983. 1800p. 1982. pap. 21.95 (ISBN 0-87866-187-5). Petersons Guides.
BIOLOGY, EXPERIMENTAL
Clarke, Geoffrey M. Statistics & Experimental Design. 200p. 1980. pap. text ed. 19.50 (ISBN 0-7131-2797-X). E Arnold.
BIOLOGY, MOLECULAR
see Molecular Biology
BIOMASS ENERGY
see also Refuse As Fuel
Grassi, G. & Palz, W., eds. Energy from Biomass. 1982. 39.50 (ISBN 90-277-1482-7, Pub. by Reidel Holland). Kluwer Boston.
Klass, Donald L. & Emert, George H., eds. Fuels from Biomass & Wastes. LC 81-68245. (Illus.). 592p. 1981. 39.95 (ISBN 0-250-40418-4). Ann Arbor Science.
Krawiec, F. Industrial Biomass Market Assessment. (Progress in Solar Energy Ser.: Suppl.). 250p. 1983. pap. text ed. 21.50x (ISBN 0-89553-102-X). Am Solar Energy.
The Potential for Production of "Hydrocarbon" Fuels from Crops in Australia. 86p. 1983. pap. 7.25 (ISBN 0-643-02931-1, CO 67, CSIRO). Unipub.
Sarkanen, Kyosti V. & Tillman, David A., eds. Progress in Biomass Conversion, Vol. 3. (Serial Publication). 304p. 1982. 24.50 (ISBN 0-12-535903-9). Acad Pr.
Schiffman, Yale M. & D-Alessio, Gregory J. Limits to Solar & Biomass Energy Growth. LC 81-48071. 1983. price not set (ISBN 0-669-05253-1). Lexington Bks.
Smith, W. Ramsay, ed. Energy from Forest Biomass. LC 82-20745. (Symposium). Date not set. 27.50 (ISBN 0-686-42980-X). Acad Pr.
White, L. P. & Plaskett, L. G. Biomass as Fuel. LC 81-66689. 211p. 1982. 29.50 (ISBN 0-686-81667-6). Acad Pr.
BIOMATERIALS
see Biomedical Materials
BIOMATHEMATICS
see also Biology–Mathematical Models; Biometry
Amari, S. & Arbib, M. A., eds. Competition & Cooperation in Neural Nets, Kyoto, Japan, 1982: Proceedings. (Lecture Notes in Biomathematics: Vol. 45). 441p. 1982. pap. 26.00 (ISBN 0-387-11574-9). Springer-Verlag.
Frehland, E. Stochastic Transport Processes in Discrete Biological Systems. (Lecture Notes in Biomathematics Ser.: Vol. 47). 169p. 1983. pap. 11.00 (ISBN 0-387-11964-7). Springer-Verlag.
Kajiya, F. & Kodama, S., eds. Comparmental Analysis. 200p. 1983. 79.25 (ISBN 3-8055-3696-8). S Karger.
Walter, E. Identifiability of State Space Models: With Applications to Transformation Systems. (Lecture Notes in Biomathematics Ser.: Vol. 46). 202p. 1983. pap. 13.50 (ISBN 0-387-11590-0). Springer-Verlag.
BIOMECHANICS
see also Human Engineering
Huiskes, R. Biomechanics: Principles & Applications. 1982. 65.00 (ISBN 90-247-3047-3, Pub. by Martinus Nijhoff Netherlands). Kluwer Boston.
Northrip, John W., et al. Analysis of Sport Motion: Anatomic & Biomechanic Perspectives. 3rd ed. 365p. 1983. pap. text ed. write for info. (ISBN 0-697-07206-1). Wm C Brown.
BIOMEDICAL ENGINEERING
see also Biomedical Materials; Medical Electronics; Medical Instruments and Apparatus; Physiological Apparatus
Humber, James H. & Almeder, Robert, eds. Biomedical Ethics Reviews 1983. (Biomedical Ethics Reviews Ser.). 224p. 1983. tentative 24.50 (ISBN 0-89603-041-5). Humana.
Matsui, Hideji & Kobayashi, Kando, eds. Biomechanics VIII, 2 vols. (International Series on Biomechanics). 1983. text ed. price not set (ISBN 0-931250-42-0). Human Kinetics.
--Biomechanics VIII, Vol. A. (International Series on Biomechanics). 1983. text ed. price not set (ISBN 0-931250-43-9). Human Kinetics.
--Biomechanics VIII, Vol. B. (International Series on Biomechanics). 1983. text ed. price not set (ISBN 0-931250-44-7). Human Kinetics.
Regier, Mary H. & Mohapatra, Ram N. Biomedical Statistics with Computing. (Medical Computing Ser.). 309p. 1982. 34.95 (ISBN 0-471-10449-3, Pub. by REs Stud Pr). Wiley.
BIOMEDICAL MATERIALS
see also Dental Materials
Harron, Frank & United Ministries in Education Health & Human Values Program. Biomedical Ethical Issues: A Digest of Law & Policy Development. LC 82-13394. 112p. 1983. pap. text ed. 4.95x (ISBN 0-300-02974-8). Yale U Pr.
BIOMETRY
see also Biomathematics; Mathematical Statistics; Sampling (Statistics)
Causton, David & Venus, Jill. Biometry of Plant Growth. 320p. 1981. text ed. 49.50 (ISBN 0-7131-2812-7). E Arnold.
Duncan, Robert C. & Knapp, Rebecca G. Introductory Biostatistics for the Health Sciences. 7th ed. 250p. 1983. 15.95 (ISBN 0-471-07869-7, Wiley Med). Wiley.
Ingelfinger. Biostatistics in Clinical Medicine. 1983. not set 24.95 (ISBN 0-02-360010-1). Macmillan.
Milton, J. S. & Tsokos, J. O. Statistical Methods in the Biological & Health Sciences. 512p. 1983. 29.95x (ISBN 0-07-042359-8, C); instr's. manual 5.95 (ISBN 0-07-042360-1). McGraw.
BIONICS
see also Artificial Intelligence; Optical Data Processing
Biotechnology Equipment & Supplies. (Reports Ser.: No. 513). 179p. 1982. 985.00 (ISBN 0-686-38954-9). Intl Res Dev.
Clerman, Robert J. & Joglekar, Rajani. Biotechnology & Energy Use. LC 77-85093. (Electrotechnology Ser.: Vol. 8). (Illus.). 189p. 1981. 39.95 (ISBN 0-250-40485-0). Ann Arbor Science.
Joglekar, Rajani & Clerman, Robert J. Biotechnology in Industry: Selected Applications & Unit Operations. LC 82-48642. (Illus.). 200p. 1983. 27.50 (ISBN 0-250-40605-5). Ann Arbor Science.
Mizrahi, Avshalom & Van Wezel, Antonius L., eds. Advances in Biotechnological Processes, Vol. 1. 360p. 1983. 58.00 (ISBN 0-8451-3200-8). A R Liss.
BIONOMICS
see Ecology
BIOPHYSICS
see Biological Physics
BIOPSY
Bonfiglio, Thomas A. Cytopathologic Interpretation of Transthoracic Fine-Needle Biopsies. (Masspn Monographs in Diagnostic Cytopathology, Vol. 4). 208p. 1983. write for info. (ISBN 0-89352-197-3). Masson Pub.
Bonk, U. E. Biopsie und Operationspraeparat. (Illus.). viii, 140p. 1983. pap. 13.25 (ISBN 3-8055-3702-6). S Karger.
BIOPSYCHOLOGY
see Psychobiology
BIORHYTHMS
see Biological Rhythms
BIOSCIENCES
see Life Sciences
BIOSCOPE
see Moving-Picture Projection
BIOSTATISTICS
see Biometry
BIOSYNTHESIS
Porter, John W. & Spurgeon, Sandra L. Biosynthesis of Isoprenoid Compounds, Vol. II. 550p. 1983. price not set (ISBN 0-471-09038-7, Pub. by Wiley-Interscience). Wiley.
Price, Charles C., ed. Synthesis of Life. LC 74-3026. (Benchmark Papers in Organic Chemistry: Vol. 1). 391p. 1974. text ed. 52.50 (ISBN 0-87933-131-3). Hutchinson Ross.
Synthesis & Fertility of Xbrassicoraphanus & Ways of Transferring Rapanus Characters to Brassica. 90p. 1983. pap. 14.50 (ISBN 90-220-0805-3, PDC256, Pudoc). Unipub.
BIOTECHNOLOGY
see Bionics; Human Engineering
BIRCH-BARK CANOES
see Indians of North America–Boats
BIRD-HOUSES
Pearce, D. W. Aviary Design & Construction. (Blandford Pet Handbooks Ser.). (Illus.). 96p. 1983. 7.50 (ISBN 0-7137-1218-X, Pub. by Blandford Pr England). Sterling.
BIRD HUNTING
see Fowling

BIRD WATCHING
Fitter. Collins Pocket Guide to Bird Watching. 29.95 (ISBN 0-686-42749-1, Collins Pub England). Greene.
Holland, John. Bird Spotting. 5th rev. ed. (Illus.). 292p. 1976. 7.50 (ISBN 0-7137-0334-2). Intl Pubns Serv.
Wilds, Claudia. Finding Birds in the National Capital Area. (Illus.). 216p. 1983. pap. 12.50 (ISBN 0-87474-959-X). Smithsonian.

BIRDS
see also Game and Game-Birds; Ornithology; Water-Birds
also names of particular birds, e.g. Robins
Allaire, Pierre. Bird Species on Mined Lands. (Illus.). 72p. (Orig.). 1982. pap. text ed. 10.00 (ISBN 0-86607-010-9). Inst Mining & Minerals.
Arndt, Thomas. Encyclopedia of Conures: The Aratingas. (Illus.). 176p. 1982. 29.95 (ISBN 0-87666-873-2, H-1042). TFH Pubns.
Brudenell & Bruce. The Birds of New Province & the Bahama Islands. 19.95 (ISBN 0-686-42758-0, Collins Pub England). Greene.
Edwards, Ernest P. A Coded Workbook of Birds of the World: Vol. 1-Non-Passerines. 2nd ed. LC 82-82891. (Illus.). xxi, 134p. 1982. pap. 10.00 plastic ring bdg. (ISBN 0-911882-07-3). E P Edwards.
Glue, David, ed. The Garden Bird Book. 224p. 1982. 39.00x (ISBN 0-333-33151-6, Pub. by Macmillan England). State Mutual Bk.
Gooders, John. Birds That Came Back. 1983. 25.00 (ISBN 0-88072-050-6). Tanager Bks.
Martin, Richard M. How to Keep Softbilled Birds in Cage or Aviary. (Illus.). 96p. 1980. 3.95 (ISBN 0-7028-8010-8). Avian Pubns.
Mikami, S., et al, eds. Avian Endocrinology: Environmental & Ecological Perspectives. 380p. 1983. 53.00 (ISBN 0-387-11871-3). Springer-Verlag.
Moon, Geoff. The Birds Around Us: New Zealand Birds; Their Habits & Habitats. (Illus.). 207p. 1983. 25.95 (ISBN 0-908592-03-5, Pub. by Heinemann Pub New Zealand). Intl Schol Bk Serv.
Nehls, Harry J. Familiar Birds of the Northwest. 2nd ed. 1983. 6.95 (ISBN 0-931686-05-9). Audobon Soc Portland.
Penny. The Birds of the Seychelles & Outlying Islands. 23.95 (ISBN 0-686-42764-5, Collins Pub England). Greene.
Peterson, Roger T. How to Know the Birds. 1982. pap. 2.50 (ISBN 0-451-09790-4, E9790, Sig). NAL.
Rogers, Cyril. How to Keep Seedeating Birds in Cage & Aviary. (Illus.). 96p. 1978. 3.95 (ISBN 0-7028-1068-1). Avian Pubns.
Rowley, Ian. Bird Life. (Illus.). 284p. 1983. pap. 12.50 (ISBN 0-00-216436-1, Pub. by W Collins Australia). Intl Schol Bk Serv.
Rutgers, A. & Norris, K. A. Encyclopedia of Aviculture, 3 vols. (Illus.). 900p. 1982. boxed set 99.95 (ISBN 0-7137-1295-3, Pub. by Blandford Pr England). Sterling.

BIRDS–BEHAVIOR
see also Birds–Eggs and Nests; Imprinting (Psychology)
Alison, Robert M. Breeding Biology & Behavior of the Oldsquaw (Clangula hyemalis L.) 52p. 1975. 3.50 (ISBN 0-943610-18-4). Am Ornithologists.
Hamilton, Robert B. Comparative Behavior of the American Avocet & the Black-Necked Stilt (Recurvirostridae) 98p. 1975. 7.50 (ISBN 0-943610-17-6). Am Ornithologists.
MacRoberts, Michael H. & MacRoberts, Barbara R. Social Organization & Behavior of the Acorn Woodpecker in Central Coastal California. 115p. 1976. 7.50 (ISBN 0-943610-21-4). Am Ornithologists.
Nolan, Val, Jr. Ecology & Behavior of the Prairie Warbler Dendroica discolor. 595p. 1978. 29.50 (ISBN 0-943610-26-5). Am Ornithologists.
Power, Harry W. Foraging Behavior of Mountain Bluebirds with Emphasis on Sexual Foraging Differences. 72p. 1980. 8.50 (ISBN 0-943610-28-1). Am Ornithologists.
Schreiber, Ralph W. Maintenance Behavior & Communication in the Brown Pelican. 78p. 1977. 6.50 (ISBN 0-943610-22-2). Am Ornithologists.
Stiles, F. Gary & Wolf, Larry L. Ecology & Evolution of Lek Mating Behavior in the Long-tailed Hermit Hummingbird. 78p. 1979. 8.50 (ISBN 0-943610-27-3). Am Ornithologists.
Stokes, Donald W. A Guide to Bird Behavior, Vol. I. (Stokes Nature Guide Ser.). (Illus.). 416p. 1983. pap. 8.70i (ISBN 0-316-81725-2). Little.
Van Tets, Gerard F. Comparative Study of Some Social Communication Patterns in the Pelecaniformes. American Ornithologists' Union, ed. 88p. 1965. 3.50 (ISBN 0-943610-02-8). Am Ornithologists.
Willis, Edwin O. Behavior of Spotted Antbirds. 162p. 1972. 9.00 (ISBN 0-943610-10-9). Am Ornithologists.
Wolf, Larry L. Species Relationships in the Avian Genus Aimophila. 220p. 1977. 12.00 (ISBN 0-943610-23-0). Am Ornithologists.

BIRDS–COLLECTION AND PRESERVATION
Bird Collection in the United States & Canada: Addenda & Corrigenda. 1976. 1.50 (ISBN 0-943610-33-8). Am Ornithologists.
Keith & Gooders. Collins Bird Guide. pap. 19.95 (ISBN 0-686-42724-6, Collins Pub England). Greene.
Martin & Ellis. Cage & Aviary Birds. pap. 16.95 (ISBN 0-686-42725-4, Collins Pub England). Greene.

BIRDS–EGGS AND NESTS
see also Bird-Houses
Grant, Gilbert S. Avian Incubation: Egg Temperature, Nest Humidity, & Behavioral Thermoregulation in a Hot Environment. 75p. 1982. 9.00 (ISBN 0-943610-30-3). Am Ornithologists.
Harrison. A Field Guide to Nests, Eggs, & Nestlings of North American Birds. 24.95 (ISBN 0-686-42754-8, Collins Pub England). Greene.
--A Field Guide to Nests, Eggs, Nestlings of British & European Birds. 29.95 (ISBN 0-686-42753-X, Collins Pub England). Greene.

BIRDS–EGGS AND NESTS–JUVENILE LITERATURE
Fitter & Richardson. Collins Pocket Guide to Nests & Eggs. 26.95 (ISBN 0-686-42751-3, Collins Pub England). Greene.

BIRDS–FOOD
Black, Robert. Nutrition of Finches & Other Cagebirds. 362p. 1981. 19.95 (ISBN 0-686-43316-5). Avian Pubns.

BIRDS–JUVENILE LITERATURE
see also Birds–Eggs and Nests–Juvenile Literature
Board, Tessa. Birds. (Insight Ser.). (gr. 4 up). 1983. PLB 8.90 (ISBN 0-531-03472-0). Watts.
McGowen, Tom. Album of Birds. (Illus.). 72p. (gr. 5up). 1982. 8.95 (ISBN 0-528-82413-9); PLB 8.97 (ISBN 0-528-80076-0). Rand.
Patterson, Y. God Made Birds. Mahany, Patricia, ed. (Happy Day Bks.). (Illus.). 24p. (ps-2). 1983. 1.29 (ISBN 0-87239-634-7, 3554). Standard Pub.
Sanger, Marjory B. Forest in the Sand. LC 82-4076. (Illus.). 160p. (gr. 7 up). 1983. 10.95 (ISBN 0-689-50248-6, McElderry Bk). Atheneum.

BIRDS–NESTS
see Birds–Eggs and Nests

BIRDS–PICTORIAL WORKS
Audubon, John J. Audubon's Birds of America Coloring Book. 48p. 1974. pap. 2.00 (ISBN 0-486-23049-X). Dover.

BIRDS–AFRICA
Brown, L. & Urban, E. K., eds. The Birds of Africa. LC 81-69594. 1982. Vol. 1. 99.00 (ISBN 0-12-137301-0); Vol. 2: 256 pgs. 42.50 (ISBN 0-12-200102-8). Acad Pr.
Cramp, Stanley, ed. Handbook of the Birds of Europe, the Middle East, & North Africa: The Birds of the Western Paleartic, Vol. III: Waders to Gulls. (Illus.). 920p. 1983. 89.00 (ISBN 0-19-857506-8). Oxford U Pr.
Heinzel & Fitter. The Birds of Britian & Europe with North Africa & the Middle East. pap. 14.95 (ISBN 0-686-42723-8, Collins Pub England). Greene.
Newman, Kenneth. Birdlife in Southern Africa. (Illus.). 252p. 1982. 38.95 (ISBN 0-86954-083-1, Pub. by Macmillan S Africa). Intl Schol Bk Serv.
Payne, Robert B. Behavior, Mimetic Songs & Song Dialects, & Relationships of the Parasitic Indigobirds (Vidua) of Africa. 333p. 1973. 12.50 (ISBN 0-943610-11-7). Am Ornithologists.
Prozesky. A Field Guide to the Birds of Southern Africa. 29.95 (ISBN 0-686-42762-9, Collins Pub England). Greene.
Serle & Morel. A Field Guide to the Birds of West Africa. 29.95 (ISBN 0-686-42763-7, Collins Pub England). Greene.
Steyn, Peter. Birds of Prey of Southern Africa. (Illus.). 309p. 1983. 42.00 (ISBN 0-88072-025-5). Tanager Bks.
Williams & Arlott. A Field Guide to the Birds of East Africa. 29.95 (ISBN 0-686-42756-4, Collins Pub England). Greene.

BIRDS–AMERICA
see also Birds–Latin-America; Birds–North America; Birds–United States
Feduccia, Alan. Evolutionary Trends in the Neotropical Ovenbirds & Woodhewers. 69p. 1973. 3.50 (ISBN 0-943610-13-3). Am Ornithologists.
Owre, Oscar T. & American Ornithologists' Union. Adaptations for Locomotion & Feeding in the Anhinga & the Double-Crested Cormorant. 138p. 1967. 6.00 (ISBN 0-943610-06-0). Am Ornithologists.
Scott, Jack D. Orphans from the Sea. 64p. 1982. 10.95 (ISBN 0-399-20858-5). Putnam Pub Group.

BIRDS–ARCTIC REGIONS
O'Donald, Peter. The Artic Skua: A Study of the Ecology & Evolution of a Seabird. LC 82-12782. (Illus.). 250p. Date not set. price not set (ISBN 0-521-23581-2). Cambridge U Pr.

BIRDS–ASIA
King & Woodcock. A Field Guide to the Birds of South East Asia. 29.95 (ISBN 0-686-42761-0, Collins Pub England). Greene.
Marshall, Joe T. Systematics of Smaller Asian Night Birds Based on Voice. 58p. 1978. 7.00 (ISBN 0-943610-25-7). Am Ornithologists.

BIRDS–AUSTRALIA
Harmon, Ian. Birdkeeping in Australia. (Illus.). 176p. 1980. 12.95 (ISBN 0-207-13422-7). Avian Pubns.

BIRDS–EUROPE
Bannerman, David & Bannerman, W. Mary. Birds of the Balearics. (Illus.). 450p. 1983. 45.00 (ISBN 0-7099-0679-X). Tanager Bks.
Cramp, Stanley, ed. Handbook of the Birds of Europe, the Middle East, & North Africa: The Birds of the Western Paleartic, Vol. III: Waders to Gulls. (Illus.). 920p. 1983. 89.00 (ISBN 0-19-857506-8). Oxford U Pr.
Harrison. A Field Guide to Nests, Eggs, Nestlings of British & European Birds. 29.95 (ISBN 0-686-42753-X, Collins Pub England). Greene.
Heinzel & Fitter. The Birds of Britian & Europe with North Africa & the Middle East. pap. 14.95 (ISBN 0-686-42723-8, Collins Pub England). Greene.
Ogilvie, M. A. Wildfowl of Britain & Europe. 1982. 16.95x (ISBN 0-19-217723-0). Oxford U Pr.
Peterson & Mountfort. A Field Guide to the Birds of Britain & Europe. 27.95 (ISBN 0-686-42752-1, Collins Pub England). Greene.
Pforr, Manfred & Limbrunner, Alfred. Breeding Birds of Europe: Vol. 2-Sandgrouse to Crows. Robertson, Iian, ed. Stoneman, Richard, tr. from Ger. (Illus.). 394p. 1983. 24.00 (ISBN 0-88072-027-1). Tanager Bks.
Prorr, Manfred & Limbrunner, Alfred. Breeding Birds of Europe: Vol. 1-Divers to Auks. Stoneman, Richard, ed. & tr. from Ger. (Illus.). 327p. 1983. 24.00 (ISBN 0-88072-026-3). Tanager Bks.
Woodcock & Heinzel. The Birds of Britian & Europe. pap. 8.95 (ISBN 0-686-42721-1, Collins Pub England). Greene.

BIRDS–GREAT BRITAIN
Fitter & Richardson. Collins Pocket Guide to British Birds. 26.95 (ISBN 0-686-42750-5, Collins Pub England). Greene.
Gooders, John. Collins British Birds. (Illus.). 384p. 1983. 39.95 (ISBN 0-00-219121-0, Collins Pub England). Greene.
Harrison. A Field Guide to Nests, Eggs, Nestlings of British & European Birds. 29.95 (ISBN 0-686-42753-X, Collins Pub England). Greene.
Heinzel & Fitter. The Birds of Britian & Europe with North Africa & the Middle East. pap. 14.95 (ISBN 0-686-42723-8, Collins Pub England). Greene.
Michelet, Jules. The Bird. 308p. 1982. 30.00x (ISBN 0-7045-0444-8, Pub. by Wildwood House). State Mutual Bk.
Peterson & Mountfort. A Field Guide to the Birds of Britain & Europe. 27.95 (ISBN 0-686-42752-1, Collins Pub England). Greene.
Prendergast, E. D. & Boys, J. V. The Birds of Dorset. (Illus.). 304p. 1983. 43.00 (ISBN 0-7153-8380-9). David & Charles.
Swaine, Christopher. Birds of Gloucestershire. 256p. 1982. text ed. 16.75x (ISBN 0-86299-012-2, Pub. by Sutton England). Humanities.
Woodcock & Heinzel. The Birds of Britian & Europe. pap. 8.95 (ISBN 0-686-42721-1, Collins Pub England). Greene.

BIRDS–INDIA
Woodcock. Birds of the Indian Sub-Continent. 21.95 (ISBN 0-686-42724-6, Collins Pub England). Greene.

BIRDS–ISLANDS OF THE ATLANTIC
Brudenell & Bruce. The Birds of New Province & the Bahama Islands. 19.95 (ISBN 0-686-42758-0, Collins Pub England). Greene.
Emlen, John T. Land Bird Communities of Grand Bahama Island: The Structure & Dynamics of an Avifauna. 129p. 1977. 9.00 (ISBN 0-943610-24-9). Am Ornithologists.

BIRDS–ISLANDS OF THE PACIFIC
Fleet, Robert R. Red-tailed Tropicbird on Kure Atoll. 64p. 1974. 5.50 (ISBN 0-943610-16-8). Am Ornithologists.
Gill, Frank B. Intra-island Variation in the Mascarene White-eye Zosterops Borbonica. 66p. 1973. 3.50 (ISBN 0-943610-12-5). Am Ornithologists.
Watling, Dick. Birds of Figi, Tonga & Somoa. (Illus.). 1983. 45.00 (ISBN 0-686-38392-3). Tanager Bks.

BIRDS–LATIN-AMERICA
Harris. A Field Guide to the Birds of the Galapagos. 25.95 (ISBN 0-686-42757-2, Collins Pub England). Greene.
Monroe, Burt L., Jr. Distributional Survey of the Birds of Honduras. 458p. 1968. 14.00 (ISBN 0-943610-07-9). Am Ornithologists.

BIRDS–NEW GUINEA
Turbott, E. G., ed. Buller's Birds of New Zealand. 206p. 1982. 150.00x (ISBN 0-7233-0022-4, Pub. by Whitcoulls New Zealand). State Mutual Bk.

BIRDS–NEW ZEALAND
Falla & Sibson. A New Guide to the Birds of New Zealand. 39.95 (ISBN 0-686-42760-2, Collins Pub England). Greene.
Falla, R. A. & Sibson, R. B. The New Guide to the Birds of New Zealand. (Illus.). 247p. 1983. 17.95 (ISBN 0-00-216928-2, Pub. by W Collins Australia). Intl Schol Bk Serv.
Lockley, Ronald. New Zealand Birds. (Illus.). 179p. 1983. 45.00 (ISBN 0-686-83935-8, Pub. by Heinemann Pub New Zealand). Intl Schol Bk Serv.
Power, Elaine. Small Birds of the New Zealand Bush. (Illus.). 27p. 1983. pap. 8.95 (ISBN 0-00-216984-3, Pub. by W Collins Australia). Intl Schol Bk Serv.

BIRDS–NORTH AMERICA
see also Birds–United States
A.O.U. Checklist of North American Birds. 6th ed. 1983. write for info. (ISBN 0-943610-32-X). Am Ornithologists.
Flack, J. A. Douglas. Bird Populations of Aspen Forests in Western North America. 97p. 1976. 7.50 (ISBN 0-943610-19-2). Am Ornithologists.
Harrison. A Field Guide to Nests, Eggs, & Nestlings of North American Birds. 24.95 (ISBN 0-686-42754-8, Collins Pub England). Greene.
Johnsgard, Paul A. Hummingbirds of North America. (Illus.). 384p. 1983. 29.95 (ISBN 0-87474-562-4). Smithsonian.
Kendeigh, S. Charles, ed. Symposium on the House Sparrow (Passer domesticus) & European Tree Sparrow (P. montanus) in North America. 121p. 1973. 6.00 (ISBN 0-943610-14-1). Am Ornithologists.
MacRoberts, Michael H. & MacRoberts, Barbara R. Social Organization & Behavior of the Acorn Woodpecker in Central Coastal California. 115p. 1976. 7.50 (ISBN 0-943610-21-4). Am Ornithologists.
Mengel, Robert M. Birds of Kentucky. American Ornithologists' Union, ed. 581p. 1965. 15.00 (ISBN 0-943610-03-6). Am Ornithologists.
Snyder, Noel F. & Wiley, James W. Sexual Size Dimorphism in Hawks & Owls of North America. 95p. 1976. 7.00 (ISBN 0-943610-20-6). Am Ornithologists.

BIRDS–NORWAY
Brusewitz, Gunnar. Wings & Seasons. Wheeler, Walston, tr. from Swedish. (Illus.). 119p. 1983. 20.00 (ISBN 0-88072-029-8). Tanager Bks.

BIRDS–UNITED STATES
Jackson, Jerome A. The Mid-South Bird Notes of Ben B. Coffey, Jr. (Special Publications: No. 1). 127p. (Orig.). 1981. pap. 10.00 (ISBN 0-686-37622-6). Mississippi Orni.
Rea, Amadeo M. Once a River: Bird Life & Habitat Changes on the Middle Gila. 270p. 1983. 24.50 (ISBN 0-8165-0799-6). U of Ariz Pr.
Weathers, Wesley W. Birds of Southern California's Deep Canyon. LC 82-13382. (Illus.). 267p. 1983. 35.00x (ISBN 0-520-04754-0). U of Cal Pr.

BIRDS, AQUATIC
see Water-Birds

BIRDS IN LITERATURE
Harting, James. The Ornithology of Shakespeare. (Illus.). 321p. 1978. 15.00x (ISBN 0-905418-26-3). Intl Pubns Serv.

BIRDS' NESTS
see Birds–Eggs and Nests

BIRDS OF PREY
see also Owls
Steyn, Peter. Birds of Prey of Southern Africa. (Illus.). 309p. 1983. 42.00 (ISBN 0-88072-025-5). Tanager Bks.

BIRMINGHAM, ALABAMA
Hoole, William S. The Birmingham Horrors. (Illus.). 272p. (Orig.). 1980. pap. 4.95 (ISBN 0-87397-151-5). Strode.

BIRMINGHAM, ENGLAND
Hilton, Rodney H. A Medieval Society: The West Midlands at the End of the Thirteenth Century. LC 82-19732. (Past & Present Publications Ser.). 315p. Date not set. price not set (ISBN 0-521-25374-8). Cambridge U Pr.

BIRTH, PREMATURE
see Infants (Premature)

BIRTH CONTROL
see also Abortion; Contraception; Family Size; Intrauterine Contraceptives
Faruqee, Rashid. Integrating Family Planning with Health Services: Does it Help? LC 82-8405. (World Bank Staff Working Papers: No. 515). (Orig.). 1982. pap. 3.00 (ISBN 0-8213-0003-2). World Bank.
Hatcher, Richard, et al. It's Your Choice: A Personal Guide to Birth Control Methods for Women... & Men, Too! Stoner, Carol, ed. (Illus.). 144p. (Orig.). 1983. pap. 7.95 (ISBN 0-87857-471-9, 05-172-1). Rodale Pr Inc.
Lewit, S., ed. Advances in Planned Parenthood, Vol. 8. (International Congress Ser.: No. 271). 1973. pap. 28.00 (ISBN 0-444-15023-4). Elsevier.
Mkangi, C. C. The Social Cost of Small Families & Land Reform: A Case Study of the Wataita of Kenya. (International Population Ser.: Vol. 2). (Illus.). 160p. 1983. 25.00 (ISBN 0-08-028952-5). Pergamon.
Reynolds, Moira D. Margaret Sanger, Leader for Birth Control. Rahmas, Sigurd C., ed. (Outstanding Personalities Ser.: No. 93). 32p. (gr. 9-12). 1982. 2.95 (ISBN 0-87157-593-0); pap. text ed. 1.95 (ISBN 0-87157-093-9). SamHar Pr.
Wilson, Yates. Family Planning on A Crowded Planet. LC 82-24160. 96p. 1983. Repr. of 1971 ed. lib. bdg. 22.50x (ISBN 0-313-22680-6, YAFP). Greenwood.

BIRTH CONTROL–RELIGIOUS ASPECTS
Ramirez de Arellano, Annette B. & Seipp, Conrad. Colonialism, Catholicism, & Contraception: A History of Birth Control in Puerto Rico. LC 82-13646. 290p. 1983. 24.00x (ISBN 0-8078-1544-6). U of NC Pr.

BIRTH CONTROL–CHINA
Kaufman, Joan. A Billion & Counting: Family Planning Campaigns & Policies in the People's Republic of China. LC 82-50312. (Illus.). 1983. pap. 7.50 (ISBN 0-911302-43-3). San Francisco Pr.

BIRTH CONTROL–GREAT BRITAIN
Banks. Feminism & Family Planning in Victorian England. 154p. 1982. 39.00x (ISBN 0-85323-281-4, Pub. by Liverpool Univ England). State Mutual Bk.

BIRTH CONTROL–INDIA
Desai, A. R. Urban Family & Family Planning in India. 224p. 1980. Repr. 22.95x (ISBN 0-940500-70-1). Asia Bk Corp.
Rele, J. R. & Kanitkar, Tara. Fertility & Family Planning in Greater Bombay. 217p. 1980. 22.95x (ISBN 0-940500-87-6, Pub by Popular Prakashan India). Asia Bk Corp.
BIRTH CONTROL–PUERTO RICO
Ramirez de Arellano, Annette B. & Seipp, Conrad. Colonialism, Catholicism, & Contraception: A History of Birth Control in Puerto Rico. LC 82-13646. 290p. 1983. 24.00x (ISBN 0-8078-1544-6). U of NC Pr.
BIRTH DEFECTS
see Abnormalities, Human
BIRTH ORDER
Ernst, C. & Angst, J. Birth Order: Its Influence on Personality. (Illus.). 370p. 1983. 29.80 (ISBN 0-387-11248-0). Springer-Verlag.
Sullivan, Barbara. First Born, Second Born. 186p. 1983. pap. 5.95 (ISBN 0-310-60380-3). Chosen Bks Pub.
Wilson, Bradford & Edington, George. First Child, Second Child: Your Birth Order Profile. 1983. pap. 3.50 (ISBN 0-8217-1144-X). Zebra.
BIRTH-RATE
see Population
BIRTH RECORDS
see Registers of Births, Deaths, Marriages, etc.
BIRTHS, REGISTERS OF
see Registers of Births, Deaths, Marriages, etc.
BISCUITS, ENGLISH
see Cookies
BISHOP, ELIZABETH
Schwartz, Lloyd & Estess, Sybil P. Elizabeth Bishop & Her Art. (Under Discussion Ser.). (Illus.). 328p. 1982. 18.50 (ISBN 0-472-09343-6); pap. 8.95 (ISBN 0-472-06343-X). U of Mich Pr.
Wyllie, Diana E. Elizabeth Bishop & Howard Nemerov: A Reference Guide. 1983. lib. bdg. 33.00 (ISBN 0-8161-8527-1, Hall Reference). G K Hall.
BISHOPS–ROME
see Popes
BISMUTH
Angino, E. D. & Long, D. T., eds. Geochemistry of Bismuth. LC 78-24291. (Benchmark Papers in Geology: Vol. 49). 432p. 1979. 53.50 (ISBN 0-87933-234-4). Hutchinson Ross.
BLACK, HUGO LAFAYETTE, 1886-1971
Hamilton, Virginia. Hugo Black: The Alabama Years. LC 75-181566. (Illus.). 352p. 1982. pap. text ed. 12.50 (ISBN 0-8173-0128-3). U of Ala Pr.
BLACK AFRICANS
see Blacks
BLACK AMERICANS
see Afro-Americans
BLACK ART (WITCHCRAFT)
see Witchcraft
BLACK CARIB INDIANS
see Indians of Central America
BLACK DEATH
Gottfried, Robert S. The Black Death. LC 82-48745. 240p. 1983. 14.95 (ISBN 0-02-912630-4). Free Pr.
BLACK ENGLISH
Sidran, Ben. Black Talk. (Quality Paperbacks Ser.). 244p. 1983. pap. 7.95 (ISBN 0-306-80184-1). Da Capo.
BLACK HILLS, SOUTH DAKOTA
Friggens, Paul. Gold & Grass: The Black Hills Story. (Illus.). 1983. price not set (ISBN 0-87108-648-4). Pruett.
BLACK HOLES (ASTRONOMY)
Chandrasekhar, S. The Mathematical Theory of Black Holes. (International Ser. of Monographs on Physics). (Illus.). 750p. 1982. text ed. 89.00 (ISBN 0-686-84053-4). Oxford U Pr.
Shapiro, Stuart L. & Teukolsky, Saul A. Black Holes, White Dwarfs, & Neutron Stars: The Physics of Compact Objects. 650p. 1983. 39.95 (ISBN 0-471-87317-9, Pub. by Wiley-Interscience). Wiley.
BLACK JACK (GAME)
see Blackjack (Game)
BLACK LITERATURE (AFRICAN)
see African Literature
BLACK LITERATURE (AMERICAN)
see American Literature–Afro-American Authors
BLACK MONKS
see Benedictines
BLACK POETRY (AFRICAN)
see African Poetry (Collections)
BLACK RACE
Here are entered theoretical works discussing the Black race from an anthropological point of view. Works on Black people outside of the United States are entered under the heading Blacks. Works on the Black people of the United States are entered under the heading Afro-Americans.
see also Blacks
McCulloch, Jock. Black Soul White Artifact: Fanon's Clinical Psychology & Social Theory. LC 82-14605. 240p. Date not set. price not set (ISBN 0-521-24700-4). Cambridge U Pr.
BLACKJACK (GAME)
Snyder, Arnold. Blackbelt in Blackjack. 120p. 1982. pap. 12.95 (ISBN 0-910575-02-9). R G Enterprises.
Uston, Ken. Million Dollar Blackjack. (Illus.). 330p. 1982. 18.95 (ISBN 0-914314-08-4). Lyle Stuart.
Wong, Stanford. Stanford Wong's Blackjack Newsletters, Vol. 4: 1982. (Illus.). 214p. (Orig.). 1982. pap. 35.00 (ISBN 0-935926-07-0). Pi Yee Pr.
BLACKS
This heading used beginning January 1976. See Negroes for earlier materials. Here are entered works on Black people outside of the United States. Works on the Black people of the United States are entered under the heading Afro-Americans. Theoretical works discussing the Black race from an anthropological point of view are entered under the heading Black Race.
see also Afro-Americans
also headings beginning with Black
Devisse, Jean & Courtes, Jean Marie. The Image of the Black in Western Art, Vol. II, Pt. 1: From the Demonic Threat to the Incarnation of Sainthood. Bugner, Ladislas, ed. (Illus.). 288p. 1983. 70.00 (ISBN 0-939594-02-1). Menil Found.
Devisse, Jean & Mollat, Michel. The Image of the Black in Western Art, Vol. II, Pt. 2: Africans in the Christian Ordinance of the World (Fourteenth to the Sixteenth Century) Bugner, Ladislas, ed. (Illus.). 336p. 1983. 80.00 (ISBN 0-939594-03-X). Menil Found.
M'Bow, Amadou-Mahtar & Vercoutter, Jean. The Image of the Black in Western Art, Vol. I: From the Pharaohs to the Fall of the Roman Empire. Bugner, Ladislas, ed. (Illus.). 352p. 1983. 65.00 (ISBN 0-939594-01-3). Menil Found.
BLACKS–HISTORY
Abrahams, Roger D. & Szwed, John F., eds. After Africa: Extracts from British Travel Accounts & Journals of the Seventeenth, Eighteenth, & Nineteenth Centuries Concerning the Slaves, Their Manners, & Customs in the British West Indies. LC 82-20110. 480p. 1983. text ed. 45.00x (ISBN 0-300-02748-6); pap. text ed. 12.95x (ISBN 0-300-03030-4). Yale U Pr.
Diggs, Ellen I. Black Chronology: From 400 B.C. to the Abolition of the Slave Trade. 1983. lib. bdg. 35.00 (ISBN 0-8161-8543-3, Hall Reference). G K Hall.
Rosof, Patricia J. & Zeisel, William. Black History. (Trends in History, Vol. 3, No. 1). 128p. 1983. text ed. 20.00 (ISBN 0-86656-135-8, B135). Haworth Pr.
BLACKS–RACE IDENTITY
This heading used beginning January 1976. See Negroes–Race Identity for earlier works.
Snowden, Frank M., Jr. Before Color Prejudice: The Ancient View of Blacks. (Illus.). 224p. 1983. text ed. 17.50x (ISBN 0-674-06380-5). Harvard U Pr.
BLACKS–SOCIAL CONDITIONS
This heading used beginning January 1976. See Negroes–Social Conditions for earlier works.
Abrahams, Roger D. & Szwed, John F., eds. After Africa: Extracts from British Travel Accounts & Journals of the Seventeenth, Eighteenth, & Nineteenth Centuries Concerning the Slaves, Their Manners, & Customs in the British West Indies. LC 82-20110. 480p. 1983. text ed. 45.00x (ISBN 0-300-02748-6); pap. text ed. 12.95x (ISBN 0-300-03030-4). Yale U Pr.
BLACKS–BRITISH WEST INDIES
Abrahams, Roger D. & Szwed, John F., eds. After Africa: Extracts from British Travel Accounts & Journals of the Seventeenth, Eighteenth, & Nineteenth Centuries Concerning the Slaves, Their Manners, & Customs in the British West Indies. LC 82-20110. 480p. 1983. text ed. 45.00x (ISBN 0-300-02748-6); pap. text ed. 12.95x (ISBN 0-300-03030-4). Yale U Pr.
BLACKS–SOUTH AFRICA
Marks, S. & Rathbone, R., eds. Industrialisation & Social Change in South Africa: African Class, Culture & Consciousness, 1870-1930. (Illus.). 368p. 1982. text ed. 35.00x (ISBN 0-582-64338-4); pap. text ed. 10.95x (ISBN 0-582-64337-6). Longman.
BLACKS–UNITED STATES
see Afro-Americans
BLADDER
see also Calculi, Urinary; Prostate Gland–Diseases
Smith & Prout. Bladder Cancer: BIMR Urology. 1983. text ed. price not set (ISBN 0-407-02358-5). Butterworth.
BLAKE, WILLIAM, 1757-1827
Blake, William. Blake's Job: William Blake's Illustrations of the Book of Job. Damon, S. Foster, ed. LC 66-13155. (Illus.). 76p. 1966. 17.50x (ISBN 0-87057-096-X, Pub. by Brown U Pr). U Pr of New Eng.
Deen, Leonard W. Conversing in Paradise: Poetic Genius & Identity-as-Community in Blake's Los. LC 82-20307. 288p. 1983. text ed. 23.00 (ISBN 0-8262-0396-5). U of Mo Pr.
Doskow, Minna. William Blake's Jerusalem. LC 81-65463. (Illus.). 388p. 1982. 37.50 (ISBN 0-8386-3090-1). Fairleigh Dickinson.
Essick, Robert N. The Separate Plates of William Blake: A Catalogue. LC 82-7588. (Illus.). 310p. 1983. 75.00x (ISBN 0-691-04011-7). Princeton U Pr.
Gilchrist, Alexander. The Life of William Blake. Todd, Ruthven, ed. (Illus.). 300p. 1983. pap. text ed. 8.95x (ISBN 0-460-01971-6, Pub. by Evman England). Biblio Dist.
Hilton, Nelson. Literal Imagination: Blake's Vision of Words. LC 81-19764. (Illus.). 400p. 1983. text ed. 30.00 (ISBN 0-520-04463-0). U of Cal Pr.
Natoli, Joseph. Twentieth Century Blake Criticism: Northrop Fyre to the Present. LC 80-9021. 375p. 1982. lib. bdg. 45.00 (ISBN 0-8240-9326-7). Garland Pub.
Punter, David. Blake, Hegel & Dialectic. (Elementa Ser.: Band XXVI). 268p. 1982. pap. text ed. 23.00x (ISBN 90-6203-694-5, Pub. by Rodopi Holland). Humanities.
Webster, Brenda. Blake's Prophetic Psychology. (Illus.). 336p. 1983. 27.50x (ISBN 0-8203-0658-4). U of Ga Pr.
Willard, Helen D., intro. by. William Blake Water-Color Drawings from the Museum of Fine Arts, Boston. (Illus.). 64p. 1954. pap. 1.25 (ISBN 0-686-83417-8). Mus Fine Arts Boston.
BLANCHING
see Bleaching
BLAZONRY
see Heraldry
BLEACHING
see also Dyes and Dyeing
Vesaas, Tarjei & Rokkan, Elizabeth. The Bleaching Yard. 156p. 1982. 14.95 (ISBN 0-7206-0560-1, Pub. by Peter Owen). Merrimack Bk Serv.
BLEEDING
see Hemorrhage
BLIMPS
see Air-Ships
BLIND
Dobree, John H. & Boulter, Eric. Blindness & Visual Handicap: The Facts. (Facts Ser.). (Illus.). 252p. 1982. 13.95x (ISBN 0-19-261328-6). Oxford U Pr.
BLIND–PERSONAL NARRATIVES
Turner, Mason. RX: Applause-Biography of a Blind Performer. 1983. pap. 5.95 (ISBN 0-8283-1879-4). Branden.
BLIND–PRINTING AND WRITING SYSTEMS
Croisdale, D. W., et al, eds. Computerised Braille Production: Today & Tomorrow. 422p. 1983. pap. 17.20 (ISBN 0-387-12057-2). Springer-Verlag.
BLIND, BOOKS FOR THE
see also Large Type Books
Recording for the Blind, Staff. A Cook's Tour. 241p. 1982. pap. 7.95x (ISBN 0-914091-19-0). Chicago Review.
BLIND, LIBRARIES FOR THE
Massis, Bruce E. & Cylke, Kurt, eds. Library Service for the Blind & Physically Handicapped: An International Approach, Vol. 2. (IFLA Publications: No. 23). 100p. 1983. 18.00 (ISBN 3-598-20385-3, Pub. by K G Saur). Shoe String.
BLIND, PHYSICAL EDUCATION FOR THE
Buell, Charles E. Physical Education for Blind Children. (Illus.). 232p. 1983. pap. text ed. 16.50x (ISBN 0-398-04816-9). C C Thomas.
Physical Education & Recreation for the Visually Impaired. 80p. 1982. 7.05 (ISBN 0-88314-139-6). AAHPERD.
BLIND, SPORTS FOR THE
see Blind, Physical Education for the
BLINDNESS
see also Color Blindness
Dobree, John H. & Boulter, Eric. Blindness & Visual Handicap: The Facts. (Facts Ser.). (Illus.). 252p. 1982. 13.95x (ISBN 0-19-261328-6). Oxford U Pr.
BLOK, ALEKSANDR ALEKSANDROVICH, 1880-1921
Chukovsky, Kornei. Alexander Blok as Man & Poet. Burgin, Diana, ed. O'Connor, Katherine, tr. LC 82-1809. 1982. 17.50 (ISBN 0-88233-485-9). Ardis Pubs.
Mochulsky, Konstantin. Aleksandr Blok. Johnson, Doris V., tr. 504p. 1983. 30.00 (ISBN 0-8143-1707-3). Wayne St U Pr.
BLOOD
see also Blood Plasma; Hemorrhage
Critser, James R., Jr. Blood Technology. (Ser.10BT-82). 1983. 100.00 (ISBN 0-88178-004-9). Lexington Data.
Gray, C. H. & James, V. H., eds. Hormones in Blood, Vol. 4. 3rd ed. Date not set. price not set (ISBN 0-12-296204-4). price not set (ISBN 0-12-296205-2). Acad Pr.
Hagen, Piet J., ed. Blood: Gift or Merchandise-Towards an International Policy. LC 82-12742. 246p. 1982. 29.50 (ISBN 0-8451-0219-2). A R Liss.
BLOOD–ANALYSIS AND CHEMISTRY
see also Anoxemia; Hyperglycemia
Fulwood, Robinson & Johnson, Clifford L. Hematological & Nutritional Biochemistries References Data of Persons 6 Months-74 Years of Age: United States, 1976-1980. Cox, Klaudia, tr. (Ser. 11: No. 232). 60p. 1982. pap. 1.95 (ISBN 0-8406-0267-7). Natl Ctr Health Stats.
Hollenberg, N. K. The Haemodynamics of Nadolol. Date not set. price not set (ISBN 0-8089-1535-5). Grune.
Russell, N. J. & Powell, G. M. Blood Biochemistry. (Biology in Medicine Ser.). 128p. 1983. text ed. 27.25x (ISBN 0-7099-0003-1, Pub. by Croom Helm Ltd England). Biblio Dist.
BLOOD–CIRCULATION–RESEARCH
see Cardiovascular Research
BLOOD–COLLECTION AND PRESERVATION
Stroup, Marjory & Treacy, Margaret. Blood Group Antigens & Antibodies. (Illus.). 255p. (Orig.). 1982. pap. text ed. 35.00 (ISBN 0-910771-00-6). Ortho Diag.
BLOOD–CORPUSCLES AND PLATELETS
see Blood Cells
BLOOD–DISEASES
see also Hemophilia; Pediatric Hematology
Bizzozero, Julius. On a New Blood Particle & Its Role in Thrombosis & Blood Coagulation. Beck, Eugen A., tr. from Ger. (Illus.). 156p. 1982. pap. text ed. 16.50 (ISBN 3-456-81182-9, Pub. by Hans Huber Switzerland). J K Burgess.
Ritzmann, Stephan E. & Daniels, Jerry C., eds. Serum Protein Abnormalities: Diagnostic & Clinical Aspects. LC 82-18001. 550p. 1982. 60.00 (ISBN 0-8451-2799-3). A R Liss.
BLOOD–GROUPS
see Blood Groups
BLOOD–PLASMA
see Blood Plasma
BLOOD–PRESSURE
see Blood Pressure
BLOOD–TRANSFUSION
see also Blood Banks; Blood Groups
Collins, John A. & Murawski, Kris, eds. Massive Transfusion in Surgery & Trauma. LC 82-18657. (Progress in Clinical & Biological Research Ser.: Vol. 108). 319p. 1982. 32.00 (ISBN 0-8451-0108-0). A R Liss.
Hauer, et al. Autotransfusion. 1981. 38.00 (ISBN 0-444-00599-4). Elsevier.
Sibinga, C. Th. & Das, P. C. Blood Transfusion & Problems of Bleeding. 1982. text ed. 39.50 (ISBN 90-247-3058-9, Pub. by Martinus Nijhoff Netherlands). Kluwer Boston.
Terasaki, Paul, ed. Blood Transfusion & Transplantation. 178p. 1982. 39.50 (ISBN 0-8089-1522-3). Grune.
BLOOD BANKS
see also Blood–Collection and Preservation
Stroup, Marjory & Treacy, Margaret. Blood Group Antigens & Antibodies. (Illus.). 255p. (Orig.). 1982. pap. text ed. 35.00 (ISBN 0-910771-00-6). Ortho Diag.
BLOOD CELL COUNT
Assendelft, Van & England, J. M. Advances in Hematological Methods: The Blood Count. 272p. 1982. 72.00 (ISBN 0-8493-6596-1). CRC Pr.
BLOOD CELLS
see also Blood Cell Count
Albertini, A. & Ekins, R. P., eds. Free Hormones in Blood: Proceedings of the Advanced Course on Free Hormone Assays & Neuropeptides, Venice, Italy, June 15-17, 1982. (Symposia of the Giovanni Lorenzini Foundation Ser.: Vol. 14). 392p. 1982. 70.25 (ISBN 0-444-80463-3, Biomedical Pr). Elsevier.
Ferrone, Soldano & Solheim, Bjarte G., eds. HLA Typing: Methodology & Clinical Aspects, 2 vols. 208p. 1982. 59.00 ea. Vol. I (ISBN 0-8493-6410-8). Vol. II (ISBN 0-8493-6411-6). CRC Pr.
Weiss, Harvey J., ed. Platelets: Pathophysiology & Antiplatelet Drug Therapy. 178p. 1982. 22.00 (ISBN 0-8451-0217-6). A R Liss.
BLOOD CHEMISTRY
see Blood–Analysis and Chemistry
BLOOD COLLECTION
see Blood–Collection and Preservation
BLOOD CORPUSCLES
see Blood Cells
BLOOD GROUPS
see also Blood–Transfusion
Lockyer, W. John. Essentials of ABO-Rh Grouping & Compatibility Testing: Theoretical Aspects & Practical Application. (Illus.). 152p. 1982. text ed. 16.50 (ISBN 0-7236-0635-8). Wright-PSG.
BLOOD PLASMA
see also Blood Banks
Drees, Thomas. Blood Plasma: The Promise & the Politics. LC 82-11617. (Illus.). 1983. 25.00 (ISBN 0-87949-225-2). Ashley Bks.
BLOOD PRESSURE
Erfurt, John C. & Foote, Andrea. Blood Pressure Control Programs in Industrial Settings. 83p. 1979. pap. 5.00 (ISBN 0-87736-334-X). U of Mich Inst Labor.
BLOOD PRESSURE, HIGH
see Hypertension
BLOOD SUBSTITUTES
see Blood Plasma
BLOOD TRANSFUSION
see Blood–Transfusion
BLOOD-VESSELS
see also Arteries
also names of organs and regions of the body, with or without the subdivision Blood Vessels
Lasjaunias, Pierre. Craniofacial & Upper Cervical Arteries: Collateral Circulation & Angiographic Protocols. 300p. 1983. lib. bdg. write for info. (ISBN 0-683-04898-8). Williams & Wilkins.
BLOOD-VESSELS–DISEASES
see also Aneurysms; Peripheral Vascular Diseases
Hallett, John W., Jr. & Brewster, David C. Manual of Patient Care in Vascular Surgery. (Spiral Manual Ser.). 262p. 1982. spiralbound 15.95 (ISBN 0-316-34050-2). Little.
BLOOD-VESSELS–GRAFTS
see Vascular Grafts

BLOOD-VESSELS–RADIOGRAPHY
see Angiography
BLOOD-VESSELS–SURGERY
Castaneda. Transluminal Angioplasty. (Illus.). 350p. 1983. write for info. (ISBN 0-86577-057-3). Thieme-Stratton.
Hallett, John W., Jr. & Brewster, David C. Manual of Patient Care in Vascular Surgery. (Spiral Manual Ser.). 262p. 1982. spiralbound 15.95 (ISBN 0-316-34050-2). Little.
Kerstein, Morris D. Aneurysms. (Illus.). 276p. 1983. lib. bdg. price not set (ISBN 0-683-04598-9). Williams & Wilkins.
Rubio. Atlas of Angioacess Surgery. 1983. 95.00 (ISBN 0-8151-7451-9). Year Bk Med.
BLOOMSBERRIES
see Bloomsbury Group
BLOOMSBURY GROUP
Mahood, Kenneth. The Secret Sketchbook of Bloomsbury Lady. (Illus.). 64p. 1983. pap. 10.95 (ISBN 0-312-70873-4). St Martin.
BLOWERS
see Compressors
BLUE COLLAR WORKERS
see Labor and Laboring Classes
BLUE JAY
Bancroft, G. Thomas & Woolfenden, Glen E. Molt of Scrub Jays & Blue Jays in Florida. 51p. 1982. write for info. (ISBN 0-943610-29-X). Am Ornithologists.
BLUE-PRINTS
Brown, Walter C. Blueprint Reading for Industry. Rev. ed. LC 82-20949. 345p. 1983. spiral bdg. 14.00 (ISBN 0-87006-429-0). Goodheart.
Hardman, William E. How To Read Shop Prints & Drawings With Blueprints. 236p. 1982. pap. text ed. 19.95 (ISBN 0-910399-01-8). Natl Tool & Mach.
Hoffman, Edward G. & Romero, Felix. Welding Blueprint Reading. 1983. pap. text ed. 19.95 (ISBN 0-534-01431-3, Breton Pubs). Wadsworth Pub.
Rohlmeier, Charles. Residential Construction: Blueprint Reading & Practices. 1983. pap. 19.95 (ISBN 0-534-01387-2, Breton). Wadsworth Pub.
Taylor, David L. Blueprint Reading for Machinists. LC 82-72423. (Illus.). 208p. 1983. pap. text ed. price not set (ISBN 0-8273-1085-4); price not set instr's guide (ISBN 0-8273-1086-2). Delmar.
Yearling, Robert A. Machine Trades Blueprint Reading. (Illus.). 320p. 1983. text ed. 18.95 (ISBN 0-13-542001-6). P-H.
BLUE SKY LAWS
see Securities
BLUEGRASS MUSIC
Creative Concepts. Bluegrass Complete: Complete Words, Music & Guitar Chords for Eighty-Nine Songs. (Illus.). 192p. (Orig.). pap. 9.95 (ISBN 0-486-24503-9). Dover.
BLUEPRINTS
see Blue-Prints
BLUES (SONGS, ETC.)
see also Spirituals (Songs)
Taft, Michael. Blues Lyric Poetry: An Anthology. LC 82-48266. 500p. 1983. lib. bdg. 75.00 (ISBN 0-686-42832-3). Garland Pub.
BLUMHARDT, CHRISTOPH, 1842-1919
Blumhardt's Battle. pap. 1.25 (ISBN 0-686-83958-7). T E Lowe.
BLUNDEN, EDMUND CHARLES, 1896-
Mallon, Thomas. Edmund Blunden. (English Authors Ser.). 158p. 1983. lib. bdg. 17.95 (ISBN 0-8057-6829-7, Twayne). G K Hall.
BOARDING-HOUSES
see Hotels, Taverns, etc.
BOARDING SCHOOLS
see also Private Schools
McBeth, Sally J. Ethnic Identity & the Boarding School Experience of West-Central Oklahoma American Indians. LC 82-21983. (Illus.). 184p. (Orig.). 1983. lib. bdg. 21.75 (ISBN 0-8191-2895-3); pap. text ed. 10.00 (ISBN 0-8191-2896-1). U Pr of Amer.
BOARDS OF DIRECTORS
see Directors of Corporations
BOARDS OF EDUCATION
see School Boards
BOARDS OF SUPERVISION (CORPORATION LAW)
see Directors of Corporations
BOAT-BUILDING
see also Ship-Building
Bingham, Bruce. The Sailor's Sketchbook. Gilbert, Jim, ed. 144p. 1983. pap. price not set (ISBN 0-915160-55-2). Seven Seas.
Rose, Pat R. The Solar Boat Book. rev. ed. 266p. 1983. 14.95 (ISBN 0-89815-089-2); pap. 8.95 (ISBN 0-89815-086-8). Ten Speed Pr.
Thomas, Barry. Building the Herreshoff Dinghy: The Manufacturer's Method. (Illus.). 72p. 1983. pap. 5.95 (ISBN 0-8289-0508-8). Greene.
Woodenboat Magazine Editors. Wooden Boat: An Appreciation of the Craft. (Illus.). 288p. 1982. 25.00 (ISBN 0-201-09280-8). A-W.
BOAT HANDLING
see Boats and Boating
BOAT MODELS
see Ship Models
BOAT RACING
see Sailboat Racing; Yacht Racing; Rowing
BOATMEN'S SONGS
see Sea Songs
BOATS, SUBMARINE
see Submarines
BOATS AND BOATING
see also Aquatic Sports; Boat-Building; Canoes and Canoeing; Hydrofoil Boats; Indians of North America–Boats; Rowing; Sailboats; Sailing; Ships; Steamboats and Steamboat Lines; Submarines; Yachts and Yachting
Andrews, Judy & Andrews, Jim. Family Boating. (Illus.). 160p. 1983. 14.95 (ISBN 0-370-30407-1, Pub by The Bodley Head); pap. 7.95 (ISBN 0-370-30473-X). Merrimack Bk Serv.
Atkin, John. Practical Boat Designs. LC 82-48618. (Illus.). 192p. 1983. 17.50 (ISBN 0-87742-160-9). Intl Marine.
Bolger, Philip C. Thirty-Odd Boats. LC 82-80403. (Illus.). 224p. 1982. 22.50 (ISBN 0-87742-152-8). Intl Marine.
Brown, Robert, ed. Boater's Safety Handbook. (Illus.). 52p. (Orig.). 1982. pap. 2.95 (ISBN 0-89886-072-5). Mountaineers.
Brown, T. Nigel, ed. Brown's Nautical Almanac, 1983. 106th ed. LC 32-280. (Illus.). 946p. 1982. 37.50x (ISBN 0-8002-3066-3). Intl Pubns Serv.
Crowley, william, ed. Rushton's Rowboats & Canoes, 1903. LC 82-48169. (Illus.). 128p. 1983. pap. 15.00 (ISBN 0-87742-164-1). Intl Marine.
Duffett, John. Boatowner's Guide to Modern Maintenance: Protecting Your Floating Investment. (Illus.). 1983. 19.95 (ISBN 0-393-03279-5). Norton.
Dye, Frank & Dye, Margaret. Open-Boat Cruising - Coastal & Inland Waters. (Illus.). 176p. (Orig.). 1982. 17.50 (ISBN 0-7153-8247-0). David & Charles.
Greenwood, John O. & Dills, Michael. Greenwood's & Dills' Lake Boats, 1983. 19th, rev. ed. 180p. 1983. price not set. Freshwater.
Guthorn, Peter J. The Sea Bright Skiff & Other Shore Boats. rev. ed. (Illus.). 256p. 1983. pap. 13.95 (ISBN 0-916838-73-0). Schiffer.
Hedley, Eugene. Boating For the Handicapped: Guidelines for the Physically Handicapped. LC 79-91181. (Illus.). 124p. 1979. 5.65 (ISBN 0-686-38820-8). Human Res Ctr.
Leather, John. Sail & Oar. LC 82-48098. (Illus.). 144p. 1982. 20.00 (ISBN 0-87742-161-7). Intl Marine.
Reed's Nautical Almanac & Coast Pilot: East Coast Edition-1983. 1983. pap. 19.95 (ISBN 0-900335-74-2, Pub. by Better Boating Assn.). Norton.
Saunders, A. E. Small Craft Piloting & Coastal Navigation. LC 81-71657. (Illus.). 287p. 1982. 19.95 (ISBN 0-686-82298-6). Van Nos Reinhold.
Sleightholme, Des. Better Boat Handling. (Illus.). 192p. 1983. 15.00 (ISBN 0-915160-30-7). Seven Seas.
--The Trouble with Cruising. (Illus.). 113p. 11.95cancelled (ISBN 0-914814-40-0). Sail Bks.
Watney, John. Cruising in British & Irish Waters. (Illus.). 224p. 1983. 23.95 (ISBN 0-7153-8402-3). David & Charles.
Woodenboat Magazine Editors. Wooden Boat: An Appreciation of the Craft. (Illus.). 288p. 1982. 25.00 (ISBN 0-201-09280-8). A-W.
BOATS AND BOATING–JUVENILE LITERATURE
Gibbons, Gail. Boat Book. LC 82-15851. (Illus.). 32p. (ps-3). 1983. reinforced binding 11.95 (ISBN 0-8234-0478-1). Holiday.
BOCCACCIO, GIOVANNI, 1313-1375
Cottino-Jones, Marga. Order from Chaos: Social & Aesthetic Harmonies in Boccaccio's Decameron. LC 82-17418. 210p. (Orig.). 1983. lib. bdg. 21.75 (ISBN 0-8191-2840-6); pap. text ed. 10.75 (ISBN 0-8191-2841-4). U Pr of Amer.
BODY, HUMAN
see also Anatomy, Human; Mind and Body
De Coursey, R. The Human Organism. 5th ed. 1980. text ed. 24.95 (ISBN 0-07-016275-1); tchr's manual avail. (ISBN 0-07-016277-8). McGraw.
Discovering the Human Body. (Discovering Science Ser.). 1983. lib. bdg. 15.96 (ISBN 0-86706-104-9, Pub. by Stonehenge). Silver.
The Human Body, 8 vols. Incl. Vol. 1. The Brain (ISBN 0-89193-601-7); Vol. 2. The Heart (ISBN 0-89193-602-5); Vol. 3. The Eye (ISBN 0-89193-603-3); Vol. 4. Blood (ISBN 0-89193-604-1); Vol. 5. Skeleton (ISBN 0-89193-605-X); Vol. 6. Reproduction (ISBN 0-89193-606-8); Vol. 7. Muscles (ISBN 0-89193-607-6); Vol. 8. Skin (ISBN 0-89193-608-4). (Illus.). 164p. 1982. Set. 15.95 (ISBN 0-686-84049-6). US News & World.
Justus, Fred. The Human Body. (Health Ser.). 24p. (gr. 3-5). 1977. wkbk. 5.00 (ISBN 0-8209-0344-2, H-5). ESP.
Overbeck, Carla. Systems of the Human Body. (Science Ser.). 24p. (gr. 5 up). 1979. wkbk. 5.00 (ISBN 0-8209-0150-4, S-12). ESP.
BODY, HUMAN–JUVENILE LITERATURE
Taylor, Ron. How the Body Works. Moore, Linda, ed. (Full Color Fact Books). (Illus.). 32p. (gr. 4-12). 1982. PLB 7.95 (ISBN 0-8219-0012-9, 35544). EMC.
Ward, Brian R. Birth & Growth. (The Human Body Ser.). (Illus.). 48p. (gr. 4 up). 1983. PLB 8.90 (ISBN 0-531-04459-9). Watts.
--Body Maintenance. (The Human Body Ser.). (Illus.). 48p. (gr. 4 up). 1983. PLB 8.90 (ISBN 0-531-04457-2). Watts.
BODY AND MIND
see Mind and Body
BODY AND SOUL (PHILOSOPHY)
see Mind and Body
BODY AND SOUL (THEOLOGY)
see Man (Theology)
BODY LANGUAGE
see Nonverbal Communication
BODY MECHANICS
see Posture
BODY SURFING
see Surfing
BODY TEMPERATURE
see also Hypothermia
Satinoff, E., ed. Thermoregulation. LC 79-10267. (Benchmark Papers in Behavior: Vol. 13). 400p. 1980. 51.50 (ISBN 0-87933-349-9). Hutchinson Ross.
BOECK'S SARCOID
see Sarcoidosis
BOEHM FLUTE
see Flute
BOEING AIRCRAFT COMPANY, SEATTLE
Taylor, Michael J., ed. Planemakers: 1 Boeing. (Planemakers Ser.). (Illus.). 160p. 1982. 17.95 (ISBN 0-86720-554-7). Sci Bks Intl.
BOEING SEVEN-O-SEVEN (JET TRANSPORTS)
Schiff, Barry J. The Boeing 707. (Illus.). 180p. 1983. pap. 7.95 (ISBN 0-8168-5653-2). Aero.
BOETHIUS, d. 524
Gibson, Margaret, ed. Boethius: His Life, Writings & Influence. (Illus.). 432p. 1982. text ed. 48.00x (ISBN 0-631-11141-7, Pub. by Basil Blackwell England). Biblio Dist.
Reiss, Edmund. Boethius. (Twayne's World Authors Ser.). 1982. lib. bdg. 18.95 (ISBN 0-8057-6519-0, Twayne). G K Hall.
BOHEMIA
Dillon, Kenneth J. King & Estates in the Bohemian Lands, 1526-1564. 206p. 1976. write for info. P Lang Pubs.
BOHEMIANISM
see also Hippies
Cook, Bruce. The Beat Generation. LC 82-20918. 248p. 1983. Repr. of 1971 ed. lib. bdg. 35.00x (ISBN 0-313-23073-0, COBG). Greenwood.
BOILERS
see also Fuel; Heating; Pressure Vessels
French, David N. Metallurgical Failures in Fossil Fired Boilers. 228p. 1983. 32.50 (ISBN 0-471-89841-4, Pub. by Wiley-Interscience). Wiley.
Hewison, C. H. Locomotive Boiler Explosions. (Illus.). 144p. 1982. 16.50 (ISBN 0-7153-8305-1). David & Charles.
BOLINGBROKE, HENRY SAINT-JOHN, 1ST VISCOUNT, 1678-1751
Varey, Simon, ed. Lord Bolingbroke: Contributions to the Craftsman. 1982. 39.95 (ISBN 0-19-822386-2). Oxford U Pr.
BOLIVIA–POLITICS AND GOVERNMENT
Nash, June. We Eat the Mines & the Mines Eat Us: Dependence & Exploitation in Bolivian Tin Mines. 363p. 1982. pap. 13.00 (ISBN 0-231-04711-8). Columbia U Pr.
BOLSHEVISM
see Communism
BOLTZMANN TRANSPORT EQUATION
see Transport Theory
BOMB RECONNAISSANCE
Here are entered works on the location, identification, and application of safety measures as protection against unexploded bombs which have been set to detonate.
Parfit, Michael. The Boys Behind the Bombs. 324p. 1983. 15.45i (ISBN 0-316-69057-0). Little.
BOMBARDMENTS WITH PARTICLES
see Collisions (Nuclear Physics)
BOMBAY
Tindall, Gillian. City of Gold: The Biography of Bombay. 1981. 40.00x (ISBN 0-686-82399-0, Pub. by M Temple Smith). State Mutual Bk.
BOMBERS
see also Heinkel One Hundred Seventy-Seven (Bombers); Kamikaze Airplanes
Birtles, Philip. Mosquito. (Illus.). 192p. 1981. 19.95. Sci Bks Intl.
Johnsen, Frederick A. Bomber Barons: History of the 5th Bomb Group. (Illus.). 28p. 1982. pap. 4.95 (ISBN 0-686-84257-X, Pub. by Bomber). Aviation.
BON-SAI
see Bonsai
BONAPARTE, LOUIS
see Napoleon 3rd, Emperor of the French, 1808-1873
BONAPARTE, NAPOLEON
see Napoleon 1st, Emperor of the French, 1769-1821
BONDING (TECHNOLOGY)
see Sealing (Technology)
BONDS
see also Debts, Public; Investments–Tables, etc.; Stocks
Fong, H. G. Bond Portfolio Analysis & Management. LC 82-73626. 225p. 1983. 32.50 (ISBN 0-87094-245-X). Dow Jones-Irwin.
Hawawini, Gabriel A., ed. Bond Duration & Immunization: Early Developments & Recent Contributions. LC 82-82490. (Accountancy in Transition Ser.). 322p. 1982. lib. bdg. 42.00 (ISBN 0-8240-5338-9). Garland Pub.
La Barre, George. Collecting Stocks & Bonds, Vol. 1. 1980. 5.00 (ISBN 0-913702-42-0). Heart Am Pr.
--Collecting Stocks & Bonds, Vol. 2. 1981. 5.00 (ISBN 0-913902-43-8). Heart Am Pr.
--Collecting Stocks & Bonds, Vol. 3. 1981. 5.00 (ISBN 0-913902-44-6). Heart Am Pr.
Sherwood, Hugh C. How to Invest in Bonds. 192p. 1983. 13.95 (ISBN 0-8027-0732-7). Walker & Co.
BONDS–TABLES, ETC.
see Investments–Tables, etc.
BONDS, CHEMICAL
see Chemical Bonds
BONE–GROWTH
Dixon, Andrew D. & Sarnat, Bernard G., eds. Factors & Mechanisms Influencing Bone Growth. LC 82-13115. (Progress in Clinical & Biological Research Ser.: Vol. 101). 657p. 1982. 96.00 (ISBN 0-8451-0101-3). A R Liss.
Katznelson, Alexander & Nerubay, Jacobo, eds. Osteosarcoma: New Trends in Diagnosis & Treatment. LC 82-4679. (Progress in Clinical & Biological Research Ser.: Vol. 99). 164p. 1982. 25.00 (ISBN 0-8451-0099-8). A R Liss.
BONEFISH
Sosin, Mark & Kreh, Lefty. Fishing the Flats. (Illus.). 160p. 1983. 14.95 (ISBN 0-8329-0278-0); pap. 8.95 (ISBN 0-8329-0280-2). Winchester Pr.
BONES
see also Cartilage; Extremities (Anatomy); Fractures; Joints; Skeleton; Skull
Elementary Science Study: Bones, Rabbit Skeleton. 1982. write for info. (ISBN 0-07-018514-X). McGraw.
BONES–DISEASES
see also Osteoporosis; X-Rays
Silbermann, M. & Slavkin, H., eds. Current Advances in Skeletogenesis: Development, Biomineralization, Mediators & Metabolic Bone Diseases (Selected Proceedings of the Fifth International Workshop on Calcified Tissues, Kiryat-Anavim, March 1982) (International Congress Ser.: No. 589). 594p. 1982. 127.75 (ISBN 0-444-90274-0). Elsevier.
BONS MOTS
see Wit and Humor
BONSAI
Dhanda, Leila. Bonsai Culture. 141p. 1980. 40.00x (ISBN 0-686-84448-3, Pub. by Oxford & I B H India). State Mutual Bk.
Shufunotomo Editors. The Essentials of Bonsai. (Illus.). 108p. 1982. 9.95. Timber.
BOOK CENSORSHIP
see Censorship
BOOK COLLECTING
see also Book-Plates; Libraries, Private
Doyle, Alfreda. Starting a Self Sufficiency Library; Suggested Places to Look for Used & Inexpensive Books. 25p. 1983. pap. text ed. 4.00 (ISBN 0-910811-32-6). Center Self.
The Official 1983 Price Guide to Old Books & Autographs. 4th ed. LC 81-81775. 512p. 1983. 9.95 (ISBN 0-87637-351-1). Hse of Collectibles.
BOOK ILLUSTRATION
see Illustration of Books
BOOK INDUSTRIES AND TRADE
see also Bookbinding; Booksellers and Bookselling; Imprints (In Books); Paper Making and Trade; Printing; Publishers and Publishing
American Book Prices Current, Vol. 86. 1975-79. 79.95 (ISBN 0-914022-11-3); index 250.00 (ISBN 0-686-82438-5). Bancroft Parkman.
Beck, Helen. How Books Get That Way: Athena Tells. (Illus.). 64p. (gr. 3-6). 1983. 9.95 (ISBN 0-940730-01-4). Athena Pr ND.
O'Hare, Joanne. Bowker Annual of Library & Book Trade Information, 1983. 55.00 (ISBN 0-686-83430-5). Bowker.
The U. S. Book Publishing Industry. 1982. 445.00 (ISBN 0-686-38433-4, 501). Busn Trend.
BOOK INDUSTRIES AND TRADE–DICTIONARIES
Peters, Jean, ed. The Bookman's Glossary. rev. ed. 200p. 1983. 21.95 (ISBN 0-8352-1686-1). Bowker.
BOOK INDUSTRIES AND TRADE–DIRECTORIES
American Book Publishing Record Annual Cumulative, 1982. 1500p. 1983. 76.50x (ISBN 0-8352-1616-0). Bowker.
Bodian, Nat G. Book Marketing Handbook, Vol. II. 2nd ed. 525p. 1983. 60.00 (ISBN 0-8352-1685-3). Bowker.
R. R. Bowker Staff. International Literary Market Place, 1983-84. new ed. 530p. 1983. pap. 55.00 (ISBN 0-8352-1576-8). Bowker.
Robinson, Ruth E. & Farudi, Daryush. Buy Books Where-Sell Books Where: A Directory of Out of Print Booksellers & Their Author-Subject Specialties. 3rd ed. (Orig.). 1982. pap. 3.95 (ISBN 0-9603556-4-2). Robinson Bks.
BOOK LISTS
see Bibliography–Best Books
BOOK OF COMMON PRAYER
see Church of England–Book of Common Prayer

BOOK-PLATES

Talbot, Clare R. Historic California in Bookplates. (Illus.). xvi, 287p. 1983. Repr. of 1963 ed. 15.95 (ISBN 0-8214-0737-6, 82-85066). Ohio U Pr.

BOOK PRICES

see Books–Prices

BOOK PRIZES

see Literary Prizes

BOOK RARITIES

see Bibliography–Rare Books

BOOK REPAIRING

see Books–Conservation and Restoration

BOOK REVIEWS

see Books–Reviews

BOOK SALES

see Books–Prices; Booksellers and Bookselling

BOOK TRADE

see Book Industries and Trade; Booksellers and Bookselling; Publishers and Publishing

BOOKBINDING

see also Book-Plates

Brenni, Vito J., compiled by. Bookbinding: A Guide to the Literature. LC 82-15810. 200p. 1983. lib. bdg. 35.00 (ISBN 0-313-23718-2, BBB/). Greenwood.

Middleton, B. C. History of English Craft Bookbinding Techniques. (Illus.). 55.00x (ISBN 0-87556-624-3). Saifer.

BOOKKEEPERS

see Accountants

BOOKKEEPING

see also Accounting; Auditing; Business Mathematics; Calculating-Machines; Cost Accounting; Financial Statements; Office Equipment and Supplies

also subdivision Accounting under specific industries, professions, trades, etc.

Brief, Richard P., ed. Four Classics on the Theory of Double Entry Bookkeeping. LC 82-82949. (Accountancy in Transition Ser.). 90p. 1982. lib. bdg. 20.00 (ISBN 0-8240-5333-8). Garland Pub.

Doyle, Dennis M. Efficient Accounting & Record Keeping. Brownstone, David, ed. LC 78-2474. (The Small Business Profit Program Ser.). 116p. 1977. pap. text ed. 5.95 (ISBN 0-471-05044-X). Wiley.

Gorham, John P. Bookkeeping Simplified & Self-Taught. LC 82-11316. (Simplified & Self-Taught Ser.). 128p. 1983. pap. 4.95 (ISBN 0-668-05456-5, 5456). Arco.

Kravitz, Wallace. Bookkeeping the Easy Way. (Easy Way Ser.). 272p. (gr. 11-12). 1983. pap. write for info. (ISBN 0-8120-2622-5). Barron.

Triple-Entry Bookkeeping & Income Momentum, Vol. 18. (Studies in Accounting Research). 53p. 1982. 6.00 (ISBN 0-86539-041-X). Am Accounting.

BOOKKEEPING–EXAMINATIONS, QUESTIONS, ETC.

Rudman, Jack. Supervising Bookkeeper. (Career Examination Ser.: C-2682). (Cloth bdg. avail. on request). pap. 12.00 (ISBN 0-8373-2682-6). Natl Learning.

BOOKKEEPING–STUDY AND TEACHING

see Accounting–Study and Teaching

BOOKMOBILES

Roberts, Don, ed. Mediamobiles. (PLR Ser.: No. 19). 124p. (Orig.). Date not set. pap. text ed. 7.00 (ISBN 0-8389-3232-0). ALA.

BOOKPLATES

see Book-Plates

BOOKS

see also Bibliography; Cataloging; Classification–Books; Copyright; Illumination of Books and Manuscripts; Illustration of Books; Imprints (In Books); Libraries; Manuscripts; Printing; Publishers and Publishing

also headings beginning with the word Book

Marquis Who's Who Publications Index to All Books, 1981-1982. LC 74-17540. 750p. 1982. 24.50 (ISBN 0-8379-1412-4). Marquis.

Szekely, Edmond B. Books, Our Eternal Companions. (Illus.). 48p. 1971. pap. 3.50 (ISBN 0-89564-064-3). IBS Intl.

BOOKS–APPRAISAL

see Bibliography–Best Books; Books and Reading; Criticism; Literature–History and Criticism

BOOKS–CENSORSHIP

see Censorship

BOOKS–COLLECTORS AND COLLECTING

see Book Collecting

BOOKS–CONSERVATION AND RESTORATION

see also Manuscripts–Conservation and Restoration

Baker, John B. & Soroka, Marguerite C., eds. Library Conservation: Preservation in Perspective. LC 78-16133. (Publications in the Informtion Sciences Ser.). 459p. 1978. 50.00 (ISBN 0-87933-332-4). Hutchinson Ross.

Harrison, Alice W. & Collister, Edward A. The Conservation of Archival & Library Materials: A Resource Guide to Audiovisual Aids. LC 82-652. 202p. 1982. 13.50 (ISBN 0-8108-1523-0). Scarecrow.

Merrill-Oldham, Jan. Conservation & Preservation of Library Materials. LC 82-1875. 1982. pap. text ed. 10.00 (ISBN 0-917590-07-4). Univ Conn Lib.

BOOKS–HISTORY

see also Incunabula; Printing–History

Vervliet, H. D. Annual Bibliography of the History of the Printed Book & Libraries. 1983. lib. bdg. 85.00 (ISBN 0-686-37696-X, Pub. by Martinus Nijhoff Netherlands). Kluwer Boston.

BOOKS–JUVENILE LITERATURE

Althea. Making a Book. (Cambridge Dinosaur Information Ser.). (Illus.). 26p. (gr. 7-10). 1983. pap. 1.50 (ISBN 0-521-27159-2). Cambridge U Pr.

BOOKS–PRESERVATION

see Books–Conservation and Restoration

BOOKS–PRICES

Erhardt, Roy. Set of Price Guides to Townsend Books. 1982. 5.00 (ISBN 0-913902-47-0). Heart Am Pr.

Hancer, Kevin. Paperback Price Guide. 2nd ed. (Illus.). 440p. 1982. pap. 9.95. Overstreet.

Heath, Wendy Y., ed. Book Auction Records: August 1980-July 1981, Vol. 78. LC 5-18641. 547p. 1981. 130.00x (ISBN 0-7129-1018-2). Intl Pubns Serv.

McGrath, Daniel F. Bookman's Price Index, Vol. 24. 780p. 1983. 115.00x (ISBN 0-8103-0624-7). Gale.

--Bookman's Price Index, Vol. 25. 800p. 1983. 115.00x (ISBN 0-8103-0638-7). Gale.

BOOKS–REPAIRING

see Books–Conservation and Restoration

BOOKS–RESTORATION

see Books–Conservation and Restoration

BOOKS–REVIEWS

Here are entered collections of reviews; Works on the technique of writing reviews are entered under the heading Book Reviewing.

RSBR Committee. Reference & Subscription Books Reviews, 1981-1982. (RSBR Ser.). 240p. 1982. pap. text ed. 20.00 (ISBN 0-8389-0380-0). ALA.

BOOKS–REVIEWS–BIBLIOGRAPHY

Matos, Antonio, ed. Guide to Reviews of Books from & about Hispanic America, 1980. LC 66-96537. 1780p. 1980. 90.00 (ISBN 0-87917-084-0). Ethridge.

BOOKS, CONDEMNED

see Condemned Books

BOOKS, FILMED

see Film Adaptations

BOOKS, ILLUSTRATED

see Illustration of Books

BOOKS, LARGE TYPE

see Large Type Books

BOOKS, RARE

see Bibliography–Rare Books

BOOKS, REFERENCE

see Reference Books

BOOKS AND READING

see also Bibliography–Best Books; Books–Reviews; Classification–Books; Libraries; Reference Books

Asheim, Lester, et al. Reading & Successful Living: The Family-School Partnership. 150p. 1983. write for info. (ISBN 0-208-02003-9, Lib Prof Pubns); pap. 11.50x (ISBN 0-208-02004-7, Lib Prof Pubns). Shoe String.

Carter, Virginia L., compiled by. How to Survey Your Readers. 48p. 1981. 10.50 (ISBN 0-89964-189-X). CASE.

Castagna, Edwin. Caught in the Act: The Decisive Reading of Some Notable Men & Women & Its Influence on Their Actions & Attitudes. LC 82-10276. 228p. 1982. 14.50 (ISBN 0-8108-1566-4). Scarecrow.

Husband, Janet. Sequels. 368p. 1982. text ed. 22.50 (ISBN 0-8389-0368-1). ALA.

Jackson, Holbrook. The Fear of Books. LC 82-15785. x, 199p. 1982. Repr. of 1932 ed. lib. bdg. 29.75x (ISBN 0-313-23738-7, JAFB). Greenwood.

Koehn, Constance, ed. Books for Public Libraries. 3rd. ed. 381p. 1981. text ed. 20.00 (ISBN 0-8389-0328-2). ALA.

Sabine, Gordon & Sabine, Patricia. Books That Made a Difference. 1983. 18.50 (ISBN 0-208-02021-7, Lib Prof Pubns); pap. 13.50x (ISBN 0-208-02022-5, Lib Prof Pubns). Shoe String.

Salmi, Ella. Southwestern Soap. (Reading Books for College Students, or Adult School Students in Grade levels). (Illus.). 50p. 1983. pap. text ed. 4.00 (ISBN 0-686-38860-7); tchr's. guide 7.50 (ISBN 0-686-38861-5); Apple II discs 25.00 (ISBN 0-686-38862-3). Mentors.

Webster, J. Reading Matters: A Practical Philosophy. 208p. Date not set. 11.00 (ISBN 0-07-084134-9). McGraw.

White, Mary Lou. Adventuring with Books. LC 81-11179. 482p. 1981. pap. text ed. 9.00 (ISBN 0-8389-3271-1). ALA.

BOOKS FOR CHILDREN

see Children'S Literature (Collections); also subdivisions under Children's Literature

BOOKS FOR THE BLIND

see Blind, Libraries for the

BOOKS OF KNOWLEDGE

see Encyclopedias and Dictionaries

BOOKSELLERS AND BOOKSELLING

see also Books–Prices; Copyright; Publishers and Publishing

Fitch, Noel R. Sylvia Beach & the Lost Generation: A History of Literary Paris in the Twenties & Thirties. (Illus.). 1983. 25.00 (ISBN 0-393-01713-3). Norton.

Heath, Wendy Y., ed. Book Auction Records: August 1980-July 1981, Vol. 78. LC 5-18641. 547p. 1981. 130.00x (ISBN 0-7129-1018-2). Intl Pubns Serv.

BOOLEAN ALGEBRA

see Algebra, Boolean

BOONE, DANIEL, 1734-1820–JUVENILE LITERATURE

Brandt, Keith. Daniel Boone: Frontier Adventures. LC 82-15915. (Illus.). 48p. (gr. 4-6). 1983. PLB 6.89 (ISBN 0-89375-843-4); pap. text ed. 1.95 (ISBN 0-89375-844-2). Troll Assocs.

Stevenson, Augusta. Daniel Boone. new ed. (Childhood of Famous Americans Ser.). (Illus.). 204p. (Orig.). (gr. 2 up). 1983. pap. 3.95 (ISBN 0-672-52752-9). Bobbs.

BOOTHE, CLARE, 1903-

Sheed, Wilfred. Clare Booth Luce. large type ed. LC 82-5871. 378p. 1982. Repr. of 1982 ed. 11.95 (ISBN 0-89621-366-8). Thorndike Pr.

BOOTS AND SHOES

see also Leather

Fairchild Market Research Division. Footwear (Men's, Women's, Children's) Includes Detail Information on the FN Magazine Survey. special ed. (Fact File Ser.). (Illus.). 50p. 1983. pap. text ed. 15.00 (ISBN 0-87005-460-0). Fairchild.

BOOTS AND SHOES–TRADE AND MANUFACTURE

The American Footwear Market. 1981. 450.00 (ISBN 0-686-38437-7, 603). Busn Trend.

Miller, Richard K. Noise Control Solutions for the Footwear Industry. 90p. pap. text ed. 45.00 (ISBN 0-89671-027-0). Southeast Acoustics.

Small-Scale Manufacture of Footwear. (Technology Ser.: No. 2). xvi, 207p. 1982. 11.40 (ISBN 92-2-103079-2). Intl Labour Office.

BORDER LIFE

see Frontier and Pioneer Life

BORING

Here are entered works relating to the operation of cutting holes in earth or rock. Material dealing with workshop operations in metal, wood, etc. is entered under Drilling and Boring.

see also Drilling Muds; Oil Well Drilling; Wells

Swindell, John G. Rudimentary Treatise on Well-Digging, Boring & Pumpwork, Eighteen Forty-Nine. (Illus.). 88p. pap. 12.50. Saifer.

BORON

Von Matuschka, A. G. Boronizing. 100p. 1981. text ed. 29.95x (ISBN 0-471-25867-9, Pub. by Wiley-Interscience). Wiley.

BORON ORGANIC COMPOUNDS

see Organoboron Compounds

BORROW, GEORGE HENRY, 1803-1881

Bigland, Eileen. In the Steps of George Borrow. 355p. 1982. Repr. of 1951 ed. lib. bdg. 50.00 (ISBN 0-89760-091-6). Telegraph Bks.

Collie, Michael. George Borrow: Eccentric. LC 82-4397. (Illus.). 250p. 1983. 39.50 (ISBN 0-521-24615-6). Cambridge U Pr.

Williams, David. A World of His Own: The Double Life of George Borrow. (Illus.). 188p. 1982. 17.95x (ISBN 0-19-211762-9). Oxford U Pr.

BORSTAL SYSTEM

see Juvenile Detention Homes

BOSTON–DESCRIPTION

Appleberg, Marilyn J. I Love Boston Guide. (Illus.). 160p. 1983. pap. 6.95 (ISBN 0-02-097300-4, Collier). Macmillan.

Cleveland, L. David. Harvard Square Restaurants & a Guidebook of History. (Illus.). 150p. (Orig.). 1983. pap. text ed. 4.95 (ISBN 0-938534-00-9). Soup to Nuts.

Davidson, Martha, et al. The Leather District & the Fort Point Channel: The Boston Photo-Documentary Project. Channing, Susan, ed. 72p. (Orig.). 1982. 5.00 (ISBN 0-932246-02-8). Artists Found.

Primack, Mark. Greater Boston Park & Recreation Guide. (Illus.). 288p. 1983. pap. 9.95 (ISBN 0-87106-979-2). Globe Pequot.

Whitehill, Walter M. Boston: Portrait of a City. (Illus.). 112p. 1964. 6.95 (ISBN 0-517-51725-6). Crown.

BOSTON–POLITICS AND GOVERNMENT

Peterson, George, et al. The Future of Boston's Capital Plant. LC 80-54775. (Illus.). 69p. (Orig.). 1981. pap. text ed. 6.00 (ISBN 0-87766-291-6). Urban Inst.

BOSTON–SOCIAL LIFE AND CUSTOMS

Nathan, Norma. Boston's Most Eligible Bachelors. (Illus.). 176p. 1982. pap. 5.95 (ISBN 0-86616-022-1). Lewis Pub Co.

BOTANIC MEDICINE

see Medicine, Botanic

BOTANICAL CHEMISTRY

Misaghi, I. J. Physiology & Biochemistry of Plant-Pathogen Interactions. 275p. 1982. 32.50x (ISBN 0-306-41059-1, Plenum Pr). Plenum Pub.

BOTANICAL SPECIMENS–COLLECTION AND PRESERVATION

see Plants–Collection and Preservation

BOTANY

see also Bulbs; Climbing Plants; Ferns; Flowers; Fresh-Water Biology; Fruit; Grafting; Growth (Plants); Insectivorous Plants; Leaves; Marine Flora; Microscope and Microscopy; Mycology; Natural History; Paleobotany; Plants; Poisonous Plants; Pollen; Seeds; Shrubs; Trees; Variation (Biology); Vegetables; Vegetation and Climate; Weeds; Wild Flowers; Woody Plants

also divisions, classes, etc. of the vegetable kingdom, e.g. Cryptograms, Fungi; also headings beginning with the word plant; and names of plants

Commonwealth Scientific & Industrial Research Institute (CSIRO) A Curious & Diverse Flora. Commonwealth Scientific & Industrial Research Institute (CSIRO) & Australian Academy of Science, eds. 1982. of slides 35.00 set (ISBN 0-686-43170-7, Pub. by CSIRO). Intl Schol Bk Serv.

Discovering Plant Life. (Discovering Science Ser.). 1983. lib. bdg. 15.96 (ISBN 0-86706-065-4, Pub. by Stonehenge). Silver.

Ellenberg, H., et al, eds. Progress in Botany, Vol. 44. (Illus.). 450p. 1983. 65.00 (ISBN 0-387-11840-3). Springer-Verlag.

Gleason & Cronquist. Manuel of Vascular Plants. 810p. 1963. text ed. write for info. Grant Pr.

Koedam, A. & Margaris, N. Aromatic Plants. 1982. text ed. 41.50 (ISBN 90-247-2720-0, Pub. by Martinus Nijhoff Netherlands). Kluwer Boston.

Li, P. H. & Sakai, A., eds. Plant Cold Hardiness & Freezing Stress: Vol. 2: Mechanisms & Crop Implications. LC 78-7038. (Symposium). 1982. 39.50 (ISBN 0-12-447602-3). Acad Pr.

The Lives of Plants: Exploring the Wonders of Botany. (Illus.). 256p. 1983. 14.95 (ISBN 0-686-83675-8, ScribT). Scribner.

Miehe, Georg. Vegetationsgeographische Untersuchungen im Dhaulagiri-und Annapurna-Himalaya, 2 vols. (Dissertationes Botanica 66). (Illus.). 500p. 1982. lib. bdg. 67.50 (ISBN 3-7682-1356-0). Lubrecht & Cramer.

Pandey, S. N. & Trivedi, P. S. Textbook of Botany: Vol. I: Algae, Fungi, Bacteria, Virus, Lichens, Mycoplasma & Elementary Plant Pathology. 5th ed. viii, 628p. 1982. text ed. 25.00x (ISBN 0-7069-1975-0, Pub. by Vikas India). Advent NY.

Pandey, S. N., et al. Textbook of Botany: Vol. II: Bryophyta, Pteridophyta, Gymnosperms & Paleobotany. 2nd ed. viii, 531p. 1981. text ed. 25.00x (ISBN 0-7069-1355-8, Pub. by Vikas India). Advent NY.

Saigo, Roy H. & Saigo, Barbara W. Botany: Principles & Applications. (Illus.). 560p. 1983. 27.95 (ISBN 0-13-080234-4). P-H.

Skellern, Claire & Rogers, Paul. Classic Botany. 208p. 1977. 19.00x (ISBN 0-7121-0255-8, Pub. by Macdonald & Evans). State Mutual Bk.

Van Der Meijden, R. Systematics & Evolution of Xantophyllum: Polygalaceae. (Leiden Botanical Ser.: Vol. 7). (Illus.). vii, 159p. 1982. pap. write for info. (ISBN 90-04-06594-6). E J Brill.

Van Reine, W. F. Prud'Homme. A Taxonomic Revision of the European Sphacelariaceae: Sphacelariales, Phaeophyceae. (Leiden Botanical Ser.: Vol. 6). (Illus.). ix, 293p. 1982. pap. write for info (ISBN 90-04-06597-0). E J Brill.

BOTANY–ANATOMY

see also Botany–Morphology; Plant Cells and Tissues

Chandurkar, P. J. Plant Anatomy. 256p. 1974. 40.00x (ISBN 0-686-84462-9, Pub. by Oxford & I B H India). State Mutual Bk.

Esau, Katherine. Anatomy of Seed Plants. 2nd ed. LC 76-41191. 550p. 1977. text ed. 29.95 (ISBN 0-471-24520-8). Wiley.

--Plant Anatomy. 2nd ed. LC 65-12713. 767p. 1965. 32.95x (ISBN 0-471-24455-4). Wiley.

BOTANY–CLASSIFICATION

see also Plants–Identification

McVaugh, Rogers. Flora Novo-Galiciana: A Descriptive Account of the Vascular Plants of Western Mexico. Anderson, William R., ed. LC 82-13537. (Graminae Ser.: Vol. 14). (Illus.). 384p. 1983. text ed. 38.00 (ISBN 0-472-04814-7). U of Mich Pr.

Stafleu & Cowan, R. S. Taxonomic Literature: LH-O, Vol. 3. 1982. 135.00 (ISBN 90-313-0444-1, Pub. by Junk Pubs Netherlands). Kluwer Boston.

Vasil'chenko, I. T. Novitates Systematicae: Plantarum Vascularium 1972, Vol. 9. 378p. 1978. 82.00 (ISBN 0-686-84461-0, Pub. by Oxford & I B H India). State Mutual Bk.

Vasil chenko, J. T. Novitates Systematicae: Plantarum Vascularium 1971, Vol. 8. 342p. 1978. 77.00x (ISBN 0-686-84460-2, Pub. by Oxford & I B H India). State Mutual Bk.

BOTANY–DICTIONARIES

Erevan University Press. A Polyglot Dictionary of Plant Names. 180p. 1981. pap. 40.00x (ISBN 0-686-82330-3, Pub. by Collets). State Mutual Bk.

BOTANY–ECOLOGY

see also Forest Ecology; Halophytes; Insectivorous Plants; Island Flora and Fauna; Plant Communities; Symbiosis

Buckley, R. Ant-Plant Interactions in Australia. 1982. text ed. 54.50 (ISBN 90-6193-684-5, Pub. by Junk Pubs Netherlands). Kluwer Boston.

Chattopadhyay, S. B. Principles & Procedures of Plant Protection. 480p. 1980. 69.00x (ISBN 0-686-84466-1, Oxford & I B H India). State Mutual Bk.

Holzner, W. & Werger, M. J. Man's Impact on Vegetation. 1983. 98.00 (ISBN 90-6193-685-3, Pub. by Junk Pubs Netherlands). Kluwer Boston.

Koopowitz, Harold & Kaye, Hilary. Plant Extinction: A Global Crisis. LC 82-62894. 256p. 1983. 16.95 (ISBN 0-913276-44-8). Stone Wall Pr.

Lange, O. L., et al, eds. Physiological Plant Ecology III: Responses to the Chemical & Biological Environment. (Encyclopedia of Plant Physiology Ser.: Vol. 12C). (Illus.). 850p. 1983. 120.00 (ISBN 0-387-10907-2). Springer-Verlag.
Misra, R. & Das, R. R. Proceedings of the School on Plant Ecology. 384p. 1971. 62.00x (ISBN 0-686-84467-X, Oxford & I B H India). State Mutual Bk.
Misra, R. C. Manual of Plant Ecology. 1980. 52.00x (ISBN 0-686-84459-9, Pub. by Oxford & I B H India). State Mutual Bk.
Rauner, Yu. L. Heat Balance of the Plant Cover. 220p. 1977. 70.00x (ISBN 0-686-84456-4, Pub. by Oxford & I B H India). State Mutual Bk.
Willson, Mary F. Plant Reproductive Ecology. 300p. 1983. 40.00 (ISBN 0-471-08362-3, Pub. by Wiley-Interscience). Wiley.

BOTANY-EMBRYOLOGY
see also Botany-Morphology; Germination; Seeds
Sharp, William R. & Evans, David A. Crop Species, Vol. 2. LC 82-73774. (Handbook of Plant Cell Culture). 550p. 1982. 49.50 (ISBN 0-02-949230-0). Free Pr.

BOTANY-FIELD WORKS
see Botany-Laboratory Manuals

BOTANY-HISTOLOGY
see Botany-Anatomy; Plant Cells and Tissues

BOTANY-HISTORY
Greene, Edward L. Landmarks of Botanical History, 2 vols. Egerton, Frank N., ed. LC 79-66057. (Illus.). 1248p. 1983. Set. text ed. 100.00 (ISBN 0-8047-1075-9). Stanford U Pr.

BOTANY-LABORATORY MANUALS
Barbour, Michael, et al. Botany: A Laboratory Manual for Weier. 5th ed. 263p. 1975. 13.50x (ISBN 0-471-04800-3). Wiley.

BOTANY-MORPHOLOGY
see also Botany-Anatomy; Botany-Embryology
Esau, Katherine. Plant Anatomy. 2nd ed. LC 65-12713. 767p. 1965. 32.95x (ISBN 0-471-24455-4). Wiley.
Shah, J. J., ed. Form, Structure & Function in Plants, Pt. 2. (Current Trends in Life Sciences Ser.: Vol. 8). (Illus.). 150p. 20.00x (ISBN 0-88065-240-3, Pub. by Messers Today & Tommorrow Printers & Publishers). Scholarly Pubns.

BOTANY-PATHOLOGY
see Plant Diseases

BOTANY-PHYSIOLOGY
see Plant Physiology

BOTANY-PHYTOGRAPHY
see Botany

BOTANY-PICTORIAL WORKS
Farr, Gerald G. Botany Illustrated. (Illus.). 52p. 1979. pap. text ed. 3.95x (ISBN 0-89641-055-2). American Pr.

BOTANY-STRUCTURE
see Botany-Anatomy

BOTANY-STUDY AND TEACHING
McFerron, Martha. Plants. (Science Ser.). 24p. (gr. 3-6). 1982. wkbk. 5.00 (ISBN 0-8209-0162-8, S-24). ESP.

BOTANY-TAXONOMY
see Botany-Classification

BOTANY-VARIATION
see Island Flora and Fauna; Variation (Biology)

BOTANY-ASIA
Chater, Hara H. & Williams, A. O. An Enumeration of the Flowering Plants of Nepal: Vol. 3, Dicotyledons. (Illus.). 226p. 1982. pap. text ed. 81.50 (ISBN 0-565-00854-4). Sabbot-Natural Hist Bks.

BOTANY-AUSTRALIA
Smith, J. M. A History of Australian Vegetation. 216p. 1981. 18.50 (ISBN 0-07-072953-0). McGraw.

BOTANY-CANADA
Batson, Wade T. Genera of the Eastern Plants. 3rd ed. LC 77-24339. 203p. 1977. pap. text ed. 11.95x (ISBN 0-471-03497-5). Wiley.

BOTANY-CANARY ISLANDS
Bramwell, David & Bramwell, Zoe. Flores Silvestres de las Islas Canarias. 364p. 1977. 50.00x (ISBN 0-686-99797-2, Pub. by Thornes England). State Mutual Bk.
--Wild Flowers of the Canary Islands. 304p. 1974. 40.00x (ISBN 0-85950-010-1, Pub. by Thornes England). State Mutual Bk.

BOTANY-CHINA
Wu Cheng Yih & H. Y. Hou, eds. The Vegetation of China, Vol. 1. 1983. 82.50 (ISBN 0-677-31080-3). Gordon.

BOTANY-EUROPE
Welten, Max, ed. Vebreitungsatlas der Farn- und Blutenpflanzen der Schweiz, 2 Vols. 1982. Vol. 1, 704pp. text ed. 48.00; Vol. 2, 752pp. text ed. 98.95 (ISBN 3-7643-1308-0). Birkhauser.

BOTANY-GREAT BRITAIN
Dandy, J. E., ed. List of British Vascular Plants: Prepared by J. E. Dandy for the British Museum (Natural History) & the Botanical Society of the British Isles. xvi, 176p. 1982. Repr. of 1958 ed. 12.50x (ISBN 0-565-00449-2, Pub. by Brit Mus Nat Hist England). Sabbot-Natural Hist Bks.
Prudhoe, Stephen. British Polyclad Turbellarians. LC 82-4508. (Synopses of the British Fauna: No. 26). (Illus.). 64p. Date not set. pap. price not set (ISBN 0-521-27076-6). Cambridge U Pr.
Rackham, Oliver. Ancient Wookland: Its History, Vegetation & Uses in England. 392p. 1980. text ed. 99.95 (ISBN 0-7131-2723-6). E Arnold.
Webb, David A. & Scannell, Mary J. Flora of Connemara & the Burren. LC 82-4425. (Illus.). 320p. Date not set. 69.50 (ISBN 0-521-23395-X). Cambridge U Pr.

BOTANY-INDIA
Beddome, R. H. The Ferns of British India, Vols. I & II. 702p. 1978. 99.00x (ISBN 0-686-84451-3, Pub. by Oxford & I B H India). State Mutual Bk.
Rayechaudhuri, S. P. & Nariani, T. K. Virus & Mycoplasm Diseases of Plants in India. 102p. 1977. 50.00x (ISBN 0-686-84449-1, Pub by Oxford & I B H India). State Mutual Bk.
Saldanha, C. J. & Nicolson, D. H. Flora of Hasson District Karnataka India. 1978p. 79.00x (ISBN 0-686-84452-1, Pub. by Oxford & I B H India). State Mutual Bk.

BOTANY-MEXICO
McVaugh, Rogers. Flora Novo-Galiciana: A Descriptive Account of the Vascular Plants of Western Mexico. Anderson, William R., ed. LC 82-13537. (Graminae Ser.: Vol. 14). (Illus.). 384p. 1983. text ed. 38.00 (ISBN 0-472-04814-7). U of Mich Pr.

BOTANY-NEW ZEALAND
Brooker, S. G. & Cambie, R. C. New Zealand Medicinal Plants. (Illus.). 117p. 1983. 36.95 (ISBN 0-86863-382-8, Pub. by Heinemann Pubs New Zealand). Intl Schol Bk Serv.
Brooker, Stanley & Cambie, Conrad. New Zealand Medicinal Plants. (Illus.). 117p. 1981. 32.50 (ISBN 0-86863-382-8, Pub. by Heinemann New Zealand). Smithsonian.

BOTANY-UNITED STATES
Barkley, T. M. Field Guide to the Common Weeds of Kansas. LC 82-21914. (Illus.). 160p. 1983. text ed. 17.95x (ISBN 0-7006-0233-X); pap. 7.95 (ISBN 0-7006-0224-0). Univ Pr KS.
Batson, Wade T. Genera of the Eastern Plants. 3rd ed. LC 77-24339. 203p. 1977. pap. text ed. 11.95x (ISBN 0-471-03497-5). Wiley.
Belzer, Thomas J. Roadside Plants of Southern California. (Illus.). 172p. 1983. pap. 7.95 (ISBN 0-87842-158-0). Mountain Pr.
Burt, Edward A. Telephoraceae of North America, 15 Pts. (Illus.). 900p. 1966. Repr. of 1926 ed. lib. bdg. 25.00x (ISBN 0-02-842320-8). Lubrecht & Cramert.
Ewan, Joseph, ed. Short History of Botany in the United States. 174p. 1969. lib. bdg. 8.50 (ISBN 0-686-37870-9). Lubrecht & Cramert.
Goebel, K. Organopgraphy of Plants, Especially of the Archegoniatae & Spermatophyta, 2 Vols. Balfour, Issac B., tr. from Ger. (Illus.). 977p. 1969. Repr. of 1905 ed. lib. bdg. 35.00 (ISBN 0-02-845320-4). Lubrecht & Cramer.
Navarro, J. Nelson. Marine Diatoms Associated with Mangrovew Prop Roots in the Indian River, Florida, USA. (Bibliotheca Phycologica 61 Ser.). (Illus.). 151p. (Orig.). 1982. pap. text ed. 22.50 (ISBN 3-7682-1337-4). Lubrecht & Cramer.
Strausbaugh, P. D. & Core, Earl L. Flora of West Virginia. LC 78-1146. (Illus.). 1079p. 1979. 25.00 (ISBN 0-89092-010-9). Seneca Bks.
Taylor, Dean W. Endangerment Status of Lupinus Dedeckerae on the Inyo National Forest, California. (Contributions Mono Basin Research Group Ser.). (Illus.). 91p. 1981. pap. 3.25 (ISBN 0-939714-02-7). Mono Basin Res.
--Plant Checklist for the Mono Basin, California. 16p. 1981. pap. 1.25 (ISBN 0-939714-01-9). Mono Basin Res.
--Plant Checklist of the Sweetwater Mountains, Mono County, California. (Contributions Mono Basin Research Group Ser.). (Illus.). 27p. 1982. pap. 3.50 (ISBN 0-939714-05-1). Mono Basin Res.
--Riparian Vegetation of the Eastern Sierra: Ecological Effects of Stream Diversion. (Contributions Mono Basin Research Group Ser.). (Illus.). 56p. 1982. pap. 3.50 (ISBN 0-939714-04-3). Mono Basin Res.
Wee, James L. Studies on the Synuraceae (Chrysophyceae) of Iowa. (Bibliotheca Phycologica 62 Ser.). 184p. (Orig.). 1982. pap. text ed. 20.00x (ISBN 3-7682-1341-2). Lubrecht & Cramer.
Winkler, David W., ed. An Ecological Study of Mono Lake, California. (Illus.). 190p. 1977. pap. 7.50 (ISBN 0-939714-00-0). Mono Basin Res.

BOTANY, FOSSIL
see Paleobotany

BOTANY, MEDICAL
see also Herbs; Materia Medica, Vegetable; Medicine, Botanic; Medicine, Medieval; Plants-Assimilation
Brooker, S. G. & Cambie, R. C. New Zealand Medicinal Plants. (Illus.). 117p. 1983. 36.95 (ISBN 0-86863-382-8, Pub. by Heinemann Pubs New Zealand). Intl Schol Bk Serv.
Brooker, Stanley & Cambie, Conrad. New Zealand Medicinal Plants. (Illus.). 117p. 1981. 32.50 (ISBN 0-86863-382-8, Pub. by Heinemann New Zealand). Smithsonian.
Jackson, Betty P. Powdered Vegetable Drugs. Snowdon, Derek, ed. 216p. 1974. 40.00x (ISBN 0-85950-005-5, Pub. by Thornes England). State Mutual Bk.
Wickham, Cnythia. Common Plants As Natural Remedies. (Illus.). 144p. 1983. pap. 9.95 (ISBN 0-584-11030-8, Pub by Salem Hse Ltd). Merrimack Bk Serv.

BOTANY, STRUCTURAL
see Botany-Anatomy

BOTANY, SYSTEMATIC
see Botany-Classification

BOTANY OF THE BIBLE
see Bible-Natural History

BOTSWANA
Hailey, William M. The Republic of South Africa & the High Commission Territories. LC 82-11865. vii, 136p. 1982. Repr. of 1963 ed. lib. bdg. 25.00x (ISBN 0-313-23625-9, HARS). Greenwood.

BOTTICELLI, SANDRO, 1447?-1510
Cox, R. The Botticelli Madonna. 1979. 9.95 (ISBN 0-07-013291-7). McGraw.

BOTTLES
Hastin, Bud. Avon Bottle Encyclopedia. 9th ed. (Illus.). 600p. 1982. 19.95. Avon Res.
Hastin, Bud & Hastin, Vickie. Bud Hastin's Avon Bottle Encyclopedia: 1982-83. (Illus.). 19.95 (ISBN 0-89145-200-1). Wallace-Homestead.
The Official 1984 Price Guide to Beer Cans & Bottles. 1st ed. LC 82-84642. 240p. 1983. pap. 2.95 (ISBN 0-87637-377-5). Hse of Collectibles.
Western World Collector's Handbook & Price Guide to Avon Bottles. (Illus.). 288p. 1982. 22.95. Avon Res.

BOTTOM DEPOSITS (OCEANOGRAPHY)
see Marine Sediments; Sedimentation and Deposition

BOUDINOT, ELIAS, d. 1839
Perdue, Theda, ed. Cherokee Editor: The Writings of Elias Boudinot. LC 82-11110. 248p. 1983. text ed. 18.95x (ISBN 0-87049-366-3). U of Tenn Pr.

BOULDER, COLORADO
Fetter, Richard. Frontier Boulder. (Illus.). 80p. (Orig.). 1983. pap. write for info. (ISBN 0-933472-72-2). Johnson Bks.

BOULDING, KENNETH, 1910-
Singell, Larry D., ed. The Collected Papers of Kenneth E. Boulding, Vol. 4. 1982. 20.00x (ISBN 0-87081-139-8). Colo Assoc.
Wilson, Vivian. Bibliography of Published Works by Kenneth E. Boulding. 1982. 10.00x (ISBN 0-87081-140-1). Colo Assoc.

BOUNDARIES
see also Geopolitics
also names of countries, states, etc. with or without subdivision Boundaries; also subdivision Territorial Question under names of wars
Downing, David. Atlas of Territorial & Border Disputes. (Illus.). 121p. 1980. 13.50x (ISBN 0-450-04804-7). Intl Pubns Serv.

BOUNDARY LAYER
Fernholz, H. & Krause, E., eds. Three-Dimensional Turbulaent Boundry Layers, Berlin FRG 1982: Proceedings. (International Union of Theoretical & Applied Mechanics Ser.). (Illus.). 389p. 1982. 39.00 (ISBN 0-387-11772-5). Springer-Verlag.

BOUNDARY VALUE PROBLEMS-NUMERICAL SOLUTIONS
Albrecht, J. & Collatz, L., eds. Numerical Treatment of Free Boundary Value Problems. (International Series of Numerical Mathematics: Vol. 58). 350p. 1982. text ed. 35.00x (ISBN 3-7643-1277-7). Birkhauser.
Brebbia, C. A., ed. Boundary Element Methods in Engineering, Southampton, England 1982: Proceedings. (Illus.). 649p. 1982. 59.00 (ISBN 0-387-11819-5). Springer-Verlag.

BOURBON WHISKEY
see Whiskey

BOURGEOISIE
see Middle Classes

BOUTIQUES
see Stores, Retail

BOWLING
Craven, Robert R., compiled by. Billiards, Bowling, Table Tennis, Pinball & Video Games: A Bibliographic Guide. LC 82-21077. 162p. 1983. lib. bdg. 29.95 (ISBN 0-313-23462-0, CBB/). Greenwood.
Falcaro, Joe & Goodman, M. Bowling for All. 3rd ed. (Illus.). 123p. 1966. 14.95x (ISBN 0-471-07141-2). Wiley.
Ideas for Bowling Instruction. 30p. 2.00 (ISBN 0-88314-103-5). AAHPERD.
Palmer, Les. Bowling. (Illus.). 54p. 1982. pap. text ed. 2.95x (ISBN 0-89641-063-3). American Pr.

BOXERS
see also China-History-1900-; Missions-China
Stanley, Charles J. Boxers. 1982. lib. bdg. 75.00 (ISBN 0-686-81932-2). Porter.

BOXERS (SPORTS)
Burchard, S. H. Sports Star: Sugar Ray Leonard. LC 82-48764. 64p. (gr. 6-10). 10.95 (ISBN 0-15-278048-3, HJ). HarBraceJ.
--Sports Star: Sugar Ray Leonard. LC 82-48764. (Illus.). 64p. (gr. 6-10). pap. 4.95 (ISBN 0-15-278049-1, VoyB). HarBraceJ.
Roberts, Randy. Papa Jack: Jack Johnson & the Era of White Hopes. LC 82-49017. 288p. 1983. 14.95 (ISBN 0-686-84093-3). Free Pr.

BOXING
Cai Longyun & Shao Shankang. Zuijiuquan: A Drunkard's Boxing. (Chinese Kung-Fu Ser.). (Illus.). 155p. 1982. pap. 6.95 (ISBN 0-686-42862-5). China Bks.
Hails, Jack. Classic Moments of Boxing. 144p. 1982. 35.00x (ISBN 0-86190-054-5, Pub. by Moorland). State Mutual Bk.
Knudson, R. R. Punch! (Illus.). 96p. 1983. pap. 1.95 (ISBN 0-380-82164-8, 82164-8, Camelot). Avon.
Liebling, A. J. The Sweet Science. 1956. 14.95 (ISBN 0-670-68653-0). Viking Pr.
Schulian, John. Writers' Fighters & Other Sweet Scientists. 300p. 1983. 12.95 (ISBN 0-8362-6704-4); pap. 7.95 (ISBN 0-8362-6703-6). Andrews & McMeel.

BOY SCOUTS
Coleman, Jerry, et al. The Scouting Report: 1983. LC 82-48225. (Illus.). 672p. (Orig.). 1983. pap. 12.45i (ISBN 0-06-091027-5, CN 1027, CN). Har-Row.

BOYS
see also Boy Scouts; Children; Church Work with Children; Youth
Rustemeyer, Ruth. Wahrnehmung Eigener Fahigkeit Bei Jungen und Madchen. 213p. (Ger.). 1982. write for info. (ISBN 3-8204-5755-0). P Lang Pubs.

BOYS-EMPLOYMENT
see Youth-Employment

BOYS-SOCIETIES AND CLUBS
see also Boy Scouts; Gangs
Albert, Burton. Clubs for Kids. 144p. (Orig.). 1983. pap. price not set (ISBN 0-345-30292-3). Ballantine.
Bricker, William R. Breaking the Youth Unemployment Cycle: The Boys Clubs of America Approach. (Vital Issues Ser.: Vol. XXXI, No. 6). 0.80 (ISBN 0-686-84144-1). Ctr Info Am.

BOYS' CLUBS
see Boys-Societies and Clubs

BOYS IN THE BIBLE
see Children in the Bible

BOYS' TOWN
see Children-Institutional Care

BRACHYGRAPHY
see Abbreviations; Shorthand

BRACKISH WATER BIOLOGY
see Marine Biology; Marine Fauna; Marine Flora

BRADLEY, OMAR NELSON, 1893-
Bradley, Omar N. & Blair, Clay. A General's Life. (Illus.). 540p. 1983. 19.95 (ISBN 0-671-41023-7). S&S.

BRADSTREET, ANNE (DUDLEY), 1612?-1672
Crowell, Pattie & Stanford, Ann. Critical Essays on Anne Bradstreet. (Critical Essays on American Literature Ser.). 330p. 1983. lib. bdg. 42.50 (ISBN 0-8161-8643-X). G K Hall.

BRADYKININ
see Kinins

BRAHMAN MYTHOLOGY
see Mythology, Hindu; Vedas

BRAHMANISM
see also Caste; Caste-India; Hinduism; Jains
Bailey, G. M. Studies in the Mythology of Brahma. 1982. 24.95x (ISBN 0-19-561411-9). Oxford U Pr.

BRAHMS, JOHANNES, 1833-1897
Kalbeck, Max, ed. Johannes Brahms: The Herzogenberg Correspondence. Bryant, Hannah, tr. LC 78-163787. 425p. Date not set. Repr. of 1909 ed. price not set. Vienna Hse.
Litzman, Berthold, ed. Letters of Clara Schumann & Johannes Brahms, 2 vols. LC 77-163792. Date not set. Repr. of 1927 ed. price not set. Vienna Hse.
McLeish, Kenneth & McLeish, Valerie. Brahms: Composers & Their World. (Illus.). 90p. (gr. 9-12). 1983. 5.95 (ISBN 0-434-95128-5, Pub. by Heinemann England). David & Charles.

BRAID
Buck, Peter. Arts & Crafts of Hawaii: Plaiting, Sec. III. (Special Publication Ser.: No. 43). (Illus.). 39p. 1957. pap. 3.00 (ISBN 0-910240-36-1). Bishop Mus.

BRAIDISM
see Hypnotism

BRAILLE BOOKS
see Blind, Books for the

BRAILLE SYSTEM
see Blind-Printing and Writing Systems

BRAIN
see also Cerebellum; Cerebral Cortex; Cerebrospinal Fluid; Dreams; Head; Hypothalamus; Memory; Mind and Body; Nervous System; Pituitary Body; Psychology; Sleep
Blakeslee, Thomas R. The Right Brain. LC 82-60690. 288p. 1983. pap. 3.50 (ISBN 0-86721-233-0). Playboy Pbks.
Boddy, John. Brain Systems & Psychological Concepts. LC 77-21203. 461p. 1978. 48.00 (ISBN 0-471-99601-7); pap. 21.95x (ISBN 0-471-99600-9, Pub. by Wiley-Interscience). Wiley.
Eccles, John, ed. Mind & Brain: The Many-Faceted Problems. (Illus.). 370p. 1982. 24.95 (ISBN 0-89226-016-5). ICF Pr.
Hart, Leslie A. Human Brain & Human Learning. 256p. 1983. text ed. 22.50x (ISBN 0-686-37692-7); pap. text ed. 12.50x (ISBN 0-582-28379-5). Longman.
Lumsden, Charles J. & Wilson, Edward O. Promethean Fire: Reflections on the Origin of Mind. (Illus.). 256p. 1983. 17.50 (ISBN 0-674-71445-8). Harvard U Pr.
Russell, Peter. The Global Brain. (Illus.). 252p. 1983. 12.95 (ISBN 0-87477-210-9); pap. 7.95 (ISBN 0-87477-248-6). J P Tarcher.

Segalowitz, Sid J. Two Sides of the Brain: Brain Lateralization Explored. 252p. 1983. 12.95 (ISBN 0-13-935296-1); pap. 6.95 (ISBN 0-13-935304-6). P-H.

Shepard. Mental Capacity. 1977. 50.00 (ISBN 0-07-000756-X); annual pocket suppl. 1979 15.00 (ISBN 0-07-000761-6). McGraw.

Stastny, F. Glucocorticoids & Brain Development. (Monographs in Neural Sciences: Vol. 9). (Illus.). viii, 200p. 1983. 54.00 (ISBN 3-8055-3626-7). S Karger.

BRAIN–ATLASES

Ford, D. H., et al. Atlas of the Human Brain. 3rd ed. 1978. 37.25 (ISBN 0-444-80008-5). Elsevier.

BRAIN–BIBLIOGRAPHY

Locke, Steven & Hornig-Rohan, Mady. Mind & Immunity: Behavioral Immunology (1976-1982)--an Annotated Bibliography. 240p. (Orig.). 1983. 35.00 (ISBN 0-910903-01-8); pap. 22.50 (ISBN 0-910903-02-6). Elliot Pr.

BRAIN–DISEASES

see also Aphasia; Brain Damage; Cerebral Edema; Cerebral Palsy; Cerebrovascular Disease; Hepatolenticular Degeneration; Nervous System–Diseases; Psychology, Pathological; Thrombosis

Desnick, Robert J. & Gatt, Shimon, eds. Gaucher Disease: A Century of Delineation & Research. LC 82-4611. (Progress in Clinical & Biological Research Ser.: Vol. 95). 764p. 1982. 76.00 (ISBN 0-8451-0095-5). A R Liss.

Philpott, William. Brain Allergies. 1980. 16.95x (ISBN 0-87983-224-X). Cancer Control Soc.

Rosenblum, M. L. & Wilson, C. B., eds. Brain Tumor Biology. (Progress in Experimental Tumor Research Ser.: Vol. 27). (Illus.). viii, 250p. 1983. bound 100.75 (ISBN 3-8055-3698-4). S Karger.

--Brain Tumor Therapy. (Progress in Experimental Tumor Research: Vol. 28). (Illus.). viii, 250p. 1983. 100.75 (ISBN 3-8055-3699-2). S Karger.

Seymour, Claire. Precipice: Learning to Live with Alzheimer's Disease. 10.00 (ISBN 0-686-84433-5). Vantage.

BRAIN–LOCALIZATION OF FUNCTIONS

Buegler, Joseph. God's Love Machine. 160p. 1983. 7.95 (ISBN 0-89962-305-0). Todd & Honeywell.

Corrick, James A. The Human Brain: Minds & Matter. LC 82-18461. (Arco How-It-Works Ser.). (Illus.). 192p. 1983. 12.95 (ISBN 0-668-05519-7). Arco.

Denny-Brown. The Cerebral Control of Movement. 222p. 1982. 50.00x (ISBN 0-85323-001-3, Pub. by Liverpool Univ England). State Mutual Bk.

Fadely, Jack L. & Hosler, Virginia N. Case Studies in Left & Right Hemisheric Functioning. (Illus.). 136p. 1983. 16.75x (ISBN 0-398-04792-8). C C Thomas.

Fulton. The Frontal Lobes & Human Behaviour. 30p. 1982. 50.00x (ISBN 0-85323-311-X, Pub. by LIverpool Univ England). State Mutual Bk.

Moore, Ernest, ed. Bases of Auditory Brain Stem Evoked Responses. 1982. 29.50 (ISBN 0-8089-1465-0). Grune.

Pribram, Karl H. Languages of the Brain: Experimental Paradoxes & Principles in Neuropsychology. 5th ed. 432p. 1982. Repr. of 1971 ed. text ed. 19.95x (ISBN 0-913412-22-8). Brandon Hse.

Segalowitz, S. J., ed. Language Functions & Brain Organization. Date not set. 43.50 (ISBN 0-12-635640-8). Acad Pr.

Woody, Charles D. Memory, Learning, & Higher Function: A Cellular View. (Illus.). 512p. 1982. 65.00 (ISBN 0-387-90525-1). Springer-Verlag.

BRAIN–RADIOGRAPHY

Gonzalez, Carlos F., et al. Computed Brain & Orbital Tomography: Technique & Interpretation. LC 76-28530. (Diagnostic & Therapeutic Radiology Ser.). 1976. 70.00x (ISBN 0-471-01692-6, Pub. by Wiley-Med). Wiley.

BRAIN–SURGERY

see also Ventriculocisternostomy

Seletz, Jeanette. Jone Brent, Neurosurgeon. LC 78-50163. 320p. 1983. 12.50 (ISBN 0-87527-136-7). Green.

BRAIN–X-RAY EXAMINATION

see Brain–Radiography

BRAIN DAMAGE

Small, Leonard. The Minimal Brain Dysfunctions: Diagnosis & Treatment. 320p. 1982. text ed. 22.95 (ISBN 0-02-929300-6). Free Pr.

BRAIN-DAMAGED CHILDREN

Polikoff, Judy. Every Loving Gift: How a Family's Courage Saved a Special Child. 256p. 1983. 14.95 (ISBN 0-399-12783-6). Putnam Pub Group.

BRAIN EDEMA

see Cerebral Edema

BRAIN FUNCTION LOCALIZATION

see Brain–Localization of Functions

BRAND, PAUL WILSON, 1914-

Wilson, Dorothy C. Ten Fingers for God. 288p. 1982. pap. 5.95 (ISBN 0-8407-5834-0). Nelson.

BRAND MANAGEMENT

see Product Management

BRAND NAMES

see Trade-Marks

BRANDEIS, LOUIS DEMBITZ, 1856-1941

Murphy, Bruce A. The Brandeis-Frankfurter Connection: The Secret Political Activities of Two Supreme Court Justices. LC 82-45546. 496p. 1983. pap. 12.95 (ISBN 0-385-18374-7, Anch). Doubleday.

BRANDS (COMMERCE)

see Trade-Marks

BRAQUE, GEORGES, 1882-1963

Chipp, Herschel B. Georges Braque: The Late Paintings 1940-1963. 1982. pap. text ed. 18.50 (ISBN 0-943044-00-6). Phillips Collect.

Mond-Fontaine, Isabelle & Carmean, E. A. Braque: Papier Colles. (Illus.). 1982. pap. 17.50 (ISBN 0-89468-056-0). Natl Gallery Art.

BRASS BAND MUSIC

see Band Music

BRASS INSTRUMENTS

see Wind Instruments

BRAUTIGAN, RICHARD

Foster, Edward H. Richard Brautigan. (United States Authors Ser.). 176p. 1983. lib. bdg. 14.95 (ISBN 0-8057-7378-9, Twayne). G K Hall.

BRAVERY

see Courage

BRAZIL

see also names of cities, towns and areas in Brazil, e.g. Rio de Janeiro; Amazon River and Valley

Enciclopedia Luso-Brasileira de Cultura, 20 vols. 18400p. (Portuguese.). Set. 1475.00 (ISBN 0-686-43251-7). Pergamon.

Hill, Lawrence F., ed. Brazil: Chapters by Manoel Cardozo & Others. LC 82-15848. (The United Nations Ser.). (Illus.). xxi, 394p. 1982. Repr. of 1947 ed. lib. bdg. 49.75x (ISBN 0-313-23503-1, HILB). Greenwood.

BRAZIL–DESCRIPTION AND TRAVEL

Brazilian Adventure. (Library of Travel Classics). 384p. pap. 8.95 (ISBN 0-87477-246-X). J P Tarcher.

Rio De Janeiro Travel Guide. (Berlitz Travel Guides). (Illus.). 1982. pap. 4.95 (ISBN 0-02-969830-8, Berlitz). Macmillan.

BRAZIL–ECONOMIC CONDITIONS

Bresser Pereira, Luis C. Development & Crisis in Brazil, 1930-1982. 275p. 1983. lib. bdg. 25.00x (ISBN 0-86531-559-0). Westview.

Dickenson, John P. Brazil. LC 81-20827. (The World's Landscapes Ser.). text ed. 28.00x (ISBN 0-686-37903-9). Longman.

Morley, Samuel. Labor Markets & Inequitable Growth: The Case of Authoritarian Capitalism in Brazil. LC 82-4488. (Illus.). 272p. Date not set. price not set (ISBN 0-521-24439-0). Cambridge U Pr.

BRAZIL–INDUSTRY

Possas, Mario L. & Coutinho, Mauricio. Multinational Enterprises, Technology & Employment in Brrazil: Three Case Studies. (Working Paper Ser.: No. 21). Date not set. price not set. Intl Labour Office.

BRAZIL–SOCIAL CONDITIONS

Batley, Richard. Power Through Bureaucracy: Urban Political Analysis in Brazil. LC 82-16872. 240p. 1982. 27.50x (ISBN 0-312-63437-4). St Martin.

Cohen, Yaveff & Converse, Phillip E. Representation & Development in Brazil, Nineteen Seventy-Two to Nineteen Seventy-Three. 2nd ed. write for info (ISBN 0-89138-950-4). ICPSR.

Dickenson, John P. Brazil. LC 81-20827. (The World's Landscapes Ser.). text ed. 28.00x (ISBN 0-686-37903-9). Longman.

BRAZILIAN LITERATURE–HISTORY AND CRITICISM

Haberly, David T. Three Sad Races: Racial Identity & National Consciousness in Brazilian Literature. LC 82-4467. (Illus.). 198p. p.n.s. (ISBN 0-521-24722-5). Cambridge U Pr.

BRAZILIAN POETRY (COLLECTIONS)

Brasil, Emanuel, ed. Brazilian Poetry, 1950-1980. Smith, William J. 160p. 25.00 (ISBN 0-686-43258-4); pap. 9.95x. Wesleyan U Pr.

BREAD

see also Baking

Carrabis, Joseph D. Mainely Bread. (Illus.). 1983. pap. 7.95 (ISBN 0-89272-161-8). Down East.

Moore, Marilyn M. Baking Your Own: Recipes & Tips for Better Breads. LC 82-61710. (Illus.). 96p. 1982. pap. 7.95 (ISBN 0-9603788-0-4). Prairie Craft.

The Southern Heritage Breads Cookbook. (Illus.). 144p. 1983. 9.95 (ISBN 0-8487-0602-1). Oxmoor Hse.

Voth, Norma J. Festive Breads of Christmas. LC 82-15731. 104p. (Orig.). 1983. pap. 3.25 (ISBN 0-8361-3319-6). Herald Pr.

BREADSTUFFS

see Grain; Wheat

BREAKERS

see Ocean Waves

BREAKFASTS

Janericco, Terence. The Book of Great Breakfasts & Brunches. 272p. 1983. 16.95 (ISBN 0-8436-2264-4). CBI Pub.

Williams, Christie. Brunch. LC 80-85004. (Illus.). 177p. (Orig.). 1981. pap. 5.95 (ISBN 0-911954-59-7). Nitty Gritty.

BREAST

Larkin, Regina & Davis, Julie. Thirty Days to a Better Bust. 1982. pap. 2.95 (ISBN 0-553-01488-9). Bantam.

McGibbon, Bernard M. Atlas of Breast Reconstruction: Following Radical Mastectomy. (Illus.). 1983. price not set (ISBN 0-8391-1704-3, 17647). Univ Park.

Tetzleff, Judith & Nama, Prabharathie G. How to Examine Your Breasts: A Guide to Breast Health Care. (Illus.). 1981. pap. 1.00 (ISBN 0-686-84300-2). Budlong.

BREAST–CANCER

Bassett, Lawrence W. & Gold, Richard H., eds. Mammography, Thermography & Ultrasound in Breast Cancer Detention. Date not set. price not set (ISBN 0-8089-1509-6). Grune.

Baum, M. & Kay, R., eds. Clinical Trails in Early Breast Cancer. (Experientia Supplementum: Vol. 41). 676p. Date not set. text ed. 49.95 (ISBN 3-7643-1358-7). Birkhauser.

Faulder, Carolyn. Breast Cancer: A Guide to It's Early Detection & Treatment. 186p. 1983. pap. 7.95 (ISBN 0-86068-287-0, Virago Pr). Merrimack Bk Serv.

Mammakarzinom. (Journal: Onkologie: Vol. 5, Suppl. 1). (Illus.). 68p. 1982. pap. 14.50 (ISBN 3-8055-3643-7). S Karger.

Pennisi, Vincent R. Women in Jeopardy from Breast Cancer. LC 81-86160. 94p. 1983. 9.95 (ISBN 0-86666-065-8). GWP.

BREAST–RADIOGRAPHY

Harper, A. Patricia, ed. Ultrasound Mammography. (Illus.). 1983. price not set (ISBN 0-8391-1807-4, 18090). Univ Park.

BREAST–SURGERY

Bostwick, John, III. Aesthetic & Reconstructive Breast Surgery. (Illus.). 748p. 1983. text ed. 155.00 (ISBN 0-8016-0731-0). Mosby.

McGibbon, Bernard M. Atlas of Breast Reconstruction: Following Radical Mastectomy. (Illus.). 1983. price not set (ISBN 0-8391-1704-3, 17647). Univ Park.

Munroe, Elizabeth A. The Shade Upon My Right Hand. 1982. 7.95 (ISBN 0-533-05359-5). Vantage.

Women Helping Women: A Guide to Organizing a Post-Mastectomy Program in Your Community. pap. 2.50 (ISBN 0-686-81725-7). NCJW.

BREAST FEEDING

Bumgarner, Norma J. Mothering Your Nursing Toddler. 2nd ed. LC 82-84383. 210p. 1982. pap. 6.50 (ISBN 0-912500-12-3). La Leche.

Llewellyn-Jones, Derek. Breast Feeding-How to Succeed: Questions & Answers for Mothers. LC 82-21051. (Illus.). 192p. 1983. 14.95 (ISBN 0-571-13003-8); pap. 5.95 (ISBN 0-571-13004-6). Faber & Faber.

Presser, Janice & Brewer, Gail S. Breastfeeding. LC 82-48736. 1983. 14.95 (ISBN 0-394-52414-4). Knopf.

Riordan, Jan. A Practical Guide to Breastfeeding. (Illus.). 370p. 1983. pap. text ed. 15.95 (ISBN 0-8016-4230-2). Mosby.

Worth, C. Breastfeeding Basics. 128p. 1983. 14.95 (ISBN 0-07-071816-4); pap. 6.95 (ISBN 0-07-071815-6). McGraw.

BREATHING

see Respiration

BREEDER REACTORS

Kessler, G. Nuclear Fission Reactors: Potential Role & Risk of Converters & Breeders. (Topics in Energy Ser.). (Illus.). 257p. 1983. 37.00 (ISBN 0-387-81713-1). Springer-Verlag.

BREEDING

see also Domestic Animals; Heredity; Heterosis; Hybridization; Plant-Breeding

also breeding of particular groups of animals, e.g. Dog Breeding

Ostrow, Marshall. Breeding Hamsters. (Illus.). 96p. 1982. 4.95 (ISBN 0-87666-935-6, KW-134). TFH Pubns.

BREEDS OF HORSES

see Horse Breeds

BREHON LAWS

see Law–Ireland

BRETON, ANDRE, 1896-1966

Bonnet, Marquerite & Chenieux-Gendron, Jacqueline. Revues Surrealistes Francaises Autour d'Andre Breton, 1948-1972. LC 82-14045. 294p. (Orig.). 1982. lib. bdg. 35.00 (ISBN 0-527-09750-0). Kraus Intl.

BREVIARIES

see Liturgies

BRIC-A-BRAC

see Art Objects

BRICKS

see also Clay

Bodel, John. Roman Brick Stamps in the Kelsey Museum. (Kelsey Museum Ser.). (Illus.). 1983. pap. text ed. 22.50 (ISBN 0-472-08039-3). U of Mich Pr.

BRIDAL CUSTOMS

see Marriage Customs and Rites

BRIDGE (GAME)

see Contract Bridge

BRIDGE CONSTRUCTION

see Bridges; Masonry; Strains and Stresses

BRIDGES

see also Girders

also names of individual bridges

Bridge Aerodynamics. 140p. 1981. 90.00x (ISBN 0-7277-0135-5, Pub. by Tech Pr). State Mutual Bk.

Welt, Suzanne F. Covered Bridges of Oregon. (Illus.). 48p. 1982. 20.00 (ISBN 0-88014-044-5). Mosaic Pr OH.

BRIDGES–JUVENILE LITERATURE

Althea. Bridges. (Cambridge Dinosaur Wingate Ser.). (Illus.). 32p. (gr. 10-12). 1983. pap. 1.95 (ISBN 0-521-27170-3). Cambridge U Pr.

BRIDGES, COVERED

see Covered Bridges

BRIDGES, SUSPENSION

Horton, Tom. Superspan. (Illus.). 96p. (Orig.). 1983. pap. 8.95 (ISBN 0-87701-277-6). Chronicle Bks.

BRIDGES, WOODEN

see also Covered Bridges

Blaser, Werner. Wooden Bridges in Switzerland (Ponts de Bois en Suisse; Schweizer Holzbrucken) 184p. 1982. 49.95 (ISBN 3-7643-1334-X). Birkhauser.

BRIDLE PATHS

see Trails

BRIEFHAND

see Shorthand

BRIGHT CHILDREN

see Gifted Children

BRIGHTNESS (ASTRONOMY)

see Photometry, Astronomical

BRINE

see Salt

BRISTOL, ENGLAND

Eason, Helena. Bristol's Historic Inns. 80p. 1982. 30.00x (ISBN 0-905459-30-X, Pub. by Redcliffe England). State Mutual Bk.

Little, Bryan. Church Treasures in Bristol. 40p. 1982. 25.00x (ISBN 0-905459-12-1, Pub. by Redcliffe England). State Mutual Bk.

--Churches in Bristol. 40p. 1982. 25.00x (ISBN 0-905459-06-7, Pub. by Redcliffe England). State Mutual Bk.

Redcliffe Press Ltd., ed. This is Bristol. 112p. 1982. 50.00x (ISBN 0-905459-28-8, Pub. by Redcliffe England). State Mutual Bk.

Shipsides, Frank & Eason, Helena. Bristol: Profile of a City. 87p. 1982. 30.00x (ISBN 0-905459-21-0, Pub. by Redcliffe England). State Mutual Bk.

BRITISH ARCHITECTURE

see Architecture–Great Britain

BRITISH COLUMBIA–DESCRIPTION AND TRAVEL

Cullins, Warren & Cullins, Laura. Zeballos, Its Gold Its People Yesterday & Today: An Historical Documentation. (Orig.). 1982. pap. 9.75 (ISBN 0-9608386-0-0). Cullins.

Douglas, Gilean. Silence Is My Homeland. LC 78-2324. (Illus.). 192p. 1978. 8.95 (ISBN 0-8117-1521-3). Stackpole.

BRITISH COLUMBIA, UNIVERSITY OF–MUSEUM OF ANTHROPOLOGY

Halpin, Marjorie M. Totem Poles: An Illustrated Guide. (Illus.). 64p. (Orig.). 1983. pap. 8.95 (ISBN 0-295-96026-4). U of Wash Pr.

BRITISH COMMONWEALTH OF NATIONS

see Commonwealth of Nations

BRITISH HONDURAS

see Belize

BRITISH IN AMERICA

Hewitt, W. P. Land & Community: European Migration to Rural Texas in the 19th Century. (Illus.). 69p. 1982. pap. text ed. 1.95 (ISBN 0-89641-101-X). American Pr.

Timmons, W. H. The Anglo-American Advance into Texas, 1810-1830. (Illus.). 46p. 1982. pap. text ed. 1.95x (ISBN 0-89641-103-6). American Pr.

BRITISH IN AUSTRALIA

Edwards, P. D. Anthony Trollope's Son in Australia: The Life & Letters of F.J.A. Trollope (1847-1910) LC 82-4928. 69p. 1983. text ed. 16.50x (ISBN 0-7022-1891-X). U of Queensland Pr.

BRITISH LEGENDS

see Legends, British

BRITISH LITERATURE

see English Literature (Collections); Irish Literature (Collections); Scottish Literature (Collections); and subdivisions under these headings, e.g. English Literature–History and Criticism

BRITISH MUSEUM

Stearn, W. T. The Natural History Museum at South Kensington: A History of the British Museum (Natural History) 1753-1980. (Illus.). 350p. 1981. 37.50x (ISBN 0-434-73600-7). Sabbot-Natural Hist Bks.

BRITISH MUSIC

see Music, British

BRITISH PAINTING

see Painting, British

BRITISH PAINTINGS

see Paintings, British

BRITISH POETRY

see English Poetry (Collections); Irish Poetry (Collections); Irish Poetry (English) (Collections); Scottish Poetry (Collections); Welsh Poetry (Collections); and subdivisions under these headings, e.g. English Poetry–History and Criticism

BRITISH PORCELAIN

see Porcelain

BRITISH PORTRAITS

see Portraits

BRITISH POTTERY

see Pottery, British

BRITISH SCIENCE

see Science, British

BRITISH SCULPTURE
see Sculpture–Great Britain
BRITTANY–DESCRIPTION AND TRAVEL
Meirion-Jones, Gwyn. The Vernacular Architecture of Brittany. 420p. 1982. text ed. 57.00x (ISBN 0-85976-060-X, Pub. by Donald England). Humanities.
Michelin Green Guide: Bretagne. (Green Guide Ser.). (Fr.). 1983. pap. write for info. (ISBN 2-06-003091-9). Michelin.
BRITTEN, BENJAMIN, 1913-1976
Brett, Philip. Benjamin Britten: Peter Grimes. LC 82-14627. (Cambridge Opera Handbooks). (Illus.). 180p. Date not set. price not set (ISBN 0-521-22916-2); pap. price not set (ISBN 0-521-29716-8). Cambridge U Pr.
White, Eric W. Benjamin Britten: His Life & Operas. rev. ed. Evans, John, ed. LC 82-10882. (Illus.). 320p. 1983. text ed. 30.00x (ISBN 0-520-04893-8); pap. text ed. 12.95x (ISBN 0-520-04894-6). U of Cal Pr.
BROADCASTING
see also Broadcasting Policy; Radio Broadcasting; Television Broadcasting
International Broadcasting Convention. 421p. 1982. pap. 64.00 (ISBN 0-85296-263-0). Inst Elect Eng.
McCavitt, William E. Radio & Television: A Selected, Annotated Bibliography Supplement One: 1977-1981. LC 82-5743. 167p. 1982. 12.00 (ISBN 0-8108-1556-7). Scarecrow.
Pegg, Mark. Broadcasting & Society Nineteen-Eighteen - Nineteen Thirty-Nine. 240p. 1983. text ed. 29.25x (ISBN 0-7099-2039-3, Pub. by Croom Helm Ltd England). Biblio Dist.
Smeyak, Paul. Broadcast News Writing. 2nd ed. LC 82-9293. (Grid Series in Advertising & Journalism). 300p. 1983. pap. text ed. 11.95 (ISBN 0-686-42906-0). Grid Pub.
BROADCASTING AND STATE
see Broadcasting Policy
BROADCASTING POLICY
Krasnow, Erwin G. & Longley, Lawrence D. The Politics of Broadcast Regulation. 3rd ed. LC 81-51850. 304p. 1982. text ed. 16.95 (ISBN 0-312-62653-3); pap. text ed. 8.95 (ISBN 0-312-62654-1). St Martin.
BROKERS
see also Stock-Exchange
New York Institute of Finance. Introduction to Brokerage Operation Department Procedures. (Illus.). 175p. 1979. 8.95 (ISBN 0-13-478982-2). NY Inst Finance.
BRONCHI
Morley, John, ed. Bronchial Hyperactivity. 1982. 22.95 (ISBN 0-12-506450-0). Acad Pr.
BRONTE, ANNE, 1820-1849
Scott, P. J. Anne Bronte: A New Critical Assessment. LC 82-22793. (Critical Studies). 208p. 1983. text ed. 27.50x (ISBN 0-389-20345-9). B&N Imports.
BRONTE, CHARLOTTE, 1816-1855
Alexander, Christine, ed. Bibliography of the Manuscripts of Charlotte Bronte. 1983. 45.00X (ISBN 0-930466-56-X). Meckler Pub.
BRONTE, EMILY JANE, 1818-1848
Barclay, Janet M., ed. Emily Bronte Criticism Nineteen Hundred to Nineteen Eighty: An Annotated Check List. 1983. 40.00X (ISBN 0-930466-63-2). Meckler Pub.
Spark, Muriel & Standford, Derek. Emily Bronte: Her Life & Work. 272p. 1982. pap. 9.95 (ISBN 0-7206-0194-0, Pub. by Peter Owen). Merrimack Bk Serv.
Visick, Mary. The Genesis of Wuthering Heights. 88p. 1982. Repr. of 1967 ed. lib. bdg. 40.00 (ISBN 0-89760-929-8). Telegraph Bks.
BRONTE FAMILY
Southwart, Elizabeth. Bronte Moors & Villages from Thorton to Haworth. 190p. 1982. Repr. of 1923 ed. lib. bdg. 65.00 (ISBN 0-89984-609-2). Century Bookbindery.
Willis, Irene C. The Brontes. 1982. lib. bdg. 34.50 (ISBN 0-686-81916-0). Porter.
BRONX (BOROUGH)
Ultan, Lloyd, et al. Devastation-Resurrection: The South Bronx. LC 79-54730. 1979. pap. 12.00 (ISBN 0-89062-139-X, Pub by Bronx Museum Arts). Pub Ctr Cult Res.
BRONZES
Brice, Donna. Step-by-Step Guide For: Making Busts & Masks (Cold-Cast Bronze or Plaster Hydrocal) LC 82-15703. (Illus.). 52p. 1983. 18.95 (ISBN 0-910733-00-7); pap. 10.95 (ISBN 0-910733-01-5). ICTL Pubns.
Frel, Jiri. The Getty Bronze. rev. ed. LC 82-81305. 58p. 1982. 10.00 (ISBN 0-89236-053-4); pap. 5.00 (ISBN 0-89236-039-9). J P Getty Mus.
Harvey, Mary. The Bronzes of Rembrandt Bugatti, 1885-1916: An Illustrated Catalogue & Biography. 112p. 1980. 40.00x (ISBN 0-906814-00-6, Pub. by Zwemmer England). State Mutual Bk.
BROOKLYN
Picture Postcards of Old Brooklyn: Twenty-Four Ready-to-Mail Views. (Illus.). 18p. (Orig.). 1983. pap. 2.50 (ISBN 0-486-24489-X). Dover.
BROOKLYN BASEBALL CLUB (NATIONAL LEAGUE)
see los Angeles Baseball Club (National League)
BROTHELS
see Prostitution
BROTHERHOOD
see Brotherliness
BROTHERLINESS
Rahner, Karl. The Love of Jesus & the Love of Neighbor. 96p. 1983. pap. 5.95 (ISBN 0-8245-0570-0). Crossroad NY.
BROWN, CHARLES BROCKDEN, 1771-1810
Axelrod, Alan. Charles Brockden Brown: An American Tale. 224p. 1983. text ed. 22.50x (ISBN 0-292-71076-3). U of Tex Pr.
BROWN COAL
see Lignite
BROWNE, THOMAS, SIR, 1605-1682
Finch, Jeremiah S. Sir Thomas Browne: A Doctor's Life of Science & Faith. 319p. 1982. Repr. of 1950 ed. lib. bdg. 40.00 (ISBN 0-89760-237-4). Telegraph Bks.
BROWNIAN MOVEMENTS
Freedman, D. Brownian Motion & Diffusion. (Illus.). 231p. 1983. Repr. of 1971 ed. 24.00 (ISBN 0-387-90805-6). Springer-Verlag.
BROWNING, ELIZABETH (BARRETT), 1806-1861
Gridley, Roy E. The Brownings & France: A Chronicle with Commentary. 320p. 1982. text ed. 38.00x (ISBN 0-485-11231-0, Althlone Pr). Humanities.
Loth, David. The Brownings: A Victorian Idyll. 289p. 1982. lib. bdg. 35.00 (ISBN 0-89760-517-9). Telegraph Bks.
BROWNING, ROBERT, 1812-1889
Anderson, Vincent P. Reaction to Religious Elements in the Poetry of Robert Browning: Introduction & Annotated Bibliography. LC 82-50407. 350p. 1983. 25.00X (ISBN 0-87875-221-8). Whitston Pub.
Gridley, Roy E. The Brownings & France: A Chronicle with Commentary. 320p. 1982. text ed. 38.00x (ISBN 0-485-11231-0, Althlone Pr). Humanities.
Loth, David. The Brownings: A Victorian Idyll. 289p. 1982. lib. bdg. 35.00 (ISBN 0-89760-517-9). Telegraph Bks.
Lounsbury, Thomas R. The Early Literary Career of Robert Browning. 205p. 1982. Repr. of 1911 ed. lib. bdg. 40.00 (ISBN 0-89984-802-8). Century Bookbindery.
Thomas, Donald. Robert Browning: A Life Within Life. 352p. 1983. 18.75 (ISBN 0-670-60090-3). Viking Pr.
BRUEGEL, PIETER, THE ELDER, 1528-1569
Roberts, Keith. Bruegel. (Phaidon Color Library). (Illus.). 84p. 1983. 27.50 (ISBN 0-7148-2225-6, Pub. by Salem Hse Ltd); pap. 18.95 (ISBN 0-7148-2239-6). Merrimack Bk Serv.
BRUNCHES
see Breakfasts; Luncheons
BRUSSELS–DESCRIPTION
Brussells Travel Guide. (Berlitz Travel Guides). (Illus.). 1982. pap. 4.95 (ISBN 0-02-969050-1, Berlitz). Macmillan.
BRYAN, WILLIAM JENNINGS, 1860-1925
Clements, Kendrick A. William Jennings Bryan: Missionary Isolationist. LC 82-8342. (Illus.). 232p. 1983. text ed. 19.95x (ISBN 0-87049-364-7). U of Tenn Pr.
BRYANT, WILLIAM CULLEN, 1794-1878
William Cullen Bryant & His America: Centennial Conference Proceedings, 1878-1973. LC 82-45233. (Hofstra University Cultural & Intercultural Studies: Vol. 4). 1982. 27.50 (ISBN 0-404-61654-2, PS1181). AMS Pr.
BUBER, MARTIN, 1878-1965
Boni, Sylvain. The Self & the Other in the Ontologies of Sartre & Buber. LC 82-20130. 202p. (Orig.). 1983. lib. bdg. 21.75 (ISBN 0-8191-2852-X); pap. text ed. 10.75 (ISBN 0-8191-2853-8). U Pr of Amer.
Friedman, Maurice. Martin Buber's Life & Work: The Middle Years, 1923-1945. (Illus.). 416p. 1983. 29.95 (ISBN 0-525-24176-0, 02908-870). Dutton.
Murphy, John W. The Social Philosophy of Martin Buber: The Social World as a Human Dimension. LC 82-21779. 176p. (Orig.). 1983. lib. bdg. 21.00 (ISBN 0-8191-2940-2); pap. text ed. 10.00 (ISBN 0-8191-2941-0). U Pr of Amer.
BUBONIC PLAGUE
see Plague
BUBONIDAE
see Owls
BUCHAN, JOHN, 1875-1940
Buchan, William. John Buchan: A Memoir. 288p. 1982. 42.50x (ISBN 0-907675-03-4, Pub. by Muller Ltd). State Mutual Bk.
BUCHNER, GEORG, 1813-1837
Hilton, J. Georg Buchner. 1982. 49.00x (ISBN 0-333-29109-3, Pub. by Macmillan England). State Mutual Bk.
Rey, William H. Georg Buchners "Dantons Tod". 121p. (Ger.). 1982. write for info. (ISBN 3-261-04933-2). P Lang Pubs.
BUCKINGHAMSHIRE, ENGLAND
Viney, Elliott & Nightingale, Pamela. Old Aylesbury. 100p. 1982. 25.00x (ISBN 0-900804-21-1, Pub. by White Crescent England). State Mutual Bk.
BUCKLEY, WILLIAM FRANK, 1925-
Buckley, William F., Jr. Overdrive: A Personal Documentary. 1982. 16.95. Doubleday.
BUDDHA
see Gautama Buddha
BUDDHISM
see also Mahayana Buddhism; Tantric Buddhism; Zen Buddhism
also headings beginning with the word Buddhist
Arnold, Edwin. The Light of Asia or, the Great Renunciation (Mahabhinishkramana) Being the Life & Teaching of Gautama, Prince of India, Founder of Buddhism. x, 176p. 1972. pap. 5.00 (ISBN 0-7100-7006-3). Routledge & Kegan.
Bahm, Archie J. The Philosophy of the Buddha. 175p. 1982. text ed. 18.95x (ISBN 0-7069-2017-1, Pub. by Vikas India). Advent NY.
Carter, John R. & Bond, George D. The Threefold Refuge in the Theravada Buddhist Tradition. 1982. 3.95 (ISBN 0-89012-030-7). Anima Pubns.
Guenther, Herbert V. Matrix of Mystery: Scientific & Humanistic Aspects of Rdzogs-chen Thought. (Illus.). 320p. 1983. pap. 15.00 (ISBN 0-87773-766-5). Great Eastern.
Hercus, L. A. Indological & Buddhist Studies. LC 81-71413. 692p. (Orig.). 1982. pap. text ed. 39.95 (ISBN 0-686-37605-6, 1187, Pub. by ANUP Australia). Bks Australia.
Klimburg-Salter, Deborah E. Buddist Art & Culture of the Hindu Kush. (Illus.). 256p. 1983. 35.00 (ISBN 0-87773-765-7). Great Eastern.
Kornfield, Jack. Living Buddhist Masters. (Illus.). 334p. 1983. pap. 10.00 (ISBN 0-87773-768-1). Great Eastern.
Poppe, Nicholas, ed. The Twelve Deeds of Buddha: A Mongolian Version of the Lalitavistara & English Translation. (Asiatische Forschungen Ser.: Band 23). Orig. Title: Mongolian. 238p. 1967. pap. 25.00x (ISBN 3-447-00120-8). Intl Pubns Serv.
Warder, Anthony K., ed. New Paths in Buddhist Research. LC 82-83594. 128p. 1983. 12.95 (ISBN 0-89386-008-5); pap. 7.95 (ISBN 0-89386-009-3). Acorn NC.
Yoshinori, Takeuchi. The Heart of Buddhism: In Search of the Timeless Spirit of Primitive Buddhism. 192p. (Orig.). 1983. 19.95 (ISBN 0-8245-0577-8). Crossroad NY.
BUDDHISM–HISTORY
Szekely, Edmond B. Pilgrim of the Himalayas. (Illus.). 32p. 1974. pap. 2.95 (ISBN 0-89564-061-9). IBS Intl.
BUDDHISM–JAPAN
LaFleur, William R. The Karma of Words: Buddhism & the Literary Arts in Medieval Japan. LC 82-45909. 232p. 1983. text ed. 25.00x (ISBN 0-520-04600-5). U of Cal Pr.
BUDDHIST ART
see Art, Buddhist
BUDDHIST DOCTRINES
Tulku, Tarthang, ed. Nyringma Edition of the sDe-dge bKa-gyur & bsTun-gyur, 120 vols. (Tibetan Buddhist Canon). 65000p. 1981. Set. 1500.00 (ISBN 0-89800-129-3). Dharma Pub.
BUDDHIST PHILOSOPHY
see Philosophy, Buddhist
BUDDHIST TANTRISM
see Tantric Buddhism
BUDDHIST THEOLOGY
see Buddhist Doctrines
BUDGERIGARS
Rogers, Cyril. Budgerigars. (Illus.). 93p. 1976. 3.95 (ISBN 0-7028-1051-7). Avian Pubns.
Videla, E., illus. Your First Budgie. (Illus.). 32p. 3.95 (ISBN 0-87666-868-6, ST-003). TFH Pubns.
BUDGET
see also Municipal Budgets; Program Budgeting; Zero-Base Budgeting
Collender, Stanley E. The Guide to the Federal Budget: Fiscal 1984 Edition. LC 82-643840. 150p. (Orig.). 1983. pap. text ed. 10.00 (ISBN 0-87766-321-1). Urban Inst.
Frederiksen, Christian P. Budgeting for Nonprofits. 57.50 (ISBN 0-686-82267-6, 42A). Public Management.
Hyde, Albert C. & Shafritz, Jay M., eds. Government Budgeting: Theory, Process, Politics. LC 78-21866. (Orig.). 1978. pap. 12.50x (ISBN 0-935610-01-4). Moore Pub IL.
Rudman, Jack. Budget Assistant (USPS) (Career Examination Ser.: C-848). (Cloth bdg. avail. on reqest). pap. 10.00 (ISBN 0-8373-0848-8). Natl Learning.
--Budget Director. (Career Examination Ser.: C-2648). (Cloth bdg. avail. on request). pap. 12.00 (ISBN 0-8373-2648-6). Natl Learning.
--Budget Supervisor. (Career Examination Ser.: C-2684). (Cloth bdg. avail. on request). pap. 12.00 (ISBN 0-8373-2684-2). Natl Learning.
--Chief Budget Examiner. (Career Examination Ser.: C-2667). (Cloth bdg. avail. on request). pap. 14.00 (ISBN 0-8373-2667-2). Natl Learning.
--Principal Budget Officer. (Career Examination Ser.: C-2685). (Cloth bdg. avail. on request). pap. 12.00 (ISBN 0-8373-2685-0). Natl Learning.
--Senior Budget Officer. (Career Examination Ser.: C-2683). (Cloth bdg. avail. on request). pap. 12.00 (ISBN 0-8373-2683-4). Natl Learning.
Schick, Allen, ed. Perspective On Budgeting (Par Classics II) LC 80-81208. 1980. 10.95 (ISBN 0-936678-01-1). Am Soc Pub Admin.
Singleton, Ralph S. & Vietor, Joan E. Budget It Right. 300p. 1983. text ed. 42.50 (ISBN 0-943728-04-5); pap. text ed. 30.00 (ISBN 0-943728-02-9). Lone Eagle Prods.
BUDGET IN BUSINESS
see also Zero-Base Budgeting
Ganong, Joan M. & Ganong, Warren L. Help with Annual Budgetary Planning & Control. (Help Series of Management Guides). 90p. 1976. pap. 13.95 (ISBN 0-933036-07-8). Ganong W L Co.
BUDGETS, MUNICIPAL
see Municipal Budgets
BUDGETS, TIME
see Time Allocation
BUFFALO BILL, 1846-1917
Cody, William. Life of Buffalo Bill. (Classics of the Old West). 1982. lib. bdg. 17.28 (ISBN 0-8094-4015-6). Silver.
BUFFETS (COOKERY)
Truax, Carol. The Woman's Day Buffet Cookbook. Date not set. pap. 6.95 (ISBN 0-449-90076-2, Columbine). Fawcett.
BUICK AUTOMOBILE
see Automobiles–Types–Buick
BUILDER'S PLANT
see Construction Equipment
BUILDING
see also Architecture; Building Sites; Building Trades; Carpentry; Ceilings; Concrete Construction; Construction Equipment; Construction Industry; Environmental Engineering (Buildings); Foundations; Girders; House Construction; Masonry; Materials; Underground Construction; Walls; Windows
Butler, Robert B. Architectural & Engineering Calculations Manual. (Illus.). 384p. 1983. 19.95 (ISBN 0-07-009363-6, P&RB). McGraw.
Fullerton, R. L. & Struct, M. I. Construction Technology Level 2, Pt. 1. 160p. 1981. 36.00x (ISBN 0-291-39653-4, Pub. by Tech Pr). State Mutual Bk.
--Construction Technology Level 2, Pt. 2. 160p. 1981. 36.00x (ISBN 0-291-39654-2, Pub. by Tech Pr). State Mutual Bk.
BUILDING–ACCOUNTING
see Construction Industry–Accounting
BUILDING–AMATEURS' MANUALS
see also Building–Handbooks, Manuals, etc.
Build Your Own Walt Disney's Cinderella Castle. 40p. 1982. pap. 9.95 (ISBN 0-399-50654-3, Perige). Putnam Pub Group.
Rose, Alan. Build Your Own Japanese Pagoda. 40p. 1982. pap. 8.95 (ISBN 0-399-50679-9, Perige). Putnam Pub Group.
--Build Your Own Saturn V. (The World on the Move Ser.). 40p. 1982. pap. 8.95 (ISBN 0-399-50681-0, Perige). Putnam Pub Group.
BUILDING–CONTRACTS AND SPECIFICATIONS
American Society of Civil Engineers, compiled by. Reducing Risk & Liability Through Better Specifications & Inspections. LC 82-70874. 168p. 1982. pap. text ed. 18.75 (ISBN 0-87262-301-7). Am Soc Civil Eng.
Aqua Group. Tenders & Contracts for Building. 100p. 1982. pap. text ed. 14.50x (ISBN 0-246-11838-5, Pub. by Granada England). Renouf.
Chudley. Construction Technology 3 Checkbook. 1982. text ed. write for info. (ISBN 0-408-00686-2); pap. text ed. 9.95 (ISBN 0-408-00604-8). Butterworth.
Cushman, R. F. & Stover, A. The McGraw-Hill Construction Form Book. 448p. 1983. 34.50 (ISBN 0-07-014995-X, P&RB). McGraw.
Snow, Dorothea J. Gardens of Love. 1982. 6.95 (ISBN 0-686-84169-7, Avalon). Bouregy.
Specification: Building Methods & Products, 5 vols. 82nd ed. LC 72-622381. (Illus., Orig.). 1980. Set. 115.00x (ISBN 0-85139-590-2). Intl Pubns Serv.
BUILDING–COSTS
see Building–Estimates
BUILDING–DETAILS
Greening. Construction Drawing. 1982. text ed. 19.95 (ISBN 0-408-00672-2); pap. text ed. 9.95 (ISBN 0-408-00646-3). Butterworth.
BUILDING–DICTIONARIES
Barry, W. R., ed. Architectural, Construction, Manufacturing & Engineering Glossary of Terms. 519p. 1979. pap. 40.00 (ISBN 0-930284-05-4). Am Assn Cost Engineers.
Stein, J. Stewart. Construction Regulations: A Glossary of Zoning Ordinances & Building Codes. 750p. 1983. 75.00 (ISBN 0-471-89776-0, Pub. by Wiley Interscience). Wiley.
BUILDING–ESTIMATES
Cook, Paul J. Estimating for the General Contractor. 225p. 1982. text ed. 32.00 (ISBN 0-911950-48-6); pap. 27.50 (ISBN 0-911950-49-4). Means.
Dell'Isola, Alphonse J. Value Engineering in the Construction Industry. 3rd ed. 376p. 1983. text ed. 34.50 (ISBN 0-442-26202-7). Van Nos Reinhold.
Godfrey, Robert S. Building Construction Cost Data, 1983. 41st ed. LC 55-20084. 400p. 1983. pap. 30.50 (ISBN 0-911950-50-8). Means.
--Historical Cost Indexes, 1983. 3rd ed. 24p. Date not set. pap. 12.25 (ISBN 0-911950-58-3). Means.
--Labor Rates for the Construction Industry, 1983. 10th ed. LC 74-75990. 300p. 1982. pap. 31.25 (ISBN 0-911950-57-5). Means.
--Means Site Work Cost Data, 1983. 2nd ed. 300p. 1983. pap. 34.75 (ISBN 0-911950-53-2). Means.
--Means Square Foot Costs, 1983. 4th ed. LC 82-643175. 350p. 1983. pap. 36.50 (ISBN 0-911950-54-0). Means.
--Means Systems Costs, 1983. 8th ed. LC 76-17689. 425p. 1983. pap. 37.50 (ISBN 0-911950-51-6). Means.

--Mechanical & Electrical Cost Data, 1983. 6th ed. LC 79-643328. 475p. 1983. pap. 34.75 (ISBN 0-911950-56-7). Means.
--Repair & Remodeling Cost Data, 1983. 4th ed. LC 80-644930. 350p. 1983. pap. 35.75 (ISBN 0-911950-55-9). Means.
--Residential-Light Commercial Cost Data, 1983. 2nd ed. 275p. 1983. pap. 33.25 (ISBN 0-911950-52-4). Means.
Lewis, Jack R. Basic Construction Estimating. (Illus.). 176p. 1983. text ed. 19.95 (ISBN 0-13-058313-8). P-H.
National Association of Home Builders. Construction Cost Control. Rev. ed. (Illus.). 64p. 1982. pap. text ed. 13.00 (ISBN 0-86718-153-2). Natl Assn Home.
Parker, Albert D. & Barrie, Donald S. Planning & Estimating Heavy Construction. 640p. 1983. 39.95 (ISBN 0-07-048489-9, P&RB). McGraw.
Pilcher, Roy. Appraisal & Control of Project Costs. (Illus.). 324p. 1982. text ed. 27.50x (ISBN 0-88133-005-1). Waveland Pr.

BUILDING–HANDBOOKS, MANUALS, ETC.
see also Building–Amateurs' Manuals
Phelps, John & Philbin. Complete Building Construction. new ed. (Audel Ser.). 1983. 19.95 (ISBN 0-672-23377-0). Bobbs.

BUILDING–HISTORY
Bassett, William B. Historic American Buildings Survey of New Jersey. (Illus.). 210p. 1977. 13.95 (ISBN 0-686-81818-0); pap. 9.95 (ISBN 0-686-81819-9). NJ Hist Soc.
Godfrey, Robert S. Historical Cost Indexes, 1983. 3rd ed. 24p. Date not set. pap. 12.25 (ISBN 0-911950-58-3). Means.

BUILDING–INSPECTION
see Building Inspection

BUILDING–LAWS AND LEGISLATION
see Building Laws

BUILDING–PRICE BOOKS
see Building–Estimates

BUILDING–SPECIFICATIONS
see Building–Contracts and Specifications

BUILDING–SUPERINTENDENCE
Rudman, Jack. Director of Custodial & Security Services. (Career Examination Ser.: C-2923). (Cloth bdg. avail. on request). pap. 14.00 (ISBN 0-8373-2923-X). Natl Learning.
--Principal Buildings Manager. (Career Examination Ser.: C-2719). (Cloth bdg. avail. on request). pap. 12.00 (ISBN 0-8373-2719-9). Natl Learning.
--Senior Superintendent of Construction. (Career Examination Ser.). (Cloth bdg. avail. on request). pap. 12.00 (ISBN 0-8373-0541-1). Natl Learning.
--Supervisor (Structures) (Career Examination Ser.: C-424). (Cloth bdg. avail. on request). pap. 12.00 (ISBN 0-8373-0424-5). Natl Learning.
--Supervisor (Structures - Group C) (Iron Work) (Career Examination Ser.: C-425). (Cloth bdg. avail. on request). pap. 12.00 (ISBN 0-8373-0425-3). Natl Learning.

BUILDING, CONCRETE
see Concrete Construction

BUILDING, EARTHQUAKE-PROOF
see Earthquakes and Building

BUILDING, HOUSE
see House Construction

BUILDING, IRON AND STEEL
see also Girders; Steel, Structural; Strength of Materials; Structures, Theory Of
Wiley, John. Structural Steel Design. 2nd ed. Tall, Lambert, ed. 892p. text ed. 49.50 (ISBN 0-89874-602-7). Krieger.

BUILDING, UNDERGROUND
see Underground Construction

BUILDING CODES
see Building Laws

BUILDING DYNAMICS
see Structural Dynamics

BUILDING EMPLOYEES
see Building-Service Employees

BUILDING INDUSTRY
see Construction Industry

BUILDING INSPECTION
see also Building Laws
American Society of Civil Engineers, compiled by. Reducing Risk & Liability Through Better Specifications & Inspections. LC 82-70874. 168p. 1982. pap. text ed. 18.75 (ISBN 0-87262-301-7). Am Soc Civil Eng.
Rudman, Jack. Supervising Building Plan Examiner. (Career Examination Ser.: C-862). (Cloth bdg. avail. on request). pap. 12.00 (ISBN 0-8373-0862-3). Natl Learning.
Schainblatt, Al & Koss, Margo. Fire Code Inspections & Fire Prevention: What Methods Lead to Success? (Illus.). 122p. (Orig.). pap. text ed. 5.00 (ISBN 0-686-84409-2). Urban Inst.
Tuck, Charles A., Jr., ed. NFPA Inspection Manual. 5th ed. LC 76-5194. (Illus.). 387p. 1982. 20.00 (ISBN 0-87765-239-2, SPP-11C). Natl Fire Prot.

BUILDING LAWS
see also Architects–Legal Status, Laws, etc.; Building–Contracts and Specifications; Building Inspection; Construction Industry–Law and Legislation; Zoning Law
American Society of Civil Engineers, compiled by. Reducing Risk & Liability Through Better Specifications & Inspections. LC 82-70874. 168p. 1982. pap. text ed. 18.75 (ISBN 0-87262-301-7). Am Soc Civil Eng.
Galbraith. Building Law Four Checkbook. 1982. 22.50 (ISBN 0-408-00677-3); pap. 9.95 (ISBN 0-408-00583-1). Butterworth.
Ryder, Virginia P. Cormorants Landing: How to Do Your Own Condo-Conversion Plus Secrets of City Hall. LC 82-90719. (Illus.). 130p. 1983. pap. 10.00 (ISBN 0-935098-02-X). Amigo Pr.
Stein, J. Stewart. Construction Regulations: A Glossary of Zoning Ordinances & Building Codes. 750p. 1983. 75.00 (ISBN 0-471-89776-0, Pub. by Wiley Interscience). Wiley.

BUILDING MATERIALS–SPECIFICATIONS
see Building–Contracts and Specifications

BUILDING REPAIR
see Buildings–Repair and Reconstruction; Dwellings–Maintenance and Repair

BUILDING SECURITY
see Burglary Protection

BUILDING-SERVICE EMPLOYEES
see also Janitors
Rudman, Jack. Assistant Director of Custodial & Security Services. (Career Examination Ser.: C-2922). (Cloth bdg. avail. on request). pap. 14.00 (ISBN 0-8373-2922-1). Natl Learning.
--Assistant Tenant Supervisor. (Career Examination Ser.: C-542). (Cloth bdg. avail. on request). pap. 10.00 (ISBN 0-8373-0542-X). Natl Learning.

BUILDING SITES
Patchett. Construction Site: Personnel 4 Checkbook. 1983. text ed. write for info. (ISBN 0-408-00688-9); pap. write for info. (ISBN 0-408-00685-4). Butterworth.
Roberts, John M. The Building Site: Planning & Practice. 288p. 1983. write for info. (ISBN 0-471-08868-4, Pub. by Wiley-Interscience). Wiley.

BUILDING SUPERINTENDENCE
see Building–Superintendence

BUILDING SUPERINTENDENTS
see Janitors

BUILDING TRADES
see also Building; Construction Industry; also Bricklayers, Carpenters, and similar headings
Arbor, Marilyn. Tools & Trades of America's Past: The Mercer Collection. 116p. 6.95 (ISBN 0-910302-12-X). Bucks Co Hist.
Langford, D. A. Direct Labour Organizations in the Construction Industry. 135p. 1982. text ed. 35.50x (ISBN 0-566-00542-5). Gower Pub Ltd.
Mainframes. 1983. 1095.00 (ISBN 0-686-37716-8, E77). Predicasts.

BUILDING TRADES–ACCOUNTING
see Construction Industry–Accounting

BUILDINGS
see also Architecture; Building; Historic Buildings also names of particular types of building and construction e.g. Dwellings; School-houses; Concrete Construction
Architectural Record Magazine. Public, Municipal & Community Buildings. 1980. 34.50 (ISBN 0-07-002351-4). McGraw.
Curran, June. Profile Your Lifestyle: Questions to Ask Yourself Before Building, Buying, or Remodeling. LC 78-72187. 159p. 1979. pap. 7.95 (ISBN 0-932370-00-4). W Kaufmann.
Jones, T. F. Building Measurement Three Checkbook. 1983. text ed. write for info. (ISBN 0-408-00652-8). Butterworth.

BUILDINGS–ACOUSTICS
see Architectural Acoustics

BUILDINGS–DETAILS
see Architecture–Details; Building–Details

BUILDINGS–ENERGY CONSERVATION
American Institute of Architects. Architect's Handbook of Energy Practice: Building Envelope. (Illus.). 42p. 1982. pap. 18.00x (ISBN 0-913962-51-1). Am Inst Arch.
--Architect's Handbook of Energy Practice: Climate & Site. (Illus.). 55p. 1982. pap. 18.00x (ISBN 0-913962-50-3). Am Inst Arch.
--Architect's Handbook of Energy Practice: Daylighting. (Illus.). 48p. 1982. pap. 18.00x (ISBN 0-913962-52-X). Am Inst Arch.
--Architect's Handbook of Energy Practice: HVAC Systems. (Illus.). 54p. 1982. pap. 18.00x (ISBN 0-913962-53-8). Am Inst Arch.
--Architect's Handbook of Energy Practice: Photovoltaics. (Illus.). 56p. 1982. pap. 18.00x (ISBN 0-913962-56-2). Am Inst Arch.
--Architect's Handbook of Energy Practice: Shading & Sun Control. (Illus.). 48p. 1982. pap. 18.00x (ISBN 0-913962-49-X). Am Inst Arch.
--Architect's Handbook of Energy Practice: Thermal Transfer Through the Envelope. (Illus.). 51p. 1982. pap. 18.00x (ISBN 0-913962-55-4). Am Inst Arch.
Dubin, Fred S. & Long, Chalmers G., Jr. Energy Conservation Standards: For Building Design, Construction & Operation. 432p. 1982. 14.95 (ISBN 0-07-017884-4). McGraw.
Harris, Jeffrey & Haggard, Keith, eds. What Works? Documenting the Results of Energy Conservation in Buildings. (Progress in Solar Energy Ser.). 1983. text ed. 50.00 Selected Papers (ISBN 0-89553-111-9); text ed. 15.00 (ISBN 0-89553-110-0). Am Solar Energy.

BUILDINGS–ENVIRONMENTAL ENGINEERING
see Environmental Engineering (Buildings)

BUILDINGS–MODELS
see Architectural Models

BUILDINGS–PROTECTION
see also Buildings–Repair and Reconstruction
Brannigan, Francis L. Building Construction for the Fire Service. 2nd ed. McKinnon, Gordon P. & Matson, Debra, eds. LC 78-178805. (Illus.). 392p. 1982. text ed. 20.00 (ISBN 0-87765-227-9, FSP-33A). Natl Fire Prot.

BUILDINGS–REPAIR AND RECONSTRUCTION
see also Architecture–Conservation and Restoration; Dwellings–Maintenance and Repair; Dwellings–Remodeling
Abrams, Lawrence & Abrams, Kathleen. Salvaging Old Barns & Houses: Tear it Down & Save Their Places. LC 82-19330. (Illus.). 128p. (Orig.). 1983. pap. 7.95 (ISBN 0-8069-7666-7). Sterling.
Godfrey, Robert S. Repair & Remodeling Cost Data, 1983. 4th ed. LC 80-644930. 350p. 1983. pap. 35.75 (ISBN 0-911950-55-9). Means.
Rains, Albert & Henderson, Laurance G., eds. With Heritage So Rich. Rev. ed. (Landmark Reprint Ser.). 200p. 1983. 12.95 (ISBN 0-89133-104-2). Preservation Pr.

BUILDINGS, FARM
see Farm Buildings

BUILDINGS, LIBRARY
see Library Architecture

BUILDINGS, MOVING OF
see Moving of Buildings, Bridges, etc.

BUILDINGS, RECONSTRUCTION OF
see Buildings–Repair and Reconstruction

BUILDINGS, RESTORATION OF
see Architecture–Conservation and Restoration

BUILDINGS, SCHOOL
see School Buildings

BULBS
Grey-Wilson, Christopher & Mathew, Brian. Bulbs: The Bulbous Plants of Europe & Their Allies. (Illus.). 1983. 32.95 (ISBN 0-686-42797-1, Collins Pub England). Greene.
Scott, George H. Bulbs: How to Select, Grow & Enjoy. 160p. 1982. pap. 7.95 (ISBN 0-89586-146-1). H P Bks.

BULGAKOV, MIKHAIL, 1891-1940
Proffer, Ellendea, ed. Bulgakov Photographic Bibliography. 140p. 1983. 22.50 (ISBN 0-88233-812-9); pap. 12.50 (ISBN 0-88233-813-7). Ardis Pubs.

BULGARIAN LANGUAGE
Foreign Service Institute. Bulgarian Basic Course. 487p. Date not set. with 23 cassettes 225.00x (ISBN 0-88432-089-8, L450). J Norton Pubs.

BULGE, BATTLE OF THE
see Ardennes, Battle of the, 1944-1945

BULL TERRIERS
see Dogs–Breeds–Bull Terriers

BULLETIN BOARDS
Bullentin Boards Should be More Than Something to Look At. 64p. (gr. k-6). 5.95 (ISBN 0-686-84808-X, GA97). Good Apple.

BULLION
see Precious Metals

BULLS
Whitlock, Ralph. Bulls Through the Ages. (Illus.). 176p. 1983. 15.95 (ISBN 0-7188-2330-3, Pub by Salem Hse Ltd). Merrimack Bk Serv.

BULLS, IRISH
see Irish Wit and Humor

BULLS AND BEARS
see Stock-Exchange

BULOW, HANS GUIDO VON, 1830-1894
Eckart, Richard, ed. Letters of Hans Von Bulow. Waller, Hannah, tr. LC 72-183503. 434p. Date not set. Repr. of 1931 ed. price not set. Vienna Hse.
Von Bulow, Marie, ed. Hans Von Bulow: The Early Correspondence. Bache, Constance, tr. LC 71-163788. 266p. Date not set. Repr. of 1869 ed. price not set. Vienna Hse.

BUNYAN, JOHN, 1628-1688
Forrest, James F. & Greaves, Richard L. John Bunyan: A Reference Guide. 1982. lib. bdg. 50.00 (ISBN 0-8161-8267-1, Hall Reference). G K Hall.

BUONARROTI, MICHELANGELO
see Michelangelo (Buonarroti, Michelangelo), 1475-1564

BUREAUCRACY
see also Civil Service
Batley, Richard. Power Through Bureaucracy: Urban Political Analysis in Brazil. LC 82-16872. 240p. 1982. 27.50x (ISBN 0-312-63437-4). St Martin.
Benveniste, Guy. Bureaucracy. 2nd ed. 240p. 1983. pap. text ed. 8.95x (ISBN 0-87835-134-5). Boyd & Fraser.
Jackson, P. M. The Political Economy of Bureaucracy. LC 82-22674. 304p. 1983. text ed. 27.50x (ISBN 0-389-20352-1). B&N Imports.
Korten, David C. & Alfonso, Felipe B., eds. Bureaucracy & the Poor: Closing the Gap. LC 82-83847. (Library of Management for Development). xiv, 258p. (Orig.). 1983. pap. write for info. (ISBN 0-931816-30-0). Kumarian Pr.
Ocko, Jonathan K. Bureaucratic Reform in Provincial China: Ting Jih-ch'ang in Restoration Kiangsu, 1867-1870. (Harvard East Asian Monographs: No. 103). 316p. 1983. text ed. 20.00x (ISBN 0-674-08617-1). Harvard U Pr.

BURGLARY PROTECTION
see also Security Systems
Cruit, Ronald L. Intruder in Your Home: How to Defend Yourself Legally With A Firearm. LC 82-42727. 288p. 1983. 17.95 (ISBN 0-686-83443-7). Stein & Day.
Maguire, Mike & Bennett, Trevor. Burglary in a Dwelling: The Offence, the Offender & the Victim, No. XLIX. Radzinowicz, Leon, ed. (Cambridge Studies in Crimonology). 204p. 1982. text ed. 40.00x (ISBN 0-435-82567-4). Heinemann Ed.

BURIAL
see also Funeral Rites and Ceremonies; Mummies; Sepulchral Monuments; Tombs
Gates, Charles. From Cremation to Inhumation: Burial Practices at Ialysos & Kameiros During the Mid-Archaic Period, ca. 625-525 B.C. (Occasional Papers: No. 11). (Illus.). 1983. pap. text ed. 9.00 (ISBN 0-917956-39-7). UCLA Arch.

BURIAL STATISTICS
see Mortality; Registers of Births, Deaths, Marriages, etc.

BURIED CITIES
see Cities and Towns, Ruined, Extinct, etc.

BURIED TREASURE
see Treasure-Trove

BURMA–DESCRIPTION AND TRAVEL
Insight Guides. Burma. (Illus.). 336p. 1983. pap. 14.95 (ISBN 0-13-090902-5). P-H.

BURMA–HISTORY
Bennett, Paul J. Conference Under the Tamarind Tree: Three Essays in Burmese History. (Illus.). 153p. 1971. 8.25 (ISBN 0-686-38050-9). Yale U SE Asia.
Ogburn, Charlton. The Marauders. LC 82-16149. 307p. 1982. pap. 6.50 (ISBN 0-688-01625-1, Quill). Morrow.

BURNEY, CHARLES, 1726-1814
Grant, Kerry S. Dr. Charles Burney as Critic & Historian of Music. Beulow, George, ed. (Studies in Musicology: No. 62). 1983. 59.95 (ISBN 0-8357-1375-X). Univ Microfilms.

BURNS, ROBERT, 1759-1796
Barke, James, ed. Poems & Songs of Robert Burns. 736p. 1983. 16.95 (ISBN 0-00-420224-4, Collins Pub England). Greene.

BURNS AND SCALDS
Burns, Kathryn A. Managing the Burn Patient: A Guide for Nurses. LC 82-62402. 1983. write for info. (ISBN 0-913590-97-5). Slack Inc.
International Burn Seminar Shanghai, June 1981. The Treatment of Research in Burns: Proceedings. Ji-Xiang Shi & Zhi-Yong Sheng, eds. 500p. 1983. 50.00x (ISBN 0-471-87328-4, Pub. by Wiley Med). Wiley.

BURR, AARON, 1756-1836
Kline, Mary-Jo & Ryan, Joanne W., eds. Political Correspondence & Public Papers of Aaron Burr, 2 vols. LC 82-61396. (Illus.). 1228p. 1983. 125.00x (ISBN 0-691-04685-9). Princeton U Pr.

BURYING GROUNDS
see Burial; Cemeteries

BUS DRIVER
see Motor Bus Drivers

BUSES
see Motor Buses

BUSHINGS
see Bearings (Machinery)

BUSINESS
see also Accounting; Advertising; Applications for Positions; Big Business; Bookkeeping; Budget in Business; Business Enterprises; Business Mathematics; Businessmen; Catalogs, Commercial; Commerce; Commercial Law; Competition; Controllership; Corporations; Credit; Customer Relations; Entrepreneur; Executives; Financial Statements; Industrial Management; Mail-Order Business; Manufactures; Marketing; Markets; New Business Enterprises; Occupations; Office Management; Profit; Purchasing; Real Estate Business; Salesmen and Salesmanship; Secretaries; Small Business; Success; Trade-Marks; Warehouses; Wealth; Women in Business
Anderson, David R. & Sweeney, Dennis J. Quantitative Methods for Business. 2nd ed. (Illus.). 656p. 1983. text ed. 26.95 (ISBN 0-314-69633-4); write for info. study guide (ISBN 0-314-71075-2); write for info. test bank (ISBN 0-314-71077-9); instrs.' manual avail. (ISBN 0-314-71076-0). West Pub.
Beauchamp, Tom L. Case Studies in Business, Society & Ethics. 256p. 1983. pap. 12.95 (ISBN 0-13-119263-9). P-H.
Bottom Line Personal, Experts, ed. The Book of Inside Information. 500p. 1982. 50.00 (ISBN 0-932648-50-9). Boardroom.
Bryant, Keith L., Jr. & Dethloff, Henry C. A History of American Business. (Illus.). 368p. 1983. pap. 15.95 (ISBN 0-13-389247-6). P-H.
Carter, Roger. Business Administration. 224p. 1982. pap. 50.00x (ISBN 0-434-90219-5, Pub. by Heinemann England). State Mutual Bk.
Chasman, Herbert. Who Gets the Business? 200p. 1983. 14.95 (ISBN 0-910580-73-1). Farnswth Pub.
Company Administration Handbook. 5th ed. 770p. 1982. text ed. 71.50x (ISBN 0-566-02352-0). Gower Pub Ltd.
Conover, Hobart & Berlye, Milton. Business Dynamics. 481p. 1982. text ed. 15.50 (ISBN 0-672-97973-X); tchr's ed. 6.67 (ISBN 0-672-97978-0); wkbk. 5.95 (ISBN 0-672-97977-2). Bobbs.

Daniel & Terrell. Business Statistics: Basic Concepts & Methodology. 1982. text ed. 28.95 (ISBN 0-686-84527-7); write for info. supplementary material. HM.
Engels, W. & Pohl, H., eds. German Yearbook on Business History, 1982. (Illus.). 186p. 1983. 15.00 (ISBN 0-387-11892-6). Springer-Verlag.
Gitman, Lawrence J., ed. Business World. McDaniel, Carl. 600p. 1982. 23.95 (ISBN 0-471-08165-5); tchr's. manual avail. (ISBN 0-471-87095-1). Wiley.
Goldstein, Arnold S. How to Save Your Business. 1983. 14.95 (ISBN 0-913864-74-9). Enterprise Del.
Hecht, Arthur & Stevens, Byron. The Business Beastiary. LC 82-42730. 96p. 1983. 14.95 (ISBN 0-8128-2908-5); pap. 7.95 (ISBN 0-8128-6176-0). Stein & Day.
Hegarty, Christopher & Goldberg, Philip. How to Manage Your Boss. 312p. 1982. pap. 9.95 (ISBN 0-931432-15-4). Whatever Pub.
Hendrick, Burton J. Age of Big Business. 1919. text ed. 8.50x (ISBN 0-686-37860-1). Elliots Bks.
Higgins, Robert C. Analysis for Financial Management. LC 82-73628. 325p. 1983. 19.95 (ISBN 0-87094-377-4). Dow Jones-Irwin.
Ivancevich, John M. & Lyon, Herbert L. Introduction to Business. 2nd ed. (Illus.). 700p. 1983. text ed. 22.95 (ISBN 0-314-69656-3); tchrs. ed avail. (ISBN 0-314-71100-7); study guide avail. (ISBN 0-314-71101-5). West Pub.
Jarvis, Ana C. & Lebredo, Raquel. Business & Economics Workbook. 256p. 1983. pap. 7.95 (ISBN 0-669-05337-6). Heath.
Kelly, Kate. How to Set Your Fees & Get Them. 79p. 1982. pap. 15.00 (ISBN 0-9603740-2-7). Visibility Ent.
Lucas, Robert E., Jr. Studies in Business-Cycle Theory. 312p. 1983. pap. 9.95x (ISBN 0-262-62044-8). MIT Pr.
Lynn, E. Russell, Jr. The Mters-Briggs Type Indicator: The Dignity of Difference. (Illus.). 1983. write for info. (ISBN 0-935652-10-8). Ctr Applications Psych.
McKnight, Daniel L., Jr. The Complete Partnership Manual & Guide with Tax, Financial & Managerial Strategies. LC 82-5799. 304p. 1982. 39.50 (ISBN 0-13-162230-7, Busn). P-H.
Morine, John. Riding the Recession: How Your Business Can Prosper Despite Shrinking Markets, High Inflation & the Ups & Downs of Today's Economy. (Illus.). 136p. 1983. 11.95 (ISBN 0-13-781062-8); pap. 5.95 (ISBN 0-13-781054-7). P-H.
Orth, Samuel P. Armies of Labor. 1919. text ed. 8.50x (ISBN 0-686-83479-8). Elliots Bks.
Petersen, Elizabeth. Maze: How Not to Go into Business. LC 82-62505. 160p. (Orig.). 1983. 14.95 (ISBN 0-9610200-0-8); pap. 9.95 (ISBN 0-9610200-1-6). MEDA Pubns.
Ramsgard, William C. Making Systems Work: The Psychology of Business Systems. LC 77-5933. 280p. Repr. of 1977 ed. text ed. 24.50 (ISBN 0-471-01522-9). Krieger.
Reekie, W. D. & Allen, D. E. Economics of Modern Business. 300p. 1983. text ed. 29.50x (ISBN 0-631-13115-9, Pub. by Basil Blackwell England). Biblio Dist.
Richards, Larry E. & LaCava, Jerry J. Business Statistics: Why & When. 2nd ed. (Illus.). 512p. 1983. text ed. 24.95 (ISBN 0-07-052276-6, C); wkbk. 15.00 (ISBN 0-07-052278-2); write for info. instr's manual (ISBN 0-07-052277-4). McGraw.
Rudman, Jack. Administrative Business Promotion Coordinator. (Career Examination Ser.: C-2599). (Cloth bdg. avail. on request). pap. 12.00 (ISBN 0-8373-2599-4). Natl Learning.
--Assistant Business Manager. (Career Examination Ser.: C-528). (Cloth bdg. avail. on request). pap. 12.00 (ISBN 0-8373-0528-4). Natl Learning.
Seltz, David D. A Treasury of Business Opportunities for the Eighties. 3rd ed. 283p. 1983. 19.95 (ISBN 0-686-84096-8). Farnswth Pub.
Senior, Patrick, pseud. Self-Solving: The Key to Making Business a Pleasure. 30p. 1982. bklet 2.00 (ISBN 0-911201-00-9). New Age Bus Bks.
Speegle, Roger & Giesecke, William B. Business World. (Illus.). 192p. (Orig.). 1983. pap. text ed. 7.95x (ISBN 0-19-503230-6). Oxford U Pr.
Stair, Lila B. Careers in Business. LC 82-73634. 170p. 1983. Repr. of 1980 ed. 12.95 (ISBN 0-87094-398-7). Dow Jones-Irwin.
Troy, Leo. Almanac of Business & Industrial Financial Ratios: 1981-1982 Edition. LC 72-181403. 373p. 1982. 16.00 (ISBN 0-13-022749-8, Busn). P-H.
Ullman, John E., ed. Social Costs in Modern Society: A Qualitative & Quantitative Assessment. LC 82-18590. (Illus.). 272p. 1983. lib. bdg. 29.95 (ISBN 0-89930-019-7, USC/, Quorum). Greenwood.
Van Oosting, James. The Business Report: Writer, Reader & Text. (Illus.). 320p. 1983. pap. 13.95 (ISBN 0-13-107581-0). P-H.
Walthall, Wylie A. & Wirth, Michael J. Getting into Business. 3rd ed. 368p. 1983. pap. text ed. 13.50 scp (ISBN 0-06-046895-5, HarpC); instr's. manual avail. (ISBN 0-06-366992-7). Har-Row.
Williamson, Robert. Business Organization. 1981. pap. 9.95 (ISBN 0-434-92262-5, Pub. by Heinemann). David & Charles.

BUSINESS–ADDRESSES, ESSAYS, LECTURES

Speegle, Roger & Giesecke, William B. Business World. (Illus.). 192p. (Orig.). 1983. pap. text ed. 7.95x (ISBN 0-19-503230-6). Oxford U Pr.

BUSINESS–BIBLIOGRAPHY

American Institute of Accountants. Library Catalogue. LC 82-48337. (Accountancy in Transition Ser.). 242p. 1982. lib. bdg. 25.00 (ISBN 0-8240-5303-6). Garland Pub.
Research Libraries of the New York Public Library & Library of Congress. Bibliographic Guide to Business & Economics: 1982. 1983. lib. bdg. 335.00 (ISBN 0-8161-6983-7, Biblio Guides). G K Hall.

BUSINESS–DATA PROCESSING

Awad, Elias M. Introduction to Computers. 2nd ed. (Illus.). 496p. 1983. text ed. 19.95 (ISBN 0-13-479444-3). P-H.
Birnbaum, Mark & Sickman, John. How to Choose Your Small Business Computer: Popular. LC 82-11665. (Microcomputer Bks.). 176p. 1982. pap. 9.95 (ISBN 0-201-10187-4). A-W.
Blumenthal, Susan. Understanding & Buying a Small Business Computer. Date not set. pap. 8.95 (ISBN 0-672-21890-9). Sams.
Clark, Roger E. Executive Visicalc: Application for the Apple. LC 82-11663. (Microcomputer Bks.-Executive). 192p. 1982. pap. 14.95 (ISBN 0-201-10242-0). A-W.
Cobb, Douglas F. VisiCalc Models for Business. LC 82-42767. 1983. pap. 14.95 (ISBN 0-88022-017-1). Que Corp.
Davis, William S. Computer & Business Information Processing. 2nd ed. LC 82-6864. (Illus.). 448p. 1983. pap. text ed. 17.95 (ISBN 0-201-11118-7). A-W.
Doswell, Andrew. Office Automation. (Information Processing). 280p. 1983. 33.95 (ISBN 0-471-10457-4, Pub. by Wiley-Interscience). Wiley.
Eliason, Alan L. Online Business Computer Applications. 336p. 1983. pap. text ed. write for info. (ISBN 0-574-21405-4, 13-4405); write for info. instr's. guide (ISBN 0-574-21406-2, 13-4406). SRA.
Finn, Nancy B. The Electronic Office. (Illus.). 144p. 1983. pap. 12.95 (ISBN 0-13-251819-8). P-H.
Fitzgerald, Jerry & Eason, Thomas. Fundamentals of Data Communications. LC 77-20842. 260p. 1978. text ed. 23.95 (ISBN 0-471-26254-4, Pub. by Wiley-Hamilton). Wiley.
Gibson, Barbara G. Personal Computers in Business: An Introduction & Buyers Guide. (Illus., Orig.). 1982. pap. 2.95 (ISBN 0-9609780-0-3). Apple Comp.
Harvard Business Review. Catching Up with the Computer Revolution. (Harvard Business Review Executive Bk. Ser.). 500p. 1983. 22.95 (ISBN 0-471-87594-5, Pub. by Wiley Interscience). Wiley.
Kilgannon, Pete. Business Data Processing & Systems Analysts. 336p. 1980. pap. text ed. 17.95 (ISBN 0-7131-2755-4). E Arnold.
Lucas, Harold. Computers in Management & Business Studies. 272p. 1979. 35.00x (ISBN 0-7121-0390-2, Pub. by Macdonald & Evans). State Mutual Bk.
McGlynn, Daniel R. McGlynn's Simplified Guide to Small Computers for Business. 250p. 1983. 14.95 (ISBN 0-471-86853-1, Pub. by Wiley Interscience). Wiley.
Myers, Stanley. RPG II & RPG III with Business Applications. 1983. text ed. 24.95 (ISBN 0-8359-6753-0). Reston.
Simplan Systems, Inc. Corporate Planning & Modeling with Simplan. 2nd ed. 598p. Date not set. pap. text ed. 25.00 (ISBN 0-201-07830-9). A-W.
SuperCalc: Super Models for Business. LC 82-42765. Date not set. pap. 14.95 (ISBN 0-88022-007-4). Que Corp.
Tomeski, Edward A. & Kleinschmidt, William. Fundamentals of Computers in Business: A Systems Approach (Student Study Guide) 1979. 8.50 (ISBN 0-8162-8735-X). Holden-Day.
Trost, Stanley R. Doing Business with SuperCalc. 300p. 1983. pap. text ed. 12.95 (ISBN 0-89588-095-4). Sybex.
Wortman, Leon. Business Problem Solving Using the IBM Pc. 416p. 1983. 27.95 (ISBN 0-89303-281-6); pap. 21.95 (ISBN 0-89303-282-4). R J Brady.

BUSINESS–DICTIONARIES

Beijing Language Institute & Beijing Institute of Foreign Trade Staff, eds. Business Chiness 500. 309p. (Orig.). 1982. pap. 4.95 (ISBN 0-8351-1039-7). China Bks.
Boardroom Reports, Editors & Experts. Encyclopedia of Practical Business. rev. ed. 400p. 1983. 50.00 (ISBN 0-932648-37-1). Boardroom.
Rosenberg, Jerry M. Dictionary of Business & Management. 2nd ed. 600p. 1983. 29.95 (ISBN 0-471-86730-6, Pub. by Wiley-Interscience). Wiley.
Sachs, Rudolf. British & American Business Terms. 144p. 1975. 20.00x (ISBN 0-7121-0242-6, Pub. by Macdonald & Evans). State Mutual Bk.
The Tampa Bay-Sun Coast Business Directory, 2 pts. 1983. Pt. 1: 960 pg. 120.00 (ISBN 0-87436-354-3). Pt. 2: 581 pg. ABC-Clio.

BUSINESS–EXAMINATIONS, QUESTIONS, ETC.

Rudman, Jack. Business Assistant. (Career Examination Ser.: C-2885). (Cloth bdg. avail. on request). pap. 10.00 (ISBN 0-8373-2885-3). Natl Learning.

BUSINESS–FORMS, BLANKS, ETC.

Prescribed Forms. (Statements on Standards for Accounting & Review Services: No. 3). 1982. pap. 1.60 (ISBN 0-686-84308-8). Am Inst CPA.

BUSINESS–INFORMATION SERVICES

Data Notes Publishing Staff. U. S. Directory of Business Start Up Fees. 1983. text ed. 59.95 50 pg. (ISBN 0-911569-13-8); pap. text ed. 29.95 160 pg. (ISBN 0-911569-08-1). Data Notes Pub.

BUSINESS–MATHEMATICAL MODELS

Meek, Gary E. & Turner, Stephen J. Statistical Analysis for Business Decisions. 768p. 1983. text ed. 27.95 (ISBN 0-395-32274-X); write for info. instr's. manual (ISBN 0-395-32825-X). HM.

BUSINESS–RECORDS

see Business Records

BUSINESS–SOCIAL ASPECTS

see Industry–Social Aspects

BUSINESS–STUDY AND TEACHING

see Business Education

BUSINESS–TAXATION

see Business Tax

BUSINESS, CHOICE OF

see Vocational Guidance

BUSINESS ADMINISTRATION

see Business

BUSINESS AND GOVERNMENT

see Industry and State

BUSINESS AND POLITICS

Magaziner, Ira C. & Reich, Robert B. Minding America's Business: The Decline & Rise of the American Economy. LC 81-13663. (Illus.). 400p. 1983. pap. 5.95 (ISBN 0-394-71538-1, Vin). Random.
Schnitzer, Martin. Contemporary Government & Business Relations. 2d ed. 608p. text ed. 21.95 (ISBN 0-395-31764-9); write for info. instr's manual (ISBN 0-395-34027-6). HM.
Ware, Edith E. Business & Politics in the Far East. 1932. text ed. 47.50x (ISBN 0-686-83497-6). Elliots Bks.

BUSINESS AND SOCIAL PROBLEMS

see Industry–Social Aspects

BUSINESS ARITHMETIC

see Business Mathematics

BUSINESS BUDGETING

see Budget in Business

BUSINESS COMMUNICATION

see Communication in Management

BUSINESS CONSULTANTS

Albert, Kenneth J. How to Solve Business Problems: The Consultant's Approach to Business Problem Solving. LC 82-14956. 224p. 1983. pap. 9.95 (ISBN 0-07-000753-5, P&RB). McGraw.
Shenson, Howard L. Consulting Handbook. 5th ed. 213p. 1982. pap. 39.00 (ISBN 0-910549-00-1). H L Shenson.
Tisdall, Patricia. Agents of Change: The Development & Practice of Management Consultancy. (Illus.). 192p. 1983. 24.95 (ISBN 0-434-91961-6, Pub. by Heinemann England). David & Charles.

BUSINESS CORPORATIONS

see Corporations

BUSINESS CORRESPONDENCE

see Commercial Correspondence

BUSINESS CYCLES

see also Business Forecasting; Economic Forecasting; Economic Stabilization

Moore, Geoffrey. Business Cycles, Inflation, & Forecasting. 2nd ed. 488p. 42.50 (ISBN 0-88410-284-X); pap. 19.95 (ISBN 0-88410-285-8). Ballinger Pub.
Paunio, W. W. The Static & the Dynamic Theory of Cycles. (A Managerical & Inventiveness Science Series Book). (Illus.). 109p. 1982. Repr. of 1924 ed. 87.85 (ISBN 0-89901-088-1). Found Class Reprints.

BUSINESS DISTRICTS, CENTRAL

see Central Business Districts

BUSINESS ECONOMICS

see Managerial Economics

BUSINESS EDUCATION

see also Accounting; Bookkeeping; Commercial Law; Penmanship; Secretaries; Shorthand; Typewriting

Hugstad, Paul. Business Schools in the Nineteen Eighties: Liberialism Versus Vocationalism. 172p. 1983. 24.95 (ISBN 0-03-060586-5). Praeger.
McKinnon, William T. Aspects of Modern Business Style. 196p. 1983. pap. 21.00 (ISBN 82-00-06444-1, Universitet). Columbia U Pr.
McNett, Ian, ed. Let's Not Reinvent the Wheel: Profiles of School-Business Collaboration. 72p. (Orig.). 1983. pap. write for info. (ISBN 0-937846-97-X). Inst Educ Lead.
Nadler, Leonard. Critical Events Training Model. LC 81-12840. (Illus.). 368p. 1982. text ed. 18.95 (ISBN 0-686-82104-1). A-W.
Norback & Company, ed. Arco's Guide to Business & Commercial Schools. (Arco Occupational Guides Ser.). 144p. 1983. lib. bdg. 11.95 (ISBN 0-668-05525-1); pap. 6.95 (ISBN 0-668-05533-2). Arco.

BUSINESS ENGLISH

see English Language–Business English

BUSINESS ENTERPRISES

Here are entered works on business concerns as legal entities.

see also Business Tax; Government Business Enterprises; International Business Enterprises; Investments, Foreign; New Business Enterprises

Conn, Charles P. An Uncommon Freedom: The Amway Experience & Why It Grows. 208p. 1983. pap. 2.95 (ISBN 0-425-05870-0). Berkley Pub.
Guroff, Gregory & Carstensen, Fred V. Entrepreneurship in Imperial Russia & the Soviet Union. LC 82-15056. 384p. 1983. 40.00x (ISBN 0-691-05376-6); pap. 12.95 (ISBN 0-691-10141-8). Princeton U Pr.
Jenkins, Michael D. & Sexton, Donald L. Starting & Operating a Business in Texas. 200p. 1983. 27.95 (ISBN 0-686-43310-6, Oasis Pr). Pub Serv Inc.
Jenkins, Michael D. & Warner, Jonathan H. Starting & Operating a Business in Florida. 200p. 1983. 27.95 (ISBN 0-916378-25-X, Oasis Pr). Pub Serv Inc.
Kuriloff, A. & Hemphill, J. How to Start Your Own Business & Succeed. Rev. ed. 1981. 21.95 (ISBN 0-07-035650-5). McGraw.
OECD Staff. International Investment & Multinational Enterprises: Mid-Term Report on the 1976 Declaration & Decisions. 80p. (Orig.). 1982. pap. 6.00 (ISBN 92-64-12349-0). OECD.
Shannon, David A. Southern Business: The Decades Ahead. (ITT Key Issues Lecture Ser.). 123p. 1981. pap. text ed. 6.50 (ISBN 0-672-97877-6). Bobbs.
Smith, Randy B. Setting Up Shop. 288p. 1983. pap. 6.95 (ISBN 0-446-37533-0). Warner Bks.
Update Publicare Research Staff. Boombusinesses U.S.A. Update: Notebook of Back Issues. 35p. 1983. 8.00 (ISBN 0-686-38889-5). Update Pub Co.
Vonkhury, Alexander. Business Speculation: Ideas, Guidelines, Techniques. (Illus., Orig.). lib. bdg. 21.00x (ISBN 0-935402-13-6); pap. 19.00 (ISBN 0-935402-14-4). Intl Comm Serv.

BUSINESS ENTERPRISES–FINANCE

Osgood, William R. Planning & Financing Your Business: A Complete Working Guide. 216p. 1983. 24.95 (ISBN 0-8436-0883-8). CBI Pub.
Paish, F. W. & Briston, R. J. Business Finance. 6th ed. 176p. 1982. 40.00x (ISBN 0-273-01768-3, Pub by Pitman Bks England). State Mutual Bk.

BUSINESS ENTERPRISES–ASIA

Law & Public Enterprise in Asia: Colloquim Report & Papers. 421p. 1976. 15.00 (ISBN 0-275-23000-7). Intl Ctr Law.

BUSINESS ENTERPRISES–GERMANY

German American Chamber of Commerce, ed. American Susidiaries of German Firms: Tochtergesellschaften Deutscher Unternehmen in USA. 15th ed. 250p. (Ger.). 1983. Spiral Bdg. 55.00 (ISBN 0-86640-009-5). German Am Chamber.

BUSINESS ESPIONAGE

see Business Intelligence

BUSINESS ETHICS

see also Business Etiquette; Business Intelligence; Competition; Success; Wealth, Ethics Of

Anderson, James L. & Cohen, Martin. The Competitive Edge. 1982. pap. 3.95 (ISBN 0-553-20358-4). Bantam.
Beauchamp, Tom L. & Bowie, Norman E. Ethical Theory & Business. 2nd ed. 640p. 1983. text ed. 22.95 (ISBN 0-13-290452-7). P-H.
Codes of Ethics in Corporations & Trade Associations & the Teaching of Ethics in Graduate Business Schools. (Opinion Research Corporation Study: No. 65302). 41p. 1.50 (ISBN 0-686-81710-9). Ethics Res Ctr.
Ellin, Joseph & Pritchard, Michael S., eds. Profits & Professional Essays in Business & Professional Ethics. (Contemporary Biomedicine, Ethics, & Society Ser.). 336p. 1983. 29.50 (ISBN 0-89603-039-3). Humana.
Fitzpatrick, M. Louise. Prologue to Professionalism. 320p. 1983. pap. text ed. 15.95 (ISBN 0-89303-773-7). R J Brady.
Lee, Gloria L. Who Gets to the Top? 160p. 1981. text ed. 33.00x (ISBN 0-566-00497-6). Gower Pub Ltd.
Natale, Samuel M. Ethics & Morals in Business. 190p. 1983. text ed. price not set (ISBN 0-89135-036-5). Religious Educ.
Opinion Research Corporation. Implementation & Enforcement Codes of Ethics in Corporations & Associations. (Opinion Research Corporation Study Ser.: No. 65334). 256p. 1980. 17.50 (ISBN 0-686-81711-7). Ethics Res Ctr.
Randolph, Robert M. Thank God It's Monday: How to Turn Work Into an Adventure. LC 82-11926. (Illus.). 249p. 1982. 15.95 (ISBN 0-87624-623-4). Inst Busn Plan.
Smoeyenbos, Milton & Almeder, Robert, eds. Business Ethics: Corporate Values & Society. 400p. 1983. pap. 12.95 (ISBN 0-87975-207-6). Prometheus Bks.
Stockdale, James B. & Hatfield, Mark O. The Ethics of Citizenship. (The Andrew R. Cecil Lectures on Moral Values in a Free Society Ser.: Vol. II). 167p. 1981. 9.95x (ISBN 0-292-72038-6). U of Tex Pr.

BUSINESS ETIQUETTE

De Feldy, L. Elizabeth. Common Sense Etiquette: For Business Women, Wives, Mistresses. (Illus.). 119p. lib. bdg. 15.00x (ISBN 0-935402-15-2); pap. 14.00 (ISBN 0-935402-16-0). Intl Comm Serv.

BUSINESS EXECUTIVES

see Executives

BUSINESS FAILURES

see Bankruptcy; Business Mortality

BUSINESS FORECASTING

Gross & Peterson. Business Forecasting. 2d ed. 1983. text ed. 27.95 (ISBN 0-686-84530-7, BS17); answer bk. avail. (BS18). HM.

Moore, Geoffrey. Business Cycles, Inflation, & Forecasting. 2nd ed. 488p. 42.50 (ISBN 0-88410-284-X); pap. 19.95 (ISBN 0-88410-285-8). Ballinger Pub.

Yavitz, Boris & Newman, William H. Strategy in Action: The Execution, Politics & Payoff of Business Planning. LC 81-71956. 1982. 19.95 (ISBN 0-02-935970-8). Free Pr.

BUSINESS FORECASTING–BIBLIOGRAPHY

Williams, Robert M., ed. UCLA Business Forecast for the Nation & California in 1983: Proceedings of an Annual Conference, December 15, 1982. 1983. 60.00x. UCLA Busn Forecasting.

BUSINESS INSURANCE

see Insurance, Business

BUSINESS INTELLIGENCE

see also Trade Secrets

Godson, Roy, ed. Analysis & Estimates. (Intelligence Requirements for the 1980's: Vol. 2). 224p. 1980. pap. 7.50 (ISBN 0-87855-827-6). Transaction Bks.

--Elements of Intelligence. (Intelligence Requirements for the 1980's: Vol. I). 124p. (Orig.). 1979. pap. 4.95 (ISBN 0-87855-826-8). Transaction Bks.

Heims, Peter. Countering Industrial Espionage. (Illus.). 290p. 1982. text ed. 29.50 (ISBN 0-905961-03-X). Sheridan.

BUSINESS LAW

see also Commercial Law; Forms (Law)

Brown, Gordon W. & Rosenberg, R. Robert. Understanding Business & Personal Law: Performance Guide. 7th ed. (Illus.). 144p. Date not set. pap. text ed. 5.80 (ISBN 0-07-053636-8, G). McGraw.

Coffinberger, Richard L. & Samuels, Linda B. Business & Its Legal Environment: Study Guide & Workbook. 176p. 1983. 8.95 (ISBN 0-13-101022-0). P-H.

Conard, Alfred F. & Knauss, Robert L. Editor's Notes to Enterprise Organization. (University Casebook Ser.). 154p. 1982. pap. text ed. write for info. (ISBN 0-88277-108-6). Foundation Pr.

Dunfee, Thomas W. & Bellace, Janice. Business & Its Legal Environment. (Illus.). 688p. 1983. text ed. 24.95 (ISBN 0-13-101006-9). P-H.

Fisher, Bruce D. & Phillips, Michael J. The Legal Environment of Business. (Illus.). 850p. 1982. text ed. 22.95 (ISBN 0-314-63172-0); write for info. study guide (ISBN 0-314-71141-4). West Pub.

Gilliam, George H. Business Entities: A Virginia Law Practice System. 350p. 1982. 75.00 (ISBN 0-87215-509-9). Michie-Bobbs.

Goldschmid, H. J. Business Disclosure: Government's Need to Know. 1979. 39.95 (ISBN 0-07-023670-4). McGraw.

Goldstein, Arnold S. EMS & the Law: A Legal Handbook for EMS Personnel. (Illus.). 224p. 1983. 16.95 (ISBN 0-89303-423-1); pap. 9.95 (ISBN 0-89303-422-3). R J Brady.

--The Small Business Legal Problem-Solver. 240p. 1983. 24.95 (ISBN 0-8436-0890-0); pap. 15.95 (ISBN 0-8436-0891-9). CBI Pub.

Henn, Harry G. Handbook of the Laws of Corporations & Other Business Enterprises. 3rd ed. LC 82-23695. (Hornbook Ser.). 1167p. 1983. text ed. write for info. (ISBN 0-314-69870-1). West Pub.

--Handbook on the Laws of Corporations & Other Business Enterprises. 3rd ed. (Handbook Ser.). 1267p. 1983. text ed. write for info. (ISBN 0-314-74292-1). West Pub.

How to Proceed in Business--Legally. 1982. pap. write for info. P-H.

Litka, Michael P. & Inman, James E. Legal Environment of Business: Public & Private Laws. 3rd ed. 1983. text ed. 25.95 (ISBN 0-471-87455-8); study guide 11.95 (ISBN 0-471-89869-4). Wiley.

Rodes, Robert E., Jr. The Legal Enterprise. 1983. price not set. U of Notre Dame Pr.

Rodriguez, Edward J. & Santoro, Anthony. The Law of Doing Business in Connecticut. 320p. 1983. write for info. (ISBN 0-88063-011-6). Butterworth Legal Pubs.

Steingold, Fred. Legal Master Guide for Small Business. 242p. 1983. 21.95 (ISBN 0-13-528422-8); pap. 9.95 (ISBN 0-13-528414-7). P-H.

Understanding Business & Consumer Law. 7th ed. 576p. 1983. 14.80 (ISBN 0-07-053635-X, G). Supplementary materials avail. McGraw.

White, Nelson H. Magick & the Law: Vol. 5, or How to Set-Up & Operate Your Own Occult Shop. LC 80-50273. (Illus.). 75p. (Orig.). 1982. pap. 10.00 (ISBN 0-939856-31-X). Tech Group.

BUSINESS LETTERS

see Commercial Correspondence

BUSINESS LIBRARIES

see also Information Storage and Retrieval Systems–Business

Campbell, Malcolm J. Case Studies in Business Information Provision. 204p. 1983. price not set (ISBN 0-85157-353-3, Pub. by Bingley England). Shoe String.

BUSINESS LITERATURE SEARCHING

see Information Storage and Retrieval Systems–Business

BUSINESS MACHINES

see Calculating-Machines; Electronic Office Machines; Office Equipment and Supplies

BUSINESS MATHEMATICS

see also Business–Mathematical Models

also subdivision Tables, etc. under economic subjects; also subdivision Tables and Ready-Reckoners under names of industries

Berenson, Mark L. & Levine, David M. Basic Business Statistics: Concepts & Applications. 2nd ed. (Illus.). 752p. 1983. text ed. 25.95 (ISBN 0-13-057620-4); study gd. & wkbk. 8.95. P-H.

Budnick, Frank S. Applied Mathematics for Business, Economics & the Social Sciences. 2nd ed. 842p. 1983. 26.50x (ISBN 0-07-008858-6); write for info. (ISBN 0-07-008859-4). McGraw.

Curtis. Practical Math for Business: 3-e. 1983. pap. text ed. 16.95 (ISBN 0-686-84525-0); Instr's. annotated ed. 17.95 (ISBN 0-686-84526-9). HM.

Duenas. Curso Basico de Matematicas Comerciales. 172p. 1982. 4.56 (ISBN 0-07-017994-8, G). McGraw.

Ellis, John T. & Beam, Victoria R. Mastering Real Estate Math in One Day. 1983. pap. 7.95 (ISBN 0-13-559666-1). P-H.

Fowler, F. Parker, Jr. Basic Mathematics for Administration. 358p. 1983. text ed. price not set (ISBN 0-89874-613-2). Krieger.

Fowler, Frank P. & Sandberg, E. W. Basic Mathematics for Administration. LC 62-15189. 339p. 1962. text ed. 26.95x (ISBN 0-471-26976-X); supp. mat. avail. (ISBN 0-471-26978-6); test avail. (ISBN 0-471-26985-9). Wiley.

Gaines, George, Jr. & Coleman, David S. Real Estate Math. 145p. (Orig.). 1980. pap. text ed. 8.95 (ISBN 0-89787-902-3). Gorsuch Scarisbrick.

Peterson, D. Mathematics for Business Decisions. 320p. 1983. 11.80x (ISBN 0-07-049620-X); write for info. instr's manual & key (ISBN 0-07-049621-8). McGraw.

Stafford, L. W. Business Mathematics. 400p. 1981. 25.00x (ISBN 0-7121-0282-5, Pub. by Macdonald & Evans). State Mutual Bk.

Tuttle, Michael D. Practical Business Math: A Performance Approach. 3rd ed. 475p. 1982. pap. text ed. write for info. (ISBN 0-697-08187-7); instrs.' manual avail. (ISBN 0-697-08188-5). Wm C Brown.

Wilton, W. B. A-Z of Business Mathematics. 192p. 1980. pap. 12.50 (ISBN 0-434-92260-9, Pub. by Heinemann). David & Charles.

BUSINESS MEN

see Businessmen

BUSINESS MERGERS

see Consolidation and Merger of Corporations

BUSINESS MORTALITY

see also Bankruptcy

Bryer, R. A. & Brignal, T. J. Accounting for British Steel: A Financial Analysis of the Failure of BSC. 303p. 1982. text ed. 37.50x (ISBN 0-686-82418-0). Gower Pub Ltd.

Oshry, Barry. Success of a Business-Failure of Its Partners. (Notes on Power Ser.). (Orig.). 1980. pap. 3.50 (ISBN 0-910411-07-7). Power & Sys.

BUSINESS PATRONAGE OF THE ARTS

see Art Patronage

BUSINESS PSYCHOLOGY

see Psychology, Industrial

BUSINESS RECORDS

see also Business–Forms, Blanks, etc.;

also specific types of business records, e.g. Financial Statements; Inventories

Copeland, Tom, ed. Basic Guide to Record Keeping & Taxes. 5th rev. ed. (Business Ideas for Family Day Care Providers Ser.). (Illus.). 40p. (Orig.). 1982. pap. 4.50 (ISBN 0-934140-07-3). Toys N Things.

Daniel, Wayne W. & Terrell, James C. Business Statistics: Basic Concepts & Methodology. LC 82-83254. 832p. 1982. text ed. 26.95 (ISBN 0-395-32601-X); write for info. instr's. resource manual (ISBN 0-395-32602-8); study guide 10.95 (ISBN 0-395-32603-6). HM.

Fritz, N. & Wirth, R. H. Supersonic Sounds: A Business Record-Keeping Practice Set. 3rd ed. 1981. text ed. 5.96 (ISBN 0-07-022562-1); tchr's manual & key avail. McGraw.

Thomas, Violet S. & Schubert, Dexter R. Records Management: Systems & Administration. 416p. 1983. text ed. 20.95 (ISBN 0-471-09094-8); write for info. (ISBN 0-471-89473-7). Wiley.

BUSINESS-REPLY MAIL

see Postal Service

BUSINESS REPORT WRITING

Baxter, Carol. Business Report Writing. 392p. 1983. text ed. 20.95x (ISBN 0-534-01392-9). Kent Pub Co.

DiGaetani, John L. & DiGaetani, Jane B. Writing out Loud: A Self-Help Guide to Clear Business Writing. LC 82-73623. 190p. 1983. 12.95 (ISBN 0-87094-374-X). Dow Jones-Irwin.

Ewing, David W. Writing for Results in Business, Government, the Sciences & the Professions. 2nd ed. LC 79-11756. 448p. 1979. 24.95 (ISBN 0-471-05036-9). Wiley.

Handy, Ralph S. & Cronk, Louise H. Handbook for Transcribers & Style Manual for Business Writers. Rev. ed. (Illus.). 104p. 1977. pap. text ed. 4.20 (ISBN 0-686-38129-7). Morrison Pub Co.

Hatch, Richard A. Business Writing. 528p. 1983. pap. text ed. write for info. (ISBN 0-574-20665-5, 13-3665); write for info. instr's. guide (ISBN 0-574-20666-3, 13-3666). SRA.

Lewis, Philip V. & Baker, William H. Business Report Writing. 2nd ed. LC 82-15436. (Grid Series in Business Communications). 350p. 1983. text ed. 25.95 (ISBN 0-88244-257-0). Grid Pub.

Markel, Michael H. & Lucier, R. J. Make Your Point: A Guide to Improving Your Business & Technical Writing. (Illus.). 156p. 1983. 12.95 (ISBN 0-13-547760-3); pap. 5.95 (ISBN 0-13-547752-2). P-H.

Rutkoskie, Alice E. & Murphree, Carolyn T. Effective Writing for Business: An Analytical Approach. 1983. 15.95 (ISBN 0-675-20049-0). Additional supplements may be obtained from publisher. Merrill.

Sussams, John. How To Write Effective Reports. 160p. 1983. 19.95 (ISBN 0-89397-145-6). Nichols Pub.

Swenson, Dan H. Business Reporting: A Management Tool. 448p. 1983. text ed. write for info. (ISBN 0-574-20675-2, 13-3675); write for info. instr's. guide (ISBN 0-574-20676-0, 13-3676). SRA.

BUSINESS RESEARCH

see Economic Research

BUSINESS SECRETS

see Trade Secrets

BUSINESS STABILIZATION

see Economic Stabilization

BUSINESS TAX

see also Licenses

Copeland, Tom, ed. Basic Guide to Record Keeping & Taxes. 5th rev. ed. (Business Ideas for Family Day Care Providers Ser.). (Illus.). 40p. (Orig.). 1982. pap. 4.50 (ISBN 0-934140-07-3). Toys N Things.

Tax Study Six: U. S. Tax Aspects of Doing Business Abroad. 1983. write for info. Am Inst CPA.

BUSINESSMEN

Honeyman, Katrina. Origins of Enterprise: Business Leadership in the Industrial Revolution. LC 82-10441. 180p. 1982. 20.00x (ISBN 0-312-58848-8). St Martin.

Ingham, John N. Biographical Dictionary of American Business Leaders. 2 vols. LC 82-6113. 2496p. 1983. lib. bdg. 195.00 (ISBN 0-313-21362-3, HC102). Greenwood.

Thomas, J. B. Shop Boy: An Autobiography. 182p. 1983. 13.95 (ISBN 0-7100-9347-0). Routledge & Kegan.

BUSINESSMEN–CORRESPONDENCE, REMINISCENCES, ETC.

Keplinger, H. F. Without Fear or Favor. Date not set. 19.95 (ISBN 0-87201-917-9). Gulf Pub.

BUSINESSMEN, AFRO-AMERICAN

see Afro-Americans in Business

BUSINESSWOMEN

see Women in Business

BUSING OF SCHOOL CHILDREN

see School Children–Transportation

BUSY WORK

see Creative Activities and Seatwork

BUTLER, JOSEPH, BP. OF DURHAM, 1692-1752

Butler, Joseph. Five Sermons. Darwell, Stephen, ed. (HPC Philosophical Classics Ser.). 88p. 1983. pap. text ed. 3.95 (ISBN 0-915145-61-8). Hackett Pub.

BUTLER, WILLIAM FRANCIS, SIR, 1838-1910

Butler, R. A. The Art of the Possible. (Illus.). 288p. 1983. Repr. of 1971 ed. 24.95 (ISBN 0-241-10896-9, Pub. by Hamish Hamilton England). David & Charles.

BUTOR, MICHEL

Hirsch, Marianne. Beyond the Single Version: Henry James, Michael Butor, Uwe Johnson. 18.00 (ISBN 0-917786-21-1). French Lit.

BUTTERFLIES

E. W. Classey Ltd., ed. Butterflies of the Oriental Region. 288p. 1982. 155.00x (ISBN 0-686-82393-1, Pub. by E W Classey England). State Mutual Bk.

--The Leipodoptera of America North of Mexico. 1982. 135.00x (ISBN 0-86096-016-1, Pub. by E W Classey England). State Mutual Bk.

Eliot, J. N. & Kawazoe, A. Blue Butterflies of the Lycaenopsis-group. (Illus.). 300p. 1983. 62.50x (ISBN 0-565-00860-9, Pub. by Brit Mus Nat Hist England). Sabbot-Natural Hist Bks.

Riley. A Field Guide to the Butterflies of the West Indies. 27.95 (0686427866, Collins Pub England). Greene.

BUTTERFLIES–AFRICA

Carcasson. The Butterflies of Africa. 29.95 (ISBN 0-686-42747-5, Collins Pub England). Greene.

BUTTERFLIES–EUROPE

Higgins & Riley. A Field Guide to the Butterflies of Britain & Europe. 29.95 (ISBN 0-686-42783-1, Collins Pub England). Greene.

Tweedie & Wilkinson. The Butterflies & Moths of Britain & Europe. pap. 8.95 (ISBN 0-686-42746-7, Collins Pub England). Greene.

BUTTERFLIES–GREAT BRITAIN

Eliot, J. N. & Kawazoe, A. Blue Butterflies of the Lycaenopsis-group. (Illus.). 300p. 1983. 62.50x (ISBN 0-565-00860-9, Pub. by Brit Mus Nat Hist England). Sabbot-Natural Hist Bks.

Higgins & Riley. A Field Guide to the Butterflies of Britain & Europe. 29.95 (ISBN 0-686-42783-1, Collins Pub England). Greene.

Tweedie & Wilkinson. The Butterflies & Moths of Britain & Europe. pap. 8.95 (ISBN 0-686-42746-7, Collins Pub England). Greene.

BUTTERFLIES–NEW ZEALAND

Gibbs, George W. New Zealand Butterflies. (Illus.). 208p. 1983. 45.00 (ISBN 0-00-216955-X, Pub. by W Collins Australia). Intl Schol Bk Serv.

BUYERS' GUIDES

see Consumer Education; Marketing (Home Economics); Shopping;

also subdivision directories under particular lines of business industry

BUYING

see Purchasing

BUYING, AUTOMOBILE

see Automobile Purchasing

BUYING, INDUSTRIAL

see Industrial Procurement

BY-PRODUCTS

see Waste Products

BYRD, HARRY FLOYD, 1887-1966

Heinemann, Ronald L. Depression & New Deal in Virginia: The Enduring Dominion. LC 82-13487. 1983. write for info. (ISBN 0-8139-0946-5). U Pr of Va.

BYRON, GEORGE GORDON NOEL BYRON, 6TH BARON, 1788-1824

Cunningham, John. The Poetics of Byron's Comedy in Don Juan. (Salzburg - Romantic Reassessment Ser.: No. 106). 242p. 1982. pap. text ed. 25.00x (ISBN 0-391-02778-6, Pub. by Salzburg Austria). Humanities.

Gilles, Maria V. Byrons Dramen. 151p. (Ger.). 1982. write for info. (ISBN 3-8204-5818-2). P Lang Pubs.

Trelaway, John E. Records of Shelley, Byron. 1983. pap. 4.95 (ISBN 0-14-043088-1). Penguin.

BYZANTINE ART

see Art, Byzantine

BYZANTINE EMPIRE–HISTORY

Justinian the Great: The Emperor & Saint. LC 82-82095. (Illus.). 1982. 14.50 (ISBN 0-914744-58-5); pap. 9.50 (ISBN 0-914744-59-3). Inst Byzantine.

Treadgold, Warren T. The Byzantine State Finances in the Eighth & Ninth Centuries. (East European Monographs: No. 121). 280p. 1982. 22.50x (ISBN 0-88033-014-7). East Eur Quarterly.

C

C ALGEBRAS

C-Bundles & Compact Transformation Groups. LC 82-11544. (Memoirs of the American Mathematical Society Ser.: No. 269). 4.00 (ISBN 0-8218-2269-1, MEMO/269). Am Math.

CABALA

see also Occult Sciences; Symbolism of Numbers

Gray, William G. Concepts of Qabalah. (The Sangreal Sodality Ser.: Vol.3). Date not set. pap. price not set (ISBN 0-87728-561-6). Weiser.

Sassoon, George. The Kabbalah Decoded. Dale, Rodney, ed. 240p. 1978. pap. 9.95 (ISBN 0-7156-1289-1). US Games Syst.

CABBALA

see Cabala

CABINET-WORK

see also Furniture Making; Kitchen Cabinets; Woodwork

Cary, Jere. Building Your Own Kitchen Cabinets. (Illus.). 1983. pap. 11.95 (ISBN 0-918804-15-9). Taunton.

Feirer. Furniture & Cabinet Making. 1983. price not set (ISBN 0-87002-388-8). Bennett Il.

CABLE TELEVISION

see Community Antenna Television; Television Relay Systems

CABLES, ELECTRIC

see Telephone Cables

CACTUS

Barthlott, W. Cacti: Botanical Aspects, Descriptions & Cultivations. Glass, Lois, tr. 384p. 1979. 40.00x (ISBN 0-85950-416-6, Pub. by Thornes England). State Mutual Bk.

CADASTRAL SURVEYS

see Real Property

CAESAR, C. JULIUS, 100 B.C.-44 B.C.

Busch, Walter. Casarismuskritik und Epische Historik. xv, 415p. (Ger.). 1982. write for info. (ISBN 3-8204-6266-X). P Lang Pubs.

CAESAREAN SECTION

see Cesarean Section

CAFES

see Hotels, Taverns, etc.; Restaurants, Lunchrooms, etc.

CAFETERIAS, ETC.

see Restaurants, Lunchrooms, etc.

CAFFEINE

American Health Research Institute, Ltd. Caffeine: A Medical & Scientific Subject Analysis & Research Index with Bibliography. Bartone, John C., ed. 120p. 1983. 29.95 (ISBN 0-941864-95-2); pap. 21.95 (ISBN 0-941864-94-4). ABBE Pubs Assn.

Goulart, Frances S. Caffeine. 240p. (Orig.). 1983. pap. 2.95 (ISBN 0-446-30581-2). Warner Bks.

CAGE, JOHN

Griffiths, Paul. Cage. (Oxford Studies of Composers). (Illus.). 56p. (Orig.). 1981. pap. 9.95 (ISBN 0-19-315450-1). Oxford U Pr.

CAIN

Coma, Anthony S. Dry Ice. 1982. 6.50 (ISBN 0-8062-1970-X). Carlton.

Kryskill, William. Check Out. 6.95 (ISBN 0-8062-1878-9). Carlton.

Standifer, Billie J. Cain: The Neolithic Link. 1982. 8.75 (ISBN 0-8062-1937-8). Carlton.

CAJUNS

Stiles, Beryl S. Cajun Odyssey: From Nova Scotia to Louisiana... with Love. (Illus.). 200p. 1982. pap. 8.99 (ISBN 0-686-37651-X). Thomson-Shore.

CAKE

see also Cake Decorating; Cookies; Pastry

Monroe, Elvira. Say Cheesecake & Smile. LC 80-54453. 168p. 1981. pap. 5.95 (ISBN 0-933174-11-X). Wide World-Tetra.

Sullivan, Marilynn C. & Sullivan, Eugene T., eds. Celebrate! Wedding Cakes. (Illus.). 192p. 1983. 12.95 (ISBN 0-912696-23-0). Wilton.

CAKE DECORATING

Farm Journal. Farm Journal's Complete Cake Decorating Book. LC 82-45540. (Illus.). 160p. 1983. 15.95 (ISBN 0-385-18376-3). Doubleday.

Lambeth, Joseph. Lambeth Method of Cake Decoration & Practical Pastries. (Illus.). 1980. 55.00x (ISBN 0-911202-24-2). Radio City.

CALAMITIES

see Disasters

CALCIUM

Godfraind, T. & Albertini, A., eds. Calcium Modulators: Proceedings of the International Symposium on Calcium Modulators, Venice, June 17-18, 1982. (Giovanni Lorenzini Foundation Ser.: Vol. 15). 380p. 1982. 68.00 (ISBN 0-444-80464-1, Biomedical Pr). Elsevier.

CALCIUM IN THE BODY

see also Calcium Metabolism

Anghileri, Leopold J. & Tuffet-Anghileri, Anne M., eds. The Role of Calcium in Biological Systems, Vol. I. 288p. 1982. 81.00 (ISBN 0-8493-6280-6). CRC Pr.

Heath & Marx. Calcium Disorders vs Clinical Endocrine Health. 1982. text ed. 59.95 (ISBN 0-407-02273-2). Butterworth.

CALCIUM METABOLISM

Campbell, Anthony K. Intracellular Calcium: Its Universal Role As Regulator. (Monographs in Molecular Biophysics & Biochemistry). 540p. 1983. write for info. (ISBN 0-471-10488-4, Pub. by Wiley-Interscience). Wiley.

CALCULATING-MACHINES

Here are entered works on calculators, as well as all mechanical computers of pre-1945 vintage. Works on modern electronic computers first developed after 1945 are entered under Computers.

see also Computation Laboratories; Computers; Cybernetics; Digital Counters; Programmable Calculators; Slide-Rule

Blackwell, Wayne W. Chemical Process Design on a Programmable Calculator. (Illus.). 416p. 1983. 32.95 (ISBN 0-07-005545-9, P&RB). McGraw.

Horsburgh, E. M., ed. Handbook of the Napier Tercentary Celebration or Modern Instruments & Methods of Calculation. (The Charles Babbage Institute Reprint Series for the History of Computing: Vol. 3). (Illus.). 1982. Repr. of 1914 ed. write for info. ltd. ed. (ISBN 0-938228-10-2). Tomash Pubs.

Saks, Mark. The Calculator Cookbook: Maximizing the Computational Power of Your Hand-Held Calculator. 320p. 1983. 22.95 (ISBN 0-13-110395-4); pap. 10.95 (ISBN 0-13-110387-3). P-H.

CALCULATING-MACHINES–JUVENILE LITERATURE

Michunas, Lynn. Kalculator Kids. (gr. 3-7). 1982. 5.95 (ISBN 0-86653-076-2, GA 410). Good Apple.

CALCULATING-MACHINES, ELECTRONIC

see Computers

CALCULATORS

see Calculating-Machines

CALCULATORS, PROGRAMMABLE

see Programmable Calculators

CALCULI, BILIARY

Dowling, R. H. & Hofmann, A. F. The Medical Treatment of Gallstones. 400p. 1982. text ed. write for info. (ISBN 0-85200-206-8, Pub. by MTP Pr England). Kluwer Boston.

Hofmann, Alan F. & Huebner, Vicky L. Bile, Bile Acid, Gallstones & Gallstone Dissolution. 340p. 1982. text ed. 39.00 (ISBN 0-85200-497-4, Pub. by MTP Pr England). Kluwer Boston.

CALCULI, URINARY

Chaussy, C., et al. Extracorporeal Shock Wave Lithotripsy. (Illus.). viii, 112p. 1982. pap. 36.00 (ISBN 3-8055-3620-8). S Karger.

CALCULUS

see also Differential Equations; Functions; Harmonic Analysis; Mathematical Analysis; Nonlinear Theories; Surfaces

Allen, G. D. & Chui, Charles K. Elements of Calculus. LC 82-12874. (Mathematics Ser.). 512p. 1983. text ed. 24.95 (ISBN 0-534-01188-8). Brooks-Cole.

Amazigo, John C. Advanced Calculus & Its Applications to the Engineering & Physical Sciences. LC 80-283. 407p. 1980. text ed. 26.95x (ISBN 0-471-04934-4). Wiley.

Anton, Howard. Calculus with Analytic Geometry. brief edition ed. LC 81-50266. 854p. 1981. text ed. 25.50 (ISBN 0-471-09443-9). Wiley.

--Calculus with Analytic Geometry. LC 79-11469. 1980. 33.95 (ISBN 0-471-03248-4); solution manual 11.95 (ISBN 0-471-04498-9). Wiley.

Apostol, T. M. Calculus: One-Variable Calculus with an Introduction to Linear Algebra, Vol. 1. 2nd ed. LC 73-20899. 666p. 1967. text ed. 30.95x (ISBN 0-471-00005-1). Wiley.

Applications of Calculus: A Workbook to Accompany Salas-Hillel. 206p. pap. 8.95 (ISBN 0-471-04852-6). Krieger.

Blakeley, Walter R. Calculus for Engineering Technology. LC 67-29017. 441p. 1968. text ed. 23.95 (ISBN 0-471-07931-6). Wiley.

Caratheodory, Constantin. Calculus of Variations & Partial Differential Equations of the First Order. 2nd ed. Brandstatter, Julius J., tr. from Ger. LC 81-71519. (Illus.). 421p. 1982. text ed. 25.00 (ISBN 0-8284-0318-X). Chelsea Pub.

Fulks, Watson. Advanced Calculus: An Introduction to Analysis. 3rd ed. LC 78-5268. 731p. 1978. text ed. 31.95 (ISBN 0-471-02195-4); avail. solutions (ISBN 0-471-05125-X). Wiley.

Larson, Roland E. & Hostetler, Robert P. Brief Calculus with Applications. 736p. Date not set. text ed. 23.95 (ISBN 0-669-04803-8). Heath.

Rice, Bernard & Strange, Jerry. Technical Math with Calculus. 1983. text ed. write for info. (ISBN 0-87150-376-X, 2801). Prindle.

Salas, S. L. & Hille, E. Calculus: One & Several Variables with Analytic Geometry, Pt. 1 & 2. 4th ed. 671p. 1982. text ed. 26.95 (ISBN 0-471-08055-1); student supp. 12.95 (ISBN 0-471-05383-X). Wiley.

Sherlock, A. J. & Roebuck, E. M. Calculus: Pure & Applied. 544p. 1982. pap. text ed. 16.95 (ISBN 0-7131-3446-1). E Arnold.

Tarasov, L. V. Calculus: Basic Concepts for High Schools. 184p. 1982. pap. 3.50 (ISBN 0-8285-2278-2, Pub. by Mir Pubs USSR). Imported Pubns.

Trim, Donald W. Calculus & Analytic Geometry. LC 82-16287. (Illus.). 960p. 1983. text ed. write for info. (ISBN 0-201-16270-9). A-W.

CALCULUS, DIFFERENTIAL

Nachbin, Leopoldo. Introduction to Functional Analysis: Banach Spaces & Different Calculus. (Pure & Applied Mathematics: Monographs & Textbooks: Vol. 60). (Illus.). 184p. 1981. 19.75 (ISBN 0-8247-6984-8). Dekker.

CALCULUS OF DIFFERENCES

see Difference Equations

CALCULUS OF VARIATIONS

see also Functional Analysis

Friedman, A. Variational Principles & Free-Boundary Problems. (Pure & Applied Mathematics Ser.). 710p. 1982. text ed. 52.50x (ISBN 0-471-86849-3, Pub. by Wiley-Interscience). Wiley.

Griffiths, P. Exterior Differential Systems & the Calculus of Variations. (Progress in Mathematics Ser.: Vol. 25). 349p. 1982. text ed. 30.00 (ISBN 3-7643-3103-8). Birkhauser.

CALDER, ALEXANDER, 1898-1976

Wattenmaker, Richard J. & Young, Christopher R. Alexander Calder. (Illus.). 48p. (Orig.). 1983. pap. 5.50 (ISBN 0-939896-05-2). Flint Inst Arts.

CALDERON DE LA BARCA, PEDRO, 1600-1681

Aycock, Wendell M. & Cravens, Sydney P., eds. Calderon de la Barca at the Tercentenary: Comparative Views, Vol. 14. LC 82-80309. (Proceedings of the Comparative Literature Symposium: Vol. 14). 195p. 1982. pap. 24.95 (ISBN 0-89672-101-9). Tex Tech Pr.

CALENDARS

see also Almanacs; Devotional Calendars

Monaco, James. The French Revolutionary Calendar. (Illus.). 32p. 1982. pap. 5.95 (ISBN 0-918432-43-X). NY Zoetrope.

CALHOUN, JOHN CALDWELL, 1782-1850

Lander, Ernest M., Jr. The Calhoun Family & Thomas Green Clemson: The Decline of a Southern Patriarch. LC 82-13568. 221p. 1983. 17.95 (ISBN 0-87249-413-6). U of SC Pr.

CALIFORNIA

see also names of cities, regions, etc. in California, e.g. San Francisco; Death Valley

Cernuda, Ralph & Lawson, Greg, photos by. California. (Illus.). 72p. (Orig., Eng., Span., Fr., Ger., Jap.). 1983. pap. 8.95 (ISBN 0-9606704-6-7). First Choice.

Jencks, Lance. The Wisdom of Southern California. 68p. (Orig.). 1982. pap. 5.95 (ISBN 0-9609678-1-8). Lindenhof Pr.

Stark, Leland A., ed. How to Live & Die with California Probate. pap. 9.95 (ISBN 0-87201-095-3). Gulf Pub.

CALIFORNIA–ANTIQUITIES

Padon, Beth, compiled by. Archaelogical Reports & Manuscripts on File at UCLA: Los Angeles, Ventura, & Orange Counties. (Occasional Papers: No. 10). 162p. 1982. pap. 8.00 (ISBN 0-917956-37-0). UCLA Arch.

Reece, Daphne. Historic Houses of California. (Illus.). 192p. (Orig.). 1983. pap. 7.95 (ISBN 0-87701-199-0). Chronicle Bks.

Sanburg, Delmer E., Jr. & Mulligan, F. K. The Archaeology of Two Northern California Sites. (Monograph Ser.: No. XXII). (Illus.). 90p. 1982. pap. 8.50 (ISBN 0-917956-41-9). UCLA Arch.

Van Tilburg, JoAnne. Ancient Images on Stone: Rock Art of the Californians. LC 82-84337. (Illus.). 128p. 1983. pap. 20.00 (ISBN 0-917956-40-0). UCLA Arch.

CALIFORNIA–BIOGRAPHY

Hafen, LeRoy R. & Hafen, Ann W., eds. The Utah Expedition, 1857-1858: A Documentary Account. LC 58-11786. (Far West & Rockies Ser.: Vol.VIII). (Illus.). 375p. 1983. Repr. of 1958 ed. 27.50 (ISBN 0-87062-035-5). A H Clark.

Holmes, Kenneth L., ed. Covered Wagon Women: Diaries & Letters from the Western Trails, 1840-1890. LC 82-72586. (Covered Wagon Women Ser.). (Illus.). 280p. 1983. 25.00 (ISBN 0-87062-146-7). A H Clark.

Phelps, William D. Alta California, 1840-1842: The Journal & Observations of William Dane Phelps. Busch, Briton C, ed. LC 82-71376. (Western Lands & Water Ser.: XIII). (Illus.). 364p. 1983. 29.50 (ISBN 0-87062-143-2). A H Clark.

CALIFORNIA–DESCRIPTION AND TRAVEL

Bristow, Linda. Bed & Breakfast: California. (Illus.). 180p. 1983. pap. 7.95 (ISBN 0-87701-196-6). Chronicle Bks.

Chapin, J. & Messick, R. California: People of a Region. 4th ed. (Our Nation, Our World Ser.). 288p. 1984. text ed. 18.48 (ISBN 0-07-010561-8); tchr's ed. 21.76 (ISBN 0-07-010562-6); blackline masters 7.20 (ISBN 0-07-010563-4). McGraw.

De Salvatierra, Juan M. Selected Letters about California. Burrus, Ernest J., tr. (Baja California Travel Ser.: No. 25). 280p. 1971. 24.00 (ISBN 0-686-84003-8). Dawsons.

Magary, Alan & Magary, Kirsten. South of San Francisco. LC 82-48520. 192p. (Orig.). 1983. pap. 5.72i (ISBN 0-06-091035-6, CN 1035, CN). Har-Row.

Moore, Kristin. Gold Country: A Pictorial Guide Through California's Historic Mother Lode. (Illus., Orig.). 1983. pap. 12.95 (ISBN 0-87701-247-4). Chronicle Bks.

Tigerman, Stanley & Lewin, Susan Grant. The California Condition: A Pregnant Architecture. Adler, Sebastian J., frwd. by. LC 82-83257. (Illus.). 104p. (Orig.). pap. 14.85 (ISBN 0-934418-15-2). La Jolla Mus Contemp Art.

Weaver, Harriet. Redwood Country: A Pictorial Guide Through California's Magnificent Redwood Forests. rev. ed. (Illus., Orig.). 1983. pap. 8.95 (ISBN 0-87701-279-2). Chronicle Bks.

CALIFORNIA–DESCRIPTION AND TRAVEL–GUIDEBOOKS

Beck, Dawn. Where To Go Dancing in Silicon Valley. LC 82-61728. 96p. 1982. pap. 4.95 (ISBN 0-9609740-0-8). Sharain Bks.

California. 1982. 8.95 (ISBN 0-933692-16-1). R Collings.

California Coastal Commission. The California Coastal Access Guide: Anniversary Ed. LC 82-45905. (Illus.). 285p. 25.00 (ISBN 0-520-04984-5). U of Cal Pr.

California Travel Guide. (Berlitz Travel Guides). (Illus.). 1982. pap. 4.95 (ISBN 0-02-969750-6, Berlitz). Macmillan.

Camaro editors. Old California: Almanac of Fairs & Festivals. (Old California Ser.: No. 1). (Illus.). 1983. pap. 3.95 (ISBN 0-913290-43-2). Camaro Pub.

--Old California: Art, Theater, & Museums. (Old California Ser.: No. 10). (Illus.). 1983. pap. 3.95 (ISBN 0-913290-51-3). Camaro Pub.

--Old California: Camping Sites, Campgrounds, & Recreation Areas. (Old California Ser.: No. 7). (Illus.). 1983. pap. 3.95 (ISBN 0-913290-48-3). Camaro Pub.

--Old California: Christmastime, Mountain Recreation, & Romantic Hide-a-Ways. (Old California Ser.: No. 12). (Illus.). 1983. pap. 3.95 (ISBN 0-913290-53-X). Camaro Pub.

--Old California: Country Inns & Historic Hotels. (Old California Ser.: No. 4). (Illus.). 1983. pap. 3.95 (ISBN 0-913290-45-9). Camaro Pub.

--Old California for Children: Picnic Spots, Haunted Houses, & Ghost Towns. (Old California Ser.: No. 6). (Illus.). 1983. pap. 3.95 (ISBN 0-913290-47-5). Camaro Pub.

--Old California: Gold Mines, Gold Mining Towns, & Country Stores. (Old California Ser.: No. 8). (Illus.). 1983. pap. 3.95 (ISBN 0-913290-49-1). Camaro Pub.

--Old California: Historical Restaurants, Wineries, & Wine Tasting. (Old California Ser.: No. 3). (Illus.). 1983. pap. 3.95 (ISBN 0-913290-44-0). Camaro Pub.

--Old California: Historical Sights & Scenic Backroads. (Old California Ser.: No. 9). (Illus.). 1983. pap. 3.95 (ISBN 0-913290-50-5). Camaro Pub.

--Old California: Visitors Guide. (Old California Ser.: No. 5). (Illus.). 1983. pap. 3.95 (ISBN 0-913290-46-7). Camaro Pub.

Chester, Carole. California & the Golden West. LC 82-61197. (Pocket Guide Ser.). (Illus.). 1983. pap. 4.95 (ISBN 0-528-84894-1). Rand.

Foster, Lee. Making the Most of the Peninsula: A California Guide to San Mateo, Santa Clara, & Santa Cruz Counties. (Illus.). 304p. (Orig.). 1983. pap. 8.95 (ISBN 0-89141-164-X). Presidio Pr.

How to Be a Total Californian. 1982. 4.95 (ISBN 0-933692-25-0). R Collings.

Levin, Bella & Whelan, Dan. City Guide, 1983: San Francisco Bay Area & Northern California. (Illus.). 312p. (Orig.). 1982. pap. 4.95 (ISBN 0-940562-10-3). Danella Pubns.

--Cityguide, Southern California: 1982-83. (Illus.). 208p. (Orig.). 1982. pap. 4.95 (ISBN 0-940562-05-7). Belldan Pubns.

Linkhart, Luther. The Trinity Alps: A Hiking & Backpacking Guide. Winnett, Thomas, ed. (Illus.). 192p. 1983. pap. 9.95 (ISBN 0-89997-024-9). Wilderness Pr.

McAuley, Milt. Hiking Trails of Malibu Creek State Park (Santa Monica Mountains) LC 82-74274. (Illus.). 112p. 1983. pap. 5.95 (ISBN 0-942568-04-4). Canyon Pub Co.

McDermott, John W. How to Get Lost & Found in California & Other Lovely Places. 1982. 9.95 (ISBN 0-686-37621-8). Orafa Pub Co.

McKinney, John. California Coastal Trails: Mexican Border to Big Sur, Vol. I. (Illus.). 240p. (Orig.). 1983. pap. 8.95 (ISBN 0-88496-198-2). Capra Pr.

Pomada, Elizabeth. Places to Go with Children in Northern California. LC 80-10140. (Illus.). 160p. (Orig.). 1981. pap. 5.95 (ISBN 0-87701-210-5). Chronicle Bks.

Rankin, Jake & Rankin, Marni. The Getaway Guide IV: Short Vacations in Southern California. LC 82-19060. (Illus.). 248p. (Orig.). 1983. pap. 9.95 (ISBN 0-686-43071-9). Pacific Search.

Reece, Daphne. Historic Houses of California. (Illus.). 192p. (Orig.). 1983. pap. 7.95 (ISBN 0-87701-199-0). Chronicle Bks.

Southern California. 1982. 8.95 (ISBN 0-933692-17-X). R Collings.

Thollander, Earl. Back Roads of California: 65 New Trips Along Country Roads. (Illus.). 1983. 19.95 (ISBN 0-517-54966-2, C N Potter Bks); pap. 9.95 (ISBN 0-517-54967-0). Crown.

--Earl Thollander's Back Roads of California. 1983. 19.95 (C N Potter Bks); pap. 9.95. Crown.

Thompson, Frances. Point Lobos: An Illustrated Walker's Handbook. LC 80-82176. (Illus.). 112p. 1980. pap. 5.00 (ISBN 0-9604542-0-9). Inkstone Books.

CALIFORNIA–GOLD DISCOVERIES

White, Stewart E. Forty-Niners. 1918. text ed. 8.50x (ISBN 0-686-83552-2). Elliots Bks.

CALIFORNIA–HISTORY

Atherton, Gertrude. California: An Intimate History. 330p. 1983. Repr. of 1914 ed. lib. bdg. 65.00 (ISBN 0-89987-041-4). Darby Bks.

Barrett, Thomas S. & Livermore, Putnam. The Conservation Easement in California. 256p. 1983. 44.95 (ISBN 0-933280-20-3); pap. 24.95 (ISBN 0-933280-19-X). Island CA.

Crouchett, Lorraine J. Filipinos in California: From the Days of the Galleon to the Present. LC 82-73374. (Illus.). 168p. 1983. 10.95x (ISBN 0-910823-00-6). Downey Place.

DiLeo, Michael & Smith, Eleanor. Two Californias: The Myths & the Realities of a State Divided Against Itself. (Illus.). 250p. (Orig.). 1983. pap. 10.95 (ISBN 0-933280-16-5). Island CA.

Hafen, LeRoy R. & Hafen, Ann W., eds. The Utah Expedition, 1857-1858: A Documentary Account. LC 58-11786. (Far West & Rockies Ser.: Vol.VIII). (Illus.). 375p. 1983. Repr. of 1958 ed. 27.50 (ISBN 0-87062-035-5). A H Clark.

Holmes, Kenneth L., ed. Covered Wagon Women: Diaries & Letters from the Western Trails, 1840-1890. LC 82-72586. (Covered Wagon Women Ser.). (Illus.). 280p. 1983. 25.00 (ISBN 0-87062-146-7). A H Clark.

Phelps, William D. Alta California, 1840-1842: The Journal & Observations of William Dane Phelps. Busch, Briton C, ed. LC 82-71376. (Western Lands & Water Ser.: XIII). (Illus.). 364p. 1983. 29.50 (ISBN 0-87062-143-2). A H Clark.

CALIFORNIA–HISTORY–SOURCES

Grove, Tami. A Collective History of the Early Years of Settlement in Surprise Valley. (ANCRR Research Paper: No. 4). 1977. 7.50 (ISBN 0-686-38933-6). Assn NC Records.

Schuman, Dewey, ed. Headlines: A History of Santa Barbara for the Pages of Its Newspapers, 1855 to 1982. (Illus.). 264p. 1982. 19.95 (ISBN 0-88496-192-3); pap. 11.95 (ISBN 0-88496-191-5). Capra Pr.

Tehama County Library. List of Northern California Holdings, Tehama County Library as of January 1, 1977. 1977. 4.50 (ISBN 0-686-38942-5). Assn NC Records.

CALIFORNIA–HISTORY, LOCAL

Boyd, W. Harland & Ludeke, John, eds. Inside Historic Kern. (Illus.). 1982. 16.95 (ISBN 0-943500-09-5). Kern Historical.

Brotherton, Jack. The Annals of Stanislaus County California. (Illus.). 260p. 1982. 22.95 (ISBN 0-934136-29-7). Western Tanager.

Colby, W. E. A Century of Transportation in Shasta County 1821-1920. (ANCRR Occasional Paper: No. 7). 105p. 1982. 7.50 (ISBN 0-686-38931-X). Assn NC Records.

Dunn, Forrest D. Butte County Place Names. (ANCRR Occasional Paper: No. 3). 122p. 1977. 6.00 (ISBN 0-686-38932-8). Assn NC Records.

Emanuels, George. Ygnacio Valley Eighteen Thirty-Four to Nineteen Seventy. (Illus.). 1982. 14.95. Diablo Bks.

CALIFORNIA-MAPS
Atlas of California. 29.95 (ISBN 0-9602544-0-4). Prof Bk Ctr Inc.
CALIFORNIA-POLITICS AND GOVERNMENT
California Legal Secretary's Resource. 4th ed. 362p. 1981. looseleaf 19.00 (ISBN 0-911110-32-1); 1983 suppl. incl. Parker & Son.
Hoeber, Thomas R., ed. California Journal Almanac of State Government & Politics, 1983-1984. (Biennial Ser.). (Illus.). 184p. (Orig.). 1983. pap. 4.95 (ISBN 0-930302-52-4). Cal Journal.
Muir, William K., Jr. Legislature: California's School of Politics. LC 82-16128. 197p. 1983. 19.00x (ISBN 0-226-54627-6). U of Chicago Pr.
Sayles, Stephen P. Clair Engle: The Forging of a Public Servant: A Study of Sacramento Valley Politics, 1933-1944. (ANCRR Occasional Publication: No. 1). 1976. 6.00 (ISBN 0-686-38940-9). Assn NC Records.
CALIFORNIA-SOCIAL CONDITIONS
Fisher, J. & Dryer, R. California Studies Program: Activity Manual. Combs, Eunice A., ed. (Illus.). 133p. (gr. 4). 1982. 49.00 (ISBN 0-943068-23-1); tchrs guide 5.00. Graphic Learning.
Melinkoff, Ellen. The Flavor of Los Angeles: How to Find the Best of the Ethnic Experience in Los Angeles. (Illus., Orig.). 1983. pap. 7.95 (ISBN 0-87701-248-2). Chronicle Bks.
Miller, Crane S. & Hyslop, Richard S. California: The Geography of Diversity. (Illus.). 334p. 1983. pap. 15.95t (ISBN 0-87484-441-X). Mayfield Pub.
CALIFORNIA-SOCIAL LIFE AND CUSTOMS
Tigerman, Stanley & Lewin, Susan Grant. The California Condition: A Pregnant Architecture. Adler, Sebastian J., frwd. by. LC 82-83257. (Illus.). 104p. (Orig.). pap. 14.85 (ISBN 0-934418-15-2). La Jolla Mus Contemp Art.
CALIFORNIA, LOWER
see Baja California
CALIFORNIA, UNIVERSITY OF
Warshow, David, ed. California: A Guide: An Illustrated History of the World's Largest University & its Environment. (Illus.). 220p. 1982. 6.95 (ISBN 0-87297-055-8). Diablo.
CALLIGRAPHIC PAINTINGS
see Letter Pictures
CALLIGRAPHY
Baker, Arthur. Arthur Baker's Foundational Calligraphy Manual. (Illus.). 96p. 1982. pap. 5.95 (ISBN 0-686-83696-0, ScribT). Scribner.
--The Calligraphic Art of Arthur Baker. (Illus.). 64p. 1983. 9.95 (ISBN 0-686-83809-2, ScribT). Scribner.
--Calligraphic Cut-Paper Designs for Artists & Craftsmen. (Pictorial Archive Ser.). (Illus.). 80p. (Orig.). 1983. pap. 2.50 (ISBN 0-486-20306-9). Dover.
--Calligraphic Swash Initials. (Illus.). 96p. (Orig.). (gr. 7 up). 1983. pap. 3.50 (ISBN 0-486-24427-X). Dover.
--Classic Roman Capitals Stroke By Stroke: An Arthur Baker Calligraphy Manual. (Illus.). 64p. (Orig.). (gr. 6 up). 1983. pap. 2.95 (ISBN 0-486-24450-4). Dover.
Casoni, Jennifer. Sincerely, Lyndon: The Handwriting of Lyndon Baines Johnson. 100p. (Orig.). 1983. pap. 14.95 (ISBN 0-9608816-1-1). Univ Autograph.
Gouies. Intro. to Calligraphy. 1980. pap. 10.00 (ISBN 0-686-84621-4, Nonpareil Bks). Godine.
CALLS (COMMERCE)
see Put and Call Transactions
CALORIMETERS AND CALORIMETRY
Calorie Guide to Brand Names. 1983. pap. 1.75 (ISBN 0-515-05909-9). Jove Pubns.
Netzer, Corrine. The Dieter's Calorie Counter. (Orig.). 1983. pap. price not set (ISBN 0-440-52086-X, Dell Trade Pbks). Dell.
CALUMNY
see Libel and Slander
CAMBISTRY
see Foreign Exchange; Money-Tables, etc.
CAMBODIA
Chandler, David P. A History of Cambodia. 225p. 1983. lib. bdg. 25.00x (ISBN 0-86531-578-7). Westview.
CAMBODIA-POLITICS AND GOVERNMENT
Chandler, David & Kiernan, Ben, eds. Revolution & its Aftermath in Kampuchea. Date not set. pap. price not set. Yale U SE Asia.
CAMBRIDGE UNIVERSITY
Needham, R. M. & Herbert, A. J. The Cambridge Distributed Computing System. 256p. 1982. pap. 25.00 (ISBN 0-201-14092-6, Adv Bk Prog). A-W.
CAMELLIA
Durrant, Tom. The Camelia Story. 168p. 1983. 47.95 (ISBN 0-686-83932-3, Pub. by Heinemann Pub New Zealand). Intl Schol Bk Serv.
CAMELS
Camels & Camel Milk. (FAO Animal Production & Health Papers: No. 26). 69p. 1982. pap. 7.50 (ISBN 92-5-101169-9, F2310, FAO). Unipub.
Gauthier-Pilters, Hilde & Dagg, Anne I. The Camel: Its Evolution, Behavior, & Relationship to Man. LC 80-23822. (Illus.). xii, 240p. 1981. pap. 8.95 (ISBN 0-226-28454-9). U of Chicago Pr.
Wilson, R. T. The Camel. (Intermediate Tropical Agriculture Ser.). (Illus.). 192p. 1983. pap. text ed. 14.95x (ISBN 0-582-77501-9). Longman.
CAMERA LENSES
see Lenses, Photographic
CAMERAS
see also Moving-Picture Cameras
American Institute of Physics Staff. The Camera. (Physics of Technology Project Ser.). 1975. pap. 7.00 (ISBN 0-07-001712-3). McGraw.
Baczynsky, Mark. Camera Repair, Restoration & Adaptation. (Illus.). 52p. 1982. pap. 9.95 (ISBN 0-89816-009-X). Embee Pr.
DiSante, Theodore. How to Select & Use Medium-Format Cameras. 192p. 1981. pap. 12.95 (ISBN 0-89586-046-5). H P Bks.
Gaunt, Leonard. Cameras. (Photographer's Library). (Illus.). 1983. pap. 12.95x (ISBN 0-240-51187-5). Focal Pr.
McKeown, James M. & McKeown, Joan C. Price Guide to Antique & Classic Still Cameras, 1983-1984. (Illus., Orig.). 1983. pap. 15.95 (ISBN 0-931838-05-3). Centennial Photo Serv.
Reynolds, Clyde. Camera Movements. (Illus.). 1983. 21.95x (ISBN 0-240-51143-3). Focal Pr.
CAMERAS-TYPES-NIKON
Wolf, John C. Nikon Guide. rev ed. (Modern Camera Guide Ser.). (Illus.). 1981. pap. 7.95 (ISBN 0-8174-5045-9, Amphoto). Watson-Guptill.
CAMERAS-TYPES-PENTAX
Reynolds, Clyde. Asahi Pentax M Series Book. (Camera Bks). (Illus.). 1983. pap. 9.95x (ISBN 0-240-51194-8). Focal Pr.
CAMORRA
see Mafia
CAMP COOKERY
see Cookery, Outdoor
CAMP COUNSELORS
Kraus, Richard & Scanlin, Margery. Introduction to Camp Counseling. (Illus.). 352p. 1983. 20.95 (ISBN 0-13-479188-6). P-H.
CAMP MANAGEMENT
see Camps
CAMPA LANGUAGE
Payne, David L. The Phonology & Morphology of Axininca Campa. Poulter, Virgil L., ed. LC 81-52739. (Publications in Linguistics: No. 66). (Illus.). 285p. 1981. pap. text ed. 11.95x (ISBN 0-88312-084-4); microfiche 3.00. Summer Inst Ling.
CAMPAIGN MANAGEMENT
Sabato, Larry J. The Rise of Political Consultants: New Ways of Winning Elections. 1983. pap. 9.95 (ISBN 0-465-07041-8). Basic.
Schwartz, Cipora. How to Run a School Board Campaign & Win. 142p. (Orig.). 1982. pap. 5.95 (ISBN 0-934460-19-1). NCCE.
CAMPAIGNS, PRESIDENTIAL
see Presidents-United States-Election
CAMPBELL, GEORGE, 1719-1796
Coeure, G. Analytic Functions & Manifolds in Infinite Dimensional Spaces. 1974. pap. 16.50 (ISBN 0-444-10621-9). Elsevier.
Narasimhan, R. Analysis on Real & Complex Manifolds. 2nd ed. 1974. 27.00 (ISBN 0-444-10452-6). Elsevier.
CAMPBELLITES
see Disciples of Christ
CAMPING
see also Backpacking; Camps; Cookery, Outdoor; Outdoor Life; Survival (After Airplane Accidents, Shipwrecks, etc.); Tourist Camps, Hostels, etc.
Bairstow, Jeffrey. Camping Year Round: A Guide to Equipment & Technique. LC 82-40019. (Illus.). 288p. (Orig.). 1983. pap. 5.95 (ISBN 0-686-43023-9, Vin). Random.
Bast, Rochelle, ed. Handbook for Senior Adult Camping. 68p. 1977. pap. 4.00 (ISBN 0-686-84032-1). U OR Ctr Leisure.
Davidson, James W. & Rugge, John. The Complete Wilderness Paddler. LC 82-40021. 288p. Date not set. pap. 5.95 (ISBN 0-394-71153-X, Vin). Random.
Goodrich, Lois. Decentralized Camping. 1982. pap. 12.50 (ISBN 0-686-83992-7). Am Camping.
Job, Glenn T., ed. Parent's Guide to Accredited Camps. 1983. pap. 4.50 (ISBN 0-87603-070-3). Am Camping.
Satterfield, Archie, Sr. & Bauer, Eddie, Sr. The Eddie Bauer Guide to Family Camping. LC 82-13923. (Illus.). 320p. 1983. 17.95 (ISBN 0-201-07776-0); pap. 8.95 (ISBN 0-201-07777-9). A-W.
YMCA Camping Centennial(Personnel) (Illus.). 37p. 1982. pap. 4.95 (ISBN 0-88035-003-2). YMCA USA.
YMCA of the USA. YMCA Camping Centennial, No. 2 Program. (YMCA Centennial Ser.). (Illus.). 48p. 1983. pap. write for info. (ISBN 0-88035-007-5). YMCA USA.
YMCA of USA. YMCA Day Camp Manual, 7 pts. (Illus.). 172p. 1982. pap. 19.95 (ISBN 0-88035-004-0). YMCA USA.
CAMPING-OUTFITS, SUPPLIES, ETC.
Satterfield, Archie, Sr. & Bauer, Eddie, Sr. The Eddie Bauer Guide to Family Camping. LC 82-13923. (Illus.). 320p. 1983. 17.95 (ISBN 0-201-07776-0); pap. 8.95 (ISBN 0-201-07777-9). A-W.
CAMPING-NORTH AMERICA
Melius, Kenneth W. National Forest Campground Guide. LC 82-51299. (Illus.). 310p. 1983. pap. 8.95 (ISBN 0-9610130-0-1). Tensleep.
VanMeer, Mary, ed. Free Campgrounds, USA. rev. ed. 600p. 1983. pap. 9.95 (ISBN 0-914788-69-8). East Woods.
Woodall's Campground Directory, 1983: Eastern Edition. pap. 7.95 (ISBN 0-671-45922-8). Woodall.
Woodall's Campground Directory, 1983: North American. pap. 12.95 (ISBN 0-671-45921-X). Woodall.
Woodall's Campground Directory, 1983: Seventeen State Editions. pap. 2.95 each (ISBN 0-686-43263-0). Woodall.
Woodall's Campground Directory, 1983: Western Edition. pap. 7.95 (ISBN 0-671-45923-6). Woodall.
CAMPS
see also Camping
Involving Impaired, Disabled & Handicapped Persons in Regular Camp Programs. 128p. 1976. 7.95 (ISBN 0-88314-109-4). AAHPERD.
Kraus, Richard & Scanlin, Margery. Introduction to Camp Counseling. (Illus.). 352p. 1983. 20.95 (ISBN 0-13-479188-6). P-H.
Lansing, Adrienne & Goldsmith, Alice. Summer Camps & Programs: Over 250 of the Best for Children Ages 8 to 18. Levy, Laurie, ed. 1983. 14.95 (ISBN 0-517-54960-3, Harmony); pap. 8.95 (ISBN 0-517-54832-1). Crown.
CAMPS-COUNSELORS
see Camp Counselors
CAMPS-WATER PROGRAMS
see Aquatic Sports
CAMPUS CULTURES
see Educational Anthropology
CANADA
see also names of cities, provinces, regions, etc. in Canada, e.g. Quebec; British Columbia; Northwest, Canadian
Callwood, June. Portrait of Canada. LC 77-25579. 1981. 14.95 (ISBN 0-385-05746-6). Doubleday.
Matthew, James S. My Fifty Years in Canada. 5.75 (ISBN 0-8062-2129-1). Carlton.
CANADA-BIOGRAPHY
Barnett, Hert E. & Fraser, Hugh, eds. Who's Who in Canada, 1982-83. LC 17-16282. (Illus.). 1608p. 1982. 75.00x (ISBN 0-919339-02-6). Intl Pubns Serv.
CANADA-CIVILIZATION
Szekely, Edmond B. Northern Summer. (Illus.). 32p. 1972. pap. 4.80 (ISBN 0-89564-030-9). IBS Intl.
CANADA-COMMERCE
Archer, M. An Introduction to Canadian Business. 4th ed. 1982. write for info. McGraw.
Overgaard, Herman O. & Crener, Maxime A. International Business: The Canadian Way. 560p. 1982. pap. text ed. 26.95 (ISBN 0-8403-2900-8). Kendall-Hunt.
CANADA-DESCRIPTION AND TRAVEL
Kraulis, J. A., ed. Canada: A Landscape Portrait. 128p. 1983. 27.50 (ISBN 0-295-96004-3, Pub. by Hurtig Pubs). U of Wash Pr.
CANADA-DESCRIPTION AND TRAVEL-GUIDEBOOKS
Birnbaum, Stephen. Canada 1983. (The Get 'em & Go Travel Guide Ser.). 1982. 11.95 (ISBN 0-395-32868-3). HM.
Fodor's Budget Canada '83. (Illus.). 272p. 1983. pap. 7.95 (ISBN 0-679-00876-4). McKay.
Kalman, Harold & Roaf, John. Exploring Ottawa: An Architectural Guide to the Nation's Capital. (Illus.). 208p. (Orig.). 1983. pap. 10.95 (ISBN 0-8020-6395-0). U of Toronto Pr.
CANADA-ECONOMIC CONDITIONS
Brennan, Mary E., ed. Canadian Conference, 14th Annual Nov. 23-27, 1981 Proceedings. 280p. (Orig.). 1982. pap. 14.00 (ISBN 0-89154-177-2). Intl Found Employ.
Melvin, James R. & Scheffman, David T. An Economic Analysis of the Impact of Rising Oil Prices on Urban Structure. (Ontario Economic Council Research Studies). 160p. (Orig.). 1983. pap. 10.50 (ISBN 0-8020-3395-4). U of Toronto Pr.
Struthers, James. No Fault of Their Own: Unemployment & the Canadian Welfare State, 1914-1941. (State & Economic Life Ser.). 264p. 1983. 31.00 (ISBN 0-8020-2480-7); pap. 12.50 (ISBN 0-8020-6502-3). U of Toronto Pr.
Wright, Becky A., ed. EDP Institute Proceedings, Dec. 13-16, 1981. 111p. (Orig.). 1982. pap. 10.00 (ISBN 0-89154-178-0). Intl Found Employ.
CANADA-EMIGRATION AND IMMIGRATION
Segal, Gary L. Immigrating to Canada: Who is Allowed? What is Required? How to do It? Rev. ed. 1983. pap. price not set (ISBN 0-88908-565-X). Self Counsel Pr.
CANADA-FOREIGN ECONOMIC RELATIONS
Hay, Keith A. Canadian Perspectives on Economic Relations with Japan. 381p. 1980. pap. text ed. 18.95x (ISBN 0-920380-72-7, Inst Res Pub Canada). Renouf.
CANADA-HISTORY
Bacchi, Carol L. Liberation Deferred? The Ideas of the English-Canadian Suffragists, 1877-1918. (Social History of Canada Ser.). 222p. 1983. 25.00x (ISBN 0-8020-2455-6); pap. 8.95 (ISBN 0-8020-6466-3). U of Toronto Pr.
Beck, J. M. Joseph Howe: Conservative Reformer 1804-1848, Vol. 1. 400p. 1983. 35.00x (ISBN 0-7735-0387-0). McGill-Queens U Pr.
--Joseph Howe: The Briton Becomes Canadian 1848-1873, Vol. 2. 448p. 1983. 37.50x (ISBN 0-7735-0388-9). McGill-Queens U Pr.
Shelton, Oscar D. Canadian Dominion. 1919. text ed. 8.50x (ISBN 0-686-83498-4). Elliots Bks.
Struthers, James. No Fault of Their Own: Unemployment & the Canadian Welfare State, 1914-1941. (State & Economic Life Ser.). 264p. 1983. 31.00 (ISBN 0-8020-2480-7); pap. 12.50 (ISBN 0-8020-6502-3). U of Toronto Pr.
CANADA-HISTORY-BIBLIOGRAPHY
Smith, Dwight L., ed. The History of Canada: An Annotated Bibliography. (Clio Bibliography Ser.: No. 10). 336p. 1983. lib. bdg. 55.00 (ISBN 0-87436-047-1). ABC-Clio.
CANADA-HISTORY-FICTION
Adair, Dennis & Rosenstock, Janet. Wildfires: The Story of Canada, Bk. IV. 336p. 3.50 (ISBN 0-380-82313-6). Avon.
CANADA-HISTORY-TO 1763 (NEW FRANCE)
Parkman, Francis. France & England in North America, 2 Vols. Levin, David, ed. LC 82-18658. 1500p. 1983. Vol. 1. each 25.00 (ISBN 0-940450-10-0). Vol. 2 (ISBN 0-940450-11-9). Literary Classics.
CANADA-HISTORY-WAR OF 1812
see United States-History-War of 1812
CANADA-INDUSTRIES
Moriei, Peter & Smith, Arthur J. Canadian Industrial Policy. 116p. (Orig.). 1982. pap. 10.00 (ISBN 0-89068-063-9). Natl Planning.
CANADA-POLITICS AND GOVERNMENT
Alexander, David G. Atlantic Canada & Confederation: Essays in Canadian Political Economy. 160p. 1983. 20.00x (ISBN 0-8020-2487-4); pap. 6.00 (ISBN 0-8020-6512-0). U of Toronto Pr.
Atkinson, Michael M. & Chandler, Marsha A., eds. The Politics of Canadian Public Policy. 320p. 1983. 30.00x (ISBN 0-8020-2485-8); pap. 12.50 (ISBN 0-8020-6517-1). U of Toronto Pr.
Beck, J. M. Joseph Howe: Conservative Reformer 1804-1848, Vol. 1. 400p. 1983. 35.00x (ISBN 0-7735-0387-0). McGill-Queens U Pr.
--Joseph Howe: The Briton Becomes Canadian 1848-1873, Vol. 2. 448p. 1983. 37.50x (ISBN 0-7735-0388-9). McGill-Queens U Pr.
Breton, Albert & Breton, Raymond. Why Disunity? 83p. 1980. pap. text ed. 6.95x (ISBN 0-920380-70-0, Inst Res Pub Canada). Renouf.
Byers, R. B., ed. Canadian Annual Review of Politics & Public Affairs, 1981. 400p. 1983. 50.00x (ISBN 0-8020-2500-5). U of Toronto Pr.
Campbell, Colin. Governments under Stress: Political Executives & Key Bureaucrats in Washington, London, & Ottawa. 384p. 1983. 25.00 (ISBN 0-8020-5622-9). U of Toronto Pr.
Fox, P. W. Politics: Canada. 5th ed. 672p. 1982. 12.95 (ISBN 0-07-548024-7). McGraw.
Kornberg, Allan & Clarke, Harold D., eds. Political Support in Canada: The Crisis Years. Duke University Center for Commonwealth & Comparative Studies. 375p. 1983. 27.50x (ISBN 0-8223-0546-1). Duke.
Marler, George C. The Admiral Issue of Canada. 566p. 1982. 35.00 (ISBN 0-933580-08-8). Am Philatelic.
Matthews, Ralph. The Creation of Regional Dependency. 336p. 1983. 40.00x (ISBN 0-8020-5617-2); pap. 12.95 (ISBN 0-8020-6510-4). U of Toronto Pr.
Penniman, Howard R., ed. Canada at the Polls, 1979 & 1980. 1982. 17.25 (ISBN 0-8447-3474-8); pap. 9.25 (ISBN 0-8447-3472-1). Am Enterprise.
CANADA-RELATIONS (GENERAL) WITH FOREIGN COUNTRIES
Pringsheim, Klaus H. Neighbors Across the Pacific: The Development of Economic & Political Relations Between Canada & Japan. LC 82-11713. (Contributions in Political Science Ser.: No. 90). 256p. 1983. lib. bdg. 29.95 (ISBN 0-313-23507-4, PRN/). Greenwood.
CANADA-SOCIAL CONDITIONS
Himelfarb, A. & Richardson, C. J. Sociology for Canadians: Images of Society. 512p. 1982. 21.95 (ISBN 0-07-548440-4). McGraw.
Lachapelle, Rejean & Henripin, Jacques. The Demolinuistic Situation in Canada: Past Trends & Future Prospects. 387p. 1982. pap. text ed. 24.95x (ISBN 0-920380-42-5, Pub. by Inst Res Pub Canada). Renouf.
CANADA-STATISTICS
Canada Yearbook, 1980-81. 74th ed. (Illus.). 1004p. 1981. 25.00 (ISBN 0-660-10014-2). Intl Pubns Serv.
CANADIAN ARCHITECTURE
see Architecture-Canada
CANADIAN AUTHORS
see Authors, Canadian
CANADIAN COMPOSERS
see Composers, Canadian
CANALS
Bryce, Iris. Canals Are My Life. (Illus.). 104p. 1982. 14.50 (ISBN 0-85937-277-4). Sheridan.
De Roquette-Buisson, Odile. The Canal Du Midi. (Illus.). 1983. 29.95 (ISBN 0-500-24115-5). Thames Hudson.
Johnson, Guy. Save the Stratford Canal! (Illus.). 168p. 1983. 17.50 (ISBN 0-7153-8424-4). David & Charles.
Owen, David. The Manchester Ship Canal. 160p. 1983. 20.00 (ISBN 0-7190-0864-6). Manchester.
Ransom, P. J. Archaeology of Canals. (Illus.). 1979. 31.50 (ISBN 0-437-14400-3, Pub. by Heinemann). David & Charles.

Shank, W. H. & Mayo. Towpaths to Tugboats,1982: A History of American Canal Engineering. 1982. 6.00 (ISBN 0-933788-40-1). Am Canal & Transport.

CANAPES

see Cookery (Appetizers); Cookery (Relishes)

CANARIES

Canaries. (Pet Care Ser.). 1983. pap. 3.95 (ISBN 0-8120-2614-4). Barron.

Dodwell, G. T. Canaries. (Illus.). 94p. 1978. 3.95 (ISBN 0-7028-1071-1). Avian Pubns.

--The Lizard Canary & Other Rare Breeds. 208p. 1982. 40.00x (ISBN 0-86230-052-5, Pub. by Saiga Pub). State Mutual Bk.

Pasca, Sue-Rhee. The T. F. H. Book of Canaries. (Illus.). 108p. 6.95 (ISBN 0-87666-819-8, HP-010). TFH Pubns.

CANARY ISLANDS

Fernandez-Armesto, Felipe. The Canary Islands after the Conquest: The Making of a Colonial Society in the Early Sixteenth Century. (Historical Monographs). (Illus.). 258p. 1982. 44.00x (ISBN 0-19-821888-5). Oxford U Pr.

CANARY PARROT

see Budgerigars

CANCER

see also Antineoplastic Agents; Carcinogenesis; Carcinogens

also subdivision Cancer or Diseases under name of organs or regions of the body

American Joint Committee on Cancer. Manual for Staging of Cancer. 2nd ed. Beahrs, Oliver H. & Myers, Max H., eds. (Illus.). 220p. 1983. pap. text ed. 17.50 (ISBN 0-686-42955-9, Lippincott Medical). Lippincott.

Ariel, Irving, ed. Progress in Clinical Cancer, Vol. 8. Date not set. price not set. Grune.

Braun, Armin C. The Biology of Cancer. 169p. 26.50 (ISBN 0-201-00318-X); pap. 19.50 (ISBN 0-201-00319-8). A-W.

Chaitow, Leon. An End to Cancer. 1978. 5.95x (ISBN 0-7225-0473-X). Cancer Control Soc.

Clark, Randolph L., ed. Year Book of Cancer 1983. 1983. 40.00 (ISBN 0-8151-1791-4). Year Bk Med.

Critser, James R. Jr., Jr. Cancer: Diagnosis & Therapy. (Ser.10CDT-82). 1983. 80.00 (ISBN 0-88178-005-7). Lexington Data.

Dallin, Lynn. Cancer Causes & Natural Controls. LC 82-13765. 1983. 19.95 (ISBN 0-87949-224-4). Ashley Bks.

Donsbach, Kurt. Metabolic Cancer Therapies. 1981. 1.95x (ISBN 0-686-37945-4). Cancer Control Soc.

Greenberg, Michael R. Urbanization & Cancer Mortality: The United States Experience, 1950-1975. (Monographs in Epidemiology & Biostatistics). (Illus.). 276p. 1983. 45.00x (ISBN 0-19-503173-3). Oxford U Pr.

International Symposium on Cancer Detection & Prevention. Abstracts: Second Symposium, Bologna, 1973. Maltoni, C., et al, eds. (International Congress Ser.: No. 275). 1973. pap. 29.00 (ISBN 0-686-43412-9). Elsevier.

International Union Against Cancer Staff. Manual of Clinical Oncology. 3rd, enl. ed. (Illus.). 370p. 1982. pap. 18.00 (ISBN 0-387-11746-6). Springer-Verlag.

Jacob, Stanley. DMSO: The True Story. 1981. 10.95x (ISBN 0-688-00716-3). Cancer Control Soc.

Jeljackzewicz, Janusz, et al, eds. Bacteria & Cancer. Date not set. 39.50 (ISBN 0-12-383820-7). Acad Pr.

Kahn, S. Benham, ed. Concepts in Cancer Medicine. Date not set. price not set (ISBN 0-8089-1486-3). Grune.

Kushi, Michio. Macrobiotic Approach to Cancer. 1981. 6.95x (ISBN 0-89529-209-2). Cancer Control Soc.

Le Cam, L. & Neyman, J., eds. Probability Models & Cancer: Proceedings of an Interdisciplinary Cancer Study Conference. 310p. 1983. 51.00 (ISBN 0-444-86514-4, North Holland). Elsevier.

Levi, S., ed. Ultrasound & Cancer: Invited Papers & Selected Free Communications Presented at the First International Symposium, Brussels, Belgium, July 23-24, 1982. (International Congress Ser.: No. 587). 384p. 1982. 88.25 (ISBN 0-444-90270-8, Excerpta Medica). Elsevier.

Livingston, Virginia. Physician's Handbook to Microbiology of Cancer. 1977. 2.00x (ISBN 0-918816-06-8). Cancer Control Soc.

Meleka, Fikri M. Dimensions of the Cancer Problem. viii, 172p. 1983. pap. 29.50 (ISBN 3-8055-3622-4). S Karger.

Mihich, Enrico, ed. Biological Responses in Cancer Progress Toward Potential Applications, Vol. 1. 300p. 1982. 37.50 (ISBN 0-306-41146-6, Plenum Pr). Plenum Pub.

Mullan, Fitzhugh. Vital Signs: A Young Doctor's Struggle with Cancer. 1983. 12.50 (ISBN 0-374-29445-3). FS&G.

Napalkov, N. P., ed. Cancer Control in the Countries of the Council of Mutual Economic Assistance. (Illus.). 742p. 1982. 40.00x (ISBN 963-05-3036-8). Intl Pubns Serv.

Nass, G., ed. Modified Nucleosides & Cancer: Workshop, Freiburg, FRG, 1981. (Recent Results in Cancer Research Ser.: Vol. 84). (Illus.). 440p. 1983. 50.50 (ISBN 0-387-12024-6). Springer-Verlag.

Phillips. Viruses Associated with Human Cancer. 896p. 1983. 95.00 (ISBN 0-8247-1738-4). Dekker.

Simone, C. B. Cancer & Nutrition: A Ten-Point Plan to Reduce Your Chances of Getting Cancer. 260p. 1983. 15.95 (ISBN 0-07-057466-9, GB). McGraw.

Sink, L. & Godden, J., eds. Conflicts in Childhood Cancer. 1976. 32.25 (ISBN 0-444-99839-X). Elsevier.

Smith & Prout. Bladder Cancer: BIMR Urology. 1983. text ed. price not set (ISBN 0-407-02358-5). Butterworth.

Stauth, Cameron. New Approach to Cancer. 1982. 6.95x (ISBN 0-942686-01-2). Cancer Control Soc.

Watson, Rita E. & Wallach, Robert C. New Choices, New Chances: A Woman's Guide to Conquering Cancer. 273p. 1983. pap. 6.95 (ISBN 0-686-42921-4). St Martin.

Weber-Stadelmann, W., ed. Adriamycin & Derivatives in Gastrointestinal Cancer. (Beitraege zur Onkologie. Contributions to Oncology Ser.: Vol. 15). (Illus.). vi, 144p. 1983. pap. 58.75 (ISBN 3-8055-3689-5). S Karger.

CANCER-CHEMOTHERAPY

Cancer Chemotherapy Drugs, Diagnostics & Instrumentation. 1982. 1195.00 (284). Predicasts.

Laszlo, John. Antiemetics & Cancer Chemotherapy. (Illus.). 200p. 1982. pap. 19.95 (ISBN 0-683-04899-6). Williams & Wilkins.

Muggia, F. M. Cancer Chemotherapy I. 1983. 69.50 (ISBN 90-247-2713-8, Pub. by Martinus Nijhoff Netherlands). Kluwer Boston.

Muggia, F. M. & Young, C. W. Anthracycline Antibiotics in Cancer Therapy. 1982. text ed. 69.50 (ISBN 0-686-37594-7, Pub. by Martinus Nijhoff Netherlands). Kluwer Boston.

Pinedo, H. M., ed. Cancer Chemotherapy 1982. (Cancer Chemotherapy Annual Ser.: No. 4). 450p. 1982. 50.00 (ISBN 0-444-90255-4, Excerpta Medica). Elsevier.

Serrou, B. & Rosenfeld, S., eds. New Immunomodulating Agents & Biological Response Modifiers. (Human Cancer Immunology Ser.: Vol. 3). 400p. 1982. 106.50 (ISBN 0-444-80401-3, Biomedical Pr). Elsevier.

Skeel, Roland T. Manual of Cancer Chemotherapy. (Spiral Manual Ser.). 279p. 1982. spiralbound 13.95 (ISBN 0-316-79572-0). Little.

CANCER-DIAGNOSIS

Cancer Chemotherapy Drugs, Diagnostics & Instrumentation. 1982. 1195.00 (284). Predicasts.

Magnus, K. Trends in Cancer Incidences: Causes & Practical Implications. 1982. 79.50 (ISBN 0-07-039501-2). McGraw.

CANCER-IMMUNOLOGICAL ASPECTS

Serrou, B. & Rosenfeld, C., eds. Current Concepts in Human Immunology & Cancer Immunomodulation: Proceedings of the International Symposium, Montpellier, France, January 18-20, 1982. (Developments in Immunology Ser.: Vol. 17). 664p. 1982. 84.95 (ISBN 0-444-80426-9, Biomedical Pr). Elsevier.

CANCER-PERSONAL NARRATIVES

see Cancer Patients-Personal Narratives

CANCER-PREVENTION

see also Cancer Education

Alderson, Michael, ed. The Prevention of Cancer. (Management of Malignant Disease Ser.: No. 4). 304p. 1982. text ed. 49.50 (ISBN 0-7131-4401-7). E Arnold.

Hassan, Mulhim A. Prevention & Control of Cancer. 240p. 1983. 11.50 (ISBN 0-682-49957-9). Exposition.

Ingall, R. F. & Mastromarino, Anthony J., eds. Prevention of Hereditary Large Bowel Cancer. LC 82-24988. (Progress in Clinical & Biological Research Ser.: Vol. 115). 278p. 1983. 30.00 (ISBN 0-8451-0115-3). A R Liss.

Kushi, Michio & East-West Foundation. The Macrobiotic Approach to Cancer. 2nd ed. (Macrobiotic Home Library Ser.). 128p. (Orig.). 1982. pap. 6.95 (ISBN 0-686-43109-X). Avery Pub.

Kushi, Michio & Jack, Alex. The Cancer-Prevention Diet. 1983. 13.95 (ISBN 0-312-11837-6). St Martin.

Rohe, Fred. Metabolic Ecology. 1982. 5.95x (ISBN 0-686-37598-X). Cancer Control Soc.

CANCER-PSYCHOLOGICAL ASPECTS

Taff, Gail A. & Friis, Robert. Stress & Cancer: An Annotated Bibliography. 60p. 1982. pap. 14.95 (ISBN 0-939552-07-8). Human Behavior.

CANCER-RESEARCH

see Cancer Research

CANCER CELLS

Boynton, Alton L. & McKeehan, Wallace L., eds. Ions, Cell Proliferation, & Cancer. LC 82-20786. 1982. 39.50 (ISBN 0-12-123050-3). Acad Pr.

CANCER EDUCATION

Ohsawa, George. Cancer & the Philosophy of the Far East. 2nd ed. Aihara, Herman, ed. 162p. 1982. pap. 7.95 (ISBN 0-918860-38-5). G Ohsawa.

CANCER NURSING

Association of Pediatric Oncology. Nursing Care of the Child With Cancer. 1982. text ed. write for info. (ISBN 0-316-04884-4). Little.

Eiseman, Ben & Steele, Glen, eds. Follow-Up of the Cancer Patient. LC 81-84767. (Illus.). 320p. 1982. text ed. 38.00 (ISBN 0-86577-021-2). Thieme-Stratton.

Yasko, Joyce. Guidelines for Cancer Care: Symptom Management. 1983. text ed. 15.00 (ISBN 0-8359-2647-8); pap. text ed. 12.95 (ISBN 0-8359-2646-X). Reston.

CANCER PATIENTS-PERSONAL NARRATIVES

Fisher, John J. Cancer Was My Copilot. 160p. 1983. 11.95 (ISBN 0-682-49978-1). Exposition.

Learning to Live Again. LC 82-18743. 252p. 1983. 16.95 (ISBN 0-03-057647-4). HR&W.

Seed, Pat. Another Day. 100p. 1983. 16.50 (ISBN 0-434-67862-7, Pub. by Heinemann England); pap. 9.95 (ISBN 0-434-68533-X). David & Charles.

Stargel, Gloria C. The Healing. (Orig.). 1982. pap. 2.50 (ISBN 0-8423-1425-3). Tyndale.

CANCER RESEARCH

Busch, Harris, ed. Methods in Cancer Research, Vol. 20. (Serial Publication). 1982. 48.50 (ISBN 0-12-147680-4). Acad Pr.

Busch, Harris & Yeoman, Lynn, eds. Methods in Cancer Research: Vol. 19, Tumor Markers. LC 66-29495. 464p. 1982. 56.00 (ISBN 0-12-147679-0); subscription 48.00 (ISBN 0-686-81714-1). Acad Pr.

Conference in Honor of Anna Goldfeder, Feb 17-19, 1982. Cell Proliferation, Cancer, & Cancer Therapy: Proceedings, Vol. 397. Baserga, Renato, ed. 328p. 1982. 65.00 (ISBN 0-89766-184-2); pap. write for info. (ISBN 0-89766-185-0). NY Acad Sci.

Greenstein, Jesse P. & Haddow, Alexander, eds. Advances in Cancer Research, Vol. 38. (Serial Publication). Date not set. price not set (ISBN 0-12-006638-6). Acad Pr.

CANDLES, LITURGICAL

see Candles and Lights

CANDLES AND LIGHTS

Dey, Charmaine. The Magic Candle. 64p. 1982. pap. 3.50 (ISBN 0-942272-00-5). Original Pubns.

CANDY

see Confectionery

CANE SUGAR

see Sugar

CANNIBALISM

Sagan, Eli. Cannibalism: Human Agression & Cultural Form. 148p. pap. 6.95 (ISBN 0-914434-24-1). Psychohistory Pr.

CANNING AND PRESERVING

Deeming, Sue & Deeming, Bill. Canning. (Illus.). 192p. 1983. pap. 7.95 (ISBN 0-89586-185-2). H P Bks.

Food Processors Institute. Canned Foods: Principles of Thermal Process Control, Acidification & Container Closure Evaluation. 4th, rev. ed. 256p. 1982. pap. 40.00 (ISBN 0-937774-07-3). Food Processors.

Wejman, Jacqueline & St. Peter, Genevieve. The Art of Preserving. rev. ed. 192p. 1983. pap. 7.95 (ISBN 0-89286-212-2). One Hund One Prods.

CANOES AND CANOEING

see also Indians of North America-Boats

Adney, Edwin T. & Chapelle, Howard I. The Bark Canoes & Skin Boats of North America. 2nd ed. (Illus.). 260p. 1983. Repr. of 1964 ed. text ed. 19.95 (ISBN 0-87474-204-8). Smithsonian.

Buck, Peter. Arts & Crafts of Hawaii: Canoes, Sec. VI. (Special Pulbication Ser.: No. 45). (Illus.). 41p. 1957. pap. 3.00 (ISBN 0-910240-39-6). Bishop Mus.

Crowley, william, ed. Rushton's Rowboats & Canoes, 1903. LC 82-48169. (Illus.). 128p. 1983. pap. 15.00 (ISBN 0-87742-164-1). Intl Marine.

Davidson, James W. & Rugge, John. The Complete Wilderness Paddler. LC 82-40021. 288p. Date not set. pap. 5.95 (ISBN 0-394-71153-X, Vin). Random.

Evans, Jay. The Kayaking Book. (Illus.). 224p. 1983. pap. 8.95 (ISBN 0-8289-0501-0). Greene.

Washburne, Randel. The Coastal Kayaker: Kayak Camping on the Alaska & B.C. Coast. (Illus.). 248p. (Orig.). 1983. pap. 9.95 (ISBN 0-914718-80-0). Pacific Search.

CANON LAW

see also Church Orders, Ancient

also special legal headings with Canon Law added in parentheses, e.g. Marriage (Canon Law)

Barr, James. Holy Scripture: Canon Authority, Criticism. LC 82-20123. 192p. 1983. 18.95 (ISBN 0-664-21395-2); pap. 9.95 (ISBN 0-664-24477-7). Westminster.

Canon Law Society of America Staff. Proceedings of the Forty-Fourth Annual Convention. (Orig.). 1983. pap. 6.00x (ISBN 0-943616-14-X). Canon Law Soc.

Kelly, Henry A. Canon Law & the Archpriest of Hita. 1983. write for info. (ISBN 0-86698-058-X). Medieval & Renaissance NY.

Manser, Anthony. Bradley's Logic. LC 82-24407. 230p. 1983. text ed. 29.95x (ISBN 0-389-20379-3). B&N Imports.

The New Canon Law: Perspectives on the Law, Religious Life & the Laity. (Orig.). 1983. pap. write for info. (ISBN 0-87125-076-4). Cath Health.

Shumacher, William A. Roman Replies, Nineteen Eighty-Two. 42p. (Orig.). 1982. pap. 3.00x (ISBN 0-943616-13-1). Canon Law Soc.

CANTEENS (RECREATION CENTERS)

see Recreation Areas

CANVAS EMBROIDERY

Feisner, Edith A. Needlepoint & Beyond: 27 Lessons in Advanced Canvas Work. (Illus.). 176p. 1983. pap. 10.95 (ISBN 0-686-83716-9, ScribT). Scribner.

Kurten, Nancy N. Needlepoint in Minature. (Illus.). 160p. 1983. pap. 10.95 (ISBN 0-686-83786-X, ScribT). Scribner.

Sorensen, Grethe. Needlepoint Designs from Oriental Rugs. (Illus.). 112p. 1983. pap. 12.95 (ISBN 0-686-83779-7, ScribT). Scribner.

Trexler, Pat. Pat's Pointers: The Needlepoint Handbook. 200p. 1982. 15.00 (ISBN 0-8362-2500-7); pap. 6.95 (ISBN 0-8362-2502-3). Andrews & McMeel.

CANVAS EMBROIDERY-PATTERNS

Lane, Maggie. Gold & Silver Needlepoint. (Illus.). 168p. 1983. 19.95 (ISBN 0-686-83805-X, ScribT). Scribner.

CANVAS WORK (NEEDLEPOINT)

see Canvas Embroidery

CAOUTCHOUC

see Rubber

CAPACITY, INDUSTRIAL

see Industrial Capacity

CAPE COD-DESCRIPTION AND TRAVEL

Green, Eugene & Sachse, William L. Names of the Land. LC 82-82167. (Illus.). 192p. (Orig.). 1983. pap. 8.95 (ISBN 0-87106-974-1). Globe Pequot.

CAPILLARITY

see also Brownian Movements; Surface Chemistry

Rowlinson, J. S. & Widom, B. Molecular Theory of Capillarity. (International Ser. of Monographs on Chemistry). (Illus.). 340p. 1982. 59.00x (ISBN 0-19-855612-8). Oxford U Pr.

CAPITAL

see also Banks and Banking; Capitalism; Interest and Usury; Investments; Profit; Saving and Investment; Wealth

Gupta, Kanhaya L. & Islam, M Anisul. Foreign Capital, Savings & Growth. 1983. lib. bdg. 34.50 (ISBN 90-277-1449-5, Pub. by Reidel Holland). Kluwer Boston.

Milgate, Murray, ed. Capital & Employment. (Studies Political Economy Ser.). Date not set. price not set (ISBN 0-12-496250-5). Acad Pr.

Sterling, Robert R. & Lemke, Kenneth W., eds. Maintenance of Capital: Financial vs Physical. LC 82-16847. 323p. 1982. 15.00 (ISBN 0-914348-32-9). Scholars Bk.

CAPITAL-TAXATION

see Capital Levy

CAPITAL AND LABOR

see Industrial Relations

CAPITAL EQUIPMENT

see Industrial Equipment

CAPITAL EXPORTS

see Foreign Exchange; Investments, Foreign

CAPITAL FORMATION

see Saving and Investment

CAPITAL GAINS TAX

see also Real Property and Taxation

Di Palma, Vera. Capital Gains Tax. 224p. 1981. 35.00x (ISBN 0-7121-0460-7, Pub. by Macdonald & Evans). State Mutual Bk.

CAPITAL IMPORTS

see Foreign Exchange; Investments, Foreign

CAPITAL INVESTMENTS

see also Art as an Investment; Replacement of Industrial Equipment

Financial Times Business Publishing Ltd., ed. Japanese Banking & Capital Markets. 1982. 150.00x (ISBN 0-686-82306-0, Pub. by Finan Times England). State Mutual Bk.

Train, John. Preserving Capital & Making It Grow. 1983. 14.95 (ISBN 0-517-54766-X, C N Potter Bks). Crown.

CAPITAL LEVY

see also Capital Gains Tax; Property Tax

Hulten, Charles R., ed. Depreciation, Inflation, & the Taxation of Income from Capital. LC 81-533061. 319p. 1981. text ed. 32.00 (ISBN 0-87766-311-4, URI 33800). Urban Inst.

CAPITAL PUNISHMENT

Laurence, John. The History of Capital Punishment. (Illus.). 230p. 1983. pap. 4.95 (ISBN 0-8065-0840-X). Citadel Pr.

Malloy, Edward A. The Ethics of Law Enforcement & Criminal Punishment. LC 82-20015. 102p. (Orig.). 1983. lib. bdg. 16.75 (ISBN 0-8191-2842-2); pap. 6.75 (ISBN 0-8191-2843-0). U Pr of Amer.

CAPITALISM

see also Capital; Christianity and Economics; Entrepreneur

Braudel, Fernand. The Wheels of Commerce: Civilization & Capitalism, 15th-18th Century Vol. 2. Reynolds, Sian, tr. from Fr. LC 82-48109. (Illus.). 720p. 1983. 33.65i (ISBN 0-06-015091-2, HarpT). Har-Row.

Cecil, Andrew R. The Third Way: Enlightened Capitalism & the Search for a New Social Order. (The Andrew R. Cecil Lectures on Moral Values in a Free Society Ser.: Vol. I). 175p. 1980. 9.95x (ISBN 0-292-78041-9). U of Tex Pr.

Dixon, Marlene & Jonas, Susanne, eds. World Capitalist Crisis & the Rise of the Right. (Contemporary Marxism Ser.). (Illus., Orig.). 1982. pap. 6.50 (ISBN 0-89935-016-X). Synthesis Pubns.

Goldwin, Robert A. & Schambra, William A., eds. How Capitalistic is the Constitution? 1982. 14.25 (ISBN 0-8447-3477-2); pap. 6.25 (ISBN 0-8447-3478-0). Am Enterprise.
Jessop, Bob. The Capitalist State: Marxist Theories & Methods. 320p. 1982. 27.50 (ISBN 0-8147-4163-0); pap. 8.50 (ISBN 0-8147-4164-9). Columbia U Pr.
Michelman, Irving S. The Roots of Capitalism in Western Civilization. LC 82-83776. 336p. 1983. 17.95 (ISBN 0-8119-0486-5). Fell.
Obrinsky, Mark. Profit Theory & Capitalism. LC 82-40482. (Illus.). 176p. 1983. 18.00x (ISBN 0-8122-7863-1); pap. 8.95x (ISBN 0-8122-1147-2). U of Pa Pr.
Pejovich, Svetozar, ed. Philosophical & Economic Foundations of Capitalism. LC 82-48047. 160p. 1982. 19.95x (ISBN 0-669-05906-4). Lexington Bks.
Shelton, Oscar D. Canadian Dominion. 1919. text ed. 8.50x (ISBN 0-686-83498-4). Elliots Bks.
Tenenbaum, Edward A. National Socialism vs. International Capitalism. 1942. text ed. 39.50x (ISBN 0-686-83630-8). Elliots Bks.

CAPITALIZATION (FINANCE)
see Corporations–Finance; Railroads–Finance; Securities; Valuation

CAPOTE, TRUMAN, 1924-
Rudisill, Marie & Simmons, James C. Truman Capote. (Illus.). 224p. 1983. 11.95 (ISBN 0-686-84633-8). Morrow.
Windham, Donald. Footnote to a Friendship: A Memoir of Truman Capote & Others. (Illus.). 1983. wrappers, ltd. ed. 25.00x (ISBN 0-917366-06-9). S Campbell.

CAR SERVICE (FREIGHT)
see Railroads–Freight

CAR WORKERS
see Railroads–Employees

CARAVAGGIO, MICHELANGELO MERISI DA, 1569-1609
Moir, Alfred. Caravaggio. (Library of Great Painters). (Illus.). 168p. 1982. 40.00 (ISBN 0-8109-0757-7). Abrams.

CARBINES
see Rifles

CARBOHYDRATE METABOLISM
Creutzfeldt, W., ed. Acarbose: Proceedings of the International Symposium on Acarbose Effects on Carbohydrate & Fat Metabolism, First, Montreux, October 8-10, 1981. (International Congress Ser.: No. 594). 588p. 1982. 81.00 (ISBN 0-444-90283-X, Excerpta Medica). Elsevier.

CARBOHYDRATES
International Symposium on Pre-Harvest Sprouting in Cereals. Proceedings. Kruger, James E. & LaBerge, Donald E., eds. 320p. 1982. lib. bdg. 22.00 (ISBN 0-86531-535-3). Westview.
Lee, C. K., et al, eds. Developments in Food Carbohydrates, Vols. 1 & 2. Vol. 1, 1977. 41.00 (ISBN 0-85334-733-6, Pub. by Applied Sci England); Vol. 2, 1980. 74.00 (ISBN 0-85334-857-X). Elsevier.
Ross, Shirley. The Complex Carbohydrate Handbook. 192p. 1981. pap. 6.95 (ISBN 0-688-00593-4). Quill NY.
Tipson, R. Stuart & Horton, Derek, eds. Advances in Carbohydrate Chemistry & Biochemistry, Vol. 41. (Serial Publication). Date not set. price not set (ISBN 0-12-007241-6); price not set Lib. ed. (ISBN 0-12-007294-7). Acad Pr.

CARBOHYDRATES IN THE BODY
see also Carbohydrate Metabolism
The New Low Carbohydrate Diet. Date not set. pap. 1.95 (ISBN 0-515-07062-9). Jove Pubns.

CARBON
see also Coal; Diamonds
Bolin, B., et al. The Global Carbon Cycle: Scope Report 13. (Scientific Committee on Problems of the Environment Ser). 491p. 1979. pap. 52.95x (ISBN 0-471-99710-2, Pub. by Wiley-Interscience). Wiley.
Thrower, Peter A., ed. Chemistry & Physics of Carbon, Vol. 18. (Illus.). 208p. 1983. 45.00 (ISBN 0-8247-1740-6). Dekker.

CARBON-ISOTOPES
Fuchs, P. L. & Bunnell, C. A. Carbon-Thirteen NMR Based Organic Spectral Problems. LC 78-20668. 309p. 1979. pap. text ed. 14.95 (ISBN 0-471-04907-7). Wiley.

CARBON COMPOUNDS
Ansell, M. F., ed. Rodd's Chemistry of Carbon Compounds, 2 pts. in 1, Suppl. Vol. 1 C & D. (Pt. A: Monocarbon Derivatives, Pt. 2: Dihydric Alcohols). 1973. 93.75 (ISBN 0-444-41072-4). Elsevier.
--Rodd's Chemistry of Carbon Compounds, 2 pts. in 1, Suppl. Vol. 1 A & B. (Pt. A: Hydrocarbons, Pt. B: Monohydric Alcohols). 1975. 72.50 (ISBN 0-444-40972-6). Elsevier.
--Rodd's Chemistry of Carbon Compounds, 3 pts. in 1, Suppl. Vol. 2 C-E. 1974. 76.75 (ISBN 0-444-41135-6). Elsevier.
--Rodd's Chemistry of Carbon Compounds, 2 pts. in 1, Suppl. Vol. 2 A & B. 1974. 93.75 (ISBN 0-444-41133-X). Elsevier.

CARBON DIOXIDE
Lemon, Edgar R. Co2 & Plants. 350p. 1983. lib. bdg. 25.00x (ISBN 0-86531-597-3). Westview.

CARBONATED BEVERAGES
see Beverages

CARBONATES
Bhattacharyya, Ajit & Friedman, Gerald M., eds. Modern Carbonate Environments. LC 82-11816. (Benchmark Papers in Geology: Vol. 74). 400p. 1982. 50.00 (ISBN 0-87933-436-3). Hutchinson Ross.

CARBONIC ACID
see Carbon Dioxide

CARBONYL COMPOUNDS
Weiner, Henry & Wermuth, Bendicht, eds. Enzymology of Carbonyl Metabolism: Aldehyde Dehydrogenase & Carbonyl Reductase. LC 82-20381. (Progress in Clinical & Biological Research Ser.: Vol. 114). 430p. 1982. 44.00 (ISBN 0-8451-0114-5). A R Liss.

CARCINOGENESIS
see also Carcinogens
Boynton, Alton L. & McKeehan, Wallace L., eds. Ions, Cell Proliferation, & Cancer. LC 82-20786. 1982. 39.50 (ISBN 0-12-123050-3). Acad Pr.
Floyd, Robert A., ed. Free Radicals & Cancer. (Illus.). 552p. 1982. 69.75 (ISBN 0-8247-1551-9). Dekker.
Harris, Curtis C. & Cerutti, Peter A., eds. Mechanisms of Chemical Carcinogenesis. LC 82-6556. (UCLA Symposia on Molecular & Cellular Biology Ser.: Vol. 2). 606p. 1982. 98.00 (ISBN 0-8451-2601-6). A R Liss.
Langenbach, Robert & Nesnow, Stephen, eds. Organ & Species Specificity in Chemical Carcinogenesis. 704p. 1983. 79.50x (ISBN 0-306-41184-9, Plenum Pr). Plenum Pub.

CARCINOGENS
Murray, Randall, ed. Mutagens & Carcinogens. 147p. 1977. 18.50x (ISBN 0-8422-4119-1). Irvington.
Nicolini, Claudio, ed. Chemical Carcinogenesis. (NATO Advanced Study Institutes Ser. A. Life Sciences). 510p. 1982. 59.50x (ISBN 0-306-41111-3, Plenum Pr). Plenum Pub.
Sugimura, Takashi & Kondo, Sohei, eds. Environmental Mutagens & Carcinogens. LC 82-15231. 784p. 1982. 80.00 (ISBN 0-8451-3007-2). A R Liss.
Vainio, H., et al. Occupational Cancer & Carcinogenesis. 1981. 49.50 (ISBN 0-07-066798-5). McGraw.

CARCINOMA
see Cancer; Tumors

CARD GAMES
see Cards

CARD SHARPING
see Cardsharping

CARD SYSTEM IN BUSINESS
see Files and Filing (Documents)

CARD TRICKS
Okal, Bill. Card Magic. LC 82-14482. (Illus.). 192p. (Orig.). 1982. pap. 7.00 (ISBN 0-910199-00-0). Paragon-Reiss.

CARDBOARD
see Paperboard

CARDIAC ARREST
see Heart Failure

CARDIAC CATHETERIZATION
Purcell, Julia Ann. Cardiac Catheterization. Hull, Nancy R., ed. (Illus.). 36p. 1982. 4.00 (ISBN 0-939838-10-9). Pritchett & Hull.

CARDIAC DISEASES
see Heart–Diseases

CARDIAC PACING
see Pacemaker, Artificial (Heart)

CARDIAC PATIENTS
see Cardiacs

CARDIAC RESUSCITATION
Dillard, Jack. Heart Stop: No Death at All. (Illus.). 42p. (Orig.). 1982. pap. write for info. (ISBN 0-940588-08-0). Hazlett Print.

CARDIACS
see also Coronary Care Units
Becker, R., et al, eds. Psychopathological & Neurological Dysfunctions Following Open-Heart Surgery, Milwaukee 1980: Proceedings. (Illus.). 384p. 1983. 57.00 (ISBN 0-387-11621-4). Springer-Verlag.
Chung, David. Anesthesia in Patients with Ischemic Heart Disease. (Current Topics in Anesthesia Ser.: No. 6). 192p. 1982. text ed. 32.50 (ISBN 0-7131-4407-6). E Arnold.
Davis & Spillman. Cardiac Rehabilitation for the Patient & Family. 1982. pap. text ed. 9.07 (ISBN 0-8359-0676-0). Reston.
Roberts, D. H. Coronary Artery Bypass Patient. 1983. 59.50 (ISBN 0-8151-7303-2). Year Bk Med.

CARDINAL VIRTUES
see Virtue and Virtues

CARDINALS
Shehan, Lawrence. A Blessing of Years: The Memoirs of Lawrence Cardinal Shehan. 1983. price not set. U of Notre Dame Pr.

CARDIOGRAPHY
An Abstract Compendium from the World Literature on the Use of Atenolol in the Management of Hypertension. (Illus.). 96p. 1982. write for info. (ISBN 0-88137-001-0). TransMedica.
Kra, Siegfried J. Basic M-Mode Echocardiography. 1982. 37.50 (ISBN 0-87488-978-2). Med Exam.
Magnani, Bruno & Hansson, Lennart, eds. Potassium, the Heart & Hypertension: A Symposium Sponsored by the Italian Society of Cardiology. LC 82-51013. (Illus.). 200p. 1982. write for info. (ISBN 0-88137-000-2). TransMedica.
Meltzer, R. S. & Roelandt, J. Contrast Echocardiography. 1982. 69.50 (ISBN 90-247-2531-3, Pub. by Martinus Nijhoff Netherlands). Kluwer Boston.
Nasser & Guiliani. Clinical Two-Dimensional Echcocardiography. 1983. 34.95t (ISBN 0-8151-3501-7). Year Bk Med.
Roelandt, J. The Practice of M-Mode & Two-Dimensional Echocardiagraphy. 1983. 59.00 (ISBN 90-247-2745-6, Pub. by Martinus Nijhoff Netherlands). Kluwer Boston.

CARDIOLOGY
see also Heart–Diseases
Baan, J. & Arntzenius, A. C. Basic & Clinical Aspects of Cardiac Dynamics. (International Congress Ser.: No. 453). (Abstracts). 1978. pap. 18.75 (ISBN 0-444-90037-3). Elsevier.
Berman, Neil D. Geriatric Cardiology. LC 81-70163. 256p. 1982. 25.95 (ISBN 0-669-04505-5). Heath.
Ferrer, M. Irene, ed. Current Cardiology, Vol. 1. (Current Ser.). 363p. 1979. 50.00 (ISBN 0-471-09478-1, Pub. by Wiley Med). Wiley.
Kaplan, Joel A., ed. Cardiac Anesthesia: Cardiovascular Pharmacology. (Clinical Cardiology Monograph: Vol. 2). write for info (ISBN 0-8089-1567-3). Grune.
Lesch, Michael, intro. by. Current Concepts in Cardiology. (Illus.). 121p. (Orig.). 1979. pap. text ed. 6.00 (ISBN 0-910133-03-4). MA Med Soc.
Loellgen, H., ed. Oberrheinisches Kardiologen-Symposium, Freiburg, May 1982: Journal: Cardiology, Vol. 70, Suppl. 1, 1983. (Illus.). vi, 118p. 1983. pap. price not set (ISBN 3-8055-3688-7). S Karger.
Phibbs, Brendan. The Human Heart: A Consumer's Guide to Cardiac Care. LC 82-2119. (Medical Library). (Illus.). 240p. 1982. pap. 8.95 (ISBN 0-452-25337-3, 3942-7). Mosby.
Proctor, Harvey W., et al, eds. Year Book of Cardiology 1983. 1983. 40.00 (ISBN 0-8151-4202-1). Year Bk Med.
Talano, James V. Textbook of Two-Dimensional Echocardiography. write for info (ISBN 0-8089-1556-8). Grune.
Vyden. Post Myocardial Infarction Management & Rehabilitation. (Cardiology Ser.). 544p. 1983. price not set (ISBN 0-8247-1799-6). Dekker.

CARDIOVASCULAR AGENTS
Cardiovascular Drugs & Instrumentation. 1982. 1195.00 (282). Predicasts.

CARDIOVASCULAR DISEASE NURSING
see also Coronary Care Units
Andreoli, Kathleen G. & Fowkes, Virginia K. Comprehensive Cardiac Care: A Text for Nurses, Physicians & Other Health Practitioners. 5th ed. (Illus.). 562p. 1983. pap. text ed. 18.95 (ISBN 0-8016-0265-3). Mosby.
Fugate, Howard. Cardiac Rehabilitation: The Road to a Healthy Heart. McCavitt, William E., ed. 92p. 1980. pap. 5.00 (ISBN 0-935648-06-2). Halldin Pub.

CARDIOVASCULAR DRUGS
see Cardiovascular Agents

CARDIOVASCULAR RESEARCH
Marker, Carolyn G. & Quigley, Edward J. Cardiovascular Assessment Update: Cardiovascular Nursing Mastery Module Program. (Illus.). 32p. 1982. pap. text ed. 12.00 (ISBN 0-916730-53-0). InterMed Comm.
Timmis, Gerald C., et al, eds. Cardiovascular Review 1983. (Monograph). 1982. 29.50. Acad Pr.

CARDIOVASCULAR SYSTEM
see also Blood-Vessels; Heart
Ghista, D. N. & Yang, W. J., eds. Cardiovascular Engineering, Part III: Diagnosis. (Advances in Cardiovascular Physics: Vol. 5). (Illus.). x, 158p. 1983. 68.50 (ISBN 3-8055-3611-9). S Karger.
Gootman. Perinatal Cardiovascular Function. 448p. 1983. 65.00 (ISBN 0-8247-1671-X). Dekker.
Hanrath, P. Cardiovascular Diagnosis by Ultrasound. 1982. 39.50 (ISBN 90-247-2692-1, Pub. by Martinus Nijhoff Netherlands). Kluwer Boston.
Nicholaides, A. International Vascular Symposium Abstracts. 320p. 1982. 39.00x (ISBN 0-686-82353-2, Pub. by Macmillan England). State Mutual Bk.
Schlaefke, M. E., et al, eds. Central Neurone Environment & the Control Systems of Breathing & Circulation. (Proceedings in Life Sciences Ser.). 275p. 1982. 35.00 (ISBN 0-387-11671-0). Springer-Verlag.

CARDIOVASCULAR SYSTEM-DISEASES
see also Cardiovascular Disease Nursing
also specific diseases, e.g. Varix
Altura, B. M. & Altura, Bella T., eds. Dietary Minerals & Cardiovascular Disease. (Journal: Magnesium: Vol. 1, No. 3-6). (Illus.). vi, 178p. 1983. pap. 78.00 (ISBN 3-8055-3682-8). S Karger.
Ghista, D. N. & Yang, W. J., eds. Cardiovascular Engineering, Part III: Diagnosis. (Advances in Cardiovascular Physics: Vol. 5). (Illus.). x, 158p. 1983. 68.50 (ISBN 3-8055-3611-9). S Karger.
Krantz, David S. & Baum, Andrew. Handbook of Psychology & Health: Cardiovascular Disorders & Behavior, No.3. 400p. 1983. text ed. write for info. (ISBN 0-89859-185-6). L Erlbaum Assocs.
Sprung, Charles L. The Pulmonary Artery Catheter: Methodology & Clinical Applications. 1983. pap. 16.95 (ISBN 0-8391-1808-2, 15520). Univ Park.
Wagner, Galen S. Myocardial Infarction. 1982. 69.50 (ISBN 90-247-2513-5, Pub. by Martinus Nijhoff Netherlands). Kluwer Boston.
Yacone, Linda A. Cardiovascular Problems. Van Meter, Margaret, ed. (RN Nursing Assessment Ser.). 160p. 1983. 10.95 (ISBN 0-87489-289-9). Med Economics.

CARDIOVASCULAR SYSTEM-RESEARCH
see Cardiovascular Research

CARDIOVASCULAR SYSTEM-SURGERY
Burakovsky, V. I. & Bockeria, L. A. Hyperbaric Oxygenation & Its Value in Cardiovascular Surgery. 343p. 1981. 11.50 (ISBN 0-8285-2282-0, Pub. by Mir Pubs USSR). Imported Pubns.
Goldstone, Jerry. Decision Making in Vascular Surgery. 240p. 1983. text ed. 30.00 (ISBN 0-941158-14-4, D1889-4). Mosby.
Pollock, J. G. Topical Reviews in Vascular Surgery, Vol. 1. (Illus.). 240p. 1982. text ed. 32.50 (ISBN 0-7236-0575-0). Wright-PSG.

CARDS
see also Card Tricks; Cardsharping
also names of card games, e.g. Cribbage, Contract Bridge
Fournier, Felix A. Playing Cards: Fournier Musuem. (Illus.). 344p. 1982. 45.00 (ISBN 0-88079-026-1). US Games Syst.
Stelzel, Christian. Magic Cards. 52p. 1982. pap. 3.95 (ISBN 0-88079-025-3). US Games Syst.
Wowk, Kathleen. Playing Cards of the World. 160p. 1982. 60.00x (ISBN 0-7188-2408-3, Pub. by Lutterworth Pr England). State Mutual Bk.
--Playing Cards of the World. (Illus.). 160p. 1982. 25.00 (ISBN 0-7188-2408-3). US Games Syst.

CARDS, GREETING
see Greeting Cards

CARDSHARPING
Robert, Williar & Houdin, William J. Card Sharper-Their Tricks Exposed or the Art of Always Winning. 158p. 1982. pap. 3.95 (ISBN 0-686-42831-5). Gamblers.

CARE OF SOULS
see Pastoral Counseling; Pastoral Theology

CAREER EDUCATION
see Vocational Education

CAREER WOMEN
see Women–Employment

CAREERS
see Occupations; Professions; Vocational Guidance

CARGO AIRCRAFT
see Transport Planes

CARGO HANDLING
George, William E. Stability & Trim for the Ship's Officer. 3rd, rev. ed. LC 82-74137. (Illus.). 400p. 1983. text ed. 15.00 (ISBN 0-87033-297-X). Cornell Maritime.
Jane's Airport Equiptment 1982-1983. (Jane's Yearbooks). (Illus.). 400p. 120.00 (ISBN 0-86720-610-1). Sci Bks Intl.

CARGO PLANES
see Transport Planes

CARIBBEAN AREA
Carim, Enver, ed. Latin America & Caribbean: 1982-83. (World of Information Ser.). 256p. pap. 24.95 (ISBN 0-911818-32-4). World Almanac.

CARIBBEAN AREA-DESCRIPTION AND TRAVEL-GUIDE-BOOKS
Baedeker. Baedeker's Caribbean. (Illus.). 250p. 1983. pap. 14.95 (ISBN 0-13-056143-6). P-H.
Birnbaum, Stephen. The Caribbean, Bermuda & the Bahamas. (Get 'em & Go Travel Guide Ser.). 1982. 11.95 (ISBN 0-686-84795-4). HM.
Zellers, Margaret. Fielding's Caribbean 1983. rev. ed. 875p. 1982. 12.00 (ISBN 0-688-01343-0). Fielding.

CARIBBEAN AREA-DISCOVERY AND EXPLORATION
see America–Discovery and Exploration

CARIBBEAN AREA-ECONOMIC CONDITIONS
Garcia, Connie & Medina, Arthur. Businessman's Guide to the Caribbean. 624p. 1983. text ed. 45.00 (ISBN 0-934642-05-2); pap. 35.00 (ISBN 0-934642-08-7). Puerto Rico Almanacs.
Kowalewski. Transnational Corporations & Caribbean Inequalities. 252p. 1982. 27.95 (ISBN 0-03-062001-5). Praeger.
Mandle, J. R. Patterns of Caribbean Development: An Interpretive Essay on Economic Change. (Carribean Studies: Vol. 2). 162p. 32.50 (ISBN 0-677-06000-9). Gordon.
Miller, E. W. & Miller, Ruby M. Middle America & the Caribbean: A Bibliography on the Third World. (Public Aministration Ser.: Bibliography P-1063). 98p. 1982. pap. 15.00 (ISBN 0-88066-213-1). Vance Biblios.

CARIBBEAN AREA-HISTORY
Williams, Eric. From Columbus to Castro: The History of the Carribean, 1492-1969. LC 82-49083. (Illus.). 608p. 1983. pap. 8.95 (ISBN 0-394-71502-0, Vin). Random.

CARIBBEAN AREA-SOCIAL CONDITIONS
Miller, E. W. & Miller, Ruby M. Middle America & the Caribbean: A Bibliography on the Third World. (Public Aministration Ser.: Bibliography P-1063). 98p. 1982. pap. 15.00 (ISBN 0-88066-213-1). Vance Biblios.

Richardson, Bonham C. Carribean Migrants: Environment & Human Survival on St. Kitts & Nevis. LC 82-7078. (Illus.). 224p. 1983. text ed. 19.95x (ISBN 0-87049-360-4); pap. text ed. 12.50x (ISBN 0-87049-361-2). U of Tenn Pr.

CARIBBEAN COOKERY

see Cookery, Caribbean

CARIBBEAN LITERATURE–HISTORY AND CRITICISM

Desnoes & Edmundo. Literatures in Transition: The Many Voices of the Caribbean Area A Symposium. Minc, Rose S., ed. LC 82-84104. 180p. (Eng. & Span.). 1983. pap. 12.95 (ISBN 0-935318-10-0). Edins Hispamerica.

Paquet, Sandra P. The Novels of George Lamming. (Studies in Caribbean Literature). 144p. (Orig.). 1983. pap. text ed. 10.00x (ISBN 0-435-91831-1). Heinemann Ed.

CARICATURE

see also Caricatures and Cartoons; Wit and Humor

Lambourne, Lionel. Introduction to Caricature. (The Victoria & Albert Museum Introductions to the Decorative Arts). (Illus.). 48p. 1983. 9.95 (ISBN 0-88045-018-5). Stemmer Hse.

CARICATURES AND CARTOONS

see also Caricature; Comic Books, Strips, Etc.; Moving-Picture Cartoons; Wit and Humor, Pictorial also American Wit and Humor, Pictorial; English Wit and Humor, Pictorial; and similar headings

Atwood, Charles. A Doughnut on the Nose is Better than Mustard on the Toes. 96p. (Orig.). 1983. pap. 3.95 (ISBN 0-89815-088-4). Ten Speed Pr.

Borgman, Jim. Smorgasborgman. Borgman, Lynn G., ed. (Illus.). 160p. (Orig.). 1982. pap. 6.95 (ISBN 0-9609632-0-0). Armadillo Pr.

Brooks, Charles, ed. Best Editorial Cartoons of the Year: 1983 Edition. LC 73-643645. 160p. 1983. pap. 9.95 (ISBN 0-88289-406-4). Pelican.

Bunker, Gary L. & Bitton, Davis. The Mormon Graphic Image, Eighteen Thirty-Four to Nineteen Fourteen: Cartoons, Caricatures, & Illustrations. (Publications in the American West: Vol. 16). (Illus.). 140p. 1983. 20.00 (ISBN 0-87480-218-0). U of Utah Pr.

Davis, Jim. Here Comes Garfield. 1982. pap. 4.95 (ISBN 0-686-82437-7). Ballantine.

Faulkner, Janette & Henderson, Robbin. Ethnic Notions: Black Images in the White Mind. (Illus.). 80p. (Orig.). pap. 11.00x (ISBN 0-686-42913-3). Berkeley Art.

Fugitt, Jack. The Big J Handbook for Artists & Cartoonists. 1983. 19.95 (ISBN 0-686-84441-6). Vantage.

Gross, S. More Gross: Cartoons. LC 82-73194. (Illus.). 128p. 1982. 10.95. Congdon & Weed.

Heller, Steven, ed. War Heads: Cartoonists Draw the Line. 1983. pap. 4.95 (ISBN 0-14-006620-9). Penguin.

Juster, Norton. Otter Nonsense. (Illus.). 64p. 1982. 8.95 (ISBN 0-399-20932-8, Philomel); pap. 3.95 (ISBN 0-399-20931-X). Putnam Pub Group.

Martin, Ted. Pavlov...Dog Pounds. 104p. 1983. pap. 3.95 (ISBN 0-8362-2050-1). Andrews & McMeel.

Millar, Jeff & Hinds, Bill. Another Day, Another 11,647.63 Dollars. 128p. 1983. pap. 5.95 (ISBN 0-8362-2016-1). Andrews & McMeel.

Rechin, Bill & Wilder, Don. There's No Escape from the Legion. 128p. 1983. pap. 1.95 (ISBN 0-449-12461-4, GM). Fawcett.

Romano, Branko E. Chicken Toons. LC 82-83844. 1982. pap. 4.00 (ISBN 0-89229-010-2). Tonatiuh-Quinto Sol Intl.

Romano, Octavio I. Word Toons. LC 82-83843. 1982. pap. 3.50 (ISBN 0-89229-011-0). Tonatiuh-Quinto Sol Intl.

Small, Ruth. Fatsy Patsy. (Illus.). 64p. 1983. 6.95 (ISBN 0-89962-329-8). Todd & Honeywell.

Tolner, J. The Gnu Book. 90p. (Orig.). 1983. pap. 5.95 (ISBN 0-939722-17-8). Pressworks.

Trudeau, Garry. It's Supposed to Be Yellow, Pinhead: Selected Cartoons from Ask for May, Settle for June, Vol. I. 128p. 1983. pap. 2.25 (ISBN 0-449-20193-7, Crest). Fawcett.

We're All in This Together: Selected Cartoons from Dr. Beagle & Mr. Hyde, Vol. II. 128p. 1983. pap. 1.95 (ISBN 0-449-20097-3, Crest). Fawcett.

Wilson, Tom. Ziggy's Big Little Book. (Illus.). 208p. 1983. pap. 3.95 (ISBN 0-8362-1990-2). Andrews & McMeel.

Wright, Patrick. Walkies. (Illus.). 64p. 1983. pap. 4.95 (ISBN 0-686-81851-2); pap. 49.50 prepack of 10. St Martin.

CARICATURES AND CARTOONS–GREAT BRITAIN

Scarfe, Gerald. Gerald Scarfe. (Illus., Orig.). 1982. pap. 12.95 (ISBN 0-500-27268-9). Thames Hudson.

CARMELITES

Eugene, P. M. I Want to See God. Clare, M. V., Sr., tr. 549p. 1982. pap. 15.00 (ISBN 0-87061-051-1). Chr Classics.

CARNEADES, 2ND CENTURY B.C.

Schutz, Alfred. Reflections on the Problem of Relevance. Zaner, Richard M., ed. LC 82-11850. xxiv, 186p. 1982. Repr. of 1970 ed. lib. bdg. 25.00x (ISBN 0-313-22820-5, SCRER). Greenwood.

CARNIVALS (CIRCUS)

see Amusement Parks

CARNIVOROUS PLANTS

see Insectivorous Plants

CAROLS

see also Christmas–Poetry; Christmas Music

Roseberry, Eric, ed. Faber Book of Carols & Christmas Songs. Date not set. pap. price not set. Faber & Faber.

CARPENTRY

see also Cabinet-Work; Walls; Woodwork

Bates, D. R. Carpentry & Joinery. (Illus.). 208p. 1982. pap. text ed. 13.95x (ISBN 0-7121-0394-5). Intl Ideas.

Feirer. Guide to Residential Carpentry. 1983. text ed. price not set (ISBN 0-87002-383-7). Bennett Il.

Rudman, Jack. Foreman (Structures - Group A) (Carpentry) (Career Examination Ser.: C-1322). (Cloth bdg. avail. on request). pap. 12.00 (ISBN 0-8373-1322-8). Natl Learning.

Step-By-Step Basic Carpentry. pap. 5.95 (ISBN 0-696-01185-9). Meredith Corp.

CARPENTRY–TOOLS

see also Saws

Roberts, Kenneth D., ed. Belcher Brothers & Co.'s Eighteen Sixty Price List of Boxwood & Ivory Rules. (Illus.). 40p. 1982. pap. text ed. 5.00 (ISBN 0-913602-51-5). K Roberts.

--The Carpenter's Slide Rule: Its History & Use. 32p. (Orig.). 1982. pap. text ed. 4.00 (ISBN 0-913602-50-7). K Roberts.

CARPETS

see also Weaving

Izmidlian, Georges. Oriental Rugs & Carpets Today: How to Choose & Enjoy Them. (Illus.). 128p. 1983. 19.95 (ISBN 0-88254-800-X); pap. 11.95 (ISBN 0-88254-801-8). Hippocrene Bks.

CARRACCI, AGOSTINO, 1577-1602

Bohlin, Diane D. Prints & Related Drawings by the Carracci Family. LC 78-31551. (Illus.). pap. 8.00 (ISBN 0-89468-047-1). Natl Gallery Art.

CARRACCI, ANNIBALE, 1560-1609

Bohlin, Diane D. Prints & Related Drawings by the Carracci Family. LC 78-31551. (Illus.). pap. 8.00 (ISBN 0-89468-047-1). Natl Gallery Art.

CARRACCI, LODOVICO, 1555-1619

Bohlin, Diane D. Prints & Related Drawings by the Carracci Family. LC 78-31551. (Illus.). pap. 8.00 (ISBN 0-89468-047-1). Natl Gallery Art.

CARRIER CONTROL SYSTEMS

International Conference, 1st, Stratford-upon-Avon, UK June 2-4, 1981. Automated Guided Vehicle Systems: Proceedings. 231p. 1981. pap. text ed. 88.00x (ISBN 0-903608-18-9). Scholium Intl.

CARRIER PIGEONS

see Pigeons

CARRIERS, AIRPLANE

see Aircraft Carriers

CARROLL, LEWIS

see Dodgson, Charles Lutwidge, 1832-1898

CARS (AUTOMOBILES)

see Automobiles

CARS, ARMORED (TANKS)

see Tanks (Military Science)

CARS, RAILROAD

see Railroads–Cars

CARS AND CAR BUILDING

see Railroads–Cars

CARSON, RACHEL LOUISE

Gartner, Carol B. Rachel Carson. LC 82-40285. (Literature & Life Ser.). 200p. 1983. 11.95 (ISBN 0-8044-5425-6); pap. 5.95 (ISBN 0-8044-6143-0). Ungar.

CARTILAGE

Hall, Brian K., ed. Cartilage: Biomedical Aspects, Vol. 3. LC 82-20566. Date not set. price not set (ISBN 0-12-319503-9). Acad Pr.

CARTOGRAPHY

Auto Carto 5: International Symposium on Computer-Assisted Cartography, Jan. 1983. 20.00 (ISBN 0-937294-44-6). ASP.

Stibble, Hugo L., ed. Cartographic Materials. LC 82-11519. 268p. 1982. text ed. 40.00 (ISBN 0-8389-0363-0). ALA.

Zogner, Lothar. Bibliogaphia Cartographica, Vol. 4. 206p. 1977. pap. 20.00 (ISBN 3-7940-3474-0, Pub. by K G Saur). Shoe String.

--Bibliographia Cartographica, Vol. 1. pap. 20.00 (ISBN 3-7940-3471-6, Pub. by K G Saur). Shoe String.

--Bibliographia Cartographica, Vol. 2. 195p. 1975. pap. 20.00 (ISBN 3-7940-3472-4, Pub. by K G Saur). Shoe String.

--Bibliographia Cartographica, Vol. 3. 209p. 1976. pap. 20.00 (ISBN 3-7940-3473-2, Pub. by K G Saur). Shoe String.

--Bibliographia Cartographica, Vol. 5. xx, 212p. 1978. pap. 20.00 (ISBN 3-598-20619-4, Pub. by K G Saur). Shoe String.

--Bibliographia Cartographica, Vol. 6. xii, 255p. 1979. pap. 27.00 (ISBN 3-598-20620-8, Pub. by K G Saur). Shoe String.

--Bibliographia Cartographica, Vol. 7. 244p. 1980. pap. 27.00 (ISBN 3-598-20622-4, Pub. by K G Saur). Shoe String.

Zogner, Redaktion L., ed. Bibliographia Cartographica, Vol. 8. xii, 223p. 1983. 28.00 (ISBN 3-598-20624-0, Pub. by K G Saur). Shoe String.

CARTONS

see Paper Coatings

CARTOON DRAWING

see Caricature

CARTOONS

see Caricatures and Cartoons

CARTULARIES

see Archives

CARUSO, ENRICO, 1873-1921

Greenfeld, Howard. Caruso. LC 82-13301. 304p. 1983. 17.95 (ISBN 0-399-12736-4). Putnam Pub Group.

Key, Pierre V. & Zirato, Bruno. Enrico Caruso: A Biography. LC 72-81091. 455p. Date not set. Repr. of 1922 ed. price not set. Vienna Hse.

CARVING (ART INDUSTRIES)

Beecroft, Glynis. Carving Techniques. LC 82-82918. (Illus.). 144p. 1983. pap. 7.95 (ISBN 0-668-05715-7, 5715). Arco.

CARY, JOYCE, 1888-1957

Majumdar, B. Joyce Cary: An Existentialist Approach. 220p. 1982. text ed. 18.50x (ISBN 0-391-02807-3). Humanities.

CASE WESTERN RESERVE UNIVERSITY–SCHOOL OF APPLIED SOCIAL SCIENCES

Runyan, William M. Life Histories & Psychobiography: Explorations in Theory & Method. (Illus.). 304p. 1982. 19.95 (ISBN 0-19-503189-X). Oxford U Pr.

CASE WORK, SOCIAL

see Social Case Work

CASH FLOW

Beehler, Paul J. Contemporary Cash Management: Principles, Practices, Perspectives. 2nd ed. (Systems & Control for Financial Management Ser.). 288p. 1983. 34.95x (ISBN 0-471-86861-2). Ronald Pr.

Cash Flow Control. 24.95 (ISBN 0-914434-20-9). Atcom.

CASHIERS

Rudman, Jack. Cashier - Cashier I. (Career Examination Ser.: C-1327). (Cloth bdg. avail. on request). pap. 10.00 (ISBN 0-8373-1327-9). Natl Learning.

--Cashier II. (Career Examination Ser.: C-2899). (Cloth bdg. avail. on request). pap. 12.00 (ISBN 0-8373-2899-3). Natl Learning.

CASSATT, MARY, 1845-1926

King, Joan. Impressionist: A Novel of Mary Cassatt. 303p. 1983. 16.95 (ISBN 0-8253-0125-4). Beaufort Bks NY.

CASSAVA

Cock, James H. Cassava. (IADS Development-Oriented Literature Ser.). 175p. 1983. lib. bdg. 18.00x (ISBN 0-86531-356-3). Westview.

CASSEROLE RECIPES

see Cookery, Casserole

CAST IRON

see also Founding

American Welding Society. Specification for Cast Iron, Welding Rods & Covered Electrodes for Welding. 1982. 8.00 (ISBN 0-686-43349-1). Am Welding.

--Specification for Steel, Low-Alloy Covered Arc Welding Electrodes: A5.5. 1981. write for info. Am Welding.

CASTAWAYS

see Survival (After Airplane Accidents, Shipwrecks, etc.)

CASTE

see also Social Classes

McGilvray, Dennis B., ed. Caste Ideology & Interaction. LC 81-18037. (Papers in Social Anthropology: No. 9). (Illus.). 258p. 1982. 34.50 (ISBN 0-521-24145-6). Cambridge U Pr.

CASTE–INDIA

see also Untouchables

Chitnis, Suma. A Long Way to Go: Report on a Survey of Scheduled Caste High School & College Students in Fifteen States in India. 350p. 1981. 39.95x (ISBN 0-940500-67-1, Pub by Allied Pubs India). Asia Bk Corp.

Chopra, P. N., ed. Religions & Communities of India. 324p. 1982. 65.00x (ISBN 0-85692-081-9, Pub. by J M Dent). State Mutual Bk.

CASTIGLIONE, BALDASSARE, CONTE, 1478-1529

Hanning, Robert W. & Rosand, David. Castiglione: The Ideal & the Real in Renaissance Culture. LC 82-6944. (Illus.). 240p. 1983. text ed. 22.50x (ISBN 0-300-02649-8). Yale U Pr.

CASTILIAN LANGUAGE

see Spanish Language

CASTING

see Founding

CASTING (FISHING)

see Fly-Casting

CASTLES

Build Your Own Walt Disney's Cinderella Castle. 40p. 1982. pap. 9.95 (ISBN 0-399-50654-3, Perige). Putnam Pub Group.

Castles of Scotland: A Collins Map. 1983. pap. 5.95 (ISBN 0-686-42793-9, Collins Pub England). Greene.

Historic Houses, Castles & Gardens in Great Britain & Ireland, 1982. LC 57-35834. (Illus.). 179p. 1982. pap. 4.50x (ISBN 0-900486-31-7). Intl Pubns Serv.

CASTLES–JUVENILE LITERATURE

Althea. Life in a Castle. (Cambridge Dinosaur Wingate Ser.). (Illus.). 32p. (gr. 10-12). 1983. pap. 1.95 (ISBN 0-521-27169-X). Cambridge U Pr.

Chisholm. Castle Times. 1983. 5.95 (ISBN 0-86020-622-X, 310031); pap. 2.95 (ISBN 0-86020-621-1, 310032). EDC.

Davison, Brian. Explore a Castle. (Illus.). 128p. (gr. 4-6). 1982. 12.50 (ISBN 0-241-10763-6, Pub. by Hamish Hamilton England). David & Charles.

CASTOR (RODENT)

see Beavers

CASTRO, FIDEL, 1927-

Castro, Fidel. Fidel Castro Speeches: Building Socialism in Cuba, Vol. 2. Taber, Michael, ed. 400p. 1983. lib. bdg. 30.00X (ISBN 0-87348-624-2); pap. 7.95X (ISBN 0-87348-650-1). Monad Pr.

CAT

see Cats

CAT, DOMESTIC

see Cats

CATABOLISM

see Metabolism

CATALAN LANGUAGE

Porqueras-Mayo, Albert, et al. The New Catalan Short Story: An Anthology. LC 82-21927. 278p. (Orig.). 1983. lib. bdg. 22.50 (ISBN 0-8191-2899-6); pap. text ed. 11.75 (ISBN 0-8191-2900-3). U Pr of Amer.

CATALOGING

see also Anglo-American Cataloging Rules; Bibliography; Classification–Books; Imprints (In Books); Indexing; Library Science; Searching, Bibliographical

Corrigan, John T., ed. Anglo-American Cataloging Rules: One Year Later. (CLA Studies in Librarianship: No. 6). (Illus.). 61p. pap. 8.00 (ISBN 0-87507-023-X). Cath Lib Assn.

Hunter, Eric & Bakewell, K. G. Cataloguing. 2nd ed. 256p. 1983. 18.50 (ISBN 0-85157-358-4, Pub. by Bingley England). Shoe String.

CATALOGING OF AUDIO-VISUAL MATERIALS

see Cataloging of Non-Book Materials

CATALOGING OF MUSIC

Research Libraries of the New York Public Library. Dictionary Catalog of the Music Collection. 2nd ed. 1983. lib. bdg. 6000.00 (ISBN 0-8161-0374-7, Hall Library). G K Hall.

CATALOGING OF NON-BOOK MATERIALS

see also cataloging of individual types of materials, e.g. Cataloging of Maps

Olson, Nancy B. A Manual of AACR2 Examples for Microcomputer Software & Video Games. Swanson, Edward, ed. 75p. 1983. pap. text ed. 7.00 (ISBN 0-936996-14-5). Soldier Creek.

CATALOGS

see Library Catalogs; also subdivision Catalogs under specific subjects, e.g. Engravings–Catalogs; Manuscripts–Catalogs

CATALOGS, COMMERCIAL

see also Advertising–Direct-Mail

Roberts, Kenneth D., ed. Belcher Brothers & Co.'s Eighteen Sixty Price List of Boxwood & Ivory Rules. (Illus.). 40p. 1982. pap. text ed. 5.00 (ISBN 0-913602-51-5). K Roberts.

Sroge, Maxwell H. The Best in Catalog-1983. 180p. 1983. 29.95 (ISBN 0-942674-03-0). Sroge M.

--Catalog Marketer Supplier's Guide, 1982. 116p. 1982. perfect bound 29.95 (ISBN 0-942674-02-2). Sroge M.

Weisinger, Thelma. One Thousand & One Valuable Things You Can Get Free. (Things You Can Get Free Ser.: No. 12). 224p. 1982. pap. 2.95 (ISBN 0-553-22662-2). Bantam.

CATALOGS, LIBRARY

see Library Catalogs

CATALOGS, PUBLISHERS'

O'Hara, Deborah A., ed. Publisher's Catalogs Annual 1982-1983. 75p. 1982. write for info (ISBN 0-930466-71-3). Meckler Pub.

CATALOGS, STAR

see Stars–Catalogs

CATALOGS, SUBJECT

see also Subject Headings

Ruecker, Norbert & Siedhoff, Thomas. Subject Catalog Film. 385p. 1983. price not set (ISBN 3-598-10414-6). K G Saur.

CATALOGS, UNION

Shaw, Graham W. & Quraishi, Salim, eds. The Bibliography of South Asian Periodicals: A Union List of Periodicals in South Asian Languages. LC 82-16454. 148p. 1983. text ed. 26.50x (ISBN 0-389-20338-6). B&N Imports.

CATALONIA

Freedman, Paul H. The Diocese of Vic: Tradition & Regeneration in Medieval Catalonia. 232p. 1983. 30.00 (ISBN 0-8135-0970-X). Rutgers U Pr.

CATALYSIS

Anderson, J. R. & Boudart, M., eds. Catalysis: Science & Technology, Vol. 3. (Illus.). 290p. 1982. 56.00 (ISBN 0-387-11634-6). Springer-Verlag.

Bell, Alexis T. & Hegedus, L. Louis, eds. Catalysis Under Transient Conditions. (ACS Symposium Ser.: No. 178). 1982. write for info. (ISBN 0-8412-0688-0). Am Chemical.

Catalysis: Science & Technology, Vol. 4. (Illus.). 280p. 1983. 56.00 (ISBN 0-387-11855-1). Springer-Verlag.

Eley, D. D. & Pines, H., eds. Advances in Catalysis, Vol. 31. (Serial Publication). 1983. 52.50 (ISBN 0-12-007831-7); 68.50 (ISBN 0-12-007888-0). Acad Pr.

Ramachandran, P. A. & Chaudhari, R. V. Three Phase Catalytic Reactors. (Topics in Chemical Engineering Ser.: Vol. 2). 530p. 1982. write for info. (ISBN 0-677-05650-8). Gordon.

Tarhan, M. Orhan. Catalytic Reactor Design. (Illus.). 352p. 1983. 36.95 (ISBN 0-07-062871-8, P&RB). McGraw.

CATALYSTS

Dehmlow, Eckhard & Dehmlow, Sigrid. Phase Transfer Catalysis. 2nd ed. Ebel, Hans F., ed. (Monographs in Modern Chemistry: Vol. 11). 1983. price not set (ISBN 3-527-25897-3). Verlag Chemie.

Figueiredo, J. L. Progress in Catalyst Deactivation. 1982. lib. bdg. 49.50 (ISBN 90-247-2690-5, Pub. by Martinus Nijhoff Netherlands). Kluwer Boston.

Tarhan, M. Orhan. Catalytic Reactor Design. (Illus.). 352p. 1983. 36.95 (ISBN 0-07-062871-8, P&RB). McGraw.

CATAMOUNTS

see Pumas

CATAPHORESIS

see Electrophoresis

CATARACT

Brooks, Dennis L. & Henley, Arthur. Don't be Afraid of Cataracts. 128p. 1983. pap. 5.95 (ISBN 0-8065-0823-X). Citadel Pr.

CATASTROPHES

see Disasters

CATAWBA INDIANS

see Indians of North America–Eastern States

CATECHETICS

see also Catechisms; Christian Education

also subdivision Catechisms and Creeds under names of Christian denominations, e.g. Catholic Church–Catechisms and Creeds

Anselm of Canterbury. Why God Became Man & The Virgin Conception & Original Sin. Colleran, Joseph M., tr. from Latin. & intro. by. LC 71-77166. 256p. (Orig.). 1982. pap. text ed. 4.95x (ISBN 0-87343-025-5). Magi Bks.

An Explanation of Dr. Martin Luther's Small Catechism. 265p. 1982. write for info. (ISBN 0-89279-043-1). Board Pub Evang.

Foley, Rita. Create! 2nd ed. (Catechist Training Ser.). 1982. 3.95 (ISBN 0-8215-1230-7). Sadlier.

CATECHETICS–CATHOLIC CHURCH

Carlson, G. R. Comment Etudier et Enselgner la Parole de Dieu. Cosson, Annie, ed. Orig. Title: Preparing to Teach God's Word. (Fr.). 1982. pap. 2.00 (ISBN 0-8297-1235-6). Life Pubs Intl.

Crawford, C. C. Survey Course in Christian Doctrine, Vol. 1 & 2. (Bible Study Textbook Ser.). 221p. (Orig.). 1970. 13.80 (ISBN 0-89900-053-3). College Pr Pub.

CATECHISMS

see also Catechetics; Creeds

also subdivision Catechisms and Creeds under names of religions, religious denominations, etc., e.g. Catholic Church–Catechisms and Creeds

Janz, Denis, ed. Three Reformation Catechisms: Catholic, Anabaptist, Lutheran. (Texts & Studies in Religion: Vol. 13). viii, 224p. 1982. 34.95x (ISBN 0-88946-800-1). E Mellen.

Lemius, J. B. Catechism of Modernism. 160p. pap. 2.00 (ISBN 0-686-81624-2). TAN Bks Pubs.

CATECHOLAMINES

Riemersma, R. A. & Oliver, M. F., eds. Catecholamines in the Non-Ischaemic & Ischaemic Myocardium: Proceedings of the Sixth Argenteuil Symposiym, Waterloo, Belgium, 1981. 260p. 1982. 89.00 (ISBN 0-444-80439-0, Biomedical Pr). Elsevier.

CATEGORIES (MATHEMATICS)

see also Functor Theory

Kamps, K. H., et al, eds. Category Theory, Applications to Algebra, Logic, & Topology: Proceedings, Gummersbach, FRG, 1981. (Lecture Notes in Mathematics Ser.: Vol. 962). 322p. 1983. pap. 16.00 (ISBN 0-387-11961-2). Springer-Verlag.

CATERERS AND CATERING

see also Breakfasts; Buffets (Cookery); Desserts; Dinners and Dining; Luncheons; Menus

Glew, G. Advances in Catering Technology. 1980. 98.50 (ISBN 0-85334-844-8, Pub. by Applied Sci England). Elsevier.

Hughes, Janet & Ireland, Brian. Costing & Calculations for Catering. 176p. 1981. 30.00x (ISBN 0-85950-493-X, Pub. by Thornes England). State Mutual Bk.

Paige, Grace. Catering Costs & Control. 1982. limp bdg. 50.00x (ISBN 0-304-29758-5, Pub. by Cassell England). State Mutual Bk.

Robins, G. V. Food Science in Catering. 1980. pap. 21.50 (ISBN 0-434-90297-7, Pub. by Heinemann). David & Charles.

Ryan, Chris. An Introduction to Hotel & Catering Economics. 288p. 1980. 35.00x (ISBN 0-85950-424-7, Pub. by Thornes England). State Mutual Bk.

CATFISHES

Humphreys Academy Patrons. Festival. (Illus.). 320p. 1983. pap. 10.95 (ISBN 0-9610058-0-7). Humphreys Acad.

Humphreys Academy Patrons, ed. Festival. (Illus.). 320p. 1983. pap. 10.95 (ISBN 0-686-82289-7). Wimmer Bks.

CATHEDRALS

see also Architecture, Gothic; also subdivision Churches under names of cities, e.g. New York (City)–Churches

Collingswood, Hermann. A Collection of Fifty-Five Dramatic Illustrations in Full Colours of the Cathedral Cities of Italy. (The Masterpieces of World Architectual Library). (Illus.). 107p. 1983. Repr. of 1911 ed. 287.75 (ISBN 0-89901-081-4). Found Class Reprints.

English Cathedrals & Churches. 24p. 1982. pap. 30.00x (ISBN 0-7141-0790-5, Pub. by Brit Mus Pubns England). State Mutual Bk.

Gallagher, Maureen. The Cathedral Book. LC 82-60592. (gr. 3-6). 1983. pap. 2.95 (ISBN 0-8091-2485-8). Paulist Pr.

Gilbert, George. The Sixty Dramatic Illustrations in Full Colours of the Cathedral Cities of England. (A Promotion of the Arts Library Bks.). (Illus.). 99p. 1983. 297.85 (ISBN 0-86650-046-4). Gloucester Art.

Levine, Lee I., ed. The Jerusalem Cathedral, Vol. 2. (Studies in the History, Archaeology, Geography & Ethnography of the Land of Israel). 300p. 1983. 25.00x (ISBN 0-8143-1715-4). Wayne St U Pr.

CATHER, WILLA SIBERT, 1873-1947

Robinson, Phyliss C. The Life of Willa Cather. 1983. 17.95 (ISBN 0-686-43267-3). Doubleday.

Robinson, Phyllis C. Willa: The Life of Willa Cather. 1983. 17.95. Doubleday.

CATHERINE 2ND, EMPRESS OF RUSSIA, 1729-1796

Batalden, Stephen K. Catherine II's Greek Prelate: Eugenios Voulgaris in Russia, 1771-1806. (East European Monographs: No. 115). 288p. 1982. 25.00x (ISBN 0-88033-006-6). East Eur Quarterly.

CATHOLIC AUTHORS

see also subdivision Catholic Authors under names of literatures, e.g. English Literature–Catholic Authors

Sonnenfeld, Albert. Crossroads: Essays on the Catholic Novelists. 15.00. French Lit.

CATHOLIC CHURCH

see also Canon Law

Griesbach, Marc F. & Carmichael, John P., eds. The ACPA in Today's Intellectual World: Proceedings, 1983, Vol. 57. LC 82-73233. 250p. 1984. pap. 8.00 (ISBN 0-918090-17-2). Am Cath Philo.

Kaschmitter, William A. The Spirituality of the Catholic Church. 980p. 1982. 30.00 (ISBN 0-912414-33-2). Lumen Christi.

Robleto, Un Adolfo. Un Vistazo a la Doctrina Romana. 128p. 1980. pap. 2.75 (ISBN 0-311-05319-X). Casa Bautista.

CATHOLIC CHURCH–ADDRESSES, ESSAYS, LECTURES

Huizing, Peter & Walf, Knut, eds. Electing Our Own Bishops. (Concilium Ser.: Vol. 137). 128p. (Orig.). 1980. pap. 5.95 (ISBN 0-8164-2279-6). Seabury.

CATHOLIC CHURCH–ASCETICISM

see Asceticism

CATHOLIC CHURCH–DIPLOMATIC RELATIONS

see Catholic Church–Relations (Diplomatic)

CATHOLIC CHURCH–DOCTRINAL AND CONTROVERSIAL WORKS

Realist. No Business Like God's Business. 239p. 1982. 10.95 (ISBN 0-533-04912-1). Vantage.

Woznicki, Andrew N. Journey to the Unknown: Catholic Doctrine on Ethnicity & Migration. 105p. (Orig.). 1982. pap. 3.95 (ISBN 0-910727-01-5). Golden Phoenix.

CATHOLIC CHURCH–FINANCE

Lunt, W. E. Financial Relations of the Papacy with England to 1327. 1967. Repr. of 1939 ed. 20.00X (ISBN 0-910956-13-8). Medieval Acad.

--Financial Relations of the Papacy with England, 1327-1534. 1962. 25.00X (ISBN 0-910956-48-0). Medieval Acad.

CATHOLIC CHURCH–FOREIGN RELATIONS

see Catholic Church–Relations (Diplomatic)

CATHOLIC CHURCH–HISTORY

see also Catholic Church in the United States–History; Counter-Reformation

also names of specific councils of the Catholic Church

Frazee, Charles A. Catholics & Sultans: The Church & the Ottoman Empire 1453-1923. LC 82-4562. 384p. Date not set. price not set (ISBN 0-521-24676-8). Cambridge U Pr.

CATHOLIC CHURCH–HISTORY–MODERN PERIOD, 1500-

Pawsey, Margaret M. The Demon of Discord: Tensions in the Catholic Church of Victoria, 1853-1864. (Illus.). 200p. 1983. 25.00 (ISBN 0-522-84249-6, Pub. by Melbourne U Pr Australia). Intl Schol Bk Serv.

CATHOLIC CHURCH–INFALLIBILITY

see also Popes–Infallibility

Kung, Hans. Infallible? An Inquiry. LC 82-45641. 288p. 1983. pap. 10.95 (ISBN 0-385-18483-2). Doubleday.

CATHOLIC CHURCH–PRAYER-BOOKS AND DEVOTIONS

Fox, Robert J. Prayerbook for Catholics. 112p. (Orig.). 1982. 6.00 (ISBN 0-931888-08-5); pap. 2.95. Christendom Pubns.

CATHOLIC CHURCH–RELATIONS–ORTHODOX EASTERN CHURCH

Chrysostomos, Archimandrite. Orthodoxy & Papism. Williams, Theodore M., ed. 70p. 1982. pap. 4.00 (ISBN 0-911165-00-2). Ctr Trad Orthodox.

CATHOLIC CHURCH–RELATIONS (DIPLOMATIC)

Lukacs, Lajos. The Vatican & Hungary 1846-1878: Reports & Correspondence on Hungary of the Apostolic Nuncios in Vienna. Kormos, Zsofia, tr. 795p. 1981. text ed. 55.00x (ISBN 963-05-2446-5, 41422, Pub. by Kultura Pr Hungary). Humanities.

CATHOLIC CHURCH AND LABOR

see Church and Labor

CATHOLIC CHURCH IN CANADA

Munnick, Harriet. Catholic Church Records of the Pacific Northwest: Vancouver & Stellamaris Mission. LC 72-83958. (Illus.). 1972. 25.00 (ISBN 0-8323-0375-5). Binford.

CATHOLIC CHURCH IN FRANCE

Kselman, Thomas A. Miracles & Prophecies in Nineteenth-Century France. (Illus.). 312p. 1983. 27.50 (ISBN 0-8135-0963-7). Rutgers U Pr.

CATHOLIC CHURCH IN IRELAND

Kerr, Donal A. Peel, Priests & Politics: Sir Robert Peel's Administration & the Roman Catholic Church in Ireland, 1841-1846. (Oxford Historical Monographs). 1982. 49.50x (ISBN 0-19-821891-5). Oxford U Pr.

CATHOLIC CHURCH IN THE UNITED STATES

Munnick, Harriet. Catholic Church Records of the Pacific Northwest: Vancouver & Stellamaris Mission. LC 72-83958. (Illus.). 1972. 25.00 (ISBN 0-8323-0375-5). Binford.

Varacalli, Joseph A. Toward the Establishment of Liberal Catholicism in America. LC 82-23811. 326p. (Orig.). 1983. lib. bdg. 23.75 (ISBN 0-8191-2974-7); pap. text ed. 13.00 (ISBN 0-8191-2975-5). U Pr of Amer.

CATHOLIC CHURCH IN THE UNITED STATES–HISTORY

Dolan, Jay P. The Immigrant Church: New York's Irish & German Catholics, 1815-1865. LC 82-23827. (Illus.). xiv, 221p. 1983. pap. text ed. 7.95x (ISBN 0-268-01151-6, 85-11511). U of Notre Dame Pr.

Hennesey, James. American Catholics: A History of the Roman Catholic Community in the United States. 414p. 1983. pap. 8.95 (ISBN 0-19-503268-3, GB 724, GB). Oxford U Pr.

CATHOLICISM

see Catholicity

CATHOLICITY

see also Ecumenical Movement

Baker, Kenneth S. Fundamentals of Catholicism, Vol. 2. LC 82-80297. 387p. (Orig.). 1983. pap. 10.95 (ISBN 0-89870-019-1). Ignatius Pr.

Kollar, Nathan R., ed. Options in Roman Catholicism: An Introduction. LC 82-21823. 224p. (Orig.). 1983. lib. bdg. 21.50 (ISBN 0-8191-2958-5); pap. text ed. 10.75 (ISBN 0-8191-2959-3). U Pr of Amer.

CATHOLICS

Burns, Robert E. Catholics on the Cutting Edge. 1983. 9.95 (ISBN 0-88347-151-5); pap. 5.95 (ISBN 0-686-83925-0). Thomas More.

Cascone, Gina. Pagan Babies & Other Catholic Memories. 160p. 1983. pap. 4.95 (ISBN 0-312-59419-4). St Martin.

Christopher, Kenneth. Ten Catholics: Lives to Remember. (Nazareth Bks). 120p. 1983. pap. 3.95 (ISBN 0-86683-715-9). Winston Pr.

Novak, Michael. Confession of a Catholic. LC 82-484236. 128p. 1983. 10.53 (ISBN 0-06-066319-7, HarpR). Har-Row.

CATHOLICS IN ENGLAND

Catholic Directory of England & Wales, 1982. 143rd ed. 681p. 1982. 27.50x (ISBN 0-904359-35-2). Intl Pubns Serv.

Hibbard, Caroline M. Charles I & the Popish Plot. LC 81-23075. 350p. 1983. 28.00x (ISBN 0-8078-1520-9). U of NC Pr.

CATIONS

Boynton, Alton L. & McKeehan, Wallace L., eds. Ions, Cell Proliferation, & Cancer. LC 82-20786. 1982. 39.50 (ISBN 0-12-123050-3). Acad Pr.

CATS

Baron, Joan. Cat Couples. LC 82-48798. 160p. (Orig.). 1983. pap. 9.57i (ISBN 0-06-090986-2, CN 986, CN). Har-Row.

Belfield, W. O. & Zucker, M. The Very Healthy Cat Book. 264p. 1983. 14.95 (ISBN 0-07-004367-1, GB); pap. 6.95 (ISBN 0-07-004354-X). McGraw.

Burden, Jean. The Woman's Day Book of Hints for Cat-Owners. Date not set. pap. 5.95 (ISBN 0-686-82631-0, Columbine). Fawcett.

Carlson, Delbert G. & Giffin, James M. Cat Owner's Home Veterinary Handbook. LC 82-23383. (Illus.). 392p. 1983. 17.95 (ISBN 0-87605-814-4). Howell Bk.

The Cat Doctor's Book of Cat Names. (Orig.). 1983. pap. 3.95 (ISBN 0-440-09232-9, Emerald). Dell.

Dale-Green, Patricia. The Archetypal Cat. 2nd ed. Orig. Title: Cult of the Cat. (Illus.). 189p. 1983. pap. 13.50 (ISBN 0-88214-700-5). Spring Pubns.

Di Francis. Cat Country: The Quest for the British Big Cat. (Illus.). 160p. 1983. 12.50 (ISBN 0-7153-8425-2). David & Charles.

Moon, Susan E. & Tracy, Susie. Pritt: The True Story of a Deaf Cat & Her Family. 96p. 1982. pap. 7.95 (ISBN 0-399-50670-5). Putnam Pub Group.

Randolph, Elizabeth. How to Be Your Cat's Best Friend. (Illus.). 224p. 1983. pap. 6.70y (ISBN 0-316-73377-6). Little.

Searle, Ronald. The Big Fat Cat Book. 1982. 12.95 (ISBN 0-316-77898-2). Little.

Suares, J. C. The Indispensable Cat. LC 82-10512. (Illus.). 1983. 29.95 (ISBN 0-941434-21-4). Stewart Tabori & Chang.

Suares, J. C. & Brown, Gene. Cat Scrapbook. (Illus.). 1982. pap. 5.95 (ISBN 0-452-25360-8, Plume). NAL.

Taber, Gladys. Amber, a Very Personal Cat. 160p. 1983. pap. 5.95 (ISBN 0-940160-20-X). Parnassus Imprints.

Urcia, Ingeborg. All About Rex Cats. (Illus.). 9.95 (ISBN 0-87666-858-9). TFH Pubns.

Wilde, Larry. The New Official Cat Lovers Joke Book. 192p. (Orig.). 1983. pap. 1.95 (ISBN 0-523-42004-8). Pinnacle Bks.

CATS–JUVENILE LITERATURE

Coffey, David. A Veterinary Surgeon's Guide for Cat Owners. (Illus.). 216p. 1983. 14.95 (ISBN 0-437-02501-2, Pub. by World's Work). David & Charles.

Hamer, Martyn. Cats. (Easy-Read Fact Bks.). (Illus.). 32p. (gr. 2-4). 1983. PLB 8.60 (ISBN 0-531-04510-2). Watts.

Hill. Cats & Kittens. 1983. 5.95 (ISBN 0-86020-645-9, 15101); pap. 2.95 (ISBN 0-86020-644-0, 15102). EDC.

Neumeyer, Peter. Dream Cat. (Orig.). 1982. pap. 2.50 (ISBN 0-914676-84-9, Pub. by Envelope Bks). Green Tiger Pr.

Rosenberg, Meir. The Jewish Cat Book: A Different Breed! LC 82-62085. (Illus.). 50p. (gr. 8-12). 1982. pap. 4.50 (ISBN 0-916288-15-3). Micah Pubns.

Stolz, Mary. Cat Walk. LC 82-47576. (Illus.). 128p. (gr. 3-7). 1983. 8.61i (ISBN 0-06-025974-4, HarpJ); PLB 8.89g (ISBN 0-06-025975-2). Har-Row.

CAT'S CRADLE

see String Figures

CATSKILL MOUNTAINS

Francis, Austin. Catskill Rivers. (Illus.). 224p. 1983. 24.95 (ISBN 0-8329-0282-9). Winchester Pr.

CATTLE

see also Beef Cattle; Cattle Trade; Cows; Dairy Cattle

also names of specific breeds, e.g. Aberdeen-Angus Cattle

Berg, Roy T. & Butterfield, Rex M. New Concepts of Cattle Growth. 240p. 1978. text ed. 16.95 (ISBN 0-424-00002-4, Pub. by Sydney U Pr). Intl Schol Bk Serv.

Reproductive Efficiency in Cattle: FAO Animal Production & Health Paper. (No. 25). 118p. 1982. pap. 9.00 (ISBN 92-5-101163-X, F2303, FAO). Unipub.

CATTLE, BEEF

see Beef Cattle

CATTLE TRADE

see also Cowboys; Ranch Life

Chrisman, Harry. The Ladder of Rivers: The Story of I. P. Olive. LC 62-22284. (Illus.). 426p. 1983. 18.95 (ISBN 0-8040-0179-0, 82-71157); pap. 9.95 (ISBN 0-8040-0845-0, 82-76164). Ohio U Pr.

Okediji, Florence A. The Cattle Industry in Northern Nigeria, 1900-1939. (African Humanities Ser.). (Illus., Orig.). 1973. pap. text ed. 2.00 (ISBN 0-941934-07-1). Ind U Afro-Amer Arts.

CATV

see Community Antenna Television

CAUGHNAWAGA INDIANS

see Indians of North America–Canada

CAUSALITY

see Causation

CAUSATION

see also Teleology

Brand, Dennis J., Jr., tr. from Span. The Book of Causes. 56p. Date not set. pap. 7.95 (ISBN 0-87462-225-5). Marquette.

James, Lawrence R. & Mulaik, Stanley A. Causal Analysis: Assumptions, Models, & Data: Studying Organizations: Innovations in Methodology. 144p. 1982. 17.95 (ISBN 0-8039-1867-4); pap. 7.95 (ISBN 0-8039-1868-2). Sage.

Schwanauer, Francis. To Make Sure is to Cohere. LC 82-17653. 94p. (Orig.). 1983. pap. text ed. 7.50 (ISBN 0-8191-2766-3). U Pr of Amer.

CAUSE AND EFFECT

see Causation

CAVALRY

Marquess of Anglesey. A History of the British Cavalry, 1872-1898, Vol. III. (Illus.). 520p. 1983. 75.00 (ISBN 0-436-27327-6, Pub. by Secker & Warburg). David & Charles.

CAVES

Trimble, Stephen. Timpanogos Cave: A Window into the Earth. Priehs, T. J. & Dodson, Carolyn, eds. LC 82-61192. 1983. pap. price not set (ISBN 0-911408-64-9). SW Pks Mnmts.

CAVITATION

Billet, M. L. & Arndt, R. E., eds. International Symposium on Cavitation Noise. 1982. 30.00 (H00231). ASME.

Hoyt, J. W., ed. Cavitation & Polyphase Flow Forum-Nineteen Eighty-Two. 65p. 1982. 20.00 (G00208). ASME.

CAYAKS

see Canoes and Canoeing

CB RADIO

see Citizens Band Radio

CBR WARFARE

see Atomic Warfare; Biological Warfare

CEILINGS
see also Mural Painting and Decoration
Better Homes & Gardens Books editors, ed. Better Homes & Gardens All About Your House: Your Walls & Ceilings. (All About your House Ser.). (Illus.). 160p. 1983. 9.95 (ISBN 0-696-02163-3). Meredith Corp.
CELESTIAL MECHANICS
see Mechanics, Celestial
CELESTIAL NAVIGATION
see Nautical Astronomy
CELL, VOLTAIC
see Electric Batteries
CELL BIOLOGY
see Cytology
CELL CULTURE
Pfeiffer, Steven. Neuroscience Approached Through Cell Culture. 248p. 1982. 75.00 (ISBN 0-8493-6340-3). CRC Pr.
CELL DIFFERENTIATION
Jaenicke, L., ed. Biochemistry of Differentiation & Morphogenosis. (Collequium Mosbach Ser.: Vol. 33). (Illus.). 301p. 1983. 37.00 (ISBN 0-387-12010-6). Springer-Verlag.
CELL MOTILITY
see Cells-Motility
CELL WALLS
see Plasma Membranes
CELLO
see Violoncello
CELLS
see also Blood Cells; Cancer Cells; Contractility (Biology); Cytology; Embryology; Epithelium; Histology; Macrophages; Membranes (Biology); Pathology, Cellular; Plant Cells and Tissues; Plasma Membranes; Protoplasm; Protozoa
Freshney, Ian R., ed. Culture of Animal Cells: A Manual of Basic Technique. LC 82-24960. 280p. 1983. write for info. (ISBN 0-8451-0223-0). A R Liss.
Horecker, Bernard & Stadtman, E., eds. Current Topics in Cellular Regulations, Vol. 22. (Serial Publication). Date not set. price not set (ISBN 0-12-152822-7); price not set Lib. ed. (ISBN 0-12-152800-6). Acad Pr.
Keebler, Catherine M. & Reagan, James W. A Manual of Cytotechnology. (Illus.). 1983. text ed. 50.00 (ISBN 0-89189-168-4, 16-3-005-00). Am Soc Clinical.
Morrow, John. Euraryotic Cell Genetics. (Cell Biology Ser.). write for info. (ISBN 0-12-507360-7). Acad Pr.
Prescott, David & Wilson, Leslie, eds. Methods in Cell Biology: Vol. 24A: The Cytoskeleton: Cytoskeletal Proteins, Isolation & Characterization. 464p. 1982. 49.00 (ISBN 0-12-564124-9). Acad Pr.
--Methods in Cell Biology: Vol. 25B: The Cytoskeleton: Biological Systems & in-Vitro Models. 448p. 1982. 47.00 (ISBN 0-12-564125-7). Acad Pr.
Sheffield, J. B. & Hilfer, S. R., eds. Cellular Communication During Ocular Development. (Cell & Developmental Biology of the Eye Ser.). (Illus.). 196p. 1983. 32.50 (ISBN 0-387-90773-4). Springer-Verlag.
CELLS-MOTILITY
Dowben, Robert M. & Shay, Jerry W., eds. Cell & Muscle Motility, Vol. 3. 295p. 1983. 39.50x (ISBN 0-306-41157-1, Plenum Pr). Plenum Pub.
Kepner, G. R., ed. Cell Membrane Permeability & Transport. LC 79-11930. (Benchmark Papers in Human Physiology: Vol. 12). 410p. 1979. 50.00 (ISBN 0-87933-352-9). Hutchinson Ross.
CELLS-PERMEABILITY
Kepner, G. R., ed. Cell Membrane Permeability & Transport. LC 79-11930. (Benchmark Papers in Human Physiology: Vol. 12). 410p. 1979. 50.00 (ISBN 0-87933-352-9). Hutchinson Ross.
CELLULAR BIOLOGY
see Cytology
CELLULAR PATHOLOGY
see Pathology, Cellular
CELLULAR THERAPY
Rafelson, M. E., ed. Cellular & Humoral Defense against Disease. (Journal: Clinical Physiology & Biochemistry: Vol. 1, No. 2-5, 1983). (Illus.). 200p. 1983. pap. price not set (ISBN 3-8055-3693-3). S Karger.
CELLULOSE
Shon, David N., ed. Graft Copolymerization of Lignocellulosic Fibers. (ACS Symposium Ser.: No. 187). 1982. write for info. (ISBN 0-8412-0721-6). Am Chemical.
CELTIC ART
see Art, Celtic
CELTIC FOLK-LORE
see Folk-Lore, Celtic
CELTIC LANGUAGES
MacLean, L. History of the Celtic Language. 288p. 1982. pap. 9.95 (ISBN 0-912526-29-7). Lib Res.
CELTS
Powell, T. G. The Celts. (Ancient Peoples & Places Ser.). (Illus.). 1983. pap. 9.95 (ISBN 0-500-27275-1). Thames Hudson.
CEMBALO
see Dulcimer
CEMENT
see also Adhesives; Concrete
Ghosh, S. N., ed. Advances in Cement Technology: Critical Reviews & Case Studies on Manufacturing, Quality Control, Optimization & Use. (Illus.). 775p. 1982. 100.00 (ISBN 0-08-028670-4). Pergamon.
CEMETERIES
see also Tombs
Arbeiter, Jean & Cirino, Linda. Permanent Addresses: A Guide to the Resting Places of Famous Americans. (Illus.). 256p. 1983. pap. 7.95 (ISBN 0-87131-402-9). M Evans.
Arnold, C. J. The Anglo-Saxon Cemeteries of the Isle of Wight. 208p. 1982. 99.00x (ISBN 0-7141-1359-X, Pub. by Brit Mus Pubns England). State Mutual Bk.
Goerge, Diana Hume & Nelson, Malcolm A. Epitaph & Icon: A Field Guide to the Old Burying Grounds of Cape Cod, Martha's Vineyard & Nantucket. (Illus.). 128p. (Orig.). 1983. 17.50 (ISBN 0-940160-21-8); pap. 12.50 (ISBN 0-940160-17-X). Parnassus Imprints.
CENA, ULTIMA
see Lord's Supper
CENSORSHIP
see also Condemned Books; Liberty of the Press
also subdivision Censorship under specific subjects, e.g. Moving Pictures-Censorship
Bryan, T. Avril. Censorship & Social Conflict in the Spanish Theatre: The Case of Alfonso Sastre. LC 82-17445. 156p. (Orig.). 1983. lib. bdg. 19.25 (ISBN 0-8191-2829-5); pap. text ed. 8.75 (ISBN 0-8191-2830-9). U Pr of Amer.
Bryson, Joseph E. & Detty, Elizabeth W. The Legal Aspects of Censorship of Public School Library & Instructional Materials. 247p. 1982. 20.00 (ISBN 0-87215-556-0). Michie-Bobbs.
Mitchell, Richard H. Censorship in Imperial Japan. LC 82-61440. 432p. 1983. 35.00x (ISBN 0-691-05384-7). Princeton U Pr.
Schopflin, George. Censorship & Political Communication. LC 82-42712. 250p. 1982. 27.50x (ISBN 0-312-12728-6). St Martin.
Sutherland, John. Offensive Literature: Decensorship in Britain, 1960-1982. LC 82-22758. 200p. 1983. text ed. 24.50x (ISBN 0-389-20354-8). B&N Imports.
CENSORSHIP OF THE PRESS
see Liberty of the Press
CENSUS
see also subdivision Census under names of countries, cities, etc. e.g. United States-Census
Goyer, Doreen S. & Domschke, Eliane. The Handbook of National Population Censuses: Latin America & the Caribbean, North America & Oceania. LC 82-9390. (Illus.). 736p. 1983. lib. bdg. 75.00 (ISBN 0-313-21352-6, GHP/). Greenwood.
Long, Sandra M. Using the Census as a Creative Teaching Resource. LC 82-60804. (Fastback Ser.: No. 184). 50p. 1982. pap. 0.75 (ISBN 0-87367-184-8). Phi Delta Kappa.
SPSS Inc. Analysis of U. S. Census Data. 144p. 1983. 16.95x (ISBN 0-07-060523-8, C). McGraw.
Surveys, Polls, Censuses, & Forcasts Directory. 300p. 1983. 150.00x (ISBN 0-8103-1692-7). Gale.
CENTRAL AMERICA
Here are entered works on Central America as a whole. For information about specific countries see names of countries, e. g. Panama.
Fagen, Richard R. & Pellicer, Olga, eds. The Future of Central America: Policy Choices for the U.S. & Mexico. LC 82-62447. 224p. 1983. text ed. 20.00x (ISBN 0-8047-1177-1); pap. text ed. 11.95x (ISBN 0-8047-1190-9). Stanford U Pr.
CENTRAL AMERICA-ANTIQUITIES
Magee, Susan F. MesoAmerican Archaeology: A Guide to the Literature & Other Information Sources. (Guides & Bibliographies Ser.: No. 12). 81p. 1981. pap. text ed. 5.95x (ISBN 0-292-75053-6). U of Tex Pr.
CENTRAL AMERICA-DESCRIPTION AND TRAVEL-GUIDEBOOKS
Barry, Tom & Wood, Beth. Dollars & Dictators: A Guide to Central America. 272p. (Orig.). 1982. pap. 5.95 (ISBN 0-686-37896-2). Resource Ctr.
CENTRAL AMERICA-DISCOVERY AND EXPLORATION
see America-Discovery and Exploration
CENTRAL AMERICA-ECONOMIC CONDITIONS
Stanford Central America Action Network, ed. Revolution in Central America. 525p. 1982. lib. bdg. 30.00 (ISBN 0-86531-540-X); pap. text ed. 13.95 (ISBN 0-86531-541-8). Westview.
CENTRAL AMERICA-FOREIGN RELATIONS
DiGiovanni, Cleto, Jr. Crisis in Central America. (Monographs in International Affairs). 1982. pap. text ed. 6.95 (ISBN 0-686-84670-2). AISI.
CENTRAL AMERICA-JUVENILE LITERATURE
Markun, Patricia M. Central America & Panama. rev. ed. (First Bks.). (Illus.). 96p. (gr. 4 up). 1983. PLB 8.90 (ISBN 0-531-04523-4). Watts.
CENTRAL AMERICA-POLITICS
Durham, William H. Scarcity & Survival in Central America: Ecological Origins of the Soccer War. LC 78-55318. (Illus.). xx, 209p. 1979. pap. 5.95 (ISBN 0-8047-1154-2, SP5); 14.50x (ISBN 0-8047-1000-7). Stanford U Pr.
Grabendorff, Wolf & Krumwiede, Heinrich. Change in Central America: Internal & External Dimensions. (Special Studies in Latin America & the Caribbean). 175p. 1983. lib. bdg. 16.50x (ISBN 0-86531-609-0). Westview.
Stanford Central America Action Network, ed. Revolution in Central America. 525p. 1982. lib. bdg. 30.00 (ISBN 0-86531-540-X); pap. text ed. 13.95 (ISBN 0-86531-541-8). Westview.
CENTRAL AMERICA-SOCIAL CONDITIONS
Durham, William H. Scarcity & Survival in Central America: Ecological Origins of the Soccer War. LC 78-55318. (Illus.). xx, 209p. 1979. pap. 5.95 (ISBN 0-8047-1154-2, SP5); 14.50x (ISBN 0-8047-1000-7). Stanford U Pr.
Flannery, Kent V., ed. The Early Mesoamerican Village. LC 82-6737. 250p. 1982. pap. 17.50 (ISBN 0-12-259852-0). Acad Pr.
Grabendorff, Wolf & Krumwiede, Heinrich. Change in Central America: Internal & External Dimensions. (Special Studies in Latin America & the Caribbean). 175p. 1983. lib. bdg. 16.50x (ISBN 0-86531-609-0). Westview.
Stanford Central America Action Network, ed. Revolution in Central America. 525p. 1982. lib. bdg. 30.00 (ISBN 0-86531-540-X); pap. text ed. 13.95 (ISBN 0-86531-541-8). Westview.
CENTRAL BANKS
see Banks and Banking, Central
CENTRAL BUSINESS DISTRICTS
Barnes, W. Anderson. Downtown Development: Plan & Implementation. LC 82-60313. (Development Component Ser.). (Illus.). 32p. 1982. pap. 10.00 (ISBN 0-87420-608-1, D21). Urban Land.
Black, J. Thomas & Morina, Michael. Downtown Office Growth & the Role of Public Transit. LC 82-50921. (Illus.). 122p. (Orig.). 1982. pap. text ed. 26.00 (ISBN 0-87420-615-4, D31). Urban Land.
O'Mara, W. Paul & Casazza, John A. Office Development Handbook. LC 82-50078. (Community Builders Handbook Ser.). (Illus.). 288p. 1982. text ed. 42.00 (ISBN 0-87420-607-3, OD1). Urban Land.
Redstone, Louis G. The New Downtowns: Rebuilding Business Districts. LC 82-17111. 356p. 1983. Repr. of 1976 ed. lib. bdg. p.n.s. (ISBN 0-89874-560-8). Krieger.
Witherspoon, Robert. Codevelopment: City Rebuilding by Business & Government. LC 82-50871. (Development Component Ser.). (Illus.). 48p. 1982. pap. 10.00 (ISBN 0-87420-614-6, D24). Urban Land.
CENTRAL NERVOUS SYSTEM
see also Brain; Spinal Cord
Bigner, Sandra H. & Johnston, William W. Cytopathology of the Central Nervous System. (Masson Monographs on Diagnostic Cytopathology, Vol. 3). 184p. 1983. price not set. Masson Pub.
Eccles. The Inhibitory Pathways of the Central Nervous System. 140p. 1982. 50.00x (ISBN 0-85323-050-1, Pub. by Liverpool Univ England). State Mutual Bk.
CENTRALIZATION IN GOVERNMENT
see Decentralization in Government
CENTRIFUGAL COMPRESSORS
see Compressors
CERAMBYCIDAE
Chemsak, John A. & Linsky, E. G. Checklist of Cerambycidae: The Longhormed Beetles. (Checklist of the Beetle of Canada United States, Mexico, Central America & the West Indies Ser.). 138p. (Orig.). 1982. pap. text ed. 18.00x (ISBN 0-937548-04-9). Plexus Pub.
CERAMIC COATING
see also Enamel and Enameling
American Welding Society. Flame Spraying of Ceramics: C2.13. 1970. 8.00 (ISBN 0-686-43373-4). Am Welding.
CERAMICS
Here are entered general works on the technology of fired earth products, or clay products intended for industrial and technical use. Works on earthenware, chinaware, and art objects are entered under Pottery or Pottery Craft.; Particular objects and types are entered under their specific names, e.g. Bricks; clay; pipe; Refractory Materials; Tiles; Vases.
see also Pottery Craft
Young, Carol M. & Dupoizat, Marie-France, eds. Vietnamese Ceramics. (Illus.). 192p. 1982. 80.00. Oxford U Pr.
CERAMICS (ART)
see Pottery
CEREAL PRODUCTS
Christensen, Edith A., ed. Approved Methods of the American Association of Cereal Chemists. 8th ed. LC 82-46081. 1200p. 1983. text ed. 140.00 member (ISBN 0-686-43049-2); text ed. 190.00 non-member (ISBN 0-913250-31-7). Am Assn Cereal Chem.
Kent, N. L. Technology of Cereals: An Introduction for Students of Food Science & Agriculture. 3rd ed. (Illus.). 200p. 1983. 40.00 (ISBN 0-08-029801-X); pap. 15.00 (ISBN 0-08-029800-1). Pergamon.
CEREALS
see Grain
CEREBELLUM
Hellige. Cerebral Hemisphere Asymmetry. 425p. 1983. 29.95 (ISBN 0-03-058638-0). Praeger.
CEREBRAL CORTEX
see also Hippocampus (Brain)
Penfield. The Excitable Cortex in Conscious Man. 54p. 1982. 50.00x (ISBN 0-85323-241-5, Pub. by Liverpool Univ England). State Mutual Bk.
CEREBRAL EDEMA
Hartmann, A. & Brock, M., eds. Treatment of Cerebral Edema. (Illus.). 176p. 1983. pap. 26.00 (ISBN 0-387-11751-2). Springer-Verlag.
CEREBRAL LOCALIZATION
see Brain-Localization of Functions
CEREBRAL PALSIED CHILDREN
Schleichkorn, Jay. Coping with Cerebral Palsy: Answers to Questions Parents Often Ask. 1983. pap. text ed. 14.95 (ISBN 0-8391-1768-X, 19186). Univ Park.
Thompson, George H., et al, eds. Comprehensive Management of Cerebral Palsy. Date not set. price not set (ISBN 0-8089-1504-5). Grune.
CEREBRAL PALSY
Hardy, James C. Cerebral Palsy. (Illus.). 288p. 1983. 20.95 (ISBN 0-13-122820-X). P-H.
Schleichkorn, Jay. Coping with Cerebral Palsy: Answers to Questions Parents Often Ask. 1983. pap. text ed. 14.95 (ISBN 0-8391-1768-X, 19186). Univ Park.
Thompson, George H., et al, eds. Comprehensive Management of Cerebral Palsy. Date not set. price not set (ISBN 0-8089-1504-5). Grune.
CEREBROSPINAL FLUID
Wood, James H., ed. Neurobiology of Cerebrospinal Fluid 2. 850p. 1983. 89.50x (ISBN 0-306-40969-0, Plenum Pr). Plenum Pub.
CEREBROVASCULAR DISEASE
see also Stroke Patients
Bergan, John J. & Yao, James S., eds. Cerebrovascular Insufficiency. Date not set. price not set (ISBN 0-8089-1540-1). Grune.
Bradac, G. B. & Oberson, R. Angiography & Computed Tomography in Cerebroarterial Occlusive Diseases. (Illus.). 290p. 1982. 68.00 (ISBN 0-387-11453-X). Springer-Verlag.
Cerebral Vascular: Diseases BIMR. 1983. text ed. price not set (ISBN 0-407-02296-1). Butterworth.
Stefanovich, Hoechst, ed. Stroke: Animal Models: Proceedings of an International Symposium held at Wiesbaden, Germany, 16 November 1981. (Illus.). 200p. 1982. 50.00 (ISBN 0-08-029799-4). Pergamon.
CEREBRUM
see Brain
CEREMONIES
see Manners and Customs; Rites and Ceremonies
CERTIFICATION OF SCHOOL SUPERINTENDENTS AND PRINCIPALS
see School Superintendents and Principals
CERTIFIED PUBLIC ACCOUNTANTS
see Accountants
CERVANTES SAAVEDRA, MIGUEL DE, 1547-1616
Johnson, Carroll B. Madness & Lust: A Psychoanalytic Approach to Don Quixote. LC 82-10916. 252p. 1983. text ed. 22.50 (ISBN 0-520-04752-4). U of Cal Pr.
Nabokov, Vladimir. Lectures on Don Quixote. Bowers, Fredson, ed. LC 82-47665. 256p. 1983. 17.95 (ISBN 0-15-149595-5). HarBraceJ.
CERVICAL VERTEBRAE
see Vertebrae, Cervical
CESAREAN SECTION
Cohen, Nancy Wainer & Estner, Lois J. Silent Knife: Cesarean Prevention & Vaginal Birth after Cesarean (VBAC) (Illus.). 480p. 1983. 29.95x (ISBN 0-89789-026-4); pap. 14.95x. J F Bergin.
Royall, Nicki. You Don't Need to Have a Repeat Cesarean. LC 82-83775. 192p. 1983. 14.95 (ISBN 0-8119-0487-3). Fell.
CESSIO BONORUM
see Bankruptcy
CESTODA
Flisser, Ana, et al, eds. Cysticercosis: Symposium. 1982. 55.00 (ISBN 0-12-260740-6). Acad Pr.
CHA-NO-YU
see Japanese Tea Ceremony
CHAGALL, MARC, 1887-
Amiel, Leon. Homage to Chagall. (Twentieth Century Art Ser.). (Illus.). 1982. 24.95 (ISBN 0-8148-0725-9). L Amiel Pub.
CHAIN REACTION PILES
see Nuclear Reactors
CHAIN-TRACK VEHICLES
see Tracklaying Vehicles
CHAIRS
see also Wheelchairs
Donovan & Green. The Wood Chair in America. LC 82-90454. (Illus.). 120p. 1982. pap. 24.95 (ISBN 0-9609844-0-2). E & S Brickel.
Stuckey, Charles. Scottburton Chairs. (Illus.). 1983. price not set. (ISBN 0-917562-25-9). Contemp Arts.
CHAMPIGNONS
see Mushrooms
CHAMPLAIN, LAKE
Palmer, Peter S. History of Lake Champlain, 1609-1814. LC 82-15422. (Illus.). 1982. Repr. of 1886 ed. write for info. (ISBN 0-916346-45-5). Harbor Hill Bks.
CHANCE
see also Probabilities

Hilliard, Joseph. How to Unlock the Secrets of Winning & Good Luck. (Orig.). 1982. pap. 5.95x (ISBN 0-934650-02-0). Sunnyside.

CHANG, TSAI

Mair, Victor H., ed. Experimental Essays on Chuang-tzu. (Asian Studies at Hawaii: No. 29). 200p. 1983. pap. 10.00x (ISBN 0-8248-0836-3). UH Pr.

CHANGE

Master Ni, Hua-Ching. The Reflecting Book of Changes. (Illus.). 825p. (Orig.). 1983. 35.00 (ISBN 0-686-84582-X); pap. 25.00 (ISBN 0-937064-04-1). SEBT.

Woodside, Alexander & Wyatt, David K., eds. Moral Order & the Question of Change: Essays on Southeast Asian Thought. LC 82-51022. (Yale University Southeast Asia Studies Monograph: No. 24). 413p. 1982. pap. 16.00x (ISBN 0-938692-02-X). Yale U SE Asia.

CHANGE (PSYCHOLOGY)

De Laurentis, Anthony C. You are Never too Old to Live: For People from 35 to 100 Who are Eager for New Challenges in Life. (Illus.). 117p. 1983. 19.75 (ISBN 0-89266-394-4). Am Classical Coll Pr.

Siegelman, Ellen Y. Personal Risk: Mastering Change in Love & Work. 240p. 1983. pap. text ed. 12.95 scp (ISBN 0-06-046136-5, HarpC). Har-Row.

CHANGE, EDUCATIONAL

see Educational Innovations

CHANGE, SOCIAL

see Social Change

CHANGE OF LIFE IN MEN

see Climacteric

CHANGE OF LIFE IN WOMEN

see Climacteric

CHANGE OF SEX

Richards, Renee & Ames, John. Second Serve: The Renee Richards Story. LC 82-48510. (Illus.). 420p. 1983. 16.95 (ISBN 0-8128-2897-6). Stein & Day.

CHANNELS (HYDRAULIC ENGINEERING)

see also Canals; Harbors; Lakes; Reservoirs; Rivers

Chermisinoff, Nicholas P. Fluid Flow: Pumps, Pipes & Channels. LC 81-68034. (Illus.). 702p. 1981. 39.95 (ISBN 0-250-40432-X). Ann Arbor Science.

CHANTEYS

see Sea Songs

CHANTYS

see Sea Songs

CHAPMAN, GEORGE, 1559?-1634

Lord, George D. Homeric Renaissance: The Odyssey of George Chapman. 1956. text ed. 14.50x (ISBN 0-686-83567-0). Elliots Bks.

CHARACTER EDUCATION

see Moral Education

CHARACTER SKETCHES–HISTORY AND CRITICISM

see Characters and Characteristics in Literature

CHARACTERS AND CHARACTERISTICS IN LITERATURE

see also Drama–Technique; Jews in Literature; Plots (Drama, Novel, etc.); Shakespeare, William, 1564-1616–Characters; Women in Literature

Price, Martin. Forms of Life: Character & Moral Imagination in the Novel. LC 82-16064. 400p. 1983. text ed. 27.50x (ISBN 0-300-02867-9). Yale U Pr.

Roback, A. A. A Bibliography of Character & Personality. 340p. 1982. Repr. of 1927 ed. lib. bdg. 85.00 (ISBN 0-89984-847-8). Century Bookbindery.

CHARADES

see also Riddles; Skits, Stunts, etc.

Charlton, James. The Charades Book. LC 82-48227. (Illus.). 160p. (Orig.). 1983. pap. 6.68i (ISBN 0-06-091025-9, CN 1025, CN). Har-Row.

CHARGED PARTICLE ACCELERATORS

see Particle Accelerators

CHARISMATA

see Gifts, Spiritual

CHARISMATIC MOVEMENT

see Pentecostalism

CHARITABLE CONTRIBUTIONS AS TAX DEDUCTIONS

see Corporations–Charitable Contributions

CHARITABLE INSTITUTIONS

see Charities

CHARITABLE USES, TRUSTS AND FOUNDATIONS

see also Endowments; Pension Trusts

Dermer, Joseph, ed. Where America's Large Foundations Make Their Grants: 1983-1984 Edition. 1983. 44.50 (ISBN 0-686-37909-8). Public Serv Materials.

Gray, D. R. Non-Private Foundations. 1978. 40.00 (ISBN 0-07-024230-5); forms suppl. avail. McGraw.

Minnesota Council on Foundations. Guide to Minnesota Foundations & Corporate Giving Programs. LC 82-21928. 136p. 1983. pap. 14.95x (ISBN 0-8166-1219-6). U of Minn Pr.

Public Service Materials Center, ed. The Survey of Grant-Making Foundations 1983-1984. 1982. 15.95 (ISBN 0-686-37910-1). Public Serv Materials.

CHARITIES

see also Charitable Uses, Trusts and Foundations; Child Welfare; Community Organizations; Corporations–Charitable Contributions; Day Care Centers; Disaster Relief; Endowments; Food Relief; Friendly Societies; Hospitals; Medical Social Work; Poor; Psychiatric Social Work; Public Welfare; Social Workers; Unemployed

also subdivision Civilian Relief under names of wars, e.g. World War, 1939-1945–Civilian Relief

Morgan, James N., et al. Results of Two National Surveys of Philanthropic Activity. 204p. 1979. pap. 12.00x (ISBN 0-87944-246-8). Inst Soc Res.

National Catholic Development Conference. Bibliography of Fund Raising & Philanthropy. 2nd ed. LC 82-81523. 1982. 22.50 (ISBN 0-9603196-1-1). Natl Cath Dev.

CHARITIES–HISTORY

Gallagher, Vera. Hearing the Cry of the Poor: The Story of the St. Vincent de Paul Society. 64p. 1983. pap. 1.50 (ISBN 0-89243-174-1). Liguori Pubns.

CHARITIES–PUBLIC RELATIONS

see Public Relations–Social Service

CHARITIES, LEGAL

see Legal Aid Societies

CHARITY

see also Altruism; Love (Theology)

Thomas Aquinas. Charity. (Summa Theologial Ser.: Vol. 34). 1975. 19.95 (ISBN 0-07-002009-4). McGraw.

CHARLEMAGNE, 742-814

Riche. Daily Life in the World of Charlemagne. 368p. 1982. 70.00x (ISBN 0-85323-124-9, Pub. by Liverpool Univ England); 39.00x (ISBN 0-85323-174-5). State Mutual Bk.

CHARLES 1ST, KING OF GREAT BRITAIN, 1600-1649

Carlton, Charles. Charles the First: The Personal Monarch. (Illus.). 432p. 1983. price not set (ISBN 0-7100-9485-X). Routledge & Kegan.

Gregg, Pauline. King Charles I. (Illus.). 508p. 1982. text ed. 24.95x (ISBN 0-460-04437-0, Pub. by J. M. Dent England). Biblio Dist.

CHARLES, PRINCE OF WALES, 1949-

Barry, Stephen. Royal Service: My Twelve Years as Valet to Prince Charles. (Illus.). 320p. 1983. 14.95 (ISBN 0-02-507490-3). Macmillan.

Hall, Trevor. Born to be King: Prince William of Wales. (Illus.). 128p. 1983. 25.00 (ISBN 0-517-39675-0). Crown.

Holden, Anthony. Prince Charles. LC 82-52176. 432p. 1983. pap. 10.95 (ISBN 0-689-70638-3, 287). Atheneum.

CHARLESTON, SOUTH CAROLINA

Simms, William G., ed. The Charleston Book: A Miscellany in Prose & Verse. (The South Caroliniana Ser.: No. 8). 432p. 1983. Repr. of 1845 ed. 25.00 (ISBN 0-87152-378-7). Reprint.

CHARTISM

Epstein, James & Thompson, Dorothy, eds. The Chartist Experience-Studies in Working-Class Radicalism & Culture 1830 to 1860. 416p. 1982. text ed. 28.00x (ISBN 0-333-32971-6, 41403, Pub. by Macmillan England); pap. text ed. 12.50x (ISBN 0-333-32972-4, 41424). Humanities.

CHATEAUX

see Castles

CHATTANOOGA

Chesney, Allen, ed. Chattanooga Album: Thirty-Two Historic Postcards. LC 82-17330. (Illus.). 16p. 1983. pap. 3.95 (ISBN 0-87049-381-7). U of Tenn Pr.

CHAUCER, GEOFFREY, d. 1400

Brewer, D. Tradition & Innovation in Chaucer. 256p. 1982. text ed. 37.00x (ISBN 0-333-28427-5, 50794, Pub. by Macmillan England). Humanities.

Hoy, Michael & Stevens, Michael. Chaucer's Major Tales. LC 82-10419. 192p. 1983. 15.00 (ISBN 0-8052-3844-1); pap. 5.95 (ISBN 0-8052-0734-1). Schocken.

Minnis, A. J. Chaucer & Pagan Antiquity. (Chaucer Studies: No. VIII). 208p. 1982. text ed. 47.50x (ISBN 0-8476-7195-X). Rowman.

Thompson. Shakespeare's Chaucer. 252p. 1982. 45.00x (ISBN 0-85323-463-9, Pub. by Liverpool Univ England). State Mutual Bk.

Wimsatt, James I. Chaucer & the Poems of "CH". (Chaucer Studies: No. IX). (Illus.). 144p. 1982. text ed. 47.50x (ISBN 0-8476-7200-X). Rowman.

CHAUCER, GEOFFREY, d. 1400–BIBLIOGRAPHY

Peck, Russell A. Chaucer's Lyrics & Anelida & Arcite: An Annoted Bibliography 1900 to 1980. (Chaucer Bibliographies Ser.). 256p. 1983. 36.00x (ISBN 0-8020-2481-5). U of Toronto Pr.

CHEATING AT CARDS

see Cardsharping

CHEESE

see also Cookery (Dairy Products)

Sherman, Steve. Cheese Sweets & Savories. 176p. 1983. pap. 8.95 (ISBN 0-8289-0498-7). Greene.

CHEEVER, JOHN

Collins, Robert G. Critical Essays on John Cheever. (Critical Essays on American Literature Ser.). 1982. lib. bdg. 32.00 (ISBN 0-8161-8623-5). G K Hall.

CHEIROMANCY

see Palmistry

CHEIROPTERA

see Bats

CHEKHOV, ANTON PAVLOVICH, 1860-1904

Chekhov, A. P. Chekhov's Poetics. Cruise, Edwina & Dragt, Donald, trs. from Rus. 1983. 27.50 (ISBN 0-88233-780-7); pap. 7.50 (ISBN 0-88233-781-5). Ardis Pubs.

Valency, Maurice. The Breaking String: The Plays of Anton Chekhov. LC 82-3369. (The Making of Modern Drama Ser.: Vol. 2). 344p. 1983. 20.00x (ISBN 0-8052-3809-3); pap. 9.95x (ISBN 0-8052-0716-3). Schocken.

CHELONIA

see Turtles

CHEMICAL ANALYSIS

see Chemistry, Analytic

CHEMICAL BONDS

see also Molecular Orbitals

Clarke, M. J., et al, eds. Structure vs. Special Properties. (Structure & Bonding Ser.: Vol. 52). (Illus.). 204p. 1982. 48.00 (ISBN 0-387-11781-4). Springer-Verlag.

CHEMICAL COMPOSITION OF THE EARTH

see Geochemistry

CHEMICAL ELEMENTS

see also Actinide Elements; Trace Elements; Valence (Theoretical Chemistry)

also names of elements

Holmes, Mike & Martin, L. H. Analysis & Design of Connection Between Elements. (Civil & Mechanical Engineering Ser.). 260p. 1983. 42.95 (ISBN 0-470-27365-8). Halsted Pr.

CHEMICAL ENGINEERING

see also Chemistry, Technical; Mechanical Engineering; Metallurgy

Chemical Engineering Magazine. Physical Properties. 1979. 49.90 (ISBN 0-07-010715-7). McGraw.

Compressors & Expanders: Selection & Application for the Process Industry. (Chemical Industries Ser.: Vol. 8). (Illus.). 328p. 1982. 37.50 (ISBN 0-8247-1854-2). Dekker.

Coulson, J. M. Chemical Engineering: An Introduction to Design, Vol. 6. (Illus.). 720p. 1983. 75.01 (ISBN 0-08-022969-7); pap. 29.50 (ISBN 0-08-022970-0). Pergamon.

Franks, Roger G. Modeling & Simulation in Chemical Engineering. LC 72-39717. 411p. 1972. 40.50x (ISBN 0-471-27535-2, Pub. by Wiley-Interscience). Wiley.

Institution of Chemical Engineers. Design Eighty-Two: Proceedings of the Symposium Organised by the Institution of Chemical Engineers at the University of Aston in Birmingham, UK, 22-23 September 1982. (Institution of Chemical Engineers Symposium Ser.: No. 76). 425p. 1982. 63.00 (ISBN 0-08-028773-5). Pergamon.

--Energy-Money, Materials & Engineering: Proceedings of the Symposium Organised by the Institution of Chemical Engineers (in Conjunction with the American Institute of Chemical Engineers & Deutsche Vereinigung fur Chemie-und Verfahrenstechnik), London, UK, 12-15 October 1982. (Institution of Chemical Engineers Symposium Ser.: No. 78). 475p. 1982. 72.00 (ISBN 0-08-028774-3). Pergamon.

--The Jubilee Chemical Engineering Symposium: Proceedings of the Symposium Organised by the Institution of Chemical Engineers, Imperial College, London, UK, April 1982. (Institution of Chemical Engineers Symposium Ser.: Vol. 73). 678p. 1982. 90.00 (ISBN 0-08-028770-0). Pergamon.

McCoy, James W. Industrial Chemical Cleaning. (Illus.). 1983. 40.00 (ISBN 0-8206-0305-8). Chem Pub.

Paulaitis, Michael E. & Penninger, Johan M. L. Chemical Engineering at Supercritical Fluid Conditions. LC 82-71529. (Illus.). 600p. 1983. 39.95 (ISBN 0-250-40564-4). Ann Arbor Science.

Prabhudesai, R. K. & Das, D. K. Chemical Engineering for Professional Engineer's Examinations. 448p. 1983. 32.50 (ISBN 0-07-050640-X, P&RB). McGraw.

Resnick, W. Process Analysis & Design for Chemical Engineers. 1980. text ed. 29.95 (ISBN 0-07-051887-4); solutions manual avail. McGraw.

CHEMICAL ENGINEERING–DATA PROCESSING

OECD. Confidentiality of Data & Chemical Control. 94p. 1982. pap. 10.00x (ISBN 92-64-12365-2). OECD.

CHEMICAL ENGINEERING–TABLES, CALCULATIONS, ETC.

Chopey, Nicholas & Hicks, Tyler G. Handbook of Chemical Engineering Calculations. (Illus.). 608p. 1983. 49.50 (ISBN 0-07-010805-6, P&RB). McGraw.

CHEMICAL EVOLUTION

Goodman, Morris, ed. Macromolecular Sequences in Systematic & Evolutionary Biology. (Monographs in Evolutionary Biology). 432p. 1982. 45.00x (ISBN 0-306-41061-3, Plenum Pr). Plenum Pub.

Price, Charles C., ed. Synthesis of Life. LC 74-3026. (Benchmark Papers in Organic Chemistry: Vol. 1). 391p. 1974. text ed. 52.50 (ISBN 0-87933-131-3). Hutchinson Ross.

CHEMICAL FORMULAE

see Chemistry–Notation

CHEMICAL GEOLOGY

see Geochemistry; Mineralogical Chemistry

CHEMICAL INDUSTRIES

Here are entered works on industries based largely on chemical processes. Material dealing with the manufacture of chemicals as such is entered under Chemicals–Manufacture and Industry.

see also Oil Industries

also names of specific industries, e.g. Soap and Soap Trade, Paper Making and Trade

Bader. Practical Quality Management in the Chemical Process Industry. (Industrial Engineering Ser.). 168p. 1983. price not set (ISBN 0-8247-1903-4). Dekker.

Bennett, Carl A. & Franklin, N. L. Statistical Analysis in Chemistry & the Chemical Industry. (Probability & Mathematical Statistics: Applied Probability & Statistics Section). 1954. 50.50 (ISBN 0-471-06633-8, Pub by Wiley-Interscience). Wiley.

Enviromental Regulation & the Chemical Industry. LC 82-83536. (Special Project Report Ser.). 122p. 1982. 8.00 (ISBN 0-89940-806-0). LBJ Sch Pub Aff.

The Specific Contribution of the Chemical Industries to the Vocational Training & Advanced Training of Manpower in Developing Countries: Report 2. Chemical Industries Committee, Ninth Session, Geneva September 21-30, 1982. iv, 1982p. 1982. 8.55 (ISBN 92-2-103055-5). Intl Labour Office.

CHEMICAL INDUSTRIES–EUROPE

Hollis, G. L., compiled by. Surfactants Europa, Vol. 1. 1982. pap. 100.00x (ISBN 0-7114-5736-0, Pub. by Macdonald & Evans). State Mutual Bk.

CHEMICAL KINETICS

see Chemical Reaction, Rate of

CHEMICAL LABORATORIES

Heasley, Victor L. & Christensen, Val J. Chemistry & Life in the Laboratory: Experiments in General, Organic & Biological Chemistry. 2nd ed. 264p. 1982. pap. text ed. 10.95x (ISBN 0-8087-4716-9). Burgess.

CHEMICAL MODELS

Kalashnikov, N. P. & Remizovich, V. S. Collisions of Fast Charged Particles in Solids. Erastov, Konstantin, tr. from Rus. 450p. 1983. price not set (ISBN 0-677-06080-7). Gordon.

CHEMICAL OCEANOGRAPHY

see also Water Chemistry

Riley, J. P. & Chester, R., eds. Chemical Oceanography, Vol. 8. write for info. (ISBN 0-12-588608-X). Acad Pr.

CHEMICAL PLANTS–TABLES, CALCULATIONS, ETC.

Quarantelli, E. L. Chemical Disasters: Preparations & Responses at the Local Level. 170p. 1983. text ed. 22.50x (ISBN 0-8290-1289-3). Irvington.

CHEMICAL PROCESSES

see also Chemical Reactions

Felder, Richard M. & Rousseau, Ronald W. Elementary Principles of Chemical Processes. LC 77-12043. 571p. 1978. text ed. 30.95x (ISBN 0-471-74330-5); solutions manual 10.95 (ISBN 0-471-03680-3). Wiley.

McKetta. Encyclopedia of Chemical Processing & Design, Vol. 18. 1983. price not set (ISBN 0-8247-2468-2). Dekker.

CHEMICAL PROCESSES–MATHEMATICAL MODELS

McKetta. Encyclopedia of Chemical Processing & Design. 1983. price not set (ISBN 0-8247-2469-0). Dekker.

CHEMICAL REACTION, CONDITIONS AND LAWS OF

Abramovitch, R. A., ed. Reactive Intermediates, Vol. 3. 615p. 1982. 59.50x (ISBN 0-306-40970-4, Plenum Pr). Plenum Pub.

CHEMICAL REACTION, RATE OF

Bamford, C. & Tipper, C., eds. Comprehensive Chemical Kinetics, Vol. 20: Complex Catalytic Processes. 1978. 119.25 (ISBN 0-444-41651-X). Elsevier.

CHEMICAL REACTIONS

see also Alkylation; Chemical Reactors; Nitroso Compounds

Adams, Roger, ed. Organic Reactions, Vol. 1. LC 42-20265. 400p. 1978. Repr. of 1942 ed. 29.50 (ISBN 0-88275-729-6). Krieger.

--Organic Reactions, Vol. 2. LC 42-20265. 470p. 1981. Repr. of 1944 ed. 29.50 (ISBN 0-89874-375-3). Krieger.

--Organic Reactions, Vol. 3. LC 42-20265. 468p. 1975. Repr. of 1946 ed. 29.50 (ISBN 0-88275-875-6). Krieger.

--Organic Reactions, Vol. 4. LC 42-20265. 438p. 1979. Repr. of 1948 ed. 29.50 (ISBN 0-88275-780-6). Krieger.

--Organic Reactions, Vol. 5. LC 42-20265. 454p. 1977. Repr. of 1949 ed. 29.50 (ISBN 0-88275-249-9). Krieger.

--Organic Reactions, Vol. 6. LC 42-20265. 526p. 1975. Repr. of 1951 ed. 29.50 (ISBN 0-88275-876-4). Krieger.

--Organic Reactions, Vol. 7. LC 42-20265. 448p. 1975. Repr. of 1953 ed. 29.50 (ISBN 0-88275-877-2). Krieger.

--Organic Reactions, Vol. 8. LC 42-20265. 446p. 1975. Repr. of 1954 ed. 29.50 (ISBN 0-88275-878-0). Krieger.

--Organic Reactions, Vol. 9. LC 42-20265. 476p. 1975. Repr. of 1957 ed. 29.50 (ISBN 0-88275-879-9). Krieger.

--Organic Reactions, Vol. 10. LC 42-20265. 572p. 1975. Repr. of 1959 ed. 29.50 (ISBN 0-88275-880-2). Krieger.

Cope, Arthur C., ed. Organic Reactions, Vol. 11. LC 42-20265. 510p. 1975. Repr. of 1960 ed. 29.50 (ISBN 0-88275-881-0). Krieger.

--Organic Reactions, Vol. 12. LC 42-20265. 546p. 1975. Repr. of 1962 ed. 29.50 (ISBN 0-88275-882-9). Krieger.

--Organic Reactions, Vol. 13. LC 42-20265. 390p. 1979. Repr. of 1962 ed. 29.50 (ISBN 0-88275-836-5). Krieger.

--Organic Reactions, Vol. 14. LC 42-20265. 506p. 1978. Repr. of 1965 ed. 29.50 (ISBN 0-88275-730-X). Krieger.

--Organic Reactions, Vol. 15. LC 42-20265. 616p. 1978. Repr. of 1967 ed. 29.50 (ISBN 0-88275-731-8). Krieger.

--Organic Reactions, Vol. 16. LC 42-20265. 456p. 1975. Repr. of 1968 ed. 29.50 (ISBN 0-88275-883-7). Krieger.

Dauben, William G. Organic Reactions, Vol. 29. 500p. 1983. 40.00 (ISBN 0-471-87490-6, Pub. by Wiley-Interscience). Wiley.

Dauben, William G., ed. Organic Reactions, Vol. 17. LC 42-20265. 346p. 1975. Repr. of 1969 ed. 29.50 (ISBN 0-88275-884-5). Krieger.

--Organic Reactions, Vol. 18. LC 42-20265. 476p. 1978. Repr. of 1970 ed. 29.50 (ISBN 0-88275-732-6). Krieger.

--Organic Reactions, Vol. 19. LC 42-20265. 446p. 1975. Repr. of 1972 ed. 29.50 (ISBN 0-88275-885-3). Krieger.

--Organic Reactions, Vol. 20. LC 42-20265. 506p. 1981. Repr. of 1973 ed. 39.50 (ISBN 0-89874-390-7). Krieger.

Daudel, R. & Pullman, A., eds. Quantum Theory of Chemical Reactions. 1982. lib. bdg. 32.50 (ISBN 90-277-1467-3, Pub. by Reidel Holland). Kluwer Boston.

Eliel, Ernest L. & Otsuka, Sei, eds. Asymmetric Reactions & Processes in Chemistry. (ACS Symposium Ser.: No. 185). 1982. write for info. (ISBN 0-8412-0717-8). Am Chemical.

Lewis, Edward S., ed. Investigation of Rates & Mechanisms of Reactions, Vol. 6, Pt.1. 3d ed. LC 74-8850. (Techniques of Chemistry Ser.). 852p. Repr. of 1974 ed. text ed. 67.50 (ISBN 0-686-84487-4). Krieger.

CHEMICAL REACTORS

Fogler, H. Scott, ed. Chemical Reactors: ACS Symposium Ser. (No. 168). 1981. write for info. (ISBN 0-8412-0658-9). Am Chemical.

Froment, Gilbert F. & Bischoff, Kenneth B. Chemical Reactor Analysis & Design. LC 78-12465. 765p. 1979. text ed. 43.95x (ISBN 0-471-02447-3). Wiley.

Ramachandran, P. A. & Chaudhari, R. V. Three Phase Catalytic Reactors. (Topics in Chemical Engineering Ser.: Vol. 2). 530p. 1982. write for info. (ISBN 0-677-05650-8). Gordon.

Tarhan, M. Orhan. Catalytic Reactor Design. (Illus.). 352p. 1983. 36.95 (ISBN 0-07-062871-8, P&RB). McGraw.

CHEMICAL REAGENTS

see Chemical Tests and Reagents

CHEMICAL STRUCTURE

see also Chemical Bonds; Stereochemistry; Valence (Theoretical Chemistry)

Clarke, M. J., et al, eds. Structure vs. Special Properties. (Structure & Bonding Ser.: Vol. 52). (Illus.). 204p. 1982. 48.00 (ISBN 0-387-11781-4). Springer-Verlag.

Dewar, M. J., et al, eds. Synthetic & Structural Problems. (Topics in Current Chemistry Ser.: Vol. 106). (Illus.). 170p. 1982. 39.00 (ISBN 0-387-11766-0). Springer-Verlag.

Koetzle, T. F., ed. Structure & Bonding: Relationships Between Quantum Chemistry & Crystallography. Date not set. pap. 7.50 (ISBN 0-937140-25-2). Polycrystal Bk Serv.

Thomas, L. C. New Chemical Structure. 1982. text ed. 36.95 (ISBN 0-471-26112-2, Pub. by Wiley-Interscience). Wiley.

CHEMICAL SYMBOLS

see Abbreviations; Chemistry–Notation

CHEMICAL TECHNOLOGY

see Chemistry, Technical

CHEMICAL TESTS AND REAGENTS

see also Ozone; Spot Tests (Chemistry)

Fieser, Louis F. & Fieser, Mary. Reagents for Organic Synthesis, 8 vols. Vol. 1, 1967. 65.00x (ISBN 0-471-25875-X); Vol. 2, 1969. 44.95x (ISBN 0-471-25876-8); Vol. 3, 1972. 42.95x (ISBN 0-471-25879-2); Vol. 4, 1974. 45.00x (ISBN 0-471-25881-4); Vol. 5, 1975. 48.50x (ISBN 0-471-25882-2); Vol. 6, 1977. 46.50x (ISBN 0-471-25873-3); Vol. 7, 1979. 44.95x (ISBN 0-471-02918-1); Vol. 8, 1980. 46.95x (ISBN 0-471-04834-8). Wiley.

CHEMICALS

see also groups of chemicals, e.g. Acids, Explosives, and individual chemical substances, e.g. Carbolic Acid

Saxena, Jitendra, ed. Hazard Assessment of Chemicals, Vol. 2. (Serial Publication). 332p. 1983. price not set (ISBN 0-12-312402-6). Acad Pr.

CHEMICALS–LAW AND LEGISLATION

OECD. Chemical Control Legislation Glossary. 170p. Date not set. pap. 13.50x (ISBN 92-64-12364-4). OECD.

CHEMICALS–MANUFACTURE AND INDUSTRY

see also Chemical Industries; Chemistry, Technical also specific chemical industries

Control of Chemicals in Importing Countries. 196p. (Orig.). 1982. pap. 12.00x (ISBN 92-64-12272-9). OECD.

Stratton, Andrew. Energy & Feedstocks in the Chemical Industry. 320p. 1981. 89.95 (ISBN 0-470-27396-8). Halsted Pr.

Valle-Riestra, J. Frank. Project Evaluation in the Chemical Process Industries. (Chemical Engineering Ser.). (Illus.). 736p. 1983. text ed. 33.50 (ISBN 0-07-066840-X, C); write for info. solutions manual (ISBN 0-07-066841-8). McGraw.

CHEMICALS–SAFETY MEASURES

Gibson, G. G. & Loannides, C., eds. Safety Evaluation of Nitrosatable Drugs & Chemicals. 275p. 1981. 90.00x (ISBN 0-85066-212-5, Pub. by Taylor & Francis). State Mutual Bk.

CHEMICULTURE

see Hydroponics

CHEMISTRY

see also Acids; Agricultural Chemistry; Alchemy; Bases, Chemistry; Biological Chemistry; Botanical Chemistry; Catalysis; Color; Combustion; Crystallization; Crystallography; Dissociation; Electrochemistry; Evaporation; Gases–Liquefaction; Geochemistry; Immunochemistry; Pharmacy; Photochemistry; Spectrum Analysis; Stereochemistry; Water Chemistry

also headings beginning with the word Chemical

Ash, M. & Ash, I. Encyclopedia of Chemical Additives Vol. 1, A-M. 1983. 75.00 (ISBN 0-8206-0299-X). Chem Pub.

Bennett, Carl A. & Franklin, N. L. Statistical Analysis in Chemistry & the Chemical Industry. (Probability & Mathematical Statistics: Applied Probability & Statistics Section). 1954. 50.50 (ISBN 0-471-06633-8, Pub by Wiley-Interscience). Wiley.

Boldyrev, V. V., et al, eds. Control of the Reactivity of Solids. (Studies in Surface Science & Catalysts: Vol. 2). 1979. 57.50 (ISBN 0-444-41800-8). Elsevier.

Brady, J. E. & Humiston, G. E. General Chemistry: Principles & Structure. 2nd ed. LC 80-14887. 779p. 1980. 27.95 (ISBN 0-471-06315-0). Wiley.

Brady, James E. & Holum, John R. Fundamentals of Chemistry. 797p. 1981. text ed. 27.95 (ISBN 0-471-05816-5); study guide avail. Wiley.

Brady, James E. & Humiston, Gerard E. General Chemistry: Principles & Structure. 2nd ed. LC 77-11045. 800p. 1978. text ed. 25.95 (ISBN 0-471-01910-0). wkbk. 8.25x (ISBN 0-471-03498-3). Wiley.

Caglioti, Luciano & Giacconi, Mirella. The Two Faces of Chemistry: The Benefits & the Risks of Chemical Technology. LC 82-12706. 230p. 1983. 17.50 (ISBN 0-262-03088-8). MIT Pr.

Chivers. Chemistry Three Checkbook. 1982. 22.50 (ISBN 0-408-00662-5); pap. text ed. 9.95 (ISBN 0-408-00658-7). Butterworth.

Dean, J. A., ed. Lange's Handbook of Chemistry. 12th ed. 1978. 41.50 (ISBN 0-07-016191-7). McGraw.

De Korosy. Approach to Chemistry. 1969. 18.50 (ISBN 0-444-19770-2). Elsevier.

Denney, Ron. Chemistry. 160p. 1982. 25.00x (ISBN 0-686-81708-7, Pub. by Muller Ltd). State Mutual Bk.

Dewar, M. J., et al, eds. Wittig Chemistry: Dedicated to Professor Dr. G. Wittig. (Topics in Current Chemistry Ser.: Vol. 109). (Illus.). 220p. 1983. 43.50 (ISBN 0-387-11907-8). Springer-Verlag.

Goldberg, E. D., ed. Atmospheric Chemistry, Berlin, 1982. (Dahlem Workshop Reports, Physical & Chemical: Vol. 4). (Illus.). 400p. 1983. 20.00 (ISBN 0-387-11651-6). Springer-Verlag.

Grant, R. A. Applied Protein Chemistry. 1980. 53.50 (ISBN 0-85334-865-0, Pub. by Applied Sci England). Elsevier.

Griffiths, P. R. Transform Techniques in Chemistry. 412p. 1978. 99.95 (ISBN 0-471-25742-7, Pub. by Wiley Heyden). Wiley.

Holum, J. R. Elements of General & Biological Chemistry: An Introduction to the Molecular Basis of Life. 6th ed. 593p. text ed. 27.95 (ISBN 0-471-09935-X); 11.95 (ISBN 0-471-08236-8); tchr's. manual avail. (ISBN 0-471-89033-2). Wiley.

Ihde, Aaron J. The Development of Modern Chemistry. (Illus.). 851p. 1983. pap. 15.00 (ISBN 0-486-64235-6). Dover.

Inagaki, Yoshio & Okazaki, Renji. Chemistry of N-Thiosulfinylamines. (Sulfur Reports: Vol. 2, No. 4). 40p. 1982. 24.50 (ISBN 3-7186-0126-5). Harwood Academic.

Katritzky, Alan R., ed. Advances in Heterocyclic Chemistry, Vol. 33. (Serial Publication). Date not set. price not set (ISBN 0-12-020633-1); price not set (ISBN 0-12-020740-0); price not set Microfiche (ISBN 0-12-020741-9). Acad Pr.

Lowman, Robert G. & Reeves, Perry B. Experimental Introductory Chemistry. 195p. 1981. pap. text ed. 4.95x (ISBN 0-89641-096-X). American Pr.

Mascetta, Joseph A. Chemistry the Easy Way. (Easy Way Ser.). 320p. (gr. 10-12). 1983. pap. write for info. (ISBN 0-8120-2624-1). Barron.

Mouton, R. P., ed. Aminoglycoside Assays: Methods & Clinical Relevance. (International Congress Ser.: No. 482). 1980. 22.00 (ISBN 0-444-90089-6). Elsevier.

Peters, Edward I. Chemical Skills. (Illus.). 416p. 1983. pap. text ed. 15.95x (ISBN 0-07-049557-2). McGraw.

Pickering, Miles. Investigations in General Chemistry. 208p. 1982. pap. text ed. write for info. (ISBN 0-87150-766-8, 4501). Grant Pr.

Rayner-Canham, Geoffrey & Last, Arthur. Foundations of Chemistry. (Illus.). 525p. 1983. text ed. 21.95 (ISBN 0-201-10284-6); Instrs' Manual avail. (ISBN 0-201-10414-8); Study Guide avail. (ISBN 0-201-10415-6); Laboratory Manual avail. (ISBN 0-201-10416-4). A-W.

Schaff, M. E. & Siebring, B. R. Basic Chemistry. 416p. 1982. pap. text ed. 19.95 (ISBN 0-8403-2802-8). Kendall-Hunt.

--Basic Chemistry: Problems Book. 64p. 1982. saddle stitched 3.95 (ISBN 0-8403-2819-2). Kendall-Hunt.

Scott, Arthur F., ed. Survey of Progress in Chemistry, Vol. 10. (Serial Publication). Date not set. price not set (ISBN 0-12-610510-3). Acad Pr.

Sharma, K. K. & Sharma, D. S. An Introduction to Practical Chemistry. 500p. 1982. text ed. 35.00x (ISBN 0-7069-1767-7, Pub. By Vikas India). Advent NY.

Veprek, S. & Venugopalan, M., eds. Plasma Chemistry, Vol. IV. (Topics in Current Chemistry Ser.: Vol. 107). (Illus.). 186p. 1983. 34.00 (ISBN 0-387-11828-4). Springer-Verlag.

Vol'pin, M. E., ed. Chemistry Reviews. Gingold, Kurt, tr. from Russian. (Soviet Scientific Reviews, Section B: Vol. 4). 378p. 1982. 157.00 (ISBN 0-686-84005-4). Harwood Academic.

Wood, E. J., ed. Strycture & Function of Invertebrate Respiratory Proteins. (Life Chemistry Reports: Supplement). 350p. 1982. 85.00 (ISBN 3-7186-0136-2). Harwood Academic.

CHEMISTRY–ADDRESSES, ESSAYS, LECTURES

Haken, H. Evolution of Order & Chaos in Physics, Chemistry, & Biology: Schloss Elmau, FRG, 1982 Proceedings. (Springer Series in Synergetics: Vol. 17). (Illus.). 287p. 1983. 32.00 (ISBN 0-387-11904-3). Springer-Verlag.

CHEMISTRY–DATA PROCESSING

Hepple, P. & Institute of Petroleum. Application of Computer Techniques in Chemical Research. 1972. 45.00 (ISBN 0-85334-488-4). Elsevier.

Institute of Petroleum. Application of Computer Techniques in Chemical Research. 1971. 59.95x (ISBN 0-471-26163-7, Pub. by Wiley Heyden). Wiley.

Lykos, Peter & Shavitt, Isaiah, eds. Supercomputers in Chemistry. (ACS Symposium Ser.: No. 173). 1981. write for info. (ISBN 0-8412-0666-X). Am Chemical.

CHEMISTRY–DICTIONARIES

Bennett, H. Encyclopedia of Chemical Trademarks & Synonyms Vol. 2, F-O. 1982. 65.00 (ISBN 0-8206-0293-0). Chem Pub.

--Encyclopedia of Chemical Trademarks & Synonyms Vol. 3, P-Z. 1983. 65.00 (ISBN 0-8206-0302-3). Chem Pub.

Bevan, S. C. A Concise Etymological Dictionary of Chemistry. 1976. 20.50 (ISBN 0-85334-653-4, Pub. by Applied Sci England). Elsevier.

Daintith, John, ed. Dictionary of Chemistry. 1982. pap. 5.72 (ISBN 0-06-463559-7, EH-559). Har-Row.

--Dictionary of Chemistry. Orig. Title: Facts on File Dictionary of Chemistry. (Illus.). 240p. 1982. pap. 5.72i (ISBN 0-06-463559-7). B&N NY.

Encyclopedia of Chemistry. 1208p. 1983. 49.50 (ISBN 0-07-045484-1, P&RB). McGraw.

Godman, Arthur. Illustrated Dictionary of Chemistry. (Illustrated Dictionaries Ser.). (Illus.). 256p. 1982. text ed. 7.95x (ISBN 0-582-55550-7). Longman.

CHEMISTRY–EXPERIMENTS

see also Chemistry, Organic–Experiments

Shakhashiri, Bassam Z., et al. Chemical Demonstrations: A Handbook for Teachers of Chemistry, Vol. 1. LC 81-70016. (Illus.). 256p. 1983. 25.00 (ISBN 0-299-08890-1). U of Wis Pr.

CHEMISTRY–JUVENILE LITERATURE

Walters, Derek. Chemistry. (Science World Ser.). 40p. (gr. 4 up). 1983. PLB 8.90 (ISBN 0-531-04581-1). Watts.

CHEMISTRY–LABORATORIES

see Chemical Laboratories

CHEMISTRY–LABORATORY MANUALS

see also Chemistry, Organic–Laboratory Manuals

Sears, Curtis & Stanitski, Conrad. Chemistry for Health-Related Sciences: Laboratory Manual. (2nd). (Illus.). 400p. 1983. pap. 13.95 (ISBN 0-686-38830-5). P H.

CHEMISTRY–LECTURE EXPERIMENTS

see Chemistry–Experiments

CHEMISTRY–MATHEMATICS

Benson, Sidney W. Chemical Calculations: An Introduction to the Use of Mathematics in Chemistry. 3rd ed. LC 76-146670. 279lp. 1971. text ed. 9.95 (ISBN 0-471-06769-5). Wiley.

Brookes, C. J., et al. Fundamentals of Mathematics: For Students of Chemistry & Allied Subjects. LC 78-26110. 496p. 1979. 67.00 (ISBN 0-471-99733-1); pap. 27.95x (ISBN 0-471-99732-3, Pub. by Wiley-Interscience). Wiley.

Franzen, H. F. Second-Order Phase Transitions & the Irreducible Representation of Space Groups. (Lecture Notes in Chemistry Ser.: Vol. 32). 98p. 1983. pap. 11.00 (ISBN 0-387-11958-2). Springer-Verlag.

CHEMISTRY–MODELS

see Chemical Models

CHEMISTRY–NOTATION

Bennett, H., ed. Chemical Formulary, Vol. 24. 1982. 35.00 (ISBN 0-8206-0291-4). Chem Pub.

--Chemical Formulary, Vol. 25. 1983. 35.00 (ISBN 0-8206-0304-X). Chem Pub.

CHEMISTRY–PROGRAMMED INSTRUCTION

Loebel, Arnold. Programmed Problem Solving for First Year Chemistry. LC 82-83359. 512p. pap. text ed. 13.95 (ISBN 0-395-32626-5). HM.

CHEMISTRY–STUDY AND TEACHING

Fraser, M. J. & Sleet, R. J. Resource Book on Chemical Education in the United Kingdom. 1975. 29.95 (ISBN 0-471-26116-5, Pub. by Wiley Heyden). Wiley.

Isenhour, T. L. & Pederson, L. G. Passing Freshman Chemistry: Prerequesite Skills & Concepts. 177p. (Orig.). 1981. pap. text ed. 9.95 spiralbound (ISBN 0-15-568230-X); instructor's manual 3.95 (ISBN 0-15-568231-8). HarBraceJ.

Loebel. Programmed Problem Solving for First Year Chemistry. 1983. text ed. 12.95 (ISBN 0-686-84542-0). HM.

Shakhashiri, Bassam Z., et al. Chemical Demonstrations: A Handbook for Teachers of Chemistry, Vol. 1. LC 81-70016. (Illus.). 256p. 1983. 25.00 (ISBN 0-299-08890-1). U of Wis Pr.

CHEMISTRY–TERMINOLOGY

Godman, Arthur. Barnes & Noble Thesaurus of Chemistry. (Illus.). 256p. (gr. 11-12). 1983. 13.41i (ISBN 0-06-015175-7); pap. 6.68i (ISBN 0-06-463578-3). B&N NY.

CHEMISTRY, AGRICULTURAL

see Agricultural Chemistry

CHEMISTRY, ANALYTIC

see also Chromatographic Analysis; Polarograph and Polarography; Radioactivation Analysis

also subdivision analysis under special subjects, e.g. Gases–Analysis; Rocks–Analysis

Analytical Chemistry in Energy Technology. Analytical Chemistry in Nuclear Technology: Proceedings of the 25th ORNL Conference. Lyon, W. S., ed. LC 81-70867. (Illus.). 402p. 1982. 29.95 (ISBN 0-250-40469-9). Ann Arbor Science.

Cheng, K. L. & Ueno, Keihei. CRC Handbook of Organic Analytical Reagents. 544p. 1982. 74.00 (ISBN 0-8493-0771-6). CRC Pr.

Counting Molecules-Approaching the Limit of Chemical Analysis. 1982. 5.00 (ISBN 0-910362-20-3). Chem Educ.

Goffer, Zvi. Archaeological Chemistry: A Sourcebook on the Applications of Chemistry to Archaeology, Vol. 55. LC 79-1425. (Chemical Analysis, Analytical Chemistry & Its Applications Ser.). 376p. 1980. 39.50x (ISBN 0-471-05156-X, Pub. by Wiley-Interscience). Wiley.

Kolthoff, I. M. & Elving, Philip J. Treatise on Analytical Chemistry, Vol. 10, Pt. 1. 372p. 1982. 65.00 (ISBN 0-471-89688-8, Pub. by Wiley-Interscience). Wiley.

--Treatise on Analytical Chemistry, Vol. 12, Pt. 1. 2nd ed. 567p. 1983. price not set (ISBN 0-471-89653-5, Pub. by Wiley-Interscience). Wiley.

--Treatise on Analytical Chemistry: Part I: Theory & Practice, Vol. 3. 2nd ed. 592p. 1983. 70.00 (ISBN 0-471-49969-2, Pub. by Wiley-Interscience). Wiley.

Pribil, R. Applied Complexometry, Vol.5. Stulikova, M., et al, trs. (Analytical Chemistry Ser.). (Illus.). 425p. 1982. 75.00 (ISBN 0-08-026277-5). Pergamon.

Royal Society of London. Recent Advances in Analytical Chemistry: Proceedings of a Royal Society Discussion Meeting held on 9 & 10 December 1981. Thomas, J. M., et al, eds. (Illus.). 219p. 1982. text ed. 70.00x (ISBN 0-85403-191-X, Pub. by Royal Soc London). Scholium Intl.

Svehla, G., ed. Wilson & Wilson's Comprehensive Analytical Chemistry Vol. 16: Chemical Microscopy, Thermomicroscopy of Organic Compounds. 514p. 1982. 138.50 (ISBN 0-444-41950-0). Elsevier.

CHEMISTRY, ANALYTIC–PROBLEMS, EXERCISES, ETC.

Brewer, Stephen. Solving Problems in Analytical Chemistry. LC 79-17164. 528p. 1980. pap. text ed. 13.95x (ISBN 0-471-04098-3). Wiley.

CHEMISTRY, ANALYTIC–QUALITATIVE

see also Spectrum Analysis; Spot Tests (Chemistry)

Kennedy, John J. Analyzing Qualitative Data: Introductory Log-Linear Analysis for Behavioral Research. 288p. 1983. 30.00 (ISBN 0-03-060422-2). Praeger.

Smith, R. & James, G. V. Analytical Sciences Monographs: The Sampling of Bulk Materials. 200p. 1982. 90.00x (ISBN 0-85186-810-X, Pub. by Royal Soc Chem England). State Mutual Bk.

CHEMISTRY, ANALYTIC–QUANTITATIVE

see also Electrochemical Analysis; Volumetric Analysis

Brown, Theodore & Le May, Eugene. Qualitative Inorganic Analysis. (Illus.). 160p. 1983. pap. 4.95 (ISBN 0-686-38828-3). P H.

CHEMISTRY, BIOLOGICAL

see Biological Chemistry

CHEMISTRY, BOTANICAL

see Botanical Chemistry

CHEMISTRY, CLINICAL

Kaiser, E. & Gabl, F., eds. Eleventh International Congress of Clinical Chemistry. (Illus.). xx, 1575p. 1982. 160.00x (ISBN 3-11-008447-3). De Gruyter.

--Sixth International Congress of Clinical Chemistry. xx, 1575p. 1982. 160.00x (ISBN 3-11-008447-3). De Gruyter.

Kaplan, Alex & Szabo, LaVerne. Clinical Chemistry: Interpretation & Techniques. 2nd ed. LC 82-17249. (Illus.). 470p. 1983. text ed. write for info. (ISBN 0-8121-0873-6). Lea & Febiger.

CHEMISTRY, INDUSTRIAL

see Chemical Engineering; Chemistry, Technical

CHEMISTRY, INORGANIC

see also Earths, Rare; Metals

also names and classes of inorganic compounds

Addison, A. W. & Cullen, W. R. Biological Aspects of Inorganic Chemistry. 410p. Repr. of 1977 ed. text ed. 35.00 (ISBN 0-471-02147-4). Krieger.

Chambers, C. & Holliday, A. K. Intermediate Chemistry: Inorganic Chemistry. new ed. 420p. 1982. text ed. 12.95 (ISBN 0-408-10822-3). Butterworth.

Davison, A., ed. Physical & Inorganic Chemistry. (Topics in Current Chemistry Ser.: Vol. III). (Illus.). 194p. 1983. 37.50 (ISBN 0-387-12065-3). Springer-Verlag.

Douglas, Bodie E. & McDaniel, D. H. Concepts & Models of Inorganic Chemistry. 510p. 1965. text ed. 31.50x (ISBN 0-471-00129-5). Wiley.

Fergusson, J. E. Inorganic Chemistry & the Earth: Chemical Resources, Their Extraction, Use & Enivironmental Impact. LC 82-15096. (Pergamon Series on Environmental Science: Vol. 6). (Illus.). 409p. 1982. 40.00 (ISBN 0-08-023995-1); pap. 19.95 (ISBN 0-08-023994-3). Pergamon.

Hill, H. A. Inorganic Biochemistry, Vol. 2. 362p. 1982. 190.00x (ISBN 0-85186-555-0, Pub. by Royal Soc Chem England). State Mutual Bk.

Holt, Smith L., ed. Inorganic Reactions in Organized Media. (ACS Symposium Ser.: No. 177). 1982. write for info. (ISBN 0-8412-0670-8). Am Chemical.

Huheey, James E. Inorganic Chemistry: Principles of Structure & Reactivity. 3rd ed. 1024p. 1983. text ed. 34.50 scp (ISBN 0-06-042987-9, HarpC); answer book avail. (ISBN 0-06-362987-9). Har-Row.

Lippard, Stephen J. Progress in Inorganic Chemistry, Vol. 30. (Progress in Inorganic Chemistry Ser.). 382p. 1983. 45.00 (ISBN 0-471-87022-6, Pub. by Wiley-Interscience). Wiley.

Mac Diarmid, A. G. Inorganic Syntheses, Vol. 17. 1977. 32.50 (ISBN 0-07-044327-0). McGraw.

Mizuike, A. Enrichment Techniques for Inorganic Trace Analysis. (Chemical Laboratory Practice). (Illus.). 144p. 1983. 29.80 (ISBN 0-387-12051-3). Springer-Verlag.

Porterfield, William W. Advanced Inorganic Chemistry. (Illus.). 650p. Date not set. text ed. 30.00 (ISBN 0-686-82179-3). A-W.

--Inorganic Chemistry: A Unified Approach. (Illus.). 768p. Date not set. text ed. 30.00 (ISBN 0-201-05660-7). A-W.

Rodymans, C. & Rabenau, A., eds. Crystal Structure & Chemical Bonding in Inorganic Chemistry. 1975. 42.75 (ISBN 0-444-10961-7). Elsevier.

Sharpe, A. G. & Emeleus, H. J., eds. Advances in Inorganic Chemistry & Radiochemistry, Vol. 26. (Serial Publication). Date not set. price not set (ISBN 0-12-023626-5); price not set lib. ed. (ISBN 0-12-023692-3); price not set microfiche (ISBN 0-12-023693-1). Acad Pr.

Sykes, A. G. Inorganic Reaction Mechanisms, Vol. 7. 460p. 1982. 250.00x (ISBN 0-85186-315-9, Pub. by Royal Soc Chem England). State Mutual Bk.

CHEMISTRY, INORGANIC–SYNTHESIS

Dewar, M. J., et al, eds. Synthetic & Structural Problems. (Topics in Current Chemistry Ser.: Vol. 106). (Illus.). 170p. 1982. 39.00 (ISBN 0-387-11766-0). Springer-Verlag.

McMurrary, John, et al, eds. Annual Reports in Organic Synthesis, Vol. 12. (Serial Publication). 1982. 26.00 (ISBN 0-12-040812-0). Acad Pr.

Pattenden, G. General & Synthetic Methods, Vol. 4. 388p. 1982. 125.00x (ISBN 0-85186-854-1, Pub. by Royal Soc Chem England). State Mutual Bk.

Wade, L. G. & O'Donnell, M. J., eds. Annual Reports in Organic Synthesis, Vol. 11. (Serial Publication). 1981. 24.00 (ISBN 0-12-040811-2). Acad Pr.

CHEMISTRY, MEDICAL AND PHARMACEUTICAL

see also Chemistry, Clinical; Disinfection and Disinfectants; Drugs; Materia Medica; Pharmacy; Poisonous Plants

Cain, C. K., ed. Annual Reports in Medicinal Chemistry, Vol. 17. (Serial Publication). 400p. 1982. 32.00 (ISBN 0-12-040517-2); membership Price 4.00 (ISBN 0-686-82449-0). Acad Pr.

Ellis, G. P. & West, G. B., eds. Progress in Medicinal Chemistry, Vols. 8 & 9. 1971-75. Vol. 8, Pt. 1. pap. 14.75 (ISBN 0-7204-7408-6); Vol. 9, Pt. 1. pap. 12.25 (ISBN 0-7204-7409-4); Vol. 9, Pt. 2. pap. 23.25 (ISBN 0-444-10578-6). Elsevier.

Ferguson, John. Biblioteca Chimica: Catalog of the Alchemical & Pharmaceutical Books in the Library of James Young, 2 vols. 1100p. 150.00 (ISBN 0-87556-493-3). Saifer.

Kligman, Albert M. & Leyden, James L., eds. Assessment of Safety & Efficacy of Topical Drugs & Cosmetics. 432p. Date not set. 39.50 (ISBN 0-8089-1527-4). Grune.

CHEMISTRY, MINERALOGICAL

see Mineralogical Chemistry

CHEMISTRY, NUCLEAR

see Nuclear Chemistry

CHEMISTRY, ORGANIC

see also Carbon Compounds; Chemistry, Physical Organic; Radicals (Chemistry); Stereochemistry; Surface Active Agents

also names of classes of organic compounds, e.g. Alkaloids; Carbohydrates; Proteins; also names of individual organic substances, e.g. Benzene

Adams, Roger, ed. Organic Reactions, Vol. 1. LC 42-20265. 400p. 1978. Repr. of 1942 ed. 29.50 (ISBN 0-88275-729-6). Krieger.

--Organic Reactions, Vol. 2. LC 42-20265. 470p. 1981. Repr. of 1944 ed. 29.50 (ISBN 0-89874-375-3). Krieger.

--Organic Reactions, Vol. 3. LC 42-20265. 468p. 1975. Repr. of 1946 ed. 29.50 (ISBN 0-88275-875-6). Krieger.

--Organic Reactions, Vol. 4. LC 42-20265. 438p. 1979. Repr. of 1948 ed. 29.50 (ISBN 0-88275-780-6). Krieger.

--Organic Reactions, Vol. 5. LC 42-20265. 454p. 1977. Repr. of 1949 ed. 29.50 (ISBN 0-88275-249-9). Krieger.

--Organic Reactions, Vol. 6. LC 42-20265. 526p. 1975. Repr. of 1951 ed. 29.50 (ISBN 0-88275-876-4). Krieger.

--Organic Reactions, Vol. 7. LC 42-20265. 448p. 1975. Repr. of 1953 ed. 29.50 (ISBN 0-88275-877-2). Krieger.

--Organic Reactions, Vol. 8. LC 42-20265. 446p. 1975. Repr. of 1954 ed. 29.50 (ISBN 0-88275-878-0). Krieger.

--Organic Reactions, Vol. 9. LC 42-20265. 476p. 1975. Repr. of 1957 ed. 29.50 (ISBN 0-88275-879-9). Krieger.

--Organic Reactions, Vol. 10. LC 42-20265. 572p. 1975. Repr. of 1959 ed. 29.50 (ISBN 0-88275-880-2). Krieger.

Baumgarten, Reuben L. Organic Chemistry: A Brief Survey. LC 74-22533. 475p. 1978. 25.95x (ISBN 0-471-06716-4). Wiley.

Bentley, K. W. & Kirby, G. W. Techniques of Chemistry: Vol. 4, 2 Pts. Elucidation of Organic Structures by Physical & Chemical Methods. 2nd ed. 689p. 1972. Pt. 1. 73.50x (ISBN 0-471-92896-8); Pt. 2, 1973, 561pgs. 75.50x (ISBN 0-471-92897-6). Wiley.

Cheng, K. L. & Ueno, Keihei. CRC Handbook of Organic Analytical Reagents. 544p. 1982. 74.00 (ISBN 0-8493-0771-6). CRC Pr.

Cope, Arthur C., ed. Organic Reactions, Vol. 11. LC 42-20265. 510p. 1975. Repr. of 1960 ed. 29.50 (ISBN 0-88275-881-0). Krieger.

--Organic Reactions, Vol. 12. LC 42-20265. 546p. 1975. Repr. of 1962 ed. 29.50 (ISBN 0-88275-882-9). Krieger.

--Organic Reactions, Vol. 13. LC 42-20265. 390p. 1979. Repr. of 1962 ed. 29.50 (ISBN 0-88275-836-5). Krieger.

--Organic Reactions, Vol. 14. LC 42-20265. 506p. 1978. Repr. of 1965 ed. 29.50 (ISBN 0-88275-730-X). Krieger.

--Organic Reactions, Vol. 15. LC 42-20265. 616p. 1978. Repr. of 1967 ed. 29.50 (ISBN 0-88275-731-8). Krieger.

--Organic Reactions, Vol. 16. LC 42-20265. 456p. 1975. Repr. of 1968 ed. 29.50 (ISBN 0-88275-883-7). Krieger.

Dauben, William G. Organic Reactions, Vol. 29. 500p. 1983. 40.00 (ISBN 0-471-87490-6, Pub. by Wiley-Interscience). Wiley.

Dauben, William G., ed. Organic Reactions, Vol. 17. LC 42-20265. 346p. 1975. Repr. of 1969 ed. 29.50 (ISBN 0-88275-884-5). Krieger.

--Organic Reactions, Vol. 18. LC 42-20265. 476p. 1978. Repr. of 1970 ed. 29.50 (ISBN 0-88275-732-6). Krieger.

--Organic Reactions, Vol. 19. LC 42-20265. 446p. 1975. Repr. of 1972 ed. 29.50 (ISBN 0-88275-885-3). Krieger.

--Organic Reactions, Vol. 20. LC 42-20265. 506p. 1981. Repr. of 1973 ed. 39.50 (ISBN 0-89874-390-7). Krieger.

Doyle, Michael P. & Mungall, William S. Experimental Organic Chemistry. LC 79-18392. 490p. 1980. text ed. 21.95 (ISBN 0-471-03383-9); avail. tchrs. manual (ISBN 0-471-08053-5). Wiley.

Fleming, I. Frontier Orbitals & Organic Chemical Reactions. LC 76-3800. 249p. 1976. 43.50x (ISBN 0-471-01820-1); pap. 17.50 (ISBN 0-471-01819-8, Pub. by Wiley-Interscience). Wiley.

Gordon, John E. How to Succeed in Organic Chemistry. LC 78-21496. (Self-Teaching Guide Ser.). 1979. pap. text ed. 9.95 (ISBN 0-471-03010-4). Wiley.

Gordon, P. F. & Gregory, P. Organic Chemistry in Colour. (Illus.). 300p. 1983. 71.50 (ISBN 0-387-11748-2). Springer-Verlag.

Hart. Organic Chemistry: A Short Course. 6th ed. 1983. text ed. 28.95 (ISBN 0-686-84540-4, CH26); write for info. supplementary materials. HM.

Hart, Harold. Organic Chemistry: A Short Course. 6th ed. LC 82-84391. 448p. 1983. text ed. 24.95 (ISBN 0-395-32611-7); write for info. supplementary materials. HM.

Herz, W., et al, eds. Progress in the Chemistry of Organic Natural Products, Vol. 42. 330p. 1983. 66.00 (ISBN 0-387-81706-9). Springer-Verlag.

Linstromberg, Walter W. & Baumgarten, Henry E. Organic Chemistry: A Brief Course. 5th ed. 448p. lib. bdg. 23.95 (ISBN 0-669-05525-5); pap. text ed. 8.95 Problems & Solutions Guide (ISBN 0-669-05526-3); pap. text ed. 10.95 Organic Experiments (ISBN 0-669-05524-7). Heath.

Loudon, G. Marc. Organic Chemistry. (Chemistry Ser.). 1200p. 1984. text ed. 34.95 (ISBN 0-201-14438-7). A-W.

Pope, Martin & Swenberg, Charles E. Electronic Processes in Organic Crystals. (Monographs on the Physics & Chemistry of Materials). (Illus.). 842p. 1982. 145.00x (ISBN 0-19-851334-8). Oxford U Pr.

Seyferth, D. & King, R., eds. Annual Surveys of Organometallic Chemistry, Vols. 1-3. 1965-68. 38.50 ea. Vol. 1, 1964 (ISBN 0-444-40527-5). Vol. 2, 1965 (ISBN 0-444-40528-3). Vol. 3, 1966 (ISBN 0-444-40529-1). Elsevier.

Shorter, John. Correlation Analysis of Organic Reactivity: With Particular Reference to Multiple Regression. LC 82-7655. 235p. 1982. 41.95 (ISBN 0-471-10479-5, Pub. by Wiley-Interscience). Wiley.

Slocum. In Place of Transition Metals in Organic Synthesis, Vol. 295. 1977. 12.00 (ISBN 0-89072-041-X). NY Acad Sci.

Wingrove & Caret. Quimica Organica. (Span.). 1983. pap. text ed. price not set (ISBN 0-06-319450-3, Pub. by HarLA Mexico). Har-Row.

CHEMISTRY, ORGANIC–EXPERIMENTS

Fieser, Louis F. & Williamson, Kenneth L. Organic Experiments. 448p. 1983. 24.95 (ISBN 0-669-05890-4). Heath.

CHEMISTRY, ORGANIC–LABORATORY MANUALS

Richey, Jane. Fundamentals of Organic Chemistry: Solutions Manual. 136p. 1983. pap. 7.95 (ISBN 0-686-38831-3). P H.

CHEMISTRY, ORGANIC–PROBLEMS, EXERCISES, ETC.

Ryles, A. P. & Smith, K. Worked Examples in Essential Organic Chemistry. 161p. 1981. text ed. 26.95x (ISBN 0-471-27972-2, Pub. by Wiley-Interscience); pap. text ed. 10.95x (ISBN 0-471-27975-7). Wiley.

CHEMISTRY, ORGANIC–SYNTHESIS

see also Biosynthesis; Plastics; Polymers and Polymerization

ApSimon, John W., ed. The Total Synthesis of Natural Products, 3 vols. LC 72-4075. 603p. 1973. Vol. 1. 59.00x (ISBN 0-471-03251-4); Vol. 2. 54.95x (ISBN 0-471-03252-2); Vol. 3. 54.95x (ISBN 0-471-02392-2, Pub. by Wiley-Interscience). Wiley.

Blatt, A. H. Organic Synthesis Collective Volumes, Vol. 2. 654p. 1943. 35.95 (ISBN 0-471-07986-3). Wiley.

Brossi, A. Organic Synthesis. LC 21-17747. (Organic Synthesis Ser.: Vol. 53). 193p. 1973. 15.95 (ISBN 0-471-10615-1). Wiley.

Buchi, George H. Organic Synthesis, Vol. 56. LC 22-17747. (Organic Synthesis Ser.). 157p. 1977. 18.95 (ISBN 0-471-02218-7, Pub. by Wiley-Interscience). Wiley.

Davies, S. G., ed. Organotransition Metal Chemistry: Applications to Organic Synthesis. (Organic Chemistry Ser.: Vol. 2). (Illus.). 428p. 1982. 85.00 (ISBN 0-08-026202-3). Pergamon.

Dewar, M. J., et al, eds. Synthetic & Structural Problems. (Topics in Current Chemistry Ser.: Vol. 106). (Illus.). 170p. 1982. 39.00 (ISBN 0-387-11766-0). Springer-Verlag.

Fleming, Ian. Selected Organic Syntheses: A Guidebook for Organic Chemists. LC 72-615. 227p. 1973. 45.95x (ISBN 0-471-26390-7); pap. 24.95 (ISBN 0-471-26391-5, Pub. by Wiley-Interscience). Wiley.

Mikhailov, B. M. & Bubnov, Yu N. Organoboron Compounds in Organic Synthesis. (Soviet Scientific Reviews Supplement Ser.). Date not set. price not set (ISBN 3-7186-0113-3). Harwood Academic.

Pattenden, G. General & Synthetic Methods, Vol. 4. 388p. 1982. 125.00x (ISBN 0-85186-854-1, Pub. by Royal Soc Chem England). State Mutual Bk.

Roberts, Ralph & Ouellette, Robert B. Industrial Applications of Electroorganic Synthesis. LC 82-71530. (Illus.). 205p. 1982. 29.95 (ISBN 0-250-40585-7). Ann Arbor Science.

Warren, Stuart. Organic Synthesis: The Disconnection Approach. 1983. 34.95x (ISBN 0-471-10160-5, Pub. by Wiley-Interscience); wkbk. avail. (ISBN 0-471-90082-6). Wiley.

CHEMISTRY, PATHOLOGICAL

see Chemistry, Medical and Pharmaceutical

CHEMISTRY, PHARMACEUTICAL

see Chemistry, Medical and Pharmaceutical

CHEMISTRY, PHYSICAL AND THEORETICAL

see also Adsorption; Atoms; Catalysis; Chemical Bonds; Chemical Reaction, Rate of; Chemical Structure; Chemistry, Physical Organic; Colloids; Crystallization; Crystallography; Dissociation; Electrochemistry; Gases–Liquefaction; Mass Transfer; Molecular Theory; Nuclear Chemistry; Nuclear Physics; Photochemistry; Polymers and Polymerization; Quantum Chemistry; Quantum Theory; Radiation Chemistry; Radiochemistry; Solid State Chemistry; Stereochemistry; Sulphur Bonding; Surface Chemistry; Thermochemistry; Thermodynamics; Valence (Theoretical Chemistry)

Alberty, Robert A. Physical Chemistry. 6th ed. 832p. 1983. text ed. 29.95 (ISBN 0-471-09284-3); solutions manual avail. (ISBN 0-471-87208-3). Wiley.

Alberty, Robert A. & Daniels, Farrington. Physical Chemistry. 5th ed. LC 78-14876. 692p. 1979. text ed. 28.95 (ISBN 0-471-02222-5); solutions manual 10.95 (ISBN 0-471-04749-X). Wiley.

--Physical Chemistry SI Version. LC 78-14876. 692p. 1980. text ed. 28.95 (ISBN 0-471-05716-9); solutions manual 12.95 (ISBN 0-471-06376-2). Wiley.

Berry, R. Stephen, et al. Physical Chemistry. LC 79-790. 1281p. 1980. comb. text ed. 38.95x (ISBN 0-471-04829-1); solutions manual 10.95 (ISBN 0-471-04844-5). Wiley.

Castellan, Gilbert W. Physical Chemistry. 3rd ed. (Chemistry Ser.). (Illus.). 960p. 1983. text ed. 28.95 (ISBN 0-201-10386-9); Solutions Manual avail. (ISBN 0-201-10387-7). A-W.

Davison, A., ed. Physical & Inorganic Chemistry. (Topics in Current Chemistry Ser.: Vol. III). (Illus.). 194p. 1983. 37.50 (ISBN 0-387-12065-3). Springer-Verlag.

Lesk, Arthur. Introduction to Physical Chemistry: Solutions manual. 100p. 1983. pap. 11.95 (ISBN 0-13-492728-1). P-H.

Levine, Ira N. Physical Chemistry. 2nd ed. (Illus.). 992p. 1983. text ed. 32.95 (ISBN 0-07-037421-X, C); solutions manual 12.95 (ISBN 0-07-037422-8). McGraw.

Morris, J. Gareth. A Biologist's Physical Chemistry. 408p. 1974. pap. text ed. 16.50 (ISBN 0-7131-2414-8). E Arnold.

Physical Methods of Chemistry: Spectroscopy & Spectrometry in the Infrared, Visible, & Ultraviolet, Vol.1, Part 3B. Weissberger, A. & Rossiter, B. W., eds. LC 45-8533. (Techniques of Chemistry Ser.). 732p. Repr. of 1972 ed. text ed. 57.50 (ISBN 0-471-92731-7). Krieger.

Sakano, Theodore & Gregory, Stephen. Basic Physical Chemistry: Solutions Manual. 192p. 1983. pap. 11.95 (ISBN 0-686-38829-1). P H.

Thomson, C. Theoretical Chemistry, Vol. 4. 189p. 1982. 140.00x (ISBN 0-85186-784-7, Pub. by Royal Soc Chem England). State Mutual Bk.

Tolk, N. H., et al, eds. Desorption Induced by Electron Transitions, DIET I. (Springer Ser. in Chemical Physics: Vol. 24). (Illus.). 305p. 1983. 29.50 (ISBN 0-387-12127-7). Springer-Verlag.

CHEMISTRY, PHYSICAL ORGANIC

Abramovitch, R. A., ed. Reactive Intermediates, Vol. 3. 615p. 1982. 59.50x (ISBN 0-306-40970-4, Plenum Pr). Plenum Pub.

Gold, V. Advances in Physical Organic Chemistry, Vol. 19. (Serial Publication). Date not set. 69.50 (ISBN 0-12-033519-0). Acad Pr.

CHEMISTRY, QUANTUM

see Quantum Chemistry

CHEMISTRY, SOIL

see Soil Chemistry

CHEMISTRY, SOLID STATE

see Solid State Chemistry

CHEMISTRY, SURFACE

see Surface Chemistry

CHEMISTRY, SYNTHETIC

see Chemistry, Inorganic–Synthesis; Chemistry, Organic–Synthesis

CHEMISTRY, TECHNICAL

see also Alloys; Animal Products; Biochemical Engineering; Bleaching; Canning and Preserving; Ceramics; Chemical Engineering; Chemical Industries; Chemical Reactors; Chemicals–Manufacture and Industry; Cleaning Compounds; Corrosion and Anti-Corrosives; Electrochemistry; Food–Analysis; Gums and Resins

also particular industries and products, e.g. Clay Industries; Dyes and Dyeing; Petroleum Products

Breck & Brown. Chemistry for Science & Engineering. 450p. Date not set. 29.95 (ISBN 0-07-092372-8). McGraw.

Halpern, M. G., ed. Polishing & Waxing Compositions: Recent Developments. LC 82-7691. (Chemical Technology Rev. 213). (Illus.). 301p. 1983. 36.00 (ISBN 0-8155-0916-2). Noyes.

Torrey, S., ed. Pre-emergence Herbicides: Recent Advances. LC 82-7954. (Chemical Technology Rev. 211). (Illus.). 335p. 1983. 48.00 (ISBN 0-8155-0914-6). Noyes.

CHEMISTRY, THEORETICAL

see Chemistry, Physical and Theoretical

CHEMISTRY OF FOOD

see Food–Analysis; Food–Composition

CHEMISTS

International Union of Pure & Applied Chemistry. Membership Lists & Report: 1982. 180p. 1982. pap. 13.00 (ISBN 0-08-029241-0). Pergamon.

CHEMOTHERAPY
see also Anti-Infective Agents; Antibiotics; Psychopharmacology;
also subdivision Chemotherapy under diseases, e.g. Cancer–Chemotheraphy
Abrams, Anne C. Clinical Drug Therapy: Rationales for Nursing Practice. (Illus.). 600p. 1983. text ed. write for info. (ISBN 0-397-54336-0, Lippincott Medical). Lippincott.
Caplan, Robert D., et al. Social Support & Patient Adherence: Experimental Survey Findings. 284p. 1980. pap. 16.00x (ISBN 0-87944-260-3). Inst Soc Res.
Cypress, Beulah K. Medication Therapy in Office Visits for Selected Diagnoses: National Ambulatory Medical Care Survey, United States, 1980. Cox, Klaudia, ed. (Ser. 13: No. 71). 65p. 1982. pap. text ed. 1.85 (ISBN 0-8406-0266-9). Natl Ctr Health Stats.
Emmerson, A. M. The Microbiology & Treatment of Life-Threatening Infections. (Antimicrobial Chemotherapy Ser.). 175p. 1982. 31.95 (ISBN 0-471-90049-4, Pub. by Res Stud Pr). Wiley.
Fox, C. Fred & Chabner, Bruce A., eds. Rational Basis for Chemotherapy. LC 82-24921. (UCLA Symposium on Molecular & Cellular Biology Ser.: Vol. 4). 524p. 1983. 54.00 (ISBN 0-8451-2603-2). A R Liss.
Hitchings, G. H., ed. Inhibition of Folate Metabolism in Chemotherapy: The Origins & Uses Of Co-trixomazole. (Handbook of Experimental Pharmacology Ser.: Vol. 64). (Illus.). 457p. 1983. 150.00 (ISBN 0-387-11782-2). Springer-Verlag.
Hollister, Leo E. Year Book of Drug Therapy 1983. 1983. 42.00 (ISBN 0-8151-4621-3). Year Bk Med.
Janke, W, ed. Response Variability to Psychotropic Drugs. (International Series in Experimental Psychology). (Illus.). 272p. 1983. 37.00 (ISBN 0-08-028907-X). Pergamon.
Koch-Weser, Jan, ed. Reprints of Articles on Drug Therapy, 6 Vols. Incl. Vol. 6. (Illus.). 215p. 1980. Repr. of 1980 ed. pap. 7.50 (ISBN 0-910133-12-3); Vol. 5. (Illus.). 1980. Repr. of 1980 ed. pap. 7.50 (ISBN 0-910133-11-5); Vol. 4. (Illus.). 141p. 1977. Repr. of 1976 ed. pap. 6.00 (ISBN 0-910133-10-7); Vol. 3. (Illus.). 197p. 1976. Repr. of 1972 ed. pap. 6.00 (ISBN 0-910133-09-3); Vol. 2. (Illus.). 167p. 1976. Repr. of 1973 ed. pap. text ed. 6.00 (ISBN 0-910133-08-5); Vol. 1. (Illus.). 163p. 1976. Repr. of 1972 ed. pap. text ed. 6.00 (ISBN 0-910133-07-7). (Orig.). pap. MA Med Soc.
Kuemmerle. Antimicrobial Chemotherapy. 1983. price not set (ISBN 0-86577-082-4). Thieme-Stratton.
--Fundamentals of Chemotherapy. Date not set. price not set (ISBN 0-86577-066-2). Thieme-Stratton.
Kuemmerle, Helmut P. Fundamentals: Clinical Chemotherapy, Vol. 1. (Illus.). 440p. 1983. price not set (ISBN 0-86577-075-1). Thieme-Stratton.
Ringler, Karin E. Coping with Chemotherapy. Nathan, Peter E., ed. (Research in Clinical Psychology Ser.: No. 6). 1983. price not set (ISBN 0-8357-1389-X). Univ Microfilms.
CHERAW INDIANS
see Indians of North America–Eastern States
CHEROKEE INDIANS
see Indians of North America–Eastern States
CHERUBIM
see Angels
CHESAPEAKE BAY
Stone, William T. & Blanchard, Fessenden. A Cruising Guide to the Chesapeake. Rev. ed. (Illus.). 1983. 19.95 (ISBN 0-396-08165-7). Dodd.
CHESS
Averbakh, Y. & Checkover, V. Comprehensive Chess Endings: Bishop Endings & Knight Endings, Vol. 1. Neat, K. P., tr. from Rus. (Russian Chess Ser.). 232p. 1983. 24.95 (ISBN 0-08-026900-1). Pergamon.
Bellin, Robert. Queen's Pawn: Veresov System. (Illus.). 96p. 1983. pap. 13.50 (ISBN 0-7134-1877-X, Pub. by Batsford England). David & Charles.
Botterill, G. S., ed. British Chess. (Chess Ser.). (Illus.). 300p. 1983. 30.01 (ISBN 0-08-024134-4). Pergamon.
Chandler, M. & Miles, A., eds. Tournament Chess. (Tournament Chess Ser.: Vol. 5). 176p. 1982. pap. 19.95 (ISBN 0-08-029720-X). Pergamon.
--Tournament Chess. 176p. 1982. pap. 19.95 (ISBN 0-08-029721-8). Pergamon.
--Tournament Chess, Vol. 4. 150p. 1982. 24.00 (ISBN 0-08-026893-5). Pergamon.
Cozens, W. H. Lessons in Chess Strategy. (Routledge Chess Handbooks). 124p. 1968. pap. 4.95 (ISBN 0-7100-5223-5). Routledge & Kegan.
Dickins, Anthony S. & Ebert, Hilmar. One Hundred Classics of the Chessboard. (Chess Ser.). 208p. 1983. 17.00 (ISBN 0-08-026921-4); pap. 9.90 (ISBN 0-08-026920-6). Pergamon.
Flesch, Janos. Planning in Chess. (Illus.). 96p. 1983. pap. 11.50 (ISBN 0-7134-1597-5, Pub. by Batsford England). David & Charles.
Griffiths, Peter. Better Chess for Club Players. (Illus.). 117p. (Orig.). 1983. pap. 7.95 (ISBN 0-7158-0788-9, Pub. by EP Publishing England). Sterling.
Levy, David & Newborn, Monroe. More Chess & Computers. 1982. pap. 19.95 (ISBN 0-914894-74-9). Computer Sci.
Marovic, D. Play the King's Indian Defense. (Pergamon Chess Ser.). (Illus.). 176p. 1983. 19.90 (ISBN 0-08-029727-7); pap. 12.90 (ISBN 0-08-029726-9). Pergamon.
Mednis, E. From the Opening into the Endgame. (Chess Ser.). (Illus.). 176p. 1983. 18.95 (ISBN 0-08-026917-6); pap. 10.95 (ISBN 0-08-026916-8). Pergamon.
Smyslov, V. V. Selected Games. LC 81-23466. (Russian Chess Ser.). 250p. 1983. 19.95 (ISBN 0-08-026912-5). Pergamon.
Taulbut, Shaun. How to Play the French Defence. (Illus.). 96p. 1983. pap. 13.50 (ISBN 0-7134-3717-0, Pub. by Batsford England). David & Charles.
CHESS–COLLECTIONS OF GAMES
Fine, Reuben. Lessons From My Games: A Passion for Chess. (Illus.). 256p. 1983. pap. 4.95 (ISBN 0-486-24429-6). Dover.
CHESS–END GAMES
Chess Visions, Inc. Staff, compiled by. Minor Piece Endgames: Yuri Averbakh Endgames Cassettes. (Illus.). 60p. 1982. 21.90 (ISBN 0-939786-03-6). Chess Visions.
Chess Visions, Inc. Staff, ed. Rook & Minor Pieces: Yuri Averbakh Endgame Cassettes. (Illus.). 56p. 1982. 21.90 (ISBN 0-939786-04-4). Chess Visions.
Hooper, David. Practical Chess Endgames. (Routledge Chess Handbooks). 152p. 1981. pap. 4.95 (ISBN 0-7100-5226-X). Routledge & Kegan.
CHESS–JUVENILE LITERATURE
Marsh, Carole. Go Queen Go! Chess for Kids. (Tomorrow's Books). (Illus.). 48p. 1983. 3.95 (ISBN 0-935326-14-6). Gallopade Pub Group.
CHESS–PICTORIAL WORKS
Garrow, Simon. The Amazing Adventures of Dan the Pawn. (Illus.). 1983. 7.25 (ISBN 0-671-46193-1). S&S.
CHESS–PROBLEMS
see Chess Problems
CHESS GAMES
see Chess–Collections of Games
CHESS PROBLEMS
Russ, Colin. Miniature Chess Problems. (Illus.). 262p. 1982. pap. 6.95 (ISBN 0-312-53370-5). St Martin.
CHEST–RADIOGRAPHY
Herman, P. G., ed. Iatrogenic Thoracic Complications. (Radiology of Iatrogenic Disorders Ser.). (Illus.). 243p. 1983. 54.90 (ISBN 0-387-90729-7). Springer-Verlag.
CHESTER PLAYS
Lumiansky, R. M. & Mills, David. The Chester Mystery Cycle: Essays & Documents. LC 82-1838. vii, 321p. 1982. 40.00x (ISBN 0-8078-1522-5). U of NC Pr.
CHEVROLET AUTOMOBILE
see Automobiles–Types–Chevrolet
CHEYENNE INDIANS
see Indians of North America–The West
CHICAGO
Algren, N. Chicago: City on the Make. 112p. 1983. pap. 5.95 (ISBN 0-07-001012-9, GB). McGraw.
CHICAGO–DESCRIPTION
Bach, Ira J. & Gray, Mary L. A Guide to Chicago's Public Sculpture. LC 82-20214. (Illus.). 384p. 1983. lib. bdg. 20.00x (ISBN 0-226-03398-8); pap. 8.95 (ISBN 0-226-03399-6). U of Chicago Pr.
Chicagoland Atlas. 1981. 29.95 (ISBN 0-933162-02-2). Creative Sales.
Chicagoland Atlas with Map Trace. 1981. 29.95 (ISBN 0-933162-03-0). Creative Sales.
Foxe, Sonja & Miles, Barbara. Essential Chicago: An Astrological Portrait of the Windy City. (Illus.). 1982. pap. 3.80 (ISBN 0-933646-21-6). Aries Pr.
Heckens, Gertrude & Friedman, Lynne. Lunching in Chicago. (Illus.). 1983. pap. 7.95 (ISBN 0-89651-426-9). Icarus.
Kelson, Allen H. & Spiselman, Anne. Chicago Magazine's Guide to Chicago. (Illus.). 416p. (Orig.). 1983. pap. 8.95 (ISBN 0-8092-5893-5). Contemp Bks.
CHICAGO–HISTORY
Dedmond, Emmett. Fabulous Chicago. rev. ed. LC 81-66024. (Illus.). 480p. 1983. pap. 9.95 (ISBN 0-689-70639-1, 288). Atheneum.
CHICAGO–SOCIAL CONDITIONS
Jones, Peter d'A., ed. Ethnic Chicago. Holli, Melvin. 1981. pap. 12.95 (ISBN 0-8028-1807-2, 1807-2). Eerdmans.
CHICANOS
see Mexican Americans
CHICKASAW INDIANS
see Indians of North America–Eastern States
CHICKENS
see Poultry
CHIEF JUSTICES
see Judges
CHILD ABUSE
Besharov, Douglas J. Protecting Abused & Neglected Children: Identification & Action. 1983. pap. text ed. price not set (ISBN 0-8391-1797-3, 17949). Univ Park.
Child Abuse. (Clinical Pediatrics Ser.). 1982. text ed. 22.50 (ISBN 0-316-60410-0). Little.
Ebeling, Nancy B. & Hill, Deborah A., eds. Child Abuse & Neglect: A Guide for Treating the Child & Family. 400p. 1982. text ed. 27.50 (ISBN 0-7236-7040-4). Wright-PSG.
Garbarino, James. Child Abuse: What Resources for Meeting the Problem? (Vital Issues, Vol. XXVIII 1978-79: No. 2). 0.60 (ISBN 0-686-81618-8). Ctr Info Am.
Gelles, Richard J. & Cornell, Claire P. International Perspectives on Family Violence. LC 82-48524. 1983. write for info. (ISBN 0-669-06199-9); pap. write for info. (ISBN 0-669-06198-0). Lexington Bks.
Giaretto, Henry. Intergrated Treatment of Child Sexual Abuse. LC 81-86712. 25.00 (ISBN 0-8314-0061-7). Sci & Behavior.
Graves, Joy D. Early Interventions in Child Abuse: The Role of the Police Officer. LC 81-85982. 125p. 1983. pap. 14.95 (ISBN 0-88247-697-1). R & E Res Assoc.
How to Kill a Child in the Easiest Way. (Analysis Ser.: No. 4). 1982. pap. 10.00 (ISBN 0-686-42839-0). Inst Analysis.
Miller, Alice. For Your Own Good: Hidden Cruelty in Childrearing & the Roots of Violence. Hannum, Hildegarde & Hannum, Hunter, trs. from German. 1983. 16.50 (ISBN 0-374-15750-2). FS&G.
Pall, Michael L. & Streit, Lois B. Let's Talk About It: The Book for Children about Child Abuse. LC 82-60527. 125p. (Orig.). (gr. 6-12). 1983. pap. 4.95 (ISBN 0-88247-682-3). R & E Res Assoc.
Reed, Robert D. How & Where to Research & Find Information about Child Abuse. LC 82-60571. 40p. (Orig.). 1983. pap. 4.50 (ISBN 0-88247-692-0). R & E Res Assoc.
Reite, Martin & Caine, Nancy, eds. Child Abuse: The Nonhuman Primate Data. (Monographs in Primatology: Vol. 1). 200p. 1983. write for info. (ISBN 0-8451-3400-0). A R Liss.
Sloan, Irving J., ed. Protection of Abused Victims: State Laws & Decisions. 1982. 35.00 (ISBN 0-379-10237-4). Oceana.
CHILD AND MOTHER
see Mother and Child
CHILD AND PARENT
see Parent and Child
CHILD BEHAVIOR
see Child Psychology; Children–Management
CHILD BIRTH
see Childbirth
CHILD CARE CENTERS
see Day Care Centers
CHILD CUSTODY
see Custody of Children
CHILD DEVELOPMENT
see also Child Psychology; Children–Growth
Ames, Louise B., et al. Your One-Year-Old: The Fun-Loving, Fussy 12-to-24-Month Old. (Illus.). 1983. pap. 5.95 (Delta). Dell.
Baldwin, Alfred L. Theories of Child Development. 2nd ed. LC 80-24517. 582p. 1980. text ed. 24.95 (ISBN 0-471-04583-7). Wiley.
Blunden, R. Social Development. (Studies in Developmental Paediatrics). (Illus.). 160p. 1982. text ed. 25.00 (ISBN 0-85200-304-8, Pub. by MTP Pr England). Kluwer Boston.
Brazelton, T. Berry. Infants & Mothers: Differences in Development. rev. ed. 1983. pap. 9.95 (ISBN 0-440-54010-0, Delta). Dell.
--Infants & Mothers: Differences in Development. rev. ed. 1983. 16.95 (ISBN 0-440-04259-3, Sey Lawr). Delacorte.
Clarke-Stewart, Alison & Koch, Joanne. Children: Development Through Adolescence. 625p. 1983. text ed. 23.95 (ISBN 0-471-03069-4); tchrs. manual avail. (ISBN 0-471-87302-0); solutions avail. (ISBN 0-471-87197-4). Wiley.
Dodson, Fitzhugh & Alexander, Ann. Your Child: Pregnancy Through Preschool. (Illus.). 416p. 1983. pap. 12.95 (ISBN 0-671-45894-9, Fireside). S&S.
Dunst, Carl J., ed. Infant & Preschool Assessment Instruments: Relability, Validity & Utility. (Illus.). 1983. text ed. price not set (ISBN 0-8391-1716-7, 17574). Univ Park.
Flake-Hobson, Carol & Robinson, Bryan E. Child Development & Relationships. (Illus.). 608p. 1983. text ed. 15.95 (ISBN 0-201-04092-1). A-W.
Goodenough, Florence L. & Anderson, John E. Experimental Child Study. 546p. 1982. Repr. of 1931 ed. lib. bdg. 45.00 (ISBN 0-8495-2134-3). Arden Lib.
Gurian, Anita & Formanek, Ruth. The Socially Competent Child: A Parent's Guide to Social Development from Infancy to Early Adolescence. 206p. 1983. 12.95 (ISBN 0-395-32205-7). HM.
Hanson, Marci J., ed. Atypical Infant Development. (Illus.). 1983. pap. text ed. price not set (ISBN 0-8391-1788-4, 18414). Univ Park.
Higgins, E. Tory & Hartup, Willard W., eds. Social Cognition & Social Development: A Sociocultural Perspective. LC 82-12897. (Cambridge Studies in Social & Emotional Development: No. 5). 352p. Date not set. price not set (ISBN 0-521-24587-7). Cambridge U Pr.
Jersild, Arthur T. Child Development & the Curriculum. 274p. 1982. Repr. of 1946 ed. lib. bdg. 50.00 (ISBN 0-89987-434-7). Darby Bks.
Jordan, Thomas E. Child Development, Information, & the Formation of Public Policy: An International Perspective. (Illus.). 316p. 1982. 24.75x (ISBN 0-398-04685-9). C C Thomas.
Kinard, Jesse & Owens, Janice B. Child Development Associate Self-Assessment Manual. (Orig.). 1983. pap. 14.95 (ISBN 0-89334-041-3). Humanics Ltd.
Linden, Wilhelm Zur. A Child is Born: Pregnancy, Birth, Early Childhood. Collis, J., ed. & tr. from Ger. 223p. 1980. pap. 6.95 (ISBN 0-85440-357-4, Pub.by Steinerbooks). Anthroposophic.
Neuschutz, Karin. The Doll Book. Schneider, Ingun, tr. from Swedish. (Illus.). 184p. (Orig.). 1983. pap. 8.95 (ISBN 0-943914-01-9, Dist. by Kampmann & Co). Larson Pubns Inc.
Overstad, Elizabeth, ed. Potpourri of Child Care & Development Pamphlets. 2nd rev. ed. 25p. lib. bdg. 14.50 (ISBN 0-934140-15-4). Toys N Things.
Ponton, Melva. Syllabus for Applied Child Development. 112p. 1982. pap. text ed. 7.95 (ISBN 0-8403-2831-1). Kendall-Hunt.
Provence, Sally & Naylor, Audrey. Early Intervention: Methods & Outcome in a Service-Centered Study. LC 82-48906. 192p. 1983. text ed. 20.00x (ISBN 0-300-02854-7). Yale U Pr.
Robertson, Audrey, ed. Infant-Toddler Growth & Development: A Guide for Training Child Care Workers. 26p. (Orig.). 1979. GBC Binding 8.95 (ISBN 0-934140-10-3). Toys N Things.
--New Parents: Guidelines for Teaching Infant-Toddler Growth & Development - Birth - 24 Months. (Illus.). 300p. (Orig.). 1982. pap. text ed. 18.95 (ISBN 0-934140-11-1). Toys N Things.
Stock, Claudette & McClure, Judith S. The Household Curriculum: A Workbook for Teaching Your Young Child to Think. LC 82-48805. (Illus.). 160p. (Orig.). 1983. pap. 6.68i (ISBN 0-06-091019-4, CN 1019, CN). Har-Row.
Wickstrom, Ralph L. Fundamental Motor Patterns. 3rd ed. LC 82-21659. (Illus.). 250p. 1983. text ed. price not set (ISBN 0-8121-0879-5). Lea & Febiger.
Wise, Francis H. Who's Boss? Training Your Baby or Child in Self-Management. Wise, Joyce M., ed. (Illus.). 235p. (Orig.). 1982. pap. 8.25 (ISBN 0-915766-58-2). Wise Pub.
Worell, Judith, ed. Psychological Development in the Elementary Years. (Educational Psychology Ser.). 504p. 39.50 (ISBN 0-12-764050-9). Acad Pr.
Yawkey, Thomas D. Child Care in Early Development & Education. LC 82-81416. 300p. 1983. pap. text ed. 13.50 (ISBN 0-87581-282-1). Peacock Pubs.
CHILD DISCIPLINE
see Discipline of Children
CHILD HEALTH
see Child Welfare; Children–Care and Hygiene
CHILD LABOR
see Youth–Employment
CHILD MENTAL HEALTH
see Child Psychiatry
CHILD NEGLECT
see Child Abuse
CHILD PLACING
see Adoption; Foster Home Care
CHILD PSYCHIATRY
see also Adolescent Psychiatry; Child Psychology; Child Psychotherapy; Mentally Handicapped Children; Mentally Ill Children
Achenbach, Thomas M. Developmental Psychopathology. (Illus.). 725p. 1974. 27.50x (ISBN 0-471-06889-6). Wiley.
Bernstein, Norman & Sussex, James, eds. Handbook of Child Psychiatry Consultation. 350p. 1983. text ed. 40.00 (ISBN 0-89335-188-1). SP Med & Sci Bks.
Greenhill, Lawrence & Shopsin, Baron, eds. Biological Influences of Child Psychiatry. 288p. 1983. text ed. 35.00 (ISBN 0-89335-192-X). SP Med & Sci Bks.
Tomb, David A. Child Psychiatry & Behavioral Pediatrics Case Studies. (Case Studies Ser.). 1982. pap. text ed. 22.50 (ISBN 0-87488-100-5). Med Exam.
CHILD PSYCHOLOGY
see also Child Psychiatry; Cognition (Child Psychology); Educational Psychology; Emotional Problems of Children; Imprinting (Psychology); Infant Psychology; Learning, Psychology of; Psychohistory; Wechsler Intelligence Scale for Children
Buntain, Ruth J. Children in the Shadows. 78p. pap. 4.95 (ISBN 0-686-82632-9). Review & Herald.
Burton, Lindy. Vulnerable Children. (International Library of Sociology). 272p. 1968. 18.00 (ISBN 0-7100-3500-4). Routledge & Kegan.
Cantor, P. Understanding a Child's World: Readings in Infancy Through Adolescence. 1977. 15.95 (ISBN 0-07-009766-6). McGraw.
Cautela, Joseph R. & Cautela, Julie. Forms for Behavior Analysis with Children. 230p. (Orig.). 1983. pap. write for info. (ISBN 0-87822-267-7, 2677). Res Press.
Clarizo, Harvey F. & McCoy, George F. Behavior Disorders in Children. 3rd ed. 672p. 1983. text ed. 18.50 scp (ISBN 0-06-041304-2, HarpC); instr's. manual avail. (ISBN 0-06-361270-4). Har-Row.
Cullinhan, Douglas & Epstein, Michael. Behavior Disorders of Children & Adolescents. (Illus.). 384p. 1983. 23.95 (ISBN 0-13-072041-0). P-H.
Damon, William. Social & Personality Development: Essays on the Growth of the Child. 504p. 1983. pap. text ed. 19.95x (ISBN 0-393-95307-6). Norton.
--Social & Personality Development: From Infancy Through Adolescence. (Illus.). 1983. 25.00 (ISBN 0-393-01742-7); pap. text ed. 12.95x04381580x (ISBN 0-393-95248-7). Norton.

Davis, Susan. Will the Real Me Please Stand Up. (Redwood Ser.). 79p. Date not set. pap. 3.95 (ISBN 0-8163-0479-3). Pacific Pr Pub Assn.

Elliot-Binns, Christopher. Too Much Tenderness: An Autobiography of Childhood & Youth. 224p. 1983. 17.50 (ISBN 0-7100-9418-3). Routledge & Kegan.

Essa, Eva. A Practical Guide to Solving Preschool Behavior Problems. LC 82-70426. (Illus.). 288p. (Orig.). 1983. pap. text ed. 10.20 (ISBN 0-8273-2082-5). Delmar.

Fowler, William. Potentials of Childhood: An Historical View of Early Experience, Vol. I. LC 80-8839. 1983. price not set (ISBN 0-669-04387-7). Lexington Bks.

Fowler, William & Ogston, Karen. Potentials of Childhood: Studies in Early Developmental Learning, Vol. II. LC 80-8839. 1983. write for info. (ISBN 0-669-06433-5). Lexington Bks.

Gelfand, Donna M. & Hartmann, Donald P. Child Behavior Analysis & Therapy. 2nd ed. (General Psychology Ser.). 1983. 35.00 (ISBN 0-08-028054-4); pap. 14.95 (ISBN 0-08-028053-6). Pergamon.

Goodenough, Florence L. & Anderson, John E. Experimental Child Study. 546p. 1982. Repr. of 1931 ed. lib. bdg. 45.00 (ISBN 0-8495-2134-3). Arden Lib.

Hersen, Michel & Ollendick, Thomas H., eds. Handbook of Child Psychopathology. 538p. 1983. 50.00x (ISBN 0-306-40938-0, Plenum Pr). Plenum Pub.

Hersov, L., ed. Children in Turmoil: Tomorrow's Parents. 256p. 1982. 30.00 (ISBN 0-08-027955-4). Pergamon.

Hetherington, E. M. & Parke, R. D. Child Psychology: A Contemporary Viewpoint. 1979. text ed. 21.95 (ISBN 0-07-028431-8); instr's. manual & study guide avail. McGraw.

Jackson, Nancy F. & Jackson, Donald A. Getting along with Others: Teaching Social Effectiveness to Children, 2 Vol. (Skill Lessons & Activities Ser.). 150p. 1983. write for info. spiral bdg. Res Press.

Kelly, Jeffrey. Solving Your Child's Behavior Problems: An Everyday Guide for Parents. 224p. 1983. 15.45 (ISBN 0-316-48696-5); pap. 6.70 (ISBN 0-316-48695-7). Little.

Knight, E. V. Critique & Society. LC 82-73478. 90p. (Orig.). pap. 6.95 (ISBN 0-931494-34-6). Brunswick Pub.

Lahey, Benjamin B. & Kazdin, Alan, eds. Advances in Clinical Child Psychology, Vol. 5. 375p. 1982. 35.00x (ISBN 0-306-41043-5, Plenum Pr). Plenum Pub.

Laquatra, Idamarie, et al. Helping Skills II: Life Development Intervention. pap. text ed. 9.95 (ISBN 0-89885-145-9); wkbk. 9.95 (ISBN 0-89885-146-7); both 14.95 (ISBN 0-89885-158-0). Human Sci Pr.

Martin, Judith. Gender-Related Behaviors of Children in Abusive Situations. LC 81-86006. 125p. (Orig.). 1983. pap. 14.95 (ISBN 0-88247-685-8). R & E Res Assoc.

Minshull, Ruth. How to Cure the Selfish, Destructive Child. (Orig.). 1980. pap. write for info. (ISBN 0-937922-07-2). SAA Pub.

Morris, Sylvia, ed. Use of Group Services in Permanency Planning for Children. LC 82-23389. (Social Work with Groups: Vol. 5, No. 4). 100p. 1983. text ed. 16.00 (ISBN 0-86656-199-4, B199). Haworth Pr.

Packard, Vance. Our Endangered Children: Growing Up in a Changing World. 352p. 1983. 17.45i (ISBN 0-316-68751-0). Little.

Palmer, James O. The Psychological Assessment of Children. 2nd ed. 750p. 1983. 40.00 (ISBN 0-471-09765-9, Pub. by Wiley-Interscience). Wiley.

Provence, Sally & Naylor, Audrey. Early Intervention: Methods & Outcome in a Service-Centered Study. LC 82-48906. 192p. 1983. text ed. 20.00x (ISBN 0-300-02854-7). Yale U Pr.

Richmond, Bert O. & Kicklighter, Richard H. Children's Adaptive Behavior Scale: Administrator's Manual. rev. ed. (Orig.). 1983. pap. 14.95 (ISBN 0-89334-040-5). Humanics Ltd.

Schultz, Edward W. & Huechert, Charles M. Childhood Stress & the School Experience. 160p. 1983. text ed. 19.95 (ISBN 0-89885-132-7); pap. text ed. 12.95 (ISBN 0-89885-151-3). Human Sci Pr.

Slater, Barbara R. & Thomas, John M. Psychodiagnostic Evaluation of Children: A Casebook Approach. 1983. pap. text ed. price not set (ISBN 0-8077-2734-2). Tchrs Coll.

Stienhauer, Paul D. & Rae-Grant, Quentin, eds. Psychological Problems of the Child in the Family: A Textbook. 1983. text ed. 29.95x (ISBN 0-465-06676-3). Basic.

Walker, C. Eugene & Roberts, Michael C. Handbook of Clinical Child Psychology. (Personality Processes Ser.). 1600p. 1983. 65.00x (ISBN 0-471-09036-0, Pub. by Wiley-Interscience). Wiley.

Wirt, Robert D., et al. Multidimensional Description of Child Personality: A Manual for the Personality Inventory for Children. LC 79-57301. 116p. 1977. pap. 10.40 (ISBN 0-87424-152-9). Western Psych.

Wise, Francis H. Who's Boss? Training Your Baby or Child in Self-Management. Wise, Joyce M., ed. (Illus.). 235p. (Orig.). 1982. pap. 8.25 (ISBN 0-915766-58-2). Wise Pub.

CHILD PSYCHOLOGY–COLLECTIONS

Silver, Richard. The Wonder of It All. LC 81-86426. 64p. 1983. pap. 5.95 (ISBN 0-686-42890-0). GWP.

CHILD PSYCHOTHERAPY

Mishne, Judith. Clinical Work with Children. 1983. text ed. 24.95 (ISBN 0-02-921630-3). Free Pr.

Morris, Richard J. & Kratochwill, Thomas R., eds. Practice of Therapy with Children: A Textbook of Methods. (General Psychology Ser.). 500p. 1983. 45.01 (ISBN 0-08-028033-1); pap. 19.50 (ISBN 0-08-028032-3). Pergamon.

Prout, H. Thompson & Brown, Douglas T. Counseling & Psychotherapy with Children & Adolescents. 1983. 19.95 (ISBN 0-936166-13-4). Mariner Pub.

CHILD REARING

see Children–Management

CHILD STUDY

see Child Development; Child Psychology

CHILD WELFARE

see also Child Abuse; Children–Hospitals; Children–Institutional Care; Children–Law; Day Care Centers; Foster Home Care; Juvenile Delinquency; Maternal and Infant Welfare; Playgrounds

Bagley, Christopher. Child Welfare & Adoption: International Perspectives. LC 82-16873. 208p. 1982. 26.00x (ISBN 0-312-13232-8). St Martin.

Baily, Thelma F. & Baily, Walter H. Child Welfare Practice: A Guide to Providing Effective Services for Children & Families. LC 82-49034. (Social & Behavioral Science Ser.). 1983. text ed. 15.95x (ISBN 0-87589-558-1). Jossey-Bass.

Children Without Justice. pap. 2.25 (ISBN 0-686-81722-2). NCJW.

Essen, Juliet & Wedge, Peter. Continuities in Childhood Disadvantage, No. 6. (SSRC DHSS Studies in Deprivation & Disadvantage). 200p. 1982. text ed. 27.00x (ISBN 0-435-82283-7). Heinemann Ed.

Hoopes, Janet L. New Publication on Adoption Offered by the Child Welfare League Prediction in Child Development: A Longitudinal Study of Adoptive & Nonadoptive Families--the Delaware Family Study. 104p. 1982. 9.50 (ISBN 0-87868-170-1). Child Welfare.

McGowan, Brenda & Meezan, William. Child Welfare: Current Dilemmas--Future Directions. LC 82-61260. 510p. 1983. text ed. 21.95 (ISBN 0-87581-287-2). Peacock Pubs.

Pardeck, John T. The Forgotten Children: A Study of the Stability & Continuity of Foster Care. LC 82-20007. (Illus.). 116p. (Orig.). 1983. lib. bdg. 18.50 (ISBN 0-8191-2844-9); pap. text ed. 8.25 (ISBN 0-8191-2845-7). U Pr of Amer.

Rudman, Jack. Coordinator of Child Support Enforcement. (Career Examination Ser.: C-927). (Cloth bdg. avail. on request). pap. 14.00 (ISBN 0-8373-0927-1). Natl Learning.

Simpkins, Mark A. What Every Woman Should Know About Child Support, Getting It! 1983. 14.95 (ISBN 0-87949-226-0). Ashley Bks.

Singer, Greta L., et al. Child Welfare Problems: Prevention, Early Identification, & Intervention. LC 82-20263. 180p. (Orig.). 1983. lib. bdg. 19.75 (ISBN 0-8191-2874-0); pap. text ed. 9.50 (ISBN 0-8191-2875-9). U Pr of Amer.

Zukerman, Erva. Child Welfare. 224p. 1982. text ed. 17.95 (ISBN 0-02-935900-7). Free Pr.

CHILD WELFARE–LAW AND LEGISLATION

see Children–Law

CHILDBIRTH

see also Labor (Obstetrics); Natural Childbirth

Ashford, Janet I. The Whole Birth Catalog. (Illus.). 325p. (Orig.). 1983. 28.95 (ISBN 0-89594-108-2); pap. 14.95 (ISBN 0-89594-107-4). Crossing Pr.

Brady, Margaret. Having a Baby Easily. (Illus.). 144p. (Orig.). 1983. pap. 6.95 (ISBN 0-7225-0668-6, Pub. by Thorsons Pubs England). Sterling.

Cohen, Nancy Wainer & Estner, Lois J. Silent Knife: Cesarean Prevention & Vaginal Birth after Cesarean (VBAC) (Illus.). 480p. 1983. 29.95x (ISBN 0-89789-026-4); pap. 14.95x. J F Bergin.

Feldman, Silvia. Choices in Childbirth. rev. ed. (Illus.). 288p. 1982. pap. 8.95 (ISBN 0-448-00953-6, G&D). Putnam Pub Group.

Freeman, R. & Pescar, S. Safe Delivery: Your Baby During High Risk Pregnancy. 320p. 1983. 7.95 (ISBN 0-07-022048-4, GB). McGraw.

Fuller, Elizabeth. Having Your First Baby after Thirty. LC 82-23548. 1983. 10.95 (ISBN 0-396-08154-1). Dodd.

McKay, Susan. Assertive Childbirth: The Future Parent's Guide to a Positive Pregnancy. (Illus.). 256p. 1983. 19.95 (ISBN 0-13-049635-9); pap. 9.95 (ISBN 0-13-049627-8). P-H.

MacMahon, Alice T. All about Childbirth. 2nd ed. LC 82-70472. (Illus.). 1982. write for info. (ISBN 0-931128-01-3). Family Pubns.

Ohasi, Wataru & Hoover, Mary. The Eastern Way of Natural Childbirth: Do-It-Yourself Shiatsu for a Healthy Pregnancy & Delivery. 224p. (Orig.). 1983. pap. 8.95 (ISBN 0-345-30089-0). Ballantine.

Rathi, M. L. & Kumar, S. Perinatal Medicine, 2 Vols. 1980-82. Vol. 1. text ed. 35.00 (ISBN 0-07-051204-3); Vol. 2. text ed. 39.50 (ISBN 0-07-051208-6). McGraw.

Salvadori, B. A. & Merialdi, A., eds. Fetal & Postnatal Outcome in EPH-Gestosis: Proceedings 13th International Meeting of the Organization Gestosis, Venice, 1981. (International Congress Ser.: No. 583). 320p. 1982. 74.50 (ISBN 0-444-90263-5, Excerpta Medica). Elsevier.

Sirota, Adair. Preparing for Childbirth: A Couple's Manual. (Illus.). 192p. (Orig.). 1983. pap. 7.95 (ISBN 0-8092-5625-8). Contemp Bks.

Sonstegard, Lois, ed. Women's Health: Childbearing, Vol. 2. Date not set. price not set (ISBN 0-8089-1508-8). Grune.

Time-Life Books, ed. A Commonsense Guide to Sex, Birth, & Babies. (Library of Health Ser.). 1983. lib. bdg. 18.60 (ISBN 0-8094-3827-5). Silver.

Vanderford, Jennifer. Joy Cometh in the Morning. LC 82-83503. (Illus.). 160p. 1983. pap. 4.95 (ISBN 0-89081-364-7). Harvest Hse.

Warshaw, Joseph B. & Hobbins, John. Perinatal Medicine in Primary Practice. 1982. 34.95 (ISBN 0-201-08294-2, Med-Nurse). A-W.

White, Gregory J. Emergency Childbirth: A Manual. (Illus.). 62p. wire-bound 4.95 (ISBN 0-686-37623-4). Police Train.

Woerth, Sheila T., et al, eds. Your Child's Birth: A Comprehensive Guide for Pregnancy, Birth, & Postpartum. (Avery's Childbirth Education Ser.). (Illus.). 96p. (Orig.). 1982. pap. 5.95 (ISBN 0-89529-182-7). Avery Pub.

Worth. Labor & Delivery. 1983. write for info. (ISBN 0-07-071818-0); pap. write for info. McGraw.

CHILDBIRTH–PSYCHOLOGY

Janov, Arthur. Imprints: The Lifelong Effects of the Birth Experience. 416p. 1983. 17.95 (ISBN 0-698-11183-4, Coward). Putnam Pub Group.

CHILDBIRTH, NATURAL

see Natural Childbirth

CHILDHOOD

see Children

CHILDREN

see also Birth Order; Boys; Church Work with Children; Day Care Centers; Education of Children; Exceptional Children; Girls; Heredity; Infants; Jewish Children; Play; Playgrounds; Stepchildren; Television and Children; Youth

Biswas, Manju. Mentally Retarded & Normal Children: A Comparative Study of Their Family Conditions. 157p. 1980. 19.95x (ISBN 0-940500-50-7, Pub. by Sterling India). Asia Bk Corp.

DesVoigne, Merritt J. Being Small Wasn't Bad at All. LC 82-90097. (Orig.). 1982. pap. 4.95x (ISBN 0-686-84843-8). Littleman.

Dittmann, Laura L. & Ramseu, Marjorie, eds. Their Future Is Now: Today Is for Children. (Illus.). 1982. pap. 5.75 (ISBN 0-87173-102-9). ACEI.

Flexner, Helen T. Quaker Childhood. 1940. text ed. 29.50x (ISBN 0-686-83718-5). Elliots Bks.

Freeman, Grace B. Children Are Poetry. 3rd ed. (Illus.). 16p. 1982. pap. 2.00 (ISBN 0-9607730-3-7). Johns Pr.

Greaney, Vincent, ed. The Rights of Children. 250p. 1983. text ed. 19.95x (ISBN 0-8290-1297-4). Irvington.

Olson, Lawrence. Costs of Children. LC 82-48173. 176p. 1982. 17.95 (ISBN 0-669-06040-2). Lexington Bks.

Ramos, Graciliano. Childhood. Oliviera, Celso D., et al, trs. 174p. 1982. 14.95 (ISBN 0-7206-0531-8, Pub. by Peter Owen). Merrimack Bk Serv.

Scheffler, Hannah N., ed. Resources for Early Childhood: An Annotated Bibliography & Guide for Educators, Librarians, & Parents. LC 81-48421. 400p. 1982. lib. bdg. 38.50 (ISBN 0-8240-9390-9). Garland Pub.

CHILDREN–AMUSEMENTS

see Amusements

CHILDREN–ASYLUMS

see Children–Institutional Care

CHILDREN–BIBLICAL TEACHING

see Children in the Bible

CHILDREN–BIOGRAPHY

see also Children in the Bible; Presidents–United States–Wives and Children

Anderson, Norman & Brown, Walter. Rescue: The Young American Medal for Bravery. (Illus.). 128p. (gr. 5 up). 1983. 10.95 (ISBN 0-8027-6487-8). Walker & Co.

CHILDREN–BOOKS AND READING

Bauer, Caroline F. This Way to Books. 376p. 1983. 30.00 (ISBN 0-8242-0678-9). Wilson.

Chambers, Aidan. Introducing Books to Children. 2nd ed. 224p. 1983. 22.00 (ISBN 0-87675-284-9); pap. 14.00 (ISBN 0-87675-285-7). Horn Bk.

Cline, Ruth K. & McBride, William G. A Guide to Literature for Young Adults: Backround, Selection, & Use. 1983. pap. text ed. 9.95x (ISBN 0-673-16030-0). Scott F.

Crago, Maureen & Crago, Hugh. Prelude to Literacy: A Young Child's Encounter with Pictures & Story. (Illus.). 320p. 1983. price not set (ISBN 0-8093-1077-5). S Ill U Pr.

Ettlinger, John R. & Spirit, Diana. Choosing Books for Young People. LC 82-11659. 238p. 1982. text ed. 25.00 (ISBN 0-8389-0366-5). ALA.

Handbook of Children's & Young People'S Literature: From 1750 to 1800. (Illus.). 880p. (Ger.). 1982. 150.00 (ISBN 0-686-38452-0). Transbooks.

Reading for Young People: The Southwest. LC 82-4002. 256p. 1982. pap. text ed. 15.00 (ISBN 0-8389-0362-2). ALA.

CHILDREN–CARE AND HYGIENE

see also Baby Sitters; Children–Diseases; Children–Nutrition; Health Education; Infants–Care and Hygiene; Nurses and Nursing; Pediatric Nursing; Physical Education for Children; School Children–Food; School Health; School Nursing

Auerbach, Stevanne. The Whole Child: A Source Book. 320p. 1982. pap. 8.95 (ISBN 0-399-50554-7, Perige). Putnam Pub Group.

Bedford, Stewart. Little Sprouts for Health & Fun. Date not set. pap. 2.95 (ISBN 0-935930-04-3). Scott Pubns CA.

Brown, Jeffrey L. The Complete Parent's Guide to Telephone Medicine: How, When & Why to Call Your Child's Doctor. 304p. 1983. pap. 3.50 (ISBN 0-425-05496-9). Berkley Pub.

Caring for Young Children: An Analysis of Education & Social Services. 231p. (Orig.). 1982. pap. 17.00x (ISBN 92-64-12315-6). OECD.

Chen, Lincoln C. & Scrimshaw, Nevin S., eds. Diarrhea & Malnutrition: Interactions, Mechanisms & Interventions. 310p. 1983. 39.50x (ISBN 0-306-41046-X, Plenum Pr). Plenum Pub.

Cohen, Jean-Pierre. Childhood: The First Six Years. (Illus.). 256p. 1983. 17.95 (ISBN 0-13-131300-2); pap. 8.95 (ISBN 0-13-131292-8). P-H.

Copeland, Tom. A Consultation in Writing. 52p. 3 ring spiral 25.00 (ISBN 0-934140-05-7). Toys N Things.

Davis, James R. Help Me, I'm Hurt: The Child-Victim Handbook. 168p. 1982. 9.95 (ISBN 0-686-84428-9); pap. text ed. 9.95 (ISBN 0-8403-2747-1). Kendall-Hunt.

Fish, Debra, ed. Home-Based Training Resouce Handbook. 2nd rev. ed. (Illus.). 392p. 1980. pap. text ed. 24.95 (ISBN 0-934140-13-8). Toys N Things.

Kane, Dorothy N. Environmental Hazards to Small Children. 336p. 1983. 25.00 (ISBN 0-89946-150-6). Oelgeschlager.

Kysar, Ardis & McLinn, Dianne. New Faces, New Spaces: Helping Children Cope with Change. 67p. (Orig.). 1980. pap. 8.95 (ISBN 0-934140-03-0). Toys N Things.

Kysar, Ardis & Overstad, Elizabeth, eds. Helping Young Children Cope with Crisis: A Guide for Training Child Care Workers. 69p. (Orig.). pap. text ed. 8.95 (ISBN 0-934140-12-X). Toys N Things.

Malina, Robert M. & Roche, Alex F., eds. Manual of Physical Status & Performance in Childhood, Vol. II. 814p. 1983. 115.00x (ISBN 0-306-41137-7, Plenum Pr). Plenum Pub.

Martin, Richard. A Parent's Guide to Childhood Symptoms: Understanding the Signals of Illness from Infancy through Adolescence. 384p. 1982. 14.95 (ISBN 0-312-59658-8). St Martin.

Middleton, Susan, ed. Blueprints: Building Educational Programs for People Who Care for Children. (Illus.). 238p. pap. 19.95 (ISBN 0-934140-16-2). Toys N Things.

Mueser, Anne & Liptay, Lynne. Talk & Toddle: A Commonsense Guide for the First Three Years. 160p. 1983. pap. 7.95 (ISBN 0-312-78430-9). St Martin.

Nicol, Jean M., ed. Calendar-Keeper 1983: A Record Keeping System for Child Care Providers. 5th ed. (Illus.). 60p. (Orig.). 1982. pap. 10.95 (ISBN 0-934140-08-1); GBC Binding 6.50 (ISBN 0-934140-06-5). Toys N Things.

Overstad, Elizabeth, ed. Potpourri of Child Care & Development Pamphlets. 2nd rev. ed. 25p. lib. bdg. 14.50 (ISBN 0-934140-15-4). Toys N Things.

Robertson, Audrey, ed. Infant-Toddler Growth & Development: A Guide for Training Child Care Workers. 26p. (Orig.). 1979. GBC Binding 8.95 (ISBN 0-934140-10-3). Toys N Things.

--New Parents: Guidelines for Teaching Infant-Toddler Growth & Development - Birth - 24 Months. (Illus.). 300p. (Orig.). 1982. pap. text ed. 18.95 (ISBN 0-934140-11-1). Toys N Things.

Robson, Kenneth S. The Borderline Child: Approaches to Etiology, Diagnosis & Treatment. (Illus.). 320p. 1983. 24.95 (ISBN 0-07-053346-6, P&RB). McGraw.

Rockwell, Robert E. & Williams, Robert A. Hug a Tree & Other Things to Do Outdoors with Young Children. 112p. 1983. pap. 7.95 (ISBN 0-87659-105-5). Gryphon Hse.

Scheffler, Hannah N., ed. Resources for Early Childhood: An Annotated Bibliography & Guide for Educators, Librarians, & Parents. LC 81-48421. 400p. 1982. lib. bdg. 38.50 (ISBN 0-8240-9390-9). Garland Pub.

Thurmond, Nancy M. Happy Mother, Happy Child. 386p. (Orig.). 1982. pap. 7.95 (ISBN 0-8423-1305-2). Tyndale.

Werner, Emmy E. Cross Cultural View of Alternate Care Givers. (Illus.). 1983. pap. price not set (ISBN 0-8391-1805-8, 17892). Univ Park.

CHILDREN–CHARITIES

see Child Welfare

CHILDREN–CLOTHING

see Children's Clothing

CHILDREN–CUSTODY

see Custody of Children

CHILDREN–DEATH AND FUTURE STATE

Buckingham, Robert W. A Special Kind of Love: Care for the Dying Child. 192p. 1983. 12.95 (ISBN 0-8264-0229-1). Continuum.

CHILDREN–DISCIPLINE
see Discipline of Children
CHILDREN–DISEASES
see also Children–Hospitals; Dentition; Infants–Diseases; Pediatric Hematology; Pediatric Nursing also names of diseases, e.g. Chicken Pox, Whooping Cough
Association of Pediatric Oncology. Nursing Care of the Child With Cancer. 1982. text ed. write for info. (ISBN 0-316-04884-4). Little.
Gershwin, M. Eric & Robbins, Dick L., eds. Musculoskeletal Diseases of Children. Date not set. price not set (ISBN 0-8089-1528-2). Grune.
Jelliffe, D. B. & Stanfield, J. P., eds. Diseases of Children in the Subtropics & Tropics. 1070p. 1978. text ed. 89.50 (ISBN 0-7131-4277-4). E Arnold.
Martin, Richard. A Parent's Guide to Childhood Symptoms: Understanding the Signals of Illness from Infancy through Adolescence. 384p. 1982. 14.95 (ISBN 0-312-59658-8). St Martin.
Sink, L. & Godden, J., eds. Conflicts in Childhood Cancer. 1976. 32.25 (ISBN 0-444-99839-X). Elsevier.
Stewart, Donald A., ed. Children with Sex Chromosome Aneuploidy: Follow-up Studies. LC 82-21657. (Birth Defects: Original Article Ser.: Vol. 18, No. 4). 251p. 1982. write for info. A R Liss.
Waddell, Charles. Faith, Hope & Luck: A Sociological Study of Children Growing Up With a Life-Threatening Illness. LC 82-24871. 104p. (Orig.). 1983. lib. bdg. 18.75 (ISBN 0-8191-3011-7); pap. text ed. 8.25 (ISBN 0-8191-3012-5). U Pr of Amer.
CHILDREN–DISEASES–PSYCHOSOMATIC ASPECTS
see Pediatrics–Psychosomatic Aspects
CHILDREN–EDUCATION
see Education of Children
CHILDREN–FOOD
see Children–Nutrition
CHILDREN–GROWTH
Damon, William. Social & Personality Development: Essays on the Growth of the Child. 504p. 1983. pap. text ed. 19.95x (ISBN 0-393-95307-6). Norton.
Elkind, David & Weiner, Irving B. Development of the Child. LC 77-14214. 728p. 1978. text ed. 28.50 (ISBN 0-471-23785-X); study guide 9.95 (ISBN 0-471-03435-5); tchrs. manual avail. (ISBN 0-471-04049-5). Wiley.
Hart, Terril H. Tender Loving Care for Your New Baby. (Illus.). 112p. (Orig.). 1983. pap. 4.95 (ISBN 0-915658-03-8). Meadowbrook Pr.
Hendry, L., ed. Growing Up & Going Out. 176p. 1983. 18.00 (ISBN 0-08-025768-2); pap. 9.50 (ISBN 0-08-025769-0). Pergamon.
Meadowbrook Press. Our Baby's First Years. (Illus.). 32p. 1983. 9.95 (ISBN 0-915658-98-4). Meadowbrook Pr.
Robertson, Audrey, ed. Infant-Toddler Growth & Development: A Guide for Training Child Care Workers. 26p. (Orig.). 1979. GBC Binding 8.95 (ISBN 0-934140-10-3). Toys N Things.
--New Parents: Guidelines for Teaching Infant-Toddler Growth & Development - Birth - 24 Months. (Illus.). 300p. (Orig.). 1982. pap. text ed. 18.95 (ISBN 0-934140-11-1). Toys N Things.
Tanner, J. M. & Whitehouse, R. H., eds. Atlas of Children's Growth: Normal Variation & Growth Disorders. LC 77-8381. 206p. 1982. 268.50 (ISBN 0-12-683340-0). Acad Pr.
CHILDREN–HEALTH
see Children–Care and Hygiene
CHILDREN–HOSPITALS
see also Child Welfare
LLoyd Hart, V. E. John Wilkes & the Founding Hospital at Aylesbury 1759-1768. 80p. 1980. text ed. 19.95x (ISBN 0-471-25860-1, Pub. by Wiley-Interscience). Wiley.
CHILDREN–HOURS OF LABOR
see Hours of Labor
CHILDREN–HYGIENE
see Children–Care and Hygiene
CHILDREN–INSTITUTIONAL CARE
see also Child Welfare; Day Care Centers
Ackland, John W. Girls in Care. 166p. 1982. text ed. 27.50x (ISBN 0-566-00511-5). Gower Pub Ltd.
Kavaler, Florence & Swire, Margaret R. Foster-Child Health Care. LC 81-47184. 1983. price not set (ISBN 0-669-04561-6). Lexington Bks.
CHILDREN–JUVENILE LITERATURE
see also names of geographic areas, countries, etc. for books about the children of those areas
Miller, Jane. Farm Counting Book. (Illus.). 32p. (ps-3). 1983. 6.95 (ISBN 0-13-304790-3). P-H.
Rosenberg, Maxine. My Friend Leslie: The Story of a Handicapped Child. LC 82-12734. (Illus.). (gr. 1-3). 1983. 9.00 (ISBN 0-688-01690-1); PLB 8.59 (ISBN 0-688-01691-X). Lothrop.
CHILDREN–LANGUAGE
see also Children–Writing
Barr, Mary & D'Aroy, Pat, eds. What's Going On? Language Learning Episode in British & American Classroom, Grades 4-13. LC 81-18119. (Illus.). 240p. 1981. pap. text ed. 9.00 (ISBN 0-86709-013-8). Boynton Cook Pubs.
Beck, M. Susan. Kidspeak: How Your Child Develops Language Skills. 144p. 1982. pap. 4.95 (ISBN 0-452-25376-4, Plume). NAL.
Beveridge, Michael, ed. Children Thinking Through Language. 280p. 1982. pap. text ed. 19.95 (ISBN 0-7131-6352-6). E Arnold.
Bloom, Lois & Lahey, Margaret. Language Development & Language Disorders. LC 77-21482. (Communication Disorders Ser.). 506p. 1978. text ed. 29.50 (ISBN 0-471-08220-1). Wiley.
Britton, James. Language & Learning. 304p. (Orig.). 1972. pap. text ed. 7.00 (ISBN 0-14-021456-9). Boynton Cook Pubs.
Burns, Paul C. & Broman, Betty. The Language Arts in Childhood Education. 5th ed. LC 82-83367. 560p. 1982. text ed. 22.95 (ISBN 0-395-32756-3, EA92); write for info. instr's manual (ISBN 0-395-32757-1; EA93). HM.
Deutsch, W., ed. The Child's Construction of Language Behavioral Development: Monographs. 408p. 1982. 39.50 (ISBN 0-12-213580-6). Acad Pr.
Eastman, Carol M. Language Planning: An Introduction. Langness, L. L. & Edgerton, Robert B., eds. (Publications in Anthropology & Related Fields Ser.). (Illus.). 288p. (Orig.). 1983. pap. text ed. 9.95x (ISBN 0-88316-552-X). Chandler & Sharp.
Fischer, Carol & Terry, Ann. Children's Language & the Language Arts. 1976. 22.50 (ISBN 0-07-021107-8). McGraw.
Hatch, Evelyn M. Psycholinguistics: A Second Language Perspective. 1983. pap. text ed. 15.95 (ISBN 0-88377-250-7). Newbury Hse.
Irwin, John V. & Wong, Seok P., eds. Phonological Development in Children 18 to 72 Months. LC 82-5893. 1983. write for info. (ISBN 0-8093-1057-0). S Ill U Pr.
Johnson, Carolyn E. & Thew, Carol L., eds. Proceedings of the Second International Congress for the Study of Child Language, Vol. I. LC 82-16145. (Illus.). 614p. (Orig.). 1983. lib. bdg. 34.50 (ISBN 0-8191-2738-8); pap. text ed. 22.50 (ISBN 0-8191-2739-6). U Pr of Amer.
Lightfoot, David. The Language Lottery: Toward a Biology of Grammars. 192p. 1983. 17.50 (ISBN 0-262-12096-8). MIT Pr.
Lowenthal, F. & Cordier, J., eds. Language & Language Acquisition. 373p. 1982. 42.50 (ISBN 0-306-41128-8, Plenum Pr). Plenum Pub.
McLaughlin, Barry. Second-Language Acquisition in Childhood. LC 75-52304. 230p. 1978. lib. bdg. 19.95 (ISBN 0-89859-180-5). L Erlbaum Assocs.
Maley, Alan & Duff, Alan. Drama Techniques in Language Learning: A Resource Book of Communication Activities for Language Teachers. (Cambridge Handbooks for Language Teachers Ser.). (Illus.). 240p. 1983. 19.95 (ISBN 0-521-24907-4); pap. 8.95 (ISBN 0-521-28868-1). Cambridge U Pr.
Miller, Peggy J. Amy, Wendy & Beth: Learning Language in South Baltimore. (Illus.). 208p. 1982. text ed. 18.95x (ISBN 0-292-70357-0). U of Tex Pr.
Moerk, Ernst L. The Mother of Eve--as a First Language Teacher. Lipsitt, Lewis P., ed. (Monographs on Infancy). 208p. 1983. text ed. 18.50 (ISBN 0-686-82460-1). Ablex Pub.
Nelson, Keith E., ed. Children's Language, Vol. 3. (Ongoing Ser.). 522p. 1982. text ed. 39.95 (ISBN 0-89859-264-X). L Erlbaum Assocs.
Oksaar. Language Acquisition in the Early Years: An Introduction to Paedolinguistics. Turfler, Katherine, tr. LC 82-42716. 240p. 1983. 30.00x (ISBN 0-686-84414-9). St Martin.
CHILDREN–LAW
see also Adoption; Custody of Children; Guardian and Ward; Juvenile Courts; Juvenile Delinquency; Parent and Child (Law); Stepchildren
Andersen, Roger W., ed. Pidginization & Creolization & Language Acquisition. 320p. 1983. pap. text ed. 20.95 (ISBN 0-88377-266-3). Newbury Hse.
Besharov, Douglas J. Protecting Abused & Neglected Children: Identification & Action. 1983. pap. text ed. price not set (ISBN 0-8391-1797-3, 17949). Univ Park.
Graves, Joy D. Early Interventions in Child Abuse: The Role of the Police Officer. LC 81-85982. 125p. 1983. pap. 14.95 (ISBN 0-88247-697-1). R & E Res Assoc.
Melton, Gay B. & Kooche, Gerald P., eds. Children's Competence to Consent. (Critical Issues in Social Justice Ser.). 286p. 1983. 29.50x (ISBN 0-306-41069-9, Plenum Pr). Plenum Pub.
Wadlington, Walter, et al. Cases & Materials on Children in the Legal System. LC 82-21114. (University Casebook Ser.). 965p. 1982. text ed. write for info. (ISBN 0-88277-101-9); write for info. tchr's manual (ISBN 0-88277-125-6). Foundation Pr.
CHILDREN–MANAGEMENT
see also Baby Sitters; Child Abuse; Children'S Questions and Answers; Discipline of Children; Moral Education; Parent and Child; Toilet Training
Baker, Pat. I Now Pronounce You Parent: What Other Books Don't Tell You About Babies. 96p. (Orig.). 1983. pap. 4.95 (ISBN 0-8010-0850-6). Baker Bk.
Bedford, Stewart. How to Teach Children Stress Management & Emotional Control: A Survival Kit for Teachers, Parents, & Kids. 1981. 29.50 (ISBN 0-935930-03-5). Scott Pubns CA.
Beebe, Brooke. Tips for Toddlers. (Orig.). 1983. pap. price not set (ISBN 0-440-58658-5, Dell Trade Pbks). Dell.
Berry, Joy W. What to Do When Your Mom Or Dad Says "Be Good While You're There!". LC 82-81202. (The Survival Series for Kids). (Illus.). 48p. (gr. 3 up). 1982. PLB 9.25 (ISBN 0-516-02570-8). Childrens.
--What to Do When Your Mom or Dad Says "Take Care of Your Clothes!". LC 82-81201. (The Surivial Series for Kids). (Illus.). 48p. (gr. 3 up). 1982. PLB 9.25 (ISBN 0-516-02573-2). Childrens.
Bradley, Martin. The Coordination of Services for Children under Five. (NFER General Ser.). 172p. 1982. pap. text ed. 15.25x (ISBN 0-7005-0507-5, NFER). Humanities.
Eyre, Linda & Eyre, Richard. Teaching Children Responsibility. LC 82-12842. (Illus.). 247p. 1982. 7.95 (ISBN 0-87747-918-6). Deseret Bk.
Fierstein, Jeff. Kid Contracts. (gr. 4-8). 1982. 3.95 (ISBN 0-86653-091-6, GA 442). Good Apple.
Fitzgerald, Hiram E. & Gage, Patricia, eds. Child Nurturance, Vol. 3: Studies of Development in Nonhuman Primates. 288p. 1982. 29.50x (ISBN 0-306-41176-8, Plenum Pr). Plenum Pub.
Fleming, Don A. How to Stop the Battle with Your Child. LC 82-90682. 144p. Date not set. pap. 7.95 (ISBN 0-9609264-0-2). D Fleming Sem.
Fontenelle, Don H. Understanding & Managing Overactive Children: A Guide for Parents & Teachers. 200p. 1983. 13.95 (ISBN 0-13-936765-9); pap. 6.95 (ISBN 0-13-936757-8). P-H.
Johnson, June. Eight-Hundred Thirty Eight Ways to Amuse a Child: Crafts, Hobbies & Creative Ideas for the Child from Six to Twelve. Rev ed. LC 82-48801. 224p. (gr. 1-6). 1983. pap. 4.76i (ISBN 0-06-091047-X, CN 1047, CN). Har-Row.
Kostelnik, Marjorie J. & Phenice, Lillian A., eds. Child Nurturance, Vol. 2: Patterns of Supplementary Parenting. 332p. 1982. 32.50x (ISBN 0-306-41175-X, Plenum Pr). Plenum Pub.
Kramer, Rita. In Defense of the Family: Raising Children in America Today. 1983. 15.50 (ISBN 0-465-03215-X). Basic.
Long, Lynette & Long, Thomas. The Handbook for Latchkey Children & Their Parents: A Complete Guide for Latchkey Kids & Their Working Parents. 1983. 16.95 (ISBN 0-87795-506-9, Pub. by Priam); pap. 7.95 (ISBN 0-87795-507-7). Arbor Hse.
Minshull, Ruth. How to Cure the Selfish, Destructive Child. (Orig.). 1980. pap. write for info. (ISBN 0-937922-07-2). SAA Pub.
--Miracles for Breakfast. rev. ed. 181p. 1982. pap. write for info. (ISBN 0-937922-01-3). SAA Pub.
Rosner, Joseph. Myths of Child Rearing. LC 82-19924. 1983. 15.50 (ISBN 0-934878-23-4); pap. 8.95 (ISBN 0-934878-29-3). Dembner Bks.
Siegel-Gorelick, Bryna. The Working Parents' Guide to Child Care. 1983. 15.45i (ISBN 0-316-79004-4); pap. 8.70i (ISBN 0-316-79003-6). Little.
Stienhauer, Paul D. & Rae-Grant, Quentin, eds. Psychological Problems of the Child in the Family: A Textbook. 1983. text ed. 29.95x (ISBN 0-465-06676-3). Basic.
Stock, Claudette & McClure, Judith S. The Household Curriculum: A Workbook for Teaching Your Young Child to Think. LC 82-48805. (Illus.). 160p. (Orig.). 1983. pap. 6.68i (ISBN 0-06-091019-4, CN 1019, CN). Har-Row.
Wilkerson, Rich. Hold Me While You Let Me Go. LC 82-83838. 196p. (Orig.). 1983. pap. 4.95 (ISBN 0-89081-370-1). Harvest Hse.
CHILDREN–MEDICAL CARE
see Pediatrics
CHILDREN–MENTAL DISORDERS
see Child Psychiatry
CHILDREN–NUTRITION
see also Infants–Nutrition; School Children–Food
Cameron, Margaret & Hofvander, Tngve. Manual on Feeding Infants & Young Children. 3rd ed. (Illus.). 240p. 1983. pap. 9.95 (ISBN 0-19-261403-7). Oxford U Pr.
Kamen, Betty & Kamen, Sid. Kids Are What They Eat: What Every Parent Needs to Know about Nutrition. LC 82-18404. (Illus.). 1983. 12.95 (ISBN 0-668-05563-4, 5563). Arco.
Kerner, John A. Manual of Pediatric Parenteral Nutrition. 550p. 1983. 29.95 (ISBN 0-471-09291-6, Pub. by Wiley Med). Wiley.
Lambert-Legace, Louise. Feeding Your Child: From Infancy to Six Years Old. LC 82-12889. 233p. 1983. pap. 9.95 (ISBN 0-8253-0119-X). Beaufort Bks NY.
Shandler, Michael & Shandler, Nina. The Complete Guide to Raising Your Child & Cookbook for Raising Your Child as a Vegetarian. 384p. 1982. pap. 3.50 (ISBN 0-345-30685-6). Ballantine.
Thurmond, Nancy M. Happy Mother, Happy Child. 386p. (Orig.). 1982. pap. 7.95 (ISBN 0-8423-1305-2). Tyndale.
Toth, Robin & Hostage, Jacqueline. Does Your Lunch Pack Punch For the Crunch & Munch Bunch? LC 82-24512. (Illus.). 160p. 1983. pap. 6.95 (ISBN 0-932620-20-5). Betterway Pubns.
CHILDREN–PRAYER-BOOKS AND DEVOTIONS
Donze, Mary T. In My Heart Room. 64p. 1982. pap. 1.50 (ISBN 0-89243-161-X). Liguori Pubns.
Grinstead, Wayne. Two Prayers: One Mile, One Miracle. (Home Mission Graded Ser.). (Illus.). 40p. (gr. 4-7). Date not set. pap. 2.00 (ISBN 0-937170-23-2). Home Mission.
Watkins, Peter & Hughes, Erica. A Book of Prayer. (Julia MacRae Ser.). 128p. (gr. 7 up). 1983. 10.95 (ISBN 0-531-04578-1, MacRae). Watts.
CHILDREN–PROTECTION
see Child Welfare
CHILDREN–PSYCHOLOGY
see Child Psychology
CHILDREN–RECREATION
see Amusements; Creative Activities and Seatwork; Games
CHILDREN–RELIGIOUS LIFE
see also Children–Prayer-Books and Devotions
Aaseng, Nate. I'm Searching, Lord, but I Need Your Light. LC 82-72644. 112p. (gr. 3-6). 1983. pap. 3.50 (ISBN 0-8066-1950-3, 10-3203). Augsburg.
Blackwell, Muriel F. Called to Teach Children. LC 82-82954. 1983. 5.95 (ISBN 0-8054-3233-7). Broadman.
Bonnici, Roberta. Your Right to Be Different. (Discovery Bks.). 48p. (YA) (gr. 9-12). pap. text ed. 1.35 (ISBN 0-88243-842-5, 02-0842). Gospel Pub.
Burgess, Beverly. Three Little Pigs: Build Your House Upon the Rock. (Orig.). (ps). 1983. pap. write for info. (ISBN 0-89274-283-6). Harrison Hse.
Cappadona, Diane A., ed. The Sacred Play of Children. 160p. 1983. pap. 9.95 (ISBN 0-8164-2427-6). Seabury.
Cavalletti, Sofia. The Religious Potential of the Child. 224p. 1982. pap. 10.95 (ISBN 0-8091-2389-4). Paulist Pr.
De Brand, Roy E. Children's Sermons for Special Occasions. LC 82-72228. (Orig.). 1983. pap. 3.95 (ISBN 0-8054-4927-2). Broadman.
Everett, Betty S. Who Am I, Lord? LC 82-72645. 112p. (Orig.). (gr. 3-6). 1983. pap. 3.50 (ISBN 0-8066-1951-1, 10-7072). Augsburg.
Miller, George A. Spontaneous Apprentices: Children & Language. 224p. 1980. 10.95 (ISBN 0-8164-9330-8). Seabury.
Reece, Colleen. Honor Bound. 176p. (gr. 3 up). 1983. 3.95 (ISBN 0-8024-0153-8). Moody.
Robinson, Edward. The Original Vision: A Study of the Religious Experience of Childhood. 192p. (Orig.). 1983. pap. 7.95 (ISBN 0-8164-2439-X). Seabury.
Rockness, Miriam H. A Time to Play: On Childhood & Creativity. 192p. 1983. pap. 5.95 (ISBN 0-310-45871-4). Zondervan.
Sledge, Linda. All Dad's Hats. (Home Mission Graded Ser.). 24p. (gr. 1-3). Date not set. pap. 2.00 (ISBN 0-937170-24-0). Home Mission.
Westerhoff, John H., III. Will Our Children Have Faith? 144p. 1983. pap. 6.95 (ISBN 0-8164-2435-7). Seabury.
CHILDREN–SPEECH
see Children–Language
CHILDREN–TRAINING
see Children–Management
CHILDREN–TRANSPORTATION
see School Children–Transportation
CHILDREN–VOCABULARY
see Children–Language
CHILDREN–WRITING
Frank Schaffer Publications. Getting Ready for Writing. (Getting Ready for Kindergarten Ser.). (Illus.). 24p. (ps-k). 1980. workbook 1.29 (ISBN 0-86734-016-9, FS 3029). Schaffer Pubns.
--Handwriting with Harvey Hippo. (Help Your Child Learn Ser.). (Illus.). 24p. (gr. 2-4). 1978. workbook 1.29 (ISBN 0-86734-009-6, FS 3010). Schaffer Pubns.
Frank Schaffer Publications, Inc. Printing with Peter Possum. (Help Your Child Learn Ser.). (Illus.). 24p. (gr. k-2). 1978. workbook 1.29 (ISBN 0-86734-006-1, FS 3007). Schaffer Pubns.
CHILDREN, ABNORMAL AND BACKWARDS
see Exceptional Children; Handicapped Children; Mentally Handicapped Children
CHILDREN, ADOPTED
see Adoption
CHILDREN, AFRO-AMERICAN
see Afro-American Children
CHILDREN, APHASIC
see Aphasia
CHILDREN, CUSTODY OF
see Custody of Children
CHILDREN, DEAF
see also Deaf–Means of Communication
Harris, George A. Broken Ears, Wounded Hearts. (Illus.). xiv, 174p. 1983. 10.95 (ISBN 0-913580-83-X). Gallaudet Coll.
Ogden, Paul W. & Lipsett, Suzanne. The Silent Garden: Understanding the Hearing-Impaired Child. 240p. 1983. pap. 7.95 (ISBN 0-8092-5571-5). Contemp Bks.
CHILDREN, EXCEPTIONAL
see Exceptional Children
CHILDREN, JEWISH
see Jewish Children
CHILDREN, PHOTOGRAPHY OF
see Photography of Children and Youth
CHILDREN, RETARDED
see Mentally Handicapped Children
CHILDREN AND DEATH
Wass, H. & Corr, C. A. Helping Children Cope with Death. 1982. 32.00 (ISBN 0-07-068427-8). McGraw.

Wass, Hannelore & Corr, Charles A., eds. Childhood & Death. LC 82-23365. (Death, Education, Aging, & Health Care). (Illus.). 400p. 1983. text ed. 24.50 (ISBN 0-89116-320-4). Hemisphere Pub.

CHILDREN AND POLITICS

Goode, Stephen. The New Federalism. (Single Title Ser.). (Illus.). 160p. (gr. 7 up). 1983. PLB 9.90 (ISBN 0-531-04501-3). Watts.

Rosenblatt, Roger. Children of War. LC 82-45366. 216p. 1983. 14.95 (ISBN 0-385-18250-3, Anchor Pr). Doubleday.

CHILDREN AND TELEVISION

see Television and Children

CHILDREN IN THE BIBLE

Bourgeois, Jean-Francois. Los Ninos de la Biblia. Maecha, Alberto, ed. Orig. Title: Les Enfants de la Bible. 40p. (Span.). (gr. 3-5). 1982. pap. write for info. (ISBN 0-942504-11-9). Overcomer Pr.

CHILDREN IN THE UNITED STATES

see also Presidents-United States-Wives and Children

Francke, Linda B. Growing Up Divorced: Children of the Eighties. 1983. 16.50 (ISBN 0-671-25516-9, Linden). S&S.

CHILDREN'S ALMANACS

see Almanacs

CHILDREN'S ART

Here are entered collections of art produced by children under fifteen years of age and or below the ninth grade in school.

DiLeo, Joseph H. Interpreting Children's Drawings. (Illus.). 212p. 1983. 25.00 (ISBN 0-87630-327-0); pap. 16.95 (ISBN 0-87630-331-9). Brunner-Mazel.

CHILDREN'S BOOKS

see Children's Literature (Collections); Illustrated Books, Children's;
also subdivisions under Children's Literature

CHILDREN'S CLOTHING

Fairchild Market Research Division. Infants' Toddlers' Girls' & Boys' (Fact File Ser.). (Illus.). 1983. pap. text ed. 12.50 (ISBN 0-87005-457-0). Fairchild.

CHILDREN'S COURTS

see Juvenile Courts

CHILDREN'S DANCES

see Dancing-Children's Dances

CHILDREN'S DISEASES

see Children-Diseases

CHILDREN'S DRAMA

see Children'S Plays

CHILDREN'S ENCYCLOPEDIAS AND DICTIONARIES

Shapiro, William E., ed. New Book of Knowledge, 21 Vols. LC 81-82202. (Illus.). 1982. write for info. (ISBN 0-7172-0513-4). Grolier Ed Corp.

CHILDREN'S HOMES

see Children-Institutional Care

CHILDREN'S HOSPITALS

see Children-Hospitals

CHILDREN'S LIBRARIES

see School Libraries

CHILDREN'S LITERATURE (COLLECTIONS)

see also Children-Books and Reading; Children's Encyclopedias and Dictionaries; Children's Plays; Children's Poetry; Children's Stories; Fairy Tales; Picture-Books for Children; Readers; Story-Telling
also subdivision Juvenile Literature under particular subjects, e.g. Astronomy-Juvenile Literature

Butler, Francelia & Pickering, Samuel, Jr. Children's Literature: Annual of the Modern Language Association Division on Children's Literature & the Children's Literature Association, No. 11. LC 79-66588. (Illus.). 224p. 1983. text ed. 20.00x (ISBN 0-300-02991-8); pap. text ed. 8.95x (ISBN 0-300-02992-6). Yale U Pr.

Green Tiger Press, ed. Books & Readers. (Illus.). 12p. 1982. pap. 2.50 (ISBN 0-914676-99-7, Pub. by Envelope Bks). Green Tiger Pr.

--Flying Horse. 12p. (Orig.). 1982. pap. 2.50 (ISBN 0-88138-005-9, Pub. by Envelope Bks). Green Tiger Pr.

Pogrebin, L. C. Stories for Free Children. 144p. 1982. 14.95 (ISBN 0-07-050389-3, GB). McGraw.

Reader's Digest Editors. Seventy Favorite Stories for Young Readers. LC 76-19444. (Illus.). 448p. 1976. 14.98 (ISBN 0-89577-031-8). RD Assn.

CHILDREN'S LITERATURE-BIBLIOGRAPHY

see also School Libraries

Larrick, Nancy. A Parent's Guide to Children's Reading. Rev., 5th ed. LC 82-24702. (Illus.). 288p. 1983. write for info. (ISBN 0-664-32705-2). Westminster.

Senick, Gerard J., ed. Children's Literature Review, Vol. 5. 350p. 1983. 56.00x (ISBN 0-8103-0330-2). Gale.

CHILDREN'S LITERATURE-BIO-BIBLIOGRAPHY

Jones, Dolores B., ed. Children's Literature Awards & Winners: A Directory of Prizes, Authors, & Illustrators. 1st ed. 1983. 65.00x (ISBN 0-8103-0171-7, Co-pub. by Neal-Schuman). Gale.

CHILDREN'S LITERATURE-HISTORY AND CRITICISM

Street, Douglas, ed. Children's Novels & the Movies. (Ungar Film Library). (Illus.). 350p. 14.95 (ISBN 0-8044-2840-9); pap. 6.95 (ISBN 0-8044-6883-4). Ungar.

CHILDREN'S LITERATURE-TECHNIQUE

Aiken, Joan. The Way to Write for Children. 112p. 1983. 10.95 (ISBN 0-312-85839-6); pap. 4.95 (ISBN 0-312-85840-X). St Martin.

CHILDREN'S PARTIES

Marzollo, Jean. Birthday Parties for Children: How to Give Them, How to Survive Them. LC 82-48234. (Illus.). 160p. 1983. pap. 4.76i (ISBN 0-06-091014-3, CN 1014, CN). Har-Row.

--Birthday Parties for Children: How to Give Them, How to Survive Them. LC 82-48234. (Illus.). 160p. 1983. 12.95 (ISBN 0-06-015119-6, HarpT); pap. 4.95 (ISBN 0-06-091014-3). Har-Row.

CHILDREN'S PLAYS

see also College and School Drama; Skits, Stunts, Etc.

Siks, Geraldine B. Drama With Children. 2nd ed. 368p. 1983. text ed. 16.95 scp (ISBN 0-06-046152-7, HarpC). Har-Row.

CHILDREN'S PLAYS-PRESENTATION, ETC.

Pierini, Francis P. Children's Theater in Elementary School. 88p. 1977. pap. 1.00 (ISBN 0-8164-0342-2). Seabury.

CHILDREN'S POETRY

see also Children's Songs; Nursery Rhymes

Dahl, Roald. Roald Dahl's Revolting Rhymes. LC 82-15263. (Illus.). 48p. 1983. 9.95 (ISBN 0-394-85422-5); lib. bdg. 9.99 (ISBN 0-394-95422-X). Knopf.

Duncan, Lois. From Spring to Spring: Poems & Photographs. LC 82-11100. 96p. (gr. 3-7). 1982. 10.95 (ISBN 0-664-32695-1). Westminster.

Heller, Rebecca, ed. My Little Book of Poems. (First Little Golden Bk.). (Illus.). 24p. (ps). 1983. 0.69 (ISBN 0-307-10142-8, Golden Press); PLB price not set (ISBN 0-307-68142-4). Western Pub.

Herzog, Barbara J. Once Upon a Rhyme. (Illus.). 48p. (Orig.). (gr. 1-3). 1983. pap. 5.98 (ISBN 0-943194-12-1). Childwrite.

Kent, Rolly, ed. Southside: Twenty-One Poems by Children from Tucson's South Side. (Illus.). 28p. 1982. pap. 5.00 (ISBN 0-9608370-1-9). Friends Tucson Library.

Lobel, Arnold. The Book of Pigericks. LC 82-47730. (Illus.). 48p. (gr. k-3). 1983. 9.57i (ISBN 0-06-023982-4, HarpJ); PLB 9.89g (ISBN 0-06-023983-2). Har-Row.

Wells, Carolyn. The Seven Ages of Childhood. (Illus.). 12p. (Orig.). 1982. pap. 2.50 (ISBN 0-914676-98-9, Pub. by Envelope Bks). Green Tiger Pr.

Zaslow, David. Pint-Sized Poetry. (ps-4). 1982. 5.95 (ISBN 0-86653-095-9, GA 435). Good Apple.

CHILDREN'S POETRY-HISTORY AND CRITICISM

Bhattacherje, M. M. Pictorial Poetry. 184p. Repr. of 1954 ed. lib. bdg. 35.00 (ISBN 0-89760-090-8). Telegraph Bks.

CHILDREN'S PRAYERS

see Children-Prayer-Books and Devotions

CHILDREN'S QUESTIONS AND ANSWERS

Adler, David. All About the Moon. LC 82-17422. (Question & Answer Bks.). (Illus.). 32p. (gr. 3-6). 1983. PLB 8.59 (ISBN 0-89375-886-8); pap. text ed. 1.95 (ISBN 0-89375-887-6). Troll Assocs.

--Amazing Magnets. LC 82-17377. (Question & Answer Bks.). (Illus.). 32p. (gr. 3-6). 1983. PLB 8.59 (ISBN 0-89375-894-9); pap. text ed. 1.95 (ISBN 0-89375-895-7). Troll Assocs.

Barrett, Judi. What's Left? LC 82-12824. (Illus.). 32p. (ps). 1983. 10.95 (ISBN 0-689-30874-4). Atheneum.

Dickinson, Jane. All About Trees. LC 82-17382. (Question & Answer Bks.). (Illus.). 32p. (gr. 3-6). 1983. PLB 8.59 (ISBN 0-89375-892-2); pap. text ed. 1.95 (ISBN 0-89375-893-0). Troll Assocs.

Hoopes, Lyn L. When I Was Little. LC 82-18207. (Illus.). 32p. (ps-3). 1983. 9.95 (ISBN 0-525-44053-4, 0966-290). Dutton.

Jefferies, Lawrence. Air, Air, Air. LC 82-15808. (Question & Answer Bks.). (Illus.). 32p. (gr. 3-6). 1983. PLB 8.59 (ISBN 0-89375-880-9); pap. text ed. 1.95 (ISBN 0-89375-881-7). Troll Assocs.

--All About Stars. LC 82-20027. (Question & Answer Bks.). (Illus.). 32p. (gr. 3-6). PLB 8.59 (ISBN 0-89375-888-4); pap. text ed. 1.95 (ISBN 0-89375-889-2). Troll Assocs.

--Amazing World of Animals. LC 82-20061. (Question & Answer Bks.). (Illus.). 32p. (gr. 3-6). 1983. PLB 8.59 (ISBN 0-89375-898-1); pap. text ed. 1.95 (ISBN 0-89375-899-X). Troll Assocs.

Knight, David C. All About Sound. LC 82-17387. (Question & Answer Bks.). (Illus.). 32p. (gr. 3-6). 1983. PLB 8.59 (ISBN 0-89375-878-7); pap. text ed. 1.95 (ISBN 0-89375-879-5). Troll Assocs.

CHILDREN'S SERMONS

Bosco, Ronald A., ed. Lessons for the Children of Godly Ancestors. LC 82-5444. 1983. 50.00 (ISBN 0-8201-1381-6). Schol Facsimiles.

CHILDREN'S SONGS

see also Nursery Rhymes

Teacher & Cookman. The Family Car Songbook. 96p. (Orig.). (gr. 4-12). 1983. lib. bdg. 12.90 (ISBN 0-89471-213-6); pap. 3.95 (ISBN 0-89471-212-8). Running Pr.

Warner, Laverne & Berry, Paulette. Tunes for Tots. (ps-2). 1982. 7.95 (ISBN 0-86653-077-0, GA 414). Good Apple.

CHILDREN'S STORIES

see also Adventure and Adventurers; Animals, Legends and Stories Of; Christmas Stories; Fairy Tales; Ghost Stories; Science Fiction (Collections); Sea Stories; Short Stories; Story-Telling; Western Stories
also subdivision Legends and Stories under names of animals, e.g. Dogs-Legends and Stories

Albright, Nancy. Do Tell! Holiday Draw & Tell Stories. (Draw & Tell Stories). (gr. 1-7). 1981. 4.50 (ISBN 0-686-38119-X). Moonlight FL.

Beckman, Delores. Who Loves Sam Grant? LC 82-18211. 160p. (gr. 5-9). 1983. 9.95 (ISBN 0-525-44055-0, 0966-290). Dutton.

Crouch, Marcus. The Whole World Storybook. (Illus.). 160p. (gr. k-4). 1983. text ed. 12.95 (ISBN 0-19-278103-0, Pub. by Oxford U Pr Childrens). Merrimack Bk Serv.

Eby, Richard E. The Amazing Lamb of God: Bedtime Stories to be Read to Children. (Illus.). 160p. 1983. 12.95 (ISBN 0-8007-1336-2). Revell.

Gorog, Judith. A Taste for Quiet: And Other Disquieting Tales. (Illus.). 124p. 1982. 9.95 (ISBN 0-399-20922-0, Philomel). Putnam Pub Group.

Peterson, Carolyn S. & Fenton, Ann D. Story Programs for Older Children. (Illus.). Date not set. price not set. Moonlight FL.

Weiss, Jacqueline S. Prizewinning Books for Children: Themes & Stereotypes in U.S. Prizewinning Prose Fiction for Children. LC 82-48624. (Libraries & Librarianship Special Ser.). 1983. write for info. (ISBN 0-669-06352-5). Lexington Bks.

Yolen, Jane. Neptune Rising: Songs & Tales of the Undersea Folk. (Illus.). 160p. 1982. 10.95 (ISBN 0-399-20918-2, Philomel). Putnam Pub Group.

CHILDREN'S THEATER

see Children's Plays-Presentation, etc.

CHILDREN'S VILLAGES

see Children-Institutional Care

CHILDREN'S WIT AND HUMOR

see Wit and Humor, Juvenile

CHILDREN'S WRITINGS

Here are entered collections and individual works written by children. Discussions of such works are entered under Children as Authors.

Krauss, Ruth. Somebody Else's Nut Tree & Other Tales From Children. (Illus.). 48p. 1983. Repr. of 1958 ed. 6.50 (ISBN 0-913660-19-1). Magic Circle Pr.

CHILE-SOCIAL CONDITIONS

Eight Years of Their Lives. 250p. 1982. pap. 15.00 (ISBN 0-88936-326-9, IDRC191, IDRC). Unipub.

McCaa, Robert. Marriage & Fertility in Chile: Demographic Turning Points in the Petorca Valley, 1840-1976. (Dellplain Latin American Studies: No. 14). 250p. 1982. softcover 20.00x (ISBN 0-86531-532-9). Westview.

CHILEAN LITERATURE

Pujals, Josefina A. El Bosque Indomado...Donde Chilla el Obsceno Pajaro de la Noche. LC 81-69533. 134p. (Orig., Span.). 1982. pap. 15.95 (ISBN 0-89729-304-5). Ediciones.

CHILIASM

see Millennium

CHIMPANZEES

De Waal, Frans. Chimpanzee Politics: Power & Sex among Apes. Milnes, Janet, tr. from Dutch. LC 82-48115. (Illus.). 224p. 1983. 15.86i (ISBN 0-06-015113-7, HarpT). Har-Row.

Plooij, Frans X. The Behavioral Development of Free-Living Chimpanzee Babies & Infants. Lipsitt, Lewis P., ed. (Monographs on Infancy). (Illus.). 208p. (Orig.). 1983. text ed. 18.50 (ISBN 0-89391-114-3). Ablex Pub.

CHINA

Chiang Kai-Shek. China's Destiny. LC 76-24849. 260p. 1976. Repr. of 1947 ed. lib. bdg. 32.50 (ISBN 0-306-70821-3). Da Capo.

China, 1980. 375.00x (ISBN 0-686-99854-5, Pub. by Metra England). State Mutual Bk.

Kampuchea, Viet Nam, China: Observations & Reflections. 17p. 1982. pap. 5.00 (ISBN 92-808-0320-4, TUNU 201, UNU). Unipub.

Pusey, James R. China & Charles Darwin. (Harvard East Asian Monographs: No. 100). 543p. 1982. text ed. 25.00x (ISBN 0-674-11735-2). Harvard U Pr.

Radiopress (Japan), ed. China Directory, 1983. 11th ed. LC 79-642283. 578p. 1982. 85.00x (ISBN 0-8002-3072-8). Intl Pubns Serv.

Sidel, Ruth & Sidel, Victor W. The Health of China. LC 81-68353. 272p. 1983. pap. 7.64 (ISBN 0-8070-2161-X, BP651). Beacon Pr.

CHINA-BIOGRAPHY

Chou, Prudence S. Lao She: The Dilemma of an Intellectual in Modern China. Date not set. price not set. Quintessence.

Ginsbourg, Sam. My First Sixty Years in China. (Illus.). 373p. 1982. pap. text ed. 5.95 (ISBN 0-8351-1109-1). China Bks.

Strassberg, Richard E. The World of K'ung Shang-Jen: A Man of Letters in Early Ch'ing China. 520p. 1983. text ed. 25.00x (ISBN 0-231-05530-7). Columbia U Pr.

Zhou Erfu. Doctor Norman Bethune. Bailey, Alison, tr. from Chinese. (Illus.). 1982. pap. write for info. (ISBN 0-8351-0997-6). China Bks.

CHINA-CHURCH HISTORY

Fitch, Janet. Foreign Devil: Reminiscences of a China Missionary Daughter, 1909-1935. (Asian Library Ser.: No. 39). 1982. 28.75x (ISBN 0-686-37543-2). Oriental Bk Store.

CHINA-CIVILIZATION

Idema, W. L., ed. Leyden Studies in Sinology: Papers Presented at the Conference held in Celebration of the 50th Anniversary of the Sinological Institute of Leyden University, December 8-12, 1982. (Sinica Leidensia Ser.: Vol. 15). (Illus.). ix, 234p. 1981. pap. write for info. (ISBN 90-04-06529-6). E J Brill.

CHINA-COMMERCE

Doing Business in Today's China. 1981. 15.00. A M Newman.

CHINA-DEFENSES

Godwin, Paul H. The Chinese Defense Establishment: Continuity & Change in the 1980s. (Special Studies on East Asia). 175p. 1983. lib. bdg. 17.50x (ISBN 0-86531-568-X). Westview.

CHINA-DESCRIPTION AND TRAVEL

Barnes, Simon. China in Focus. (The "In Focus" Ser.). (Illus.). 64p. (Orig.). 1981. pap. 5.95 (ISBN 962-7031-12-7). C E Tuttle.

Congwen, Shen. Recollections of West Hunan. Yang, Gladys, tr. from Chinese. 196p. (Orig.). 1982. pap. 4.95 (ISBN 0-295-96016-7, Pub. by Chinese Lit Beijing). U of Wash Pr.

Kaplan, Fredric M. & Dekeijzer, Arne J. The China Guidebook 1983. X ed. (Illus.). 528p. (Orig.). pap. 12.95 (ISBN 0-932030-15-7). Eurasia Pr NJ.

Lai, T. C. Kweilin. (Illus.). 96p. 8.95 (ISBN 0-86519-023-2). LEE PUBS GROUP.

--Visiting China: A Cultured Guide. 248p. 1983. 12.95 (ISBN 0-686-42997-4, Swindon Hong Kong). Hippocrene Bks.

Liu, Henry. Travel Aid to China. 110p. 1982. 10.00 (ISBN 0-533-04985-7). Vantage.

Pannell, Clifton W. & Ma, Laurence J. C. China: The Geography of Development & Modernization. (Scripts Series in Geography). 390p. 49.95 (ISBN 0-470-27376-3); pap. 19.95 (ISBN 0-470-27377-1). Halsted Pr.

Reid, Daniel P. The Complete Guide to China. (The Complete Asian Guide Ser.). (Illus.). 126p. 1981. pap. 6.95 (ISBN 962-7031-03-8, Pub. by CFW Pubns Hong Kong). C E Tuttle.

Snow, Lois W. Edgar Snow's China. LC 82-49084. (Illus.). 304p. 1983. pap. 11.95 (ISBN 0-394-71500-4, Vin). Random.

Xianshi, Fu. Mount Taishan. Nianpei, Li, tr. from Chinese. (Illus.). 37p. (Orig.). 1982. pap. 0.95 (ISBN 0-8351-1040-0). China Bks.

CHINA-DESCRIPTION AND TRAVEL-1949-

National Geographic Society. Journey into China. (Illus.). 1982. write for info. Natl Geog.

Schwartz, Brian. China off the Beaten Track. (Illus.). 256p. 1983. pap. 10.95 (ISBN 0-312-13304-9). St Martin.

Spender, Stephen & Hockney, David. China Diary. 1983. 28.50 (ISBN 0-686-42992-3). Abrams.

CHINA-ECONOMIC CONDITIONS

China from Mao to Deng: The Politics & Economics of Socialist Development. (Illus.). 100p. (Orig.). 1983. text ed. 17.50 (ISBN 0-87332-240-1); pap. text ed. 8.95 (ISBN 0-87332-244-4). M E Sharpe.

China's Foreign Economic Legislation, Vol. 1. 289p. 1982. pap. 5.95 (ISBN 0-8351-0983-6). China Bks.

Dixin, Xu, et al. China's Search for Economic Growth. (Illus.). 217p. (Orig.). 1982. pap. 5.95 (ISBN 0-8351-0974-7). China Bks.

CHINA-ECONOMIC CONDITIONS-1949-

Feutchwant & Hussain. The Chinese Economic Reforms. LC 82-10703. 384p. 1982. 32.50x (ISBN 0-312-13385-5). St Martin.

CHINA-FOREIGN RELATIONS

Rossabi, Morris, ed. China among Equals: The Middle Kingdom & Its Neighbors, 10th-14th Centuries. LC 81-11486. 400p. 1983. text ed. 28.50x (ISBN 0-520-04383-9); pap. text ed. 12.50x (ISBN 0-520-04562-9). U of Cal Pr.

Zhou Guo, ed. China & the World, No. 2. (China & the World Ser.). 123p. 1982. pap. 1.95 (ISBN 0-8351-1115-6). China Bks.

CHINA-FOREIGN RELATIONS-1949-

Glaudue, E. Ted, Jr. China's Perception of Global Politics. LC 82-13572. 258p. 1983. lib. bdg. 23.50 (ISBN 0-8191-2700-0); pap. text ed. 11.50 (ISBN 0-8191-2701-9). U Pr of Amer.

CHINA-FOREIGN RELATIONS-JAPAN

Bedeski, Robert E. The Fragile Entente: The Nineteen Seventy-Eight Japan-China Peace Treaty in a Global Context. (Replica Edition Ser.). 235p. 1983. softcover 18.50x (ISBN 0-86531-944-8). Westview.

CHINA-FOREIGN RELATIONS-UNITED STATES

Hsiao. Sino-American Normalization. 300p. 1983. 27.95 (ISBN 0-03-058022-6); pap. 9.95 (ISBN 0-03-058023-4). Praeger.

Hunt, Michael H. The Making of a Special Relationship: The United States & China to 1914. LC 82-9753. 480p. 1983. 27.50x (ISBN 0-231-05516-1). Columbia U Pr.

Sutter, Robert G. The China Quandary: Domestic Determinants of U. S. - China Policy, 1972-1982. 250p. 1983. lib. bdg. 22.50x (ISBN 0-86531-579-5). Westview.

Tien, Hung-Mao, ed. Mainland China, Taiwan, & U. S. Policy. LC 82-14155. 212p. 1983. 25.00 (ISBN 0-89946-151-4). Oelgeschlager.

Tucker, Nancy B. Patterns in the Dust: Chinese-American Relations & the Recognition Controversy, 1949-1950. Leuchtenburg, William E., ed. (Contemporary American History Ser.). 400p. 1983. text ed. 30.00 (ISBN 0-231-05362-2); pap. 15.00 (ISBN 0-231-05363-0). Columbia U Pr.

Woodcock, Leonard. China-United States Relations in Transition. LC 82-12135. 25p. 1982. 1.25 (ISBN 0-934742-21-9, Inst Study Diplomacy). Geo U Sch For Serv.

CHINA-HISTORIOGRAPHY

Meskill, John T., intro. by. The Pattern of Chinese History: Cycles, Development or Stagnation. LC 82-18378. (Problems in Asian Civilizations Ser.). xx, 108p. 1983. Repr. of 1965 ed. lib. bdg. 27.50x (ISBN 0-313-23739-5, MEPC). Greenwood.

CHINA-HISTORY

Here are entered general works on Chinese history. Smaller periods are listed chronologically at the end of the History subject headings.

Bush, Richard. China Briefing, 1982. 125p. 1982. lib. bdg. 14.50x (ISBN 0-86531-516-7); pap. text ed. 6.95x (ISBN 0-86531-517-5). Westview.

Cochran, Sherman & Hsieh, Andrew C. K., trs. One Day in China: May 21, 1936. LC 82-48901. 304p. 1983. text ed. 19.95x (ISBN 0-300-02834-2). Yale U Pr.

CHINA-HISTORY-EARLY TO 1643

Ames, Roger T. The Art of Rulership: A Study in Ancient Chinese Political Thought. LC 82-25917. 1983. 25.00x (ISBN 0-8248-0825-8). UH Pr.

Pirazzoli-t'Serstevens, Michele. The Han Dynasty. LC 82-50109. (Illus.). 224p. 1982. 50.00 (ISBN 0-8478-0438-0). Rizzoli Intl.

CHINA-HISTORY-1900-

Chiang, Monlin. Tides From the West: A Chinese Autobiography. 1947. text ed. 23.50x (ISBN 0-686-83825-4). Elliots Bks.

Restarick, Henry B. Sun Yat Sen, Liberator of China. 1931. text ed. 14.50x (ISBN 0-686-83796-7). Elliots Bks.

CHINA-HISTORY-1949-

China: An Uncensored Look. LC 79-63789. 254p. 1983. pap. 4.95 (ISBN 0-933256-41-8). Second Chance.

Gerside, Roger. Coming Alive: China After Mao. 1982. pap. 4.50 (ISBN 0-451-62087-9, ME2087, Ment). NAL.

CHINA-HISTORY, MILITARY

Li, Sun. Stormy Years. Yang, Gladys, tr. from Chinese. 437p. 1982. pap. 6.96 (ISBN 0-686-84097-6). China Bks.

CHINA-INTELLECTUAL LIFE-1949-

Yee, Lee, ed. The New Realism: Writings from China after the Cultural Revolution. 280p. 1983. 22.50 (ISBN 0-88254-794-1); pap. 14.95 (ISBN 0-88254-810-7). Hippocrene Bks.

CHINA-JUVENILE LITERATURE

Lawson, Don. The Long March: Red China under Chairman Mao. LC 82-45580. (Illus.). 160p. (YA) (gr. 7 up). 1983. 10.10i (ISBN 0-690-04271-X, TYC-J); PLB 10.89g (ISBN 0-690-04272-8). Harper Row.

Newlon, Clarke. China: The Rise to World Power. LC 82-46000. 224p. (gr. 7 up). 1983. PLB 10.95 (ISBN 0-396-08136-3). Dodd.

CHINA-KINGS AND RULERS

The Emperors of China. LC 81-51333. (Treasures of the World Ser.). lib. bdg. 26.60 (ISBN 0-86706-056-5, Pub. by Stonehenge). Silver.

CHINA-MAPS

Cartographic Publishing House Staff, ed. Map of the People's Republic of China-Relief. 1981. pap. 3.95 (ISBN 0-8351-1035-4). China Bks.

CHINA-NAVY

Leonard, Jane K. Wie Yuan & China's Rediscovery of the Maritime World. (Duke Press Policy Studies). 250p. 1983. 35.00 (ISBN 0-8223-0549-6). Duke.

Muller, David G., Jr. China as a Maritime Power. (Special Studies on East Asia). 300p. 1983. price not set (ISBN 0-86531-098-X). Westview.

CHINA-POLITICS AND GOVERNMENT

Ames, Roger T. The Art of Rulership: A Study in Ancient Chinese Political Thought. LC 82-25917. 1983. 25.00x (ISBN 0-8248-0825-8). UH Pr.

China from Mao to Deng: The Politics & Economics of Socialist Development. (Illus.). 100p. (Orig.). 1983. text ed. 17.50 (ISBN 0-87332-240-1); pap. text ed. 8.95 (ISBN 0-87332-244-4). M E Sharpe.

Dardess, John W. Confucianism & Autocracy: Professional Elites in the Founding of the Ming Dynasty. LC 82-4822. 400p. 1983. text ed. 35.00x (ISBN 0-520-04659-5). U of Cal Pr.

Marcy, Sam. China, Suppression of the Left. 111p. 1977. pap. 2.00 (ISBN 0-686-84043-7). WV Pubs.

Marcy, Sam & Griswold, Deirdre. China, the Struggle Within. 2nd ed. 116p. 1972. pap. 2.00 (ISBN 0-89567-079-8). WV Pubs.

Thaxton, Ralph. China Turned Rightside Up: Revolutionary Legitimacy in the Peasant World. LC 82-40165. (Illus.). 312p. 1983. text ed. 27.50x (ISBN 0-300-02707-9). Yale U Pr.

CHINA-POLITICS AND GOVERNMENT-1949-

Brady, J. P., ed. Justice & Politics in People's China: Legal Order of Continuing Revolution. Date not set. 33.00 (ISBN 0-12-124750-3). Acad Pr.

Gardner, John. Chinese Politics & the Succession to Mao. (Illus.). 217p. 1982. text ed. 20.00x (ISBN 0-8419-0808-7); pap. text ed. 14.00x (ISBN 0-8419-0809-5). Holmes & Meier.

Short, Philip. The Dragon & the Bear: Inside China & Russia Today. LC 82-12427. (Illus.). 504p. 1983. 19.95 (ISBN 0-688-01524-7). Morrow.

Siu, Helen & Stern, Zelda, eds. Mao's Harvest: Voices from China's New Generation. LC 82-14300. (Illus.). 384p. 1983. 17.95 (ISBN 0-19-503274-8). Oxford U Pr.

The Twelfth National Congress of CPC. 157p. (Orig.). 1982. pap. 2.95 (ISBN 0-8351-1045-1). China Bks.

Whyte, Martin K. Small Groups & Political Ritual in China. 288p. 1983. pap. text ed. 8.95x (ISBN 0-520-04941-1, CAMPUS 157). U of Cal Pr.

CHINA-POPULATION

Eberhard, Wolfram. China's Minorities: Yesterday & Today. 192p. 1982. pap. text ed. 8.95x (ISBN 0-534-01080-6). Wadsworth Pub.

CHINA-RELIGION

Fung, Raymond, ed. Households of God on China's Soil. LC 82-18974. 96p. (Orig.). 1983. pap. 5.95 (ISBN 0-88344-189-6). Orbis Bks.

CHINA-SOCIAL CONDITIONS

Chiang, Monlin. Tides From the West: A Chinese Autobiography. 1947. text ed. 23.50x (ISBN 0-686-83825-4). Elliots Bks.

Greenblat, Sidney L. Social Interaction in Chinese Society. Wilson, Richard & Wilson, Amy A., eds. 272p. 1982. 29.95 (ISBN 0-03-058021-8). Praeger.

McKnight, Brian E. Village & Bureaucracy in Southern Sung China. LC 72-159834. xii, 220p. 1971. pap. 6.95 (ISBN 0-226-56060-0). U of Chicago Pr.

CHINA-SOCIAL CONDITIONS-1949-

Stacey, Judith. Patriarchy & Socialist Revolution in China. LC 82-8482. 330p. 1983. text ed. 28.50x (ISBN 0-520-04825-3). U of Cal Pr.

Thaxton, Ralph. China Turned Rightside Up: Revolutionary Legitimacy in the Peasant World. 27.50 (ISBN 0-686-42817-X). Yale U Pr.

CHINA-SOCIAL LIFE AND CUSTOMS

Bonavia, David. The Chinese. rev. ed. 1983. pap. 4.95 (ISBN 0-14-022394-0, Pelican). Penguin.

Chao, Paul. Chinese Kinship. 220p. 1983. 30.00 (ISBN 0-7103-0020-4). Routledge & Kegan.

Chinese Experts & Staff of the Peoples. The Chinese Way to A Long & Healthy Life. Medical Publishing House, Beijin, China, ed. (Illus.). 224p. 1983. 14.95 (ISBN 0-88254-792-5). Hippocrene Bks.

Crook, David & Crook, Isabel. Revolution in a Chinese Village: Ten Mile Inn. (International Library of Sociology). 190p. 1979. 20.00 (ISBN 0-7100-3393-1). Routledge & Kegan.

Eberhard, Wolfram. Life & Thought of Ordinary Chinese: Collected Essays. (East Asian Folklore & Social Life Monographs: Vol. 106). 230p. 1982. 18.00 (ISBN 0-89986-337-X). Oriental Bk Store.

Lai, T. C. Things Chinese. (Illus.). 213p. 12.95 (ISBN 0-86519-096-8). Lee Pubs Group.

Levy, Howard S. & Kawatani, Michiko, trs. Japan's Dirty Old Man: Sex Adventures of Hirota Kicchomu. 1979. 15.00 (ISBN 0-686-37541-6). Oriental Bk Store.

Seaman, Gary. Temple Organization in a Chinese Village. (Asian Folklore & Social Life Monographs: Vol. 101). 173p. 1978. 14.50 (ISBN 0-89986-332-9). Oriental Bk Store.

CHINA (PORCELAIN)

see Porcelain

CHINA PAINTING

Southwell, Sheila. Painting China & Porcelain. (Illus.). 104p. 1983. pap. 7.50 (ISBN 0-7137-1341-0, Pub. by Blandford Pr England). Sterling.

CHINAWARE

see Porcelain; Pottery

CHINCHILLAS

Denham, Ken. Guinea Pigs & Chinchillas. (Illus.). 93p. 1977. pap. 3.95 (ISBN 0-7028-1075-4). Avian Pubns.

CHINESE ARCHITECTURE

see Architecture-China

CHINESE ART

see Art, Chinese

CHINESE DRAMA-TRANSLATIONS INTO ENGLISH

Gunn, Edward M., ed. Twentieth Century Chinese Drama: An Anthology. (Midland Bks.). (Illus.). 560p. (Orig.). 1983. 22.50x (ISBN 0-253-36109-5); pap. 15.00x (ISBN 0-253-20310-4). Ind U Pr.

CHINESE FICTION

see also Short Stories, Chinese

Lanyun, Liu. Golden Millet Dream & Other Stories. Fanqin, Yu & Mingjie, Wang, trs. from Span. (The Chinese-English Readers). (Illus.). 296p. (Orig.). 1982. pap. 4.95 (ISBN 0-8351-1102-4). China Bks.

CHINESE FLOWER ARRANGEMENT

see Flower Arrangement, Chinese

CHINESE FOLK-LORE

see Folk-Lore, Chinese

CHINESE IN FOREIGN COUNTRIES

Richardson, Peter. Chinese Mine Labour in the Transvaal. 287p. 1982. text ed. 31.50x (ISBN 0-333-27222-6, Pub. by Macmillan England). Humanities.

CHINESE IN THE UNITED STATES

Reed, Karen L. The Chinese in Tehama County: 1860-1890. (ANCRR Research Paper: No. 6). 1980. 4.00 (ISBN 0-686-38938-7). Assn NC Records.

CHINESE LANGUAGE

Berlitz Editors. Chinese for Travel Cassettepack. 1983. 14.95 (ISBN 0-02-962210-7, Berlitz); cassette incl. Macmillan.

Gassmann, Robert H. Zur Syntax Von Einbettungsstrukturen Im Klassischen Chinesisch. 227p. (Ger.). 1982. write for info. (ISBN 3-261-05002-0). P Lang Pubs.

Hsu Ying & Brown, J. Marvin. Speaking Chinese in China. LC 82-48904. 1983. text ed. 35.00 (ISBN 0-300-02955-1); pap. text ed. 9.95x (ISBN 0-300-03032-0). Yale U Pr.

Lai, T. C. More Chinese Sayings. 86p. 1983. 6.95 (ISBN 0-686-42996-6, Swindon Hong Kong). Hippocrene Bks.

--Selected Chinese Sayings. 198p. 1983. pap. 4.95 (ISBN 0-686-42995-8, Swindon Hong Kong). Hippocrene Bks.

Liang, James C. & DeFrancis, John. Varieties of Spoken Standard Chinese, Vol. I: A Speaker from Tianjin. 120p. 1982. pap. 14.00x (ISBN 0-686-37586-6). Foris Pubns.

CHINESE LANGUAGE-CONVERSATION AND PHRASE BOOKS

Armstrong, Virginia W. L. Guest of China: English-Chinese Phrases. (Illus.). 120p. 1982. pap. 10.00x (ISBN 2-88089-000-4). A Robinson.

Getting By in Chinese. (Getting By Language Ser.). 90p. 1983. pap. 2.95 (ISBN 0-8120-2665-9). Barron.

Lai, T. C. Chinese Couplets. 13p. 1983. pap. 6.95 (ISBN 0-686-43000-X, Swindon Hong Kong). Hippocrene Bks.

CHINESE LANGUAGE-DICTIONARIES

Beijing Language Institute & Beijing Institute of Foreign Trade Staff, eds. Business Chiness 500. 309p. (Orig.). 1982. pap. 4.95 (ISBN 0-8351-1039-7). China Bks.

Chinese-English Translation Assistance Group. Chinese Dictionaries: An Extensive Bibliography of Dictionaries in Chinese & Other Languages. LC 82-923. 49.95 (ISBN 0-313-23505-8). Greenwood.

Collier, David. Chinese-English Dictionary of Colloquial Terms Used in Modern Chinese Literature. 10.75 (ISBN 0-686-38037-1). Far Eastern Pubns.

English-Chinese Dictionary of Medicine. 1675p. 1979. text ed. 24.95 (ISBN 0-8351-1048-6). China Bks.

Getting By in Chinese. (Getting By Language Ser.). 90p. 1983. pap. 2.95 (ISBN 0-8120-2665-9). Barron.

Zhou Long Ru. English-Chinese Dictionary of Abbreviation & Acronyms. 1290p. 1980. 9.95 (ISBN 0-8351-1106-7). China Bks.

CHINESE LANGUAGE-GRAMMAR

Chu, Show-Chih R. Chinese Grammar & English Grammar: A Comparative Study. 417p. 1982. 12.95 (ISBN 0-686-37976-4); pap. 10.95 (ISBN 0-686-37977-2). Inst Sino-Amer.

Show-Chih Rai Chu. Chinese Grammer & English Grammer: A Comparative Study. 417p. 1982. 12.95 (ISBN 0-686-37710-9); pap. 10.95 (ISBN 0-686-37711-7). Inst Sino Amer.

CHINESE LANGUAGE-PRIMERS

see Primers, Chinese

CHINESE LANGUAGE-READERS

Beijing Language Institute. Elementary Chinese-Supplement. (Elementary Chinese Readers). 277p. 1982. pap. 4.95 (ISBN 0-8351-1038-9). China Bks.

Beijing Language Institute Staff, ed. Annotated Chinese Proverbs. (Elementary Chinese Readers). (Illus.). 178p. (Orig.). 1982. pap. 4.95 (ISBN 0-8351-1100-8). China Bks.

Fenn, H. C. & Tewksbury, M. G. Read Chinese, Vol. 1. 236p. Date not set. includes 4 cassettes 55.00x (ISBN 0-88432-090-1, M300). J Norton Pubs.

--Read Chinese, Vol. 2. 267p. Date not set. includes 3 cassettes 45.00x (ISBN 0-88432-091-X, M310). J Norton Pubs.

CHINESE LANGUAGE-VOCABULARY

Tan Huay Peng. Fun with Chinese Characters. (Vol. I). (Illus.). 192p. 1982. pap. 5.95 (ISBN 9971-4-6072-6). Hippocrene Bks.

--Fun with Chinese Characters. (Vol. 2). (Illus.). 160p. 1983. pap. 5.95 (ISBN 0-686-42987-7). Hippocrene Bks.

CHINESE LANGUAGE-WRITING

Willetts, William. Chinese Calligraphy: Its History & Aesthetic Motivation. (Illus.). 276p. 1981. 49.00x (ISBN 0-19-580478-3). Oxford U Pr.

CHINESE LEGENDS

see Legends, Chinese

CHINESE LITERATURE (COLLECTIONS)

Cao, Xueqin. The Story of the Stone (The Dream of the Red Chamber), Vol. 1: The Golden Days. Hawkes, David, tr. from Chinese. LC 78-20279. (Chinese Literature in Translation Ser.). 544p. 1979. 25.00x (ISBN 0-253-19261-7). Ind U Pr.

--The Story of the Stone (The Dream of the Red Chamber), Vol. 2: The Crab-Flower Club. Hawkes, David, tr. from Chinese. LC 78-20279. (Chinese Literature in Translation Ser.). 608p. 1979. 25.00x (ISBN 0-253-19262-5). Ind U Pr.

CHINESE LITERATURE-TRANSLATIONS INTO ENGLISH

Cao, Xueqin. The Story of the Stone (The Dream of the Red Chamber), Vol. 1: The Golden Days. Hawkes, David, tr. from Chinese. LC 78-20279. (Chinese Literature in Translation Ser.). 544p. 1979. 25.00x (ISBN 0-253-19261-7). Ind U Pr.

--The Story of the Stone (The Dream of the Red Chamber), Vol. 2: The Crab-Flower Club. Hawkes, David, tr. from Chinese. LC 78-20279. (Chinese Literature in Translation Ser.). 608p. 1979. 25.00x (ISBN 0-253-19262-5). Ind U Pr.

Link, Perry, ed. Stubborn Weeds: Chinese Literature after the Cultural Revolution. LC 82-48268. 320p. 1983. 22.50x (ISBN 0-253-35512-5). Ind U Pr.

CHINESE MUSIC

see Music, Chinese

CHINESE PAINTING

see Painting, Chinese

CHINESE PAINTINGS

see Paintings, Chinese

CHINESE PHILOSOPHY

see Philosophy, Chinese

CHINESE POETRY-HISTORY AND CRITICISM

Liu, James J. Y. The Art of Chinese Poetry. LC 62-7475. (Midway Reprint Ser.). xii, 164p. 1962. pap. write for info. (ISBN 0-226-48685-0). U of Chicago Pr.

CHINESE POETRY-TRANSLATIONS INTO ENGLISH

Alley, Rewi, tr. Folk Poems From China's Minority. (Illus.). 147p. 1982. 5.95 (ISBN 0-8351-1104-0); pap. 4.95 (ISBN 0-8351-1105-9). China Bks.

Liang, Cecilia. Chinese Folk Poetry. 108p. Date not set. pap. 4.00 (ISBN 0-686-37600-5). Beyond Baroque.

Qing, Ai. The Black Eel. Xianyi, Yang & Friend, Robert C., trs. from Chinese. (Illus.). 103p. (Orig.). 1982. pap. 2.95 (ISBN 0-8351-1043-5). China Bks.

Wu-chi Liu & Yucheng Lo, Irving, eds. Sunflower Splendor. (Anchor Literary Library). 1983. pap. 6.95 (ISBN 0-686-42702-5, Anch). Doubleday.

CHINESE POTTERY

see Pottery, Chinese

CHINESE QUESTION

see China-History

CHIRICO, GIORGIO DE, 1888-

Lanchner, Carolyn & Rosenstock, Laura. Four Modern Masters: De Chirico, Ernst, Magritte, & Miro. (Illus.). 122p. 1982. pap. 14.95 (ISBN 0-686-83914-5, 28738-6). U of Chicago Pr.

CHIROGRAPHY

see Penmanship; Writing

CHIROMANCY

see Palmistry

CHIROPRACTIC

Upledger, John & Vredevoogd, Jon. Craniosacral Therapy. (Illus.). 381p. 1983. 39.95 (ISBN 0-939616-01-7). Eastland.

CHIROPTERA

see Bats

CHIROTHERAPY

see Massage

CHIVALRY

see also Civilization, Medieval; Courtly Love; Feudalism; Heraldry; Tournaments

Funcken, Liliane & Funcken, Fred. Arms & Uniforms: The Age of Chivalry, 3 vols. 112p. 1983. 17.95 set (ISBN 0-686-84587-0). Vol. I (ISBN 0-13-046284-5). Vol. II (ISBN 0-13-046318-3). Vol. III (ISBN 0-13-046334-5). pap. 8.95 set (ISBN 0-686-84588-9). Vol. I (ISBN 0-13-046276-4). Vol. II (ISBN 0-13-046292-6). Vol. III (ISBN 0-13-046326-4). P-H.

CHIVALRY-ROMANCES

see Romances

CHLAMYDOPHORIDAE

see Armadillos

CHLOROPLASTS

Edelman, M. & Hallick, R. B., eds. Methods in Chloroplast Molecular Biology. 1152p. 1982. 183.00 (ISBN 0-444-80368-8, Biomedical Pr). Elsevier.

CHOCOLATE

see also Cookery (Chocolate)

Rubinstein, Helge. The Ultimate Chocolate Cake: One Hundred Eleven Other Chocolate Indulgences. (Illus.). 336p. 1983. 14.95 (ISBN 0-312-92851-3). Congdon & Weed.

CHOCTAW INDIANS

see Indians of North America-Eastern States

CHOICE (PSYCHOLOGY)

see also Decision-Making

Estes. Models of Learning, Memory & Choice. 410p. 1982. 29.95 (ISBN 0-03-059266-6). Praeger.

Fuchs, Victor. How We Live. (Illus.). 320p. 1983. 17.50 (ISBN 0-674-41225-7). Harvard U Pr.

Sen, Amartya K. Choice, Welfare & Measurement. 440p. 1983. 37.50x (ISBN 0-262-19214-4). MIT Pr.

CHOICE OF BOOKS

see Bibliography-Best Books; Books and Reading

CHOICE OF COLLEGE

see College, Choice of

CHOICE OF PROFESSION

see Vocational Guidance

CHOIRS (MUSIC)

see also Choral Music

Nardone, Nancy K., ed. Secular Choral Music in Print: 1982 Supplement. (Music-In-Print Ser.). 179p. 1982. lib. bdg. 48.00 (ISBN 0-88478-013-9). Musicdata.

White, J. Perry. Twentieth Century Choral Music: An Annotated Bibliography of Music Suitable for Use by High School Choirs. LC 82-10239. x, 153p. 1982. 17.50 (ISBN 0-8108-1568-0). Scarecrow.

CHOLELITHIASIS

see Calculi, Biliary

CHOLESTEROL, DIETARY
see Low-Cholesterol Diet
CHOMSKSY, NOAM
Noam Chomsky on the Generative Enterprise: A Discussion with Riny Huybregts & Henk van Riemsdijk. 136p. 1982. pap. 18.00x (ISBN 90-70176-70-X). Foris Pubns.
CHOPIN, FRYDERYK FRANCISZEK, 1810-1849
Jonson, G. C. Handbook to Chopin's Works. 278p. 1983. pap. 7.25 (ISBN 0-88072-004-2). Tanager Bks.
Opienski, Henryk, ed. Chopin: Collected Letters. Voynich, E. L., tr. LC 79-163798. 424p. Date not set. Repr. of 1931 ed. price not set. Vienna Hse.
CHORAL MUSIC
Here are entered works on choral music. Collections of choral compositions are entered under Choruses.
see also Choirs (Music); Motet; Part-Songs
Roe, Paul F. Choral Music Education. 2nd ed. (Illus.). 352p. 1983. text ed. 21.95 (ISBN 0-13-133322-4). P-H.
Whitlock, Ruth. Choral Insights. (Orig.). 1982. pap. text ed. 1.45 student bk., 15 p. (ISBN 0-8497-4154-8, V71S); tchr's ed., 31 p. 3.45 (ISBN 0-8497-4153-X, V71T). Kjos.
--Choral Insights: Renaissance Edition. Anderson, Linda A., ed. (Orig.). 1982. pap. text ed. 1.45 student ed., 16 p. (ISBN 0-8497-4155-6, V72S); tchr's ed., 31 p. 3.45 (ISBN 0-8497-4156-4, V72T). Kjos.
Wright, Cynthia. Alphabet Soup. 60p. (Orig.). 1981. pap. text ed. 8.95 (ISBN 0-8497-5900-5). Kjos.
CHORAL MUSIC-BIBLIOGRAPHY
Laster, James, compiled by. Catalogue of Choral Music Arranged in Biblical Order. LC 82-16745. 269p. 1983. 22.50 (ISBN 0-8108-1592-3). Scarecrow.
CHOREOGRAPHY
see also Ballet
Simmonds, Harvey, ed. Choreography by George Balanchine. LC 82-83072. 75.00 (ISBN 0-87130-050-8). Eakins.
CHORUSES
White, J. Perry. Twentieth Century Choral Music: An Annotated Bibliography of Music Suitable for Use by High School Choirs. LC 82-10239. x, 153p. 1982. 17.50 (ISBN 0-8108-1568-0). Scarecrow.
CHRESTOMATHIES
see Readers
CHRIST
see Jesus Christ
CHRISTENING
see Baptism
CHRISTIAN ART AND SYMBOLISM
see also Art and Religion; Bible-Pictures, Illustrations, etc.; Cathedrals; Church Architecture; Church Decoration and Ornament; Emblems; Icons; Illumination of Books and Manuscripts; Mosaics; Symbolism in the Bible; Symbolism of Numbers
also subdivision Art under various subjects, e.g. Jesus Christ-Art
Bettey, J. H. & Taylor, C. W. Sacred & Satiric: Medieval Stone Carving in the West Country: With Illustrations from Churches in Avon, Gloucestershire, Somerset & Wiltshire. 1982. 39.00x (ISBN 0-686-82403-2, Pub. by Redcliffe England). State Mutual Bk.
Cope, Gilbert. Symbolism in the Bible & the Church. 1959. 10.00 (ISBN 0-8022-0300-0). Philos Lib.
Maldonado, Luis & Power, David, eds. Symbol & Art in Worship. (Concilium Ser.: Vol. 132). 128p. (Orig.). 1980. pap. 5.95 (ISBN 0-8164-2274-5). Seabury.
Van Voss, M. Heerma. Agypten, die 21: Dynastie. (Iconography of Relifions Ser.: XVI/9). (Illus.). viii, 18p. 1982. pap. write for info. (ISBN 90-04-06826-0). E J Brill.
The Vatican Collections: The Papacy & Art. 1983. 75.00 (ISBN 0-686-42992-3). Abrams.
Vatican Curators. The Vatican: Spirit & Art of Christian Rome. 1983. 75.00 (ISBN 0-686-42994-X). Abrams.
CHRISTIAN BIOGRAPHY
see also Apostles; Cardinals; Clergy; Fathers of the Church; Missionaries; Monasticism and Religious Orders; Popes; Puritans; Saints; Theologians
Blair, Charles & Sherrill, John. The Man Who Could Do No Wrong. 1982. pap. 3.50 (ISBN 0-8423-4002-5). Tyndale.
BOyer, Orlando. Biografias de Grandes Cristianos: Tomo 1. Carrodeguas, Andy & Marosi, Esteban, eds. Kjellgreen, Shily, tr. 160p. (Span.). 1983. pap. 2.00 (ISBN 0-8297-1342-5). Life Pubs Intl.
--Biografias de Grandes Cristianos: Tomo 2. Carrodeguas, Andy & Marosi, Esteban, eds. Kjellgreen, Shily, tr. 176p. (Span.). 1983. pap. 2.00 (ISBN 0-8297-1343-3). Life Pubs Intl.
Brights, Bill. Manual del Maestro. Carrodeguas, Andy & Marosi, Estenan, eds. 533p. (Span.). 1982. Repr. text ed. 6.25 (ISBN 0-8297-1395-6). Life Pubs Intl.
Cho, Paul Y. Guupos Familiares y el Crecimiento de la I Glesia. Carrodeguas, Andy, ed. Lacy, Susana B., tr. 204p. (Span.). 1982. pap. 2.25 (ISBN 0-8297-1347-6). Life Pubs Intl.
Christopher, Kenneth. Ten Catholics: Lives to Remember. (Nazareth Bks). 120p. 1983. pap. 3.95 (ISBN 0-86683-715-9). Winston Pr.
Delaney, John J. Pocket Dictionary of Saints. LC 82-45479. 528p. 1983. pap. 5.95 (ISBN 0-385-18274-0, Im). Doubleday.
--Saints Are Now: Eight Portraits of Modern Sanctity. LC 82-45866. 224p. 1983. pap. 4.50 (ISBN 0-385-17356-3, Im). Doubleday.
Dyer, Donita. Bright Promise. 176p. 1983. pap. 5.95 (ISBN 0-310-45751-3). Zondervan.
Eareckson, Joni. Joni. Arcangeli, Gianfranco, ed. 203p. (Ital.). 1981. pap. 1.60 (ISBN 0-8297-1022-1). Life Pubs Intl.
Estes, James M. Christian Magistrate & State Church: The Reforming Career of Johannes Brenz. 208p. 1982. 27.50x (ISBN 0-8020-5589-3). U of Toronto Pr.
Fleischer, David & Freedman, David M. Death of an American: The Killing of John Singer. (Illus.). 248p. 1983. 14.95 (ISBN 0-8264-0231-3). Crossroad NY.
Graham, Franklinn & Lockerbie, Jeanette. Bob Pierce: This One Thing I Do. 1983. 9.95 (ISBN 0-8499-0097-2). Word Bks.
Haig, J. A. Headmaster. 1982. 4.95 (ISBN 0-941478-06-8). Paraclete Pr.
Haines, J. Harry. Ten Hands for God. 80p. (Orig.). 1983. pap. 3.50 (ISBN 0-8358-0449-6). Upper Room.
Jaeger, Marietta. The Lost Child. 128p. 1983. pap. 4.95 (ISBN 0-310-45811-0). Zondervan.
Johnson, A. Wetherall. Created for Commitment. Date not set. 9.95 (ISBN 0-8423-0484-3). Tyndale.
Massey, Marilyn C. Christ Unmasked: The Meaning of "The Life of Jesus" in German Politics. LC 82-8547. (Studies in Religion Ser.). xi, 175p. 1982. 23.00x (ISBN 0-8078-1524-1). U of NC Pr.
Mother Teresa. Words to Love By. LC 82-73373. (Illus.). 80p. (Orig.). 1983. pap. 4.95 (ISBN 0-87793-261-1). Ave Maria.
Nason, Michael & Nason, Donna. Robert Schuller: The Inside Story. Date not set. 8.95 (ISBN 0-8499-0300-9). Word Pub.
Petersen, William J. Martin Luther Had a Wife. 1983. pap. 2.95 (ISBN 0-8423-4104-8). Tyndale.
--Timoteo, el Hombre Fiel. Carrodeguas, Andy & Marosi, Esteban, eds. Calderon, Wilfredo, tr. 218p. (Span.). 1982. pap. 2.50 (ISBN 0-8297-1250-X). Life Pubs Intl.
Phillips, Carolyn. Michelle. Date not set. 3.25 (ISBN 0-88113-205-5). Edit Betania.
Riley, Jeannie C. & Buckingham, Jamie. From Harper Valley to the Mountain Top. (Epiphany Bks.). (Illus.). 1983. pap. 2.75 (ISBN 0-345-30481-0). Ballantine.
Roberts, Pattie & Andrews, Sherry. Patti Roberts. 1983. 8.95 (ISBN 0-8499-0346-7). Word Bks.
Rudolph, L. C. Francis Asbury. 240p. (Orig.). 1983. pap. 7.95 (ISBN 0-687-13461-7). Abingdon.
Showers, Ralph. Reach for a Rainbow. 1983. 8.95 (ISBN 0-8499-0342-4). Word Bks.
Taylor, Herbert J. The Herbert J. Taylor Story. 128p. 1983. pap. 3.95 (ISBN 0-87784-836-X). Inter-Varsity.
Van Buskirk, Robert & Bauer, Fred. Tailwind: My Story. 1983. 8.95 (ISBN 0-8499-0341-6). Word Bks.
Van Halsema, Thea. Three Men Came to Heidelberg. (Christian Biography Ser.). 96p. 1982. pap. 3.95 (ISBN 0-8010-9289-2). Baker Bk.
Volio, Maria F. Confesion de un Alma Idolatra. 152p. (Orig.). 1982. pap. 3.25 (ISBN 0-89922-218-8). Edit Caribe.
Whipple, Edwin P. Recollections of Eminent Men with Other Papers. 397p. 1982. Repr. of 1886 ed. lib. bdg. 45.00 (ISBN 0-8495-5840-9). Arden Lib.
White, Mel. Mike Douglas: When the Going Gets Tough. 1982. 9.95 (ISBN 0-8499-0318-1). Word Pub.
Ziglar, Zig. Confessions of a Happy Christian. 199p. 1982. pap. 5.95 (ISBN 0-88289-400-5). Pelican.
CHRISTIAN BIOGRAPHY-JUVENILE LITERATURE
McDowell, Mary. Never Too Late. 2nd ed. LC 82-82811. 160p. 1983. pap. 4.95 (ISBN 0-89081-365-5). Harvest Hse.
Thornton, Andre & Janssen, Al. Triumph Born of Tragedy. LC 82-82812. 176p. (Orig.). 1983. pap. 4.95 (ISBN 0-89081-367-1). Harvest Hse.
Watson, Jean. Watchmaker's Daughter: The Life of Corrie ten Boom for Young People. (Illus.). 160p. (gr. 5-8). 1983. pap. 5.95 (ISBN 0-8007-5116-7, Power Bks). Revell.
CHRISTIAN CIVILIZATION
see Civilization, Christian
CHRISTIAN COMMUNICATION
see Communication (Theology)
CHRISTIAN CONVERTS
see Converts
CHRISTIAN DEVOTIONAL CALENDARS
see Devotional Calendars
CHRISTIAN DEVOTIONAL LITERATURE
see Devotional Literature
CHRISTIAN DOCTRINE
see Theology, Doctrinal
CHRISTIAN DOCTRINE (CATHOLIC CHURCH)
see Catechetics-Catholic Church
CHRISTIAN EDUCATION
Here are entered works dealing with instruction in the Christian religion in schools and private life; Works on the relation of the church to education in general, and works on the history of the part that the church has taken in secular education are entered under Church and education.
see also Bible-Study; Catechetics; Catechisms; Christian Leadership; Church Schools; Theology-Study and Teaching; Week-Day Church Schools
Cherne, J. The Learning Disabled Child in Your Church School. (09). 1983. pap. 3.50 (ISBN 0-570-03883-9). Concordia.
Episcopal Church. Prayer Book Guide to Christian Education. 224p. 1983. pap. 9.95 (ISBN 0-8164-2422-5). Seabury.
Foster, Robert D. The Navigator: Experiences & Teachings of Dawson Trotman. 1983. pap. 3.95 (ISBN 0-89109-495-4). NavPress.
Gangel, Kenneth O. & Benson, Warren S. Christian Education: Its History & Philosophy. 1983. 16.95 (ISBN 0-8024-3561-0). Moody.
Knight, George R. Philosophy & Education: An Introduction in Christian Perspective. (Illus.). xii, 244p. 1980. pap. text ed. 8.95 (ISBN 0-943872-79-0). Andrews Univ Pr.
Lee, Rachel G. Learning Centers for Better Christian Education. 80p. 1982. pap. 7.95 (ISBN 0-8170-0927-2). Judson.
Moore, Mary E. Education for Continuity & Change: A New Model for Christian Religious Education. 224p. (Orig.). 1983. pap. 11.50 (ISBN 0-687-11523-X). Abingdon.
Neville, Gwen K. & Westerhoff, John H., III. Learning Through Liturgy. 189p. 1983. pap. 6.95 (ISBN 0-8164-2423-3). Seabury.
Seymour, Jack L. From Sunday School to Church School: Continuities in Protestant Church Education in the United States, 1860-1929. LC 82-15977. 188p. 1982. lib. bdg. 22.00 (ISBN 0-8191-2726-4); pap. text ed. 10.00 (ISBN 0-8191-2727-2). U Pr of Amer.
Sylwester, R. The Puppet & the Word. LC 12-2966. 1982. pap. 4.95 (ISBN 0-570-03873-1). Concordia.
Weber, Hans-Ruedi. Experiments with Bible Study. LC 82-13398. 336p. 1983. pap. 12.95 (ISBN 0-664-24461-0). Westminster.
CHRISTIAN ETHICS
see also Christian Life; Christianity and Economics; Commandments, Ten; Fear of God; Love (Theology); Pastoral Medicine; Sin; Sins; Social Ethics; Virtue and Virtues
also subdivision Moral and Religious Aspects under specific subjects, e.g. Amusements-Moral and Religious Aspects
Beach, Waldo & Niebuhr, H. Richard, eds. Christian Ethics-Sources of the Living Tradition. 2nd ed. 550p. 1973. text ed. 23.95x (ISBN 0-471-07007-6). Wiley.
Bonino, Jose M. Toward a Christian Political Ethics. LC 82-48541. 144p. 1983. pap. 5.95 (ISBN 0-8006-1697-9, 1-1697). Fortress.
Brill, Earl H. The Christain Moral Vision. (Church's Teaching Ser.: Vol. 6). 254p. 1979. 5.95 (ISBN 0-8164-0423-2); pap. 3.95 (ISBN 0-8164-2219-2). Seabury.
Cecil, Andrew R. The Third Way: Enlightened Capitalism & the Search for a New Social Order. (The Andrew R. Cecil Lectures on Moral Values in a Free Society Ser.: Vol. I). 175p. 1980. 9.95x (ISBN 0-292-78041-9). U of Tex Pr.
Curran, Charles E. Moral Theology: A Continuing Journey. LC 81-23160. xiv, 238p. 1983. pap. text ed. 6.95 (ISBN 0-268-01351-9, 85-13517). U of Notre Dame Pr.
Elizondo, Virgil & Greinacher, Norbert, eds. Church & Peace. (Concilium 1983: Vol. 164). 128p. (Orig.). 1983. pap. 6.95 (ISBN 0-8164-2444-6). Seabury.
Ellison, Marvin M. The Center Cannot Hold: The Search for a Global Economy of Justice. LC 82-23795. 330p. (Orig.). 1983. lib. bdg. 24.75 (ISBN 0-8191-2963-1); pap. text ed. 13.75 (ISBN 0-8191-2964-X). U Pr of Amer.
Gardner, E. Clinton. Christocentrism in Christian Social Ethics: A Depth Study of Eight Modern Protestants. LC 82-21843. 264p. (Orig.). 1983. lib. bdg. 22.50 (ISBN 0-8191-2954-2); pap. text ed. 11.75 (ISBN 0-8191-2955-0). U Pr of Amer.
Hughes, Philip E. Christian Ethics in Secular Society: An Introduction to Christian Ethics. 240p. 1983. 13.95 (ISBN 0-8010-4267-4). Baker Bk.
Laurie, Greg. God's Design for Christian Dating. 2nd ed. LC 82-83836. 96p. (YA) (gr. 10-12). 1983. pap. 1.95 (ISBN 0-89081-373-6). Harvest Hse.
Long, Edward L., Jr. A Survey of Recent Christian Ethics. 1982. 12.95x (ISBN 0-19-503159-8); pap. 7.95x (ISBN 0-19-503160-1). Oxford U Pr.
Mieth, Dietmar & Pohier, Marie, eds. Christian Ethics & Economics. (Concilium Ser. Vol. 140). 128p. (Orig.). 1980. pap. 5.95 (ISBN 0-8164-2282-6). Seabury.
Rossi, Philip. Together Toward Hope: A Journey to Moral Theology. 1983. price not set. U of Notre Dame Pr.
Simmons, Paul D. Birth & Death: Bioethical Decision-Making. LC 82-20160. (Biblical Perspectives on Current Issues). 276p. 1983. pap. price not set (ISBN 0-664-24463-7). Westminster.
Staton, Knofel. Check Your Morality. Underwood, Jon, ed. 194p. (Orig.). 1983. pap. 3.95 (ISBN 0-87239-630-4, 39971). Standard Pub.
Willimon, William H. The Service of God. 240p. 1983. 10.95 (ISBN 0-687-38094-4). Abingdon.
CHRISTIAN EVIDENCES
see Apologetics
CHRISTIAN GIVING
see Stewardship, Christian
CHRISTIAN HYMNS
see Hymns
CHRISTIAN LEADERSHIP
see also Church Officers
Barber, Cyril J. Nehemias, Dinamica de un Lider. Carrodeguas, Andy & Marosi, Esteban, eds. Taracido, Frank, tr. from Eng. Orig. Title: Nehemiah & the Dynamics of Effective Leadership. 174p. (Span.). 1982. pap. 3.00 (ISBN 0-8297-1206-2). Life Pubs Intl.
Hepburn, Daisy. Lead, Follow or Get Out of the Way. 1983. resource manual 2.95 (ISBN 0-8307-0872-3). Regal.
Le Peau, Andrew T. Paths of Leadership. 132p. (Orig.). 1983. pap. 3.95 (ISBN 0-87784-806-8). Inter-Varsity.
CHRISTIAN LEGENDS
see Legends, Christian
CHRISTIAN LIFE
see also Asceticism; Christian Education; Christian Ethics; Conduct of Life; Conversion; Devotional Exercises; Faith; Family-Religious Life; Prayer; Revivals; Sanctification; Spiritual Life; Stewardship, Christian
also subdivision Religious Life under classes of persons and institutions, e.g. Children-Religious Life
Ackland, Donald F. Broadman Comments, July-September, 1983. (Orig.). 1983. pap. 2.35 (ISBN 0-8054-1479-7). Broadman.
Ahrens, Herman C., Jr. Life with Your Parents. 24p. 1983. pap. 1.25 (ISBN 0-8298-0667-9). Pilgrim NY.
Ahrens, Herman, Jr. Feeling Good About Yourself. 24p. (Orig.). 1983. pap. 1.25 (ISBN 0-8298-0644-X). Pilgrim NY.
Allbritton, Cliff. How to Get Married: And Stay That Way. LC 82-71219. (Orig.). 1983. pap. 4.95 (ISBN 0-8054-5653-8). Broadman.
Anderson, William. Journeying in His Light. 160p. 1982. wire coil 4.25 (ISBN 0-697-01858-X). Wm C Brown.
Arp, Dave & Arp, Claudia. Ten Dates for Mates. 176p. 1983. pap. 6.95 (ISBN 0-8407-5845-6). Nelson.
Arts, Herwig. With Your Whole Soul: On the Christian Experience of God. LC 82-61419. 192p. 1983. pap. 7.95 (ISBN 0-8091-2517-X). Paulist Pr.
Augsburger, David. From Here to Maturity. 1982. pap. 2.50 (ISBN 0-8423-0938-1). Tyndale.
Baer, Louis S. Better Health with Fewer Pills. LC 82-8394. 132p. 1982. pap. 5.95 (ISBN 0-664-24425-4). Westminster.
Balch, Dianne. All Joy. 175p. 1982. pap. 4.95 (ISBN 0-86605-098-1). Here's Life.
Baur, Francis. Life in Abundance: A Contemporary Spirituality. 240p. 1983. pap. 7.95 (ISBN 0-8091-2507-2). Paulist Pr.
Biegert, John E. Mirando Hacia Arriba en Medio de la Enfermedad. 24p. (Orig., Span.). 1983. pap. 1.25 (ISBN 0-8298-0663-6). Pilgrim NY.
Billheimer, Paul E. Destined for the Cross. 1982. pap. 3.95 (ISBN 0-8423-0604-8). Tyndale.
Bisagno, John R. Life Without Compromise. LC 81-71253. 1983. 3.25 (ISBN 0-8054-1503-3). Broadman.
Bliitchington, W. Peter. Sex Roles & the Christian Family. 1983. pap. 5.95 (ISBN 0-8423-5896-X); wkbk. 2.95 (ISBN 0-8423-5897-8). Tyndale.
Blitchington, Peter & Cruise, Robert J. Understanding Your Temperament: A Self-Analysis with a Christian Viewpoint. 38p. (Orig.). 1979. pap. 2.95 (ISBN 0-943872-67-7). Andrews Univ Pr.
Boa, Kenneth & Moody, Larry. I'm Glad You Asked. 1982. pap. 5.95 (ISBN 0-88207-354-0). Victor Bks.
Botterweck, C. Michael. A Test of Faith: Challenges of Modern Day Christians. 304p. (Orig.). 1983. pap. 8.95 (ISBN 0-686-37684-6). Gregory Pub.
Bradley, Gerard T. Face the Light. 1982. 8.95 (ISBN 0-533-05448-6). Vantage.
Broadus, Loren. How to Stop Procrastinating & Start Living. LC 82-72641. 128p. 1983. pap. 4.95 (ISBN 0-8066-1947-3, 10-3178). Augsburg.
Brown, Stephen. If God Is In Charge. 180p. 1983. pap. 4.95 (ISBN 0-8407-5844-8). Nelson.
Bruster, Bill G. & Dale, Robert D. How to Encourage Others. LC 82-70868. (Orig.). 1983. pap. 6.95 (ISBN 0-8054-2247-1). Broadman.
Bucheli, Fausto & Maxson, Robin. Hostage. 208p. (Orig.). 1982. pap. 6.95 (ISBN 0-310-45631-2). Zondervan.
Bunyan, John. Young Christian's Pilgrimage. Rev. ed. Wright, Christopher, ed. 1982. pap. 4.95 (ISBN 0-88270-534-2). Bridge Pub.
Burns, Jim. Putting God First. (Illus.). 64p. (gr. 7-10). 1983. wkbk. 3.95 (ISBN 0-89081-366-3). Harvest Hse.
Campbell, Alexander. Heroes Then, Heroes Now. (Illus.). 89p. (Orig.). 1981. pap. 12.95 (ISBN 0-940754-08-8). Ed Ministries.
--Live with Moses. 90p. (Orig.). 1982. pap. 12.95 (ISBN 0-940754-13-4). Ed Ministries.

--Stories of Jesus, Stories of Now. 80p. (Orig.). (gr. 1-6). 1980. pap. 12.95 (ISBN 0-940754-04-5). Ed Ministries.
Campbell, R. K. Essentials of the Christian Life. 46p. pap. 0.40 (ISBN 0-88172-008-9). Believers Bkshelf.
Caraman, Phillip, ed. Saints & Ourselves: A Selection of Saints Lives. 226p. 1982. pap. 6.95 (ISBN 0-89283-123-5). Servant.
Carroll, Anne Kristin. Together Forever: For Healthy Marriages, or for Strained, or Broken Ones. 256p. (Orig.). 1982. pap. 7.95 (ISBN 0-310-45021-7). Zondervan.
Cavnar, Rebecca. Winning at Losing: A Complete Program for Losing Weight & Keeping it off. (Illus.). 150p. 1983. pap. 4.95 (ISBN 0-686-82582-9). Servant.
Chambers, Oswald. Daily Thought for Disciples. 256p. 1983. pap. 5.95 (ISBN 0-310-22401-2). Zondervan.
Cole, C. Donald. Christian Perspectives on Controversial Issues. 128p. (Orig.). 1983. pap. 2.95 (ISBN 0-686-82149-1). Moody.
Collier, Philip E. It Seems to Me. 1982. 3.95 (ISBN 0-86544-019-0). Salvation Army.
Collins, Charlotte. Not Healed? LC 82-73707. 1983. pap. text ed. 2.50 (ISBN 0-932050-15-8). New Puritan.
Collins, Gary R. Beyond Easy Believism. 1982. 8.95 (ISBN 0-8499-0332-7). Word Pub.
Cornwall, Judson. La Fe No Fingida. Carrodeguas, Andy & Marosi, Esteban, eds. Oyola, Eliezar, tr. from Eng. Orig. Title: Unfeigned Faith. 201p. (Span.). 1982. pap. 2.25 (ISBN 0-8297-1174-0). Life Pubs Intl.
Corwith, Bonnie. Transitions of a Purple Rabbit. 1983. 7.95 (ISBN 0-533-05463-X). Vantage.
Cox, Edward F. Twelve for Twelve. 64p. 1982. pap. 3.50 (ISBN 0-8341-0787-2). Beacon Hill.
Crabb, Lawrence J., Jr. The Marriage Builder: A Blueprint for Couples & Counselors. 176p. 1982. 8.95 (ISBN 0-310-22580-9). Zondervan.
Culliton, Joseph. Non-Violence-Central to Christian Spirituality: Perspectives from Scriptures to the Present. LC 82-7964. (Toronto Studies in Theology: Vol. 8). 312p. 1982. 39.95x (ISBN 0-88946-964-4). E Mellen.
Culton, Martha. This is That. (Illus.). 1983. 6.95 (ISBN 0-533-05647-0). Vantage.
Darey-Bembe, Francoise & Bembe, John P. Day by Day with God. 1982. 4.95 (ISBN 0-8215-9908-9). Sadlier.
Davis, Earl C. Somebody Cares. LC 81-71255. 1983. 6.95 (ISBN 0-8054-5211-7). Broadman.
Day, N. R. Your Faith Is Growing! 51p. (Orig.). 1981. pap. 5.45 (ISBN 0-940754-10-X). Ed Ministries.
Day, N. Raymond. From Palm Sunday to Easter. 45p. (Orig.). 1979. pap. 5.45 (ISBN 0-940754-01-0). Ed Ministries.
Deal, William S. What Every Young Christian Should Know. 1982. write for info. Crusade Pubs.
DeMarco, Donald. The Anesthetic Society. 182p. (Orig.). 1982. pap. 5.95 (ISBN 0-931888-09-3). Christendom Pubns.
Dowsett, Dick. God, That's Not Fair. 1982. pap. 2.95 (ISBN 0-85363-148-4). OMF Bks.
Drakeford, John W. The Awesome Power of the Listening Heart. 192p. 1982. pap. 5.95 (ISBN 0-310-70261-5). Zondervan.
Duckworth, Robin. This is the Word of the Lord: Year C. The Year of Luke. 180p. (Orig.). 1982. pap. 9.95 (ISBN 0-19-826666-9). Oxford U Pr.
Dunning, H. Ray. Fruit of the Spirit. 1982. pap. 2.95 (ISBN 0-8341-0806-2). Beacon Hill.
Duquoc, Christian & Floristan, Casiano, eds. Christian Experience. (Concilium Ser.: Vol. 139). 128p. (Orig.). 1980. pap. 5.95 (ISBN 0-8164-2281-8). Seabury.
Eareckson, Joni & Estes, Steve. A Step Further. 192p. 1982. mass market pb 3.95 (ISBN 0-310-23972-9). Zondervan.
Edwards, Gene. Our Mission. (Orig.). 1983. pap. 4.95 (ISBN 0-940232-11-1). Christian Bks.
Edwards, Judson. A Matter of Choice. Date not set. 3.25 (ISBN 0-8054-5204-4). Broadman.
Ellis, Joyce. The Big Split. rev. ed. 128p. 1983. pap. 4.95 (ISBN 0-8024-0190-2). Moody.
Evans, Gary T. & Hayes, Richard E. Equipping God's People. (Church's Teaching Ser.: Introductory). 80p. 1979. pap. 1.25 (ISBN 0-8164-2238-9). Seabury.
Fearon, Mary & Hirstein, Sandra J. Wonder-Filled. 1983. pap. write for info. Wm C Brown.
Ferm, Dean W. Alternative Lifestyles Confront the Church. 144p. 1983. pap. 8.95 (ISBN 0-8164-2394-6). Seabury.
Fischer, Kathleen R. The Inner Rainbow: The Imagination in Christian Life. 160p. 1983. pap. 5.95 (ISBN 0-8091-2498-X). Paulist Pr.
Forbes, Cheryl. The Religion of Power. 176p. 1983. 9.95 (ISBN 0-310-45770-X). Zondervan.
Forliti, John E. Reverence for Life & Family Program. write for info.. Wm C Brown.
Fosdick, Harry E. The Meaning of Service. 224p. 1983. pap. 3.75 (ISBN 0-687-23961-3). Abingdon.
Fulghum, Thomas. Tommy: The Comeback Kid. 1983. text ed. 8.95 (ISBN 0-88207-649-3). Victor Bks.
Gandy, Tilly H. Of Cabbages & Kings. 1983. 6.50 (ISBN 0-8062-2138-0). Carlton.
Grant, Brian W. From Sin to Wholeness. LC 81-16122. 1982. pap. write for info (ISBN 0-664-24399-1). Westminster.
Grant, Dave. The Ultimate Power. 192p. 1983. 9.95 (ISBN 0-8007-1337-0). Revell.
Grant, Wilson W. The Caring Father. LC 82-72990. (Orig.). 1983. pap. 5.95 (ISBN 0-8054-5654-6). Broadman.
Guest Book. (Illus.). 48p. 1983. padded cover 8.50 (ISBN 0-8007-1346-X). Revell.
Hald, Marie M. Jesus Jewels. 112p. 1983. 5.00 (ISBN 0-682-49963-3). Exposition.
Halpin, Marlene. Imagine That! 144p. 1982. pap. 4.50 (ISBN 0-697-01812-1); videotapes avail. Wm C Brown.
Haney, David. El Senor y Sus Laicos. Martinez, Jose Luis, ed. Orig. Title: The Lord & His Laity. 84p. (Span.). Date not set. pap. price not set (ISBN 0-311-09095-8). Casa Bautista.
Harakas, S. S. Toward Transfigured Life. 1983. pap. 9.95 (ISBN 0-937032-28-X). Light&Life Pub Co MN.
Hartley, Fred. One Hundred Percent. 160p. (Orig.). 1983. pap. 5.95 (ISBN 0-8007-5112-4, Power Bks). Revell.
Hathrill, Robert. The Bell Ringer. 1983. 8.95 (ISBN 0-533-05631-4). Vantage.
Hayes, Norvel. God's Boot Camp. 32p. 1983. pap. 1.75 (ISBN 0-686-83913-7). Harrison Hse.
Hendershot, Kathy. Obedience: The Road to Reality. 176p. (Orig.). 1982. pap. 3.00 (ISBN 0-911567-00-3). Christian Mini.
Hickey, Marilyn. Fear Free Faith Filled. 176p. 1982. pap. 3.25 (ISBN 0-89274-259-3). Harrison Hse.
Hollis, Marcia & Hollis, Reginald. The Godswept Heart. 96p. 1983. pap. 5.95 (ISBN 0-8164-2410-1). Seabury.
Holmes, Urban T. & Westerhoff, John H. Christain Believing. (Church's Teaching Ser.: Vol. I). 144p. 1979. 5.95 (ISBN 0-8164-0418-6); pap. 3.95 (ISBN 0-8164-2214-1). Seabury.
Hong, Edna. The Way of the Sacred Tree. LC 82-72643. 192p. 1983. pap. 8.95 (ISBN 0-8066-1949-X, 10-6958). Augsburg.
Hook & Boren. Los Pequenos Eschuchan a Dios. Carrodeguas, Andy & Marosi, Esteban, eds. Powell, David, tr. from Eng. Orig. Title: Little Ones Listen to God. 132p. (Span.). (gr. k-3). 1982. pap. 2.50 (ISBN 0-8297-1331-X). Life Pubs Intl.
Hosmer, Rachel & Jones, Alan. Living in the Spirit. (Church's Teaching Ser.: Vol. 7). 272p. 1979. 5.95 (ISBN 0-8164-0424-0); pap. 3.95 (ISBN 0-8164-2220-6). Seabury.
Hunt, Gladys. Relationships. (Fisherman Bible Studyguides Ser.). 80p. 1983. saddle stitched 2.50 (ISBN 0-87788-721-7). Shaw Pubs.
Jackson, Neta. A New Way to Live. LC 82-83392. 104p. (Orig.). 1982. pap. 4.95 (ISBN 0-8361-3323-4). Herald Pr.
Jess, John D. Reflections for Busy People. 1982. pap. 3.95 (ISBN 0-8423-5399-2). Tyndale.
Jobe, Bobbie C. Striving for Holiness. write for info. (ISBN 0-89137-423-X). Quality Pubns.
Jones, James A. I Never Thought It Would Be This Way. 5.95 (ISBN 0-89137-533-3). Quality Pubns.
Jones, Larry. Practice to Win. Date not set. pap. 3.95 (ISBN 0-8423-4887-5). Tyndale.
Jordan, Jerry M. One More Brown Bag. 53p. 1983. pap. 5.95 (ISBN 0-8298-0645-8). Pilgrim NY.
Karssen, Gien. Getting the Most Out of Being Single. rev. ed. LC 82-62240. 1983. pap. 3.95 (ISBN 0-89109-505-5). NavPress.
Keller, W. Phillip. Lessons from a Sheepdog. 1983. 6.95 (ISBN 0-8499-0335-1). Word Pub.
Kennedy, John. Torch of the Testimony. (Orig.). Date not set. pap. 6.95 (ISBN 0-940232-12-X). Christian Bks.
Killinger, John. The Cup & the Waterfall. LC 82-61421. 1983. pap. 3.95 (ISBN 0-8091-2515-3). Paulist Pr.
Kilpatrick, William K. Psychological Seduction. 228p. 1983. pap. 5.95 (ISBN 0-8407-5843-X). Nelson.
Kinzer, Mark. Taming the Tongue: Why Christians Should Care about What They Say. (Living as a Christian Ser.). 1982. pap. 2.50 (ISBN 0-89283-165-0). Servant.
Klopsch, Louis. Daily Light on the Daily Path. 384p. 1983. 6.95 (ISBN 0-8407-5278-4). Nelson.
Klug, Ron. Growing in Joy: God's Way to Increase Joy in All of Life. LC 82-72637. 128p. 1983. pap. 4.95 (ISBN 0-8066-1943-0, 10-2902). Augsburg.
Landorf, Joyce. Irregular People. 1982. 8.95 (ISBN 0-8499-0291-6). Word Pub.
Landsman, Michael. Doubling your Ability through God. 58p. 1982. pap. 1.95 (ISBN 0-89274-266-6). Harrison Hse.
Lane, Denis. Keeping Body & Soul Together. 1982. pap. 2.75 (ISBN 0-85363-144-1). OMF Bks.
Larsen, Gaylord. Trouble Crossing the Pyrenees. 1983. pap. 6.95 (ISBN 0-8307-0880-4). Regal.
Lawrence, Deborah & Villanueva, Aggie. Chase the Wind. 256p. 1983. pap. 5.95 (ISBN 0-8407-5840-5). Nelson.
Learning to Love. 1982. 3.00 (ISBN 0-89858-040-4). Fill the Gap.
Lee, Betsy. Miracle in the Making. LC 82-72647. 128p. (Orig.). 1983. pap. 4.95 (ISBN 0-8066-1954-6, 10-4451). Augsburg.
L'Engle, Madeleine. A Circle of Quiet. (The Crosswicks Journal Trilogy). 246p. 1977. pap. 6.95 (ISBN 0-8164-2260-5); Three Volume Set. 19.95 (ISBN 0-8164-2617-1). Seabury.
Lester, Andrew D. Coping with Your Anger: A Christian Guide. LC 82-24730. 120p. 1983. pap. 5.95 (ISBN 0-664-24471-8). Westminster.
Lindsey, Hal. Compte a Rebours D'Harmaguedon. Cosson, Annie, ed. Remoussin, Philippe, tr. from Eng. Orig. Title: The 1980's, Countdown to Armageddon. 192p. (Fr.). 1982. pap. 2.25 (ISBN 0-8297-1327-1). Life Pubs Intl.
Lyden, Kathryn C. The Struggle to Become a Butterfly. (Illus.). 87p. (Orig.). 1982. pap. 2.50 spiral bound (ISBN 0-9609152-0-6). K C Lyden.
McCarty, Michele. Becoming. 1983. pap. write for info. (ISBN 0-697-01856-3); program manual avail. (ISBN 0-697-01857-1). Wm C Brown.
McCauley, George. The Unfinished Image. 1983. 10.95 (ISBN 0-8215-9903-8). Sadlier.
McCauley, Michael F. In the Name of the Father. 1983. 12.95 (ISBN 0-88347-147-7). Thomas More.
McFadden, Jim. The Fear Factor: Everyone Has it, You Can Master It. (Living As a Christian Ser.). (Orig.). 1983. pap. write for info. (ISBN 0-89283-159-6). Servant.
Mackes, Shy. The Overcoming Power. LC 82-73708. 1983. pap. text ed. 5.00 (ISBN 0-932050-17-4). New Puritan.
Mackey, James P. The Christian Experience of God As Trinity. 320p. 1983. 17.50 (ISBN 0-8245-0561-1). Crossroad NY.
Mahoney, Ralph. Drawing Closer to God. 60p. 1982. pap. 2.95 (ISBN 0-930756-72-X). Women's Aglow.
Mandrell, Louise & Collins, Ace. The Mandrell Family Album. (Illus.). 168p. 1983. 14.95 (ISBN 0-8407-4109-X). Nelson.
Meister, Charles W. The Year of the Lord: A. D. Eighteen Forty-Four. LC 82-23976. 272p. 1983. lib. bdg. 18.95x (ISBN 0-89950-037-4). McFarland & Co.
Menconi, Jan. The Battle for the Mind. 48p. 1983. study guide 3.95 (ISBN 0-8007-1341-9). Revell.
Miller, Ted, ed. On Meeting Life's Challenges. LC 82-4824. (Christian Reader Ser.). 128p. (Orig.). 1983. pap. 5.72i (ISBN 0-06-061388-2, HarpR). Harper Row.
Monty, Shirlee. May's Boy. (Illus.). 186p. 1983. pap. 4.95 (ISBN 0-8407-5784-0). Nelson.
Muggeridge, Malcolm & Thornhill, Alan. Sentenced to Life: A Parable in Three Acts. 132p. 1983. pap. 3.95 (ISBN 0-8407-5839-1). Nelson.
Nelson, Stanley A., compiled by. A Journey in Becoming. (Orig.). 1983. pap. 4.50 (ISBN 0-8054-6320-8). Broadman.
Ness, Alex W. Pioneering. LC 82-73706. 1983. pap. text ed. 5.00 (ISBN 0-932050-14-X). New Puritan.
Newhouse, Flower A. Here Are Your Answers, Vol. III. Boult, Pamela & Boult, Pamela, eds. 150p. 1983. write for info. (ISBN 0-910378-18-5). Christward.
Niven, Marian. The Doctor of Souls. (The Seekers Trilogy Ser.). 348p. 1977. 10.95 (ISBN 0-8164-0098-9). Seabury.
--The Inheritors. (Seekers Trilogy Ser.). 224p. 1977. 8.95 (ISBN 0-8164-0097-0); The Seekers Trilogy 3 Vol. Set. 27.00 (ISBN 0-8164-0514-X). Seabury.
Ortlund, Raymond C. Be a New Christian All Your Life. 192p. 1983. 6.95 (ISBN 0-8007-5119-1, Power Bks). Revell.
Osborne, Cecil G. The Art of Getting Along With People. 192p. 1982. pap. 3.95 (ISBN 0-310-30612-4). Zondervan.
Our Christian Wedding Guest Book. (Illus.). 48p. 1983. padded cover 8.50 (ISBN 0-8007-1345-1). Revell.
Owens, Virginia S. A Feast of Families. 160p. 1983. 9.95 (ISBN 0-310-45850-1). Zondervan.
Parker, Helen. Light on a Dark Trail. LC 82-71560. 1982. pap. 4.95 (ISBN 0-8054-5430-6). Broadman.
Pegram, Don R. America: Christian or Pagan. 1982. pap. 1.00 (ISBN 0-89265-082-6). Randall Hse.
--Sheep Among Wolves. 1982. pap. 1.00 (ISBN 0-89265-084-2). Randall Hse.
Pocketpac Bks. Promises for the Golden Years. 96p. 1983. pap. 1.95 (ISBN 0-87788-320-3). Shaw Pubs.
Price, Eugenia. No Pat Answers. 144p. 1983. pap. 4.95 (ISBN 0-310-31331-7). Zondervan.
--A Woman's Choice. 192p. 1983. pap. 5.95 (ISBN 0-310-31381-3). Zondervan.
Rader, Rosemary. Breaking Boundaries: Male-Female Friendship in Early Christian Communities. (Theological Inquiries Ser.). 144p. 1983. pap. 6.95 (ISBN 0-8091-2506-4). Paulist Pr.
Rice, Barbara. The Power of a Woman's Love. 160p. 1982. 8.95 (ISBN 0-8007-1342-7). Revell.
Richards, Lawrence O. The Word Parents Handbook. 1983. 8.95 (ISBN 0-8499-0328-9). Word Bks.
Rinehart, Stacy & Rinehart, Paula. Choices: Finding God's Way in Dating, Sex, Singleness & Marriage. LC 82-62071. 1983. pap. 3.95 (ISBN 0-89109-494-6). NavPress.
Roberts, Lois H. Now It Is Time. LC 82-71221. 1983. 5.95 (ISBN 0-8054-7228-2). Broadman.
Rogers, Dale E. Let Us Love. 1982. 7.95 (ISBN 0-8499-0298-3). Word Pub.
Ross, Maggie. Fire of Your Life. LC 82-61420. 128p. 1983. pap. 4.95 (ISBN 0-8091-2513-7). Paulist Pr.
Rossi, Michael. The Wisest Fools. 168p. 1983. 9.95 (ISBN 0-8407-5285-7); pap. 4.95 (ISBN 0-8407-5842-1). Nelson.
Rowlands, Gerald. How to Be Alive in the Spirit. (Aglow Cornerstone Ser.). 38p. 1982. pap. 2.00 (ISBN 0-930756-69-X). Women's Aglow.
Ruyle, Gene. Making a Life: Career Choices & the Life Process. 128p. (Orig.). 1983. pap. price not set (ISBN 0-8164-2408-X). Seabury.
Ryan, Thomas P. Tales of Christian Unity: The Adventures of an Ecumenical Pilgrim. LC 82-60748. 224p. 1983. pap. 8.95 (ISBN 0-8091-2502-1). Paulist Pr.
Sager, Harold G. Rebel for God. 1983. 5.75 (ISBN 0-8062-1868-1). Carlton.
Sanders, Rostelle. When the Working Men Rise & Shine. 1984. 4.95 (ISBN 0-8062-2136-4). Carlton.
Sanford, John A. The Man Who Lost His Shadow. LC 82-62414. 1983. 5.95 (ISBN 0-8091-0337-0). Paulist Pr.
Savelle, Jerry. If Satan Can't Steal Your Joy, He Can't Have Your Goods. 160p. 1983. pap. 2.95 (ISBN 0-686-83912-9). Harrison Hse.
--Living in Divine Prosperity. 256p. 1983. pap. 3.95 (ISBN 0-89274-247-X). Harrison Hse.
--Sowing in Famine. 32p. (Orig.). 1982. pap. 1.50 (ISBN 0-686-83911-0). Harrison Hse.
Sayler, Mary H. Why Are You Home, Dad? (gr. 1-6). 1983. 4.95 (ISBN 0-8054-4276-6). Broadman.
Schaeffer, Edith. Common Sense Christian Living. 272p. 1983. 14.95 (ISBN 0-8407-5280-6). Nelson.
Schmidt, Jerry A. Do You Hear What You're Thinking? 1983. pap. 4.50 (ISBN 0-88207-381-8). Victor Bks.
Schuller, Robert H. Tough Times Never Last, But Tough People Do. (Illus.). 224p. 1983. 12.95 (ISBN 0-8407-5287-3). Nelson.
The Seabury Diary 1983. 144p. 1982. pap. 4.95 (ISBN 0-8164-2378-4). Seabury.
Senn, Frank C. Christian Worship & Its Cultural Setting. LC 82-48587. 160p. 1983. pap. 8.95 (ISBN 0-8006-1700-2, 1-1700). Fortress.
Shaw, Jean W. TV: Friend or Foe? 1983. pap. cancelled (ISBN 0-8054-5652-X). Broadman.
Sheen, Fulton J. On Being Human. LC 81-43373. 400p. 1983. pap. text ed. 5.95 (ISBN 0-385-18469-7, Im). Doubleday.
Simons, George F. How Big Is a Person? LC 82-61423. 72p. 1983. 3.95 (ISBN 0-8091-0336-2). Paulist Pr.
Smith, Charles E. Commitment: The Cement of Love. LC 82-71915. (Orig.). 1983. pap. 4.50 (ISBN 0-8054-5651-1). Broadman.
Smoke, Jim. Every Single Day. 256p. 1983. 6.95 (ISBN 0-8007-5120-5, Power Bks). Revell.
Sproul, R. C. Basic Training: Plain Talk on the Key Truths of the Faith. 176p. (Orig.). 1982. pap. 5.95 (ISBN 0-310-44921-9). Zondervan.
Staton, Knofel. Check Your Homelife. Sparks, Judith A., ed. 176p. (Orig.). 1983. pap. 4.95 (ISBN 0-87239-649-5, 39973). Standard Pub.
--Check Your Life in Christ. Root, Orrin, ed. 160p. (Orig.). 1983. pap. 2.95 (ISBN 0-87239-666-5, 41018). Standard Pub.
--What to Do Till Jesus Comes. LC 81-14594. 112p. 1983. pap. 2.25 (ISBN 0-87239-481-6, 41016). Standard Pub.
Storrer, Carol M. & Hesterman, Vicki. Walking Home. LC 82-72636. 160p. (Orig.). 1983. pap. 6.95 (ISBN 0-8066-1942-2, 10-6922). Augsburg.
Strauss, Richard. Gane la Batalla de Su Mente. Carrodeguas, Andy & Marosi, Esteban, eds. Taracido, Frank, tr. from Eng. Orig. Title: Win the Battle for Your Mind. 167p. (Span.). 1982. pap. 2.00 (ISBN 0-8297-1262-3). Life Pubs Intl.
Stugard, Christine. Living Bread. (Illus.). 200p. (Orig.). 1983. pap. 4.95 (ISBN 0-88028-023-9). Forward Movement.
Sumrall, Lester. My Story to His Glory. 192p. 1983. pap. 4.95 (ISBN 0-8407-5837-5). Nelson.
Sutton, Hilton. The Devil Ain't What He Used to Be. 80p. (Orig.). 1983. pap. 1.95 (ISBN 0-686-83910-2). Harrison Hse.
Sweeting, George. Catch the Spirit of Love. 120p. 1983. pap. 3.95 (ISBN 0-88207-108-4). Victor Bks.
Swindoll, Charles R. Starting Over: Fresh Hope for the Road Ahead. LC 82-24636. 1983. pap. 4.95 (ISBN 0-88070-015-7). Multnomah.
Tengbom, M. Help for Families of the Terminally Ill. (Trauma Bks.: Ser. 2). 1983. pap. 2.50 ea. (ISBN 0-570-08256-0); Set. pap. 9.15. Concordia.
The Three D Cookbook. 1982. 9.95 (ISBN 0-941478-01-7). Paraclete Pr.
Timmons, Tim. Maximum Marriage. rev. & updated ed. 160p. pap. 5.95 (ISBN 0-8007-5106-X, Power Bks). Revell.
To Move in Faith. (Youth Elect Ser.). 32p. (Orig.). 1983. pap. 2.75 (ISBN 0-8298-0673-3). Pilgrim NY.
Tully, Mary Jo. Blessed Be. 96p. 1982. pap. 3.50 (ISBN 0-697-01822-9). Wm C Brown.
--Church: A Faith Filled - People. 96p. 1982. pap. 3.50 (ISBN 0-697-01823-7). Wm C Brown.
Vanderford, Jennifer. Joy Cometh in the Morning. LC 82-83503. (Illus.). 160p. 1983. pap. 4.95 (ISBN 0-89081-364-7). Harvest Hse.
Van Impe, Rexella. Satisfied. 160p. 1983. pap. 4.95 (ISBN 0-8407-5841-3). Nelson.
Van Zeller, Hubert. The Trodden Road. 173p. 1982. 4.00 (ISBN 0-8198-7326-8, SP0773); pap. 3.00 (ISBN 0-8198-7327-6). Dghtrs St Paul.

Wallace, John. Control in Conflict. LC 82-72227. (Orig.). 1983. pap. 4.95 (ISBN 0-8054-3001-6). Broadman.

Ward, Elaine. After My House Burned Down. 88p. (Orig.). 1982. pap. 6.95 (ISBN 0-940754-11-8). Ed Ministries.

--Be & Say a Fingerplay. 71p. (Orig.). 1982. pap. 5.95 (ISBN 0-940754-12-6). Ed Ministries.

--Being-in-Creation. 80p. (Orig.). 1983. pap. 9.95 (ISBN 0-940754-14-2). Ed Ministries.

--Feelings Grow Too! 81p. (Orig.). 1981. pap. 9.95 (ISBN 0-940754-07-X). Ed Ministries.

Ward, Frances. Keep the Fruit on the Table. 48p. 1982. pap. 1.95 (ISBN 0-88144-006-X, CPS-006). Christian Pub.

Way, Robert. The Garden of the Beloved. 80p. 1983. pap. 3.95 (ISBN 0-8091-2534-X). Paulist Pr.

Whiston, Lionel A. For Those in Love: Making Your Marriage Last a Lifetime. 128p. 1983. 9.95 (ISBN 0-687-13285-1). Abingdon.

Wicks, Robert J. Christian Introspection: Self-Ministry Through Self-Understanding. 128p. 1983. pap. 7.95 (ISBN 0-8245-0583-2). Crossroad NY.

Wilkerson, Rich. Hold Me While You Let Me Go. LC 82-83838. 196p. (Orig.). 1983. pap. 4.95 (ISBN 0-89081-370-1). Harvest Hse.

Wilkins, Ronald J. Christian Living: The Challenge of Response. 72p. 1978. pap. 3.25 (ISBN 0-697-01686-2); tchrs. manual 3.75 (ISBN 0-697-01689-7); tests 9.95 (ISBN 0-686-84110-7). Wm C Brown.

Williams, Pat & Jenkins, Jerry. The Power Within You. LC 82-24825. 196p. 1983. price not set (ISBN 0-664-27008-5, Bridgebooks Publciations). Westminster.

Williams, Rowan. The Truce of God. 128p. (Orig.). 1983. pap. 3.95 (ISBN 0-8298-0660-1). Pilgrim NY.

Willis, John R. A History of Christian Thought, Vol. II. 400p. 1983. 18.00 (ISBN 0-682-49973-0). Exposition.

Wise, Karen. Confessions of a Totaled Woman. 128p. 1983. pap. 3.95 (ISBN 0-8407-5785-9). Nelson.

Wolfe, Fred H. The Divine Pattern. 1983. pap. 5.95 (ISBN 0-8054-5244-3). Broadman.

Woodward, Thomas B. To Celebrate. 144p. (Orig.). 1973. pap. 3.95 (ISBN 0-8164-5705-0). Seabury.

Worthington, Lowell. Forty-Five & Satisfied. write for info. (ISBN 0-89137-313-6). Quality Pubns.

Wright, Norm. Celebration of Marriage. LC 82-83835. (Illus.). 160p. (Orig.). 1983. pap. 4.95 (ISBN 0-89081-327-2). Harvest Hse.

Yohn, Rick. Getting Control of Your Life. 168p. (How to Overcome Temptation.). 1983. pap. 3.95 (ISBN 0-8407-5836-7). Nelson.

Ziglar, Zig. Confessions of a Happy Christian. 192p. 1982. pap. 2.75 (ISBN 0-553-22739-4). Bantam.

CHRISTIAN LIFE–BIOGRAPHY

see Christian Biography

CHRISTIAN LIFE–CATHOLIC AUTHORS

Talafous, Don. The Risk in Believing. LC 82-17250. 160p. 1982. pap. 6.50 (ISBN 0-8146-1280-6). Liturgical Pr.

CHRISTIAN LIFE–LUTHERAN AUTHORS

Juel, Donald H. Living a Biblical Faith. Date not set. price not set. Geneva Divinity.

--Living a Biblical Faith, Vol. 6. LC 82-8652. (Library of Living Faith Ser.). 118p. 1982. pap. 5.95 (ISBN 0-664-24429-7). Westminster.

CHRISTIAN LIFE–STORIES

Von Eschen, Jessie M. Pot of Gold. 1983. 7.95 (ISBN 0-8062-2135-6). Carlton.

CHRISTIAN LIFE–STUDY AND TEACHING

Hartman, Doug & Sutherland, Doug. Guidebook to Discipleship. 2nd ed. LC 76-20398. (Illus.). 176p. 1983. pap. 4.95 (ISBN 0-89081-062-1). Harvest Hse.

Littauer, Florence. Christian Leader's & Speaker's Seminar. 100p. 1983. lab manual 69.95 (ISBN 0-89081-369-8). Harvest Hse.

CHRISTIAN LITERATURE

see also Christianity and Literature; Christianity in Literature; Devotional Literature

Matin, Ralph P. Carmen Christi: Philippians 2: 5-11 in Recent Interpretations & in the Setting of Early Christian Worship. 378p. 1983. pap. 7.95 (ISBN 0-8028-1960-5). Eerdmans.

CHRISTIAN LITERATURE, EARLY

Whittaker, Molly, ed. Tatian: Oratorio ad Graecos & Fragments. (Early Christian Texts). 1982. 27.50x (ISBN 0-19-826809-2). Oxford U Pr.

CHRISTIAN MINISTRY

see Clergy–Office

CHRISTIAN NAMES

see Names, Personal

CHRISTIAN PRIESTHOOD

see Priesthood

CHRISTIAN REFORMED CHURCH

Schaap, James C. CRC Family Portrait: Sketches of Ordinary Christians in a 125-Year-Old Church. 275p. (Orig.). 1982. pap. 4.35 (ISBN 0-933140-60-6). Bd of Pubns CRC.

CHRISTIAN SOCIALISM

see Socialism, Christian

CHRISTIAN SOCIOLOGY

see Sociology, Christian

CHRISTIAN STEWARDSHIP

see Stewardship, Christian

CHRISTIAN SYMBOLISM

see Christian Art and Symbolism

CHRISTIAN THEOLOGIANS

see Theologians

CHRISTIAN YEAR

see Church Year

CHRISTIANITY

see also Catholicity; Church; Civilization, Christian; Ecumenical Movement; God; Homosexuality and Christianity; Jesus Christ; Jews; Miracles; Missions; Protestantism; Reformation; Socialism, Christian; Sociology, Christian; Theology; Women in Christianity also headings beginning with the word Christian and Church; and names of Christian churches and sects, e.g. Catholic Church, Lutheran Church, Huguenots

Bacon, Banjamin W. Non-Resistance: Christian or Pagan. 1918. pap. text ed. 19.50x (ISBN 0-686-83649-9). Elliots Bks.

Bacon, Benjamin W. Christianity, Old & New. 1914. text ed. 24.50x (ISBN 0-686-83503-4). Elliots Bks.

Brown, Leslie. The Indian Christians of St. Thomas: An Account of the Ancient Syrian Church of Malabar. LC 81-21766. (Illus.). 330p. 1982. 34.50 (ISBN 0-521-21258-8). Cambridge U Pr.

Brown, Marvin L., Jr. The Wisdom of Christendom. 131p. 1982. pap. 5.95. Edenwood Hse.

Butt, Howard & Wright, Elliott. At the Edge of Hope: Christain Laity in Paradox. 223p. 1979. 3.00 (ISBN 0-8164-0414-3); pap. 1.00 (ISBN 0-8164-2614-7). Seabury.

Carmody, Denise L. & Carmody, John T. Christianity: An Introduction. 288p. 1982. pap. text ed. 11.95x (ISBN 0-534-01181-0). Wadsworth Pub.

Carmody, John. The Heart of the Christian Matter: An Ecumenical Approach. 304p. (Orig.). 1983. pap. 11.95 (ISBN 0-687-16765-5). Abingdon.

Clarke, William N. Immortality. 1920. text ed. 24.50x (ISBN 0-686-83578-6). Elliots Bks.

Coleman, William. Une Douzaine de Chretiens Audacieux. Cosson, Annie, ed. Martin, Marie T., tr. from Eng. 160p. (Fr.). 1983. pap. 2.00 (ISBN 0-8297-1240-2). Life Pubs Intl.

De Young, Garry. The Meaning of Christianity. 96p. 1982. text ed. 9.95x ten or more bks. (ISBN 0-686-81748-6); pap. 7.95x (ISBN 0-686-81749-4); tchrs' ed. 7.95 (ISBN 0-686-81750-8). De Young Pr.

Dwyer, John C. Son of Man & Son of God: A New Language for Faith. 160p. 1983. pap. 7.95 (ISBN 0-8091-2505-6). Paulist Pr.

Frank, S. L. Go with Us. 1946. text ed. 29.50x (ISBN 0-686-83560-3). Elliots Bks.

Gogan, Brian. The Commom Corps of Christendom: Ecclesiological Themes in the Writing of Sir Thomas More. (Studies in the History of Christian Thought Ser.: Vol. 26). xii, 404p. 1982. write for info. (ISBN 90-04-06508-3). E J Brill.

Grider, J. Kenneth. Born Again & Growing. 118p. 1982. pap. 3.50 (ISBN 0-8341-0758-9). Beacon Hill.

Hohlt, David T. Heaven Can't Wait: We've Seen Too Much of Hell. 1983. 8.95 (ISBN 0-533-05599-7). Vantage.

Joy, Donald M., ed. Moral Development Foundations: Judeo-Christian Alternatives to Piaget-Kohlberg. 240p. (Orig.). 1983. pap. 12.95 (ISBN 0-687-27177-0). Abingdon.

Kyker, Rex, compiled by. I Am Born Again. (Undenominational Christianity Ser.: Vol. 2). 94p. (Orig.). 1983. pap. 2.95 (ISBN 0-88027-110-8). Firm Foun Pub.

Oberhammer, Gerhard, ed. Epiphanie des Heils: Zur Heilsgegenwart in Indischer und Christlicher Religion. Arbeitsdokumentation Eines Symposiums. (Publications of the De Nobili Research Library: Vol. 9). 256p. 1982. pap. write for info. (ISBN 90-04-06881-3). E J Brill.

Theodore Thornton Munger: New England Minister. 1913. text ed. 65.00x (ISBN 0-686-83814-9). Elliots Bks.

Torrey, Charles G. Apocalypse of John. 1958. text ed. 29.50x (ISBN 0-686-83474-7). Elliots Bks.

Trace, Arthur. Christianity & the Intellectuals. 208p. (Orig.). 1982. 12.95 (ISBN 0-89385-019-5); pap. 4.95 (ISBN 0-89385-018-7). Sugden.

Way of Life. 160p. 1983. 7.95 (ISBN 0-686-82587-X). Todd & Honeywell.

CHRISTIANITY–APOLOGETIC WORKS

see Apologetics

CHRISTIANITY–BIBLIOGRAPHY

Christian Periodical Index: Annual & Quarterlies. 32.00 (ISBN 0-686-31592-8). Assn Chr Libs.

Christian Periodical Index 1976-1978. Cumulated vol. 35.00x (ISBN 0-686-37453-3). Assn Chr Libs.

CHRISTIANITY–BIOGRAPHY

see Christian Biography

CHRISTIANITY–COMMUNICATION

see Communication (Theology)

CHRISTIANITY–EVIDENCES

see Apologetics

CHRISTIANITY–HISTORY

see Church History

CHRISTIANITY–ORIGIN

North, Gary. Unconditional Surrender: God's Program for Victory. 2nd ed. LC 82-84385. 280p. 1983. pap. text ed. 9.95 (ISBN 0-939404-06-0). Geneva Divinity.

CHRISTIANITY–PHILOSOPHY

Altizer, Thomas J. The Descent into Hell: A Study of the Radical Reversal of the Christain Consciousness. 222p. 1979. pap. 6.95 (ISBN 0-8164-1194-8). Seabury.

Blamires, Harry. On Christian Truth. 168p. (Orig.). 1983. pap. 4.95 (ISBN 0-89283-130-8). Servant.

Farrer, Austin. Finite & Infinite: A Philosophical Essay. 312p. (Orig.). 1979. pap. 8.95 (ISBN 0-8164-2001-7). Seabury.

Hunt, Dave. Peace, Prosperity & the Coming Holocaust. LC 82-84069. 224p. 1983. pap. 6.95 (ISBN 0-89081-331-0). Harvest Hse.

Kierkegaard, Soren. Fear & Trembling & Repetition, 2 vols. in 1. Hong, Howard V. & Hong, Edna H., eds. Hong, Howard V. & Hong, Edna H., trs. LC 82-9006. (Kierkegaard's Writings Ser.: No. VI). 432p. 1983. 32.50x (ISBN 0-691-07237-X); pap. 6.95 (ISBN 0-691-02026-4). Princeton U Pr.

Ouweneel, W. J. What Is the Christian's Hope? 53p. pap. 2.45 (ISBN 0-88172-116-6). Believers Bkshelf.

Schaff, Philip. The Creeds of Christendom, 3 vols. 1983. price not set (ISBN 0-8010-8232-3). Baker Bk.

Smedes, Lewis B. Union with Christ: A Biblical View of the New Life in Jesus Christ. rev. ed. Orig. Title: All Things Made New. 208p. 1983. pap. 4.95 (ISBN 0-8028-1963-X). Eerdmans.

CHRISTIANITY–PSYCHOLOGY

Handford, Elizabeth R. Woman in Despair: A Christian Guide to Self-Repair. 132p. 1983. 9.95 (ISBN 0-13-961797-3); pap. 4.95 (ISBN 0-13-961789-2). P-H.

Hurding, Roger F. Christian Care & Counseling: A Practical Guide. (Illus.). 128p. (Orig.). 1983. pap. 4.95 (ISBN 0-8192-1321-7). Morehouse.

Koteskey, Ronald L. General Psychology for Christian Counselors. 308p. (Orig.). 1983. pap. 10.95 (ISBN 0-687-14044-7). Abingdon.

Rollins, Wayne G. Jung & The Bible. LC 82-48091. 156p. 1983. pap. 9.50 (ISBN 0-8042-1117-5). John Knox.

CHRISTIANITY–RENEWAL

see Church Renewal

CHRISTIANITY–17TH CENTURY

Wirt, Sherwood. Spiritual Disciplines: Devotional Writings from the Great Christians Leaders of the Seventheenth Century. 180p. 1983. pap. 7.95 (ISBN 0-89107-277-2, Crossway Bks). Good News.

CHRISTIANITY–20TH CENTURY

Bussell, Harold L. Unholy Devotion: Why Cults Lure Christians. 160p. 1983. pap. 4.95 (ISBN 0-310-37251-8). Zondervan.

CHRISTIANITY AND COMMUNISM

see Communism and Christianity

CHRISTIANITY AND CULTURE

Bussell, Harold L. Unholy Devotion: Why Cults Lure Christians. 160p. 1983. pap. 4.95 (ISBN 0-310-37251-8). Zondervan.

CHRISTIANITY AND ECONOMICS

see also Church and Labor; Communism and Christianity; Socialism, Christian; Sociology, Christian; Stewardship, Christian

Ellison, Marvin M. The Center Cannot Hold: The Search for a Global Economy of Justice. LC 82-23795. 330p. (Orig.). 1983. lib. bdg. 24.75 (ISBN 0-8191-2963-1); pap. text ed. 13.75 (ISBN 0-8191-2964-X). U Pr of Amer.

Vogt, Virgil. Treasure in Heaven: The Biblical Teaching about Money, Finances, & Possessions. (Orig.). 1983. pap. write for info. (ISBN 0-89283-114-6). Servant.

CHRISTIANITY AND LAW

see Religion and Law

CHRISTIANITY AND LITERATURE

see also Christian Literature; Christianity in Literature

Sinfield, Alan. Literature in Protestant England 1560-1660. LC 82-18408. 168p. 1983. text ed. 23.50x (ISBN 0-389-20341-6). B&N Imports.

CHRISTIANITY AND MEDICINE

see Medicine and Religion

CHRISTIANITY AND OTHER RELIGIONS

see also Paganism

Camps, Arnulf. Partners in Dialogue: Christianity & Other World Religions. Drury, John, tr. from Dutch. LC 82-18798. 272p. (Orig.). 1983. pap. 10.95 (ISBN 0-88344-378-3). Orbis Bks.

Griffiths, Bede. The Cosmic Revelation. 128p. 1983. pap. 6.95 (ISBN 0-87243-119-3). Templegate.

Marks, Stanley J. The Two Christs; Or, the Decline & Fall of Christianity. 1983. pap. 14.95 (ISBN 0-686-38796-1). Bur Intl Aff.

Oxtoby, Willard G. The Meaning of Other Faiths, Vol. 10. Mulder, John C., ed. LC 83-1090. (Library of Living Faith). 120p. (Orig.). 1983. pap. price not set (ISBN 0-664-24443-2). Westminster.

CHRISTIANITY AND OTHER RELIGIONS–ISLAM

Goldsmith, Martin. Islam & Christian Witness. 160p. 1983. pap. 4.95 (ISBN 0-87784-809-2). Inter-Varsity.

CHRISTIANITY AND OTHER RELIGIONS–JUDAISM

see also Missions to Jews

Davies, W. D. Jewish & Pauline Studies. LC 82-48620. 432p. 1983. text ed. 29.95 (ISBN 0-8006-0694-9). Fortress.

Friedman, Jerome. The Most Ancient Testimony: Sixteenth-Century Christian-Hebraica in the Age of Renaissance Nostalgia. LC 82-18830. x, 279p. 1983. text ed. 24.95 (ISBN 0-8214-0700-7, 82-84697). Ohio U Pr.

Rosen, Moishe. Y'shua. 128p. (Orig.). 1983. pap. 2.95 (ISBN 0-8024-9842-6). Moody.

Wyschogrod, Michael. The Body of Faith: The Corporeal Election of Israel. 320p. (Orig.). 1983. pap. price not set (ISBN 0-8164-2479-9). Seabury.

CHRISTIANITY AND PHILOSOPHY

see Philosophy and Religion

CHRISTIANITY AND POLITICS

Bonino, Jose M. Toward a Christian Political Ethics. LC 82-48541. 144p. 1983. pap. 5.95 (ISBN 0-8006-1697-9, 1-1697). Fortress.

CHRISTIANITY AND SCIENCE

see Religion and Science

CHRISTIANITY AND THE WORLD

see Church and the World

CHRISTIANITY AND WAR

see War and Religion

CHRISTIANITY IN (AFRICA, ASIA, ETC.)

see Christians in (Africa, Asia, etc.)

CHRISTIANITY IN LITERATURE

Chernaik, Warren L. The Poet's Time: Politics & Religion in the Work of Andrew Marvell. LC 82-4395. 250p. Date not set. 37.50 (ISBN 0-521-24773-X). Cambridge U Pr.

Flieger, Velyn. Splintered Light: Logos & Languages in Tolkien's World. 144p. 1983. pap. 6.95 (ISBN 0-8028-1955-9). Eerdmans.

CHRISTIANS IN CHINA

Brown, G. Thompson. Christianity in the People's Republic of China. LC 82-49018. 240p. 1983. pap. 6.95 (ISBN 0-8042-1484-0). John Knox.

Wing-hung Lam. Chinese Theology in Construction. LC 81-15483. 320p. 1983. pap. 11.95x (ISBN 0-87808-180-1). William Carey Lib.

CHRISTIE, AGATHA (MILLER), 1891-1976

Osborne, Charles. The Life & Crimes of Agatha Cristie. (Rainbow Bks.). (Illus.). 256p. 1983. 17.95 (ISBN 0-03-062784-2). HR&W.

CHRISTMAS

see also Christmas Decorations

Bacher, June M. Great Gifts of Christmas Joy. 96p. 1983. pap. 4.95 (ISBN 0-8054-5707-0). Broadman.

A Christmas Together-John Denver & the Muppets. 5.95 (ISBN 0-89524-073-4). Cherry Lane.

Favish, Melody. Christmas in Scandinavia. (Illus.). 160p. 1982. write for info. Trollpost.

Ingersoll, Robert G. A Christmas Sermon. 30p. pap. 3.00 (ISBN 0-686-83986-2). Am Atheist.

McCullough, Bonnie & Cooper, Bev. Seventy-Six Ways to Get Organized for Christmas & Make it Special, Too. (Illus.). 96p. 1982. pap. 3.95 (ISBN 0-312-71327-4); pap. 39.50 ppk. of 10. St Martin.

Peterkin, Julia. A Plantation Christmas. LC 34-41450. 1972. 6.95 (ISBN 0-910220-41-7). Berg.

Sparks, Judy, ed. Christmas Programs for the Church. (No. 16). 64p. 1983. pap. 2.95 (ISBN 0-87239-614-2). Standard Pub.

--Standard Christmas Program Book, No. 44. 48p. 1983. pap. 1.95 (ISBN 0-87239-621-5). Standard Pub.

CHRISTMAS–BIBLIOGRAPHY

Reader's Digest Editors. The Book of Christmas. LC 73-84158. (Illus.). 304p. 1973. 14.98 (ISBN 0-89577-013-X). RD Assn.

Samuelson, Sue. Christmas: An Annotated Bibliography of Analytical Scholarship. Dundes, Alan, ed. LC 82-48083. (Garland Folklore Bibliographies Ser.). 200p. 1982. lib. bdg. 25.00 (ISBN 0-8240-9263-5). Garland Pub.

CHRISTMAS–DRAMA

see Christmas Plays

CHRISTMAS–JUVENILE LITERATURE

Chapman, Jean. The Sugar-Plum Christmas Book. (Teacher Resource Collections Ser.). (Illus.). 190p. 1982. lib. bdg. 17.25 (ISBN 0-516-08952-8). Childrens.

Elson, Diane. A Christmas Book. (Illus.). 104p. (gr. 6 up). 1982. 11.00 (ISBN 0-437-37703-2, Pub. by World's Work). David & Charles.

Herda, D. J. Christmas. (First Bks.). (Illus.). 72p. (gr. 4 up). 1983. PLB 8.90 (ISBN 0-531-04524-2). Watts.

Hunt, Roderick. Oxford Christmas Book for Children. (Illus.). 160p. 1982. 10.95 (ISBN 0-19-278104-9, Pub. by Oxford U Pr Childrens). Merrimack Bk Serv.

Nedobeck, Don. Nedobeck's Twelve Days of Christmas. (Illus.). 32p. (gr. k-6). 1982. 3.25 (ISBN 0-8249-8043-3). Ideals.

CHRISTMAS–POETRY

see also Carols

Herzog, Barbara J. My Night Before Christmas. (Illus.). 16p. (Orig.). (gr. 1-3). 1983. pap. 3.98 (ISBN 0-943194-13-X). Childwrite.

CHRISTMAS–SONGS AND MUSIC

see Christmas Music

CHRISTMAS BOOKS

see Christmas; Christmas Plays; Christmas Stories

CHRISTMAS CARDS

see also Greeting Cards

Menendez, Albert J. Christmas in the White House. (Illus.). 160p. 1983. write for info. (ISBN 0-664-21392-8). Westminster.

CHRISTMAS CAROLS

see Carols

CHRISTMAS COOKERY

Clancy, John. John Clancy's Christmas Cookbook. (Illus.). 1982. 17.50 (ISBN 0-87851-207-1). Hearst Bks.

Menendez, Albert J. Christmas in the White House. (Illus.). 160p. 1983. write for info. (ISBN 0-664-21392-8). Westminster.

Voth, Norma J. Festive Breads of Christmas. LC 82-15731. 104p. (Orig.). 1983. pap. 3.25 (ISBN 0-8361-3319-6). Herald Pr.

CHRISTMAS DECORATIONS
see also Christmas Trees
Better Homes & Gardens Books editors, ed. Better Homes & Gardens Christmas Crafts to Make Ahead. (Illus.). 80p. 1983. 5.95 (ISBN 0-696-00885-8). Meredith Corp.
Chilton Staff, ed. McCall's Big Book of Christmas Knit & Crochet. LC 82-70537. 304p. (Orig.). 1982. pap. 12.95 (ISBN 0-8019-7252-3). Chilton.
Sibbett, Ed, Jr. Christmas Cut & Use Stencils. 64p. 1978. pap. 3.25 (ISBN 0-486-23636-6). Dover.
Smereczynska, Anastasia, compiled by. How to Make Christmas Tree Ornaments. Jarymowycz, Mary, tr. from Ukranian. (Illus.). 80p. (Orig.). 1982. 6.00 (ISBN 0-686-38965-4). UNWLA.
Sterbenz, Carol E. & Johnson, Nancy. The Decorated Tree: Recreating Traditional Christmas Ornaments. LC 82-1774. (Illus.). 168p. 1982. 22.50 (ISBN 0-8109-0805-0). Abrams.

CHRISTMAS MUSIC
see also Carols
Roseberry, Eric, ed. Faber Book of Carols & Christmas Songs. Date not set. pap. price not set. Faber & Faber.

CHRISTMAS PLAYS
Schoer, Karl J., compiled by. Christmas Plays From Oberufer. 3rd ed. Harwood, A. C., tr. & intro. by. 64p. 1973. pap. 3.50 (ISBN 0-85440-279-9, Pub. by Steinerbooks). Anthroposophic.
Wyatt, Isabel. A Man, A Maiden, & A Tree: A Christmas Mystery Play. (Illus.). 64p. (Orig.). pap. 2.95 (ISBN 0-88010-056-7, Pub. by Michael Pr. England). Anthroposophic.

CHRISTMAS SERMONS
Hagin, Kenneth E. Must Christmas Suffer? 1982. pap. 1.50 (ISBN 0-89276-404-X). Hagin Ministry.
Haskett, William P. Grandpa Haskett Presents: Original New Christmas Stories for the Young & Young-at-Heart. Haskett, M. R., ed. (Illus.). 20p. (Orig.). 1982. pap. 3.00g (ISBN 0-9609724-0-4). Haskett Spec.

CHRISTMAS STORIES
Fowler, Roe. Christmas Was. 88p. 1982. pap. 6.95 (ISBN 0-686-38093-2). Fig Leaf Pr.
Henry, O. The Gift of the Magi. (Picture Book Studio Ser.). (Illus.). 32p. 1982. 11.95 (ISBN 0-907234-17-8). Neugebauer Pr.
Peterson, Carolyn S. Christmas Story Programs. (Illus.). 1981. 7.00 (ISBN 0-686-38109-2). Moonlight FL.

CHRISTMAS TREES
see also Christmas Decorations
Smereczynska, Anastasia, compiled by. How to Make Christmas Tree Ornaments. Jarymowycz, Mary, tr. from Ukranian. (Illus.). 80p. (Orig.). 1982. 6.00 (ISBN 0-686-38965-4). UNWLA.
Sterbenz, Carol E. & Johnson, Nancy. The Decorated Tree: Recreating Traditional Christmas Ornaments. LC 82-1774. (Illus.). 168p. 1982. 22.50 (ISBN 0-8109-0805-0). Abrams.
Triggs, Matt. Christmas Tree Taxation. LC 82-62548. 75p. 1982. pap. 25.00 (ISBN 0-910744-06-8). Media Awards.

CHRISTMAS TREES–JUVENILE LITERATURE
Marbach, Ethel. A Christmas Tree For All Seasons. (Illus.). 12p. (Orig.). 1982. pap. 2.50 (ISBN 0-914676-60-1, Pub. by Envelope Bks). Green Tiger Pr.
Neumeyer, Peter. Fenstermachers's Boulder. (Illus.). 12p. (Orig.). pap. 2.50 (ISBN 0-914676-61-X, Pub. by Envelope Bks). Green Tiger Pr.

CHRISTOLOGY
see Jesus Christ

CHROMATIC ABERRATION (OPTICS)
see Lenses

CHROMATIC VISION
see Color Vision

CHROMATICS
see Color

CHROMATOGRAPHIC ANALYSIS
see also Gas Chromatography; Liquid Chromatography; Thin Layer Chromatography
Cern, J. M., ed. Perturbative Quantum Chromodynamics. (Physics Reports Reprint Book Ser.: Vol. 5). 836p. 1982. 76.75 (ISBN 0-444-86420-2, North Holland). Elsevier.
Fiechter, A., ed. Chromatography. (Advances in Biochemical Engineering Ser.: Vol. 25). (Illus.). 145p. 1983. 25.00 (ISBN 0-387-11829-2). Springer-Verlag.
Giddings. Advances in Chromatography, Vol. 21. 368p. 1983. write for info. (ISBN 0-8247-1679-5). Dekker.
Horvath, Csaba, ed. High-Performance Liquid Chromatography: Advances & Perspectives, Vol. 3. 220p. 1983. price not set (ISBN 0-12-312203-1). Acad Pr.
Huber, J., ed. Proceedings: First Symposium. (Journal of Chromatography Ser.: Vol. 83). 1973. 64.00 (ISBN 0-444-41170-4). Elsevier.
Irwin, William J. Analytical Pyrolysis: A Comprehensive Guide. (Chromatographic Science Ser.: Vol. 22). (Illus.). 600p. 1982. 69.50 (ISBN 0-686-82221-8). Dekker.

CHROMATOGRAPHY, THIN LAYER
see Thin Layer Chromatography

CHROMOPHOTOGRAPHY
see Color Photography
Grafton, Carol B. Victorian Color Vignettes & Illustrations for Artists & Craftsmen: 344 Antique Chromolithographs. (Illus.). 48p. (Orig.). 1983. pap. 4.95 (ISBN 0-486-24477-6). Dover.

CHROMOSOMES
see also Genetics; Human Chromosomes; Linkage (Genetics); Sex Chromosomes; Translocation (Genetics)
Bonne-Tamir, Batsheva & Cohen, Tirza, eds. Human Genetics, Part A: The Unfolding Genome. LC 82-17230. (Progress in Clinical & Biological Research Ser.: Vol. 103A). 531p. 1982. 88.00 (ISBN 0-8451-0168-4). A R Liss.
Epstein, Henry F. & Wolf, Stewart, eds. Genetic Analysis of the Chromosome: Studies of Duchenne Muscular Dystrophy & Related Disorders, Vol. 154. (Advances in Experimental Medicine & Biology). 222p. 1982. 37.50x (ISBN 0-306-41129-6, Plenum Pr). Plenum Pub.
Lee, Sherry, et al. Chromosomes & Genes: An Interracial Anthology. 54p. (Orig.). 1982. pap. 3.50 (ISBN 0-940248-12-3). Guild Pr.
Mueller, D. Sister Chromatid Exchange Test. (Illus.). 120p. 1983. 16.50 (ISBN 0-86577-069-7). Thieme-Stratton.
Sharma, Archana. The Chromosomes. 286p. 1976. 50.00x (ISBN 0-686-84450-5, Pub. by Oxford & I B H India). State Mutual Bk.

CHRONIC DISEASES
Kaslow, Arthur. Freedom from Chronic Disease. 1979. 10.95x (ISBN 0-87477-112-9). Cancer Control Soc.
Kotarba, Joseph A. Chronic Pain. (Sociological Observations Ser.: Vol. 13). 256p. 1982. 25.00 (ISBN 0-8039-1880-1); pap. 12.50 (ISBN 0-8039-1881-X). Sage.
Petty, Thomas L. Prescribing Home Oxygen for COPD. 128p. 9.95 (ISBN 0-86577-078-6). Thieme-Stratton.
University of Wisconsin. Center for Health Sciences. Strategies to Promote Self-Management of Chronic Disease. LC 82-11533. 128p. 1982. pap. 14.00 (ISBN 0-87258-380-5, AHA-070150). Am Hospital.

CHRONOLOGY, HEBREW
see Chronology, Jewish

CHRONOLOGY, JEWISH
Thiele, Edwin. The Mysterious Numbers of the Hebrew Kings. 256p. 1982. 12.95 (ISBN 0-310-36010-2). Zondervan.

CHRONOMETRY, MENTAL
see Time Perception

CHRONOPHOTOGRAPHY
see Cinematography

CHRYSANTHEMUMS
Beijing Bureau of Parks & Gardens, Staff. Chinese Chrysanthemums. (Illus.). 74p. (Orig.). 1981. pap. 13.95 (ISBN 0-8351-0965-8). China Bks.

CHURCH
see also Christianity; Church Work; Ecumenical Movement; Jesus Christ–Mystical Body; Mission of the Church
Althoff, Karl F. The Magna Charta of the Christian Church. Grimm, Werner, tr. from Ger. 19p. 1982. pap. 3.00 (ISBN 0-919924-15-8, Pub. by Steiner Book Centre Canada). Anthroposophic.
Hayford, Jack. The Church on the Way. 200p. 1983. 9.95 (ISBN 0-310-60370-6). Chosen Bks Pub.
Holmes, Urban T. & Westerhoff, John H., III. The Church's Teaching Series, 9 Vols. 1979. Set. 45.45 (ISBN 0-8164-0453-4); Set. pap. 24.95 (ISBN 0-8164-2271-0). Seabury.
Schaeffer, Jerry. Churches Don't Grow on Trees. (Home Mission Graded Ser.). 39p. (gr. 8-12). Date not set. pap. 1.50 (ISBN 0-937170-51-8). Home Mission.
Shenk, Wilbert R. Exploring Church Growth. 336p. 1983. pap. 12.95 (ISBN 0-8028-1962-1). Eerdmans.
Storsz. Understanding My Church. Date not set. text ed. write for info (ISBN 0-87509-325-6); price not set leader's guide. Chr Pubns.
Thompson, Phyllis F. Sodbuster: Five Stories of Church Planters. (Home Mission Graded Ser.). (Illus.). 136p. Date not set. pap. 2.50 (ISBN 0-937170-50-X). Home Mission.
Zikmund, Barbara B. & Mulder, John C. Discovering the Church. LC 82-23870. (Library of Living Faith). 120p. 1983. pap. price not set (ISBN 0-664-24441-6). Westminster.

CHURCH–BIBLICAL TEACHING
Gallaway, Ira. Drifted Astray: Returning the Church to Witness & Ministry. 160p. (Orig.). 1983. pap. 6.95 (ISBN 0-687-11186-2). Abingdon.

CHURCH–JUVENILE LITERATURE
Concept Books Series, No. 4. (gr. 1-4). 1983. Set. pap. 12.95 (ISBN 0-570-08528-4). Concordia.
Matthews, C. S. The Church: Learning about God's People. (Concept Bks.: Ser. 4). 1983. pap. 3.50 (ISBN 0-570-08525-X); Set. pap. 12.95. Concordia.

CHURCH–MISSION
see Mission of the Church

CHURCH–PUBLIC OPINION
Redemptorist Pastoral Publication. Questions People Ask. 80p. 1982. pap. 2.50 (ISBN 0-89243-167-9). Liguori Pubns.

CHURCH–REFORM
see Church Renewal

CHURCH–UNITY
Smyth, Norman & Walker, Williston. Approaches Toward Church Unity. 1919. text ed. 24.50x (ISBN 0-686-37862-8). Elliots Bks.

CHURCH ADMINISTRATION
see Church Management

CHURCH AND EDUCATION IN GREAT BRITAIN
Brothers. Church & School. 196p. 1982. 39.00x (ISBN 0-85323-021-8, Pub. by Liverpool Univ England). State Mutual Bk.

CHURCH AND HOMOSEXUALITY
see Homosexuality and Christianity

CHURCH AND LABOR
see also Christianity and Economics; Church and Social Problems; Work (Theology)
Catherwood, Fred. On the Job: The Christian 9 to 5. 192p. 1983. pap. 5.95 (ISBN 0-310-37261-5). Zondervan.
Day, Dorothy. Loaves & Fishes: The Story of the Catholic Worker Movement. LC 82-48433. (Illus.). 240p. 1983. pap. 6.68i (ISBN 0-06-061771-3, HarpR). Har-Row.

CHURCH AND SLAVERY
see Slavery and the Church

CHURCH AND SOCIAL PROBLEMS
see also Church and Labor; Civilization, Christian; Slavery and the Church; Socialism, Christian; Sociology, Christian
Derr, Thomas S. Barriers to Ecumenism: The Holy See & the World Council on Social Questions. LC 82-18761. 128p. (Orig.). 1983. pap. 7.95 (ISBN 0-88344-031-8). Orbis Bks.
Evans, Robert A. & Evans, Alice F. Human Rights: A Dialogue Between the First & Third Worlds. LC 82-18780. 272p. (Orig.). 1983. pap. 19.95 (ISBN 0-88344-194-2). Orbis Bks.

CHURCH AND SOCIAL PROBLEMS–UNITED STATES
Benestad, J. Brian. The Pursuit of a Just Social Order: Policy Statements of the U. S. Catholic Bishops, 1966-80. LC 82-18326. 220p. (Orig.). 1982. 12.00 (ISBN 0-89633-060-5); pap. 7.00 (ISBN 0-89633-061-3). Ethics & Public Policy.

CHURCH AND SOCIETY
see Church and the World

CHURCH AND STATE
see also Christianity and Politics; Government, Resistance To; Nationalism and Religion; Religion and State; Religious Liberty; Taxation, Exemption From
Constitutional Problems in Church State Relations: A Symposium. LC 75-155825. vi, 84p. 1971. Repr. of 1966 ed. lib. bdg. 19.50 (ISBN 0-306-70131-6). Da Capo.
Heyer, Robert, ed. Nuclear Disarmament: Key Statements of Popes, Bishops, Councils & Churches. 1982. pap. 7.95 (ISBN 0-8091-2456-4). Paulist Pr.

CHURCH AND STATE–CHURCH OF ENGLAND
see Church and State in Great Britain

CHURCH AND STATE IN GREAT BRITAIN
Here are entered works dealing not only with church and state in England, Scotland and Ireland, or in any two of them, but also works dealing with England alone.
see also Puritans
Jones, Norman. Faith by Statute: Parliament & the Settlement of Religion, 1559. (Royal Historical Society Studies in History: No. 32). 246p. 1982. text ed. 33.25x (ISBN 0-391-02689-5, Pub. by Swiftbks England). Humanities.

CHURCH AND STATE IN IRELAND
Titley, E. B. Church, State, & the Control of Schooling in Ireland, 1900-1944. 232p. 1983. 27.50x (ISBN 0-7735-0394-3). McGill-Queens U Pr.

CHURCH AND STATE IN THE UNITED STATES
Miller, Robert T. & Flowers, Ronald B. Toward Benevolent Neutrality: Church, State, & the Supreme Court. rev. ed. 726p. 1982. 25.00 (ISBN 0-918954-28-2). Markham Pr Fund.

CHURCH AND THE WORLD
Here are entered works on the position and responsibilities of the Christian church in secular society.
see also Christianity and Economics; Christianity and Politics; Church and Social Problems; History (Theology); Sociology, Christian
Folk, Jerry. Worldly Christians. LC 82-72652. 144p. 1983. pap. 6.50 (10-7343). Augsburg.
Holmes, Arthur F. Contours of a World View. Henry, Carl F., ed. (Studies in a Christian World View: Vol. 1). 256p. 1983. pap. 8.95 (ISBN 0-8028-1957-5). Eerdmans.
Shelley, Bruce. What is the Church? God's People. 132p. 1983. pap. 4.50 (ISBN 0-88207-105-X). Victor Bks.
Snyder, Howard A. Liberating the Church: The Ecology of Church & Kingdom. 280p. (Orig.). 1982. pap. 6.95 (ISBN 0-87784-385-6); cloth 12.95 (ISBN 0-87784-894-7). Inter-Varsity.
Spong, John S. Into the Whirlwind: The Future of the Church. 192p. 1983. price not set (ISBN 0-8164-0539-5). Seabury.

CHURCH AND WAR
see War and Religion

CHURCH ARCHITECTURE
see also Abbeys; Architecture, Gothic; Cathedrals; Church Decoration and Ornament
Architectural Record Magazine. Religious Buildings. 1980. 36.50 (ISBN 0-07-002342-5). McGraw.

CHURCH ARCHITECTURE–GERMANY
Harries, Karsten. The Bavarian Rococo Church: Between Faith & Aestheticism. LC 82-1116. (Illus.). 304p. 1983. text ed. 37.00x (ISBN 0-300-02720-6). Yale U Pr.

CHURCH ARCHITECTURE–GREAT BRITAIN
English Cathedrals & Churches. 24p. 1982. pap. 30.00x (ISBN 0-7141-0790-5, Pub. by Brit Mus Pubns England). State Mutual Bk.

CHURCH ARCHITECTURE–UNITED STATES
Kennedy, Roger G. American Churches. (Illus.). 296p. 50.00 (ISBN 0-941434-17-6, IBM 8005). Stewart Tabori & Chang.

CHURCH BIOGRAPHY
see Christian Biography

CHURCH BUILDINGS
see Church Architecture; Churches

CHURCH DECORATION AND ORNAMENT
see also Christian Art and Symbolism; Glass Painting and Staining; Mosaics; Mural Painting and Decoration
Snyder, Bernadette M. & Terry, Hazelmai M. Decorations for Forty-Four Parish Celebrations: Enhancing Worship Experiences Tastefully & Simply. (Illus., Orig.). 1982. pap. 9.95 (ISBN 0-89622-167-9). Twenty-Third.

CHURCH DISCIPLINE
see also Asceticism; Church Orders, Ancient; Marriage, Mixed; Penance
also subdivision Discipline under names of religions, religious denominations, etc., e.g. Catholic Church–Discipline
Foster, Richard J. Celebration of Discipline Study Guide. LC 77-20444. 96p. (Orig.). 1983. pap. 3.80i (ISBN 0-06-062833-2, HarpR). Har-Row.

CHURCH FACILITIES
Bowman, Ray, ed. Church Building Sourcebook, No. 2. 264p. 1982. 39.95 (ISBN 0-8341-0759-7). Beacon Hill.

CHURCH FATHERS
see Fathers of the Church

CHURCH HISTORY
This heading is subdivided first according to subject matter, e.g. Church History–Philosophy, and second, chronologically, according to the period of history covered.
see also Abbeys; Church and State; Creeds; Fathers of the Church; Miracles; Missions; Monasticism and Religious Orders; Papacy; Popes; Protestantism; Reformation; Revivals; Sects
also subdivision Church History under names of countries; names of denominations, sects, churches, councils, etc.; headings beginning with the word Christian
The Church of Stiled the Great 1881-1981: The Heart of Little Italy. LC 81-67378. (Illus.). 136p. 1982. 25.00 (ISBN 0-9607014-0-0). Church St Leo.
Dawes, Walter A. Christianity Four Thousand Years Before Jesus. Dawes, Kathleen A., ed. (Illus.). 63p. (Orig.). 1982. pap. 4.95 (ISBN 0-938792-17-2). New Capernaum.
Dekar, Paul R. & Ban, Joseph D., eds. In the Great Tradition. 240p. 1982. 25.00 (ISBN 0-8170-0972-8). Judson.
Drobner, Hubertus R. Grefor von Nyssa: Die drei Tage Zwischen Tod und Auferstehung unseres Hern Jesus Christus. (Philosophia Patrum: Vol. 5). x, 252p. 1982. write for info. (ISBN 90-04-06553-9). E J Brill.
Fulks, Clay. Christianity: A Continuing Calamity. 31p. Date not set. pap. 3.00 (ISBN 0-686-83977-3). Am Atheist.
General Conference Youth Department. Church Heritage: A Course in Church History. pap. 2.50 (ISBN 0-686-82636-1). Review & Herald.
Glisson, Jerry & Taylor, Jack R. The Church in a Storm. (Orig.). 1983. pap. 5.95. Broadman.
Gonzalez, Justo L. La Era de los Dogmas y las Dudas. (Y hasta lo ultimo de la tierra Ser.: Tomo No. 8). (Illus.). 224p. (Orig.). 1983. pap. 4.95 (ISBN 0-89922-171-8). Edit Caribe.
Hawkins, Elza M. From Now to Pentecost: A Mirrored View of Development in Christianity. 260p. (Orig.). 1982. pap. 11.00 (ISBN 971-10-0038-5, Pub. by New Day Philippines). Cellar.
Lawson, LeRoy. The New Testament Church Then & Now Workbook. 48p. 1983. pap. 1.75 (ISBN 0-87239-609-6, 88586). Standard Pub.
Maner, Robert E. Making the Small Church Grow. 101p. 1982. pap. 2.95 (ISBN 0-8341-0741-4). Beacon Hill.
Marks, Stanley J. The Two Christs; Or, the Decline & Fall of Christianity. 1983. pap. 14.95 (ISBN 0-686-38796-]). Bur Intl Aff.
Montgomery, John W. History & Christianity. 128p. pap. 2.95 (ISBN 0-89840-045-7). Heres Life.
Morland, Samuel. History of the Evangelical Churches of the Valleys of Piemont. 1983. 32.00 (ISBN 0-686-42929-X). Church History.
Pannenberg, Wolfhart. The Church. LC 82-23768. 189p. 1983. pap. write for info. (ISBN 0-664-24460-2). Westminster.
Pollet, J. V., ed. Julius Pflug: Correspondance. (Suppl.). (Illus.). vi, 316p. 1982. write for info (ISBN 90-04-06752-3). E J Brill.
Sisemore, John T. Church Growth Through the Sunday School. (Orig.). 1983. pap. 5.95 (ISBN 0-8054-6237-6). Broadman.

Stock, Ursula. Die Bedeutung der Sakramente in Luthers Sermonen von 1519. (Studies in the History of Christian Thought Ser.: Vol. 27). viii, 383p. 1982. write for info. (ISBN 90-04-06536-9). E J Brill.

Walker, Sheila S. The Religious Revolution in the Ivory Coast: The Prophet Harris & the Harrist Church. LC 81-13010. (Studies in Religion). xvii, 206p. 1983. 29.95x (ISBN 0-8078-1503-9). U of NC Pr.

Wantland, William C. Foundations of the Faith. LC 82-61889. 176p. (Orig.). 1983. pap. 6.95 (ISBN 0-8192-1320-9). Morehouse.

Wiersbe, David & Wiersbe, Warren. Making Sense of the Ministry. 128p. (Orig.). 1983. pap. 5.95 (ISBN 0-686-82021-5). Moody.

Wilbur, Ruth E. & Wilbur, C. Keith. Bid Us God Speed: The History of the Edwards Church, Northhampton, Massachusetts 1833-1983. LC 82-22347. (Illus.). 120p. 1983. 12.95 (ISBN 0-914016-93-8). Phoenix Pub.

CHURCH HISTORY–OUTLINES, SYLLABI, ETC.

North, Gary. The Theology of Christian Resistance. LC 82-84286. (Christianity & Civilization Ser.: No. 2). 388p. (Orig.). 1983. pap. 9.95 (ISBN 0-939404-05-2). Geneva Divinity.

CHURCH HISTORY–PRIMITIVE AND EARLY CHURCH, ca. 30-600

see also Apostles; Church Orders, Ancient; Fathers of the Church

Bellini, Enzo, et al. The Church Established, 180-381. Drury, John, ed. & tr. from Ital. (An Illustrated History of the Church). (Illus.). 126p. 16.95 (ISBN 0-03-056824-2). Winston Pr.

Volz, Carl A. Faith & Practice in the Early Church. LC 82-72654. 224p. 1983. pap. 9.95 (ISBN 0-8066-1961-9, 10-2177). Augsburg.

CHURCH HISTORY–MIDDLE AGES, 600-1500

see also Monasticism and Religious Orders–Middle Ages, 600-1500; Papacy; Reformation–Early Movements; Waldenses

Bellini, Enzo. The Middle Ages, 900-1300. Drury, John, ed. & tr. from Ital. (An Illustrated History of the Church). 126p. 16.95 (ISBN 0-03-056828-5). Winston Pr.

Bellini, Enzo, et al. The Church in the Age of Humanism, 1300-1500. Drury, John, ed. & tr. (An Illustrated History of the Church). 126p. 16.95 (ISBN 0-03-056829-3). Winston Pr.

Damian, Peter. Book of Gomorrah: An Eleventh-Century Treaties Against Clerical Homosexual Practices. Payer, Pierre J., tr. 120p. 1982. pap. text ed. 7.50x (ISBN 0-88920-123-4, 40794, Pub. by Wilfred Laurier U Pr Canada). Humanities.

CHURCH HISTORY–REFORMATION, 1517-1648

see Reformation

CHURCH HISTORY–19TH CENTURY

Martin, Roger H. Evangelicals United: Ecumenical Stirrings in Pre-Victorian Britain, 1795-1830. LC 82-10784. (Studies in Evangelicalism: No. 4). 244p. 1983. 17.50 (ISBN 0-8108-1586-9). Scarecrow.

CHURCH HISTORY–20TH CENTURY

Chaney, Charles. Church Planting in America at the End of the Twentieth Century. 128p. 1982. pap. 6.95 (ISBN 0-8423-0279-4). Tyndale.

Hitchcock, James. The New Enthusiasts: And What They Are Doing to the Catholic Church. 168p. 1982. pap. 7.95 (ISBN 0-88347-150-7). Thomas More.

CHURCH LEADERSHIP

see Christian Leadership

CHURCH LIBRARIES

see Libraries, Church

CHURCH MANAGEMENT

Bowen, Van S. A Vestry Member's Guide. rev. ed. 80p. 1983. pap. 3.95 (ISBN 0-8164-2464-0). Seabury.

Williams, George M. Improving Parish Management: Working Smarter, Not Harder. 112p. pap. 9.95 (ISBN 0-89622-176-8). Twenty-Third.

CHURCH MEMBERSHIP

see also Baptism; Church Discipline; Lord's Supper

Schaller, Lyle E. Growing Plans: Strategies to Increase your Church's Membership. 176p. 1983. pap. 6.95 (ISBN 0-687-15962-8). Abingdon.

CHURCH MUSIC

see also Carols; Choirs (Music); Choral Music; Christmas Music; Hymns; Liturgies; Motet; Psalmody

Arnold, Denis. Monteverdi Church Music. LC 81-71298. (BBC Music Guides Ser.). 64p. (Orig.). 1983. pap. 4.95 (ISBN 0-295-95923-1). U of Wash Pr.

Hamill, Paul, ed. The Church Music Handbook 1983-4: Annual Planning Guide for the Music of the Church. 80p. (Orig.). 1983. pap. 5.95 (ISBN 0-8298-0672-5). Pilgrim NY.

CHURCH MUSIC–BIBLIOGRAPHY

Laster, James, compiled by. Catalogue of Choral Music Arranged in Biblical Order. LC 82-16745. 269p. 1983. 22.50 (ISBN 0-8108-1592-3). Scarecrow.

CHURCH OF CHRIST OF LATTER-DAY SAINTS

see Mormons and Mormonism

CHURCH OF ENGLAND

see also Church and State in Great Britain; Marprelate Controversy; Puritans

Smyth, Norman. Story of Church Unity: The Lambeth Conference of Anglican Bishops & the Congregational-Episcopal Approaches. 1923. text ed. 29.50x (ISBN 0-686-83788-6). Elliots Bks.

CHURCH OF ENGLAND–BIOGRAPHY

Smith, Martin L., ed. Benson of Cowley. 153p. 1983. pap. 8.00 (ISBN 0-936384-12-3). Cowley Pubns.

CHURCH OF ENGLAND–BOOK OF COMMON PRAYER

Episcopal Church. Prayer Book Guide to Christian Education. 224p. 1983. pap. 9.95 (ISBN 0-8164-2422-5). Seabury.

CHURCH OF ENGLAND–DOCTRINAL AND CONTROVERSIAL WORKS

McAdoo, Henry R. The Unity of Anglicanism: Catholic & Reformed. 48p. 1983. pap. write for info. (ISBN 0-8192-1324-1). Morehouse.

CHURCH OF ENGLAND–HISTORY

Jagger, Peter J. Clouded Witness: Initiation in the Church of England in the Mid-Victorian Period 1850-1875. (Pittsburgh Theological Monographs New Ser.: No. 1). vii, 221p. (Orig.). 1982. pap. 16.50 (ISBN 0-915138-51-4). Pickwick.

CHURCH OF ENGLAND–LITURGY AND RITUAL

see also Church of England–Book of Common Prayer

Cuming, Geoffrey. A History of Anglican Liturgy. 450p. 1982. 50.00x (ISBN 0-333-30661-9, Pub. by Macmillan England). State Mutual Bk.

CHURCH OF ENGLAND–RELATIONS

McAdoo, Henry R. The Unity of Anglicanism: Catholic & Reformed. 48p. 1983. pap. write for info. (ISBN 0-8192-1324-1). Morehouse.

CHURCH OF THE NEW JERUSALEM

see New Jerusalem Church

CHURCH OFFICERS

see also Church Ushers; Deacons; Installation Service (Church Officers)

Wiebe, Ronald W. & Rowlison, Bruce A. Let's Talk About Church Staff Relationships. 64p. 1983. pap. 3.95 (ISBN 0-938462-12-1). Green Leaf CA.

CHURCH ORDERS, ANCIENT

see also Canon Law

Bailey, Sherwin. Canonical Houses of Wells. 192p. 1982. text ed. 18.75x (ISBN 0-904387-91-7, Pub. by Sutton England). Humanities.

CHURCH ORNAMENT

see Church Decoration and Ornament

CHURCH RECORDS AND REGISTERS

see Registers of Births, Deaths, Marriages, etc.

CHURCH REFORM

see Church Renewal

CHURCH RENEWAL

see also Counter-Reformation; Mission of the Church; Reformation–Early Movements

Haney, David. Renueva Mi Iglesia. Martinez, Jose Luis, ed. Kratzig, Guillermo, tr. Orig. Title: Renew My Church. 104p. (Span.). Date not set. pap. price not set (ISBN 0-311-17025-0). Casa Bautista.

Snyder, Howard A. Liberating the Church: The Ecology of Church & Kingdom. 280p. (Orig.). 1982. pap. 6.95 (ISBN 0-87784-385-6); cloth 12.95 (ISBN 0-87784-894-7). Inter-Varsity.

Suenens, Leon-Joseph. Renewal & the Powers of Darkness. 120p. (Orig.). 1983. pap. 4.95 (ISBN 0-89283-125-1). Servant.

CHURCH SCHOOLS

see also Week-Day Church Schools

also subdivision Education under names of religious denominations, e.g. Lutheran Church–Education

Phillips, Harold R. & Firth, Robert E., eds. Cases in Denominational Administration: A Management Casebook for Decision-Making. vi, 314p. 1978. pap. text ed. 4.95 (ISBN 0-943872-75-8). Andrews Univ Pr.

Twomley, Dale E. Parochiaid & the Courts. (Andrews University Monographs, Studies in Education: Vol. 2). x, 165p. 1979. 3.95 (ISBN 0-943872-51-0). Andrews Univ Pr.

CHURCH STAFF

see Church Officers

CHURCH USHERS

Elford, Homer J. A Guide to Church Ushering. 64p. (Orig.). 1983. pap. 4.50 (ISBN 0-687-16243-2). Abingdon.

CHURCH WORK

see also Christian Leadership; Church and Social Problems; Church Management; Church Officers; Church Ushers; Christian Leadership; City Clergy; City Missions; Evangelistic Work; Pastoral Counseling; Revivals; Sunday-Schools

Bavarel, Michel. New Communities, New Ministries: The Church Resurgent in Africa, Asia, & Latin America. Martin, Francis, tr. from Fr. LC 82-22318. Orig. Title: Chretienes Du Bout Du Monde. 128p. (Orig.). 1983. pap. 5.95 (ISBN 0-88344-337-6). Orbis Bks.

Clasper, Paul D. The Yogi, the Commissar & the Third World Church. 92p. (Orig.). 1982. pap. 5.75 (ISBN 0-686-37580-7, Pub. by New Day Philippines). Cellar.

Dudley, Carl S., ed. Building Effective Ministry: Theory & Practice in the Local Church. LC 82-48411. 256p. 1983. pap. 8.61 (ISBN 0-06-062102-8, HarpR). Har-Row.

Fabella, Virginia & Torres, Sergio, eds. Irruption of the Third World: Challenge to Theology. LC 82-18851. 304p. (Orig.). 1983. pap. 10.95 (ISBN 0-88344-216-7). Orbis Bks.

Haney, David. El Ministerio de Todo Creyente. Martinez, Jose Luis, ed. Kratzig, Guillermo, tr. Orig. Title: The Idea of Laity. 200p. Date not set. pap. price not set (ISBN 0-311-09099-0). Casa Bautista.

Hutchinson, Robert. What One Christian Can Do About Hunger in America. LC 82-18199. xii, 115p. (Orig.). 1982. pap. 5.95 (ISBN 0-8190-0651-3, FC 145). Fides Claretian.

Johnson, Daniel L. Starting Right, Staying Strong: A Guide to Effective Ministry. LC 82-22383. 108p. (Orig.). 1983. pap. 5.95 (ISBN 0-8298-0648-2). Pilgrim NY.

Maness, Bill. Recreation Ministry: A Guide for all Congregations. LC 81-85324. 102p. 1983. pap. 11.95 (ISBN 0-8042-1186-8). John Knox.

Nee, Watchman. The Church & the Work, 3 Vols. Kaung, Stephen, tr. 550p. (Chinese.). 1982. 27.00 (ISBN 0-935008-57-8); pap. text ed. 15.00 (ISBN 0-935008-58-6). Christian Fellow Pubs.

Oduyoye, Modupe. Sons of the Gods & Daughters of Men: An Afro-Asiatic Interpretation of Genesis 1-11. 96p. (Orig.). 1983. pap. price not set (ISBN 0-88344-467-4). Orbis Bks.

Seraydarian, Patricia M. The Church Secretary's Handbook. 159p. 1982. pap. 5.95 (ISBN 0-8423-0281-6). Tyndale.

Sider, Ronald J., ed. Evangelicals & Development: Toward a Theology of Social Change. LC 82-6970. (Contemporary Issues in Social Ethics Ser.). 1982. pap. 6.95 (ISBN 0-664-24445-9). Westminster.

CHURCH WORK–VOCATIONAL GUIDANCE

see Church Work As a Profession

CHURCH WORK AS A PROFESSION

Little, Sara. To Set One's Heart: Belief & Teaching in the Church. LC 82-49020. 160p. 1983. pap. 7.50 (ISBN 0-8042-1442-5). John Knox.

CHURCH WORK WITH ADULTS

see Church Work

CHURCH WORK WITH ALCOHOLICS

Marsh, Jack. You Can Help the Alcoholic: A Christian Plan for Intervention. LC 82-74499. 88p. (Orig.). 1983. pap. 2.95 (ISBN 0-87793-270-0). Ave Maria.

CHURCH WORK WITH CHILDREN

Lang, June & Carl, Angela. Twenty-Six Children's Church Programs: Getting to Know Jesus. (Illus.). 112p. 1983. pap. 6.95 (ISBN 0-87239-608-8, 3378). Standard Pub.

CHURCH WORK WITH FAMILIES

Weekly, James. The Tangerine Flavored Peanut Butter Gang: Your Family Growth Workbook. Meyer, Sheila, ed. LC 82-62574. (Illus.). 145p. (Orig.). 1983. pap. text ed. write for info. (ISBN 0-916260-21-6). Meriwether Pub.

CHURCH YEAR

see also Christmas; Easter; Lent

Hessel, Dieter T., ed. Social Themes of the Christian Year: A Commentary on the Lectionary. 276p. (Orig.). 1983. pap. price not set (ISBN 0-664-24472-6). Westminster.

CHURCHES

see also Cathedrals; Church Architecture; Church Decoration and Ornament; Parishes

also names of individual churches; subdivision Churches under names of cities

Adams, Jennifer A. The Solar Church. Hoffman, Douglas R., ed. 288p. (Orig.). 1982. pap. 9.95 (ISBN 0-8298-0482-X). Pilgrim NY.

CHURCHES–LIBRARIES

see Libraries, Church

CHURCHES–MANAGEMENT

see Church Management

CHURCHES–CANADA

Jacquet, Constant H., Jr. Yearbook of American & Canadian Churches, 1983. 304p. (Orig.). 1983. pap. 17.95 (ISBN 0-687-46638-5). Abingdon.

CHURCHES–GREAT BRITAIN

Kilmister, Anthony, ed. The Good Church Guide. 320p. 1982. 39.00x (ISBN 0-85634-120-7, Pub. by Muller Ltd). State Mutual Bk.

Little, Bryan. Church Treasures in Bristol. 40p. 1982. 25.00x (ISBN 0-905459-12-1, Pub. by Redcliffe England). State Mutual Bk.

--Churches in Bristol. 40p. 1982. 25.00x (ISBN 0-905459-06-7, Pub. by Redcliffe England). State Mutual Bk.

Verey, David. Cotswold Churches. 189p. 1982. pap. text ed. 9.00x (ISBN 0-904387-78-X, 61040, Pub. by Sutton England). Humanities.

CHURCHES–UNITED STATES

Jacquet, Constant H., Jr. Yearbook of American & Canadian Churches, 1983. 304p. (Orig.). 1983. pap. 17.95 (ISBN 0-687-46638-5). Abingdon.

CHURCHILL, RANDOLPH HENRY SPENCER, LORD, 1849-1895

Foster, R. F. Lord Randolph Churchill: A Political Life. (Illus.). 448p. 1983. pap. 15.95 (ISBN 0-19-822756-6). Oxford U Pr.

CHURCHILL, WINSTON LEONARD SPENCER, SIR, 1874-1965

Kersaudy, Francois. Churchill & DeGaulle. LC 81-69154. 480p. 1983. pap. 11.95 (ISBN 0-689-70641-3, 290). Atheneum.

Manchester, William. The Last Lion: Winston Spencer Churchill Visions of Glory, 1874-1932. LC 82-24972. (Illus.). 1983. 25.00i (ISBN 0-316-54503-1). Little.

Neilson, Francis. The Churchill Legend: Winston Churchill as Fraud, Fakir & War-Monger. 1983. lib. bdg. 79.95 (ISBN 0-87700-001-8). Revisionist Pr.

Thompson, Kenneth W. Winston Churchill's World View: Statesmanship & Power. LC 82-4699. 368p. 1983. text ed. 25.00x (ISBN 0-8071-1045-0). La State U Pr.

CHURCHYARDS

see Cemeteries

CHWEE LANGUAGE

see Twi Language

CHWI LANGUAGE

see Twi Language

CIA

see United States–Central Intelligence Agency

CICERO, MARCUS TULLIUS, 106-43 B.C.

Tyrrell, Robert Y., ed. Cicero in His Letters. 1983. 11.50 (ISBN 0-89241-347-6). Caratzas Bros.

CIGARETTE HABIT

see Smoking

CIGARETTE MANUFACTURE AND TRADE

Reuijl, Jan C. On the Determination of Advertising Effectiveness: An Empirical Study of the German Cigarette Market. 1982. lib. bdg. 30.00 (ISBN 0-89838-125-8). Kluwer-Nijhoff.

CILIATA

Elliot, Alfred M. Biology of Tetrahymena. LC 73-12911. 508p. 1973. text ed. 62.00 (ISBN 0-87933-013-9). Hutchinson Ross.

CINCINNATI

Hughes, Jon C. The Tanyard Murder: On the Case with Lafcadio Hearn. LC 82-20280. (Illus.). 138p. (Orig.). 1983. lib. bdg. 19.50 (ISBN 0-8191-2833-3); pap. text ed. 8.25 (ISBN 0-8191-2834-1). U Pr of Amer.

CINCINNATI FOOTBALL CLUB (AMERICAN LEAGUE)

Collett, Ritter. Super Stripes: Paul Brown & the Super Bowl Bengals. LC 82-83268. (Illus.). 224p. 1982. 13.95 (ISBN 0-913428-34-5). Landfall Pr.

CINEMA

see Moving-Pictures

CINEMATOGRAPHY

see also Cinematography, Trick; Moving-Picture Cameras

Almendros, Nestor. A Man with a Camera. Belash, Rachel P., tr. from French. Truffaut, Francois, pref. by. (Illus.). 280p. 1982. 14.50 (ISBN 0-374-20172-2). FS&G.

Beaver, Frank. Dictionary of Film Terms. (Illus.). 320p. 1983. text ed. 15.95 (ISBN 0-07-004216-0, C); pap. text ed. 9.95 (ISBN 0-07-004212-8). McGraw.

Coe, Brian. The History of Movie Photography. (Illus.). 176p. 1982. 19.95 (ISBN 0-904069-38-9). NY Zoetrope.

Skvorecky, Josef. Contemporary Czech Cinematography: Jiri Menzel & the History of the "Closely Watched Trains". (East European Monographs: No. 118). 144p. 1982. 17.50x (ISBN 0-88033-011-2). East Eur Quarterly.

CINEMATOGRAPHY–SPECIAL EFFECTS

see Cinematography, Trick

CINEMATOGRAPHY, TRICK

Clark, Frank P. Special Effects in Motion Pictures. (Illus.). 238p. 1982. pap. text ed. 20.00 (ISBN 0-940690-00-4). Soc Motion Pic & TV Engrs.

CINESIOLOGY

see Kinesiology

CIPHERS

see also Abbreviations; Cryptography; Writing

Beker, Henry & Piper, Fred. Cipher Systems: The Protection of Communications. 350p. 1983. 34.95 (ISBN 0-471-89192-4, Pub. by Wiley-Interscience). Wiley.

CIRCLE–JUVENILE LITERATURE

Hoban, Tana. Round & Round & Round. LC 82-11984. (Illus.). 32p. (gr. k-3). 1983. 9.00 (ISBN 0-688-01813-0); PLB 8.59 (ISBN 0-688-01814-9). Greenwillow.

CIRCUITS, ELECTRIC

see Electric Circuits

CIRCUITS, INTEGRATED

see Integrated Circuits

CIRCULAR FUNCTIONS

see Trigonometrical Functions

CIRCULATION, PULMONARY

see Pulmonary Circulation

CIRCULATORY SYSTEM

see Cardiovascular System

CIRCUS

see also Amusement Parks

Kelley, F. Beverly. It Was Better Than Work. Franzwa, Gregory M., ed. LC 82-24556. xii, 287p. 1983. 14.95 (ISBN 0-935284-25-7). Patrice Pr.

CIRCUS–JUVENILE LITERATURE

Daniel, Becky. I Can Draw a Circus. (ps-3). 1982. 5.95 (ISBN 0-86653-082-7, GA 428). Good Apple.

West, Robin. The Greatest Show On Earth: How to Create Your Own Circus. LC 83-23580. (Illus.). 64p. (gr. k-3). 1983. PLB 8.95 (ISBN 0-87614-212-9). Carolrhoda Bks.

CITATION OF LEGAL AUTHORITIES

Teply, Larry L. Legal Research & Citation: Programmed Materials. 326p. 1982. 9.95 (ISBN 0-314-65784-3). West Pub.

CITIES AND TOWNS

see also Community; Education, Urban; Markets; Parks; Sociology, Urban; Urbanization; Villages also headings beginning with the word City, Municipal and Urban; names of individual cities and towns

Bush-Brown, Albert. Skidmore, Owings & Merrill: Architecture & Urbanism, 1974-1982. (Illus.). 400p. 1983. 49.95 (ISBN 0-8038-0401-6). Architectural.

Carter, Harold. The Study of Urban Geography. 434p. 1981. pap. text ed. 14.95 (ISBN 0-7131-6235-X). E Arnold.

Crosby, Robert W., ed. Cities & Regions As Nonlinear Decision Systems. (AAAS Selected Symposium: No. 77). 200p. 1983. lib. bdg. 25.00 (ISBN 0-86531-530-2). Westview.

Doyle, Alfreda C. Survival Suggestions for Urban Dwellers. 26p. 1983. pap. text ed. 6.95 (ISBN 0-910811-23-7). Center Self.

Shaffer, Carolyn & Fielder, Erica. Nature & the City: An Explorer's Guide for Kids & Grownups. (Illus.). 112p. (Orig.). Date not set. pap. 6.95 (ISBN 0-938530-12-7, 12-7). Lexikos.

Tanghe, J. & Vlaeminck, S., eds. Cities for Living In? A Case for Urbanism & Guidelines for Re-Urbanization. (Illus.). 384p. 1983. 45.00 (ISBN 0-08-025238-9); pap. 22.50 (ISBN 0-08-025237-0). Pergamon.

Young, Margaret W. Cities of the World: Supplement. 1983. pap. 65.00x (ISBN 0-8103-1110-0). Gale.

CITIES AND TOWNS–BEAUTIFICATION

see Urban Beautification

CITIES AND TOWNS–GROWTH

see also Suburbs

Golany, Gideon. International Urban Growth Policies: New-Town Contributions. LC 77-28274. 460p. 1978. 58.00x (ISBN 0-471-03748-6, Pub. by Wiley-Interscience). Wiley.

CITIES AND TOWNS–HISTORY

see also Cities and Towns, Ancient

Castells, Manuel. The City & the Grassroots: A Cross-Cultural Theory of Urban Social Movements. LC 82-40099. (California Ser. in Urban Development: Vol. 2). (Illus.). 600p. 1983. 38.50x (ISBN 0-520-04756-7). U of Cal Pr.

Dyos, H. J. Exploring the Urban Past: Essays in Urban History. Cannadine, David & Reeder, David, eds. LC 82-1209. (Illus.). 320p. 1982. 39.50 (ISBN 0-521-24624-5); pap. 12.95 (ISBN 0-521-28848-7). Cambridge U Pr.

CITIES AND TOWNS–JUVENILE LITERATURE

Bentley, John & Charlton, Bill. Finding Out about Villages. (Finding Out about Ser.). (Illus.). 48p. (gr. 5-8). 1983. 12.50 (ISBN 0-7134-4291-3, Pub. by Batsford England). David & Charles.

Ferguson, Sheila. Village & Town Life. (History in Focus Ser.). (Illus.). 72p. (gr. 7-12). 1983. 14.95 (ISBN 0-7134-4301-4, Pub. by Batsford England). David & Charles.

CITIES AND TOWNS–PLANNING

see City Planning

CITIES AND TOWNS–RESEARCH

see Municipal Research

CITIES AND TOWNS–SURVEYING

see Surveying

CITIES AND TOWNS–CANADA

Melvin, James R. & Scheffman, David T. An Economic Analysis of the Impact of Rising Oil Prices on Urban Structure. (Ontario Economic Council Research Studies). 160p. (Orig.). 1983. pap. 10.50 (ISBN 0-8020-3395-4). U of Toronto Pr.

CITIES AND TOWNS–GREAT BRITAIN

Cannadine, David, ed. Patricians, Power & Politics in Nineteenth Century Towns. LC 82-42544. 240p. 1982. 35.00x (ISBN 0-312-59803-3). St Martin.

Dony, John G. & Dyer, James. The Story of Luton. 160p. 1982. 35.00x (ISBN 0-900804-11-4, Pub. by White Crescent England). State Mutual Bk.

Twaddle, W. Old Dunstable. 64p. 1982. 25.00x (ISBN 0-900804-08-4, Pub. by White Crescent England). State Mutual Bk.

Viney, Elliott & Nightingale, Pamela. Old Aylesbury. 100p. 1982. 25.00x (ISBN 0-900804-21-1, Pub. by White Crescent England). State Mutual Bk.

White, Harold. Luton Past & Present. 152p. 1982. 35.00x (ISBN 0-900804-20-3, Pub. by White Crescent England). State Mutual Bk.

Wildman, Richard. Bygone Bedford. 96p. 1982. 25.00x (ISBN 0-900804-09-2, Pub. by White Crescent England). State Mutual Bk.

CITIES AND TOWNS–GREECE

Drews, Robert. Basileus: The Evidence for Kingship in Geometric Greece. LC 82-10915. (Yale Classical Monographs: No. 4). 160p. 1983. text ed. 18.50x (ISBN 0-300-02831-8). Yale U Pr.

CITIES AND TOWNS–ITALY

Tobriner, Stephen. The Genesis of Noto: An Eighteenth-Century Sicilian City. 296p. 1981. 150.00x (ISBN 0-302-00543-9, Pub. by Zwemmer England). State Mutual Bk.

CITIES AND TOWNS–UNITED STATES

Bane, Michael & Moore, Ellen. Tampa: Yesterday, Today & Tomorrow. (Illus.). 180p. (Orig.). 1982. 19.95 (ISBN 0-9609530-0-0); pap. 12.95 (ISBN 0-9609530-2-7). Mishler & King.

Bender, Thomas. Toward an Urban Vision: Ideas & Institutions in Nineteenth-Century America. LC 82-47980. 296p. (Orig.). 1982. pap. text ed. 7.50x (ISBN 0-8018-2925-9). Johns Hopkins.

Hales, Peter B. Silver Cities: The Photography of American Urbanization. 1983. write for info. (ISBN 0-87722-299-1). Temple U Pr.

McCarthy, Kenneth G., Jr., ed. Hattiesburg: A Pictorial History. LC 82-10868. (Illus.). 240p. 1982. 25.00 (ISBN 0-87805-169-4). U Pr of Miss.

Pulitzer. The American City: An Urban Odyssey to 11 U. S. Cities. (Illus.). 192p. 1983. pap. 9.95 (ISBN 0-517-54591-8). Crown.

Shumsky, Neil L. & Crimmins, Timothy, eds. Urban America: A Historical Bibliography. LC 82-24292. (Clio Bibliography Ser.: No. 11). 422p. 1982. lib. bdg. 55.00 (ISBN 0-87436-038-2). ABC-Clio.

Stein. Towards New Towns for America. 264p. 1982. 32.00x (ISBN 0-85323-163-X, Pub. by Liverpool Univ England). State Mutual Bk.

Wolensky, Robert P. & Miller, Edward J. The Small City & Regional Community: Proceedings of the 1982 Conference, Vol. V. LC 79-644450. viii, 450p. 1982. pap. text ed. 14.50 (ISBN 0-932310-04-4). UWSP Found Pr.

CITIES AND TOWNS, ANCIENT

see also names of ancient cities, e.g. Pompeii

Drews, Robert. Basileus: The Evidence for Kingship in Geometric Greece. LC 82-10915. (Yale Classical Monographs: No. 4). 160p. 1983. text ed. 18.50x (ISBN 0-300-02831-8). Yale U Pr.

Matheson, Susan B. Dura-Europos: The Ancient City & the Yale Collection. (Illus.). 42p. 1983. pap. 3.00 (ISBN 0-8143-1752-9, Dist. by the Yale Univ. Art Gallery). Wayne St U Pr.

CITIES AND TOWNS, MOVEMENT TO

see Cities and Towns–Growth; Urbanization

CITIES AND TOWNS, RUINED, EXTINCT, ETC.

see also Excavations (Archaeology)

Bartlett, John. Jericho. 128p. 1982. 35.00x (ISBN 0-7188-2456-3, Pub. by Lutterworth Pr England). State Mutual Bk.

Fox, Theron. Utah Treasure Hunter's Ghost Town Guide. (Illus.). 1983. pap. 2.50. Nevada Pubns.

CITIZENS' ASSOCIATIONS

Durrance, Joan. Armed for Action: The Power of an Informed Citizenry. 250p. lib. bdg. 24.95 (ISBN 0-918212-71-5). Neal-Schuman.

CITIZENS BAND RADIO

Judd. Questions & Answers: CB Radio. (Illus.). 1982. pap. 6.95 (ISBN 0-408-01216-1). Focal Pr.

CITIZENS RADIO SERVICE

see Citizens Band Radio

CITIZENSHIP

see also Aliens; Patriotism; Self-Determination, National; Suffrage

Garbe, Detlef. Burgerbeteiligung. iv, 248p. (Ger.). 1982. write for info. (ISBN 3-8204-5840-9). P Lang Pubs.

Paz, Carlos F. Preparacion para el Examen de Ciudadania. (Illus.). 144p. (Orig.). 1983. pap. 3.95 (ISBN 0-668-05677-0, 5677). Arco.

Whitlock, Marlene. Basic Skills Citizenship Workbook. (Basic Skills Workbooks). 32p. (gr. 3-6). 1983. 0.99 (ISBN 0-8209-0539-9, SSW-3). ESP.

--Developing Citizenship. (Social Studies). 24p. (gr. 3-6). 1979. wkbk. 5.00 (ISBN 0-8209-0254-3, SS-21). ESP.

CITY AND TOWN LIFE

Bohme, Gunther. Urbanitat. 116p. (Ger.). 1982. write for info. (ISBN 3-8204-7025-5). P Lang Pubs.

Center for Self-Sufficiency Research Division. Making the Switch from City Living to Small Town Living: A Reference. 55p. Date not set. pap. text ed. 8.95 (ISBN 0-910811-06-7). Center Self.

Davis, Peter. Hometown. 1983. pap. price not set (ISBN 0-671-47059-0, Touchstone Bks). S&S.

DiPrima, Richard. The City & Its Problems. LC 80-70425. 89p. (Orig.). 1980. pap. text ed. 3.95 (ISBN 0-86652-004-X). Educ Indus.

Gans, Herbert J. The Urban Villagers. (Illus.). 456p. 1982. pap. text ed. write for info. Free Pr.

Ribalta, Marta, ed. Habitat: City Living, No. 4. (Illus.). 91p. 1982. pap. 9.95 (ISBN 84-7031-035-6, Pub. by Editorial Blume Spain). Intl Schol Bk Serv.

Roberts, Glenys. Metropolitan Myths. 176p. 1982. 16.95 (ISBN 0-575-03154-9, Pub by Gollancz England); pap. 12.50 (ISBN 0-575-03232-4, Pub. by Gollancz England). David & Charles.

CITY BEAUTIFICATION

see Urban Beautification

CITY CLERGY

Ellison, Craig. The Urban Mission: Essays on the Building of a Comprehensive Model for Evangelical Urban Ministry. LC 82-23764. 230p. 1983. pap. text ed. 10.75 (ISBN 0-8191-2968-2). U Pr of Amer.

CITY GOVERNMENT

see Municipal Government

CITY LIFE

see City and Town Life

CITY MISSIONS

Ellison, Craig. The Urban Mission: Essays on the Building of a Comprehensive Model for Evangelical Urban Ministry. LC 82-23764. 230p. 1983. pap. text ed. 10.75 (ISBN 0-8191-2968-2). U Pr of Amer.

CITY PLANNING

see also Central Business Districts; Community Development; Housing; Industries, Location of; Municipal Research; Parks; Playgrounds; Regional Planning; Social Surveys; Space (Architecture); Store Location; Suburbs; Urban Beautification; Urban Renewal; Urban Transportation

Adrian, C. R. & Press, C. Governing Urban America. 5th ed. 1977. 26.50 (ISBN 0-07-000446-3). McGraw.

Agranoff, Robert, ed. Human Services on a Limited Budget. (Practical Management Ser.). (Illus.). 224p. (Orig.). 1983. pap. 19.50 (ISBN 0-87326-038-4). Intl City Mgt.

Anglin, R. L., Jr., ed. Energy & the Man Built Environment. LC 81-67745. 728p. 1982. pap. text ed. 47.00 (ISBN 0-87262-297-5). Am Soc Civil Eng.

Ashihara, Yoshinobu & Riggs, Lynne E. The Aesthetic Townscape. (Illus.). 196p. 1983. 20.00 (ISBN 0-262-01069-0). MIT Pr.

Barnes, W. Anderson. Downtown Development: Plan & Implementation. LC 82-60313. (Development Component Ser.). (Illus.). 32p. 1982. pap. 10.00 (ISBN 0-87420-608-1, D21). Urban Land.

A Big Atlas of Town Plans. 96p. 1983. pap. 9.95 (ISBN 0-86145-111-2, Pub. by Auto Assn-British Tourist Authority England). Merrimack Bk Serv.

Black, J. Thomas & Morina, Michael. Downtown Office Growth & the Role of Public Transit. LC 82-50921. (Illus.). 122p. (Orig.). 1982. pap. text ed. 26.00 (ISBN 0-87420-615-4, D31). Urban Land.

Community Applications of Density Design, Cost. (Illus.). 32p. (Orig.). 1983. pap. write for info. (ISBN 0-86718-159-1). Natl Assn Home.

Financing Urban Development in Developing Countries. (UNCRD Working Paper: No. 82-6). 56p. 1983. pap. 6.00 (ISBN 0-686-43294-0, CRD 141, UNCRD). Unipub.

Forrest, Ray & Henderson, Jeff. Urban Political Economy & Social Theory. 220p. 1982. text ed. 32.00x (ISBN 0-566-00493-3). Gower Pub Ltd.

Friedland, Roger. Power & Crisis in the City, Corporations, Unions & Urban Policy. LC 82-10368. 292p. 1983. 19.95 (ISBN 0-8052-3838-7). Schocken.

Gallion, Arthur B. & Eisner, Simon. The Urban Pattern: City Planning & Design. 4th ed. 464p. 1982. pap. 14.95 (ISBN 0-442-22926-7). Van Nos Reinhold.

Gappert, Gary & Knight, Richard V. Cities of the Twenty First Century. (Urban Affairs Annual Reviews: Vol. 23). (Illus.). 320p. 1982. 25.00 (ISBN 0-8039-1910-7); pap. 12.50 (ISBN 0-8039-1911-5). Sage.

Grove & Creswell. City Landscape. 1982. text ed. 65.00 (ISBN 0-408-01165-3). Butterworth.

LaConte, P. & Gibson, J. E. Human & Energy Factors: Factors in Urban Planning; A Systems Approach. 1982. 50.00 (ISBN 90-247-2688-3, Pub. by Martinus Nijhoff Netherlands). Kluwer Boston.

Lynch, Kevin. A Theory of Good City Form. (Illus.). 514p. 1981. 25.00 (ISBN 0-262-12085-2). MIT Pr.

Matzer, John F., Jr., ed. Capital Financing Strategies. (Practical Management Ser.). (Illus.). 224p. (Orig.). 1983. pap. 19.50 (ISBN 0-87326-037-6). Intl City Mgt.

OECD Staff. Improving the Management of Urban Research: City University Co-Operation. (OECD Urban Management Studies: No. 5). 158p. (Orig.). 1982. pap. 9.00x (ISBN 92-64-12294-X). OECD.

Paris, C., ed. Critical Readings in Planning Theory. (Urban & Regional Planning Ser.: Vol. 27). (Illus.). 260p. 1982. 27.00 (ISBN 0-08-024681-8); 15.00 (ISBN 0-08-024680-X). Pergamon.

Peterson, George, et al. The Future of Boston's Capital Plant. LC 80-54775. (Illus.). 69p. (Orig.). 1981. pap. text ed. 6.00 (ISBN 0-87766-291-6). Urban Inst.

--The Future of Oakland's Capital Plant. LC 80-54776. 80p. (Orig.). 1981. pap. text ed. 6.00 (ISBN 0-87766-290-8). Urban Inst.

Planning & the Civil Engineer. 170p. 1982. 90.00x (ISBN 0-7277-0152-5, Pub. by Telford England). State Mutual Bk.

Redstone, Louis G. The New Downtowns: Rebuilding Business Districts. LC 82-17111. 356p. 1983. Repr. of 1976 ed. lib. bdg. p.n.s. (ISBN 0-89874-560-8). Krieger.

Richardson, R. C. & James, T. B., eds. The Urban Experience: A Sourcebook. 224p. 1983. 25.00 (ISBN 0-7190-0900-6). Manchester.

Sarin, Madhu. Urban Planning in the Third World: The Chandigarh Experience. 240p. 1982. 31.00 (ISBN 0-7201-1637-6, Pub. by Mansell England). Wilson.

Siemon, Charles L. & Larsen, Wendy U. Vested Rights: Balancing Public & Private Development Expectations. LC 82-50897. 106p. (Orig.). 1982. pap. text ed. 42.00 (ISBN 0-87420-612-X, VO1). Urban Land.

Sim, Duncan. Change in the City Centre. 124p. 1982. text ed. 29.50x (ISBN 0-566-00405-4). Gower Pub Ltd.

Stout, Gary & Vitt, Joseph E. Public Incentives & Financial Techniques for Codevelopment. LC 82-50705. (Development Component Ser.). (Illus.). 26p. 1982. pap. 10.00 (ISBN 0-87420-610-3, D23). Urban Land.

Weicher, John C. & Yap, Lorene. Metropolitan Housing Needs for the 1980's. LC 81-70526. 138p. text ed. 16.50 (ISBN 0-87766-308-4, URI 33500). Urban Inst.

Witherspoon, Robert. Codevelopment: City Rebuilding by Business & Government. LC 82-50871. (Development Component Ser.). (Illus.). 48p. 1982. pap. 10.00 (ISBN 0-87420-614-6, D24). Urban Land.

Wynne, George G. Winning Designs: Vol. 4, The Competitions Renaissance. (Learning from Abroad Ser.). 60p. 1981. pap. text ed. 3.95x (ISBN 0-87855-893-4). Transaction Bks.

CITY PLANNING–BRAZIL

Batley, Richard. Power Through Bureaucracy: Urban Political Analysis in Brazil. LC 82-16872. 240p. 1982. 27.50x (ISBN 0-312-63437-4). St Martin.

CITY PLANNING–UNITED STATES

Ferebee, Ann, ed. Education for Urban Design. (Urban Design Selections Ser.). 183p. 1982. pap. 20.00 (ISBN 0-942468-00-7). Inst Urban Des.

Gibson, J. E. Designing the New City: A Systematic Approach. LC 76-44899. (Systems Engineering & Analysis Ser.). 288p. 1977. 39.95x (ISBN 0-471-29752-6, Pub. by Wiley-Interscience). Wiley.

Golany, Gideon, adapted by. Urban Planning for Arid Zones: American Experiences & Directions. LC 77-10472. 245p. 1978. 42.50x (ISBN 0-471-02948-3, Pub. by Wiley-Interscience). Wiley.

Lefcoe, George, ed. Urban Land Policy for the Reagan Years: The Message for State & Local Governments. LC 82-48492. (A Lincoln Institute of Land Policy Bk.). 240p. 1983. 28.95x (ISBN 0-669-06157-3). Lexington Bks.

Nathan, Richard P. & Webman, Jerry A. The Urban Development Action Grant Program. 125p. 1980. pap. text ed. 7.95 (ISBN 0-938882-01-5, Dist. by Transaction Bks). PURRC.

Rasmussen, David W. & Struyk, Raymond J. A Housing Strategy for the City of Detroit: Policy Perspectives Based on Economic Analysis. LC 81-51874. (Illus.). 81p. (Orig.). 1981. pap. text ed. 9.00 (ISBN 0-87766-300-9, URI 32500). Urban Inst.

Taebel, Del & Smith, Ann. Innovation in Texas Cities. 94p. (Orig.). 1982. pap. 10.00 (ISBN 0-936440-45-7). Inst Urban Studies.

CITY SCHOOLS

see Education, Urban

CITY SURVEYING

see Surveying

CITY TRAFFIC

Olsson, Marie. Parking Discounts & Car Pool Formation in Seattle. 115p. (Orig.). 1980. pap. text ed. 3.50 (ISBN 0-87766-226-6). Urban Inst.

Wynne, George G. Traffic Restraints in Residential Areas, Vol. II. (Learning from Abroad Ser.). 48p. 1980. pap. 5.95 (ISBN 0-87855-845-4). Transaction Bks.

CITY TRANSIT

see Local Transit

CITY TRANSPORTATION

see Urban Transportation

CITY UNIVERSITY OF NEW YORK

Marshak, Robert E. Academic Renewal in the 1970's: Memoirs of a City College President. LC 82-16111. 300p. (Orig.). 1983. lib. bdg. 23.25 (ISBN 0-8191-2779-5); pap. text ed. 11.25 (ISBN 0-8191-2780-9). U Pr of Amer.

CIVIC PLANNING

see City Planning

CIVIL AERONAUTICS

see Aeronautics, Commercial

CIVIL AVIATION

see Aeronautics, Commercial

CIVIL DEFENSE

see also Atomic Bomb–Safety Measures; Bomb Reconnaissance; Disaster Relief

also subdivision Civil Defense under names of countries, cities, etc., e.g. Great Britain–Civil Defense

Jakovljevic, B. New International Status of Civil Defence. 1982. lib. bdg. 34.50 (ISBN 90-247-2567-4, Pub. by Martinus Nijhoff Netherlands). Kluwer Boston.

Royal United Services Institute for Defence Studies (Rusi), Whitehall, London, UK. Rusi & Brassey's Defence Yearbook Nineteen Hundred-Eighty-Three. 93rd ed. (Rusi & Brassey's Defence Yearbook Ser.). 400p. 1983. 50.00 (ISBN 0-08-028346-2); pap. 20.00 (ISBN 0-08-028347-0). Pergamon.

CIVIL DISOBEDIENCE

see Government, Resistance to

CIVIL DISORDERS

see Riots

CIVIL ENGINEERING

see also Bridges; Canals; Dams; Drainage; Foundations; Hydraulic Engineering; Irrigation; Marine Engineering; Masonry; Mechanical Engineering; Mining Engineering; Piling (Civil Engineering); Railroad Engineering; Reclamation of Land; Rivers; Roads; Sanitary Engineering; Steel, Structural; Strength of Materials; Structural Dynamics; Surveying; Tunnels and Tunneling; Walls; Water-Supply Engineering

also subdivision Public Works under names of countries, cities, etc. e.g. United States–Public Works

American Society of Civil Engineers. ASCE Combined Index, 1981. 212p. 1982. pap. text ed. 20.00 (ISBN 0-87262-314-9). Am Soc Civil Eng.

American Society of Civil Engineers, compiled by. Evaluation, Maintenance & Upgrading of Wood Structures. LC 82-72779. 440p. 1982. pap. text ed. 13.00 (ISBN 0-87262-317-3). Am Soc Civil Eng.

--Transactions of the American Society of Civil Engineers, Vol. 146, 1981. 1056p. 1982. pap. text ed. 52.50 (ISBN 0-87262-309-2). Am Soc Civil Eng.

Friedlander, S. K. Smoke, Dust & Haze: Fundamentals of Aerosol Behavior. LC 76-26928. 317p. 1977. 35.50 (ISBN 0-471-01468-0, Pub. by Wiley Interscience). Wiley.

Future Needs in Civil Engineering Education. 166p. 1982. 90.00x (ISBN 0-7277-0153-3, Pub. by Telford England). State Mutual Bk.

Haswell. Civil Engineering: Contracts. 1982. text ed. 29.95 (ISBN 0-408-00526-2). Butterworth.

Judson, David, ed. Caving & Potholding Manual. (Illus.). 224p. 1983. 23.95 (ISBN 0-7153-8155-5). David & Charles.

Monismith, Carl L. Addressing Societal Needs of the 1980's Through Civil Engineering Research. LC 82-70765. 336p. 1982. pap. text ed. 34.75 (ISBN 0-87262-300-9). Am Soc Civil Eng.

Planning & the Civil Engineer. 170p. 1982. 90.00x (ISBN 0-7277-0152-5, Pub. by Telford England). State Mutual Bk.

Plate, E., ed. Engineering Methodology. (Studies in Wind Engineering & Industrial Aerodynamics: No. 1). 740p. 1982. 149.00 (ISBN 0-444-41972-1). Elsevier.

Sharp, B. B. Water Hammer: Problems & Solutions. 152p. 1981. text ed. 26.50 (ISBN 0-7131-3427-5). E Arnold.

CIVIL ENGINEERING–DATA PROCESSING

Cope, R. & Sawko, F. Computer Methods for Civil Engineering. 336p. 1982. 19.00 (ISBN 0-07-084129-2). McGraw.

CIVIL ENGINEERING–DICTIONARIES

Paulus, Andre. Civil Engineering in French. 192p. 1982. 90.00x (ISBN 0-7277-0138-X, Pub. by Telford England). State Mutual Bk.

CIVIL ENGINEERING–ESTIMATES AND COSTS

see Engineering–Estimates and Costs

CIVIL ENGINEERING–EXAMINATIONS, QUESTIONS, ETC.

Raphael, Coleman & Lindskog, Robert. Preparing for the Civil Engineering Professional Examination. LC 82-24270. (Civil Engineering Ser.). 248p. 1983. pap. 17.95 (ISBN 0-910554-41-2). Eng Pr.

Rudman, Jack. Bridge Maintenance Supervisor I. (Career Examination Ser.: C-855). (Cloth bdg. avail. on request). pap. 12.00 (ISBN 0-8373-0855-0). Natl Learning.

--Bridge Maintenance Supervisor II. (Career Examination Ser.: C-856). (Cloth bdg. avail. on request). pap. 12.00 (ISBN 0-8373-0856-9). Natl Learning.

--Bridge Maintenance Supervisor III. (Career Examination Ser.: C-857). (Cloth bdg. avil. on request). pap. 14.00 (ISBN 0-8373-0857-7). Natl Learning.

--Junior Civil Engineer Trainee. (Career Examination Ser.: C-212). (Cloth bdg. avail. on request). pap. 10.00 (ISBN 0-8373-0212-9). Natl Learning.

CIVIL ENGINEERING–HANDBOOKS, MANUALS, ETC.

Seelye, E. E. Data Book for Civil Engineers: Design, Vol. 1. 3rd ed. 670p. 1960. text ed. 85.50x (ISBN 0-471-77286-0, Pub. by Wiley-Interscience). Wiley.

CIVIL ENGINEERING–MANAGEMENT

see Engineering–Management

CIVIL ENGINEERING–STUDY AND TEACHING

see Engineering–Study and Teaching

CIVIL ENGINEERS

Skempton, A. W. John Smeaton FRS. 288p. 1981. 69.00x (ISBN 0-7277-0088-X, Pub. by Telford England). State Mutual Bk.

CIVIL GOVERNMENT

see Political Science

CIVIL LAW

see also Liability (Law); Roman Law

Kraftds, Melvin D. Using Experts in Civil Cases. 2nd ed. 356p. 1982. text ed. 45.00 (ISBN 0-686-81879-2, H3-2965). PLI.

CIVIL LAW–ROME

see Roman Law

CIVIL LAW–SCOTLAND

Walker, David M. Principles of Scottish Private Law, Vol. II. 3rd ed. 680p. 1983. 55.00 (ISBN 0-19-876133-3). Oxford U Pr.

--Principles of Scottish Private Law, Vol. 1. 1982. 58.00 (ISBN 0-19-876132-5). Oxford U Pr.

CIVIL LAW (ISLAMIC LAW)

see Islamic Law

CIVIL LAW (JEWISH LAW)

see Jewish Law

CIVIL LAW (ROMAN LAW)

see Roman Law

CIVIL LAW SYSTEMS

Sumpter, Jerry L. Civil Trial Strategy & Technique Notebook. 650p. looseleaf bound 148.00 (ISBN 0-935506-02-0). Carnegie Pr.

CIVIL LIBERTY

see Liberty

CIVIL-MILITARY RELATIONS

see Militarism

CIVIL PROCEDURE

see also Actions and Defenses; Appellate Procedure; Arbitration and Award; Compromise (Law); Instructions to Juries; Jury; Pleading; Pre-Trial Procedure; Probate Law and Practice; Trial Practice

Boyd, T. Munford & Graves, Edward S. Virginia Civil Procedure. 700p. 1982. 65.00 (ISBN 0-87215-424-6). Michie-Bobbs.

CIVIL RIGHTS

see also Due Process of Law; Freedom of Information; Liberty; Liberty of Speech; Liberty of the Press; Natural Law; Race Discrimination; Religious Liberty

Bullock, Charles S., III & Lamb, Charles M. Implementation of Civil Rights Policy. (Political Science Ser.). 250p. 1983. pap. text ed. 12.95 (ISBN 0-534-01259-0). Brooks-Cole.

Evans, Robert A. & Evans, Alice F. Human Rights: A Dialogue Between the First & Third Worlds. LC 82-18780. 272p. (Orig.). 1983. pap. 19.95 (ISBN 0-88344-194-2). Orbis Bks.

Eze, Osita C. Human Rights in Africa: Some Selected Problems. LC 82-16809. 310p. 1982. 22.50x (ISBN 0-312-39962-6). St Martin.

Gastil, Raymond D. Freedom in the World: Political Rights & Civil Liberties 1982. LC 80-66430. (Freedom House Annual Ser.). (Illus.). 416p. 1982. lib. bdg. 35.00 (ISBN 0-313-23178-8, FR82). Greenwood.

Greaney, Vincent, ed. The Rights of Children. 250p. 1983. text ed. 19.95x (ISBN 0-8290-1297-4). Irvington.

Kavaas, Igor I. & Granier, Jacqueline P., eds. Human Rights, the Helsinki Accords & the United States, 3 vols in 9. LC 82-81319. 1982. lib. bdg. 360.00 (ISBN 0-89941-152-5). W S Hein.

Kim, Dong Soo & Kim, Byong-suh, eds. Human Rights in Minority Perspectives. xviii, 292p. 1979. 8.00 (ISBN 0-932014-04-6). AKCS.

Phillips, Wendell. Wendell Phillips on Civil Rights & Freedom. 2nd ed. Filler, Louis, ed. LC 82-17343. 252p. 1983. pap. text ed. 10.25 (ISBN 0-8191-2793-0). U Pr of Amer.

Plattner, Mark F. Human Rights in Our Time: History, Theory, Policy. 175p. 1983. 18.50x (ISBN 0-86531-606-6). Westview.

Rotunda, Ronald D. Six Justices on Civil Rights. 1983. lib. bdg. 22.50 (ISBN 0-379-20044-9). Oceana.

Shepard. Civil Rights & Civil Liberties Litigation: A Guide to S1983. 1979. 50.00 (ISBN 0-07-045856-1). McGraw.

Vacca, Richard S. & Hudgins, H. C. Liability of School Officials & Administrators for Civil Rights Torts. 327p. 1982. 20.00 (ISBN 0-87215-561-7). Michie-Bobbs.

Wasby, Stephen L. Civil Liberties: Policy & Policy Making. 271p. 1976. pap. 9.95 (ISBN 0-8093-0817-7). Lexington Bks.

CIVIL RIGHTS–GREAT BRITAIN

Anderson, Gerald D. Fascists, Communists, & the National Government: Civil Liberties in Great Britain, 1931-1937. LC 82-10985. 256p. 1983. text ed. 20.00x (ISBN 0-8262-0388-4). U of Mo Pr.

CIVIL RIGHTS–INDIA

Benoyendranath, Banerjea. The Practice of Freedom. 1983. 9.00x (ISBN 0-8364-0918-3, Pub. by Minerva India). South Asia Bks.

CIVIL RIGHTS–UKRAINE

The Ukrainian Helsinki Group: Five Years of Struggle in Defense of Rights. LC 81-85108. 45p. 1981. pap. 1.50 (ISBN 0-914834-46-0). Smoloskyp.

CIVIL RIGHTS–UNITED STATES

see also Afro-Americans–Civil Rights; United States–Constitution

Bollier, David. Liberty & Justice for Some: Defending a Free Society from the Radical Right's Holy War on Democracy. LC 82-51019. 336p. (Orig.). 1982. pap. 8.95 (ISBN 0-8044-6060-4, Co-pub. by People for Amer Way). Ungar.

Executive Director's Testimony before the Subcommittee on Civil & Constitutional Rights of the House Judiciary Committee on June 23, 1981. 1981. 1.00 (ISBN 0-686-38013-4). Voter Ed Proj.

Faulk, John H. Fear on Trial. rev. ed. 256p. 1983. 17.50 (ISBN 0-292-72443-8); pap. 7.95 (ISBN 0-292-72442-X). U of Tex Pr.

Kavaas, Igor I. & Granier, Jacqueline P., eds. Human Rights, the Helsinki Accords & the United States, 3 vols in 9. LC 82-81319. 1982. lib. bdg. 360.00 (ISBN 0-89941-152-5). W S Hein.

McClosky, Herbert & Brill, Alida. Dimensions of Tolerance: What Americans Believe about Civil Liberties. LC 82-72959. 450p. 1983. 27.50x (ISBN 0-87154-591-8). Russell Sage.

McNeil, Genna R. Groundwork: Charles Hamilton Houston & the Struggle for Civil Rights. LC 82-40483. (Illus.). 320p. 1983. 27.50x (ISBN 0-8122-7878-X). U of Pa Pr.

CIVIL RIGHTS (INTERNATIONAL LAW)

Daviss, Diana V., ed. Bibliography of Human Rights. Date not set. looseleaf 85.00 (ISBN 0-379-20816-4). Oceana.

Kavaas, Igor I. & Granier, Jacqueline P., eds. Human Rights, the Helsinki Accords & the United States, 3 vols in 9. LC 82-81319. 1982. lib. bdg. 360.00 (ISBN 0-89941-152-5). W S Hein.

Robertson, A. H. Human Rights in the World: An Introduction to the International Protection of Human Rights. LC 82-10238. 1982. 22.50x (ISBN 0-312-39961-8). St Martin.

Sieghart, Paul. The International Law of Human Rights. 600p. 1983. 74.00 (ISBN 0-19-876096-5). Oxford U Pr.

CIVIL SERVICE

see also Administrative Law; Bureaucracy; Collective Bargaining–Government Employees; Municipal Officials and Employees

also subdivision Officials and Employees–Appointments, Qualifications, Tenure, etc. under the names of countries, cities, etc. e.g. United States–Officials and Employees–Appointments, Qualifications, Tenure, etc.

Gretton, John & Harrison, Anthony, eds. How Much are Public Servants Worth? 44p. 1983. pap. text ed. 12.00x (ISBN 0-631-13251-1, Pub. by Basil Blackwell England). Biblio Dist.

Hoogehboom, Ari A. Outlawing the Spoils: A History of the Civil Service Movement, 1865-1883. LC 82-15507. xi, 306p. 1982. Repr. of 1968 ed. lib. bdg. 35.00x (ISBN 0-313-22821-3, H00S). Greenwood.

Kershen, Harry, ed. Labor-Management Relations among Government Employees. (Public Sector Contemporary Issues Ser.: Vol. 2). 224p. 1983. pap. text ed. 13.95X (ISBN 0-89503-033-0). Baywood Pub.

Levine, Marvin A. Personnel Management for Public Sector Employees. (Illus.). 500p. 1983. text ed. 24.95x (ISBN 0-89832-023-2). Brighton Pub Co.

Morgan, Nicole S. No-Where to Go? 100p. 1981. pap. text ed. 8.95x (ISBN 0-920380-90-5, Pub. by Inst Res Pub Canada). Renouf.

CIVIL SERVICE–EXAMINATIONS

see Civil Service Examinations

CIVIL SERVICE–POSITIONS

see Civil Service Positions

CIVIL SERVICE–VOCATIONAL GUIDANCE

see Civil Service Positions

CIVIL SERVICE EXAMINATIONS

Here are entered general works and works on United States civil service examinations. Examinations for specific cities in the United States or for countries other than the United States are entered under the appropriate subdivisions.

Rudman, Jack. Junior Administration Assistant. (Career Examination Ser.: C-832). (Cloth bdg. avail. on request). pap. 8.00 (ISBN 0-8373-0832-1). Natl Learning.

CIVIL SERVICE POSITIONS

Grayson, Fred N. The Office Handbook for Civil Service Employers. LC 82-18480. 288p. 1983. pap. 8.00 (ISBN 0-668-05605-3). Arco.

CIVIL SERVICE REFORM

see also Patronage, Political

Suleiman, Ezra N., ed. Higher Civil Servants in the Policy Making Process. 350p. 1983. text ed. price not set (ISBN 0-8419-0847-8). Holmes & Meier.

CIVIL WAR–GREAT BRITAIN

see Great Britain–History–Puritan Revolution, 1642-1660

CIVIL WAR–UNITED STATES

see United States–History–Civil War, 1861-1865

CIVIL WRONGS

see Torts

CIVILIAN DEFENSE

see Civil Defense

CIVILIZATION–HISTORY

see also Civilization, Ancient; Civilization, Medieval

Taylor, Henry O. Ancient Ideals: A Study of Intellectual & Spiritual Growth from Early Times to the Establishment of Christianity, 2 Vols. 430p. 1982. Repr. of 1900 ed. Set. lib. bdg. 100.00 (ISBN 0-686-81834-2). Telegraph Bks.

Thapar, Romila. From Lineage to State: Social Formations of the Mid-First Millenium B.C. in the Ganges Valley. 1982. pap. 15.00x (ISBN 0-19-561394-5). Oxford U Pr.

CIVILIZATION–JUVENILE LITERATURE

Hauptly, Denis J. The Journey From the Past: A History of the Western World. LC 82-13740. (Illus.). 240p. (gr. 5-9). 1983. 12.95 (ISBN 0-689-30973-2). Atheneum.

Szekely, Edmond B. & Bordeaux, Norma N. Messengers from Ancient Civilizations. (Illus.). 44p. (gr. 5 up). 1974. pap. 3.50 (ISBN 0-89564-068-6). IBS Intl.

CIVILIZATION–PHILOSOPHY

see also Philosophical Anthropology

Shils, Edward. Tradition. LC 80-21643. viii, 334p. 1981. pap. 10.95 (ISBN 0-226-75326-3). U of Chicago Pr.

CIVILIZATION, AMERICAN

see America–Civilization; Latin America–Civilization; United States–Civilization

CIVILIZATION, ANCIENT

DeBurgh, W. G. Legacy of the Ancient World. 576p. 1971. Repr. 30.00x (ISBN 0-7121-1210-3, Pub. by Macdonald & Evans). State Mutual Bk.

Gibson, Michael & Box, Sue. Discovering Ancient Mysteries. (Full Color Fact Books). (Illus.). 32p. (gr. 4-12). 1982. PLB 7.95 (ISBN 0-8219-0015-3). EMC.

Hackett, Neil J. Ancient World to Eight Hundred. LC 78-67276. Date not set. pap. text ed. 2.95x (ISBN 0-88273-319-2). Forum Pr IL.

Szekeley, Edmond B. Death of the New World. (Illus.). 48p. 1973. pap. 4.80 (ISBN 0-89564-026-0). Ibs Intl.

Szekely, Edmond B. The Greatness in the Smallness. (Illus.). 192p. 1978. pap. 7.50 (ISBN 0-89564-052-X). IBS Intl.

Taylor, Henry O. Ancient Ideals: A Study of Intellectual & Spiritual Growth from Early Times to the Establishment of Christianity, 2 Vols. 430p. 1982. Repr. of 1900 ed. Set. lib. bdg. 100.00 (ISBN 0-686-81834-2). Telegraph Bks.

CIVILIZATION, CHRISTIAN

see also Christianity and Culture; Church and Social Problems

Palma, Robert J. Karl Barth's Free Theology of Culture. (Pittsburgh Theological Monographs New Ser.: No. 2). 1983. pap. write for info. (ISBN 0-915138-54-9). Pickwick.

CIVILIZATION, GERMANIC

Bernstein, Eckhard. German Humanism. (World Authors Ser.). 176p. 1983. lib. bdg. 18.95 (ISBN 0-8057-6537-9, Twayne). G K Hall.

Bock, C. V. & Riley, V. J. Theses in Germanic Studies, 1972-1977. 57p. 1980. 35.00x (ISBN 0-85457-081-0, Pub. by Inst Germanic Stud England). State Mutual Bk.

Knight, K. G. & Norman, F. Hauptmann Centenary Lectures. 167p. 1964. 60.00x (ISBN 0-85457-021-7, Pub. by Inst Germanic Stud England). State Mutual Bk.

Norman, F. Theses in Germanic Studies, 1903-1961. 46p. 1962. 25.00x (ISBN 0-85457-015-2, Pub. by Inst Germanic Stud England). State Mutual Bk.

Prawer, S. S. & Riley, V. J. Theses in Germanic Studies, 1962-67. 18p. 1968. 25.00x (ISBN 0-85457-032-2, Pub. by Inst Germanic Stud England). State Mutual Bk.

Robson-Scott, W. D. & Riley, V. J. Theses in Germanic Studies, 1967-72. 18p. 1973. 20.00x (ISBN 0-85457-055-1, Pub. by Inst Germanic Stud England). State Mutual Bk.

CIVILIZATION, GREEK

see also Civilization, Mycenaean; Hellenism

Murray, Oswyn. Early Greece. (Illus.). 320p. 1982. pap. 8.95 (ISBN 0-8047-1185-2). Stanford U Pr.

Royal National Foundation. Athens Civilization: The Past & the Future. 1968. 6.50 (ISBN 0-444-40747-2). Elsevier.

CIVILIZATION, ISLAMIC

Beg, M. A. S. Fine Arts in Islamic Civilisation. 5.95 (ISBN 0-686-83581-6). Kazi Pubns.

Irving, T. B. Tide of Islam. 5.95 (ISBN 0-686-83887-4). Kazi Pubns.

Some Aspects of Islamic Culture. 3.00 (ISBN 0-686-83584-0). Kazi Pubns.

Vryonis, Speros, ed. Islam & Cultural Change in the Middle Ages: Fourth Giogio Levi Della Vida Biennial Conference, May 11-13, 1973 (University of California, Los Angeles) 150p. (Orig.). pap. 45.00x (ISBN 3-447-01608-6). Intl Pubns Serv.

Wisdom of Islamic Culture. 5.95 (ISBN 0-686-83585-9). Kazi Pubns.

CIVILIZATION, MEDIEVAL

see also Art, Medieval; Chivalry; Feudalism; Monasticism and Religious Orders; Renaissance

Alexander, James W. Medieval World. LC 78-67276. 1979. pap. text ed. 3.25x (ISBN 0-88273-320-6). Forum Pr IL.

Cook, William R. & Herzman, Ronald B. The Medieval World View: An Introduction. (Illus.). 320p. 1982. 14.95x (ISBN 0-19-503089-3); pap. 6.95x (ISBN 0-19-503090-7). Oxford U Pr.

Wood, Charles T. The Quest for Eternity: Medieval Manners & Morals. LC 82-40476. (Illus.). 176p. 1983. pap. 8.95 (ISBN 0-87451-259-X). U Pr of New Eng.

CIVILIZATION, MODERN–20TH CENTURY

Hickey, Denis. Home from Exile: An Approach to Post-Existentialist Philosophizing. LC 82-20059. 504p. (Orig.). (gr. 2-5). 1983. lib. bdg. 29.50 (ISBN 0-8191-2848-1); pap. text ed. 17.75 (ISBN 0-8191-2849-X). U Pr of Amer.

Sack, John. Fingerprint: The Autobiography of An American Man. Date not set. 13.95 (ISBN 0-394-50197-7). Random.

CIVILIZATION, MODERN–1950-

Berman, Marshall. All That is Solid Melts into Air. 1983. pap. 6.75 (ISBN 0-671-45700-4, Touchstone Bks). S&S.

CIVILIZATION, MUSLIM

see Civilization, Islamic

CIVILIZATION, MYCENAEAN

Taylour, William. The Myceneans. rev. ed. (Ancient Peoples & Places Ser.). (Illus.). 1983. 19.95 (ISBN 0-500-02103-1). Thames Hudson.

CIVILIZATION AND MACHINERY

see Technology and Civilization

CIVILIZATION AND SCIENCE

see Science and Civilization

CIVILIZATION AND TECHNOLOGY

see Technology and Civilization

CLAIMS

Rudman, Jack. Administrative Claim Examiner. (Career Examination Ser.: C-2600). (Cloth bdg. avail. on request). pap. 12.00 (ISBN 0-8373-2600-1). Natl Learning.

CLAIRVOYANCE

see also Extrasensory Perception; Hypnotism

Steiner, Rudolf. Links Between the Living & the Dead: Transformation of Earthly Forces into Clairvoyance. Osmond, D. S. & Davy, C., trs. 64p. 1973. pap. 3.00 (ISBN 0-85440-273-X, Pub. by Steinerbooks). Anthroposophic.

CLARINET

Pino, DAvid. The Clarinet & Clairnet Playing. 03/1983 ed. (Illus.). 320p. pap. 9.95 (ISBN 0-686-83740-1, ScribT). Scribner.

Russianoff, Leon. Clarinet Method, Bk. II. 1982. pap. 14.95 (ISBN 0-02-872250-7). Schirmer Bks.

CLASS CONFLICT

see Social Conflict

CLASS DISTINCTION
see Social Classes
CLASS STRUGGLE
see Social Conflict
CLASSES (MATHEMATICS)
see Set Theory
CLASSES, SOCIAL
see Social Classes
CLASSICAL ATLASES
see Classical Geography
CLASSICAL DANCING
see Modern Dance
CLASSICAL FIELD THEORY
see Field Theory (Physics)
CLASSICAL GEOGRAPHY
Tabula Imperii Romani: Condate-Glevum-Londinium-Lutetia (Southern England & Northern France) (Tabula Imperii Romani Ser.). (Illus.). 88p. 1983. 27.50 (ISBN 0-19-726020-9). Oxford U Pr.
CLASSICAL LITERATURE (COLLECTIONS)
Here are entered collections of works in both Greek and Latin. for English Translations see subdivision Translations into English.
see also Latin Literature (Collections)
Race, William H. The Classical Priamel from Homer to Boethius. (Mnemosyne: Suppl. 74). xii, 171p. 1982. pap. write for info. (ISBN 90-04-06515-6). E J Brill.
CLASSICAL LITERATURE–BIBLIOGRAPHY
Halton, Thomas P. & O'Leary, Catherine S. Classical Scholarship: An Annotated Bibliography. LC 82-48984. 1983. lib. bdg. price not set (ISBN 0-527-37436-9). Kraus Intl.
Wellington, Jean S., ed. Dictionary of Bibliographic Abbreviations Found in the Scholarship of Classical Studies & Related Disciplines. LC 82-21068. 416p. 1983. lib. bdg. 45.00 (ISBN 0-313-23523-6, WLC/). Greenwood.
CLASSICAL LITERATURE–HISTORY AND CRITICISM
Clark, Howard, ed. Twentieth Century Interpretations of the Odyssey. 132p. 1983. 9.95 (ISBN 0-13-934851-4); pap. 4.95 (ISBN 0-13-934844-1). P-H.
Michael, I. The Treatment of Classical Material in the Libro de Alexandre. 1970. 22.00 (ISBN 0-7190-1247-3). Manchester.
Moskalew, Walter. Formular Language & Poetic Design in the Aneid. (Mnemosyne: Suppl. 73). xi, 273p. 1982. pap. write for info. (ISBN 90-04-06580-6). E J Brill.
Plowden, G. F. C. Pope on Classic Ground. LC 82-14413. 184p. 1983. text ed. 20.95x (ISBN 0-8214-0664-7, 82-84333). Ohio U Pr.
Tacitus. Empire & Emperors. Tingay, Graham, ed. LC 82-14616. (Illus.). 112p. Date not set. pap. 4.95 (ISBN 0-521-28190-3). Cambridge U Pr.
CLASSICAL MYTHOLOGY
see Mythology, Classical
CLASSIFICATION–BOOKS
see also Classification, Dewey Decimal; Classification, Library of Congress
American National Standards Institute, Z39 on Library Work & Information Sciences. American National Standards Identification Code for the Book Industry. 1980. 5.00 (ISBN 0-686-38030-4, Z39.43). ANSI.
American National Standards Institute Z39 on Library Work & Information Sciences. American National Standards Order Form for Single Titles of Library Materials in 3-Inch by 5-Inch Format. 1982. 6.00 (ISBN 0-686-38032-0, Z39.30). ANSI.
American National Standards Institute. American National Standards Serial Holdings Statement at the Summary Level. 1980. 7.00 (ISBN 0-686-38029-0, Z39.42). ANSI.
CLASSIFICATION–BOOKS–BIBLIOGRAPHY
Carrol, Frieda, compiled by. Bibliotheca Press Subject Notebook with Bibliographic Information. 300p. 1983. notebook 35.00 (ISBN 0-939476-64-9). Biblio Pr GA.
CLASSIFICATION–BOOKS–LAW
Dershem, Larry D., ed. Library of Congress Classification Class K, Subclass KF Law of the United States Cumulative Index. (AALL Publication Ser.: No. 18). vii, 326p. 1982. loose-leaf 35.00x (ISBN 0-8377-0115-5). Rothman.
CLASSIFICATION–BOOKS–SCIENCE
Lancaster, F. W. Libraries & Librarians in on Age of Electronics. LC 82-81403. (Illus.). ix, 229p. 1982. text ed. 22.50 (ISBN 0-87815-040-4). Info Resources.
CLASSIFICATION–BOTANY
see Botany–Classification
CLASSIFICATION–PLANTS
see Botany–Classification
CLASSIFICATION, DEWEY DECIMAL
Shaw, Marie-Jose. The Dewey Decimal Classification. (Sound Filmstrip Kits Ser.). (gr. 4-8). 1981. tchrs ed. 24.00 (ISBN 0-8209-0447-3, FCW-24). ESP.
CLASSIFICATION, LIBRARY OF CONGRESS
Dershem, Larry D., ed. Library of Congress Classification Class K, Subclass KF Law of the United States Cumulative Index. (AALL Publication Ser.: No. 18). vii, 326p. 1982. loose-leaf 35.00x (ISBN 0-8377-0115-5). Rothman.
CLASSROOM MANAGEMENT
Axelrod, Saul. Behavior Modification for the Classroom Teacher. 2nd ed. (Illus.). 272p. 1983. pap. text ed. 13.50x (ISBN 0-07-002572-X, C). McGraw.
Bettencourt, Vladimir. New Discoveries in the Psychology of Management. (Research Center for Economic Psychology Library). (Illus.). 148p. 1983. 59.75 (ISBN 0-86654-061-X). Inst Econ Finan.
Charles, C. M. Elementary Classroom Management: A Handbook for Excellence in Teaching. Akers, Lane, ed. (Illus.). 452p. (Orig.). 1983. pap. text ed. 12.50x (ISBN 0-582-28349-3). Longman.
Kriedler, William. Classroom Management. 1983. pap. text ed. 9.95 (ISBN 0-673-15642-7). Scott F.
Tuccillo, John. Housing & Investment in an Inflationary World: Theory & Evidence. (Illus.). 55p. (Orig.). 1980. pap. text ed. 5.50 (ISBN 0-87766-281-9). Urban Inst.
Yonker, Tom. But Teach, You Ain't Listenin', or How to Cope with Violence in a Public School Classroom. LC 82-60524. 125p. (Orig.). 1983. pap. 9.95 (ISBN 0-88247-678-5). R & E Res Assoc.
CLAY
see also Bricks; Ceramics; Particles
The Infrared Spectra Handbook of Minerals & Clays. 1982. 225.00 (ISBN 0-686-84522-6). Sadtler Res.
Van Olphen, H., ed. International Clay Conference, 1981: Proceedings of the VII International Clay Conference, Bologna & Pavia, Italy, September 6-12, 1981. (Developments in Sedimentology Ser.: No. 35). 828p. 1982. 85.00 (ISBN 0-444-42096-7). Elsevier.
CLEANING COMPOUNDS
see also Detergents, Synthetic; Soap and Soap Trade
The Market For Soap & Detergents. 1981. 395.00 (ISBN 0-686-38438-5, 699). Busn Trend.
Milwidsky, B. & Gabriel, D. Detergent Analysis. 1982. 69.00x (ISBN 0-7114-5735-2, Pub. by Macdonald Bk). State Mutual Bk.
CLEANING PREPARATIONS
see Cleaning Compounds
CLEANLINESS
see Baths; Sanitation
CLEANSERS (COMPOUNDS)
see Cleaning Compounds
CLEFT PALATE
McWilliams, Betty J. & Morris, Hughlett H. Cleft Palate Speech. 300p. 1983. text ed. 28.00 (ISBN 0-941158-11-X, D3339-7). Mosby.
CLEMENS, SAMUEL LANGHORNE, 1835-1910
Kaplan, Justin. Mr. Clemens & Mark Twain. 1983. pap. write for info. (ISBN 0-671-47071-X, Touchstone Bks). S&S.
Liljegren, S. B. Revolt Against Romanticism in American Literature as Evidenced in the Work of S. L. Clemens. 59p. pap. 12.50 (ISBN 0-87556-576-X). Saifer.
Norton, Charles A. Writing Tom Sawyer: The Adventures of Mark Twain's Classic. 210p. 1983. lib. bdg. 18.95x (ISBN 0-89950-067-6). McFarland & Co.
Paine, Albert B. A Short Life View of Mark Twain. 344p. 1982. Repr. of 1920 ed. lib. bdg. 25.00 (ISBN 0-89984-829-X). Century Bookbindery.
CLERGY
see also City Clergy; Deacons; Monasticism and Religious Orders; Pastoral Theology; Priests; Theologians; Women Clergy
also subdivision Clergy under church denominations, e.g. Church of England–Clergy
Baxter, Richard. The Reformed Pastor: A Pattern for Personal Growth & Ministry. rev. ed. Houston, James M., ed. LC 82-18825. (Classics of Faith & Devotion Ser.). 150p. 1983. 9.95 (ISBN 0-88070-003-3). Multnomah.
Goodenough, Simon. The Country Parson. (Illus.). 192p. 1983. 19.95 (ISBN 0-7153-8238-1). David & Charles.
Hagin, Kenneth E. Godliness Is Profitable. 1982. pap. 0.50 (ISBN 0-89276-256-X). Hagin Ministry.
--The Ministry Gifts Study Guide. 1981. pap. 10.00 spiral bdg. (ISBN 0-89276-092-3). Hagin Ministry.
Oates, Wayne E. The Christian Pastor. Rev. 3rd ed. LC 82-4933. 1982. pap. 9.95 (ISBN 0-664-24372-X). Westminster.
Patsavos, L. J. & Charles, G. J. The Role of the Priest & the Apostolate of the Laity. Vaporis, N. M., ed. (Clergy Seminar Lectures Ser.). 63p. (Orig.). 1983. pap. 3.00 (ISBN 0-916586-57-X). Holy Cross Orthodox.
Tracy, David & Cobb, John B., Jr. Talking About God: Doing Theology in the Context of Modern Pluralism. 144p. 1983. 6.95 (ISBN 0-8164-2458-6). Seabury.
CLERGY–CORRESPONDENCE, REMINISCENCES, ETC.
see also subdivision Clergy–Correspondence, Reminiscences, etc. under particular denominations, e.g. Catholic Church–Clergy–Correspondence, Reminiscences, etc.
Smith, John C. From Colonialism to World Community: The Church's Pilgrimage. LC 82-12138. 1982. pap. 8.95 (ISBN 0-664-24452-1). Westminster.
CLERGY–MAJOR ORDERS
see Clergy
CLERGY–OFFICE
Pittenger, Norman. The Ministry of All Christians. 96p. 1983. pap. write for info. (ISBN 0-8192-1323-3). Morehouse.
CLERGY–RELIGIOUS LIFE
see also Retreats; Spiritual Direction
Krueger, Catherine M. Mother Was a Bachelor. 1983. 10.00 (ISBN 0-533-05496-6). Vantage.
Loetscher, Lefferts A. Facing the Enlightenment & Pietism: Archibald Alexander & the Founding of Princeton Theological Seminary. LC 82-11995. (Contributions to the Study of Religion Ser.: No. 8). 352p. 1983. lib. bdg. 35.00 (ISBN 0-313-23677-1, LOE/). Greenwood.
O'Meara, Thomas F. Theology of Ministry: Charism within Culture. LC 82-60588. 1983. pap. 8.95 (ISBN 0-8091-2487-4). Paulist Pr.
CLERGY–SALARIES, PENSIONS, ETC.
Simon, John M. Abingdon Clergy Tax Record Book, 1983. 80p. (Orig.). 1983. pap. 5.95 (ISBN 0-687-00386-5). Abingdon.
Waterhouse. Abingdon Clergy Income Tax Guide, 1983: For 1982 Returns. Rev. ed. 96p. (Orig.). 1983. pap. 4.95 (ISBN 0-687-00384-9). Abingdon.
CLERGY–GREAT BRITAIN
Moore, Aubrey. A Son of the Rectory. 160p. 1982. text ed. 16.75x (ISBN 0-86299-035-1, Pub. by Sutton England); pap. text ed. 8.50x (ISBN 0-86299-036-X). Humanities.
CLERGY–RUSSIA
Freeze, Gregory. The Parish Clergy in Nineteenth-Century Russia: Crisis, Reform, Counter-Reform. LC 82-61361. 552p. 1983. 50.00x (ISBN 0-691-05381-2). Princeton U Pr.
CLERGY–SCOTLAND
Brown, Stewart J. Thomas Chalmers & Godly Commonwealth in Scotland. (Illus.). 368p. 1983. 55.00 (ISBN 0-19-213114-1). Oxford U Pr.
CLERGY, CITY
see City Clergy
CLERICAL EMPLOYEES
see Clerks
CLERICAL MEDICINE
see Pastoral Medicine
CLERKS
see also Office Practice; Receptionists
Rudman, Jack. Administrative Services Clerk. (Career Examination Ser.: C-2869). (Cloth bdg. avail. on request). pap. 10.00 (ISBN 0-8373-2869-1). Natl Learning.
--Senior Office Assistant. (Career Examination Ser.: C-2594). (Cloth bdg. avail. on request). pap. 10.00 (ISBN 0-8373-2594-3). Natl Learning.
Steinberg, Eve P. How to Get a Clerical Job in Government. LC 82-16263. 224p. 1983. pap. 8.00 (ISBN 0-686-82499-7, 5647). Arco.
CLERKS–EXAMINATIONS, QUESTIONS, ETC.
Rudman, Jack. Commissary Clerk I. (Career Examination Ser.: C-216). (Cloth bdg. avail. on request). pap. 8.00 (ISBN 0-8373-0216-1). Natl Learning.
--Commissary Clerk II. (Career Examination Ser.: C-217). (Cloth bdg. avail. on request). pap. 8.00 (ISBN 0-8373-0217-X). Natl Learning.
--Commissary Clerk III. (Career Examination Ser.: C-218). (Cloth bdg. avail. on request). pap. 10.00 (ISBN 0-8373-0218-8). Natl Learning.
--Commissary Clerk IV. (Career Examination Ser.: C-219). (Cloth bdg. avail. on request). pap. 10.00 (ISBN 0-8373-0219-6). Natl Learning.
--Principal Administrative Services Clerk. (Career Examination Ser.: C-2871). (Cloth bdg. avail. on request). pap. 12.00 (ISBN 0-8373-2871-3). Natl Learning.
--Principal Office Assistant. (Career Examination Ser.: C-2595). pap. 12.00 (ISBN 0-8373-2595-1); avail. Natl Learning.
--Recording Clerk. (Career Examination Ser.: C-2914). (Cloth bdg. avail. on request). pap. 10.00 (ISBN 0-8373-2914-0). Natl Learning.
--Senior Clerk-Stenographer. (Career Examination Ser.: C-2633). (Cloth bdg. avail. on request). pap. 10.00 (ISBN 0-8373-2633-8). Natl Learning.
CLERKS OF COURT
Rudman, Jack. Associate Court Clerk. (Career Examination Ser.: C-2587). (Cloth bdg. avail. on request). pap. 12.00 (ISBN 0-8373-2587-0). Natl Learning.
CLEVELAND, GROVER, PRES. U. S., 1837-1908
Ford, Henry J. Cleveland Era. 1919. text ed. 8.50x (ISBN 0-686-83504-2). Elliots Bks.
CLEVELAND
DeLuca, Michael & Michaelides, Stephen. Dining In--Cleveland. (Dining In--Ser.). (Illus.). 190p. 1982. pap. 8.95 (ISBN 0-89716-034-7). Peanut Butter.
Lynch, Kevin W. A Woman's Guide to Cleveland Men. 224p. 1982. pap. 5.95 (ISBN 0-911671-00-5). Lynch Group Pub.
CLIMACTERIC
Van Keep, Pieter A. & Utian, Wulf H., eds. The Controversial Climacteric. (Illus.). 200p. 1982. text ed. 25.00 (ISBN 0-85200-410-9, Pub. by MTP Pr England). Kluwer Boston.
CLIMATE
see Climatology
CLIMATE, INFLUENCE OF
see Man-Influence of Environment
CLIMATOLOGY
see also Dendrochronology; Meteorology; Paleoclimatology; Vegetation and Climate; Weather also names of countries, cities, etc. with or without the subdivision Climate
Griffiths, John F. Climate & the Environment: The Atmospheric Impact on Man. LC 76-5801. (Westview Environmental Studies Ser.: Vol. 2). 1976. pap. text ed. 11.00 (ISBN 0-236-40022-3). Westview.
McCormac, Billy M., ed. Solar-Terrestrial Influences on Weather & Climate. 1983. 19.50x (ISBN 0-87081-138-X). Colo Assoc.
Muller, Manfred J. Selected Climatic Data for a Global Set of Standard Stations for Vegetation Science. 1982. 87.00 (ISBN 90-6193-945-3, Pub. by Junk Pubs. Netherlands). Kluwer Boston.
Sulman, Felix G. Short & Long Term Changes in Climate, Vol. I. 224p. 1982. 59.50 (ISBN 0-686-84131-X). CRC Pr.
--Short & Long Term Changes in Climate, Vol. II. 184p. 1982. 59.50 (ISBN 0-8493-6421-3). CRC Pr.
Thran, P. & Brockhuizen, S., eds. Agro-Climatic Atlas of Europe. (Agro-Ecological Atlas Ser.: Vol. 1). 1965. 202.25 (ISBN 0-444-40569-0). Elsevier.
Updegraffe, Imelda & Updegraffe, Robert. Continents & Climates. (Turning Points Ser.). (Illus.). 24p. 1983. pap. 3.50 (ISBN 0-14-049188-0, Puffin). Penguin.
Watson, Donald & Labs, Kenneth. Climatic Design: Energy Efficient Buildings Principles & Practices. (Illus.). 288p. 1983. 29.95 (ISBN 0-07-068478-2, P&RB). McGraw.
CLIMATOLOGY, AGRICULTURAL
see Crops and Climate
CLIMBING PLANTS
Darwin, Charles R. The Movement & Habits of Climbing Plants. LC 72-3896. (Illus.). viii, 208p. write for info. (ISBN 0-404-08411-7). AMS Pr.
CLINICAL CHEMISTRY
see Chemistry, Clinical
CLINICAL ENDOCRINOLOGY
see also Pediatric Endocrinology
Carlson, Harold E. Endocrinology. (UCLA Series of Internal Medicine Today: A Comprehensive Postgraduate Library). 328p. 1983. 35.00 (ISBN 0-471-09553-2, Pub. By Wiley Med). Wiley.
CLINICAL ENGINEERING
see Biomedical Engineering
CLINICAL ENZYMOLOGY
Colowick, Sidney P. & Kaplan, Sidney O., eds. Methods in Enzymology: Polyamines, Vol. 94. Date not set. price not set (ISBN 0-12-181994-9). Acad Pr.
Kaldor. Clinical Enzymology. 256p. 1983. 27.50 (ISBN 0-03-063217-X). Praeger.
Usdin, E. & Weiner, N. Function & Regulation of Monoamine Enzymes: Basic & Clinical Aspects. 1982. 159.00x (ISBN 0-686-42941-9, Pub. by Macmillan England). State Mutual Bk.
Weiner, Henry & Wermuth, Bendicht, eds. Enzymology of Carbonyl Metabolism: Aldehyde Dehydrogenase & Carbonyl Reductase. LC 82-20381. (Progress in Clinical & Biological Research Ser.: Vol. 114). 430p. 1982. 44.00 (ISBN 0-8451-0114-5). A R Liss.
CLINICAL LABORATORY TECHNICIANS
see Medical Technologists
CLINICAL MEDICINE
see Medicine, Clinical
CLINICAL PARASITOLOGY
see Medical Parasitology
CLINICAL PHYSIOLOGY
see Physiology, Pathological
CLINICAL PSYCHOLOGY
see also Psychological Tests
also names of specific psychological tests
Cohen, S. I. & Ross, R. N. Handbook of Clinical Psychobiology & Pathology, 2 Vols. Date not set. Vol. 1. 25.00 (ISBN 0-07-011621-0); Vol. 2. 35.00 (ISBN 0-07-011622-9). McGraw.
Feldmann, H. Kompendium der Medizinischen Psychologie. (Illus.). viii, 264p. 1983. pap. 12.00 (ISBN 3-8055-3673-9). S Karger.
Hersen, Michel & Kazdin, Alan E., eds. The Clinical Psychology Handbook. (General Psychology Ser.: No. 120). 1000p. Date not set. 100.00 (ISBN 0-08-028058-7); before 7/83 75.00 (ISBN 0-686-82630-2). Pergamon.
Manuso, James S. Occupational Clinical Psychology. 350p. 1983. 35.95 (ISBN 0-03-059006-X). Praeger.
Norton, James C. Introduction to Medical Psychology. 416p. 1982. text ed. 22.95 (ISBN 0-02-923290-2). Free Pr.
Sundberg, Norman & Tyler, Leona. Introduction to Clinical Psychology: Perspectives, Issues, & Contributions to Human Service. (Illus.). 512p. 1983. 23.95 (ISBN 0-13-479451-6). P-H.
Walker, C. E., ed. The Handbook of Clinical Psychology: Theory, Research & Practice, Vol. I. (The Dorsey Professional Ser.). 425p. 1983. 35.00 (ISBN 0-87094-319-7). Dow Jones-Irwin.
--The Handbook of Clinical Psychology: Theory, Research & Practice, Vol. II. (The Dorsey Professional Ser.). 425p. 1983. 35.00 (ISBN 0-87094-411-8). Dow Jones-Irwin.
CLINICAL RADIOLOGY
see Radiology, Medical
CLINICAL RECORDS
see Medical Records
CLIPPING OF DOGS
see Dog Grooming

CLOCK AND WATCH MAKERS

Chandlee, Edward E. Six Quaker Clockmakers. (Illus.). 260p. Repr. of 1943 ed. 12.95 (ISBN 0-686-81726-5). New Eng Pub.

CLOCKS AND WATCHES

see also Time Measurements

Illinois Watch Co: 1923 Material & Price List. Repr. 5.00 (ISBN 0-913902-46-2). Heart Am Pr.

Maurice, Klaus & Mayr, Otto. The Clockwork Universe: German Clocks & Automata 1550-1650. LC 80-16780. (Illus.). 331p. 1980. 19.95 (ISBN 0-87474-628-0). Smithsonian.

Research in Outdoor Education: Summaries of Doctoral Studies. 8.95 (ISBN 0-88314-220-1). AAHPERD.

Shugart, Cooksey & Engle, Tom. Complete Guide to American Pocket Watches. 3rd ed. (Illus.). 320p. 1983. pap. 9.95 (ISBN 0-517-54916-6). Overstreet.

--The Complete Guide to American Pocket Watches 1983: Pocket Watches from 1809-1950. 1983. pap. 9.95 (ISBN 0-517-54916-6, Harmony). Crown.

Townsend, George. Everything You Wanted TO Know About American Watches & Didn't Know Who to Ask. 1974. 8.00 (ISBN 0-913902-38-1). Heart Am Pr.

--Watch That Made the Dollar Famous. 1974. 8.00 (ISBN 0-913702-39-0). Heart Am Pr.

Waterbury Clock Co. Waterbury Clocks: The Complete Illustrated Catalog of 1983. 2nd ed. (Illus.). 128p. 1983. pap. 5.00 (ISBN 0-486-24460-1). Dover.

Weaver. Electoral & Electronic Clocks & Watches. 1982. text ed. 29.95 (ISBN 0-408-01140-8). Butterworth.

CLOCKS AND WATCHES–REPAIRING AND ADJUSTING

Barder, Richard C. Grandfather Clocks: The English Country Longcase, 1660-1830. (Illus.). 192p. 1983. 31.50 (ISBN 0-7153-8314-0). David & Charles.

Vernon, John. The Grandfather Clock Maintenance Manual. (Illus.). 104p. 1983. 14.95 (ISBN 0-7153-8438-4). David & Charles.

CLONING

see also Plant Propagation

Hyde, Margaret O. Cloning & the New Genetics. (Illus.). 128p. (gr. 5-11). 1983. 10.95 (ISBN 0-89490-084-6). Enslow Pubs.

CLOSE-UP PHOTOGRAPHY

see Photography, Close-Up

CLOTH

see Textile Fabrics

CLOTHING

see Clothing and Dress; Costume

CLOTHING, DOLL

see Doll Clothes

CLOTHING, MEN'S

see Men's Clothing

CLOTHING AND DRESS

Here are entered works dealing with clothing as a covering for the body and works on the art of dress. Descriptive and historical works on the costumes of particular countries, nations, or periods are entered under Costume.

see also Children's Clothing; Costume; Costume Design; Dress Accessories; Dressmaking; Fashion; Men's Clothing; Models, Fashion; Tailoring; Trousers

Buck, Peter. Arts & Crafts of Hawaii: Clothing, Sec. V. (Special Publication Ser.: No. 45). (Illus.). 97p. 1957. pap. 3.00 (ISBN 0-910240-38-8). Bishop Mus.

Fairchild Market Research Division. Infants' Toddlers' Girls' & Boys' (Fact File Ser.). (Illus.). 1983. pap. text ed. 12.50 (ISBN 0-87005-457-0). Fairchild.

--Women's Coats, Suits, Rainwear, Furs. (Fact File Ser.). (Illus.). 50p. 1983. pap. text ed. 12.50 (ISBN 0-87005-459-7). Fairchild.

Irick, Tina. The First Price Guide to Antique & Vintage Clothes: Styles for Women. (Illus.). 128p. 1983. pap. 13.95 (ISBN 0-525-48050-1, 01354-410). Dutton.

Lyle & Brinkley. Contemporary Clothing. 1983. text ed. write for info. (ISBN 0-87002-381-0). Bennett Il.

Maeder, Edward, et al. An Elegant Art: Fashion & Fantasy in the Eighteenth Century. Freshman, Phil, ed. (Illus.). 256p. (Orig.). 1983. 45.00 (ISBN 0-8109-0864-6); pap. 16.95 (ISBN 0-87587-111-9). LA Co Art Mus.

Packard, Sidney & Winters, Arthur. Fashion Buying & Merchandising. 2nd ed. (Illus.). 390p. 1983. text ed. 16.50 (ISBN 0-87005-445-7). Fairchild.

Rosen, Selma. Children's Clothing: Designing, Selecting Fabrics, Patternmaking, Sewing. LC 82-83319. (Illus.). 150p. 1983. text ed. 15.00. Fairchild.

Williams-Mitchell, Christobel. Dressed for the Job: The Story of Occupational Costume. (Illus.). 144p. 1983. 16.95 (ISBN 0-7137-1020-9, Pub. by Blandford Pr England). Sterling.

Wilson, R. Turner. The Mode in Costume. (Illus.). 480p. 1983. pap. 13.95 (ISBN 0-686-83797-5, ScribT). Scribner.

CLOTHING AND DRESS–JUVENILE LITERATURE

Hare, Lorraine. Who Needs Her? LC 82-13899. (Illus.). 32p. (gr. 2-5). 1983. 9.95 (ISBN 0-689-50268-0, McElderry Bk). Atheneum.

CLOTHING AND DRESS–REPAIRING

Kennett, Frances. The Collector's Book of Fashion. (Illus.). 1983. 22.50 (ISBN 0-517-54860-7). Crown.

CLOTHING AND DRESS IN ART

see Costume in Art

CLOUD PHYSICS

Agee, E. M. & Assai, T., eds. Cloud Dynamics. 1982. 49.50 (ISBN 90-277-1458-4, Pub. by Reidel Holland). Kluwer Boston.

COACHING

see also Roads

Holmes, Oliver W. & Rohrbach, Peter T. Stagecoach East: Stagecoach Days in the East from the Colonial period to the Civil War. (Illus.). 240p. 1983. text ed. 17.50x (ISBN 0-87474-522-5). Smithsonian.

Maurer, Stephen G., ed. Grand Canyon by Stage. (Illus.). 24p. (Orig.). 1982. pap. 3.85 (ISBN 0-910467-00-5). Heritage Assocs.

COACHING (ATHLETICS)

see also Football Coaching; Soccer Coaching; Track-Athletics Coaching

Leggett, Les. The Philosophy of Coaching. (Illus.). 256p. 1983. text ed. 19.75 (ISBN 0-398-04784-7). C C Thomas.

COAL

see also Coal Mines and Mining; Lignite

Blaustein, Bernard D. & Bockrath, Bradley C., eds. New Approaches in Coal Chemistry. (ACS Symposium Ser.: No. 169). 1981. write for info. (ISBN 0-8412-0659-7). Am Chemical.

Chadwick, M. J. & Lindman, N., eds. Environmental Implications of Expanded Coal Utilization. LC 81-23560. (Illus.). 304p. 1982. 55.00 (ISBN 0-08-028734-4). Pergamon.

Coal Pyrolysis. (Coal Science & Technology Ser.: No. 4). 168p. 1982. 53.25 (ISBN 0-444-42107-6). Elsevier.

Dryden, I. G., ed. Coal Science, Vol. 1. (Serial Publication). 304p. 1982. 32.50 (ISBN 0-12-150701-7). Acad Pr.

Edgar, Thomas F. Coal Processing & Population Control Handbook. 1983. text ed. 45.00 (ISBN 0-87201-122-4). Gulf Pub.

Hellman, Caroline J. C. & Hellman, Richard. The Competitive Economics of Nuclear & Coal Power. LC 82-47500. 208p. 1982. 23.95x (ISBN 0-669-05533-6). Lexington Bks.

OECD. Coal Liquification: A Technology Review. 70p. (Orig.). 1982. pap. 9.25x (ISBN 92-64-12377-6). OECD.

OECD Staff. The Use of Coal in Industry. 445p. (Orig.). 1982. pap. 44.00x (ISBN 92-64-12308-3). OECD.

Shannon, Robert H. Handbook of Coal-Based Electric Power Generation: The Technology, Utilization, Application & Economics of Coal for Generating Electric Power. LC 82-7916. (Illus.). 372p. 1983. 45.00 (ISBN 0-8155-0907-3). Noyes.

Sheahan, Richard. Coal Conversion Decisionmaking: Industry Notebook. 250p. 1982. Wkbk. 48.00 (ISBN 0-86587-101-9). Gov Insts.

COAL–COMBUSTION

see Combustion

COAL LANDS

see Coal

COAL MINERS–GREAT BRITAIN

Douglass, David & Krieger, Joel. A Miner's Life. 116p. (Orig.). 1983. pap. 8.95 (ISBN 0-7100-9473-6). Routledge & Kegan.

COAL MINES AND MINING

Barat, Morton S. The Union & the Coal Industry. LC 82-25141. (Yale Studies in Economics: Vol. 4). xvii, 170p. 1983. Repr. of 1955 ed. lib. bdg. 29.75x (ISBN 0-313-23698-4, BAUC). Greenwood.

Brant, Russell A. Coal Resources of the Princess District, Kentucky. Pettit, Rhonda & Cobb, James, eds. (Energy Resource Ser.). (Illus.). 50p. (Orig.). 1982. pap. text ed. 10.00 (ISBN 0-86607-011-7). Inst Mining & Minerals.

Coal Age Magazine. Coal Age Operating Handbook of Underground Mining. 1977. 25.90 (ISBN 0-07-011457-9). McGraw.

--Operating Handbook of Coal Surface Mining. 1978. 25.90 (ISBN 0-07-011458-7). McGraw.

Crickmer, D. F. & Zegeer, D. A., eds. Elements of Practical Coal Mining. 2nd ed. LC 79-57346. (Illus.). 847p. 1981. 44.00x (ISBN 0-89520-270-0, 270-0). Soc Mining Eng.

Houghton-Alico, Doann & Dunning, Marcy. Mining Industry Permitting Guidelines: Coal Exploration & Production - the Western Region. 450p. 1982. 650.00 (ISBN 0-86531-463-2). Westview.

Quirk. Coal Models & Use in Government Planning. 288p. 1982. 29.95 (ISBN 0-03-061576-3). Praeger.

COAL MINES AND MINING–GREAT BRITAIN

British Coal-Mining Industrty During the War. (Economic & Social History of the World War Ser.). 1923. text ed. 65.00x (ISBN 0-686-37864-4). Elliots Bks.

COAL OIL

see Petroleum

COAL TRADE

Crow, Michael M., ed. High Sulfur Coal Exports: An International Analysis. 1983. write for info. (ISBN 0-8093-1122-4). S Ill U Pr.

OECD Staff & IEA Staff. Coal Prospects & Policies in IEA Countries, 1981 Review. 170p. (Orig.). 1982. pap. 17.00x (ISBN 92-64-12336-9). OECD.

COAST CHANGES

see also Sedimentation and Deposition; Shore Lines; Shore Protection

Coastal Discharges: Engineering Aspects & Experience. 224p. 1981. 99.00x (ISBN 0-7277-0124-X, Pub. by Telford England). State Mutual Bk.

COAST PROTECTION

see Shore Protection

COAST PROTECTIVE WORKS

see Shore Protection

COASTAL ECOLOGY

see Seashore Ecology

COASTAL SIGNALS

see Signals and Signaling

COASTAL ZONE MANAGEMENT

see also Marine Pollution; Shore Protection

United Nations Department of International Economic & Social Affairs, Ocean Economics & Technology Branch. Coastal Area Management & Development. 196p. 1982. 40.00 (ISBN 0-08-023393-7). Pergamon.

COASTS

see also Coast Changes; Coastal Zone Management; Estuaries; Ocean Waves; Seashore; Shore Protection; Territorial Waters

Beer, T. Environmental Oceanography: An Introduction to the Behaviour of Coastal Waters. (PIL Ser.). (Illus.). 109p. 1983. 40.00 (ISBN 0-08-026291-0); pap. 14.00 (ISBN 0-08-026290-2). Pergamon.

Swift, D. J. & Palmer, Harold D., eds. Coastal Sedimentation. LC 78-18696. (Benchmark Papers in Geology Ser.: Vol. 42). 339p. 1978. 48.50 (ISBN 0-87933-330-8). Hutchinson Ross.

COATED PAPER

see Paper Coatings

COATINGS, PROTECTIVE

see Protective Coatings

COATS OF ARMS

see Heraldry

COBOL (COMPUTER PROGRAM LANGUAGE)

Ashley, Ruth. ANS Cobol. 2nd ed. LC 78-27717. (Self-Teaching Guide Ser.). 265p. 1979. pap. text ed. 9.50 (ISBN 0-471-05136-5). Wiley.

--Structured Cobol. LC 79-27340. (Self-Teaching Guides Ser.). 295p. 1980. pap. text ed. 10.95 (ISBN 0-471-05362-7). Wiley.

Ashley, Ruth & Fernandez, Judi. COBOL for Microcomputers. (Self-Teaching Guide Ser.). 288p. 1983. pap. text ed. 10.95 (ISBN 0-471-87241-5). Wiley.

Carver, D. Keith. Structured COBOL for Microcomputers. LC 82-20573. (Computer Science Ser.). 418p. 1983. pap. text ed. 17.95 (ISBN 0-534-01421-6). Brooks-Cole.

Clary, Wayne. OS Debugging for the COBOL Programmer. Eckols, Steve & Taylor, Judy, eds. LC 80-84122. (Illus.). 312p. (Orig.). 1981. pap. text ed. 20.00 (ISBN 0-911625-10-0). M Murach & Assoc.

Davis, G. B. & Olson, M. H. Elementary Structured COBOL: A Step by Step Approach. 3rd ed. 416p. 1983. 14.95 (ISBN 0-07-015788-X); write for info. inst's manual (ISBN 0-07-015789-8). McGraw.

Feingold, Carl. Fundamentals of Structured COBOL Programming. 4th ed. 720p. 1983. pap. text ed. write for info. (ISBN 0-697-08173-7); write for info. (ISBN 0-697-08185-0); write for info. (ISBN 0-697-08186-9). Wm C Brown.

Horn & Gleason. Beginning Structured COBOL. 450p. 1983. pap. text ed. 21.95x (ISBN 0-87835-133-7). Boyd & Fraser.

Kant, Sharad. Practical Approach to Cobol Programming. 250p. 1983. 19.95 (ISBN 0-470-27392-5). Halsted Pr.

Kudlick, Michael D. & Ledin, George, Jr. The COBOL Programmer's Book of Rules. (Computer Technology Ser.). (Illus.). 224p. pap. 14.95 (ISBN 0-534-97923-8). Lifetime Learn.

Lowe, Doug. VSAM for the COBOL Programmer. Murach, Mike, ed. (Illus.). 150p. 1982. pap. text ed. 15.00 (ISBN 0-911625-12-7). M Murach & Assoc.

McNitt, Lawrence. Invitation to COBOL for the TRS-80. (Illus.). 330p. 1983. text ed. 15.00 (ISBN 0-89433-209-0). Petrocelli.

Murach, Mike & Noll, Paul. Structured ANS COBOL, 2 pts. Incl. Pt. 1. A Course for Novices. 498p; Pt. 2. An Advanced Course. 458p. (Illus.). 1979. pap. text ed. 20.00 ea. (ISBN 0-911625-13-5). M Murach & Assoc.

Noll, Paul. Structured Programming for the COBOL Programmer. Taylor, Judy, ed. LC 77-85445. (Illus.). 239p. (Orig.). 1977. pap. text ed. 15.00 (ISBN 0-911625-03-8). M Murach & Assoc.

Noll, Paul & Murach, Mike. Structured ANS COBOL Advisor's Guide. 320p. (Orig.). 1980. 3 ring bdr. 100.00 (ISBN 0-911625-09-7). M Murach & Assoc.

Parkin, Andrew. COBOL for Students. 224p. 1982. pap. text ed. 14.95 (ISBN 0-7131-3477-1). E Arnold.

--COBOL Workbook. 80p. 1981. pap. text ed. 8.95 (ISBN 0-7131-3438-0). E Arnold.

Philippakis, Andreas & Kazmier, Leonard. Program Design Concepts with Application in COBOL. (Illus.). 240p. 1983. text ed. 24.95 (ISBN 0-07-049808-3, C). McGraw.

Pollack, Morris & Geist, Harry. Structured COBOL Programming. 340p. (Orig.). 1982. pap. text ed. 19.95 (ISBN 0-672-97690-0). Bobbs.

Popkin, Gary S. Advanced Structured COBOL. 512p. 1983. pap. text ed. 23.95x (ISBN 0-534-01394-5). Kent Pub Co.

COBRA (AUTOMOBILE)

see Automobiles–Types–Cobra

COCHIN CHINA

see Vietnam

COCHITI INDIANS

see Indians of North America–Southwest, New

COCKATEELS

Low, Rosemary. How to Keep Parrots, Cockatiels & Macaws in Cage or Aviary. (Illus.). 96p. 1980. 3.95 (ISBN 0-7028-1029-0). Avian Pubns.

COCKER SPANIEL

see Dogs–Breeds–Cocker Spaniel

COCKTAILS

Chester, Helen. Cocktails. (Illus.). 80p. 1983. pap. 4.95 (ISBN 0-312-14634-5). St Martin.

COCONUT-PALM

Thampan, P. K. Handbook of Coconut Palm. 311p. 1981. 63.00x (ISBN 0-686-84455-6, Pub. by Oxford & I B H India). State Mutual Bk.

CODES, ERROR CORRECTING

see Error-Correcting Codes (Information Theory)

CODETERMINATION (INDUSTRIAL RELATIONS)

see Employees' Representation in Management

CODICILS

see Wills

CODING THEORY

see also Error-Correcting Codes (Information Theory); Programming (Electronic Computers)

Blake, Ian F., ed. Algebraic Coding Theory: History & Development. LC 73-9627. (Benchmark Papers in Electrical Engineering & Computer Science: Vol. 3). 413p. 1973. 49.50 (ISBN 0-87933-038-4). Hutchinson Ross.

CODY, WILLIAM FREDERICK, 1846-1917

see Buffalo Bill, 1846-1917

COEFFICIENT OF EXPANSION

see Gases

COENZYMES

Everse, Johannes, et al, eds. The Pyridine Nucleotide Coenzymes. 416p. 1982. 46.00 (ISBN 0-12-244750-6). Acad Pr.

COEXISTENCE

see United States–Foreign Relations–Russia; World Politics–1945-

COFFEE HOUSES

Boettcher, Jurgen. Coffee Houses of Europe. (Illus.). 1983. 29.95 (ISBN 0-500-54063-2). Thames Hudson.

COFFEE TRADE

Bergad, Laird W. Coffee & the Growth of Agrarian Capitalism in Nineteenth-Century Puerto Rico. LC 82-61354. (Illus.). 264p. 1983. 25.00x (ISBN 0-691-07646-4); pap. 12.50 (ISBN 0-691-10139-6). Princeton U Pr.

COG-WHEELS

see Gearing

COGNITION

see also Knowledge, Theory Of; Perception

Anderson, John R. The Architecture of Cognition. (Cognitive Science Ser.: No. 5). (Illus.). 352p. 1983. text ed. 25.00x (ISBN 0-674-04425-8). Harvard U Pr.

Brainerd, Charles J., ed. Recent Advances in Cognitive-Developmental Theory, Progress in Cognitive Developmental Research. (Springer Series in Cognitive Development). (Illus.). 288p. 1983. 29.95 (ISBN 0-387-90767-X). Springer-Verlag.

Broadbent, D. E. & Weiskrantz, L., eds. The Neuropsychology of Cognitive Function: Proceedings of a Royal Society Discussion Meeting, November 18-19, 1981. (RSL Philosophical Transcriptions of the Royal Society of London, Ser. B: Vol. 298, No. 1089). (Illus.). 230p. 1982. text ed. 68.00x (ISBN 0-85403-190-1, Pub. by Royal Soc London). Scholium Intl.

Dillon, Ronna F. & Schmeck, Ronald R., eds. Individual Differences in Cognition, Vol. 1. Date not set. 34.00 (ISBN 0-12-216401-6). Acad Pr.

Ellis, Henry C. & Hunt, R. Reed. Fundamentals of Human Memory & Cognition. 3rd ed. 350p. 1983. pap. text ed. write for info. (ISBN 0-697-06554-5); instr's. manual avail. (ISBN 0-697-06555-3). Wm C Brown.

Emery, Gary. Own Your Own Life: How the New Cognitive Therapy Can Make You Feel Wonderful. 1982. 15.95 (ISBN 0-453-00428-8, H428). NAL.

Fodor, Jerry A. Representations: Philosophical Essays on the Foundations of Cognitive Science. 356p. 1983. pap. 9.95x (ISBN 0-262-56027-5). MIT Pr.

Guidano, V. F. & Liotti, G. Cognitive Processes of Emotional Disorders. LC 83-13188. (Psychology & Psychotherapy Ser.). 347p. 1983. text ed. 24.50x (ISBN 0-89862-006-6). Guilford Pr.

Higgins, E. Tory & Hartup, Willard W., eds. Social Cognition & Social Development: A Sociocultural Perspective. LC 82-12897. (Cambridge Studies in Social & Emotional Development: No. 5). 352p. Date not set. price not set (ISBN 0-521-24587-7). Cambridge U Pr.

Kaplan. Cognition & Environment. 304p. 1982. 29.95 (ISBN 0-03-062344-8); pap. 13.95 (ISBN 0-03-062346-4). Praeger.

Malatesha, Rattihalli N. Neuropsychology & Cognition. 1982. lib. bdg. 135.00 (ISBN 90-247-2752-9, Pub. by Martinus Nijhoff Netherlands). Kluwer Boston.

Olson, David R. & Bialystok, Ellen. Spatial Cognition: The Structure & Development of Mental Representations of Spatial Relations. 256p. 1983. text ed. price not set (ISBN 0-89859-252-6). L Erlbaum Assocs.

Saljo, Roger. Learning & Understanding. (Goteborg Studies in Educational Sciences: No. 41). 212p. 1982. pap. text ed. 17.25x (ISBN 91-7346-106-7, Pub. by Acta-Universitatis Sweden). Humanities.

Serafica, Felicisima C. Social-Cognitive Development in Context. LC 82-2933. 283p. 1982. text ed. 24.50x (ISBN 0-89862-623-4). Guilford Pr.

Steingart, Irving. Cognition as Pathological Play in Borderline-Narcissistic Personalities. 256p. 1983. text ed. 25.00 (ISBN 0-89335-179-2). SP Med & Sci Bks.

Thatcher, Robert W. & John, E. Roy. Functional Neuroscience: Foundations of Cognitive Processes, Vol. 1. 400p. 1977. text ed. 29.95 (ISBN 0-89859-141-4). L Erlbaum Assocs.

Tighe, Thomas J., ed. Perception, Cognition & Development: Interactional Analyses. Shepp, Bryan E. 400p. 1983. text ed. 39.95 (ISBN 0-89859-254-2). L Erlbaum Assocs.

Wertheimer, Max. Productive Thinking: Enlarged Edition. LC 82-10913. (Phoenix Ser.). 328p. 1982. pap. 8.95 (ISBN 0-226-89376-6). U of Chicago Pr.

COGNITION (CHILD PSYCHOLOGY)

Ault, Ruth L. Children's Cognitive Development. 2nd ed. (Illus.). 1982. 15.00x (ISBN 0-19-503183-0); pap. 6.00 (ISBN 0-19-503184-9). Oxford U Pr.

Cohen, Gillian, ed. Psychology of Cognition. 2nd ed. Date not set. price not set (ISBN 0-12-178760-5); pap. price not set (ISBN 0-12-178762-1). Acad Pr.

Tronick, Edward Z., ed. Social Interchange in Infancy: Affect, Cognition & Communication. (Illus.). 240p. 1982. 29.95 (ISBN 0-8391-1510-5, 17493). Univ Park.

COHOMOLOGY THEORY

see Homology Theory

COIFFURE

see Hairdressing

COINAGE

see also Currency Question; Gold; Money; Silver Question

Edmund's United States Coin Prices. (Orig.). 1983. pap. 2.50 (ISBN 0-440-02438-2). Dell.

COINS

Here are entered lists of coins, specimens, etc. Works about coins are entered under the heading numismatics.

see also Gold Coins

also names of coins

Coin Yearbook, 1983. 16th ed. LC 74-644812. (Illus.). 386p. 1982. pap. 13.50x (ISBN 0-901265-18-7). Intl Pubns Serv.

Frank, Alan R. & McFarland, Thomas. Coin Skills Curriculum. (Illus.). 100p. (Orig.). 1983. pap. text ed. write for info. (ISBN 0-936104-28-7, 0360). Pro Ed.

Hoberman, J. Art of Coins & Their Photography. 1982. lib. bdg. 75.00 (ISBN 0-686-43399-8). S J Durst.

Reinfeld, Fred & Hobson, Burton. Catalogue of the World's Most Popular Coins. 11th ed. (Illus.). 544p. 1983. 24.95 (ISBN 0-8069-6078-7); lib. bdg. 29.49 (ISBN 0-8069-6079-5); pap. 16.95 (ISBN 0-8069-7708-6). Sterling.

COINS, AMERICAN

U. S. Coins & Currency. (What's It Worth Ser.). Date not set. pap. 2.95 (ISBN 0-440-09209-4). Dell.

Wilhite, Bob & Lemke, Bob. Standard Guide to U. S. Coin & Paper Money Valuations. 9th ed. LC 79-67100. (Illus.). 1982. pap. 2.25 (ISBN 0-87341-025-4). Krause Pubns.

Yeoman, R. S. Handbook of United States Coins. 40th, rev. ed. Bressett, Kenneth E., ed. (Illus.). 224p. 1982. 3.50 (ISBN 0-307-01983-7, Pub. by Whitman Coin Products). Western Pub.

COINS, ANCIENT

Betlyon, John. The Coinage & Mints of Phoenicia: The Pre-Alexandrine Period. (Harvard Semitic Monographs). 184p. 1982. 18.75 (ISBN 0-686-42951-6, 04-00-26). Scholars Pr CA.

COINS, ARABIC

Betlyon, John. The Coinage & Mints of Phoenicia: The Pre-Alexandrine Period. (Harvard Semitic Monographs). 184p. 1982. 18.75 (ISBN 0-686-42951-6, 04-00-26). Scholars Pr CA.

COINS, GREEK

Miller, Michael F. Classical Greek & Roman Coins: The Investor's Handbook. LC 81-69260. (Illus.). 224p. 1982. 17.95 (ISBN 0-9607106-0-4). Altara Group.

COINS, INDIC

Kosambi, Damodar D. Indian Numismatics. (Illus.). 159p. 1981. text ed. 25.00x (ISBN 0-86131-018-7, Pub. by Orient Longman Ltd India). Apt Bks.

COINS, IRISH

Finn, P. Irish Coin Values. pap. 4.00 (ISBN 0-686-43400-5, Pub. by Spink & Son England). S J Durst.

COINS, ROMAN

Banti, Alberto & Simonetti, L. Corpus Nummorum Romanorum (Roman Imperial, 18 Vol. 1978. Set. 750.00 (ISBN 0-686-37929-2). Numismatic Fine Arts.

Seaby, B. A. Roman Silver Coins: Gordian III to Postumus, Vol. IV. 4th ed. 1982. 22.50 (ISBN 0-686-37931-4). Numismatic Fine Arts.

--Roman Silver Coins: Pertinax, to Balbinus & Pupienus, Vol. III. 4th ed. 1982. 22.50 (ISBN 0-686-37930-6). Numismatic Fine Arts.

COLD WAR

see World Politics-1945-

COLDEN, CADWALLADER, 1688-1776

Fingerhut, Eugene R. Survivor: Cadwallader Colden II in Revolutionary America. LC 82-20092. (Illus.). 200p. (Orig.). 1983. lib. bdg. 21.75 (ISBN 0-8191-2868-6); pap. text ed. 10.50 (ISBN 0-8191-2869-4). U Pr of Amer.

COLDITZ, GERMAN CASTLE

Baybutt, Ron. Camera in Colditz. (Illus.). 128p. 1983. 14.45i (ISBN 0-316-08394-1). Little.

COLERIDGE, SAMUEL TAYLOR, 1772-1834

Beyer, Werner W. The Enchanted Forest: Coleridge, Wordsworth. 273p. 1982. Repr. of 1963 ed. lib. bdg. 35.00 (ISBN 0-686-81684-6). Century Bookbindery.

Dekker, George. Coleridge & the Literature of Sensibility. (Critical Studies). 270p. 1978. text ed. 20.00x (ISBN 0-686-83548-4). B&N Imports.

Vlasopolos, Anca. The Symbolic Method of Coleridge, Baudelaire, & Yeats. 232p. 1983. 17.95x (ISBN 0-8143-1730-8). Wayne St U Pr.

Wallace, C. M. The Design of Biographia Literaria. 176p. 1983. text ed. 25.00 (ISBN 0-04-800016-7). Allen Unwin.

Wise, Thomas J. Coleridgeiana. 1982. lib. bdg. 34.50 (ISBN 0-686-81925-X). Porter.

COLET, LOUISE (REVOIL), 1810-1876

Jackson, Joseph F. Louise Colet et Ses Amis Litteraires. 1937. text ed. 16.50x (ISBN 0-686-83609-X). Elliots Bks.

COLETTE, SIDONIE GABRIELLE, 1873-1954

Stewart, Joan Hinde. Colette. (World Authors Ser.). 198p. 1983. lib. bdg. 13.95 (ISBN 0-8057-6527-1, Twayne). G K Hall.

COLITIS

Goodman, Michael J. & Sparberg, Marshall. Ulcerative Colitis. LC 78-8686. (Clinical Gastroenterology Monographs). 1978. 39.95x (ISBN 0-471-48895-X, Pub. by Wiley Medical). Wiley.

COLLAGE

Ragbourne, Jo. Seed Collage. (Illus.). 1983. 16.95 (ISBN 0-85936-241-8, Pub. by Midas Bks England). Hippocrene Bks.

COLLAGEN

Furthmayr, Heinz, ed. Immunochemistry of the Extracellular Matrix, 2 Vols. 1982. Vol. I, 272 pp. 75.00 (ISBN 0-8493-6196-6); Vol. II, 280 pp. 59.50 (ISBN 0-8493-6197-4). CRC Pr.

Woodhead-Galloway, John. Collagen: The Anatomy of Protein. (Studies in Biology: No. 117). 64p. 1979. pap. text ed. 8.95 (ISBN 0-7131-2783-X). E Arnold.

COLLECTING

see Collectors and Collecting

COLLECTING OF ACCOUNTS

How to Get Blood from a Turnip. 19.95 (ISBN 0-930566-25-4). FMA Bus.

Paulsen, Timothy. Collection Techniques for the Small Business: A Practical Guide to Collection Overdue Accounts. 2nd ed. (Illus.). 112p. 1983. pap. write for info. (ISBN 0-88908-559-5). Self Counsel Pr.

Samuel, Arthur F. & Pustilnick, Robert A. Collections: A Virginia Law Practice Systems. 657p. 1982. looseleaf with forms 75.00 (ISBN 0-87215-506-4). Michie-Bobbs.

COLLECTION LETTERS

see Collecting of Accounts

COLLECTION OF BLOOD

see Blood-Collection and Preservation

COLLECTIVE BARGAINING

see also Arbitration, Industrial; Employees' Representation in Management; Labor Contract; Strikes and Lockouts; Trade-Unions

Allen, Robert E. & Keaveny, Timothy J. Contemporary Labor Relations. 672p. 1983. text ed. 24.95 (ISBN 0-686-82182-3). A-W.

Bogenschneider, Duane, ed. A Directory to Collective Bargaining Agreements: Private Sector, 1981. 275p. 1982. reference bk. 100.00 (ISBN 0-667-00643-5). Microfilming Corp.

Willman, Paul. Fairness, Collective Bargaining, & Income Policy. (Illus.). 208p. 1982. 34.95x (ISBN 0-19-827252-9). Oxford U Pr.

COLLECTIVE BARGAINING-CIVIL SERVICE

see Collective Bargaining-Government Employees

COLLECTIVE BARGAINING-EDUCATION

Cooper, Bruce S. Collective Bargaining, Strikes, & Financial Costs in Public Education: A Comparative Review. LC 81-71248. xix, 120p. (Orig.). 1982. pap. 7.85 (ISBN 0-86552-079-8). U of Oreg ERIC.

COLLECTIVE BARGAINING-GOVERNMENT EMPLOYEES

Kershen, Harry, ed. Collective Bargaining by Government Workers: The Public Employee. (Public Sector Contemporary Issues Ser.: Vol. 3). 264p. 1983. pap. text ed. 16.50 (ISBN 0-89503-032-2). Baywood Pub.

Nyman, Tore. A Guide to the Teaching of Collective Bargaining. 91p. 1981. 2.85 (ISBN 0-686-84631-1). Intl Labour Office.

COLLECTIVE PSYCHOTHERAPY

see Group Psychotherapy

COLLECTIVE SECURITY

see Security, International

COLLECTIVE SETTLEMENTS

Berger, Bennett M. The Survival of a Counterculture: Ideological Work & Everyday Life Among Rural Communards. 278p. 1983. pap. 8.95 (ISBN 0-520-04950-0, CAL 579). U of Cal Pr.

COLLECTIVE SETTLEMENTS-ISRAEL

Palgi, Michal & Rosner, Menachem. Sexual Equality: The Israeli Kibbutz Tests the Theories. 337p. 1982. lib. bdg. 27.50 (ISBN 0-8482-5676-X). Norwood Edns.

COLLECTORS AND COLLECTING

see also Antiques; Book Collecting; Hobbies; Phonorecord Collecting

also names of objects collected, e.g. Postage-Stamps-Collectors and Collecting

Arnall, Franklin M. The Padlock Collector. 4th ed. (Illus.). 140p. 1982. pap. 8.95 (ISBN 0-914638-03-3). Collector.

Cranor, Rosalind. Elvis Collectibles. 368p. Date not set. 12.95 (ISBN 0-89145-205-2). Collector Bks.

Rainwater, Dorothy T. & Felger, Donna H. A Collector's Guide to Spoons Around the World. 2nd ed. (Illus.). 19.95 (ISBN 0-686-84756-3). Schiffer.

Schweiter, John C. The ABC of Doll Collecting. LC 81-8764. (Illus.). 160p. 1983. pap. 8.95 (ISBN 0-8069-7696-9). Sterling.

Sugar, Bert R., ed. American & National League Baseball Card Classics. 1982. pap. 2.95 ea. (ISBN 0-486-24308-7). Dover.

COLLEGE, CHOICE OF

Data Notes Publishing Staff. Directory of Colleges that Offer Credit for Life Experience. 300p. 1983. text ed. 49.95 (ISBN 0-911569-07-3). Data Notes Pub.

Manski, Charles F. & Wise, David A. College Choice in America. (Illus.). 272p. 1983. text ed. 22.50x (ISBN 0-674-14125-3). Harvard U Pr.

Shanahan, William F. College: Yes or No? The High School Student's Career Decision-Making Handbook. LC 82-6775. 256p. (gr. 9 up). 1983. lib. bdg. 12.95 (ISBN 0-668-05589-8); pap. 7.95 (ISBN 0-668-05590-1). Arco.

COLLEGE ADMINISTRATORS

Rudman, Jack. College Administrative Associate. (Career Examination Ser.: C-2658). (Cloth bdg. avail. on request). pap. 10.00 (ISBN 0-8373-2658-3). Natl Learning.

COLLEGE ADMISSION

see Universities and Colleges-Admission

COLLEGE AND SCHOOL DRAMA

see also Children's Plays; Drama in Education; Skits, Stunts, etc.

Wilder, Rosilyn. A Space Where Anything Can Happen: Creative Drama in a Middle School. LC 77-82855. (Illus.). 184p. 1977. 12.95 (ISBN 0-932720-69-2); pap. text ed. 6.95 (ISBN 0-932720-70-6). New Plays Bks.

COLLEGE AND SCHOOL JOURNALISM

Harwood, William N. Writing & Editing School News. 2nd & rev. ed. (Illus.). 364p. (gr. 10-12). 1983. pap. 8.40 (ISBN 0-931054-11-7). Clark Pub.

COLLEGE ATHLETICS

see Athletics; Track-Athletics

COLLEGE COSTS

Kohl, Kenneth & Kohl, Irene. Financing College Education. 3rd ed. LC 82-48232. 288p. 1983. pap. 5.72i (ISBN 0-06-090994-3, CN 994, CN). Har-Row.

COLLEGE CREDITS

Data Notes Publishing Staff. Directory of Colleges that Offer Credit for Life Experience. 300p. 1983. text ed. 49.95 (ISBN 0-911569-07-3). Data Notes Pub.

COLLEGE DEGREES

see Degrees, Academic

COLLEGE DROPOUTS

see Dropouts

COLLEGE ENTRANCE REQUIREMENTS

see Universities and Colleges-Admission

COLLEGE FACULTY

see College Teachers; Universities and Colleges-Faculty

COLLEGE GRADUATES

Ginn, Robert J. The College Graduate's Career Guide. 256p. 1982. pap. 5.95 (ISBN 0-686-83719-3, ScribT). Scribner.

COLLEGE LIBRARIES

see Libraries, University and College

COLLEGE LIFE

see College Students

COLLEGE PLAYS

see College and School Drama

COLLEGE PRESIDENTS

see Universities and Colleges-Administration

COLLEGE READERS

Here are entered selections of reading material in the English language, literary as well as non-literary, compiled for teaching rhetoric, comprehension and related topics on the college level; General literary selections are entered under appropriate literature headings, e. g. American Literature.

Barry, Vincent. Good Reason for Writing: A Text with Readings. 400p. 1982. pap. text ed. 12.95x (ISBN 0-534-01232-9). Wadsworth Pub.

Bartholomy, David. Sometimes You Just Have to Stand Naked: A Guide to Interesting Writing. (Illus.). 224p. 1983. pap. text ed. 8.95 (ISBN 0-13-822593-1). P-H.

Brinegar, Bonnie C. & Skates, Craig B. Technical Writing: A Guide with Models. 1982. text ed. 13.95x (ISBN 0-673-15410-6). Scott F.

Fencl, Shirley & Jager, Susan G. The Two R's: Paragraph to Essay. LC 78-16026. 1979. pap. text ed. 14.50x (ISBN 0-673-15723-7). Scott F.

McCuen, JoRay & Winkler, Anthony C. From Idea to Essay: A Rhetoric, Reader & Handbook. 3rd ed. 432p. 1982. pap. text ed. write for info. (ISBN 0-574-22085-2, 13-5085); write for info. answer bk (ISBN 0-574-22086-0, 13-5086). SRA.

COLLEGE STUDENT ORIENTATION

Orque, Modesta S. & Bloch, Bobbie. Ethnic Nursing Care: A Multi-Cultural Approach. (Illus.). 414p. 1983. pap. text ed. 14.95 (ISBN 0-8016-3742-2). Mosby.

Schimmels, Cliff. How to Survive & Thrive in College. 160p. 1983. pap. 5.95 (ISBN 0-8007-5104-3, Power Bks). Revell.

Shepherd. College Study Skills. 1983. pap. text ed. 10.95 (ISBN 0-686-84577-3, RD02); instr's. manual avail. (RD03). HM.

COLLEGE STUDENTS

Yale University Division of Student Mental Hygiene Staff. Psychosocial Problems of College Men. Wedge, Bryant M., ed. 1958. text ed. 13.50x (ISBN 0-686-83715-0). Elliots Bks.

COLLEGE STUDENTS-CONDUCT OF LIFE

Dumond, Michael, ed. Coping with Life after High School. (Personal Adjustment Ser.). 1983. lib. bdg. 7.97 (ISBN 0-8239-0606-X). Rosen Pr.

Gruneau, Richard S. Class, Sports, & Social Development. LC 82-21896. 192p. 1983. lib. bdg. 18.50 (ISBN 0-87023-387-4). U of Mass Pr.

Harvey, Harriet. Stories Parents Seldom Hear: College Students Write about Their Lives & Families. 1983. pap. 10.95 (ISBN 0-440-58262-8, Delta). Dell.

Ottens, Allen J. Coping with Academic Anxiety. (Personal Adjustment Ser.). 140p. 1983. lib. bdg. 7.97 (ISBN 0-8239-0607-8). Rosen Pr.

COLLEGE STUDENTS-ORIENTATION

see College Student Orientation

COLLEGE STUDENTS-POLITICAL ACTIVITY

see also geographic subdivisions for books on political activities in specific countries

The Student Nonviolent Coordinating Committee Papers, 1959-1972. 132p. 1982. reference bk. 25.00 (ISBN 0-667-00665-6). Microfilming Corp.

COLLEGE TEACHERS

see also Universities and Colleges-Faculty

Husen, T. An Incurable Academic: Memoirs of a Professor. (Illus.). 138p. 1983. 30.00 (ISBN 0-08-027925-2). Pergamon.

Krannich, Ronald L. & Bants, William J. Moving Out of Education: The Educator's Guide To Career Management & Change. 264p. 1981. 14.95 (ISBN 0-940010-00-3). Impact VA.

COLLEGE TEACHING AS A PROFESSION

Krannich, Ronald L. & Bants, William J. Moving Out of Education: The Educator's Guide To Career Management & Change. 264p. 1981. 14.95 (ISBN 0-940010-00-3). Impact VA.

COLLEGE THEATRICALS

see College and School Drama

COLLEGES

see Universities and Colleges

COLLEGES, AFRO-AMERICAN

see Afro-American Universities and Colleges

COLLIE (DOG)

see Dogs-Breeds-Collies

COLLISIONS (NUCLEAR PHYSICS)

see also Ionization; Radiation; Scattering (Physics)

also names of particles, e.g. Electrons, Neutrons, Protons

Bowman, J. M., ed. Molecular Collision Dynamics. (Topics in Current Physics Ser.: Vol. 33). (Illus.). 180p. 1983. 19.00 (ISBN 0-387-12014-9). Springer-Verlag.

Bransden, B. H. Atomic Collision Theory. 2nd ed. (Illus.). 500p. 1970. text ed. 29.95 (ISBN 0-8053-1181-5). Benjamin-Cummings.

Brouillard, F., ed. Physics of Ion-Ion & Electron-Ion Collisions. (NATO ASI Series B, Physics: Vol. 83). 535p. 1983. 69.50x (ISBN 0-306-41105-9, Plenum Pr). Plenum Pub.

Conference on the Physics of Electronic & Atomic Collisions: Proceedings, Tenth, Paris, 1977, 2 Vols. 1978. Set. pap. 104.75 (ISBN 0-444-85101-1). Elsevier.

Hinze, Jugen, ed. Electron-Atom & Electron Molecule Collisions. (Physics of Atoms & Molecules Ser.). 362p. 1983. 49.50x (ISBN 0-306-41188-1, Plenum Pr). Plenum Pub.

Madurga, G. & Lozano, M. Heavy-Ion Colision, La Rabida, Spain, 1982: Proceedings. (Lecture Notes in Physics: Vol. 168). 429p. 1983. pap. 21.00 (ISBN 0-387-11945-0). Springer-Verlag.

Rahman, N. K. & Guidotti, C., eds. Photon-Assisted Collisions & Related Topics. 377p. 1982. 63.50 (ISBN 0-686-84008-9). Harwood Academic.

COLLISIONS, AUTOMOBILE

see Traffic Accidents

COLLISIONS AT SEA

see also Shipwrecks

Cockcroft, A. N. & Lameijer, J. N. Guide to the Collision Avoidance Rules. 3rd ed. (Illus.). 240p. 1982. text ed. 17.50x (ISBN 0-540-07278-8). Sheridan.

COLLOIDS

see also Particles; Rheology

Dickinson, E. & Stainsby, G. Colloids in Food. (Illus.). xiv, 532p. 1982. 98.50 (ISBN 0-85334-153-2, Pub. by Applied Sci England). Elsevier.

COLLOQUIAL ENGLISH

see English Language–Conversation and Phrase Books; English Language–Spoken English

COLOMBIA

Kline, Harvey F. Columbia. (Nations of Contemporary Latin America). 144p. 1983. lib. bdg. 16.50 (ISBN 0-89158-941-4). Westview.

COLOMBIA–ECONOMIC CONDITIONS

Lombard, Francois J. The Foreign Investment Screening Process in L.D.C.'s: The Case of Columbia, 1967-1975. (Replica Edition Ser.). 171p. 1979. softcover 25.00x (ISBN 0-89158-399-8). Westview.

Marsh, Robin R. Development Strategies in Rural Colombia: The Case of Caaueta. LC 82-620032. (Latin American Studies: Vol. 55). 1983. text ed. write for info. (ISBN 0-87903-055-0). UCLA Lat Am Ctr.

COLOMBO, CRISTOFORO

see Columbus, Christopher (Cristoforo Colombo), 1446-1506

COLON (ANATOMY)

see also Colitis; Megacolon

Bustos-Fernandez, Luis, ed. Colon: Structure & Function. (Topics in Gastroenterology Ser.). 326p. 1983. 39.50x (ISBN 0-306-41056-7, Plenum Pr). Plenum Pub.

Miller, R. E. & Skucas, J. Radiological Examination of the Colon. 1983. 128.00 (ISBN 90-247-2666-2, Pub. by Martinus Nijhoff Netherlands). Kluwer Boston.

COLON (ANATOMY)–DISEASES

Kasper, W. & Goebell, H., eds. Colon & Nutrition. (Illus.). 350p. 1982. text ed. 75.00 (ISBN 0-85200-444-3, Pub. by MTP Pr England). Kluwer Boston.

Malt, R. A. & Williamson, R., eds. Colonic Carcinogenesis. (Illus.). 406p. 1981. text ed. 65.00 (ISBN 0-85200-443-5, Pub. by MTP Pr England). Kluwer Boston.

COLONIAL AFFAIRS

see Colonies

COLONIALISM

see Colonies; Imperialism

COLONIES

see also Colonies in America; Emigration and Immigration

also subdivision Colonies under names of countries, e.g. France–Colonies

Fish, Carl R. Path of Empire. 1919. text ed. 8.50x (ISBN 0-686-83685-5). Elliots Bks.

Ostrander, Gilman H. Early Colonial Thought. 1970. pap. text ed. 1.95x (ISBN 0-88273-221-8). Forum Pr IL.

COLONIES–ADMINISTRATION

see also subdivision Colonies–administration under names of countries, e.g. Great Britain–Colonies–Administration

Niven, Rex. Nigerian Kaleidoscope: Memoirs of a Colonial Servant. 1982. 25.00 (ISBN 0-208-02008-X, Archon Bks). Shoe String.

COLONIES IN AMERICA

Speth, Linda & Hirsch, Alison D. Women, Family, & Community in Colonial America: Two Perspectives. LC 82-23326. (Women & History Ser.: No. 4). 85p. 1983. text ed. 20.00 (ISBN 0-86656-191-9). Haworth Pr.

COLONITIS

see Colitis

COLOR

see also Colors; Dyes and Dyeing

Sinclair, R. S. Numerical Problems in Colour Physics. 1982. 27.00 (ISBN 0-686-81691-9, Pub. by Soc Dyers & Colour). State Mutual Bk.

COLOR–JUVENILE LITERATURE

Kentner, Bernice. A Rainbow in Your Eyes-Yes You Can Find Your Colors & for Others Too. (Illus.). 146p. 1982. 14.95x (ISBN 0-941522-01-6). Ken Kra Pubs.

Peyo, pseud. Coloring Magic with Painter Smurf. (Illus.). 16p. (ps-3). 1983. 1.25 (ISBN 0-394-85621-X). Random.

Walt Disney Productions. Goofy's Book of Colors. LC 82-18630. (Disney's Wonderful World of Reading: No. 52). (Illus.). 32p. 1983. 4.95 (ISBN 0-394-85734-8); PLB 4.99 (ISBN 0-394-95734-2). Random.

COLOR BLINDNESS

Verriest, G. Colour Vision Deficiencies VI. 1982. text ed. 99.50 (ISBN 90-6193-729-9, Pub. by Junk Pubs Netherlands). Kluwer Boston.

COLOR DISCRIMINATION

see Color Vision

COLOR OF MAN

see also Hair

Rushton. Visual Pigments in Man. 48p. 1982. 50.00x (ISBN 0-85323-223-7, Pub. by Liverpool Univ England). State Mutual Bk.

COLOR PERCEPTION

see Color Vision

COLOR PHOTOGRAPHY

Deyl, Z., et al. Bibliography of Column Chromatography, 1967-1970, & Survey of Applications. 1973. 88.00 (ISBN 0-444-41008-2). Elsevier.

Hayes, John P. Philadelphia in Color. (Illus., Orig.). 1983. 7.95 (ISBN 0-8038-5898-1). Hastings.

Hedgecoe, John. The Art of Color Photography. 1983. pap. 14.95 (ISBN 0-671-46096-X). S&S.

Knapman, C. E. Developments in Chromatography, Vols. 1 & 2. 1978-80. Vol. 1. 33.00 (ISBN 0-85334-748-4, Pub. by Applied Sci England); Vol. 2. 33.00 (ISBN 0-85334-871-5). Elsevier.

COLOR PHOTOGRAPHY–PRINTING PROCESSES

Krause, Peter & Shull, Henry. Complete Guide to Cibachrome Printing, Vol. 14. 160p. 1982. pap. 14.95 (ISBN 0-89586-176-3). H P Bks.

COLOR PRINTS (PHOTOGRAPHY)

see Color Photography–Printing Processes

COLOR SENSE

see Color Vision

COLOR TELEVISION

Reddihough & Knight. Questions & Answers: Color TV. 2nd ed. (Illus.). 1975. pap. 4.95 (ISBN 0-408-00162-3). Focal Pr.

Trundell. Questions & Answers: Color TV. 3rd ed. (Illus.). 1983. pap. write for info. (ISBN 0-408-01305-2). Focal Pr.

COLOR TELEVISION–JUVENILE LITERATURE

see Television–Juvenile Literature

COLOR VISION

see also Color Blindness

Graham, Clarence H., et al, eds. Vision & Visual Perception. LC 65-12711. 1965. 69.95x (ISBN 0-471-32170-2). Wiley.

Verriest, G. Colour Vision Deficiencies VI. 1982. text ed. 99.50 (ISBN 90-6193-729-9, Pub. by Junk Pubs Netherlands). Kluwer Boston.

Zrenner, E. Neurophysiological Aspects of Color Vision in Primates. (Studies of Brain Function: Vol. 9). (Illus.). 218p. 1983. 37.00 (ISBN 0-387-11653-2). Springer-Verlag.

COLORADO

see also names of cities, towns, etc. in Colorado

Lawson, Greg, photos by. Colorado. (Illus.). 72p. (Orig., Eng., Span., Fr., Ger.). 1983. pap. 8.95 (ISBN 0-9606704-5-9). First Choice.

COLORADO–DESCRIPTION AND TRAVEL

Bancroft, Caroline. Grand Lake: From Utes to Yachts. (Bancroft Booklet Ser.). (Illus.). 40p. (Orig.). 1982. pap. 2.50 (ISBN 0-933472-68-4). Johnson Bks.

Cole, Michael & Frampton, Susan. Dining In--Vail. (Dining In--Ser.). (Illus.). 1983. pap. 8.95 (ISBN 0-89716-059-2). Peanut Butter.

Fetter, Richard. Frontier Boulder. (Illus.). 80p. (Orig.). 1983. pap. write for info. (ISBN 0-933472-72-2). Johnson Bks.

Gregory, Lee. Colorado Scenic Guide: Northern Region. (Illus.). 240p. (Orig.). 1983. pap. price not set (ISBN 0-933472-73-0). Johnson Bks.

Martin, Bob. Hiking Trails of Central Colorado. (Illus.). 1983. pap. price not set (ISBN 0-87108-635-2). Pruett.

Massey, Penelope P., ed. Colorado. (Travel Ser.). (Illus.). 72p. (Orig.). 1982. write for info. (ISBN 0-938440-09-8). Colourpicture.

Wheat, Doug. Floater's Guide to Colorado. (Illus.). 256p. 1983. 8.95 (ISBN 0-934318-16-6). Falcon Pr MT.

Whitney, Gleaves. Colorado Front Range: A Landscape Divided. (Illus.). 120p. (Orig.). 1983. pap. price not set (ISBN 0-933472-71-4). Johnson Bks.

COLORADO–HISTORY

Digerness, David S. The Mineral Belt: Georgetown, Mining, Colorado Central Railroad, Vol. III. (Illus.). 416p. 49.00 (ISBN 0-686-84503-X). Sundance.

COLORADO RIVER AND VALLEY

Stanton, Robert B. Colorado River Controversies. Chalfant, James M. & Stone, Julius F., eds. LC 82-60295. (Illus.). 310p. 1982. pap. 12.95 (ISBN 0-916370-09-7). Westwater.

COLORED GLASS

see Glass, Colored

COLORED PEOPLE (U. S.)

see Afro-Americans

COLORING MATTER

see also Pigments

Harley, R. Artist's Pigments Circa, Sixteen Hundred to Eighteen Thirty-Five. 1970. 12.50 (ISBN 0-444-19652-8). Elsevier.

COLORS

see also Color

Bullrich, Kurt. Die Farbigen Dammerungserscheinngen. 100p. 1982. 17.95 (ISBN 3-7643-1355-2). Birkhauser.

Colour Index. 3rd, Rev. ed. 1982. 650.00x (ISBN 0-686-81698-6, Pub. by Soc Dyers & Colour). State Mutual Bk.

Colour Index: Supplement, Vol. 5. Rev. ed. 1982. 210.00x (ISBN 0-686-81697-8, Pub. by Soc Dyers & Colour). State Mutual Bk.

Cravens, Dorras. Reading Colors. (ps-1). 1981. 5.95 (ISBN 0-86653-018-5, GA247). Good Apple.

COLOSTOMY

Schindler, Margaret. Living with a Colostomy. (Illus.). 128p. (Orig.). 1983. pap. 6.95 (ISBN 0-7225-0681-3, Pub. by Thorsons Pubs England). Sterling.

COLT REVOLVER

Cochran, Keith. Colts Peacemaker. (Illus.). 1982. 4.95 (ISBN 0-910156-07-7). Art & Ref.

COLUMBAE

see Pigeons

COLUMBIA RIVER AND VALLEY

Woodward, John. The Ancient Painted Images of the Columbia Gorge. (Illus.). 100p. (Orig.). 1982. pap. 39.95 (ISBN 0-916552-28-4). Acoma Bks.

COLUMBIDAE

see Pigeons

COLUMBUS, CHRISTOPHER (CRISTOFORO COLOMBO), 1446-1506

Morison, Samuel E. Admiral of the Ocean Sea: A Life of Christopher Columbus. (Illus.). 680p. pap. text ed. 9.95X (ISBN 0-930350-37-5). NE U Pr.

COLUMBUS, CHRISTOPHER (CRISTOFORO COLOMBO), 1446-1506–JUVENILE LITERATURE

Weil, Lisl. I, Christopher Columbus. LC 82-16323. (Illus.). 48p. (gr. k-4). 1983. 10.95 (ISBN 0-689-30965-1). Atheneum.

COLUMNISTS

see Journalists

COMANCHE INDIANS

see Indians of North America–The West

COMBAT VEHICLES

see Armored Vehicles, Military

COMBINATIONS OF LABOR

see Strikes and Lockouts

COMBINATORIAL ANALYSIS

see also Graph Theory

Anderson, Ian. A First Course in Combinatorial Mathematics. (Illus.). 132p. 1979. pap. text ed. 9.95x (ISBN 0-19-859617-0). Oxford U Pr.

Berge, C. & Bresson, D., eds. Combinatorial Mathematics: Proceedings of the International Colloquium on Graph Theory & Combinatorics, Marseille-Luminy, June, 1981. (North-Holland Mathematics Studies: Vol. 75). 660p. 1983. 106.50 (ISBN 0-444-86512-8, North Holland). Elsevier.

Billington, E. J., et al, eds. Combinatorial Mathematics IX, Brisbane, Australia: Proceedings, 1981. (Lecture Notes in Mathematics Ser.: Vol. 952). 443p. 1983. pap. 23.00 (ISBN 0-387-11601-X). Springer-Verlag.

Bogart, Kenneth P. Introductory Combinatorics. 400p. 1983. text ed. 24.95 (ISBN 0-273-01923-6). Pitman Pub MA.

Chandler, B. & Magnus, W. History of Combinatorial Group Theory: A Case Study of the History of Ideas. (Studies in the History of Mathematics & Physical Sciences: Vol. 9). (Illus.). 234p. 1983. 46.00 (ISBN 0-387-90749-1). Springer-Verlag.

Jungnickel, D. H. & Vedder, K., eds. Combinatorial Theory: Proceedings, Schloss Rauischholzhausen, FRG, 1982. (Lecture Notes in Mathematics Ser.: Vol. 969). 326p. 1983. pap. 16.00 (ISBN 0-387-11971-X). Springer-Verlag.

COMBUSTION

see also Flame; Fuel

Chigier, N. A., ed. Progress in Energy & Combustion Science, Vol. 7. (Illus.). 316p. 1982. 130.00 (ISBN 0-08-029124-4). Pergamon.

COMBUSTION GASES

see also Automobiles–Motors–Exhaust Gas

Hudson, John L. & Rochelle, Gary T., eds. Flue Gas Desulfurization. (ACS Symposium Ser.: No. 188). 1982. write for info. (ISBN 0-8412-0722-4). Am Chemical.

COMEDIANS

Costello, Chris & Strait, Raymond. Lou's on First: The Biography of Lou Costello. (Illus.). 384p. 1983. pap. 6.95 (ISBN 0-312-49914-0). St Martin.

Lenburg, Jeff. Dudley Moore: An Informal Biography. (Illus.). 144p. (Orig.). 1982. pap. 9.95 (ISBN 0-933328-56-7). Delilah Bks.

Mason, Jackie. Jackie Mason's America. 192p. 1983. 12.00 (ISBN 0-8184-0338-1). Lyle Stuart.

COMEDIANS–CORRESPONDENCE, REMINISCENCES, ETC.

Brenner, David. Soft Pretzels with Mustard. (Illus.). 1983. 14.95 (ISBN 0-87795-442-9). Arbor Hse.

Paar, Jack. P. S. Jack Paar. LC 82-45938. (Illus.). 360p. 1983. 14.95 (ISBN 0-385-18743-2). Doubleday.

COMEDY

Badalato, Billy & Richards, Charlie R. Comedy Realm. 140p. (Orig.). (gr. 5-12). 1982. pap. 10.50 (ISBN 0-9609224-0-7). Comedy Writ.

Bareiss, Karl-Heinz. Comoedia. 525p. (Ger.). 1982. write for info. (ISBN 3-8204-5986-3). P Lang Pubs.

Corneille. L' Illusion Comique. 2nd ed. Marks, J., ed. (Modern French Texts Ser.). 1969. pap. write for info. (ISBN 0-7190-0323-7). Manchester.

Gewitz, Arthur. Restoration Adaptations of Early 17th Century Comedies. LC 82-15937. 214p. 1983. lib. bdg. 23.00 (ISBN 0-8191-2722-1); pap. text ed. 10.75 (ISBN 0-8191-2723-X). U Pr of Amer.

Grawe, Paul H. Comedy in Space, Time, & the Imagination. LC 82-10603. 368p. 1983. text ed. 27.95 (ISBN 0-88229-631-0). Nelson-Hall.

Grote, David. The End of Comedy: Sit-Com & the Comedic Tradition. 208p. 1983. 19.50 (ISBN 0-208-01991-X, Archon Bks). Shoe String.

Hampton, Christopher. Philanthropist: A Bourgeois Comedy. 78p. 1970. pap. 3.95 (ISBN 0-571-09527-5). Faber & Faber.

Price. The Unfortunate Comedy. 208p. 1982. 40.00x (ISBN 0-85323-000-5, Pub. by Liverpool Univ England). State Mutual Bk.

Whitelaw, Denny. Slightly Sexy, Comedy from Europe. (Illus.). 120p. 1982. pap. 15.00 (ISBN 0-940178-14-1). Sitare Inc.

COMETS

Periodic comets are entered under the name of the discoverer, e.g. Halley's Comet.

Brandt, John C. & Chapman, Robert D. Introduction to Comets. LC 76-47207. 256p. 1982. pap. 11.95 (ISBN 0-521-27218-1). Cambridge U Pr.

Marsden, Brian G. Catalog of Cometary Orbits. 128p. 1983. pap. text ed. 10.00 (ISBN 0-89490-095-1). Enslow Pubs.

COMFORT, STANDARD OF

see Cost and Standard of Living

COMIC BOOKS, STRIPS, ETC.

see also Newspapers–Sections, Columns, etc.

Barrier, Michael. Carl Barks & the Art of the Comic Book. (Illus.). 228p. 1982. 49.95 (ISBN 0-9607652-0-4). M Lilien.

Davies, Andrew. Marmalade & Rufus. 1983. 8.95 (ISBN 0-517-54632-9). Crown.

Eternally Mad. (Mad Ser.: No. 62). (Illus.). 192p. (Orig.). 1983. pap. 1.95 (ISBN 0-446-30587-1). Warner Bks.

The Official 1983 Price Guide to Comic & Science Fiction Books. 6th ed. LC 81-81799. 544p. 1983. 9.95 (ISBN 0-87637-353-8). Hse of Collectibles.

Olshevsky, George. The Amazing Spider-Man & Other Titles. rev. ed. (The Marvel Comics Index Ser.: Pt. 1). (Illus.). 300p. 1983. 12.95 (ISBN 0-943348-21-8); pap. 8.95 (ISBN 0-943348-01-3). G Olshevsky.

--The Marvel Comics Index Series. rev. ed. (Illus.). 1982. Set. write for info. (ISBN 0-943348-20-X); Set. pap. write for info. (ISBN 0-943348-00-5). G Olshevsky.

Overstreet, Robert M. Comic Book Price Guide. 13th ed. (Illus.). 600p. 1983. pap. 9.95 (ISBN 0-517-54915-8). Overstreet.

--The Comic Book Price Guide, No. 13. 1983. pap. 9.95 (ISBN 0-517-54915-8, Harmony). Crown.

Schulz, Charles M. It's Chow Time, Snoopy! Selected Cartoons from Dr. Beagle & Mr. Hyde, Vol. I. (Illus.). 128p. 1983. pap. 1.95 (ISBN 0-449-20096-5, Crest). Fawcett.

COMIC BOOKS, STRIPS, ETC.–HISTORY AND CRITICISM

Miss Buxley: Sexism in Beetle Bailey? 96p. 1982. pap. 4.95 (ISBN 0-940420-01-5). Comicana Bks.

COMIC LITERATURE

see Comedy

COMIC OPERA

see Opera

COMIC STRIPS

see Comic Books, Strips, etc.

COMINTERN

see Communist International

COMITIA

see Rome–Politics and Government

COMMANDMENTS, TEN

Quesnell, Quentin. Cycle A: The Commandments. (The Gospel in the Church). 210p. 1983. pap. 7.95 (ISBN 0-8245-0568-9). Crossroad NY.

Teaching the Ten Commandments. 20p. 1982. pap. 7.55 (ISBN 0-88479-035-5). Arena Lettres.

COMMANDMENTS, TEN–JUVENILE LITERATURE

Truitt, G. A. The Ten Commandments: Learning about God's Law. (Concept Bks.: Ser. 4). 1983. pap. 3.50 (ISBN 0-570-08527-6). Concordia.

COMMENSALISM

see Symbiosis

COMMENTARIES, BIBLICAL

see Bible–Commentaries

COMMENTATORS

see Journalists

COMMERCE

see also Balance of Trade; Barter; Business; Business Mathematics; Businessmen; Central Business Districts; Competition, International; Exchange; Export Credit; Export Marketing; Foreign Exchange; Freight and Freightage; Harbors; Inland Navigation; Insurance, Marine; International Business Enterprises; Investments, Foreign; Maritime Law; Markets; Merchant Marine; Money; Neutrality; Purchasing; Retail Trade; Shipping; Trade-Marks; Trade Routes; Transportation; Warehouses; Wholesale Trade

also subdivision Commerce under names of countries, cities, etc.; names of articles of commerce, e.g. Cotton, Leather, Lumber; headings beginning with the word Commercial

Conference of European Statisticians. Correspondence Table Between the Standard International Trade Classification of the United Nations (SITC) & the Standard Foreign Trade Classification of the Council for Mutual Economic Assistance (SFTC). 22.00 (ISBN 0-686-43224-X, E/R.82.II.E.10). UN.

Data Notes Publishing Staff, compiled by. The Foreign Trade Index. 55p. Date not set. pap. cancelled (ISBN 0-686-37652-8). Data Notes Pub.
Gartside, L. Commerce. 576p. 1977. 29.00x (ISBN 0-7121-0349-X, Pub. by Macdonald & Evans). State Mutual Bk.
Golt, Sidney. World Trade Issues in the Mid-1980s. (British-North American Committee Ser.). 112p. 1982. pap. 7.00 (ISBN 0-902594-42-7, BN32-NPA198). Natl Planning.
Hufbauer, Gary C. & Erb, Joanna S. Subsidies in International Trade. 200p. 1983. 20.00 (ISBN 0-88132-004-8). Inst Intl Eco.
Hulbert, Archer B. Path of Inland Commerce. 1920. text ed. 8.50x (ISBN 0-686-83686-3). Elliots Bks.
Keir, Malcolm. March of Commerce. 1927. text ed. 22.50x. Elliots Bks.
Lall, Sanjaya. Developing Countries as Exporters of Technology & Capital Goods. 134p. 1982. text ed. 31.50x (ISBN 0-333-28844-0, 50921, Pub. by Macmillan England). Humanities.
OECD. Controls on International Capital Movements: The Experience with Controls on Int.Financial Credits, Loans, & Deposits. 130p. 1982. pap. 11.00 (ISBN 92-64-12376-8). OECD.
Sau, Ranjit. Trade, Capital & Underdevelopment: Towards a Marxist Theory. (Illus.). 1982. 15.00x (ISBN 0-19-561209-4). Oxford U Pr.
Shekhar, K. C. & Nair, R. R. Elements of Commerce. 225p. 1982. text ed. 20.00x (ISBN 0-7069-2020-1, Pub. by Vikas India). Advent NY.
United Nations Conference on Contracts for the International Sale of Goods. Official Records. 33.00 (ISBN 0-686-84908-6, E.82.V.5). UN.
Whiting, D. P. International Trade & Payments. 160p. 1978. 30.00x (ISBN 0-7121-0952-8, Pub. by Macdonald & Evans). State Mutual Bk.
Williams, A. O. International Trade & Investment: A Managerial Approach. 461p. 1982. text ed. 29.95x (ISBN 0-471-03293-X). Ronald Pr.
Williamson, Oliver E. Markets & Hierarchies: A Study in the Internal Organizations. 320p. 1983. pap. text ed. 11.95 (ISBN 0-02-934780-7). Free Pr.
Woolcock, Stephen. Western Policies on East-West Trade. (Chatham House Papers Ser.: No. 15). 96p. (Orig.). 1982. pap. 10.00 (ISBN 0-7100-9314-4). Routledge & Kegan.

COMMERCE–DICTIONARIES
Hanson, J. L. A Dictionary of Economics & Commerce. 480p. 1977. 29.00x (ISBN 0-7121-0424-0, Pub. by Macdonald & Evans). State Mutual Bk.

COMMERCE–DIRECTORIES
Marconi's International Register. 83rd ed. 1982. 70.00 (ISBN 0-916446-08-5). Tele Cable.
Pacific Islands Business & Trade Directory, 1982: With a Special Australian & New Zealand Exporters Section. 27th ed. LC 72-622889. (Illus.). 724p. (Orig.). 1982. pap. 45.00x (ISBN 0-8002-3106-6). Intl Pubns Serv.
Swiss Office for the Development of Trade, Geneva. Swiss Export Products & Services Directory, 1983-85. 14th ed. LC 53-19872. 920p. 1982. 65.00x (ISBN 0-8002-3059-0). Intl Pubns Serv.

COMMERCE–HISTORY
Braudel, Fernand. The Wheels of Commerce: Civilization & Capitalism, 15th-18th Century Vol. 2. Reynolds, Sian, tr. from Fr. LC 82-48109. (Illus.). 720p. 1983. 33.65i (ISBN 0-06-015091-2, HarpT). Har-Row.
Fleure, H. J. & Peake, Harold. Merchant Ventures in Bronze. (Corridors of Time Ser.: No. 7). 1931. text ed. 24.50x (ISBN 0-686-83625-1). Elliots Bks.

COMMERCE–STATISTICS
see Commercial Statistics

COMMERCIAL AERONAUTICS
see Aeronautics, Commercial

COMMERCIAL ARBITRATION
see Arbitration and Award

COMMERCIAL ARITHMETIC
see Business Mathematics

COMMERCIAL ART
Dempsey, Mike, ed. Pipe Dreams: Early Advertising Art from the Imperial Tobacco Company. (Illus.). 96p. 1983. pap. 11.95 (ISBN 0-907516-12-2, Pub by Michael Joseph). Merrimack Bk Serv.
Dept. of Advertising Design, Mohawk Valley Community College. Signature One, A Graphics Annual. (Illus.). 32p. 1983. pap. 7.95 (ISBN 0-86610-126-8). Meridian Pub.
Gawain, Shakti. Creative Visualization. 144p. 1982. pap. 3.50 (ISBN 0-553-22689-4). Bantam.

COMMERCIAL ART–YEARBOOKS
Print Casebooks, 6 vols. Incl. Vol. 1. The Best in Advertising. LC 75-649579 (ISBN 0-915734-34-6); Vol. 2. The Best in Annual Reports. LC 75-649581 (ISBN 0-915734-35-4); Vol. 3. The Best in Environmental Graphics. LC 75-649585 (ISBN 0-915734-36-2); Vol. 4. The Best in Exhibition Design. LC 76-39580 (ISBN 0-915734-37-0); Vol. 5. The Best in Packaging. LC 75-649583 (ISBN 0-915734-38-9); Vol. 6. The Best in Covers & Posters. LC 75-649580 (ISBN 0-915734-39-7). Set. 99.50 (ISBN 0-915734-33-8); 17.95 ea. R C Pubns.

COMMERCIAL ART AS A PROFESSION
Craig, James. Graphic Design Career Guide: How to Get a Job & Establish a Career in Design. (Illus.). 176p. (Orig.). 1983. pap. 14.95 (ISBN 0-8230-2151-3). Watson-Guptill.

COMMERCIAL AVIATION
see Aeronautics, Commercial

COMMERCIAL CATALOGS
see Catalogs, Commercial

COMMERCIAL CORNERS
see Stock-Exchange

COMMERCIAL CORRESPONDENCE
see also Advertising–Direct-Mail; English Language–Business English
Carlsen, Robert D. Handbook & Portfolio of Successful Sales Proposals. LC 82-15085. 506p. looseleaf bdg. 125.00 (ISBN 0-13-380808-4, Busn). P-H.
Carrol, Frieda. New & Useful Forms, Stationery, & Greetings To Duplicate & Use. 50p. Date not set. pap. text ed. 10.95 (ISBN 0-939476-84-3). Biblio Pr GA.
Craz, Albert G. & Mavragis, Edward P. Writing: The Business Letter. (Writing Ser.). 68p. 1981. wkbk. 3.95 (ISBN 0-9602800-1-4). Comp Pr.
Duenas. Curso Basico de Correspondencia Comercial. 120p. 1982. 4.56 (ISBN 0-07-017995-6, G). McGraw.
Gartside, L. Modern Business Correspondence. 480p. 1979. 30.00x (ISBN 0-7121-1392-4, Pub. by Macdonald & Evans). State Mutual Bk.
Hatch, Richard A. Business Writing. 528p. 1983. pap. text ed. write for info. (ISBN 0-574-20665-5, 13-3665); write for info. instr's. guide (ISBN 0-574-20666-3, 13-3666). SRA.
Hunsinger. Correspondencia Comercial Moderna. 4th ed. 232p. 1982. 9.00 (ISBN 0-07-031282-6, G). McGraw.
Love, C. & Tinervia, J. Commercial Correspondence: For Students of English as a Second Language. 2nd ed. 1980. text ed. 7.25 (ISBN 0-07-038785-0). McGraw.
Markel, Michael H. & Lucier, R. J. Make Your Point: A Guide to Improving Your Business & Technical Writing. (Illus.). 156p. 1983. 12.95 (ISBN 0-13-547760-3); pap. 5.95 (ISBN 0-13-547752-2). P-H.

COMMERCIAL CORRESPONDENCE, GERMAN
Gartside, L. Der Englische Geschaftsbrief. 512p. 1977. 45.00x (ISBN 0-7121-0422-4, Pub. by Macdonald & Evans). State Mutual Bk.

COMMERCIAL CORRESPONDENCE, SPANISH
Jackson, Mary H. Guide to Correspondence in Spanish. 64p. 1981. 25.00x (ISBN 0-85950-335-6, Pub. by Thornes England). State Mutual Bk.

COMMERCIAL CREDIT
see Credit

COMMERCIAL DESIGN
see Commercial Art

COMMERCIAL DOCUMENTS
see also Legal Documents; Negotiable Instruments
American Railroad Stock Certificates. 28.50. StanGib Ltd.

COMMERCIAL EDUCATION
see Business Education

COMMERCIAL EMPLOYEES
see Clerks

COMMERCIAL ETHICS
see Business Ethics

COMMERCIAL FISHING
see Fisheries

COMMERCIAL LAW
Here are entered general works and works on commercial law in the United States. For commercial law of other countries, see subdivisions below.
see also Accounting–Law; Antitrust Law; Arbitration and Award; Auctions; Banking Law; Bankruptcy; Brokers; Business; Business Enterprises; Business Law; Clerks; Collecting of Accounts; Contracts; Corporation Law; Debt; Debtor and Creditor; Foreign Exchange; Foreign Trade Regulation; Forms (Law); Insurance Law; Landlord and Tenant; Leases; Licenses; Liquidation; Maritime Law; Mortgages; Negotiable Instruments; Partnership; Real Property; Sales; Trade-Marks; Trade Regulation; Trusts and Trustees; Vendors and Purchasers; Warehouses
Becker, U. Dictionary of Commercial Law. 992p. 1980. 175.00x (ISBN 0-7121-5489-2, Pub. by Macdonald & Evans). State Mutual Bk.
Commercial Business & Trade Laws, 6 vols. Incl. India. Rosen, Robert C. LC 82-61002 (ISBN 0-379-22401-1); Nigeria. Aguda, T. A., ed. LC 82-80770 (ISBN 0-379-23001-1); Peoples' Republic of China. Chu, Franklin D., ed. LC 82-6512; Soviet Union & Mongolia. Butler, William E. LC 81-85376 (ISBN 0-379-22501-8); United Kingdom, 2 vols. Simmonds, Kenneth, ed. LC 81-38330 (ISBN 0-379-22201-9). 1982. 125.00 ea. Oceana.
Frankel, Lionel H. & McDonnell, Julian B. Commercial Transactions: Payment Systems. (Contemporary Legal Education Ser.). 322p. 1982. pap. text ed. 11.00 (ISBN 0-686-84215-4). Michie-Bobbs.
--Commercial Transactions: Sales. (Contemporary Legal Education Ser.). 463p. pap. text ed. 15.00 (ISBN 0-87215-470-X). Michie-Bobbs.
--Commercial Transactions: Secured Financing. (Contemporary Legal Education Ser.). 389p. 1982. pap. text ed. 14.00 (ISBN 0-87215-468-8). Michie-Bobbs.
Hermann, A. H. Conflicts of National Laws with International Business Activity: Issues of Extraterritoriality. (British-North America Committee Ser.). 104p. 1982. pap. 6.00 (ISBN 0-902594-41-9, BN30-NPA195). Natl Planning.
Keesee, Allen P. Commercial Laws of the Middle East, 8 vols. Incl. Algeria. LC 80-18047. 1981; Egypt, Arab Republic of Egypt. 1981 (ISBN 0-379-20467-3); Iran. Vafai, G. H. 1982 (ISBN 0-379-22904-8); Kuwait. 1980 (ISBN 0-379-22905-6); Oman. 1982 (ISBN 0-379-22906-4); United Arab Emirates. 1982; Saudi Arabia. 1981 (ISBN 0-379-22907-2); Sudan. 1981 (ISBN 0-379-22908-0). 1980. Set. 760.00 (ISBN 0-379-22900-5); 125.00 ea. Oceana.
Lorimer, James J. & Perlet, Harry F., Jr. The Legal Environment of Insurance, 2 Vols. LC 81-66114. 823p. 1981. Vol. 1. text ed. 18.00 (ISBN 0-89463-026-1); Vol. 2. text ed. 18.00 (ISBN 0-686-82668-X). Am Inst Property.
Schwartz, Alan & Scott, Robert E. Commercial Transactions Principles & Policies. (University Casebook Ser.). 1104p. 1982. text ed. write for info. tchr's manual (ISBN 0-88277-121-3); pap. write for info. Foundation Pr.
Smith, Len Young & Gale, Roberson G. Smith & Roberson's Essentials of Business Law. (Illus.). 1008p. 1982. text ed. 23.95 (ISBN 0-314-69680-6); tchrs.' manual avail. (ISBN 0-314-71127-9); study guide avail. (ISBN 0-314-71145-7); transparency masters avail. (ISBN 0-314-71128-7). West Pub.
Trakman, Leon E. The Law Merchant: The Evolution of Commercial Law. LC 82-15067. xi, 195p. 1983. text ed. 35.00x (ISBN 0-8377-1207-6). Rothman.

COMMERCIAL LAW–EXAMINATIONS, QUESTIONS, ETC.
Ficek, Edmund. Comprehensive CPA Business Law Review. 1st ed. (Illus.). 640p. 1983. text ed. 26.95 (ISBN 0-07-020671-6, C); instr's. manual 10.95 (ISBN 0-07-020672-4). McGraw.

COMMERCIAL LAW–STUDY AND TEACHING
Epstein, David G. & Martin, James A. Basic Uniform Commercial Code Teaching Materials. 2d ed. (American Casebook Ser.). 589p. 1983. text ed. write for info. (ISBN 0-314-71764-1). West Pub.

COMMERCIAL PAPER
see Negotiable Instruments

COMMERCIAL PHOTOGRAPHY
see Photography, Commercial

COMMERCIAL POLICY
see also Commercial Treaties; Commodity Control; Export Credit; Foreign Trade Regulation
also subdivision Commerce or Commercial Policy under names of countries
Baldwin, Robert E. The Inefficacy of Trade Policy. LC 82-23425. (Essays in International Finance Ser.: No. 150). 1982. pap. text ed. 2.50x (ISBN 0-88165-057-9). Princeton U Int Finan Econ.
De Alessi, Louis. Some Economic Aspects of Government Ownership & Regulation: Essays From Economia Pubblica. (LEC Occasional Paper). 50p. 1982. pap. 3.00 (ISBN 0-916770-12-5). Law & Econ U Miami.
Greenaway, David. Trade Policy & the New Protectionism. LC 82-10621. 232p. 1982. 25.00x (ISBN 0-312-81213-2). St Martin.
Rojas. Redaccion Comercial Estructurada. 2nd ed. 200p. 1982. 9.12 (ISBN 0-07-053566-3). McGraw.

COMMERCIAL PRODUCTS
see also Animal Products; Commodity Control; Commodity Exchanges; Display of Merchandise; Forest Products; Manufactures; Marine Resources; New Products; Raw Materials
also names of individual products
Bohlinger, Maryanne Smith. Merchandise Buying: A Practical Guide. 2nd ed. 570p. 1982. pap. text ed. write for info. (ISBN 0-697-08086-2). Wm C Brown.
Gould, Bruce G. How to Make Money in Commodities. 2nd ed. (Illus.). 186p. (Orig.). 1982. pap. 7.95x (ISBN 0-918706-09-2). B Gould Pubns.
Gregory, C. A. Gifts & Commodities. (Studies in Political Economy: Vol. 2). 37.00 (ISBN 0-12-301460-3); pap. 16.00 (ISBN 0-12-301462-X). Acad Pr.
Seidel, Andrew D. & Ginsberg, Philip M. Commodities Trading: Analysis & Operations. (Illus.). 448p. 1982. text ed. 39.95 (ISBN 0-13-152678-2). P-H.

COMMERCIAL PRODUCTS–SAFETY MEASURES
see Product Safety

COMMERCIAL RECORDS
see Business Records

COMMERCIAL ROUTES
see Trade Routes

COMMERCIAL SCHOOLS
see Business Education

COMMERCIAL SECRETS
see Trade Secrets

COMMERCIAL STATISTICS
see also subdivision Commerce under names of countries, cities, etc. e.g. France–Commerce
Foreign Trade Statistics for Africa. (Ser. "B", Trade by Commodity: No. 31). 4.00 (ISBN 0-686-84898-5, E/F.78.II.U.3). UN.
Handbook of International Trade & Development Statistics: Supplement 1981. 33.00 (ISBN 0-686-84903-5, E/F.82.II.D.11). UN.
McClave, James T. & Benson, P. George. A First Course in Business Statistics. 2nd ed. (Illus.). 1983. text ed. 24.95 (ISBN 0-89517-043-4). Dellen Pub.
Mansfield, Edwin. Statistics for Business & Economics: Methods & Applications. 2nd ed. 1983. text ed. 22.95x (ISBN 0-393-95293-2); write for info. Problems & Case Studies (ISBN 0-393-95333-5); write for info. solutions manual; write for info. test item file. Norton.
OECD. Historical Statistics of Foreign Trade, 1956-1980. 104p. (Orig., Eng. & Fr.). 1982. pap. 11.00x (ISBN 92-64-02352-6). OECD.

COMMERCIAL TREATIES
Glick, Leslie A. Multilateral Trade Negotiations. 400p. Date not set. text ed. 48.50x (ISBN 0-86598-036-5). Allanheld.

COMMERCIALS, RADIO
see Radio Advertising

COMMERCIALS, TELEVISION
see Television Advertising

COMMISSIONS, INDEPENDENT REGULATORY
see Independent Regulatory Commissions

COMMISSIONS OF INQUIRY
see Governmental Investigations

COMMISSIONS OF THE FEDERAL GOVERNMENT
see Independent Regulatory Commissions

COMMODITIES
see Commercial Products

COMMODITY CONTROL
Ainsworth, Ralph M. Basic Principles of Successful Commodity Futures Speculation. (Illus.). 174p. 1983. 117.45 (ISBN 0-86654-069-5). Inst Econ Finan.

COMMODITY EXCHANGES
see also Commercial Products; Marketing; Markets; Put and Call Transactions
Cubberley, William. The Commodity Market Today. 62p. (Orig.). 1979. pap. 11.00 (ISBN 0-686-37422-3). Future Pub TN.
Ernst, Ervin. International Commodity Agreements. 1982. lib. bdg. 29.00 (ISBN 90-247-2648-4, Pub. by Martinus Nijhoff Netherlands). Kluwer Boston.
Gould, Bruce. Bruce Gould on Commodoties, Vol. 3. 213p. 1977. 14.00 (ISBN 0-686-84396-7). B Gould Pubns.
--Bruce Gould on Commodoties, Vol. 4. 213p. 1978. 14.00 (ISBN 0-686-84397-5). B Gould Pubns.
--Bruce Gould on Commodoties, Vol. 5. 213p. 1978. 14.00 (ISBN 0-686-84398-3). B Gould Pubns.
--Bruce Gould on Commodoties, Vol. 6. 213p. 1979. 14.00 (ISBN 0-686-84399-1). B Gould Pubns.
Gould, Bruce G. Bruce Gould on Commodities. 213p. 1983. Vol. 1, Pt. 1 & 2. pap. 12.95 ea. Vol. 1, Pt. 1 (ISBN 0-918706-05-X). Vol. 1, Pt. 2 (ISBN 0-918706-07-6). B Gould Pubns.
--Bruce Gould on Commodities. 1983. Vol. 3, Pt. 1, 231 pgs. pap. 12.95 (ISBN 0-918706-10-6); Vol. 3, Pt. 2, 244 pgs. pap. 12.95 (ISBN 0-918706-12-2). B Gould Pubns.
--Bruce Gould on Commodities. (Illus.). 218p. 1983. pap. 12.95 ea. Vol. 2, Pt. 1 (ISBN 0-918706-08-4). Vol. 2, Pt. 2 (ISBN 0-918706-06-8). B Gould Pubns.
--Bruce Gould On Commodoties, Vol. 2. 213p. 1977. 14.00 (ISBN 0-686-84395-9). B Gould Pubns.
--Commodity Trading Manual. 128p. 1983. pap. 65.00 (ISBN 0-918706-11-4). B Gould Pubns.
Horn, Frederick F. & Farah, Victor W. Trading in Commodity Futures. 2nd ed. LC 78-27235. (Illus.). 373p. 1979. 18.95 (ISBN 0-13-925941-4). NY Inst Finance.
Marasco, Michael C., ed. The Complete Commodity Futures Directory. 2nd ed. 250p. 1982. 3 ring binder 49.00 (ISBN 0-9610034-0-5). Christopher Res.
Prast, William G. & Lax, Howard L. Oil-Futures Markets: An Introduction. LC 82-48622. 1983. write for info. (ISBN 0-669-06354-1). Lexington Bks.
Spurga, Ronald C. A Practical Guide to the Commodities Markets. 204p. 1983. 19.95 (ISBN 0-13-690644-3); pap. 9.95 (ISBN 0-13-690636-2). P-H.

COMMON BUSINESS ORIENTED LANGUAGE
see COBOL (Computer Program Language)

COMMON LAW PLEADING
see Pleading

COMMON MARKET COUNTRIES
see European Economic Community

COMMON SCHOOLS
see Public Schools

COMMON SENSE
Paine, Thomas. Common Sense. (Penguin American Library). 1982. pap. 2.95 (ISBN 0-14-039016-2). Penguin.
Pugsley, John A. The Alpha Strategy. 2nd ed. LC 81-50893. 1981. 13.95 (ISBN 0-936906-04-9). Stratford Pr.

COMMONS (SOCIAL ORDER)
see Labor and Laboring Classes; Middle Classes; Proletariat

COMMONWEALTH, THE
see State, The

COMMONWEALTH OF NATIONS
see also Great Britain–Colonies

Mansergh, Nicholas. The Commonwealth Experience, 2 vols. rev. ed. Incl. Vol. 1. The Durham Report to the Anglo-Irish Treaty. 27.50x (ISBN 0-8020-2491-2); pap. 12.95 (ISBN 0-8020-6515-5); Vol. 2. From British to Multiracial Commonwealth. 27.50 (ISBN 0-8020-2492-0); pap. 12.95 (ISBN 0-8020-6516-3). 1982. 50.00x (ISBN 0-8020-2477-7); Set. pap. 25.00 (ISBN 0-8020-6497-3). U of Toronto Pr.

COMMUNAL SETTLEMENTS
see Collective Settlements

COMMUNES (CHINA)

Crook, David & Crook, Isabel. The First Years of Yangyi Commune. (International Library of Sociology). 288p. 1979. 22.50 (ISBN 0-7100-3463-6). Routledge & Kegan.

COMMUNICABLE DISEASES
see also Animals As Carriers of Disease; Bacteria, Pathogenic; Bacteriology; Biological Warfare; Disinfection and Disinfectants; Dust; Epidemiology; Immunity; Medicine, Preventive; Vaccination; Virus Diseases
also names of communicable diseases, e.g. Chicken-Pox, Malarial Fever

Anderson, R. C. & May, R. M., eds. Population Biology of Infectious Diseases: Berlin 1982. (Dahlem Workshop Reports: Vol. 25). (Illus.). 320p. 1982. 18.00 (ISBN 0-387-11650-8). Springer-Verlag.

Case, Laurel, ed. Guide to the Management of Infectious Diseases. X ed. (Mongraphs in Family Medicine). Date not set. price not set (ISBN 0-8089-1506-1). Grune.

Chase, Allan. Magic Shots: A Human & Scientific Account of the Long & Continuing Struggle to Eradicate Infectious Diseases by Vaccination. LC 82-12505. 600p. 1982. 19.95 (ISBN 0-688-00787-2). Morrow.

Emmerson, A. M. The Microbiology & Treatment of Life-Threatening Infections. (Antimicrobial Chemotherapy Ser.). 175p. 1982. 31.95 (ISBN 0-471-90049-4, Pub. by Res Stud Pr). Wiley.

Freedman, Lawrence R. Infective Endocarditis & Other Intravascular Infections. (Current Topics in Infectious Diseases Ser.). (Illus.). 250p. 1982. 35.00x (ISBN 0-306-40937-2, Plenum Med Bk). Plenum Pub.

Kass, Edward H. & Platt, Richard. Current Therapy of Infectious Disease. 400p. 1983. text ed. 44.00 (ISBN 0-941158-06-3, D2621-8). Mosby.

Meyer, Richard D. Practical Infectious Diseases. (Family Practice Today: A Comprehensive Postgraduate Library). 264p. 1983. 14.95 (ISBN 0-471-09565-6, Pub. by Wiley Med). Wiley.

Patent, Dorothy H. Germs! (Illus.). 40p. (gr. 3-7). 1983. reinforced binding 9.95 (ISBN 0-8234-0481-1). Holiday.

COMMUNICABLE DISEASES–LAW AND LEGISLATION
see Public Health Laws

COMMUNICATION
Here are entered works on human communication, including both the primary techniques of language, pictures, etc., and the secondary techniques which facilitate the process, such as the press and radio.
see also Communications Research; Cybernetics; Information Science; Information Theory; Intercultural Communication; Language and Languages; Mass Media; Nonverbal Communication; Oral Communication; Persuasion (Psychology); Popular Culture; Symbolism in Communication

Arnold, William E. Crisis Communication. (Illus.). 90p. (Orig.). 1980. pap. text ed. 6.95 (ISBN 0-89787-302-5). Gorsuch Scarisbrick.

Barker, Larry & Edwards, Renee. Intrapersonal Communication. (Comm Comp Ser.). (Illus.). 52p. 1979. pap. text ed. 2.95 (ISBN 0-89787-301-7). Gorsuch Scarisbrick.

Berko, Roy M. & Wolvin, Andrew D. This Business of Communicating. 2nd ed. 250p. 1983. pap. text ed. write for info. (ISBN 0-697-04227-8); instrs' manual avail. (ISBN 0-697-04232-4). Wm C Brown.

Bolton. General & Communications Studies, No. I, II. 1983. No. I. text ed. write for info. (ISBN 0-408-01195-5); No. II. text ed. write for info. (ISBN 0-408-01197-1). Butterworth.

Brooks, William D. & Scafe, Marla G. Verbal Language & Communication. (Comm Comp Ser.). (Illus.). 32p. 1980. pap. text ed. 2.95 (ISBN 0-686-84490-4). Gorsuch Scarisbrick.

Burgoon, Michael, ed. Communication Yearbook Six: An Annual Review Published for the International Commucation Association. LC 76-45943. (Communication Yearbook Ser.: Vol. 6). 968p. 1982. 45.00 (ISBN 0-8039-1862-3). Sage.

Carlson, Faith. Alternate Methods of Communication. 1981. pap. text ed. 3.95x (ISBN 0-8134-2237-X). Interstate.

Cheatham, T. Richard. Communication & Law Enforcement. (Procom Ser.). 1983. pap. text ed. 7.95 (ISBN 0-673-15556-0). Scott F.

Communications, Bk.III. (Ed-Lab Experiment Manual Ser.). (Illus.). (gr. 9-12). 1982. lab manual 11.50 (ISBN 0-86711-026-0). CES Industries.

Communications Nineteen Eighty-Two. (IEE Conference Publications: No. 209). 328p. 1982. pap. 68.00 (ISBN 0-85296-258-4). Inst Elect Eng.

Davidson, C. W. Transmission Lines For Communications. LC 78-4546. 218p. 1982. 19.95x (ISBN 0-470-27358-5). Halsted Pr.

Discovering Communications. (Discovering Science Ser.). 1982. lib. bdg. 15.96 (ISBN 0-86706-057-3, Pub. by Stonehenge). Silver.

Fabun, Don. Communications: The Transfer of Meaning. (Illus.). 1983. 4.50 (ISBN 0-686-84070-4). Intl Gen Semantics.

Feagans, Lynne & Garvey, Catherine. The Origins & Growth of Communication. 432p. 1983. 37.50 (ISBN 0-89391-164-X). Ablex Pub.

Goldstein, M. & Waldman, S., eds. The Creative Black Book: 1983, 3 vols. (Illus.). 1175p. 1983. Set. 70.00 (ISBN 0-916098-07-9). Friendly Pubns.

Goodall, H. Lloyd, Jr. Human Communication: Creating Reality. 255p. 1983. pap. write for info. (ISBN 0-697-04216-2); instr's. manual avail. (ISBN 0-697-04224-3). Wm C Brown.

Goss, Blaine. Communication in Everyday Life. 320p. 1982. pap. text ed. 13.95x (ISBN 0-534-01215-9). Wadsworth Pub.

Graff, Robert. Communications for National Development: Roles, Methods, Values (Published for the Salzburg Seminar) 196p. 1983. text ed. 22.50 (ISBN 0-89946-161-1). Oelgeschlager.

Hart, Roderick P. Public Communication. 2nd ed. 368p. 1983. text ed. 13.50 scp (ISBN 0-06-042687-X, HarpC); instr's. manual avail. (ISBN 0-06-362667-5). Har-Row.

Hellweg, Susan A. & Samovar, Larry A. Organizational Communication. (Comm Comp Ser.). (Illus.). 60p. 1981. pap. text ed. 2.95 (ISBN 0-89787-310-6). Gorsuch Scarisbrick.

Huyler, Jean W. Crisis Communications & Communicating About Negotiations. rev., 2nd ed. Orig. Title: Crisis Communications. 92p. pap. 8.95x (ISBN 0-941554-03-1). EdCom.

Johannesen, Richard L. Ethics in Human Communications. 2nd ed. 244p. 1983. pap. text ed. 8.95X (ISBN 0-88133-009-4). Waveland Pr.

Johnson, Bonnie M. Communication: The Process of Organizing. 404p. 1981. pap. text ed. 12.95x (ISBN 0-89641-089-7). American Pr.

Krevolin, Nathan. Communication Systems & Procedures for the Modern Office. (Illus.). 464p. 1983. 21.95 (ISBN 0-13-153668-0). P-H.

Lewis, Byron A. & Pucelik, R. Frank. Magic Demystified: A Pragmatic Guide to Communication & Change. (Illus.). 164p. 1982. pap. 12.95 (ISBN 0-943920-00-0). Metamorphous Pr.

Lewis, Michael & Rosenblum, Leonard A. Interaction, Conversation & the Development of Language. LC 82-21225. 344p. 1983. Repr. of 1977 ed. lib. bdg. write for info. (ISBN 0-89874-588-8). Krieger.

Marcy, Sam. Poland: Behind the Crisis. 168p. 1982. pap. 3.95 (ISBN 0-89567-076-3). WV Pubs.

Miller, Gary M. Modern Electronic Communications. 2nd ed. (Illus.). 592p. 1983. text ed. 26.95 (ISBN 0-13-593152-5). P-H.

The Right to Communicate: A Status Report. (Reports & Papers on Mass Communication: No. 94). 53p. 1982. pap. 5.00 (ISBN 92-3-101991-0, U1238, UNESCO). Unipub.

Slack & Mueller. A Propos! Communication et Culture: Un Debut. 1985. text ed. 22.95 (ISBN 0-686-84591-9, FR34); write for info. supplementary materials. HM.

Tompkins, Phillip K. Communication as Action: An Introduction to Rehtoric & Communication. 272p. 1982. text ed. 15.95x (ISBN 0-534-01157-8). Wadsworth Pub.

COMMUNICATION (THEOLOGY)
see also Evangelistic Work

Kraft, Charles H. Communication Theory for Christian Witness. 256p. (Orig.). 1983. pap. 11.95 (ISBN 0-687-09224-8). Abingdon.

COMMUNICATION–JUVENILE LITERATURE

Arnold, Caroline. How Do We Communicate? (Easy-Read Community Bks.). (Illus.). 32p. (gr. k-3). 1983. PLB 7.90 (ISBN 0-531-04505-6). Watts.

COMMUNICATION–PSYCHOLOGICAL ASPECTS
see also Interpersonal Communication

Londgren, Richard E. Communication by Objectives: A Guide to Productive & Cost-Effective Public Relations & Marketing. (Illus.). 208p. 1983. 16.95 (ISBN 0-13-153650-8); pap. 7.95 (ISBN 0-13-153643-5). P-H.

COMMUNICATION–RESEARCH
see Communications Research

COMMUNICATION–SOCIAL ASPECTS

Mytton, Graham. The Sociology of Communications: Changing Patterns in Africa. 220p. 1982. pap. text ed. 16.95 (ISBN 0-7131-8080-3). E Arnold.

Slack, Anne & Mueller, Marlies. A Propos! Communication et Culture: Un Debut. LC 82-82509. 1983. 23.95 (ISBN 0-395-32728-8); write for info. supplementary materials. HM.

COMMUNICATION–STUDY AND TEACHING

Corner, J. & Hawthorn, J. Communication Studies: An Introductory Reader. 256p. 1980. pap. text ed. 13.95 (ISBN 0-7131-6278-3). E Arnold.

Patty, Catherine. Communications. (Social Studies). 24p. (gr. 5-8). 1979. wkbk. 5.00 (ISBN 0-8209-0250-0, SS-17). ESP.

Zuckman, Harvey L. & Gaynes, Martin J. Mass Communications in a Nutshell. 2nd ed. LC 82-20029. 473p. 1982. pap. text ed. 6.95 (ISBN 0-314-69869-8). West Pub.

COMMUNICATION, BUSINESS
see Communication in Management

COMMUNICATION, EMPLOYEE
see Communication in Personnel Management

COMMUNICATION, INTERCULTURAL
see Intercultural Communication

COMMUNICATION AMONG ANIMALS
see Animal Communication

COMMUNICATION IN EDUCATION
see also Education

Butler, Matilda & Paisley, William J. Knowledge Utilization Systems in Education. (Illus.). 320p. 1983. 27.50 (ISBN 0-8039-1944-1). Sage.

Cooper, Pamela J. Speech Communication for the Classroom Teacher. (Illus.). 296p. (Orig.). 1980. pap. text ed. 15.95 (ISBN 0-89787-303-3). Gorsuch Scarisbrick.

Idol-Maestas, Lorna. Special Educator's Consultation Handbook. 350p. 1982. 27.50 (ISBN 0-89443-926-X). Aspen Systems.

Organizing Educational Broadcasting. 302p. 1982. pap. 37.25 (ISBN 92-3-101878-7, U1184, UNESCO). Unipub.

COMMUNICATION IN INDUSTRY
see Communication in Management

COMMUNICATION IN MANAGEMENT
see also Business Report Writing; Communication in Personnel Management

Baird, John E., Jr. & Rittof, David J. Quality Circles: Facilitator's Manual. (Illus.). 247p. (Orig.). 1983. pap. 34.95X (ISBN 0-88133-010-8). Waveland Pr.

Baird, John W. & Stull, James B. Business Communication: A Problem-Solving Approach. (Illus.). 416p. 1983. text ed. 21.95x (ISBN 0-07-003281-5, C); write for info. instr's manual (ISBN 0-07-003282-3); write for info. wkbk. (ISBN 0-07-003283-1). McGraw.

Berko, Roy M. & Wolvin, Andrew D. This Business of Communicating. 2nd ed. 250p. 1983. pap. text ed. write for info. (ISBN 0-697-04227-8); instrs' manual avail. (ISBN 0-697-04232-4). Wm C Brown.

Bradley, Patricia H. & Baird, John E., Jr. Communication for Business & the Professions. 2nd ed. 360p. 1983. pap. text ed. Write for info. (ISBN 0-697-04223-5); instrs.' manual avail. (ISBN 0-697-04233-2). Wm C Brown.

Chappell, R. T. & Read, W. L. Business Communications. 232p. 1980. 30.00x (ISBN 0-7121-0272-8, Pub. by Macdonald & Evans). State Mutual Bk.

Douglis, Philip N. Pictures for Organizations. LC 82-60042. (Communications Library). (Illus.). 233p. (Orig.). 1982. pap. 35.00 (ISBN 0-931368-10-3). Ragan Comm.

Dumaine, Deborah. Write to the Top: Writing for Corporate Success. LC 82-40145. 1983. pap. 7.95 (ISBN 0-394-71226-9). Random.

Foseco Minsep Group. The Business Traveller's Handbook: How to Get along with People in 100 Countries. 300p. 1983. 14.95 (ISBN 0-13-107797-X); pap. 7.95 (ISBN 0-13-107789-9). P-H.

Glatthorn, Allan A. & Adams, Herbert R. Listening Your Way to Management Success. (Goals Ser.). 1983. pap. text ed. 7.95 (ISBN 0-673-15802-0). Scott F.

Goldhaber, Gerald. Organizational Communication. 3rd ed. 450p. 1983. text ed. write for info. (ISBN 0-697-04219-7); instrs.' manual avail. (ISBN 0-697-04220-0). Wm C Brown.

Gorden, William I. & Miller, John R. Managing Your Communication: In & For the Organization. (Illus.). 280p. 1983. pap. 9.95x (ISBN 0-88133-007-8). Waveland Pr.

Hatch, Richard A. Business Communication. 608p. 1983. text ed. write for info. (ISBN 0-574-20660-4, 13-3660); write for info. instr's. guide (ISBN 0-574-20661-2, 13-3661). SRA.

Londgren, Richard E. Communication by Objectives: A Guide to Productive & Cost-Effective Public Relations & Marketing. (Illus.). 208p. 1983. 16.95 (ISBN 0-13-153650-8); pap. 7.95 (ISBN 0-13-153643-5). P-H.

Mancuso, Joseph R. How to Prepare & Present a Business Plan. (Illus.). 316p. 1983. 19.95 (ISBN 0-13-430629-5); pap. 9.95 (ISBN 0-13-430611-2). P-H.

Pace, R. Wayne. Organizational Communication: Foundations for Human Resource Development. (Illus.). 352p. 1983. text ed. 18.95 (ISBN 0-13-641324-2). P-H.

Phillips, Bonnie D. Business Communication. 2nd ed. LC 82-73090. (Illus.). 272p. 1983. text ed. 16.00 (ISBN 0-8273-2188-0); wkbk. 5.20 (ISBN 0-8273-2190-2); cassette 12.00 (ISBN 0-8273-2192-9); instr's guide 4.20 (ISBN 0-8273-2191-0). Delmar.

Ragan Report Workshop. Workshops Notebook. Ragan, Lawrence & Lange, Catherine, eds. (Communications Library). 78p. 1982. three-ring binder 25.00 (ISBN 0-931368-11-1). Ragan Comm.

Sparrow, W. Keats & Pickett, Nell Ann, eds. Technical & Business Communication in Two-Year Programs. (Orig.). 1983. pap. write for info. (ISBN 0-8141-5298-8). NCTE.

Timm, Paul R. & Jones, Christopher G. Business Communication: Getting Results. 312p. 1983. 22.95 (ISBN 0-13-091793-1). P-H.

Wildavsky, Aaron, ed. The Policy Organization. (Managing Information Ser.: Vol. 5). (Illus.). 224p. 1983. 25.00 (ISBN 0-8039-1912-3); pap. 12.50 (ISBN 0-8039-1913-1). Sage.

COMMUNICATION IN MEDICINE
see also Health Education; Medical Libraries

Peterson, H. E. & Isaksson, A. J., eds. Communication Networks in Health Care: Proceedings of the IFIP-IMIA Working Conference on Communication Networks in Health Care, Ulvsunda Palace, Sweden, 14-18 June, 1982. 366p. 1982. 49.00 (ISBN 0-444-86513-6, North Holland). Elsevier.

COMMUNICATION IN PERSONNEL MANAGEMENT

Cummings, H. Wayland & Long, Larry W. Managing Communication in Organizations: An Introduction. 361p. 1982. pap. text ed. 15.95x (ISBN 0-89787-314-9). Gorsuch Scarisbrick.

Sarnoff, Dorothy. Make the Most of Your Best. LC 82-11927. 240p. 1983. pap. 7.95 (ISBN 0-03-062376-6). HR&W.

Smith, Robert E. Workrights: How to Draw the Line Without Losing Your Job. 236p. 1983. 14.95 (ISBN 0-525-24179-5, 01451-440); pap. 8.95 (ISBN 0-525-48047-1, 0801-240). Dutton.

COMMUNICATION IN RESEARCH
see Communication in Science

COMMUNICATION IN SCIENCE
see also Communication in Medicine; Communication of Technical Information; Science–Information Services; Scientific Libraries

Olsen, L. & Ruchin, T. Principles of Communications for Science & Technology. 432p. 1983. 16.95x (ISBN 0-07-047821-X). McGraw.

COMMUNICATION IN THE SOCIAL SCIENCES

Edwards, Dan W. Communication Skills for the Helping Professions. 112p. 1983. 16.75x (ISBN 0-398-04766-9). C C Thomas.

Tannenbaum, Percy H. & Kostrich, Leslie J. Turned-On TV - Turned-Off Voters: Policy Options for Election Projections. (People & Communication Ser.: Vol. 15). 244p. 1983. 25.00 (ISBN 0-8039-1929-8). Sage.

COMMUNICATION OF TECHNICAL INFORMATION
see also Technical Libraries; Technical Writing

Miller, Gary M. Modern Electronic Communications. 2nd ed. (Illus.). 592p. 1983. text ed. 26.95 (ISBN 0-13-593152-5). P-H.

Olsen, L. & Ruchin, T. Principles of Communications for Science & Technology. 432p. 1983. 16.95x (ISBN 0-07-047821-X). McGraw.

Sparrow, W. Keats & Pickett, Nell Ann, eds. Technical & Business Communication in Two-Year Programs. (Orig.). 1983. pap. write for info. (ISBN 0-8141-5298-8). NCTE.

COMMUNICATION SATELLITES
see Artificial Satellites in Telecommunication

COMMUNICATION SKILLS (ELEMENTARY EDUCATION)
see English Language–Study and Teaching (Elementary)

COMMUNICATION THEORY
see Information Theory

COMMUNICATIONS, MILITARY
see also Signals and Signaling

Raggett, R. J., ed. Jane's Military Communications, 1982. (Jane's Yearbooks). (Illus.). 650p. 1982. 140.00 (ISBN 0-86720-615-2). Sci Bks Intl.

--Jane's Military Communications, 1983. 4th ed. (Jane's Yearbooks). (Illus.). 720p. 1983. 140.00x (ISBN 0-86720-646-2). Sci Bks Intl.

COMMUNICATIONS RELAY SYSTEMS
see Artificial Satellites in Telecommunication

COMMUNICATIONS RESEARCH

Dervin, Brenda & Voigt, Melvin J., eds. Progress in Communication Sciences, Vol. 4. 304p. 1983. text ed. 32.50 (ISBN 0-89391-102-X). Ablex Pub.

Singh, Indu. Telematics in the Year Two Thousand. Voigt, Melvin J., ed. (Communication & Information Science Ser.). 224p. 1983. text ed. 24.95 (ISBN 0-89391-137-2). Ablex Pub.

COMMUNICATIONS SYSTEMS, POLICE
see Police Communication Systems

COMMUNICATIVE DISORDERS

Boyce, Nancy L. & Larson, Vicki L. Adolescents' Communication: Development & Disorders. 250p. 1983. three-ring binder 15.95 (ISBN 0-9610370-0-8). Thinking Ink Pr.

Lasky, Elaine Z. & Katz, Jack, eds. Central Auditory Processing Disorders: Problems of Speech, Language & Learning. (Illus.). 1983. 29.95 (ISBN 0-8391-1802-3, 18368). Univ Park.

Perkins. Language Handicaps in Adults. (Current Therapy of Communication Disorders Ser.: Vol. 3). 1983. price not set (ISBN 0-86577-090-5). Thieme-Stratton.

Perkins, William. Dysarthria & Apraxia: Current Therapy of Communication Disorders, Vol. 2. (Illus.). 128p. 1983. write for info. (ISBN 0-86577-086-7). Thieme-Stratton.

Pilotta, Joseph J. Women in Organizations: Barriers & Breakthroughs. 101p. (Orig.). 1983. pap. text ed. 4.95x (ISBN 0-88133-008-6). Waveland Pr.

Tibbits, Donald F. Language Disorders in Adolescents. LC 82-71669. (Cliffs Speech & Hearing Ser.). 120p. (Orig.). 1982. pap. text ed. 4.95 (ISBN 0-8220-1832-2). Cliffs.

Weinberg, Bernd & Meitus, Irv J., eds. AN Introduction to Diagnosis of Speech & Language Disorders. 1983. pap. text ed. price not set (ISBN 0-8391-1810-4, 18430). Univ Park.

Winitz, Harris, ed. Treating Language Disorders: For Clinicians by Clinicians. 1983. pap. text ed. price not set (ISBN 0-8391-1813-9, 19674). Univ Park.

COMMUNION

see Lord's Supper

COMMUNISM

Here are entered general works. For works on communism in specific countries, see subdivisions below.

see also Collective Settlements; Communist International; Communists; Marxian Economics; Nationalism and Socialism; Socialism; Tribes and Tribal System; Women and Socialism

Adelman, Jonathan R., ed. Terror & Communist Politics: The Role of the Secret Police in Communist States. (Special Study). 300p. 1983. lib. bdg. 25.00 (ISBN 0-86531-293-1). Westview.

Chilcote, Ronald H., ed. Dependency & Marxism: Toward a Resolution of the Debate. (Latin American Perpsective Ser.: No. 1). 179p. 1982. lib. bdg. 18.95 (ISBN 0-86531-457-8); pap. text ed. 9.95 (ISBN 0-86531-458-6). Westview.

Counts, George S. Bolshevism, Fascism & Capitalism. 1932. text ed. 12.50x (ISBN 0-686-83492-5). Elliots Bks.

Dunayavskaya, Raya. Rosa Luxemburg, Women's Liberation & Marx's Philosophy of Revolution. 260p. 1982. text ed. 19.95x (ISBN 0-391-02569-4, Pub. by Harvester England); pap. text ed. 10.95x (ISBN 0-391-02793-X). Humanities.

Jessop, Bob. The Capitalist State: Marxist Theories & Methods. 320p. 1982. 27.50 (ISBN 0-8147-4163-0); pap. 8.50 (ISBN 0-8147-4164-9). Columbia U Pr.

Marx, Karl & Engles, Friedrich. Harold J. Laski on the Communist Manifesto. 1982. pap. 2.25 (ISBN 0-451-62125-5, ME2125, Ment). NAL.

Nelson, Daniel N., ed. Communism & the Politics of Inequalities. LC 81-48525. 1983. write for info. (ISBN 0-669-05415-1). Lexington Bks.

Novoselov, S. P. Problems of the Communist Movement. 336p. 1981. pap. 6.00 (ISBN 0-8285-2276-6, Pub. by Progress Pubs USSR). Imported Pubns.

Plato. Philebus. Waterfield, Robin A., tr. from Gr. 1983. pap. 3.95 (ISBN 0-14-044395-9). Penguin.

Suvorov, L. N. Marxist Philosophy at the Leninist Stage. 245p. 1982. 6.95 (ISBN 0-8285-2424-6, Pub. by Progress Pubs USSR). Imported Pubns.

Troung Tien Dat. The Red Dragon. 1983. 15.95 (ISBN 0-533-05578-4). Vantage.

Whetten, Lawrence L., ed. The Present State of Communist Internationalism. 1983. price not set (ISBN 0-669-05582-4). Lexington Bks.

COMMUNISM–HISTORY

Chase-Dunn, Christopher K. Socialist States in the World-System. (Sage Focus Editions). 320p. 1982. 25.00 (ISBN 0-8039-1878-X); pap. 12.50 (ISBN 0-8039-1879-8). Sage.

Marx, Karl. The Communist Manifesto. (Illus.). 1983. 3.25 (ISBN 0-7178-0600-6). Intl Pub Co.

Saltman, Richard B. The Social & Political Thought of Michael Bakunin. LC 82-9348. (Contributions in Political Science Ser.: No. 88). 256p. 1983. lib. bdg. 35.00 (ISBN 0-313-23378-0, SPB/). Greenwood.

COMMUNISM–HISTORY–SOURCES

Szajkowski. Documents in Communist Affairs, 1977. 1982. text ed. 39.95 (ISBN 0-408-10818-5). Butterworth.

--Documents in Communist Affairs, 1979. 1982. text ed. 52.50 (ISBN 0-408-10819-3). Butterworth.

COMMUNISM–AFRICA

Dadoo, Y. M., et al. South African Communist Speak, 1915-1980. 474p. 1981. pap. 25.00x (ISBN 0-686-83901-3, Pub. by Inkuleko). Imported Pubns.

COMMUNISM–ASIA

see also Communism–China; Communism–India

Arnold, Anthony. Afghanistan's Two-Party Communism: Parcham & Khalq. (Publication Ser.: No. 279). 260p. 1983. pap. 10.95 (ISBN 0-8179-7792-9). Hoover Inst Pr.

COMMUNISM–CHINA

Shalom, Stephen R. The Human Costs of Chinese Communism: Propaganda Versus Reality. (Occasional Paper Arizona State Univ., Center for Asian Studies Ser.: No. 15). 200p. 1983. pap. 4.00 (ISBN 0-939252-11-2). ASU Ctr Asian.

Thaxton, Ralph. China Turned Rightside Up: Revolutionary Legitimacy in the Peasant World. LC 82-40165. (Illus.). 312p. 1983. text ed. 27.50x (ISBN 0-300-02707-9). Yale U Pr.

COMMUNISM–EUROPE

Lindemann, Albert S. A History of European Socialism. LC 82-40167. 416p. 1983. text ed. 25.00x (ISBN 0-300-02797-4). Yale U Pr.

Marcy, Sam. Eurocommunism, New Form of Reformism. 52p. 1978. pap. 1.00 (ISBN 0-89567-026-7). WV Pubs.

COMMUNISM–FRANCE

Wall, Irwin M. French Communism in the Era of Stalin: The Quest for Unity & Integration, 1945-1962. LC 82-20970. (Contributions in Political Science Ser.: No. 97). 280p. 1983. lib. bdg. 29.95 (ISBN 0-313-23662-3, WFC/). Greenwood.

COMMUNISM–GREAT BRITAIN

Northedge, F. S. & Wells, A. Britain & Soviet Communism: The Impact of a Revolution. 280p. 1982. text ed. 31.50x (ISBN 0-333-27192-0, 41036, Pub. by Macmillan England); pap. text ed. 15.50x (ISBN 0-333-27193-9, 41104). Humanities.

Winstanley, Gerrard. The Law of Freedom & Other Writings. Hill, Christopher, ed. LC 82-14604. (Past & Present Publications Ser.). 395p. Date not set. price not set (ISBN 0-521-25299-7). Cambridge U Pr.

COMMUNISM–INDIA

Charles, K. J. Total Development: Essays Toward an Integration of Marxian & Gandhian Perspectives. 1983. text ed. write for info. (ISBN 0-7069-2075-9, Pub. by Vikas India). Advent NY.

COMMUNISM–ITALY

Piccone, Paul. Italian Marxism. LC 82-1474. 225p. 1983. text ed. 19.95x (ISBN 0-520-04798-2). U of Cal Pr.

Ruscoe, James. On the Threshold of Government: The Italian Communist 1976-1981. LC 81-14622. 304p. 1982. 27.50x (ISBN 0-312-58457-1). St Martin.

COMMUNISM–LATIN AMERICA

Dulles, John W. Brazilian Communism 1935-1945: Repression during World Upheaval. (Illus.). 311p. 1983. text ed. 25.00x (ISBN 0-292-70741-X). U of Tex Pr.

COMMUNISM–RUSSIA

Northedge, F. S. & Wells, A. Britain & Soviet Communism: The Impact of a Revolution. 280p. 1982. text ed. 31.50x (ISBN 0-333-27192-0, 41036, Pub. by Macmillan England); pap. text ed. 15.50x (ISBN 0-333-27193-9, 41104). Humanities.

O'Neill, William L. The Great Schism: Stalinism & the American Intellectuals. (Illus.). 447p. 17.95 (ISBN 0-686-43340-8). S&S.

Ustinov, D. F. Serving the Homeland & the Cause of Communism. (World Leaders Speeches & Writings Ser.). 96p. 1982. 30.00 (ISBN 0-08-028174-5). Pergamon.

Venturi, Franco. Roots of Revolution: A History of the Populist & Socialist Movements in Nineteenth-Century Russia. Haskell, Francis, tr. xxxviii, 850p. 1960. pap. 14.95 (ISBN 0-226-85270-9). U of Chicago Pr.

COMMUNISM–UNITED STATES

Hoxa, Enver. Party of Labor of Albania, Report Submitted to the 8th Congress. 82p. 1981. pap. 2.00 (ISBN 0-86714-021-6). Marxist-Leninist.

Kurland, Gerald R. Communism & the Red Scare: Topics of Our Times Ser. Rahmas, Sigurd C., ed. (No. 18). 32p. (Orig.). 1982. 2.95x (ISBN 0-87157-819-0); pap. text ed. 1.95 (ISBN 0-87157-319-9). SamHar Pr.

Marxist-Leninist Party, U. S. A. El Avance del Movimiento Revolucionario Require de una Enconada Lucha Contra la Socialdemocracia y el Liquidacionismo. 93p. (Span.). pap. 1.00 (ISBN 0-86714-023-2). Marxist-Leninist.

--Songbook: Down with Ronald Reagan, Chieftain of Capitalist Reaction & Other Songs of Revolutionary Struggle & Socialism. (Illus.). 84p. 1982. pap. 1.00 (ISBN 0-86714-024-0). Marxist-Leninist.

--La Verdad sobre las Relaciones entre el Partido Marxista de los EUA y el Partido Communista del Canada. 86p. (Span.). 1982. pap. 1.00 (ISBN 0-86714-022-4). Marxist-Leninist.

Naison, Mark. Communists in Harlem During the Depression. Meier, August, ed. LC 82-10848. (Blacks in the New World Ser.). 360p. 19.95 (ISBN 0-252-00644-5). U of Ill Pr.

O'Neill, William L. The Great Schism: Stalinism & the American Intellectuals. (Illus.). 447p. 17.95 (ISBN 0-686-43340-8). S&S.

Selcraig, James T. The Red Scare in the Midwest, 1945-1955: A State & Local Study. Berkhofer, Robert, ed. LC 82-17545. (Studies in American History & Culture: No. 36). 226p. 1982. 39.95 (ISBN 0-8357-1380-6, Pub. by UMI Res Pr). Univ Microfilms.

COMMUNISM AND CHRISTIANITY

Turner, Denys. Marxism & Christianity. LC 82-22713. 250p. 1983. text ed. 25.00x (ISBN 0-389-20351-3). B&N Imports.

COMMUNIST COUNTRIES–BIBLIOGRAPHY

Research Libraries of the New York Public Library & Library of Congress. Bibliographic Guide to Soviet & East European Studies: 1982. 1983. lib. bdg. 350.00 (ISBN 0-8161-6980-2, Biblio Guides). G K Hall.

COMMUNIST COUNTRIES–ECONOMIC CONDITIONS

Schnytzer, Adi. Stalinist Economic Strategy in Practice: The Case of Albania. (Economies of the World Ser.). (Illus.). 180p. 1983. 34.95 (ISBN 0-686-84829-2). Oxford U Pr.

COMMUNIST COUNTRIES–POLITICS AND GOVERNMENT

Bertsch, Gary K. Power & Policy in Communist Systems. 2nd ed. LC 81-19715. 192p. 1982. text ed. 10.95 (ISBN 0-471-09005-0). Wiley.

White, Stephen & Gardner, John. Communist Political Systems: An Introduction. LC 82-6021. 304p. 1982. 20.00x (ISBN 0-686-81984-5). St Martin.

COMMUNIST INTERNATIONAL

Carr, Edward H. Twilight of the Comintern, 1930-1935. 436p. 1983. 22.50 (ISBN 0-394-52512-4). Pantheon.

COMMUNIST PARTY OF RUSSIA

Lowenhardt, John. The Soviet Politburo. LC 81-8759. 192p. 1982. 20.00x (ISBN 0-312-74843-4). St Martin.

Miller, Robert F. & Rigby, T. H. Twenty Sixth Congress of the CPSU in Current Political Perspective. (Department of Political Science, Research School of Social Sciences Ser.: Occasional Paper No. 16). 94p. (Orig.). pap. text ed. 9.95 (ISBN 0-909779-03-1, 1184, Pub. by ANUP Australia). Bks Australia.

COMMUNISTIC SETTLEMENTS

see Collective Settlements

COMMUNISTS

Chernin, Kim. In My Mother's House. LC 82-19514. 320p. 1983. 14.95 (ISBN 0-89919-167-3). Ticknor & Fields.

Foster, Jane. An Unamerican Lady. (Illus.). 254p. 1983. pap. 7.95 (ISBN 0-686-38853-4, Pub by Sidgwick & Jackson). Merrimack Bk Serv.

Patolichev, N. S. Measures of Maturity - My Early Life. (World Leaders Speeches & Writings). (Illus.). 320p. 1983. 50.00 (ISBN 0-08-024545-5). Pergamon.

COMMUNITY

see also Community Life; Community Organizations

Clear, Todd R. & O'Leary, Vincent. Controlling the Offenders in the Community: Reforming the Community Supervision Function. LC 81-47444. 208p. 1982. 29.95x (ISBN 0-669-04633-7). Lexington Bks.

Kamenka, Eugene. Community As a Social Idea. LC 82-16850. 180p. 1983. 22.50x (ISBN 0-312-15302-3). St Martin.

Liao, Wen Kwei. The Individual & the Community: A Historical Analysis of the Motivating Factors of Social Conduct. 313p. 1982. Repr. of 1933 ed. text ed. 50.00 (ISBN 0-8495-3266-3). Arden Lib.

Speth, Linda & Hirsch, Alison D. Women, Family, & Community in Colonial America: Two Perspectives. LC 82-23326. (Women & History Ser.: No. 4). 85p. 1983. text ed. 20.00 (ISBN 0-86656-191-9). Haworth Pr.

COMMUNITY ANTENNA TELEVISION

see also Television Relay Systems

Crossed Wires (Cable TV) 100p. 1982. 12.50 (ISBN 0-686-81764-8). Ctr Analysis Public Issues.

Eastman, Susan Tyler & Klein, Robert. Strategies in Broadcast & Cable Promotion: Commercial Television, Radio, Cable, Pay Television, Public Television. 352p. 1982. pap. text ed. 13.95x (ISBN 0-534-01156-X). Wadsworth Pub.

Gay, Tim, ed. Cable Contacts Yearbook, 1983. 1982. deluxe ed. 170.00 (ISBN 0-935224-16-5). Larimi Comm.

Pagano, Anne L., ed. Cable Advertising Directory, 1982. 508p. 1982. pap. 30.00 (ISBN 0-940272-06-7). Natl Cable.

Roman, James. Cablemania: The Cable Television Source Book. (Illus.). 240p. 1983. 18.95 (ISBN 0-13-110106-4); pap. 9.95 (ISBN 0-13-110098-X). P-H.

COMMUNITY CHESTS

see Federations, Financial (Social Service)

COMMUNITY COLLEGES

Gleazer, Edmund J., Jr. Community Colleges: What Is Their Promise & Future Place in America? (Vital Issues, Vol. XXIX 1979-80: No. 1). 0.50 (ISBN 0-686-81606-4). Ctr Info Am.

COMMUNITY COUNCILS

see Community Organizations

COMMUNITY DEVELOPMENT

see also City Planning; Technical Assistance

Alliband, Terry. Voluntary Agencies in Rural Community Development. (Library of Management for Development). 128p. 1983. pap. write for info. (ISBN 0-931816-28-9). Kumarian Pr.

Blackard, M. Kay & Barsh, Elizabeth T. Reaching Out: Achieving Community Involvement with Developmentally Disabled Children. 72p. 1982. pap. text ed. 9.95 (ISBN 0-911227-00-8). Willoughby Wessington.

Loehr, William & Powelson, John P. Threat to Development: Pitfalls of the NIE. (Special Study in Social, Political, & Economic Developmen). 160p. 1982. lib. bdg. 22.00X (ISBN 0-86531-128-5); pap. text ed. 10.00 (ISBN 0-86531-129-3). Westview.

Martelli, L. & Graham, A. Communities. (Our Nation, Our World Ser.). (gr. 3). 1983. 11.96 (ISBN 0-07-039943-3); supplementary materials avail. McGraw.

Marzuki, S. & Dilts, R. Bintang Anda: A Game Process for Community Development. (Technical Note Ser.: No. 18). 21p. (Orig.). 1982. pap. 1.00 (ISBN 0-686-84116-6). Ctr Intl Ed U of MA.

Mico, Paul R. Developing Your Community-Based Organization: With Special Emphasis on Community Economic Development Organizations & Community Action Agencies. LC 80-53828. (Illus.). 160p. 1981. pap. text ed. 7.95 (ISBN 0-89914-004-1). Third Party Pub.

Murphy, Kathleen J. Macroproject Development in the Third World: An Analysis of Transnational Partnerships. (Replica Edition). 150p. 1982. softcover 17.00x (ISBN 0-86531-939-1). Westview.

O'Mara, W. Paul & Casazza, John A. Office Development Handbook. LC 82-50078. (Community Builders Handbook Ser.). (Illus.). 288p. 1982. text ed. 42.00 (ISBN 0-87420-607-3, OD1). Urban Land.

Omer, Salima M. Institution Building & Comprehensive Social Development. LC 82-20229. 290p. (Orig.). 1983. 22.75 (ISBN 0-8191-2870-8); pap. 11.75 (ISBN 0-8191-2871-6). U Pr of Amer.

Raitz, Karl B. & Ulack, Richard. Land, People, & Development in Appalachia. 375p. 1983. lib. bdg. 30.00x (ISBN 0-86531-075-0). Westview.

Rudman, Jack. Assistant Community Development Project Supervisor. (Career Examination Ser.: C-907). (Cloth bdg. avail. on request). pap. 12.00 (ISBN 0-8373-0907-7). Natl Learning.

--Community Development Assistant. (Career Examination Ser.: C-904). (Cloth bdg. avail. on request). pap. 10.00 (ISBN 0-8373-0904-2). Natl Learning.

--Community Development Housing Analyst. (Career Examination Ser.: C-905). (Cloth bdg. avail. on request). pap. 12.00 (ISBN 0-8373-0905-0). Natl Learning.

--Community Development Program Analyst. (Career Examination Ser.: C-903). (Cloth bdg. avail. on request). pap. 12.00 (ISBN 0-8373-0903-4). Natl Learning.

--Community Development Program Technician. (Career Examination Ser.: C-902). (Cloth bdg. avail. on request). pap. 10.00 (ISBN 0-8373-0902-6). Natl Learning.

--Community Development Project Director. (Career Examination Ser.: C-909). (Cloth bdg. avail. on request). pap. 14.00 (ISBN 0-8373-0909-3). Natl Learning.

--Community Development Project Supervisor. (Career Examination Ser.: C-908). (Cloth bdg. avail. on request). pap. 12.00 (ISBN 0-8373-0908-5). Natl Learning.

--Community Improvement Coordinator. (Career Examination Ser.: C-906). (Cloth bdg. avail. on request). pap. 12.00 (ISBN 0-8373-0906-9). Natl Learning.

--Community Service Worker. (Career Examination Ser.: C-2675). (Cloth bdg. avail. on request). pap. 10.00 (ISBN 0-8373-2675-3). Natl Learning.

--Senior Neighborhood Aide. (Career Examination Ser.: C-2911). (Cloth bdg. avail. on request). pap. 12.00 (ISBN 0-8373-2911-6). Natl Learning.

School for Community Action: Serving the Many Faces of Families in the Eighties, No. 7. pap. 4.75 (ISBN 0-686-81720-6). NCJW.

Stout, Gary & Vitt, Joseph E. Public Incentives & Financial Techniques for Codevelopment. LC 82-50705. (Development Component Ser.). (Illus.). 26p. 1982. pap. 10.00 (ISBN 0-87420-610-3, D23). Urban Land.

Technologies for Rural Development. 174p. 1982. pap. 13.25 (ISBN 92-3-101971-6, U1227, UNESCO). Unipub.

Turner, John E., et al. Community Development & Rational Choice: A Korean Study, Vol. 20, Bk. 1. (Monograph Series in World Affairs). 120p. (Orig.). 1983. pap. 5.00 (ISBN 0-87940-072-2). U of Denver Intl.

COMMUNITY HEALTH

see Public Health

COMMUNITY JUNIOR COLLEGES

see Community Colleges

COMMUNITY LIFE

see also Community Development; Community Organizations; Social Isolation; Social Participation

Brooks, Bearl. Our Neighborhood. (Social Studies Ser.). 24p. (gr. 2). 1979. wkbk. 5.00 (ISBN 0-8209-0235-7, SS-2). ESP.

Krieger, Susan. The Mirror Dance: Identity in a Women's Community. 1983. write for info. (ISBN 0-87722-304-1). Temple U Pr.

Patty, Catherine. Community Spirit. (Social Studies). 24p. (gr. 3-5). 1976. wkbk. 5.00 (ISBN 0-8209-0251-9, SS-18). ESP.

Yarrington, Roger. Community Relations Handbook. (Public Communication Ser.). (Illus.). 224p. 1983. text ed. 24.95x (ISBN 0-582-28088-5); pap. text ed. 12.95x (ISBN 0-582-28087-7). Longman.

COMMUNITY MENTAL HEALTH SERVICES

American Psychiatric Association & Task Force on Community Residential Services. A Typology of Community Residential Services. LC 82-24467. (APA Task Force Report Ser.: No. 21). (Illus.). 64p. 1982. pap. 5.00x (ISBN 0-89042-221-4, 42-221-4). Am Psychiatric.

Bicknell & Sines. Community Mental Handicap Nursing. 1983. pap. text ed. 12.95 (ISBN 0-06-318246-7, Pub. by Har-Row Ltd England). Har-Row.

Biegel, David E. & Naparstek, Arthur J. Neighborhood Networks for Humane Mental Health Care. 238p. 1982. 24.50x (ISBN 0-306-41051-6, Plenum Pr). Plenum Pub.

Glasscote, R. M., et al. Preventing Mental Illness: Efforts & Attitudes. LC 80-65220. 138p. 1980. 10.00x (ISBN 0-89042-503-5). Am Psychiatric.

Menolascino, Frank J. & McCann, Brian, eds. Mental Health & Mental Retardation: Bridging the Gap. (Illus.). 272p. 1983. pap. text ed. 27.50 (ISBN 0-8391-1784-1, 19593). Univ Park.

Wagenfeld, Morton O. & Lemkau, Paul V., eds. Public Mental Health. (Studies in Community Mental Health). (Illus.). 288p. 1982. 25.00 (ISBN 0-8039-1120-3); pap. 12.50 (ISBN 0-8039-1224-2). Sage.

Wodarski, John S. Rural Community Mental Health Practice. 288p. 1983. pap. text ed. 24.50 (ISBN 0-8391-1785-X, 19402). Univ Park.

COMMUNITY ORGANIZATIONS

see also Federations, Financial (Social Service); Urban Renewal

Biklen, Douglas P. Community Organizing: Theory & Practice. 336p. 1983. text ed. 23.95 (ISBN 0-13-153676-1). P-H.

Blackard, M. Kay & Barsh, Elizabeth T. Reaching Out: Achieving Community Involvement with Developmentally Disabled Children. 72p. 1982. pap. text ed. 9.95 (ISBN 0-911227-00-8). Willoughby Wessington.

Burghardt, Steven. Organizing for Community Action. (Sage Human Services Guides: Vol. 27). 120p. 1982. pap. 7.00 (ISBN 0-8039-0206-9). Sage.

Cunningham, James V. & Kotler, Milton. Building Neighborhood Organizations. 224p. 1983. text ed. 15.95x (ISBN 0-268-00668-7); pap. text ed. 7.95x (ISBN 0-268-00669-5). U of Notre Dame Pr.

Ecklein, J. L. & Lauffer, A. Community Organizers & Social Planners: A Volume of Cases & Illustrative Materials. LC 75-171912. (Community Organization Ser.). 378p. 1972. pap. 21.95x (ISBN 0-471-22980-6). Wiley.

Leighton, Neil & Stalley, Richard. Rights & Responsibilities. (Community Care Practice Handbooks Ser.). vii, 62p. (Orig.). 1982. pap. text ed. 7.95x (ISBN 0-435-82515-1). Heinemann Ed.

Mico, Paul R. Developing Your Community-Based Organization: With Special Emphasis on Community Economic Development Organizations & Community Action Agencies. LC 80-53828. (Illus.). 160p. 1981. pap. text ed. 7.95 (ISBN 0-89914-004-1). Third Party Pub.

COMMUNITY SONG-BOOKS

see Songs

COMMUNITY SURVEYS

see Social Surveys

COMPACTS, INTERSTATE

see Interstate Agreements

COMPANIES

see Corporations; Partnership

COMPANIES, HOLDING

see Holding Companies

COMPANIES, INSURANCE

see Insurance Companies

COMPANY INSURANCE

see Insurance, Business

COMPANY LAW

see Corporation Law

COMPANY MAGAZINES

see Employees' Magazines, Handbooks, etc.

COMPANY MEETINGS

see Corporate Meetings

COMPANY PUBLICATIONS

see Employees' Magazines, Handbooks, etc.

COMPARATIVE BEHAVIOR

see Psychology, Comparative

COMPARATIVE ECONOMICS

Mueller, Dennis C., ed. The Political Economy of Growth. LC 81-15955. 296p. 1983. text ed. 23.50x (ISBN 0-300-02658-7). Yale U Pr.

Salisbury, Gregorius. The Essence of the Supply-Side Economics for the Benefit of Politicians & Businessmen. (Research Center for Economic Psychology Library). (Illus.). 121p. 1983. 39.75 (ISBN 0-86654-060-1). Inst Econ Finan.

COMPARATIVE EDUCATION

see also Intercultural Education

Clark, Burton R. The Higher Education System: Academic Organization in Cross-National Perspective. LC 82-13521. 1983. text ed. 24.95x (ISBN 0-520-04841-5). U of Cal Pr.

COMPARATIVE GOVERNMENT

see also subdivision Politics and Government under names of countries, cities, etc.

Bertsch, Gary K., et al. Comparing Political Systems: Power & Policy in Three Worlds. LC 77-27575. 515p. 1978. text ed. 21.95 (ISBN 0-471-02674-3). Wiley.

Calvert, Peter. Politics, Power & Revolution: A Comparative Analysis of Contemporary Gov't. LC 82-16879. 208p. 1982. 22.50x (ISBN 0-312-62954-0). St Martin.

Hague, R. & Harrop, M. Comparative Government. 256p. 1982. text ed. 22.95x (ISBN 0-333-25636-0, 40592, Pub. by Macmillan England); pap. text ed. 9.95x (ISBN 0-333-25637-9, 40707). Humanities.

Hogwood, Brian & Peters, Guy. Policy Dynamics. LC 82-10330. 304p. 1982. 27.50x (ISBN 0-312-62014-4). St Martin.

Hollander, Paul. The Many Faces of Socialism: Essays in Comparative Sociology & Politics. 371p. 1983. 29.95 (ISBN 0-87855-480-7). Transaction Bks.

COMPARATIVE LAW

Here are entered works on the comparison of various systems of law as a method of legal study and research. Comparative studies of individual legal topics or branches of the law are entered under the respective headings applying to these subjects.

see also Law–History and Criticism

Barton, John H., et al. Law in Radically Different Cultures. LC 82-24802. (American Casebook Ser.). 960p. 1983. text ed. write for info. (ISBN 0-314-70396-9). West Pub.

Peteri, Zoltan & Lamm, Vanda, eds. General Reports to the Tenth International Congress of Comparative Law, 8 Vols. 1050p. 1981. 395.00x (ISBN 0-569-08701-5, Pub. by Collets). State Mutual Bk.

Rotondi, M. Aims & Methods of Comparative Law, 2 vols. LC 72-181274. 1973. 18.00 ea. (ISBN 0-379-00026-1). Oceana.

COMPARATIVE LITERATURE

see Literature, Comparative

COMPARATIVE MORPHOLOGY

see Morphology

COMPARATIVE PATHOLOGY

see Pathology, Comparative

COMPARATIVE PHYSIOLOGY

see Physiology, Comparative

COMPARATIVE POLITICS

see Comparative Government

COMPARATIVE PSYCHOLOGY

see Psychology, Comparative

COMPARATIVE RELIGION

see Christianity and Other Religions; Religions

COMPASSION (ETHICS)

see Sympathy

COMPENSATION

see Pensions; Wages

COMPENSATION (PHYSIOLOGY)

see Adaptation (Physiology)

COMPENSATION, DEFERRED

see Deferred Compensation

COMPENSATION FOR VICTIMS OF CRIME

see Reparation

COMPETITION

see also Laissez-Faire; Oligopolies; Supply and Demand

Agar, Herbert & Tate, Allen, eds. Who Owns America? A New Declaration of Independence. LC 82-24752. 352p. 1983. pap. text ed. 12.75 (ISBN 0-8191-2767-1). U Pr of Amer.

Korah, V. Competition Law of Britain & the Common Market. 1982. lib. bdg. 59.00 (ISBN 0-686-37430-4, Pub. by Martinus Nijhoff Netherlands). Kluwer Boston.

Mas-Colell, Andrew, ed. Noncooperative Approaches to the Theory of Perfect Competition. LC 82-13936. 1982. 25.00 (ISBN 0-12-476750-8). Acad Pr.

Porter, Michael E. Cases in Competitive Strategy. (Illus.). 400p. 1982. text ed. 22.50 (ISBN 0-02-925410-8). Free Pr.

COMPETITION, INTERNATIONAL

see also Commercial Treaties; International Cooperation; War–Economic Aspects

Walker, William & Lonnroth, Mans. Nuclear Power Struggles: Industrial Competition & Proliferation Control. (Illus.). 192p. 1983. text ed. 24.00x (ISBN 0-04-338104-9). Allen Unwin.

COMPETITIONS

see Rewards (Prizes, etc.)

COMPETITIVE EXAMINATIONS

see Civil Service Examinations

COMPILING (ELECTRONIC COMPUTERS)

see also Electronic Data Processing; Electronic Digital Computers–Programming

Davie, J. T. & Morrison, R. Recursive Descent Compiling. LC 81-6778. (Computers & Their Applications). 195p. 1982. pap. 29.95x (ISBN 0-470-27361-5). Halsted Pr.

Kastens, U., et al. GAG: A Practical Compiler Generator. (Lecture Notes in Computer Science: Vol. 141). 156p. 1983. pap. 10.00 (ISBN 0-387-11591-9). Springer-Verlag.

Tremblay, J. P. & Sorenson, P. G. The Theory & Practice of Compiler Writing. Date not set. price not set (ISBN 0-07-065161-2); supplementary materials avail. McGraw.

COMPLEXES

Eells, J., ed. Complex Analysis Trieste: Proceedings, 1981. (Lecture Notes in Mathematics Ser.: Vol. 950). 428p. 1983. pap. 20.50 (ISBN 0-387-11596-X). Springer-Verlag.

Miller, Joel S., ed. Extended Linear Chain Compounds. (Vol. 3). 549p. 1982. 55.00x (ISBN 0-306-40941-0, Plenum Pr). Plenum Pub.

COMPLEXION

see Beauty, Personal; Color of Man; Cosmetics

COMPOSERS

Ensor, Wendy-Ann. More Heroes & Heroines in Music. (Illus.). 48p. 1983. pap. 5.00 laminated (ISBN 0-19-321106-8); cassette 18.00 (ISBN 0-19-321107-6). Oxford U Pr.

Green, Mildred D. Black Women Composers: A Genesis. (Music Ser.). 174p. 1983. lib. bdg. 18.95 (ISBN 0-8057-9450-6, Twayne). G K Hall.

McLeish, Kenneth & McLeish, Valerie. Composers & Their Music. (Illus.). 32p. pap. 4.75 laminated (ISBN 0-19-321438-5). Oxford U Pr.

Thomson, John M. A Distant Music: The Life & Times of Alfred Hill 1870-1960. (Illus.). 1982. 39.00 (ISBN 0-19-558051-6). Oxford U Pr.

COMPOSERS–CORRESPONDENCE, REMINISCENCES, ETC.

see Musicians–Correspondence, Reminiscences, etc.

COMPOSERS–DICTIONARIES

see Music–Bio-Bibliography

COMPOSERS, AMERICAN

Butterworth, Neil. A Dictionary of American Composers. LC 81-43331. 600p. 1983. lib. bdg. 75.00 (ISBN 0-8240-9311-9). Garland Pub.

Carmichael, Hoagy. The Stardust Road. LC 82-48583. (Midland Bks.). (Illus.). 160p. 1983. pap. 6.95 (ISBN 0-253-20269-8). Ind U Pr.

Rorem, Ned. The Paris & New York Diaries of Ned Rorem. LC 82-73718. 464p. 1983. pap. 15.00 (ISBN 0-86547-109-6). N Point Pr.

COMPOSERS, BRITISH

Bridge, Frederick. Twelve Good Musicians: From John Bull to Henry Purcell. 152p. 1983. pap. 6.50 (ISBN 0-88072-001-8). Tanager Bks.

COMPOSERS, CANADIAN

Adams, Stephen. R. Murray Schafer. (Canadian Composers Ser.). 248p. 1983. 27.50x (ISBN 0-8020-5571-0). U of Toronto Pr.

Eastman, Sheila & McGee, Timothy J. Barbara Pentland. (Canadian Composers Ser.). 284p. 1983. 30.00x (ISBN 0-8020-5562-1). U of Toronto Pr.

COMPOSERS, GERMAN

Osborne, Charles, ed. Richard Wagner: Stories & Essays. 187p. 16.00x (ISBN 0-912050-43-8, Library Press). Open Court.

COMPOSITE MATERIALS

Grayson, Martin. Encyclopedia of Composite Materials & Components, Vol. 2. 1200p. 1983. 49.50 (ISBN 0-471-87357-8, Pub. by Wiley-Interscience). Wiley.

Piatti, G. Advances in Composite Materials. 1978. 98.50 (ISBN 0-85334-770-0, Pub. by Applied Sci England). Elsevier.

Schwartz, Mel M. Composite Materials Handbook. (Illus.). 704p. 1983. 34.50 (ISBN 0-07-055743-8, P&RB). McGraw.

COMPOSITES, FIBROUS

see Fibrous Composites

COMPOSITION (MUSIC)

see also Instrumentation and Orchestration; Music, Popular (Songs, etc.)–Writing and Publishing

Henning, Fritz. Concept & Composition: The Basis of Successful Art. 208p. 1983. 22.50 (ISBN 0-89134-059-9); pap. 11.95 (ISBN 0-89134-060-2). North Light Pub.

Schoenberg & Strang, eds. Fundamentals of Music Composition. 8.95 (ISBN 0-686-84403-3). Faber & Faber.

Von Gunden, Heidi. The Music of Pauline Oliveros. LC 82-21443. 206p. 1983. 15.00 (ISBN 0-8108-1600-8). Scarecrow.

COMPOSITION (PHOTOGRAPHY)

Grill, Tom & Scanlon, Mark. Photographic Composition: Guidelines for Total Image Control Through Effective Design. 144p. 1983. 22.50 (ISBN 0-8174-5419-5, Amphoto). Watson-Guptill.

COMPOSITION (PRINTING)

see Type-Setting

COMPOSITION (RHETORIC)

see Letter-Writing; Rhetoric;

also subdivision Composition and Exercises under names of languages

COMPREHENSIVE HEALTH CARE DELIVERY ORGANIZATIONS

see Health Maintenance Organizations

COMPRESSORS

see also Refrigeration and Refrigerating Machinery

Narayanan, R., ed. Axially Compressed Structures. 300p. 1982. 61.50 (ISBN 0-85334-139-7, Pub. by Applied Sci England). Elsevier.

Pumps & Compressors. 1982. 445.00 (ISBN 0-686-38424-5, A210). Busn Trend.

COMPROMISE (LAW)

see also Arbitration and Award

Edwards, Mary F., ed. Settlement & Plea Bargaining. 388p. 1981. pap. 35.00 (ISBN 0-941916-02-2). Assn Trial Ed.

How to Win, Delay, Reduce or Eliminate Lawsuits for Money Without a Lawyer. 19.95 (ISBN 0-686-38781-3). FMA Bus.

Williams, Gerald R. Legal Negotiation & Settlement. LC 82-19975. 207p. 1983. pap. text ed. write for info. (ISBN 0-314-68093-4); tchrs.' manual avail. (ISBN 0-314-73521-6). West Pub.

COMPTROLLERSHIP

see Controllership

COMPULSION (PSYCHOLOGY)

see Obsessive-Compulsive Neuroses

COMPULSORY MILITARY SERVICE

see Military Service, Compulsory

COMPULSORY SCHOOL ATTENDANCE

see Educational Law and Legislation

COMPUTATION LABORATORIES

Hoie, T. A. Performance Control: Service & Resource Control in Complex IBM Computing Centres. (Illus.). 252p. 1983. 42.75 (ISBN 0-444-86517-9, North Holland). Elsevier.

COMPUTATIONAL LINGUISTICS

see Programming Languages (Electronic Computers)

COMPUTER ARCHITECTURE

see also Computer Engineering

Peeters, Paul & Meijer, Anton. Computer Network Architectures. 1983. text ed. 27.95 (ISBN 0-914894-41-2). Computer Sci.

Thurber, Kenneth J. & Patton, Peter C. Computer-System Requirements: Techniques & Examples. LC 79-7184. 128p. 1982. 15.95x (ISBN 0-669-02958-0). Lexington Bks.

COMPUTER-ASSISTED INSTRUCTION

Baker, Justine. Microcomputers in the Classroom. LC 82-60799. (Fastback Ser.: No. 179). 50p. 1982. pap. 0.75 (ISBN 0-87367-179-1). Phi Delta Kappa.

Goldberg, Kenneth P. & Sherwood, Robert D. Microcomputers & Parents. (Education Ser.). 224p. 1983. pap. text ed. 8.50 (ISBN 0-471-87278-4). Wiley.

Wilkinson, Alex C., ed. Classroom Computers & Cognitive Science. (Educational Technology Ser.). Date not set. write for info. (ISBN 0-12-752070-8). Acad Pr.

COMPUTER CENTERS

see Computation Laboratories

COMPUTER CIRCUITS

see Computers–Circuits

COMPUTER CONTROL

see Automation

COMPUTER DEBUGGING

see Debugging (Electronic Computers)

COMPUTER DEPARTMENT SECURITY MEASURES

see Electronic Data Processing Departments–Security Measures

COMPUTER ENGINEERING

see also Computer Architecture

Badre, Albert & Shneiderman, Ben, eds. Directions in Human-Computer Interaction. 240p. 1982. text ed. 27.50 (ISBN 0-89391-144-5). Ablex Pub.

Engineering Staff of Archive. Streaming. (Illus.). 196p. (Orig.). pap. 14.95 (ISBN 0-9608810-0-X). Archive Corp.

Kudlick, Michael D. Assembly Language Programming for the IBM Systems 360 & 370 for OS-DOS. 2nd ed. 560p. 1983. pap. text ed. write for info. (ISBN 0-697-08166-4); solutions manual avail. (ISBN 0-697-08184-2). Wm C Brown.

Levin, Paul. Construction Computer Applications Directory. 3rd ed. Layman, Donald & Young, Nancy A., eds. 600p. 135.00 (ISBN 0-686-42716-5). Constr Ind Pr.

Lewart, Cass. Science & Engineering for the IBM-PC. (Illus.). 150p. 1983. 18.95 (ISBN 0-13-794925-1); pap. 12.95 (ISBN 0-13-794917-0). P-H.

Sumner, F., ed. Supercomputer Systems Technology: Design & Application. (Computer State of the Art Report: Ser.10 No.6). (Illus.). 400p. 1982. 445.00 (ISBN 0-08-028569-4). Pergamon.

Townsent. Digital Computer & Design. 2nd ed. 1982. text ed. 39.95 (ISBN 0-408-01158-0); pap. text ed. 24.95 (ISBN 0-408-01155-6). Butterworth.

U. S. Third-Party Maintnance Market for Computer Datacom Equipment. (Reports Ser.: No. 512). 145p. 1982. 985.00 (ISBN 0-686-38953-0). Intl Res Dev.

COMPUTER GRAPHICS

Bedworth. Computer Animation. 1983. write for info. (ISBN 0-07-004269-1). McGraw.

Cassidy, Pat & Close, Jim. Computer Graphics & Games for Kids: Apple II. (Illus.). 200p. 1983. 17.95 (ISBN 0-13-164533-1); pap. 11.95 (ISBN 0-13-164517-X). P-H.

Color Computer Graphics. (Illus.). 128p. Date not set. 9.95 (ISBN 0-86668-012-8). ARCsoft.

Consentino, John. Computer Graphics Marketplace. 2nd ed. 64p. 1983. pap. 25.00 (ISBN 0-89774-086-6). Oryx Pr.

Foundyller, Charles M. U. S. Directory of Systems & Vendors, 1982: CAD-CAM Computer Graphics: Survey & Buyers Guide. rev. ed. Murphy, Jane A., ed. (Illus.). 374p. 1982. spiral 185.00 (ISBN 0-938484-08-7). Daratech.

Fu, K. S. & Kunii, T. L., eds. Picture Engineering. (Springer Series in Information Sciences: Vol. 6). (Illus.). 320p. 1982. 29.50 (ISBN 0-387-11822-5). Springer-Verlag.

Goetsch, David L. Introduction to Computer Aided Drafting. (Illus.). 272p. 1983. text ed. 20.95 (ISBN 0-13-479287-4). P-H.

Goldstein, Larry J. The Graphics Generator: Business & Technical Graphics for the IBM Personal Computer. (Illus.). 155p. 1982. 60.00 (ISBN 0-89303-266-2). R J Brady.

Grillo, John P. & Robertson, J. D. Introduction to Graphics for the IBM Personal Computer. (Microcomputer Power Ser.). 165p. 1983. pap. write for info. (ISBN 0-697-09989-X); diskette avail. (ISBN 0-697-09990-3). Wm C Brown.

Hearn, D. Donald & Baker, M. Pauline. Microcomputer Graphics: Techniques & Applications. (Illus.). 272p. 1983. text ed. 24.95 (ISBN 0-13-580670-4); pap. text ed. 18.95 (ISBN 0-13-580662-3). P-H.

Hubbard, Stuart W. The Computer Graphics Glossary. 1983. price not set (ISBN 0-89774-072-6). Oryx Pr.

Infotech Ltd., ed. Computer Graphics, 2 vols. Incl. Vol. 1-Analysis. 247p; Vol. 2-Invited Papers. 301p. (Illus.). 1980. Set. 355.00x (ISBN 0-8002-3034-5). Intl Pubns Serv.

Inman, Don & Inman, Kurt. Assembly Language Graphics for the TRS-80 Color Computer. 1982. text ed. 19.95 (ISBN 0-8359-0318-4); pap. text ed. 14.95 (ISBN 0-8359-0317-6). Reston.

Jarett, Irwin M. Computer Graphics & Reporting Financial Data. 250p. 1983. price not set (ISBN 0-471-86761-6). Ronald Pr.

Luehrmann, A. & Peckham, H. Hands On BASIC: For the Atari 400 & 800 Computer. 448p. 1983. 22.95 (ISBN 0-07-049177-1). McGraw.

Neundorf, Norman. Computer-Aided Drawing Using the Tektronix Graphic System. (Illus.). 320p. 1983. 16.95 (ISBN 0-13-164723-7). P-H.

COMPUTER INDUSTRY

see also Computers

Duncan, Doris G. & Aviel, S. David. Computers & Remote Computing Services. LC 82-20094. (Illus.). 258p. (Orig.). 1983. lib. bdg. 22.50 (ISBN 0-8191-2881-3); pap. text ed. 11.50 (ISBN 0-8191-2882-1). U Pr of Amer.

Japanese Computers, Nineteen Eighty-Two. 400p. 1983. 250.00x (ISBN 0-686-38411-3). Sci & Tech Pr.

Wild, Victor. Your Fortune in the Microcomputer Business: Getting Started, Vol. I. (Illus.). 304p. 1982. pap. 15.95 (ISBN 0-938444-04-2). Wildfire Pub.

--Your Fortune in the Microcomputer Business: Growth, Survival, Success, Vol. II. (Illus.). 256p. 1982. pap. 15.95 (ISBN 0-938444-05-0). Wildfire Pub.

COMPUTER INDUSTRY–DIRECTORIES

Computing Marketplace. 1982. pap. text ed. 63.00x (ISBN 0-566-03401-8). Gower Pub Ltd.

Gilman, Kenneth & Public Management Institute Staff. Computer Resource Guide for Nonprofits. 175.00 (ISBN 0-686-82256-0, 68A). Public Management.

Stern, Michael, compiled by. National Computer Services Register Winter 1983. 300p. 1982. pap. 15.95 (ISBN 0-943816-03-3). Spex Intl.

COMPUTER INPUT-OUTPUT EQUIPMENT

see also Automatic Speech Recognition; Computer Storage Devices; Computers–Optical Equipment; Information Display Systems

Ingraham, Curtis. CP-M DiskGuide. (DiskGuides Ser.). 32p. (Orig.). 1983. pap. 8.95 (ISBN 0-931988-97-7). Osborne-McGraw.

Mazur, Ken, ed. The Creative TRS-Eighty. (Illus.). 250p. 1983. pap. 15.95 (ISBN 0-916688-36-4). Creative Comp.

COMPUTER LANGUAGES

see Programming Languages (Electronic Computers)

COMPUTER MATHEMATICS

see Numerical Analysis

COMPUTER MEMORY SYSTEMS

see Computer Storage Devices

COMPUTER PROGRAM LANGUAGES

see Programming Languages (Electronic Computers)

COMPUTER PROGRAMMING

see Programming (Electronic Computers)

COMPUTER PROGRAMMING MANAGEMENT

Claybrook, Billy G. File Management Techniques. 300p. 1983. text ed. 15.95 (ISBN 0-471-04596-9); solutions bk. avail. (ISBN 0-471-87575-9). Wiley.

Ejiogu, Lem O. Effective Structured Programming. (Illus.). 292p. 1983. 24.95 (ISBN 0-89433-205-8). Petrocelli.

Kelly, Derek A. Documenting Computer Application Systems. (Illus.). 192p. 1983. 19.95 (ISBN 0-89433-206-6). Petrocelli.

Stair, Ralph M., Jr. Learning to Live with Computers: Advice for Managers. LC 82-73408. 190p. 1983. 19.95 (ISBN 0-87094-383-9). Dow Jones-Irwin.

Wallis, J. Software Portability. 1982. 100.00x (ISBN 0-333-31035-7, Pub. by Macmillan England). State Mutual Bk.

COMPUTER PROGRAMS

Abelson, H. Logo for the Apple II. 1982. 14.95 (ISBN 0-07-000426-9). McGraw.

Ashley, Ruth & Fernandez, Judi. PC Dos: Using the IBM PC Operating System A Self Teaching Guide. 188p. 1983. pap. text ed. 14.95 (ISBN 0-471-89718-3). Wiley.

Berner, Jeff. The Foolproof Guide to SCRIPSIT. 225p. 1983. pap. text ed. 11.95 (ISBN 0-89588-098-9). Sybex.

Bundy, Alan. The Computer Modelling of Mathematical Reasoning. Date not set. price not set (ISBN 0-12-141252-0). Acad Pr.

Castlewitz, David M. VisiCalc Made Easy. 160p. (Orig.). 1983. pap. 12.95 (ISBN 0-931988-89-6). Osborne-McGraw.

The Color Computer Songbook. (Illus.). 96p. Date not set. 7.95 (ISBN 0-86668-011-X). ARCsoft.

David, H. The Statistical Package STATCAT: Source Programs & User Manual. 800p. 1982. 102.25 (ISBN 0-444-86453-9, North Holland). Elsevier.

Davis, Steve. Programs for the T.I. Home Computer. LC 82-90783. 150p. (Orig.). (gr. 5 up). 1983. pap. 14.95 (ISBN 0-911061-00-2). S Davis Pub.

Davis, William S. Operating Systems. 2nd ed. LC 82-3926. (Illus.). 448p. 1983. text ed. 19.95 (ISBN 0-201-11116-0). A-W.

Dennon. CP-M Revealed. Date not set. 12.95 (ISBN 0-686-81999-3, 5204). Hayden.

Ejiogu, Lem O. Effective Structured Programming. (Illus.). 292p. 1983. 24.95 (ISBN 0-89433-205-8). Petrocelli.

Gehani, Narain. ADA: An Advanced Introduction. (Software Ser.). (Illus.). 336p. 1983. pap. text ed. 21.95 (ISBN 0-13-003962-4). P-H.

Gourlay, Alastair & Walsh, James. Fifty 1K-2K Games for the Timex-Sinclair 1000 & ZX81. 1983. text ed. 16.95 (ISBN 0-8359-1979-X); pap. text ed. 10.95 (ISBN 0-8359-1978-1). Reston.

Hartnell, Tim & Ramshaw, Mark. Zap! Pow! Boom! Arcade Games for the VIC-20. 1983. text ed. 17.95 (ISBN 0-8359-9539-9); pap. text ed. 12.95 (ISBN 0-8359-9538-0). Reston.

Hergert, Douglas. Mastering VisiCalc. 224p. 1982. pap. text ed. 11.95 (ISBN 0-89588-090-3). Sybex.

Hewlett-Packard Co. Series Eighty Software Catalog. 2nd ed. 1982. pap. 12.95 (ISBN 0-8359-6983-5). Reston.

Higgins, David. Designing Structured Programs. (Illus.). 240p. 1983. pap. text ed. 14.95 (ISBN 0-13-201418-1). P-H.

Hughes. Systems Programming Under CP-M80. 1982. text ed. 21.95 (ISBN 0-8359-7457-X); pap. text ed. 15.95 (ISBN 0-8359-7456-1). Reston.

IFAC. Control of Distributed Parameter Systems: Proceedings of the 3rd IFAC Symposium, 29 June-2 July 1982. Babary, J. P. & Letty, L. le, eds. 550p. 1983. 145.00 (ISBN 0-08-029361-1). Pergamon.

International Computer Programs, Inc. ICP Software Directory - United Kingdom: Software Products, Services & Suppliers. Spangler, Richard J., ed. 1982. pap. 125.00 (ISBN 0-88094-012-3). Intl Computer.

--ICP Software Directory: Cross Industry Applications. rev. ed. Spangler, Richard J., ed. 1983. pap. 150.00 (ISBN 0-686-82214-5). Intl Computer.

--ICP Software Directory: Directory of Business Applications for Microcomputers. (Illus.). 320p. 1983. 26.95 (ISBN 0-89303-533-5); pap. 19.95 (ISBN 0-89303-532-7). R J Brady.

--ICP Software Directory: Industry Specific Applications. rev. ed. Spangler, Richard J., ed. 1983. pap. 150.00 (ISBN 0-88094-015-8). Intl Computer.

--ICP Software Directory: Software Product & Service Suppliers. rev. ed. Spangler, Richard J., ed. 1983. pap. 150.00 (ISBN 0-88094-016-6). Intl Computer.

--ICP Software Directory: Systems Software. rev. ed. Spangler, Richard J., ed. 1983. pap. 150.00 (ISBN 0-88094-013-1). Intl Computer.

Kelly, Derek A. Documenting Computer Application Systems. (Illus.). 192p. 1983. 19.95 (ISBN 0-89433-206-6). Petrocelli.

Kerr, Elaine B. & Hiltz, Starr R. Computer-Mediated Communication Systems: Status & Evaluation. (Human Communication Research Ser.). 1982. 26.50 (ISBN 0-12-404980-X). Acad Pr.

Leventhal, Lance A. & Sayville, Winthrop. Z Eighty Assembly Language Subroutines. 550p. (Orig.). 1983. pap. 15.95 (ISBN 0-931988-91-8). Osborne-McGraw.

Loftin, Richard, ed. Sell Your Software! 400p. (Orig.). 1983. pap. 24.95 (ISBN 0-940758-25-3). Finan Data Corp.

Melbourne House Publishers. Thirty Programs for the Timex PC 1000. 192p. 1983. 15.95 (ISBN 0-13-919019-8); pap. 9.95 (ISBN 0-13-919001-5). P-H.

Miller, Alan R. The Best of CP-M Software. 250p. 1983. pap. 11.95 (ISBN 0-89588-100-4). Sybex.

Muller, Robert, ed. Computer Software Protection. 113p. 1981. text ed. 48.00x (ISBN 0-566-03418-2). Gower Pub Ltd.

My Buttons Are Blue & Other Love Poems from the Digital Heart of an Electronic Computer. (Illus.). 96p. Date not set. 4.95 (ISBN 0-86668-013-6). ARCsoft.

North, Alan. Thirty-One New Atari Computer Programs for Home, School & Office. new ed. (Illus.). 96p. (Orig.). 1982. pap. 8.95 (ISBN 0-86668-018-7). ARCsoft.

Page, Edward. Thirty Seven Timex 1000-Sinclair ZX-81 Computer Programs for Home, School & Office. (Illus.). 96p. (Orig.). 1982. pap. 8.95 (ISBN 0-86668-021-7). ARCsoft.

Sachs, Jonathan & Meyer, Rick. The HHC User Guide. 200p. (Orig.). 1983. pap. 14.95 (ISBN 0-931988-87-X). Osborne-McGraw.

Schmucker, Kurt J. Fuzzy Sets, Natural Language Computation & Risk Analysis. 1983. text ed. price not set (ISBN 0-914894-83-8). Computer Sci.

Shooman, M. L. Software Engineering: Reliability, Development & Management. 1982. text ed. 34.95 (ISBN 0-07-057021-3); instr's manual avail. McGraw.

Stanton, Jeffrey & Dickey, John, eds. The Addison-Wesley Book of Apple Computer Software 1983. (Microbooks Ser. Popular). 402p. 1982. pap. text ed. 19.95 (ISBN 0-201-10285-4). A-W.

Summe, Richard, intro. by. Expansion & Software Guide for the IBM PC. 264p. 1982. pap. 19.95 (ISBN 0-88022-019-8). Que Corp.

SuperCalc: Super Models for Business. LC 82-42765. Date not set. pap. 14.95 (ISBN 0-88022-007-4). Que Corp.

Texas Instruments Learning Center Staff. Texas Instruments Awareness Program for Children: Activity Book. Rev. ed. (Illus.). 40p. (gr. 3-10). 1982. pap. text ed. 5.95 (ISBN 0-89512-068-2). Tex Instr Inc.

Thirty-Five Practical Programs for the CASIO Pocket Computer. (Illus.). 96p. Date not set. 8.95 (ISBN 0-86668-014-4). ARCsoft.

Trost, Stanley R. Doing Business with SuperCalc. 300p. 1983. pap. text ed. 12.95 (ISBN 0-89588-095-4). Sybex.

Trost, Stanley R. & Pomernacki, Charles. VisiCalc for Science & Engineering. 225p. 1983. pap. text ed. 13.95 (ISBN 0-89588-096-2). Sybex.

Wallis, J. Software Portability. 1982. 100.00x (ISBN 0-333-31035-7, Pub. by Macmillan England). State Mutual Bk.

White, Fred. Thirty-Three New Apple Computer Programs for Home, School & Office. new ed. (Illus.). 96p. (Orig.). 1982. pap. 8.95 (ISBN 0-86668-016-0). ARCsoft.

Whitehouse, Gary, et al. IIE Microsoftware: Economic Analysis. 1981. 140.00, 175.00 non-members (ISBN 0-89806-013-3). Inst Indus Eng.

--IIE Microsoftware: Production Control. 1981. 140.00, 175.00 non-members (ISBN 0-89806-012-5). Inst Indus Eng.

--IIE Microsoftware: Project Management. 1981. 140.00, 175.00 non-members (ISBN 0-89806-030-3). Inst Indus Eng.

--IIE Microsoftware: Work Measurement. 1982. 140.00, 175.00 non-members (ISBN 0-89806-035-4). Inst Indus Eng.

Wilson, David A. IBM PC DiskGuide. (DiskGuides Ser.). 32p. (Orig.). 1983. pap. text ed. 8.95 (ISBN 0-931988-94-2). Osborne-McGraw.

--VisiCalc DiskGuide. (DiskGuides Ser.). 32p. (Orig.). 1983. pap. 6.95 (ISBN 0-931988-98-5). Osborne-McGraw.

Zimmerman, Steven & Conrad, Leo. Practical Programs for Your Pocket Computer: For the TRS-80TM, Pc-1, and Sharp 1211. (Microcomputer Power Ser.). 224p. 1983. pap. write for info. (ISBN 0-697-09975-X). Wm C Brown.

COMPUTER SECURITY MEASURES

see Electronic Data Processing Departments–Security Measures

COMPUTER SIMULATION, DIGITAL

see Digital Computer Simulation

COMPUTER SOFTWARE

see Computer Programs; Programming (Electronic Computers); Programming Languages (Electronic Computers);

also similar headings

COMPUTER STORAGE DEVICES

Electronics Magazine. Memory Design: Microcomputers to Mainframes. 1978. 29.00 (ISBN 0-07-019154-9). McGraw.

Ferrari, Domenico & Serazzi, Guiseppe. Measurement & Tuning of Computer Systems. (Illus.). 624p. 1983. text ed. 35.00 (ISBN 0-13-568519-2). P-H.

U. S. Magnetic Storage Devices. 1982. 995.00 (ISBN 0-686-37718-4, E76). Predicasts.

COMPUTERS

Here are entered works on modern electronic computers first developed after 1945. Works on calculators, as well as all mechanical computers of pre-1945 vintage, are entered under Calculating-Machines.

see also Computation Laboratories; Electronic Data Processing; Electronic Digital Computers; Information Storage and Retrieval Systems; Minicomputers

also headings beginning with the word Computer

Alder, Alfred A. My Computer & I Make Money. 250p. 1983. pap. 13.95 (ISBN 0-88056-105-X). Dilithium Pr.

American Machinist Magazine. Computers in Manufacturing. 300p. 1983. 33.95 (ISBN 0-07-001548-1, P&RB). McGraw.

Anderson, Ron & Atkins, Walter J., Jr. The Rest of Eighty. (Illus.). 1983. write for info. Green.

Arnold, Robert R., et al. Modern Data Processing. 3rd ed. LC 77-14941. 435p. 1978. 25.95x (ISBN 0-471-03361-8); wkbk. 11.95 (ISBN 0-471-03362-6); avail. tchrs. manual (ISBN 0-471-03405-3). Wiley.

Atkin, J. K. Computer Science. 272p. 1981. 19.00 (ISBN 0-7121-0396-1, Pub. by Macdonald & Evans). State Mutual Bk.

Auerbach, ed. Best Computer Papers, 1979. (Annual Computer Papers Ser.). 1980. 49.00 (ISBN 0-444-00350-9). Elsevier.

--Best Computer Papers, 1980. (Annual Computer Papers Ser.). 1980. 58.00 (ISBN 0-444-00447-5). Elsevier.

Baczynsky, Mark. How to Make a Comfortable Living with Your Computer. 1983. pap. 4.95 (ISBN 0-89816-010-3). Embee Pr.

Bentley, Colin. Computer Project Management. 112p. 1983. 29.95 (ISBN 0-471-26208-0, Pub. by Wiley-Interscience). Wiley.

Bic, Lubomir. Micos Handbook. 1983. text ed. price not set (ISBN 0-914894-76-5). Computer Sci.

Bishop, Peter. Comprehensive Computer Studies. 200p. 1981. pap. text ed. 12.95 (ISBN 0-7131-0371-X). E Arnold.

Blumenthal, Howard J. Everyone's Guide to Personal Computers. (Orig.). 1983. pap. 5.95 (ISBN 0-345-30218-4). Ballantine.

Booth, Taylor L. Digital Network & Computer Systems. 2nd ed. LC 77-10832. 592p. 1978. text ed. 30.95 (ISBN 0-471-08842-0); tchrs. manual avail. (ISBN 0-471-03049-X). Wiley.

Bosworth. Codes, Ciphers, & Computers: An Introduction to Information Security. Date not set. 13.95 (ISBN 0-686-82006-1, 5149). Hayden.

Bove, Tony & Finkel, LeRoy. The TRS-80 TM Model III User's Guide. 252p. 1983. pap. 12.95 (ISBN 0-471-86242-8). Wiley.

Boyer, Dean. Computer Word Processing: Do You Want It? 148p. 1981. pap. 14.95 (ISBN 0-88022-000-7, 81-52571). Que Corp.

Bradbeer, Robin. The Personal Computer Book. 2nd ed. 240p. 1982. text ed. 23.50x (ISBN 0-566-03445-X). Gower Pub Ltd.

Bradbeer, Robin & DeBono, Peter. The Beginners Guide to Computers: Everything you Need to Know About the New Technology. (Illus.). 208p. 1982. 19.95 (ISBN 0-201-11208-6); pap. 9.95 (ISBN 0-201-11209-4). A-W.

Brechner, Irv. Getting into Computers: A Career Guide to Today's Hottest New Field. 224p. (Orig.). 1983. pap. 4.95 (ISBN 0-345-30172-2). Ballantine.

Brickman. Solving the Computer Contract Dilemma: A How-To Book for Decision Makers. Date not set. 20.00 (ISBN 0-686-82000-2, 6259). Hayden.

Busald, Gerald. An Introduction to Computer Terminals. 64p. 1982. pap. text ed. 4.50 (ISBN 0-8403-2788-9). Kendall-Hunt.

Ceruzzi, Paul E. Reckoners: The Prehistory of the Digital Computer, From Relays to the Stored Program Concept, 1935-1945. LC 82-20980. (Contributions to the Study of Computer Science Ser.: No. 1). (Illus.). 240p. 1983. lib. bdg. 29.95 (ISBN 0-313-23382-9, CED/). Greenwood.

Computer Control of Transport. 61p. (Orig.). 1981. pap. text ed. 24.00x (ISBN 0-85825-149-3, Pub. by Inst Engineering Australia). Renouf.

Computers & Related Equipment: Thailand. 75.00 (ISBN 0-686-38463-6). Info Gatekeepers.

Connor, Ursula. How to select & Buy a Personal computer: For Small Business, for Department Heads, for the Home, for Self-Employed Professionals. 1983. pap. 9.95 (ISBN 0-686-81787-7). Devin.

Consumer Guides Editors. An Easy-to-Understand Guide to Home Computers. 1982. pap. 3.95 (ISBN 0-686-84861-6, AE2031, Sig). NAL.

Cooke, D. & Craven, A. H. Basic Statistical Computing. 176p. 1982. pap. text ed. 13.95 (ISBN 0-7131-3441-0). E Arnold.

Cremers, A. B. & Kriegel, H. P., eds. Theoretical Computer Science: Proceedings, Dortmund, FRG, 1983. (Lecture Notes in Computer Science Ser.: Vol. 145). 367p. 1983. pap. 16.50 (ISBN 0-387-11973-6). Springer-Verlag.

Discovering Computers. LC 81-51991. (Discovering Science Ser.). lib. bdg. 15.96 (Pub. by Stonehenge). Silver.

Dwyer, Thomas A. & Critchfield, Margot. CP-M & the Personal Computer: Popular. LC 82-20703. (Microcomputer Bks.). 280p. 1982. pap. 16.95 (ISBN 0-201-10355-9). A-W.

Electronics Magazine. Personal Computing: Hardware & Software Basics. 1979. 26.95 (ISBN 0-07-019151-4). McGraw.

Evans, David J., ed. Preconditioning Methods: Analysis & Application. (Topics in Computer Mathematics Ser.: Vol. 1). 1982. write for info. (ISBN 0-677-16320-7). Gordon.

Freedman, Alan & Morrison, Irma Lee. The Computer Coloring Book: It's Not Just a Coloring Book. 80p. 1983. pap. 6.95 (ISBN 0-13-164632-X). P-H.

Gabriel, Peter & Gabriel, Rosemarie. Game Techniques in Applesoft B A S I C. 1983. pap. 12.95 (ISBN 0-8159-5617-7). Devin.

Garetz, Mark. Bits, Bytes & Buzzwords. 110p. (Orig.). 1983. pap. 7.95 (ISBN 0-88056-111-4). Dilithium Pr.

Gecsei, Jan. Architecture of Videotex Systems. (Illus.). 320p. 1983. 29.95 (ISBN 0-13-044776-5). P H.

Giarratano, Joseph. Foundations of Computer Technology. Date not set. pap. 22.95 (ISBN 0-672-21814-3). Sams.

--Modern Computer Concepts. Date not set. pap. 22.95 (ISBN 0-672-21815-1). Sams.

Gilman, Kenneth & Public Management Institute Staff. Computers for Nonprofits. 47.50 (ISBN 0-686-82255-2, 58A). Public Management.

Graham, Neill. The Mind Tool: Computers & Their Impact on Society. 3rd ed. (Illus.). 410p. 1983. pap. text ed. 13.95 (ISBN 0-314-69650-4); study manual avail. (ISBN 0-314-71093-0); instrs.' manual avail. (ISBN 0-314-71094-9). West Pub.

Guidelines for General Systems Specifications for a Computer System. 6.00 (ISBN 0-686-42707-6). Am Inst CPA.

Harris, Sidney. What's So Funny about Computers? LC 82-21227. (Illus.). 128p. 1983. pap. 6.95 (ISBN 0-86576-049-7). W Kaufmann.

Harvard Business Review. Catching Up with the Computer Revolution. (Harvard Business Review Executive Bk. Ser.). 500p. 1983. 22.95 (ISBN 0-471-87594-5, Pub. by Wiley Interscience). Wiley.

Hayward. Computers for Film Makers. (Illus.). 1983. 31.95 (ISBN 0-240-51049-6). Focal Pr.

Heller, Rachelle & Martin, Dianne. Bits 'n Bytes About Computing for Everyone. write for info. (ISBN 0-914894-92-7). Computer Sci.

--Bits 'n Bytes Gazette. write for info. (ISBN 0-914894-88-9). Computer Sci.

Helms, H. L. The McGraw-Hill Computer Handbook. 1200p. 1983. 79.50 (ISBN 0-07-027972-1, P&RB). McGraw.

Henderson, Richard. A Practical Guide to Performance Appraisal. 2nd ed. 1983. text ed. 15.00 (ISBN 0-8359-5576-1). Reston.
Hickman. Get More from your Personal Computer. 1983. text ed. 13.50 (ISBN 0-408-01131-9). Butterworth.
Japanese Computers, Nineteen Eighty-Two. 400p. 1983. 250.00x (ISBN 0-686-38411-3). Sci & Tech Pr.
Johnson, T. B. & Barnes, R. J., eds. Application of Computers & Operations in the Mineral Industry: 17th International Symposium. LC 82-70016. (Illus.). 806p. 1982. text ed. 35.00x (ISBN 0-89520-293-X). Soc Mining Eng.
Khalil, H. M. & Carberry, M. S. Introductory Computer Science Textbook. 1983. text ed. p.n.s. Computer Sci.
Kleinman, A. Handbook of Personal Computer Terms. 1982. pap. 9.95 (ISBN 0-686-81783-4). Devin.
Kolve, Carolee K. How to Buy (& Survive!) Your First Computer. (Illus.). 224p. 1983. 14.95 (ISBN 0-07-035130-9). McGraw.
Lee, G. From Hardware to Software: An Introduction to Computers. 1982. 40.00x (ISBN 0-333-24363-3, Pub. by Macmillan England). State Mutual Bk.
Levy, Henry M. Capability-Based Computer Systems. 200p. 1983. 25.00 (ISBN 0-932376-22-3). Digital Pr.
Lewis, Ted. Thirty Two Visicalc Worksheets. Rev. ed. 150p. 1982. pap. 19.95 (ISBN 0-88056-085-1). Dilithium Pr.
Lias, Ed. Income from Your Home Computer: Thirty Ways to Make Extra Money. 1982. text ed. 17.95 (ISBN 0-8359-3047-5); pap. text ed. 12.95 (ISBN 0-8359-3046-7). Reston.
Lindelof, E. T. Cobra: The Computer-Designed Bidding System. (Master Bridge Ser.). 320p. 1983. 34.00 (ISBN 0-575-02987-0, Pub. by Gollancz England). David & Charles.
Logsdon. How to Cope with Computers. 1983. pap. 10.95 (ISBN 0-686-82003-7, 5193). Hayden.
Lord, Norman W. & Giragosian, Paul A. Advanced Computers: Parallel & Biochip Processors. (Illus.). 170p. 29.50 (ISBN 0-686-84668-0). Ann Arbor Science.
Luebbert, William F. The Guide to What's Where in the Apple. 1982. 9.95 (ISBN 0-938222-10-4). Micro Ink.
--What's Where in the Apple...Plus...the All New Guide to What's Where. 1982. 24.95 (ISBN 0-938222-09-0). Micro Ink.
Luedtke, Peter & Luedtke, Rainer. Your First Business Computer. 250p. 1983. 22.00 (ISBN 0-932376-26-6); pap. 15.00 (ISBN 0-932376-27-4). Digital Pr.
McGilton, Henry & McGilton, Rachel. Introducing the UNIX System. Guty, Stephen G., ed. (Illus.). 352p. 1983. 18.95 (ISBN 0-07-045001-3, P&RB). McGraw.
Mandell, Steven L. Computers & Data Processing Today. (Illus.). 350p. 1983. pap. text ed. 15.95 (ISBN 0-314-69663-6); instrs.' manual avail. (ISBN 0-314-71105-8); study guide avail. (ISBN 0-314-71106-6). West Pub.
--Computers & Data Processing Today with PASCAL. (Illus.). 450p. 1983. pap. text ed. 8.95 (ISBN 0-314-70647-X). West Pub.
Mau, Ernest E. Create Word Games With Your Microcomputer. (Illus.). 304p. 1982. pap. 14.95 (ISBN 0-8104-6251-6). Hayden.
Mazlack, L. J. PL-C Essentials. text ed. 18.95 (ISBN 0-07-041170-0). McGraw.
Merkle, Ralph C. Secrecy, Authentication & Public Key Systems. Stone, Harold, ed. LC 82-17611. (Computer Science Systems Programming Ser.: No. 18). 112p. 1982. 34.95 (ISBN 0-8357-1384-9). Univ Microfilms.
Micro Staff, ed. MICRO on the Apple, Vol. 3. 1982. softcover 24.95 (ISBN 0-938222-08-2). Micro Ink.
Network Interfaces for Personal Computers & Office Workstations. (Reports Ser.: No. 509). 357p. 1982. 1850.00 (ISBN 0-686-38951-4). Intl Res Dev.
Norusis, M. J. SPSS-X Introducing Statistics Guide. 1983. write for info. (ISBN 0-07-046549-5). McGraw.
Palmer, D. C. & Morris, B. D. Computing Science. 400p. 1980. pap. text ed. 19.95 (ISBN 0-7131-2538-1). E Arnold.
Proceedings of the Third Caltech Conference on VLSI. write for info. (ISBN 0-914894-86-2). Computer Sci.
Rembold & Armbruster. Inter, Technology for Computer: Controlled Manufacturing Processes. (Manufacturing Engineering & Materials Processing Ser.). 360p. 1983. not set 48.50 (ISBN 0-8247-1836-4). Dekker.
Rudman, Jack. Computer Operator Trainee. (Career Examination Ser.: C-878). (Cloth bdg. avail. on request). pap. 10.00 (ISBN 0-8373-0878-X). Natl Learning.
--Computer Science. (Graduate Record Examination Ser.). 21.95 (ISBN 0-8373-5271-1); pap. 13.95 (ISBN 0-8373-5221-5). Natl Learning.
--Computer Specialist (Applications Programming) (Career Examination Ser.: C-2871). (Cloth bdg. avail. on request). pap. 12.00 (ISBN 0-8373-2874-8). Natl Learning.
--Computer Specialist (Data Base Administration) (Career Examination Ser.: C-2876). (Cloth bdg. avail. on request). pap. 12.00 (ISBN 0-8373-2876-4). Natl Learning.
--Computer Specialist (Systems Programming) (Career Examination Ser.: C-2875). (Cloth bdg. avail. on request). pap. write for info. (ISBN 0-8373-2875-6). Natl Learning.
Ryan, Michael A. The PET Index. 194p. 1982. text ed. 32.00x (ISBN 0-686-42829-3). Gower Pub Ltd.
Segal, Hillel & Berst, Jesse. How to Manage Your Small Computer: Without Frustration. (Illus.). 1983. text ed. 22.95 (ISBN 0-13-423665-3); pap. text ed. 14.95 (ISBN 0-13-423681-5). P-H.
Seidel, Robert J., ed. Computer Literacy: Issues & Directions for 1985. LC 82-1677. 308p. 1982. 23.00 (ISBN 0-12-634960-6). Acad Pr.
Sikonowiz, Walter. Guide to the IBM Personal Computer. (Illus.). 352p. 1983. pap. text ed. 19.95 (ISBN 0-07-057484-7, P&RB). McGraw.
Sime, Max S. & Coombs, Michael J., eds. Designing for Human-Computer Communication. write for info. (ISBN 0-12-643820-X). Acad Pr.
Siminoff, Jonathan. The Timex Personal Computer Made Simple. 1982. pap. 3.50 (ISBN 0-451-12138-4, AE2138, Sig). NAL.
Sloan, M. E. Computer Hardware & Organization. 2nd ed. 500p. 1983. text ed. write for info. (ISBN 0-574-21425-9, 13-4425); write for info. instr's. guide (ISBN 0-574-21426-7). SRA.
Smith, Brian R. The Small Computer in Small Business. 1983. pap. 9.95 (ISBN 0-86616-024-8). Greene.
Software for the IBM-PC & Other 8088-86 Computers. 6.95 (ISBN 0-910085-07-2). Info Res MI.
Spencer, Donald A. Computer Literacy Test Questions. 1983. 6.95x (ISBN 0-89218-074-9). Camelot Pub.
Spencer, Donald D. Computer Poster Book. 1982. 14.95x (ISBN 0-89218-067-6). Camelot Pub.
--Famous People of Computing: A Book of Posters. 1982. 12.95x (ISBN 0-89218-068-4). Camelot Pub.
--An Introduction to Computers: Developing Computer Literacy. 1983. 18.95 (ISBN 0-675-20030-X). Additional supplements may be obtained from publisher. Merrill.
--Visual Masters for Teaching about Computers. 2d ed. 1982. 9.95x (ISBN 0-89218-050-1). Camelot Pub.
Statistical Software. 5.95 (ISBN 0-910085-02-1). Info Res MI.
Strackbein, Ray & Strackbein, Dorothy B. Computers & Data Processing Simplified & Self-Taught. LC 82-11664. (Simplified & Self-Taught Ser.). (Illus.). 128p. 1983. lib. bdg. 9.95 (ISBN 0-668-05553-7); pap. 4.95 (ISBN 0-668-05549-9). Arco.
Suen, Ching Y. & DeMori, Renato, eds. Computer Analysis & Perception: Visual Signals, Vol. 1. 176p. 1982. 57.00 (ISBN 0-8493-6305-5). CRC Pr.
Teicholz, Eric. McGraw-Hill A-E Computer Systems Update: Selecting & Acquiring a Low-Cost CAD System for Design & Drafting. 280p. 1983. 240.00 (ISBN 0-07-063402-5, P&RB). McGraw.
Timex-Sinclair One Thousand. LC 82-42768. Date not set. pap. 9.95 (ISBN 0-88022-016-3). Que Corp.
Tourlakis. Computability. 1983. text ed. 27.95 (ISBN 0-8359-0876-3). Reston.
Twenty-Two Computer Profiles. 7.95 (ISBN 0-910085-08-0). Info Res MI.
Tymon, Frank & Tymon, Tim. How to Program Computer Games for Fun & Profit. 300p. 1983. pap. price not set. Dilithium Pr.
Uffenbeck, John E. Hardware Interfacing with the TRS-80. 01/1983 ed. (Illus.). 240p. text ed. 19.95 (ISBN 0-13-383877-3); pap. 13.95 (ISBN 0-13-383869-2). P-H.
U. S. Third-Party Maintnance Market for Computer Datacom Equipment. (Reports Ser.: No. 512). 145p. 1982. 985.00 (ISBN 0-686-38953-0). Intl Res Dev.
Victor, John. Everything You Always Wanted to Understand about Personal Computers: But Did Not Know How to Ask. 1982. pap. 9.95 (ISBN 0-686-81780-X); pap. 19.95 audio & cassette (ISBN 0-686-81781-8). Devin.
Weiss, Eberhard. Input-Output Modellgenerator. 284p. 1982. write for info. (ISBN 3-8204-5808-5). P Lang Pubs.
The Whole Computer Catalog. (Orig.). 1983. pap. 19.95 (ISBN 0-440-03665-8, Emerald). Dell.
Wolfe, Philip M., et al. A Practical Guide to Selecting Small Business Computers. 1982. pap. text ed. 16.00 (ISBN 0-89806-033-8); pap. text ed. 8.00 members. Inst Indus Eng.
Woodwell, Donald R. Automating Your Financial Portfolio: An Investor's Guide to Personal Computers. LC 82-73637. 220p. 1983. 17.50 (ISBN 0-87094-399-5). Dow Jones-Irwin.
Young, S. J. An Introduction to ADA. (Computers & Their Applications Ser.). 320p. 1983. 69.95x (ISBN 0-470-27551-0); pap. 29.95x (ISBN 0-470-27350-X). Halsted Pr.
Yovits, Marshall, ed. Advances in Computers, Vol. 22. (Serial Publication). Date not set. price not set (ISBN 0-12-012122-0); price not set lib. ed. (ISBN 0-12-012192-1); price not set microfiche (ISBN 0-12-012193-X). Acad Pr.

COMPUTERS–APPRAISAL
see Computers–Valuation

COMPUTERS–CIRCUITS
Uhr, Leonard, ed. Algorithm-Structured Computer Arrays & Networks: Architectures & Processes for Images, Percepts, Models, Information. Date not set. price not set (ISBN 0-12-706960-7). Acad Pr.
Zarrella, John. Designing with the 8088 Microprocessor. 180p. (Orig.). 1983. pap. write for info. (ISBN 0-935230-07-6). Microcomputer Appns.

COMPUTERS–DEBUGGING
see Debugging (Electronic Computers)

COMPUTERS–DESIGN AND CONSTRUCTION
see Computer Engineering

COMPUTERS–DICTIONARIES
Anderson, R. G. Dictionary of Data Processing & Computer Terms. 112p. 1982. pap. text ed. 9.95x (ISBN 0-7121-0429-1). Intl Ideas.
Dictionary of Japanese Microcomputer. 30p. 1983. 30.00x (ISBN 0-686-38826-7). Sci & Tech Pr.
Directory of Japanese Computers. 400p. 1983. 250.00x (ISBN 0-686-38825-9). Sci & Tech Pr.
Freedman, Alan. The Computer Glossary: It's Not Just a Glossary. 3rd ed. (Illus.). 320p. Date not set. price not set (ISBN 0-941878-02-3). Computer Lang.
Freedman, Alan & Morrison, Irma L. The Computer Glossary: It's Not Just a Glossary. 320p. 1983. pap. 14.95 (ISBN 0-686-38832-1). P H.
Giarratano, Joseph C. Timex-Sinclair One Thousand Pocket Dictionary. 1983. pap. 4.95 (ISBN 0-88022-028-7). Que Corp.
Spencer, Donald D. Illustrated Computer Dictionary for Young People. LC 81-21795. (Illus.). 1982. 8.95x (ISBN 0-89218-052-8). Camelot Pub.

COMPUTERS–DIRECTORIES
Computer Services. 1982. 1095.00 (E74). Predicasts.
Digital Research, Inc. CP-M Compatible Software Catalog. 2nd ed. Date not set. pap. 12.95 (ISBN 0-88022-018-X). Que Corp.
Forrest, E. & Johnson, R. H. CAE, CAD, CAD-CAM Service Bureaus: Directory, Review, & Outlook, 1983. (Illus.). 130p. 1983. spiral bdg. 150.00 (ISBN 0-938484-09-5). Daratech.
International Computer Programs, Inc. ICP Software Directory: Cross Industry Applications. rev. ed. Spangler, Richard J., ed. 1983. pap. 150.00 (ISBN 0-686-82214-5). Intl Computer.
--ICP Software Directory: Industry Specific Applications. rev. ed. Spangler, Richard J., ed. 1983. pap. 150.00 (ISBN 0-88094-015-8). Intl Computer.
--ICP Software Directory: Software Product & Service Suppliers. rev. ed. Spangler, Richard J., ed. 1983. pap. 150.00 (ISBN 0-88094-016-6). Intl Computer.
--ICP Software Directory: Systems Software. rev. ed. Spangler, Richard J., ed. 1983. pap. 150.00 (ISBN 0-88094-013-1). Intl Computer.
Kelman, Peter & Key, Newton E., eds. Classroom Computer News Directory of Educational Computing Resources, 1983. (Illus.). 160p. (Orig.). 1982. pap. 14.95 (ISBN 0-9607970-0-9). Intentional Ed.
Levin, Paul. Construction Computer Applications Directory. 3rd ed. Layman, Donald & Young, Nancy A., eds. 600p. 135.00 (ISBN 0-686-42716-5). Constr Ind Pr.
Merrill, Martha, ed. New England Directory for Computer Professionals, 1983. 214p. (Orig.). 1982. pap. text ed. 28.50 (ISBN 0-686-37958-6). Bradford Co.
Stern, Michael. National Computer Services Register, 1983: Small Computers, North American Edition. 350p. 1983. pap. 39.95 (ISBN 0-911345-00-0). Datanet Pub.

COMPUTERS–HANDBOOKS, MANUALS, ETC.
Abrahams, et al. An Introduction to BASIC Programming for Small Computers. 96p. 1983. text ed. 5.96x (ISBN 0-7715-0790-9); tchr's manual 5.96x (ISBN 0-7715-0791-7). Forkner.
Arneson, D. J. The Official Computer Hater's Handbook. (Orig.). 1983. pap. price not set (ISBN 0-440-56619-3, Dell Trade Pbks). Dell.
Barnett, Nancy B. & Baker, John T. Texas Instruments Compact Computer Forty User's Guide. 336p. (Orig.). 1983. pap. 14.95 (ISBN 0-89512-057-7). Tex Instr Inc.
Billing Systems for Health Professionals. 7.95 (ISBN 0-910085-05-6). Info Res MI.
Choosing a Word Processor. 17.95 (ISBN 0-910085-00-5); comparison tables 6.95, (ISBN 0-910085-01-3). Info Res MI.
Commodore Computer Staff. User's Guide. Date not set. pap. 12.95 (ISBN 0-672-22010-5). Sams.
Dennon. CP-M Revealed. Date not set. 12.95 (ISBN 0-686-81999-3, 5204). Hayden.
Electronic Spread Sheets. 5.95 (ISBN 0-910085-04-8). Info Res MI.
Fernandes, Judi N. & Ashley, Ruth. CP-M Eighty-Six for the IBM Personal Computer. (A Self-Teaching & Wiley IBM PC Ser.). 331p. 1983. pap. text ed. 14.95 (ISBN 0-471-89719-1). Wiley.
Giarratano, Joseph C. Timex-Sinclair One Thousand User's Guide, Vol. II. 1983. pap. 12.95 (ISBN 0-88022-029-5). Que Corp.
Grillo, John P. & Robertson, J. D. Data & File Management for the IBM Personal Computer. (Microcomputer Power Ser.). 240p. 1983. pap. write for info. (ISBN 0-697-09987-3); diskette avail. (ISBN 0-697-09988-1). Wm C Brown.
--Users Guide with Applications for the IBM Personal Computer. (Microcomputer Power Ser.). 330p. 1983. pap. write for info. (ISBN 0-697-09985-7); diskette avail. (ISBN 0-697-09986-5). Wm C Brown.
Grosswirth, Marvin. Beginner's Guide to Small Computers. updated ed. Amyx, Richard, rev. by. LC 82-45324. (Illus.). 144p. 1983. pap. 7.95 (ISBN 0-385-17931-6, Dolp). Doubleday.
Hergert, Douglas. Your Timex Sinclair 1000 & ZX81. 176p. 1982. pap. 6.95 (ISBN 0-89588-099-7). Sybex.
Horsburgh, E. M., ed. Handbook of the Napier Tercentary Celebration or Modern Instruments & Methods of Calculation. (The Charles Babbage Institute Reprint Series for the History of Computing: Vol. 3). (Illus.). 1982. Repr. of 1914 ed. write for info. ltd. ed. (ISBN 0-938228-10-2). Tomash Pubs.
Kelley, James E., Jr. The IBM Personal Computer User's Guide. 352p. 1983. spiral bdg., shrink-wrapped, incl. a programmed floppy disk 29.95 (ISBN 0-440-03946-0, Banbury). Dell.
Lindley, Craig A. & McCarthy, Nan. The TRS Eighty & Z-Eighty Assembly Language Library. (Illus.). 1983. pap. write for info. LooseleafBinder (ISBN 0-88006-060-3). Green.
Lipman, Matthew & Sharp, Ann M. Wondering at the World: Instructional Manual to Accompany KIO & GUS. (Philosophy for Children Ser.). 400p. 1983. 40.00 (ISBN 0-916834-20-4). Inst Adv Philo.
Long, Larry. Managers Guide to Computers & Information Systems. (Illus.). 400p. 1983. text ed. 25.00 (ISBN 0-13-549394-3). P-H.
Morse, Peter & Adamson, Ian. Computerlab. 1983. pap. price not set (ISBN 0-671-47069-8, Touchstone Bks). S&S.
Mosher, Doug. Your Color Computer. 350p. 1983. pap. text ed. 12.95 (ISBN 0-89588-097-0). Sybex.
Munzert, Alfred. Test Your Computer IQ. Levy, Valerie, ed. (Test Yourself Ser.). (Orig.). 1983. pap. 4.95 (ISBN 0-671-47171-6). Monarch Pr.
SAS Institute, Inc. SAS ETS User's Guide, 1982 Edition. (Orig.). 1983. pap. text ed. 14.95 (ISBN 0-917382-38-2). SAS Inst.
SAS Institute Inc. SAS User's Guide: Basics, 1982 Edition. 923p. (Orig.). 1982. pap. 14.95 (ISBN 0-917382-36-6). SAS Inst.
SAS Institute, Inc. SAS User's Guide: Statistics, 1982 Edition. 584p. (Orig.). 1982. pap. 14.95 (ISBN 0-917382-37-4). SAS Inst.
Sinclair, Ian R. & McCarty, Nan. Inside Your Computer. (Illus.). 1983. write for info. (ISBN 0-88006-058-1). Green.
Software for the IBM-PC & Other 8088-86 Computers. 6.95 (ISBN 0-910085-07-2). Info Res MI.
Stewart, Ian & Jones, Robin. Timex Sinclair One-Thousand: Programs, Games, & Graphics. 100p. 1982. pap. 10.95 (ISBN 3-7643-3080-5). Birkhauser.
Van Trees, James & Wolenik, Robert. A Buyer's Guide to Home Computers. 288p. (Orig.). 1983. pap. 3.75 (ISBN 0-523-41992-9). Pinnacle Bks.
Willoughby, William E. & Jacobs, Nancy F. The ABC's of the IBM. 100p. 1983. pap. 5.95 (ISBN 0-89588-102-0). Sybex.
Wolfe, Philip M., et al. A Practical Guide to Selecting Small Business Computers. 1982. pap. text ed. 16.00 (ISBN 0-89806-033-8); pap. text ed. 8.00 members. Inst Indus Eng.
Zimmerman, Steven & Conrad, Leo. Osborne User's Guide: Applications & Programming. (Illus.). 264p. 1982. text ed. 19.95 (ISBN 0-89303-207-7); pap. 14.95 (ISBN 0-89303-206-9). R J Brady.

COMPUTERS–JUVENILE LITERATURE
Boren, Sharon. An Apple in the Classroom. 170p. (gr. 3-8). 1983. pap. 7.95 (ISBN 0-88056-119-X). Dilithium Pr.
Colgren, John. The Computer Revolution. (gr. 4-8). 1982. 5.95 (ISBN 0-86653-067-3, GA 421). Good Apple.
D'Ignazio, Fred. Messner's Introduction to the Computer. (Illus.). 288p. (gr. 9-12). 1983. PLB 9.79 (ISBN 0-671-42267-7). Messner.
--The Star Wars Question & Answer Book about Computers. LC 82-19030. (Illus.). 64p. (gr. 4-8). 1983. PLB 7.99 (ISBN 0-394-95686-9); pap. 4.95 (ISBN 0-394-85686-4). Random.
Hellman, Hal. Computer Basics. (Illus.). 48p. (gr. 3-7). 1983. pap. 8.95 (ISBN 0-13-164574-9). P-H.
Horn, Cárin E. & Collins, Carroll L. Com-Lit: Computer Literacy for Kids. 1983. write for info. Sterling Swift.
Larsen, Sally G. Computers for Kids: Commodore VIC-20 Edition. (Illus.). 88p. (gr. 4-10). 1983. pap. 4.95 (ISBN 0-916688-42-9). Creative Comp.
Marsh, Carole. Bugs & Bytes: Computer for Kids. (Tomorrow's Books). (Illus.). 56p. 1983. 5.95 (ISBN 0-935326-15-4). Gallopade Pub Group.
Math, Irwin. Bits & Pieces: Understanding & Building Computing Devices. (Illus.). 96p. (gr. 7 up). 1983. 12.95 (ISBN 0-684-17879-6). Scribner.
Spencer, Donald D. Understanding Computers. (gr. 9-12). 1982. 13.95x (ISBN 0-89218-057-9); instr's. guide 12.95x (ISBN 0-89218-059-5); student wkbk. 5.95x (ISBN 0-89218-058-7). Camelot Pub.

COMPUTERS–LAW AND LEGISLATION
Brooks, Daniel T., et al. Computer Law 1982: Aquiring Computer Goods & Services, 2 vols. LC 82-61508. (Commercial Law & Practice Course Handbook Ser.). 1370p. 1982. 30.00 (A6-4041). PLI.
Danziger, James N. & Dutton, William H. Computers & Politics. 320p. 1983. pap. 15.00 (ISBN 0-231-04889-0). Columbia U Pr.
Turi, Leonard F. OEM & Turnkey Contracts. 178p. 1982. 59.95 (ISBN 0-935506-09-8). Carnegie Pr.
COMPUTERS–MEMORY SYSTEMS
see Computer Storage Devices
COMPUTERS–MORAL AND RELIGIOUS ASPECTS
Card, Stuart K. & Moran, Thomas P. The Psychology of Human-Computer Interaction. 464p. 1983. text ed. write for info. (ISBN 0-89859-243-7). L Erlbaum Assocs.
Green, Thomas & Payne, Stephen J., eds. The Psychology of Computer Use. (Computer & People Ser.). Date not set. price not set (ISBN 0-12-297420-4). Acad Pr.
COMPUTERS–OPTICAL EQUIPMENT
see also Information Display Systems; Optical Data Processing
Barrett, R. Developments in Optical Disc Technology & the Implications for Information Storage & Retrieval. 80p. 1981. pap. 170.00x (ISBN 0-905984-71-4, Pub. by Brit Lib England). State Mutual Bk.
Biotechnology Equipment & Supplies. (Reports Ser.: No. 513). 179p. 1982. 985.00 (ISBN 0-686-38954-9). Intl Res Dev.
COMPUTERS–PROGRAMMING
see Programming (Electronic Computers)
COMPUTERS–STORAGE DEVICES
see Computer Storage Devices
COMPUTERS–TIME-SHARING SYSTEMS
Shoenberg, Isaac J. Mathematical Time Exposures. 200p. 1983. write for info. (ISBN 0-88385-438-4). Math Assn.
COMPUTERS–VALUATION
Grimes, Dennis & Kelly, Brian. The Personal Computer Buyers Guide. 350p. (Orig.). 1983. 14.95 (ISBN 0-88410-917-8). Ballinger Pub.
COMPUTERS, ELECTRONIC
see Computers; Electronic Digital Computers
COMPUTERS AND CIVILIZATION
Graham, Neill. The Mind Tool: Computers & Their Impact on Society. 3rd ed. (Illus.). 410p. 1983. pap. text ed. 13.95 (ISBN 0-314-69650-4); study manual avail. (ISBN 0-314-71093-0); instrs.' manual avail. (ISBN 0-314-71094-9). West Pub.
Masuda, Yoneji. The Information Society: As Post-Industrial Society. (Illus.). 178p. 1980. pap. text ed. 12.50x (ISBN 0-930242-15-7). Transaction Bks.
Van Tassel, Dennie & Van Tassel, Cynthia L. The Compleat Computer. 2nd ed. 280p. 1983. pap. text ed. write for info. (ISBN 0-574-21415-1, 13-4415). SRA.
COMPUTING MACHINES
see Calculating-Machines
COMPUTING MACHINES (COMPUTERS)
see Computers
COMTE, AUGUSTE, 1798-1857
Norhausberber, Rudolph C. The Historical-Philosophical Significance of Comte, Darwin, Marx & Freud. (Human Development Library Book). (Illus.). 139p. 1983. 59.85 (ISBN 0-89266-392-8). Am Classical Coll Pr.
CONAN DOYLE, ARTHUR, SIR
see Doyle, Arthur Conan, Sir, 1859-1930
CONCENTRATION CAMPS
Eitinger, Leo. Psychological & Medical Effects on Concentration Camps. 122p. 1982. lib. bdg. 15.00 (ISBN 0-8482-0747-5). Norwood Edns.
Hart, Kitty. Return to Auschwitz. LC 81-69155. 200p. 1983. pap. 7.95 (ISBN 0-689-70637-5, 283). Atheneum.
Mendelsohn, J. The Final Solution in the Extermination Camps & the Aftermath. LC 81-80320. (The Holocaust Ser.). 250p. 1982. lib. bdg. 50.00 (ISBN 0-8240-4886-5). Garland Pub.
Mendelsohn, John. Medical Experiments on Jewish Inmates of Concentration Camps. LC 81-80317. (The Holocaust Ser.). 282p. 1982. lib. bdg. 50.00 (ISBN 0-8240-4883-0). Garland Pub.
CONCEPTION–PREVENTION
see Contraception
CONCEPTUALISM
Scholnick, Ellin K. New Trends in Conceptual Representation: Challanges to Piaget's Theory? (Jean Piaget Symposium). 320p. 1983. text ed. write for info. (ISBN 0-89859-260-7). L Erlbaum Assocs.
CONCERT OF EUROPE
Echard, William E. Napoleon III & the Concert of Europe. LC 82-12660. 325p. 1983. text ed. 32.50x (ISBN 0-8071-1056-6). La State U Pr.
CONCHOLOGY
see Mollusks; Shells
CONCORDANCES
see also Bible-Concordances; Indexes; also subdivision Concordances under names of authors, e.g. Shakespeare, William-Concordances
Kasten, Lloyd & Anderson, Jean. Concordance to the Celestina (1499) 338p. 1976. 12.50 (ISBN 0-942260-10-4). Hispanic Seminary.
CONCORDE (JET TRANSPORTS)
Owen, Ken. Concorde. (Illus.). 240p. 1982. 24.95 (ISBN 0-86720-630-6). Sci Bks Intl.
CONCRETE
see also Cement; Gunite; Reinforced Concrete
Broms, Bengt B. Precast Piling Practice. 126p. 1981. 65.00x (ISBN 0-7277-0121-5, Pub. by Telford England). State Mutual Bk.
Bungey, John H. Testing of Concrete in Structures. 1982. 39.00X (ISBN 0-412-00231-0, Pub. by Chapman & Hall England). Methuen Inc.
Fookes, P. J. & Collis, L. Concrete in the Middle East, Pt. I. 1982. pap. 4.00 (ISBN 0-86310-001-5). Scholium Intl.
Fookes, P. J. & Pollock, D. J. Concrete in the Middle East, Pt. II. 1982. pap. 15.00 (ISBN 0-86310-007-4). Scholium Intl.
Lydon, F. D. Concrete Mix Design. 2nd ed. (Illus.). xii, 196p. 1983. 45.00 (ISBN 0-85334-162-1, Pub. by Applied Sci England). Elsevier.
--Developments in Concrete Technology, Vol. 1. 1979. 53.50 (ISBN 0-85334-855-3, Pub. by Applied Sci England). Elsevier.
Residential Concrete. (Illus.). 142p. 1983. pap. write for info. (ISBN 0-86718-158-3). Natl Assn Home.
Richardson, J. G. Precast Concrete Production. 1977. pap. 32.50 (ISBN 0-7210-0912-3). Scholium Intl.
Survey of Concrete Research in Australia: A Report on Information Subjects Allied to Concrete. 86p. (Orig.). 1979. pap. text ed. 18.00x (ISBN 0-85825-108-6, Pub. by Inst Engineering Australia). Renouf.
Wittman, F. H., ed. Autoclaved Aerated Concrete: Moisture & Properties. (Developments in Civil Engineering Ser.: No. 6). 380p. 1982. 81.00 (ISBN 0-444-42117-3). Elsevier.
CONCRETE, REINFORCED
see Reinforced Concrete
CONCRETE BUILDING
see Concrete Construction
CONCRETE CONSTRUCTION
see also Grouting; Precast Concrete Construction; Prestressed Concrete Construction; Reinforced Concrete; Reinforced Concrete Construction
American Society of Civil Engineers, compiled by. Finite Element Analysis of Reinforced Concrete. LC 82-71691. 560p. 1982. pap. text ed. 39.00. Am Soc Civil Eng.
Jones. Concrete Technology. 1982. text ed. 22.50 (ISBN 0-408-00673-0); pap. text ed. 9.95 (ISBN 0-408-00643-9). Butterworth.
Koll, F. & Cohen, Edward. Handbook of Structural Concrete. 1936p. 1983. 85.86 (ISBN 0-07-011573-7, P&RB). McGraw.
Ricouard, M. J. Formwork for Concrete Construction. 1982. 60.00x (ISBN 0-686-42939-7, Pub. by Macmillan England). State Mutual Bk.
Ruesck, H., et al. Creep & Shrinkage: Their Effect on the Behavior of Concrete Structures. (Illus.). 304p. 1983. 60.00 (ISBN 0-387-90669-X). Springer-Verlag.
CONCRETE CONSTRUCTION, PRECAST
see Precast Concrete Construction
CONCRETE CONSTRUCTION, PREFABRICATED
see Precast Concrete Construction
CONCRETE CONSTRUCTION, TILT-UP
see Precast Concrete Construction
CONDEMNATION OF LAND
see Eminent Domain
CONDEMNED BOOKS
see also Censorship; Liberty of the Press
Jackson, Holbrook. The Fear of Books. LC 82-15785. x, 199p. 1982. Repr. of 1932 ed. lib. bdg. 29.75x (ISBN 0-313-23738-7, JAFB). Greenwood.
Speculator Morum. Bibliotheca Arcana: Brief Notices of Books that have been Secretly Printed, Prohibited by Law, Seized, Anathematized, Burnt or Bowdlerized. 189p. 1982. 60.00x (ISBN 0-284-79523-2, Pub. by C Skilton Scotland). State Mutual Bk.
CONDITIONED RESPONSE
Pavlov, I. P. Lectures on Conditioned Reflexes. Gray, Jeffrey, ed. (Classics of Psychology & Psychiatry Ser.). 640p. 1983. Repr. of 1928 ed. write for info. (ISBN 0-904014-43-6). F Pinter Pubs.
CONDOMINIUM (CIVIL LAW)
see Condominium (Housing)
CONDOMINIUM (HOUSING)
Casazza, John A. Condominium Conversions. LC 82-70139. (Illus.). 157p. 1982. pap. text ed. 26.00 (ISBN 0-87420-606-5, C19). Urban Land.
Giese, Lester J. Budget Builder I for Condominium Associations. LC 82-90784. 63p. 1982. 21.95 (ISBN 0-910049-01-7). Condo Mgmt.
--Condominium Reserve Builder. 1983. pap. text ed. 32.50 (ISBN 0-910049-02-5). Condo Mgmt.
Ludy, Andrew. Condominium Ownership: A Buyer's Guide. (Illus.). 128p. 1982. pap. 7.95 (ISBN 0-943912-00-8). Landing Pr.
Rosen, Kenneth D. Condominium Conversions: Ken Rosen's Success Formula for Big Profits. LC 82-11251. 233p. 1983. 19.95 (ISBN 0-13-167049-2, Busn). P-H.
Ryder, Virginia P. Cormorants Landing: How to Do Your Own Condo-Conversion Plus Secrets of City Hall. LC 82-90719. (Illus.). 130p. 1983. pap. 10.00 (ISBN 0-935098-02-X). Amigo Pr.
Shapiro, Eugene. The Condo & Co-op Book: A Game Plan for Winning the Condo-Co-op Conversion Battle. 186p. 1983. 14.95 (ISBN 0-13-167171-5); pap. 6.95 (ISBN 0-13-167163-4). P-H.
CONDOMINIUM (REAL PROPERTY)
see Condominium (Housing)
CONDORCET, MARIE JEAN ANTOINE NICOLAS CARITAT, MARQUIS DE, 1743-1794
Baker, Keith M. Condorcet: From Natural Philosophy to Social Mathematics. LC 74-5725. 538p. 1982. 15.00x (ISBN 0-226-03533-6). U of Chicago Pr.
CONDORS
Andrews, Michael A. The Flight of the Condor: A Wildlife Exploration of the Andes. LC 81-48533. (Illus.). 158p. 1982. 22.50 (ISBN 0-316-03958-6). Little.
CONDUCT OF LIFE
see also Altruism; Anger; Business Ethics; Charity; Christian Life; Courage; Courtesy; Culture; Ethics; Family Life Education; Friendship; Habit; Interpersonal Relations; Justice; Love; Obedience; Patriotism; Self-Control; Self-Culture; Self-Respect; Sharing; Simplicity; Spiritual Life; Success; Sympathy; Temperance; Virtue and Virtues
also subdivision Conduct of Life under names of classes of persons, e.g. Youth-Conduct of Life
Afraid to Live, Afraid to Die. 5.95 (ISBN 0-89486-147-6). Hazelden.
Apgar, Kathryn & Riley, Donald P. Life Education in the Workplace: How to Design, Lead & Market Employee Seminars. 184p. 1982. 17.95 (ISBN 0-87304-197-6). Family Serv.
Bach, George & Goldberg, Herb. Creative Aggression: The Art of Creative Living. LC 82-45621. 432p. 1983. pap. 8.95 (ISBN 0-385-18442-5, Anch). Doubleday.
Ballard, Juliet B. The Art of Living. 251p. 1982. pap. 7.95 (ISBN 0-87604-144-6). ARE Pr.
Baudhuin, John & Hawks, Linda. Living Longer, Living Better. 144p. 1983. pap. 6.95 (ISBN 0-86683-671-3). Winston Pr.
Baxter, Batsell B. & Hazelip, Harold. Anchors in Troubled Waters. Abr. ed. LC 82-50267. (Journey Adult Ser.). 124p. pap. text ed. 2.95 (ISBN 0-8344-0120-7). Sweet.
Boswell, Thomas. How Life Imitates the World Series. (Penguin Sports Library). 1983. pap. 4.95 (ISBN 0-14-006469-9). Penguin.
Butler, Samuel. Life & Habit. 320p. 1982. 30.00x (ISBN 0-7045-0425-1, Pub. by Wildwood House). State Mutual Bk.
Buzan, Tony. The Brain User's Guide: A Handbook for Sorting out Your Life. (Illus.). 128p. 1983. pap. 7.95 (ISBN 0-525-48045-5, 0772-230). Dutton.
Corder, George E. Your Brain-Image Power: How to Selfsex & Imagize Your Way to Super-Successful Living. LC 82-90505. 200p. 1983. lib. bdg. 25.00 (ISBN 0-9609246-0-4). Brain-Image.
Dingoian, George. The Tide is Turning. LC 81-86207. 64p. 1983. pap. 4.95 (ISBN 0-86666-037-2). GWP.
Dixon. I Can Manage. 1983. write for info. (ISBN 0-07-072902-6). McGraw.
Each Day a New Beginning. 5.95 (ISBN 0-89486-161-1). Hazelden.
Farina, Richard. Been Down So Long It Looks Like Up to Me. 1983. pap. 4.95 (ISBN 0-14-006536-9). Penguin.
Felder, David W. The Best Investment: Land In a Loving Community. LC 86-61882. (Illus.). 176p. 1983. pap. 8.50 (ISBN 0-910959-00-5). Wellington Pr.
Gambill, Henrietta. Self-Control. LC 82-1201. (What is It? Ser.). 32p. (gr. k-3). 1982. PLB 6.50 (ISBN 0-89565-225-0). Childs World.
Ganton, Doris. Drive On. Date not set. pap. 7.00 (ISBN 0-87980-393-2). Wilshire.
Goodman, Lisl M. Death & the Creative Life. 1983. pap. 5.95 (ISBN 0-14-006275-0). Penguin.
Goot, Mary V. A Life Planning Guide for Women. 128p. 1982. pap. 9.95x (ISBN 0-88946-512-6). E Mellen.
Guisewite, Cathy. How to Get Rich, Fall in Love, Lose Weight, & Solve All Your Problems by Saying "No". LC 82-72412. (Illus.). 60p. (Orig.). 1983. pap. 2.95 (ISBN 0-8362-1986-4). Andrews & McMeel.
Hanson, R. Galen. A New Day Still Dawning: A Sequel to Surgery in Personal Experience & a Reaffirmation of the Joy of Living. 70p. 1983. 5.50 (ISBN 0-682-49937-4). Exposition.
Hofstadter, Douglas R. & Dennett, Daniel C., eds. The Mind's I: Fantasies & Reflections of Self & Soul. 368p. 1982. pap. 8.95 (ISBN 0-553-01412-9). Bantam.
Hume, David. An Enquiry Concerning the Principles of Morals. Schneewind, J. B., ed. LC 82-11679. (HPC Philosophical Classics Ser.). 132p. lib. bdg. 13.50 (ISBN 0-915145-46-4); pap. text ed. 2.95 (ISBN 0-915145-45-6). Hackett Pub.
Jones, Larry. Build a Brand New You. 1983. pap. 2.50 (ISBN 0-686-82529-2). Tyndale.
Kerns, Phil. Fake It Til You Make It. (Illus.). 182p. (Orig.). pap. 5.95 (ISBN 0-9609908-0-1). Victory Pr.
Kistler, Edgar P. Your Life on Planet Earth. 1982. 8.75 (ISBN 0-8062-1923-8). Carlton.
Landers, Ann. Since You Asked Me. 206p. 1983. pap. 5.95 (ISBN 0-13-810531-6). P-H.
Leichtman, Robert R. & Japikse, Carl. The Art of Living, Vol. III. LC 81-69186. (Illus.). 250p. (Orig.). 1982. pap. 5.00 (ISBN 0-89804-034-5). Ariel OH.
Leonard, Jim & Laut, Phil. Rebirthing: The Science of Enjoying all of Your Life. 90p. (Orig.). 1983. pap. 5.00 (ISBN 0-686-84663-X). Trinity Pubns.
Mullen, Tom. Funny Things Happen on the Way to the Cemetery. 1983. 7.95 (ISBN 0-686-84763-6). Word Bks.
Nelson, Bill & Schmidt, Bill. Stick With It! (Illus.). 112p. (Orig.). 1983. pap. 3.95 (ISBN 0-936750-08-1). Wetherall.
Olivier, Tanya. How to Survive When Your Husband or Wife Walks Out, Vol. I. Thuvenet, Renee, ed. LC 82-84063. 154p. (Orig.). 1983. pap. 10.95 (ISBN 0-686-38459-8). Ferrucci.
Pond, Mimi. The Valley Girls Guide to Life. (Orig.). 1982. pap. 2.95 (ISBN 0-440-59334-4, Dell Trade Pbks). Dell.
Quennell, Peter. Customs & Characters: Contemporary Portraits. 1983. 16.00i (ISBN 0-686-82203-X). Little.
Rajneesh, Bhagwan Shree. Don't Look Before You Leap. Rajneesh Foundation International, ed. 232p. 1983. pap. 12.95 (ISBN 0-88050-554-0). Rajneesh Found Intl.
--Love, Life, Laughter. Rajneesh Foundation International, ed. 64p. 1983. pap. 3.95 (ISBN 0-88050-696-2). Rajneesh Found Intl.
Richards, John & Richards, Mary. Experiencing Self-Mastery. 64p. (Orig.). 1983. pap. 3.95 (ISBN 0-942044-02-9). Polestar.
Robinson, Ras. A New You. 67p. (Orig.). 1982. pap. 2.00 (ISBN 0-937778-06-0, MB 21). Fulness Hse.
Sea, Beth. I Am what I Am-Human. (Illus.). 40p. (Orig.). Date not set. pap. 3.50 (ISBN 0-9608796-0-9). B S Beaulieu.
Seabury, David. How to Live With Yourself. 104p. 1972. pap. 3.95 (ISBN 0-911336-39-7). Sci of Mind.
Spock, Marjorie. In Celebration of the Human Heart. 1982. pap. 5.95 (ISBN 0-916786-65-X). St George Bk Serv.
Stortz, Margaret R. Start Living Every Day of Your Life: How to Use the Science of Mind. 96p. 1981. pap. 2.95 (ISBN 0-911336-87-7). Sci of Mind.
Varenhorst, Barbara B. Real Friends: Becoming the Friend You'd Like to Have. LC 82-48412. (Illus.). 160p. (Orig.). 1983. pap. 5.72 (ISBN 0-06-250890-3, HarpR). Har-Row.
Wright, P. Wayne. Positive Power. 1983. 7.95 (ISBN 0-533-05596-2). Vantage.
Zitko, Howard J. World University Insights: With Your Future in Mind. Orig. Title: New Age Perspectives in Questions & Answers. 208p. 1980. pap. 6.20 (ISBN 0-941902-01-3). World Univ AZ.
CONDUCTING
see also Conductors (Music); Music–Performance; Orchestra
Matheopoulos, Helena. Maestro: Encounters with Conductors of Today. LC 82-48125. (Illus.). 512p. 1983. 24.95 (ISBN 0-06-015103-X, HarpT). Har-Row.
Parker, Robert. Carlos Chavez: Mexico's Modern-Day Orpheus. (Music Ser.). 192p. 1983. lib. bdg. 21.95 (ISBN 0-8057-9455-7, Twayne). G K Hall.
CONDUCTORS (MUSIC)
see also Conducting
Ensor, Wendy-Ann. More Heroes & Heroines in Music. (Illus.). 48p. 1983. pap. 5.00 laminated (ISBN 0-19-321106-8); cassette 18.00 (ISBN 0-19-321107-6). Oxford U Pr.
Russell, John. Erich Kleiber: A Memoir. (Illus.). ix, 256p. 1981. Repr. of 1957 ed. lib. bdg. 27.00 (ISBN 0-686-42958-3). Da Capo.
CONFECTIONERY
see also Cake Decorating; Ice Cream, Ices, etc.; Snack Foods
Brand, Mildred. Candy & Candy Molding. (Illus.). 64p. 1982. pap. 3.25 (ISBN 0-686-83999-4). Ideals.
The Candy Market. 1981. 450.00 (ISBN 0-686-38420-2, 104). Busn Trend.
CONFEDERATE STATES OF AMERICA–BIBLIOGRAPHY
Confederate Imprints: A Reel Index to the Microfilm Collection. 1974. 15.00 (ISBN 0-89235-051-2). Res Pubns Conn.
CONFEDERATE STATES OF AMERICA–HISTORY
Stephenson, Nathaniel W. Day of the Confederacy. 1919. text ed. 8.50x (ISBN 0-686-83524-7). Elliots Bks.
CONFEDERATE STATES OF AMERICA–REGIMENTAL HISTORIES
see United States–History–Civil War, 1861-1865–Regimental Histories
CONFERENCES
see Congresses and Conventions; Forums (Discussion and Debate); Meetings
CONFESSIONS OF FAITH
see Creeds
CONFIGURATION (PSYCHOLOGY)
see Gestalt Psychology
CONFLAGRATIONS
see Fires

CONFLICT (PSYCHOLOGY)
Antrieb und Hemmung bei Toetungsdelikten. (Schriftenreihe des Instituts fuer Konfliktforschung: Heft 9). x, 124p. 1982. pap. 12.00 (ISBN 3-8055-3604-6). S Karger.
Taylor. The Future of Conflict. 122p. 1983. 6.95 (ISBN 0-03-061951-3). Praeger.
CONFLICT OF CULTURES
see Culture Conflict
CONFLICT OF INTERESTS (PUBLIC OFFICE)
Federal Conflict of Interest Laws as Applied to Government Service by Parteners & Employees of Accounting Firms. 1981. pap. 8.00 (ISBN 0-686-84283-9). Am Inst CPA.
CONFLICT OF LAWS
see also Aliens; Jurisdiction (International Law); Public Policy (Law)
Institute for the Study of Conflict, London. Annual of Power & Conflict, 1981-82. 11th ed. LC 77-370326. 485p. 1982. 77.50x (ISBN 0-8002-3061-2). Intl Pubns Serv.
Moffatt, Hancock. Torts in the Conflict of Laws. LC 42-36734. (Michigan Legal Studies). lviii, 288p. 1982. Repr. of 1942 ed. lib. bdg. 30.00 (ISBN 0-89941-166-5). W S Hein.
Rosenthal, Douglas E. & Knighton, William M. National Laws & International Commerce: The Problem of Extraterritoriality. (Chatham House Papers Ser.: No. 17). 96p. (Orig.). 1982. pap. 10.00 (ISBN 0-7100-9338-1). Routledge & Kegan.
Summer Institute on International & Comparative Law. Lectures on the Conflict of Laws & International Contracts. LC 51-62311. (Michigan Legal Studies). xiv, 200p. 1982. Repr. of 1951 ed. lib. bdg. write for info. (ISBN 0-89941-177-0). W S Hein.
CONFORMITY
see also Deviant Behavior; Persuasion (Psychology); Social Values
Kirk, Russell. Enemies of the Permanent Things: Observations of Abnormity in Literature & Politics. 316p. pap. 8.95 (ISBN 0-89385-021-7). Sugden.
Sack, John. Fingerprint: The Autobiography of An American Man. Date not set. 13.95 (ISBN 0-394-50197-7). Random.
CONFUCIUS AND CONFUCIANISM
Confucius. The Most Compelling Sayings by Confucius. Lynall, Leonard D., tr. (Most Meaningful Classics in World Culture Ser.). (Illus.). 166p. 1983. 83.45 (ISBN 0-89266-387-1). Am Classical Coll Pr.
--The Wisdom of Confucius. Yutang, Lin, ed. 5.95 (ISBN 0-394-60426-1). Modern Lib.
CONGENITAL ABNORMALITIES
see Abnormalities, Human
CONGO
Thornton, John. The Kingdom of Kongo: Civil War & Transition, 1641-1718. LC 82-70549. (Illus.). 224p. 1983. 25.00 (ISBN 0-299-09290-9). U of Wis Pr.
CONGREGATIONAL CHURCHES
Smyth, Norman. Story of Church Unity: The Lambeth Conference of Anglican Bishops & the Congregational-Episcopal Approaches. 1923. text ed. 29.50x (ISBN 0-686-83788-6). Elliots Bks.
CONGRESSES AND CONVENTIONS
see also International Organization; Treaties; also names of particular congresses
Bennett, Gregory R. Successful Convention Management. (Illus., Orig.). 1983. write for info. (ISBN 0-916732-59-2); pap. text ed. write for info. (ISBN 0-916732-58-4). Starmont Hse.
Congressional Information Service, Inc. Staff. CIS-Index 1975 Annual, 2 Vols. 220.00 (ISBN 0-912380-32-2). Cong Info.
--CIS-Index 1981 Annual, 2 Vols. LC 79-158879. 370.00 (ISBN 0-686-84194-8). Cong Info.
Ellis, William & Seidel, Frank. How to Win the Conference. 214p. 1982. 6.95 (ISBN 0-13-439489-5). P-H.
Murray, Sheila L. How to Organize & Manage a Seminar: What to Do & When to Do It. 204p. 1983. 13.95 (ISBN 0-13-425199-7); pap. 6.95 (ISBN 0-13-425181-4). P-H.
Research Libraries of the New York Public Library & Library of Congress. Bibliographic Guide to Conference Publications: 1982. 1983. lib. bdg. 180.00 (ISBN 0-8161-6969-1, Biblio Guides). G K Hall.
CONGRESSIONAL INVESTIGATIONS
see Governmental Investigations
CONGRESSMEN
see Legislators
CONGRUENCES AND RESIDUES
see also Numbers, Theory of
Stevens, Glenn H. Arithmetic on Modular Curves. (Progress in Mathematics Ser.: 20). 1982. text ed. 15.00 (ISBN 3-7643-3088-0). Birkhauser.
CONIFERAE
Harrison, Charles R. Ornamental Conifers. (Illus.). 224p. 1982. Repr. of 1975 ed. pap. text ed. 37.50 (ISBN 0-7153-6848-6). David & Charles.
Ouden, P. den & Boom, B. K. Manual of Cultivated Conifers: Hardy in the Cold & Warm Temperature Zone. 1982. text ed. 59.00 (ISBN 90-247-2148-2, Pub. by Martinus Nijhoff); pap. text ed. 37.00 (ISBN 90-247-2644-1). Kluwer Boston.
CONJURING
Here are entered works on modern (parlor) magic, legerdemain, prestidigitation, etc. Works dealing with occult science (supernatural arts) are entered under the heading Magic.
see also Card Tricks; Magic; Medicine-Man
Moulton, H. J. Houdini's History of Magic in Boston, 1792-1915. (Illus.). 176p. 1983. 35.00 (ISBN 0-916638-27-8). Meyerbooks.
CONNECTICUT
see also names of cities, counties, etc. in Connecticut
Bernstein, Charles S., ed. Connecticut Real Estate Statutes. 480p. 1983. write for info. looseleaf binder (ISBN 0-88063-007-8). Butterworth Legal Pubs.
Rodriguez, Edward J. & Santoro, Anthony. The Law of Doing Business in Connecticut. 320p. 1983. write for info. (ISBN 0-88063-011-6). Butterworth Legal Pubs.
CONNECTICUT-DESCRIPTION AND TRAVEL
Boyle, Michael J., ed. Boyle's Connecticut Almanac & Guide: 1983. (Illus.). 96p. (Orig.). 1982. pap. 2.95 (ISBN 0-911097-00-7). M Boyle Pub.
Connecticut in Color: Thirty-Two Full Color Pages of Conneticut Attractions. (Illus.). 64p. 1983. price not set. Spoonwood Pr.
Cooley, Susan D. Country Walks in Connecticut: A Guide to the Nature Conservancy Preserves. (Illus.). 224p. (Orig.). 1982. pap. 6.95 (ISBN 0-910146-41-1). Appalach Mtn.
CONNECTICUT-HISTORY
Bickford, Christopher P. Farmington in Connecticut. LC 82-18575. (Illus.). 496p. 1982. 19.95 (ISBN 0-914016-92-X). Phoenix Pub.
Swigart, Edmund K. The Prehistory of the Indians of Western Connecticut. (Occasional Paper Ser.: No. One). 49p. pap. text ed. write for info. (ISBN 0-936322-02-0). Am Indian Arch.
CONNECTICUT-POLITICS AND GOVERNMENT
Caron, Denis R. Connecticut Foreclosures: An Attorney's Manual of Practice & Procedure. 2nd ed. 229p. 1982. 35.00 (ISBN 0-910051-00-3). CT Law Trib.
CONNECTIVE TISSUES
see also Collagen
Wagner, Bernard M. & Fleischmajer, Paul. Connective Tissue & Diseases of Connective Tissue. (International Academy of Pathology: No. 24). (Illus.). 246p. 1983. lib. bdg. price not set (ISBN 0-683-08601-4). Williams & Wilkins.
CONNECTIVE TISSUES-DISEASES
Wagner, Bernard M. & Fleischmajer, Paul. Connective Tissue & Diseases of Connective Tissue. (International Academy of Pathology: No. 24). (Illus.). 246p. 1983. lib. bdg. price not set (ISBN 0-683-08601-4). Williams & Wilkins.
CONQUISTADORS
see America-Discovery and Exploration
CONRAD, JOSEPH, 1857-1924
Conrad, Joseph. A Personal Record. LC 82-73728. xvii, 220p. 1982. pap. 6.95 (ISBN 0-910395-05-5). Marlboro Pr.
Wilson, Edward A. Joseph Conrad. 1982. lib. bdg. 34.50 (ISBN 0-686-81917-9). Porter.
CONSCIENCE
see also Free Will and Determinism
Debus, Michael. The Search for Identity, Conscience & Rebirth. 1982. pap. 2.50 (ISBN 0-903540-59-2). St George Bk Serv.
CONSCIENTIOUS OBJECTORS
Jones, T. Canby. The Biblical Basis of Conscientious Objection. 0.50 (ISBN 0-910082-09-X). Am Pr Serv Comm.
CONSCIOUS AUTOMATA
Book, W. J., ed. Robotics Research & Advanced Applications. 1982. 50.00 (H00236). ASME.
Flora, Philip C., ed. Robotics Industry Directory, 1983. (Illus.). 250p. 1983. pap. 50.00 (ISBN 0-910747-02-4). Tech Data Corp.
Industrial Robots, International Symposium, Twelfth. Proceedings of the Twelfth International Symposium on Industrial Robots: Paris, June 9-11, 1982. 540p. 1982. 101.00 (ISBN 0-444-86471-7, North Holland). Elsevier.
Industrial Robots, 12th Intl. Symposium. Bd. with Industrial Robot Technology, 6th International Conference, June 1982, Paris, France, Proceedings. (Illus.). 540p. 1982. text ed. 115.00x (ISBN 0-903608-24-3, Pub. by IFSPUBS). Scholium Intl.
Japan Industrial Robot Association. The Robotics Industry of Japan: Today & Tomorrow. 592p. 1982. pap. 525.00 (ISBN 0-13-782102-6). P-H.
Pugh, A., ed. Robot Vision. (International Trends in Manufacturing Technology Ser.). 356p. 1983. 47.50 (ISBN 0-387-12073-4). Springer-Verlag.
Robot Vision & Sensory Controls: Proc. of the 2nd International Conference, Stuttgart, Germany November 1982. (Illus.). 386p. 1982. pap. text ed. 80.00x (ISBN 0-903608-29-4, Pub. by IFSPUBS). Scholium Intl.
CONSCIOUSNESS
see also Belief and Doubt; Conscious Automata; Gestalt Psychology; Knowledge, Theory of; Personality; Self; Subconsciousness
Childs, Michael. An Introduction to Mastery. (Orig.). 1982. pap. 10.00 (ISBN 0-910247-00-5). Source Unlimited.
Clark, John H. A Map of Mental States. (Illus.). 224p. 1983. pap. price not set (ISBN 0-7100-9235-0). Routledge & Kegan.
Crescimanno, Russell. Culture, Consciousness, & Beyond: An Introduction. LC 82-17425. 102p. (Orig.). lib. bdg. 18.75 (ISBN 0-8191-2811-2); pap. text ed. 8.00 (ISBN 0-8191-2812-0). U Pr of Amer.
Davidson, Richard J. & Schwartz, Gary E., eds. Consciousness & Self-Regulation: Advances in Research & Theory, Vol. 3. 225p. 1982. 25.00x (ISBN 0-306-41214-4, Plenum Pr). Plenum Pub.
Gross, Sri D. Consciousness: The Key to Life. LC 82-81647. (Orig.). 1982. pap. 5.95 (ISBN 0-914766-82-1, 0114). IWP Pub.
Ong, Walter J. Interfaces of the Word: Studies in the Evolution of Consciousness & Culture. LC 77-3124. 352p. 1982. pap. 8.95x (ISBN 0-8014-9240-8). Cornell U Pr.
Penfield. The Excitable Cortex in Conscious Man. 54p. 1982. 50.00x (ISBN 0-85323-241-5, Pub. by Liverpool Univ England). State Mutual Bk.
Steiner, Rudolf. The Evolution of Consciousness. Watkin, V. E. & Davy, C., trs. from Ger. 199p. 1979. pap. 7.95 (ISBN 0-85440-351-5, Pub. by Steinerbooks). Anthroposophic.
CONSCIOUSNESS, MULTIPLE
see Personality, Disorders of
CONSCIOUSNESS EXPANDING DRUGS
see Hallucinogenic Drugs
CONSCRIPTION, MILITARY
see Military Service, Compulsory
CONSERVATION EDUCATION
see Conservation of Natural Resources-Study and Teaching
CONSERVATION OF BOOKS
see Books-Conservation and Restoration
CONSERVATION OF BUILDINGS
see Architecture-Conservation and Restoration
CONSERVATION OF ENERGY RESOURCES
see Energy Conservation
CONSERVATION OF MANUSCRIPTS
see Manuscripts-Conservation and Restoration
CONSERVATION OF NATURAL RESOURCES
see also Energy Conservation; Human Ecology; Nature Conservation; Reclamation of Land; Recycling (Waste, etc.); Soil Conservation; Water; Wildlife Conservation
Allman, S. Andean & Kopp, O. W. Environmental Education: A Promise for the Future. 196p. 1981. pap. text ed. 8.95x (ISBN 0-89641-085-4). American Pr.
Andrews, Suzanna, et al, eds. The World Environment Handbook: A Directory of Government Natural Resource Management Agencies in 144 Countries. 144p. (Orig.). 1982. pap. write for info. (ISBN 0-910499-00-4). World Env Ctr.
Congressional Quarterly Inc. Staff. Earth, Energy & Environment. LC 81-12621. (Editorial Research Reports Ser.). 212p. 1977. pap. 7.50 (ISBN 0-87187-107-6). Congr Quarterly.
Cooley, Susan D. Country Walks in Connecticut: A Guide to the Nature Conservancy Preserves. (Illus.). 224p. (Orig.). 1982. pap. 6.95 (ISBN 0-910146-41-1). Appalach Mtn.
Ford, Phyllis M. Principles & Practices of Outdoor-Environment Education. LC 80-23200. 348p. 1981. text ed. 20.95 (ISBN 0-471-04768-6). Wiley.
Forest History Society. Encyclopedia of American Forest & Conservation History, 2 vols. Davis, Richard C., ed. 1983. lib. bdg. 150.00X (ISBN 0-02-919750-3). Macmillan.
Frenkiel, Francois N. & Goodall, David W. Simulation Modeling of Environmental Problems: Scope Report 9. LC 77-92369. (Scientific Committee on Problems of the Environment). 112p. 1978. 15.00x (ISBN 0-471-99580-0, Pub. by Wiley-Interscience). Wiley.
Glantz, Micheal H. & Thompson, J. Dana, eds. Resource Management & Environmental Uncertainty: Lessons from Coastal Upwelling Fisheries. LC 80-16645. (Advances in Environmental Science & Technology Ser.). 491p. 1980. 51.50x (ISBN 0-471-05984-6, Pub. by Wiley-Interscience). Wiley.
Gordimer, Nadine. The Conservationist. 1983. pap. 4.95 (ISBN 0-14-004716-6). Penguin.
Greenwald, Carol. Conservation of Our Natural Resources. (Science Ser.). 24p. (gr. 5 up). 1979. wkbk. 5.00 (ISBN 0-8209-0149-0, S-11). ESP.
Hersey, Jerry. Pollution & Our Environment. (Science Ser.). 24p. (gr. 7 up). 1977. wkbk. 5.00 (ISBN 0-8209-0154-7, S-16). ESP.
Instrumentation & Measurement for Environmental Sciences. 2nd ed. LC 82-73892. 223p. 1982. pap. 24.50 (ISBN 0-916150-48-8). Am Soc Ag Eng.
Purdom, P. Walton & Anderson, Stanley H. Environmental Science: Managing the Environment. 1983. text ed. 23.95 (ISBN 0-675-20009-1). Additional supplements may be obtained from publisher. Merrill.
Russell, Stuart H. Resource Recovery Economics: Methods for Feasibility Analysis. (Pollution Engineering & Technology Ser.: Vol. 22). (Illus.). 312p. 1982. 39.75 (ISBN 0-8247-1726-0). Dekker.
Taylor, Dean W. Endangerment Status of Lupinus Dedeckerae on the Inyo National Forest, California. (Contributions Mono Basin Research Group Ser.). (Illus.). 91p. 1981. pap. 3.25 (ISBN 0-939714-02-7). Mono Basin Res.
--Plant Checklist for the Mono Basin, California. 16p. 1981. pap. 1.25 (ISBN 0-939714-01-9). Mono Basin Res.
--Plant Checklist of the Sweetwater Mountains, Mono County, California. (Contributions Mono Basin Research Group Ser.). (Illus.). 27p. 1982. pap. 3.50 (ISBN 0-939714-05-1). Mono Basin Res.
--Riparian Vegetation of the Eastern Sierra: Ecological Effects of Stream Diversion. (Contributions Mono Basin Research Group Ser.). (Illus.). 56p. 1982. pap. 3.50 (ISBN 0-939714-04-3). Mono Basin Res.
Winkler, David W., ed. An Ecological Study of Mono Lake, California. (Illus.). 190p. 1977. pap. 7.50 (ISBN 0-939714-00-0). Mono Basin Res.
CONSERVATION OF NATURAL RESOURCES-STUDY AND TEACHING
Donaldson, George & Swan, Malcom. Administration of Eco-Education: A Handbook for Administrators of Environmental-Conservation-Outdoor Education Programs. 136p. 7.50 (ISBN 0-88314-008-X). AAHPERD.
Hackley, Sharon & Hackley, Mike. Environmental Science: Activities with Plants of the Southwest. (Illus.). 64p. 1982. workbook 6.95 (ISBN 0-9607366-6-2, KP112). Kino Pubns.
Meeker, Joseph W. The Comedy of Survival: In Search of an Environmental Ethic. (Illus.). 174p. 1980. pap. 7.95 (ISBN 0-917270-03-7). Finn Hill.
CONSERVATION OF NATURE
see Nature Conservation
CONSERVATION OF POWER RESOURCES
see Energy Conservation
CONSERVATION OF RESOURCES
see Conservation of Natural Resources
CONSERVATION OF THE SOIL
see Soil Conservation
CONSERVATION OF WATER
see Water-Conservation
CONSERVATION OF WILDLIFE
see Wildlife Conservation
CONSERVATISM
Bollier, David. Liberty & Justice for Some: Defending a Free Society from the Radical Right's Holy War on Democracy. LC 82-51019. 336p. (Orig.). 1982. pap. 8.95 (ISBN 0-8044-6060-4, Co-pub. by People for Amer Way). Ungar.
Clepper, H. Origins of American Conservation. 493p. Repr. of 1966 ed. text ed. 25.95 (ISBN 0-471-06850-0). Krieger.
Dixon, Marlene & Jonas, Susanne, eds. World Capitalist Crisis & the Rise of the Right. (Contemporary Marxism Ser.). (Illus., Orig.). 1982. pap. 6.50 (ISBN 0-89935-016-X). Synthesis Pubns.
Dworkin, Andrea. Right-Wing Women: The Politics of Domesticated Females. 256p. 1983. 14.95 (ISBN 0-698-11171-0, Coward). Putnam Pub Group.
--Right-Wing Women: The Politics of Domesticated Females. 256p. 1983. pap. 6.95 (ISBN 0-399-50671-3, Perige). Putnam Pub Group.
Kolkey, Jonathan M. The New Right, Nineteen Sixty to Nineteen Sixty-Eight: With Epilogue, 1969-1980. LC 82-23821. 416p. (Orig.). 1983. lib. bdg. 26.75 (ISBN 0-8191-2993-3); pap. text ed. 15.50 (ISBN 0-8191-2994-1). U Pr of Amer.
Medsger, Betty. Framed: The New Right Attack on Chief Justice Rose Bird & the Courts. 320p. 1983. 17.95 (ISBN 0-8298-0655-5). Pilgrim NY.
CONSERVATIVE PARTY (GREAT BRITAIN)
Norton, Philip & Aughey, Arthur. Conservatives & Conservatism. 1981. 50.00x (ISBN 0-85117-211-3, Pub. by M Temple Smith); pap. 35.00x (ISBN 0-85117-212-1). State Mutual Bk.
CONSERVATORIES
see Greenhouses
CONSOLIDATION AND MERGER OF CORPORATIONS
see also Railroads-Consolidation
Andrews, William D. & Surrey, Stanley S., eds. Proposals of the American Law Institute on Corporate Acquisitions & Dispositions & Reporter's Study on Corporate Distributions. LC 82-71580. (Federal Income Tax Project Ser.: Subchapter C). 551p. 1983. 65.00 (ISBN 0-686-82168-8, 5650). Am Law Inst.
Brozen, Yale. Mergers in Perspective. 1982. 14.95 (ISBN 0-8447-3489-6); pap. 6.95 (ISBN 0-8447-3483-7). Am Enterprise.
Goldberg, Walter H. Mergers: Motives, Modes, Methods. 350p. 1983. 29.50 (ISBN 0-89397-155-3). Nichols Pub.
CONSTABLE, JOHN, 1776-1837
Sunderland, Joan. Constable. (Phaidon Color Library). (Illus.). 84p. Date not set. 25.00 (ISBN 0-7148-2158-6, Pub. by Salem Hse Ltd); pap. 17.95 (ISBN 0-7148-2132-2). Merrimack Bk Serv.
CONSTELLATIONS
see also Stars; also names of constellations
Berger, Paul & Wadden, Douglas, eds. Photographic Constellations. (Illus., Orig.). 1983. pap. write for info. (ISBN 0-935558-10-1). Henry Art.
Vautier, Ghislaine & McLeish, Kenneth. The Way of the Stars: Greek Legends of the Constellations. (Illus.). 32p. Date not set.. 9.95 (ISBN 0-521-25061-7). Cambridge U Pr.
CONSTITUTIONAL HISTORY
see also Democracy; Political Science; Representative Government and Representation

also subdivision Constitutional History under names of countries, states, etc. e.g. Great Britian–Constitutional History

Conley, Patrick T. Rhode Island Constitutional Development, 1636-1775: A Survey. 35p. 1968. pap. 2.75 (ISBN 0-917012-42-9). RI Pubns Soc.

CONSTITUTIONAL LAW

see also Administrative Law; Citizenship; Civil Rights; Democracy; Due Process of Law; Eminent Domain; Federal Government; Judicial Review; Law–Interpretation and Construction; Legislation; Legislative Bodies; Legislative Power; Natural Law; Police Power; Representative Government and Representation; Suffrage; War and Emergency Powers also subdivision Constitutional Law under names of countries, e.g. United States–Constitutional Law

Ladenson, Robert F. A Philosophy of Free Expression & Its Constitutional Applications. LC 82-18106. (Philosophy & Society Ser.). 224p. 1983. text ed. 34.50x (ISBN 0-8476-6761-8). Rowman.

Phillips, Michael J. The Dilemma of Individualism: Status, Liberty, & American Constitutional Law. LC 82-15580. (Contributions in American Studies: No. 67). 240p. 1983. lib. bdg. 29.95 (ISBN 0-313-23690-9, KF4749). Greenwood.

CONSTITUTIONAL LAW–HISTORY

see Constitutional History

CONSTITUTIONAL LIMITATIONS

see Constitutional Law

CONSTITUTIONS

see also Constitutional History; Constitutional Law; Representative Government and Representation; also subdivision Constitutional Law under names of countries, states, etc.

Ducat, Craig R. & Chase, Harold W. Constitutional Interpretation. 3rd ed. 1550p. 1983. text ed. 27.95 (ISBN 0-314-69640-7). West Pub.

Eidlin, Fred. Constitutional Democracy: Essays in Comparative Politics. (Replica Edition Ser.). 350p. 1983. softcover 20.00x (ISBN 0-86531-948-0). Westview.

CONSTRUCTION

see Architecture; Building; Engineering

CONSTRUCTION, CONCRETE

see Concrete Construction

CONSTRUCTION, HOUSE

see House Construction

CONSTRUCTION AND INTERPRETATION (LAW)

see Law–Interpretation and Construction

CONSTRUCTION AND INTERPRETATION OF STATUTES

see Law–Interpretation and Construction

CONSTRUCTION EQUIPMENT

see also Pumping Machinery

Douglas, J. Construction Equipment Policy. 1975. text ed. 28.95 (ISBN 0-07-017658-2); instr's manual avail. (ISBN 0-07-017659-0). McGraw.

The Markets for Construction Machinery. 1981. 450.00 (ISBN 0-686-38427-X, 241). Busn Trend.

Schexnayder, C. J. Construction Equipment & Techniques for the Eighties. LC 81-71797. 404p. 1982. pap. text ed. 29.50 (ISBN 0-87262-293-2). Am Soc Civil Eng.

Shuttleworth, Riley & Verma, Kiran. Mechanical & Electrical Systems for Construction. (Construction Ser.). (Illus.). 736p. 1984. text ed. 32.95x (ISBN 0-07-057215-1, C). McGraw.

CONSTRUCTION INDUSTRY

Here are entered works dealing comprehensively with the construction business, including finance, planning, management, and skills.

see also Building; Building Trades

American Institute of Architects. AIA Metric Building & Construction Guide. Braybrooke, Susan, ed. LC 78-31997. 150p. 1980. 29.50x (ISBN 0-471-03812-1); pap. 19.50x (ISBN 0-471-03813-X, Pub. by Wiley-Interscience). Wiley.

Banz, Hans. Building Construction Details: Practical Drawings. 272p. pap. 14.95 (ISBN 0-442-21325-5). Van Nos Reinhold.

Berger & Associates Cost Consultants, Inc. The Berger Building & Design Cost File, 1983: General Construction Trades, Vol. 1. LC 83-70008. 477p. 1983. pap. 36.75 (ISBN 0-942564-02-2). Building Cost File.

Chudley. Construction Technology 2 Checkbook. Date not set. pap. text ed. 8.95. Butterworth.

--Construction Technology 4 Checkbook. 1983. text ed. write for info.; pap. text ed. write for info. (ISBN 0-408-00605-6). Butterworth.

Civitello, Andrew M., Jr. Construction Operations Manual of Policies & Procedures. LC 82-16156. 300p. 1983. looseleaf bdg. 149.50 (ISBN 0-13-168773-5, Busn). P-H.

Construction Management: The Jobs of the Superintendent. (Illus., Orig.). 1983. pap. write for info. (ISBN 0-86718-160-5). Natl Assn Home.

Davies. Construction Site: Production 4 Checkbook. 1982. text ed. 22.50 (ISBN 0-408-00675-7); pap. 12.50 (ISBN 0-408-00656-0). Butterworth.

Fullerton, R. L. & Struct, M. I. Construction Technology Level 2, Pt. 1. 160p. 1981. 36.00x (ISBN 0-291-39653-4, Pub. by Tech Pr). State Mutual Bk.

--Construction Technology Level 2, Pt. 2. 160p. 1981. 36.00x (ISBN 0-291-39654-2, Pub. by Tech Pr). State Mutual Bk.

Rudman, Jack. Federal Construction Project Coordinator. (Career Examination Ser.: C-2879). (Cloth bdg. avail. on request). pap. 14.00 (ISBN 0-8373-2879-9). Natl Learning.

Vance, Mary. Mortgage & Construction Finance: A Bibliography. (Architecture Ser.: Bibliography A-778). 57p. 1982. pap. 8.25 (ISBN 0-88066-202-6). Vance Biblios.

CONSTRUCTION INDUSTRY–ACCOUNTING

Berger & Associates Cost Consultants, Inc. The Berger Building & Design Cost File, 1983: General Construction Trades, Vol. 1. LC 83-70008. 477p. 1983. pap. 36.75 (ISBN 0-942564-02-2). Building Cost File.

Coombs, W. E. & Palmer, W. J. A Handbook of Construction Accounting & Financial Management. 3rd ed. 576p. 1983. 37.50 (ISBN 0-07-012611-9). McGraw.

Watson. Construction Cost Estimating. 1983. write for info. (ISBN 0-07-068450-2). McGraw.

CONSTRUCTION INDUSTRY–CONTRACTS AND SPECIFICATIONS

see Building–Contracts and Specifications

CONSTRUCTION INDUSTRY–ESTIMATES

see Building–Estimates

CONSTRUCTION INDUSTRY–LAW AND LEGISLATION

Shepard. California Construction Law Manual. 2nd ed. 1977. 42.00 (ISBN 0-07-000223-1). McGraw.

CONSTRUCTION INDUSTRY–MANAGEMENT

see also Building–Superintendence

Anderson, S. D. & Woodhead, R. W. Project Manpower Management: Management Process in Construction Practice. LC 80-22090. 264p. 1981. 39.95x (ISBN 0-471-95979-0, Pub. by Wiley-Interscience). Wiley.

Fisk, E. R. Construction Project Administration. 434p. 1982. text ed. 28.95 (ISBN 0-471-09186-3). Wiley.

Goldhaber, Stanley, et al. Construction Management: Principles & Practices. LC 76-58397. (Construction Management & Engineering Ser.). 450p. 1977. 39.95x (ISBN 0-471-44270-4, Pub. by Wiley-Interscience). Wiley.

Kern, Dale R., ed. Engineering & Construction Projects: The Emerging Management Roles. LC 82-70492. 336p. 1982. pap. text ed. 28.50 (ISBN 0-87262-299-1). Am Soc Civil Eng.

Management of Small Construction Firms. 240p. 1982. pap. 14.75 (ISBN 92-833-1474-3, APO126, APO). Unipub.

Volpe, S. P. Construction Management Practices. 181p. Repr. of 1972 ed. text ed. 24.50 (ISBN 0-471-91010-4). Krieger.

CONSTRUCTION MACHINERY

see Construction Equipment

CONSULAR SERVICE

see Diplomatic and Consular Service

CONSULATES

see Diplomatic and Consular Service

CONSULTANTS, BUSINESS

see Business Consultants

CONSULTATION, PSYCHIATRIC

see Psychiatric Consultation

CONSUMER ADVERTISING

see Advertising

CONSUMER BEHAVIOR

see Consumers

CONSUMER CREDIT

Chatterton, William A. Consumer & Small Business Bankruptcy: A Complete Working Guide. LC 82-12040. 256p. 1982. text ed. 89.50 (ISBN 0-87624-101-1). Inst Busn Plan.

Nunlist, Robert A. & Seibert, Joseph C. Industrial & Consumer Credit Management. 320p. 1983. text ed. 25.95 (ISBN 0-88244-258-9). Grid Pub.

CONSUMER EDUCATION

Here are entered works on the selection and most efficient use of consumer goods and services, as well as works on means and methods of educating the consumer.

see also Consumers; Consumption (Economics); Home Economics; Marketing (Home Economics); Shopping; also specific consumer problems, e.g. Food adulturation and Inspection; Installment Plan; Labels

Abate, Susan & Lucia, Nancy. Consumer Power: Classroom Resources for Consumer Education. 1983. pap. text ed. 14.95 (ISBN 0-673-16594-9). Scott F.

Best Report Staff, ed. The Book of Bests. 1983. 14.95 (ISBN 0-89696-196-6). Dodd.

Consumer Guide: 1983 Buying Guide. 1983. pap. 3.95 (ISBN 0-451-12088-4, AE2088, Sig). NAL.

Consumer Guide: 1983 Cars. 1983. pap. 3.95 (ISBN 0-451-12089-2, AE2089, Sig). NAL.

Consumers Union. Consumer Reports Buying Guide 1983. 400p. 1982. pap. 3.50 (ISBN 0-385-18349-6). Doubleday.

Cornacchia, Harold J. & Barrett, Stephen. Shopping for Health Care: The Essential Guide to Products & Services. 1982. pap. 9.95 (ISBN 0-452-25366-7, Plume). NAL.

Data Notes Publishing Staff. Aluminum Recycling: Data Notes. 30p. 1983. pap. text ed. 9.95 (ISBN 0-911569-40-5). Data Notes Pub.

--Automobile Recycling: Data Notes. 30p. pap. text ed. 9.95 (ISBN 0-911569-50-2). Data Notes Pub.

--Clothing Recycling: Data Notes. 1983. pap. text ed. 9.95 (ISBN 0-911569-49-9). Data Notes Pub.

--Directory of Flea Market Directories, Books, References. 200p. 1983. pap. text ed. 14.95 (ISBN 0-911569-57-X). Data Notes Pub.

--Equipment Recycling: Data Notes. 30p. 1983. pap. text ed. 9.95 (ISBN 0-911569-48-0). Data Notes Pub.

--Furniture Recycling: Data Notes. 30p. 1983. pap. 9.95 (ISBN 0-911569-45-6). Data Notes Pub.

--Glass Recycling: Data Notes. 30p. 1983. pap. text ed. 9.95 (ISBN 0-911569-42-1). Data Notes Pub.

--Kitchen Recycling: Data Notes. 35p. 1983. pap. text ed. 9.95 (ISBN 0-911569-51-0). Data Notes Pub.

--Metal Recycling: Data Notes. 30p. 1983. pap. text ed. 9.95 (ISBN 0-911569-44-8). Data Notes Pub.

--Paper Recycling: Data Notes. 30p. 1983. pap. text ed. 9.95 (ISBN 0-911569-41-3). Data Notes Pub.

--Rubber Recycling: Data Notes. 30p. 1983. pap. text ed. 9.95 (ISBN 0-911569-43-X). Data Notes Pub.

--Shelter Recycling: Data Notes. 30p. 1983. pap. text ed. 9.95 (ISBN 0-911569-46-4). Data Notes Pub.

--Wood Recycling: Data Notes. 30p. 1983. pap. text ed. 9.95 (ISBN 0-911569-47-2). Data Notes Pub.

Earle, Anitra. How to Live Fairly Elegantly on Virtually Nothing...in Los Angeles. LC 82-161492. 100p. (Orig.). 1982. pap. 7.95 (ISBN 0-910795-00-2). Ondine Pr.

Ellis, Iris. S. O. S.-Save on Shopping. (Orig.). Date not set. pap. price not set (ISBN 0-440-58398-5, Dell Trade Pbks). Dell.

Fowler, Gus. Getting What You Pay For. LC 82-74187. (Illus.). 248p. 1983. 10.95 (ISBN 0-9610432-1-0); pap. 9.95 (ISBN 0-9610432-0-2). Amistad Brands.

Fritchman, June & Solomon, Karey. Living Lean off the Fat of the Land. 224p. (Orig.). 1983. pap. 8.95 (ISBN 0-943914-03-5, Dist. by Kampmann & Co). Larson Pubns Inc.

Gillis, Jack. The Car Book: 1983 Models. (Illus.). 104p. 1983. pap. 6.95 (ISBN 0-525-48049-8, 0675-200). Dutton.

Goldberg, Joan R. You Can Afford a Beautiful Wedding. 160p. 1983. pap. 6.95 (ISBN 0-8092-5631-2). Contemp Bks.

Greenfield, Michael M. Consumer Transactions. (University Casebook Ser.). 729p. 1983. text ed. write for info. (ISBN 0-88277-110-8). Foundation Pr.

--Statutory Supplement to Consumer Transactions. (University Casebook Ser.). 576p. 1983. pap. text ed. write for info. (ISBN 0-88277-114-0). Foundation Pr.

Gruber, Barbara. Barbara Jean's Household Money Tips: Hundreds of Ideas for Saving Money on Food, Clothing, Decorating. 256p. 1983. pap. 7.95 (ISBN 0-525-93294-1, 0772-230). Dutton.

Husak, G. & Pahre, P. The Money Series, 11 bks. Incl. Banking. 25p. pap. text ed. 2.00 (ISBN 0-910839-18-2); Buying a House. 32p. pap. text ed. 2.00 (ISBN 0-910839-20-4); Buying Furniture for Your Home. 46p. pap. text ed. 3.00 (ISBN 0-910839-13-1); Finding a Place to Live. 28p. pap. text ed. 2.50 (ISBN 0-910839-14-X); How to Borrow Money. 39p. pap. text ed. 2.50 (ISBN 0-910839-17-4); How to Budget Your Money. 23p. pap. text ed. 2.50 (ISBN 0-910839-16-6); How to Buy Clothes. 44p. pap. text ed. 3.00 (ISBN 0-910839-12-3); How to Buy Food. 40p. pap. text ed. 3.00 (ISBN 0-910839-11-5); Insurance. 40p. pap. text ed. 2.00 (ISBN 0-910839-19-0); Where to Get Medical Help. 33p. pap. text ed. 2.50 (ISBN 0-910839-15-8). (Illus.). 28p. (gr. 7-12). 1977. tchrs' ed. 2.00 (ISBN 0-910839-21-2). Hopewell.

Kalian, Robert & Kalian, Linda. A Few Thousand of the Best Free Things in America. (Illus.). 1982. pap. 3.50. Roblin Enterprises.

King, C. D. What's That You're Eating? Food Label Language & What it Means to you. Grubb, Mary L & Grubb, John D., eds. LC 82-90187. (Illus.). 62p. 1982. pap. 3.95 (ISBN 0-9608862-0-6). C King.

Lane, Hana, ed. The World Almanac Consumer Survival Kit. 62p. (Orig.). 1983. pap. 1.50 (ISBN 0-911818-37-5). World Almanac.

Luckey, Camilla. You Can Live on Half Your Income. 192p. (Orig.). 1982. mass market pb 3.95 (ISBN 0-310-45582-0). Zondervan.

Nash, M. J. How to Save a Fortune Using Refunds & Coupons. (Orig.). 1982. pap. 5.95x (ISBN 0-934650-03-9). Sunnyside.

Newton, Harry. One Hundred-One-Saving Secrets Your Phone Company Won't Tell You. 96p. (Orig.). 1982. pap. text ed. 10.95 (ISBN 0-936648-15-5). Telecom Lib.

Pagana, Kathleen D. & Pagana, Timothy J. Understanding Medical Testing. (Medical Library). (Illus.). 272p. 1983. pap. price not set (ISBN 0-452-25404-3, 3778-3). Mosby.

Rudman, Jack. Consumer Frauds Representative. (Career Examination Ser.: C-876). (Cloth bdg. avail. on request). pap. 10.00 (ISBN 0-8373-0876-3). Natl Learning.

Trainers' Manual: Staff Training-Consumer Co-Operatives. 98p. 1981. 17.00 (ISBN 92-2-102226-9). Intl Labour Office.

Update Publicare Research Staff. Refunding Update: Notebook of Back Issues. 35p. 1983. pap. text ed. 8.00 (ISBN 0-686-38895-X). Update Pub Co.

Weatherman, H. M. Book One, Price Trends. (Illus.). 144p. 1983. pap. 5.50 (ISBN 0-913074-18-7). Weatherman.

Weatherman, Hazel M. Decorated Tumbler "PriceGuy". 128p. 1983. pap. 4.00 (ISBN 0-913074-19-5). Weatherman.

Weathermen, Hazel M. Book Two, Price Trends. (Illus.). 304p. 1982. pap. 10.50 (ISBN 0-913074-17-9). Weatherman.

CONSUMER ORGANIZATIONS

see Cooperative Societies

CONSUMER PRICE INDEX

see Cost and Standard of Living

CONSUMER PRODUCTS

see Commercial Products

CONSUMER PROTECTION

see also Consumer Education; Drugs–Adulteration and Analysis; Food Adulteration and Inspection; Product Safety

Greenfield, Michael M. Consumer Transactions. (University Casebook Ser.). 729p. 1983. text ed. write for info. (ISBN 0-88277-110-8). Foundation Pr.

--Statutory Supplement to Consumer Transactions. (University Casebook Ser.). 576p. 1983. pap. text ed. write for info. (ISBN 0-88277-114-0). Foundation Pr.

A Promise Unfulfilled: Consumer Protection. 50p. 1982. 8.00 (ISBN 0-686-81773-7). Ctr Analysis Public Issues.

Rudman, Jack. Consumer Frauds Representative. (Career Examination Ser.: C-876). (Cloth bdg. avail. on request). pap. 10.00 (ISBN 0-8373-0876-3). Natl Learning.

--Senior Consumer Affairs Investigator: Career Examination Ser. (C-2376). (Cloth bdg. avail. on request). pap. 12.00 (ISBN 0-8373-2376-2). Natl Learning.

--Senior Consumer Frauds Representative. (Career Examination Ser.: C-877). (Cloth bdg. avail. on request). pap. 12.00 (ISBN 0-8373-0877-1). Natl Learning.

Siegel, Mark A. & Jacobs, Nancy R., eds. Consumer Regulation Needed Protection or Too Much Bureaucracy. Rev. ed. (Instructional Aides Ser.). 80p. 1982. pap. text ed. 11.95 (ISBN 0-936474-23-8). Instruct Aides TX.

CONSUMER PROTECTION–LAW AND LEGISLATION

Samuel, G. H. Cases in Consumer Law. 312p. 1979. 29.00x (ISBN 0-7121-0377-5, Pub. by Macdonald & Evans). State Mutual Bk.

CONSUMERS

Here are entered works on consumer behavior. Consumers' guides are entered under Consumer Education; works on the economic theory of consumption under Consumption (economics).

see also Consumer Education; Consumer Protection; Consumption (Economics); Cooperation

Consumers Union. Top Tips from Consumer Reports: How to Do Things Better, Faster, Cheaper. 320p. (Orig.). 1983. pap. 6.70 (ISBN 0-316-15344-3). Little.

Redden, Kenneth R. & McClellan, James. Federal Regulation of Consumer-Creditor Relations: Federal Law Library. 666p. 1982. 45.00 (ISBN 0-87215-441-6). Michie-Bobbs.

Schiffman, Leon G. & Kanuk, Leslie L. Consumer Behavior. 2nd ed. 592p. 1982. 25.95 (ISBN 0-13-168880-4). P-H.

Uusitalo, Liisa. Consumer Behavior & Environmental Quality. LC 82-10686. 156p. 1982. 25.00x (ISBN 0-312-16606-0). St Martin.

CONSUMERS' GOODS

see Manufactures

CONSUMPTION (ECONOMICS)

Works designed to inform and educate the consumer are entered under the heading Consumer Education. Works on consumer behavior are entered under the heading Consumers.

see also Consumer Education; Market Surveys; Marketing; Supply and Demand

Phelps, L. Applied Consumption Analysis. 1974. 37.50 (ISBN 0-444-10663-4); pap. 18.00 (ISBN 0-444-10714-2). Elsevier.

CONTACT LENSES

Critser, James R., Jr. Prosthetics & Contact Lens. 126p. 1982. 80.00 (ISBN 0-914428-96-9, 10PC-81). Lexington Data.

McGregor, Ian P. & Gardner, Alvin F. Contact Lens Guidelines. (Allied Health Professions Monograph Ser.). 1983. write for info. (ISBN 0-87527-321-1). Green.

CONTACT PRINTS

see Blue-Prints

CONTACTORS, ELECTRIC

see Electric Contactors

CONTAGIOUS DISEASES

see Communicable Diseases

CONTAINER INDUSTRY

see also Paper Box Industry

Containerisation International Yearbook 1982. 13th ed. LC 70-617164. (Illus.). 634p. 1982. 75.00x (ISBN 0-85223-231-4). Intl Pubns Serv.

Diernisse, Villy. Retort Pouch: New Growth Industry. (Illus.). 191p. 1981. 950.00x (ISBN 0-910211-00-0). Laal Co.

CONTAINER TRANSPORTATION

see Containerization

CONTAINERIZATION
Ernst, Edgar. Fahrplanerstellung und Umlaufdisposition Im Containerschiffsverkehr. 136p. (Ger.). 1982. write for info. (ISBN 3-8204-5822-0). P Lang Pubs.
Finlay, Patrick, ed. Jane's Freight Containers 1983. 15th ed. (Jane's Yearbooks). (Illus.). 640p. 1983. 140.00x (ISBN 0-86720-642-X). Sci Bks Intl.
CONTAINERS, PRESSURIZED
see *Pressure Vessels*
CONTAMINATION OF ENVIRONMENT
see *Pollution*
CONTEMPLATION (HINDUISM)
see *Samadhi*
CONTEMPORARY ART
see *Art, Modern–20th Century*
CONTEMPT OF THE WORLD
see *Asceticism*
CONTESTS
see *Rewards (Prizes, etc.)*
CONTINENTAL CONGRESS
see *United States–Continental Congress*
CONTINENTAL DISPLACEMENT
see *Continental Drift*
CONTINENTAL DRIFT
see also *Submarine Geology*
Miller, Russell. Continents in Collision. (Planet Earth Ser.). 1983. lib. bdg. 19.92 (ISBN 0-8094-4325-2, Pub. by Time-Life). Silver.
CONTINENTS
see also *Continental Drift*
Updegraffe, Imelda & Updegraffe, Robert. Continents & Climates. (Turning Points Ser.). (Illus.). 24p. 1983. pap. 3.50 (ISBN 0-14-049188-0, Puffin). Penguin.
CONTINGENT FEES
see *Lawyers–Fees*
CONTINUING EDUCATION CENTERS
Data Notes Publishing Staff. One Thousand & More Places to Look for Continuing Education. 200p. 1983. text ed. 49.95 (ISBN 0-911569-05-7). Data Notes Pub.
Lenz, E. Creating & Marketing Programs in Continuing Education. 1980. 18.95 (ISBN 0-07-037190-3). McGraw.
CONTINUUM MECHANICS
see also *Field Theory (Physics); Fluid Mechanics; Magnetohydrodynamics; Sound*
Santilli, R. M. Foundations of Theoretical Mechanics II: Birkhoffian Generalization of Hamiltonian Mechanics. (Texts & Monographs in Physics). 370p. 1983. 66.00 (ISBN 0-387-09482-2). Springer-Verlag.
Ziegler. An Introduction to Thermomechanics. (Series in Applied Mathematics & Mechanics: Vol. 21). Date not set. 68.00 (ISBN 0-444-86503-9, North Holland). Elsevier.
CONTINUUM PHYSICS
see *Field Theory (Physics)*
CONTRACEPTION
see also *Birth Control; Contraceptives; Sterilization (Birth Control)*
Hatcher, Richard, et al. It's Your Choice: A Personal Guide to Birth Control Methods for Women... & Men, Too! Stoner, Carol, ed. (Illus.). 144p. (Orig.). 1983. pap. 7.95 (ISBN 0-87857-471-9, 05-172-1). Rodale Pr Inc.
Hatcher, Robert A. & Josephs, Nancy. It's Your Choice: A Personal Guide to Birth Control Methods for Women... & Men Too! (Illus.). 140p. 1983. text ed. 16.95x. Irvington.
Langley, L. L., ed. Contraception. LC 73-4256. (Benchmark Papers in Human Physiology: Vol. 2). 500p. 1973. text ed. 55.00 (ISBN 0-87933-025-2). Hutchinson Ross.
Ramirez de Arellano, Annette B. & Seipp, Conrad. Colonialism, Catholicism, & Contraception: A History of Birth Control in Puerto Rico. LC 82-13646. 290p. 1983. 24.00x (ISBN 0-8078-1544-6). U of NC Pr.
Stevens, Ella. Sex Education: Contraception. (Michigan Learning Module Ser.). 1979. write for info. (ISBN 0-914004-37-9). Ulrich.
CONTRACEPTIVES
see also *Oral Contraceptives*
Harper, Michael J. Birth Control Technologies: Prospects by the Year 2000. (Illus.). 288p. 1983. text ed. 27.50x (ISBN 0-292-70739-8). U of Tex Pr.
Hatcher, Richard, et al. It's Your Choice: A Personal Guide to Birth Control Methods for Women... & Men, Too! Stoner, Carol, ed. (Illus.). 144p. (Orig.). 1983. pap. 7.95 (ISBN 0-87857-471-9, 05-172-1). Rodale Pr Inc.
Kleinman, Robert L., ed. Directory of Contraceptives-Repertoire des Contraceptifs-Guia de Anticonceptivos. 3rd ed. (International Planned Parenthood Federation Medical Publications). 95p. (Orig., Eng., Fr. & Span.). 1981. pap. 12.50x (ISBN 0-86089-043-0). Intl Pubns Serv.
McDaniel, Edwin B., ed. Second Asian Regional Workshop on Injectable Contraceptives. (Illus.). 93p. 1982. pap. 5.00 (ISBN 0-942716-04-3). World Neigh.
CONTRACEPTIVES, ORAL
see *Oral Contraceptives*

CONTRACT BRIDGE
Kelsey, Hugh. Start Bridge the Easy Way. (Master Bridge Ser.). 96p. 1983. pap. 8.95 (ISBN 0-575-03254-5, Pub. by Gollancz England). David & Charles.
Klinger, Ron. World Championship Pairs Bridge. 160p. 1983. 16.50 (ISBN 0-575-03233-2, Pub. by Gollancz England). David & Charles.
Lawrence, Mike. The Complete Book on Hand Evaluation in Contract Bridge. 1983. pap. 8.95 (ISBN 0-939460-28-9). M Hardy.
McVey, Mary A. Bridge Basics: An Introduction to the Game. 2d ed. 120p. 1982. pap. 5.50x (ISBN 0-910475-01-6). KET.
Mollo, Victor. Bridge a la Carte. 144p. 1983. 16.95 (ISBN 0-7207-1385-4, Pub by Michael Joseph). Merrimack Bk Serv.
North, Freddie. Bridge with Aunt Agatha. 208p. 1983. 14.95 (ISBN 0-571-13012-7); pap. 7.95 (ISBN 0-571-13014-3). Faber & Faber.
Reese, Terence & Bird, David. Bridge: The Modern Game. 256p. 1983. 15.95 (ISBN 0-571-13053-4). Faber & Faber.
Sharif, Omar. Omar Sharif's Life in Bridge. Reese, Terence, tr. from French. 144p. 1983. pap. 6.95 (ISBN 0-571-13098-4). Faber & Faber.
Squire, Norman. A Guide to Bridge Conventions. 2nd ed. 100p. 1979. pap. 4.95 (ISBN 0-7156-1426-6). US Games Syst.
Squires, Norman. Squeeze Play Simplified. 184p. 1979. pap. 5.95 (ISBN 0-7156-1348-0). US Games Syst.
CONTRACT BRIDGE–PROGRAMMED INSTRUCTION
Marsh, Carole. Six Puppy Feet: Bridge for Kids. (Tomorrow's Bks.). (Illus.). 48p. 1983. 3.95 (ISBN 0-935326-13-8). Gallopade Pub Group.
CONTRACT RESEARCH
see *Research and Development Contracts*
CONTRACTILITY (BIOLOGY)
Stracher, Alfred, ed. Muscle & Non-Muscle Motility, Vol. 1. LC 82-11567. (Molecular Biology Ser.). Date not set. price not set (ISBN 0-12-673001-6); price not set Vol. 2 (ISBN 0-12-673002-4). Acad Pr.
CONTRACTING PARTIES TO THE GENERAL AGREEMENT ON TARIFFS AND TRADE
Gatt Status of Legal Instruments. 120p. 1983. pap. 6.50 (ISBN 0-686-42850-1, G154, GATT). Unipub.
Hanson, Gote. Social Clauses & International Trade. LC 82-42563. 1982. 22.50x (ISBN 0-312-73162-0). St Martin.
CONTRACTIONS
see *Abbreviations; Ciphers*
CONTRACTORS OPERATIONS–ACCOUNTING
see *Construction Industry–Accounting*
CONTRACTS
see also *Authors and Publishers; Compromise (Law); Debtor and Creditor; Labor Contract; Leases; Liability (Law); Mortgages; Negotiable Instruments; Partnership; Public Contracts; Research and Development Contracts; Sales*
also subdivision Contracts and Specifications under particular subjects, e.g. Building–Contracts and Specifications
Hirsch, William J. The Contracts Management Deskbook: For Buyers & Sellers in Business, Industry, & Government. 256p. 1983. 29.95 (ISBN 0-8144-5759-2). Am Mgmt Assns.
Lakin, Leonard & Beane, Leona. Materials in the Law of Business Contracts. 352p. 1982. pap. text ed. 9.50 (ISBN 0-8403-2825-7). Kendall-Hunt.
McGonagle, John J. Business Agreements: A Complete Guide to Oral & Written Contracts. LC 82-71298. (Illus.). 256p. 1982. 27.50 (ISBN 0-8019-7223-X). Chilton.
Norris, Jeffrey A. Contract Compliance under the Reagan Administration: A Practitioner's Guide to Current Use of the OFCCP Compliance Manual. 520p. (Orig.). 1982. pap. 24.95 (ISBN 0-937856-05-3). Equal Employ.
North, P. M., ed. Contract Conflicts: The EEC Convention on the Law Applicable to Contractual Obligations; a Comparative Study. 404p. 1982. 49.00 (ISBN 0-686-82017-7, North Holland). Elsevier.
Rudman, Jack. Contracts Examiner. (Career Examination Ser.: C-888). (Cloth bdg. avail. on request). pap. 10.00 (ISBN 0-8373-0888-7). Natl Learning.
--Contracts Technician. (Career Examination Ser.: C-834). (Cloth bdg. avail. on request). pap. 10.00 (ISBN 0-8373-0834-8). Natl Learning.
Sawyer, J. G. & Gillott, C. A. The FIDIC Conditions Digest of Contractual Relationships & Responsibilities. 120p. 1981. pap. 50.00x (ISBN 0-7277-0127-4, Pub. by Telford England). State Mutual Bk.
Silberberg, H. The German Standard Contracts Act. 124p. 1979. 75.00 (ISBN 0-7121-5485-X, Pub. by Macdonald & Evans). State Mutual Bk.
Summer Institute on International & Comparative Law. Lectures on the Conflict of Laws & International Contracts. LC 51-62311. (Michigan Legal Studies). xiv, 200p. 1982. Repr. of 1951 ed. lib. bdg. write for info. (ISBN 0-89941-177-0). W S Hein.
Suter, Erich. Contracts at Work. 276p. 1982. pap. text ed. 33.50x (ISBN 0-85292-297-3, Pub by Inst Personnel Mgmt England). Renouf.

CONTRACTS–FORMS
Adams, Paul. The Complete Legal Guide for Your Small Business. LC 81-11445. (Small Business Management Ser.). 218p. 1982. 19.95 (ISBN 0-471-09436-6). Ronald Pr.
CONTRACTS, GOVERNMENT
see *Public Contracts*
CONTRACTS, PUBLIC
see *Public Contracts*
CONTRACTUAL LIMITATIONS
see *Contracts*
CONTRAHOMOLOGY THEORY
see *Homology Theory*
CONTRARIETY
see *Opposition, Theory of*
CONTRITION
see *Penance*
CONTROL (PSYCHOLOGY)
Forbes, Cheryl. The Religion of Power. 176p. 1983. 9.95 (ISBN 0-310-45770-X). Zondervan.
CONTROL, INVENTORY
see *Inventory Control*
CONTROL, PRODUCTION
see *Production Control*
CONTROL BIOPHYSICS
see *Biological Control Systems*
CONTROL ENGINEERING
see *Automatic Control*
CONTROL EQUIPMENT
see *Automatic Control*
CONTROL OF FUMES
see *Fume Control*
CONTROL OF INDUSTRIAL PROCESSES
see *Process Control*
CONTROL OF PESTS
see *Pest Control*
CONTROL SYSTEMS, BIOLOGICAL
see *Biological Control Systems*
CONTROL SYSTEMS, CARRIER
see *Carrier Control Systems*
CONTROL THEORY
see also *Automatic Control; Biological Control Systems*
Apte, Y. S. Linear Multivariable Control Theory. 1982. 9.95x (ISBN 0-07-451512-8). McGraw.
Bell, D. J. & Cook, P. A., eds. Design of Modern Control Systems. (IEE Control Engineering Ser.: No. 20). 400p. 1982. pap. 49.50 (ISBN 0-906048-74-5). Inst Elect Eng.
Findeisen, W., et al. Control & Coordination in Hierarchical Systems. (IIASA International Ser. on Applied Systems Analysis: No. 9). 469p. 1980. 63.95x (ISBN 0-471-27742-8). Wiley.
Gupta, Someshwar C. & Hasdorff, Lawrence. Fundamentals of Automatic Control. LC 82-20338. 602p. 1983. Repr. of 1970 ed. lib. bdg. write for info. (ISBN 0-89874-578-0). Krieger.
Leigh, J. R. Applied Control Theory. (IEE Control Engineering Ser.: No. 18). 192p. 1982. 56.00 (ISBN 0-906048-72-9). Inst Elect Eng.
Murata, Yasuo. Optimal Control Methods for Linear Discrete-Time Economic Systems. (Illus.). 175p. 1982. 34.00 (ISBN 0-387-90709-2). Springer-Verlag.
Tzafestas, S. G., ed. Distributed Parameter Control Systems: Theory & Application. (International Series on Systems & Control: Vol. 6). 525p. 1982. 60.00 (ISBN 0-08-027624-5). Pergamon.
CONTROLLED ACCESS HIGHWAYS
see *Express Highways*
CONTROLLED FUSION
World Survey of Major Activities in Controlled Fusion Research, 1982 Edition, Special Supplement 1982. 419p. 1983. pap. 49.00 (ISBN 92-0-139082-3, ISP23/82, IAEA). Unipub.
CONTROLLED RELEASE PREPARATIONS
see *Delayed-Action Preparations*
CONTROLLERS, ELECTRIC
see *Electric Controllers*
CONTROLLERSHIP
see also *Accounting; Auditing; Budget in Business*
Jones, Graham. Financial Practice & Control. 250p. 1982. pap. text ed. 12.95x (ISBN 0-7121-0640-5). Intl Ideas.
CONUNDRUMS
see *Riddles*
CONVENTIONS
see *Treaties*
CONVENTIONS (CONGRESSES)
see *Congresses and Conventions*
CONVENTIONS, POLITICAL
see *Political Conventions*
CONVERGENCE
see also *Asymptotic Expansions*
Ferrar, W. L. A Textbook of Convergence. (Illus.). 200p. 1980. Repr. of 1938 ed. 15.95x (ISBN 0-19-853176-1). Oxford U Pr.
CONVERSATION
Adler, Mortimer J. How to Speak-How to Listen: A Guide to Pleasurable & Profitable Conversation. (Illus.). 288p. 1983. 12.95 (ISBN 0-02-500570-7). Macmillan.
Kleiser, Grenville. How to Improve Your Conversation: An Aid to Social & Business Success. 267p. 1982. Repr. of 1932 ed. lib. bdg. 25.00 (ISBN 0-8495-3136-5). Arden Lib.
Lehrer, Adrienne. Wine & Conversation. LC 82-48538. 256p. 1983. 25.00x (ISBN 0-253-36550-3). Ind U Pr.

Walters, Barbara. How to Talk with Practically Anybody about Practically Anything. LC 82-45618. 216p. 1983. pap. 6.95 (ISBN 0-385-18334-8, Dolp). Doubleday.
CONVERSION
see also *Christianity–Psychology; Converts; Grace (Theology); Salvation*
Brancaforte, Benito. Guzman de Alfarache: conversion o proceso de degradacion? vi, 230p. 1980. 11.00 (ISBN 0-942260-14-7). Hispanic Seminary.
CONVERSION OF WASTE PRODUCTS
see *Recycling (Waste, etc.); Salvage (Waste, etc.)*
CONVERT MAKING
see *Evangelistic Work*
CONVERTER REACTORS
see *Breeder Reactors*
CONVERTS
see also *Buddhist converts, Muslim converts, etc. for works on converts to religions other than Christianity*
Fox, James. Comeback: An Actor's Direction. 224p. 1983. 9.95 (ISBN 0-8028-3585-6). Eerdmans.
Simonsen, Sharon. God Never Slept. (Daybreak Ser.). 78p. Date not set. pap. 3.95 (ISBN 0-8163-0472-6). Pacific Pr Pub Assn.
CONVEYING MACHINERY
American Chain Association, compiled by. Chains for Power Transmission & Materials Handling: Design & Applications Handbook. (Mechanical Engineering Ser.: Vol. 18). (Illus.). 368p. 1982. 35.00 (ISBN 0-8247-1701-5). Dekker.
CONVICTION
see *Belief and Doubt; Truth*
CONVICTS
see *Prisoners*
COOK, JAMES, 1728-1779
Bott, Elizabeth. Tongan Society at the Time of Captain Cook's Visits: Discussions with Her Majesty Queen Salote Tupou. 187p. 1983. pap. text ed. 15.00x (ISBN 0-8248-0864-9). UH Pr.
COOK-BOOKS
see *Cookery*
COOKERY
see also *Baking; Bread; Breakfasts; Cake; Canning and Preserving; Caterers and Catering; Christmas Cookery; Confectionery; Cookery, Casserole; Desserts; Diet; Dinners and Dining; Food; Food Processor Cookery; Luncheons; Menus; Pastry; Quantity Cookery; Salads; Sandwiches; Sauces; Souffles; Soups; Vegetarian Cookery*
Ackerman, Carolyn. Cooking with Kids. 76p. 1982. pap. 5.50 (ISBN 0-87659-104-7). Gryphon Hse.
Adams, Charlotte. The ABC's of Cooking. LC 82-45139. (Illus.). 256p. 1983. 12.95 (ISBN 0-385-18512-X). Doubleday.
Aihara, Cornellia, intro. by. The Do of Cooking. 230p. 1982. pap. 19.95 (ISBN 0-918860-39-3). G Ohsawa.
Arant, Olive G., illus. Magic: The Cookbook of the Junior League of Birmingham. 2nd ed. LC 81-85953. (Illus.). 348p. 1982. 9.95 (ISBN 0-686-38454-7). Jr League Birm.
Armentani, Andy & Donatelli, Gary. The Monday Night Football Cookbook & Restaurant Guide. LC 82-71965. (Illus.). 176p. 1982. pap. 9.95 (ISBN 0-8019-7270-1). Chilton.
Bates, William. The Computer Cookbook. (Illus.). 1983. 21.95 (ISBN 0-13-164558-7); pap. 12.95 (ISBN 0-13-165167-6). P-H.
Beeton, Isabella M. Mrs. Beeton's Cookery & Household Management. Rev. ed. LC 64-3849. (Illus.). 1606p. 1982. Repr. of 1980 ed. 37.50x (ISBN 0-7063-5743-4). Intl Pubns Serv.
Benenson, Sharen. The New York Botanical Garden Cookbook. (Illus.). 256p. 1982. 16.95 (ISBN 0-686-83750-9). Hastings.
Benham, Phyllis S. Woodstove Cookery Cookbook: Soups, Stews, Chowders & Home-Made Breads, Vol. 2. 54p. 1981. pap. 3.95 (ISBN 0-686-81745-1). Country Cooking.
Better Homes & Gardens Books editors, ed. Better Homes & Gardens My Recipe Collection. (Illus.). 142p. 1983. 12.95 (ISBN 0-696-01070-4). Meredith Corp.
--Better Homes & Gardens My Turn to Cook. (Illus.). 96p. 1983. pap. 4.95 (ISBN 0-696-00875-0). Meredith Corp.
Better Homes & Gardens Editors. Better Homes & Gardens New Cook Book. 960p. 1982. pap. 4.50 (ISBN 0-553-22528-6). Bantam.
Bibliotheca Press Staff. Cookbooks & Recipes for Almost Nothing & More. 75p. 1983. pap. text ed. 9.95 (ISBN 0-939476-67-3). Biblio Pr GA.
Bingham, Joan & Riccio, Dolores. The Smart Shopper's Guide to Food Buying & Preparation. 320p. 1983. pap. 6.95 (ISBN 0-686-83711-8, ScribT). Scribner.
Bornschlegel, Ruth. More Fast & Fresh. LC 82-824814. (Illus.). 240p. 1983. pap. 14.95 (ISBN 0-686-42800-5, HarpT). Har-Row.
Brown, Mary K. Aunt Mary's Kitchen Cookbook. (Illus.). 224p. 1983. pap. 6.95 (ISBN 0-02-009320-9, Collier). Macmillan.
Brown, Richard & Cook, Melva. Special Occasion Cookbook. 1983. 9.95 (ISBN 0-8054-7001-8). Broadman.
Buckminster Staff. Synergetic Stew: Explorations in Dymaxion Dining. 120p. (Orig.). 1982. 6.95 (ISBN 0-911573-00-3). Buckminster Fuller.

Burbach, Hal. Especially for Him. LC 82-50937. (Illus.). 236p. (Orig.). 1982. pap. 7.95 (ISBN 0-942320-03-4). WRC Pub.

Burmeister, Jill & Hutchinson, Rosemary, eds. Better Homes & Gardens Complete Quick & Easy Cook Book. 1983. 24.95 (ISBN 0-696-00725-8). Meredith Corp.

Cadwallader, Sharon. The Living Kitchen. LC 82-10763. (Tools for Today Ser.). (Illus.). 128p. (Orig.). 1983. pap. 7.95 (ISBN 0-87156-326-6). Sierra.

--The Living Kitchen. (Tools for Today Ser.). 1983. pap. 6.95 (ISBN 0-686-84928-0). Sierra.

Calwallader, S. Sharing in the Kitchen. 1979. pap. 5.95 (ISBN 0-07-009528-0). McGraw.

Capossela, Jim & Capossela, Josephine. Festive Christmas Recipes. 36p. 1982. pap. 1.95 (ISBN 0-942990-04-8). Northeast Sportsmans.

Center for Self-Sufficiency Research Division. The Alternative Cooking Facilities Cookbook. 50p. 1983. pap. text ed. 12.95 (ISBN 0-910811-08-3). Center Self.

--Made from Scratch: A Reference on Cooking, Crafts, etc. 50p. Date not set. pap. text ed. 14.95 (ISBN 0-910811-07-5). Center Self.

Center For Self Sufficiency Research Division Staff. One Thousand & More Places to Find Free & Almost Free Recipes. 200p. 1983. pap. text ed. 12.95 (ISBN 0-910811-13-X). Center Self.

Cioffredi, Peg & Cioffredi, Terry. These Guys Can Cook! 96p. (Orig.). 1982. pap. 4.95 (ISBN 0-686-82510-1). Elijah Pr.

Claiborne, Craig & Franey, Pierre. The Spiral Cooking Course. (Illus.). 128p. 1982. 15.95 (ISBN 0-686-82376-1, Perige); spiral bdg. 9.95 (ISBN 0-399-50586-5). Putnam Pub Group.

Consumer Guide Publications International Editors. Favorite Brands Name Recipes, Soups & Sandwiches. 144p. (Orig.). 1982. pap. 2.50 (ISBN 0-449-24571-3, Crest). Fawcett.

Cookbook Committee of Lutheran General Hospital. Cooking in General. 350p. 1978. 10.00 (ISBN 0-686-82545-4). Serv League IL.

Cooking & Memories. (People's Place Booklet Ser.: No. 5). (Illus.). 96p. (Orig.). 1983. pap. write for info. Good Bks PA.

Corbett, Tiffany K. & Taylor, Susan H., eds. For Hospitality's Sake. LC 81-86664. (Illus.). 275p. 1982. pap. 8.95 (ISBN 0-9608052-0-6). Summit Jr Fort.

Dannenbaum, Julie. More Fast & Fresh. LC 82-48114. (Illus.). 256p. 1983. 14.37i (ISBN 0-06-015084-X, HarpT). Har-Row.

Don't Lick the Spoon Before You Put it in the Pot. 1982. 7.50 (ISBN 0-939418-46-0). Ferguson-Florissant.

Eckley, Mary & Norton, Mary J. McCall's Cooking School. 1982. pap. 7.95 (ISBN 0-394-73281-2). Random.

Edge, Nellie. May I Have That Recipe? Martin, Paul J., ed. LC 82-61483. (Illus.). 132p. (Orig.). 1982. pap. 7.95 (ISBN 0-918146-24-0). Peninsula WA.

Elliot, Sharon. The Busy People's Naturally Nutritious Decidedly Delicious Fast Food Book. LC 83-3055. (Illus.). 120p. (Orig.). 1983. pap. 6.95 (ISBN 0-8069-7732-9). Sterling.

Ewalt, Norma & Huth, Tom. Decadent Dinners & Lascivious Lunches. LC 82-71880. (Illus.). 320p. 1982. 10.95 (ISBN 0-686-82435-0). Clear Creek.

Family Circle Holiday Cookbook. (Illus.). 128p. 1982. pap. 5.95 (ISBN 0-8249-3014-2). Ideals.

First You Make a Roux. 20th ed. 48p. pap. 2.50 (ISBN 0-9608412-0-2). Lafayette Mus.

Franey, Pierre. The New York Times More 60-Minute Gourmet. 1983. pap. 7.95 (ISBN 0-449-90038-X, Columbine). Fawcett.

Fuller, John & Renold, Edward. Chef's Compendium of Professional Recipes. 1972. 14.95 (ISBN 0-434-90583-6, Pub. by Heinemann). David & Charles.

Gottsegen, Katherine. Cooking Is an Act of Love. (Illus.). 165p. (Orig.). 1983. 8.95 (ISBN 0-686-38740-6). Buckminster Pr.

Grant, Rose. Fast & Delicious Cookbook. LC 81-81484. (Illus.). 183p. (Orig.). 1981. pap. 5.95 (ISBN 0-911954-62-7). Nitty Gritty.

Grosser, Arthus E. The Cookbook Decoder. 304p. 1983. pap. 3.50 (ISBN 0-446-30605-3). Warner Bks.

Hall, Maureen & Reilly, Cari. The Gut Course in College Cookery. LC 82-61570. (Illus.). 250p. 1982. 9.95 (ISBN 0-910963-00-2). Mercury Bks.

Hecht, Helen. Cuisine for All Seasons. LC 82-73033. 320p. 1983. 12.95 (ISBN 0-689-11351-X). Atheneum.

Hildebrandt, Rita. The Rita & Timonthy Hildebrandt Fantasy Cookbook. new ed. 128p. 1983. 14.95 (ISBN 0-672-52703-0). Bobbs.

The I'm in the Mood For Cookbook. 1982. 11.95 (ISBN 0-911974-29-6). Hopkinson.

Johnson, Carlean. Six Ingredients or Less. (Illus.). 224p. pap. 8.95 (ISBN 0-942878-00-0). C J Bks.

Jones, Jeanne & Swajeski, Donna. The Love in the Afternoon Cookbook: Recipes from Your Favorite ABC-TV Soap Operas - Ryans Hope, One Life to Live, All My Children, General Hospital. (Illus.). 192p. 1983. pap. 7.95 (ISBN 0-87131-405-3). M Evans.

Junior League of San Antonio. Flavors: The Junior League of San Antonio. LC 77-88731. (Illus.). 426p. 1982. 14.95 (ISBN 0-9610416-0-9). Jr League Antonio.

Junior League of Tyler, Inc., ed. Cooking Through Rose Colored Glasses. (Illus.). 426p. 1975. pap. 7.95 (ISBN 0-9607122-0-8). Jr League Tyler.

Kay, Sophie. One-Dish Meals. (Illus.). 64p. 1982. pap. 3.25 (ISBN 0-8249-3012-6). Ideals.

Kennedy, E. Cooking for Love...& Money. 176p. 1982. 10.95 (ISBN 0-932620-12-4, Pub. by Betterway Pubns); pap. 6.95 (ISBN 0-932620-11-6). Berkshire Traveller.

The Kitchen Aid Cookbook. 1983. 12.95 (ISBN 0-911974-30-X). Hopkinson.

Klungness, Elizabeth J. & Klungness, James G. The Nongolfer's Cookbook. (Illus.). 160p. Date not set. pap. 5.95 (ISBN 0-910431-00-0). Tower Ent.

Kowtaluk, Helen. The Cook's Problem Solver. 296p. (Orig.). 1983. pap. 8.95 (ISBN 0-910469-00-8). IAM Ent.

Kump, Peter. Quiche & Pate. LC 82-47862. (Great American Cooking Schools Ser.). (Illus.). 84p. 1982. 8.61i (ISBN 0-06-015067-X, HarpT). Har-Row.

Lamm, Joanne. The Quarter of Six Cookbook. 96p. 1982. 4.95 (ISBN 0-932128-03-3). Lamm Morada.

Langley, Nadine. Your Favorite Recipes. 225p. (Orig.). 1982. pap. 5.00 (ISBN 0-932970-32-X). Prinit Pr.

Leith, Prudence & Waldegrave, Caroline. Leith's Cookery Course: A Guide to Perfect Cooking. (Illus.). 1982. 24.95 (ISBN 0-233-97153-X, Pub. by Salem Hse Ltd). Merrimack Bk Serv.

Louis, Dorothy. My Father, the Chef. (Illus.). 148p. (Orig.). 1978. pap. 6.00 (ISBN 0-9609624-0-9). Bookworm NY.

Lovelace, Alice. The Kitchen Survival Almanac. Johnson, Sylvia L. & Lanier, Linda K., eds. (Illus.). 500p. (Orig.). Date not set. pap. 9.95 (ISBN 0-942050-04-5). Southern-Lite.

Mannix, Jeffrey. Food Combining: The Revolutionary Diet Plan for Health & Longevity. 160p. 1983. 13.95 (ISBN 0-8092-5662-2). Contemp Bks.

Martland, Richard E. & Welsby, Derek A. Basic Cookery. 1980. pap. 12.50 (ISBN 0-434-92232-3, Pub. by Heinemann). David & Charles.

Media Publications Staff. More of the World's Best Recipes. Everest, Anne, ed. 1983. pap. 12.95 (ISBN 0-943214-04-1). Media Pubns.

Meyman, Jay. The Gourmet Guide to Water Cookery. 128p. 1983. pap. 4.95 (ISBN 0-380-81935-X, 81935-X). Avon.

Mitchell, Susan. Thirty Minute Meals. Coolman, Anne L., ed. LC 82-82158. (Illus.). 96p. 1982. pap. 5.95 (ISBN 0-89721-006-9). Ortho.

Morgan, Jinx & Morgan, Jefferson. Two Cooks In One Kitchen. LC 81-43573. 256p. 1983. 19.95 (ISBN 0-385-17462-4). Doubleday.

Muhaiyaddeen, Bawa M. A Tasty Economical Cookbook, Vol. 2. Toomey, Lauren, ed. (Illus.). 166p. 1983. price not set spiral (ISBN 0-914390-22-8). Fellowship Pr Pa.

Munson, Shirley & Nelson, Jo. Cooking with Apples. LC 75-18210. 128p. (Orig.). 1975. pap. 3.95 (ISBN 0-89795-016-X). Farm Journal.

Naxon, Jan L. & Rosenthal, Beth E. Dallas Entrees: A Restaurant Guide & Celebrity Cookbook (with a Primer to California Wines) 144p. (Orig.). 1982. pap. 5.95 (ISBN 0-910163-00-6). Artichoke Pub.

New Alchemy Staff. Gardening for All Seasons: How to Feed Your Family from Your Own Garden Twelve Months a Year. (Illus.). 320p. 1983. pap. 10.95 (ISBN 0-931790-56-5). Brick Hse Pub.

New Junior Cook Book. pap. 5.95 (ISBN 0-696-01145-X). Meredith Corp.

Nitty Gritty Productions, ed. Family Favorites. (Illus.). 192p. (Orig.). 1981. pap. 4.95 (ISBN 0-911954-61-9). Nitty Gritty.

--My Cookbook. (Illus.). 192p. (Orig.). 1981. pap. 4.95 (ISBN 0-911954-60-0). Nitty Gritty.

O'Connor, Hyla. Cooking on Your Wood Stove. (Illus.). 78p. 1981. pap. 5.95 (ISBN 0-9608050-0-1). Turkey Hill Pr.

Olney, Judith. Summer Food. LC 77-15870. 272p. 1983. pap. 7.95 (ISBN 0-689-70643-X, 292). Atheneum.

Patten, Marguerite. Marguerite Patten's Sunday Lunch Cookbook. (Illus.). 120p. 14.95 (ISBN 0-7153-8381-7). David & Charles.

Price, Christene, ed. Food for the Senses: Recipes & Artwork from the Esalen Community. (Illus.). 120p. (Orig.). 1982. pap. 5.95. C Price.

Pryor, Harold, ed. James K. Polk Cookbook. Armstrong, Emma P. LC 78-60329. (Illus.). 254p. 1978. pap. 7.95 (ISBN 0-9607668-0-4). James K Polk.

Redman, Scott. Real Men Don't Cook Quiche: The Real Man's Cookbook. Feirstein, Bruce, ed. (Illus., Orig.). 1982. pap. 3.95 (ISBN 0-671-46308-X). PB.

Regent House, ed. Sugarless Recipes Cookbook. 88p. 1983. pap. 7.95 (ISBN 0-911238-71-9). Regent House.

Riggs, Karen B. The Preppy Chef. (Illus.). 237p. 1982. 7.00 (ISBN 0-686-37893-8). Riggs.

Rosencrans, Joyce. A Cook for All Seasons. (Illus.). 320p. (Orig.). 1982. pap. 7.95x (ISBN 0-933002-02-5). Cin Post.

Ross, Bow. Cooking Amid Chaos. 1983. pap. 7.95 (ISBN 0-89272-168-5). Down East.

Sax, Richard & Ricketts, David. Cooking Great Meals Every Day: Techniques, Recipes & Variations. 320p. 1982. 15.95 (ISBN 0-394-51601-X). Random.

Senderens, Alain. The Three-Star Recipes of Alain Senderens. Hyman, Philip & Hyman, Mary, trs. LC 82-6488. (Illus.). 352p. 1982. 22.50 (ISBN 0-688-00728-7). Morrow.

Shepard, Judith. More Food of My Friends: Their Favorite Recipes. LC 82-84010. 176p. (Orig.). 1983. pap. 8.95 (ISBN 0-932966-29-2). Permanent Pr.

Smith, Cathy. Food One Hundred One: A Student Guide to Quick & Easy Cooking. (Illus.). 155p. 1982. 7.95 (ISBN 0-914718-75-4). Pacific Search.

Solomon, C. The Complete Curry Cookbook. 13.95 (ISBN 0-07-059639-5). McGraw.

Stat, Bob & Stat, Susan. Complete Chocolate Chip Cookie Book. (Illus.). 128p. 1982. pap. 4.95 (ISBN 0-440-01273-2, Banbury). Dell.

Stendahl. The Full Flavor Cookbook. LC 82-184519. (Illus.). 160p. 1983. pap. 6.95 (ISBN 0-89709-043-8). Liberty Pub.

Sunset Books & Sunset Magazine, ed. Easy Basics for Good Cooking. LC 82-81368. (Illus.). 192p. (Orig.). 1982. pap. 9.95 (ISBN 0-376-02093-8). Sunset-Lane.

--Favorite Recipes I. 2nd ed. LC 82-81373. 128p. 1982. pap. 5.95 (ISBN 0-376-02177-2). Sunset-Lane.

--Favorite Recipes II. LC 82-81400. (Illus.). 160p. (Orig.). 1982. pap. 5.95 (ISBN 0-376-02154-3). Sunset-Lane.

Swendson. A Couple of Cooks. pap. 5.95 (ISBN 0-686-81678-1). Corona Pub.

Swenson, Gwen & Cunningham, Susan. The Mid-Life Crisis Cookbook. Rev. ed. (Illus.). 40p. (Orig.). 1982. pap. 4.50 (ISBN 0-9609806-1-X). Mid Life.

Taber, Gladys. Stillmeadow Cook Book. 336p. 1983. pap. 9.95 (ISBN 0-940160-18-8). Parnassus Imprints.

Tausch, Gerry. Glamour in the Kitchen: Recipes & Memoirs of a West Point Wife. Tausch, Roland D., ed. LC 82-82681. (Illus.). 152p. 1982. 9.95 (ISBN 0-686-82513-6). Gerosota Pub.

Thackeray, Helen & Brown, Beth. Mormon Family Cookbook. LC 82-73085. (Illus.). 180p. 1982. 12.95 (ISBN 0-87747-930-5). Deseret Bk.

Thirty-Two Meals in Minutes. 1983. 4.95 (ISBN 0-8120-5522-5). Barron.

Thirty-Two Warm Weather Suppers. 1983. 4.95 (ISBN 0-8120-5531-4). Barron.

Toaster Oven Cook Book. pap. 5.95 (ISBN 0-696-01175-1). Meredith Corp.

Tole World Magazine Staff. Tole World Cook Book. Swant, Dale, ed. (Illus.). 220p. (Orig.). 1982. pap. 9.95 (ISBN 0-943470-02-1). Daisy Pub WA.

Trupin, Judy. A Concoctionist Cookbook. 1982. pap. 4.50 (ISBN 0-934834-32-6). White Pine.

Urvater, Michele. Fine Fresh Food--Fast. LC 82-48679. (Illus.). 80p. 1983. 8.61i (ISBN 0-06-015170-6, HarpT). Har-Row.

Virgil M. Hancher Auditorium, The University of Iowa. Entertaining Arts: Menus & Recipes from Performers & Patrons. LC 82-81567. (Illus.). 258p. 1982. spiral bdg. 14.70 (ISBN 0-941016-06-4). Penfield.

Von Welanetz, Diana & Von Welanetz, Paul. The Von Welanetz Guide to Ethnic Ingredients. LC 82-10470. (Illus.). 496p. 1982. 20.00 (ISBN 0-87477-225-7). J P Tarcher.

Washington Opera Womens Committee, ed. The Washington Cookbook. 200p. 1982. pap. write for info. (ISBN 0-9610542-0-4). Wash Opera.

Wilk, Janet. Holiday Cooking for Kids. (Illus.). 64p. 1982. pap. 3.25. Ideals.

Wood, Morrison. With a Jug of Wine. 1983. pap. 9.25 (ISBN 0-374-51773-8). FS&G.

Young, Pam & Jones, Peggy. The Sidetracked Sisters Catch Up on the Kitchen. 224p. 1983. pap. 6.95 (ISBN 0-446-37526-8). Warner Bks.

COOKERY-BIBLIOGRAPHY

Update Publicare Research Staff. Almost Free Cookbooks & Recipes Update: Notebook of Back Issues. 35p. 1983. pap. text ed. 8.00 (ISBN 0-686-38886-0). Update Pub Co.

COOKERY-GARNISHES AND GARNISHING

see Cookery (Garnishes)

COOKERY-JUVENILE LITERATURE

Deming, Mary & Haddard, Joyce. Follow the Sun: International Cookbook for Young People. LC 82-61563. (Illus.). 96p. (gr. 4-12). 1982. pap. 6.50 (ISBN 0-9609188-0-9). Sun Scope.

Glovach, Linda. The Little Witch's Spring Holiday Book. (Illus.). 48p. (ps-4). 8.95 (ISBN 0-13-538108-8). P-H.

Jackson, Jonathan. The Teenage Chef. LC 82-20144. (Illus.). 96p. (gr. 12 up). 1983. 10.95 (ISBN 0-7232-6219-5); pap. 5.95 (ISBN 0-7232-6248-9). Warne.

Johnson, Evelyne & Santoro, Christopher. A First Cookbook for Children: With Illustrations to Color. (Illus.). 48p. (Orig.). (gr. 4 up). 1983. pap. 2.25 (ISBN 0-486-24275-7). Dover.

Littlejohn, Patricia & Stokes, Susan. Nutritious Nibbles for Kids & Others. (Illus.). 79p. (Orig.). 1981. pap. 6.95 (ISBN 0-9607374-0-5). Palasam Pub.

Moore, Eva. The Great Banana Cookbook for Boys & Girls. (Illus.). 48p. (gr. 1-4). 1983. 10.50 (ISBN 0-89919-150-9, Clarion). HM.

Sue, John. The How-to Cookbook. (Illus.). 32p. 1982. pap. 6.95 (ISBN 0-399-20890-9, Philomel). Putnam Pub Group.

--The Time to Eat Cookbook. (Illus.). 32p. 1982. pap. 6.95 (ISBN 0-399-20898-4, Philomel). Putnam Pub Group.

Wishik, Cindy. Kids Dish It...Sugar-Free. (Illus.). 160p. 1982. pap. 8.95 (ISBN 0-918146-22-4). Peninsula WA.

COOKERY-PICTORIAL WORKS

Cornwell, Stephen & Cornwell, Debbra. Cooking in the Nude: For Playful Gourmets. (Illus.). 64p. 1982. pap. 3.95 (ISBN 0-943678-00-5). Wellton Bks.

COOKERY-REDUCING RECIPES

Barker, Louisa & Poe, Tina. The Diet Cookbook. 45p. (Orig.). 1983. pap. 6.50 (ISBN 0-943938-00-7). Res Assocs.

Caloric Microwave Cookbook. 1982. write for info (ISBN 0-87502-105-0). Benjamin Co.

Kulick, Florence & Matthews, Florence. The Hamptons Health Spa Diet Cookbook. 224p. (Orig.). 1983. pap. 8.95 (ISBN 0-932966-28-4). Permanent Pr.

Pomeroy, Ruth F., ed. Redbook's Wise Woman's Diet Cookbook. 310p. 1983. 14.95 (ISBN 0-453-00436-9). NAL.

Rossant, Colette. Colette's Slim Cuisine. (Illus.). 256p. 1983. 14.95 (ISBN 0-688-01937-4). Morrow.

COOKERY-VOCATIONAL GUIDANCE

Silverman, Dee. How to Turn Your Kitchen Talents Into Extra Cash. 101p. 1980. pap. text ed. write for info. (ISBN 0-938908-00-6). Opportunity Knocks.

COOKERY (APPETIZERS)

Hors D'Oeuvre. LC 82-657. (Good Cook Ser.). lib. bdg. 19.96 (ISBN 0-8094-2942-X, Pub. by Time-Life). Silver.

Lee, Gary. Wok Appetizers & Light Snacks. (Illus.). 182p. (Orig.). 1982. pap. 5.95 (ISBN 0-911954-67-8). Nitty Gritty.

Rockdale Temple Sisterhood. In the Beginning: A Collection of Hors D'oeuvres. rev. ed. Bd. with And Beginning Again: More Hors D'oeuvres for Cooks Who Love in the Beginning. 1982. pap. 13.95 slipcased (ISBN 0-9602338-2-2). Rockdale Ridge.

Uvezian, Sonia. The Complete International Appetizer CookBook. LC 82-40015. 288p. 1983. 14.95 (ISBN 0-8128-2877-1). Stein & Day.

COOKERY (BEAN CURD)

Shurtleff, William & Aoyagi, Akiko. The Book of Tofu. LC 74-31629. (Soyfoods Ser.). (Illus.). 336p. 1975. pap. 9.95 (ISBN 0-933332-09-2). Soyfoods Center.

COOKERY (BEEF)

Farm Journal's Food Editors. Farm Journal's Ground Beef Roundup. LC 82-12107. 128p. (Orig.). 1982. pap. 3.95 (ISBN 0-686-84082-8). Farm Journal.

Nickerson, Doyne & Nickerson, Dorothy. New Three Hundred Sixty-Five Ways to Cook Hamburger & Other Ground Meat. LC 82-45262. (Illus.). 240p. 1983. 12.95 (ISBN 0-385-18068-3). Doubleday.

COOKERY (BEER)

DeHaven, Kent C. & DeHaven, Charlotte. What's on Tap. (Illus., Orig.). 1982. pap. write for info. Trends & Custom.

COOKERY (BUTTERMILK)

see Cookery (Dairy Products)

COOKERY (CEREALS)

Ramp, Wilma, compiled by. Fantastic Oatmeal Recipes. 64p. pap. 3.75 (ISBN 0-9603858-3-5). Penfield.

COOKERY (CHEESE)

see Cookery (Dairy Products)

COOKERY (CHICKEN)

Dyer, Ceil. Chicken Cookery. (Illus.). 160p. 1983. pap. 7.95 (ISBN 0-89586-054-6). H P Bks.

Farm Journal's Food Editors. Chicken Twice a Week. LC 76-12306. 128p. (Orig.). 1976. pap. 2.95 (ISBN 0-89795-019-4). Farm Journal.

Gohlke, Annette, ed. Chicken Country Style. LC 81-85696. 84p. 1982. pap. 2.95 (ISBN 0-89821-040-2). Reiman Assocs.

COOKERY (CHOCOLATE)

Larsen, Phyllis. Ghirardelli Original Chocolate Cookbook. 2nd ed. Allen, Vera, ed. (Orig.). 4.95 (ISBN 0-9610218-0-2). Ghirardelli Choc.

Rubinstein, Helge. The Ultimate Chocolate Cake: One Hundred Eleven Other Chocolate Indulgences. (Illus.). 336p. 1983. 14.95 (ISBN 0-312-92851-3). Congdon & Weed.

COOKERY (DAIRY PRODUCTS)

Sherman, Steve. Cheese Sweets & Savories. 176p. 1983. pap. 8.95 (ISBN 0-8289-0498-7). Greene.

COOKERY (EGGS)

Byrd, Anne. Omelettes & Souffles. LC 82-47860. (Great American Cooking Schools Ser.). (Illus.). 84p. 1982. 8.61i (ISBN 0-06-015065-3, HarpT). Har-Row.

Seranne, Ann. The Complete Book of Egg Cookery. 224p. 1983. 14.95 (ISBN 0-02-609620-X). Macmillan.

COOKERY (FISH)

see Cookery (Sea Food)

COOKERY (FRUIT)

Ballantyne, Janet. Desserts from the Garden. Chesman, Andrea, ed. (Illus.). 144p. (Orig.). 1983. pap. 5.95 (ISBN 0-88266-322-4). Garden Way Pub.

Fielder, Mildred. Wild Fruits: An Illustrated Field Guide & Cookbook. (Illus.). 288p. (Orig.). 1983. pap. 9.95 (ISBN 0-8092-5614-2). Contemp Bks.

Gohlke, Annette, ed. Cherry Delights. LC 82-50004. 68p. 1982. pap. 2.95 (ISBN 0-89821-041-0). Reiman Assocs.

Gorman, Marion. Cooking with Fruit. Gerras, Charles, ed. (Illus.). 320p. 1983. 14.95 (ISBN 0-87857-414-X, 07-003-0). Rodale Pr Inc.

Graham, Winifred. The Vegetarian Treasure Chest. Fraser, Lisa, ed. Orig. Title: The Vegetable, Fruit & Nut Cookbook. 224p. 1983. pap. 6.95 (ISBN 0-930356-33-0). Quicksilver Prod.

McCreary, Susan A., ed. Strawberry Sportcake. (Illus.). 96p. 1982. pap. 4.00 (ISBN 0-686-37646-3). Strawberry Works.

Munson, Shirley & Nelson, Jo. Cooking with Apples. LC 75-18210. 128p. (Orig.). 1975. pap. 3.95 (ISBN 0-89795-016-X). Farm Journal.

Rare Fruit Council International Staff. Tropical Fruit Recipes. (Illus.). 176p. Date not set. pap. 10.95 (ISBN 0-686-84236-7). Banyan Bks.

COOKERY (GAME)

MacIlquham, Frances. Complete Fish & Game Cookery of North America. (Illus.). 304p. 1983. 29.95 (ISBN 0-8329-0284-5). Winchester Pr.

Pederson, Rolf A. Rolf's Collection of Wild Game Recipes: Vol. I: Upland Game Birds. Carlson, Nancy, ed. 174p. (Orig.). 1982. pap. 9.95 (ISBN 0-910579-00-8). Rolfs Gall.

COOKERY (GARNISHES)

see also Cookery (Relishes)

Good, Phyllis P. & Pellman, Rachel T., eds. Jams, Jellies & Relishes: From Amish & Mennonite Kitchens. (Pennsylvania Dutch Cookbooks Ser.). (Illus., Orig.). 1983. pap. 1.95 (ISBN 0-934672-14-8). Good Bks PA.

Haydock, Yukiko & Haydock, Bob. More Japanese Garnishes. LC 82-15563. (Illus.). 128p. 1983. 15.95 (ISBN 0-03-063611-6). HR&W.

Sauces & Dressings. 1982. 450.00 (ISBN 0-686-38414-8, 155). Busn Trend.

COOKERY (GROUND BEEF)

see Cookery (Beef)

COOKERY (HAMBURGER)

see Cookery (Beef)

COOKERY (HERBS AND SPICES)

Clairborne, Craig. Cooking with Herbs & Spices. LC 82-48224. (Illus.). 376p. 1983. pap. 7.64i (ISBN 0-06-090998-6, CN 998, CN). Har-Row.

Culinary Herbs. 1982. 2.25 (ISBN 0-686-38720-1). Bklyn Botanic.

Doeser, Linda & Richardson, Rosamond. The Little Garlic Book. (Illus.). 64p. 1983. 5.95 (ISBN 0-312-48864-5). St Martin.

--The Little Pepper Book. (Illus.). 64p. 1983. 5.95 (ISBN 0-312-48864-5). St Martin.

Townsend, Doris M. How to Cook With Herbs, Spices & Flavorings. 160p. 1982. pap. 6.95 (ISBN 0-89586-192-5). H P Bks.

COOKERY (HONEY)

Honey Recipes from Amana. 32p. pap. 2.45 (ISBN 0-941016-00-5). Penfield.

COOKERY (MACARONI)

Beard, James. Beard on Pasta. LC 82-48727. 1983. 13.95 (ISBN 0-394-52291-5). Knopf.

Better Homes & Gardens Books editors, ed. Better Homes & Gardens Pasta Cook Book. (Illus.). 96p. 1983. 5.95 (ISBN 0-696-00855-6). Meredith Corp.

Gohlke, Annette, ed. Pasta, Please. LC 82-50005. 68p. 1982. pap. 2.95 (ISBN 0-89821-042-9). Reiman Assocs.

Middione, Carlo. Pasta! Cooking It, Loving It. LC 82-47861. (Great American Cooking Schools Ser.). (Illus.). 84p. 1982. 8.61i (ISBN 0-06-015068-8, HarpT). Har-Row.

COOKERY (MEAT)

see also Cookery, Barbecue; Cookery (Game)

Variety Meats. LC 82-10380. (Good Cook Ser.). lib. bdg. 19.96 (ISBN 0-8094-2951-9, Pub. by Time-Life). Silver.

COOKERY (MILK)

see Cookery (Dairy Products)

COOKERY (NATURAL FOODS)

Albright, Nancy. Natural Foods Epicure: The No Salt, No Sugar, No Artificial Ingredients, All Natural Foods Cookbook. Gerras, Charles, ed. (Orig.). 1983. pap. 10.95 (ISBN 0-87857-468-9, 03-545-1). Rodale Pr Inc.

Frompovich, Catherine J. Natural & Nutritious Cooking Course. 94p. 1982. lab manual 50.00 (ISBN 0-935322-21-3). C J Frompovich.

Geiskopf, Susann & Toomay, Melinda. Fast & Natural Cuisine. Bass, M., ed. (Illus.). 300p. (Orig.). 1983. pap. 6.95 (ISBN 0-930356-38-1). Quicksilver Prod.

Hunt, Janet. Simple & Speedy Wholefood Cooking. (Illus.). 128p. (Orig.). 1983. pap. 3.95 (ISBN 0-7225-0752-6, Pub. by Thorsons Pubs England). Sterling.

McCrone, Carole N. & Rose-Hancock, Marga, eds. Fresh, Fast, & Fabulous. 190p. 1982. pap. 8.95 (ISBN 0-89716-122-X). Peanut Butter.

Mayo, Patricia T. The Sugarless Baking Book: The Natural Way to Prepare America's Favorite Breads, Pies, Cakes, Puddings & Desserts. LC 82-42757. (Illus.). 116p. (Orig.). 1983. pap. 4.95 (ISBN 0-394-71429-6). Shambhala Pubns.

One Hundred & One Productions. The Whole World Cookbook. (Illus.). 512p. 1983. pap. 14.95 (ISBN 0-686-83735-5, ScribT). Scribner.

Ridgeway, Donald G. The Healthy Peasant Gourmet. LC 82-90747. (Illus.). 220p. 1983. 12.95 (ISBN 0-910361-01-0); pap. 7.95 (ISBN 0-910361-00-2). Earth Basics.

Turnball, Yvonne. Living Cookbook. 396p. 1983. looseleaf bdg. 14.95 (ISBN 0-686-42983-4). Bethany Hse.

COOKERY (NOODLES)

see Cookery (Macaroni)

COOKERY (NUTS)

Graham, Winifred. The Vegetarian Treasure Chest. Fraser, Lisa, ed. Orig. Title: The Vegetable, Fruit & Nut Cookbook. 224p. 1983. pap. 6.95 (ISBN 0-930356-33-0). Quicksilver Prod.

COOKERY (RELISHES)

Chesman, Andrea. Pickles & Relishes: One Hundred Thirty Recipes, Apple to Zucchini. (Illus.). 160p. (Orig.). 1983. pap. 5.95 (ISBN 0-88266-321-6). Garden Way Pub.

Good, Phyllis P. & Pellman, Rachel T., eds. Jams, Jellies & Relishes: From Amish & Mennonite Kitchens. (Pennsylvania Dutch Cookbooks Ser.). (Illus., Orig.). 1983. pap. 1.95 (ISBN 0-934672-14-8). Good Bks PA.

McCrachen, Betsy. Farm Journal's Homemade Pickles & Relishes. LC 76-14048. 128p. (Orig.). 1976. pap. 3.95 (ISBN 0-89795-018-6). Farm Journal.

COOKERY (RICE)

An International Survey of Methods Used for Evaluation of the Cooking & Eating Qualities of Milled Rice. (IRRI Research Paper Ser.: No. 77). 28p. 1983. pap. 5.00 (ISBN 0-686-42853-6, R177, IRRI). Unipub.

COOKERY (SEA FOOD)

Carstarphen, Dee. Maverick Sea Fare, A Caribbean Cook Book. LC 78-107177. 60p. Date not set. pap. 5.95 (ISBN 0-686-84293-6). Banyan Bks.

Classy Conch Cooking. (Illus.). 28p. Date not set. pap. 3.00 (ISBN 0-686-84219-7). Banyan Bks.

Cronin, Isaac. The International Squid Cookbook. (Illus.). 96p. 1981. pap. 6.95 (ISBN 0-915572-61-3). Aris Bks.

Cronin, Isaac & Harlow, Jay. The California Seafood Cookbook. (Illus.). 300p. 1983. 16.95 (ISBN 0-943186-04-8); pap. 10.95 (ISBN 0-943186-03-X). Aris Bks.

Emmons, Vicki. Simply Seafood. (Illus.). 224p. (Orig.). 1983. pap. 4.95 (ISBN 0-89933-043-6). DeLorme Pub.

Flagg, William G. The Clam Lover's Cookbook. 3rd ed. (Illus.). 160p. (Orig.). 1983. pap. 6.95 (ISBN 0-88427-054-8, Dist. by Everest Hse). North River.

How to Clean a Mess of Fish Without Making a Mess of the Fish: Secrets from the Pros. LC 78-58346. (Illus.). 1978. pap. 1.95 (ISBN 0-686-37908-X). Normark Corp.

Humphreys Academy Patrons. Festival. (Illus.). 320p. 1983. pap. 10.95 (ISBN 0-9610058-0-7). Humphreys Acad.

Humphreys Academy Patrons, ed. Festival. (Illus.). 320p. 1983. pap. 10.95 (ISBN 0-686-82289-7). Wimmer Bks.

MacIlquham, Frances. Complete Fish & Game Cookery of North America. (Illus.). 304p. 1983. 29.95 (ISBN 0-8329-0284-5). Winchester Pr.

Ross, S. The Seafood Cookbook. 1978. 12.95 (ISBN 0-07-053881-6). McGraw.

Thirty-Two Seafood Suppers. 1983. 4.95 (ISBN 0-8120-5530-6). Barron.

COOKERY (SMOKED FOODS)

Waldron, Maggie. Barbeque & Smoke Cookery. rev. ed. (Illus.). 192p. 1983. pap. 7.95 (ISBN 0-89286-211-4). One Hund One Prods.

COOKERY (SOUR CREAM AND MILK)

see Cookery (Dairy Products)

COOKERY (SOYBEANS)

Shurtleff, William & Aoyagi, Akiko. The Book of Kudzu. LC 77-74891. 104p. 1977. pap. 4.95 (ISBN 0-933332-11-4). Soyfoods Center.

--The Book of Miso. LC 76-19599. (Soyfoods Ser.). (Illus.). 256p. 1976. pap. 8.95 (ISBN 0-933332-10-6). Soyfoods Center.

--The Book of Miso. rev. ed. (Illus.). 256p. 14.95 (ISBN 0-89815-098-1); pap. 9.95 (ISBN 0-89815-097-3). Ten Speed Pr.

--The Book of Tofu. LC 74-31629. (Soyfoods Ser.). (Illus.). 336p. 1975. pap. 9.95 (ISBN 0-933332-09-2). Soyfoods Center.

COOKERY (SPAGHETTI)

see Cookery (Macaroni)

COOKERY (VEGETABLES)

Bibliotheca Press Research Dept. Almost Meat: Nutritional Foods that Can Be Prepared to Taste Like Meat. 50p. 1983. pap. 8.95 (ISBN 0-939476-60-6). Biblio Pr GA.

Bibliotheca Press Staff. Directory of Vegetarian Cookbooks. 70p. 1983. pap. text ed. 9.95 (ISBN 0-939476-68-1). Biblio Pr GA.

Brenner, Shauna C. & Smoot, Shields. The Vegetable Lover's Cookbook. (Illus.). 128p. (Orig.). 1983. pap. 7.95 (ISBN 0-8092-5642-8). Contemp Bks.

Burpee, Lois. Lois Burpee's Gardener's Companion & Cookbook. LC 82-47736. (Illus.). 256p. 1983. 14.37i (ISBN 0-06-038021-7, HarpT). Har-Row.

Colbin, Annemarie. The Book of Whole Meals: A Seasonal Guide to Assembling Balanced Vegetarian Breakfasts, Lunches & Dinners. 240p. (Orig.). 1983. pap. 7.95 (ISBN 0-345-30982-0). Ballantine.

Doeser, Linda & Richardson, Rosamond. The Little Green Avocado Book. (Illus.). 64p. 1983. 5.95 (ISBN 0-312-48862-9). St Martin.

Hillman, Libby. Fresh Garden Vegetables. LC 82-48667. (Great American Cooking School Ser.). (Illus.). 80p. 1983. 8.61i (ISBN 0-06-015157-9, HarpT). Har-Row.

Landin, Judy. The Well Dressed Salad. (Illus.). 32p. (Orig.). 1981. pap. 2.00 (ISBN 0-9609266-0-7). GNK Pr.

Mayer, Paul. Fresh Vegetable. rev. ed. (Illus.). 192p. 1982. pap. 5.95 (ISBN 0-911954-34-1). Nitty Gritty.

Pappas, Lou S. Vegetable Cookery. (Illus.). 192p. 1982. pap. 7.95 (ISBN 0-89586-193-3). H P Bks.

Rasmus, Lucy. The Carrot Cookbook, 57 Recipes. (Illus.). 1982. pap. 2.50 (ISBN 0-933646-17-8). Aries Pr.

Uberoi, Pritam. Pure Vegetarian Indian Cookery. 167p. 1981. pap. 9.95 (ISBN 0-940500-61-2, Pub. by Sterling India). Asia Bk Corp.

COOKERY (VERMICELLI)

see Cookery (Macaroni)

COOKERY (WINE)

Hebert, Malcolm. Wine Lovers Cookbook. 128p. 1983. pap. 6.95 (ISBN 0-932664-29-6). Wine Appreciation.

COOKERY, AMERICAN

see also Cookery, Creole

Alaska Magazine, ed. Alaska Wild Berry Guide & Cookbook. (Illus.). 216p. 1983. pap. 13.95 (ISBN 0-88240-229-3). Alaska Northwest.

American Cancer Society. Show Me Missouri Four Seasons Cookbook, 1983. 1983. pap. 6.00 (ISBN 0-686-43081-6). Am Cancer MO.

Atwood, Valdine, ed. Maine D.A.R. Cook Book. LC 82-73245. 310p. (Orig.). 1982. pap. 7.00 (ISBN 0-941216-04-7). Cay-bel.

Bailey, Lee. Country Weekends. 1983. 18.95 (C N Potter Bks). Crown.

Blue Lake-Deerhaven Cookbook Staff. A Texas Hill Country Cookbook. 8th ed. (Illus.). 406p. 1982. pap. 10.95 (ISBN 0-9609210-0-1). Blue Haven.

Bowman, Dee. Southwestern Cooking Recipes. 16p. pap. 2.00x (ISBN 0-943462-05-3). CaseCo.

Broili, June. Nevada Cookery: Table Traditions & Tales of the Sagebrush State. Browder, Robyn, ed. LC 82-14771. (Regional Cookbook Ser.). (Illus.). 300p. (Orig.). 1983. pap. 8.95 (ISBN 0-89865-255-3). Donning Co.

Buck, Peter. Arts & Crafts of Hawaii: Food, Sec. I. (Special Publication Ser.: No. 45). (Illus.). 83p. 1957. pap. 4.50 (ISBN 0-910240-34-5). Bishop Mus.

Camaro editors. Old California: Cooking, Recipes, & Menus. (Old California Ser.: No. 11). (Illus.). 1983. pap. 3.95 (ISBN 0-913290-52-1). Camaro Pub.

Cameron, Sheila M. More of the Best From New Mexico Kitchens. King, Scottie, ed. LC 82-62076. (Illus.). 160p. (Orig.). 1982. pap. 5.95 (ISBN 0-937206-02-4, Pub. by NM Magazine). U of NM Pr.

Clegg, Holly Berkowitz & Jarrett, Beverly. From a Louisiana Kitchen. (Illus.). 256p. 1983. pap. 9.95 (ISBN 0-686-82622-1). Wimmer Bks.

Crabtree, Catherine G. Ala Texas: Restaurant Recipes. 1983. pap. 9.95 (ISBN 0-937070-04-1). Crabtree.

DeBolt, Margaret W. Georgia Sampler Cookbook. Browder, Robyn, ed. LC 82-19841. (Regional Cookbook Ser.). (Illus.). 300p. (Orig.). 1983. pap. 8.95 (ISBN 0-89865-283-9). Donning Co.

Dobbins, Joann H. Pineapple Gold. 304p. 1983. pap. 10.95 (ISBN 0-9610540-0-X). Wimmer Bks.

DuSablon, Mary Anna. Cincinnati Recipe Treasury: Queen City's Culinary Heritage. Browder, Robyn, ed. LC 82-14773. (Regional Cookbook Ser.). (Illus.). 300p. 1983. pap. 8.95 (ISBN 0-89865-247-2). Donning Co.

Engelken, David & Huth, Tricia. Undiscovered Denver Dining. (Illus.). 84p. 1982. pap. 3.95 (ISBN 0-9610064-0-4). Undiscovered.

Fannin County Historical Commission. Tempting Traditions. Jones, Barbara C., ed. 280p. (Orig.). 1982. pap. 11.95 (ISBN 0-686-38456-3). Fannin County.

Farr, Sidney S. More than Moonshine: Appalachian Recipes & Recollections. LC 82-13524. 176p. 1983. 11.95 (ISBN 0-8229-3475-2); pap. 4.95 (ISBN 0-8229-5347-1). U of Pittsburgh Pr.

Fauntleroy, Fran, ed. Houston Epicure 1982-83. (Epicure Ser.). 160p. 1982. pap. 5.95 (ISBN 0-89716-114-9). Peanut Butter.

Foster, Pearl B. Mrs. Foster's Creative American Cookery. (Illus.). Date not set. 17.50 (ISBN 0-671-44303-8). S&S.

Fournier, Priscilla. American Wok Cookery. LC 82-50569. 64p. (Orig.). 1982. pap. 2.98 (ISBN 0-686-82681-7). WRC Pub.

Gaede, Sarah R. The Pirate's House Cookbook. (Illus.). 224p. 1982. pap. 10.95 (ISBN 0-939114-61-5). Wimmer Bks.

Goldbeck, Nikki & Goldbeck, David. Nikki & David Goldbeck's American Wholefoods Cuisine. (Illus.). 608p. 1983. 19.95 (ISBN 0-686-84824-1). NAL.

Good, Phyllis P. & Pellman, Rachel T., eds. Cakes: From Amish & Mennonite Kitchens. (Pennsylvania Dutch Cookbooks Ser.). (Illus., Orig.). 1983. pap. 1.95 (ISBN 0-934672-12-1). Good Bks PA.

--Candies, Beverages & Snacks: From Amish & Mennonite Kitchens. (Pennsylvania Dutch Cookbooks Ser.). (Illus., Orig.). 1983. pap. 1.95 (ISBN 0-934672-16-4). Good Bks PA.

--Casseroles: From Amish & Mennonite Kitchens. (Pennsylvania Dutch Cookbooks Ser.). (Illus., Orig.). 1983. pap. 1.95 (ISBN 0-934672-11-3). Good Bks PA.

Harrell, Pauline C. & Chase, Charlotte. Arrowhead Farm: 300 Years of New England Husbandry & Cooking. (Illus.). 240p. 1983. 16.95 (ISBN 0-914378-98-8); pap. 10.95. Countryman.

Heathwood Hall Parents Guild. Palmetto Pantry. (Illus.). 242p. 1983. pap. 9.50 (ISBN 0-686-82273-0). Wimmer Bks.

Holmes, Thomas, Jr. Bayou Cook Book. (Illus.). 185p. 1983. Pelican.

Holst, Phyllis. Recipes from Hidden Hills, Tried & True. 36p. pap. 3.95 (ISBN 0-941016-02-1). Penfield.

Hurshell, Jennifer, ed. Aspen Epicure. (Epicure Ser.). 1982. pap. 2.95 (ISBN 0-89716-116-5). Peanut Butter.

--Portland Epicure 1982-83. (Epicure Ser.). 112p. 1982. pap. 5.95 (ISBN 0-89716-094-0). Peanut Butter.

Jasmin, Barbara Dalia, ed. The Captain's Lady: Cookbook-Personal Journal Circa Massachusetts 1837-1917, Vol. II. LC 82-90816. (Illus.). 192p. pap. 10.95 (ISBN 0-9609534-0-X). Captains Lady.

Junaluska Historical Society. Junaluska Joy. Cornwell, Mary & Cornwell, Ada, eds. (Illus.). 388p. 1982. pap. 9.95 (ISBN 0-686-82093-2). Wimmer Bks.

Junior League of Nashville. Nashville Encore. McInnis, Donna, ed. 502p. 1982. pap. 12.50 (ISBN 0-939114-68-2). Wimmer Bks.

Junior Welfare League of Enid, OK., Inc. & Sailors, Ruth A. Stir-Ups. (Cookbook Ser.). 1982. pap. 12.95 (ISBN 0-9609340-0-6). Jr Welfare Enid.

Kafka, Barbara. American Food & California Wine. LC 82-47863. (The Great American Cooking Schools Ser.). (Illus.). 84p. 1982. 8.61i (ISBN 0-06-015066-1, HarpT). Har-Row.

King, Louise T. & Wirker, Stewart. The Martha's Vineyard Cookbook. 320p. 1983. pap. 8.95 (ISBN 0-686-42851-X). Globe Pequot.

Kropotkin, Marjorie & Kropotkin, Igor. The Inn Cookbook: New England. 288p. 1983. 18.45 (ISBN 0-316-50473-4); pap. 9.70i (ISBN 0-316-50474-2). Little.

Liffring-Zug, Joan, compiled by. The American Gothic Cookbook. 72p. pap. 4.75 (ISBN 0-9603858-0-0). Penfield.

--Recipes from Our Annual Fourth of July Potluck Picnic for Friends & Relations. 36p. pap. 2.45 (ISBN 0-9603858-1-9). Penfield.

Maryland Chapter Arthritis Foundation. Beyond Beer & Crabs: Cooking in Maryland. Streich, Marianne, ed. (Illus.). 192p. (Orig.). 1982. pap. 6.50. Wimmer Bks.

Mynatt, Elaine S., ed. Koinonia Cooking. (Illus.). 149p. (Orig.). 1982. pap. 6.00 (ISBN 0-911175-00-8). Elm Pubs.

Nusom, Lynn. The New Mexico Cookbook. Browder, Robyn, ed. LC 82-17730. (Regional Cookbook Ser.). (Illus.). 250p. pap. 7.95 (ISBN 0-89865-249-9). Donning Co.

Palmer, Elsie & Oeltien, Jody. Eating the Oregon Way. LC 82-73683. (Illus.). 180p. (Orig.). pap. 7.95 (ISBN 0-686-38722-8). Berry Patch.

Reid, Robert, ed. Country Inns of America Cookbook. (Illus.). 180p. 1982. 24.95 (ISBN 0-686-82288-9). HR&W.

Reingold, Carmel B. California Cuisine. 192p. 1983. pap. 5.95 (ISBN 0-380-82156-7, 82156). Avon.

Richardson Woman's Club. The Texas Experience: Friendship & Food Texas Style, A Cookbook from the Richardson Woman's Club. Dennis, Ivanette, ed. (Illus.). 373p. 1982. lib. bdg. 12.95 (ISBN 0-9609416-0-6). Hart Graphics.

Rothenbuehler, Mary L., ed. Family Secrets: Recipes from Grandma Fowler's Kitchen. (Illus.). 1981. pap. 2.25 (ISBN 0-939010-00-3). Zephyr Pr.

Sanchez, Irene B. & Yund, Gloria S. Comida Sabrosa: Home-Style Southwestern Cooking. (Illus.). 128p. 1982. 14.95 (ISBN 0-8263-0636-5). U of NM Pr.

Savannah Junior Auxiliary. Savannah: Proud As A Peacock. Barker, Carol & Patrick, Lynn, eds. 320p. 1982. pap. 9.95 (ISBN 0-939114-45-3). Savannah Jr Aux.

Shell, Ella Jo. Recipes From Our Front Porch. (Illus.). 152p. 1982. pap. 10.00 (ISBN 0-939114-65-8). Wimmer Bks.

Sokolov, Raymond. Fading Feast: A Compendium of Disappearing American Regional Foods. (Illus.). 288p. 1983. pap. 6.95 (ISBN 0-525-48030-7, 0674-210, Obelisk). Dutton.

Stehle, Audrey P. & Ingram, Marilyn, eds. The Southern Heritage Cakes Cookbook. LC 82-62141. (The Southern Heritage Cookbook Library). (Illus.). 144p. 1983. 9.57i (ISBN 0-8487-0601-3). Oxmoor Hse.

--The Southern Heritage Company's Coming Cookbook. LC 82-62140. (The Southern Heritage Cookbook Library). (Illus.). 144p. 1983. 9.57i (ISBN 0-8487-0603-X). Oxmoor Hse.
--The Southern Heritage Poultry Cookbook. LC 82-62142. (The Southern Heritage Cookbook Library). (Illus.). 144p. 1983. 9.57i (ISBN 0-8487-0604-8). Oxmoor Hse.
Talmadge, Betty. Lovejoy Plantation Cookbook. 1983. 8.95 (ISBN 0-931948-44-4). Peachtree Pubs.
The Junior League of Tulsa Inc. Cook's Collage: Favorite Fore of the Junior League of Tulsa. 352p. 1978. 9.95 (ISBN 0-9604368-0-4). Jr. League Tulsa.
Theriot, Jude. La Meilleure de la Louisiane: The Best of Louisiana. (Illus.). 361p. 1983. Repr. of 1980 ed. spiral 10.95 (ISBN 0-88289-407-2). Pelican.
Thibodaux Service League Members. Louisiana Legacy: A Rich Tradition of Artistry with Food & Joy in Life. Lynch, Gloria E. & Silverberg, Katherine D., eds. LC 82-50498. (Illus.). 288p. 1982. 11.95 (ISBN 0-9608800-0-3). Thibodaux.
Three Hundred Years of Carolina Cooking. LC 76-124563. (Illus.). 318p. 1970. 9.95 (ISBN 0-9608172-0-4). Jr League Greenville.
Thwaite, Jean & Smith, Susan. Chef's Secrets from Great Restaurants in California. (Chef's Secrets Cookbooks Ser.). (Illus.). 270p. 1983. 11.95 (ISBN 0-939944-24-3). Marmac Pub.
--Chef's Secrets from Great Restaurants in Louisiana: 1984 World Exposition Edition. (Chef's Secrets Cookbooks Ser.). (Illus.). 270p. 1983. 11.95 (ISBN 0-939944-25-1). Marmac Pub.
--Chef's Secrets from Great Restaurants in Pennsylvania. (Chef's Secrets Cookbooks Ser.). (Illus.). 270p. 1983. 11.95 (ISBN 0-939944-26-X). Marmac Pub.
Thwaite, Jean & Nicholson, Diana, eds. Chefs' Secrets from Great Restaurants in Georgia. (Cookbook Ser.). (Illus.). 248p. 11.95 (ISBN 0-939944-06-5). Marmac Pub.
Touchstone, Billie L. Redneck Country Cookin' 100p. (Orig.). 1982. pap. 3.95 (ISBN 0-941186-03-2). Twin Oaks LA.
Vollstedt, Maryana. Whats for Dinner in the Northwest? (Illus.). 144p. (Orig.). 1982. pap. 5.95 (ISBN 0-910983-14-3). Cookbook Fact.
Walker, Nancy P. Southern Legacies. Stone, Nancy W. & Stone, William E., eds. (Illus.). 256p. 1982. pap. 9.95 (ISBN 0-939114-75-5). Wimmer Bks.
Weaver, William W. Sauerkraut Yankees: Pennsylvania German Food & Foodways. LC 82-40488. (Illus.). 224p. (Orig.). 1983. 25.00x (ISBN 0-8122-7868-2); pap. 12.50 (ISBN 0-8122-1145-6). U of Pa Pr.
Weiner, Melissa R. & Ruffner, Budge. Arizona Territorial Cookbook: The Food & Lifestyles of a Frontier. Browder, Robyn, ed. LC 82-2489. (Regional Cookbook Ser.). (Illus.). 232p. Date not set. pap. 8.95 (ISBN 0-89865-312-6, AACR2). Donning Co.
Wolf, Elliott, ed. Sun Valley Epicure. (Epicure Ser.). 1982. pap. 2.95 (ISBN 0-89716-118-1). Peanut Butter.
--Vail Epicure. (Epicure Ser.). 1982. pap. 2.95 (ISBN 0-89716-117-3). Peanut Butter.
Woodward, Sandra K. Norfolk Cookery Book: The Culinary Heritage of a Southern Seaport. Friedman, Donna R., ed. LC 81-15302. (Regional Cookbook Ser.). (Illus.). 224p. (Orig.). 1981. pap. 6.95 (ISBN 0-89865-164-6, AACR2). Donning Co.
Worstman, Gail L. Gail Worstman's Goodtime Hardtimes Cookbook. LC 82-81587. 165p. 1982. pap. 8.95 (ISBN 0-933686-01-3). Gray Beard.
Ziemann, Hugo & Gillette, F. L. The Original White House Cookbook. 619p. 1983. 16.95 (ISBN 0-8159-6413-7). Devin.

COOKERY, AMISH
see Cookery, American

COOKERY, BARBECUE
see also Cookery, Outdoor
All Time Favorite Barbeque Recipes. pap. 5.95 (ISBN 0-696-01100-X). Meredith Corp.
Charmglow. The Complete Barbecue Cookbook: Recipes for the Gas Grill & Water Smoker. (Illus.). 192p. 1983. 14.95 (ISBN 0-8092-5554-5). Contemp Bks.
Thirty-Two Barbecues. 1983. 4.95 (ISBN 0-8120-5517-9). Barron.

COOKERY, CAMP
see Cookery, Outdoor

COOKERY, CARIBBEAN
Ortiz, Elisabeth L. The Complete Book of Caribbean Cooking. 448p. 1983. pap. 7.95 (ISBN 0-87131-409-6). M Evans.

COOKERY, CASSEROLE
see also Electric Cookery, Slow
All Time Favorite Casserole Recipes. pap. 5.95 (ISBN 0-696-01105-0). Meredith Corp.
Crockery Cooker Cook Book. pap. 5.95 (ISBN 0-696-01020-8). Meredith Corp.

COOKERY, CHINESE
Chen, Joyce. Joyce Chen Cook Book. LC 82-49008. (Illus.). 224p. 1983. pap. 7.12i (ISBN 0-06-464060-4, BN 4060). B&N NY.
Claiborne, Craig & Lee, Virginia. The Chinese Cookbook. LC 82-48827. (Illus.). 476p. (Orig.). 1983. pap. 9.56i (ISBN 0-06-464063-9, BN 4063). B&N NY.
Hong Kong & China Gas Chinese Cookbook. (Illus.). 319p. 39.95 (ISBN 0-686-38769-4). NW Intl.
Hoy, Sharon W. Cuisine of China. LC 80-70735. (Illus.). 310p. 1982. 15.95 (ISBN 0-9607508-1-9). Benshaw Pub.
Lai, T. C. Chinese Food for Thought. (Illus.). 96p. 9.95 (ISBN 0-86519-094-1). Lee Pubs Group.
Law, Ruth. Dim Sum: Fast & Festive Chinese Cooking. (Illus.). 256p. 1982. pap. 9.95 (ISBN 0-8092-5881-1). Contemp Bks.
Lefebvre, G. Godchaux. Wok Cooking, Vol. 1. (Audio Cassette Cooking School Library). 16p. 1982. pap. text ed. 12.95x (ISBN 0-910327-01-7). Cuisine Con.
More from Your Wok. pap. 5.95 (ISBN 0-696-01125-5). Meredith Corp.
Piazza, Gail. World of Wok Cookery. LC 82-71462. (Illus.). 144p. 1982. pap. 5.95 (ISBN 0-916752-59-3). Dorison Hse.
Suitin, L. Cook Chinese. (Golden Asia Cookbooks). (Illus.). 152p. 1983. pap. 21.95 (ISBN 9971-65-076-2). Hippocrene Bks.
Wong, Ting & Schulman, Sylvia. More Long-Life Chinese Cooking from Madame Wong. (Illus.). 320p. 1983. pap. 7.95 (ISBN 0-8092-5609-6). Contemp Bks.

COOKERY, CREOLE
Carstarphen, Dee. Maverick Sea Fare, A Caribbean Cook Book. LC 78-107177. 60p. Date not set. pap. 5.95 (ISBN 0-686-84293-6). Banyan Bks.
Ockman, Rita. Cajun Bits Cooking Ease. 1983. 5.75 (ISBN 0-8062-2134-8). Carlton.
Theriot, Jude. La Meilleure de la Louisiane: The Best of Louisiana. (Illus.). 361p. 1983. Repr. of 1980 ed. spiral 10.95 (ISBN 0-88289-407-2). Pelican.
Thibodaux Service League Members. Louisiana Legacy: A Rich Tradition of Artistry with Food & Joy in Life. Lynch, Gloria E. & Silverberg, Katherine D., eds. LC 82-50498. (Illus.). 288p. 1982. 11.95 (ISBN 0-9608800-0-3). Thibodaux.

COOKERY, CZECH
Martin, Pat, compiled by. The Czech Book: Recipes & Traditions. (Illus.). 60p. pap. 4.75 (ISBN 0-9603858-6-X). Penfield.

COOKERY, DANISH
McDonald, Julie J. Delectably Danish: Recipes & Reflections. 64p. pap. 5.75 (ISBN 0-941016-04-8). Penfield.

COOKERY, DUTCH
Morgan, Jan. From Holland with Love: Delicious Dutch Recipes. (Illus.). 91p. 1980. 12.50x (ISBN 0-911268-48-0). Rogers Bk.

COOKERY, FRENCH
Carley, Eliane. Classics from a French Kitchen: Delicious Recipes, both Ancient & Modern, Together with Savory History & Gastronomic Lore in the Grand Tradition of the Cuisine of France. 1983. 14.95 (ISBN 0-517-54919-0). Crown.
Didier, Jean, ed. Le Bottin Gourmand. (Illus.). 1176p. (Orig., Fr.). 1982. pap. 40.00x (ISBN 2-7039-0505-X). Intl Pubns Serv.
Larrieu, Jean-Claude. Montastruc: Seen by its Cooking. (Illus.). 128p. 1983. 27.50 (ISBN 0-937950-05-X). Xavier-Moreau.

COOKERY, INDIC
Abdulla, Ummi. Malabar Muslim Cookery. 112p. 1981. pap. text ed. 4.25x (ISBN 0-86131-241-4, Pub. by Orient Ltd India). Apt Bks.
Indian Cooking. 1983. price not set (ISBN 0-8120-5467-9). Barron.
Tyabji, Surayya. Mirch Masala. 92p. 1981. pap. text ed. 3.95x (ISBN 0-86131-205-8, Pub. by Orient Longman Ltd India). Apt Bks.
Uberoi, Pritam. Non-Vegetarian Indian Cookery. 203p. (Orig.). 1981. pap. 9.95x (ISBN 0-940500-62-0, Pub by S Chand India). Asia Bk Corp.
--Pure Vegetarian Indian Cookery. 167p. 1981. pap. 9.95 (ISBN 0-940500-61-2, Pub. by Sterling India). Asia Bk Corp.

COOKERY, INDONESIAN
Brackman, Agnes D. Cook Indonesian. (Golden Asia Cookbooks Ser.). 128p. 1982. pap. 21.95 (ISBN 9971-65-077-0). Hippocrene Bks.

COOKERY, INTERNATIONAL
Bibliotheca Press Staff, ed. The Cultural & Ethnic Cookbook Index. 60p. 1983. pap. 9.95 (ISBN 0-939476-69-X). Biblio Pr GA.
Ethnic Foods. 1982. 495.00 (ISBN 0-686-38419-9, 151). Busn Trend.
Kriin, Vera, ed. Sheraton World Cookbook. 304p. (Orig.). 1983. pap. 9.95 (ISBN 0-672-52761-8). Bobbs.
Kuper, Jessica, ed. The Anthropologists' Cookbook. (Illus.). 208p. 14.95 (ISBN 0-7100-8583-4). Routledge & Kegan.
Philip, Thangam E. Modern Cookery for Teaching & the Trade, Vol. 1. 3rd ed. (Illus.). 1062p. 1981. pap. text ed. 30.00x (ISBN 0-86131-284-8, Pub. by Orient Longman Ltd India). Apt Bks.
--Modern Cookery for Teaching & the Trade, Vol. 2. (Illus.). 824p. 1982. pap. text ed. 30.00x (ISBN 0-86125-158-X, Pub. by Orient Longman Ltd India). Apt Bks.
Rozin, Elisabeth. Ethnic Cuisine: The Flavor-Principle Cookbook. 320p. 1983. 14.95 (ISBN 0-8289-0497-9). Greene.
Sousanis, Marti E. The Art of Filo Cookbook. Virbila, Sherry, ed. (Illus.). 160p. (Orig.). 1983. pap. 7.95 (ISBN 0-943186-05-6). Aris Bks.
Zabriskie, Sherry L. & Zabriskie, George A. Empanadas: with Calzones, Pasties, Pierogis, Piroshkis, Samones, & other International Turnovers. 1983. pap. 5.95 (ISBN 0-517-54756-2, C N Potter Bks). Crown.

COOKERY, IRANIAN
Ghanoonparvar, Mohammad R. Persian Cuisine: Book One, Traditional Foods. LC 82-61281. (Illus.). 248p. (Orig.). 1982. write for info. (ISBN 0-939214-11-3); pap. 12.95 (ISBN 0-939214-10-5). Mazda Pubs.

COOKERY, IRISH
Murphy, John. Traditional Irish Recipes. (Illus.). 74p. 1982. 14.95 (ISBN 0-904651-63-0, Pub. by Salem Hse Ltd.). Merrimack Bk Serv.

COOKERY, ITALIAN
The Classic Cuisine of Sicily. 1983. write for info (ISBN 0-8120-5483-0). Barron.
Hazelton, Nika. The Regional Italian Kitchen. (Illus.). 370p. 1983. pap. 7.95 (ISBN 0-87131-413-4). M Evans.
Martini, Anna. Mondadori Regional Italian Cookbook. 1983. 18.95 (ISBN 0-517-54873-9, Harmony). Crown.
Pasquale, Bruno, Jr. The Great Chicago-Style Pizza Cookbook. (Illus.). 128p. 1983. pap. 6.95 (ISBN 0-686-42922-2). Contemp Bks.

COOKERY, JAPANESE
Green, Karen. Japanese Cooking for the American Table. (Illus.). 174p. 1982. 14.95 (ISBN 0-686-84175-1). J P Tarcher.
Haydock, Yukiko & Haydock, Bob. More Japanese Garnishes. LC 82-15563. (Illus.). 128p. 1983. 15.95 (ISBN 0-03-063611-6). HR&W.
Kumagai, Kenji. The Sushi Handbook. (Illus., Orig.). 1983. pap. 8.95 (ISBN 0-89346-211-X). Heian Intl.
Midwest Plan Service. Solar Livestock Housing Handbook. 1st ed. (Illus., Orig.). 1983. pap. 4.00 (ISBN 0-89373-056-4, MWPS-23). Midwest Plan Serv.

COOKERY, MEXICAN
Aaron, Jan & Salom, Georgine S. The Art of Mexican Cooking. 1982. pap. 2.95 (ISBN 0-451-11433-7, AE1433, Sig). NAL.
Arias, Toby & Frassanito, Elaine. Fiesta Mexicana. (Illus.). 90p. 1982. pap. 6.95 (ISBN 0-9609942-0-3). T & E Ent.
Curry. The World of Mexican Cooking. pap. 4.95 (ISBN 0-686-81679-X). Corona Pub.
Douglas, Jim. Santa Fe Cookery: Traditional New Mexican Recipes. 1982. 8.95 (ISBN 0-385-27753-9). Dial.
Mexican Cook Book. pap. 5.95 (ISBN 0-696-01030-5). Meredith Corp.
Wallace, George & Wallace, Inger. Authentic Mexican Cooking. rev. ed. LC 72-177202. 181p. 1982. pap. 5.95 (ISBN 0-911954-70-8). Nitty Gritty.

COOKERY, MICROWAVE
see Microwave Cookery

COOKERY, NEAR EAST
Dosti, Rose. Middle Eastern Cooking. (Illus.). 192p. 1982. pap. 9.95 (ISBN 0-89586-184-4). H P Bks.

COOKERY, NORWEGIAN
Roalson, Louise, ed. Notably Norwegian: Recipes, Festivals, Folk Arts. LC 82-81569. (Illus.). 88p. 1982. pap. 5.95 (ISBN 0-941016-05-6). Penfield.

COOKERY, ORIENTAL
Oriental Cook Book. pap. 5.95 (ISBN 0-696-01045-3). Meredith Corp.
Tan, Terry. The Oriental Kitchen. (Golden Asia Cookbooks Ser.). (Illus.). 336p. 1983. 49.50 (ISBN 0-686-42991-5). Hippocrene Bks.
Wong, Benita M. The Culinary Art of Modern Taiwan. (East Asian Folklore & Social Life Monographs: Vol. 104). 24p. 1980. 11.50 (ISBN 0-89986-335-3). Oriental Bk Store.

COOKERY, OUTDOOR
see also Cookery, Barbecue
Krenzel, Kathleen & Heckendorf, Robyn. The Sporting Life Gourmet. (Illus.). 74p. (Orig.). 1980. 9.95x (ISBN 0-9605410-0-4). R Louis Pub.
Outdoor Cooking. LC 82-16735. (Good Cook Ser.). lib. bdg. 19.96 (Pub. by Time-Life). Silver.
Scott, Herschel L., Jr. Dehydrator Gourmet. LC 82-61641. (Western Backpacking Ser.). (Illus.). 65p. (Orig.). 1983. pap. 3.95 (ISBN 0-88083-003-4). Poverty Hill Pr.

COOKERY, PENNSYLVANIA GERMAN
see Cookery, American

COOKERY, PHILIPPINE
Alejandro, Reynaldo. The Philippine Cookbook. (Illus.). 288p. 1983. 17.95 (ISBN 0-698-11174-5, Coward). Putnam Pub Group.

COOKERY, PUERTO RICAN
Valldejuli, Carmen A. Puerto Rican Cookery. (Illus.). 389p. 1983. Repr. of 1977 ed. 11.95 (ISBN 0-88289-411-0). Pelican.

COOKERY, QUANTITY
see Quantity Cookery

COOKERY, SOUTHERN
see Cookery, American

COOKERY, VEGETARIAN
see Vegetarian Cookery

COOKERY, VIENNESE
Gronner, Georgina. Viennese Desserts Made Easy. (Illus.). 128p. (Orig.). 1983. pap. 7.95 (ISBN 0-8092-5621-5). Contemp Bks.

COOKERY FOR ALLERGICS
Autry, Gloria D. & Allen, T. D. The Color Coded Allergy Cookbook. new ed. 400p. 1983. 16.95 (ISBN 0-672-52746-4). Bobbs.
Goulart, Frances S. One Hundred & One Allergy-Free Desserts. 1983. pap. 7.95 (ISBN 0-671-45785-3, Wallaby). S&S.
Little, Billie. Recipes for Allergies. 304p. 1983. pap. 3.95. Bantam.
Powers, Margaret. Gluten Free & Good. (Orig.). Date not set. pap. 7.95 (ISBN 0-9610140-0-8). Old Town Pr.
Roth, June. The Allergic Gourmet. (Illus.). 288p. 1983. 14.95 (ISBN 0-8092-5612-6). Contemp Bks.

COOKERY FOR DIABETICS
Barbour, Pamela G. & Spivey, Morma G. The Exchange Cookbook for Diabetic & Weight Control Programs. Davidson, Paul C., ed. LC 82-83512. (Illus.). 198p. (Orig.). 1982. pap. 9.95 (ISBN 0-9610028-0-8). G&G Pub.
Majors, Judith S. Sugar Free...Sweets & Treats. LC 82-73049. 1982. pap. 4.95 (ISBN 0-9602238-6-X). Apple Pr.

COOKERY FOR INSTITUTIONS, ETC.
see Quantity Cookery

COOKERY FOR LARGE NUMBERS
see Quantity Cookery

COOKERY FOR THE SICK
see also Cookery for Allergics; Cookery for Diabetics; Diet in Disease; Low-Fat Diet; Salt-Free Diet; Sugar-Free Diet
Schell, Merle. Tasting Good: The International Salt-Free Diet Cookbook. 1982. pap. 7.95 (ISBN 0-452-25364-0, Z5364, Plume). NAL.

COOKIES
Better Homes & Gardens Books editors, ed. Better Homes & Gardens Cookies for Kids. (Illus.). 96p. 1983. pap. 4.95 (ISBN 0-696-00865-3). Meredith Corp.
Cookies & Crackers. LC 82-5839. (Good Cook Ser.). lib. bdg. 19.96 (ISBN 0-8094-2938-1, Pub. by Time-Life). Silver.
Gohlke, Annette, ed. Bar Cookie Bonanza. LC 82-60453. 68p. 1982. pap. 2.95 (ISBN 0-89821-044-5). Reiman Assocs.
Homemade Cookies. pap. 5.95 (ISBN 0-696-01140-9). Meredith Corp.
Houston, Julie. The Woman's Day Great American Cookie Book. Date not set. pap. 5.95 (ISBN 0-449-90032-0, Columbine). Fawcett.
Riecken, Susan. A Baker's Dozen: A Sampler of Early American Cookie Cut-Outs with Recipes. (Illus.). 1982. pap. 3.95 (ISBN 0-942820-01-0). Steam Pr MA.
Stat, Bob & Stat, Susan. Complete Chocolate Chip Cookie Book. (Illus.). 128p. 1982. pap. 4.95 (ISBN 0-440-01273-2, Banbury). Dell.
Van Ness, Lottye G. The Cookie Connection. LC 81-81356. 315p. (Orig.). 1981. pap. 7.95 laminated (ISBN 0-9608648-0-6, CC-2). Van Ness LOTCO.

COOKING UTENSILS
see Kitchen Utensils

COOLEY'S ANEMIA
see Thalassemia

COOLIE LABOR
see Chinese in Foreign Countries

COOLING APPLIANCES
see Refrigeration and Refrigerating Machinery

COOLING-TOWERS
Baker, Donald R. Cooling Tower Performance. (Illus.). 1983. 40.00 (ISBN 0-8206-0300-7). Chem Pub.

COOPER, JAMES FENIMORE, 1789-1851
Cooper, James F., ed. Correspondence of James Fenimore-Cooper, 2 Vols. 776p. 1983. Repr. of 1922 ed. lib. bdg. 200.00 set (ISBN 0-89760-167-X). Telegraph Bks.

COOPERATION
Here are entered works on the theory and history of cooperation and the cooperative movement.
see also Agriculture, Cooperative; Banks and Banking, Cooperative; Collective Settlements; Cooperative Societies; International Cooperation; Profit-Sharing; Trade-Unions
Material & Techniques for Co-Operative Management Training: Project Preparation & Appraisal. 130p. 1981. 20.00 (ISBN 92-2-102446-6). Intl Labour Office.

COOPERATION, INTELLECTUAL
see Intellectual Cooperation

COOPERATION, INTERNATIONAL
see International Cooperation

COOPERATION, INTERSTATE
see Interstate Agreements

COOPERATION, LIBRARY
see Library Cooperation

COOPERATIVE AGRICULTURE
see Agriculture, Cooperative

COOPERATIVE ASSOCIATIONS
see Cooperative Societies

COOPERATIVE BANKS
see Banks and Banking, Cooperative

COOPERATIVE DISTRIBUTION
see Cooperation; Cooperative Societies

COOPERATIVE PRODUCTION
see Cooperation; Cooperative Societies

COOPERATIVE SOCIETIES
Here are entered works dealing specifically with the nature and organization of cooperative enterprises and the laws governing them. Works on the theory and history of cooperation and the cooperative movement are entered under the heading Cooperation.
see also Agriculture, Cooperative; Banks and Banking, Cooperative; Federations, Financial (Social Service)
Doyle, Kathleen E. & Hoover, Jan. Cooperative Law for California Retail Consumer Co-Ops. 316p. 1982. pap. text ed. 7.00 (ISBN 0-686-82421-0). Calif Dept Co.
Whyte, William F. & Hammer, Tove H. Worker Participation & Ownership: Cooperative Strategies for Strengthening Local Economies. LC 82-23413. (ILR Paperback Ser.). 168p. (Orig.). 1983. pap. price not set (ISBN 0-87546-097-6). ILR Pr.
COOPERATIVE STORES
see Cooperative Societies
COPENHAGEN
Fodor's Stockholm, Copenhagen, Oslo, Helsinki & Reykjavik. (Illus.). 144p. 1983. pap. 5.95 (ISBN 0-679-00966-3). McKay.
COPPER
Owen, Charles A., Jr. Biological Aspects of Copper: Occurrence, Assay & Interrelationships. LC 82-7931. (Copper in Biology & Medicine Ser.). 156p. 1983. 28.00 (ISBN 0-8155-0918-9). Noyes.
COPPER IN THE BODY
Owen, Charles A., Jr. Biological Aspects of Copper: Occurrence, Assay & Interrelationships. LC 82-7931. (Copper in Biology & Medicine Ser.). 156p. 1983. 28.00 (ISBN 0-8155-0918-9). Noyes.
COPPER INDUSTRY AND TRADE
Harris. The Copper King. 212p. 1982. 49.00x (ISBN 0-85323-111-7, Pub. by Liverpool Univ England). State Mutual Bk.
COPPER RIVER REGION, ALASKA
Hahable, William S. Alaska's Copper River: The 18th & 19th Centuries. LC 82-71377. (Alaska Historical Commission Series in History: No. 21). (Illus.). 110p. (Orig.). 1982. pap. text ed. write for info. (ISBN 0-943712-10-6). Alaska Hist.
COPTIC CHURCH
Abdel-Massih, Ernest. The Life & Miracles of Pope Kirillos VI. 139p. (Orig.). 1982. pap. text ed. 3.00 (ISBN 0-932098-20-7). St Mark Coptic Orthodox.
COPTIC LANGUAGE
see also Egyptian Language
Smith, Richard H. A Concise Coptic-English Lexicon. 96p. 1983. 10.95 (ISBN 0-8028-3581-3). Eerdmans.
COPTS
Abdel-Massih, Ernest. The Life & Miracles of Pope Kirillos VI. 139p. (Orig.). 1982. pap. text ed. 3.00 (ISBN 0-932098-20-7). St Mark Coptic Orthodox.
COPY, ADVERTISING
see Advertising Copy
COPY-BOOKS
see Penmanship–Copy-Books; Writing
COPY WRITING
see Advertising Copy
COPYRIGHT
see also Authors and Publishers; Trade-Marks
Goldstein, Paul. Copyright, Patent, Trademark & Related State Doctrines: Cases & Materials on the Law of Intellectual Property. 2nd ed. (University Casebook Ser.). 183p. 1982. write for info. tchrs. manual (ISBN 0-88277-105-1). Foundation Pr.
COPYRIGHT–MUSIC
ASCAP Staff, ed. American Society of Composers, Authors, & Publishers Copyright Law Symposium, No. 29. 250p. 1983. 20.00 (ISBN 0-231-05554-4). Columbia U Pr.
--American Society of Composers, Authors, & Publishers Copyright Law Symposium, No. 30. (ASCAP Copyright Symposium Ser.). 200p. 1983. text ed. 20.00x (ISBN 0-231-05582-X). Columbia U Pr.
Erickson, J. Gunnar & Hearn, Edward R. Musician's Guide to Copyright. rev. ed. 160p. 12.95 (ISBN 0-686-83667-7, ScribT). Scribner.
COPYRIGHT–UNITED STATES
Latman, Alan & Gorman, Robert A. Copyright for the Eighties. (Contemporary Legal Education Ser.). 622p. 1981. text ed. 26.50 (ISBN 0-87215-403-3). Michie-Bobbs.
Latman, Alan & Lightstone, James F., eds. Kaminstein Legislative History Project: A Compendium & Analytical Index of Materials Leading to the Copyright Act of 1976, Vol. II; Sections 109-114. LC 81-5953. xxxviii, 490p. 1982. text ed. 95.00x (ISBN 0-8377-0732-3). Rothman.
CORAL REEFS AND ISLANDS
Darwin, Charles R. The Structure & Distribution of Coral Reefs. 3rd ed. LC 73-147085. (Illus.). xx, 344p. 1972. write for info. (ISBN 0-404-08402-8). AMS Pr.
Endean, Robert. Australia's Great Barrier Reef. (Illus.). 348p. 1983. text ed. 29.95x (ISBN 0-7022-1678-X). U of Queensland Pr.
Sheppard, Charles. Natural History of the Coral Reef. (Illus.). 160p. 1983. 16.95 (ISBN 0-7137-1268-6, Pub. by Blandford Pr England). Sterling.
CORDOVAN LEATHER
see Leather Work
CORE CURRICULUM
see Education–Curricula
CORN
Dudley, J. W., ed. Severly Generators of Selection for Oil & Protein in Maize. 1974. 10.00 (ISBN 0-89118-502-X). Crop Sci Soc Am.
Inglett, George E., ed. Maize: Recent Progress in Chemistry & Technology. LC 82-20711. 1982. 23.50 (ISBN 0-12-370940-7). Acad Pr.
Technical Guideline for Maize Seed Technology. 192p. 1982. pap. 15.00 (ISBN 92-5-101190-7, F2323, FAO). Unipub.
CORNEA–DISEASES
Grayson, Merrill. Diseases of the Cornea. (Illus.). 640p. 1983. text ed. 89.50 (ISBN 0-686-43076-X). Mosby.
CORNELL UNIVERSITY
Margulis, Daniel, ed. A Century at Cornell. (Illus.). 232p. 1980. 19.95 (ISBN 0-938304-00-3). Cornell Daily.
CORNERS, COMMERCIAL
see Stock-Exchange
CORNU AMMONIS
see Hippocampus (Brain)
CORNWALL, ENGLAND–ANTIQUITIES
Clare, Tom. Archaeological Sites of Devon & Cornwall. 160p. 1982. 50.00x (ISBN 0-86190-057-X, Pub. by Moorland). State Mutual Bk.
CORNWALL, ENGLAND–DESCRIPTION AND TRAVEL
Baker, Denys V., ed. A View From Land's End: Writers Against a Cornish Background. 1982. 39.00x (ISBN 0-686-82341-9, Pub. by W Kimber). State Mutual Bk.
Baring-Gould, S. A Book of Cornwall. 304p. 1982. 30.00x (ISBN 0-7045-0419-7, Pub. by Wildwood House). State Mutual BK.
Darke, Jo. Cornish Landscapes. (Illus.). 64p. 1983. 12.50 (ISBN 0-7134-4187-9, Pub. by Batsford England). David & Charles.
CORNWALL, ENGLAND–SOCIAL LIFE AND CUSTOMS
Jenkin, Hamilton. Cornwall & Its People. (Illus.). 224p. 1983. 27.50 (ISBN 0-7153-4702-0). David & Charles.
CORONA, SOLAR
see Sun
CORONA DISCHARGE PHOTOGRAPHY
see Kirlian Photography
CORONARY ARTERIES
Chahine, Robert A., ed. Coronary Artery Spasm. (Illus.). 300p. 1983. monograph 34.50 (ISBN 0-87993-192-2). Futura Pub.
Kalsner, Stanley, ed. The Coronary Artery. (Illus.). 784p. 1982. text ed. 75.00 (ISBN 0-19-520398-4). Oxford U Pr.
CORONARY ARTERIES–DISEASES
see Coronary Heart Disease
CORONARY ARTERIOSCLEROSIS
see Coronary Heart Disease
CORONARY CARE UNITS
Andreoli, Kathleen G. & Fowkes, Virginia K. Comprehensive Cardiac Care: A Text for Nurses, Physicians & Other Health Practitioners. 5th ed. (Illus.). 562p. 1983. pap. text ed. 18.95 (ISBN 0-8016-0265-3). Mosby.
Meltzer, Lawrence. Intensive Coronary Care: A Manual for Nurses. 4th ed. Incl. Deal, Jacquelyn. pap. text ed. 11.95 wkbk (ISBN 0-89303-248-4). 416p. 1983. text ed. 21.95 (ISBN 0-89303-247-6). R J Brady.
CORONARY HEART DISEASE
see also Angina Pectoris; Heart–Infarction
Adgey, A. J. Acute Phase of Ischemic Heart Disease & Myocardial Infarction. 1982. text ed. 49.50 (ISBN 90-247-2675-1, Pub. by Martinus Nijhoff Netherlands). Kluwer Boston.
Goldberg, Sheldon, et al, eds. Coronary Artery Spasm & Thrombosis: Clinical Aspects. (Cardiovascular Clinics Ser.: Vol. 14: No. 1). (Illus.). 255p. 1983. text ed. 40.00 (ISBN 0-8036-4161-3, 4161-3). Davis Co.
Hammermeister, Karl E. Coronary Bypass Surgery. 464p. 1983. 43.50 (ISBN 0-03-059588-6). Praeger.
Kalsner, Stanley, ed. The Coronary Artery. (Illus.). 784p. 1982. text ed. 75.00 (ISBN 0-19-520398-4). Oxford U Pr.
Martin, Wayne. We Can Do Without Heart Attacks. 1983. 9.75 (ISBN 0-8062-1974-2). Carlton.
CORONARY THROMBOSIS
see Coronary Heart Disease
CORPORAL PUNISHMENT
see also School Discipline
Newman, Graeme R. Just & Painful: An Unbeatable Case for the Corporal Punishment of Criminals. (Illus.). 210p. (Orig.). 1983. text ed. 22.00 (ISBN 0-911577-00-9); pap. 9.95 (ISBN 0-911577-01-7). Harrow & Heston.
CORPORATE FINANCE
see Corporations–Finance
CORPORATE INSURANCE
see Insurance, Business
CORPORATE MEETINGS
Carnes, William T. Effective Meetings for Busy People: Let's Decide It & Go Home. 368p. 1983. pap. 9.95 (ISBN 0-07-010118-3, P&RB). McGraw.
CORPORATE MERGERS
see Consolidation and Merger of Corporations
CORPORATE PLANNING
Ackoff, R. L. Concept of Corporate Planning. LC 74-100318. 158p. 1969. 19.95 (ISBN 0-471-00290-9, Pub. by Wiley-Interscience). Wiley.
Ackoff, Russell L. Creating the Corporate Future: Plan or Be Planned for. LC 80-28005. 297p. 1981. 18.95 (ISBN 0-471-09009-3). Wiley.
Amara, Roy C. & Lipinski, Andrew J. Business Planning for an Uncertain Future: Scenarios & Strategies. 250p. 25.00 (ISBN 0-686-84789-X). Work in Amer.
Camillus, John C. The Practice of Strategic Planning. (League Exchange Ser.: No. 124). 79p. 1980. 5.95 (ISBN 0-686-38163-7, 21-1803). Natl League Nurse.
Corporations & the Environment: Symposium on Corporate Environmental Decision Making. 184p. 1981. 12.95 (ISBN 0-686-84019-4); pap. 7.95 (ISBN 0-86576-019-5). W Kaufmann.
Henderson, Bruce D. Henderson on Corporate Strategy. 1982. pap. 3.50 (ISBN 0-451-62127-1, ME2127, Ment). NAL.
Hussey, D. E., ed. The Truth About Corporate Planning: International Research into the Practice of Planning. (Illus.). 388p. 1983. 35.00 (ISBN 0-08-025833-6). Pergamon.
Hussey, David. Corporate Planning: Theory & Practice. 2nd ed. 468p. 35.00 (ISBN 0-686-84784-9). Work in Amer.
Tavel, Charles. The Third Industrial Age: Strategy for Business Survival. 356p. 25.00 (ISBN 0-686-84792-X). Work in Amer.
Wheelen, Thomas L. & Hunger, J. David. Strategic Management & Business Policy. LC 82-13886. 944p. 1983. text ed. 23.95 (ISBN 0-201-09011-2); instrs' manual 400 pg. avail. (ISBN 0-201-09012-0). A-W.
CORPORATION ACCOUNTING
see Corporations–Accounting
CORPORATION DIRECTORS
see Directors of Corporations
CORPORATION EXECUTIVES
see Executives
CORPORATION FINANCE
see Corporations–Finance
CORPORATION INCOME TAX
see Corporations–Taxation
CORPORATION LAW
Here are entered general works, and works on the United States For works on other countries, see local subdivisions below.
see also Bonds; Consolidation and Merger of Corporations; Corporate Meetings; Corporations, Nonprofit; Directors of Corporations; Limited Partnership; Liquidation; Public Utilities; Securities; Stocks
Berle, Adolf A., Jr. & Means, Gardiner C. The Modern Corporation & Private Property. xiii, 396p. 1982. Repr. of 1933 ed. lib. bdg. 30.00 (ISBN 0-89941-183-5). W S Hein.
Carrol, Freida, compiled by. Directory of Registering Agents Services for Delaware Incorporators. 150p. 1983. pap. text ed. 19.95 (ISBN 0-939476-87-8). Biblio Pr GA.
Conard, Alfred F., et al. Corporations-Cases, Statutes & Analysis. 2nd ed. LC 82-15888. (University Casebook Ser.). 805p. 1982. text ed. write for info. Foundation Pr.
--Editor's Notes to Corporations. 2nd ed. (University Casebook Ser.). 99p. 1982. pap. write for info. (ISBN 0-88277-117-5). Foundation Pr.
Henn, Harry G. Handbook on the Laws of Corporations & Other Business Enterprises. 3rd ed. (Handbook Ser.). 1267p. 1983. text ed. write for info. (ISBN 0-314-74292-1). West Pub.
Levinson, Daniel R. Personal Liability of Managers & Supervisors for Corporate EEO Policies & Decisions. LC 82-84264. (EEAC Monograph Ser.). 52p. (Orig.). 1982. pap. 6.95 (ISBN 0-937856-06-1). Equal Employ.
Rohrlich, Chester. Law & Practice in Corporate Control. vii, 268p. 1982. Repr. of 1933 ed. lib. bdg. 30.00 (ISBN 0-89941-184-3). W S Hein.
Samuel, Horace B. Shareholders Money. LC 82-48371. (Accountancy in Transition Ser.). 410p. 1982. lib. bdg. 40.00 (ISBN 0-8240-5328-1). Garland Pub.
Steinberg, Marc I. Corporate Internal Affairs: A Corporate & Securities Law Perspective. LC 82-16619. 296p. 1983. lib. bdg. 35.00 (ISBN 0-89930-039-1, SCS/, Quorum). Greenwood.
Williams, Phillip G. How to Form Your Own Illinois Corporation Before the Inc. Dries: A Step-by-Step Guide, with Forms. 136p. (Orig.). 1983. lib. bdg. 9.95 (ISBN 0-936284-25-0); pap. 9.95 (ISBN 0-936284-26-9). P Gaines Co.
CORPORATION LAW–FORMS
Riley, Michael. Massachusetts Legal Forms-Probate. 175p. 1983. write for info. looseleaf binder (ISBN 0-88063-013-2). Butterworth Legal Pubs.
Walsh, Joseph. Massachusetts Legal Forms-Corporations. 175p. 1983. write for info. looseleaf binder (ISBN 0-88063-015-9). Butterworth Legal Pubs.
CORPORATION LAW–GERMANY
Mueller, Rudolf & Schneider, Hannes. The German Antitrust Law. 296p. 1981. 77.00x (ISBN 0-7121-5481-7, Pub. by Macdonald & Evans). State Mutual Bk.
Olivier, M. C. The Private Company in Germany. 128p. 1976. 35.00x (ISBN 0-7121-1665-6, Pub. by Macdonald & Evans). State Mutual Bk.
CORPORATION LAW–GREAT BRITAIN
Jordan & Sons Ltd. Gore-Browne on Companies: Main Work & Three Supplements. 43rd ed. 1982. 350.00x (ISBN 0-686-82304-4, Pub. by Jordan & Sons England); 3rd supplement 65.00. State Mutual Bk.
CORPORATION MEETINGS
see Corporate Meetings
CORPORATION TAX
see Corporations–Taxation
CORPORATIONS
Here are entered works on business associations organized as legal persons. For works dealing with United States corporations see the subdivision United States which follows.
see also Bonds; Corporate Meetings; Corporate Planning; Cooperative Societies; Corporation Law; Directors of Corporations; Holding Companies; International Business Enterprises; Public Utilities; Securities; Stocks
Clinard, Marshall B. & Yeager, Peter C. Corporate Crime. LC 80-2156. Date not set. Repr. of 1980 ed. write for info. (ISBN 0-02-906420-1). Free Pr.
De Mott, D. A. Corporations at the Crossroads: Governance & Reform. 1979. 47.95 (ISBN 0-07-016330-8). McGraw.
Groening, W. A. The Modern Corporate Manager: Responsibility & Regulation. 1981. 25.95 (ISBN 0-07-024940-7). McGraw.
How to Form Your Own Corporation. 19.95 (ISBN 0-930566-27-0). FMA Bus.
Monsen, R. J. & Walters, K. D. Nationalized Companies: A Threat to American Business. 192p. 1983. 17.95 (ISBN 0-07-071569-6, GB). McGraw.
Musoff, Lloyd D. Uncle Sam's Private, Profitseeking Corporations: Comsat, Fannie Mae, Amtrak, & Conrail. LC 81-48687. 144p. 1982. 18.95x (ISBN 0-669-05532-8). Lexington Bks.
Nikolai, Lorin A., et al. The Measurement of Corporate Environmental Activity. 105p. pap. 12.95 (ISBN 0-86641-054-6, 7684). Natl Assn Accts.
Palia, Kyamas A. & Hitt, Michael A. Grand Corporate Strategy & Critical Functions: Interactive Effects of Organizational Dimensions. 236p. 1982. 26.95 (ISBN 0-03-061734-0). Praeger.
Peterson, Walter F. An Industrial Heritage: Allis-Chalmers Corporation. LC 76-57456. (Illus.). 448p. 1978. 17.50 (ISBN 0-938076-02-7). Milwaukee County.
Vested, I. M. The Confidential Memos of I. M. Vested. LC 82-60688. 208p. 1983. pap. 2.95 (ISBN 0-86721-231-4). Playboy Pbks.
Wyman, Harold E. & Ketz, J. Edward. Managing Corporate Energy Needs: The Role of Management Accounting. 116p. pap. 12.95 (ISBN 0-86641-029-5, 82136). Natl Assn Accts.
CORPORATIONS–ACCOUNTING
Chambers, R. J. Accounting is Disarray: A Case for the Reform of Company Accounts. LC 82-48354. (Accountancy in Transition Ser.). 258p. 1982. lib. bdg. 25.00 (ISBN 0-8240-5307-9). Garland pub.
Fremgen, James M. & Liao, Shu S. The Allocation of Corporate Indirect Costs. 103p. pap. 12.95 (ISBN 0-86641-006-6). Natl Assn Accts.
Joo, Jalaleddin S. An Empirical Evaluation of FASB 33 "Financial Reporting & Changing Prices". Farmer, Richard N., ed. LC 82-16062. (Research for Business Decisions Ser.: No. 55). 114p. 1982. 34.95 (ISBN 0-8357-1385-7). Univ Microfilms.
Reid, Walter & Myddleton, D. R. The Meaning of Company Acounts. 3rd ed. 354p. 1982. text ed. 47.50x (ISBN 0-566-02284-2). Gower Pub Ltd.
CORPORATIONS–CHARITABLE CONTRIBUTIONS
The Corporate Five Hundred: Directory of Corporate Philanthropy. 2nd ed. 1983. 195.00 (ISBN 0-686-82262-5). Public Management.
CORPORATIONS–CONSOLIDATION
see Consolidation and Merger of Corporations
CORPORATIONS–DIRECTORIES
Sardell, William. Modern Corporation Checklists. 1982. 56.00 (ISBN 0-88262-797-X). Warren.
CORPORATIONS–FINANCE
see also Cash Flow; Corporations–Taxation
Archer, Stephen N. & D'Ambrosio, Charles A. The Theory of Business Finance: A Book of Readings. 3rd ed. 720p. 1983. pap. 23.95 (ISBN 0-02-304150-1). Macmillan.
Arthur Andersen & Co. Interest Rate Futures: The Corporate Decision. LC 82-82392. 1982. 4.50 (ISBN 0-910586-46-2). Finan Exec.
Block, Stanley B. & Hirt, Geoffrey A. Introduction to Finance. LC 80-69851. Orig. Title: Foundation of Financial Management. 289p. 1980. Repr. of 1978 ed. text ed. 14.00 (ISBN 0-89463-030-X). Am Inst Property.
Copeland, Thomas E. & Weston, J. Fred. Financial Theory & Corporate Policy. 2nd ed. LC 82-11662. (Illus.). 704p. 1983. text ed. 26.95 (ISBN 0-201-10291-9). A-W.
Donaldson, Elvin F., et al. Corporate Finance. 4th ed. 689p. 1975. 30.50x (ISBN 0-471-06562-5); instrs'. manual 3.00 (ISBN 0-471-07459-4). Wiley.
Samuel, Horace B. Shareholders Money. LC 82-48371. (Accountancy in Transition Ser.). 410p. 1982. lib. bdg. 40.00 (ISBN 0-8240-5328-1). Garland Pub.
Vichas, Robert P. New Encyclopedia Dictionary of Systems & Procedures. LC 82-11275. 680p. 1983. 65.00 (ISBN 0-13-612705-3, Busn). P-H.

CORPORATIONS–LAWS AND LEGISLATION
see Corporation Law
CORPORATIONS–MEETINGS
see Corporate Meetings
CORPORATIONS–MERGER
see Consolidation and Merger of Corporations
CORPORATIONS–RECORDS AND CORRESPONDENCE
see Business Records
CORPORATIONS–TAXATION
see also Corporations–Charitable Contributions

Massachusetts Bar Association Staff & Massachusetts Society of Certified Public Accountants Staff. Massachusetts Corporate Tax Manual with 1982 Supplement. 300p. 1983. write for info. looseleaf binder (ISBN 0-88063-021-3). Butterworth Legal Pubs.

Paley, Stephen H., et al. Professional Corporations: An Advanced Tax Planning Program, 1982. LC 82-61269. (Tax Law & Estate Planning Course Handbook Ser.). 863p. 1982. pap. 30.00 (J4-3512). PLI.

Shepard. International Corporation Taxation. 1980. 70.00 (ISBN 0-07-050537-3). McGraw.

CORPORATIONS–AUSTRALIA

Jobson's Year Book of Public Companies of Australia & New Zealand, 1982. 54th ed. LC 72-200962. 630p. 1982. 130.00x (ISBN 0-8002-3053-1). Intl Pubns Serv.

CORPORATIONS–EUROPE

Olivier, M. C. The Private Company in Germany. 128p. 1976. 35.00x (ISBN 0-7121-1665-6, Pub. by Macdonald & Evans). State Mutual Bk.

CORPORATIONS–GREAT BRITAIN

Britian's Top Two Thousand Private Companies, 1982. 2nd ed. 264p. 1982. pap. 90.00x (ISBN 0-686-81686-2). Gale.

British Security Companies. 85p. 1982. 275.00x (ISBN 0-85938-162-5, Pub. by Jordan & Sons England). State Mutual Bk.

Bryer, R. A. & Brignal, T. J. Accounting for British Steel: A Financial Analysis of the Failure of BSC. 303p. 1982. text ed. 37.50x (ISBN 0-686-82418-0). Gower Pub Ltd.

Flanders, Dennis. The Great Livery Companies of the City of London. 120p. 1982. 75.00x (ISBN 0-284-98512-0, Pub. by C Skilton Scotland). State Mutual Bk.

Glyn-Jones, Anne. Small Firms in a Country Town. 88p. 1982. 30.00x (ISBN 0-85989-138-0, Pub. by Exeter Univ England). State Mutual Bk.

Jordan & Sons Ltd. Gore-Browne on Companies: Main Work & Three Supplements. 43rd ed. 1982. 350.00x (ISBN 0-686-82304-4, Pub. by Jordan & Sons England); 3rd supplement 65.00. State Mutual Bk.

CORPORATIONS–UNITED STATES

Agar, Herbert & Tate, Allen, eds. Who Owns America? A New Declaration of Independence. LC 82-24752. 352p. 1983. pap. text ed. 12.75 (ISBN 0-8191-2767-1). U Pr of Amer.

Lipset, Seymour M. & Schneider, William. The Confidence Gap: Business, Labor & Government in the Public Mind. LC 82-70720. (Studies of the Modern Corporation). (Illus.). 496p. 1983. text ed. 29.95 (ISBN 0-02-919230-7). Free Pr.

Mancuso, Anthony & Honigsberg, Peter. California Professional Corporations Handbook. (Orig.). 1982. pap. 19.95 (ISBN 0-917316-46-0). Nolo Pr.

Schlumberger, Anne G. The Schlumberger Adventure. LC 82-8830. (Illus.). 135p. 1983. 22.50 (ISBN 0-668-05644-4, 5644). Arco.

CORPORATIONS, BUSINESS
see Corporations
CORPORATIONS, GOVERNMENT–CANADA

Tupper, Allan & Doern, G. Bruce, eds. Public Corporations & Public Policy in Canada. 398p. 1981. pap. text ed. 16.95x (ISBN 0-920380-51-4, Inst Res Pub Canada). Renouf.

CORPORATIONS, MEMBERSHIP
see Corporations, Nonprofit
CORPORATIONS, NONPROFIT

Certain Nonprofit Organizations: Industry Audit Guide. 1981. pap. 8.50 (ISBN 0-686-84274-X). Am Inst CPA.

Council of New York Law Associates & Volunteer Lawyers for the Arts, eds. New York Not-for-Profit Organization Manual. rev. ed. 190p. 1982. pap. 20.00 (ISBN 0-686-37424-X). Coun NY Law.

The Directory of Grants for Nonprofit Management Support. 69.00 (ISBN 0-686-82263-3, 62A). Public Management.

Frederiksen, Christian P. Budgeting for Nonprofits. 57.50 (ISBN 0-686-82267-6, 42A). Public Management.

--Nonprofit Financial Management. 57.50 (ISBN 0-686-82266-8, 41A). Public Management.

Gambino, Anthony J. & Reardon, Thomas. Financial Planning & Evaluation for the Nonprofit Organization. 170p. pap. 14.95 (ISBN 0-86641-003-1, 81125). Natl Assn Accts.

Gilman, Kenneth & Public Management Institute Staff. Computer Resource Guide for Nonprofits. 175.00 (ISBN 0-686-82256-0, 68A). Public Management.

--Computers for Nonprofits. 47.50 (ISBN 0-686-82255-2, 58A). Public Management.

Gross, Malvern J. & Warshauer, William. Financial & Accounting Guide for Nonprofit Organizations. 3rd ed. 568p. 1983. price not set (ISBN 0-471-87113-3). Ronald Pr.

Hennessey, Paul. Managing Non-Profit Agencies For Results. 42.00 (ISBN 0-686-38900-X). Public Serv Materials.

Listro, John P. Accounting for Nonprofit Organizations. 112p. 1983. pap. text ed. 9.95 (ISBN 0-8403-2912-1). Kendall-Hunt.

Northeast Midwest Institute, compiled by. Guide to Government resources for Economic Development, 1983: A Handbook for Non-Profit Agencies & Municipalities. 19.95 (ISBN 0-686-38891-7). Public Serv Materials.

Salamon, Lester M. & Abramson, Alan J. The Federal Budget & the Nonprofit Sector. (The Nonprofit Sector Ser.). 116p. (Orig.). 1982. pap. text ed. 11.50 (ISBN 0-87766-318-1, 34400). Urban Inst.

Upshur, Carole. How to Set up a Non-Profit Organization. 252p. 1982. 18.95 (ISBN 0-13-433755-7); pap. 9.95 (ISBN 0-13-433748-4). P-H.

Vargo, Richard J. & Dierks, Paul A. Readings & Cases in Governmental & Nonprofit Accounting. LC 82-70506. 272p. 1983. pap. text ed. 13.95x (ISBN 0-931920-37-X). Dame Pubns.

White, Michelle J. Nonprofit Firms in a Three Sector Economy. LC 81-52791. (Coupe Ser.: No. 6). (Illus.). 181p. (Orig.). 1981. pap. 10.00 (ISBN 0-87766-312-2, URI 32700). Urban Inst.

Young, Dennis R. If Not for Profit, for What? A Behavioral Theory of the Nonprofit Sector Based on Entrepreneurship. Simon, John, frwd. by. LC 82-48482. 192p. 1983. 20.95x (ISBN 0-669-06154-9). Lexington Bks.

CORPULENCE
see Obesity
CORPUSCLES, BLOOD
see Blood Cells
CORPUSCULAR THEORY OF MATTER
see Electrons
CORRECTION OFFICER
see Correctional Personnel
CORRECTIONAL PERSONNEL

American Correctional Association. Correctional Career Logbook. 52p. (Orig.). Date not set. pap. 4.50 (ISBN 0-942974-01-8). Am Correctional.

--Correctional Personnel Compensation & Benefits. Rev. ed. 36p. Date not set. pap. 5.00 (ISBN 0-942974-06-9). Am Correctional.

--Legal Responsibility & Authority of Correctional Officers. Rev. ed. 64p. Date not set. pap. 3.50 (ISBN 0-942974-11-5). Am Correctional.

American Correctional Association Staff. An Administrator's Guide to Conditions of Confinement Litigation. 22p. (Orig.). 1979. text ed. 3.50 (ISBN 0-942974-12-3). Am Correctional.

--Classification. (Series 1: No. 4). 83p. (Orig.). 1981. pap. 5.00 (ISBN 0-942974-21-2). Am Correctional.

--Classification as a Management Tool: Theories & Models for Decision-Makers. 155p. (Orig.). 1981. pap. 9.00 (ISBN 0-942974-40-9). Am Correctional.

--Correctional Management. 40p. (Orig.). 1981. pap. 5.00 (ISBN 0-686-37661-7). Am Correctional.

Rudman, Jack. Correction Counselor. (Career Examination Ser.: C-2593). (Cloth bdg. avail. on request). pap. 12.00 (ISBN 0-8373-2593-5). Natl Learning.

--Correction Officer I. (Career Examination Ser.: C-837). (Cloth bdg. avail. on request). pap. 10.00 (ISBN 0-8373-0837-2). Natl Learning.

--Correction Officer II. (Career Examination Ser.: C-838). (Cloth bdg. avail. on request). pap. 10.00 (ISBN 0-686-84416-5). Natl Learning.

--Correction Officer III. (Career Examination Ser.: C-839). (Cloth bdg. avail. on request). pap. 12.00 (ISBN 0-8373-0839-9). Natl Learning.

--Correction Officer IV. (Career Examination Ser.: C-840). (Cloth bdg. avail. on request). pap. 12.00 (ISBN 0-8373-0840-2). Natl Learning.

Weisz, Michael & Crane, Richard. Defenses to Civil Rights Actions Against Correctional Employees. 35p. (Orig.). 1980. pap. 2.00 (ISBN 0-942974-14-X). Am Correctional.

CORRECTIONAL SERVICES
see Corrections
CORRECTIONS
see also Correctional Personnel; Imprisonment; Parole; Probation; Punishment; Rehabilitation of Criminals

American Correctional Association. Correctional Law: An Updated Bibliography of Selected Books & Articles. Rev. ed. 44p. Date not set. pap. 4.00 (ISBN 0-942974-15-8). Am Correctional.

--Directory of Juvenile & Adult: Correctional Departments, Institutions, Agencies & Paroling Authorities. Rev. ed. 400p. Date not set. pap. 25.00 (ISBN 0-942974-03-4). Am Correctional.

--Korrectional Kartoon for the Captive Audience. (Illus.). 32p. (Orig.). Date not set. pap. 4.00 (ISBN 0-942974-00-X). Am Correctional.

--Proceedings: One Hundred & Eleventh Annual Congress of Correction of the American Correctional Association. 192p. (Orig.). Date not set. pap. 10.00 (ISBN 0-942974-09-3). Am Correctional.

American Correctional Association Staff. Classification. (Series 1: No. 4). 83p. (Orig.). 1981. pap. 5.00 (ISBN 0-942974-21-2). Am Correctional.

--Classification as a Management Tool: Theories & Models for Decision-Makers. 155p. (Orig.). 1981. pap. 9.00 (ISBN 0-942974-40-9). Am Correctional.

--Community Corrections. (Series 1: No. 5). 79p. (Orig.). 1981. pap. 5.00 (ISBN 0-942974-20-4). Am Correctional.

--Correctional Management. 40p. (Orig.). 1981. pap. 5.00 (ISBN 0-686-37661-7). Am Correctional.

--Corrections & Public Awareness. (Series 2: No. 1). 25p. (Orig.). 1981. pap. 3.50 (ISBN 0-942974-22-0). Am Correctional.

--Guidelines for the Development of Policies & Procedures-Adult Community Residential Services. 220p. (Orig.). 1981. pap. 15.00 (ISBN 0-942974-32-8). Am Correctional.

--Guidelines for the Development of Policies & Procedures-Adult Correctional Institutions. 500p. (Orig.). 1981. pap. 20.00 (ISBN 0-942974-30-1). Am Correctional.

--Model Correctional Rules & Regulations. rev. ed. 50p. 1979. pap. 4.50 (ISBN 0-942974-13-1). Am Correctional.

--Standards for Adult Community Residential Services. 2nd ed. 65p. 1980. pap. 7.50 (ISBN 0-942974-27-1). Am Correctional.

--Standards for Adult Correctional Institutions. 2nd ed. 163p. 1981. pap. 10.00 (ISBN 0-942974-25-5). Am Correctional.

--Standards for Adult Local Detention Facilities. 2nd ed. 142p. 1981. pap. 10.00 (ISBN 0-942974-26-3). Am Correctional.

--Standards for Correctional Industries. 32p. (Orig.). 1981. pap. 5.00 (ISBN 0-942974-39-5). Am Correctional.

--Standards for the Administration of Correctional Agencies. 42p. (Orig.). 1979. pap. 5.00 (ISBN 0-942974-38-7). Am Correctional.

Doig, Jameson, ed. Issues and Realities in Corrections: A Symposium. 1982. pap. 6.00 (ISBN 0-918592-58-5). Policy Studies.

Fox, Vernon. Correctional Institutions. (Illus.). 336p. 1983. 21.95 (ISBN 0-13-178228-2). P-H.

Issues in Correctional Recreation. (Leisure Today Ser.). 32p. 1.50 (ISBN 0-88314-116-7). AAHPERD.

U. S. Dept of Justice, Bureau of Justice Statistics. Survey of Inmates of State Correctional Facilities, 1979. 1982. write for info. (ISBN 0-89138-941-5). ICPSR.

Weisz, Michael & Crane, Richard. Defenses to Civil Rights Actions Against Correctional Employees. 35p. (Orig.). 1980. pap. 2.00 (ISBN 0-942974-14-X). Am Correctional.

Wines, Frederick H. Punishment & Reformation. (Historical Foundations of Forensic Psychiatry & Psychology Ser.). xii, 481p. 1983. Repr. of 1919 ed. lib. bdg. 45.00 (ISBN 0-306-76184-X). Da Capo.

CORRECTIONS EMPLOYEES
see Correctional Personnel
CORRECTIVE TEACHING
see Remedial Teaching
CORRELATION OF FORCES
see Force and Energy
CORRESPONDENCE
see Commercial Correspondence; Letter-Writing; Letters
CORRESPONDENT BANKS
see Banks and Banking
CORRESPONDENTS, FOREIGN
see Journalists
CORROSION AND ANTI-CORROSIVES
see also Paint; Protective Coatings

American Water Works Association. Corrosion Control. (AWWA Handbooks-Proceedings Ser.). (Illus.). 70p. 1982. pap. 10.20 (ISBN 0-89867-283-X). Am Water Wks Assn.

Carter. Corrosion Testing for Metal Finishing. 1982. text ed. 24.95 (ISBN 0-408-01194-7). Butterworth.

Parker, Marshall. Pipe Line Corrosion & Cathodic Protection. 2nd ed. 1982. text ed. 18.95x (ISBN 0-87201-148-8). Gulf Pub.

Parkins, R. N., ed. Corrosion Processes. 320p. 1982. 61.50 (ISBN 0-85334-147-8, Pub. by Applied Sci England). Elsevier.

Seymour, R. B. Plastics vs. Corrosives. (Society of Plastics Engineers Monographs). 285p. 1982. text ed. 47.50x (ISBN 0-471-08182-5, Pub. by Wiley-Interscience). Wiley.

CORSAIRS
see Pirates
CORSICA

Ramsay, Robert. The Corsican Time-Bomb. 176p. 1982. 26.50 (ISBN 0-7190-0893-X). Manchester.

CORTEX, CEREBRAL
see Cerebral Cortex
CORTICOSTEROIDS
see Adrenocortical Hormones
CORVETTE (AUTOMOBILE)
see Automobiles–Types–Corvette
COSBY, BILL, 1938-

Woods, Harold & Woods, Geraldine. Bill Cosby: Making America Laugh & Learn. Schneider, Thomas, ed. (Taking Part Ser.). (Illus.). 48p. (gr. 3 up). 1983. PLB 7.95 (ISBN 0-87518-240-2). Dillon Pr.

COSMETICS
see also Beauty, Personal; Beauty Culture

Alexander, Jerome & Elins, Roberta. Be Your Own Makeup Artist: Jerome Alexander's Complete Makeup Workshop. LC 82-48107. (Illus.). 128p. 1983. 14.95 (ISBN 0-06-015088-2, HarpT). Harper-Row.

Balsam, M. S. & Sagarin, Edward, eds. Cosmetics: Science & Technology, 3 vols. 2nd ed. LC 75-177888. Set. 188.50x (ISBN 0-471-04650-7); Vol. 1, 1972, 605 Pgs. 67.50x (ISBN 0-471-04646-9); Vol. 2, 1972, 691 Pgs. 75.50x (ISBN 0-471-04647-7); Vol. 3, 1974, 787 Pgs. 67.50x (ISBN 0-471-04649-3, Pub. by Wiley-Interscience). Wiley.

Directory of Cosmetic & Toiletry Ingredients. 2d ed. 365p. 1982. pap. 985.00 (ISBN 0-686-84482-3). Kline.

Gallant, Ann. Cosmetic Camouflage: The Practice & Techniques. 352p. 1982. 35.00x (ISBN 0-85950-489-1, Pub. by Thornes England). State Mutual Bk.

Gunn, Fenja. The Artificial Face: A History of Cosmetics. (Illus.). 220p. (gr. 6 up). 1983. pap. 9.95 (ISBN 0-88254-795-X). Hippocrene Bks.

Wilkinson, J. B. & Moore, R. J., eds. Harry's Cosmeticology. 1982. 160.00x (ISBN 0-7114-5679-8, Pub. by Macdonald & Evans). State Mutual Bk.

COSMETOLOGY
see Beauty Culture
COSMIC HARMONY
see Harmony of the Spheres
COSMOGONY
see also Creation; Nebulae

Davies, Paul. The Edge of Infinity. 1983. pap. 6.95 (ISBN 0-671-46062-5, Touchstone Bks). S&S.

COSMOGONY, BIBLICAL
see Creation
COSMOLOGY
see also Astronomy; Creation; Earth; Harmony of the Spheres; Life on Other Planets; Philosophy; Space Sciences; Teleology; Theosophy

Caillat, Collette. Jain Cosmology. (Illus.). 192p. 1982. 55.00 (ISBN 0-517-54662-0, Harmony). Crown.

Cronin, Vincent. The View from Planet Earth: Man Looks at the Cosmos. LC 82-16654. (Illus.). 384p. 1983. pap. 6.95 (ISBN 0-688-01479-8). Quill NY.

Islam, Jumal N. The Ultimate Fate of the Universe. LC 82-14558. 150p. Date not set. price not set (ISBN 0-521-24814-0). Cambridge U Pr.

Narlikar, Jayant V. Introduction to Cosmology. (Illus.). 484p. 1983. text ed. 29.00 (ISBN 0-86720-015-4). Sci Bks Intl.

Novikov, Igor D. Evolution of the Universe. LC 82-9475. 180p. Date not set. price not set (ISBN 0-521-24129-4). Cambridge U Pr.

Szekely, Edmond B. Cosmos, Man & Society. 152p. 1973. pap. 5.80 (ISBN 0-89564-070-8). IBS Intl.

--The Cosmotherapy of the Essenes. (Illus.). 64p. 1975. pap. 3.50 (ISBN 0-89564-012-0). IBS Intl.

--The Discovery of the Essene Gospel of Peace: The Essenes & the Vatican. (Illus.). 96p. 1977. pap. 4.80 (ISBN 0-89564-004-X). IBS Intl.

Tracy, David & Lash, Nicholas. Cosmology & Theology. (Concilium 1983: Vol. 166). 128p. (Orig.). 1983. pap. 6.95 (ISBN 0-8164-2446-2). Seabury.

Van Der Merwe, Alwyn, ed. Old & New Questions in Physics, Cosmology, Philosophy, & Theoretical Biology: Essays in Honor of Wolfgang Yourgrau. 905p. 1983. 95.00x (ISBN 0-306-40962-3, Plenum Pr). Plenum Pub.

Wolfendale, A. W., ed. Progress in Cosmology. 1982. 54.50 (ISBN 90-277-1441-X, Pub. by Reidel Holland). Kluwer Boston.

COSMOLOGY–JUVENILE LITERATURE

Asimov, Isaac. How Did We Find Out About the Universe? (History of Science Ser.). (Illus.). 64p. (gr. 5-8). 1983. 7.95 (ISBN 0-8027-6476-2); lib. bdg. 8.85 (ISBN 0-8027-6477-0). Walker & Co.

COSMOLOGY, BIBLICAL
see Creation
COSMONAUTS
see Astronauts
COST
see also Value
also names of various activities or industries, with or without the subdivisions Cost of Construction, Cost of Operation, Costs, or Estimates and Costs

Belkaoui, Ahmed. Cost Accounting: A Multidimensional Emphasis. 656p. 1983. text ed. 29.95 (ISBN 0-03-061121-0). Dryden Pr.

Harper, W. M. Cost Accounting. (Cost & Management Accounting Ser.: Vol. 1). 250p. 1982. pap. text ed. 13.95 (ISBN 0-7121-0468-2). Intl Ideas.

--Management Accounting (Cost & Management Accounting, Vol. 2. 250p. 1982. pap. text ed. 13.95x (ISBN 0-7121-0469-0). Intl Ideas.

COST ACCOUNTING
see also Managerial Accounting

Davidson, S. & Weil, R. Handbook of Cost Accounting. 1978. 38.50 (ISBN 0-07-015452-X). McGraw.

Harper, W. M. Cost Accounting. (Cost & Management Accounting Ser.: Vol. 1). 250p. 1982. pap. text ed. 13.95 (ISBN 0-7121-0468-2). Intl Ideas.

--Management Accounting (Cost & Management Accounting, Vol. 2. 250p. 1982. pap. text ed. 13.95x (ISBN 0-7121-0469-0). Intl Ideas.

Sullivan, Kenneth M. Practical Computer Cost Accounting. 304p. 1983. text ed. 24.95 (ISBN 0-442-27961-2). Van Nos Reinhold.
Walker, C. J. Principles of Cost Accounting. 3rd ed. 352p. 1982. pap. text ed. 23.50x (ISBN 0-7121-1757-1). Intl Ideas.

COST AND STANDARD OF LIVING
see also Food Prices; Homelessness; Rent; Wages
Cebula, Richard J. Geographic Living-Cost Differentials. LC 82-48096. 208p. 1983. 27.95x (ISBN 0-669-05968-4). Lexington Bks.
O'Kane, Monica. Living With Adult Children. (Illus.). 208p. (Orig.). 1981. 9.95 (ISBN 0-933656-21-1); pap. 4.95 (ISBN 0-933656-20-3). Trinity Pub Hse.

COST CONTROL
see also Cost Accounting; Value Analysis (Cost Control)
National Association of Home Builders. Construction Cost Control. Rev. ed. (Illus.). 64p. 1982. pap. text ed. 13.00 (ISBN 0-86718-153-2). Natl Assn Home.

COST OF LIVING
see Cost and Standard of Living

COST OF MEDICAL CARE
see Medical Care, Cost of

COST REDUCTION
see Cost Control

COSTA RICA–POLITICS AND GOVERNMENT
Ameringer. Democracy in Costa Rica. 154p. 1982. 20.95 (ISBN 0-03-062158-5). Praeger.

COSTS
see Cost

COSTUME
see also Arms and Armor; Clothing and Dress; Cosmetics; Dressmaking; Fashion; Jewelry; Make-Up, Theatrical; Men's Clothing; Wigs and Wigmakers also individual articles of apparel, e.g. Hosiery; Gloves
O'Donnol, Shirley M. American Costume, 1915-1970: A Source Book for the Stage Costumer. Barton, Lucy, frwd. by. LC 81-48390. (Illus.). 288p. 1982. 27.50 (ISBN 0-253-30589-6). Ind U Pr.
Ross, Heather C. The Art of Arabian Costume. 1982. 59.00x (ISBN 0-907513-00-X, Pub. by Cave Pubns England). State Mutual Bk.
--The Art of Arabian Costume: A Saudi Arabian Profile. (Illus.). 188p. 1982. 50.00 (ISBN 0-7103-0031-X, Kegan Paul). Routledge & Kegan.

COSTUME–HISTORY
Costumes of Religious Orders of the Middle Ages. 300p. Date not set. pap. 35.00 (ISBN 0-87556-491-7). Saifer.
Ginsburg, Madeleine. Victorian Dress. (Illus.). 192p. 1983. text ed. 35.00 (ISBN 0-8419-0838-9). Holmes & Meier.
Harte, N. B. & Pointing, K. G. Cloth & Clothing in Medieval Europe: Essays in Memory of Professor E. M. Carus-Wilson. 448p. 1982. 50.00 (ISBN 0-435-32382-2, Pub. by Heinemann England). State Mutual Bk.
Laver, James. Costume & Fashion: A Concise History. rev. ed. (World of Art Ser.). (Illus.). 322p. 1983. pap. 9.95 (ISBN 0-19-520390-9, GB). Oxford U Pr.
Sichel, Marion. History of Children's Costume. (Costume Reference Ser.). (Illus.). 72p. 1983. 10.95 (ISBN 0-8238-0259-0). Plays.

COSTUME–GREAT BRITAIN
Ginsburg, Madeleine. Victorian Dress. (Illus.). 192p. 1983. text ed. 35.00 (ISBN 0-8419-0838-9). Holmes & Meier.
Williams-Mitchell, Christobel. Dressed for the Job: The Story of Occupational Costume. (Illus.). 144p. 1983. 16.95 (ISBN 0-7137-1020-9, Pub. by Blandford Pr England). Sterling.

COSTUME, ANCIENT
see Costume–History

COSTUME, MEDIEVAL
see Costume–History

COSTUME, MILITARY
see Uniforms, Military

COSTUME, THEATRICAL
see Costume

COSTUME DESIGN
Brockman, Helen L. Theory of Fashion Design. LC 65-25852. 268p. 1965. 26.50x (ISBN 0-471-10586-4). Wiley.
Ingham, Rosemary & Covey, Liz. The Costume Designer's Handbook: A Complete Guide for Amateur & Professional Costume Designers. 272p. 1983. 24.95 (ISBN 0-13-181289-0); pap. 12.95 (ISBN 0-13-181271-8). P-H.

COSTUME IN ART
Maeder, Edward, et al. An Elegant Art: Fashion & Fantasy in the Eighteenth Century. Freshman, Phil, ed. (Illus.). 256p. (Orig.). 1983. 45.00 (ISBN 0-8109-0864-6); pap. 16.95 (ISBN 0-87587-111-9). LA Co Art Mus.

COT DEATH
see Sudden Death in Infants

COTENANCY
see Condominium (Housing)

COTTAGE INDUSTRIES
see also Artisans; Home Labor
Allal, M. & Chuta, E. Cottage Industries & Handicrafts: Some Guidelines for Employment Promotion. 200p. 11.40 (ISBN 92-2-103029-6). Intl Labour Office.

COTTON
see also Fibers
Henderson, Herbert D. Cotton Control Board. (Economic & Social History of the World War Ser.). 1922. text ed. 39.50x (ISBN 0-686-83513-1). Elliots Bks.

COTTON GROWING
King, W. J. Cotton in the Gambia: Report on the Cotton Development Project 1975 to 1978. 1980. 35.00x (ISBN 0-85135-109-3, Pub. by Centre Overseas Research). State Mutual Bk.
Tunstall, J. P. & King, W. J. The Gumbia Cotton Handbook. 1979. 40.00x (ISBN 0-85135-100-X, Pub. by Centre Overseas Research). State Mutual Bk.

COTTON MANUFACTURE
see also Textile Industry
Montalvo, Joseph G., Jr., ed. Cotton Dust-Controlling: An Occupational Health Hazard. (ACS Symposium Ser.: NO. 189). 1982. write for info. (ISBN 0-8412-0716-X). Am Chemical.

COTTON TRADE
Bush, George S. An American Harvest: The Story of Weil Brothers-Cotton. LC 82-9797. 495p. 25.00 (ISBN 0-13-027458-5, Busn). P-H.

COTYLEDON (ANATOMY)
see Placenta

COUGARS
see Pumas

COUNCILS AND SYNODS, ECUMENICAL
see also names of Councils and Synods, e.g. Vatican Council, 2nd.
Derr, Thomas S. Barriers to Ecumenism: The Holy See & the World Council on Social Questions. LC 82-18761. 128p. (Orig.). 1983. pap. 7.95 (ISBN 0-88344-031-8). Orbis Bks.

COUNSELING
see also Employee Counseling; Genetic Counseling; Group Counseling; Interviewing; Marriage Counseling; Pastoral Counseling; Personnel Service in Education; Social Case Work; Vocational Guidance
Auvenshine, Charles D. & Noffsinger, Anne-Russell L. Counseling: Issues & Procedures in the Human Services. (Illus.). 1983. pap. text ed. price not set (ISBN 0-8391-1793-0, 14230). Univ Park.
Blocher, Donald H. & Biggs, Donald A. Counseling Psychology in Community Settings. 304p. 1983. text ed. 23.95 (ISBN 0-8261-3680-X). Springer Pub.
Bloom, Martin. The Paradox of Helping: Introduction to the Philosophy of Scientific Practice. LC 74-13524. 283p. 1975. text ed. 25.95x (ISBN 0-471-08235-X). Wiley.
Complete Guide to Consulting. 100p. 1982. pap. 3.00 (ISBN 0-686-37417-7). Ideals PA.
Dienhart, John W. A Cognitive Approach to the Ethics of Counseling Psychology. LC 82-17393. 152p. (Orig.). 1983. lib. bdg. 18.75 (ISBN 0-8191-2817-1); pap. text ed. 8.50 (ISBN 0-8191-2818-X). U Pr of Amer.
Drapela, Victor J. The Counselor as Consultant & Supervisor. (Illus.). 176p. 1983. 17.50x (ISBN 0-398-04789-8). C C Thomas.
Harper, Frederick D. & Bruce, Gail C. Counseling Techniques: An Outline & Overview. 270p. 1983. pap. text ed. price not set (ISBN 0-935392-04-1). Douglas Pubs.
Jackins, Harvey. Fundamentals of Co-Counseling Manual: Greek Translation. Anastassatos, Popi, tr. (Greek.). 1979. pap. 5.00 (ISBN 0-911214-71-2). Rational Isl.
--Fundamentals of Co-Counseling Manual: Hebrew Translation. (Orig., Hebrew.). 1979. pap. 5.00 (ISBN 0-911214-70-4). Rational Isl.
Koteskey, Ronald L. General Psychology for Christian Counselors. 308p. (Orig.). 1983. pap. 10.95 (ISBN 0-687-14044-7). Abingdon.
Ohlsen, Merle. Introduction to Counseling. LC 82-61587. 520p. 1983. text ed. 17.95 (ISBN 0-87581-290-2). Peacock Pubs.
Patterson, Lewis E. & Eisenberg, Sheldon. The Counseling Process. 3rd ed. LC 82-82906. 304p. 1982. pap. text ed. 14.95 (ISBN 0-395-33165-X). HM.
Riccardi, Vincent M. & Kurtz, Susanne M. Communication & Counseling in Health Care. 1983. pap. text ed. 14.75x (ISBN 0-398-04825-8). C C Thomas.
Wicks, Robert J. Helping Others: Ways of Listening, Sharing & Counseling. 1982. 14.95 (ISBN 0-89876-040-2). Gardner Pr.

COUNSELING–STUDY AND TEACHING
McMaster, John M. Skills in Social & Educational Caring. 148p. 1982. text ed. 32.00x (ISBN 0-566-00385-6). Gower Pub Ltd.

COUNSELING, EMPLOYEE
see Employee Counseling

COUNSELING, PASTORAL
see Pastoral Counseling

COUNSELORS, CAMP
see Camp Counselors

COUNTER-REFORMATION
see also Jesuits; Reformation
Wright, A. D. Counter Reformation. LC 82-3210. 344p. 1982. 25.00x (ISBN 0-312-17021-1). St Martin.

COUNTERESPIONAGE
see Intelligence Service

COUNTERINTELLIGENCE
see Intelligence Service

COUNTERS, DIGITAL
see Digital Counters

COUNTING
see Numeration

COUNTING DEVICES, DIGITAL
see Digital Counters

COUNTRY AND WESTERN MUSIC
see Country Music

COUNTRY HOMES
see also Second Homes
Clemenson, Heather. English Country Houses & Landed Estates. LC 82-3298. (Illus.). 256p. 1982. 30.00x (ISBN 0-312-25414-8). St Martin.

COUNTRY LIFE
see also Farm Life; Farmers; Outdoor Life; Rural Conditions
Barrette, Roy. A Countryman's Journal: Views of Life & Nature from a Maine Coastal Farm. (Illus.). 7.50 (ISBN 0-686-84139-5). Down East.
Center for Self-Sufficiency Research Division. Making the Switch from City Living to Country Living: A Bibliography. 55p. Date not set. pap. text ed. 8.95 (ISBN 0-910811-05-9). Center Self.
Clare, John. Clare's Countryside. (Illus.). 1981. 19.95 (ISBN 0-434-98013-7, Pub. by W Heinemann). David & Charles.
Drabble, Phil. Country Matters. (Illus.). 216p. 1983. 15.95 (ISBN 0-7181-2177-5, Pub by Michael Joseph). Merrimack Bk Serv.
Henke, Emerson O. Accounting for Nonprofit Organizations. 3rd ed. 228p. 1983. pap. text ed. 11.95x (ISBN 0-534-01429-1). Kent Pub Co.
Liddell, Viola G. With a Southern Accent. LC 82-10893. 272p. 1982. pap. 8.95 (ISBN 0-8173-0130-5). U of Ala Pr.
McKenzie, William H. Mountain to Mill. LC 82-18862. (Illus.). 1982. 32.95 (ISBN 0-936206-16-0). MAC Pub Inc.
Mwaniki, Nyaga. Pastoral Societies & Resistance to Change: A Re-evaluation. (Graduate Student Paper Competition Ser.: No. 3). 40p. (Orig.). 1980. pap. text ed. 2.00 (ISBN 0-941934-32-2). Ind U Afro-Amer Arts.
Ribalta, Marta, ed. Habitat: Living in the Country, No. 5. (Illus.). 181p. 1982. pap. 9.95 (ISBN 84-7031-046-1, Pub. by Editorial Blume Spain). Intl Schol Bk Serv.

COUNTRY LIFE–GREAT BRITAIN
Dodd, A. E. & Dodd, E. M. Peakland Roads & Trackways. 192p. 1982. 40.00x (ISBN 0-86190-066-9, Pub. by Moorland). State Mutual Bk.
Sancha, Sheila. The Luttrell Village: Country Life in the Middle Ages. LC 82-45585. (Illus.). 64p. (gr. 6-9). 1983. 12.45i (ISBN 0-690-04323-6, TYC-J); PLB 12.89g (ISBN 0-690-04324-4). Har-Row.
Thackrah, J. R. Making of the Yorkshire Dales. 160p. 1982. 50.00x (ISBN 0-86190-070-7, Pub. by Moorland). State Mutual Bk.

COUNTRY MUSIC
Reader's Digest Editors. The Reader's Digest Country & Western Songbook. (Illus.). 252p. 1983. Lie-flat spiral bdg. 20.50 (ISBN 0-89577-147-0, Pub. by RD Assn). Random.
Robbins, Johnny. You Can Be A Country Music Songwriter. (Illus.). 84p. 1982. pap. 4.95 (ISBN 0-9609748-0-6). Green Block.

COUNTY FINANCE
see Local Finance

COUNTY GOVERNMENT
May, George W. History of Massac County, Illinois. (Illus.). 232p. 1983. Repr. of 1955 ed. 6.00x (ISBN 0-9605566-4-8). G W May.

COUPERIN, FRANCOIS, 1668-1733
Tunley, David. Couperin. LC 81-71302. (BBC Music Guides Ser.). 104p. (Orig.). 1983. pap. 5.95 (ISBN 0-295-95924-X). U of Wash Pr.

COUPLES PSYCHOTHERAPY
see Family Psychotherapy

COURAGE
see also Fear; Heroes
Thomas Aquinas. Courage. (Summa Theologial Ser.: Vol. 42). 1966. 11.95 (ISBN 0-07-002017-5). McGraw.

COURSES OF STUDY
see Education–Curricula

COURT ADMINISTRATION
Neely, Richard. How Courts Govern America. LC 81-1048. 256p. 1983. pap. 7.95 (ISBN 0-300-02980-2). Yale U Pr.
Winsor, Ernest. Using the Indigent Court Costs Law. Spriggs, Marshall T., ed. (Tools of the Trade for Massachusetts Lawyers Ser.). (Illus.). 25p. (Orig.). 1983. pap. 0.00p.n.s. (ISBN 0-910001-02-2). MA Poverty Law.

COURT AND COURTIERS
see Courts and Courtiers

COURT CLERKS
see Clerks of Court

COURT FOOLS
see Fools and Jesters

COURT MANAGEMENT
see Court Administration

COURT REPORTS
see Law Reports, Digests, etc.

COURT RULES
see also Pleading
Publisher's Editorial Staff. District of Columbia Court Rules, 2 vols. 1981. 35.00 (ISBN 0-87215-414-9). Michie-Bobbs.

COURTESY
see also Conduct of Life
Baronian, Hagop. The Perils of Politeness. Antreassian, Jack, tr. from Armenian. (Illus.). 160p. (Orig.). 1983. pap. 7.50 (ISBN 0-935102-10-8). Ashod Pr.
Hanning, Robert W. & Rosand, David. Castiglione: The Ideal & the Real in Renaissance Culture. LC 82-6944. (Illus.). 240p. 1983. text ed. 22.50x (ISBN 0-300-02649-8). Yale U Pr.

COURTIERS
see Courts and Courtiers

COURTLY LOVE
see also Chivalry; Love
O'Donoghue, Bernard. The Courtly Love Tradition. LC 82-18180. (Literature in Context Ser.). 320p. 1983. text ed. 25.00x (ISBN 0-389-20347-5); pap. text ed. 8.95x (ISBN 0-389-20348-3). B&N Imports.

COURTS
Here are entered works on courts in general and in the United states; For works on courts in foreign countries see appropriate subdivision, e.g. Courts–Great Britain.
see also Appellate Procedure; Arbitration and Award; Civil Procedure; Court Rules; Criminal Procedure; Judges; Judicial Review; Jury; Justice, Administration Of; Juvenile Courts; Psychology, Forensic; Vigilance Committees
Birkby, Robert H. The Court & Public Policy. 435p. 1983. pap. 13.95 (ISBN 0-87187-248-X). Congr Quarterly.
Campos, German J. The Argentine Supreme Court: The Court of Constitutional Guarantees. Brisk, William J., tr. from Span. viii, 143p. 1982. pap. 15.00x (ISBN 9-500621-14-2). Rothman.
Cooper, Frank E. Administrative Agencies & the Courts. LC 51-62547. (Michigan Legal Studies). xxv, 470p. 1982. Repr. of 1951 ed. lib. bdg. 35.00 (ISBN 0-89941-171-1). W S Hein.
Donovan, J. W. Tact in Court Containing Sketches of Cases Won by Skill, Wit, Art, Tact, Courage & Eloquence with Practical Illustrations in Letters of Lawyers Giving Their Best Rules for Winning Cases. 3rd rev. ed. 135p. 1983. Repr. of 1886 ed. lib. bdg. 20.00x (ISBN 0-8377-0517-7). Rothman.
Gardner, Linda. The Texas Supreme Court: An Index of Selected Sources on the Court & Its Members, 1836 to 1981. (Tarlton Law Library Legal Bibliography Ser.: No. 25). 142p. 1982. pap. 15.00 (ISBN 0-935630-08-2). U of Tex Tarlton Law Lib.
Judson, Frederick N. The Judiciary & the People. (William Storrs Lectures). 270p. 1982. Repr. of 1913 ed. lib. bdg. 24.00x (ISBN 0-8377-0740-4). Rothman.
Kelman, Alistair & Sizer, Richard. The Computer in Court. 104p. 1982. text ed. 33.50x (ISBN 0-566-03419-0). Gower Pub Ltd.
Neely, Richard. How Courts Govern America. LC 81-1048. 256p. 1983. pap. 7.95 (ISBN 0-300-02980-2). Yale U Pr.
--How Courts Govern America. pap. 7.95 (ISBN 0-686-42823-4, Y-455). Yale U Pr.
Redish, Martin H. Federal Courts: Cases, Comments & Questions. LC 82-24763. 871p. 1983. text ed. 24.95 (ISBN 0-314-71146-5). West Pub.
Wright, Charles A. Handbook on the Law of Federal Courts. 4th ed. (Hornbook Ser.). 900p. 1983. write for info (ISBN 0-314-74293-X). West Pub.

COURTS–ADMINISTRATION
see Court Administration

COURTS–EUROPE
Usher, John. European Court Practice. (European Practice Books). 300p. 1983. lib. bdg. 50.00 (ISBN 0-379-20714-1). Oceana.

COURTS–GREAT BRITAIN
Atiyah, P. S. Law & Modern Society. 240p. 1983. 22.00 (ISBN 0-19-219166-7). Oxford U Pr.
Duman, Daniel. The Judicial Bench in England. (Royal Historical Society-Studies in History: No. 29). 208p. 1982. text ed. 33.75x (ISBN 0-901050-80-6, Pub. by Swiftbks England). Humanities.
Judson, Frederick N. The Judiciary & the People. (William Storrs Lectures). 270p. 1982. Repr. of 1913 ed. lib. bdg. 24.00x (ISBN 0-8377-0740-4). Rothman.

COURTS, JEWISH
Goodenough, Erwin R. Jurisprudence of the Jewish Courts in Egypt. 1929. text ed. 75.00x (ISBN 0-686-83604-9). Elliots Bks.

COURTS AND COURTIERS
see also Fools and Jesters; Kings and Rulers; Princes also subdivision Courts and Courtiers under names of countries, e.g. Great Britain–Court and Courtiers
Hanning, Robert W. & Rosand, David. Castiglione: The Ideal & the Real in Renaissance Culture. LC 82-6944. (Illus.). 240p. 1983. text ed. 22.50x (ISBN 0-300-02649-8). Yale U Pr.

COVENANTS (THEOLOGY)
see also Grace (Theology); Salvation
Hagin, Kenneth E. A Better Covenant. 1981. pap. 0.50 (ISBN 0-89276-251-9). Hagin Ministry.

COVERED BRIDGES
Ziegler, Phil. Sentinels of Time. (Illus.). 1983. pap. 8.95t (ISBN 0-89272-160-X). Down East.

COVERLETS
Kurita, Valerie. The Second Big Book of Afghans. 168p. 1982. 16.95 (ISBN 0-442-24863-6). Van Nos Reinhold.

COW
see Cows

COWBOY SLANG
see Cowboys–Language
COWBOYS
see also Ranch Life; Rodeos
Dary, Davis. Cowboy Culture. 1982. pap. 7.95 (ISBN 0-380-60632-1). Avon.
COWBOYS–JUVENILE LITERATURE
Artman, John. Cowboys: An Activity Book. (gr. 4-8). 1982. 5.95 (ISBN 0-86653-068-1, GA 417). Good Apple.
COWBOYS–LANGUAGE
Potter, Edgar R. Cowboy Slang. Rev. ed. 192p. 1983. pap. 9.95 (ISBN 0-87842-155-6). Mountain Pr.
COWPER, WILLIAM, 1731-1800
Cowper, William. The Letters & Prose Writings of William Cowper, Vol. III: Letters, 1787-1791. King, James & Ryskamp, Charles, eds. (Illus.). 1982. 79.00x (ISBN 0-19-812608-5). Oxford U Pr.
Hutchings, William. William Cowper: A Critical Study. 208p. 1983. text ed. 25.25x (ISBN 0-7099-1249-8, Pub. by Croom Helm Ltd England). Biblio Dist.
COWS
see also Cattle; Dairying;
also particular breeds of cattle
Karg, H. & Schallenberger, E. Factors Influencing Fertility in the Post-Partum Cow. 1982. 76.00 (ISBN 90-247-2715-4, Pub. by Martinus Nijhoff Netherlands). Kluwer Boston.
COYOTES
Cadieux, Charles L. Coyotes: Predators & Survivors. (Illus.). 224p. 1983. 16.95 (ISBN 0-913276-42-1). Stone Wall Pr.
COZZENS, JAMES GOULD, 1903-
Bruccoli, Matthew J. James Gould Cozzens: A Life Apart. 384p. 19.95 (ISBN 0-15-146048-5). HarBraceJ.
CRAFTS (HANDICRAFTS)
see Handicraft
CRAFTSMEN
see Artisans
CRAMMING
see Study, Method of
CRANE, HART, 1899-1932
Schwartz, Joseph. Hart Crane: A Reference Guide. 251p. 1983. 36.00 (ISBN 0-8161-8493-3). G K Hall.
CRANE, STEPHEN, 1871-1900
Wolford, Chester L. The Anger of Stephen Crane: Fiction & the Epic Tradition. LC 82-8491. (Illus.). xviii, 169p. 1983. 15.95x (ISBN 0-8032-4717-6). U of Nebr Pr.
CRANIUM
see Skull
CRAPS (GAME)
Spira, Robert. Craps: Pressing Your Luck. 32p. (Orig.). 1982. pap. 2.00 (ISBN 0-911455-01-9). Quartz Pr.
CRATER LAKE NATIONAL PARK
Schaffer, Jeffrey P. Crater Lake National Park & Vicinity. Winnett, Thomas, ed. (Illus.). 160p. (Orig.). 1983. pap. 8.95 (ISBN 0-89997-020-6). Wilderness Pr.
CRAYFISH
see Crustacea
CREATION
see also Cosmology; Earth; Evolution; Geology; God; Man
Baker, Ralph. Reality. 1982. 7.95 (ISBN 0-533-05434-6). Vantage.
Chittick, Donald E. Philosophies in Conflict: The Creation-Evolution Controversy. 1983. price not set (ISBN 0-88070-019-X). Multnomah.
Francuch, Peter D. Four Concepts of the Spiritual Structure of Creation. LC 82-62630. 150p. 1983. pap. 5.00 (ISBN 0-939386-05-4). Spiritual Advisory.
Friar, Wayne & Davis, Percival. A Case for Creation. 3rd ed. (Illus.). 1983. pap. 5.95 (ISBN 0-8024-0176-7). Moody.
L'Engle, Madeleine. And It Was Good. 1983. 9.95; pap. 5.95 (ISBN 0-87788-046-8). Shaw Pubs.
Long, Charles H. Alpha: The Myths of Creation. LC 82-21532. (AAR-SP Classics in Religious Studies). 320p. 1982. Repr. of 1963 ed. 13.50x (ISBN 0-89130-604-8, 00-05-04). Scholars Pr CA.
Szekely, Edmond B. The Essene Book of Creation. (Illus.). 86p. 1975. pap. 4.50 (ISBN 0-89564-005-8). IBS Intl.
--The Essene Code of Life. (Illus.). 44p. 1978. pap. 3.50 (ISBN 0-89564-013-9). IBS Intl.
Tracy, David & Lash, Nicholas. Cosmology & Theology. (Concilium 1983: Vol. 166). 128p. (Orig.). 1983. pap. 6.95 (ISBN 0-8164-2446-2). Seabury.
CREATION–JUVENILE LITERATURE
Taylor, Kenneth R. What High School Students Should Know about Creation. (YA) (gr. 9-12). 1983. pap. 2.50 (ISBN 0-8423-7872-3). Tyndale.
CREATION (LITERARY, ARTISTIC, ETC.)
see also Creative Ability; Creative Writing; Inspiration; Planning
Fifield, William. In Search of Genius. LC 82-8193. 1982. 13.95 (ISBN 0-688-03717-8). Morrow.
Getzels, Jacob W. & Csikszentmihalyi, Mihaly. The Creative Vision: A Longitudinal Study of Problem Finding in Art. LC 76-16862. 304p. 1976. 31.95x (ISBN 0-471-01486-9, Pub. by Wiley-Interscience). Wiley.
Perkins, D. N. The Mind's Best Work: A New Psychology of Creative Thinking. 328p. 1983. pap. 7.95 (ISBN 0-674-57624-1). Harvard U Pr.
Rosenberg, Harold. Art on the Edge: Creators & Situations. LC 82-24807. (Illus.). xiv, 304p. 1983. pap. 8.95 (ISBN 0-226-72674-6). U of Chicago Pr.
Rothenberg, Albert. The Emerging Goddess: The Creative Process in Art, Science, & other Fields. LC 78-26486. (Illus.). 440p. 1982. pap. 10.95 (ISBN 0-226-72949-4). U of Chicago Pr.
CREATIVE ABILITY
see also Creation (Literary, Artistic, etc.)
Buzan, Tony. Use Both Sides of Your Brain. rev. ed. (Illus.). 160p. 1983. pap. 7.25 (ISBN 0-525-48011-0, 0704-210). Dutton.
Fleming, Spencer. How to Develop the Creative Powers of your Imagination. (Human Development Library Book). (Illus.). 63p. (Orig.). 1983. pap. 6.95 (ISBN 0-89266-388-X). Am Classical Coll Pr.
Novikov, V. Artistic Truths & Dialectics of Creative Work. 342p. 1981. 10.00 (ISBN 0-8285-2296-0, Pub. by Progress Pubs USSR). Imported Pubns.
Sandblom, Philip. Creativity & Disease. (Illus.). 139p. 1982. 12.50 (ISBN 0-89313-066-4). G F Stickley.
Tichumanatman, D. Letters on Creativity: A Universalist Guidebook. 1982. pap. 5.00 (ISBN 0-686-37641-2). All In All.
CREATIVE ACTIVITIES AND SEATWORK
see also Paper Work
Armour, Richard. Educated Guesses: Light-Serious Suggestions for Parents & Teachers. LC 82-17670. 192p. (Orig.). 1983. 9.95 (ISBN 0-88007-126-5); pap. 5.95 (ISBN 0-88007-127-3). Woodbridge Pr.
Bizer, Linda & Nathan, Beverly. Discovering New Worlds. Lawrence, Leslie & Weingartner, Ronald, eds. (Bright Beginnings I). (Illus.). 48p. (Orig.). (gr. k-2). pap. 1.69 (ISBN 0-88049-023-3, 7386). Milton Bradley Co.
--Learning My Letters. Lawrence, Leslie & Weingartner, Ronald, eds. (Bright Beginnings I). (Illus.). 48p. (Orig.). (gr. k-2). pap. 1.69 (ISBN 0-88049-021-7, 7384). Milton Bradley Co.
--Learning My Numbers. Lawrence, Leslie & Weingartner, Ronald, eds. (Bright Beginnings I). (Illus.). 48p. (Orig.). (gr. k-2). pap. 1.69 (ISBN 0-88049-025-X, 7388). Milton Bradley Co.
--Put Together Take Away. Lawrence, Leslie & Weingartner, Ronald, eds. (Bright Beginnings I). (Illus.). 48p. (Orig.). (gr. k-2). pap. 1.69 (ISBN 0-88049-026-8, 7389). Milton Bradley Co.
--Spell Well. Lawrence, Leslie & Weingartner, Ronald, eds. (Bright Beginnings I). (Illus.). 48p. (Orig.). (gr. k-2). pap. 1.69 (ISBN 0-88049-028-4, 7391). Milton Bradley Co.
--Understanding What I Read. Lawrence, Leslie & Weingartner, Ronald, eds. (Bright Beginnings I). (Illus.). 48p. (Orig.). (gr. k-2). pap. 1.69 (ISBN 0-88049-024-1, 7387). Milton Bradley Co.
--Writing My Letters & Numbers. Lawrence, Leslie & Weingartner, Ronald, eds. (Bright Beginnings I). (Illus.). 48p. (Orig.). (gr. k-2). pap. 1.69 (ISBN 0-88049-027-6, 7390). Milton Bradley Co.
Brown, Osa. The Metropolitan Museum of Art Activity Book. (Illus.). 96p. (gr. 5-9). 1983. 6.95 (ISBN 0-394-85241-9). Random.
Falk, Cathy. Year-Round Preschool Activity Patterns. Bennett, Marian, ed. 48p. (Orig.). (ps-k). 1983. pap. 4.50 (ISBN 0-87239-680-0, 2141). Standard Pub.
Fearn, Leif. The First First I Think. 91p. (gr. 1-3). 1981. 6.50 (ISBN 0-940444-14-3). Kabyn.
Fearn, Leif & Garner, Irene A. Maneras de Divertirme con Mi Mente. (Illus.). 182p. (gr. 3-9). 1982. 6.50 (ISBN 0-940444-16-X). Kabyn.
Feshbach, Norma & Feshbach, Seymour. Learning to Care: Classroom Activities for Social & Affective Development. 1983. pap. text ed. 9.95 (ISBN 0-673-15804-7). Scott F.
Forte, Imogene. The Kids' Stuff Book of Patterns, Projects, & Plans to Perk Up Early Learning Programs. LC 82-83051. (Illus.). 200p. (ps-1). 1982. pap. text ed. 9.95 (ISBN 0-86530-054-2, IP 54-2). Incentive Pubs.
Frank Schaffer Publications. Beginning Activities with Pencil & Paper. (Getting Ready for Kindergarten Ser.). (Illus.). 24p. (ps-k). 1980. workbook 1.29 (ISBN 0-86734-017-7, FS 3030). Schaffer Pubns.
--Beginning Activities with Shapes. (Getting Ready for Kindergarten Ser.). (Illus.). 24p. (ps-k). 1980. workbook 1.29 (ISBN 0-86734-013-4, FS 3026). Schaffer Pubns.
--Beginning Activities with the Alphabet. (Getting Ready for Kindergarten Ser.). (Illus.). 24p. (ps-k). 1980. workbook 1.29 (ISBN 0-86734-015-0, FS 3028). Schaffer Pubns.
--Following Directions. (Helping Your Child Learn Ser.). (Illus.). 24p. (gr. 2-4). 1978. workbook 1.29 (ISBN 0-86734-008-8, FS 3009). Schaffer Pubns.
--Getting Ready for Kindergarten. (Help Your Child Learn Ser.). (Illus.). 24p. (ps-k). 1978. workbook 1.29 (ISBN 0-86734-000-2, FS 3001). Schaffer Pubns.
--Getting Ready for Math. (Getting Ready for Kindergarten Ser.). (Illus.). 24p. (ps-k). 1980. 1.29 (ISBN 0-86734-020-7, FS 3033). Schaffer Pubns.
Guenther, John. Fun with the Funnies: Fifty Motivating Activities for Language Arts, Writing, & Social Studies, Grades 4-6. 1983. pap. text ed. 7.95 (ISBN 0-673-15637-0). Scott F.
Kaufman, Tanya & Wishny, Judith. School Events. Piltch, Benjamin, ed. 64p. (gr. 2-5). 1982. 4.00 (ISBN 0-934618-04-6). Skyview Pub.
Kelley, Barbara & Tomacci, Toni M. The Vacations & Weekends Learning Guide: Ideas & Activities to Help Children Learn Throughout the Year. 208p. 1983. 14.95 (ISBN 0-13-940130-X); pap. 8.95 (ISBN 0-13-940122-9). P-H.
Kinsman, Barbara. I've Been Thinking. Lawrence, Leslie & Weingartner, Ronald, eds. (Bright Beginnings I). (Illus.). 48p. (Orig.). (gr. 1-3). pap. 1.69 (ISBN 0-88049-032-2, 7395). Milton Bradley Co.
--Numbers for All Reasons. Lawrence, Leslie & Wiengartner, Ronald, eds. (Bright Beginnings I). (Illus.). 48p. (Orig.). (gr. 1-3). pap. 1.69 (ISBN 0-88049-031-4, 7394). Milton Bradley Co.
Lamping, Ed. The Awareness Book. (Illus.). 40p. (gr. 3-6). 1982. 5.00 (ISBN 0-940444-15-1). Kabyn.
Lipson, Greta & Bolkosky, Sidney. Mighty Myth. (gr. 5-12). 1982. 9.95 (ISBN 0-86653-064-9, GA 419). Good Apple.
Mapes, Lola R. Name Games. 80p. (gr. 3-5). 1983. pap. text ed. 5.95 (ISBN 0-86530-077-1, IP 77-1). Incentive Pubs.
Melsom, Andrew. House Party Games & Amusements for the Upper Class & Other Folks. Orig. Title: Are You There, Moriarty? (Illus.). 114p. 1983. pap. 4.76i (ISBN 0-06-463577-5, EH 577). B&N NY.
Nelson, Bonnie E. Science Activities for Children Three to Nine Years Old. 102p. 1982. 20.00 (ISBN 0-931642-12-4). Lintel.
Peyo, pseud. The Smurf Activity Book. Schwarz, Rae P. (Illus.). 64p. (gr. 1-5). 1983. 3.95 (ISBN 0-394-85383-0). Random.
Polkinghorn, Anne T. & Toohey, Catherine. Creative Encounters: Activities to Expand Children's Responses to Literature. 120p. 1983. lib. bdg. 15.00 (ISBN 0-87287-371-4). Libs Unl.
Shaw, Jackie. You Can Do-Things By Yourself. 72p. (gr. 1-4). 1977. pap. 4.00 (ISBN 0-941284-00-X). Deco Design Studio.
Taylor, Jane. What We Hear. Lawrence, Leslie & Weingartner, Ronald, eds. (Bright Beginnings I). (Illus.). 48p. (Orig.). (gr. k-2). pap. 1.69 (ISBN 0-88049-030-6, 7393). Milton Bradley Co.
--What We See. Lawrence, Leslie & Weingartner, Ronald, eds. (Bright Beginnings I). (Illus.). 48p. (Orig.). (gr. k-2). pap. 1.69 (ISBN 0-88049-029-2, 7392). Milton Bradley Co.
Toole, Amy L. & Boehm, Ellen. Off to a Good Start: Four Hundred Sixty-Four Readiness Activities for Reading, Math Social Studies, & Science. (Illus.). 224p. 1983. 16.95 (ISBN 0-8027-9179-4). Walker & Co.
Westland, Cor & Knight, Jane. Playing, Living, Learning: A Worldwide Perspective on Children's Opportunities to Play. LC 81-69902. (Illus.). 211p. (Orig.). 1982. pap. 13.95x (ISBN 0-910251-02-9). Venture Pub PA.
CREATIVE WRITING
Brashers, Charles. Creative Writing Handbook. 1982. pap. 3.95 (ISBN 0-933362-04-8). Assoc Creative Writers.
Grady, Denice. Basic Skills Creative Writing Workbook. (Basic Skills Workbooks). 32p. (gr. 5-9). 1983. 0.99 (ISBN 0-8209-0549-6, EW-3). ESP.
Hammond, E. Teaching Writing. 168p. 1983. 10.95x (ISBN 0-07-025893-7). McGraw.
Leonard, Robert J. & De Beer, Peter H. Composition Practice Book: Survival Kit Individual Student Workbooks. 96p. 1982. pap. 2.95x (ISBN 0-87628-778-X). Ctr Appl Res.
Quigley, Pat. Creative Writing: A Handbook for Teaching Classes Wherever Adults Gather. (Illus.). 98p. 1982. pap. 6.95 (ISBN 0-932910-40-8). Potentials Development.
Thill, Carol J. Creative Writing. 218p. 1982. pap. text ed. 10.95x (ISBN 0-911337-00-8). Acad Pub Amer.
Vesey, Caulean. Write Your Way to Success with the Paragraph System. (Illus.). 206p. (Orig.). 1982. pap. 9.95 (ISBN 0-9609582-0-7). Excel Pr.
CREATIVE WRITING (ELEMENTARY EDUCATION)
Grady, Denice. Creative Writing. (Language Arts Ser.). 24p. (gr. 3-5). 1977. wkbk. 5.00 (ISBN 0-8209-0326-4, LA-12). ESP.
Warren, Barbara L. Capture Creativity. 40p. (gr. k-12). 1982. pap. 69.95 (ISBN 0-88450-200-7, 47000). Communication Skill.
CREATIVITY
see Creation (Literary, Artistic, etc.); Creative Ability
CRECHES (DAY NURSERIES)
see Day Care Centers
CREDIT
see also Agricultural Credit; Banks and Banking; Collecting of Accounts; Consumer Credit; Debt; Debts, Public; Export Credit; Loans
Davis, L. J. Bad Money. 224p. 1982. 12.95 (ISBN 0-312-06524-8). St Martin.
Virmani, Arvind. The Nature of Credit Markets in Less Developed Countries: A Framework for Policy Analysis. LC 82-11087. (World Bank Staff Working Papers: No. 524). (Orig.). 1982. pap. text ed. 5.00 (ISBN 0-8213-0019-9). World Bank.
CREDIT, AGRICULTURAL
see Agricultural Credit
CREDIT, CONSUMER
see Consumer Credit
CREDIT, EXPORT
see Export Credit
CREDIT COOPERATIVES
see Banks and Banking, Cooperative
CREDIT FONCIER
see Agricultural Credit
CREDIT UNIONS
see Banks and Banking, Cooperative
CREDITOR
see Debtor and Creditor
CREEDS
see also Apostles' Creed; Catechisms
also subdivision Catechisms and Creeds under names of religions, religious denominations, etc. e.g. Catholic Church–Catechisms and Creeds
Creed. 20p. 1980. pap. 7.55 (ISBN 0-88479-026-6). Arena Lettres.
CREEK INDIANS
see Indians of North America–Eastern States
CREEP OF MATERIALS
see Materials–Creep;
also subdivision Creep under names of specific materials, e.g. Concrete–Creep
CREOLE DIALECTS
Baker, Philip & Corne, Chris. Isle de France Creole: Affinities & Origins. viii, 299p. 23.50 (ISBN 0-89720-049-7); pap. 15.50 (ISBN 0-89720-048-9). Karoma.
Woolford, Ellen & Washabaugh, William, eds. The Social Context of Creolization. 149p. 1982. 15.50 (ISBN 0-89720-045-4); pap. 12.50 (ISBN 0-89720-046-2). Karoma.
CRESTS
see Heraldry
CRETACEOUS PERIOD
see Geology, Stratigraphic–Cretaceous
CREWEL WORK
see Embroidery
CRIB DEATH
see Sudden Death in Infants
CRICKET
Brown, Lionel H. Victor Trumper & the 1922 Australians. 1981. 24.95 (ISBN 0-436-07107-X, Pub. by Secker & Warburg). David & Charles.
Lillywhite, Fred & Marlar, Robin. English Crieketers Trip to Canada & the U. S. A. 1859. 1980. 12.50 (ISBN 0-437-08930-4, Pub. by World's Work). David & Charles.
Rippon, Anton. Classic Moments of the Ashes. 144p. 1982. 35.00x (ISBN 0-86190-051-0, Pub. by Moorland). State Mutual Bk.
--Cricket Around the World. 144p. 1982. 35.00x (ISBN 0-86190-055-3, Pub. by Moorland). State Mutual Bk.
CRIME AND CRIMINALS
Here are entered general works. For books dealing with crime and criminals in specific areas see the appropriate geographic subdivision, e.g. Crime and Criminals–United States.
see also Anarchism and Anarchists; Assassination; Crime Prevention; Drug Abuse and Crime; Female Offenders; Gangs; Prisoners–Education; Organized Crime; White Collar Crimes
also headings beginning with the word Criminal
American Health Research Institute, Ltd. Crime Research Index For, 1983: With Medical Subject Analysis & Bibliography. Bartone, John C., ed. 120p. 1983. 29.95 (ISBN 0-88164-036-0); pap. 21.95 (ISBN 0-88164-037-9). ABBE Pubs Assn.
Cullen, Francis T., Jr. Theories of Crime & Deviance: Accounting for Form & Content. 224p. Date not set. text ed. 27.50x (ISBN 0-86598-073-X). Allanheld.
Greenwald, Carol. Crime & Punishment. (Social Studies). 24p. (gr. 7 up). 1977. wkbk. 5.00 (ISBN 0-8209-0252-7, SS-19). ESP.
Hagan, John, ed. Quantitative Criminology: Innovations & Applications. (Research Progress Series in Criminology: Vol. 24). 160p. 1982. 18.95 (ISBN 0-8039-0948-9); pap. 8.95 (ISBN 0-8039-0949-7). Sage.
Harding, John. Victims & Offenders: Needs & Responsibilities. 54p. 1982. pap. 7.25 (ISBN 0-7199-1083-8, Pub. by Bedford England). Renouf.
Houdini, Harry. The Right Way to do Wrong: An Expose of Successful Criminals. 96p. 1983. 12.95 (ISBN 0-943224-01-2); lib. bdg. 13.95 (ISBN 0-943224-02-0); pap. 6.95 (ISBN 0-943224-03-9). Presto Bks.
Jacoby, Joseph E., ed. Classics of Criminology. LC 79-15697. (Classics Ser.). (Orig.). 1979. pap. 11.00x (ISBN 0-935610-08-1). Moore Pub IL.
Johnson, Elmer H., ed. International Handbook of Contemporary Developments in Criminology, Vol. I: General Issues & the Americas; Volume II, Europe, Africa, the Middle East & Asia, 2 Vols. LC 82-6164. (Illus.). lib. bdg. 95.00 (ISBN 0-313-21059-4, JCR/). Greenwood.
Maguire, Mike & Bennett, Trevor. Burglary in a Dwelling: The Offence, the Offender & the Victim, No. XLIX. Radzinowicz, Leon, ed. (Cambridge Studies in Crimonology). 204p. 1982. text ed. 40.00x (ISBN 0-435-82567-4). Heinemann Ed.
Man Without Qualities: Into the Millenium, The Criminals , Vol. 3. 1979. 19.95 (ISBN 0-436-29802-3, Pub by Secker & Warburg). David & Charles.
Man Without Qualities: The Like of it Now Happens, Vol. 1. 1979. 19.95 (ISBN 0-436-29800-7, Pub by Secker & Warburg). David & Charles.

Man Without Qualities: The Like of it Now Happens, Vol. 2. 1979. 19.95 (ISBN 0-436-29801-5, Pub by Secker & Warburg). David & Charles.
Murdoch, Derrick. Disappearances. LC 82-45302. (Illus.). 192p. 1983. 14.95 (ISBN 0-385-17711-9). Doubleday.
Pepinsky, Harold E., ed. Rethinking Criminology: New Premises, New Directions. (Research Progress Series in Criminology: Vol. 27). 152p. 1982. 18.95 (ISBN 0-8039-1891-7); pap. 8.95 (ISBN 0-686-82380-X). Sage.
Schreiber, Flora R. The Shoemaker. 1983. write for info. (ISBN 0-671-22652-5). S&S.
Shoham, Giora S. & Rahav, Giora. The Mark of Cain: The Stigma Theory of Crime & Social Deviance. LC 82-3173. 240p. 1982. 27.50x (ISBN 0-312-51446-8). St Martin.
Siegel, Larry J. Criminology. 650p. 1983. text ed. write for info. (ISBN 0-314-69678-4). West Pub.
Siegel, Mark A. & Jacobs, Nancy R., eds. Crime: A Serious American Problem. rev. ed. (Instructional Aides Ser.). 88p. 1982. pap. 11.95 (ISBN 0-936474-24-6). Instruct Aides TX.
Thomas, Charles W. & Hepburn, John R. Crime, Criminal Law & Criminology. 600p. 1983. pap. text ed. write for info. (ISBN 0-697-08220-2); instrs' manual avail. (ISBN 0-697-08221-0). Wm C Brown.
White, William A. Crimes & Criminals. (Historical Foundations of Forensic Psychiatry & Psychology Ser.). viii, 276p. 1983. lib. bdg. 29.50 (ISBN 0-306-76179-3). Da Capo.

CRIME AND CRIMINALS–ADDRESSES, ESSAYS, LECTURES

Doyle, A. Conan. Strange Studies from Life & Other Narratives: The Complete True Crime Writings of Sir Arthur Conan Doyle. (Conan Doyle Centennial Ser.). 96p. 1983. 11.95 (ISBN 0-934468-49-4). Gaslight.

CRIME AND CRIMINALS–BIBLIOGRAPHY

Wilson, James Q., ed. Crime & Public Policy. 400p. 1983. 22.95 (ISBN 0-917616-52-9); pap. 8.95 (ISBN 0-917616-51-0). ICS Pr.

CRIME AND CRIMINALS–BIOGRAPHY

Stout, Steve. The Starved Rock Murders. (Illus.). 210p. 1982. pap. 6.95 (ISBN 0-686-43142-1). Utica Hse.
Wright, William. The Von Bulow Affair. 384p. 1983. 16.95 (ISBN 0-440-09166-7). Delacorte.

CRIME AND CRIMINALS–IDENTIFICATION

Taylor, Lawrence. Eyewitness Identification. 304p. 1982. 35.00 (ISBN 0-686-84228-6). Michie-Bobbs.

CRIME AND CRIMINALS–AUSTRALIA

Sturma, Michael. Vice in a Vicious Society: Crime & Convicts in Mid-Nineteenth Century New South Wales. LC 82-8636. (Illus.). 224p. 1983. text ed. 32.50x (ISBN 0-7022-1911-8). U of Queensland Pr.

CRIME AND CRIMINALS–FRANCE

Wright, Gordon. Between the Guillotine & Liberty: Two Centuries of the Crime Problem in France. (Illus.). 288p. 1983. 19.95 (ISBN 0-19-503243-8). Oxford U Pr.

CRIME AND CRIMINALS–UNITED STATES

Cox, Robert V. Deadly Pursuit. LC 77-76773. 192p. 1977. 8.95 (ISBN 0-8117-0481-5). Stackpole.
Howard, Clark. Brothers In Blood. 320p. 1983. 16.95 (ISBN 0-312-10610-6, Pub. by Marek). St Martin.
Jenkins, Herbert T. Crime in Georgia: Interviews with Georgia Top Law Enforcement Officials. Jenkins, James, ed. LC 82-73850. 217p. 1982. pap. write for info. (ISBN 0-89937-035-7). Ctr Res Soc Chg.
Michaud, Stephen G. & Aynesworth, Hugh. The Only Living Witness. (Illus.). 464p. 1983. 16.95 (ISBN 0-671-44961-3, Linden). S&S.
Research & Forecasts, Inc. & Friedberg, Ardy. America Afraid: How Fear of Crime Changes the Way We Live. 256p. 1983. 15.95 (ISBN 0-453-00425-3, H425). NAL.
Sanders, William B. Criminology. LC 82-11332. 512p. 1983. text ed. write for info. (ISBN 0-201-07765-5). A-W.

CRIME AND CRIMINALS, SEXUAL

see Sex Crimes

CRIME AND DRUG ABUSE

see Drug Abuse and Crime

CRIME DETECTION

see Criminal Investigation

CRIME PREVENTION

see also Burglary Protection; Criminal Psychology; Electronics in Crime Prevention

American Correctional Association Staff. Corrections & Public Awareness. (Series 2: No. 1). 25p. (Orig.). 1981. pap. 3.50 (ISBN 0-942974-22-0). Am Correctional.
Dintino, Justin J. & Martens, Frederick T. Police Intelligence Systems in Crime Control: Maintaining a Delicate Balance in a Liberal Democracy. (Illus.). 143p. 1983. text ed. price not set (ISBN 0-398-04830-4). C C Thomas.
Sliwa, Curtis & Alliance of Guardian Angels, Inc. Street-Smart: The Guardian Angel Guide to Safe Living. LC 82-16238. (Illus.). 192p. 1982. pap. 5.95 (ISBN 0-686-82142-4). A-W.

CRIME STORIES

see Detective and Mystery Stories

CRIME STORIES (COLLECTIONS)

see Detective and Mystery Stories (Collections)

CRIME SYNDICATES

see Gangs; Organized Crime

CRIMES AND MISDEMEANORS

see Criminal Law

CRIMINAL COURTS

see also Criminal Procedure; Jury; Juvenile Courts

Feeley, Malcolm M. Court Reform On Trial: Why Simple Solutions Fail (A Twentieth Century Fund Report) 200p. 1983. 14.95 (ISBN 0-465-01437-2). Basic.

CRIMINAL INVESTIGATION

see also Crime and Criminals–Identification; Detectives; Legal Documents; Medical Jurisprudence; Police Questioning

Horgan, J. J. Criminal Investigation. 2nd ed. 1979. text ed. 21.95 (ISBN 0-07-030334-7); instr's. manual avail. McGraw.
Morris, Jack. Crime Analysis Charting. (Illus.). 70p. 1982. 9.95 (ISBN 0-686-37558-0). Palmer Pub CA.
Pena, Manuel S. Practical Criminal Investigation. LC 82-70470. (Illus.). 425p. 1982. text ed. 15.95 (ISBN 0-942728-08-4); pap. 12.95 (ISBN 0-942728-00-9). Custom Pub Co.
Smith, Edward R. Practical Guide for Private Investigators. 144p. 1982. pap. 8.95 (ISBN 0-87364-255-4). Paladin Ent.
Vandiver, James V. Criminal Investigation: A Guide to Techniques & Solutions. LC 82-10554. 408p. 1983. 27.50 (ISBN 0-8108-1576-1). Scarecrow.
Whitehouse, Jack E. How & Where to Find the Facts: Researching Criminology. LC 82-61338. 125p. (Orig.). 1983. pap. 6.95 (ISBN 0-88247-695-5). R & E Res Assoc.
--How & Where to Find the Facts: Researching Corrections Including Probation & Parole. LC 82-61337. 125p. (Orig.). 1983. pap. 6.95 (ISBN 0-88247-694-7). R & E Res Assoc.

CRIMINAL JUSTICE, ADMINISTRATION OF

see also Crime and Criminals; Criminal Investigation; Criminal Law; Criminal Procedure; Impeachments; Juvenile Courts; Juvenile Delinquency; Law Enforcement; Parole; Police; Prisons; Probation; Punishment; Rehabilitation of Criminals

Bensinger, Gad J. A Graphic Overview of the Organization & Process of the Criminal Justice System in Chicago & Cook County. (Illus.). 112p. 7.00 (ISBN 0-942854-02-0). Criminal Jus Dept.
Edelstein, C. D. & Wicks, R. J. An Introduction to Criminal Justice. 1977. text ed. 17.95 (ISBN 0-07-018980-3); instr's manual & key avail. McGraw.
Jones. Criminal Justice Administration. (Annuals of Public Adminstrations Ser.). 144p. 1983. 32.75 (ISBN 0-8247-1808-9). Dekker.
Letman, Sloan T. Criminal Justice: The Main Issues. Bracey, Dorothy H., intro. by. LC 82-23928. 1983. lib. bdg. 15.95x (ISBN 0-89950-039-0). McFarland & Co.
McGuigan, Patrick B. & Rader, Randall R., eds. Criminal Justice Reform. 1983. 14.00 (ISBN 0-89526-841-8). Regnery-Gateway.
Malinowski, B. Crime & Punishment in Primitive Societies. (A Science of Man Library Book). (Illus.). 131p. 1983. Repr. of 1926 ed. 98.75 (ISBN 0-89901-080-6). Found Class Reprints.
Morash, Merry, ed. Implementing Criminal Justice Policies: Common Problems & their Sources. (Sage Research Progress Series in Criminology: Vol. 26). 160p. 1982. 18.95 (ISBN 0-8039-1884-4); pap. 8.95 (ISBN 0-8039-1885-2). Sage.
Sanders, William B. Criminology. LC 82-11332. 512p. 1983. text ed. write for info. (ISBN 0-201-07765-5). A-W.
Schlueter, David A. Military Criminal Justice: Practice & Procedure. 425p. 1982. 35.00 (ISBN 0-87215-417-3). Michie-Bobbs.
Tonry, Michael & Morris, Norval, eds. Crime & Justice: An Annual Review of Research, Vol. 4. LC 82-13435. 344p. 1983. 25.00 (ISBN 0-226-80797-5). U of Chicago Pr.

CRIMINAL LAW

see also Abortion; Adultery; Arson; Capital Punishment; Criminal Justice, Administration of; Criminal Liability; Criminal Procedure; Fraud; Gambling; Homicide; Infanticide; Libel and Slander; Murder; Parole; Probation; Punishment; Rape; Reparation; Riots; Sex Crimes; Suicide; Tax Evasion; Traffic Violations

American Health Research Institute, Ltd. Medical Jurisprudence & Criminal Law: A Medical Subject Analysis with Research Index & Bibliography. Bartone, John C., ed. 120p. 1983. 29.95 (ISBN 0-88164-008-5); pap. 21.95 (ISBN 0-88164-009-3). ABBE Pubs Assn.
Becker, Loftus E. & Goldstein, Joseph. Supplement to Criminal Law: Theory & Process. 1983. pap. 9.95x (ISBN 0-02-912320-8). Free Pr.
Lillich, Richard B. International Aspects of Criminal Law: Enforcing United States Law in the World Community. 215p. 1981. 19.50 (ISBN 0-87215-388-6). Michie-Bobbs.
Nelken, D., ed. The Limits of the Legal Process: A Study of Landlords, Law & Crime. Date not set. price not set (ISBN 0-12-515280-9). Acad Pr.
Perkins, Rollin M. & Boyce, Ronald N. Criminal Law. 3rd ed. LC 82-15976. (University Textbook Ser.). 1269p. 1982. text ed. write for info. (ISBN 0-88277-067-5). Foundation Pr.
Samaha, Joel. Criminal Law. (Illus.). 466p. 1982. text ed. 15.95 (ISBN 0-314-69675-X). West Pub.
Thomas, Charles W. & Hepburn, John R. Crime, Criminal Law & Criminology. 600p. 1983. pap. text ed. write for info. (ISBN 0-697-08220-2); instrs' manual avail. (ISBN 0-697-08221-0). Wm C Brown.

CRIMINAL LAW–PLEADING AND PROCEDURE

see Criminal Procedure

CRIMINAL LIABILITY

Winslade, William J. & Ross, Judith W. The Insanity Plea. 240p. 1983. 14.95 (ISBN 0-684-17897-4). Scribner.

CRIMINAL PROCEDURE

see also Appellate Procedure; Criminal Law; Extradition; Instructions to Juries; Jury; Parole; Pleading; Probation; Psychology, Forensic; Sentences (Criminal Procedure); Trial Practice; Trials

Andrews, J. A. Human Rights in Criminal Procedure. 1982. lib. bdg. 85.00 (ISBN 90-247-2552-6, Pub. by Martinus Nijhoff Netherlands). Kluwer Boston.
California Superior Court Criminal Trial Judges' Deskbook: 1982 Edition. LC 82-11114. 1982. write for info. West Pub.

CRIMINAL PROCEDURE–GREAT BRITAIN

Graham, Michael H. Tightening the Reins of Justice in America: A Comparative Analysis of the Criminal Jury Trail in England & the United States. LC 82-12029. (Contributions in Legal Studies: No. 26). (Illus.). 376p. 1983. lib. bdg. 35.00 (ISBN 0-313-23598-8, GJA/). Greenwood.

CRIMINAL PSYCHOLOGY

see also Forensic Psychiatry; Prison Psychology; Psychology, Forensic; Psychology, Pathological; Sex Crimes

American Health Research Institute, Ltd. Criminal Psychology: A Medical Subject Analysis & Research Index with Bibliography. Bartone, John C., ed. 120p. 1983. 29.95 (ISBN 0-88164-024-7); pap. 21.95 (ISBN 0-88164-025-5). ABBE Pubs Assn.
Bartol, Curt R. Psychology & American Law. 384p. 1982. text ed. 22.95x (ISBN 0-534-01217-5). Wadsworth Pub.
Briggs, L. Vernon. The Manner of Man that Kills. (Historical Foundations of Forensic Psychiatry & Psychology Ser.). (Illus.). 444p. 1983. Repr. of 1921 ed. lib. bdg. 45.00 (ISBN 0-306-76182-3). Da Capo.
Eysenck, H. J. Crime & Personality. 3rd, rev. ed. 222p. 1977. 18.95 (ISBN 0-7100-8487-0). Routledge & Kegan.
Healy, William & Bronner, Augusta F. Delinquents & Criminals. (Historical Foundations of Forensic Psychiatry & Psychology Ser.). x, 317p. 1983. Repr. of 1928 ed. lib. bdg. 32.50 (ISBN 0-306-76187-4). Da Capo.
Lange, Johannes. Crime & Destiny. Haldane, Charlotte, tr. from Ger. (Historical Foundations of Forensic Psychiatry & Psychology Ser.). 250p. 1983. Repr. of 1930 ed. lib. bdg. 25.00 (ISBN 0-306-76209-9). Da Capo.
Murchison, Carl. Criminal Intelligence. (Historical Foundations of Forensic Psychiatry & Psychology Ser.). 291p. 1983. Repr. of 1926 ed. lib. bdg. 29.50 (ISBN 0-306-76183-1). Da Capo.
Sliwa, Curtis & Alliance of Guardian Angels, Inc. Street-Smart: The Guardian Angel Guide to Safe Living. LC 82-16238. (Illus.). 192p. 1982. pap. 5.95 (ISBN 0-686-82142-4). A-W.
Smith, M. Hamblin. The Psychology of the Criminal. (Historical Foundations of Forensic Psychiatry & Psychology Ser.). viii, 182p. 1983. Repr. of 1922 ed. lib. bdg. 22.50 (ISBN 0-306-76176-9). Da Capo.
Wooden, Wayne S. & Parker, Jay. Men Behind Bars: Sexual Exploitation in Prison. 250p. 1982. 15.95x (ISBN 0-306-41074-5, Plenum Pr). Plenum Pub.

CRIMINAL RESPONSIBILITY

see Criminal Liability

CRIMINALS

see Crime and Criminals

CRIMINALS, REHABILITATION OF

see Rehabilitation of Criminals

CRIMINOLOGY

see Crime and Criminals

CRIPPLE CREEK, COLORADO

McFarland, E. M. The Cripple Creek Road: A Midland Terminal Guide & Data Book. (Illus.). 1983. price not set (ISBN 0-87108-647-6). Pruett.

CRIPPLED CHILDREN

see Physically Handicapped Children

CRIPPLES

see Physically Handicapped

CRISIS INTERVENTION (PSYCHIATRY)

Aguilera, Donna C. & Messick, Janice M. Crisis Intervention: Therapy for Psychological Emergencies. (Mosby Medical Library). 1982. pap. 7.95 (ISBN 0-452-25369-1, Plume). NAL.
Greenstone, James L. & Levton, Sharon C. Crisis Intervention: A Handbook for Interveners. 224p. 1982. pap. text ed. 19.95 (ISBN 0-8403-2739-0). Kendall-Hunt.
Hawton, Keith & Catalan, Jose. Attempted Suicide: A Practical Guide to its Nature & Management. (Illus.). 150p. 1982. 14.95 (ISBN 0-19-261289-1). Oxford U Pr.

CRISIS THEOLOGY

see Dialectical Theology

CRITICAL CARE UNITS

see Intensive Care Units

CRITICAL PATH ANALYSIS

Brennan, J. Applications of Critical Path Techniques. 1968. 22.50 (ISBN 0-444-19976-4). Elsevier.

CRITICISM

Here are entered works on the principles of criticism in general and of literary criticism in particular. Criticism in a specific field is entered under the appropriate heading, e.g. Art Criticism; English Literature–History and Criticism; English Poetry–History and Criticism; Literature–History and Criticism; Music–History and Criticism. Criticism of the work of an individual is entered under the name of the individual.

see also Bible–Criticism, Interpretation, etc.; Books–Reviews; Esthetics; Hermeneutics; Literature–History and Criticism; Moving-Picture Criticism

also Criticism in specific fields e.g. Art Criticism; English Literature–History and Criticism; also names of individuals, with or without the subdivision Criticism and Interpretation

Amirthanayagam, G. & Harrex, S. C., eds. Only Connect: Literary Perspectives East & West. 335p. 1981. pap. text ed. 19.95x (ISBN 0-7258-0197-2, Pub. by Flinders U Australia). Humanities.
Benda, Julien. Belphegor. Lawson, S. J., tr. from Fr. LC 82-73432. 165p. Repr. of 1929 ed. lib. bdg. 15.00 (ISBN 0-88116-000-8). Brenner Bks.
Birenbaum, Harvey. Tragedy & Innocence. LC 82-23828. (Illus.). 176p. (Orig.). 1983. lib. bdg. 20.75 (ISBN 0-8191-2991-7); pap. text ed. 9.75 (ISBN 0-8191-2992-5). U Pr of Amer.
Bloom, Harold. The Breaking of the Vessels. LC 81-12975. xiv, 108p. 1982. pap. 4.95 (ISBN 0-226-06044-6). U of Chicago Pr.
Craige, Betty J., ed. Relativism in the Arts. LC 82-4726. 216p. text ed. 19.00x (ISBN 0-8203-0625-8). U of Ga Pr.
De Man, Paul. Blindness & Insight: Essays in the Rhetoric of Contemporary Criticism. 2nd, rev. ed. (Theory & History of Literature Ser.: Vol. 7). 288p. 1983. 29.50x (ISBN 0-8166-1134-3); pap. 12.95 (ISBN 0-8166-1135-1). U of Minn Pr.
Leavis, F. R. The Critic as Anti-Philosopher. Singh, G., ed. Bd. with Essays & Papers. LC 82-13580. 208p. 1983. text ed. 16.00x (ISBN 0-8203-0656-8). U of Ga Pr.
Lewisohn, Ludwig. A Modern Book of Criticism. 210p. 1982. Repr. of 1919 ed. lib. bdg. 25.00 (ISBN 0-89760-515-2). Telegraph Bks.
Oates, J. C. Shandyism & Sentiment, Seventy Sixty to Eighteen Hundred. 60p. 1982. Repr. of 1968 ed. lib. bdg. 10.00 (ISBN 0-89760-633-7). Telegraph Bks.
Rannie, David W. The Elements of Style: An Introduction to Literary Criticism. 312p. 1982. Repr. of 1960 ed. lib. bdg. 40.00 (ISBN 0-89760-775-9). Telegraph Bks.
Reeves, James. The Critical Sense: Practical Criticism of Prose & of Poetry. 159p. 1982. Repr. of 1956 ed. lib. bdg. 25.00 (ISBN 0-8495-4700-8). Arden Lib.
Roberts, Michael. T. E. Hulme. 356p. 1982. Repr. of 1938 ed. text ed. 21.00x (ISBN 0-85635-411-2, 61258, Pub. by Carcanet New Pr England). Humanities.
Rodway, Allan. The Craft of Criticism. LC 82-4499. 192p. 1982. 32.50 (ISBN 0-521-23320-8); pap. 9.95 (ISBN 0-521-29909-8). Cambridge U Pr.
Shafer, Robert. Paul Elmermoore & American Criticism. 1935. text ed. 19.50x (ISBN 0-686-83688-X). Elliots Bks.
Shaffer, E. S. Comparative Criticism: A Yearbook, Vol. 4. (Illus.). 320p. 1982. 49.50 (ISBN 0-521-24578-8). Cambridge U Pr.
Tinker, Chauncey B. Good Estate of Poetry. 1929. text ed. 9.50x (ISBN 0-686-83561-1). Elliots Bks.

CRITICISM–ADDRESSES, ESSAYS, LECTURES

Arac, Johnathan, et al, eds. The Yale Critics: Deconstruction in America. LC 83-1127. (Theory & History of Literature Ser.: Vol. 6). 288p. 1983. 29.50x (ISBN 0-8166-1201-3); pap. 12.95 (ISBN 0-8166-1206-4). U of Minn Pr.
Cook, Eleanor & Hosek, Chaviva, eds. Centre & Labyrinth: Essays in Honour of Northrop Frye. 328p. 1982. 35.00x (ISBN 0-8020-2496-3). U of Toronto Pr.
Paz, Octavio. Alternating Current. 256p. 1983. 14.95 (ISBN 0-394-53212-0); pap. 7.95 (ISBN 0-394-62470-X). Seaver Bks.
Said, Edward W. The World, the Text, & the Critic. 352p. 1983. 20.00x (ISBN 0-674-96186-2). Harvard U Pr.

CRITICISM–GREAT BRITAIN

Garrett, William. Charles Wentworth Dilke. (World Authors Ser.). 1982. lib. bdg. 17.95 (ISBN 0-8057-6792-4, Twayne). G K Hall.

CRITICISM (PHILOSOPHY)

Battersby, James J. Elder Olson: An Annotated Bibliography. LC 82-48273. 250p. 1982. lib. bdg. 30.00 (ISBN 0-8240-9254-6). Garland Pub.
Wexler, Philip. Critical Social Psychology. (Critical Social Thought Ser.). 176p. 1983. 17.50 (ISBN 0-7100-9194-X). Routledge & Kegan.

CRITICISM, TEXTUAL

McGann, Jerome J. A Critique of Modern Textual Criticism. 144p. 1983. lib. bdg. 12.00x (ISBN 0-226-55851-7). U of Chicago Pr.

CROATIAN LANGUAGE

see Serbo-Croatian Language

CROATO-SERBIAN LANGUAGE
see Serbo-Croatian Language
CROCHETING
see also Beadwork; Lace and Lace Making
Chilton Staff, ed. McCall's Big Book of Christmas Knit & Crochet. LC 82-70537. 304p. (Orig.). 1982. pap. 12.95 (ISBN 0-8019-7252-3). Chilton.
--McCall's Big Book of Knit Crochet. LC 82-70538. (Illus.). 304p. (Orig.). 1982. pap. 12.95 (ISBN 0-8019-7253-1). Chilton.
Lep, Annette. Crocheting Baby Blankets & Carriage Covers. (Illus.). 48p. (Orig.). 1983. pap. 2.25 (ISBN 0-486-24480-6). Dover.
Suzuki, Yoko. Elegant Crochet Laces. (Illus.). 100p. (Orig.). 1983. pap. 6.95 (ISBN 0-87040-528-4). Kodansha.
CROCKERY
see Pottery
CROCKERY COOKERY, ELECTRIC
see Electric Cookery, Slow
CROCKETT, DAVID, 1786-1836
Bishop, Lee. Davy Crockett: Frontier Fighter. (American Explorer Ser.: No. 11). (Orig.). 1983. pap. 2.95 (ISBN 0-440-01695-9). Dell.
CROCKETT, DAVID, 1786-1836-JUVENILE LITERATURE
Santrey, Laurence. Davy Crockett: Young Pioneer. LC 82-16040. (Illus.). 48p. (gr. 4-6). 1983. PLB 6.89 (ISBN 0-89375-847-7); pap. text ed. 1.95 (ISBN 0-89375-848-5). Troll Assocs.
CRONIN, ARCHIBALD JOSEPH, 1896-
Salwak, Dale. A. J. Cronin: A Reference Guide. 1983. lib. bdg. 28.00 (ISBN 0-8161-8595-6, Hall Reference). G K Hall.
CROP ESTIMATING
see Agricultural Estimating and Reporting
CROP YIELDS
see also Agricultural Estimating and Reporting; Crops and Climate
The Effect of Meteorological Factors on Crop Yields & Methods of Forecasting the Yield. (Technical Note Ser.: No. 174). 54p. 1982. pap. 7.00 (ISBN 92-63-10566-9, W540, WMO). Unipub.
CROPS
see Agriculture; Field Crops; Plants, Cultivated
CROPS AND CLIMATE
see also Crop Yields; Vegetation and Climate
Kilmer, Victor J., ed. Handbook of Soils & Climate in Agriculture. 456p. 1982. 94.00 (ISBN 0-686-84130-1). CRC Pr.
CROQUET
Osborn, Jack R. & Kornbluth, Jesse. Winning Croquet: From Backyard to Greensward. 1983. price not set (ISBN 0-671-47276-3). S&S.
CROSBY, BING
Crosby, Kathryn. My Life With Bing. LC 82-74361. (Illus.). 358p. 1983. 29.95 (ISBN 0-938728-01-6). Collage Inc.
CROSS-COUNTRY RUNNING
see Running
CROSS-COUNTRY SKIING
Jeneid, Michael & Martens, Tom. Five Easy Turns: A Guide to Cross-Country Ski Turns. (Illus.). 72p. 1980. pap. 7.95 (ISBN 0-9610410-0-5). Nordic Ski.
Satterfield, Archie & Bauer, Eddie. The Eddie Bauer Guide to Cross-Country Skiing. (Illus.). 256p. 1982. 17.95 (ISBN 0-201-07774-4); pap. 8.95 (ISBN 0-201-07775-2). A-W.
Woodward, Robert. The Technique Book for Cross-Country Skiing. LC 82-83918. (Illus.). 176p. (Orig.). 1983. pap. 6.95 (ISBN 0-88011-123-2). Leisure Pr.
CROSS-EXAMINATION
see also Evidence (Law); Witnesses
Reynolds, William. The Theory of the Law of Evidence as Established in the United States & of the Conduct of the Examination of Witnesses. 3rd ed. xix, 206p. 1983. Repr. of 1897 ed. lib. bdg. 22.50x (ISBN 0-8377-1039-1). Rothman.
CROSS-EYE
see Strabismus
CROSS-STITCH
see also Samplers
Lindberg, Jana H. Counted Cross-Stitch Designs for All Seasons. (Illus.). 96p. 1983. 15.95 (ISBN 0-686-83666-9, ScribT). Scribner.
Nihon Vogue Staff. Lovely Cross Stich Designs. (Illus.). 84p. (Orig.). 1983. pap. 6.95 (ISBN 0-87040-529-2). Kodansha.
Ondori Staff. Elegant Cross-Stich Embroidery. (Illus.). 100p. (Orig.). 1983. pap. 9.50 (ISBN 0-87040-538-1). Japan Pubns.
--Embroidery & Cross-Stich for Framing. (Illus.). 100p. (Orig.). 1983. pap. 9.50 (ISBN 0-87040-537-3). Japan Pubns.
CROSS-WORD PUZZLES
see Crossword Puzzles
CROSSWORD PUZZLES
Associated Press, ed. The Associated Press Sunday Crossword Puzzle Book. (Illus.). 96p. (Orig.). 1983. 4.95 (ISBN 0-8092-5573-1). Contemp Bks.
Bell, Irene W. Literature Cross-A-Word Book II: Crossword Learning Experiences with Historical Fiction Mystery & Detective Stories, & Newbery Award Winners. (Illus.). 96p. 1982. pap. 12.50 (ISBN 0-89774-070-X). Oryx Pr.
Crossword Puzzles II. 18p. 1981. pap. 7.55 (ISBN 0-88479-033-9). Arena Lettres.
Crowther, Jonathan. Intermediate Crosswords, for Learners of English as a Foreign Language. 46p. 1980. pap. 3.25x (ISBN 0-19-581751-6). Oxford U Pr.
Diagram Group. Crossword Puzzles: How to Make Your Own. 160p. 1982. pap. 7.95 (ISBN 0-312-17689-9). St Martin.
Ettenson, Herb, ed. The Puzzle Lover's Daily Crossword, No. 6. 128p. (Orig.). 1983. pap. 1.75 (ISBN 0-425-05857-3). Berkley Pub.
Hill, Norman. Webster's Red Seal Crossword Dictionary. 272p. 1982. pap. 2.75 (ISBN 0-446-31055-7). Warner Bks.
Justus, Fred. Crossword Puzzles. (Puzzles Ser.). 24p. (gr. 5). 1980. wkbk. 5.00 (ISBN 0-8209-0295-0, PU-9). ESP.
--Crossword Puzzles Using Rhyming Words. (Puzzles Ser.). 24p. (gr. 5-7). 1980. wkbk. 5.00 (ISBN 0-8209-0299-3, PU-13). ESP.
Manchester, Richard B. Grab a Pencil Book of Crossword Puzzles. (Grab a Pencil Ser.). 256p. (Orig.). 1983. pap. 4.95 (ISBN 0-89104-326-8, A & W Visual Library). A & W Pubs.
Moore, Rosalind, ed. Dell Crossword Puzzles, No. 45. (Orig.). 1983. pap. 2.50 (ISBN 0-440-11901-4). Dell.
Preston, Charles. Signet Crossword Puzzle Book, No. 6. 1982. pap. 1.75 (ISBN 0-451-11473-6, AE1473, Sig). NAL.
Preston, Charles, ed. Dow Jones-Irwin Crosswords for the Serious, Bk. 11. 48p. (Orig.). 1983. pap. 3.95 (ISBN 0-87094-372-3). Dow Jones-Irwin.
--Dow Jones-Irwin Crosswords for the Serious, Bk. 12. 48p. (Orig.). 1983. pap. 3.95 (ISBN 0-87094-373-1). Dow Jones-Irwin.
--Dow Jones-Irwin Crosswords for the Serious, Bk. 13. 48p. (Orig.). 1983. pap. 3.95 (ISBN 0-87094-407-X). Dow Jones-Irwin.
--Dow Jones-Irwin Crosswords for the Serious, Bk. 14. 48p. (Orig.). 1983. pap. 3.95 (ISBN 0-87094-408-8). Dow Jones-Irwin.
--Dow Jones-Irwin Crosswords for the Serious, Bk. 15. 48p. (Orig.). 1983. pap. 3.95 (ISBN 0-87094-409-6). Dow Jones-Irwin.
--Dow Jones-Irwin Crosswords for the Serious, Bk. 16. 48p. (Orig.). 1983. pap. 3.95 (ISBN 0-87094-410-X). Dow Jones-Irwin.
--Signet Crossword Puzzle Book, No. 7. 1982. pap. 1.75 (ISBN 0-451-11570-8, AE1570, Sig). NAL.
Rosen, Mel, ed. Crosswords: From the Nation's Expert Puzzle Constructors, Fifty Stimulating Stumpers Guaranteed to Challenge & Tantalize any Crossword Connoisseur. 122p. (Orig.). 1983. lib. bdg. 12.90 (ISBN 0-89471-197-0); pap. 4.95 (ISBN 0-89471-196-2). Running Pr.
Weng, Will. The New York Times Crossword Puzzles Omnibus, Vol. 2. 1982. pap. 8.95 (ISBN 0-8129-1018-4). Times Bks.
CROSSWORD PUZZLES-GLOSSARIES, VOCABULARIES, ETC.
Rafferty, Kathleen, ed. The Dell Crossword Dictionary. 1983. pap. 5.95 (ISBN 0-440-56314-3, Dell Trade Pbks). Dell.
Room, Adrian. Dictionary of Cryptic Crossword Clues. 288p. 1983. price not set (ISBN 0-7100-9415-9). Routledge & Kegan.
Webster's New World Crossword Puzzle Dictionary. 1983. pap. write for info. (ISBN 0-671-46870-7). S&S.
CROW INDIANS
see Indians of North America-The West
CROWDS
see also Riots
LeBow, Gustave. The Crowd. LC 26-6009. 1969. pap. 4.95 (ISBN 0-910220-16-6). Berg.
CROWLEY, ALEISTER
Regardie, Israel & Stephensen, P. R. The Legend of Aleister Crowley. 175p. 1983. pap. 9.95 (ISBN 0-941404-20-X). Falcon Pr Az.
CROWN JEWELS
Feinberg, Karen. Crown Jewels. LC 82-60559. (Illus.). 64p. 1982. 24.00 (ISBN 0-88014-055-0). Mosaic Pr OH.
CRUCIFIXION OF CHRIST
see Jesus Christ-Crucifixion
CRUDE OIL
see Petroleum
CRUELTY TO CHILDREN
see Child Abuse
CRUSADES-LATER, 13TH, 14TH, AND 15TH CENTURIES
Housley, Norman. The Italian Crusade: The Papal-Angevin Alliance & the Crusades Against Christian Lay Powers, 1254-1343. (Illus.). 308p. 1982. 44.00x (ISBN 0-19-821925-3). Oxford U Pr.
CRUSTACEA
see also Ostracoda
Bliss, Dorothy, ed. The Biology of Crustacea: Vol. 7: Behavior & Ecology of Crustacea. Date not set. price not set (ISBN 0-12-106407-7). Acad Pr.
Bliss, Dorothy E., ed. The Biology of Crustacea: Environmental Adaptations, Vol. 8. Date not set. price not set (ISBN 0-12-106408-5). Acad Pr.
Bliss, Dorothy E. & Provenzano, J., eds. Biology of the Crustacea: Vol. 6, Economic Aspects: Pathobiology, Culture & Fisheries. LC 82-4058. Date not set. 39.00 (ISBN 0-12-106406-9). Acad Pr.
Chapman, M. A. & Lewis, M. H. An Introduction to the Freshwater Crustacea of New Zealand. (Illus.). 261p. 1983. 19.95 (ISBN 0-00-216905-3, Pub. by W Collins Australia). Intl Schol Bk Serv.
Morgan, Mark D. Ecology of Mysidacea. 1982. text ed. 54.50 (ISBN 90-6193-761-2, Pub. by Junk Pubs Netherlands). Kluwer Boston.
CRYOGENICS
see Low Temperature Engineering; Refrigeration and Refrigerating Machinery
CRYPTANALYSIS
see Cryptography
CRYPTESTHESIA
see Extrasensory Perception
CRYPTOGAMS, VASCULAR
see Pteridophyta
CRYPTOGRAPHY
see also Ciphers
Bosworth. Codes, Ciphers, & Computers: An Introduction to Information Security. Date not set. 13.95 (ISBN 0-686-82006-1, 5149). Hayden.
Foster. Cryptanalysis for Microcomputers. Date not set. 14.95 (ISBN 0-686-82007-X, 5174). Hayden.
CRYSTAL GROWTH
see Crystals-Growth
CRYSTALLINE SEMICONDUCTORS
see Semiconductors
CRYSTALLIZATION
see also Crystals-Growth
Nyvlt, Jaroslav. Industrial Crystallisation: The Present State of the Art. 2nd ed. 1983. pap. write for info. (ISBN 0-89573-069-3). Verlag-Chemie.
Rudman, Reuben, ed. Diffraction Aspects of Orientationally Disordered (Plastic) Crystals. Date not set. pap. 10.00 (ISBN 0-937140-26-0). Polycrystal Bk Serv.
CRYSTALLOGRAPHY
see also Crystals; Geology; Mineralogy; Oscillators, Crystal; Pyro- and Piezo-Electricity
also names of minerals
Brown, F. C. & Noriaki Itoh, eds. Recombination-Induced Defect Formation in Crystals. (Semiconductors & Insulators Ser.: Special Issue). 300p. 1983. write for info. (ISBN 0-677-40365-8). Gordon.
Epstein, A. J. & Conwell, E. M., eds. Low-Dimensional Conductors. (Molecular Crystals & Liquid Crystals Ser.: Vols. 77, 79, 81, 83, 85, & 86). 2078p. 1982. 620.00 (ISBN 0-677-16405-X). Gordon.
Jaswon, M. A. & Rose, M. A. Crystal Symmetry: The Theory of Colour Crystallography. (Mathematics & Its Applications Ser.). 150p. 1983. 47.95x (ISBN 0-470-27353-4). Halsted Pr.
Koetzle, T. F., ed. Structure & Bonding: Relationships Between Quantum Chemistry & Crystallography. Date not set. pap. 7.50 (ISBN 0-937140-25-2). Polycrystal Bk Serv.
Smith, J. V. Geometrical & Structural Crystallography. (Smith-Wylie Intermediate Geology Ser.). 450p. 1982. text ed. 29.95 (ISBN 0-471-86168-5). Wiley.
CRYSTALS
see also Oscillators, Crystal; Semiconductors
also names of particular types of crystals
Business Communications Staff. Synthetic Crystals. 1983. 1250.00 (ISBN 0-89336-350-2, C-039). BCC.
Decius, J. C. & Hexter, R. M. Molecular Vibrations in Crystals. 1977. 47.50 (ISBN 0-07-016227-1). McGraw.
Freyhardt, H. C. Analytical Methods: High-Melting Metals. (Crystals, Growth, Properties, & Applications Ser.: Vol. 7). (Illus.). 150p. 1982. 42.00 (ISBN 0-387-11790-3). Springer-Verlag.
Freyhardt, H. C., ed. Silicon-Chemical Etching. (Crystals-Growth, Properties & Applications Ser.: Vol. 8). (Illus.). 255p. 1983. 55.00 (ISBN 0-387-11862-4). Springer-Verlag.
Pokrovsky, V. L. & Talapov, A. L. Theory of Incommensurate Crystals. (Soviet Scientific Reviews Supplement Ser. Physics: Vol. 1). 140p. 1983. 77.50 (ISBN 3-7186-0134-6). Harwood Academic.
CRYSTALS-DEFECTS
Kofstad, Per. Nonstoichiometry, Diffusion & Electrical Conductivity in Binary Metal Oxides. LC 82-20336. 394p. 1983. Repr. of 1972 ed. lib. bdg. write for info. (ISBN 0-89874-569-1). Krieger.
Mura, T. Micromechanics of Defects in Solids. 1982. lib. bdg. 98.00 (ISBN 90-247-2560-7, Pub. by Martinus Nijhoff Netherlands). Kluwer Boston.
CRYSTALS-ELECTRIC PROPERTIES
Pope, Martin & Swenberg, Charles E. Electronic Processes in Organic Crystals. (Monographs on the Physics & Chemistry of Materials). (Illus.). 842p. 1982. 145.00x (ISBN 0-19-851334-8). Oxford U Pr.
CRYSTALS-GROWTH
Gilman, John J. Art & Science of Growing Crystals. LC 63-11432. (Science & Technology of Materials Ser.). 493p. 1963. 63.50x (ISBN 0-471-30177-9, Pub. by Wiley-Interscience). Wiley.
CRYSTALS-MODELS
Rousseau, D. L. Vibrational Models & Point Groups in Crystals. 40p. 1982. text ed. 21.95 (ISBN 0-471-26143-2). Wiley.
CRYSTALS, LIQUID
see Liquid Crystals
CUB SCOUTS
see Boy Scouts
CUBA-HISTORY
Betancourt, Juan, ed. From the Palm Tree: The Cuban Revolution in Retrospect. 224p. 1983. 12.00 (ISBN 0-8184-0344-6). Lyle Stuart.
Lubian, Rafael & Arias, M. M. Marti en los Campos de Cuba Libre. (Illus.). 186p. (Span.). 1982. pap. 9.95 (ISBN 0-89729-319-3). Ediciones.
Perez, Louis A., Jr. Cuba Between Empires, Eighteen Seventy-Eight to Nineteen Two. LC 82-11059. (Pitt Latin American Ser.). 465p. 1983. 34.95 (ISBN 0-8229-3472-8). U of Pittsburgh Pr.
CUBA-POLITICS AND GOVERNMENT
Castro, Fidel. Fidel Castro Speeches: Building Socialism in Cuba, Vol. 2. Taber, Michael, ed. 400p. 1983. lib. bdg. 30.00X (ISBN 0-87348-624-2); pap. 7.95X (ISBN 0-87348-650-1). Monad Pr.
CUBA-SOCIAL CONDITIONS
Montaner, Carlos A. Cuba: Claves Para Una Conciencia En Crisis. 154p. 1982. pap. text ed. 9.95x (ISBN 0-686-84095-X). Transaction Bks.
CUBA-SOCIAL LIFE AND CUSTOMS
Boswell, Thomas D. & Curtis, James R. The Cuban-American Experience: Culture, Images and Perspectives. 250p. 1983. text ed. 29.50x (ISBN 0-86598-116-7). Allanheld.
CUBAN INTERVENTION, 1906-1909
see Cuba-History
CUBAN LITERATURE (COLLECTIONS)
Desnoes, Edmundo, ed. Los Dispositivos en la flor (Cuban literatura desde la revolucion) 557p. (Span.). 1981. pap. 12.00 (ISBN 0-910061-03-3). Ediciones Norte.
CUBAN QUESTION, 1895-1898
see Cuba-History
CUBANS IN THE UNITED STATES
Boswell, Thomas D. & Curtis, James R. The Cuban-American Experience: Culture, Images and Perspectives. 250p. 1983. text ed. 29.50x (ISBN 0-86598-116-7). Allanheld.
CUBO-FUTURISM
see Futurism
CULDOSCOPY
Logan-Edwards, R. Manual of Laparoscopy & Culdoscopy. new ed. 160p. 1983. text ed. write for info. (ISBN 0-407-00195-6). Butterworth.
CULTIVATED PLANTS
see Plants, Cultivated
CULTS
Here are entered works on groups or movements whose system of religious beliefs or practices differs significantly from the major world religions and which are often gathered around a specific diety or person. Works on the major world religions are entered under Religions. Works on religious groups whose adherents recognize special teachings or practices which fall within the normative bounds of the major world religions are entered under Sects.
see also Sects
Appel, Willa. Cults in America. LC 82-15538. 228p. 1983. 15.95 (ISBN 0-03-054836-5). HR&W.
Bussell, Harold L. Unholy Devotion: Why Cults Lure Christians. 160p. 1983. pap. 4.95 (ISBN 0-310-37251-8). Zondervan.
Daly, Lloyd W. Iohannis Philoponi: De Vocabulis Quae Diversum Signification Exhibent Secundum Differentiam Accentus. LC 81-72156. (Memoirs Ser.: Vol. 151). 1983. 20.00 (ISBN 0-87169-151-5). Am Philos.
Das, H. C. Tantricism: A Study of the Yogini Cult. (Illus.). 88p. 1981. text ed. 21.50x (ISBN 0-391-02791-3, 41007, Pub. by Sterling India). Humanities.
Enroth, Ronald, et al. A Guide to Cults & New Religions. 200p. (Orig.). 1983. pap. 5.95 (ISBN 0-87784-837-8). Inter-Varsity.
Larson, Bob. Larson's Book of Cults. 1982. 7.95 (ISBN 0-8423-2104-7). Tyndale.
Streiker, Lowell D. Cults: The Continuing Threat. 144p. 1983. pap. 2.95 (ISBN 0-687-10069-0). Abingdon.
CULTURAL ANTHROPOLOGY
see Ethnology
CULTURAL CHANGE
see Social Change
CULTURAL EVOLUTION
see Social Change; Social Evolution
CULTURAL EXCHANGE PROGRAMS
see Cultural Relations; Exchange of Persons Programs; Intellectual Cooperation
CULTURAL RELATIONS
see also Exchange of Persons Programs;
also subdivision Relations (General) under names of countries, e.g. United States-Relations (General) with Latin America
Landis, Dan & Brislin, Richard W., eds. Handbook of Intercultural Training: Issues in Training Methodology, Vol. II. (Pergamon General Psychology Ser.: No. 116). (Illus.). 400p. 1983. 40.00 (ISBN 0-08-027534-6). Pergamon.
CULTURE
see also Biculturalism; Education; Educational Anthropology; Humanism; Intercultural Communication; Popular Culture; Self-Culture; Social Evolution; United States-Popular Culture
Anyanwu, K. C. The American Experts & the Academic Market: A Comparative Study of Cultural Philosophy. 128p. 1983. 5.00 (ISBN 0-682-49976-5). Exposition.

Horning, A. S. Readings in Contemporary Culture. 1979. text ed. 5.62 (ISBN 0-07-030352-5). McGraw.
Lewis, Mumford. The Golden Day: A Study in American Literature & Culture. LC 82-24199. xxx, 144p. 1983. Repr. of 1957 ed. lib. bdg. 22.50x (ISBN 0-313-23845-6, MUG0). Greenwood.
McCready, William C., ed. Culture, Ethnicity, & Identity: Current Issues in Research. LC 82-22651. Date not set. price not set (ISBN 0-12-482920-1). Acad Pr.
Slack & Mueller. A Propos! Communication et Culture: Un Debut. 1985. text ed. 22.95 (ISBN 0-686-84591-9, FR34); write for info. supplementary materials. HM.
CULTURE, EVOLUTION OF
see Social Evolution
CULTURE AND CHRISTIANITY
see Christianity and Culture
CULTURE AND EDUCATION
see Educational Anthropology
CULTURE CONFLICT
see also Marriage, Mixed; Miscegenation
Taylor, William J., Jr. & Maaranen, Steven A., eds. The Future of Conflict in the Nineteen Eighties. LC 82-48474. 1983. write for info. (ISBN 0-669-06145-X). Lexington Bks.
CULTURE MEDIA (MICROBIOLOGY)
see Microbiology–Cultures and Culture Media
CULTURE OF CELLS
see Cell Culture
CULTUS, DISPARITY OF
see Marriage, Mixed
CULTUS, EGYPTIAN
Baines, J. Fecundity Figures: Egyptian Personification & the Iconology of a Genre. 200p. 1982. text ed. 75.00x (ISBN 0-85668-087-7, 40651, Pub. by Aris & Phillips England). Humanities.
CUMBERLAND RIVER AND VALLEY
Head, K. Maynard. Brogans, Clothespins & a Twist of Tobacco. (Illus.). 160p. (Orig.). 1983. 8.95 (ISBN 0-89769-077-X); pap. 4.95 (ISBN 0-89769-050-8). Pine Mntn.
CUNEIFORM INSCRIPTIONS
Clay, Albert T. Neo-Babylonian Letters From Erech. 1920. text ed. 26.50x (ISBN 0-686-83634-0). Elliots Bks.
Goetze, Albrecht. Old Babylonian Omen Texts. 1947. text ed. 29.50x (ISBN 0-686-83651-0). Elliots Bks.
Hackman, George G., ed. Temple Documents of the Third Dynasty of Ur From Umma. 1937. text ed. 27.50x (ISBN 0-686-83806-8). Elliots Bks.
Tremayne, Archibald. Records From Erech, Time of Cyrus & Cambyses. 1926. text ed. 29.50x (ISBN 0-686-83726-6). Elliots Bks.
CUPS AND SAUCERS
see Porcelain; Pottery
CURE OF SOULS
see Pastoral Counseling; Pastoral Theology
CURIE, MARIE (SKLODOWSKA) (MME. PIERRE CURIE), 1867-1934–JUVENILE LITERATURE
Brandt, Keith. Marie Curie: Brave Scientist. LC 82-16092. (Illus.). 48p. (gr. 4-6). 1983. PLB 6.89 (ISBN 0-89375-855-8); pap. text ed. 1.95 (ISBN 0-89375-856-6). Troll Assocs.
CURIOSA
see also subdivision Curiosa and Miscellany under names of persons, and under particular subjects
Ferguson, John. Bibliographical Notes on Histories & Inventions & Books of Secrets, 2 vols. in 1. Date not set. 75.00 (ISBN 0-87556-494-1). Saifer.
CURIOSITIES AND WONDERS
A general and miscellaneous form heading, not to be confused with Curiosa which stands for literary and bibliographical curiosities.
Best Report Staff, ed. The Book of Bests. 1983. 14.95 (ISBN 0-89696-196-6). Dodd.
Gunning, Thomas G. Unexplained Mysteries. LC 82-19950. (High Interest, Low Vocabulary Ser.). (Illus.). 128p. (gr. 4 up). 1983. 8.95 (ISBN 0-396-08122-3). Dodd.
McWhirter, Norris. Guinness Book of World Records 1984. LC 64-4984. (Illus.). 544p. 1983. 12.95 (ISBN 0-8069-0256-6); lib. bdg. 15.69 (ISBN 0-8069-0257-4). Sterling.
Michell, John & Rickard, J. M. Living Wonders: Mysteries & Curiosities of the Animal World. (Illus., Orig.). 1983. pap. 9.95 (ISBN 0-500-27263-8). Thames Hudson.
Nowlan, Robert A. The College of Trivial Knowledge. 160p. 1983. 12.95 (ISBN 0-686-84638-9). Morrow.
--The College of Trivial Knowledge. 160p. pap. 6.95 (ISBN 0-688-02072-0). Quill NY.
Ripley's Believe It or Not, No. 33. 1982. pap. 2.25 (ISBN 0-451-12214-3, AE2214, Sig). NAL.
Signs & Wonders Today. 1983. Repr. write for info. Creation Hse.
Slater, Barbara & Slater, Ron. Tracking Down Trivia. (gr. 5-12). 1982. 4.95 (ISBN 0-86653-078-9, GA 423). Good Apple.
Stover, Doug. Encyclopedia of Amazing but True Facts. 1982. pap. 3.50 (ISBN 0-451-11559-7, AE1559, Sig). NAL.
Wallechinsky, David & Wallace, Amy. The Book of Lists, No. 3. 512p. 1983. 15.95 (ISBN 0-688-01647-2). Morrow.
Wilson, Craig M. YHWH...Is Not a Radio Station in Minneapolis: And Other Things Everyone Should Know. LC 82-48405. (Illus.). 96p. (Orig.). 1983. pap. 4.76 (ISBN 0-06-069432-7, HarpR). Har-Row.
World Almanac Editors. The World Almanac Book of the Strange, No. 2. 1982. pap. 3.50 (ISBN 0-451-11890-1, AE1890, Sig). NAL.
CURIOSITY
Voss, Hans-Georg & Keller, Heide, eds. Curiosity & Exploration: Theories & Results. LC 82-22705. Date not set. price not set (ISBN 0-12-728080-4). Acad Pr.
CURRENCY
see Money
CURRENCY DEVALUATION
see Currency Question
CURRENCY QUESTION
see also Banks and Banking, Central; Finance; Finance, Public; Foreign Exchange Problem; Gold; Inflation (Finance); Monetary Policy; Money; Paper Money; Precious Metals; Silver; Silver Question
Aliber, Robert Z. The International Money Game. 4th, rev. ed. 350p. 1983. 15.00 (ISBN 0-465-03377-6); pap. 8.95 (ISBN 0-465-03379-2). Basic.
Basagni, Fabio. International Monetary Relations After Jamaica. (The Atlantic Papers: No. 76/4). (Orig.). 1977. pap. text ed. 4.75x (ISBN 0-686-83641-3). Allanheld.
Bergsten, C. Fred & Williamson, John. The Multiple Reserve Currency System & International Monetary Reform. (Policy Analyses in International Economics Ser.: No. 4). 1983. 6.00 (ISBN 0-88132-003-X). Inst Intl Eco.
Dreyer, Jacob S., et al, eds. International Monetary System: A Time of Turbulence. 1982. 29.95 (ISBN 0-8447-2228-6); pap. 14.95 (ISBN 0-8447-2227-8). Am Enterprise.
Illustrations of Foreign Currency Translation. (Financial Report Survey Ser.: No. 24). 1982. pap. 9.50 (ISBN 0-686-84298-7). Am Inst CPA.
CURRENT METERS (FLUD DYNAMICS)
see Flow Meters
CURRENTS, ALTERNATING
see Electric Currents, Alternating
CURRENTS, DIRECT
see Electric Currents, Direct
CURRICULA (COURSES OF STUDY)
see Education–Curricula
CURRICULUM DEVELOPMENT
see Curriculum Planning
CURRICULUM PLANNING
ASBO's School Facilities Council Division Staff. Schoolhouse Planning. 1980. 8.50 (ISBN 0-910170-12-6). Assn Sch Busn.
Bellon, Jerry & HAndler, Janet R. Curriculum Development & Evaluation: A Design for Improvement. 96p. 1982. pap. text ed. 7.95 (ISBN 0-8403-2720-X). Kendall-Hunt.
Brown, Janet F., ed. Curriculum Planning for Young Children. 267p. 1982. pap. text ed. 5.50 (ISBN 0-912674-83-0). Natl Assn Child Ed.
Elbaz, Freema. Teacher Thinking: A Study of Practical Knowledge. LC 82-14418. 224p. 1983. 24.50 (ISBN 0-89397-144-8). Nichols Pub.
Goodson, Ivor. School Subjects & Curriculum Change. (Curriculum Policy & Research Ser.). 222p. 1983. text ed. 32.00x (ISBN 0-7099-1104-1, Pub. by Croom Helm Ltd England). Biblio Dist.
Jersild, Arthur T. Child Development & the Curriculum. 274p. 1982. Repr. of 1946 ed. lib. bdg. 50.00 (ISBN 0-89987-434-7). Darby Bks.
Madaus, G. & Scriven, M. S. Conceptual Issues in Evaluation. (Evaluation & Education in Human Services Ser.). 1983. lib. bdg. 38.00 (ISBN 0-89838-123-1). Kluwer Nijhoff.
Zenger, Sharon K. & Zenger, Weldon. Curriculum Planning: A Ten Step Process. LC 82-60521. 150p. (Orig.). 1983. pap. 12.95 (ISBN 0-88247-675-0). R & E Res Assoc.
CURSOLARI, BATTLE OF, 1571
see Lepanto, Battle of, 1571
CURTAIN WALLS
see Walls
CURTAINS
see Drapery
CURVED SURFACES
see Surfaces
CURVES, ALGEBRAIC
see also Geometry, Algebraic
Steklov Institute of Mathematics & Kuz'mina, G. V. Moduli of Families of Curves & Quadratic Differentials. LC 82-8902. (Proceedings of the Steklov Institute of Mathematics). 76.00 (ISBN 0-8218-3040-6, STEKLO-1982-1). Am Math.
CUSTER, GEORGE ARMSTRONG, 1839-1876
Urwin, Gregory J. Custer Victorious: The Civil War Battles of General George Armstrong Custer. LC 81-65873. (Illus.). 312p. 1982. 29.50 (ISBN 0-8386-3113-4). Fairleigh Dickinson.
Varnum, Charles & Carroll, John M. I, Varnum: The Autobiographical Reminiscences of Custer's Chief of Scouts. LC 82-70693. (Hidden Springs of Custeriana: VII). (Illus.). 194p. 1982. 45.00 (ISBN 0-87062-142-4). A H Clark.
CUSTODIANS
see Janitors
CUSTODY OF CHILDREN
Abrahms, Sally. Children in the Crossfire: The Tragedy of Parental Kidnapping. LC 82-73030. 320p. 1983. 12.95 (ISBN 0-689-11339-0). Atheneum.
Berger, Stuart. Divorce Without Victims. 200p. 1983. 12.95 (ISBN 0-395-33115-3). HM.
Bienenfeld, Florence. Child Custody. 1983. 9.95. Sci & Behavior.
Franks, Maurice R. Winning Custody. LC 82-24114. 185p. 1983. 16.95 (ISBN 0-13-961011-1, Busn); pap. 7.95 (ISBN 0-13-961003-0). P-H.
Kiefer, Louis J. How to Win Custody. LC 82-14153. 308p. 1982. pap. 8.95 (ISBN 0-346-12579-0). Cornerstone.
Meyers & Lakin. Who Will Take the Children? new ed. 228p. 1983. 13.95 (ISBN 0-672-52739-1). Bobbs.
Schnell, Barry T. The Child Support Survivor's Guide. LC 82-73099. 174p. 1983. pap. price not set. Consumer Aware.
CUSTOMER RELATIONS
see also Customer Service
Gold, Carol S. Solid Gold Customer Relations: A Professional Resource Guide. 122p. 1983. 10.95 (ISBN 0-13-822338-6); pap. 5.95 (ISBN 0-13-822320-3). P-H.
CUSTOMER SERVICE
Toch, Hans & Grant, J. Douglas. Change Through Participation: Humanizing Human Service Settings. (Library of Social Research). (Illus.). 240p. 1982. 22.00 (ISBN 0-8039-1886-0); pap. 10.95 (ISBN 0-8039-1887-9). Sage.
CUSTOMS, SOCIAL
see Manners and Customs;
also subdivision Social Life and Customs under ethnic groups, e.g. Indians, Jews, and under names of countries, cities, etc.
CUTANEOUS DISEASES
see Skin–Diseases
CUTIS
see Skin
CUTTING MACHINES
see also Metal-Cutting Tools
Modern Trends in Cutting Tools. LC 82-61010. 265p. 1982. 32.00 (ISBN 0-87263-109-5). SME.
CUTTING OF GEMS
see Gem Cutting
CUTTING OF METALS
see Metal-Cutting
CYBERNETICS
see also Biological Control Systems; Bionics; Computers; Conscious Automata; Information Theory; System Analysis; Systems Engineering
Morecki, A. & Ekiel, J. Cybernetic Systems of Limb Movements in Man, Animals & Robots. LC 82-15717. 250p. 1983. 79.95x (ISBN 0-470-27374-7). Halsted Pr.
Progress in Cybernetics & Systems Research, Vol. 9. 1982. 110.00 (ISBN 0-07-065069-1). McGraw.
Progress in Cybernetics & Systems Research, Vol. 10. 1982. 110.00 (ISBN 0-07-065070-5). McGraw.
Progress in Cybernetics & Systems Research, Vol. 11. 1982. 110.00 (ISBN 0-07-065071-3). McGraw.
Rosenberg, M. J. The Cybernetics of Art. (Studies in Cybernetics: Vol. 4). 206p. 1982. 42.50 (ISBN 0-677-05970-1). Gordon.
Sime, Max S. & Coombs, Michael J., eds. Designing for Human-Computer Communication. write for info. (ISBN 0-12-643820-X). Acad Pr.
Strank, R. H. Management Principles & Practice. (Studies in Cybernetics: Vol. 3). 150p. 1982. write for info. Gordon.
Trappl, R. Progress in Cybernetics & Systems Research, Vol. 8. 1982. 110.00 (ISBN 0-07-065068-3). McGraw.
Trappl, R., ed. Cybernetics & Systems Research: Proceedings of the Sixth European Meeting, Organized by the Austrian Society for Cybernetic Studies, University of Vienna, 1982. 984p. 1982. 127.75 (ISBN 0-444-86488-1, North Holland). Elsevier.
CYCLES (BICYCLES)
see Bicycles and Tricycles
CYCLES IN BIOLOGY
see Biological Rhythms
CYCLIC COMPOUNDS
see also Heterocyclic Compounds
Hiraoka, M. Crown Compounds: Their Characteristics & Applications. (Studies in Organic Chemistry: No. 12). 276p. 1982. 76.75 (ISBN 0-444-99692-3). Elsevier.
CYCLING
see also Bicycles and Tricycles; Motorcycles; Motorcycling
Bagg, Lyman H. Ten Thousand Miles on a Bicycle. rev. ed. 911p. 1982. 20.00x (ISBN 0-9610060-0-5). E Rosenblatt.
Basic Bicycling. 4.50 (ISBN 0-686-84042-9). AAHPERD.
Colling, Gene. Bicyclist's Guide to Yellowstone National Park. (Illus.). 64p. 1983. pap. 4.95 (ISBN 0-934318-15-8). Falcon Pr MT.
Faria, I. E. & Cavanagh, P. R. The Physiology & Biomechanics of Cycling. 179p. 1978. 17.95x (ISBN 0-471-25490-8). Wiley.
Forester, John. Effective Cycling: Instructors Manual. (Illus.). 158p. 1982. pap. 6.00 (ISBN 0-940558-02-5). CCF.
George, Robert F., photos by. Velo-News Cyclist's Training Diary. (Illus.). 176p. (Orig.). 1982. pap. 6.95 (ISBN 0-686-82523-3). Velo-News.
Nixdorf, Bert. Hikes & Bike Rides for the Delaware Valley & Southern New Jersey: With Emphasis on the Pine Barrens, No. 1. (Illus.). 140p. (Orig.). pap. 5.50 (ISBN 0-9610474-0-2). B Nixdorf.
Petersen, Grant. Roads of Alameda, Contra Costa & Marin Counties: A Topographic Guide for Bicylists. 200p. Date not set. pap. 5.95 (ISBN 0-930588-07-X). Heyday Bks.
Roth, Mark & Walters, Sally. Twenty Bicycle Tours in the Finger Lakes: Scenic Route to Central New York's Best Waterfalls, Wineries, Beacher & Parks. (Twenty Bicycle Tours Ser.). (Illus.). 160p. (Orig.). 1983. pap. 6.95 (ISBN 0-942440-09-9). Backcountry Pubns.
Schneider, Bill. Bicyclist's Guide to Glacier National Park. (Illus.). 48p. 1983. pap. 3.95 (ISBN 0-934318-17-4). Falcon Pr MT.
Velo-news Editors. Ten Years of Championship Bicycle Racing. (Illus.). 128p. (Orig.). 1983. specialty trade 14.95 (ISBN 0-686-42828-5). Velo-News.
Whatmore, John. The CTC Book of Cycling: The Cyclists' Touring Club of Britain. (Illus.). 256p. 1983. 24.95 (ISBN 0-7153-8370-1). David & Charles.
Woollett, Mick. Racing Bikes. (Illus.). 64p. 1983. pap. 4.95 (ISBN 0-7134-1294-1, Pub. by Batsford England). David & Charles.
CYCLOHEXANE
Szejtli, J. Cyclodextrins & Their Inclusion Complexes. Nogradi, M. & Horvath, K., trs. from Hungarian. (Illus.). 296p. 1982. 35.00x (ISBN 963-05-2850-9). Intl Pubns Serv.
CYCLOIDS, MIXED (CHEMISTRY)
see Heterocyclic Compounds
CYCLOPEDIAS
see Encyclopedias and Dictionaries
CYPRUS–ANTIQUITIES
Feltenburg, E. J. Vrysi: A Subterranean Settlement in Cyprus - Excavations of Ayios Epiktitos, 1969-1973. (Illus.). 132p. 1983. pap. text ed. 31.50x (ISBN 0-85668-217-9, Pub. by Aris & Phillips England). Humanities.
Kapera, Z. J. Kinyras: Bibliography of Ancient Cyprus for the Year 1979. (Studies in Mediterranean Archaeology Pocketbooks Ser.: No. 18). 68p. 1982. pap. text ed. 23.00x (ISBN 91-86098-06-3, Pub. by Astroms Sweden). Humanities.
Kromholz, Susan F. The Bronze Age Necropolis at Ayia Paraskevi (Nicosia) Unpublished Tombs in the Cyprus Museum. (Studies in Mediterranean Archaeology: No. 17). 360p. 1982. pap. text ed. 34.50x (ISBN 91-86098-01-2, Pub. by Astroms Sweden). Humanities.
CYPRUS–HISTORY
Oberling, Pierre. The Road to Bellapais: The Turkish Cypriot Exodus to Northern Cyprus. (Brooklyn College Studies on Society in Change). 288p. 1982. 25.00x (ISBN 0-88033-000-7). East Eur Quarterly.
CYSTIC FIBROSIS
Quinton, P. M. & Martinez, J. R., eds. Fluid & Electrolyte Anormalities in Exocrine Glands in Cystic Fibrosis. (Illus.). 1982. 18.75 (ISBN 0-911302-45-X). San Francisco Pr.
CYSTOSCOPY
see Bladder
CYSTOSTOMY
see Bladder
CYSTS
see also Tumors
Flisser, Ana, et al, eds. Cysticercosis: Symposium. 1982. 55.00 (ISBN 0-12-260740-6). Acad Pr.
CYTOCHEMISTRY
see also Histochemistry
Cuello, A. C. Immunohistochemistry. (IBRO Handbook Ser.: Methods in the Neurosciences). 500p. 1982. write for info. (ISBN 0-471-10245-8, Pub. by Wiley-Interscience); pap. write for info. (ISBN 0-471-90052-4). Wiley.
CYTOGENETICS
Jotterand-Bellomo, Martine & Klinger, H. P., eds. The Robert Malthey Dedication. (Cytogenetics & Cell Genetics Ser.: Vol. 34, Nos. 1-2). (Illus.). iv, 188p. 1982. pap. 96.00 (ISBN 3-8055-3650-X). S Karger.
Shay, Jerry W., ed. Techniques in Somatic Cell Genetics. (Illus.). 568p. 1982. 49.50x (ISBN 0-306-41040-0, Plenum Pr). Plenum Pub.
CYTOLOGY
see also Cell Differentiation; Cells; Cytochemistry; Cytogenetics; Plant Cells and Tissues
Alberts, Bruce & Bray, Dennis. Molecular Biology of the Cell. LC 82-15692. 1250p. 1983. lib. bdg. 29.95 (ISBN 0-8240-7282-0). Garland Pub.
Bigner, Sandra H. & Johnston, William W. Cytopathology of the Central Nervous System. (Masson Monographs on Diagnostic Cytopathology, Vol. 3). 184p. 1983. price not set. Masson Pub.
Bourne, Geoffrey & Danielli, James, eds. International Review of Cytology. LC 52-5203. (Serial Publication). 1982. 37.00 ea. Vol. 74 (ISBN 0-12-364474-7). Vol. 75 (ISBN 0-12-364475-5). Acad Pr.
--International Review of Cytology Supplement, No. 14. (Serial Publication). Date not set. 44.00 (ISBN 0-12-364375-9). Acad Pr.

Bradley, Stanley E. & Purcell, Elizabeth F., eds. The Paracellular Pathway. (Illus.). 382p. 1982. pap. 15.00 (ISBN 0-914362-37-2). J Macy Foun.
Bregman, Allyn A. Laboratory Investigations in Cell Biology. 250p. 1982. pap. text ed. 14.95 (ISBN 0-471-86241-X). Wiley.
Campbell, Anthony K. Intracellular Calcium: Its Universal Role As Regulator. (Monographs in Molecular Biophysics & Biochemistry). 540p. 1983. write for info. (ISBN 0-471-10488-4, Pub. by Wiley-Interscience). Wiley.
Clayton, R. M. & Truman, D. E., eds. Stability & Switching in Cellular Differentiation. (Advances in Experimental Medicine & Biology). 484p. 1982. 62.50x (ISBN 0-306-41181-4, Plenum Pr). Plenum Pub.
Danielli, James F., ed. International Review of Cytology Supplement: Vol. 15: Aspects of Cell Regulation. Date not set. price not set (ISBN 0-12-364376-7). Acad Pr.
Elliot, Alfred M. Biology of Tetrahymena. LC 73-12911. 508p. 1973. text ed. 62.00 (ISBN 0-87933-013-9). Hutchinson Ross.
Federoff, S. & Hertz, L., eds. Advances in Cellular Neurobiology, Vol. 3. (Serial Publication). 448p. 1982. 56.00 (ISBN 0-12-008303-5). Acad Pr.
Frazier, William A. & Glaser, Luis, eds. Cellular Recognition. LC 82-6555. (UCLA Symposia on Molecular & Cellular Biology Ser.: Vol. 3). 966p. 1982. 152.00 (ISBN 0-8451-2602-4). A R Liss.
Gompel, Claude. Atlas of Diagnostic Cytology. LC 77-27068. 1978. text ed. 80.00x (ISBN 0-471-02278-0, Pub. by Wiley Medical). Wiley.
Ingraham, John L. & Maaloe, Ole. Growth of the Bacterial Cell. (Illus.). 375p. 1983. text ed. write for info. (ISBN 0-87893-352-2). Sinauer Assoc.
Le-Douarin, Nicole. The Neural Crest. LC 82-1183. (Developmental & Cell Biology Ser.: No. 12). (Illus.). 200p. 1983. 65.00 (ISBN 0-521-24770-5). Cambridge U Pr.
Linsk, Joseph A. & Franzen, Sixten, eds. Clinical Aspiration Cytology. (Illus.). 386p. 1983. text ed. 59.00 (ISBN 0-397-50504-3, Lippincott Medical). Lippincott.
LLoyd, C. & Ress, D. A., eds. Cellular Controls in Differentiation. LC 81-6783. 336p. 1982. 25.50 (ISBN 0-12-453580-1). Acad Pr.
McIntosh, J. Richard & Satir, Birgit H., eds. Modern Cell Biology: Spatial Organization of Eukaryotic Cells. (Modern Cell Biology Ser.: Vol. 2). 550p. 1983. 50.00 (ISBN 0-8451-3301-2). A R Liss.
Moscona, Aron A. & Monroy, Alberto, eds. Current Topics in Developmental Biology: Vol. 18: Genome Function, Cell Interactions, & Differentiation. (Serial Publication). Date not set. price not set (ISBN 0-12-153118-X). Acad Pr.
O'Malley, Bert W., ed. Gene Regulation: UCLA Symposium Molecular Cellular Biology. LC 82-20709. (Vol. 26). 1982. 36.50 (ISBN 0-12-525960-3). Acad Pr.
Reich, J. G. & Selkov, E. Energy Metabolism of the Cell: A Theoretical Treatise. LC 81-66389. 352p. 1982. 74.00 (ISBN 0-12-585920-1). Acad Pr.
Sakai, Hikoichi & Mohri, Hideo, eds. Biological Functions of Microtubules & Related Structure: Proceedings, 13th Oji International Seminar, Tokyo, Japan, December, 1981. LC 82-11609. 1982. 32.00 (ISBN 0-12-615080-X). Acad Pr.
Satir, Birgit, ed. Modern Cell Biology. (Modern Cell Biology Ser.: Vol. 1). 216p. 1983. 34.00 (ISBN 0-8451-3300-4). A R Liss.
Segel, L. A., ed. Mathematical Models of Molecular & Cellular Biology. LC 79-52854. (Illus.). 767p. Date not set. pap. price not set (ISBN 0-521-27054-5). Cambridge U Pr.
Trump, Benjamin F. & Arstila, A. U., eds. Pathobiology of Cell Membranes, Vol. 3. Date not set. price not set (ISBN 0-12-701503-5). Acad Pr.

CYTOPATHOLOGY
see Pathology, Cellular

CYTOPLASM
see Protoplasm

CYTOTOXIC DRUGS
see Antineoplastic Agents

CZECH LITERATURE
Liehm, Antonin & Kussi, Peter, eds. The Writing on the Wall: An Anthology of Contemporary Czech Literature. 256p. 1983. 29.95 (ISBN 0-943828-53-8); pap. 12.95 (ISBN 0-943828-54-6). Karz-Cohl Pub.

CZECH LITERATURE–HISTORY AND CRITICISM
Milosz, Czeslaw. Poeticheskii Traktat. Gorbanevskaya, Natalia, tr. from Polish. 64p. 1982. text ed. write for info. (ISBN 0-88233-828-5); pap. text ed. 4.50 (ISBN 0-88233-829-3). Ardis Pubs.

CZECHOSLOVAKIA–ANTIQUITIES
Magocsi, Paul R. Vienna Nineteen Eighty-Two: Wooden Churches in the Carpathians, Holzkirchen in den Karpaten, the Photographs of Florian Zapletal. (Illus.). 176p. (Ger. & Eng.). 1982. 24.95 (ISBN 0-686-38725-2, Pub. by Wm Braumuller Univ Vlg Vienna). Res Ctr.

CZECHOSLOVAKIA–BIOGRAPHY
Buechner, Thomas & Warmus, William. Czechoslovakia Diary. 16p. 1980. pap. 3.00 (ISBN 0-87290-102-5). Corning.

CZECHOSLOVAKIA–HISTORY
Janics, Kalman. Czechoslovak Policy & the Hungarian Minority, 1945-1948. 288p. 1982. 25.00 (ISBN 0-686-82241-2). Columbia U Pr.
Magocsi, Paul R. Vienna Nineteen Eighty-Two: The Rusyn-Ukrainians of Czechoslovakia, An Historical Survey. (Bausteine Zur Ethnopolitischen Forschung: Ethnos Vol. 6). (Illus.). 94p. (Orig.). 1982. pap. 7.95 (ISBN 3-7003-0312-2, Pub. by Wm Braumuller Univ Vlg Vienna). Res Ctr.

CZECHOSLOVAKIA–HISTORY–INTERVENTION, 1968-
Marcy, Sam. Czechoslovakia Nineteen Sixty-Eight: The Class Character of the Events. 62p. 1978. pap. 1.50 (ISBN 0-89567-002-X). WV Pubs.

CZECHOSLOVAKIA–POLITICS AND GOVERNMENT
Janics, Kalman. Czechoslovak Policy & the Hungarian Minority: 1945-1948. Borsody, Stephen, tr. from Hungarian. & intro. by. LC 80-67487. (Brooklyn College Studies on Society in Change). 288p. 1982. 25.00x (ISBN 0-914710-99-0). East Eur Quarterly.

D

DACTYLOLOGY
see Deaf–Means of Communication

DADAISM
see also Letter Pictures
Motherwell, Robert, ed. The Dada Painters & Poets: An Anthology. 2nd ed. (Documents of 20th Century Art). 1981. lib. bdg. 40.00 (ISBN 0-8057-9951-6, Twayne). G K Hall.
Rothenberg, Jerome. That Dada Strain. LC 82-18827. 96p. 1983. pap. 7.25 (ISBN 0-8112-0860-5, NDP550). New Directions.

DAHLIAS
Damp, Phillip. Growing Dahlias. (Illus.). 139p. 1982. 12.95 (ISBN 0-7099-0800-8). Timber.

DAILY READINGS (SPIRITUAL EXERCISES)
see Devotional Calendars

DAIRIES
see Dairying

DAIRY CATTLE
Broster, W. H. & Swan, Henry. Feeding Strategy for the High Yielding Dairy Cow. 432p. 1979. text ed. 45.00x (ISBN 0-258-97126-6, Pub. by Granada England). Renouf.
Etgen, William M. & Reaves, Paul M. Dairy Cattle Feeding & Management. 6th ed. LC 63-20646. 638p. 1978. text ed. 34.95 (ISBN 0-471-71199-3). Wiley.

DAIRY CHEMISTRY
see Dairy Products–Analysis and Examination

DAIRY INDUSTRY
see Dairying

DAIRY PRODUCTS
see also Dairying;
also names of specific dairy products, e.g. milk, cheese, etc.
Diary Products. 1981. 395.00 (ISBN 0-686-38421-0, 106). Busn Trend.
OECD Staff. Milk, Milk Products & Egg Balances in OECD Member Countries, 1975-1980. 112p. (Orig.). 1982. pap. 12.50x (ISBN 92-64-02324-0). OECD.

DAIRY PRODUCTS–ANALYSIS AND EXAMINATION
Fox, P. F., ed. Developments in Dairy Chemistry, Vol. 1: Proteins. (Illus.). x, 405p. 1982. 90.25 (ISBN 0-85334-142-7, Pub. by Applied Sci England). Elsevier.

DAIRYING
see also Cheese; Cows; Dairy Cattle; Dairy Products; Milk
Baker, Frank H., ed. Dairy Science Handbook: International Stockmen's School Handbooks, Vol. 15. 500p. 1982. lib. bdg. 35.00X (ISBN 0-86531-508-6, Pub. in Cooperation with Winrock International). Westview.
Manchester, Alden C. The Public Role in the Dairy Economy: How & Why Governments Intervene in the Dairy Business. (Special Studies in Agriculture-Aquaculture Science & Policy). 304p. 1983. price not set (ISBN 0-86531-590-6). Westview.

DAKOTA INDIANS
see Indians of North America–The West

DALLAS
Ingram, Marilyn W. & Folse, Lois J. Dining In--Dallas. (Dining In--Ser.). 200p. 1982. pap. 8.95 (ISBN 0-89716-113-0). Peanut Butter.

DALLES, FORT
Knuth, Priscilla. Picturesque Frontier: The Army's Fort Dalles. 2nd ed. (Illus.). 112p. 1983. pap. write for info. (ISBN 0-87595-140-6, Western Imprints). Oreg Hist Soc.

DALMATIAN LANGUAGE (SLAVIC)
see Serbo-Croatian Language

DAMPIER, WILLIAM, 1652-1715
Dampier, William. Voyage to New Holland. 256p. 1982. text ed. 22.50x (ISBN 0-904387-75-5, Pub. by Alan Sutton England); pap. text ed. 10.50x (ISBN 0-86299-006-8). Humanities.

DAMS
see also Flood Dams and Reservoirs
also particular dams, e.g. Grand Coulee Dam
Dams & Earthquake. 304p. 1981. 129.00x (ISBN 0-7277-0123-1, Pub. by Telford England). State Mutual Bk.
Parker, Albert D. & Barrie, Donald S. Planning & Estimating Heavy Construction. 640p. 1983. 39.95 (ISBN 0-07-048489-9, P&RB). McGraw.

DANCE MUSIC
see also Jazz Music
Kuppuswamy, Gowry. Indian Dance & Music Literature: A Select Bibliography. 1982. 12.00x (ISBN 0-8364-0903-5, Pub. by Biblia Impex). South Asia Bks.
Saxena, S. K. Aesthetical Essays: Studies in Aesthetics; Hindustani Music & Kathak Dance. 1982. 18.00x (ISBN 0-8364-0898-5, Pub. by Chanakya). South Asia Bks.

DANCE OF DEATH
Chick, Edson. Dances of Death: Wedekind, Brecht, Durrenmatt, & the Satiric Tradition. (Studies in German Literature, Linguistics, & Culture: Vol. 19). (Illus.). 190p. 1983. 16.95x (ISBN 0-938100-04-1). Camden Hse.
Eichenberg, Fritz. Dance of Death. (Illus.). 136p. 1983. 25.95 (ISBN 0-89659-339-8). Abbeville Pr.

DANCE PRODUCTION
A Guide to Dance Production: "On With the Show" 92p. 8.95 (ISBN 0-88314-000-4). AAHPERD.

DANCE THERAPY
Completed Research in Health, Physical Education, Recreation & Dance, Vol.19. 1977. 9.25 (ISBN 0-88314-044-6). AAHPERD.
Completed Research in Health, Physical Education, Recreation & Dance, Vol. 20. 1978. write for info. (ISBN 0-88314-045-4). AAHPERD.
Completed Research in Health, Physical Education, Recreation & Dance, Vol. 24. 1983. 10.95 (ISBN 0-686-38056-8). AAHPERD.
Dance for Physically Disabled Persons: A Manual for Teaching Ballroom, Square & Folk Dances to Users of Wheelchairs & Crutches. 128p. 1976. 7.95 (ISBN 0-88314-056-X). AAHPERD.

DANCERS
Barnes, Clive. Nureyev. (Illus.). 272p. 1982. 35.00 (ISBN 0-9609736-2-1). Helene Obolensky Ent.
Cohen-Stratyner, Barbara. Biographical Dictionary of Dance. 1982. lib. bdg. 75.00x (ISBN 0-02-870260-3). Schirmer Bks.
Crickmay, Anthony. Dancers. LC 81-48551. (Illus.). 128p. 1982. 50.00 (ISBN 0-688-01239-6). Morrow.
Jacobi, Lotte. Theatre & Dance Photographs. 46p. (Orig.). 1982. pap. 10.95 (ISBN 0-914378-93-7). Countryman.
Zola, Meguido. Karen Kain. (Picture Life Ser.). 48p. (gr. k-3). 1983. PLB 7.90 (ISBN 0-531-04598-6). Watts.

DANCING
see also Ballet; Choreography; Dance Music; Dancers; Jazz Dance; Modern Dance; Square Dancing
also names of dances
Aesthetics & Dance. 40p. 6.95 (ISBN 0-88314-009-8). AAHPERD.
Almeida, Bira. Capoeira: A Brazilian Art Form. 2nd ed. (Illus.). 152p. 1982. pap. 7.95 (ISBN 0-938190-09-1). North Atlantic.
Associated Press, ed. The Associated Press Sunday Crossword Puzzle Book. (Illus.). 96p. (Orig.). 1983. 4.95 (ISBN 0-8092-5573-1). Contemp Bks.
Completed Research in Health, Physical Education, Recreation & Dance, Vol. 22. 1980. 9.25 (ISBN 0-686-38058-4). AAHPERD.
Copeland, Roger & Cohen, Marshall. What is Dance? Readings in Theory & Criticism. (Illus.). 512p. 1983. pap. 10.95 (ISBN 0-19-503197-0, GB 720, GB). Oxford U Pr.
Copeland, Roger & Cohen, Roger. What is Dance? Readings in Theory & Criticism. (Illus.). 512p. 1983. 29.95 (ISBN 0-19-503217-9). Oxford U Pr.
D'Amboise, Jaques & Cooke, Hope. Teaching the Magic of Dance. (Illus.). 1983. price not set (ISBN 0-671-47026-4). S&S.
Dancing: A Guide for the Dancer You Can Be. 350p. 9.95 (ISBN 0-201-04957-0). AAHPERD.
Focus on Dance: Vol. 10 Religion & Dance. 96p. 9.95 (ISBN 0-88314-074-8). AAHPERD.
Focus on Dance: Vol. 8, Dance Heritage. 96p. 8.25 (ISBN 0-88314-073-X). AAHPERD.
Focus on Dance: Vol. 9 Dance for the Handicapped. 104p. 8.25 (ISBN 0-88314-071-3). AAHPERD.
Kisselle & Mazzeo. Aerobic Dance: A Way to Fitness. (Illus.). 192p. 1983. pap. text ed. 7.95x (ISBN 0-89582-094-3). Morton Pub.
McLeish, Kenneth & McLeish, Valerie. Singing & Dancing. (Illus.). 32p. pap. 4.75 laminated (ISBN 0-19-321436-9). Oxford U Pr.
Neal, Larry L., ed. The Next Fifty Years: Health, Physical Education, Recreation, Dance. 179p. 1971. pap. 3.50 (ISBN 0-686-84034-8). U OR Ctr Leisure.
Polley, Maxine. Dance Aerobics: Two. 160p. 1983. pap. 6.95 (ISBN 0-89037-256-X). Anderson World.
Research on Dance, Vol. III. 176p. 7.95 (ISBN 0-88314-153-1). AAHPERD.
Sexuality & the Dance. 32p. 4.95 (ISBN 0-88314-171-X). AAHPERD.

DANCING–BIBLIOGRAPHY
Research Libraries of the New york Public Library & Library of Congress. Bibliographic Guide to Dance: 1982. 1983. lib. bdg. 195.00 (ISBN 0-8161-6970-5, Biblio Guides). G K Hall.

DANCING–CHILDREN'S DANCES
Book of Worldwide Games & Dances. 160p. 8.95 (ISBN 0-88314-102-7). AAHPERD.
Crane, Debra J. & Berson, Misha, eds. Young Stages: A Guide to Theatre & Dance for Youth in the San Francisco Bay Area. LC 82-51320. (Illus.). 72p. (Orig.). 1982. pap. 5.00 (ISBN 0-9605896-1-9). Theatre Ctr Bay.

DANCING–HISTORY
Focus on Dance: Vol. 8, Dance Heritage. 96p. 8.25 (ISBN 0-88314-073-X). AAHPERD.

DANCING–JUVENILE LITERATURE
Finney, Shan. Dance. (First Bks.). (Illus.). 72p. (gr. 4 up). 1983. PLB 8.90 (ISBN 0-531-04525-0). Watts.

DANCING–LIBRARIES AND MUSEUMS
see Music Libraries

DANCING–PICTORIAL WORKS
Fehl, Fred. Stars of the Ballet & Dance in Performance Photographs. (Illus.). 144p. (Orig.). (gr. 6 up). 1983. pap. 8.95 (ISBN 0-486-24492-X). Dover.

DANCING–STUDY AND TEACHING
Carroll, Joan & Lofthouse, Peter. Creative Dance for Boys. 72p. 1972. 30.00x (ISBN 0-7121-0318-X, Pub. by Macdonald & Evans). State Mutual Bk.
Preston-Dunlop, Valerie. A Handbook for Dance in Education. 256p. 1980. 29.00x (ISBN 0-7121-0815-7, Pub. by Macdonald & Evans). State Mutual Bk.

DANCING–THERAPEUTIC USE
see Dance Therapy

DANCING–VOCATIONAL GUIDANCE
Costa, Ray. How to Be a Male Exotic Dancer. (Illus.). 114p. (Orig.). pap. text ed. 9.95 (ISBN 0-686-38733-3). Costa.

DANCING–INDIA
Kuppuswamy, Gowry. Indian Dance & Music Literature: A Select Bibliography. 1982. 12.00x (ISBN 0-8364-0903-5, Pub. by Biblia Impex). South Asia Bks.
Rao, Krishna. A Dictionary of Bharata Natya. (Illus.). 100p. 1980. text ed. 15.95x (ISBN 0-86131-155-8, Pub. by Orient Longman Ltd India). Apt Bks.
Saxena, S. K. Aesthetical Essays: Studies in Aesthetics; Hindustani Music & Kathak Dance. 1982. 18.00x (ISBN 0-8364-0898-5, Pub. by Chanakya). South Asia Bks.
Wade, Bonnie C., ed. Performing Arts in India: Essays on Music, Dance & Drama. LC 82-20141. (Monograph Ser.: No. 21). (Illus.). 270p. 1983. lib. bdg. 21.75 (ISBN 0-8191-2872-4); pap. text ed. 11.00 (ISBN 0-8191-2873-2). U Pr of Amer.

DANCING–ISLANDS OF THE PACIFIC
Hopkins, Jerry. The Hula. (Illus.). 194p. 1982. 35.00 (ISBN 9971-925-07-9). Lee Pubs Group.
McLean, Mervyn. Supplement: An Annotated Bibliography of Oceanic Music & Dance. 74p. 1982. pap. text ed. 8.00x (ISBN 0-8248-0862-2). UH Pr.

DANCING–LATIN AMERICA
Romain, Elizabeth. Popular Variations in Latin-American Dancing. rev. ed. 68p. (gr. 10 up). 1983. pap. text ed. 10.50x (ISBN 0-392-16896-0, SpS). Sportshelf.

DANCING–SCOTLAND
Barrett & Ovenden. The Seacoast. pap. 8.95 (ISBN 0-686-42741-6, Collins Pub England). Greene.
Cambell, Andrew & Martine, Roddy. The Swinging Sporran: A Lighthearted Guide to the Basic Steps of Scottish Reels & Country Dances. (Illus.). 120p. 1982. 10.95 (ISBN 0-904505-88-X, Pub. by Salem Hse Ltd.). Merrimack Bk Serv.

DANCING–UNITED STATES
Mazo, Joseph H. Prime Movers: The Makers of Modern Dance in America. LC 82-62346. (Illus.). 322p. 1983. pap. text ed. 12.95x (ISBN 0-916622-27-4). Princeton Bk Co.
Murphy, Edward. Western Dancing. (Illus.). 64p. 1983. 7.95 (ISBN 0-686-82404-0). Todd & Honeywell.

DANCING AS A PROFESSION
see Dancing–Vocational Guidance

DANIEL, SAMUEL, 1562-1619
Michel, Lawrence. Tragedy of Philotas by Samuel Daniel. 1949. text ed. 14.50x (ISBN 0-686-83831-9). Elliots Bks.

DANIELS, JONATHAN, 1902-
Eagles, Charles W. Jonathan Daniels & Race Relations: The Evolution of a Southern Liberal. LC 82-2756. (Twentieth-Century American Ser.). 254p. 1982. text ed. 24.50x (ISBN 0-87049-356-6); pap. text ed. 11.95x (ISBN 0-87049-357-4). U of Tenn Pr.

DANISH LANGUAGE
Berlitz Editors. Danish for Travel Cassettepack. 1983. 14.95 (ISBN 0-02-962970-5, Berlitz); cassette incl. Macmillan.
Frickelton, Annelise & Dierrsen, Gunther. It's Fun to Speak Danish. 48p. Date not set. includes 5 cassettes 75.00 (ISBN 0-88432-092-8, DAI). J Norton Pubs.

DANISH LITERATURE
Schroeder, Carol. A Bibliography of Danish Literature in English Translation, 1950-1980. 197p. 1982. 19.95x (ISBN 87-7429-044-4). Nordic Bks.

DANO-NORWEGIAN LANGUAGE
see Danish Language; Norwegian Language

DANSE MACABRE
see Dance of Death

DANTE ALIGHIERI, 1265-1321
Borges, Jorge L., et al. Dante Studies, Vol. I: Dante in the Twentieth Century. Date not set. 15.00; lea. 25.00; leather ltd. ed. 50.00. Branden.
Gardner, Edmund G. Dante. 166p. 1982. Repr. of 1912 ed. lib. bdg. 20.00 (ISBN 0-8495-2132-7). Arden Lib.
Harris, W. T. The Mythology of Plato & Dante & the Future Life. (The Essential Library of the Great Philosophers). (Illus.). 107p. 1983. Repr. of 1896 ed. 71.85 (ISBN 0-89901-091-1). Found Class Reprints.
Oelsner, Herman. The Influence of Dante on Modern Thought: Being the Le Bas Prize Essay, 1894. 120p. 1982. Repr. of 1895 ed. lib. bdg. 45.00 (ISBN 0-89984-363-8). Century Bookbindery.
Ralphs, S. Dante's Journey to the Centre. 1972. 9.50 (ISBN 0-7190-1254-6). Manchester.
DANTE IN FICTION, DRAMA, POETRY, ETC.
Giammati, A. Bartlett, ed. Dante in America: The First Two Centuries. 1983. 20.00 (ISBN 0-86698-059-8). Medieval Renaissance.
Nandakumar, P. Dante & Sri Aurobindo. 160p. 1981. 12.00x (ISBN 0-391-02391-8). Humanities.
DANTON, GEORGES JACQUES, 1759-1794
Wendel, Hermann. Danton: Dictator of the French Revolution. 1935. text ed. 49.50x (ISBN 0-686-83522-0). Elliots Bks.
DANUBE RIVER AND VALLEY
Frucht, Richard C. Dunarea Noastra: Romania, the Great Powers, & the Danube Question, 1914-1921. (East European Monographs: No. 113). 256p. 1982. 22.50x (ISBN 0-88033-007-4). East Eur Quarterly.
DARDANELLES CAMPAIGN, 1915
see European War, 1914-1918–Campaigns
DARIO, RUBEN, 1867-1916
see Sarmiento, Felix Ruben Garcia, 1867-1916
DARK AGES
see Europe–History–392-814
DARK ROOMS
see Photography–Studios and Dark Rooms
DARKROOM TECHNIQUE IN PHOTOGRAPHY
see Photography–Processing
DARWIN, CHARLES ROBERT, 1809-1882
Brent, Peter. Charles Darwin: A Man of Enlarged Curiosity. (Illus.). 560p. 1983. pap. 9.25x (ISBN 0-393-30109-5). Norton.
Darwin, Charles R. The Life & Letters of Charles Darwin, 2 Vols. Darwin, Francis, ed. LC 72-3904. (Illus.). 1972. write for info. (ISBN 0-404-08417-6). AMS Pr.
Norhausberber, Rudolph C. The Historical-Philosophical Significance of Comte, Darwin, Marx & Freud. (Human Development Library Book). (Illus.). 139p. 1983. 59.85 (ISBN 0-89266-392-8). Am Classical Coll Pr.
Parodiz, J. J. Darwin in the New World. (Illus.). 143p. 1982. pap. text ed. 12.00x (ISBN 90-04-06546-6, Pub. by Brill Holland). Humanities.
Pusey, James R. China & Charles Darwin. (Harvard East Asian Monographs: No. 100). 543p. 1982. text ed. 25.00x (ISBN 0-674-11735-2). Harvard U Pr.
DARWINISM
see Evolution
DASYPODIDAE
see Armadillos
DATA BASE MANAGEMENT
Akoak, J., ed. Management of Distributed Data Processing: Proceedings of the International Conference, Paris, France, June 23-26, 1982. 294p. 1982. 40.50 (ISBN 0-444-86458-X, North Holland). Elsevier.
Atre, Shakuntala. Data Base Structured Techniques to Designing Performance & Management: With Case Studies. LC 80-14808. (Business Data Processing Ser.). 442p. 1980. 31.95x (ISBN 0-471-05267-1, Pub. by Wiley-Interscience). Wiley.
Brooner, Ernie. Microcomputer Data-Base Management. Date not set. pap. 12.95 (ISBN 0-672-21875-5). Sams.
Chase, Leslie. Proven Techniques for Increasing Database Use. 1983. 49.95 (ISBN 0-942774-09-4). Info Indus.
Chorafas, Dimitri N. Databases Management Systems for Distributed Computer & Networks. (Illus.). 240p. 1983. 24.95 (ISBN 0-89433-184-1). Petrocelli.
Computer-Readable Data Bases: A Directory & Data Sourcebook. 1500p. 1982. 120.00 (ISBN 0-686-43328-9). Knowledge Industry Pubns.
Gradwell, D. J., ed. Database: The Second Generation. (Computer State of the Art Report, Series 10: No. 7). (Illus.). 662p. 1982. 445.00 (ISBN 0-08-028570-8). Pergamon.
Kruglinski, David. Data Base Management Systems: A Guide to Microcomputer Software. 272p. (Orig.). 1982. pap. 16.95 (ISBN 0-931988-84-5). Osborne-McGraw.
Loomis, Mary E. Data Management & File Processing. (Software Ser.). (Illus.). 544p. 1983. 28.95 (ISBN 0-13-196477-1). P-H.
Martin, James. Managing the Data Base Environment. (Illus.). 720p. 1983. text ed. 35.00 (ISBN 0-13-550582-8). P-H.
Norusis, M. J. SPSS-X Statistical Guide. 820p. 1983. 15.95 (ISBN 0-07-046548-7). McGraw.
Perry, William E. Ensuring Data Base Integrity. 300p. 1983. write for info (ISBN 0-471-86526-5). Ronald Pr.
Robinson, Hugh. Database Analysis & Design. 375p. 1981. pap. text ed. 26.50x (ISBN 0-686-81668-4, Pub. by Studentlitteratur). Renouf.
Rudman, Jack. Data Base Manager. (Career Examination Ser.: C-2873). (Cloth bdg. avail. on request). pap. 14.00 (ISBN 0-8373-2873-X). Natl Learning.
--Data Control Assistant. (Career Examination Ser.: C-2889). (Cloth bdg. avail. on request). pap. 10.00 (ISBN 0-8373-2889-6). Natl Learning.
--Data Control Specialist. (Career Examination Ser.: C-901). (Cloth bdg. avail. on request). pap. 12.00 (ISBN 0-8373-0901-8). Natl Learning.
Schmidt, J. W. & Brodie, M. L., eds. Relational Database Systems: Analysis & Comparison. 618p. 1983. 19.80 (ISBN 0-387-12032-7). Springer-Verlag.
SPSS, Inc. SPSS-X Data Management. 256p. 1983. 16.95x (ISBN 0-07-046547-9). McGraw.
--SPSS-X User's Guide. 864p. 1983. 28.95x (ISBN 0-07-046550-9, C). McGraw.
Stire, Tom G., ed. Process Control Computer Systems: Guide for Managers. LC 82-70705. (Illus.). 296p. 1982. 29.95 (ISBN 0-686-82280-3). Ann Arbor Science.
Thompson, Treva L. Systems Project Management: Principles & Guidelines. LC 82-80833. 200p. Date not set. 14.50 (ISBN 0-942898-00-1). Halpern & Simon.
Tremblay, J. P. & Sorenson, P. G. An Introduction to Data Structures with Applications. 2nd ed. 736p. 1982. 22.00x (ISBN 0-07-065157-4). McGraw.
Ullman, Jeffrey. Principles of Database Systems. 2nd ed. 1982. text ed. 24.95 (ISBN 0-914894-36-6). Computer Sci.
Wiederhold, Gio. Database Design. 2nd ed. Munson, Eric, ed. (Computer Science Ser.). (Illus.). 784p. 1983. text ed. 32.00 (ISBN 0-07-070132-6, C). McGraw.
DATA DISPLAY SYSTEMS
see Information Display Systems
DATA PROCESSING
see Electronic Data Processing; Information Storage and Retrieval Systems
DATA SMOOTHING FILTERS
see Digital Filters (Mathematics)
DATA TERMINALS (COMPUTERS)
see Computer Input-Output Equipment
DATA TRANSMISSION SYSTEMS
see also Library Information Networks; Telemeter
Davis, George R. The Local Network Handbook. (Illus.). 1982. pap. text ed. 26.95 (ISBN 0-07-015823-1, P&RB). McGraw.
Gallager, R. G. Information Theory & Reliable Communication. LC 68-26850. 588p. 1968. 41.95x (ISBN 0-471-29048-3). Wiley.
Kellejian, Robert. Applied Electronic Communication: Circuits, Systems, Transmission. rev. ed. 608p. 1982. 25.95 (ISBN 0-574-21580-8, 13-4580); instr's. guide 3.95 (ISBN 0-574-21581-6). SRA.
Lee, Alfred M. Electronic-Message Transfer & its Implications. LC 82-47683. 224p. 1983. 23.95x (ISBN 0-669-05555-7). Lexington Bks.
Lucky, R. W. & Salz, J. Principles of Data Communication. LC 82-14857. 1983. Repr. of 1968 ed. lib. bdg. p.n.s. (ISBN 0-89874-550-0). Krieger.
Money. Teletext & Viewdata. (Illus.). 1979. pap. 15.95 (ISBN 0-408-00378-2). Focal Pr.
DATE
Date Production & Protection. (FAO Plant Production & Protection Papers: No. 35). 294p. 1982. pap. 22.50 (ISBN 92-5-101121-4, F213, FAO). Unipub.
DATE ETIQUETTE
see Dating (Social Customs)
DATES, BOOKS OF
see Calendars
DATING (SOCIAL CUSTOMS)
Cahn, Julie. The Dating Book. Schneider, Meg, ed. (Just For Teens). 160p. 1983. pap. 3.50 (ISBN 0-671-46277-6). Wanderer Bks.
--The Dating Book. (Teen Survival Library). 160p. (gr. 9-12). 1983. PLB 9.29 (ISBN 0-671-46742-5). Messner.
Casey, W. W. How to Meet Men (For Ladies Only) 16p. pap. 3.00x (ISBN 0-943462-01-0). CaseCo.
Christie, Les. Dating & Mating: From a Christian View. Underwood, Jon, ed. (Illus.). 80p. (Orig.). 1983. pap. 2.95 (ISBN 0-87239-643-6, 39972). Standard Pub.
Diebel, Don. The Complete Guide to Meeting Women. 180p. 1983. pap. 8.95 (ISBN 0-937164-01-1). Gemini Pub Co.
Koestlime, Henry. Dating for Singles Over Thirty. LC 82-62514. 112p. (Orig.). 1983. pap. 6.50 (ISBN 0-935834-10-9). Rainbow-Betty.
Laurie, Greg. God's Design for Christian Dating. 2nd ed. LC 82-83836. 96p. (YA) (gr. 10-12). 1983. pap. 1.95 (ISBN 0-89081-373-6). Harvest Hse.
Lynch, Kevin W. A Woman's Guide to Cleveland Men. 224p. 1982. pap. 5.95 (ISBN 0-911671-00-5). Lynch Group Pub.
Rinehart, Stacy & Rinehart, Paula. Choices: Finding God's Way in Dating, Sex, Singleness & Marriage. LC 82-62071. 1983. pap. 3.95 (ISBN 0-89109-494-6). NavPress.
Weber, Eric & Cochran, Molly. How to Pick Up Women. 1980. text ed. 12.95 (ISBN 0-914094-14-9). Symphony.
What Men Know About Women. (Blank Books Ser.). 128p. 1982. cancelled 0.00 (ISBN 0-939944-15-4). Marmac Pub.
What Women Know About Men. (Blank Books Ser.). 128p. 1982. cancelled 0.00 (ISBN 0-939944-16-2). Marmac Pub.
Wild, Victor. The Complete Book of How to Succeed with Women. (Illus.). 208p. (Orig.). 1981. pap. 11.95 (ISBN 0-938444-01-8). Wildfire Pub.
DATING, RADIOACTIVE
see Radioactive Dating
DATING OF ROCKS
see Geological Time
DATSUN (AUTOMOBILE)
see Automobiles, Foreign–Types–Datsun
D'AVENANT, WILLIAM, SIR, 1606-1668
Spencer, Christopher. Davenant's MacBeth From the Yale Manuscript. 1961. text ed. 39.50x (ISBN 0-686-83523-9). Elliots Bks.
DA VINCI, LEONARDO
see Leonardo Da Vinci, 1452-1519
DAY CAMPS
see Camps
DAY CARE CENTERS
see also Nursery Schools
Copeland, Tom, ed. Basic Guide to Record Keeping & Taxes. 5th rev. ed. (Business Ideas for Family Day Care Providers Ser.). (Illus.). 40p. (Orig.). 1982. pap. 4.50 (ISBN 0-934140-07-3). Toys N Things.
Eichenberger, Shirley. Mother's Day Out. LC 82-42762. 1983. 12.95 (ISBN 0-911391-25-8); pap. 10.95 (ISBN 0-911391-26-6). Oak Hill KS.
Ispa, Jean. Exploring Careers in Child Care Services. (Careers in Depth Ser.). 140p. 1983. lib. bdg. 7.97 (ISBN 0-8239-0556-X). Rosen Pr.
McMurray, Georgia L. & Kazanjian, Dolores P. Day Care & the Working Poor: The Struggle for Self-Sufficiency. LC 82-199119. 140p. 1982. pap. 7.50 (ISBN 0-88156-001-4). Comm Serv Soc NY.
Morgan, Gwen G. Managing the Day Care Dollars: A Financial Handbook. LC 82-50691. 112p. (Orig.). 1982. pap. 7.95 (ISBN 0-942820-02-9). Steam Pr MA.
Murphy, Karen. A House Full of Kids: Running a Successful Day Care Business in Your Own Home. LC 82-73961. 320p. (Orig.). 1983. 14.37 (ISBN 0-8070-2302-7); pap. 9.57 (ISBN 0-8070-2303-5). Beacon Pr.
Windows on Day Care. pap. 2.25 (ISBN 0-686-81721-4). NCJW.
YMCA of USA. YMCA School Age Child Care. 165p. 1982. pap. 50.00 (ISBN 0-686-83762-2, 0-88350067). YMCA USA.
DAY DREAMS
see Fantasy
DAY NURSERIES
see Day Care Centers
DAY OF JUDGMENT
see Judgment Day
DAYLIGHT
Robbins, Claude L. & Hunter, Kerri C. Daylighting Availability Data for Selected Cities in the United States. (Progress in Solar Energy Ser.: Suppl.). 275p. 1983. pap. text ed. 21.00 (ISBN 0-89553-140-2). Am Solar Energy.
--Hourly Availability of Sunlight in the United States. 150p. 1983. pap. text ed. 13.50 (ISBN 0-89553-141-0). Am Solar Energy.
--A Method for Predicting Energy Savings Attributed to Daylighting. (Progress in Solar Energy Ser.: Suppl.). 225p. 1983. pap. text ed. 18.00 (ISBN 0-89553-139-9). Am Solar Energy.
DAYS
see also Anniversaries; Festivals; Holidays
also names of special day, e.g. Christmas
Craig, Helen. Mouse House Days of the Week. LC 82-60211. (Illus.). 30p. (ps-1). 1983. 2.95 (ISBN 0-394-85286-9). Random.
DEACONS
see also Church Officers
Kleiber, Kenneth & Lemire, Deacon H. Deacons: Permanent or Passing? 70p. 1982. 6.95 (ISBN 0-911519-02-5). Richelieu Court.
DEAD SEA SCROLLS
see also Essenes; Qumran Community
Szekely, Edmond B. The Teachings of the Essenes from Enoch to the Dead Sea Scrolls. (Illus.). 112p. 1981. pap. 4.80 (ISBN 0-89564-006-6). IBS Intl.
DEAF
see also Children, Deaf
Craig, William N. & Collins, James L. New Vistas for Competitive Employment of Deaf. (Monograph: No. 2). 110p. 1970. pap. text ed. 3.00 (ISBN 0-914494-04-X). Am Deaf & Rehab.
Levine, Edna S., ed. The Preparation of Psychological Service Providers to the Deaf. (Monograph: No. 4). 1977. pap. text ed. 4.00 (ISBN 0-914494-05-8). Am Deaf & Rehab.
DEAF–MEANS OF COMMUNICATION
Jackson, Timothy. Friends Are for Signing. (Illus.). 34p. (Orig.). (YA) (gr. 7-9). 1982. pap. 1.95x (ISBN 0-913072-51-6). Natl Assn Deaf.
DEAF MUTES
see Deaf
DEAFNESS
Here are entered works on the lack of sense of hearing, including the lack combined with the inability to speak, i.e. deaf-mutism. Works on the inability to speak whether from any functional or physical case other than deafness are entered under Mutism.
see also Ear; Hearing
Wright, M. I. Pathology of Deafness. 188p. 1971. 17.00 (ISBN 0-7190-0418-7). Manchester.
DEAFNESS IN CHILDREN
see Children, Deaf
DEAN'S WOODS
Phelps, Humphrey. The Forest of Dean. 192p. 1982. pap. text ed. 8.25x (ISBN 0-904387-86-0, Pub. by Sutton England). Humanities.
DEATH
see also Children and Death; Future Life; Hell; Immortalism; Mortality; Terminal Care
Epting, Franz R. & Neimeyer, Robert A., eds. Personal Meanings of Death. (Death Education, Aging & Health Care Ser.). (Illus.). 200p. 1983. text ed. 24.95 (ISBN 0-89116-363-8). Hemisphere Pub.
Fruehling, James A. Sourcebook on Death & Dying. LC 82-82013. 788p. 1982. write for info. (ISBN 0-8379-5801-6). Marquis.
Goodman, Lisl M. Death & the Creative Life. 1983. pap. 5.95 (ISBN 0-14-006275-0). Penguin.
Griffin, Graeme M. & Tobin, Des. In the Midst of Life: The Australian Response to Death. (Illus.). 191p. 1983. pap. 9.95 (ISBN 0-522-84248-8, Pub. by Melbourne U Pr). Intl Schol Bk Serv.
Hafen, Brent Q. Faces of Death: Grief, Dying, Euthanasia, Suicide. 276p. 1983. pap. text ed. 10.00x (ISBN 0-89582-092-7). Morton Pub.
Lodo, Venerable L. Bardo Teachings: The Way of Death & Rebirth. Clark, Nancy & Parke, Caroline M., eds. (Illus.). 76p. 1982. pap. text ed. 5.95 (ISBN 0-910165-00-9). KDK Pubns.
Szekely, Edmond B. The Conquest of Death. 68p. 1973. pap. 2.95 (ISBN 0-89564-043-0). IBS Intl.
DEATH–BIBLIOGRAPHY
Enright, D. J., ed. The Oxford Book of Death. 320p. 1983. 19.95 (ISBN 0-19-214129-5). Oxford U Pr.
DEATH–CAUSES
see also Mortality; Suicide
Chamblee, Ronald F. & Evans, Marchsll C. Transax: The NCHS System for Producing Multiple Cause-of-Death Statistics, 1968-78. Madison, Eddie, ed. 55p. 1982. pap. text ed. 1.75 (ISBN 0-8406-0269-3). Natl Ctr Health Stats.
DEATH–JUVENILE LITERATURE
Miner, Jane C. A Man's Pride: Losing a Father. Schroeder, Howard, ed. LC 82-1380. (Crisis Ser.). (Illus.). 64p. (gr. 4-5). 1982. lib. bdg. 7.95 (ISBN 0-89686-168-6). Crestwood Hse.
DEATH–PSYCHOLOGY
see also Children and Death
DeSpelder, Lynne A. & Strickland, Albert L. The Last Dance: Encountering Death & Dying. 457p. 1983. text ed. 16.95 (ISBN 0-87484-535-1). Mayfield Pub.
Epting, Franz R. & Neimeyer, Robert A., eds. Personal Meanings of Death. (Death Education, Aging & Health Care Ser.). (Illus.). 200p. 1983. text ed. 24.95 (ISBN 0-89116-363-8). Hemisphere Pub.
Lee, Jung Y. Death Overcome: Towards a Convergence of Eastern & Western Views. LC 82-20192. 98p. (Orig.). 1983. lib. bdg. 17.25 (ISBN 0-8191-2902-X); pap. text ed. 7.25 (ISBN 0-8191-2901-1). U Pr of Amer.
Morgan, Ernest. Dealing Creatively with Death: A Manual of Death Education & Simple Burial. 10th Rev. ed. 96p. Date not set. pap. price not set (ISBN 0-914064-25-8). Celo Pr.
DEATH–RELIGIOUS AND MORAL ASPECTS
Evely, Louis. In the Face of Death. 112p. 1979. 7.95 (ISBN 0-686-83909-9). Seabury.
Hill, Brennan. The Near-Death Experience: A Christian Approach. 66p. 1981. pap. 3.50 (ISBN 0-697-01756-7). Wm C Brown.
Hill, Dick. Death & Dying. 4.25 (ISBN 0-89137-532-5). Quality Pubns.
Liguori, Alphonsus. Preparation for Death. pap. 4.00 (ISBN 0-686-81628-5). TAN Bks Pubs.
Partridge, Jeannette. Losing a Loved One. 2.00 (ISBN 0-686-84350-9). Olympus Pub Co.
DEATH, DANCE OF
see Dance of Death
DEATH, MERCY
see Euthanasia
DEATH AND CHILDREN
see Children and Death
DEATH DUTIES
see Inheritance and Transfer Tax
DEATH-MASKS
see Masks (Sculpture)
DEATH OF CHILDREN
see Children–Death and Future State
DEATH PENALTY
see Capital Punishment
DEATH RATE
see Mortality
DEATHS, REGISTERS OF
see Registers of Births, Deaths, Marriages, Etc.
DEBATES AND DEBATING
see also Forums (Discussion and Debate); Oratory; Parliamentary Practice

Hensley, Dana & Prentice, Diana. Mastering Competitive Debate. rev. ed. 190p. 1982. pap. text ed. 7.03 (ISBN 0-931054-08-7). Clark Pub.
Patterson, J. W. & Zarefsky, David. Contemporary Debate. LC 82-82020. 356p. 1982. pap. text ed. 19.95 (ISBN 0-395-32641-9). HM.
Sanders, Gerald H. Introduction to Contemporary Academic Debate. 2nd ed. LC 82-50791. 157p. 1983. pap. 7.95x (ISBN 0-917974-94-8). Waveland Pr.

DEBENTURES
see Bonds

DEBT
see also Bankruptcy; Collecting of Accounts; Credit; Debtor and Creditor
Rogers, Harry E. The Debt Relief Kit. 200p. (Orig.). 1983. pap. 9.95 (ISBN 0-937464-04-X). Lawkits.

DEBTOR AND CREDITOR
see also Bankruptcy; Compromise (Law)
Spencer, Natalie, compiled by. References for Debtor's or Bill Payor's; Data Notes. 75p. Date not set. 12.95 (ISBN 0-686-37648-X). Data Notes Pub.

DEBTS, PUBLIC
Here are entered works on internal public debts as well as works on both internal and external public debts Works dealing with external public debts only are entered under the heading Debts, External.
see also Bonds
Anderson, William G. The Price of Liberty: The Public Debt of the American Revolution. LC 82-17420. 1983. 20.00x (ISBN 0-8139-0975-9). U Pr of Va.

DEBUGGING (ELECTRONIC COMPUTERS)
see also Computer Programming Management
Clary, Wayne. OS Debugging for the COBOL Programmer. Eckols, Steve & Taylor, Judy, eds. LC 80-84122. (Illus.). 312p. (Orig.). 1981. pap. text ed. 20.00 (ISBN 0-911625-10-0). M Murach & Assoc.

DEBUSSY, CLAUDE, 1862-1918
Orledge, Robert. Debussy & the Theatre. LC 82-1348. (Illus.). 350p. 1983. 49.50 (ISBN 0-521-22807-7). Cambridge U Pr.
Till, Nicholas. Debussy: His Life & Times. (Illus.). 150p. 1983. 16.95 (ISBN 0-88254-808-5, Pub. by Midas Bks England). Hippocrene Bks.
Wenk, Arthur B. Claude Debussy & Twentieth Century Music. (Music Ser.). 184p. 1983. lib. bdg. 21.95 (ISBN 0-8057-9454-9, Twayne). G K Hall.

DECALOGUE
see Commandments, Ten

DECEDENTS' ESTATES
Hughes, Theodore E. & Klein, David. A Family Guide to Estate Planning, Funeral Arrangements, & Settling an Estate After Death. 240p. 1983. 13.95 (ISBN 0-686-83669-3, ScribT). Scribner.

DECEIT
see Fraud

DECENTRALIZATION IN GOVERNMENT
see also Federal Government; Local Government; Public Administration
Stewart, John. Local Government: The Conditions of Local Choice. (Institute of Local Government Studies). 216p. 1983. text ed. 28.50x (ISBN 0-04-352102-9); pap. text ed. 12.95x (ISBN 0-04-352103-7). Allen Unwin.

DECIDABILITY THEORY
see Goedel's Theorem

DECIMAL SYSTEM-PROGRAMMED INSTRUCTION
Loose, Frances F. Decimals & Percentages. (Illus.). 96p. (gr. 4-6). 1977. 7.00 (ISBN 0-89039-200-5); answer key incl. Ann Arbor Pubs.

DECISION (PSYCHOLOGY)
see Decision-Making

DECISION-MAKING
see also Choice (Psychology); Statistical Decision
Avery, Michel, et al. Building United Judgement: A Handbook for Consensus Decision Making. 124p. (Orig.). 1981. pap. text ed. 5.00 (ISBN 0-941492-01-X). Ctr Conflict Resol.
Brest, Levinson. Processes of Constitutional Decisionmaking. 2nd ed. LC 81-86686. 1983. text ed. cancelled (ISBN 0-316-10794-8). Little.
Collingridge, David. Critical Decision Making: A New Theory of Social Choice. LC 82-6017. 1982. 25.00x (ISBN 0-312-17418-7). St Martin.
Easton, Allan. Decision Making: A Short Course in Problem Solving for Professionals. (Professional Development Programs Ser.). 352p. 1976. Set. text ed. 29.95x (ISBN 0-471-01700-0). Wiley.
Gallagher, C. A. & Watson, H. J. Quantitative Methods for Business Decisions. 1980. text ed. 27.95 (ISBN 0-07-022751-9); supplementary materials avail. McGraw.
Gupta, M. M. & Sanchez, E., eds. Approximate Reasoning in Decision Analysis. 480p. 1982. 68.50 (ISBN 0-444-86492-X, North Holland). Elsevier.
Holbrook, Stephen F. Effective Decision Making. revised ed. 45p. 1983. pap. text ed. 9.90 (ISBN 0-686-42968-0). PMA.
House, William C. Decision Support Systems. 250p. pap. 15.00 (ISBN 0-89433-208-2). Petrocelli.
Johnson, Luke T. Decision Making in the Church: A Biblical Model. LC 82-17675. 112p. 1983. pap. 5.95 (ISBN 0-8006-1694-4). Fortress.
Moody, Paul. Decision Making: Proven Methods for Better Decisions. LC 82-17196. (Illus.). 256p. 1983. 24.95 (ISBN 0-07-042868-9, P&RB). McGraw.
A New Way to Decision Making. 290p. (Eng. & Ger.). 1981. pap. 16.00 (ISBN 0-89192-349-7). Transbooks.
Presentations for Decision Makers. (Management Development Ser.). (Illus.). 175p. 1983. 20.00 (ISBN 0-534-02704-0). Lifetime Learn.
Shilling, Dana. Making Wise Decisions: Plaintext Forms for Analyzing Your Options in Financial, Legal, Health, & Consumer Markets. 256p. (Orig.). 1982. pap. 8.00 (ISBN 0-688-01941-2). Quill NY.
Wagner, Thomas A. Kognitive Problemlosungsbarrieren Bei Entscheidungsprozessen In der Unternehmung. vi, 250p. (Ger.). 1982. write for info. (ISBN 3-8204-5774-7). P Lang Pubs.
Watson, S. R., ed. The Practice of Decision Making. 100p. 1983. 15.50 (ISBN 0-08-028162-1). Pergamon.

DECISION-MAKING-MATHEMATICAL MODELS
see also Critical Path Analysis
Schellenberger, R. & Boseman, G. MANSYM III: A Dynamic Management Simulator with Decision Support System. (Management Ser.). 94p. 1982. pap. text ed. 12.95 (ISBN 0-471-08581-2); tchrs. manual 6.00 (ISBN 0-471-86815-9). Wiley.
Srivastava, U. K. & Shenov, G. V. Quantitative Techniques for Managerial Decision Making: Concepts, Illustrations, & Problems. LC 82-21242. 968p. 1983. 29.95 (ISBN 0-470-27375-5). Wiley.

DECISION-MAKING (ETHICS)
Larsen, Sandy & Larsen, Dale. Choices: Picking Your Way Through the Ethical Jungle. (Young Fisherman Bible Studyguides). (Illus.). 80p. (Orig.). (gr. 2-12). 1983. saddle-stitched student ed. 2.95 (ISBN 0-87788-113-8); tchr's. ed. 3.95 (ISBN 0-87788-114-6). Shaw Pubs.
Price, Eugenia. A Woman's Choice. 192p. 1983. pap. 5.95 (ISBN 0-310-31381-3). Zondervan.

DECISION-MAKING, JUDICIAL
see Judicial Process

DECISION PROBLEMS
see Statistical Decision

DECISION PROCESSES
see Decision-Making

DECLAMATION
see Public Speaking

DECLARATION OF INDEPENDENCE
see United States-Declaration of Independence

DECLARATIONS (LAW)
see Pleading

DECORATION, INTERIOR
see Interior Decoration

DECORATION AND ORNAMENT
see also Alphabets; Antiques; Art, Decorative; Art Objects; Bronzes; Carpets; Carving (Art Industries); China Painting; Church Decoration and Ornament; Decoupage; Design; Design, Decorative; Embroidery; Enamel and Enameling; Flower Arrangement; Folk Art; Furniture; Gems; Glass Painting and Staining; Illumination of Books and Manuscripts; Illustration of Books; Interior Decoration; Jewelry; Leather Work; Lettering; Metal-Work; Mosaics; Mural Painting and Decoration; Painting; Pottery; Sculpture; Stencil Work; Table Setting and Decoration; Textile Design; Wood-Carving
Baker, Arthur. Calligraphic Cut-Paper Designs for Artists & Craftsmen. (Pictorial Archive Ser.). (Illus.). 80p. (Orig.). 1983. pap. 2.50 (ISBN 0-486-20306-9). Dover.
Menten, Ted. Ready-to Use Art Nouveau Borders. (Illus.). 64p. (Orig.). 1983. pap. 2.95 (ISBN 0-486-24431-8). Dover.
Veasey, William. Blue Ribbon Pattern Series, Bk. 1: Full Size Decorative Patterns. (Illus.). 63p. 1982. 14.95 (ISBN 0-916838-71-4). Schiffer.
Ward, James. Historic Ornament: A Treatise on Decorative Art & Architectural Ornament. (Illus.). 858p. 1983. pap. 9.95 (ISBN 0-686-38395-8). Tanager Bks.

DECORATION AND ORNAMENT-ART DECO
see Art Deco

DECORATION AND ORNAMENT-ASIA
Lane, Maggie. Gold & Silver Needlepoint. (Illus.). 168p. 1983. 19.95 (ISBN 0-686-83805-X, ScribT). Scribner.

DECORATION AND ORNAMENT-EUROPE
Southard, Edna C. Decorative Arts of the Russian Royalty. LC 82-61597. (Illus.). 32p. 1982. pap. 3.00 (ISBN 0-940784-04-1). Miami Univ Art.

DECORATION AND ORNAMENT-UNITED STATES
Bishop, Robert & Coblentz, Patricia. American Decorative Arts: 360 Years of Creative Design. (Illus.). 395p. 1982. 65.00 (ISBN 0-8109-0692-9). Abrams.

DECORATION AND ORNAMENT, ARCHITECTURAL
Chapman, Linda L., et al. Louis H. Sullivan Architectural Ornament Collection: Southern Illinois University at Edwardsville. LC 81-51083. (Illus.). 79p. (Orig.). 1981. pap. 10.00 (ISBN 0-89062-136-5, Pub by Southern Illinois Univ Edwardsville). Pub Ctr Cult Res.
Jensen, Robert & Conway, Patricia. Ornamentalism: The New Decorativeness in Architecture & Design. (Illus.). 312p. 1982. 40.00 (ISBN 0-517-54383-4, C N Potter Bks). Crown.
McArdle, Alma deC. & McArdle, Deirdred B. Carpenter Gothic: Nineteenth Century Ornamented Houses of New England. (Illus.). 160p. 1983. pap. 14.95 (ISBN 0-8230-7101-4, Whitney Lib). Watson-Guptill.
Meier, Richard. Shards by Frank Stella, Text by Richard Meier. (Illus., Orig.). 1982. pap. 5.95 (ISBN 0-902825-19-4). Petersburg Pr.
Robertson, J. C. The Basic Principles of Architectural Design. (Illus.). 127p. 1983. 47.25 (ISBN 0-86650-058-8). Gloucester Art.
Ward, James. Historic Ornament: A Treatise on Decorative Art & Architectural Ornament. (Illus.). 858p. 1983. pap. 9.95 (ISBN 0-686-38395-8). Tanager Bks.

DECORATION OF FOOD
see Cookery (Garnishes)

DECORATIONS OF HONOR
see also Heraldry; Medals;
also names of particular medals, e.g. Medal of Honor
Campbell, Burt L. Marine Badges & Insignia of the World: Including Marines, Commandos & Navel Infantrymen. (Illus.). 160p. 1983. 16.95 (ISBN 0-7137-1138-8, Pub. by Blandford Pr England). Sterling.
Chalif, Don & Bender, Roger J. Military Pilot & Aircrew Badges of the World: 1870 to Present, Vol. 1. (Illus.). 224p. 1982. 24.95 (ISBN 0-912138-26-2). Bender Pub CA.
Davis, Brian L. Badges & Insignia of the Third Reich 1933-1945. (Illus.). 160p. 1983. 16.95 (ISBN 0-7137-1130-2, Pub. by Blandford Pr England). Sterling.
Olson, David V. Badges & Distinctive Insignia of the Kingdom of Saudi Arabia. 186p. 1981. pap. 10.00 (ISBN 0-686-84348-7). Olson QMD.
Royal Saudi Air Force: Badges & Distinctive Insignia of the Kingdom of Saudi Arabia, Vol. II. 1982. 10.00 (ISBN 0-686-83747-9). Olson QMD.

DECORATIVE ARTS
see Art, Decorative; Art Industries and Trade; Decoration and Ornament; Design, Decorative; Interior Decoration
also the specific subjects referred to under these headings

DECORATIVE DESIGN
see Design, Decorative

DECORATIVE LIGHTING
see Lighting, Architectural and Decorative

DECOUPAGE
Baker, Arthur. Calligraphic Cut-Paper Designs for Artists & Craftsmen. (Pictorial Archive Ser.). (Illus.). 80p. (Orig.). 1983. pap. 2.50 (ISBN 0-486-20306-9). Dover.
Rawlings, Eleanor H., ed. The Cornucopia of Design & Illustration for Decoupage & Other Arts & Crafts. (Illus.). 160p. (Orig.). 1983. pap. 6.95 (ISBN 0-486-24486-5). Dover.

DECOYS (HUNTING)
Fleckenstein, Henry, Jr. New Jersey Decoys. (Illus.). 240p. 1983. text ed. 37.50 (ISBN 0-916838-75-7). Schiffer.
Guyette, Dale & Guyette, Gary. Decoys of Maritime Canada. (Illus.). 204p. 1983. text ed. 35.00 (ISBN 0-916838-76-5). Schiffer.
Luckey, Carl F. Collecting Antique American Bird Decoys: Identification & Value Guide. (Illus.). 208p. 1983. pap. 14.95 (ISBN 0-89689-043-0). Bks Americana.
Veasey, William. Head Patterns. (Blue Ribbon Pattern Ser.: Book III). (Illus.). 64p. 1983. pap. 14.95 (ISBN 0-916838-78-1). Schiffer.
--Miniature Decoy Patterns. (Blue Ribbon Pattern Ser.: Bk. II). (Illus.). 64p. (Orig.). 1983. pap. 14.95 (ISBN 0-916838-77-3). Schiffer.

DECUBITUS
see Bed-Sores

DEDUCTION (LOGIC)
see Logic

DEDUCTIVE LOGIC
see Logic

DEEP-SEA DEPOSITS
see Marine Sediments; Sedimentation and Deposition

DEEP-SEA EXPLORATION
see Marine Biology; Marine Fauna; Marine Flora

DEEP SEA FISHING
see Salt-Water Fishing

DEER
see also Elk
Ahlstrom, Mark. The Whitetail. Schroeder, Howard, ed. (Wildlife Habits & Habitat Ser.). (Illus.). 48p. (gr. 4-5). 1983. lib. bdg. 8.95 (ISBN 0-89686-224-0). Crestwood Hse.
Goss, Richard J., ed. Deer Antlers: Regeneration, Function, & Evolution. LC 82-22795. (Monograph). Date not set. price not set (ISBN 0-12-293080-0). Acad Pr.

DEFAMATION
see Libel and Slander

DEFECTIVE SPEECH
see Speech, Disorders Of

DEFECTS, BIRTH
see Abnormalities, Human

DEFENSE (LAW)
see Actions and Defenses

DEFENSE (MILITARY SCIENCE)
see Attack and Defense (Military Science)

DEFENSE, CIVIL
see Civil Defense

DEFENSE, PERCEPTUAL
see Perception

DEFENSE ECONOMICS
see Disarmament-Economic Aspects; War-Economic Aspects

DEFENSE RESEARCH
see Military Research

DEFENSES
see Industrial Mobilization

DEFERRED COMPENSATION
Hansman, Robert J. & Larrabee, John W. Deferred Compensation: The New Methodology for Executive Reward. LC 82-48596. 1983. write for info. (ISBN 0-669-06329-0). Lexington Bks.

DEFOE, DANIEL, 1661?-1731
Boardman, Michael. Defoe & the Usage of Narrative. 195p. 1982. text ed. 22.50x (ISBN 0-8135-0961-0). Rutgers U Pr.
Novak, Maximillian E. Realism, Myth, & History in Defoe's Fiction. LC 82-11141. xviii, 170p. 1983. 16.95x (ISBN 0-8032-3307-8). U of Nebr Pr.

DEFORMATIONS (MECHANICS)
see also Continuum Mechanics; Fracture Mechanics; Materials-Creep; Plasticity; Rheology; Strains and Stresses
Frost, H. J. & Ashby, M. F. Deformation-Mechanism Maps: The Plasticity & Creep of Metals & Ceramics. (Illus.): 184p. 1982. 45.00 (ISBN 0-08-029338-7); pap. 25.00 (ISBN 0-08-029337-9). Pergamon.

DEFORMATIONS, CONTINUOUS
see Homotopy Theory

DEFORMITIES
see Abnormalities, Human

DEGAS, HILAIRE GERMAIN EDGAR, 1834-1917
Roberts, Keith. Degas. (Phaidon Color Library). (Illus.). 84p. 1983. 27.50 (ISBN 0-7148-2226-4, Pub. by Salem Hse Ltd); pap. 18.95 (ISBN 0-7148-2240-X). Merrimack Bk Serv.

DE GAULLE, CHARLES
see Gaulle, Charles De, Pres. France, 1890-1970

DEGENERATION, HEPATOLENTICULAR
see Hepatolenticular Degeneration

DEGREES, ACADEMIC
Bear, John. How to Get the Degree You Want. LC 82-905. 256p. (Orig.). 1982. pap. 9.95 (ISBN 0-89815-080-9). Ten Speed Pr.
Engineering & Technology Degrees, 1980, 3 pts. Set. 150.00 (ISBN 0-87615-031-8, 201-80); Pt. I. 35.00 (ISBN 0-87615-041-5, 201A-80); Pt. II. 100.00 (ISBN 0-87615-051-2, 201B-80); Pt. III. 35.00 (ISBN 0-87615-061-X, 201C-80). AAES.

DEGREES OF LATITUDE AND LONGITUDE
see Geodesy

DEHYDROFROZEN FOOD
see Food, Frozen

DEITIES
see Gods

DEJECTION
see Depression, Mental

DELAWARE-HISTORY
Reynolds, Hazel W. Flower of Caroon Manor. 438p. 1982. 16.50 (ISBN 0-9608106-0-9). H W Reynolds.

DELAWARE INDIANS
see Indians of North America-Eastern States

DELAWARE RIVER AND VALLEY
Brandywine Conservancy, Inc. Historic Preservation in the Lower Delaware Valley. 150p. 1983. write for info. Brandywine Conserv.
Nixdorf, Bert. Hikes & Bike Rides for the Delaware Valley & Southern New Jersey: With Emphasis on the Pine Barrens, No. 1. (Illus.). 140p. (Orig.). pap. 5.50 (ISBN 0-9610474-0-2). B Nixdorf.

DELAYED-ACTION PREPARATIONS
Roseman, Mansdorf. Controlled Released Delivery Systems. 400p. 1983. 57.50 (ISBN 0-8247-1728-7). Dekker.

DELINQUENCY, JUVENILE
see Juvenile Delinquency

DELINQUENT WOMEN
see Female Offenders

DELIVERY, ABDOMINAL
see Cesarean Section

DELIVERY (OBSTETRICS)
see Labor (Obstetrics)

DELPHINIDAE
see Dolphins

DELUSIONS
see Superstition; Witchcraft

DEMAND AND SUPPLY
see Supply and Demand

DEMENTIA PRAECOX
see Schizophrenia

DEMILUNES OF HEIDENHAIN
see Salivary Glands

DEMOCRACY
see also Despotism; Equality; Federal Government; Liberty; Representative Government and Representation; Socialism; Suffrage
Aberbach, Joel D. & Putnam, Robert D. Bureaucrats & Politicians in Western Democracies. 324p. 1982. pap. text ed. 9.95x (ISBN 0-674-08627-9). Harvard U Pr.

Adams, Pauline & Thornton, Emma S. A Populist Assualt: Sarah E. Van de Vort Emery on American Democracy 1862-1895. LC 82-60665. (Illus.). 146p. 1982. 13.95 (ISBN 0-87972-203-7); pap. 6.95 (ISBN 0-87972-204-5). Bowling Green Univ.

Clor, Harry M. The Mass Media & Democracy. 1974. pap. 10.50 (ISBN 0-395-30789-9). HM.

Danielson, Michael N. & Murphy, Walter F. American Democracy. 10th ed. (Illus.). 608p. 1983. text ed. price not set (ISBN 0-8419-0839-7). Holmes & Meier.

Democracy & Free Enterprise as Negative Utopia in America, 1980-1982. (Analysis Ser.: No. 10). 1983. pap. 10.00 (ISBN 0-686-42849-8). Inst Analysis.

Edwards, John. Christian Cordoba: The City & its Region in the Late Middle Ages. LC 81-24213. (Cambridge, Iberian & Latin American Studies). 256p. 1982. 47.50 (ISBN 0-521-24320-3). Cambridge U Pr.

Eidlin, Fred. Constitutional Democracy: Essays in Comparative Politics. (Replica Edition Ser.). 350p. 1983. softcover 20.00x (ISBN 0-86531-948-0). Westview.

Garrison, Julie. Democracy in the U. S. A. (Social Studies). 24p. (gr. 6-9). 1980. wkbk. 5.00 (ISBN 0-8209-0246-2, SS-13). ESP.

Groth, Alexander J. Major Ideologies: An Interpretative of Democracy, Socialism & Nationalism. LC 82-18755. 256p. 1983. Repr. of 1971 ed. text ed. write for info. (ISBN 0-89874-579-9). Krieger.

Herz, John H. From Dictatorship to Democracy: Coping with the Legacies of Authoritarianism & Totalitarianism. LC 82-12002. (Contributions in Political Science Ser.: No. 92). (Illus.). 376p. 1983. lib. bdg. 35.00 (ISBN 0-313-23636-4, HDD/). Greenwood.

Hindess, Barry. Parliamentary Democracy & Socialist Politics. 200p. 1983. pap. 10.95 (ISBN 0-7100-9319-5). Routledge & Kegan.

Kann, Mark E., ed. The Future of American Democracy: Views from the Left. 1983. write for info. (ISBN 0-87722-288-6). Temple U Pr.

Lebedoff, David. The New Elite: The Death of Democracy. 208p. 1983. pap. 8.95 (ISBN 0-8092-5617-7). Contemp Bks.

Lindenfeld, Frank & Rothschild-Whitt, Joyce, eds. Workplace Democracy & Social Change. LC 82-80137. 456p. 1982. 20.00 (ISBN 0-87558-101-3, Pub. by Extending Hor Bks); pap. 12.00 (ISBN 0-87558-102-1). Porter Sargent.

Marriott, John A. Dictatorship & Democracy. 231p. 1982. Repr. of 1935 ed. lib. bdg. 30.00 (ISBN 0-8495-3937-4). Arden Lib.

Nordlinger, Eric A. On the Autonomy of the Democratic State. (Center for International Affairs Ser.). 247p. 1982. pap. text ed. 7.95x (ISBN 0-674-63409-8). Harvard U Pr.

Ostrander, Gilman M. Romantic Democracy. 1970. pap. text ed. 1.95x (ISBN 0-88273-223-4). Forum Pr IL.

A Serious Breach of National Security as Occurred: Some Game!!! (Analysis Ser.: No. 9). 1982. pap. 10.00 (ISBN 0-686-42844-7). Inst Analysis.

Tocqueville, Alexis. Alexis de Tocqueville on Democracy, Revolution, & Society. Stone, John, et al, eds. LC 79-21204. (Heritage of Sociology Ser.). 392p. 1982. pap. 7.95 (ISBN 0-226-80527-1). U of Chicago Pr.

DEMOCRACY–ADDRESSES, ESSAYS, LECTURES

Goldwin, Robert A. & Schambra, William A., eds. How Capitalistic is the Constitution? 1982. 14.25 (ISBN 0-8447-3477-2); pap. 6.25 (ISBN 0-8447-3478-0). Am Enterprise.

DEMOCRACY IN EDUCATION

see Self-Government (In Education)

DEMOCRATIC PARTY

Baker, Jean H. Affairs of Party: The Political Culture of Northern Democrats in the Mid-19th Century. (Illus.). 368p. 1983. 39.50x (ISBN 0-8014-1513-6); pap. 14.95x (ISBN 0-8014-9883-X). Cornell U Pr.

DEMOGRAPHY

see also Fertility, Human; Geopolitics; Mortality; Population

also subdivision Population under names of countries

Correa, Hector & El Torky, Mohamed A. The Biological & Social Determinants of the Demographic Transition. LC 82-16042. (Illus.). 298p. (Orig.). 1983. lib. bdg. 24.25 (ISBN 0-8191-2754-X); pap. text ed. 12.75 (ISBN 0-8191-2755-8). U Pr of Amer.

Demographic Indicators of Countries: Estimates & Projections as Assessed in 1980. 40.00 (ISBN 0-686-43219-3, E.82.XIII.5). UN.

Mosk, Carl, ed. Patriarchy & Fertility: The Evolution of Natality in Japan & Sweden 1880-1960. (Population & Social Structure: Advances in Historical Demography). Date not set. price not set (ISBN 0-12-508480-3). Acad Pr.

Schnell, George A. & Monmonier, Mark S. The Study of Population: A Geographic Approach. 362p. Date not set. text ed. 24.95 (ISBN 0-675-20046-6). Merrill.

United Nations. Demographic Year Book 1980. 65.00 (ISBN 0-686-84891-8, E/F.81.XIII.1). UN.

DEMOGRAPHY–BIBLIOGRAPHY

Infomap Inc. Atlas of Demographics: U. S. by County. (Illus.). 60p. 1982. 195.00 (ISBN 0-910471-00-2). Infomap Inc.

United Nations. Demographic Yearbook, 1980. 32nd ed. LC 50-641. (Illus.). 973p. 1982. 65.00x (ISBN 0-8002-3062-0). Intl Pubns Serv.

DEMONOLOGY

see also Apparitions; Devil; Exorcism; Magic; Occult Sciences; Superstition; Witchcraft

Kapferer, Bruce. A Celebration of Demons. LC 81-48677. (Illus.). 352p. (Orig.). 1983. 32.50x (ISBN 0-253-31326-0); pap. 18.50x (ISBN 0-253-20304-X). Ind U Pr.

Sumrall, Lester. Questions & Answers on Demon Powers. (Orig.). 1983. pap. 3.50 (ISBN 0-89274-261-5). Harrison Hse.

DEMURRER

see Pleading

DENDROCHRONOLOGY

Libby, Leona M. Past Climates: Tree Thermometers, Commodities & People. 157p. 1983. text ed. 25.00x (ISBN 0-292-73019-5). U of Tex Pr.

Webb, George E. Tree Rings & Telescopes: The Scientific Career of A. E. Douglass. 250p. 1983. 19.50x (ISBN 0-8165-0798-8). U of Ariz Pr.

DENDROLOGY

see Trees

DENMARK–DESCRIPTION AND TRAVEL

Copenhagen Travel Guide. (Berlitz Travel Guides). (Illus.). 1982. pap. 4.95 (ISBN 0-02-969070-6, Berlitz). Macmillan.

Fodor's Stockholm, Copenhagen, Oslo, Helsinki & Reykjavik. (Illus.). 144p. 1983. pap. 5.95 (ISBN 0-679-00966-3). McKay.

Rutherford, G. K. The Physical Environment of the Faeroe Islands. 1982. 39.50 (ISBN 90-6193-099-5, Pub. by Junk Pubs Netherlands). Kluwer Boston.

DENMARK–HISTORY

Roesdahl, Else. Viking Age Denmark. 272p. 1982. 60.00x (ISBN 0-7141-8027-0, Pub. by Brit Mus Pubns England). State Mutual Bk.

DENOMINATIONAL SCHOOLS

see Church Schools

DENOMINATIONS, RELIGIOUS

see Religions; Sects;

also particuliar denominations and sects

DENTAL ANATOMY

see Teeth

DENTAL CARE

Bishop, Eric. Dental Insurance: The What, the Why, & the How of Dental Benefits. 224p. 1983. 29.95 (ISBN 0-07-005471-1, P&RB). McGraw.

Frandsen, Asger, ed. Dental Health Care in Scandinavia. (Illus.). 260p. (Orig.). 1982. 14.00 (ISBN 0-931386-46-2). Quint Pub Co.

DENTAL FEES

see also Medical Fees

Felmeister, Charles J. & Tulman, Michael M. Personalized Guide to Financial Planning. Snyder, Thomas L., ed. (Dental Practice Management Ser.). 136p. 1982. pap. text ed. 12.95 (ISBN 0-8016-4713-4). Mosby.

Kudrle, Robert T. & Meskin, Lawrence, eds. Reducing the Cost of Dental Care. 240p. 1982. 25.00x (ISBN 0-8166-1118-1). U of Minn Pr.

Rates & Data: Dental Publications. 5.00 (ISBN 0-934510-22-9, K029). Am Dental.

DENTAL HYGIENE

Here are entered works on dental hygiene as practiced by dental hygienists. Works on dental hygiene for the layman are entered under Teeth–Care and Hygiene.

Wilkins, Esther M. Clinical Practice of the Dental Hygienist: The True Role of the Dental Hygienist As Dental Health Educator & Clinical Operator for Specific Preventive Techniques. 5th ed. LC 82-8966. (Illus.). 913p. 1983. 37.50 (ISBN 0-8121-0844-2). Lea & Febiger.

Yes, You Can Teach Dental Health. 56p. 3.95 (ISBN 0-88314-213-9). AAHPERD.

DENTAL HYGIENISTS

Wilkins, Esther M. Clinical Practice of the Dental Hygienist: The True Role of the Dental Hygienist As Dental Health Educator & Clinical Operator for Specific Preventive Techniques. 5th ed. LC 82-8966. (Illus.). 913p. 1983. 37.50 (ISBN 0-8121-0844-2). Lea & Febiger.

DENTAL JURISPRUDENCE

Motley, Wilma E. Ethics, Jurisprudence & History for the Dental Hygienist. 3rd ed. LC 82-23926. (Illus.). 200p. 1983. text ed. price not set (ISBN 0-8121-0870-1). Lea & Febiger.

DENTAL LABORATORY TECHNICIANS

see Dental Technicians

DENTAL MATERIALS

Craig, Robert G. & O'Brien, William J. Dental Materials: Properties & Manipulation. 3rd ed. Powers, John M., ed. (Illus.). 327p. 1983. pap. text ed. 15.95 (ISBN 0-8016-1084-2). Mosby.

DENTAL MEDICINE

see Teeth–Diseases

DENTAL MICROBIOLOGY

see Mouth–Microbiology

DENTAL ORTHOPEDICS

see Orthodontics

DENTAL PATHOLOGY

see Teeth–Diseases

DENTAL PERSONNEL

see also Dentists

Snyder, Thomas L. & Domer, Larry R. Personalized Guide to Practice Evaluation. Felmeister, Charles J., ed. (Dental Practice Management Ser.). 216p. 1982. pap. text ed. 12.95 (ISBN 0-8016-4715-0). Mosby.

DENTAL PROSTHESIS

see Prosthodontics

DENTAL RESEARCH

Chilton Staff. Design & Analysis of Dental-Oral Research. 2nd ed. 460p. 1982. 44.50 (ISBN 0-03-056157-4). Praeger.

DENTAL SURGERY

see Dentistry; Dentistry, Operative; Mouth–Surgery

DENTAL TECHNICIANS

Motley, Wilma E. Ethics, Jurisprudence & History for the Dental Hygienist. 3rd ed. LC 82-23926. (Illus.). 200p. 1983. text ed. price not set (ISBN 0-8121-0870-1). Lea & Febiger.

Reap, Charles A., Jr. Complete Handbook for Dental Auxiliaries. (Illus.). 150p. 1981. pap. 18.00 (ISBN 0-931386-44-6). Quint Pub Co.

Woodall, Irene R. Legal, Ethical & Management Aspects of the Dental Care System. 2nd ed. LC 82-8198. (Illus.). 285p. 1983. pap. text ed. 14.50 (ISBN 0-8016-5683-4). Mosby.

DENTISTRY

see also Dental Jurisprudence; Diagnosis, Radioscopic; Endodontics; Hypnotism–Therapeutic Use; Mouth; Orthodontics; Pedodontia; Prosthodontics; Teeth

Ashley, Ruth & Kirby, Tess. Dental Anatomy & Terminology. LC 76-49088. (Self-Teaching Guides). 242p. 1977. text ed. 4.95x (ISBN 0-471-01348-X). Wiley.

Computers in Dental Practice. 9.00 (ISBN 0-934510-12-1, J006). Am Dental.

Domer, Larry R. & Bauer, Jeffrey C. Personalized Guide to Establishing Associateships & Partnerships. Snyder, Thomas L. & Felmeister, Charles J., eds. (Dental Practice Management Ser.). (Illus.). 168p. 1982. pap. text ed. 12.95 (ISBN 0-8016-4714-2). Mosby.

Gangarosa, Louis P. Iontophoresis in Dental Practice. (Illus.). 144p. 1983. text ed. 48.00 (ISBN 0-931386-52-7). Quint Pub Co.

Hale, Merle L., ed. Year Book of Dentistry 1983. 1983. 40.00 (ISBN 0-8151-4093-2). Year Bk Med.

Lange, Brian M. & Entwistle, Beverly M. Dental Management of the Handicapped & Approaches for Dental Auxiliaries. (Illus.). 150p. 1982. text ed. write for info. (ISBN 0-8121-0884-1). Lea & Febiger.

Lucia, Victor O. Modern Gnathological Concepts. (Illus.). 1983. text ed. 160.00 (ISBN 0-86715-105-6). Quint Pub Co.

Scully, C. & Cawson, R. A. Medical Problems in Dentistry. (Illus.). 528p. 1982. pap. 33.50 (ISBN 0-7236-0607-2). Wright-PSG.

Simonsen, Richard & Thompson, Van. Etched Cast Restorations: Clinical & Laboratory Techniques. (Illus.). 180p. 1982. text ed. 46.00 (ISBN 0-86715-120-X). Quint Pub Co.

Speaker's Guide for Dental Professionals. 5.00 (ISBN 0-934510-14-8, W012). Am Dental.

DENTISTRY–FEES

see Dental Fees

DENTISTRY–HISTORY

Motley, Wilma E. Ethics, Jurisprudence & History for the Dental Hygienist. 3rd ed. LC 82-23926. (Illus.). 200p. 1983. text ed. price not set (ISBN 0-8121-0870-1). Lea & Febiger.

Woodforde, John. The Strange Story of False Teeth. 152p. 1983. pap. 8.95 (ISBN 0-7100-9307-1). Routledge & Kegan.

DENTISTRY–JURISPRUDENCE

see Dental Jurisprudence

DENTISTRY–JUVENILE LITERATURE

The Tooth Chicken. 4 copies 5.00 (ISBN 0-934510-24-5, W013). Am Dental.

DENTISTRY–PRACTICE

Computers in Dental Practice. 9.00 (ISBN 0-934510-12-1, J006). Am Dental.

DENTISTRY–PSYCHOLOGICAL ASPECTS

Bosmajian, C. Perry & Bosmajian, Linda S. Personalized Guide to Stress Evaluation. Snyder, Thomas L. & Felmeister, Charles J., eds. LC 82-8182. (Dental Practice Management Ser.). (Illus.). 103p. 1983. pap. text ed. 12.95 (ISBN 0-8016-4724-X). Mosby.

DENTISTRY–RESEARCH

see Dental Research

DENTISTRY–STUDY AND TEACHING

D.A.E. Project University of Washington. D.A.E Project: Instructional Materials for Dental Health Professions, 25 Bks. Incl. Bk. 1. Establish Patient Relationships. 9.95x (ISBN 0-8077-6041-2); Bk. 2. Self-Care One. 7.95x (ISBN 0-8077-6042-0); Vol. 3. Self-Care Two. 7.95x (ISBN 0-8077-6043-9); Vol. 4. Coronal Polish. 9.95x (ISBN 0-8077-6044-7); Vol. 5. Topical Fluoride. 6.95x (ISBN 0-8077-6045-5); Vol. 6. Normal Radiographic Landmarks. 8.95x (ISBN 0-8077-6046-3); Vol. 7. Oral Inspection. 5.95x (ISBN 0-8077-6047-1); Vol. 8. Oral Inspection. 4.95x (ISBN 0-8077-6048-X); Margination: Overhang Removal. 8.95x (ISBN 0-8077-6049-8); Vol. 10. Root Planning. 5.95x (ISBN 0-8077-6050-1); Vol. 11. Take Study Model Impressions. 7.95x (ISBN 0-8077-6051-X); Vol. 12. Pour & Separate Models. 5.95x (ISBN 0-8077-6052-8); Vol. 13. Trim & Finish Models. 4.95x (ISBN 0-8077-6053-6); Vol. 14. Instrument Transfer One. 6.95x (ISBN 0-8077-6054-4); Vol. 15. Instrument Transfer: Restorative. 6.95x (ISBN 0-8077-6055-2); Vol. 16. Instrument Transfer: Endodontics. 4.95x (ISBN 0-8077-6056-0); Vol. 17. Instrument Transfer: Oral Surgery. 6.95x (ISBN 0-8077-6057-9); Vol. 18. Instrument Transfer: Periodontics. 6.95x (ISBN 0-8077-6058-7); Vol. 19. Maintain Operating Field. 6.95x (ISBN 0-8077-6059-5); Vol. 20. Rubber Dam. 8.50x (ISBN 0-8077-6060-9); Vol. 21. Microbiology. 5.95x (ISBN 0-8077-6061-7); Vol. 22. Sterilization & Disinfection. 8.50x (ISBN 0-8077-6062-5); Vol. 23. Dental Handpieces. 4.95x (ISBN 0-8077-6063-3); Vol. 24. Maintain Equipment & Operatory. 9.95x (ISBN 0-8077-6064-1); Vol. 25. Maintain Sterilization & Laboratory Equipment. 6.95x (ISBN 0-8077-6065-X); Faculty Guide & Test Items 9.95x (ISBN 0-8077-6066-8). 1982. Tchrs Coll.

Dickson, Murray. Where There Is No Dentist. Blake, Michael, ed. LC 82-84067. (Illus.). 192p. (Orig.). 1983. pap. 5.00 (ISBN 0-942364-05-8). Hesperian Found.

DENTISTRY–VOCATIONAL GUIDANCE

Rickert, Jessica A., ed. Exploring Careers in Dentistry. (Careers in Depth Ser.). 140p. 1983. lib. bdg. 7.97 (ISBN 0-8239-0604-3). Rosen Pr.

DENTISTRY, FORENSIC

see Dental Jurisprudence

DENTISTRY, OPERATIVE

Here are entered works on that field of dentistry concerned with restoring diseased or defective teeth to a state of normal function, health and aesthetics.

Messing, J. J. Operative Dental Surgery. 2nd ed. 1982. 79.00x (ISBN 0-333-31040-3, Pub. by Macmillan England). State Mutual Bk.

Scharer, Peter & Rinn, L. A., eds. Esthetic Guidelines for Restorative Dentistry. Koehler, Henry M., tr. from Ger. (Illus.). 236p. 1982. text ed. 72.00 (ISBN 0-86715-111-0). Quint Pub Co.

DENTISTRY, PROSTHETIC

see Prosthodontics

DENTISTRY, PSYCHOSOMATIC

see Dentistry–Psychological Aspects

DENTISTRY, RESTORATIVE

see Dentistry, Operative

DENTISTS

see also Dental Hygienists; Dentistry–Vocational Guidance

Felmeister, Charles J. & Tulman, Michael M. Personalized Guide to Financial Planning. Snyder, Thomas L., ed. (Dental Practice Management Ser.). 136p. 1982. pap. text ed. 12.95 (ISBN 0-8016-4713-4). Mosby.

Haver, Jurgen F. Personalized Guide to Marketing Strategy. Snyder, Thomas L. & Felmeister, Charles J., eds. (Dental Practice Management Ser.). (Illus.). 118p. 1983. pap. text ed. 12.95 (ISBN 0-8016-4725-8). Mosby.

DENTISTS–FEES

see Dental Fees

DENTITION

see also Teeth

Hurzeler, Johannes. Contribution a L'odontologie et a la Phylogenese du Genre Pliopithecus Gervais. Bd. with Die Primatenfunde aus der miozanen Spaltenfullung von neudorf an der March, Devin ska Nova Ves, Tschechoslowakei. Zapfe, Helmuth. 1961. LC 78-72721. 1954. 79.50 (ISBN 0-404-18296-8). AMS Pr.

DENTURES

see Prosthodontics

DENVER–HISTORY

Brettell, Richard R. Historic Denver: The Architects & the Architecture, 1858-1893. 1979. pap. 14.95 (ISBN 0-914248-00-6). Hist Denver.

West, William A. & Etter, Don D. Curtis Park: A Denver Neighborhood. 1980. 9.95 (ISBN 0-87081-077-4). Hist Denver.

DEONTOLOGY

see Ethics

DEOXYRIBONUCLEIC ACID

Beljanski, M. The Regulation of DNA Replication & Transcription. (Experimental Biology & Medicine Ser.: Vol. 8). x, 180p. 1983. pap. 70.25 (ISBN 3-8055-3631-3). S Karger.

De Recondo, A. M., ed. New Approaches in Eukaryotic DNA Replication. 375p. 1983. 47.50x (ISBN 0-306-41182-2, Plenum Pr). Plenum Pub.

Friedberg & Hanawalt. DNA Repair. 296p. 1983. price not set (ISBN 0-8247-1805-4). Dekker.

Kaplan, Albert S. Organization & Replication of Viral DNA. 208p. 1982. 67.00 (ISBN 0-8493-6405-1). CRC Pr.

Structures of DNA. LC 34-8174. (Cold Spring Harbor Symposia on Quantitative Biology: Vol. 47). 1250p. 1983. 140.00x (ISBN 0-87969-046-1). Cold Spring Harbor.

DEPENDENCIES

see Colonies

DEPENDENCY (PSYCHOLOGY)

Glatt, M. M. & Marks, J., eds. The Dependence Phenomenon. 300p. 1982. 38.00 (ISBN 0-942068-03-3). Bogden & Son.

DEPOSITION AND SEDIMENTATION

see Sedimentation and Deposition

DEPOSITS, DEEP-SEA

see Marine Sediments; Sedimentation and Deposition

DEPRAVITY

see Sin, Original

DEPRESSED CLASSES OF INDIA

see Untouchables

DEPRESSION, MENTAL

see also Manic-Depressive Psychoses

Baldessarini, Ross J. Biomedical Aspects of Depression & Its Treatment. LC 82-22659. (Illus.). 140p. 1983. casebound 18.00x (ISBN 0-88048-004-1). Am Psychiatric.

Hafen, Brent Q. & Brog, Molly J. Emotional Survival. 114p. 1983. 11.95 (ISBN 0-13-274480-5); pap. 5.95 (ISBN 0-13-274472-4). P-H.

Klerman, Gerald & Weissman, Myrna. Interpersonal Psychotherapy of Depression. 1983. text ed. 20.95x (ISBN 0-465-03396-2). Basic.

Lavender, John A. Beat the Blues. 1982. pap. 5.95 (ISBN 0-8423-0128-3). Tyndale.

Levitt, Eugene E. & Lubin, Bernard. Depression: Concepts, Controversies & Some New Facts. 2nd ed. 208p. 1983. text ed. write for info. (ISBN 0-89859-278-X). L Erlbaum Assocs.

McKnew, Donald H., Jr., et al. Why Isn't Johnny Crying? Coping with Depression in Children. 1983. 15.50 (ISBN 0-393-01724-9). Norton.

Mendlewicz, J. & Van Pragg, H. M. Management of Depressions with Monomine Precursors. (Advances in Biological Psychiatry: Vol. 10). (Illus.). viii, 200p. 1983. pap. 57.00 (ISBN 3-8055-3645-3). S Karger.

Morgan, Marie. Breaking Through: How to Overcome Housewives' Depression. 204p. 1983. pap. 9.95 (ISBN 0-86683-697-7). Winston Pr.

Morrison, Helen L., ed. Children of Depressed Parents: Risk Identification & Intervention. Date not set. price not set (ISBN 0-8089-1545-2). Grune.

Official Satellite Symposium, International Congress of Pharmacology, Nagasaki, Japan, 8th 30-31 July 1982. New Vistas in Depression: Proceedings. Langer, S. Z., et al, eds. (Illus.). 339p. 1982. 60.00 (ISBN 0-08-027388-2). Pergamon.

Petti, Theodore, ed. Childhood Depression. LC 83-580. (Journal of Children in Contemporary Society Ser.: Vol. 15, No. 2). 104p. 1983. text ed. 20.00 (ISBN 0-917724-95-X, B95). Haworth Pr.

Rowe, D. The Experience of Depression. 275p. 1978. text ed. 49.95x (ISBN 0-471-99554-1, Pub. by Wiley-Interscience). Wiley.

Soubrier, J. P. & Vedrinne, J., eds. Depression & Suicide: Medical, Psychological & Socio-Cultural Aspects, Proceedings of the XI Congress of the International Association for Suicide Prevention, Paris, July 5-9, 1981. (Illus.). 912p. 1983. 100.00 (ISBN 0-08-027080-8); pap. 60.00 (ISBN 0-08-027081-6). Pergamon.

Stefanis, C. N. Recent Advances In Depression. 152p. 1983. 18.00 (ISBN 0-08-027954-6). Pergamon.

DEPRESSIONS–1929

Heinemann, Ronald L. Depression & New Deal in Virginia: The Enduring Dominion. LC 82-13487. 1983. write for info. (ISBN 0-8139-0946-5). U Pr of Va.

Stevens, Irving L. Fishbones: Hoboing in the 1930's. LC 82-90088. (Illus.). 136p. (Orig.). 1982. pap. 7.95 (ISBN 0-9609208-0-3). Moosehead Prods.

DEPRESSIVE PSYCHOSES

see Depression, Mental

DERMATITIS

see Skin–Diseases

DERMATOLOGY

see also Skin–Diseases

Barry. Dermatological Formation. (Drugs & the Pharmaceutical Science Ser.). 472p. 1983. price not set (ISBN 0-8247-1729-5). Dekker.

Dahl, Mark V. Common Office Dermatology. Date not set. price not set (ISBN 0-8089-1497-9). Grune.

Dobson, Richard L. Year Book of Dermatology 1983. 1983. 40.00 (ISBN 0-8151-2669-7). Year Bk Med.

Goldberg, Audrey G. Care of the Skin. (Illus.). 1975. pap. 13.95 (ISBN 0-434-90672-7, Pub. by Heinemann). David & Charles.

Laude, Theresita & Russo, Raymond M. Dermatologic Disorders in Dark-Skinned Children & Adolescents. 1983. text ed. price not set (ISBN 0-87488-409-8). Med Exam.

Marks, R. & Plewig, G., eds. Stratum Corneum. (Illus.). 300p. 1983. pap. 35.00 (ISBN 0-387-11704-0). Springer-Verlag.

Nasemann, T. & Sauerbrey, W. Fundamentals of Dermatology. (Illus.). 416p. 1983. pap. 24.90 (ISBN 0-387-90738-6). Springer-Verlag.

Ortonne, Jean-Paul & Mosher, David B. Vitiligo & Other Hypomelanoses of Hair & Skin. (Topics in Dermatology Ser.). 680p. 1983. 79.50x (ISBN 0-306-40974-7, Plenum Med Bk). Plenum Pub.

Reeves, John & Maibach, Howard. Clinical Dermatology Illustrated. 250p. 1983. text ed. write for info. (ISBN 0-86792-010-6, Pub by Adis Pr Australia). Wright-PSG.

Steigleder. Pocket Atlas of Dermatology. (Flexi-Bk.). 1983. write for info. (ISBN 0-86577-092-1). Thieme-Stratton.

Vasarinsh. Clinical Dermatology: Diagnosis & Treatment. 1982. text ed. 49.95 (ISBN 0-409-95013-0). Butterworth.

Wilkinson, D. S. Nursing & Management of Skin Diseases: A Guide to Practical Dermatology for Doctors & Nurses. 4th ed. 403p. 1977. 16.95 (ISBN 0-571-04875-7); pap. 11.95 (ISBN 0-571-04876-5). Faber & Faber.

DESCARTES, RENE, 1596-1650

Federico, P. J. Descartes on Polyhedra: A Study of the "De Solidorum Elementis". (Sources in the History of Mathematics & Physical Sciences: Vol. 4). (Illus.). 144p. 1983. 36.00 (ISBN 0-387-90760-2). Springer-Verlag.

Jean, B. & Mouret, F. Montaigne, Descartes et Pascal. 1971. pap. 10.00 (ISBN 0-7190-0422-5). Manchester.

DESCENT

see Genealogy; Heredity

DESCRIPTIVE GEOMETRY

see Geometry, Descriptive

DESEGREGATION

see also Segregation

Hawley, Willis D., ed. Strategies for Effective Desegration: Lessons from Research. LC 82-47968. 224p. 1982. 23.95x (ISBN 0-669-05722-3); pap. 13.95 (ISBN 0-669-06376-2). Lexington Bks.

DESEGREGATION IN EDUCATION

see School Integration

DESERT FAUNA

Wallwork, John N. Desert Soil Fauna. 304p. 1982. 37.50 (ISBN 0-03-055306-7). Praeger.

DESERTS

see also names of deserts e.g.; Kalahari Desert, Sahara Desert; also headings beginning with the word Desert

Farm Journal's Food Editors. Farm Journal's Molded Salads, Desserts. LC 76-10410. 128p. (Orig.). 1976. pap. 3.95 (ISBN 0-89795-017-8). Farm Journal.

Good, Phyllis P. & Pellman, Rachel T., eds. Desserts: From Amish & Mennonite Kitchens. (Pennsylvania Dutch Cookbooks Ser.). (Illus., Orig.). 1983. pap. 1.95 (ISBN 0-934672-13-X). Good Bks PA.

Monroe, Elvira. Say Cheesecake & Smile. LC 80-54453. 168p. 1981. pap. 5.95 (ISBN 0-933174-11-X). Wide World-Tetra.

Waloff, Z. Field Studies on Solitary & Transient Desert Locusts in the Red Sea Area. 1963. 35.00 (ISBN 0-85135-040-2, Pub. by Centre Overseas Research). State Mutual Bk.

West, N. E. & Skujins, J., eds. Nitrogen in Desert Ecosystems. LC 78-17672. (US-IBP Synthesis Ser.: Vol. 9). 307p. 1978. 31.50 (ISBN 0-87933-333-2). Hutchinson Ross.

DESIGN

see also Costume Design; Furniture Design; Pattern-Making; Printing–Layout and Typography; Textile Design

Beitler, Ethel J. & Lockhart, Bill C. Design for You. 2nd ed. LC 73-76050. 247p. 1969. 26.95x (ISBN 0-471-06337-1). Wiley.

Burden, Ernest E. Design Presentation: Techniques for Marketing & Project Presentation. (Illus.). 256p. 1983. 34.95 (ISBN 0-07-008931-0, P&RB). McGraw.

De Sausmarez, Maurice. Basic Design. 96p. 1982. 30.00x (ISBN 0-906969-22-0, Pub. by Benn Pubns). State Mutual Bk.

Holdridge, Barbara. Aubrey Beardsley Designs from the Age of Chivalry. (The International Design Libary). (Illus.). 48p. (Orig.). 1983. pap. 2.95 (ISBN 0-88045-022-3). Stemmer Hse.

McFadden, David, ed. Scandinavian Modern Design: Eighteen Eighty to Nineteen Eighty. LC 82-8899. (Illus.). 288p. 1982. 45.00 (ISBN 0-8109-1643-6). Abrams.

Mckillip, Rebecca. Art Nouveau Abstract Designs. (The International Design Library). (Illus.). 48p. (Orig.). 1983. pap. 2.95 (ISBN 0-88045-023-1). Stemmer Hse.

Orr, Anne. Favorite Charted Designs by Anne Orr. 40p. (Orig.). 1983. pap. 2.75 (ISBN 0-486-24484-9). Dover.

Pye, David. Nature & Aesthetics of Design. 160p. 1982. pap. 9.95 (ISBN 0-442-27379-7). Van Nos Reinhold.

Reigeluth, Charles M. Instructional Design Theories & Models: An Overview of Their Current Status. 432p. 1983. text ed. write for info. (ISBN 0-89859-275-5). L Erlbaum Assocs.

Shoch, J. Design & Performance of Local Computer Networks. Date not set. price not set (ISBN 0-07-056984-3). McGraw.

Sprieregen, P. Design Competitions. 1979. 36.50 (ISBN 0-07-060381-2). McGraw.

Strong's Book of Designs. 92p. 1982. Repr. of 1910 ed. 39.50 (ISBN 0-911380-61-2). Signs of Times.

Travers, David. Preparing Design Office Brochures: A Handbook. 2nd ed. (Illus.). 1982. pap. 10.75 (ISBN 0-931228-08-5). Arts & Arch.

Uttal, William R. Visual Form Detection in Three Dimensional Space. (MacEachram Lectures). 160p. 1983. text ed. write for info. (ISBN 0-89859-289-5). L Erlbaum Assocs.

Weiss, Rita. The Artist's & Craftsman's Guide to Reducing, Enlarging & Transferring Designs. (General Crafts Ser.). 64p. (Orig.). Date not set. pap. 3.25 (ISBN 0-486-24142-4). Dover.

DESIGN (PHILOSOPHY)

see Teleology

DESIGN, ARCHITECTURAL

see Architecture–Designs and Plans; Architecture–Details; Decoration and Ornament, Architectural

DESIGN, DECORATIVE

see also Art, Decorative; Carving (Art Industries); Decoration and Ornament; Decoupage; Drawing; Folk Art; Glass, Ornamental; Illumination of Books and Manuscripts; Lettering; Textile Design

Grafton, Carol B. Banners, Ribbons & Scrolls: An Archive For Artists & Designers, Five Hundred & Three Copyright Free Designs. (Illus.). 96p. (Orig.). 1983. pap. 4.00 (ISBN 0-486-24443-1). Dover.

Heller, Ruth. Creative Coloring-Geometric Designs. (Creative Coloring Pandabacks Ser.). (Illus.). 32p. 1982. pap. 1.50 (ISBN 0-448-49632-1, G&D). Putnam Pub Group.

--Creative Coloring-Seashells. (Creative Coloring Pandabacks Ser.). 32p. 1982. pap. 1.50 (ISBN 0-448-49629-1, G&D). Putnam Pub Group.

--Creative Coloring-Simple Designs. (Creative Coloring Pandabacks Ser.). 32p. 1982. pap. 1.50 (ISBN 0-448-49630-5, G&D). Putnam Pub Group.

--Creative Coloring-Super Designs. (Creative Coloring Pandabacks Ser.). (Illus.). 32p. 1982. pap. 1.50 (ISBN 0-448-49631-3, G&D). Putnam Pub Group.

Rettich, Judi. Pennsylvania Dutch Designs for Hand Coloring: Create Your Own Decorative Awards, Certificates & Notepaper. (Illus.). 48p. (Orig.). 1983. pap. 2.25 (ISBN 0-486-24496-2). Dover.

Veasey, William. Blue Ribbon Pattern Series, Bk. 1: Full Size Decorative Patterns. (Illus.). 63p. 1982. 14.95 (ISBN 0-916838-71-4). Schiffer.

DESIGN, DECORATIVE–PLANT FORMS

Seguy, E. A. The Spectacular Color Floral Designs of E.A. Seguy. (Illus.). 48p. (Orig.). 1983. pap. 2.95 (ISBN 0-486-24488-1). Dover.

DESIGN, ENGINEERING

see Engineering Design

DESIGN, INDUSTRIAL

see also Engineering Design; Environmental Engineering; Human Engineering; Mechanical Drawing; Value Analysis (Cost Control)

Caplan, Ralph. By Design: Why There are No Locks on the Bathroom Doors in the Hotel Louis XIV & Other Object Lessons. (Illus.). 192p. 1982. 16.95 (ISBN 0-312-11085-5). St Martin.

Pulos, Arthur J. American Design Ethic: A History of Industrial Design. (Illus.). 576p. 1983. 50.00 (ISBN 0-262-16085-4). MIT Pr.

DESIGN OF EXPERIMENTS

see Experimental Design

DESIGN PERCEPTION

see Pattern Perception

DESIGNED GENETIC CHANGE

see Genetic Engineering

DESIGNS, FLORAL

see Design, Decorative–Plant Forms

DESMIDIEAE

Croasdale, Hannah & Bicudo, Carlos E. A Synopsis of North American Desmids, Part II; Desmidiaceae: Placodermae Section 5, The Filamentous Genera. LC 70-183418. (Illus.). vi, 122p. 1983. 26.50x (ISBN 0-8032-3661-1). U of Nebr Pr.

DE SOTO, HERNANDO

see Soto, Hernando De, 1500?-1542

DESOXYRIBONUCLEIC ACID

see Deoxyribonucleic Acid

DESPOTISM

see also Authority; Democracy; Dictators; Kings and Rulers

Herz, John H. From Dictatorship to Democracy: Coping with the Legacies of Authoritarianism & Totalitarianism. LC 82-12002. (Contributions in Political Science Ser.: No. 92). (Illus.). 376p. 1983. lib. bdg. 35.00 (ISBN 0-313-23636-4, HDD/). Greenwood.

Treasure, Geoffrey. Cardinal Richelieu & the Development of Absolutism. 316p. 1982. 7.50 (ISBN 0-85683-065-8, Pub. by Shepheard-Walwyn). Flatiron Book Dist.

DESSERTS

see also Ice Cream, Ices, etc.

Goulart, Frances S. One Hundred & One Allergy-Free Desserts. 1983. pap. 7.95 (ISBN 0-671-45785-3, Wallaby). S&S.

Gronner, Georgina. Viennese Desserts Made Easy. (Illus.). 128p. (Orig.). 1983. pap. 7.95 (ISBN 0-8092-5621-5). Contemp Bks.

Hirsch, Sylvia. Miss Grimble Presents: Delicious Deserts. (Illus.). 256p. 1983. 14.95 (ISBN 0-02-551860-7). Macmillan.

DESTITUTION

see Poverty

DESTROYERS (WARSHIPS)

see Warships

DESTRUCTION OF PROPERTY

see Vandalism

DESTRUCTION OF THE JEWS (1939-1945)

see Holocaust, Jewish (1939-1945)

DETAILS, ARCHITECTURAL

see Architecture–Details

DETECTIVE AND MYSTERY STORIES

see also Ghost Stories; Horror Tales

Bellairs, John. The Curse of the Blue Figurine. LC 82-73217. (Illus.). 224p. (gr. 5 up). 1983. 10.95 (ISBN 0-8037-1119-0, 01063-320); lib. bdg. 10.89 (ISBN 0-8037-1265-0). Dial Bks Young.

Bond, Ann S. Adam & Noah & the Cops. LC 82-21181. (Illus.). 160p. (gr. 3-6). 1983. 8.95 (ISBN 0-395-33225-7). HM.

Symons, Julian. The Tigers of Subtopia & other Stories. 221p. 1983. 14.75 (ISBN 0-670-71283-3). Viking Pr.

DETECTIVE AND MYSTERY STORIES (COLLECTIONS)

see also Ghost Stories; Horror Tales

Asimov, Isaac & Greenberg, Martin H., eds. Miniature Mysteries: 100 Malicious Little Mystery Stories. LC 80-28667. 1983. pap. 9.95 (ISBN 0-8008-5252-4). Taplinger.

Harris, Herbert, ed. John Creasey's Crime Collection 1982. 192p. 1982. 12.95 (ISBN 0-312-44296-3). St Martin.

MacLean, A. D., ed. Winter's Tales Twenty-Eight. 224p. 1983. 11.95 (ISBN 0-312-88421-4). St Martin.

Pronzini, Bill, ed. The Arbor House Treasure of Detective & Mystery Stories from the Great Pulps. 1983. 15.95 (ISBN 0-87795-451-8). Arbor Hse.

Reader's Digest Editors. Great Short Tales of Mystery & Terror. LC 80-52212. (Illus.). 640p. 1982. 14.98 (ISBN 0-89577-091-1). RD Assn.

--Great Stories of Mystery & Suspense, 2 Vols. LC 73-76284. (Open-ended Ser.). 1294p. 1981. Set. 15.99 (ISBN 0-89577-083-0). RD Assn.

Watson, Hilary. Winter's Crimes Fourteen. 224p. 1983. 11.95 (ISBN 0-312-88241-6). St Martin.

DETECTIVE AND MYSTERY STORIES–BIBLIOGRAPHY

Hagemann, E. R. A Comprehensive Index to Black Mask, 1920-1951. 236p. 1982. 15.95 (ISBN 0-87972-201-0); pap. 8.95 (ISBN 0-87972-202-9). Bowling Green Univ.

Hitching, Francis. World Atlas of Mysteries. (Illus.). 256p. 1980. 21.75x (ISBN 0-330-25683-1). Intl Pubns Serv.

DETECTIVE AND MYSTERY STORIES–HISTORY AND CRITICISM

Cassiday, Bruce, ed. Roots of Detection: The Art of Deduction before Sherlock Holmes. (Recognitions). 225p. 1983. 12.95 (ISBN 0-8044-2113-7); pap. 6.95 (ISBN 0-8044-6065-5). Ungar.

Most, Glenn W. & Stowe, William W., eds. The Poetics of Murder: Detective Fiction & Literary Theory. 416p. cloth 22.95 (ISBN 0-15-172280-3). HarBraceJ.

--The Poetics of Murder: Detective Fiction & Literary Theory. 416p. pap. 9.95 (ISBN 0-15-672312-3, Harv). HarBraceJ.

Mystery Story Problems: Multiplication & Division Problems. (Mystery Story Problems Ser.). 1981. 12.50 (ISBN 0-88488-205-5); of ten 59.00 set (ISBN 0-88488-229-2, 10454). Creative Pubns.

DETECTIVE AND MYSTERY STORIES–TECHNIQUE

Bendel, Stephanie B. Making Crime Pay: A Practical Guide to Mystery Writing. (Illus.). 204p. 1983. 13.95 (ISBN 0-13-545939-7); pap. 5.95 (ISBN 0-13-545921-4). P-H.

Queen, Ellery, ed. Ellery Queen's Lost Ladies. 288p. 1983. 12.95 (ISBN 0-385-27915-9). Davis Pubns.

DETECTIVES

see also Criminal Investigation; Police; Secret Service

Regency International Directory of Private Investigators, Private Detectives, Debt Collecting Agencies 1981-1982. 15th ed. LC 68-45751. 400p. 1980. text ed. 37.50x (ISBN 0-900618-63-9). Intl Pubns Serv.

DETENTE

Chand, Attar. Disarmament, Detente & World Peace: A Bibliography with Selected Abstracts, 1916-1981. 167p. 1982. 22.95x (ISBN 0-940500-49-3, Pub. by Sterling India). Asia Bk Corp.

DETENTION CAMPS

see Concentration Camps

DETENTION HOMES, JUVENILE

see Juvenile Detention Homes

DETERGENTS

see Cleaning Compounds

DETERGENTS, SYNTHETIC

Milwidsky, B. & Gabriel, D. Detergent Analysis. 1982. 69.00x (ISBN 0-7114-5735-2, Pub. by Macdonald Bk). State Mutual Bk.

DETERMINISM AND INDETERMINISM

see Free Will and Determinism

DETERRENCE (STRATEGY)

Barnaby, Frank & Thomas, Geoffrey, eds. The Nuclear Arms Race: Control or Catastrophe. LC 81-21282. 265p. 1982. 25.00x (ISBN 0-312-57974-8). St Martin.

Brookes, Andrew. V Force: The History of Britain's Airborne Deterrent. (Illus.). 173p. 1983. 19.95 (ISBN 0-86720-639-X). Sci Bks Intl.

Carlton, David & Schaerf, Carlo, eds. The Arms Race in the Nineteen Eighties. LC 81-21303. 256p. 1982. 27.50x (ISBN 0-312-04946-3). St Martin.

DETROIT

Kannan. Downsizing Detroit. 202p. 1982. 28.95 (ISBN 0-03-060597-0). Praeger.

DETROIT-HISTORY

Brown, Stanley H. A Tale of Two Cities: Houston & Detroit. (Illus.). 1983. 16.95 (ISBN 0-87795-486-0). Arbor Hse.

DEVALUATION OF CURRENCY

see Currency Question

DEVELOPMENT (BIOLOGY)

see Developmental Biology

DEVELOPMENT, CHILD

see Child Development

DEVELOPMENTAL ABNORMALITIES

see Abnormalities, Human

DEVELOPMENTAL BIOLOGY

see also Aging; Child Development; Embryology; Growth; Psychobiology

Chandebois, Rosine & Faber, J. Automation in Animal Development. (Monographs in Developmental Biology: Vol. 16). (Illus.). iv, 150p. 1983. 69.50 (ISBN 3-8055-3666-6). S Karger.

Scott, J. P., ed. Critical Periods. LC 78-632. (Benchmark Papers in Animal Behavior: Vol. 12). 381p. 1978. 48.50 (ISBN 0-87933-119-4). Hutchinson Ross.

DEVELOPMENTAL DYSLEXIA

see Reading Disability

DEVELOPMENTAL PSYCHOLOGY

Here are entered works on the psychological development of the individual from infancy to old age. Works on the evolutionary psychology of man in terms of origin and development, whether in the individual or in the species, are entered under Genetic Psychology.

see also Child Psychology

Beard, Ruth M. An Outline of Piaget's Developmental Psychology. (Student's Library of Education). 144p. 1976. pap. 6.95 (ISBN 0-7100-6344-X). Routledge & Kegan.

Droege, Thomas A. Faith Passages & Patterns. LC 82-48544. (Lead Bks.). 128p. 1983. pap. 3.95 (ISBN 0-8006-1602-2, 1-1602). Fortress.

Freiberg, Karen L. Human Development: A Life-Span Approach. 2nd ed. LC 82-24736. 600p. 1983. text ed. 20.95 (ISBN 0-534-01413-5). Brooks-Cole.

Kagan, Jerome & Moss, Howard. Birth to Maturity. LC 62-19148. 1983. text ed. 25.00x (ISBN 0-300-02998-5); pap. 8.95 (ISBN 0-300-03029-0). Yale U Pr.

Lerner, Richard M., ed. Developmental Psychology: Historical & Philosophical Perspectives. 288p. 1983. text ed. 24.95 (ISBN 0-89859-247-X). L Erlbaum Assocs.

Martlew, Margaret. The Psychology of Written Language: A Developmental Approach. 432p. 1983. 49.95 (ISBN 0-471-10291-1, Pub. by Wiley-Interscience). Wiley.

DEVIANT BEHAVIOR

see also Crime and Criminals; Conformity

Cullen, Francis T., Jr. Theories of Crime & Deviance: Accounting for Form & Content. 224p. Date not set. text ed. 27.50x (ISBN 0-86598-073-X). Allanheld.

Gagne, Eve E. School Behavior & School Discipline: Coping with Deviant Behavior in the Schools. LC 82-15912. 176p. 1983. lib. bdg. 20.75 (ISBN 0-8191-2748-5); pap. text ed. 10.00 (ISBN 0-8191-2749-3). U Pr of Amer.

Little, Craig B. Understanding Deviance. LC 82-61588. 256p. 1983. pap. text ed. 10.95 (ISBN 0-87581-289-9). Peacock Pubs.

Shoham, Giora S. & Rahav, Giora. The Mark of Cain: The Stigma Theory of Crime & Social Deviance. LC 82-3173. 240p. 1982. 27.50x (ISBN 0-312-51446-8). St Martin.

Thio, Alex. Deviant Behavior. 2nd ed. 480p. 1983. text ed. 22.95 (ISBN 0-395-32584-6); write for info. instr's manual (ISBN 0-395-32585-4). HM.

DEVIATION, SEXUAL

see Sexual Deviation

DEVIL

see also Demonology

Delaporte. The Devil: Does He Exist & What Does He Do? 212p. pap. 4.00 (ISBN 0-686-81625-0). TAN Bks Pubs.

DEVON, ENGLAND

Cooke, Michael. The Ancient Curse of the Baskervilles. LC 82-83499. 96p. pap. 4.95 (ISBN 0-934468-14-1). Gaslight.

Durrance, E. M. & Laming, D. J. The Geology of Devon. 416p. 1982. 75.00x (ISBN 0-85989-153-4, Pub. by Exeter Univ England). State Mutual Bk.

Glyn-Jones, Anne. Small Firms in a Country Town. 88p. 1982. 30.00x (ISBN 0-85989-138-0, Pub. by Exeter Univ England). State Mutual Bk.

Greenbow, Desna. Devon Mill: The Restoration of a Corn Mill. 44p. 1982. 25.00x (ISBN 0-284-98624-0, Pub. by C Skilton Scotland). State Mutual Bk.

DEVON, ENGLAND-ANTIQUITIES

Clare, Tom. Archaeological Sites of Devon & Cornwall. 160p. 1982. 50.00x (ISBN 0-86190-057-X, Pub. by Moorland). State Mutual Bk.

DEVONIAN PERIOD

see Geology, Stratigraphic-Devonian

DEVOTIONAL CALENDARS

Cook, Leah, ed. Devotion for Every Day, 183-84. 384p. 1983. pap. 3.95 (ISBN 0-87239-618-5). Standard Pub.

--Devotion for Every Day, 1983-84. large type ed. 384p. 1983. pap. 5.95 (ISBN 0-87239-619-3). Standard Pub.

The Seabury Diary 1984. 144p. 1983. pap. 4.95 (ISBN 0-8164-2463-2). Seabury.

DEVOTIONAL EXERCISES

see also Church Music; Devotional Calendars; Hymns; Liturgies; Lord's Prayer; Lord's Supper; Meditations; Prayer

also subdivision Prayer-books and devotions under particular denominations; children's prayers; women-prayerbooks and devotions, etc.

Allen, R. Earl. Good Morning, Lord: Devotionals for Times of Sorrow. (Good Morning, Lord Ser.). 96p. 1983. 4.95 (ISBN 0-8010-0191-9). Baker Bk.

Caulfield, Sean. Under the Broom Tree. LC 82-60593. 80p. 1983. pap. 3.95 (ISBN 0-8091-2493-9). Paulist Pr.

Hembree, Ron. Good Morning, Lord: Devotions for New Christians. (Good Morning, Lord Ser.). 96p. 1983. 4.95 (ISBN 0-8010-4271-2). Baker Bk.

Rey, Greta. Good Morning, Lord: Devotions for Young Teens. (Good Morning, Lord Ser.). 96p. 1983. 4.95 (ISBN 0-8010-7719-2). Baker Bk.

Wood, Robert. Thirty Days Are Not Enough: More Images for Meditative Journaling. 112p. (Orig.). 1983. pap. 3.75 (ISBN 0-8358-0445-3). Upper Room.

DEVOTIONAL LITERATURE

see also Religious Literature;

also subdivision Devotional Literature under specific subjects, e.g. Jesus christ-devotional Literature

Adair, James R. & Miller, Ted. Escape from Darkness. 156p. 1982. pap. 4.95 (ISBN 0-88207-318-4). Victor Bks.

Adams, Judith. Against the Gates of Hell. 152p. pap. 2.50 (ISBN 0-87509-232-2). Chr Pubns.

Balthasar, Hans Urs von. The Glory of the Lord: A Theological Aesthetics-Seeing the Form, Vol. 1. 656p. (Orig.). 1983. 30.00 (ISBN 0-8245-0579-4). Crossroad NY.

Beatty, David. He That Wins Souls is Wise. 1982. pap. 0.75 (ISBN 0-88144-005-1, CPS-005). Christian Pub.

Brent, Bill. Unto Perfection. 90p. 1983. pap. 6.95 (ISBN 0-913408-82-4). Friends United.

Burke, Albert L. He That Hath an Ear. 101p. (Orig.). 1982. pap. 3.50 (ISBN 0-9608662-0-5). Eleventh Hour.

Castle, Tony, ed. The New Book of Christian Quotations. 272p. 1983. pap. 9.95 (ISBN 0-8245-0551-4). Crossroad NY.

Clakson, Margaret. Destined for Glory: The Meaning of Suffering. 144p. 1983. pap. 4.95 (ISBN 0-8028-1953-2). Eerdmans.

Doherty, Catherine De Hueck. Urodivoi: Fools for Good. 112p. 1983. 9.95 (ISBN 0-8245-0553-0). Crossroad NY.

Edman, V. E. & Laidlaw, R. A. The Fullness of the Spirit. 36p. pap. 0.85 (ISBN 0-87509-083-4). Chr Pubns.

Eight Keys to Spiritual & Physical Health. 96p. 1982. pap. 3.95 (ISBN 0-89221-092-3, Pub. by SonLife). New Leaf.

Erdman, V. R. Signs of Christ's Second Coming. 29p. pap. 0.85 (ISBN 0-87509-130-X). Chr Pubns.

Eugene, P. M. I Am a Daughter of the Church. Clare, M. V., Sr., tr. 667p. 1982. pap. 15.00 (ISBN 0-87061-050-3). Chr Classics.

Freligh, Harold M. Say unto This Mountain. 40p. 1966. pap. 1.00 (ISBN 0-87509-128-8). Chr Pubns.

Gratton, Carolyn. Trusting: Theory & Practice. 256p. 1983. pap. 9.95 (ISBN 0-8245-0548-4). Crossroad NY.

Hall, Roger L., ed. The Happy Journey: Thirty-Five Shaker Spirituals Compiled by Miss Clara Endicott Sears. LC 81-69875. (Illus.). 60p. (Orig.). 1982. 8.00 (ISBN 0-941632-00-8). Fruitlands Mus.

Halverstadt, Robert. God's Word for Your Healing. 1982. pap. 1.75 (ISBN 0-88144-003-5, CPS-003). Christian Pub.

--God's Word for Your Prosperity. 1982. pap. 1.75 (ISBN 0-88144-002-7, CPS-002). Christian Pub.

--Your New Birth. 1982. pap. 0.75 (ISBN 0-88144-001-9, CPS-001). Christian Pub.

Havner, Vance. Pleasant Paths. (Direction Bks.). 96p. 1983. pap. 2.95 (ISBN 0-8010-4268-2). Baker Bk.

Holmes, Marjorie. To Help You Through the Hurting. LC 81-43571. (Illus.). 120p. 1983. 7.95 (ISBN 0-385-17842-5). Doubleday.

Jacobs, Mildred Spires. Come Unto Me. (Illus.). 56p. (Orig.). (gr. 5-6). 1982. pap. 2.95 (ISBN 0-9609612-0-8). Enrichment.

Kaplan, David & Phillips, Marcia. Smiles. (Inspirational Ser.). (Illus.). 100p. 1982. pap. 4.95 (ISBN 0-939944-05-7). Marmac Pub.

Kelsey, Morton T. Companions on the Inner Way: The Art of Spiritual Guidance. 250p. 1983. 17.50 (ISBN 0-8245-0585-9); pap. 8.95 (ISBN 0-8245-0560-3). Crossroad NY.

Kenyon, Don J. The Double Mind. 95p. 1981. pap. 2.50 (ISBN 0-87509-288-8). Chr Pubns.

Kupferle, Mary L. God Never Fails. 141p. 1983. pap. 4.50 (ISBN 0-87516-513-3). De Vorss.

Lemmons, Reuel & Bannister, John. Unto Us a Child is Born. Kyker, Rex, compiled by. 126p. (Orig.). 1982. pap. 2.95 (ISBN 0-88027-109-4). Firm Foun Pub.

Mackey, James P. The Christian Experience of God As Trinity. 320p. 1983. 17.50 (ISBN 0-8245-0561-1). Crossroad NY.

Marshall, Howad I. Biblical Inspiration. 128p. 1983. pap. 4.95 (ISBN 0-8028-1959-1). Eerdmans.

Meloon, Walter. Men Alive. Enlow, David, ed. 120p. 1982. pap. 3.95 (ISBN 0-87509-320-5). Chr Pubns.

Meyers, Carol L. & O'Connor, M., eds. The Word of the Lord Shall Go Forth: Essays in Honor of David Noel Freedman in Celebration of His Sixtieth Birthday. 1983. text ed. price not set (ISBN 0-89757-507-5, Pub. by Am Sch Orient Res). Eisenbrauns.

Morantte, M. P. God Is in the Heart: Poetical & Symbolical Essays. (Illus.). 78p. (Orig.). 1982. pap. 4.75 (ISBN 971-10-0040-7, Pub. by New Day Philippines). Cellar.

Murray, Andrew. Jesus Himself. 27p. 1966. pap. 0.85 (ISBN 0-87509-096-6). Chr Pubns.

Neel, Peg. How To Pray According to God's Word. 72p. 1982. pap. 2.25 (ISBN 0-88144-004-3, CPS-004). Christian Pub.

Owens, Virginia S. And the Trees Clap Their Hands: Faith, Perception & the New Physics. 160p. 1983. pap. 6.95 (ISBN 0-8028-1949-4). Eerdmans.

Pierson, A. T. The Holy Care of the Body. 1966. pap. 0.45 (ISBN 0-87509-093-1). Chr Pubns.

Pollard, T. E. Fullness of Humanity: Christ's Humanness & Ours. 128p. 1982. text ed. 19.95x (ISBN 0-907459-10-2, Pub. by Almond Pr England); pap. text ed. 9.95x (ISBN 0-907459-11-0, Pub. by Almond Pr England). Eisenbrauns.

Pudaite, Mawii. Beyond the Next Mountain. 160p. (Orig.). 1982. pap. 5.95 (ISBN 0-8423-0154-2). Tyndale.

Schillebeeckx, Edward. God among Us: The Gospel Proclaimed. 278p. 1983. 12.95 (ISBN 0-8245-0575-1). Crossroad NY.

Simpson, A. B. Is Life Worth Living? 30p. pap. 1.00 (ISBN 0-87509-045-1). Chr Pubns.

Sinclair, Keith V., ed. French Devotional Texts of the Middle Ages: A Bibliographic Manuscript Guide, First Supplement. LC 82-11773. 246p. 1982. lib. bdg. 65.00 (ISBN 0-313-23664-X, SIF/). Greenwood.

Wallace, Joyce. A Closer Walk. LC 82-99994. 128p. 1982. pap. 4.50 (ISBN 0-686-38098-3). Foun Christ Serv.

Walters, Richard P. Forgive & Be Free: Healing the Wounds of Past & Present. 144p. 1983. pap. 4.95 (ISBN 0-310-42611-1). Zondervan.

Ward, Frances. Keep the Fruit on the Table. 48p. 1982. pap. 1.95 (ISBN 0-88144-006-X, CPS-006). Christian Pub.

Welch, Reuben. We Really Do Need Each Other. 112p. 1982. pap. 5.95 (ISBN 0-310-70221-6). Zondervan.

Wheat, Ed. Amor que no se apaga. Date not set. 2.50 (ISBN 0-88113-010-9). Edit Betania.

Wicks, Robert J. Christian Introspection: Self-Ministry Through Self-Understanding. 128p. 1983. pap. 7.95 (ISBN 0-8245-0583-2). Crossroad NY.

DEVOTIONAL LITERATURE (SELECTIONS: EXTRACTS, ETC.)

Daily Light on the Daily Path: From the New International Version. 384p. 1983. pap. 8.95 (ISBN 0-310-23117-5). Zondervan.

Shedd, Charlie. Devotions for Dieters. 1983. 8.95 (ISBN 0-8499-0330-0). Word Bks.

DEVOTIONAL THEOLOGY

see Devotional Exercises; Devotional Literature; Meditations; Prayers;

also subdivision Prayer-Books and Devotions under names of Christian denominations, religious orders, classes of persons, etc.

DEVOTIONAL YEARBOOKS

see Devotional Calendars

DEVOTIONS

see Devotional Exercises

DE VRIES, PETER

Bowden, J. H. Peter De Vries. (United States Authors Ser.). 177p. 1983. lib. bdg. 15.95 (ISBN 0-8057-7388-6, Twayne). G K Hall.

DEWEY, JOHN, 1859-1952

Bullert, Gary. The Politics of John Dewey. 275p. 1983. 19.95 (ISBN 0-87975-208-4). Prometheus Bks.

Meyer, Samuel, ed. Dewey & Russell: An Exchange. 1983. 9.95 (ISBN 0-8022-2406-7). Philos Lib.

DEWEY DECIMAL CLASSIFICATION

see Classification, Dewey Decimal

DEXTERITY

see Motor Ability

DHARMA

Macy, Joanna. Dharma & Development: Religion As Resource in the Sarvodaya Movement. LC 82-83015. (K. P. Monograph: No. 2). 104p. 1983. pap. 6.75x (ISBN 0-931816-11-4); 13.75x (ISBN 0-931816-74-2). Kumarian Pr.

Rama, Frederick Lenz. The Wheel of Dharma. Blank, Nina, et al, eds. LC 82-83343. (Illus.). 112p. (Orig.). 1982. pap. text ed. 5.00 (ISBN 0-941868-01-X). Lakshmi.

DHYANA (SECT)

see Zen Buddhism

DIABETES

Addanki, Sam & Kindrick, Shirley A. Renewed Health for Diabetics & Obese People. Brennan, R. O., ed. (Orig.). 1982. pap. 3.50 (ISBN 0-9609896-0-9). Nu-Diet.

Anderson, James. Diabetes. 288p. 1983. pap. 3.50 (ISBN 0-446-30593-6). Warner Bks.

Berstein, Richard K. Diabetes: The Glucograf Method for Normalizing Blood Sugar. (Illus.). 320p. 1981. 14.95 (ISBN 0-517-54155-6). Crown.

Craig, Oman. Childhood Diabetes: The Facts. (The Facts Ser.). (Illus.). 126p. 1982. 12.95 (ISBN 0-19-261330-8). Oxford U Pr.

Developing Programs to Control & Prevent Diabetes: An Analysis of the Problems. LC 80-85242. (Policy Research Project Report Ser.: No. 43). 140p. 1982. 7.95 (ISBN 0-89940-645-9). LBJ Sch Pub Aff.

Eschwege, E., ed. Advances in Diabetes Epidemiology: Proceedings of the International Symposium on the Advances in Diabetes Epidemiology, Abbaye de Fontevraud, France, 3-7 May 1982. (INSERM Symposium Ser.: No. 22). 408p. Date not set. 81.00 (ISBN 0-444-80453-6, Biomedical Pr). Elsevier.

Friedman, Eli A., ed. Diabetic Renal-Retinal Syndrome II: Prevention & Management. Date not set. price not set (ISBN 0-8089-1539-8). Grune.

International Diabetes Federation. Abstracts: Eighth Congress. Hoet, J., et al, eds. (International Congress Ser.: No. 280). 1973. pap. 29.50 (ISBN 0-444-15064-1). Elsevier.

Kahn, Ada P. Diabetes. (Help Yourself to Health Ser.). 96p. (Orig.). 1983. pap. 3.95 (ISBN 0-8092-5601-0). Contemp Bks.

Keen, Harry & Jarrett, John. Complications of Diabetes. 344p. 1982. text ed. 64.50 (ISBN 0-7131-4409-2). E Arnold.

O'Brien, Charles J. A Joyful Diabetic. (Illus.). 144p. 1983. 7.95 (ISBN 0-89962-323-9). Todd & Honeywell.

DIABETIC DIET

see Cookery for Diabetics

DIABETIC RETINOPATHY

see also Diabetes; Retina-Diseases

Little, Hunter & Jack, Robert L. Diabetic Retinopathy: Pathogenesis & Treatment. (Illus.). 568p. 1983. write for info. (ISBN 0-86577-076-X). Thieme-Stratton.

DIACONATE

see Deacons

DIAGHILEV, SERGEI PAVLOVICH, 1872-1929

Buckle, Richard. In the Wake of Diaghilev. LC 82-12096. (Illus.). 400p. 1983. 19.95 (ISBN 0-03-062493-2). HR&W.

DIAGNOSIS

see also Body Temperature; Diagnosis, Differential; Diagnosis, Radioscopic; Endoscope and Endoscopy; Medical History Taking; Medicine, Clinical; Microscopy, Medical; Pain; Pathology; Reflexes; Veterinary Medicine-Diagnosis

also subdivisions Diseases-Diagnosis or Diseases under names of organs and regions of the body, e.g. Lungs-diseases-diagnosis; also subdivisions Diagnosis under particular diseases, e.g. Tuberculosis-Diagnosis

Business Communications Staff. Medical Diagnostic Reagents & O Products. 1983. 1250.00 (ISBN 0-89336-352-9, C-045). BCC.

Chadwick, Maureen V. Mycobacteria. (Institute of Medical Laboratory Sciences Monographs). 128p. 1982. pap. text ed. write for info. (ISBN 0-7236-0595-5). Wright-PSG.

Critser, James R., Jr. Clinical Assays. (Ser.10CA-82). 1983. 100.00 (ISBN 0-88178-003-0). Lexington Data.

--Medical Diagnostic Apparatus: Systems. (Ser.10DAS-82). 1983. 100.00 (ISBN 0-88178-006-5). Lexington Data.

Galen, P. S. & Gambino, S. R. Beyond Normality: The Predictive Value & Efficiency of Medical Diagnosis. LC 75-25915. 237p. 1975. 32.95x (ISBN 0-471-29047-5, Pub. by Wiley Medical). Wiley.

Heusghem, Camille & Albert, Adelin, eds. Advanced Interpretation of Clinical Laboratory Data. (Clinical & Biochemical Analysis Ser.: Vol. 13). (Illus.). 448p. 1982. 55.00 (ISBN 0-8247-1744-9). Dekker.

International Immunodiagnostic Testing Markets. 1983. 995.00 (ISBN 0-686-37714-1, 290). Predicasts.

Johannessen, Jan V. Diagnostic Electron Microscopy. 210p. 1982. text ed. 34.50 (ISBN 0-07-032543-X, Co-Pub. by Hemisphere Pub). McGraw.

Kerr, Donald A. & Ash, Major M., Jr. Oral Diagnosis. 6th ed. LC 82-6291. (Illus.). 383p. 1983. text ed. 32.50 (ISBN 0-8016-2656-0). Mosby.

Kovac, Alexander & Kozarek, Richard. Guide to Diagnostic Imaging: Vol. III - The Pancreas. 1983. write for info. (ISBN 0-87488-415-2). Med Exam.

Lodewick, L. & Gunn, A. D. The Physical Examination. 270p. 1982. text ed. 35.00 (ISBN 0-85200-395-1, Pub. by MTP Pr England). Kluwer Boston.

Pagana, Kathleen D. & Pagana, Timothy J. Understanding Medical Testing. (Medical Library). (Illus.). 272p. 1983. pap. price not set (ISBN 0-452-25404-3, 3778-3). Mosby.

Tilkian, Sarko M. & Conover, Mary B. Clinical Implications of Laboratory Tests. 3rd ed. (Illus.). 494p. 1983. pap. text ed. 13.95 (ISBN 0-8016-4960-9). Mosby.

Trump, B. F. & Jones, R. T. Diagnostic Electron Microscopy, Vol. 1. (Diagnostic Electron Microscopy Ser.). 346p. 1978. text ed. 65.00 (ISBN 0-471-89196-7, Pub. by Wiley Med). Wiley.

Valasek, V. F. Diagnostic Tests & Nursing Implications. 704p. 1983. 13.95x (ISBN 0-07-066805-1). McGraw.

Widmann, Frances K. Clinical Interpretation of Laboratory Tests. 9th ed. LC 82-14927. (Illus.). 605p. 1983. pap. text ed. 18.95 (ISBN 0-8036-9323-0). Davis Co.

DIAGNOSIS, DIFFERENTIAL

Beck, Eric R., et al. Differential Diagnosis: Internal Medicine. LC 82-71362. (Illus.). 229p. (Orig.). 1983. pap. text ed. 14.50x (ISBN 0-668-05622-3, 5622). Arco.

Colby, Kenneth M. & Spar, James E. The Fundamental Crisis in Psychiatry: Unreliability of Diagnosis. 236p. 1983. 24.75x (ISBN 0-398-04788-X). C C Thomas.

Horny, J. Differentialdiagnostisches Kompendium. 3rd ed. xvi, 260p. 1982. pap. 17.00 (ISBN 3-8055-3627-5). S Karger.

DIAGNOSIS, RADIOSCOPIC

see also Angiography; Pediatric Radiology; X-Rays also subdivision names of organs with or without the subdivision Radiography

Naidech, Howard J. & Damon, Lorraine. Radiologic Technology Examination Review. LC 82-13908. (Illus.). 288p. (Orig.). 1983. pap. text ed. 12.95 (ISBN 0-668-05366-6, 5366). Arco.

Sherwood, T., et al. Roads to Radiology: An Imaging Guide to Medicine & Surgery. (Illus.). 96p. 1983. pap. 16.00 (ISBN 0-387-11801-2). Springer-Verlag.

Sowby, F. D. & International Commission on Radiology Protection, eds. Protection of the Patient in Diagnostic Radiology: ICRP Publication, No. 34. 88p. 1982. pap. 25.00 (ISBN 0-08-029797-8). Pergamon.

Thijssen, H. O., ed. Liber Amicorum Presented to Prof. Dr. Wm. Penn. (Journal: Diagnostic Imaging: Vol. 52, No. 2-3). (Illus.). ii, 108p. 1983. pap. 45.50 (ISBN 3-8055-3671-2). S Karger.

Wackenheim, A. Radiodiagnosis of the Vertebrae in Adults: 125 Exercises for Students & Practitioners. (Exercises in Radiological Diagnosis Ser.). (Illus.). 176p. 1983. pap. 14.80 (ISBN 0-387-11681-8). Springer-Verlag.

DIAGNOSIS, ULTRASONIC

see also Ultrasonics in Medicine

Goldberg, Barry B. Abdominal Gray Scale Ultrasonography. LC 77-5889. (Diagnostic & Therapuetic Radiology Ser.). 372p. 1977. 55.00x (ISBN 0-471-01510-5, Pub. by Wiley Med). Wiley.

Reba, Richard & Goodenough, David J. Diagnostic Imaging Medicine. 1983. 87.00 (ISBN 90-247-2798-7, Pub. by Martinus Nijhoff Netherlands). Kluwer Boston.

Zwiebel, William J., ed. Introduction to Vascular Ultrasonography. Date not set. price not set (ISBN 0-8089-1531-2). Grune.

DIAGNOSIS, VETERINARY

see Veterinary Medicine–Diagnosis

DIAGNOSTIC PSYCHOLOGICAL TESTING

see Clinical Psychology

DIAGNOSTIC ULTRASONICS

see Diagnosis, Ultrasonic

DIALECTIC

Mueller, Gustav E. Dialectic: A Way Into & Within Philosophy. Keyes, C. D., ed. 234p. 1983. pap. text ed. 11.00 (ISBN 0-8191-2691-8). U Pr of Amer.

Punter, David. Blake, Hegel & Dialectic. (Elementa Ser.: Band XXVI). 268p. 1982. pap. text ed. 23.00x (ISBN 90-6203-694-5, Pub. by Rodopi Holland). Humanities.

DIALECTIC (LOGIC)

see Logic

DIALECTIC (RELIGION)

see Dialectical Theology

DIALECTIC LOGIC

see Logic

DIALECTICAL THEOLOGY

Rumscheidt, Martin, ed. Footnotes to a Theology: The Karl Barth Colloquim of 1972. 151p. 1974. pap. text ed. 5.25x (ISBN 0-919812-02-3, Pub. by Laurier U Pr). Humanities.

Szekely, Edmond B. The Dialectical Method of Thinking. (Illus.). 40p. 1973. pap. 2.95 (ISBN 0-89564-063-5). IBS Intl.

DIALECTS

see Creole Dialects; Franco-Provencal Dialects also subdivisions Dialects; Idioms, Corrections, Errors; Provincialisms under names of languages

DIALOGUE

see also Drama

Barth, E. M. & Krabbe, E. C., eds. From Axiom to Dialogue: Foundations of Communication Ser. xi, 337p. 1982. 69.00x (ISBN 3-11-008489-9). De Gruyter.

DIALOGUE SERMONS

Freed, Harvey G. Chapel Talks, Sermons & Debates. 1983. pap. 6.95 (ISBN 0-89225-269-3). Gospel Advocate.

DIALOGUES

see also Drama

Tasso, Torquato. Tasso's Dialogues: A Selection, With the Discourse on the Art of the Dialogue. Lord, Carnes & Trafton, Dain A., trs. LC 81-12937. (Bibliateca Italiana Ser.). 288p. 1983. 18.50x (ISBN 0-520-04464-9). U of Cal Pr.

DIAMOND DRILLING

see Boring

DIAMONDS

see also Gems

Lenzen. Diamonds & Diamond Grading. 1983. text ed. 59.95 (ISBN 0-408-00547-5). Butterworth.

DIANA, PRINCESS OF WALES, 1961-

Butler, Lucy. Diana: The Fairy Tale Princess. (YA) (gr. 5-12). 1983. 8.95. Summit Bks.

Hall, Trevor. Born to be King: Prince William of Wales. (Illus.). 128p. 1983. 25.00 (ISBN 0-517-39675-0). Crown.

Junor, Penny. Diana, Princess of Wales. LC 82-45832. (Illus.). 224p. 1983. 14.95 (ISBN 0-385-19007-7). Doubleday.

DIARIES

see also Autobiographies; also American Diaries, English Diaries, etc.

Potter, Beatrix. The Peter Rabbit Diary. (Illus.). 90p. 1983. 3.95 (ISBN 0-7232-2982-1). Warne.

Sassoon, Seigfried. Siegfried Sassoon Diaries, 1920-1922. Hart-Davis, Rupert, ed. Date not set. pap. 18.95 (ISBN 0-571-11685-X). Faber & Faber.

Sassoon, Siegfried. Siegfried Sassoon Diaries, 1915-1918. Hart-Davis, Rupert, ed. 296p. 1983. 19.95 (ISBN 0-571-11997-2). Faber & Faber.

Zimmerman, William. A Book of Questions: To Keep Thoughts & Feelings. 270p. 1983. write for info. (ISBN 0-935966-02-1); pap. write for info. (ISBN 0-935966-01-3). Guarionex Pr.

DIARRHEA

Chen, Lincoln C. & Scrimshaw, Nevin S., eds. Diarrhea & Malnutrition: Interactions, Mechanisms & Interventions. 310p. 1983. 39.50x (ISBN 0-306-41046-X, Plenum Pr). Plenum Pub.

DIASPORA OF THE JEWS

see Jews–Diaspora

DICE

Mendelsohn, Martin. One Hundred Thousand Rolls of the Dice. LC 82-84680. 100p. 1982. pap. 9.95 (ISBN 0-89650-500-6). Gamblers.

DICHROISM

Mason, S. F. Molecular Optical Activity & the Chiral Discriminations. LC 82-1125. (Illus.). 250p. 1982. 39.50 (ISBN 0-521-24702-0). Cambridge U Pr.

DICKENS, CHARLES, 1812-1870

Perkins, Donald. Charles Dickens: A New Perspective. 1982. 15.95 (ISBN 0-903540-53-3, Pub. by Floris Books). St George Bk Serv.

Slater, Michael. Dickens & Women. LC 82-62351. (Illus.). 512p. 1983. 28.50x (ISBN 0-8047-1180-1). Stanford U Pr.

DICKINSON, EMILY ELIZABETH, 1830-1886

Anderson, Charles R. Emily Dickinson's Poetry: Stairway of Surprise. LC 82-15844. (Illus.). xvii, 334p. 1982. Repr. of 1963 ed. lib. bdg. 35.00x (ISBN 0-313-23733-6, ANED). Greenwood.

Juhasz, Suzanne, intro. by. Feminist Critics Read Emily Dickinson. LC 82-48265. 192p. 1983. 17.50x (ISBN 0-253-32170-0). Ind U Pr.

DICOTYLEDONS

Chater, Hara H. & Williams, A. O. An Enumeration of the Flowering Plants of Nepal: Vol. 3, Dicotyledons. (Illus.). 226p. 1982. pap. text ed. 81.50 (ISBN 0-565-00854-4). Sabbot-Natural Hist Bks.

DICTATORS

see also Despotism

Marriott, John A. Dictatorship & Democracy. 231p. 1982. Repr. of 1935 ed. lib. bdg. 30.00 (ISBN 0-8495-3937-4). Arden Lib.

DICTATYPY

see Stenotypy

DICTIONARIES

see Encyclopedias and Dictionaries; also particular languages or subjects with or without the subdivision dictionaries

The American Heritage Dictionary. rev. ed. 1983. pap. price not set (ISBN 0-440-50079-6, Dell Trade Pbks). Dell.

DICTIONARIES, PICTURE

see Picture Dictionaries

DICTIONARIES, RHYMING

see English Language–Rime–Dictionaries

DIDACTICS

see Teaching

DIDEROT, DENIS, 1713-1784

Seznec, Jean, ed. Diderot: Salons, Vol. III, Seventeen Sixty-Seven. 2nd ed. (Illus.). 1982. 110.00 (ISBN 0-19-817372-5). Oxford U Pr.

DIE CASTING

Allsop, D. F. Pressure Diecasting: The Technology of the Casting & the Die, Pt. 2. (Materials Engineering Practice Ser.). (Illus.). 200p. 1983. 27.50 (ISBN 0-08-027615-6); pap. 13.00 (ISBN 0-08-027614-8). Pergamon.

Kaye & Street. Die Casting Metallurgy. 1982. text ed. 49.95 (ISBN 0-408-10717-0). Butterworth.

DIEPPE RAID, 1942

Whitehead, William & Macarthey-Filgate, Terence. Dieppe Nineteen Forty-Two: Echoes of Disaster. 192p. 1982. 39.25x (ISBN 0-86267-006-3, Pub. by R Drew Pub). State Mutual Bk.

DIESEL ENGINE

see Diesel Motor

DIESEL LOCOMOTIVE ENGINES

see Diesel Locomotives

DIESEL LOCOMOTIVES

Harris, Ken. World Diesel Locomotives. (Illus.). 160p. 1982. 19.95 (ISBN 0-86720-625-X). Sci Bks Intl.

Kirkland, John F. & Sebree, Mac. Dawn of the Diesel Age. 200p. 1983. price not set (ISBN 0-916374-52-1). Interurban.

Schulz, E. J. Diesel Mechanics. 2nd ed. 496p. 1983. 24.95x (ISBN 0-07-055639-3, G). McGraw.

DIESEL MOTOR

see also Automobiles–Motors

Black, Perry O. & Scahill. Diesel Engine Manual. new ed. (Audel Ser.). 1983. 12.95 (ISBN 0-672-23371-1). Bobbs.

Toboldt, Bill. Diesel: Fundamentals, Service, Repair. Rev. ed. LC 82-14319. (Illus.). 1983. text ed. 14.00 (ISBN 0-87006-424-X). Goodheart.

DIET

see also Beverages; Cookery; Cookery–Reducing Recipes; Dieticians; Food; Food, Dietetic; Food, Raw; Food Habits; Low-Fat Diet; Menus; Nutrition; Reducing Diets; School Children–Food; Therapeutics, Physiological; Vegetarianism

Abravanel, Eliott D. & King, Elizabeth A. Dr. Abravanel's Body Type Diet & Lifetime Nutrition Plan. (Illus.). 256p. 1983. 12.95 (ISBN 0-553-05036-2). Bantam.

Barrile, Jackie. Confessions of a Closet Eater. 1983. 12.95 (ISBN 0-941018-09-1). P Hanson.

Better Homes & Gardens Books editors, ed. Better Homes & Gardens Calorie-Counter's Cook Book. rev. ed. (Illus.). 96p. 1983. 5.95 (ISBN 0-696-00835-1). Meredith Corp.

Bruno, Frank J. Think Yourself Thin. (PBN Ser.). 265p. 1974. pap. 2.25 (ISBN 0-06-465024-3, 5024). B&N NY.

Corson, Helen B. Does Your Diet Work? LC 80-8427. (Illus.). 105p. (Orig.). 1980. pap. 7.95 (ISBN 0-9605358-0-2). MIND.

Dachslager, Howard & Yayashi, Masato. Learning BASIC Programming: A Systematic Approach. 280p. 1983. pap. text ed. 18.95 (ISBN 0-534-01422-4). Brooks-Cole.

Dennison, Darwin. The Dine System: The Nutrition Plan for Better Health. 1982. pap. 8.95 (ISBN 0-452-25367-5, Plume). NAL.

Ferguson, Sybil. The Diet Center Program: Lose Weight Fast & Keep It Off Forever. 424p. 1983. 14.45i (ISBN 0-316-27901-3). Little.

Guisewite, Cathy. Eat Your Way to a Better Relationship. LC 82-72420. 60p. (Orig.). 1983. pap. 2.95 (ISBN 0-8362-1987-2). Andrews & McMeel.

Hostage, Jacqueline. Jackie's Diet & Nutrition Charts. 128p. 1982. pap. 5.95 (ISBN 0-932620-10-8, Pub. by Betterway Pubns). Berkshire Traveller.

Hui, Yiu H. Human Nutrition & Diet Therapy. LC 82-20136. 900p. 1983. text ed. 25.00 (ISBN 0-534-01336-8). Brooks-Cole.

Kushi, Michio & Jack, Alex. The Cancer-Prevention Diet. 1983. 13.95 (ISBN 0-312-11837-6). St Martin.

Lanz, Sally J. An Introduction to the Profession of Dietetics. LC 82-18683. (Illus.). 160p. 1983. pap. price not set (ISBN 0-8121-0883-3). Lea & Febiger.

Osborn, S. The American Guide to Diet & Health. 352p. 1982. 24.95 (ISBN 0-07-069074-X, GB); pap. 12.95 (ISBN 0-07-069072-3). McGraw.

Partee, Phillip E. The Layman's Guide to Buying & Eating a Natural Balanced Diet. 130p. (Orig.). 1983. pap. 3.95x (ISBN 0-686-84761-X). Sprout Pubns.

Reingold, Carmel B. The Lifelong Anti-Cancer Diet. 1982. pap. 3.50 (ISBN 0-451-12220-8, AE2220, Sig). NAL.

Rohe, Fred. Fred Rohe's Complete Book of Natural Foods. LC 82-50282. (Illus.). 448p. (Orig.). 1983. pap. 10.95 (ISBN 0-394-71240-4). Shambhala Pubns.

Shapiro, Jacqueline R. & Swaybill, Marion L. Sexibody Diet & Exercise Program. 1982. text ed. 10.95 (ISBN 0-914094-19-X). Symphony.

DIET, LOW SUGAR

see Sugar-Free Diet

DIET, MACROBIOTIC

see Macrobiotic Diet

DIET IN DISEASE

see also Cookery–Reducing Recipes; Cookery for Diabetics; Cookery for the Sick; Dieticians; Food, Dietetic; High-Fiber Diet; Low-Cholesterol Diet; Low-Fat Diet; Salt-Free Diet; Sugar-Free Diet

Frederick, Carlton. Carlton Frederick's Nutrition Guide for the Prevention & Cure of Common Ailments & Diseses. LC 82-10705. (Illus.). 194p. Date not set. pap. 8.95 (ISBN 0-671-44509-X, Fireside). S&S.

Fredericks, Carl. Carlton Frederick's Nutrition Guide for Prevention & Cure of Common Ailments & Disease. 1982. 8.95x. Cancer Control Soc.

Roth, June. Living Better with a Special Diet. LC 82-11652. 276p. 1983. lib. bdg. 12.95 (ISBN 0-668-05718-1); pap. 7.95 (ISBN 0-668-05651-7). Arco.

Stern, Ellen & Michaels, Jonathan. The Good Heart Diet Cookbook. 256p. 1983. pap. 6.95 (ISBN 0-446-37547-0). Warner Bks.

Szekely, Edmond B. The Preventive Diet for Heart & Overweight. (Illus.). 48p. 1977. pap. 3.50 (ISBN 0-89564-040-6). IBS Intl.

Wentworth, Josie A. Migraine Prevention Cookbook. LC 82-45277. (Illus.). 216p. 1983. 13.95 (ISBN 0-385-18052-7). Doubleday.

Whitney, Eleanor N. & Cataldo, Corrine. Understanding Normal & Clinical Nutrition. (Illus.). 1000p. 1983. text ed. 26.95 (ISBN 0-314-69685-7); tchrs.' manual avail. (ISBN 0-314-71137-6). West Pub.

Winick, M. Nutrition in Health & Disease. 261p. 1980. text ed. 24.95x (ISBN 0-471-05713-4, Pub. by Wiley-Interscience). Wiley.

Winters, R. W. & Greene, H. L., eds. Nutritional Support of the Seriously Ill Patient, Vol. 1. LC 82-18426. (Bristol-Myers Nutrition Symposia Ser.). Date not set. price not set (ISBN 0-12-759801-4). Acad Pr.

DIET THERAPY

see Diet in Disease

DIETARIES

see also Food

American Dietetic Association. Abstracts 1982: Sixty-Fifth Annual Meeting of The American Dietetic Association in San Antonio, Texas. 240p. 1982. pap. 8.50 (ISBN 0-88091-007-0). Am Dietetic Assn.

DIETARY FIBER

see High-Fiber Diet

DIETETIC FOOD

see Food, Dietetic

DIETETICS

see Diet; Diet in Disease; Nutrition

DIETICIANS

Lanz, Sally J. An Introduction to the Profession of Dietetics. LC 82-18683. (Illus.). 160p. 1983. pap. price not set (ISBN 0-8121-0883-3). Lea & Febiger.

DIETING

see Reducing

DIETING FOR WEIGHT LOSS

see Reducing Diets

DIFFERENCE EQUATIONS

see also Asymptotic Expansions

Goldberg, Samuel. Introduction to Difference Equations: With Illustrative Examples from Economics, Psychology & Sociology. LC 58-10223. (Illus.). 1958. pap. 18.50x (ISBN 0-471-31051-4). Wiley.

DIFFERENTIAL CALCULUS

see Calculus, Differential

DIFFERENTIAL DIAGNOSIS

see Diagnosis, Differential

DIFFERENTIAL EQUATIONS

see also Differential Operators; Functions; Surfaces

Arnold, V. I. Geometrical Methods in the Theory of Ordinary Differential Equations. (Grundlehren der Mathematischen Wissenschaften: Vol. 250). (Illus.). 384p. 1983. 36.00 (ISBN 0-387-90681-9). Springer-Verlag.

Birkhoff, Garrett & Gian-Carlo Rota. Ordinary Differential Equations. 3rd ed. LC 78-8304. 350p. 1978. text ed. 31.95x (ISBN 0-471-07411-X). Wiley.

Boyce, William E. & Di Prima, Richard C. Elementary Differential Equations. 3rd ed. LC 75-35565. 497p. 1977. text ed. 26.50 (ISBN 0-471-09339-4). Wiley.

Boyce, William E. & DiPrima, Richard C. Elementary Differential Equations & Boundary Value Problems. 3rd ed. LC 75-45093. 638p. 1977. 26.50 (ISBN 0-471-09334-3). Wiley.

--Introduction to Differential Equations. 310p. 1970. text ed. 22.95x (ISBN 0-471-09338-6). Wiley.

De Figueiredo, D. G., ed. Differential Equations, Sao Paulo, Brazil, 1981: Proceedings. (Lecture Notes in Mathematics: Vol. 957). 301p. 1983. pap. 16.00 (ISBN 0-387-11951-5). Springer-Verlag.

Differential Geometry & Differential Equations: Proceedings of the 1980 Conference in Beijing, The People's Republic of China. 1744p. 1982. 325.00 (ISBN 0-677-31120-6). Gordon.

Dwork, Bernard. Lectures on P-Adic Differential Equations. (Grundlehron der Mathematischen Wissenschaften Ser.: Vol. 253). (Illus.). 304p. 1982. 46.00 (ISBN 0-387-90714-9). Springer-Verlag.

Haberman, Richard. Elementary Applied Partial Differential Equations. (Illus.). 560p. 1983. text ed. 34.95 (ISBN 0-13-252833-9). P-H.

Hannsgen, Kenneth B. & Herdman, Terry L., eds. Volterra & Functional Differential Equations. (Lecture Notes in Pure & Applied Mathematics: Vol. 81). (Illus.). 352p. 1982. 45.00 (ISBN 0-8247-1721-X). Dekker.

Hartman, P. Ordinary Differential Equations. 2nd ed. 1982. text ed. 29.95 (ISBN 3-7643-3068-6). Birkhauser.

Levitan, B. M. & Zhikov, V. V. Almost Periodic Functions & Differential Equations. Longdon, L. V., tr. LC 82-4352. 150p. 1983. 34.50 (ISBN 0-521-24407-2). Cambridge U Pr.

Littman, Walter, ed. Studies in Partial Differential Equations. (MAA Studies in Mathematics Ser.: No. 23). 200p. Date not set. price not set (ISBN 0-88385-125-3). Math Assn.

Lucas, W. F., ed. Modules in Applied Mathematics: Differential Equation Models, Vol. 1. (Illus.). 400p. 1982. 28.00 (ISBN 0-387-90695-9). Springer-Verlag.

McCann, Roger C. Introduction to Ordinary Differential Equations. 448p. 1982. text ed. 24.95 (ISBN 0-15-543485-3, HC); answer manual 4.95 (ISBN 0-15-543486-1). HarBraceJ.

Martin, Robert E., Jr. Ordinary Differential Equations. (Illus.). 496p. 1983. text ed. 27.95x (ISBN 0-07-040687-1, C); instr's. manual 7.00 (ISBN 0-07-040688-X). McGraw.
Mikhlin & Smolitskii. Approximate Methods for Solution of Differential & Integral Equations. 1967. 20.00 (ISBN 0-444-00022-4). Elsevier.
Ordinary & Partial Differential Equations: Proceedings, Dundee, Scotland, 1982. (Lecture Notes in Mathematics Ser.: Vol. 964). 726p. 1983. pap. 32.00 (ISBN 0-387-11968-X). Springer-Verlag.
Pandit, S. G. & Deo, S. G. Differential Systems Involving Impulses. (Lecture Notes in Mathematics Ser.: Vol. 954). 102p. 1983. pap. 8.00 (ISBN 0-387-11606-0). Springer-Verlag.
Sanchez, David A. & Allen, Richard C., Jr. Differential Equations: An Introduction. LC 82-16326. (Illus.). 512p. Date not set. text ed. 22.95 (ISBN 0-201-07760-4). A-W.
Sixteen Papers on Differential Equations. LC 82-20595. (AMS Translations Ser.: No. 2 vol. 118). 70.00 (ISBN 0-8218-3073-2, TRANS/2/118). Am Math.
Zauderer, Erich. Partial Differential Equations of Applied Mathematics. (Pure & Applied Mathematics Ser.). 600p. 1983. 42.50x (ISBN 0-471-87517-1, Pub. by Wiley-Interscience). Wiley.
Zuev, V. E. & Naats, I. E. Inverse Problems of Lidar Sensing of the Atmosphere. (Springer Ser. in Optical Sciences: Vol. 29). (Illus.). 260p. 1983. 41.00 (ISBN 0-387-10913-7). Springer-Verlag.

DIFFERENTIAL EQUATIONS, ELLIPTIC
Agmon, Samuel. Lectures on Exponential Decay of Solutions of Second-Order Elliptic Equations. LC 82-14978. (Mathematical Notes Ser.: No. 29). 118p. 1983. 10.50 (ISBN 0-691-08318-5). Princeton U Pr.
Rempel, S. & Schulze, B. W. Index Theory of Elliptic Boundary Problems. 394p. 1982. text ed. 48.95. Birkhauser.

DIFFERENTIAL EQUATIONS, LINEAR
see also Differential Equations, Elliptic
Feschenko, S., et al, eds. Asymptotic Methods in the Theory of Linear Differential Equations. 1968. 17.50 (ISBN 0-444-00026-7). Elsevier.
Hinze, J., ed. Numerical Integration of Differential Equations & Large Linear Systems: Proceedings, Bielfeld, FRG, 1980. (Lecture Notes in Mathematics Ser.: Vol. 968). 412p. 1983. pap. 20.00 (ISBN 0-387-11970-1). Springer-Verlag.
Krein, S. G. Linear Equations in Banach Spaces. 128p. Date not set. text ed. 14.95x (ISBN 3-7643-3101-1). Birkhauser.
Rabenstein, Albert. Elementary Differential Equations with Linear Algebra. 3rd ed. 518p. 1982. text ed. 21.95 (ISBN 0-12-573945-1); avail. Instr's Manual 2.50 (ISBN 0-12-573946-X). Acad Pr.
Yakubovich, V. A. & Starzhinskii, V. M. Linear Differential Equations with Periodic Coefficients, 2 vols. 775p. Repr. of 1975 ed. text ed. 56.75 (ISBN 0-470-96953-9). Krieger.

DIFFERENTIAL EQUATIONS, NONLINEAR
Hagedorn, Peter. Non-Linear Oscillations. (Engineering Science Ser.). (Illus.). 308p. 1982. pap. 19.95 (ISBN 0-19-856156-3). Oxford U Pr.
Sparrow, C. The Lorenz Equations: Bifurcations, Chaos, & Strange Attractors. (Applied Mathematical Sciences Ser.: Vol. 41). (Illus.). 288p. 1983. 19.80 (ISBN 0-387-90775-0). Springer-Verlag.

DIFFERENTIAL EQUATIONS, PARTIAL
see also Differential Equations, Elliptic; Harmonic Functions
Chazarain, J. & Piriou, A. Introduction to the Theory of Linear Partial Differential Equations. (Studies in Mathematics & Its Applications: Vol. 14). 560p. 1982. 74.50 (ISBN 0-444-86452-0, North Holland). Elsevier.
Garabedian, Paul R. Partial Differential Equations. LC 64-11505. 672p. 1964. 39.95x (ISBN 0-471-29088-2). Wiley.
Price, P. F. & Simon, L. M., eds. Miniconference on Partial Equations. new ed. 133p. (Orig.). pap. text ed. 13.95 (ISBN 0-86784-123-0, 1246, Pub. by ANUP Australia). Bks Australia.

DIFFERENTIAL GEOMETRY
see Geometry, Differential

DIFFERENTIAL OPERATORS
see also Differential Equations
Arsene, Gr., ed. Invariant Subspaces & Other Topics. (Operator Theory: Advances & Applications Ser.: No. 6). 229p. Date not set. text ed. 26.95 (ISBN 3-7643-1360-9). Birkhauser.
Hoermander, L. The Analysis of Linear Partial Differential Operators II: Differential Operators with Constant Coefficients. (Illus.). 380p. 1983. 49.50 (ISBN 0-387-12139-0). Springer-Verlag.
--The Analysis of Linear Partial Differential Operators I: Distribution Theory & Fourier Analysis. (Grundlehren der Mathematischen Wissenschaften: Vol. 256). (Illus.). 380p. 1983. 39.00 (ISBN 0-387-12104-8). Springer-Verlag.

DIFFERENTIAL THERMAL ANALYSIS
see Thermal Analysis

DIFFERENTIATION OF CELLS
see Cell Differentiation

DIFFRACTION
Northover, F. Applied Diffraction Theory. 1971. 45.00 (ISBN 0-444-00085-2). Elsevier.

DIFFUSION
see also Biological Transport; Colloids; Gases; Light-Scattering; Mass Transfer; Matter-Properties
Watts, Richard J. Elementary Principles of Diffusion: Theory & the Chain Reaction. (Illus.). 307p. (Orig.). 1982. pap. 25.00x (ISBN 0-9609112-0-0). Desperation Pr.

DIFFUSION OF INNOVATIONS
see also Technology Transfer
Rogers, Everett M. Diffusion of Innovations. 3rd ed. (Illus.). 512p. 1982. text ed. 18.95 (ISBN 0-02-926650-5). Free Pr.

DIGESTION
see also Bile; Diet; Dyspepsia; Enzymes; Food; Metabolism, Disorders Of; Nutrition
Goebell, H., ed. European Pancreatic Club: EPC XIV Meeting, Essen Sept.-Oct. 1982, Abstracts. (Journal: Digestion: Vol. 25, No. 1). 80p. 1982. pap. 34.75 (ISBN 3-8055-3633-X). S Karger.
Stafford, D. A. Anaerobic Digestion. 1980. 94.50 (ISBN 0-85334-904-5, Pub. by Applied Sci England). Elsevier.

DIGESTIVE ORGANS-DISEASES
Weber-Stadelmann, W., ed. Adriamycin & Derivatives in Gastrointestinal Cancer. (Beitraege zur Onkologie. Contributions to Oncology Ser.: Vol. 15). (Illus.). vi, 144p. 1983. pap. 58.75 (ISBN 3-8055-3689-5). S Karger.

DIGESTS OF CASES (LAW)
see Law Reports, Digests, Etc.

DIGGERS
see Levellers

DIGITAL COMPUTER CIRCUITS
see Electronic Digital Computers-Circuits

DIGITAL COMPUTER SIMULATION
see also Artificial Intelligence
Deo, Narsingh. System Simulation with Digital Computer. (Illus.). 224p. 1983. pap. 17.95 (ISBN 0-13-881789-8). P-H.
Franks, Roger G. Modeling & Simulation in Chemical Engineering. LC 72-39717. 411p. 1972. 40.50x (ISBN 0-471-27535-2, Pub. by Wiley-Interscience). Wiley.
Heathkit-Zenith Educational Systems. Digital Techniques. 480p. 1983. 21.95 (ISBN 0-13-214049-7); pap. 14.95 (ISBN 0-13-214031-4). P-H.
Lewis, P. Enterprise Sandwich Shops: A Market Simulation Apple II Plus (on Apple with Applesoft) Version. 1982. 199.00 (ISBN 0-07-037536-4, G). McGraw.
Mitrani, I. Simulation Techniques for Discrete Event Systems. LC 82-4549. (Cambridge Computer Science Texts Ser.: No. 14). (Illus.). 200p. 1983. 29.95 (ISBN 0-521-23885-4); pap. 11.95 (ISBN 0-521-28282-9). Cambridge U Pr.
Schoemaker, S., ed. Computer Networks & Simulation II. 326p. 1982. 51.00 (ISBN 0-444-86438-5, North Holland). Elsevier.
Smith, Gaylord. The Briton Manufacturing Company: A Microcomputer Simulation. user's guide scp 8.00 (ISBN 0-06-046314-7, HarpC); complete package scp 225.00 (ISBN 0-06-046313-9). Har-Row.

DIGITAL COMPUTERS, ELECTRONIC
see Electronic Digital Computers

DIGITAL COUNTERS
Frenzel, Louis E. Digital Counter Handbook. 1981. pap. 10.95 (ISBN 0-672-21758-9). Sams.

DIGITAL ELECTRONICS
Booth, Taylor L. Digital Network & Computer Systems. 2nd ed. LC 77-10832. 592p. 1978. text ed. 30.95 (ISBN 0-471-08842-0); tchrs. manual avail. (ISBN 0-471-03049-X). Wiley.
Gold, Bernard & Rader, Charles M. Digital Processing of Signals. LC 82-14072. 282p. 1983. Repr. of 1969 ed. lib. bdg. p.n.s. (ISBN 0-89874-548-9). Krieger.
Hodges, David A. & Jackson, Horace G. Analysis & Design of Digital Integrated Circuits. (Series in Electrical Engineering). (Illus.). 448p. 1983. 29.50x (ISBN 0-07-029153-5, C); text ed. 15.00 (ISBN 0-07-029154-3). McGraw.
Kasper, Joseph & Feller, Steven. Digital Integrated Circuits. 197p. 1983. 19.95 (ISBN 0-13-213587-6); pap. 12.95 (ISBN 0-13-213579-5). P-H.
Kershaw, John K. Digital Electronics: Logic & Systems. 2nd ed. 1983. text ed. 27.95 (ISBN 0-534-01471-2, Breton Pubs). Wadsworth Pub.
Rohde, Ulrich L. Digital PLL Frequency Synthesizers: Theory & Design. (Illus.). 608p. 1983. text ed. 49.95 (ISBN 0-13-214239-2). P-H.
Warring, R. H. Understanding Digital Electronics. 128p. 1982. 39.00x (ISBN 0-7188-2521-7, Pub. by Lutterworth Pr England). State Mutual Bk.

DIGITAL FILTERS (MATHEMATICS)
Nussbaumer, H. Fast Fourier Transform & Convolution Algorithms. 2nd ed. (Springer Series in Information Sciences). (Illus.). 280p. 1982. pap. 28.00 (ISBN 0-686-82318-4). Springer-Verlag.

DIGITAL SIMULATION
see Digital Computer Simulation

DIMETHYL SULFOXIDE
Biological Actions of Dimethyl Sulfoxide, Vol.23. 508p. 1975. pap. 27.00 (ISBN 0-89766-155-9, Jacob & Herschler Pub.). NY Acad Sci.

DINE, JAMES
Belloli, Jay. Jim Dine: The Summers Collection. (Illus.). 28p. 1974. 4.50x (ISBN 0-686-99817-0). La Jolla Mus Contemp Art.

DINING
see Dinners and Dining

DINING CARS
see Railroads-Cars

DINING ESTABLISHMENTS
see Restaurants, Lunchrooms, Etc.

DINKA (NILOTIC TRIBE)
Ryle, J. Warriors of the White Nile: The Dinka. (Peoples of the Wild Ser.). 1982. 15.96 (ISBN 0-7054-0700-4, Pub. by Time-Life). Silver.

DINNERS AND DINING
see also Buffets (Cookery); Cookery; Desserts; Food; Menus
Cole, Michael & Frampton, Susan. Dining In--Vail. (Dining In--Ser.). (Illus.). 1983. pap. 8.95 (ISBN 0-89716-059-2). Peanut Butter.
Curtis, Donald R., ed. Indianapolis Dining Guide, 1983. (Illus.). 272p. (Orig.). 1982. pap. 6.95 (ISBN 0-9607968-1-9). Indytype.
Ewalt, Norma & Huth, Tom. Decadent Dinners & Lascivious Lunches. LC 82-71880. (Illus.). 320p. 1982. 10.95 (ISBN 0-686-82435-0). Clear Creek.
Golos, Natalie & Golbitz, Frances G. If This Is Tuesday It Must Be Chicken or How to Rotate Your Food for Better Health. Martin, Joan, ed. LC 81-13509. 109p. (Orig.). 1981. pap. 6.95 (ISBN 0-941962-00-8). Human Eco Res.
Hauser, Joan, ed. Manhattan Epicure. (Epicure Ser.). 160p. 1983. pap. 8.95 (ISBN 0-89716-123-8). Peanut Butter.
Nagasawa, Kimiko & Condon, Camy. Eating Cheap in Japan. (Illus.). 104p. (Orig.). 1972. pap. 7.50 (ISBN 0-8048-1401-5, Pub. by Shufunotomo Co Ltd Japan). C E Tuttle.
Wolf, Elliott, ed. Seattle Epicure. (Epicure Ser.). 1983. pap. 5.95 (ISBN 0-89716-115-7). Peanut Butter.

DINOSAURIA
Holler, Rich. Dinosaur Era. (Science Ser.). 24p. (gr. 3-9). 1979. wkbk. 5.00 (ISBN 0-8209-0159-8, S-21). ESP.
McGinnis, Helen J. Carnegie's Dinosaurs. Jacobs, Martina M., et al, eds. LC 82-70212. (Illus.). 120p. (Orig.). 1982. pap. 8.50 (ISBN 0-911239-00-6). Carnegie Board.

DINOSAURIA-JUVENILE LITERATURE
Lambert, Mark. Fifty Facts About Dinosaurs. (Fifty Facts About Ser.). (Illus.). 32p. (gr. 4-6). 1983. PLB 8.90 (ISBN 0-531-09209-7). Watts.
Lampton, Christopher. Dinosaurs & the Age of Reptiles. (First Bk.). (Illus.). 96p. (gr. 4 up). 1983. PLB 8.90 (ISBN 0-531-04526-9). Watts.
Wolf, Donald D. & Wolf, Margot L. Dinosaurs. (Matter of Fact Books Ser.). (Illus.). 64p. 1982. pap. 3.95 (ISBN 0-448-04084-0, G&D). Putnam Pub Group.

DIOCESAN SCHOOLS
see Church Schools

DIPLOMACY
see also Diplomatic and Consular Service; Diplomatic Negotiations in International Disputes; Diplomats; Treaties
also subdivision Foreign Relations under names of countries, e.g. United States-Foreign Relations
Borisov, C. B. & Dubinin, Y. V. Modern Diplomacy of Capitalist Powers. (World Leaders Speeches & Writings Ser.). 396p. 1983. 50.00 (ISBN 0-08-028173-7). Pergamon.
De Callieres. On the Manner of Negotiating with Princes. Whyte, A. F., tr. from Fr. LC 82-21800. 160p. 1983. pap. text ed. 8.75 (ISBN 0-8191-2923-2). U Pr of Amer.
Herz, Martin F., ed. Contacts with the Opposition: A Symposium. LC 79-91020. 72p. 1979. 3.00 (ISBN 0-934742-03-0, Inst Study Diplomacy). Geo U Sch For Serv.
Jones, Kenneth P. U. S. Diplomats in Europe Nineteen Hundred Nineteen-Nineteen Hundred Forty-One. (Illus.). 240p. 1983. Repr. lib. bdg. 35.00 (ISBN 0-87436-349-7); pap. text ed. 12.75 (ISBN 0-87436-351-9). ABC-Clio.
Kimball, Warren F., ed. American Diplomacy in the Twentieth Century. LC 78-81060. 1980. pap. text ed. 6.95 (ISBN 0-88273-020-7). Forum Pr IL.
Martin, Edwin M. Conference Diplomacy-A Case Study: The World Food Conference, Rome, 1974. LC 79-91018. 58p. 1979. 3.00 (ISBN 0-934742-01-4, Inst Study Diplomacy). Geo U Sch For Serv.
Papadopoulos, A. Multilateral Diplomacy Within the Commonwealth. 1982. lib. bdg. 39.50 (ISBN 90-247-2568-2, Pub. by Martinus Nijhoff Netherlands). Kluwer Boston.
Watson, A. Diplomacy: The Dialogue Between the States. 240p. 1982. 19.95 (ISBN 0-07-068461-8). McGraw.
Wilkowski, Jean M. Conference Diplomacy II A Case Study: The UN Conference on Science & Technology for Development, Vienna, 1979. LC 82-12103. 56p. 1982. 4.00 (ISBN 0-934742-20-0, Inst Study Diplomacy). Geo U Sch For Serv.

DIPLOMACY-DICTIONARIES
Barakat, Gamal. English-Arabic Dictionary of Diplomacy & Related Terminology. 1982. 25.00x (ISBN 0-86685-290-5). Intl Bk Ctr.

DIPLOMACY-HISTORY
see also Treaties
Gaddis, John L. Russia, the Soviet Union & the United States: An Interpretive History. LC 77-12763. (America & the World Ser.). 309p. 1978. pap. text ed. 11.50x (ISBN 0-471-28911-6). Cloth ed. 12.95 o.p. Wiley.
Jones, Raymond A. The British Diplomatic Service, 1815-1914. 315p. 1982. text ed. 11.50x (ISBN 0-88920-124-2, 40810, Pub. by Laurier U Pr). Humanities.

DIPLOMATIC AND CONSULAR SERVICE
see also Ambassadors; Diplomacy; Diplomats
also subdivisions Diplomatic and Consular Service, or Politics and Government under names of countries, e.g. United States-Diplomatic and Consular Service
Berman, Susan. Your Career in the Foreign Service. (Arco's Career Guide Ser.). (Illus.). 128p. 1983. lib. bdg. 7.95 (ISBN 0-668-05510-3); pap. 4.50 (ISBN 0-668-05517-0). Arco.
Berman, Susanna. Your Career in the International Field. (Arco's Career Guidance Ser.). (Illus.). 128p. 1983. lib. bdg. 7.95 (ISBN 0-668-05507-3); pap. 4.50 (ISBN 0-668-05515-4). Arco.

DIPLOMATIC NEGOTIATIONS IN INTERNATIONAL DISPUTES
De Callieres. On the Manner of Negotiating with Princes. Whyte, A. F., tr. from Fr. LC 82-21800. 160p. 1983. pap. text ed. 8.75 (ISBN 0-8191-2923-2). U Pr of Amer.
Herz, Martin F. David Bruce's "Long Telegram" of July 3, 1951. LC 78-71946. 26p. 1978. 1.50 (ISBN 0-686-83450-X, Inst Study Diplomacy). Geo U Sch For Serv.
--Making the World a Less Dangerous Place: Lessons learned from a Career in Diplomacy. LC 81-86226. 24p. 1981. 1.25 (ISBN 0-934742-15-4, Inst Study Diplomacy). Geo U Sch For Serv.
Ikle, Fred C. How Nations Negotiate. LC 76-8398. 264p. 1982. Repr. of 1964 ed. 20.00 (ISBN 0-527-44220-8, Inst Study Diplomacy). Geo U Sch For Serv.

DIPLOMATIC PROTESTS
see Diplomacy

DIPLOMATS
see also Ambassadors; Diplomatic and Consular Service
Diplomacy: The Role of the Wife: A Symposium. LC 81-917. 88p. 1981. 4.50 (ISBN 0-934742-10-3, Inst Study Diplomacy). Geo U Sch For Serv.
Faber, Richard. The Brave Courtier: Sir William Temple. 176p. 1983. 29.95 (ISBN 0-571-11982-4). Faber & Faber.
Herz, Martin F. David Bruce's "Long Telegram" of July 3, 1951. LC 78-71946. 26p. 1978. 1.50 (ISBN 0-686-83450-X, Inst Study Diplomacy). Geo U Sch For Serv.
Herz, Martin F. & Krogh, Peter F. Two Hundred Fifteen Days in the Life of an American Ambassador. LC 81-13346. 1981. 9.85 (ISBN 0-934742-12-X, Inst Study Diplomacy). Geo U Sch For Serv.

DIPSOMANIA
see Alcoholism

DIPTERA
see also Fleas; Flies;
also particular kinds of flies, gnats, etc. e.g. Mosquitoes
Stone, Alan, et al, eds. A Catalog of the Diptera of America North of Mexico. 2nd printing ed. 1700p. 1983. Repr. of 1965 ed. text ed. 37.50x (ISBN 0-87474-890-9). Smithsonian.

DIRECT ADVERTISING
see Advertising-Direct-Mail

DIRECT CURRENTS
see Electric Currents, Direct

DIRECT ENERGY CONVERSION
see also Controlled Fusion; Fuel Cells; Photoelectric Cells; Solar Batteries
Intersociety Energy Conversion Engineering Conference, 16th. Proceeding, 3 Vols. 2608p. 1981. Set. 165.00 (H00179). ASME.
Sorensen, Harry A. Energy Conversion Systems. 750p. 1983. text ed. 30.95 (ISBN 0-471-08872-2); price not set solutions manual (ISBN 0-471-87156-7). Wiley.

DIRECT-MAIL ADVERTISING
see Advertising-Direct-Mail

DIRECT TAXATION
see Income Tax; Taxation

DIRECTION, SENSE OF
see Orientation

DIRECTION, SPIRITUAL
see Spiritual Direction

DIRECTORIES
Here are entered works on the history, description, and bibliography of directories and directory-making. Specific directories are listed under the subdivision Directories under names of places and subjects, e.g. Schools-Directories; New York (City)-Directories.
Loomis, Kristin S. & Spaeth, Steven E., eds. National Directory of Addresses & Telephone Numbers: 1983 Edition. LC 81-52822. 1982. pap. 24.95 (ISBN 0-940994-25-9). Concord Ref Bks.

DIRECTORS, MOVING-PICTURE
see Moving-Picture Producers and Directors

DIRECTORS OF CORPORATIONS
see also Corporate Meetings
Mills, Geoffrey. On the Board. 232p. 1982. text ed. 35.50x (ISBN 0-900488-61-1). Gower Pub Ltd.
Trost, Arty & Rauner, Judy A. Gaining Momentum for Board Action. LC 82-17202. (Illus.). 104p. (Orig.). 1983. pap. 10.50x (ISBN 0-9604594-1-3). Marlborough Pubns.

White, Lawrence J. Corporate Governance in the 1980s: New Roles & Images for Directors & Executives. (Seven Springs Studies). 1981. pap. 3.00 (ISBN 0-943006-04-X). Seven Springs.

DIRECTORS OF RELIGIOUS EDUCATION

Baker's Record Book for Ministers. 64p. (Orig.). 1983. pap. 2.95 (ISBN 0-8010-0851-4). Baker Bk.

DIRIGIBLE BALLOONS

see Air-Ships

DISABILITY, READING

see Reading Disability

DISABILITY EVALUATION

see also Industrial Accidents

Colverd, Edward C. & Less, Menahem. Teaching Driver Education To The Physically Disabled: A Sample Course. 40p. 1978. 4.25 (ISBN 0-686-38805-4). Human Res Ctr.

Less, Menahem & Colverd, Edward C. Evaluating Driving Potential of Persons With Physical Disabilities. LC 78-62052. (Illus.). 36p. 1978. 4.25 (ISBN 0-686-38803-8). Human Res Ctr.

Rudman, Jack. Senior Services Disability Analyst. (Career Examination Ser.: C-859). (Cloth bdg. avail. on request). pap. 10.00 (ISBN 0-8373-0859-3). Natl Learning.

Singleton, W. T. & Debney, L. M., eds. Occupational Disability. (Illus.). 307p. 1982. 36.80 (ISBN 0-942068-02-5). Bogden & Son.

DISABILITY INSURANCE

see Insurance, Disability

DISABLED

see Handicapped

DISARMAMENT

see also Arbitration, International; Atomic Weapons and Disarmament; Militarism; Peace; Security, International

Albert, Michael & Dellinger, Dave, eds. Mobilizing for Survival. 300p. 1983. 20.00 (ISBN 0-89608-176-1); pap. 7.50 (ISBN 0-89608-175-3). South End Pr.

Bender, David L., ed. The Arms Race: Opposing Viewpoints. (Opposing Viewpoints Ser.). 1982. lib. bdg. 10.95 (ISBN 0-89908-339-0); pap. 5.95 (ISBN 0-89908-314-5). Greenhaven.

Chand, Attar. Disarmament, Detente & World Peace: A Bibliography with Selected Abstracts, 1916-1981. 167p. 1982. 22.95x (ISBN 0-940500-49-3, Pub. by Sterling India). Asia Bk Corp.

Dumas, Lloyd J. The Political Economy of Arms Reduction: Reversing Economic Delay. (AAAS Selected Symposium 80 Ser.). 162p. 1982. lib. bdg. 17.50x (ISBN 0-86531-405-5). Westview.

Ferguson, John. Disarmament: The Unanswerable Case. 112p. 1982. pap. 8.95 (ISBN 0-434-25707-9, Pub by Heinemann, England). David & Charles.

Heyer, Robert, ed. Nuclear Disarmament: Key Statements of Popes, Bishops, Councils & Churches. 1982. pap. 7.95 (ISBN 0-8091-2456-4). Paulist Pr.

United Nations. Disarmament: A Periodic Review by the United Nations, Vol. V, No. 1. 1982. 5.00 (ISBN 0-686-84895-0, E.82.IX.5). UN.

The United Nations Disarmament Yearbook: 1981, Vol. 6. 458p. 1982. pap. 35.00 (ISBN 0-686-82550-0, UN 82/9/6, UN). Unipub.

DISARMAMENT-ECONOMIC ASPECTS

Hartley, Keith. NATO Arms Co-Operation: A Study in Economics & Politics. 240p. 1983. text ed. 35.00x (ISBN 0-04-341022-7). Allen Unwin.

Tuomi & Vayrynen. Militarization & Arms Production. LC 82-16882. 320p. 1983. 30.00x (ISBN 0-312-53255-5). St Martin.

DISARMAMENT AND ATOMIC WEAPONS

see Atomic Weapons and Disarmament

DISASTER RELIEF

see also Civil Defense; Emergency Medical Services

Green, S. International Disaster Relief: Toward a Responsive System. 1977. 14.95 (ISBN 0-07-024287-9); pap. 3.95 (ISBN 0-07-024288-7). McGraw.

Models Rules for Disaster Relief Operations. 5.00 (ISBN 0-686-84893-4, E.82.XV.PE/8). UN.

DISASTERS

see also Accidents; Fires; Natural Disasters; Shipwrecks

Drabek, Thomas E. & Key, William H. Conquering Disaster: Family Recovery & Long Term Consequences. 485p. 1983. text ed. 39.50x (ISBN 0-8290-1000-9). Irvington.

DISCIPLES, TWELVE

see Apostles

DISCIPLES OF CHRIST

Borsh, Frederick H. Power in Weakness: New Hearing for Gospel Stories of Healing & Discipleship. LC 82-15997. 160p. 1983. pap. 8.95 (ISBN 0-8006-1703-7, 1-1703). Fortress.

Torrey, Charles G. Apocalypse of John. 1958. text ed. 29.50x (ISBN 0-686-83474-7). Elliots Bks.

DISCIPLESHIP

see Christian Life

DISCIPLINE, ECCLESIASTICAL

see Church Discipline

DISCIPLINE, INDUSTRIAL

see Labor Discipline

DISCIPLINE, LABOR

see Labor Discipline

DISCIPLINE, MENTAL

see Mental Discipline

DISCIPLINE, SCHOOL

see School Discipline

DISCIPLINE OF CHILDREN

see also School Discipline

Gibson, Janice T. Discipline Is Not a Dirty Word. 1983. 12.95 (ISBN 0-86616-027-2); pap. 7.95 (ISBN 0-686-42867-6). Greene.

Grey, Loren. Discipline Without Fear. 192p. 1982. pap. 6.00 (ISBN 0-939654-02-4). Social Interest.

--Discipline Without Tyranny. 192p. 1982. pap. 6.00 (ISBN 0-939654-03-2). Social Interest.

Larlham, Hattie. Dear Children. 152p. 1983. 9.95 (ISBN 0-8361-3325-0). Herald Pr.

Sabatino, David & Mann, Lester. Discipline & Behavioral Management: A Handbook of Tactics, Strategies & Programs. 300p. 1983. price not set (ISBN 0-89443-933-2). Aspen Systems.

DISCO DANCING

The Art of Disco Dancing. 176p. 9.75 (ISBN 0-88314-019-5). AAHPERD.

Morton, Pamela. Basics of Disco Dancing. (Illus.). 67p. 1981. pap. text ed. 2.95x (ISBN 0-89641-084-6). American Pr.

DISCOURSES

see Speeches, Addresses, etc.

DISCOVERERS

see Discoveries (In Geography); Explorers

DISCOVERIES (IN GEOGRAPHY)

see also Antarctic Regions; Arctic Regions; Explorers; Geography–History; Scientific Expeditions; Voyages and Travels

also subdivision Discovery and Exploration under names of countries, etc.

Grant, Neil & Jones, Jo. Discovering the World. (Full Color Fact Books). (Illus.). 32p. (gr. 4-12). 1982. PLB 7.95 (ISBN 0-8219-0011-0, 35548). EMC.

DISCOVERIES (IN SCIENCE)

see Industrial Arts; Inventions; Patents; Science

DISCRETE TIME SYSTEMS

see also Feedback Control Systems

Goessel, M. Nonlinear Time-Discrete Systems: A General Approach by Nonlinear Superposition. (Lecture Notes in Control & Information Science: Vol. 41). 112p. 1983. pap. 8.00 (ISBN 0-387-11914-0). Springer-Verlag.

Lucas, W. F., et al, eds. Modules in Applied Mathematics, Vol. 3: Discrete & System Models. (Illus.). 416p. 1983. 28.00 (ISBN 0-387-90724-6). Springer-Verlag.

Moroney, Paul. Issues in the Implementation of Digital Feedback Compensators. (Signal Processing, Optimization, & Control Ser.). (Illus.). 224p. 1983. 30.00x (ISBN 0-262-13185-4). MIT Pr.

DISCRIMINATION

Here are entered general works on social discrimination based on race, religion, sex, social minority status, or other factors.

see also Civil Rights; Discrimination in Employment; Minorities; Race Discrimination; Segregation; Sex Discrimination; Toleration

Rabier, Jacques-Rene & Inglehart, Ronald. Euro-Barometer 13: Regional Development & Integration, April 1980. LC 82-81760. 1982. write for info. (ISBN 0-89138-937-7, ICPSR 7957). ICPSR.

Readon, Betty. Discrimination, Vol. 2: No. 2. 111p. Date not set. 5.00 (ISBN 0-686-43044-1). Decade Media.

Shepard. Statistical Proof of Discrimination. 1980. 50.00 (ISBN 0-07-003470-2). McGraw.

DISCRIMINATION, RACE

see Race Discrimination

DISCRIMINATION, SEXUAL

see Sex Discrimination

DISCRIMINATION AGAINST WOMEN

see Sex Discrimination

DISCRIMINATION IN EMPLOYMENT

see also Age and Employment;

also subdivision Employment under names of social or racial groups, e.g. Afro-Americans–Employment; Women–Employment: etc

Parcel, Toby L. & Mueller, Charles W., eds. Ascription & Labor Markets: Race & Sex Difference in Earnings. LC 82-22741. (Quantitative Studies Social Relations (Monograph)). Date not set. price not set (ISBN 0-12-545020-6). Acad Pr.

Pepper, William F. & Kennedy, Florynce R. Sex Discrimination in Employment. 337p. 1982. 25.00 (ISBN 0-87215-331-2). Michie-Bobbs.

Sulton, Cynthia G. & Wolfe, Randy P. Equal Employment Opportunity & Affirmative Action: A Sourcebook for Court Managers. LC 82-8291. 64p. 1982. 10.00 (ISBN 0-89656-057-0). Natl Ctr St Courts.

Torrington, Derek & Hitner, Trevor. Management & the Multi-Racial Work Force. 117p. 1982. text ed. 34.00x (ISBN 0-566-00585-9). Gower Pub Ltd.

Wood, Mary A. & Gee, E. Gordon. Fair Employment Practice & Standards, Cases & Materials. (Contemporary Legal Education Ser.). 896p. 1982. text ed. 32.50 (ISBN 0-87215-498-X); 6.00 (ISBN 0-87215-553-6). Michie-Bobbs.

DISCRIMINATION IN EMPLOYMENT-LAW AND LEGISLATION

Friedman, Joel Wm. & Strickler, George M., Jr. Cases & Materials on the Law of Employment Discrimination. LC 82-21016. (University Casebook Ser.). 865p. 1982. text ed. write for info. (ISBN 0-88277-096-9). Foundation Pr.

DISCS

see Phonorecords

DISEASE (PATHOLOGY)

see Pathology

DISEASE, DIET IN

see Diet in Disease

DISEASE GERMS

see Bacteria, Pathogenic

DISEASE WARFARE

see Biological Warfare

DISEASES-CAUSES AND THEORIES OF CAUSATION

see also Accidents; Bacteria, Pathogenic; Communicable Diseases; Heredity; Infection; Traumatism

Beard, Howard. New Approach to Etiology Diagnosis, Treatment & Prevention of the Degenerative Diseases. 1965. 10.00x (ISBN 0-943080-14-2). Cancer Control Soc.

Cockburn, Eve & Cockburn, Aiden. Mummies, Diseases & Ancient Cultures. Abridged ed. LC 79-25682. (Illus.). 256p. Date not set. price not set (ISBN 0-521-27237-8). Cambridge U Pr.

Crowley, Leonard V. Introduction to Human Disease. 700p. 1983. text ed. 23.95 (ISBN 0-534-01264-7). Brooks-Cole.

Hudson, Robert P. Disease & It's Control: The Shaping of Modern Thought. LC 82-21135. (Contributions in Medical History: No. 12). 288p. 1983. lib. bdg. 29.95 (ISBN 0-313-23806-5, HHD/). Greenwood.

Sheppard, John R. & Anderson, V. Elving, eds. Membranes & Genetic Disease. LC 82-12672. (Progress in Clinical & Biological Research Ser.: Vol. 97). 422p. 1982. 68.00 (ISBN 0-8451-0097-1). A R Liss.

DISEASES-PREVENTION

see Medicine, Preventive

DISEASES-TRANSMISSION

see also Animals As Carriers of Disease; Communicable Diseases

Bulla & Cheng. Pathobiology of Invertebrate Vectors of Disease, Vol. 266. 1975. 64.00 (ISBN 0-89072-020-7). NY Acad Sci.

Locke, Steven & Hornig-Rohan, Mady. Mind & Immunity: Behavioral Immunology (1976-1982)--an Annotated Bibliography. 240p. (Orig.). 1983. 35.00 (ISBN 0-910903-01-8); pap. 22.50 (ISBN 0-910903-02-6). Elliot Pr.

DISEASES, CHRONIC

see Chronic Diseases

DISEASES, COMMUNICABLE

see Communicable Diseases

DISEASES, IATROGENIC

see Iatrogenic Diseases

DISEASES, MENTAL

see Mental Illness; Psychology, Pathological

DISEASES, OCCUPATIONAL

see Occupational Diseases

DISEASES OF ANIMALS

see Veterinary Medicine

DISEASES OF CHILDREN

see Children–Diseases; Infants–Diseases

DISEASES OF OCCUPATIONS

see Occupational Diseases

DISEASES OF PLANTS

see Plant Diseases

DISEASES OF THE BLOOD, DISEASES OF THE BRAIN, DISEASES OF THE HEART

see subdivision Diseases under specific subjects, e.g. Blood–Diseases; Brain–Diseases

DISEASES OF WOMEN

see Women–Diseases

DISINFECTION AND DISINFECTANTS

see also Sterilization

Block, Seymor S., ed. Disinfection, Sterilization & Preservation. 3rd ed. LC 82-24002. (Illus.). 1500p. 1983. text ed. price not set (ISBN 0-8121-0863-9). Lea & Febiger.

DISK RECORDING

see Phonorecords; Sound–Recording and Reproducing

DISMISSAL OF EMPLOYEES

see Employees, Dismissal Of

DISORDERS OF NUTRITION

see Nutrition Disorders

DISORDERS OF PERSONALITY

see Personality, Disorders Of

DISORDERS OF SPEECH

see Speech, Disorders Of

DISPARITY OF CULTUS

see Marriage, Mixed

DISPATCHING OF AIRPLANES

see Airplanes–Dispatching

DISPERSION

Meyer, Richard E., ed. Theory of Dispersed Multiphase Flow. (Symposium). Date not set. 28.00 (ISBN 0-12-493120-0). Acad Pr.

Tadros, T. F., ed. Effects of Polymers on Dispersion Properties. LC 81-68982. 432p. 1982. 36.00 (ISBN 0-12-682620-X). Acad Pr.

DISPERSION OF THE JEWS

see Jews–Diaspora

DISPERSOIDS

see Colloids

DISPLAY OF MERCHANDISE

see also Packaging

also names of articles manufactured; names of industries and trades

Colborne, Robert. Fundamentals of Merchandise Presentation. LC 82-61469. (Illus.). 208p. 1983. 18.00 (ISBN 0-911380-59-0). Signs of Times.

DISPLAY SYSTEMS, INFORMATION

see Information Display Systems

DISPOSAL OF REFUSE

see Refuse and Refuse Disposal

DISRAELI, BENJAMIN

see Beaconsfield, Benjamin Disraeli, 1st Earl of, 1804-1881

DISRAELI, ISAAC, 1766-1848

Frietzsche, Arthur H. The Monstrous Clever Young Man: The Novelist Disraeli & His Heroes. 60p. 1982. Repr. of 1959 ed. lib. bdg. 10.00 (ISBN 0-8495-1735-4). Arden Lib.

Raymond, E. T. Disraeli: Alien Patriot. 346p. 1982. Repr. of 1925 ed. lib. bdg. 50.00 (ISBN 0-89987-723-0). Darby Bks.

DISSECTION

Cuello, A. C. Brain Microdissection Techniques. 160p. 1983. write for info. (ISBN 0-471-10523-6, Pub. by Wiley-Interscience); pap. 24.95 (ISBN 0-471-90019-2, Pub. by Wiley-Interscience). Wiley.

Mizeres, N. J. Methods of Dissection. 176p. 1982. pap. 14.95 (ISBN 0-444-00721-0, Biomedical Pr). Elsevier.

DISSERTATIONS, ACADEMIC

see also Report Writing

Balian, Edward S. How to Design, Analyze, & Write Doctoral Research: The Practical Guidebook. LC 82-20164. (Illus.). 268p. (Orig.). 1983. lib. bdg. 22.75 (ISBN 0-8191-2879-1); pap. text ed. 11.75 (ISBN 0-8191-2880-5). U Pr of Amer.

Kugler, Paul. The Alchemy of Discourse: An Archetypal Approach to Language. 144p. 1982. 21.50 (ISBN 0-8387-5020-6). Bucknell U Pr.

Madsen, David. Successful Dissertations & Theses: A Guide to Graduate Student Research from Proposal to Completion. LC 82-49039. 1983. text ed. 12.95x (ISBN 0-87589-555-7). Jossey-Bass.

Mason, Abelle. Understanding Academic Lectures. (Illus.). 208p. 1983. pap. text ed. 9.95 (ISBN 0-13-936419-6). P-H.

Mauch & Birch. Guide to the Successful Thesis & Dissertation, Vol. 19. (Library & Informations Ser.). 352p. 1983. price not set (ISBN 0-8247-1800-3). Dekker.

Witt, Robert E. Marketing Doctoral Dissertation Abstracts, 1981. (Bibliography Ser.). 138p. 1982. pap. 11.00 (ISBN 0-686-83902-1). Am Mktg.

DISSOCIATION

Perrin, D. D., ed. Ionisation Constants of Inorganic Acids & Bases in Aqueous Solution, No.29. 2nd ed. (Chemical Data Ser.). 194p. 1982. 50.00 (ISBN 0-08-029214-3). Pergamon.

DISSOCIATION OF PERSONALITY

see Personality, Disorders Of

DISTRIBUTION, COOPERATIVE

see Cooperation; Cooperative Societies

DISTRIBUTION OF GOODS, PHYSICAL

see Physical Distribution of Goods

DISTRIBUTION OF INCOME

see Income

DISTRIBUTION OF WEALTH

see Wealth

DISTRIBUTIONS, THEORY OF (FUNCTIONAL ANALYSIS)

Friedlander, F. G. Introduction to the Theory of Distributions. LC 82-4504. 150p. 1983. 34.50 (ISBN 0-521-24300-9); pap. 14.95 (ISBN 0-521-28591-7). Cambridge U Pr.

Hoermander, L. The Analysis of Linear Partial Differential Operators I: Distribution Theory & Fourier Analysis. (Grundlehren der Mathematischen Wissenschaften: Vol. 256). (Illus.). 380p. 1983. 39.00 (ISBN 0-387-12104-8). Springer-Verlag.

DISTRICT NURSES

see Nurses and Nursing

DIVERSIFICATION IN INDUSTRY

OECD Staff. Product Durability & Product Life Extension: Their Contribution to Solid Waste Management. 129p. (Orig.). 1982. pap. 10.00x (ISBN 92-64-12293-1). OECD.

DIVES AND LAZARUS (PARABLE)

see Jesus Christ–Parables

DIVINE HEALING

see Faith-Cure; Miracles

DIVING

see also Swimming

Diving Rulebook, 1981. Date not set. 4.50 (ISBN 0-686-43033-6). AAU Pubns.

DIVING, SKIN

see Skin Diving

DIVINITY OF CHRIST

see Jesus Christ–Divinity

DIVISION

Mock, Valerie E. Division Drill. (Learning Workbooks Mathematics). (gr. 3-5). pap. 1.50 (ISBN 0-686-38848-8). Pitman.

DIVISION OF LABOR

see also Machinery in Industry

Dixon, Marlene & Jonas, Susanne, eds. The New Nomads: From Immigrant Labor to Transnational Working Class. LC 82-10356. (Contemporary Marxism Ser.). (Illus.). 165p. (Orig.). 1982. pap. 6.50 (ISBN 0-89935-018-6). Synthesis Pubns.

DIVISION OF POWERS
see Federal Government

DIVORCE
see also Divorcees; Custody of Children; Remarriage

Cantor, Dorothy W. & Drake, Ellen A. Divorced Parents & Their Children: A Guide for Mental Health Professionals. 1983. text ed. 19.95 (ISBN 0-8261-3560-9). Springer Pub.

Cauhape, Elizabeth. Fresh Starts: Men & Women after Divorce. 227p. 1983. 16.50 (ISBN 0-465-02553-6). Basic.

Correu, Larry M. Beyond the Broken Marriage. LC 82-13661. 144p. 1982. pap. 7.95 (ISBN 0-664-24446-7). Westminster.

Coulson, Robert. Fighting Fair. 224p. 1983. price not set. Free Pr.

Elliot, Elisabeth. What God Has Joined. 32p. 1983. Repr. 1.50 (ISBN 0-89107-276-4). Good News.

Fisher, Bruce. When Your Relationship Ends. 1981. pap. text ed. 6.00 (ISBN 0-9607250-0-8). Family Relations.

Francke, Linda B. Growing Up Divorced: Children of the Eighties. 1983. 16.50 (ISBN 0-671-25516-9, Linden). S&S.

Jacobson, Gerald. The Multiple Crises of Marital Separation & Divorce. (Seminars in Psychiatry Ser.). Date not set. price not set (ISBN 0-8089-1483-9). Grune.

Johnson, Margaret. Divorce Is A Family Affair. 128p. 1983. pap. 4.95 (ISBN 0-310-45831-5). Zondervan.

Kerpelman, Leonard. Divorce: A Man's Guide. 1983. price not set (ISBN 0-89651-151-0). Icarus.

Lamar, Kristena A. Divorce Guide for Oregon. 2nd ed. (Illus.). 120p. 1982. pap. 8.95 (ISBN 0-88908-813-6). Self Counsel Pr.

McNamara, Lynne & Morrison, Jennifer. Separation, Divorce & After. LC 82-2718. 192p. 1983. pap. 9.95 (ISBN 0-7022-1931-2). U of Queensland Pr.

Mumford, Amy R. When Divorce Ends Your Marriage...It Hurts. (Accent Expressions Ser.). (Illus.). 24p. (Orig.). 1982. 4.95 (ISBN 0-89636-099-7). Accent Bks.

Paylor, Neil & Head, Barry. Scences From A Divorce: A Book for Friends & Relatives of a Divorcing Family. 120p. 1983. pap. 6.95 (ISBN 0-86683-635-7). Winston Pr.

Pennington, Lucinda. The Hundred Forty-Nine Ways to Profit from Your Divorce. new ed. 228p. 1983. 12.95 (ISBN 0-672-52744-8). Bobbs.

Shapiro, Daniel Z. Thinking Divorce-Consider the Shocking Personal & Financial Reality. 125p. (Orig.). 1983. pap. price not set (ISBN 0-930256-11-5). Almar.

Weber, Eric & Simring, Steven S. How to Win Back the One You Love. 192p. 1983. 11.95 (ISBN 0-02-624700-3). Macmillan.

Wilkie, Jane. The Divorced Woman's Handbook: An Outline for Starting the First Year Alone. (Illus.). 1980. pap. 4.95 (ISBN 0-688-08607-1). Quill NY.

DIVORCE–BIBLICAL TEACHING

Woodrow, Ralph. Divorce & Remarriage: What Does the Bible Really Say? LC 82-99960. (Illus.). 1982. pap. 3.95 (ISBN 0-916938-06-9). R Woodrow.

DIVORCE–JUVENILE LITERATURE

Coleman, William L. What Children Need to Know When Parents Get Divorced. 128p. (gr. k-5). 1983. pap. 3.95 (ISBN 0-87123-612-5). Bethany Hse.

Miner, Jane C. Split Decision: Facing Divorce. Schroeder, Howard, ed. LC 82-1406. (Crisis Ser.). (Illus.). 64p. (gr. 4-5). 1982. lib. bdg. 7.95 (ISBN 0-89686-170-8). Crestwood Hse.

DIVORCE–GREAT BRITAIN

Ambrose, Peter & Harper, John. Surviving Divorce: Fathers & the Child. 226p. 1983. text ed. 24.95x (ISBN 0-86598-122-1). Rowman.

Search, Gay. Surviving Divorce: A British Handbook for Men. (Illus.). 128p. 1983. 16.50 (ISBN 0-241-10954-X, Pub. by Hamish Hamilton England). David & Charles.

DIVORCEES
see also Single-Parent Family

Cantor, Dorothy W. & Drake, Ellen A. Divorced Parents & Their Children: A Guide for Mental Health Professionals. 1983. text ed. 19.95 (ISBN 0-8261-3560-9). Springer Pub.

Jensen, Marilyn. Formerly Married: Learning to Live with Yourself. 120p. 1983. price not set (ISBN 0-664-27010-7). Westminster.

DIZZINESS
see Vertigo

DNA
see Deoxyribonucleic Acid

DO-IT-YOURSELF WORK
see specific fields of activity for do-it-yourself manuals in such fields, e.g. House Painting; Interior Decoration

DOCTOR-PATIENT RELATIONSHIP
see Physician and Patient

DOCTORS
see Physicians

DOCTORS' DEGREES
see Degrees, Academic

DOCTORS IN ART
see Medicine and Art

DOCTRINAL ANTHROPOLOGY
see Man (Theology)

DOCTRINAL THEOLOGY
see Theology, Doctrinal

DOCTRINE, CHRISTIAN (CATHOLIC CHURCH)
see Catechetics–Catholic Church

DOCTRINES
see Dogma; Theology, Doctrinal

DOCUMENTARY FILMS
see Moving-Pictures, Documentary

DOCUMENTARY PHOTOGRAPHY
see Photography, Documentary

DOCUMENTATION
see also Abstracting and Indexing Services; Archives; Bibliography; Cataloging; Classification–Books; Files and Filing (Documents); Indexing; Information Services; Information Storage and Retrieval Systems; Library Science; Museums; Translating Services

Technical Documentation Standards: For Computer Programmes & Computer Based Systems Used in Engineering. 133p. 1981. 165.00x (ISBN 0-85012-247-3, Pub. by Telford England). State Mutual Bk.

DOCUMENTS
see also Archives; Government Publications; Legal Documents

Norman, Adrian. Electronic Document Delivery: The Artemis Concept. 226p. 1982. 45.00 (ISBN 0-686-82554-3). Knowledge Indus.

DOCUMENTS, CONSERVATION OF
see Archives; Manuscripts–Conservation and Restoration

DOCUMENTS, IDENTIFICATION OF
see Legal Documents

DODGERS (BASEBALL CLUB)
see los Angeles Baseball Club (National League)

DODGSON, CHARLES LUTWIDGE, 1832-1898

Carroll, Lewis. The Philosopher's Alice: Alice's Adventures in Wonderland & Through the Looking-Glass. (Illus.). 256p. 1983. pap. 7.95 (ISBN 0-312-60518-8). St Martin.

DOG
see Dogs

DOG FOOD
see Dogs–Food

DOG GROOMING

Kohl, Sam & Goldstein, Catherine. The All Breed Dog Grooming Guide. LC 82-18446. (Illus.). 272p. 1983. spiral bdg. 16.95 (ISBN 0-668-05573-1, 5573). Arco.

Migliorini, Mario. Schnauzer Grooming Made Easy. (Illus.). 96p. 1983. spiral 9.95 (ISBN 0-668-05419-0, 5419). Arco.

DOG-SHOWS
see also Dog Grooming

Harmar, Hilary. Dogs: How to Train & Show Them. (Illus.). 192p. 1983. 22.50 (ISBN 0-7153-8323-X). David & Charles.

DOGMA
see also Theology, Doctrinal

Hyatt, Christopher S. & Slaughter, S. L. Dogma Daze. 40p. 1982. pap. 2.95 (ISBN 0-941404-22-6). Falcon Pr Az.

DOGMATIC THEOLOGY
see Theology, Doctrinal

DOGS
Here are entered works on dogs in general. For works on specific breeds of dogs see subdivision breeds, further subdivided by specific names, e.g. Dogs–Breeds–Dalmatians.
see also Dog-Shows; Hunting Dogs; Working Dogs

Baker, S. Games Dogs Play. Date not set. pap. 5.95 (ISBN 0-07-003452-4). McGraw.

Belfield, Wendel & Zucker, Martin. How to Have a Healthier Dog. 1982. pap. 2.95 (ISBN 0-451-11833-2, AE1833, Sig). NAL.

Caras, Roger. A Celebration of Dogs. 1982. 14.95 (ISBN 0-8129-1029-X). Times Bks.

Coffey, David. A Veterinary Surgeon's Guide to Dogs. (Illus.). 199p. 1980. 14.95 (ISBN 0-437-02500-4, Pub. by World's Work). David & Charles.

Dog Control Officer. (Career Examination Ser.: C-547). (Cloth bdg. avail. on request). pap. 10.00 (ISBN 0-8373-0547-0). Natl Learning.

Hull, Raymond. Man's Best Friend. (Illus.). 180p. 1982. Repr. of 1975 ed. pap. 5.97 (ISBN 0-88254-706-2). Hippocrene Bks.

Patient Care Publications. Your Dog: An Owner's Manual. (Illus.). 128p. 1983. pap. 6.95 (ISBN 0-686-82185-8, 5704). Arco.

Rudman, Jack. Dog Warden. (Career Examination Ser.: C-2645). (Cloth bdg. avail. on request). pap. 10.00 (ISBN 0-8373-2645-1). Natl Learning.

DOGS–BREEDS

Tortora, Daniel F. The Right Dog For You: Choosing a Breed that Matches Your Personality, Family & Lifestyle. (Illus.). 384p. 1983. pap. 8.95 (ISBN 0-671-47247-X, Fireside). S&S.

DOGS–BREEDS–BEAGLES

Schaeppi, U. The Neurologic Examination of Beagle Dogs in Toxicity Tests. (Lectures in Toxicology Ser.: No. 18). (Illus.). 1982. 60.00 (ISBN 0-08-029787-0). Pergamon.

DOGS–BREEDS–BULL TERRIERS

Horner, Tom. All About the Bull Terrier. (All About Ser.). (Illus.). 150p. 1983. 12.95 (ISBN 0-7207-1086-3, Pub by Michael Joseph). Merrimack Bk Serv.

DOGS–BREEDS–COCKER SPANIEL

Brearley, Joan M. The Book of the Cocker Spaniel. (Illus.). 300p. 1982. 29.95 (ISBN 0-87666-737-X, H-1034). TFH Pubns.

DOGS–BREEDS–COLLIES

Collie Club of America. The New Collie. LC 82-19049. 304p. 1983. 14.95 (ISBN 0-87605-130-1). Howell Bk.

DOGS–BREEDS–JACK RUSSELL TERRIER

Tottenham, Katherine & Nicholas, Anna K. This Is the Jack Russell Terrier. (Illus.). 192p. 1982. 19.95 (ISBN 0-87666-746-9, H-1053). TFH Pubns.

DOGS–BREEDS–ST. BERNARD

Weil, Martin. Saint Bernards. (Illus.). 1982. 4.95 (ISBN 0-87666-727-2, KW-109). TFH Pubns.

DOGS–BREEDS–SCOTTISH TERRIERS

T.F.H. Staff. Scottish Terrier. (Illus.). 128p. 1982. 4.95 (ISBN 0-87666-728-0, KW-103). TFH Pubns.

DOGS–BREEDS–STAFFORDSHIRE TERRIER

Morley, W. M. & Nicholas, Anna K. This Is the Staffordshire Bull Terrier. (Illus.). 192p. 1982. 19.95 (ISBN 0-87666-745-0, H-1054). TFH Pubns.

DOGS–DICTIONARIES

Spira, Harold R. Canine Terminology. (Illus.). 147p. 1983. 29.95 (ISBN 0-06-312047-X, Dist. by Har-Row). Howell Bk.

DOGS–EXHIBITIONS
see Dog-Shows

DOGS–FOOD

Edney, A. T., ed. Dog & Cat Nutrition: A Handbook for Students, Veterinarians, Breeders & Owners. (Illus.). 124p. 1982. 24.00 (ISBN 0-08-028891-X); pap. 12.00 (ISBN 0-08-028890-1). Pergamon.

DOGS–GROOMING
see Dog Grooming

DOGS–JUVENILE LITERATURE

Clements. Dog & Puppies. 1983. 5.95 (ISBN 0-86020-647-5, 15111); pap. 2.95 (ISBN 0-86020-646-7, 15112). EDC.

Gackenbach, Dick. Claude the Dog. 32p. (ps-2). 1974. 7.95 (ISBN 0-395-28792-8, Clarion). HM.

DOGS–LAWS AND LEGISLATION

Rudman, Jack. Senior Dog Warden. (Career Examination Ser.: C-2646). (Cloth bdg. avail. on request). pap. 12.00 (ISBN 0-8373-2646-X). Natl Learning.

DOGS–PSYCHOLOGY

Baker, S. Games Dogs Play. Date not set. pap. 5.95 (ISBN 0-07-003452-4). McGraw.

DOGS–TRAINING

Douglas, James. Gundog Training. (Illus.). 144p. 1983. 17.50 (ISBN 0-7153-8336-1). David & Charles.

Haggerty, Arthur J. & Benjamin, Carol L. Dog Tricks. LC 77-16919. (Illus.). 160p. 1982. Repr. 9.95 (ISBN 0-87605-517-X). Howell Bk.

Harmar, Hilary. Dogs: How to Train & Show Them. (Illus.). 192p. 1983. 22.50 (ISBN 0-7153-8323-X). David & Charles.

Keim, Abe. Complete Guide: How to Raise, Train & Sell Puppies Successfully. Printing, Lelli, ed. 104p. (Orig.). Date not set. pap. price not set. A Keim.

Mulvany, Mollie. All About Obedience Training. (All About Ser.). (Illus.). 150p. 1983. 12.95 (ISBN 0-7207-1089-8, Pub by Michael Joseph). Merrimack Bk Serv.

Radcliffe, Talbot. Spaniels for Sport. 136p. 1983. text ed. 8.95 (ISBN 0-571-08772-8). Faber & Faber.

Volhard, Joachim J. & Fisher, Gail T. Training Your Dog: The Step-by-Step Manual. LC 82-21327. (Illus.). 240p. 1983. 12.95 (ISBN 0-87605-775-X). Howell Bk.

DOLL CLOTHES

Knitting & Crocheting for Antique Dolls, 3 vols. 32p. 1981. pap. 3.95 ea. Vol. 1 (ISBN 0-87588-179-3). Vol. 2 (ISBN 0-87588-180-7). Vol. 3 (ISBN 0-87588-181-5). Hobby Hse.

McKee, Carol. Lenci Clothes. 124p. 1982. 17.95 (ISBN 0-87588-191-2). Hobby Hse.

Ulseth, Shannon. Antique Children's Fashions. 126p. 1982. pap. 12.95 (ISBN 0-87588-192-0). Hobby Hse.

Welker, Lauren. Fashions to Fit Ginny & Jill. 32p. 1982. pap. 4.95 (ISBN 0-87588-183-1). Hobby Hse.

DOLL-HOUSES

Baggett, Glick. Dollhouse Kit & Dining Room Accessories. 30p. pap. 1.95 (ISBN 0-87588-150-5). Hobby Hse.

--Dollhouse Lamps & Chandeliers. 30p. pap. 1.95 (ISBN 0-87588-149-1). Hobby Hse.

Byfield, Magdelina. In a Miniature Garden. 64p. pap. 6.95 (ISBN 0-87588-175-0). Hobby Hse.

Dodge, Venus & Dodge, Martin. The Doll's House Do-It Yourself Book. LC 82-19486. (Illus.). 224p. 1983. 16.95 (ISBN 0-8069-5484-1); pap. 9.95 (ISBN 0-8069-7710-8). Sterling.

Maidment, Patricia. How to Make & Furnish A Dollhouse for a Hundred Dollars or Less. new ed. 192p. 1983. 16.95 (ISBN 0-672-52742-1); pap. 10.95 (ISBN 0-672-52745-6). Bobbs.

DOLL MAKING
see Dollmaking

DOLLMAKING

Neuschutz, Karin. The Doll Book. Schneider, Ingun, tr. from Swedish. (Illus.). 184p. (Orig.). 1983. pap. 8.95 (ISBN 0-943914-01-9, Dist. by Kampmann & Co). Larson Pubns Inc.

DOLLS
see also Doll-Houses; Dollmaking; Katcinas

Axe, John. Collectible Black Dolls. 48p. 1978. pap. 4.95 (ISBN 0-87588-138-6). Hobby Hse.

--The Encyclopedia of Celebrity Dolls. 420p. 1983. 27.50 (ISBN 0-87588-186-6). Hobby Hse.

Axe, John, ed. Collecting Modern Dolls. 64p. 1981. pap. 7.95 (ISBN 0-87588-178-5). Hobby Hse.

Baggett, Glick. Dollhouse Kit & Dining Room Accessories. 30p. pap. 1.95 (ISBN 0-87588-150-5). Hobby Hse.

Doll Collector's Manual. 1983. 12.95 (ISBN 0-686-42808-0). Hobby Hse.

Felger, Donna, ed. Doll Catalog. 3rd ed. 254p. 1982. pap. 8.95 (ISBN 0-87588-188-2). Hobby Hse.

Foulke, Jan. Blue Book of Dolls & Values. 5th ed. 364p. 1982. pap. 12.95 (ISBN 0-87588-189-0). Hobby Hse.

Haines, E. Early American Brides. 150p. 1982. pap. 12.95 (ISBN 0-87588-176-9). Hobby Hse.

Heyerdahl, V., ed. Best of the Doll Reader. 250p. 1980. pap. 9.95 (ISBN 0-87588-187-4). Hobby Hse.

Hillier, Mary. Pollock's Dictionary of English Dolls. 1983. 19.95 (ISBN 0-517-54922-0). Crown.

Hoyer, Mary. Mary Hoyer & Her Dolls. 232p. 1982. 17.95 (ISBN 0-87588-182-3). Hobby Hse.

Lutz, Nancie A. The Doll Directory: Including Miniatures. (Illus.). 180p. (Orig.). lib. bdg. 29.00 (ISBN 0-940070-17-0); pap. 9.50 (ISBN 0-940070-16-2). Doll Works.

Neuschutz, Karin. The Doll Book. Schneider, Ingun, tr. from Swedish. (Illus.). 184p. (Orig.). 1983. pap. 8.95 (ISBN 0-943914-01-9, Dist. by Kampmann & Co). Larson Pubns Inc.

The Official 1983 Price Guide to Dolls. 1st ed. LC 82-84647. 240p. 1983. pap. 2.95 (ISBN 0-87637-316-3). Hse of Collectibles.

Price Guide for Madame Alexander Dolls. 4th ed. 1983. 8.00 (ISBN 0-686-84006-2). R Shoemaker.

Schweiter, John C. The ABC of Doll Collecting. LC 81-8764. (Illus.). 160p. 1983. pap. 8.95 (ISBN 0-8069-7696-9). Sterling.

Seeley, Mildred & Seeley, Colleen. Doll Collecting for Fun & Profit. LC 82-84016. (Illus.). 144p. 1983. 14.95 (ISBN 0-89586-207-7). H P Bks.

Smith, Patricia. Effanbee Dolls. 248p. Date not set. 19.95 (ISBN 0-89145-202-8). Collector Bks.

Uhl, Marjorie V. Madame Alexander Dolls Are Made With Love. Ltd. ed. (Illus.). 164p. 40.00 (ISBN 0-9608590-1-2). From Me.

--Madame Alexander Dolls on Review. LC 81-90052. (Illus.). 231p. 1981. 29.95 (ISBN 0-9608590-0-4). From Me.

Waugh, Carol-Lynn. Petite Portraits. 224p. 1982. pap. 12.95 (ISBN 0-87588-190-4). Hobby Hse.

DOLLS–HISTORY

Foulke, Jan. Kestner: King of Dollmakers. 5th ed. 236p. 1982. 19.95 (ISBN 0-87588-185-8). Hobby Hse.

DOLLS–JUVENILE LITERATURE

Horwitz, Joshua. Doll Hospital. LC 82-14508. (Illus.). 56p. (gr. 3-7). 1983. 10.95 (ISBN 0-394-85332-6); PLB 10.99 (ISBN 0-394-95332-0). Pantheon.

DOLLS' CLOTHES
see Doll Clothes

DOLPHINS
see also Porpoises

Cousteau, Jacques-Yves & Diola, Philippe. Dolphins. (Undersea Discoveries Ser.). (Illus.). 304p. 1983. pap. 10.95 (ISBN 0-89104-076-5, A & W Visual Library). A & W Pubs.

Dobbs, Horace. Follow the Wild Dolphins. LC 82-5712. (Illus.). 292p. 1982. 15.95 (ISBN 0-312-29752-1). St Martin.

Purves, P. E. & Pilleri, G., eds. Echolocation in Whales & Dolphins. write for info. (ISBN 0-12-567960-2). Acad Pr.

DOMAIN, EMINENT
see Eminent Domain

DOMESTIC ANIMALS
see also Animals, Treatment of; Cats; Cattle; Cows; Dogs; Goats; Horses; Livestock; Pets; Sheep; Swine

Ewer, T. K. Practical Animal Husbandry. (Illus.). 265p. 1982. text ed. 25.00 (ISBN 0-7236-0635-8). Wright-PSG.

Hammond, J., Jr. & Robinson, T. Hammond's Farm Animals. 350p. 1982. pap. text ed. 35.00 (ISBN 0-686-38087-8). E Arnold.

Lazarus, Pat. Keep Your Pet Healthy the Natural Way. 224p. 1983. 12.95 (ISBN 0-672-52726-X). Bobbs.

DOMESTIC ANIMALS–ANATOMY
see Veterinary Anatomy

DOMESTIC ANIMALS–DISEASES
see Veterinary Medicine

DOMESTIC ANIMALS–JUVENILE LITERATURE

Miller, Jane. Farm Counting Book. (Illus.). 32p. (ps-3). 1983. 6.95 (ISBN 0-13-304790-3). P-H.

DOMESTIC ANIMALS–LAW

Favre, David S. & Loring, Murray, eds. Animal Law. LC 82-23130. 296p. 1983. lib. bdg. 35.00 (ISBN 0-89930-021-9, LAL/, Quorum). Greenwood.

DOMESTIC APPLIANCES
see Household Appliances

DOMESTIC ARCHITECTURE
see Architecture, Domestic

DOMESTIC ECONOMY
see Home Economics

DOMESTIC JURISDICTION
see Jurisdiction (International Law)

DOMESTIC RELATIONS
see also Children–Law; Family; Guardian and Ward; Husband and Wife; Parent and Child (Law)

Areen, Judith. Cases & Materials on Family Law: 1983 Supplement. (University Casebook Ser.). 393p. 1982. pap. text ed. write for info. (ISBN 0-88277-107-8). Foundation Pr.

Bean, L. Lee. Domestic Relations: A Virginia Law Practice System. 400p. 1982. 75.00 (ISBN 0-87215-508-0). Michie-Bobbs.

Domestic Violence. pap. 3.50 (ISBN 0-686-81724-9). NCJW.
Finkelhor, David & Gelles, Richard J., eds. The Dark Side of Families: Current Family Violence Research. 384p. 1983. 29.95 (ISBN 0-8039-1934-4); pap. 14.95 (ISBN 0-8039-1935-2). Sage.
Hunt, Jeanne, ed. Being A Loving Wife. LC 82-48422. (Christian Reader Ser.). 128p. (Orig.). 1983. pap. 5.72i (ISBN 0-06-061386-6, HarpR). Har-Row.
Redden, Kenneth L. Federal Regulation of Family Law. (Federal Law Library). 457p. 1982. 40.00 (ISBN 0-87215-558-7). Michie-Bobbs.
Van Arsdale, Robert S. The Unknown Domestic Life of Primitive Men & Women. (The Great Currents of History Library Bks). (Illus.). 147p. 1983. 67.45 (ISBN 0-89266-384-7). Am Classical Coll Pr.
Weyrauch, Walter O. & Katz, Sanford N. American Family Law in Transition. 650p. 1983. text ed. 35.00 (ISBN 0-87179-390-3). BNA.

DOMESTIC SCIENCE
see Home Economics

DOMESTICATION
see Domestic Animals; Plants, Cultivated

DOMESTICS
see Servants

DOMINICAN REPUBLIC-FOREIGN RELATIONS-UNITED STATES
Bracey, Audrey. Resolution of the Dominican Crisis, 1965: A Study in Mediation. LC 80-27239. 64p. 1980. 3.50 (ISBN 0-934742-04-9, Inst Study Diplomacy). Geo U Sch For Serv.
Calder, Bruce J. The Impact of Intervention: The Dominican Republic During the U. S. Occupation of 1916-1924. (Texas Pan American Ser.). (Illus.). 352p. 1983. text ed. 22.50x (ISBN 0-292-73830-7). U of Tex Pr.

DOMINICAN REPUBLIC-HISTORY
Bracey, Audrey. Resolution of the Dominican Crisis, 1965: A Study in Mediation. LC 80-27239. 64p. 1980. 3.50 (ISBN 0-934742-04-9, Inst Study Diplomacy). Geo U Sch For Serv.

DOMINION OF THE SEA
see Maritime Law

DOMINIONS, BRITISH
see Commonwealth of Nations

DON JUAN
see Juan, Don

DONATELLO I.E., DONATO DI NICCOLO DI BETTO BARDI, 1386?-1466
Greenhalgh, Michael. Donatello & His Sources. (Illus.). 200p. 1982. text ed. 54.50x (ISBN 0-8419-0827-3). Holmes & Meier.
Lightbown, Ronald W. Donatello & Michelozzo: An Artistic Partnership & Its Patrons in the Early Renaissance, 2 vols. (Illus.). 460p. 1980. 74.00x (ISBN 0-19-921024-1). Oxford U Pr.

DONATIONS
see Charitable Uses, Trusts and Foundations; Endowments; Gifts

DOOMSDAY
see Judgment Day

DOOR PORTERS
see Dummy Board Figures

DOPING IN SPORTS
Taylor, William N. Anabolic Steroids & the Athlete. LC 82-17269. (Illus.). 128p. 1982. pap. 13.95x (ISBN 0-89950-055-2). McFarland & Co.

DORSET, ENGLAND
Mervyn, P. Memoirs of a Mis-spent Youth. 1982. 38.00x (ISBN 0-686-99795-6, Pub. by Sycamore Pr England). State Mutual Bk.

DORSET, ENGLAND-DESCRIPTION AND TRAVEL-GUIDEBOOKS
Treves, Frederick. Highways & Byways of Dorset. 376p. 1982. 30.00x (ISBN 0-7045-0430-8, Pub. by Wildwood House). State Mutual Bk.

DOSIMETRY
see Drugs-Dosage; Radiation Dosimetry

DOSTOEVSKII, FEDOR MIKHAILOVICH, 1821-1881
Jones, Malcolm V. & Terry, Garth M., eds. New Essays on Dostoyevsky. LC 82-14566. 256p. Date not set. 39.50 (ISBN 0-521-24890-6). Cambridge U Pr.

DOUBLE CONSCIOUSNESS
see Personality, Disorders Of

DOUBLE EMPLOYMENT
see Supplementary Employment

DOUBLE ENTRY BOOKKEEPING
see Bookkeeping

DOUBLE STARS
see Stars, Double

DOUBT
see Belief and Doubt

DOUGLAS, WILLIAM ORVILLE, 1898-
Douglas, William O. Go East, Young Man: The Early Years. LC 81-4196. (Illus.). 544p. pap. 7.95 (ISBN 0-394-71165-3, Vin). Random.

DOUGLASS, FREDERICK, 1817?-1895
Santrey, Laurence. Young Frederick Douglass: Fight for Freedom. LC 82-15993. (Illus.). 48p. (gr. 4-6). 1983. PLB 6.89 (ISBN 0-89375-857-4); pap. text ed. 1.95 (ISBN 0-89375-858-2). Troll Assocs.

DOVES
see Pigeons

DOYLE, ARTHUR CONAN, SIR, 1859-1930
Redmond, Donald A. Sherlock Homes, a Study in Sources. 375p. 1982. 24.95 (ISBN 0-7735-0391-9). McGill-Queens U Pr.

DRAFT, MILITARY
see Military Service, Compulsory

DRAFT HORSES
Lavine, Sigmund A. & Casey, Brigid. Wonders of Draft Horses. LC 82-46002. (Wonders Ser.). (Illus.). 80p. (gr. 4 up). 1983. PLB 9.95 (ISBN 0-396-08138-X). Dodd.
Miller, Lynn R. Work Horse Handbook. (Illus.). 224p. 1983. pap. 12.95 (ISBN 0-686-83703-7, ScribT). Scribner.

DRAFTING, ELECTRONIC
see Electronic Drafting

DRAFTING, MECHANICAL
see Mechanical Drawing

DRAINAGE
Here are entered only works relating to land drainage, as distinguished from sewerage and house drainage.
see also Marshes; Moors and Heaths; Sewerage
Advances in Drainage. LC 82-73786. 177p. 1982. pap. 18.50 (ISBN 0-916150-47-X). Am Soc Ag Eng.
Bumli, George R., ed. Principles of Project Formulation for Irrigation & Drainage Projects. LC 82-73505. 132p. 1982. pap. text ed. 15.75 (ISBN 0-87262-345-9). Am Soc Civil Eng.
Kruse, E. G. & Burdick, C. R., eds. Environmentally Sound Water & Soil Management. LC 82-72213. 544p. 1982. pap. text ed. 42.50 (ISBN 0-87262-312-2). Am Soc Civil Eng.
Lysimeters. (FAO Irrigation & Drainage Paper: No. 39). 68p. 1982. pap. 7.50 (ISBN 92-5-101186-9, F2330, FAO). Unipub.
Port Sines Investigating Panel. Failure of the Breakwater at Port Sines, Portugal. LC 82-70493. 296p. 1982. pap. text ed. 22.00 (ISBN 0-686-82486-5). Am Soc Civil Eng.
Vertical Drains. 100p. 1982. 90.00x (ISBN 0-7277-0102-9, Pub. by Telford England). State Mutual Bk.

DRAINAGE, HOUSE
see also Plumbing; Sanitary Engineering; Sewerage
Briggs Amasco Ltd. Flat Roofing: A Guide to Good Practice. (Illus.). 216p. 1982. pap. 33.95 (ISBN 0-9507919-0-3, Pub. by RIBA). Intl Schol Bk Serv.

DRAMA
Here are entered works dealing with the subject of the drama in general. Works on the history and criticism of the drama are entered under Drama-History and Criticism. Collections of drama are entered under Drama-Collections. Collections of drama of specific nationalities are entered as English Drama, French Drama, etc.
see also Acting; Ballet; Characters and Characteristics in Literature; Children's Plays; Christmas Plays; College and School Drama; Comedy; Dialogue; Dramatists; Masques; Mysteries and Miracle-Plays; Opera; Puppets and Puppet-Plays; Skits, Stunts, etc.; Television Plays; Theater; Tragedy
also drama of specific nationalities, e.g. English Drama, French Drama; subdivision Drama under special subjects and names of persons, e.g. Indians of North America-Drama; Lincoln, Abraham, Pres., United States-drama
De Rohan, Pierre, ed. Federal Theatre Plays: 3 Plays. LC 72-2386. (Illus.). 1973. lib. bdg. 22.50 (ISBN 0-306-70494-3). Da Capo.
Hampton, Christopher. Tales from Hollywood. 96p. (Orig.). 1983. pap. 7.95 (ISBN 0-571-11883-6). Faber & Faber.
Ross, Beverly & Durgin, Jean. Junior Broadway. LC 82-23983. (Illus.). 225p. (Orig.). 1983. pap. 13.95x (ISBN 0-89950-033-1). McFarland & Co.

DRAMA-BIOGRAPHY
see Dramatists

DRAMA-COLLECTIONS
Beadle, Richard, ed. The York Cycle of Plays. 600p. 1982. text ed. 98.50 (ISBN 0-7131-6326-7). E Arnold.
A Book of Short Plays XV-XX Centuries. 299p. 1982. Repr. of 1940 ed. lib. bdg. 35.00 (ISBN 0-89984-016-7). Century Bookbindery.

DRAMA-COLLECTIONS-20TH CENTURY
Foster, Rick, ed. West Coast Plays, No. 11-12. (Illus.). 369p. (Orig.). 1982. pap. 9.95 (ISBN 0-934782-11-3). West Coast Plays.
Foundation of the Dramatists Guild Editors. The Young Playwrights Festival Collection. 256p. 1983. pap. 3.95 (ISBN 0-380-83642-4, Bard). Avon.

DRAMA-HISTORY AND CRITICISM
see also Music-Yearbooks; Theater-United States
also similar headings
Borras, A. A., ed. The Theatre & Hispanic Life: Essays in Honour of Neale H. Taylor. 97p. 1982. text ed. 11.50x (ISBN 0-88920-129-3, Pub. by Wilfred Laurier U Pr Canada). Humanities.
Hartigan, Karelisa V. All the World... Drama Past & Present. LC 82-40207. 148p. 1983. lib. bdg. 20.00 (ISBN 0-8191-2711-6); pap. text ed. 8.25 (ISBN 0-8191-2712-4). U Pr of Amer.
Kermode, Frank, ed. Shakespeare, Spenser, Donne: Renaissance Essays. 304p. 1971. 18.95 (ISBN 0-7100-7003-9). Routledge & Kegan.
Kimberling, C. Ronald. Kenneth Burke's Dramatism & Popular Arts. LC 81-85522. 108p. 1982. 11.95 (ISBN 0-87972-195-2); pap. 5.95 (ISBN 0-87972-196-0). Bowling Green Univ.
Saunders, Jeraldine. Cruise Diary. (Illus.). 1982. 9.95 (ISBN 0-686-84160-3). J P Tarcher.
Vinson, James & Kirkpatrick, Daniel, eds. Contemporary Dramatists. 3rd ed. LC 82-22994. 1024p. 1982. 55.00x (ISBN 0-312-16664-8). St Martin.
White, Kenneth, ed. Alogical Modern Drama. (Faux Titre Band Ser.: No. 10). 68p. 1982. pap. text ed. 9.25x (ISBN 90-6203-784-4, Pub. by Rodopi Holland). Humanities.

DRAMA-HISTORY AND CRITICISM-20TH CENTURY
Esslin, Martin. Theatre of the Absurd. 1983. pap. 5.95 (ISBN 0-14-020929-8, Pelican). Penguin.
Rosen, Carol. Plays of Impasse: The Institutional Setting in Contemporary Drama. LC 82-61381. (Illus.). 304p. 1983. 20.00x (ISBN 0-691-06565-9). Princeton U Pr.
Skinner, Dana R. Our Changing Theatre. 327p. 1982. Repr. of 1931 ed. lib. bdg. 35.00 (ISBN 0-8495-4967-1). Arden Lib.

DRAMA-OUTLINES, SYLLABI, ETC.
Calandra, Denis. Comedy of Errors Notes. Bd. with Love's Labour's Lost & The Two Gentlemen of Verona Notes. 88p. (Orig.). 1982. pap. 2.75 (ISBN 0-8220-0010-5). Cliffs.

DRAMA-PRODUCTION AND DIRECTION
see Theater-Production and Direction

DRAMA-SELECTIONS
see Drama-Collections

DRAMA-STUDY AND TEACHING
see also Drama in Education
Ball, David. Backwards & Forwards: A Technical Manual for Reading Plays. 128p. (Orig.). 1983. pap. price not set (ISBN 0-8093-1110-0). S Ill U Pr.
Peachment, Brian. Educated Drama. 232p. 1976. 29.00x (ISBN 0-7121-0552-2, Pub. by Macdonald & Evans). State Mutual Bk.
Wooton, Margaret, ed. New Directions in Drama Teaching. 224p. (Orig.). 1982. pap. text ed. 15.00x (ISBN 0-435-18927-1). Heinemann Ed.

DRAMA-TECHNIQUE
see also Plots (Drama, Novel, Etc.)
Averett, Tanner F. Basic Drama Projects. 4th ed. (Illus.). 286p. 1982. pap. text ed. 7.50 (ISBN 0-931054-06-0). Clark Pub.

DRAMA, ACADEMIC
see College and School Drama

DRAMA, MODERN
see Drama; Drama-Collections-20th Century

DRAMA IN EDUCATION
see also Acting; College and School Drama; Schools-Exercises and Recreations; Theater
Jackson, Tony, ed. Learning Through Theatre: Essays & Casebooks on Theatre in Education. 240p. 1982. 20.00 (ISBN 0-7190-0789-5). Manchester.
Peachment, Brian. Educated Drama. 232p. 1976. 29.00x (ISBN 0-7121-0552-2, Pub. by Macdonald & Evans). State Mutual Bk.
Stewig, John W. Informal Drama in the Elementary Language Arts Program. (Orig.). 1983. pap. text ed. write for info. Tchrs Coll.

DRAMATIC MUSIC
see Musical Revue, Comedy, Etc.; Opera

DRAMATISTS
Johnson, Robert K. Neil Simon. (United States Authors Ser.). 228p. 1983. lib. bdg. 15.95 (ISBN 0-8057-7387-8, Twayne). G K Hall.
Thompson, Laurie. Stig Dagerman. (World Authors Ser.: No. 676). 166p. 1983. lib. bdg. 19.95 (ISBN 0-8057-6523-9, Twayne). G K Hall.
Vinson, James & Kirkpatrick, Daniel, eds. Contemporary Dramatists. 3rd ed. LC 82-22994. 1024p. 1982. 55.00x (ISBN 0-312-16664-8). St Martin.

DRAMATURGY
see Drama-Technique

DRAMSHOPS
see Hotels, Taverns, etc.

DRAPERY
Center for Self Sufficiency Research Division Staff. Guide to Craft, Quilt, Drapery, Etc. Pattern Sources. 35p. 1983. pap. text ed. 15.95 (ISBN 0-910811-31-8). Center Self.
Neal. Custom Draperies in Interior Design. 1982. 24.95 (ISBN 0-444-00640-0). Elsevier.

DRAW-POKER
see Poker

DRAWING
see also Anatomy, Artistic; Architectural Drawing; Caricature; Design, Decorative; Drawing, Psychology of; Drawings; Fashion Drawing; Graphic Methods; Illustration of Books; Mechanical Drawing; Painting; Pastel Drawing; Pencil Drawing; Perspective; Portrait Drawing
also Birds in Art; Dogs-Pictures, Illustrations, Etc., and similar headings
Hill, Adrian. What Shall We Draw? (Illus.). 80p. 1983. 8.95 (ISBN 0-87523-202-7). Emerson.
Jacobs, Valerie. Black & White Shaded Drawing. (Illus.). 64p. 1975. pap. 5.50 (ISBN 0-85440-295-0, Pub. by Steinerbooks). Anthroposophic.
Pignatti, Terisio. Master Drawings: From Cave Art to Picasso. (Illus.). 400p. 1982. 65.00 (ISBN 0-8109-1663-0). Abrams.
Probyn, Peter, ed. The Complete Drawing Book. (Illus.). 400p. 1970. 25.00 (ISBN 0-8230-0780-4). Watson-Guptill.

DRAWING-HISTORY
Pignatti, Terisio. Master Drawings: From Cave Art to Picasso. (Illus.). 400p. 1982. 65.00 (ISBN 0-8109-1663-0). Abrams.
Rose, Bernice. A Century of Modern Drawing. 160p. 1982. 40.00x (ISBN 0-7141-0791-3, Pub. by Brit Mus Pubns England). State Mutual Bk.

DRAWING-INSTRUCTION
see also Airbrush Art; Commercial Art
also special subjects of instruction, e.g. Figure Drawing; Flower Painting and Illustration; Birds Art; and similar headings; also subdivision Pictures, Illustrations, etc. under names of animals, e.g. Cats-Pictures, Illustrations, etc.
Appleton, George A. The Louvre Complete Treatise in Charcoal Drawing with the Lessons by M. Allonge. (The Promotion of the Arts Library Bk.). (Illus.). 139p. 1983. Repr. of 1880 ed. 49.75 (ISBN 0-89901-098-9). Found Class Reprints.
Crawford, Marjorie F. Kinder Art Drawing. (Illus.). 57p. 1982. 7.00 (ISBN 0-9610102-0-7). Edutech.
Gordon, Louise. How to Draw the Human Head: Techniques & Anatomy. (Illus.). 1983. pap. 6.95 (ISBN 0-14-046560-X). Penguin.
Kaupelis, Robert. Learning to Draw: A Creative Approach to Drawing. (Illus.). 144p. (Orig.). 1983. pap. text ed. 12.95 (ISBN 0-8230-2676-0). Watson-Guptill.

DRAWING-INSTRUCTION-JUVENILE LITERATURE
Baker, Darrel. Bugs Bunny & Friends. (How to Draw Ser.: No. 2150). (Illus.). 48p. (gr. 2-5). 1983. pap. 0.99 (ISBN 0-307-20150-3). Western Pub.
Boldman, Craig & Boldman, Craig. Comic Characters. (How to Draw Ser.: No. 2152). (Illus.). 48p. 1983. pap. 0.99 (ISBN 0-307-20152-X). Western Pub.
Frame, Paul. Drawing Sharks, Whales, Dolphins & Seals. (How-to-Draw Ser.). (Illus.). 64p. (gr. 4-6). 1983. PLB 8.90 (ISBN 0-531-04541-2). Watts.
Mickey Mouse & Friends. (How to Draw Ser.: No. 2153). (Illus.). 48p. (gr. 2-5). 1983. pap. 0.99 (ISBN 0-307-20153-8). Western Pub.
Super Heroes. (How to Draw Ser.: No. 2154). (Illus.). 48p. (gr. 2-5). pap. 0.99 (ISBN 0-307-20154-6). Western Pub.
Winchester, Linda. Fun Animals. (How to Draw Ser.: No. 2151). (Illus.). 48p. (gr. 2-5). 1983. pap. 0.99 (ISBN 0-307-20151-1). Western Pub.
Woody Woodpecker & Friends. (How to Draw Ser.: No. 2155). (Illus.). 48p. (gr. 2-5). 1983. pap. 0.99 (ISBN 0-307-20155-4). Western Pub.

DRAWING, ARCHITECTURAL
see Architectural Drawing

DRAWING, PSYCHOLOGY OF
see also Graphology
Selfe, Lorna, ed. Normal & Anomalous Representationl Drawing Ability in Children. Date not set. price not set (ISBN 0-12-635760-9). Acad Pr.

DRAWINGS
see also Etchings; Lithographs
Brophy, Brigid. The Prince & the Wild Geese. (Illus.). 64p. 1983. 10.95 (ISBN 0-312-64551-1). St Martin.
Eighteenth Century Drawings from the Collection of Mrs. Gertrude Laughlin Chanler. 1982. pap. 5.00 (ISBN 0-89468-026-9). Natl Gallery Art.
Labor, Brian. Dublin: Ninety Drawings by Brian Labor. 1983. pap. 11.95 (ISBN 0-7100-9497-3). Routledge & Kegan.
Leunig, Mary. There's No Place Like Home: Drawings. 1983. pap. 6.95 (ISBN 0-14-006443-5). Penguin.

DRAWINGS-CATALOGS
Bean, Jacob & Turcic, Lawrence. Fifteenth & Sixteenth Century Drawings in the Metropolitan Museum of Art. Preuss, Anne M., ed. (Illus.). 332p. 1982. 35.00 (ISBN 0-87099-314-3); pap. 19.95 (ISBN 0-87099-315-1). Metro Mus Art.

DRAWINGS-EXHIBITIONS
Dickson, Joanne, ed. Manuel Neri: Sculpture & Drawings. LC 80-71065. (Illus.). 28p. (Orig.). 1981. pap. 5.95 (ISBN 0-932216-11-0). Seattle Art.

DRAWINGS, AMERICAN
Crown, Patricia. Drawings by E. F. Burney. LC 82-21300. (Illus.). 80p. 1982. pap. 7.50 (ISBN 0-87328-124-1). Huntington Lib.

DRAWINGS, EUROPEAN
Here are entered works on European artists as a whole, as well as those on artists of specific European countries.
Lloyd, C. H. Durer to Cezanne: Northern European Drawings from the Ashmolean. 152p. 49.00x (ISBN 0-900090-89-8, Pub. by Ashmolean Mus Oxford). State Mutual Bk.

DRAWINGS, FRENCH
Goddad, Don, ed. Watercolors & Drawings of the French Impressionists & Their Parisian Contemporaries. Korneitchouk, Ursula, tr. from Ger. LC 81-20558. 1982. pap. text ed. 60.00 (ISBN 0-8109-1103-5). Abrams.

DRAWINGS, GERMAN
Bailey, C. J. Nineteenth Century German Drawings from the Ashmolean. 55.00x (ISBN 0-900090-96-0, Pub. by Ashmolean Mus Oxford). State Mutual Bk.

DRAWINGS, ITALIAN
Ames-Lewis, Francis. Drawing in Early Renaissance Italy. pap. 14.95 (ISBN 0-686-42818-8, Y-447). Yale U Pr.

--Drawings in Early Renaissance Italy. LC 81-40434. (Illus.). 208p. 1983. pap. 14.95 (ISBN 0-300-02978-0, Y-447). Yale U Pr.

Gere, J. A. & Pouncey, Philip. Italian Drawings: Five Artists Working in Rome c.1550-c.1640. 176p. 1982. 395.00x (ISBN 0-7141-0783-2, Pub. by Brit Mus Pubns England). State Mutual Bk.

Szabo, George. Masterpieces of Italian Drawing in the Robert Lehman Collection: The Metropolitan Museum of Art. (Illus.). 264p. 1983. 50.00 (ISBN 0-933920-35-0). Hudson Hills.

DREADNOUGHTS

see Warships

DREAMS

see also Fantasy; Psychoanalysis; Sleep

Bergson, Henri. Dreams. Slosson, Edwin E., tr. 62p. 1982. Repr. of 1914 ed. lib. bdg. 35.00 (ISBN 0-89987-092-9). Darby Bks.

De Saint-Denys, Hervey. Dreams & How to Guide Them. Schatzman, Morton, ed. 174p. 1982. text ed. 13.50x (ISBN 0-7156-1584-X, Pub. by Duckworth England). Biblio Dist.

Kirsch, James. The Reluctant Prophet: An Exploration of Prophecy & Dreams. LC 72-96516. 214p. 1973. 7.50 (ISBN 0-8202-0156-1). Sherbourne.

McGuire, William, ed. Dream Analysis: C. J. Jung Seminars, Vol. 1. LC 82-42787. (Bollingen Ser.: No. XCIX-1). (Illus.). 500p. 1983. 30.00 (ISBN 0-691-09896-4). Princeton U Pr.

The Mystic Dream Book: Two Thousand Five Hundred Dreams Explained. 186p. 1983. pap. 2.50 (ISBN 0-668-05733-5, 5733). Arco.

Reid, Clyde H. Dreams: Discovering Your Inner Teacher. 144p. 1983. pap. 7.95 (ISBN 0-86683-703-5). Winston Pr.

Scott, Charles, ed. On Dreaming: An Encounter with Medard Boss. LC 82-21429. (Scholars Press General Series). 124p. 1982. pap. text ed. 9.95 (ISBN 0-89130-603-X, 00-03-06). Scholars Pr CA.

Taylor, Jeremy. Dream Work: Techniques for Discovering the Creative Power of Dreams. LC 82-62411. 1983. pap. 8.95 (ISBN 0-8091-2525-0). Paulist Pr.

DREISER, THEODORE, 1871-1945

Hussman, Lawrence E. Dreiser & His Fiction: A Twentieth-Century Quest. LC 82-40493. 224p. 1983. 22.50x (ISBN 0-8122-7875-5). U of Pa Pr.

DREPANOCYTIC ANEMIA

see Sickle Cell Anemia

DRESS

see Clothing and Dress

DRESS ACCESSORIES

Fairchild Market Research Division. Fashions Accessories (Men's & Women's) (Fact File Ser.). (Illus.). 55p. 1983. pap. text ed. 12.50 (ISBN 0-87005-456-2). Fairchild.

DRESS DESIGN

see Costume Design

DRESSAGE

see Horsemanship

DRESSINGS (SURGERY)

see Bandages and Bandaging

DRESSINGS, SURGICAL

see Bandages and Bandaging

DRESSMAKING

see also Doll Clothes; Needlework; Sewing

Cardy, Lynn & Dart, Alan. Maternity Clothes: Simple Patterns to Make while You Wait. 128p. 1982. 30.00x (ISBN 0-7135-1312-8, Pub. by Bell & Hyman England). State Mutual Bk.

Ladbury, Ann. The Dressmaker's Dictionary. LC 82-8725. (Illus.). 360p. 1983. 19.95 (ISBN 0-668-05653-3, 5653). Arco.

DREYFUS, ALFRED, 1859-1935

Dreyfus, Alfred & Dreyfus, Pierre. Dreyfus Case. 1937. text ed. 49.50x (ISBN 0-686-83527-1). Elliots Bks.

DRIFT, CONTINENTAL

see Continental Drift

DRIFTING OF CONTINENTS

see Continental Drift

DRILLING, OIL WELL

see Oil Well Drilling

DRILLING AND BORING

Here are entered works relating to the drilling and boring of holes in metal, wood, other materials, as carried on in workshops, etc., for building and constructive purposes.

Kennedy, John L. Fundamentals of Drilling. 252p. 1982. 32.50x (ISBN 0-87814-200-2). Pennwell Pub.

DRILLING MUDS

Love, W. W. Disposal Systems. (Mud Equipment Manual Ser.: No. 11). 1982. pap. 10.75x (ISBN 0-87201-623-4). Gulf Pub.

Love, W. W. & Brandt, Louis. Shale Shakers. (Mud Equipment Manual Ser.: No. 3). 1982. pap. text ed. 10.75 (ISBN 0-87201-615-3). Gulf Pub.

Ormsby, George. Hydrocyclones. (Mud Equipment Manual Ser.: No. 6). 1982. pap. text ed. 10.75 (ISBN 0-87201-618-8). Gulf Pub.

Ormsby, George S. Mud Systems Arrangements. (Mud Equipment Manual Ser.: No. 2). 1982. pap. text ed. 10.75 (ISBN 0-87201-614-5). Gulf Pub.

Robinson, L. H., ed. Mud Cleaners & Combination Separators. (Mud Equipment Manual Ser.: No. 7). 1982. pap. text ed. 10.75 (ISBN 0-87201-619-6). Gulf Pub.

White, Doug. Agitation & Addition. (Mud Pump Manual Ser.: No. 9). 1982. pap. 10.75x (ISBN 0-87201-621-8). Gulf Pub.

DRINK INDUSTRY

see Beverage Industry

DRINKING AND YOUTH

see Alcohol and Youth

DRINKS

see Beverages

DRIVERS' TESTS, AUTOMOBILE

see Automobile Drivers' Tests

DRIVING, AUTOMOBILE

see Automobile Driving

DRIVING TESTS, AUTOMOBILE

see Automobile Drivers' Tests

DROMEDARIES

see Camels

DROP TESTS (CHEMISTRY)

see Spot Tests (Chemistry)

DROPOUTS

Price, Melvia. The Drop-Out Epidemic: Discussion of Educational Problems, Particularly for Minorities. 1983. pap. 6.95 (ISBN 0-937196-04-5). Sunset Prods.

DRUG ABUSE

see also Alcoholism; Hallucinogenic Drugs; Marihuana; Narcotic Habit

American Health Research Institute, Ltd. Drug Addiction, Substance Abuse & Narcotic Dependence: A Medical Subject Analysis & Research Index With Bibliography. Bartone, John C., ed. 120p. 1983. 29.95 (ISBN 0-88164-006-9); pap. 21.95 (ISBN 0-88164-007-7). ABBE Pubs Assn.

Baker, Joe. Coping with Drug Abuse: A Lifeline for Parents. LC 82-12723. (Illus.). 60p. 1982. pap. 9.95 (ISBN 0-943690-00-5). DARE.

Bargmann, Eve & Wolfe, Sidney M. Stopping Valium: And Ativan, Centrax, Dalmane, Librium, Paxipam, Restoril, Serax, Tranxene, Xanax. 1983. pap. 5.95 (ISBN 0-446-37582-9). Warner Bks.

Burns, Hugh J. The Parents Guide to Teenage Drug Abuse. 1983. pap. 3.95 (ISBN 0-932972-02-0). Sprout Pubns.

DeVries, Martin & Berg, Robert L. The Use & Abuse of Medicine. 316p. 1982. 34.95 (ISBN 0-03-061702-2). Praeger.

Giannini, A. James & Slaby, Andrew E. Emergency Guide to Overdose & Detoxification. 1983. pap. text ed. price not set (ISBN 0-87488-182-X). Med Exam.

Hobbing, Peter. Strafwurdigkeit der Selbstverletzung der Drogenkonsum Im Deutschen und Brasilianischen Recht. xv, 400p. (Ger.). 1982. write for info. (ISBN 3-8204-6278-3). P Lang Pubs.

Krivanek, Jara A. Drug Problems, People Problems: Causes, Treatment & Prevention. 256p. 1983. text ed. 28.50x (ISBN 0-86861-364-9); pap. 10.95 (ISBN 0-86861-372-X). Allen Unwin.

Nurco. Ex-Addicts' Self-Help Groups: Potential & Pitfalls. 160p. 1983. 25.95 (ISBN 0-03-063346-X). Praeger.

Parssinen, Terry M. Secret Passions, Secret Remedies: Narcotic Drugs in British Society, 1820 to 1930. LC 82-15571. (Illus.). 250p. 1983. text ed. 17.50 (ISBN 0-89727-043-6). Inst Study Human.

Ray, Oakley. Drugs, Society & Human Behavior. 3rd ed. LC 82-8203. (Illus.). 512p. 1983. pap. text ed. 17.95 (ISBN 0-8016-4092-X). Mosby.

Research Developments in Drug & Alcohol Use. Proceedings, Vol. 362. 244p. 1981. 49.00 (ISBN 0-89766-117-6, Millman Pub); pap. write for info. (ISBN 0-89766-118-4). NY Acad Sci.

Rudman, Jack. Drug Abuse Rehabilitation Counselor. (Career Examination Ser.: C-2929). (Cloth bdg. avail. on request). pap. 12.00 (ISBN 0-8373-2929-9). Natl Learning.

--Senior Drug Abuse Rehabilitation Counselor. (Career Examination Ser.: C-2928). (Cloth bdg. avail. on request). pap. 12.00 (ISBN 0-8373-2928-0). Natl Learning.

Serban, George, ed. Social & Medical Aspects of Drug Abuse. 288p. 1983. text ed. 35.00 (ISBN 0-89335-191-1). SP Med & Sci Bks.

Shouse, Dennis, et al. Handbook for Volunteers in Substance Abuse Agencies. 32p. 1983. pap. 9.95x pkg. of 4 (ISBN 0-918452-40-6). Learning Pubns.

Sloman, Larry. Reefer Madness: A of Marijuana in America. (Illus.). 360p. 1983. pap. 8.95 (ISBN 0-394-62446-7, Ever). Grove.

Stafford, Peter. Psychedelics Encyclopedia. (Illus.). 400p. 1982. pap. 12.95 (ISBN 0-87477-231-1). J P Tarcher.

Stimmel, Barry, ed. Evaluation of Drug Treatment Programs. LC 82-21194. (Advances in Alcohol & Substance Abuse Ser.: Vol. 2, No 1). 108p. 1983. text ed. 14.95 (ISBN 0-86656-194-3, B194). Haworth Pr.

Vesell & Braude. Interactions of Drug Abuse, Vol. 281. 1976. 32.00 (ISBN 0-89072-027-4). NY Acad Sci.

DRUG ABUSE AND CRIME

Vernon, Sidney. Happiness & Discipline: A Survey of Drugs, Crime & Law. Salter, Thomas, ed. (Illus.). 100p. 1983. 9.95 (ISBN 0-943150-04-3); pap. 6.95 (ISBN 0-943150-05-1). Rovern Pr.

--Reach for Charisma: A Personal Guide for Body Language Use. Salter, Thomas, ed. (Illus.). 50p. (Orig.). 1983. 11.95 (ISBN 0-943150-08-6); pap. 6.95 (ISBN 0-943150-03-5); plastic comb bdg. 6.95 (ISBN 0-943150-07-8). Rovern Pr.

DRUG ADDICTION

see Drug Abuse; Narcotic Habit

DRUG ADULTERATION

see Drugs–Adulteration and Analysis

DRUG HABIT

see Drug Abuse; Narcotic Habit

DRUG INDUSTRY

see Drug Trade

DRUG METABOLISM

Smith, et al. PCP: Problems & Prevention. 1982. pap. text ed. 15.95 (ISBN 0-8403-2809-5). Kendall-Hunt.

DRUG RESEARCH

see Pharmaceutical Research

DRUG RESISTANCE IN MICRO-ORGANISMS

see also Micro-Organisms; Pharmacology

Mitsuhashi, S. Drug Resistance in Bacteria. 380p. 35.00 (ISBN 0-86577-085-9). Thieme-Stratton.

DRUG THERAPY

see Chemotherapy

DRUG TRADE

Bell, Bryan, ed. World Directory of Pharmaceutical Manufacturers. 4th ed. 316p. (Orig.). 1982. pap. 250.00x (ISBN 0-906184-03-7). Intl Pubns Serv.

Indian Pharmaceutical Guide, 1982. 20th ed. 1592p. 1982. 60.00x (ISBN 0-8002-3036-1). Intl Pubns Serv.

Japan Pharmaceutical Association, ed. Modern Pharmaceuticals of Japan, 1981. 6th ed. LC 73-165508. (Illus.). 128p. 1980. pap. 35.00x (ISBN 0-8002-3064-7). Intl Pubns Serv.

Pharmaceutical Packaging & Drug Delivery Systems. 1982. 1195.00 (283). Predicasts.

Pradhan, Suesh B. International Pharmaceutical Marketing. LC 82-15022. 352p. 1983. lib. bdg. 49.95 (ISBN 0-89930-009-X, PPH/, Quorum). Greenwood.

Smith, Mickey C., ed. Principles of Pharmaceutical Marketing. 3rd ed. LC 82-6624. (Illus.). 529p. 1983. text ed. write for info. (ISBN 0-8121-0858-2). Lea & Febiger.

DRUG TRADE–LAW AND LEGISLATION

see Pharmacy–Laws and Legislation

DRUGS

see also Botany, Medical; Doping in Sports; Drug Metabolism; Materia Medica; Medicine–Formulae, Receipts, Prescriptions; Pharmacology; Pharmacy also names of particular drugs and groups of drugs, e.g. Narcotics, Stimulants

American Health Research Institute, Ltd. World Survey of Drug & Narcotic Control: A Medical Subject Analysis & Research Index with Bibliography. Bartone, John C., ed. 120p. 1983. 29.95 (ISBN 0-88164-014-X); pap. 21.95 (ISBN 0-88164-015-8). ABBE Pubs Assn.

Bindra, Jasjit S. & Lednicer, Daniel. Chronicles of Drug Discovery, Vol. 2. 300p. 1983. 32.50 (ISBN 0-471-89135-5, Pub. by Wiley-Interscience). Wiley.

Drugs & Pharmaceuticals. 1982. 1195.00 (279). Predicasts.

Gibson, G. G. & Loannides, C., eds. Safety Evaluation of Nitrosatable Drugs & Chemicals. 275p. 1981. 90.00x (ISBN 0-85066-212-5, Pub. by Taylor & Francis). State Mutual Bk.

Goldberg, Eugene P. Targeted Drugs. (Polymers in Biology & Medicine Ser.). 300p. 1983. 50.00 (ISBN 0-471-04884-4, Pub. by Wiley-Interscience). Wiley.

Lomax, P. & Schoenbaum, E. Enivironment, Drugs & Thermoregulation: International Symposium on the Pharmacology of Thermoregulation, 5th, Saint-Paul-de-Vence, November 1982. (Illus.). xvi, 224p. 1983. 47.50 (ISBN 3-8055-3654-2). S Karger.

Manell, P. & Johansson, S. G., eds. The Impact of Computer Technology on Drug Information: Proceedings of the IFIP-IMIA Working Conference, Uppsala, Sweden, October 26-28, 1981. 262p. 1982. 34.00 (ISBN 0-444-86451-2, North Holland). Elsevier.

Modell, Walter. Drugs in Current Use & New Drugs 1983. 29th ed. 1983. pap. text ed. 10.95 (ISBN 0-8261-0162-3). Springer Pub.

Scientific Research (SIR), ed. Drugs Studies in CVD & PVD: Proceedings of the International Symposium, Geneva, May 25-26, 1981. (Illus.). 250p. 1982. 41.00 (ISBN 0-08-027084-0). Pergamon.

Trissel, L. A. Pocket Guide to Injectable Drugs. 159p. 1981. pap. text ed. 13.50 (ISBN 0-471-09131-6, Pub. by Wiley Med). Wiley.

Weil, Andrew & Rosen, Winifred. Chocolate to Morphine: Understanding Mind-Active Drugs. LC 82-12112. (Illus.). 250p. 1983. 14.95 (ISBN 0-395-33108-0); pap. 8.95 (ISBN 0-686-42997-4). HM.

Witters-Jones, Patricia & Witters, Weldon. Drugs & Society: A Biological Perspective. LC 82-21738. 400p. 1983. pap. text ed. 14.95 (ISBN 0-534-01412-7). Brooks-Cole.

Woods, Arthur. Dangerous Drugs. 1931. text ed. 29.50x (ISBN 0-686-83520-4). Elliots Bks.

Zimmerman, David R. The Essential Guide to Nonprescription Drugs. LC 82-48139. (Illus.). 704p. 1983. pap. 10.53i (ISBN 0-06-091023-2, CN 1023, CN). Har-Row.

--The Essential Guide to Nonprescription Drugs. (Illus.). 704p. 1983. 27.50 (ISBN 0-06-014915-9, HarpT). Har-Row.

DRUGS–ADULTERATION AND ANALYSIS

Florey, Klaus, ed. Analytical Profiles of Drug Subsubstances, Vol. II. LC 70-187259. 1982. 39.00 (ISBN 0-12-260811-9). Acad Pr.

Mills, et al. Instrumental Data for Drug Analysis, Vol. 1. 1982. 95.00 (ISBN 0-444-00718-0). Elsevier.

DRUGS–BIBLIOGRAPHY

Hopkins, S. J. Principal Drugs: An Alphabetical Guide to Modern Therapeutic Agents. 7th ed. 192p. (Orig.). 1983. pap. 3.95 (ISBN 0-571-18063-9). Faber & Faber.

DRUGS–DICTIONARIES

Graa, Albert, ed. Vocabularium Pharmaceuticum. 2nd ed. 125p. 1964. text ed. 13.50x (ISBN 0-8002-3024-8). Intl Pubns Serv.

Nursing Drug Handbook 83. 1000p. 1983. 17.95 (ISBN 0-916730-54-9). Intermed Comm.

Silverman, Harold M., et al. The Pill Book. 2nd ed. LC 82-90322. 620p. 1982. 19.95 (ISBN 0-553-05013-3); pap. 9.95 (ISBN 0-553-01377-7). Bantam.

USAN & the USP Dictionary of Drug Names: 1983. 1982. 35.00 (ISBN 0-686-37681-1). USPC.

DRUGS–DOSAGE

Fleischman, Marjorie R. Dosage Calculation: Method & Workbook. (League Exchange Ser.: No. 106). 106p. 1975. 5.95 (ISBN 0-686-38188-2, 20-1560). Natl League Nurse.

Florence, A. T. & Attwood, D. Physicochemical Principles of Pharmacy. 1982. 29.95x (ISBN 0-412-00131-4). Methuen Inc.

Pirie, Susan. Drug Calculations. 48p. 1982. 25.00x (ISBN 0-85950-367-4, Pub. by Thornes England). State Mutual Bk.

Thompson, Margaret J. Workbook in the Calculation of Solutions & Dosage for Student Nurses. 80p. 1982. pap. text ed. 5.95 (ISBN 0-8403-2744-7). Kendall-Hunt.

Wartak, Joseph. Drug Dosage & Administration: Modern Theory & Practice. (Illus.). 208p. 1983. pap. text ed. 32.50 (ISBN 0-8391-1786-8, 19445). Univ Park.

DRUGS–PHYSIOLOGICAL EFFECT

Garrett & Hirtz. Drug Fate & Metabolism, Vol. 4. 408p. 1983. price not set (ISBN 0-8247-1849-6). Dekker.

Goldberg, Morton E., ed. Pharmacological & Biochemical Properties of Drug Substances, Vol. 2. 257p. 1977. 36.00 (ISBN 0-917330-25-0). Am Pharm Assn.

Goldstein, Avram, et al. Principles of Drug Action: The Basis of Pharmacology. 2nd ed. LC 73-15871. 1974. 46.00x (ISBN 0-471-31260-6, Pub. by Wiley-Medical). Wiley.

Ray, Oakley. Drugs, Society & Human Behavior. 3rd ed. LC 82-8203. (Illus.). 512p. 1983. pap. text ed. 17.95 (ISBN 0-8016-4092-X). Mosby.

Smith, et al. PCP: Problems & Prevention. 1982. pap. text ed. 15.95 (ISBN 0-8403-2809-5). Kendall-Hunt.

Stafford, Peter. Psychedelics Encyclopedia. (Illus.). 400p. 1982. pap. 12.95 (ISBN 0-87477-231-1). J P Tarcher.

Stern, Leo. Drug Use in Pregnancy. 300p. 1983. text ed. write for info. (ISBN 0-86792-011-4, Pub by Adis Pr Australia). Wright-PSG.

Topliss, John G., ed. Quantitative Structure-Activity Relationships of Drugs. Date not set. price not set (ISBN 0-12-695150-0). Acad Pr.

DRUGS–PSYCHOLOGICAL ASPECTS

Drew, L. R. & Stolz, P., eds. Man, Drugs & Society: Current Perspectives. new ed. 474p. (Orig.). 1982. pap. text ed. 25.95 (ISBN 0-909190-12-7, 1242, Pub. by ANUP Australia). Bks Australia.

DRUGS–RESEARCH

see Pharmaceutical Research

DRUGS–STANDARDS

see also Biological Assay

Auriche, M. & Burke, J., eds. Drug Safety: Proceeding of the Fourth International Congress of Pharmaceutical Physicians by the Association des Medecins de l'Industrie Pharmaceutique (AMPI) under the Auspices of the International Federation of the Association of the Pharmaceutical Physicians (IFAPP) in Paris, April 1981. 320p. 1982. 60.50 (ISBN 0-08-027073-5); pap. 36.00 (ISBN 0-08-027074-3). Pergamon.

DRUGS–TESTING

Testing Drugs for the Aging Brain. (Journal: Gerontology: Vol. 28, Suppl. 2). (Illus.). vi, 58p. 1983. pap. 33.00 (ISBN 3-8055-3659-3). S Karger.

DRUGS, ANTINEOPLASTIC

see Antineoplastic Agents

DRUGS, CARDIOVASCULAR

see Cardiovascular Agents

DRUGS, CYTOTOXIC

see Antineoplastic Agents

DRUGS, DERMATOLOGIC

see Dermatology

DRUGS AND YOUTH

see also Narcotics and Youth

Burns, Hugh J. The Parents Guide to Teenage Drug Abuse. 1983. pap. 3.95 (ISBN 0-932972-02-0). Sprout Pubns.

Jackson, Bruce & Jackson, Michael. Doing Drugs. 320p. 1983. pap. 6.95 (ISBN 0-686-42931-1, Pub. by Marek). St Martin.

DRUM
Vennum, Thomas, Jr. The Ojibwa Dance Drum: Its History & Construction. (Folklife Ser.: Vol. 2). (Illus.). 320p. (Orig.). 1983. pap. 12.50x (ISBN 0-87474-941-7). Smithsonian.
DRUNKARDS
see Alcoholics
DRUNKENNESS
see Alcoholics; Alcoholism; Temperance
DUAL EMPLOYMENT
see Supplementary Employment
DUBLIN
Labor, Brian. Dublin: Ninety Drawings by Brian Labor. 1983. pap. 11.95 (ISBN 0-7100-9497-3). Routledge & Kegan.
O'Dwyer, Frederick. Lost Dublin. (Illus.). 152p. 1982. pap. 17.95 (ISBN 0-7171-1047-8, Pub. by Salem Hse Ltd). Merrimack Bk Serv.
DUBUFFET, JEAN, 1901-
Ratcliff, Carter. Jean Dubuffet, Partitions 1980-1981; Psycho-Sites 1981. (Illus.). 36p. (Orig.). 1982. pap. text ed. 16.50 (ISBN 0-938608-10-X). Pace Gallery Pubns.
DUCHAMP, MARCEL, 1887-1968
Matisse, Paul, ed. Marcel Duchamp, Notes. (Documents of Twentieth Century Art). (Illus.). 270p. 1983. lib. bdg. 65.00 (ISBN 0-8057-9955-9, Twayne). G K Hall.
DUCKS–JUVENILE LITERATURE
Kelty, Jean McClure. If You Have a Duck. (Illus.). 104p. 1982. write for info. G Whittell Mem.
Nentl, Jerolyn. The Mallard. Schroeder, Howard, ed. (Wildlife Habits & Habitat Ser.). (Illus.). 48p. (gr. 4-5). 1983. lib. bdg. 8.95 (ISBN 0-89686-221-6). Crestwood Hse.
DUCTLESS GLANDS
see Endocrine Glands
DUE PROCESS OF LAW
Auerbach, Jerold S. Justice Without Law? (Illus.). 224p. 1983. 16.95 (ISBN 0-19-503175-X). Oxford U Pr.
DUERER, ALBRECHT, 1471-1528
Heaton, Mary M. K. The Life of Albrecht Durer of Nuremberg. (Illus.). 373p. 1983. pap. 8.75 (ISBN 0-686-38398-2). Tanager Bks.
DULCIMER
Adams, Jane I. Are You Ready for More on the Dulcimore? 84p. 1982. pap. 8.95 (ISBN 0-941126-04-8). Meadowlark.
Baehr, Tom. A Pleasant Addiction. (Illus.). 48p. (Orig.). 1982. 5.95 (ISBN 0-9608842-1-1). Hogfiddle Pr.
Larkin, Bryant. Larkin's Dulcimer Book. (Illus.). 103p. 1982. pap. 6.95 (ISBN 0-943644-00-3); cassette 6.95; Set. 12.95. Ivory Pal.
May, Dorothy. Dulcimer Classics. (Illus.). 48p. (Orig.). 1980. pap. 2.95 (ISBN 0-941126-02-1). Meadowlark.
DUMAS, ALEXANDRE, 1802-1870
Lucas-Dubreton, J. The Fourth Musketeer: The Life of Alexander Dumas. Darnton, Maida C., tr. 276p. Repr. of 1928 ed. lib. bdg. 35.00 (ISBN 0-89984-812-5). Century Bookbindery.
DU MAURIER, GEORGE LOUIS PALMELLA BUSSON, 1834-1896
Kelly, Richard. George DuMaurier. (English Authors Ser.). 200p. 1983. lib. bdg. 16.95 (ISBN 0-8057-6841-6, Twayne). G K Hall.
DUMB (DEAF MUTES)
see Deaf
DUMMY BOARD FIGURES
Lucky, Carl F. Hummel Figurines & Plates: A Collectors Identification & Value Guide. 5th ed. (Illus.). 370p. 1983. pap. 9.95 (ISBN 0-89689-042-2). Bks Americana.
DUNGEONS
see Prisons
DUNHAM, KATHERINE–JUVENILE LITERATURE
Haskins, James. Katherine Dunham. (Illus.). 176p. 1982. 10.95 (ISBN 0-698-20549-9, Coward). Putnam Pub Group.
DURATION, INTUITION OF
see Time Perception
DURER, ALBRECHT, 1471-1528
see Duerer, Albrecht, 1471-1528
DURKHEIM, EMILE, 1858-1917
Besnard, Philippe, ed. The Sociological Domain: The Durkheimians & the Founding of French Sociology. LC 82-9485. (Illus.). 336p. Date not set. price not set (ISBN 0-521-23876-5). Cambridge U Pr.
Taylor, Steve. Durkeheim & the Study of Suicide. (Contemporary Social Theory Ser.). 240p. 1982. 35.00x (ISBN 0-333-28645-6, Pub. by Macmillan England). State Mutual Bk.
--Durkheim & the Study of Suicide. LC 82-6001. 240p. 1982. 22.50x (ISBN 0-312-22266-1). St Martin.
DURUM WHEAT
see Wheat
DUST
Nagy & Verakis. Development & Control of Dust Explosions. (Occupational Safety & Health Ser.). 352p. 1983. price not set (ISBN 0-8247-7004-8). Dekker.
DUTCH ART
see Art, Dutch
DUTCH IN THE UNITED STATES
Swierenga, Robert P. Dutch Immigrants in U.S. Ship Passenger Manifests, 1820-1880: An Alphabetical Listing by Household Heads & Independent Persons, 2 Vols. LC 82-23078. 1328p. 1983. lib. bdg. 125.00 set (ISBN 0-8420-2206-6). Scholarly Res Inc.
DUTCH LANGUAGE
Berlitz Editors. Dutch for Travel Cassettepack. 1983. 14.95 (ISBN 0-02-962950-0, Berlitz); cassette incl. Macmillan.
Donaldson, B. C. Dutch Reference Grammar. 324p. 1981. 45.00x (ISBN 90-247-2354-X, Pub. by Thornes England). State Mutual Bk.
Knopper, Rob, ed. Woordstructurr. 140p. (Dutch.). pap. 13.75x (ISBN 90-70176-56-4). Foris Pubns.
Renkema, Jan, ed. Taalschat. 108p. (Dutch.). pap. 8.60x (ISBN 0-686-37588-2). Foris Pubns.
Schoenmaker, Anneke. Praatpaal: Dutch for Beginners. 160p. 1981. 32.00x (ISBN 0-85950-474-3, Pub. by Thornes England). State Mutual Bk.
Shetter, William Z. Introduction to Dutch: A Practical Grammar. 220p. 1981. 35.00x (ISBN 90-247-2116-4, Pub. by Thornes England). State Mutual Bk.
Smith, Jacob & Meijer, Reinder P. Dutch Grammar & Reader. 2nd ed. 224p. 1978. 32.00x (ISBN 0-85950-022-5, Pub. by Thornes England). State Mutual Bk.
Van Eemeren, Grootendorst. Regels voor Redilijke Discussies. 496p. (Dutch.). Date not set. 19.50x (ISBN 0-686-37587-4); pap. price not set. Foris Pubns.
Williams, Jelly K. A Dutch Reader. 112p. 1981. 32.00x (ISBN 0-85950-349-6, Pub. by Thornes England). State Mutual Bk.
DUTCH LANGUAGE–DICTIONARIES
Claes, Frans M., compiled by. A Bibliography of Netherlandic Dictionaries: Dutch-Flemish. (Orig.). 1980. lib. bdg. 50.00 (ISBN 0-686-83480-1). Kraus Intl.
DUTCH LITERATURE–HISTORY AND CRITICISM
Meijer, Reinder P. Literature of the Low Countries. 416p. 1978. 40.00x (ISBN 0-85950-099-3, Pub. by Thornes England). State Mutual Bk.
DUTCH PAINTINGS
see Paintings, Dutch
DUTIES
see Taxation
DUTIES OF MEMBERS OF CONGRESS
see United States–Congress–Powers and Duties
DWARF TREES
see Bonsai
DWELLINGS
see also Apartment Houses; Architecture, Domestic; Bathrooms; Country Homes; House Construction; Kitchens; Lake-Dwellers and Lake-Dwellings; Solar Houses
Better Homes & Gardens Books editors, ed. Better Homes & Gardens All About Your House: Stretching your Living Space. (All About your House Ser.). (Illus.). 160p. 1983. 9.95 (ISBN 0-696-02162-5). Meredith Corp.
--Better Homes & Gardens All About Your House: Your Kitchen. (All About your House Ser.). 160p. 1983. 9.95 (ISBN 0-696-02161-7). Meredith Corp.
--Better Homes & Gardens All About Your House: Your Walls & Ceilings. (All About your House Ser.). (Illus.). 160p. 1983. 9.95 (ISBN 0-696-02163-3). Meredith Corp.
--Better Homes & Gardens Step-by-Step Cabinets & Shelves. (Illus.). 1983. pap. 5.95 (ISBN 0-696-01065-8). Meredith Corp.
Morton, R., et al. The Home, It's Furnishings & Equipment. 1979. text ed. 20.84 (ISBN 0-07-043417-4); tchr's manual avail. McGraw.
One Sixty-Six Low Medium Cost Homes. 96p. Date not set. 2.00 (ISBN 0-918894-14-X). Home Planners.
Schwartz, Helen. The New Jersey House. (Illus.). 238p. 1983. 25.00 (ISBN 0-8135-0965-3); pap. 14.95 (ISBN 0-8135-0990-4). Rutgers U Pr.
DWELLINGS–ENERGY CONSERVATION
Chapman, Keeler C. & Traister, John E. Homes for the Nineteen-Eighties: An Energy & Construction Design Aid. LC 82-5929. (Illus.). 256p. pap. 16.95 (ISBN 0-8306-1425-7). TAB Bks.
Energy Alternatives. (Home Repair & Improvement Ser.). 1982. lib. bdg. 15.96 (ISBN 0-8094-3495-4, Pub. by Time-Life). Silver.
Energy-Efficient Construction Methods. (Illus.). 1982. pap. 12.95 (ISBN 0-918984-01-7). Solarvision.
Heat Saving Home Insulation. (Illus.). 1982. pap. 9.95 (ISBN 0-918984-03-3). Solarvision.
Scheller, William G. Energy Saving Home Improvements. 1979. pap. 8.95 (ISBN 0-672-21605-1). Sams.
Shurcliff, William. Superinsulated Houses. 1982. pap. 7.95 (ISBN 0-931790-25-5). Brick Hse Pub.
DWELLINGS–HEATING AND VENTILATION
see Heating
DWELLINGS–JUVENILE LITERATURE
Althea. Building a House. (Cambridge Dinosaur Information Ser.). (Illus.). 26p. (gr. 7-10). 1983. pap. 1.50 (ISBN 0-521-27152-5). Cambridge U Pr.
DWELLINGS–MAINTENANCE AND REPAIR
see also Buildings–Repair and Reconstruction
Baum, Herman. The House Doctor's Guide to Simple Home Repair. 240p. 1983. pap. 2.95 (ISBN 0-523-41270-3). Pinnacle Bks.
Bragdon, Allen D., ed. The Homeowner's Complete Manual of Repair & Improvement. LC 82-18184. (Illus.). 576p. 1983. 19.95 (ISBN 0-668-05737-8, 5737). Arco.
Briggs Amasco Ltd. Flat Roofing: A Guide to Good Practice. (Illus.). 216p. 1982. pap. 33.95 (ISBN 0-9507919-0-3, Pub. by RIBA). Intl Schol Bk Serv.
Cleaning. LC 82-5717. (Home Repair & Improvement Ser.). lib. bdg. 15.96 (ISBN 0-8094-3491-1, Pub. by Time-Life). Silver.
Cobb, H. H. Improvements that Increase the Value of Your House. 1981. pap. 6.95 (ISBN 0-07-011488-9). McGraw.
Energy Alternatives. (Home Repair & Improvement Ser.). 1982. lib. bdg. 15.96 (ISBN 0-8094-3495-4, Pub. by Time-Life). Silver.
Hinde, Thomas. Cottage Book: Manual of Maintenance, Repair, Construction. 1979. 18.95 (ISBN 0-686-84202-2, Pub. by W Heineman). David & Charles.
Mills, Richard G. Jackie's Home Repair & Maintenance Charts. Hostage, Jacqueline, ed. LC 82-25290. (Illus.). 128p. 1983. pap. 5.95 plastic comb bdg. (ISBN 0-932620-18-3). Betterway Pubns.
Proulx, E. Annie. Plan & Make Your Own Fences & Gates, Walkways, Walls & Drives. Halpin, Anne, ed. (Illus.). 224p. 1983. 16.95 (ISBN 0-87857-452-2, 14-048-0); pap. 11.95 (ISBN 0-87857-453-0, 14-048-1). Rodale Pr Inc.
Weiss. Home Maintenance. rev. ed. 1983. text ed. 15.20 (ISBN 0-87002-386-1). Bennett IL.
DWELLINGS–REMODELING
see also Buildings–Repair and Reconstruction
Abrams, Lawrence & Abrams, Kathleen. Salvaging Old Barns & Houses: Tear it Down & Save Their Places. LC 82-19330. (Illus.). 128p. (Orig.). 1983. pap. 7.95 (ISBN 0-8069-7666-7). Sterling.
Hutchins, Nigel. Restoring Old Houses. 240p. 1982. pap. 19.95 (ISBN 0-7706-0021-2). Van Nos Reinhold.
Reader's Digest Editors. Home Improvements Manual. LC 81-84488. (Illus.). 384p. 1983. 21.50 (ISBN 0-89577-132-2, Pub. by RD Assn). Random.
Reed, Mortimer. Complete Guide to Residential Remodeling. (Illus.). 320p. 1983. 28.95 (ISBN 0-13-160663-8); pap. 14.95 (ISBN 0-13-160671-9). P-H.
Rural Home Modifications for Survival (Retreat Security) (Economic & Survival Ser.). (Illus.). 65p. (Orig.). 1981. pap. 15.00 (ISBN 0-939856-22-0). Tech Group.
Schram, Joseph & Boeschen, John. Children's Rooms & Play Areas. (Do-It-Yourself Bks.). (Illus.). 96p. 1982. pap. 3.95 (ISBN 0-8249-6119-6). Ideals.
Sunset Books & Sunset Magazine, ed. Bedroom & Bath Storage. LC 81-82870. (Illus.). 80p. (Orig.). 1982. pap. 3.95 (ISBN 0-376-01120-3). Sunset-Lane.
--Flooring: Do it Yourself. LC 81-82872. (Illus.). 112p. (Orig.). 1982. pap. 4.95 (ISBN 0-376-01141-6). Sunset-Lane.
--Home Lighting. LC 82-81371. (Illus.). 96p. (Orig.). 1982. pap. 4.95 (ISBN 0-376-01312-5). Sunset-Lane.
--Solar Remodeling. LC 82-81372. (Illus.). 96p. (Orig.). 1982. pap. 4.95 (ISBN 0-376-01534-9). Sunset-Lane.
--Wallcoverings. LC 82-81370. (Illus.). 96p. (Orig.). 1982. pap. 4.95 (ISBN 0-376-01673-6). Sunset-Lane.
--Windows & Skylights. LC 81-82871. (Illus.). 112p. (Orig.). 1982. pap. 4.95 (ISBN 0-376-01751-1). Sunset-Lane.
DYEING
see Dyes and Dyeing
DYES AND DYEING
see also Bleaching; Coloring Matter
Advances in Preparation, Coloration & Finishing. 1982. 60.00x (ISBN 0-686-81693-5, Pub. by Soc Dyers & Colour). State Mutual Bk.
Bliss, Anne. A Handbook of Dyes from Natural Materials. (Illus.). 192p. 1983. pap. 9.95 (ISBN 0-686-83790-8, ScribT). Scribner.
Colour Index. 3rd, Rev. ed. 1982. 650.00x (ISBN 0-686-81698-6, Pub. by Soc Dyers & Colour). State Mutual Bk.
Colour Index: Supplement, Vol. 5. Rev. ed. 1982. 210.00x (ISBN 0-686-81697-8, Pub. by Soc Dyers & Colour). State Mutual Bk.
Efficiency & Control of Coloration Process. 1982. 35.00x (ISBN 0-686-81695-1, Pub. by Soc Dyers & Colour). State Mutual Bk.
Gittinger, Mattiebelle. Master Dyers to the World: Technique & Trade in Early Indian Dyed Cotton Textiles. McEuen, Caroline K., ed. (Illus.). 208p. 1982. pap. 20.00 (ISBN 0-87405-020-0). Textile Mus.
Goodwin, Jill. A Dyer's Manual. (Illus.). 128p. 1983. 17.95 (ISBN 0-7207-1327-7, Pub by Michael Joseph). Merrimack Bk Serv.
Ponting, Ken. A Dictionary of Dyes & Dyeing. 216p. 1982. 35.00x (ISBN 0-7135-1311-X, Pub. by Bell & Hyman England). State Mutual Bk.
Progress & Productivity in Coloration. 1982. 60.00x (ISBN 0-686-81692-7, Pub. by Soc Dyers & Colour). State Mutual Bk.
Sinclair, R. S. Numerical Problems in Colour Physics. 1982. 27.00 (ISBN 0-686-81691-9, Pub. by Soc Dyers & Colour). State Mutual Bk.
Standard Methods for the Determination of the Colour Fastness of Textiles & Leather. 1982. 75.00x (ISBN 0-686-81696-X, Pub. by Soc Dyers & Colour). State Mutual Bk.
Wada, Yoshiko. Shibori: Japanese Shaped Resist Dyeing. LC 82-48789. (Illus.). 296p. 1983. 65.00 (ISBN 0-87011-559-6). Kodansha.
DYING PATIENT
see Terminal Care
DYLAN, BOB, 1941-
Dorman, James E. Recorded Dylan: A Critical Review & Discography. LC 82-60706. (Illus., Orig.). 1982. pap. 5.95 (ISBN 0-943564-00-X). Soma Pr Cal.
DYNAMIC DISPLAY SYSTEMS
see Information Display Systems
DYNAMIC PROGRAMMING
Gresser, Ion, ed. Interferon Eighty-Two. (Serial Publication). Date not set. 18.50 (ISBN 0-12-302253-3). Acad Pr.
DYNAMICS
see also Aerodynamics; Control Theory; Force and Energy; Hydrodynamics; Kinematics; Mechanics; Motion; Perturbation (Mathematics); Physics; Plasma Dynamics; Quantum Theory; Rotational Motion; Statics; Thermodynamics
Abraham, Ralph & Shaw, Chris. Dynamics, the Geometry of Behavior. LC 81-71616. (Visual Mathematics Ser.). (Illus.). 240p. 1982. pap. text ed. 29.00x (ISBN 0-942344-01-4). Pt. 1, Periodic Behavior. Pts. 2 & 3 Future. Aerial Pr.
AIP Conference, 88th, La Jolla Institute, 1981. Mathematical Methods in Hydrodynamics & Integrability in Dynamical Systems: Proceedings. Tabor, Michael & Treves, Yvain M., eds. LC 82-72462. 352p. 1982. lib. bdg. 34.00 (ISBN 0-88318-187-8). Am Inst Physics.
Bednarek, A. R. & Cesari, L., eds. Dynamical Systems: Symposium, II. 1982. 49.00 (ISBN 0-12-084720-5). Acad Pr.
Ginsberg, Jerry H. & Genin, Joseph. Dynamics. LC 76-40409. 1977. text ed. 22.95x (ISBN 0-471-29606-6). Wiley.
Palm, William J. Modeling, Analysis & Control of Dynamic Systems. 800p. 1983. text ed. 36.95 (ISBN 0-471-05800-9); solutions manual avail. (ISBN 0-471-89887-2). Wiley.
Percival, Ian C. & Richards, Derek. Introduction to Dynamics. LC 82-15514. (Illus.). 240p. 1983. 34.50 (ISBN 0-521-23680-0); pap. 14.95 (ISBN 0-521-28149-0). Cambridge U Pr.
Rosenberg, R. & Karnopp, D. Introduction to Physical Systems Dynamics. 512p. 1983. 32.95x (ISBN 0-07-053905-7, C); solutions manual 9.95 (ISBN 0-07-053906-5). McGraw.
Sandor, Bela I. & Schlack, A. L. Learning & Review Aid for Dynamics: To Go With Engineering Mechanics. 144p. (Orig.). 1983. pap. 9.95 (ISBN 0-13-278952-3). P-H.
Smith, C. E. Applied Mechanics-Dynamics. 2nd ed. 518p. 1982. text ed. 27.95x (ISBN 0-471-02966-1). Wiley.
Sudarshan, E. C. & Mukunda, N. Classical Dynamics: A Modern Perspective. LC 82-21237. 630p. 1983. Repr. of 1974 ed. lib. bdg. write for info. (ISBN 0-89874-583-7). Krieger.
Sundermeyer, K. Constrained Dynamics, with Applications to Yang-Mills Theory, General Relativity, Classical Spin, Duel String Model. (Lecture Notes in Physics: Vol. 169). 318p. 1983. pap. 13.00 (ISBN 0-686-83753-3). Springer-Verlag.
DYNAMICS, MOLECULAR
see Molecular Dynamics
DYNAMICS, STRUCTURAL
see Structural Dynamics
DYNAMICS AND STATICS (SOCIAL SCIENCES)
see Statics and Dynamics (Social Sciences)
DYSKINESIA
American Psychiatric Association. Tardive Dyskinesia, Task Force Report Eighteen. LC 80-65372. (Monographs). (Illus.). 1980. 11.00 (ISBN 0-89042-218-4, 42-218-4). Am Psychiatric.
DYSLEXIA
see also Reading Disability
Goldberg, Herman, et al. Dyslexia: Interdisciplinary Approaches to Reading Disabilities. Date not set. price not set (ISBN 0-8089-1484-7). Grune.
Miles, T. R. Dyslexia: The Pattern of Difficulties. 256p. 1982. 27.50x (ISBN 0-398-04747-2). C C Thomas.
DYSLEXIA, DEVELOPMENTAL
see Reading Disability
DYSPEPSIA
see also Pancreas
Roth, June. Living Better with a Special Diet. LC 82-11652. 276p. 1983. lib. bdg. 12.95 (ISBN 0-668-05718-1); pap. 7.95 (ISBN 0-668-05651-7). Arco.

E

EAR
see also Hearing
Keidel, Wolfgang D. The Physiological Basis of Hearing. (Illus.). 272p. 1983. 25.00 (ISBN 0-86577-072-7). Thieme-Stratton.

EARHART, AMELIA, 1898-1937

Backus, Jean L. Letters From Amelia: An Intimate Portrait of Amelia Earhart. LC 81-68356. (Illus.). 262p. 1983. pap. 9.57 (ISBN 0-8070-6703-2, BP 655). Beacon Pr.

Sabin, Francene. Amelia Earhart: Adventure in the Sky. LC 82-15987. (Illus.). 48p. (gr. 4-6). 1983. PLB 6.89 (ISBN 0-89375-839-6); pap. text ed. 1.95 (ISBN 0-89375-840-X). Troll Assocs.

EARLY CHRISTIAN LITERATURE

see Christian Literature, Early

EARLY MAN

see Fossil Man

EARLY MAN IN THE AMERICAS

see Paleo-Indians

EARLY PRINTED BOOKS

see Bibliography-Rare Books; Incunabula

EARTH

see also Antarctic Regions; Arctic Regions; Atmosphere; Climatology; Cosmogony; Cosmology; Creation; Earthquakes; Geodesy; Geography; Geology; Geophysics; Glacial Epoch; Meteorology; Ocean; Oceanography; Physical Geography

Allen, Oliver. Atmosphere. (Planet Earth Ser.). 1983. lib. bdg. 19.92 (ISBN 0-8094-4337-6, Pub. by Time-Life). Silver.

Daily Planet Almanac. 1982. pap. 3.95 (ISBN 0-380-80838-2, 80838-2). Avon.

Earth's Resources. (Today's World Ser.). (Illus.). 1983. cancelled (ISBN 0-7134-4459-2, Pub by Batsford England). David & Charles.

Jackson, Donald. Underground Worlds. (Planet Earth Ser.). 1982. lib. bdg. 19.92 (ISBN 0-8094-4321-X, Pub. by Time-Life). Silver.

Miller, Russell. Continents in Collision. (Planet Earth Ser.). 1983. lib. bdg. 19.92 (ISBN 0-8094-4325-2, Pub. by Time-Life). Silver.

Reader's Digest Editors. Marvels & Mysteries of the World Around Us. LC 72-77610. (Illus.). 320p. 1972. 15.99 (ISBN 0-89577-012-1). RD Assn.

Royal Society Discussion Meeting, January 27-28, 1982, Proceedings. The Earth's Core: Its Structure, Evolution & Magnetic Field. Runcorn, S. K. & Creer, K. M., eds. (Illus.). 289p. 1982. text ed. 87.00x (ISBN 0-85403-192-8, Pub. by Royal Soc London). Scholium Intl.

Wyllie, Peter J. The Dynamic Earth: Textbook in Geosciences. LC 82-21239. 432p. 1983. Repr. of 1971 ed. lib. bdg. write for info. (ISBN 0-89874-584-5). Krieger.

EARTH-CHEMICAL COMPOSITION

see Geochemistry

EARTH-JUVENILE LITERATURE

Lye, Keith & Moore, Linda. All About our Earth. (Full Color Fact Books). (Illus.). 32p. (gr. 4-12). 1982. PLB 7.95 (ISBN 0-8219-0013-7, 35546). EMC.

EARTH, EFFECT OF MAN ON

see Man-Influence on Nature

EARTH SCIENCE

see Earth; Earth Sciences; Geology; Physical Geography

EARTH SCIENCES

see also Atmosphere; Climatology; Geochemistry; Geography; Geology; Geology-Graphic Methods; Geophysics; Hydrology; Meteorology; Oceanography

Bacheller, Martin A., ed. The Whole Earth Atlas: New Census Edition. (Illus.). 256p. 1983. pap. 8.95 (ISBN 0-8437-2499-4). Hammond Inc.

Benton, Floria. Hollow Earth Mysteries & the Polar Shift. 100p. (Orig.). pap. 9.95 (ISBN 0-911306-25-0). G Barker Bks.

Discovering Earth Science. (Discovering Science Ser.). 1983. lib. bdg. 15.96 (ISBN 0-86706-116-2, Pub. by Stonehenge). Silver.

Martelli, L. & Graham, A. Earth's Regions. (Our Nation, Our World Ser.). (gr. 4). Date not set. text ed. 13.72 (ISBN 0-07-039944-1); tchr's. ed. 25.00 (ISBN 0-07-039954-9); suppl. materials avail. McGraw.

Yoxall, W. H. Dynamic Models in Earth-Science Instruction. LC 82-4385. (Illus.). 200p. Date not set. price not set (ISBN 0-521-24262-2). Cambridge U Pr.

EARTH SCIENCES-BIBLIOGRAPHY

Porter, Roy S. The History of the Earth Sciences: An Annotated Bibliography. LC 81-43367. 250p. 1983. lib. bdg. 30.00 (ISBN 0-8240-9267-8). Garland Pub.

Wetherill, G. W., et al, eds. Annual Review of Earth & Planetary Sciences, Vol. 11. LC 72-82137. (Illus.). 500p. 1983. text ed. 44.00 (ISBN 0-8243-2011-5). Andrews & McMeel.

EARTHENWARE

see Pottery

EARTHQUAKES

see also Seismic Waves; Seismology; Seismometry

Crosson, R. S., et al. Compilation of Earthquake Hypo-Centers in Western Washington: 1977. (Information Circular Ser.: No. 66). (Illus.). 1979. 0.50 (ISBN 0-686-38467-9). Geologic Pubns.

Dams & Earthquake. 304p. 1981. 129.00x (ISBN 0-7277-0123-1, Pub. by Telford England). State Mutual Bk.

Golden, Frederic. The Trembling Earth: Probing & Predicting Quakes. (Illus.). 176p. (gr. 7 up). 1983. 11.95 (ISBN 0-684-17884-2, ScribJ). Scribner.

Updegraffe, Imelda & Updegraffe, Robert. Earthquakes & Volcanoes. (Turning Points Ser.). (Illus.). 24p. 1983. pap. 3.50 (ISBN 0-14-049190-2, Puffin). Penguin.

Walker, Bryce. Earthquake. LC 81-16662. (Planet Earth Ser.). lib. bdg. 19.92 (ISBN 0-8094-4301-5, Pub. by Time-Life). Silver.

EARTHQUAKES AND BUILDING

Krishna, Jai & Chandrasekaran, A. R. Elements of Earthquake Engineering. 260p. Date not set. 12.95 (ISBN 0-9605004-2-1, Pub. by Sarita Prakashan India). Eng Pubns.

EARTHS, RARE

see also kinds of rare earths, e.g. Cerium

Gschneidner, K. A. & Eyring, L., eds. Handbook of the Physics & Chemistry of Rare Earths, Vol. 5: Rare Earth Handbook. 700p. 1983. 149.00 (ISBN 0-444-86375-3, North Holland). Elsevier.

EARTHWORMS

Workshop on the Role of Earthworms in the Stabilization of Organic Residues, 2 vols. 70.00 set (ISBN 0-686-84201-4). Beech Leaf.

Workshop on the Role of Earthworms in the Stabilization of Organic Residues, 2 Vols. Set. 70.00 (ISBN 0-686-43051-4). Beech Leaf.

EAST (NEAR EAST)

see Near East

EAST ASIA-POLITICS

Weinstein, Martin E., ed. Northeast Asian Security after Vietnam. LC 82-1909. 192p. 1982. 17.50 (ISBN 0-252-00966-5). U of Ill Pr.

EAST INDIAN PHILOSOPHY

see Philosophy, Indic

EAST PAKISTAN

see Pakistan

EASTER

see also Jesus Christ-Resurrection

Berger, Gilda. Easter & Other Spring Holidays. (First Bks.). (Illus.). 72p. (gr. 4 up). 1983. PLB 8.90 (ISBN 0-531-04547-1). Watts.

Ellebracht, Mary P. Easter Passage: The RCIA Experience. 204p. 1983. pap. 11.95 (ISBN 0-86683-693-4). Winston Pr.

Merry, Eleanor C. Easter: The Legends & the Fact. Merry, Eleanor C., tr. (Illus.). 153p. 1967. 5.25 (ISBN 0-88010-048-6, Pub. by New Knowledge Bks England). Anthroposophic.

Reeder, Rachel, ed. Liturgy: Easter's Fifty Days. (Journal of The Liturgical Conference: Vol. 3, No. 1). (Illus.). 72p. 1982. pap. text ed. 7.95 (ISBN 0-918208-29-7). Liturgical Conf.

EASTER-PRAYER-BOOKS AND DEVOTIONS

Berger & Hollerweger, eds. Celebrating the Easter Vigil. O'Connell, Matthew J., tr. 160p. (Ger.). 1983. pap. 9.95 (ISBN 0-916134-56-3). Pueblo Pub Co.

EASTER-SERMONS

Steinke, Peter L. Preaching the Theology of the Cross: Sermons & Worship Ideas for Lent & Easter. LC 82-72638. 128p. (Orig.). 1983. pap. 5.95 (ISBN 0-8066-1944-9, 10-5144). Augsburg.

EASTER CAROLS

see Carols

EASTER ISLAND

Thomson, William J. Te Pito Te Henua, or Easter Island. (The Americas Collection Ser.). (Illus.). 108p. 1982. pap. 14.95 (ISBN 0-936332-14-X). Falcon Hill Pr.

EASTERN CHURCHES

see also Orthodox Eastern Church

Kucharek, Casimar. Our Faith. De Vinck, Jose M., ed. LC 82-73784. 350p. 1983. 15.75 (ISBN 0-911726-43-8). Alleluia Pr.

EASTERN EUROPE

see Europe, Eastern

EASTERN ORTHODOX CHURCH

see Orthodox Eastern Church

EASTERN STATES-DESCRIPTION AND TRAVEL-GUIDEBOOKS

Weiner, Neal O. & Schwartz, David M. The Interstate Gourmet: Mid-Atlantic States, Vol. 2. (Illus.). 256p. 1983. pap. 5.95 (ISBN 0-671-44993-1). Summit Bks.

EATING

see Dinners and Dining

EBONITE

see Rubber

ECCLESIASTICAL ARCHITECTURE

see Church Architecture

ECCLESIASTICAL ART

see Christian Art and Symbolism

ECCLESIASTICAL BIOGRAPHY

see Christian Biography

ECCLESIASTICAL DECORATION AND ORNAMENT

see Church Decoration and Ornament

ECCLESIASTICAL DISCIPLINE

see Church Discipline

ECCLESIASTICAL HISTORY

see Church History

ECCLESIASTICAL OFFICE

see Clergy-Office

ECCLESIASTICAL RITES AND CEREMONIES

see Liturgies; Rites and Ceremonies; Sacraments

ECCLESIASTICAL THEOLOGY

see Church

ECCLESIASTICAL YEAR

see Church Year

ECHINOCOCCOSIS

Echinococcosis-Hydatidosis Surveillance, Prevention & Control. (FAO Animal Production & Health Paper: No. 29). 147p. 1982. pap. 11.50 (ISBN 92-5-101205-9, F2343, FAO). Unipub.

ECHO RANGING

see Sonar

ECOLOGY

see also Animal Ecology; Animal Populations; Aquatic Ecology; Botany-Ecology; Conservation of Natural Resources; Forest Ecology; Fresh-Water Ecology; Geographical Distribution of Animals and Plants; Grassland Ecology; Human Ecology; Marine Ecology; Paleoecology; Radioecology

Barrett, Thomas S. & Livermore, Putnam. The Conservation Easement in California. 256p. 1983. 44.95 (ISBN 0-933280-20-3); pap. 24.95 (ISBN 0-933280-19-X). Island CA.

Battocletti, Joseph H. Electromagnetism, Man, & the Environment. LC 76-7905. (Westview Environmental Studies Ser.). 1976. 17.50 (ISBN 0-89158-612-1). Westview.

Benton, Allen H. & Werner, William, Jr. Manual of Field Biology & Ecology. 6th ed. 208p. 1982. 14.95x (ISBN 0-8087-4086-5). Burgess.

Brehaut, Roger N. Ecology of Rocky Shores. (Studies in Biology: No. 139). 64p. 1982. pap. text ed. 8.95 (ISBN 0-7131-2839-9). E Arnold.

Clapham, W. B., Jr. Natural Ecosystems. 2nd ed. 256p. 1983. pap. 11.95 (ISBN 0-686-38033-9). Macmillan.

Cragg, J. B. Advances in Ecological Research, Vol. 13. (Serial Publication). write for info. (ISBN 0-12-013913-8). Acad Pr.

Cragg, J. B., ed. Advances in Ecological Research, Vol. 12. (Serial Publication). 1982. 35.50 (ISBN 0-12-013912-X). Acad Pr.

Cronon, William. Changes in the Land. (Illus.). 1982. 14.50 (ISBN 0-8090-3405-0); pap. 6.75 (ISBN 0-8090-0158-6). Hill & Wang.

Discovering Ecology. LC 81-52420. (Discovering Science Ser.). lib. bdg. 15.96 (ISBN 0-86706-062-X, Pub. by Stonehenge). Silver.

Dussart, Bernard H. Man-Made Lakes As Modified Ecosystems: Scope Report 2. (Scientific Committee on Problems of the Environment Ser.). 76p. 1972. pap. 8.00x (ISBN 0-471-99595-9, Pub. by Wiley-Interscience). Wiley.

Edwards, R. W. & Brooker, M. P. The Ecology of the Wye. 1982. text ed. 41.50 (ISBN 90-6193-103-7, Pub. by Junk Pubs Netherlands). Kluwer Boston.

Ellen, Roy. Environment, Subsistence & System. LC 81-18035. (Themes in the Social Sciences). (Illus.). 340p. 1982. 39.50 (ISBN 0-521-24458-7); pap. 12.95 (ISBN 0-521-28703-0). Cambridge U Pr.

Felins, Yehuda. Nature & Man in the Bible: Chapters in Biblical Ecology. 1982. 25.00x (ISBN 0-900689-19-6). Bloch.

Florman, Samuel. Blaming Technology: The Irrational Search for Scapegoats. 224p. pap. 6.95 (ISBN 0-312-08363-7). St Martin.

Fontaine, Thomas D., III & Bartell, Steven M., eds. Dynamics of Lotic Ecosystems. LC 82-48641. (Illus.). 450p. 1983. 24.50 (ISBN 0-250-40612-8). Ann Arbor Science.

Frenkiel, Francois N. & Goodall, David W. Simulation Modeling of Environmental Problems: Scope Report 9. LC 77-92369. (Scientific Committee on Problems of the Environment). 112p. 1978. 15.00x (ISBN 0-471-99580-0, Pub. by Wiley-Interscience). Wiley.

Kruger, F. J., et al, eds. Mediterranean-Type Ecosystems: The Role of Nutrients. (Ecological Studies: Vol. 43). (Illus.). 530p. 1983. 39.50 (ISBN 0-387-12158-7). Springer-Verlag.

McKinney, John. California Coastal Trails: Mexican Border to Big Sur, Vol. I. (Illus.). 240p. (Orig.). 1983. pap. 8.95 (ISBN 0-88496-198-2). Capra Pr.

McMullen, R. Environmental Science. 1982. 55.00x (ISBN 0-333-32755-1, Pub. by Macmillan England). State Mutual Bk.

Mayer, Garry F., pref. by. Ecological Stress & the New York Bight: Science & Management. LC 82-71795. (Illus.). x, 717p. (Orig.). 1982. pap. text ed. 10.00 (ISBN 0-9608990-0-6). Estuarine Res.

Millar. Ciona. 128p. 1982. 39.00x (ISBN 0-85323-031-5, Pub. by Liverpool Univ England). State Mutual Bk.

Morgan, Mark D. Ecology of Mysidacea. 1982. text ed. 54.50 (ISBN 90-6193-761-2, Pub. by Junk Pubs Netherlands). Kluwer Boston.

OECD Staff. Economic & Ecological Interdependence. 86p. (Orig.). 1982. pap. 6.50 (ISBN 92-64-12311-3). OECD.

Packham, John R. & Harding, David J. Ecology of Woodland Processes. 256p. 1982. pap. text ed. 19.95 (ISBN 0-7131-2834-8). E Arnold.

Purdom, P. Walton & Anderson, Stanley H. Ecosystems & Human Affairs. 1980. pap. text ed. 6.50 (ISBN 0-675-08035-5). Merrill.

Risser, P. G. The True Prairie Ecosystem. LC 79-19857. (The US-IBP Synthesis Ser.: Vol. 16). 544p. 1981. 31.50 (ISBN 0-87933-361-8). Hutchinson Ross.

Rohe, Fred. Metabolic Ecology. 1982. 5.95x (ISBN 0-686-37598-X). Cancer Control Soc.

Schell, Jonathan. The Fate of the Earth. large type ed. LC 82-10299. 405p. 1982. Repr. of 1982 ed. 10.95 (ISBN 0-89621-380-3). Thorndike Pr.

Shugart, H. H. & O'Neill, R. V., eds. Systems Ecology. LC 79-970. (Benchmark Papers in Ecology: Vol. 9). 368p. 1979. 43.00 (ISBN 0-87933-347-2). Hutchinson Ross.

Shuval, Hillel I. Environmental Quality & Exology, Vol. II. 400p. 1983. pap. text ed. 44.00 (ISBN 0-86689-020-3). Balaban Intl Sci Serv.

Sumner, William G. Earth Hunger & Other Essays. 1913. text ed. 18.50x (ISBN 0-686-83530-1). Elliots Bks.

West, N. E. & Skujins, J., eds. Nitrogen in Desert Ecosystems. LC 78-17672. (US-IBP Synthesis Ser.: Vol. 9). 307p. 1978. 31.50 (ISBN 0-87933-333-2). Hutchinson Ross.

Williamson, Mark. Island Populations. (Illus.). 298p. 1983. pap. 19.95 (ISBN 0-19-854139-2). Oxford U Pr.

Winkler, David W., ed. An Ecological Study of Mono Lake, California. (Illus.). 190p. 1977. pap. 7.50 (ISBN 0-939714-00-0). Mono Basin Res.

ECOLOGY-JUVENILE LITERATURE

Szekely, Edmond B. Brother Tree. (Illus.). 32p. 1977. pap. 3.50 (ISBN 0-89564-074-0). IBS Intl.

ECOLOGY-STUDY AND TEACHING

Ford, Phyllis. Eco-Acts. rev. 2nd ed. 200p. 1982. 10.00 (ISBN 0-686-84023-2). U OR Ctr Leisure.

ECOLOGY, HUMAN

see Human Ecology

ECONOMETRICS

see also Economics, Mathematical; Statistics

Bridge, J. Applied Econometrics. 1971. 29.50 (ISBN 0-444-10098-9). Elsevier.

Chow, Gregory C. Econometrics. 416p. 1983. text ed. 29.95x (ISBN 0-07-010847-1, C). McGraw.

Goldberger, Arthur S. Econometric Theory. LC 64-10370. (Probability & Mathematical Statistics Ser.). (Illus.). 1964. 32.95x (ISBN 0-471-31101-4). Wiley.

Greenberg, Edward & Webster, Charles E. Advanced Econometrics: A Bridge to the Current Literature. (Probability & Mathematical Statistics Ser.). 352p. 1983. text ed. 34.95 (ISBN 0-471-09077-8). Wiley.

Griliches, A. & Intriligator, M. D., eds. Handbook of Econometrics, 3 Vols. 1200p. 1983. Set. 198.00 (ISBN 0-444-86188-2, North Holland); 65.00 ea. Vol. 1 (ISBN 0-444-86185-8). Vol. 2 (ISBN 0-444-86186-6). Vol. 3 (ISBN 0-444-86187-4). Elsevier.

Gruber, J., ed. Econometric Decision Models: Proceedings, Hagen, FRG, 1981. (Lecture Notes in Economics & Mathematical Systems Ser.: Vol. 208). (Illus.). 364p. 1983. pap. 24.50 (ISBN 0-387-11554-4). Springer-Verlag.

Hildenbrand, Werner, ed. Advances in Econometrics. LC 81-18171. (Econometric Society Monograph in Quantitative Economics). 282p. 1983. 39.50 (ISBN 0-521-24572-9). Cambridge U Pr.

Maddala, G. S. Econometrics. 1977. 30.95 (ISBN 0-07-039412-1). McGraw.

--Limited-Dependent & Qualitative Variables in Economometrics. LC 82-9554. (Econometric Society Monographs in Quantitative Economics 3). 416p. Date not set. 39.50 (ISBN 0-521-24143-X). Cambridge U Pr.

Migliaro, Al & Jain, Chaman L. An Executive's Guide to Econometric Forecasting. 74p. 1983. pap. 24.95 (ISBN 0-932126-10-3). Graceway.

Shapiro, Harold T. & Fulton, George A. A Regional Econometric Forecasting System: Major Economic Areas of Michigan. 1983. 35.00 (ISBN 0-472-10035-1). U of Mich Pr.

Szego, Giorgio, ed. New Quantitative Techniques for Economic Analysis: Economic Theory, Econometrics & Mathematical Economics Ser. 1982. 49.50 (ISBN 0-12-680760-4). Acad Pr.

ECONOMIC ANTHROPOLOGY

Singh, K. S. Economies of the Tribes & Their Transformation. 400p. 1982. text ed. 41.00x (ISBN 0-391-02786-7, 40956, Pub. by Concept India). Humanities.

ECONOMIC ASSISTANCE

see also Loans; Reconstruction (1939-1951); Technical Assistance

McDonald, John W. The North-South Dialogue & the United Nations. LC 82-1039. 24p. 1982. 1.25 (ISBN 0-934742-16-2, Inst Study Diplomacy). Geo U Sch For Serv.

Mikesell, Raymond F. & Kilmarx, Robert A. The Economics of Foreign Aid & Self-Sustaining Development. 106p. 1983. lib. bdg. 17.50x (ISBN 0-86531-577-9). Westview.

Thompson, Kenneth W. Foreign Assistance: A View from the Private Sector. LC 82-25091. 170p. 1983. pap. text ed. 8.75 (ISBN 0-8191-2713-2). U Pr of Amer.

ECONOMIC ASSISTANCE, DOMESTIC

see also Community Development; Grants-In-Aid; Subsidies; Unemployed

Johnson, Harriette C. & Goldberg, Gertrude S. Government Money for Everyday People. 1982. pap. 10.00 (ISBN 0-536-03867-8). Adelphi Univ.

ECONOMIC CONCENTRATION

see Oligopolies

ECONOMIC CONDITIONS

see Economic History

ECONOMIC CYCLES

see Business Cycles

ECONOMIC DEVELOPMENT

Here are entered general works on the theory and policy of economic development. Works restricted to a particular area are entered under the name of the area. see also Industrialization; Saving and Investment; Underdeveloped Areas

Chatterji, Manas. Management & Regional Science for Economic Development. 1982. lib. bdg. 30.00 (ISBN 0-89838-108-8). Kluwer-Nijhoff.

Chilcote, Ronald H. & Johnson, Dale L., eds. Theories of Development: Mode of Production or Dependency? (Class, State & Development Ser.: Vol. 2). (Illus.). 272p. 1983. 25.00 (ISBN 0-8039-1925-5); pap. 12.50 (ISBN 0-8039-1926-3). Sage.

Different Theories & Practices of Development. 258p. 1982. pap. 30.00 (ISBN 92-3-102002-1, U1225, UNESCO). Unipub.

Elusive Development. 265p. pap. 11.00 (ISBN 0-686-82537-3, SD 034, UN Res Inst). Unipub.

Gilbert, Alan, ed. Development Planning & Spatial Structure. LC 75-30804. 207p. 1976. 34.50x (ISBN 0-471-29904-9, Pub. by Wiley-Interscience). Wiley.

Gillis, Malcolm, et al. Economic Development. 650p. text ed. 21.95x (ISBN 0-393-95253-3). Norton.

Hammergren, Linn. Development & the Politics of Administrative Reform: Lessons from Latin America. (Replica Edition Ser.). 220p. 1983. softcover 19.00x (ISBN 0-86531-956-1). Westview.

Hammond, R. Air Survey in Economic Development. 1967. 10.00 (ISBN 0-444-19916-0). Elsevier.

Handbook of International Trade & Development Statistics: Supplement 1981. 33.00 (ISBN 0-686-84903-5, E/F.82.II.D.11). UN.

Higgott, Richard A. Political Development Theory: The Contemporary Debate. LC 82-42718. 140p. 1983. 18.95x (ISBN 0-312-62225-2). St Martin.

Jhingan, M. L. The Economics of Development & Planning. 15th ed. 600p. 1982. text ed. 40.00x (ISBN 0-7069-2057-0, Pub. by Vikas India). Advent NY.

Kindleberger, C. & Herrick, Bruce. Economic Development. 4th ed. 560p. 1983. 25.95x (ISBN 0-07-034584-8). McGraw.

Kristensen. Development in Rich & Poor Countries. 2nd ed. 152p. 1982. 20.95 (ISBN 0-03-059053-1). Praeger.

Leonard, David K. & Marshall, Dale R., eds. Institutions of Rural Development for the Poor: Decentralization & Organizational Linkages. LC 82-15651. (Research Ser.: No. 49). xii, 237p. 1982. pap. 11.50x (ISBN 0-87725-149-5). U of Cal Intl St.

Loehr, William & Powelson, John P. Threat to Development: Pitfalls of the NIE. (Special Study in Social, Political, & Economic Developmen). 160p. 1982. lib. bdg. 22.00X (ISBN 0-86531-128-5); pap. text ed. 10.00 (ISBN 0-86531-129-3). Westview.

Manual for the Preparation of Records in Development-Information Systems: Recommended Methods for Development-Information Systems. 272p. 1983. pap. 20.00 (ISBN 0-88936-354-4, IDRC TS40, IDRC). Unipub.

Mico, Paul R. Developing Your Community-Based Organization: With Special Emphasis on Community Economic Development Organizations & Community Action Agencies. LC 80-53828. (Illus.). 160p. 1981. pap. text ed. 7.95 (ISBN 0-89914-004-1). Third Party Pub.

Mikesell, Raymond F. & Kilmarx, Robert A. The Economics of Foreign Aid & Self-Sustaining Development. 106p. 1983. lib. bdg. 17.50x (ISBN 0-86531-577-9). Westview.

Mueller, Dennis C., ed. The Political Economy of Growth. LC 81-15955. 296p. 1983. text ed. 23.50x (ISBN 0-300-02658-7). Yale U Pr.

Nektarios, Miltiadis. Public Pensions, Capital Formation, & Economic Growth. Replica ed. 175p. 1982. softcover 20.00 (ISBN 0-86531-936-7). Westview.

Nieuwenhuijze, C. A. van. Development Begins at Home: Problems & Prospects of the Sociology of Development. LC 82-304. (Illus.). 352p. 1982. 27.50 (ISBN 0-08-027415-3). Pergamon.

Northeast Midwest Institute, compiled by. Guide to Government resources for Economic Development, 1983: A Handbook for Non-Profit Agencies & Municipalities. 19.95 (ISBN 0-686-38891-7). Public Serv Materials.

Obudho, R. A. & Taylor, D. R. F. The Spatial Structure of Development. (Replica Edition Ser.). 315p. 1979. softcover 32.50x (ISBN 0-89158-597-4). Westview.

Pasinetti, Luigi. Structural Change & Economic Growth. LC 80-41496. 296p. Date not set. pap. 14.95 (ISBN 0-521-27410-9). Cambridge U Pr.

Planned Development & Self-Management. (UNCRD Working Paper: No. 82-8). 15p. 1983. pap. 6.00 (ISBN 0-686-43298-3, CRD 145, UNCRD). Unipub.

Ramanathan, R. Introduction to The Theory of Economic Growth. (Lecture Notes in Economics & Mathematical Systems: Vol. 205). (Illus.). 347p. 1983. pap. 23.00 (ISBN 0-387-11943-4). Springer-Verlag.

Regional Development Dialogue, Vol. 3, No. 1. 242p. 1982. pap. 16.75 (ISBN 0-686-84617-6, CRD139, UNCRD). Unipub.

Research & Development Systems in Rural Settings: Background on the Project. 85p. 1982. pap. 5.00 (ISBN 92-808-0363-8, TUNU207, UNU). Unipub.

Roman, Zoltan. Productivity & Economic Growth. Lukacs, Laszlo, tr. from Hungarian. LC 82-173070. (Illus.). 276p. 1982. 30.00x (ISBN 963-05-2786-3). Intl Pubns Serv.

Rudman, Jack. Development Specialist. (Career Examination Ser.: C-923). (Cloth bdg. avail. on request). pap. 12.00 (ISBN 0-8373-0923-9). Natl Learning.

--Economic Opportunity Program Specialist. (Career Examination Ser.: C-2545). (Cloth bdg. avail. on request). pap. 12.00 (ISBN 0-8373-2545-5). Natl Learning.

--Principal Developmental Specialist. (Career Examination Ser.: C-925). (Cloth bdg. avail. on request). pap. 14.00 (ISBN 0-8373-0925-5). Natl Learning.

Victoria, Pablo. Foundations of Economic Development: Intelligence vs. Capital. (Illus.). 128p. 1983. 7.50 (ISBN 0-682-49932-3). Exposition.

World Bank. IDA in Retrospect: The First Two Decades of the International Development Association. (Illus.). 142p. 1982. 17.95 (ISBN 0-19-520407-7); pap. 6.00 (ISBN 0-19-520408-5). Oxford U Pr.

ECONOMIC DEVELOPMENT-ADDRESSES, ESSAYS, LECTURES

Dobb, Maurice. An Essay on Economic Growth & Planning. 119p. 1977. 10.75 (ISBN 0-7100-1284-5). Routledge & Kegan.

ECONOMIC DEVELOPMENT-SOCIAL ASPECTS

Correa, Hector & El Torky, Mohamed A. The Biological & Social Determinants of the Demographic Transition. LC 82-16042. (Illus.). 298p. (Orig.). 1983. lib. bdg. 24.25 (ISBN 0-8191-2754-X); pap. text ed. 12.75 (ISBN 0-8191-2755-8). U Pr of Amer.

Swanson, Jon C. Emigration & Economic Development. LC 79-5155. (Replica Edition Ser.). 125p. 1979. softcover 16.00x (ISBN 0-89158-690-3). Westview.

ECONOMIC ENTOMOLOGY

see Insects, Injurious and Beneficial

ECONOMIC FORECASTING

see also Business Forecasting; Economic Indicators

Bird, Caroline. The Good Years: Your Life in the 21st Century. 288p. 1983. 15.95 (01549-460). Dutton.

Faaland, Just. Population & the World Economy in the 21st Century. LC 82-10579. 272p. 1982. 32.50x (ISBN 0-312-63123-5). St Martin.

Migliaro, Al & Jain, Chaman L. An Executive's Guide to Econometric Forecasting. 74p. 1983. pap. 24.95 (ISBN 0-932126-10-3). Graceway.

Shapiro, Harold T. & Fulton, George A. A Regional Econometric Forecasting System: Major Economic Areas of Michigan. 1983. 35.00 (ISBN 0-472-10035-1). U of Mich Pr.

Shvyrkov, V. V. Statistical Science in Economic Forecasting. (Illus.). 212p. (Orig.). 1983. pap. 18.30 wkbk. (ISBN 0-942004-04-3). G Throwkoff.

ECONOMIC GROWTH

see Economic Development

ECONOMIC HISTORY

see also subdivision Economic conditions under names of countries, regions, cities, etc. Also Automation-Economic aspects

Beenstock, Michael. The World Economy in Transition. 240p. 1983. text ed. 25.00x (ISBN 0-04-339033-1). Allen Unwin.

Fay, Stephan. Beyond Greed. 1983. pap. 6.95 (ISBN 0-14-006688-8). Penguin.

Hughes, Jonathan R. American Economic History. 1983. text ed. 24.95x (ISBN 0-673-15338-X). Scott F.

Kenwood, A. G. & Lougheed, A. L. The Growth of the International Economy, 1820-1980: An Introductory Text. 320p. 1983. pap. text ed. 12.95x (ISBN 0-04-330332-3). Allen Unwin.

Nove, Alec. The Economics of Feasible Socialism. 272p. 1983. text ed. 29.50x (ISBN 0-04-335048-8); pap. text ed. 9.95x (ISBN 0-04-335049-6). Allen Unwin.

Richardson, Peter. Chinese Mine Labour in the Transvaal. 287p. 1982. text ed. 31.50x (ISBN 0-333-27222-6, Pub. by Macmillan England). Humanities.

Slaven, A. & Aldcroft, D., eds. Business, Banking & Urban History: Essays in Honour of S. G. Checkland. 235p. 1982. text ed. 31.50x (ISBN 0-85976-083-9, 40292, Pub. by Donald Scotland). Humanities.

Stigler, George J. Essays in the History of Economics. LC 65-14426. (Phoenix Ser.). viii, 392p. Date not set. pap. 9.95 (ISBN 0-226-77427-9). U of Chicago Pr.

World Economic Survey 1981-1982. 9.00 (ISBN 0-686-84910-8, E.82.II.C.1). UN.

ECONOMIC HISTORY-20TH CENTURY

Faaland, Just. Population & the World Economy in the 21st Century. LC 82-10579. 272p. 1982. 32.50x (ISBN 0-312-63123-5). St Martin.

Overy, R. The Nazi Economic Recovery Nineteen Thirty-two to Nineteen Thirty-eight. (Studies in Economic & Social History). 80p. 1982. pap. text ed. 4.75x (ISBN 0-333-31119-1, Pub. by Macmillan England). Humanities.

ECONOMIC INDICATORS

Lynn, E. Russell, Jr. The Mters-Briggs Type Indicator: The Dignity of Difference. (Illus.). 1983. write for info. (ISBN 0-935652-10-8). Ctr Applications Psych.

Powers, Mary G. Measures of Socio-Economic Status: Current Issues. (AAAS Selected Symposium 81). 205p. 1982. lib. bdg. 20.00x (ISBN 0-86531-395-4). Westview.

ECONOMIC INTEGRATION, INTERNATIONAL

see International Economic Integration

ECONOMIC POISONS

see Pesticides

ECONOMIC POLICY

see also Agriculture and State; Commercial Policy; Comparative Economics; Economic Assistance; Economic Assistance, Domestic; Economic Development; Economic Security; Economic Stabilization; Fiscal Policy; Full Employment Policies; Government Ownership; Government Spending Policy; Industrial Laws and Legislation; Industrial Mobilization; Industrialization; Industry and State; Inflation (Finance); International Economic Relations; Labor Supply; Laissez-Faire; Land Reform; Manpower Policy; Monetary Policy; Social Policy; Subsidies; Technical Assistance; Unemployed; Wage-Price Policy; Welfare Economics

also subdivisions Commercial Policy and Economic Policy under names of countries

Anderson, James E. Economic Regulatory Policies. 241p. 1976. pap. 9.95 (ISBN 0-8093-0818-5). Lexington Bks.

Boes, D., et al, eds. Public Production: International Seminar in Public Economics, Bonn, FRG 1981. (Journal of Economics Supplementum: Vol. 2). (Illus.). 222p. 1983. pap. 62.00 (ISBN 0-387-81726-3). Springer-Verlag.

Bray, Jeremy. Production, Purpose & Structure. LC 82-42603. 1982. 19.95x (ISBN 0-312-64778-6). St Martin.

Chakravarty, Sukhamoy. Alternative Approaches to a Theory of Economic Growth: Marx, Marshall & Schumpeter. (R. C. Dutt Lectures on Political Economy Ser.: 1980). 1982. pap. text ed. 4.95x (ISBN 0-86131-355-0, Pub. by Orient Longman Ltd India). Apt Bks.

Foreman-Peck, James. A History of the World Economy: Economic Relations Since 1850. LC 82-24295. 320p. 1983. text ed. 27.50 (ISBN 0-389-20337-8). B&N Imports.

Gowland, D. H. Modern Economic Analysis. new ed. 224p. (Orig.). 1982. text ed. write for info.; pap. write for info. (ISBN 0-408-10772-3). Butterworth.

Hughes-Hallett, Andrew & Rees, Hedley. Quantitative Economic Policies & Interactive Planning: A Reconstruction of the Theory of Economic Policy. LC 82-4204. 370p. Date not set. 49.50 (ISBN 0-521-23718-1). Cambridge U Pr.

Lavoie, Don C. National Economic Planning: What Is Left? 175p. 1983. pap. 6.95 (ISBN 0-932790-35-6). Cato Inst.

Law & Economics Center of Emory University. Supreme Court Economic Review, Vol. I. Aranson, Peter H., ed. 1983. 29.95X (ISBN 0-02-918160-7). Macmillan.

Marcy, Sam. Anatomy of the Economic Crisis. 120p. 1982. pap. 3.25 (ISBN 0-89567-077-1). WV Pubs.

Mueller, Dennis C., ed. The Political Economy of Growth. LC 81-15955. 296p. 1983. text ed. 23.50x (ISBN 0-300-02658-7). Yale U Pr.

Myrdal, Gunnar. Beyond the Welfare State: Economic Planning & Its International Implications. LC 82-15819. xiii, 287p. 1982. Repr. of 1960 ed. lib. bdg. 35.00x (ISBN 0-313-23697-6, MYBW). Greenwood.

O'Driscoll, Gerald P. Inflation or Deflation? Prospects for Capital Formation, Employment, & Economic Recovery. (Pacific Institute). 1983. write for info. (ISBN 0-88410-930-5). Ballinger Pub.

OECD Staff. International Aspects of Inflation. The Hidden Economy. (OECD Occasional Studies). (Orig.). 1982. pap. 14.50x (ISBN 92-64-12330-X). OECD.

--OECD Economic Outlook, No. 31. 150p. 1982. pap. 11.00 (ISBN 0-686-37445-2). OECD.

--OECD Economic Outlook Historical Statistics, 1960-1980. 150p. (Orig.). 1982. pap. 11.00x (ISBN 92-64-02325-9). OECD.

Purcell, L. E., ed. Economic Recovery Tax Act: Implications for State Finances. 20p. 1982. pap. 5.00 (ISBN 0-87292-030-5). Coun State Govts.

Ritter, Lawrence S. & Silber, William L. Principles of Money, Banking, & Financial Markets. 1983. text ed. 23.95x (ISBN 0-686-82533-0); write for info. (ISBN 0-465-06345-4); wkbk. 10.00. Basic.

Rousseau, Jean-Jacques. Of the Social Contract & Discourse on the Origin of Inequality & Discourse on Political Economy. Cress, Donald A., tr. from Fr. (HPC Philosophical Classics Ser.). 288p. 1983. lib. bdg. 15.95 (ISBN 0-915145-57-X); pap. text ed. 4.95 (ISBN 0-915145-56-1). Hackett Pub.

Stone, Alan. The Political Economy of Public Policy. (Sage Yearbooks in Politics & Public Policy: Vol. 10). 256p. 1982. 25.00 (ISBN 0-8039-1795-3); pap. 12.50 (ISBN 0-8039-1796-1). Sage.

Townsend, Alan R. The Impact of Recession: On Industry, Employment & the Regions, 1976-1981. 224p. 1983. text ed. 30.00x (ISBN 0-7099-2417-8, Pub. by Croom Helm Ltd England). Biblio Dist.

Williamson, John. The Open Economy & the World Economy: A Textbook in International Economics. 1983. text ed. 23.95x (ISBN 0-465-05287-8). Basic.

ECONOMIC POLICY-MATHEMATICAL MODELS

Multiregional Economic Modeling: Practice & Prospect. (Studies in Regional Science & Urban Economics: Vol. 9). 336p. 1983. 55.75 (ISBN 0-444-86485-7, North Holland). Elsevier.

ECONOMIC RELATIONS, FOREIGN

see International Economic Relations

ECONOMIC RESEARCH

see also Economic Surveys; Market Surveys

Laumer, Helmut & Ziegler, Maria, eds. International Research on Business Cycle Surveys: Papers Presented at the 15th Conference Proceedings, Athens, 1981. 499p. 1982. text ed. 63.00x (ISBN 0-566-00439-9). Gower Pub Ltd.

Washington Information Workbook. 6th ed. 65.00 (ISBN 0-934940-12-6). Wash Res.

ECONOMIC SECURITY

see also Full Employment Policies; Old Age Pensions; Public Welfare; Social Security; Wages; Wages-Minimum Wage

Anell, Lars. Recession, the Western Economies & the Changing World Order. 181p. 1982. pap. 9.50 (ISBN 0-86187-243-6). F Pinter Pubs.

How to Survive & Prosper in the Next American Depression, War or Revolution. 13.95 (ISBN 0-686-38782-1). FMA Bus.

ECONOMIC STABILIZATION

Calmfors, Lars. Long-Run Effects of Short-Run Stabilization Policy. 276p. 1983. text ed. 30.75x (ISBN 0-333-33172-9, Pub. by Macmillan England). Humanities.

ECONOMIC STATISTICS

see Economic History (for collections of statistics), Statistics (for works on the theory and methodology of economic statistics)

ECONOMIC SURVEYS

see also Market Surveys

Bendavid-Val, Avron. Regional & Local Economic Analysis for Practicioners. new ed. (Illus.). 208p. 1983. 29.95 (ISBN 0-03-062912-8); pap. 13.95 (ISBN 0-03-062913-6). Praeger.

ECONOMIC THEORY

see Economics

ECONOMIC UNION

see International Economic Integration

ECONOMICS

see also Balance of Trade; Banks and Banking; Barter; Business; Capital; Capitalism; Christianity and Economics; Commerce; Comparative Economics; Competition; Consumption (Economics); Cooperation; Cost; Cost and Standard of Living; Credit; Debt; Debts, Public; Demography; Division of Labor; Econometrics; Economic Development; Economic Forecasting; Economic History; Economic Policy; Employment (Economic Theory); Entrepreneur; Exchange; Finance; Finance, Public; Government Ownership; Gross National Product; Income; Individualism; Industry; Interest and Usury; Keynesian Economics; Labor and Laboring Classes; Labor Economics; Laissez-Faire; Land Use; Macroeconomics; Managerial Economics; Manufactures; Marxian Economics; Microeconomics; Money; Population; Profit; Property; Rent; Risk; Saving and Investment; Self-Interest; Socialism; Space in Economics; Statics and Dynamics (Social Sciences); Statistics; Supply and Demand; Taxation; Transportation; Value; Wages; Wealth; Welfare Economics

Allen, Polly R. & Kenen, Peter B. Asset Markets & Exchange Rates: Modeling an Open Economy. LC 79-16874. 352p. Date not set. pap. 17.95 (ISBN 0-521-27406-0). Cambridge U Pr.

Anthony, T. M. The Way Out. LC 82-72166. (Illus.). 141p. (Orig.). 1982. pap. 5.95 (ISBN 0-89305-042-3). Anna Pub.

Ayres, R. U. Resources, Environment, & Economics: Applications of the Materials-Energy Balance Principle. 207p. Repr. of 1978 ed. text ed. 40.00 (ISBN 0-471-02627-1). Krieger.

Banks, Arthur S., et al. Economic Handbook of the World: 1982. 640p. 1982. 44.95 (ISBN 0-07-003692-6, P&RB). McGraw.

Baranzini, Mauro. Advances In Economic Theory. LC 82-42613. 330p. 1982. 35.00 (ISBN 0-312-00636-5). St Martin.

Bartlett, Ronald & Wolfson, Marty. Galbraiths Garbled Economics. (Illus.). 1974. pap. 1.95 (ISBN 0-916114-03-1). Wolfson.

Bates, James & Parkinson, J. R., eds. Business Economics. (Illus.). 36p. 1982. text ed. 22.50x (ISBN 0-631-13146-9, Pub. by Basil Blackwell England); pap. text ed. 9.50x (ISBN 0-631-13147-7, Pub. by Basil Blackwell England). Biblio Dist.

Budnick, Frank S Applied Mathematics for Business, Economics & the Social Sciences. 2nd ed. 842p. 1983. 26.50x (ISBN 0-07-008858-6); write for info. (ISBN 0-07-008859-4). McGraw.

Davis, J. Morton. How to Make the Economy Succeed. LC 82-15776. 336p. 1983. 14.95 (ISBN 0-87663-402-1). Universe.

Dornbusch, Rudiger & Fischer, Stanley. Economics. (Illus.). 1008p. 1983. 25.95x (ISBN 0-07-017757-0); study guide 10.95 (ISBN 0-07-017759-7); instr's. manual 8.95 (ISBN 0-07-017758-9); transparency masters 8.95 (ISBN 0-07-017764-3). McGraw.

Dumont, Louis. From Mandeville to Marx: The Genesis & Triumph of Economic Ideology. LC 76-8087. (Midway Reprint Ser.). 236p. 1977. pap. write for info. (ISBN 0-226-16966-9). U of Chicago Pr.

Evans, Michael K. The Truth About Supply-Side Economics. 230p. 1983. 17.95 (ISBN 0-465-08778-7). Basic.

Federal Reserve Bank of Atlanta & Emory University Law & Economics Center. Supply-Side Economics in the Nineteen Eighties: Conference Proceedings. LC 82-15025. (Illus.). 572p. 1982. lib. bdg. 35.00 (ISBN 0-89930-045-6, FSU/, Quorum). Greenwood.

Friedman, Milton. Bright Promises, Dismal Performance: An Economist's Protests. 272p. 16.95 (ISBN 0-15-114152-5). HarBraceJ.

--Bright Promises, Dismal Performance: An Economist's Protest. 272p. pap. 5.95 (ISBN 0-15-614161-2, Harv). HarBraceJ.

Gordon, Alan. Economics & Social Policy: An Introduction. (Illus.). 224p. 1982. text ed. 24.95x (ISBN 0-85520-527-X, Pub. by Martin Robertson England). Biblio Dist.

Greenwald, Douglas, et al. The McGraw-Hill Dictionary of Modern Economics. 3rd ed. (Illus.). 656p. 1983. 49.95 (ISBN 0-07-024376-X, P&RB). McGraw.

Harbury, C. D., ed. Workbook in Introductory Economics. 3rd ed. (Illus.). 176p. 1982. 7.00 (ISBN 0-08-027442-0). Pergamon.

Hawken, Paul. The Nest Economy. (Illus.). 252p. 1983. 12.95 (ISBN 0-686-84860-8). HR&W.

Heertje, Arnold, et al. Economics. 480p. 1983. pap. text ed. 18.95 (ISBN 0-03-059336-0). Dryden Pr.

Heilbroner, Robert L. & Thurow, Lester C. The Economic Problem: (Second CPCU Edition) 6th ed. LC 80-16631. 670p. 1981. Repr. of 1981 ed. text ed. 22.00 (ISBN 0-89463-032-6). Am Inst Property.

Heyne, Paul T. The Economic Way of Thinking. 4th ed. 208p. 1983. text ed. write for info. (ISBN 0-574-19425-8); write for info. tchr's ed. (ISBN 0-574-19426-6); write for info. student guide (ISBN 0-574-19427-4). SRA.

Hodgetts, R. & Smart, T. Essentials of Economics & Free Enterprise. (gr. 9-12). 1982. pap. text ed. 19.60 (ISBN 0-201-03958-3); manual 21.20 (ISBN 0-201-03959-1). A-W.

Jarvis, Ana C. & Lebredo, Raquel. Business & Economics Workbook. 256p. 1983. pap. 7.95 (ISBN 0-669-05337-6). Heath.

Jhingan, M. L. The Economics of Development & Planning. 15th ed. 600p. 1982. text ed. 40.00x (ISBN 0-7069-2057-0, Pub. by Vikas India). Advent NY.

Khiel, Alois. Kommunailwirtschaft und Wirtschaftsordnung. 161p. (Ger.). 1982. write for info. (ISBN 3-8204-5788-7). P Lang Pubs.

Kornai, Janos. Growth, Shortage & Efficiency: A Macrodynamic Model of the Socialist Economy. 142p. 1983. text ed. 19.50x (ISBN 0-520-04901-2). U of Cal Pr.

Kozma, Ferenc. Economy Integration & Economic Strategy. 1982. lib. bdg. 48.00 (ISBN 90-247-2649-2, Pub. by Martinus Nijhoff Netherlands). Kluwer Boston.

Kreinin, Mordechai. Economics: An Introductory Text. (Illus.). 544p. 1983. pap. text ed. 19.95 (ISBN 0-13-224261-3). P-H.

Lauber. The Politics of Economic Policy. 128p. 1983. write for info. Praeger.

Lee, Dwight R. & McNown, Robert F. Economics in Our Time: Concepts & Issues. 2nd ed. 224p. 1983. pap. text ed. write for info. (ISBN 0-574-19435-5, 13-2435); write for info. instr's. guide (ISBN 0-574-19436-3). SRA.

McKenzie, George. Measuring Economic Welfare: New Methods. LC 82-4422. 208p. Date not set. 32.50 (ISBN 0-521-24862-0). Cambridge U Pr.

McKenzie, Richard B. The Limits of Economic Science. 1982. lib. bdg. 23.00 (ISBN 0-89838-116-9). Kluwer-Nijhoff.

McPhalle, David B. The Adam Smith's Theory of Economic Psychology. (The Most Meaningful Classics in World Culture Ser.). (Illus.). 117p. 1983. 49.75 (ISBN 0-89266-376-6). Am Classical Coll Pr.

Miernyk, William H. Illusions of Conventional Economics. 1982. 6.95 (ISBN 0-937058-14-9). West Va U Pr.

Miller, Roger L. & Pulsinelli, Robert W. Understanding Economics. (Illus.). 1983. text ed. 19.95 (ISBN 0-314-69669-5); instrs.' manual avail. (ISBN 0-314-71114-7); study guide avail. (ISBN 0-314-71143-0). West Pub.

Moffat, Robert E. Money & Wealth in the Affluent Society: Some Pratical Realities. 1983. 11.95 (ISBN 0-533-05607-1). Vantage.

Nyilas, Jozsef. The World Economy & Its Main Developmental Tendencies. 1982. lib. bdg. 49.50 (ISBN 0-686-38405-9, Pub. by Martinus Nijhoff Netherlands). Kluwer Boston.

Perelman, Michael. Classical Political Economy: Primitive Accumulation & the Social Division of Labor. 224p. 1983. text ed. 25.95x (ISBN 0-86598-095-0). Allanheld.

Porter, Roger. Presidential Decision Making: The Economic Policy Board. LC 80-10165. 272p. 1982. pap. 9.95 (ISBN 0-521-27112-6). Cambridge U Pr.

Salvatore, D. Schaum's Outline of International Economics. 2nd ed. 256p. 1983. 7.95 (ISBN 0-07-050640-X, P&RB). McGraw.

Shefrin, Steven M. Rational Expectations. LC 82-19747. (Cambridge Surveys of Economic Literature Ser.). 215p. Date not set. 29.95 (ISBN 0-521-24310-6); pap. 8.95 (ISBN 0-521-28595-X). Cambridge U Pr.

Smith, Adam. The Wealth of Nations. Cannan, Edwin, ed. & intro. by. 9.95 (ISBN 0-394-60409-1). Modern Lib.

--Wealth of Nations. LC 37-3720. 1976. 24.95 (ISBN 0-910220-79-4). Berg.

Smith, Charles W. The Mind of the Market. LC 82-48235. 224p. 1983. pap. 5.72i (ISBN 0-06-090993-5, CN 993, CN). Har-Row.

Solow, Robert & Brown, E. Carey, eds. Paul Samuelson & Modern Economic Theory. 350p. 1983. 27.00 (ISBN 0-07-059667-0, C). McGraw.

Sorel, George. Social Foundation of Contemporary Economy. Stanley, John L., ed. 270p. 1983. Repr. 39.95 (ISBN 0-87855-482-3). Transaction Bks.

Spiegel, Henry W. The Growth of Economic Thought. rev. ed. 880p. 1983. text ed. 37.50 (ISBN 0-8223-0550-X); pap. text ed. 22.50 (ISBN 0-8223-0551-8). Duke.

Stegmueller, W., et al, eds. Philosophy of Economics, Munich, Federal Republic of Germany, 1981: Proceedings. (Studies in Contemporary Economics: Vol. 2). (Illus.). 306p. 1983. pap. 21.00 (ISBN 0-387-11927-2). Springer-Verlag.

Toch, Henry. Economics for Professional Studies. 240p. 1979. 29.00x (ISBN 0-7121-0568-9, Pub. by Macdonald & Evans). State Mutual Bk.

Tuccille, Jerome. Inside the Underground Economy. 158p. 1982. pap. 2.50 (ISBN 0-451-11648-8, AE1648, Sig). NAL.

Ullman, John E., ed. Social Costs in Modern Society: A Qualitative & Quantitative Assessment. LC 82-18590. (Illus.). 272p. 1983. lib. bdg. 29.95 (ISBN 0-89930-019-7, USC/, Quorum). Greenwood.

Weidenaar, Dennis J. & Weiler, Emanuel. Economics: An Introduction to the World Around You. 3rd ed. LC 82-11477. 512p. Date not set. pap. text ed. 17.95 (ISBN 0-201-08271-3). A-W.

Witker. Derecho Economico. (Span.). 1983. pap. text ed. write for info. (ISBN 0-06-319370-1, Pub. by HarLA Mexico). Har-Row.

ECONOMICS–ADDRESSES, ESSAYS, AND LECTURES

American Institute, ed. Reading in Economics. LC 81-66115. 189p. 1981. pap. 10.00 (ISBN 0-89463-028-8). Am Inst Property.

Colander, David C., ed. Selected Economic Writings of Abba P. Lerner. (Selected Economic Writings Ser.). 752p. 1983. text ed. 65.00X (ISBN 0-8147-1385-8). NYU Pr.

Dutta, M. & Hartline, Jessie, eds. Essays in Regional Economic Studies. LC 82-71901. 336p. 1983. 27.50 (ISBN 0-89386-005-0). Acorn NC.

Gersovitz, Mark, ed. Selected Economic Writings of W. Arthur Lewis. (Selected Economic Writings Ser.). 832p. 1983. text ed. 65.00X (ISBN 0-686-82268-4). NYU Pr.

Hill, Ivan, ed. Ethical Basis of Economic Freedom. LC 87-5829. 325p. 1980. pap. 15.95 (ISBN 0-686-81709-5). Ethics Res Ctr.

Needy, Charles W., ed. Classics of Economics. (Classics Ser.). (Orig.). 1980. pap. 12.50x (ISBN 0-935610-12-X). Moore Pub IL.

Samuelson, Paul. Economics from the Heart: A Samuelson Sampler. 320p. cloth 19.95 (ISBN 0-15-127487-8). HarBraceJ.

--Economics from the Heart: A Samuelson Sampler. 320p. pap. 6.95 (ISBN 0-15-627551-1, Harv). HarBraceJ.

Stigler, George J. Essays in the History of Economics. LC 65-14426. (Phoenix Ser.). viii, 392p. Date not set. pap. 9.95 (ISBN 0-226-77427-9). U of Chicago Pr.

ECONOMICS–BIBLIOGRAPHY

Bulkley, Mildred E. Bibliographical Survey of Contemporary Sources for the Economic & Social History of the World War. 1922. text ed. 75.00x (ISBN 0-686-83490-9). Elliots Bks.

Goldsmiths'-Kress Library of Economic Literature: A Consolidated Guide to the Microfilm Collection, 7 vols. 950.00 (ISBN 0-89235-077-6). Res Pubns Conn.

Research Libraries of the New York Public Library & Library of Congress. Bibliographic Guide to Business & Economics: 1982. 1983. lib. bdg. 335.00 (ISBN 0-8161-6983-7, Biblio Guides). G K Hall.

Stewart, Frances. Work, Income & Inequality. LC 81-24065. 304p. 1982. 32.50x (ISBN 0-312-88943-7). St Martin.

ECONOMICS–COLLECTED WORKS

Canney, M., et al, eds. The Catalogue of the Goldsmiths' Library of Economic Literature, Vol. 1. 838p. 1970. Repr. of 1967 ed. text ed. 100.00x (ISBN 0-485-15014-X, Athlone Pr). Humanities.

--The Catalogue of the Goldsmiths' Library of Economic Literature, Vol. 2. 772p. 1975. text ed. 100.00x (ISBN 0-485-15015-8, Athlone Pr). Humanities.

--The Catalogue of the Goldsmiths' Library of Economic Literature, Vol. 3. 336p. 1982. text ed. 120.00x (ISBN 0-485-15012-3, Athlone Pr). Humanities.

ECONOMICS–DICTIONARIES

Blaug, Mark & Sturges, Paul, eds. Who's Who in Economics: A Biographical Dictionary of Major Economics, 1700-1981. 416p. 1983. 65.00x (ISBN 0-262-02188-9). MIT Pr.

Hanson, J. L. A Dictionary of Economics & Commerce. 480p. 1977. 29.00x (ISBN 0-7121-0424-0, Pub. by Macdonald & Evans). State Mutual Bk.

Taylor, Philip A. A New Dictionary of Economics. 2nd ed. 321p. (Orig.). 1969. pap. 10.00 (ISBN 0-7100-7812-9). Routledge & Kegan.

Zahn, Hans E. Glossaries of Financial & Economic Terms: English-German. 530p. 1977. 100.00 (ISBN 0-7121-5492-2, Pub. by Macdonald & Evans). State Mutual Bk.

ECONOMICS–HISTORY

Blaug, Mark & Sturges, Paul, eds. Who's Who in Economics: A Biographical Dictionary of Major Economics, 1700-1981. 416p. 1983. 65.00x (ISBN 0-262-02188-9). MIT Pr.

Moody, John. Masters of Capital. 1919. text ed. 8.50x (ISBN 0-686-83619-7). Elliots Bks.

O'Brien, D. P. & Darnell, A. C. Authorship Puzzles in the History of Economics: A Statistical Approach. 230p. 1982. text ed. 37.00x (ISBN 0-333-30078-5, Pub. by Macmillan England). Humanities.

Obrinsky, Mark. Profit Theory & Capitalism. LC 82-40482. (Illus.). 176p. 1983. 18.00x (ISBN 0-8122-7863-1); pap. 8.95x (ISBN 0-8122-1147-2). U of Pa Pr.

Puth, Robert C. American Economic History. 485p. 1983. 25.95 (ISBN 0-03-050556-9). Dryden Pr.

Schlesinger, Reuben & Wolfson, Marty. Todays Economic Issues. (Illus.). 1974. pap. 5.95 (ISBN 0-916114-04-X). Wolfson.

Shackleton, J. R. & Locksley, Gareth. Twelve Contemporary Economists. LC 81-2403. 263p. 1982. pap. 17.95x (ISBN 0-470-27367-4). Halsted Pr.

ECONOMICS–INFORMATION SERVICES

Data Notes Publishing Staff. Directory of Refunding Periodicals, Books, Clubs, Associations. 200p. 1983. text ed. 29.95 (ISBN 0-911569-06-5). Data Notes Pub.

ECONOMICS–JUVENILE LITERATURE

Marsh, Carole. The Teddy Bear Company: Easy Economics for Kids. (Tomorrow's Books). (Illus.). 62p. 1983. 5.95 (ISBN 0-935326-16-2). Gallopade Pub Group.

--The Teddy Bear's Annual Report: Tomorrow's Books. (Illus.). 48p. 1983. 7.95 (ISBN 0-935326-26-X). Gallopade Pub Group.

ECONOMICS–MATHEMATICAL MODELS

see also Agriculture–Economic Aspects–Mathematical Models

Goldberger, Arthur S. Econometric Theory. LC 64-10370. (Probability & Mathematical Statistics Ser.). (Illus.). 1964. 32.95x (ISBN 0-471-31101-4). Wiley.

Katzner, Donald W. Analysis Without Measurement. LC 82-4469. 366p. Date not set. price not set (ISBN 0-521-24847-7). Cambridge U Pr.

Whiteman, Charles H. Linear Rational Expaectations Models: A User's Guide. 130p. 1983. 19.50 (ISBN 0-8166-1181-5); pap. 9.95 (ISBN 0-8166-1179-3). U of Minn Pr.

ECONOMICS–METHODOLOGY

see also Economics, Mathematical

Katzner, Donald W. Analysis Without Measurement. LC 82-4469. 366p. Date not set. price not set (ISBN 0-521-24847-7). Cambridge U Pr.

ECONOMICS–MISCELLANEA

Fox, C. J., Jr. C. J. Understanding. 261p. 1982. 10.95 (ISBN 0-89962-286-0). Todd & Honeywell.

Hawken, Paul. The Next Economy. (Illus.). 252p. Date not set. 12.95 (ISBN 0-03-062631-5). HR&W.

ECONOMICS–MORAL AND RELIGIOUS ASPECTS

Finn, James, ed. Global Economics & Religion. 277p. 1983. 26.95 (ISBN 0-87855-477-7). Transaction Bks.

Skurski, Roger. New Directions in Economic Justice. 304p. 1983. text ed. 20.95x (ISBN 0-268-01460-4); pap. text ed. 10.95x (ISBN 0-268-01461-2). U of Notre Dame Pr.

ECONOMICS–RESEARCH

see Economic Research

ECONOMICS, COMPARATIVE

see Comparative Economics

ECONOMICS, INTERNATIONAL

see also International Economic Relations

World Bank. World Development Report, 1982. (Illus.). 182p. (Orig.). 1982. 20.00x (ISBN 0-19-503224-1); pap. 8.00 (ISBN 0-19-503225-X). Oxford U Pr.

ECONOMICS, MATHEMATICAL

see also Economics–Mathematical Models; Interindustry Economics

Chiang, A. Fundamental Methods of Mathematical Economics. 3rd ed. 736p. 1983. 23.95 (ISBN 0-07-010813-7). McGraw.

Debreu, Gerard. Mathematical Economics: Twenty Papers of Gerard Debreu. LC 82-12875. (Econometric Society Monographs in Pure Theory). 320p. Date not set. price not set (ISBN 0-521-23736-X). Cambridge U Pr.

Kim. Competitive Economics: Equilibrium & Arbitration. Date not set. price not set (ISBN 0-444-86497-0). Elsevier.

Paelinck, J. H. Qualitative & Quantitative Mathematical Economics. 1982. lib. bdg. 34.50 (ISBN 90-247-2623-9, Pub. by Martinus Nijhoff Netherlands). Kluwer Boston.

Shvyrkov, V. V. Statistical Science in Economics. (Volume II). (Illus.). 207p. (Orig.). 1983. wkbk. 19.10 (0686387597). G Throwkoff.

Wiseman, Jack. Beyond Positive Economics? LC 82-16874. 232p. 1982. 25.00x (ISBN 0-312-07780-7). St Martin.

ECONOMICS, PRIMITIVE

see Economic Anthropology

ECONOMICS AND CHRISTIANITY

see Christianity and Economics

ECONOMICS AND ISLAM

see Islam and Economics

ECONOMICS OF WAR

see War–Economic Aspects

ECONOMY, ENGINEERING

see Engineering Economy

ECUADOR

Man, J. Jungle Nomads of Equador: The Waorani. (Peoples of the Wild Ser.). 1982. write for info. (ISBN 0-7054-0704-7, Pub. by Time-Life). Silver.

ECUMENICAL COUNCILS AND SYNODS

see Councils and Synods, Ecumenical

ECUMENICAL MOVEMENT

Geffre, Claude & Jossua, Jean-Pierre. Indifference to Religion. (Concilium 1983: Vol. 165). 128p. (Orig.). 1983. pap. 6.95 (ISBN 0-8164-2445-4). Seabury.

Martin, Roger H. Evangelicals United: Ecumenical Stirrings in Pre-Victorian Britain, 1795-1830. LC 82-10784. (Studies in Evangelicalism: No. 4). 244p. 1983. 17.50 (ISBN 0-8108-1586-9). Scarecrow.

Schellman, James M. Ecumenical Services of Prayer: Consultation on Common Texts. 80p. 1982. pap. 1.95 (ISBN 0-8091-5180-4). Paulist Pr.

Smith, John C. From Colonialism to World Community: The Church's Pilgrimage. LC 82-12138. 1982. pap. 8.95 (ISBN 0-664-24452-1). Westminster.

Smyth, Norman. Story of Church Unity: The Lambeth Conference of Anglican Bishops & the Congregational-Episcopal Approaches. 1923. text ed. 29.50x (ISBN 0-686-83788-6). Elliots Bks.

ECZEMA

MacKie, Roan M. Eczema & Dermatitis. LC 82-11390. (Positive Health Guides Ser.). (Illus.). 112p. 1983. lib. bdg. 12.95 (ISBN 0-668-05629-0); pap. 7.95 (ISBN 0-668-05634-7). Arco.

EDEMA

see Cerebral Edema

EDIBLE OILS AND FATS

see Oils and Fats, Edible

EDIBLE PLANTS

see Plants, Edible

EDINBURGH

Duke of Edinburgh, frwd. by. Harpers Handbook to Edinburgh. 322p. 1982. pap. 12.95 (ISBN 0-907686-01-X, Pub. by Auto Assn-British Tourist Authority England). Merrimack Bk Serv.

Gordon-Smith, W. Edinburgh. (Illus.). 128p. 1983. 22.95 (ISBN 0-686-42794-7, Collins Pub England). Greene.

EDISON, THOMAS ALVA, 1847-1931

Hodgkins, John B. Thomas A. Edison & Major Frank McLaughlin: Their Quest for Gold in Butte County. (ANCRR Research Paper: No. 5). 1979. 6.00 (ISBN 0-686-38937-9). Assn NC Records.

Sabin, Louis. Thomas Alva Edison: Young Inventor. LC 82-15889. (Illus.). 48p. (gr. 4-6). 1983. PLB 6.89 (ISBN 0-89375-841-8); pap. text ed. 1.95 (ISBN 0-89375-842-6). Troll Assocs.

Wachorst, Wyn. Thomas Alva Edison: An American Myth. (Illus.). 256p. 1981. 15.00 (ISBN 0-262-23108-5). MIT Pr.

EDISON, THOMAS ALVA, 1847-1931–JUVENILE LITERATURE

Guthridge, Sue. Thomas A. Edison. new ed. (Childhood of Famous Americans). (Illus.). 204p. (Orig.). (gr. 2 up). 1983. pap. 3.95 (ISBN 0-672-52751-0). Bobbs.

EDITORS (JOURNALISM)

see Journalists

EDUCATION

see also Adult Education; Books and Reading; Business Education; Christian Education; Communication in Education; Culture; Drama in Education; Education and State; Education of Children; Education of the Aged; Education of Women; Home and School; Illiteracy; Inefficiency, Intellectual; Learning, Psychology of; Libraries; Library Education; Mental Discipline; Military Education; Moral Education; Moving-Pictures in Education; Nature Study; Physical Education and Training; Prisoners–Education; Private Schools; Professional Education; Public Schools; Religious Education; Religious Education of Adolescents; Role Playing; Schools; Self-Culture; Self-Government (In Education); Socialization; Students; Study, Method of; Teachers; Teaching; Technical Education; Television in Education; Universities and Colleges; Vocational Education; Youth also subdivision Study and Teaching under special subjects; subdivision Education under names of denominations, sects, etc., e.g. Catholic Church–Education, and under special classes of people and social groups, e.g. Deaf–Education; and headings beginning with the word Educational

Alternatives Notebook & Supplement. pap. 8.00 (ISBN 0-934338-11-6). NAIS.

Alwine, Nevin S., ed. Readings for Foundation of Education. 121p. 1969. pap. text ed. 9.95x (ISBN 0-8290-1310-5). Irvington.

Ballantine, Jeanne H. The Sociology of Education: A Systematic Analysis. (Illus.). 400p. 1983. 21.95 (ISBN 0-13-820860-3). P-H.

Barton, Len & Walker, Stephen. Race, Class & Education. 256p. 1983. text ed. 27.25 (ISBN 0-7099-0683-8, Pub. by Croom Helm Ltd England). Biblio Dist.

Conroy, Barbara. Learning Packaged to Go: A Directory & Guide to Staff Development & Training Packages. 1983. price not set (ISBN 0-89774-065-3). Oryx Pr.

Crowfoot, James & Bryant, Bunyan. Action for Educational Equity: A Guide for Parents & Members of Community Groups. 184p. (Orig.). 1982. pap. text ed. 9.00 (ISBN 0-917754-19-0). Inst Responsive.

Furntratt, Ernst & Moller, Christine. Lernprinzip Erfolg. viii, 235p. (Ger.). 1982. write for info. (ISBN 3-8204-5836-0). P Lang Pubs.

Gotz, Ignacio L. No Schools. 198p. 1971. pap. text ed. 10.95x (ISBN 0-8422-0163-7). Irvington.

Helmer, Karl. Weltordnung und Bildung. 254p. (Ger.). 1982. write for info. (ISBN 3-8204-5839-5). P Lang Pubs.

Hill, Clyde M., ed. Educational Progress & School Administration: Symposium By a Number of His Former Associates Written As a Tribute to Frank Ellsworth Spauling. 1936. text ed. 49.50x (ISBN 0-686-83532-8). Elliots Bks.

Lazar, Irving. As the Twig Is Bent: Lasting Effects of Early Education. (Consortium for Longitudinal Studies). 469p. 1983. text ed. write for info. (ISBN 0-89859-271-2). L Erlbaum Assocs.

Lotz, Klaus. Normbegrundung Als Legitimation Fur Padagogisches Argumentieren und Entscheiden. 274p. (Ger.). 1982. write for info. (ISBN 3-8204-5819-0). P Lang Pubs.

Patty, Catherine. Developing Citizenship. (Sound Filmstrip Kits Ser.). (gr. 3-6). 1981. tchrs ed. 24.00 (ISBN 0-8209-0439-2, FCW-16). ESP.

Shaw, Marie-Jose. The Dewey Decimal Classification. (Sound Filmstrip Kits Ser.). (gr. 4-8). 1981. tchrs ed. 24.00 (ISBN 0-8209-0447-3, FCW-24). ESP.

--The Dictionary. (Sound Filmstrip Kits Ser.). (gr. 3-6). 1981. tchrs ed. 24.00 (ISBN 0-8209-0441-4, FCW-18). ESP.

Slosson, Edwin E. American Spirit in Education. 1921. text ed. 8.50x (ISBN 0-686-83467-4). Elliots Bks.

Standard Education Almanac, 1981-82. 14th ed. LC 68-3442. 656p. 1981. write for info. (ISBN 0-8379-2108-2). Marquis.

Steiner, Rudolf. A Modern Art of Education. 3rd ed. Darrell, Jesse, tr. from Ger. 233p. 1981. 16.95 (ISBN 0-85440-261-6, Pub. by Steinerbooks); pap. 11.95 (ISBN 0-85440-262-4). Anthroposophic.

Sturo, Edmund. Conquering Academic Failure: A Guide for Parents, Students & Educators. LC 81-85805. (Illus.). 112p. 1983. pap. 5.95 (ISBN 0-86666-060-7). GWP.

EDUCATION–ADDRESSES, ESSAYS, LECTURES

Cruickshank, William M. & Tash, Eli, eds. Academics & Beyond: The Best of ACLD, Vol. 4. (The Best of ACLD Ser.). 256p. pap. text ed. 13.95 (ISBN 0-8156-2272-4). Syracuse U Pr.

Dewey, John. Middle Works, Eighteen Ninety-Nine to Nineteen Twenty-Four, Vols. 13-15. Incl. Vol. 13. 30.00x (ISBN 0-8093-1083-X); Vol. 14. 22.50x (ISBN 0-8093-1084-8); Vol. 15. 25.00x (ISBN 0-8093-1085-6). LC 76-7231. 1983. S Ill U Pr.

McCormick, Richard P. & Schlatter, Richard, eds. The Selected Speeches of Mason Gross. 160p. 1980. 14.95 (ISBN 0-87855-388-6). Transaction Bks.

Report of the Second National Conference on PPBES in Education. 0.69 (ISBN 0-686-84134-4). Assn Sch Busn.

White, Roger & Brockington, Dave. Tales Out of School. (Routledge Education Bks.). 148p. 1983. write for info. (ISBN 0-7100-9448-5); pap. 7.95 (ISBN 0-7100-9445-0). Routledge & Kegan.

EDUCATION–AIMS AND OBJECTIVES

see also Educational Equalization; Educational Planning; Educational Sociology

Giroux, Henry A. Theory & Resistance in Education: A Pedagogy for the Opposition. Freire, Paulo, frwd. by. 256p. 1983. text ed. 24.95x; pap. text ed. 12.95. J F Bergin.

Hechinger, Grace & Hechinger, Fred M. Restoring Confidence in Public Education. (Seven Springs Studies). 1982. pap. 3.00 (ISBN 0-943006-01-5). Seven Springs.

Jackson, Brian. Streaming: An Educational System in Miniature. 156p. 1964. pap. 8.95 (ISBN 0-7100-3926-3). Routledge & Kegan.

McBeath, Ron & Sleeman, Phillip, eds. Trends & Practices. (Instructional Media & Technology Ser.: Vol. 1). 210p. (Orig.). 1983. pap. text ed. 11.50 (ISBN 0-89503-041-1). Baywood Pub.

Mann, Pete M. Correspondence Models for Educators. LC 82-80826. 105p. (Orig.). 1982. pap. 6.95x (ISBN 0-89950-065-X). McFarland & Co.

Mursell, James L. Human Values in Music Education. 388p. 1982. Repr. of 1934 ed. lib. bdg. 35.00 (ISBN 0-89987-646-3). Darby Bks.

Peters, R. s., ed. The Concept of Education. 226p. 1970. pap. 8.95 (ISBN 0-7100-7658-4). Routledge & Kegan.

Sturo, Edmund. Conquering Academic Failure: A Guide for Parents, Students & Educators. LC 81-85805. (Illus.). 112p. 1983. pap. 5.95 (ISBN 0-86666-060-7). GWP.

Wallenfeldt, E. C. American Higher Education: Servant of the People or of Special Interests? LC 82-15837. (Contributions to the Study of Education: No. 9). 256p. 1983. lib. bdg. 29.95 (ISBN 0-313-23469-8). Greenwood.

Wyant. Of Principals & Projects. 1980. 5.00 (ISBN 0-686-38075-4). Assn Tchr Ed.

EDUCATION–BIBLIOGRAPHY

Research Libraries of the New york Public Library & Library of Congress. Bibliographic Guide to Education: 1982. 1983. lib. bdg. 135.00 (ISBN 0-8161-6971-3, Biblio Guides). G K Hall.

EDUCATION–COSTS

Here are entered works on institutional costs in the field of education.

Costs at U. S. Educational Institutions 1982-83. 238p. 1982. pap. 20.00 (ISBN 0-686-84615-X, IIE36, IIE). Unipub.

The Economics of New Educational Media: Volume 3: Cost & Effectiveness Overview & Synthesis. 150p. 1982. pap. 13.25 (ISBN 92-3-101997-X, UNESCO). Unipub.

Paying for Your Education: A Guide for Adult Learners. (Illus.). 160p. (Orig.). 1983. pap. 7.95 (ISBN 0-87447-152-4). College Bd.

EDUCATION–CURRICULA

Works on the curriculum of a particular denomination, sect, or order are entered under name of denominations, etc., with subdivision Education.

see also Articulation (Education)

also subdivision Curricula under various subdivisions of Education, e.g. Education, Secondary–Curricula; also heading Universities and colleges; also subdivision Study and Teaching under special subjects

Curriculum Development. (Occasional Papers: No. 9). 19p. 1982. pap. 5.00 (ISBN 0-686-84627-3, UB109, UNESCO Regional Office). Unipub.

Fenstermacher, Gary D. & Goodlad, John I., eds. Individual Differences in the Common Curriculum: National Society for the Study of Education 82nd Yearbook, Pt. 1. LC 82-62381. 350p. 1983. lib. bdg. 18.00x (ISBN 0-226-60135-8). U of Chicago Pr.

Romiszowski, A. J. Producing Instructional Systems. 350p. 1983. 33.50 (ISBN 0-89397-085-9). Nichols Pub.

EDUCATION–DATA PROCESSING

see also Computer-Assisted Instruction

Corporate Monitor, Inc. Educational Software Directory. 1982. pap. text ed. 22.50 (ISBN 0-87287-352-8). Libs Unl.

McCredie, John, ed. Campus Computing Strategies. 320p. 1983. 21.00 (ISBN 0-932376-20-7). Digital Pr.

Nibeck, Richard G., intro. by. Learning With Microcomputers Readings form Instructional Innovator-5. 80p. Date not set. pap. 10.95 (ISBN 0-89240-042-0). Assn Ed Comm Tech.

Smith, I. C. Microcomputers in Education. LC 81-20176. (Computers & Their Applications Ser.). 212p. 1982. 34.95 (ISBN 0-470-27362-3). Halsted Pr.

EDUCATION–DIRECTORIES

Moody, Douglas, ed. Patterson's Schools Classified, 1983. 225p. (Orig.). 1983. pap. 6.00x (ISBN 0-910536-32-5). Ed Direct.

Woodbury, Marda. A Guide to Sources of Educational Information. 2nd ed. LC 82-80549. xiii, 430p. 1982. text ed. 37.50 (ISBN 0-87815-041-2). Info Resources.

EDUCATION–ECONOMIC ASPECTS

see also Education–Finance

Gift Reporting Standards & Management Reports for Educational Institutions. 24p. 1981. 10.00 (ISBN 0-89964-185-7). CASE.

Majumdar, Tapas. Investment in Education & Social Choice. LC 82-12829. (Illus.). 160p. Date not set. 29.95 (ISBN 0-521-25143-5). Cambridge U Pr.

EDUCATION–EXAMINATIONS, QUESTIONS, ETC.

Madaus, George F., ed. The Courts, Validity & Minimum Competency Testing. (Evaluation in Education & Human Services Ser.). 1982. lib. bdg. 20.00 (ISBN 0-89838-113-4). Kluwer-Nijhoff.

Rudman, Jack. Education Program Assistant. (Career Examination Ser.: C-865). (Cloth bdg. avail. on request). pap. 12.00 (ISBN 0-8373-0865-8). Natl Learning.

--Education Supervisor. (Career Examination Ser.: C-2508). (Cloth bdg. avail. on request). pap. 12.00 (ISBN 0-8373-2508-0). Natl Learning.

--Education Supervisor (Developmental Disabilities) (Career Examination Ser.: C-2511). (Cloth bdg. avail. on request). pap. 12.00 (ISBN 0-8373-2511-0). Natl Learning.

--Education Supervisor (Special Subjects) (Career Examination Ser.: C-2509). pap. 12.00 (ISBN 0-8373-2509-9); avail. Natl Learning.

--Education Supervisor (Vocational) (Career Examination Ser.: C-2510). (Cloth bdg. avail. on request). pap. 12.00 (ISBN 0-8373-2510-2). Natl Learning.

EDUCATION–EXPERIMENTAL METHODS

see also Educational Innovations; Imprinting (Psychology); Open Plan Schools

Partee, Linda. Attribute Pattern Boards. (Illus.). 80p. 1982. 12.95 (ISBN 0-9607366-4-6, KP114). Kino Pubns.

Wade, Theodore E., Jr., et al. School at Home: A Guide for Parents Teaching Their Own Children. rev. ed. 275p. 1983. 11.00 (ISBN 0-930192-12-5); pap. 7.95 (ISBN 0-930192-13-3). Gazelle Pubns.

EDUCATION–FEDERAL AID

see Federal Aid to Education

EDUCATION–FINANCE

see also College Costs; Education–Costs; Educational Equalization; Federal Aid to Education

ASBO's Student Activity Research Committee. Internal Auditing for Student Activity Funds. 1981. 5.95 (ISBN 0-910170-18-5). Assn Sch Busn.

Certificate of Excellence in Financial Reporting by School Systems. 1980. 5.95 (ISBN 0-910170-13-4). Assn Sch Busn.

Congressional Quarterly Inc. Staff. Education in America: Quality vs. Cost. LC 81-12621. (Editorial Research Reports Ser.). 208p. 1981. pap. 7.95 (ISBN 0-87187-212-9). Congr Quarterly.

Dembowski. A Handbook for School District Financial Management. 1982. 11.95 (ISBN 0-910170-24-X). Assn Sch Busn.

League of Women Voters of Minnesota. How Will We Pay for Our Schools? Financing Public Education in Minnesota (K-12) (Illus.). 59p. (Orig.). 1982. pap. text ed. 5.00 (ISBN 0-939816-02-4). LWV MN.

Linnell, Robert. Dollars & Scholars. Clark, Henry B. & Dillon, Kristine E., eds. (Orig.). 1982. 12.00 (ISBN 0-88474-106-0); pap. 8.00 (ISBN 0-686-82258-7). U of S Cal Pr.

Odden, Allan & Webb, Dean, eds. School Finance & School Improvement: Linkages in the 1980's. (American Education Finance Association). 1983. price not set prof ref (ISBN 0-88410-399-4). Ballinger Pub.

Rudman, Jack. School Finance Manager. (Career Examination Ser.: C-2886). (Cloth bdg. avail. on request). pap. 12.00 (ISBN 0-8373-2886-1). Natl Learning.

School Accounting, Budgeting & Finance Challenges: ASBO's 66th Annual Meeting & Exhibits Special Sessions. 1981. 6.50 (ISBN 0-910170-22-3). Assn Sch Busn.

Schug, Mark C. Economic Education Across the Curriculum. LC 82-60803. (Fastback Ser.: No. 183). 50p. 1982. pap. 0.75 (ISBN 0-87367-183-X). Phi Delta Kappa.

Seymour, Harold J. Campanas para Obtencion de Fondus. 194p. 1964. 9.50 (ISBN 0-686-82669-8). CASE.

Working Papers for Financial & Managerial Accounting for Elementary & Secondary School Systems. 1977. 5.00 (ISBN 0-910170-03-7). Assn Sch Busn.

EDUCATION–HISTORY

Here are entered general works on the history of education. For works on history of specific areas see the geographical subdivisions which follow.

see also Comparative Education

Brownhill, R. J. Education & the Nature of Knowledge. (New Patterns of Learning Ser.). 144p. 1983. text ed. 27.25x (ISBN 0-7099-0654-4, Pub. by Croom Helm Ltd England). Biblio Dist.

Hadley, Morris. Arthur Twining Hadley. 1948. text ed. 39.50x (ISBN 0-686-83481-X). Elliots Bks.

Monroe, Paul. Source Book of the History of Education for the Greek & Rowan Period. 515p. 1982. Repr. of 1948 ed. lib. bdg. 65.00 (ISBN 0-8495-3940-4). Arden Lib.

EDUCATION–HISTORY–SOURCES

World of Learning Nineteen Eighty-two to Nineteen Eighty-three. 2 vols. 33rd ed. 2110p. 1983. 150.00x set (ISBN 0-686-84916-7, Pub. by Europa England). Gale.

EDUCATION–INTEGRATION

see School Integration

EDUCATION–JUVENILE LITERATURE

Fisher, Leonard E. The Schools. LC 82-18710. (Nineteenth Century America Ser.). (Illus.). 64p. (gr. 5 up). 1983. reinforced binding 10.95 (ISBN 0-8234-0477-3). Holiday.

EDUCATION–LAWS AND LEGISLATION

see Educational Law and Legislation

EDUCATION–PERIODICALS

Elam, Stanley, compiled by. A User's Index to the Phi Delta Kappan, 1970-81. LC 82-61909. 150p. 1982. pap. 7.00 (ISBN 0-87367-785-4). Phi Delta Kappa.

Manera, Elizabeth S. & Wright, Robert E. Annotated Writer's Guide to Professional Educational Journals. 188p. 1982. pap. 9.95 (ISBN 0-9609782-0-8). Bobets.

EDUCATION–PERSONNEL SERVICE

see Personnel Service in Education; Personnel Service in Higher Education

EDUCATION–PHILOSOPHY

see also Educational Anthropology

Apple, Michael & Weis, Lois, eds. Ideology & Practice in Schooling. 1983. write for info. (ISBN 0-87722-295-9). Temple U Pr.

Giroux, Henry A. Theory & Resistance in Education: A Pedagogy for the Opposition. Freire, Paulo, frwd. by. 256p. 1983. text ed. 24.95x; pap. text ed. 12.95. J F Bergin.

Kelly, Eugene W. Beyond Schooling: Education in a Broader Context. LC 82-60798. (Fastback Ser.: No. 177). 50p. 1982. pap. 0.75 (ISBN 0-87367-177-5). Phi Delta Kappa.

Kleinig, John. Philosophical Issues in Education. LC 82-50084. 1982. 29.95x (ISBN 0-312-60524-2). St Martin.

Knight, George R. Philosophy & Education: An Introduction in Christian Perspective. (Illus.). xii, 244p. 1980. pap. text ed. 8.95 (ISBN 0-943872-79-0). Andrews Univ Pr.

Nathan, Joe. Free to Teach: Achieving Equity & Excellence in Schools. 224p. 1983. 14.95 (ISBN 0-8298-0657-1). Pilgrim NY.

O'Hare, Padraic, ed. Education for Peace & Justice. LC 82-48412. 224p. (Orig.). 1983. pap. 9.57 (ISBN 0-06-066361-8, HarpR). Har-Row.

Powell, J. P. Philosophy of Education. 3rd ed. 1974. pap. 8.50 (ISBN 0-7190-0597-3). Manchester.

Rodriguez, Fred. Education in a Multicultural Society. LC 82-23755. 172p. (Orig.). 1983. lib. bdg. 21.75 (ISBN 0-8191-2977-1); pap. text ed. 10.50 (ISBN 0-8191-2978-X). U Pr of Amer.

Scheffler, Israel. Reason & Teaching. LC 72-86641. 214p. lib. bdg. 17.50x (ISBN 0-672-51854-6); pap. text ed. 5.95x (ISBN 0-672-61253-4). Hackett Pub.

Schneider, Manfred. Erziehung der Erzieher? 253p. (Ger.). 1982. write for info. (ISBN 3-8204-6997-4). P Lang Pubs.

Spangler, Mary M. Principles of Education: A Study of Aristotelian Thomism Contrasted with Other Philosophies. LC 82-24757. 306p. (Orig.). lib. bdg. 23.50 (ISBN 0-8191-3015-X); pap. text ed. 12.50 (ISBN 0-8191-3016-8). U Pr of Amer.

Strike, Kenneth. Liberty & Learning. LC 82-5723. 192p. 1982. 20.00x (ISBN 0-312-48353-8). St Martin.

EDUCATION–PSYCHOLOGY

see Educational Psychology

EDUCATION–RESEARCH

see Educational Research

EDUCATION–SEGREGATION

see Segregation in Education

EDUCATION–STATISTICAL METHODS

see Educational Statistics

EDUCATION–STATISTICS

Wright, B. D. & Mayers, P. L. Interactive Statistics for Education. Date not set. price not set (ISBN 0-07-072081-9). McGraw.

EDUCATION–STUDY AND TEACHING

Blumenfeld, Samuel L. Alpha-Phonics: A Primer for Beginning Readers. 160p. (Orig.). 1983. pap. 19.95 (ISBN 0-686-83942-0); 19.95 (ISBN 0-8159-6916-3). Devin.

Bolam, Ray, ed. School-Focused in-Service Training. (Heinemann Organization in Schools Ser.). x, 246p. 1983. pap. text ed. 25.00x (ISBN 0-435-80090-6). Heinemann Ed.

Griffin, Gary A., ed. Staff Development, Pt. II. LC 82-62382. (The National Society for the Study of Education 82nd Yearbook). 275p. 1983. lib. bdg. 16.00x (ISBN 0-226-60136-6). U of Chicago Pr.

Knowles, Malcolm M. Self-Directed Learning: A Guide for Learners & Teachers. 144p. 1975. pap. 6.95 (ISBN 0-695-81116-9). Follett.

Lawson, Robert F. & Schnell, R. L., eds. Education Studies: Foundations of Policy. LC 82-21924. 468p. (Orig.). 1983. lib. bdg. 29.75 (ISBN 0-8191-2919-4); pap. text ed. 17.25 (ISBN 0-8191-2920-8). U Pr of Amer.

Rodriguez, Fred. Mainstreaming a Multicultural Concept into Teacher Education Guidelines for Teacher Trainers. LC 82-60529. 125p. (Orig.). 1983. pap. 12.95 (ISBN 0-88247-688-2). R & E Res Assoc.

Wallace, Michael. Teaching Vocabulary, No. 10. Geddes, Marion & Sturtridge, Gillian, eds. (Practical Language Teaching Ser.). 144p. (Orig.). 1983. pap. text ed. 7.50x (ISBN 0-435-28974-8). Heinemann Ed.

EDUCATION–UNDERDEVELOPED AREAS

Mandi, Peter. Education & Economic Growth in the Developing Countries. 225p. 1981. text ed. 25.00x (ISBN 963-05-2781-2, 50012, Pub. by Kultura Pr Hungary). Humanities.

Population Education in Non-Formal Education & Development Programmes. 260p. 1981. pap. 12.25 (ISBN 0-686-82543-8, UB107, UNESCO Regional Office). Unipub.

Swift, Digby G. Physics for Rural Development: A Sourcebook for Teachers & Extension Workers in Developing Countries. 272p. 1983. 21.90 (ISBN 0-471-10364-0, Pub. by Wiley-Interscience). Wiley.

EDUCATION–YEAR-BOOKS

Griffin, Gary A., ed. Staff Development, Pt. II. LC 82-62382. (The National Society for the Study of Education 82nd Yearbook). 275p. 1983. lib. bdg. 16.00x (ISBN 0-226-60136-6). U of Chicago Pr.

EDUCATION–AFRICA

Liebenow, J. Gus. Agriculture, Education, & Rural Transformation: With Particular Reference to East Africa. (African Humanities Ser.). 31p. (Orig.). 1969. pap. text ed. 2.00 (ISBN 0-941934-00-4). Ind U Afro-Amer Arts.

Lutsenburg Maas, Jacob van & Criel, Geert. Primary School Participation & Its Internal Distribution in Eastern Africa. LC 82-10839. (World Bank Staff Working Papers: No. 511). (Orig.). 1982. pap. text ed. 5.00 (ISBN 0-8213-0055-5). World Bank.

Richmond, Edmun B. New Directions in Language Teaching in Sub-Saharan Africa: A Seven-Country Study of Current Policies & Programs for Teaching Official & National Languages & Adult Functional Literacy. LC 82-23831. (Illus.). 74p. (Orig.). 1983. pap. text ed. 6.50 (ISBN 0-8191-2980-1, Co-pub. by Ctr Applied Ling). U Pr of Amer.

EDUCATION–ASIA

In-Service Primary Teacher Education in Asia. 100p. 1982. pap. 7.00 (ISBN 0-686-82542-X, UB105, UNESCO Regional Office). Unipub.

EDUCATION–CANADA

Holmes, Brian. International Handbook of Education Systems: Europe & Canada, Vol. 1. 800p. 1983. write for info. (ISBN 0-471-90078-8, Pub. by Wiley-Interscience). Wiley.

EDUCATION–CEYLON

Peiris, Kamala. Tiny Sapling-Sturdy Tree: Primary Education Reforms of the 1970's in Sri Lanka. 1983. write for info. (Universitet). Columbia U Pr.

EDUCATION–EUROPE

Holmes, Brian. International Handbook of Education Systems: Europe & Canada, Vol. 1. 800p. 1983. write for info. (ISBN 0-471-90078-8, Pub. by Wiley-Interscience). Wiley.

Van der Eyken, Willem. The Education of Three to Eight Year Olds in Europe in the Eighties. (NFER European Trends Reports). 168p. 1982. pap. text ed. 11.75x (ISBN 0-85633-237-2, NFER). Humanities.

EDUCATION–GERMANY

Albisetti, James C. Secondary School Reform in Imperial Germany. LC 82-12223. 392p. 1983. 35.00x (ISBN 0-691-05373-1). Princeton U Pr.

Pyenson, Lewis. Mathematics, Physical Reality, & Neohumanism in Nineteenth & Early Twentieth Century German Education. LC 82-72156. (Memoirs Ser.: Vol. 150). 1983. pap. text ed. 10.00 (ISBN 0-87169-150-7). Am Philos.

EDUCATION–GREAT BRITAIN

Cohen, L. & Thomas, J., eds. Educational Research in Britain Nineteen Seventy to Nineteen Eighty. (NFER Research Publications Ser.). 567p. 1982. text ed. 105.00x (ISBN 0-85633-243-7, NFER). Humanities.

EDUCATION–INDIA

Haq, Ehsanul. Education & Political Culture in India. 176p. 1981. 22.50x (ISBN 0-940500-54-X, Pub. by Sterling India). Asia Bk Corp.

Mohanty, Jagganath. Indian Education in the Emerging Society. 205p. 1982. 24.95x (ISBN 0-940500-52-3, Pub. by Sterling India). Asia Bk Corp.

Saxena, Sateshwari. Educational Planning in India: A Study in Approach & Methodology. LC 79-900462. (Illus.). 202p. 1979. 14.00x (ISBN 0-8002-0394-1). Intl Pubns Serv.

EDUCATION–ISRAEL

Jaffe, Eliezer D. Israelis in Institutions: Studies in Child Placement, Practice & Policy. (Special Aspects of Education Ser.: Vol. 2). 324p. 1982. 52.75 (ISBN 0-677-05960-4). Gordon.

EDUCATION–JAPAN

Association of International Education, Japan. ABC's of Study in Japan, 1982-83. (Illus.). 154p. (Orig.). 1981. pap. 5.00x (ISBN 0-8002-3041-8). Intl Pubns Serv.

Passin, Herbert. Society & Education in Japan. LC 82-48167. 347p. 1982. pap. 6.25 (ISBN 0-87011-554-5). Kodansha.

EDUCATION–LATIN AMERICA

Educational Networks in Latin America: Their Role in Production, Diffusion, & Use of Educational Knowledge. 44p. 1983. pap. 7.50 (ISBN 0-88936-350-1, IDRC TS 39, IDRC). Unipub.

El Financiamiento de la Educacion Superior en Latino America. 49p. 1981. 9.50 (ISBN 0-686-82672-8). CASE.

EDUCATION–NIGERIA

Bray, Mark. Universal Primary Education in Nigeria: A Study of Kano State. 272p. (Orig.). 1982. pap. write for info. (ISBN 0-7100-0933-X). Routledge & Kegan.

EDUCATION–RUSSIA

Shatsky, S. Teacher's Experience. 342p. 1981. 8.00 (ISBN 0-8285-2158-1, Pub. by Progress Pubs USSR). Imported Pubns.

EDUCATION–UNITED STATES

Angell, James R. American Education. 1937. text ed. 19.50x (ISBN 0-686-83461-5). Elliots Bks.

Arons, S. Compelling Belief: The Culture of American Schooling. 256p. 19.95 (ISBN 0-07-002326-3). McGraw.

Flesch, Rudolf. Johnny Still Can't Read: A New Look at the Scandal of Our Schools. LC 80-8686. 224p. 1983. pap. 4.76i (ISBN 0-06-091031-3, CN 1031, CN). Har-Row.

Graham, Patricia A. Community & Class in American Education: 1865 to 1918. LC 84-562. 268p. Repr. of 1974 ed. text ed. 11.50 (ISBN 0-471-32091-9). Krieger.

Johanningmeir, Edwin V. Americans & Their Schools. 328p. 1980. pap. 15.50 (ISBN 0-395-30640-X). HM.

Vega, Jose E. Education, Politics, & Bilingualism in Texas. 262p. (Orig.). 1983. lib. bdg. 21.50 (ISBN 0-8191-2985-2); pap. text ed. 11.50 (ISBN 0-8191-2986-0). U Pr of Amer.

EDUCATION–UNITED STATES–FINANCE

see also Federal Aid to Education

Costs at U. S. Educational Institutions 1982-83. 238p. 1982. pap. 20.00 (ISBN 0-686-84615-X, IIE36, IIE). Unipub.

Garber, Lee O. & Hubbard, Ben C. Law, Finance, & the Teacher in Illinois. 1983. write for info. (ISBN 0-8134-2252-3). Interstate.

EDUCATION–UNITED STATES–HISTORY

Hill, Clyde M., ed. Educational Progress & School Administration: Symposium By a Number of His Former Associates Written As a Tribute to Frank Ellsworth Spauling. 1936. text ed. 49.50x (ISBN 0-686-83532-8). Elliots Bks.

Kaestle, Carl. Pillars of the Republic: Common Schools & American Society, 1790-1860. Foner, Eric, ed. 1983. 17.50 (ISBN 0-8090-7620-9); pap. 7.25 (ISBN 0-8090-0154-3). Hill & Wang.

Makepeace, LeRoy M. Sherman Thatcher & His School. 1941. text ed. 49.50x (ISBN 0-686-83739-8). Elliots Bks.

EDUCATION, ART

see Art-Study and Teaching

EDUCATION, BILINGUAL

Baker, Keith A., ed. Bilingual Education: A Reappraisal of Federal Policy. Kenter, Adriana A. LC 82-48040. 272p. 1982. 21.95x (ISBN 0-669-05885-8). Lexington Bks.

Cohen, L. & Manion, L. Multicultural Classrooms: Perspectives for Teachers. 256p. 1983. text ed. 27.25x (ISBN 0-7099-0719-2, Pub. by Croom Helm Ltd England). Biblio Dist.

Cox, Barbara G. & Macaulay, Janet. Nuevas Fronteras-New Frontiers: Un Programa de Aprendizaje Bilingue para Ninos-A Bilingual Early Learning Program. LC 81-81331. 1982. 636.00 (ISBN 0-08-028280-6). Pergamon.

Millier, Jane. Many Voices: Bilingualism Culture, & Education. 250p. 1983. price not set; pap. price not set (ISBN 0-7100-9341-1). Routledge & Kegan.

Vega, Jose E. Education, Politics, & Bilingualism in Texas. 262p. (Orig.). 1983. lib. bdg. 21.50 (ISBN 0-8191-2985-2); pap. text ed. 11.50 (ISBN 0-8191-2986-0). U Pr of Amer.

EDUCATION, BUSINESS

see Business Education

EDUCATION, CHARACTER

see Moral Education

EDUCATION, CHRISTIAN

see Religious Education

EDUCATION, COMPARATIVE

see Comparative Education

EDUCATION, ELEMENTARY

see also Creative Activities and Seatwork; Education of Children;

also subdivision Study and Teaching (Elementary) under special subjects, e.g. Science-Study and Teaching (Elementary)

Brooks, Bearl. Jumbo Cursive Handwriting Yearbook. (Jumbo Handwriting Ser.). 96p. (gr. 3). 1978. wkbk. 14.00 (ISBN 0-8209-0019-2, JHWY-3). ESP.

--Learning to Tell Time. (Early Education Ser.). 24p. (ps-2). 1979. wkbk. 5.00 (ISBN 0-8209-0207-1, K-9). ESP.

--My Fifth Grade Yearbook. (My Yearbook Ser.). 832p. (gr. 5). 1981. 14.00 (ISBN 0-8209-0085-0, MFG-5). ESP.

--My First Grade Yearbook. (My Yearbook Ser.). 544p. (gr. 1). 1979. 14.00 (ISBN 0-8209-0081-8, MFG-1). ESP.

--My Kindergarten Yearbook. (My Yearbook Ser.). 544p. (gr. k). 1980. 14.00 (ISBN 0-8209-0080-X, MKY_K). ESP.

--My Second Grade Yearbook. (My Yearbook Ser.). 640p. (gr. 2). 1979. 14.00 (ISBN 0-8209-0082-6, MSG-2). ESP.

--My Sixth Grade Yearbook. (My Yearbook Ser.). 832p. 1981. 14.00 (ISBN 0-8209-0086-9, MSG-6). ESP.

--My Third Grade Yearbook. (My Yearbook Ser.). 768p. (gr. 3). 1979. 14.00 (ISBN 0-8209-0083-4, MTG-3). ESP.

Brooks, Pearl. Basic Skills Handwriting Workbook: Grade 1. (Basic Skills Workbooks). 32p. 1982. tchrs' ed. 0.99 (ISBN 0-8209-0370-1, CHW-1). ESP.

--Basic Skills Handwriting Workbook: Grade 2. (Basic Skills Workbooks). 32p. 1982. tchr's ed. 0.99 (ISBN 0-8209-0371-X, CHW-2). ESP.

--Basic Skills Handwriting Workbook: Grade 3. (Basic Skills Workbooks). 32p. 1982. tchr's ed. 0.99 (ISBN 0-8209-0372-8, CHW-3). ESP.

Camp, Diana Van. Basic Skills Human Body Workbook: Grade 5. (Basic Skills Workbooks). 32p. 1982. tchrs' ed. 0.99 (ISBN 0-8209-0420-1, HBW-F). ESP.

--Basic Skills Human Body Workbook: Grade 8. (Basic Skills Workbook). 32p. 1982. tchrs' ed. 0.99 (ISBN 0-8209-0423-6, HBW-I). ESP.

--Basic Skills Human Workbook: Grade 7. (Basic Skills Workbook). 32p. 1982. tchrs' ed. 0.99 (ISBN 0-8209-0422-8, HBW-H). ESP.

--Basic Skills Human Workbooks: Grade 6. (Basic Skills Workbooks). 32p. 1982. tchrs' ed. 0.99 (ISBN 0-8209-0421-X, HBW-G). ESP.

Dittmar, Mark. Jumbo Art Yearbook: Grade 3 & 4. (Jumbo Art Ser.). 96p. (gr. 3-4). 1981. wkbk. 14.00 (ISBN 0-8209-0046-X, JAY-34). ESP.

--Jumbo Art Yearbook: Grade 5 & 6. (Jumbo Art Ser.). 96p. (gr. 5-6). 1981. wkbk. 14.00 (ISBN 0-8209-0047-8, JAY-56). ESP.

--Jumbo Art Yearbook: Grade 7 & 8. (Jumbo Art Ser.). 96p. (gr. 7-8). 1982. wkbk. 14.00 (ISBN 0-8209-0048-6, JAY-78). ESP.

Doyle, Walter & Good, Thomas L., eds. Focus on Teaching: Readings from the Elementary School Journal. 290p. 1983. lib. bdg. 22.00x (ISBN 0-226-16177-3); pap. 8.95 (ISBN 0-226-16178-1). U of Chicago Pr.

Galton, Maurice & Willcocks, John, eds. Moving from the Primary Classroom. 260p. (Orig.). 1983. pap. price not set (ISBN 0-7100-9343-8). Routledge & Kegan.

Hayes, Marilyn. Basic Skills Health Workbook: Grade 3. (Basic Skills Workbooks). 32p. 1982. tchrs' ed. 0.99 (ISBN 0-686-38397-4, HW-D). ESP.

--Basic Skills Health Workbook: Grade 4. (Basic Skills Workbooks). 32p. 1982. tchrs' ed. 0.99 (ISBN 0-8209-0414-7, HW-E). ESP.

--Basic Skills Health Workbook: Grade 5. (Basic Skills Workbooks). 32p. 1982. tchrs' ed. 0.99 (ISBN 0-8209-0415-5, HW-F). ESP.

Hobson, Libby. What's Music All About? (Music Ser.). 24p. (gr. 3-6). 1977. wkbk. 5.00 (ISBN 0-8209-0272-1, MU-1). ESP.

Houston, Jack. Basic Skills Health Workbook: Grade 7. (Basic Skills Workbook). 32p. 1982. tchrs' ed. 0.99 (ISBN 0-8209-0417-1, HW-H). ESP.

--Basic Skills Health Workbook: Grade 8. (Basic Skills Workbook). 32p. 1982. tchrs' ed. 0.99 (ISBN 0-8209-0418-X, HW-I). ESP.

--Basic Skills Health Workbooks: Grade 6. (Basic Skills Workbooks). 32p. 1982. tchrs' ed. 0.99 (ISBN 0-8209-0416-3, HW-G). ESP.

In-Service Primary Teacher Education in Asia. 100p. 1982. pap. 7.00 (ISBN 0-686-82542-X, UB105, UNESCO Regional Office). Unipub.

Jose-Shaw, Marie. Memory Development. (Sound Filmstrip Kits Ser.). 1p. (gr. 4-8). 1981. 24.00 (ISBN 0-8209-0448-1, FCW-25). ESP.

Justus, Fred. Basic Skills Visual Discrimination Workbook. (Basic Skills Workbooks). 32p. (gr. 1-2). 1983. 0.99 (ISBN 0-8209-0544-5, PW-4). ESP.

--Basic Skills Vocabulary Workbook: Grade 1. (Basic Skills Workbooks). 32p. (gr. 1). 1982. wkbk. 0.99 (ISBN 0-8209-0377-9, VW-B). ESP.

--The Human Body. (Health Ser.). 24p. (gr. 3-5). 1977. wkbk. 5.00 (ISBN 0-8209-0344-2, H-5). ESP.

--Spatial Relationships. (Early Education Ser.). 24p. (gr. k-1). 1981. wkbk. 5.00 (ISBN 0-8209-0221-7, K-23). ESP.

--Thinking Development. (Early Education Ser.). 24p. (gr. k). 1981. wkbk. 5.00 (ISBN 0-8209-0213-6, K-15). ESP.

McMasters, Dale. Using the Library. (Language Arts Ser.). 24p. (gr. 4-8). 1979. wkbk. 5.00 (ISBN 0-8209-0307-8, LIB-1). ESP.

Minton, Janis. Understanding Instructions. (Language Arts Ser.). 24p. (gr. 3-6). 1979. wkbk. 5.00 (ISBN 0-8209-0322-1, LA-8). ESP.

--Understanding Maps. (Social Studies Ser.). 24p. (gr. 4-7). 1979. wkbk. 5.00 (ISBN 0-8209-0257-8, SS-24). ESP.

My Fourth Grade Yearbook. (My Yearbook Ser.). 832p. (gr. 4). 1979. 14.00 (ISBN 0-8209-0084-2, MFG-4). ESP.

Overbeck, Carla. Systems of the Human Body. (Science Ser.). 24p. (gr. 5 up). 1979. wkbk. 5.00 (ISBN 0-8209-0150-4, S-12). ESP.

Patty, Catherine. Electricity. (Sound Filmstrip Kits Ser.). (gr. 3-6). 1981. tchrs ed. 24.00 (ISBN 0-8209-0437-6, FCW-14). ESP.

--The Healthy Body. (Sound Filmstrip Kits Ser.). (gr. 3-6). 1980. tchrs ed. 24.00 (ISBN 0-8209-0431-7, FCW-8). ESP.

--The Human Body. (Sound Filmstrip Kits Ser.). (gr. 3-6). 1980. tchrs ed. 24.00 (ISBN 0-8209-0428-7, FCW-5). ESP.

--Life's Senses. (Science Ser.). 24p. (gr. 4-8). 1979. wkbk. 5.00 (ISBN 0-8209-0152-0, S-14). ESP.

--Using the Encyclopedia. (Language Arts Ser.). 24p. (gr. 5-9). 1979. wkbk. 5.00 (ISBN 0-8209-0313-2, UE-1). ESP.

Shaw, Marie-Jose. Basic Skills Vocabulary Workbook: Grade 2. (Basic Skills Workbooks). 32p. (gr. 2). 1982. wkbk. 0.99 (ISBN 0-8209-0378-7, VW-C). ESP.

--Basic Skills Vocabulary Workbook: Grade 3. (Basic Skills Workbooks). 32p. (gr. 3). 1982. wkbk. 0.99 (ISBN 0-8209-0379-5, VW-D). ESP.

--Basic Skills Vocabulary Workbook: Grade 4. (Basic Skills Workbooks). 32p. (gr. 4). 1982. wkbk. 0.99 (ISBN 0-8209-0380-9, VW-E). ESP.

--Basic Skills Vocabulary Workbook: Grade 5. (Basic Skills Workbooks). 32p. (gr. 5). 1982. wkbk. 0.99 (ISBN 0-8209-0381-7, VW-F). ESP.

--Basic Skills Vocabulary Workbook: Grade 6. (Basic Skills Workbooks). 32p. (gr. 6). 1982. wkbk. 0.99 (ISBN 0-8209-0382-5, VW-G). ESP.

--The Encyclopedia. (Sound Filmstrip Kits Ser.). (gr. 3-6). 1981. tchrs ed. 24.00 (ISBN 0-8209-0442-2, FCW-19). ESP.

--Energy & Man. (Sound Filmstrip Kits Ser.). (gr. 3-6). 1981. 24.00 (ISBN 0-8209-0435-X, FCW-12). ESP.

--First Aid. (Sound Filmstrip Kits Ser.). (gr. 3-6). 1981. tchrs ed. 24.00 (ISBN 0-8209-0434-1, FCW-11). ESP.

--Following Directions. (Sound Filmstrip Kits Ser.). (gr. 2-4). 1981. tchrs ed. 24.00 (ISBN 0-8209-0449-X, FCW-26). ESP.

--Mr. Fish Talks About Subjects. (English Sound Filmstrip Kits Ser.). 1p. (gr. 4). 1980. 24.00 (ISBN 0-8209-0482-1, FCW4E-9). ESP.

Spiess, Gesine. Zum Rollenspieleinsatz In der Grundschule. 338p. (Ger.). 1982. write for info. (ISBN 3-8204-5831-X). P Lang Pubs.

Spodek, Bernard, ed. Handbook of Research in Early Childhood Education. LC 81-71152. (Illus.). 640p. 1982. text ed. 49.95 (ISBN 0-02-930570-5). Free Pr.

Van Camp, Diana. Jumbo Nutrition Yearbook: Grade 2. (Jumbo Nutrition Ser.). 96p. (gr. 2). 1981. 14.00 (ISBN 0-8209-0041-9, JNY 2). ESP.

Vaughn, James E. Impact: Grades Five to Six. (Impact Ser.). 24p. 1979. wkbk. 5.00 (ISBN 0-8209-0348-5, IM-56). ESP.

--Impact: Grades Seven to Eight. (Impact Ser.). 24p. 1979. wkbk. 5.00 (ISBN 0-8209-0349-3, IM-78). ESP.

--Impact: Grades Three to Four. (Impact Ser.). 24p. 1979. wkbk. 5.00 (ISBN 0-8209-0347-7, IM-34). ESP.

Vaughn, Jim. Jumbo Algebra Yearbook. (Jumbo Math Ser.). 96p. (gr. 9). 1981. wkbk. 14.00 (ISBN 0-8209-0038-9, JMY-9). ESP.

--Jumbo Early Childhood Readiness Yearbook. (Jumbo Social Studies Ser.). 96p. (gr. k). 1982. wkbk. 14.00 (ISBN 0-8209-0074-5, JECR-R). ESP.

Walker, Mary Lou. Rhythm, Time, & Value. (Music Ser.). 24p. (gr. 3 up). 1980. wkbk. 5.00 (ISBN 0-8209-0278-0, MU-7). ESP.

--Treble Clef & Notes. (Music Ser.). 24p. (gr. 1 up). 1980. wkbk. 5.00 (ISBN 0-8209-0274-8, MU-3). ESP.

Whitlock, Marlene. Listening Skills. (Early Education Ser.). 24p. (gr. 1-3). 1977. wkbk. 5.00 (ISBN 0-8209-0209-8, K-11). ESP.

Yarbo, Peggy. Reference Materials. (Language Arts Ser.). 24p. (gr. 5-9). 1980. wkbk. 5.00 (ISBN 0-8209-0314-0, RM-1). ESP.

EDUCATION, ELEMENTARY–CURRICULA

Elementary Teachers Guide to Free Curriculum Materials. 39th ed. Date not set. 19.00 (ISBN 0-686-38443-1). Pro Ed.

EDUCATION, ETHICAL

see Moral Education; Religious Education

EDUCATION, HIGHER

see also Degrees, Academic; Education, Humanistic; Junior Colleges; Professional Education; Technical Education; Universities and Colleges; Universities and Colleges–Graduate Work

also subdivision Study and Teaching (Higher) under special subjects, e.g. English Language–Study and Teaching (Higher)

Clark, Burton R. The Higher Education System: Academic Organization in Cross-National Perspective. LC 82-13521. 1983. text ed. 24.95x (ISBN 0-520-04841-5). U of Cal Pr.

Ellner, Carolyn L. & Barnes, Carol P. Studies in Post-Secondary Teaching: Experimental Results, Theoretical Interpretations, & New Perspectives. LC 82-47853. 1982. write for info. (ISBN 0-669-05656-1). Lexington Bks.

Fuentes, Epifanio. Knowledge Versus the College Mind. 1983. 5.95 (ISBN 0-686-84437-8). Vantage.

Fulton, O. & Gordon, A. Higher Education & Manpower Planning: A Comparative Study of Planned & Market Economies. 127p. 1982. 11.40 (ISBN 92-2-102973-5). Intl Labour Office.

Gambino, Anthony J. Planning & Control in Higher Education. 114p. pap. 12.95 (ISBN 0-86641-027-9, 79111). Natl Assn Accts.

Jarausch, Konrad. The Transformation of Higher Learning, Eighteen Sixty to Nineteen Thirty: Expansion, Diversification, Social Opening, & Professionalization in England, Germany, Russia, & the United States. LC 82-17629. 376p. 1983. lib. bdg. 30.00x (ISBN 0-226-39367-4). U of Chicago Pr.

Yearbook of Higher Education, 1981-82. 13th ed. LC 69-18308. 814p. 1981. write for info. Marquis.

EDUCATION, HIGHER–CURRICULA

Carnegie Foundation for the Advancement of Teaching Staff. The Control of the Campus: A Report on the Governance of Higher Education. LC 82-18772. 128p. 1982. pap. text ed. 6.95 (ISBN 0-931050-21-9). Carnegie Found Adv Teach.

EDUCATION, HIGHER–PERSONNEL SERVICE

see Personnel Service in Higher Education

EDUCATION, HIGHER-AFRICA
Maliyamkono, T. L. & Ishumi, A. G. Higher Education & Development in Eastern Africa. (Eastern Africa Universities Research Project Ser.). 336p. 1982. text ed. 40.00x (ISBN 0-435-89580-X). Heinemann Ed.

EDUCATION, HIGHER-EUROPE
Jarausch, Konrad. The Transformation of Higher Learning, Eighteen Sixty to Nineteen Thirty: Expansion, Diversification, Social Opening, & Professionalization in England, Germany, Russia, & the United States. LC 82-17629. 376p. 1983. lib. bdg. 30.00x (ISBN 0-226-39367-4). U of Chicago Pr.

EDUCATION, HIGHER-GREAT BRITAIN
British Qualifications. 13th ed. 897p. 1982. 42.50x (ISBN 0-85038-579-2). Intl Pubns Serv.
Engel, A. J. From Clergyman to Don: The Rise of the Academic Profession in Nineteenth-Century Oxford. 336p. 1983. 55.00 (ISBN 0-19-822606-3). Oxford U Pr.

EDUCATION, HUMANISTIC
see also Humanism
Catlin, Daniel, Jr. Liberal Education at Yale: The Yale College Course of Study 1945-1978. LC 82-17576. 264p. (Orig.). 1983. lib. bdg. 24.00 (ISBN 0-8191-2796-5); pap. text ed. 11.75 (ISBN 0-8191-2797-3). U Pr of Amer.
Dill, Stephen H. Integrated Studies: Challenges to the College Curriculum. LC 82-17511. (Illus.). 158p. (Orig.). 1983. lib. bdg. 19.50 (ISBN 0-8191-2794-9); pap. text ed. 9.25 (ISBN 0-8191-2795-7). U Pr of Amer.

EDUCATION, INDUSTRIAL
see Technical Education

EDUCATION, INTERCULTURAL
see Intercultural Education

EDUCATION, LIBERAL
see Education, Humanistic

EDUCATION, MILITARY
see Military Education

EDUCATION, MORAL
see Moral Education

EDUCATION, MUSICAL
see Music-Instruction and Study

EDUCATION, OUTDOOR
see Outdoor Education

EDUCATION, PHYSICAL
see Physical Education and Training

EDUCATION, PRESCHOOL
see also Education of Children; Nursery Schools
Berson, Minnie, ed. Opening, Mixing, Matching. (Illus.). 44p. 1.50x (ISBN 0-87173-003-0). ACEI.
Dwight, Theodore. Sketches of Scenery & Manners in the United States. LC 82-10258. 1983. 30.00x (ISBN 0-8201-1383-2). Schol Facsimiles.
Lall, Geeta R. & Lall, Bernard M. Comparative Early Childhood Education. 168p. 1983. 16.75x (ISBN 0-398-04777-4). C C Thomas.
Lombardo, Victor S. & Lombardo, Edith F. Developing & Administering Early Childhood Programs. (Illus.). 224p. 1983. 23.50x (ISBN 0-398-04773-1). C C Thomas.
Paget, Kathleen & Brackett, Bruce, eds. The Psychoeducational Assessment of Pre-School Children. Date not set. price not set (ISBN 0-8089-1475-8). Grune.
Stavely, A. L. Where is Beradino? 96p. 1982. 8.95 (ISBN 0-89756-011-6). Two Rivers.
Whordley, Derek & Doster, Rebecca J. Humanics National Orientation to Preschool Assessment. 200p. (Orig.). 1983. pap. 14.95 (ISBN 0-89334-031-6). Humanics Ltd.
Young, F. A. & McCann, W. P. Samuel Wilderspin & the Infant School Movement. 228p. 1983. text ed. 34.50x (ISBN 0-7099-2903-X, Pub. by Croom Helm Ltd England). Biblio Dist.

EDUCATION, PRIMARY
see also Creative Activities and Seatwork; Education of Children; Readiness for School
Brooks, Bearl. Beginning Sounds. (Early Education Ser.). 24p. (ps-1). 1978. wkbk. 5.00 (ISBN 0-8209-0204-7, K-6). ESP.
--Following Directions. (Early Education Ser.). 24p. (ps-3). 1980. wkbk. 5.00 (ISBN 0-8209-0208-X, K-10). ESP.
--Learning to Think. (Early Education Ser.). 24p. (gr. k). 1979. wkbk. 5.00 (ISBN 0-8209-0205-5, K-7). ESP.
--Nonreading Exercises. (Early Education Ser.). 24p. (ps-1). 1975. wkbk. 5.00 (ISBN 0-8209-0202-0, K-4). ESP.
Hayes, Marilyn. Basic Skills Seeing Differences Workbook. (Basic Skills Workbooks). 32p. (gr. k-1). 1983. 0.99 (ISBN 0-8209-0588-7, EEW-11). ESP.
--Seeing Differences. (Early Education Ser.). 24p. (gr. k). 1982. wkbk. 5.00 (ISBN 0-8209-0210-1, K-12). ESP.
Justus, Fred. Basic Skills Seatwork Workbook. (Basic Skills Workbooks). 32p. (gr. k-1). 1983. 0.99 (ISBN 0-8209-0550-X, EEW-1). ESP.
--Beginner's Seatwork. (Early Education Ser.). 24p. (ps-1). 1979. wkbk. 5.00 (K-3). ESP.
--Getting a Head Start in School. (Early Education Ser.). 24p. (gr. 1-2). 1975. wkbk. 5.00 (ISBN 0-8209-0206-3, K-8). ESP.
--Learning Directions. (Early Education Ser.). 24p. (gr. 1). 1981. wkbk. 5.00 (ISBN 0-8209-0225-X, K-27). ESP.
--Things & Words. (Early Education Ser.). 24p. (ps-1). 1978. wkbk. 5.00 (ISBN 0-8209-0203-9, K-5). ESP.
--Things Around Us. (Science Ser.). 24p. (ps). 1975. wkbk. 5.00 (ISBN 0-8209-0138-5, S-R). ESP.
Leatzow, Nancy & Neuhauser, Carol. Creating Discipline in the Early Childhood Classroom. (Illus., Orig.). 1983. pap. text ed. 8.95 (ISBN 0-8425-2112-7). BYU Clark Law.

EDUCATION, PRIMARY-CURRICULA
Integrating Subject Areas in Primary Education Curriculum. 71p. 1983. pap. 7.00 (ISBN 0-686-84914-0, UB 114, UNESCO Regional Office). Unipub.

EDUCATION, PROFESSIONAL
see Professional Education

EDUCATION, RELIGIOUS
see Religious Education

EDUCATION, RURAL
Darnell, Frank & Simpson, Patricia. Rural Education: In Pursuit of Excellence. 244p. 1982. pap. 29.95 (ISBN 0-686-84840-3, Pub. by CSIRO Australia). Intl Schol Bk Serv.

EDUCATION, SCIENTIFIC
see Science-Study and Teaching

EDUCATION, SECONDARY
see also Private Schools; Public Schools also subdivision Study and Teaching (Secondary) under special subjects, e.g. Science-Study and Teaching (Secondary)
Albisetti, James C. Secondary School Reform in Imperial Germany. LC 82-12223. 392p. 1983. 35.00x (ISBN 0-691-05373-1). Princeton U Pr.
Epstein, Joyce L. & Karweit, Nancy L., eds. Friends in School: Patterns of Selection & Influence in Secondary Schools. LC 82-22822. Date not set. price not set (ISBN 0-12-240540-4). Acad Pr.
Houston, Jack. Basic Skills Health Workbook: Grade 9. (Basic Skills Workbooks). 32p. (YA) 1982. tchr's ed. 0.99 (HW-J). ESP.
Rudman, Jack. Intermediate Schools. (Teachers Lesson Plan Bk.: IS-1). (gr. 5-8). pap. 3.95 (ISBN 0-686-84419-X). Natl Learning.
--Junior High School. (Teachers Lesson Plan Bk.: J-1). (gr. 7-9). pap. 3.95 (ISBN 0-686-84420-3). Natl Learning.
Vaghn, Jim. Jumbo Geometry Yearbook. (Jumbo Math Ser.). 96p. (gr. 10). 1981. wkbk. 14.00 (ISBN 0-8209-0039-7, JMY-10). ESP.
Vaughn, Jim. Basic Skills Workbooks: Grade 10. (Basic Skills Workbooks). 32p. (gr. 10). 1982. wkbk. 0.99 (ISBN 0-8209-0397-3, MW-K). ESP.

EDUCATION, SECONDARY-AIMS AND OBJECTIVES
Johnson, Daphne & Ransom, Elizabeth. Family & School. 192p. 1983. text ed. 24.50x (ISBN 0-7099-2236-1, Pub. by Croom Helm Ltd England). Biblio Dist.

EDUCATION, TECHNICAL
see Technical Education

EDUCATION, THEOLOGICAL
see Religious Education; Theology-Study and Teaching

EDUCATION, URBAN
Goodenow, Ronald K. & Ravitch, Diane, eds. Community Studies in Urban Educational History. 360p. 1983. text ed. 40.00x (ISBN 0-8419-0850-8). Holmes & Meier.
Vahey, Esther J. Micro Wave the Easy Way Vol. II. (Audio Cassette Cooking School Library). 16p. 1982. pap. text ed. 12.95x. Cuisine Con.
Weinberg, Meyer. The Search for Quality Integrated Education: Policy & Research on Minority Students in School & College. LC 82-12016. (Contributions to the Study of Education: No. 7). (Illus.). 320p. 1983. lib. bdg. 35.00 (ISBN 0-313-23714-X, LC214). Greenwood.

EDUCATION, VISUAL
see Visual Education

EDUCATION, VOCATIONAL
see Vocational Education

EDUCATION AND ANTHROPOLOGY
see Educational Anthropology

EDUCATION AND SOCIOLOGY
see Educational Sociology

EDUCATION AND STATE
see also Art and State; Endowments; Federal Aid to Education; State Encouragement of Science, Literature, and Art
Ahier, John & Flude, Michael, eds. Contemporary Education Policy. 304p. 1983. pap. text ed. 19.50x (ISBN 0-7099-0512-2, Pub. by Croom Helm Ltd England). Biblio Dist.
Busshoff, Ludger. Das Zehn Bildungsjahr Unter Bildungspolitischem Aspekt. 234p. (Ger.). 1982. write for info. (ISBN 3-8204-7044-1). P Lang Pubs.
Fagerlind, I. & Saha, L. Education & National Development: A Comparative Perspective. (Illus.). 200p. 1983. 32.00 (ISBN 0-08-028915-0); pap. 13.00 (ISBN 0-08-030202-5). Pergamon.
McNett, Ian, ed. Early Alert: The Impact of Federal Education on the States. 64p. (Orig.). 1983. pap. write for info. (ISBN 0-937846-99-6). Inst Educ Lead.
OECD. Reviews of National Policies for Education: Finland. 120p. 1982. pap. 13.00 (ISBN 92-64-12371-7). OECD.
OECD Staff. Review of National Policies for Education: Greece. 122p. (Orig.). 1982. pap. 9.00x (ISBN 92-64-12334-2). OECD.
Sherman, Joel D. & Kutner, Mark A., eds. New Dimensions of the Federal-State Partnership in Education. 168p. (Orig.). 1983. pap. write for info. (ISBN 0-937846-98-8). Inst Educ Lead.

EDUCATION AS A PROFESSION
Turner, J. D. & Rushton, J., eds. Education for the Professionals. 1976. 14.00 (ISBN 0-7190-0641-4). Manchester.

EDUCATION FOR LIBRARIANSHIP
see Library Education

EDUCATION OF ADULTS
see Adult Education

EDUCATION OF CHILDREN
see also Education, Elementary; Education, Preschool; Education, Primary; Physical Education for Children; School Social Work; Schools
Cataldo, Christine Z. Infant & Toddler Programs: A Guide to Very Early Childhood Education. LC 82-11418. (Illus.). 240p. Date not set. pap. text ed. 9.95 (ISBN 0-201-11020-2). A-W.
Duke, Robert E. Why Children Fail & How You Can Help Them: Meditation-Therapy. 130p. 1983. 16.95x (ISBN 0-686-84047-X). Irvington.
Feeney, Stephanie & Christensen, Doris. Who Am I in the Lives of Children? An Introduction to Teaching Young Children. 416p. 1983. text ed. 19.95 (ISBN 0-675-20056-3). Additional supplements may be obtained from publisher. Merrill.
Katz, Lilian, ed. Current Topics in Early Childhood Education, Vol. 4. 256p. 1982. text ed. 27.50 (ISBN 0-89391-109-7); pap. text ed. 16.95 (ISBN 0-89391-110-0). Ablex Pub.
Monroe, Walter S. Directing Learning in the Elementary School. 480p. 1982. Repr. of 1932 ed. lib. bdg. 45.00 (ISBN 0-89987-648-X). Darby Bks.
Quisenberry, James D., ed. & intro. by. Changing Family Lifestyles: Their Effect on Children. (Illus.). 64p. 1982. pap. 5.75 (ISBN 0-87173-100-2). ACEI.
Rice, Mary F. & Flatter, Charles H. Help Me Learn: A Handbook for Teaching Young Children. 192p. 1979. 13.95 (ISBN 0-13-386292-5); pap. 6.95 (ISBN 0-13-386284-4). P-H.
Saracho, Olivia N. & Spodek, Bernard, eds. Understanding the Multicultural Experience in Early Childhood Education. 1983. pap. text ed. write for info. Natl Assn Child Ed.
Scheffler, Hannah N., ed. Resources for Early Childhood: An Annotated Bibliography & Guide for Educators, Librarians, & Parents. LC 81-48421. 400p. 1982. lib. bdg. 38.50 (ISBN 0-8240-9390-9). Garland Pub.
Schickedanz, Judith & York, Mary. Strategies for Teaching Young Children. 2nd ed. (Illus.). 416p. 1983. 22.95 (ISBN 0-13-851139-X). P-H.
Steiner, Rudolf. The Education of the Child. 4th impr. of 2nd ed. Adams, George & Adams, Mary, trs. from Ger. 48p. 1981. pap. 3.00 (ISBN 0-85440-030-3, Pub. by Steinerbooks). Anthroposophic.
They Have to Be Carefully Taught. 161p. 1981. 9.95 (ISBN 0-88314-191-4). AAHPERD.
Zigmond, Naomi & Vallecorsa, Ada. Assessment for Instructional Planning: A Guide for Teachers of Children & Adolescents. (Illus.). 400p. 1983. 23.95 (ISBN 0-13-049643-X). P-H.

EDUCATION OF CRIMINALS
see Prisoners-Education

EDUCATION OF GIRLS
see Education of Women

EDUCATION OF PRISONERS
see Prisoners-Education

EDUCATION OF THE AGED
Deichman, Elizabeth S. & Evans, Patricia L. A Teaching Guide for Working with the Elderly. 27p. 1980. pap. text ed. 4.95 (ISBN 0-932910-24-6, 124). Potentials Development.
Peterson, David A. Facilitating Education for Older Learners. LC 82-49041. (Higher Education Ser.). 1983. text ed. price not set (ISBN 0-87589-565-4). Jossey-Bass.

EDUCATION OF WOMEN
Blade, Melinda K. Education of Italian Renaissance Women. rev. ed. LC 82-1190. (Woman in History Ser.: Vol. 21B). (Illus.). 86p. 1983. lib. bdg. 15.95 (ISBN 0-86663-070-8); pap. text ed. 8.95 (ISBN 0-86663-071-6). Ide Hse.
Women's Education in a Rural Environment. 105p. 1982. pap. 13.75 (ISBN 0-686-84626-5, UB112, UNESCO Regional Office). Unipub.

EDUCATIONAL ADMINISTRATION
see School Management and Organization; Universities and Colleges-Administration

EDUCATIONAL AIMS AND OBJECTIVES
see Education-Aims and Objectives

EDUCATIONAL ANTHROPOLOGY
Gaff, Jerry G. General Education Today: A Critical Analysis of Controversies, Practices & Reforms. LC 82-49037. 1983. text ed. price not set (ISBN 0-87589-560-3). Jossey-Bass.
Rodriguez, Fred. Education in a Multicultural Society. LC 82-23755. 172p. (Orig.). 1983. lib. bdg. 21.75 (ISBN 0-8191-2977-1); pap. text ed. 10.50 (ISBN 0-8191-2978-X). U Pr of Amer.
Rushton, J. & Turner, J. D., eds. Education & Deprivation. 1975. 12.00 (ISBN 0-7190-0624-4). Manchester.

EDUCATIONAL CHANGE
see Educational Innovations

EDUCATIONAL ENDOWMENTS
see Endowments

EDUCATIONAL EQUALIZATION
Appleton, Nicholas & Benevento, Nicole. Cultural Pluralism in Education: Theoretical Foundations. (Illus.). 288p. (Orig.). 1983. pap. text ed. 12.95 (ISBN 0-582-28233-0). Longman.
Majumdar, Tapas. Investment in Education & Social Choice. LC 82-12829. (Illus.). 160p. Date not set. 29.95 (ISBN 0-521-25143-5). Cambridge U Pr.
Weinberg, Meyer. The Search for Quality Integrated Education: Policy & Research on Minority Students in School & College. LC 82-12016. (Contributions to the Study of Education: No. 7). (Illus.). 320p. 1983. lib. bdg. 35.00 (ISBN 0-313-23714-X, LC214). Greenwood.

EDUCATIONAL EXCHANGES
see also Exchange of Persons Programs
Jenkins, Hugh M. Educating Students from Other Nations: American Colleges & Universities in International Educational Interchange. LC 82-49043. (Higher Education Ser.). 1983. text ed. price not set (ISBN 0-87589-559-X). Jossey-Bass.

EDUCATIONAL FACILITIES
see School Facilities

EDUCATIONAL GAMES
Kelley, Barbara & Tomacci, Toni M. The Vacations & Weekends Learning Guide: Ideas & Activities to Help Children Learn Throughout the Year. 208p. 1983. 14.95 (ISBN 0-13-940130-X); pap. 8.95 (ISBN 0-13-940122-9). P-H.

EDUCATIONAL GUIDANCE
see Personnel Service in Education

EDUCATIONAL INNOVATIONS
see also Education-Experimental Methods; Educational Technology; Non-Formal Education
Bisignano, Joseph & Bisignano, Judith. Creating Your Future: Level 3. (Illus.). 72p. 1982. workbook 6.95 (ISBN 0-9607366-9-7, KP109). Kino Pubns.
Cera, Mary J. & Bisignano, Judith. Creating Your Future: Level 1. (Illus.). 72p. 1982. 6.95 (ISBN 0-910141-00-2, KP107). Kino Pubns.
Robinson, Marilyn & Bisignano, Judith. Creating Your Future: Level 2. (Illus.). 72p. 1982. 6.95g (ISBN 0-9607366-8-9, KP108). Kino Pubns.
Supporting Innovations in Education: Preparing Administrators, Supervisors & Other Key Personnel. 86p. 1981. pap. 5.25 (ISBN 0-686-81853-9, UB103, UNESCO). Unipub.

EDUCATIONAL LAW AND LEGISLATION
see also School Discipline; School Management and Organization; Segregation in Education
Bickel, Robert D. & Young, Parker, eds. The College Administrator & the Courts. Date not set. price not set. Coll Admin Pubns.
Gallant, Claire B. Mediation in Special Education Disputes. LC 82-60764. 104p. (Orig.) 1982. pap. 6.95 (ISBN 0-87101-105-0, NASW CODE: CBS-097-C). Natl Assn Soc Wkrs.
Garber, Lee O. & Hubbard, Ben C. Law, Finance, & the Teacher in Illinois. 1983. write for info. (ISBN 0-8134-2252-3). Interstate.
Goldberg, Steven S. Special Education Law: A Guide for Parents, Advocates, & Educators. (Critical Topics in Law & Society). 244p. 1982. 24.50x (ISBN 0-306-40848-1, Plenum Pr). Plenum Pub.
McDaniel, Thomas R. The Teacher's Dilemma: Essays of School Law & School Discipline. LC 82-21743. (Illus.). 158p. (Orig.) 1983. lib. bdg. 19.75 (ISBN 0-8191-2944-5); pap. text ed. 9.75 (ISBN 0-8191-2945-3). U Pr of Amer.
O'Reilly, Robert C. & Green, Edward T. School Law for the Practitioner. LC 82-11982. (Contributions to the Study of Education Ser.: No. 6). (Illus.). 320p. 1983. lib. bdg. 35.00 (ISBN 0-313-23639-9, ORS/). Greenwood.
Vega, Jose E. Education, Politics, & Bilingualism in Texas. 262p. (Orig.). 1983. lib. bdg. 21.50 (ISBN 0-8191-2985-2); pap. text ed. 11.50 (ISBN 0-8191-2986-0). U Pr of Amer.

EDUCATIONAL LITERATURE SEARCHING
see Information Storage and Retrieval Systems-Education

EDUCATIONAL MEASUREMENTS
see Educational Tests and Measurements

EDUCATIONAL PLANNING
see also Educational Innovations; School Management and Organization
Saxena, Sateshwari. Educational Planning in India: A Study in Approach & Methodology. LC 79-900462. (Illus.). 202p. 1979. 14.00x (ISBN 0-8002-0394-1). Intl Pubns Serv.

EDUCATIONAL POLICY
see Education and State

EDUCATIONAL PSYCHOLOGY
see also Abstraction; Achievement Motivation; Child Psychology; Imagination; Intelligence Levels; Learning, Psychology Of; Listening; Memory; Perception; Psychology, Applied; School Psychologists; Subconsciousness; Thought and Thinking
Bergan, John R. & Dunn, James A. Psychology & Education: A Science for Instruction. LC 75-14321. 542p. 1976. text ed. 32.95 (ISBN 0-471-06910-8); tchrs. manual avail. (ISBN 0-471-06911-6). Wiley.

Cory, Herbert E. The Intellectuals & the Wage Works: A Study in Educational Psychoanalysis. 273p. 1982. Repr. of 1919 ed. lib. bdg. 50.00 (ISBN 0-686-81846-6). Darby Bks.
Crescimanno, Russell. Culture, Consciousness, & Beyond: An Introduction. LC 82-17425. 102p. (Orig.). lib. bdg. 18.75 (ISBN 0-8191-2811-2); pap. text ed. 8.00 (ISBN 0-8191-2812-0). U Pr of Amer.
Golay, Keith J. Learning Patterns & Temperament Styles: A Systematic Guide to Maximizing Student Achievement. LC 82-62144. 109p. (Orig.). 1982. pap. text ed. 8.95 (ISBN 0-686-38240-4). Manas Sys.
Grob, Paul & Brown, Nina W., eds. Readings in Education & Psychology. 333p. 1969. pap. text ed. 12.95x (ISBN 0-686-84056-9). Irvington.
Hudgins, Bryce B. Educational Psychology. LC 82-81417. 690p. 1983. pap. text ed. 14.95 (ISBN 0-87581-283-X). Peacock Pubs.
Koerner, Thomas F., ed. Student Learning Styles & Brain Behavior. 256p. (Orig.). 1982. pap. text ed. 10.00 (ISBN 0-88210-142-0). Natl Assn Principals.
Kratochwill, Thomas R., ed. Advances in School Psychology, Vol.3. 400p. 1983. text ed. write for info. (ISBN 0-89859-280-1). L Erlbaum Assocs.
Monroe, Walter S. Directing Learning in the Elementary School. 480p. 1982. Repr. of 1932 ed. lib. bdg. 45.00 (ISBN 0-89987-648-X). Darby Bks.
Ogden, Robert M. Psychology & Education. 350p. 1982. Repr. of 1932 ed. lib. bdg. 40.00 (ISBN 0-89984-364-6). Century Bookbindery.
Sahakian, William S. An Introduction to the Psychology of Learning. LC 82-81418. 526p. 1983. text ed. 19.95 (ISBN 0-87581-284-8). Peacock Pubs.

EDUCATIONAL RESEARCH
Cohen, L. & Thomas, J., eds. Educational Research in Britain Nineteen Seventy to Nineteen Eighty. (NFER Research Publications Ser.). 567p. 1982. text ed. 105.00x (ISBN 0-85633-243-7, NFER). Humanities.
Hauser-Cram, Penny & Carrozza-Martin, Fay, eds. Essays on Educational Research: Methodology, Testing & Application. LC 82-84690. (Reprint Ser.: No. 16). 1983. 16.95 (ISBN 0-916690-19-9). Harvard Educ Rev.
Lagemann, Ellen C. Private Power for the Public Good: A History of the Carnegie Foundation for the Advancement of Teaching. 272p. 1982. 17.95 (ISBN 0-8195-5085-X). Wesleyan U Pr.
Lindenmann, Walter K. Attitude & Opinion Research. 2nd ed. 83p. 1981. 14.50 (ISBN 0-89964-196-2). CASE.
Long, Sandra M. Using the Census as a Creative Teaching Resource. LC 82-60804. (Fastback Ser.: No. 184). 50p. 1982. pap. 0.75 (ISBN 0-87367-184-8). Phi Delta Kappa.
McMaster, John M. Skills in Social & Educational Caring. 148p. 1982. text ed. 32.00x (ISBN 0-566-00385-6). Gower Pub Ltd.
McMaster, John M., ed. Methods in Social & Educational Caring. 140p. 1982. text ed. 32.00x (ISBN 0-566-00386-4). Gower Pub Ltd.
Travers, Robert M. How Research Has Changed American Schools: A History from 1840 to the Present. (Illus.). xii, 600p. 1983. lib. bdg. 25.00 (ISBN 0-686-38132-7). Mythos Pr.
Van Dalen, D. B. Understanding Educational Research. 4th ed. 1978. text ed. 26.50 (ISBN 0-07-066883-3). McGraw.

EDUCATIONAL SECRETARIES
see School Secretaries

EDUCATIONAL SOCIOLOGY
see also Education–Aims and Objectives; Socially Handicapped Children–Education
Whiteside, Tom. Sociology of Educational Innovation. 1978. pap. 5.95x (ISBN 0-416-55830-5). Methuen Inc.

EDUCATIONAL STATISTICS
Garrett, Henry E. Statistics in Psychology & Education. LC 82-15599. xii, 491p. 1982. Repr. of 1966 ed. lib. bdg. 45.00x (ISBN 0-313-23653-4, GAST). Greenwood.

EDUCATIONAL SURVEYS
Here are entered works on the technique of conducting school surveys, evaluating school efficiency, etc. Specific surveys are entered under the name of the school or subject surveyed.
Madaus, G. & Scriven, M. S. Conceptual Issues in Evaluation. (Evaluation & Education in Human Services Ser.). 1983. lib. bdg. 38.00 (ISBN 0-89838-123-1). Kluwer Nijhoff.

EDUCATIONAL TECHNOLOGY
see also Audio-Visual Education; Computer-Assisted Instruction; Teaching-Aids and Devices
Understanding Educational Technology. LC 80-730588. 1982. 26.95 (ISBN 0-686-84126-3); members 20.95 (ISBN 0-686-84127-1). Assn Ed Comm Tech.

EDUCATIONAL TELEVISION
see Television in Education

EDUCATIONAL TESTS AND MEASUREMENTS
see also Ability–Testing; Grading and Marking (Students); Personality Tests; Psychological Tests also names of specific tests, or subdivision Examinations, Questions, Etc. under subjects
Friedman, Carol A. & Meade, Andre T. Reading & Writing Skills Workbook for the GED Test. LC 82-18400. (Arco's Preparation for the GED Examination Ser.). 256p. 1983. pap. 5.95 (ISBN 0-668-05540-5). Arco.
Serebriakoff, Victor & Langer, Steven. Test Your Child's I.Q. 1982. pap. 1.95 (ISBN 0-451-11461-2, AJ1461, Sig). NAL.

EDUCATORS–UNITED STATES
Harlan, Louis R. Booker T. Washington: The Wizard of Tuskegee, 1901-1915. (Illus.). 540p. 1983. 24.95 (ISBN 0-19-503202-0). Oxford U Pr.

EDWARD 3RD, KING OF ENGLAND, 1312-1377
Hewitt, H. J. The Organisation of War under Edward III, 1338-62. 1966. 19.00 (ISBN 0-7190-0066-1). Manchester.
Vale, Juliet. Edward III & Chivalry: Chivalric Society & Its Context, 1270-1350. 256p. 1983. text ed. 49.50x (ISBN 0-85115-170-1, Pub. by Boydell & Brewer). Biblio Dist.

EDWARD 8TH, KING OF GREAT BRITAIN, 1894-1972
Bloch, Michael. The Duke of Windsor's War: The Windsors in the Bahamas, 1940-1945. 388p. 1983. 16.95 (ISBN 0-698-11177-X, Coward). Putnam Pub Group.

EELWORMS
see Nematoda

EFFECT AND CAUSE
see Causation

EFFICIENCY, PERSONAL
see Success

EFFICIENCY ENGINEERS
see Business Consultants

EFFICIENCY RATING
see Employees, Rating Of; Teachers, Rating Of

EFFIGIES, SEPULCHRAL
see Sepulchral Monuments

EFFORT
see Struggle

EGG (BIOLOGY)
see Embryology

EGO (PSYCHOLOGY)
see also Identity (Psychology); Regression (Psychology)
Striner, Max. Ego & Its Own. Byington, Steven, tr. from Ger. (Illus.). 366p. 1982. pap. 7.95 (ISBN 0-946061-00-9). Left Bank.

EGYPT–ANTIQUITIES
Bierbrier, Morris. Tomb Builders of the Pharoahs. 160p. 1982. 75.00x (ISBN 0-7141-8044-0, Pub. by Brit Mus Pubns England). State Mutual Bk.
Fahim, Hussein M. Egyptian Nubians: Resettlement & Years of Coping. (Illus.). xiv, 197p. 1983. 20.00x (ISBN 0-87480-215-6). U of Utah Pr.
Groll, Sarah I. Egyptological Studies. (Scripta Hierosolymitana Ser.: No. XXVIII). (Illus.). 537p. 1983. text ed. 53.50x (ISBN 0-85668-911-4, Pub. by Aris & Phillips England). Humanities.
Handlist to Howard Carter's Catalogue of Objects in Tutankamun's Tomb, Vol. 1. (Tutankamun's Tomb Ser.). 1963. text ed. 24.00x (ISBN 0-900416-06-8). Humanities.
James, T. G., ed. Excavating in Egypt: The Egypt Exploration Society 1882-1982. 194p. 1982. 45.00x (ISBN 0-7141-0932-0, Pub. by Brit Mus Pubns England). State Mutual Bk.
Kitchen. Suppiluliuma & the Amarna Pharoahs. 72p. 1982. 50.00x (ISBN 0-85323-133-8, Pub. by Liverpool Univ England). State Mutual Bk.
Page, Anthea. Ancient Egypt Figured Ostraca in the Petrie Collection. (Illus.). 120p. 1983. pap. text ed. 31.50x (ISBN 0-85668-216-0, Pub. by Aris & Phillips). Humanities.
The Pharaohs. LC 81-52543. (Treasures of the World Ser.). lib. bdg. 26.60 (ISBN 0-86706-067-0, Pub. by Stonehenge). Silver.
Stone, Michael. The Armenian Inscriptions from the Sinai. (Armenian Texts & Studies: No. 6). (Illus.). 275p. 1983. text ed. 28.50x (ISBN 0-674-04626-9). Harvard U Pr.

EGYPT–CIVILIZATION
Clayton, Peter A. The Rediscovery of Ancient Egypt: Artists & Travellers in the 19th Century. (Illus.). 1983. 37.50 (ISBN 0-500-01284-9). Thames Hudson.

EGYPT–DESCRIPTION AND TRAVEL
Cox, Thorton. Thorton Cox Travel Guide to Egypt. (Thorton Cox Travel Guides). (Illus.). 120p. 1983. pap. 6.95 (ISBN 0-88254-809-3, Pub. by Geographia England). Hippocrene Bks.
Harvard Student Agencies. Let's Go Greece, Israel, & Egypt. (The Let's Go Ser.). (Illus.). 474p. 1983. pap. 7.95 (ISBN 0-312-48213-2). St Martin.

EGYPT–ECONOMIC CONDITIONS
Page, John, Jr. Shadow Prices for Trade Strategy & Investment Planning in Egypt. LC 82-8594. (World Bank Staff Working Papers: No. 521). (Orig.). 1982. pap. 5.00 (ISBN 0-8213-0009-1). World Bank.
Waterbury, John. The Egypt of Nasser & Sadat: The Political Economy of Two Regimes. LC 82-61393. (Princeton Studies on the Near East). (Illus.). 496p. 1983. 45.00x (ISBN 0-691-07650-2); pap. 12.50 (ISBN 0-691-10147-7). Princeton U Pr.

EGYPT–FOREIGN RELATIONS
The Egyptian Policy in the Arab World: Intervention in Yemen, 1962-1967 Case Study. LC 82-23812. (Illus.). 412p. (Orig.). 1983. lib. bdg. 26.75 (ISBN 0-8191-2997-6); pap. text ed. 15.50 (ISBN 0-8191-2998-4). U Pr of Amer.
McMullen, Christopher J. Resolution of the Yemen Crisis, 1963: A Case Study in Mediation. LC 80-25944. 56p. 1980. 3.00 (ISBN 0-934742-07-3, Inst Study Diplomacy). Geo U Sch For Serv.

EGYPT–HISTORY
Murname, William J. Guide to Ancient Egypt. 1983. pap. price not set (ISBN 0-14-046326-7). Penguin.

EGYPT–HISTORY–TO 640
Rawlsinson, George. History of Ancient Egypt, 2 Vols. 312p. 1982. Repr. of 1876 ed. lib. bdg. 150.00 set (ISBN 0-89760-754-6). Telegraph Bks.

EGYPT–POLITICS AND GOVERNMENT
Cooper, Mark N. The Transformation of Egypt. LC 82-15317. 288p. 1982. text ed. 22.50x (ISBN 0-8018-2836-8). Johns Hopkins.

EGYPTIAN ARCHITECTURE
see Architecture–Egypt

EGYPTIAN ART
see Art, Egyptian

EGYPTIAN CULTUS
see Cultus, Egyptian

EGYPTIAN HIEROGLYPHICS
see Egyptian Language–Writing, Hieroglyphic

EGYPTIAN LANGUAGE
see also Coptic Language
Arnett, William S. The Predynastic Origin of Egyptian Hieroglyphs: Evidence for the Development of Rudimentary Forms of Hieroglyphs in Upper Egypt in the Fourth Millennium B.C. LC 82-17562. (Illus.). 176p. (Orig.). 1983. lib. bdg. 19.00 (ISBN 0-8191-2775-2); pap. text ed. 8.25 (ISBN 0-8191-2776-0). U Pr of Amer.

EGYPTIAN LANGUAGE–INSCRIPTIONS
Lemesurier, Peter. The Great Pyramid Decoded. 1982. 30.00x (ISBN 0-85955-015-X, Pub. by Element Bks). State Mutual Bk.

EGYPTIAN LANGUAGE–WRITING, HIEROGLYPHIC
Arnett, William S. The Predynastic Origin of Egyptian Hieroglyphs: Evidence for the Development of Rudimentary Forms of Hieroglyphs in Upper Egypt in the Fourth Millennium B.C. LC 82-17562. (Illus.). 176p. (Orig.). 1983. lib. bdg. 19.00 (ISBN 0-8191-2775-2); pap. text ed. 8.25 (ISBN 0-8191-2776-0). U Pr of Amer.
Bierbrier, M. L. Hieroglyphic Texts from Egyptian Stelae etc. in the British Museum, Pt. X. 152p. 1982. 99.00x (ISBN 0-7141-0926-6, Pub. by Brot Mus Pubns England). State Mutual Bk.
Manniche, Lise. The Prince Who Knew His Fate: An Ancient Egyptian Story Translated from Hieroglyphs. 40p. 1982. 30.00x (ISBN 0-7141-8043-2, Pub. by Brit Mus Pubns England). State Mutual Bk.

EGYPTIAN MYTHOLOGY
see Mythology, Egyptian

EGYPTIAN STUDIES
see Egyptology

EGYPTOLOGY
Baines, J. Fecundity Figures: Egyptian Personification & the Iconology of a Genre. 200p. 1982. text ed. 75.00x (ISBN 0-85668-087-7, 40651, Pub. by Aris & Phillips England). Humanities.

EICHMANN, ADOLF, 1906-1962
Von Lang, Jochen, ed. Eichmann Interrogated: Transcripts from the Archives of the Israeli Police. Manheim, Ralph, tr. from German. 1983. 15.50 (ISBN 0-374-14666-7). FS&G.

EIGENVALUES
Cullum, J. K. & Willoughby, R. A. Lanczos Algorithms for Large, Symmetric Eigenvalue Computations. (Progress in Scientific Computing Ser.). Date not set. text ed. price not set (ISBN 3-7643-3058-9). Birkhauser.
Gourlay, A. R. & Watson, G. A. Computational Methods for Matrix Eigenproblems. LC 73-2783. 1979. pap. text ed. 14.95x (ISBN 0-471-27586-7, Pub. by Wiley-Interscience). Wiley.

EIGHTEENTH CENTURY
see also Enlightenment
Payne, Harry, ed. Studies in Eighteenth-Century Culture, Vol. 12. (SECC Ser.). (Illus.). 256p. 1983. text ed. 25.00 (ISBN 0-299-09270-4). U of Wis Pr.

EIKONS
see Icons

EINSTEIN, ALBERT, 1879-1955
White, Kenneth S. Einstein & Modern French Drama: An Analogy. LC 82-21789. 132p. (Orig.). 1983. lib. bdg. 17.75 (ISBN 0-8191-2942-9); pap. text ed. 7.75 (ISBN 0-8191-2943-7). U Pr of Amer.

EINSTEIN, ALBERT, 1879-1955–JUVENILE LITERATURE
Dank, Milton. Albert Einstein. (Impact Biography Ser.). (Illus.). 128p. (gr. 7up). 1983. PLB 8.90 (ISBN 0-531-04587-0). Watts.

EISENHOWER, DWIGHT DAVID, PRES. U. S., 1890-1969
Davis, Lester & Davis, Irene. Ike & Mamie. large type ed. LC 82-5869. (Illus.). 410p. 1982. Repr. of 1981 ed. 12.95 (ISBN 0-686-82639-6). Thorndike Pr.
Ferrell, Robert H., ed. The Diary of James C. Hagerty: Eisenhower in Mid-Course, 1954-1955. LC 82-48477. (Illus.). 256p. 1983. 17.50x (ISBN 0-253-11625-2). Ind U Pr.

EISENHOWER, IDA ELIZABETH (STOVER), 1886-1946
Davis, Lester & Davis, Irene. Ike & Mamie. large type ed. LC 82-5869. (Illus.). 410p. 1982. Repr. of 1981 ed. 12.95 (ISBN 0-686-82639-6). Thorndike Pr.

EL DORADO
The Kings of El Dorado. (Treasures of the World Ser.). 1983. lib. bdg. 26.60 (ISBN 0-86706-081-6, Pub. by Stonehenge). Silver.

EL PASO, TEXAS
Egloff, Fred R. El Paso Lawman: G. W. Campbell. (The Early West Ser.). (Illus.). 144p. 1982. 12.95 (ISBN 0-932702-22-8); pap. 7.95 (ISBN 0-932702-24-4); leatherbound collectors ed. 75.00 (ISBN 0-932702-23-6). Creative Texas.

EL SALVADOR
see Salvador

ELASTICITY
see also Continuum Mechanics; Plasticity; Shells; Strains and Stresses; Strength of Materials
Carlson, D. & Shield, R., eds. Finite Elasticity. 1982. lib. bdg. 79.00 (ISBN 90-247-2629-8, Pub. by Martinus Nijhoff Netherlands). Kluwer Boston.
Saada, Adel S. Elasticity Theory & Applications. LC 82-17171. 660p. 1983. Repr. of 1974 ed. lib. bdg. write for info. (ISBN 0-89874-559-4). Krieger.
Sokolnikoff, I. S. Mathematical Theory of Elasticity. LC 82-14844. 488p. 1982. Repr. of 1956 ed. lib. bdg. 29.50 (ISBN 0-89874-555-1). Krieger.
Timoshenko, Stephen P. History of Strength of Materials: With a Brief Account of the History of Theory of Elasticity & Theory of Structure. (Illus.). 452p. 1983. pap. 8.95 (ISBN 0-486-61187-6). Dover.

ELECTION DISTRICTS
see also Apportionment (Election Law)
Jewell, Malcolm E., ed. The Politics of Reapportionment. LC 82-18695. (The Atherton Press Political Science Ser.). xii, 334p. 1982. Repr. of 1962 ed. lib. bdg. 39.75x (ISBN 0-313-23317-9, JERA). Greenwood.

ELECTIONS
see also Campaign Management; Election Districts; Presidents–United States–Election; Representative Government and Representation; Suffrage; Voters, Registration Of; Voting; Women–Suffrage also subdivision Election or Elections under subjects, e.g. Presidents–United States–election; Great Britain–Parliament–Elections
Alexander, Herbert E. & Haggerty, Brian A. Financing the Nineteen-Eighty Election. LC 82-48863. 1983. price not set (ISBN 0-669-06375-4). Lexington Bks.
Sabato, Larry J. The Rise of Political Consultants: New Ways of Winning Elections. 1983. pap. 9.95 (ISBN 0-465-07041-8). Basic.
Tannenbaum, Percy H. & Kostrich, Leslie J. Turned-On TV - Turned-Off Voters: Policy Options for Election Projections. (People & Communication Ser.: Vol. 15). 244p. 1983. 25.00 (ISBN 0-8039-1929-8). Sage.
Trilling, Richard J. Party Image & Electoral Behavior. LC 76-24794. 250p. Repr. of 1976 ed. text ed. 23.50 (ISBN 0-471-88935-0). Krieger.
Wald, Kenneth D. Crosses on the Ballot: Patterns of British Voter Alignment Since 1885. LC 82-61392. 290p. 1983. 25.00x (ISBN 0-691-07652-9). Princeton U Pr.

ELECTIONS–RUSSIA
Emmons, Terrence. The Formation of Political Parties & the First National Elections in Russia. (Illus.). 576p. 1983. text ed. 42.50x (ISBN 0-674-30935-9). Harvard U Pr.

ELECTIONS–UNITED STATES
see also Afro-Americans–Politics and Suffrage; Presidents–United States–Election; United States–Congress–Elections
Alexander, Stan & Broussard, Sharon. An Analysis of the 1973 Atlanta Elections. 1973. 3.00 (ISBN 0-686-38001-0). Voter Ed Proj.
CBS News & New York Times. CBS News-The New York Times Election Surveys 1980, 2 vols. LC 82-81160. 1982. Set. write for info. (ISBN 0-89138-931-8, ICPSR 7812); Vol. I. write for info. (ISBN 0-89138-933-4); Vol. II. write for info. (ISBN 0-89138-932-6). ICPSR.
Kiewiet, D. Roderick. Macroeconomics & Micropolitics: The Electoral Effects of Economic Issues. LC 82-21985. (Illus.). 160p. 1983. lib. bdg. 16.00x (ISBN 0-226-43532-6). U of Chicago Pr.
Miller, Warren & Miller, Arthur. American National Election Study, 1976. LC 82-81969. Repr. of 1977 ed. write for info. (ISBN 0-89138-929-6, ICPSR 7381). ICPSR.
Miller, Warren, et al. American National Election Study, 1972. LC 82-81968. 1982. Repr. of 1975 ed. write for info. (ISBN 0-89138-928-8, ICPSR 7010). ICPSR.
Miller, Warren E. & National Election Studies Center for Political Studies. American National Election Study, 1980, 4 vols. LC 82-82378. 1982. Set. write for info. (ISBN 0-89138-925-3, ICPSR 7763); Vol. I, Pre & Post Election Surveys. write for info. (ISBN 0-89138-921-0); Vol. II, Major Panel File. write for info. (ISBN 0-89138-922-9); Appendix A, Contextual Data. write for info. (ISBN 0-89138-923-7); Appendix B, Notes & Questionnaires. write for info. (ISBN 0-89138-924-5). ICPSR.

Rooks, Charles S. The Atlanta Elections of Nineteen Sixty-nine. 1970. 4.00 (ISBN 0-686-37998-5). Voter Ed Proj.
Worcester, Robert M. & Harrop, Martin, eds. Political Communications: The General Election Campaign of 1979. (Illus.). 208p. 1982. text ed. 37.50x (ISBN 0-04-324007-0). Allen Unwin.

ELECTIONS–UNITED STATES–CAMPAIGN FUNDS

Alexander, Herbert E. Parties, Pacs & Political Finance Reform: How & Why has Election Financing Reform Gone Awry? What to do About it? (Vital Issues Ser.: Vol. XXXII, No. 1). 0.80 (ISBN 0-686-84152-2). Ctr Info Am.

ELECTORAL COLLEGE

see Presidents–United States–Election

ELECTRIC APPARATUS AND APPLIANCES

see also Household Appliances; Recording Instruments; Remote Control; Storage Batteries
World Appliances. 1983. 995.00 (ISBN 0-686-37717-6, 288). Predicasts.

ELECTRIC ARC WELDING

see Electric Welding

ELECTRIC BASS

see Guitar

ELECTRIC BATTERIES

see also Fuel Cells; Solar Batteries; Storage Batteries
Bagshaw, Norman E. Batteries on Ships. (Battery Applications Bk.). 215p. 1983. write for info. (ISBN 0-471-90021-4). Res Stud Pr.
Crompton, T. R. Small Batteries: Primary Cells, Vol. 2. LC 81-11495. 224p. 1983. 64.95x (ISBN 0-470-27356-9). Halsted Pr.

ELECTRIC CIRCUITS

see also Electric Contactors; Electric Networks; Electronic Circuits; Printed Circuits; Radio Circuits
Basi, Santokh. Semiconductor Pulse & Switching Circuits. LC 79-15379. (Electronic Technology Ser.). 538p. 1980. text ed. 23.95x (ISBN 0-471-05539-5); avail. solutions manual (ISBN 0-471-05831-9). Wiley.
Brown, R. G., et al. Lines, Waves & Antennas: The Transmission of Electric Energy. 2nd ed. (Illus.). 471p. 1973. text ed. 22.50 (ISBN 0-8260-1431-3). Wiley.
Edminister, J. Schaum's Outline of Electric Circuits. 2nd ed. (Schaum Outline Ser.). 304p. 1983. pap. 6.95 (ISBN 0-07-018984-6, SP). McGraw.
Electronics Magazine. Circuits for Electronic Engineers. 1977. 39.90 (ISBN 0-07-019157-3). McGraw.
Floyd, Thomas L. Electric Circuits: Electron Flow Version. 1983. text ed. 24.95 (ISBN 0-675-20037-7). Additional supplements may be obtained from publisher. Merrill.
Nilsson, James W. Electric Circuits. 1983. pap. text ed. solutions manual avail. A-W.
Reeves, Thomas C. The Life & Times of Joe McCarthy. LC 79-3730. 1981. 19.95. Stein & Day.
Ridsdale, R. E. Electric Circuits. 2nd ed. 736p. 1983. 24.95x (ISBN 0-07-052948-5, G). McGraw.
Tocci, Ronald J. Introduction to Electric Circuit Analysis. 2nd ed. 1983. text ed. 25.95 (ISBN 0-675-20002-4). Additional supplements may be obtained from publisher. Merrill.

ELECTRIC COMMUNICATION

see Telecommunication

ELECTRIC CONTACTORS

Here are entered works on devices for repeatedly establishing and interrupting an electric circuit.
CES Industries, Inc. Staff. Contactor Sensor Operation. (Ed-Lab Experiment Manual Ser.). (Illus.). (gr. 9-12). 1982. write for info. lab manual (ISBN 0-86711-063-5). CES Industries.

ELECTRIC CONTROLLERS

see also Remote Control
Rexford, Kenneth. Electrical Control for Machines. 2nd ed. 384p. 1983. pap. text ed. 24.00 (ISBN 0-8273-2175-9); lab manual 8.00 (ISBN 0-8273-2177-5); write for info. instr's guide (ISBN 0-8273-2176-7). Delmar.

ELECTRIC COOKERY, SLOW

Pappas, Lou. Extra-Special Crockery Pot Recipes. rev. ed. LC 75-9644. (Illus.). 192p. 1982. pap. 5.95 (ISBN 0-911954-69-4). Nitty Gritty.

ELECTRIC CROCKERY COOKERY

see Electric Cookery, Slow

ELECTRIC CURRENTS, ALTERNATING

Kittel, Joseph P. Understanding DC & AC Circuits Through Analogies. LC 79-65896. (Illus.). viii, 416p. (Orig.). 1983. pap. text ed. 14.95 (ISBN 0-9603198-0-8). B Royal Pr.

ELECTRIC CURRENTS, DIRECT

Kittel, Joseph P. Understanding DC & AC Circuits Through Analogies. LC 79-65896. (Illus.). viii, 416p. (Orig.). 1983. pap. text ed. 14.95 (ISBN 0-9603198-0-8). B Royal Pr.

ELECTRIC DISCHARGES THROUGH GASES

see also Plasma (Ionized Gases); Vacuum; X-Rays
Kunhardt, Erich E. & Luessen, Lawrence H., eds. Electrical Breakdown & Discharges in Gases, Pt. A: Fundamental Processes & Breakdown. (NATO ASI Series B, Physics: Vol. 89a). 475p. 1983. 65.00x (ISBN 0-306-41194-6, Plenum Pr). Plenum Pub.
--Electrical Breakdown & Discharges in Gases, Pt. B: Macroscopic Processes & Discharges. (NATO ASI Series B, Physics: Vol. 89b). 469p. 1983. 65.00x (ISBN 0-306-41195-4, Plenum Pr). Plenum Pub.

ELECTRIC ENGINEERING

see also Electric Apparatus and Appliances; Electric Machinery; Electric Power Distribution; Electric Power Systems; Electricity in Mining; Radio; Telephone
Alley, Charles L. & Atwood, Kenneth W. Electronic Engineering. 3rd ed. LC 72-8520. 838p. 1973. text ed. 35.95x (ISBN 0-471-02450-3). Wiley.
Berger & Associates Cost Consultants, Inc. The Berger Building & Design Cost File, 1983: Mechanical, Electrical Trades, Vol. 2. LC 83-70008. 207p. 1983. pap. 26.45 (ISBN 0-942564-04-9). Building Cost File.
Bose, N. K. Multidimensional Systems: Theory & Applications. (IEEE Reprint Ser.). 295p. 1979. 35.95x (ISBN 0-471-05214-0); (Pub. by Wiley-Interscience). Wiley.
Boylestad, Robert & Nashelsky, Louis. Electricity, Electronics, & Electromagnetics: Principles & Applications. 2nd ed. (Illus.). 544p. 1983. 21.95 (ISBN 0-13-248146-4). P-H.
Chirlian, Paul M. Introduction to Fourth. 350p. (Orig.). 1982. pap. write for info. (ISBN 0-916460-36-3). Matrix Pub.
Davis, B. D. Electrical & Electronic Technologies: A Chronology of Events & Inventors from 1900 to 1940. LC 82-16739. 220p. 1983. 16.00 (ISBN 0-8108-1590-7). Scarecrow.
Developments in Design & Performance of EHV Switching Equipment. (IEE Conference Publication Ser.: 182). 134p. 1979. 40.50 (ISBN 0-85296-211-8). Inst Elect Eng.
Egan, William F. Frequency Synthesis by Phase-Lock. LC 80-16917. 279p. 1981. text ed. 32.50x (ISBN 0-471-08202-3, Pub. by Wiley-Interscience). Wiley.
Electrical Installations in Buildings. (IEE Conference Publications: No. 211). 58p. 1982. pap. 25.00 (ISBN 0-85296-261-4). Inst Elect Eng.
Faber, Rodney B. Applied Electricity & Electronics for Technology. LC 77-15037. (Electronics Technology Ser.). 348p. 1978. text ed. 21.95 (ISBN 0-471-25022-8); avail. solutions (ISBN 0-471-03699-4). Wiley.
Ferguson, R. Comparative Risks of Electricity Generating Fuel Systems in the UK. 216p. 1981. 66.00 (ISBN 0-906048-66-4). Inst Elect Eng.
Fitzgerald, A. E., et al. Basic Electrical Engineering. 1981. text ed. 34.95 (ISBN 0-07-021154-X); instr's manual avail. McGraw.
Flurscheim, C. H., ed. Power Circuit Breaker Theory & Design. (IEE Power Ser.: No. 1). 602p. 1982. 61.00 (ISBN 0-906048-70-2). Inst Elect Eng.
Future Energy Concepts. (IEE Conference Publication Ser.: No. 192). 360p. 1981. 81.50 (ISBN 0-85296-229-0). Inst Elect Eng.
Gagliardi, Robert. Introduction to Communications Engineering. LC 77-18531. 508p. 1978. 40.00x (ISBN 0-471-03099-6, Pub. by Wiley-Interscience). Wiley.
Knable, Alvin H. Electrical Power Systems Engineering: Problems & Solutions. LC 82-14801. 256p. 1983. lib. bdg. 22.50 (ISBN 0-89874-549-7). Krieger.
Laithwaite, L. & Freris, T. Electrical Energy: Its Generation, Transmission & Use. 365p. 1982. 20.95 (ISBN 0-07-084109-8). McGraw.
McPartlnd, Joseph F. Handbook of Practical Electrical Design. Crawford, Harold B., ed. (Illus.). 672p. 1983. 24.50 (ISBN 0-07-045695-X, P&RB). McGraw.
Meland, Sam. Electrical Project Management. (Illus.). 320p. 1983. 32.50 (ISBN 0-07-041338-X, P&RB). McGraw.
Middleton, Robert & Meyers. Practical Electricity. new ed. (Audel Ser.). 1983. 13.95 (ISBN 0-672-23375-4). Bobbs.
Naidu, N. S. & Kamaraju, V. High Voltage Engineering. 384p. Date not set. 4.00 (ISBN 0-07-451786-4). McGraw.
Neidle. Electrical Installation for Technology. 2nd ed. 1983. text ed. write for info. (ISBN 0-408-01146-7). Butterworth.
Pratley, J. B. Study Notes for Technicians: Electrical & Electronic Principles, Vol. 1. 96p. 1982. 7.00 (ISBN 0-07-084661-8). McGraw.
Robinson, Enders A. Times Series Analysis & Applications. LC 81-81825. (Illus.). 628p. 1981. 25.00 (ISBN 0-910835-00-4). Goose Pond Pr.
Roe, L. B. Practical Electrical Project Engineering. 1978. 30.25 (ISBN 0-07-053392-X). McGraw.
Seely, Samuel & Poularikas, Alexander. Electrical Engineering: Introduction & Concepts. 650p. 1981. text ed. 26.95 (ISBN 0-916460-31-2). Matrix Pub.
Turner. Electronic Engineers Reference Book. 5th ed. 1983. text ed. price not set. Butterworth.
Wright, A. & Newberry, P. G. Electric Fuses. (IEE Power Ser.: No. 2). 208p. 1982. pap. 36.00 (ISBN 0-906048-78-8). Inst Elect Eng.

ELECTRIC ENGINEERING–APPARATUS AND APPLIANCES

see Electric Apparatus and Appliances

ELECTRIC ENGINEERING–ESTIMATES

Belt, E. R. Complete Electrical Estimating Course, 4 vols. 1976. Complete Course. 59.50 (ISBN 0-07-095030-X); Vol. 1: Electrical Estimating. 24.95 (ISBN 0-07-004454-6); Vol. 2: Electrical Pricing Units & Procedures. 24.95 (ISBN 0-07-004455-4); Vol. 3: Pricing Forms. 21.50 (ISBN 0-07-004456-2); Vol. 4: Take-Off Forms. 21.50 (ISBN 0-07-004457-0); study guide & final exam 12.00 (ISBN 0-07-004458-9). McGraw.
Tyler, Edward J. Estimating Electrical Construction. 272p. 1983. pap. 19.00 (ISBN 0-910460-99-X). Craftsman.

ELECTRIC ENGINEERING–EXAMINATIONS, QUESTIONS, ETC.

Constance, J. D. Electrical Engineering for Professional Engineers Examinations. 3rd ed. 1981. 18.95 (ISBN 0-07-012455-8). McGraw.

ELECTRIC ENGINEERING–HANDBOOKS, MANUALS, ETC.

Osborn, Richard W. & Flach, George W. Tapping in to the NECR. Osborn, Richard W., ed. LC 82-82124. (Illus.). 178p. 1982. pap. text ed. 8.50 (ISBN 0-87765-226-0, NEC-QUE). Natl Fire Prot.

ELECTRIC ENGINEERING–MATHEMATICS

Blake, Ian F., ed. Algebraic Coding Theory: History & Development. LC 73-9627. (Benchmark Papers in Electrical Engineering & Computer Science: Vol. 3). 413p. 1973. 49.50 (ISBN 0-87933-038-4). Hutchinson Ross.

ELECTRIC ENGINEERING–SAFETY MEASURES

ISA Electrical Safety Standards. LC 81-86097. (ISA Standards Mini-Standards Bks.). 104p. 1982. pap. text ed. 25.00x (ISBN 0-87664-641-0). Instru Soc.

ELECTRIC ENGINEERING–VOCATIONAL GUIDANCE

see Engineering–Vocational Guidance

ELECTRIC ENGINEERING MATHEMATICS

see Electric Engineering–Mathematics

ELECTRIC HOUSEHOLD APPLIANCES

see Household Appliances

ELECTRIC LIGHT

see Photometry

ELECTRIC LIGHT AND POWER INDUSTRY

see Electric Utilities

ELECTRIC LIGHT IN PHOTOGRAPHY

see Photography–Portraits–Lighting and Posing

ELECTRIC LIGHTING–RATES

see Electric Utilities–Rates

ELECTRIC LOCOMOTIVES

Harris, Ken. World Electric Locomotives. (Illus.). 160p. 1981. 17.95 (ISBN 0-86720-569-5). Sci Bks Intl.

ELECTRIC MACHINERY

see also Electric Controllers; Electric Motors; Electric Transformers; Electricity in Mining
Electrical Machines: Design & Applications. (IEE Conference Publications: No. 213). 272p. 1982. pap. 51.00 (ISBN 0-85296-260-6). Inst Elect Eng.

ELECTRIC MOTORS

see also Electric Transformers; Electricity in Mining
Acarnley, P. P. Stepping Motors: A Guide to Modern Theory & Practice. (IEE Control Engineering Ser.: No. 19). 160p. 1982. casebound 41.00 (ISBN 0-906048-83-4); pap. 25.00 (ISBN 0-906048-75-3). Inst Elect Eng.
Anderson, Edwin P. & Miller, Rex. Electric Motors. new ed. (Audel Ser.). 1983. 12.95 (ISBN 0-672-23376-2). Bobbs.
Drives-Motors-Controls Nineteen Eighty-Two: Proceedings of the First European Conference Held in Leeds, England, June 29-July 1, 1982. (PPL Conference Publications: No. 19). 160p. 1982. pap. 39.00 (ISBN 0-906048-85-0, Pub. by Peregrinus England). Inst Elect Eng.
Jordan, Howard E. Energy Efficient Electric Motors & Their Applications. 176p. 1983. text ed. 24.50 (ISBN 0-442-24523-8). Van Nos Reinhold.
Yang, S. J. Low-Noise Electrical Motors. (Monographs in Electrical & Electronic Engineering). (Illus.). 112p. 1981. 34.50x (ISBN 0-19-859332-5). Oxford U Pr.

ELECTRIC NETWORKS

Balabanian, Norman & Bickart, Theodore. Electrical Network Theory. LC 82-21224. 954p. 1983. Repr. of 1969 ed. lib. bdg. 59.50 (ISBN 0-89874-581-0). Krieger.
Brown, R. G., et al. Lines, Waves & Antennas: The Transmission of Electric Energy. 2nd ed. (Illus.). 471p. 1973. text ed. 22.50 (ISBN 0-8260-1431-3). Wiley.
Uhr, Leonard, ed. Algorithm-Structured Computer Arrays & Networks: Architectures & Processes for Images, Percepts, Models, Information. Date not set. price not set (ISBN 0-12-706960-7). Acad Pr.

ELECTRIC POWER

Shannon, Robert H. Handbook of Coal-Based Electric Power Generation: The Technology, Utilization, Application & Economics of Coal for Generating Electric Power. LC 82-7916. (Illus.). 372p. 1983. 45.00 (ISBN 0-8155-0907-3). Noyes.

ELECTRIC POWER–RATES

see Electric Utilities–Rates

ELECTRIC POWER DISTRIBUTION

see also Electric Networks; Electric Power Transmission; Electric Utilities; Electric Wiring
Bowers, B. A History of Electric Light & Power. (IEE History of Technology Ser.: No. 3). 304p. 1982. 71.00 (ISBN 0-906048-68-0); pap. 43.50 (ISBN 0-906048-71-0). Inst Elect Eng.
Electricity Distribution (CIRED 1981) 6th International Conference on Electricity Distribution. (IEE Conference Publication Ser.: No. 197). 1981. 89.00 (ISBN 0-85296-239-8); Eng. Version, 371p. 89.00 (ISBN 0-85296-238-X). Fr. Version, 387p. Inst Elect Eng.
Knable, Alvin H. Electrical Power Systems Engineering: Problems & Solutions. LC 82-14801. 256p. 1983. lib. bdg. 22.50 (ISBN 0-89874-549-7). Krieger.
Pansini, Anthony J. & Seale, Arthur C., Jr. Electrical Distribution Engineering. (Illus.). 464p. 1983. 45.95 (ISBN 0-07-048454-6, P&RB). McGraw.
Power System Protection, Vol. II. (Illus.). 344p. 1981. 69.00 (ISBN 0-906048-53-2). Inst Elect Eng.
Power System Protection, Vol. III. (Illus.). 496p. 1981. 69.00 (ISBN 0-906048-54-0). Inst Elect Eng.
Power System Protection Principles & Components, Vol. 1. (Illus.). 544p. 1981. 78.50 (ISBN 0-906048-47-8). Inst Elect Eng.
Progress in Cables & Overhead Lines for 220kV & Above. (IEE Conference Publication Ser.: No. 176). 324p. 1979. 58.75 (ISBN 0-85296-207-X). Inst Elect Eng.
Rolls, T. B. Power Distribution in Industrial Installations, VIII. rev. ed. (IEE Monograph Ser.: No. 10). (Illus.). 100p. 1972. pap. 21.75 (ISBN 0-906048-29-X). Inst Elect Eng.
Seidman, Arthur H. & Mahrous, Haroun. Handbook of Electric Power Calculations. 608p. 1983. 29.50 (ISBN 0-07-056061-7, P&RB). McGraw.
Sources & Effects of Power System Disturbances. (IEE Conference Publication Ser.: No. 210). 313p. 1982. 68.00 (ISBN 0-85296-257-6). Inst Elect Eng.

ELECTRIC POWER DISTRIBUTION–DATA PROCESSING

Off-Line Electronic Data Processing for Electricity Distribution. 337p. 1981. 70.00 (ISBN 0-686-37421-5). Inst Elect Eng.

ELECTRIC POWER IN MINING

see Electricity in Mining

ELECTRIC POWER INDUSTRY

see Electric Utilities

ELECTRIC POWER POOLING

see Electric Utilities

ELECTRIC POWER SYSTEMS

Here are entered works on the complex assemblage of equipment and circuits for generating, transmitting, transforming, and distributing electric energy.
see also Electric Power Distribution; Electric Power Transmission
Husain, Ashfaq. Electral Power System. (Illus.). 400p. 1982. text ed. 35.00x (ISBN 0-7069-1765-0, Pub. by Vikas India). Advent NY.
Knable, Alvin H. Electrical Power Systems Engineering: Problems & Solutions. LC 82-14801. 256p. 1983. lib. bdg. 22.50 (ISBN 0-89874-549-7). Krieger.
Traister, John E. Handbook of Power Generation: Transformers & Generators. (Illus.). 272p. 1982. 19.95 (ISBN 0-13-380816-5). P-H.

ELECTRIC POWER TRANSMISSION

see also Electric Power Distribution
Eaton, J. Robert & Cohen, Edwin. Electric Power Transmission Systems. 2nd ed. (Illus.). 432p. 1983. 24.95 (ISBN 0-13-247304-6). P-H.
Graneau, Peter. Underground Power Transmission: The Science, Technology, & Economics of High Voltage Cables. LC 79-15746. 1979. 47.50x (ISBN 0-471-05757-6, Pub. by Wiley-Interscience). Wiley.
Weedy, B. M. Underground Transmission of Electric Power. 294p. 1979. text ed. 59.95x (ISBN 0-471-27700-2, Pub. by Wiley-Interscience). Wiley.

ELECTRIC RAILROADS

see also Electric Locomotives
Myers, Johnnie J. Texas Electric Railway: Bulletin No. 121. King, LeRoy O., Jr., ed. LC 82-71474. (Illus.). 256p. 1982. 36.00 (ISBN 0-915348-21-7). Central Electric.

ELECTRIC RAILROADS–CARS

Sachs, Bernard J. & Nixon, George F. Balitimore Streetcars 1905-1963: The Semi-Convertible Era. (Orig.). 1982. pap. 14.95 (ISBN 0-9609638-0-4). Baltimore Streetcar.

ELECTRIC RELAYS

CES Industries, Inc. Staff. Relay Module. (Ed-Lab Experiment Manual Ser.). (Illus.). (gr. 9-12). 1981. write for info. lab manual. CES Industries.

ELECTRIC SIGNAL THEORY

see Signal Theory (Telecommunication)

ELECTRIC TOOLS, PORTABLE

see Power Tools

ELECTRIC TOYS

O'Brien, Richard. American Premium Guide to Electric Trains: Identifications & Values. 304p. (Orig.). 1982. pap. 10.95 (ISBN 0-89689-038-4). Bks Americana.

ELECTRIC TRANSFORMERS

Lowden. Transformer Design Manual. 1983. write for info. (ISBN 0-07-038841-5). McGraw.

ELECTRIC UTILITIES

Here are entered economic works on the sale and distribution of electricity for lighting and power purposes. Technical works are entered under Electric Engineering; Electric Lighting; Electric power Etc.
Hellman, Caroline J. C. & Hellman, Richard. The Competitive Economics of Nuclear & Coal Power. LC 82-47500. 208p. 1982. 23.95x (ISBN 0-669-05533-6). Lexington Bks.

Murphy, Frederic H. & Soyster, Allen L. Economic Behavior of Electric Utilities. 1983. 29.95 (ISBN 0-13-224089-0). P-H.

Nicholson, H. Structure of Interconnected Systems. (Illus.). 258p. 1978. 35.75 (ISBN 0-901223-69-7). Inst Elect Eng.

Rustebakke, Homer M. Electric Utility Systems & Practices. 375p. 1983. 44.95 (ISBN 0-471-04890-9, Pub. by Wiley-Interscience). Wiley.

ELECTRIC UTILITIES–RATES

Godfrey, Robert S. Means Systems Costs, 1983. 8th ed. LC 76-17689. 425p. 1983. pap. 37.50 (ISBN 0-911950-51-6). Means.

--Mechanical & Electrical Cost Data, 1983. 6th ed. LC 79-643328. 475p. 1983. pap. 34.75 (ISBN 0-911950-56-7). Means.

ELECTRIC WAVES

see also Electromagnetic Waves; Electrooptics; Signal Theory (Telecommunication); Wave Guides

Brown, R. G., et al. Lines, Waves & Antennas: The Transmission of Electric Energy. 2nd ed. (Illus.). 471p. 1973. text ed. 22.50 (ISBN 0-8260-1431-3). Wiley.

ELECTRIC WELDING

American Welding Society. Arc Welding Safety & Health. 1982. wkbk. 45.00 (ISBN 0-686-43376-9); instr's manual 17.50 (ISBN 0-686-43377-7); cassettes & slides 125.00 (ISBN 0-686-43378-5). Am Welding.

--Recommendations for Arc Welded Joints in Clad Steel Construction. 66p. 1969. 4.00 (ISBN 0-686-43359-9). Am Welding.

--Recommended Practices for Air Carbon-Arc Grouping & Cutting: C5.3. 1982. 8.00 (ISBN 0-686-43370-X). Am Welding.

--Recommended Practices for Electrogas Welding: C5.7. 1981. 8.00 (ISBN 0-686-43372-6). Am Welding.

--Recommended Practices for Gas Tungsten Arc Welding: C5.5. 1980. 8.00 (ISBN 0-686-43375-0). Am Welding.

--Specification for Steel, Carbon, Covered Arc Welding Electrodes: A5.1. 1981. 8.00 (ISBN 0-686-43345-9). Am Welding.

--Specification for Steel, Low-Alloy Electrodes & Fluxes for Submerged Arc Welding: A5.23. 1980. 8.00 (ISBN 0-686-43380-7). Am Welding.

--Specification for Steel, Low-Alloy Filler Metals for Gas Shielded Arc Welding: A5.28. 1979. 8.00 (ISBN 0-686-43352-1). Am Welding.

--Specification for Steel, Low-Alloy Flux Cored Arc Welding Electrodes: A5.29. 1980. 8.00 (ISBN 0-686-43360-2). Am Welding.

--Specification for Steels, Consumables Used for Electroslag Welding of Carbon & High Strength Low Alloy: A5.25. 1978. 8.00 (ISBN 0-686-43354-8). Am Welding.

--Specification for Steels, Consumables Used for Electrogas Welding of Carbon & High Strength Low Alloy: A5.26. 1978. 8.00 (ISBN 0-686-43356-4). Am Welding.

ELECTRIC WIRING

Electrical Wiring Fundamentals. (Contemporary Construction Ser.). 1981. text ed. 13.40 (ISBN 0-07-067561-9); tchr's. manual & key 2.00 (ISBN 0-07-067562-7). McGraw.

Fallon. Electric Wiring: Domestic. 8th ed. 1983. text ed. price not set (ISBN 0-408-00392-8). Butterworth.

Guillou. Beginners Guide to Electric Wiring. 3rd ed. 1982. text ed. 9.95 (ISBN 0-408-01130-0). Butterworth.

Shuler, Charles, ed. Residential Wiring. (Basic Skills in Electricity & Electronics Ser.). Date not set. text ed. price not set (ISBN 0-07-053354-7); price not set tchr's. manual (ISBN 0-07-053356-3); price not set activity manual (ISBN 0-07-053355-5). McGraw.

Starr, William. Electrical Wiring & Design: A Practical Approach. (Electronic Technology Ser.). 432p. 1983. text ed. 21.95 (ISBN 0-471-05131-4); write for info. tchr's. ed. (ISBN 0-471-89527-X). Wiley.

Step-By-Step Basic Wiring. pap. 5.95 (ISBN 0-696-01090-9). Meredith Corp.

ELECTRICAL ENGINEERING

see Electric Engineering

ELECTRICIANS

Thurkauf, Ernest A. One Small Lifetime. 1983. 11.95 (ISBN 0-533-05508-3). Vantage.

ELECTRICITY

see also Electrons; Magnetism; Telephone; Thermoelectricity; X-Rays

also headings beginning with Electric and Electro

Bird, May. Electrical Science: No. 3-Checkbook. 1981. text ed. 18.95 (ISBN 0-408-00657-9); pap. text ed. 8.95 (ISBN 0-408-00626-9). Butterworth.

Davis, B. D. Electrical & Electronic Technologies: A Chronology of Events & Inventors from 1900 to 1940. LC 82-16739. 220p. 1983. 16.00 (ISBN 0-8108-1590-7). Scarecrow.

Davis, Barry. Understanding DC Power Supplies. (Illus.). 240p. 1983. 18.95 (ISBN 0-13-936831-0); pap. 12.95 (ISBN 0-13-936823-X). P-H.

DeFrance, Joseph J. Electrical Fundamentals. 2nd ed. (Illus.). 672p. 1983. text ed. 25.95 (ISBN 0-13-247262-7). P-H.

Electrical Safety in Hazardous Environments. 241p. 1982. pap. 65.00 (ISBN 0-85296-267-3). Inst Elect Eng.

International Electric Energy Conference, 1980. 358p. (Orig.). 1980. pap. text ed. 45.00x (ISBN 0-85825-137-X, Pub. by Inst Engineering Australia). Renouf.

Jones, Peter. Residential Electricity. 416p. 1983. 24.95 (ISBN 0-13-774638-5); pap. 14.95 (ISBN 0-13-774620-2). P-H.

Marson, Ron. Electricity. (Science with Simple Things Ser.: No. 32). (Illus.). 80p. 1983. pap. text ed. 12.95 (ISBN 0-941008-32-0). Tops Learning.

Metering Apparatus & Tariffs for Electricity Supply. 229p. 1982. pap. 65.00 (ISBN 0-85296-265-7). Inst Elect Eng.

Patty, Catherine. Electricity. (Sound Filmstrip Kits Ser.). (gr. 3-6). 1981. tchrs ed. 24.00 (ISBN 0-8209-0437-6, FCW-14). ESP.

Smith, Sharon. Electricity. (Science Ser.). 24p. (gr. 5-9). 1977. wkbk. 5.00 (ISBN 0-8209-0157-1, S-19). ESP.

Thomson, Joseph J. Electricity & Matter. 1911. text ed. 32.50x (ISBN 0-686-83533-6). Elliots Bks.

ELECTRICITY–APPARATUS AND APPLIANCES

see Electric Apparatus and Appliances

ELECTRICITY–DISCHARGES THROUGH GASES

see Electric Discharges through Gases

ELECTRICITY–DISTRIBUTION

see Electric Power Distribution

ELECTRICITY–HISTORY

Lurkis, Alexander. The Power Brink. (Illus.). 207p. (Orig.). 1982. 13.95x (ISBN 0-9609492-1-6); pap. 9.95x (ISBN 0-9609492-0-8). Icare Pr.

ELECTRICITY–TRANSMISSION

see Electric Power Transmission

ELECTRICITY, ANIMAL

see Electrophysiology

ELECTRICITY, MEDICAL

see Electrotherapeutics

ELECTRICITY, PIEZO-

see Pyro- and Piezo-Electricity

ELECTRICITY, PYRO-

see Pyro- and Piezo-Electricity

ELECTRICITY IN MINING

see also Mining Engineering

Mular, Andrew L. & Jergensen, Gerald V., III, eds. Design & Installation of Communication Circuits. LC 82-71992. (Illus.). 1022p. 1982. 40.00x (ISBN 0-89520-401-0). Soc Mining Eng.

ELECTRICITY ON SHIPS

Bagshaw, Norman E. Batteries on Ships. (Battery Applications Bk.). 215p. 1983. write for info. (ISBN 0-471-90021-4). Res Stud Pr.

ELECTROBIOLOGY

see Electrophysiology

ELECTROCARDIOGRAPHY

Garson, Arthur, Jr. The Electrocardiogram in Infants & Children: A Systematic Approach. (Illus.). 250p. 1983. text ed. price not set (ISBN 0-8121-0872-8). Lea & Febiger.

Marriott, Henry J. Practical Electrocardiography. 7th ed. (Illus.). 560p. 1983. text ed. price not set (ISBN 0-683-05574-7). Williams & Wilkins.

Roelandt, J. & Hugenholtz, P. G. Long-Term Ambulatory Electrocardiography. 1982. text ed. 39.50 (ISBN 90-247-2664-6, Pub. by Martinus Nijhoff Netherlands). Kluwer Boston.

ELECTROCHEMICAL ANALYSIS

see also Polarograph and Polarography

Weinberg, Norman L., ed. Technique of Electroorganic Synthesis. LC 73-18447. (Techniques of Chemistry Ser.). 928p. Repr. of 1974 ed. text ed. 74.50 (ISBN 0-686-84485-8). Krieger.

ELECTROCHEMICAL DEVICES

see Fuel Cells

ELECTROCHEMISTRY

see also Electric Batteries; Electrochemical Analysis; Electrometallurgy; Fuel Cells

Bard, Lund. Encyclopedia of Electrochemistry of the Elements, Vol. 9B. 1983. price not set (ISBN 0-8247-2519-0). Dekker.

Bockris, J. O'M & Conway, Brian E., eds. Comprehensive Treatise in Electrochemistry, Vol. 6: Electrodiscs-Transport. LC 82-13144. 546p. 1982. 67.50x (ISBN 0-306-40942-9, Plenum Pr). Plenum Pub.

Business Communications Staff. New Commercial Opportunities in Electrochemistry. 1983. 1500.00 (ISBN 0-89336-351-0, C-044). BCC.

Ferrone, Soldano & David, Chella S. IA Antigens. 1982. Vol. I, Mice. 73.50 (ISBN 0-8493-6461-2); Vol. II, Man & Other Species. 55.00 (ISBN 0-8493-6462-0). CRC Pr.

Gerischer, Heinz & Tobias, Charles W., eds. Advances in Electrochemistry & Electrochemical Engineering. LC 61-15021. Vol. 10, 1977. 51.95x (ISBN 0-471-87527-9, Pub. by Wiley-Interscience); Vol. 11, 1978. 48.50x (ISBN 0-471-87528-7). Wiley.

Meites, Louis & Zuman, Petr. CRC Handbook of Organic Electrochemistry, Vol. 5. 472p. 1982. 75.00 (ISBN 0-8493-7225-9). CRC Pr.

ELECTRODES

American Welding Society. Specification for Cast Iron, Welding Rods & Covered Electrodes for Welding. 1982. 8.00 (ISBN 0-686-43349-1). Am Welding.

--Specification for Steel, Carbon, Covered Arc Welding Electrodes: A5.1. 1981. 8.00 (ISBN 0-686-43345-9). Am Welding.

--Specification for Steel, Low-Alloy Covered Arc Welding Electrodes: A5.5. 1981. write for info. Am Welding.

--Specification for Steel, Low-Alloy Electrodes & Fluxes for Submerged Arc Welding: A5.23. 1980. 8.00 (ISBN 0-686-43380-7). Am Welding.

--Specification for Steel, Low-Alloy Flux Cored Arc Welding Electrodes: A5.29. 1980. 8.00 (ISBN 0-686-43360-2). Am Welding.

--Specification for Surface Welding Rods & Electrodes. 1980. Composite. 8.00 (ISBN 0-686-43346-7, A5.21); Solid. 8.00 (ISBN 0-686-43347-5, A5.13). Am Welding.

--Specification for Zirconium & Zirconium Alloy Bare Welding Rods & Electrodes: A 5.24. 1979. 8.00 (ISBN 0-686-43343-2). Am Welding.

ELECTROENCEPHALOGRAPHY–BIBLIOGRAPHY

Brazier, M. Bibliography of Electroencephalography, Vol. 1. 1950. 12.25 (ISBN 0-444-40081-8). Elsevier.

ELECTROGRAPHY

see Kirlian Photography

ELECTROLYTIC ANALYSIS

see Electrochemical Analysis

ELECTROMAGNETIC INTERACTIONS

Breuer, Reinhard & Lechleitner, Hans. The EMP Factor: The Twenty-Minute War. Orig. Title: Der Lautlose Schlag. (Illus.). 150p. (Orig.). 1983. pap. 6.95 (ISBN 0-914842-99-4). Madrona Pubs.

ELECTROMAGNETIC THEORY

see also Electric Waves; Electromagnetic Waves; Electrons; Field Theory (Physics); Light

Klimontovich, Yu L. The Kinetic Theory of Electromagnetic Processes. (Springer Series in Synergetics: Vol. 10). 320p. 1983. 44.50 (ISBN 0-387-11458-0). Springer-Verlag.

ELECTROMAGNETIC WAVES

Button, Kenneth J., ed. Infrared & Millimeter Waves: Electromagnetic Waves in Matter, Vol. 8. LC 79-6949. Date not set. price not set (ISBN 0-12-147708-8). Acad Pr.

ELECTROMAGNETICS

see Electromagnetism

ELECTROMAGNETISM

see also Magnetohydrodynamics

Battocletti, Joseph H. Electromagnetism, Man, & the Environment. LC 76-7905. (Westview Environmental Studies Ser.). 1976. 17.50 (ISBN 0-89158-612-1). Westview.

Grant, I. S. & Phillips, W. R. Electromagnetism. LC 73-17668. (Manchester Physics Ser). 1975. pap. 23.00x (ISBN 0-471-32246-6, Pub. by Wiley-Interscience). Wiley.

Jayawant, B. V. Electromagnetic Levitation & Suspension Techniques. 144p. 1981. pap. text ed. 24.50 (ISBN 0-7131-3428-3). E Arnold.

Klimontovich, Yu L. The Kinetic Theory of Electromagnetic Processes. (Springer Series in Synergetics: Vol. 10). 320p. 1983. 44.50 (ISBN 0-387-11458-0). Springer-Verlag.

Lucas, Georges. Transfer Theory for Trapped Electromagnetic Energy. 74p. 1982. 16.95x (ISBN 0-471-10500-7, Pub. by Wiley-Interscience). Wiley.

Mitter, H., ed. Electroweak Interactions, Schladming (Graz), Austria 1982: Proceedings. (Acta Physia Austriaca Supplementum: Vol. 24). (Illus.). 474p. 1983. 38.00 (ISBN 0-387-81729-8). Springer-Verlag.

Shen, Liang & Kong, J. A. Applied Electromagnetism. (Electrical Engineering Ser.). 584p. 1983. text ed. 33.95 (ISBN 0-534-01358-9). Brooks-Cole.

Teplitz, Doris, ed. Electromagnetism: Paths to Research. 375p. 1982. 55.00x (ISBN 0-306-41047-8, Plenum Pr). Plenum Pub.

ELECTROMETALLURGY

Hellwege, K. H., ed. Metals: Phonon States, Electron States, & Fermi States, Subvolume B: Phonon States of Alloys; Electron States & Fermi Surfaces of Strained Elements. (Landolt-Boernstein--Numerical Data & Functional Relationships in Science & Technology, New Ser.: Group III, Vol. 13). (Illus.). 410p. 1983. 289.00 (ISBN 0-387-10661-8). Springer-Verlag.

ELECTROMOTIVE FORCE

see also Polarograph and Polarography

Alcock, C. B., ed. Electromotive Force Measurements in High-Temperature Systems. 227p. 1968. 28.75 (ISBN 0-686-38299-4). IMM North Am.

ELECTRON CIRCUITS–DESIGN

see Electronic Circuit Design

ELECTRON COLLISIONS

see Collisions (Nuclear Physics)

ELECTRON MICROSCOPE

Cosslett, V. E. & Barer, R., eds. Advances in Optical & Electron Microscopy, Vol. 8. (Serial Publication). 281p. 1982. 58.00 (ISBN 0-12-029908-9). Acad Pr.

EMSA Annual Meeting, 41st, 1983. Electron Microscopy Society of America: Proceedings. 1983. 45.00 (ISBN 0-911302-47-6). San Francisco Pr.

Geiss, R. H., ed. Analytical Electron Microscopy: 1981. (Illus.). 1981. 25.00 (ISBN 0-911302-42-5). San Francisco Pr.

Griffith, J. D. Electron Microscopy in Biology, Vol. 2. 349p. 1982. text ed. 85.00x (ISBN 0-471-05526-3, Pub. by Wiley-Interscience). Wiley.

Hafez, E. S. & Kenemans, P. An Atlas of Human Reproduction: By Scanning Electron Microscopy. 300p. 1982. text ed. 60.00 (ISBN 0-85200-411-7, Pub. by MTP Pr England). Kluwer Boston.

Johannessen, J. V. Electron Microscopy in Human Medicine, Vol. 7: Digestive System. 1980. text ed. 69.00 (ISBN 0-07-032507-3). McGraw.

Johannessen, J. V., ed. Electron Microscopy in Human Medicine, Vol. 11: The Skin - Special Applications. Date not set. text ed. price not set (ISBN 0-07-032510-3). McGraw.

Johannessen, Jan V. Diagnostic Electron Microscopy. 210p. 1982. text ed. 34.50 (ISBN 0-07-032543-X, Co-Pub. by Hemisphere Pub). McGraw.

Johari, Om & Albrecht, R. M, eds. Scanning Electron Microscopy 1981, Vol. IV. LC 72-626068. viii, 312p. 1982. 53.00 (ISBN 0-931288-20-7). SEM Inc.

Johari, Om & Zaluzec, N. J., eds. Scanning Electron Microscopy 1981, Vol. I. (Illus.). xiv, 666p. 1982. 53.00 (ISBN 0-931288-17-7); Set of 4 parts 109.00 (ISBN 0-931288-21-5). SEM Inc.

Trump, B. F. & Jones, R. T. Diagnostic Electron Microscopy, Vol. 1. (Diagnostic Electron Microscopy Ser.). 346p. 1978. text ed. 65.00 (ISBN 0-471-89196-7, Pub. by Wiley Med). Wiley.

Trump, Benjamin F. & Jones, Raymond T., eds. Diagnostic Electron Microscopy, Vol. 4. (Diagnostic Electron Microscopy Ser.). 544p. 1983. 65.00 (ISBN 0-471-05149-7, Pub. by Wiley Med). Wiley.

ELECTRON OPTICS

see also Electron Microscope; Electronics; Image Converters; Ion Flow Dynamics

Siemens Teams of Authors. Optoelectronics: Liquid-Crystal Display. (Siemens Team of Authors Ser.). 1981. text ed. 57.00x (ISBN 0-471-26125-4, Pub. by Wiley Heyden). Wiley.

--Optoelects Components. (Siemens Team of Authors Ser.). 1981. text ed. 45.95 (ISBN 0-471-26132-7, Pub. by Wiley Heyden). Wiley.

ELECTRON PARAMAGNETIC RESONANCE

Ayscough, P. B. Electron Spin Resonance, Vol. 6. 372p. 1982. 195.00x (ISBN 0-85186-801-0, Pub. by Royal Soc Chem England). State Mutual Bk.

Gordy, Walter. Theory & Applications of Electron Spin Resonance. LC 79-12377. (Techniques of Chemistry Ser.: Vol. 15). 1980. 48.00 (ISBN 0-471-93162-4, Pub. by Wiley-Interscience). Wiley.

ELECTRON RESONANCE

see Electron Paramagnetic Resonance

ELECTRON SPECTROSCOPY

Carlson, T. A. X-Ray Photoelectron Spectroscopy. LC 77-28499. (Benchmark Papers in Physical Chemistry & Chemical Physics: Vol. 2). 341p. 1978. 51.00 (ISBN 0-87933-325-1). Hutchinson Ross.

ELECTRON SPIN RESONANCE

see Electron Paramagnetic Resonance

ELECTRONIC ANALOG COMPUTERS–INPUT-OUTPUT EQUIPMENT

see Computer Input-Output Equipment

ELECTRONIC APPARATUS AND APPLIANCES

see also Antennas (Electronics); Computers; Electronic Control; Electronic Instruments; Electronic Office Machines; Electronic Toys; Industrial Electronics; Microwave Devices; Printed Circuits; Transducers

Business Communications Staff. Electronic Sensors. 1983. 1250.00 (ISBN 0-89336-354-5, G-076). BCC.

--Emerging Local Area Network Business. 1983. 1250.00 (ISBN 0-89336-349-9, G-074). BCC.

CES Industries, Inc. Staff. Counter-Timer Module: Troubleshooting System. (Ed-Lab Experiment Manual Ser.). (Illus.). (gr. 9-12). 1982. write for info. lab manual (ISBN 0-86711-031-7). CES Industries.

Floyd, Thomas L. Essentials of Electronic Devices. 1983. pap. text ed. 7.95 (ISBN 0-675-20062-8). Merrill.

Kelley, David & Donway, Roger. Laissez Parler: Freedom in the Electronic Media. (Studies in Social Philosophy & Policy: No. 1). 96p. 1982. pap. 4.00 (ISBN 0-935756-99-X). BGSU Dept Phil.

Lenk, John D. Handbook of Advanced Troubleshooting. (Illus.). 352p. 1983. text ed. 22.95 (ISBN 0-13-372391-7). P-H.

Tocci, Ronale J. Electronic Devices: Conventional Flow Version. 3rd ed. 1983. text ed. 23.95 (ISBN 0-675-20063-6). Merrill.

ELECTRONIC APPARATUS AND APPLIANCES–DRAWING

see Electronic Drafting

ELECTRONIC APPARATUS AND APPLIANCES–TESTING

Davis, B. P. The Economics of Automatic Testing: Electronics Components & Sub-Assemblies. 320p. 1982. 42.50 (ISBN 0-07-084584-0, P&RB). McGraw.

Heathkit-Zenith Educational Systems. Electronic Test Equipment. 512p. 1983. 21.95 (ISBN 0-13-252205-5); pap. 14.95 (ISBN 0-13-252197-0). P-H.

ELECTRONIC BRAINS

see Artificial Intelligence; Computers; Conscious Automata

ELECTRONIC CALCULATING-MACHINES

see Computers

ELECTRONIC CIRCUIT DESIGN

Lindsey, Darry. The Design & Drafting of Printed Circuits. 2nd ed. (Illus.). 400p. 1983. 45.95 (ISBN 0-07-037844-4, P&RB). McGraw.

ELECTRONIC CIRCUITS

see also Computers–Circuits; Electronic Digital Computers–Circuits; Integrated Circuits; Printed Circuits; Semiconductors

Current Electronic Components Industry in Japan. (Japanese Industry Studies: No. J77). 155p. 1980. 310.00. Intl Res Dev.

Heathkit-Zenith Educational Systems. Electronics Circuits. 352p. 1983. 19.95 (ISBN 0-13-250183-X); pap. 12.95 (ISBN 0-13-250175-9). P-H.

Klein, Barry. Electronic Music Circuits. Date not set. pap. 16.95 (ISBN 0-686-82323-0). Sams.

ELECTRONIC COMPUTER–DEBUGGING

see Debugging (Electronic Computers)

ELECTRONIC COMPUTER–PROGRAMMING

see Programming (Electronic Computers)

ELECTRONIC COMPUTERS

see Computers

ELECTRONIC CONTROL

Schmitt, N. M. & Farwell, R. F. Understanding Electronic Control of Automation Systems. LC 81-85603. (Understanding Ser.). (Illus.). 280p. 1983. pap. 6.95 (ISBN 0-89512-052-6). Tex Instr Inc.

ELECTRONIC DATA PROCESSING

see also Artificial Intelligence; Compiling (Electronic Computers); Data Transmission Systems; Debugging (Electronic Computers); Data Base Management; Office Practice; Optical Data Processing; Programming (Electronic Computers); Programming Languages (Electronic Computers); Real-Time Data Processing also subdivision Data Processing under subjects, e.g. Business–Data Processing

Ahmed, Nasir & Natarajan, T. Discrete Time Systems & Signals. 1983. text ed. 25.95 (ISBN 0-8359-1375-9); solution manual incl. Reston.

Akoak, J., ed. Management of Distributed Data Processing: Proceedings of the International Conference, Paris, France, June 23-26, 1982. 294p. 1982. 40.50 (ISBN 0-444-86458-X, North Holland). Elsevier.

Alkins, Arthur C. Fundamentals of Data Processing. (Plaid Ser.). 200p. 1983. pap. 8.95 (ISBN 0-87094-389-8). Dow Jones-Irwin.

Arnold, Robert R., et al. Modern Data Processing. 3rd ed. LC 77-14941. 435p. 1978. 25.95x (ISBN 0-471-03361-8); wkbk. 11.95 (ISBN 0-471-03362-6); avail. tchrs. manual (ISBN 0-471-03405-3). Wiley.

Becker, Jack D. Introduction to Business Data Processing: Supplement. 216p. 1982. pap. text ed. 11.95 (ISBN 0-8403-2829-X). Kendall-Hunt.

Bentley, Colin. Computer Project Management. 112p. 1983. 29.95 (ISBN 0-471-26208-0, Pub. by Wiley-Interscience). Wiley.

Bures, Jan & Krekule, Ivan. Practical Guide to Computer Applications in Neurosciences. 1983. 42.95 (ISBN 0-471-10012-9, Pub. by Wiley-Interscience). Wiley.

Burril, Claude W. & Ellsworth, Leon W. Quality Data Processing. LC 79-9623. (Data Processing Handbook). (Illus.). 208p. 1982. text ed. 25.00 (ISBN 0-935310-01-0). Burrill-Ellsworth.

Callahan, John J. Needed: Professional Management in Data Processing. (Illus.). 240p. 1983. 25.00 (ISBN 0-13-610956-X). P-H.

Carter, Ruth C. & Bruntjien, Scott. Data Conversion. 130p. 1983. 34.50 (ISBN 0-86729-047-1); pap. 27.50 (ISBN 0-86729-046-3). Knowledge Indus.

Data Processing the Easy Way. 1983. pap. price not set (ISBN 0-8120-2627-6). Barron.

Date, C. J. Introduction to Database Systems. LC 82-3900. 480p. Date not set. text ed. 25.95 (ISBN 0-201-14474-3). A-W.

Disney, R. & Ott, T., eds. Applied Probability--Computer Science: The Interface, 2 Vols. (Progress in Computer Science). 1982. text ed. 34.00x ea. Vol. 2, 532pp (ISBN 3-7643-3067-8). Vol. 3, 514pp (ISBN 3-7643-3093-7). Birkhauser.

Ellzey, Roy. Data Structures for Computer Information Systems. 288p. 1982. pap. 21.95 (ISBN 0-574-21400-3, 13-4400); 4.95 (ISBN 0-574-21402-X). SRA.

Encarnacao, J., ed. File Structures & Data Bases for CAD: Proceedings of the IFIP-WG 5-2 Working Conference, Seeheim, Federal Republic of Germany, September 14-16, 1981. 372p. 1982. 51.25 (ISBN 0-444-86462-8, North Holland). Elsevier.

Farvour, James L. TRSDOS 2.3 Decoded & Other Mysteries. (TRS-80 Information Ser.: Vol. VI). 300p. (Orig.). 1982. pap. 29.95 (ISBN 0-936200-07-3). IJG Inc.

Fernandez, Judi N. Using CPM. Ashley, Ruth, ed. LC 80-36673. (Self-Teaching Guides Ser.). 243p. 1980. pap. text ed. 12.95 (ISBN 0-471-08011-X). Wiley.

Finn, Nancy B. The Electronic Office. (Illus.). 144p. 1983. pap. 12.95 (ISBN 0-13-251819-8). P-H.

Fry. Data Processing. 1983. text ed. price not set (ISBN 0-408-01171-8). Butterworth.

Fuori, William M. & Tedesco, Dominick. Introduction to Information Processing: Study Guide. (Illus.). 80p. 1983. pap. 2.95 (ISBN 0-13-484659-1). P H.

Gantt, Michael D. & Gatza, James. Computers in Insurance. LC 80-67525. 150p. 1981. pap. 7.00 (ISBN 0-89463-029-6). Am Inst Property.

Gonzalez, Harvey J. & Fein, Lois. Datatran: A Comprehensive & Practical System for Developing & Maintaining Data Processing Systems. (Illus.). 432p. 1983. text ed. 32.50 (ISBN 0-13-196493-3). P-H.

Gray, P. A Student Guide to IFPS. 384p. 1983. 14.95 (ISBN 0-07-024322-0, C). McGraw.

Hannula, Reino. Computers & Programming: A System Three Sixty-Three Seventy Assembler Language Approach. LC 73-9192. 1983. pap. 21.00 (ISBN 0-9605044-1-9). Quality Hill.

Hanson, R. N. & Rigby, D. S. Gregg Keyboarding for Information Processing: Apple Version. 1982. 200.00 (ISBN 0-07-026109-1). McGraw.

Huber, Norman F. Data Communications: The Business Aspects. 356p. 1982. looseleaf bound 49.95 (ISBN 0-935506-05-5). Carnegie Pr.

Huges, Patricia & Ochi, Kaz. The Power of Visiplot-Visicalc-Visifile. 154p. 1982. pap. 14.95 (ISBN 0-13-687368-5). P-H.

Kellejian, Robert. Applied Electronic Communication: Circuits, Systems, Transmission. rev. ed. 608p. 1982. 25.95 (ISBN 0-574-21580-8, 13-4580); instr's. guide 3.95 (ISBN 0-574-21581-6). SRA.

Kent, W. Data & Reality: Basic Assumptions in Data Processing Reconsidered. 1978. 34.00 (ISBN 0-444-85187-9). Elsevier.

Kroenke, David M. Database Processing: Fundamentals, Design, Implementation. 2nd ed. 448p. 1982. text ed. write for info. (ISBN 0-574-21320-1, 13-4320); write for info. instr's. guide (ISBN 0-574-21321-X, 13-4321). SRA.

Logsdon. How to Cope with Computers. 1983. pap. 10.95 (ISBN 0-686-82003-7, 5193). Hayden.

Lucas, Henry C. Coping with Computers: A Manager's Guide to Controlling Information Processing. (Illus.). 192p. 1982. 14.95 (ISBN 0-02-919310-9). Free Pr.

Mandell, Steven L. Computers & Data Processing Today. (Illus.). 350p. 1983. pap. text ed. 15.95 (ISBN 0-314-69663-6); instrs.' manual avail. (ISBN 0-314-71105-8); study guide avail. (ISBN 0-314-71106-6). West Pub.

--Computers & Data Processing Today with PASCAL. (Illus.). 450p. 1983. pap. text ed. 8.95 (ISBN 0-314-70647-X). West Pub.

Miller, Boulton B. Computers & Data Processing. Woltering, Denise M. & Oberthaler, James V., eds. (Illus.). 335p. 1982. 12.95 (ISBN 0-915234-06-8); pap. text ed. 7.95 (ISBN 0-915234-05-X). Bainbridge.

Needham, R. M. & Herbert, A. J. The Cambridge Distributed Computing System. 256p. 1982. pap. 25.00 (ISBN 0-201-14092-6, Adv Bk Prog). A-W.

Page, E. S. & Wilson, L. B. Information Representation & Manipulation Using PASCAL. LC 82-4505. (Cambridge Computer Science Texts: No. 15). (Illus.). 275p. Date not set. price not set (ISBN 0-521-24954-6); pap. price not set (ISBN 0-521-27096-0). Cambridge U Pr.

Philips, J. P. & Dacons, J. C. Organic Electronic Spectral Data. 1152p. Repr. of 1976 ed. text ed. 54.50 (ISBN 0-471-02305-1). Krieger.

--Organic Electronic Spectral Data, Vol. 11. 1072p. Repr. of 1975 ed. text ed. 49.50 (ISBN 0-471-68802-9). Krieger.

Popkin, Gary S. & Pike, Arthur M. Introduction to Data Processing. 2nd ed. (Illus.). 1981. 20.95 (ISBN 0-395-29483-5). HM.

Robichaud, Beryl & Muscat, Eugene. Data Processing Work Kit. 2nd ed. 96p. (gr. 9-12). 1983. practice set 7.96 (ISBN 0-07-053207-9, C); instr's manual & key 2.50 (ISBN 0-07-053206-0). McGraw.

Rudman, Jack. Principal Data Entry Machine Operator. (Career Examination Ser.: C-2866). (Cloth bdg. avail. on request). pap. 12.00 (ISBN 0-8373-2866-7). Natl Learning.

SPSS Inc. SPSS-X Analysis of SMF Data. 144p. 1983. 16.95x (ISBN 0-07-060522-X, C). McGraw.

Stern, R. A. & Stern, N. Concepts of Information Processing with Basic. 216p. 1982. pap. text ed. 13.95 (ISBN 0-471-87617-8). Wiley.

Strackbein, Ray & Strackbein, Dorothy B. Computers & Data Processing Simplified & Self-Taught. LC 82-11664. (Simplified & Self-Taught Ser.). (Illus.). 128p. 1983. lib. bdg. 9.95 (ISBN 0-668-05553-7); pap. 4.95 (ISBN 0-668-05549-9). Arco.

Ten Thousand Data Processor Patent Abstracts, 1931-1982, Vol. 7: 1981-82. (Illus.). 295p. Date not set. 89.00 (ISBN 0-935714-15-4). Patent Data.

Thompson, Treva L. The Comprehensive System Procedure Desk Book. LC 82-80832. 350p. Date not set. 24.95 (ISBN 0-942898-01-X). Halpern & Simon.

--VSAM Performance & System Fine-Tuning Quick Reference Handbook. LC 82-83606. 150p. Date not set. 17.50 (ISBN 0-942898-02-8). Halpern & Simon.

Wagner, Michael J. Machine Language Disk I-O & Other Mysteries. (TRS-80 Information Ser.: Vol. V). 272p. (Orig.). 1982. pap. 29.95 (ISBN 0-936200-06-5). IJG Inc.

Weaver, David H. Videotex Journalism: Teletext, Viewdata, & the News. 160p. 1983. text ed. write for info. (ISBN 0-89859-263-1). L Erlbaum Assocs.

Wigander, K. & Svenson, A. Structured Analysis & Design of Information Systems. 288p. 1983. 29.95 (ISBN 0-07-015061-3, P&RB). McGraw.

Wilhelm, Carl & Amkreutz, Johann, eds. Dictionary of Data Processing, 2 Vols. 2nd ed. 1349p. 1981. Set. 105.00 (ISBN 3-921899-25-7). Intl Pubns Serv.

Williams, Robert. The Power of Multiplan. 168p. 1982. pap. 14.95 (ISBN 0-13-687343-X). P-H.

ELECTRONIC DATA PROCESSING–AUDITING

Andersen, Anker. Budgeting for Data Processing. 45p. pap. 4.95 (ISBN 0-86641-089-9, 82141). Natl Assn Accts.

Frielink, A. Auditing Automatic Data Processing. 1961. 9.75 (ISBN 0-444-40249-7). Elsevier.

Nolan, Richard L. Management Accounting & Control of Data Processing. 190p. pap. 14.95 (ISBN 0-86641-045-7, 7793). Natl Assn Accts.

ELECTRONIC DATA PROCESSING–DICTIONARIES

Anderson, R. G. Dictionary of Data Processing & Computer Terms. 112p. 1982. pap. text ed. 9.95x (ISBN 0-7121-0429-1). Intl Ideas.

Meadows, A. J. & Gordon, M., eds. The Random House Dictionary of New Information Technology. LC 82-40026. 200p. Date not set. pap. 7.95 (ISBN 0-394-71202-1, Vin). Random.

Shain, M. & Longley, D. A Dictionary of Information Technology. 1982. 75.00x (ISBN 0-686-42940-0, Pub. by Macmillan England). State Mutual Bk.

ELECTRONIC DATA PROCESSING–EXAMINATIONS

Rudman, Jack. Computer Associate (Applications Programming) (Career Examination Ser.: C-2470). (Cloth bdg. avail. on request). pap. 12.00 (ISBN 0-8373-2470-X). Natl Learning.

--Computer Associate (Operations) (Career Examination Ser.: C-2471). (Cloth bdg. avail. on request). pap. 12.00 (ISBN 0-8373-2471-8). Natl Learning.

--Computer Associate (Systems Programming) (Career Examination Ser.). (Cloth bdg. avail. on request). pap. 12.00 (ISBN 0-8373-2472-6). Natl Learning.

--Computer Associate (Technical Support) (Career Examination Ser.: C-2473). (Cloth bdg. avail. on request). pap. 12.00 (ISBN 0-8373-2473-4). Natl Learning.

--Data Processing Clerk I. (Career Examination Ser.: C-536). (Cloth bdg. avail. on request). pap. 10.00 (ISBN 0-8373-0536-5). Natl Learning.

--Data Processing Clerk II. (Career Examination Ser.: C-537). (Cloth bdg. avail. on request). pap. 12.00 (ISBN 0-8373-0537-3). Natl Learning.

--Data Processing Clerk III. (Career Examination Ser.: C-538). (Cloth bdg. avail. on request). pap. 12.00 (ISBN 0-8373-0538-1). Natl Learning.

ELECTRONIC DATA PROCESSING–VOCATIONAL GUIDANCE

Peterson's Guide to Engineering, Science, & Computer Jobs 1983. 4th Ed. ed. 787p. pap. 12.95 (ISBN 0-87866-204-9, 2049). Peterson's Guides.

Winkler, Connie. The Computer Careers Handbook. LC 82-18460. (Illus.). 176p. 1983. lib. bdg. 12.95 (ISBN 0-668-05528-6); pap. 7.95 (ISBN 0-668-05530-8). Arco.

ELECTRONIC DATA PROCESSING DEPARTMENTS–MANAGEMENT

Chandor, Anthony. Choosing & Keeping Computer Staff. LC 76-357362. (Illus.). 203p. 1976. 17.50 (ISBN 0-04-658217-7). Intl Pubns Serv.

Fisher, P. S. & Slonim, Jacob. Advances in Distributed Processing Management, Vol. 2. (Advances in Library EDP Management Ser.). 200p. 1983. price not set (ISBN 0-471-26232-3, Pub. by Wiley Heyden). Wiley.

Thompson, Treva L. Information Processing Job Description for Personnel Officers. LC 82-83717. 100p. Date not set. 10.50 (ISBN 0-942898-03-6). Halpern & Simon.

ELECTRONIC DATA PROCESSING DEPARTMENTS–SECURITY MEASURES

Eason, Thomas S. & Webb, Douglas. Nine Steps to Effective EDP Loss Control. 240p. 1983. 21.00 (ISBN 0-932376-25-8). Digital Pr.

Leiss, Ernst L. Principles of Data Security. (Foundations of Computer Science Ser.). 200p. 1982. 25.00x (ISBN 0-306-41098-2, Plenum Pr). Plenum Pub.

National Computing Centre (Manchester) Computing Practice: Security Aspects. 53p. (Orig.). 1979. pap. 25.00x (ISBN 0-85012-215-5). Intl Pubns Serv.

ELECTRONIC DATA PROCESSING IN PROGRAMMED INSTRUCTION

see Computer-Assisted Instruction

ELECTRONIC DIGITAL COMPUTERS

see also Computer-Assisted Instruction; Computer Graphics; Digital Computer Simulation; Error-Correcting Codes (Information Theory); Minicomputers; Time-Sharing Computer Systems

Bencar, Gary R. Computers for Small Business: A Step by Step Guide on How to Buy. (Illus.). 148p. 1983. pap. 11.95 (ISBN 0-935222-05-7). La Cumbre.

Booth, Taylor L. Digital Network & Computer Systems. 2nd ed. LC 77-10832. 592p. 1978. text ed. 30.95 (ISBN 0-471-08842-0); tchrs. manual avail. (ISBN 0-471-03049-X). Wiley.

Hall, Douglas V. Microprocessors & Digital Systems. 2nd ed. (Illus.). 480p. 1983. 22.05 (ISBN 0-07-025552-0, G). McGraw.

Kline, Raymond. Structured Digital Design Including MSI-LSI Components & Microprocessors. (Illus.). 544p. 1983. text ed. 28.95 (ISBN 0-13-854554-5). P-H.

Townsent. Digital Computer & Design. 2nd ed. 1982. text ed. 39.95 (ISBN 0-408-01158-0); pap. text ed. 24.95 (ISBN 0-408-01155-6). Butterworth.

ELECTRONIC DIGITAL COMPUTERS–CIRCUITS

Middleton, Robert G. Digital Logic Circuits: Tests & Analysis. Date not set. pap. 16.95 (ISBN 0-672-21799-6). Sams.

--Understanding Digital Logic Circuits. Date not set. pap. 18.95 (ISBN 0-672-21867-4). Sams.

Tocci, Ronald J. Fundamentals of Pulse & Digital Circuits. 3rd ed. 1983. text ed. 22.95 (ISBN 0-675-20033-4). Additional supplements may be obtained from publisher. Merrill.

ELECTRONIC DIGITAL COMPUTERS–DESIGN AND CONSTRUCTION

Peatman, J. B. Digital Hardware Design. 1980. 33.50 (ISBN 0-07-049132-1). McGraw.

Rajaraman, V. & Radhakrishnan, T. An Introduction to Digital Computer Design. 2nd ed. (Illus.). 416p. 1983. pap. 19.95 (ISBN 0-13-480657-3). P-H.

ELECTRONIC DIGITAL COMPUTERS–INPUT-OUTPUT EQUIPMENT

see Computer Input-Output Equipment

ELECTRONIC DIGITAL COMPUTERS–MEMORY SYSTEMS

see Computer Storage Devices

ELECTRONIC DIGITAL COMPUTERS–PROGRAMMING

see also Compiling (Electronic Computers); Computer Programs; Data Base Management also names of specific computers, with or without the subdivision programming

Booth, Taylor L. & Chien, Yi-Tzuu. Computing: Fundamentals & Applications. LC 73-20157. 497p. 1974. 29.95x (ISBN 0-471-08847-1). Wiley.

Daniels, Alan & Yeates, Don. Design & Analysis of Software Systems. 257p. 1983. pap. 15.00 (ISBN 0-89433-212-0). Petrocelli.

Disney, R. & Ott, T., eds. Applied Probability--Computer Science: The Interface, 2 Vols. (Progress in Computer Science). 1982. text ed. 34.00x ea. Vol. 2, 532pp (ISBN 3-7643-3067-8). Vol. 3, 514pp (ISBN 3-7643-3093-7). Birkhauser.

Gilbert, Philip. Software Design & Development. 608p. 1983. text ed. write for info. (ISBN 0-574-21430-5, 13-4430); write for info. instr's. guide (ISBN 0-574-21431-3, 13-4431). SRA.

Leeson, Marjorie M. Programming Logic. 320p. 1983. pap. text ed. write for info. (ISBN 0-574-21420-8, 13-4420); write for info. instr's. guide (ISBN 0-574-21421-6, 13-4421). SRA.

Rohl, J. S. Writing PASCAL Programs. LC 82-14591. (Cambridge Computer Science Texts Ser.: No. 16). 250p. Date not set. 24.95 (ISBN 0-521-25077-3); pap. 11.95 (ISBN 0-521-27196-7). Cambridge U Pr.

ELECTRONIC DRAFTING

Lindsey, Darry. The Design & Drafting of Printed Circuits. 2nd ed. (Illus.). 400p. 1983. 45.95 (ISBN 0-07-037844-4, P&RB). McGraw.

ELECTRONIC GAMES

see Electronic Toys

ELECTRONIC INDUSTRIES

see also names of individual industries and products, e.g. Television Industry; Electron Tubes

McLean, Mick. The Japanese Electronics Challenge. LC 82-42710. 170p. 1982. 27.50x (ISBN 0-312-44066-9). St Martin.

Profile of Electronic Components Manufacturers in Japan. (Japanese Industry Studies: No. J78). 172p. 1981. 280.00 (ISBN 0-686-38963-8). Intl Res Dev.

U. S. Magnetic Storage Devices. 1982. 995.00 (ISBN 0-686-37718-4, E76). Predicasts.

ELECTRONIC INSTRUMENTS

see also Astronautical Instruments; Electronic Apparatus and Appliances; Electronic Measurements also specific electronic instruments, e.g. Cathode Ray Oscillograph

Advances in Instrumentation: Proceedings of the 37th ISA Conference & Exhibit, 3 pts, Vol. 37. LC 52-29277. (Orig.). 1982. pap. text ed. 35.00x ea. Pt. 1; 510 p (ISBN 0-87664-700-X). Pt. 2; 541 p (ISBN 0-87664-701-8). Pt. 3; 644 p (ISBN 0-87664-702-6). Set. pap. text ed. 95.00x (ISBN 0-87664-709-3). Instru Soc.

Carter, Forrest L., ed. Molecular Electronic Devices. 424p. 1982. 65.00 (ISBN 0-8247-1676-0). Dekker.

Fike, J. L. & Friend, G. E. Understanding Telephone Electronics. (Understanding Ser.). (Illus.). 272p. 1983. pap. 6.95 (ISBN 0-686-84797-0, 7141). Tex Instr Inc.

Instrumentation Symbols & Identification: ISA Standard S5.1. 60p. (Sp.). 1982. pap. text ed. 17.00x (ISBN 0-87664-727-1). Instru Soc.

ISA Directory of Instrumentation 1982-83: Includes ISA Standards S5.1, S20 & S51.1, Vol. 4. 1417p. 1982. text ed. 95.00 (ISBN 0-87664-657-7). Instru Soc.

ISA Symbol Standards. LC 81-86096. (ISA Standards Mini-Reference Bks.). 128p. 1982. pap. text ed. 20.00x (ISBN 0-87664-642-9). Instru Soc.

ISA Terminology Standards. LC 81-86098. (ISA Standards Mini-References Bks.). 104p. 1982. pap. text ed. 12.00 (ISBN 0-87664-643-7). Instru Soc.

Moore, Ralph L., ed. Basic Instrumentation Lecture Notes & Study Guide, 2 vols. (Orig.). 1983. pap. text ed. 27.95 ea. Vol. 1; Measurement Fundamentals. 178p (ISBN 0-87664-633-X). Vol. 2; Process Analyzers & Recorders. 116p (ISBN 0-87664-677-1). Set. pap. text ed. 50.00x (ISBN 0-87664-678-X); Vol. 1. slides 445.00 (ISBN 0-686-83972-2); Vol. 2. slides 380.00 (ISBN 0-686-83973-0); Vol. 1. transparencies 510.00 (ISBN 0-686-83974-9); Vol. 2. transparencies 440.00 (ISBN 0-686-83975-7). Instru Soc.

Patton, Joseph D., Jr. Preventative Maintenance. LC 82-48557. 1982. text ed. 29.95x (ISBN 0-87664-718-2); pap. text ed. 19.95x (ISBN 0-87664-639-9). Instru Soc.

ELECTRONIC MEASUREMENTS

see also Telemeter

Heiserman, Russell L. Electrical & Electronic Measuring Instruments. 208p. 1983. pap. text ed. 16.95 (ISBN 0-471-86178-2). Wiley.

Wolf, Stanley. Guide to Electronic Measurements & Laboratory Practice. 2nd ed. (Illus.). 480p. 1983. text ed. 26.95 (ISBN 0-13-369652-9). P-H.

ELECTRONIC MUSIC

Consumer Electronics Group. New World of Audio: A Music Lover's Guide. Date not set. pap. 8.95 (ISBN 0-672-21946-8). Sams.

Klein, Barry. Electronic Music Circuits. Date not set. pap. 16.95 (ISBN 0-686-82323-0). Sams.

ELECTRONIC NAVIGATION

see Electronics in Navigation

ELECTRONIC NOISE

Ambrozy, Andras. Electronic Noise. (Series in Electrical Engineering). (Illus.). 284p. 1982. text ed. 34.00x (ISBN 0-07-001124-9, C). McGraw.

Connor, F. R. Noise. (Introductory Topics in Electronics & Telecommunications). 144p. 1982. pap. text ed. 9.95 (ISBN 0-7131-3459-3). E Arnold.

ELECTRONIC OFFICE MACHINES

see also Computers; Office Practice

Cohen, Aaron & Cohen, Elaine. Planning the Electronic Office. (Illus.). 288p. Date not set. 29.95 (ISBN 0-07-011583-4, P&RB). McGraw.

Donohue, Brian. How to Buy an Office Computer or Word Processor. (Illus.). 256p. 1983. 17.95 (ISBN 0-13-403113-X); pap. 8.95 (ISBN 0-13-403105-9). P-H.

ELECTRONIC OPTICS

see Electron Optics

ELECTRONIC TOYS

see also Video Games

Buchbaum, W. H. & Mauro, R. Microprocessor-Based Electronic Games. 304p. 1983. 9.95 (ISBN 0-07-008722-9). McGraw.

Buchsbaum, W. H. & Mauro, R. Electronic Games: Design, Programming, Troubleshooting. 1979. 26.95 (ISBN 0-07-008721-0). McGraw.

ELECTRONICS

see also Cybernetics; Electronic Apparatus and Appliances; Electronic Circuits; Electronic Industries; Electronic Instruments; Electronics in Aeronautics; Electronics in Navigation; High-Fidelity Sound Systems; Industrial Electronics; Medical Electronics; Microelectronics; Modulation (Electronics); Oscillators, Crystal; Particle Accelerators; Semiconductors

Bird, B. M. & King, K. G. Power Electronics. 300p. 1983. price not set (ISBN 0-471-10430-2, Pub. by Wiley-Interscience); pap. price not set (ISBN 0-471-90051-6, Pub. by Wiley-Interscience). Wiley.

Blitzer, Richard. Basic Electricity for Electronics. LC 73-20102. 727p. 1974. text ed. 25.95x (ISBN 0-471-08160-4). Wiley.

Boylestad, Robert & Nashelsky, Louis. Electricity, Electronics, & Electromagnetics: Principles & Applications. 2nd ed. (Illus.). 544p. 1983. 21.95 (ISBN 0-13-248146-4). P-H.

Brant, Carroll A. Electronics for Communication. 800p. 1983. text ed. write for info. (ISBN 0-574-21575-1, 13-4575); write for info. instr's. guide (ISBN 0-574-21576-X, 13-4576). SRA.

Brophy, James J. Basic Electronics for Scientists. 4th ed. (Illus.). 464p. 1982. text ed. 34.95x (ISBN 0-07-008133-6, C); instructor's manual avail. (ISBN 0-07-008134-4). McGraw.

CES Industries, Inc. Staff. Basic Electronics Trainer. (Ed-Lab Experiment Manual Ser.). (Illus.). (gr. 9-12). 1982. write for info. lab manual. CES Industries.

--DC-AC Electronics Program. (Ed-Lab Experiment Manual Ser.). (Illus.). (gr. 9-12). 1982. write for info. lab manual (ISBN 0-86711-062-7). CES Industries.

--Fault Location & System. (Ed-Lab Experiment Manual Ser.). (Illus.). (gr. 9-12). 1982. write for info. lab manual (ISBN 0-86711-060-0). CES Industries.

Connor, F. R. Signals. (Introductory Topics in Electronics & Telecommunication). 144p. 1982. pap. text ed. 9.95 (ISBN 0-7131-3458-5). E Arnold.

Davis, B. D. Electrical & Electronic Technologies: A Chronology of Events & Inventors from 1900 to 1940. LC 82-16739. 220p. 1983. 16.00 (ISBN 0-8108-1590-7). Scarecrow.

Einspruch, Norman, ed. VLSI Electronics: Microstructure Science. 1982. Vol. 4. write for info. (ISBN 0-12-234104-X); Vol. 6. write for info. (ISBN 0-12-234106-6). Acad Pr.

Faber, Rodney B. Applied Electricity & Electronics for Technology. LC 77-15037. (Electronics Technology Ser.). 348p. 1978. text ed. 21.95 (ISBN 0-471-25022-8); avail. solutions (ISBN 0-471-03699-4). Wiley.

Fairchild Market Research Division. Personal Electronics. special ed. (Fact File Ser.). (Illus.). 50p. 1983. pap. text ed. 15.00 (ISBN 0-87005-458-9). Fairchild.

The Future of the Electronics & Telecommunications Industries in Australia. 93p. (Orig.). 1978. pap. text ed. 18.00x (ISBN 0-85825-099-3, Pub. by Inst Engineering Australia). Renouf.

Giacoletto, L. J. Electronics Designer's Handbook. 2nd ed. 1977. 76.50 (ISBN 0-07-023149-4). McGraw.

Heathkit-Zenith Educational Systems. AC Electronics. (Spectrum Fundamentals of Electronics Ser.). (Illus.). 280p. 1983. 19.95 (ISBN 0-13-002121-0); pap. 12.95 (ISBN 0-13-002113-X). P-H.

--DC Electronics. (Spectrum Fundamentals of Electronics Ser.). 279p. 1983. 19.95 (ISBN 0-13-198192-7); pap. 12.95 (ISBN 0-13-198184-6). P-H.

--Electronic Communications. (Spectrum Fundamentals of Electronics Ser.). (Illus.). 300p. 1983. 19.95 (ISBN 0-13-250423-5); pap. 12.95 (ISBN 0-13-250415-4). P-H.

Heiserman, Russell L. Electronic Equipment Wiring & Assembly. LC 82-13678. 98p. 1983. pap. text ed. 14.95 (ISBN 0-471-86176-6). Wiley.

Japan Electronics Almanac, 1982. 276p. (Orig.). 1982. pap. 37.50x (ISBN 0-8002-3019-1). Intl Pubns Serv.

Japan Electronics Buyer's Guide, 1982. 1233p. 1982. pap. 81.00x (ISBN 0-8002-3013-2). Intl Pubns Serv.

Jowett, C. E. Materials & Process in Electronics. 329p. 1982. text ed. 43.50x (ISBN 0-09-145100-0). Sheridan.

Klinger, David S., ed. Ultrasensitive Spectroscopic Techniques. LC 82-18417. (Quantum Electronics Ser.). Date not set. 55.00 (ISBN 0-12-414980-4). Acad Pr.

Larson, Boyd. Power Control Electronics. 2nd ed. (Illus.). 176p. 1982. text ed. 21.95 (ISBN 0-13-687186-0). P-H.

Local Government Engineering. 384p. (Orig.). 1981. pap. text ed. 37.50x (ISBN 0-85825-153-1, Pub. by Inst Engineering Australia). Renouf.

Marton, C. & Septier, A., eds. Advances in Electronics & Electron Physics Supplement, No. 13C. (Serial Publication). 544p. 1983. price not set (ISBN 0-12-014576-6). Acad Pr.

Marton, L., ed. Advances in Electronics & Electron Physics, Vol. 60. (Serial Publication). 424p. Date not set. 60.00 (ISBN 0-12-014660-6). Acad Pr.

Miller, Gary M. Modern Electronic Communications. 2nd ed. (Illus.). 592p. 1983. text ed. 26.95 (ISBN 0-13-593152-5). P-H.

Olsen. Electronics a Course Book for Students: 2nd. Limp. 1982. text ed. 42.50 (ISBN 0-408-01193-9); pap. text ed. 24.95 (ISBN 0-408-00491-6). Butterworth.

Penketh. Electronic Power Control for Technical Paper. 1982. pap. text ed. 14.95 (ISBN 0-408-01154-8). Butterworth.

Pratley, J. B. Study Notes for Technicians: Electrical & Electronic Principles, Vol. 1. 96p. 1982. 7.00 (ISBN 0-07-084661-8). McGraw.

Sinclair, Ian R. Electronics for the Service Engineer, Vol. 1. 176p. 1980. 40.00x (ISBN 0-291-39638-0, Pub. by Tech Pr). State Mutual Bk.

Supreme Publications Master Index. 49p. Date not set. pap. 9.00 (ISBN 0-938630-21-0). Ars Electronics.

Zbar, Paul B. & Malvino, Albert P. Basic Electronics: A Text-Lab Manual. 5th ed. (EIA Basic Electricity-Electronics Ser.). (Illus.). 352p. 1983. pap. text ed. 13.50 (ISBN 0-07-072803-8, G); write for info. instr's guide (ISBN 0-07-072804-6). McGraw.

ELECTRONICS-AMATEURS' MANUALS

Mims, Forrest. The Forrest Mims Circuit Scrapbook. Helms, Harry L., ed. (Illus.). 170p. 1982. pap. 14.95 (ISBN 0-07-042389-X, P&RB). McGraw.

ELECTRONICS-APPARATUS AND APPLIANCES

see Electronic Apparatus and Appliances

ELECTRONICS-DICTIONARIES

Markus, J. Electronics Dictionary. 4th ed. 1978. 32.95 (ISBN 0-07-040431-3). McGraw.

ELECTRONICS-DRAFTING

see Electronic Drafting

ELECTRONICS-HANDBOOKS, MANUALS, ETC.

Draper, C. R., ed. Production of Printed Circuits & Electronics Assemblies & Metal Finishing in the Electronics Industry. LC 77-492006. (Illus.). 468p. 1969. 35.00x (ISBN 0-85218-028-4). Intl Pubns Serv.

Electronics. (Equipment Planning Guide Ser.: No. 10). 276p. 1981. pap. 23.00 (ISBN 92-2-102588-8, ILO 196, ILO). Unipub.

Ginsberg, Gerlad L. A User's Guide to Selecting Electronic Components. LC 80-25197. 249p. 1981. 33.50x (ISBN 0-471-08308-9, Pub. by Wiley-Interscience). Wiley.

Greene, Bob. Twenty Five Quick-N-Easy Electronics Projects. 96p. (Orig.). 1982. pap. 4.95 (ISBN 0-86668-023-3). ARCsoft.

ELECTRONICS-LABORATORY MANUALS

Veley, Victory & Dulin, John. Lab Experiments for Modern Electronics: A First Course. (Illus.). 256p. 1983. pap. text ed. 13.95 (ISBN 0-13-593103-7). P-H.

ELECTRONICS IN AERONAUTICS

Wilson, Michael, ed. Jane's Avionics, 1982-1983. (Jane's Yearbooks). (Illus.). 400p. 1982. 110.00 (ISBN 0-86720-611-X). Sci Bks Intl.

ELECTRONICS IN CRIME PREVENTION

La Mont, M. Dean. Understanding Electronic Security Systems. LC 82-50800. (Understanding Ser.). (Illus.). 128p. 1982. pap. 6.95 (ISBN 0-686-84790-3, 7201). Tex Instr Inc.

ELECTRONICS IN INDUSTRY

see Industrial Electronics

ELECTRONICS IN MEDICINE

see Medical Electronics

ELECTRONICS IN NAVIGATION

see also Radar in Navigation; Sonar

Keys, Gerry. Practical Navigation by Calculator. (Illus.). 176p. 1982. pap. text ed. 14.95x (ISBN 0-540-07410-1). Sheridan.

ELECTRONS

see also Electric Discharges through Gases; Electromagnetic Theory; Electron Paramagnetic Resonance; Electronics; Molecular Orbitals; Neutrons; Photoelectricity; Plasma (Ionized Gases); Positron Annihilation; Protons

Ibach, H. & Mills, L. Electron Energy Loss Spectroscopy & Surgace Vibrations. LC 81-22938. 384p. 1982. 49.00 (ISBN 0-12-369350-0). Acad Pr.

Marton, L., ed. Advances in Electronics & Electron Physics, Vol. 60. (Serial Publication). 424p. Date not set. 60.00 (ISBN 0-12-014660-6). Acad Pr.

ELECTRONYSTAGMOGRAPHY

Stockwell, Charles. Eng Workbook. 1983. pap. text ed. write for info. (ISBN 0-8391-1743-4, 17566). Univ Park.

ELECTROOPTICS

International Conference, Brighton, United Kingsom, March 1982 & Jerrard. Electro-Optics Laser International, 82: Proceedings. 1982. text ed. write for info. (ISBN 0-408-01235-8). Butterworth.

ELECTROPHONIC MUSIC

see Electronic Music

ELECTROPHORESIS

Deyl, Z. & Crambach, A., eds. Electrophoresis: Pt. B-Applications. (Journal of Chromatography Library: Vol. 18). 462p. 1983. 95.75 (ISBN 0-444-42114-9). Elsevier.

Deyl, Z., et al. Bibliography of Electrophoresis, 1968-1972, & Survey of Applications, Vol. 4. (Journal of Chromatography Ser.). 1976. 85.00 (ISBN 0-444-41225-5). Elsevier.

Gaal, O., et al. Electrophoresis in the Separation of Biological Macromolecules. LC 77-28502. 422p. 1980. 80.00x (ISBN 0-471-99602-5, Pub. by Wiley-Interscience). Wiley.

Lowenthal, A. Agar Gel Electrophoresis in Neurology. 1964. 18.00 (ISBN 0-444-40377-9). Elsevier.

Smith, M. W., et al. Bibliography of Electrophoretic Studies of Biochemical Variation in Natural Vertebrate Populations. 105p. 1982. 19.95 (ISBN 0-89672-106-X); pap. 8.00 (ISBN 0-89672-105-1); looseleaf 5.00 (ISBN 0-89672-104-3). Tex Tech Pr.

Wieme. Agar Gel Electophoresis. 1960. 22.10 (ISBN 0-444-40638-7). Elsevier.

ELECTROPHYSIOLOGY

see also Muscle; Nerves

John, E. Roy. Functional Neuroscience, Neurometrics: Clinical Applications of Quantitative Electrophysiology, Vol. 2. 320p. 1977. text ed. 29.95 (ISBN 0-89859-125-2). L Erlbaum Assocs.

Langford, T. E. Electricity Generation & the Ecology of Natural Waters. 376p. 1982. 90.00x (ISBN 0-85323-334-9, Pub. by Liverpool Univ England). State Mutual Bk.

Milazzo, G. Topics in Bioelectrochemistry & Bioenergetics, Vol. 5. 350p. 1983. 90.00x (ISBN 0-471-10531-7, Pub. by Wiley-Interscience). Wiley.

ELECTROTHERAPEUTICS

see also Radiotherapy

Stillwell, G. Keith. Therapeutic Electricity & Ultraviolet Radiation. 3rd ed. (Illus.). 361p. 1983. lib. bdg. price not set (ISBN 0-683-07979-4). Williams & Wilkins.

ELEMENTARY EDUCATION

see Education, Elementary

ELEMENTARY PARTICLES (PHYSICS)

see Particles (Nuclear Physics)

ELEMENTARY SCHOOL TEACHING

Stephens, Thomas M. & Hartman, A. Carol. Teaching Children Basic Skills: A Circiculum Handbook. 512p. 1983. pap. text ed. 17.95 (ISBN 0-675-20013-X). Merrill.

ELEMENTS, CHEMICAL

see Chemical Elements

ELEPHANTS

Elephants & Rhinos in Africa: A Time for Decision. 36p. 1983. pap. 10.00 (ISBN 2-88032-208-1, IUCN 113, IUCN). Unipub.

ELEVATORS

Safety Code for Elevators & Escalators: Handbook on A17.1. 372p. 1981. 50.00 (A00112). ASME.

ELIOT, GEORGE, PSEUD., I.E. MARIAN EVANS, AFTERWARDS CROSS, 1819-1880

Browning, Oscar. Life of George Eliot. Robertson, Eric S., ed. 174p. 1982. Repr. of 1892 ed. lib. bdg. 20.00 (ISBN 0-89984-087-6). Century Bookbindery.

Hardy, Barbara. Particularities: Readings in George Eliot. 204p. 1983. text ed. 20.95x (ISBN 0-8214-0741-4, 82-85108); pap. 10.95 (ISBN 0-8214-0742-2, 82-85116). Ohio U Pr.

Hardy, Barbara, ed. Critical Essays on George Eliot. 282p. 1979. Repr. 22.00 (ISBN 0-7100-6758-5). Routledge & Kegan.

ELIOT, THOMAS STEARNS, 1888-1965

Behr, Caroline. T. S. Eliot: A Chronology of His Life & Works. LC 82-16716. 250p. 1982. 25.00x (ISBN 0-686-84435-1). St Martin.

Delank, Claudia. Die Struktur des Zylklus "Four Quartets" Von T. S. Eliot. 327p. (Ger.). 1982. write for info. (ISBN 3-8204-5810-7). P Lang Pubs.

Dwivedi, A. N. T. S. Eliot's Major Poems: An Indian Interpretation. (Salzburg-Poetic Drama: Vol. 61). 145p. 1982. pap. text ed. 25.00x (ISBN 0-391-02731-X, Pub. by Salzburg Austria). Humanities.

Greene, Edward J. T. S. Eliot, et la France. 248p. 1982. Repr. lib. bdg. 75.00 (ISBN 0-89760-252-8). Telegraph Bks.

Kirk, Russell. Eliot & His Age: T. S. Eliot's Moral Imagination in the Twentieth Century. 490p. 1983. pap. 9.95 (ISBN 0-89385-020-9). Sugden.

Martin, P. W. Experiment in Depth: A Study of the Work of Jung, Eliot & Toynbee. 275p. 1982. Repr. of 1955 ed. lib. bdg. 40.00 (ISBN 0-89987-649-8). Darby Bks.

Tomlinson, Charles. Poetry & Metamorphosis. LC 82-19893. 112p. Date not set. 19.95 (ISBN 0-521-24848-5). Cambridge U Pr.

Williamson, George C. The Talent of T. S. Eliot. lib. bdg. 34.50 (ISBN 0-686-81914-4). Porter.

Williamson, Hugh R. Th Poetry of T. S. Eliot. 1982. lib. bdg. 34.50 (ISBN 0-686-81915-2). Porter.

Wood, Douglas K. Men Against Time: Nicolas Berdyaev, T. S. Eliot, Aldous Huxley, & C. G. Jung. LC 82-526. x, 254p. 1982. text ed. 22.50x (ISBN 0-7006-0222-4). Univ Pr KS.

ELITE (SOCIAL SCIENCES)

Jenkins, Philip. The Making of a Ruling Class: The Glamorgan Gentry 1640-1790. LC 82-14703. 336p. Date not set. 44.50 (ISBN 0-521-25003-X). Cambridge U Pr.

Nelson, Daniel N., ed. Communism & the Politics of Inequalities. LC 81-48525. 1983. write for info. (ISBN 0-669-05415-1). Lexington Bks.

Zweigenhaft. Jews in Protestant Establishment. 144p. 1982. 23.95 (ISBN 0-03-062607-2); pap. 10.95 (ISBN 0-03-062606-4). Praeger.

ELIZABETH, QUEEN OF ENGLAND, 1533-1603

Erickson, Carolly. The First Elizabeth. 464p. 1983. 19.95 (ISBN 0-671-41746-0). Summit Bks.

Naunton, Robert. Fragmenta Regalia: Sixteen Thirty. Arber, Edward, ed. 272p. Date not set. pap. 17.50 (ISBN 0-87556-577-8). Saifer.

ELK

Houston, Douglas. The Northern Yellowstone Elk: Ecology & Management. LC 82-70079. 1982. 48.00x (ISBN 0-02-949450-8). Free Pr.

ELLIPTIC DIFFERENTIAL EQUATIONS

see Differential Equations, Elliptic

ELLIPTIC FUNCTIONS

see Functions, Elliptic

ELLIS ISLAND, NEW YORK

Bolino, August C. Ellis Island Source Book. (Illus.). 224p. 1983. 15.00 (ISBN 0-89962-331-X). Todd & Honeywell.

Stewart, Fred M. Ellis Island. Golbitz, Pat, ed. LC 82-14301. 384p. 1983. 15.95 (ISBN 0-688-01622-7). Morrow.

ELVES

see Fairies

EMANCIPATION OF SLAVES

see Slavery in the United States–Emancipation

EMANCIPATION OF WOMEN

see Women's Rights

EMBASSIES

see Ambassadors; Diplomatic and Consular Service

EMBLEMS

see also Christian Art and Symbolism; Heraldry; Mottoes; Seals (Numismatics)

Jenner, Thomas. Emblem Books of Thomas Jenner. 1983. write for info. (ISBN 0-8201-1389-1). Schol Facsimiles.

EMBROIDERY

see also Beadwork; Canvas Embroidery; Needlework; Samplers

Johnson, Beryl. Advanced Embroidery Techniques. (Illus.). 144p. 1983. 22.50 (ISBN 0-7134-0085-4, Pub. by Batsford England). David & Charles.

Ondori Staff. Elegant Cross-Stich Embroidery. (Illus.). 100p. (Orig.). 1983. pap. 9.50 (ISBN 0-87040-538-1). Japan Pubns.

--Embroidery & Cross-Stich for Framing. (Illus.). 100p. (Orig.). 1983. pap. 9.50 (ISBN 0-87040-537-3). Japan Pubns.

Sestay, Catherine J. Needlework: A Selected Bibliography with Special Reference to Embroidery & Needlepoint. LC 82-5806. 162p. 1982. 12.00 (ISBN 0-8108-1554-0). Scarecrow.

Workbasket Magazine Staff, ed. Aunt Ellen's Embroidery Handbook: A Treasury of Techniques & Designs. LC 82-60950. (Illus.). 64p. (Orig.). 1983. pap. 2.95 (ISBN 0-86675-331-1, 3311). Mod Handcraft.

EMBROIDERY, INDIAN
see Indians of North America–Art

EMBRYOLOGY
see also Cells; Developmental Biology; Fetus; Genetics; Morphogenesis; Placenta; Protoplasm; Reproduction

Muramatsu, Takashi, et al, eds. Teratocarcinoma & Embryonic Cell Interactions. 1982. 36.00 (ISBN 0-12-511180-0). Acad Pr.

EMBRYOLOGY–INSECTS

Popov, G. B. Ecological Studies on Ovipostion by Swarms of the Desert Locust (Schistocerca Gregaria Forskal) in Eastern Africa. 1958. 35.00x (ISBN 0-85135-029-1, Pub. by Centre Overseas Research). State Mutual Bk.

--Studies on Oviposition, Egg Development & Mortality in Oedaleus Senegalenis: Krauss, Orthoptera, Acridoidea in the Sahel. 1980. 35.00x (ISBN 0-85135-111-5, Pub. by Centre Overseas Research). State Mutual Bk.

Stower, W. J. & Popov, G. B. Oviposition Behavior & Egg Mortality of the Desert Locust (Schistocerca Gregaria Forskal) on the Coast of Eritrea. 1958. 35.00x (ISBN 0-85135-037-2, Pub. by Centre Overseas Research). State Mutual Bk.

EMBRYOLOGY (BOTANY)
see Botany–Embryology

EMBRYOLOGY, HUMAN
see also Fertilization in Vitro, Human

Gartner, Leslie P. Essentials of Oral Histology & Embryology. LC 82-90755. (Illus.). 120p. 1982. pap. text ed. 8.75 (ISBN 0-910841-00-4). Jen Hse Pub Co.

EMBRYOLOGY, VEGETABLE
see Botany–Embryology

EMERGENCIES
see Accidents; First Aid in Illness and Injury; Medical Emergencies

EMERGENCY COMMUNICATION SYSTEMS
see also Radio; Telephone

Rudman, Jack. Emergency Communications Specialist. (Career Examination Ser.: C-2878). (Cloth bdg. avail. on request). pap. 12.00 (ISBN 0-8373-2878-0). Natl Learning.

EMERGENCY MEDICAL SERVICES

American Health Research Institute, Ltd. Medical Emergencies: A Medical Subject Analysis & Research Index with Bibliography. Bartone, John C., ed. 120p. 1983. 29.95 (ISBN 0-88164-004-2); pap. 21.95 (ISBN 0-88164-005-0). ABBE Pubs Assn.

Bassuk, Ellen L. & Fox, Sandra S. Behavioral Emergencies: A Field Guide for EMT's & Paramedics. 1983. pap. text ed. write for info. (ISBN 0-316-08330-5); instrs.' manual avail. (ISBN 0-316-08331-3). Little.

Bergeron, J. D. Self-Instructional Workbook for Emergency Care. 3rd ed. (Illus.). 224p. 1982. pap. text ed. 7.95 (ISBN 0-89303-186-0). R J Brady.

Caroline, Nancy L. Emergency Care in the Streets. 1983. pap. write for info. (ISBN 0-316-12875-9). Little.

--Emergency Medical Treatment: A Text for EMT-As & EMT-Intermediates. 1982. pap. text ed. 13.95 (ISBN 0-316-12872-4); wkbk. 8.95 (ISBN 0-316-12873-2); answer 3.95 (ISBN 0-316-12874-0). Little.

Georgopoulos, Basil S. & Cook, Robert A. A Comparative Study of the Organization & Performance of Hospital Emergency Services. 512p. 1980. pap. 20.00x (ISBN 0-87944-253-0). Inst Soc Res.

Hutchinson, Sally A. Survival Practices of Rescue Workers: Hidden Dimensions of Watchful Readiness. LC 82-20097. 114p. (Orig.). 1983. lib. bdg. 18.50 (ISBN 0-8191-2889-9); pap. text ed. 8.00 (ISBN 0-8191-2890-2). U Pr of Amer.

Jensen, Steven A. Paramedic Handbook. 120p. 1983. pap. write for info. (ISBN 0-940122-05-7). Mosby.

McNeil, E. L. Airborne Care of the Ill & Injured. (Illus.). 208p. 1983. pap. 14.95 (ISBN 0-387-90754-8). Springer-Verlag.

Robertson, Audrey. Health, Safety & First Aid: A Guide for Training Child Care Workers. 115p. (Orig.). 1980. pap. 11.95 (ISBN 0-934140-04-9). Toys N Things.

Rosen, Peter & Baker, Frank J. Emergency Medicine: Concepts & Clinical Practice, 2 vols. (Illus.). 2016p. 1983. text ed. 99.95 (ISBN 0-8016-3057-6). Mosby.

Systech Corporation. Emergency Medical Services Communications Design Manual. 1980. 50.00 (ISBN 0-686-37969-1). Info Gatekeepers.

Wagner, David K., et al, eds. Year Book of Emergency Medicine 1983. 1983. 40.00 (ISBN 0-686-83756-8). Year Bk Med.

Wilkins, Earle W., Jr. MGH Textbook of Emergency Medicine. 2nd ed. (Illus.). 1056p. 1983. text ed. price not set (ISBN 0-683-09084-4). Williams & Wilkins.

Wills, Sheryle L. & Tremblay, Sharyn F., eds. Critical Care Review for Nurses. (Illus.). 495p. 1983. pap. write for info. (ISBN 0-940122-06-5). Mosby.

EMERGENCY NURSING

Caroline, Nancy L. Emergency Medical Treatment: A Text for EMT-As & EMT-Intermediates. 1982. pap. text ed. 13.95 (ISBN 0-316-12872-4); wkbk. 8.95 (ISBN 0-316-12873-2); answer 3.95 (ISBN 0-316-12874-0). Little.

Lanros, Nedell E. Review Manual for Certification: Emergency Nursing. 1982. pap. text ed. 13.95 (ISBN 0-89303-244-1). R J Brady.

EMERGENCY POWERS
see War and Emergency Powers

EMERGENCY RELIEF
see Disaster Relief

EMERSON, RALPH WALDO, 1803-1882

Burkholder, Robert E. & Myerson, Joel, eds. Critical Essays on Ralph Waldo Emerson. (Critical Essays in American Literature Ser.). 618p. 1983. lib. bdg. 60.00 (ISBN 0-8161-8305-8). G K Hall.

Faulkner, Florence. A Challenge for Two. 1982. 6.95 (ISBN 0-686-84158-1, Avalon). Bouregy.

Hutch, Richard A. Emerson's Optics: Biographical Process & the Dawn of Religious Leadership. 380p. (Orig.). 1983. lib. bdg. 27.25 (ISBN 0-8191-3005-2); pap. text ed. 15.75 (ISBN 0-8191-3006-0). U Pr of Amer.

EMIGRATION AND IMMIGRATION
see also Aliens; Anthropo-Geography; Migration, Internal; Population Transfers; Refugees
also subdivision Emigration and Immigration under names of countries; and names of special nationalities, e.g. Americans in Foreign Countries, British in Asia

Frank, Mary, ed. Children & Families of Newcomers to the United States. (Journal of Children in Contemporary Society, Vol. 15, No. 3). 128p. text ed. 19.95 (ISBN 0-86656-181-1, B181). Haworth Pr.

Kritz, Mary, ed. U. S. Immigration & Refugee Policy. LC 82-47513. 448p. 1982. 23.95xc (ISBN 0-669-05543-3). Lexington Bks.

Mattelart, Armand. Transnationals & the Third World: The Struggle for Culture. Buxton, David, tr. from French. (Illus.). 224p. 1983. text ed. 22.95x (ISBN 0-89789-030-2). J F Bergin.

Orth, Samuel P. Our Foreigners. 1920. text ed. 8.50x (ISBN 0-686-83670-7). Elliots Bks.

Papademetriou, Demetrios G. & Miller, Mark J., eds. The Unavoidable Issue: U. S. Immigration Policy in the 1980's. LC 82-15650. 328p. 1983. text ed. 20.00x (ISBN 0-89727-047-9). Inst Study Human.

Swanson, Jon C. Emigration & Economic Development. LC 79-5155. (Replica Edition Ser.). 125p. 1979. softcover 16.00x (ISBN 0-89158-690-3). Westview.

EMIGRATION AND IMMIGRATION LAW

Marshall, F. Ray. Illegal Immigration: The Problem, the Solutions. 1982. pap. text ed. 2.50 (ISBN 0-935776-02-8). F A I R.

EMINENT DOMAIN

Gelin, Jacques B. & Miller, David W. The Federal Law of Eminent Domain. (Federal Law Library). 605p. 1982. 40.00 (ISBN 0-87215-558-7). Michie-Bobbs.

EMISSION CONTROL DEVICES (MOTOR VEHICLES)
see Motor Vehicles–Pollution Control Devices

EMOTIONAL HEALTH
see Mental Health

EMOTIONAL PROBLEMS OF CHILDREN

Petti, Theodore, ed. Childhood Depression. LC 83-580. (Journal of Children in Contemporary Society Ser.: Vol. 15, No. 2). 104p. 1983. text ed. 20.00 (ISBN 0-917724-95-X, B95). Haworth Pr.

EMOTIONAL STRESS
see Stress (Psychology)

EMOTIONALLY DISTURBED CHILDREN
see Mentally Ill Children

EMOTIONS
see also Anger; Anxiety; Attitude (Psychology); Belief and Doubt; Control (Psychology); Emotional Problems of Children; Fear; Joy and Sorrow; Love; Pain; Sympathy; Temperament

Buck, Ross W. Human Motivation & Emotion. LC 75-37893. 529p. 1976. text ed. 26.95x (ISBN 0-471-11570-3). Wiley.

Darwin, Charles. The Expression of Emotion in Man & Animals. Rachman, S. J., ed. (Classics in Psychology & Psychiatry Ser.). 432p. 1983. Repr. of 1872 ed. write for info. (ISBN 0-904014-39-8). F Pinter Pubs.

Lutzer, Erwin. Managing Your Emotions. 180p. 1983. pap. 4.95 (ISBN 0-88207-386-9). Victor Bks.

Minshull, Ruth. Ups & Downs. 103p. 1980. pap. write for info. (ISBN 0-937922-05-6). SAA Pub.

Plutchik, Robert & Kellerman, Henry, eds. Emotion: Theory, Research & Experience, Vol. 2. 340p. 1983. price not set (ISBN 0-12-558702-3). Acad Pr.

Solomon, Robert C. The Passions. xxv, 448p. 1983. text ed. 22.95x (ISBN 0-268-01551-1); pap. text ed. 9.95x (ISBN 0-268-01552-X). U of Notre Dame Pr.

Tengbom, Mildred. I Wish I Felt Good All the Time. 128p. (Orig.). 1983. pap. 4.95 (ISBN 0-87123-281-2). Bethany Hse.

Zimolzak, Chester E. & Stansfield, Charles A. The Human Landscape. 2nd ed. 448p. 1983. text ed. 25.95 (ISBN 0-675-20043-1). Additional supplements may be obtained from publisher. Merrill.

EMPLOYEE BENEFITS
see Non-Wage Payments

EMPLOYEE COMMUNICATION
see Communication in Personnel Management

EMPLOYEE COUNSELING

Apgar, Kathryn & Riley, Donald P. Life Education in the Workplace: How to Design, Lead & Market Employee Seminars. 184p. 1982. 17.95 (ISBN 0-87304-197-6). Family Serv.

EMPLOYEE-EMPLOYER RELATIONS
see Industrial Relations

EMPLOYEE OWNERSHIP

Conte, Michael, et al. Employee Ownership. 70p. 1981. pap. 8.00x (ISBN 0-87944-255-7). Inst Soc Res.

EMPLOYEE PENSION TRUSTS
see Pension Trusts

EMPLOYEE TURNOVER
see Labor Turnover

EMPLOYEES, CLERICAL
see Clerks

EMPLOYEES, DISMISSAL OF

Barbash, Joseph & Feerick, John D. Unjust Dismissal & At Will Employment. (Litigation & Administrative Practice Course Handbook Ser.). 343p. 1982. pap. 30.00 (H4-4885). PLI.

EMPLOYEES, RATING OF
see also Ability-Testing; Performance Standards; Teachers, Rating Of

Dailey, Charles A. & Madsen, Ann M. How to Evaluate People in Business: The Track-Record Method of Making Correct Judgments. LC 82-16233. 240p. 1983. pap. 9.95 (ISBN 0-07-015087-7, P&RB). McGraw.

Fournies, Ferdinand F. Performance Appraisal: Design Manual. (Illus.). 326p. 1983. 96.45 (ISBN 0-917472-09-8). F Fournies.

Ganong, Joan M. & Ganong, Warren L. Help with Performance Appraisal: A Results-Oriented Approach. (Help Series of Management Guides). 115p. 1981. pap. 11.50 (ISBN 0-933036-25-6). Ganong W L Co.

EMPLOYEES, RECRUITING OF
see Recruiting of Employees

EMPLOYEES, SUPERVISION OF
see Supervision of Employees

EMPLOYEES, TRAINING OF
Here are entered works on the training of employees on the job. Works on retraining persons with obsolete vocational skills are entered under Occupational Retraining. Works on vocational instruction within the standard educational system are entered under Vocational Education. Works on the vocationally oriented process of endowing people with a skill after either completion or termination of their formal education are entered under Occupational Training.
see also Apprentices; Executives, Training Of; Technical Education

Trainers' Manual: Staff Training-Consumer Co-Operatives. 98p. 1981. 17.00 (ISBN 92-2-102226-9). Intl Labour Office.

EMPLOYEES' MAGAZINES, HANDBOOKS, ETC.

Arnold, Edmund C. Editing the Organizational Publication. LC 82-60043. (Communications Library). 283p. (Orig.). 1982. pap. 25.00 (ISBN 0-931368-09-X); pap. text ed. 18.75 (ISBN 0-686-82102-5). Ragan Comm.

EMPLOYEES' REPRESENTATION IN MANAGEMENT
see also Employee Ownership

Basagni, Fabio & Sauzey, Francois. Employee Participation & Company Reform. (The Atlantic Papers: No. 75/4). (Orig.). 1976. pap. text ed. 4.75x (ISBN 0-686-83643-X). Allanheld.

Ireland & Law. The Economics of the Labor-Managed Enterprises. LC 82-42615. 240p. 1982. 25.00x (ISBN 0-312-23431-7). St Martin.

EMPLOYER-EMPLOYEE RELATIONS
see Industrial Relations

EMPLOYERS' LIABILITY
see also Industrial Accidents; Occupational Diseases; Personal Injuries; Workmen's Compensation

Deterrence & Compensation: Legal Liability in Occupational Safety & Health. 76p. 1982. pap. 10.00 (ISBN 92-2-103010-5, ILO 194, ILO). Unipub.

Griffes, Ernest J., ed. Employee Benefits Programs: Management, Planning & Control. 250p. 1983. 30.00 (ISBN 0-686-83835-1). Dow Jones-Irwin.

EMPLOYMENT (ECONOMIC THEORY)
see also Job Vacancies; Manpower Policy

Arnold, Ulli. Strategische Beschaffungspolitik. 311p. (Ger.). 1982. write for info. (ISBN 3-8204-5842-5). P Lang Pubs.

Bibliography of Published Research of the World Employment Programme. 4th ed. vii, 106p. 1982. 8.55 (ISBN 92-2-103074-1). Intl Labour Office.

Milgate, Murray, ed. Capital & Employment. (Studies Political Economy Ser.). Date not set. price not set (ISBN 0-12-496250-5). Acad Pr.

Pierson, John H. Full Employment. 1941. text ed. 39.50x (ISBN 0-686-83556-5). Elliots Bks.

EMPLOYMENT, PART-TIME
see Part-Time Employment

EMPLOYMENT, SUPPLEMENTARY
see Supplementary Employment

EMPLOYMENT, TEMPORARY
see Temporary Employment

EMPLOYMENT AGENCIES
see also Job Vacancies; Labor Supply

Price, Jonathan. How to Find Work. 267p. 1983. pap. 3.50 (ISBN 0-451-12070-1, Sig). NAL.

EMPLOYMENT AND AGE
see Age and Employment

EMPLOYMENT DISCRIMINATION
see Discrimination in Employment

EMPLOYMENT EXCHANGES
see Employment Agencies

EMPLOYMENT IN FOREIGN COUNTRIES
see Americans in Foreign Countries–Employment

EMPLOYMENT INTERVIEWING

Munro, John. Employment Interviewing. 224p. 1978. 30.00x (ISBN 0-7121-0570-0, Pub. by Macdonald & Evans). State Mutual Bk.

Price, Jonathan. How to Find Work. 267p. 1983. pap. 3.50 (ISBN 0-451-12070-1, Sig). NAL.

EMPLOYMENT MANAGEMENT
see Personnel Management

EMPLOYMENT OF WOMEN
see Women–Employment

EMPLOYMENT OF YOUTH
see Youth–Employment

EMPLOYMENT OFFICES
see Employment Agencies

ENAMEL AND ENAMELING

Campbell, Marian. An Introduction to Medieval Enamels. (The Victoria & Albert Museum Introductions to the Decorative Arts). (Illus.). 48p. 9.95 (ISBN 0-88045-021-5). Stemmer Hse.

ENAMEL PAINTS
see Paint; Painting, Industrial

ENAMELED WARE
see also Transfer Printing

Hackenbroch, Yvonne & Hawes, Vivian. The Markus Collection of European Ceramics & Enamels. (Illus.). 220p. 1983. write for info. Mus Fine Arts Boston.

ENCEPHALOGRAPHY
see Brain–Radiography

ENCOUNTER GROUPS
see Group Relations Training

ENCULTURATION
see Socialization

ENCYCLOPEDIAS AND DICTIONARIES
Encyclopedias and dictionaries of a particular subject are entered under the subject with subdivisions Dictionaries, Dictionaries, Juvenile or, in the case of countries, cities, etc. or ethnic groups, dictionaries and encyclopedias e.g. Botany–Dictionaries; Catholic Church–Dictionaries Juvenile.
see also Children's Encyclopedias and Dictionaries; Handbooks, Vade-Mecums, etc.; Picture Dictionaries; Questions and Answers
also particular subjects with or without the subdivision Dictionaries

The American Heritage Dictionary. rev. ed. 1983. pap. price not set (ISBN 0-440-10068-2). Dell.

Begeron, Leandre. The Quebecois Dictionary. 206p. 1983. 28.00 (ISBN 0-89490-092-7); pap. 17.95 (ISBN 0-89490-093-5). Enslow Pubs.

Full Color Fact Books. Incl. How the Body Works; All about Space; All About Our Earth; All About Knights; Discovering the World; Discovering Ancient Mysteries. (Illus.). (YA) (gr. 4-12). 1982. PLB 7.95 ea. EMC.

McMasters, Dale. Basic Skills Dictionary Workbook. (Basic Skills Workbooks). 32p. (gr. 4-7). 1983. 0.99 (ISBN 0-8209-0536-4, DW-1). ESP.

--The Dictionary. (Language Arts Ser.). 24p. (gr. 6 up). 1980. wkbk. 5.00 (ISBN 0-8209-0308-6, D-1). ESP.

Patty, Catherine. Basic Skills Encyclopedia Workbook. (Basic Skills Workbooks). 32p. (gr. 5-9). 1983. 0.99 (ISBN 0-8209-0537-2, UEW-1). ESP.

--Using the Encyclopedia. (Language Arts Ser.). 24p. (gr. 5-9). 1979. wkbk. 5.00 (ISBN 0-8209-0313-2, UE-1). ESP.

Pugmire, Roger L. How to Use Your Dictionary. 88p. 1980. 15.00x (ISBN 0-7121-2163-3, Pub. by Macdonald & Evans). State Mutual Bk.

Room, Adrian. Room's Dictionary of Distinguishables & Confusibles, 2 vols. 1981. 19.95 (ISBN 0-7100-9472-8). Routledge & Kegan.

RSBR Committee. Purchasing an Encyclopedia. 24p. 1982. pap. text ed. 3.00 (ISBN 0-8389-3236-3). ALA.

Shaw, Marie-Jose. The Dictionary. (Sound Filmstrip Kits Ser.). (gr. 3-6). 1981. tchrs ed. 24.00 (ISBN 0-8209-0441-4, FCW-18). ESP.

--The Encyclopedia. (Sound Filmstrip Kits Ser.). (gr. 3-6). 1981. tchrs ed. 24.00 (ISBN 0-8209-0442-2, FCW-19). ESP.

The World Book Encyclopedia, 22 Vols. LC 82-60049. (Illus.). 14200p. (gr. 4-12). 1983. PLB write for info. (ISBN 0-7166-0083-8). World Bk.

END OF THE WORLD
see also Antichrist; Judgment Day

Campbell, Roger F. A Place to Hide. 108p. 1983. pap. 3.95 (ISBN 0-88207-383-4). Victor Bks.

Davies, Kirk. Earth's Final Hours. 330p. (Orig.). 1982. pap. 9.95 (ISBN 0-9609174-0-3). Pacific Inst.

Lerner, Robert E. The Powers of Prophecy: The Cedar of Lebanon Vision from the Mongol Onslaught to the Dawn of the Enlightenment. LC 82-4824. 256p. 1983. text ed. 32.50x (ISBN 0-520-04461-4). U of Cal Pr.

ENDANGERED SPECIES
see Rare Animals

ENDEAVOR
see Struggle

ENDLESS PUNISHMENT
see Hell

ENDOCRINE GLANDS
see also Hormones; Hypothalamus; Pancreas; Pituitary Body; Thyroid Gland

Davies, Terry F. Autoimmune Endocrine Disease. 500p. 1983. write for info. (ISBN 0-471-09778-0, Pub. by Wiley-Interscience). Wiley.

Korenman. Endocrine Aspects of Aging. (Current Endocrinology Ser.: Vol. 6). 1982. 39.95 (ISBN 0-444-00681-8). Elsevier.

Williams. Current Endocrine Concepts. 252p. 1982. 37.50 (ISBN 0-03-062119-4). Praeger.

ENDOCRINE GYNECOLOGY

Speroff, Leon, et al. Clinical Gynecological Endocrinology & Infertilty. 450p. 1983. lib. bdg. price not set (ISBN 0-683-07895-X). Williams & Wilkins.

ENDOCRINOLOGY
see also Clinical Endocrinology; Endocrine Glands; Endocrine Gynecology; Gonadotropin; Hormones; Neuroendocrinology; Pancreas; Pediatric Endocrinology; Pituitary Body; Rejuvenation; Testicle; Thyroid Gland

Cohen, Margo P. & Foa, Piero P., eds. Special Topics in Endocrinology & Metabolism, Vol. 4. (Special Topics in Endocrinology & Metabolism). 251p. 1982. 38.00 (ISBN 0-8451-0703-8). A R Liss.

Heath & Marx. Calcium Disorders vs Clinical Endocrine Health. 1982. text ed. 59.95 (ISBN 0-407-02273-2). Butterworth.

Highnam, K. & Hill, L. Comparative Endocrinology of the Invertebrates. 2nd ed. 1977. 36.00 (ISBN 0-444-19497-5). Elsevier.

Johnson, Thompson. Endocrine Surgery: BIMR 2. 1983. text ed. 39.95 (ISBN 0-407-02317-8). Butterworth.

Jubiz, W. Endocrinology: A Logical Approach for Clinicians. 1980. 18.95 (ISBN 0-07-033066-2). McGraw.

Krieger, Dorothy T. & Bardin, C. Wayne, eds. Current Therapy in Endocrinology. 420p. 1983. 44.00 (ISBN 0-941158-04-7, D2755-9). Mosby.

Martini, L. & James, V. H., eds. Current Topics in Experimental Endocrinology, Vol. 4. (Serial Publication). Date not set. price not set (ISBN 0-12-153204-6). Acad Pr.

Martini, Luciano & James, V. H., eds. Current Topics in Experimental Endocrinology: Vol. 5: Fetal Endocrinology & Metabolism. (Serial Publication). Date not set. price not set (ISBN 0-12-153205-4). Acad Pr.

Medvei, V. C. A History of Endocrinology. (Illus.). 900p. 1982. text ed. 95.00 (ISBN 0-85200-245-9, Pub. by MTP Pr England). Kluwer Boston.

Mikami, S., et al, eds. Avian Endocrinology: Environmental & Ecological Perspectives. 380p. 1983. 53.00 (ISBN 0-387-11871-3). Springer-Verlag.

Pinchera, A. & Vanhaelst, L., eds. Autoimmunity & Endocrine Diseases. (Jounal: Hormone Research: Vol. 16, No. 5). (Illus.). 84p. 1982. pap. 24.75 (ISBN 3-8055-3658-5). S Karger.

Scanes, C. G. & Ottinger, M. A. Aspect of Avian Endocrinology: Practical & Theoretical Implications. (Graduate Studies: No. 26). 411p. 1982. 59.95 (ISBN 0-89672-103-5); pap. 29.95 (ISBN 0-89672-102-7). Tex Tech Pr.

Schwartz, Theodore B. Year Book of Endocrinology 1983. 1983. 40.00 (ISBN 0-8151-7725-9). Year Bk Med.

ENDODONTICS

Harty, F. J. Endodontics in Clinical Practice. 2nd ed. (Illus.). 296p. 1982. pap. text ed. 19.95 (ISBN 0-7236-0643-9). Wright-PSG.

Schroeder, Andre. Endodontics-Science & Practice: A Textbook for Student & Practitioners. (Illus.). 286p. 1981. vinyl bound 64.00 (ISBN 0-931386-36-5). Quint Pub Co.

ENDOGENOUS RHYTHMS
see Biological Rhythms

ENDOMETRIUM

Semm, Kurt & Greenblatt, Robert B. Genital Endometriosis in Infertility. 110p. 15.95 (ISBN 0-86577-059-X). Thieme-Stratton.

ENDOSCOPE AND ENDOSCOPY

Draf, W. Endoscopy of the Paranasal Sinuses: Technique-Typical Findings-Theraputic Possibilities. Pohl, W. E., tr. from Ger. (Illus.). 112p. 1983. 27.50 (ISBN 0-387-11258-8). Springer-Verlag.

ENDOTHELIUM

Nossel, Hymie & Vogel, Henry J., eds. Pathobiology of the Endothelial Cell. (P & S Biomedical Sciences Symposia Ser.). 1982. 63.00 (ISBN 0-12-521980-6). Acad Pr.

ENDOTOXIN

Watson, Stanley W. & Levin, Jack, eds. Endotoxins & Their Detection with the Limulus Amebocyte Lysate Test. LC 82-8967. (Progress in Clinical & Biological Research Ser.: Vol. 93). 438p. 1982. 44.00 (ISBN 0-8451-0093-9). A R Liss.

ENDOWED CHARITIES
see Charitable Uses, Trusts and Foundations; Charities; Endowments

ENDOWMENTS
Here are entered general works on endowed institutions, endowment funds and donations to such funds. Works on the legal structure of endowments are entered under the heading Charitable Uses, trusts and Foundations.
see also Charitable Uses, Trusts and Foundations; Charities

Arnove, Robert F., ed. Philanthropy & Cultural Imperialism: The Foundations at Home & Abroad. LC 82-48055. (Midland Bks.: No. 303). 488p. 1982. pap. 10.95x (ISBN 0-253-20303-1). Ind U Pr.

Fink, Norman S. & Metzler, Howard C. The Costs & Benefits of Deferred Giving. 24.50 (ISBN 0-686-38899-2). Public Serv Materials.

Foundation Center. Corporate Foundation Profiles. 512p. (Orig.). 1983. pap. text ed. 50.00 (ISBN 0-87954-075-3). Foundation Ctr.

Lagemann, Ellen C. Private Power for the Public Good: A History of the Carnegie Foundation for the Advancement of Teaching. 272p. 1982. 17.95 (ISBN 0-8195-5085-X). Wesleyan U Pr.

Staff of Public Management Institute. How to Build a Big Endowment. 590p. 75.00 (ISBN 0-686-38885-2). Public Serv Materials.

Williamson, J. Peter. Foundation Investment Strategies: New Possibilities in the 1981 Tax Law. (Seven Springs Studies). 1981. pap. 3.00 (ISBN 0-943006-05-8). Seven Springs.

ENDURANCE, PHYSICAL
see Physical Fitness

ENEMY ALIENS
see Aliens

ENERGY
see Force and Energy; Power Resources

ENERGY, BIOMASS
see Biomass Energy

ENERGY AND STATE
see Energy Policy

ENERGY CONSERVATION
Here are entered general works on the conservation of all forms of energy. Works on the conservation of a specific form of energy are entered under that form, e.g. Petroleum Conservation. Works on the conservation of energy as a physical concept are entered under Force and Energy.
see also Architecture and Energy Conservation; Energy Policy; Recycling (Waste, etc.)

Barnett, A. & Bell, R. M. Rural Energy & the Third World: A Review of Social Science Research & Technology Policy Problems. (Illus.). 302p. 1982. 36.00 (ISBN 0-08-028953-3); 18.00 (ISBN 0-08-028954-1). Pergamon.

Cousins, K. Residential Conservation Service Inspector-Installer Examination Guide. (Progress in Solar Energy Supplements SERI Ser.). 60p. 1983. pap. text ed. 9.00x (ISBN 0-89553-087-2). Am Solar Energy.

Cowan, H. J. Predictive Methods for the Energy Conserving Design of Buildings. (Illus.). 128p. 1983. pap. 33.50 (ISBN 0-08-029838-9). Pergamon.

Coxon, DeWayne. Energy Bootstrapping in Israel. 90p. 1983. 11.95 (ISBN 0-910213-03-8); pap. 6.95 (ISBN 0-910213-02-X). Jordan Pub.

Energy Bibliography & Index, Vol. 2. 1280p. 1979. 295.00 (ISBN 0-87201-970-5). Gulf Pub.

Energy Management & Conservation: Special Session on Energy Management at the 66th ASBO Annual Meeting & Exhibits. 1981. 7.50. Assn Sch Busn.

Farhar-Pilgrim, Barbara & Unseld, Charles T. America's Solar Potential: A National Consumer Study. Shama, Avraham, ed. (Studies in Energy Conservation & Solar Energy). 464p. 1982. 35.00 (ISBN 0-03-061696-4). Praeger.

Field-Proven Programs to Conserve Energy in Schools: ASBO's 65th Annual Meeting Mini-workshops on Energy & Energy Management. 1980. 5.95. Assn Sch Busn.

Fields, P. Computer Assisted Home Energy Management. Date not set. pap. 15.95 (ISBN 0-686-82319-2). Sams.

Greenberger, Martin. Caught Unawares: The Energy Decade in Retrospect. 400p. 1983. prof ref. 24.50 (ISBN 0-88410-916-X). Ballinger Pub.

Inhaber, Herbert. Energy Risk Assessment. 408p. 1982. 67.50 (ISBN 0-677-05980-9). Gordon.

International Seminar on Energy Conservation & Use of Renewable Energies in the Bio-Industries, Trinity College, Oxford, UK, 2nd 6-10 Sept. 1982. Energy Conservation & Use of Renewable Energies in the Bio-Industries: Proceedings. Vogt, F., ed. (Illus.). 750p. 1982. 100.00 (ISBN 0-08-029781-1). Pergamon.

Mitchell, J. W. Energy Engineering. 420p. 1983. write for info. (ISBN 0-471-08772-6, Pub. by Wiley-Interscience). Wiley.

Robbins, Claude L. & Hunter, Kerri C. A Method for Predicting Energy Savings Attributed to Daylighting. (Progress in Solar Energy Ser.: Suppl.). 225p. 1983. pap. text ed. 18.00 (ISBN 0-89553-139-9). Am Solar Energy.

Scheller, William G. Energy Saving Home Improvements. 1979. pap. 8.95 (ISBN 0-672-21605-1). Sams.

Shaw, Marie-Jose. Energy & Man. (Sound Filmstrip Kits Ser.). (gr. 3-6). 1981. 24.00 (ISBN 0-8209-0435-X, FCW-12). ESP.

United Nations Educational Scientific & Cultural Organization. International Directory of New & Renewable Energy Information Sources & 467p. 1983. pap. text ed. 35.00 (ISBN 0-89553-142-9). Am Solar Energy.

Wadden, Richard A. Energy Utilization & Environmental Health: Methods for Prediction & Evaluation of Impact on Human Health. LC 78-9688. 216p. Repr. of 1978 ed. text ed. 29.50 (ISBN 0-686-84496-3). Krieger.

ENERGY CONVERSION, DIRECT
see Direct Energy Conversion

ENERGY CONVERSION, MICROBIAL
see Biomass Energy

ENERGY POLICY
see also Energy Conservation

Barbour. Energy & American Values. 256p. 1982. 27.95 (ISBN 0-03-062468-1); pap. 12.95 (ISBN 0-03-062469-X). Praeger.

Chubb, John E. Interest Groups & the Bureaucracy: The Politics of Energy. LC 82-60106. (Illus.). 336p. 1983. 29.50x (ISBN 0-8047-1158-5). Stanford U Pr.

Deudney, Daniel & Flavin, Christopher. Renewable Energy: The Power to Choose. 1983. 18.95 (ISBN 0-393-01710-9). Norton.

Energy Policy in Perspective: Solutions, Problems, & Prospects. LC 81-85675. (Symposia Ser.). 74p. 1982. 5.95 (ISBN 0-686-37946-2). LBJ Sch Pub Aff.

Energy User Series, 3 Vols. 1979. pap. 60.00 (ISBN 0-86587-028-4). Gov Insts.

Foell, Wesley K. Management of Energy-Environment Systems: Methods & Case Studies. LC 78-13617. (International Institute Series on Applied Systems Analysis). 487p. 1979. 49.95x (ISBN 0-471-99721-8, Pub. by Wiley-Interscience). Wiley.

Ghosh, Arabinda. OPEC, The Petroleum Industry, & United States Energy Policy. LC 82-13245. (Illus.). 296p. 1983. lib. bdg. 35.00 (ISBN 0-89930-010-3, HD9566, Quorum). Greenwood.

Horwich, George & Mitchell, Edward J., eds. Policies for Coping with Oil Supply Disruptions. 1982. 16.95 (ISBN 0-8447-2241-3); pap. 8.95 (ISBN 0-8447-2240-5). Am Enterprise.

Lovins, Amory & Lovins, Hunter. Brittle Power: Energy Strategy for National Security. 512p. 1983. pap. 8.95 (ISBN 0-931790-49-2). Brick Hse Pub.

MacAvoy, Paul W. Energy Policy: An Economic Analysis. pap. text ed. 4.95x (ISBN 0-393-95321-1). Norton.

MacLean, Douglas & Brown, Peter G., eds. Energy & the Future. LC 82-18609. 224p. 1983. text ed. 35.95x (ISBN 0-8476-7149-6); pap. text ed. 18.50x (ISBN 0-8476-7225-5). Rowman.

Nax, Beunab & Burt, Barbara J., eds. The Social Constraints on Energy-Policy Implementation. LC 81-48613. 1983. write for info. (ISBN 0-669-05466-6). Lexington Bks.

Purcell, Edward L. The States & Energy Siting, Vol. I. 70p. 1982. pap. 8.00 (ISBN 0-87292-026-7). Coun State Govts.

Purcell, L. E., ed. The States & Energy Siting, Vol. II. 150p. 1982. pap. 8.00 (ISBN 0-87292-027-5). Coun State Govts.

Thrall, Robert M. & Thompson, Russell G., eds. Large-Scale Energy Models: Prospects & Potential. (AAAS Selected Synposium 73). 350p. 1982. lib. bdg. 25.00x (ISBN 0-86531-408-X). Westview.

Toward a Renewable Energy Future: The Urban Potential, Austin, Texas. LC 81-82253. (Policy Research Project Report Ser.: No. 44). 139p. 1982. 8.50 (ISBN 0-89940-646-7). LBJ Sch Pub Aff.

Zillman, Donald N. & Lattman, Laurence H. Energy Law. LC 82-20933. (University Casebook Ser.). 852p. 1982. text ed. write for info. (ISBN 0-88277-076-4). Foundation Pr.

ENERGY RECOVERY FROM WASTE
see Refuse As Fuel

ENERGY RESOURCES
see Power Resources

ENFORCEMENT OF LAW
see Law Enforcement

ENGINEERING
see also Agricultural Engineering; Architecture; Bioengineering; Biomedical Engineering; Boring; Bridges; Canals; Chemical Engineering; Civil Engineering; Dams; Drainage; Electric Engineering; Engineers; Engines; Environmental Engineering; Girders; Harbors; Hydraulic Engineering; Irrigation; Low Temperature Engineering; Machinery; Marine Engineering; Masonry; Mechanical Drawing; Mechanical Engineering; Mechanics; Mensuration; Mining Engineering; Nuclear Engineering; Plant Engineering; Railroad Engineering; Reclamation of Land; Reliability (Engineering); Reservoirs; Rivers; Roads; Sanitary Engineering; Statics; Strength of Materials; Structural Engineering; Surveying; Systems Engineering; Tolerance (Engineering); Tunnels and Tunneling; Ventilation; Walls; Water-Supply Engineering

Austin, Ellis H. Drilling Engineering Handbook. (Short Course Handbooks). (Illus.). 288p. 1983. text ed. 29.00 (ISBN 0-934634-46-7); pap. text ed. 22.00 (ISBN 0-934634-54-8). Intl Human Res.

Bailey, Robert L. Disciplined Creativity for Engineers. LC 78-50310. (Illus.). 614p. 1982. pap. 19.95 (ISBN 0-250-40615-2). Ann Arbor Science.

Bird, May. Engineering Science Three Checkbook. 1983. text ed. price not set (ISBN 0-408-00624-2). Butterworth.

--Engineering Science Two Checkbook. 1982. text ed. 24.95 (ISBN 0-408-00691-9); pap. text ed. 12.50 (ISBN 0-408-00627-7). Butterworth.

Bragg, S. L., frwd. by. Engineering Challenges in the 1980's, Vol. 2. (Proceedings of the Engineering Section of the British Association for the Advancement of Science Ser.). 103p. 1982. text ed. 60.00 (ISBN 0-89116-349-2, Pub. by Cambridge Info & Res Serv England). Hemisphere Pub.

Coastal & Ocean Engineering, 1978: Managing the Coast. (Australian Conference: No. 4). 246p. (Orig.). 1978. pap. text ed. 31.50x (ISBN 0-85825-100-0, Pub. by Inst Engineering Australia). Renouf.

Control Engineering, 1982 Conference: Merging of Technology & Theory to Solve Industrial Automation Problems. 247p. (Orig.). 1982. pap. text ed. 42.00x (ISBN 0-85825-168-X, Pub. by Inst Engineering Australia). Renouf.

Digital Systems Design: 1980 Conference. 91p. (Orig.). 1980. pap. text ed. 24.00 (ISBN 0-85825-127-2, Pub. by Inst Engineering Australia). Renouf.

Directory of Engineering Societies & Related Organizations. 10th ed. 32.00 (ISBN 0-87615-002-4, 101-82). AAES.

Dyball, G. E. Mathematics for Technician Engineers: Levels 4 & 5. 384p. 1983. write for info. (ISBN 0-07-084664-2). McGraw.

Engineering & Technology Enrollments: Fall 1982, 2 pts. 1983. Set. 100.00 (ISBN 0-87615-074-1, 207-83); Pt. I. 60.00 (ISBN 0-87615-084-9, 207A-83); Pt. II. 60.00 (ISBN 0-87615-094-6, 207B-83). AAES.

Engineering Conference, 1981, 2 vols. (Canberra Conferences Ser.). 486p. (Orig.). 1981. pap. text ed. 45.00x (ISBN 0-85825-143-4, Pub. by Inst Engineering Australia). Renouf.

The Engineering Conference, 1982. 261p. (Orig.). 1982. pap. text ed. 37.50x (Pub. by Inst Engineering Australia). Renouf.

Engineering Equipment Users Association Staff. Systematic Fault Diagnosis. (Illus.). 168p. 1982. text ed. 38.00x (ISBN 0-7114-5739-5). Longman.

Hibbeler, R. C. Engineering Mechanics: Statics. 3rd ed. 448p. 1983. text ed. 25.95 (ISBN 0-02-354300-0). Macmillan.

Hobart: Changing Society: A Challenge for Engineering. 261p. (Orig.). 1982. pap. text ed. 37.50x (Pub. by Inst Engineering Australia). Renouf.

Krishna, Jai & Chandrasekaran, A. R. Elements of Earthquake Engineering. 260p. Date not set. 12.95 (ISBN 0-9605004-2-1, Pub. by Sarita Prakashan India). Eng Pubns.

Lewart, Cass. Science & Engineering Sourcebook. 96p. 1982. 17.95 (ISBN 0-13-795229-5); pap. 9.95 (ISBN 0-13-795211-2). P-H.

Maunder, L., frwd. by. Engineering Challenges in the 1980's, Vol. 1. (Proceedings of the Engineering Section of the British Association for the Advancement of Science Ser.). (Illus.). 192p. 1982. text ed. 69.95 (ISBN 0-89116-348-4, Pub. by Cambridge Info & Res Serv England). Hemisphere Pub.

OECD Staff. The Engineering Industries in OECD Member Countries, 1976-1979. 93p. 1982. pap. 10.00 (ISBN 92-64-02283-X). OECD.

Proceedings: Conference on Engineering Personnel, Houston 1980. 60.00 (ISBN 0-87615-023-7, 136-80). AAES.

Ravindran, A. & Ragsdell, K. M. Engineering Optimization: Methods & Application. 550p. 1983. 44.95 (ISBN 0-471-05579-4, Pub. by Wiley Interscience). Wiley.

Rigby, G. R., intro. by. Expanding Horizons in Chemical Engineering. (Chemeca Ser.). 241p. (Orig.). 1979. pap. text ed. 54.00x (ISBN 0-85825-116-7, Pub. by Inst Engineering Australia). Renouf.

Ryland's Directory of the Engineering Industry, 1982-83. 48th ed. 900p. 1982. pap. 60.00x (ISBN 0-86108-104-8). Intl Pubns Serv.

Schaub, J. H. & Dickison, S. K. Engineering & the Humanities. 503p. 1982. text ed. 29.95x (ISBN 0-471-08909-5, Pub. by Wiley-Interscience). Wiley.

Seddiqui, Fred R. Engineering Functions: Concerns of the Industry. 1983. 20.00 (ISBN 0-533-05497-4). Vantage.

Shepherd, F. A. Advance Engineering Surveying. 288p. 1982. pap. text ed. 24.95 (ISBN 0-7131-3416-X). E Arnold.

Silvester, Richard, intro. by. Coastal & Ocean Engineering: Offshore Structures. (Australian Conference: No. 5). 471p. (Orig.). 1981. pap. text ed. 37.50x (ISBN 0-85825-159-0, Pub. by Inst Engineering Australia). Renouf.

Who's Who in Engineering. 5th ed. 85.00 (ISBN 0-87615-013-X, 107-82). AAES.

ENGINEERING-AUTHORSHIP
see Technical Writing

ENGINEERING–CONTRACTS AND SPECIFICATIONS

Ohno, Y., ed. Requirements Engineering Environments: Proceedings of the International Symposium on Current Issues of Requirements Engineering Environments, Sept. 20-21, 1982, Kyoto, Japan. 174p. 1983. 42.75 (ISBN 0-444-86533-0, North Holland). Elsevier.

Patil, B. S. Civil Engineering Contracts & Estimates. (Illus.). 586p. 1981. pap. text ed. 20.00 (ISBN 0-86125-036-2, Pub. by Orient Longman Ltd India). Apt Bks.

ENGINEERING–DATA PROCESSING

Computer Engineering Div., ASME. Computer in Engineering Nineteen Eighty-Two: Vol. 3-Mesh Generation; Finite Elements; Computers in Structural Optimization; Computers in the Engineering Workplace; Computers in Energy Systems; Personal Computing, 4 Vol. Set. 1982. 60.00 ea. (G00217); 200.00 set (G00219). ASME.

--Computers In Engineering, 1982: Vol. 1-Computer-Aided Design, Manugacturing, & Simulation, 4 Vol. Set. 1982. 60.00 (G00215); 200.00 set (G00215). ASME.

--Computers In Engineering 1982: Vol. 1-Robots & Robotics, 4 Vols. 1982. 60.00 (G00216); 200.00 set (G00219). ASME.

Computer in Engineering: Vol. 4-Process Control, State-of-the-Art Printing, Technology, Software Engineering & Management, Stastistical Modelling & Reliability Techniques. (Computers in Education Ser.). 1982. 60.00 (G00218). ASME.

ENGINEERING–DESIGN

see Engineering Design

ENGINEERING–DICTIONARIES

Barry, W. R., ed. Architectural, Construction, Manufacturing & Engineering Glossary of Terms. 519p. 1979. pap. 40.00 (ISBN 0-930284-05-4). Am Assn Cost Engineers.

Ernst, Richard. Comprehensive Dictionary of Engineering & Technology: French-English. 1982. 69.00 (ISBN 0-19-520414-X). Oxford U Pr.

Parker, Sybil P., ed. McGraw-Hill Encyclopedia of Engineering. (Illus.). 1272p. Date not set. 57.50 (ISBN 0-07-045486-8, P&RB). McGraw.

ENGINEERING–ESTIMATES AND COSTS

see also Engineering Economy

American Telephone & Telegraph Co. Engineering Economy: A Manager's Guide to Economic Decision Making. 3rd ed. 1977. 43.50 (ISBN 0-07-001530-9). McGraw.

Barry, W. R., ed. Architectural, Construction, Manufacturing & Engineering Glossary of Terms. 519p. 1979. pap. 40.00 (ISBN 0-930284-05-4). Am Assn Cost Engineers.

Humphreys, K. K. & McMillan, B. G., eds. AACE Publications Index, 1979-1981, Vol. 2. 54p. 1982. pap. 25.00 (ISBN 0-930284-16-X). Am Assn Cost Engineers.

--Transactions of the American Association of Cost Engineers. (Illus.). 334p. 1982. 48.50 (ISBN 0-930284-15-1); pap. 38.50 (ISBN 0-930284-14-3). Am Assn Cost Engineers.

Patil, B. S. Civil Engineering Contracts & Estimates. (Illus.). 586p. 1981. pap. text ed. 20.00 (ISBN 0-86125-036-2, Pub. by Orient Longman Ltd India). Apt Bks.

Sides, C. M., ed. Transactions of the American Association of Cost Engineers, 1979. (Illus.). 28p. 1979. pap. 30.00 (ISBN 0-930284-03-8). Am Assn Cost Engineers.

ENGINEERING–EXAMINATIONS, QUESTIONS, ETC.

LaLonde, W. S. Professional Engineers Examination Questions & Answers. 4th ed. 544p. 1983. 35.00 (ISBN 0-07-036099-5, P&RB). McGraw.

Levinson, Irving J. Preparing for the Engineer-In-Training Examination. LC 82-18251. 242p. 1983. pap. 12.95 (ISBN 0-910554-40-4). Eng Pr.

ENGINEERING–GRAPHIC METHODS

see Engineering Graphics

ENGINEERING–HANDBOOKS, MANUALS, ETC.

Gieck, Kurt. Engineering Formulas. 4th ed. 260p. 1983. 16.95 (ISBN 0-07-023219-9, P&RB). McGraw.

Midwest Plan Service Engineers Staff. Structures & Environment Handbook. 11th ed. (Illus.). 700p. 1983. pap. text ed. price not set (ISBN 0-89373-057-2). Midwest Plan Serv.

Transamerica Delaval Inc. Transamerica Delaval Engineering Handbook. 4th ed. Welch, Harry & Crawford, Harold B., eds. (Illus.). 640p. 1983. 39.50 (ISBN 0-07-016250-6, P&RB). McGraw.

ENGINEERING–HISTORY

Corbett, Arthur. History of the Institution of Engineers: Australia 1919-1969. 288p. 1973. text ed. 19.50x (ISBN 0-207-12516-3, Pub. by Inst Engineering Australia). Renouf.

The Protection of the Engineering Heritage: Brisbane, Austalia, May 1982. 92p. (Orig.). 1982. pap. text ed. 27.00x (ISBN 0-85825-164-7, Pub. by Inst Engineering Australia). Renouf.

ENGINEERING–LAW AND LEGISLATION

see Engineering Law

ENGINEERING–MANAGEMENT

American Society of Civil Engineers, compiled by. ASCE Salary Survey 1981. LC 82-73522. 80p. 1982. pap. text ed. 12.00 (ISBN 0-87262-347-5). Am Soc Civil Eng.

Baird, Bruce F. The Engineering Manager: How to Manage People & Make Decisions. (Illus.). 224p. 1983. 22.50 (ISBN 0-534-97925-4). Lifetime Learn.

Engineering Management Conference, Melbourne, Australia, March 1979. Engineering Management Update. 78p. (Orig.). 1979. pap. text ed. 24.00x (ISBN 0-85825-105-1, Pub. by Inst Engineering Australia). Renouf.

Hajek, V. Management of Engineering Projects. 2nd ed. 1977. 27.50 (ISBN 0-07-025534-2). McGraw.

Kern, Dale R., ed. Engineering & Construction Projects: The Emerging Management Roles. LC 82-70492. 336p. 1982. pap. text ed. 28.50 (ISBN 0-87262-299-1). Am Soc Civil Eng.

King, J. R., ed. Managing Liability. LC 82-70764. 96p. 1982. pap. text ed. 16.00 (ISBN 0-87262-304-1). Am Soc Civil Eng.

ENGINEERING–MATERIALS

see Materials

ENGINEERING–PROBLEMS, EXERCISES, ETC.

Hartley, T. C. & O'Bryant, D. C. Problems in Engineering. (Graphics Ser.: No. 31). 1975. pap. 7.20 (ISBN 0-87563-109-6). Stipes.

ENGINEERING–STATISTICAL METHODS

Ang, A. H. & Tang, W. H. Probability Concepts in Engineering Planning & Design, Vol. 1. LC 75-5892. 409p. 1975. text ed. 30.50x (ISBN 0-471-03200-X). Wiley.

--Probability Concepts in Engineering Planning & Design, Vol. 2. 1982. 15.95 (ISBN 0-471-03201-8). Wiley.

ENGINEERING–STATISTICS

Wilson, C. Applied Statistics for Engineers. 1972. 24.75 (ISBN 0-85334-529-5, Pub. by Applied Sci England). Elsevier.

ENGINEERING–STUDY AND TEACHING

Engineering & Technology Enrollments, Fall 1980, 2 pts. 100.00 (ISBN 0-87615-072-5, 207-81). AAES.

Engineering & Technology Enrollments: Fall 1981, 2 pts. Set. 100.00 (ISBN 0-87615-072-5, 207-81); Pt. I. 60.00 (ISBN 0-87615-082-2, 207A-81); Pt. II. 60.00 (ISBN 0-87615-092-X, 207B-81). AAES.

Engineering Education: 1978 Conference. 192p. (Orig.). 1978. pap. text ed. 30.00x (ISBN 0-85825-094-2, Pub. by Inst Engineering Australia). Renouf.

Engineering Education: 1980 Conference. 205p. (Orig.). 1980. pap. text ed. 45.00x (ISBN 0-85825-134-5, Pub. by Inst Engineering Australia). Renouf.

Engineering Education, 1982 Conference-Whither Engineering Education. 157p. (Orig.). 1982. pap. text ed. 37.50x (ISBN 0-85825-171-X, Pub. by Inst Engineering Australia). Renouf.

Future Needs in Civil Engineering Education. 166p. 1982. 90.00x (ISBN 0-7277-0153-3, Pub. by Telford England). State Mutual Bk.

Houghton, E. I. & Carruthers, N. B. Aerodynamics for Engineering Students. 704p. 1982. pap. text ed. 39.50 (ISBN 0-7131-3433-X). E Arnold.

Ready, Barbara C., ed. Peterson's Annual Guides to Graduate Study: Engineering & Applied Sciences, 1983. 800p. 1982. pap. 17.95 (ISBN 0-87866-189-1). Petersons Guides.

ENGINEERING–TABLES, CALCULATIONS, ETC.

Greck, K. Engineering Formulas. 3rd ed. 1979. 15.95 (ISBN 0-07-023216-4). McGraw.

Greer, A. Tables, Data & Formulae for Engineers. 96p. 1977. 25.00x (ISBN 0-85950-023-3, Pub. by Thornes England). State Mutual Bk.

ENGINEERING–VOCATIONAL GUIDANCE

Engineering & Technology Degrees, 1980, 3 pts. Set. 150.00 (ISBN 0-87615-031-8, 201-80); Pt. I. 35.00 (ISBN 0-87615-041-5, 201A-80); Pt. II. 100.00 (ISBN 0-87615-051-2, 201B-80); Pt. III. 35.00 (ISBN 0-87615-061-X, 201C-80). AAES.

Engineering & Technology Enrollments, Fall 1980, 2 pts. 100.00 (ISBN 0-87615-072-5, 207-81). AAES.

Engineering & Technology Enrollments: Fall 1981, 2 pts. Set. 100.00 (ISBN 0-87615-072-5, 207-81); Pt. I. 60.00 (ISBN 0-87615-082-2, 207A-81); Pt. II. 60.00 (ISBN 0-87615-092-X, 207B-81). AAES.

Engineering Manpower Commission. Demand for Engineers, 1981. (Illus.). 1982. 35.00x (ISBN 0-87615-112-8, 231-82). AAES.

Engineering Personnel: Proceedings of Conference on Engineering Personnel, Houston, 1980. 60.00 (ISBN 0-87615-023-7, 136-80). AAES.

Engineering Personnel: Proceedings of Industry Advisory Committee on Engineering Personnel, Atlanta, January, 1979. 50.00 (ISBN 0-87615-021-0, 111-79). AAES.

Engineers' Salaries: Special Industry Report 1980. 100.00 (ISBN 0-87615-121-7, 301-80). AAES.

Engineers' Salaries: Special Industry Report 1981. 100.00 (ISBN 0-87615-122-5, 301-81). AAES.

Peterson's Guide to Engineering, Science, & Computer Jobs 1983. 4th Ed. ed. 787p. pap. 12.95 (ISBN 0-87866-204-9, 2049). Peterson's Guides.

A Pilot Study of the Demand for Engineers 1980. 15.00 (ISBN 0-87615-111-X, 231-80). AAES.

Placement of Engineering & Technology Graduates 1981. 35.00 (ISBN 0-87615-102-0, 210-82). AAES.

Rudman, Jack. Administrative Engineer. (Career Examination Ser.: C-2601). (Cloth bdg. avail. on request). pap. 12.00 (ISBN 0-8373-2601-X). Natl Learning.

--Assistanf Tower Engineer. (Career Examination Ser.: C-211). (Cloth bdg. avail. on request). pap. 12.00 (ISBN 0-8373-0211-0). Natl Learning.

--Engineering Materials Technician. (Career Examination Ser.: C-315). (Cloth bdg. avail. on request). pap. 10.00 (ISBN 0-8373-0315-X). Natl Learning.

--Senior Engineering Materials Technician. (Career Examination Ser.: C-316). (Cloth bdg. avail. on request). pap. 12.00 (ISBN 0-8373-0316-8). Natl Learning.

Salaries of Engineers in Education 1981. 20.00 (ISBN 0-87615-152-7, 307-82). AAES.

Salaries of Engineers in Education 1982. 1982. 20.00 (ISBN 0-87615-153-5, 307-82A). AAES.

Shanahan, William F. Resumes for Engineers: A Resume Preparation & Job-Getting Guide. 128p. 1983. lib. bdg. 11.95 (ISBN 0-668-05664-9); pap. 6.95 (ISBN 0-668-05668-1). Arco.

Smith, Ralph J. & Butler, Blaine. Engineering as a Career. 4th rev. ed. (Illus.). 352p. 1983. pap. text ed. 15.95x (ISBN 0-07-058788-4, C); write for info. instr's manual (ISBN 0-07-058789-2). McGraw.

Survey of Employment Practices among Employers of Engineers 1981. 25.00 (ISBN 0-87615-172-1, 510-82). AAES.

ENGINEERING, AGRICULTURAL

see Agricultural Engineering

ENGINEERING, ARCHITECTURAL

see Building; Building, Iron and Steel; Strains and Stresses; Strength of Materials; Structures, Theory of

ENGINEERING, BIOMEDICAL

see Biomedical Engineering

ENGINEERING, CHEMICAL

see Chemical Engineering

ENGINEERING, CIVIL

see Civil Engineering

ENGINEERING, CLINICAL

see Biomedical Engineering

ENGINEERING, ELECTRICAL

see Electric Engineering

ENGINEERING, GENETIC

see Genetic Engineering

ENGINEERING, HYDRAULIC

see Hydraulic Engineering

ENGINEERING, INDUSTRIAL

see Industrial Engineering

ENGINEERING, MARINE

see Marine Engineering

ENGINEERING, MECHANICAL

see Mechanical Engineering; Mechanics, Applied

ENGINEERING, MEDICAL

see Biomedical Engineering

ENGINEERING, MINING

see Mining Engineering

ENGINEERING, MUNICIPAL

see Municipal Engineering

ENGINEERING, RAILROAD

see Railroad Engineering

ENGINEERING, SANITARY

see Sanitary Engineering

ENGINEERING, STRUCTURAL

see Structural Engineering

ENGINEERING, TRAFFIC

see Traffic Engineering

ENGINEERING, WATER-SUPPLY

see Water-Supply Engineering

ENGINEERING ANALYSIS

see Engineering Mathematics

ENGINEERING CYBERNETICS

see Automation

ENGINEERING DESIGN

see also Materials; Structural Design; Systems Engineering;
also subdivisions Design and Design and Construction under special subjects, e.g. Machinery–Design; Automobiles–Design and Construction

Cullum. Handbook of Engineering Design. text ed. write for info (ISBN 0-408-00558-0). Butterworth.

Earle, James H. Engineering Design Graphics. 4th ed. LC 82-6709. 704p. 1983. text ed. 27.95 (ISBN 0-201-11318-X). A-W.

Eastman Kodak Company. Designing for People at Work. (Engineering Ser.). (Illus.). 600p. 1983. 49.95 (ISBN 0-686-82248-X). Lifetime Learn.

Engineering Staff of Texas Instruments. The MOS Memory Data Book for Design Engineers, 1982. Rev. ed. 296p. pap. 8.35 (ISBN 0-89512-112-3, LCC7061). Tex Instr Inc.

Faupel, J. H. & Fisher, F. E. Engineering Design: A Synthesis of Stress Analysis & Materials Engineering. 2nd ed. LC 80-16727. 1056p. 1981. 45.50x (ISBN 0-471-03381-2, Pub. by Wiley-Interscience). Wiley.

Seelye, E. E. Data Book for Civil Engineers: Design, Vol. 1. 3rd ed. 670p. 1960. text ed. 85.50x (ISBN 0-471-77286-0, Pub. by Wiley-Interscience). Wiley.

ENGINEERING DESIGN–DATA PROCESSING

see also Computer Graphics

Besant, C. B. Computer-Aided Design & Manufacture. 2nd ed. LC 79-40971. (Engineering Science Ser.). 228p. 1983. 54.95 (ISBN 0-470-27372-0); pap. 24.95 (ISBN 0-470-27373-9). Halsted Pr.

ENGINEERING DRAWING

see Mechanical Drawing

ENGINEERING DRAWINGS

Besterfield & O'Hagan. Technical Sketching for Engineers, Technologists & Technicians. 1983. text ed. 19.95 (ISBN 0-8359-7540-1). Reston.

Huth, Mark. Understanding Construction Drawings. (Illus.). 304p. 1983. pap. text ed. 14.60 (ISBN 0-8273-1584-8); instr's guide 2.96 (ISBN 0-8273-1585-6). Delmar.

Thomas, M. A Guide to the Preparation of Civil Engineering Drawings. 1982. 65.00x (ISBN 0-333-28081-4, Pub. by Macmillan England). State Mutual Bk.

Wirshing, J. R. & Wirshing, R. H. Civil Engineering Drafting. 352p. 1983. pap. 14.95x (ISBN 0-07-071127-5, G). McGraw.

Yearling, Robert A. Machine Trades Blueprint Reading. (Illus.). 320p. 1983. text ed. 18.95 (ISBN 0-13-542001-6). P-H.

ENGINEERING ECONOMY

see also Replacement of Industrial Equipment

Engineers' Salaries: Special Industry Report 1980. 100.00 (ISBN 0-87615-121-7, 301-80). AAES.

Engineers' Salaries: Special Industry Report 1981. 100.00 (ISBN 0-87615-122-5, 301-81). AAES.

Leech, D. J. Economics & Financial Studies for Engineers. 260p. 1982. 49.95x (ISBN 0-470-27351-8); pap. 23.95x (ISBN 0-470-27352-6). Halsted Pr.

Stone, P. A. Building Economy: Design, Production & Organisation. 3rd ed. 250p. 1982. 45.00 (ISBN 0-08-028677-1); 17.00 (ISBN 0-08-028678-X). Pergamon.

ENGINEERING ETHICS

Martin, Michael & Schinzinger, Roland. Ethics in Engineering. 1st ed. (Illus.). 336p. 1983. pap. text ed. 17.95 (ISBN 0-07-040701-0, C); write for info. instr's manual (ISBN 0-07-040702-9). McGraw.

ENGINEERING GEOLOGY

see also Rock Mechanics

Harvey, John C. Geology for Geotechnical Engineers. (Illus.). 136p. 1983. 24.95 (ISBN 0-521-24629-6); pap. 9.95 (ISBN 0-521-28862-2). Cambridge U Pr.

ENGINEERING GRAPHICS

see also Computer Graphics;
also subdivision Graphic Methods under specific subjects

Earle, James H. Engineering Design Graphics. 4th ed. LC 82-6709. 704p. 1983. text ed. 27.95 (ISBN 0-201-11318-X). A-W.

ENGINEERING GRAPHICS–DATA PROCESSING

see Computer Graphics

ENGINEERING LAW

see also Engineering–Contracts and Specifications

Hinkel, Daniel F. & Dick, Richard J. Indiana Mechanic's Lien Law. 221p. 1982. 25.00 (ISBN 0-87215-416-5). Michie-Bobbs.

ENGINEERING LITERATURE

see Technical Literature

ENGINEERING LITERATURE SEARCHING

see Information Storage and Retrieval Systems–Engineering

ENGINEERING MATERIALS

see Materials

ENGINEERING MATHEMATICS

see also Electric Engineering–Mathematics; Engineering–Statistical Methods; Mechanics, Applied; Structures, Theory of

Bajpai, A. C., et al. Engineering Mathematics. LC 73-21230. 793p. 1974. pap. text ed. 22.95x (ISBN 0-471-04376-1, Pub. by Wiley-Interscience). Wiley.

Bajpai, Avi C., et al. Advanced Engineering Mathematics. LC 77-2198. 578p. 1977. 55.00 (ISBN 0-471-99521-5); pap. 22.95x (ISBN 0-471-99520-7). Wiley.

Bird, May. Engineering Mathematics & Science 3 Checkbook. 1981. pap. text ed. 8.95 (ISBN 0-408-00625-0). Butterworth.

Blakeley, Walter R. Calculus for Engineering Technology. LC 67-29017. 441p. 1968. text ed. 23.95 (ISBN 0-471-07931-6). Wiley.

Brebbia, C. A., ed. Boundary Element Methods in Engineering, Southampton, England 1982: Proceedings. (Illus.). 649p. 1982. 59.00 (ISBN 0-387-11819-5). Springer-Verlag.

Crandall, Stephen H. Engineering Analysis. LC 82-20335. 428p. 1983. Repr. of 1956 ed. lib. bdg. write for info. (ISBN 0-89874-577-2). Krieger.

Glowinski, R. & Lions, J. L., eds. Computing Methods in Applied Sciences & Engineering V: Proceedings of the Fifth International Symposium, Versailles, France, December 14-18, 1981, Vol. 5. 626p. 1982. 102.25 (ISBN 0-444-86450-4). Elsevier.

Goodson, Carole E. & Miertschin, Susan. Technical Mathematics with Applications. 960p. 1983. 22.95x (ISBN 0-471-08244-9); tchr's. manual avail. (ISBN 0-471-89526-1); study guide avail. (ISBN 0-471-87578-3). Wiley.

Kreyszig, Erwin. Advanced Engineering Mathematics. 5th ed. 1100p. 1983. text ed. 36.95 (ISBN 0-471-86251-7); tchrs.' manual avail. (ISBN 0-471-89855-4). Wiley.

Nustad, Harry L. & Wesner, Terry H. Essentials of Technical Mathematics. 600p. 1983. text ed. write for info. (ISBN 0-697-08551-1); instrs' manual avail. (ISBN 0-697-08553-8); wkbk. avail. (ISBN 0-697-08552-X). Wm C Brown.

Tuma, J. J. Engineering Mathematics Handbook. 2nd ed. 1979. text ed. 31.25 (ISBN 0-07-065429-8). McGraw.

ENGINEERING STATISTICS

see Engineering–Statistical Methods

ENGINEERING TOLERANCES

see Tolerance (Engineering)

ENGINEERS
see also Civil Engineers; Engineering–Vocational Guidance; Inventors; Technologists

Engineering Manpower Commission. Demand for Engineers, 1981. (Illus.). 1982. 35.00x (ISBN 0-87615-112-8, 231-82). AAES.
--Professional Income of Engineers, 1982. (Illus.). 1982. 35.00 (ISBN 0-87615-134-9, 302-82). AAES.
Engineering Personnel: Proceedings of Conference on Engineering Personnel, Houston, 1980. 60.00 (ISBN 0-87615-023-7, 136-80). AAES.
Engineering Personnel: Proceedings of Industry Advisory Committee on Engineering Personnel, Atlanta, January, 1979. 50.00 (ISBN 0-87615-021-0, 111-79). AAES.
Modern Scientists & Engineers, 3 vols. 1980. 135.00 (ISBN 0-07-045266-0). McGraw.
Professional Income of Engineers 1980. 35.00 (ISBN 0-87615-132-2, 302-80). AAES.
Professional Income of Engineers 1981. 35.00 (ISBN 0-87615-133-0, 302-81). AAES.
Salaries of Engineering Technicians & Technologies 1981. 100.00 (ISBN 0-87615-142-X, 304-82). AAES.
Salaries of Engineers in Education 1981. 20.00 (ISBN 0-87615-152-7, 307-82). AAES.
Salaries of Engineers in Education 1982. 1982. 20.00 (ISBN 0-87615-153-5, 307-82A). AAES.
Survey of Employment Practices among Employers of Engineers 1981. 25.00 (ISBN 0-87615-172-1, 510-82). AAES.

ENGINEERS–LEGAL STATUS, LAWS, ETC.
see Engineering Law

ENGINES
see also Fuel; Gas and Oil Engines; Locomotives; Pumping Machinery; Tractors

Small Engines. LC 82-10304. (Home Repair & Improvement). lib. bdg. 15.96 (ISBN 0-8094-3511-X, Pub. by Time-Life). Silver.

ENGLAND
see also Great Britain;
also specific countries, cities and geographic areas in England

Blake, Robert, ed. The English World: History, Character & People. LC 82-1788. (Illus.). 268p. 1982. 50.00 (ISBN 0-8109-0865-4). Abrams.

ENGLAND–ANTIQUITIES

Barrett, William. The History & Antiquities of the City of Bristol. 704p. 1982. text ed. 75.00x (ISBN 0-904387-48-8, Pub. by Sutton England). Humanities.
Clare, Tom. Archaeological Sites of Devon & Cornwall. 160p. 1982. 50.00x (ISBN 0-86190-057-X, Pub. by Moorland). State Mutual Bk.
Dellheim, Charles. The Face of the Past: The Preservation of the Medieval Inheritance in Victorian England. LC 82-4486. (Illus.). 225p. 1983. 29.95 (ISBN 0-521-23645-2). Cambridge U Pr.
Forde-Johnston. Hillforts of the Iron Age in England & Wales. 370p. 1982. 90.00x (ISBN 0-85323-381-0, Pub. by Liverpool Univ England). State Mutual Bk.
Gray, Irvine. Antiquaries of Gloucestershire & Bristol. 208p. 1981. text ed. 18.00x (ISBN 0-900197-14-5, Pub. by Sutton England). Humanities.
MacGregor, Arthur. Anglo-Scandinavian Finds from Lloyds Bank, Pavement & Other Sites. (Archaeology of York-Small Finds 17-3). 174p. 1982. pap. text ed. 15.00x (ISBN 0-906780-02-0, 40256, Pub. by Coun Brit Archaeology England). Humanities.

ENGLAND–CIVILIZATION
see Great Britain–Civilization

ENGLAND–DESCRIPTION AND TRAVEL
see also Great Britain–Description and Travel; Great Britain–Historic Houses, etc.

Biggs, Howard. The River Medway. 160p. 1982. 35.00x (ISBN 0-86138-005-3, Pub. by Terence Dalton England). State Mutual Bk.
Fitzgerald, R. S. Liverpool Road Station, Manchester. 1980. 20.00 (ISBN 0-7190-0765-8); pap. 9.50 (ISBN 0-7190-0790-9). Manchester.
Smith, William. The Particular Description of England in 1588. (Illus.). 124p. 1982. text ed. 76.00x (ISBN 0-86299-015-7, Pub. by Sutton England). Humanities.
Spiers, M. Victoria Park, Manchester. 1976. 21.00 (ISBN 0-7190-1333-X). Manchester.
Steinbicker, Earl. DayTrips from London by Rail, Bus or Car. (Illus.). 256p. (Orig.). 1983. pap. 8.95 (ISBN 0-8038-1581-6). Hastings.

ENGLAND–DESCRIPTION AND TRAVEL–GUIDEBOOKS

Watkins, Paul. X Devon. (Golden Hart Guides Ser.). (Illus.). 96p. 1983. pap. 3.95 (ISBN 0-283-98911-4, Pub by Sidgwick & Jackson). Merrimack Bk Serv.

ENGLAND–GENEALOGY
see Great Britain–Genealogy

ENGLAND–HISTORY
see Great Britain–History

ENGLAND–SOCIAL CONDITIONS
see Great Britain–Social Conditions

ENGLAND–SOCIAL LIFE AND CUSTOMS
see also Great Britain–Social Life and Customs

Davis, Norman, ed. The Paston Letters. (The World's Classics Ser.). (Illus.). 320p. 1983. pap. 6.95 (ISBN 0-19-281615-2, GB). Oxford U Pr.
Kasterine, Omitri. England & the English. 1981. 24.95 (ISBN 0-437-08050-1, Pub. by World's Work). David & Charles.
Storch, Robert D., ed. Popular Culture & Custom in Nineteenth-Century England. LC 82-3302. 232p. 1982. 27.50x (ISBN 0-312-63033-6). St Martin.
Williams, Alfred. Round about Middle Thames: Glimpses of Rural Victorian Life. 192p. 1982. text ed. 8.50x (ISBN 0-86299-032-7, Pub. by Sutton England). Humanities.

ENGLAND, CHURCH OF
see Church of England

ENGLISH ARCHITECTURE
see Architecture–Great Britain

ENGLISH ART
see Art, British

ENGLISH AS A FOREIGN LANGUAGE
see English Language–Study and Teaching–Foreign Students

ENGLISH COMPOSERS
see Composers, British

ENGLISH DRAMA (COLLECTIONS)
see also Mysteries and Miracle-Plays

Beaumont, Francis & Fletcher, John. The Dramatic Works in the Beaumont & Fletcher Canon: Vol. V, The Mad Lover, The Loyal Subject, The Humorous Lieutenant, Women Pleased, The Island Princess. Bowers, Fredson, ed. LC 66-74421. 600p. Date not set. 89.50 (ISBN 0-521-20061-X). Cambridge U Pr.

ENGLISH DRAMA (COLLECTIONS)–RESTORATION, 1660-1700

Baillie, William M., ed. A Choice Ternary of English Plays: Gratiae Theatrales, 1662. 1983. write for info. (ISBN 0-86698-054-7). Medieval & Renaissance NY.

ENGLISH DRAMA–BIBLIOGRAPHY

Summers, Montague. A Bibliography of Restoration Drama. 2nd ed. 94p. 1982. 30.00x (ISBN 0-284-98554-6, Pub. by C Skilton Scotland). State Mutual Bk.

ENGLISH DRAMA–EXAMINATIONS, QUESTIONS, ETC.
see English Literature–Examinations, Questions, etc.

ENGLISH DRAMA–HISTORY AND CRITICISM

Hunter. Dramatic Identities & Cultural Tradition. 376p. 1982. 60.00x (ISBN 0-85323-443-4, Pub. by Liverpool Univ England). State Mutual Bk.
Manmohan, Mehra. Harley Granville Barker: A Critical Study of the Major Plays. 1982. 16.00x (ISBN 0-686-38375-3). South Asia Bks.
Price. The Unfortunate Comedy. 208p. 1982. 40.00x (ISBN 0-85323-000-5, Pub. by Liverpool Univ England). State Mutual Bk.

ENGLISH DRAMA–HISTORY AND CRITICISM–TO 1500

Lumiansky, R. M. & Mills, David. The Chester Mystery Cycle: Essays & Documents. LC 82-1838. vii, 321p. 1982. 40.00x (ISBN 0-8078-1522-5). U of NC Pr.

ENGLISH DRAMA–HISTORY AND CRITICISM–EARLY MODERN AND ELIZABETHAN, 1500-1600

Gair, Reavley. The Children of Paul's: The Story of a Theatre Company, 1553-1608. LC 82-4185. (Illus.). 232p. 1982. 34.50 (ISBN 0-521-24360-2). Cambridge U Pr.
Ure. Elizabethan & Jacobean Drama. 262p. 1982. 50.00x (ISBN 0-85323-142-7, Pub. by Liverpool Univ England). State Mutual Bk.

ENGLISH DRAMA–HISTORY AND CRITICISM–RESTORATION, 1660-1700

Powell, Jocelyn. Restoration Theatre Production. (Theatre Production Studies). (Illus.). 240p. 1983. write for info. (ISBN 0-7100-9321-7). Routledge & Kegan.
Summers, Montague. A Bibliography of Restoration Drama. 2nd ed. 94p. 1982. 30.00x (ISBN 0-284-98554-6, Pub. by C Skilton Scotland). State Mutual Bk.
Sutherland, Sarah P. Masques in Jacobean Tragedy. LC 81-69122. 1982. 24.50 (ISBN 0-404-62279-8). AMS Pr.

ENGLISH DRAMA–HISTORY AND CRITICISM–18TH CENTURY

Hume, Robert D. The Rakish Stage: Studies in English Drama, 1660-1800. 1983. price not set (ISBN 0-8093-1100-3). S Ill U Pr.
Kenny, Shirley S. & Backscheider, P. R., eds. The Performers & Their Plays. LC 78-66655. (Eighteenth Century English Drama Ser.). lib. bdg. 50.00 (ISBN 0-8240-3577-1). Garland Pub.
Liesenfeld, Vincent J. & Backscheider, P. R., eds. The Stage & the Licensing Act, 1729-1739. LC 78-66661. (Eighteenth Century English Drama Ser.). lib. bdg. 50.00 (ISBN 0-8240-3576-3). Garland Pub.

ENGLISH DRAMA–HISTORY AND CRITICISM–20TH CENTURY

Brown, John R. A Short Guide to Modern British Drama. LC 82-22699. 150p. 1983. pap. text ed. 7.95x (ISBN 0-389-20353-X). B&N Imports.
Durand, Loup. The Angkor Massacre. Lane, Helen R., tr. from Fr. 416p. 1983. 15.95 (ISBN 0-688-00487-3). Morrow.

ENGLISH DRAMA–STUDY AND TEACHING
see English Literature–Study and Teaching

ENGLISH ESSAYS
Here are entered only collections of essays by several authors.

Britton, James. Prospect & Retrospect: Selected Essays of James Britton. Pradl, Gordon M., ed. LC 82-14608. 224p. 1982. pap. text ed. 9.00 (ISBN 0-686-38081-9). Boynton Cook Pubs.
Dixon-Hunt, John & Holland, Faith M., eds. The Ruskin Polygon. 266p. 1982. 30.00 (ISBN 0-7190-0834-4). Manchester.
Dorsch, T. S., ed. Essays & Studies-1972. (Essays & Studies: Vol. 25). 125p. 1972. text ed. 12.50 (ISBN 0-391-00231-7). Humanities.
Ellrodt, Robert, ed. Essays & Studies-1975. (Essays & Studies: Vol. 28). 122p. 1975. text ed. 15.00x (ISBN 0-7195-3232-9, Pub. by Murray England). Humanities.
Harris, Bernard, ed. Essays & Studies-1971. (Essays & Studies: Vol. 24). 122p. 1971. text ed. 12.50 (ISBN 0-7195-2325-7, Pub. by Murray England). Humanities.
Holroyd, Michael, ed. Essays by Diverse Hands XLII. (Royal Society of Literature Ser.). 208p. 1983. text ed. 22.50x (ISBN 0-85115-173-6, Pub. by Boydell & Brewer). Biblio Dist.
Lawlor, John, ed. Essays & Studies-1973. (Essays & Studies: Vol. 26). 112p. 1973. text ed. 12.50x (ISBN 0-391-00279-1). Humanities.
Merchant, W. M., ed. Essays & Studies-1977. (Essays & Studies: Vol. 30). 109p. 1977. text ed. 15.00x (ISBN 0-391-00701-7). Humanities.
Redmond, J., et al, eds. Year's Work in English Studies 1979. (Year's Work in English Studies: Vol. 60). 519p. 1982. text ed. 43.75x (ISBN 0-391-02623-2, Pub. by Murray England). Humanities.
Robson, W. W., ed. Essays & Studies-1978. (Essays & Studies: Vol. 31). 130p. 1978. text ed. 18.00x (ISBN 0-391-00838-2). Humanities.
Sisson, C. H. Anglican Essays. 208p. 1983. text ed. 14.75x (ISBN 0-85635-456-2, Pub. by Carcanet New Pr England). Humanities.

ENGLISH FICTION–BIBLIOGRAPHY

Rice, Thomas J., ed. English Fiction, 1900-1950: A Guide to Information Sources, Vol. 2. (American Literature, English Literature, & World Literature in English Information Guide Ser.: Vol. 21). 627p. 1983. 42.00x (ISBN 0-8103-1505-X). Gale.

ENGLISH FICTION–HISTORY AND CRITICISM

Ermarth, Elizabeth. Realism & Consensus in the English Novel. LC 82-61360. 304p. 1983. 25.00x (ISBN 0-691-06560-8). Princeton U Pr.
Levine, George. The Realistic Imagination: English Fiction from Frankenstein to Lady Chatterley. LC 80-17444. 358p. 1981. pap. 10.95 (ISBN 0-226-47551-4). U of Chicago Pr.

ENGLISH FICTION–HISTORY AND CRITICISM–EARLY MODERN 1500-1700

Davis, Lennard J. Factual Fictions: The Origins of the English Novel. LC 82-12815. 272p. 1983. 24.00x (ISBN 0-231-05420-3); pap. 12.50x (ISBN 0-231-05421-1). Columbia U Pr.
Timko, Michael & Kaplan, Fred, eds. Dickens Studies Annual: Essays on Victorian Fiction, Vol. 10. (Illus.). 1982. 32.50 (ISBN 0-404-18530-4). AMS Pr.

ENGLISH FICTION–HISTORY AND CRITICISM–19TH CENTURY

Barickman, Richard, et al. Corrupt Relations: Dickens, Thackeray, Trollope, Collins & the Victorian Sexual System. 1982. 25.00 (ISBN 0-686-82110-6). Columbia U Pr.
Davis, Earle. The Flint & the Flame: The Artistry of Charles Dickens. 333p. 1982. Repr. of 1964 ed. lib. bdg. 35.00 (ISBN 0-89760-142-4). Telegraph Bks.
Fyfe, Thomas A., compiled by. Who's Who in Dickens: A Complete Dickens Repertory in Dickens' Own Words. 355p. 1982. Repr. of 1912 ed. lib. bdg. 45.00 (ISBN 0-89987-278-6). Darby Bks.
Leclaire, Lucien. A General Analytical Bibliography of the Regional Novelists of the British Isles: 1800-1950. 399p. 1983. Repr. of 1954 ed. lib. bdg. 100.00 (ISBN 0-89984-811-7). Century Bookbindery.
Stirling, Monica. The Fine & the Wicked: The Life & Times of Ouida. 223p. 1982. Repr. of 1958 ed. lib. bdg. 30.00 (ISBN 0-89760-850-X). Telegraph Bks.

ENGLISH FICTION–HISTORY AND CRITICISM–20TH CENTURY

Batchelor, Roy. Edwardian Novelists. 1982. 25.00 (ISBN 0-312-23907-6). St Martin.
Leclaire, Lucien. A General Analytical Bibliography of the Regional Novelists of the British Isles: 1800-1950. 399p. 1983. Repr. of 1954 ed. lib. bdg. 100.00 (ISBN 0-89984-811-7). Century Bookbindery.

ENGLISH FOLK-LORE
see Folk-Lore, English

ENGLISH IN AMERICA
see British in America

ENGLISH IN AUSTRALIA
see British in Australia

ENGLISH LANGUAGE
see also Basic English; COBOL (Computer Program Language)

Abbs, Peter. English Within the Arts. 148p. (Orig.). 1983. pap. 8.50 (ISBN 0-89874-599-3). Krieger.
Bernstein, Theodore M. Dos, Don'ts & Maybes of the English Language. 1982. pap. 8.95 (ISBN 0-8129-6321-0). Times Bks.
Collins, Beverly & Mees, Inger. Working with the Sounds of English & Dutch. vii, 72p. 1982. pap. write for info. (ISBN 90-04-06836-8). E J Brill.
Fieldhouse, Harry. Everyman's Good English Guide. 283p. 1983. 15.95 (ISBN 0-686-38410-5, Pub. by Evman England). Biblio Dist.
Ft. Myer School Staff. Instant Pep for Language. 1983. 5.50 (ISBN 0-686-84077-1). Intl Gen Semantics.
Holmes, Keith D. The Sound of English. Set. tchrs guide 25.00 (ISBN 0-9608250-4-5); per set, 4 disc recordings 25.00 (ISBN 0-9608250-3-7). Educ Serv Pub.
Justus, Fred. Beginning Language. (English Ser.). 24p. (ps). 1978. wkbk. 5.00 (ISBN 0-8209-0172-5, E-R). ESP.
--English at Work: Grade Eight. (English Ser.). 24p. 1977. wkbk. 5.00 (ISBN 0-8209-0180-6, E-8). ESP.
--English at Work: Grade Five. (English Ser.). 24p. 1980. wkbk. 5.00 (ISBN 0-8209-0177-6, E-5). ESP.
--English at Work: Grade Seven. (English Ser.). 24p. 1979. wkbk. 5.00 (ISBN 0-8209-0179-2, E-7). ESP.
--English at Work: Grade Six. (English Ser.). 24p. 1979. wkbk. 5.00 (ISBN 0-8209-0178-4, E-6). ESP.
--Learning English: Grade 1. (English Ser.). 24p. 1975. wkbk. 5.00 (ISBN 0-8209-0173-3, E-1). ESP.
--Learning English: Grade 2. (English Ser.). 24p. 1978. wkbk. 5.00 (ISBN 0-8209-0174-1, E-2). ESP.
--Learning English: Grade 3. (English Ser.). 24p. 1980. 5.00 (ISBN 0-8209-0175-X, E-3). ESP.
--Learning English: Grade 4. (English Ser.). 24p. 1980. wkbk. 5.00 (ISBN 0-8209-0176-8, E-4). ESP.
Kachru, B. The Other Tongue: English Across Culture. (World Language English Ser.). 358p. 1983. pap. 13.95 (ISBN 0-08-029469-3). Pergamon.
Lass, Norman J., ed. Speech & Language: Advances in Basic Research & Practice. (Serial Publication: Vol. 9). Date not set. price not set (ISBN 0-12-608609-5). Acad Pr.
Lodwig, Robert R. Career English. LC 80-24831. 200p. (Orig.). 1981. pap. text ed. 7.25x (ISBN 0-686-84386-X). Boynton Cook Pubs.
Quirk, Randolph. Style & Communication in the English Language. 160p. 1982. pap. text ed. 12.95 (ISBN 0-7131-6260-0). E Arnold.
Shaw, Marie-Jose. Jumbo English Yearbook: Grade 10. (Jumbo English Ser.). (gr. 10). 1979. wkbk. 14.00 (ISBN 0-8209-0008-7, JEY-8). ESP.
Vaughn, James E. Impact: Grades Eleven to Twelve. (Impact Ser.). 24p. 1979. wkbk. 5.00 (ISBN 0-8209-0350-7, IM-1112). ESP.

ENGLISH LANGUAGE–TO 1100
see Anglo-Saxon Language

ENGLISH LANGUAGE–MIDDLE ENGLISH, 1100-1500

Brooks, G. L. An Introduction of Old English. 1955. pap. 5.50 (ISBN 0-7190-0569-8). Manchester.
Mitchell, Bruce & Robinson, Fred C. A Guide to Old English: Revised With Texts & Glossary. 286p. 1982. 35.00x (ISBN 0-8020-2489-0); pap. 15.00 (ISBN 0-8020-6513-9). U of Toronto Pr.

ENGLISH LANGUAGE–MIDDLE ENGLISH, 1100-1500–GLOSSARIES

Meritt, Herbert Dean. Old English Glosses: A Collection. 135p. 1982. Repr. of 1945 ed. lib. bdg. 30.00 (ISBN 0-89760-580-2). Telegraph Bks.

ENGLISH LANGUAGE–ABBREVIATIONS
see Abbreviations

ENGLISH LANGUAGE–ACRONYMS
see Acronyms

ENGLISH LANGUAGE–ALPHABET

Haas, W., ed. Alphabets for English. 1969. 14.50 (ISBN 0-7190-0391-1). Manchester.
Herzog, Barbara J. ABC! Animals & Me! (Illus.). 32p. (Orig.). (gr. 1-2). 1983. pap. 4.98 (ISBN 0-943194-15-6). Childwrite.

ENGLISH LANGUAGE–ANALYSIS AND PARSING
see English Language–Grammar

ENGLISH LANGUAGE–ANTONYMS
see English Language–Synonyms and Antonyms

ENGLISH LANGUAGE–BUSINESS ENGLISH

Cypert, Samuel A. Writing Effective Business Letters, Memos, Proposals, & Reports. 192p. 1983. 12.95 (ISBN 0-8092-5605-3). Contemp Bks.
Dow, Roger W. Business English. LC 78-18253. 451p. 1979. 17.95 (ISBN 0-471-36661-7); wkbk. 8.95 (ISBN 0-471-04959-X); avail. tchrs. manual (ISBN 0-471-05251-5). Wiley.
Dunlop, I. & Schrand, H. Communication for Business: Materials for Reading Comprehension & Discussion. (Materials for Language Practice Ser.). (Illus.). 110p. 1982. pap. 4.95 (ISBN 0-08-029438-3). Pergamon.
Gartside, L. English for Business Studies. 416p. 1981. 30.00x (ISBN 0-7121-0582-4, Pub. by Macdonald & Evans). State Mutual Bk.
Guffey, Mary E. Business English. 352p. 1983. pap. text ed. 19.95x (ISBN 0-534-01396-1). Kent Pub Co.
Henderson, G. L. & Voiles, P. R. Business English Essentials. 6th ed. 1980. 10.85 (ISBN 0-07-027984-5); tchr's ed. avail. McGraw.
Hoban, Y. Instrumental English: English for the Secretary. 1982. text ed. 6.96 (ISBN 0-07-004522-4). McGraw.

Holtz, H. Persuasive Writing: Communicating Effectively in Business. 288p. 1983. 14.95 (ISBN 0-07-029627-8); pap. 6.95 (ISBN 0-07-029630-8). McGraw.

Hudson, Randolph H. & McGuire, Gertrude M., eds. Business Writing: Concepts & Applications. (Illus.). 332p. 1983. pap. text ed. 16.95x (ISBN 0-935732-06-3). Roxbury Pub Co.

Lindsell, Sheryl L. The Secretary's Quick Reference Manual. LC 82-8888. 288p. (Orig.). 1983. pap. 2.95 (ISBN 0-668-05595-2, 5595). Arco.

McCauley, Rosemarie & Slocum, Keith. Business Spelling & Word Power. 2nd ed. 336p. 1983. pap. text ed. 10.95 (ISBN 0-672-97975-6); instr's. guide 3.33 (ISBN 0-672-97976-4). Bobbs.

Markel, Michael H. & Lucier, R. J. Make Your Point: A Guide to Improving Your Business & Technical Writing. (Illus.). 156p. 1983. 12.95 (ISBN 0-13-547760-3); pap. 5.95 (ISBN 0-13-547752-2). P-H.

Ryckman, W. G. The Art of Writing Clearly. (Plaid Ser.). 90p. 1983. pap. 7.95 (ISBN 0-87094-388-X). Dow Jones-Irwin.

ENGLISH LANGUAGE–COMPOSITION AND EXERCISES

Here are entered works of an elementary character containing exercises in, and treatises on English composition. More advanced works on English composition are entered under the headings English Language–Rhetoric and English Language–Style.

see also English Language–Grammar; English Language–Rhetoric; English Language–Style; English Language–Text-Books for Foreigners

Adams, Anne & Bebensee, Elisabeth L. Success in Reading & Writing: Grade 6. 1983. text ed. 15.95 (ISBN 0-673-16586-8). Scott F.

Bennett, Barbara. Words Take Wing: A Teaching Guide to Creative Writing for Children. 260p. 1983. text ed. 15.00 (ISBN 0-8138-1932-6). Iowa St U Pr.

Black, Ann N. & Smith, Jo R. Ten Tools of Language-Written. 2nd ed. (Illus.). 166p. (gr. 11-12). 1982. pap. text ed. 12.60x (ISBN 0-910513-00-7). Mayfield Printing.

Camp, Gerald, ed. Teaching Writing: Essays from the Bay Area Writing Project. 336p. (Orig.). 1983. pap. text ed. 7.80x (ISBN 0-86709-081-2). Boynton Cook Pubs.

Cornelius, L. A. Grammar & Composition for Schools. 390p. 1981. pap. text ed. 5.95x (ISBN 0-86131-291-0, Pub. by Orient Longman Ltd India). Apt Bks.

Craz, Albert G. & Mavragis, Edward P. Writing: The Composition. (Writing Ser.). 66p. 1981. wkbk. 3.95 (ISBN 0-9602800-3-0). Comp Pr.

Fawcett & Sandberg. Grassroots. 2d ed. 1982. pap. text ed. 11.95 (ISBN 0-686-84574-9, RM96); instr's. annotated ed. 12.95 (ISBN 0-686-84575-7, RM95). HM.

Forte, Imogene. Write about It Series, 3 vols. Incl. Beginning Readers. 80p. (gr. k-1). pap. text ed. 5.95 (ISBN 0-86530-044-5); Primary. 80p. (gr. 2-4). pap. text ed. 5.95 (ISBN 0-86530-045-3); Middle Grades. 80p. (gr. 4-6). 1983. pap. text ed. 5.95 (ISBN 0-86530-046-1). (Illus.). (gr. k-6). 1983. pap. text ed. 16.95 set (ISBN 0-86530-043-7, IP 43-7). Incentive Pubns.

Friedman, Carol A. & Meade, Andre T. Reading & Writing Skills Workbook for the GED Test. LC 82-18400. (Arco's Preparation for the GED Examination Ser.). 256p. 1983. pap. 5.95 (ISBN 0-668-05540-5). Arco.

Graves, Donald. Writing: Teachers & Children at Work. 312p. (Orig.). 1982. pap. text ed. 10.00x (ISBN 0-435-08203-5). Heinemann Ed.

Guth, H. P. Advanced Composition. (American English Today Ser.). 1980. text ed. 7.36 (ISBN 0-07-025013-8). McGraw.

--Basic Composition Two. (American English Today Ser.). 1980. text ed. 7.36 (ISBN 0-07-025012-X). McGraw.

Hopper, Vincent F. & Gale, Cedric. Essentials of Writing. 3rd ed. 168p. 1983. pap. 3.95 (ISBN 0-8120-2265-3). Barron.

Howley, Robert C. & Simon, Sidney B. Composition for Personal Growth: A Teacher's Handbook of Meaningful Student Writing Experiences. 184p. (Orig.). 1983. pap. 9.95 (ISBN 0-913636-15-0). Educ Res MA.

Knight, Tanis & Lewin, Larry. Open the Deck. Carmichael, Standrod, ed. (Writing Program Ser.). 1982. pap. 4.50 (ISBN 0-933282-07-9). Stack the Deck.

Leonard, Robert J. & De Beer, Peter H. A Survival Kit for Teachers of Composition: Skill-by-Skill Writing Improvement Program. 1982. comb-bound 19.95x (ISBN 0-87628-777-1). Ctr Appl Res.

Pauk, Walter. Six-Way Paragraphs, Advanced Level. (gr. 8-12). 1983. pap. text ed. price not set (ISBN 0-89061-303-6); price not set. Jamestown Pubs.

--Six-Way Paragraphs, Middle Level. (gr. 4-8). 1983. pap. price not set (ISBN 0-89061-302-8). Jamestown Pubs.

Price, Bren T. Basic Composition Activities Kit. 232p. 1982. comb-bound 22.50X (ISBN 0-87628-169-2). Ctr Appl Res.

Schultz, John. Writing from Start to Finish. LC 82-14595. 408p. 1982. 13.50x (ISBN 0-86709-039-1). Boynton Cook Pubs.

Spargo, Edward. Skills Drills, Book 1. (Skills Drills Ser.). 100p. 1983. price not set spirit masters (ISBN 0-89061-321-4); price not set reproducibles (ISBN 0-89061-324-9). Jamestown Pubs.

--Skills Drills, Book 2. (Skills Drills Ser.). 100p. 1983. price not set spirit masters (ISBN 0-89061-322-2); price not set reproducibles (ISBN 0-89061-350-8). Jamestown Pubs.

--Skills Drills, Book 3. (Skills Drills Ser.). 100p. 1983. price not set spirit masters (ISBN 0-89061-323-0); price not set reproducibles (ISBN 0-89061-351-6). Jamestown Pubs.

Swaim, Gary D. Learning Composition Skills. (Language Arts Ser.). 24p. (gr. 4-9). 1980. wkbk. 5.00 (ISBN 0-8209-0316-7, LA-2). ESP.

Van Becker, Nell S. & Van Becker, David. Journal to Essay: A Sequential Program in Composition. 192p. 1982. pap. text ed. 12.95 (ISBN 0-8403-2719-6). Kendall-Hunt.

Yeager, David C. The Writing Discovery Book: New Ways to Improve Writing Skills, Grade 4-8. 1982. pap. text ed. 8.95 (ISBN 0-673-15647-8). Scott F.

ENGLISH LANGUAGE–COMPOSITION AND EXERCISES–PROGRAMMED INSTRUCTION

see English Language–Programmed Instruction

ENGLISH LANGUAGE–CONVERSATION AND PHRASE BOOKS

Berlitz Editors. English for Arabic Phrasebook. 1982. pap. 4.95 (ISBN 0-02-965540-4, Berlitz). Macmillan.

--English for Japanese Travellers. Date not set. 4.95 (ISBN 0-02-966850-6, Berlitz). Macmillan.

Kimbrough, Victoria & Palmer, Michael. Odyssey: A Communicative Course in English. Incl. 128p. teacher's manual 5.50 (ISBN 0-582-79835-3); 32p. student's workbook 2.30 (ISBN 0-582-79850-7). 96p. (Orig.). (gr. 7-12). 1983. pap. text ed. 3.90 (ISBN 0-582-79811-6). Longman.

Silverson, Sarah & Smith, Jan. Speak Easy. 1982. with 3-4inch Umatic Videocassettes 395.00x (ISBN 0-88432-113-4); with Betamax Videocassette 380.00x (ISBN 0-88432-114-2); with VHS videocassette 380.00x (ISBN 0-88432-115-0); manual 4.95x (ISBN 0-88432-085-5). J Norton Pubs.

ENGLISH LANGUAGE–DIAGRAMING

see English Language–Grammar

ENGLISH LANGUAGE–DIALECTS

The New Zealand Dictionary. 1339p. 1983. 9.95 (ISBN 0-86863-373-9, Pub. by Heinemann Pubs New Zealand). Intl Schol Bk Serv.

ENGLISH LANGUAGE–DICTIONARIES

see also English Language–Dictionaries, Juvenile; also subdivisions Etymology; Glossaries, Vocabularies, etc.; Idioms, Corrections, Errors; Rime; Synonyms and Antonyms; Terms and Phrases under English Language

Beeching, Cyril L. A Dictionary of Eponyms. 2nd ed. 160p. 1983. price not set (ISBN 0-85157-329-0, Pub. by Bingley England). Shoe String.

Bornstein, Harry & Saulnier, Karen L., eds. The Comprehensive Signed English Dictionary. LC 82-21044. (Illus.). x, 454p. 1983. 27.95 (ISBN 0-913580-81-3). Gallaudet Coll.

Burridge, Shirley, ed. Oxford Elementary Learner's Dictionary of English. (Illus.). 304p. (Orig.). 1981. pap. text ed. 9.95x (ISBN 0-19-431253-4). Oxford U Pr.

Ciardi, John. A Second Browser's Dictionary: Native's Guide to the Unknown American Language. LC 82-48658. 420p. 1983. 16.30i (ISBN 0-06-015125-0, HarpT). Har-Row.

Cowie, A. P. & Mackin, Ronald. Oxford Dictionary of Current Idiomatic English: Verbs with Prepositions & Particles, Vol. 1. 1975. 13.95x (ISBN 0-19-431145-7). Oxford U Pr.

Dictionary of American Idioms Workbook, Vol. 2. 1984. pap. price not set (ISBN 0-8120-2515-6). Barron.

DuGran, Claurene. Wordsmanship: A Dictionary. 1982. Repr. pap. 2.95 (ISBN 0-671-45468-4). WSP.

Evans, Ivor H., ed. Brewer's Dictionary of Phrase & Fable. 1248p. 1982. 50.00x (ISBN 0-304-30706-8, Pub. by Cassell England). State Mutual Bk.

Fowler, H. W. A Dictionary of Modern English Usage. 2nd ed. Gowers, Ernest, ed. 748p. 1983. pap. 8.95 (ISBN 0-19-281389-7, GB 725, GB). Oxford U Pr.

Guinagh, Kevin, tr. & compiled by. Dictionary of Foreign Phrases & Abbreviations. 3rd ed. 288p. 1982. 28.00 (ISBN 0-8242-0675-4). Wilson.

Guralnik, David. Webster's New World Dictionary of the American Language. 704p. 1982. pap. 2.95 (ISBN 0-446-31051-4). Warner Bks.

Lewis, Norman. The New Roget's Thesaurus in Dictionary Form. rev. ed. LC 77-24457. 552p. 8.95 (ISBN 0-399-12678-3); Thumb-indexed ed. 9.95 (ISBN 0-399-12679-1). Putnam Pub Group.

Macmillan Very First Dictionary: A Magic World of Words. LC 82-22901. (Illus.). 280p. (gr. k-2). 1983. 10.95 (ISBN 0-02-761730-0). Macmillan.

New World Dictionary Editors. Misspeller's Dictionary. 1983. write for info. (ISBN 0-671-46864-2). S&S.

Nunberg, Geoffrey, ed. The American Heritage Dictionary. 1982. 13.95 (ISBN 0-686-81876-8). HM.

Paikeday, Thomas, ed. The New York Times Everyday Dictionary. 1982. 12.95 (ISBN 0-8129-0910-0). Times Bks.

Seeing Essential English: Elementary Dictionary. 9.95 (ISBN 0-87108-231-4). Pruett.

Silvet, J. Estonian-English Dictionary. 2nd ed. 508p. 1980. 55.00x (ISBN 0-686-82326-5, Pub. by Collets). State Mutual Bk.

Wyld, Henry C., ed. The Universal Dictionary of the English Langauge. rev. ed. 1447p. 1978. 45.00 (ISBN 0-7100-2333-2). Routledge & Kegan.

ENGLISH LANGUAGE–DICTIONARIES–ARABIC

Abdeen, Adnan. English-Arabic Dictionary for Accounting & Finance. LC 79-41213. 1981. 23.95x (ISBN 0-471-27673-1, Pub. by Wiley-Interscience). Wiley.

ENGLISH LANGUAGE–DICTIONARIES–CHINESE

English-Chinese Dictionary of Medicine. 1675p. 1979. text ed. 24.95 (ISBN 0-8351-1048-6). China Bks.

Zhou Long Ru. English-Chinese Dictionary of Abbreviation & Acronyms. 1290p. 1980. 9.95 (ISBN 0-8351-1106-7). China Bks.

ENGLISH LANGUAGE–DICTIONARIES–ESKIMO

Wells, Roger, Jr., compiled by. English-Eskimo & Eskimo-English Vocabularies. Kelly, John W., tr. LC 82-51153. 72p. 1982. pap. 6.95 (ISBN 0-8048-1403-1). C E Tuttle.

ENGLISH LANGUAGE–DICTIONARIES–GREEK

Megali Amerikaniki Encyclopedia, 21 Vols. 750p. (Greek.). 925.00 (ISBN 0-686-43252-5). Pergamon.

ENGLISH LANGUAGE–DICTIONARIES–HUNGARIAN

Orszagh, Laszlo, ed. English-Hungarian Dictionary. 13th ed. 608p. 1982. 6.25x (ISBN 963-05-2975-0). Intl Pubns Serv.

ENGLISH LANGUAGE–DICTIONARIES–JAPANESE

Getting By in English for Japanese. 90p. 1983. pap. price not set (ISBN 0-8120-2659-4). Barron.

ENGLISH LANGUAGE–DICTIONARIES–LATIN

Woodhouse, S. C., ed. Latin-English & English-Latin Dictionary. (Routledge Pocket Dictionaries Ser.). 496p. (Orig.). 1982. pap. 8.95 (ISBN 0-7100-9267-9). Routledge & Kegan.

ENGLISH LANGUAGE–DICTIONARIES–LATVIAN

Raskevics, J., et al. English-Latvian-Russian Dictionary. 718p. 1977. 50.00x (ISBN 0-686-82324-9, Pub. by Collets). State Mutual Bk.

ENGLISH LANGUAGE–DICTIONARIES–POLISH

Pogonowski, Iwo. Concise Polish-English-English-Polish Dictionary. 436p. (Orig.). 1983. pap. 3.95 (ISBN 0-88254-799-2). Hippocrene Bks.

ENGLISH LANGUAGE–DICTIONARIES–POLYGLOT

Graa, Albert, ed. Vocabularium Pharmaceuticum. 2nd ed. 125p. 1964. text ed. 13.50x (ISBN 0-8002-3024-8). Intl Pubns Serv.

ENGLISH LANGUAGE–DICTIONARIES–RUSSIAN

Olev, Kulno. English-Estonian-Russian Maritime Dictionary. 560p. 1981. 60.00x (ISBN 0-686-82322-2, Pub. by Collets). State Mutual Bk.

Parsons, Charles. Russian-English Dictionary of Irovat' Verbs. 34p. (Orig.). 1982. 10.00x (ISBN 0-917564-14-6). Translation Research.

Wilson, E. A. The Modern Russian Dictionary for English Speakers: English-Russian. LC 81-12141. 1200p. 1982. 39.50 (ISBN 0-08-020554-2). Pergamon.

ENGLISH LANGUAGE–DICTIONARIES–SANSKRIT

Williams, Monier, ed. Sanskirt-English Dictionary: Etymologically & Philologically Arranged with Special Reference to Cognate Indo-European Languages. LC 73-495007. 1333p. 1981. Repr. of 1899 ed. 50.00x (ISBN 0-8002-0204-X). Intl Pubns serv.

ENGLISH LANGUAGE–DICTIONARIES–SERBO-CROATIAN

Simic, Z. Yugoslavian Dictionary: English-Serbocroatian. 446p. 1977. pap. text ed. 6.50x (ISBN 0-89918-784-6). Vanous.

Verbic, S. Yugoslavin Mining Dictionary: English-Serbo-English. 527p. 1981. pap. text ed. 25.00x (ISBN 0-89918-783-8). Vanous.

ENGLISH LANGUAGE–DICTIONARIES–SPANISH

Di Benedetto, Ubaldo, ed. New Comprehensive English-Spanish, Spanish-English Dictionary, 2 Vols. 3100p. 1977. Set. 60.00x (ISBN 84-7166-211-6). Intl Pubns Serv.

Simeone, Joseph F. Complete Spanish-English Reference Guide. 1983. 11.95 (ISBN 0-533-05530-X). Vantage.

ENGLISH LANGUAGE–DICTIONARIES, JUVENILE

Barnhart, Clarence L. & Barnhart, Robert K., eds. The World Book Dictionary, 2 Vols. LC 82-45610. (Illus.). 2554p. (gr. 4-12). 1983. lib. bdg. write for info. (ISBN 0-7166-0283-0). World Bk.

Schimpff, Jill W. Open Sesame Picture Dictionary: Featuring Jim Henson's Sesame Street Muppets, Children's Television Workshop. 84p. 1982. pap. text ed. 4.95x (ISBN 0-19-503035-4). Oxford U Pr.

ENGLISH LANGUAGE–ERRORS

see English Language–Idioms, Corrections, Errors

ENGLISH LANGUAGE–ETYMOLOGY

Conway, R. S. The Making of Latin: An Introduction to Latin, Greek & English Etymology. 1983. 20.00 (ISBN 0-89241-335-2); pap. 12.50 (ISBN 0-89241-341-7). Caratzas Bros.

Sherk, William. Five Hundred Years of New Words. LC 82-45307. (Illus.). 200p. 1983. pap. 9.95 (ISBN 0-385-17902-2). Doubleday.

ENGLISH LANGUAGE–EXAMINATIONS, QUESTIONS, ETC.

Berkley, Sandra. Delta's Oral Placement Test Teacher's Manual. 16p. (Orig.). 1982. pap. text ed. 6.95 (ISBN 0-937354-04-X). Delta Systems.

Berkley, Sandra & Moore, Gary W. Delta's Oral Placement Test. 62p. (Orig.). 1982. pap. text ed. 18.95 (ISBN 0-937354-05-8). Delta Systems.

Getting Ready for the High School Equivalency Exam in English. 2nd & rev. ed. (gr. 12). 1983. pap. text ed. 3.95 (ISBN 0-8120-2429-X). Barron.

Rafter, Rosalie & Alaia, Cheri. Practice RCT Writing Exam, No. 3. of 20 5.50 set (ISBN 0-937820-24-5). Westsea Pub.

--Practice RCT Writing Exam, No. 4. 1982. of 20 5.50 set (ISBN 0-937820-29-6). Westsea Pub.

Scholastic Testing Service Editors. Practice for High School Competency Test in English: Reading & Writing Skills. (Illus.). 160p. 1983. pap. 4.95 (ISBN 0-668-05550-2, 5550). Arco.

ENGLISH LANGUAGE–EXERCISES

see English Language–Composition and Exercises

ENGLISH LANGUAGE–FOREIGN WORDS AND PHRASES

Guinagh, Kevin, tr. & compiled by. Dictionary of Foreign Phrases & Abbreviations. 3rd ed. 288p. 1982. 28.00 (ISBN 0-8242-0675-4). Wilson.

ENGLISH LANGUAGE–GLOSSARIES, VOCABULARIES, ETC.

see also Crossword Puzzles–Glossaries, Vocabularies, etc.

Bliss, A. J. A Dictionary of Foreign Words & Phrases in Current English. 400p. 1983. 18.00 (ISBN 0-7100-1092-3); pap. 9.95 (ISBN 0-7100-9521-X). Routledge & Kegan.

Bornstein, Scott. Vocabulary Mastery. (Illus.). 272p. (YA) (gr. 9-12). 1982. 19.95 (ISBN 0-9602610-1-X). Bornstein Memory.

Norback, C. & Norback, P. The Must Words: The 6000 Most Important Words for a Successful & Profitable Vocabulary. 312p. 1983. pap. 5.95 (ISBN 0-07-047141-X, GB). McGraw.

Reader's Digest Editors. Success with Words. LC 82-62542. 704p. 1983. 20.97 (ISBN 0-89577-168-3, Pub. by RD Assn). Random.

Richards, J. C. Words in Action One: A Basic Illustrated English Vocabulary. (Illus.). 102p. (Orig.). 1978. pap. 6.50x (ISBN 0-19-581666-8). Oxford U Pr.

--Words in Action Three: A Basic Illustrated English Vocabulary. (Illus.). 132p. (Orig.). 1978. pap. 6.50x. Oxford U Pr.

--Words in Action Two: A Basic Illustrated English Vocabulary. (Illus.). 110p. (Orig.). 1978. pap. 6.50x (ISBN 0-19-581698-6). Oxford U Pr.

Schonberg, James. The Comparative Trilby Glossary, French-English. 60p. 1983. Repr. of 1895 ed. lib. bdg. 30.00 (ISBN 0-89984-614-9). Century Bookbindery.

Schweitzer, Burton L. & Aarons, Howell. Word Attack: An Individualized Approach. 1980. text ed. 8.95 (ISBN 0-675-08187-4). Additional supplements may be obtained from publisher. Merrill.

Sisson, A. F. Sisson's Word & Expression Locater. 371p. 1966. 17.95 (ISBN 0-13-810671-1, Busn). P-H.

ENGLISH LANGUAGE–GRAMMAR

see also English Language–Text-Books for Foreigners

Bates, Myrtle & Stern, Renee. The Grammar Game. (Illus.). 368p. (Orig.). 1983. pap. text ed. 8.95 (ISBN 0-686-82307-9); instr's. guide 3.33 (ISBN 0-686-82308-7). Bobbs.

Bell, Laurel & Garthwiate, Elloyse M. Accelerated Grammar. 1982. pap. text ed. 17.95 (ISBN 0-8403-2778-1). Kendall-Hunt.

Bullions, Peter. The Principles of English Grammar. LC 82-10418. (American Linguistics Ser.). 1983. 30.00x (ISBN 0-8201-1386-7). Schol Facsimiles.

Cornelius, L. A. Grammar & Composition for Schools. 390p. 1981. pap. text ed. 5.95x (ISBN 0-86131-291-0, Pub. by Orient Longman Ltd India). Apt Bks.

Cory, Beverly. Grammar & Usage. (Learning Workbooks Language Arts). (gr. 4-6). pap. 1.50 (ISBN 0-8224-4179-9). Pitman.

Folse, Keith S. English Structure Practices. 384p. 1983. pap. text ed. 6.95x (ISBN 0-472-08034-2). U of Mich Pr.

Goudiss, Maria H. Wordstar in Everyday English. 1983. pap. 9.95 (ISBN 0-8159-7221-0). Devin.

Greene, Samuel S. An Analysis of the English Language. LC 82-10272. (American Linguistics Ser.). 1983. Repr. of 1874 ed. 40.00 (ISBN 0-8201-1384-0). Schol Facsimiles.

Justus, Fred. Grammar Crossword Puzzles. (Puzzles Ser.). 24p. (gr. 5-9). 1980. wkbk. 5.00 (ISBN 0-8209-0288-8, PU-2). ESP.

Konsler, Runelle. Capitalization Critters & Punctuation Pals. (gr. 2-5). 1982. 7.95 (ISBN 0-86653-090-8, GA 441). Good Apple.

Lacey, C. Hightown Grammar. 1970. pap. 7.00 (ISBN 0-7190-0485-3). Manchester.

Lakritz, Joyce. Verbal Workbook for the ACT. LC 82-11644. 192p. 1983. pap. 6.00 (ISBN 0-668-05348-8, 5348). Arco.

Lubker, Robert. Von der Syntax Des Englischen Verbs In Seinen Finiten Formen. 430p. (Ger.). 1982. write for info. (ISBN 3-8204-6158-2). P Lang Pubs.

Molinsky, Steven J. & Bliss, Bill. Line by Line: Reading English Through Grammar Stories, Bk. 1. (Illus.). 208p. 1983. pap. text ed. 6.95 (ISBN 0-13-537076-0). P-H.

--Side by Side: English Grammar Through Guided Conversation 1A. 128p. 1983. pap. text ed. 3.95 (ISBN 0-13-809715-1); wkbk. 2.50 (ISBN 0-13-809525-6). P-H.

--Side by Side: English Grammar Through Guided Conversation 1B. 128p. 1983. pap. text ed. 3.95 (ISBN 0-13-809723-2); wkbk. 2.50 (ISBN 0-13-809582-5). P-H.

--Side by Side: English Grammar Through Guided Conversations 2A. 128p. 1983. pap. text ed. 3.95 (ISBN 0-13-809772-0); wkbk. 2.50 (ISBN 0-13-809640-6). P-H.

--Side by Side: English Grammar Through Guided Conversation 2B. 128p. 1983. pap. text ed. 3.95 (ISBN 0-13-809798-4); pap. 2.50 wkbk. (ISBN 0-13-809699-6). P-H.

Prevocational English: Text 2. 1971. text ed. 6.95 (ISBN 0-88499-037-0); wkbk. 5.95 (ISBN 0-88499-038-9). Inst Mod Lang.

Schachter, Paul & Otanes, Fe T. Tagalog Reference Grammar. (California Library Reprint Ser.). 600p. 1983. text ed. 35.00x (ISBN 0-520-04943-8, CLRS 122). U of Cal Pr.

Shaw, Marie-Jose. Direct & Indirect Objects. (English Sound Filmstrip Kits Ser.). (gr. 5). 1980. tchrs ed. 24.00 (ISBN 0-8209-0505-4, FCW5E-12). ESP.

--Direct Objects. (English Sound Filmstrips Kits Ser.). (gr. 4). 1979. tchrs ed. 24.00 (ISBN 0-8209-0483-X, FCW4E-10). ESP.

Show-Chih Rai Chu. Chinese Grammer & English Grammer: A Comparative Study. 417p. 1982. 12.95 (ISBN 0-686-37710-9); pap. 10.95 (ISBN 0-686-37711-7). Inst Sino Amer.

Wolfson, Nessa. CHP: The Conversational Historical Present in American English Narrative. 130p. 1982. 29.50x (ISBN 90-70176-61-0); pap. 19.50x (ISBN 90-70176-60-2). Foris Pubns.

ENGLISH LANGUAGE–GRAMMAR–PROGRAMMED INSTRUCTION

see English Language–Programmed Instruction

ENGLISH LANGUAGE–GRAMMAR, COMPARATIVE

Chu, Show-Chih R. Chinese Grammar & English Grammar: A Comparative Study. 417p. 1982. 12.95 (ISBN 0-686-37976-4); pap. 10.95 (ISBN 0-686-37977-2). Inst Sino-Amer.

ENGLISH LANGUAGE–GRAMMAR, HISTORICAL

Cox, M. History of Sir John Deane's Grammar School, Northwich. 1976. 25.00 (ISBN 0-7190-1282-1). Manchester.

ENGLISH LANGUAGE–GRAMMAR, 1950-

Fencl, Shirley & Jager, Susan G. The Two R's: Paragraph to Essay. LC 78-16026. 1979. pap. text ed. 14.50x (ISBN 0-673-15723-7). Scott F.

ENGLISH LANGUAGE–HISTORY

Baron, Dennis E. Going Native: The Regeneration of Saxon English. (Publications of the American Dialect Society (PADS): No. 69). 63p. (Orig.). 1982. pap. text ed. 4.80 (ISBN 0-8173-0011-2). U of Ala Pr.

Bourcier, George. An Introduction to the History of the English Language: From the Middle Ages to Modern Times. Clark, Cecily, tr. 232p. 1981. 55.00x (ISBN 0-85950-482-4, Pub. by Thornes England). State Mutual Bk.

Eagleson, Robert D., ed. English in the Eighties. 176p. (Orig.). 1982. pap. text ed. 10.25 (ISBN 0-909955-40-9). Boynton Cook Pubs.

Markman, Alan M. & Steinberg, Erwin R. Exercises in the History of English. LC 82-23769. 100p. 1983. pap. text ed. 7.25 (ISBN 0-8191-2971-2). U Pr of Amer.

Sherk, William. Five Hundred Years of New Words. LC 82-45307. (Illus.). 200p. 1983. pap. 9.95 (ISBN 0-385-17902-2). Doubleday.

ENGLISH LANGUAGE–IDIOMS, CORRECTIONS, ERRORS

Cowie, A. P. & Mackin, Ronald. Oxford Dictionary of Current Idiomatic English: Verbs with Prepositions & Particles, Vol. 1. 1975. 13.95x (ISBN 0-19-431145-7). Oxford U Pr.

ENGLISH LANGUAGE–METRICS AND RHYTHMICS

see English Language–Style

ENGLISH LANGUAGE–ORTHOGRAPHY AND SPELLING

see also Spellers

Brooks, Bearl. Basic Spelling: Grade One. (Spelling Ser.). 24p. 1979. wkbk. 5.00 (ISBN 0-8209-0165-2, SP-1). ESP.

--Basic Spelling: Grade Three. (Spelling Ser.). 24p. 1977. wkbk. 5.00 (ISBN 0-8209-0167-9, SP-3). ESP.

--Basic Spelling: Grade Two. (Spelling Ser.). 24p. 1979. wkbk. 5.00 (ISBN 0-8209-0166-0, SP-2). ESP.

Cory, Beverly. Phonics & Spelling. (Learning Workbooks Language Arts). (gr. 4-6). pap. 1.50 (ISBN 0-8224-4176-4). Pitman.

--Word Structure. (Learning Workbooks Language Arts). (gr. 4-6). pap. 1.50 (ISBN 0-8224-4177-2). Pitman.

The Good Apple Spelling Book. 107p. (gr. 3-8). 7.95 (ISBN 0-686-84801-2, GA60). Good Apple.

Kottmeyer, William & Claus, Audrey. Basic Goals in Spelling, 4 Levels. 7th ed. Incl. Level 1. 160p. pap. text ed. 4.64 (ISBN 0-07-034651-8, W); tchr's. ed. 16.60 (ISBN 0-07-034661-5, W); Level 2. 192p. text ed. 9.32 (ISBN 0-07-034632-1, W); pap. text ed. 4.64 (ISBN 0-07-034652-6, W); tchr's. ed. 16.60 (ISBN 0-07-034662-3); Level 3. 192p. text ed. 9.32 (ISBN 0-07-034633-X, W); pap. text ed. 4.64 (ISBN 0-07-034653-4, W); tchr's. ed. 16.60 (ISBN 0-07-034663-1); Level 4. 192p. text ed. 9.32 (ISBN 0-07-034634-8, W); pap. text ed. 4.76 (ISBN 0-07-034654-2, W); tchr's. ed. 17.20 (ISBN 0-07-034664-X). (Illus.). Date not set. McGraw.

New World Dictionary Editors. Misspeller's Dictionary. 1983. write for info. (ISBN 0-671-46864-2). S&S.

Read, et al. Continuous Progress in Spelling. (gr. 4-12). pap. 3.18 activity bk. (ISBN 0-8372-4382-3); tchr's manual 5.28 (ISBN 0-8372-4381-5); suppl. materials avail. Bowmar-Noble.

Scragg, D. G. A History of English Spelling. 1975. pap. 7.00 (ISBN 0-7190-0639-2). Manchester.

Shady, Raymond C. & Shand, G. B., eds. Play-Texts in Old Spelling. LC 81-69123. 1982. 24.50 (ISBN 0-404-62276-3). AMS Pr.

Shaw, Marie. Basic Skills Spelling Tests Workbook. (Basic Skills Workbooks). 32p. (gr. 5-6). 1983. 0.99 (ISBN 0-8209-0567-4, STW-2). ESP.

--Basic Skills Spelling Tests Workbook. (Basic Skills Workbooks). 32p. (gr. 3-4). 1983. 0.99 (ISBN 0-8209-0566-6, STW-1). ESP.

ENGLISH LANGUAGE–ORTHOGRAPHY AND SPELLING–PROGRAMMED INSTRUCTION

Brooks, Bearl. Alphabet. (Early Education Ser.). 26p. (ps-1). 1979. wkbk. 5.00 (ISBN 0-8209-0199-7, K-1). ESP.

--Writing Letters & Words. (Handwriting). 24p. (gr. k-1). 1980. wkbk. 5.00 (ISBN 0-8209-0268-3, W-0). ESP.

Hayes, Marilyn. Alphabet & Words. (Early Education Ser.). 24p. (gr. 1). 1982. wkbk. 5.00 (ISBN 0-8209-0214-4, K-16). ESP.

Justus, Fred. Alphabet Sequence. (Early Education Ser.). 24p. (gr. 1). 1980. wkbk. 5.00 (ISBN 0-686-42826-9). ESP.

--Writing Capital & Small Letters. (Early Education Ser.). 24p. (gr. 1). 1981. wkbk. 5.00 (ISBN 0-8209-0223-3, K-25). ESP.

Shaw, Marie. Spelling Tests: Grade 3. Incl. Grade 4. wkbk. 5.00 (ISBN 0-8209-0169-5, ST-4); Grade 5. wkbk. 5.00 (ISBN 0-8209-0170-9, ST-5); Grade 6. wkbk. 5.00 (ISBN 0-8209-0171-7, ST-6). (Spelling Ser.). 24p. 1979. wkbk. 5.00 (ISBN 0-8209-0168-7, ST-3). ESP.

Swaim, Gary D. Write Right Correctly. (Language Arts Ser.). 24p. (gr. 4-9). 1977. wkbk. 5.00 (ISBN 0-8209-0315-9, LA-1). ESP.

ENGLISH LANGUAGE–PARSING

see English Language–Grammar

ENGLISH LANGUAGE–PHONETICS

see also Reading (Elementary)–Phonetic Method

Cory, Beverly. Phonics & Spelling. (Learning Workbooks Language Arts). (gr. 4-6). pap. 1.50 (ISBN 0-8224-4176-4). Pitman.

Van der Hulst, Harry & Smith, Norval, eds. The Structure of Phonological Representation: Pt. Two. 265p. 1983. 35.00x (ISBN 90-70176-59-9); pap. 21.00x (ISBN 90-70176-58-0). Foris Pubns.

ENGLISH LANGUAGE–PHRASES AND TERMS

see English Language–Terms and Phrases

ENGLISH LANGUAGE–PRIMERS

see Readers

ENGLISH LANGUAGE–PROGRAMMED INSTRUCTION

Culp. Keys to Good Language, Levels 2-6. (gr. 2-6). Level 2. pap. 1.83 (ISBN 0-8372-4300-9); Levels 3-6. pap. 2.67 ea.; tchr's ed. 2.19 (ISBN 0-8372-4301-7); Levels 3-6. tchr's eds. 3.39 ea.; dupl. masters avail. Bowmar-Noble.

Guidebook to Better English, 4 Bks. (gr. 6-12). pap. 2.97 ea. Bk. 1 (ISBN 0-8372-4355-6). Bk. 2 (ISBN 0-8372-4359-9). Bk. 3 (ISBN 0-8372-4363-7). Bk. 4 (ISBN 0-8372-4367-X). tchr's handbk. 1.38 (ISBN 0-8372-4371-8); dupl. masters avail. Bowmar-Noble.

Stewart, et al. Keys to English Mastery, 6 Levels. (gr. 7-12). pap. 3.39 ea.; tchr's eds. 3.96 ea.; dupl. masters 21.12 ea. Bowmar-Noble.

Watkins, Floyd C., et al. Practical English Workbook. 312p. 1982. pap. text ed. 8.95 (ISBN 0-395-33187-0); write for info. instr's. manual (ISBN 0-395-33186-2). HM.

Woodford, P. & Kernan, D. Bridges to English, 6 bks. Rebrisz, J., ed. Incl. Bk. 1 (ISBN 0-07-034481-7). tchr's manual (ISBN 0-07-034482-5); wkbk. (ISBN 0-07-034483-3); Bk. 2 (ISBN 0-07-034487-6). tchr's manual (ISBN 0-07-034488-4); wkbk. (ISBN 0-07-034489-2); Bk. 3 (ISBN 0-07-034493-0). tchr's manual (ISBN 0-07-034494-9); wkbk. (ISBN 0-07-034495-7); Bk. 4 (ISBN 0-07-034499-X). tchr's manual (ISBN 0-07-034500-7); wkbk. (ISBN 0-07-034501-5); Bk. 5 (ISBN 0-07-034505-8). tchr's manual (ISBN 0-07-034506-6); wkbk. (ISBN 0-07-034507-4); Bk. 6 (ISBN 0-07-034511-2). tchr's manual (ISBN 0-07-034512-0); wkbk. (ISBN 0-07-034513-9). (Illus.). 1981. pap. text ed. 4.00 ea.; tchr's manual 2.00 ea.; wkbk. 3.52 ea.; tests 30.00 ea.; cassettes & cue cards avail. McGraw.

ENGLISH LANGUAGE–PRONUNCIATION

Here are entered works on the pronunciation of words (as distinct from that of particular sounds or letters) especially with reference to best usage.

Baker, Ann. Introducing English Pronunciation: A Teacher's Guide to Tree or Three? & Ship or Sheep. 1982. 7.95 (ISBN 0-686-81782-6). Cambridge U Pr.

Kurath, Hans & McDavid, Raven I., Jr. The Pronunciation of English in the Atlantic States: Based Upon the Collections of the Linguistic Atlas of the Eastern United States. LC 60-5671. (Illus.). 384p. 1983. pap. text ed. 25.00 (ISBN 0-8173-0129-1). U of Ala Pr.

Lane, Richard. Lane's English Pronunciation Guide. LC 79-90622. (Illus.). 64p. 1979. pap. text ed. 4.95 (ISBN 0-686-83962-5). Lane Pr.

Marzollo, Jean & Savage, Beth. Letter Sounds. (Learning Workbooks Language Arts). (gr. k-2). pap. 1.50 (ISBN 0-8224-4175-6). Pitman.

Minn, Loretta. Teach Speech. (gr. 3-7). 1982. 5.95 (ISBN 0-86653-058-4, GA 418). Good Apple.

ENGLISH LANGUAGE–PRONUNCIATION BY FOREIGNERS

Trudgill, Peter & Hannah, Jean. International English: A Guide to the Varieties of Standard English. 144p. 1982. pap. text ed. 9.95 (ISBN 0-7131-6362-3). E Arnold.

ENGLISH LANGUAGE–PUNCTUATION

Brooks, Bearl. Basic Skills Punctuation Workbook. (Basic Skills Workbooks). 32p. (gr. 4-7). 1983. 0.99 (ISBN 0-8209-0548-8, EW-4). ESP.

--Understanding Punctuation: Grades 4-7. (English Ser.). 24p. (gr. 4-7). 1979. wkbk. 5.00 (ISBN 0-8209-0186-5, E-15). ESP.

Gordon, Karen E. The Well-Tempered Sentence: A Punctuation Handbook for the Innocent, the Eager, & the Doomed. LC 82-19704. (Illus.). 96p. 1983. 7.95 (ISBN 0-89919-170-3). Ticknor & Fields.

ENGLISH LANGUAGE–READERS

see Readers

ENGLISH LANGUAGE–REVERSE DICTIONARIES

see English Language–Synonyms and Antonyms

ENGLISH LANGUAGE–RHETORIC

see also English Language–Composition and Exercises; English Language–Style

Barry, Vincent. Good Reason for Writing: A Text with Readings. 400p. 1982. pap. text ed. 12.95x (ISBN 0-534-01232-9). Wadsworth Pub.

Bartholomy, David. Sometimes You Just Have to Stand Naked: A Guide to Interesting Writing. (Illus.). 224p. 1983. pap. text ed. 8.95 (ISBN 0-13-822593-1). P-H.

Brannon, Lil & Knight, Melinda. Writers Writing. LC 82-14587. 192p. (Orig.). 1982. pap. text ed. 7.75 (ISBN 0-86709-045-6). Boynton Cook Pubs.

Brinegar, Bonnie C. & Skates, Craig B. Technical Writing: A Guide with Models. 1982. text ed. 13.95x (ISBN 0-673-15410-6). Scott F.

Butler, Eugenia W. & Hickman, Mary A. Correct Writing. 3rd ed. 384p. 1983. pap. 11.95 (ISBN 0-669-05437-2). Heath.

Canavan, P J. Paragraphs & Themes. 4th ed. 510p. 1983. pap. text ed. 12.95 (ISBN 0-669-05273-6). Heath.

Case, Doug & Davey, John. Developing Writing Skills in English. 1982. pap. text ed. 4.00x (ISBN 0-435-28021-X); tchr's. ed. 6.00x (ISBN 0-435-28022-8); wkbk. 2.00x (ISBN 0-435-28023-6). Heinemann Ed.

Clifford, John & Waterhouse, Robert. Sentence Combining: Shaping Ideas for Better Style. 224p. (Orig.). 1983. pap. text ed. 6.95 (ISBN 0-672-61605-X); instr's. guide 3.33 (ISBN 0-672-61604-1). Bobbs.

Donald, Robert & Moore, James. Writing Clear Paragraphs. 2nd ed. (Illus.). 272p. 1983. pap. text ed. 10.95 (ISBN 0-13-970004-8). P-H.

Elbow, Peter. Writing with Power: Techniques for Mastering the Writing Process. 396p. 1981. 22.50x (ISBN 0-19-502912-7). Oxford U Pr.

Emig, Janet. The Web of Meaning: Essays on Writing, Teaching, Learning, & Thinking. Goswami, Dixie & Butler, Maureen, eds. 192p. (Orig.). 1983. pap. text ed. 8.50x (ISBN 0-86709-047-2). Boynton Cook Pubs.

Ewald, Helen R. Writing As Process: Invention & Convention. 1983. 9.95 (ISBN 0-675-20014-8). Additional supplements may be obtained from publisher. Merrill.

Fencl, Shirley & Jager, Susan G. The Two R's: Paragraph to Essay. LC 78-16026. 1979. pap. text ed. 14.50x (ISBN 0-673-15723-7). Scott F.

Fishman, Judith. Responding to Prose: A Reader for Writers. (Illus.). 480p. (Orig.). 1982. pap. text ed. 9.95 (ISBN 0-672-61569-X); instr's. guide 3.33 (ISBN 0-672-61566-5). Bobbs.

Gayley, Henry. How to Write for Development. 50p. 1981. 14.50 (ISBN 0-89964-186-5). CASE.

Gilbert, Marilyn B. Clear Writing. LC 70-38627. (Self-Teaching Guides Ser.). 336p. (Orig., Prog. Bk.). 1972. pap. 7.95 (ISBN 0-471-29896-4). Wiley.

Hammond, E. Teaching Writing. 168p. 1983. 10.95x (ISBN 0-07-025893-7). McGraw.

Kiefer, Kathleen E. Making Writing Work: Effective Paragraphs. 224p. 1983. pap. text ed. 9.95 (ISBN 0-07-034541-4, C); instructor's manual 4.95 (ISBN 0-07-034542-2). McGraw.

Lewis, Stephen C. & Forte, M. Cecile. Writing Through Reading. (Illus.). 372p. 1983. pap. text ed. 11.95 (ISBN 0-13-971630-0). P-H.

Lipman, Michael & Joyner, Russell. How to Write Clearly: Guidelines & Exercises for Clear Writing. 1983. pap. 1.60 (ISBN 0-686-84057-7). Intl Gen Semantics.

McCuen, JoRay & Winkler, Anthony C. From Idea to Essay: A Rhetoric, Reader & Handbook. 3rd ed. 432p. 1982. pap. text ed. write for info. (ISBN 0-574-22085-2, 13-5085); write for info. answer bk (ISBN 0-574-22086-0, 13-5086). SRA.

McDavid, Virginia & Creswell, Thomas J. Today's English: Keys to Basic Writing. 464p. 1983. pap. text ed. 10.95 scp (ISBN 0-06-044351-0, HarpC); instr's manual avail. (ISBN 0-06-361410-3). Har-Row.

Martin, Nancy. Selected Essays. 192p. (Orig.). 1983. pap. text ed. 8.50x (ISBN 0-86709-069-3). Boynton Cook Pubs.

Mattson, Marylu & Leshing, Sophia. Help Yourself: A Guide To Writing & Rewriting. 320p. 1983. pap. text ed. 9.95 (ISBN 0-675-20027-X). Additional supplements may be obtained from publisher. Merrill.

Murray, Donald M. Learning By Teaching: Selected Articles on Writing & Teaching. LC 82-20558. 192p. 1982. pap. text ed. 8.25x (ISBN 0-86709-025-1). Boynton Cook Pubs.

Neman, Beth S. Writing Effectively. 504p. 1983. text ed. 13.95 (ISBN 0-675-20047-4); tchr's ed. 13.95 (ISBN 0-675-20053-9). Additional supplements may be obtained from publisher. Merrill.

Paulston, Christina B. & Henderson, Robert T. Writing: Communicative Activities in English. (Illus.). 288p. 1983. pap. text ed. 9.95 (ISBN 0-13-970277-6). P-H.

Rico, Gabriele L. Writing the Natural Way: Using Right-Brain Techniques to Release Your Expressive Powers. (Illus.). 272p. 1983. 15.95 (ISBN 0-87477-186-2); pap. 9.95 (ISBN 0-87477-236-2). J P Tarcher.

Taylor, Maureen. Writing to Communicate: A Rhetoric, Reader, & Handbook for College Writers. 392p. 1982. pap. text ed. 13.95x (ISBN 0-534-01196-9). Wadsworth Pub.

ENGLISH LANGUAGE–RIME–DICTIONARIES

Walker, J. Walker's Rhyming Dictionary of the English Language: In Which the Whole Language is Arranged According to its Terminations. rev. & enl. ed. 558p. 1979. Repr. of 1924 ed. 14.95 (ISBN 0-7100-2247-6). Routledge & Kegan.

ENGLISH LANGUAGE–SEMANTICS

Bloom, Lois & Lahey, Margaret. Language Development & Language Disorders. LC 77-21482. (Communication Disorders Ser.). 506p. 1978. text ed. 29.50 (ISBN 0-471-08220-1). Wiley.

Globus, Leo & Globus, Helen. The Wee Wisdom Record. 1983. 6.50 (ISBN 0-686-84074-7). Intl Gen Semantics.

Holmes, Stewart. Meaning in Language. 1983. 6.50 (ISBN 0-686-84069-0). Intl Gen Semantics.

Joohnson, Kenneth & Senatore, John. Nothing Never Happens. 1983. 17.75 (ISBN 0-686-84063-1). Intl Gen Semantics.

Minteer, Catherine. Words & What They Do To You. 1983. 5.50 (ISBN 0-686-84067-4). Intl Gen Semantics.

Morain, Mary, ed. Classroom Exercises in General Semantics. 1983. 5.50 (ISBN 0-686-84071-2). Intl Gen Semantics.

Potter, Robert R. Making Sense: Exploring Semantics & Critical Thinking. 1983. 8.50 (ISBN 0-686-84072-0). Intl Gen Semantics.

Webber, Irma. It Looks Like This. 1983. 5.50 (ISBN 0-686-84075-5); pap. 4.00 (ISBN 0-686-84076-3). Intl Gen Semantics.

What Everyone Should Know About Semantics. 1983. pap. 1.25 (ISBN 0-686-84068-2). Intl Gen Semantics.

ENGLISH LANGUAGE–SENTENCES

Aston, Melba. Developing Sentence Skills. (English Ser.). 24p. (gr. 4-7). 1980. wkbk. 5.00 (ISBN 0-8209-0182-2, E-10). ESP.

Folse, Keith S. English Structure Practices. 384p. 1983. pap. text ed. 6.95x (ISBN 0-472-08034-2). U of Mich Pr.

Gordon, Karen E. The Well-Tempered Sentence: A Punctuation Handbook for the Innocent, the Eager, & the Doomed. LC 82-19704. (Illus.). 96p. 1983. 7.95 (ISBN 0-89919-170-3). Ticknor & Fields.

ENGLISH LANGUAGE–SLANG

see also English Language–Terms and Phrases

Elting, John R. & Cragg, Dan. A Dictionary of Soldier Talk. 480p. 1983. 24.95 (ISBN 0-686-83680-4, ScribT). Scribner.

ENGLISH LANGUAGE–SLANG–DICTIONARIES

Spears, Richard A. Slang & Euphemism: Abridged Edition. 1982. pap. 4.50 (ISBN 0-451-11889-8, AE1889, Sig). NAL.

ENGLISH LANGUAGE–SOCIAL ASPECTS

Goldberg, Adele & Robson, David. Smalltalk-Eighty: The Language & its Implementation. (Illus.). 544p. Date not set. text ed. price not set (ISBN 0-201-11371-6). A-W.

ENGLISH LANGUAGE–SPELLERS

see Spellers

ENGLISH LANGUAGE–SPELLING

see English Language–Orthography and Spelling

ENGLISH LANGUAGE–SPOKEN ENGLISH

Coe, Marguerite. Basic Skills Parts of Speech Workbook. (Basic Skills Workbooks). 32p. (gr. 5-9). 1983. 0.99 (ISBN 0-8209-0547-X, EW-2). ESP.

Lass, Norman J., ed. Speech & Language: Advances in Basic Research & Practice. (Serial Publication: Vol. 9). Date not set. price not set (ISBN 0-12-608609-5). Acad Pr.

Tannen, Deborah. Conversational Style. Wallat, Cynthia & Green, Judith, eds. (Language & Learning for Human Service Professions Ser.). 196p. 1983. text ed. 19.95 (ISBN 0-89391-188-7); pap. text ed. 11.50 (ISBN 0-89391-200-X). Ablex Pub.

ENGLISH LANGUAGE–STUDY AND TEACHING

Bellafiore, Joseph. Essentials of English. 3rd ed. (Orig.). (gr. 9-12). 1983. pap. text ed. write for info. (ISBN 0-87720-448-9). AMSCO Sch.

Cole, Jack & Cole, Martha. Language Lessons for the Special Education Classroom. 200p. 1983. price not set (ISBN 0-89443-932-4). Aspen Systems.

Dubin, F. & Olshtain, E. Facilitating Language Learning: A Guidebook for the ESL-EFL Teacher. 1977. pap. 5.50 (ISBN 0-07-017877-1). McGraw.

ELS International. New Ways to English, 3 bks. 1974. pap. text ed. 4.75 ea.; Student Text I. pap. text ed. Avail. (ISBN 0-89318-001-7); Student Text II. pap. text ed. Avail (ISBN 0-89318-002-5); Student Text III. pap. text ed. avail (ISBN 0-89318-003-3); 5.50 (ISBN 0-89318-000-9); Cassettes 1 60.00 (ISBN 0-89318-004-1); Cassettes 2 60.00 (ISBN 0-89318-005-X); Cassettes 3 60.00 (ISBN 0-89318-006-8). ELS Intl.

English Nine Hundred Series, Bk. 1. 1964. pap. 3.25 (ISBN 0-02-971140-1); wkbk. 2.00 (ISBN 0-02-971210-6). Macmillan.

English Nine Hundred Series, Bk. 2. 1964. pap. 3.25 (ISBN 0-02-971150-9); wkbk. 2.00 (ISBN 0-02-971220-3). Macmillan.

English Nine Hundred Series, Bk. 3. 1964. pap. 3.25 (ISBN 0-02-971160-6); wkbk. 2.00 (ISBN 0-02-971230-0). Macmillan.

English Nine Hundred Series, Bk. 4. 1964. pap. 3.25 (ISBN 0-02-971170-3); wkbk. 2.25 (ISBN 0-02-971240-8). Macmillan.

English Nine Hundred Series, Bk. 6. 1964. pap. 3.25 (ISBN 0-02-971190-8); wkbk. 2.25 (ISBN 0-02-971260-2). Macmillan.

Karshen, S., ed. The Natural Approach: Language Acquisition in the Classroom. Terrell, T. (Language Teaching Methodology Ser.). (Illus.). 160p. 1982. 11.95 (ISBN 0-08-028651-8). Pergamon.

Keltner, Autumn & Howard, Leann. Basic English for Adult Competency: Teacher's Edition. 112p. 1983. pap. text ed. 10.95 (ISBN 0-13-060426-7). P-H.

Mangrum, Charles T. Learning to Study: Study Skills-Strategies Book F. (Learning to Study Ser.). 1983. pap. text ed. 3.95 (ISBN 0-89061-287-0); tchr's ed 5.25 (ISBN 0-89061-293-5). Jamestown Pubs.

--Learning to Study: Study Skills-Study Strategies Book B-C. (Learning to Study Ser.). 80p. 1983. pap. text ed. 3.95 (ISBN 0-89061-284-6); tchr's ed 5.25 (ISBN 0-89061-290-0). Jamestown Pubs.

--Learning to Study: Study Skills-Study Strategies Book D. (Learning to Study Ser.). 80p. 1983. pap. text ed. 3.95 (ISBN 0-89061-285-4); tchr's ed 5.25 (ISBN 0-89061-291-9). Jamestown Pubs.

--Learning to Study: Study Skills-Study Strategies Book E. (Learning to Study Ser.). 96p. 1983. pap. text ed. 3.95 (ISBN 0-89061-286-2); tchr's ed 5.25 (ISBN 0-89061-292-7). Jamestown Pubs.

--Learning to Study: Study Skills-Study Strategies Book G. (Learning to Study Ser.). 96p. 1983. pap. text ed. 3.95 (ISBN 0-89061-288-9); tchr's ed 5.25 (ISBN 0-89061-294-3). Jamestown Pubs.

--Learning to Study: Study Skills-Study Strategies Book H. (Learning to Study Ser.). 96p. 1983. pap. text ed. 3.95 (ISBN 0-89061-289-7); tchr's ed 5.25 (ISBN 0-89061-295-1). Jamestown Pubs.

Martin, Nancy, ed. Writing Across the Curriculum Pamphlets. 160p. (Orig.). 1983. pap. text ed. 8.00x (ISBN 0-86709-101-0). Boynton Cook Pubs.

Murray, Donald M. Learning By Teaching: Selected Articles on Writing & Teaching. LC 82-20558. 192p. 1982. pap. text ed. 8.25x (ISBN 0-86709-025-1). Boynton Cook Pubs.

National Council of Teachers of English. English for Tomorrow: Student's Edition, 3 Bks. 3rd ed. 1983. Bk. 1. 4.38 ea. (ISBN 0-07-046581-9). Bk. 2 (ISBN 0-07-046582-7). Bk. 3 (ISBN 0-07-046583-5). McGraw.

Thomas, James L., ed. Cartoons & Comics in the Classroom: A Reference for Teachers & Librarians. LC 82-17957. 182p. 1983. lib. bdg. 18.50 (ISBN 0-87287-357-9). Libs Unl.

Turbill, Jan, ed. No Better Way to Teach Writing. 96p. (Orig.). 1982. pap. text ed. 6.00x (ISBN 0-909955-39-5, 00568). Heinemann Ed.

Yunus, Noor A. Preparing & Using Aids for English Language Teaching. (Illus.). 120p. (Orig.). 1981. pap. text ed. 7.95 (ISBN 0-19-581809-1). Oxford U Pr.

ENGLISH LANGUAGE–STUDY AND TEACHING–AUDIO-VISUAL AIDS

Shaw, Marie-Jose. Combining Forms: Grade 5. (English Sound Filmstrip Kits Ser.). (gr. 5). 1980. tchrs ed. 24.00 (ISBN 0-8209-0512-7, FCW5E-19). ESP.

--Combining Forms: Grade 6. (English Sound Filmstrip Kits Ser.). (gr. 6). 1980. tchrs ed. 24.00 (ISBN 0-8209-0532-1, FCW6E-19). ESP.

--Commands. (English Sound Filmstrip Kits Ser.). (gr. 3). 1979. tchrs ed. 24.00 (ISBN 0-8209-0466-X, FCW3E-13). ESP.

--Compounding Sentence Parts. (English Sound Filmstrip Kits Ser.). (gr. 5). 1980. tchrs ed. 24.00 (ISBN 0-8209-0508-9, FCW5E-15). ESP.

--Conjunctions & Interjections. (English Sound Filmstrip Kits Ser.). (gr. 6). 1980. tchrs ed. 24.00 (ISBN 0-8209-0520-8, FCW6E-7). ESP.

--Conjunctions & Prepositions. (English Sound Filmstrip Kits Ser.). (gr. 5). 1980. tchrs ed. 24.00 (ISBN 0-8209-0501-1, FCW5E-8). ESP.

--Direct & Indirect Objects. (English Sound Filmstrip Kits Ser.). (gr. 5). 1980. tchrs ed. 24.00 (ISBN 0-8209-0505-4, FCW5E-12). ESP.

--Direct Objects. (English Sound Filmstrips Kits Ser.). (gr. 4). 1979. tchrs ed. 24.00 (ISBN 0-8209-0483-X, FCW4E-10). ESP.

--Four Kinds of Sentences: Grade 4. (English Sound Filmstrip Kits Ser.). (gr. 4). 1979. tchrs ed. 24.00 (ISBN 0-8209-0486-4, FCW4E-13). ESP.

--Four Kinds of Sentences: Grade 5. (English Sound Filmstrip Kits Ser.). (gr. 5). 1980. tchrs ed. 24.00 (ISBN 0-8209-0509-7, FCW5E-16). ESP.

--Four Sentence Patterns. (English Sound Filmstrip Kits Ser.). (gr. 6). 1980. tchrs ed. 24.00 (ISBN 0-8209-0528-3, FCW6E-15). ESP.

--Four Sentence Types. (English Sound Filmstrip Kits Ser.). (gr. 6). 1980. tchrs ed. 24.00 (ISBN 0-8209-0529-1, FCW6E-16). ESP.

--How to Make Comparisons. (English Sound Filmstrip Kits Ser.). (gr. 6). 1980. tchrs ed. 24.00 (ISBN 0-8209-0519-4, FCW6E-6). ESP.

--Indirect Objects. (English Sound Filmstrip Kits Ser.). (gr. 4). 1979. tchrs ed. 24.00 (ISBN 0-8209-0484-8, FCW4E-11). ESP.

--Mr. Tense. (English Sound Filmstrip Kits Ser.). 1p. (gr. 4). 1980. 24.00 (ISBN 0-8209-0480-5, FCW4E-7). ESP.

--Pronouns. (English Sound Filmstrip Kits Ser.). 1p. (gr. 6). 1980. 24.00 (ISBN 0-8209-0515-1, FCW6E-2). ESP.

ENGLISH LANGUAGE–STUDY AND TEACHING–FOREIGN STUDENTS

Allen, H. B. & Campbell, R. N. Teaching English as a Second Language: A Book of Readings. 2nd ed. 1975. pap. 6.50 (ISBN 0-07-001072-2). McGraw.

Allen, Virginia F. Techniques in Teaching Vocabulary. (Illus.). 128p. (Orig.). 1983. pap. 3.95x (ISBN 0-19-503231-4). Oxford U Pr.

Blance & Cook. Monstruo, 12 bks, Set 1. Incl. Monstruo busca un amigo (ISBN 0-8372-1163-8); Monstruo busca una Casa (ISBN 0-8372-1161-1); Monstruo conoce a la Senorita Monstruo (ISBN 0-8372-1164-6); Monstruo da una Fiesta (ISBN 0-8372-1170-0); Monstruo en la Escuela (ISBN 0-8372-1169-7); Monstruo en el Autobus; Monstruo limpia su Casa (ISBN 0-8372-1162-X); Monstruo va a la Escuela; Monstruo va al Museo (ISBN 0-8372-1166-2); Monstruo va al Zoologico (ISBN 0-8372-1171-9); Monstruo viene a la Ciudad (ISBN 0-8372-1160-3); Monstruo y la Sombrilla Magica (ISBN 0-8372-1165-4). (gr. k-4). pap. 1.74 ea.; pap. 19.50 1 of ea. title with tchr's. guide (ISBN 0-8372-1173-5); tchr's. guide 1.50 (ISBN 0-8372-0707-X); filmstrips & tapes avail. Bowmar-Noble.

Carter, Candy & Committee on Classroom Practices, eds. Non-Native & Nonstandard Dialect Students: Classroom Practices in Teaching English, 1982-1983. LC 82-14502. (Classroom Practices in Teaching English Ser.). 112p. 1982. pap. 7.00 (ISBN 0-8141-3351-7, 33517). NCTE.

Cook, V. J. & Esnol, A. English for Life Book I Francophone: Livre de l'eleve. (Pergamon Institute of English Courses Ser.). (Illus.). 151p. 1983. pap. 5.95 (ISBN 0-08-024580-3). Pergamon.

Cook, V. J., et al. English for Life Book I Francophone Teachers' Guide: Guide du Professeur. (Pergamon Institute of English Courses Ser.). 64p. 1983. pap. 2.95 (ISBN 0-08-024582-X). Pergamon.

Donaldson, Judy P. Transcultural Picture Word List: For Teaching English to Children from any of Twelve Language Backgrounds, Vol. II. LC 78-58532. 204p. (Orig.). pap. text ed. 15.95x (ISBN 0-918452-38-4). Learning Pubns.

Finocchiaro, Mary & Brumfit, Christopher. The Functional-Notional Approach: From Theory to Practice. (Illus.). 320p. (Orig.). 1983. pap. text ed. 10.95x (ISBN 0-19-502744-2). Oxford U Pr.

Huffman, Franklin E. & Proum, Im. English for Speakers of Khmer. LC 82-48905. 608p. 1983. text ed. 30.00 (ISBN 0-300-02895-4); pap. text ed. 10.95x (ISBN 0-300-03031-2). Yale U Pr.

Lane, Richard. Lane's English As a Second Language. (English As a Second Language Ser.: Bk. 2). (Illus.). 83p. 1981. pap. text ed. 4.95 (ISBN 0-686-83956-0). Lane Pr.

--Lane's English As a Second Language. (English As a Second Language Ser.: Bk. 3). (Illus.). 82p. 1981. pap. text ed. 4.95 (ISBN 0-686-83957-9). Lane Pr.

--Lane's English As a Second Language. (Language As a Second Language Ser.: Bk. 4). (Illus.). 84p. 1981. pap. text ed. 4.95 (ISBN 0-686-83959-5). Lane Pr.

--Lane's English As a Second Language. (English Language Ser.: Bk. 6). (Illus.). 105p. 1981. pap. text ed. 4.95 (ISBN 0-686-83961-7). Lane Pr.

--Lane's English Pronunciation Guide. LC 79-90622. (Illus.). 64p. 1979. pap. text ed. 4.95 (ISBN 0-686-83962-5). Lane Pr.

Raimes, Ann. Techniques in Teaching Writing. (Teaching Techniques in English as a Second or Foreign Language Ser.). (Illus.). 128p. (Orig.). 1983. pap. text ed. 3.95x (ISBN 0-19-503250-0). Oxford U Pr.

Robinett. Teaching English to Speakers of Other Languages: Substance & Technique. 1979. 8.95 (ISBN 0-07-053179-X). McGraw.

Sesma, Candido. Multilingual E.S.L. Textbook in 17 Languages. 150p. 6.95 (ISBN 0-933146-00-0). Orbis Pubns.

Smith, Wm. Flint & Medley, Frank. Noticiario: Segundo Nivel. (Noticiario Ser.). 184p. 1982. pap. text ed. 8.95 (ISBN 0-88377-219-1). Newbury Hse.

Smith, Wm. Flint & Nieman, Linda. Noticiario: Tercer Nivel. (Noticiario Ser.). 176p. 1982. pap. text ed. 8.95 (ISBN 0-88377-277-9). Newbury Hse.

Velazquez, Clara V. English As a Second Language, Vol. I. 240p. 1982. pap. text ed. 12.95 (ISBN 0-8403-2859-1). Kendall-Hunt.

Young, Lynne & Fitzgerald, Brigid. Listening & Learning: Lectures, Modules I-V. 176p. 1982. pap. text ed. 5.95. Module I. Module II. Module III (ISBN 0-88377-723-1). Module IV. Module V. tchrs manual 3.95. Newbury Hse.

ENGLISH LANGUAGE–STUDY AND TEACHING (ELEMENTARY)

Brooks, Bearl. Understanding Punctuation: Grades 4-7. (English Ser.). 24p. (gr. 4-7). 1979. wkbk. 5.00 (ISBN 0-8209-0186-5, E-15). ESP.

--Writing Letters & Words. (Handwriting). 24p. (gr. k-1). 1980. wkbk. 5.00 (ISBN 0-8209-0268-3, W-0). ESP.

Brooks, Bearl, et al. Jumbo Word Games Yearbook. (Jumbo Vocabulary Ser.). 96p. (gr. 3). 1980. 14.00 (ISBN 0-8209-0059-1, JWG 1). ESP.

Eberle, Bob. Chip In. (gr. 3-8). 1982. 7.95 (ISBN 0-86653-050-9, GA 416). Good Apple.

Gagnon, Constance. Help! for Preschoolers. (ps). 1982. 3.95 (ISBN 0-86653-061-4, GA 412). Good Apple.

Guadarrama, Argelia A. Steps to English Kindergarten Teacher's Manual. 128p. 1983. pap. text ed. 7.68 (ISBN 0-07-033110-3, W); kit 266.64 (ISBN 0-07-033100-6). McGraw.

Hayes, Marilyn. Words We Use. (Early Education Ser.). 24p. (gr. 1). 5.00 (ISBN 0-8209-0218-7, K-20). ESP.

Justus, Fred. Jumbo Vocabulary Development Yearbook: Grade 1. (Jumbo Vocabulary Ser.). 96p. (gr. 1). 1979. 14.00 (ISBN 0-8209-0050-8, JVDY 1). ESP.

--Jumbo Vocabulary Development Yearbook: Grade 2. (Jumbo Vocabulary Ser.). 96p. (gr. 2). 1980. 14.00 (ISBN 0-8209-0051-6, JVDY 2). ESP.

--Jumbo Vocabulary Fun Yearbook. (Jumbo Vocabulary Ser.). 96p. (gr. 3). 1980. 14.00 (ISBN 0-8209-0058-3, JVFY 3). ESP.

--Think & Write. (Early Education Ser.). 24p. (gr. 1). 1982. wkbk. 5.00 (ISBN 0-8209-0220-9, K-22). ESP.

--Visual Discrimination. (Language Arts Ser.). 24p. (gr. 1-2). 1979. wkbk. 5.00 (ISBN 0-8209-0319-1, LA-5). ESP.

--Word Picture Puzzles. (Puzzles Ser.). 24p. (gr. 1). 1980. wkbk. 5.00 (ISBN 0-8209-0296-9, PU-10). ESP.

--Word Scan Puzzles. (Puzzles Ser.). 24p. (gr. 3). 1980. wkbk. 5.00 (ISBN 0-8209-0297-7, PU-11). ESP.

--Writing Capital & Small Letters. (Early Education Ser.). 24p. (gr. 1). 1981. wkbk. 5.00 (ISBN 0-8209-0223-3, K-25). ESP.

McMaster, Dale. Vocabulary Development. (Language Arts Ser.). 24p. (gr. 6-9). 1976. wkbk. 5.00 (ISBN 0-8209-0312-4, VD-4). ESP.

McMasters, Dale. Vocabulary Study. (Language Arts Ser.). 24p. (gr. 5-7). 1976. wkbk. 5.00 (ISBN 0-8209-0311-6, VD-3). ESP.

Moberg, Goran. Writing in Groups: Techniques for Good Writing Without Drills. (Illus.). 210p. 1983. pap. text ed. 12.95 (ISBN 0-911683-00-3). Writing Con.

Nelson, Keith E., ed. Children's Language, Vol. 3. (Ongoing Ser.). 522p. 1982. text ed. 39.95 (ISBN 0-89859-264-X). L Erlbaum Assocs.

Shaw, Marie. Spelling Tests: Grade 3. Incl. Grade 4. wkbk. 5.00 (ISBN 0-8209-0169-5, ST-4); Grade 5. wkbk. 5.00 (ISBN 0-8209-0170-9, ST-5); Grade 6. wkbk. 5.00 (ISBN 0-8209-0171-7, ST-6). (Spelling Ser.). 24p. 1979. wkbk. 5.00 (ISBN 0-8209-0168-7, ST-3). ESP.

Shaw, Marie-Jose. Basic Skills English Workbook: Grade 2. (Basic Skills Workbooks). 32p. 1982. tchrs' ed. 0.99 (ISBN 0-8209-0351-5, EW-C). ESP.

--Basic Skills English Workbook: Grade 3. (Basic Skills Worbooks). wkbk. 0.99 (ISBN 0-8209-0352-3, EW-D). ESP.

--Basic Skills English Workbook: Grade 4. (Basic Skills Workbooks). 32p. 1982. wkbk. 0.99 (ISBN 0-686-38394-X). ESP.

--Basic Skills English Workbook: Grade 5. (Basic Skills Workbooks). 32p. 1982. wkbk. 0.99 (ISBN 0-8209-0354-X, EW-F). ESP.

--Basic Skills English Workbook: Grade 6. (Basic Skills Workbook). 32p. 1982. wkbk. 0.99 (ISBN 0-8209-0355-8, EW-G). ESP.

--Basic Skills English Workbook: Grade 7. (Basic Skills Workbooks). 32p. 1982. wkbk. 0.99 (ISBN 0-8209-0356-6, EW-H). ESP.

--Basic Skills English Workbook: Grade 8. (Basic Skills Workbooks). 32p. 1982. wkbk. 0.99 (ISBN 0-8209-0357-4, EW-I). ESP.

--Combining Forms: Grade 5. (English Sound Filmstrip Kits Ser.). (gr. 5). 1980. tchrs ed. 24.00 (ISBN 0-8209-0512-7, FCW5E-19). ESP.

--Combining Forms: Grade 6. (English Sound Filmstrip Kits Ser.). (gr. 6). 1980. tchrs ed. 24.00 (ISBN 0-8209-0532-1, FCW6E-19). ESP.

--Did-Done, Ran-Run, & Saw-Seen. (English Sound Filmstrip Kits Ser.). (gr. 3). 1980. tchrs ed. 24.00 (ISBN 0-8209-0471-6, FCW3E-18). ESP.

--Four Kinds of Sentences: Grade 4. (English Sound Filmstrip Kits Ser.). (gr. 4). 1979. tchrs ed. 24.00 (ISBN 0-8209-0486-4, FCW4E-13). ESP.

--Four Kinds of Sentences: Grade 5. (English Sound Filmstrip Kits Ser.). (gr. 5). 1980. tchrs ed. 24.00 (ISBN 0-8209-0509-7, FCW5E-16). ESP.

--Four Sentence Patterns. (English Sound Filmstrip Kits Ser.). (gr. 6). 1980. tchrs ed. 24.00 (ISBN 0-8209-0528-3, FCW6E-15). ESP.

--Four Sentence Types. (English Sound Filmstrip Kits Ser.). (gr. 6). 1980. tchrs ed. 24.00 (ISBN 0-8209-0529-1, FCW6E-16). ESP.

--How to Make Comparisons. (English Sound Filmstrip Kits Ser.). (gr. 6). 1980. tchrs ed. 24.00 (ISBN 0-8209-0519-4, FCW6E-6). ESP.

--Indirect Objects. (English Sound Filmstrip Kits Ser.). (gr. 4). 1979. tchrs ed. 24.00 (ISBN 0-8209-0484-8, FCW4E-11). ESP.

--Jumbo English Yearbook: Grade 2. (Jumbo English Ser.). 96p. (gr. 2). 1980. wkbk. 14.00 (ISBN 0-8209-0000-1, JEY-0). ESP.

--Jumbo English Yearbook: Grade 3. (Jumbo English Ser.). 96p. (gr. 3). 1977. wkbk. 14.00 (ISBN 0-8209-0001-X, JEY-1). ESP.

--Jumbo English Yearbook: Grade 4. (Jumbo English Ser.). (gr. 4). 1977. wkbk. 14.00 (ISBN 0-8209-0002-8, JEY-2). ESP.

--Jumbo English Yearbook: Grade 5. (Jumbo English Ser.). (gr. 5). 1977. wkbk. 14.00 (ISBN 0-8209-0003-6, JEY-3). ESP.

--Jumbo English Yearbook: Grade 6. (Jumbo English Ser.). (gr. 6). 1977. wkbk. 14.00 (ISBN 0-8209-0004-4, JEY-4). ESP.

--Jumbo English Yearbook: Grade 7. (Jumbo English Ser.). (gr. 7). 1982. wkbk. 14.00 (ISBN 0-8209-0005-2, JEY-5). ESP.

--Jumbo English Yearbook: Grade 8. (Jumbo English Ser.). (gr. 8). 1979. wkbk. 14.00 (ISBN 0-8209-0006-0, JEY-6). ESP.

--Jumbo Spelling Yearbook: Grade 3. (Jumbo Spelling Ser.). 96p. (gr. 3). 1979. 14.00 (ISBN 0-8209-0020-6, JSPY 3). ESP.

--Jumbo Spelling Yearbook: Grade 4. (Jumbo Spelling Ser.). 96p. (gr. 4). 1979. 14.00 (ISBN 0-8209-0021-4, JSPY 4). ESP.

--Jumbo Spelling Yearbook: Grade 5. (Jumbo Spelling Ser.). 96p. (gr. 5). 1980. 14.00 (ISBN 0-686-38407-5, JSPY 5). ESP.

--Jumbo Spelling Yearbook: Grade 6. (Jumbo Spelling Ser.). 96p. (gr. 6). 1980. 14.00 (ISBN 0-8209-0023-0, JSPY 6). ESP.

--Jumbo Vocabulary Development Yearbook: Grade 3. (Jumbo Vocabulary Ser.). 96p. (gr. 3). 1980. 14.00 (ISBN 0-8209-0052-4, JVDY 3). ESP.

--Jumbo Vocabulary Development Yearbook: Grade 4. (Jumbo Vocabulary Ser.). 96p. (gr. 4). 1980. 14.00 (ISBN 0-8209-0053-2, JVDY 4). ESP.

--Jumbo Vocabulary Development Yearbook: Grade 5. (Jumbo Vocabulary Ser.). 96p. (gr. 5). 1981. 14.00 (ISBN 0-8209-0054-0, JVDY 5). ESP.

--Mr. Tense. (English Sound Filmstrip Kits Ser.). 1p. (gr. 4). 1980. 24.00 (ISBN 0-8209-0480-5, FCW4E-7). ESP.

--Pronouns. (English Sound Filmstrip Kits Ser.). 1p. (gr. 6). 1980. 24.00 (ISBN 0-8209-0515-1, FCW6E-2). ESP.

Sheppard, Valerie & Premazon, Judith. Carnival of Language Fun. (gr. 4-8). 1982. 5.95 (ISBN 0-86653-085-1, GA 431). Good Apple.

Strohm, Sally. Word Signals. (English Ser.). 24p. (gr. 4-7). 1979. wkbk. 5.00 (ISBN 0-8209-0185-7, E-13). ESP.

Swaim, Gary D. Write Right Correctly. (Language Arts Ser.). 24p. (gr. 4-9). 1977. wkbk. 5.00 (ISBN 0-8209-0315-9, LA-1). ESP.

Vaughn, Jim. Jumbo Vocabulary Development Yearbook: Grade 7. (Jumbo Vocabulary Ser.). 96p. (gr. 7-9). 1981. 14.00 (ISBN 0-8209-0056-7, JVDY J). ESP.

ENGLISH LANGUAGE–STUDY AND TEACHING (HIGHER)

College English Placement Test. write for info. (RivEd). HM.

ENGLISH LANGUAGE–STUDY AND TEACHING (SECONDARY)

McDonald, Bruce & Orsinsi, Leslie. Basic Language Skills Through Film: An Instructional Program for Secondary Students. 300p. 1983. lib. bdg. 22.50 (ISBN 0-87287-368-4). Libs Unl.

Shaw, Marie-Jose. Basic Skills English Workbook: Grade 10. (Basic Skills Workbooks). 32p. 1982. wkbk. 0.99 (ISBN 0-8209-0359-0, EW-K). ESP.

--Basic Skills English Workbook: Grade 11. (Basic Skills Workbooks). 32p. 1982. wkbk. 0.99 (EW-L). ESP.

--Basic Skills English Workbook: Grade 12. (Basic Skills Workbooks). 32p. 1982. wkbk. 0.99 (ISBN 0-8209-0361-2, EW-M). ESP.

--Basic Skills English Workbook: Grade 9. (Basic Skills Workbooks). 32p. 1982. wkbk. 0.99 (ISBN 0-8209-0358-2, EW-J). ESP.

--Jumbo English Yearbook: Grade 11. (Jumbo English Ser.). (gr. 11). 1982. wkbk. 14.00 (ISBN 0-8209-0009-5, JEY-9). ESP.

--Jumbo English Yearbook: Grade 12. (Jumbo English Ser.). (gr. 12). 1982. wkbk. 14.00 (ISBN 0-8209-0010-9, JEY-10). ESP.

--Jumbo English Yearbook: Grade 9. (Jumbo English Ser.). (gr. 9). 1979. wkbk. 14.00 (ISBN 0-8209-0007-9, JEY-7). ESP.

Vaughn, Jim. Jumbo Vocabulary Development Yearbook: Grade 10. (Jumbo Vocabulary Ser.). 96p. (gr. 10-12). 1981. 14.00 (ISBN 0-8209-0057-5, JVDY S). ESP.

ENGLISH LANGUAGE–STYLE

Boyle, Joe, intro. by. The Federal Way with Words. 1982. 15.00 (ISBN 0-9609194-0-6). Twain Pub.

Cleary, J. B. & Lacombe, J. M. English Style Skill Builders: A Self-Improvement Program for Transcribers & Typists. 1980. text ed. 9.96 (ISBN 0-07-011305-X); tchr's manual & key 7.55 (ISBN 0-07-011306-8). McGraw.

Howell, John B. Style Manuals of the English Speaking World: A Guide. 1983. price not set (ISBN 0-89774-089-0). Oryx Pr.

ENGLISH LANGUAGE–SYNONYMS AND ANTONYMS

Devlin. A Dictionary of Synonyms & Antonyms. 384p. 1982. pap. 2.95 (ISBN 0-446-31028-X). Warner Bks.

Hillman, Priscilla. The Merry Mouse Book of Opposites. LC 82-45292. (Illus.). 14p. (gr. k-3). 1983. 3.95 (ISBN 0-385-17918-9). Doubleday.

McMillan, Bruce. Here a Chick, There a Chick. LC 82-20348. (Illus.). 28p. (ps-1). 1983. 10.50 (ISBN 0-688-02000-3); PLB 10.08 (ISBN 0-688-02001-1). Lothrop.

ENGLISH LANGUAGE–SYNTAX

Gibson, Ralph. Syntax. LC 82-83708. (Illus.). 80p. 1983. 24.95 (ISBN 0-912810-39-4). Lustrum Pr.

Klein-Andreu, Flora, ed. Discourse Perspectives on Syntax. Date not set. price not set (ISBN 0-12-413720-2). Acad Pr.

ENGLISH LANGUAGE–TERMS AND PHRASES

see also English Language–Slang

Armstrong, Virginia W. L. Guest of China: English-Chinese Phrases. (Illus.). 120p. 1982. pap. 10.00x (ISBN 2-88089-000-4). A Robinson.

Evans, Ivor H., ed. Brewer's Dictionary of Phrase & Fable. 1248p. 1982. 50.00x (ISBN 0-304-30706-8, Pub. by Cassell England). State Mutual Bk.

Terban, Marvin. In a Pickle & other Funny Idioms. (Illus.). 64p. (gr. 1-4). 1983. 11.50 (ISBN 0-89919-153-3, Clarion); pap. 3.95 (ISBN 0-89919-164-9). HM.

ENGLISH LANGUAGE–TEXT-BOOKS FOR FOREIGNERS

Babin, Edith H. & Cordes, Carole V. TOEFL (Test of English as a Foreign Language) 3rd ed. 288p. 1983. pap. 7.95 (ISBN 0-668-05446-8); cassette 7.95 (ISBN 0-668-05743-2). Arco.

Black, John W. American Speech for Foreign Students. 2nd ed. (Illus.). 408p. 1983. spiral 28.75x (ISBN 0-398-03999-2). C C Thomas.

Bull, Richard H. & Ide, Sachiko. English Made Polite. 2nd ed. (Illus.). 264p. (Orig.). 1981. pap. text ed. 6.50x (ISBN 0-19-581710-9). Oxford U Pr.

Crowther, Jonathan. Intermediate Crosswords, for Learners of English as a Foreign Language. 46p. 1980. pap. 3.25x (ISBN 0-19-581751-6). Oxford U Pr.

Dunlop, I. & Schrand, H. Communication for Business: Materials for Reading Comprehension & Discussion. (Materials for Language Practice Ser.). (Illus.). 110p. 1982. pap. 4.95 (ISBN 0-08-029438-3). Pergamon.

Graham, Carolyn. The Electric Elephant & Other Stories. (Illus.). 128p. (Orig.). 1982. pap. text ed. 4.95x (ISBN 0-19-503229-2). Oxford U Pr.

Gregg, Joan Y. & Russel, Joan. Past, Present, & Future: A Reading-Writing Text. 384p. 1982. pap. text ed. 12.95x (ISBN 0-534-01218-3). Wadsworth Pub.

Huffman, Franklin E. & Proum, Im. English for Speakers of Khmer. LC 82-48905. 608p. 1983. text ed. 30.00 (ISBN 0-300-02895-4); pap. text ed. 10.95x (ISBN 0-300-03031-2). Yale U Pr.

Keltner, Autumn & Howard, Leann. Basic English for Adult Competency. 112p. 1983. pap. text ed. 4.95 (ISBN 0-13-060418-6). P-H.

Sesma, Candido. Multilingual E.S.L. Textbook in 17 Languages. 150p. 6.95 (ISBN 0-933146-00-0). Orbis Pubns.

Smith, Wm. Flint & Medley, Frank. Noticiario: Segundo Nivel. (Noticiario Ser.). 184p. 1982. pap. text ed. 8.95 (ISBN 0-88377-219-1). Newbury Hse.

Smith, Wm. Flint & Nieman, Linda. Noticiario: Tercer Nivel. (Noticiario Ser.). 176p. 1982. pap. text ed. 8.95 (ISBN 0-88377-277-9). Newbury Hse.

Stricherz, Gregory. English Made Casual. 210p. 1980. pap. text ed. 6.50x (ISBN 0-19-581880-6). Oxford U Pr.

Young, Lynne & Fitzgerald, Brigid. Listening & Learning: Lectures, Modules I-V. 176p. 1982. pap. text ed. 5.95. Module I. Module II. Module III (ISBN 0-88377-723-1). Module IV. Module V. tchrs manual 3.95. Newbury Hse.

ENGLISH LANGUAGE–USAGE

Morrison, Leger R. & Birt, Robert F. Guide to Confused Words. xxvi, 272p. (Orig.). 1972. pap. 6.55 (ISBN 0-686-38127-0). Morrison Pub Co.

Robinson, Pauline. Using English: International Edition. (Illus.). 224p. 1983. pap. text ed. 10.00x (ISBN 0-631-12953-7, Pub. by Basil Blackwell England). Biblio Dist.

--Using English Today: Teacher's Book. (Illus.). 224p. 1983. pap. text ed. 7.95x (ISBN 0-631-12585-X, Pub. by Basil Blackwell). Biblio Dist.

Swan, Michael. Practical English Usage. 560p. (Orig.). 1980. pap. 9.95x (ISBN 0-19-431185-6). Oxford U Pr.

Vizetelly, Frank H. How to Use English. 658p. 1982. Repr. of 1933 ed. lib. bdg. 45.00 (ISBN 0-8495-5532-9). Arden Lib.

ENGLISH LANGUAGE–VOCABULARIES

see English Language–Glossaries, Vocabularies, etc.

ENGLISH LANGUAGE–VOCABULARY

see Vocabulary

ENGLISH LANGUAGE–VOWELS

Phillips, Jean A. For Better Reading: Lots You Need to Know about Short Vowels. (Illus.). 56p. 1981. pap. write for info. (ISBN 0-911305-00-9). J Phillips Pub Co.

--For Better Reading: Lots You Need to Know about Vowels. (Illus.). 58p. 1982. pap. 3.88 (ISBN 0-911305-01-7). J Phillips Pub Co.

ENGLISH LANGUAGE–WORDS–HISTORY

Haddad, Raymond. English Words of Arabic Origin. (Illus.). 140p. 500.00 (ISBN 0-9608594-0-3); abridged. 75.00. Genie Ent.

Reader's Digest Editors. Use the Right Word. LC 72-8783. 726p. 1968. 14.98 (ISBN 0-89577-025-3). RD Assn.

Weekley, Ernest. Something About Words. 233p. 1982. Repr. of 1935 ed. lib. bdg. 35.00 (ISBN 0-89760-942-5). Telegraph Bks.

ENGLISH LANGUAGE IN FOREIGN COUNTRIES

Trudgill, Peter & Hannah, Jean. International English: A Guide to the Varieties of Standard English. 144p. 1982. pap. text ed. 9.95 (ISBN 0-7131-6362-3). E Arnold.

ENGLISH LETTERS

Daudet, A. Bi-Linguals French-English Lettres De Mon Moulin, A. Daudet. Mansion, J. E., tr. from Fr. (Harrap's Bilingual Ser.). 62p. 1955. 5.00 (ISBN 0-911268-42-1). Rogers Bk.

Douglas, Alfred. Oscar Wilde & Myself. 306p. 1983. Repr. of 1914 ed. lib. bdg. 45.00 (ISBN 0-686-38783-X). Century Bookbindery.

Gibson, Donald, ed. A Parson in the Vale of White Horse: George Woodward's Letters from East Hendred, 1753-61. 192p. 1982. pap. text ed. 8.25x (ISBN 0-86299-025-4, Pub. by Sutton England). Humanities.

Smith, G. C., ed. The Boole-DeMorgan Correspondence, 1842-1864. (Logic Guides Ser.). (Illus.). 162p. 1982. 44.00x (ISBN 0-19-853183-4). Oxford U Pr.

ENGLISH LETTERS–HISTORY AND CRITICISM

Abbott, John L. John Hawkesworth, Eighteenth-Century Man of Letters. 316p. 1982. text ed. 22.50 (ISBN 0-299-08610-0). U of Wis Pr.

ENGLISH LITERATURE (COLLECTIONS)

see also College Readers

Barnes, William. A Prose Anthology. Hearl, Trevor, ed. 384p. 1983. text ed. 21.00x (ISBN 0-85635-407-4, Pub. by Carcanet Pr England). Humanities.

Ford, Boris, ed. From Dickens to Hardy. 1983. pap. 5.95 (ISBN 0-14-022269-3, Pelican). Penguin.

ENGLISH LITERATURE (COLLECTIONS)–MIDDLE ENGLISH (1100-1500)

Leslie, R. F., ed. The Wanderer. (Old & Middle English Text Ser.). 1966. pap. 5.00 (ISBN 0-7190-0120-X). Manchester.

Swanton, M. J., ed. The Dream of the Rood. (Old & Middle English Text Ser.). 1970. pap. 6.00 (ISBN 0-7190-0440-3). Manchester.

ENGLISH LITERATURE (COLLECTIONS)–EARLY MODERN, 1500-1700

Axton, Marie. Three Tudor Classical Interludes: Thersites, Jacke Jugeler & Horestes. (Tudor Interludes Ser.: No. III). 246p. 1982. text ed. 47.50x (ISBN 0-8476-7193-3). Rowman.

ENGLISH LITERATURE (COLLECTIONS)–20TH CENTURY

Blackburn, Alex, ed. Writers Forum 8, 1982. LC 78-649046. pap. 8.95 (ISBN 0-9602992-2-X). U CO at Colorado Springs.

Happel, Edward, ed. Fountain of Youth. (The Best of U.S. College Magazines Ser.). (Illus.). 100p. (Orig.). 1982. pap. 4.95 (ISBN 0-910127-00-X). Student Ed Assoc.

ENGLISH LITERATURE (SELECTIONS: EXTRACTS, ETC.)

Brittain, Robert, ed. The Booklover's Almanac. 432p. 1982. 39.00x (ISBN 0-284-79527-5, Pub. by C Skilton Scotland). State Mutual Bk.

ENGLISH LITERATURE–BIBLIOGRAPHY–CATALOGS

Gatton, John S., et al. The W. Hugh Peal Collection at the University of Kentucky. (The Kentucky Review Ser.: Vol. IV, No. 1). 237p. 1982. pap. text ed. 3.50 (ISBN 0-910123-00-4). U KY Lib Assocs.

ENGLISH LITERATURE–EXAMINATIONS, QUESTIONS, ETC.

Williams, J. David. Questions That Count: British Literature to 1750. LC 82-15893. 98p. (Orig.). 1983. lib. bdg. 18.50 (ISBN 0-8191-2742-6); pap. text ed. 4.25 (ISBN 0-8191-2743-4). U Pr of Amer.

ENGLISH LITERATURE–HISTORY AND CRITICISM

Buchan, John, ed. A History of English Literature: From Chaucer to the end of the 19th Century. 675p. 1982. Repr. of 1923 ed. lib. bdg. 45.00 (ISBN 0-686-81843-1). Darby Bks.

Diekstra, Frans. Early & Middle English Literature. (Dutch Quarterly Review of Anglo-American Letters: Vol. 11, 1981/4). 80p. 1981. pap. text ed. 9.25x (ISBN 90-6203-933-2, Pub. by Rodopi England). Humanities.

Essays & Reviews: (Macaulay, James Wordsworth, Byron. 2 Vols. 421p. 1982. Repr. of 1885 ed. Set. lib. bdg. 100.00 (ISBN 0-8495-5842-5). Arden Lib.

Frietzsche, Arthur H. Disraeli's Religion: The Treatment of Religion in Disraeli's Novels. 62p. 1982. Repr. of 1961 ed. lib. bdg. 10.00 (ISBN 0-8495-1718-4). Arden Lib.

--The Monstrous Clever Young Man: The Novelist Disraeli & His Heroes. 60p. 1982. Repr. of 1959 ed. lib. bdg. 10.00 (ISBN 0-8495-1735-4). Arden Lib.

Halleck, Reuben P. Halleck's New English Literature. 647p. 1982. Repr. of 1913 ed. lib. bdg. 30.00 (ISBN 0-8495-2434-2). Arden Lib.

Moody, William V. & Lovett, Robert M. A First View of English Literature. 386p. 1982. Repr. of 1911 ed. lib. bdg. 40.00 (ISBN 0-89760-582-9). Telegraph Bks.

Morley, Henry. English Writers: An Attempt Towards a History of English Literature. 2 Vols. 1982. Repr. of 1887 ed. lib. bdg. 450.00 (ISBN 0-8495-3942-0, SET). Arden Lib.

Oliphant, Lancelot. Great Comic Scenes from English Literature. 259p. 1982. Repr. of 1930 ed. lib. bdg. 40.00 (ISBN 0-89760-632-9). Telegraph Bks.

Powell, Lawrence C. Southwest Classics: The Creative Literature of the Arid Lands--Essays on the Books & Their Writers. 384p. 1982. pap. 9.95 (ISBN 0-8165-0795-3). U of Ariz Pr.

Scherer, Edmond. Essays on English Literature. Saintsbury, George, tr. 272p. 1982. Repr. of 1891 ed. lib. bdg. 4.00 (ISBN 0-8495-4966-3). Arden Lib.

Spitzer, Leo. Essays on English & American Literature. Hatcher, Anna, ed. 307p. 1983. Repr. of 1968 ed. 15.00 (ISBN 0-87752-227-8). Gordian.

ENGLISH LITERATURE–HISTORY AND CRITICISM–ADDRESSES, ESSAYS AND LECTURES

Brewer, J. S. & Wace, Henry. English Studies, or Essays in English History & Literature. 448p. 1982. Repr. of 1881 ed. lib. bdg. 75.00 (ISBN 0-8495-0611-5). Arden Lib.

Bushrui, S., ed. Essays & Studies,1982. (Essays & Studies: No. 35). 123p. 1982. text ed. 18.00x (ISBN 0-391-02622-4, 20098). Humanities.

Kappeler, Susanne & Bryson, Norman, eds. Teaching the Text. 200p. (Orig.). 1983. pap. price not set (ISBN 0-7100-9412-4). Routledge & Kegan.

ENGLISH LITERATURE–HISTORY AND CRITICISM–MIDDLE ENGLISH (1100-1500)

Beranek, Bernard. Annuale Mediaevele, Vol. 21. 138p. 1982. 13.50x (ISBN 0-686-82238-2). Humanities.

Diekstra, Frans. Early & Middle English Literature. (Dutch Quarterly Review of Anglo-American Letters: Vol. 11, 1981/4). 80p. 1981. pap. text ed. 9.25x (ISBN 90-6203-933-2, Pub. by Rodopi England). Humanities.

DiMarco, Vincent. Piers Plowman: A Reference Guide. 1982. lib. bdg. 45.00 (ISBN 0-8161-8309-0, Hall Reference). G K Hall.

Frantzen, Allen J. The Literature of Penance in Anglo-Saxon England. 395p. Date not set. 27.50x (ISBN 0-8135-0955-6). Rutgers U Pr.

Grabes, Herbert. The Mutable Glass: Mirror Imagery in Titles & Texts of the Middle Ages & the English Renaissance. Collier, Gordon, tr. LC 82-4263. (Illus.). 532p. 79.00 (ISBN 0-521-22203-6). Cambridge U Pr.

Knapp, Peggy A., ed. Assays: Critical Approaches to Medieval & Renaissance Texts, Vol. II. 160p. 1983. 14.95x (ISBN 0-8229-3468-X). U of Pittsburgh Pr.

ENGLISH LITERATURE–HISTORY AND CRITICISM–EARLY MODERN, 1500-1700

Derrick, Thomas, et al, eds. Thomas Wilson's Arte Rhetorique: An Old Spelling Critical Edition. LC 81-47031. (Garland English Texts Ser.). 804p. 1982. lib. bdg. 75.00 (ISBN 0-8240-9408-5). Garland Pub.

Grabes, Herbert. The Mutable Glass: Mirror Imagery in Titles & Texts of the Middle Ages & the English Renaissance. Collier, Gordon, tr. LC 82-4263. (Illus.). 532p. 79.00 (ISBN 0-521-22203-6). Cambridge U Pr.

Hippisley, J. H. Chapters on Early English Literature. 344p. 1982. Repr. of 1837 ed. lib. bdg. 75.00 (ISBN 0-8495-2433-4). Arden Lib.

Knapp, Peggy A., ed. Assays: Critical Approaches to Medieval & Renaissance Texts, Vol. II. 160p. 1983. 14.95x (ISBN 0-8229-3468-X). U of Pittsburgh Pr.

Roston, Murray. Sixteenth-Century English Literature. (History of Literature Ser.). (Illus.). 235p. 1983. 28.50 (ISBN 0-8052-3825-5). Schocken.

Sinfield, Alan. Literature in Protestant England 1560-1660. LC 82-18408. 168p. 1983. text ed. 23.50x (ISBN 0-389-20341-6). B&N Imports.

Thomas, Helen S. An Enterlude Called Lusty Iuuentus. Liuely Describing the Frailtie of Youth, or Nature Prone to Vyce: By Grace & Good Councell Traynable to Vertue, by R. Wever. An Old Spelling Critical Edition. LC 80-9008. (Garland English Texts Ser.). 1982. lib. bdg. 35.00 (ISBN 0-8240-9406-9). Garland Pub.

Whipple, Edwin P. The Literature of the Age of Elizabeth. 364p. 1982. Repr. of 1869 ed. lib. bdg. 50.00 (ISBN 0-8495-5841-7). Arden Lib.

ENGLISH LITERATURE–HISTORY AND CRITICISM–18TH CENTURY

Eagleton, Terry. The Rape of Clarissa: Writing, Sexuality & Class-Struggle in Richardson. 128p. 1983. 25.00x (ISBN 0-8166-1204-8); pap. 9.95 (ISBN 0-8166-1209-9). U of Minn Pr.

Keener, Frederick M. The Chain of Becoming: The Philosophical Tale, the Novel & a Neglected Realism of the Enlightenment: Swift, Montesquieu, Voltaire, Johnson & Austen. LC 82-12878. 376p. 1983. 30.00x (ISBN 0-231-04001-6); pap. 15.00 (ISBN 0-231-05573-0). Columbia U Pr.

Rivers, Isabel, ed. Books & their Readers in Eighteenth-Century England. LC 82-7317. 1982. 30.00x (ISBN 0-312-09248-2). St Martin.

Speck, W. A. Society & Literature in England 1700-1760. 220p. 1982. 40.00x (ISBN 0-7171-0977-1, Pub. by Macmillan England). State Mutual Bk.

Williams, Raymond. The English Novel from Dickens to Lawrence. 196p. 1983. pap. text ed. 7.95x (ISBN 0-391-02815-4). Humanities.

ENGLISH LITERATURE–HISTORY AND CRITICISM–19TH CENTURY

Cosslett, Tess. The Scientific Movement & Victorian Literature. LC 82-10284. 1982. 22.50x (ISBN 0-312-70298-1). St Martin.

Earls, Michael. Manuscripts & Memories: Chapters in Our Literary Tradition. 275p. 1982. Repr. of 1935 ed. lib. bdg. 45.00 (ISBN 0-686-81683-8). Century Bookbindery.

Hasan, Noorul. Thomas Hardy: The Sociological Imagination. 200p. 1982. text ed. 21.00x (ISBN 0-333-32628-8, Pub. by Macmillan England). Humanities.

Levine, Richard A. The Victorian Experience: The Novelists. LC 75-15338. 272p. 1983. pap. 10.95 (ISBN 0-8214-0747-3, 82-85165). Ohio U Pr.

Meisel, Martin. Realizations: Narrative, Pictorial, & Theatrical Arts of the Nineteenth Century. LC 82-12292. (Illus.). 416p. 1983. 45.00x (ISBN 0-691-06553-5). Princeton U Pr.

Putzell-Korah, S. The Evolving Consciousness: An Hegelian Reading of the Novels of George Eliot. (Salzburg-Romantic Reassessment Ser.: No. 29). 140p. 1982. pap. text ed. 25.00x (ISBN 0-391-02777-8, Pub. by Salzburg Austria). Humanities.

Williams, Raymond. The English Novel from Dickens to Lawrence. 196p. 1983. pap. text ed. 7.95x (ISBN 0-391-02815-4). Humanities.

ENGLISH LITERATURE–HISTORY AND CRITICISM–20TH CENTURY

see also Bloomsbury Group

Benkovitz, Miriam J., ed. A Bibliography of Ronald Firbank. 2nd ed. 122p. 1982. text ed. 42.00x (ISBN 0-19-818188-4). Oxford U Pr.

Connolly, Cyril. Enemies of Promise. 268p. 1983. cancelled 13.95 (ISBN 0-89255-077-5); pap. 6.95 (ISBN 0-89255-078-3). Persea Bks.

McCallum, Pamela. Literature & Method: Towards a Critique of I. A. Richards, T. S. Eliot & F. R. Leavis. (Literature & Society Ser.). 288p. 1982. text ed. 42.00x (ISBN 0-391-02795-6). Humanities.

Vinson, James & Kirkpatrick, D. L., eds. Twentieth-Century Romance & Gothic Writers. 898p. 1982. 75.00x (ISBN 0-8103-0226-8, Pub. by Macmillan England). Gale.

Wilson, Edmund. The Fourties: From Notebooks & Diaries of the Period. Edel, Leon, ed. & intro. by. LC 82-21028. (Illus.). 1983. 22.50 (ISBN 0-374-15762-6). FS&G.

ENGLISH LITERATURE-IRISH AUTHORS-HISTORY AND CRITICISM

Cronin, Anthony. Heritage Now: Irish Literature in the English Language. 215p. 1983. 17.95x (ISBN 0-312-36993-X). St Martin.

ENGLISH LITERATURE-STUDY AND TEACHING

Coody, Betty. Using Literature with Young Children. 3rd ed. 220p. 1983. pap. write for info. (ISBN 0-697-06068-3). Wm C Brown.

ENGLISH LITERATURE-STYLE

see English Language-Style

ENGLISH LITERATURE-TRANSLATIONS FROM FOREIGN LITERATURE

O'Donoghue, Bernard. The Courtly Love Tradition. LC 82-18180. (Literature in Context Ser.). 320p. 1983. text ed. 25.00x (ISBN 0-389-20347-5); pap. text ed. 8.95x (ISBN 0-389-20348-3). B&N Imports.

ENGLISH LITERATURE-AUSTRALIA

see Australian Literature (Collections)

ENGLISH LITERATURE-NEW ZEALAND

see New Zealand Literature (Collections)

ENGLISH MUSIC

see Music, English

ENGLISH NEWSPAPERS-HISTORY

Brendon, Piers. The Life & Death of the Press Barons. LC 82-73017. 288p. 1983. 14.95 (ISBN 0-689-11341-2). Atheneum.

ENGLISH PAINTING

see Painting, British

ENGLISH PAINTINGS

see Paintings, British

ENGLISH PHILOLOGY

Shipley, Joseph T. In Praise of English: The Growth & Use of Language. 1982. 8.95 (ISBN 0-8129-6325-3). Times Bks.

ENGLISH PHILOSOPHERS

see Philosophers-Great Britain

ENGLISH PHILOSOPHY

see Philosophy, British

ENGLISH POETRY (COLLECTIONS)

see also American Poetry (Collections); Poetry

Herbert, David, ed. Everyman's Book of Evergreen Verse. 396p. 1983. pap. text ed. 7.95x (ISBN 0-460-01246-0, Pub. by Evman England). Biblio Dist.

Hieatt, Constance B., ed. Beowolf & Other Old English Poems. (Bantam Classics Ser.). 192p. (YA) (gr. 9-12). 1982. pap. 1.95 (ISBN 0-553-21109-9). Bantam.

ENGLISH POETRY (COLLECTIONS)-EARLY MODERN, 1500-1700

Brougham, Eleanor M. Corn from Olde Fieldes: An Anthology of English Poems from the 14th to the 17th Century with Biographical Notes. 294p. 1982. Repr. of 1918 ed. lib. bdg. 40.00 (ISBN 0-89760-095-9). Telegraph Bks.

ENGLISH POETRY (COLLECTIONS)-19TH CENTURY

Roper, Derek, ed. Wordsworth & Coleridge: Lyrical Ballads 1805. 432p. 1979. 29.00x (ISBN 0-7121-0140-3, Pub. by Macdonald & Evans). State Mutual Bk.

Sharp, Amy. Victorian Poets. 207p. 1982. Repr. of 1891 ed. lib. bdg. 35.00 (ISBN 0-89987-792-3). Darby Bks.

ENGLISH POETRY (COLLECTIONS)-20TH CENTURY

Editorial Board, Grange Book Co., ed. The World's Best Poetry: Supplement One: Twentieth Century English & American Verse, 1900-1929. (The Granger Anthology Ser.: No. I). 400p. 1983. 39.50 (ISBN 0-89609-236-4). Granger Bk.

ENGLISH POETRY-EXAMINATIONS, QUESTIONS, ETC.

see English Literature-Examinations, Questions, etc.

ENGLISH POETRY-EXPLICATION

Rodway, Allan. The Craft of Criticism. LC 82-4499. 192p. 1982. 32.50 (ISBN 0-521-23320-8); pap. 9.95 (ISBN 0-521-29909-8). Cambridge U Pr.

ENGLISH POETRY-HISTORY AND CRITICISM

Bentley, Clerihew. The First Clerihews. (Illus.). 59p. 1983. 14.95 (ISBN 0-19-212980-5). Oxford U Pr.

Kent, Charles W., ed. Elene: An Old English Poem. 149p. 1982. lib. bdg. 35.00 (ISBN 0-89760-433-4). Telegraph Bks.

Sambrook, A. J. English Pastoral Poetry. (English Authors Ser.). 163p. 1983. lib. bdg. 16.95 (ISBN 0-8057-6834-3, Twayne). G K Hall.

Thomas, Donald. Robert Browning: A Life Within Life. 352p. 1983. 18.75 (ISBN 0-670-60090-3). Viking Pr.

ENGLISH POETRY-HISTORY AND CRITICISM-MIDDLE ENGLISH (1100-1500)

Edwards, A. S. Stephen Hawes. (English Authors Ser.: No. 354). 152p. 1983. lib. bdg. 18.95 (ISBN 0-8057-6840-8, Twayne). G K Hall.

Lawton, David A., ed. Middle English Alliterative Poetry & Its Literary Background. 224p. 1983. text ed. 49.50x (ISBN 0-85991-097-0, Pub. by Boydell & Brewer). Biblio Dist.

ENGLISH POETRY-HISTORY AND CRITICISM-EARLY MODERN, 1500-1700

Edwards, A. S. Stephen Hawes. (English Authors Ser.: No. 354). 152p. 1983. lib. bdg. 18.95 (ISBN 0-8057-6840-8, Twayne). G K Hall.

Guillory, John. Poetic Authority: Spenser, Milton, & Literary History. 224p. 1983. text ed. 25.00x (ISBN 0-231-05540-4); pap. 12.50x (ISBN 0-231-05541-2). Columbia U Pr.

Hollingworth, Brian, ed. Songs of the People: Lancashire Dialect Poetry of the Industrial Revolution. 176p. 1982. pap. 6.50 (ISBN 0-7190-0906-5). Manchester.

Moore, Dennis. The Politics of Spenser's Complaints & Sidney's Philsides Poems. (Salzburg - Elizabethean Studies: No. 101). 196p. 1982. pap. text ed. 25.00x (ISBN 0-391-02783-2, Pub. by Salzburg Austria). Humanities.

Nichols. The Poetry of Sir Philip Sydney. 192p. 1982. 39.00x (ISBN 0-85323-351-9, Pub. by Liverpool Univ England). State Mutual Bk.

ENGLISH POETRY-HISTORY AND CRITICISM-19TH CENTURY

Cunningham, John. The Poetics of Byron's Comedy in Don Juan. (Salzburg - Romantic Reassessment Ser.: No. 106). 242p. 1982. pap. text ed. 25.00x (ISBN 0-391-02778-6, Pub. by Salzburg Austria). Humanities.

Hogg, James, ed. Stylistic Media of Byron's Satire. (Salzburg - Romantic Reassessment Ser.: Vol. 81, No. 3). 83p. 1982. pap. text ed. 25.00x (ISBN 0-391-02804-9, Pub. by Salzburg Austria). Humanities.

Levine, Richard A., ed. The Victorian Experience: The Poets. LC 81-4020. x, 202p. 1983. pap. 10.95 (ISBN 0-8214-0748-1, 82-85173). Ohio U Pr.

Natoli, Joseph. Twentieth Century Blake Criticism: Northrop Fyre to the Present. LC 80-9021. 375p. 1982. lib. bdg. 45.00 (ISBN 0-8240-9326-7). Garland Pub.

ENGLISH POETRY-HISTORY AND CRITICISM-20TH CENTURY

Hogg, James. The Peter Russell Seminar, 1981-82. (Salzburg - Poetic Drama Ser.: No. 72). 143p. 1982. pap. text ed. 25.00x (ISBN 0-391-02776-X, Pub. by Salzburg Austria). Humanities.

Sisson, C. H. English Poetry Nineteen Hundred to Nineteen Fifty: An Assessment. 274p. 1981. Repr. of 1971 ed. text ed. 21.00x (ISBN 0-85635-393-0, 90202, Pub. by Carcanet New Pr England). Humanities.

Weatherhead, A. Kingsley. The British Dissonance: Essays on Ten Contemporary Poets. LC 82-17319. 224p. 1983. text ed. 21.00x (ISBN 0-8262-0391-4). U of Mo Pr.

ENGLISH POETRY-SCOTTISH AUTHORS

see Scottish Poetry (Collections); also subdivisions under Scottish Poetry

ENGLISH POETRY-STUDY AND TEACHING

see English Literature-Study and Teaching

ENGLISH PORCELAIN

see Porcelain

ENGLISH POTTERY

see Pottery, English

ENGLISH PROSE LITERATURE-HISTORY AND CRITICISM

Levine, Richard A., ed. The Victorian Experience: The Prose Writers. LC 81-22492. 239p. 1983. pap. 10.95 (ISBN 0-8214-0707-4, 82-84762). Ohio U Pr.

Siebenschuh, William R. Fictional Techniques & Factual Works. LC 82-8373. 200p. 1983. text ed. 18.00x (ISBN 0-8203-0636-3). U of Ga Pr.

Stevenson, Catherine B. Victorian Women Travel Writers in Africa. (English Authors Ser.). 184p. 1982. lib. bdg. 17.95 (ISBN 0-8057-6835-1, Twayne). G K Hall.

ENGLISH PROSE LITERATURE-HISTORY AND CRITICISM-EARLY MODERN, 1500-1700

Clark, Sandra. Elizabethan Pamphleteers: Popular Moralistic Pamphlets, 1580-1640. LC 81-72064. (Illus.). 320p. 1982. 30.00 (ISBN 0-8386-3173-8). Fairleigh Dickinson.

ENGLISH SCHOOL CERTIFICATE EXAMINATION

see High School Equivalency Examination

ENGLISH SCULPTURE

see Sculpture-Great Britain

ENGLISH SONGS

see Songs, English

ENGLISH WIT AND HUMOR-ART, SCIENCES, ETC.

Thompson, John O., ed. Monty Python: Complete & Utter Theory of the Grotesque. (Illus.). 58p. 1982. pap. 7.95 (ISBN 0-85170-119-1). NY Zoetrope.

ENGRAVERS

Bryans Dictionary of Painters & Engravers, 5 Vols. Date not set. 200.00 (ISBN 0-686-43124-3). Apollo.

Fielding, Mantle. Dictionary of American Painters, Sculptors & Engravers. 1974. 30.00 (ISBN 0-913274-03-8). Apollo.

Harper. Early Painters & Engravers in Canada. 1981. 75.00 (ISBN 0-686-43128-6). Apollo.

Young. Dictionary of American Artists, Sculptors, & Engravers. 1968. 60.00 (ISBN 0-686-43150-2). Apollo.

ENHARMONIC ORGAN

see Organ

ENIGMAS

see Curiosities and Wonders; History-Curiosa and Miscellany; Riddles

ENLIGHTENMENT

Manuel, Frank E. The Changing of the Gods. 180p. 1983. text ed. 14.00x (ISBN 0-87451-254-9). U Pr of New Eng.

Rama, Swami. Enlightenment Without God (Mandukya Upanishad) LC 82-83391. 144p. (Orig.). 1982. pap. 4.95 (ISBN 0-89389-084-7). Himalayan Intl Inst.

ENSEMBLES (MATHEMATICS)

see Set Theory

ENTEROPATHY

see Intestines-Diseases

ENTERPRISE (AIRCRAFT CARRIER, CVA N 65)

Ewing, Steve. U. S. S. Enterprise (CV-Six), the Most Decorated Ship of World War II: A Pictorial History. (Illus.). 132p. 1982. 7.95. Pictorial Hist.

ENTERPRISES

see Business Enterprises; Entrepreneur

ENTERTAINING

see also Amusements; Buffets (Cookery); Children's Parties; Dinners and Dining; Games; Luncheons

Casual Entertaining. pap. 5.95 (ISBN 0-696-01135-2). Meredith Corp.

Historic Huntsville Foundation. Huntsville Entertains. King, Shelbie, ed. 480p. 1983. pap. 13.95 (ISBN 0-686-43262-2). Wimmer Bks.

Scott, Blackie. It's Fun to Entertain. 200p. 1983. 8.95 (ISBN 0-931948-42-8). Peachtree Pubns.

Virgil M. Hancher Auditorium, The University of Iowa. Entertaining Arts: Menus & Recipes from Performers & Patrons. LC 82-81567. (Illus.). 258p. 1982. spiral bdg. 14.70 (ISBN 0-941016-06-4). Penfield.

ENTHUSIASM

Melton, James E. Vital Enthusiam. LC 82-81903. 232p. 1982. 12.95 (ISBN 0-9604752-1-4). Global Pubns CA.

ENTOMOLOGICAL RESEARCH

Dirsh, V. A. Morphometrical Studies on Phases of the Desert Locust (Schistocerca Gregaria Forskal) 1953. 35.00x (ISBN 0-85135-066-6, Pub. by Centre Overseas Research). State Mutual Bk.

ENTOMOLOGY

see also Entomological Research

Mittler, T. E., et al, eds. Annual Review of Entomology, Vol. 28. (Illus.). 1983. text ed. 27.00 (ISBN 0-8243-0128-5). Annual Reviews.

ENTOMOLOGY-JUVENILE LITERATURE

see Insects-Juvenile Literature

ENTOMOLOGY, ECONOMIC

see Insects, Injurious and Beneficial

ENTRANCE EXAMINATIONS

see Universities and Colleges-Examinations

ENTREPRENEUR

see also Business Enterprises; Capitalism; New Business Enterprises; Profit

Backman, Jules. Entrepreneurship & the Outlook for America. 1982. text ed. 12.95 (ISBN 0-02-922940-5). Free Pr.

Frontiers of Entrepreneurship Research, Vol. III. 1983. write for info. (ISBN 0-910897-03-4). Babson College.

Greene, Bill. Think Like a Tycoon. Date not set. pap. 5.95 (ISBN 0-449-90068-1, Columbine). Fawcett.

Guroff, Gregory & Carstensen, Fred V. Entrepreneurship in Imperial Russia & the Soviet Union. LC 82-15056. 384p. 1983. 40.00x (ISBN 0-691-05376-6); pap. 12.95 (ISBN 0-691-10141-8). Princeton U Pr.

Honeyman, Katrina. Origins of Enterprise: Business Leadership in the Industrial Revolution. LC 82-10441. 180p. 1982. 20.00x (ISBN 0-312-58848-8). St Martin.

The Practice of Entrepreneurship. 196p. 1982. pap. 11.50 (ISBN 92-2-102846-1, ILO198, ILO). Unipub.

Silver, A. David. The Entrepreneurial Life: How to Go for It & Get It. 288p. 1983. 22.95 (ISBN 0-471-87382-9). Ronald Pr.

Vesper, Karl H., ed. Frontiers of Entrepreneurship Research: 1982. 634p. 1982. pap. 25.00 (ISBN 0-910897-02-6). Babson College.

Webb, Terry & Quince, Thelma, eds. Small Business Research: The Development of Entrepreneurs. 218p. 1982. text ed. 34.00x (ISBN 0-566-00381-3). Gower Pub Ltd.

Welsh, John & White, Jerry. The Entrepreneur's Master Planning Guide: How to Launch A Successful New Business. (Illus.). 408p. 1983. 24.95 (ISBN 0-13-282814-6); pap. 11.95 (ISBN 0-13-282806-5). P-H.

Young, Dennis R. If Not for Profit, for What? A Behavioral Theory of the Nonprofit Sector Based on Entrepreneurship. Simon, John, frwd. by. LC 82-48482. 192p. 1983. 20.95x (ISBN 0-669-06154-9). Lexington Bks.

ENTROPY

Christensen, R. Belief & Behavior. Date not set. price not set (ISBN 0-938876-16-3). Entropy ltd.

--Entropy Minimax Sourcebook, Vol. VII: Data Distributions. Date not set. price not set (ISBN 0-938876-17-1). Entropy Ltd.

Collie, C. H. Kinetic Theory & Entropy. LC 81-8332. (Illus.). 416p. 1983. pap. text ed. 22.00x (ISBN 0-582-44368-7). Longman.

Starosciak, Jane. Entropy & the Speed of Light. 1982. pap. 7.50 (ISBN 0-686-38085-1). K Starosciak.

ENVIRONMENT

see Adaptation (Biology); Ecology; Human Ecology; Anthropo-Geography; Man-Influence of Environment; Man-Influence on Nature

ENVIRONMENT, HUMAN

see Human Ecology

ENVIRONMENT AND STATE

see Environmental Policy

ENVIRONMENTAL, SPACE

see Space Environment

ENVIRONMENTAL CONTROL

see Environmental Engineering; Environmental Law; Environmental Policy

ENVIRONMENTAL EDUCATION

see Conservation of Natural Resources-Study and Teaching; Ecology-Study and Teaching

ENVIRONMENTAL ENGINEERING

see also Environmental Health; Environmental Policy; Environmental Protection; Human Engineering; Lighting; Noise Control; Pollution; Sanitary Engineering

Camougis, G. Environmental Biology for Engineers: A Guide to Environmental Assessment. 1980. 24.50 (ISBN 0-07-009677-5). McGraw.

Dyer, Jon C. & Mignone, Nicholas A. Handbook of Industrial Residues. LC 82-19082. (Environment Engineering Ser.). (Illus.). 453p. 1983. 54.00 (ISBN 0-8155-0924-3). Noyes.

Environmental Engineering, Eighty One. 210p. (Orig.). 1981. pap. text ed. 37.50x (Pub. by Inst Engineering Australia). Renouf.

Environmental Enquiry: Proceedings. 103p. (Orig.). 1978. pap. 24.00x (ISBN 0-85825-152-3, Pub. by Inst Engineering Australia). Renouf.

Francis, Chester & Auerbach, Stanley I., eds. Environment & Solid Wastes: Characterization, Treatment, & Disposal. LC 82-71528. (Illus.). 450p. 1983. 49.95 (ISBN 0-250-40583-0). Ann Arbor Science.

Integrated Physical, Socio-Economic & Environmental Planning. 196p. 1982. pap. 21.00 (ISBN 0-907567-19-3, TYP111, Tycooly Intl). Unipub.

Johnson, Walter K., ed. National Conference on Environmental Engineering, 1982. LC 82-72214. 784p. 1982. pap. text ed. 56.00 (ISBN 0-87262-311-4). Am Soc Civil Eng.

Justus, Fred. Our Environment. (Science Ser.). 24p. (gr. 2). 1979. wkbk. 5.00 (ISBN 0-8209-0140-7, S-2). ESP.

McGraw Pub. Co. Encyclopedia of Environmental Science. 2nd ed. 1980. 44.50 (ISBN 0-07-045264-4). McGraw.

McMullen, R. Environmental Science. 1982. 55.00x (ISBN 0-333-32755-1, Pub. by Macmillan England). State Mutual Bk.

Moriarty, F., ed. Ecotoxicology: The Study of Pollutants in Exosystems. Date not set. price not set (ISBN 0-12-506760-7). Acad Pr.

Pritchard. Environmental Science Four Checkbook. 1982. text ed. 22.50 (ISBN 0-408-00663-3); pap. text ed. 12.50 (ISBN 0-408-00608-0). Butterworth.

Rudman, Jack. Environmental Analyst. (Career Examination Ser.: C-2659). (Cloth bdg. avail. on request). pap. 10.00 (ISBN 0-8373-2659-1). Natl Learning.

--Environmental Planner. (Career Examination Ser.: C-2662). (Cloth bdg. avail. on request). pap. 10.00 (ISBN 0-8373-2662-1). Natl Learning.

--Principal Environmental Analyst. (Career Examination Ser.: C-2661). (Cloth bdg. avail. on request). pap. 12.00 (ISBN 0-8373-2661-3). Natl Learning.

--Principal Environmental Planner. (Career Examination Ser.: C-2664). (Cloth bdg. avail. on request). pap. 12.00 (ISBN 0-8373-2664-8). Natl Learning.

--Senior Environmental Analyst. (Career Examination Ser.: C-2660). (Cloth bdg. avail. on request). pap. 12.00 (ISBN 0-8373-2660-5). Natl Learning.

--Senior Environmental Planner. (Career Examination Ser.: C-2663). (Cloth bdg. avail. on request). pap. 12.00 (ISBN 0-8373-2663-X). Natl Learning.

Second International Congress on Analytical Techniques in Environmental Chemistry. Analytical Techniques in Environmental Chemistry 2: Proceedings of the Second International Congress, Barcelona, Spain, November 1981. Albaiges, J., ed. LC 82-15047. (Series on Environmental Science: Vol. 7). (Illus.). 482p. 1982. 75.00 (ISBN 0-08-028740-9). Pergamon.

ENVIRONMENTAL ENGINEERING (BUILDINGS)

see also Architectural Acoustics; Ventilation

Canadian Government. Winning Low Energy Building Designs. 651p. 1980. text ed. 35.00x (ISBN 0-660-50675-0, Pub. by Inst Engineering Australia). Renouf.

Coates, D. F. Rock Mechanics Principles. 442p. 1981. pap. text ed. 26.40 (ISBN 0-660-10933-6, Pub. by Inst Engineering Australia). Renouf.

Grant, Donald P. Design by Objectives: Multiple Objective Design Analysis & Evaluation in Architectural, Environmental & Product Design. LC 82-73290. 50p. (Orig.). 1982. pap. text ed. 4.00 (ISBN 0-910821-00-3). Design Meth.

Rapoport, Amos. The Meaning of the Built Environment: A Non-Verbal Communication Approach. 200p. 1982. 25.00 (ISBN 0-8039-1892-5); pap. 12.50 (ISBN 0-8039-1893-3). Sage.

ENVIRONMENTAL HEALTH
see also Environmental Engineering; Environmentally Induced Diseases; Man-Influence of Environment; Pollution; Public Health

Frick, G. William. Environmental Glossary. 2nd ed. LC 82-83908. 310p. 1982. text ed. 28.00 (ISBN 0-686-38762-7). Gov Insts.

Leaverton. Environmental Epidemiology. 192p. 1982. 23.50 (ISBN 0-03-061716-2). Praeger.

Rom, William N., ed. Environmental & Occupational Medicine. 1982. text ed. 68.50 (ISBN 0-316-75560-5). Little.

Rudman, Jack. Environmental Health Technician. (Career Examination Ser.: C-2652). (Cloth bdg. avail. on request). pap. 10.00 (ISBN 0-8373-2652-4). Natl Learning.

Travis, Curtis C. & Etnier, Elizabeth L., eds. Health Risks of Energy Technologies. (AAAS Selected Symposium: No. 82). 291p. 1982. lib. bdg. 25.00 (ISBN 0-86531-520-5). Westview.

ENVIRONMENTAL HEALTH ENGINEERING
see Sanitary Engineering

ENVIRONMENTAL LAW
see also Air-Pollution-Laws and Legislation; Natural Resources-Law and Legislation

Arbuckle, J. Gordon & Frick, G. William. Environmental Law Handbook. 7th ed. 450p. 1983. text ed. 39.50 (ISBN 0-86587-098-5). Gov Insts.

Denney, Richard J. & Biles, Blake A. European Environmental Laws & Regulations Notebook. 160p. 1982. Wkbk. 48.00 (ISBN 0-86587-104-3). Gov Insts.

Dworkin, Daniel M. Environmental Sciences in Developing Countries: Scope Report 4. 70p. 1978. pap. 8.00x (ISBN 0-471-99597-5). Wiley.

Eicher, George J. The Enviromental Control Department in Industry & Government: It's Organization & Operation. 165p. 1982. 38.50 (ISBN 0-9607390-0-9). Words Pr.

Environmental Resources Ltd., ed. The Law & Practice Relating to Pollution Control in the Member States of the European Communities, 10 vols. 1982. Set. 850.00 (ISBN 0-686-82384-2, Pub. by Graham & Trotman England); 90.00x ea. State Mutual Bk.

Firestone, David B. & Reed, Frank C. Environmental Law for Non-Lawyers. LC 82-70697. (Illus.). 300p. 1983. 36.00 (ISBN 0-250-40529-6). Ann Arbor Science.

Frick, G. William. Environmental Compliance Audits Manuel. 99p. 1982. Wkbk. 38.00 (ISBN 0-86587-099-3). Gov Insts.

Lake. Environmental Regulation. 160p. 1982. 20.95 (ISBN 0-03-062761-3). Praeger.

Olson, Jim. Michigan Environmental Law: A Citizens Guide in the 1980's. 344p. 1981. pap. 19.95 (ISBN 0-943806-01-1). Greenprint Pr.

Rose, Jerome G. Legal Foundations of Environmental Planning. 488p. 1983. text ed. 22.95x (ISBN 0-88285-090-3, Dist. by Transaction Bks). Ctr Urban Pol Res.

Selected Environmental Law Statutes: 1983 Edition. 768p. 1982. pap. write for info. (ISBN 0-314-70395-0). West Pub.

Sullivan, Thomas F. Environmental Statutes, 1982 Edition. 601p. 1982. pap. text ed. 19.95 (ISBN 0-86587-110-8). Gov Insts.

--TSCA Inspection Manuel Part I. 300p. 1982. pap. text ed. 35.00 (ISBN 0-686-38763-5). Gov Insts.

--U. S. Epa Guidebook. (Illus.). 166p. pap. 28.00 (ISBN 0-86587-057-8). Gov Insts.

Taylor, Serge. Making Bureaucracies Think: The Evironmental Impact Statement Strategy of Administrative Reform. LC 81-84456. 320p. 1983. pap. 29.50x (ISBN 0-8047-1152-6). Stanford U Pr.

ENVIRONMENTAL MANAGEMENT
see Environmental Engineering; Environmental Policy

ENVIRONMENTAL POLICY
see also Environmental Law

Andrews, Suzanna, et al, eds. The World Environment Handbook: A Directory of Government Natural Resource Management Agencies in 144 Countries. 144p. (Orig.). 1982. pap. write for info. (ISBN 0-910499-00-4). World Env Ctr.

Congressional Quarterly Inc. Staff. Environmental Issues: Prospects & Problems. LC 82-4975. (Editorial Research Reports Ser.). 168p. 1982. pap. 7.95 (ISBN 0-87187-238-2). Congr Quarterly.

Dasgupta, Partha. The Control of Resources. (Illus.). 240p. 1983. text ed. 22.50x (ISBN 0-674-16980-8). Harvard U Pr.

Eicher, George J. The Enviromental Control Department in Industry & Government: It's Organization & Operation. 165p. 1982. 38.50 (ISBN 0-9607390-0-9). Words Pr.

Environmental Resources Ltd., ed. The Law & Practice Relating to Pollution Control in the Member States of the European Communities, 10 vols. 1982. Set. 850.00 (ISBN 0-686-82384-2, Pub. by Graham & Trotman England); 90.00x ea. State Mutual Bk.

Foell, Wesley K. Management of Energy-Environment Systems: Methods & Case Studies. LC 78-13617. (International Institute Series on Applied Systems Analysis). 487p. 1979. 49.95x (ISBN 0-471-99721-8, Pub. by Wiley-Interscience). Wiley.

Freeman, A. Myrick, et al. The Economics of Environmental Policy. LC 72-7249. 184p. 1973. pap. text ed. 12.95x (ISBN 0-471-27786-X). Cloth ed. 7.25 o.p. Wiley.

Frick, G. William. Environmental Glossary. 2nd ed. LC 82-83908. 310p. 1982. text ed. 28.00 (ISBN 0-686-38762-7). Gov Insts.

Goodin, Robert E. The Politics of Rational Man. LC 75-35616. 240p. 1976. 38.95x (ISBN 0-471-31360-2, Pub. by Wiley-Interscience). Wiley.

Healy, Robert G. America's Industrial Future: An Environment Perspective. LC 82-19941. 49p. (Orig.). 1982. pap. 5.00 (ISBN 0-89164-073-8). Conservation Foun.

Integrated Physical, Socio-Economic & Environmental Planning. 196p. 1982. pap. 21.00 (ISBN 0-907567-19-3, TYP111, Tycooly Intl). Unipub.

Jordan, Terry G. Environment & Environmental Perceptions in Texas. Rosenbaum, Robert J., ed. (Texas History Ser.). (Illus.). 36p. 1981. pap. text ed. 1.95x (ISBN 0-89641-059-5). American Pr.

Lowe, J. & Lewis, D. Total Environmental Control: The Economics of Cross-Media Pollution Transfers. LC 82-9827. (Illus.). 134p. 1982. 21.50 (ISBN 0-08-026276-7). Pergamon.

Lowe, Philip & Goyder, Jane. Environmental Groups in Politics. (Resource Management Ser.: No. 6). (Illus.). 240p. 1983. text ed. 30.00x (ISBN 0-04-329043-4); pap. text ed. 13.95x (ISBN 0-04-329044-2). Allen Unwin.

Nikolai, Lorin A., et al. The Measurement of Corporate Environmental Activity. 105p. pap. 12.95 (ISBN 0-86641-054-6, 7684). Natl Assn Accts.

Reese, Craig E. Deregulation & Environmental Quality: The Use of Tax Policy to Control Pollution in North America & Western Europe. LC 82-11266. (Illus.). 480p. 1983. lib. bdg. 45.00 (ISBN 0-89930-018-9, RDE/, Quorum). Greenwood.

Scherer, Donald & Attig, Thomas. Ethics & the Environment. (Illus.). 1983. pap. 9.95 (ISBN 0-13-290163-9). P-H.

Schrepfer, Susan R. The Fight to Save the Redwoods: A History of Environmental Reform, 1917-1978. LC 81-69828. (Illus.). 352p. 1983. 22.50 (ISBN 0-299-08850-2). U of Wis Pr.

Taylor, Serge. Making Bureaucracies Think: The Evironmental Impact Statement Strategy of Administrative Reform. LC 81-84456. 320p. 1983. pap. 29.50x (ISBN 0-8047-1152-6). Stanford U Pr.

ENVIRONMENTAL POLLUTION
see Pollution

ENVIRONMENTAL PROTECTION
see also Conservation of Natural Resources; Environmental Engineering; Environmental Law; Environmental Policy

Auerbach & Geehr. Management of Wilderness & Environmental Emergency. 1983. price not set (ISBN 0-02-304630-9). Macmillan.

Downing, Paul, ed. Cross-National Comparisons in Environmentals Protection. (Orig.). 1982. pap. 6.00 (ISBN 0-918592-57-7). Policy Studies.

Huisingh, Donald & Bailey, Vicki, eds. Making Pollution Prevention Pay: Ecology with Economy as Policy. 168p. 1982. 25.00 (ISBN 0-08-029417-0). Pergamon.

Lowe, J. & Lewis, D. Total Environmental Control: The Economics of Cross-Media Pollution Transfers. LC 82-9827. (Illus.). 134p. 1982. 21.50 (ISBN 0-08-026276-7). Pergamon.

ReVelle, Charles & ReVelle, Penny. The Environment: Issues & Choices. 762p. 1981. text ed. write for info (ISBN 0-87150-758-7). Grant Pr.

Schrepfer, Susan R. The Fight to Save the Redwoods: A History of Environmental Reform, 1917-1978. LC 81-69828. (Illus.). 352p. 1983. 22.50 (ISBN 0-299-08850-2). U of Wis Pr.

Shepard. Environmental Protection: The Legal Framework. 1981. 60.00 (ISBN 0-07-057883-4). McGraw.

Sullivan, Thomas F. TSCA Inspection Manuel Part I. 300p. 1982. pap. text ed. 35.00 (ISBN 0-686-38763-5). Gov Insts.

--U. S. Epa Guidebook. (Illus.). 166p. pap. 28.00 (ISBN 0-86587-057-8). Gov Insts.

Uusitalo, Liisa. Consumer Behavior & Environmental Quality. LC 82-10686. 156p. 1982. 25.00x (ISBN 0-312-16606-0). St Martin.

ENVIRONMENTAL RADIOACTIVITY
see Radioecology

ENVIRONMENTAL STUDIES
see Conservation of Natural Resources-Study and Teaching

ENVIRONMENTALLY INDUCED DISEASES

Davis, Steven A. How to Stay Healthy in an Unhealthy World. LC 82-12581. 288p. 1983. 12.50 (ISBN 0-688-01574-3). Morrow.

Evans, Gary. Environmental Stress. LC 82-1336. (Illus.). 400p. 1983. 34.50 (ISBN 0-521-24636-9). Cambridge U Pr.

Kolber, Alan R. & Wong, Thomas K., eds. In Vitro Toxicity Testing of Environmental Agents, Current & Future Possibilities: Part A-Survey of Test Systems. (NATO Conference Ser.: No. I, Ecology). 574p. 1983. 69.50x (ISBN 0-306-41123-7, Plenum Pr). Plenum Pub.

--In Vitro Toxicity Testing of Environmental Agents, Current & Future Possibilities: Part B-Development of Risk Assessment Guidelines. (NATO Conference Series I, Ecology: Vol. 5B). 566p. 1983. 69.50x (ISBN 0-306-41124-5). Plenum Pub.

ENZYMES
see also Clinical Enzymology; Coenzymes; Pancreas also names of enzymes, e.g. Diastase, Pepsin

Chibata, Ichiro & Fukui, Saburo, eds. Enzyme Engineering, Vol. 6. 560p. 1982. 59.50x (ISBN 0-306-41121-0, Plenum Pr). Plenum Pub.

Colowick, S. & Langone, John, eds. Methods in Enzymology: Immunological Techniques, Vol. 84, Pt. D. LC 82-1678. 736p. 1982. 65.00 (ISBN 0-12-181984-1). Acad Pr.

Colowick, Sidney P. & Kaplan, Nathan O., eds. Methods in Enzymology: Vol. 91, Pt. 1: Enzyme Structure. Date not set. 69.00 (ISBN 0-12-181991-4). Acad Pr.

Howell, Edward. Enzyme Nutrition. 160p. 1983. pap. 7.95 (ISBN 0-686-43191-X). Avery Pub.

Purich, Daniel L., ed. Contemporary Enzyme Kinetics & Mechanisms. LC 82-16265. Date not set. price not set (ISBN 0-12-568050-3). Acad Pr.

Usdin, E. & Weiner, N. Function & Regulation of Monoamine Enzymes: Basic & Clinical Aspects. 1982. 159.00x (ISBN 0-686-42941-9, Pub. by Macmillan England). State Mutual Bk.

Wiseman, Alan. Topics in Enzyme & Fermentation Biotechnology, Vol. 7. LC 77-511. 345p. 1982. 84.95 (ISBN 0-470-27366-6). Halsted Pr.

Zaborsky, Oskar. Immobiljzed Enzymes. 190p. 1984. text ed. write for info. (ISBN 0-89874-611-6). Krieger.

ENZYMOLOGY, CLINICAL
see Clinical Enzymology

EPHEMERIDAE
see May-Flies

EPIC LITERATURE

Calin, William. A Muse for Heroes: Nine Centuries of the Epic in France. (Romance Ser.). 504p. 1983. 47.50x (ISBN 0-8020-5599-0). U of Toronto Pr.

Lord, George D. Trials of the Self: Heroic Ordeals in the Epic Tradition. 1983. 27.50 (ISBN 0-208-02013-6, Archon). Shoe String.

EPIDAURUS-ANTIQUITIES

Burford. The Greek Temple Builders at Epidauros. 274p. 1982. 50.00x (ISBN 0-85323-080-3, Pub. by Liverpool Univ England). State Mutual Bk.

EPIDEMIC HEPATITIS
see Hepatitis, Infectious

EPIDEMIOLOGY

Chiazze, Leonard, Jr. & Lundin, Frank E., eds. Methods & Issues in Occupational & Environmental Epidemiology. LC 82-72346. (Illus.). 225p. 1982. 39.95 (ISBN 0-250-40576-8). Ann Arbor Science.

Eschwege, E., ed. Advances in Diabetes Epidemiology: Proceedings of the International Symposium on the Advances in Diabetes Epidemiology, Abbaye de Fontevraud, France, 3-7 May 1982. (INSERM Symposium Ser.: No. 22). 408p. Date not set. 81.00 (ISBN 0-444-80453-6, Biomedical Pr). Elsevier.

Kleinbaum, David G. & Kupper, Lawrence L. Solutions Manual for Epidemiologic Research: Principles & Quantitative Methods. (Research Methods Ser.). 58p. 1982. pap. 4.95 (ISBN 0-534-97935-1). Lifetime Learn.

EPIDERMIS
see Skin

EPILEPSY

Dreifuss. Childhood Epilepsy. 1983. text ed. 35.00 (ISBN 0-7236-7039-0). Wright-PSG.

Speckmann, E. J. & Elger, C. E., eds. Epilepsy & Motor System. (Illus.). 359p. pap. text ed. 27.50 (ISBN 0-8067-1821-8). Urban & S.

Sterman, M. B. & Shouse, Margaret N., eds. Sleep & Epilepsy: Symposium. LC 82-11657. 1982. 39.00 (ISBN 0-12-666360-2). Acad Pr.

EPISCOPAL CHURCH
see Church of England; Protestant Episcopal Church in the U. S. A.

EPISTEMOLOGY
see Knowledge, Theory Of

EPITHELIUM

Sawyer. Epithelial-Mesenchymal Interactions. 270p. 1983. 32.95 (ISBN 0-03-060326-9). Praeger.

EQUAL EMPLOYMENT OPPORTUNITY
see Discrimination in Employment

EQUAL OPPORTUNITY IN EMPLOYMENT
see Discrimination in Employment

EQUALITY
see also Democracy; Individualism; Liberty; Social Classes; Socialism

Fishkin, James S. Justice, Equal Opportunity & the Family. LC 82-10939. 208p. 1983. text ed. 18.95x (ISBN 0-300-02865-2). Yale U Pr.

Lee, K. Wayne. Equality Without Regimentation: An Introduction to Mutualism. LC 82-62539. 240p. 1983. pap. 9.50 (ISBN 0-88100-020-5). New Tide.

Mooney, Christopher F. Inequality & the American Conscience: Justice Through the Judicial System. (Woodstock Studies). 144p. 1983. pap. 5.95 (ISBN 0-8091-2500-5). Paulist Pr.

Nelson, Daniel N., ed. Communism & the Politics of Inequalities. LC 81-48525. 1983. write for info. (ISBN 0-669-05415-1). Lexington Bks.

Robbins, David & Caldwell, Lesley, eds. Rethinking Social Inequality. 263p. 1982. text ed. 36.50x (ISBN 0-566-00557-3). Gower Pub Ltd.

Schniedewind, Nancy & Davidson, Ellen. Open Minds to Equality. (Illus.). 272p. 1983. pap. 16.95 (ISBN 0-13-637264-3). P-H.

Stasz, Clarice. The American Nightmare: Why Inequality Persists. LC 80-6191. 233p. 1983. pap. 7.95 (ISBN 0-8052-0709-0). Schocken.

Walzer, Michael. The Spheres of Justice: A Defense of Pluralism & Equality. LC 82-72409. 356p. 1983. 19.95 (ISBN 0-465-08190-8). Basic.

EQUALITY OF STATES

Nelson, Daniel N., ed. Communism & the Politics of Inequalities. LC 81-48525. 1983. write for info. (ISBN 0-669-05415-1). Lexington Bks.

EQUATIONS

Struppa, Daniele C. The Fundamental Principle for Sysytems of Convolution Equations. LC 82-20614. (Memoirs of the American Mathematical Society Ser.: No. 273). 10.00 (ISBN 0-8218-2273-X, MEMO/273). Am Math.

EQUATIONS-NUMERICAL SOLUTIONS

Jain, M. K. Numerical Solution of Differential Equations. 2nd ed. 1983. 29.95 (ISBN 0-470-27389-5). Halsted Pr.

EQUATIONS, DIFFERENCE
see Difference Equations

EQUATIONS, DIFFERENTIAL
see Differential Equations

EQUATIONS, INTEGRAL
see Integral Equations

EQUATIONS, QUADRATIC

Steklov Institute of Mathematics & Kuz'mina, G. V. Moduli of Families of Curves & Quadratic Differentials. LC 82-8902. (Proceedings of the Steklov Institute of Mathematics). 76.00 (ISBN 0-8218-3040-6, STEKLO-1982-1). Am Math.

EQUESTRIANISM
see Horsemanship

EQUILIBRIUM (SOCIAL SCIENCES)
see Statics and Dynamics (Social Sciences)

EQUILIBRIUM, THERMAL
see Thermodynamics

EQUILIBRIUM, VAPOR-LIQUID
see Vapor-Liquid Equilibrium

EQUILIBRIUM THEORY OF TIDES
see Tides

EQUIPMENT, INDUSTRIAL
see Industrial Equipment

EQUIPMENT, POLLUTION CONTROL
see Pollution Control Equipment

EQUIPMENT LEASING
see Industrial Equipment Leases

EQUITATION
see Horsemanship

EQUIVALENCY EXAMINATION, HIGH SCHOOL
see High School Equivalency Examination

ERASMUS, DESIDERIUS, d. 1536

Devereux, E. J. Renaissance English Translations of Erasmus: A Bibliography to 1700. (Erasmus Ser.). 256p. 1983. 35.00x (ISBN 0-8020-2411-4). U of Toronto Pr.

ERGODIC THEORY

Katok, A., ed. Ergodic Theory & Dynamical Systems Eleven. (Progress in Mathematics Ser.: Vol. 21). 210p. 1982. text ed. 15.00x (ISBN 3-7643-3096-1). Birkhauser.

Petersen, Karl. Ergodic Theory. LC 82-4473. (Cambridge Studies in Advanced Mathematics: No. 2). (Illus.). 320p. Date not set. price not set (ISBN 0-521-23632-0). Cambridge U Pr.

ERGONOMICS
see Human Engineering

ERLANG TRAFFIC FORMULA
see Queuing Theory

ERNST, MAX, 1891-

Lanchner, Carolyn & Rosenstock, Laura. Four Modern Masters: De Chirico, Ernst, Magritte, & Miro. (Illus.). 122p. 1982. pap. 14.95 (ISBN 0-686-83914-5, 28738-6). U of Chicago Pr.

Speis, Werner. Loplop: The Artist in the Third Person. Gabriel, J. W., tr. from Ger. (Illus.). 200p. 1983. 50.00 (ISBN 0-8076-1065-8). Braziller.

EROSION
see also Coast Changes; Geomorphology; Glaciers; Sedimentation and Deposition; Valleys; Weathering

Laronne, Jonathan & Mosley, M. Paul, eds. Erosion & Sediment Yield. LC 81-6456. (Benchmark Papers in Geology: Vol. 63). 400p. 1982. 47.00 (ISBN 0-87933-409-6). Hutchinson Ross.

EROSION CONTROL
see Soil Conservation

EROTIC ART
see also Nude in Art

Benedict, Brad, ed. The Blue Book. (Illus.). 96p. 1983. 13.95 (ISBN 0-394-62439-4, E857, Ever). Grove.

EROTIC LITERATURE
see also Liberty of the Press; Literature, Immoral; Sex in Literature

Kearney, Patrick J. A History of Erotic Literature. 216p. 1982. 75.00x (ISBN 0-333-34126-0, Pub. by Macmillan England). State Mutual Bk.

ERROR-CORRECTING CODES (INFORMATION THEORY)

Blahut, Richard E. Theory & Practice of Error Control Codes. LC 82-11441. (Illus.). 512p. Date not set. text ed. price not set (ISBN 0-201-10102-5). A-W.

ERRORS
Cipra, Barry. Mistakes---& How to Avoid Them. 70p. Date not set. pap. text ed. price not set (ISBN 3-7643-3083-X). Birkhauser.
ERRORS, LOGICAL
see Fallacies (Logic)
ERRORS, THEORY OF
see also Graphic Methods; Probabilities; Sampling (Statistics)
Muthu, S. K. Probability & Errors: For the Physical Sciences. 568p. 1982. text ed. 35.00x (ISBN 0-86131-137-X, Pub. by Orient Longman Ltd India). Apt Bks.
ERTE
Erte. Erte: Things I Remember. (Illus.). 208p. 1983. 22.50 (ISBN 0-7206-0124-X, Pub by Peter Owen). Merrimack Bk Serv.
ERYTHROPOIESIS
Dunn, C. D. Current Concepts in Erythropoiesis. 1983. 59.00 (ISBN 0-471-90033-8, Pub. by Wiley Med). Wiley.
ESALEN INSTITUTE
Price, Christene, ed. Food for the Senses: Recipes & Artwork from the Esalen Community. (Illus.). 120p. (Orig.). 1982. pap. 5.95. C Price.
ESCALATORS
Safety Code for Elevators & Escalators: Handbook on A17.1. 372p. 1981. 50.00 (A00112). ASME.
ESKIMO LANGUAGE
Wells, Roger, Jr., compiled by. English-Eskimo & Eskimo-English Vocabularies. Kelly, John W., tr. LC 82-51153. 72p. 1982. pap. 6.95 (ISBN 0-8048-1403-1). C E Tuttle.
ESKIMOS
see also Aleuts
Freuchen, Peter. Arctic Adventure: My Life in the Frozen North. 467p. 1982. Repr. of 1935 ed. lib. bdg. 35.00 (ISBN 0-89987-269-7). Darby Bks.
Green, Rayna. Native American Women: A Contextual Bibliography. LC 82-48571. 160p. 1983. 19.50x (ISBN 0-253-33976-6). Ind U Pr.
Herbert, Wally. Hunters of the Polar North: The Eskimos. (Peoples of the Wild Ser.). 1981. 15.96 (ISBN 0-7054-0701-2, Pub. by Time-Life). Silver.
Nelson, Richard K. Shadow of a the Hunter: Stories of Eskimo Life. LC 80-11091. (Illus.). xiv, 282p. 1980. pap. 7.95 (ISBN 0-686-84090-9). U of Chicago Pr.
ESKIMOS–ALASKA
Jamison, P. L. & Seguras, S. L., eds. The Eskimo of Northwestern Alaska: A Biological Perspective. LC 77-18941. (US-IBP Synthesis Ser.: Vol. 8). 319p. 1978. 46.00 (ISBN 0-87933-319-7). Hutchinson Ross.
Nelson, Edward W. The Eskimo About Bering Strait. (Classics of Smithsonian Anthropology Ser.). (Illus.). 520p. 1982. pap. text ed. 17.50x (ISBN 0-87474-671-X). Smithsonian.
ESOPHAGUS–DISEASES
Pfeiffer, Carl J. Cancer of the Esophagus. 176p. 1982. 51.50 (ISBN 0-8493-6213-X). CRC Pr.
ESP
see Extrasensory Perception; Psychical Research
ESPERANTO (ARTIFICIAL LANGUAGE)
Forster, Peter G. The Esperanto Movement. (Contributions to the Sociology of Language Ser.: No. 32). xiv, 413p. 1982. 60.00 (ISBN 90-279-3399-5). Mouton.
ESPIONAGE
see also Spies
West, Nigel. The Circus: MI5 Operations, 1945-1972. LC 82-42928. 384p. 1983. 16.95 (ISBN 0-686-42920-6). Stein & Day.
ESPIONAGE, BUSINESS
see Business Intelligence
ESPIONAGE, JAPANESE
Deacon, Richard. Kempei Tai: A History of the Japanese Secret Service. LC 82-20564. (Illus.). 306p. 14.95 (ISBN 0-8253-0131-9). Beaufort Bks NY.
ESPIONAGE STORIES
see Spy Stories
ESSAYS
see also English Essays; French Essays; and similar headings; and subdivision Addresses, Essays, Lectures under specific subjects
Blau, J. L. Pragmatism & Other Essays. 1983. pap. 3.95 (ISBN 0-686-37708-7). WSP.
Frye, Northrop. Spiritus Mundi: Essays on Literature, Myth, & Society. LC 76-12364. (Midland Bks.: No. 289). 320p. 1983. pap. 7.95 (ISBN 0-253-20289-2). Ind U Pr.
Levi, Isaac & Parsons, Charles, eds. How Many Questions? Essays in Honor of Sidney Morgenbesser. 448p. 30.00 (ISBN 0-686-83521-2); pap. text ed. 12.50 (ISBN 0-915145-58-8). Hackett Pub.
Mathews, Wiliam. The Great Conversers, & Other Essays. 304p. 1982. Repr. of 1878 ed. lib. bdg. 50.00 (ISBN 0-89987-644-7). Darby Bks.
Paul, E. V. Essays of Yesterday: A Collection of Literary Essays. 160p. 1983. text ed. 16.95x (ISBN 0-7069-1753-7, Pub. by Vikas India). Advent NY.
Stilman, Leon. Collected Essays. 250p. Date not set. 22.00 (ISBN 0-88233-794-7). Ardis Pubs.
Vidal, Gore. The Second American Revolution. LC 82-40425. 288p. 1983. pap. 5.95 (ISBN 0-394-71379-6, Vin). Random.
ESSENES
see also Dead Sea Scrolls; Qumran Community
Ginsburg, Christian D. The Essenes: Their History & Doctrines & The Kabbalah: Its Doctrines, Development & Literature. 246p. 1970. 15.00 (ISBN 0-7100-1449-X). Routledge & Kegan.
Szekely, Edmond B. The Cosmotherapy of the Essenes. (Illus.). 64p. 1975. pap. 3.50 (ISBN 0-89564-012-0). IBS Intl.
--The Discovery of the Essene Gospel of Peace: The Essenes & the Vatican. (Illus.). 96p. 1977. pap. 4.80 (ISBN 0-89564-004-X). IBS Intl.
--The Essene Book of Asha: Journey to the Cosmic Ocean. (Illus.). 140p. 1976. pap. 7.50 (ISBN 0-89564-008-2). IBS Intl.
--The Essene Book of Creation. (Illus.). 86p. 1975. pap. 4.50 (ISBN 0-89564-005-8). IBS Intl.
--The Essene Code of Life. (Illus.). 44p. 1978. pap. 3.50 (ISBN 0-89564-013-9). IBS Intl.
--The Essene Communions with the Infinite. (Illus.). 64p. 1979. pap. 3.95 (ISBN 0-89564-009-0). IBS Intl.
--The Essene Gospel of Peace, Bk. 1. (Illus.). 72p. 1981. pap. 1.00 (ISBN 0-89564-000-7). IBS Intl.
--The Essene Gospel of Peace, Bk. 2. (Illus.). 132p. 1981. pap. 5.80 (ISBN 0-89564-001-5). IBS Intl.
--The Essene Gospel of Peace, Bk. 3: Lost Scrolls of the Essene Brotherhood. (Illus.). 144p. 1981. pap. 5.60 (ISBN 0-89564-002-3). IBS Intl.
--The Essene Gospel of Peace, Bk. 4: Teachings of the Elect. (Illus.). 40p. 1981. pap. 4.50 (ISBN 0-89564-003-1). IBS Intl.
--The Essene Jesus. (Illus.). 72p. 1977. pap. 4.50 (ISBN 0-89564-007-4). IBS Intl.
--The Essene Origins of Christianity. (Illus.). 184p. 1981. pap. 8.50 (ISBN 0-89564-015-5). IBS Intl.
--The Essene Science of Life. (Illus.). 64p. 1976. pap. 3.50 (ISBN 0-89564-010-4). IBS Intl.
--The Essene Teachings of Zarathurstra. (Illus.). 32p. 1974. pap. 2.95 (ISBN 0-89564-016-3). IBS Intl.
--The Essene Way: Biogenic Living. (Illus.). 200p. 1981. pap. 8.80 (ISBN 0-89564-019-8). IBS Intl.
--The Essene Way: World Pictures & Cosmic Symbols. (Illus.). 40p. 1978. pap. 1.80 (ISBN 0-89564-050-3). IBS Intl.
--The Essenes, by Josephus & His Contemporaries. (Illus.). 32p. 1981. pap. 2.95 (ISBN 0-89564-014-7). IBS Intl.
--The Fiery Chariots. (Illus.). 96p. 1971. pap. 4.80 (ISBN 0-89564-017-1). IBS Intl.
--The First Essene. (Illus.). 240p. 1981. pap. 9.50 (ISBN 0-89564-018-X). IBS Intl.
--I Came Back Tomorrow. (Illus.). 32p. 1976. pap. 3.50 (ISBN 0-89564-073-2). IBS Intl.
--The Teachings of the Essenes from Enoch to the Dead Sea Scrolls. (Illus.). 112p. 1981. pap. 4.80 (ISBN 0-89564-006-6). IBS Intl.
ESSEX, ENGLAND
Hunt, William. The Puritan Movement: The Coming of Revolution in an English County. (Harvard Historical Studies: No. 102). (Illus.). 384p. 1983. text ed. 36.00x (ISBN 0-674-73903-5). Harvard U Pr.
ESTATE PLANNING
see also Estates (Law); Inheritance and Transfer Tax; Insurance; Investments; Tax Planning; Taxation; Trusts and Trustees
Cannon, Gwenda L. Financial & Estate Planning Applications, 2 Vols. (Huebner School Ser.). (Illus.). 463p. (Orig.). 1983. Vol. 1. pap. text ed. 32.00 (ISBN 0-943590-05-1); Vol. 2. pap. text ed. 32.00 (ISBN 0-943590-06-X). E Mellen.
Holzman, Robert S. Estate Planning: The New Golden Opportunities. LC 82-12942. 250p. 1982. 50.00 (ISBN 0-932648-31-2). Boardroom.
Hood & Shors. Closely Held Corporations in Estate Planning. LC 81-86293. 1982. write for info. (ISBN 0-316-37218-8). Little.
Hughes, Theodore E. & Klein, David. A Family Guide to Estate Planning, Funeral Arrangements, & Settling an Estate After Death. 240p. 1983. 13.95 (ISBN 0-686-83669-3, ScribT). Scribner.
Kahn, Waggoner. Provisions of the Internal Revenue Code & Treasury Regulations Pertaining to the Federal Taxation of Gifts, Trusts, & Estates 1983. 1983. pap. write for info. Little.
Keir, Jack C. & Lundy, Carl P. Fundamentals of Estate Planning. 4th, rev. ed. 1982. pap. 8.95 (ISBN 0-87863-037-6). Farnswth Pub.
Kurtz, Sheldon F. Problems, Cases & Other Materials on Family Estate Planning. LC 82-21920. (American Casebook Ser.). 853p. 1982. text ed. 23.95 (ISBN 0-314-69313-0); tchrs.' manual avail. (ISBN 0-314-72900-3). West Pub.
Shepard. Estate Planning for Farmers & Ranchers. 1980. 65.00 (ISBN 0-07-033500-1). McGraw.
--International Estate Planning. 1981. 80.00 (ISBN 0-07-046430-8). McGraw.
ESTATE PLANNING–GREAT BRITAIN
Wordie, Ross. Estate Management in Eighteenth-Century England. (Royal Historical Society-Studies in History: No. 30). 303p. 1982. text ed. 42.00x (ISBN 0-901050-85-7, Pub. by Swiftbks England). Humanities.
ESTATE PLANNING–UNITED STATES
Crumbley, D. L. & Milam, Edward E. Estate Planning in the '80s. 224p. 1983. 15.95 (ISBN 0-8144-5758-4). Am Mgmt.
Esperti, Robert A. & Peterson, Renno L. The Handbook of Estate Planning. (Illus.). 304p. 1983. 29.95 (ISBN 0-07-019668-0, P&RB). McGraw.
Gertz, Elmer, et al. A Guide to Estate Planning. LC 82-10790. 128p. (Orig.). 1983. pap. 9.95 (ISBN 0-8093-1103-8). S Ill U Pr.
ESTATES (LAW)
see also Decedents' Estates; Estate Planning
Averill, Lawrence H. Estate Valuation Handbook. (Tax Library Ser.). 448p. 1983. 65.00 (ISBN 0-471-89859-7). Wiley.
Soled, Alex J. Federal Income of Estates & Beneficiaries. LC 82-73532. 915p. (Orig.). 1982. compression binder 79.00 (ISBN 0-940024-01-2). Chancery Pubs.
ESTATES OF DECEDENTS
see Decedents' Estates
ESTERS
Sadtler Spectra Handbook of Esters NMR. 1982. 2.85 (ISBN 0-8456-0079-6). Sadtler Res.
Sadtler's Spectra Handbook of Esters Ir. 285.00 (ISBN 0-8456-0078-8). Sadtler Res.
ESTHER, FEAST OF
see Purim (Feast of Esther)
ESTHETICS
see also Art; Art–Philosophy; Color; Criticism; Dadaism; Expressionism (Art); Impressionism (Art); Literature–Esthetics; Literature–Psychology; Music–Philosophy and Esthetics; Painting; Poetry; Realism in Literature; Romanticism; Sculpture; Surrealism; Symmetry; Values
Arts & Aesthetics: An Agenda for the Future. 430p. 14.95 (ISBN 0-686-84058-5). AAHPERD.
Aschenbrenner, Karl. Analysis of Appraisive Characterization. 1983. lib. bdg. 48.00 (ISBN 90-277-1452-5, Pub. by Reidel Holland). Kluwer Boston.
Balthasar, Hans Urs von. The Glory of the Lord: A Theological Aesthetics-Seeing the Form, Vol. 1. 656p. (Orig.). 1983. 30.00 (ISBN 0-8245-0579-4). Crossroad NY.
Fisher, John, ed. Essays on Aesthetics: Perspectives on the Work of Monroe C. Beardsley. 1983. write for info. (ISBN 0-87722-287-8). Temple U Pr.
Gardner, Howard. The Arts & Human Development. LC 72-13404. (Illus.). 395p. 1973. 35.95x (ISBN 0-471-29145-5, Pub. by Wiley-Interscience). Wiley.
Heyl, Bernard C. New Bearings in Esthetics & Art Criticism: A Study in Semantics & Evaluation. 1943. text ed. 13.50x (ISBN 0-686-83646-4). Elliots Bks.
Kant, Immanuel. The Idea & the Ideal of Beauty. (Illus.). 121p. 1983. 79.85 (ISBN 0-89901-107-1). Found Class Reprints.
Kentner, Bernice. Tie Me up with Rainbows: A Guide to Beauty & Color. (Illus.). 126p. 1983. pap. 9.95 (ISBN 0-941522-02-4, 788-156). Ken Kra Pubs.
Moore, Richard. That Cunning Alphabet: Melville's Aesthetics of Nature. (Costerus New Ser.: No. 35). 232p. 1982. pap. text ed. 18.50x (ISBN 90-6203-734-8, Pub. by Rodopi Holland). Humanities.
Wolff, Janet. Aesthetics & the Sociology of Art. (Controversies in Sociology Ser.: No. 14). 128p. 1983. text ed. 22.50x (ISBN 0-04-301152-7); pap. text ed. 8.95x (ISBN 0-04-301153-5). Allen Unwin.
ESTIMATES
see subdivision Estimates and Estimates and Costs under technical subjects, e.g. Building–Estimates; Engineering–Estimates and Costs
ESTIMATION OF DISABILITY
see Disability Evaluation
ESTIMATION THEORY
see also Decision-Making
Lehmann, Erich L. Theory of Point Estimation. (Wiley Series in Probability & Mathematical Statistics Ser.). 525p. 1983. 45.00x (ISBN 0-471-05849-1, Pub. by Wiley-Interscience). Wiley.
Vapnik, Vladimir N. Estimation of Dependences Based on Empirical Data Dependences. (Springer Series in Statistics). (Illus.). 432p. 1982. 56.00 (ISBN 0-387-90733-5). Springer-Verlag.
ESTONIAN LANGUAGE
Olev, Kulno. English-Estonian-Russian Maritime Dictionary. 560p. 1981. 60.00x (ISBN 0-686-82322-2, Pub. by Collets). State Mutual Bk.
Silvet, J. Estonian-English Dictionary. 2nd ed. 508p. 1980. 55.00x (ISBN 0-686-82326-5, Pub. by Collets). State Mutual Bk.
ESTRANGEMENT (PHILOSOPHY)
see Alienation (Philosophy)
ESTRANGEMENT (SOCIAL PSYCHOLOGY)
see Alienation (Social Psychology)
ESTROGEN
Berry, C. L. The Effects of Estrogen Administration on the Male Breast. (Lectures in Toxicology Ser.: No. 15). (Illus.). 1982. 60.00 (ISBN 0-08-029791-9). Pergamon.
ESTUARIES
see also names of specific rivers
Kennedy, Victor S., ed. Esturarine Comparisons: Symposium. 1982. 37.00 (ISBN 0-12-404070-5). Acad Pr.
ETCHING
see also Etchings
Collie, M. J., ed. Etching Compositions & Processes. LC 82-7894. (Chemical Technology Rev. 210). (Illus.). 308p. 1983. 42.00 (ISBN 0-8155-0913-8). Noyes.
ETCHINGS
Saunders, Boyd & Saunders, Stephanie, eds. The Etchings of James Fowler Cooper. (Illus.). 196p. 1982. 70.00 (ISBN 0-686-82615-9). U of SC Pr.
ETERNAL LIFE
see Future Life
ETERNAL PUNISHMENT
see Hell
ETHANES
Hayduk, W. & Kertes, eds. Ethane. (Solubility Data Ser.: Vol. 9). 286p. 1982. 100.00 (ISBN 0-08-026230-9). Pergamon.
ETHANOL
see Alcohol
ETHER (ANESTHETIC)
Mangold, H. K. & Paltavy, F., eds. Ether Lipids: Biomedical Aspects. LC 82-11619. Date not set. price not set (ISBN 0-12-468780-6). Acad Pr.
ETHERS
Hiraoka, M. Crown Compounds: Their Characteristics & Applications. (Studies in Organic Chemistry: No. 12). 276p. 1982. 76.75 (ISBN 0-444-99692-3). Elsevier.
ETHICAL EDUCATION
see Moral Education; Religious Education
ETHICAL RELATIVISM
Hollis, Martin & Lukes, Steven, eds. Rationality & Relativism. 320p. 1983. 25.00x (ISBN 0-262-08130-X); pap. 12.50x (ISBN 0-262-58061-6). MIT Pr.
ETHICAL THEOLOGY
see Christian Ethics
ETHICS
see also Altruism; Anger; Animals, Treatment of; Asceticism; Business Ethics; Charity; Christian Ethics; Christian Life; Conduct of Life; Conscience; Courage; Courtesy; Crime and Criminals; Decision-Making (Ethics); Divorce; Engineering Ethics; Ethical Relativism; Free Will and Determinism; Friendship; Gambling; Good and Evil; Habit; Happiness; Hedonism; Joy and Sorrow; Justice; Legal Ethics; Literature and Morals; Love; Medical Ethics; Moral Education; Natural Law; Obedience; Patriotism; Peace; Political Ethics; Professional Ethics; Responsibility; Secularism; Self-Interest; Self-Realization; Self-Respect; Sexual Ethics; Simplicity; Sin; Sins; Social Problems; Spiritual Life; Spirituality; Success; Suicide; Sympathy; Temperance; Utilitarianism; Values; Virtue and Virtues; War; Wealth, Ethics of
also subdivision Moral and Religious Aspects under specific subjects, e.g. Atomic Warfare–Moral and Religious Aspects
Amato, Joseph A. Ethics: Living or Dead? Themes in Contemporary Values. 1982. 10.50 (ISBN 0-916620-62-X). Portals Pr.
Anselme, Michel. Freedom & Morality: A Nonsubjective Moral Code. Wald, Susan, tr. from Fr. 1983. 15.00 (ISBN 0-8022-2414-8). Philos Lib.
Bond, E. J. Reason & Value. LC 82-4564. (Cambridge Studies in Philosophy). 220p. Date not set. p.n.s. (ISBN 0-521-24571-0); pap. p.n.s. (ISBN 0-521-27079-0). Cambridge U Pr.
Callahan, Daniel & Jennings, Bruce, eds. Ethics, The Social Sciences & Policy Analysis. (The Hastings Center Series in Ethics). 370p. 1983. 29.50x (ISBN 0-306-41143-1, Plenum Pr). Plenum Pub.
Kant, Immanuel. Perpetual Peace & Other Essays on Politics, History, & Morals. Humphrey, Ted, ed. & tr. from Ger. LC 82-11748. (HPC Philosophical Classics Ser.). 152p. 1982. lib. bdg. 13.50 (ISBN 0-915145-48-0); pap. text ed. 2.95 (ISBN 0-915145-47-2). Hackett Pub.
Kupperman, Joel J. The Foundations of Morality. (Unwin Education Bks.). 176p. 1983. text ed. 25.00x (ISBN 0-04-370124-8); pap. text ed. 9.95x (ISBN 0-04-370125-6). Allen Unwin.
Larsen, Sandy & Larsen, Dale. Choices: Picking Your Way Through the Ethical Jungle. (Young Fisherman Bible Studyguides). (Illus.). 80p. (Orig.). (gr. 2-12). 1983. saddle-stitched student ed. 2.95 (ISBN 0-87788-113-8); tchr's. ed. 3.95 (ISBN 0-87788-114-6). Shaw Pubs.
ETHICS–ADDRESSES, ESSAYS, LECTURES
Hill, Ivan, ed. Ethical Basis of Economic Freedom. LC 87-5829. 325p. 1980. pap. 15.95 (ISBN 0-686-81709-5). Ethics Res Ctr.
Warnock, G. J. Morality & Language. LC 82-18171. 240p. 1983. text ed. 35.00x (ISBN 0-389-20349-1). B&N Imports.
ETHICS, CHRISTIAN
see Christian Ethics
ETHICS, COMMERCIAL
see Business Ethics
ETHICS, ENGINEERING
see Engineering Ethics
ETHICS, HUMANISTIC
see Humanistic Ethics
ETHICS, LEGAL
see Legal Ethics
ETHICS, MEDICAL
see Medical Ethics
ETHICS, MODERN–20TH CENTURY
Hill, Ivan. Common Sense & Everyday Ethics. 36p. 1980. write for info. Ethics Res Ctr.
Ouden, Bernard D. A Symposium on Ethics: The Role of Moral Values in Contemporary Thought. 104p. (Orig.). 1983. lib. bdg. 18.75 (ISBN 0-8191-2763-9); pap. text ed. 8.00 (ISBN 0-8191-2764-7). U Pr of Amer.
ETHICS, POLITICAL
see Political Ethics
ETHICS, PRACTICAL
see Conduct of Life; Ethics

ETHICS, SEXUAL
see Sexual Ethics
ETHICS, SOCIAL
see Social Ethics
ETHICS AND LAW
see Law and Ethics
ETHICS OF DECISION MAKING
see Decision-Making (Ethics)
ETHICS OF WEALTH
see Wealth, Ethics Of
ETHIOPIA-ECONOMIC CONDITIONS
Participation of a Rural Community in the Identification of Technological Problems in Ethiopia. 61p. 1982. pap. 5.00 (ISBN 92-808-0366-2, TUNU 206, UNU). Unipub.
ETHIOPIAN LITERATURE
Kane, Thomas L. Ethiopian Literature in Amharic. 304p. (Orig.). 1975. pap. 37.50 (ISBN 3-447-01675-2). Intl Pubns Serv.
ETHNIC GROUPS
Here are entered theoretical works on groups of people who are bound together by common ties of ancestry and culture. Works on the subjective sense of belonging to an individual ethnic group are entered under Ethnicity. Works on all or several of the ethnic groups located in a particular region or country are entered under Ethnology with appropriate local subdivisions, e.g. ethnology-Indonesia. Works on individual ethnic groups are entered under the name of the group, e.g. Italian Americans.
see also Ethnicity; Minorities; Race Relations
Glazer, Nathan & Ueda, Reed. How Ethnic Groups are Presented: A Study of Six American History Textbooks. 1982. pap. write for info. (ISBN 0-89633-064-8). Ethics & Public Policy.
ETHNIC IDENTITY
see Ethnicity
ETHNIC PSYCHOLOGY
see Ethnopsychology
ETHNICITY
Here are entered works on the subjective sense of belonging to an individual ethnic group. Works on groups of people who are bond together by common ties of ancestry and culture are entered under Ethnic groups.
see also Blacks-Race Identity; Pluralism (Social Sciences)
Allen, Irving L. The Language of Ethnic Conflict. 168p. 1983. 20.00x (ISBN 0-231-05556-0); pap. 9.50x (ISBN 0-231-05557-9). Columbia U Pr.
Appleton, Nicholas & Benevento, Nicole. Cultural Pluralism in Education: Theoretical Foundations. (Illus.). 288p. (Orig.). 1983. pap. text ed. 12.95 (ISBN 0-582-28233-0). Longman.
Jones, Peter d'A., ed. Ethnic Chicago. Holli, Melvin. 1981. pap. 12.95 (ISBN 0-8028-1807-2, 1807-2). Eerdmans.
McCready, William C., ed. Culture, Ethnicity, & Identity: Current Issues in Research. LC 82-22651. Date not set. price not set (ISBN 0-12-482920-1). Acad Pr.
Parker, James H. Ethnic Identity: The Case of the French Americans. LC 82-23718. (Illus.). 80p. (Orig.). 1983. lib. bdg. 16.50 (ISBN 0-8191-2981-X); pap. text ed. 6.75 (ISBN 0-8191-2982-8). U Pr of Amer.
Sowell, Thomas. Ethnic America: A History. 353p. 1983. pap. 9.50 (ISBN 0-465-02075-5). Basic.
Warner, William L. Social Systems of American Ethnic Groups. 1945. text ed. 25.00x (ISBN 0-686-83770-3). Elliots Bks.
ETHNOBOTANY
Jain, S. K. Glimpses of Indian Ethnobotany. 344p. 1980. 69.00 (ISBN 0-686-84454-8, Pub. by Oxford & I B H India). State Mutual Bk.
ETHNOGRAPHY
see Ethnology
ETHNOLOGY
see also Anthropo-Geography; Archaeology; Cannibalism; Color of Man; Costume; Ethnic Groups; Ethnicity; Ethnomusicology; Ethnopsychology; Folk-Lore; Kinship; Language and Languages; Man, Prehistoric; Manners and Customs; Native Races; Race Relations; Socialization; Urban Anthropology also individual ethnic groups and peoples, e.g. Indo-Europeans; Caucasian Race; Bantus
Adams, Robert M. Decadent Societies. LC 82-73710. 208p. 1983. 15.00 (ISBN 0-86547-103-7). N Point Pr.
Alland, Alexander. To Be Human: An Introduction to Cultural Anthropology. LC 80-17252. 388p. 1981. text ed. 16.95 (ISBN 0-471-06213-8). Wiley.
Boon, James A. Other Tribes, Other Scribes: Symbolic Anthropology in the Comparative Study of Cultures, Histories, Religions & Texts. LC 82-9516. (Illus.). 320p. 1983. 27.50 (ISBN 0-521-25081-1); pap. 9.95 (ISBN 0-521-27197-5). Cambridge U Pr.
Hooton, Ernest A. Indians of Pecos Pueblo. 1930. text ed. 175.00x (ISBN 0-686-83582-4). Elliots Bks.
ETHNOLOGY-ADDRESSES, ESSAYS, LECTURES
Lawless, Robert & Sutlive, Vinson H., Jr., eds. Fieldwork: The Human Experience. (Library of Anthropology). 132p. 1983. 29.50 (ISBN 0-677-16460-2). Gordon.
ETHNOLOGY-METHODOLOGY
Boon, James A. Other Tribes, Other Scribes: Symbolic Anthropology in the Comparative Study of Cultures, Histories, Religions & Texts. LC 82-9516. (Illus.). 320p. 1983. 27.50 (ISBN 0-521-25081-1); pap. 9.95 (ISBN 0-521-27197-5). Cambridge U Pr.
Mehan, Hugh & Wood, Houston. The Reality of Ethnomethodology. LC 82-20885. 274p. 1983. Repr. of 1975 ed. lib. bdg. write for info. (ISBN 0-89874-586-1). Krieger.
ETHNOLOGY-CENTRAL AMERICA
Sherzer, Joel. Kuna Ways of Speaking: An Ethnographic Perspective. (Texas Linguistic Ser.). 288p. 1983. 22.50 (ISBN 0-292-74305-X). U of Tex Pr.
ETHNOLOGY-GREAT BRITAIN
Kuper, Adam. Anthropology & Anthropologists: The Modern British School. Rev. ed. 220p. 1983. pap. price not set. Routledge & Kegan.
MacDougall, Hugh A. Racial Myth in English History: Trojans, Teutons, & Anglo-Saxons. LC 81-69941. 160p. 1983. pap. text ed. 6.50x (ISBN 0-87451-229-8). U Pr of New Eng.
ETHNOLOGY-INDIA
see also Untouchables
Singh, K. S., ed. Tribal Movements in India, Vol. 1. 1982. 25.00X (ISBN 0-8364-0901-9, Pub. by Manohar India). South Asia Bks.
ETHNOLOGY-TROBRIAND ISLANDS
Weiner, Annette B. Women of Value, Men of Renown: New Perspectives in Trobriand Exchange. (Texas Press Sourcebooks in Anthropology: No. 11). (Illus.). 321p. 1983. pap. text ed. 8.95x (ISBN 0-292-79019-8). U of Tex Pr.
ETHNOLOGY-UNITED STATES
see also Afro-Americans; Asian Americans; Irish Americans; Italian Americans
Josey, E. J. & DeLoach, Marva L., eds. Ethnic Collections in Libraries. 1983. 24.95 (ISBN 0-918212-63-4). Neal-Schuman.
Justus, Fred. The Melting Pot. (Social Studies Ser.). 24p. (gr. 5-9). 1978. wkbk. 5.00 (ISBN 0-8209-0255-1, SS-22). ESP.
McGoldrick, Monica & Pearce, John, eds. Ethnicity & Family Therapy. LC 81-20198. (Guilford Family Therapy Ser.). 600p. 1982. text ed. 29.50x (ISBN 0-89862-040-6). Guilford Pr.
ETHNOLOGY-WEST INDIES
Layng, Anthony. The Carib Reserve: Identity & Security in the West Indies. LC 82-21739. (Illus.). 200p. (Orig.). 1983. lib. bdg. 20.75 (ISBN 0-8191-2808-2); pap. text ed. 9.75 (ISBN 0-8191-2809-0). U Pr of Amer.
ETHNOMUSICOLOGY
Nettl, Bruno. The Study of Ethnomusicology: Twenty-Nine Issues & Concepts. LC 82-7065. 426p. 1983. 37.50 (ISBN 0-252-00986-X); pap. 12.50 (ISBN 0-252-01039-6). U of Ill Pr.
ETHNOPSYCHOLOGY
see also Culture Conflict; Psychology, Applied; Race Awareness; Social Psychology
Hsu, Francis L. Rugged Individualism Reconsidered: Essays in Psychological Anthropology. LC 82-13687. 544p. 1983. text ed. 34.50x (ISBN 0-87049-370-1); pap. text ed. 14.95x (ISBN 0-87049-371-X). U of Tenn Pr.
ETHOLOGY
see Ethics; Human Behavior
ETHOLOGY (ZOOLOGY)
see Animals, Habits and Behavior of
ETHOLOGY, COMPARATIVE
see Psychology, Comparative
ETHYL ALCOHOL
see Alcohol
ETIOLOGY
see Diseases-Causes and Theories of Causation
ETIQUETTE, BUSINESS
see Business Etiquette
ETIQUETTE, OFFICE
see Business Etiquette
ETIQUETTE, TELEPHONE
see Telephone Etiquette
EUCALYPTUS
Boland, D. J., et al. Eucalyptus Seed. (Illus.). 191p. 1980. pap. 25.00 (ISBN 0-643-02586-3). Sabbot-Natural Hist Bks.
EUCHARIST
see Lord's Supper
EUCLID, ca. 323-285 B.C.
Smith, Thomas. Euclid: His Life & His System. (The Essential Library of the Great Philosophers). (Illus.). 113p. 1983. Repr. of 1902 ed. 67.85 (ISBN 0-89901-092-X). Found Class Reprints.
EUCLID'S ALGORITHM
see Algorithms
EUDEMONISM
see Hedonism
EURIPIDES, d. 406 B.C.-CRITICISM, TEXTUAL
Mastronarde, Donald J. & Bremer, Jan M. The Textural Tradition of Euripides' Phoinissai. LC 82-13492. (Publications in Classical Studies: Vol. 27). 464p. 1982. pap. text ed. 30.50x (ISBN 0-520-09664-9). U of Cal Pr.
EUROPE
see also Europe, Eastern; European Economic Community also names of countries, cities and geographic areas in Europe
Prologue: The Eurocentric State of the Discipline. 64p. 1982. pap. 5.00 (ISBN 92-808-0385-9, TUNU 204, UNU). Unipub.
Schindler, Maria. Europe: A Cosmic Picture. Fletcher, John, ed. Gorge, Peter, tr. from Ger. (Illus.). 240p. 1975. 18.95 (ISBN 0-88010-041-9, Pub. by New Knowledge Bks England). Anthroposophic.
EUROPE-CIVILIZATION
Monaco, Paul. Modern European Culture & Consciousness, Eighteen Seventy through Nineteen Seventy: Interdisciplinary Perspectives in Social History. LC 82-10487. 182p. 1983. 30.50 (ISBN 0-87395-702-4); pap. 8.95 (ISBN 0-87395-703-2). State U NY Pr.
EUROPE-CLIMATE
Thran, P. & Brockhuizen, S., eds. Agro-Climatic Atlas of Europe. (Agro-Ecological Atlas Ser.: Vol. 1). 1965. 202.25 (ISBN 0-444-40569-0). Elsevier.
EUROPE-DEFENSES
Kennedy, Robert & Weinstein, John M., eds. The Defense of the West: Strategic & European Security Issues Reappraised. 350p. 1983. price not set (ISBN 0-86531-612-0). Westview.
Lefever, Ernest W. & Hunt, E. Stephen, eds. The Apocalyptic Premise: Nuclear Arms Debated. LC 82-18315. 429p. (Orig.). 1982. 14.00 (ISBN 0-89633-062-1); pap. 9.00 (ISBN 0-89633-063-X). Ethics & Public Policy.
Mako, William P. U. S. Ground Forces & the Defense of Central Europe. LC 82-45977. (Studies in Defense Policy). 200p. 1983. 22.95; pap. 8.95 (ISBN 0-8157-5443-4). Brookings.
EUROPE-DESCRIPTION AND TRAVEL
Burtschi, Mary. European Journey. (Illus.). 93p. pap. 5.95 (ISBN 0-686-84842-X). Little Brick Hse.
DeCombray, Richard. Goodbye Europe. LC 82-45122. 216p. 1983. 13.95 (ISBN 0-385-18097-7). Doubleday.
EUROPE-DESCRIPTION AND TRAVEL-GUIDEBOOKS
All of Europe at Low Cost. 1978. 5.95 (ISBN 0-686-42896-X). Harian.
Birnbaum, Stephen. Europe. (Get 'em & Go Travel Guide Ser.). 1982. 13.95 (ISBN 0-395-32870-5). HM.
Business Travel Guide to Europe. (Berlitz Travel Guides). (Illus.). 1982. pap. 4.95 (ISBN 0-02-964990-0, Berlitz). Macmillan.
Europe on Twenty-Five Dollars a Day, 1983-84. pap. 9.25 (ISBN 0-671-45419-6). Frommer-Pasmantier.
Europe Through the Back Door. 3rd ed. 5.95 (ISBN 0-686-82506-3). Signpost Bk Pub.
Fielding, Temple. Fielding's Europe 1983. 1982. 12.95 (ISBN 0-688-01346-5). Morrow.
Fodor's Eastern Europe 1983. 512p. 1983. traveltex 14.95 (ISBN 0-679-00907-8). McKay.
Harvard Student Agencies. Let's Go Europe. (Let's Go Ser.). (Illus.). 825p. 1983. pap. 8.95 (ISBN 0-312-48211-6). St Martin.
Rand McNally Road Atlas & City Guide of Europe. 1983. pap. 12.95 (ISBN 0-528-84320-6). Rand.
Rubinstein, Hilary. Europe's Wonderful Little Hotels & Inns. 5th ed. (Illus.). 608p. 1983. pap. 14.95 (ISBN 0-312-92193-4). Congdon & Weed.
Simpson, Norman T. Country Inns & Back Roads: Continental Europe. 3rd ed. LC 78-51115. 380p. (Orig.). 1983. pap. 8.95 (ISBN 0-912944-76-5). Berkshire Traveller.
Travellers Guide to Europe. 396p. 1983. pap. 10.95 (ISBN 0-86145-087-6, Pub. by Auto Assn-British Tourist Authority England). Merrimack Bk Serv.
Walsh, Ken. The Backpacker's Guide to Europe. (Illus.). 288p. (Orig.). 1982. pap. 4.95 (ISBN 0-8329-0270-5). New Century.
Welles, Sigourney. The Best Bed & Breakfast in the World. LC 82-83265. 348p. 1983. pap. 9.95 (ISBN 0-914788-65-5). East Woods.
Zellers, Margaret. Fielding's Sightseeing Guide to Europe Exploring Off the Beaten Path. 495p. pap. 9.95 (ISBN 0-688-03813-5). Fielding.
EUROPE-ECONOMIC CONDITIONS
Boltho, Andrea. The European Economy: Growth & Crisis. (Illus.). 650p. 1982. 49.00 (ISBN 0-19-877119-3); pap. 19.95 (ISBN 0-19-877118-5). Oxford U Pr.
Dennell, R., ed. European Economic Prehistory: A New Approach. Date not set. price not set (ISBN 0-12-209180-9). Acad Pr.
Economic Survey of Europe in 1980. 243p. 1983. pap. 17.00 (ISBN 0-686-43280-0, UN 81/2E1, UN). Unipub.
Franzmeyer, Fritz. Approaches to Industrial Policy Within the EC & Its Impact on European Integration. 167p. 1982. text ed. 40.00x (ISBN 0-566-00358-9). Gower Pub Ltd.
Hager, Wolfgang. Europe's Economic Security. (The Atlantic Papers: No. 75/3). 78p. (Orig.). 1976. pap. text ed. 4.75x (ISBN 0-686-83635-9). Allanheld.
Kane, Daniel. The Eurodollar Market & the Years of Crisis. LC 82-16828. 224p. 1983. 25.00x (ISBN 0-312-26735-5). St Martin.
Life-Styles Environment & Development: A European Perspective. (UNEP Reports & Proceedings Ser.: No. 4). 627p. 1983. pap. 14.50 (ISBN 92-807-1049-4, UNEP 071, UNEP). Unipub.
Mathias, Peter & Postan, Michael, eds. Cambridge Economic History of Europe: The Industrial Economies: Capital, Labour & Enterprise, Part 1: Britain, France, Germany & Scandinavia. 1982. 19.95 (ISBN 0-521-28800-2). Cambridge U Pr.
--Cambridge Economic History of Europe: The Industrial Economies: Capital, Labour, & Enterprise, Part 2: The United States, Japan, & Russia. 1982. 17.95 (ISBN 0-521-28801-0). Cambridge U Pr.
O'Brien, Patrick. Railways & the Economic Development of Western Europe: 1830-1914. LC 81-23261. 356p. 1982. 30.00x (ISBN 0-312-66277-7). St Martin.
United Nations. Economic Survey of Europe. 1980. pap. 17.00 (ISBN 0-686-84901-9, E.81.II.E.1). UN.
Who Owns Whom: Continental Europe, 1982, 2 vols. 21st ed. 2734p. 1982. Set. 285.00x (ISBN 0-900625-59-7). Intl Pubns Serv.
EUROPE-FOREIGN RELATIONS
Jenkins, Roy. The Role of the European Community in World Affairs. LC 81-13340. 20p. 1981. 1.25 (ISBN 0-934742-09-X, Inst Study Diplomacy). Geo U Sch For Serv.
Kissinger, Henry A. The Troubled Partnership: A Re-appraisal of the Atlantic Alliance. LC 82-15533. xii, 266p. 1982. Repr. of 1965 ed. lib. bdg. 25.00x (ISBN 0-313-23219-9, KIPA). Greenwood.
Laqueur, Walter. America, Europe, & the Soviet Union: Selected Essays. 1983. 22.95 (ISBN 0-87855-362-2). Transaction Bks.
Porter, Bernard. Britain Europe & the World, 1850 to 1982: Illusions of Grandeur. 184p. text ed. 19.50x (ISBN 0-04-909011-9). Allen Unwin.
Van Oudenaren, John. The United States & Europe: Issues to Resolve. (Seven Springs Studies). 1981. pap. 3.00 (ISBN 0-943006-02-3). Seven Springs.
EUROPE-HISTORICAL GEOGRAPHY
Anderson, Malcolm. Frontier Regions in Western Europe. 144p. 1983. text ed. 30.00 (ISBN 0-7146-3217-1, Pub. by Frank Cass). Biblio Dist.
EUROPE-HISTORY
Here are entered general works on European history. For works covering shorter periods of time see chronological subdivisions below.
Bartholomew, J. G. A Literary Historical Atlas of Europe. 253p. 1983. Repr. of 1982 ed. lib. bdg. 30.00 (ISBN 0-89984-092-2). Century Bookbindery.
Best, Geoffrey. War & Society in Revolutionary Europe 1770-1870. LC 82-3261. 336p. 1982. 27.50x (ISBN 0-312-85551-6). St Martin.
Chatelain, Alfred V. Ancient Europe in the Vision of the Rarest Available Steel Engravings. (Illus.). 99p. Repr. of 1887 ed. 227.75 (ISBN 0-89901-112-8). Found Class Reprints.
Dennell, R., ed. European Economic Prehistory: A New Approach. Date not set. price not set (ISBN 0-12-209180-9). Acad Pr.
Hackett, Neil J., et al. World of Europe to Fifteen Hundred, Vol. 1. 1979. pap. text ed. 10.85x. Forum Pr IL.
Jensen, DeLamar, et al. World of Europe to Eighteen Fifteen, Vol. 2. 1979. pap. text ed. 10.95x. Forum Pr IL.
Mathias, Peter & Postan, Michael, eds. Cambridge Economic History of Europe: The Industrial Economies: Capital, Labour, & Enterprise, Part 2: The United States, Japan, & Russia. 1982. 17.95 (ISBN 0-521-28801-0). Cambridge U Pr.
Pinkney, David H. World of Europe Since Eighteen Fifteen, Vol. 3. 1979. pap. text ed. 10.95x (ISBN 0-88273-332-X). Forum Pr IL.
Simons, Walter. Evolution of International Public Law in Europe Since Grotius. 1931. text ed. 29.50x (ISBN 0-686-83542-5). Elliots Bks.
EUROPE-HISTORY-392-814
see also Rome-History-Empire, 30 B.C.-476 a.D.
Randers-Pherson, Justine D. Barbarians & Romans: The Birth Struggle of Europe, A.D. 400-700. LC 82-20025. (Illus.). 416p. 1983. 29.50 (ISBN 0-8061-1818-0). U of Okla Pr.
Stafford, Pauline. Queens, Concubines, & Dowagers: The King's Wife in the Early Middle Ages. LC 82-13368. (Illus.). 264p. 1983. text ed. 22.50 (ISBN 0-8203-0639-8). U of Ga Pr.
EUROPE-HISTORY-476-1492
see also Middle Ages-History; Twelfth Century; Fourteenth Century; Fifteenth Century
Riche. Daily Life in the World of Charlemagne. 368p. 1982. 70.00x (ISBN 0-85323-124-9, Pub. by Liverpool Univ England); 39.00x (ISBN 0-85323-174-5). State Mutual Bk.
EUROPE-HISTORY-1492-1648
Headley, John M. The Emperor & His Chancellor: A Study of the Imperial Chancellery of Gattinara. LC 82-4525. (Cambridge Studies in Early Modern History). 208p. Date not set. 42.50 (ISBN 0-521-24444-7). Cambridge U Pr.
EUROPE-HISTORY-17TH CENTURY
Gillis, John R. The Development of European Society Seventeen Seventy to Eighteen Seventy. LC 82-20234. (Illus.). 316p. 1983. pap. text ed. 11.75 (ISBN 0-8191-2898-8). U Pr of Amer.
EUROPE-HISTORY-1648-1789
Aston, Trevor, ed. Crisis in Europe 1560-1660: Essays from "Past & Present". 376p. 1980. pap. 7.95 (ISBN 0-7100-6889-1). Routledge & Kegan.

Childs, John. Armies & Warfare in Europe, 1648-1789. 208p. 1982. text ed. 22.50x (ISBN 0-8419-0820-6). Holmes & Meier.
Mckay, Derek & Scott, H. M. The Rise of the Great Powers: The Great Powers & European States Systems, 1648-1815. LC 82-159. 1983. text ed. 23.00x (ISBN 0-582-48553-3); pap. text ed. 11.95x (ISBN 0-686-37799-0). Longman.

EUROPE-HISTORY-18TH CENTURY

Gillis, John R. The Development of European Society Seventeen Seventy to Eighteen Seventy. LC 82-20234. (Illus.). 316p. 1983. pap. text ed. 11.75 (ISBN 0-8191-2898-8). U Pr of Amer.

EUROPE-HISTORY-19TH CENTURY

Mowat, R. B. Europe in the Age of Napoleon. 80p. 1982. Repr. of 1927 ed. lib. bdg. 25.00 (ISBN 0-89987-588-2). Darby Bks.

EUROPE-HISTORY-20TH CENTURY

Thompson, Paul. Our Common History. 334p. 1982. text ed. 19.95x (ISBN 0-391-02606-2). Humanities.
Weber, Eugene, ed. Twentieth Century Europe. 1980. pap. text ed. 6.95 (ISBN 0-88273-199-8). Forum Pr IL.

EUROPE-HISTORY-1918-1945

Aubert, Louis. Reconstruction of Europe. 1925. text ed. 37.50x (ISBN 0-686-83724-X). Elliots Bks.
Siverson, J. W. Europe Nineteen Thirty-Seven. 1982. 5.75 (ISBN 0-8062-1953-X). Carlton.

EUROPE-INDUSTRY

Washington Researchers. European Markets: A Guide to Company & Industry Information Sources. 500p. 1983. pap. text ed. 150.00 (ISBN 0-934940-17-7). Wash Res.

EUROPE-INTELLECTUAL LIFE

Bartholomew, J. G. A Literary Historical Atlas of Europe. 253p. 1983. Repr. of 1982 ed. lib. bdg. 30.00 (ISBN 0-89984-092-2). Century Bookbindery.

EUROPE-MILITARY POLICY

Best, Geoffrey. War & Society in Revolutionary Europe 1770-1870. LC 82-3261. 336p. 1982. 27.50x (ISBN 0-312-85551-6). St Martin.
Childs, John. Armies & Warfare in Europe, 1648-1789. 208p. 1982. text ed. 22.50x (ISBN 0-8419-0820-6). Holmes & Meier.
Nunn, Frederick M. Yesterday's Soldiers: European Military Professionalism in South America, 1890-1940. LC 82-6961. xiv, 358p. 1983. 26.95x (ISBN 0-8032-3305-1). U of Nebr Pr.

EUROPE-POLITICS AND GOVERNMENT

Berger, Suzanne, ed. Religion in West European Politics. 200p. 1982. text ed. 29.50x (ISBN 0-7146-3218-X, F Cass Co). Biblio Dist.
Berghe, Guido V. Political Rights for European Citizens. 245p. (Orig.). 1982. text ed. 38.00 (ISBN 0-566-00524-7). Gower Pub Ltd.
Brazini, Luigi. The Europeans. 1983. price not set (ISBN 0-671-24578-3). S&S.

EUROPE-POLITICS AND GOVERNMENT-1945-

McKay, David. Planning & Politics in Western Europe. LC 81-21233. 256p. 1982. 27.50x (ISBN 0-312-61399-7). St Martin.

EUROPE-RELIGION

Berger, Suzanne, ed. Religion in West European Politics. 200p. 1982. text ed. 29.50x (ISBN 0-7146-3218-X, F Cass Co). Biblio Dist.

EUROPE-SOCIAL CONDITIONS

Washington, Booker T. & Park, Robert E. The Man Farthest Down: A Record of Observation & Study in Europe. (Social Science Classics, Black Classics). 1983. pap. 19.95 (ISBN 0-87855-933-7). Transaction Bks.

EUROPE-SOCIAL LIFE AND CUSTOMS

Brazini, Luigi. The Europeans. 1983. price not set (ISBN 0-671-24578-3). S&S.
Gillis, John R. The Development of European Society Seventeen Seventy to Eighteen Seventy. LC 82-20234. (Illus.). 316p. 1983. pap. text ed. 11.75 (ISBN 0-8191-2898-8). U Pr of Amer.
MacDonald, William W., et al, eds. European Traditions in the Twentieth Century. LC 79-52456. 1979. pap. text ed. 10.95x (ISBN 0-88273-375-3). Forum Pr IL.

EUROPE, EASTERN

Buchholz, Arnold, ed. Soviet & East European Studies in the International Framework. LC 82-62037. 96p. 1982. 15.00 (ISBN 0-941320-08-1). Transnatl Pubs.

EUROPE, EASTERN-ECONOMIC CONDITIONS

D'Angelo, Edward, et al. Contemporary East European Marxism, Vol. II. (Praxis: Vol. 7). 275p. 1982. pap. text ed. 27.75x (ISBN 0-391-02788-3). Humanities.
Drewnowski, Jan, ed. Crisis in the East European Economy: The Spread of the Polish. LC 82-42560. 1982. 20.00x (ISBN 0-312-17314-8). St Martin.
Kaser, M. C. The Economic History of Eastern Europe 1919-1975. (Illus.). 1982. 65.00x (ISBN 0-19-828445-4). Oxford U Pr.

EUROPE, EASTERN-FOREIGN RELATIONS

Sodaro & Wolchik. Foreign & Domestic Policy in Eastern Europe in the 1980's: Trends & Prospects. LC 82-3265. 192p. 1983. 25.00x (ISBN 0-312-29843-9). St Martin.

EUROPE, EASTERN-HISTORY

Rothenberg, Gunther E. & Kiraly, Bela K. East Central European Society & War in Pre-Revolutionary Eighteenth Century. (Brooklyn College Studies on Society in Change). 574p. 1982. 35.00x (ISBN 0-686-82237-4). East Eur Quarterly.
Sukiennicki, Wiktor. East Central Europe in World War I: From Foreign Domination to National Freedom. (Brooklyn College Studies on Society in Change). 1050p. 1982. 45.00x (ISBN 0-88033-012-0, Dist. by Columbia University Press). East Eur Quarterly.

EUROPE, EASTERN-POLITICS AND GOVERNMENT

D'Angelo, Edward, et al. Contemporary East European Marxism, Vol. II. (Praxis: Vol. 7). 275p. 1982. pap. text ed. 27.75x (ISBN 0-391-02788-3). Humanities.
Schopflin, George. Censorship & Political Communication. LC 82-42712. 250p. 1982. 27.50x (ISBN 0-312-12728-6). St Martin.
Sodaro & Wolchik. Foreign & Domestic Policy in Eastern Europe in the 1980's: Trends & Prospects. LC 82-3265. 192p. 1983. 25.00x (ISBN 0-312-29843-9). St Martin.

EUROPEAN ARCHITECTURE

see Architecture-Europe

EUROPEAN ART

see Art, European

EUROPEAN COMMON MARKET (1955-)

see European Economic Community

EUROPEAN CONCERT

see Concert of Europe

EUROPEAN COOPERATION

Lodge, Juliet. Institutions & Policies of the European Community. LC 81-23271. 320p. 1982. 32.50 (ISBN 0-312-41887-6). St Martin.

EUROPEAN DRAWINGS

see Drawings, European

EUROPEAN ECONOMIC COMMUNITY

Balekjian, Wahe H. Legal Aspects of Foreign Investment in the European Economic Community. LC 67-15827. 356p. 1967. 10.80 (ISBN 0-379-00312-0). Oceana.
Cawthra, Bruce I. Industrial Property Rights in the European Economic Community. 1973 ed. 250p. 27.00 (ISBN 0-686-37377-4). Beekman Pubs.
Kurland, Gerald R. Creation of the Common Market. Rahmas, Sigurd C., ed. (Topics of Our Times Ser.: No. 16). 32p. (Orig.). 1982. 2.95x (ISBN 0-87157-817-4); pap. text ed. 1.95 (ISBN 0-87157-317-2). SamHar Pr.
Lodge, Juliet. Institutions & Policies of the European Community. LC 81-23271. 320p. 1982. 32.50 (ISBN 0-312-41887-6). St Martin.
McAllister, Ian. Regional Development & the European Economic Community: A Canadian Perspective. 243p. 1982. pap. 13.95x (ISBN 0-920380-59-X, Pub. by Inst Res Pub Canada). Renouf.
Moss, Joanna. The Lome Conventions & Their Implications for the United States. Replica ed. 225p. 1982. softcover 19.50 (ISBN 0-86531-935-9). Westview.
National Accounts: Vol. II Detailed Tables, 1963-1980. 316p. (Orig., Eng. & Fr.). 1982. pap. 22.00 (ISBN 92-64-02329-1). OECD.
Pinder, David. Regional Economic Development & Policy: Theory & Practice in the European Community. 144p. 1983. text ed. 24.95x (ISBN 0-04-320153-9); pap. text ed. 10.95x (ISBN 0-04-320152-0). Allen Unwin.
Rabier, Jacques-Rene & Inglehart, Ronald. Euro-Barometer 14: Trust in the European Community, October 1980. LC 82-81761. write for info. (ISBN 0-89138-936-9, ICPSR 7958). ICPSR.
--Euro-Barometer 15: Membership in the European Community, April 1981. LC 82-81762. 1982. write for info. (ISBN 0-89138-935-0, ICPSR 7959). ICPSR.
Revenue Statistics of OECD Countries: 1965-1981. 210p. (Orig., Eng. & Fr.). 1982. pap. 17.50x (ISBN 92-64-02328-3). OECD.
Seers, Dudley & Vaitsos, Constantine, eds. The Second Enlargement of the EEC: The Integration of the Unequal Partners. 312p. 1982. 60.00x (ISBN 0-333-29189-1, Pub. by Macmillan England). State Mutual Bk.
Ziebe, Jurgen. Der Erwerb Eigener Aktien und Eigener GmbH-Geschaftsanteile In Den Staaten der Europaischen Gemeinschaft. 179p. (Ger.). 1982. write for info. (ISBN 3-8204-7112-X). P Lang Pubs.

EUROPEAN ECONOMIC COMMUNITY-BIBLIOGRAPHY

Paxton, John. A Dictionary of the European Communities. 2nd ed. LC 82-10375. 290p. 1982. 27.50x (ISBN 0-312-20099-4). St Martin.

EUROPEAN ECONOMIC COMMUNITY-GREAT BRITAIN

Bailey, R. The European Connection: Britain's Relationship with the European Community. (Illus.). 250p. 1983. 21.00 (ISBN 0-08-026775-0); pap. 14.00 (ISBN 0-08-026774-2). Pergamon.
Korah, V. Competition Law of Britain & the Common Market. 1982. lib. bdg. 59.00 (ISBN 0-686-37430-4, Pub. by Martinus Nijhoff Netherlands). Kluwer Boston.

EUROPEAN FOLK-LORE

see Folk-Lore, European

EUROPEAN MUSIC

see Music, European

EUROPEAN PAINTINGS

see Paintings, European

EUROPEAN PORCELAIN

see Porcelain

EUROPEAN POTTERY

see Pottery, European

EUROPEAN WAR, 1914-1918

Auge-Laribe, Michel & Pinot, Pierre. Agriculture & Food Supply in France During the War. (Economic & Social History of the World War Ser.). 1927. text ed. 75.00x (ISBN 0-686-83458-5). Elliots Bks.
Seymour, Charles. Woodrow Wilson & the World War. 1921. text ed. 8.50x (ISBN 0-686-83860-2). Elliots Bks.
Smith, A. W. Captain Departed. 1935. text ed. 24.50 (ISBN 0-686-83500-X). Elliots Bks.
Trade Unionism & Munitions. (Economic & Social History of the World War Ser.). 1924. text ed. 49.50x (ISBN 0-686-83830-0). Elliots Bks.

EUROPEAN WAR, 1914-1918-AERIAL OPERATIONS

Aders, Gebhard. History of the German Night Fighter Force 1917-1945. (Illus.). 360p. 1980. 19.95 (ISBN 0-86720-581-4). Sci Bks Intl.
America's First Eagles: The Official History of the Air Service in W.W.I. (Illus.). 352p. 1983. 19.95 (ISBN 0-912138-24-6). Bender Pub CA.
Winter, Denis. The First of the Few: Fighter Pilots of the First World War. LC 82-13478. (Illus.). 224p. 17.50 (ISBN 0-8203-0642-8). U of Ga Pr.

EUROPEAN WAR, 1914-1918-BIBLIOGRAPHY

Bulkley, Mildred E. Bibliographical Survey of Contemporary Sources for the Economic & Social History of the World War. 1922. text ed. 75.00x (ISBN 0-686-83490-9). Elliots Bks.

EUROPEAN WAR, 1914-1918-BIOGRAPHY

Bowerman, Guy E. The Compensations of War: The Diary of an Ambulance Driver During the Great War. Carnes, Mark C., ed. 200p. 1983. 9.95 (ISBN 0-292-71074-7). U of Tex Pr.
Lewis, Cecil. Sagittarius Rising. 1983. 17.95 (ISBN 0-434-80600-5, Pub. by Heinemann England). David & Charles.

EUROPEAN WAR, 1914-1918-CAMPAIGNS

Moorehead, Alan. Gallipoli. (War Library). 352p. 1982. pap. 3.50 (ISBN 0-345-30772-0). Ballantine.

EUROPEAN WAR, 1914-1918-COMMERCE

see European War, 1914-1918-Economic Aspects

EUROPEAN WAR, 1914-1918-ECONOMIC ASPECTS

Here are entered works on the condition and prospects of commerce and industry as affected by the war.

Dearle, Norman B. Economic Chronicle of the Great War For Great Britain & Ireland: 1914-1919. (Economic & Social History of the World War Ser.). 1929. text ed. 65.00x (ISBN 0-686-83531-X). Elliots Bks.
Henderson, Herbert D. Cotton Control Board. (Economic & Social History of the World War Ser.). 1922. text ed. 39.50x (ISBN 0-686-83513-1). Elliots Bks.

EUROPEAN WAR, 1914-1918-EMBARGOES

see European War, 1914-1918-Economic Aspects

EUROPEAN WAR, 1914-1918-GERMAN PROPAGANDA

see Propaganda, German

EUROPEAN WAR, 1914-1918-NEUTRALITY OF THE UNITED STATES

see United States-Neutrality

EUROPEAN WAR, 1914-1918-PERSONAL NARRATIVES

Morrison, Elton J. My Experiences Overseas in World War I. 1982. 7.95 (ISBN 0-533-05483-4). Vantage.
Sassoon, Siegfried. Memoirs of an Infantry Officer. 236p. 1965. pap. 6.95 (ISBN 0-571-06410-8). Faber & Faber.

EUROPEAN WAR, 1914-1918-FRANCE

Cobb, Richard. French & Germans, Germans & French: A Personal Interpretation of France under Two Occupations; 1914-1918, 1940-1944. LC 82-40472. (Tauber Institute Ser.: No. 2). 208p. 1983. 14.00 (ISBN 0-87451-225-5). U Pr of New Eng.
Stevenson, D. French War Aims Against Germany, Nineteen Fourteen to Nineteen Nineteen. (Illus.). 320p. 1982. 49.00x (ISBN 0-19-822574-1). Oxford U Pr.

EUROPEAN WAR, 1914-1918-GERMANY

Stevenson, D. French War Aims Against Germany, Nineteen Fourteen to Nineteen Nineteen. (Illus.). 320p. 1982. 49.00x (ISBN 0-19-822574-1). Oxford U Pr.

EUROPEAN WAR, 1914-1918-GREAT BRITAIN

Dearle, Norman B. Economic Chronicle of the Great War For Great Britain & Ireland: 1914-1919. (Economic & Social History of the World War Ser.). 1929. text ed. 65.00x (ISBN 0-686-83531-X). Elliots Bks.

EUROPEAN WAR, 1914-1918-UNITED STATES

The New Jersey Historical Society Collection of World War I Posters. (Illus.). 87p. 1976. pap. 10.00 (ISBN 0-686-81826-1). NJ Hist Soc.

EUROPEAN WAR, 1939-1945

see World War, 1939-1945

EUTHANASIA

Ferman, Edward L., ed. The Best from Fantasy & Science Fiction. 24th ed. 2.95 (ISBN 0-441-05485-4, Pub. by Ace Science Fiction). Ace Bks.
Hensley, Jeffrey. The Zero People. 310p. 1983. pap. 7.95 (ISBN 0-89283-126-X). Servant.

EVALUATION, JOB

see Job Evaluation

EVALUATION OF LITERATURE

see Bibliography-Best Books; Books and Reading; Criticism; Literature-History and Criticism

EVALUATION OF SCHOOLS

see Educational Surveys

EVANGELICAL AND REFORMED CHURCH

Morland, Samuel. History of the Evangelical Churches of the Valleys of Piemont. 1983. 32.00 (ISBN 0-686-42929-X). Church History.

EVANGELICAL LUTHERAN SYNOD OF MISSOURI, OHIO, AND OTHER STATES

Eisenberg, C. G. History of the First Dakota-District of the Evangelical-Lutheran Synod of Iowa & Other States. Richter, Anton H., tr. from Ger. LC 82-17645. 268p. (Orig.). 1983. lib. bdg. 23.25 (ISBN 0-8191-2798-1); pap. text ed. 12.00 (ISBN 0-8191-2799-X). U Pr of Amer.

EVANGELICAL RELIGION

see Evangelicalism

EVANGELICALISM

see also Fundamentalism; Pietism

Aldrich, Joseph C. Life-Style Evangelism: Study Guide. 1983. pap. price not set (ISBN 0-88070-020-3). Multnomah.
Altschuler, Glenn C. & Saltzgaber, Jan M. Revivalism, Social Conscience, & Community in the Burned-Over District: The Trial of Rhoda Bement. (Illus.). 184p. 1983. 22.50x (ISBN 0-8014-1541-1); pap. 7.95x (ISBN 0-8014-9246-7). Cornell U Pr.
Brestin, Dee. Finders Keepers: Small Group Evangelism. 1983. 8.95 (ISBN 0-87788-259-2); pap. 5.95. Shaw Pubs.
Cassidy, Michael. Bursting the Wineskins. 1983. 9.95; pap. 5.95 (ISBN 0-87788-094-8). Shaw Pubs.
DeWitt, David. Beyond the Basics. 1983. pap. 5.95 (ISBN 0-8024-0178-3). Moody.
Henry, Carl F. God, Revelation & Authority, Vol. 6, Part 2. (The God Who Stands & Stays Ser.). 1983. 19.95 (ISBN 0-8499-0333-5). Word Pub.
Hunter, James D. American Evangelicalism: Conservative Religion & the Quandary of Modernity. LC 82-317. 166p. 1983. 27.50x (ISBN 0-8135-0960-2); pap. 9.95x (ISBN 0-8135-0985-8). Rutgers U Pr.
Johnson, Ben C. An Evangelism Primer. LC 82-49021. 120p. 1983. pap. 4.95 (ISBN 0-8042-2039-5). John Knox.
Martin, Roger H. Evangelicals United: Ecumenical Stirrings in Pre-Victorian Britain, 1795-1830. LC 82-10784. (Studies in Evangelicalism: No. 4). 244p. 1983. 17.50 (ISBN 0-8108-1586-9). Scarecrow.
Moore, William C., ed. The Evangelical Sunday School Teacher's Guide 1983-1984. 448p. (Orig.). 1983. pap. 6.95 (ISBN 0-8007-1348-6). Revell.
Neighbour, Ralph. Contacto con el Espiritu. Martinez, Jose L., ed. Kratzig, Guillermo, tr. Orig. Title: The Touch of the Spirit. 120p. (Span.). Date not set. pap. price not set (ISBN 0-311-09098-2). Casa Bautista.
Nicholls, Bruce & Kantzer, Kenneth. In Word & Deed. 224p. 1983. pap. 10.95 (ISBN 0-8028-1965-6). Eerdmans.
Sider, Ronald J., ed. Evangelicals & Development: Toward a Theology of Social Change. LC 82-6970. (Contemporary Issues in Social Ethics Ser.). 1982. pap. 6.95 (ISBN 0-664-24445-9). Westminster.
Tozer, A. W. Worship: The Missing Jewel of the Evangelical Church. 30p. 1979. bklet 1.00 (ISBN 0-87509-219-5). Chr Pubns.

EVANGELISTIC WORK

see also Communication (Theology); Conversion; Missions; Revivals; Salvation Army

Conn, Harvie. Evangelism: Doing Justice & Preaching Grace. 112p. (Orig.). 1982. pap. 3.95 (ISBN 0-310-45311-9). Zondervan.

EVANGELISTS

Altschuler, Glenn C. & Saltzgaber, Jan M. Revivalism, Social Conscience, & Community in the Burned-Over District: The Trial of Rhoda Bement. (Illus.). 184p. 1983. 22.50x (ISBN 0-8014-1541-1); pap. 7.95x (ISBN 0-8014-9246-7). Cornell U Pr.

EVAPORATION

Hall, Vivian S. & Spencer, Margaret R. Bibliography of Evaporites, Brines & Salt. 1983. write for info. (ISBN 0-89774-042-4). Oryx Pr.

EVARTS, WILLIAM MAXWELL, 1818-1901

Dyer, Brainerd. The Public Career of William M. Evarts. LC 72-87565. 279p. 1969. Repr. of 1933 ed. lib. bdg. 35.00 (ISBN 0-686-42966-4). Da Capo.

EVASION, FISCAL

see Tax Evasion

EVERLASTING PUNISHMENT

see Hell

EVIDENCE (LAW)

see also Cross-Examination; Medical Jurisprudence; Psychology, Forensic; Witnesses

Brandis, Henry. Brandis on North Carolina Evidence, 2 vols. 1982. 80.00 (ISBN 0-87215-447-5). Michie-Bobbs.
Curzon, L. B. Law of Evidence. 288p. 1978. 39.00x (ISBN 0-7121-1244-8, Pub. by Macdonald & Evans). State Mutual Bk.
Kelman, Alistair & Sizer, Richard. The Computer in Court. 104p. 1982. text ed. 33.50x (ISBN 0-566-03419-0). Gower Pub Ltd.
Tanford, J. Alexander & Quinlan, Richard M. Indiana Trial Evidence Manual. 393p. 1982. 30.00 (ISBN 0-87215-497-1). Michie-Bobbs.

Waltz, Jon R. & Kaplan, John. Evidence: Making the Record. LC 82-13634. (University Casebook Ser.). 83p. 1982. pap. text ed. write for info. (ISBN 0-88277-075-6). Foundation Pr.

Weinstein, Jack B., et al. Cases & Materials on Evidence. 7th ed. LC 82-21049. (University Casebook Ser.). 1543p. 1982. text ed. write for info. (ISBN 0-88277-074-8). Foundation Pr.

White, Jeffrey R., ed. The Trial Lawyer & the Federal Rules of Evidence. 630p. 1980. 15.00 (ISBN 0-941916-03-0). Assn Trial Ed.

EVIDENCES, CHRISTIAN
see Apologetics

EVIDENCES OF CHRISTIANITY
see Apologetics

EVIDENCES OF THE BIBLE
see Bible–Evidences, Authority, etc.

EVIL
see Good and Evil

EVIL SPIRITS
see Demonology

EVOLUTION
see also Adaptation (Biology); Biology; Color of Man; Creation; Embryology; Genetic Psychology; Genetics; Heredity; Holism; Human Evolution; Island Flora and Fauna; Life–Origin; Man–Influence of Environment; Man–Origin; Natural Selection; Origin of Species; Statics and Dynamics (Social Sciences); Variation (Biology)

Barigozzi, Claudio, ed. Mechanisms of Speciation. LC 82-13014. (Progress in Clinical & Biological Research Ser.: Vol. 96). 560p. 1982. 88.00 (ISBN 0-8451-0096-3). A R Liss.

Berry, R. J. Neo-Darwinism. (Studies in Biology: No. 144). 72p. 1982. pap. text ed. 8.95 (ISBN 0-7131-2849-6). E Arnold.

Bradshaw, A. D. & McNeilly, D. T. Evolution & Pollution. (Studies in Biology: No. 130). 80p. 1981. pap. text ed. 8.95 (ISBN 0-7131-2818-6). E Arnold.

Darwin, Charles. The Origin of Species & the Descent of Man. 8.95 (ISBN 0-394-60398-2). Modern Lib.
--Origin of the Species. 1982. pap. 3.95 (ISBN 0-14-043205-1). Penguin.

Dover, G. A. & Flavell, R. B., eds. Genome Evolution. (Systematics Association Ser.: Vol. 20). 388p. 1982. 33.50 (ISBN 0-12-221380-7); pap. 17.50 (ISBN 0-12-221382-3). Acad Pr.

Eisen, Sydney & Lightman, Bernard. Victorian Science & Religion: A Bibliography of Works on Ideas & Institutions with Emphasis on Evolution, Belief & Unbelief, Published from c.1900 to 1975. 1983. price not set (ISBN 0-208-02010-1, Archon Bks). Shoe String.

Futuyma, Douglas J. & Slatkin, Montgomery, eds. Coevolution. LC 82-19496. (Illus.). 400p. 1983. text ed. write for info. (ISBN 0-87893-228-3); pap. text ed. write for info. (ISBN 0-87893-229-1). Sinauer Assoc.

Hecht, Max K. & Wallace, Bruce, eds. Evolutionary Biology. (Vol.15). 440p. 49.50x (ISBN 0-306-41042-7, Plenum Pr). Plenum Pub.

Holz, Harald. Evolution und Geist. 560p. 1981. write for info. (ISBN 3-8204-6107-8). P Lang Pubs.

Jastrow, Robert. The Enchanted Loom. 1983. pap. write for info. (ISBN 0-671-47068-X, Touchstone Bks). S&S.

Kueppers, B. O. Molecular Theory of Evolution: Outline of a Physico-Chemical Theory of the Origin of Life. (Illus.). 321p. 1983. 32.00 (ISBN 0-387-12080-7). Springer-Verlag.

March, Robert H. Physics for Poets. (Illus.). 304p. 1983. pap. 7.95 (ISBN 0-8092-5532-4). Contemp Bks.

Minkoff, Eli C. Evolutionary Biology. (Biology Ser.). (Illus.). 650p. 1983. text ed. 22.95 (ISBN 0-201-15890-6); Instrs' Manual avail. (ISBN 0-201-15891-4). A-W.

Moorhead, Paul S. & Kaplan, Martin M., eds. Mathematical Challenges to the Neo-Darwinian Interpretation of Evolution. rev. ed. (Illus.). 176p. 1983. pap. 19.95 (ISBN 0-915520-60-5). Ross-Erikson.

Nagle, James J. Heredity & Human Affairs. 3rd ed. (Illus.). 448p. 1983. text ed. 18.95 (ISBN 0-8016-3626-4). Mosby.

Oldroyd, David R. & Langham, Ian G. The Wilder Domain of Evolutionary Thought. 1983. lib. bdg. 54.50 (ISBN 90-277-1477-0, Pub. by Reidel Holland). Kluwer Boston.

Sauvani, Karl P. The Group of Seventy-Seven: Evolution, Structure, Organization. LC 81-3998. 232p. 1981. 22.50 (ISBN 0-379-00964-1); pap. 10.00 (ISBN 0-686-84382-7). Oceana.

Schopf, J. William, ed. Earth's Earliest Biosphere: Its Origin & Evolution. LC 82-61383. (Illus.). 1000p. 1983. 60.00 (ISBN 0-691-08323-1); pap. 22.50 (ISBN 0-691-02375-1). Princeton U Pr.

Sims, Reginald W. & Price, James H., eds. Evolution, Time & Space. Date not set. price not set (ISBN 0-12-644550-8). Acad Pr.

Smith, John M. Evolution & the Theory of Games. 200p. 1982. 34.50 (ISBN 0-521-24673-3); pap. 11.95 (ISBN 0-521-28884-3). Cambridge U Pr.

Thompson, Adell. Biology, Zoology, & Genetics: Evolution Model vs. Creation Model. LC 82-21995. (Illus.). 144p. (Orig.). 1983. lib. bdg. 18.00 (ISBN 0-8191-2921-6); pap. text ed. 8.25 (ISBN 0-8191-2922-4). U Pr of Amer.

Thomson, J. Arthur. Concerning Evolution. 1925. text ed. 32.50x (ISBN 0-686-83508-5). Elliots Bks.

Wilson, M. Emett. Relativity of Survival & Evolution. 1983. 10.00 (ISBN 0-533-05584-9). Vantage.

EVOLUTION–ADDRESSES, ESSAYS, LECTURES

Bajema, Carl J., ed. Natural Selection Theory: From the Speculations of the Greeks to the Quantitative Measurements of the Biometricians. LC 82-15633. (Benchmark Papers in Systematic and Evolutionary Biology: Vol. 5). 400p. 1983. 42.00 (ISBN 0-87933-412-6). Hutchinson Ross.

EVOLUTION–JUVENILE LITERATURE

Althea. How Life Began. (Cambridge Dinosaur Information Ser.). (Illus.). 26p. (gr. 7-10). 1983. pap. 1.50 (ISBN 0-521-27167-3). Cambridge U Pr.

Taylor, Kenneth R. What High School Students Should Know about Evolution. 70p. (YA) (gr. 9-12). 1983. pap. 2.50 (ISBN 0-8423-7873-1). Tyndale.

EVOLUTIONARY PSYCHOLOGY
see Genetic Psychology

EX LIBRIS
see Book-Plates

EX-SERVICE MEN
see Veterans

EXAMINATION OF THE BLOOD
see Blood–Analysis and Chemistry

EXAMINATION OF WITNESSES
see Cross-Examination

EXAMINATIONS, MEDICAL
see Diagnosis

EXAMINATIONS, PREPARATION FOR
see Study, Method Of

EXCAVATIONS (ARCHAEOLOGY)
see also Archaeology
also subdivision Antiquities under names of countries, etc., names of sites of archeological excavations, e.g. Medinet-Abu

Bartlett, John. Jericho. 128p. 1982. 35.00x (ISBN 0-7188-2456-3, Pub. by Lutterworth Pr England). State Mutual Bk.

EXCAVATIONS (ARCHAEOLOGY)–AFRICA

James, T. G., ed. Excavating in Egypt: The Egypt Exploration Society 1882-1982. 194p. 1982. 45.00x (ISBN 0-7141-0932-0, Pub. by Brit Mus Pubns England). State Mutual Bk.

EXCAVATIONS (ARCHAEOLOGY)–ASIA

Moorey, Roger. Excavation in Palestine. 1982. 35.00x (ISBN 0-7188-2432-6, Pub. by Lutterworth Pr England). State Mutual Bk.

EXCAVATIONS (ARCHAEOLOGY)–EUROPE

McDonald, William A. & Coulson, William D., eds. Excavations at Nichoria in Southwest Greece, Vol. III: The Dark Age & Byzantine Occupation. LC 78-3198. (Illus.). 544p. 1983. 49.50x (ISBN 0-8166-1144-0). U of Minn Pr.

Tomlinson, R. A. Epiduaros. (Illus.). 96p. 1983. 12.50 (ISBN 0-292-72044-0). U of Tex Pr.

Topal, Judit. The Southern Cemetery of Matricia. 106p. 1981. 90.00x (ISBN 0-569-08702-3, Pub. by Collets). State Mutual Bk.

EXCAVATIONS (ARCHAEOLOGY)–GREAT BRITAIN

MacGregor, Arthur. Anglo-Scandinavian Finds from Lloyds Bank, Pavement & Other Sites. (Archaeology of York-Small Finds 17-3). 174p. 1982. pap. text ed. 15.00x (ISBN 0-906780-02-0, 40256, Pub. by Coun Brit Archaeology England). Humanities.

EXCAVATIONS (ARCHAEOLOGY)–NORTH AMERICA

Andrews, Peter P. & Layhe, Robert, eds. Excavations on Black Mesa, Nineteen Eighty: A Descriptive Report. LC 82-72189. (Research Paper Ser.: No. 24). Date not set. price not set (ISBN 0-88104-003-7). S Ill U Pr.

Autry, William O., Jr. An Archaeological, Architectural, & Historic Cultural Resources Reconnaissance of the Northeast Metropolitan Nashville Transportation Corridor. (Illus.). vii, 120p. (Orig.). 1982. pap. 12.00 (ISBN 0-940148-04-8). TARA.

Autry, William O., Jr., et al. Archaeological Investigations at the Tennessee Valley Authority Hartsville Nuclear Plants Off-Site Borrow Areas: The Taylor Tract. (T.A.R.A. Report Ser.: No. 2). (Illus.). 125p. (Orig.). 1983. pap. price not set (ISBN 0-940148-03-X). TARA.

Lopinot, Neal H. & Hutto, M. Denise. Archaeological Investigations at the Kingfish Site, St. Clair County, Illinois. LC 82-50285. (Research Paper Ser.: No. 25). Date not set. price not set (ISBN 0-88104-001-0). S Ill U Pr.

Oakley, Carey, ed. Archaeological Investigations in the Gainesville Lake Area of the Tennessee-Tombigee Waterway, 5 vols. Incl. Vol. I. The Gainseville Lake Area Excavations. Jenkins, Ned J. & Ensor, H. Blaine. xiv, 157p. (Orig.). 1981. pap. text ed. 21.00x (ISBN 0-8173-0157-7); Vol. II. Gainesville Lake Area Ceramic Description & Chronology. Jenkins, Ned J. xx, 445p. (Orig.). 1981. pap. text ed. 46.00x (ISBN 0-8173-0158-5); Vol. III. Gainesville Lake Area Lithics: Chronology, Technology & Use. Ensor, H. Blaine. xiii, 303p. (Orig.). 1981. pap. text ed. 36.00x (ISBN 0-8173-0159-3); Vol. IV. Biocultural Studies in the Gainesville Lake Area. Caddell, Gloria M., et al. v, 334p. (Orig.). 1981. pap. text ed. 28.50x (ISBN 0-8173-0160-7); Vol. V. Archaeology of the Gainesville Lake Area. Jenkins, Ned. J. xv, 258p. (Orig.). 1982. pap. text ed. 23.50x (ISBN 0-8173-0161-5). (Illus.). 1981-82. Set. pap. text ed. 153.25x (ISBN 0-8173-0156-9). U of Ala Pr.

EXCAVATIONS (ARCHAEOLOGY)–SOUTH AMERICA

Terada, Kazuo, ed. Excavations at Huacaloma in the North Highlands of Peru, 1979: Report No. 2 of the Japanese Scientific Expedition to Nuclear America. (Illus.). 300p. 1982. text ed. 79.50 (ISBN 0-86008-315-2, Pub. by U of Tokyo Japan). Columbia U Pr.

EXCEPTIONAL CHILDREN
see also Gifted Children; Handicapped Children

Clark, Barbara. Growing up Gifted. 544p. 1983. pap. text ed. 21.95 (ISBN 0-675-20060-1). Merrill.

Holowinsky, Ivan Z. Psychology & Education of Exceptional Children & Adolescents: United States & International Perspectives. LC 82-61527. 352p. 1983. text ed. 22.95x (ISBN 0-916622-26-6). Princeton Bk Co.

Howell, Kenneth W. & Kaplan, Joseph S. Evaluating Exceptional Children: A Task Analysis Approach. 320p. 1979. text ed. 23.95 (ISBN 0-675-08389-3). Additional supplements may be obtained from publisher. Merrill.

Identifying Children with Special Needs: A Practical Guide to Developmental Screening. 2nd ed. LC 78-58531. 1983. text ed. 19.95x (ISBN 0-918452-39-2). Learning Pubns.

Paget, Kathleen & Brackett, Bruce, eds. The Psychoeducational Assessment of Pre-School Children. Date not set. price not set (ISBN 0-8089-1475-8). Grune.

Paul, James L., ed. The Exceptional Child: A Guidebook for Churches & Community Agencies. LC 82-16914. 176p. text ed. 22.00x (ISBN 0-8156-2287-2); pap. text ed. 12.95x (ISBN 0-8156-2288-0). Syracuse U Pr.

Payne, James S. & Kauffman, James M. Exceptional Children in Focus. 160p. 1983. pap. text ed. 10.95 (ISBN 0-675-20041-5). Merrill.

EXCEPTIONAL CHILDREN–EDUCATION
see also Teachers of Exceptional Children

Holowinsky, Ivan Z. Psychology & Education of Exceptional Children & Adolescents: United States & International Perspectives. LC 82-61527. 352p. 1983. text ed. 22.95x (ISBN 0-916622-26-6). Princeton Bk Co.

Horn, John L. The Education of Exceptional Children: A Consideration of Public School Problems & Policies in the Field of Differentiated Education. 343p. 1982. Repr. of 1929 ed. lib. bdg. 40.00 (ISBN 0-686-37943-8). Darby Bks.

Kirk, Samuel A. & Gallagher, James J. Educating Exceptional Children. 4th ed. 560p. 1983. text ed. 22.95 (ISBN 0-395-32772-5); write for info. instr's. manual (ISBN 0-395-32774-1); study guide 8.95 (ISBN 0-395-32773-3). HM.

EXCHANGE
see also Balance of Trade; Commerce; Money; Supply and Demand; Value

Williamson, John. The Exchange Rate System. (Policy Analyses in International Economics Ser.: No. 7). 1983. 6.00 (ISBN 0-88132-012-9). Inst Intl Eco.

EXCHANGE (BARTER)
see Barter

EXCHANGE, FOREIGN
see Foreign Exchange

EXCHANGE ADSORPTION
see Ion Exchange

EXCHANGE OF PERSONS PROGRAMS
see also Educational Exchanges
also subdivision relations (General) under names of countries, e.g. United States–Relations (General) with Latin America

Muller, Ronald E. Revitalizing the U. S. & World Economy: Would a Global Marshall Plan Work? (Vital Issues, Vol. XXX 1980-81: No. 10). 0.60 (ISBN 0-686-81605-6). Ctr Info Am.

EXCHANGE OF POPULATION
see Population Transfers

EXCHANGE OF PRISONERS OF WAR
see Prisoners of War

EXCHANGE PROGRAMS (INTERNATIONAL)
see Exchange of Persons Programs

EXCHANGES, COMMODITY
see Commodity Exchanges

EXCHANGES, EDUCATIONAL
see Educational Exchanges

EXCHANGES, PRODUCE
see Commodity Exchanges

EXCHANGES, STOCK
see Stock-Exchange

EXCISE
see Internal Revenue Law

EXCITATION, NUCLEAR
see Nuclear Excitation

EXECUTIVE ABILITY
see also Leadership; Management; Personnel Management; Planning

Bothwell, Lin K. The Art of Leadership: Skill-Building Techniques that Produce Results. (Illus.). 272p. 1983. 18.95 (ISBN 0-13-047100-3); pap. 9.95 (ISBN 0-13-047092-9). P-H.

Bourland, Gary N. An Executive Primer: The Management Club. 15p. 1983. spiral 5.95x (ISBN 0-9609350-0-2). Management Club.

Peters, Thomas J. & Waterman, Robert H., Jr. In Search of Excellence: Lessons from America's Best Run Companies. LC 82-47530. (Illus.). 384p. 1982. 19.18i (ISBN 0-06-015042-4, HarpT). Har-Row.

Vance, Charles C. Manager Today, Executive Tomorrow. LC 82-14865. 240p. 1983. Repr. of 1974 ed. lib. bdg. write for info. (ISBN 0-89874-554-3). Krieger.

EXECUTIVE AGENCIES
see Administrative Agencies

EXECUTIVE COMPENSATION
see Executives–Salaries, Pensions, etc.

EXECUTIVE INVESTIGATIONS
see Governmental Investigations

EXECUTIVES
see also Executive Ability; Personnel Management

Cawood, Diana. Assertiveness for Managers. 200p. (Orig.). 1983. pap. price not set (ISBN 0-88908-562-5). Self Counsel Pr.

Elliott, Charles. Mr. Anonymous: Robert W. Woodruff of Coca-Cola. (Illus.). 316p. 1982. 14.95 (ISBN 0-87797-062-9). Cherokee.

Fiedorek, Mary B. & Jewell, Diana L. Executive Style: Looking It... Living It. (Illus.). 256p. 1983. 12.95 (ISBN 0-8329-0254-3). New Century.

Heiser, Dick. Personal Computers for Managers. 1983. pap. 14.95 (ISBN 0-88022-031-7). Que Corp.

Lee, Gloria L. Who Gets to the Top? 160p. 1981. text ed. 33.00x (ISBN 0-566-00497-6). Gower Pub Ltd.

Moore, Carol-Lynne. Executives in Action. 2nd ed. 112p. 1982. pap. 13.50x (ISBN 0-7121-0176-4). Intl Ideas.

Steiner, George. The New CEO. LC 82-48599. (Studies of the Modern Corporation-Graduate School of Business-Columbia Univ). 160p. 1983. write for info. (ISBN 0-02-931250-7). Free Pr.

White, Lawrence J. Corporate Governance in the 1980s: New Roles & Images for Directors & Executives. (Seven Springs Studies). 1981. pap. 3.00 (ISBN 0-943006-04-X). Seven Springs.

EXECUTIVES–RECRUITING

Dudeney, Charles. A Guide to Executive Re-Employment. 192p. 1972. 29.00 (ISBN 0-7121-1972-8, Pub. by Macdonald & Evans). State Mutual Bk.

Miner, John B. The Human Constraint: The Coming Shortage of Managerial Talent. 1974. text ed. 12.50x (ISBN 0-87179-215-X). Organizat Mea.

Wilkinson, William R. Executive Musical Chairs. 176p. 1983. 15.00 (ISBN 0-911735-00-3). Warrington.

EXECUTIVES–SALARIES, PENSIONS, ETC.

Hansman, Robert J. & Larrabee, John W. Deferred Compensation: The New Methodology for Executive Reward. LC 82-48596. 1983. write for info. (ISBN 0-669-06329-0). Lexington Bks.

EXECUTIVES, TRAINING OF

Boyle, Denis & Bradick, Bill. The Challenge of Change: Developing Business Leaders for the 1980s. 45p. 1961. pap. text ed. 10.00x (ISBN 0-566-02283-4). Gower Pub Ltd.

Dyer, William G. Contemporary Issues in Management & Organization Development. LC 82-8732. 224p. 1982. text ed. 15.95 (ISBN 0-201-10348-6). A-W.

EXECUTIVES' WIVES

Finch, Janet. Married to the Job: Wives' Incorporation in Men's Work. 170p. 1983. text ed. 18.95x (ISBN 0-04-301149-7). Allen Unwin.

EXEMPTION FROM MILITARY SERVICE
see Military Service, Compulsory

EXEMPTION FROM TAXATION
see Taxation, Exemption From

EXERCISE
see also Exercise Therapy; Gymnastics; Isometric Exercise; Physical Education and Training; Physical Fitness; Yoga, Hatha
also particular types of exercise, e.g. Fencing, Rowing, Running

Anthony, Douglas. Do it In Bed: An Exercise Program. LC 82-90978. (Illus.). 96p. 1983. pap. 5.95 (ISBN 0-911433-00-7). HealthRight.

Cedeno & Lazar. The Exercise Plus Pregnancy Program: Exercises for Before, During & After Pregnancy. (Illus.). 192p. 1980. pap. 4.95 (ISBN 0-688-08697-7). Quill NY.

Costanzo, Christie. Mommy & Me Exercises the Kidnastics Program. (Illus.). 72p. (Orig.). 1983. pap. 5.95 (ISBN 0-917982-28-2). Cougar Bks.

Dunphy, Pat & Wolf, Michael. The Sexy Stomach: How to Get it & How to Keep it. LC 82-83928. (Illus.). 64p. (Orig.). 1983. pap. 4.95 (ISBN 0-88011-096-1). Leisure Pr.

Eason, Robert, ed. Adapted Physical Activity: From Theory to Implementation. Proceedings of the 3rd International Symposium on Adapted Physical Activities. 1983. text ed. price not set (ISBN 0-931250-40-4). Human Kinetics.
Fit Magazine Editors. Breast Care. (Fit Self-Improvement Ser.). 96p. 1983. pap. 7.95 (ISBN 0-89037-259-4). Anderson World.
--Figure Maintenance. (Fit Self-Improvement Ser.). 96p. 1983. pap. 7.95 (ISBN 0-89037-255-1). Anderson World.
--Legs & Thifgs. (Fit Self-Improvement Ser.). 96p. 1983. pap. 7.95 (ISBN 0-89037-260-8). Anderson World.
Getchell, Bud. Physical Fitness: A Way of Life. 2nd ed. LC 78-13094. 1979. pap. text ed. 12.95 (ISBN 0-471-04037-1); avail tchr's manual (ISBN 0-471-04985-9). Wiley.
--Physical Fitness: A Way of Life. 3rd ed. LC 82-17654. 258p. 1983. text ed. 12.95 (ISBN 0-471-09635-0). Wiley.
Knuttgen, Howard, ed. Biochemistry of Exericise. (International Series on Sport Sciences). 1983. text ed. price not set (ISBN 0-931250-41-2). Human Kinetics.
Moncure, Jane B. Healthkins Exercise! LC 82-14712. (Healthkins Ser.). (Illus.). 32p. (ps-2). 1982. lib. bdg. 6.05 (ISBN 0-89565-241-2). Childs World.
Peterson, Susan L. The Women's Stretching Book. LC 82-83927. (Illus.). 144p. (Orig.). 1983. pap. 6.95 (ISBN 0-88011-095-3). Leisure Pr.
Prudden, Suzy. Exercise Program for Young Children. LC 82-40506. (Illus.). 192p. 1983. pap. 6.95 (ISBN 0-89480-371-9). Workman Pub.
Shapiro, Jacqueline R. & Swaybill, Marion L. Sexibody Diet & Exercise Program. 1982. text ed. 10.95 (ISBN 0-914094-19-X). Symphony.
Sorenson, Jacki & Bruns, Bill. Jacki Sorenson's Aerobic Lifestyles. 1983. 15.95 (ISBN 0-671-45616-4, Poseidon). PB.
Sorine, Stephanie. The French Riviera Body Book. (Illus.). 128p. 1983. 12.95 (ISBN 0-312-30527-3). St Martin.
Springer, Jeanne A. Fitness for You: A Head-to-Toe Stretching Strengthening & Body-Toning Exercise Program for Women. LC 82-90713. (Illus.). 68p. (Orig.). 1982. pap. 3.95 (ISBN 0-9609394-0-7). Kelane Pub.
Yanker, Gary D. The Complete Book of Exercise Walking. (Illus.). 288p. (Orig.). 1983. pap. 8.95 (ISBN 0-8092-5535-9). Contemp Bks.

EXERCISE–PHYSIOLOGICAL EFFECT
Galbo, H. Hormonal & Metabolic Adaption to Exercise. (Illus.). 120p. 1982. 21.00 (ISBN 0-86577-065-4). Thieme-Stratton.
Katch, Frank I. & McArdle, William D. Nutrition, Weight Control, & Exercise. LC 82-25873. (Illus.). 300p. 1983. text ed. price not set (ISBN 0-8121-0867-1). Lea & Febiger.
Lamb, David R. Physiology of Exercises: Responses & Adaptations. 2nd ed. 464p. 1983. text ed. 20.95 (ISBN 0-02-367210-2); lab manual 9.95 (ISBN 0-02-367220-X). Macmillan.

EXERCISE, DEVOTIONAL
see Devotional Exercises

EXERCISE, SPIRITUAL
see Spiritual Exercises

EXERCISE THERAPY
see also Mechanotherapy
Lowe, Carl & Nechas, Jim. Body Healing. (Illus.). 440p. 1983. 21.95 (ISBN 0-87857-441-7, 05-024-0). Rodale Pr Inc.

EXERCISES, DEVOTIONAL
see Devotional Exercises

EXERCISES, SPIRITUAL
see Spiritual Exercises

EXHAUST CONTROL DEVICES (MOTOR VEHICLES)
see Motor Vehicles–Pollution Control Devices

EXHAUST GAS, AUTOMOBILE
see Automobiles–Motors–Exhaust Gas

EXHAUSTERS
see Compressors

EXHAUSTION
see Fatigue

EXHIBITIONS
see also Fairs
also particular exhibitions, e.g. Chicago–World's Columbian Exposition, 1893; exhibitions under special subjects, e.g. Paintings–Exhibitions
Trade & Professional Exhibits Directory, 3 Pts. 300p. 1983. pap. 75.00x (ISBN 0-8103-1109-7). Gale.

EXHIBITS
see Exhibitions

EXISTENTIALISM
Blackham, H. J. Six Existentialist Thinkers. 179p. 1965. pap. 7.95 (ISBN 0-7100-4611-1). Routledge & Kegan.
Harbert, David L. Existence, Knowing, & Philosophical Systems. LC 82-17565. 226p. (Orig.). 1983. lib. bdg. 21.75 (ISBN 0-8191-2804-X); pap. text ed. 10.25 (ISBN 0-8191-2805-8). U Pr of Amer.
Hayim, Gila J. The Existential Sociology of Jean-Paul Sartre. LC 80-10131. 176p. 1982. pap. text ed. 7.00 (ISBN 0-87023-381-5). U of Mass Pr.
Solomon, Robert C. Existentialism. 1974. pap. 5.95 (ISBN 0-686-38912-3, Mod LibC). Modern Lib.
Wilson, Colin. The New Existentialism. 188p. 1983. pap. 8.95 (ISBN 0-7045-0415-4, Pub by Salem Hse Ltd). Merrimack Bk Serv.

EXOBIOLOGY
see Life on Other Planets

EXODONTIA
see Teeth–Extraction

EXODUS, THE
Jacobson, Howard. The Exagoge of Ezekiel. LC 82-4410. 240p. 1983. 44.50 (ISBN 0-521-24580-X). Cambridge U Pr.

EXORCISM
see also Demonology; Witchcraft
Kapferer, Bruce. A Celebration of Demons. LC 81-48677. (Illus.). 352p. (Orig.). 1983. 32.50x (ISBN 0-253-31326-0); pap. 18.50x (ISBN 0-253-20304-X). Ind U Pr.

EXPANSION (U. S. POLITICS)
see Imperialism; United States–Territorial Expansion

EXPANSION OF GASES
see Gases

EXPEDITIONS, ANTARCTIC
see Antarctic Regions;
also names of expeditions, and names of explorers

EXPEDITIONS, ARCTIC
see Arctic Regions;
also names of expeditions, and names of explorers

EXPEDITIONS, SCIENTIFIC
see Scientific Expeditions

EXPENDITURES, PUBLIC
see also Budget; Government Spending Policy
Adler, Jack. A Consumer's Guide to Travel. LC 82-22195. 240p. (Orig.). 1983. pap. 8.95 (ISBN 0-88496-194-X). Capra Pr.
Annan, Bill & Hinchcliffe, Keith. Planning Policy Analysis & Public Spending: Theory & the Papua New Guinea Practice. 168p. 1982. text ed. 35.00x (ISBN 0-566-00496-8). Gower Pub Ltd.
Collender, Stanley E. The Guide to the Federal Budget: Fiscal 1984 Edition. LC 82-643840. 150p. (Orig.). 1983. pap. text ed. 10.00 (ISBN 0-87766-321-1). Urban Inst.
Haveman, Robert & Margolis, Julius. Public Expenditure & Policy Analysis. 3rd ed. LC 82-81354. 608p. pap. text ed. 18.95 (ISBN 0-686-82250-1). HM.

EXPERIENCE
see also Pragmatism; Wisdom
Harbert, David L. Existence, Knowing, & Philosophical Systems. LC 82-17565. 226p. (Orig.). 1983. lib. bdg. 21.75 (ISBN 0-8191-2804-X); pap. text ed. 10.25 (ISBN 0-8191-2805-8). U Pr of Amer.
Peele, Stanton. The Science of Experience: A Direction for Psychology. LC 81-48555. 1983. price not set (ISBN 0-669-05420-8). Lexington Bks.
Powell, Ralph A. Freely Chosen Reality. LC 82-21943. 194p. (Orig.). 1983. lib. bdg. 21.50 (ISBN 0-8191-2924-0); pap. text ed. 10.25 (ISBN 0-8191-2925-9). U Pr of Amer.

EXPERIENCE (RELIGION)
Hicks, Roy. Another Look at the Rapture. 120p. (Orig.). 1982. pap. 3.95 (ISBN 0-89274-246-1). Harrison Hse.
White, Sharon. The Man Who Talked With Angels. 226p. (Orig.). 1982. pap. 5.95 (ISBN 0-89221-088-5, Pub. by SonLife). New Leaf.

EXPERIMENTAL BIOLOGY
see Biology, Experimental

EXPERIMENTAL DESIGN
Brownlee, Kenneth A. Statistical Theory & Methodology in Science & Engineering. 2nd ed. 590p. 1965. 39.95x (ISBN 0-471-11355-7). Wiley.

EXPERIMENTAL METHODS IN EDUCATION
see Education–Experimental Methods

EXPERIMENTAL PATHOLOGY
see Pathology, Experimental

EXPERIMENTAL PSYCHIATRY
see Psychiatric Research

EXPERIMENTAL PSYCHOLOGY
see Psychology, Experimental

EXPERIMENTAL SURGERY
see Surgery, Experimental

EXPERIMENTATION ON MAN, MEDICAL
see Human Experimentation in Medicine

EXPLORATION, SUBMARINE
see Underwater Exploration

EXPLORATION, UNDERWATER (ARCHAEOLOGY)
see Underwater Archaeology

EXPLORATION OF SPACE
see Outer Space–Exploration

EXPLORATION OF THE DEEP SEA
see Marine Biology; Marine Fauna; Marine Flora

EXPLORERS
see also Discoveries (In Geography); Travelers; Voyages and Travels;
also subdivisions Description and Travel and Discovery and Exploration under names of continents, countries, etc.
Dampier, William. Voyage to New Holland. 256p. 1982. text ed. 22.50x (ISBN 0-904387-75-5, Pub. by Alan Sutton England); pap. text ed. 10.50x (ISBN 0-86299-006-8). Humanities.
Limb, Sue & Cordingley, Patrick. Captain Oates: Soldier & Explorer. (Illus.). 176p. 1982. 31.50 (ISBN 0-7134-2693-4, Pub. by Batsford England). David & Charles.
Richman, Irving B. Spanish Conquerors. 1919. text ed. 8.50x (ISBN 0-686-83782-7). Elliots Bks.

EXPLORERS–JUVENILE LITERATURE
Sandak, Cass R. Explorers & Discovery. (A Reference First Bk.). (Illus.). 96p. (gr. 4 up). 1983. PLB 8.90 (ISBN 0-531-04537-4). Watts.
Weil, Lisl. I, Christopher Columbus. LC 82-16323. (Illus.). 48p. (gr. k-4). 1983. 10.95 (ISBN 0-689-30965-1). Atheneum.

EXPLOSIONS
see also Shock Waves
Hewison, C. H. Locomotive Boiler Explosions. (Illus.). 144p. 1982. 16.50 (ISBN 0-7153-8305-1). David & Charles.

EXPORT AND IMPORT CONTROLS
see Foreign Trade Regulation

EXPORT CREDIT
OECD Staff. Export Credit Financing Systems in OECD Member Countries. 252p. (Orig.). 1982. pap. 12.50x (ISBN 92-64-12291-5). OECD.

EXPORT MARKETING
Allen, P. The Practice of Exporting. 240p. 1977. 29.00x (ISBN 0-7121-1658-3, Pub. by Macdonald & Evans). State Mutual Bk.
American Chamber of Commerce in Japan. Exporting to Japan. 1982. 10.00 (ISBN 0-686-37954-3). A M Newman.
U. S. Dept. of Commerce. A Basic Guide to Exporting. 1981. 50.00 (ISBN 0-686-37968-3). Info Gatekeepers.
Walsh, L. S. International Marketing. 272p. 1981. 30.00x (ISBN 0-7121-0968-4, Pub. by Macdonald & Evans). State Mutual Bk.

EXPORTS
see Commerce

EXPOSITIONS
see Exhibitions

EXPRESS HIGHWAYS
Brodsly, David. L. A. Freeway: An Appreciative Essay. (Illus.). 188p. 1983. pap. 8.95 (ISBN 0-520-04546-7, CAL 535). U of Cal Pr.
Kundell, James E. & White, Fred C. Prime Farmland in Georgia. 49p. 1982. pap. 6.50 (ISBN 0-89854-081-X). U of GA Inst Govt.

EXPRESSION (PHILOSOPHY)
Ladenson, Robert F. A Philosophy of Free Expression & Its Constitutional Applications. LC 82-18106. (Philosophy & Society Ser.). 224p. 1983. text ed. 34.50x (ISBN 0-8476-6761-8). Rowman.

EXPRESSIONISM (ART)
Muller, Kurt. Konventionen und Tendenzen der Gesellschaftskritik Im Expressionistischen Amerikanischen Drama der Zwanziger Jahre. 250p. (Ger.). 1977. write for info. (ISBN 3-261-02201-9). P Lang Pubs.

EXPRESSWAYS
see Express Highways

EXPROPRIATION
see Eminent Domain

EXPULSION
see United States–Emigration and Immigration

EXTEMPORIZATION (MUSIC)
see Improvisation (Music)

EXTERIOR BALLISTICS
see Ballistics

EXTERMINATION
see Insect Control; Pest Control;
also names of specific pests, with or without the subdivision extermination

EXTERMINATION, JEWISH (1939-1945)
see Holocaust, Jewish (1939-1945)

EXTINCT ANIMALS
see also Paleontology; Rare Animals
Cuppy, Will. How to Become Extinct. LC 82-17649. (Illus.). 114p. 1941. pap. 4.95 (ISBN 0-226-12826-1). U of Chicago Pr.
McGowan, Christopher. The Successful Dragons: A Natural History of Extinct Reptiles. (Illus.). 282p. 1983. 29.95 (ISBN 0-88866-618-7). Samuel Stevens.
Oliveros, Chuck. The Pterodactyl in the Wilderness. 56p. (Orig.). 1983. pap. 3.00 (ISBN 0-911757-00-7). Dead Angel.

EXTINCT CITIES
see Cities and Towns, Ruined, Extinct, etc.

EXTRACTION (DENTISTRY)
see Teeth–Extraction

EXTRA-CURRICULAR, ACTIVITIES
see Student Activities

EXTRADITION
Bassiouni, M. C., ed. International Extradition: U. S. Law & Practice, Release 1, Binder 1. 1983. looseleaf 85.00 (ISBN 0-379-20746-X). Oceana.

EXTRAGALACTIC NEBULAE
see Galaxies

EXTRASENSORY PERCEPTION
see also Psychical Research
Deigh, Khigh, ed. The Golden Oracle: The Ancient Chinese Way to Prosperity. LC 82-18471. (Illus.). 176p. 1983. 11.95 (ISBN 0-668-05661-4). Arco.
Mintz, Elizabeth & Schmeidler, R. The Psychic Thread: Paranormal & Transpersonal Aspects of Psychotherapy. 240p. 1983. 24.95 (ISBN 0-89885-139-4). Human Sci Pr.

EXTRATERRESTRIAL ENVIRONMENT
see Space Environment

EXTRATERRESTRIAL LIFE
see Life on Other Planets

EXTRATERRITORIALITY
Rosenthal, Douglas E. & Knighton, William M. National Laws & International Commerce: The Problem of Extraterritoriality. (Chatham House Papers Ser.: No. 17). 96p. (Orig.). 1982. pap. 10.00 (ISBN 0-7100-9338-1). Routledge & Kegan.

EXTREMITIES (ANATOMY)
see also Leg
Fallon, John F. & Caplan, Arnold I., eds. Limb Development & Regeneration, Pt. A. LC 82-20391. (Progress in Clinical & Biological Research Ser.: Vol. 110A). 639p. 1982. 68.00 (ISBN 0-8451-0170-6). A R Liss.
Kelley, Robert O. & Goetnick, Paul F., eds. Limb Development & Regeneration, Pt. B. LC 82-20391. (Progress in Clinical & Biological Research Ser.: Vol. 110B). 434p. 1982. 46.00 (ISBN 0-8451-0171-4). A R Liss.

EXTRINSIC EVIDENCE
see Evidence (Law)

EYE
see also Retina; Vision
Sheffield, J. B. & Hilfer, S. R., eds. Cellular Communication During Ocular Development. (Cell & Developmental Biology of the Eye Ser.). (Illus.). 196p. 1983. 32.50 (ISBN 0-387-90773-4). Springer-Verlag.

EYE-CARE AND HYGIENE
Lee, Howard W. Eye Care: What You Need to Know before You See the Eye Doctor. 250p. 1982. pap. 6.95 (ISBN 0-914091-16-6). Chicago Review.

EYE–DISEASES AND DEFECTS
see also Blindness; Color Blindness; Glaucoma; Nystagmus; Ophthalmology; Retina–Diseases; Strabismus; Uvea–Diseases; Veterinary Ophthalmology
Cotlier, Edward & Maumenee, Irene H., eds. Genetic Eye Diseases: Retinitis Pigmentosa & Other Inherited Eye Disorders. LC 82-13049. (Birth Defects; Original Article Ser.: Vol. 18, No. 6). 746p. 1982. 76.00 (ISBN 0-8451-1050-0). A R Liss.
Peiffer, Robert L., Jr. Comparative Ophthalmic Pathology. (Illus.). 448p. 1983. 60.00x (ISBN 0-398-04780-4). C C Thomas.

EYE–EXAMINATION
Fuller, Dwain & Hutton, William, eds. Presurgical Evaluation of Eyes with Opaque Media. Date not set. 39.50 (ISBN 0-8089-1470-7). Grune.

EYE–JUVENILE LITERATURE
Doty, Roy. Eye Fooled You. (Illus.). 48p. (gr. 3-7). 1983. pap. 2.95 (ISBN 0-02-042980-0, Collier). Macmillan.

EYE–MOVEMENTS
Gonzalez, Caleb. Strabismus & Ocular Motility. (Illus.). 298p. 1983. lib. bdg. price not set (ISBN 0-683-03629-7). Williams & Wilkins.
Roucoux, A. & Crommelinck, M. Physiological & Pathological Aspects of Eye Movements. 1983. 76.00 (ISBN 90-619-3730-2, Pub. by Junk Pubs Netherlands). Kluwer Boston.

EYE–SURGERY
Smith, Byron C. & Bosniak, Stephen L., eds. Advances in Ophthalmic Plastic & Reconstructive Surgery. (Illus.). 278p. 1983. 60.00 (ISBN 0-08-029656-4). Pergamon.
Stern, Walter H., ed. Vitrectomy Techniques for the Anterior Segment Surgeon: A Practical Approach. (Current Opthamology Monographs). write for info. Grune.

EYO LANGUAGE
see Yoruba Language

EZEKIEL, THE PROPHET
Jacobson, Howard. The Exagoge of Ezekiel. LC 82-4410. 240p. 1983. 44.50 (ISBN 0-521-24580-X). Cambridge U Pr.

F

F-FIFTY-ONE (FIGHTER PLANES)
see Mustang (Fighter Planes)

FABLES
see also Animals, Legends and Stories Of; Bestiaries; Folk-Lore; Parables; Romances
Kennerly, Karen, ed. Hesitant Wolf, Scrupulous Fox: Fables Selected from World Literature. LC 82-3328. (Illus.). 352p. 1983. pap. 9.95 (ISBN 0-8052-0717-1). Schocken.

FABRI, FELIX, 1441-1502
Fabri, Felix. The Wanderings of Felix Fabri: Circa 1480-1483 A.D, 2 Vols. Stewart, Aubrey, tr. LC 74-141802. Set. 65.00 (ISBN 0-404-09140-7); Vol. 9-10 (Vol. 2, Pts. 1-2) 32.50 (ISBN 0-686-81995-0); 32.50 (ISBN 0-686-81996-9). AMS Pr.

FABRICS
see Textile Fabrics

FACE
see also Beauty, Personal; Mouth; Physiognomy
Gartner, Leslie P. Essentials of Oral Histology & Embryology. LC 82-90755. (Illus.). 120p. 1982. pap. text ed. 8.75 (ISBN 0-910841-00-4). Jen Hse Pub Co.
Garvy, John W., Jr. Five Phase Facial Diagnosis. Liebermann, Jeremiah, ed. (Five Phase Energetics Ser.: No. 3). (Illus., Orig.). 1982. pap. 3.00 (ISBN 0-943450-02-0). Wellbeing Bks.

Imber, Gerald & Kurtin, Stephen B. Face Care: The Plan for Looking Younger Longer. 228p. 1983. 14.95 (ISBN 0-89479-127-3). A & W Pubs.

Kushi, Michio. Your Face Never Lies: An Introduction to Oriental Diagnosis. (The Macrobiotic Home Library). 144p. 1983. pap. 7.95 (ISBN 0-89529-214-9). Avery Pub.

FACETIAE

see Wit and Humor;

see American Wit and Humor, English Wit and Humor, and similar headings subdivided by subject, e.g. American Wit and Humor-Sports

FACTOR ANALYSIS

Gorsuch, Richard L. Factor Analysis. 2nd ed. 375p. 1983. text ed. write for info. (ISBN 0-89859-202-X). L Erlbaum Assocs.

FACTORIES

see also Mills and Mill-Work; Workshops

also headings beginning with the word Factory

Low, J. D. & Warner, William L. Social System of the Modern Factory: The Strike, a Social Analysis. 1947. text ed. 15.50x (ISBN 0-686-83772-X). Elliots Bks.

FACTORIES-DESIGN AND CONSTRUCTION

Apple, J. M. Plant Layout & Materials Handling. 3rd ed. LC 77-75127. (Illus.). 600p. 1977. 27.95x (ISBN 0-471-07171-4). Wiley.

FACTORIES-LAW AND LEGISLATION

see Factory Laws and Legislation

FACTORIES-MAINTENANCE AND REPAIR

see Plant Maintenance

FACTORIES-MANAGEMENT

see Factory Management

FACTORIES-NOISE

see Industrial Noise

FACTORY AND TRADE WASTE

see also Pollution; Refuse and Refuse Disposal

Bell, John M., ed. Thirty-Seven Purdue University Industrial Waste Conference, 1982. LC 77-84415. (Illus.). 1000p. 1983. 69.95 (ISBN 0-250-40592-X). Ann Arbor Science.

Brown, Michael D. & Reilly, Thomas C. Solid Waste Transfer Fundamentals. LC 81-66617. (Illus.). 1981. 19.95 (ISBN 0-250-40426-5). Ann Arbor Science.

Crandall, Robert W. Controlling Industrial Pollution: The Economics & Politics of Clean Air. LC 82-45982. 220p. 1983. 24.95 (ISBN 0-8157-1604-4); pap. 9.95 (ISBN 0-8157-1603-6). Brookings.

Feder & Burrell. Impact of Seafood Cannery Waste on the Benthic Biota & Adjacent Waters at Dutch Harbor Alaska. (IMS Report Ser.: No. R82-1). write for info. U of AK Inst Marine.

Industrial Wastewater Control Program for Municipal Agencies. (Manual of Practice, Operations & Maintenance: No. 4). 166p. (Orig.). 1982. pap. text ed. 18.00 (ISBN 0-943244-37-4). Water Pollution.

Lowe, J. & Lewis, D. Total Environmental Control: The Economics of Cross-Media Pollution Transfers. LC 82-9827. (Illus.). 134p. 1982. 21.50 (ISBN 0-08-026276-7). Pergamon.

Mayer, Garry F., pref. by. Ecological Stress & the New York Bight: Science & Management. LC 82-71795. (Illus.). x, 717p. (Orig.). 1982. pap. text ed. 10.00 (ISBN 0-9608990-0-6). Estuarine Res.

Mid-Atlantic Conference. Industrial Waste: Proceedings of the 14th Mid-Atlantic Conference. Alleman, James E. & Kavanagh, Joseph T., eds. LC 81-65971. (Illus.). 612p. 1982. 39.95 (ISBN 0-250-40510-5). Ann Arbor Science.

OECD Staff. Product Durability & Product Life Extension: Their Contribution to Solid Waste Management. 129p. (Orig.). 1982. pap. 10.00x (ISBN 92-64-12293-1). OECD.

Pratt, Alan, ed. Directory of Waste Disposal & Recovery. 232p. 1978. 60.00x (ISBN 0-686-99829-4, Pub. by Graham & Trotman England). State Mutual Bk.

Vance, Mary. Industrial Waste Disposal: A Bibliography. (Public Administration Ser.: Bibliography). 1982. pap. 8.25 (ISBN 0-88066-153-4). Vance Biblios.

FACTORY BUILDINGS

see Factories

FACTORY DESIGN

see Factories-Design and Construction

FACTORY LAWS AND LEGISLATION

see also Employers' Liability; Industrial Accidents; Labor Laws and Legislation

Deterrence & Compensation: Legal Liability in Occupational Safety & Health. 76p. 1982. pap. 10.00 (ISBN 92-2-103010-5, ILO 194, ILO). Unipub.

FACTORY LAYOUT

see Factories-Design and Construction

FACTORY MANAGEMENT

see also Assembly-Line Methods; Industrial Engineering; Office Management; Personnel Management; Plant Engineering; Production Control; Production Engineering; Quality Control

APICS Cirriculum & Certification Program Council Committee, ed. Shop Floor Controls Reprints. 165p. 1973. 13.50 (ISBN 0-935406-17-4). Am Prod & Inventory.

FACTORY NOISE

see Industrial Noise

FACTORY WASTE

see Factory and Trade Waste

FACULTY (EDUCATION)

see College Teachers; Teachers; Universities and Colleges-Faculty

FAIENCE

see Pottery

FAILURE OF SOLIDS

see Fracture Mechanics

FAIR EMPLOYMENT PRACTICE

see Discrimination in Employment

FAIRIES

Croker, Thomas C. Fairy Legends & Tradition of the South Ireland. LC 82-5885. 1983. 50.00 (ISBN 0-8201-1380-8). Schol Facsimiles.

Gardner, Edward L. Fairies. LC 82-42707. (Illus.). 53p. 1983. pap. 5.75 (ISBN 0-8356-0569-8, Quest). Theos Pub Hse.

Keightley, Thomas. The Fairy Mythology. 560p. 1982. 30.00x (Pub. by Wildwood House). State Mutual Bk.

Poortvliet, Rien & Huygen, Wil. Secrets of the Gnomes. LC 82-3948. (Illus.). 200p. 1982. 19.95 (ISBN 0-8109-1614-2). Abrams.

FAIRS

see also Exhibitions; Markets

Gale, Janice & Gale, Stephen. Guide to Fairs, Festivals & Fun Events. (Illus.). 190p. Date not set. pap. 6.95 (ISBN 0-686-84245-6). Banyan Bks.

Primack, Phil. The New England Fair. LC 81-86607. (Illus.). 286p. (Orig.). 1982. pap. 9.95 (ISBN 0-87106-970-9). Globe Pequot.

FAIRY TALES

see also Folk-Lore; Legends; Tales

Brothers Grimm. The Devil with the Three Golden Hairs. LC 82-12735. (Illus.). 40p. (gr. k-3). 1983. 10.95 (ISBN 0-394-85560-4); lib. bdg. 10.99 (ISBN 0-394-95560-9). Knopf.

--Favorite Tales from Grimm. (Illus.). (gr. 1 up). 1982. 15.95 (ISBN 0-590-07791-0, Four Winds). Schol Bk Serv.

--Little Red Riding Hood. Hyman, Trina S., retold by. & illus. LC 82-7700. (Illus.). 32p. (ps-3). 1982. reinforced binding 13.95 (ISBN 0-8234-0470-6). Holiday.

--Snow White. LC 82-20960. (Illus.). 24p. (ps-3). 1983. PLB 11.95 (ISBN 0-571-12518-2). Faber & Faber.

Caraway, Caren. Hansel & Gretel. 32p. (ps up). 1982. pap. 2.95 (ISBN 0-88045-017-7). Stemmer Hse.

Croker, Thomas C. Fairy Legends & Tradition of the South Ireland. LC 82-5885. 1983. 50.00 (ISBN 0-8201-1380-8). Schol Facsimiles.

Dahl, Roald. Roald Dahl's Revolting Rhymes. LC 82-15263. (Illus.). 48p. 1983. 9.95 (ISBN 0-394-85422-5); lib. bdg. 9.99 (ISBN 0-394-95422-X). Knopf.

Evans, C. S. Cinderella. (Illus.). 1982. 14.95 (ISBN 0-434-95862-X, Pub. by Heinemann). David & Charles.

Gipson, Morrell. Favorite Nursery Tales. LC 82-45304. (Illus.). 32p. 1983. 9.95a (ISBN 0-385-17960-X); PLB (ISBN 0-385-17961-8). Doubleday.

Grahame, Kenneth. The Wind in the Willows. Green, Peter, ed. (The World's Classics Ser.). 224p. 1983. pap. 3.95 (ISBN 0-19-281640-3, GB). Oxford U Pr.

Hall, Nancy C. Macmillan Fairy Tale Alphabet Book. LC 82-20905. (Illus.). 64p. 1983. 9.95 (ISBN 0-02-741960-6). Macmillan.

Hoban, Russell. The Flight of Bembel Rudzuk. 32p. 1982. 6.95 (ISBN 0-399-20888-7, Philomel). Putnam Pub Group.

Hyman, Trina S., as told by. The Sleeping Beauty. 48p. (gr. 1 up). 1983. pap. 5.70i (ISBN 0-316-38708-8). Little.

Keigwin, R. P., ed. Hans Christian Andersen: Eighty Fairy Tales. Date not set. 14.95 (ISBN 0-686-37608-0). Pantheon.

North, Carol. The Three Bears. LC 82-82650. (First Little Golden Bk.). (Illus.). 24p. (ps). 1983. 0.69 (ISBN 0-307-10147-9, Golden Pr); PLB price not set (ISBN 0-307-68147-5). Western Pub.

Rackham, Arthur, illus. Grimm Fairy Tales. (Illus.). 1982. 14.95 (ISBN 0-434-95862-X, Pub. by Heinemann). David & Charles.

FAITH

see also Atheism; Faith and Reason; Salvation; Sanctification; Skepticism; Trust in God; Truth

Chubb, J. Faith Possesses Understanding: A Suggestion for a New Direction in Rational Theology. 200p. 1982. text ed. 14.00x (ISBN 0-391-02756-5, Pub. by Concept India). Humanities.

Collingwood, Guillermo. Las Dos Naturalezas del Creyente. 2nd ed. Bennett, Gordon H., ed. Bautista, Sara, tr. from Eng. (La Serie Diamante). (Illus.). 52p. (Span.). 1982. pap. 0.85 (ISBN 0-942504-03-8). Overcomer Pr.

Crawford, C. C. What the Bible Says about Faith. LC 82-72621. (What the Bible Says Ser.). 380p. 1982. 13.50 (ISBN 0-89900-089-4). College Pr Pub.

Day, N. R. David's Faithfulness. 85p. (Orig.). 1979. pap. 6.95 (ISBN 0-940754-02-9). Ed Ministries.

Droege, Thomas A. Faith Passages & Patterns. LC 82-48544. (Lead Bks.). 128p. 1983. pap. 3.95 (ISBN 0-8006-1602-2, 1-1602). Fortress.

Faith Development in the Adult Life Cycle. 1983. 9.95 (ISBN 0-8215-9899-6). Sadlier.

Faith's Cooperating Powers. 1979. 1.25 (ISBN 0-89858-028-5). Fill the Gap.

Faith's Definition. 1981. 1.25 (ISBN 0-89858-019-6). Fill the Gap.

Faith's Destroyers. 1981. 1.25 (ISBN 0-89858-020-X). Fill the Gap.

Faith's Prayer Sequence. 1979. 1.25 (ISBN 0-89858-029-3). Fill the Gap.

Faith's Steadfastness. 1981. 1.25 (ISBN 0-89858-021-8). Fill the Gap.

Ferguson, John. Gods Many, Lords Many. 128p. 1982. 39.00x (ISBN 0-7188-2496-2, Pub. by Lutterworth Pr England). State Mutual Bk.

Fishelis, Avraham. Bastion of Faith. 3rd ed. 256p. 1980. 9.00 (ISBN 0-9605560-1-X). A Fishelis.

Gutting, Gary. Religious Belief & Religious Skepticism. LC 82-50287. xi, 192p. 1983. pap. text ed. 9.95x (ISBN 0-268-01618-6, 85-16189). U of Notre Dame Pr.

Hagin, Kenneth E. Having Faith in Your Faith. 1981. pap. 0.50 (ISBN 0-89276-252-7). Hagin Ministry.

--New Thresholds of Faith. 1972. pap. 2.50 (ISBN 0-89276-070-2). Hagin Ministry.

Hagin, Kenneth, Jr. Faith Takes Back What the Devil's Stolen. 1982. pap. 0.50 (ISBN 0-89276-709-X). Hagin Ministry.

Hayes, Norvel. How to Protect Your Faith. 80p. 1983. pap. 2.95 (ISBN 0-89274-279-8). Harrison Hse.

Heil, Ruth. My Child Within: A Young Woman's Reflections on Becoming Pregnant, Being Pregnant & Giving Birth. 128p. 1983. pap. 5.95 (ISBN 0-89107-268-3). Good News.

Hodges, Zane C. The Gospel Under Siege: A Study on Faith & Works. 125p. (Orig.). 1981. pap. 4.95 (ISBN 0-9607576-0-0). Redencion Viva.

Holbrook, D. L. God Needs Strong Men. 3.75 (ISBN 0-89137-530-9). Quality Pubns.

Horden, William. Experience & Faith. LC 82-72653. 160p. 1983. pap. 8.95 (ISBN 0-8066-1960-0, 10-2133). Augsburg.

Ingersall, Robert G. Faith or Agnosticism. 24p. Date not set. pap. 3.00 (ISBN 0-686-83985-4). Am Atheist.

Kazee, Buell H. Faith is the Victory. 1983. pap. 4.95 (ISBN 0-8423-0844-X). Tyndale.

McCurley, Foster R. Ancient Myths & Biblical Faith. LC 82-48589. 208p. 1983. pap. 11.95 (ISBN 0-8006-1696-0, 1-1696). Fortress.

Meyer, Charles R. Religious Belief in a Scientific World. 1983. 12.95 (ISBN 0-88347-152-3). Thomas More.

O'Connor, Francine. ABC'S of Faith, Bk. 5. 32p. (gr. 1-4). 1982. pap. 1.75 (ISBN 0-89243-165-2). Liguori Pubns.

Pedraz, Juan L. I Wish I Could Believe. Attanasio, Salvatore, tr. from Span. LC 82-20606. 216p. (Orig.). 1983. pap. 7.95 (ISBN 0-8189-0445-3). Alba.

Price, Eugenia. No Pat Answers. 144p. 1983. pap. 4.95 (ISBN 0-310-31331-7). Zondervan.

Requirements for Faithfulness. 1981. 1.25 (ISBN 0-89858-030-7). Fill the Gap.

Richardson, W. Christian Doctrine: The Faith...Once Delivered. LC 82-25598. (Christian Activities Ser.). 448p. 1983. pap. 9.95 (ISBN 0-87239-610-X). Standard Pub.

Savelle, Jerry. Energizing Your Faith. Date not set. pap. price not set (ISBN 0-89274-285-2, HH-285). Harrison Hse.

--Nature of Faith. Date not set. pap. price not set (ISBN 0-89274-284-4, HH-284). Harrison Hse.

Steidl, G. S. By Faith. 48p. pap. 2.25 (ISBN 0-88172-127-1). Believers Bkshelf.

Thomas Aquinas. Faith. (Summa Theologial Ser.: Vol. 31). 1975. 19.95 (ISBN 0-07-002006-X). McGraw.

Ujka, Mary. The Cross Gives Me Courage. 132p. (Orig.). 1983. pap. 5.95 (ISBN 0-87973-618-6, 618). Our Sunday Visitor.

Waltz, Alan K. To Proclaim the Faith. 144p. 1983. pap. 3.95 (ISBN 0-687-42252-3). Abingdon.

Westerhoff, John H., III. Will Our Children Have Faith? 144p. 1983. pap. 6.95 (ISBN 0-8164-2435-7). Seabury.

Wolf, Barbara & Wolf, Frederick B. Exploring Faith & Life: A Journey in Faith for Junior High - Manual for Clergy & Leaders. 64p. (Orig.). 1983. pap. 3.95 (ISBN 0-8164-2437-3). Seabury.

--Exploring Faith & Life: A Journey in Faith for Junior High - Manual for Sponsors. 32p. (Orig.). 1983. pap. 2.95 (ISBN 0-8164-2436-5). Seabury.

Yates, Miles & Charles, John. Believing in God. 1982. pap. 1.70 (ISBN 0-88028-021-2). Forward Movement.

FAITH, CONFESSIONS OF

see Creeds

FAITH AND REASON

see also Philosophy and Religion; Religion and Science

Towns, Elmer L. Say-It-Faith. 1982. pap. 4.95 (ISBN 0-8423-5825-0). Tyndale.

FAITH-CURE

see also Medicine, Magic, Mystic, and Spagiric; Mental Healing; Miracles

Hayes, Norvel. God's Power Through the Laying On of Hands. 45p. 1982. pap. 1.95 (ISBN 0-89274-280-1). Harrison Hse.

--Your Faith Can Heal You. 78p. 1982. pap. 2.50 (ISBN 0-89274-273-9). Harrison Hse.

Heijkoop, H. L. Faith Healing & Speaking in Tongues. 40p. pap. 2.00 (ISBN 0-88172-083-6). Believers Bkshelf.

Holmes, Fenwicke L. The Faith That Heals. 100p. 4.00 (ISBN 0-686-38218-8). Sun Bks.

Landorf, Joyce. Irregular People. 1982. 8.95 (ISBN 0-8499-0291-6). Word Pub.

Lynch, Richard. Health & Spiritual Healing. 140p. 5.50 (ISBN 0-686-38221-8). Sun Bks.

Talbot, Alice-Mary M. Faith Healing in Late Byzantium: The Posthumous Miracles of Patriarch Athanasios I of Constaninople by Theoktistos the Stoudite. Vaporis, N. M., ed. (The Archbishop Iakovos Library of Ecclesiastical & Historical Sources). 160p. (Orig.). 1983. 17.00 (ISBN 0-916586-92-8); pap. 12.00 (ISBN 0-916586-93-6). Hellenic College Pr.

FAITH HEALING

see Faith-Cure

FALKLAND ISLANDS

Calvert, Peter. The Falklands Crisis. LC 82-42611. 1982. 20.00x (ISBN 0-312-27964-7). St Martin.

Goebel, Julius. The Struggle for the Falkland Islands: A Study in Legal & Diplomatic History. 512p. 1982. text ed. 35.00x (ISBN 0-300-02943-8); pap. text ed. 10.95x (ISBN 0-300-02945-4, Y-445). Yale U Pr.

Harris, Robert. Gotcha! The Media, the Government & the Falklands Crisis. 176p. (Orig.). 1983. pap. 5.95 (ISBN 0-571-13052-6). Faber & Faber.

Hoffmann, Fritz L. & Hoffmann, Olga M. Sovereignty in Dispute: The Falklands-Malvinas. (Special Studies on Latin America & the Caribbean). 150p. 1983. lib. bdg. 18.50x (ISBN 0-86531-605-8). Westview.

Linklater & Sunday Times of London Insight Team. War in the Falklands: The Full Story. LC 82-48612. (Illus.). 320p. 1982. 14.95 (ISBN 0-06-015082-3, HarpT). Har-Row.

Woods, Robin W. Falkland Island Birds. (Illus.). 1982. 15.00 (ISBN 0-904614-07-7). Buteo.

FALLA, MANUEL DE, 1876-1946

Crichton, Ronald. Falla. LC 81-71303. (BBC Music Guides Ser.). 104p. (Orig.). 1983. pap. 5.95 (ISBN 0-295-95926-6). U of Wash Pr.

FALLACIES (LOGIC)

Buridan, John. John Buridan on Self-Reference: Chapter Eight of Buridan's Sophismata, with a Translation, an Introduction, & a Philosophical Commentary. Hughes, G. E., ed. LC 81-15465. 272p. 1982. 39.50 (ISBN 0-521-24086-7); pap. 12.95 (ISBN 0-521-28864-9). Cambridge U Pr.

FAMILY

see also Birth Order; Children; Church Work with Families; Divorce; Domestic Relations; Family Life Education; Family Size; Fathers; Foster Home Care; Grandparents; Heredity, Human; Kinship; Marriage; Mothers; Parent and Child; Single-Parent Family; Tribes and Tribal System; Twins; Widows

Aldous, Joan. Family Careers: Developmental Change in Families. LC 77-15043. 358p. 1978. text ed. 21.95 (ISBN 0-471-02046-X). Wiley.

--Her & His Paychecks: Life in Dual Earner Families. (Sage Focus Editions). (Illus.). 232p. 1982. 22.00 (ISBN 0-8039-1882-8); pap. 10.95 (ISBN 0-8039-1883-6). Sage.

Barrett, Michele & McIntosh, Mary. The Anti-Social Family. 164p. 1983. 18.50 (ISBN 0-686-37927-6); pap. 7.50 (ISBN 0-686-37928-4). Schocken.

Biswas, Manju. Mentally Retarded & Normal Children: A Comparative Study of Their Family Conditions. 157p. 1980. 19.95x (ISBN 0-940500-50-7, Pub. by Sterling India). Asia Bk Corp.

Cates, Judith N. & Sussman, Marvin B., eds. Family Systems & Inheritance Patterns. LC 82-15790. (Marriage & Family Review Ser.: Vol. 5, No. 3). 128p. 1983. text ed. 19.95 (ISBN 0-86656-158-7, B158). Haworth Pr.

Charles, J. Norman & Charles, Sharon. Vida Abundante en Familia. Carrodeguas, Andy & Marosi, Esteban, eds. Romanenghi de Powell, Elsa R., tr. 192p. (Span.). 1982. pap. 2.25 (ISBN 0-8297-1317-4). Life Pubs Intl.

Christian, Esther. Family Enrichment: A Manual for Promoting Family Togetherness. Sorenson, Don L., ed. LC 82-70356. 160p. 1982. pap. text ed. 5.95x (ISBN 0-932796-12-5). Ed Media Corp.

Congressional Quarterly Inc. Changing American Family. LC 79-12753. (Editorial Research Reports). 216p. 1979. pap. 7.50 (ISBN 0-87187-149-1). Congr Quarterly.

Curran, Dolores. Traits of a Healthy Family: Fifteen Traits Commonly Found in Healthy Families by Those Who Work With Them. LC 82-70489. 300p. 1983. 14.95 (ISBN 0-86683-643-8). Winston Pr.

Denton, Wallace & Denton, Juanita H. Creative Couples: The Growth Factor in Marriage. LC 82-17439. 156p. 1983. pap. 8.95 (ISBN 0-664-24453-X). Westminster.

Divas, Mireille. I'm a Year Old Now. (Illus.). 176p. 1983. 15.95 (ISBN 0-13-451344-4); pap. 7.95 (ISBN 0-13-451336-3). P-H.

Ember, Melvin. Marriage, Family, & Kinship: Comparative Studies of Social Organization. LC 82-83702. 425p. 1983. 30.00 (ISBN 0-87536-113-7); pap. 15.00 (ISBN 0-87536-114-5). HRAFP.

Finkelhor, David & Gelles, Richard J., eds. The Dark Side of Families: Current Family Violence Research. 384p. 1983. 29.95 (ISBN 0-8039-1934-4); pap. 14.95 (ISBN 0-8039-1935-2). Sage.

Fishkin, James S. Justice, Equal Opportunity & the Family. LC 82-10939. 208p. 1983. text ed. 18.95x (ISBN 0-300-02865-2). Yale U Pr.

Geerken, Michael & Grove, Walter. At Home & at Work: The Family's Allocation of Labor. (New Perspectives on Family Ser.). 200p. 1983. 22.00 (ISBN 0-8039-1940-9); pap. 10.95 (ISBN 0-8039-1941-7). Sage.

Getz, Gene A. Dimensions de la Famille, Les. Cosson, Annie, ed. Audfray, Annie, tr. from Eng. Orig. Title: The Measure of a Family. 190p. (Fr.). 1982. pap. 2.25 (ISBN 0-8297-1053-1). Life Pubs Intl.

Hunter. Families Under the Flag: A Review of Military Family Literature. 320p. 1982. 33.95 (ISBN 0-03-062014-7). Praeger.

James, Gene, ed. The Unification Church & The Family. (Conference Ser.: No. 17). 1983. pap. text ed. price not set (ISBN 0-932894-17-8). Unif Theol Seminary.

Lamb, Michael E. & Sagi, Abraham, eds. Fatherhood & Family Policy. 288p. 1983. text ed. 24.95 (ISBN 0-89859-190-2). L Erlbaum Assocs.

Macklin, Eleanor D. & Rubin, Roger H. Contemporary Families & Alternative Lifestyles: Handbook on Research & Theory. 416p. 1982. 29.95 (ISBN 0-8039-1053-3). Sage.

Moch, Leslie P. & Stark, Gary D., eds. Essays on the Family & Historical Change. LC 82-45900. (Walter Prescott Webb Memorial Lectures Ser.: No. 17). 136p. 1983. 17.50x (ISBN 0-89096-151-4). Tex A&M Univ Pr.

O'Kane, Monica L. Living with Adult Children: A Helpful Guide for Parents & Grown Children Sharing the Same Roof. (Illus.). 190p. 1982. 9.95 (ISBN 0-9609198-1-3); pap. 4.95 (ISBN 0-9609198-0-5). Diction Bks.

Olson, David H. & Miller, Brent C., eds. Family Study Review Yearbook. (Family Study Review Yearbooks). (Illus.). 768p. 1983. 37.50 (ISBN 0-8039-1924-7). Sage.

Owens, Virginia S. A Feast of Families. 160p. 1983. 9.95 (ISBN 0-310-45850-1). Zondervan.

Quisenberry, James D., ed. & intro. by. Changing Family Lifestyles: Their Effect on Children. (Illus.). 64p. 1982. pap. 5.75 (ISBN 0-87173-100-2). ACEI.

Rich, Shelley, illus. The Family Bond: A Woman's Place. 72p. 1977. pap. text ed. 3.00 (ISBN 0-686-43396-3). N Grey Inc.

Royal Society of Medicine. Family Matters-Perspectives on the Family & Social Policy: Proceedings of the Symposium on Priority for the Family, Royal Society of Medicine, London, November 3-5, 1981. Franklin, A. White, ed. 160p. 1983. 19.95 (ISBN 0-08-028928-2). Pergamon.

Satir, Virginia M. Peoplemaking. LC 73-188143. 1972. 9.95 (ISBN 0-8314-0031-5); pap. 7.95. Sci & Behavior.

Scanzoni, John. Is Family Possible? Theory & Policy for the 21st Century. (Sage Library of Social Research). 224p. 1983. 22.00 (ISBN 0-8039-1920-4); pap. 10.95 (ISBN 0-8039-1921-2). Sage.

Segalen, Martine. Love & Power in the Peasant Family. Matthews, Martine, tr. LC 82-50495. (Illus.). 224p. 1983. 21.00x (ISBN 0-226-74451-5). U of Chicago Pr.

Strong, Bryan & DeVault, Christine. The Marriage & Family Experience. 2nd ed. (Illus.). 600p. 1983. text ed. 20.95 (ISBN 0-314-69682-2). West Pub.

Weinbaum, Batya. Picture of Patriarchy. 200p. 1982. 17.50 (ISBN 0-89608-161-3); pap. 7.00 (ISBN 0-89608-162-1). South End Pr.

FAMILY–HISTORY

Berger, Brigitte & Berger, Peter L. War Over the Family: Capturing the Middle Ground. LC 82-45237. 240p. 1984. pap. price not set (ISBN 0-385-18006-3, Anch). Doubleday.

--War Over the Family: Capturing the Middle Ground. 240p. 1983. 14.95 (ISBN 0-385-18001-2, Anchor Pr). Doubleday.

British Family Research Committee. Families in Britain. 350p. 1983. pap. 25.00 (ISBN 0-7100-9236-9). Routledge & Kegan.

Cohen, Steven M. & Hyman, Paula, eds. The Evolving Jewish Family. 256p. 1983. text ed. 30.00x (ISBN 0-8419-0860-5). Holmes & Meier.

Hodgson, Pat. Home Life. (History in Focus Ser.). (Illus.). 72p. (gr. 7-12). 1982. 14.95 (Pub by Batsford England). David & Charles.

Mintz, Steven. A Prison of Expectations: The Family in Victorian Culture. 232p. 1983. text ed. 25.00X (ISBN 0-8147-5388-4). NYU Pr.

Speth, Linda & Hirsch, Alison D. Women, Family, & Community in Colonial America: Two Perspectives. LC 82-23326. (Women & History Ser.: No. 4). 85p. 1983. text ed. 20.00 (ISBN 0-86656-191-9). Haworth Pr.

Wilson, Sylvia E. Huyck Family in America. 736p. 1982. 35.00x (ISBN 0-932334-54-7). Heart of the Lakes.

FAMILY–JUVENILE LITERATURE

Hermes, Patricia. Who Will Take Care of Me? LC 82-48757. 128p. (gr. 8-12). 10.95 (ISBN 0-15-296265-4, HJ). HarBraceJ.

York, Christopher C. The Ram & the Black Sheep. (Daring Relations Involving Families & Their Black Sheep). (Illus.). 175p. 1983. 49.95x (ISBN 0-8187-0050-5). C C York.

FAMILY–LAW

see Domestic Relations

FAMILY–PRAYER-BOOKS AND DEVOTIONS

Crisi, J. Bruce. What to Do When the Family Hurts. 1982. pap. 5.95 (ISBN 0-8423-7996-7). Tyndale.

Robertson, John M. Roots & Wings: Prayers & Promises for Parents. 84p. 1983. pap. 2.50 (ISBN 0-8423-5712-2). Tyndale.

FAMILY–RECREATION

see Family Recreation

FAMILY–RELIGIOUS LIFE

see also Religious Education–Home Training

Anderson, Joan W. Dear World: Don't Spin So Fast, I'm Having Trouble Hanging On. LC 82-73131. 160p. 1982. pap. 4.95 (ISBN 0-87029-188-2, 20280-4). Abbey.

Bird, Lois & Bird, Joseph. To Live As a Family. LC 81-43392. 288p. 1983. pap. 5.50 (ISBN 0-385-19020-4, Im). Doubleday.

Clulow, C. F. To Have & to Hold: Marriage, the First Baby, & Preparing Couples for Parenthood. 168p. 1982. 16.50 (ISBN 0-08-028470-1); pap. 9.50 (ISBN 0-08-028471-X). Pergamon.

Coletti, Mina S. & Giesea, Roberta. Family Idea, Bk. 2. LC 82-14612. 279p. 1982. pap. 5.95 (ISBN 0-87747-925-9). Deseret Bk.

Connolly, Paul H. Building Family: An Act of Faith. LC 82-74073. 96p. 1982. pap. 4.95 (ISBN 0-87029-186-6, 20277-0). Abbey.

Cowles, C. S. Family Journey Into Joy. 168p. 1982. pap. 3.95 (ISBN 0-8341-0803-8). Beacon Hill.

Forliti, John E. Reverence for Life & Family Program. write for info.. Wm C Brown.

Getting in Touch with Yourself-And Your Parents. 1982. pap. 4.25 (ISBN 0-686-82559-4). St Anthony Mess Pr.

Gibson, Dennis L. Live, Grow & Be Free: A Guide to Self-Parenting. 136p. 1982. pap. 4.95 (ISBN 0-89840-031-7). Here's Life.

Hickey, Marilyn. God's Covenant for Your Family. 140p. (Orig.). 1982. pap. 4.95 (ISBN 0-89274-245-3). Harrison Hse.

Hunt, Jeanne, ed. Being A Loving Wife. LC 82-48422. (Christian Reader Ser.). 128p. (Orig.). 1983. pap. 5.72i (ISBN 0-06-061386-6, HarpR). Har-Row.

--Raising a Joyful Family. LC 82-4823. (Christian Reader Ser.). 128p. (Orig.). 1983. pap. 5.72i (ISBN 0-06-061387-4, HarpR). Har-Row.

Leonard, Joe, Jr. Planning Family Ministry: A Guide for the Teaching Church. 64p. 1982. pap. 3.95 (ISBN 0-8170-0971-X). Judson.

Lutzer, Erwin & Orr, Bill. If I Could Change My Mom & Dad. 128p. 1983. pap. 3.50 (ISBN 0-8024-0174-0). Moody.

Owens, Virginia S. A Feast of Families. 160p. 1983. 9.95 (ISBN 0-310-45850-1). Zondervan.

Popoff, Peter. America's Family Crisis. Tanner, Don, ed. LC 82-82843. 80p. 1982. pap. 2.00 (ISBN 0-938544-15-2). Faith Messenger.

Voigt, Tracy. The Relatives. (Orig.). (gr. 10 up). 1982. pap. write for info. T Voigt.

FAMILY–CHINA

Chao, Paul. Chinese Kinship. 220p. 1983. 30.00 (ISBN 0-7103-0020-4). Routledge & Kegan.

Stacey, Judith. Patriarchy & Socialist Revolution in China. LC 82-8482. 330p. 1983. text ed. 28.50x (ISBN 0-520-04825-3). U of Cal Pr.

FAMILY–GREAT BRITAIN

Barrett, Michele & McIntosh, Mary. The Anti-Social Family. 160p. 1982. 18.50 (ISBN 0-8052-7134-1, Pub. by NLB England); pap. 7.50 (ISBN 0-686-38371-0). Nichols Pub.

British Family Research Committee. Families in Britain. 350p. 1983. pap. 25.00 (ISBN 0-7100-9236-9). Routledge & Kegan.

Family Welfare Association. Guide to the Social Services (U.K.) 1982. 70th ed. LC 55-33805. 326p. (Orig.). 1982. pap. 16.50x (ISBN 0-900954-15-9). Intl Pubns Serv.

Gittens, Diana. Fair Sex: Family Size & Structure in Britain, 1930-39. LC 81-21248. 256p. 1982. 27.50x (ISBN 0-312-27962-0). St Martin.

FAMILY–WALES

Rosser, Colin & Harris, C. C. The Family & Social Change: A Study of Family & Kinship in a South Wales Town. (International Library of Sociology). 256p. 1983. pap. 10.95 (ISBN 0-7100-9434-5). Routledge & Kegan.

FAMILY CASE WORK

see Family Social Work

FAMILY COURTS

see Juvenile Courts

FAMILY FUN

see Family Recreation

FAMILY GROUP THERAPY

see Family Psychotherapy

FAMILY HISTORIES

see subdivision genealogy under countries, e.g., United States–Genealogy; and individual families, e.g. Lee Family

FAMILY LAW

see Domestic Relations

FAMILY LIFE EDUCATION

see also Counseling; Finance, Personal; Home Economics; Interpersonal Relations; Marriage Counseling; Sex Instruction

Figley, Charles R. & McCubbin, Hamilton I., eds. Stress & the Family: Coping with Catastrophe, Vol. II. 300p. 1983. price not set (ISBN 0-87630-332-7). Brunner-Mazel.

Fleischman, Matthew J. & Horne, Arthur M. Troubled Families: A Treatment Program. 250p. (Orig.). 1983. pap. text ed. price not set (ISBN 0-87822-296-0). Res Press.

McCubbin, Hamilton I. & Figley, Charles R., eds. Stress & the Family: Coping with Normative Transitions, Vol. I. 300p. 1983. price not set (ISBN 0-87630-321-1). Brunner-Mazel.

Sullender, R. Scott. Family Enrichment Workshops: Leader's Manual. 125p. (Orig.). 1982. pap. 12.95 (ISBN 0-940754-17-7). Ed Ministries.

FAMILY MEDICINE

American Health Research Institute, Ltd. Family Practice: A Medical Subject Analysis & Research Index With Bibliography. Bartone, John C., ed. 120p. 1983. 29.95 (ISBN 0-88164-000-X); pap. 21.95 (ISBN 0-88164-001-8). ABBE Pubs Assn.

Doherty, William J. & Baird, Macaran A. Family Therapy & Family Medicine. LC 82-3135. (Family Therapy Ser.). 285p. 1983. text ed. 22.50x (ISBN 0-89862-041-4, G35). Guilford Pr.

Frey, John, ed. Common Dilemmas in Family Medicine. 420p. 1982. 25.80 (ISBN 0-942068-04-1). Bogden & Son.

Fry, J., ed. The Beecham Manual for Family Practice. 300p. 1982. text ed. 29.00 (ISBN 0-85200-456-7, Pub. by MTP Pr England). Kluwer Boston.

Gray, D. Pereira. Training for General Practice. 352p. 1981. 49.00x (ISBN 0-7121-2004-1, Pub. by Macdonald & Evans). State Mutual Bk.

Hess, Joseph W., et al, eds. Family Practice & Preventitive Medicine: Health Promotion in Primary Care. LC 82-15718. 304p. 1983. text ed. 29.95x (ISBN 0-89885-131-9). Human Sci Pr.

Modell, Michael & Boyd, Robert. Paediatric Problems in General Practice. (Illus.). 1982. pap. 23.95x (ISBN 0-19-261264-6). Oxford U Pr.

Rakel, Robert E., ed. Year Book of Family Practice 1983. 1983. 41.00 (ISBN 0-8151-7024-6). Year Bk Med.

Taylor, R. B., et al, eds. Fundamentals of Family Medicine. (Illus.). 488p. 1983. pap. 34.50 (ISBN 0-387-90705-X). Springer-Verlag.

Taylor, R. E., ed. Family Medicine-Principles & Practice. 2nd ed. (Illus.). 2021p. 1983. 69.50 (ISBN 0-387-90718-1). Springer-Verlag.

World Book Inc. & Tressler, Arthur G., eds. Medical Update 1983: The World Book Family Health Annual. (Illus.). 272p. 1982. lib. bdg. write for info. (ISBN 0-7166-1183-X). World Bk.

FAMILY PLANNING

see Birth Control

FAMILY PRACTICE (MEDICINE)

see Family Medicine

FAMILY PSYCHOTHERAPY

Anderson, Carol & Stewart, Susan. Mastering Resistance: A Practical Guide to Family Therapy. (Family Therapy Ser.). 251p. 1983. text ed. 20.00x (ISBN 0-89862-044-9, G36). Guilford Pr.

Andolfi, Maurizio & Angelo, Claude. Behind the Family Mask: Therapeutic Change in Rigid Family Systems. 184p. 1983. 17.50 (ISBN 0-87630-330-0). Brunner-Mazel.

Boss, Allan. Family Therapy. LC 82-15555. (Family Therapy Ser.). 253p. 1983. 20.00x (ISBN 0-89862-045-7). Guilford Pr.

Broderick, Carlfred B. The Theraputic Triangle: A Sourcebook on Marital Therapy. (Illus.). 200p. 1983. 20.00 (ISBN 0-8039-1943-3). Sage.

Cantor, Dorothy W. & Drake, Ellen A. Divorced Parents & Their Children: A Guide for Mental Health Professionals. 1983. text ed. 19.95 (ISBN 0-8261-3560-9). Springer Pub.

De Shazer, Steve. Patterns of Brief Family Therapy. LC 81-7239. (Guilford Family Therapy Ser.). 1982. 17.50 (ISBN 0-89862-038-4). Guilford Pr.

Dobson, James. Dr. Dobson Answers Your Questions. 1983. 12.50 (ISBN 0-8423-0652-8). Tyndale.

Doherty, William J. & Baird, Macaran A. Family Therapy & Family Medicine. LC 82-3135. (Family Therapy Ser.). 285p. 1983. text ed. 22.50x (ISBN 0-89862-041-4, G35). Guilford Pr.

Franks, Cyril M., ed. The New Developments in Behavior Therapy: From Research to Clinical Application. (Supplement to Child & Family Behavior Therapy Ser.: Vol. 4). 525p. 1983. pap. text ed. 20.00 (ISBN 0-86656-178-1, B178). Haworth Pr.

Hansen, James C., et al, eds. Family Therapy Collections, Collection V: Sexual Issues in Family Therapy. 200p. 1983. price not set (ISBN 0-89443-605-8). Aspen Systems.

Kadis, Leslie B. & McClendon, Ruth A. Chocolate Pudding & Other Approaches to Intensive Family Therapy. 1983. 12.95. Sci & Behavior.

Kenney, Bradford. Aesthetics of Change. (Guilford Family Therapy Ser.). 227p. 1983. 19.50x (ISBN 0-89862-043-0). Guilford Pr.

L'Abate, Luciano. Family Psychology: Theory, Therapy, & Training. LC 82-20255. 328p. (Orig.). 1983. lib. bdg. 25.75 (ISBN 0-8191-2883-X); pap. text ed. 13.75 (ISBN 0-8191-2884-8). U Pr of Amer.

McGoldrick, Monica & Pearce, John, eds. Ethnicity & Family Therapy. LC 81-20198. (Guilford Family Therapy Ser.). 600p. 1982. text ed. 29.50x (ISBN 0-89862-040-6). Guilford Pr.

Nelson, Judith C. Family Treatment: An Integrative Approach. 304p. 1983. 22.95 (ISBN 0-13-301895-4). P-H.

Rudestam, Kjell E. & Frankel, Mark. Treating the Multiproblem Family: A Casebook. LC 82-19739. (Psychology Ser.). 320p. 1983. pap. text ed. 12.95 (ISBN 0-534-01300-7). Brooks-Cole.

Sager, Clifford J., et al. Treating the Remarried Family. LC 82-17811. 450p. 1983. 35.00 (ISBN 0-87630-323-8). Brunner-Mazel.

Saunders, Susan & Anderson, Ann M. Violent Individuals & Families: A Handbook for Practitioners. (Illus.). 256p. 1983. text ed. write for info (ISBN 0-398-04833-9). C C Thomas.

Sullender, R. Scott. Family Enrichment Workshops (Participant's Books) 70p. 1982. pap. 7.50 (ISBN 0-940754-16-9). Ed Ministries.

FAMILY RECREATION

Satterfield, Archie, Sr. & Bauer, Eddie, Sr. The Eddie Bauer Guide to Family Camping. LC 82-13923. (Illus.). 320p. 1983. 17.95 (ISBN 0-201-07776-0); pap. 8.95 (ISBN 0-201-07777-9). A-W.

FAMILY SIZE

see also Birth Control

Gittens, Diana. Fair Sex: Family Size & Structure in Britain, 1930-39. LC 81-21248. 256p. 1982. 27.50x (ISBN 0-312-27962-0). St Martin.

FAMILY SOCIAL WORK

see also Family Life Education; Marriage Counseling

Fenton, Joan, ed. Directory of Member Agencies, 1983. rev. ed. 104p. 1983. pap. 11.00 (ISBN 0-87304-200-X). Family Serv.

FAMILY THERAPY

see Family Psychotherapy

FAMILY WORSHIP

see Family–Prayer-Books and Devotions; Family–Religious Life

FAMINES

Appleby. Famine in Tudor & Stuart England. 262p. 1982. 50.00x (ISBN 0-85323-014-5, Pub. by Liverpool Univ England). State Mutual Bk.

Watts, Michael J. Silent Violence: Food, Famine, & Peasantry in Northern Nigeria. LC 82-13384. (Illus.). 500p. 1983. text ed. 38.50x (ISBN 0-520-04323-5). U of Cal Pr.

FANCY DRESS

see Costume

FANON, FRANTZ, 1925-1961

Gendzier, Irene L. Frantz Fanon: A Critical Study. 2nd ed. 312p. (Orig.). 1983. pap. 8.95 (ISBN 0-394-62453-X, Ever). Grove.

McCulloch, Jock. Black Soul White Artifact: Fanon's Clinical Psychology & Social Theory. LC 82-14605. 240p. Date not set. price not set (ISBN 0-521-24700-4). Cambridge U Pr.

Onwuanibe, Richard C. A Critique of Revolutionary Humanism: Frantz Fanon. 400p. 1983. write for info. (ISBN 0-87527-296-7). Green.

FANTASTIC FICTION

see also Ghost Stories; Science Fiction (Collections); Supernatural in Literature

Asimov, Isaac. The Best Fantasy of the Nineteenth Century. Waugh, Charles G. & Greenberg, Martin H., eds. 357p. 1982. 15.95 (ISBN 0-686-82284-6). Beaufort Bks NY.

Salmonson, Jessica A., ed. Heroic Visions. pap. 2.95 (ISBN 0-441-32821-0, Pub. by Ace Science Fiction). Ace Bks.

FANTASTIC FICTION–HISTORY AND CRITICISM

Beauchamp, Gorman. Reader's Guide to Jack London. Schlobin, Roger C., ed. (Reader's Guides to Contemporary Science Fiction & Fantasy Authors Ser.: Vol. 15). (Illus., Orig.). 1983. 10.95x (ISBN 0-916732-40-1); pap. text ed. 4.95x (ISBN 0-916732-39-8). Starmont Hse.

Clareson, Thomas D. Reader's Guide to Robert Silverberg. Schlobin, Roger C., ed. (Reader's Guides to Contemporary Science Fiction & Fantasy Authors Ser.: Vol. 18). (Illus., Orig.). 1983. 11.95x (ISBN 0-916732-48-7); pap. text ed. 5.95x (ISBN 0-916732-47-9). Starmont Hse.

Collings, Michael R. Reader's Guide to Piers Anthony. Schlobin, Roger C., ed. (Reader's Guides to Contemporary Science Fiction & Fantasy Authors Ser.: Vol. 20). (Illus., Orig.). 1983. 10.95x (ISBN 0-916732-53-3); pap. text ed. 4.95x (ISBN 0-916732-52-5). Starmont Hse.

Elliot, Jeffrey M. Reader's Guide to A. E. van Vogt. Schlobin, Roger C., ed. (Reader's Guides to Contemporary Science Fiction & Fantasy Authors Ser.: Vol. 17). (Illus., Orig.). 1983. 10.95x (ISBN 0-916732-46-0); pap. text ed. 4.95x (ISBN 0-916732-45-2). Starmont Hse.

Garber, Eric & Paleo, Lyn. Uranian Worlds: A Reader's Guide to Alternative Sexuality in Science Fiction & Fantasy. 1983. lib. bdg. 28.50 (ISBN 0-8161-8573-5, Hall Reference). G K Hall.

Hassler, Donald M. Reader's Guide to Hal Clement. Schlobin, Roger C., ed. (Reader's Guides to Contemporary Science Fiction & Fantasy Authors Ser.: Vol. 11). (Illus., Orig.). 1982. 10.95x (ISBN 0-916732-30-4); pap. text ed. 4.95x (ISBN 0-916732-27-4). Starmont Hse.

Hassler, Donald M., ed. Patterns of the Fantastic: Academic Programming at Chicon IV. (Illus.). 1983. 11.95x (ISBN 0-916732-63-0); pap. 5.95x text ed. (ISBN 0-916732-62-2). Starmont Hse.

Kinnaird, John. Reader's Guide to Olaf Stapledon. Schlobin, Roger C., ed. (Reader's Guides to Contemporary Science Fiction & Fantasy Authors Ser.: Vol. 21). (Illus., Orig.). 1983. 10.95x (ISBN 0-916732-55-X); pap. text ed. 4.95x (ISBN 0-916732-54-1). Starmont Hse.

Manlove, C. N. The Impulse of Fantasy Literature. LC 82-15335. xiii, 174p. 1983. 17.50 (ISBN 0-87338-273-0). Kent St U Pr.

Pierce, Hazel. Reader's Guide to Philip K. Dick. Schlobin, Roger C., ed. (Reader's Guides to Contemporary Science Fiction & Fantasy Authors Ser.: Vol. 12). (Illus., Orig.). 1982. 10.95x (ISBN 0-916732-34-7); pap. text ed. 4.95x (ISBN 0-916732-33-9). Starmont Hse.

Slusser, George E., et al, eds. Coordinates: Placing Science Fiction & Fantasy. (Alternatives Ser.). 264p. 1983. price not set (ISBN 0-8093-1105-4). S Ill U Pr.

Tymn, Marshall B., compiled by. The Teacher's Guide to Fantastic Literature. (Illus., Orig.). 1983. write for info. (ISBN 0-916732-61-4); pap. text ed. write for info. (ISBN 0-916732-60-6). Starmont Hse.

Weedman, Jane B. Reader's Guide to Samuel R. Delany. Schlobin, Roger C., ed. LC 82-5545. (Reader's Guides to Contemporary Science Fiction & Fantasy Authors Ser.: Vol. 10). (Illus., Orig.). 1982. 10.95x (ISBN 0-916732-28-2); pap. text ed. 4.95x (ISBN 0-916732-25-8). Starmont Hse.

Winter, Douglas E. Reader's Guide to Stephen King. Schlobin, Roger C., ed. (Reader's Guides to Contemporary Science Fiction & Fantasy Authors Ser.: Vol. 16). (Illus., Orig.). 1982. 11.95x (ISBN 0-916732-44-4); pap. text ed. 5.95x (ISBN 0-916732-43-6). Starmont Hse.

Wolfe, Gary K. Reader's Guide to David Lindsay. Schlobin, Roger C., ed. LC 82-5563. (Reader's Guides to Contemporary Science Fiction & Fantasy Authors Ser.: Vol. 9). (Illus., Orig.). 1982. 10.95x (ISBN 0-916732-29-0); pap. text ed. 4.95x (ISBN 0-916732-26-6). Starmont Hse.

FANTASY

Gilman, Dorothy. Maze in the Heart of the Castle. LC 82-45198. 192p. (gr. 7). 1983. 11.95 (ISBN 0-385-17817-4). Doubleday.

Hammond, Bernice. Hokus-Pokus the Goodwill Pixie. Davis, Audrey, ed. (Illus.). 110p. 1981. text ed. 10.50 (ISBN 0-9609398-0-6). Assn Preserv.

Mayhar, Ardath. Lords of the Triple Moons. LC 82-16241. 156p. (gr. 6 up). 1983. 10.95 (ISBN 0-689-30978-3, Argo). Atheneum.

Norton, Mary. The Borrowers Avenged. (Illus.). (gr. 3 up). Date not set. 12.95 (ISBN 0-15-210530-1). HarBraceJ.

Warren, Sandra. If I Were a Table. (gr. 1-6). 1982. 5.95 (ISBN 0-86653-089-4, GA 440). Good Apple.

FANTIN-LATOUR, IGNACE HENRI JEAN THEODORE, 1836-1904

Druick, Douglas & Hoog, Michel. Henri Fantin-Latour. (Illus.). 350p. 1983. pap. price not set (56351-0). U of Chicago Pr.

Layton, Gustave. The Dreamy, Romantic & Symbolic Art by Fantin-Latour. (Art Library of the Great Masters). (Illus.). 133p. 1983. 59.85 (ISBN 0-86650-057-X). Gloucester Art.

FAO

see Food and Agriculture Organization of the United Nations

FARE, BILLS OF

see Menus

FARINACEOUS PRODUCTS

see Starch

FARM ANIMALS

see Domestic Animals

FARM BUILDINGS

see also Agricultural Engineering; Architecture, Domestic; Livestock–Housing

Woodforde, John. Farm Buildings in England & Wales. (Illus.). 176p. 1983. 15.95 (ISBN 0-7100-9275-X). Routledge & Kegan.

FARM CROPS

see Field Crops

FARM IMPLEMENTS

see Agricultural Implements

FARM LABORERS

see Agricultural Laborers

FARM LIFE

see also Country Life; Rural Conditions

Holman, L. Bruce. Holman's Harvest from Down on the Farm. (Illus.). 117p. 1982. 9.95 (ISBN 0-686-83875-0). Harvest Pr.

Horne, Field, ed. The Diary of Mary Cooper: Life on a Long Island Farm 1768-1773. LC 81-38405. (Illus.). 84p. (Orig.). 1981. pap. 10.00 (ISBN 0-89062-108-X, Pub by Oyster Bay Historical Society). Pub Ctr Cult Res.

FARM LIFE–JUVENILE LITERATURE

Graham-Cameron, M. The Farmer. (Cambridge Dinosaur Information Ser.). (Illus.). 26p. (gr. 7-10). 1983. pap. 1.50 (ISBN 0-521-27162-2). Cambridge U Pr.

FARM MACHINERY

see Agricultural Machinery

FARM MANAGEMENT

Baum, Kenneth H & Schertz, Lyle P. Modeling Farm Decisions for Policy Analysis. 500p. 1983. lib. bdg. 20.00x (ISBN 0-86531-589-2). Westview.

Doane's Farm Management Guide. 15th ed. LC 82-71964. (Illus.). 336p. (gr. 10-12). 1982. pap. 9.95 (ISBN 0-932250-19-X); write for info. Doane-Western.

Warren, Martyn. Financial Management for Farmers: The Basic Techniques of Money-Farming. 288p. 1982. 55.00X (ISBN 0-09-148930-X, Pub. by Hutchinson); pap. 40.00x (ISBN 0-09-148931-8). State Mutual Bk.

FARM MECHANICS

see Agricultural Engineering

FARM PRODUCE–MARKETING

Here are entered works on the marketing of farm produce from the point of view of the farmer.

see also Field Crops; Food Industry and Trade also subdivision Marketing under specific commodities, e.g. Eggs–Marketing

Carrol, Frieda. Directory of Farmer's Markets in the U. S. & Some Other Countries. 60p. Date not set. pap. text ed. 10.95 (ISBN 0-939476-78-9). Biblio Pr GA.

FARM SHOPS

see Agricultural Machinery

FARM TOOLS

see Agricultural Implements

FARMERS

see also Agricultural Laborers; Farm Life; Farm Management; Peasantry

Cole, Ethel. American Farmer. (Social Studies). 24p. (gr. 5-9). 1976. wkbk. 5.00 (ISBN 0-8209-0245-4, SS-12). ESP.

Shepard. Estate Planning for Farmers & Ranchers. 1980. 65.00 (ISBN 0-07-033500-1). McGraw.

FARMERS' COOPERATIVES

see Agriculture, Cooperative

FARMING

see Agriculture

FARMS

see also Farm Management; Plantations

Agricultural Land: Assessment, Taxation & Representation. (Bibliographic Ser.). 44p. 1981. 7.50 (ISBN 0-686-84054-2). Intl Assess.

Kundell, James E. & White, Fred C. Prime Farmland in Georgia. 49p. 1982. pap. 6.50 (ISBN 0-89854-081-X). U of GA Inst Govt.

Vince, John. Old Farms: An Illustrated Guide. LC 82-10698. (Illus.). 160p. (Orig.). 1983. pap. 11.95 (ISBN 0-8052-0729-5). Schocken.

FARMS–ACCOUNTING

see Agriculture–Accounting

FARMS–VALUATION

Misplaced Hopes, Misspent Millions (Farmland Assessments) 45p. 1982. 7.00 (ISBN 0-686-81769-9). Ctr Analysis Public Issues.

FARRAGUT, DAVID GLASGOW, 1801-1870

Barnes, James. David G. Farragut. 132p. 1982. Repr. of 1899 ed. lib. bdg. 25.00 (ISBN 0-686-81844-X). Darby Bks.

FARRIERY

see Horses; Veterinary Medicine; Veterinary Surgery

FASCISM

see also National Socialism

Gross, Bertram. Friendly Fascism: The New Face of Power in America. 350p. 1982. pap. 8.00 (ISBN 0-89608-149-4). South End Pr.

Osborne, Harrison. In Defense of Fascism: A New Critical Evaluation of the Fascist Experience in Modern History. (Illus.). 108p. 1983. Repr. of 1957 ed. 74.85 (ISBN 0-89901-109-8). Found Class Reprints.

Payne, Stanley G. Fascism: A Comparative Approach Toward a Definition. LC 79-5415. 248p. 1983. pap. 6.95 (ISBN 0-299-08064-1). U of Wis Pr.

Raushenbush, Stephen. March of Fascism. 1939. text ed. 39.50x (ISBN 0-686-83616-2). Elliots Bks.

FASCISM–ITALY

Von Bertholdi, Franz W. Considerations on the Phenomenon of Italian Fascism & the Evaluation of the Principle of Authority. (The Great Currents of History Library Bks). (Illus.). 137p. 1983. 77.55 (ISBN 0-89266-382-0). Am Classical Coll Pr.

FASHION

see also Clothing and Dress; Costume; Costume Design; Dressmaking; Men's Clothing; Tailoring

Barthes, Ronald. The Fashion System. Ward, Matthew & Howard, Richard, trs. from Fr. 1983. 20.50 (ISBN 0-8090-4437-4). Hill & Wang.

Kennett, Frances. The Collector's Book of Fashion. (Illus.). 1983. 22.50 (ISBN 0-517-54860-7). Crown.

Packard, Sidney & Winters, Arthur. Fashion Buying & Merchandising. 2nd ed. (Illus.). 390p. 1983. text ed. 16.50 (ISBN 0-87005-445-7). Fairchild.

FASHION–HISTORY

Feeny, Maura. A La Mode: Womens Fashion in French Art, 1850-1900. 44p. 1982. pap. 4.00 (ISBN 0-686-37427-4). S & F Clark.

Kennett, Frances. The Collector's Book of Fashion. (Illus.). 1983. 22.50 (ISBN 0-517-54860-7). Crown.

Laver, James. Costume & Fashion: A Concise History. rev. ed. (World of Art Ser.). (Illus.). 322p. 1983. pap. 9.95 (ISBN 0-19-520390-9, GB). Oxford U Pr.

Olvin, Joann. High Fashion in the Gilded Age. 64p. 1982. 12.95 (ISBN 0-686-81964-0). Stemmer Hse.

Wilson, R. Turner. The Mode in Costume. (Illus.). 480p. 1983. pap. 13.95 (ISBN 0-686-83797-5, ScribT). Scribner.

FASHION DESIGN

see Costume Design

FASHION DRAWING

Westerman, Maxine. Elementary Fashion Design & Trade Sketching. 2nd ed. (Illus.). 1983. text ed. 13.50 (ISBN 0-87005-438-4). Fairchild.

FASHION MODELS

see Models, Fashion

FASHION PHOTOGRAPHY

Farber, Robert. Professional Fashion Photography: New, Updated Edition of an AMPHOTO Bestseller. Rev. ed. 1983. pap. 14.95 (ISBN 0-8174-5549-3, Amphoto). Watson-Guptill.

FASHIONABLE SOCIETY

see Upper Classes

FAST-RESPONSE DATA PROCESSING

see Real-Time Data Processing

FASTENERS

see also Sealing (Technology)

Jones, Peter. Fasteners, Joints & Adhesives: A Guide to Engineering Solid Constructions. 416p. 1983. 24.95 (ISBN 0-13-307694-6); pap. 14.95 (ISBN 0-13-307686-5). P-H.

FASTER READING

see Rapid Reading

FASTING

Hagin, Kenneth E. A Commonsense Guide to Fasting. 1981. pap. 1.50 (ISBN 0-89276-403-1). Hagin Ministry.

Szekely, Edmond B. The Essene Science of Fasting & the Art of Sobriety. (Illus.). 48p. 1981. pap. 3.50 (ISBN 0-89564-011-2). IBS Intl.

FAT METABOLISM

Creutzfeldt, W., ed. Acarbose: Proceedings of the International Symposium on Acarbose Effects on Carbohydrate & Fat Metabolism, First, Montreux, October 8-10, 1981. (International Congress Ser.: No. 594). 588p. 1982. 81.00 (ISBN 0-444-90283-X, Excerpta Medica). Elsevier.

FATHER AND CHILD

Franks, Maurice R. Winning Custody. LC 82-24114. 185p. 1983. 16.95 (ISBN 0-13-961011-1, Busn); pap. 7.95 (ISBN 0-13-961003-0). P-H.

Gosse, Edmund. Father & Son. 1983. pap. 3.95 (ISBN 0-14-000700-8). Penguin.

Hichman, Martha W. When can Daddy Come Home? (Illus.). 48p. 1983. 9.50 (ISBN 0-687-44969-3). Abingdon.

Siebenschuh, William R. Fictional Techniques & Factual Works. LC 82-8373. 200p. 1983. text ed. 18.00x (ISBN 0-8203-0636-3). U of Ga Pr.

FATHERS

see also Adolescent Parents; Grandparents; Stepfathers

Bitman, Sam & Zalk, Sue R. Expectant Fathers. (Orig.). 1981. pap. 6.95 (ISBN 0-345-28746-0). Ballantine.

Feirstein, Frederick. Fathering. 55p. 1982. pap. 4.95 (ISBN 0-918222-33-8). Apple Wood.

Grant, Wilson W. The Caring Father. LC 82-72990. (Orig.). 1983. pap. 5.95 (ISBN 0-8054-5654-6). Broadman.

Gresh, Sean. Becoming a Father: A Handbook for Expectant Fathers. 192p. 1982. pap. 2.95 (ISBN 0-553-22744-0). Bantam.

Lamb, Michael E. & Sagi, Abraham, eds. Fatherhood & Family Policy. 288p. 1983. text ed. 24.95 (ISBN 0-89859-190-2). L Erlbaum Assocs.

Miller, Ted, ed. On Being a Caring Father. LC 82-48421. 128p. (Orig.). 1983. pap. 5.72i (ISBN 0-06-061384-X, HarpR). Har-Row.

Osborn, Lois. My Dad is Really Something. Tucker, Kathleen, ed. (Concept Bks.). (Illus.). 32p. (gr. 1-3). 1983. PLB 7.50 (ISBN 0-8075-5329-8). A Whitman.

Sayers, Robert. Fathering: It's Not the Same. (Illus.). 95p. 1983. pap. 10.95 (ISBN 0-686-38770-8). Nurtury Fam.

Shechtman, Stephen & Singer, Wenda G. Real Men Enjoy their Kids: How to Spend Quality Time with the Children in Your Life. LC 82-24317. 176p. (Orig.). 1983. pap. 6.95 (ISBN 0-687-35598-2). Abingdon.

Silver, Gerald A. & Silver, Myrna. Weekend Fathers. LC 81-51695. 1981. 13.95 (ISBN 0-936906-06-5). Stratford Pr.

Simon, Norma. I Wish I Had My Father. Tucker, Kathleen, ed. (Concept Bks.). (Illus.). 32p. (gr. 1-4). 1983. PLB 7.50 (ISBN 0-8075-3522-2). A Whitman.

Stanley, Hugh P. The Challenge of Fatherhood. LC 82-73132. 96p. (Orig.). 1982. pap. 2.45 (ISBN 0-87029-185-8, 20279-6). Abbey.

Woolfolk, William & Cross, Donna W. Daddy's Little Girl: The Unspoken Bargain Between Fathers & Their Daughters. 220p. 1983. pap. 5.95 (ISBN 0-13-196279-5). P-H.

FATHERS OF THE CHURCH

Here are entered works on the life and thought of the Fathers of the Church, a term that embraces the leaders of the early church to the time of Gregory the Great in the West and John of Damascus in the east. Works on their writing are entered under the heading Christian Literature, Early.

Meijering, E. P. Hilary of Poitiers on the Trinity: De Trinitate 1, 1-19, 2, 3. (Philosophia Patrum: Vol. 6). ix, 199p. 1982. write for info. (ISBN 90-04-06734-5). E J Brill.

FATIGUE

Ribner, Richard & Cherian, Thyparambil C. Living Without Fatigue. 1983. pap. 7.95 (ISBN 0-8159-6117-0). Devin.

FATIGUE OF MATERIALS

see Materials–Fatigue

FATNESS

see Obesity

FATS

see Oils and Fats

FATTY ACID METABOLISM

Hornstra, G. Dietary Fats, Prostanoids & Arterial Thrombosis. 1983. 48.00 (ISBN 90-247-2667-0, Pub. by Martinus Nijhoff Netherlands). Kluwer Boston.

FAULKNER, WILLIAM, 1897-1962

Bleikasten, Andre. William Faulkner's The Sound & the Fury: Selected Criticism. LC 81-43365. 242p. 1982. lib. bdg. 30.00 (ISBN 0-8240-9269-4). Garland Pub.

Kinney, Arthur F. Critical Essays on William Faulkner: The Compson Family. (Critical Essays on American Literature Ser.). 1982. lib. bdg. 32.00 (ISBN 0-8161-8464-X). G K Hall.

Peters, Erskine. William Faulkner: The Yoknapatawpha World & Black Being. 265p. 1982. lib. bdg. 25.00 (ISBN 0-8482-5675-1). Norwood Edns.

Pitavy, Francois. William Faulkner's Light in August: A Critical Casebook. LC 81-48416. 300p. 1982. lib. bdg. 40.00 (ISBN 0-8240-9385-2). Garland Pub.

Ruppersburg, Hugh M. Voice & Eye in Faulkner's Fiction. LC 82-17347. 200p. 1983. text ed. 16.00x (ISBN 0-8203-0627-4). U of Ga Pr.

Serafin, Joan M. Faulkner's Uses of the Classics. (Studies in Modern Literature: No. 1). 208p. 1983. 34.95 (ISBN 0-8357-1397-0, Pub. by UMI Res Pr). Univ Microfilms.

Sundquist, Eric J. Faulkner: The House Divided. LC 82-8923. 256p. 1983. 16.95q (ISBN 0-8018-2898-8). Johns Hopkins.

Wasson, Ben. Count No'Count: Flashbacks to Faulkner. (Center for the Study of Southern Culture Ser.). (Illus.). 208p. 1983. 12.95 (ISBN 0-87805-162-7). U Pr of Miss.

FAUNA

see Animals; Fresh-Water Biology; Zoology

FAUNA, PREHISTORIC

see Paleontology

FBI

see United States–Federal Bureau of Investigation

FEAR

see also Agoraphobia; Anxiety; Courage; Phobias

Donahue, Bob & Donahue, Marilyn. Things That Go Bump in the Night, & Other Fears. (YA) 1983. pap. 3.95 (ISBN 0-686-82528-4). Tyndale.

Freeman, Lucy. Fight Against Fears. 368p. 1983. pap. 3.50 (ISBN 0-446-30329-1). Warner Bks.

McFadden, Jim. The Fear Factor: Everyone Has it, You Can Master It. (Living As a Christian Ser.). (Orig.). 1983. pap. write for info. (ISBN 0-89283-159-6). Servant.

FEAR OF GOD

Burke, Dennis. Understanding the Fear of the Lord. 1982. pap. 1.50 (ISBN 0-686-83915-3). Harrison Hse.

FEAST OF ESTHER

see Purim (Feast of Esther)

FECUNDITY

see Fertility

FEDERAL AID TO EDUCATION

see also Educational Equalization

Lefever, Ernest W. & English, Raymond. Scholars, Dollars & Public Policy: New Frontiers in Corporate Giving. LC 82-25126. 62p. (Orig.). 1983. pap. 4.00 (ISBN 0-89633-065-6). Ethics & Public Policy.

Twomley, Dale E. Parochiaid & the Courts. (Andrews University Monographs, Studies in Education: Vol. 2). x, 165p. 1979. 3.95 (ISBN 0-943872-51-0). Andrews Univ Pr.

FEDERAL AID TO THE ARTS

Larson, Gary O. The Reluctant Patron: The United States Government & the Arts, 1943-1965. LC 82-40492. (Illus.). 320p. (Orig.). 1983. 30.00x (ISBN 0-8122-7876-3); pap. 12.95 (ISBN 0-8122-1144-8). U of Pa Pr.

Millsaps, Daniel & Washington International Arts Letter Editors. National Directory of Arts Support by Private Foundations. 5th ed. LC 77-79730. (The Arts Patronage Ser.: No. 12). 340p. (Orig.). 1983. 79.95 (ISBN 0-912072-13-X). Wash Intl Arts.

--National Directory of Grants & Aid to Individuals in the Arts. 5th ed. LC 70-112695. (The Arts Patronage Ser.: No. 11). 254p. (Orig.). 1983. 15.95 (ISBN 0-912072-12-1). Wash Intl Arts.

FEDERAL BUREAU OF INVESTIGATION

see United States–Federal Bureau of Investigation

FEDERAL CORPORATION TAX

see Corporations–Taxation

FEDERAL GOVERNMENT

see also Decentralization in Government; Democracy; Grants-In-Aid; Intergovernmental Fiscal Relations; Intergovernmental Tax Relations; Legislative Power; State Governments also subdivision Constitution and subdivision Politics and Government under names of federal states, e.g. United States–Constitution; France–Politics and Government

Hay, Peter & Rotunda, Ronald D. The United States Federal System: Legal Integration in the American Federal Experience. (Studies in Comparative Law: No. 22). Date not set. lib. bdg. 35.00 (ISBN 0-379-20800-8). Oceana.

Press, Charles & VerBurg, Kenneth. State & Community Governments in the Federal System. 2nd ed. 600p. 1983. text ed. write for info. (ISBN 0-471-86979-1); write for info. tchr's ed. (ISBN 0-471-87199-0). Wiley.

FEDERAL GRANTS FOR EDUCATION
see Federal Aid to Education

FEDERAL GRANTS FOR THE ARTS
see Federal Aid to the Arts

FEDERAL REVENUE SHARING
see Intergovernmental Fiscal Relations; Intergovernmental Tax Relations

FEDERAL-STATE FISCAL RELATIONS
see Intergovernmental Fiscal Relations

FEDERAL-STATE RELATIONS
see Federal Government

FEDERAL-STATE TAX RELATIONS
see Intergovernmental Tax Relations

FEDERAL THEOLOGY
see Covenants (Theology)

FEDERALISM
see Federal Government

FEDERATION, INTERNATIONAL
see International Organization

FEDERATIONS, FINANCIAL (SOCIAL SERVICE)

Brownrigg, W. G. Out of the Red: Strategies for Effective Corporate Fundraising. (Illus.). 176p. 1983. pap. 12.95 (ISBN 0-915400-43-X). Am Council Arts.

FEDERATIONS FOR CHARITY AND PHILANTHROPY
see Federations, Financial (Social Service)

FEE SYSTEM (TAXATION)
see Taxation

FEEBLE MINDED
see Mental Deficiency; Mentally Handicapped

FEED
see Feeds

FEEDBACK CONTROL SYSTEMS
see also Adaptive Control Systems; Biological Control Systems

Callier, F. M. & Desoer, C. A. Multivariable Feedback Systems. (Springer Texts in Electrical Engineering). (Illus.). 275p. 1983. 36.00 (ISBN 0-387-90768-8); pap. 19.50 (ISBN 0-387-90759-9). Springer-Verlag.

Hung, Y. S. & MacFarlane, A. G. Multivariable Feedback: A Quasi-Classical Approach. (Lecture Notes in Control & Information Sciences: Vol. 40). 182p. 1983. pap. 9.50 (ISBN 0-387-11902-7). Springer-Verlag.

Moroney, Paul. Issues in the Implementation of Digital Feedback Compensators. (Signal Processing, Optimization, & Control Ser.). (Illus.). 224p. 1983. 30.00x (ISBN 0-262-13185-4). MIT Pr.

Nordholt, E. H. Design of High Performance Negative-Feedback Amplifiers. (Studies in Electric & Electronic Engineering: Vol. 7). Date not set. 57.50 (ISBN 0-444-42140-8). Elsevier.

Owens, D. H. Feedback & Multivariable Systems. (IEE Control Engineering Ser.). (Illus.). 320p. 1978. casebound 47.75 (ISBN 0-906048-03-6). Inst Elect Eng.

FEEDING
see Animal Nutrition

FEEDING BEHAVIOR
see Animals, Food Habits of

FEEDS
see also Animal Nutrition; Forage Plants
also subdivision Feeding and Feeds under names of animals and groups of animals, e.g. Poultry–Feeding and Feeds

Broster, W. H. & Swan, Henry. Feeding Strategy for the High Yielding Dairy Cow. 432p. 1979. text ed. 45.00x (ISBN 0-258-97126-6, Pub. by Granada England). Renouf.

FEELING
see Perception; Touch

FEELINGS
see Emotions

FEES, LEGAL
see Lawyers–Fees

FEES, MEDICAL
see Medical Fees

FEET
see Foot

FELONY
see Criminal Law

FEMALE
see Women

FEMALE OFFENDERS
see also Reformatories for Women

Gora. The New Female Criminal. 160p. 1982. 21.95 (ISBN 0-03-062007-4). Praeger.

Mukherjee, Satyanshu K. & Scutt, Jocelynne A., eds. Women & Crime. 208p. 1982. pap. text ed. 12.50x (ISBN 0-86861-067-4). Allen Unwin.

Spaulding, Edith R. An Experimental Study of Psychopathic Delinquent Women. (Historical Foundations of Forensic Psychiatry & Psychology Ser.). (Illus.). xviii, 368p. 1983. Repr. of 1923 ed. lib. bdg. 45.00 (ISBN 0-306-76185-8). Da Capo.

FEMALE STUDIES
see Women'S Studies

FEMININITY (PSYCHOLOGY)
see also Sex (Psychology)

Jillson, Joyce. Real Women Don't Pump Gas: A Guide to All That Is Divinely Feminine. (Illus., Orig.). 1982. pap. 3.95 (ISBN 0-671-46309-8). PB.

Mollenkott, Virginia R. The Divine Feminine: The Biblical Imagery of God As Female. 144p. 1983. 12.95 (ISBN 0-8245-0565-4). Crossroad NY.

Murray, Meg M., ed. Face to Face: Fathers, Mothers, Masters, Monsters--Essays for a Nonsexist Future. LC 82-11708. (Contributions in Women's Studies: No. 36). 360p. 1983. lib. bdg. 29.95 (ISBN 0-313-23044-7, MFF/). Greenwood.

FEMINISM
see also Sex Discrimination; Women–History; Women–Legal Status, Laws, etc.; Women's Rights; Women–Social Conditions

Banks. Feminism & Family Planning in Victorian England. 154p. 1982. 39.00x (ISBN 0-85323-281-4, Pub. by Liverpool Univ England). State Mutual Bk.

Bradshaw, J., ed. The Women's Liberation Movement: Europe & North America. 100p. 1982. 19.00 (ISBN 0-08-028932-0). Pergamon.

Brunt & Rowen, eds. Feminism, Culture & Politics. 190p. 1982. text ed. 21.00x (ISBN 0-85315-543-7, Pub. by Lawrence & Wishart Ltd England). Humanities.

Charvet, John. Feminism. (Modern Ideologies Ser.). 168p. 1982. text ed. 15.00x (ISBN 0-460-10255-9, Pub. by J. M. Dent England); pap. text ed. 7.95x (ISBN 0-460-11255-4, Pub. by J. M. Dent England). Biblio Dist.

Dixon, Marlene. Women in Class Struggle. 3rd ed. 175p. 1983. pap. 7.95 (ISBN 0-89935-021-6). Synthesis Pubns.

Eichenbaum, Luise & Orbach, Susie. Understanding Women: A Feminist Psychoanalytic Approach. 1983. 15.50 (ISBN 0-465-08864-3). Basic.

Friedan, Betty. The Second Stage. 352p. 1982. pap. 5.95 (ISBN 0-671-45951-1). Summit Bks.

Frye, Marilyn. The Politics of Reality: Essays in Feminist Theory. 150p. 1983. 14.95 (ISBN 0-89594-100-7); pap. 6.95 (ISBN 0-89594-099-X). Crossing Pr.

Gallop, J. Feminism & Psychoanalysis: The Daughters Seduction. 1982. 55.00x (ISBN 0-333-29471-8, Pub. by Macmillan England). State Mutual Bk.

Holbrook, D. L. & Holbrook, Becky T. Lib Movement-God's Way. 3.75 (ISBN 0-89137-419-1). Quality Pubns.

Howe, Florence, ed. Dialogue on Difference. 224p. 1983. 8.95 (ISBN 0-935312-22-6). Feminist Pr.

Johnson, Sonia. From Housewife to Heretic. LC 80-2964. 408p. 1983. pap. 8.95 (ISBN 0-385-17494-2, Anch). Doubleday.

Kelly, Mary. Post-Partum Document. (Illus.). 172p. (Orig.). 1983. pap. price not set (ISBN 0-7100-9495-7). Routledge & Kegan.

McElroy, Wendy, ed. Freedom, Feminism, & the State. 357p. 1982. pap. 7.95 (ISBN 0-932790-32-1). Cato Inst.

Rothschild, Joan, ed. Machina ex Dea: Feminist Perspectives on Technology. (Athene Ser.). 250p. 1983. 27.50 (ISBN 0-08-029404-9); pap. 10.95 (ISBN 0-08-029403-0). Pergamon.

Scharf, Lois & Jensen, Joan M., eds. Decades of Discontent: The Women's Movement 1920-1940. LC 81-4243. (Contributions in Women's Studies: No. 28). 352p. 1983. lib. bdg. 35.00 (ISBN 0-313-22694-6). Greenwood.

Sievers, Sharon L. Flowers in Salt: The Beginnings of Feminist Consciousness in Modern Japan. LC 82-60104. (Illus.). 256p. 1983. 22.50x (ISBN 0-8047-1165-8). Stanford U Pr.

Simpson, Hilary. D. H. Lawrence & Feminism. 174p. 1982. text ed. write for info (ISBN 0-87580-090-4). N Ill U Pr.

Stanley, Liz & Wise, Sue. Breaking Out: Feminist Consciousness & Feminist Research. 192p. (Orig.). 1983. pap. price not set (ISBN 0-7100-9315-2). Routledge & Kegan.

Taylor, Barbara. Eve & the New Jerusalem: Socialism & Feminism in the Nineteenth Century. 315p. 1983. pap. 9.95 (ISBN 0-686-37899-7). Pantheon.

Thorp, Margaret. Female Persuasion: Six Strong-Minded Women. 1949. text ed. 16.50x (ISBN 0-686-83549-2). Elliots Bks.

Women, Reason & Nature: Some Philosophical Problems with Feminism. LC 82-12207. 165p. 1982. 17.50 (ISBN 0-691-07274-4). Princeton U Pr.

FEMINISM AND LITERATURE

Barickman, Richard, et al. Corrupt Relations: Dickens, Thackeray, Trollope, Collins & the Victorian Sexual System. 1982. 25.00 (ISBN 0-686-82110-6). Columbia U Pr.

Hanscombe, Gillian E. The Art of Life: Dorothy Richardson & the Development of Feminist Consciousness. 200p. 1983. text ed. 20.95x (ISBN 0-8214-0739-2, 82-85082); pap. 10.95 (ISBN 0-8214-0740-6, 82-85090). Ohio U Pr.

FEMINIST STUDIES
see Women'S Studies

FENCES
see also Gates

Chamberlin, Susan & Pollock, Susan. Fences, Gates & Walls. 1983. pap. 9.95 (ISBN 0-89586-189-5). H P Bks.

Hanson, Michael L. Pocket Handbook for Hi-Tensile Fencing. (Illus.). 58p. (Orig.). 1982. write for info. Agri-Fence.

FENCING

Curry, Nancy L. Fencing. LC 82-83919. (Illus.). 144p. (Orig.). 1983. pap. 6.95 (ISBN 0-918438-99-3). Leisure Pr.

FERLINGHETTI, LAWRENCE, 1919-

Smith, Larry. Lawrence Ferlinghetti: Poet-at-Large. LC 82-10835. 144p. 1983. 22.50 (ISBN 0-8093-1101-1); pap. 9.95 (ISBN 0-8093-1102-X). S Ill U Pr.

FERMENTS
see Enzymes

FERN ALLIES
see Pteridophyta

FERNS

Beddome, R. H. The Ferns of British India, Vols. I & II. 702p. 1978. 99.00x (ISBN 0-686-84451-3, Pub. by Oxford & I B H India). State Mutual Bk.

Page, C. N. The Ferns of Britain & Ireland. LC 82-1126. (Illus.). 450p. Date not set. price not set (ISBN 0-521-23213-9); pap. price not set (ISBN 0-521-29872-5). Cambridge U Pr.

FERRARI (AUTOMOBILE)
see Automobiles, Foreign–Types–Ferrari

FERRATES
see Ferrites (Magnetic Materials)

FERRITES (MAGNETIC MATERIALS)

Hellwege, K. H., ed. Magnetic & Other Properties of Xides & Related Compounds: Hexagonal Ferrites. Special Lanthanide & Actinide Compounds. (Landolt-Boernstein Ser.: Group III, Vol. 12, Pt. C). (Illus.). 650p. 1983. 408.00 (ISBN 0-387-10137-3). Springer-Verlag.

FERROCEMENT
see Reinforced Concrete

FERROUS METAL INDUSTRIES
see Iron Industry and Trade; Steel Industry and Trade

FERTILITY
see also Heterosis

Bongaarts, John & Potter, Robert G., eds. Fertility, Biology & Behavior: An Analysis of the Proximate Determinants (Monograph) (Studies in Population). 216p. 1983. price not set (ISBN 0-12-114380-5). Acad Pr.

Drayson, James E. Herd Bull Fertility. (Illus.). 160p. (Orig.). 1982. pap. 9.95 (ISBN 0-934318-08-5). J E Drayson.

Hartmann, John F., ed. Mechanism & Control of Animal Fertilization. (Cell Biology Ser.). Date not set. price not set (ISBN 0-12-328520-8). Acad Pr.

Muldoon, Thomas G. & Mahesh, Virendra B., eds. Recent Advances in Fertility Research, Pt. A: Developments in Reproductive Endocrinology. LC 82-20327. (Progress in Clinical & Biological Research Ser.: Vol. 112A). 340p. 1982. 36.00 (ISBN 0-8451-0172-2). A R Liss.

FERTILITY, HUMAN
see also subdivision Population under names of countries

Barker, Graham H. Your Search for Fertility: A Sympathetic Guide to Achieving Pregnancy for Childless Couples. Bronson, Richard A., frwd. by. LC 82-61676. 208p. 1983. pap. 5.95 (ISBN 0-688-01593-X). Quill NY.

Garcia, Celso-Ramon & Mastroianni, Luigi, Jr. Current Therapy of Infertility, 1982-1983. 256p. 1982. text ed. 32.00 (ISBN 0-941158-02-0, D1738-3). Mosby.

Mosk, Carl, ed. Patriarchy & Fertility: The Evolution of Natality in Japan & Sweden 1880-1960. (Population & Social Structure: Advances in Historical Demography). Date not set. price not set (ISBN 0-12-508480-3). Acad Pr.

FERTILIZATION IN VITRO, HUMAN

Smith, Roberta H. In Vitro: Propagation of Kalanchoe. (Avery's Plant Tissue Culture Ser.). (Illus.). 16p. (Orig.). 1982. pap. text ed. 2.95 (ISBN 0-89529-163-0). Avery Pub.

FERTILIZER INDUSTRY

Transnational Corporations in the Fertilizer Industry. 8.00 (ISBN 0-686-43222-3, E.82.II.A.10). UN.

FERTILIZERS AND MANURES
see also Agricultural Chemistry; Humus; Nitrates; Phosphates; Salt

Cooke, G. W. Fertilizing for Maximum Yield. 3rd ed. 473p. 1982. 32.50 (ISBN 0-02-949310-2). Free Pr.

Crop Response to the Supply of Macronutrients. 46p. 1982. pap. 6.75 (ISBN 90-220-0807-X, PDC247, Pudoc). Unipub.

FAO Fertilizer Yearbook 1981, Vol. 31. (FAO Statistics Ser.: No. 42). 144p. 1983. 24.50 (ISBN 92-5-001208-X, F2345, FAO). Unipub.

Hagin, Josef & Tucker, Billy. Fertilization of Dryland & Irrigated Soils. (Advanced Series in Agricultural Sciences: Vol. 12). (Illus.). 210p. 1982. 39.50 (ISBN 0-387-11121-2). Springer-Verlag.

Martinez, Adolfo & Diamond, Ray B. Fertilizer Use Statistics in Crop Production. LC 82-15856. (Technical Bulletin Ser.: No. T-24). 37p. (Orig.). 1982. pap. text ed. 4.00 (ISBN 0-88090-042-3). Intl Fertilizer.

Thompson, M. K., ed. IFDC Annual Report, 1981. (Circular Ser.: S-5). 60p. (Orig.). 1982. pap. text ed. 4.00. Intl Fertilizer.

FESTIVALS
see also Anniversaries; Holidays; Music Festivals; Tournaments
also names of particular festivals, e.g. Christmas; Hanukkah (Feast of Lights)

Gale, Janice & Gale, Stephen. Guide to Fairs, Festivals & Fun Events. (Illus.). 190p. Date not set. pap. 6.95 (ISBN 0-686-84245-6). Banyan Bks.

Gilbert, Elizabeth R. Fairs & Festivals: A Smithsonian Guide to Celebrations in Maryland, Virginia, & Washington, D.C. LC 82-600152. (Illus.). 160p. 1982. pap. 4.50 (ISBN 0-87474-473-3). Smithsonian.

Simon, Erika. Festivals of Attica: An Archaeological Commentary. 160p. 1983. text ed. 21.50 (ISBN 0-299-09180-5). U of Wis Pr.

Welbon, Guy & Yocum, Glenn, eds. Festivals in South India & Sri Lanka. 1982. 25.00X (ISBN 0-8364-0900-0, Pub.by Manohar India). South Asia Bks.

FETICIDE
see Abortion

FETUS
see also Obstetrics

Martini, Luciano & James, V. H., eds. Current Topics in Experimental Endocrinology: Vol. 5: Fetal Endocrinology & Metabolism. (Serial Publication). Date not set. price not set (ISBN 0-12-153205-4). Acad Pr.

Miler, I. The Immunity of the Foetus & Newborn Infant. 1983. 41.50 (ISBN 90-247-2610-7, Pub. by Martinus Nijhoff Netherlands). Kluwer Boston.

FEUDAL CASTLES
see Castles

FEUDALISM
see also Chivalry; Peasantry

Bell, Andrew. A History of Feudalism: British & Continental. 360p. 1982. Repr. of 1863 ed. lib. bdg. 75.00 (ISBN 0-686-81829-6). Darby Bks.

FEUERBACH, LUDWIG ANDREAS, 1804-1872

Wartofsky, Marx. Feuerbach. LC 76-9180. 480p. 1982. pap. 14.95 (ISBN 0-521-28929-7). Cambridge U Pr.

FEVER
see also Body Temperature

Murray, Henry W., ed. Fever of Undetermined Origin. (Illus.). 350p. Date not set. price not set monograph (ISBN 0-87993-194-9). Futura Pub.

FIAT (AUTOMOBILE)
see Automobiles, Foreign–Types–Fiat

FIAT MONEY
see Currency Question; Paper Money

FIBER IN THE DIET
see High-Fiber Diet

FIBER OPTICS

Boyd, W. T. Fiber Optics Communications: Experiments & Projects. Date not set. pap. 15.95 (ISBN 0-672-21834-8). Sams.

Ezekiel, S. & Arditty, H. J., eds. Fiber-Optic Rotation Sensors, Cambridge, MA: Proceedings, 1981. (Springer Series in Optical Sciences Ser.: Vol. 32). (Illus.). 440p. 1983. 33.00 (ISBN 0-387-11791-1). Springer-Verlag.

Future Systems, Inc. Optical Fiber Communications: Current Systems & Future Developments. (Illus.). 135p. (Orig.). 1982. pap. 45.00x (ISBN 0-940520-47-8). Monegon Ltd.

Information Gatekeepers, Inc. The Second European Fiber Optics & Communications Exposition, 2 vols. 1982. pap. 125.00 (ISBN 0-686-38470-9). Info Gatekeepers.

--The Sixth International Fiber Optics & Communications Exposition. 1982. 125.00 (ISBN 0-686-38469-5). Info Gatekeepers.

Keiser, Gerd. Optical Fiber Communications. (Series in Electrical Engineering). (Illus.). 336p. 1983. text ed. 35.00 (ISBN 0-07-033467-6, C); solutions manual 18.00 (ISBN 0-07-033468-4). McGraw.

FIBER PLANTS
see Fibers

FIBERS
see also Cotton; Fibrous Composites; Linen; Paper; Silk

Fiberarts Magazine Staff, ed. The Fiberarts Design Book. LC 80-67315. (Illus.). 176p. (Orig.). 1980. 24.95 (ISBN 0-937274-00-3); pap. 15.95 (ISBN 0-937274-01-1). Lark Bks.

Report of the Seventeenth Session of the Intergovernmental Group on Jute, Kenaf & Allied Fibres. pap. 7.50 (ISBN 0-686-82540-3, F2318, FAO). Unipub.

FIBRIN AND FIBRINOGEN

Henschen, A. & Graeff, H., eds. Fibrinogen. (Illus.). x, 400p. 1982. 67.50x (ISBN 3-11-008543-7). De Gruyter.

FIBROCYSTIC DISEASE OF PANCREAS
see Cystic Fibrosis

FIBROSIS, CYSTIC
see Cystic Fibrosis

FIBROUS COMPOSITES
see also Reinforced Plastics

Nachmias, Vivianne T. Microfilaments. Head, J. J., ed. LC 82-73999. (Carolina Biology Readers Ser.). (Illus.). 16p. 1983. pap. text ed. 1.60 (ISBN 0-89278-330-3, 45-9730). Carolina Biological.

FICINO, MARSILIO, 1433-1499
Ficino, Marsilio. The Letters of Marsilio Ficino, Vol. 2. School of Economic Science, London, Language Dept., tr. from Lat. 121p. 1978. 16.00 (ISBN 0-85683-036-4). Spring Pubns.
--The Letters of Marsilio Ficino, Vol. 3. School of Economic Science, London, Language Dept., tr. from Lat. 162p. 1981. 16.00 (ISBN 0-85683-045-3). Spring Pubns.
--The Letters of Marsilo Ficino, Vol. 1. School of Economic Science, London, Language Dept., tr. from Lat. 248p. 1975. 16.00 (ISBN 0-85683-010-0). Spring Pubns.
FICTION
see also Baseball Stories; Children's Stories; Detective and Mystery Stories; Fables; Fairy Tales; Fantastic Fiction; Folk-Lore; Ghost Stories; Historical Fiction; Horror Tales; Legends; Romances; Romanticism; Science Fiction (Collections); Sea Stories; Short Stories; Spy Stories; Tales; Western Stories
also American Fiction, English Fiction, French Fiction, and similar headings; and subdivision Fiction under historical events and characters, etc. e.g. Gettysburg, Battle of, 1863–Fiction; Napolean 1st, Emperor of the French, 1769-1821–Fiction; World War, 1939-1945–Fiction
Bernardin de Saint-Pierre, Jacques-Henri. Paul & Virginia. 110p. 1983. 14.95 (ISBN 0-7206-0598-9, Pub by Peter Owen). Merrimack Bk Serv.
Morris, William, ed. The Novel on Blue Paper. 79p. 1982. pap. 4.50 (ISBN 0-904526-51-8, Pub. by Journeyman England). Lawrence Hill.
Simpson, George & Burger, Neal. Severed Ties. (Orig.). 1983. pap. 3.50 (ISBN 0-440-17705-7). Dell.
Upfield, Arthur W. The House of Cain. Farmer, Philip Jose, intro. by. (Illus.). 296p. 1983. Repr. of 1928 ed. 20.00x (ISBN 0-9609986-0-8). D McMillan.
FICTION (COLLECTIONS)
Lynch, Richard & Rae, Helen, eds. Signal Fire 1982. (Signal Fire Ser.). (Illus.). 104p. (Orig.). 1982. pap. 3.95 (ISBN 0-941588-13-0). Creative Assoc.
FICTION–AUTHORSHIP
Gordon, Lois. Robert Coover: The Universal Fictionmaking Process. (Crosscurrents-Modern Critques-New Issues Ser.). 208p. 1983. 15.95x (ISBN 0-8093-1092-9). S Ill U Pr.
Stevenson, John. Writing Commercial Fiction. 128p. 1983. 12.95 (ISBN 0-13-971689-0, Reward); pap. 6.95 (ISBN 0-13-971671-8). P-H.
Wolfe, Thomas. The Autobiography of an American Novelist. Field, Leslie, ed. (Illus.). 128p. 1983. text ed. 15.00x (ISBN 0-674-05316-8); pap. text ed. 5.95x (ISBN 0-674-05317-6). Harvard U Pr.
FICTION–BIBLIOGRAPHY
Fredette, Jean. Fiction Writer's Market 1983-84. 2nd ed. 672p. 1983. 17.95 (ISBN 0-89879-108-1). Writers Digest.
FICTION–HISTORY AND CRITICISM
Dillard, Annie. Living by Fiction. LC 81-47882. 192p. 1983. pap. 4.76i (ISBN 0-06-091044-5, CN 1044, CN). Har-Row.
Figes, E. Sex & Subterfuge: Women Novelists to 1850. 1982. 50.00x (ISBN 0-333-29208-1, Pub. by Macmillan England). State Mutual Bk.
Fitzgerald, Edward & Hemmant, Lynette. Rubaiyat of Omar Khayam. 1979. 8.95 (ISBN 0-437-40120-0, Pub. by World's Work). David & Charles.
Hagg, Thomas. The Novel in Antiquity. LC 82-45906. (Illus.). 288p. 1983. text ed. 30.00x (ISBN 0-520-04923-3). U of Cal Pr.
Novak, Maximillian E. Realism, Myth, & History in Defoe's Fiction. LC 82-11141. xviii, 170p. 1983. 16.95x (ISBN 0-8032-3307-8). U of Nebr Pr.
Price, Martin. Forms of Life: Character & Moral Imagination in the Novel. LC 82-16064. 400p. 1983. text ed. 27.50x (ISBN 0-300-02867-9). Yale U Pr.
Servodidio, Mirella & Welles, Marcia L., eds. From Fiction to Metafiction: Essays in Honor of Carmen Martin Gaite. LC 82-61181. 200p. (Orig.). 1983. pap. 25.00 (ISBN 0-89295-023-4). Society Sp & Sp-Am.
Stone, William W. Balzac, James & the Realistic Novel. LC 82-61388. 224p. 1983. 19.50x (ISBN 0-691-06567-5). Princeton U Pr.
FICTION–HISTORY AND CRITICISM–BIBLIOGRAPHY
Fitzgerald, Louise S. & Kearney, Elizabeth I. The Continental Novel: A Checklist of Criticism in English 1967-1980. LC 82-20454. 510p. 1983. 29.50 (ISBN 0-8108-1598-2). Scarecrow.
FICTION–HISTORY AND CRITICISM–20TH CENTURY
Deduck, Patricia A. Realism, Reality & the Fictional Theory of Alain Robbe-Grillet & Anais Nin. LC 82-13549. 118p. 1982. lib. bdg. 19.00 (ISBN 0-8191-2719-1); pap. text ed. 8.25 (ISBN 0-8191-2720-5). U Pr of Amer.
Staley, T. F. Twentieth-Century Women Novelists. 1982. 70.00x (ISBN 0-686-42935-4, Pub. by Macmillan England). State Mutual Bk.
FICTION–STORIES, PLOTS, ETC.
see Plots (Drama, Novel, etc.)
FICTION–TECHNIQUE
see also Detective and Mystery Stories–Technique; Plots (Drama, Novel, etc.)
Berman, Jan. Fiction Writing. (Learning Workbooks Language Arts). (gr. 4-6). pap. 1.50 (ISBN 0-8224-4182-9). Pitman.

FICTION, HISTORICAL
see Historical Fiction
FICTITIOUS NAMES
see Anonyms and Pseudonyms
FIDDLE
see Violin
FIDUCIA
see Trusts and Trustees
FIEFS
see Feudalism
FIELD, NATHAN, 1587-1620?
Nathan Field: The Actor-Playwright. 1928. pap. text ed. 10.00x (ISBN 0-686-83629-4). Elliots Bks.
FIELD ATHLETICS
see Track-Athletics
FIELD BIOLOGY
see Biology–Field Work
FIELD CROPS
see also Forage Plants; Grain; Horticulture; Tropical Crops
also names of specific crops, e.g. Cotton, Hay
Fogg, H. Witham. Salad Crops all Year Round. (Illus.). 200p. 1983. 19.95 (ISBN 0-7153-8411-2). David & Charles.
Lockhart, J. A. & Wiseman, A. J. Introduction to Crop Husbandry. 5th ed. (Illus.). 300p. 1983. 40.00 (ISBN 0-08-029793-5); pap. 16.00 (ISBN 0-08-029792-7). Pergamon.
Wang, Jaw-Kai, ed. Taro: A Review of "Colocasia Esculenta" & Its Potentials. LC 82-21903. (Illus.). 416p. 1983. text ed. 35.00x (ISBN 0-8248-0841-X). UH Pr.
FIELD HOCKEY
Field Hockey. (Scorebooks Ser.). 2.95 (ISBN 0-88314-167-1). AAHPERD.
Johnson, Dewayne & Parks, Barbara A. Field Hockey. (Illus.). 79p. 1983. pap. text ed. 2.95x (ISBN 0-89641-091-9). American Pr.
FIELD SPORTS
see Hunting; Sports
FIELD THEORY (PHYSICS)
see also Continuum Mechanics; Electromagnetic Theory; Magnetic Fields
Adamson, Iain T. An Introduction to Field Theory. 2nd ed. LC 82-1164. 192p. 1982. 19.95 (ISBN 0-521-24388-2); pap. 9.95 (ISBN 0-521-28658-1). Cambridge U Pr.
Garczynski, W., ed. Gauge Field Theories: Theoretical Studies & Computer Stimulations. (Studies in High Energy Physics: Vol. 4). Date not set. price not set (ISBN 3-7186-0121-4). Harwood Academic.
FIELD WORK (BIOLOGY)
see Biology–Field Work
FIELD WORK (EDUCATIONAL METHOD)
see also School Excursions
Redleaf, Rhoda, ed. Field Trips: An Adventure in Learning. (Illus.). 75p. (Orig.). 1980. pap. text ed. 8.95 (ISBN 0-934140-14-6). Toys N Things.
FIELD WORK (SOCIAL SERVICE)
see Social Service–Field Work
FIFTEENTH CENTURY
Wolff, Martha, ed. Anonymous Masters of the Fifteenth Century. (Illus.). 1983. 120.00 (ISBN 0-89835-023-9). Abaris Bks.
FIFTH COLUMN
see Subversive Activities
FIGHTER PLANES
see also Hurricane (Fighter Planes); Mustang (Fighter Planes); Spitfire (Fighter Planes)
Aders, Gebhard. History of the German Night Fighter Force 1917-1945. (Illus.). 360p. 1980. 19.95 (ISBN 0-86720-581-4). Sci Bks Intl.
Davis, Larry. P-Fifty-One Mustang in Color. (Fighting Colors Ser.). (Illus.). 32p. 1982. softcover 5.95 (ISBN 0-89747-135-0, 6505). Squad Sig Pubns.
Demand, Carlo. Airplanes of the Second World War Coloring Book. 48p. 1981. pap. 2.00 (ISBN 0-486-24107-6). Dover.
--Airplanes of World War I Coloring Book. 48p. 1979. pap. 1.75 (ISBN 0-486-23807-5). Dover.
Drendel, Lou. F-Sixteeen Falcon in Action. (Aircraft in Action Ser.). (Illus.). 50p. 1982. saddlestitch 4.95 (ISBN 0-89747-133-4). Squad Sig Pubns.
--Phantom II, A Pictorial History of the McDonnell-Douglas F-4 Phantom II. (Illus.). 64p. 1982. 6.95 (ISBN 0-89747-062-1). Squad Sig Pubns.
Miller, Jay. Aerograph: General Dynamics F-16 Fighting Falcon, No.1. (Illus.). 116p. 1982. pap. 14.95 (ISBN 0-686-43364-5, Pub. by Aero Fax Inc.). Aviation.
Moyes, Philip J. Modern U. S. Fighters. (Aerodata International Ser.). (Illus.). 120p. 1982. 9.95 (ISBN 0-89747-125-3, 6203). Squad Sig Pubns.
Stern, Rob. SB2C Helldiver in Action. (Aircraft in Action Ser.). (Illus.). 50p. 1982. saddlestitch 4.95 (ISBN 0-89747-128-8, 1054). Squad Sig Pubns.
Winter, Denis. The First of the Few: Fighter Pilots of the First World War. LC 82-13478. (Illus.). 224p. 17.50 (ISBN 0-8203-0642-8). U of Ga Pr.
FIGHTING
see Boxing; Karate; Military Art and Science; Naval Art and Science; Tournaments; War
FIGHTING, HAND-TO-HAND
see Hand-To-Hand Fighting
FIGURE SKATING
see Skating
FIGURINES
see Bronzes; Dolls; Dummy Board Figures; Ivories

FIJI ISLANDS
McDermott, John W. How to Get Lost & Found in Fiji. 3rd ed. 1981. 9.95 (ISBN 0-686-37616-1). Orafa Pub Co.
Rural Workers' Organisations in Fiji. 50p. 1982. 6.85 (ISBN 92-2-103004-0). Intl Labour Office.
Siers, James. Fiji in Colour. (Illus.). 124p. 1982. cancelled (ISBN 0-908582-52-8, Pub by Salem Hse Ltd.). Merrimack Bk Serv.
Stanner, W. E. The South Seas in Transition: A Study of Post-War Rehabilitation & Reconstruction in Three British Pacific Dependencies. LC 82-15534. xiv, 448p. 1982. Repr. of 1953 ed. lib. bdg. 39.75x (ISBN 0-313-23661-5, STSOS). Greenwood.
FILAMENT REINFORCED COMPOSITES
see Fibrous Composites
FILES AND FILING (DOCUMENTS)
see also Indexing
Rudman, Jack. Chief File Clerk. (Career Examination Ser.: C-453). (Cloth bdg. avail. on request). pap. 12.00 (ISBN 0-8373-0453-9). Natl Learning.
FILICINEAE
see Ferns
FILING SYSTEMS
see Files and Filing (Documents)
FILIPINOS IN THE UNITED STATES
Crouchett, Lorraine J. Filipinos in California: From the Days of the Galleon to the Present. LC 82-73374. (Illus.). 168p. 1983. 10.95x (ISBN 0-910823-00-6). Downey Place.
FILLERS (IN PAPER, PAINT, ETC.)
American Welding Society. Specification for Silver, Aluminum, Gold, Cobalt, Copper, Magnesium & Nickel Alloys Brazing Filler Metal. 1981. 8.00 (ISBN 0-686-43351-3). Am Welding.
FILM ACTORS
see Moving-Picture Actors and Actresses
FILM ADAPTATIONS
Harwell, Richard, ed. Gone With the Wind as Book & Film. (Illus.). 300p. 1983. 19.95 (ISBN 0-686-82616-7). U of SC Pr.
Millichap, Joseph R. Steinbeck & Film. LC 82-42502. (Ungar Film Library). (Illus.). 200p. 1983. 12.95 (ISBN 0-8044-2630-9); pap. 6.95 (ISBN 0-8044-6500-2). Ungar.
Street, Douglas, ed. Children's Novels & the Movies. (Ungar Film Library). (Illus.). 350p. 14.95 (ISBN 0-8044-2840-9); pap. 6.95 (ISBN 0-8044-6883-4). Ungar.
FILM AUTHORSHIP
see Moving-Picture Authorship
FILM EDITING (CINEMATOGRAPHY)
see Moving-Pictures–Editing
FILM MUSIC
see Moving-Picture Music
FILM STARS
see Moving-Picture Actors and Actresses
FILMS
see Moving-Pictures; Photography–Films
FILMS, METALLIC
see Metallic Films
FILMS, THIN
see Thin Films
FILMS FROM BOOKS
see Film Adaptations
FILTERS, DIGITAL (MATHEMATICS)
see Digital Filters (Mathematics)
FILTERS AND FILTRATION
Cheremisinoff, Nicholas P. & Azbel, David S., eds. Liquid Filtration. LC 82-46063. (Illus.). 400p. 1983. 49.95 (ISBN 0-250-40600-4). Ann Arbor Science.
FINAL CAUSE
see Causation; Teleology
FINANCE
see also Bankruptcy; Banks and Banking; Bonds; Budget in Business; Business Mathematics; Capital; Commerce; Controllership; Credit; Currency Question; Finance, Personal; Finance, Public; Foreign Exchange; Income; Inflation (Finance); Insurance; Interest and Usury; International Finance; Investments; Loans; Money; Profit; Saving and Investment; Securities; Stock-Exchange; Wealth
also subdivision Finance under special subjects, e.g. Corporations–Finance; Railroads–Finance
Altman, Edward I. Financial Handbook. 5th ed. LC 81-10473. 1344p. 1981. 55.00x (ISBN 0-471-07727-5, Pub. by Ronald Pr). Wiley.
Beehler, Paul J. Contemporary Cash Management: Principles, Practices, Perspectives. 2nd ed. (Systems & Control for Financial Management Ser.). 288p. 1983. 34.95x (ISBN 0-471-86861-2). Ronald Pr.
Browning, Edgar K. & Browning, Jacqueline M. Public Finance & the Price System. 2nd ed. 500p. 1983. text ed. 24.95 (ISBN 0-686-84132-8). Macmillan.
Cannon, Gwenda L. Financial & Estate Planning Applications, 2 Vols. (Huebner School Ser.). (Illus.). 463p. (Orig.). 1983. Vol. 1. pap. text ed. 32.00 (ISBN 0-943590-05-1); Vol. 2. pap. text ed. 32.00 (ISBN 0-943590-06-X). E Mellen.
Carrol, Freida. Creative Financing for Education, Housing, Automobiles, Vacations, Medical Care Etc. 60p. 1983. pap. text ed. 29.95 (ISBN 0-939476-58-4). Biblio Pr GA.
Cerami, Charles A. More Profits, Less Risk: Your New Financial Strategy. LC 82-7775. 240p. 1982. 14.95 (ISBN 0-07-010324-0). McGraw.

Copeland, Thomas E. & Weston, J. Fred. Financial Theory & Corporate Policy. 2nd ed. LC 82-11662. (Illus.). 704p. 1983. text ed. 26.95 (ISBN 0-201-10291-9). A-W.
Data Notes Publishing Staff, compiled by. Creative Financing Data Notes. 65p. Date not set. 15.95 (ISBN 0-686-37650-1). Data Notes Pub.
Donaldson. The Medium-Term Loan Market. LC 82-42619. 176p. 1982. 25.00x (ISBN 0-312-52820-5). St Martin.
Financial Times Business Publishing Ltd., ed. Offshore Financial Centres. 1982. 159.00x (ISBN 0-902998-41-2, Pub. by Finan Times England). State Mutual Bk.
Gart, Alan. The Insider's Guide to the Financial Services Revolution. (Illus.). 192p. 1983. 24.95 (ISBN 0-07-022891-4, P&RB). McGraw.
Gourgues, Harold W., Jr. Financial Planning Handbook. 416p. 1983. 34.95 (ISBN 0-13-316398-9). NY Inst Finance.
Harvard Business Review. Financial Management. (Harvard Business Review Executive Bk. Ser.). 550p. 1983. 22.95 (ISBN 0-471-87598-8, Pub. by Wiley Interscience). Wiley.
Havrilesky, Thomas M. & Schweitzer, Robert, eds. Contemporary Developments in Financial Institutions & Markets. LC 82-19901. (Illus.). 450p. 1983. pap. 18.95 (ISBN 0-88295-409-1). Harlan Davidson.
Higgins, Robert C. Analysis for Financial Management. LC 82-73628. 325p. 1983. 19.95 (ISBN 0-87094-377-4). Dow Jones-Irwin.
Jones, Graham. Financial Practice & Control. 250p. 1982. pap. text ed. 12.95x (ISBN 0-7121-0640-5). Intl Ideas.
Kapany, Narinder S., ed. Finance & Utilization of Solar Energy: Supplement. (Progress in Solar Energy Ser.). 1983. pap. text ed. 45.00 (ISBN 0-89553-121-6). Am Solar Energy.
Levin, Dick. Buy Low, Sell High, Collect Early & Pay Late: The Manager's Guide to Financial Survival. (Illus.). 224p. 1983. 15.95 (ISBN 0-13-109439-4). P-H.
Lewis, R. & Pendrill, D. Advanced Financial Accounting. 528p. 1981. 50.00x (ISBN 0-273-01640-7, Pub. by Pitman Bks England). State Mutual Bk.
McGee, Robert W. Fundamentals of Accounting & Finance: A Handbook for Business & Professional People. (Illus.). 216p. 1983. 14.95 (ISBN 0-13-332437-0); pap. 6.95 (ISBN 0-13-332429-X). P-H.
Mettling, Stephen R. Buydown Agreements. (Creative Financing Skill Development Ser.). 26p. 1982. pap. 7.95 (ISBN 0-88462-134-0). Real Estate Ed Co.
--Selling Creative Financing. (Creative Financing Skill Development Ser.). 30p. 1982. pap. 7.95 (ISBN 0-88462-139-1). Real Estate Ed Co.
Richards, Judith W. Fundamentals of Development Finance: A Practitioner's Guide. 224p. 1983. 31.95 (ISBN 0-03-062191-7). Praeger.
Rudman, Jack. Financial Analyst. (Career Examination Ser.: C-2642). (Cloth bdg. avail. on request). pap. 10.00 (ISBN 0-8373-2642-7). Natl Learning.
--Fiscal Manager. (Career Examination Ser.: C-2686). (Cloth bdg. avail. on request). pap. 12.00 (ISBN 0-8373-2686-9). Natl Learning.
FINANCE–DICTIONARIES
Ewald, Peter K. Encyclopedia of Finance & Investment Terms. 1983. pap. price not set (ISBN 0-8120-2522-9). Barron.
Zahn, Hans E. Glossaries of Financial & Economic Terms: English-German. 530p. 1977. 100.00 (ISBN 0-7121-5492-2, Pub. by Macdonald & Evans). State Mutual Bk.
FINANCE–RESEARCH
see Financial Research
FINANCE–ASIA
Skully, Michael T., ed. Financial Institutions & Markets in the Far East: A Study of China, Hong Kong, Japan, South Korea & Taiwan. LC 82-5652. 240p. 1982. 27.50x (ISBN 0-312-28961-8). St Martin.
FINANCE–CHINA
Byrd, William. China's Financial System: The Changing Role of Banks. (Replica Edition Ser.). 150p. 1982. softcover 17.00x (ISBN 0-86531-943-X). Westview.
FINANCE–GREAT BRITAIN
Lee, S. Y. Financial Structures & Monetary Policy. 300p. 1982. 49.00x (ISBN 0-333-28617-0, Pub. by Macmillan England). State Mutual Bk.
FINANCE–INDIA
Goldsmith, Raymond W. The Financial Development of India. LC 82-7094. 264p. 1983. text ed. 35.00x (ISBN 0-300-02030-9). Yale U Pr.
FINANCE–JAPAN
Financial Times Business Publishing Ltd., ed. Japanese Banking & Capital Markets. 1982. 150.00x (ISBN 0-686-82306-0, Pub. by Finan Times England). State Mutual Bk.
Goldsmith, Raymond W. The Financial Development of Japan. LC 82-8378. 256p. 1983. text ed. 30.00x (ISBN 0-300-02933-0). Yale U Pr.
FINANCE–SWITZERLAND
Dafflon, Bernard. Federal Finance in Theory & Practice with Special Reference to Switzerland. 176p. 1977. 90.00x (ISBN 0-7121-5624-0, Pub. by Macdonald & Evans). State Mutual Bk.
FINANCE, INTERNATIONAL
see International Finance

FINANCE, LOCAL
see Local Finance
FINANCE, MUNICIPAL
see Municipal Finance
FINANCE, PERSONAL
see also Consumer Credit; Estate Planning; Insurance; Investments
Bailard, Thomas E. & Biehl, David L. Personal Money Management. 4th ed. 640p. 1983. text ed. write for info. (ISBN 0-574-19525-4, 13-2525); write for info. instr's guide (ISBN 0-574-19526-2, 13-2526); write for info. study guide (ISBN 0-574-19527-0, 13-2527). SRA.
Brien, Mimi. Moneywise. 1982. pap. 3.50 (ISBN 0-686-82381-8). Bantam.
Burnett, Neil. Turning Assets into Prosperity: How to Trade Your Way to Financial Success. 206p. 1982. pap. 6.95 (ISBN 0-940986-03-5). ValuWrite.
Chakrapani, Chuck. Financial Freedom on Five Dollars a Day. (Orig.). 1983. pap. write for info. (ISBN 0-88908-564-1). Self Counsel Pr.
Cobleigh, Ira W. Double Your Dollars in 600 Days. 224p. 1979. 9.95 (ISBN 0-517-53777-X, Harmony). Crown.
Colman, Carol. Love & Money: What Your Finances Say About Your Personal Relationships. 300p. 1983. 15.95 (ISBN 0-698-11189-3, Coward). Putnam Pub Group.
Doyle, Alfreda, compiled by. Refrences on Prosperity. 35p. 1983. pap. 6.95 (ISBN 0-939476-62-2). Biblio Pr GA.
Easy Ways To Make Money. (Blank Books Ser.). 128p. 1982. cancelled (ISBN 0-939944-17-0). Marmac Pub.
Flumiani, Carlo M. How to Select a Stock with the Power to make you Wealthy Almost Overnight. (New Stock Market Library Book). (Illus.). 61p. (Orig.). 1983. pap. 6.95 (ISBN 0-89266-390-1). Am Classical Coll Pr.
--Three Ways for an Investor with very Little Money to make a Killing in the Stock Market. 04/1983 ed. (New Stock Market Library Book). (Illus.). 69p. (Orig.). pap. 6.95 (ISBN 0-89266-391-X). Am Classical Coll Pr.
Fowler, Gus. Getting What You Pay For. LC 82-74187. (Illus.). 248p. 1983. 10.95 (ISBN 0-9610432-1-0); pap. 9.95 (ISBN 0-9610432-0-2). Amistad Brands.
Fritchman, June & Solomon, Karey. Living Lean off the Fat of the Land. 224p. (Orig.). 1983. pap. 8.95 (ISBN 0-943914-03-5, Dist. by Kampmann & Co). Larson Pubns Inc.
German, Don & German, Joan. The Only Money Book for the Middle Class. LC 82-14236. (Illus.). 320p. 1983. 13.95 (ISBN 0-688-01567-0). Morrow.
Gould, Bruce G. The Most Dangerous Money Book Ever Written. 444p. (Orig.). 1983. pap. 100.00 (ISBN 0-918706-13-0). B Gould Pubns.
Kriyananda, Swami. How to use Money for Your Own Highest Good. 48p. 1981. pap. write for info. (ISBN 0-916124-22-3). Ananda.
Miller, Roger L. & Power, Fred B. Personal Finance Today. 2nd ed. (Illus.). 500p. 1983. text ed. 22.95 (ISBN 0-314-69668-7); instrs.' manual avail. (ISBN 0-314-71112-0); student guide avail. (ISBN 0-314-71113-9). West Pub.
Money-Yours & Mine. 175p. 1982. pap. 5.00 (ISBN 0-686-37414-2). Ideals PA.
Nelson, W. How to Profit from the Money Revolution. 92p. 1983. 12.95 (ISBN 0-07-046217-8, GB). McGraw.
Porter, Sylvia. Sylvia Porter's Your Own Money. 768p. 1983. 12.95 (ISBN 0-380-83527-4). Avon.
Roll, Richard J. & Young, G. Douglas. Getting Yours. 1983. pap. 6.95 (ISBN 0-440-53005-9, Delta). Dell.
Ross, Lanson. Total Life Prosperity. 170p. (Orig.). 1982. pap. 4.95 (ISBN 0-8423-7293-8). Tyndale.
Simon, Sam & Waz, Joe. Reverse the Charges: How to Save Money on Your Phone Bill. 3rd ed. 1982. pap. 4.95 (ISBN 0-943444-00-4). NCCB.
Skousen, Mark. Mark Skousen's Guide to Financial Privacy. 1983. write for info (ISBN 0-671-47060-4). S&S.
Stadt, R. W. Personal & Family Finance. 256p. 1983. 7.95 (ISBN 0-07-000403-X, G). McGraw.
Taussig, F. W. The Psychology of Money Making & How to Master It. (The Library of Scientific Psychology). (Illus.). 121p. 1983. 49.85 (ISBN 0-89266-381-2). Am Classical Coll Pr.
Thomas, Rick. The Money Manager: A Personal Finance Simulation. 1983. ring binder 74.95 (ISBN 0-88408-166-4); pap. 5.95 student manual (ISBN 0-88408-167-2). Sterling Swift.
Tremont, Stuart. How Even a Superficial Knowledge of Charts May Help You to Double, Treble, Quadruple your Stock Market Profits. (New Stock Market Library Book). (Illus.). 67p. (Orig.). 1983. pap. 6.95 (ISBN 0-89266-389-8). Am Classical Coll Pr.
Woodwell, Donald R. Automating Your Financial Portfolio: An Investor's Guide to Personal Computers. LC 82-73637. 220p. 1983. 17.50 (ISBN 0-87094-399-5). Dow Jones-Irwin.
FINANCE, PRIMITIVE
see Economic Anthropology

FINANCE, PUBLIC
see also Bonds; Budget; Claims; Currency Question; Debts, Public; Expenditures, Public; Fiscal Policy; Government Spending Policy; Grants-In-Aid; Intergovernmental Fiscal Relations; Loans; Local Finance; Money; Municipal Finance; Paper Money; Taxation
also subdivision Finance under special subjects, e.g. Education–Finance; World War, 1939-1945–Finance
Bhatia, H. L. Public Finance. 8th ed. 400p. 1982. text ed. 40.00x (ISBN 0-7069-2055-4, Pub. by Vikas India). Advent NY.
Congress of the International Institute of Public Finance Tokyo, 37th, 1981. Public Finance & Growth: Proceedings. Stolper, Wolfgang, ed. 320p. 1983. 30.00x (ISBN 0-8143-1751-0). Wayne St U Pr.
Davey, Kenneth. Financing Regional Government: International Practices & Their Relevance to the Third World. (Public Administration in Developing Countries Ser.). 208p. 1983. 24.95 (ISBN 0-471-10356-X, Pub. by Wiley-Interscience). Wiley.
Davis, J. Ronnie & Meyer, Charles W. Principles of Public Finance. (Illus.). 448p. 1983. 23.95 (ISBN 0-13-709881-2). P-H.
Fuchs, Hans-Ulrich. Zur Lehre Vom Allgemeinen Bankvertrag. xxi, 212p. (Ger.). 1982. write for info. (ISBN 3-8204-7120-0). P Lang Pubs.
Golembiewski & Rabin. Public Budgeting & Finance. (Public Adminstration & Public Policy Ser.). 400p. 1983. price not set (ISBN 0-8247-1668-X). Dekker.
Hayes, Frederick O., et al. Linkages: Improving Financial Management in Local Government. LC 82-60180. 184p. (Orig.). 1982. pap. text ed. 12.00 (ISBN 0-87766-313-0, 33700). Urban Inst.
Holcombe, Randall G. Public Finance & Political Process. LC 82-10803. (Political & Social Economy Ser.). 208p. 1983. price not set (ISBN 0-8093-1082-1). S Ill U Pr.
Hulten, Charles R., ed. Depreciation, Inflation, & the Taxation of Income from Capital. LC 81-533061. 319p. 1981. text ed. 32.00 (ISBN 0-87766-311-4, URI 33800). Urban Inst.
Hyman, David N. Public Finance: A Contemporary Application of Theory to Policy. 689p. 1983. 28.95 (ISBN 0-686-43099-9). Dryden Pr.
Rabin, Lynch. Handbook on Public Budgeting & Financial Management. (Public Adminstration & Public Policy Ser.). 720p. 1983. 99.75 (ISBN 0-8247-1253-6). Dekker.
Ritter, Lawrence S. & Silber, William L. Principles of Money, Banking, & Financial Markets. 1983. text ed. 23.95x (ISBN 0-686-82533-0); write for info. (ISBN 0-465-06345-4); wkbk. 10.00. Basic.
FINANCE, PUBLIC–ACCOUNTING
see also Tax Accounting
Accounting & Reporting by State & Local Governments. 1981. pap. 7.50 (ISBN 0-686-84203-0). Am Inst CPA.
American Water Works Association. Financial Planning & the Use of Financial Information for General Management Personnel. (AWWA Handbooks-Proceedings Ser.). (Illus.). 80p. 1982. pap. 10.20 (ISBN 0-89867-277-5). Am Water Wks Assn.
Copeland, Ronald M. & Ingram, Robert W. Municipal Financial Reporting & Disclosure Quality. LC 82-11580. (Illus.). 156p. Date not set. pap. text ed. 4.76 (ISBN 0-201-10197-1). A-W.
Magann, Julia H. Municipal Financial Disclosure: An Empirical Investigation. Farmer, Richard N., ed. LC 82-4905. (Research for Business Decisions: No. 58). 1983. write for info. (ISBN 0-8357-1394-6). Univ Microfilms.
Rudman, Jack. Principal Financial Analyst. (Career Examination Ser.: C-2644). (Cloth bdg. avail. on request). pap. 12.00 (ISBN 0-8373-2644-3). Natl Learning.
Vargo, Richard J. & Dierks, Paul A. Readings & Cases in Governmental & Nonprofit Accounting. LC 82-70506. 272p. 1983. pap. text ed. 13.95x (ISBN 0-931920-37-X). Dame Pubns.
FINANCE, PUBLIC–LAW
Wharton School of Finance & Commerce, University of Pennsylvania. A Study of Mutual Funds: Report of the Committee on Interstate & Foreign Commerce-(87th Congress, 2nd Session, House Report No. 2274) LC 62-62400. xxxiii, 595p. 1982. Repr. of 1962 ed. lib. bdg. 38.50 (ISBN 0-89941-181-9). W. S. Hein.
FINANCE, PUBLIC–EUROPE
Dafflon, Bernard. Federal Finance in Theory & Practice with Special Reference to Switzerland. 176p. 1977. 90.00x (ISBN 0-7121-5624-0, Pub. by Macdonald & Evans). State Mutual Bk.
FINANCE, PUBLIC–INDIA
Wallich, Christine. State Finances in India. LC 82-11087. (World Bank Staff Working Papers: No. 523). (Orig.). 1982. pap. 3.00 (ISBN 0-8213-0013-X). World Bank.
FINANCE, PUBLIC–LATIN AMERICA
TePaske, John J. & Klein, Herbert S. The Royal Treasuries of the Spanish Empire in America, 3 vols. LC 82-2457. 1982. Set. 125.00 (ISBN 0-8223-0486-4); Vol. I: Peru. 590 p. 55.00 (ISBN 0-8223-0530-5); Vol. II: Peru (Bolivia), 446 p. 45.00 (ISBN 0-686-81650-1); Vol. III: Chile & the Rio de la Plata, 434 p. 45.00 (ISBN 0-8223-0532-1). Duke.

FINANCE, PUBLIC–UNITED STATES
Adler, Jack. A Consumer's Guide to Travel. LC 82-22195. 240p. (Orig.). 1983. pap. 8.95 (ISBN 0-88496-194-X). Capra Pr.
FINANCIAL ACCOUNTING
see Accounting
FINANCIAL INSTITUTIONS
see also Banks and Banking; Insurance Companies; Investment Trusts
Havrilesky, Thomas M. & Schweitzer, Robert, eds. Contemporary Developments in Financial Institutions & Markets. LC 82-19901. (Illus.). 450p. 1983. pap. 18.95 (ISBN 0-88295-409-1). Harlan Davidson.
FINANCIAL NEWS
see Newspapers–Sections, Columns, etc.
FINANCIAL RESEARCH
Rudman, Jack. Senior Financial Analyst. (Career Examination Ser.: C-2643). (Cloth bdg. avail. on request). pap. 12.00 (ISBN 0-8373-2643-5). Natl Learning.
FINANCIAL STATEMENTS
see also subdivision Accounting under special subjects, e.g. Agriculture–Accounting
Anderson, Anker. Graphing Financial Information. 50p. pap. 4.95 (ISBN 0-86641-086-4, 82138). Natl Assn Accts.
Backer, Morton & Gosman, Martin L. Financial Reporting & Business Liquidity. 305p. pap. 24.95 (ISBN 0-86641-020-1, 78110). Natl Assn Accts.
Couchman, Charles B. The Balance Sheet. LC 82-48355. (Accountancy in Transition Ser.). 300p. 1982. lib. bdg. 30.00 (ISBN 0-8240-5308-7). Garland Pub.
Dean, G. W. & Wells, M. C., eds. Forerunners of Realizable Values Accounting in Financial Reporting. LC 82-82486. (Accountancy in Transition Ser.). 342p. 1982. lib. bdg. 45.00 (ISBN 0-8240-5334-6). Garland Pub.
Finney, H. A. Consolidated Statements. LC 82-48362. (Accountancy in Transition Ser.). 242p. 1982. lib. bdg. 25.00 (ISBN 0-8240-5313-3). Garland Pub.
Langer, Steven, ed. Accounting-Financial Report. 3rd ed. 1982. pap. 85.00 ea. Pt. I: Public Accounting Firms (ISBN 0-916506-71-1). Pt. II: Industry, Government, & Education, Non-Profit (ISBN 0-916506-72-X). Abbott Langer Assocs.
Newlove, George H. Consolidated Balance Sheets. LC 82-48380. (Accountancy in Transition Ser.). 309p. 1982. lib. bdg. 30.00 (ISBN 0-8240-5325-7). Garland Pub.
O'Malia, Thomas J. Banker's Guide to Financial Statements. 2nd ed. LC 82-8786. 348p. 1982. 42.00 (ISBN 0-87267-038-4). Bankers.
Reporting on Compiled Financial Statements. (Statements on Standards for Accounting & Review Services Ser.: No. 5). 1982. pap. 1.60 (ISBN 0-686-84312-6). Am Inst CPA.
Robson, T. B. Consolidated & Other Group Accounts. 2nd ed. LC 82-48381. (Accountancy in Transition Ser.). 156p. 1982. lib. bdg. 20.00 (ISBN 0-8240-5326-5). Garland Pub.
FINCHES
Black, Robert. Nutrition of Finches & Other Cagebirds. 362p. 1981. 19.95 (ISBN 0-686-43316-5). Avian Pubns.
--Problems with Finches. (Illus.). 108p. 1980. pap. 9.95 (ISBN 0-686-43315-7). Avian Pubns.
Immelman, Klaus. Australian Finches. (Illus.). 224p. 1982. 32.95 (ISBN 0-207-14165-7). Avian Pubns.
Lack, David. Darwin's Finches. Boag, P. & Ratcliffe, L., eds. LC 82-19856. (Cambridge Science Classics). (Illus.). 240p. Date not set. price not set (ISBN 0-521-25243-1); pap. price not set (ISBN 0-521-27242-4). Cambridge U Pr.
Rogers, Cyril. Zebra Finches. (Illus.). 94p. 1977. pap. 3.95 (ISBN 0-7028-1085-1). Avian Pubns.
FINDING LISTS
see Library Catalogs
FINE ARTS
see Art; Arts, the
FINGER ALPHABET
see Deaf–Means of Communication
FINISHING, FURNITURE
see Furniture Finishing
FINITE DIFFERENCES
see Difference Equations
FINITE ELEMENT METHOD
Atluri, S. N. & Gallagher, R. H. Hybrid & Mixed Finite Element Methods. (Numerical Methods in Engineering). 450p. 1983. 69.95 (ISBN 0-471-10486-8, Pub. by Wiley-Interscience). Wiley.
Chinese Mechanical Engineering Society & Chinese Society of Theoretical & Applied Mechanics, eds. Finite Element Methods: Proceedings of the 1981 Symposium, Hefei, People's Republic of China. 400p. 1982. write for info. (ISBN 0-677-31020-X). Gordon.
Glowinski, R., et al. Energy Methods in Finite Element Analysis. LC 78-13642. (Numerical Methods in Engineering Ser.). 361p. 1979. 67.00x (ISBN 0-471-99723-4, Pub. by Wiley-Interscience). Wiley.
Kawai, T., ed. Finite Element Flow Analysis: Proceedings of the Fourth International Symposium on Finite Element Methods in Flow Problems, Held at Chuo University, Tokyo, July, 1982. 1096p. 1982. 95.00 (North Holland). Elsevier.

FINITE NUMBER SYSTEMS
see Modules (Algebra)
FINLAND
Central Statistical Office of Finland. Statistical Yearbook of Finland-Suomen Tilastollimen Vuosikirja-Statistisk Arsbok for Finland. 77th ed. Laakso, Elia, ed. LC 59-42150. (Illus.). 517p. (Eng., Finnish & Swedish.). 1982. vinyl 38.00x (ISBN 0-8002-3068-X). Intl Pubns Serv.
FINNISH LANGUAGE
Aaltio, Maija-Hellikki. Finnish for Foreigners, 2 vols. Date not set. Vol. 1. includes 5 cassettes 85.00x (ISBN 0-88432-093-6, FN01); Vol. II. includes 4 cassettes 60.00x (ISBN 0-88432-094-4, FN10). J Norton Pubs.
Berlitz Editors. Finnish for Travel Cassettepack. 1983. 14.95 (ISBN 0-02-962960-8, Berlitz); cassette incl. Macmillan.
FIRE–JUVENILE LITERATURE
Satchwell, John. Fire. LC 82-9434. (Illus.). 32p. (gr. k-4). 1983. 9.95 (ISBN 0-8037-2288-5, 0966-290). Dial Bks Young.
FIRE COMPANIES
see Fire Departments
FIRE DEPARTMENTS
Fire Service Resource Directory for Microcomputers. LC 82-62577. 92p. 1982. pap. text ed. 8.00 (ISBN 0-87765-251-1, FSP-65). Natl Fire Prot.
Small Community Fire Departments: Organization & Operations. LC 82-61905. (Illus.). 76p. 1982. pap. text ed. 9.50 (ISBN 0-686-83431-3, FSP-58). Natl Fire Prot.
Smalley, James. Funding Sources for Fire Departments. LC 82-62452. 75p. 1982. pap. text ed. 15.00 (ISBN 0-87765-246-5, FSP-60). Natl Fire Prot.
Weaver, Betsy & Frederick, Gary E. Hands, Horses & Engines: A Centennial History of the Baltimore County Fire Service. Campbell, Colin A., ed. (Illus.). 160p. 1982. 16.95 (ISBN 0-9608952-0-5). Baltimore CFSCC.
FIRE EXTINCTION
see also Forest Fires
Gold, David T. Fire Brigade Training Manual: Emergency Forces Training for Work Environments. Carwile, Ruth, ed. LC 82-82125. (Illus.). 236p. 1982. pap. text ed. 17.00 (ISBN 0-87765-224-4, SPP-73); training manual 21.50 (SPP-73M). Natl Fire Prot.
Klevan, Jacob B. Modeling of Available Egress Time from Assembly Spaces or Estimating the Advance of the Fire Threat. Date not set. 4.65 (ISBN 0-686-37666-8, TR 82-2). Society Fire Protect.
Nao, T. Van. Forest Fire Prevention & Control. 1982. text ed. 39.50 (ISBN 90-247-3050-3, Pub. by Martinus Nijhoff). Kluwer Boston.
FIRE EXTINCTION–EXAMINATIONS, QUESTIONS, ETC.
Rudman, Jack. Administrative Fire Alarm Dispatcher. (Career Examination Ser.: C-2602). (Cloth bdg. avail. on request). pap. 12.00 (ISBN 0-8373-2602-8). Natl Learning.
--Administrative Fire Marshall (Uniformed) (Career Examination Ser.: C-2603). (Cloth bdg. avail. on request). pap. 12.00 (ISBN 0-8373-2603-6). Natl Learning.
FIRE FIGHTING
see Fire Extinction
FIRE LOSSES
see Fires
FIRE PREVENTION
see also Fire Extinction; Forest Fires
also subdivision Fires and Fire Prevention under various classes of institutions and buildings, e.g. Schools–Fires and Fire Prevention
Bare, William K. Fundamentals of Fire Prevention. LC 76-23221. (Fire Science Ser.). 213p. 1977. text ed. 18.95 (ISBN 0-471-04835-6). Wiley.
--Introduction to Fire Science & Fire Prevention. LC 77-14002. (Fire Science Ser.). 290p. 1978. text ed. 19.95x (ISBN 0-471-01708-6); tchrs. manual (ISBN 0-471-03779-6). Wiley.
Belles, Donald W. Fire Hazard Analysis from Plastic Insulation in Exterior Walls of Buildings. Date not set. 5.35 (ISBN 0-686-37665-X, TR 82-1). Society Fire Protect.
Blair, William. Fire! Survival & Prevention. (Illus.). 192p. (Orig.). 1983. pap. 2.84i (ISBN 0-06-465147-9, P-BN 5147). B&N NY.
Brannigan, Francis L. Building Construction for the Fire Service. 2nd ed. McKinnon, Gordon P. & Matson, Debra, eds. LC 78-178805. (Illus.). 392p. 1982. text ed. 20.00 (ISBN 0-87765-227-9, FSP-33A). Natl Fire Prot.
Campbell, John A. Adding Logic to Fire Prevention Systems. Date not set. 4.65 (ISBN 0-686-37669-2, TR 82-5). Society Fire Protect.
DeCicco, Paul R. Life Safety Considerations in Atrium Buildings. Date not set. 4.35 (ISBN 0-686-37667-6, TR 82-3). Society Fire Protect.
DiNenno, Philip J. Simplified Radiation Heat Transfer Calculations from Large Open Hydrocarbon Fires. Date not set. 5.35 (ISBN 0-686-37674-9, TR 82-9). Society Fire Protect.
Fire Safety Educator's Handbook: A Comprehensive Guide to Planning, Designing, & Implementing Firesafety Programs. LC 82-62828. 150p. 1983. 19.00 (ISBN 0-87765-231-7, FSP-61). Natl Fire Prot.

Fire Safety in Boarding Homes. LC 82-61904. 82p. 1982. pap. text ed. 10.50 (ISBN 0-87765-236-8, SPP-76). Natl Fire Prot.

Glenn, Gary & Glenn, Peggy. Don't Get Burned: A Family Fire-Safety Guide. (Illus.). 210p. (Orig.). 1982. pap. 7.95 (ISBN 0-936930-81-0). Aames-Allen.

Gold, David T. Fire Brigade Training Manual: Emergency Forces Training for Work Environments. Carwile, Ruth, ed. LC 82-82125. (Illus.). 236p. 1982. pap. text ed. 17.00 (ISBN 0-87765-224-4, SPP-73); training manual 21.50 (SPP-73M). Natl Fire Prot.

Heskestad, Gunnar. Engineering Relations for Fire Plumes. Date not set. 4.65 (ISBN 0-686-37673-0, TR 82-8). Society Fire Protect.

Klevan, Jacob B. Modeling of Available Egress Time from Assembly Spaces or Estimating the Advance of the Fire Threat. Date not set. 4.65 (ISBN 0-686-37666-8, TR 82-2). Society Fire Protect.

Moulton, Gene. Conducting Fire Inspections: A Guidebook for Field Use. LC 82-61920. 302p. 1982. 18.00 (ISBN 0-87765-230-9, SPP-75). Natl Fire Prot.

Mowrer, David S. Costing Data for Fire Protection in Complex Industrial Occupancies. Date not set. 4.65 (ISBN 0-686-37671-4, TR 82-7). Society Fire Protect.

Nao, T. Van. Forest Fire Prevention & Control. 1982. text ed. 39.50 (ISBN 90-247-3050-3, Pub. by Martinus Nijhoff). Kluwer Boston.

Osborn, Richard W. & Flach, George W. Tapping in to the NECR. Osborn, Richard W., ed. LC 82-82124. (Illus.). 178p. 1982. pap. text ed. 8.50 (ISBN 0-87765-226-0, NEC-QUE). Natl Fire Prot.

Schainblatt, Al & Koss, Margo. Fire Code Inspections & Fire Prevention: What Methods Lead to Success? (Illus.). 122p. (Orig.). pap. text ed. 5.00 (ISBN 0-686-84409-2). Urban Inst.

Smith, Dennis. Dennis Smith's Fire Safety Book: Everything You Need to Know to Save Your Life. 1983. pap. 2.95 (ISBN 0-686-43213-4). Bantam.

Thornberry, Richard P. Designing Stair Pressurization Systems. Date not set. 4.65 (ISBN 0-686-37668-4, TR 82-4). Society Fire Protect.

Transue, Ralph E. Impact of Modern Electronics on Fire Protection. Date not set. 3.35 (ISBN 0-686-37670-6, TR 82-6). Society Fire Protect.

Tuck, Charles A., Jr., ed. NFPA Inspection Manual. 5th ed. LC 76-5194. (Illus.). 387p. 1982. 20.00 (ISBN 0-87765-239-2, SPP-11C). Natl Fire Prot.

FIREARMS

see also Rifles; Shot-Guns

also names of specific kinds of firearms, e.g. Colt Revolver; Machine Guns; Mauser Rifle; Winchester Rifle

Cameron, Frank & Campione, Frank. Micro Guns. (Illus.). 48p. 1982. 24.00 (ISBN 0-88014-049-6). Mosaic Pr OH.

The Compleat Gunner: 1672. 250p. Date not set. 17.50 (ISBN 0-87556-430-5). Saifer.

Daw, George. Gun Patents 1864. 1982. 15.00x (ISBN 0-87556-251-5). Saifer.

Irwin, John R. Guns & Gunmaking Tools of Southern Appalachia. 2nd ed. (Illus.). 120p. 1983. pap. 9.95 (ISBN 0-916838-81-1). Schiffer.

Shelsby, Earl, ed. NRA Gunsmithing Guide: Updated. rev. ed. (Illus.). 336p. (Orig.). 1980. pap. text ed. 11.95 (ISBN 0-935998-47-0). Natl Rifle Assn.

Smith, W. H. Basic Manual of Military Small Arms. (Illus.). 216p. 1979. Repr. of 1943 ed. 22.95 (ISBN 0-8117-0409-2). Stackpole.

FIREARMS-COLLECTORS AND COLLECTING

The Official 1983 Price Guide to Antique & Modern Firearms. 3rd ed. LC 81-81803. 544p. 1983. 9.95 (ISBN 0-87637-363-5). Hse of Collectibles.

The Official 1984 Price Guide to Collector Handguns. 1st ed. LC 82-84634. 544p. 1983. 9.95 (ISBN 0-87637-367-8). Hse of Collectibles.

FIREARMS-IDENTIFICATION

Baer, Larry L. The Parker Gun. 29.95 (ISBN 0-686-43087-5). Gun Room.

Brooker, R. E., Jr. British Military Pistols 1603-1888. 22.95 (ISBN 0-686-43082-4). Gun Room.

Brophy, William S. The Krag Rifle. 29.95 (ISBN 0-686-43084-0). Gun Room.

--L. C. Smith Shotguns. 29.95 (ISBN 0-686-43085-9). Gun Room.

Garton, George. Colt's SAA Post-War Models. 21.95 (ISBN 0-686-43083-2). Gun Room.

Ruth, Larry. M I Carbine. pap. 15.00 (ISBN 0-686-43086-7). Gun Room.

FIREARMS-LAWS AND REGULATIONS

Cruit, Ronald L. Intruder in Your Home: How to Defend Yourself Legally With A Firearm. LC 82-42727. 288p. 1983. 17.95 (ISBN 0-686-83443-7). Stein & Day.

FIREARMS CONTROL

see Firearms-Laws and Regulations

FIREBOARDS

see Dummy Board Figures

FIRES

see also Fire Departments; Fire Extinction; Fire Prevention; Forest Fires

also subdivision Fires and Fire Prevention under various classes of institutions and buildings, e.g. Schools-Fires and Fire Prevention; Particular conflagrations are entered under names of place, e.g. London-Fire, 1666

DiNenno, Philip J. Simplified Radiation Heat Transfer Calculations from Large Open Hydrocarbon Fires. Date not set. 5.35 (ISBN 0-686-37674-9, TR 82-9). Society Fire Protect.

Hotel Fires Behind the Headlines. LC 82-51056. 161p. 1982. pap. text ed. 13.50 (ISBN 0-87765-228-7, SPP-74). Natl Fire Prot.

Investigation Report on the Westchase Hilton Hotel Fire. LC 82-61906. 64p. 1982. pap. text ed. 10.00 (ISBN 0-87765-238-4, LS-7). Natl Fire Prot.

Klevan, Jacob B. Modeling of Available Egress Time from Assembly Spaces or Estimating the Advance of the Fire Threat. Date not set. 4.65 (ISBN 0-686-37666-8, TR 82-2). Society Fire Protect.

FIREWORKS

Anderson, Norman D. & Brown, Walter R. Fireworks! Pyrotechnics on Display. LC 82-45995. (Illus.). 96p. (gr. 4 up). 1983. PLB 8.95 (ISBN 0-396-08142-8). Dodd.

Brenner, Martha. Fireworks! (Illus.). 128p. (gr. 3-7). 1983. PLB 9.95 (ISBN 0-8038-2400-9). Hastings.

FIRMS

see Business Enterprises

FIRST AID IN ILLNESS AND INJURY

see also Accidents; Ambulances; Bandages and Bandaging; Burns and Scalds; Emergency Medical Services; Medical Emergencies

Bergeron, Dave. First Responder: Self-Instructional Workbook. (Illus.). 166p. 1982. 5.95 (ISBN 0-89303-227-1). R J Brady.

Bergeron, J. D. Self-Instructional Workbook for Emergency Care. 3rd ed. (Illus.). 224p. 1982. pap. text ed. 7.95 (ISBN 0-89303-186-0). R J Brady.

Freeman, Lory. What Would You Do If? A Children's Guide to First Aid. (ps-3). 1983. PLB 9.95 (ISBN 0-943990-00-9); pap. 4.95 (ISBN 0-943990-01-7). Parenting Pr.

Justus, Fred. Basic Skills First Aid Workbook. (Basic Skills Workbooks). 32p. (gr. 5-9). 1983. 0.99 (ISBN 0-8209-0576-3, HW-3). ESP.

--First Aid. (Science Ser.). 24p. (gr. 5-9). 1980. wkbk. 5.00 (ISBN 0-8209-0164-4, FA-1). ESP.

Lefevre, M. J., ed. First Aid Manual for Chemical Accidents: For Use with Nonpharmaceutical Chemicals. Solvay American Corporation & Becker, Ernest I., trs. from Fr. LC 80-17518. 218p. 1980. pap. 16.50 (ISBN 0-87933-395-2). Hutchinson Ross.

Robertson, Audrey. Health, Safety & First Aid: A Guide for Training Child Care Workers. 115p. (Orig.). 1980. pap. 11.95 (ISBN 0-934140-04-9). Toys N Things.

Shaw, Marie-Jose. First Aid. (Sound Filmstrip Kits Ser.). (gr. 3-6). 1981. tchrs ed. 24.00 (ISBN 0-8209-0434-1, FCW-11). ESP.

Wolfe, Bob & Wolfe, Diane. Emergency Room. LC 82-19878. (Illus.). 40p. (gr. 1-4). 1983. PLB 7.95g (ISBN 0-87614-206-4). Carolrhoda Bks.

FISCAL EVASION

see Tax Evasion

FISCAL POLICY

see also Monetary Policy

Brems, Hans. Fiscal Theory: Government, Inflation, & Growth. LC 82-47905. 1983. price not set (ISBN 0-669-05688-X). Lexington Bks.

Hansen, Alvin. Monetary Theory & Fiscal Policy. LC 82-20924. ix, 236p. 1983. Repr. of 1949 ed. lib. bdg. 29.75x (ISBN 0-313-23736-0, HAMT). Greenwood.

Hyman, David N. Public Finance: A Contemporary Application of Theory to Policy. 689p. 1983. 28.95 (ISBN 0-686-43099-9). Dryden Pr.

Lewis, Alan. The Psychology of Taxation. LC 82-10656. 224p. 1982. 25.00x (ISBN 0-312-65330-1). St Martin.

Reese, Craig E. Deregulation & Environmental Quality: The Use of Tax Policy to Control Pollution in North America & Western Europe. LC 82-11266. (Illus.). 480p. 1983. lib. bdg. 45.00 (ISBN 0-89930-018-9, RDE/, Quorum). Greenwood.

Wagner, Richard E. & Tollison, Robert D. Balanced Budgets, Fiscal Responsibility & the Constitution. 109p. 1982. pap. 6.00 (ISBN 0-932790-36-4). Cato Inst.

FISCAL POLICY-GREAT BRITAIN

Beer, Samuel H. Treasury Control: The Co-ordination of Financial & Economic Policy in Great Britain. LC 82-11843. viii, 138p. 1982. Repr. of 1957 ed. lib. bdg. 25.00x (ISBN 0-313-23626-7, BETRC). Greenwood.

FISCAL RELATIONS, INTERGOVERNMENTAL

see Intergovernmental Fiscal Relations

FISH

see Fishes

FISH BY-PRODUCTS

see Fishery Products

FISH-CULTURE

see also Aquariums; Fish Ponds

Better Freshwater Fish Farming: The Pond. (Better Farming Ser.: No. 29). 43p. 1981. pap. 5.00 (ISBN 92-5-101127-3, F2316, FAO). Unipub.

Introduction to the Use of Sonar Systems for Estimating Fish Biomass. 89p. 1982. pap. 8.00 (ISBN 92-5-101161-3, F2301, FAO). Unipub.

Proceedings of the Symposium on the Development & Exploitation of Artificial Lakes. (FAO Fisheries Report Ser.: No. 273). 17p. 1983. pap. 7.50 (ISBN 92-5-001246-2, F2347, FAO). Unipub.

Report of the Technical Consultation on Methodologies Used for Fish Age-Rearing. (FAO Fisheries Report Ser.: No. 257). 104p. 1982. pap. 8.00 (ISBN 92-5-001207-1, F2305, FAO). Unipub.

Schoitz & Dahlstrom. Collins Guide to Aquarium Fishes & Plants. 29.95 (ISBN 0-686-42787-4, Collins Pub England). Greene.

FISH FARMING

see Fish-Culture

FISH HATCHERIES

see Fish-Culture

FISH LAW

see Fishery Law and Legislation

FISH PONDS

Better Freshwater Fish Farming: The Pond. (Better Farming Ser.: No. 29). 43p. 1981. pap. 5.00 (ISBN 92-5-101127-3, F2316, FAO). Unipub.

FISH TRADE

see also Fishery Products

Fish by Catch...Bonus from the Sea. 163p. 1982. pap. 18.00 (ISBN 0-88936-336-6, IDRC 198, IDRC). Unipub.

International Labour Office. Small-scale Processing of Fish. (Technology Series Technical Memorandum: No. 3). xi, 118p. (Orig.). 1982. pap. 8.55 (ISBN 92-2-103205-1). Intl Labour Office.

FISH WASTE

see Fishery Products

FISHERIES

see also Fish Trade; Fishes

Brown, E. Evan. World Fish Farming: Cultivation & Economics. 2nd ed. (Illus.). 1983. text ed. 27.00 (ISBN 0-87055-427-1). AVI.

Fish by Catch...Bonus from the Sea. 163p. 1982. pap. 18.00 (ISBN 0-88936-336-6, IDRC 198, IDRC). Unipub.

German, Andrew W. Down on T Wharf: The Boston Fisheries as Seen Through The Photographs of Henry D. Fisher. (American Maritime Library: Vol. 10). (Illus.). 168p. 1982. 24.00 (ISBN 0-913372-26-9). Mystic Seaport.

Manual of Methods in Aquatic Environment Research: Toxicity Tests, Pt. 6. (FAO Fisheries Technical Papers: No. 185). 23p. 1982. pap. 7.50 (ISBN 92-5-101178-8, F2312, FAO). Unipub.

Maril, Robert L. Texas Shrimpers: Community, Capitalism, & the Sea. LC 82-45897. (Illus.). 256p. 1983. 18.00x (ISBN 0-89096-147-6). Tex A&M Univ Pr.

Paquette, Gerald N. Fish Quality Improvement: A Manual for Plant Operators. Practical Everyday Procedures to Benefit Performance & Quality. LC 82-24677. (Orig.). 1983. pap. text ed. 17.50x (ISBN 0-943738-05-9). Osprey Bks.

Proceedings of the Symposium on the Development & Exploitation of Artificial Lakes. (FAO Fisheries Report Ser.: No. 273). 17p. 1983. pap. 7.50 (ISBN 92-5-001246-2, F2347, FAO). Unipub.

Report of the Technical Consultation on Methodologies Used for Fish Age-Rearing. (FAO Fisheries Report Ser.: No. 257). 104p. 1982. pap. 8.00 (ISBN 92-5-001207-1, F2305, FAO). Unipub.

Review of Fisheries in OECD Member Countries, 1981. 278p. (Orig.). 1982. pap. 13.50 (ISBN 92-64-12346-6). OECD.

Squid Jigging from Small Boats. 74p. 1982. pap. 19.00 (ISBN 0-85238-122-0, FN99, FNB). Unipub.

FISHERIES-EQUIPMENT AND SUPPLIES

see also Fishing-Implements and Appliances

Netting Materials for Fishing Gear. 175p. 1982. pap. 25.25 (ISBN 0-85238-118-2, FN 98, FNB). Unipub.

FISHERIES-LAW

see Fishery Law and Legislation

FISHERIES-AFRICA

Report of the FAO Expert Consultation on Fish Technology in Africa. (FAO Fisheries Report Ser.: No. 268). 19p. 1982. pap. 7.50 (ISBN 92-5-101236-9, F2337, FAO). Unipub.

Report of the First Session of the Sub-Committee for the Development & Management of the Fisheries of Lake Victoria. (FAO Fisheries Reports Ser.: No. 262). 71p. 1982. pap. 7.50 (ISBN 92-5-101189-3, F2376, FAO). Unipub.

FISHERIES-EUROPE

EIFAC Experiments on Pelagic Fish Stock Assessment by Accoustic Methods in Lake Konnevesi, Finland, No. 14, (EIFAC Occasional Paper). 16p. 1983. pap. 7.50 (ISBN 92-5-101234-2, F2349, FAO). Unipub.

Report of the Second Session of the Working Party on Fishery Statistics: Fishery Committee for the Eastern Atlantic (CECAF) (FAO Fisheries Report Ser.: No. 265). 80p. 1982. pap. 7.50 (ISBN 92-5-101215-6, F2339, FAO). Unipub.

Report of the Second Technical Consultation on Stock Assessment in the Balearic & Gulf of Lions Statistical Division. (FAO Fisheries Report Ser.: No. 263). 165p. 1982. pap. 12.75 (ISBN 92-5-001211-X, F2304, FAO). Unipub.

Report of the Twelfth Session of the European Inland Fisheries Advisory Commission. (FAO Fisheries Report Ser.: No. 267). 41p. 1983. pap. 7.50 (ISBN 92-5-101250-4, F2353, FAO). Unipub.

FISHERIES-GREAT BRITAIN

FAO Fisheries Technology Service & Hamabe, Mototsugu, eds. Squid Jigging from Small Boats. 84p. 1982. 42.95x (ISBN 0-85238-122-0, Pub. by Fishing News England). State Mutual Bk.

FISHERIES-INDIA

Report of the First Session of the Committee for the Development & Management of Fisheries in the Bay of Bengal. (FAO Fisheries Report Ser.: No. 260). 15p. 1982. pap. 7.50 (ISBN 92-5-101195-8, F2300, FAO). Unipub.

FISHERIES-LATIN AMERICA

Report of the Second Session of the Commission for Island Fisheries of Latin America. (FAO Fisheries Report Ser.: No. 261). 39p. 1982. pap. 7.50 (ISBN 92-5-101191-5, F2309, FAO). Unipub.

FISHERMEN

Maril, Robert L. Texas Shrimpers: Community, Capitalism, & the Sea. LC 82-45897. (Illus.). 256p. 1983. 18.00x (ISBN 0-89096-147-6). Tex A&M Univ Pr.

Olivier, Julien. Prende Le Large: Big Jim Cote Pecheur. (Oral History Ser.). (Illus.). 107p. (Fr.). (gr. 9-10). 1981. pap. 2.50x (ISBN 0-911409-08-4). Natl Mat Dev.

FISHERY LAW AND LEGISLATION

Fisheries Regulations under Extended Jurisdiction & International Law. (FAO Fisheries Technical Papers: No. 223). 23p. 1983. pap. 7.50 (ISBN 92-5-101231-8, F2341, FAO). Unipub.

Index to the Proceedings of the International Association of Fish & Wildlife Agencies: 1976 Through 1980. Date not set. price not set (ISBN 0-932108-06-7). IAFWA.

International Association of Fish & Wildlife Agencies. Proceedings of the Sixty-Ninth Convention. Blouch, Ralph I., ed. (Orig.). 1980. pap. 11.00 (ISBN 0-932108-04-0). IAFWA.

Proceedings of the Seventy-First Convention: International Association of Fish & Wildlife Agencies 1982. Date not set. 13.00 (ISBN 0-932108-07-5). IAFWA.

FISHERY METHODS

see Fisheries

FISHERY PRODUCTS

see also Canning and Preserving

OECD Staff. International Trade in Fish Products: Effects on the 200-Mile Limit. 192p. (Orig.). 1982. pap. 17.50 (ISBN 92-64-12318-0). OECD.

FISHES

see also Aquariums; Fish-Culture; Fisheries; Fishing; Tropical Fish

also names of classes, orders, etc. of fishes, e.g. Bass, salmon

Allen, Gerald R. Butterfly & Angelfishes of the World: Vol. 2, Atlantic Ocean, Caribbean Sea, Red Sea, Indo-Pacific. LC 78-17351. 352p. 1980. 39.95 (ISBN 0-471-05618-9, Pub. by Wiley-Interscience). Wiley.

Bagenal, T. B. Ageing of Fish. 240p. 1982. 40.00 (ISBN 0-686-84445-9, Pub. by Gresham England). State Mutual Bk.

Proceedings of the Seventieth Convention: International Association of Fish & Wildlife Agencies. 1981. 13.00 (ISBN 0-932108-05-9). IAFWA.

FISHES-PHYSIOLOGY

Reproductive Physiology of Fish. 256p. 1983. 34.50 (ISBN 90-220-0818-5, PDC251, Pudoc). Unipub.

FISHES-PICTORIAL WORKS

Greenberg, Idaz. Hawaiian Fishwatcher's Field Guide. (Illus.). 1983. plastic card 3.95x (ISBN 0-913008-13-3). Seahawk Pr.

FISHES-AUSTRALIA

Allen, G. R. A Field Guide to Inland Fishes of Western Australia. (Illus.). 92p. 1982. pap. 15.00 (ISBN 0-7244-8409-4, Pub. by U of West Austral Pr). Intl Schol Bk Serv.

Weil, Martin. Puli. (Illus.). 128p. 1982. 4.95 (ISBN 0-87666-740-X, KW-141). TFH Pubns.

FISHES-EUROPE

Miller & Nicholls. The Fishes of Britain & Europe. pap. 8.95 (ISBN 0-686-42748-3, Collins Pub England). Greene.

Muus & Dahlstrom. Collins Guide to the Fresh Water Fishes of Britain & Europe. 29.95 (ISBN 0-686-42788-2, Collins Pub England). Greene.

--Collins Guide to the Sea Fishes of Britain & Northwestern Europe. 29.95 (ISBN 0-686-42789-0, Collins Pub England). Greene.

FISHES-GREAT BRITAIN

Miller & Nicholls. The Fishes of Britain & Europe. pap. 8.95 (ISBN 0-686-42748-3, Collins Pub England). Greene.

Muus & Dahlstrom. Collins Guide to the Fresh Water Fishes of Britain & Europe. 29.95 (ISBN 0-686-42788-2, Collins Pub England). Greene.

--Collins Guide to the Sea Fishes of Britain & Northwestern Europe. 29.95 (ISBN 0-686-42789-0, Collins Pub England). Greene.

FISHES-NEW ZEALAND

Ayling, Tony & Cox, Geoffrey J. The Collins Guide to the Sea Fishes of New Zealand. (Illus.). 384p. 1983. 19.95 (ISBN 0-00-216987-8, Pub. by W Collins Australia). Intl Schol Bk Serv.

FISHES-NORTH AMERICA

MacIlquham, Frances. Complete Fish & Game Cookery of North America. (Illus.). 304p. 1983. 29.95 (ISBN 0-8329-0284-5). Winchester Pr.

Ono, Dane R. & Williams, James D. Vanishing Fishes of North America. (Illus.). 272p. 1983. 27.50 (ISBN 0-913276-43-X). Stone Wall Pr.

FISHES-PACIFIC OCEAN

Greenberg, Idaz. Hawaiian Fishwatcher's Field Guide. (Illus.). 1983. plastic card 3.95x (ISBN 0-913008-13-3). Seahawk Pr.

Springer, Victor G. Pacific plate Biogeography, with Special Reference to Shorefishes. LC 82-600146. (Contributions to Zoology Ser.: No. 367). (Illus.). 182p. 1982. pap. text ed. 7.95x (ISBN 0-87474-883-6). Smithsonian.

FISHES-TROPICS

see also Tropical Fish

Weil, Martin. Puli. (Illus.). 128p. 1982. 4.95 (ISBN 0-87666-740-X, KW-141). TFH Pubns.

FISHES, TROPICAL

see Tropical Fish

FISHING

see also Bait; Bass Fishing; Fishery Law and Legislation; Fly-Casting; Fly Fishing; Salmon Fishing; Salt-Water Fishing; Shark Fishing; Trout Fishing

Beard, Henry & McKie, Roy. Fishing. 96p. 1983. 8.95 (ISBN 0-89480-357-3); pap. 4.95 (ISBN 0-89480-355-7). Workman Pub.

Heaps, Ian & Mitchell, Colin. Ian Heaps on Fishing. 128p. 1982. 25.00x (ISBN 0-907675-02-6, Pub. by Muller Ltd). State Mutual Bk.

Nathan, Bill, ed. The Sea Fisherman's Bedside Book. (Illus.). 166p. 1982. text ed. 12.95x (ISBN 0-7156-1537-8, Pub. by Duckworth England). Biblio Dist.

Sternberg, Dick. Fishing with Live Bait. 160p. 1983. 16.95 (ISBN 0-307-46635-3, Golden Pr). Western Pr.

Wisner, Bill. The Fishermen's Sourcebook. (Illus.). 352p. 1983. 24.95 (ISBN 0-02-630570-4). Macmillan.

Woolner, Frank & Lyman, Hal. Striped Bass Fishing. 192p. 1983. 15.95 (ISBN 0-8329-0279-9); pap. 9.95 (ISBN 0-8329-0281-0). Winchester Pr.

Zenanko, Tom. Walleye Fishing Today. Zenanko, Tom, ed. (Illus.). 212p. (Orig.). 1982. pap. 9.95 (ISBN 0-9610296-0-9). Zenanko Outdoors.

FISHING-IMPLEMENTS AND APPLIANCES

Definition & Classification of Fishing Gear Categories. (FAO Fisheries Technical Papers: No. 222). 51p. 1982. pap. 7.50 (ISBN 92-5-101219-9, F2314, FAO). Unipub.

Netting Materials for Fishing Gear. 175p. 1982. pap. 25.25 (ISBN 0-85238-118-2, FN 98, FNB). Unipub.

FISHING-ATLANTIC OCEAN

Allen, Richard B., ed. Atlantic Fishermans Handbook. (Illus.). 482p. (Orig.). 1982. pap. 12.95 (ISBN 0-9608932-0-2). Fisheries Comm.

Warner, William. Distant Water: The Fate of the North Atlantic Fisherman. (Illus.). 352p. 1983. 17.45i (ISBN 0-316-92328-1). Little.

FISHING-AUSTRALIA

Encyclopedia of Australian Fishing, 12 vols. (Illus.). 1981. Set. 135.00x (ISBN 0-85835-412-8). Intl Pubns Serv.

Gould, Peter. The Complete Taupo Fishing Guide. (Illus.). 248p. 1982. 19.95 (ISBN 0-00-216969-X, Pub. by W Collins Australia). Intl Schol Bk Serv.

FISHING-GREAT BRITAIN

Darling, John. Sea Anglers' Guide to Britian & Ireland. 160p. 1982. 60.00x (ISBN 0-7188-2509-8, Pub. by Lutterworth Pr England); pap. 40.00x (ISBN 0-7188-2510-1). State Mutual Bk.

FISHING-HAWAII

Buck, Peter. Arts & Crafts of Hawaii: Fishing, Sec. VII. (Special Publication Ser.: No. 45). (Illus.). 78p. 1957. pap. 4.50 (ISBN 0-910240-40-X). Bishop Mus.

FISHING-NEW ZEALAND

Forrester, Rex. Trout Fishing in New Zealand. 204p. 1982. 40.00x (ISBN 0-7233-0612-5, Pub. by Whitcoulls New Zealand). State Mutual Bk.

FISHING-UNITED STATES

Knapp, Ken. Idaho Fishing Guide. 320p. 1983. pap. 9.95 (ISBN 0-87842-156-4). Mountain Pr.

Sample, Mike. Angler's Guide to Montana. (Illus.). 256p. (Orig.). 1983. pap. 8.95 (ISBN 0-934318-13-1). Falcon Pr MT.

Sosin, Mark & Kreh, Lefty. Fishing the Flats. (Illus.). 160p. 1983. 14.95 (ISBN 0-8329-0278-0); pap. 8.95 (ISBN 0-8329-0280-2). Winchester Pr.

FISHING LURES

Sternberg, Dick. Fishing with Live Bait. 160p. 1983. 16.95 (ISBN 0-307-46635-3, Golden Pr). Western Pr.

FISHING REGULATIONS

see Fishery Law and Legislation

FISHPONDS

see Fish Ponds

FISSION DATING METHOD

see Radioactive Dating

FITS (ENGINEERING)

see Tolerance (Engineering)

FITZGERALD, EDWARD, 1809-1883

Sisson, C. H. Edward Fitzgerald: A Life. 192p. 1983. pap. text ed. 8.50x (ISBN 0-85635-465-1, Pub. by Carcanet New Pr England). Humanities.

FITZGERALD, FRANCIS SCOTT KEY, 1896-1940

Bryer, Jackson R. The Critical Reputation of F. Scott Fitzgerald: Supplement I through 1981. 2nd ed. 464p. 1983. price not set (ISBN 0-208-01489-6, Archon). Shoe String.

FIVE YEAR PLAN (RUSSIA)

see Russia-Economic Policy

FIXED IDEAS

see Hysteria; Obsessive-Compulsive Neuroses

FIXED WING AIRCRAFT

see Airplanes

FIXTURES (MECHANICAL DEVICES)

see Jigs and Fixtures

FLAGELLATION

see Corporal Punishment

FLAME

Buckmaster, J. D. & Ludford, G. S. S. Theory of Laminar Flames. LC 81-21573. (Cambridge Monographs on Mechanics & Applied Mathematics Ser.). (Illus.). 250p. 1982. 49.50 (ISBN 0-521-23929-X). Cambridge U Pr.

FLASKS

see Bottles

FLAT RACING

see Horse-Racing

FLATWORMS

see Platyhelminthes

FLAUBERT, GUSTAVE, 1821-1880

Wetherill, P. M., ed. Flaubert: La Dimension du Texte. 288p. (Fr.). 1982. pap. 12.50 (ISBN 0-7190-0842-5). Manchester.

FLEAS

Hopkins, G. H. & Rothschild, M. An Illustrated Catalogue of the Rothschild Collection of Fleas, Vol. V: Leptopsyllidae & Ancistropsyllidae. 530p. 1971. 180.00x (ISBN 0-686-82366-4, Pub. by Brit Mus England). State Mutual Bk.

--An Illustrated Catalogue of the Rothschild Collection of Fleas, Vol. IV: Hystrichopsyllidae (Tenophthalminae, Dinopsyllinae & Listropsyllinae) 594p. 1966. 175.00x (ISBN 0-686-82367-2, Pub. by Brit Mus England). State Mutual Bk.

--An Illustrated Catalogue of the Rothschild Collection of Fleas, Vol. III: Hystrichopsyllidae (Acedestiinae, Anamiopsyllinae, Histrichopsyllinae, Neopsyllinae, Rhadinopsyllinae & Stenoponiinae) 559p. 1962. 125.00x (ISBN 0-686-82369-9, Pub. by Brit Mus England). State Mutual Bk.

--An Illustrated Catalogue of the Rothschild Collection of Fleas, Vol. II: Coptopsyllidae, Verminpsyllidae, Sephanociridae, Tschnopsyllidae, Hypsophthalmidae & Xiphiopsyllidae. 446p. 1956. 110.00x (ISBN 0-686-82370-2, Pu b. by Brit Mus England). State Mutual Bk.

--An Illustrated Catalogue of the Rothschild Collection of Fleas, Vol. I: Tungidae & Pulicidae. 362p. 1953. 90.00x (ISBN 0-686-82372-9, Pub. by Brit Mus England). State Mutual Bk.

Mardon, D. K. An Illustrated Catalogue of the Rothschild Collection of Fleas, Vol. VI: Pygiopsyllidae. 298p. 1981. 200.00x (ISBN 0-686-82365-6, Pub. by Brit Mus England). State Mutual Bk.

FLEMISH LANGUAGE

see Dutch Language

FLIES

see also Tsetse-Flies

Ashburner, M. & Carson, H. L., eds. The Genetics & Biology of Drosophila. Date not set. price not set (ISBN 0-12-064947-0). Acad Pr.

Griffiths, G. C. Flies of the Nearctic Region Vol. VIII: Cyclorrhapha II (Schizophora. Calyptratae, Pt. 2 Anthomyiidae, No. 1. (Illus.). 160p. (Orig.). 1982. pap. text ed. 53.76 (ISBN 3-510-70004-X). Lubrecht & Cramer.

FLIGHT

see also Aeronautics; Flying-Machines; Stability of Airplanes

Dalton. The Miracle of Flight. 1977. 16.95 (ISBN 0-07-015207-1). McGraw.

Etkin, Bernard. Dynamics of Atmospheric Flight. LC 73-165946. (Illus.). 579p. 1972. text ed. 39.95x (ISBN 0-471-24620-4). Wiley.

--Dynamics of Flight Stability & Control. 2nd ed. LC 81-13058. 370p. 1982. text ed. 29.95x (ISBN 0-471-08936-2). Wiley.

McCollister, J. Philosophy of Flight. 170p. 1980. pap. 10.95 (ISBN 0-686-43358-0, Pub. by JSB Enterprises). Aviation.

FLIGHT-JUVENILE LITERATURE

Barnes, Caroline. The Star Wars Book about Flight. LC 82-20423. (Illus.). 32p. (gr. 3-8). 1983. pap. 1.25 (ISBN 0-394-85689-9). Random.

FLIGHT-MEDICAL ASPECTS

see Aviation Medicine

FLIGHT-PHYSIOLOGICAL ASPECTS

Ehret, Charles F. & Scanlon, Lynne W. Overcoming Jet Lag. 192p. (Orig.). 1983. pap. 4.95 (ISBN 0-425-05877-8). Berkley Pub.

Kowet, Don. The Jet Set Jet Lag Book: How to Rest Your Mind & Body & Beat the Fatigue & Confusion of Jet Lag. 1983. pap. 4.95 (ISBN 0-517-54895-X). Crown.

FLIGHT TRAINING

Explanations to the Flight Instructor: Airplane Written Test Guide (AP 472B) (Illus.). 80p. (Orig.). 1980. pap. 7.50 (ISBN 0-941272-21-4). Astro Pubs.

FLOGGING

see Corporal Punishment

FLOOD CONTROL

see also Flood Dams and Reservoirs

Australian Rainfall & Runoff Flood Analysis & Design. 159p. (Orig.). 1977. pap. text ed. 27.00x (ISBN 0-85825-077-2, Pub. by Inst Engineering Australia). Renouf.

Baker, V. R., ed. Catastrophic Flooding: The Origin of the Channeled Scabland. LC 79-22901. (Benchmark Papers in Geology: Vol. 55). 384p. 46.00 (ISBN 0-87933-360-X). Hutchinson Ross.

FLOOD DAMS AND RESERVOIRS

Baker, V. R., ed. Catastrophic Flooding: The Origin of the Channeled Scabland. LC 79-22901. (Benchmark Papers in Geology: Vol. 55). 384p. 46.00 (ISBN 0-87933-360-X). Hutchinson Ross.

FLOOD PROTECTION

see Flood Control

FLOODS

see also Flood Control; Reclamation of Land; Rivers; also subdivision floods under names of rivers, cities, etc.

CLark, Champ. Flood. LC 81-18545. (Planet Earth Ser.). lib. bdg. 19.92 (ISBN 0-8094-4309-0, Pub. by Time-Life). Silver.

FLOOR COVERINGS

see also Carpets

Sunset Books & Sunset Magazine, ed. Flooring: Do it Yourself. LC 81-82872. (Illus.). 112p. (Orig.). 1982. pap. 4.95 (ISBN 0-376-01141-6). Sunset-Lane.

FLOOR MATERIALS

see Flooring

FLOORING

see also Floor Coverings

Sunset Books & Sunset Magazine, ed. Flooring: Do it Yourself. LC 81-82872. (Illus.). 112p. (Orig.). 1982. pap. 4.95 (ISBN 0-376-01141-6). Sunset-Lane.

FLORA

see Botany; Plants

FLORAL DECORATION

see Flower Arrangement

FLORAL DESIGN

see Design, Decorative-Plant Forms

FLORENCE-DESCRIPTION-GUIDEBOOKS

Borsook, Eve. Companion Guide to Florence. (Illus.). 400p. 1983. 16.95 (ISBN 0-13-154484-5); pap. 8.95 (ISBN 0-13-154476-4). P-H.

Holler, Anne. Florencewalks. LC 82-1107. (Illus.). 224p. 1983. pap. 9.95 (ISBN 0-03-059938-5). New Republic.

FLORENCE-HISTORY

Brucker, Gene A. Renaissance Florence. rev. ed. LC 82-40097. (Illus.). 320p. 1983. text ed. 25.00x (ISBN 0-520-04919-5); pap. 7.95x (ISBN 0-520-04695-1). U of Cal Pr.

Stephens, J. N. The Fall of the Florentine Republic 1512-1530. (Oxford-Warburg Studies). 300p. 1983. 39.50 (ISBN 0-19-822599-7). Oxford U Pr.

FLORIDA

see also names of cities, towns, and geographic areas in Florida, e.g. Miami; Everglades

Peters, Thelma. Biscayne Country, 1870-1926. (Illus.). 300p. Date not set. pap. 14.95 (ISBN 0-686-84304-5). Banyan Bks.

FLORIDA-DESCRIPTION AND TRAVEL

Bane, Michael & Moore, Ellen. Tampa: Yesterday, Today & Tomorrow. (Illus.). 180p. (Orig.). 1982. 19.95 (ISBN 0-9609530-0-0); pap. 12.95 (ISBN 0-9609530-2-7). Mishler & King.

French, Seth, ed. Semi-Tropical Florida: Its Climate, Soil & Productions, with a Sketch of Its History, Natural Features & Social Condition, Being a Manual of Reliable Information Concerning the Resources of the State, & the Inducements Which It Offers to Persons. LC 82-62496. (Historic Byways of Florida Ser.: Vol. VII). (Illus.). 60p. 1982. pap. 5.95 (ISBN 0-941948-07-2). St Johns-Oklawaha.

Niedhauk, Charlotte A. Charlotte's Story. 224p. 1983. pap. 10.00 (ISBN 0-682-49938-2). Exposition.

Sehlinger, Bob & Finley, John. Southern Florida Attractions: A Consumer Guide. (Illus.). 140p. 1982. pap. 3.95 (ISBN 0-89732-017-4). Menasha Ridge.

Smiley, Nixon. Crowder Tales. (Illus.). 169p. Date not set. 5.95 (ISBN 0-686-84216-2). Banyan Bks.

Washington, Ray. Cracker Florida. 160p. 1982. pap. 7.95 (ISBN 0-686-84275-8). Banyan Bks.

FLORIDA-DESCRIPTION AND TRAVEL-GUIDEBOOKS

Conch Train Tour. (Illus.). 28p. Date not set. pap. 3.00 (ISBN 0-686-84220-0). Banyan Bks.

Florida Travel Guide. (Berlitz Travel Guides). (Illus.). 1982. pap. 4.95 (ISBN 0-02-969780-8, Berlitz). Macmillan.

Hemingway House. (Illus.). 28p. Date not set. pap. 3.00 (ISBN 0-686-84221-9). Banyan Bks.

Insight Guides. Florida. (Illus.). 456p. 1983. pap. 14.95 (ISBN 0-13-322412-0). P-H.

Kornberg, Patti. But It Is in Brevard. Stewart, Sally A. & Hellmich, Nanci, eds. (Illus.). 216p. (Orig.). Date not set. pap. 4.95 (ISBN 0-686-82539-X). P Kornberg.

Livingston, Elizabeth & Starbuck, Carol. Miami for Kids: A Family Guide to Greater Miami Including Everglades National Park & the Florida Keys. LC 81-65980. 80p. Date not set. pap. 4.95 (ISBN 0-686-84246-4). Banyan Bks.

Norman Ford's Florida. 1983. 5.95 (ISBN 0-686-42888-9). Harian.

Pierce, Eleanor B. Tampa for Children of All Ages. McCaskey, Mary J., ed. LC 80-82486. (Illus.). 124p. Date not set. pap. 5.95 (ISBN 0-686-84249-9). Banyan Bks.

Sex After Forty. (Blank Books Ser.). 128p. 1982. cancelled (ISBN 0-939944-07-3). Marmac Pub.

The Thomas Cook Travel Guide to Miami-Ft. Lauderdale. (Orig.). Date not set. pap. 3.95 (ISBN 0-440-18887-3). Dell.

Tolf, Robert. Discover Florida: A Guide to Unique Sites & Sights. (Illus.). 143p. pap. 5.95 (ISBN 0-686-84224-3). Banyan Bks.

--Discover Fort Lauderdale's Top Twelve Restaurants. (Florida Keepsake Ser.: No. 2). (Illus.). 28p. 3.00 (ISBN 0-686-84230-8). Banyan Bks.

FLORIDA-HISTORY

Burghard, August. Half a Century in Florida. (Illus.). 263p. Date not set. 25.00 (ISBN 0-686-84226-X). Banyan Bks.

Hickox, Ron G. U. S. Military Edged Weapons of the Second Seminole War 1835-1842. LC 82-62494. (Historic Byways of Florida Ser.: Vol. IX). (Illus.). 100p. 1982. pap. 10.95 (ISBN 0-941948-09-9). St Johns-Oklawaha.

Johnson, A. J., illus. Eighteen Sixty-Three A. J. Johnson Map of Florida. (Illus.). 1p. Date not set. Repr. of 1863 ed. map 2.95 (ISBN 0-941948-13-7). St Johns-Oklawaha.

King, Carl. Model T Days: Florida or Bust. 1983. 12.95 (ISBN 0-932298-37-0). Copple Hse.

Mitchell, S. Augustus, illus. Eighteen Seventy-Two S. Augustus Mitchell Map of Florida. (Illus.). 1p. Date not set. Repr. of 1872 ed. map 2.95 (ISBN 0-941948-14-5). St Johns-Oklawaha.

Schenck, Noella L. Winter Park's Old Alabama Hotel. (Illus., Orig.). 1982. pap. 6.95 (ISBN 0-89305-043-1). Anna Pub.

Smith, Joseph B. The Plot to Steal Florida: James Madison's Phony War. 1983. 15.95 (ISBN 0-87795-477-1). Arbor Hse.

FLORIDA-JUVENILE LITERATURE

Sanger, Marjory B. Forest in the Sand. LC 82-4076. (Illus.). 160p. (gr. 7 up). 1983. 10.95 (ISBN 0-689-50248-6, McElderry Bk). Atheneum.

FLORIDA-MAPS

Johnson, A. J., illus. Eighteen Sixty-Three A. J. Johnson Map of Florida. (Illus.). 1p. Date not set. Repr. of 1863 ed. map 2.95 (ISBN 0-941948-13-7). St Johns-Oklawaha.

Mitchell, S. Augustus, illus. Eighteen Seventy-Two S. Augustus Mitchell Map of Florida. (Illus.). 1p. Date not set. Repr. of 1872 ed. map 2.95 (ISBN 0-941948-14-5). St Johns-Oklawaha.

FLORIDA-POLITICS AND GOVERNMENT

Langley, Michael. State of Florida's Procurement Policies & Minority Business Enterprises. 1980. 1.00 (ISBN 0-686-38006-1). Voter Ed Proj.

FLORIDA-SOCIAL LIFE AND CUSTOMS

King, Carl. Model T Days: Florida or Bust. 1983. 12.95 (ISBN 0-932298-37-0). Copple Hse.

FLORIDA KEYS

Stevenson, George B. Keyguide to Key West & the Florida Keys. (Illus.). 64p. Date not set. pap. 3.50 (ISBN 0-686-84251-0). Banyan Bks.

FLORISTS

Pfahl, Peter B. & Pfahl, P. Blair, Jr. The Retail Florist Business. 4th ed. 500p. 1983. 19.35 (ISBN 0-8134-2250-7); text ed. 14.50x (ISBN 0-686-83989-7). Interstate.

FLOUR MILLS

Greenbow, Desna. Devon Mill: The Restoration of a Corn Mill. 44p. 1982. 25.00x (ISBN 0-284-98624-0, Pub. by C Skilton Scotland). State Mutual Bk.

FLOW, MULTIPHASE

see Multiphase Flow

FLOW, TWO-PHASE

see Two-Phase Flow

FLOW CHARTS

Asanuma, T. Flow Visualization. 1979. 69.50 (ISBN 0-07-002378-6). McGraw.

FLOW DIAGRAMS

see Flow Charts

FLOW METERS

Scott, R. W. Developments in Flow Measurement, Vol. 1. 1982. 74.00 (ISBN 0-85334-976-2, Pub. by Applied Sci England). Elsevier.

FLOW OF WATER

see Hydraulics

FLOW PROCESS CHARTS

see Flow Charts

FLOWCHARTS

see Flow Charts

FLOWER ARRANGEMENT

Jekyll, Gertrude. Flower Decoration in the House. (Illus.). 1982. 29.50 (ISBN 0-907462-31-6). Antique Collect.

Johnson, Marion. A Personal Bouquet: An Idea Book for Miniature Flower Arrangements. 1983. 12.95 (ISBN 0-517-54788-0, C N Potter Bks). Crown.

Kennedy, Scott. Making Pressed Flower Pictures. (Illus.). 120p. 1982. pap. 5.95 (ISBN 0-486-24422-9). Dover.

Vagg, Daphne. Flower Arrangements Through the Year. (Illus.). 64p. 1983. pap. 4.95 (ISBN 0-7134-3732-4, Pub. by Batsford England). David & Charles.

--Flowers for the Table. (Illus.). 120p. 1983. 22.50 (ISBN 0-7134-4176-3, Pub. by Batsford England). David & Charles.

FLOWER ARRANGEMENT, CHINESE

Huang Su Huei. Meditations on Nature: The Art of Flower Arrangement. Simonds, Nina, tr. (Illus.). 184p. 1975. 12.95 (ISBN 0-941676-06-4). Wei-Chuan's Cooking.

FLOWER ARRANGEMENT, JAPANESE

Sparnon, Norman. Creative Japanese Flower Arrangement. Stuart, Isla, ed. (Illus.). 133p. 1982. 15.00 (ISBN 0-8048-1404-X, Pub. by Shufunmoto Co Ltd Japan). C E Tuttle.

FLOWER GARDENING

see also Wild Flower Gardening

Browne, Roland A. The Rose-Lover's Guide: A Practical Handbook for Rose Gardening. LC 73-92067. (Illus.). 256p. 1983. pap. 9.95 (ISBN 0-689-70642-1, 291). Atheneum.

Moggi, Guido, et al. Simon & Schuster's Guide to Garden Flowers. Schuler, Stanley, ed. (Illus.). 1983. price not set (ISBN 0-671-46674-7); pap. price not set (ISBN 0-671-46678-X). S&S.

Sackville-West, V. V. Sackville-West's Garden Book. LC 68-8261. (Illus.). 256p. 1983. pap. 9.95 (ISBN 0-689-70647-2, 295). Atheneum.

Snyder, Leon C. Flowers for Northern Gardens. (Illus.). 464p. 1983. 25.00 (ISBN 0-8166-1229-3). U of Minn Pr.

FLOWERING OF PLANTS

see Plants, Flowering Of

FLOWERING PLANTS

see Angiosperms

FLOWERS

see also Botany; Flower Arrangement; Flower Gardening; Plants; Plants, Flowering of; Wild Flowers; Window-Gardening

also names of flowers, e.g. Carnations, Roses, Violets

Blundell. A Guide to the Flowers of Kenya. 34.95 (ISBN 0-686-42770-X, Collins Pub England). Greene.

Cameron, Elizabeth. A Floral ABC. (Illus.). 64p. 1983. 7.95 (ISBN 0-688-01821-1). Morrow.

Croft, J. R. & Kanis, A. Handbooks of the Flora of Papua New Guinea, Vol. II. (Illus.). 276p. 1982. text ed. 37.50 (ISBN 0-522-84204-6, Pub. by Melbourne U Pr Australia). Intl Schol Bk Serv.

Darwin, Charles R. The Different Forms of Flowers on Plants of the Same Species. LC 72-3900. (Illus.). viii, 352p. 1972. write for info. (ISBN 0-404-08414-1). AMS Pr.

Durant, Mary. Who Named the Daisy? Who Named the Rose? A Roving Dictionary of North American Wildflowers. (Illus.). 224p. 1983. pap. 8.95 (ISBN 0-312-92944-7). Congdon & Weed.

Fahy, Everett. Metropolitan Flowers. Allison, Ellyn, ed. (Illus.). 112p. 1982. 14.95 (ISBN 0-87099-310-0). Metro Mus Art.

Flower Essence Society. The Flower Essence Journal, Issue 1. rev. ed. Katz, Richard A., ed. (Illus.). 36p. 1982. pap. 3.00 (ISBN 0-943986-01-X). Gold Circle.

--The Flower Essence Journal, Issue 2. rev. ed. Katz, Richard A., ed. (Illus.). 36p. 1983. pap. 3.00 (ISBN 0-943986-02-8). Gold Circle.

--The Flower Essence Journal, Issue 3. rev. ed. Katz, Richard A., ed. (Illus.). 48p. 1982. pap. 3.00 (ISBN 0-943986-03-6). Gold Circle.

Grey-Wilson & Blamey. The Alpine Flowers of Britain & Europe. pap. 19.95 (ISBN 0-686-42736-X, Collins Pub England). Greene.

Miller, Millie. Saguaroc: The Desert Flower Book. new ed. (Orig.). 1982. pap. 4.95 (ISBN 0-933472-69-2). Johnson Bks.

Moggi, Guido, et al. Simon & Schuster's Guide to Garden Flowers. Schuler, Stanley, ed. (Illus.). 1983. price not set (ISBN 0-671-46674-7); pap. price not set (ISBN 0-671-46678-X). S&S.

Okun, Sheila. A Book of Cut Flowers. (Illus.). 144p. 1983. 10.00 (ISBN 0-688-01971-4). Morrow.

Oldham, Kathleen I. The Annals of Flowerland. 1982. 7.95 (ISBN 0-533-05235-1). Vantage.

FLOWERS (IN RELIGION, FOLK-LORE, ETC.)

Ewart, Neil & O'Connell, Nina. The Lore of Flowers. 192p. 1983. 19.95 (ISBN 0-7137-1176-0, Pub. by Blandford Pr England). Sterling.

FLOWERS–ARRANGEMENT

see Flower Arrangement

FLOWERS–DRYING

Scott, Margaret K. & Beazley, Mary. Pressed Flowers Through the Seasons. (Illus.). 120p. 1983. 19.95 (ISBN 0-7134-4039-2, Pub. by Batsford England). David & Charles.

FLOWERS–PICTORIAL WORKS

Fahy, Everett. Metropolitan Flowers. Allison, Ellyn, ed. (Illus.). 112p. (Orig.). 1982. 29.50 (ISBN 0-8109-1317-8). Abrams.

Tropical Flowers of the World Coloring Book. 48p. 1981. pap. 2.00 (ISBN 0-486-24206-4). Dover.

FLOWERS, WILD

see Wild Flowers

FLOWMETERS

see Flow Meters

FLU

see Influenza

FLUID DYNAMICS

see also Aerodynamics; Boundary Layer; Hydrodynamics; Ion Flow Dynamics; Magnetohydrodynamics; Mass Transfer; Multiphase Flow; Shock Waves

Cheremisinoff, Nicholas P. & Azbel, David S. Fluid Mechanics & Unit Operations. LC 82-48638. (Illus.). 1100p. 1983. 49.95 (ISBN 0-250-40541-5). Ann Arbor Science.

Cheremisinoff, Nicholas P. & Gupta, Ramesh, eds. Handbook of Fluids In Motion. LC 82-70706. (Illus.). 1200p. 1983. 79.95 (ISBN 0-250-40458-3). Ann Arbor Science.

Fluidics Quarterly: The Journal of Fluid Control, Vol. 14. (Illus.). 1982. 125.00 (ISBN 0-88232-073-4). Delbridge Pub Co.

Fluidics Quarterly: The Journal of Fluid Control, Vol. 15. (Illus.). 1983. 125.00 (ISBN 0-88232-078-5). Delbridge Pub Co.

Krause, E., ed. Eighth International Conference on Numerical Methods in Fluid Dynamics, Aachen, FRG, 1982: Proceedings. (Lecture Notes in Physics Ser.: Vol. 170). 569p. 1983. pap. 27.20 (ISBN 0-387-11948-5). Springer-Verlag.

Morton, K. M. & Baines, M. J., eds. Numerical Methods for Fluid Dynamics. LC 82-11627. Date not set. 55.50 (ISBN 0-12-508360-2). Acad Pr.

Pedlosky, J. Geophysical Fluid Dynamics: Springer Study Edition. (Illus.). 624p. 1983. pap. 26.00 (ISBN 0-387-90745-9). Springer-Verlag.

Roe, P. L. Numerical Methods in Aeronautical Fluid Dynamics. (IMA Conference Ser.). Date not set. 55.50 (ISBN 0-12-592520-4). Acad Pr.

Shapiro, Ascher H. The Dynamics & Thermodynamics of Compressible Fluid Flow, Vol. 2. LC 82-17967. 550p. 1983. Repr. of 1954 ed. lib. bdg. price not set (ISBN 0-89874-566-7). Krieger.

Shin, Y. W. & Moody, F. J., eds. Fluid Transients & Fluid-Structure Interaction. (PVP Ser.: Vol. 64). 381p. 1982. 60.00 (H00221). ASME.

Symposium on Thermophysical Properties, 8th. Thermophysical Properties of Fluids: Proceedings, 2 Vols, Vol. 1. 1981. 65.00 (I00151). ASME.

FLUID MECHANICS

see also Fluid Dynamics; Fluids; Hydraulic Engineering; Hydraulics; Hydrodynamics

Bacon, Stephens. Fluid Mechanics for Tech 3-4. 1983. text ed. 14.95 (ISBN 0-408-01115-7). Butterworth.

Bober, William & Kenyon, Richard A. Fluid Mechanics. LC 79-12977. 558p. 1980. 34.95x (ISBN 0-471-04886-0); solutions manual avail. (ISBN 0-471-04999-9). Wiley.

Chermisinoff, Nicholas P. Fluid Flow: Pumps, Pipes & Channels. LC 81-68034. (Illus.). 702p. 1981. 39.95 (ISBN 0-250-40432-X). Ann Arbor Science.

Dyke, Van M. & Wehausen, J. V., eds. Annual Review of Fluid Mechanics, Vol. 15. LC 74-80866. (Illus.). 1983. text ed. 28.00 (ISBN 0-8243-0715-1). Annual Reviews.

Fox, Robert W. & McDonald, Alan T. Introduction to Fluid Mechanics. 2nd ed. LC 77-20839. 684p. 1978. text ed. 30.95x (ISBN 0-471-01909-7). Wiley.

Haase, W., ed. Recent Contributions to Fluid Mechanics. (Illus.). 338p. 1983. 23.00 (ISBN 0-387-11940-X). Springer-Verlag.

Pletcher, R. H., et al. Computational Fluid Mechanics & Heat Transfer. 1983. price not set (ISBN 0-07-050328-1). McGraw.

Verruijt, A. Grounderwater Flow. 2nd ed. (Illus.). 145p. 1982. text ed. 33.50x (ISBN 0-333-32958-9); pap. text ed. 17.50 (ISBN 0-333-32959-7). Scholium Intl.

Webb, D. R. & Papadakis, C. N., eds. Small Hydro Power Fluid Machinery. 1982. 40.00 (H00233). ASME.

Zierep, Juergen & Oertel, Herbert, Jr., eds. Convective Transport & Instability Phenomena. (Illus.). 577p. 1982. text ed. 65.00 (ISBN 3-7650-1114-2). Sheridan.

FLUID METERS

see Flow Meters

FLUID THERAPY

Aloia, Roland C., ed. Membrane Fluidity in Biology: Vol. 1: Concepts of Membrane Structure. 1982. 43.00 (ISBN 0-12-053001-5). Acad Pr.

Loblay, R. H. & Tiller, D. J. Fluid, Electrolyte & Acid-Base Disturbances: A Practical Guide for Interns. 144p. 1976. text ed. 14.95 (ISBN 0-471-25861-X, Pub. by Wiley Med). Wiley.

Winters, Robert W. Principles of Pediatric Fluid Therapy. 2nd ed. 1982. pap. text ed. 16.95 (ISBN 0-316-94738-5). Little.

FLUIDS

see also Fluid Dynamics; Fluid Mechanics; Gases; Hydraulic Engineering; Liquids

Cheremisinoff, Nicholas P. & Azbel, David S., eds. Liquid Filtration. LC 82-46063. (Illus.). 400p. 1983. 49.95 (ISBN 0-250-40600-4). Ann Arbor Science.

Gallagher, R. H., et al, eds. Finite Elements in Fluids, 3 vols. Incl. Vol. 1. Viscous Flow & Hydrodynamics. 290p. 1975. 67.00x (ISBN 0-471-29045-9); Vol. 2. Mathematical Foundations, Aerodynamics, & Lubrication. 287p. 1975. 67.00x (ISBN 0-471-29046-7); Vol. 3. 1978. 67.00x (ISBN 0-471-99630-0). LC 74-13573 (Pub. by Wiley-Interscience). Wiley.

Metheny, Norma & Snively, W. D., Jr. Nurses' Handbook of Fluid Balance. 4th ed. (Illus.). 512p. 1983. text ed. price not set (ISBN 0-397-54381-6, Lippincott Medical). Lippincott.

FLUIDS–THERAPEUTIC USE

see Fluid Therapy

FLUIDS, DRILLING

see Drilling Muds

FLUORESCENCE

Wehry, E. L. Modern Fluorescence Spectroscopy. 713p. 1976. text ed. 178.00x (ISBN 0-471-26079-7, Pub. by Wiley-Interscience). Wiley.

FLUORINE–PHYSIOLOGICAL EFFECT

Murray, J. J. & Rugg-Gunn, A. J. Fluorides in Cavities Prevention: Dental Practitioner Handbook, No. 20. 1982. text ed. 22.50 (ISBN 0-7236-0644-7). Wright-PSG.

FLUTE

Harrison, Howard. How to Play the Flute. (Illus.). 112p. 1983. 17.50 (ISBN 0-241-10875-6, Pub. by Hamish Hamilton England); pap. 9.95 (ISBN 0-241-10876-4). David & Charles.

FLUXIONS

see Calculus

FLY

see Flies

FLY-CASTING

Ferris, George. Flycasting: Techniques for the Flyfisherman. (Illus.). 56p. 1977. pap. 3.95 (ISBN 0-686-42805-6, Pub. by Heinemann Pubs New Zealand). Intl Schol Bk Serv.

Kreh, Lefty. Fly Fishing in Salt Water. write for info. N Lyons Bks.

Kreh, Lefty & Sosin, Mark. Practical Fishing Knots. write for info. N Lyons Bks.

Lyons, Nick, ed. Art Flick's Master Fly-Tying Guide. write for info. N Lyons Bks.

--Art Flick's New Streamside Guide. write for info. N Lyons Bks.

Marinaro, vincent. In the Ring of the Rise. write for info. N Lyons Bks.

--A Modern Dry-Fly Code. write for info. N Lyons Bks.

Pfeiffer, C. Boyd. Tackle Craft. write for info. N Lyons Bks.

Swisher, Doug & Richards, Carl. Fly-Fishing Strategy. write for info. N Lyons Bks.

--Selective Trout. write for info. N Lyons Bks.

Veniard, John. Fly Tying Problems. write for info. N Lyons Bks.

FLY FISHING

see also Fly-Casting

Bark, Voss. West Country Fly Fishing. (Illus.). 192p. 1983. 22.50 (ISBN 0-7134-1882-6, Pub. by Batsford England). David & Charles.

Cooper, Gwen & Haas, Evelyn. Wade a Little Deeper Dear. 1978. pap. 4.50 (ISBN 0-87735-044-2). Wade Bks.

Ferris, George. Fly Fishing in New Zealand. (Illus.). 116p. 1976. 6.95 (ISBN 0-686-42803-X, Pub. by Heinemann Pubs New Zealand). Intl Schol Bk Serv.

McClane, A. J. The Practical Fly Fisherman. 288p. 1983. pap. 7.95 (ISBN 0-13-689380-5, Reward). P-H.

Schwiebert, Ernest. Trout Strategies: Observations on Modern Fly Fishing, Including Tested Methods of Matching the Hatch, Fishing the Nymph, Bucktails & Streamers, Wet & Dry Flies; & Techniques for Eastern & Western Lakes, Ponds, Rivers & Streams--Drawn from the Author's Masterwork "Trout". (Illus.). 288p. 1983. pap. 10.95 (ISBN 0-525-48052-8, 01064-310). Dutton.

FLYING

see Flight

FLYING BOMBS

see V-Two Rocket

FLYING CLASSES

see Flight Training

FLYING-MACHINES

see also Aeronautics; Airplanes; Autogiros; Helicopters

Taylor, Michael. Fantastic Flying Machines. (Illus.). 144p. 1982. 12.95 (ISBN 0-86720-552-0). Sci Bks Intl.

FLYING SAUCERS

Denaerde, Stefan & Stevens, Wendelle C. UFO... Contact from Planet Iarga. Lodge, Jim, tr. from Dutch. (UFO Fact Bks.). Orig. Title: Buitenaardse Beschaving. (Illus.). 368p. 1982. lib. bdg. 15.95 (ISBN 0-9608558-1-5). UFO Photo.

Klass, Philip J. UFOs: The Public Deceived. 250p. 1983. 17.95 (ISBN 0-87975-203-3). Prometheus Bks.

Sanchez-Ocejo, Virgilio & Stevens, Wendelle C. UFO Contact from Undersea. (UFO Factbooks). (Illus.). 190p. 1982. lib. bdg. 14.95 (ISBN 0-9608558-0-7). UFO Photo.

Stevens, Wendelle & Herrmann, William J. UFO...Contact from Reticulum. (UFO Factbooks). (Illus.). 398p. 1981. lib. bdg. 16.95 (ISBN 0-686-84864-0). UFO Photo.

Stevens, Wendelle C. UFO Contact from the Pleiades. (UFO Factbooks). (Illus.). 542p. 1982. lib. bdg. 17.95 (ISBN 0-9608558-2-3). UFO Photo.

Stevens, Wendelle C. & Dong, Paul. UFOs Over Modern China. (UFO Factbks.). (Illus.). 452p. 1983. lib. bdg. 17.95 (ISBN 0-9608558-3-1). UFO Photo.

Whiteside, I. W. Sharon's UFO Code for Outer Space. 64p. (Orig.). 1983. pap. 4.00 (ISBN 0-682-49969-2). Exposition.

FLYING SAUCERS (GAME)

see Frisbee (Game)

FOAMED MATERIALS

Business Communications Staff. Structural Foam. 1982. 1750.00 (ISBN 0-686-84696-6, P-006). BCC.

FODDER

see Feeds

FOETUS

see Fetus

FOLIAGE

see Leaves

FOLK ART

see also Art Industries and Trade

Bishop, Robert & Weissman, Judith R. Folk Art: Painting, Sculpture & Country Objects. LC 82-48945. 13.95 (ISBN 0-394-71493-8). Knopf.

Ferris, William. Local Color: A Sense of Place in Folk Art. 272p. 1983. 19.95 (ISBN 0-07-020652-X); pap. 11.95 (ISBN 0-07-020651-1). McGraw.

Vaughan, Betty A. Folk Art Painting: A Bit of the Past & Present. (Illus.). 52p. 1981. pap. 7.95 (ISBN 0-9605172-0-0). BETOM Pubns.

FOLK ART–AFRICA

Ross, Heather C. The Art of Bedouin Jewellery. 1982. 59.00x (ISBN 0-907513-01-8, Pub. by Cave Pubns England). State Mutual Bk.

FOLK ART–ASIA

Rubel, Mary. Double Happiness: Getting More from Chinese Popular Art. (Illus.). 172p. (Orig.). 1981. pap. 6.98 (ISBN 0-9609154-0-0). Magaru Enterprises.

FOLK ART–NORWAY

Roalson, Louise, ed. Notably Norwegian: Recipes, Festivals, Folk Arts. LC 82-81569. (Illus.). 88p. 1982. pap. 5.95 (ISBN 0-941016-05-6). Penfield.

FOLK ART–RUMANIA

Dancu, Juliana & Dancu, Dumitru. Romanian Icons on Glass. (Illus.). 179p. 1983. 13.50x (ISBN 0-8143-1711-1). Wayne St U Pr.

FOLK COSTUME

see Costume

FOLK CUSTOMS

see Manners and Customs

FOLK-LORE

see also Animals, Legends and Stories Of; Devil; Fables; Fairies; Fairy Tales; Folk Music; Folk-Songs; Ghosts; Grail; Halloween; Legends; Marriage Customs and Rites; Myth; Mythology; Nursery Rhymes; Proverbs; Riddles; Story-Telling; Superstition; Tales; Werewolves; Witchcraft

Cohen, Daniel. Southern Fried Rat & Other Gruesome Tales. (Illus.). 128p. 1983. 9.95 (ISBN 0-87131-400-2). M Evans.

Grant, Charles L. The Dodd, Mead Gallery of Horror. 1983. 15.95 (ISBN 0-396-08160-6). Dodd.

Waters, Donald J. Strange Ways & Sweet Dreams: Afro-American Folklore from the Hampton Institute. 466p. 1983. lib. bdg. 49.95 (ISBN 0-8161-9022-4, Univ Bks). G K Hall.

FOLK-LORE–BIBLIOGRAPHY

Georges, Robert A. & Stern, Stephen. American & Canadian Immigrant & Ethnic Folklore: An Annnotated Bibliography. LC 80-9019. (Folklore Bibliographies Ser.). 300p. 1982. lib. bdg. 35.00 (ISBN 0-8240-9307-0). Garland Pub.

Wrigglesworth, Hazel J., tr. An Anthology of Ilianen Manobo Folktales. (San Carlos Humanities Ser.: No. 11). 299p. 1982. 15.75 (ISBN 0-686-37561-0, Pub. by San Carlos Philippines); pap. 12.00 (ISBN 0-686-37562-9). Cellar.

FOLK-LORE–JUVENILE LITERATURE

Bendick, Jeanne. Scare a Ghost, Tame a Monster. LC 82-23696. (Illus.). 120p. (gr. 3-6). 1983. price not set (ISBN 0-664-32701-X). Westminster.

Chandler, Robert, tr. The Magic Ring & other Russian Folktales. (Illus.). 90p. (gr. 2-6). 1983. pap. 2.95 (ISBN 0-571-13006-2). Faber & Faber.

FOLK-LORE, AFRICAN

White, Paul. Fabulas de la Selva. Orig. Title: Jungle Doctor's Fables. 80p. Date not set. pap. price not set (ISBN 0-311-39000-5). Casa Bautista.

FOLK-LORE, AFRO-AMERICAN

see Afro-American Folk-Lore

FOLK-LORE, AMERICAN

Aldrich, Lawson. The Cheechako: Facts, Fables & Recipes. LC 82-72999. 192p. 1982. pap. 7.95 (ISBN 0-89272-156-1). Down East.

Binner, Vinal O. American Folktales One: A Structured Reader. 1966. pap. text ed. 8.50 scp (ISBN 0-690-00704-6, HarpC). Har-Row.

Breihan, Carl W. Gunslingers. (Illus.). 300p. 1983. 12.95 (ISBN 0-89769-076-1); pap. 6.95 (ISBN 0-89769-048-6). Pine Mntn.

Glimm, James Y. Flatlanders & Ridgerunners: Folktales from the Mountains of Northern Pennsylvania. LC 82-10895. (Illus.). 240p. 1983. 11.95 (ISBN 0-8229-3471-X); pap. 5.95 (ISBN 0-8229-5345-5). U of Pittsburgh Pr.

McCrary, Blanche. The Redneck Way of Knowledge. 1983. pap. 4.95 (ISBN 0-14-006725-6). Penguin.

Mittlefehldt, Pamela. Minnesota Folklife: An Annotated Bibliography. Sherarts, I. Karon, ed. LC 79-23255. 42p. (Orig.). 1979. pap. 3.50 (ISBN 0-935288-00-7). Minn Hist.

Ortiz y Pino, Jose, III. Curandero. Hausman, Gerald, ed. LC 82-19507. (Illus.). 128p. 1982. pap. 7.95 (ISBN 0-86534-020-X). Sunstone Pr.

Russell, Bert. Calked Boots & Other Northwest Writings. 4th ed. (Folklore). 1979. pap. 5.95 (ISBN 0-930344-00-6); 8.95 (ISBN 0-930344-03-0). Lacon Pubs.

Sessions, Thelma A. Country Folk Ain't So Bad. 72p. 1983. 5.50 (ISBN 0-682-49956-0). Exposition.

Virgines, George. Western Legends & Lore. (Illus.). 128p. 1983. 12.95 (ISBN 0-686-81870-9); pap. 6.95 (ISBN 0-686-81871-7). Pine Mntn.

FOLK-LORE, ASIAN

Bagshawe, L. E., tr. The Maniyadanabon of Shin Sandalinka. 152p. 1981. 7.00 (ISBN 0-87727-115-1). Cornell SE Asia.

Huynh Sanh Thong. The Tale of Kieu: A Bilingual Edition of Nauyen Du's "Truyen Kieu". Huynh, Sanh T., tr. LC 82-10979. 256p. (Chinese & Eng.). 1983. text ed. 17.50x (ISBN 0-300-02873-3). Yale U Pr.

Toth, Marian D. Tales From Thailand: Folklore, Culture, & History. LC 77-125563. (Illus.). 184p. 1983. 14.50 (ISBN 0-8048-0563-6). C E Tuttle.

FOLK-LORE, CELTIC

Rys, John. Celtic Folklore: Welsh & Manx, Vol. II. 317p. 1982. pap. 8.95 (ISBN 0-7045-0410-3, Pub. by Salem Hse Ltd.). Merrimack Bk Serv.

--Celtic Folklore: Welsh & Manx, Vol. I. 400p. 1982. pap. 9.95 (ISBN 0-7045-0405-7, Pub. by Salem Hse Ltd.). Merrimack Bk Serv.

FOLK-LORE, CHINESE

Bender, Mark, tr. Seventh Sister & Teh Serpent. (Illus.). 65p. 1982. pap. 2.95 (ISBN 0-8351-1044-3). China Bks.

Gigliesi, Primerose & Friend, Robert, trs. from Chinese. The Effendi & the Pregnant Pot. (Illus.). 88p. (Orig.). 1982. pap. 2.25 (ISBN 0-8351-1027-3). China Bks.

The Magic Knife: Folk Tales from China, No. 5. (Illus.). 142p. (Orig.). 1982. pap. 2.50 (ISBN 0-8351-0971-2). China Bks.

The Seven Sister-Folk Tales, No. 6. (Chinese Folk Tales' Ser.). (Illus.). 122p. 1982. pap. 2.95 (ISBN 0-8351-1037-0). China Bks.

Shoushen, Jin. Beijing Legends. Yang, Gladys, tr. (Illus.). 141p. (Orig.). 1982. pap. 2.95 (ISBN 0-8351-1042-7). China Bks.

FOLK-LORE, ENGLISH

Leger-Gordon, Ruth. The Witchcraft & Folklore of Dartmoor. 192p. 1982. pap. text ed. 8.25x (ISBN 0-86299-021-1, 51426, Pub. by Sutton England). Humanities.

Marples, Morris. White Horses & Other Hill Figures. 224p. 1982. pap. text ed. 9.00x (ISBN 0-904387-59-3, 61083, Pub. by Sutton England). Humanities.

FOLK-LORE, EUROPEAN

Mediaeval Tales. Morley, Henry, intro. by. 287p. 1982. Repr. of 1884 ed. lib. bdg. 40.00 (ISBN 0-89984-807-9). Century Bookbinding.

Shoehmelian, O. Three Apples from Heaven: Armenian Folk Tales. Avakian, Arra & Bond, Harold, eds. Shoehmelian, O., tr. from Armenian. (Illus.). 150p. (Orig.). 1982. pap. 6.95 (ISBN 0-933706-23-5). Ararat Pr.

FOLK-LORE, GERMAN

See, Carolyn. Rhine Maidens. 1983. pap. 4.95 (ISBN 0-14-006361-7). Penguin.

FOLK-LORE, HUNGARIAN

Domotor, Tekla. Hungarian Folk Beliefs. LC 82-48163. (Illus.). 324p. 1983. 17.50x (ISBN 0-253-32876-4). Ind U Pr.

FOLK-LORE, INDIAN

Here are entered works on the folk-lore of the American Indians; Collections of Indan tales, legends, or myths are entered under Indians of North America–Legends; Indians of South America–Legends; etc.

Holsinger, Rosemary. Shasta Indian Tales. (Illus.). 48p. 1982. lib. bdg. 8.95 (ISBN 0-87961-128-6); pap. 3.95 (ISBN 0-87961-129-4). Naturegraph.

Walker, Deward E., Jr. Myths of Idaho Indians. 1979. 10.95 (ISBN 0-89301-066-9). U Pr of Idaho.

Walking Night Bear. How the Creator Gave Us the Herbs. (Illus.). 48p. (gr. 3-6). 1983. lib. bdg. price not set (ISBN 0-943986-22-2); pap. 5.95 (ISBN 0-943986-21-4). Gold Circle.

FOLK-LORE, IRISH

Dunne, John J. & O'Connor, Lawrence. Haunted Ireland: Her Romantic & Mysterious Ghosts. (Illus.). 115p. pap. 8.95 (ISBN 0-904651-30-4, Pub. by Salem Hse Ltd). Merrimack Bk Serv.

Logan, Patrick. The Old Gods: The Facts about Irish Fairies. 125p. 1982. 12.95 (ISBN 0-904651-82-7, Pub. by Salem Hse Ltd.); pap. 6.95 (ISBN 0-904651-83-5, Pub. by Salem Hse Ltd.). Merrimack Bk Serv.

Messenger, Betty. Picking Up the Linen Threads. 1982. 40.00x (ISBN 0-85640-210-9, Pub. by Blackstaff Pr). State Mutual Bk.

FOLK-LORE, ITALIAN

Scarpato, Maria & Fattoross, Camille. The Simpleton of Naples & Other Italian Folktales. LC 82-81946. (Illus.). 96p. (gr. 3-8). 1983. 13.95 (ISBN 0-88100-010-8). Capricorn Bks.

FOLK-LORE, JEWISH

Haut, Irwin H. The Talmud as Law or Literature: An Analysis of David W. Halivni's Mekorot Umasorot. x, 83p. pap. 6.95 (ISBN 0-87203-107-1). Hermon.

Patai, Raphael. On Jewish Folklore. 524p. 1983. 27.50x (ISBN 0-8143-1707-3). Wayne St U Pr.

Schwartz, Howard. Elijah's Violin & Other Jewish Fairy Tales. LC 82-48133. (Illus.). 272p. 1983. 14.95 (ISBN 0-06-015108-0, HarpT). Har-Row.

FOLK-LORE, MEDICAL

see Folk Medicine

FOLK-LORE, MEXICAN

Gomez, Ermilo A. Canek: History & Legend of a Maya Hero. 80p. 1983. pap. 2.50 (ISBN 0-380-61937-7, 61937, Bard). Avon.

FOLK-LORE, RUSSIAN

Komarovich, V. L., ed. Kitezhskaia Legenda: Opyt Izuchenilia Mestnykh Legend. (Monuments of Early Russian Literature: Vol. 5). 184p. (Russian.). 1982. pap. 9.50 (ISBN 0-686-84208-1). Berkeley Slavic.

Zoshchenko, Mikhail. Rasskazy Nazara Il'icha, Gospodina Sinebriukhova. 89p. (Russian.). 1982. pap. 3.50 (ISBN 0-933884-33-8). Berkeley Slavic.

FOLK-LORE, SCOTTISH

Warner, Gerald. Tales of the Scottish Highlands. 192p. 1982. 11.50 (ISBN 0-85683-060-7, Pub. by Shepheard-Walwyn); pap. 5.95 (ISBN 0-85683-061-5). Flatiron Book Dist.

FOLK-LORE OF DAYS

see Days

FOLK-LORE OF FLOWERS

see Flowers (In Religion, Folk-Lore, etc.)

FOLK-LORE OF INITIATIONS

see Initiations (In Religion, Folk-Lore, etc.)

FOLK-LORE OF THE SEA

Beck, Horace. Folklore & the Sea. (Illus.). 480p. 1983. pap. 10.95 (ISBN 0-8289-0499-5). Greene.

FOLK MEDICINE

Ash, Michael. The Handbook of Natural Healing. 1982. 25.00x (ISBN 0-906186-00-5, Pub. by Element Bks). State Mutual Bk.

Austin, Phylis A. & Thrash, Agatha M. Natural Remedies: A Manual. 283p. (Orig.). 1983. pap. price not set (ISBN 0-942658-05-1). Yuchi Pines.

Boulos, Loutfy. Medicinal Plants of North Africa. Ayensu, Edward S., ed. LC 82-20412. (Medicinal Plants of the World Ser.: No. 3). (Illus.). 300p. 1983. 29.95 (ISBN 0-917256-16-6). Ref Pubns.

Gimlette, John D. Malay Poisons & Charm Cures. 3rd ed. (Oxford in Asia Paperbacks Ser.). 328p. 1982. pap. 13.95 (ISBN 0-19-638150-9). Oxford U Pr.

Jarvis, D. C. Folk Medicine. Date not set. pap. 5.95 (ISBN 0-449-90066-5, Columbine). Fawcett.

LaArta, Moulton. Nature's Medicine Chest, Set 4. 96p. 1975. 5.50 (ISBN 0-935596-07-0). Gluten Co.

LeArta, Moulton. Nature's Medicine Chest, 6 bks. Set. 32.00 (ISBN 0-935596-10-0). Gluten Co.

--Nature's Medicine Chest, Set 2. 96p. 1975. 5.00 (ISBN 0-935596-05-4). Gluten Co.

--Nature's Medicine Chest, Set 3. 96p. 1976. 5.50 (ISBN 0-935596-06-2). Gluten Co.

--Nature's Medicine Chest, Set 5. 96p. 1976. 5.50 (ISBN 0-935596-08-9). Gluten Co.

--Nature's Medicine Chest, Set 6. 96p. 1977. 5.50 (ISBN 0-935596-09-7). Gluten Co.

Moulton, LeArta. Nature's Medicine Chest, Set 1. 96p. 1974. 5.00 (ISBN 0-935596-04-6). Gluten Co.

Seidle, Helmut A. Medizinische Sprichwortr Im Englischen und Deutschen. 410p. (Ger.). 1981. write for info. (ISBN 3-8204-5985-5). P Lang Pubs.

FOLK MUSIC

see also Country Music; Folk-Songs

Cuthbert, John A. West Virginia Folk Music. 185p. 1982. 10.00 (ISBN 0-937058-12-2). West Virginia U Pr.

List, George. Music & Poetry in a Colombian Village: A Tri-Cultural Heritage. LC 82-48534. (Illus.). 640p. 1983. 35.00x (ISBN 0-253-33951-0). Ind U Pr.

FOLK-PSYCHOLOGY

see Ethnopsychology

FOLK-SONGS

see also Carols; Folk-Lore; National Songs

Maddox, Irene, ed. Campfire Songs. 192p. 1983. pap. 7.95 (ISBN 0-914788-68-X). East Woods.

FOLK-SONGS–JUVENILE LITERATURE

Douillard, Jeanne & Snow, Suzanne. Chasons de Chez-Nous. (Illus.). 61p. (Fr., Music). (gr. k-6). 1978. pap. text ed. 1.00x (ISBN 0-911409-01-7). Natl Mat Dev.

FOLK-SONGS, AMERICAN

Cuthbert, John A. West Virginia Folk Music. 185p. 1982. 10.00 (ISBN 0-937058-12-2). West Virginia U Pr.

Gainer, Patrick W. Folk Songs from the West Virginia Hills. LC 75-38967. 236p. 1982. pap. 8.98 (ISBN 0-686-84022-4). Seneca Bks.

Karpeles, Maud & Sharp, Cecil J., eds. Eighty Appalachian Folk Songs. LC 82-24252. 112p. 1983. pap. 5.95 (ISBN 0-571-10049-X). Faber & Faber.

Owens, William A. Sing Me a Song. 1983. 8.95xtape (ISBN 0-292-77574-1). U of Tex Pr.

Palmer, Roy, ed. Folk Songs Collected by Ralph Vaughan Williams. 256p. 1983. text ed. 21.95x (ISBN 0-460-04558-X, Pub by J M Dent England). Biblio Dist.

FOLK-SONGS, ASIAN

Graham, David C. The Tribal Songs & Tales of the Ch'uan-Miao. (Asian Folklore & Social Life Monographs: Vol. 102). 1980. 20.50 (ISBN 0-89986-333-7). Oriental Bk Store.

FOLK-SONGS, SPANISH

List, George. Music & Poetry in a Colombian Village: A Tri-Cultural Heritage. LC 82-48534. (Illus.). 640p. 1983. 35.00x (ISBN 0-253-33951-0). Ind U Pr.

FOLK-TALES

see Folk-Lore; Legends; Tales

FOLKWAYS

see Manners and Customs

FONDA, HENRY

Goldstein, Norm & Associated Press. Henry Fonda. LC 82-48627. (Illus.). 124p. 1982. pap. 7.70 (ISBN 0-03-063353-2, Owl Bks). HR&W.

Teichmann, Howard. Fonda: My Life. large type ed. LC 82-5983. (Illus.). 697p. 1982. Repr. of 1981 ed. 13.95 (ISBN 0-89621-370-6). Thorndike Pr.

FONTANEL

see Skull

FOOD

see also Animals, Food Habits of; Beverages; Cookery; Diet; Dietaries; Food, Natural; Fruit; Grain; Markets; Meat; Nutrition; Nuts; Sea Food; Vegetables; Vegetarianism

also headings beginning with the word Food; also particular foods and beverages, e.g. Bread, Milk; also subdivision Food under subjects, e.g. Fishes–Food; Indians of North America–Food

Cadwallader, Sharon. The Living Kitchen. (Tools for Today Ser.). 1983. pap. 6.95 (ISBN 0-686-84928-0). Sierra.

Fairchild Books Special Projects Division. SN Distribution Study of Grocery Store Sales 1983. (Illus.). 300p. 1983. pap. 35.00 (ISBN 0-87005-444-9). Fairchild.

Food & Nutrition Group. Feed, Need, Greed. Tafler, Sue & Phillips, Connie, eds. (Illus.). 108p. (Orig.). 1980. pap. 5.00 (ISBN 0-9607314-0-7); tchr's. ed. 5.00 (ISBN 0-686-84488-2). Sci People.

Food Combining Made Easy Chart. 1981. pap. 3.95 (ISBN 0-9603532-2-4). Ten Talents.

Fox, Brian A. & Cameron, Allan G. Food Science: A Chemical Approach. 382p. 1982. pap. 13.50x (ISBN 0-8448-1451-2). Crane-Russak Co.

Ganmaster. Food Irradiation Now. 1982. 22.00 (ISBN 90-247-2763-4, Pub. by Martinus Nijhoff Netherlands). Kluwer Boston.

Garvy, John W., Jr. The Five Phases of Food: How To Begin. 2nd ed. Liebermann, Jeremiah, ed. (Five Phase Energetics Ser.: No. 1). (Illus.). 1982. pap. 3.00 (ISBN 0-943450-03-9). Wellbeing Bks.

Golos, Natalie & Golbitz, Frances G. If This Is Tuesday It Must Be Chicken or How to Rotate Your Food for Better Health. Martin, Joan, ed. LC 81-13509. 109p. (Orig.). 1981. pap. 6.95 (ISBN 0-941962-00-8). Human Eco Res.

Kumagai, Kenji. The Sushi Handbook. (Illus., Orig.). 1983. pap. 8.95 (ISBN 0-89346-211-X). Heian Intl.

Lehman, S. C. Nutrition & Food Preparation & Preventive Care & Maintenance. (Lifeworks Ser.). 1981. text ed. 5.80 (ISBN 0-07-037094-X). McGraw.

Mass Merchandised Healthy Foods: Market Trends. 140p. 1982. 975.00 (ISBN 0-686-43330-0). Knowledge Indus.

Morris, Jane. The Food Book Activity Guide. 128p. (Orig.). 1983. wkbk. 3.80 (ISBN 0-87006-425-8). Goodheart.

Sourcebook on Food & Nutrition. 3rd ed. LC 82-82014. 549p. 1982. 49.50 (ISBN 0-8379-4503-8). Marquis.

Szekely, Edmond B. The Book of the Living Foods. (Illus.). 56p. 1977. pap. 3.50 (ISBN 0-89564-039-2). IBS Intl.

FOOD–ANALYSIS

see also Food–Composition

King, R. D. Developments in Food Analysis, Vols. 1 & 2. Vol. 1, 1978. 69.75 (ISBN 0-85334-755-7, Pub. by Applied Sci England); Vol. 2, 1980. 49.25 (ISBN 0-85334-921-5). Elsevier.

Lessof, M. H. Clinical Reations to Food. 1983. 17.50 (ISBN 0-471-10436-1, Pub. by Wiley Med). Wiley.

FOOD–COMPOSITION

see also Food–Analysis

Breimer, T. Environmental Factors & Cultural Measures Affecting the Nitrate of Spinach. 1982. pap. text ed. 22.00 (ISBN 90-247-3053-8, Pub. by Martinus Nijhoff Netherlands). Kluwer Boston.

Iglesias, Hector A. & Chirife, Jorge, eds. Handbook of Food Isotherms: Water Sorption Parameters for Food & Food Components (Monographs) (Food Science & Technology Ser.). 1982. 49.00 (ISBN 0-12-370380-8). Acad Pr.

FOOD–DICTIONARIES

Esser, William L. Dictionary of Hygienic Food. (Illus.). 1982. pap. 3.50 (ISBN 0-686-84404-1). Natural Hygiene.

FOOD–FREEZING

see Food, Frozen

FOOD–INSPECTION

see Food Adulteration and Inspection

FOOD–MICROBIOLOGY

see also Food Poisoning

Davies, R. Developments in Food Microbiology, Vol. 1. 1982. 49.25 (ISBN 0-85334-999-1, Pub. by Applied Sci England). Elsevier.

Lessof, M. H. Clinical Reations to Food. 1983. 17.50 (ISBN 0-471-10436-1, Pub. by Wiley Med). Wiley.

Microbial Ecology of Foods. 1982. Vol. 1. pap. text ed. 19.50 (ISBN 0-12-363521-7); Vol. 2: Food Commodities. pap. text ed. 29.50 (ISBN 0-12-363522-5). Acad Pr.

Walford, J., ed. Developments in Food Colours, Vol. 1. 1980. 45.00 (ISBN 0-85334-881-2, Pub. by Applied Sci England). Elsevier.

FOOD–PACKAGING

Food Processing & Packaging Equipment. 1982. 450.00 (ISBN 0-686-38425-3, 212). Busn Trend.

Palling, S. J., ed. Developments in Food Packaging, Vol. 1. 1980. 45.00 (ISBN 0-85334-917-7, Pub. by Applied Sci England). Elsevier.

FOOD–PRESERVATION

see also Canning and Preserving; Fishery Products; Food, Frozen

Center for Self-Sufficiency Research Division, compiled by. The Food Preservation Index. 50p. 1982. pap. text ed. 12.95 (ISBN 0-910811-10-5). Center Self.

Food Processing & Packaging Equipment. 1982. 450.00 (ISBN 0-686-38425-3, 212). Busn Trend.

Spicer, A. Advances in Preconcentration & Dehydration of Food. 1974. 67.75 (ISBN 0-85334-599-6). Elsevier.

Thorne, S., ed. Developments in Food Preservation, Vol. 1. 1981. 67.75 (ISBN 0-85334-979-7, Pub. by Applied Sci England). Elsevier.

Tilbury, R. H., ed. Developments in Food Preservatives, Vol. 1. 1980. 39.00 (ISBN 0-85334-918-5, Pub. by Applied Sci England). Elsevier.

FOOD–PRICES

see Food Prices

FOOD–RADIATION EFFECTS

see Food, Effect of Radiation on

FOOD, CHEMISTRY OF

see Food–Analysis; Food–Composition

FOOD, COST OF

see Cost and Standard of Living

FOOD, DIETETIC

Aspartame: A Summary & Annotated Bibliography. (Illus.). 20p. 1982. pap. 3.50 (ISBN 0-88091-006-2). Am Dietetic Assn.

FOOD, EFFECT OF RADIATION ON

Training Manual on Food Irradiation: Technology & Techniques. (Technical Reports Ser.: No. 114). 205p. 1982. pap. 26.75 (ISBN 92-0-115082-2, IDC114/2, IAEA). Unipub.

FOOD, FROZEN

Glanfield, P. Applied Cook-Freezing. 1980. 35.00 (ISBN 0-85334-888-X, Pub. by Applied Sci England). Elsevier.

FOOD, HEALTH

see Food, Natural

FOOD, NATURAL

see also Cookery (Natural Foods)

Center for Self Sufficiency Research Division Staff. International Directory of Herb, Health, Vitamin & Natural Food Catalogs. 200p. 1983. pap. text ed. 15.95 (ISBN 0-910811-36-9). Center Self.

Clute, Robin & Andersen, Sigrid. Juel Andersen's Carob Primer. 50p. (Orig.). 1983. pap. 3.95 (ISBN 0-916870-60-X). Creative Arts Bk.

Nakamura, Hiroshi. Spirulina: Food for a Hungry World; A Pioneer's Story in Aquaculture. Hills, Christopher, ed. Wargo, Robert, tr. from Japanese. (Illus.). 224p. (Orig.). 1982. pap. 10.95 (ISBN 0-916438-47-3). Univ of Trees.

Rohe, Fred. Fred Rohe's Complete Book of Natural Foods. LC 82-50282. (Illus.). 448p. (Orig.). 1983. pap. 10.95 (ISBN 0-394-71240-4). Shambhala Pubns.

Walker, Norman W. Pure & Simple Natural Weight Control. LC 81-11080. 1981. pap. 4.95 (ISBN 0-89019-078-X). O'Sullivan Woodside.

FOOD, ORGANICALLY GROWN

see Food, Natural

FOOD, PURE

see Food Adulteration and Inspection

FOOD, RAW

see also Vegetarianism

Szekely, Edmond B. Treasury of Raw Foods. (Illus.). 48p. 1981. pap. 2.95 (ISBN 0-89564-042-2). IBS Intl.

FOOD, SMOKED

see Cookery (Smoked Foods)

FOOD ADULTERATION AND INSPECTION

Knutson, Ronald & Penn, J. B. Agricultural & Food Policy. (Illus.). 384p. 1983. text ed. 25.95 (ISBN 0-13-018911-1). P-H.

Mycotoxin Surveillance. (FAO Food & Nutrition Papers: No. 21). 68p. 1982. pap. 7.50 (ISBN 92-5-101180-X, F2306, FAO). Unipub.

Pesticide Residues in Food, 1981 Report. (FAO Plant Production & Protection Papers: No. 37). 69p. 1982. pap. 7.50 (ISBN 92-5-101202-4, FAO). Unipub.

Rudman, Jack. Food Inspector. (Career Examination Ser.: C-2543). (Cloth bdg. avail. on request). pap. 8.00 (ISBN 0-8373-2543-9). Natl Learning.

FOOD AID PROGRAMS

see Food Relief

FOOD ALLERGY

see Allergy

FOOD AND AGRICULTURE ORGANIZATION OF THE UNITED NATIONS

Organization & Structure of FAO. (FAO Terminology Bulletin Ser.: No. 15, Rev. 4). 158p. 1983. pap. 12.00 (ISBN 92-5-001240-3, F2346, FAO). Unipub.

FOOD CHEMISTRY

see Food–Analysis; Food–Composition

FOOD CONTROL

see Food Supply

FOOD CUSTOMS

see Food Habits

FOOD DECORATION

see Cookery (Garnishes)

FOOD FOR INVALIDS

see Cookery for the Sick

FOOD FOR SCHOOL CHILDREN
see School Children-Food

FOOD HABITS
see also Diet; Nutrition

Boskind-White, Marlene & White, William C. Bulimarexia: The Binge-Purge Cycle. 1983. 15.00 (ISBN 0-393-01650-1). Norton.

Cauwels, Janice M. Bulimia: The Binge-Purge Compulsion. LC 82-45538. 288p. 1983. 14.95 (ISBN 0-385-18377-1). Doubleday.

FOOD HABITS OF ANIMALS
see Animals, Food Habits of

FOOD HANDLING

Leichtman, Robert R. Nikola Tesla Returns. (From Heaven to Earth Ser.). (Illus.). 104p. (Orig.). 1980. pap. 3.00 (ISBN 0-89804-060-4). Ariel OH.

Troller, John A., ed. Sanitation in Food Processing. LC 82-16291. (Food Science & Technology Ser.). Date not set. price not set (ISBN 0-12-700660-5). Acad Pr.

FOOD INDUSTRY AND TRADE
see also Food Prices; Food Supply; Snack Foods also individual processed food and processing industries, e.g. Cheese and Dairying; Meat Industry and Trade

Coons, Kenelm. Seafood Seasons-How to Plan Profitable Purchasing of Fish & Shellfish: A Guide to Natural Cycles & Regulatory Controls for the Seafood Buyer. Dore, Ian, ed. (Osprey Seafood Handbooks). 1983. 48.00 (ISBN 0-943738-02-4); pap. 40.00 (ISBN 0-943738-03-2). Osprey Bks.

Davis, Bernard. Food Commodities--Catering, Processing, Storing. 1978. pap. 16.50 (ISBN 0-434-90297-7, Pub. by Heinemann). David & Charles.

Earle, R. L. Unit Operations in Food Processing. 2nd ed. (Illus.). 220p. 1983. 40.00 (ISBN 0-08-025537-X); pap. 19.95 (ISBN 0-08-025536-1). Pergamon.

Food Processors Institute. Guide for Waste Management in the Food Processing Industry, 2 vols, Vol. 1. Katsuyama, Allen M., ed. Incl. Vol. II. Warrick, Louis F., ed. 555p. pap. text ed. 15.00 (ISBN 0-937774-01-4). LC 79-115086. 276p. 1979. pap. text ed. 50.00 (ISBN 0-937774-00-6). Food Processors.

Food Products & Drink Industries, Second Tripartite Technical Meeting, Geneva, 1978. Appropriate Technology for Employment Creation in the Food Processing & Drink Industries of Developing Countries: Report III. 88p. 1978. 8.55 (ISBN 92-2-101880-6, FAD/2/III). Intl Labour Office.

Gunstone, F. D. & Norris, F. D. Lipids in Foods: Chemistry, Biochemistry & Application Technology. 175p. 1983. 40.01 (ISBN 0-08-025499-3); pap. 18.01 (ISBN 0-08-025498-5). Pergamon.

King, C. D. What's That You're Eating? Food Label Language & What it Means to you. Grubb, Mary L & Grubb, John D., eds. LC 82-90187. (Illus.). 62p. 1982. pap. 3.95 (ISBN 0-9608862-0-6). C King.

MacFarlane. Automatic Control of Food Manufacturing Processes. Date not set. price not set (ISBN 0-85334-200-8). Elsevier.

Marks, Nolan. On the Spot Repair Manual for Commercial Food Equipment. (Illus.). 80p. 1982. pap. write for info. (ISBN 0-941712-01-X). INtl Pub Corp OH.

Miller, Duncan & Soranna, Morag. OECD Directory of Food Policy Institutes. new ed. 98p. 1982. pap. text ed. 29.95. Butterworth.

Miller, Richard K. Noise Control Solutions for the Food Industry. (Illus.). 110p. text ed. 45.00 (ISBN 0-89671-034-3). Southeast Acoustics.

--Noise Control Solutions for the Food Industry, Vol. II. (Illus.). 120p. 1981. pap. text ed. 45.00 (ISBN 0-89671-024-6). Southeast Acoustics.

Saguy. Applications of Computers in Food Research & Food Industry. (Food Science Ser.). 504p. 1983. price not set (ISBN 0-8247-1383-4). Dekker.

Wright, Becky A., ed. Food Industry Institute Proceedings April 18-21, 1982. 99p. (Orig.). 1982. pap. 10.00 (ISBN 0-89154-197-7). Intl Found Employ.

FOOD INSPECTION
see Food Adulteration and Inspection

FOOD OF ANIMALS
see Animals, Food Habits of

FOOD PLANTS
see Plants, Edible

FOOD POISONING

Mycotoxin Surveillance. (FAO Food & Nutrition Papers: No. 21). 68p. 1982. pap. 7.50 (ISBN 92-5-101180-X, F2306, FAO). Unipub.

FOOD PRESERVATION
see Food-Preservation

FOOD PRICES

Cinnamon, Pamela A. & Swanson, Marilyn A. Everything About Exchange Values for Foods. LC 81-53064. 1981. 3.50 (ISBN 0-89301-083-9). U Pr of Idaho.

FOOD PROCESSING
see Food Industry and Trade

FOOD PROCESSOR COOKERY

Food Processor Cook Book. pap. 5.95 (ISBN 0-686-43156-1). Meredith Corp.

Lefebvre, G. G. & Vahey, Esther J. Using Your Food Processor. (Audio Cassette Cooking School Library). (Illus., Orig.). 1982. pap. 12.95 (ISBN 0-910327-03-3). Cuisine Con.

Ramsay, Laura. Food Processor Cooking-Naturally. (Illus.). 176p. 1983. pap. 8.95 (ISBN 0-686-38406-7). Contemp Bks.

FOOD RELIEF

Harbert, Lloyd & Scandizzo, Pasquale L. Food Distribution & Nutrition Intervention: The Case of Chile. LC 82-8370. (World Bank Staff Working Papers: No. 512). (Orig.). 1982. pap. text ed. 5.00 (ISBN 0-8213-0001-6). World Bank.

Hutchinson, Robert. What One Christian Can Do About Hunger in America. LC 82-18199. xii, 115p. (Orig.). 1982. pap. 5.95 (ISBN 0-8190-0651-3, FC 145). Fides Claretian.

Miller, Duncan & Soranna, Morag, eds. Directory of Food Policy Institutes. Date not set. 29.95 (ISBN 0-686-37446-0). OECD.

Scandizzo, Pasguale L. & Swamy, Gurushri. Benefits & Costs of Food Distribution Policies: The India Case. LC 82-8543. (World Bank Staff Working Papers: No. 509). (Orig.). 1982. pap. 3.00 (ISBN 0-8213-0011-3). World Bank.

World Food Programme: Report of the Thirteenth Session of the United Nations-FAO Committee on Food Aid Policies & Programmes. 73p. 1982. pap. 7.50 (ISBN 92-5-101237-7, F2348, FAO). Unipub.

FOOD SANITATION
see Food Handling

FOOD SERVICE
Here are entered works on quantity preparation and service of food for outside the home. Works dealing solely with quantity food preparation are entered under Quantity Cookery.
see also Caterers and Catering; Quantity Cookery; Restaurants, Lunchrooms, Etc.

Davis, Bernard. Food Commodities--Catering, Processing, Storing. 1978. pap. 16.50 (ISBN 0-434-90297-7, Pub. by Heinemann). David & Charles.

Directory of Food & Nutrition Information Services & Resources. Date not set. price not set. Oryx Pr.

Gottlieb, Leon. Foodservice-Hospitality Advertising & Promotion. 363p. 1982. text ed. 18.50 (ISBN 0-672-97868-7); Tchr's Ed. 3.33 (ISBN 0-672-97869-5). Bobbs.

Minor, Lewis J. L. J. Minor Foodservice Standards Series: Nutritional Standards, Vol. 1. (Illus.). 1983. text ed. 20.00 (ISBN 0-87055-425-5). AVI.

--L. J. Minor Foodservice Standards Series: Sanitation, Safety, Environmental Standards, Vol. 2. (Illus.). 1983. text ed. 20.00 (ISBN 0-87055-428-X). AVI.

FOOD SERVICE-VOCATIONAL GUIDANCE

Morton, Alexander C. The Official Career Guide to Food Service & Hospitality Management. (Illus.). 128p. 1983. pap. 7.95 (ISBN 0-686-82173-4). Arco.

FOOD STAMP PLAN
see Food Relief

FOOD SUBSTITUTES

Business Communications Staff. New Diet, Meal Replacement & Substitute Foods. 1983. 1250.00 (ISBN 0-89336-353-7, GA-052). BCC.

FOOD SUPPLY
see also Famines; Food-Preservation; Food Industry and Trade; Meat Industry and Trade

Auge-Laribe, Michel & Pinot, Pierre. Agriculture & Food Supply in France During the War. (Economic & Social History of the World War Ser.). 1927. text ed. 75.00x (ISBN 0-686-83458-5). Elliots Bks.

McAlpin, Michelle B. Subject to Famine: Food Crisis & Economic Change in Western India, 1860-1920. LC 82-61376. 320p. 1983. 35.00x (ISBN 0-691-05385-5). Princeton U Pr.

Oswalt, Wendell H. An Anthropological Analysis of Food-Getting Technology. 328p. 1983. Repr. of 1976 ed. text ed. price not set (ISBN 0-89874-606-X). Krieger.

Ramachandran, L. Food Planning: Some Vital Aspects. 392p. 1982. 22.95x (ISBN 0-940500-68-X, Pub by Allied Pubs India). Asia Bk Corp.

The State of Food & Agriculture 1981. 177p. 1983. pap. 32.50 (ISBN 92-5-101201-6, F2266, FAO). Unipub.

Underwood, Barbara A., ed. Nutrition Intervention Strategies in National Development. 394p. 1983. price not set (ISBN 0-12-709080-0). Acad Pr.

Wright, Richard. American Hunger. LC 76-47248. 160p. 1983. pap. 4.76i (ISBN 0-06-090991-9, CN 991, CN). Har-Row.

FOOD TRADE
see Farm Produce-Marketing; Food Industry and Trade

FOOLS AND JESTERS

Goldsmith. Wise Fools in Shakespeare. 136p. 1982. 40.00x (ISBN 0-85323-263-6, Pub. by Liverpool Univ England). State Mutual Bk.

FOOT

Bryant, Ina. Foot Reflexology. LC 81-11016. 1981. pap. 4.95 (ISBN 0-89019-076-3). O'Sullivan Woodside.

Kaplan, Charles & Natale, Peter, eds. Paddings & Strappings of the Foot. LC 82-82871. (Illus.). 256p. 1982. pap. 31.00 (ISBN 0-87993-185-X). Futura Pub.

FOOT RACING
see Running

FOOT TRAILS
see Trails

FOOTBALL
see also Football Coaching; Rugby Football; Soccer

Benjamin, Don-Paul. Wait 'Til Next Year: The Football Fan's Handbook. (Illus.). 20p. (Orig.). 1982. pap. 2.00 (ISBN 0-932624-05-7). Elevation Pr.

Campbell, Jim. The Second Offical NFL Trivia Book. 1982. pap. 2.25 (ISBN 0-451-11789-1, AE1789, Sig). NAL.

Creative Services Division. The Official NFL Encyclopedia of Pro Football. 1982. 27.95 (ISBN 0-453-00431-8, H431). NAL.

Dickey, Glenn. America Has a Better Team: The Story of Bill Walsh & San Francisco's World Champion 49ers. rev. ed. (Illus.). 192p. 1982. 14.95 (ISBN 0-936602-66-X); pap. 9.95 (ISBN 0-936602-65-1). Harbor Pub CA.

Football Schedule 1982. 1982. 1.95 (ISBN 0-89204-095-5). Sporting News.

Great Moments in Football by An American Housewife. (Blank Books Ser.). 128p. 1982. cancelled (ISBN 0-939944-23-5). Marmac Pub.

Koppett, Leonard. Forty-Niner Fever! (Illus.). 256p. 1982. pap. 3.95 (ISBN 0-86576-044-6). W Kaufmann.

NFL, compiled by. The NFL Media Information Book 1983. (Illus.). 182p. 1983. pap. 7.95 (ISBN 0-89480-367-0). Workman Pub.

Wurman, Richard S., ed. Football-Access. (Access Sports Ser.). (Illus.). 1982. pap. 4.95 (ISBN 0-9604858-1-3). Access Pr.

FOOTBALL-DEFENSE

Roche, Charles. Football's Stunting Defenses. LC 82-6321. 181p. 1982. 14.95 (ISBN 0-13-324020-7, Parker). P-H.

FOOTBALL-HISTORY

Slattery, David. Washington Redskins: A Pictorial History. LC 77-15328. (Illus.). 168p. 1977. 14.95 (ISBN 0-686-84393-2). JCP Corp VA.

FOOTBALL-JUVENILE LITERATURE

Aaseng, Nate. Football: You Are the Coach. LC 82-269. (You Are the Coach Ser.). (Illus.). 104p. (gr. 4up). 1983. PLB 8.95g (ISBN 0-8225-1551-2). Lerner Pubns.

Hollander, Zander, ed. Strange but True Football Stories. LC 82-13237. (Random House Sports Library). (Illus.). 144p. (gr. 5-10). 1983. pap. 1.95 (ISBN 0-394-85632-5). Random.

FOOTBALL COACHING

Roche, Charles. Football's Stunting Defenses. LC 82-6321. 181p. 1982. 14.95 (ISBN 0-13-324020-7, Parker). P-H.

FOOTPATHS
see Trails

FOOTWEAR
see Boots and Shoes

FORAGE PLANTS
see also Cactus; Corn; Grasses; Legumes; Rape (Plant)

Forage Evaluation: Concepts & Techniques. 582p. 1981. 45.00 (ISBN 0-686-84866-7, CO 68, CSIRO). Unipub.

FORAMINIFERA

Catalogue of Index Foraminifera, 3 vols. (Illus.). 1967. Set. 75.00 (ISBN 0-686-84240-5). Am Mus Natl Hist.

Catalogue of Index Smaller Foraminifera, 3 vols. (Illus.). 1969. Set. 75.00 (ISBN 0-686-84241-3). Am Mus Natl Hist.

Murray, J. Atlas of British Recent Foraminiferids. 1972. 24.50 (ISBN 0-444-19594-7). Elsevier.

Tjalsma, R. C. & Lohmann, G. P. Paleocene-Eocene Bathyal & Abyssal Foraminifera from the Atlantic Basin. (Micropaleontology Special Publications Ser.: No. 4). 1982. 45.00 (ISBN 0-686-84256-1). Am Mus Natl Hist.

FORBIDDEN-COMBINATION CHECK
see Error-Correcting Codes (Information Theory)

FORCE AND ENERGY
see also Dynamics; High Pressure Research; Mass (Physics); Mechanics; Motion; Quantum Theory

Bryant, Raymond C. & McGorray, J. J. Managing Energy for Buildings: Mid-Atlantic Energy Conference Proceedings. LC 82-84596. 400p. 1983. text ed. 40.00 (ISBN 0-86587-109-4). Gov Insts.

Bryant, Raymond C. & McGorray, J. J., eds. Managing Energy for Industry: Mid-Atlantic Energy Conference Proceedings. LC 82-84596. (Illus.). 270p. 1983. 40.00 (ISBN 0-86587-108-6). Gov Insts.

Gibson, Duncan. Energy Graphics. (Illus.). 144p. 1983. 19.95 (ISBN 0-13-277624-3). P-H.

Gunther, Bernard. Energy Ecstasy & Your Seven Vital Shakras. 200p. (Orig.). 1983. pap. 9.95 (ISBN 0-87877-066-6). Newcastle Pub.

Sih, G. & Czoboly, E. Absorbed Specific Energy & or Strain Energy Density Criterion. 1982. lib. bdg. 65.00 (ISBN 90-247-2598-4, Pub. by Martinus Nijhoff Netherlands). Kluwer Boston.

FORCE AND ENERGY-JUVENILE LITERATURE

Adler, David. Wonders of Energy. LC 82-20042. (Question & Answer Bks.). (Illus.). 32p. (gr. 3-6). 1983. PLB 8.59 (ISBN 0-89375-884-1); pap. text ed. 1.95 (ISBN 0-89375-885-X). Troll Assocs.

FORCE PUMPS
see Pumping Machinery

FORD, GERALD, PRES. U. S., 1913-

Hartmann, R. T. Palace Politics: An Inside Account of the Ford Years. 1980. 15.95 (ISBN 0-07-026951-3). McGraw.

FORD AUTOMOBILE
see Automobiles-Types-Ford

FORD MOTOR COMPANY

Sheller, Roscoe. Me & the Model T. (Illus.). 1982. pap. 7.95 (ISBN 0-686-84255-3). Binford.

FORECASTING

Chambers, John C., et al. An Executive's Guide to Forecasting. 320p. 1983. Repr. of 1974 ed. text ed. price not set (ISBN 0-89874-585-3). Krieger.

Chaney, Earlyne C. Revelations of Things to Come. (Illus.). 156p. 1982. pap. 13.95 (ISBN 0-918936-12-8). Astara.

Curtis, R. K. Evolution or Extinction: The Choice Before Us-A Systems Approach to the Study of the Future. 420p. 1982. 50.00 (ISBN 0-08-027933-3); pap. 25.00 (ISBN 0-08-027932-5). Pergamon.

De Rougemont, D. The Future Is Our Concern. (Systems Science & World Order Library). 254p. 1983. 45.00 (ISBN 0-08-027395-5); pap. 16.00 (ISBN 0-08-027394-7). Pergamon.

Goodman, Nelson. Fact, Fiction & Forecast. 4th ed. 176p. 1983. text ed. 10.00x (ISBN 0-674-29070-4); pap. text ed. 4.95x (ISBN 0-674-29071-2). Harvard U Pr.

Hofstadter, Dan, tr. Nostradamus: The Future Foretold. (Illus.). 64p. 1983. 3.95 (ISBN 0-88088-451-7). Peter Pauper.

Roberts, H. V. Forecasting. Date not set. price not set (ISBN 0-07-053136-6). McGraw.

The World Restored Not Destroyed. 132p. 1982. 9.95 (ISBN 0-9608002-0-4). Quest Prods.

FORECASTING, BUSINESS
see Business Forecasting

FORECASTING, ECONOMIC
see Economic Forecasting

FORECASTING, TECHNOLOGICAL
see Technological Forecasting

FORECASTING THEORY
see Prediction Theory

FOREIGN ACCENT
see English Language-Pronunciation by Foreigners

FOREIGN AFFAIRS
see International Relations;
see subdivisions Foreign Relations under names of countries

FOREIGN AID PROGRAM
see Economic Assistance; Technical Assistance

FOREIGN ASSISTANCE
see Economic Assistance

FOREIGN AUTOMOBILES
see Automobiles, Foreign

FOREIGN COMMERCE
see Commerce

FOREIGN ECONOMIC RELATIONS
see International Economic Relations

FOREIGN EXCHANGE
see also Balance of Payments; Foreign Exchange Problem

Argy, Victor. Exchange-Rate Management in Theory & Practice. LC 82-12015. (Princeton Studies in International Finance: No. 50). 1982. pap. text ed. 4.50x (ISBN 0-88165-221-0). Princeton U Int Finan Econ.

Batchelor, Roy A. & Wood, Geoffrey E., eds. Exchange Rate Policy. LC 81-23262. 265p. 1982. 27.50x (ISBN 0-312-27389-4). St Martin.

Bell, Steven & Kettell, Brian. Foreign Exchange Market Handbook. 250p. 1982. 92.00x (ISBN 0-86010-385-4, Pub. by Graham & Trotman England). State Mutual Bk.

Bindon, Kathleen R. Inventories & Foreign Currency Translation Requirements. Farmer, Richard N., ed. LC 82-21729. (Research for Business Decisions Ser.). 1983. write for info. (ISBN 0-8357-1391-1). Univ Microfilms.

Coninx, Raymond G. Foreign Exchange Dealer's Handbook. LC 82-81900. 1982. 20.00x (ISBN 0-87551-350-6). Pick Pub.

Kettell, Brian & Bell, Steven. Foreign Exchange Handbook. LC 82-23053. (Illus.). 250p. 1983. lib. bdg. 39.95 (ISBN 0-89930-054-5, KFM/, Quorum). Greenwood.

Krueger, Anne O. Exchange Rate Determination. LC 82-14649. (Cambridge Surveys of Economic Literature Ser.). (Illus.). 240p. Date not set. price not set (ISBN 0-521-25304-7); pap. price not set (ISBN 0-521-27301-3). Cambridge U Pr.

Rabin, Alan A. & Yeager, Leland B. Monetary Approaches to the Balance of Payments & Exchange Rates. LC 82-15587. (Essays in International Finance Ser.: No. 148). 1982. pap. text ed. 2.50x (ISBN 0-88165-055-2). Princeton U Int Finan Econ.

Walmsley, Julian. The Foreign Exchange Handbook: A User's Guide. 425p. 1983. 39.95x (ISBN 0-471-86388-2, Pub. by Wiley-Interscience). Wiley.

Weisweiller, R. L. Introduction to Foreign Exchange. 172p. (Orig.). 1983. 17.50 (ISBN 0-85941-220-2); pap. 9.95 (ISBN 0-85941-234-2). Woodhead.

FOREIGN EXCHANGE-TABLES, ETC.
see Money-Tables, etc.

FOREIGN EXCHANGE PROBLEM

Wonnacott, Paul. U. S. Intervention in the Exchange Market for DM, 1977-80. (Princeton Studies in International Finance: No. 51). 1982. pap. text ed. 4.50x (ISBN 0-88165-222-9). Princeton U Int Finan Econ.

FOREIGN INVESTMENTS
see Investments, Foreign

FOREIGN LOANS
see Loans, Foreign

FOREIGN POLICY
see International Relations
FOREIGN POPULATION
see Emigration and Immigration
FOREIGN RELATIONS
see International Relations
FOREIGN TRADE
see Commerce
FOREIGN TRADE POLICY
see Commercial Policy
FOREIGN TRADE REGULATION
see also Commercial Treaties

Austrian Export Directory: Export-Adressbuch von Osterreich 1982/83. 1982/83 ed. LC 52-24185. 501p. (Orig., Eng., Fr., & Span.). 1982. pap. 45.00x (ISBN 0-8002-3043-4). Intl Pubns Serv.

Baron, David P., ed. The Export-Import Bank: An Economic Analysis. (Mathematical Economics, Econometrics & Economic Theory Monograph). Date not set. price not set (ISBN 0-12-079080-7). Acad Pr.

Hillman, Jordan J. The Export-Import Bank at Work: Promotional Financing in the Public Sector. LC 82-11204. (Illus.). 288p. 1982. lib. bdg. 35.00 (ISBN 0-89930-040-5, HIE/, Quorum). Greenwood.

Rosenthal, Douglas E. & Knighton, William M. National Laws & International Commerce: The Problem of Extraterritoriality. (Chatham House Papers Ser.: No. 17). 96p. (Orig.). 1982. pap. 10.00 (ISBN 0-7100-9338-1). Routledge & Kegan.

FOREIGNERS
see Aliens
FORENAMES
see Names, Personal
FORENSIC DENTISTRY
see Dental Jurisprudence
FORENSIC MEDICINE
see Medical Jurisprudence
FORENSIC ORATIONS

Re, Edward D. Breif Writing & Oral Argument. 5th Rev. ed. 484p. 1983. lib. bdg. 17.50 (ISBN 0-379-01050-X). Oceana.

FORENSIC PSYCHIATRY
Here are entered works on psychiatry as applied in courts of law. Works on the legal status of persons of unsound mind are entered under the heading Insanity-Jurisprudence.

Cook, Earleen H. The Insane or Mentally Impaired Defendant: A Selected Bibliography. (Public Administration Ser.). 57p. 1983. pap. 8.25 (ISBN 0-88066-355-3). Vance Biblios.

Freedman, Lawrence Z., intro. by. By Reason of Insanity: Essays on Psychiatry & the Law. 250p. 1983. PLB 24.95 (ISBN 0-8420-2203-1). Scholarly Res Inc.

Guy, William A. The Factors of the Unsound Mind. (Historical Foundations of Forensic Psychiatry & Psychology Ser.). xx, 232p. 1983. Repr. of 1881 ed. lib. bdg. 25.00 (ISBN 0-306-76186-6). Da Capo.

Ray, Isaac. A Treatise on the Medical Jurisprudence of Insanity. (Historical Foundations of Forensic Psychiatry & Psychology Ser.). xvi, 480p. 1983. Repr. of 1838 ed. lib. bdg. 45.00 (ISBN 0-306-76181-5). Da Capo.

Williams, Caleb. Observations on the Criminal Responsibility of the Insane. (Historical Foundations of Forensic Psychiatry & Psychology Ser.). 148p. 1983. Repr. of 1856 ed. lib. bdg. 19.50 (ISBN 0-306-76178-5). Da Capo.

Winslow, Forbes. The Plea of Insanity in Criminal Cases. (Historical Foundations of Forensic Psychiatry & Psychology Ser.). vii, 78p. 1983. Repr. of 1843 ed. lib. bdg. 17.50 (ISBN 0-306-76180-7). Da Capo.

FORENSIC PSYCHOLOGY
see Psychology, Forensic
FOREST ECOLOGY
see also Woody Plants

Edmonds, Robert L., ed. Analysis of Coniferous Forest Ecosystems in the Western United States. LC 80-26699. (US-IBP Synthesis Ser.: Vol. 14). 448p. 1982. 44.00 (ISBN 0-87933-382-0). Hutchinson Ross.

Puri & Meher. Indian Forest Ecology. 2nd. Ed. ed. 179.00x (ISBN 0-686-84457-2, Pub. by Oxford & I B H India). State Mutual Bk.

Sattoo, T. & Madgwick, H. I. Forest Biomass. 1982. 35.00 (ISBN 90-247-2710-3, Pub. by Martinus Nijhoff Netherlands). Kluwer Boston.

Zlotin, R. I. & Khodashova, K. S., eds. The Role of Animals in Biological Cycling of Forest-Steppe Ecosystems. Lewus, William & Grant, W. E., trs. from Russian. LC 80-12228. 240p. 1980. 22.50 (ISBN 0-87933-377-4). Hutchinson Ross.

FOREST ENTOMOLOGY
see Entomology
FOREST FIRES

Nao, T. Van. Forest Fire Prevention & Control. 1982. text ed. 39.50 (ISBN 90-247-3050-3, Pub. by Martinus Nijhoff). Kluwer Boston.

FOREST INDUSTRIES
see Wood-Using Industries
FOREST MANAGEMENT
see Forests and Forestry
FOREST PLANTING
see Forests and Forestry
FOREST PRODUCTS
see also Gums and Resins; Lumber Trade; Rubber; Timber; Wood; Wood-Pulp; Wood-Using Industries

Classification & Definitions of Forest Products. (FAO Forestry Paper: No. 32). 201p. 1982. pap. 18.50 (ISBN 92-5-001209-8, F2325, FAO). Unipub.

Estimated Production of Pulp, Paper & Paperboard in Certain Countries in 1981. 30p. 1982. pap. 7.50 (ISBN 0-686-84613-3, F2327, FAO). Unipub.

FOREST REPRODUCTION
see Forests and Forestry
FOREST RESERVES
see also Forests and Forestry; National Parks and Reserves; Wilderness Areas

Melius, Kenneth W. National Forest Campground Guide. LC 82-51299. (Illus.). 310p. 1983. pap. 8.95 (ISBN 0-9610130-0-1). Tensleep.

FORESTATION
see Forests and Forestry
FORESTS, NATIONAL
see Forest Reserves
FORESTS AND FORESTRY
see also Botany-Ecology; Flood Control; Hardwoods; Landscape Gardening; Lumber Trade; Lumbering; Pruning; Trees; Wood

Forest History Society. Encyclopedia of American Forest & Conservation History, 2 vols. Davis, Richard C., ed. 1983. lib. bdg. 150.00X (ISBN 0-02-919750-3). Macmillan.

Frome, Michael. The Forest Service. (Federal Departments, Agencies, & Systems). 300p. 1983. lib. bdg. 25.00 (ISBN 0-86531-177-3). Westview.

Jahn, G. Application of Vegetation Science to Forestry. 1982. 79.50 (ISBN 90-6193-193-2, Pub. by Junk Pubs Netherlands). KLuwer Boston.

Prakash, Ram & Khanna, L. S. Theory & Practice of Silvicultural Systems. 263p. 1979. text ed. 10.00 (ISBN 0-686-38950-6, Pub. by Intl Bk Dist). Intl Schol Bk Serv.

Purcell, L. E., ed. Forest Resource Management in the States. 112p. 1982. pap. 8.00 (ISBN 0-87292-028-3). Coun State Govts.

Rigby, G. R., intro. by. Expanding Horizons in Chemical Engineering. (Chemeca Ser.). 241p. (Orig.). 1979. pap. text ed. 54.00x (ISBN 0-85825-116-7, Pub. by Inst Engineering Australia). Renouf.

Rudman, Jack. Urban Forester. (Career Examination Ser.: C-2905). (Cloth bdg. avail. on request). pap. 12.00 (ISBN 0-8373-2905-1). Natl Learning.

Schwab, Judith L. Recreation as a Forest Product. (Public Administration Ser.: Bibliography P 1096). 57p. 1982. pap. 8.25 (ISBN 0-88066-286-7). Vance Biblios.

Smith, W. Ramsay, ed. Energy from Forest Biomass. LC 82-20745. (Symposium). Date not set. 27.50 (ISBN 0-686-42980-X). Acad Pr.

Young, R. A. Introduction to Forest Science. 554p. 1982. text ed. 26.50 (ISBN 0-471-06438-6). Wiley.

FORESTS AND FORESTRY-ECOLOGY
see Forest Ecology
FORESTS AND FORESTRY-VOCATIONAL GUIDANCE

Nyland, Ralph & Larson, Charles. Forestry & Its Career Opportunities. 4th ed. (Illus.). 400p. 1983. text ed. 28.95x (ISBN 0-07-056979-7). McGraw.

FORESTS AND FORESTRY-ASIA

Hamilton, Lawrence S., ed. Forest & Watershed Development & Conservation in Asia & the Pacific. (Special Studies in Natural Resources & Energy Management). 650p. 1982. lib. bdg. 25.00 (ISBN 0-86531-534-5). Westview.

FORESTS AND FORESTRY-INDIA

Puri & Meher. Indian Forest Ecology. 2nd. Ed. ed. 179.00x (ISBN 0-686-84457-2, Pub. by Oxford & I B H India). State Mutual Bk.

FORESTS AND FORESTRY-INDONESIA

Indonesian Forestry Abstracts Dutch Literature until about 1960. 657p. 1983. 105.25 (ISBN 90-220-0800-2, PDC257, Pudoc). Unipub.

FORESTS AND FORESTRY-NORTH AMERICA

Edmonds, Robert L., ed. Analysis of Coniferous Forest Ecosystems in the Western United States. LC 80-26699. (US-IBP Synthesis Ser.: Vol. 14). 448p. 1982. 44.00 (ISBN 0-87933-382-0). Hutchinson Ross.

FORESTS AND FORESTRY-TROPICS

The Pulping & Paper Making Potential of Tropical Hardwoods: Mixed Species from the Gogol Timber Area, Papua New Guinea, Vol. VI. 32p. 1979. 6.00 (ISBN 0-643-00339-8, CO64, CSIRO). Unipub.

FORGERY OF WORKS OF ART

Dutton, Denis. The Forger's Art: Forgery & the Philosophy of Art. LC 82-11029. (Illus.). 250p. 1983. 22.50 (ISBN 0-520-04341-3). U of Cal Pr.

FORGETFULNESS
see Memory
FORGIVENESS OF SIN
see also Penance

Du Plessis, David. Forgiveness: God Has No Grandsons. 1974. 0.95 (ISBN 0-88270-203-3). Bridge Pub.

Mackintosh, Carlos H. El Perdon de los Pecados. 2nd ed. Bennett, Gordon H., ed. Bautista, Sara, tr. from Eng. (La Serie Diamante). 36p. (Span.). 1982. pap. 0.85 (ISBN 0-942504-02-X). Overcomer Pr.

FORM (PHILOSOPHY)
see also Structuralism

Edwards, Lawrence. The Field of Form. 1982. pap. 19.95 (ISBN 0-903540-50-9). St George Bk Serv.

FORM IN BIOLOGY
see Morphology
FORM PSYCHOLOGY
see Gestalt Psychology
FORMAL GARDENS
see Gardens
FORMICIDAE
see Ants
FORMOSA
see Taiwan
FORMS (BUSINESS)
see Business-Forms, Blanks, etc.
FORMS (LAW)
Here are entered works on and collections of legal forms in general. Forms relating to special topics or branches of law are entered under the specific heading.
see also Contracts-Forms; Legal Composition

Wolcotts-Legal Forms. California Notary's Journal. 202p. 1982. 11.95 (ISBN 0-910531-00-5); pap. 7.95 (ISBN 0-910531-01-3). Wolcotts.

FORMS, QUADRATIC

Weil, A. Adeles & Algebraic Groups. (Progress in Mathematics Ser.: Vol. 23). 126p. 1982. text ed. 10.00x (ISBN 3-7643-3092-9). Birkhauser.

FORMULA TRANSLATION (COMPUTER PROGRAM LANGUAGE)
see FORTRAN (Computer Program Language)
FORMULARIES
see Medicine-Formulae, Receipts, Prescriptions
FORSTER, EDWARD MORGAN, 1879-1970

E. M. Forster: The Personal Voice. 1983. pap. 7.95 (ISBN 0-7100-9496-5). Routledge & Kegan.

Scott, P. J. E. M. Forster: Our Permanent Contemporary. (Critical Studies). (Illus.). 208p. 1983. text ed. 26.50x (ISBN 0-389-20368-8). B&N Imports.

FORSYTH, PETER TAYLOR, 1848-1921

Pitt, Clifford S. Church, Ministry & Sacraments: A Critical Evaluation of the Thought of Peter Taylor Forsyth. LC 82-24817. 360p. (Orig.). 1983. lib. bdg. 25.00 (ISBN 0-8191-3027-3); pap. text ed. 14.00 (ISBN 0-8191-3028-1). U Pr of Amer.

FORT DALLES
see Dalles, Fort
FORT LAUDERDALE

Tolf, Robert. Discover Fort Lauderdale's Top Twelve Restaurants. (Florida Keepsake Ser.: No. 2). (Illus.). 28p. 3.00 (ISBN 0-686-84230-8). Banyan Bks.

FORT LAUDERDALE, FLORIDA-HISTORY

Kirk, Cooper. William Lauderdale, General Andrew Jackson's Warrior. (Illus.). 300p. 1982. 14.95 (ISBN 0-686-84231-6). Banyan Bks.

FORTIFICATION
see also Castles
also subdivision Defenses under countries, e.g. Great Britain-Defenses; also names of specific forts, e.g. Fort Ticonderoga

Altshuler, Constance W. Starting with Defiance: Nineteenth Century Arizona Military Posts. (Historical Monograph: No. 7). (Illus.). 88p. 1982. 10.00 (ISBN 0-910037-19-1); pap. 6.00 (ISBN 0-910037-20-5). AZ Hist Soc.

Hogg, Ian. The History of Fortification. (Illus.). 256p. 1983. 32.50 (ISBN 0-312-37852-1). St Martin.

FORTRAN (COMPUTER PROGRAM LANGUAGE)

Brown, Gary D. FORTRAN to PL-I Dictionary: PL-I to FORTRAN Dictionary. LC 82-21283. 218p. 1983. Repr. of 1975 ed. lib. bdg. write for info. (ISBN 0-89874-587-X). Krieger.

Cassel & Swanson. FORTRAN Made Easy. text ed. 19.95 (ISBN 0-8359-2090-9). Reston.

Etter, D. M. Structured FORTRAN 77 for Engineers & Scientists. 1982. 19.95 (ISBN 0-8053-2520-4, 32520). Benjamin-Cummings.

Forsythe, Alexandra I., et al. Computer Science: Programming in FORTRAN IV with WATFOR-WATFIV. LC 74-96044. 210p. 1975. pap. 9.50x (ISBN 0-471-26685-X). Wiley.

Friedmann, J., et al. Fortran IV. 2nd ed. (Self Teaching Guide Ser.). 499p. 1980. pap. 12.95 (ISBN 0-471-07771-2). Wiley.

Holoien, Martin O. & Behforooz, Ali. Problem Solving & Structured Programming with FORTRAN 77. LC 82-24436. 560p. 1983. pap. text ed. 18.95 (ISBN 0-534-01275-2). Brooks-Cole.

Law, Victor J. ANSI FORTRAN 77: An Introduction to Software Design. 400p. 1983. pap. text ed. write for info (ISBN 0-697-08167-2); instr's manual avail. (ISBN 0-697-08175-3); wkbk. avail. (ISBN 0-697-08176-1). Wm C Brown.

McNitt, Lawrence. Invitation to FORTRAN for the TRS-80. (Illus.). 240p. 1983. pap. 15.00 (ISBN 0-89433-210-4). Petrocelli.

Metcalf, Michael. FORTRAM Optimization. (APIC Studies in Data Processing: Vol. 17). write for info. (ISBN 0-12-492480-8). Acad Pr.

Monro, Donald M. Fortran Seventy-Seven. 368p. 1982. pap. text ed. 19.95 (ISBN 0-7131-2794-5). E Arnold.

Page, Rex & Didday, Richard. FORTRAN Seventy-Seven for Humans. 2nd ed. (Illus.). 500p. 1983. pap. text ed. 14.95 (ISBN 0-314-69672-5). West Pub.

Perrott, Ronald & Allison, Donald. PASCAL for FORTRAN Programmers. 1983. text ed. p.n.s. (ISBN 0-914894-09-9). Computer Sci.

Rao, P. V. Computer Programming in Fortran & Other Languages. 1982. 3.00x (ISBN 0-07-096569-2). McGraw.

Rule, Wilfred P. FORTRAN Seventy-Seven: A Practical Approach. 448p. 1983. text ed. write for info. (ISBN 0-87150-390-5, 8030). Prindle.

Starkey, J. Denbigh & Ross, Rockford. Fundamental Programming: FORTRAN. 352p. 1982. pap. text ed. write for info. (ISBN 0-314-71812-5). West Pub.

FORTRAN (COMPUTER PROGRAM LANGUAGE)-PROGRAMMED INSTRUCTION

Spencer, Donald D. Visual Masters for Teaching FORTRAN Programming. 1978. 9.95x (ISBN 0-89218-035-8). Camelot Pub.

FORTS
see Fortification
FORTUNE
see also Chance; Probabilities; Success

Your Big Book of Luck & Fortune. (Illus.). 192p. 1983. pap. 2.95 (ISBN 0-668-05732-7, 5732). Arco.

FORTUNES
see Income; Wealth
FORUMS (DISCUSSION AND DEBATE)

Burgett, Gordon L. How To Set Up & Market Your Own Seminar or Workshop. (Illus.). 120p. 1983. 19.95 (ISBN 0-9605078-4-1). Successful Sem.

FOSSIL BOTANY
see Paleobotany
FOSSIL MAN
see also Australopithecines

Hrdlicka, Ales. The Most Ancient Skeletal Remains of Man. 2nd ed. Bd. with The Skeletal Remains of Early Man. Hrdlicka, Ales. 1930. LC 78-72697. 1916. 80.00 (ISBN 0-404-18268-2, -). AMS Pr.

Reichs, Kathleen J., ed. Hominid Origins: Inquiries Past & Present. LC 82-20161. (Illus.). 278p. (Orig.). 1983. lib. bdg. 22.50 (ISBN 0-8191-2864-3); pap. text ed. 11.75 (ISBN 0-8191-2865-1). U Pr of Amer.

FOSSILS
see Paleontology
FOSTER, STEPHEN COLLINS, 1826-1864

Howard, John Tasker. Stephen Foster, America's Throubadour. 445p. 1982. Repr. of 1943 ed. lib. bdg. 50.00 (ISBN 0-8495-2436-9). Arden Lib.

FOSTER CARE, INSTITUTIONAL
see Children-Institutional Care
FOSTER DAY CARE
see Day Care Centers
FOSTER HOME CARE
see also Adoption; Children-Institutional Care

Fitzgerald, John & Murcer, Bill. Building New Families: Through Adoption & Fostering. (The Practice of Social Work Ser.: No. 10). 44p. 1982. text ed. 25.00x (ISBN 0-631-13148-5, Pub. by Basil Blackwell England); pap. text ed. 9.95x (ISBN 0-631-13193-0, Pub. by Basil Blackwell England). Biblio Dist.

Pardeck, John T. The Forgotten Children: A Study of the Stability & Continuity of Foster Care. LC 82-20007. (Illus.). 116p. (Orig.). 1983. lib. bdg. 18.50 (ISBN 0-8191-2844-9); pap. text ed. 8.25 (ISBN 0-8191-2845-7). U Pr of Amer.

FOUNDATIONS
see also Concrete; Masonry; Piling (Civil Engineering); Soil Mechanics; Walls

Bowles, J. E. Foundation Analysis & Design. 2nd ed. 1977. text ed. 34.50 (ISBN 0-07-006750-3). McGraw.

The Foundation Directory: Supplement. 8th ed. 408p. (Orig.). 1982. pap. text ed. 20.00 (ISBN 0-87954-074-5). Foundation Ctr.

Hanna, Thomas H. Foundations in Tension: Ground Anchors. (Illus.). 700p. 1983. 54.95 (ISBN 0-07-026017-6). McGraw.

Myslivec, A. & Kysela, Z. Bearing Capacity of Building Foundations. (Developments in Geotechnical Engineering: Vol. 21). 1978. 53.25 (ISBN 0-444-99794-6). Elsevier.

Young, F. E., ed. Piles & Foundations. 328p. 1981. 90.00x (ISBN 0-7277-0118-5, Pub. by Telford England). State Mutual Bk.

FOUNDATIONS (ENDOWMENTS)
see Charitable Uses, Trusts and Foundations; Endowments
FOUNDING
see also Die Casting; Metal-Work; Pattern-Making; Type and Type-Founding

Harper, J. D. Small Scale Foundries for Developing Countries: A Guide to Process Selection. (Illus.). 66p. (Orig.). 1981. pap. 9.50x (ISBN 0-903031-78-7, Pub. by Intermediate Tech England). Intermediate Tech.

FOUNDRY PRACTICE
see Founding
FOURIER ANALYSIS
see also Fourier Transformations

Salem, Raphael & Carleson, Lennart. Algebraic Numbers & Fourier Analysis & Selected Problems on Exceptional Set. LC 82-20053. (Wadsworth Mathematics Ser.). 224p. Repr. 29.95 (ISBN 0-534-98049-X). Wadsworth Pub.

FOURIER TRANSFORMATIONS
see also Digital Filters (Mathematics)

Gaskill, Jack D. Linear Systems, Fourier Transforms & Optics. LC 78-1118. (Pure & Applied Optics Ser.). 1978. 39.95x (ISBN 0-471-29288-5, Pub. by Wiley-Interscience). Wiley.

Nussbaumer, H. Fast Fourier Transform & Convolution Algorithms. 2nd ed. (Springer Series in Information Sciences). (Illus.). 280p. 1982. pap. 28.00 (ISBN 0-686-82318-4). Springer-Verlag.

FOURTEENTH CENTURY

Cooke, Thomas D., ed. The Present State of Scholarship in Fourteen Century Literature. (Illus.). 304p. 1983. 23.80 (ISBN 0-8262-0379-5). U of MO Pr.

FOURTH DIMENSION

Here are entered only philosophical and imaginative works. Mathematical works are entered under the heading Hyperspace.

see also Space and Time

Henderson, Linda D. The Fourth Dimension & Non-Euclidean Geometry in Modern Art. LC 82-15076. (Illus.). 496p. 1983. 55.00x (ISBN 0-686-43212-6); pap. 16.50 (ISBN 0-691-10142-6). Princeton U Pr.

FOURTH OF JULY

Giblin, James C. Fireworks, Pinics, & Flags: The Story of the Fourth of July Symbols. (Illus.). 96p. (gr. 3-6). 1983. 10.50 (ISBN 0-89919-146-0, Clarion); pap. 3.95 (ISBN 0-89919-174-6). HM.

FOWLES, JOHN

McSweeney, Kerry. Four Contemporary Novelists: Angus Wilson, Brian Moore, John Fowles, V. S. Naipaul. 232p. 1983. 24.95 (ISBN 0-7735-0399-4). McGill-Queens U Pr.

FOWLING

see also Decoys (Hunting)

Harbour, Dave. Hunting the American Wild Turkey. LC 74-31449. (Illus.). 258p. 1974. 14.95 (ISBN 0-8117-0863-2). Stackpole.

FOWLS

see Poultry

FOX

see Foxes

FOXE, JOHN, 1516-1587

Wooden, Warren W. John Foxe. (English Authors Ser.). 176p. 1983. lib. bdg. 17.95 (ISBN 0-8057-6830-0, Twayne). G K Hall.

FOXES

Ahlstrom, Mark. The Foxes. Schroeder, Howard, ed. (Wildlife Habits & Habitat Ser.). (Illus.). 48p. (gr. 4-5). 1983. lib. bdg. 8.95 (ISBN 0-89686-220-8). Crestwood Hse.

FRACTIONS

Mock, Valerie E. Fractions Drill. (Learning Workbooks Mathematics). (gr. 3-5). pap. 1.50 (ISBN 0-8224-4188-8). Pitman.

FRACTURE MECHANICS

see also Materials-Fatigue

Broek, David. Elementary Engineering Fracture Mechanics. 1982. lib. bdg. 69.00 (ISBN 90-247-2580-1, Pub. by Martinus Nijhoff Netherlands); pap. 29.50 (ISBN 90-247-2656-5, Pub. by Martinus Nijhoff Netherlands). Kluwer Boston.

Chell, G. G., ed. Developments in Fracture Mechanics, Vols. 1 & 2. Vol. 1, 1979. 53.50 (ISBN 0-85334-858-8, Pub. by Applied Sci England); Vol. 2, 1981. 59.50 (ISBN 0-85334-973-8). Elsevier.

Hertzberg, Richard W. Deformation & Fracture Mechanics of Engineering Materials. 2d ed. 725p. 1983. 36.95 (ISBN 0-686-84628-1). Wiley.

Sih, G. C. & Francois, D., eds. Progress in Fracture Mechanics: Fracture Mechanics Research & Technological Activities of Nations Around the World. (International Series on Strength & Fracture of Materials). (Illus.). 96p. 1983. 19.95 (ISBN 0-08-028691-7). Pergamon.

FRACTURE OF SOLIDS

see Fracture Mechanics

FRACTURES

see also Bones; Surgery; X-Rays

also subdivision Fracture or Wounds and injuries under particular bones etc. e.g. Skull-Wounds and Injuries

Brooker, Andrew F. & Cooney, William P., 3rd. Prinicples of External Fixation. 300p. 1983. lib. bdg. price not set (ISBN 0-683-01065-4). Williams & Wilkins.

Difficult Fractures in Children. 1983. text ed. 39.95 (ISBN 0-407-02346-1). Butterworth.

FRAGONARD, JEAN HONORE, 1732-1806

Williams, Eunice. Drawings by Fragonard in North American Collections. LC 78-22017. (Illus.). pap. 5.00 (ISBN 0-89468-036-6). Natl Gallery Art.

FRAMES (STRUCTURES)

see Structural Frames

FRAMING OF PICTURES

see Picture Frames and Framing

FRANCE

see also names of cities, towns and geographic areas in France

Ardagh, John. France in the 1980s. 672p. 1983. pap. 7.95 (ISBN 0-14-022409-2, Pelican). Penguin.

FRANCE-BIOGRAPHY

Stendhal, Henry B. The Life of Henri Brulard. Phillips, Catherine A., tr. from Fr. 361p. 1982. Repr. of 1925 ed. lib. bdg. 40.00 (ISBN 0-89984-091-4). Century Bookbindery.

FRANCE-CHURCH HISTORY

Cheney, C. R. From Becket to Langton. 1956. 19.00 (ISBN 0-7190-0064-5). Manchester.

McManners, J. French Ecclesiastical Society under the Ancien Regime. 1960. 28.50 (ISBN 0-7190-0340-7). Manchester.

McManners, John. The French Revolution & the Church. LC 82-15532. x, 161p. 1982. Repr. of 1969 ed. lib. bdg. 22.50x (ISBN 0-313-23074-9, MCFR). Greenwood.

FRANCE-DESCRIPTION AND TRAVEL

De Roquette-Buisson, Odile. The Canal Du Midi. (Illus.). 1983. 29.95 (ISBN 0-500-24115-5). Thames Hudson.

Harper, Mike. Through France to the Med. 216p. 1982. 40.00x (ISBN 0-85614-034-1, Pub. by Gentry England). State Mutual Bk.

FRANCE-DESCRIPTION AND TRAVEL-GUIDEBOOKS

Binns, Richard. Hidden France. (Illus.). 160p. 1983. 8.95 (ISBN 0-89919-157-6). Ticknor & Fields.

Duo Publishing. French Farm & Holiday Guide. 1982. pap. 12.95. Bradt Ent.

French Riviera Travel Guide. (Berlitz Travel Guides). (Illus.). 1982. pap. 4.95 (ISBN 0-02-969220-2, Berlitz). Macmillan.

Harvard Student Agencies. Let's Go France. (Let's Go Ser.). (Illus.). 380p. 1983. pap. 7.95 (ISBN 0-312-48212-4). St Martin.

Loire Valley Travel Guide. (Berlitz Travel Guides). (Illus.). 1982. pap. 4.95 (ISBN 0-02-969310-1, Berlitz). Macmillan.

Lyall, Archibald. Companion Guide to the South of France. (Illus.). 272p. 1983. 15.95 (ISBN 0-13-154641-4); pap. 7.95 (ISBN 0-13-154633-3). P-H.

Michelin Green Guide: Chateaux de la Loire. (Green Guide Ser.). (Fr.). 1983. pap. write for info. (ISBN 2-06-003181-8). Michelin.

Michelin Green Guide: Pyrenees. (Green Guide Ser.). (Fr.). 1983. pap. write for info. (ISBN 2-06-003661-5). Michelin.

FRANCE-ECONOMIC CONDITIONS

Cohen, Gourevitch. France in the Troubled World Economy. 1982. text ed. 39.95 (ISBN 0-408-10787-1). Butterworth.

Institut national de la statistique et des etudes economiques. Annuaire Statistique de la France 1980: Statistical Yearbook of France 1980. 85th ed. LC 7-39039. (Illus.). 913p. (Fr.). 1980. 80.00x (ISBN 0-8002-3010-8). Intl Pubns Serv.

--Annuaire Statistique de la France 1981: Statistical Yearbook of France 1981. 86th ed. LC 7-39079. (Illus.). 862p. (Fr.). 1981. 80.00x (ISBN 0-8002-3011-6). Intl Pubns Serv.

Jennings, Robert M. & Trout, Andrew P. The Tontine: From the Reign of Louis XIV to the French Revolutionary Era. LC 82-81028. (S. S. Huebner Foundation Monograph Ser.). 96p. (Orig.). 1982. pap. 14.95 (ISBN 0-918930-12-X). Huebner Foun Insur.

FRANCE-ECONOMIC POLICY

Baum, Warren C. The French Economy & the State. LC 82-15539. xvi, 391p. 1982. lib. bdg. 39.95 (ISBN 0-313-23650-X, BAFE). Greenwood.

Estrin, Saul & Holmes, Peter. French Planning in Theory & Practice. 224p. 1983. text ed. 29.50x (ISBN 0-04-339028-5). Allen Unwin.

FRANCE-FOREIGN RELATIONS

Cohen, Gourevitch. France in the Troubled World Economy. 1982. text ed. 39.95 (ISBN 0-408-10787-1). Butterworth.

Echard, William E. Napoleon III & the Concert of Europe. LC 82-12660. 325p. 1983. text ed. 32.50x (ISBN 0-8071-1056-6). La State U Pr.

FRANCE-FOREIGN RELATIONS-ALGERIA

Sullivan, Antony. Robert Thomas Bugeaud, France & Algeria 1784-1849: Politics, Power & the Good Society. 1983. 24.50 (ISBN 0-208-01969-3, Archon Bks). Shoe String.

FRANCE-FOREIGN RELATIONS-GERMANY

Stevenson, D. French War Aims Against Germany, Nineteen Fourteen to Nineteen Nineteen. (Illus.). 320p. 1982. 49.00x (ISBN 0-19-822574-1). Oxford U Pr.

FRANCE-FOREIGN RELATIONS-UNITED STATES

Dougherty, Patricia. American Diplomats & the Franco-Prussian War: Perceptions from Paris & Berlin. LC 80-250000089. 42p. 1980. 2.50 (ISBN 0-934742-06-5, Inst Study Diplomacy). Geo U Sch For Serv.

Egan, Clifford L. Neither Peace nor War: Franco-American Relations, 1803 to 1812. LC 82-17272. (Illus.). 288p. 1983. text ed. 30.00 (ISBN 0-8071-1076-0). La State U Pr.

Munro, William B. Crusaders of New France. 1918. text ed. 8.50x (ISBN 0-686-83519-0). Elliots Bks.

Wrong, George M. Conquest of New France. 1918. text ed. 8.50x (ISBN 0-686-83510-7). Elliots Bks.

FRANCE-HISTORY

Best, Geoffrey. War & Society in Revolutionary Europe 1770-1870. LC 82-3261. 336p. 1982. 27.50x (ISBN 0-312-85551-6). St Martin.

De Bertier de Sauvigny, G. & Pinkney, David H. History of France. rev. & enl. ed. Friguglietti, James, tr. LC 82-20978. (Illus.). 350p. 1983. text ed. 28.50 (ISBN 0-88273-426-1); pap. 17.95 (ISBN 0-88273-425-3). Forum Pr Il.

James, Edward. The Origins of France: From Clovis to the Capetians, AD 500-1000. LC 82-10691. 288p. 1982. 25.00x (ISBN 0-312-58862-3). St Martin.

Vercel, Roger. Bertrand of Brittany: Biography of Messire du Guesclin. Saunders, M., tr. 1934. text ed. 39.50x (ISBN 0-686-83487-9). Elliots Bks.

FRANCE-HISTORY-MEDIEVAL PERIOD, 987-1515

Here are entered works on the medieval period as whole as well as those on any part of this period.

Bloch, Howard R. Etymologies & Genealogies: A Literary Anthropology of the French Middle Ages. LC 82-20036. 296p. 1983. lib. bdg. 29.00x (ISBN 0-226-05981-2). U of Chicago Pr.

Highfield, J. R. & Jeffs, Robin, eds. The Crown & Local Communities in England & France in the Fifteenth Century. 192p. 1981. text ed. 20.25x (ISBN 0-904387-67-4, 61065); pap. text ed. 11.25x (ISBN 0-904387-79-8, 61090). Humanities.

FRANCE-HISTORY-BOURBONS, 1589-1789

Here are entered works on the history of France from 1589 to 1789 as a whole as well as those on any portion of it. For books about individual kings, etc. see under the names of kings etc. e.g. Louis 12th King of France; Richelieu.

Necker, Jacques M. The Famous Financial Statement Submitted by M. Necker to Louis XVI of France in 1781 on the Conditions of the Country Just Prior to the French Revolution. (The Most Meaningful Classics in World Culture Ser.). 105p. 1983. Repr. of 1781 ed. 117.00 (ISBN 0-89901-101-2). Found Class Reprints.

FRANCE-HISTORY-17TH CENTURY

see France-History-Bourbons, 1589-1789

FRANCE-HISTORY-1789-1815

Glover, Michael. The Napoleonic Wars: An Illustrated History 1792-1815. (Illus.). 240p. 1982. pap. 14.95 (ISBN 0-88254-710-0). Hippocrene Bks.

FRANCE-HISTORY-REVOLUTION, 1789-1799

Burke, Edward. Reflections on Revolution in France. 1982. pap. 3.50 (ISBN 0-14-043204-3). Penguin.

Fox, Charles J. Speeches During the French Revolution. 415p. 1982. Repr. of 1924 ed. lib. bdg. 20.00 (ISBN 0-89984-210-0). Century Bookbindery.

Freyer, Grattan, ed. Bishop Stock's "Narrative" of the Year of the French: 1798. LC 82-71112. (Illus.). 118p. 1982. 9.00 (ISBN 0-906462-07-X, Pub. by Irish Humanities Ireland); pap. 5.00 (ISBN 0-906462-08-8). Dufour.

Hazen, Charles D. The French Revolution & Napoleon. 385p. 1982. Repr. of 1917 ed. lib. bdg. 50.00 (ISBN 0-89987-390-1). Darby Bks.

McManners, John. The French Revolution & the Church. LC 82-15532. x, 161p. 1982. Repr. of 1969 ed. lib. bdg. 22.50x (ISBN 0-313-23074-9, MCFR). Greenwood.

Manceron, Claude. The French Revolution IV: Toward the Brink. LC 82-47836. 1983. 20.00 (ISBN 0-394-51533-1). Knopf.

--Toward the Brink: The French Revolution Vol. 4. LC 82-47836. (Illus.). 480p. 1983. 20.00 (ISBN 0-394-51533-1). Knopf.

FRANCE-HISTORY-REVOLUTION, 1789-1799-CAUSES AND CHARACTER

Hampson, Norman. Will & Circumstance: Montesquieu, Rousseau, & the French Revolution. LC 82-40455. 208p. 1983. 17.50x (ISBN 0-8061-1843-1). U of Okla Pr.

FRANCE-HISTORY-REVOLUTION, 1789-1799-PHILOSOPHY

see France-History-Revolution, 1789-1799-Causes and Character

FRANCE-HISTORY-REVOLUTION, 1789-1799-PICTORIAL WORKS

Paulson, Ronald. Representations of Revolution, 1789-1820. LC 82-13458. (Illus.). 416p. 1983. text ed. 29.95x (ISBN 0-300-02864-4). Yale U Pr.

FRANCE-HISTORY-FRANCO-GERMAN WAR, 1870-1871

see Franco-German War, 1870-1871

FRANCE-HISTORY-THIRD REPUBLIC, 1870-1940

Lissagaray, P. O. History of the Commune of 1871. Aveling, Eleanor M., tr. LC 82-73427. 500p. Repr. of 1898 ed. lib. bdg. 37.50x (ISBN 0-88116-007-5). Brenner Bks.

FRANCE-HISTORY-GERMAN OCCUPATION, 1940-1945

Cobb, Richard. French & Germans, Germans & French: A Personal Interpretation of France under Two Occupations; 1914-1918, 1940-1944. LC 82-40472. (Tauber Institute Ser.: No. 2). 208p. 1983. 14.00 (ISBN 0-87451-225-5). U Pr of New Eng.

FRANCE-HISTORY-1945-

Ardagh, John. France in the 1980's. 720p. 1983. 37.50 (ISBN 0-436-01747-4, Pub. by Secker & Warburg). David & Charles.

FRANCE-HISTORY, MILITARY

Parker, Harold T. Three Napoleonic Battles. (Illus.). 280p. 1983. pap. 9.95 (ISBN 0-8223-0547-X). Duke.

Rogers, H. C. Napoleon's Army. (Illus.). 192p. 1982. pap. 8.95 (ISBN 0-88254-709-7). Hippocrene Bks.

FRANCE-INTELLECTUAL LIFE

Berstein, Samuel. French Political & Intellectual History. 224p. 1983. pap. 24.95 (ISBN 0-87855-938-8). Transaction Bks.

Hansen, Eric C. Disaffection & Decadence: A Crisis in French Intellectual Thought 1848-1898. LC 82-17326. 304p. (Orig.). 1983. lib. bdg. 22.50 (ISBN 0-8191-2821-X); pap. text ed. 12.25 (ISBN 0-8191-2822-8). U Pr of Amer.

FRANCE-KINGS AND RULERS

The French Kings. (Treasures of the World Ser.). 1982. lib. bdg. 26.60 (ISBN 0-686-42796-3, Pub. by Stonehenge). Silver.

FRANCE-LAWS, STATUTES, ETC.

Boutmy, Emile. Studies in Constitutional Law: France-England-United States. 2nd ed. Dicey, E. M., tr. xiv, 183p. 1982. Repr. of 1891 ed. lib. bdg. 22.50x (ISBN 0-8377-0332-8). Rothman.

FRANCE-POLITICS AND GOVERNMENT

Berstein, Samuel. French Political & Intellectual History. 224p. 1983. pap. 24.95 (ISBN 0-87855-938-8). Transaction Bks.

Cerny, Philip G., ed. Social Movements & Protest in France. 270p. 1982. pap. 12.00 (ISBN 0-86187-214-2). F Pinter Pubs.

Lloyd, Howell. The State, France, & the Sixteenth Century. (Early Modern Europe Today Ser.). 256p. 1983. text ed. 25.00x (ISBN 0-04-940066-5). Allen Unwin.

FRANCE-POLITICS AND GOVERNMENT-1958-

Kuisel, Richard F. Capitalism & the State in Modern France: Renovation & Economic Management in the Twentieth Century. LC 81-616. (Cambridge Paperback Library Ser.). 344p. Date not set. pap. 14.95 (ISBN 0-521-27378-1). Cambridge U Pr.

Nugent, Neill & Lowe, David. The Left in France. 190p. 1982. 50.00x (ISBN 0-333-24135-5, Pub. by Macmillan England). State Mutual Bk.

Wilson, F. French Political Parties under the Fifth Republic. 256p. 1982. 26.95 (ISBN 0-03-062046-5). Praeger.

FRANCE-RELIGION

see France-Church History

FRANCE-SOCIAL CONDITIONS

Hantrais, L. Contemporary French Society. 1982. 50.00x (ISBN 0-333-28062-8, Pub. by Macmillan England). State Mutual Bk.

FRANCE-SOCIAL LIFE AND CUSTOMS

Hantrais, L. Contemporary French Society. 1982. 50.00x (ISBN 0-333-28062-8, Pub. by Macmillan England). State Mutual Bk.

FRANCESCO D'ASSISI, SAINT, 1182-1226

Works of the Seraphic Father St. Francis of Assisi: Translated by a Religious of the Order. 269p. 1982. Repr. of 1890 ed. lib. bdg. 40.00 (ISBN 0-89984-015-9). Century Bookbindery.

FRANCESCO D'ASSISI, SAINT, 1182-1226-JUVENILE LITERATURE

Ross, Elizabeth & Ross, Gerald. How St. Francis Tamed the Wolf. (Illus.). 32p. (ps). 1983. bds. 8.95 (ISBN 0-370-30506-X, Pub by The Bodley Head). Merrimack Bk Serv.

FRANCHISE

see Elections; Suffrage

FRANCHISES (RETAIL TRADE)

Coltman, Michael M. Franchising in the U.S. Pros & Cons. 148p. 1982. pap. text ed. 5.95 (ISBN 0-88908-909-4). Self Counsel Pr.

FRANCHISES, TAXATION OF

see Corporations-Taxation

FRANCIS OF ASSISI, SAINT

see Francesco D'Assisi, Saint, 1182-1226

FRANCIS OF SALES

see Francois De Sales, Saint, Bishop of Geneva, 1567-1622

FRANCISCANS

O'Neill, Daniel. Troubadour for the Lord: The Story of John Michael Talbot. 192p. 1983. 9.95 (ISBN 0-8245-0567-0). Crossroad NY.

FRANCO-GERMAN WAR, 1870-1871

see also Paris-History

Dougherty, Patricia. American Diplomats & the Franco-Prussian War: Perceptions from Paris & Berlin. LC 80-250000089. 42p. 1980. 2.50 (ISBN 0-934742-06-5, Inst Study Diplomacy). Geo U Sch For Serv.

FRANCO-PROVENCAL DIALECTS

Esperet, Eric. Langage et Origine Sociale Des Eleves. 2nd ed. 281p. (Fr.). 1982. write for info. (ISBN 3-261-04754-2). P Lang Pubs.

FRANCO-PRUSSIAN WAR, 1870-1871

see Franco-German War, 1870-1871

FRANCOIS DE SALES, SAINT, BISHOP OF GENEVA, 1567-1622

Bregy, Katherine. The Story of Saint Francis de Sales: Patron of Catholic Writers. 108p. 1982. Repr. of 1958 ed. lib. bdg. 35.00 (ISBN 0-686-81682-X). Century Bookbindery.

FRANKFURTER, FELIX, 1882-1965

Murphy, Bruce A. The Brandeis-Frankfurter Connection: The Secret Political Activities of Two Supreme Court Justices. LC 82-45546. 496p. 1983. pap. 12.95 (ISBN 0-385-18374-7, Anch). Doubleday.

FRANKLIN, BENJAMIN, 1706-1790

Clark, Ronald W. Benjamin Franklin: A Biography. LC 82-40115. (Illus.). 480p. 1983. 22.95 (ISBN 0-394-50222-1). Random.

Franklin, Benjamin. The Papers of Benjamin Franklin, Vol. 23: October Twenty-Seventh, Seventeen Seventy-Six, Through April Thirtieth, Seventeen Seventy-Seven. Willcox, William B. & Arnold, Douglas M., eds. LC 59-12697. 752p. 1983. text ed. 45.00x (ISBN 0-300-02897-0). Yale U Pr.

James, Marquis. They Had Their Hour: Benjamin Franklin, Thomas Jefferson. 324p. 1982. Repr. of 1926 ed. lib. bdg. 40.00 (ISBN 0-8495-2802-X). Arden Lib.

Randall, Willard. A Little Revenge: Benjamin Franklin & His Son. 1983. 18.00i (ISBN 0-316-73364-4). Little.

FRANKLIN, BENJAMIN, 1706-1790–BIBLIOGRAPHY

Buxbaum, Melvin H. Benjamin Franklin, 1721-1906: A Reference Guide. 334p. 1983. 35.00 (ISBN 0-8161-7985-9, Hall Reference). G K Hall.

FRANKLIN, BENJAMIN, 1706-1790–JUVENILE LITERATURE

Stevens, Bryna. Ben Franklin's Glass Harmonica. LC 82-9715. (Carolrhoda On My Own Bks). (Illus.). 48p. (gr. 1-4). 1983. PLB 6.95g (ISBN 0-87614-202-1). Carolrhoda Bks.

FRATERNAL BENEFIT SOCIETIES

see Friendly Societies

FRATERNAL ORGANIZATIONS

see Friendly Societies

FRAUD

McClintick, David. Stealing from the Rich: The Story of the Swindle of the Century. 348p. 1983. pap. 6.95 (ISBN 0-688-01967-6). Quill NY.

FREAKS

see Monsters

FREDERICK, THE GREAT, KING OF PRUSSIA

see Friedrich 2nd, Der Grosse, King of Prussia, 1712-1786

FREDHOLM'S EQUATION

see Integral Equations

FREE AGENCY

see Free Will and Determinism

FREE COINAGE

see Currency Question; Silver Question

FREE DIVING

see Skin Diving

FREE ENTERPRISE

see Laissez-Faire

FREE MATERIAL

Hendrickson, Marilyn & Hendrickson, Robert. Two Thousand & One Free Things for the Garden. 256p. 1983. 16.95 (ISBN 0-312-82746-6); pap. 7.95 (ISBN 0-312-82747-4). St Martin.

FREE SPEECH

see Liberty of Speech

FREE WILL AND DETERMINISM

see also Decision-Making (Ethics); Freedom (Theology); God-Will; Responsibility

Powell, Ralph A. Freely Chosen Reality. LC 82-21943. 194p. (Orig.). 1983. lib. bdg. 21.50 (ISBN 0-8191-2924-0); pap. text ed. 10.25 (ISBN 0-8191-2925-9). U Pr of Amer.

Watson, Gary. Free Will. 200p. 1982. pap. 7.95 (ISBN 0-19-875054-4). Oxford U Pr.

FREEBOOTERS

see Pirates

FREEDOM

see Liberty; Slavery

FREEDOM (THEOLOGY)

Shaw, Graham. The Cost of Authority: Manipulation & Freedom in the New Testament. LC 82-48545. 320p. 1983. pap. 16.95 (ISBN 0-8006-1707-X). Fortress.

FREEDOM OF DECISION (ETHICS)

see Decision-Making (Ethics)

FREEDOM OF INFORMATION

see also Government and the Press; Government Information; Liberty of Speech; Liberty of the Press; Moving-Pictures-Censorship; Radio Broadcasting

Adler, Allan & Halperin, Morton H., eds. The Litigation Under the Federal Freedom of Information Act & Privacy Act, 1983 Edition. LC 82-72706. 350p. 1982. pap. 30.00 (ISBN 0-86566-025-5). Ctr Natl Security.

Hendricks, Evan. Former Secrets: Government Records Made Public Through the Freedom of Information Act. Shaker, Peggy, ed. 204p. 1982. pap. 15.00 (ISBN 0-910175-01-2). Campaign Political.

FREEDOM OF RELIGION

see Religious Liberty

FREEDOM OF SPEECH

see Liberty of Speech

FREEDOM OF THE PRESS

see Liberty of the Press

FREEDOM OF THE WILL

see Free Will and Determinism

FREEDOM OF WORSHIP

see Religious Liberty

FREEHOLD

see Real Property

FREEMASONS

Bede, Elbert. Five Fifteen-Minute Talks. 1981. Repr. of 1972 ed. 4.50 (ISBN 0-686-43321-1). Macoy Pub.

--Three-Five-Seven Minute Talks on Freemasonry. 1981. Repr. of 1978 ed. 4.00 (ISBN 0-686-43320-3). Macoy Pub.

Freemasonry-Humanum Genus. 32p. pap. 0.50 (ISBN 0-686-81638-2). TAN Bks Pubs.

Hilburn, May S. Golden Tributes: Fraternal Ceremonies. 1982. Repr. of 1977 ed. text ed. 8.75 (ISBN 0-686-43323-8). Macoy Pub.

Landon, H. C. Mozart & the Masons: New Light Shed on the Lodge "Crowned Hope". (Illus.). 1983. 10.95 (ISBN 0-500-55014-X). Thames Hudson.

Reid, Elmer T. Practical Guide for Royal Arch Chapter Officers & Companions. (Illus.). 1980. Repr. of 1970 ed. 3.95 (ISBN 0-686-43318-1). Macoy Pub.

Roberts, Allen E. House Undivided: The Story of Freemasonry & the Civil War. 1982. Repr. of 1976 ed. 12.50 (ISBN 0-686-43324-6). Macoy Pub.

Steinmetz, George H. Freemasonry: Its Hidden Meaning. 1982. Repr. of 1976 ed. 9.50 (ISBN 0-686-43322-X). Macoy Pub.

Wathen, James F. Is the Order of St. John Masonic? 84p. 1973. pap. 3.50 (ISBN 0-686-81626-9). TAN Bks Pubs.

FREEMASONS–HISTORY

Landon, H. C. Mozart & the Masons: New Light Shed on the Lodge "Crowned Hope". (Illus.). 1983. 10.95 (ISBN 0-500-55014-X). Thames Hudson.

FREEMASONS–NEGRO

Mason, Joseph & Cox, Andrew. Great Black Men of Masonry: Qualitative Black Achievers Who Were Freemasons. 211p. 1982. 15.00 (ISBN 0-686-82377-X); pap. 8.00 (ISBN 0-686-82378-8). Blue Diamond.

FREEWAYS

see Express Highways

FREEZING

see Refrigeration and Refrigerating Machinery

FREEZING OF FOOD

see Food, Frozen

FREIGHT AND FREIGHTAGE

see also Railroads–Freight

Clark, Merrian E., ed. Ford's Freighter Travel Guide: Summer 1983. 61st ed. LC 54-3845. (Illus.). 144p. 1983. pap. 6.95 (ISBN 0-916486-70-2). M Clark.

Finaly, Patrick, ed. Jane's Freight Containers, 1982. (Jane's Yearbooks). (Illus.). 640p. 1982. 140.00 (ISBN 0-86720-613-6). Sci Bks Intl.

Moffat, Bruce. Forty Feet Below: The Story of Chicago's Freight Tunnels. Walker, Jim, ed. (Special Ser.: No. 82). (Illus.). 84p. 1982. 9.95 (ISBN 0-916374-54-8). Interurban.

Official Freight Forwarders Directory 1982: Offizielles Spediteur Adressbuch - Annuaire Officiel des Transitaires. 950p. 1981. pap. text ed. 67.50x (ISBN 3-87154-161-3). Intl Pubns Serv.

Stevenson, Arthur J. The New York-Newark Air Freight System. LC 82-160111. (Research Papers: Nos. 199-200). (Illus.). 440p. 1982. pap. 16.00x (ISBN 0-89065-106-X). U Chicago Dept Geog.

FREIGHT HANDLING

see Freight and Freightage; Railroads–Freight

FREIGHT PLANES

see Transport Planes

FREIGHT RATES

see Freight and Freightage

FREIGHTERS

Kane, Robert B. & Kane, Barbara W. Frieghter Voyaging. LC 82-51070. (Illus.). 120p. (Orig.). 1982. pap. 7.95 (ISBN 0-910711-00-3). Voyaging Pr.

FRENCH ART

see Art, French

FRENCH AUTHORS

see Authors, French

FRENCH DRAMA–HISTORY AND CRITICISM

Francois, Carlo. Raison et Deraison dans le Theatre de Pierre Corneille. (Fr.). 15.00 (ISBN 0-917786-17-3). French Lit.

Lyons, John D. A Theatre of Disguise: Studies in French Baroque Drama (1630-1660) 14.00 (ISBN 0-917786-25-4). French Lit.

White, Kenneth S. Einstein & Modern French Drama: An Analogy. LC 82-21789. 132p. (Orig.). 1983. lib. bdg. 17.75 (ISBN 0-8191-2942-9); pap. text ed. 7.75 (ISBN 0-8191-2943-7). U Pr of Amer.

FRENCH DRAMA–TRANSLATIONS INTO ENGLISH

Mandel, Oscar, tr. from Fr. Five Comedies of Medieval France. LC 82-13499. 158p. 1982. pap. text ed. 8.00 (ISBN 0-8191-2668-3). U Pr of Amer.

FRENCH DRAWINGS

see Drawings, French

FRENCH ESSAYS

Joubert, Joseph. The Notebooks of Joseph Joubert: A Selection. Auster, Paul, ed. & tr. from Fr. LC 82-73711. 176p. 1983. pap. 13.50 (ISBN 0-86547-108-8). N Point Pr.

Yale French Studies. Montaigne: Essays in Reading, No. 64. Defaux, Gerard, ed. (Yale French Studies). 264p. (Orig.). 1983. pap. text ed. 10.95x (ISBN 0-300-02977-2). Yale U Pr.

FRENCH FARCES–HISTORY AND CRITICISM

Babcock, Arthur E. Portraits of Artists: Reflexivity in Gidean Fiction, 1902-1936. 16.00 (ISBN 0-917786-26-2). French Lit.

FRENCH FICTION–HISTORY AND CRITICISM

Bond, David. The Fiction of Andre Pieyre de Mandiargues. LC 82-5894. 176p. 1982. text ed. 22.00x (ISBN 0-8156-2265-1); pap. text ed. 12.95x (ISBN 0-8156-2283-X). Syracuse U Pr.

Flannigan, Arthur. Les Desordres De L'Amour: Madame De Villedieu: A Critical Edition. LC 82-16138. (Illus.). 130p. 1983. lib. bdg. 19.00 (ISBN 0-8191-2730-2); pap. text ed. 8.25 (ISBN 0-8191-2731-0). U Pr of Amer.

--Me De Villedieu's Les Desordres Del L'amour: History, Literature & the Nouvelle Historique. LC 81-43835. 206p. 1983. lib. bdg. 22.50 (ISBN 0-8191-2696-9); pap. text ed. 10.75 (ISBN 0-8191-2697-7). U Pr of Amer.

FRENCH IN FOREIGN COUNTRIES

Parker, James H. Ethnic Identity: The Case of the French Americans. LC 82-23718. (Illus.). 80p. (Orig.). 1983. lib. bdg. 16.50 (ISBN 0-8191-2981-X); pap. text ed. 6.75 (ISBN 0-8191-2982-8). U Pr of Amer.

FRENCH LANGUAGE

Benamou, Michel & Carduner, Jean. Le Moulin a paroles. 2nd ed. LC 71-126958. (Illus.). 336p. (Fr.). 1975. pap. text ed. 11.95x (ISBN 0-471-06450-5). Wiley.

Dietiker, Simone R. En Bonne Forme. 3rd ed. 416p. 1983. pap. 15.95 (ISBN 0-669-05255-8). Heath.

Schorr, Natalie G. En Revue: Le Francais Par le Journalisme. 272p. 1983. pap. 9.95 (ISBN 0-686-82409-1). Heath.

FRENCH LANGUAGE–ABBREVIATIONS

see Abbreviations

FRENCH LANGUAGE–COMPOSITION AND EXERCISES

Benamou, Michel & Carduner, Jean. Le Moulin a paroles. 2nd ed. LC 71-126958. (Illus.). 336p. (Fr.). 1975. pap. text ed. 11.95x (ISBN 0-471-06450-5). Wiley.

McArthur, D. G. Les Constructions Verbales du Francais Contemporain. 1971. 12.00 (ISBN 0-7190-1250-3). Manchester.

FRENCH LANGUAGE–CONVERSATION AND PHRASE BOOKS

see also French Language–Self Instruction

Berlitz Editors. French for Spanish Travellers. 1977. pap. 4.95 (ISBN 0-02-966610-4, Berlitz). Macmillan.

--French for Travel Cassettepack. 1983. 14.95 (ISBN 0-02-962190-9, Berlitz); cassette incl. Macmillan.

Hart. Speedy French: To Get You There & Back. (Speedy Language Ser.). 24p. (Orig., Fr.). 1976. pap. 1.75 (ISBN 0-9602838-1-1). Baja Bks.

Lexus. The French Travelmate. LC 82-83997. 128p. 1983. pap. 1.95 (ISBN 0-307-46602-7, Golden Pr). Western Pub.

Rooks, George. Conversations sans Fin. 136p. 1983. pap. text ed. 7.95 (ISBN 0-88377-278-7). Newbury Hse.

Traveler's French. (EH Ser.). (Fr.). 1980. pap. 17.95 (ISBN 0-686-37987-X, 610). B&N NY.

FRENCH LANGUAGE–DIALECTS

Yale French Studies. The Language of Difference: Writing in Quebec(ois, No. 65. Sarkonak, Ralph, ed. (Yale French Studies). 1983. pap. text ed. 10.95x (ISBN 0-300-03025-8). Yale U Pr.

FRENCH LANGUAGE–DICTIONARIES

Armstrong, Virginia W. Our Science Book. Bodle, Marie, tr. from Fr. (Illus.). 27p. (gr. 2-5). 1982. pap. 6.00x (ISBN 2-88089-001-2). A Robinson.

Dictionnaire Vidal, 1982. 58th ed. 1168p. (Fr.). 1982. 75.00x (ISBN 2-85091-058-9). Intl Pubns Serv.

Paulus, Andre. Civil Engineering in French. 192p. 1982. 90.00x (ISBN 0-7277-0138-X, Pub. by Telford England). State Mutual Bk.

FRENCH LANGUAGE–EXAMINATIONS, QUESTIONS, ETC.

Foreign Service Institute. French & Spanish Testing Kit. 140p. Date not set. with 8 cassettes 95.00x (ISBN 0-88432-060-X, X100). J Norton Pubs.

Rudman, Jack. Foreign Language: French. (Regents External Degree Ser.: REDP-27). 17.95 (ISBN 0-8373-5677-6); pap. 9.95 (ISBN 0-8373-5627-X). Natl Learning.

FRENCH LANGUAGE–GLOSSARIES, VOCABULARIES, ETC.

Schonberg, James. The Comparative Trilby Glossary, French-English. 60p. 1983. Repr. of 1895 ed. lib. bdg. 30.00 (ISBN 0-89984-614-9). Century Bookbindery.

FRENCH LANGUAGE–GRAMMAR

Benamou, Michel & Carduner, Jean. Le Moulin a paroles. 2nd ed. LC 71-126958. (Illus.). 336p. (Fr.). 1975. pap. text ed. 11.95x (ISBN 0-471-06450-5). Wiley.

FRENCH LANGUAGE–MORPHOLOGY

Andereggen, Anton. Etude Philologique du Jugement Dernier (Lo Jutgamen General), Drame Provencal du XVe Siecle. Williman, Joseph P., ed. LC 82-80909. 386p. 1983. lib. bdg. 40.00 (ISBN 0-938942-02-6). Pacific Gallery.

FRENCH LANGUAGE–PHONETICS

Andereggen, Anton. Etude Philologique du Jugement Dernier (Lo Jutgamen General), Drame Provencal du XVe Siecle. Williman, Joseph P., ed. LC 82-80909. 386p. 1983. lib. bdg. 40.00 (ISBN 0-938942-02-6). Pacific Gallery.

FRENCH LANGUAGE–SELF INSTRUCTION

see also French Language–Conversation and Phrase Books

Berlitz French for Your Trip. 192p. 1982. 8.95 (ISBN 0-02-965160-3, Berlitz). Macmillan.

Kendris, Christopher. French the Easy Way, Bk. 1. (Easy Way Ser.). 160p. (gr. 9-12). 1982. pap. 5.95 (ISBN 0-8120-2635-7). Barron.

FRENCH LANGUAGE–STUDY AND TEACHING

Adrienne. Fast French. 1983. 15.50 (ISBN 0-393-01705-2); pap. 6.95 (ISBN 0-393-30105-2). Norton.

Bull, Vivien & Guillet-Rydell, Mireille. A Vous de Choisir: Traditional & Self-Paced Learning in French. LC 82-23781. (Illus.). 342p. (Orig.). 1983. pap. text ed. 13.50 (ISBN 0-8191-2915-1). U Pr of Amer.

Gourevitch, D. & Stadler, E. M. Premiers Textes Litteraires. 2nd ed. LC 74-83346. 242p. 1975. text ed. 11.50x (ISBN 0-471-00811-7). Wiley.

Politzer, Robert L. Teaching French: An Introduction to Applied Linguistics. 2nd ed. LC 65-14561. 1965. text ed. 20.95x (ISBN 0-471-00430-8). Wiley.

FRENCH LANGUAGE–SYNTAX

Andereggen, Anton. Etude Philologique du Jugement Dernier (Lo Jutgamen General), Drame Provencal du XVe Siecle. Williman, Joseph P., ed. LC 82-80909. 386p. 1983. lib. bdg. 40.00 (ISBN 0-938942-02-6). Pacific Gallery.

FRENCH LETTERS

Daudet, A. Bi-Linguals French-English Lettres De Mon Moulin, A. Daudet. Mansion, J. E., tr. from Fr. (Harrap's Bilingual Ser.). 62p. 1955. 5.00 (ISBN 0-911268-42-1). Rogers Bk.

Proust, Marcel. Marcel Proust: Selected Letters, 1880-1903. Kolb, Philip, ed. Manheim, Ralph, tr. LC 81-43567. 456p. 1983. 19.95 (ISBN 0-385-14394-X). Doubleday.

Saint-Martin, Louis Claude de. Theosophic Correspondence between Louis Claude de Saint-Martin & Kirchberger, Baron de Liebistorf. Penny, Edward B., tr. from Fr. LC 82-61304. xxxii, 326p. Repr. of 1949 ed. 13.75 (ISBN 0-911500-62-6). Theos U Pr.

FRENCH LITERATURE (COLLECTIONS)

Here are entered collections of French Literature in French. For translations into English see subdivision Translations into English.

Allain, Mathe & Ancelet, Barry, eds. Litterature Francais de la Louisiana. (Anthologie Ser.). (Illus.). 360p. (Fr.). (gr. 10 up). 1981. pap. text ed. 7.00x (ISBN 0-911409-34-3). Natl Mat Dev.

Feuillerat, Albert. Baudelaire et la Belle aux Cheveux D'or. 1941. text ed. 32.50x (ISBN 0-686-83483-6). Elliots Bks.

Gerould, Daniel, ed. Gallant & Libertine: Divertissements & Parades from Eighteenth Century France. LC 82-62099. 1983. 18.95 (ISBN 0-933826-48-6); pap. 7.95 (ISBN 0-933826-49-4). Performing Arts.

O'Gorman, Richard, ed. Les Braies au Cordelier: Anonymous Fabliau of the Thirteenth Century. 1983. 16.00 (ISBN 0-917786-35-1). French Lit.

Santerre, Richard. Litterature Franco-Americaine de la Nouvelle: Angle Terre. (Anthologie Tome Ser.: No. 4). (Illus.). 215p. (Fr.). (gr. 10 up). 1980. pap. text ed. 5.50x (ISBN 0-911409-28-9). Natl Mat Dev.

Santerre, Richard, ed. Litterature Franco-Americaine de la Nouvelle: Angle Terre. (Anthologie Tome Ser.: No. 9). (Illus.). 365p. (Fr.). (gr. 10 up). 1981. pap. text ed. 5.50x (ISBN 0-911409-33-5). Natl Mat Dev.

--Litterature Franco-Americaine de la Nouvelle: Angle Terre. (Anthologie Tome Ser.: No. 1). (Illus.). 320p. (Fr.). (gr. 10 up). 1980. pap. text ed. 5.50x (ISBN 0-911409-25-4). Natl Mat Dev.

--Litterature Franco-Americaine de la Nouvelle: Angle Terre. (Anthologie Tome Ser.: No. 2). (Illus.). 250p. (Fr.). (gr. 10 up). 1980. pap. text ed. 5.50x (ISBN 0-911409-26-2). Natl Mat Dev.

--Litterature Franco-Americaine de la Nouvelle: Angle Terre. (Anthologie Tome Ser.: No. 3). (Illus.). 260p. (Fr.). (gr. 10 up). 1980. pap. text ed. 5.50x (ISBN 0-911409-27-0). Natl Mat Dev.

--Litterature Franco-Americaine de la Nouvelle: Angle Terre. (Anthologie Tome Ser.: No. 5). (Illus.). 378p. (Fr.). (gr. 10 up). 1981. pap. text ed. 5.50x (ISBN 0-911409-29-7). Natl Mat Dev.

--Litterature Franco-Americaine de la Nouvelle: Angle Terre. (Anthologie Tome Ser.: No. 6). (Illus.). 328p. (Fr.). (gr. 10 up). 1981. pap. text ed. 5.50x (ISBN 0-911409-30-0). Natl Mat Dev.

--Litterature Franco-Americaine de la Nouvelle: Angle Terre. (Anthologie Tome Ser.: No. 7). (Illus.). 294p. (Fr.). (gr. 10 up). 1981. pap. text ed. 5.50x (ISBN 0-911409-31-9). Natl Mat Dev.

--Litterature Franco-Americaine de la Nouvelle: Angle Terre. (Anthologie Tome Ser.: No. 8). (Illus.). 360p. (Fr.). (gr. 10 up). 1981. pap. text ed. 5.50 (ISBN 0-911409-32-7). Natl Mat Dev.

Vajda, M., ed. Le Tournant Du Siecle Des Lumieres 1780-1820. (Comparative Literature Ser.: No. 3). 684p. (Fr.). 1982. text ed. 39.50x (ISBN 0-686-43088-3, Pub. by Kultura Pr Hungary). Humanities.

FRENCH LITERATURE (COLLECTIONS)–TO 1500

De Blois, Pierre. Hystore Job: Adaptation en Vers Francaise du Compenonm in Job de Pierre de Blois. Bates, Robert C., ed. 1937. text ed. 14.50x (ISBN 0-686-83574-3). Elliots Bks.

Theobaldus of Provins Saint. Two Old French Poems on Saint Thibaut. Hill, Raymond T., ed. 1936. text ed. 9.50x (ISBN 0-686-83834-3). Elliots Bks.

FRENCH LITERATURE–AFRICAN AUTHORS

see African Literature (French)

FRENCH LITERATURE–BIBLIOGRAPHY

Hall, H. Gaston & Brooks, Richard A., eds. A Critical Bibliography of French Literature: Vol. III-A, the Seventeenth Century, Supplement. 464p. 1983. text ed. 65.00x (ISBN 0-8156-2275-9). Syracuse U Pr.

FRENCH LITERATURE–HISTORY AND CRITICISM

Braun, Sidney D. Andre Suares: Hero among Heroes. 11.00 (ISBN 0-686-38460-1). French Lit.

Calin, William. A Muse for Heroes: Nine Centuries of the Epic in France. (Romance Ser.). 504p. 1983. 47.50x (ISBN 0-8020-5599-0). U of Toronto Pr.

Conferences de litterature francaise: XVIe siecle. 1983. 15.00 (ISBN 0-686-83919-6). C de Bussy.

DiPietro, John C. Structures in Beckett's Watt. 12.00 (ISBN 0-917786-22-X). French Lit.

Durham, Carolyn A. L' Art Romanesque de Raymond Roussell. (Fr.). 15.00 (ISBN 0-686-38461-X). French Lit.

Gould, Karen L. Claude Simon's Mythic Muse. 16.00. French Lit.

Green, Mary J. Louis Guilloux: An Artisan of Language. 17.00 (ISBN 0-917786-15-7). French Lit.

Hines, Thomas M. Le Reve et l'Action: Une Etude de l'Homme a Cheval de Drieu la Rochelle. 14.00 (ISBN 0-917786-02-5). French Lit.

Lacy, Norris J. & Nash, Jerry C., eds. Essays in Early French Literature, Presented to Barbara M. Craig. 17.00 (ISBN 0-917786-28-9). French Lit.

Litvack, Frances. Le Droigt du Seigneur in Eurpoean & American Literature. 18.00. French Lit.

Poe, Elizabeth W. From Poetry to Prose in Old Provencal. 1983. 16.00 (ISBN 0-917786-33-5). French Lit.

Sankovitch, Tilde. Jodelle et la Creation du Masque: Etude Structurale et Normative de l'Eugene. (Fr.). 15.00 (ISBN 0-917786-11-4). French Lit.

Zuurdeeg, Atie D. Narrative Techniques & Their Effects in la Morte le Roi Artu. 12.00 (ISBN 0-917786-19-X). French Lit.

FRENCH LITERATURE–HISTORY AND CRITICISM–TO 1500

Bloch, Howard R. Etymologies & Genealogies: A Literary Anthropology of the French Middle Ages. LC 82-20036. 296p. 1983. lib. bdg. 29.00x (ISBN 0-226-05981-2). U of Chicago Pr.

FRENCH LITERATURE–HISTORY AND CRITICISM–17TH CENTURY

Flannigan, Arthur. Les Desordres De L'Amour: Madame De Villedieu: A Critical Edition. LC 82-16138. (Illus.). 130p. 1983. lib. bdg. 19.00 (ISBN 0-8191-2730-2); pap. text ed. 8.25 (ISBN 0-8191-2731-0). U Pr of Amer.

--Me De Villedieu's Les Desordres Del L'amour: History, Literature & the Nouvelle Historique. LC 81-43835. 206p. 1983. lib. bdg. 22.50 (ISBN 0-8191-2696-9); pap. text ed. 10.75 (ISBN 0-8191-2697-7). U Pr of Amer.

Hall, H. Gaston & Brooks, Richard A., eds. A Critical Bibliography of French Literature: Vol. III-A, the Seventeenth Century, Supplement. 464p. 1983. text ed. 65.00x (ISBN 0-8156-2275-9). Syracuse U Pr.

FRENCH LITERATURE–HISTORY AND CRITICISM–18TH CENTURY

Lynch, Lawrence W. Eighteenth Century French Novelists & the Novel. 17.00 (ISBN 0-917786-16-5). French Lit.

FRENCH LITERATURE–HISTORY AND CRITICISM–20TH CENTURY

Bond, David. The Fiction of Andre Pieyre de Mandiargues. LC 82-5894. 176p. 1982. text ed. 22.00x (ISBN 0-8156-2265-1); pap. text ed. 12.95x (ISBN 0-8156-2283-X). Syracuse U Pr.

Bree, Germine. Twentieth-Century French Literature, 1920-1970. Guiney, Louise, tr. LC 82-15980. (Illus.). 352p. 1983. lib. bdg. 25.00x (ISBN 0-226-07195-2). U of Chicago Pr.

Davis, James B. La Quete de Paul Gadenne: Une Morale pour Notre Epoque. (Fr.). 12.00 (ISBN 0-917786-18-1). French Lit.

FRENCH LITERATURE–TRANSLATIONS INTO ENGLISH

Benedeit. The Anglo-Norman Voyage of St. Brendan. Short, I. & Merrilees, B., eds. (Medieval French Text Ser.). 1979. pap. 6.00 (ISBN 0-7190-0735-6). Manchester.

Constant, Benjamin. Adolphe. 2nd ed. Rudler, G., ed. (Modern French Texts Ser.). 1941. pap. write for info. (ISBN 0-7190-0142-0). Manchester.

Danon, Samuel & Rosenburg, Samuel N., trs. from Fr. Ami & Amile. 10.00 (ISBN 0-917786-20-3). French Lit.

Martin, Mary L. The Fables of Marie de France: An English Translation. 16.00 (ISBN 0-917786-34-3). French Lit.

FRENCH NATIONAL CHARACTERISTICS

see National Characteristics, French

FRENCH PAINTING

see Painting, French

FRENCH PAINTINGS

see Paintings, French

FRENCH PHILOSOPHY

see Philosophy, French

FRENCH POETRY (COLLECTIONS)

Here are entered collections of Poetry in French. For translations into English see subdivision Translations into English.

see also Romances

De Lamartine. Poemes Choisis. Barbier, J. L., ed. (Modern French Text Ser.). 1921. pap. write for info. (ISBN 0-7190-0147-1). Manchester.

FRENCH POETRY–HISTORY AND CRITICISM

Cameron, Keith. A Concordance of Agrippa d'Aubigne's "Les Traigques". 400p. 1982. 95.00x (ISBN 0-85989-143-7, Pub. by Exeter Univ England). State Mutual Bk.

Caws, Mary A. & Riffaterre, Hermine, eds. The Prose Poem in France: Theory & Practice. 256p. 1983. 25.00x (ISBN 0-231-05434-3); pap. 12.50x (ISBN 0-231-05435-1). Columbia U Pr.

Fowlie, Wallace. Characters from Proust: Poems. 65p. 1983. text ed. 13.95 (ISBN 0-8071-1070-1); pap. 5.95 (ISBN 0-8071-1071-X). La State U Pr.

Stirling, William, tr. From Machault to Malherbe Thirteenth to Seventeenth Century. 230p. 1982. Repr. of 1947 ed. lib. bdg. 45.00 (ISBN 0-89760-017-7). Telegraph Bks.

FRENCH REVOLUTION

see France–History–Revolution, 1789-1799

FRENCH SCULPTURE

see Sculpture–France

FRENCH SONGS

see Songs, French

FRENCH WIT AND HUMOR, PICTORAL

Monaco, James. The French Revolutionary Calendar. (Illus.). 32p. 1982. pap. 5.95 (ISBN 0-918432-43-X). NY Zoetrope.

FRESCO PAINTING

see Mural Painting and Decoration

FRESH-WATER BIOLOGY

see also Aquarium Plants; Aquariums; Fresh-Water Fauna; Limnology

Edmondson, W. T., et al. Freshwater Biology. 2nd ed. LC 59-6781. (Illus.). 1248p. 1959. 79.95x (ISBN 0-471-23298-X). Wiley.

Headstrom, Richard. Adventures with Freshwater Animals. (Illus.). 217p. (gr. 5 up). 1983. pap. 5.00 (ISBN 0-486-24453-9). Dover.

McLarney, William. The Freshwater Aquaculture Book: A Handbook for Small Scale Fish Culture. (Illus.). 600p. 1983. 38.50 (ISBN 0-88930-046-1, Pub. by Cloudburst Canada). Madrona Pubs.

FRESH-WATER ECOLOGY

see also Marsh Ecology; Pond Ecology

Furtado, J. I. & Mori, S. Tasek Bera: The Ecology of a Freshwater Swamp. 1982. text ed. 79.00 (ISBN 90-6193-100-2, Pub. by Junk Pubs Netherlands). Kluwer Boston.

Snow, John. Secrets of Ponds & Lakes. Jack, Susan, ed. (Secrets of Ser.). (Illus.). 96p. (Orig.). 1982. pap. 5.95 (ISBN 0-930096-30-4). G Gannett.

FRESH-WATER FAUNA

see also Aquariums

Holdich, D. M. & Jones, J. A. Tanaids. LC 82-12761. (Synopses of the British Fauna Ser.: No. 27). (Illus.). 64p. Date not set. 29.95 (ISBN 0-521-27203-3). Cambridge U Pr.

FREUD, SIGMUND, 1856-1939

Berliner, Arthur K. Psychoanalysis & Society: The Social Thought of Sigmund Freud. LC 82-21932. 216p. (Orig.). 1983. lib. bdg. 20.75 (ISBN 0-8191-2893-7); pap. text ed. 10.50 (ISBN 0-8191-2894-5). U Pr of Amer.

Bettelheim, Bruno. Freud & Man's Soul. LC 82-47809. 112p. 1983. 11.95 (ISBN 0-394-52481-0). Knopf.

Freud, Sigmund. The Basic Writings of Sigmund Freud. Brill, A. A., ed. & intro. by. 12.95 (ISBN 0-394-60400-8). Modern Lib.

Gabriel, Yiannis. Freud & Society. (International Library of Group Psychotherapy & Group Process). 330p. 1983. price not set (ISBN 0-7100-9410-8). Routledge & Kegan.

Norhausberber, Rudolph C. The Historical-Philosophical Significance of Comte, Darwin, Marx & Freud. (Human Development Library Book). (Illus.). 139p. 1983. 59.85 (ISBN 0-89266-392-8). Am Classical Coll Pr.

FRIARS, GRAY

see Franciscans

FRIARS MINOR

see Franciscans

FRICTION

see also Bearings (Machinery); Lubrication and Lubricants

Lubrication, Friction & Wear. 332p. (Orig.). 1980. pap. text ed. 60.00x (ISBN 0-85825-148-5, Pub. by Inst Engineering Australia). Renouf.

FRIEDRICH 2ND, DER GROSSE, KING OF PRUSSIA, 1712-1786

Duffy, Christopher. Royal Adversaries: The Armies of Frederick the Great & Maria Theresa. (Illus.). 572p. boxed set 32.00 (ISBN 0-88254-713-5). Hippocrene Bks.

FRIENDLINESS

see Friendship

FRIENDLY SOCIETIES

Lapomarda, Vincent A. The Knights of Columbus in Massachusetts. 158p. (Orig.). 1982. 12.00 (ISBN 0-9608258-0-0); pap. 10.00 (ISBN 0-9608258-1-9). Mass State.

FRIENDS, SOCIETY OF

Fisher, Sidney G. Quaker Colonies. 1919. text ed. 8.50x (ISBN 0-686-83720-7). Elliots Bks.

Flexner, Helen T. Quaker Childhood. 1940. text ed. 29.50x (ISBN 0-686-83718-5). Elliots Bks.

Hilty, Hiram. North Carolina Quakers & Slavery. 120p. 1983. write for info. (ISBN 0-913408-84-0); pap. 7.95 (ISBN 0-913408-83-2). Friends United.

FRIENDSHIP

see also Love; Sympathy

Cutler, Julian S. Seasons of Friendship. 1983. 3.95 (ISBN 0-8378-2032-4). Gibson.

Gurian, Anita & Formanek, Ruth. The Socially Competent Child: A Parent's Guide to Social Development from Infancy to Early Adolescence. 206p. 1983. 12.95 (ISBN 0-395-32205-7). HM.

Miller, Stuart. Men & Friendship. LC 82-18718. 206p. 1983. 13.95 (ISBN 0-395-33103-X). HM.

Peck, Robert Newton. Soup in the Saddle. LC 82-14010. (Illus.). 96p. (gr. 3-6). 1983. 9.95 (ISBN 0-394-85294-X); lib. bdg. 9.99 (ISBN 0-394-95294-4). Knopf.

Rabinowich, Ellen. Underneath I'm Different. LC 82-14919. 192p. (gr. 7 up). 1983. 12.95 (ISBN 0-440-09253-1). Delacorte.

Richardson Woman's Club. The Texas Experience: Friendship & Food Texas Style, A Cookbook from the Richardson Woman's Club. Dennis, Ivanette, ed. (Illus.). 373p. 1982. lib. bdg. 12.95 (ISBN 0-9609416-0-6). Hart Graphics.

Smith, David W. The Friendless American Male. LC 82-21518. 1983. pap. 4.95 (ISBN 0-8307-0863-4, 5417309). Regal.

Stein, Shifra. You're A Great Friend! 1982. 5.50 (ISBN 0-8378-1712-9). Gibson.

Varenhorst, Barbara B. Real Friends: Becoming the Friend You'd Like to Have. LC 82-48412. (Illus.). 160p. (Orig.). 1983. pap. 5.72 (ISBN 0-06-250890-3, HarpR). Har-Row.

FRINGE BENEFITS

see Non-Wage Payments

FRINGILLIDAE

see Finches

FRISBEE (GAME)

Monroe, Tom. The Frisbee Book. LC 82-83937. (Illus.). 176p. (Orig.). 1983. pap. 7.95 (ISBN 0-88011-105-4). Leisure Pr.

Ultimate: Fundamentals of the Sport. LC 81-90610. 104p. (Orig.). 1982. pap. 7.95 (ISBN 0-686-37953-5). Rev Pubs.

FRISBIE (GAME)

see Frisbee (Game)

FRISCH, MAX, 1911-

Frisch, Max. Sketchbook, Nineteen Forty-Six to Nineteen Forty-Nine. Skelton, Geoffrey, tr. 320p. pap. 8.95 (ISBN 0-15-682746-8, Harv). HarBraceJ.

--Sketchbook, Nineteen Sixty-Six to Nineteen Seventy-One. Skelton, Geoffrey, tr. 343p. pap. 8.95 (ISBN 0-15-682747-6, Harv). HarBraceJ.

FROGS

Bohensky, Fred. Photo Manual & Dissection Guide of the Frog. (Avery's Anatomy Ser.). (Illus.). 88p. (Orig.). 1982. lab manual 4.95x (ISBN 0-89529-162-2). Avery Pub.

Tyler, Michael J. Frogs. (Illus.). 256p. 1983. pap. 12.50 (ISBN 0-00-216450-7, Pub. by W Collins Australia). Intl Schol Bk Serv.

FRONTIER AND PIONEER LIFE

see also Cowboys; Overland Journeys to the Pacific; Pioneers; Ranch Life; West

Gravel-Kellogg, Orlentha, ed. Bloom on the Land: A Prairie Pioneer Experience. LC 81-90537. (Illus.). 608p. 1982. 25.00x (ISBN 0-9608684-0-2). Gravel-Kellogg.

Hafen, LeRoy R. & Hafen, Ann W., eds. The Utah Expedition, 1857-1858: A Documentary Account. LC 58-11786. (Far West & Rockies Ser.: Vol.VIII). (Illus.). 375p. 1983. Repr. of 1958 ed. 27.50 (ISBN 0-87062-035-5). A H Clark.

Hafen, Mary A. Recollections of a Handcart Pioneer of 1860: A Woman's Life on the Mormon Frontier. (Illus.). 117p. 1983. 10.95x (ISBN 0-8032-2325-0); pap. 4.50 (ISBN 0-8032-7219-7, BB 841, Bison). U of Nebr Pr.

Holmes, Kenneth L., ed. Covered Wagon Women: Diaries & Letters from the Western Trails, 1840-1890. LC 82-72586. (Covered Wagon Women Ser.). (Illus.). 280p. 1983. 25.00 (ISBN 0-87062-146-7). A H Clark.

Hough, Emerson. Passing of the Frontier. 1918. text ed. 8.50x (ISBN 0-686-83683-9). Elliots Bks.

Phelps, William D. Alta California, 1840-1842: The Journal & Observations of William Dane Phelps. Busch, Briton C, ed. LC 82-71376. (Western Lands & Water Ser.: XIII). (Illus.). 364p. 1983. 29.50 (ISBN 0-87062-143-2). A H Clark.

Walton, Nancy. Famous Pioneers. (Social Studies). 24p. (gr. 5-9). 1979. wkbk. 5.00 (ISBN 0-8209-0253-5, SS-20). ESP.

Young, Paul E. Back Trail of an Old Cowboy. Yost, Nellie S., ed. LC 82-7096. vi, 229p. 1983. 14.95 (ISBN 0-8032-4901-2). U of Nebr Pr.

FRONTIER AND PIONEER LIFE–JUVENILE LITERATURE

Perez, Robert H. Southwest Borderlands: Veins of Silver & Gold. (Illus.). 160p. (YA) (gr. 10-12). 1982. pap. text ed. 7.50 (ISBN 0-940870-13-4); tchr's man. 2.50 (ISBN 0-940870-14-2). U of AZ Ed Mat.

FRONTIER AND PIONEER LIFE–SOUTHWEST, NEW

Martin, Patricia P. & Bernal, Louis C. Images & Conversations: Mexican Americans Recall a Southwestern Past. 1983. 25.00 (ISBN 0-8165-0801-1); pap. 12.50 (ISBN 0-8165-0803-8). U of Ariz Pr.

Walker, Dale. Buckey O'Neill: The Story of a Rough Rider. 220p. 1983. pap. 9.50 (ISBN 0-8165-0805-4). U of Ariz Pr.

FRONTIER AND PIONEER LIFE–TEXAS

Egloff, Fred R. El Paso Lawman: G. W. Campbell. (The Early West Ser.). (Illus.). 144p. 1982. 12.95 (ISBN 0-932702-22-8); pap. 7.95 (ISBN 0-932702-24-4); leatherbound collectors ed. 75.00 (ISBN 0-932702-23-6). Creative Texas.

FRONTIER AND PIONEER LIFE–THE WEST

see also Frontier and Pioneer Life–Southwest, New

Bagley, Helen G. Sand in My Shoe: Homestead Days in Twentynine Palms. 2nd ed. Weight, Harold & Weight, Lucile, eds. LC 77-94990. (Illus.). 269p. 1980. Repr. of 1978 ed. 11.95 (ISBN 0-912714-08-5). Homestead Pub.

Barton, Lois. Spencer Butte Pioneers: One Hundred Years on the Sunny Side of the Butte 1850-1950. Mills, Charlotte & Northwest Matrix, eds. LC 82-61837. (Illus.). 144p. 1982. pap. write for info. (ISBN 0-9609420-0-9). S Butte Pr.

Bourke, John G. On the Border with Crook. (Classics of the Old West Ser.). 1980. lib. bdg. 17.28 (ISBN 0-8094-3584-5). Silver.

Carrington. Ab-Sa-Ra-Ka, Land of Massacre. (Classics of the Old West Ser.). 1983. lib. bdg. 17.28 (ISBN 0-686-42740-8). Silver.

Cody, William. Life of Buffalo Bill. (Classics of the Old West). 1982. lib. bdg. 17.28 (ISBN 0-8094-4015-6). Silver.

Conard, Howard. Uncle Dick Wootton. LC 80-22533. (Classics of the Old West Ser.). lib. bdg. 17.28 (ISBN 0-8094-3951-4). Silver.

DeBarthe, Frank. Life & Adventures of Frank Grouard. (Classics of the Old West Ser.). 1982. lib. bdg. 17.28 (ISBN 0-8094-4007-5). Silver.

Delano, A. Life on the Plains & at the Diggings. LC 81-16565. (Classics of the Old West). lib. bdg. 17.28 (ISBN 0-8094-3987-5). Silver.

Dellenbaugh, Frederick. The Romance of the Colorado River. LC 82-3339. (Classics of the Old West Ser.). lib. bdg. 17.28 (ISBN 0-8094-4003-2). Silver.

Dimsdale, Thomas. Vigilantes of Montana. LC 80-29395. (Classics of the Old West Ser.). lib. bdg. 17.28 (ISBN 0-8094-3959-X). Silver.

Garrard, Lewis. Wah-To-Yah & the Taos Trail. (Classics of the Old West Ser.). 1982. lib. bdg. 17.28 (ISBN 0-8094-4011-3). Silver.

Grant, Blanche. When Old Trails Were New: The Story of Taos. LC 63-21230. 348p. 1983. Repr. of 1963 ed. softcover 12.00 (ISBN 0-87380-140-7). Rio Grande.

Hamilton, William. My Sixty Years on the Plains Trapping, Trading & Indian Fighting. LC 82-17547. (Classics of the Old West). lib. bdg. 17.28 (ISBN 0-8094-4030-X). Silver.

Irving, Washington. A Tour of the Praries. (Classics of the Old West Ser.). 1983. lib. bdg. 17.28 (ISBN 0-8094-4034-2). Silver.

Marryat, Frank. Mountains & Molehills. (Classics of the Old West). 1982. lib. bdg. 17.28 (ISBN 0-8094-3999-9). Silver.

Murphy, Lawrence R. Lucien Bonaparte Maxwell: The Napoleon of the Southwest. LC 82-40454. (Illus.). 280p. 1983. 19.95 (ISBN 0-8061-1807-5). U of Okla Pr.

Ruxton, George. Life in the Far West. (Classics of the Old West). 1983. lib. bdg. 17.28 (ISBN 0-8094-4046-6). Silver.

Sage, Rufus B. Rocky Mountain Life: Or, Startling Scenes & Perilous Adventures in the Far West During an Expedition of Three Years. LC 82-20165. (Illus.). 351p. 1983. 23.50x (ISBN 0-8032-4142-9); pap. 7.50 (ISBN 0-8032-9137-X, BB 835, Bison). U of Nebr Pr.

Stratton, R. B. Captivity of the Oatman Girls. LC 81-18247. (Classics of the Old West Ser.). lib. bdg. 17.28 (ISBN 0-8094-3991-3). Silver.

Twain, Mark. Roughing It. (Classics of the Old West Ser.). 1982. lib. bdg. 17.28 (ISBN 0-8094-3995-6). Silver.

FRONTIER AND PIONEER LIFE–THE WEST–FICTION

Tuska, Jon & Piekarski, Vicki. Encyclopedia of Frontier & Western Fiction. (Illus.). 384p. 1983. 24.95 (ISBN 0-07-065587-1, P&RB). McGraw.

FRONTIERS

see Boundaries

FROST, ROBERT, 1874-1963

Gerber, Philip L., ed. Critical Essays on Robert Frost. (Critical Essays on American Literature Ser.). 1982. lib. bdg. 28.50 (ISBN 0-8161-8442-9). G K Hall.

Trikha, M. Robert Frost: Poetry of Clarifications. 224p. 1982. text ed. 11.00x (ISBN 0-391-02751-4, Pub. by Heinemann India). Humanities.

FROZEN FOOD

see Food, Frozen

FROZEN STARS

see Black Holes (Astronomy)

FRUIT

see also Berries; Cookery (Fruit)

also particular fruits, e.g. Apple, Orange

English, Sandal. Fruits of the Desert. 181p. (Orig.). 1981. pap. 6.75 (ISBN 0-9607758-0-3). Ariz Daily Star.

Jacob, John & Jacob, Meera. Fruit & Vegatable Carving. revised ed. 99p. 1983. 25.00 (ISBN 0-686-42989-3). Hippocrene Bks.

Teranishi, Roy & Barrera-Benitez, Heriberto, eds. Quality of Selected Fruits & Vegetables of North America. (ACS Symposium Ser.: No. 170). 1981. write for info. (ISBN 0-8412-0662-7). Am Chemical.

FRUIT–DISEASES AND PESTS

see also Insects, Injurious and Beneficial; Plant Diseases

also subdivision Diseases and Pests under particular fruits, and names of diseases and pests

Croft, B. A. & Hoyt, S. C. Integrated Management of Insect Pests of Pome & Stone Fruit. (Environemental Science & Technology Texts & Monographs). 464p. 1983. 52.50 (ISBN 0-471-05334-1, Pub. by Wiley-Interscience). Wiley.

FRUIT–PESTS

see Fruit–Diseases and Pests

FRUIT PESTS

see Fruit–Diseases and Pests

FRUIT TREES

Stebbins, Robert L. & Walheim, Lance. Western Fruit, Berries & Nuts: How to Select, Grow & Enjoy. (Illus.). 192p. (Orig.). pap. 7.95 (ISBN 0-89586-078-3). H P Bks.

FRUITS

see Fruit

FRYE, NORTHROP

Denham, Robert. Northrop Frye: A Supplementary Bibliography. 67p. (Orig.). 1979. pap. 5.00 (ISBN 0-931182-02-6). Iron Mtn Pr.

FUCHSIA

Barnes, Bill. New A to Z on Fuchsias. (Illus.). Date not set. pap. 9.95. Natl Fuchsia.

Jennings, K. & Miller, V. Growing Fuchsias. (Illus.). 170p. 1982. 14.95 (ISBN 0-85664-890-6). Timber.

FUEL

see also Biomass Energy; Coal; Heating; Lignite; Liquid Fuels; Petroleum As Fuel; Synthetic Fuels

Bisio, Attilio. Encyclopedia of Energy Technology. 4000p. 1983. Set. 350.00 (ISBN 0-471-89039-1, Pub. by Wiley-Interscience). Wiley.

The Potential for Production of "Hydrocarbon" Fuels from Crops in Australia. 86p. 1983. pap. 7.25 (ISBN 0-643-02931-1, CO 67, CSIRO). Unipub.

Semenza, G. Of Oxygen, Fuels & Living Matter, Vol. 2, Pt. 2. (Evolving Life Sciences: Recollections on Scientific Ideas & Events Ser.). 508p. 1982. text ed. 65.00x (ISBN 0-471-27924-2, Pub. by Wiley-Interscience). Wiley.

Thompson, R., ed. Energy & Chemistry. 368p. 1982. 55.00x (ISBN 0-85186-845-2, Pub. by Royal Soc Chem England). State Mutual Bk.

FUEL CELLS

Linden, D. Handbook of Batteries & Fuel Cells. 1024p. 1983. 49.50 (ISBN 0-07-037874-6, P&RB). McGraw.

FUEL ELEMENTS

see Nuclear Fuel Elements

FUEL OIL

see Petroleum As Fuel

FUENTES, CARLOS

Faris, Wendy B. Carlos Fuentes. LC 82-40281. (Literature & Life Ser.). 220p. 1983. 14.50 (ISBN 0-8044-2193-5). Ungar.

FULFILLMENT (ETHICS)

see Self-Realization

FULL EMPLOYMENT POLICIES

see also Employment Agencies; Government Spending Policy; Labor Supply; Unemployed

Ginsburg, Helen. Full Employment & Public Policy: The United States & Sweden. LC 76-55536. 256p. 1983. 24.95x (ISBN 0-669-01318-8). Lexington Bks.

FUME CONTROL

American Welding Society. The Facts About Fumes. 1976. 13.00 (ISBN 0-686-43387-4). Am Welding.

--Welding Fume Control: A Demonstration Project. 65p. 1982. 20.00 (ISBN 0-686-43388-2). Am Welding.

--Welding Fume Control with Mechanical Ventilation. 1981. 8.00 (ISBN 0-686-43342-4). Am Welding.

FUNCTION TESTS (MEDICINE)

see also Pulmonary Function Tests

Galen, P. S. & Gambino, S. R. Beyond Normality: The Predictive Value & Efficiency of Medical Diagnosis. LC 75-25915. 237p. 1975. 32.95x (ISBN 0-471-29047-5, Pub. by Wiley Medical). Wiley.

FUNCTION TESTS, PULMONARY

see Pulmonary Function Tests

FUNCTIONAL ANALYSIS

see also Approximation Theory; Digital Filters (Mathematics); Distributions, Theory of (Functional Analysis); Functor Theory; Integral Equations; Perturbation (Mathematics); Spectral Theory (Mathematics); Topological Algebras; Vector Spaces

Functional Analysis, Dubrovnik Yugoalavia: Proceedings, 1981. (Lecture Notes in Mathematics Ser.: Vol. 948). 239p. 1983. pap. 12.00 (ISBN 0-387-11594-3). Springer-Verlag.

Goffman, Casper & Pedrick, George. First Course in Functional Analysis. 2nd ed. LC 82-74164. 242p. 1983. text ed. 14.95 (ISBN 0-8284-0319-8). Chelsea Pub.

Groetsch, Charles W. Elements of Applicable Functional Analysis. (Pure & Applied Mathematics: Monographs & Textbooks: Vol. 55). (Illus.). 320p. 1980. 28.75 (ISBN 0-8247-6986-4). Dekker.

Johnstone, Peter. Stone Spaces. LC 82-4506. (Cambridge Studies in Advanced Mathematics: No. 3). 300p. Date not set. price not set (ISBN 0-521-23893-5). Cambridge U Pr.

Nachbin, Leopoldo. Introduction to Functional Analysis: Banach Spaces & Different Calculus. (Pure & Applied Mathematics: Monographs & Textbooks: Vol. 60). (Illus.). 184p. 1981. 19.75 (ISBN 0-8247-6984-8). Dekker.

Prolla, J. B. Approximation Theory & Functional Analysis. (Proceedings). 1979. 64.00 (ISBN 0-444-85264-6). Elsevier.

Wouk, A. A Course of Applied Functional Analysis. (Pure & Applied Mathematics Ser.). 443p. 1979. text ed. 41.50x (ISBN 0-471-96238-4, Pub. by Wiley-Interscience). Wiley.

FUNCTIONAL CALCULUS

see Functional Analysis

FUNCTIONALS

see Functional Analysis

FUNCTIONS

see also Asymptotic Expansions; Calculus; Convergence; Distributions, Theory of (Functional Analysis); Riemann Surfaces

Fisher, Stephen D. Function Theory on Planar Domains: A Second Course in Complex Analysis. (Pure & Applied Mathematics Series of Texts, Monographs). 400p. 1983. 37.50 (ISBN 0-471-87314-4, Pub. by Wiley-Interscience). Wiley.

Martinet, Jean. Singularities of Smooth Functions & Maps. Simon, C. P., tr. LC 81-18034. (London Mathematical Society Lecture Note Ser.: No. 58). 180p. 1982. pap. 19.95 (ISBN 0-521-23398-4). Cambridge U Pr.

FUNCTIONS (FUNCTIONAL ANALYSIS)

see Distributions, Theory of (Functional Analysis)

FUNCTIONS, ALGEBRAIC

Kadison, Richard V., ed. Operations Algebras & Applications, 2 pts. (Proceedings of Symposia in Pure Mathematics Ser.: Vol. 38). Set. 80.00 (ISBN 0-8218-1445-1, PSPUM/38); Part one. 46.00 (ISBN 0-8218-1441-9, PSPUM/38.1); 46.00 (ISBN 0-8218-1444-3, PSPUM/38.2). Am Math.

FUNCTIONS, ALMOST PERIODIC

see Almost Periodic Functions

FUNCTIONS, CIRCULAR

see Trigonometrical Functions

FUNCTIONS, ELLIPTIC

see also Functions of Complex Variables

Gubert, Robert P., ed. Plane Ellipticity & Related Problems. LC 82-11562. (Contemporary Mathematics Ser.: Vol. 2). 19.00 (ISBN 0-8218-5012-1, CONTM/11). Am Math.

FUNCTIONS, GENERALIZED

see Distributions, Theory of (Functional Analysis)

FUNCTIONS, HARMONIC

see Harmonic Functions

FUNCTIONS, POTENTIAL

see Differential Equations, Partial; Harmonic Analysis

FUNCTIONS, THETA

Mumford, David. Tata Lecture Notes on Theta Functions, 2 Vols. (Progress in Mathematics Ser.). 1983. Vol. 1, 220p. text ed. 15.00 (ISBN 3-7643-3109-7); Vol. 2, 200pp. text ed. 17.50 (ISBN 3-7643-3110-0). Birkhauser.

FUNCTIONS, TRANSCENDENTAL

see also names of specific transcendental functions, e.g. Bellel Functions; Functions, Gamma

Marichev, O. I. Handbook of Integral Transforms of Higher Transcendental Functions: Theory & Algorithmic Tables. (Mathematics & Its Applications). 350p. 1983. 79.95x (ISBN 0-470-27364-X). Halsted Pr.

FUNCTIONS, TRIGONOMETRICAL

see Trigonometrical Functions

FUNCTIONS OF COMPLEX VARIABLES

see also Banach Spaces; Functions, Elliptic; Functions of Real Variables

Jameson, G. J. First Course Complex Functions. 1970. pap. 11.95x (ISBN 0-412-09710-9, Pub. by Chapman & Hill England). Methuen Inc.

Wunsch, A. David. Complex Variables with Applications. LC 82-16288. (Illus.). 416p. 1983. text ed. 20.95 (ISBN 0-201-08885-1). A-W.

FUNCTIONS OF REAL VARIABLES

see also Functions of Complex Variables

Fischer, E. Intermediate Real Analysis. (Undergraduate Texts in Mathematics Ser.). (Illus.). 770p. 1983. 28.00 (ISBN 0-387-90721-1). Springer-Verlag.

Goldberg, Richard R. Methods of Real Analysis. 2nd ed. LC 75-30615. 1976. text ed. 31.95x (ISBN 0-471-31065-4). Wiley.

FUNCTOR THEORY

see also Categories (Mathematics)

Kamps, K. H., et al, eds. Category Theory, Applications to Algebra, Logic, & Topology: Proceedings, Gummersbach, FRG, 1981. (Lecture Notes in Mathematics Ser.: Vol. 962). 322p. 1983. pap. 16.00 (ISBN 0-387-11961-2). Springer-Verlag.

FUNCTORIAL REPRESENTATION

see Functor Theory

FUND RAISING

see also Federations, Financial (Social Service)

Brakeley, George A., Jr. Tested Ways to Successful Fund Raising. 19.95 (ISBN 0-686-38896-8). Public Serv Materials.

Brownrigg, W. G. Out of the Red: Strategies for Effective Corporate Fundraising. (Illus.). 176p. 1983. pap. 12.95 (ISBN 0-915400-43-X). Am Council Arts.

Doyle, A. C. Fundraiser's Workbook: Based on Guide for Fundraisers. 8.95 (ISBN 0-939476-76-2). Biblio Pr GA.

Fundraising Market Place, 3 pts. 1st ed. 1983. Set. pap. 125.00x (ISBN 0-8103-0411-2, Pub. by K G Saur). Gale.

Hay, J. Thomas. Five Hundred & Thirty-Four Ways to Raise Money. 256p. 1983. 15.95 (ISBN 0-671-47167-8); pap. 7.95 (ISBN 0-671-47286-0). S&S.

National Catholic Development Conference. Bibliography of Fund Raising & Philanthropy. 2nd ed. LC 82-81523. 1982. 22.50 (ISBN 0-9603196-1-1). Natl Cath Dev.

Schneiter, Paul H. & Nelson, Donald T. The Thirteen Most Common Fund-Raising Mistakes & How to Avoid Them. Kalish, Susan E., ed. LC 82-51251. (Illus.). 95p. (Orig.). 1982. pap. 14.95 (ISBN 0-914756-53-2). Taft Corp.

FUNDAMENTAL THEOLOGY

see Apologetics

FUNDAMENTALISM

see also Evangelicalism

Thomas, Ray. Planting & Growing a Fundamental Church. 1979. 7.95 (ISBN 0-89265-055-9). Randall Hse.

FUNDS

see Finance

FUNERAL DIRECTORS

see Undertakers and Undertaking

FUNERAL RITES AND CEREMONIES

Bloch, Maurice & Parry, Jonathan, eds. Death & the Regeneration of Life. LC 82-9467. 256p. 1982. 29.50 (ISBN 0-521-24875-2); pap. 8.95 (ISBN 0-521-27037-5). Cambridge U Pr.

Buck, Peter. Arts & Crafts of Hawaii: Death & Burial, Sec. XIII. (Special Publication Ser.: No. 45). (Illus.). 26p. 1957. pap. 2.00 (ISBN 0-910240-46-9). Bishop Mus.

FUNGAL TOXINS

see Mycotoxins

FUNGI

see also Ascomycetes; Bacteriology; Lichens; Mushrooms; Soil Micro-Organisms

Gupta, J. S. Textbook of Fungi. 305p. 1981. 60.00x (ISBN 0-686-84469-6, Pub. by Oxford & I B H India). State Mutual Bk.

Nilsson, S. T., ed. Atlas of Airborne Fungal Spores in Europe. (Illus.). 145p. 1983. 50.00 (ISBN 0-387-11900-0). Springer-Verlag.

Ross, I. K. Biology of the Fungi. 1979. 28.50 (ISBN 0-07-053870-0). McGraw.

Smith. Fungal Differentiations. (Mycology Ser.). 600p. 1983. price not set (ISBN 0-8247-1734-1). Dekker.

Stevenson, G. Biology of Fungi. 1970. 12.00 (ISBN 0-444-19674-9). Elsevier.

FUNGICIDES

Page, B. G. & Thomson, W. T. Insecticide, Herbicide Fungicide Quick Guide, 1983. 140p. Date not set. pap. 12.00 (ISBN 0-913702-20-X). Thomson Pub CA.

FUNGOUS DISEASES

see Medical Mycology

FUNNIES

see Comic Books, Strips, etc.

FUR-BEARING ANIMALS

see also Fur Trade

also Names of Fur-Bearing Animals

Deems, Eugene F., Jr. & Pursley, Duane. North American Furbearers: A Contemporary Reference. (Illus.). 217p. 1983. text ed. 14.00 (ISBN 0-932108-08-3). Intl Assn Fish & Wildlife.

North American Furbearers: A Contemporary Referencee. 1983. 14.00 (ISBN 0-932108-08-3). IAFWA.

FUR TRADE

Francis, Daniel & Morantz, Toby. Partners in Furs: A History of the Fur Trade in Eastern James Bay, 1600-1870. 200p. 1983. 25.00x (ISBN 0-7735-0385-4); pap. 9.95 (ISBN 0-7735-0386-2). McGill-Queens U Pr.

Grant, Blanche. When Old Trails Were New: The Story of Taos. LC 63-21230. 348p. 1983. Repr. of 1963 ed. softcover 12.00 (ISBN 0-87380-140-7). Rio Grande.

Holm, Bill, annotations by. Soft Gold: The Fur Trade & Cultural Exchange on the Northwest Coast of America. LC 82-81739. (Illus.). 312p. (Orig.). 1982. 29.95 (ISBN 0-87595-107-4, Western Imprints); pap. 19.95 (ISBN 0-87595-108-2, Western Imprints). Oreg Hist Soc.

Van Kirk, Sylvia. Many Tender Ties: Women in Fur-Trade Society, Sixteen Seventy to Eighteen Seventy. LC 82-40457. (Illus.). 303p. 1983. 22.50x (ISBN 0-8061-1842-3); pap. 9.95x (ISBN 0-8061-1847-4). U of Okla Pr.

Vaughn, Thomas & Holm, Bill. Soft Gold: The Fur Trade & Cultural Exchange on the Northwest Coast of America. (Illus.). 320p. 1982. 29.95 (ISBN 0-295-96002-7, Pub. by Oreg Hist Soc). U of Wash Pr.

FUR TRADE–JUVENILE LITERATURE

Kozlak, Chet, illus. A Great Lakes Fur Trade Coloring Book. Belanger, Jean-Pierre, tr. 32p. (Eng. & Fr.). 1981. pap. 2.00 (ISBN 0-87351-154-9). Minn Hist.

FURNITURE

see also Chairs; Implements, Utensils, etc.; Interior Decoration; Library Fittings and Supplies; Mirrors; Schools–Furniture, Equipment, etc.; Upholstery; Wood-Carving

Blaser, Werner. Folding Chairs, Klappstuehle. 110p. 1982. 17.95 (ISBN 3-7643-1357-9). Birkhauser.

Data Notes Publishing Staff. Furniture Recycling: Data Notes. 30p. 1983. pap. 9.95 (ISBN 0-911569-45-6). Data Notes Pub.

Household Furniture. 1982. 450.00 (ISBN 0-686-38439-3, A403). Busn Trend.

McGriffin, Robert F., Jr. Furniture Care & Conservation. (Illus.). 256p. 1983. text ed. write for info. (ISBN 0-910050-62-7). AASLH.

Ribalta, Marta, ed. Habitat: Furniture, No. 6. (Illus.). 269p. 1982. pap. 9.95 (ISBN 84-7031-059-3, Pub. by Editorial Blume Spain). Intl Schol Bk Serv.

FURNITURE–BUILDING

see Furniture Making

FURNITURE–CATALOGS

Mason, J. W. Furniture Trade Catalog of J. W. Mason & Co. (Illus.). 116p. Date not set. pap. 25.00 (ISBN 0-87556-495-X). Saifer.

FURNITURE–DESIGN

see Furniture Design

FURNITURE–DICTIONARIES

VonZweck, Dina. Woman's Day Dictionary of Furniture. 1983. pap. 4.95 (ISBN 0-8065-0842-6). Citadel Pr.

FURNITURE–HISTORY

Clarke, Rosy. Antique Japanese Furniture: A Guide to Evaluating & Restoring. LC 82-21916. (Illus.). 168p. (Orig.). 1983. pap. 17.50 (ISBN 0-8348-0178-7). Weatherhill.

Voss, Thomas M. Antique American Country Furniture. LC 82-48009. (Illus.). 384p. 1983. pap. 7.95 (ISBN 0-06-464061-2, BN 4061). B&N NY.

FURNITURE–REPAIRING

see also Furniture Finishing

Grotz, George. From Gunk to Glow: The Gentle Art of Refinishing Antiques & Other Furniture. 1983. pap. 4.95 (ISBN 0-440-53053-9, Delta). Dell.

Jackson, Albert & Day, David. Better Than New: A Practical Guide to Renovating Furniture. LC 83-370. (Illus.). 144p. (Orig.). 1983. pap. 8.95 (ISBN 0-8069-7730-2). Sterling.

Learoyd, Stan. Conservation & Restoration of Antique Furniture. (Illus.). 140p. (Orig.). 1983. pap. 9.95 (ISBN 0-8069-7682-9). Sterling.

Salazar, Tristan. The Complete Book of Furniture Restoration. (Illus.). 160p. 1982. 20.00 (ISBN 0-312-15630-8). St Martin.

FURNITURE–RESTORATION

see Furniture–Repairing; Furniture Finishing

FURNITURE–UNITED STATES

Donovan & Green. The Wood Chair in America. LC 82-90454. (Illus.). 120p. 1982. pap. 24.95 (ISBN 0-9609844-0-2). E & S Brickel.

Madigan, Mary Jean & Colgan, Susan, eds. Early American Furniture: From Settlement to City Aspects of Form, Style, & Regional Design from 1620-1830. 160p. 1983. 25.00 (ISBN 0-8230-8007-2, Art & Antiques). Watson-Guptill.

Melchor, Jim & Lohr, Gordon. Eastern Shore, Virginia, Raised-Panel Furniture, 1730-1830. LC 82-72773. (Illus.). 136p. (Orig.). 1982. pap. 20.00 (ISBN 0-940744-39-2). Chrysler Museum.

Whitford, Mary M. Price Guide to Furniture Made in America: 1875-1905. 16p. 1982. pap. text ed. 5.00 (ISBN 0-916838-70-6). Schiffer.

FURNITURE BUILDING

see Furniture Making

FURNITURE DESIGN

Gottshall, Franklin H. Provincial Furniture, Design & Construction. (Illus.). 1983. 24.95 (ISBN 0-517-54930-1). Crown.

Page, Marian. Furniture Designed by Architects. (Illus.). 224p. 1983. pap. 14.95 (ISBN 0-8230-7181-2, Whitney Lib). Watson-Guptill.

FURNITURE FINISHING

Grotz, George. From Gunk to Glow: The Gentle Art of Refinishing Antiques & Other Furniture. 1983. pap. 4.95 (ISBN 0-440-53053-9, Delta). Dell.

Salazar, Tristan. The Complete Book of Furniture Restoration. (Illus.). 160p. 1982. 20.00 (ISBN 0-312-15630-8). St Martin.

FURNITURE INDUSTRY AND TRADE

Household Furniture. 1982. 450.00 (ISBN 0-686-38439-3, A403). Busn Trend.

FURNITURE MAKING

see also Cabinet-Work; Furniture–Repairing; Furniture; Upholstery

Feirer. Furniture & Cabinet Making. 1983. price not set (ISBN 0-87002-388-8). Bennett Il.

Gottshall, Franklin H. Provincial Furniture, Design & Construction. (Illus.). 1983. 24.95 (ISBN 0-517-54930-1). Crown.

Marlow, A. W. The Early American Furnituremaker's Manual. LC 72-91257. 144p. 1983. pap. 8.95 (ISBN 0-8128-6184-1). Stein & Day.

Staff of the Family Handyman Magazine. Early American Furniture-Making Handbook. (Illus.). 162p. pap. 9.95 (ISBN 0-686-83795-9, ScribT). Scribner.

FUSED SALTS

Lovering, David G., ed. Molten Salt Technology. 550p. 1982. 65.00x (ISBN 0-306-41076-1, Plenum Pr). Plenum Pub.

FUSION OF CORPORATIONS
see Consolidation and Merger of Corporations
FUSION REACTIONS, CONTROLLED
see Controlled Fusion
FUTURE LIFE
see also Children-Death and Future State; Immortality; Resurrection; Soul; Spiritualism
Evans, Louis H. Your Thrilling Future. 1982. pap. 4.95 (ISBN 0-8423-8573-8). Tyndale.
Harris, W. T. The Mythology of Plato & Dante & the Future Life. (The Essential Library of the Great Philosophers). (Illus.). 107p. 1983. Repr. of 1896 ed. 71.85 (ISBN 0-89901-091-1). Found Class Reprints.
Phillips, John. Exploring the Future. 400p. 1983. 14.95 (ISBN 0-8407-5275-X). Nelson.
Rossier, H. Que Pasa Despues de la Muerte? 2nd ed. Bennett, Gordon H., ed. Bautista, Sara, tr. from Eng. (La Serie Diamante). (Illus.). 36p. (Span.). 1982. pap. 0.85 (ISBN 0-942504-07-0). Overcomer Pr.
Smith, Malcolm. Life Beyond Life. 1978. 1.25 (ISBN 0-88270-317-X). Bridge Pub.
ST. Johns, A. R. No Good-byes: My Search Into Life Beyond Death. 1981. 10.95 (ISBN 0-07-054450-6). McGraw.
FUTURE TIME PERSPECTIVE
see Time Perspective
FUTURES
see Commodity Exchanges
FUTURISM
Toffler, Alvin. Previews & Premises. 192p. 1983. 11.95 (ISBN 0-688-01910-2). Morrow.

G

GABLE, CLARK, 1901-1960
Scagnetti, Jack. The Life & Loves of Gable. 1982. pap. 8.95 (ISBN 0-8246-0279-X). Jonathan David.
GADGETS
see Implements, Utensils, etc.
GAELS
see Celts
GAGES
Aitchison, Ian J. An Informal Introduction to Gauge Field Theories. LC 81-21753. (Illus.). 150p. 1982. 22.50 (ISBN 0-521-24540-0). Cambridge U Pr.
GAGING
Leader, Elliot & Predazzi, Enrico. An Introduction to Gauge Theories & the "New Physics". LC 81-3860. (Illus.). 400p. 1982. 65.00 (ISBN 0-521-23375-5); pap. 27.50 (ISBN 0-521-29937-3). Cambridge U Pr.
GAINSBOROUGH, THOMAS, 1727-1788
Rothschild, M. The Life & Art of Thomas Gainsborough. (The Great Art Masters of the World). (Illus.). 102p. 1983. 97.75 (ISBN 0-86650-044-8). Gloucester Art.
GALAPAGOS ISLANDS
Otterman, Lillian. Clinker Islands. LC 81-86431. (Illus.). 1983. pap. 8.95 (ISBN 0-86666-109-3). GWP.
GALAXIES
Barker, Edmund S. Webb Society Deep-Sky Observer's Handbook: Vol. 4, Galaxies. Glyn-Jones, Kenneth, ed. 250p. 1982. 40.00x (ISBN 0-7188-2527-6, Pub. by Lutterworth Pr England). State Mutual Bk.
Palumbo, Giorgio G. Catalogue of Radial Velocities of Galaxies. 550p. 1982. write for info. (ISBN 0-677-06090-4). Gordon.
Sandage, Allan & Sandage, Mary, eds. Galaxies & the Universe, Vol. IX. LC 74-7559. (Stars & Stellar Systems Midway Reprint Ser.). (Illus.). 818p. 1983. pap. text ed. 40.00x (ISBN 0-226-45970-5). U of Chicago Pr.
Shapley, Harlow. Inner Metagalaxy. 1957. text ed. 39.50x (ISBN 0-686-83589-1). Elliots Bks.
GALES
see Storms; Winds
GALICIA-BIBLIOGRAPHY
Magocsi, Paul R. Galicia: A Historical Survey & Bibliographic Guide. (Illus.). 336p. 1983. 19.50x (ISBN 0-8020-2482-3). U of Toronto Pr.
GALL
see Bile
GALL-BLADDER-CALCULI
see Calculi, Biliary
GALL-STONES
see Calculi, Biliary
GALLERIES (ART)
see Art Museums
GALLIPOLI CAMPAIGN, 1915
see European War, 1914-1918-Campaigns
GALUTH
see Jews-Diaspora
GALVANIC BATTERIES
see Electric Batteries
GALVANISM
see Electricity
GALVANOPLASTY
see Electrometallurgy
GAMBLING
see also Blackjack (Game); Cards; Cardsharping; Dice; Horse Race Betting; Probabilities
Barnhart, Russell T. Gamblers of Yesteryear. LC 82-83031. (Illus.). 280p. (Orig.). 1983. pap. 14.95 (ISBN 0-89650-708-4). Gamblers.
Davidowitz, Steve. Betting Thoroughbreds: A Professional's Guide for the Horseplayer. Rev. ed. (Illus.). 232p. 1983. pap. 7.25 (ISBN 0-525-48046-3, 0772-230). Dutton.
Kallick, Maureen, et al. Survey of American Gambling Attitudes & Behavior. 560p. 1979. pap. 22.00x (ISBN 0-87944-245-X). Inst Soc Res.
Karlins, Marvin. Psyching Out Vegas. (Illus.). 280p. 1983. 12.00 (ISBN 0-914314-03-3). Lyle Stuart.
Lake, Hank. How to Win at Atlantic City, Las Vegas & Caribbean Gaming. (Illus.). 71p. 1982. pap. 3.95 (ISBN 0-938512-05-6). Brigadoon.
McClure, Wayne. Keno Winning Ways. Rev. ed. LC 82-83487. (Illus.). 234p. 1983. pap. 8.95 (ISBN 0-89650-780-7). Gamblers.
Mendelsohn, Martin. One Hundred Thousand Rolls of the Dice. LC 82-84680. 100p. 1982. pap. 9.95 (ISBN 0-89650-500-6). Gamblers.
Patterson, Jerry L. & Jaye, Walter. Casino Gambling: Winning Techniques for Craps, Roulette, Baccarat & Blackjack. 224p. 1983. pap. 6.95 (ISBN 0-399-50656-X, Perige). Putnam Pub Group.
Quinn, James. The Literature of Thoroughbred Handicapping 1965-1982: A Selective Review for the Practioner. LC 82-84680. (Illus.). 176p. 1983. pap. 9.95 (ISBN 0-89650-794-7). Gamblers.
Robert, Williar & Houdin, William J. Card Sharper-Their Tricks Exposed or the Art of Always Winning. 158p. 1982. pap. 3.95 (ISBN 0-686-42831-5). Gamblers.
Sklansky, David. Getting the Best of It. 224p. (Orig.). 1982. pap. 9.95 (ISBN 0-89650-721-1). Gamblers.
GAME AND GAME-BIRDS
see also Cookery (Meat); Decoys (Hunting); Dogs-Training; Fowling; Hunting; Sports; Water-Birds; Waterfowl
also Particular Animals and Birds, e.g. Deer, Grouse, Rabbits, Woodcock
Harbour, Dave. Advanced Wild Turkey Hunting & World Records. (Illus.). 264p. 1983. 19.95 (ISBN 0-8329-0286-1, Pub. by Winchester Pr.). New Century.
--Hunting the American Wild Turkey. LC 74-31449. (Illus.). 258p. 1974. 14.95 (ISBN 0-8117-0863-2). Stackpole.
Nesbitt, W. H., ed. Eighteenth Boone & Crockett Big Game Awards, 1980-1982. (Illus.). 250p. 1983. 19.50 (ISBN 0-940864-05-3). Boone & Crockett.
Nesbitt, W. H. & Wright, Philip L., eds. Records at North American Big Game. 8th ed. xii, 412p. 1981. leather, ltd. ed. 195.00x (ISBN 0-940864-01-0). Boone & Crockett.
Robbins, Charles T., ed. Wildlife Feeding & Nutrition. LC 82-13720. Date not set. price not set (ISBN 0-12-589380-9). Acad Pr.
GAME AND GAME-BIRDS-NORTH AMERICA
Leopold, A. Starker & Gutierrez, Ralph J. North American Game Birds & Mammals. (Illus.). 208p. 1983. pap. 10.95 (ISBN 0-686-83783-5, ScribT). Scribner.
MacIlquham, Frances. Complete Fish & Game Cookery of North America. (Illus.). 304p. 1983. 29.95 (ISBN 0-8329-0284-5). Winchester Pr.
Southard, Doris. North American Game Birds & Mammals. (Illus.). 224p. 1983. pap. 10.95 (ISBN 0-686-83781-9, ScribT). Scribner.
GAME MANAGEMENT
see Wildlife Management
GAME THEORY
see also Decision-Making; Statistical Decision
Ankeny, Nesmith C. Poker Strategy: Winning With Game Theory. (Illus.). 208p. 1982. pap. 4.95 (ISBN 0-399-50669-1, Perige). Putnam Pub Group.
Colman, A. Game Theory & Experimental Games: The Study of Strategic Interaction. (International Ser. in Experimental Social Psychology: Vol. 4). 300p. 1982. 38.00 (ISBN 0-08-026070-5); pap. 17.95 (ISBN 0-08-026069-1). Pergamon.
GAMES
see also Amusements; Bible Games and Puzzles; Cards; Children's Parties; Dancing-Children's Dances; Games for Travelers; Indoor Games; Mathematical Recreations; Olympic Games; Play; Puzzles; Schools-Exercises and Recreations; Sports; Video Games
also specific games, e.g. Baseball, Contract Bridge, Tennis
Book of Worldwide Games & Dances. 160p. 8.95 (ISBN 0-88314-102-7). AAHPERD.
Braunlich, Tom. The Official Book of Penter: The Classic Game of Skill. 128p. (Orig.). 1983. pap. 7.95 (ISBN 0-8092-5522-7). Contemp Bks.
--Pente Strategy Book I. Date not set. pap. 3.50 (ISBN 0-9609414-0-1). Pente Games.
--Pente Strategy Book II. Date not set. pap. 4.00 (ISBN 0-9609414-1-X). Pente Games.
Buck, Peter. Arts & Crafts of Hawaii: Games & Recreation, VIII. (Special Publication Ser.: No. 45). (Illus.). 32p. 1957. pap. 3.00 (ISBN 0-910240-41-8). Bishop Mus.
Cooper, Rosaleen & Palmer, Ann. Games from an Edwardian Childhood. (Illus.). 96p. 1982. 9.95 (ISBN 0-7153-8317-5). David & Charles.
Craven, Robert R., compiled by. Billiards, Bowling, Table Tennis, Pinball & Video Games: A Bibliographic Guide. LC 82-21077. 162p. 1983. lib. bdg. 29.95 (ISBN 0-313-23462-0, CBB/). Greenwood.
Donnelly, R. H., et al. Active Games & Contests. 2nd ed. 672p. 1958. 21.95 (ISBN 0-471-07088-2). Wiley.
Hacken, Sara. Games & Puzzles for Mormon Youth. 64p. 1982. 4.95 (ISBN 0-87747-932-1). Deseret Bk.
Harris, Frank W. Games. rev. ed. (Illus.). 89p. 1983. pap. 6.95 (ISBN 0-686-42928-1). F Harris.
Holiday Game Book. 1982. 9.95 (ISBN 0-939418-47-9). Ferguson-Florissant.
How to Win at Zaxxon. (Orig.). 1982. pap. 2.25 (ISBN 0-671-46749-2). Pb.
Mauldon, E. & Redfern, H. B. Games Teaching. 144p. 1981. 30.00x (ISBN 0-7121-0739-8, Pub. by Macdonald & Evans). State Mutual Bk.
Melsom, Andrew. House Party Games & Amusements for the Upper Class & Other Folks. Orig. Title: Are You There, Moriarty? (Illus.). 114p. 1983. pap. 4.76i (ISBN 0-06-463577-5, EH 577). B&N NY.
Mood, Dale & Musker, Frank F. Sports & Recreational Activities for Men & Women. 8th ed. (Illus.). 442p. 1983. pap. text ed. 14.95 (ISBN 0-8016-0290-4). Mosby.
Morris, Scot. Omni Games. (Illus.). 192p. 1983. pap. 9.95 (ISBN 0-03-060297-1). HR&W.
Nomura, Yoko. Pinch & Ouch: Acting Games. 43p. 1982. pap. text ed. 4.00 (ISBN 0-940264-14-5). Lingual Hse Pub.
Patterns for Holiday Games. 1982. 2.75 (ISBN 0-939418-48-7). Ferguson-Florissant.
Sanborn, Jane, ed. Bag of Tricks. (Illus.). 87p. (Orig.). 1983. pap. 6.95 (ISBN 0-910715-02-5). Search Public.
The U. S. Toy & Game Industry. 1982. 495.00 (ISBN 0-686-38432-6, 502). Busn Trend.
Williams, Kit. Masquerade: The Answers & Clues Explained. LC 82-40502. 48p. 1983. pap. 3.95 (ISBN 0-89480-369-7). Workman Pub.
GAMES-COMPUTER PROGRAMS
Gabriele, Rosemarie. Game Techniques in Applesoft BASIC. 1983. pap. 12.95 (ISBN 0-686-83945-5). Devin.
Mau. Create Word Puzzles with Your Microcomputer. 14.95 (ISBN 0-686-82004-5, 6251). Hayden.
GAMES-JUVENILE LITERATURE
Gawron, Marlene E. Busy Bodies: Finger Plays & Action Rhymes. (Illus.). (ps-1). 1981. 4.50 (ISBN 0-686-38123-8). Moonlight FL.
Hand, Phyllis. The Name of the Game Is... Learning. (gr. 2-6). 1982. 9.95 (ISBN 0-86653-096-7, GA 436). Good Apple.
Reich, Ali. Jump Rope Jingles. LC 82-13317. (Annie Hummingbird Bks.). (Illus.). 16p. (ps-8). 1983. pap. 1.25 saddle-wire (ISBN 0-394-85674-0). Random.
GAMES, OLYMPIC
see Olympic Games
GAMES, THEORY OF
see Game Theory
GAMES FOR TRAVELERS
Harwood, Michael. Games to Play in the Car. (Illus.). 96p. 1983. pap. 6.95 (ISBN 0-312-92239-6). Congdon & Weed.
GAMES OF CHANCE
see Gambling
GAMING
see Gambling
GANDHI, INDIRA (NEHRU), 1917-
Deol, D. Charisma & Commitment: The Mind & Political Thinking of Indira Gandhi. 136p. 1981. 12.95x (ISBN 0-940500-56-6, Pub. by Sterling India). Asia Bk Corp.
GANDHI, MOHANDAS KARAMCHAND, 1869-1948
Attenborough, Richard. In Search of Gandhi. (Illus.). 240p. 1983. 17.95 (ISBN 0-8329-0237-3). New Century.
Attenborough, Richard, intro. by. The Words of Gandhi. LC 82-14403. (Illus.). 111p. 1982. 8.95 (ISBN 0-937858-14-5). Newmarket.
Briley, John. Gandhi: Screenplay for the Film by Richard Attenborough. 192p. 1983. 6.95 (ISBN 0-394-62471-8, E856, Ever). Grove.
Fischer, Louis. The Essential Gandhi. LC 82-48890. 1983. pap. 4.95 (ISBN 0-394-71466-0, Vin). Random.
--The Life of Mahatma Gandhi. 1983. pap. 8.95 (ISBN 0-06-091038-0, CN1038, CN). Har-Row.
Gandhi: An Autobiography, Mohandas Gandhi, 1957. Date not set. pap. 8.61 (ISBN 0-8070-5981-1, BP 35). Beacon Pr.
Gaur, V. P. Mahatma Gandhi: A Study of His Message of Mpm-Violence. 145p. 1977. 12.95x (ISBN 0-940500-60-4, Pub. by Sterling India). Asia Bk Corp.
Gold, Gerald. Gandhi: A Pictorical Biography. (Illus.). 192p. 1983. 16.95 (ISBN 0-937858-27-7); pap. 9.95 (ISBN 0-937858-20-X). Newmarket.
Green, Martin. Tolstoy & Gandhi, Men of Peace (A Biography) 500p. 1983. 23.50 (ISBN 0-465-08631-4). Basic.
Homer, Jack A., ed. Gandhi Reader: A Resourcebook of his Life & Writings. 316p. 1983. 5.95 (ISBN 0-394-62472-6, E279, Ever). Grove.
Kytle, Calvin. Gandhi: Soldier of Nonviolence. LC 82-10633. (Illus.). 208p. 1983. 13.95 (ISBN 0-932020-18-6); pap. 8.95 (ISBN 0-932020-19-4). Seven Locks Pr.
Shirer, William L. Ghandi: A Memoir. 1982. pap. 3.95 (ISBN 0-671-46147-8). WSP.
GANDHI, MOHANDAS KARAMCHAND, 1869-1948-JUVENILE LITERATURE
Cheney, Glenn A. Mohandas Gandhi. (Impact Biography Ser.). (Illus.). 128p. (gr. 7 up). 1983. PLB 8.90 (ISBN 0-531-04600-1). Watts.
GANGES RIVER
Abbas, B. M. The Ganges Water Dispute. 160p. 1982. text ed. 27.50x (ISBN 0-7069-2080-5, Pub. by Vikas India). Advent NY.
GANGLIA, NERVOUS
see Nerves
GANGS
Muhlbauer. The Losers: Gang Delinquency in American Suburbs. 160p. 1983. 19.95 (ISBN 0-03-060313-7). Praeger.
GANGSTERS
see Gangs
GAOLS
see Prisons
GARBAGE
see Refuse and Refuse Disposal
GARCIA LORCA, FEDERICO, 1899-1936
Cobb, Carl W., tr. from Span. Lorca's Romancero Gitano: A Ballad Translation & Critical Study. LC 82-17454. 136p. 1983. text ed. 15.00x (ISBN 0-87805-177-5). U Pr of Miss.
GARDEN ARCHITECTURE
see Architecture, Domestic; Landscape Gardening
GARDEN PESTS
see also Insects, Injurious and Beneficial; Plant Diseases
Carr, Anna. Rodale's Color Handbook of Garden Insects. (Illus.). 256p. 1983. pap. 10.95 (ISBN 0-87857-460-3, 01-637-1). Rodale Pr Inc.
Logsdon, Gene. Wildlife in Your Garden: Or Dealing with Deer, Rabbits, Raccoons, Moles, Crows, Sparrows, & Other of Nature's Creatures in Ways That Keep Them Around but Away from Your Fruits & Vegetables. Wallace, Dan, ed. (Illus.). 416p. 1983. 16.95 (ISBN 0-87857-454-9, 01-028-0). Rodale Pr Inc.
GARDENING
Here are entered general works. For works dealing with gardening in specific countries see the geographic subdivisions which follow. Works dealing with specific areas of the United states, e.g. Southern States are entered under the subdivision United States.
see also Bulbs; Climbing Plants; Flower Gardening; Garden Pests; Gardens; Grafting; Greenhouses; Herbs; Horticulture; Insects, Injurious and Beneficial; Landscape Gardening; Organic Gardening; Plant Propagation; Plants, Ornamental; Pruning; Vegetable Gardening; Weeds; Window-Gardening
Baker, Jarry. The Impatient Gardener. 288p. (Orig.). 1983. pap. 6.95 (ISBN 0-345-30949-9). Ballantine.
Baldwin, Ian & Stanley, John. The Garden Centre Manuel. (Illus.). 250p. 1982. pap. text ed. 29.95 (ISBN 0-686-84094-1). Timber.
Ball, Jeff. The Self-Sufficient Suburban Gardener: A Step-by-Step Planning & Management Guide to Backyard Food Production. Halpin, Anne, ed. (Illus.). 256p. 1983. 14.95 (ISBN 0-87857-457-3, 01-083-0). Rodale Pr Inc.
Bartholmew, Mel. Square Foot Gardening. (Illus.). 360p. 14.95 (ISBN 0-87857-340-2); pap. 11.95 (ISBN 0-87857-341-0). Rodale Pr Inc.
Beckett, Kenneth A. & Carr, David. The Contained Garden: A Complete Illustrated Guide to Growing Plants, Flowers, Fruits, & Vegetables Outdoors in Pots. (Illus.). 168p. 1983. 26.00 (ISBN 0-670-23960-7, Studio); pap. 12.95 (ISBN 0-670-23961-5). Viking Pr.
Boston Urban Gardeners. A Handbook of Community Gardening. (Illus.). 192p. 1983. pap. 7.95 (ISBN 0-686-37894-6). CribT.
Burpee, Lois. Lois Burpee's Gardener's Companion & Cookbook. LC 82-47736. (Illus.). 256p. 1983. 14.37i (ISBN 0-06-038021-7, HarpT). Har-Row.
Center for Self-Sufficiency Staff, ed. Plant Your Own Fruits & Vegetables & More. 50p. 1983. pap. text ed. cancelled (ISBN 0-686-82426-1). Center Self.
Chamberlin, Susan. Hedges, Screens & Espaliers: How to Select, Grow & Enjoy. 176p. 1982. pap. 9.95 (ISBN 0-89586-190-9). H P Bks.
The Ed Hume Gardening Book. LC 82-48231. (Illus.). 192p. (Orig.). 1983. pap. 12.45i (ISBN 0-06-091028-3, CN 1028, CN). Har-Row.
Fitz, Franklin H. A Gardener's Guide to Propagating Food Plants. (Illus.). 160p. 1983. 10.95 (ISBN 0-684-17655-6, ScribT). Scribner.
Foster, Raymond. The Garden in Autumn & Winter. (Illus.). 192p. 1983. 24.95 (ISBN 0-7153-8416-3). David & Charles.
--The Gardener's Guide to Rare, Exotic, & Difficult Plants. (Illus.). 208p. 1983. 27.50 (ISBN 0-7153-8293-4). David & Charles.
Fryer, Lee. The Bio-Gardener's Bible: Building Super-Fertile Soil. (Illus.). 288p. 1982. 14.95 (ISBN 0-686-82061-4); pap. 9.95 (ISBN 0-8019-7289-2). Chilton.
Gardener's Catalog People. The Gardener's Catalog, No. 2. rev. ed. (Illus.). 320p. 1983. pap. 12.95 (ISBN 0-688-01238-8). Quill NY.
Graham, Sharon K. One Thousand & One Tips for Successful Gardening: Easy Ways to Grow the Best Vegetables, Fruits, Herbs, Flowers & Houseplants. 160p. 1983. 6.95 (ISBN 0-525-93278-X, 0675-200). Dutton.

Hatchett, David. Country House Garden. (Illus.). 192p. 1983. 23.95 (ISBN 0-7153-8250-0). David & Charles.

Hendrickson, Marilyn & Hendrickson, Robert. Two Thousand & One Free Things for the Garden. 256p. 1983. 16.95 (ISBN 0-312-82746-6); pap. 7.95 (ISBN 0-312-82747-4). St Martin.

James, Theodore, Jr. The Gourmet Garden: How to Grow Vegetables, Fruits & Herbs for Today's Cuisine. (Illus.). 256p. 1983. 15.95 (ISBN 0-525-93264-X, 01549-460); pap. 9.95 (ISBN 0-525-48044-7, 0966-290). Dutton.

Jekyll, Gertrude. A Gardener's Testament. (Illus.). 336p. 1982. 29.50 (ISBN 0-907462-29-4). Antique Collect.

--Home & the Garden. (Illus.). 390p. 1982. 29.50 (ISBN 0-907462-18-9). Antique Collect.

--Wall, Water & Woodland Gardens. (Illus.). 380p. 1982. 29.50 (ISBN 0-907462-26-X). Antique Collect.

Langston, Jack M. Lexigrow: A New & Easy Gardening Concept. LC 82-90041. (Illus.). 160p. (Orig.). 1982. pap. 8.95 (ISBN 0-910387-00-1). Lexigrow Intl.

Massingham, Betty. A Century of Gardeners. (Illus.). 288p. 1983. 24.95 (ISBN 0-571-11811-9). Faber & Faber.

Pearson, Robert, ed. The Wisley Book of Gardening. (Illus.). 1983. 25.95 (ISBN 0-393-01676-5). Norton.

Proulx, E. Annie. The Gardener's Journal & Record Book. Halpin, Anne, ed. (Illus.). 208p. 1983. 15.95 (ISBN 0-87857-461-1, 01-162-0); pap. 9.95 (ISBN 0-87857-462-X, 01-162-1). Rodale Pr Inc.

Raymond, Dick. Garden Way's Joy of Gardening. Thabault, George, ed. (Illus.). 384p. 1983. 25.00 (ISBN 0-88266-320-8); pap. 17.95 (ISBN 0-88266-319-4). Garden Way Pub.

Reader's Digest Editors. Illustrated Guide to Gardening. LC 77-85145. (Illus.). 672p. 1978. 22.50 (ISBN 0-89577-046-6, Pub. by RD Assn). Random.

Scott, George H. Bulbs: How to Select, Grow & Enjoy. 160p. 1982. pap. 7.95 (ISBN 0-89586-146-1). H P Bks.

Seifert, Anne & Hoyt, Fred. Hydroponic Home Gardening: Made Easy! (Illus.). 120p. (Orig.). 1983. pap. 4.50 (ISBN 0-943584-00-0). Varnes Pubs.

Sinnes, A. Cort. Easy Maintenance Gardening. Burke, Ken, ed. LC 82-82160. (Illus.). 96p. 1982. pap. 5.95 (ISBN 0-89721-004-2). Ortho.

--Shade Gardening. Burke, Ken, ed. LC 82-82159. (Illus.). 96p. (Orig.). 1982. pap. 5.95 (ISBN 0-89721-005-0). Ortho.

Stephenson, Ashley. The Garden Planner. (Illus.). 258p. 1983. 25.00 (ISBN 0-312-31688-7); pap. 12.95 (ISBN 0-312-31689-5). St Martin.

Sunset Books & Sunset Magazine Editors. Gardener's Answer Book. LC 82-83214. (Illus.). 160p. 1983. pap. 7.95 (ISBN 0-376-03186-7). Sunset-Lane.

Szekely, Edmond B. The Ecological Health Garden & the Book of Survival. (Illus.). 80p. 1978. pap. 4.50 (ISBN 0-89564-072-4). IBS Intl.

Teacher, Lawrence, ed. The Gardener's Notebook: A Personal Journal. (Illus.). 96p. (Orig.). 1983. lib. bdg. 12.90 (ISBN 0-89471-205-5); pap. 4.95 (ISBN 0-89471-204-7). Running Pr.

Wright, Tom. Large Gardens & Parks: Maintenance, Management & Design. 194p. (Orig.). 1982. text ed. 35.50x (ISBN 0-246-11402-9, Pub by Granada England). Renouf.

GARDENING-JUVENILE LITERATURE

Glovach, Linda. The Little Witch's Spring Holiday Book. (Illus.). 48p. (ps-4). 8.95 (ISBN 0-13-538108-8). P-H.

GARDENING-GREAT BRITAIN

Chatto, Beth. The Damp Garden. 224p. 1982. 40.00x (ISBN 0-460-04551-2, Pub. by J M Dent). State Mutual Bk.

Historic Houses, Castles & Gardens in Great Britain & Ireland, 1982. LC 57-35834. (Illus.). 179p. 1982. pap. 4.50x (ISBN 0-900486-31-7). Intl Pubns Serv.

Martin, Peter. Pursuing Innocent Pleasures: The Gardening World of Alexander Pope. 1983. price not set (ISBN 0-208-02011-X, Archon Bks). Shoe String.

Pearkes, Gillian. Vinegrowing in Britain. 224p. 1982. 40.00x (ISBN 0-460-04393-5, Pub. by J M Dent England). State Mutual Bk.

Thomas, Edward. In Pursuit of Spring. 302p. 1982. 30.00x (ISBN 0-7045-0423-5, Pub. by Wildwood House). State Mutual Bk.

GARDENING-UNITED STATES

David Fairchild's the World Was My Garden. LC 82-72427. (Illus.). 494p. 1982. Repr. 20.00 (ISBN 0-686-84310-X). Banyan Bks.

Kriegel, John. Houston Home & Garden's Complete Guide to Houston Gardening. 425p. 1983. 24.95 (ISBN 0-940672-08-1). Shearer Pub.

Mac Perry's Florida Lawn & Garden Care. LC 77-9038. (Illus.). 160p. 1982. pap. 7.95 (ISBN 0-686-84278-2). Banyan Bks.

Marson, Chuck. Great Plains Gardening. (Illus.). 208p. 1983. pap. 6.95 (ISBN 0-941974-01-4). Baranski Pub Corp.

Marson, Chuck & Parker, Roy. In Your Own Backyard: A Gardener's Guide & the Great Plains. (Illus.). 208p. (Orig.). 1983. pap. 6.95 (ISBN 0-941974-01-4). Baranski Pub Corp.

Neal, Marie C. In Gardens of Hawaii. rev. ed. (Special Publication Ser.: No. 50). (Illus.). 944p. 1965. 25.00 (ISBN 0-910240-33-7). Bishop Mus.

Wyatt, Roy. Cuttings from a Country Garden. 1983. 11.95 (ISBN 0-932298-35-4). Copple Hse.

GARDENS

see also Rock Gardens

Binney, William R. The Architectural Characteristics & Types of Spanish Gardens. (The Masterpieces of World Architecture Library). (Illus.). 129p. 1983. 87.45 (ISBN 0-86650-045-6). Gloucester Art.

Jekyll, Gertrude. Children & Gardens. (Illus.). 192p. 1982. 29.50 (ISBN 0-907462-27-8). Antique Collect.

Lennard, Erica. Classic Gardens. LC 83-80908. (Illus.). 128p. 1982. 27.95 (ISBN 0-912810-38-6). Lustrum Pr.

Lewis, Sherwood A. The Illustrated Book of American Gardens. (An American Culture Library Book). (Illus.). 117p. 1983. 67.85 (ISBN 0-86650-050-2). Gloucester Art.

Saville, Diana. Walled Gardens: Their Planting & Design. (Illus.). 168p. 1982. 42.00 (ISBN 0-7134-1494-4, Pub. by Batsford England). David & Charles.

GARDENS-EUROPE

Kaden, Vera. The Illustration of Plants & Gardens, 1500-1850. (Illus.). 113p. 1982. pap. 15.00 (ISBN 0-686-43333-5). Intl Pubns Serv.

GARDENS-GREAT BRITAIN

Fleming, Laurence & Gore, Alan. The English Garden. (Illus.). 256p. 1983. pap. 10.95 (ISBN 0-7181-2191-0, Pub by Michael Joseph). Merrimack Bk Serv.

Jekyll, Gertrude. Lilies for English Gardens. (Illus.). 156p. 1982. 29.50 (ISBN 0-907462-28-6). Antique Collect.

Sidwell, Ron. West Midland Gardens. 252p. 1981. text ed. 18.00x (ISBN 0-904387-71-2, 61110, Pub. by Sutton England). Humanities.

GARFIELD, JAMES ABRAM, PRES. U. S., 1831-1881

Brown, Harry J. & Williams, Frederick D., eds. The Diary of James A. Garfield, Vol. IV: 1878-1881. 1982. 40.00 (ISBN 0-87013-221-0). Mich St U Pr.

GARLIC

Doeser, Linda & Richardson, Rosamond. The Little Garlic Book. (Illus.). 64p. 1983. 5.95 (ISBN 0-312-48864-5). St Martin.

GARNISHES IN COOKERY

see Cookery (Garnishes)

GARRETT, PATRICK FLOYD, 1850-1908

Metz, Leon C. Pat Garrett: The Story of a Western Lawman. LC 72-9261. (Illus.). 328p. 1983. pap. 9.95 (ISBN 0-8061-1838-5). U of Okla Pr.

GAS, NATURAL

see also Boring; Gas Industry; Oil Fields

Maull, Hanns W. Natural Gas & Economic Security. (The Atlantic Papers: No. 43). 60p. (Orig.). 1981. pap. text ed. 6.50X (ISBN 0-86598-082-9). Allanheld.

OECD Staff. Natural Gas Prospects to 2000. 173p. 1982. pap. 24.00 (ISBN 92-64-12309-1). OECD.

GAS, NATURAL-LAW AND LEGISLATION

see also Oil and Gas Leases

Hemingway, Richard W. The Law of Oil & Gas. 2nd ed. (Hornbook Ser.). 507p. 1983. text ed. price not set (ISBN 0-314-71558-4). West Pub.

Russell, Jeremy L. Geopolitics of Natural Gas. 176p. 1983. prof ref 24.50x (ISBN 0-88410-610-1). Ballinger Pub.

GAS AND OIL ENGINES

see also Diesel Motor

Benson, Rowland S. Thermodynamics & Gas Dynamics of Internal Combustion Engines, Vol. 1. Horlock, J. H. & Winterbone, D., eds. (Illus.). 600p. 1982. text ed. 125.00x (ISBN 0-19-856210-1). Oxford U Pr.

Brown, Arlen D. & Strickland, R. Mack. Tractor & Small Engine Maintenance. 5th ed. 350p. 1983. 15.65 (ISBN 0-8134-2258-2); text ed. 11.75x (ISBN 0-686-83991-9). Interstate.

A Guide to Transformer Maintenance. write for info (ISBN 0-939320-00-2). Myers Inc.

Hickling, Robert & Kamal, Mounir M. Engine Noise: Excitation, Vibration, & Radiation. (General Motors Research Symposia Ser.). 490p. 1982. 62.50x (ISBN 0-306-41168-7, Plenum Pr). PLenum Pub.

Myers, S. D. Gas-in-Oil Analysis vs. All Other Methods. (TMI Evaluates Ser.). 72p. 1980. 10.00 (ISBN 0-939320-02-9). Myers Inc.

--Transformer Oil Treatment vs. Transformer Desludging. (TMI Evaluates Ser.). 72p. 1980. 10.00 (ISBN 0-939320-03-7). Myers Inc.

--What to Do about Askarel (PCB) Transformers. (TMI Evaluates Ser.). 106p. 1980. 10.00 (ISBN 0-939320-05-3). Myers Inc.

S. D. Myers, Inc. TMI Evaluates Series, 10 bks. Date not set. write for info. (ISBN 0-939320-04-5). Myers Inc.

Uzkan, T., ed. Flows in Internal Combustion Engines. 1982. 24.00 (H00245). ASME.

Watson, N. & Janota, M. S. Turbocharging the Internal Combustion Engine. 608p. 1982. 84.95 (ISBN 0-471-87072-2, Pub. by Wiley-Interscience). Wiley.

--Turbocharging the Internal Combustion Engine. 1982. 125.00x (ISBN 0-333-24290-4, Pub. by Macmillan England). State Mutual Bk.

GAS AND OIL LEASES

see Oil and Gas Leases

GAS CHROMATOGRAPHY

Schupp, Orion E., ed. Gas Chromatography. (Technique of Organic Chemistry Ser.: Vol. 13). 437p. Repr. of 1968 ed. text ed. 36.50 (ISBN 0-470-93263-5). Krieger.

GAS ENGINES

see Gas and Oil Engines

GAS INDUSTRY

Here are entered general works on industries based on natural or manufactured gas.

see also Gas, Natural

also other headings beginning with the word Gas

Guiliano, Francis A., ed. Introduction to Oil & Gas Technology. 2nd ed. (Short Course Handbooks). (Illus.). 194p. 1981. text ed. 29.00 (ISBN 0-934634-48-3); pap. text ed. 21.00. Intl Human Res.

Knowles, Ruth S. The First Pictorial History of the American Oil & Gas Industry, 1859-1983. (Illus.). 177p. 1983. 15.95 (ISBN 0-8214-0693-0, 82-84622). Ohio U Pr.

Metal Structures in the Mining, Gas & Oil Industries: Metal Stuctures Conferences, 1978. 114p. (Orig.). 1978. pap. text ed. 31.50 (ISBN 0-85825-104-3, Pub. by Inst Engineering Australia). Renouf.

GAS LEASES

see Oil and Gas Leases

GAS LIQUID CHROMATOGRAPHY

see Gas Chromatography

GAS-TURBINES

Sawyer, John W., ed. Sawyer's Gas Turbine Engineering Handbook, 3 Vols. Incl. Vol. I. Theory & Design. 42.50 (ISBN 0-937506-05-2); Vol. II. Applications. 42.50 (ISBN 0-937506-06-0). LC 74-140403. 1976. Set. 85.00x (ISBN 0-937506-04-4). Turbo Intl Pubn.

GASEOUS PLASMA

see Plasma (Ionized Gases)

GASES

see also Combustion Gases

also Specific gases, e.g. Acetyelene, Helium, Hydrogen, Nitrogen, Oxygen

Henzel, D. S., et al. Handbook for Flue Gas Desulfurization Scrubbing with Limestone. LC 82-7926. (Pollution Technology Rev. 94). (Illus.). 424p. 1983. 44.00 (ISBN 0-8155-0912-X). Noyes.

Jeans, James S. An Introduction to the Kinetic Theory of Gases. LC 40-3353. (Cambridge Science Classics). 319p. 1982. pap. 15.95 (ISBN 0-521-09232-9). Cambridge U Pr.

Reintjes, John F., ed. Nonlinear Optical Parametric Processes in Liquids & Gases. LC 82-11603. Date not set. price not set (ISBN 0-12-585980-5). Acad Pr.

Ruch, Walter E. Chemical Detection of Gaseous Pollutants: An Annotated Bibliography. LC 66-29577. 180p. 1982. 24.00 (ISBN 0-250-40099-5). Ann Arbor Science.

GASES-DIFFUSION

see Diffusion

GASES-LIQUEFACTION

see also Hydrogen

Vargaftik, N. B. Handbook of Physical Properties of Liquids & Gases: Pure Substances & Mixtures. 2nd ed. LC 82-25857. 1983. text ed. 59.95 (ISBN 0-89116-356-5). Hemisphere Pub.

GASES, ELECTRIC DISCHARGES THROUGH

see Electric Discharges through Gases

GASES, KINETIC THEORY OF

Collie, C. H. Kinetic Theory & Entropy. LC 81-8332. (Illus.). 416p. 1983. pap. text ed. 22.00x (ISBN 0-582-44368-7). Longman.

Klimontovich, Yu L. Kinetic Theory of Nonideal Gases & Nonideal Plasmas, Vol. 105. Bakescu, R., tr. LC 82-9044. (International Series in Natural Philosophy). (Illus.). 328p. 1982. 65.00 (ISBN 0-08-021671-4). Pergamon.

GASOLINE ENGINES

see Gas and Oil Engines

GASTRIN

Borsy, J. Symposium on Gastrin & It's Antagonists, Vol. 3. (Hungarian Pharmacological Society, First Congress Ser.). (Illus.). 153p. 1973. 10.00 (ISBN 0-8002-3045-0). Intl Pubns Serv.

GASTROENTEROLOGY

see also Intestines; Stomach

Alexander-Williams, J. Large Intestine. new ed. (BIMR Gastroenterolgy Ser.: vol. 3). 1983. text ed. price not set (ISBN 0-407-02289-9). Butterworth.

Bongiovanni, G. Manual of Clinical Gastroenterology. 598p. 1982. 13.95 (ISBN 0-07-006471-7). McGraw.

Csomos, G. Clinical Hepatology: History-Present State-Outlook. (Illus.). 430p. 1982. 42.00 (ISBN 0-387-11838-1). Springer-Verlag.

Galambos. Gastroenterology Appraisal for Patient Care. text ed. write for info (ISBN 0-409-95024-6). Butterworth.

Gitnick, Gary L. Gastroenterology. (Internal Medicine Today: A Comprehensive Postgraduate Library). 424p. 1983. 35.00 (ISBN 0-471-09566-4, Pub. by Wiley Med). Wiley.

Jerzy, George B. & Sherlock, Paul, eds. Progress in Gastroenterology. (Vol. 4). write for info. Grune.

Sernka, Thomas J. & Jacobson, Eugene D. Gastrointestinal Physiology: The Essentials. 2nd ed. 184p. 1983. pap. text ed. write for info. (ISBN 0-683-07721-X). Williams & Wilkins.

Silverberg, Mervin. Advanced Textbook of Pediatric Gastroenterology. (Advanced Textbook Ser.). 1982. pap. text ed. 32.50 (ISBN 0-87488-657-0). Med Exam.

Silverman, Arnold & Roy, Claude C. Pediatric Clinical Gastroenterology. 3rd ed. (Illus.). 978p. 1983. text ed. 66.00 (ISBN 0-8016-4623-5). Mosby.

Spiro. Clinical Gastroenterology. 3rd ed. 1983. 85.00 (ISBN 0-02-415250-1). Macmillan.

Stern, Robert M. & Davis, Christopher M., eds. Gastric Motility: A Selectively Annotated Bibliography. LC 82-12173. 208p. 1982. 19.50 (ISBN 0-87933-430-4). Hutchinson Ross.

Strum, Williamson B. Gastroenterology Assistant's Handbook. Gardner, Alvin F., ed. (Allied Professions Monograph Ser.). 224p. 1983. 28.50 (ISBN 0-87527-292-4). Green.

Yetiv, Jack & Bianchine, Joseph R. Recent Advances in Clinical Therapeutics: Psychopharmacology, Neuropharmacology, Gastrointestinal Therapeutics. (Vol. 2). write for info (ISBN 0-8089-1542-8). Grune.

GASTROINTESTINAL TRACT

see Alimentary Canal

GATES

Chamberlin, Susan & Pollock, Susan. Fences, Gates & Walls. 1983. pap. 9.95 (ISBN 0-89586-189-5). H P Bks.

GATT

see Contracting Parties to the General Agreement on Tariffs and Trade

GATTI-CASAZZA, GIULIO, 1869-1940

Taubman, Howard, pref. by. Gatti-Casazza, Giulio: Memories of the Opera. LC 71-183334. (Illus.). 356p. Date not set. Repr. of 1941 ed. price not set. Vienna Hse.

GAUDI Y CORNET, ANTONIO, 1852-1926

Martinell, Cesar. Gaudi: His LIfe, His Theories, His Work. Ribalta, Marta, ed. (Illus.). 127p. 1982. pap. 12.95 (ISBN 84-7031-218-9, Pub. by Editorial Blume Spain). Intl Schol Bk Serv.

GAUGES

see Gages

GAUGING

see Gaging

GAULLE, CHARLES DE, PRES. FRANCE, 1890-1970

Kersaudy, Francois. Churchill & DeGaulle. LC 81-69154. 480p. 1983. pap. 11.95 (ISBN 0-689-70641-3, 290). Atheneum.

Ledwidge, Bernard. De Gaulle. (Illus.). 448p. 1983. 17.95 (ISBN 0-312-19127-8). St Martin.

GAUSSIAN NOISE

see Random Noise Theory

GAUTAMA BUDDHA

Szekely, Edmond B. The Living Buddha. (Illus.). 70p. 1977. pap. 4.50 (ISBN 0-89564-059-7). IBS Intl.

GAY LIB

see Gay Liberation Movement

GAY LIBERATION MOVEMENT

D'Emilio, John. Sexual Politics, Sexual Communities: The Making of a Homosexual Minority in the United States 1940-1970. LC 82-16000. 262p. 1983. 20.00 (ISBN 0-226-14265-5). U of Chicago Pr.

Rueda, Enrique. Homosexual Network: Private Lives & Public Policy. 740p. 1983. 24.95 (ISBN 0-8159-5715-7); pap. 11.95 (ISBN 0-8159-5714-9). Devin.

GAZETTEERS

see Geography-Dictionaries

GEARING

see also Automobiles-Steering Gear; Mechanical Movements

Smith, James D. Gears & Their Vibration: A Basic Approach to Understanding Gear Noise. (Mechanical Engineering Ser.: Vol. 17). (Illus.). 192p. 1983. 29.50 (ISBN 0-8247-1797-X). Dekker.

GEARS

see Gearing

GED TESTS

see General Educational Development Tests

GELEE, CLAUDE, CALLED CLAUDE LORRAIN, 1600-1682

Russell, H. Diane. Claude Lorrain: A Tercentery Exhibition. 1982. pap. 29.95 (ISBN 0-89468-057-9). Natl Gallery Art.

GELS

see Colloids

GEM CUTTING

Vargas, Glenn & Vargas, Martha. Diagrams For Faceting, Vol. II. (Illus.). 1983. 15.00 (ISBN 0-686-82596-9). Glenn Vargas.

GEMMATION (BOTANY)

see Plants-Reproduction

GEMS

Here are entered books on engraved stones and jewels, interesting from the point of view of antiquities or art. Works on mineralogical interest are entered under Precious Stones.

see also Crown Jewels; Jewelry

Read. Dictionary of Gemmology. 1982. text ed. 34.95 (ISBN 0-408-00571-8). Butterworth.

--Gemmological Instruments. 2nd ed. 1983. text ed. price not set (ISBN 0-408-01190-4). Butterworth.

Webster & Anderson. Gems. 4th ed. 1983. text ed. price not set (ISBN 0-408-01148-3). Butterworth.

GEMSTONE COLLECTING

see Mineralogy-Collectors and Collecting

GENEALOGICAL RESEARCH

see Genealogy

GENEALOGY
see also Biography; Heraldry; Pensions, Military; Registers of Births, Deaths, Marriages, etc.; Wills also names of families, e.g. Adams Family; and names of places with or without the subdivision Genealogy, e.g. United States - Genealogy

Croom, Emily A. Unpuzzling Your Past: A Basic Guide to Genealogy. LC 82-24514. (Illus.). 128p. 1983. pap. 7.95 (ISBN 0-932620-21-3). Betterway Pubns.

Field, D. M. Step-by-Step Guide to Tracing Your Ancestors. 64p. 1983. 9.95 (ISBN 0-7095-1228-7, Pub. by Auto Assn-British Tourist Authority England). Merrimack Bk Serv.

Guide to Genealogical Research in the National Archives. (Illus.). 21.00 (ISBN 0-911333-00-2); pap. 17.00 (ISBN 0-911333-01-0). Natl Archives.

Haggerty, Charles E. Nuzum Family History. Rev. ed. (Illus.). 400p. 1983. lib. bdg. 30.00x (ISBN 0-686-43327-0). D G Nuzum.

Harvey, Richard. Genealogy for Librarians. 200p. 1983. 19.50 (Pub. by Bingley England). Shoe String.

Mason, James H. The Dudley Genealogies. LC 82-62705. 200p. 1983. 20.00 (ISBN 0-9609032-1-6). J H Mason.

Mayhew, Catherine M. Genealogical Periodical Annual Index, Vol. 18, 1979. Towle, Laird C., ed. xiv, 179p. 1982. 15.00 (ISBN 0-917890-24-8). Heritage Bk.

Olivier, Julien. Souches et Racines. (Illus.). 175p. (Fr.). 1981. pap. text ed. 4.50 (ISBN 0-911409-09-2). Natl Mat Dev.

Reeves, Emma B. Reeves Review, Book II. LC 82-61874. (Illus.). 504p. 1982. lib. bdg. 30.00 (ISBN 0-911013-00-8). E B Reeves.

Saperetti, Claudio. Assur 14446: Le Altre Famiglie. LC 82-50981. (Cuneiform Texas Ser.: Vol. 3). 196p. 1982. pap. 13.50 (ISBN 0-89003-118-5). Undena Pubns.

Sheppard, Walter L., Jr. Ancestry of Edward Carleton & Ellen Newton His Wife. (Illus.). 860p. 1978. text ed. write for info. (ISBN 0-9607610-2-0). W L Sheppard.

Trossbach, J. E. Fourteen Generations of Trossbach's, 1470-1982. 4th ed. 130p. 1982. 16.00 (ISBN 0-686-43300-9). J E Trossbach.

GENEALOGY-BIBLIOGRAPHY

Ericson, Jack T. Genealogy & Local History: Title List, Parts 2 & 3. 85p. 1981. write for info. Microfilming Corp.

GENEALOGY-RESEARCH
see Genealogy

GENEALOGY-SOURCES

Harvey, Richard. Genealogy for Librarians. 200p. 1983. 19.50 (Pub. by Bingley England). Shoe String.

GENERAL AGREEMENT ON TARIFFS AND TRADE
see Contracting Parties to the General Agreement on Tariffs and Trade

GENERAL EDUCATION
see Education, Humanistic

GENERAL EDUCATIONAL DEVELOPMENT TESTS
see also High School Equivalency Examination

Herring, Chuck & Herring, Judy. Offical GED Handbook. rev. ed. (The GED Institute's Offical GED Preparation Ser.). Orig. Title: The GED Handbook. (Illus.). 96p. (gr. 8-12). 1982. write for info (ISBN 0-937128-06-6). GED Inst.

Herzog, David A. Mathematics Workbook for the GED Test. LC 82-20571. (Arco's Preparation for the GED Examination Ser.). 256p. 1983. pap. 5.95 (ISBN 0-668-05542-1). Arco.

GENERAL JUDGMENT
see Judgment Day

GENERAL PRACTICE (MEDICINE)
see Family Medicine

GENERAL PROPERTY TAX
see Property Tax

GENERAL STAFFS
see Armies-Staffs

GENERALIZED FUNCTIONS
see Distributions, Theory of (Functional Analysis)

GENERALS
see also Military Biography

Reed, Thomas S. A Profile of Brigadire General Alfred N. A. Duffie. 1982. 11.00 (ISBN 0-89126-109-5). MA AH Pub.

Richardson, Frank M. Mars Without Venus: Study of Some Homosexual Generals. 188p. 1982. 14.95 (ISBN 0-85158-148-X, Pub. by Salem Hse Ltd.). Merrimack Bk Serv.

Urwin, Gregory J. Custer Victorious: The Civil War Battles of General George Armstrong Custer. LC 81-65873. (Illus.). 312p. 1982. 29.50 (ISBN 0-8386-3113-4). Fairleigh Dickinson.

GENERALS-CORRESPONDENCE, REMINISCENCES, ETC.

Beverley, George H. Pioneer in the U. S. Air Corps: The Memoirs of Brigadier General George H. Beverley. 1982. pap. 9.95x (ISBN 0-89745-029-9). Sunflower U Pr.

GENERATION
see Reproduction

GENERATIVE GRAMMAR

Noam Chomsky on the Generative Enterprise: A Discussion with Riny Huybregts & Henk van Riemsdijk. 136p. 1982. pap. 18.00x (ISBN 90-70176-70-X). Foris Pubns.

GENERATIVE ORGANS-ABNORMITIES AND DEFORMITIES

Hadziselimovic, F. Cryptorchidism: Management & Implications. (Illus.). 135p. 1983. 49.00 (ISBN 0-387-11881-0). Springer-Verlag.

GENERATIVE ORGANS-DISEASES

Nisbet, Ian C. & Karch, Nathan J. Chemical Hazards to Human Reproduction. LC 82-14441. (Illus.). 245p. 1983. 28.00 (ISBN 0-8155-0931-6). Noyes.

GENES
see Heredity

GENET, JEAN, 1910-

Coe, Richard. The Vision of Jean Genet. 344p. 1983. 17.95 (ISBN 0-7206-0080-4, Pub by Peter Owen). Merrimack Bk Serv.

GENETIC COUNSELING

Applebaum, Eleanor G. & Firestein, Stephen. A Genetic Counseling Casebook. LC 82-48605. 320p. 1983. price not set (ISBN 0-02-931300-7). Free Pr.

Dillon, Lawrence S. The Inconstant Gene. 568p. 1982. 65.00x (ISBN 0-306-41084-2, Plenum Pr). Plenum Pub.

Fuhrmann, W. & Vogel, F. Genetic Counseling. 3rd ed. Kurth-Scherer, S., tr. from Ger. (Illus.). 188p. 1983. pap. 15.95 (ISBN 0-387-90715-7). Springer-Verlag.

GENETIC ENGINEERING
see also Cloning

Cherfas, Jeremy. Man Made Life: An Overview of the Science, Technology & Commerce of Genetic Engineering. 279p. 1983. 15.95 (ISBN 0-394-52926-X). Pantheon.

Gassen, Hans G. & Lang, Anne, eds. Chemical & Enzymatic Synthesis of Gene Fragments: A Laboratory Manual. (Illus.). 259p. 1982. 41.10x (ISBN 0-89573-068-5). Verlag-Chemie.

Harsanyi, Zsolt & Hutton, Richard. Genetic Prophecy: Beyond the Double Helix. 288p. 1982. pap. 3.95 (ISBN 0-553-22601-0). Bantam.

Huang, P. C. & Kuo, T. T., eds. Genetic Engineering Techniques: Recent Developments (Symposium) LC 82-20687. Date not set. 28.50 (ISBN 0-12-358250-4). Acad Pr.

Levin, Morris A., et al. Applied Genetic Engineering: Future Trends & Problems. LC 82-14401. (Illus.). 191p. 1983. 24.00 (ISBN 0-8155-0925-1). Noyes.

Moraczewski, Albert S., ed. Genetic Medicine & Engineering: Ethical & Social Dimensions. (Orig.). 1983. pap. write for info. (ISBN 0-87125-077-2). Cath Health.

Williamson, R., ed. Genetic Engineering, Vol. 3. (Serial Publication). 192p. 1982. 22.00 (ISBN 0-12-270303-0). Acad Pr.

GENETIC PSYCHOLOGY
Here are entered works on the evolutionary psychology of man in terms of origin and development, whether in the individual or in the species. Works on the psychological development of the individual from infancy to old age are entered under Developmental Psychology.
see also Culture Conflict; Intelligence Levels; Sociobiology

Lumsden, Charles J. & Wilson, Edward O. Promethean Fire: Reflections on the Origin of Mind. (Illus.). 256p. 1983. 17.50 (ISBN 0-674-71445-8). Harvard U Pr.

GENETIC SURGERY
see Genetic Engineering

GENETICS
see also Adaptation (Biology); Biology; Chromosomes; Cytogenetics; Evolution; Genetic Psychology; Heredity; Human Genetics; Linkage (Genetics); Mutation (Biology); Natural Selection; Origin of Species; Population Genetics; Radiogenetics; Translocation (Genetics); Variation (Biology)

Avers, Charlotte. Genetics, Revised Edition. 657p. 1980. text ed. write for info (ISBN 0-87150-759-5). Grant Pr.

Brewer, George J. & Sing, Charles F. Genetics. (Biology Ser.). (Illus.). 575p. 1983. text ed. 24.95 (ISBN 0-201-10138-6); Courseware avail.; Solutions Manual avail. A-W.

Crow, James F. Genetics Notes: An Introduction to Genetics. 8th ed. 352p. 1982. pap. text ed. write for info. (ISBN 0-8087-4805-X). Burgess.

Current Concepts in Genetics. (Illus.). 117p. (Orig.). 1980. pap. text ed. 6.00 (ISBN 0-910133-02-6). MA Med Soc.

Daniel, William & Fleiszar, Kathleen. Genetics & Variation. (Illus.). 471p. text ed. 21.80 (ISBN 0-87563-220-3). Stipes.

Demerec, M., ed. Advances in Genetics, Vol. 21. LC 47-30313. (Serial Publication). 384p. 1982. 36.00 (ISBN 0-12-017621-1). Acad Pr.

Discovering Genetics. LC 81-52419. (Discovering Science Ser.). lib. bdg. 15.96 (ISBN 0-86706-061-1, Pub. by Stonehenge). Silver.

Dover, G. A. & Flavell, R. B., eds. Genome Evolution. (Systematics Association Ser.: Vol. 20). 388p. 1982. 33.50 (ISBN 0-12-221380-7); pap. 17.50 (ISBN 0-12-221382-3). Acad Pr.

Durand, P. & O'Brien, J. S., eds. Genetic Errors of Glycoprotein Metabolism. (Illus.). 220p. 1983. 33.50 (ISBN 0-387-12066-1). Springer-Verlag.

Epstein, Henry F. & Wolf, Stewart, eds. Genetic Analysis of the Chromosome: Studies of Duchenne Muscular Dystrophy & Related Disorders. Vol. 154. (Advances in Experimental Medicine & Biology). 222p. 1982. 37.50x (ISBN 0-306-41129-6, Plenum Pr). Plenum Pub.

Gardner, Eldon J. & Snustad, D. Peter. Principles of Genetics. 6th ed. LC 80-12114. 688p. 1981. text ed. 27.95 (ISBN 0-471-04412-1). Wiley.

Hyde, Margaret O. Cloning & the New Genetics. (Illus.). 128p. (gr. 5-11). 1983. 10.95 (ISBN 0-89490-084-6). Enslow Pubs.

Jaenicke, L., ed. Biochemistry of Differentiation & Morphogenosis. (Collequium Mosbach Ser.: Vol. 33). (Illus.). 301p. 1983. 37.00 (ISBN 0-387-12010-6). Springer-Verlag.

Klug, William S. & Cummings, Michael R. Concepts of Genetics. 1983. text ed. 22.95 (ISBN 0-675-20010-5). Additional supplements may be obtained from publisher. Merrill.

Lakovaara, Seppo, ed. Advances in Genetics, Development & Evolution of Drosophila. LC 82-9154. 480p. 1982. 57.50x (ISBN 0-306-41106-7, Plenum Pr). Plenum Pub.

Lebacqz, Karen. Genetics, Ethics & Parenthood. 128p. (Orig.). 1983. pap. 7.95 (ISBN 0-8298-0671-7). Pilgrim NY.

Lewin, Benjamin. Genes. 800p. 1983. text ed. 31.95 (ISBN 0-471-09316-5); lab. manual avail. (ISBN 0-471-89851-1). Wiley.

Moraczewski, Albert S., ed. Genetic Medicine & Engineering: Ethical & Social Dimensions. (Orig.). 1983. pap. write for info. (ISBN 0-87125-077-2). Cath Health.

Nei, Masatoshi & Koehn, Richard K., eds. Evolution of Genes & Proteins. (Illus.). 380p. 1983. price not set (ISBN 0-87893-603-3); pap. price not set (ISBN 0-87893-604-1). Sinauer Assoc.

Steiner, Walter & Tabachnick, WAlter, eds. Recent Development in the Genetics of Insect Disease Vectors. (Illus.). 665p. text ed. 26.00 (ISBN 0-87563-224-6). Stipes.

Tsukada, Y., ed. Genetic Approaches to Development Neurobiology. 269p. 1983. 43.00 (ISBN 0-387-11872-1). Springer-Verlag.

Wiesner, E. & Willer, S. Lexikon der Genetik der Hundekrankheiten. (Illus.). 480p. 1983. 29.50 (ISBN 3-8055-3616-X). S. Karger.

Zaleski, Marek B., et al. Immunogenetics. 512p. 1983. text ed. 34.95 (ISBN 0-273-01925-2). Pitman Pub MA.

GENITO-URINARY ORGANS

Magee, Michael C. Basic Science for the Practicing Urologist. LC 82-4561. (Illus.). 250p. Date not set. price not set (ISBN 0-521-24567-2). Cambridge U Pr.

GENITO-URINARY ORGANS-DISEASES
see also Gynecology; Urinary Organs-Diseases

Kane, H. H. The Bicycle as a Factor in Genito Urinary Diseases, Prostratis, Prostatorrhea, or Prostatic Catarrh. 24p. Date not set. pap. 5.00 (ISBN 0-87556-575-1). Saifer.

GENIUS
see also Creation (Literary, Artistic, etc.); Creative Ability; Gifted Children

Albert, R. S., ed. Genius & Eminence: The Social Psychology of Creativity & Exceptional Achievement. (International Series in Experimental Social Psychology). 300p. 1983. 35.00 (ISBN 0-08-028105-2). Pergamon.

GENIUS AND INSANITY
see Genius

GENTZ, FRIEDRICH VON, 1764-1832

Mann, Golo. Secretary of Europe: The Life of Fredrich Gentz, Enemy of Napoleon. 1946. text ed. 18.50x (ISBN 0-686-83734-7). Elliots Bks.

GEOCHEMISTRY
see also Chemical Oceanography; Geothermal Resources; Mineralogical Chemistry

Akimoto, S. & Manghnani, M. H. High Pressure Research in Geophysics. 1982. 113.00 (ISBN 90-277-1439-8, Pub. by Reidel Holland). Kluwer Boston.

Angino, E. D. & Long, D. T., eds. Geochemistry of Bismuth. LC 78-24291. (Benchmark Papers in Geology: Vol. 49). 432p. 1979. 53.50 (ISBN 0-87933-234-4). Hutchinson Ross.

Back, William, ed. Chemical Hydrogeology. Freeze, Allan. LC 81-11853. (Benchmark Papers in Geology Ser.: Vol. 73). 432p. 1983. 49.00 (ISBN 0-87933-440-1). Hutchinson Ross.

Bjorov, Malvin. Advances in Organic Geochemistry, 1981. 1000p. 1983. write for info. (ISBN 0-471-26229-3, Pub. by Wiley Heyden). Wiley.

Windley, B. F. & Nagvi, S. M. Archaean Geochemistry. (Proceedings). 1978. 66.00 (ISBN 0-444-41718-4). Elsevier.

GEOCHRONOLOGY
see Geological Time

GEODESY
see also Area Measurement; Gravity; Isostasy; Surveying

Postnikov, M. M. The Variational Theory of Geodesics. Scripta Technica Inc., tr. from Rus. 200p. 1983. pap. 4.50 (ISBN 0-486-63166-4). Dover.

GEODYNAMICS
see also Earthquakes; Rock Mechanics

Akimoto, S. & Manghnani, M. H. High Pressure Research in Geophysics. 1982. 113.00 (ISBN 90-277-1439-8, Pub. by Reidel Holland). Kluwer Boston.

Geodynamics in South-West Pacific. 428p. 1977. 199.00x (ISBN 2-7108-0317-8, Pub. by Graham & Trotman England). State Mutual Bk.

Wyllie, Peter J. The Dynamic Earth: Textbook in Geosciences. LC 82-21239. 432p. 1983. Repr. of 1971 ed. lib. bdg. write for info. (ISBN 0-89874-584-5). Krieger.

GEOGNOSY
see Geology

GEOGRAPHERS

Concept-Research & Reference Division, ed. Who's Who of Indian Geographers. 139p. 1982. text ed. 15.25x (ISBN 0-391-02808-1, Pub. by Concept India). Humanities.

GEOGRAPHICAL ATLASES
see Atlases

GEOGRAPHICAL BOUNDARIES
see Boundaries

GEOGRAPHICAL DICTIONARIES
see Geography-Dictionaries

GEOGRAPHICAL DISTRIBUTION OF ANIMALS AND PLANTS
see also Forest Ecology also subdivisions Geographical Distribution or Migration under names of organisms, e.g. Fishes-Geographical Distribution; Birds-Migration

Brown, James H. & Gibson, Arthur C. Biogeography. (Illus.). 992p. 1983. text ed. 32.95 (ISBN 0-8016-0824-4). Mosby.

Browne, Janet. The Secular Ark: Studies in the History of Biogeography. LC 82-17497. (Illus.). 272p. 1983. text ed. 27.50x (ISBN 0-300-02460-6). Yale U Pr.

Sauer, Jonathan D. Cayman Islands Seashore Vegetation: A Study in Comparative Biogeography. LC 82-2608. (Publications in Geographical Sciences: Vol. 25). 166p. 1983. pap. 16.00x (ISBN 0-520-09656-8). U of Cal Pr.

Springer, Victor G. Pacific plate Biogeography, with Special Reference to Shorefishes. LC 82-600146. (Contributions to Zoology Ser.: No. 367). (Illus.). 182p. 1982. pap. text ed. 7.95x (ISBN 0-87474-883-6). Smithsonian.

GEOGRAPHICAL DISTRIBUTION OF MAN
see Anthropo-Geography; Ethnology

GEOGRAPHICAL DISTRIBUTION OF PLANTS AND ANIMALS
see Geographical Distribution of Animals and Plants

GEOGRAPHICAL NAMES
see Names, Geographical

GEOGRAPHICAL RESEARCH

Amedeo, Douglas & Golledge, Reginald G. Introduction to Scientific Reasoning in Geography. LC 75-1411. 431p. 1975. text ed. 34.95x (ISBN 0-471-02537-2). Wiley.

GEOGRAPHY
see also Anthropo-Geography; Atlases; Boundaries; Classical Geography; Discoveries (In Geography); Ethnology; Geographers; Geographical Research; Man-Influence of Environment; Maps; Physical Geography; Voyages and Travels also subdivision Description and Travel under names of countries, e.g. France-Description and Travel; and subdivision Description, Geography under names of countries of antiquity, e.g. Greece-Description, Geography; and subdivision Maps under names of places, e.g. France-Maps

Boardman, David. Graphicacy & Geography Teaching. 208p. 1983. pap. text ed. 19.50x (ISBN 0-7099-0644-7, Pub. by Croom Helm Ltd England). Biblio Dist.

Haggett, Peter. Geography: A Modern Synthesis. 3rd. rev. ed. 640p. 1983. text ed. 23.50 scp (ISBN 0-06-042579-2, HarpC); instr's. manual avail. (ISBN 0-06-362693-4); scp study guide 8.50 (ISBN 0-06-042729-9). Har-Row.

Mitchell & Draper. Relevance & Ethics in Geography. LC 81-19386. (Illus.). 256p. 1982. text ed. 28.00 (ISBN 0-582-30035-5). Longman.

Pacione, Michael, ed. Progress in Rural Geography. LC 82-22756. (Illus.). 268p. 1983. text ed. 26.95x (ISBN 0-389-20358-0). B&N Imports.

--Progress in Urban Geography. LC 82-22757. 296p. 1983. text ed. 26.95x (ISBN 0-389-20357-2). B&N Imports.

Scott, James. Yearbook Forty-Three, Nineteen Eighty-One, Association of Pacific Coast Geographers. LC 37-13376. (Illus.). 176p. 1982. pap. text ed. 7.00 (ISBN 0-87071-243-8). Oreg St U Pr.

Warner, Gerald. Homelands of the Clans. 320p. 1983. 19.95 (ISBN 0-00-411128-1, Collins Pub England). Greene.

GEOGRAPHY-ATLASES
see Atlases

GEOGRAPHY-BIBLIOGRAPHY

Heinemann Educational Bk. Ltd., ed. The Catalogue of the Alpine Club Library. 750p. 1982. 195.00x (ISBN 0-686-82314-1, Pub. by Heinemann England). State Mutual Bk.

Steer, Francis W. A Catalogue of Sussex Estate & Tithe Award Maps, Vol. 1. 240p. 1962. 40.00x (ISBN 0-686-82392-3). State Mutual Bk.

GEOGRAPHY-DICTIONARIES
International Geographical Union, ed. Orbis Geographicus, 1980-84: World Directory of Geography. 5th ed. 962p. (Orig.). 1982. pap. 50.00x (ISBN 0-686-84541-2). Intl Pubns Serv.
GEOGRAPHY-EARLY WORKS
see Classical Geography
GEOGRAPHY-GAZETTEERS
see Geography-Dictionaries
GEOGRAPHY-HISTORY
see also Discoveries (In Geography)
Crump, Donald J., ed. Preserving America's Past. LC 81-48076. (Special Publications: No. 17). 200p. 1983. 6.95 (ISBN 0-87044-415-8); lib. bdg. 8.50 (ISBN 0-87044-420-4). Natl Geog.
Eckel, Edwin B. The Geographical Society of America: Life History of a Learned Society. LC 82-15412. (Memoir Ser.: No. 155). (Illus.). 1982. 24.50x (ISBN 0-8137-1155-X). Geol Soc.
GEOGRAPHY-MATHEMATICAL MODELS
Cotter, C. Astronomical & Mathematical Foundations of Geography. 1966. 9.00 (ISBN 0-444-19960-8). Elsevier.
Killen, James E. Mathematical Programming Methods for Geographers & Planners. LC 82-42839. 384p. 1983. 35.00x (ISBN 0-312-50133-1). St Martin.
Norcliffe, G. B. Inferential Statistics for Geographers. (Illus.). 272p. 1983. text ed. 15.00x (ISBN 0-686-84478-5). Sheridan.
GEOGRAPHY-METHODOLOGY
Estes, John E. & Senger, Leslie W. Remote Sensing: Techniques for Environmental Analysis. LC 73-8601. 340p. 1974. 24.95x (ISBN 0-471-24595-X). Wiley.
GEOGRAPHY-RESEARCH
see Geographical Research
GEORGRAPHY-STATISTICS
see Geography-Tables, Etc.
GEOGRAPHY-STUDY AND TEACHING
Cullup, Michael. Reading Geographies. 96p. 1982. pap. text ed. 7.00x (ISBN 0-85635-429-5, 51124, Pub. by Carcanet Pr England). Humanities.
GEOGRAPHY-TABLES, ETC.
Norcliffe, G. B. Inferential Statistics for Geographers. (Illus.). 272p. 1983. text ed. 15.00x (ISBN 0-686-84478-5). Sheridan.
GEOGRAPHY, CLASSICAL
see Classical Geography
GEOGRAPHY, PHYSICAL
see Physical Geography
GEOGRAPHY, POLITICAL
see also Boundaries; Cities and Towns; Geopolitics
Busteed, Mervyn, ed. Developments in Political Geography. Date not set. price not set (ISBN 0-12-148420-3). Acad Pr.
Johnston, R. J. Geography & the State. LC 82-10483. 304p. 1982. 27.50x (ISBN 0-312-32172-4). St Martin.
GEOGRAPHY, SOCIAL
see Anthropo-Geography
GEOGRAPHY, URBAN
see Cities and Towns
GEOLOGICAL CHEMISTRY
see Geochemistry
GEOLOGICAL EROSION
see Erosion
GEOLOGICAL MAPS
see Geology-Maps
GEOLOGICAL OCEANOGRAPHY
see Submarine Geology
GEOLOGICAL PHYSICS
see Geophysics
GEOLOGICAL RESEARCH
Mitchell & Draper. Relevance & Ethics in Geography. LC 81-19386. (Illus.). 256p. 1982. text ed. 28.00 (ISBN 0-582-30035-5). Longman.
Schreyer, W., ed. High-Pressure Researches in Geoscience: Behavior & Properties of Earth Materials at High Pressure & Temperatures. (Illus.). 545p. 1983. 86.50x (ISBN 3-510-65111-1). Lubrecht & Cramer.
GEOLOGICAL TIME
see also Paleoclimatology; Radioactive Dating
Givens, Donald R. Processional Papers in Archiometric Dating. 66p. 1982. pap. 8.00 (ISBN 0-940604-02-7). Intl Inst Adv Stud.
GEOLOGY
see also Caves; Continents; Coral Reefs and Islands; Creation; Crystallography; Earth; Earthquakes; Erosion; Geophysics; Glaciers; Hydrogeology; Mineralogy; Mountains; Natural History; Oceanography; Paleoclimatology; Paleontology; Petroleum-Geology; Petrology; Physical Geography; Rocks; Sedimentation and Deposition; Submarine Geology; Volcanoes; Weathering
Angins, E. & Billings, K. Atomic Absorption Spectrometry in Geology. 2nd ed. 1973. 16.75 (ISBN 0-444-41036-8). Elsevier.
Bell. Fundamentals of Engineering Geology. 1983. text ed. write for info. (ISBN 0-408-01169-6). Butterworth.
Faure, Gunter. Principles of Isotope Geology. LC 77-4479. (Intermediate Geology Ser.). 464p. 1977. text ed. 36.95 (ISBN 0-471-25665-X). Wiley.
Flint, Richard F. & Skinner, Brian J. Physical Geology. 2nd ed. LC 76-23206. 671p. 1977. text ed. 26.95 (ISBN 0-471-26442-3); study guide 7.50 (ISBN 0-471-02593-3); tchrs.' manual avail. (ISBN 0-471-03075-9). Wiley.
Foster, Robert J. General Geology. 4th ed. 672p. 1983. text ed. 26.95 (ISBN 0-675-20020-2). Merrill.
Gregory, Herbert E. Military Geology & Topography. 1918. text ed. 39.50x (ISBN 0-686-83626-X). Elliots Bks.
Harvey, John C. Geology for Geotechnical Engineers. (Illus.). 136p. 1983. 24.95 (ISBN 0-521-24629-6); pap. 9.95 (ISBN 0-521-28862-2). Cambridge U Pr.
Hobson, G. D. Developments in Petroleum Geology, Vols. 1 & 2. Vol. 1, 1977. 74.00 (ISBN 0-85334-745-X, Pub. by Applied Sci England); Vol. 2, 1980. 74.00 (ISBN 0-85334-907-X). Elsevier.
Leveson, David J. A Sense of the Earth. LC 82-11437. (Illus.). 176p. 18.00 (ISBN 0-404-19149-5). AMS Pr.
Long, Leon E. Geology. (Illus.). 526p. 1982. pap. text ed. 18.95x (ISBN 0-89641-110-9). American Pr.
McCall, G. J., ed. Ophiolitic & Related Melanges. LC 81-13490. (Benchmark Papers in Geology Ser.: Vol. 66). 464p. 1983. 56.00 (ISBN 0-87933-421-5, Pub. by Van Nos Reinhold). Hutchinson Ross.
Mulvihill, John, ed. Bibliography & Index of Geology: Users Guide. 160p. (Orig.). 1982. pap. text ed. write for info. (ISBN 0-913312-66-5). Am Geol.
Spencer, Edgar W. Physical Geology. (Biology Ser.). (Illus.). 656p. 1983. text ed. 26.95 (ISBN 0-201-06423-5); Laboratory Manual avail.; Instrs's Manual avail.; Study Guide avail. A-W.
Tank, Ronald W., ed. Environmental Geology: Text & Readings. 570p. 1983. pap. 16.95 (ISBN 0-19-503288-8). Oxford U Pr.
Whitlow. Geotechnics Four Checkbook. 1983. text ed. price not set (ISBN 0-408-00676-5); pap. text ed. price not set (ISBN 0-408-00631-5). Butterworth.
GEOLOGY-BIBLIOGRAPHY
Hazen, R. M. & Hazen, M. Hindle, eds. American Geological Literature 1669-1850. LC 79-25898. 448p. 1980. 36.50 (ISBN 0-87933-371-5). Hutchinson Ross.
GEOLOGY-DICTIONARIES
Godman, A. Illustrated Dictionary of Geology. (Illustrated Dictionaries Ser.). (Illus.). 192p. 1982. text ed. 7.95x (ISBN 0-582-55549-3). Longman.
Watt, Alec. Barnes & Noble Thesaurus of Geology. (Illus.). 192p. (gr. 11-12). 1983. 13.41i (ISBN 0-06-015177-3); pap. 6.68i (ISBN 0-06-463579-1). B&N NY.
GEOLOGY-GRAPHIC METHODS
Directory of Geoscience Departments. 200p. (Orig.). 1982. pap. 16.50 (ISBN 0-913312-67-3). Am Geol.
GEOLOGY-HISTORY
Harrington, John W. & Gallagher, Janice. Dance of the Continents: Adventures with Rocks & Time. (Illus.). 224p. 1983. 13.95 (ISBN 0-87477-168-4); pap. 9.50 (ISBN 0-87477-247-8). J P Tarcher.
GEOLOGY-JUVENILE LITERATURE
Dixon, Dougal. Geology. (Science World Ser.). (Illus.). 40p. (gr. 4 up). 1983. PLB 8.90 (ISBN 0-531-04582-X). Watts.
GEOLOGY-LABORATORY MANUALS
McPhater, Donald. Well-Site Geologists Handbook. MacTiernan, Brian, ed. 96p. 1983. 19.95x (ISBN 0-87814-217-7). Pennwell Pub.
GEOLOGY-MAPS
Concise World Atlas of Geology & Mineral Deposits. 110p. 1982. 52.00x (ISBN 0-900117-28-1, Pub. by Mining Journal England). State Mutual Bk.
GEOLOGY-MATHEMATICAL MODELS
Martins, J. B., ed. Numerical Methods in Geomechanics. 1982. 69.50 (ISBN 90-277-1461-4, Pub. by Reidel Holland). Kluwer Boston.
GEOLOGY-RESEARCH
see Geological Research
GEOLOGY-STATISTICS
Cubitt, J. M. & Henley, S., eds. Statistical Analysis in Geology. LC 78-17368. (Benchmark Papers in Geology Ser.: Vol. 37). 340p. 1978. 48.50 (ISBN 0-87933-335-9). Hutchinson Ross.
GEOLOGY-GREAT BRITAIN
Durrance, E. M. & Laming, D. J. The Geology of Devon. 416p. 1982. 75.00x (ISBN 0-85989-153-4, Pub. by Exeter Univ England). State Mutual Bk.
GEOLOGY-HAWAII
Macdonald, Gordon & Macdonald, Kyselka. Anatomy of an Island: A Geological History of Oahu. (Special Publication Ser.: No. 55). (Illus.). 37p. 1967. pap. 3.25 (ISBN 0-910240-14-0). Bishop Mus.
GEOLOGY-NORTH AMERICA
Hazen, R. M., ed. North American Geology: Early Writings. LC 79-708. (Benchmark Papers in Geology: Vol. 51). 356p. 1979. 46.50 (ISBN 0-87933-345-6). Hutchinson Ross.
Leviton, A. E. & Rodda, P. U., eds. Frontiers of Geological Exploration of Western North America. 248p. (Orig.). 1982. 16.95 (ISBN 0-934394-03-2). AAASPD.
McPhee, John. In Suspect Terrain. 1983. 12.95 (ISBN 0-374-17650-7). FS&G.
Palmer, A. R., ed. Perspectives in Regional Geological Synthesis: Planning for the Geology of North America. LC 82-9331. (DNAG Special Pub. Ser.: No. 1). (Illus.). 1982. 7.50x (ISBN 0-8137-5201-9). Geol Soc.
GEOLOGY-PACIFIC AREA
Geodynamics in South-West Pacific. 428p. 1977. 199.00x (ISBN 2-7108-0317-8, Pub. by Graham & Trotman England). State Mutual Bk.
GEOLOGY-UNITED STATES
Here are entered works on the geology of the United States as a whole, together with works on individual states or specific areas.
Baumgardner, Robert W., et al. Report of Investigations No. 114: The Wink Sink, a Salt Dissolution & Collapse Feature, Winker County, Texas. (Illus.). 38p. 1982. 1.50 (ISBN 0-686-37544-0). U of Tex Econ Geology.
Caran, S. C., et al. Geological Circular 82-1: Lineament Analysis & Inference of Geologic Structure-Examples from the Balcones-Quachita Trend of Texas. 11p. 1982. Repr. 1.00 (ISBN 0-686-37545-9). U of Tex Econ Geology.
Collins, Edward W. Geological Circular 82-3: Surficial Evidence of Tectonic Activity & Erosion Rates, Palestine, Keechi, & Oakwood Salt Domes, East Texas. (Illus.). 39p. 1982. 1.75 (ISBN 0-686-37547-5). U of Tex Econ Geology.
Galloway, William E. & Henry, Christopher D. Report of Investigations No. 113: Depositional Framework, Hydrostratigraphy, & Uranium Mineralization of the Oakville Sandstone (Miocene), Texas Coastal Plain. (Illus.). 51p. 1982. 2.50 (ISBN 0-686-37542-4). U of Tex Econ Geology.
Manson, Connie J., ed. Index to Geologic & Geophysical Mapping of Washington. (Information Circular Ser.: No. 73). (Illus.). 63p. 4.00 (ISBN 0-686-38468-7). Geologic Pubns.
Merrill, George P. First One Hundred Years of American Geology. (Illus.). 773p. 1969. Repr. of 1924 ed. lib. bdg. 15.75 (ISBN 0-686-37867-9). Lubrecht & Cramer.
Moen, Wayne S. Silver Occurrences of Washington. (Bulletin Ser.: No. 69). (Illus.). 188p. 1976. 4.00 (ISBN 0-686-38464-4). Geologic Pubns.
Morey, G. B. & Balaban, Nancy. Bibliography of Minnesota Geology, 1951-1980. (Bulletin: No. 46). 1981. 10.00 (ISBN 0-934938-01-6). Minn Geol Survey.
Snodk, J. R., et al. A Cross-Section of Nevada-Style Thrust in Northeast Washington. (Reports of Investigations: No. 25). (Illus.). 1981. 0.50 (ISBN 0-686-38466-0). Geologic Pubns.
Tewalt, Susan J., et al. Geological Circular 82-2: Detailed Evaluation of Two Texas Lignite Deposits of Fluvial & Deltaic Origins. (Illus.). 12p. 1982. Repr. 1.00 (ISBN 0-686-37546-7). U of Tex Econ Geology.
Wold, Richard J. & Hinz, William J., eds. Geology & Tectonics of the Lake Superior Basin. LC 82-15425. (Memoir Ser.: No. 156). (Illus.). 1982. 38.50x (ISBN 0-8137-1156-8). Geol Soc.
GEOLOGY, CHEMICAL
see Geochemistry; Mineralogical Chemistry
GEOLOGY, DYNAMIC
see Geodynamics
GEOLOGY, HISTORICAL
see Geology, Stratigraphic; Paleontology
GEOLOGY, STRATIGRAPHIC
see also Glacial Epoch; Paleontology; Paleontology, Stratigraphic
Dunbar, Carl O. & Waage, Karl M. Historical Geology. 3rd ed. LC 72-89681. (Illus.). 556p. 1969. text ed. 28.95x (ISBN 0-471-22507-X). Wiley.
GEOLOGY, STRATIGRAPHIC-CRETACEOUS
Pessagno, E. A., Jr. Radiolarian Zonation & Stratigraphy of the Upper Cretaceous Portion of the Great Valley Sequence, California Coast Ranges. (Micropaleontology Special Publications Ser.: No. 2). 95p. 1976. 20.00 (ISBN 0-686-84250-2). Am Mus Natl Hist.
Renz, O. The Cretaceous Amonites of Venezuela. (Illus.). 216p. 1982. 69.95x (ISBN 3-7643-1364-1). Birkhauser.
Schlanger, S. O. & Cita, M. B., eds. Nature & Origin of Cretaceous Carbonrich Facies. write for info. (ISBN 0-12-624950-4). Acad Pr.
GEOLOGY, STRATIGRAPHIC-DEVONIAN
Murphy, Michael & Matti, Jonathan C. Lower Devonian Conodonts - Hesperius-Kindlei Zones. LC 82-8638. (Publications in Geological Sciences: Vol. 123). 94p. Date not set. pap. text ed. 8.25 (ISBN 0-520-09661-4). U of Cal Pr.
GEOLOGY, STRATIGRAPHIC-PLEISTOCENE
Porter, Stephen C., ed. Late Quaternary Environments of the United States, Volume 1: The Late Pleistocene. (Illus.). 480p. 1983. 45.00x (ISBN 0-8166-1169-6). U of Minn Pr.
GEOLOGY, STRATIGRAPHIC-PLIOCENE
May, Julian. The Saga of Pliocene Exile: The Nonborn King, Vol. 3. (Illus.). 395p. 1983. 16.95 (ISBN 0-686-82648-5). HM.
GEOLOGY, STRATIGRAPHIC-QUATERNARY
see also Geology, Stratigraphic-Pleistocene
Flint, Richard F. Glacial & Quaternary Geology. LC 74-141198. (Illus.). 892p. 1971. 40.95x (ISBN 0-471-26435-0). Wiley.
McCalpin, James P. Quaternary Geology & Neotectonics of the West Flank of the Northern Sangre de Cristo Mountains, South-Central Colorado. Raese, Jon Wl & Goldberg, J. H., eds. (Colorado School of Mines Quarterly: Vol. 77, No. 3). 100p. 1982. pap. text ed. 12.00 (ISBN 0-686-82132-7). Colo Sch Mines.
Porter, Stephen C., ed. Late Quaternary Environments of the United States, Volume 1: The Late Pleistocene. (Illus.). 480p. 1983. 45.00x (ISBN 0-8166-1169-6). U of Minn Pr.
Wright, Herbert E., Jr., ed. Late Quaternary Environments of the United States, Volume 2: The Holocene. (Illus.). 384p. 1983. 45.00x (ISBN 0-8166-1171-8). U of Minn Pr.
GEOLOGY, STRUCTURAL
see also Geomorphology; Mountains
Baker, Wallace H., ed. Grouting in Geotechnical Engineering. LC 81-71798. 1032p. 1982. pap. text ed. 69.00 (ISBN 0-87262-295-9). Am Soc Civil Eng.
Lee, J. S. Introduction to Geomechanics. 2nd ed. 140p. 1983. 58.75 (ISBN 0-677-31070-6). Gordon.
McCall, G. J., ed. Astroblemes-Cryptoexplosion Structures. LC 79-10991. (Benchmark Papers in Geology: Vol. 50). 437p. 1979. 55.00 (ISBN 0-87933-342-1). Hutchinson Ross.
Matsumoto, T. Age & Nature of the Circum-Pacific Orogenesis. 1967. 42.50 (ISBN 0-686-43415-3). Elsevier.
Yong, R. N. & Selig, E. T., eds. Application of Plasticity & Generalized Stress-Strain in Geotechnical Engineering. LC 81-71796. 360p. 1982. pap. text ed. 27.25 (ISBN 0-87262-294-0). Am Soc Civil Eng.
GEOLOGY, SUBMARINE
see Submarine Geology
GEOLOGY AND RELIGION
see Religion and Science
GEOMETRY
see also Complexes; Surfaces; Topology; Transformations (Mathematics); Trigonometry
Hudspeth, Mary Kay. Introductory Geometry. (Illus.). 576p. Date not set. pap. text ed. 16.95 (ISBN 0-201-10690-6). A-W.
Lang, Serge & Murrow, Gene. Geometry. (Illus.). 464p. 1982. pap. text ed. 24.00 (ISBN 0-387-90727-0). Springer-Verlag.
Meserve, Bruce E. Fundamental Concepts of Geometry. (Illus.). 352p. 1983. Repr. of 1955 ed. pap. 6.50 (ISBN 0-486-63415-9). Dover.
Mitchell, Robert & Prickel, Donald. Number Power Four: Geometry. (Number Power Ser.). 176p. (Orig.). 1983. pap. 4.95 (ISBN 0-8092-5517-0). Contemp Bks.
Pedoe, Dan. Geometry & the Visual Arts. (Illus.). 353p. 1983. pap. 6.00 (ISBN 0-486-24458-X). Dover.
Postnikov, M. Lectures in Geometry: Linear Algebra & Differential Geometry. 319p. 1982. 8.45 (ISBN 0-8285-2461-0, Pub. by Mir Pubs USSR). Imported Pubns.
Young, J. W. Projective Geometry. (Carus Monograph: No. 4). 185p. 1930. 16.50 (ISBN 0-88385-004-4). Math Assn.
GEOMETRY-JUVENILE LITERATURE
Amir-Moez, Ali R. & Menzel, Donald H. Fun with Numbers: Lines & Angles. (Handbooks Ser.). (gr. 3-6). 1981. pap. 1.95 (ISBN 0-87534-179-9). Highlights.
GEOMETRY-STUDY AND TEACHING
Drooyan, Irving & Wooton, William. Elementary Algebra with Geometry. LC 75-35736. 334p. 1976. text ed. 22.95x (ISBN 0-471-22245-3). Wiley.
Husserl, E. Studien zur Arithmetik und Geometrie. 1983. 91.50 (ISBN 90-247-2497-X, Pub. by Martinus Nijhoff Netherlands). Kluwer Boston.
Vaghn, Jim. Jumbo Geometry Yearbook. (Jumbo Math Ser.). 96p. (gr. 10). 1981. wkbk. 14.00 (ISBN 0-8209-0039-7, JMY-10). ESP.
GEOMETRY, ALGEBRAIC
see also Algebraic Spaces; Curves, Algebraic; Geometry, Analytic; Surfaces; Surfaces, Algebraic; Topology; Transformations (Mathematics)
Kunz, E. Introduction to Commutative Algebra & Algebraic Geometry. Date not set. text ed. price not set (ISBN 3-7643-3065-1). Birkhauser.
GEOMETRY, ANALYTIC
see also Surfaces
Anton, Howard. Calculus with Analytic Geometry. brief edition ed. LC 81-50266. 854p. 1981. text ed. 25.50 (ISBN 0-471-09443-9). Wiley.
--Calculus with Analytic Geometry. LC 79-11469. 1980. 33.95 (ISBN 0-471-03248-4); solution manual 11.95 (ISBN 0-471-04498-9). Wiley.
Bugrov, Y. S. & Nikolsky, S. M. Fundamentals of Linear Algebra & Analytical Geometry. 189p. 1982. pap. 3.45 (ISBN 0-8285-2445-9, Pub. by Mir Pubs USSR). Imported Pubns.
Salas, S. L. & Hille, E. Calculus: One & Several Variables with Analytic Geometry, Pt. 1 & 2. 4th ed. 671p. 1982. text ed. 26.95 (ISBN 0-471-08055-1); student supp. 12.95 (ISBN 0-471-05383-X). Wiley.
Trim, Donald W. Calculus & Analytic Geometry. LC 82-16287. (Illus.). 960p. 1983. text ed. write for info. (ISBN 0-201-16270-9). A-W.
GEOMETRY, DESCRIPTIVE
see also Engineering Graphics; Perspective
Lamit, Gary. Descriptive Geometry. (Illus.). 464p. 1983. 21.95 (ISBN 0-13-199802-1); pap. 14.95 (ISBN 0-13-199828-5). P-H.
GEOMETRY, DIFFERENTIAL
see also Geometry, Riemannian; Surfaces; Transformations (Mathematics)

Arnold, V. I. Geometrical Methods in the Theory of Ordinary Differential Equations. (Grundlehren der Mathematischen Wissenschaften: Vol. 250). (Illus.). 384p. 1983. 36.00 (ISBN 0-387-90681-9). Springer-Verlag.

Buchin, Su. Affine Differential Geometry. 1982. write for info. (ISBN 0-677-31060-9). Gordon.

Prakash, N. Differential Geometry: An Integrated Approach. 1982. 7.00x (ISBN 0-07-096560-9). McGraw.

GEOMETRY, DIFFERENTIAL-PROJECTIVE

Asten, H. Keller-von. Encounters with the Infinite: Geometrical Experiences Through Active Comtemplation. Juhr, Gerald, tr. from Germ. (Illus.). 364p. 1971. 19.95 (ISBN 0-88010-040-0, Pub. by Verlag Walter Keller Switzerland). Anthroposophic.

GEOMETRY, ENUMERATIVE

see also Surfaces

Barz, P. Le & Hervier, Y., eds. Enumerative Geometry & Classical Algebra. (Progress in Mathematics Ser.: Vol. 24). 246p. 1982. text ed. 20.00 (ISBN 3-7643-3106-2). Birkhauser.

GEOMETRY, MODERN

see also Geometry, Projective

Rees, E. G. Notes in Geometry. (Universitexts Ser.). (Illus.). 109p. 1983. pap. 14.00 (ISBN 0-387-12053-X). Springer-Verlag.

GEOMETRY, NON-EUCLIDEAN

see also Geometry, Riemannian

Henderson, Linda D. The Fourth Dimension & Non-Euclidean Geometry in Modern Art. LC 82-15076. (Illus.). 496p. 1983. 55.00x (ISBN 0-686-43212-6); pap. 16.50 (ISBN 0-691-10142-6). Princeton U Pr.

GEOMETRY, PLANE

see also Area Measurement

Hughes, D. R. & Piper, F. C. Projective Planes. 2nd ed. (Graduate Texts in Mathematics: Vol. 6). 291p. 1982. 32.00 (ISBN 0-387-90043-8). Springer-Verlag.

Lacret-Subirat, Fabian. Lacret Plane Geometry: Grade 9-12. 2nd ed. (Illus.). 478p. 1983. 13.75 (ISBN 0-686-43022-0); s.p. 8.00 (ISBN 0-943144-05-1). Lacret Pub.

GEOMETRY, PROJECTIVE

Hughes, D. R. & Piper, F. C. Projective Planes. 2nd ed. (Graduate Texts in Mathematics: Vol. 6). 291p. 1982. 32.00 (ISBN 0-387-90043-8). Springer-Verlag.

GEOMETRY, PROJECTIVE DIFFERENTIAL

see Geometry, Differential-Projective

GEOMETRY, RIEMANNIAN

Willmore, T. J. Total Curvature in Riemannian Geometry. (Mathematics & Its Applications Ser.). 168p. 1982. 39.95x (ISBN 0-470-27354-2). Halsted Pr.

GEOMORPHOLOGY

see also Erosion; Landforms; Physical Geography

Goudie, A. S. & Pye, K., eds. Chemical Sediments & Geomorphology. Date not set. price not set (ISBN 0-12-293480-6). Acad Pr.

GEOPHYSICAL RESEARCH

Fitch, A. A., ed. Developments in Geophysical Exploration Methods, Vol. 3. (Illus.). 320p. 1982. 57.50 (ISBN 0-85334-126-5, Pub. by Applied Sci England). Elsevier.

GEOPHYSICS

see also Continents; Geodynamics; Geology; Geophysical Research; Magnetism; Magnetohydrodynamics; Meteorology; Oceanography; Seismology

Akimoto, S. & Manghnani, M. H. High Pressure Research in Geophysics. 1982. 113.00 (ISBN 90-277-1439-8, Pub. by Reidel Holland). Kluwer Boston.

Bates, C. C. & Gaskell, T. F. Geophysics in the Affairs of Man: A Personalized History of Exploration Geophysics & Its Allied Sciences of Seismology & Oceanography. (Illus.). 536p. 1982. 60.00 (ISBN 0-08-024026-7); pap. 25.00 (ISBN 0-08-024025-9). Pergamon.

Bradford, James N. Escape Route: Surviving the Earth Changes. 120p. 1983. pap. 6.50 (ISBN 0-89540-135-5, SB-135). Sun Pub.

Fitch, A. A., ed. Developments in Geophysical Exploration Methods, Vol. 2. 1981. 41.00 (ISBN 0-85334-930-4, Pub. by Applied Sci England). Elsevier.

Foster, Robert J. Physical Geology. 4th ed. 460p. 1983. text ed. 24.95 (ISBN 0-675-20021-0). Additional supplments may be obtained from publisher. Merrill.

Kleyn, A. H. Seismic Reflection Interpretation. (Illus.). xii, 265p. 1983. 57.50 (ISBN 0-85334-161-3, Pub. by Applied Sci England). Elsevier.

Nelson, H. Royce, Jr. New Technologies in Exploration Geophysics. 1983. text ed. 29.95x (ISBN 0-87201-321-9). Gulf Pub.

Pedlosky, J. Geophysical Fluid Dynamics: Springer Study Edition. (Illus.). 624p. 1983. pap. 26.00 (ISBN 0-387-90745-9). Springer-Verlag.

Robinson, Enders A. Migration of Geophysical Data. LC 82-82537. (Illus.). 224p. 1982. text ed. 34.00 (ISBN 0-934634-14-9). Intl Human Res.

Saltzman, Barry, ed. Advances in Geophysics, Vol. 25. (Serial Publication). Date not set. price not set (ISBN 0-12-018825-2); price not set lib. ed. (ISBN 0-12-018886-4) (ISBN 0-12-018887-2). Acad Pr.

GEOPOLITICS

see also Anthropo-Geography; Boundaries; Demography; World Politics

Johnston, R. J. Geography & the State. LC 82-10483. 304p. 1982. 27.50x (ISBN 0-312-32172-4). St Martin.

Russell, Jeremy L. Geopolitics of Natural Gas. 176p. 1983. prof ref 24.50x (ISBN 0-88410-610-1). Ballinger Pub.

GEORGE, HENRY, 1839-1897

Thomas, John L. Alternative America: Henry George, Edward Bellamy, Henry Demarest Lloyd & the Adversary Tradition. (Illus.). 416p. 1983. 25.00x (ISBN 0-674-01676-9). Harvard U Pr.

GEORGETOWN, COLORADO

Digerness, David S. The Mineral Belt: Georgetown, Mining, Colorado Central Railroad, Vol. III. (Illus.). 416p. 49.00 (ISBN 0-686-84503-X). Sundance.

GEORGETOWN, D. C.

Mitchell, Mary. Glimpses of Georgetown, Past & Present. LC 82-62163. (Illus.). 96p. 1983. pap. 12.50. Road St Pr.

GEORGIA-DESCRIPTION AND TRAVEL

Smith, Susan H. Marmac Guide to Atlanta. 2nd ed. Nicholson, Diana M., ed. (Marmac Guide Ser.). (Illus.). 296p. 1983. pap. 6.95 (ISBN 0-939944-27-8). Marmac Pub.

GEORGIA-GENEALOGY

Dorsey, James E. Georgia Genealogy & Local History: A Bibliography. LC 82-7594. 416p. 1983. 27.50 (ISBN 0-87152-359-0); pap. 20.00 (ISBN 0-87152-363-9). Reprint.

Dorsey, James E. & Derden, John K. Montgomery County, Georgia: A Source Book of Genealogy & History. 256p. 1983. price not set (ISBN 0-87152-377-9); pap. 20.00 (ISBN 0-87152-376-0). Reprint.

GEORGIA-HISTORY

Buechler, Sandra. Sesquicentennial of Effingham County. (Illus.). 808p. 1982. 75.00 (ISBN 0-9609598-0-7). Banbury Pub Co.

Cook, James F. Governors of Georgia. (Illus.). 320p. 1979. 12.95 (ISBN 0-686-83449-6). Strode.

Dorsey, James E. Georgia Genealogy & Local History: A Bibliography. LC 82-7594. 416p. 1983. 27.50 (ISBN 0-87152-359-0); pap. 20.00 (ISBN 0-87152-363-9). Reprint.

Hepburn, Lawrence R. The Georgia History Book. 212p. (gr. 8-9). 1982. text ed. 11.95 (ISBN 0-89854-080-1). U of GA Inst Govt.

Shavin, Norman & Galphin, Bruce. Atlanta: Triumph of a People. (Illus.). 456p. 1982. 29.95 (ISBN 0-910719-00-4). Capricorn Corp.

Wingo, Bruce. Georgia in American Society. 1982. 14.95 (ISBN 0-932298-38-9). Copple Hse.

GEORGIA-POLITICS AND GOVERNMENT

Alexander, Stan & Broussard, Sharon. An Analysis of the 1973 Atlanta Elections. 1973. 3.00 (ISBN 0-686-38001-0). Voter Ed Proj.

Cook, James F. Governors of Georgia. (Illus.). 320p. 1979. 12.95 (ISBN 0-686-83449-6). Strode.

Farouk, Brimah K. Georgia State Senate District Thirty-Five Democratic Primaries of 1982. 1982. 1.00 (ISBN 0-686-38025-8). Voter Ed Proj.

Lewis, John. Election Law Changes in Cities & Counties in Georgia. 1976. 1.00 (ISBN 0-686-38002-9). Voter Ed Proj.

Rooks, Charles S. The Atlanta Elections of Nineteen Sixty-nine. 1970. 4.00 (ISBN 0-686-37998-5). Voter Ed Proj.

GEOSCIENCE

see Earth Sciences; Geology-Graphic Methods

GEOTECHNIQUE

see Rock Mechanics; Soil Mechanics

GEOTECTONICS

see Geology, Structural

GEOTHERMAL RESOURCES

Geothermal Resources Council, ed. Fractures in Geothermal Resevoirs: Presented August 27-28, Honolulu, Hawaii. (Special Report Ser.: No. 12). (Illus.). 174p. (Orig.). 1982. pap. 15.00 (ISBN 0-934412-12-X). Geothermal.

--Geothermal Potential of the Cascade Mountain Range: Exploration & Development. (Special Report Ser.: No. 10). (Illus.). 79p. (Orig.). 1981. pap. 12.00 (ISBN 0-934412-10-3). Geothermal.

Grant, Malcolm A., et al. Geothermal Reservoir Engineering. LC 82-4105. (Energy Science & Technology Ser.). Date not set. 45.00 (ISBN 0-12-295620-6). Acad Pr.

Huttrer, Gerald W. & Roesner, Raymond E., eds. Geothermal Energy: The International Success Story. (Transaction Ser.: Vol. 5). (Illus.). 749p. 1981. 30.00 (ISBN 0-934412-55-3). Geothermal.

Johnson, Willard E. & Sherwood, Peter B., eds. Geothermal Energy: Turn on the Power! (Transactions Ser.: Vol. 6). (Illus.). 546p. 1982. 33.00 (ISBN 0-934412-56-1). Geothermal.

GERBILS

Smith, K. W. Hamsters & Gerbils. (Illus.). 93p. 1977. pap. 3.95 (ISBN 0-7028-1082-7). Avian Pubns.

GERIATRIC NURSING

Understanding the Aging Process & the Institutionalized Elderly Person. 1976. Instructor's Guide, 102p. 7.95 (ISBN 0-686-38195-5, 38-1616); Instructive Program, 140p. 6.95 (ISBN 0-686-38196-3, 38-1615); Resident Care Guides, 26p. 1.95 (ISBN 0-686-38197-1, 38-1615S). Natl League Nurse.

GERIATRIC PHARMACOLOGY

see Geriatrics-Formulae, Receipts, Prescriptions

GERIATRICS

see also Aged-Care and Hygiene; Aged-Medical Care

Beaver, Marion L. Human Service Practice with the Elderly. (Illus.). 256p. 1983. 19.95 (ISBN 0-686-38827-5). P H.

Blumenthal, Herman T., ed. Handbook of the Diseases of Aging. 512p. 1983. text ed. 36.50 (ISBN 0-442-21566-5). Van Nos Reinhold.

Feldman. Nutrition in the Middle & Later Years. (Illus.). 352p. 1982. text ed. 29.50 (ISBN 0-7236-7046-3). Wright-PSG.

Gibson, Mary J. & Heath, Angela, eds. International Survey of Peroidicals in Gerontology. 2nd ed. 53p. (Orig.). 1982. pap. text ed. 10.00 (ISBN 0-910473-02-1). Intl Fed Ageing.

Ham. Geriatrics. 464p. 1983. text ed. price not set (ISBN 0-7236-7052-8). Wright-PSG.

Lopez, Martita A. & Hoyer, William J. Behavioral Gerontology. 225p. 1983. 25.00 (ISBN 0-08-028040-4); pap. 12.95 (ISBN 0-08-028039-0). Pergamon.

Oral Health Care for the Geriatric Patient in a Long Term Care Facility. 5.25 (ISBN 0-934510-13-X, J010). Am Dental.

Platt, D., ed. Geriatrics II: Digestive, Endocrine, Kidney Urogenital, Hematologic, Respiratory Systems, Rehabilitation, Nutrition & Drug Treatment. (Illus.). 490p. 1983. 70.00 (ISBN 0-387-10982-X). Springer-Verlag.

Sherouse, Deborah L. Professional's Handbook on Geriatric Alcoholism. (Illus.). 288p. 1983. text ed. price not set (ISBN 0-398-04828-2). C C Thomas.

Taylor, Rex & Gilmore, Anne, eds. Current Trends in British Gerontology. 230p. 1982. text ed. 35.00x (ISBN 0-566-00495-X). Gower Pub Ltd.

Wilcock, G. K. & Gray, J. A. Geriatric Problems in General Practice. (General Practice Ser.). 1982. 26.95x (ISBN 0-19-261313-8). Oxford U Pr.

GERIATRICS-FORMULAE, RECEIPTS, PRESCRIPTIONS

Gerson, Cyrelle K. & Beavers, Eleanor, eds. Rational Geriatric Drug Therapy: An Interdisciplinary Approach. 2 vols. 1979. pap. text ed. 25.00 (ISBN 0-917330-43-9). Am Pharm Assn.

Oppeneer, Joan E. & Vervoren, Thora M. Gerontological Pharmacology: A Resource for Health Practitioners. (Illus.). 208p. 1983. pap. 13.95 (ISBN 0-8016-3739-2). Mosby.

Vestal, R. E., ed. Drug Therapy in the Elderly. 300p. 1982. text ed. write for info. (ISBN 0-86792-008-4, Pub by Adis Pr Australia). Wright-PSG.

Wheatley, David, ed. Psychopharmacology of Old Age. (British Association for Psychopharmacology Monographs). (Illus.). 1982. 29.50 (ISBN 0-19-261373-1). Oxford U Pr.

GERM THEORY

see Life-Origin

GERM WARFARE

see Biological Warfare

GERMAN ARCHITECTURE

see Architecture-Germany

GERMAN ART

see Art, German

GERMAN AUTHORS

see Authors, German

GERMAN DRAMA-HISTORY AND CRITICISM

Aikin, Judith P. German Baroque Drama. (World Authors Ser.). 1982. lib. bdg. 17.95 (ISBN 0-8057-6477-1, Twayne). G K Hall.

International Brecht Society. Beyond Brecht: Brecht Yearbook, Vol. 11. Fuegi, John & Bahr, Gisela, eds. 250p. 1982. 20.00 (ISBN 0-8143-1735-9). Wayne St U Pr.

Speirs, Ronald. Brecht's Early Plays. 224p. 1982. text ed. 35.00x (ISBN 0-391-02554-6). Humanities.

GERMAN DRAMA-TRANSLATIONS INTO ENGLISH

Goethe. Torquato Tasso. Prudhoe, J., tr. from Ger. (Classic of Drama in English Translation). 1979. pap. 6.50 (ISBN 0-7190-0720-8). Manchester.

Schiller. Wilhelm Tell. Prudhoe, J., tr. from Ger. (Classics of Drama in English Translation Ser.). 1970. pap. 6.50 (ISBN 0-7190-0426-8). Manchester.

GERMAN DRAWINGS

see Drawings, German

GERMAN FICTION

Here are entered collections of German fiction in German. For translations into English see subdivision Translations into English.

Rose, William, ed. The History of the Damnable Life & Deserved Death of Doctor John Faustus: Together with the Second Report of Faustus Containing His Appearances and the Deeds of Wagner, 1592. 327p. 1982. Repr. of 1982 ed. lib. bdg. 40.00 (ISBN 0-8495-1717-6). Arden Lib.

GERMAN FICTION-HISTORY AND CRITICISM

Blackall, Eric A. The Novels of the German Romantics. LC 82-22104. (Illus.). 320p. 1983. 34.50x (ISBN 0-8014-1523-3); pap. 14.95 (ISBN 0-8014-9885-6). Cornell U Pr.

Ryan, Judith. The Uncompleted Past: Postwar German Novels & the Third Reich. 272p. 1983. 24.00x (ISBN 0-8143-1728-6). Wayne St U Pr.

GERMAN FICTION-TRANSLATIONS INTO ENGLISH

Thomas, J. W., tr. from Ger. The Best Novellas of Medieval Germany. (Studies in German Literature, Linguistics, & Culture: Vol. 17). (Illus.). 160p. 1983. 15.00x (ISBN 0-938100-10-6). Camden Hse.

GERMAN FOLK-LORE

see Folk-Lore, German

GERMAN HEBREW

see Yiddish Language

GERMAN LANGUAGE

see also Low German Language

Bicknese. Hier und Heute: Lesen Leicht Gemacht. 1983. pap. text ed. price not set. HM.

Curts, Paul. Luther's Variations in Sentence Arrangement From the Modern Literary Usage With Primary Reference to the Position of the Verb. 1910. pap. text ed. 29.50x (ISBN 0-686-83611-1). Elliots Bks.

Komar, Kathleen L. Pattern & Chaos: A Structural Analysis of Novels by Doeblin, Koeppen, Dos Passos, & Faulkner. LC 82-73875. (Studies in German Literature, Linguistics, & Culture: Vol. 14). (Illus.). 160p. 1983. 20.00x (ISBN 0-938100-19-X). Camden Hse.

Landwehr, Gotz. Studien Zu Den Germanischen Volksrechten Gedachtnisschrift Fur Wilhelm Ebel. 217p. (Ger.). 1982. write for info. (ISBN 3-8204-6412-3). P Lang Pubs.

Moeller & Liedloff. Kaleidoskop: Kultur, Literatur und Grammatik. text ed. 16.95 (ISBN 0-686-84589-7, GR15); instr's. annotated ed. 17.95 (ISBN 0-686-84590-0, GR12); write for info. supplementary materials. HM.

Rychener, Hans. Freude Am Wort Gutes Deutsch: Guter Stil. 282p. (Ger.). 1982. write for info. (ISBN 3-261-04984-7). P Lang Pubs.

Scherer, Thomas. Phraseologie Im Schulalter. 174p. (Ger.). 1982. write for info. (ISBN 3-261-05015-2). P Lang Pubs.

GERMAN LANGUAGE-CONVERSATION AND PHRASE BOOKS

see also German Language-Self-Instruction

Berlitz Editors. German for Travel Cassettepack. 1983. 14.95 (ISBN 0-02-962200-X, Berlitz); cassette incl. Macmillan.

Hart, Babe. Speedy German: To Get You There & Back. Hart, Babe, ed. & tr. (Speedy Language Ser.). (Illus.). 24p. (Ital.). 1977. pap. 1.75 (ISBN 0-9602838-3-8). Baja Bks.

Traveler's German. (EH). (Gr.). 1980. pap. 17.95 (ISBN 0-686-37989-6, 611). B&N NY.

GERMAN LANGUAGE-DIALECTS

Keller, R. E. German Dialects. 408p. 1961. pap. 10.00 (ISBN 0-7190-0762-3). Manchester.

GERMAN LANGUAGE-DICTIONARIES-ENGLISH

Bicknese, Gunther. Hier und Heute: Lessen Leicht Gemacht. LC 82-84304. 96p. 1983. pap. text ed. 7.95 (ISBN 0-395-33249-4). HM.

GERMAN LANGUAGE-EXAMINATIONS, QUESTIONS, ETC.

Rudman, Jack. Foreign Language: German. (Regents External Degree Ser.: REDP-28). 17.95 (ISBN 0-8373-5678-4); pap. 9.95 (ISBN 0-8373-5628-8). Natl Learning.

GERMAN LANGUAGE-GRAMMAR

Politzer, Robert L. Workbook to Accompany Active Review of German. 108p. pap. text ed. 7.95 (ISBN 0-686-84495-5). Krieger.

GERMAN LANGUAGE-GRAMMAR, COMPARATIVE

Lohnes, Walter F. & Hopkins, Edwin A., eds. The Contrastive Grammar of English & German. xx, 231p. 1982. pap. 19.50 (ISBN 0-89720-052-7). Karoma.

GERMAN LANGUAGE-SELF-INSTRUCTION

see also German Language-Conversation and Phrase Books

Berlitz German for Your Trip. 192p. 1982. 8.95 (ISBN 0-02-965170-0, Berlitz). Macmillan.

GERMAN LITERATURE (COLLECTIONS)

Here are entered works in German. For translations into English see subdivision Translations into English.

Stokes, Richard, ed. Gefunden: An Anthology of German Literature. 192p. (Orig.). 1981. pap. text ed. 7.50x (ISBN 0-435-38860-6). Heinemann Ed.

GERMAN LITERATURE-BIBLIOGRAPHY

Newman, L. M. German Language & Literature: Select Bibliography of Reference Books. 2nd. enl. ed. 175p. 1979. 30.00x (ISBN 0-85457-077-2, Pub. by Inst Germanic Stud England). State Mutual Bk.

GERMAN LITERATURE-HISTORY AND CRITICISM

Beckmann, Till. Studien Zur Bestimmung Des Lebens In Meister Eckharts Deutschen Predigten. 244p. (Ger.). 1982. write for info. (ISBN 3-8204-5708-9). P Lang Pubs.

Bernstein, Eckhard. German Humanism. (World Authors Ser.). 176p. 1983. lib. bdg. 18.95 (ISBN 0-8057-6537-9, Twayne). G K Hall.

Gajek, Bernhard & Wedel, Erwin. Gebrauchsliteratur-Interferenz-Kontrastivitat Beitrage Zur Polnischen und Deutschen Literatur-und Sprachwissenschaft. 390p. (Ger.). 1982. write for info. (ISBN 3-8204-7089-1). P Lang Pubs.

Hammer, Carl, ed. Studies in German Literature. LC 82-15862. (Louisiana State University Studies: Humanities Ser.: No. 13). xviii, 172p. 1982. Repr. of 1963 ed. lib. bdg. 35.00x (ISBN 0-313-23735-2, HASGL). Greenwood.

Kleiss, Peter. Georg Herweghs Literaturkritik. 172p. (Ger.). 1982. write for info. (ISBN 3-8204-6292-9). P Lang Pubs.

Klohn, Sabine. Helene Simon. 650p. (Ger.). 1982. write for info (ISBN 3-8204-6249-X). P Lang Pubs.

Komar, Kathleen L. Pattern & Chaos: A Structural Analysis of Novels by Doeblin, Koeppen, Dos Passos, & Faulkner. LC 82-73875. (Studies in German Literature, Linguistics, & Culture: Vol. 14). (Illus.). 160p. 1983. 20.00x (ISBN 0-938100-19-X). Camden Hse.

Krahenmann, Heidi. Das Gegensatzliche In Heinrich Federers Leben und Werk. 318p. (Ger.). 1982. write for info. (ISBN 3-261-05012-8). P Lang Pubs.

Murdoch, Brian O. Old High German Literature. (World Authors Ser.). 169p. 1983. lib. bdg. 18.95 (ISBN 0-8057-6535-2, Twayne). G K Hall.

Schrader, Richard J. God's Handiwork: Images of Women in Early Germanic Literature. LC 82-21005. (Contributions in Women's Studies: No. 41). 144p. 1983. lib. bdg. 23.95 (ISBN 0-313-23666-6, SGH/). Greenwood.

Stehle, Claudia. Individualitat und Romanform. 186p. (Ger.). 1982. write for info. (ISBN 3-8204-5727-5). P Lang Pubs.

Timmermann, Waltraud. Studien Zur Allegorischen Bildlichkeit In Den Parabolae Bernhards Von Clairvaux. 305p. (Ger.). 1982. write for info. (ISBN 3-8204-6274-0). P Lang Pubs.

Wissemann, Michael. Die Parther In der Augusteischen Dichtung. 186p. (Ger.). 1982. write for info. (ISBN 3-8204-5948-0). P Lang Pubs.

GERMAN LITERATURE-HISTORY AND CRITICISM-EARLY MODERN, 1500-1700

Voigt, Jurgen. Ritter, Harlekin und Henker. 486p. (Ger.). 1982. write for info. (ISBN 3-8204-5952-9). P Lang Pubs.

GERMAN LITERATURE-HISTORY AND CRITICISM-18TH CENTURY

Lange, Victor. Classical Age of German Literature, 1740-1815. 256p. (Orig.). 1983. text ed. 26.00x (ISBN 0-8419-0853-2); pap. text ed. 17.50x (ISBN 0-8419-0854-0). Holmes & Meier.

GERMAN LITERATURE-HISTORY AND CRITICISM-19TH CENTURY

Hamburger, Michael. German Literature from Nietzsche to the Present Day, Vol. 1. 320p. 1983. text ed. 21.00x (ISBN 0-85635-467-8, Pub. by Carcanet New Pr England). Humanities.

Heiderich, Manfred W. The German Novel of Eighteen Hundred: A Study of Popular Prose Fiction. 347p. 1982. write for info. (ISBN 3-261-04803-4). P Lang Pubs.

Lange, Victor. Classical Age of German Literature, 1740-1815. 256p. (Orig.). 1983. text ed. 26.00x (ISBN 0-8419-0853-2); pap. text ed. 17.50x (ISBN 0-8419-0854-0). Holmes & Meier.

GERMAN LITERATURE-HISTORY AND CRITICISM-20TH CENTURY

Elstun, Esther N. Richard Beer-Hoffmann: His Life & Work. Strelka, Joseph P., ed. LC 82-14990. (Penn State Studies in German Literature). 225p. 1983. 17.95x (ISBN 0-271-00335-9). Pa St U Pr.

Hamburger, Michael. German Literature from Nietzsche to the Present Day, Vol. 1. 320p. 1983. text ed. 21.00x (ISBN 0-85635-467-8, Pub. by Carcanet New Pr England). Humanities.

GERMAN NATIONAL CHARACTERISTICS

see National Characteristics, German

GERMAN OCCUPATION OF DENMARK, 1940-1945

see Denmark-History

GERMAN PHILOLOGY

Bernstein, Eckhard. German Humanism. (World Authors Ser.). 176p. 1983. lib. bdg. 18.95 (ISBN 0-8057-6537-9, Twayne). G K Hall.

GERMAN PHILOSOPHY

see Philosophy, German

GERMAN POETRY-MIDDLE HIGH GERMAN, 1050-1500-HISTORY AND CRITICISM

Sayce, Olive. The Medieval German Lyric, Eleven Fifty-Thirteen Hundred: The Development of Its Themes & Forms in Their European Context. 540p. 1982. 83.00x (ISBN 0-19-815772-X). Oxford U Pr.

GERMAN PORCELAIN

see Porcelain

GERMAN POTTERY

see Pottery, German

GERMAN PROPAGANDA

see Propaganda, German

GERMAN SOUTHWEST AFRICA

see Namibia

GERMAN TALES

see Tales, German

GERMANIC CIVILIZATION

see Civilization, Germanic

GERMANIC LANGUAGES

see also Anglo-Saxon Language; Danish Language; Dutch Language; English Language; German Language; Low German Language; Norwegian Language; Scandinavian Languages

Moller, Hermann. Vergleichendes Indogermanisch-Semitisches Worterbuch. 316p. 1982. Repr. of 1911 ed. lib. bdg. 150.00 (ISBN 0-89984-810-9). Century Bookbindery.

GERMANIC LEGENDS

see Legends, Germanic

GERMANS

Dundes, Alan. German National Character: An Anthropological Study, or Life Is Like a Chicken Coop Ladder. (Illus.). 176p. 1983. 16.00x (ISBN 0-231-05494-7). Columbia U Pr.

GERMANS IN THE UNITED STATES

see also Pennsylvania Germans

Dolan, Jay P. The Immigrant Church: New York's Irish & German Catholics, 1815-1865. LC 82-23827. (Illus.). xiv, 221p. 1983. pap. text ed. 7.95x (ISBN 0-268-01151-6, 85-11511). U of Notre Dame Pr.

Schweizer, Niklaus R. Hawaii & the German Speaking Peoples. (Illus.). 232p. (Orig.). pap. 15.00 (ISBN 0-914916-60-2). Topgallant.

GERMANY

Here are entered works on Germany for the pre-1949 period, the Territories under Allied Occupation, and East Germany and West Germany, collectively, for the post-1949 period.

De Stael. Germany, 2 vols. Wight, O. W., tr. LC 82-73430. 845p. Repr. of 1864 ed. lib. bdg. 65.00x (ISBN 0-88116-010-5). Brenner Bks.

International Film Bureau Inc., ed. Deutsche Kulturfilme. (European Studies-Germany). 32p. 1982. 3.00x (ISBN 0-8354-2547-9). Intl Film.

Koss, Gerhard. Names of Germany. (International Library of Names). 250p. 1983. text ed. 24.50x (ISBN 0-8290-1285-0). Irvington.

GERMANY-AIR FORCE

Aders, Gebhard. History of the German Night Fighter Force 1917-1945. (Illus.). 360p. 1980. 19.95 (ISBN 0-86720-581-4). Sci Bks Intl.

Cooper, Matthew. The German Air Force Nineteen Thirty-Three to Nineteen Forty-Five: An Anatomy of Failure. (Illus.). 375p. 1981. 19.95 (ISBN 0-86720-565-2). Sci Bks Intl.

Stahl, P. W., ed. KG Two Hundred. (Illus.). 224p. 1981. 19.95 (ISBN 0-86720-564-4). Sci Bks IntL.

GERMANY-BIBLIOGRAPHY

Hans-Albrecht, Koch, ed. International Bibliography of German Studies, 1980, Vol. 1. 854p. 1981. 120.00x (ISBN 3-598-10405-7, Pub. by K G Saur). Gale.

--International Bibliography of German Studies, 1981, Vol. 2. 800p. 1983. 120.00x (ISBN 0-686-82085-1, Pub. by K G Saur). Gale.

GERMANY-BIOGRAPHY

Maier, Mathilde. All the Gardens of My Life. 1983. 7.95 (ISBN 0-533-05486-9). Vantage.

Stritzke, Barbara. Marieluise Fleisser: Pionere In Ingolstadt. 111p. (Ger.). 1982. write for info. (ISBN 3-8204-5975-8). P Lang Pubs.

GERMANY-CIVILIZATION

Abish, Walter. How German Is It. 195p. 1982. text ed. 14.75x (ISBN 0-85635-396-5, Pub. by Carcanet Pr England). Humanities.

Komar, Kathleen L. Pattern & Chaos: A Structural Analysis of Novels by Doeblin, Koeppen, Dos Passos, & Faulkner. LC 82-73875. (Studies in German Literature, Linguistics, & Culture: Vol. 14). (Illus.). 160p. 1983. 20.00x (ISBN 0-938100-19-X). Camden Hse.

GERMANY-COMMERCE

Export Directory of German Industries 1982. 29th ed. LC 57-16210. 1500p. (Orig.). 1982. 55.00x (ISBN 0-8002-3016-7). Intl Pubns Serv.

Kriegsmann, Klaus-Peter & Neu, Axel D. Globale Regionale und Sektorale Wettbewerbsfahigkeit der Deutschen Wirtschaft. x, 295p. (Ger.). 1982. write for info. (ISBN 3-8204-5809-3). P Lang Pubs.

GERMANY-CONSTITUTIONAL HISTORY

Oestreich, Gerhard. Neostoicism & the Early Modern State. Oestreich, B. & Koenigsberger, H. G., eds. LC 81-12285. (Cambridge Studies in Early Modern History Ser.). 272p. 1982. 49.50 (ISBN 0-521-24202-9). Cambridge U Pr.

GERMANY-DESCRIPTION AND TRAVEL

Jackson, J. H. Stars in the Night: Report on a Visit to Germany. 1950. 1.50 (ISBN 0-686-42986-9). Townsend Pr.

GERMANY-ECONOMIC CONDITIONS

Wilkens, Herbert. The Two German Economies. 180p. 1981. text ed. 44.50x (ISBN 0-566-00304-X). Gower Pub Ltd.

GERMANY-EMIGRATION AND IMMIGRATION

Jackman, Jarrell C. & Borden, Carla M., eds. The Muses Flee Hitler: Cultural Transfer & Adaptation, 1930-1945. (Illus.). 340p. 1983. 17.50 (ISBN 0-87474-554-3); pap. 8.95 (ISBN 0-87474-555-1). Smithsonian.

GERMANY-FOREIGN RELATIONS

Mendelsohn, John. The Crystal Night Pogrom. LC 81-80331. (The Holocaust Ser.). 325p. 1982. lib. bdg. 50.00 (ISBN 0-8240-4877-6). Garland Pub.

Weinberg, Gerhard L. The Foreign Policy of Hitler's Germany: Diplomatic Revolution in Europe, 1933-1936. LC 70-124733. xii, 398p. 1970. pap. 10.95 (ISBN 0-226-88513-5). U of Chicago Pr.

GERMANY-FOREIGN RELATIONS-UNITED STATES

Dougherty, Patricia. American Diplomats & the Franco-Prussian War: Perceptions from Paris & Berlin. LC 80-250000089. 42p. 1980. 2.50 (ISBN 0-934742-06-5, Inst Study Diplomacy). Geo U Sch For Serv.

Miller, Marvin D. Wunderlich's Salute: The Interrelationship of the German-American Bund, Camp Siegfried, Yaphank, Long Island, & the Young Siegfrieds & Their Relations with American & Nazi Institutions. LC 82-62515. (Illus.). 270p. 1983. pap. write for info. (ISBN 0-9610466-0-0). Malamud-Rose.

GERMANY-HISTORY

Wehrli, Christoph. Mittelaterliche Uberlieferungen Von Dagobert I. 386p. (Ger.). 1982. write for info (ISBN 3-261-04914-6). P Lang Pubs.

GERMANY-HISTORY-SOURCES

Smith, Clifford Neal. Eighteenth-Century Emigrants from Kreis Simmern (Hunsrueck), Rheinland-Pfalz, Germany, to Central Europe, Pfalzdorf am Niederrhein, & North America. (German-American Genealogical Research Monograph: No. 15). 25p. (Orig.). 1982. pap. 10.00 (ISBN 0-915162-15-6). Westland Pubns.

GERMANY-HISTORY-TO 1517

DuBoulay, F. R. H. Germany Thirteen Fifty to Fifteen Hundred. 200p. 1982. text ed. 26.25x (ISBN 0-485-11220-5, Althlone Pr). Humanities.

GERMANY-HISTORY-FRANCO-GERMAN WAR, 1870-1871

see Franco-German War, 1870-1871

GERMANY-HISTORY-1933-1945

Fromm, Hermann. Deutschland in der Offentlichen Kriegszieldiskussion Grossbritanniens 1939-1945. 167p. 1982. write for info. P Lang Pubs.

Mendelsohn, John. Propaganda & Aryanization, 1938-1944. LC 81-80312. (The Holocaust Ser.). 255p. 1982. lib. bdg. 50.00 (ISBN 0-8240-4878-4). Garland Pub.

Tournier, Jacques M. Extermination as a Policy of Political & Military Power in Nazi Germany & the Middle East. (The Great Currents of History Library Book). (Illus.). 135p. 1983. 87.45 (ISBN 0-86722-020-1). Inst Econ Pol.

Wellner, Cathryn J. Witness to War: A Thematic Guide to Young Adult Literature on World War II, 1965-1981. LC 82-5600. 287p. 1982. 17.00 (ISBN 0-8108-1552-4). Scarecrow.

GERMANY-HISTORY, MILITARY

Cooper, Matthew. The German Air Force Nineteen Thirty-Three to Nineteen Forty-Five: An Anatomy of Failure. (Illus.). 375p. 1981. 19.95 (ISBN 0-86720-565-2). Sci Bks Intl.

Tournier, Jacques M. Extermination as a Policy of Political & Military Power in Nazi Germany & the Middle East. (The Great Currents of History Library Book). (Illus.). 135p. 1983. 87.45 (ISBN 0-86722-020-1). Inst Econ Pol.

GERMANY-IMPRINTS

German Books in Print, 1982-83: Authors, Titles, Keywords, 4 Vols. 12th ed. 7000p. 1982. 280.00 (ISBN 0-686-82084-3, Pub. by K G Saur). Gale.

ISBN Register German Books in Print, 1982-83. 12th ed. 600p. 1982. 130.00x (ISBN 0-686-82081-9, Pub. by K G Saur). Gale.

Subject Guide to German Books in Print, 1982-83, 3 Vols. 5th ed. 6000p. 1982. 250.00x (ISBN 0-686-82083-5, Pub. by K G Saur). Gale.

GERMANY-INDUSTRY

Who Makes Machinery? West Germany, 1982. 44th ed. LC 53-30391. 884p. 1982. pap. 15.00x (ISBN 3-87362-019-7). Intl Pubns serv.

GERMANY-INTELLECTUAL LIFE

Reuter, Helmut H. Der Intellektuelle und die Politik. 234p. (Ger.). 1982. write for info. (ISBN 3-8204-5769-0). P Lang Pubs.

GERMANY-POLITICS AND GOVERNMENT

Johnson, N. State & Government in the Federal Republic of Germany: The Executive at Work. (Governments of Western Europe Ser.). 240p. 1983. 35.00 (ISBN 0-08-030188-6); pap. 17.50 (ISBN 0-08-030190-8). Pergamon.

Oestreich, Gerhard. Neostoicism & the Early Modern State. Oestreich, B. & Koenigsberger, H. G., eds. LC 81-12285. (Cambridge Studies in Early Modern History Ser.). 272p. 1982. 49.50 (ISBN 0-521-24202-9). Cambridge U Pr.

The Old Reich: Essays on German Political Institutions, 1495-1806. xii, 165p. 1974. write for info. P Lang Pubs.

Reuter, Helmut H. Der Intellektuelle und die Politik. 234p. (Ger.). 1982. write for info. (ISBN 3-8204-5769-0). P Lang Pubs.

Smith, Gordon. Democracy in Western Germany: Parties & Politics in the Federal Republic. 2nd ed. 180p. (Orig.). 1983. pap. text ed. 8.50x (ISBN 0-686-82618-3). Holmes & Meier.

GERMANY-POLITICS AND GOVERNMENT-1789-1900

Massey, Marilyn C. Christ Unmasked: The Meaning of "The Life of Jesus" in German Politics. LC 82-8547. (Studies in Religion Ser.). xi, 175p. 1982. 23.00x (ISBN 0-8078-1524-1). U of NC Pr.

GERMANY-POLITICS AND GOVERNMENT-1871-1918

Hughes, Judith M. Emotion & High Politics: Personal Relations in Late Nineteenth-Century Britain & Germany. LC 82-4737. 232p. 1983. 28.50x (ISBN 0-520-04691-9). U of Cal Pr.

GERMANY-POLITICS AND GOVERNMENT-20TH CENTURY

Bendersky, Joseph W. Carl Schmitt, Theorist for the Reich. LC 82-61353. 336p. 1983. 27.50x (ISBN 0-691-05380-4). Princeton U Pr.

Schorske, Carl E. German Social Democracy, Nineteen Five to Nineteen Eighteen: The Development of the Great Schism. (Harvard Historical Studies: No. 65). 384p. 1983. pap. text ed. 4.95x (ISBN 0-674-35125-8). Harvard U Pr.

GERMANY-POLITICS AND GOVERNMENT-1918-1933

Grill, Johnpeter H. The Nazi Movement in Baden, 1920-1945. LC 82-13383. xvii, 720p. 1983. 32.00x (ISBN 0-8078-1472-5). U of NC Pr.

Schulz, Birger. Der Republikanische Richterbund (1921-1933) 211p. (Ger.). 1982. write for info. (ISBN 3-8204-7122-7). P Lang Pubs.

Stachura, Peter D. Gregor Strasser & the Rise of Nazism. 208p. 1983. text ed. 19.50x (ISBN 0-04-943027-0). Allen Unwin.

GERMANY-POLITICS AND GOVERNMENT-1933-1945

Angolia, John R. For Fuhrer & Fatherland: Military Awards of the Third Reich. 1978. 19.00 (ISBN 0-686-82440-7). Quaker.

Friedlander, Saul. Reflections on Nazism. Weyr, Thomas, tr. from Fr. LC 82-48117. 160p. 1983. 11.49i (ISBN 0-06-015097-1, HarpT). Har-Row.

Grill, Johnpeter H. The Nazi Movement in Baden, 1920-1945. LC 82-13383. xvii, 720p. 1983. 32.00x (ISBN 0-8078-1472-5). U of NC Pr.

Stachura, Peter D. Gregor Strasser & the Rise of Nazism. 208p. 1983. text ed. 19.50x (ISBN 0-04-943027-0). Allen Unwin.

Weinberg, Gerhard L. The Foreign Policy of Hitler's Germany: Diplomatic Revolution in Europe, 1933-1936. LC 70-124733. xii, 398p. 1970. pap. 10.95 (ISBN 0-226-88513-5). U of Chicago Pr.

GERMANY-POLITICS AND GOVERNMENT-1945-

Donhoff, Marion. Foe Into Friend: The Makers of the New Germany from Konrad Adenaver to Helmut Schmidt. LC 82-10381. 214p. 1982. 18.50x (ISBN 0-312-29692-4). St Martin.

Goren, Simon L., tr. from German. German Civil Code & the Introductory Act to the German Civil Code & the Marriage Law of the Federal Republic of Germany: 1981 Supplement. LC 75-7935. v, 73p. 1982. pap. text ed. 12.50x (ISBN 0-8377-0615-7). Rothman.

Vale, Michel & Steinke, Rudolf, eds. Germany Debates Security: The NATO Alliance at the Crossroads. Vale, Michel, tr. from Ger. 228p. 1983. 25.00 (ISBN 0-87332-243-6). M E Sharpe.

GERMANY-RELIGION

Hollerbach, Marion. Das Religionsgesprach Als Mittel Der Konfessionellen Und Politischen Auseinandersetzung Im Deutschland Des 16. Jahrhunderts. (Ger.). 1982. write for info (ISBN 3-8204-7015-8). P Lang Pubs.

GERMANY-SOCIAL CONDITIONS

Kater, Michael H. The Nazi Party: A Social Profile of Members & Leaders, 1919-1945. (Illus.). 400p. 1983. text ed. 25.00x (ISBN 0-674-60655-8). Harvard U Pr.

Russ, J. German Festivals & Customs. 180p. 1982. pap. text ed. 16.75x (ISBN 0-85496-365-0, 41266, Pub. by Wolff Pubs England). Humanities.

GERMANY, EAST-ECONOMIC CONDITIONS

Wilkens, Herbert. The Two German Economies. 180p. 1981. text ed. 44.50x (ISBN 0-566-00304-X). Gower Pub Ltd.

GERMANY, EAST-POLITICS AND GOVERNMENT

Scharf, C. Bradley. Politics & Social Change in East Germany: An Evaluation of Socialist Democracy. (Westview Special Studies on the Soviet Union & Eastern Europe). 215p. 1983. lib. bdg. 18.50x; pap. text ed. price not set (ISBN 0-86531-451-9). Westview.

Von Beyme, Klaus, ed. Policy Making in the German Democratic Republic. LC 82-5544. 220p. 1982. 25.00x (ISBN 0-312-62032-2). St Martin.

GERMANY, WEST-POLITICS AND GOVERNMENT

Braunthal, Gerard. The West German Social Democrats, 1969-1982: Profile of a Party in Power. (Replica Edition Ser.). 400p. 1983. softcover 25.00x (ISBN 0-86531-958-8). Westview.

Markovits, Andrei S., ed. The Political Economy of West Germany: Modell Deutschland. 240p. 1982. 27.95 (ISBN 0-03-060617-9). Praeger.

GERMANY, WEST-SOCIAL CONDITIONS

Markovits, Andrei S., ed. The Political Economy of West Germany: Modell Deutschland. 240p. 1982. 27.95 (ISBN 0-03-060617-9). Praeger.

GERMICIDES

see Disinfection and Disinfectants; Fungicides

GERMINATION
Black, M. & Bewley, J. D. Physiology & Biochemistry of Seeds in Relation to Germination: Viability, Dormancy, & Environmental Control, Vol. 2. (Illus.). 380p. 1982. 54.00 (ISBN 0-387-11656-7). Springer-Verlag.
GERMS
see Bacteria; Bacteriology; Micro-Organisms
GERONTOLOGY
see Aged; Geriatrics
GESTAGENS
see Progestational Hormones
GESTALT PSYCHOLOGY
Wertheimer, Max. Productive Thinking: Enlarged Edition. LC 82-10913. (Phoenix Ser.). 328p. 1982. pap. 8.95 (ISBN 0-226-89376-6). U of Chicago Pr.
GESTATION
see Pregnancy
GESTURE LANGUAGE
see Deaf-Means of Communication
GETTY (J. PAUL) MUSEUM
Thompson, David L. Mummy Portraits in the J. Paul Getty Museum. LC 82-81303. 70p. 1982. pap. 16.95 (ISBN 0-89236-038-0). J P Getty Mus.
GHANA-HISTORY
Chazan, Naomi H. An Anatomy of Ghanaian Politics: Managing Political Recession, 1969-1982. (Special Study on Africa). 350p. 1982. lib. bdg. 25.00 (ISBN 0-86531-439-X). Westview.
GHANA-POLITICS AND GOVERNMENT
Chazan, Naomi H. An Anatomy of Ghanaian Politics: Managing Political Recession, 1969-1982. (Special Study on Africa). 350p. 1982. lib. bdg. 25.00 (ISBN 0-86531-439-X). Westview.
Maier, D. J. Priests & Power: The Case of the Dente Shrine in Nineteenth-Century Ghana. LC 82-48582. (Illus.). 272p. 1983. 18.50x (ISBN 0-253-34602-9). Ind U Pr.
Rooney, David. Sir Charles Arden-Clarke. 236p. 1982. text ed. 22.50 (ISBN 0-89874-598-5). Krieger.
GHANA-RELIGION
Maier, D. J. Priests & Power: The Case of the Dente Shrine in Nineteenth-Century Ghana. LC 82-48582. (Illus.). 272p. 1983. 18.50x (ISBN 0-253-34602-9). Ind U Pr.
GHANDI, MAHATMA
see Gandhi, Mohandas Karamchand, 1869-1948
GHOST STORIES
see also Horror Tales
Bleiler, Everett. A Treasury of Victorian Ghost Stories. 368p. 1983. pap. 7.95 (ISBN 0-686-83713-4, ScribT). Scribner.
Jones, Louis C. Things That Go Bump in the Night. (York State Bks.). (Illus.). 220p. 1983. pap. 9.95 (ISBN 0-8156-0184-0). Syracuse U Pr.
GHOST TOWNS
see Cities and Towns, Ruined, Extinct, etc.
GHOSTS
see also Apparitions; Demonology; Poltergeists; Psychical Research; Spiritualism; Superstition
Abbott, G. Ghosts of the Tower of London. (Illus.). 85p. pap. 4.95 (ISBN 0-434-00595-9, Pub. by Heinemann). David & Charles.
Aoams, Charles J., III. Ghost Stories of Berks County (Pennsylvania) 215p. 1982. pap. 5.95 (ISBN 0-9610008-0-5). C J Adams.
Bendick, Jeanne. Scare a Ghost, Tame a Monster. LC 82-23696. (Illus.). 120p. (gr. 3-6). 1983. price not set (ISBN 0-664-32701-X). Westminster.
MacKenzie, Andrew. Hauntings & Apparitions. 12p. 1982. 40.00x (ISBN 0-434-44051-5, Pub. by Heinemann England). State Mutual Bk.
GIANNUZZI'S SEMILUNAR BODIES
see Salivary Glands
GIBRAN, KAHLIL, 1883-1931
Mutlak, Suheil. In Memory of Kahil Gibran. 1982. 12.00x (ISBN 0-86685-295-6). Intl Bk Ctr.
GIFT OF TONGUES
see Glossolalia
GIFT TAX
see Gifts-Taxation
GIFTED CHILDREN
Feldman, Ruth D. Whatever Happened to the Quiz Kids? Perils & Profits of Growing Up Gifted. (Illus.). 375p. 1982. 12.95 (ISBN 0-914091-17-4). Chicago Review.
Galbraith, Judy. The Gifted Kids Survival Guide. (Illus., Orig.). (gr. 6-12). 1983. pap. price not set (ISBN 0-936750-07-3). Wetherall.
Pascoe, Victoria. The Golden Journey. 1983. 7.95 (ISBN 0-533-05551-2). Vantage.
Perlmutter, Marion, ed. Development & Policy Concerning Children with Special Needs. (Minnesota Symposium on Child Psychology Ser.: Vol. 16). 272p. 1983. text ed. write for info. (ISBN 0-89859-261-5). L Erlbaum Assocs.
GIFTED CHILDREN-EDUCATION
Gallagher, James J. Leadership Unit: The Use of Teacher-Scholar Teams to Develop Units for the Gifted. (Illus.). 138p. 1982. pap. 12.50 tchr's ed (ISBN 0-89824-036-0). Trillium Pr.
Gallagher, James J., ed. Gifted Children: Reaching their Potential. 440p. (Orig.). 1979. pap. 14.00 (ISBN 0-89824-012-3). Trillium Pr.
Kramer, Alan H., ed. Gifted Children: Challenging their Potential. 331p. (Orig.). 1981. pap. 14.00 (ISBN 0-89824-027-1). Trillium Pr.
Moore, Linda P. Does This Mean My Kid's a Genius? How to Identify, Educate, Motivate & Live with the Gifted Child. 1982. pap. 6.95 (ISBN 0-452-25375-6, Plume). NAL.
Webb, James T. & Meckstroth, Betty. Guiding the Gifted Child. LC 82-9939. 262p. 1982. pap. 11.95 (ISBN 0-910707-00-6). Ohio Psych Pub.
GIFTED CHILDREN-EDUCATION-DIRECTORIES
Clendening, Corinne P. & Davies, Ruth A. Challenging the Gifted Child. (Serving Special Populations Ser.). 1983. 32.50 (ISBN 0-8352-1682-9). Bowker.
GIFTS
Doyle, Alfreda C. Survival Suggestions for the Holidays & Other Gift Giving Occassions. 26p. 1983. pap. text ed. 6.95 (ISBN 0-910811-28-8). Center Self.
Gregory, C. A. Gifts & Commodities. (Studies in Political Economy: Vol. 2). 37.00 (ISBN 0-12-301460-3); pap. 16.00 (ISBN 0-12-301462-X). Acad Pr.
King, J. Greatest Gift Guide Ever. (Illus.). 190p. 1982. pap. 5.95 (ISBN 0-932620-15-9, Pub. by Betterway Pubns). Berkshire Traveller.
GIFTS-TAXATION
see also Real Property and Taxation
Crumbley, D. L. & Milam, Edward E. Estate Planning in the '80s. 224p. 1983. 15.95 (ISBN 0-8144-5758-4). Am Mgmt.
McNulty, John K. Federal Estate & Gift Taxation in a Nutshell. 3rd ed. LC 82-24726. (Nutshell Ser.). 493p. 1983. pap. text ed. 7.95 (ISBN 0-314-71766-8). West Pub.
GIFTS, SPIRITUAL
see also Fear of God; Glossolalia; Prophecy (Christianity)
Fearon, Mary & Hirstein, Sandra J. Celebrating the Gift of Forgiveness. 64p. 1982. pap. 2.75 (ISBN 0-697-01792-3); program manual 6.95 (ISBN 0-697-01793-1). Wm C Brown.
Gangel, Kenneth O. Unwrap Your Spiritual Gifts. 120p. 1983. pap. 4.50 (ISBN 0-88207-102-5). Victor Bks.
Hagin, Kenneth E. Concerning Spiritual Gifts. 1974. pap. 2.50 (ISBN 0-89276-072-9). Hagin Ministry.
McRae, William. The Dynamics of Spiritual Gifts. 144p. 1983. pap. 4.95 (ISBN 0-310-29091-0). Zondervan.
Mallone, George, et al. Those Controversial Gifts. 168p. (Orig.). 1983. pap. 4.95 (ISBN 0-87784-823-8). Inter-Varsity.
GILA RIVER AND VALLEY
Rea, Amadeo M. Once a River: Bird Life & Habitat Changes on the Middle Gila. 270p. 1983. 24.50 (ISBN 0-8165-0799-6). U of Ariz Pr.
GILBERT ISLANDS
Macdonald, Barrie. Cinderellas of the Empire. LC 81-68450. 335p. (Orig.). 1982. pap. text ed. 29.95 (ISBN 0-7081-1616-7, 1183, Pub. by ANUP Australia). Bks Australia.
GINGER
Ronay, Nadja. Ginger. LC 82-170230. 62p. 1981. 17.95 (ISBN 0-943516-00-5). Magnolia Pubns Inc.
GINGERBREAD
see Cake
GIPSIES
Borrow, George. Romano Lavo-Lil: A Book of the Gypsy. 192p. 1982. pap. text ed. 6.25x (ISBN 0-86299-024-6, Pub. by Alan Sutton England). Humanities.
Okely, Judith. The Traveller-Gypsies. LC 82-9478. (Illus.). 228p. 1983. 34.50 (ISBN 0-521-24641-5); pap. 10.95 (ISBN 0-521-28870-3). Cambridge U Pr.
GIRAFFES
Wildlife Education, Ltd. Giraffes. Wexo, John B., ed. (Zoobooks). (Illus.). 20p. (Orig.). 1982. pap. 1.50 (ISBN 0-937934-09-7). Wildlife Educ.
GIRDERS
see also Bridges; Building, Iron and Steel; Steel, Structural
Gorman, D. J. Free Vibration Analysis of Beams & Shafts. LC 74-20504. 448p. 1975. 49.95x (ISBN 0-471-31770-5, Pub. by Wiley-Interscience). Wiley.
GIRLS
see also Adolescent Girls; Children; Church Work with Children; Education of Women; Women; Youth
Reese, Lyn & Wilkinson, Jean. I'm on My Way Running. 384p. 4.95 (ISBN 0-380-83022-1, Discus). Avon.
Rustemeyer, Ruth. Wahrnehmung Eigener Fahigkeit Bei Jungen und Madchen. 213p. (Ger.). 1982. write for info. (ISBN 3-8204-5755-0). P Lang Pubs.
GIRLS-EDUCATION
see Education of Women
GIRLS-EMPLOYMENT
see Education of Women; Youth-Employment
GIRLS-SOCIETIES AND CLUBS
see also Gangs
Albert, Burton. Clubs for Kids. 144p. (Orig.). 1983. pap. price not set (ISBN 0-345-30292-3). Ballantine.
GIRLS' CLUBS
see Girls-Societies and Clubs
GIRLS IN THE BIBLE
see Children in the Bible
GISSING, GEORGE ROBERT, 1857-1903
Selig, Robert L. George Gissing. (English Authors Ser.). 192p. 1983. lib. bdg. 15.95 (ISBN 0-8057-6831-9, Twayne). G K Hall.
GIVE-AWAYS
see Free Material
GIVING, CHRISTIAN
see Stewardship, Christian
GLACIAL EPOCH
see also Geology, Stratigraphic-Pleistocene
Chorlton, Windsor. Ice Ages. (Planet Earth Ser.). 1983. lib. bdg. 19.92 (ISBN 0-8094-4329-5, Pub. by Time-Life). Silver.
Daly, Reginald D. Changing World of the Ice Age. 1934. text ed. 19.50 (ISBN 0-686-83502-6). Elliots Bks.
Noone, Richard W. Ice: The Ultimate Disaster. LC 82-73265. (Illus.). 384p. 1982. 19.95 (ISBN 0-910285-00-4). Astraea Pub.
GLACIER NATIONAL PARK
Raup, Omer B. & Earhart, Robert L. Geology Along Going-to-the-Sun Road Glacier National Park Montana. LC 82-84746. (Illus.). 64p. 1983. pap. 4.95 (ISBN 0-934318-11-5). Falcon Pr MT.
Schneider, Bill. Bicyclist's Guide to Glacier National Park. (Illus.). 48p. 1983. pap. 3.95 (ISBN 0-934318-17-4). Falcon Pr MT.
GLACIERS
see also Erosion
Andrews, John T., ed. Glacial Isostasy. LC 73-12624. (Benchmark Papers in Geology: Vol. 10). 491p. 1974. text ed. 54.00 (ISBN 0-87933-051-1). Hutchinson Ross.
Bailey, Ronald. Glacier. (Planet Earth Ser.). 1982. lib. bdg. 19.92 (ISBN 0-8094-4317-1, Pub. by Time-Life). Silver.
Cunningham, Frank. James David Forbes: Pioneer Scottish Glaciologist. 475p. 1983. 60.00x (ISBN 0-7073-0320-6, Pub. by Scottish Academic Pr Scotland). Columbia U Pr.
Zumbuhl, H. J. The Fluctuations of the Grindenwald Glaciers in the Written & Illustrated Sources of the 12th to 19th Centuries. 278p. 1980. text ed. 67.10x (ISBN 3-7643-1199-1). Birkhauser.
GLACIOLOGY
see Glaciers
GLADES COUNTY, FLORIDA-HISTORY
Glades County Commissioners & Bass, Billy O. Glades County, Florida History. Wright, Betty, ed. LC 82-61321. (A Pioneer Heritage Presentation Ser.). 208p. 1983. pap. 10.00 (ISBN 0-935834-09-5). Rainbow Betty.
GLADNESS
see Happiness
GLADSTONE, WILLIAM EWART, 1809-1898
Gladstone, William E. The Gladstone Diaries: Vol. 7, January 1869-June 1871. Matthew, H. C., ed. (Illus.). 642p. 1982. 79.00x (ISBN 0-19-822445-1). Oxford U Pr.
--The Gladstone Diaries: Vol. 8, July 1871-December 1874. Matthew, H. C., ed. (Illus.). 620p. 1982. 79.00x (ISBN 0-19-822639-X). Oxford U Pr.
Guedalla, Philip. Gladstone & Palmerston: Being the Correspondence of Lord Palmerston with Mr. Gladstone, 1851-1865. 367p. 1982. Repr. of 1928 ed. lib. bdg. 40.00 (ISBN 0-89987-314-6). Darby Bks.
GLAND OF INTERNAL SECRETION
see Endocrine Glands
GLANDS
see also Cystic Fibrosis; Endocrine Glands; Secretion; also particular glands, e.g. Carotid Gland, Kidneys
Berman. The Glands Regulating Personality: A Study of the Glands of Internal Secretion in Relation to the Types of Human Nature. 341p. 1983. Repr. of 1933 ed. lib. bdg. 40.00 (ISBN 0-89760-051-7). Telegraph Bks.
Himalayan International Institute. Joints & Glands Exercises. 2nd ed. Ballentine, Rudolph M., ed. (Illus.). 90p. (Orig.). 1982. pap. 3.95 (ISBN 0-89389-083-9). Himalayan Intl Inst.
GLANDS, DUCTLESS
see Endocrine Glands
GLANDS, MAMMARY
see Mammary Glands
GLANDS, SALIVARY
see Salivary Glands
GLASGOW, ELLEN ANDERSON GHOLSON, 1874-1945
Raper, J. R. Without Shelter: The Career of Ellen Glasgow. LC 82-15863. (Southern Literary Studies). xii, 273p. 1982. Repr. of 1971 ed. lib. bdg. 39.75x (ISBN 0-313-23742-5, RAWS). Greenwood.
GLASGOW, SCOTLAND
Bryant, B. & Bryant, R. Change & Conflict: A Study of Community Work in Glasgow. 250p. 1983. 21.00 (ISBN 0-08-028475-2); pap. 11.50 (ISBN 0-08-028480-9). Pergamon.
Corrace, Douglas & Bond, Edward. Glasgow. (Illus.). 128p. 1983. 22.95 (ISBN 0-00-435667-5, Collins Pub England). Greene.
Gibb, A. Glasgow: The Making of a City. 224p. 1983. text ed. 25.25 (ISBN 0-7099-0161-5, Pub. by Croom Helm Ltd England). Biblio Dist.
GLASS, HUGH, 1780-1833
Neihardt, John G. The Song of Three Friends & the Song of Hugh Glass. 335p. 1982. Repr. of 1941 ed. lib. bdg. 25.00 (ISBN 0-89984-360-3). Century Bookbindery.
GLASS
see also Glassware
Berlye, Milton K. Encyclopedia of Working with Glass. 1983. 29.95 (ISBN 0-89696-193-1). Dodd.
Data Notes Publishing Staff. Glass Recycling: Data Notes. 30p. 1983. pap. text ed. 9.95 (ISBN 0-911569-42-1). Data Notes Pub.
Journal of Glass Studies, Vol. 24. LC 59-12390. (Illus.). 175p. 1982. 20.00 (ISBN 0-87290-024-X). Corning.
Uhlmann, D. R. & Kreidl, N. J., eds. Glass: Science & Technology: Vol. 1: Glass Systems & Glass Ceramics. 424p. 1983. price not set (ISBN 0-12-706701-9); price not set subscription price. Acad Pr.
GLASS-COLLECTORS AND COLLECTING
see Glassware
GLASS, COLORED
see also Glass Painting and Staining
Caviness, Madeline H. Stained Glass before 1540: An Annotated Bibliography. 1983. lib. bdg. 45.00 (ISBN 0-8161-8332-5, Hall Reference). G K Hall.
Rath, Wilhelm. The Imagery of the Goetheanum Windows. Mann, William, tr. from German. (Illus.). 30p. 1976. 12.50 (ISBN 0-85440-300-0, Pub. by Steinerbooks). Anthroposophic.
GLASS, ORNAMENTAL
see also Glass, Colored; Glass Painting and Staining
Piche, Thomas. Art Nouveau Glass & Pottery. Meyer, Faith, ed. (Illus.). 16p. (Orig.). 1982. pap. text ed. 4.00 (ISBN 0-932660-06-1). U of NI Dept Art.
GLASS, PRESSED
see Pressed Glass
GLASS, STAINED
see Glass Painting and Staining
GLASS MANUFACTURE
see also Mirrors; Optical Instruments
Miller, Richard K. Noise Control Solutions for the Glass Industry. 120p. pap. text ed. 90.00 (ISBN 0-89671-016-5). Southeast Acoustics.
GLASS MANUFACTURE-GREAT BRITAIN
Murray, Sheilagh. The Peacock & the Lions. (Illus.). 240p. 1983. 25.00 (ISBN 0-686-84463-7, Oriel). Routledge & Kegan.
GLASS PAINTING AND STAINING
see also Glass, Colored
Caviness, Madeline H. Stained Glass before 1540: An Annotated Bibliography. 1983. lib. bdg. 45.00 (ISBN 0-8161-8332-5, Hall Reference). G K Hall.
Evans, David. A Bibliography of Stained Glass. 214p. 1983. text ed. 75.00x (ISBN 0-85991-087-3, Pub by Boydell & Brewer). Biblio Dist.
French, Jennie. Design for Stained Glass. 168p. 1982. pap. 9.95 (ISBN 0-442-22449-4). Van Nos Reinhold.
Hungness, Carl. Who's Who in Stained Glass. 284p. 1983. pap. 9.95 (ISBN 0-915088-34-7). C Hungness.
Kedda, Helena. Stained Glass Cook Book. (Illus.). 56p. (Orig.). 1982. pap. 4.95 (ISBN 0-9608958-0-9). Paw-Print.
Mortimer, Richard L. Stained Glass Menagerie. (Illus.). 96p. (Orig.). 1982. pap. 7.95 (ISBN 0-9608356-0-1). Glass Art.
Sibbett, Ed, Jr. Easy-to-Make Stained Glass Panels: With Full-Size Templates for 32 Projects. (Illus.). 64p. (Orig.). 1983. pap. 3.95 (ISBN 0-486-24448-2). Dover.
Tom Stained Glass Artisans. Challenging Projects in Stained Glass. LC 82-18437. (Illus.). 1983. pap. 7.95 (ISBN 0-668-05581-2). Arco.
Tom Studio Artisans. Getting Started in Stained Glass. LC 82-18438. (Illus.). 144p. 1983. pap. 7.95 (ISBN 0-668-05577-4). Arco.
Wood, Paul W. Stained Glass Crafting. LC 67-27750. (Illus.). 104p. 1983. pap. 7.95 (ISBN 0-8069-7724-8). Sterling.
GLASSWARE
see also Bottles; Pressed Glass
Lucky, Carl F. Depression: Era Glassware. (Identification & Value Guide Ser.). (Illus.). 200p. 1983. pap. 9.95 (ISBN 0-89689-040-6). Bks Americana.
Mehlman, Felice. Phaidon Guide to Glass. (Illus.). 256p. 1983. 12.95 (ISBN 0-13-662023-X); pap. 6.95 (ISBN 0-13-662015-9). P-H.
New Glass Review, No. 2. (Illus.). 16p. 1981. pap. 5.00 (ISBN 0-87290-101-7). Corning.
New Glass Review, No. 4. (Illus.). 32p. 1983. pap. 5.00 (ISBN 0-87290-108-4). Corning.
GLASSWARE-COLLECTORS AND COLLECTING
Kovel, Ralph & Kovel, Terry. The Kovels' Illustrated Price Guide to Depression Glass & American Dinnerware. (Illus.). 1983. pap. 10.95 (ISBN 0-517-54974-3). Crown.
GLASSWARE-DICTIONARIES
VonZweck, Dina. Woman's Day Dictionary of Glass. 1983. pap. 4.95 (ISBN 0-8065-0841-8). Citadel Pr.
GLASSWARE-PRICES
Weatherman, Hazel M. Decorated Tumbler "PriceGuy". 128p. 1983. pap. 4.00 (ISBN 0-913074-19-5). Weatherman.
GLASSWARE-GREAT BRITAIN
Wakefield, Hugh. Nineteenth Century British Glass. 2nd ed. (Monographs on Glass). (Illus.). 176p. 1982. 49.95 (ISBN 0-571-18054-X). Faber & Faber.
GLASSWARE-SPAIN
Frothingham, A. W. Hispanic Glass. (Illus.). 1941. pap. 3.00 (ISBN 0-87535-052-6). Hispanic Soc.

GLASSWARE-UNITED STATES
Florence, Gene. Elegant Glassware of the Depression Era. 160p. Date not set. 17.95 (ISBN 0-89145-220-6). Collector Bks.
--Pocket Guide to Depression Glass. 3rd ed. 160p. Date not set. 9.95 (ISBN 0-89145-209-5). Collector Bks.
Madigan, Mary J. Steuben Glass: An American Tradition in Crystal. LC 81-22907. (Illus.). 320p. 1982. 55.00 (ISBN 0-8109-1642-8). Abrams.

GLASTONBURY ABBEY
Capt, Raymond E. The Traditions of Glastonbury. LC 82-72525. (Illus.). 128p. 1983. pap. 5.00 (ISBN 0-934666-10-5). Artisan Sales.

GLAUCOMA
Clayman, Henry M. & Jaffe, Norman S. Intraocular Lens Implantation: Techniques & Complications. LC 82-8267. (Illus.). 300p. 1983. text ed. 59.50 (ISBN 0-8016-1080-X). Mosby.
Kolker, Allan E. & Hetherington, John, Jr. Becker-Shaffer's Diagnosis & Therapy of the Glaucomas. (Illus.). 576p. 1983. text ed. 55.00 (ISBN 0-8016-2723-0). Mosby.

GLENCOE MASSACRE, 1692
Linklater, Magnus. Massacre: The Story of Glencoe. (Illus.). 160p. 1983. 24.95 (ISBN 0-00-435669-1, Collins Pub England). Greene.

GLOBAL SATELLITE COMMUNICATIONS SYSTEMS
see Artificial Satellites in Telecommunication

GLOBE THEATER
see Southwark, England-Globe Theatre

GLOBULAR PROTEINS
see Proteins

GLOSSOLALIA
Cook, Bob. Speaking in Tongues: Is That All There Is? (Discovery Bks.). 48p. (YA) (gr. 9-12). 1982. pap. text ed. 1.35 (ISBN 0-88243-932-4, 02-0932). Gospel Pub.
Heijkoop, H. L. Faith Healing & Speaking in Tongues. 40p. pap. 2.00 (ISBN 0-88172-083-6). Believers Bkshelf.
Pegram, Don R. Why We Do Not Speak in Tongues. 1982. pap. 1.00 (ISBN 0-89265-086-9). Randall Hse.

GLOUCESTER, ENGLAND
McWhirr, Alan. Roman Gloucestershire. 224p. 1982. text ed. 18.00x (ISBN 0-904387-63-1, Pub. by Sutton England); pap. text ed. 9.00x (ISBN 0-904387-60-7). Humanities.
Mander, Nicholas, ed. Gloucestershire: A Concise Guide. (Illus.). 192p. 1982. pap. text ed. 9.00x (ISBN 0-904387-72-0, Pub. by Sutton England). Humanities.

GLOVES
Hansen, Robin. Fox & Geese & Fences: A Collection of Maine Traditional Mittens. (Illus.). 64p. 1983. pap. 4.95t (ISBN 0-89272-162-6). Down East.

GLYCOGEN
Horowitz, Martin, ed. The Glycoconjugates: Glyconproteins, Glycolipides & Proteoglycans. LC 77-4086. 392p. 1982. 49.50 ea. Vol. III: Pt. A: 392 pgs (ISBN 0-12-356103-5). Vol. IV: Pt. B: 82-45134: 384 pgs (ISBN 0-12-356104-3). subscription 42.00 (ISBN 0-686-81649-8). Acad Pr.
Makita, Akira & Handa, Shizuo, eds. New Vistas in Glycolipid Research. (Advances in Experimental Medicine & Biology Ser.: Vol. 152). 504p. 1982. 62.50x (ISBN 0-306-41108-3, Plenum Pr). Plenum Pub.

GLYCOSIDES
Horowitz, Martin, ed. The Glycoconjugates: Glyconproteins, Glycolipides & Proteoglycans. LC 77-4086. 392p. 1982. 49.50 ea. Vol. III: Pt. A: 392 pgs (ISBN 0-12-356103-5). Vol. IV: Pt. B: 82-45134: 384 pgs (ISBN 0-12-356104-3). subscription 42.00 (ISBN 0-686-81649-8). Acad Pr.

GNOMES
see Fairies

GNOMES (MAXIMS)
see Aphorisms and Apothegms; Proverbs

GNOSTICISM
Mead, G. R. Fragments of a Faith Forgotten, 3 Vols. 1982. Vol 1, 192pp. text ed. 13.50 (ISBN 0-7224-0211-2); Vol 2, 302pp. text ed. 18.95 (ISBN 0-7224-0212-0); Vol 3, 216pp. text ed. 13.50 (ISBN 0-7224-0213-9). Robinson & Watkins.

GOA-BIBLIOGRAPHY
Scholberg, Henry. Bibliography of Goa & the Portuguese in India. 1982. 55.00x (ISBN 0-8364-0896-9, Pub. by Promilla). South Asia Bks.

GOATS
Baker, Frank H., ed. Sheep & Goat Handbook: International Stockmen's School Handbooks, Vol. 3. 600p. 1982. lib. bdg. 35.00 (ISBN 0-86531-510-8, Pub. with Winrock International). Westview.
Sheep & Goat Breeds of India. (FAO Animal Production & Health Paper: No. 30). 189p. 1982. pap. 14.50 (ISBN 92-5-101212-1, F2340, FAO). Unipub.

GOBLINS
see Fairies

GOD
see also Agnosticism; Atheism; Causation; Christianity; Creation; Fear of God; Holy Spirit; Jesus Christ; Metaphysics; Myth; Mythology; Ontology; Providence and Government of God; Rationalism; Religion; Teleology; Theodicy; Theology; Trinity; Trust in God
Cohen, I. L. Urim & Thumim: The Secret of God. Murphy, G., ed. (Illus.). 280p. 1983. 16.95 (ISBN 0-910891-00-1). New Research.
Eaton, Jeffrey C., ed. For God & Clarity: New Essays in Honor of Austin Ferrer. Loades, Ann. (Pittsburgh Theological Monographs New Series: No. 4). 1983. pap. write for info. (ISBN 0-915138-52-2). Pickwick.
Freddoso, Alfred J., ed. The Existence & Nature of God. 1983. price not set. U of Notre Dame Pr.
Halverstadt, Robert. God's Word for Your Healing. 1982. pap. 1.75 (ISBN 0-88144-003-5, CPS-003). Christian Pub.
--God's Word for Your Prosperity. 1982. pap. 1.75 (ISBN 0-88144-002-7, CPS-002). Christian Pub.
Henry, Patrick & Stransky, Thomas F. God on Our Minds. LC 81-70593. 176p. 1982. pap. 6.95 (ISBN 0-8146-1249-0). Liturgical Pr.
Knight, George A. I Am: This is my Name. 96p. 1983. pap. 4.95 (ISBN 0-8028-1958-3). Eerdmans.
Kupferle, Mary L. God Never Fails. 141p. 1983. pap. 4.50 (ISBN 0-87516-513-3). De Vorss.
Martell, Dwane K. The Enigma of God & Man's Proclivity to Evil. (Institute for Religious Research Library Books). (Illus.). 77p. 1983. 37.75 (ISBN 0-89920-049-4). Am Inst Psych.
Moltmann-Wendel, Elisabeth & Moltmann, Jurgen. Humanity in God. (Illus.). 160p. 1983. 13.95 (ISBN 0-8298-0662-8); pap. 7.95 (ISBN 0-8298-0670-9). Pilgrim NY.
Showers, Renald E. What on Earth Is God Doing? Satan's Conflict with God. 48p. 1983. pap. 3.50 study guide (ISBN 0-87213-785-6). Loizeaux.
Sontag, Frederick & Bryant, M. Darrol, eds. God: The Contemporary Discussion. LC 82-70771. (Conference Ser.: No. 12). vi, 419p. (Orig.). 1982. pap. text ed. 12.95 (ISBN 0-932894-12-7). Unif Theol Seminary.

GOD-ATTRIBUTES
see also Providence and Government of God
Davis, Stephen. Logic & the Nature of God. LC 81-18464. 200p. 1983. 22.50x (ISBN 0-312-49448-3). St Martin.
Davis, Stephen T. Logic & the Nature of God. 200p. 1983. 9.95 (ISBN 0-8028-3321-7). Eerdmans.

GOD-BIBLICAL TEACHING
Zimmerli, Walther. I Am Yahweh. Brueggemann, Walter, ed. Scott, Doug, tr. from German. LC 81-85326. 160p. Date not set. 15.95 (ISBN 0-8042-0519-1). John Knox.

GOD-FEAR
see Fear of God

GOD-KNOWABLENESS
Steiner, Rudolf. The Change in the Path to Supersensible Knowledge. 22p. 1982. pap. 2.75 (ISBN 0-919924-18-2, Pub. by Steiner Book Centre Canada). Anthroposophic.
--Knowledge of the Higher Worlds: How Is It Achieved? 6th ed. Davy, Charles & Osmond, D. S., trs. from Ger. 222p. 1976. pap. 5.50 (ISBN 0-85440-221-7, Pub. by Steinerbooks). Anthroposophic.

GOD-LOVE
Here are entered works on God's love toward man. Works on the love and worship which man accords to God are entered under the heading God-Worship and Love.
Bernard of Clairvaux & William of St. Thierry. The Love of God. Houston, James M., ed. (Classics of Faith & Devotion). Orig. Title: Life & Works of St. Bernard. 1983. 9.95 (ISBN 0-88070-017-3). Multnomah.
Chapian, Marie. Love & Be Loved. 192p. 1983. pap. 5.95 (ISBN 0-8007-5092-6, Power Bks). Revell.
Hayes, Norvel. God's Medicine of Faith: The Word. 96p. 1983. pap. 2.25 (ISBN 0-89274-278-X). Harrison Hse.
Solomon, Charles R. The Rejection Syndrome. 144p. 1982. pap. 4.95 (ISBN 0-8423-5417-4). Tyndale.

GOD-MISCELLANEA
Parrott, Bob W. God's Sense of Humor. 1983. 17.50 (ISBN 0-8022-2421-0). Philos Lib.

GOD-OMNIPOTENCE
Coffman, Carl. Unto a Perfect Man. 4th ed. 1982. pap. 7.95 (ISBN 0-943872-83-9). Andrews Univ Pr.

GOD-PERMISSIVE WILL
see Theodicy

GOD-PROMISES
Bulle, Florence. God Wants You Rich: And Other Enticing Doctrines. 192p. (Orig.). 1983. pap. 4.95 (ISBN 0-87123-264-2). Bethany Hse.

GOD-PROOF
Brady, Jules M. A Philosopher's Search for the Infinite. 96p. 1983. 10.00 (ISBN 0-8022-2410-5). Philos Lib.
Detacuden, Nam U. The Simplest Explanation of God Ever Explained. 240p. 1983. 13.50 (ISBN 0-682-49951-X). Exposition.
Visser't Hooft, W. A. The Fatherhood of God in an Age of Emancipation. LC 82-13404. 180p. 1983. pap. 7.95 (ISBN 0-664-24462-9). Westminster.

GOD-PROVIDENCE AND GOVERNMENT
see Providence and Government of God

GOD-WILL
Friesen, Garry & Maxson, Robin. Decision Making & the Will of God: Study Guide. (Critical Concern Ser.). 1983. pap. price not set (ISBN 0-88070-021-1). Multnomah.
McKeever, Jim. How You Can Know the Will of God. 24p. 1982. 1.00 (ISBN 0-86694-095-2). Omega Pubns OR.

GOD-WILL, PERMISSIVE
see Theodicy

GOD-WORSHIP AND LOVE
see also Fear of God
Chapian, Marie. Love & Be Loved. 192p. 1983. pap. 5.95 (ISBN 0-8007-5092-6, Power Bks). Revell.
Hagin, Kenneth E. In Him. 1975. pap. 0.50 (ISBN 0-89276-052-4). Hagin Ministry.
--The New Birth. 1975. pap. 0.50 (ISBN 0-89276-050-8). Hagin Ministry.
--Turning Hopeless Situations Around. 1981. pap. 1.00 (ISBN 0-89276-022-2). Hagin Ministry.
--Why do People Fall under the Power? 1981. pap. 0.50 (ISBN 0-89276-254-3). Hagin Ministry.
--Why Tongues? 1975. pap. 0.50 (ISBN 0-89276-051-6). Hagin Ministry.
--ZOE: The God-Kind of Life. 1981. pap. 2.50 (ISBN 0-89276-402-3). Hagin Ministry.
Hagin, Kenneth, Jr. Itching Ears. 1982. pap. 0.50 (ISBN 0-89276-711-1). Hagin Ministry.
--The Prison Door Is Open: What Are You Still Doing Inside? 1982. pap. 0.50 (ISBN 0-89276-710-3). Hagin Ministry.
--Where Do We Go from Here? 1982. pap. 0.50 (ISBN 0-89276-712-X). Hagin Ministry.
Welch, Reuben. We Really Do Need Each Other. 112p. 1982. pap. 5.95 (ISBN 0-310-70221-6). Zondervan.

GOD, FEAR OF
see Fear of God

GOD AND MAN, MYSTICAL UNION OF
see Mystical Union

GODDESSES, MOTHER
see Mother-Goddesses

GODEL'S THEOREM
see Goedel's Theorem

GODS
see also Mother-Goddesses; Myth; Mythology; Religions
Simon, Erika. Festivals of Attica: An Archaeological Commentary. 160p. 1983. text ed. 21.50 (ISBN 0-299-09180-5). U of Wis Pr.
Von Daniken, Erich. Pathways to the Gods: The Stones of Kiribati. Heron, Michael, tr. from Ger. (Illus.). 288p. 1982. 16.95 (ISBN 0-399-12751-8). Putnam Pub Group.

GOEBBELS, JOSEPH, 1897-1945
Heiber, Helmut. Goebbels: A Biography. Dickinson, John K., tr. from Ger. (Quality Paperbacks Ser.). (Illus.). 393p. 1983. pap. 9.95 (ISBN 0-306-80187-6). Da Capo.

GOEDEL'S THEOREM
Mostowski, Andrej. Sentences Undecidable in Formalized Arithmetic: An Exposition of the Theory of Kurt Godel. LC 82-11886. (Studies in Logic & the Foundations of Mathematics). viii, 117p. 1982. Repr. of 1952 ed. lib. bdg. 25.00x (ISBN 0-313-23151-6, MOSU). Greenwood.

GOETHE, JOHANN WOLFGANG VON, 1749-1832
Ludwig, Emil. Genius & Character: Shakespeare, Voltaire, Goethe, Balzac. 330p. 1982. Repr. of 1927 ed. lib. bdg. 35.00 (ISBN 0-8495-3267-1). Arden Lib.
Steiner, Rudolph. Spiritual-Scientific Basis of Goethe's Work. 1982. pap. 2.50 (ISBN 0-916786-66-8). St George Bk Serv.

GOGH, VINCENT VAN
see Van Gogh, Vincent, 1853-1890

GOGOL, NIKOLAI VASILEVICH, 1809-1852
Franz, Philip. Gogol Bibliography. 300p. 1983. 30.00 (ISBN 0-88233-809-9). Ardis Pubs.
Woodward, James B. The Symbolic Art of Gogol: Essays on His Short Fiction. 131p. 1982. 11.95 (ISBN 0-89357-093-1). Slavica.

GOLD
see also Alchemy; Coinage; Currency Question; Gold Mines and Mining; Jewelry; Money; Silver Question
Merriman, Raymond. The Gold Book: Geocosmic Correlations to Gold Price Cycles. Robertson, Arlene, ed. 320p. (Orig.). 1982. pap. 50.00 (ISBN 0-930706-13-7). Seek-It Pubns.
Rogers, James H. America Weighs Her Gold. 1931. text ed. 29.50x (ISBN 0-686-83460-7). Elliots Bks.

GOLD-HISTORY
Jackson, Joseph H. Anybody's Gold. LC 70-133990. (Illus.). 320p. (Orig.). 1982. pap. 7.95 (ISBN 0-87701-273-3). Chronicle Bks.

GOLD-THERAPEUTIC USE
Schattenkirchner, M. & Mueller, W., eds. Gold Therapy. (Rheumatology Ser.: Vol. 8). (Illus.). viii, 200p. 1983. 78.00 (ISBN 3-8055-3630-5). S Karger.

GOLD COINS
Bowers, David Q. United States Gold Coins: An Illustrated History. (Illus.). 415p. 1982. 35.00 (ISBN 0-914490-21-4). Bowers & Ruddy.
Gold Coins & Bullion. (What's it Worth Ser.). Date not set. pap. 2.95 (ISBN 0-440-02880-9). Dell.

GOLD CURE
see Alcoholism-Treatment

GOLD MINES AND MINING
see also California-Gold Discoveries; Prospecting
Schlitt, W. J. & Larson, W. C., eds. Gold & Silver Leaching, Recovery & Economics. LC 81-68558. (Illus.). 148p. 1981. pap. text ed. 20.00x (ISBN 0-89520-289-1). Soc Mining Eng.
Volcanogenic Gold Deposits. 1982. 82.60 (ISBN 0-942218-19-1). Minobras.

GOLD MINES AND MINING-AFRICA, SOUTH
Richardson, Peter. Chinese Mine Labour in the Transvaal. 287p. 1982. text ed. 31.50x (ISBN 0-333-27222-6, Pub. by Macmillan England). Humanities.
Yudelman, David. The Emergence of Modern South Africa: State, Capital, & the Incorporation of Organized Labor on the South African Gold Fields, 1902-1939. LC 82-9375. (Contributions in Comparative Colonial Studies: No. 13). (Illus.). 288p. 1983. lib. bdg. 35.00 (ISBN 0-313-23170-2, YMS/). Greenwood.

GOLDEN HAMSTER
see Hamsters

GOLDFISH
Videla, E. Your First Goldfish. (Illus.). 32p. 1982. 3.95 (ISBN 0-87666-574-1, ST-002). TFH Pubns.

GOLDSMITH, OLIVER, 1728-1774
Forster, John. The Life & Adventures of Oliver Goldsmith: A Biography, 4 bks. 704p. 1982. Repr. of 1848 ed. Set. lib. bdg. 100.00 (ISBN 0-89984-209-7). Century Bookbindery.

GOLF
see also Swing (Golf)
Alexander, Arch. The Joy of Golf. 341p. 1982. write for info. (ISBN 0-941760-00-6). Pendulum Bks.
Anthony, Ann. The Diary of a Mad Golf Wife or How to Begin. (Illus.). 96p. 1983. pap. 5.95 (ISBN 0-911433-02-3). HealthRight.
Dobereiner, Peter. Golf Rules Explained. (Illus.). 160p. 1982. Repr. of 1980 ed. 12.50 (ISBN 0-7153-8081-8). David & Charles.
Dobreiner, Peter. Down the Nineteenth Fairway. LC 82-73279. 256p. 1983. 12.95 (ISBN 0-689-11380-3). Atheneum.
Hobbs, Michael, compiled by. In Celebration of Golf. (Illus.). 224p. 1983. 19.95 (ISBN 0-684-17800-1, ScribT). Scribner.
Jacobs, John & Bowden, Ken. Practical Golf. LC 82-73277. 192p. 1983. pap. 10.95 (ISBN 0-689-70634-0). Atheneum.
Kaskie, Shirli. A Woman's Golf Game. (Illus.). 208p. 1983. pap. 7.95 (ISBN 0-8092-5756-4). Contemp Bks.
Low, George & Barkow, Al. The Master of Putting. LC 82-73018. 160p. 1983. 12.95 (ISBN 0-689-11355-2). Atheneum.
McDougal, Stan. World's Greatest Golf Jokes. 1983. pap. 4.95 (ISBN 0-8065-0831-0). Citadel Pr.
Plimpton, George. The Bogey Man. (Penguin Sports Library). 306p. 1983. pap. 5.95 (ISBN 0-14-006430-3). Penguin.

GONADOTROPIN
Flamigni, C. & Givens, J. R., eds. The Gonadotropins. (Serono Symposium Ser.: No. 42). 512p. 1982. 58.50 (ISBN 0-12-258550-X). Acad Pr.

GOOD AND EVIL
see also Providence and Government of God; Sin; Theodicy
Deffner, Donald. I Hear Two Voices, God! 1983. pap. 4.95 (ISBN 0-570-03882-0). Concordia.
Hebblethwaite, Brian. Evil, Suffering & Reflection. 132p. 1976. pap. 2.00 (ISBN 0-8164-1237-5). Seabury.
Martell, Dwane K. The Enigma of God & Man's Proclivity to Evil. (Institute for Religious Research Library Books). (Illus.). 77p. 1983. 37.75 (ISBN 0-89920-049-4). Am Inst Psych.
Serrano, Miguel. The Serpent of Paradise. pap. 7.95 (ISBN 0-7100-7785-8). Routledge & Kegan.

GOOD SAMARITAN (PARABLE)
see Jesus Christ-Parables

GOTHIC ARCHITECTURE
see Architecture, Gothic

GOTHIC LITERATURE
Summers, Montague. The Gothic Quest. 448p. 1982. 55.00x (ISBN 0-284-79521-6, Pub. by C Skilton Scotland). State Mutual Bk.

GOTHIC PAINTING
see Painting, Gothic

GOUT
see also Arthritis
Emmerson, Bryan T. Hyperuricaemia & Gout in Clinical Practice. 120p. 1982. text ed. 16.00 (ISBN 0-86792-006-8). Wright-PSG.

GOVERNMENT
see Political Science
also subdivision Politics and Government under names of countries, states, etc., e.g. United States-Politics and government; New York (state) State Politics and Government

GOVERNMENT, COMPARATIVE
see Comparative Government

GOVERNMENT, RESISTANCE TO
see also Anomy; Revolutions
Bennett, James T. & DiLorenzo, Thomas J. Underground Government: The Off-Budget Public Sector. 184p. 1983. pap. 8.95 (ISBN 0-932790-37-2). Cato Inst.
Deitrich, Jeff. Reluctant Resister. (Illus.). 1983. 17.00 (ISBN 0-87775-156-0); pap. 6.00 (ISBN 0-87775-157-9). Unicorn Pr.

GOVERNMENT ACCOUNTING
see Finance, Public-Accounting

GOVERNMENT AGENCIES
see Administrative Agencies

GOVERNMENT AND BUSINESS
see Industry and State

GOVERNMENT AND THE PRESS
Harris, Robert. Gotcha! The Media, the Government & the Falklands Crisis. 176p. (Orig.). 1983. pap. 5.95 (ISBN 0-571-13052-6). Faber & Faber.
GOVERNMENT BUSINESS ENTERPRISES
see also Government Ownership
Schnitzer. Contemporary Government & Business Relations. 2d ed. text ed. 21.95 (ISBN 0-686-84539-0, BS46); instr's manual avail. HM.
Stanbury. Managing Public Enterprises. 320p. 1982. 29.95 (ISBN 0-03-061977-7). Praeger.
GOVERNMENT CENTRALIZATION
see Decentralization in Government
GOVERNMENT CONTRACTS
see Public Contracts
GOVERNMENT DECENTRALIZATION
see Decentralization in Government
GOVERNMENT DOCUMENTS
see Government Publications
GOVERNMENT EMPLOYEES
see Civil Service
GOVERNMENT EXPENDITURES
see Expenditures, Public
GOVERNMENT HOUSING
see Public Housing
GOVERNMENT INFORMATION
see also Government and the Press
Hendricks, Evan. Former Secrets: Government Records Made Public Through the Freedom of Information Act. Shaker, Peggy, ed. 204p. 1982. pap. 15.00 (ISBN 0-910175-01-2). Campaign Political.
Richardson, John, Jr. Graduate Research in Government Information, 1928-1982. Date not set. write for info. (ISBN 0-89774-063-7). Oryx Pr.
Robertson, K. G. Public Secrets: A Study in the Development of Government Secrets. 224p. 1982. 50.00x (ISBN 0-333-32008-5, Pub. by Macmillan England). State Mutual Bk.
GOVERNMENT INVESTIGATIONS
see Governmental Investigations
GOVERNMENT JOBS
see Civil Service Positions
GOVERNMENT LITIGATION
Brown, C. Christopher. Introduction to Maryland Civil Litigation. 258p. 1982. 30.00 (ISBN 0-87215-528-5). Michie-Bobbs.
Church, Randolph W. Appellate Litigation: A Virginia Law Practice System. 250p. 1982. looseleaf with forms 75.00 (ISBN 0-87215-510-2). Michie-Bobbs.
Schwarzer, William W. Managing Antitrust & Other Complex Litigation. 465p. 1982. 35.00 (ISBN 0-686-84229-4). Michie-Bobbs.
GOVERNMENT OWNERSHIP
De Alessi, Louis. Some Economic Aspects of Government Ownership & Regulation: Essays From Economia Pubblica. (LEC Occasional Paper). 50p. 1982. pap. 3.00 (ISBN 0-916770-12-5). Law & Econ U Miami.
GOVERNMENT POSITIONS
see Civil Service Positions
GOVERNMENT PRICE REGULATION
see Price Regulation
GOVERNMENT PUBLICATIONS
Research Libraries of the New York Public Library & Library of Congress. Bibliographic Guide to Government Publications-Foriegn: 1982. 1983. lib. bdg. 295.00 (ISBN 0-8161-6972-1, Biblio Guides). G K Hall.
--Bibliographic Guide to Government Publications-U. S. 1982. 1983. lib. bdg. 295.00 (ISBN 0-8161-6973-X, Biblio Guides). G K Hall.
GOVERNMENT PURCHASING
see also Eminent Domain; Public Contracts
Council of State Governments Staff, ed. State & Local Government Purchasing. 2nd ed. 750p. (Orig.). 1982. pap. 21.00 (ISBN 0-87292-033-X). Coun State Govts.
Hudlin, Richard A. & Brimah, K. Farouk. State of Mississippi's Procurement Policies & Minority Business Enterprises. 1981. 1.00 (ISBN 0-686-38010-X). Voter Ed Proj.
Hudlin, Richard A. & Farouk, Brimah K. State of North Carolina's Procurement Policies & Minority Business Enterprises. 1981. 1.00 (ISBN 0-686-38011-8). Voter Ed Proj.
Langley, Michael. State of Florida's Procurement Policies & Minority Business Enterprises. 1980. 1.00 (ISBN 0-686-38006-1). Voter Ed Proj.
--State of North Carolina's Procurement Policies & Minority Business Enterprises. 1980. 1.00 (ISBN 0-686-38008-8). Voter Ed Proj.
--Supreme Court Says Minority Enterprises Must be Given a Piece of the Action. 1980. 1.00 (ISBN 0-686-38005-3). Voter Ed Proj.
GOVERNMENT RECORDS
see Public Records
GOVERNMENT REGULATION OF COMMERCE
see Commercial Policy; Industrial Laws and Legislation; Industry and State; Trade Regulation
GOVERNMENT SECRECY
see Government Information
GOVERNMENT SPENDING POLICY
see also Expenditures, Public
also subdivision Appropriations and Expenditures under names of countries (for descriptive and statistical works on government spending)
Collender, Stanley E. The Guide to the Federal Budget: Fiscal 1984 Edition. LC 82-643840. 150p. (Orig.). 1983. pap. text ed. 10.00 (ISBN 0-87766-321-1). Urban Inst.
Haveman, Robert & Margolis, Julius. Public Expenditure & Policy Analysis. 3rd ed. LC 82-81354. 608p. pap. text ed. 18.95 (ISBN 0-686-82250-1). HM.
Nichols, Egbert R. & Roskam, William E, eds. Pump-Priming Theory of Government Spending. 482p. 1982. Repr. of 1939 ed. lib. bdg. 65.00 (ISBN 0-89984-809-5). Century Bookbindery.
GOVERNMENT SUPPORT OF SCIENCE, LITERATURE, AND ART
see State Encouragement of Science, Literature, and Art
GOVERNMENT SURVEYS
see Surveys
GOVERNMENTAL INVESTIGATIONS
see also Criminal Investigation; Police
No Holds Barred: The Final Congressional Testimony of Admiral Hyman Rickover. 103p. 1982. 1.50 (ISBN 0-936758-07-4). Ctr Responsive Law.
GOVERNOR SHIRLEY'S WAR
see United States-History-King George's War, 1744-1748
GOVERNORS-UNITED STATES
Cook, James F. Governors of Georgia. (Illus.). 320p. 1979. 12.95 (ISBN 0-686-83449-6). Strode.
Raimo, John, ed. Biographical Directory of the Governors of the United States, 1978-1982. 1983. 45.00X (ISBN 0-930466-62-4). Meckler Pub.
GOYA Y LUCIENTES, FRANCISCO JOSE DE, 1746-1828
Harris, Tomas. Goya: Lithographs & Engravings, 2 vols. (Illus.). 1983. Repr. of 1964 ed. Vol. 1: 472 p. 175.00 set (ISBN 0-915346-72-9). Vol. 2: 248 p. A Wofsy Fine Arts.
Licht, Fred. Goya: The Origins of the Modern Temper in Art. (Icon Edition). (Illus.). 288p. 1983. pap. 11.49i (ISBN 0-06-430123-0, IN-123, HarpT). Har-Row.
GRACE (THEOLOGY)
see also Covenants (Theology)
Hagin, Kenneth E. Five Hindrances to Growth in Grace. 1981. pap. 0.50 (ISBN 0-89276-253-5). Hagin Ministry.
Steiner, Rudlof. The Concepts of Original Sin & Grace. Osmond, D. S., tr. from Ger. 32p. 1973. pap. 1.95 (ISBN 0-85440-275-6, Pub. by Steinerbooks). Anthroposophic.
Twombly, Gerald & Kennedy, Timothy. A Taste of Grace, Vol. 1. (Illus.). 182p. 1982. pap. 7.50 (ISBN 0-910219-04-4). Little People.
GRACE, PRINCESS OF MONACO, 1929-
Hart-Davis, Phyllida. Grace: The Story of a Princess. (Illus.). 144p. 1982. pap. 9.95 (ISBN 0-312-34209-8). St Martin.
GRACE, GIFTS OF
see Gifts, Spiritual
GRADED SCHOOLS
see Grading and Marking (Students)
GRADING AND MARKING (STUDENTS)
Smith, Grey. Better Grades in Ten Minutes. rev. ed. 49p. 1983. pap. text ed. 4.95 (ISBN 0-686-84030-5). WordShop Pubns.
GRADUATE WORK
see Universities and Colleges-Graduate Work
GRAFTING
see also Plant Propagation
Johnston, Patricia I., ed. Perspectives on a Grafted Tree. (Illus.). 1983. 12.95 (ISBN 0-9609504-0-0). Perspect Indiana.
GRAIL
Ihle, Sandra N. Malory's Grail Quest: Invention & Adaptation in Medieval Prose Romance. LC 82-70554. (Illus.). 224p. 1983. text ed. 22.50 (ISBN 0-299-09240-2). U of Wis Pr.
Steiner, Rudolf. The Holy Grail: From the Works of Rudolf Steiner. Roboz, Steven, ed. 40p. 1979. pap. 2.95 (ISBN 0-88010-049-4, Pub. by Steiner Book Centre Canada). Anthroposophic.
GRAIN
Kent, N. L. Technology of Cereals: An Introduction for Students of Food Science & Agriculture. 3rd ed. (Illus.). 200p. 1983. 40.00 (ISBN 0-08-029801-X); pap. 15.00 (ISBN 0-08-029800-1). Pergamon.
Peryt, T., ed. Coated Grains. (Illus.). 600p. 1983. 58.00 (ISBN 0-387-12071-8). Springer-Verlag.
Thran, P. & Brockhuizen, S., eds. Agro-Climatic Atlas of Europe. (Agro-Ecological Atlas Ser.: Vol. 1). 1965. 202.25 (ISBN 0-444-40569-0). Elsevier.
GRAIN-BREEDING
see also Rice Breeding
Cereal Aphid Population, Biology, Simulation & Prediction. 91p. 1983. pap. 14.50 (ISBN 90-220-0804-5, PDC252, Pudoc). Unipub.
GRAIN-DISEASES AND PESTS
Judenko, E. Analytical Method for Assessing Yield Losses Caused by Pests on Cereal Crops with & Without Pesticides. 1973. 35.00x (ISBN 0-85135-061-5, Pub. by Centre Overseas Research). State Mutual Bk.
GRAIN-STORAGE
China: Grain Storage Structures. (FAO Agricultural Services Bulletin Ser.: No. 49). 113p. 1982. pap. 14.50 (ISBN 92-5-101154-0, F2311, FAO). Unipub.
GRAIN PESTS
see Grain-Diseases and Pests
GRAMMAR, GENERATIVE
see Generative Grammar
GRAMMAR, TRANSFORMATIONAL
see Generative Grammar
GRAMMAR SCHOOLS
see Public Schools
GRAMOPHONE
see Phonograph
GRAND CANYON
Fodor's Grand Canyon. (Illus.). 224p. 1983. traveltex 8.95 (ISBN 0-679-00917-5). McKay.
Grand Canyon: Shrine of the Ages. 1982. 7.95 (ISBN 0-933692-22-6). R Collings.
Maurer, Stephen G., ed. Grand Canyon by Stage. (Illus.). 24p. (Orig.). 1982. pap. 3.85 (ISBN 0-910467-00-5). Heritage Assocs.
GRAND LAKE, COLORADO
Bancroft, Caroline. Grand Lake: From Utes to Yachts. (Bancroft Booklet Ser.). (Illus.). 40p. (Orig.). 1982. pap. 2.50 (ISBN 0-933472-68-4). Johnson Bks.
GRANDPARENTS
Ashley, Nova. Call Me Grandma! 1982. 5.50 (ISBN 0-8378-1716-1). Gibson.
Kivnick, Helen Q. The Meaning of Grandparenthood. Nathan, Peter, ed. LC 82-17567. (Studies in Clinical Psychology: No. 3). 252p. 1982. 39.95 (ISBN 0-8357-1383-0). Univ Microfilms.
Rogers, Dale E. & Carlson, Carole C. Grandparents Can. 128p. 1983. 7.95 (ISBN 0-8007-1343-5). Revell.
GRANITE
Twidale, C. R. Granite Landforms. 372p. 1982. 115.00 (ISBN 0-444-42116-5). Elsevier.
GRANT, ULYSSES SIMPSON, PRES. U. S., 1822-1885
Frassanito, William A. Grant & Lee: The Virginia Campaigns, 1864-1865. (Illus.). 448p. 1983. 19.95 (ISBN 0-686-83857-2, ScribT). Scribner.
Porter, Horace. Campaigning with Grant. LC 81-14445. (Collector's Library of the Civil War). 26.60 (ISBN 0-8094-4200-0). Silver.
GRANTS
see Subsidies
GRANTS-IN-AID
see also Economic Assistance, Domestic; Research Grants;
also subdivision Finance under particular subjects, e.g. Education-Finance
Conrad, Daniel L. The Quick Proposal Workbook. 119p. 13.95 (ISBN 0-686-82294-3, 37A). Public Management.
Conrad, Daniel L. & Public Management Institute Staff. The New Grants Planner. rev. ed. 400p. 47.50 (ISBN 0-686-82257-9, 30B). Public Management.
The Directory of Grants for Nonprofit Management Support. 69.00 (ISBN 0-686-82263-3, 62A). Public Management.
The Grant Writer's Handbook, 2 vols. Vol. I. 37.50 (ISBN 0-686-82259-5, 31A); Vol. II. 37.50 (ISBN 0-686-82260-9, 31B). Public Management.
Lefferts, Robert. The Basic Handbook of Grants Management. 300p. 1983. 20.95 (ISBN 0-465-00600-0). Basic.
Margolin, Judith B. The Individual's Guide to Grants. 300p. 1983. 15.95x (ISBN 0-306-41309-4, Plenum Pr). Plenum Pub.
Public Management Institute Staff. Grants Administration. 75.00 (ISBN 0-686-82261-7, 33A). Public Management.
--How to Get Corporate Grants. 47.50 (ISBN 0-686-82254-4, 80A). Public Management.
Rubin, Mary. How to Get Money for Research. 96p. 1983. 5.95 (ISBN 0-935312-18-8). Feminist Pr.
Smith, Craig W. & Skjei, Eric W. Getting Grants. 14.00 (ISBN 0-686-38890-9). Public Serv Materials.
White, Virginia, ed. Grant Proposals That Succeeded. (Nonprofit Management & Finance). 230p. 1982. 22.50x (ISBN 0-306-40873-2, Plenum Pr). Plenum Pub.
Williams, Cortez H. The Complete Grants Reference Book: Writing the Proposal, Getting the Money, & Managing the Project. 300p. Date not set. 24.95 (ISBN 0-13-159780-9); pap. 14.95 (ISBN 0-13-159772-8). P-H.
GRANTS-IN-AID, INTERNATIONAL
see Economic Assistance
GRANULOMA BENIGNUM
see Sarcoidosis
GRANVILLE-BARKER, HARLEY GRANVILLE, 1877-1946
Salenius, Elmer W. Harley Granville-Barker. (English Authors Ser.). 1982. lib. bdg. 17.95 (ISBN 0-8057-6801-7, Twayne). G K Hall.
GRAPES
Jackson, David & Schuster, Danny. Grape Growing & Wine Making: A Handbook for Cool Climates. (Illus.). 194p. 1981. 27.50 (ISBN 0-9607896-0-X). Altarinda Bks.
GRAPH THEORY
see also Network Analysis (Planning)
Bollabas, B., ed. Graph Theory: Proceedings of the Conference on Graph Theory, Cambridge. (North-Holland Mathematics Studies: Vol. 62). 202p. 1982. 42.75 (ISBN 0-444-86449-0, North Holland). Elsevier.
GRAPHIC ARTS
see also Bookbinding; Commercial Art; Drawing; Painting; Printing; Prints
Castleman, Riva. Prints from Blocks: Gaugin to Now. (Illus.). 84p. 1983. pap. 8.95 (ISBN 0-87070-561-X). Museum Mod Art.
Craig, James. Graphic Design Career Guide: How to Get a Job & Establish a Career in Design. (Illus.). 176p. (Orig.). 1983. pap. 14.95 (ISBN 0-8230-2151-3). Watson-Guptill.
Dennis, Ervin A. & Jenkins, John D. Comprehensive Graphic Arts. 2nd ed. (Illus.). 576p. 1983. text ed. 26.95 (ISBN 0-672-97681-1); instr's guide 6.67 (ISBN 0-672-97682-X); wkbk. 5.95 (ISBN 0-672-98447-4). Bobbs.
Ediciones Poligrafa, Barcelona - Redfern Gallery, London. (Illus.). 66p. 1983. pap. 60.00 (ISBN 0-8390-0304-8). Allanheld & Schram.
Fry, Edmund. Pantographia: Excerpts form the Original Work. 37p. 1982. pap. 2.95 (ISBN 0-912526-31-9). Lib Res.
Graphics Arts Trade Journals International Inc. Export Grafics USA, 1982-83. Humphrey, G. A. & Miura, Lydia, eds. (Illus.). 106p. (Orig.). 1982. pap. 6.00 (ISBN 0-910762-10-4). Graph Arts Trade.
Greenaway, D. S. & Warman, E. A., eds. Eurographics Eighty-Two: Proceedings of the International Conference & Exhibition, U.M.I.S.T., Manchester, U.K., 1982. 396p. 1982. 55.75 (ISBN 0-444-86480-6, North Holland). Elsevier.
Japan Graphic Designers Association. Graphic Design in Japan, Vol. 2. (Graphic Design in Japan Ser.). (Illus.). 288p. 1983. 59.50 (ISBN 0-87011-552-9). Kodansha.
Jussim, Estelle. Visual Communication & the Graphic Arts. pap. 24.95 (ISBN 0-8352-1674-8). Bowker.
Klika, Thom. Ten Thousand Rainbows. (Illus.). 80p. 1983. pap. 6.95 (ISBN 0-312-79096-1); pap. 69.50 prepack of 10 (ISBN 0-312-79098-8). St Martin.
Levine, Jack. The Complete Graphic Work of Jack Levine. (Fine Art Ser.). (Illus.). 112p. (Orig.). 1983. pap. 6.00 (ISBN 0-486-24481-4). Dover.
Pattison, Polly. How to Design a Nameplate: A Guide for Art Directors & Editors. LC 81-86058. (Communications Library). 64p. 1982. pap. 18.00 (ISBN 0-931368-07-3). Ragan Comm.
Rudman, Jack. Graphic Arts Specialist. (Career Examination Ser.: C-2672). (Cloth bdg. avail. on request). pap. 10.00 (ISBN 0-8373-2672-9). Natl Learning.
--Illustrator Aide. (Career Examination Ser.: C-2930). (Cloth bdg. avail. on request). pap. 10.00 (ISBN 0-8373-2930-2). Natl Learning.
Sawamura, Kaichi, intro. by. Graphic Arts Japan, 1981-82. 23rd ed. LC 64-43886. (Illus.). 170p. (Orig.). 1982. pap. 37.50x (ISBN 0-8002-3065-5). Intl Pubns Serv.
Stewart, M. M., et al. Basic Graphic Arts. 624p. 1983. 15.96 (ISBN 0-07-061420-2, G). McGraw.
Stitt, F. A. Systems Graphics: Breakthroughs in Drawing Production & Project Management for Architects, Designers & Engineers. 224p. 1983. 34.95 (ISBN 0-07-061551-9, P&RB). McGraw.
Vermeersch, LaVonne F. & Southwick, Charles E. Practical Problems in Mathematics for Graphic Arts. Rev. ed. LC 82-72128. (Illus.). 176p. 1983. pap. text ed. 7.00 (ISBN 0-8273-2100-7); Instr's Guide avail. (ISBN 0-8273-2101-5). Delmar.
GRAPHIC ARTS-BIBLIOGRAPHY
Chicago Talent Sourcebook. (Illus.). 410p. Date not set. pap. 35.00 (ISBN 0-942454-01-4). Chicago Talent.
GRAPHIC ARTS-TECHNIQUE
Baumgartner, Victor. Graphic Games: From Pattern to Composition. (Illus.). 160p. 1983. text ed. 12.95 (ISBN 0-13-363333-0). P-H.
Henrion, F. H. Top Graphic Design. (Illus.). 180p. 1983. 67.50 (ISBN 0-8038-7227-5). Hastings.
Luehrmann, A. & Peckham, H. Hands On BASIC: For the Atari 400 & 800 Computer. 448p. 1983. 22.95 (ISBN 0-07-049177-1). McGraw.
GRAPHIC ARTS-YEARBOOKS
Graphic Arts Green Book: 1983 Midwest Edition. 500p. 1983. pap. 60.00 (ISBN 0-910880-16-6). Lewis.
Graphic Arts Trade Journals Int'l. Inc. Export Graficas U. S. A. 1983-84. Miura, Lydia, ed. (Illus.). 115p. (Span.). 1983. pap. 15.00 (ISBN 0-910762-11-2). Graphic Arts Trade.
Scott, Alexis, ed. The Workbook: California Edition. (Illus.). 700p. 1977. Set. 33.95 (ISBN 0-911113-00-2). Scott & Daughters.
GRAPHIC DATA PROCESSING
see Computer Graphics
GRAPHIC DIFFERENTIATION
see Numerical Integration
GRAPHIC METHODS
see also Flow Charts
also subdivision Graphic Methods under specific subjects, e.g. Statistics-Graphic Methods
Boardman, David. Graphicacy & Geography Teaching. 208p. 1983. pap. text ed. 19.50x (ISBN 0-7099-0644-7, Pub. by Croom Helm Ltd England). Biblio Dist.

Graphic Flow Diagrams for Distributed Control-Shared Display Instrumentation, Logic & Computer Systems: ISA Standard S5.3. 15p. 1982. pap. text ed. 10.00 (ISBN 0-87664-707-7). Instru Soc.

Mitchell, Robert & Prickel, Donald. Number Power Five: Graphs, Tables, Schedules & Maps. (Number Power Ser.). 176p. (Orig.). 1983. pap. 4.95 (ISBN 0-8092-5516-2). Contemp Bks.

GRAPHICS, COMPUTER
see Computer Graphics

GRAPHICS, ENGINEERING
see Engineering Graphics

GRAPHOLOGY
see also Drawing, Psychology Of

Green, James & Lewis, David. The Hidden Language of Your Handwriting: The Remarkable New Science of Graphonomy & What It Reveals about Personality & Health & Emotions. 256p. 1983. pap. 5.95 (ISBN 0-89104-330-6, A & W Visual Library). A & W Pubs.

GRAPHOLOGY–DICTIONARIES

Westergaard, Marjorie. Directory of Handwriting Analysts. 5th ed. LC 82-640893. 88p. 1983. pap. text ed. 8.95 (ISBN 0-9609578-5-5). M Westergaard.

GRAPHOPHONE
see Phonograph

GRAPHS
see Graphic Methods

GRASS, GUNTER, 1927-

Mews, Siegfried, ed. The Fisherman & His Wife. LC 81-69878. 1982. 29.50 (ISBN 0-404-61582-1). AMS Pr.

GRASS PARAKEET
see Budgerigars

GRASSES
see also Forage Plants; Grasslands
also names of grasses

Gould, Frank W. & Shaw, Robert B. Grass Systematics. 2nd ed. LC 82-45894. (Illus.). 416p. 1983. pap. text ed. 15.00 (ISBN 0-89096-153-0). Tex A&M Univ Pr.

Hunter, Peter J. Peter Hunter's Guide to Grasses, Clovers, & Weeds. (Illus.). 80p. pap. 5.95 (ISBN 0-938670-02-6). By Hand & Foot.

GRASSES–DISEASES AND PESTS

Smiley, R. W., ed. Compendium of Turfgrass Diseases. LC 82-73593. (Ninth in Compendium Ser.). (Illus.). 100p. 1983. pap. 12.00 member (ISBN 0-89054-049-7); pap. 15.00 nonmember (ISBN 0-686-82687-6). Am Phytopathological Soc.

GRASSHOPPERS
see Locusts

GRASSLAND ECOLOGY

Huntley, B. J. & Walker, B. H., eds. Ecology of Tropical Savannas. (Ecological Studies: Vol. 42). (Illus.). 669p. 1983. 49.00 (ISBN 0-387-11885-3). Springer-Verlag.

GRASSLANDS
see also Prairies; Steppes

Arnolds, Eef. Ecology & Coenology of Macrofungi in Grasslands & Moist Heathlands in Drenthe, the Netherlands. (Illus.). 510p. (Orig.). 1982. Pt. 2. lib. bdg. 80.00x; Pt. 3 Taxonomy. lib. bdg. 90.00 (ISBN 3-7682-1346-3). Lubrecht & Cramer.

GRATEFUL DEAD

Jackson, Blair. The Grateful Dead: The Music Never Stopped. (Illus.). 160p. (Orig.). 1983. pap. 9.95 (ISBN 0-933328-61-3). Delilah Bks.

GRAVEL (PATHOLOGY)
see Calculi, Urinary

GRAVES, ROBERT, 1895-

Seymour-Smith, Martin. Robert Graves: His Life & Work. (Illus.). 624p. 1983. 22.50 (ISBN 0-03-022171-4). HR&W.

Weinzinger, Anita. Graves As a Critic. (Salzburg - Poetic Drama Ser.: No. 79). 141p. 1982. pap. text ed. 25.00x (ISBN 0-391-02803-0, Pub. by Salzburg Austria). Humanities.

GRAVES
see Burial; Funeral Rites and Ceremonies; Sepulchral Monuments; Tombs

GRAVESTONES
see Sepulchral Monuments

GRAVEYARDS
see Cemeteries

GRAVIMETRIC ANALYSIS
see Chemistry, Analytic–Quantitative

GRAVITY

Ferrara, S. & Taylor, J. G., eds. Supergravity Nineteen Eighty One. LC 82-1204. 512p. 1982. 44.50 (ISBN 0-521-24738-1). Cambridge U Pr.

Lagerwerff, Ellen B. & Perlroth, Karen A. Mensendieck Your Posture, Encountering Gravity the Correct & Beautiful Way. Rev. ed. LC 72-97093. (Illus.). 1982. pap. 10.00 (ISBN 0-686-84332-0). Aries Pr.

Wess, Julius & Bagger, Jonathan. Supersummetry & Supergravity. (Princeton Series in Physics). 192p. 1983. 40.00 (ISBN 0-691-08327-4); pap. 12.50 (ISBN 0-691-08326-6). Princeton U Pr.

GRAY, JOHN HENRY, 1866-1934

Cevasco, G. A. John Gray. (English Authors Ser.). 1982. lib. bdg. 17.95 (ISBN 0-8057-6839-4, Twayne). G K Hall.

GRAY FRIARS
see Franciscans

GREASE
see Lubrication and Lubricants; Oils and Fats

GREAT BARRIER REEF, AUSTRALIA

Endean, Robert. Australia's Great Barrier Reef. (Illus.). 348p. 1983. text ed. 29.95x (ISBN 0-7022-1678-X). U of Queensland Pr.

GREAT BRITAIN
see also Commonwealth of Nations; England;
also names of cities, districts, and geographical areas in Great Britain

Davies, Hunter & Herrmann, Frank. Great Britain. (Illus.). 288p. 1983. 31.50 (ISBN 0-241-10755-5, Pub. by Hamish Hamilton England). David & Charles.

Gamble, Andrew. Britain in Decline: Economic Policy, Political Strategy, & the British State. LC 81-683554. 312p. 1983. pap. 8.61 (ISBN 0-8070-4701-5, BP649). Beacon Pr.

GREAT BRITAIN–ANTIQUITIES

Bassett, S. R. Saffron Walden: Excavations & Research 1972-1980. (CBA Research Report: No. 45). 134p. 1982. pap. text ed. 38.00x (ISBN 0-906780-15-2, 41417, Pub. by Coun Brit Archaelolgy England). Humanities.

Case, H. J. & Whittle, A. W., eds. Settlement Patterns in the Oxford Region: The Abingdon Causewayed Enclosure & Other Sites. (CBA Research Report: No. 44). 170p. 1982. pap. text ed. 38.00x (ISBN 0-906780-14-4, 41438, Pub. by Coun Brit Archaeology England). Humanities.

Dyer, James. The Penguin Guide to Prehistoric England & Wales. (Illus.). 400p. 1983. pap. 7.95 (ISBN 0-14-046351-8). Penguin.

Leach, Peter, ed. Archaeology in Kent to AD 1500. (CBA Research Report: No. 48). 144p. 1982. pap. text ed. 31.50x (ISBN 0-906780-18-7, 50019, Pub. by Coun Brit Archaeology England). Humanities.

Shoesmith. Excavations on & Close to the Defences: Hereford City Excavations, Vol. 2. (CBA Research Report: No. 46). 120p. 1982. pap. text ed. 31.50x (ISBN 0-906780-16-0, 41410, Pub. by Coun Brit Archaeology England). Humanities.

GREAT BRITAIN–BIOGRAPHY

Crisp, Quentin. How to Become a Virgin. 192p. 1983. pap. 6.95 (ISBN 0-312-39543-4). St Martin.

Dew, Desmond. Let's Try It This Way. 1983. 13.95 (ISBN 0-533-05383-8). Vantage.

Gailey, Harry A. Clifford: Imperial Proconsul. 215p. (Orig.). 1982. pap. text ed. 11.50 (ISBN 0-86036-189-6). Krieger.

Gethyn-Jones, Eric. George Thorpe & the Berkeley Company. 296p. 1982. text ed. 18.00x (ISBN 0-904387-83-6, Pub. by Sutton England). Humanities.

Gray, Lawrence V. Simian Horizons. 1983. 10.95 (ISBN 0-533-05546-6). Vantage.

Greaves, Richard & Zaller, Robert, eds. Biographical Dictionary of British Radicals in the Seventeenth Century, Vol. 2. 352p. 1982. text ed. 75.00x (ISBN 0-7108-0430-X, Pub. by Harvester England). Humanities.

Johnson, Joan. Excellent Cassandra: The Life & Times of the Dutchess of Chandos. 160p. 1981. text ed. 18.00x (ISBN 0-904387-76-3, 61071, Pub. by Sutton England). Humanities.

Olien, Diana D. Morpeth: A Victorian Public Career. LC 82-23820. 538p. (Orig.). 1983. lib. bdg. 29.75 (ISBN 0-8191-2989-5); pap. text ed. 18.75 (ISBN 0-8191-2990-9). U Pr of Amer.

Rowse, A. L. Eminent Elizabethans. LC 82-13484. (Illus.). 240p. 1983. 19.00 (ISBN 0-8203-0649-5). U of Ga Pr.

Tarling, Peter N. The Burthen, the Risk & the Glory: A Biography of Sir James Brook. 350p. 1982. 39.00 (ISBN 0-19-582508-X). Oxford U Pr.

Temple, Cliff. Daley Thompson. (Profiles Ser.). (Illus.). 64p. (gr. 4-6). 1983. 7.95 (ISBN 0-241-10932-9, Pub. by Hamish Hamilton England). David & Charles.

GREAT BRITAIN–CHURCH HISTORY–19TH CENTURY

Martin, Roger H. Evangelicals United: Ecumenical Stirrings in Pre-Victorian Britain, 1795-1830. LC 82-10784. (Studies in Evangelicalism: No. 4). 244p. 1983. 17.50 (ISBN 0-8108-1586-9). Scarecrow.

GREAT BRITAIN–CIVILIZATION

Keene, D. J. Winchester Studies, Vol. 2: Survey of Medieval Winchester. (Illus.). 750p. 1982. 169.00 (ISBN 0-19-813181-X). Oxford U Pr.

GREAT BRITAIN–COLONIAL OFFICE

Lee, J. M. & Petter, Martin. The Colonial Office: War & Development Policy. 1981. 60.00x (ISBN 0-686-82395-8, Pub. by M Temple Smith). State Mutual Bk.

GREAT BRITAIN–COLONIES
see also Commonwealth of Nations

Constantine, Stephen. The Making of British Colonial Development Policy 1914-1940. 200p. 1983. text ed. 32.50 (ISBN 0-7146-3204-X, F Cass Co). Biblio Dist.

GREAT BRITAIN–COLONIES–AMERICA

Quinn, David B. & Quinn, Alison M. The First Colonists: Documents on the Planting of the First English Settlements in North America, 1584-1590. 199p. 1982. pap. 5.00 (ISBN 0-86526-195-4). NC Archives.

GREAT BRITAIN–COMMERCE

The United Kingdom Marketing Handbook 1982-83. 460p. 1982. 42.50x (ISBN 0-903617-14-5). Intl Pubns Serv.

GREAT BRITAIN–CONSTITUTIONAL LAW

Boutmy, Emile. Studies in Constitutional Law: France-England-United States. 2nd ed. Dicey, E. M., tr. xiv, 183p. 1982. Repr. of 1891 ed. lib. bdg. 22.50x (ISBN 0-8377-0332-8). Rothman.

Dicey, Albert V. Introduction to the Study of the Law of the Constitution. LC 81-82778. 586p. 1982. 15.00X (ISBN 0-86597-002-5); pap. 7.00X (ISBN 0-86597-003-3). Liberty Fund.

Smith, Thomas. De Republica Anglorum. Dewar, Mary, ed. LC 81-21634. (Cambridge Studies in the History & Theory of Politics). 192p. 1982. 39.50 (ISBN 0-521-24109-X). Cambridge U Pr.

GREAT BRITAIN–COURT AND COURTIERS
see also Great Britain–Kings and Rulers

Naunton, Robert. Fragmenta Regalia: Sixteen Thirty. Arber, Edward, ed. 272p. Date not set. pap. 17.50 (ISBN 0-87556-577-8). Saifer.

GREAT BRITAIN–COURTS

Maitland, F. W., ed. Bracton's Note Book: A Collection of Cases Decided in the King's Courts During the Reign of Henry the Third, Annotated by a Lawyer of That Time, Seemingly by Henry of Bratton, 3 Vols. 1983. Repr. of 1887 ed. lib. bdg. 145.00x (ISBN 0-8377-0334-4). Rothman.

GREAT BRITAIN–DEFENSES

Chichester, Michael & Wilkinson, John. The Uncertain Ally. 264p. 1982. text ed. 38.00x (ISBN 0-566-00534-4). Gower Pub Ltd.

Ekoko, A. E. British Defence Strategy in Western Africa 1880-1914. 200p. 1983. text ed. 30.00x (ISBN 0-7146-3219-8, F Cass Co). Biblio Dist.

GREAT BRITAIN–DESCRIPTION AND TRAVEL
see also England–Description and Travel; Scotland–Description and Travel; Wales–Description and Travel

Acland, C. H. D. The Country Life Picture Book of the Lake District. (Illus.). 1983. 19.95 (ISBN 0-393-01733-8, Country Life). Norton.

Catholic Directory of England & Wales, 1982. 143rd ed. 681p. 1982. 27.50x (ISBN 0-904359-35-2). Intl Pubns Serv.

Colwell, Maggie. West of England Market Towns. (Illus.). 192p. 1983. 17.50 (ISBN 0-7134-2780-9, Pub. by Batsford England). David & Charles.

Darke, Jo. Lake District Landscapes. (Illus.). 64p. 1983. 12.50 (ISBN 0-7134-4185-2, Pub. by Batsford England). David & Charles.

--South Coast Landscapes. (Illus.). 64p. 1983. 12.50 (ISBN 0-7134-4189-5, Pub. by Batsford England). David & Charles.

Ferguson & King. Guide to Antique Shops in Britain 1983. (Illus.). 1983. 16.00. Apollo.

Gray, Michael & James, Francis. Marlborough in Old Photographs. 128p. 1982. pap. text ed. 8.25x (ISBN 0-86299-018-1, Pub. by Sutton England). Humanities.

Hudson, W. H. The Lands End. 307p. 1982. 30.00x (ISBN 0-7045-0420-0, Pub. by Wildwood House). State Mutual Bk.

Jeffries & Mabey, Richard. The Open Air. 270p. 1982. 30.00x (ISBN 0-686-81704-4, Pub. by Wildwood House). State Mutual Bk.

King, W. J. The British Isles. 576p. 1975. 35.00x (ISBN 0-7121-0246-9, Pub. by Macdonald & Evans). State Mutual Bk.

Mander, Nicholas, ed. Gloucestershire: A Concise Guide. (Illus.). 192p. 1982. pap. text ed. 9.00x (ISBN 0-904387-72-0, Pub. by Sutton England). Humanities.

Thomas, Edward. The Icknield Way. 320p. 1982. 30.00x (ISBN 0-7045-0407-3, Pub. by Wildwood House). State Mutual Bk.

Uttley, David. Marlborough in Colour. 64p. 1982. text ed. 13.75x (ISBN 0-86299-033-5, Pub. by Sutton England). Humanities.

Williams, Howard. The Diary of a Rowing Tour from Oxford to London in 1875. (Illus.). 168p. 1982. text ed. 16.75x (ISBN 0-904387-69-0, Pub. by Sutton England); pap. text ed. 8.25x (ISBN 0-904387-70-4, 61182). Humanities.

Winter, Gordon. The Country Life Picture Book of Britain. (Illus.). 1983. 19.95 (ISBN 0-393-01735-4, Pub. by Country Life). Norton.

GREAT BRITAIN–DESCRIPTION AND TRAVEL–GUIDEBOOKS
see also Restaurants, Lunchrooms, etc.–Great Britain

Ashe, Geoffrey. A Guidebook to Arthurian Britain. (Longman Travellers Ser.). (Illus.). 1983. text ed. 15.95x (ISBN 0-582-50282-9). Longman.

Automobile Association of England Staff. Discovering Britain. 1983. 24.95 (ISBN 0-393-01741-9). Norton.

Birnbaum, Stephen. Great Britain & Ireland 1983. (Get 'em & Go Travel Guide Ser.). 1982. 11.95 (ISBN 0-395-32871-3). HM.

BTA Commended: Country Hotels, Guesthouses & Restaurants. 100p. 1983. pap. 5.95 (ISBN 0-7095-1293-7, Pub. by Auto Assn-British Tourist Authority England). Merrimack Bk Serv.

Camping & Caravanning in Britain. 224p. 1983. pap. 8.95 (ISBN 0-86145-136-8, Pub. by Auto Assn-British Tourist Authority England). Merrimack Bk Serv.

Freethy, Ron. The Naturalist's Guide to the British Coastline. (Illus.). 192p. 1983. 22.50 (ISBN 0-7153-8342-6). David & Charles.

Goldring, Patrick. Britain by Train. 208p. 1983. pap. 5.95 (ISBN 0-600-20669-6, Pub. by Auto Assn-British Tourist Authority England). Merrimack Bk Serv.

Harvard Student Agencies. Let's Go Britain & Ireland. (The Let's Go Ser.). (Illus.). 450p. 1983. pap. 7.95 (ISBN 0-312-48210-8). St Martin.

Hudson, Kenneth, ed. The Good Museums Guide: The Best Museums & Art Galleries in the British Isles. 320p. 1982. 30.00x (ISBN 0-333-32763-2, Pub. by Macmillan England). State Mutual Bk.

Nicholson, Robert. Nicholson's Historic Britain. 1983. pap. 12.95 (ISBN 0-686-38866-6). Merrimack Bk Serv.

Parry, Keith. The Resorts of the Lancashire Coast. (Illus.). 200p. (Orig.). 1983. 19.95 (ISBN 0-7153-8304-3). David & Charles.

Rand McNally Road Atlas of Britain. 1983. pap. 12.95 (ISBN 0-528-84433-4). Rand.

Self-Catering in Britain. 272p. 1983. pap. 8.95 (ISBN 0-86145-138-4, Pub. by Auto Assn-British Tourist Authority England). Merrimack Bk Serv.

Stately Homes, Museums, Castles & Gardens in Great Britain. 272p. 1983. pap. 8.95 (ISBN 0-686-38447-4, Pub. by Auto Assn-British Tourist Authority England). Merrimack Bk Serv.

Watkins, Paul. Traditional Britain. (Golden Hart Guides Ser.). (Illus.). 96p. 1983. pap. 3.95 (ISBN 0-283-98913-0, Pub by Sidgwick & Jackson). Merrimack Bk Serv.

Watney, John. Cruising in British & Irish Waters. (Illus.). 224p. 1983. 23.95 (ISBN 0-7153-8402-3). David & Charles.

Where to Stay, 1983: East Anglia. 130p. 1983. pap. 3.50 (ISBN 0-86143-087-5, Pub. by Auto Assn-British Tourist Authority England). Merrimack Bk Serv.

Where to Stay, 1983: East Midlands. 98p. 1983. pap. 3.50 (ISBN 0-86143-085-9, Pub. by Auto Assn-British Tourist Authority England). Merrimack Bk Serv.

Where to Stay, 1983: Heart of England. 138p. 1983. pap. 3.50 (ISBN 0-86143-084-0, Pub. by Auto Assn-British Tourist Authority England). Merrimack Bk Serv.

Where to Stay, 1983: North-West England. 82p. 1983. pap. 3.50 (ISBN 0-86143-082-4, Pub. by Auto Assn-British Tourist Authority England). Merrimack Bk Serv.

Where to Stay, 1983: Northumbria. 82p. 1983. pap. 3.50 (ISBN 0-86143-081-6, Pub. by Auto Assn-British Tourist Authority England). Merrimack Bk Serv.

Where to Stay, 1983: South of England. 122p. 1983. pap. 3.50 (ISBN 0-86143-090-5, Pub. by Auto Assn-British Tourist Authority England). Merrimack Bk Serv.

Winks, Robin W. An American's Guide to Britain. rev. ed. (Illus.). 464p. 1983. 14.95 (ISBN 0-686-83849-1, ScribT). Scribner.

GREAT BRITAIN–DESCRIPTION AND TRAVEL–HISTORY

Keates, Jonathan. Companion Guide to the Shakespeare Country. (Illus.). 352p. 1983. 15.95 (ISBN 0-13-154625-2); pap. 7.95 (ISBN 0-13-154617-1). P-H.

GREAT BRITAIN–ECONOMIC CONDITIONS

Aaronovitch, S. & Smith, R. The Political Economy of British Capitalism: A Marxist Analysis. 416p. 1982. 17.00 (ISBN 0-07-084121-7). McGraw.

Ashley, Maurice. The People of England: A Short Short Social & Economic History. (Illus.). 214p. 1983. text ed. 20.00x (ISBN 0-8071-1105-8). La State U Pr.

Booth, P. H. W. The Financial Administration of the Lordship & Country of Chester, 1272-1377. 192p. 1982. 20.00 (ISBN 0-7190-1337-2). Manchester.

Bowles, Roger. Law & the Economy. 256p. 1983. text ed. 29.50x (ISBN 0-85520-465-6, Pub. by Martin Robertson England). Biblio Dist.

Crouzet, Francois. The Victorian Economy. Forster, A. S., tr. 400p. 1982. text ed. 32.50x (ISBN 0-231-05542-0); pap. 16.00x (ISBN 0-231-05543-9). Columbia U Pr.

Feinstein, Charles. The Managed Economy: Essays in British Economic Policy & Performance Since 1929. 310p. 1983. 39.95 (ISBN 0-19-828289-3); pap. 17.95 (ISBN 0-19-828290-7). Oxford U Pr.

Gregg, Pauline. Social & Economic History of Britain, 1760-1980. 8th ed. (Illus.). 636p. (Orig.). 1982. 22.50x (ISBN 0-245-53938-7). Intl Pubns Serv.

Harbury, C. D., ed. Workbook in Introductory Economics. 3rd ed. (Illus.). 176p. 1982. 7.00 (ISBN 0-08-027442-0). Pergamon.

Kay, John, ed. Budget, Nineteen Eighty-Two. (Illus.). 156p. 1982. text ed. 15.00x (ISBN 0-631-13153-1, Pub. by Basil Blackwell England); pap. text ed. 6.50x (ISBN 0-631-13154-X, Pub. by Basil Blackwell England). Biblio Dist.

Laux. In First Gear. 251p. 1982. 50.00x (ISBN 0-85323-213-X, Pub. by Liverpool Univ England). State Mutual Bk.

Taylor, B., ed. British Planning Databook. (Illus.). 168p. 1983. 40.00 (ISBN 0-08-028170-2). Pergamon.

GREAT BRITAIN–ECONOMIC CONDITIONS–1945-

Taylor, B., ed. British Planning Databook. (Illus.). 168p. 1983. 40.00 (ISBN 0-08-028170-2). Pergamon.

GREAT BRITAIN–ECONOMIC POLICY

Booth, P. H. W. The Financial Administration of the Lordship & Country of Chester, 1272-1377. 192p. 1982. 20.00 (ISBN 0-7190-1337-2). Manchester.

Feinstein, Charles. The Managed Economy: Essays in British Economic Policy & Performance Since 1929. 310p. 1983. 39.95 (ISBN 0-19-828289-3); pap. 17.95 (ISBN 0-19-828290-7). Oxford U Pr.

GREAT BRITAIN-ECONOMIC POLICY-1945-

Beer, Samuel H. Treasury Control: The Co-ordination of Financial & Economic Policy in Great Britain. LC 82-11843. viii, 138p. 1982. Repr. of 1957 ed. lib. bdg. 25.00x (ISBN 0-313-23626-7, BETRC). Greenwood.

GREAT BRITAIN-FOREIGN RELATIONS

Alexander, G. M. The Prelude to the Truman Doctrine: British Policy in Greece, 1944-47. 1982. 46.00x (ISBN 0-19-822653-5). Oxford U Pr.

Barros, James. Britain, Greece & the Politics of Sanctions. (Royal Historical Society, Studies in History: No. 33). 248p. 1982. text ed. 30.00x (ISBN 0-391-02690-9, Pub. by Swiftbks England). Humanities.

Searight, Sarah. The British in the Middle East. (Illus.). 290p. 1982. 21.95 (ISBN 0-85692-018-5, Pub. by Salem Hse Ltd). Merrimack Bk Serv.

Willert, Arthur. Aspects of British Foreign Policyy. 1928. text ed. 29.50x (ISBN 0-686-83482-8). Elliots Bks.

GREAT BRITAIN-FOREIGN RELATIONS-19TH CENTURY

Jones, Raymond A. The British Diplomatic Service, 1815-1914. 315p. 1982. text ed. 11.50x (ISBN 0-88920-124-2, 40810, Pub. by Laurier U Pr). Humanities.

Porter, Bernard. Britain Europe & the World, 1850 to 1982: Illusions of Grandeur. 184p. text ed. 19.50x (ISBN 0-04-909011-9). Allen Unwin.

GREAT BRITAIN-FOREIGN RELATIONS-20TH CENTURY

Jones, Raymond A. The British Diplomatic Service, 1815-1914. 315p. 1982. text ed. 11.50x (ISBN 0-88920-124-2, 40810, Pub. by Laurier U Pr). Humanities.

Porter, Bernard. Britain Europe & the World, 1850 to 1982: Illusions of Grandeur. 184p. text ed. 19.50x (ISBN 0-04-909011-9). Allen Unwin.

GREAT BRITAIN-FOREIGN RELATIONS-ARGENTINE REPUBLIC

Calvert, Peter. The Falklands Crisis. LC 82-42611. 1982. 20.00x (ISBN 0-312-27964-7). St Martin.

Goebel, Julius. The Struggle for the Falkland Islands: A Study in Legal & Diplomatic History. 512p. 1982. text ed. 35.00x (ISBN 0-300-02943-8); pap. text ed. 10.95x (ISBN 0-300-02945-4, Y-445). Yale U Pr.

GREAT BRITAIN-FOREIGN RELATIONS-CHINA

Wong, John Y. Anglo-Chinese Relations, 1838-1860: A Calendar of Documents in British Foreign Office Records. (British Academy Oriental Documents Ser.). 400p. 1983. 36.00 (ISBN 0-19-726014-4). Oxford U Pr.

GREAT BRITAIN-FOREIGN RELATIONS-INDIA

Kamerkar, Mani. British Paramountcy: British-Baroda Relations, 1818-1848. 253p. 1980. 34.50 (ISBN 0-940500-75-2, Pub by Popular Prakashan India). Asia Bk Corp.

GREAT BRITAIN-FOREIGN RELATIONS-IRELAND

Rea, Desmond, ed. Northern Ireland, the Republic of Ireland & Great Britain: Problems of Political Co-Operation. 300p. 1982. 50.00x (Pub. by Macmillan England). State Mutual Bk.

GREAT BRITAIN-FOREIGN RELATIONS-NEAR EAST

Abadi, Jacob. Britain's Withdrawal from the Middle East: The Economic & Strategic Imperatives (1947-1971) (Leaders, Politics, & Social Change in the Islamic World: No. 4). 275p. 1983. 26.00 (ISBN 0-940670-19-4). Kingston Pr.

Leatherdale, Clive. Britain & Saudi Arabia 1925-1939: An Imperial Oasis. 200p. 1983. text ed. 37.50x (ISBN 0-7146-3220-1, F Cass Co). Biblio Dist.

GREAT BRITAIN-FOREIGN RELATIONS-UNITED STATES

Russett, Bruce M. Community & Contention: Britain & America in the Twentieth Century. LC 82-20952. xii, 252p. 1983. Repr. of 1963 ed. lib. bdg. 29.75x (ISBN 0-313-23792-1, RUCC). Greenwood.

GREAT BRITAIN-GENEALOGY

Bankes, J. & Kerridge, E. The Early Records of the Bankes Family at Winstanley. 1973. 19.00 (ISBN 0-7190-1158-2). Manchester.

Fairbairn, James. Fairbairn's Crests of the Families of Great Britain & Ireland. LC 68-25887. (Illus.). 800p. 1968. 32.30 (ISBN 0-8048-0177-0). C E Tuttle.

GREAT BRITAIN-GENTRY

Jenkins, Philip. The Making of a Ruling Class: The Glamorgan Gentry 1640-1790. LC 82-14703. 336p. Date not set. 44.50 (ISBN 0-521-25003-X). Cambridge U Pr.

GREAT BRITAIN-GOVERNMENT PUBLICATIONS

Butcher, David. Official Publications in Britain. 160p. 1983. 18.50 (ISBN 0-85157-351-7, Pub. by Bingley England). Shoe String.

GREAT BRITAIN-HISTORIC HOUSES, ETC.

Carver, M. O. H. Two Town Houses in Medieval Shrewsbury. 144p. 1982. pap. text ed. 25.25x (ISBN 0-86299-023-8, Pub. by Alan Sutton England). Humanities.

Sauvain, Philip. Britain's Living Heritage. (Illus.). 128p. 1982. 19.95 (ISBN 0-7134-3813-4, Pub. by Batsford England). David & Charles.

GREAT BRITAIN-HISTORIOGRAPHY

Rein, G. A. Sir John Robert Seeley: A Study of the Historian. Herkless, John L., ed. 1983. 25.00 (ISBN 0-89341-550-2). Longwood Pr.

GREAT BRITAIN-HISTORY

Here are entered works on the history of Great Britain as a whole. For works on specific periods see the period subdivisions.

Aubrey, John. Brief Lives (Modern English Version) Barber, Richard, ed. LC 82-24416. 200p. 1983. text ed. 22.50x (ISBN 0-389-20366-1). B&N Imports.

Elton, G., ed. Annual Bibliography of British & Irish History 1981. 196p. 1982. text ed. 37.50x (ISBN 0-391-02728-X, Pub. by Harvester England). Humanities.

Fowles, John. A Short History of Lime Regis. (Illus.). 56p. 1983. 13.00 (ISBN 0-316-28987-6). Little.

Gregg, Pauline. Social & Economic History of Britain, 1760-1980. 8th ed. (Illus.). 636p. (Orig.). 1982. 22.50x (ISBN 0-245-53938-7). Intl Pubns Serv.

Hawkins, Desmond. Avalon & Sedgemoor. 192p. 1982. pap. text ed. 9.50x (ISBN 0-86299-016-5, 10011, Pub. by Sutton England). Humanities.

Jenkins, Philip. The Making of a Ruling Class: The Glamorgan Gentry 1640-1790. LC 82-14703. 336p. Date not set. 44.50 (ISBN 0-521-25003-X). Cambridge U Pr.

Kenyon, J. P., ed. A Dictionary of British History. LC 82-42759. 415p. 1983. 20.00 (ISBN 0-8128-2910-7). Stein & Day.

Rordorf, Willy & Schneider, Andre. L'Evolution Du Concept De Tradition Dans l'Englise Ancienne. xxxii, 208p. (Fr.). 1982. write for info. P Lang Pubs.

Squibb, George D. Precedence in England & Wales. 158p. 1981. 34.50x (ISBN 0-19-825389-3). Oxford U Pr.

Worcester, Dean K., Jr. Life & Times of Thomas Turner of East Hoathly. 1948. text ed. 29.50x (ISBN 0-686-83607-3). Elliots Bks.

GREAT BRITAIN-HISTORY-ADDRESSES, ESSAYS, LECTURES

Brewer, J. S. & Wace, Henry. English Studies, or Essays in English History & Literature. 448p. 1982. Repr. of 1881 ed. lib. bdg. 75.00 (ISBN 0-8495-0611-5). Arden Lib.

GREAT BRITAIN-HISTORY-SOURCES

see also subdivision sources for various period subdivisions which follow, e.g., Great Britain-History-Medieval Period, 1066-1485-Sources; Great Britain-History-Sources

Blakeley, Brian L. & Collins, Jacquelin. Documents in English History: Early Times to the Present. LC 74-18264. 467p. 1975. pap. text ed. 16.50x (ISBN 0-471-07946-4). Wiley.

Gairdner, James. The Early Chronicles of England. 328p. 1982. Repr. lib. bdg. 50.00 (ISBN 0-8495-2133-5). Arden Lib.

GREAT BRITAIN-HISTORY-TO 449

Here are entered works on the early history of great britain to the end of the roman occupation as a whole, as well as books on parts of the period, such as the roman occupation.

Holder, P. A., ed. The Roman Army in Britain. LC 82-3332. (Illus.). 137p. 1982. 20.00x (ISBN 0-312-68961-6). St Martin.

MacDougall, Hugh A. Racial Myth in English History: Trojans, Teutons, & Anglo-Saxons. LC 81-69941. 160p. 1983. pap. text ed. 6.50x (ISBN 0-87451-229-8). U Pr of New Eng.

GREAT BRITAIN-HISTORY-TO 1485

Here are entered works on the History of Great Britain to 1485 as a whole.

McGregor, Patricia. Odiham Castle Twelve Hundred to Fifteen Hundred. 192p. 1982. text ed. 18.75x (ISBN 0-86299-030-0, Pub. by Sutton England). Humanities.

Smith, Lacey B. A History of England, Vol. I: The Making of England 55 B. C. to 1399. 4th ed. Hollister, C. W., ed. 320p. 1983. pap. text ed. 10.95 (ISBN 0-669-04377-X). Heath.

GREAT BRITAIN-HISTORY-ANGLO-SAXON PERIOD, 449-1066

Here are entered works on the Anglo-Saxon period whether as a whole or portions of the period. For works on specific rulers of this period see the name of the ruler.

Clemoes, Peter, ed. Anglo Saxon England II. LC 78-190423. (Illus.). 350p. Date not set. price not set (ISBN 0-521-24918-X). Cambridge U Pr.

GREAT BRITAIN-HISTORY-MEDIEVAL PERIOD, 1066-1485

Here are entered works on the Medieval period as a whole as well as those on parts of the period.

Bennett, Michael J. Community, Class & Careerism: Cheshire & Lancashire in the Age of Sir Gawain & the Green Knight. LC 82-4354. (Cambridge Studies in Medieval Life & Thought: No. 18). (Illus.). 312p. Date not set. price not set (ISBN 0-521-24744-6). Cambridge U Pr.

Highfield, J. R. & Jeffs, Robin, eds. The Crown & Local Communities in England & France in the Fifteenth Century. 192p. 1981. text ed. 20.25x (ISBN 0-904387-67-4, 61065); pap. text ed. 11.25x (ISBN 0-904387-79-8, 61090). Humanities.

Lowerson, J. R., ed. Southern History, 1982, Vol. 4. 320p. 1983. text ed. 28.25x (ISBN 0-904387-93-3, Pub. by Sutton England); pap. text ed. 17.00x (ISBN 0-904387-94-1). Humanities.

Price, Mary R. A Portrait of Britain in the Middle Ages 1066-1485. 256p. 1982. Repr. of 1951 ed. lib. bdg. 30.00 (ISBN 0-8495-4413-0). Arden Lib.

Saul, Nigel. A Companion to Medieval England. (Illus.). 320p. 1983. text ed. 27.50x (ISBN 0-389-20359-9). B&N Imports.

Skelton, R. A. & Harvey, P. D. Local Maps & Plans from Medieval England. (Illus.). 344p. 1982. 25.00x (ISBN 0-19-822363-3). Oxford U Pr.

Smith, Lacey B., ed. A History of England Vol. II: This Realm of England 1399 to 1688. 4th ed. 336p. 1983. pap. text ed. 10.95 (ISBN 0-669-04378-8). Heath.

Treharne, R. F. The Baronial Plan of Reform, 1258-1263. 1932. 31.00 (ISBN 0-7190-0397-0). Manchester.

GREAT BRITAIN-HISTORY-MEDIEVAL PERIOD, 1066-1485-SOURCES

Davies, R. Trevor, tr. from Lat. & Fr. Documents Illustrating the History of Civilization in Medieval England: 1066-1500. 413p. 1982. Repr. of 1926 ed. lib. bdg. 50.00 (ISBN 0-8495-1140-2). Arden Lib.

Davis, Norman, ed. The Paston Letters. (The World's Classics Ser.). (Illus.). 320p. 1983. pap. 6.95 (ISBN 0-19-281615-2, GB). Oxford U Pr.

GREAT BRITAIN-HISTORY-MODERN PERIOD, 1485-

Highfield, J. R. & Jeffs, Robin, eds. The Crown & Local Communities in England & France in the Fifteenth Century. 192p. 1981. text ed. 20.25x (ISBN 0-904387-67-4, 61065); pap. text ed. 11.25x (ISBN 0-904387-79-8, 61090). Humanities.

Lowerson, J. R., ed. Southern History, 1982, Vol. 4. 320p. 1983. text ed. 28.25x (ISBN 0-904387-93-3, Pub. by Sutton England); pap. text ed. 17.00x (ISBN 0-904387-94-1). Humanities.

Walker, Eric A. British Empire: Its Structure & Spirit, 1497-1953. 2nd ed. 1953. text ed. 39.50x (ISBN 0-686-83494-1). Elliots Bks.

GREAT BRITAIN-HISTORY-TUDORS-1485-1603

Here are entered works on the period between 1485 and 1603 as a whole, as well as those on any part except the reign of Elizabeth, for which see Great Britain-History-Elizabeth-1558-1603.

Appleby. Famine in Tudor & Stuart England. 262p. 1982. 50.00x (ISBN 0-85323-014-5, Pub. by Liverpool Univ England). State Mutual Bk.

Elton, G. R. Essays on Tudor & Stuart Politics & Government: Vol. 3, Papers & Reviews 1973-1981. LC 73-79305. 512p. Date not set. 49.50 (ISBN 0-521-24893-0). Cambridge U Pr.

Guth, Delloyd J. & McKenna, John W. Tudor Rule & Revolution. LC 82-4266. 400p. p.n.s. (ISBN 0-521-24841-8). Cambridge U Pr.

Smith, Lacey B., ed. A History of England Vol. II: This Realm of England 1399 to 1688. 4th ed. 336p. 1983. pap. text ed. 10.95 (ISBN 0-669-04378-8). Heath.

GREAT BRITAIN-HISTORY-16TH CENTURY

see Great Britain-History-Tudors-1485-1603

GREAT BRITAIN-HISTORY-ELIZABETH, 1558-1603

Erickson, Carolly. The First Elizabeth. 464p. 1983. 19.95 (ISBN 0-671-41746-0). Summit Bks.

Hogg, James, ed. Elizabethan Miscellany, Vol. 3. (Salzburg-Elizabethan & Renaissance Ser.: Vol. 71: 2). 117p. 1981. pap. text ed. 25.00x (ISBN 0-391-02813-8, Pub. by Salzburg Austria). Humanities.

GREAT BRITAIN-HISTORY-17TH CENTURY

see Great Britain-History-Stuarts, 1603-1714

GREAT BRITAIN-HISTORY-STUARTS, 1603-1714

Here are entered works on England in the Stuart period as a whole or in part, except for the subdivisions listed immediately below.

Appleby. Famine in Tudor & Stuart England. 262p. 1982. 50.00x (ISBN 0-85323-014-5, Pub. by Liverpool Univ England). State Mutual Bk.

Blackwood, B. G. The Lancashire Gentry & the Great Rebellion, 1640-60. 1978. 24.00 (ISBN 0-7190-1334-8). Manchester.

Elton, G. R. Essays on Tudor & Stuart Politics & Government: Vol. 3, Papers & Reviews 1973-1981. LC 73-79305. 512p. Date not set. 49.50 (ISBN 0-521-24893-0). Cambridge U Pr.

Gregg, Pauline. King Charles I. (Illus.). 508p. 1982. text ed. 24.95x (ISBN 0-460-04437-0, Pub. by J. M. Dent England). Biblio Dist.

Hogg, James, ed. Elizabethan Miscellany, Vol. 3. (Salzburg-Elizabethan & Renaissance Ser.: Vol. 71: 2). 117p. 1981. pap. text ed. 25.00x (ISBN 0-391-02813-8, Pub. by Salzburg Austria). Humanities.

Larkin, James F., ed. Stuart Royal Proclamations: Volume II: Royal Proclamations of King Charles I, 1625-46. 1144p. 1983. 154.00 (ISBN 0-19-822466-4). Oxford U Pr.

Shapiro, Barbara J. Probability & Certainty in Seventeenth Century England: A Study of the Relationships Between Natural Science, Religion, History, Law, Literature. LC 82-61385. 368p. 1983. 35.00x (ISBN 0-691-05379-0). Princeton U Pr.

Smith, Lacey B., ed. A History of England Vol. II: This Realm of England 1399 to 1688. 4th ed. 336p. 1983. pap. text ed. 10.95 (ISBN 0-669-04378-8). Heath.

GREAT BRITAIN-HISTORY-PURITAN REVOLUTION, 1642-1660

Blackwood, B. G. The Lancashire Gentry & the Great Rebellion, 1640-60. 1978. 24.00 (ISBN 0-7190-1334-8). Manchester.

D'Ewes, Simonds. Journal of Sir Simonds D'Ewes From the First Recess of the Long Parliament to the Withdrawal of King Charles From London. Coates, Willson H., ed. 1942. text ed. 24.50x (ISBN 0-686-83599-9). Elliots Bks.

Hunt, William. The Puritan Movement: The Coming of Revolution in an English County. (Harvard Historical Studies: No. 102). (Illus.). 384p. 1983. text ed. 36.00x (ISBN 0-674-73903-5). Harvard U Pr.

GREAT BRITAIN-HISTORY-CIVIL WAR, 1642-1649

see Great Britain-History-Puritan Revolution, 1642-1660

GREAT BRITAIN-HISTORY-RESTORATION, 1660-1688

Draper, Maurice L. Restoration Studies, Vol. II. 1983. pap. 13.00 (ISBN 0-8309-0362-3). Herald Hse.

GREAT BRITAIN-HISTORY-1689-1714

Reed, Michael. The Georgian Triumph: Seventeen Hundred to Eighteen Thirty. (Making of Britain Ser.). (Illus.). 224p. 1983. 24.95 (ISBN 0-7100-9414-0). Routledge & Kegan.

Willcox, William B. & Arnstein, Walter L. A History of England Vol. III: The Age of Aristocracy 1688 to 1830. 4th ed. Smith, Lacey B., ed. 304p. 1983. pap. text ed. 10.95 (ISBN 0-669-04379-6). Heath.

GREAT BRITAIN-HISTORY-18TH CENTURY

Porter, Roy. English Society in the 18th Century. 1983. pap. 5.95 (ISBN 0-14-022099-2, Pelican). Penguin.

Wells, Roger. Insurrection: The British Experience, 1795-1803. 256p. 1982. text ed. 30.00x (ISBN 0-86299-019-X, 40155, Pub. by Sutton England). Humanities.

GREAT BRITAIN-HISTORY-1714-1837

Here are entered works on the period between 1714 and 1837 as a whole or in part.

Reed, Michael. The Georgian Triumph: Seventeen Hundred to Eighteen Thirty. (Making of Britain Ser.). (Illus.). 224p. 1983. 24.95 (ISBN 0-7100-9414-0). Routledge & Kegan.

Sanderson, Michael. Education, Economic Change & Society in England, 1780-1870. (Studies in Economic & Social Theory). 88p. 1983. pap. text ed. 6.25x (ISBN 0-333-32569-9, Pub. by Macmillan England). Humanities.

Willcox, William B. & Arnstein, Walter L. A History of England Vol. III: The Age of Aristocracy 1688 to 1830. 4th ed. Smith, Lacey B., ed. 304p. 1983. pap. text ed. 10.95 (ISBN 0-669-04379-6). Heath.

GREAT BRITAIN-HISTORY-19TH CENTURY

Here are entered works on the nineteenth century as a whole or any part except the reign of Victoria, for which see Great Britain-History-Victoria, 1837-1901.

Arnstein, Walter L. A History of England, Vol. IV: Britain Yesterday & Today 1830 to Present. Smith, Lacey B., ed. 304p. 1983. pap. text ed. 10.95 (ISBN 0-669-04380-X). Heath.

Ford, Colin & Harrison, Brian. A Hundred Years Ago: Britain in the 1880s in Words & Photographs. (Illus.). 344p. 1983. text ed. 25.00x (ISBN 0-674-42626-6). Harvard U Pr.

Heyck, T. W. The Transformation of Intellectual Life in Victorian England. LC 82-840. 262p. 1982. 25.00x (ISBN 0-312-81427-5). St Martin.

GREAT BRITAIN-HISTORY-VICTORIA, 1837-1901

Burrow, J. W. A Liberal Descent: Victorian Historians & the English Past. LC 81-3912. 318p. Date not set. pap. 14.95 (ISBN 0-521-27482-6). Cambridge U Pr.

Daunton, Martin. House & Home in the Victorian City. 400p. 1983. text ed. 55.00x (ISBN 0-8419-0836-2). Holmes & Meier.

Duman, Daniel. The Judicial Bench in England. (Royal Historical Society-Studies in History: No. 29). 208p. 1982. text ed. 33.75x (ISBN 0-901050-80-6, Pub. by Swiftbks England). Humanities.

Pluckrose, Henry. Victorian Britain: History Around Us. 80p. 1982. 30.00x (ISBN 0-7135-1290-3, Pub. by Bell & Hyman England). State Mutual Bk.

Sanderson, Michael. Education, Economic Change & Society in England, 1780-1870. (Studies in Economic & Social Theory). 88p. 1983. pap. text ed. 6.25x (ISBN 0-333-32569-9, Pub. by Macmillan England). Humanities.

Williams, Alfred. Round about Middle Thames: Glimpses of Rural Victorian Life. 192p. 1982. text ed. 8.50x (ISBN 0-86299-032-7, Pub. by Sutton England). Humanities.

GREAT BRITAIN-HISTORY-CRIMEAN WAR, 1853-1856

Evans, S. The Slow Rapprochement: Britain & Turkey in the Age of Kemal Ataturk, 1919-38. 123p. 1982. pap. text ed. 8.00x (ISBN 0-906719-04-6, Pub. by Eothen Pr England). Humanities.

GREAT BRITAIN-HISTORY-20TH CENTURY

Arnstein, Walter L. A History of England, Vol. IV: Britain Yesterday & Today 1830 to Present. Smith, Lacey B., ed. 304p. 1983. pap. text ed. 10.95 (ISBN 0-669-04380-X). Heath.

Carr, E. H. The Twenty Years' Crisis Nineteen Nineteen to Nineteen Thirty-Nine. 244p. 1981. Repr. of 1939 ed. text ed. 18.95x (ISBN 0-333-06913-7, Pub. by Macmillan England). Humanities.
Castle, H. G. Fire over England. (Illus.). 254p. 1982. 22.50 (ISBN 0-436-08900-9, Pub. by Secker & Warburg). David & Charles.
Henderson, Herbert D. Cotton Control Board. (Economic & Social History of the World War Ser.). 1922. text ed. 39.50x (ISBN 0-686-83513-1). Elliots Bks.
Kingsford, Peter. The Hunger Marchers in Britain, 1920-1940. 230p. 1982. text ed. 26.50x (ISBN 0-85315-555-0, Pub. by Lawrence & Wishart Ltd England). Humanities.
Leatherdale, Clive. Britain & Saudi Arabia 1925-1939: An Imperial Oasis. 200p. 1983. text ed. 37.50x (ISBN 0-7146-3220-1, F Cass Co). Biblio Dist.
Proceedings of the British Academy, 1980, Vol. LXVI. (Illus.). 504p. 1982. 110.00x (ISBN 0-19-726013-6). Oxford U Pr.
Proceedings of the British Academy, 1981, Vol. LXVII. (Illus.). 400p. 1982. 99.00 (ISBN 0-19-726015-2). Oxford U Pr.
Robbins, Keith. The Eclipse of a Great Power: Modern Britain 1870-1975. LC 81-18608. (Illus.). 304p. 1983. text ed. 33.00x (ISBN 0-582-48971-7); pap. text ed. 14.95x (ISBN 0-582-48972-5). Longman.
Stewart, Angus, ed. Contemporary Britain. 220p. (Orig.). 1983. pap. price not set (ISBN 0-7100-9406-X). Routledge & Kegan.

GREAT BRITAIN–HISTORY, NAVAL
see also Armada, 1588; Great Britain–Navy
Doughty, Martin. Merchant Shipping & War. (Royal Historical Society, Studies in History: No. 31). 218p. 1982. text ed. 30.00x (ISBN 0-391-02688-7). Humanities.
Harding, Steven. Grey Ghost: RMS Queen Mary at War. (Illus.). 92p. 1982. 8.95 (ISBN 0-933126-26-3). Pictorial Hist.
Wettern, Desmond. The Decline of British Sea Power. (Illus.). 224p. 1982. 29.95 (ISBN 0-86720-627-6). Sci Bks Intl.

GREAT BRITAIN–IMPRINTS
Butcher, David. Official Publications in Britain. 160p. 1983. 18.50 (ISBN 0-85157-351-7, Pub. by Bingley England). Shoe String.

GREAT BRITAIN–INDUSTRY
Johnson. The Social Evolution of Industrial Britain. 188p. 1982. 49.00x (ISBN 0-85323-073-0, Pub. by Liverpool Univ England). State Mutual Bk.
Utton, M. A. The Political Economy of Big Business. LC 82-10739. 272p. 1982. 32.50x (ISBN 0-312-62255-4). St Martin.

GREAT BRITAIN–INDUSTRY–HISTORY
Honeyman, Katrina. Origins of Enterprise: Business Leadership in the Industrial Revolution. LC 82-10441. 180p. 1982. 20.00x (ISBN 0-312-58848-8). St Martin.
Mantoux, Paul. The Industrial Revolution in the Eighteenth Century: An Outline of the Beginnings of the Modern Factory System in England. LC 82-20219. iv, 528p. 1983. pap. 12.50 (ISBN 0-226-50384-4). U of Chicago Pr.
Trinder, Barrie. The Making of the Industrial Landscape. (Illus.). 288p. 1982. text ed. 24.95x (ISBN 0-460-04427-3, Pub. by J. M. Dent England). Biblio Dist.

GREAT BRITAIN–INTELLECTUAL LIFE
Shapiro, Barbara J. Probability & Certainty in Seventeenth Century England: A Study of the Relationships Between Natural Science, Religion, History, Law, Literature. LC 82-61385. 368p. 1983. 35.00x (ISBN 0-691-05379-0). Princeton U Pr.

GREAT BRITAIN–KINGS AND RULERS
Brown, Craig & Cunliffe, Lesley. The Book of Royal Lists. 292p. (Orig.). 1983. 15.95 (ISBN 0-671-46507-4); pap. 7.95 (ISBN 0-671-47282-8). Summit Bks.
Erickson, Carolly. The First Elizabeth. 464p. 1983. 19.95 (ISBN 0-671-41746-0). Summit Bks.
Gregg, Pauline. King Charles I. (Illus.). 508p. 1982. text ed. 24.95x (ISBN 0-460-04437-0, Pub. by J. M. Dent England). Biblio Dist.

GREAT BRITAIN–MAPS
Skelton, R. A. & Harvey, P. D. Local Maps & Plans from Medieval England. (Illus.). 344p. 1982. 25.00x (ISBN 0-19-822363-3). Oxford U Pr.

GREAT BRITAIN–MILITARY POLICY
Beckett, Ian & Gooch, John, eds. Politicians & Defence: Studies in the Formulation of British Defence Policy. 224p. 1982. 20.00 (ISBN 0-7190-0818-2). Manchester.
Smith, E. D. Britain's Brigade of Gurkhas. (Illus.). 291p. 1983. 22.50 (ISBN 0-436-47510-3, Pub. by Secker & Warburg). David & Charles.

GREAT BRITAIN–NATIONAL HEALTH SERVICE
Ham, C. Health Policy in Britain: The Politics & Organization of the NHS. 208p. 1982. text ed. 23.25x (ISBN 0-333-30737-2, Pub. by Macmillan England). Humanities.

GREAT BRITAIN–NAVY
see also Great Britain–History, Naval
Moore, John E. Warships of the Royal Navy. rev. ed. (Illus.). 128p. 1981. 19.50 (ISBN 0-86720-566-0). Sci Bks Intl.

GREAT BRITAIN–NAVY–HISTORY
Carew, Anthony. The Lower Deck of the Royal Navy, 1900-39: The Invergordon Mutiny in Perspective. 256p. 1982. 25.00 (ISBN 0-7190-0841-7). Manchester.
Ellis, Paul. Aircraft of the Royal Navy. (Illus.). 192p. 1982. 17.95 (ISBN 0-86720-556-3). Sci Bks Intl.
Pack, A. J. Nelson's Blood. LC 82-61669. 1982. 14.95 (ISBN 0-87021-944-8). Naval Inst Pr.
Wettern, Desmond. The Decline of British Sea Power. (Illus.). 224p. 1982. 29.95 (ISBN 0-86720-627-6). Sci Bks Intl.

GREAT BRITAIN–NOBILITY
Cannadine, David, ed. Patricians, Power & Politics in Nineteenth Century Towns. LC 82-42544. 240p. 1982. 35.00x (ISBN 0-312-59803-3). St Martin.
Cavendish, Arthur M. The Guidebook to British Nobility: The History of the Great English Families. (The Memoirs Collections of Significant Historical Personalities Ser.). (Illus.). 99p. 1983. 79.85 (ISBN 0-89901-086-5). Found Class Reprints.

GREAT BRITAIN–PARLIAMENT
Cruickshanks, Eveline, ed. Parliamentary History, 1982, Vol. 1. 256p. 1983. text ed. 28.25x (ISBN 0-86299-013-0, Pub. by Sutton England); pap. text ed. 17.00x (ISBN 0-86299-014-9). Humanities.

GREAT BRITAIN–PARLIAMENT–HOUSE OF COMMONS
Bindoff, S. T., ed. The House of Commons 1509-1558: The History of Parliament, 3-Vols. (Parliament Ser.). (700 Pgs. ea. vol.). 1983. Set. 250.00 (ISBN 0-436-04282-7, Pub by Secker & Warburg). David & Charles.

GREAT BRITAIN–PEERAGE
Cokayne, G. E. The Complete Peerage - Of England, Scotland, Ireland, Great Britain & the United Kingdom, Extant, Extinct or Dormant, 6 Vols. 2850p. Repr. Set. text ed. 675.00x (ISBN 0-904387-82-8, Pub. by Alan Sutton England). Humanities.

GREAT BRITAIN–POLITICS AND GOVERNMENT
see also Great Britain–Parliament
Aaronovitch, S. & Smith, R. The Political Economy of British Capitalism: A Marxist Analysis. 416p. 1982. 17.00 (ISBN 0-07-084121-7). McGraw.
Badger, John. British Destiny. 1983. pap. 8.00 (ISBN 0-906158-30-3). Pendragon Hse.
Brennan, Tom. Politics & Government in Britain. 2nd ed. LC 82-4145. (Illus.). 352p. 1982. pap. 14.95 (ISBN 0-521-28600-X). Cambridge U Pr.
Checkland, Sydney. British Public Policy Seventeen Seventy Six To Nineteen Thirty-Nine: An Economic & Social Perspective. LC 82-9552. 432p. price not set (ISBN 0-521-24596-6); pap. price not set (ISBN 0-521-27086-3). Cambridge U Pr.
Cross, J. A. Lord Swinton. 320p. 1983. 45.00 (ISBN 0-19-822602-0). Oxford U Pr.
Madgwick, Peter & Rose, Richard, eds. The Territorial Dimension in United Kingdom Politics. 256p. 1982. text ed. 42.00x (ISBN 0-333-29403-3, Pub. by Macmillan England). Humanities.
Norton, Philip & Aughey, Arthur. Conservatives & Conservatism. 1981. 50.00x (ISBN 0-85117-211-3, Pub. by M Temple Smith); pap. 35.00x (ISBN 0-85117-212-1). State Mutual Bk.
Pimlott, Ben & Cook, Chris, eds. Trade Unions in British Politics. 320p. (Orig.). 1982. pap. text ed. 13.95 (ISBN 0-582-49184-3). Longman.
Pooley, Beverley J. The Evolution of British Planning Legislation. LC 63-63300. (Michigan Legal Publications Ser.). 100p. 1982. Repr. of 1960 ed. lib. bdg. 26.00 (ISBN 0-89941-173-8). W S Hein.
Richard, Ivor. We, the British. LC 80-2623. 264p. 1983. 16.95 (ISBN 0-385-14531-4). Doubleday.

GREAT BRITAIN–POLITICS AND GOVERNMENT–1485-1603
Smith, Thomas. De Republica Anglorum. Dewar, Mary, ed. LC 81-21634. (Cambridge Studies in the History & Theory of Politics). 192p. 1982. 39.50 (ISBN 0-521-24109-X). Cambridge U Pr.

GREAT BRITAIN–POLITICS AND GOVERNMENT–1603-1714
Baxter, Stephen, ed. England's Rise to Greatness, 1660-1763. LC 82-40095. (Clark Library Professorship Ser.). (Illus.). 400p. 1983. text ed. 30.00x (ISBN 0-520-04572-6). U of Cal Pr.
Elton, G. R. Essays on Tudor & Stuart Politics & Government: Vol. 3, Papers & Reviews 1973-1981. LC 73-79305. 512p. Date not set. 49.50 (ISBN 0-521-24893-0). Cambridge U Pr.

GREAT BRITAIN–POLITICS AND GOVERNMENT–18TH CENTURY
Baxter, Stephen, ed. England's Rise to Greatness, 1660-1763. LC 82-40095. (Clark Library Professorship Ser.). (Illus.). 400p. 1983. text ed. 30.00x (ISBN 0-520-04572-6). U of Cal Pr.

GREAT BRITAIN–POLITICS AND GOVERNMENT–19TH CENTURY
Duman, Daniel. The Judicial Bench in England. (Royal Historical Society-Studies in History: No. 29). 208p. 1982. text ed. 33.75x (ISBN 0-901050-80-6, Pub. by Swiftbks England). Humanities.
Duschinsky, Michael P. British Political Finance, 1830-1980. 1981. 17.95; pap. 10.50 (ISBN 0-8447-3452-7). Am Enterprise.
Harrison, Brian. Peaceable Kingdom: Stability & Change in Modern Britain. 400p. 1982. 39.95x (ISBN 0-19-822603-9). Oxford U Pr.
Hibbert, Christopher. The Court of St. James's: The Monarch at Work from Victoria to Elizabeth II. LC 82-62185. (Illus.). 288p. 1983. pap. 6.95 (ISBN 0-688-01602-2). Quill NY.
Hughes, Judith M. Emotion & High Politics: Personal Relations in Late Nineteenth-Century Britain & Germany. LC 82-4737. 232p. 1983. 28.50x (ISBN 0-520-04691-9). U of Cal Pr.

GREAT BRITAIN–POLITICS AND GOVERNMENT–1837-1901
Porter, Bernard. Britain Europe & the World, 1850 to 1982: Illusions of Grandeur. 184p. text ed. 19.50x (ISBN 0-04-909011-9). Allen Unwin.

GREAT BRITAIN–POLITICS AND GOVERNMENT–20TH CENTURY
Beckett, Ian & Gooch, John, eds. Politicians & Defence: Studies in the Formulation of British Defence Policy. 224p. 1982. 20.00 (ISBN 0-7190-0818-2). Manchester.
Cregier, Don M. Chiefs Without Indians: Asquith, Lloyd George, & the Liberal Remnant, 1916-1935. LC 82-17546. (Illus.). 330p. (Orig.). 1983. lib. bdg. 23.50 (ISBN 0-8191-2806-6); pap. text ed. 12.50 (ISBN 0-8191-2807-4). U Pr of Amer.
Duschinsky, Michael P. British Political Finance, 1830-1980. 1981. 17.95; pap. 10.50 (ISBN 0-8447-3452-7). Am Enterprise.
Harrison, Brian. Peaceable Kingdom: Stability & Change in Modern Britain. 400p. 1982. 39.95x (ISBN 0-19-822603-9). Oxford U Pr.
Hibbert, Christopher. The Court of St. James's: The Monarch at Work from Victoria to Elizabeth II. LC 82-62185. (Illus.). 288p. 1983. pap. 6.95 (ISBN 0-688-01602-2). Quill NY.
Weekly Political Intelligence Summaries 1939-1947: Great Britain, Foreign Office, 16 vols. LC 82-49004. (Orig.). 1983. Set. lib. bdg. 960.00 (ISBN 0-527-35749-9). Kraus Intl.

GREAT BRITAIN–POLITICS AND GOVERNMENT–1945-
Barker, Anthony, ed. Quangos in Britain: Government & the Networks of Public Policy-Making. 200p. 1982. 49.00x (ISBN 0-333-29468-8, Pub. by Macmillan England). State Mutual Bk.
Birch, Anthony H. The British System of Government. 6th ed. 298p. 1982. pap. text ed. 7.95x (ISBN 0-04-320154-7). Allen Unwin.
Campbell, Colin. Governments under Stress: Political Executives & Key Bureaucrats in Washington, London, & Ottawa. 384p. 1983. 25.00 (ISBN 0-8020-5622-9). U of Toronto Pr.
Hall, S. & Jacques, M. The Politics of Thatcherism. 265p. 1983. text ed. 23.00x (ISBN 0-85315-553-4, Pub. by Lawrence & Wishart Ltd England). Humanities.
Jones, B. & Kavanagh, D. British Politics Today. 155p. 1979. pap. 3.50 (ISBN 0-7190-0736-4). Manchester.
Rose, Richard & McAllister, Ian. United Kingdom Facts. 160p. 1982. 80.00x (ISBN 0-333-25341-8, Pub. by Macmillan England). State Mutual Bk.

GREAT BRITAIN–POPULATION
Barker, Theo & Drake, Michael, eds. Population & Society in Britain, 1850-1980. 240p. 1982. 30.00 (ISBN 0-8147-1043-3). Columbia U Pr.
Coleman, D. A., ed. Demography of Immigrants & Minority Groups in the United Kingdom. Date not set. pap. price not set (ISBN 0-12-179780-5). Acad Pr.

GREAT BRITAIN–RELIGION
Haigh, C. Last Days of the Lancashire: Monasteries & the Pilgrimage of Grace. 182p. 1969. 19.00 (ISBN 0-7190-1150-7). Manchester.
Leech, Joseph. Rural Rides of the Bristol Churchgoer. 348p. 1982. text ed. 20.25x (ISBN 0-904387-50-X, Pub. by Sutton England); pap. text ed. 11.25x (ISBN 0-904387-68-2). Humanities.
Martin, Roger H. Evangelicals United: Ecumenical Stirrings in Pre-Victorian Britain, 1795-1830. LC 82-10784. (Studies in Evangelicalism: No. 4). 244p. 1983. 17.50 (ISBN 0-8108-1586-9). Scarecrow.
Pattison, Mark. Essays & Reviews: Tendencies of Religious Thought in England. Jowett, Benjamin, ed. 434p. 1982. Repr. of 1861 ed. lib. bdg. 75.00 (ISBN 0-686-83993-5). Darby Bks.
Wark, K. R. Elizabethan Recusancy in Cheshire. 1971. 18.50 (ISBN 0-7190-1154-X). Manchester.

GREAT BRITAIN–ROYAL AIR FORCE
Bowyer, Chaz. History of the RAF. (Illus.). 224p. 1982. 11.98 (ISBN 0-8119-0519-5, Pub. by Bison Bks.). Fell.
Brookes, Andrew. V Force: The History of Britain's Airborne Deterrent. (Illus.). 173p. 1983. 19.95 (ISBN 0-86720-639-X). Sci Bks Intl.
Donne, Michael & Fowler, Cynthia. Per Ardua Ad Astra: Seventy Years of the RFC & RAF. 192p. 1982. 39.00x (ISBN 0-584-11022-7, Pub. by Muller Ltd). State Mutual Bk.
--The Wings of Britain. 192p. 1982. 50.00x (ISBN 0-584-11022-7, Pub. by Muller Ltd). State Mutual Bk.
Winter, Denis. The First of the Few: Fighter Pilots of the First World War. LC 82-13478. (Illus.). 224p. 17.50 (ISBN 0-8203-0642-8). U of Ga Pr.
Wortley, Rothesay S. Letters from a Flying Officer. (Illus.). 192p. 1982. pap. text ed. 8.25x (ISBN 0-86299-017-3, Pub. by Sutton England). Humanities.

GREAT BRITAIN–ROYAL HOUSEHOLD
Brown, Craig & Cunliffe, Lesley. The Book of Royal Lists. 292p. (Orig.). 1983. 15.95 (ISBN 0-671-46507-4); pap. 7.95 (ISBN 0-671-47282-8). Summit Bks.

GREAT BRITAIN–SOCIAL CONDITIONS
American Water Works Association. Basic Management Principles for Small Water Systems. (AWWA Handbooks-General Ser.). (Illus.). 132p. 1982. pap. 18.20 (ISBN 0-89867-280-5). Am Water Wks Assn.
Ashley, Maurice. The People of England: A Short Short Social & Economic History. (Illus.). 214p. 1983. text ed. 20.00x (ISBN 0-8071-1105-8). La State U Pr.
Barker, Theo & Drake, Michael, eds. Population & Society in Britain, 1850-1980. 240p. 1982. 30.00 (ISBN 0-8147-1043-3). Columbia U Pr.
Harrison, Brian. Peaceable Kingdom: Stability & Change in Modern Britain. 400p. 1982. 39.95x (ISBN 0-19-822603-9). Oxford U Pr.
Hilton, Rodney H. A Medieval Society: The West Midlands at the End of the Thirteenth Century. LC 82-19732. (Past & Present Publications Ser.). 315p. Date not set. price not set (ISBN 0-521-25374-8). Cambridge U Pr.
Jones, Catherine & Stevenson, June, eds. The Yearbook of Social Policy in Britain 1980-1981. 239p. 1982. 35.00 (ISBN 0-7100-9083-8). Routledge & Kegan.
Marwick, Arthur. British Society Since '45. 1983. pap. cancelled (ISBN 0-14-021906-4, Pelican). Penguin.
Orr, Willie. Deer Forests, Landlords & Crofters. 226p. 1982. text ed. 31.50x (ISBN 0-85976-081-2, Pub. by Donald England). Humanities.
Spender, Humphrey. Worktown People: Photographs from Northern England, 1937-1938. Mulford, Jeremy, ed. (Illus.). 128p. 1982. 14.95 (ISBN 0-905046-20-X). Falling Wall.
Stevenson, June & Jones, Catherine. Yearbook of Social Policy in Britain 1982. 260p. 1983. price not set (ISBN 0-7100-9537-6). Routledge & Kegan.

GREAT BRITAIN–SOCIAL LIFE AND CUSTOMS
see also England–Social Life and Customs
Ford, Colin & Harrison, Brian. A Hundred Years Ago: Britain in the 1880s in Words & Photographs. (Illus.). 344p. 1983. text ed. 25.00x (ISBN 0-674-42626-6). Harvard U Pr.
Frankenberg, Ronald, ed. Custom & Conflict in British Society. 361p. 1982. text ed. 21.00x (ISBN 0-7190-0855-7, 40671, Pub. by Manchester England). Humanities.
Hills, C. A. Growing Up in the Nineteen Fifties. (Growing Up Ser.). (Illus.). 72p. (gr. 7-12). 1983. 14.95 (ISBN 0-7134-1367-0, Pub. by Batsford England). David & Charles.
Tames, Richard. Growing Up in the Nineteen Sixties. (Growing Up Ser.). (Illus.). 72p. (gr. 7-12). 1983. 14.95 (ISBN 0-7134-1342-5, Pub. by Batsford England). David & Charles.

GREAT BRITAIN–TREASURY
Beer, Samuel H. Treasury Control: The Co-ordination of Financial & Economic Policy in Great Britain. LC 82-11843. viii, 138p. 1982. Repr. of 1957 ed. lib. bdg. 25.00x (ISBN 0-313-23626-7, BETRC). Greenwood.

GREAT BRITAIN–WAR CABINET
British War Budgets. (Economic & Social History of the World War Ser.). 1926. text ed. 75.00x (ISBN 0-686-83495-X). Elliots Bks.

GREAT LAKES–HISTORY
Feltner, Charles E. & Feltner, Jeri B. Great Lakes Maritime History: Bibliography & Sources of Information. LC 82-51175. 124p. 1982. 14.95 (ISBN 0-9609014-1-8); pap. 9.95 (ISBN 0-9609014-0-X). Seajay.

GREAT NORTHERN RAILWAY
Dorin, Patrick C. The Great Northern Railway: Lines East. (Illus.). 192p. Date not set. 24.95 (ISBN 0-87564-541-0). Superior Pub.

GREAT PLAINS
Barr, Claude A. Jewels of the Plains: Wild Flowers of the Great Plains Grasslands & Hills. LC 82-13691. 256p. 1983. 19.95 (ISBN 0-8166-1127-0). U of Minn Pr.

GREATER VEHICLE
see Mahayana Buddhism

GREATNESS
see Genius

GREECE–ANTIQUITIES
Andronicos, Manolis. The Acropolis: The Monuments & the Museum. (Athenon Illustrated Guides Ser.). (Illus.). 80p. 1983. pap. 14.00 (ISBN 0-88332-310-9, 8245, Pub. by Ekdotike Athenon Greecee). Larousse.
--Delphi. (Athenon Illustrated Guides Ser.). (Illus.). 80p. 1983. pap. 8.00 (ISBN 0-88332-298-6, Pub. by Ekdotike Athenon Greece). Larousse.
--National Museum. (Athenon Illustrated Guides Ser.). (Illus.). 96p. 1983. pap. 8.00 (ISBN 0-88332-296-X, 8240, Pub. by Ekdotike Athenon Greece). Larousse.
--Olympia. (Athenon Illustrated Guides Ser.). (Illus.). 80p. 1983. pap. 8.00 (ISBN 0-88332-300-1, 8242, Pub. by Ekdotike Athenon Greece). Larousse.
Iakovidis, S. E. Mycenae-Epidaurus. (Athenon Illustrated Guides Ser.). (Illus.). 160p. 1983. pap. 12.00 (ISBN 0-88332-302-8, 8239, Pub. by Ekdotike Athenon Greece). Larousse.

Kadas, Sotiris. Mount Athos. (Athenon Illustrated Guides Ser.). (Illus.). 200p. 1983. pap. 16.00 (ISBN 0-88332-304-4, 8237, Pub. by Ekdotike Athenon Greece). Larousse.

Karageorghis, Vassos. Cypress Museum & Archaeological Sites of Cypurs. (Athenon Illustrated Guides Ser.). (Illus.). 56p. 1983. pap. 9.00 (ISBN 0-88332-312-5, 8247, Pub. by Ekdotike Athenon Greece). Larousse.

Karouzou, Semni. The National Museum. (Athenon Illustrated Guides Ser.). (Illus.). 174p. 1983. pap. 12.00 (ISBN 0-88332-297-8, 8241, Pub by Ekdotike Athenon Greece). Larousse.

Karpodini-Dimitriadi, E. Greece. (Athenon Illustrated Guides Ser.). (Illus.). 212p. 1983. pap. 20.00 (ISBN 0-686-43392-0, 8234, Pub. by Ekdotike Athenon Greece). Larousse.

--The Peloponnese. (Athenon Illustrated Guides Ser.). (Illus.). 208p. 1983. pap. 20.00 (ISBN 0-88332-306-0, 8243, Pub. by Ekdotike Athenon Greece). Larousse.

McDonald, William A. & Coulson, William D., eds. Excavations at Nichoria in Southwest Greece, Vol. III: The Dark Age & Byzantine Occupation. LC 78-3198. (Illus.). 544p. 1983. 49.50x (ISBN 0-8166-1144-0). U of Minn Pr.

MacKendrick, Paul. The Greek Stones Speak: The Story of Archaeology in Greek Lands. 2nd ed. (Illus.). 576p. 1983. pap. 9.95 (ISBN 0-393-30111-7). Norton.

Mylonas, George E. Mycenae. (Athenon Illustrated Guides Ser.). (Illus.). 96p. 1983. pap. 10.00 (ISBN 0-88332-305-2, 8238, Pub. by Ekdotike Greece). Larousse.

Papahatzis, Nicos. Ancient Corinth. (Athenon Illustrated Guides Ser.). (Illus.). 112p. 1983. pap. 10.00 (ISBN 0-88332-303-6, Pub. by Ekdotike Athenon Greece). Larousse.

Rhodes. (Athenon Illustrated Guides Ser.). (Illus.). 1983. pap. 10.00 (ISBN 0-88332-309-5, Pub. by Ekdotike Athenon Greece). Larousse.

Tataki, A. B. Rhodes: Lindos-Kamiros-Filerimos. (Athenon Illustrated Guides Ser.). (Illus.). 110p. 1983. pap. 14.00 (ISBN 0-686-43397-1, 8248, Pub. by Ekdotike Athenon Greece). Larousse.

Tomlinson, R. A. Epiduaros. (Illus.). 96p. 1983. 12.50 (ISBN 0-292-72044-0). U of Tex Pr.

GREECE-CIVILIZATION

see Civilization, Greek

GREECE-DESCRIPTION, GEOGRAPHY

Andronicos, Manolis. The Acropolis: The Monuments & the Museum. (Athenon Illustrated Guides Ser.). (Illus.). 80p. 1983. pap. 14.00 (ISBN 0-88332-310-9, 8245, Pub. by Ekdotike Athenon Greecee). Larousse.

--Delphi. (Athenon Illustrated Guides Ser.). (Illus.). 80p. 1983. pap. 8.00 (ISBN 0-88332-298-6, Pub. by Ekdotike Athenon Greece). Larousse.

--Herakleion Museum. (Athenon Illustrated Guides Ser.). (Illus.). 80p. 1983. pap. 8.00 (ISBN 0-686-43393-9, 8235, Pub. by Ekdotike Athenon Greece). Larousse.

--National Museum. (Athenon Illustrated Guides Ser.). (Illus.). 96p. 1983. pap. 8.00 (ISBN 0-88332-296-X, 8240, Pub. by Ekdotike Athenon Greece). Larousse.

--Olympia. (Athenon Illustrated Guides Ser.). (Illus.). 80p. 1983. pap. 8.00 (ISBN 0-88332-300-1, 8242, Pub. by Ekdotike Athenon Greece). Larousse.

Bradford, Ernle. Companion Guide to the Greek Islands. (Illus.). 320p. 1983. 15.95 (ISBN 0-13-154500-0); pap. 7.95 (ISBN 0-13-154492-6). P-H.

Douskou, Iris. Athens: The City & It's Museums. (Athenon Illustrated Guides Ser.). (Illus.). 112p. 1983. pap. 14.00 (ISBN 0-88332-313-3, Pub. by Ekdotike Athenon Greece). Larousse.

Hooker, J. T. Mycanean Greece. (States & Cities of Ancient Greece Ser.). 330p. 1977. 25.00 (ISBN 0-7100-8379-3). Routledge & Kegan.

Iakovidis, S. E. Mycenae-Epidaurus. (Athenon Illustrated Guides Ser.). (Illus.). 160p. 1983. pap. 12.00 (ISBN 0-88332-302-8, 8239, Pub. by Ekdotike Athenon Greece). Larousse.

Kadas, Sotiris. Mount Athos. (Athenon Illustrated Guides Ser.). (Illus.). 200p. 1983. pap. 16.00 (ISBN 0-88332-304-4, 8237, Pub. by Ekdotike Athenon Greece). Larousse.

Karageorghis, Vassos. Cypress Museum & Archaeological Sites of Cypurs. (Athenon Illustrated Guides Ser.). (Illus.). 56p. 1983. pap. 9.00 (ISBN 0-88332-312-5, 8247, Pub. by Ekdotike Athenon Greece). Larousse.

Karouzou, Semni. The National Museum. (Athenon Illustrated Guides Ser.). (Illus.). 174p. 1983. pap. 12.00 (ISBN 0-88332-297-8, 8241, Pub by Ekdotike Athenon Greece). Larousse.

Karpodini-Dimitriadi, E. Greece. (Athenon Illustrated Guides Ser.). (Illus.). 212p. 1983. pap. 20.00 (ISBN 0-686-43392-0, 8234, Pub. by Ekdotike Athenon Greece). Larousse.

--The Peloponnese. (Athenon Illustrated Guides Ser.). (Illus.). 208p. 1983. pap. 20.00 (ISBN 0-88332-306-0, 8243, Pub. by Ekdotike Athenon Greece). Larousse.

Michailidou, Anna. Knossos. (Athenon Illustrated Guides Ser.). (Illus.). 128p. 1983. pap. 12.00 (ISBN 0-686-43394-7, 8236, Pub. by Ekdotike Athenon Greece). Larousse.

Mylonas, George E. Mycenae. (Athenon Illustrated Guides Ser.). (Illus.). 96p. 1983. pap. 10.00 (ISBN 0-88332-305-2, 8238, Pub. by Ekdotike Greece). Larousse.

Papahatzis, Nicos. Ancient Corinth. (Athenon Illustrated Guides Ser.). (Illus.). 112p. 1983. pap. 10.00 (ISBN 0-88332-303-6, Pub. by Ekdotike Athenon Greece). Larousse.

Pritchett, Kendrick W. Studies in Ancient Greek Topography. LC 65-65210. (Publications in Classical Studies: Vol. 28). 374p. 1982. pap. text ed. 30.00x (ISBN 0-520-09660-6). U of Cal Pr.

Rhodes. (Athenon Illustrated Guides Ser.). (Illus.). 1983. pap. 10.00 (ISBN 0-88332-309-5, Pub. by Ekdotike Athenon Greece). Larousse.

Tataki, A. B. Rhodes: Lindos-Kamiros-Filerimos. (Athenon Illustrated Guides Ser.). (Illus.). 110p. 1983. pap. 14.00 (ISBN 0-686-43397-1, 8248, Pub. by Ekdotike Athenon Greece). Larousse.

Themelis, Petros G. The Delphi Museum. (Athenon Illustrated Guides Ser.). (Illus.). 104p. 1983. pap. 10.00 (ISBN 0-88332-299-4, Pub. by Ekdotike Athenon Greece). Larousse.

GREECE-ECONOMIC CONDITIONS

Garnsey, Peter & Hopkins, Keith, eds. Trade in the Ancient Economy. LC 81-13652. 250p. 1983. text ed. 32.00x (ISBN 0-520-04803-2). U of Cal Pr.

GREECE-FOREIGN RELATIONS

Alexander, G. M. The Prelude to the Truman Doctrine: British Policy in Greece, 1944-47. 1982. 46.00x (ISBN 0-19-822653-5). Oxford U Pr.

Zapantis, Andrew L. Greek-Soviet Relations, 1917-1941. (East European Monographs: No. 96). 640p. 1982. 35.00x (ISBN 0-88033-004-X). East Eur Quarterly.

GREECE-HISTORY

Drews, Robert. Basileus: The Evidence for Kingship in Geometric Greece. LC 82-10915. (Yale Classical Monographs: No. 4). 160p. 1983. text ed. 18.50x (ISBN 0-300-02831-8). Yale U Pr.

Gullath, Brigitte. Untersuchungen Zur Geschichte Boiotiens In Der Zeit Alexanders Und Der Diadochen. 249p. 1982. write for info (ISBN 3-8204-7026-3). P Lang Pubs.

Westlake, H. D. Timoleon & His Relations with Tyrants. 1952. 12.00 (ISBN 0-7190-1217-1). Manchester.

Zapantis, Andrew L. Greek-Soviet Relations, 1917-1941. (East European Monographs: No. 96). 640p. 1982. 35.00x (ISBN 0-88033-004-X). East Eur Quarterly.

GREECE-HISTORY-SOURCES

Crawford, Michael & Whitehead, David, eds. Archaic & Classical Greece: A Selection of Ancient Sources in Translation. LC 82-4355. 700p. Date not set. price not set (ISBN 0-521-22775-5); pap. price not set (ISBN 0-521-29638-2). Cambridge U Pr.

GREECE-POLITICS AND GOVERNMENT

Alexander, G. M. The Prelude to the Truman Doctrine: British Policy in Greece, 1944-47. 1982. 46.00x (ISBN 0-19-822653-5). Oxford U Pr.

GREECE-RELIGION

Simon, Erika. Festivals of Attica: An Archaeologieal Commentary. 160p. 1983. text ed. 21.50 (ISBN 0-299-09180-5). U of Wis Pr.

GREECE-SOCIAL LIFE AND CUSTOMS

Doumanis, Mariella, ed. Mothering in Greece: Behavioral Development. Date not set. price not set. Acad Pr.

Simon, Erika. Festivals of Attica: An Archaeological Commentary. 160p. 1983. text ed. 21.50 (ISBN 0-299-09180-5). U of Wis Pr.

GREECE, MODERN-ANTIQUITIES

Andronicos, Manolis. The Acropolis: The Monuments & the Museum. (Athenon Illustrated Guides Ser.). (Illus.). 80p. 1983. pap. 14.00 (ISBN 0-88332-310-9, 8245, Pub. by Ekdotike Athenon Greecee). Larousse.

--Delphi. (Athenon Illustrated Guides Ser.). (Illus.). 80p. 1983. pap. 8.00 (ISBN 0-88332-298-6, Pub. by Ekdotike Athenon Greece). Larousse.

--National Museum. (Athenon Illustrated Guides Ser.). (Illus.). 96p. 1983. pap. 8.00 (ISBN 0-88332-296-X, 8240, Pub. by Ekdotike Athenon Greece). Larousse.

--Olympia. (Athenon Illustrated Guides Ser.). (Illus.). 80p. 1983. pap. 8.00 (ISBN 0-88332-300-1, 8242, Pub. by Ekdotike Athenon Greece). Larousse.

Iakovidis, S. E. Mycenae-Epidaurus. (Athenon Illustrated Guides Ser.). (Illus.). 160p. 1983. pap. 12.00 (ISBN 0-88332-302-8, 8239, Pub. by Ekdotike Athenon Greece). Larousse.

Kadas, Sotiris. Mount Athos. (Athenon Illustrated Guides Ser.). (Illus.). 200p. 1983. pap. 16.00 (ISBN 0-88332-304-4, 8237, Pub. by Ekdotike Athenon Greece). Larousse.

Karageorghis, Vassos. Cypress Museum & Archaeological Sites of Cypurs. (Athenon Illustrated Guides Ser.). (Illus.). 56p. 1983. pap. 9.00 (ISBN 0-88332-312-5, 8247, Pub. by Ekdotike Athenon Greece). Larousse.

Karouzou, Semni. The National Museum. (Athenon Illustrated Guides Ser.). (Illus.). 174p. 1983. pap. 12.00 (ISBN 0-88332-297-8, 8241, Pub by Ekdotike Athenon Greece). Larousse.

Karpodini-Dimitriadi, E. Greece. (Athenon Illustrated Guides Ser.). (Illus.). 212p. 1983. pap. 20.00 (ISBN 0-686-43392-0, 8234, Pub. by Ekdotike Athenon Greece). Larousse.

--The Peloponnese. (Athenon Illustrated Guides Ser.). (Illus.). 208p. 1983. pap. 20.00 (ISBN 0-88332-306-0, 8243, Pub. by Ekdotike Athenon Greece). Larousse.

Mylonas, George E. Mycenae. (Athenon Illustrated Guides Ser.). (Illus.). 96p. 1983. pap. 10.00 (ISBN 0-88332-305-2, 8238, Pub. by Ekdotike Greece). Larousse.

Papahatzis, Nicos. Ancient Corinth. (Athenon Illustrated Guides Ser.). (Illus.). 112p. 1983. pap. 10.00 (ISBN 0-88332-303-6, Pub. by Ekdotike Athenon Greece). Larousse.

Rhodes. (Athenon Illustrated Guides Ser.). (Illus.). 1983. pap. 10.00 (ISBN 0-88332-309-5, Pub. by Ekdotike Athenon Greece). Larousse.

Tataki, A. B. Rhodes: Lindos-Kamiros-Filerimos. (Athenon Illustrated Guides Ser.). (Illus.). 110p. 1983. pap. 14.00 (ISBN 0-686-43397-1, 8248, Pub. by Ekdotike Athenon Greece). Larousse.

GREECE, MODERN-DESCRIPTION AND TRAVEL

Ebdon, John. Ebdon's Iliad. (Illus.). 192p. 1983. 17.50 (ISBN 0-434-22196-1, Pub. by Heineman England). David & Charles.

GREECE, MODERN-DESCRIPTION AND TRAVEL-GUIDEBOOKS

Andronicos, Manolis. The Acropolis: The Monuments & the Museum. (Athenon Illustrated Guides Ser.). (Illus.). 80p. 1983. pap. 14.00 (ISBN 0-88332-310-9, 8245, Pub. by Ekdotike Athenon Greecee). Larousse.

--Delphi. (Athenon Illustrated Guides Ser.). (Illus.). 80p. 1983. pap. 8.00 (ISBN 0-88332-298-6, Pub. by Ekdotike Athenon Greece). Larousse.

--Herakleion Museum. (Athenon Illustrated Guides Ser.). (Illus.). 80p. 1983. pap. 8.00 (ISBN 0-686-43393-9, 8235, Pub. by Ekdotike Athenon Greece). Larousse.

--National Museum. (Athenon Illustrated Guides Ser.). (Illus.). 96p. 1983. pap. 8.00 (ISBN 0-88332-296-X, 8240, Pub. by Ekdotike Athenon Greece). Larousse.

--Olympia. (Athenon Illustrated Guides Ser.). (Illus.). 80p. 1983. pap. 8.00 (ISBN 0-88332-300-1, 8242, Pub. by Ekdotike Athenon Greece). Larousse.

Bradford, Ernle. Companion Guide to the Greek Islands. (Illus.). 320p. 1983. 15.95 (ISBN 0-13-154500-0); pap. 7.95 (ISBN 0-13-154492-6). P-H.

De Jongh, Brian. Companion Guide to Mainland Greece. (Illus.). 456p. 1983. 16.95 (ISBN 0-13-154567-1); pap. 8.95 (ISBN 0-13-154559-0). P-H.

Douskou, Iris. Athens: The City & It's Museums. (Athenon Illustrated Guides Ser.). (Illus.). 112p. 1983. pap. 14.00 (ISBN 0-88332-313-3, Pub. by Ekdotike Athenon Greece). Larousse.

Greek Island Travel Guide. (Berlitz Travel Guides). (Illus.). 1982. pap. 4.95 (ISBN 0-02-969720-4, Berlitz). Macmillan.

Harvard Student Agencies. Let's Go Greece, Israel, & Egypt. (The Let's Go Ser.). (Illus.). 474p. 1983. pap. 7.95 (ISBN 0-312-48213-2). St Martin.

Iakovidis, S. E. Mycenae-Epidaurus. (Athenon Illustrated Guides Ser.). (Illus.). 160p. 1983. pap. 12.00 (ISBN 0-88332-302-8, 8239, Pub. by Ekdotike Athenon Greece). Larousse.

Kadas, Sotiris. Mount Athos. (Athenon Illustrated Guides Ser.). (Illus.). 200p. 1983. pap. 16.00 (ISBN 0-88332-304-4, 8237, Pub. by Ekdotike Athenon Greece). Larousse.

Karageorghis, Vassos. Cypress Museum & Archaeological Sites of Cypurs. (Athenon Illustrated Guides Ser.). (Illus.). 56p. 1983. pap. 9.00 (ISBN 0-88332-312-5, 8247, Pub. by Ekdotike Athenon Greece). Larousse.

Karouzou, Semni. The National Museum. (Athenon Illustrated Guides Ser.). (Illus.). 174p. 1983. pap. 12.00 (ISBN 0-88332-297-8, 8241, Pub by Ekdotike Athenon Greece). Larousse.

Karpodini-Dimitriadi, E. Greece. (Athenon Illustrated Guides Ser.). (Illus.). 212p. 1983. pap. 20.00 (ISBN 0-686-43392-0, 8234, Pub. by Ekdotike Athenon Greece). Larousse.

--The Peloponnese. (Athenon Illustrated Guides Ser.). (Illus.). 208p. 1983. pap. 20.00 (ISBN 0-88332-306-0, 8243, Pub. by Ekdotike Athenon Greece). Larousse.

Michailidou, Anna. Knossos. (Athenon Illustrated Guides Ser.). (Illus.). 128p. 1983. pap. 12.00 (ISBN 0-686-43394-7, 8236, Pub. by Ekdotike Athenon Greece). Larousse.

Michelin Green Guide: Greece. (Green Guide Ser.). (Fr.). 1983. pap. write for info. (ISBN 2-0600-5190-8). Michelin.

Mylonas, George E. Mycenae. (Athenon Illustrated Guides Ser.). (Illus.). 96p. 1983. pap. 10.00 (ISBN 0-88332-305-2, 8238, Pub. by Ekdotike Greece). Larousse.

Papahatzis, Nicos. Ancient Corinth. (Athenon Illustrated Guides Ser.). (Illus.). 112p. 1983. pap. 10.00 (ISBN 0-88332-303-6, Pub. by Ekdotike Athenon Greece). Larousse.

Rhodes. (Athenon Illustrated Guides Ser.). (Illus.). 1983. pap. 10.00 (ISBN 0-88332-309-5, Pub. by Ekdotike Athenon Greece). Larousse.

Tataki, A. B. Rhodes: Lindos-Kamiros-Filerimos. (Athenon Illustrated Guides Ser.). (Illus.). 110p. 1983. pap. 14.00 (ISBN 0-686-43397-1, 8248, Pub. by Ekdotike Athenon Greece). Larousse.

Themelis, Petros G. The Delphi Museum. (Athenon Illustrated Guides Ser.). (Illus.). 104p. 1983. pap. 10.00 (ISBN 0-88332-299-4, Pub. by Ekdotike Athenon Greece). Larousse.

GREECE, MODERN-FOREIGN RELATIONS

Barros, James. Britain, Greece & the Politics of Sanctions. (Royal Historical Society, Studies in History: No. 33). 248p. 1982. text ed. 30.00x (ISBN 0-391-02690-9, Pub. by Swiftbks England). Humanities.

GREECE, MODERN-POLITICS AND GOVERNMENT

Mavrogordatos, George T. Stillborn Republic: Social Strategies in Greece, 1922-1936. LC 82-2781. 416p. 1983. text ed. 40.00x (ISBN 0-520-04358-8). U of Cal Pr.

Woodhouse, C. M. Karamanlis: The Restorer of Greek Democracy. (Illus.). 1982. 44.00x (ISBN 0-19-822584-9). Oxford U Pr.

GREECE, MODERN-SOCIAL CONDITIONS

Mavrogordatos, George T. Stillborn Republic: Social Strategies in Greece, 1922-1936. LC 82-2781. 416p. 1983. text ed. 40.00x (ISBN 0-520-04358-8). U of Cal Pr.

GREEK AMERICANS

Papanikolas, Zeese. Buried Unsung: Louis Tikas & the Ludlow Massacre. LC 82-13475. (University of Utah Publications in the American West: Vol. 14). (Illus.). 331p. 1982. 20.00 (ISBN 0-87480-211-3). U of Utah Pr.

GREEK ART

see Art, Greek

GREEK CHURCH

see Orthodox Eastern Church, Greek

GREEK CIVILIZATION

see Civilization, Greek; Hellenism

GREEK DRAMA (COLLECTIONS)

Aeschylus & Sophocles. An Anthology of Greek Tragedy. Cook, Albert & Dolin, Edwin, eds. Sylvester, William & Sugg, Alfred, trs. (Dunquin Series: No. 15). (Illus.). 445p. 1983. pap. 14.50 (ISBN 0-88214-215-1). Spring Pubns.

GREEK DRAMA-HISTORY AND CRITICISM

Lesky, Albin. Greek Tragic Poetry. LC 82-1886. 528p. 1983. text ed. 50.00x (ISBN 0-300-02647-1). Yale U Pr.

Wecklein, N., ed. Prometheus Bound, & the Fragments of Prometheus Loosed. 1981. 25.00 (ISBN 0-89241-358-1); pap. 12.50 (ISBN 0-89241-126-0). Caratzas Bros.

GREEK DRAMA-TRANSLATIONS INTO ENGLISH

Aeschylus & Sophocles. An Anthology of Greek Tragedy. Cook, Albert & Dolin, Edwin, eds. Sylvester, William & Sugg, Alfred, trs. (Dunquin Series: No. 15). (Illus.). 445p. 1983. pap. 14.50 (ISBN 0-88214-215-1). Spring Pubns.

Harrison, Tony, tr. Aeschylus: The Oresteia. 126p. 1982. pap. text ed. 6.95x (ISBN 0-8476-4766-8). Rowman.

GREEK LANGUAGE

see also Hellenism

Berlitz Greek for Your Trip. 192p. 1982. 8.95 (ISBN 0-02-965480-7, Berlitz). Macmillan.

Conway, R. S. The Making of Latin: An Introduction to Latin, Greek & English Etymology. 1983. 20.00 (ISBN 0-89241-335-2); pap. 12.50 (ISBN 0-89241-341-7). Caratzas Bros.

An Etymology of Latin & Greek. xix, 252p. 1983. 25.00 (ISBN 0-89241-334-4); pap. 12.50 (ISBN 0-89241-340-9). Caratzas Bros.

GREEK LANGUAGE-CONVERSATION AND PHRASE BOOKS

Found, James. Basic Greek in Thirty Minutes A Day. 128p. 1983. pap. 4.95 (ISBN 0-87123-285-5). Bethany Hse.

Getting By in Greek. (Getting By Language Ser.). 90p. 1983. pap. 2.95 (ISBN 0-8120-2663-2). Barron.

Hart, Babe. Speedy Greek. Hart, Babe, ed. & illus. (Speedy Language Ser.). (Illus.). 24p. (Orig.). 1983. pap. 1.75 (ISBN 0-9602838-8-9). Baja Bks.

GREEK LANGUAGE-DICTIONARIES

Getting By in Greek. (Getting By Language Ser.). 90p. 1983. pap. 2.95 (ISBN 0-8120-2663-2). Barron.

GREEK LANGUAGE-METRICS AND RHYTHMICS

West, M. L. Greek Metre. (Illus.). 1982. 35.00 (ISBN 0-19-814018-5). Oxford U Pr.

GREEK LANGUAGE-PRONUNCIATION

Daitz, Stephen G. Pronunciation of Ancient Greek: A Practical Guide. 10p. Date not set. with 2 cassettes 19.95x (ISBN 0-88432-083-9, S23660). J Norton Pubs.

GREEK LANGUAGE-SYNTAX

Blank, David. Ancient Philosophy & Grammar: The Syntax of Appolonius Dyscolus. LC 82-5751. (American Philological Association, American Classical Studies). 136p. 1982. pap. 11.25 (ISBN 0-89130-580-7, 40 04 10). Scholars Pr CA.

GREEK LANGUAGE, MODERN

Farmakides, Anne. Advanced Modern Greek. LC 82-48914. 400p. 1983. pap. text ed. 22.50x (ISBN 0-300-03023-1). Yale U Pr.

--A Manual of Modern Greek, Vol. I. LC 82-48915. 304p. 1983. pap. text ed. 16.95x (ISBN 0-300-03019-3). Yale U Pr.

--A Manual of Modern Greek, Vol. II. LC 82-48916. 304p. 1983. pap. text ed. 14.95x (ISBN 0-300-03020-7). Yale U Pr.

GREEK LANGUAGE, MODERN–CONVERSATION AND PHRASE BOOKS
Berlitz Editors. Greek for Travel Cassettepack. 1983. 14.95 (ISBN 0-02-962940-3, Berlitz); cassette incl. Macmillan.
Lexus. The Greek Travelmate. LC 82-83993. 128p. 1983. pap. 1.95 (ISBN 0-307-46605-1, Golden Pr). Western Pub.
GREEK LANGUAGE, MODERN–READERS
Farmakides, Anne. Modern Greek Reader, No. I. LC 82-48913. 278p. 1983. pap. text ed. 14.95x (ISBN 0-300-03021-5). Yale U Pr.
--Modern Greek Reader, No. II. LC 82-48913. 260p. 1983. pap. text ed. 14.95 (ISBN 0-300-03022-3). Yale U Pr.
GREEK LAW
see Law, Greek
GREEK LITERATURE–HISTORY AND CRITICISM
Aylen, Leo. Greek Tragedy & the Modern World. 1983. Repr. of 1964 ed. text ed. 24.50x (ISBN 0-8290-1299-0). Irvington.
Bain, David. Masters, Servants, & Orders in Greek Tragedy: Some Aspects of Dramatic Technique & Convention. 84p. 1982. 15.00 (ISBN 0-7190-1296-1). Manchester.
Gadamer, Hans-Georg. Dialogue & Dialectic: Eight Hermeneutical Studies on Plato. Smith, P. Christopher, tr. LC 79-18887. 224p. 1983. pap. text ed. 7.95x (ISBN 0-300-02983-7). Yale U Pr.
MacCary, W. T. Childlike Achilles: Ontogeny & Phylogeny in the Iliad. LC 82-4458. 304p. 1982. text ed. 25.00 (ISBN 0-686-82113-0). Columbia U Pr.
Neo-Hellenika IV. 242p. 1981. 30.00 (ISBN 0-932242-01-4). Ctr Neo Hellenic.
Quinn, T. J. Athens & Samos, Lesbos & Chios: 478-404 B. C. 11/1982 ed. 112p. 17.50 (ISBN 0-7190-1295-3). Manchester.
Sowa, Cora A. Traditional Themes & the Homeric Hymns. 250p. 1982. 39.00x (ISBN 0-86516-018-X). Bolchazy-Carducci.
Winans, Samuel R. Xenophon: Symposium. 95p. Date not set. Repr. of 1881 ed. 6.00x (ISBN 0-86516-020-1). Bolchazy-Carducci.
GREEK LITERATURE–TRANSLATIONS INTO ENGLISH
Butterworth, Charles E., tr. Averroe's Middle Commentaries on Aristotle's Categories & De Interpretations. LC 82-61359. 192p. 1983. 17.50 (ISBN 0-691-07276-0). Princeton U Pr.
GREEK LITERATURE, MODERN–TRANSLATIONS INTO ENGLISH
Frantzeskakis, Ion F., ed. Zygos. Cullen, Timothy & Duckworth, Eddie, trs. from Greek. (Illus.). 216p. 1982. pap. 9.95 (ISBN 0-686-83954-4, Pub. by Zygos Greece). Intl Schol Bk Serv.
GREEK MATHEMATICS
see Mathematics, Greek
GREEK ORATIONS
Jebb, R. C., ed. Selections from the Attic Orators: Antiphon, Andocides, Lysias, Isocrates & Isaeus. 1983. 25.00 (ISBN 0-89241-360-3); pap. 12.50 (ISBN 0-89241-129-5). Caratzas Bros.
GREEK PHILOSOPHY
see Philosophy, Ancient
GREEK POETRY (COLLECTIONS)
Here are entered collections in the Greek Language. For English translations see subdivision Translations into English.
Tyler, Henry M., ed. Selections from the Greek Lyric Poets. 1983. 25.00 (ISBN 0-89241-363-8); pap. 12.50 (ISBN 0-89241-120-1). Caratzas Bros.
GREEK RHETORIC
see Rhetoric, Ancient
GREEK SCULPTURE
see Sculpture, Greek
GREEKS
Vryonis, Speros, Jr. A Brief History of the Greek-American Community of St. George, Memphis, Tennessee 1962-1982. LC 82-50980. (Byzantina Kai Metabyzantina Ser.: Vol. 3). 130p. 1982. 17.50x (ISBN 0-89003-126-6); pap. 12.50x (ISBN 0-89003-127-4). Undena Pubns.
GREEN BELTS
see Greenbelts
GREEN BERETS
see United States–Army
GREENBELTS
Munton, Richard. London's Green Belt: Containment in Practice. (London Research Ser. in Geography: No. 3). (Illus.). 184p. 1983. text ed. 24.95x (ISBN 0-04-333020-7). Allen Unwin.
GREENE, GRAHAM, 1904-
Allain, Marie-Francoise. The Other Man: Conversations with Graham Greene. 1983. price not set (ISBN 0-671-44767-X). S&S.
GREENHEAD
see Striped Bass
GREENHOUSES
Hellyer, Arthur. Dobics Book of Greenhouses. (Illus.). 1981. pap. 12.50 (ISBN 0-434-32626-7, Pub. by Heinemann). David & Charles.
Marier, Donald & Stoiaken, Larry. Alternative Sources of Energy Housing-Greenhouses, No. 59. (Orig.). 1983. pap. 3.50 (ISBN 0-917328-49-3). ASEI.
Plastic Greenhouses for Warm Climates. (FAO Agricultural Services Bulletin Ser.: No. 48). 17p. 1982. pap. 7.50 (ISBN 0-686-81864-4, F2302, FAO). Unipub.
Walls, Ian. Modern Greenhouse Methods: Flowers & Plants. 220p. 1982. 31.00x (ISBN 0-584-10386-7, Pub. by Muller Ltd). State Mutual Bk.
--Modern Greenhouse Methods: Vegetables. 220p. 1982. 31.00x (ISBN 0-584-10388-3, Pub. by Muller Ltd). State Mutual Bk.
GREENLAND
Anderson, Madelyn. Greenland: Island at the Top of the World. LC 82-46003. (Illus.). 128p. (gr. 5 up). 1983. PLB 9.95 (ISBN 0-396-08139-8). Dodd.
GREENLAND–DESCRIPTION AND TRAVEL
Freuchen, Peter. Arctic Adventure: My Life in the Frozen North. 467p. 1982. Repr. of 1935 ed. lib. bdg. 35.00 (ISBN 0-89987-269-7). Darby Bks.
Kpomassie, Tete-Michel. An African in Greenland. Kirkup, James, tr. (Illus.). 224p. 14.95 (ISBN 0-15-105589-0). HarBraceJ.
GREENLAND–HISTORY
The History of Greenland: 1782-1808, Vol. 3. 486p. 1983. 40.00x (ISBN 0-7735-0409-5). McGill-Queens U Pr.
GREENLANDIC LANGUAGE
see Eskimo Language
GREETING CARDS
Doyle, Alfreda. Unusual & Different Greeting Cards & Forms to Duplicate. 45p. 1983. pap. text ed. 9.95 (ISBN 0-939476-59-2). Biblio Pr GA.
GREY FRIARS
see Franciscans
GRIEVANCE PROCEDURES
Briggs, Steven. The Municipal Grievance Process. (Monograph & Research Ser.: No. 34). 350p. 1983. price not set (ISBN 0-89215-118-8). U Cal LA Indus Rel.
GRIFFITH, DAVID WARK, 1875-1948
D. W. Griffith Papers, 1897-1954. 190p. 1982. reference bk. 9.95 (ISBN 0-667-00673-7). Microfilming Corp.
GRIPPE
see Influenza
GRIST-MILLS
see Flour Mills
GRISTLE
see Cartilage
GROCERIES–PACKAGING
see Food–Packaging
GROCERY TRADE
Hawes, Jon M. Retailing Strategies for Generic Brand Grocery Products. Farmer, Richard, ed. LC 82-17631. (Research for Business Decisions Ser.: No. 54). 190p. 1982. 39.95 (ISBN 0-8357-1376-8). Univ Microfilms.
GROOMING, PERSONAL
see Beauty, Personal
GROOMING FOR WOMEN
see Beauty, Personal
GROOMING OF DOGS
see Dog Grooming
GROS VENTRE INDIANS
see Indians of North America–The West
GROSS NATIONAL PRODUCT
see also Income; National Income
Modigliani & Hemming. The Determinants of National Savings & Wealth: Proceedings of a Conference Held by International Economic Association in Bergamo, Italy. LC 82-10377. 305p. 1982. 35.00x (ISBN 0-312-19590-7). St Martin.
GROSSETESTE, ROBERT, BP. OF LINCOLN, 1175-1253
Marrone, Steven P. William Auvergne & Robert Grosseteste: New Ideas of Truth in the Early Thirteenth Century. LC 82-61375. 328p. 1983. 32.50 (ISBN 0-691-05383-9). Princeton U Pr.
GROTIUS, HUGO, 1583-1645
Gellinek, Christian. Hugo Grotius. (World Authors Ser.: No. 680). 176p. 1983. lib. bdg. 19.95 (ISBN 0-8057-6525-5, Twayne). G K Hall.
GROTTOES
see Caves
GROUND COVER PLANTS
Ortho Books Staff. All About Ground Covers. Burke, Ken, ed. LC 82-82157. (Illus.). 112p. 1982. pap. 5.95 (ISBN 0-89721-010-7). Ortho.
GROUND-RENT
see Rent
GROUND WATER
see Water, Underground
GROUP COUNSELING
see also Group Psychotherapy; Self-Help Groups
Grayson, Ellis S. The Elements of Short-Term Group Counseling. rev. ed. (Illus.). 112p. (Orig.). 1978. pap. 5.00 (ISBN 0-942974-10-7). Am Correctional.
GROUP DISCUSSION
see Forums (Discussion and Debate)
GROUP DYNAMICS
see Social Groups
GROUP GUIDANCE IN EDUCATION
McMaster, John M., ed. Methods in Social & Educational Caring. 140p. 1982. text ed. 32.00x (ISBN 0-566-00386-4). Gower Pub Ltd.
GROUP INDENTITY, ETHNIC
see Ethnicity
GROUP INSURANCE
see Insurance, Group
GROUP MEDICAL PRACTICE
see also Health Maintenance Organizations
Domer, Larry R. & Bauer, Jeffrey C. Personalized Guide to Establishing Associateships & Partnerships. Snyder, Thomas L. & Felmeister, Charles J., eds. (Dental Practice Management Ser.). (Illus.). 168p. 1982. pap. text ed. 12.95 (ISBN 0-8016-4714-2). Mosby.
GROUP MEDICAL PRACTICE, PREPAID
see Health Maintenance Organizations
GROUP PSYCHOTHERAPY
see also Family Psychotherapy
Bovill, Diana. Tutorial Therapy: Teaching Neurotics to Treat Themselves. (Illus.). 200p. 1982. text ed. 25.00 (ISBN 0-85200-451-6, Pub. by MTP Pr England). Kluwer Boston.
Lindenberg, Steven P. Group Psychotherapy with People who Are Dying. (Illus.). 400p. 1983. text ed. 24.75x (ISBN 0-398-04814-2). C C Thomas.
Pines, Malcolm, ed. The Evolution of Group Analysis. (International Library of Group Psychotherapy & Group Process). 280p. 1983. price not set (ISBN 0-7100-9290-3). Routledge & Kegan.
Yalom, Irvin D. Inpatient Group Psychotherapy. 1983. text ed. 16.95x (ISBN 0-465-03298-2). Basic.
GROUP PSYCHOTHERAPY–STUDY AND TEACHING
Bradford, Leland P., et al, eds. T-Group Theory & Laboratory Method: Innovation in Re-Education. LC 64-11499. 498p. 1964. 32.95x (ISBN 0-471-09510-9). Wiley.
GROUP RELATIONS TRAINING
Adams, Robert, ed. The New Times Network: Groups & Centres for Personal Growth. 192p. 1983. pap. 8.95 (ISBN 0-7100-9355-1). Routledge & Kegan.
Baird, John E., Jr. Quality Circles: Leaders Manual. 256p. 1982. pap. 11.95. Waveland Pr.
Johnson, David W. & Johnson, Frank P. Joining Together: Group Theory & Group Skills. 2nd ed. LC 74-23698. 480p. 1982. 17.95 (ISBN 0-13-510396-7). P-H.
LeCroy, Craig W., ed. Social Skills Training for Children & Youth. (Child & Youth Services Ser.: Vol. 5, No. 3 & 4). 184p. 1983. text ed. 19.95 (ISBN 0-86656-184-6, B184). Haworth Pr.
Napier & Gershenfeld. Making Groups Work: A Guide for Group Leaders. 1983. pap. text ed. 16.95 (ISBN 0-686-84567-6). HM.
Napier, Rodney & Gershenfeld, Matti. Making Groups Work: A Guide for Group Leaders. LC 82-82242. 304p. 1983. pap. text ed. 17.95 (ISBN 0-395-29705-2). HM.
GROUP REPRESENTATION (MATHEMATICS)
see Representations of Groups
GROUP THEATER
Clurman, Harold. The Fervent Years: The Group Theatre & the Thirties. (Quality Paperbacks Ser.). (Illus.). 352p. 1983. pap. 8.95 (ISBN 0-306-80186-8). Da Capo.
GROUP WORK, SOCIAL
see Social Group Work
GROUPS, AGE
see Age Groups
GROUPS, ETHNIC
see Ethnic Groups
GROUPS, LIE
see Lie Groups
GROUPS, REPRESENTATION THEORY OF
see Representations of Groups
GROUPS, SELF-HELP
see Self-Help Groups
GROUPS, SMALL
see Small Groups
GROUPS, SOCIAL
see Social Groups
GROUPS, THEORY OF
see also Algebra, Boolean; Categories (Mathematics); Fourier Transformations; Lattice Theory; Representations of Groups; Transformation Groups; Transformations (Mathematics)
Beyl, F. R. & Tappe, J. Group Extensions, Representations, & the Schur Multiplicator. (Lecture Notes in Mathematics Ser.: Vol. 958). 278p. 1983. pap. 13.50 (ISBN 0-387-11954-X). Springer-Verlag.
Campbell, C. M. & Robertson, E. F., eds. Groups: St. Andrew's 1981. LC 82-4427. (London Mathematical Society Lecture Note Ser.: No. 71). 360p. 1982. pap. 34.50 (ISBN 0-521-28974-2). Cambridge U Pr.
Carrell, J. B., ed. Group Actions & Vector Fields: Vancouver, Canada, 1981, Proceedings. (Lecture Notes in Mathematics: Vol. 956). 144p. 1983. pap. 8.00 (ISBN 0-387-11946-9). Springer-Verlag.
Carrell, James B., et al. Topics in the Theory of Algebraic Groups. LC 82-17329. (Notre Dame Mathematical Lectures Ser.: No. 10a). 192p. (Orig.). 1982. pap. text ed. 9.95x (ISBN 0-268-01843-X, 85-18433). U of Notre Dame Pr.
Gallo, D. M. & Porter, R. M., eds. Kleinian Groups & Related Topics: Proceedings, Oaxtepec, Mexico, 1981. (Lecture Notes in Mathematics Ser.: Vol. 971). 117p. 1983. pap. 8.50 (ISBN 0-387-11975-2). Springer-Verlag.
GROUPS, TOPOLOGICAL
see Topological Groups
GROUPS OF TRANSFORMATIONS
see Transformation Groups
GROUTING
Baker, Wallace H., ed. Grouting in Geotechnical Engineering. LC 81-71798. 1032p. 1982. pap. text ed. 69.00 (ISBN 0-87262-295-9). Am Soc Civil Eng.
GROWTH
see also Developmental Biology; Growth (Plants); Heterosis
also subdivision Growth under subjects, e.g. Bone–Growth; cities and towns - growth
Dale, John E. The Growth of Leaves. (No. 137). 64p. 1982. pap. text ed. 8.95 (ISBN 0-7131-2836-4). E Arnold.
Dale, John E. & Milthorpe, Frederick L. The Growth & Functioning of Leaves. LC 82-4377. (Illus.). 550p. Date not set. price not set (ISBN 0-521-23761-0). Cambridge U Pr.
Hoffman, Joseph F & Giebisch, Gerhard H., eds. Membranes in Growth & Development. LC 82-7178. (Progress in Clinical & Biological Research Ser.: Vol. 91). 644p. 1982. 94.00 (ISBN 0-8451-0091-2). A R Liss.
Madaras, Lynda. What's Happening to My Body? The Growing-Up Book for Mothers & Daughters. (Illus.). 192p. (gr. 4 up). 1983. 14.95 (ISBN 0-937858-25-0); pap. 7.95 (ISBN 0-937858-21-8). Newmarket.
Perez-Polo, J. Regino & De Vellis, Jean, eds. Growth & Trophic Factors. LC 83-954. (Progress in Clinical & Biological Research Ser.: Vol. 118). 472p. 1983. 45.00 (ISBN 0-8451-0118-8). A R Liss.
GROWTH (PLANTS)
see also Growth Promoting Substances; Heterosis
Causton, David & Venus, Jill. Biometry of Plant Growth. 320p. 1981. text ed. 49.50 (ISBN 0-7131-2812-7). E Arnold.
Charles-Edwards, D., ed. Physiological Determinants of Crop Growth. Date not set. 26.00 (ISBN 0-12-169360-0). Acad Pr.
Donahue, Roy & Miller, John. Soils: An Introduction to Soils & Plant Growth. 5th ed. (Illus.). 656p. 1983. text ed. 27.95 (ISBN 0-13-822288-6). P-H.
Fletcher, W. W. & Kirkwood, R. C. Herbicide Plant Growth Regulation. 1982. 49.95x (ISBN 0-412-00271-X, Pub. by Chapman & Hall England). Methuen Inc.
Johnson, J. C., ed. Plant Growth Regulators & Herbicide Antagonists: Recent Advances. LC 82-7966. (Chemical Technology Rev. 212). (Illus.). 303p. 1983. 45.00 (ISBN 0-8155-0915-4). Noyes.
Kozlowski, T. T. & Riker, A. J., eds. Water Deficits & Plant Growth: Additional Woody Crop Plants. (Vol. 7). Date not set. price not set (ISBN 0-12-424157-3). Acad Pr.
Simulation of Plant Growth & Crop Production. 308p. 1982. pap. 33.75 (ISBN 90-220-0809-6, PDC250, Pudoc). Unipub.
Wareing, P. F., ed. Plant Growth Substances. 1982. write for info. (ISBN 0-12-735380-1). Acad Pr.
Whatley, F. R. & Whatley, J. M. Light & Plant Life. (Studies in Biology: No. 124). 96p. 1980. pap. text ed. 8.95 (ISBN 0-7131-2785-6). E Arnold.
GROWTH HORMONE
see Somatotropin
GROWTH PROMOTING SUBSTANCES
Crop Response to the Supply of Macronutrients. 46p. 1982. pap. 6.75 (ISBN 90-220-0807-X, PDC247, Pudoc). Unipub.
McLaren. Chemical Manipulation of Crop Growth. 1982. text ed. 89.95 (ISBN 0-408-10767-7). Butterworth.
GUARDIAN AND WARD
see also Adoption; Custody of Children; Parent and Child (Law)
Goode, John W., Jr. & Barrows, Suzanne S., eds. Texas Guardianship Manual. LC 82-61569. 791p. 1982. law bk. binder 65.00 (ISBN 0-938160-31-1, 6335). State Bar TX.
GUATEMALA–ANTIQUITIES
Coe, William R. & Haviland, William A. Introduction to the Archaeology of Tikal, Guatemala. LC 82-21799. (Tikal Reports Ser.: No. 12). (Illus.). xii, 100p. 1982. 20.00 (ISBN 0-934718-43-1). Univ Mus of U PA.
Haviland, William A. Excavations in Small Residential Groups of Tikal: Group 4F-1 & 4F-2. (Tikal Reports Ser.: No. 19). 1983. price not set. Univ Mus of U PA.
Jones, Christopher & Satterthwaite, Linton. The Monuments & Inscriptions of Tikal, Pt. A: The Carved Monuments. LC 83-1086. (Tikal Reports Ser.: No. 33). (Illus.). 364p. 1982. 55.00 (ISBN 0-934718-07-5). Univ Mus of U PA.
Puleston, Dennis E. The Settlement Survey of Tikal. (Tikal Reports Ser.: No. 13). 1983. write for info. Univ Mus of U PA.
GUATEMALA–ECONOMIC CONDITIONS
McCreerdy, David. Development & the State in Reforma Guatemala, 1871-1885. (Latin American Series, Ohio University Papers in International Studies). (Illus.). 93p. (Orig.). 1982. pap. text ed. 13.00 (ISBN 0-89680-113-6, Ohio U Ctr Intl). Ohio U Pr.
GUATEMALA–HISTORY
Fried, Jonathan L. & Gettlemen, Marvin, eds. Guatemala in Rebellion: Unfinished History. 360p. (Orig.). 1983. pap. 7.95 (ISBN 0-394-62455-6, Ever). Grove.

GUATEMALA–POLITICS AND GOVERNMENT
Raushenbush, Richard. The Terrorist War in Guatemala. LC 82-14167. 82p. (Orig.). pap. 5.00 (ISBN 0-910637-05-9). Coun Inter Ed.
GUESTS
see Entertaining
GUIDANCE, STUDENT
see Personnel Service in Education; Vocational Guidance
GUIDANCE, VOCATIONAL
see Vocational Guidance
GUIDANCE IN EDUCATION
see Personnel Service in Education
GUIDE-BOOKS
see Voyages and Travels–Guidebooks
GUIDE-POSTS
see Signs and Signboards
GUIDEBOOKS
see Travel
GUIDED MISSILES
see also Ballistic Missiles
also names of specific missiles
Bellany, Ian & Blacker, Coit D., eds. Antiballistic Missile Defence in the 1980s. 200p. 1983. text ed. 30.00 (ISBN 0-7146-3207-4, F Cass Co). Biblio Dist.
Betts, Richard. Cruise Missiles & U. S. Policy. LC 82-72704. 61p. 1982. pap. 5.95 (ISBN 0-8157-0933-1). Brookings.
Kennedy, Gregory P. Vengeance Weapon 2: The V-2 Guided Missile. (Illus.). 144p. 1983. pap. text ed. 9.95x (ISBN 0-87474-573-X). Smithsonian.
GUIDED MISSILES–JUVENILE LITERATURE
Cave, Ron & Cave, Joyce. What About... Missiles. (What About Ser.). (Illus.). 32p. (gr. k-3). 1983. PLB 7.90 (ISBN 0-531-03469-0). Watts.
GUILLAUMIN, JEAN BAPTISTE ARMAND, 1841-1927
Marshall, Peter. Jean Baptiste Anteine Guillemet Eighteen Hundred Forty-One to Nineteen Hundred Eighteen. (Illus.). 63p. 1983. 20.00 (ISBN 0-8390-0303-X). Allanheld & Schram.
GUINEA-PIGS
Denham, Ken. Guinea Pigs & Chinchillas. (Illus.). 93p. 1977. pap. 3.95 (ISBN 0-7028-1075-4). Avian Pubns.
Guinea Pigs. (Pet Care Ser.). 1983. pap. 3.95 (ISBN 0-8120-2629-2). Barron.
GUITAR
Martin, Will. Everybody's Guitar Manual: How to Buy, Maintain & Repair an Acoustic Guitar. (Illus.). 96p. (Orig.). 1983. pap. 7.50 (ISBN 0-912528-30-3). John Muir.
GUITAR–INSTRUCTION AND STUDY
Doubtfire, Stanley. Make Your Own Classical Guitar. LC 82-16860. (Illus.). 128p. 1983. Repr. of 1981 ed. 17.95 (ISBN 0-8052-3833-6). Schocken.
Green Note Music Publications Staff. Improvising Blues Guitar, Vol. 3. (Guitar Transcription Ser.). 1982. pap. 7.95 (ISBN 0-912910-12-7). Green Note Music.
--Improvising Rock Guitar, Vol. 4. (Guitar Transcription Ser.). 1982. pap. 7.95 (ISBN 0-912910-13-5). Green Note Music.
Hamann, Donald L. Introduction to the Classical Guitar: An Ensemble Approach for the Classroom. LC 82-16100. (Illus.). 148p. (Orig.). 1983. lib. bdg. 19.75 (ISBN 0-8191-2758-2); pap. text ed. 8.25 (ISBN 0-8191-2759-0). U Pr of Amer.
Silverman, Jerry. How to Play Better Guitar. LC 79-180109. pap. 7.95 (ISBN 0-385-00579-2). Doubleday.
GUJRI LANGUAGE
see Urdu Language
GULF STATES
The Gulf States. 1981. 375.00x (ISBN 0-686-99852-9, Pub. by Metra England). State Mutual Bk.
GUM ELASTIC
see Rubber
GUMS AND RESINS
Ash, M. & Ash, I. Encyclopedia of Plastics, Polymers & Resins Vol. 1, A-G. 1981. 75.00 (ISBN 0-8206-0290-6). Chem Pub.
--Encyclopedia of Plastics, Polymers & Resins Vol. 2, H-P. 1982. 75.00 (ISBN 0-8206-0296-5). Chem Pub.
--Encyclopedia of Plastics, Polymers & Resins Vol. 3, Q-Z. 1983. 75.00 (ISBN 0-8206-0303-1). Chem Pub.
Davidson, R. L. Handbook of Water-Soluble Gums & Resins. 1980. 47.75 (ISBN 0-07-015471-6). McGraw.
GUN CONTROL
see Firearms–Laws and Regulations
GUN DOGS
see Hunting Dogs
GUNITE
Ryan, T. F. Gunite, a Handbook for Engineers. 1973. pap. 14.50 (ISBN 0-7210-0820-8). Scholium Intl.
GUNNING
see Hunting
GUNS
see Firearms; Rifles; Shot-Guns
GUNSHOT WOUNDS
American Health Research Institute, Ltd. Gunshot Wounds in Crime & Medicine: A Medical Subject Analysis & Research Index With Bibliography. Bartone, John C., ed. 120p. 1983. 29.95 (ISBN 0-941864-82-0); pap. 21.95 (ISBN 0-941864-83-9). ABBE Pubs Assn.
GUNSMITHING
Irwin, John R. Guns & Gunmaking Tools of Southern Appalachia. 2nd ed. (Illus.). 120p. 1983. pap. 9.95 (ISBN 0-916838-81-1). Schiffer.
Shelsby, Earl, ed. NRA Gunsmithing Guide: Updated. rev. ed. (Illus.). 336p. (Orig.). 1980. pap. text ed. 11.95 (ISBN 0-935998-47-0). Natl Rifle Assn.
GUNTER'S LINE
see Slide-Rule
GURDJIEFF, GEORGE IVANOVITCH, 1872-1949
Ridley, Gustave. From Boredom to Bliss. Campbell, Jean, ed. (Illus.). 24p. (Orig.). 1983. pap. 6.95 (ISBN 0-9610544-0-9). Harmonious Pr.
GURJARI LANGUAGE
see Urdu Language
GUYANA
Braveboy-Wagner, Jacqueline A. The Venezuela-Guyana Border Dispute: Britain's Colonial Legacy in Latin America. (Replica Edition Ser.). 200p. 1983. softcover 20.00x (ISBN 0-86531-953-7). Westview.
GYMNASIUMS
Dietrich, John & Waggoner, Susan. The Complete Health Club Handbook. (Orig.). 1983. pap. price not set (ISBN 0-671-47027-2). S&S.
GYMNASTICS
see also Exercise; Gymnastics for Women; Physical Education and Training; Schools–Exercises and Recreations
Brown, James R. & Wardell, David B. Teaching & Coaching Gymnastics for Men & Women. 441p. 1980. text ed. 23.95x (ISBN 0-471-10798-0). Wiley.
Smith, Tony. Gymnastics: A Mechanical Understanding. (Illus.). 192p. 1983. text ed. 15.00 (ISBN 0-8419-0829-X). Holmes & Meier.
GYMNASTICS–JUVENILE LITERATURE
Traetta, John & Traetta, MaryJean. Gymnastics Basics. (Illus.). 48p. (ps-7). 1983. pap. 3.95 (ISBN 0-13-371740-2). P-H.
GYMNASTICS–STUDY AND TEACHING
Holbrook, Jennifer K. Gymnastics: A Movement Activity. 116p. 1975. 29.00 (ISBN 0-7121-0717-7, Pub. by Macdonald & Evans). State Mutual Bk.
GYMNASTICS, MEDICAL
see Exercise Therapy
GYMNASTICS FOR WOMEN
Brown, James R. & Wardell, David B. Teaching & Coaching Gymnastics for Men & Women. 441p. 1980. text ed. 23.95x (ISBN 0-471-10798-0). Wiley.
Sands, William A. Modern Women's Gymnastics. (Illus.). 104p. (Orig.). 1983. pap. 6.95 (ISBN 0-8069-7686-1). Sterling.
GYNECOLOGIC ENDOCRINOLOGY
see Endocrine Gynecology
GYNECOLOGIC NURSING
Sonstegard, Lois, ed. Women's Health: Ambulatory Care, Vol. 1. 368p. 1982. 24.50 (ISBN 0-8089-1501-0). Grune.
GYNECOLOGY
see also Endocrine Gynecology; Gynecologic Nursing; Women–Diseases
Benson, Ralph C., ed. Current Obstetric & Gynecologic Diagnosis & Treatment. 4th ed. 1050p. 1982. 25.00 (ISBN 0-87041-213-2). Lange.
Bongiovanni, Alfred M., ed. Adolescent Gynecology: A Guide for Clinicians. 275p. 1983. 32.50x (ISBN 0-306-41203-9, Plenum Pr). Plenum Pub.
Clayton, Stanley & Lewis, T. L. Gynecology by Ten Teachers. 396p. 1981. pap. text ed. 19.50 (ISBN 0-7131-4394-0). E Arnold.
Dreher, E., ed. Schweizerische Gesellschaft fuer Gynaekologie und Geburtshilfe unter Mitkirkung der Schweizerischen Gesellschaft fuer. Medizinische Genetik. Bericht ueber die Jahresversammlung, Zuerich, 1982. (Journal-Gynaekologische Rundschau: Vol. 22, Suppl. 3). (Illus.). iv, 104p. 1983. pap. 23.50 (ISBN 3-8055-3656-9). S Karger.
Gitsch, E. & Reinold, E., eds. Jahrestagung der Oesterreichischen Gesellschaft fuer Gynaekologie und Geburtshilfe, Bad Ischl, Juni 1982. (Journal: Gynaekologische Rundschau: Vol. 22, Supplement 1). (Illus.). vi, 190p. 1982. pap. 30.00 (ISBN 3-8055-3625-9). S Karger.
Hale, Ralph W. & Krieger, John A. Concise Textbook of Gynecology. (Concise Textbook Ser.). 1982. pap. text ed. 21.00 (ISBN 0-87488-585-X). Med Exam.
Hibbard, Lester T. & Gibbons, William. Handbook of Gynecologic Emergencies. 2nd ed. 1982. pap. 13.95 (ISBN 0-87488-640-6). Med Exam.
Huang, C. L. & Daniels, V. G., eds. Companion to Gynaecology. (Companion Ser.). 120p. 1982. text ed. 18.00 (ISBN 0-85200-379-X, Pub. by MTP Pr England). Kluwer Boston.
Pitkin, Roy M., ed. Year Book of Obstetrics & Gynecology 1983. 1983. 35.00 (ISBN 0-8151-6692-3). Year Bk Med.
Ruettgers, H., ed. Trichomoniasis. (Journal: Gynaekologische Rundschau: Vol. 22, Supplement 2). (Illus.). iv, 88p. 1983. pap. 17.00 (ISBN 3-8055-3646-1). S Karger.
Saik, Richard P. Vagotomy Testing. LC 82-83471. (Illus.). 176p. 1983. monograph 22.50 (ISBN 0-87993-189-2). Futura Pub.
Sheppard, Bruce D. & Sheppard, Carroll A. The Complete Guide to Women's Health. LC 82-14802. (Illus.). 421p. 1982. 19.95 (ISBN 0-936166-07-X). Mariner Pub.
Ulmsten, U., ed. Female Stress Incontinence. (Contributions to Gynecology & Obstetrics: Vol. 10). (Illus.). viii, 120p. 1983. pap. 57.50 (ISBN 3-8055-3665-8). S Karger.
Vontver, Louis A. Obstetrics & Gynecology Review. 3rd ed. LC 82-8773. (Illus.). 320p. 1983. pap. text ed. 10.00 (ISBN 0-668-05484-0, 5484). Arco.
Willson, J. Robert & Carrington, Elsie R. Obstetrics & Gynecology. 7th ed. (Illus.). 800p. 1983. text ed. 39.95 (ISBN 0-8016-5597-8). Mosby.
Wynn, Ralpf M. Obstetrics & Gynecology. 3rd ed. LC 82-20879. (Illus.). 310p. 1982. text ed. write for info. (ISBN 0-8121-0875-2). Lea & Febiger.
GYNECOLOGY, OPERATIVE
Nichols, David H. Clinical Problems, Injuries & Complications of Gynecologic Surgery. (Illus.). 300p. 1983. lib. bdg. write for info. (ISBN 0-683-06495-9). Williams & Wilkins.
Schwartz, Ronald O. Common Female Problems & their Surgical Correction: Facts for Men & Women. LC 82-11248. (Illus.). 96p. (Orig.). Date not set. pap. text ed. 2.95 (ISBN 0-9609222-0-2). Med-Ed.
GYPSIES
see Gipsies
GYRODYNAMICS
see Rotational Motion
GYROPLANES
see Autogiros

H

HABIT
see also Instinct
Levison, Peter K. & Gerstein, Dean R., eds. Commonalities in Substance Abuse & Habitual Behavior. LC 82-48537. 384p. 1983. 33.95x (ISBN 0-669-06293-6). Lexington Bks.
HABITS OF ANIMALS
see Animals, Habits and Behavior Of
HADES
see Future Life; Hell
HADRONS
Leader, Elliot & Predazzi, Enrico. An Introduction to Gauge Theories & the "New Physics". LC 81-3860. (Illus.). 400p. 1982. 65.00 (ISBN 0-521-23375-5); pap. 27.50 (ISBN 0-521-29937-3). Cambridge U Pr.
Mukunda, N., et al. Relativistic Models of Extended Hadrons Obeying a Mas-Spin Trajectory Constraint. (Lecture Notes in Physics: Vol. 165). 163p. 1983. pap. 8.50 (ISBN 0-387-11586-2). Springer-Verlag.
HAECKEL, ERNST HEINRICH PHILIPP AUGUST, 1834-1919
DeGrood, David. Haeckel's Theory of the Unity of Nature. (Praxis: Vol.8). 100p. 1982. pap. text ed. 11.50x (ISBN 90-6032-216-9). Humanities.
HAEMOSTASIS
see Hemostasis
HAENDEL, GEORG FRIEDRICH, 1685-1759
Hayward, Christopher. Handel: His Life & Times. (Midas Composer's Life & Times Ser.). (Illus.). 150p. (gr. 7 up). 1983. 16.95 (ISBN 0-88254-807-7). Hippocrene Bks.
HAIKU
Henderson, Harold G., tr. An Introduction to Haiku: An Anthology of Poems & Poets from Basho to Shiki. (Anchor Literary Library). 1983. pap. 4.95 (ISBN 0-686-42703-3, Anch). Doubleday.
Zolbrod, Leon M. Haiku Painting. LC 82-48792. (Great Japanese Art Ser.). (Illus.). 48p. 1983. 18.95 (ISBN 0-87011-560-X). Kodansha.
HAIKU–HISTORY AND CRITICISM
Sato, Hirosaki. One Hundred Frogs: From Renga to Haiku to English. LC 82-17505. (Illus.). 300p. 1983. pap. 14.95 (ISBN 0-8348-0176-0). Weatherhill.
HAIR
see also Wigs and Wigmakers
Huffaker, Sandy. The Bald Book: Miracle Cures & More. (Illus.). 64p. 1983. pap. 3.95 (ISBN 0-87131-401-0). M Evans.
Michael, George & Lindsay, Ray. George Michael's Complete Hair Program for Men. LC 82-45114. (Illus.). 192p. 1983. 14.95 (ISBN 0-385-17450-0). Doubleday.
Ortonne, Jean-Paul & Mosher, David B. Vitiligo & Other Hypomelanoses of Hair & Skin. (Topics in Dermatology Ser.). 680p. 1983. 79.50x (ISBN 0-306-40974-7, Plenum Med Bk). Plenum Pub.
Passwater, Richard. Hair Analysis. 1982. 10.95x (ISBN 0-686-37942-X). Cancer Control Soc.
HAIR–DISEASES
see also Baldness
Salter, Mary & Sturtivant, Doreen. Health for Hairdressers: Notes for Hairdressing Students & Apprentices. 144p. 1981. pap. 25.00x (ISBN 0-291-39613-5, Pub. by Tech Pr). State Mutual Bk.
HAIRDRESSING
see also Costume
Jeremiah, Rosemary W. How You Can Make Money in the Hairdressing Business. 112p. 1982. 29.00x (ISBN 0-85950-330-5, Pub. by Thornes England). State Mutual Bk.
Mayhew, John. Hair Techniques & Alternatives to Baldness. (Illus.). 250p. 1983. 29.95 (ISBN 0-932426-25-5). Trado-Medic.
Palladino, Leo & Perry, John. Hairdressing Management. 352p. 1982. 40.00x (ISBN 0-85950-338-0, Pub. by Thornes England). State Mutual Bk.
Salter, Mary & Sturtivant, Doreen. Health for Hairdressers: Notes for Hairdressing Students & Apprentices. 144p. 1981. pap. 25.00x (ISBN 0-291-39613-5, Pub. by Tech Pr). State Mutual Bk.
HAITI
Price-Mars, Jean. So Spoke the Uncle. Shannon, Magdaline W., tr. from Fr. (Illus.). 240p. 1983. 16.00x (ISBN 0-89410-389-X); pap. 7.00x (ISBN 0-89410-390-3). Three Continents.
Vibrancy or the Weight of Inertia: A Testimonial to Haitian Original Creative Expression Across Endogenous or Exogenous Constraints. 14p. 1982. pap. 5.00 (ISBN 92-808-0270-4, TUNU 200, UNU). Unipub.
HALACHA
see Jewish Law; Talmud
HALITE
see Salt
HALLOWEEN
Herda, D. J. Halloween. (First Bks.). (Illus.). 72p. (gr. 4 up). 1983. PLB 8.90 (ISBN 0-531-04527-7). Watts.
Strand, Julie & Boggs, Juanita. Sing a Song of Halloween: With Communication, Arts & Nutrition Activities. (Illus.). 133p. 1982. pap. text ed. 10.95 (ISBN 0-910817-00-6). Collaborative Learn.
Walker, Mark. The Great Halloween Book. LC 82-184276. (Illus.). 160p. 1983. pap. 6.95 (ISBN 0-89709-038-1). Liberty Pub.
HALLUCINOGENIC DRUGS
Stafford, Peter. Psychedelics Encyclopedia. (Illus.). 400p. 1982. pap. 12.95 (ISBN 0-87477-231-1). J P Tarcher.
HALOPHYTES
Sen, D. N. Contributions to the Ecology of Halophytes. 1982. 69.50 (ISBN 90-6193-942-9, Pub. by Junk Pubs Netherlands). Kluwer Boston.
HAMBURGER
see Cookery (Beef)
HAMMARSKJOLD, DAG HJALMAR AGNE CARL, 1905-1961
Hammarskjold, Dag. Markings. (Epiphany Bks.). 1983. pap. 2.95 (ISBN 0-345-30699-6). Ballantine.
HAMMERED STRINGED INSTRUMENTS
see Stringed Instruments
HAMMETT, DASHIELL, 1894-1961
Nolan, William F. Dashiell Hammett: A Life on the Edge. 1983. price not set. Congdon & Weed.
--Hammett: A Life at the Edge. (Illus.). 288p. 1983. 14.95 (ISBN 0-312-92281-7). Congdon & Weed.
HAMPSHIRE, ENGLAND–DESCRIPTION AND TRAVEL
Innes, Kathleen E. Hampshire Pilgrimages: Men & Women Who Have Sojourned in Hampshire (Jane Austen, Charlotte Mary Yonge, William Cobbett. 60p. 1982. Repr. of 1982 ed. lib. bdg. 40.00 (ISBN 0-89984-927-X). Century Bookbindery.
HAMSTERS
Ostrow, Marshall. Breeding Hamsters. (Illus.). 96p. 1982. 4.95 (ISBN 0-87666-935-6, KW-134). TFH Pubns.
Smith, K. W. Hamsters & Gerbils. (Illus.). 93p. 1977. pap. 3.95 (ISBN 0-7028-1082-7). Avian Pubns.
HAND–WOUNDS AND INJURIES
Sandzen, S. C. Color Atlas of Acute Hand Injuries. 1980. 115.00 (ISBN 0-07-054671-1). McGraw.
HAND SHADOWS
see Shadow-Pictures
HAND-TO-HAND FIGHTING
see also Self-Defense
Aoki, Hiroyuki. Shintaido, a New Art of Movement & Life Expression. Thompson, Michael & Ito, Haruyoshi, trs. from Japanese. LC 82-80496. (Illus.). 120p. 1982. pap. 8.95 (ISBN 0-942634-00-4). Shintaido.
Chong, Jun. Kicking Strategy: The Art of Korean Sparring. LC 82-83443. (Illus.). 99p. (Orig.). 1983. pap. 5.95 (ISBN 0-86568-037-X, 351). Unique Pubns.
Croucher, Michael & Reid, Howard. The Fighting Arts. (Illus.). 1983. price not set (ISBN 0-671-47158-9). S&S.
Herbert, Anthony B. A Military Manual of Self Defense: A Complete Guide to Hand-to-Hand Combat. (Illus.). 280p. 1983. 19.95 (ISBN 0-88254-708-9). Hippocrene Bks.
Kim, Ashida. Ninja Death Touch. (Illus.). 108p. 1982. pap. 10.00 (ISBN 0-87364-257-0). Paladin Ent.
Sang Kyu Shim. The Making of a Martial Artist. (Illus.). 1980. 9.95 (ISBN 0-942062-01-9); pap. 6.95 (ISBN 0-942062-02-7). S K Shim Pub.
HAND WEAVING
Bogdonoff, Nancy D., ed. Handwoven Textiles of Early New England. LC 75-5582. (Illus.). 192p. 1975. pap. 9.95 (ISBN 0-8117-2069-1). Stackpole.
Sutton, Ann. The Structure of Weaving. LC 82-84398. (Illus.). 192p. 1983. 27.95 (ISBN 0-937274-08-9). Lark Bks.

HANDBALL
see also Racquetball
Leve, Mort & Lewis, Fred. Percentage Handball. LC 82-83942. 160p. (Orig.). 1983. pap. 7.95 (ISBN 0-88011-111-9). Leisure Pr.

HANDBOOKS, VADE-MECUMS, ETC.
see also Recipes;
also subdivision Handbooks, Manuals, etc. under subjects
Doyle, A. Self-Sufficiency & Back to Basics Workbook. 60p. Date not set. 9.95 (ISBN 0-939476-81-9). Biblio Pr GA.
Doyle, A. C. Self-Sufficiency Workbook. 50p. 1983. 10.95 (ISBN 0-939476-77-0). Biblio Pr GA.
Frost, David & Deakin, Michael. David Frost's Book of the World's Worst Decisions. (Illus.). 1983. 9.95 (ISBN 0-517-54977-8). Crown.

HANDEL, GEORG FRIEDRICH, 1685-1759
see Haendel, Georg Friedrich, 1685-1759

HANDICAPPED
see also Disability Evaluation; Mentally Handicapped; Physical Education for Handicapped Persons; Physically Handicapped; Sick
Darnbrough, A. & Kinrade, F. Directory for the Disabled: A Handbook of Information & Opportunities for Disabled & Handicapped People. X ed. 242p. 1981. pap. text ed. 15.00 (ISBN 0-85941-184-2). Verry.
Greer, John G. & Anderson, Robert M. Strategies for Helping Severely & Multiply Handicapped Citizens. (Illus.). 448p. 1982. text ed. 18.95 (ISBN 0-8391-1692-6, 16918). Univ Park.
Howell, Kenneth. Working with the Handicapped. 250p. 1983. pap. text ed. 8.95 (ISBN 0-675-20050-4). Merrill.
Lange, Brian M. & Entwistle, Beverly M. Dental Management of the Handicapped & Approaches for Dental Auxiliaries. (Illus.). 150p. 1982. text ed. write for info. (ISBN 0-8121-0884-1). Lea & Febiger.
Office of Technical Assessment, Congress of the U. S. Technology & Handicapped People. 1983. text ed. price not set (ISBN 0-8261-4510-8). Springer Pub.
Pensis, Nancy T. & Maloney, Mary Ann. Mealtimes for People with Handicaps: A Guide for Parents, Paraprofessionals, & Allied Health Professionals. 142p. 1983. pap. text ed. write for info. (ISBN 0-398-04819-3). C C Thomas.
Polak, J. B. & Hupkes, G., eds. Vervoer Voor Gehandicapten: Illusie of Realiteit? 340p. (Dutch.). pap. 17.50x (ISBN 90-70176-62-9). Foris Pubns.
Raviv, J., ed. Uses of Computers in Aiding the Disabled: Proceedings of the IFIP-IMIA Working Conference, Haifa, Israel, November 3-5, 1981. 446p. 1982. 55.50 (ISBN 0-444-86436-9, North Holland). Elsevier.
Rudman, Jack. Developmental Disabilities Program Aide. (Career Examination Ser.: C-864). (Cloth bdg. avail. on request). pap. 10.00 (ISBN 0-8373-0864-X). Natl Learning.
Schroedel, John G. Attitudes Toward Persons With Disabilities: A Compendium of Related Literature. LC 78-62049. 182p. 1978. 8.25 (ISBN 0-686-38794-5). Human Res Ctr.
Seidl, Frederick & Applebaum, Robert. Delivering In-Home Services to the Aged & Disabled: The Wisconsin Experiment. LC 81-48068. (Illus.). 1983. write for info. (ISBN 0-669-05243-4). Lexington Bks.
Valletutti, J. & Bender, Michael. Teaching Interpersonal & Community Living Skills: A Curriculum Model for Handicapped Adolescents & Adults. 288p. 1982. pap. text ed. 19.95 (ISBN 0-8391-1748-5, 18341). Univ Park.
Yuker, Harold E. & Block, J. Richard. Challenging Barriers to Change: Attitudes Towards the Disabled. LC 79-84738. 68p. 1979. 4.75 (ISBN 0-686-42976-1). Human res Ctr.

HANDICAPPED–BIOGRAPHY
Brightman, Alan J., ed. Negotiating the Mainstream: Personal Accounts of the Disabled Experience in Contemporary Society. (Illus.). 1983. pap. text ed. price not set (ISBN 0-8391-1791-4, 17981). Univ Park.
Woodall, Corbett. Disjointed Life. 1980. pap. 9.95 (ISBN 0-434-87796-4, Pub. by Heinemann). David & Charles.

HANDICAPPED–EDUCATION
Cohen, James S. & Stieglitz, Maria N. Career Education For Physically Disabled Students: Classroom Business Ventures. LC 79-91614. (Illus.). 50p. 1980. 5.00 (ISBN 0-686-38798-8). Human Res Ctr.
Fiscus, Edward D. & Mandell, Colleen J. Developing Individualized Education Programs (IEP) (Illus.). 350p. 1983. pap. text ed. 9.95 (ISBN 0-314-69648-2); write for info. instr's. manual (ISBN 0-314-72292-0). West Pub.
Jowett, S. Young Disabled People: Their Further Education, Training & Employment. 148p. 1982. pap. text ed. 15.25x (ISBN 0-7005-0508-3, NFER). Humanities.
Mount, Marianne & Shea, Victoria. How to Arrange the Environment to Stimulate and Teach Pre-Language Skills in the Severley Handicapped. 1982. pap. 3.95 (ISBN 0-686-84109-3). H & H Ent.
--How to Recognize & Assess Pre-Language Skills in the Severely Handicapped. 1982. pap. 3.95 (ISBN 0-89079-070-1). H & H Ent.
Palmer, John T. Career Education For Physically Disabled Students: Development As A Lifetime Activity. LC 80-82642. 64p. 1980. 6.50 (ISBN 0-686-38799-6). Human Res Ctr.
Reams, Bernard D., Jr., ed. Education of the Handicapped: Legislative Histories & Administrative Documents, V.1-55, 55. LC 82-81360. (Legislative Histories of the Law of the Handicapped Ser.: Part two). 1982. lib. bdg. 1925.00x (ISBN 0-89941-157-6). W S Hein.
Sailor & Guess. Severely Handicapped Students: An Instructional Design. 1982. text ed. 24.95 (ISBN 0-686-84566-8). HM.
Snell, Martha E. Systematic Instruction of the Moderately & Severely Handicapped. 2nd ed. 550p. (pb). 1983. pap. 23.95 (ISBN 0-675-20035-0). Merrill.
Stieglitz, Maria. Career Education For Physically Disabled Students: Career Awareness Curriculum. LC 80-83986. (Illus.). 100p. (gr. k-8). 1981. 9.75 (ISBN 0-686-38797-X). Human Res Ctr.
--Career Education For Physically Disabled Students: Self-Concept Curriculum. LC 80-82643. (Illus.). 96p. (gr. k-3). 1981. 9.75 (ISBN 0-686-38800-3). Human Res Ctr.
Stieglitz, Maria & Cohen, James S. Career Education For Physically Disabled Students: Speaker's Bureau. LC 79-93340. (Illus.). 62p. 1980. 6.50 (ISBN 0-686-38801-1). Human Res Ctr.

HANDICAPPED–EMPLOYMENT
Bozza, Linda. Ready, Willing & Able: What You Should Know About Workers With Disabilities. Lindberg, Charles A., ed. LC 79-118229. (Illus.). 44p. 1979. 3.25 (ISBN 0-686-42977-X). Humana.
Co-operatives for the Disabled: Organisation & Development. iii, 230p. 1981. 5.70 (ISBN 92-2-101929-2). Intl Labour Office.
Desmond, Margaret G. Modifying the Work Environment for the Physically Disabled: An Accessibility Checklist for Employers. LC 80-83500. (Illus.). 128p. 1981. 8.95 (ISBN 0-686-38822-4). Human Res Ctr.
Jacobsen, Richard J. & Avellani, Pamela B. A Review of Placement Services Within a Comprehensive Rehabilitation Framework: Survey Report. LC 78-72067. 76p. 1978. 8.25 (ISBN 0-686-38818-6). Human Res Ctr.
Jowett, S. Young Disabled People: Their Further Education, Training & Employment. 148p. 1982. pap. text ed. 15.25x (ISBN 0-7005-0508-3, NFER). Humanities.
Lewis, Adele & Marks, Edith. Job Hunting for the Disabled. 1983. pap. 7.95 (ISBN 0-8120-2487-7). Barron.
McCarthy, Henry & Smart, Lana. Affirmative Action in Action: Strategies for Enchancing Employment Prospects of Qualified Handicapped Individuals. LC 79-90291. 40p. 1979. 3.75 (ISBN 0-686-38808-9). Human Res Ctr.
Modifying the Work Environment for the Physically Disabled Employee, 2 pts. Incl. Pt. 1. Washam, Veronica; Pt. 2. Desmond, Margaret G. (Illus.). 128p. 1981. 16.00 set (ISBN 0-686-38823-2). Human Res Ctr.
Schroedel, John G. & Jacobsen, Richard J. Employer Attitudes Towards Hiring Persons With Disabilities: A Labor Market Research Model. LC 78-70971. 60p. 1978. 5.75 (ISBN 0-686-42975-3). Human Res Ctr.
Smart, Lana. Recruiting Qualified Disabled Workers: An Employer's Directory to Placement Services in the Greater New York Area. LC 79-92836. 160p. 1980. 5.59 (ISBN 0-686-38817-8). Human Res Ctr.
Smart, Lana, compiled by. Recruting Qualified Disabled Workers: An Employer's Directory to Placement Services in the Greater New York Area. LC 79-92836. 160p. 1980. 5.95 (ISBN 0-686-38815-1). Human Res Ctr.
Stieglitz, Maria N. & Cohen, James S. Career Education For Physically Disabled Students: A Bibliography. LC 79-89057. 152p. 1980. 11.25 (ISBN 0-686-42978-8). Human Res Ctr.
Vandergoot, David & Swirsky, Jessica. A Review of Placement Services Within a Comprehensive Rehabilitation Framework: Technical Report. LC 78-72067. 60p. 1979. 5.25 (ISBN 0-686-38819-4). Human Res Ctr.
Veatch, Deborah. How to Get the Job you Really Want. 174p. 1982. pap. text ed. 10.95x (ISBN 0-913072-50-8). Natl Assn Deaf.
Walker, Alan. Unqualified & Underemployed: Handicapped Young People & the Labour Market. 240p. 1981. 39.00x (ISBN 0-333-32189-8, Pub. by Macmillan England). State Mutual Bk.

HANDICAPPED–RECREATION
Croucher, N. Outdoor Pursuits for Disabled People. 180p. 1981. pap. text ed. 13.00x (ISBN 0-85941-186-9). Verry.
Fairchild, Effie L. & Neal, Larry L., eds. Common-Unity in the Community: A Forward-Looking Program of Recreation & Leisure Service for the Handicapped. 114p. 1975. pap. 4.50 (ISBN 0-686-84031-3). U OR Ctr Leisure.
Fe, Lu. God Bless Our HUD Home: Downtowner Congregate Housing. 1983. 7.95 (ISBN 0-533-05597-0). Vantage.
Focus on Dance: Vol. 9 Dance for the Handicapped. 104p. 8.25 (ISBN 0-88314-071-3). AAHPERD.
Hedley, Eugene. Boating For the Handicapped: Guidelines for the Physically Handicapped. LC 79-91181. (Illus.). 124p. 1979. 5.65 (ISBN 0-686-38820-8). Human Res Ctr.
Weller, B. Helping Sick Children Play. 1982. 25.00x (ISBN 0-7020-0792-7, Pub. by Cassell England). State Mutual Bk.

HANDICAPPED–REHABILITATION
see Rehabilitation; Vocational Rehabilitation

HANDICAPPED CHILDREN
see also Aphasia; Brain-Damaged Children; Mentally Handicapped Children; Physically Handicapped Children
Bentley, John E. Problem Children: An Introduction to the Study of Handicapped Children in the Light of Their Psychological & Social Status. 437p. 1982. Repr. of 1936 ed. lib. bdg. 40.00 (ISBN 0-89760-094-0). Telegraph Bks.
Cox, T. Disadvantaged Eleven Year Olds. 140p. 1983. 18.90 (ISBN 0-08-028911-8). Pergamon.
Froman, Katherine. Chance to Grow. 1983. 13.95 (ISBN 0-89696-192-3). Dodd.
--The Chance to Grow. 224p. 1983. 13.95 (ISBN 0-89696-192-3). Everest Hse.
Goldberg, Steven S. Special Education Law: A Guide for Parents, Advocates, & Educators. (Critical Topics in Law & Society). 244p. 1982. 24.50x (ISBN 0-306-40848-1, Plenum Pr). Plenum Pub.
Hawkins, Robert P. & McGinnis, Lyn D. The School & Home Enrichment Program for Severely Handicapped Children. 350p. 1983. price not set (ISBN 0-87822-297-9). Res Press.
Keele, Doman K. The Developmentally Disabled Child: A Manual for Primary Physicians. (Illus.). 250p. 1983. text ed. 19.95 (ISBN 0-87489-271-6). Med Economics.
Michaelis, Carol T. Coping with Handicapped Infants & Children: A Handbook for Parents & Professionals. (Illus.). 1983. pap. text ed. price not set (ISBN 0-8391-1598-9, 17663). Univ Park.
Newson, Elizabeth & Hipgrave, Tony. Getting Through to Your Handicapped Child: A Handbook for Parents, Foster-Parents, Teachers & Anyone Caring for Handicapped Children. LC 82-4310. 144p. 1983. pap. 7.95 (ISBN 0-521-27056-1). Cambridge U Pr.
Paul, James L., ed. The Exceptional Child: A Guidebook for Churches & Community Agencies. LC 82-16914. 176p. text ed. 22.00x (ISBN 0-8156-2287-2); pap. text ed. 12.95x (ISBN 0-8156-2288-0). Syracuse U Pr.
Schwede, Olga. An Early Childhood Activity Program for Handicapped Children. 1977. pap. 7.95 (ISBN 0-914420-59-3). Exceptional Pr Inc.
Seligman, Milton. A Guide to Understanding & Treating the Family with a Handicapped Child. write for info (ISBN 0-8089-1561-4). Grune.
Wheeler, Bonnie. Challenged Parenting: A Practical Handbook for Parents of Children with Handicaps. 210p. 1983. pap. 6.95 (ISBN 0-8307-0835-9, 5316502). Regal.

HANDICAPPED CHILDREN–EDUCATION
Garwood, S. Gray. Educating Young Handicapped Children. 2nd ed. 1983. write for info. (ISBN 0-89443-929-4). Aspen Systems.
Meier, Marie. The Development & Evaluation of A Pre-School Curriculum For Severely Disabled Children. 44p. 1970. 1.50 (ISBN 0-686-38802-X). Human Res Ctr.
Sailor, Wayne & Guess, Doug. Severely Handicapped Students: An Instructional design. LC 82-83289. 448p. 1982. text ed. 24.95 (ISBN 0-395-32788-1). HM.
Seligman, Milton. A Guide to Understanding & Treating the Family with a Handicapped Child. write for info (ISBN 0-8089-1561-4). Grune.

HANDICAPPED CHILDREN–REHABILITATION
Moore, Gary T. & Cohen, U. Designing Environments for Handicapped Children: A Design Guide & Case Study. LC 79-89670. 1979. write for info. U of Wis Ctr Arch-Urban.

HANDICAPPING
see Horse Race Betting

HANDICRAFT
see also Artisans; Basket Making; Beadwork; Bookbinding; China Painting; Creative Activities and Seatwork; Decoration and Ornament; Design, Decorative; Embroidery; Enamel and Enameling; Folk Art; Furniture; Glass Painting and Staining; Illumination of Books and Manuscripts; Industrial Arts; Jewelry; Lace and Lace Making; Leather Work; Metal-Work; Models and Modelmaking; Mosaics; Mural Painting and Decoration; Needlework; Occupational Therapy; Occupations; Paper Work; Pottery; Pottery Craft; Stencil Work; Wood-Carving
Baldwin, Ed & Baldwin, Stevie. Scrap Fabric Crafts. (Illus.). 160p. 1982. pap. 7.95 (ISBN 0-89586-168-2). H P Bks.
Boyles, Margaret. Margaret Boyles' Craft Designs for Babies. 1983. write for info (ISBN 0-671-43902-2). S&S.
Brokering, L. Thirty Six Creative Ideas for Children in the Church School. LC 12-2958. 1982. pap. 4.50 (ISBN 0-570-03865-0). Concordia.
Buck, Peter. Arts & Crafts of Hawaii: Index, Sec. XIV. (Special Publication Ser.: No. 45). 19p. 1957. pap. 1.50 (ISBN 0-910240-47-7). Bishop Mus.
--Arts & Crafts of Hawaii: Ornaments & Personal Adornment, Sec. XII. (Special Publication Ser.: No. 45). (Illus.). 40p. 1957. pap. 3.50 (ISBN 0-910240-45-0). Bishop Mus.
Bumbalough, Marine. Puppet Pillows. (Illus.). 18p. 1982. pap. 4.00 (ISBN 0-943574-13-7). That Patchwork.
Burdette, Kay. Fabric Painting in Tole, Bk. 1. (Illus., Orig.). 1982. pap. 7.95 (ISBN 0-941284-16-6). Deco Design Studio.
Center for Self Sufficiency Research Division Staff. Guide to Craft, Quilt, Drapery, Etc. Pattern Sources. 35p. 1983. pap. text ed. 15.95 (ISBN 0-910811-31-8). Center Self.
Center for Self-Sufficiency Research Division. Made from Scratch: A Reference on Cooking, Crafts, etc. 50p. Date not set. pap. text ed. 14.95 (ISBN 0-910811-07-5). Center Self.
Doyle, Alfreda. How to Make Simple Potpourri to Give as Gifts. 35p. 1983. pap. 7.95 (ISBN 0-939476-61-4). Biblio Pr GA.
Espejel, Carlos. Mexican Folk Crafts. (Illus.). 237p. 1982. 35.00 (ISBN 84-7031-058-5, Pub. by Editorial Blume Spain). Intl Schol Bk Serv.
Evrard, Gwen. Homespun Crafts from Scraps. (Illus.). 168p. 1983. 17.95 (ISBN 0-8329-0253-5). New Century.
Friend, Diane & Nicholson, Dale. Bridal Sewing & Crafts. (Illus.). 72p. 1983. pap. 2.50 (ISBN 0-918178-31-2). Simplicity.
Fry, Eric C. The Book of Knots & Ropework: Practical & Decorative. (Illus.). 176p. 1983. 10.95 (ISBN 0-517-54885-2); pap. 4.95 (ISBN 0-517-54886-0). Crown.
Graff, Michelle & Reese, Loretta. Thirty-Four Craft Stick Projects. LC 82-61453. (Illus.). 48p. 1983. pap. 3.50 (ISBN 0-87239-622-3, 2104). Standard Pub.
Johnson, June. Eight-Hundred Thirty Eight Ways to Amuse a Child: Crafts, Hobbies & Creative Ideas for the Child from Six to Twelve. Rev ed. LC 82-48801. 224p. (gr. 1-6). 1983. pap. 4.76i (ISBN 0-06-091047-X, CN 1047, CN). Har-Row.
Manners, John. Irish Crafts & Craftsmen. (Illus.). 130p. 1983. pap. 7.95 (ISBN 0-904651-92-4, Pub by Salem Hse Ltd). Merrimack Bk Serv.
Page, Linda & Wigginton, Eliot, eds. The Foxfire Calendar, 1984: Things You Can Make with Little or No Money. (Illus.). 24p. 1983. 5.95 (ISBN 0-525-93293-3, 0577-180). Dutton.
Pearce, G. L. The Pioneer Craftsmen of New Zealand. (Illus.). 256p. 1982. 29.95 (ISBN 0-00-216986-X, Pub. by W Collins Australia). Intl Schol Bk Serv.
Pearson, Katherine. American Crafts for the Home. (Illus.). 240p. 1983. 35.00 (ISBN 0-941434-30-3). Stewart Tabori & Chang.
Pelauzy, M. A. & Roca, F. Catala. Spanish Folk Crafts. (Illus.). 240p. 1982. 35.00 (ISBN 84-7031-060-7, Pub. by Editorial Blume Spain). Intl Schol Bk Serv.
Randolph, Elizabeth, ed. Baby Book. (Illus.). 72p. (Orig.). 1982. pap. 2.50 (ISBN 0-918178-30-4). Simplicity.
Shaw, Jackie. Freehanding with Jackie. (Illus.). 48p. (Orig.). 1980. pap. 6.50 (ISBN 0-941284-12-3). Deco Design Studio.
--Rock 'N Tole. (Orig.). 1980. pap. 8.50 (ISBN 0-941284-10-7). Deco Design Studio.
Sterbenz, Carol E. & Johnson, Nancy. The Decorated Tree: Recreating Traditional Christmas Ornaments. LC 82-1774. (Illus.). 168p. 1982. 22.50 (ISBN 0-8109-0805-0). Abrams.
Thirty Five Handicraft Projects for Children. LC 12-2957. 1982. pap. 4.50 (ISBN 0-570-03864-2). Concordia.
U-Bild Enterprises. Patterns for Better Living, 1983-84 Edition. 112p. 1982. pap. 2.95 (ISBN 0-910495-00-9). U-Bild.
Watkins, Paul. British Crafts. (Golden Hart Guides Ser.). (Illus.). 96p. 1983. pap. 3.95 (ISBN 0-283-98914-9, Pub by Sidgwick & Jackson). Merrimack Bk Serv.
Watt, Alexander. The Art of Papermaking. (Illus.). 240p. Date not set. pap. 20.00 (ISBN 0-87556-581-6). Saifer.
Workbench Magazine staff. The Workbench Treasury of Occasional & End Table Projects. LC 82-18769. (Illus.). 56p. (Orig.). 1983. pap. 3.95 (ISBN 0-86675-006-1, 61). Mod Handcraft.
Yates, Raymond F. & Yates, Marguerite W. Early American Crafts & Hobbies. LC 82-48834. (Illus.). 224p. 1983. pap. 5.72i (ISBN 0-06-463575-9, EH 575). B&N NY.

HANDICRAFT–JUVENILE LITERATURE
Glovach, Linda. The Little Witch's Spring Holiday Book. (Illus.). 48p. (ps-4). 8.95 (ISBN 0-13-538108-8). P-H.
Jordan, Ethel T. Scissor Magic. (ps-4). 1982. 5.95 (ISBN 0-86653-097-5, GA 424). Good Apple.
Martin, Toy. Pre-School Crafts Book. (Illus.). 64p. (Orig.). (gr. k-1). 1983. pap. 3.95 (ISBN 0-7137-1330-5, Pub. by Blandford Pr England). Sterling.
Vollmar, Karen & Fischer, Eileen. Kiddie Krafts. (ps-4). 1982. 4.95 (ISBN 0-86653-059-2, GA 413). Good Apple.
Volpe, Nancee. Good Apple & Seasonal Arts & Crafts. (gr. 3-7). 1982. 9.95 (ISBN 0-86653-087-8, GA 438). Good Apple.

HANDLING OF FOOD
see Food Handling

HANDLING OF MATERIALS
see Materials Handling
HANDWRITING
see Autographs; Graphology; Penmanship; Writing
HANGING ROOFS
see Roofs, Suspension
HANSEN'S DISEASE
see Leprosy
HAPPINESS
see also Joy and Sorrow; Mental Health
Ellis, Albert & Becker, Irving. Guide to Personal Happiness. Date not set. pap. 5.00 (ISBN 0-87980-395-9). Wilshire.
Fischer, Michael W. Verheissungen des Glucks. 251p. (Ger.). 1982. write for info. (ISBN 3-8204-6251-1). P Lang Pubs.
Klaas, Joe. The Twelve Steps to Happiness. 4.95 (ISBN 0-89486-156-5). Hazelden.
Lefson, Edward. All the Happiness... 1982. pap. write for info. (ISBN 0-937922-04-8). SAA Pub.
Le Gallienne, Richard. The Highway to Happiness. 154p. 1982. Repr. of 1913 ed. lib. bdg. 30.00 (ISBN 0-89987-317-0). Darby Bks.
Schmidt-Neubauer, Joachim. Die Bedeutung des Gluckseligkeitsbegriffes fur die Dramentheorie und -Praxis der Aufklarung und Des Sturm und Drang. 164p. (Ger.). 1982. write for info. (ISBN 3-261-05011-X). P Lang Pubs.
HAPTICS
see Touch
HARBORS
see also Pilots and Pilotage; Shore Protection
Bushnell, Rick B. Northwest Waters: Harbors. (Illus.). 122p. pap. write for info. (ISBN 0-941368-01-7). Pub Enterprises.
HARBORS–UNITED STATES
Levitt, James H. For Want of Trade: Shipping & the New Jersey Ports, 1680-1783, Vol. 17. 224p. 1981. 19.95 (ISBN 0-911020-03-9). NJ Hist Soc.
HARD OF HEARING CHILDREN
see Children, Deaf
HARD WOODS
see Hardwoods
HARDWOODS
see also names of hardwoods, e.g. Mahogany
The Pulping & Paper Making Potential of Tropical Hardwoods: Mixed Species from the Gogol Timber Area, Papua New Guinea, Vol. VI. 32p. 1979. 6.00 (ISBN 0-643-00339-8, CO64, CSIRO). Unipub.
Usher, M. B. & Ocloo, J. K. The Natural Resistance of Eighty-Five West African Hardwood Timbers to Attack by Termites & Micro-Organisms. 1979. 35.00x (ISBN 0-85135-103-4, Pub. by Centre Overseas Research). State Mutual Bk.
HARDY, OLIVER, 1892-1957
Scagnetti, Jack. The Laurel & Hardy Scrapbook. 1982. pap. 8.95 (ISBN 0-8246-0278-1). Jonathan David.
HARDY, THOMAS, 1840-1928
Das, Manas M. The Rooted Alien: A Study of Hardy's Poetic Sensibility. 160p. 1982. text ed. 13.75x (ISBN 0-391-02805-7). Humanities.
Hawkins, Desmond. Concerning Agnes-Thomas Hardy's "Good Little Pupil". (Illus.). 160p. 1982. text ed. 16.75x (ISBN 0-904387-97-6, Pub. by Sutton England). Humanities.
Springer, Marlene. Hardy's Use of Allusion. LC 82-21977. 22.50x (ISBN 0-7006-0231-3). Univ Pr KS.
Taylor, R. The Neglected Hardy: Thomas Hardy's Lesser Novels. 1982. 59.00x (ISBN 0-686-42949-4, Pub. by Macmillan England). State Mutual Bk.
HARE KRISHNA SECT
Gelberg, Steven, ed. Hare Krishna Hare Krishna: Five Distinguished Scholars in Religion Discuss the Krishna Movement in the West. (Grove Press Eastern Philosophy & Literature Ser.). 224p. (Orig.). 1983. pap. 7.95 (ISBN 0-394-62454-8, Ever). Grove.
HARES
see also Rabbits
Bare, Colleen S. Rabbits & Hares. LC 82-45992. (Illus.). 80p. (gr. 4 up). 1983. PLB 9.95 (ISBN 0-396-08127-4). Dodd.
HARIJANS
see Untouchables
HARMONIC ANALYSIS
see also Fourier Transformations; Harmonic Functions; Time-Series Analysis
Beckner, William, et al, eds. Conference on Harmonic Analysis in Honor of Antoni Zygmund. LC 82-11172. (Mathematics Ser.: Vols. I & II). 837p. 1983. 79.95 (ISBN 0-534-98043-0). Wadsworth Pub.
Knill, R. J., et al, eds. Harmonic Maps, Tulane: 1980, Proceedings. (Lecture Notes in Mathematics Ser.: Vol. 949). 158p. 1983. pap. 10.00 (ISBN 0-387-11595-1). Springer-Verlag.
HARMONIC FUNCTIONS
see also Harmonic Analysis
Chao, J. A. & Woyczynski, W. A., eds. Martingale Theory in Harmonic Analysis & Banach Spaces, Cleveland, Ohio 1981: Proceedings. (Lecture Notes in Mathematics: Vol. 939). 225p. 1982. pap. 12.00 (ISBN 0-387-11569-2). Springer-Verlag.
HARMONICA, MOUTH
see Mouth-Organ
HARMONY (COSMOLOGY)
see Harmony of the Spheres
HARMONY OF THE SPHERES
Szekely, Edmond B. Cosmos, Man & Society. 152p. 1973. pap. 5.80 (ISBN 0-89564-070-8). IBS Intl.
HARNESS MAKING AND TRADE
Gorzalka, Ann L. The Saddlemakers of Sheridan County, Wyoming. 1983. price not set (ISBN 0-87108-634-4). Pruett.
HARP
Woods, Sylvia. The Harp of Brandiswhiere: A Suite for Celtic Harp. Snyder, Don, ed. (Illus.). 64p. 1982. pap. 9.95 (ISBN 0-9602990-2-5). Woods Bks.
HATHA YOGA
see Yoga, Hatha
HAUNTED HOUSES
see Ghosts
HAUPTMANN, GERHARD JOHANN ROBERT, 1862-1946
Maurer, Warren. Gerhart Hauptmann. (World Authors Ser.). 1982. lib. bdg. 17.95 (ISBN 0-8057-6517-4, Twayne). G K Hall.
HAUSA LANGUAGE
Foreign Service Institute. Hausa Basic Course. 420p. Date not set. with 15 cassettes 175.00x (ISBN 0-88432-109-6, HA1). J Norton Pubs.
HAVASUPAI INDIANS
see Indians of North America–Southwest, New
HAWAII
Bauer, Helen. Hawaii: The Aloha State. rev. ed. (Illus.). 192p. (gr. 4-7). 1982. 12.95 (ISBN 0-935848-13-4); pap. 9.95 (ISBN 0-935848-15-0). Bess Pr.
Brown, David T. Hawaii Recalls. (Illus.). 130p. (Orig.). 1982. 19.95 (ISBN 0-9607938-3-6); pap. 9.95 (ISBN 0-9607938-2-8). Editions Ltd.
Morgan, Joseph R. Hawaii. (Geographics of the U. S.). 275p. 1983. lib. bdg. 35.00 (ISBN 0-89158-942-2); pap. 18.00 (ISBN 0-86531-488-8). Westview.
HAWAII–BIOGRAPHY
Singletary, Milly. Hilo Hattie: A Legend in our Time. (Illus.). 191p. ltd. ed. 10.95 (ISBN 0-9601256-5-5); pap. 5.95 (ISBN 0-9601256-6-3). Sunset Pubns.
HAWAII–DESCRIPTION AND TRAVEL
Hawaiian Journey. Date not set. price not set (ISBN 0-935180-04-4). Mutual Pub HI.
Reflections. Date not set. price not set (ISBN 0-935180-05-2). Mutual Pub HI.
HAWAII–DESCRIPTION AND TRAVEL–GUIDEBOOKS
Birnbaum, Stephen. Hawaii 1983. (Get 'em & Go Travel Guide Ser.). 1982. 11.95 (ISBN 0-395-32872-1). HM.
Fodor's Budget Hawaii '83. 192p. 1983. pap. 6.95 (ISBN 0-679-00882-9). McKay.
Insight Guides. Hawaii. (Illus.). 418p. 1983. 18.95 (ISBN 0-13-384651-2); pap. 14.95 (ISBN 0-13-384529-X). P-H.
Wurman, Richard S., ed. Hawaii-Access. (Access Guidebook Ser.). (Illus.). 1982. pap. 9.95 (ISBN 0-9604858-4-8). Access Pr.
HAWAII–HISTORY
Baker, Ray J. Hawaiian Yesterdays. Van Dyke, Robert E. & Ronck, Ronn, eds. 256p. 1982. 28.95 (ISBN 0-935180-03-6). Mutual Pub HI.
Devaney, Dennis M. & Kelly, Marion. Kaneohe: A History of Change. rev. ed. (Illus.). 300p. 1982. Repr. of 1976 ed. pap. 14.95 (ISBN 0-935848-14-2). Bess Pr.
Gregg, David L. The Diaries of David Lawrence Gregg, 1853-1858: An American Diplomat in Hawaii. King, Pauline, ed. LC 82-80764. (Illus.). 605p. 1982. 25.00x (ISBN 0-8248-0861-4). UH Pr.
Handy, E. S. & Handy, E. G. Native Planters of Old Hawaii: Their Life, Lore & Environment. LC 78-119560. (Bulletin Ser.: No. 223). (Illus.). 641p. 1972. pap. 22.00 (ISBN 0-910240-11-6). Bishop Mus.
The Island of Lanai: A Survey of Native Culture. rev. ed. (Bulletin Ser.: No. 12). (Illus.). 129p. 1969. pap. 5.00 (ISBN 0-910240-07-8). Bishop Mus.
Kamakau, S. M. Ka Po'e Kahiko: The People of Old. Barrere, Dorothy B., ed. Pukui, Mary K., tr. (Special Publication Ser.: No. 51). (Illus.). 174p. 1964. pap. 8.00 (ISBN 0-910240-32-9). Bishop Mus.
Papa, John. Fragments of Hawaiian History. rev. ed. Barrere, Dorothy B., ed. Pukui, Mary K., tr. (Special Publication Ser.: No. 70). (Illus.). 212p. 1982. pap. 8.00 (ISBN 0-910240-31-0). Bishop Mus.
HAWAII–POPULATION
Schweizer, Niklaus R. Hawaii & the German Speaking Peoples. (Illus.). 232p. (Orig.). pap. 15.00 (ISBN 0-914916-60-2). Topgallant.
HAWAII–RELIGION
Buck, Peter. Arts & Crafts of Hawaii: Religion, Sec. XI. (Special Publication Ser.: No. 45). (Illus.). 77p. 1957. pap. 4.50 (ISBN 0-910240-44-2). Bishop Mus.
Phaigh, Bethal. Gestalt & the Wisdom of the Kahunas. LC 82-50928. 144p. 1983. pap. 5.95 (ISBN 0-87516-498-6). De Vorss.
HAWKESWORTH, JOHN, 1715?-1773
Abbott, John L. John Hawkesworth, Eighteenth-Century Man of Letters. 316p. 1982. text ed. 22.50 (ISBN 0-299-08610-0). U of Wis Pr.
HAWTHORNE, NATHANIEL, 1804-1864
Gollin, Rita. Nathaniel Hawthorne: An Iconography. 105p. 1983. 25.00 (ISBN 0-87580-087-4). N Ill U Pr.
Martin, Terence. Nathaniel Hawthorne. rev. ed. (United States Authors Ser.). 233p. 1983. lib. bdg. 13.95 (ISBN 0-8057-7384-3, Twayne). G K Hall.
Montgomery, Marion. Why Hawthorne Was Melancholy: Vol. III, of the Trilogy, the Prophetic Poet & the Spirit of the Age. 486p. 1983. 19.95 (ISBN 0-89385-027-6). Sugden.
HAYDN, JOSEPH, 1732-1809
Geiringer, Karl & Geiringer, Irene. Haydn: A Creative Life in Music. rev., 3rd ed. (Illus.). 416p. 1983. pap. 8.95 (ISBN 0-520-04317-0, CAL 613). U of Cal Pr.
Landon, H. C., et al. The Haydn Yearbook, Vol. XIII. LC 63-3879. 256p. 1983. pap. 25.00x (ISBN 0-253-37113-9). Ind U Pr.
Larsen, Jens P. & Feder, Georg. The New Grove Haydn. (New Grove Composer Biography Ser.). (Illus.). 1983. 15.95 (ISBN 0-393-01681-1); pap. 7.95 (ISBN 0-393-30085-4). Norton.
HAYWOOD, WILLIAM DUDLEY, 1869-1928
Haywood, William D. Bill Haywood's Book: The Autobiography of William D. Haywood. LC 82-25134. 368p. 1983. Repr. of 1929 ed. lib. bdg. 35.00x (ISBN 0-313-23842-1, HABI). Greenwood.
HAYWORTH, RITA
Hill, James. Rita Hayworth. 1983. 14.95 (ISBN 0-671-43273-7). S&S.
HAZARDOUS SUBSTANCES
Cope, C. B. & Fuller, W. H. The Scientific Management of Hazardous Wastes. LC 82-14650. (Illus.). 375p. Date not set. 69.50 (ISBN 0-521-25100-1). Cambridge U Pr.
Exner, Jurgen H., ed. Detoxication of Hazardous Waste. LC 82-70696. (Illus.). 350p. 1982. 37.50 (ISBN 0-250-40521-0). Ann Arbor Science.
Highland, Joseph H. Hazardous Waste: What is Being Done to Control Its Disposal? (Vital Issues Ser.: Vol. XXXI, No. IV). 0.80 (ISBN 0-686-84137-9). Ctr Info Am.
Parr, James F., et al, eds. Land Treatment of Hazardous Wastes. LC 82-14402. (Illus.). 422p. 1983. 45.00 (ISBN 0-8155-0926-X). Noyes.
Saxena, Jitendra, ed. Hazard Assessment of Chemicals, Vol. 2. (Serial Publication). 332p. 1983. price not set (ISBN 0-12-312402-6). Acad Pr.
Shuckrow, Alan J., et al. Hazardous Waste Leachate Management Manual. LC 82-7924. (Pollution Technology Rev. 92). (Illus.). 379p. 1983. 36.00 (ISBN 0-8155-0910-3). Noyes.
Sweeney, Thomas L. & Bhatt, Harasiddhiprasad D., eds. Hazardous Waste Management for the Eighties. LC 82-71532. (Illus.). 553p. 1982. 39.95 (ISBN 0-250-40429-X). Ann Arbor Science.
Watson, Thomas & Davidson, Jeffrey. Hazardous Wastes Handbook. 4th ed. 500p. 1982. Wkbk. 95.00 (ISBN 0-86587-097-7). Gov Insts.
Young, R. E. Control in Hazardous Environments. (IEE Control Engineering Ser.: No. 17). 128p. 1982. pap. 30.00 (ISBN 0-906048-69-9). Inst Elect Eng.
HAZLITT, WILLIAM, 1778-1830
Mackerness, E. D., ed. Hazlitt-the Spirit of the Age. 448p. 1969. 25.00x (ISBN 0-7121-0143-8, Pub. by Macdonald & Evans). State Mutual Bk.
HEAD
see also Brain; Ear; Eye; Face; Hair; Mouth; Skull
Lang, J. Clinical Anatomy of the Head: Neurocranium, Orbita, Craniocervical Regions. (Illus.). 489p. 1983. 490.00 (ISBN 0-387-11014-3). Springer-Verlag.
HEAD–RADIOGRAPHY
Tsai, Fong Y. & Hieshima, Grant B. Neuroradiology of Head Trauma. (Illus.). 1983. price not set (ISBN 0-8391-1776-0, 13668). Univ Park.
HEAD–WOUNDS AND INJURIES
Shapiro, Kenneth, ed. Pediatric Head Trauma. LC 82-84516. (Illus.). 1983. price not set monograph (ISBN 0-87993-191-4). Futura Pub.
Tsai, Fong Y. & Hieshima, Grant B. Neuroradiology of Head Trauma. (Illus.). 1983. price not set (ISBN 0-8391-1776-0, 13668). Univ Park.
HEAD-GEAR
see Costume
HEAD NURSE
see Nursing Service Administration
HEADACHE
see also Migraine
Kahn, Ada P. Headaches. (Help Yourself to Health Ser.). 96p. (Orig.). 1983. pap. 3.95 (ISBN 0-8092-5600-2). Contemp Bks.
Lance, James W. Mechanisms & Management of Headache. 4th ed. 264p. 1982. text ed. 39.95 (ISBN 0-407-26458-2). Butterworth.
HEADDRESS
see Hairdressing
HEADINGS, SUBJECT
see Subject Headings
HEADS OF STATE
see also Statesmen
Gardner, John. Chinese Politics & the Succession to Mao. (Illus.). 217p. 1982. text ed. 20.00x (ISBN 0-8419-0808-7); pap. text ed. 14.00x (ISBN 0-8419-0809-5). Holmes & Meier.
HEALING (IN RELIGION, FOLK-LORE, ETC.)
see also Faith-Cure
Hagin, Kenneth E. How to Keep Your Healing. 1980. pap. 0.50 (ISBN 0-89276-059-1). Hagin Ministry.
Hagin, Kenneth, Jr. Healing: A Forever-Settled Subject. 1981. pap. 0.50 (ISBN 0-89276-707-3). Hagin Ministry.
Jensen, Bernard. Iridology: Science & Practice in the Healing Arts, Vol. II. 608p. 1982. write for info. (ISBN 0-9608360-6-3). B Jensen.
McCrossan, T. J. Bodily Healing & the Atonement. 1982. pap. 3.50 (ISBN 0-89276-505-4). Hagin Ministry.
Riesser, Paul C. & Riesser, Teri K. The Holistic Healers. 168p. (Orig.). 1983. pap. 5.95 (ISBN 0-87784-814-9). Inter-Varsity.
HEALING, MENTAL
see Mental Healing
HEALING, PSYCHIC
see Mental Healing
HEALTH
Here are entered works on optimal physical, mental, and social well-being, as well as how to achieve and preserve it. Works on personal body care and cleanliness are entered under Hygiene. Works on muscular efficiency and physical endurance are entered under Physical fitness.
see also Diet; Environmental Health; Exercise; Health Education; Longevity; Mental Health; Nutrition; Physical Fitness; Public Health; Relaxation; Sleep; Temperance
also subdivision Care and Hygiene under parts of the body, or under age groups dependent on the assistance of others, e.g. Eye–Care and Hygiene; Infants–Care and Hygiene; and subdivision Health and Hygiene under classes of persons or ethnic groups, e.g. Students–Health and Hygiene; Afro-Americans–Health and Hygiene
Baer, Louis S. Better Health with Fewer Pills. LC 82-8394. 132p. 1982. pap. 5.95 (ISBN 0-664-24425-4). Westminster.
Brannin, Marilyn. Your Body in Mind. 192p. 1983. pap. 2.95 (ISBN 0-345-29787-3). Ballantine.
Cember, Herman. Introduction to Health Physics. 2nd ed. (Illus.). 475p. 1983. 35.00 (ISBN 0-08-030129-0). Pergamon.
Completed Research in Health, Physical Education, Recreation & Dance, Vol.19. 1977. 9.25 (ISBN 0-88314-044-6). AAHPERD.
Completed Research in Health, Physical Education, Recreation & Dance, Vol. 20. 1978. write for info. (ISBN 0-88314-045-4). AAHPERD.
Completed Research in Health, Physical Education, Recreation & Dance, Vol. 22. 1980. 9.25 (ISBN 0-686-38058-4). AAHPERD.
Completed Research in Health, Physical Education, Recreation & Dance, Vol. 24. 1983. 10.95 (ISBN 0-686-38056-8). AAHPERD.
Davis, Steven A. How to Stay Healthy in an Unhealthy World. LC 82-12581. 288p. 1983. 12.50 (ISBN 0-688-01574-3). Morrow.
Dintiman, George B. & Greenberg, Jerrold S. Health Through Discovery. 2nd ed. LC 82-11421. 608p. 1983. pap. text ed. 16.95 (ISBN 0-686-82162-9). A-W.
Douglass, William C. & Walker, Morton. DMSO: The New Healing Power. (Illus.). 1983. 14.95 (ISBN 0-8159-5315-1). Devin.
Dunton, Sabina & Miller, Kathy A. CounSELFile. McNeely, Richard A., ed. LC 82-50626. (Illus.). 150p. (Orig.). 1982. 25.00 (ISBN 0-943562-50-3); incl. 3-ring notebk. 28.00. Well Aware.
Fassbender, William. You & Your Health. 2nd ed. LC 79-12472. 479p. 1980. text ed. 16.95 (ISBN 0-471-04936-0); tchrs' manual 7.00 (ISBN 0-471-06384-3). Wiley.
Grupenhoff, John T., ed. National Health Directory, 1983. 600p. 1983. price not set (ISBN 0-89443-811-5). Aspen Systems.
Harron, Frank & Burnside, John. Health & Human Values: A Guide to Making Your Own Decisions. 24.95 (ISBN 0-686-42812-9); pap. 6.95 (ISBN 0-686-42813-7, Y-448). Yale U Pr.
Harron, Frank, et al. Health & Human Values: Making Your Own Decisions. 185p. 1983. 24.95 (ISBN 0-686-83922-6); pap. 6.95 (ISBN 0-686-83923-4). Yale U Pr.
Horne, Ross. Health Revolution. 1980. 8.95 (ISBN 0-9594423-0-8). Cancer Control Soc.
Lynch, L. R. Educational Approaches to High Level Wellness: An Annotated Bibliography. 1982. pap. 4.95 (ISBN 0-935872-01-9). R Bernard.
Moore, Michael C. & Moore, Lynda J. A Complete Handbook of Holistic Health. 253p. 1983. 17.95 (ISBN 0-13-168914-2); pap. 8.95 (ISBN 0-13-168906-1). P-H.
Muller, Frederick, ed. The Healthy Body: The Diagram Group. 526p. 1982. 39.00x (ISBN 0-584-11031-6, Pub. by Muller Ltd). State Mutual Bk.
Neal, Larry L., ed. The Next Fifty Years: Health, Physical Education, Recreation, Dance. 179p. 1971. pap. 3.50 (ISBN 0-686-84034-8). U OR Ctr Leisure.
Osborn, S. The American Guide to Diet & Health. 352p. 1982. 24.95 (ISBN 0-07-069074-X, GB); pap. 12.95 (ISBN 0-07-069072-3). McGraw.
Simmers, Louise M. Diversified Health Occupations. LC 82-73084. (Illus.). 480p. (Orig.). 1983. text ed. 20.00 (ISBN 0-8273-2288-7); write for info. set wkbk. (ISBN 0-8273-2289-5); write for info. instr's guide (ISBN 0-8273-2290-9). Delmar.
Small, Lucile J. Not by Prescription. 64p. pap. 2.95 (ISBN 0-686-82633-7). Review & Herald.
Szekely, Edmond B. Creative Exercises for Health & Beauty. (Illus.). 48p. 1976. pap. 3.50 (ISBN 0-89564-048-1). IBS Intl.
Taylor, T Geoffrey. Nutrition & Health. (Studies in Biology: No. 141). 64p. 1982. pap. text ed. 8.95 (ISBN 0-7131-2840-2). E Arnold.

Thompson & Cox. Steps to Better Health: Common Problems & What to Do About Them. 1983. pap. 9.95 (ISBN 0-8359-7077-9). Reston.
Towards Better Health & Nutrition. 83p. 1981. pap. 7.00 (ISBN 0-686-81852-0, UB97, UNESCO). Unipub.
Wilson, Margery. Double Your Energy & Live Without Fatigue. 240p. 1983. pap. 5.95 (ISBN 0-13-218917-8, Reward). P-H.

HEALTH-BIBLIOGRAPHY
McClure, Susan H., ed. Health Care, 1980: A Bibliographic Guide to the Documents Update. 30p. 1982. 25.00 (ISBN 0-667-00635-4). Microfilming Corp.

HEALTH-DICTIONARIES
Reader's Digest Editors. Family Health Guide & Medical Encyclopedia. rev ed. LC 76-23541. (Illus.). 640p. 1976. 16.98 (ISBN 0-89577-032-6). RD Assn.

HEALTH-JUVENILE LITERATURE
Moncure, Jane B. Healthkins Help. LC 82-14713. (Healthkins Ser.). (Illus.). 32p. (ps-2). 1982. lib. bdg. 6.95 (ISBN 0-89565-242-0). Childs World.

HEALTH-READERS
see Readers-Health

HEALTH-STUDY AND TEACHING
see Health Education

HEALTH, COMMUNITY
see Public Health

HEALTH, INDUSTRIAL
see Industrial Health

HEALTH, MENTAL
see Mental Health

HEALTH, PUBLIC
see Public Health

HEALTH, PUBLIC-ADMINISTRATION
see Public Health Administration

HEALTH, RURAL
Childs, Alan W. & Melton, Gary B., eds. Rural Psychology. 455p. 1982. 39.50x (ISBN 0-306-41045-1, Plenum Pr). Plenum Pub.
Rosenblatt, R. A. & Moscovice, I. S. Rural Health Care. (Health Services Ser.). 301p. 1982. text ed. 19.95 (ISBN 0-471-05419-4, Pub. by Wiley Med). Wiley.
Steltzer, Ulli. Health in the Highlands: The Chimaltenango Development Program of Guatemala. LC 82-48872. (Illus.). 128p. 1983. 30.00 (ISBN 0-295-95994-0); pap. 0.00 (ISBN 0-295-96024-8). U of Wash Pr.

HEALTH ADMINISTRATION
see Public Health Administration

HEALTH CARE
see Medical Care

HEALTH CARE ADMINISTRATION
see Public Health Administration

HEALTH CARE DELIVERY ORGANIZATIONS, COMPREHENSIVE
see Health Maintenance Organizations

HEALTH COMMUNICATION
see Communication in Medicine

HEALTH EDUCATION
see also Cancer Education; School Health
Brooks, Bearl. Basic Skills Healthy Body Workbook. (Basic Skills Workbooks). 32p. (gr. 6-7). 1983. 0.99 (ISBN 0-8209-0575-5, HW-2). ESP.
--Health & Fun. (Health Ser.). 24p. (gr. 2-4). 1979. wkbk. 5.00 (ISBN 0-8209-0343-4, H-4). ESP.
--Health & Good Manners. (Health Ser.). 24p. (gr. 2-3). 1979. wkbk. 5.00 (ISBN 0-8209-0342-6, H-3). ESP.
--Health & Safety. (Health Ser.). 24p. (gr. 1-2). 1979. wkbk. 5.00 (ISBN 0-8209-0341-8, H-2). ESP.
--Health Habits. (Health Ser.). 24p. (gr. 1-2). 1980. wkbk. 5.00 (ISBN 0-8209-0340-X, H-1). ESP.
--The Healthy Body. (Health Ser.). 24p. (gr. 4-6). 1977. wkbk. 5.00 (ISBN 0-8209-0345-0, H-6). ESP.
Cole, Clara. Personal Health. (Health Ser.). 24p. (gr. 4-9). 1979. wkbk. 5.00 (ISBN 0-8209-0346-9, H-7). ESP.
Evaluation Instruments in Health Education. 64p. 5.95 (ISBN 0-88314-069-1). AAHPERD.
Galli, Nicholas. Foundations & Principles of Health Education. LC 77-21586. 389p. 1978. text ed. 23.95x (ISBN 0-471-29065-3). Wiley.
Hayes, Marilyn. Basic Skills Health Workbook: Grade 3. (Basic Skills Workbooks). 32p. 1982. tchrs' ed. 0.99 (ISBN 0-686-38397-4, HW-D). ESP.
--Basic Skills Health Workbook: Grade 4. (Basic Skills Workbooks). 32p. 1982. tchrs' ed. 0.99 (ISBN 0-8209-0414-7, HW-E). ESP.
--Basic Skills Health Workbook: Grade 5. (Basic Skills Workbooks). 32p. 1982. tchrs' ed. 0.99 (ISBN 0-8209-0415-5, HW-F). ESP.
--Basic Skills Nutrition Workbook: Grade 5. (Basic Skills Workbooks). 32p. (gr. 5). tchrs' ed. 0.99 (ISBN 0-8209-0411-2, NW-F). ESP.
--Jumbo Health Yearbook: Grade 3. (Jumbo Health Ser.). 96p. (gr. 3). 1978. 14.00 (ISBN 0-8209-0063-X, JHY 3). ESP.
--Jumbo Health Yearbook: Grade 4. (Jumbo Health Ser.). 96p. (gr. 4). 1979. 14.00 (ISBN 0-8209-0064-8, JHY 4). ESP.
--Jumbo Nutrition Yearbook: Grade 4. (Jumbo Nutrition Ser.). 96p. (gr. 4). 1981. 14.00 (ISBN 0-8209-0043-5, JNY 4). ESP.
--Jumbo Nutrition Yearbook: Grade 5. (Jumbo Nutrition Ser.). 96p. (gr. 5). 1981. 14.00 (ISBN 0-8209-0044-3, JNY 5). ESP.
Haynes, Marilyn. Basic Skills Nutrition Workbook: Grade 4. (Basic Skills Workbooks). 32p. (gr. 4). tchrs' ed. 0.99 (ISBN 0-8209-0410-4, NW-E). ESP.
Health Education Completed Research, Vol. II. 400p. 17.50 (ISBN 0-88314-096-9). AAHPERD.
Health Education Completed Research, Vol. III. 1983. write for info. (ISBN 0-88314-222-8). AAHPERD.
Health Education Teaching Ideas: Elementary. 1982. write for info. (ISBN 0-88314-223-6). AAHPERD.
Houston, Jack. Basic Skills Health Workbook: Grade 7. (Basic Skills Workbook). 32p. 1982. tchrs' ed. 0.99 (ISBN 0-8209-0417-1, HW-H). ESP.
--Basic Skills Health WorkBook: Grade 8. (Basic Skills Workbook). 32p. 1982. tchrs' ed. 0.99 (ISBN 0-8209-0418-X, HW-I). ESP.
--Basic Skills Health Workbook: Grade 9. (Basic Skills Workbooks). 32p. (YA) 1982. tchr's ed. 0.99 (HW-J). ESP.
--Basic Skills Health Workbooks: Grade 6. (Basic Skills Workbooks). 32p. 1982. tchrs' ed. 0.99 (ISBN 0-8209-0416-3, HW-G). ESP.
--Jumbo Health Yearbook: Grade 5. (Jumbo Health Ser.). 96p. (gr. 5). 1979. 14.00 (ISBN 0-8209-0065-6, JHY 5). ESP.
--Jumbo Health Yearbook: Grade 6. (Jumbo Health Ser.). 96p. (gr. 6). 1979. 14.00 (ISBN 0-8209-0066-4, JHY 6). ESP.
--Jumbo Health Yearbook: Grade 7. (Jumbo Health Ser.). 96p. (gr. 7). 1979. 14.00 (ISBN 0-8209-0067-2, JHY 7). ESP.
--Jumbo Health Yearbook: Grade 8. (Jumbo Health Ser.). 96p. (gr. 8). 1979. 14.00 (ISBN 0-8209-0068-0, JHY 8). ESP.
Husak, Glen. How to Buy & Use Medicine. (The Health Ser.). (Illus.). 45p. (gr. 7-12). 1981. pap. text ed. 3.00 (ISBN 0-910839-24-7). Hopewell.
Londos, Eutychia G. AV Health: Current Publications of the United States Government. LC 82-10366. 240p. 1982. 17.50 (ISBN 0-8108-1571-0). Scarecrow.
Pahre, P. & Stewart, J. Going to the Doctor. (The Health Ser.). (Illus.). 65p. (gr. 7-12). 1981. pap. text ed. 3.00 (ISBN 0-910839-23-9). Hopewell.
Patty, Catherine. The Healthy Body. (Sound Filmstrip Kits Ser.). (gr. 3-6). 1980. tchrs ed. 24.00 (ISBN 0-8209-0431-7, FCW-8). ESP.
Rudman, Jack. Elementary Schools. (Teachers Lesson Plan Bk.: E-1). (ps-6). pap. 3.95 (ISBN 0-686-84418-1). Natl Learning A.
Runswick, H. Health Education: Practical Teaching Techniques. (Topics in Community Health). 120p. 1975. text ed. 9.95 (ISBN 0-471-26003-7, Pub. by Wiley Med). Wiley.
Shaw, Marie-Jose. Basic Skills Spelling Workbook: Grade 3. (Basic Skills Workbooks). 32p. (gr. 3). 1982. wkbk. 0.99 (ISBN 0-8209-0373-6, SPW-D). ESP.
--Basic Skills Spelling Workbook: Grade 5. (Basic Skills Workbooks). 32p. (gr. 5). 1982. wkbk. 0.99 (ISBN 0-8209-0375-2, SPW-F). ESP.
--Basic Skills Spelling Workbook: Grade 6. (Basic Skills Workbooks). 32p. (gr. 6). 1982. wkbk. 0.99 (ISBN 0-8209-0376-0, SPW-G). ESP.
Teaching Occupational Health & Safety at the Secondary & College Level. 144p. 10.95 (ISBN 0-88314-187-6). AAHPERD.
Van Camp, Diana. Basic Skills Nutrition Workbook: Grade 2. (Basis Skills Workbooks). 32p. (gr. 2). 1982. tchrs' ed. 0.99 (ISBN 0-8209-0408-2, NW-C). ESP.
--Jumbo Human Body Yearbook: Grade 5. (Jumbo Human Body Ser.). 96p. (gr. 5). 1980. 14.00 (ISBN 0-8209-0070-2, JHBY 5). ESP.
--Jumbo Human Body Yearbook: Grade 6. (Jumbo Human Body Ser.). 96p. (gr. 6). 1980. 14.00 (ISBN 0-8209-0071-0, JHBY 6). ESP.
--Jumbo Human Body Yearbook: Grade 7. (Jumbo Human Body Ser.). 96p. (gr. 7). 1980. 14.00 (ISBN 0-8209-0072-9, JHBY 7). ESP.
--Jumbo Human Body Yearbook: Grade 8. (Jumbo Human Body Ser.). 96p. (gr. 8). 1982. 14.00 (ISBN 0-8209-0073-7, JHBY 8). ESP.
VanCamp, Marilyn. Jumbo Nutrition Yearbook: Grade 3. (Jumbo Nutrition Ser.). 96p. (gr. 3). 1981. 14.00 (ISBN 0-8209-0042-7, JNY 3). ESP.
Vaughn, James E. Basic Skills Vocabulary Workbook: Junior High. (Basic Skills Workbooks). 32p. (gr. 7-9). 1982. wkbk. 0.99 (ISBN 0-8209-0383-3, VW-H). ESP.
--Basic Skills Vocabulary Workbook: Senior High. (Basic Skills Workbooks). 32p. (gr. 9-12). 1982. wkbk. 0.99 (ISBN 0-8209-0384-1, VW-I). ESP.

HEALTH FACILITIES
see also Health Resorts, Watering-Places, Etc.
AHA Clearinghouse for Hospital Management Engineering. Health Facility Design Using Quantitative Techniques: A Collection of Case Studies. 148p. 1982. pap. 18.75 (ISBN 0-87258-397-X, AHA-043170). Am Hospital.
Dietrich, John & Waggoner, Susan. The Complete Health Club Handbook. (Orig.). 1983. pap. price not set (ISBN 0-671-47027-2). S&S.

HEALTH FOOD
see Food, Natural

HEALTH INSURANCE
see Insurance, Health

HEALTH MAINTENANCE ORGANIZATIONS
Center for Self Sufficiency Research Division Staff. Health Care Alternatives. 60p. 1983. pap. 15.95 (ISBN 0-910811-37-7). Center Self.

HEALTH OF CHILDREN
see Children-Care and Hygiene

HEALTH OF INFANTS
see Infants-Care and Hygiene

HEALTH OF WOMEN
see Women-Health and Hygiene

HEALTH OF WORKERS
see Industrial Health

HEALTH PROFESSIONS
see Medical Personnel

HEALTH RECORDS
see Medical Records

HEALTH RESORTS, WATERING-PLACES, ETC.
Babcock, Judy & Kennedy, Judy. The Spa Book: A Guided, Personal Tour of Health Resorts & Beauty Spas for Men & Women. LC 82-18249. (Illus.). 288p. 1983. 14.95 (ISBN 0-517-54950-6). Crown.

HEALTH RESORTS, WATERING-PLACES, ETC.-DIRECTORIES
Wilkens, Emily. More Secrets from the Super Spas. LC 82-19918. (Illus.). 1983. 17.50 (ISBN 0-934878-24-2); pap. 9.95 (ISBN 0-934878-25-0). Dembner Bks.

HEALTH SCIENCES ADMINISTRATION
see Public Health Administration

HEALTH SERVICES
see Public Health

HEALTH SURVEYS
Cypress, Beulah K. Medication Therapy in Office Visits for Selected Diagnoses: National Ambulatory Medical Care Survey, United States, 1980. Cox, Klaudia, ed. (Ser. 13: No. 71). 65p. 1982. pap. text ed. 1.85 (ISBN 0-8406-0266-9). Natl Ctr Health Stats.
Landis, J. Richard & Eklund, Stephen A. A Statistical Methodology for Analyzing Data from a Complex Survey: The First National Health & Nutrition Examination Survey. Cox, Klaudia, ed. (No. 92). 50p. 1982. pap. 1.75 (ISBN 0-686-81990-X). Natl Ctr Health Stats.
National Center for Health Statistics. Health Interview Survey, 1975. LC 82-80685. write for info. (ISBN 0-89138-926-1, ICPSR 7672). ICPSR.

HEALTH THOUGHTS
see Mental Healing

HEALTHS, DRINKING OF
see Toasts

HEARING
see also Audiometry; Deafness; Ear
Claussen, Paulette M. Speech-Language-Hearing Update: The Standard Reference Guide, Vol. 5, No. 2. 790p. 1982. 40.00 (ISBN 0-686-84041-0). Update Pubns AZ.
--Speech-Language-Hearing Update: The Standard Reference Guide, Vol. 6, No. 1. 80p. 1982. 40.00 (ISBN 0-943002-02-8). Update Pubns AZ.
Glattke, Theodore J. Auditory Evoked Potentials. 1983. pap. 16.95 (ISBN 0-686-82638-8, 14710). Univ Park.
Keidel, Wolfgang D. The Physiological Basis of Hearing. (Illus.). 272p. 1983. 25.00 (ISBN 0-86577-072-7). Thieme-Stratton.
Lasky, Elaine Z. & Katz, Jack, eds. Central Auditory Processing Disorders: Problems of Speech, Language & Learning. (Illus.). 1983. 29.95 (ISBN 0-8391-1802-3, 18368). Univ Park.
Lutman, M. E. & Haggard, M. P., eds. Hearing Science & Hearing Disorders. Date not set. 28.00 (ISBN 0-12-460440-4). Acad Pr.
Moore, B. C. An Introduction to the Psychology of Hearing. 2nd ed. LC 81-69595. 27.00 (ISBN 0-12-505620-6); pap. 11.00 (ISBN 0-12-505622-2). Acad Pr.
Murphy, Wendy B. Touch, Smell, Taste, Sight & Hearing. LC 82-5738. (Library of Health). lib. bdg. 18.60 (ISBN 0-8094-3799-6, Pub. by Time-Life). Silver.

HEARING-TESTING
see Audiometry

HEARING DISORDERS
see also Deafness
Shea, John J. & Akens, David S. Hearing Help. (Illus.). 112p. 1979. 7.95 (ISBN 0-87397-128-0). Strode.
Sundstrom, Susan. Understanding Hearing Loss & What Can Be Done To Help. 64p. 1983. pap. text ed. 2.95x (ISBN 0-8134-2266-3). Interstate.

HEARING DISORDERS IN CHILDREN
see also Children, Deaf
Daniels, Paul R. Teaching the Gifted Learning Disabled Child. 400p. 1983. 26.50 (ISBN 0-89443-928-6). Aspen Systems.

HEARING-IMPAIRED CHILDREN
see Children, Deaf

HEART
see also Cardiography
Davies. Conduction System of the Heart. 1982. text ed. 99.95 (ISBN 0-407-00133-6). Butterworth.

HEART-DISEASES
see also Cardiacs; Cardiology; Heart-Radiography; Heart Failure
Amsterdam, Ezra A. & Holmes, Ann M. Take Care of Your Heart. (Illus.). 256p. 1983. 14.95 (ISBN 0-87196-731-6). Facts on File.
Dembroski, T. M. & Schmidt, T. H., eds. Biobehavioral Bases of Coronary Heart Disease. (Karger Biobehavioral Medicine Ser.: Vol. 2). (Illus.). 530p. 1983. 95.25 (ISBN 3-8055-3629-1). S Karger.
Dillard, Jack. Heart Stop: No Death at All. (Illus.). 42p. (Orig.). 1982. pap. write for info. (ISBN 0-940588-08-0). Hazlett Print.
Elkayam, Uri & Gleicher, Norbert, eds. Cardiac Problems in Pregnancy: Diagnosis & Management of Maternal & Fetal Disease. LC 82-9938. 638p. 1982. 85.00 (ISBN 0-8451-0216-8). A R Liss.
Phibbs, Brendan. The Human Heart: A Consumer's Guide to Cardiac Care. LC 82-2119. (Medical Library). (Illus.). 240p. 1982. pap. 8.95 (ISBN 0-452-25337-3, 3942-7). Mosby.
Simkin, Peter A. Heart & Rheumatic Disease, Vol. 2. new ed. (BIMR Rheumatology Ser.). 320p. 1983. text ed. price not set (ISBN 0-407-02353-4). Butterworth.
Spaet, Theodore, ed. Progress in Hemostasis & Thrombosis, Vol. 6. X ed. write for info. (ISBN 0-8089-1493-6). Grune.
Tucker, Bernard L., ed. Second Clinical Conference on Congential Heart Disease. 448p. 1982. 29.50 (ISBN 0-8089-1507-X). Grune.

HEART-DISEASES-DIAGNOSIS
see also Cardiac Catheterization; Cardiography; Electrocardiography
Osbakken, Mary D., et al. Techniques, Diagnostics & Advances in Nuclear Cardiology. (Illus.). 344p. 1983. text ed. 53.50x (ISBN 0-398-04772-3). C C Thomas.
Roelandt, J. & Hugenholtz, P. G. Long-Term Ambulatory Electrocardiography. 1982. text ed. 39.50 (ISBN 90-247-2664-6, Pub. by Martinus Nijhoff Netherlands). Kluwer Boston.

HEART-DISEASES-PREVENTION
Gruberg, Edward & Raymond, Stephen. Beyond Cholesterol. 208p. 1983. pap. 4.95 (ISBN 0-686-42893-5). St Martin.
Szekeres, L. & Papp, J. Gy., eds. Symposium on Drugs & Heart Metabolism, Vol. 2. (Hungarian Pharmacological Society, First Congress Ser.). (Illus.). 369p. 1973. 25.00x (ISBN 0-8002-3044-2). Intl Pubns Serv.

HEART-INFARCTION
Adgey, A. J. Acute Phase of Ischemic Heart Disease & Myocardial Infarction. 1982. text ed. 49.50 (ISBN 90-247-2675-1, Pub. by Martinus Nijhoff Netherlands). Kluwer Boston.
Destevens, George, ed. Myocardial Infarction & Cardiac Death. LC 82-11547. Date not set. price not set (ISBN 0-12-212160-0). Acad Pr.
Kirchhoff, Karin T. Coronary Precautions: A Diffusion Survey. Kalisch, Philip & Kalisch, Beatrice, eds. LC 82-17613. (Studies in Nursing Management: No. 8). 128p. 1982. 34.95 (ISBN 0-8357-1377-6). Univ Microfilms.

HEART-JUVENILE LITERATURE
Silverstein, Alvin & Silverstein, Virginia. Heartbeats: Your Body, Your Heart. LC 82-48465. (Illus.). 48p. (gr. 3-5). 1983. 9.57i (ISBN 0-397-32037-X, JBL-J); PLB 9.89g (ISBN 0-397-32038-8). Har-Row.

HEART-RADIOGRAPHY
Hipona, Florencio, ed. Heart. (Multiple Imaging Procedures Ser.: Vol. 5). Date not set. price not set (ISBN 0-8089-1485-5). Grune.

HEART-SURGERY
see also Cardiac Catheterization
Becker, R., et al, eds. Psychopathological & Neurological Dysfunctions Following Open-Heart Surgery, Milwaukee 1980: Proceedings. (Illus.). 384p. 1983. 57.00 (ISBN 0-387-11621-4). Springer-Verlag.
Bharati, Saroja & Lev, Maurice. Cardiac Surgery & the Conduction System. 108p. 1983. 59.50 (ISBN 0-471-08147-7, Pub. by Wiley Med). Wiley.
Dillard & Millar. Atlas of Cardiac Surgery. 1983. price not set (ISBN 0-02-329530-9). Macmillan.
Hochman, Gloria. Heart Bypass: What Every Patient Must Know. 368p. 1983. pap. 7.95 (ISBN 0-345-30902-2). Ballantine.
Holden, M. P. A Practice of Cardiothoracic Surgery. (Illus.). 448p. 1982. text ed. 49.50 (ISBN 0-7236-0626-9). Wright-PSG.
Reinfeld, Nyles V. Open Heart Surgery: A Second Chance. 192p. 1983. 14.00 (ISBN 0-13-637520-0); pap. 6.95 (ISBN 0-13-637512-X). P-H.
Utley, Joe R. Pathophysiology & Techniques of Cardiopulmonary Bypass, Vol. II. (Illus.). 274p. 1983. lib. bdg. price not set (ISBN 0-683-08502-6). Williams & Wilkins.
Wallace, Gordon. The Valiant Heart. 201p. 1982. 12.95 (ISBN 0-942078-01-2). R Tanner Assocs Inc.

HEART ATTACK
see Coronary Heart Disease; Heart-Diseases; Heart-Infarction

HEART CATHETERIZATION
see Cardiac Catheterization

HEART FAILURE
see also Cardiac Resuscitation
Dillard, Jack. Heart Stop: No Death at All. (Illus.). 42p. (Orig.). 1982. pap. write for info. (ISBN 0-940588-08-0). Hazlett Print.
Just, H. & Bussmann, W. D., eds. Vasidilators in Chronic Heart Failure. (Illus.). 240p. 1983. 22.00 (ISBN 0-387-11616-8). Springer-Verlag.

Michaelson, Cydney R., ed. Congestive Heart Failure. (Illus.). 592p. 1983. text ed. 24.95 (ISBN 0-8016-3443-1). Mosby.

HEART PATIENTS

see Cardiacs

HEARTFIELD, JOHN

Kahn, Douglas. John Heartfield: The Cutting Edge. 150p. (Orig.). 1983. 15.95 (ISBN 0-934378-27-4); pap. 7.95 (ISBN 0-934378-28-2). Tanam Pr.

HEAT-PHYSIOLOGICAL EFFECT

Bicherx, Haim I. & Bruley, Duane F., eds. Hyperthermia. (Advances in Experimental Medicine & Biology: Vol. 157). 200p. 1982. 37.50 (ISBN 0-306-41172-5, Plenum Pr). Plenum Pub.

HEAT-TRANSMISSION

see also Heat Exchangers

Barlow, A. Analysis of the Absorption Process & of Desicdant Cooling Systems: A Pseudo-Steady State Model for Coupled Heat & Mass Transfer. (Progress in Solar Energy Supplements Ser.). 160p. 1983. pap. text ed. 15.00x (ISBN 0-89553-069-4). Am Solar Energy.

Beck, J. V. & Yao, L. S., eds. Heat Transfer in Porous Media. (HTD Ser.: Vol. 22). 1982. 24.00 (H00250). ASME.

DiNenno, Philip J. Simplified Radiation Heat Transfer Calculations from Large Open Hydrocarbon Fires. Date not set. 5.35 (ISBN 0-686-37674-9, TR 82-9). Society Fire Protect.

Hausen, Helmuth. Heat Transfer: In Counterflow, Parallel Flow & Cross.Flow. 2nd ed. Wilmott, A. J. & Sayer, M. S., trs. from Ger. (Illus.). 544p. 1982. 59.50 (ISBN 0-07-027215-8, P&RB). McGraw.

Kakac, Sadik & Yener, Yaman. Convective Heat Transfer. (Illus.). 512p. (Orig.). 1982. pap. text ed. 20.00 (ISBN 0-89116-347-6). Hemisphere Pub.

--Convective Heat Transfer. (Illus.). 512p. (Orig.). 1982. pap. text ed. 19.95 (ISBN 0-89116-347-6, Pub. by Middle East Tech U Turkey). Hemisphere Pub.

--Heat Conduction. (Illus.). 431p. (Orig.). 1982. pap. text ed. 20.00 (ISBN 0-89116-346-8, Pub. by Middle East Tech U Turkey). Hemisphere Pub.

Manrique. Transferencia de Calor. 216p. (Span.). 1982. pap. text ed. write for info. (ISBN 0-06-315514-1, Pub. by HarLA Mexcio). Har-Row.

Pletcher, R. H., et al. Computational Fluid Mechanics & Heat Transfer. 1983. price not set (ISBN 0-07-050328-1). McGraw.

Wakao, N. & Kaguei, S. Heat & Mass Transfer in Packed Beds. (Topics in Chemical Engineering Ser.: Vol. 1). 360p. 1982. write for info. Gordon.

Zaric, Z. Structure of Turbulence in Heat & Mass Transfer. 1982. 90.00 (ISBN 0-07-072731-7). McGraw.

HEAT EXCHANGERS

Chisholm, D., ed. Developments in Heat Exchanger Technology, Vol. 1. 1980. 65.75 (ISBN 0-85334-913-4, Pub. by Applied Sci England). Elsevier.

Kakak, S., et al. Heat Exchangers: Thermal-Hydraulic Fundamentals & Design. 1981. 60.00 (ISBN 0-07-033284-3). McGraw.

Shurcliff, William A. Air to Air Heat Exchanges for Houses. 224p. 1982. pap. 12.95 (ISBN 0-931790-40-9). Brick Hse Pub.

Walker, R. G. Industrial Heat Exchangers. 1982. 41.50 (ISBN 0-07-067814-6). McGraw.

HEAT INSULATING MATERIALS

see Insulation (Heat)

HEAT PIPES

Here are entered works on heat transfer cylinders that absorb heat at one end by vaporization of a liquid and release heat by condensation of the liquid at the other end. Works on pipes which are components of heating installations in structures are entered under Heating-Pipes.

American Welding Society. Local Heat Treatment of Welds in Piping & Tubing: D10.10. 1975. 8.00 (ISBN 0-686-43381-5). Am Welding.

Dunn, F. D. Heat Pipes. 3rd ed. (Illus.). 320p. 1982. 49.50 (ISBN 0-08-029356-5); pap. 20.00 (ISBN 0-08-029355-7). Pergamon.

HEAT PUMPS

OECD. Heat Pump Systems: A Technology Review. 200p. 1982. pap. 19.50 (ISBN 92-64-12378-4). OECD.

Swisher, J. Heat Pump Demonstration Analysis. (Progress in Solar Energy Supplements Ser.). 200p. 1982. pap. text ed. 16.50x (ISBN 0-89553-067-8). Am Solar Energy.

HEAT STRESS (BIOLOGY)

see Heat-Physiological Effect

HEAT TRANSFER

see Heat-Transmission

HEATHENISM

see Paganism

HEATHS

see Moors and Heaths

HEATING

see also Boilers; Fuel; Insulation (Heat); Solar Heating; Stoves; Ventilation

El Khashab, A. G. Heating Ventilating & Air-Conditioning Systems Estimating Manual. 2nd ed. 320p. 1983. 37.50 (ISBN 0-07-034536-8, P&RB). McGraw.

Heating, Air Conditioning & Refrigeration Equipment. 1981. 695.00 (ISBN 0-686-38426-1, 203). Busn Trend.

Meador, Roy. Cogeneration & District Heating. LC 81-67258. (Illus.). 203p. 1981. 19.95 (ISBN 0-250-40420-6). Ann Arbor Science.

Swenson, S. D. Heating Technology: Principles Equipment & Application. text ed. 23.95 (ISBN 0-534-01481-X, Breton Pubs). Wadsworth Pub.

Teng, Derek P. Heating & Ventilating: A Handbook of Fitting Craft Practice. 216p. 1980. 40.00x (ISBN 0-85950-051-9, Pub. by Thornes England). State Mutual Bk.

HEAVY IONS

Madurga, G. & Lozano, M. Heavy-Ion Colision, La Rabida, Spain, 1982: Proceedings. (Lecture Notes in Physics: Vol. 168). 429p. 1983. pap. 21.00 (ISBN 0-387-11945-0). Springer-Verlag.

HEBREW ART

see Art, Jewish

HEBREW CHRONOLOGY

see Chronology, Jewish

HEBREW LANGUAGE

see also Yiddish Language

Bergman, Bella. Hebrew Level Two. (Illus.). 243p. 1983. pap. text ed. 5.95 (ISBN 0-87441-360-5). Behrman.

Friedman, Jerome. The Most Ancient Testimony: Sixteenth-Century Christian-Hebraica in the Age of Renaissance Nostalgia. LC 82-18830. x, 279p. 1983. text ed. 24.95 (ISBN 0-8214-0700-7, 82-84697). Ohio U Pr.

McFall, Leslie. The Enigma of the Hebrew Verbal System: Solutions from Ewald to the Present Day. (Historic Texts & Interpreters in Biblical Scholarship Ser.: No. 2). 272p. 1983. text ed. 29.95x (ISBN 0-907459-20-X, Pub. by Almond Pr England); pap. 16.95 (ISBN 0-907459-21-8). Eisenbrauns.

Shachter-Haham, Mayer, ed. Compound of Hebrew. 776p. 1982. text ed. 15.00 (ISBN 0-686-38112-2). K Sefer.

Shipman, Chris. Exercise: The New Language of Love. LC 82-83946. (Illus.). 176p. (Orig.). 1983. pap. 7.95 (ISBN 0-88011-113-5). Leisure Pr.

Simon, Ethelyn & Stahl, Nanette. The First Hebrew Primer for Adults. 2nd ed. 320p. (Orig.). 1983. pap. text ed. 14.95 (ISBN 0-939144-05-0). EKS Pub Co.

Tarnor, Pearl & Tarnor, Norman. Biddur Program III to Hebrew & Heritage. 128p. 1983. pap. text ed. 3.50 (ISBN 0-87441-359-1). Behrman.

--Siddur Program, II to Hebrew & Heritage. (Illus.). 128p. 1982. pap. text ed. 3.50 (ISBN 0-87441-330-3). Behrman.

HEBREW LANGUAGE-CONVERSATION AND PHRASE BOOKS

Berlitz Editors. Hebrew for Travel Cassettepack. 1983. 14.95 (ISBN 0-02-962890-3, Berlitz); cassette incl. Macmillan.

Getting By in Hebrew. (Getting By Language Ser.). 90p. 1983. pap. 2.95 (ISBN 0-8120-2662-4). Barron.

Strauss, Ruby G. & Schuller, Ahuva. I Can Read Hebrew. (Illus.). 64p. (gr. 1-2). 1982. 2.50x (ISBN 0-87441-358-3). Behrman.

HEBREW LANGUAGE-DICTIONARIES

Even-Shosan, Abraham, ed. Condensed Hebrew Dictionary. (Illus.). 824p. (Hebrew.). 1982. text ed. 35.00 (ISBN 0-686-38120-3). K Sefer.

Even-Shoshan, Abraham, ed. The Dictionary for School. (Illus.). 728p. (Hebrew.). 1982. text ed. 10.00 (ISBN 0-686-38116-5). K Sefer.

--The Student's Dictionary. (Illus.). 592p. (Hebrew.). 1982. text ed. 12.00 (ISBN 0-686-38121-1). K Sefer.

Getting By in Hebrew. (Getting By Language Ser.). 90p. 1983. pap. 2.95 (ISBN 0-8120-2662-4). Barron.

HEBREW LANGUAGE-DICTIONARIES-ENGLISH

Even-Shoshan, Abraham, ed. The Complete Hebrew Dictionary in Seven Volumes. (Illus.). 3236p. (Eng. & Hebrew.). text ed. 70.00 (ISBN 0-686-42964-8). K Sefer.

--The Complete Hebrew Dictionary in Three Volumes. (Illus.). 1664p. (Eng. & Hebrew.). text ed. 70.00 (ISBN 0-686-42959-1). K Sefer.

Kamrat, Mordechai & Samuel, Edwin, eds. Roots: A Hebrew-English Word List. (Illus.). 308p. 1982. pap. text ed. 7.50 (ISBN 0-686-38122-X). K Sefer.

Levenston, Edward A. & Sivan, Reuban, eds. The Megiddo Modern Dictionary: English-Hebrew, Hebrew-English, 3 Vols. 1983. 75.00 (ISBN 0-686-43009-3, Carta Maps & Guides Pub Isreal). Hippocrene Bks.

HEBREW LANGUAGE-READERS

Rosenberg, Amye. Sam the Detective's Reading Readiness Book. (Illus.). 63p. (ps). 1982. pap. text ed. 3.50 (ISBN 0-87441-361-3). Behrman.

Simon, Ethelyn & Stahl, Nanette. The First Hebrew Primer for Adults. 2nd ed. 320p. 1983. lib. bdg. 34.95 (ISBN 0-939144-06-9). EKS Pub Co.

HEBREW LANGUAGE-TEXTBOOKS FOR CHILDREN

Sivan, Audrey J. Can You Help This Puppy Find His Family? An Educational Aid for Learning Verb Tenses in Hebrew. (gr. 3up). 1983. pap. write for info. (ISBN 0-86628-044-8). Ridgefield Pub.

HEBREW LAW

see Jewish Law

HEBREW LITERATURE

see also Apocalyptic Literature; Cabala; Talmud

Amram, David. Makers of Hebrew Books in Italy. 350p. Date not set. 60.00 (ISBN 0-87556-013-X). Saifer.

Fishelis, Avraham. Kol Rom, Vol. I. 3rd ed. 208p. (Hebrew.). 5.50 (ISBN 0-9605560-0-1). A Fishelis.

--Kol Rom, Vol. II. 292p. (Hebrew.). 6.50 (ISBN 0-9605560-2-8). A Fishelis.

--Kol Rom, Vol. III. 431p. (Hebrew.). 12.00 (ISBN 0-9605560-3-6). A Fishelis.

Millgram, Abraham E. An Anthology of Medieval Hebrew Literature. 469p. 1982. lib. bdg. 100.00 (ISBN 0-89760-019-3). Telegraph Bks.

HEBREW LITERATURE-TRANSLATIONS INTO ENGLISH

Lelchuk, Alan & Shaked, Gerson, eds. Eight Great Hebrew Short Stories. 1983. pap. 7.95 (ISBN 0-452-00605-8, Mer). NAL.

HEBREW PRIMERS

see Hebrew Language-Textbooks for Children

HEBREWS

see Jews

HEDONISM

see also Altruism; Happiness; Self-Interest; Utilitarianism

Rashdall, Hastings. A Comparative Analysis of Psychological Hedonism & Rationalistic Utilitarianism. (Science of Man Library). (Illus.). 143p. 1983. 79.65 (ISBN 0-89266-385-5). Am Classical Coll Pr.

Safouan, Moustafa. Pleasure & Being: Hedonism from a Psychoanalytic Point of View. Thom, Martin, tr. LC 82-16819. 150p. 1982. 20.00x (ISBN 0-312-61700-3). St Martin.

HEGEL, GEORG WILHELM FRIEDRICH, 1770-1831

Kainz, Howard P. Hegel's Phenomenology: The Evolution of Ethical & Religious Consciousness to the Dialectical Standpoint. 260p. 1983. text ed. 23.95x (ISBN 0-8214-0677-9, 82-84457); pap. 12.95 (ISBN 0-8214-0738-4, 82-85074). Ohio U Pr.

Mure, Geoffrey R. An Introduction to Hegel. LC 82-15853. xviii, 180p. 1982. Repr. of 1940 ed. lib. bdg. 29.75x (ISBN 0-313-23741-7, MUIH). Greenwood.

Punter, David. Blake, Hegel & Dialectic. (Elementa Ser.: Band XXVI). 268p. 1982. pap. text ed. 23.00x (ISBN 90-6203-694-5, Pub. by Rodopi Holland). Humanities.

Wall, Kevin. Relation in Hegel. LC 82-23775. 118p. 1983. pap. text ed. 8.50 (ISBN 0-8191-2976-3). U Pr of Amer.

White, Alan. Absolute Knowledge: Hegel & the Problem of Metaphysics. 190p. 1983. text ed. 22.95x (ISBN 0-8214-0717-1, 82-84861); pap. 11.95 (ISBN 0-8214-0718-X, 82-84879). Ohio U Pr.

HEIDEGGER, MARTIN, 1889-1976

Eisenbeis, Walter. The Key Ideas of Martin Heidegger's Treatise, Being & Time. LC 82-23874. 172p. (Orig.). 1983. lib. bdg. 20.75 (ISBN 0-8191-3009-5); pap. text ed. 10.00 (ISBN 0-8191-3010-9). U Pr of Amer.

Fandozzi, Phillip R. Nihilism & Technology: A Heideggerian Investigation. LC 82-17337. 158p. (Orig.). 1983. lib. bdg. 19.25 (ISBN 0-8191-2825-2); pap. text ed. 8.75 (ISBN 0-8191-2826-0). U Pr of Amer.

Fell, Joseph P. Heidegger & Sartre: An Essay on Being & Place. 517p. 1983. pap. 15.00 (ISBN 0-231-04555-7). Columbia U Pr.

Grassi, Ernesto. Heidegger & the Question of Renaissance Humanism: Four Studies, Vol. 24. Krois, John M., tr. 110p. 1983. 11.00 (ISBN 0-86698-062-8). Medieval & Renaissance NY.

Guignon, Charles B. Heidegger & the Problem of Knowledge. 380p. 1983. text ed. 30.00 (ISBN 0-915145-21-9). Hackett Pub.

Marx, Werner. Heidegger Memorial Lectures. 125p. 1982. 10.00x (ISBN 0-8207-0154-8). Humanities.

HEINE, HEINRICH, 1797-1856

Fullner, Bernd. Heinrich Heine In Deutschen Literaturgeschichten. 340p. (Ger.). 1982. write for info. (ISBN 3-8204-7016-6). P Lang Pubs.

Spencer, Hanna. Heinrich Heine. (World Authors Ser.: No. 669). 1982. lib. bdg. 13.95 (ISBN 0-8057-6516-6, Twayne). G K Hall.

HEINKEL ONE HUNDRED SEVENTY-SEVEN (BOMBERS)

Nowarre, Heinz. Heinkel HE III: A Documentary History. (Illus.). 192p. 1981. 19.95 (ISBN 0-86720-585-7). Sci Bks Intl.

HELICOPTERS

Harrison, P. G. Military Helicopters. (Battlefields Weapons Systems & Technology Ser.: Vol. XI). 200p. 1983. 26.00 (ISBN 0-08-029958-X); pap. 13.00 (ISBN 0-08-029959-8). Pergamon.

Knight, S. Rotorcraft-Helicopter Private: Commercial FAA Written Test Guide. 150p. 1982. 19.95X (ISBN 0-686-43382-3, Progressive Pilot Sem.). Aviation.

Young, Warren. The Helicopters. (Epic of Flight Ser.). 1982. lib. bdg. 19.96 (ISBN 0-8094-3351-6, Pub. by Time-Life). Silver.

HELICOPTERS, USED

see Used Aircraft

HELIOCHROMY

see Color Photography

HELIUM

Benneman, K. H. & Ketterson, J. B., eds. The Physics of Solid and Liquid Helium, Pt.1. 600p. Repr. of 1976 ed. text ed. 46.50 (ISBN 0-471-06600-1). Krieger.

--The Physics of Solid and Liquid Helium, Pt. 2. LC 75-20235. 760p. Repr. of 1978 ed. text ed. 80.95 (ISBN 0-471-06601-X). Krieger.

Sheffer, H. R. Cycles. Schroeder, Howard, ed. (Movin' On Ser.). (Illus.). 48p. (Orig.). (gr. 5-6). 1983. lib. bdg. 7.95 (ISBN 0-89686-199-6). Crestwood Hse.

HELL

Adams, Judith. Against the Gates of Hell. 152p. pap. 2.50 (ISBN 0-87509-232-2). Chr Pubns.

Fudge, Edward. The Fire that Consumes: A Biblical & History Study of Final Punishment. Date not set. 19.95 (ISBN 0-89890-018-2). Providential Pr.

Hagin, Kenneth E. I Went to Hell. 1982. pap. 0.50 (ISBN 0-89276-257-8). Hagin Ministry.

Teller, Woolsey & Gauvin, Marshall. Hell, A Christian Doctrine. (Illus.). 47p. 1983. pap. 3.00 (ISBN 0-910309-01-9). Am Atheist.

HELLENISM

Barnes, Jonathan, et al. Science & Speculation. LC 82-4221. (Studies in Hellinistic Theory & Practice). 352p. Date not set. 44.50 (ISBN 0-521-24689-X). Cambridge U Pr.

HELVETIUS, CLAUDE ADRIEN, 1715-1771

Smith, David W. Helvetius: A Study in Persecution. LC 82-15841. (Illus.). viii, 250p. 1982. lib. bdg. 35.00x (ISBN 0-313-23744-1, SMHL). Greenwood.

HEMATOLOGY

see also Blood; Pediatric Hematology

Brain, Michael C. & McCulloch, Peter B. Current Therapy in Hematology-Oncology. 400p. 1983. text ed. 44.00 (ISBN 0-941158-05-5, D07809). Mosby.

Ferrone, Soldano & Solheim, Bjarte G., eds. HLA Typing: Methodology & Clinical Aspects, 2 vols. 208p. 1982. 59.00 ea. Vol. I (ISBN 0-8493-6410-8). Vol. II (ISBN 0-8493-6411-6). CRC Pr.

Fulwood, Robinson & Johnson, Clifford L. Hematological & Nutritional Biochemistries References Data of Persons 6 Months-74 Years of Age: United States, 1976-1980. Cox, Klaudia, tr. (Ser. 11: No. 232). 60p. 1982. pap. 1.95 (ISBN 0-8406-0267-7). Natl Ctr Health Stats.

Hocking, William G. Practical Hematology. (Family Practice Today: A Comprehensive Postgraduate Library). 355p. 1983. 35.00 (ISBN 0-471-09563-X, Pub. by Wiley Med). Wiley.

Roath, S., ed. Topical Reviews in Haematology, Vol. 2. (Illus.). 240p. 1982. text ed. 32.50 (ISBN 0-7236-0615-3). Wright-PSG.

Williams, W. Hematology: PreTest Self-Assessment & Review. 240p. Date not set. 31.95 (ISBN 0-07-051930-7). McGraw-Pretest.

HEMATOPHILA

see Hemophilia

HEMATOPOIETIC SYSTEM

see also Reticulo-Endothelial System

Marchesi, Vincent T. & Gallo, Robert C., eds. Differentiation & Function of Hematopoietic Cell Surfaces. LC 82-6557. (UCLA Symposia on Molecular & Cellular Biology Ser.: Vol. 1). 320p. 1982. 56.00 (ISBN 0-8451-2600-8). A R Liss.

HEMIC CELLS

see Blood Cells

HEMINGWAY, ERNEST, 1899-1961

Hotchner, A. E. Papa Hemingway: The Ecstasy & Sorrow. (Illus.). 352p. 1983. Repr. 16.95 (ISBN 0-688-02041-0). Morrow.

--Papa Hemingway: The Ecstasy & Sorrow. (Illus.). 352p. 1982. pap. 8.95 (ISBN 0-688-02042-9). Quill NY.

Kert, Bernice. The Hemingway Women. (Illus.). 1983. 20.00 (ISBN 0-393-01720-6). Norton.

Reynolds, Michael S. Critical Essays on Ernest Hemingway's "In Our Time". (Critical Essays in American Literature Ser.). 330p. 1983. lib. bdg. 32.00 (ISBN 0-8161-8637-5). G K Hall.

Svoboda, Frederic J. Hemingway & the Sun Also Rises: The Crafting of a Style. LC 82-20026. (Illus.). 216p. 1983. text ed. 19.95x (ISBN 0-7006-0228-3). Univ Pr KS.

HEMOPHILIA

Forbes, C. D. Unresolved Problems in Haemophilia. (Illus.). 245p. 1981. text ed. 29.95 (ISBN 0-85200-388-9, Pub. by MTP Pr England). Kluwer Boston.

HEMORRHAGE

see also Hemostasis

Sibinga, C. Th. & Das, P. C. Blood Transfusion & Problems of Bleeding. 1982. text ed. 39.50 (ISBN 90-247-3058-9, Pub. by Martinus Nijhoff Netherlands). Kluwer Boston.

HEMORRHAGIC DIATHESIS

see Hemophilia

HEMORRHOIDS

Holt, Robert L. Hemorrhoids: A Cure & Preventative. LC 77-86391. (Illus.). 1978. pap. 7.95 (ISBN 0-930926-01-3). Calif Health.

HEMOSTASIS

see also Hemorrhage

Sharp, Alan A. Hemostasis & Thrombosis. new ed. (BIMR Hematology Ser.: vol. 1). 1983. text ed. price not set (ISBN 0-407-02335-6). Butterworth.

HENS

see Poultry

HEORTOLOGY
see Church Year
HEPATITIS, INFECTIOUS
Beker, Simon, ed. Diagnostic Procedures in the Evaluation of Hepatic Diseases. LC 82-20324. (Laboratory & Research Methods in Biology & Medicine Ser.: Vol. 7). 620p. 1983. write for info. (ISBN 0-8451-1656-8). A R Liss.
HEPATOLENTICULAR DEGENERATION
Epstein. Kidney in Liver Disease. 1982. 75.00 (ISBN 0-444-00655-9). Elsevier.
HERALDIC BOOK-PLATES
see Book-Plates
HERALDRY
see also Chivalry; Decorations of Honor; Emblems; Genealogy; Mottoes; Nobility; Seals (Numismatics)
Manning, Alan. The Argentaye Tract: A Critical Edition. (Toronto Medieval Texts & Translations). (Illus.). 132p. 1983. 30.00x (ISBN 0-8020-5590-7). U of Toronto Pr.
HERALDRY–IRELAND
De Breffny, Brian. Irish Family Names: Arms, Origins, & Locations. 50.00x (ISBN 0-7171-1225-X). State Mutual Bk.
HERBAGE
see Grasses
HERBALS
see Botany, Medical; Herbs; Materia Medica, Vegetable; Medicine, Medieval
HERBICIDES
Bovey, Rodney W. & Young, Alvin L. The Science of Two, Four, Five-T & Associated Phenoxy Herbicides. 462p. 1980. 47.95x (ISBN 0-471-05134-9, Pub. by Wiley-Interscience). Wiley.
Eagle, D. J. & Caverly, D. J. Diagnosis of Herbicide Damage to Crops. (Illus.). 1981. 35.00 (ISBN 0-8206-0294-9). Chem Pub.
Johnson, J. C., ed. Plant Growth Regulators & Herbicide Antagonists: Recent Advances. LC 82-7966. (Chemical Technology Rev. 212). (Illus.). 303p. 1983. 45.00 (ISBN 0-8155-0915-4). Noyes.
Moreland, Donald E. & St. John, Judith B., eds. Biochemical Responses by Herbicides. (ACS Symposium Ser.: No. 181). 1982. write for info. (ISBN 0-8412-0699-6). Am Chemical.
Page, B. G. & Thomson, W. T. Insecticide, Herbicide Fungicide Quick Guide, 1983. 140p. Date not set. pap. 12.00 (ISBN 0-913702-20-X). Thomson Pub CA.
Torrey, S., ed. Pre-emergence Herbicides: Recent Advances. LC 82-7954. (Chemical Technology Rev. 211). (Illus.). 335p. 1983. 48.00 (ISBN 0-8155-0914-6). Noyes.
Van Strum, Carol. A Bitter Fog: Herbicides & Human Rights. LC 82-16821. 320p. 1983. 14.95 (ISBN 0-87156-329-0). Sierra.
Wilcox, Fred A. Waiting for an Army to Die: The Tragedy of Agent Orange. LC 82-42791. 256p. 1983. pap. 7.95 (ISBN 0-394-71518-7, Vin). Random.
HERBIVORA
see also names of herbivorous animals
Denno, Robert F. & McClure, Mark S., eds. Variable Plants & Herbivores in Natureal & Managed Systems. Date not set. price not set (ISBN 0-12-209160-4). Acad Pr.
HERBS
see also Botany, Medical; Cookery (Herbs and Spices); Materia Medica, Vegetable; Medicine, Medieval
Campbell, Mary M. & Greely, Deborah W., eds. A Basket of Herbs. (Illus.). 1983. text ed. 10.95 (ISBN 0-8289-0500-2). Greene.
Center for Self Sufficiency Research Division Staff. International Directory of Herb, Health, Vitamin & Natural Food Catalogs. 200p. 1983. pap. text ed. 15.95 (ISBN 0-910811-36-9). Center Self.
Center for Self-Sufficiency Staff, compiled by. Herbs: A Bibliography Index. 35p. Date not set. pap. text ed. 8.95 (ISBN 0-910811-04-0). Center Self.
Conrow, Robert & Hecksel, Arlene. Herbal Pathfinders: A Sourcebook for the Herbal Renaissance. (Illus.). 320p. 1983. pap. 9.95 (ISBN 0-88007-128-1). Woodbridge Pr.
Culpeper, Nicholas. Culpeper's Color Herbal. (Illus.). 224p. (Orig.). 1983. pap. 12.95 (ISBN 0-8069-7690-X). Sterling.
Leyel, C. F. THe Truth About Herbs. 106p. 4.50 (ISBN 0-686-38236-6). Sun-Bks.
Miller, Richard A. The Magical & Ritual Use of Herbs. 144p. 1983. pap. 5.95 (ISBN 0-89281-047-5). Destiny Bks.
Riva, Anna. Modern Herbal Spellbook. (Illus.). 1974. pap. 3.00 (ISBN 0-943832-03-9). Intl Imports.
Simon, James & Chadwick. Herbs: An Indexed Bibliography of Last Decade, 1971-1980. (The Scientific Literature on Selected Temperate Herb, Aromatic, & Medicine Plants Ser.). 1983. 49.50 (ISBN 0-208-01990-1, Archon Bks). Shoe String.
Szekely, Edmond B. The Book of Herbs. (Illus.). 48p. 1981. pap. 2.95 (ISBN 0-89564-044-9). IBS Intl.
Tierra, Michael, ed. Way of Herbs. 1983. pap. 3.50 (ISBN 0-686-37705-2). WSP.
HERBS–THERAPEUTIC USE
see Botany, Medical; Materia Medica, Vegetable; Medicine, Medieval
HERCULES
Richardson, I. M. The Adventures of Hercules. LC 82-16557. (Illus.). 32p. (gr. 4-8). 1983. PLB 8.79 (ISBN 0-89375-865-5); pap. text ed. 2.50 (ISBN 0-89375-866-3). Troll Assocs.
HEREDITARY METABOLIC DISORDERS
see Metabolism, Inborn Errors of
HEREDITY
see also Biometry; Blood Groups; Chromosomes; Evolution; Hybridization; Genetics; Linkage (Genetics); Natural Selection; Population Genetics; Variation (Biology)
Galton, Francis. Hereditary Genius. Eysenck, H. J., ed. (Classics in Psychology & Psychiatry Ser.). 432p. 1983. Repr. of 1869 ed. write for info. (ISBN 0-904014-40-1). F Pinter Pubs.
Lee, Sherry, et al. Chromosomes & Genes: An Interracial Anthology. 54p. (Orig.). 1982. pap. 3.50 (ISBN 0-940248-12-3). Guild Pr.
O'Malley, Bert W., ed. Gene Regulation: UCLA Symposium Molecular Cellular Biology. LC 82-20709. (Vol. 26). 1982. 36.50 (ISBN 0-12-525960-3). Acad Pr.
Pierce, Carl W. & Cullen, Susan E., eds. Ir Genes: Past, Present, & Future. (Experimental Biology & Medicine Ser.). (Illus.). 640p. 1983. 64.50 (ISBN 0-89603-050-4). Humana.
HEREDITY, HUMAN
see also Human Genetics
Gardner, Eldon J. Human Heredity. 460p. 1983. text ed. 20.95 (ISBN 0-471-08376-3). Wiley.
HERMENEUTICS
Flinn, Frank K., ed. Hermeneutics & Horizons: The Shape of the Future. LC 82-50053. (Conference Ser.: No. 11). xvii, 445p. (Orig.). 1982. pap. text ed. 11.95 (ISBN 0-932894-11-9). Unif Theol Seminary.
Pannenberg, Wolfhart. Basic Questions in Theology, Vol. I. LC 82-15984. 257p. 1983. pap. write for info. (ISBN 0-664-24466-1). Westminster.
HERMENEUTICS, BIBLICAL
see Bible–Hermeneutics
HERMETIC ART AND PHILOSOPHY
see Alchemy; Astrology; Magic; Occult Sciences
HERO-WORSHIP
see Heroes
HEROES
see also Courage; Explorers; Mythology; Saints
also particular civilian and military awards, e.g. Nobel Prizes, Medal of Honor
Carlyle, Thomas. The Psychological Theory of the Hero in History & in Politics. (The Essential Library of the Great Philosophers Ser.). (Illus.). 121p. 1983. 61.85 (ISBN 0-686-82208-0). Am Inst Psych.
Linenthal, Edward T. Changing Images of the Warrior Hero in America: A History of Popular Symbolism. (Studies in American Religion: Vol. 6). 296p. 1983. 39.95 (ISBN 0-88946-921-0). E Mellen.
Mitchell, Meredith. Heroes & Victims. Sternback-Scott, Sisa & Smith, Lindsay, eds. 1983. 16.95 (ISBN 0-938434-18-7); pap. 11.95 (ISBN 0-938434-15-2). Sigo Pr.
HEROES IN LITERATURE
Brommer, Frank. The Twelve Labors of the Hero in Ancient Art & Literature. Schwarz, S. J., tr. (Illus.). 128p. lib. bdg. 20.00x (ISBN 0-89241-375-1). Caratzas Bros.
HEROIN
Kaplan, John. The Hardest Drug: Heroin & Public Policy. LC 82-17514. (Studies in Crime & Justice). 1983. 20.00. U of Chicago Pr.
HEROINES
see Women; Women in Literature; Women in the Bible
HEROISM
see Courage; Heroes
HERPES SIMPLEX VIRUS
Kennedy, Raymond. Herpes: How to Live with It, How to Treat It, How Not to Treat It. 1983. pap. 10.95 (ISBN 0-911411-12-7). Am Med Pub.
Landow, R. K. Herpes in Focus. (Illus.). 288p. 1983. 17.95 (ISBN 0-8065-0837-X). Citadel Pr.
Langston, Deborah P. Living with Herpes. LC 82-45627. (Illus.). 216p. 1983. pap. 7.95 (ISBN 0-385-18410-7, Dolp). Doubleday.
Pan, Charlene. Herpes Simplex: A Complete Cure. 110p. 1982. pap. 5.00 (ISBN 0-940178-12-5). Sitare Inc.
Roizman, Bernard, ed. The Herpes Viruses. LC 82-15034. (The Viruses: Vol.1). 1982. 39.50x (ISBN 0-686-83976-5, Plenum Pr). Plenum Pub.
HERRICK, ROBERT, 1591-1674
Hageman, Elizabeth H. Robert Herrick: A Reference Guide. 1983. lib. bdg. 34.00 (ISBN 0-8161-8012-1, Hall Reference). G K Hall.
HERSEY, JOHN, 1914-
Huse, Nancy L. The Survival Tales of John Hersey. LC 82-50825. 220p. 1983. 18.50X (ISBN 0-87875-238-2). Whitston Pub.
HERTFORDSHIRE, ENGLAND
Meadows, Eric G. Pictorial Guide to Hertfordshire. 160p. 1982. 25.00x (ISBN 0-900804-22-X, Pub. by White Crescent England). State Mutual Bk.
HERTZIAN WAVES
see Electric Waves
HESSE, HERMANN, 1877-1962
Marrer-Tising, Carlee. The Reception of Herman Hesse by the Youth in the United States: A Thematic Analysis. 487p. 1982. write for info. (ISBN 3-261-05006-3). P Lang Pubs.
HETEROCERA
see Moths
HETEROCYCLIC COMPOUNDS
Ellis, G. P. Chromenes, Chromanones, & Chromones: Chemistry of Heterocyclic Compounds-A Series of Monographs. (Vol. 31). 1196p. 1977. 212.95x (ISBN 0-471-38212-4). Wiley.
Finley, K. T. Triazoles. (Chemistry of Heterocyclic Compounds, Series of Monographs: Vol. 39). 349p. 1980. 126.50x (ISBN 0-471-07827-1). Wiley.
Katritzky, A. R. & Boulton, A. J., eds. Advances in Heterocyclic Chemistry Supplement, No. 2. 432p. 1982. 59.50 (ISBN 0-12-020652-8); 77.50 (ISBN 0-12-020693-5); 42.00 (ISBN 0-12-020694-3). Acad Pr.
Katritzky, Alan R., ed. Advances in Heterocyclic Chemistry, Vol. 33. (Serial Publication). Date not set. price not set (ISBN 0-12-020633-1); price not set (ISBN 0-12-020740-0); price not set Microfiche (ISBN 0-12-020741-9). Acad Pr.
Rosowsky, Andre. Azepines, Pt. 2. (Chemistry of Heterocyclic Compounds). 850p. 1983. 175.00 (ISBN 0-471-89592-X, Pub. by Wiley-Interscience). Wiley.
--Azepines: Heterocyclic Compounds. (Series of Monographs: Pt. 1). 700p. 1983. 150.00 (ISBN 0-471-01878-3, Pub. by Wiley-Interscience). Wiley.
HETEROGENESIS
see Life–Origin
HETEROSIS
Frankel, R., ed. Heterosis. (Monographs on Theoretical & Applied Genetics: Vol. 6). (Illus.). 320p. 1983. 33.50 (ISBN 0-387-12125-0). Springer-Verlag.
HEXAPODA
see Insects
HI-FI SYSTEMS
see High-Fidelity Sound Systems
HIDATSA INDIANS
see Indians of North America–The West
HIERATIC INSCRIPTIONS
see Egyptian Language–Inscriptions
HIERONYMUS, SAINT
see Jerome, Saint (Hieronymus, Saint)
HIGH BLOOD PRESSURE
see Hypertension
HIGH ENERGY FORMING
Schroeder, J. W., ed. High Energy Rate Fabrication. (PVP Ser.: Vol. 70). 1982. 20.00 (H00246). ASME.
HIGH-FIBER DIET
Eyton, Audrey. The F-Plan Diet. LC 82-17969. 256p. 1983. 12.95 (ISBN 0-517-54934-4). Crown.
The Natural High-Fiber Diet. Date not set. pap. 1.75 (ISBN 0-515-05913-7). Jove Pubns.
HIGH-FIDELITY SOUND SYSTEMS
see also Stereophonic Sound Systems
Brown. Questions & Answers: Hi-Fi. (Illus.). 1974. pap. 4.95 (ISBN 0-408-00151-8). Focal Pr.
HIGH-FREQUENCY INDUCTION HEATING
see Induction Heating
HIGH INTRAOCULAR PRESSURE
see Glaucoma
HIGH JUMPING
see Jumping
HIGH PRESSURE RESEARCH
Akimoto, S. & Manghnani, M. H. High Pressure Research in Geophysics. 1982. 113.00 (ISBN 90-277-1439-8, Pub. by Reidel Holland). Kluwer Boston.
HIGH-RESIDUE DIET
see High-Fiber Diet
HIGH SCHOOL EQUIVALENCY EXAMINATION
see also General Educational Development Tests
Barasch, Seymour. High School Equivalency Diploma Test. LC 81-1618. (Arco's Preparation for the GED Examination Ser.). 480p. 1983. lib. bdg. 12.95 (ISBN 0-668-05375-5); pap. 6.95 (ISBN 0-668-05382-8). Arco.
Rudman, Jack. High School Equivalency Diplomacy Examination. (Career Examination Ser.: CS-50). (Cloth bdg. avail. on request). pap. 13.95 (ISBN 0-686-84423-8). Natl Learning.
HIGH SCHOOL STUDENTS
Belting, Paul E. & Clevenger, A. W. The High School at Work. 441p. 1982. Repr. of 1939 ed. lib. bdg. 30.00 (ISBN 0-89760-093-2). Telegraph Bks.
Herzog, A. Regula & Bachman, Jerald G. Sex Roles Attitudes Among High School Seniors: Views about Work & Family Roles. 272p. 1982. pap. 16.00x (ISBN 0-87944-275-1). Inst Soc Res.
Soutter, John C. Survive! (Orig.). (gr. 9-12). 1983. pap. 3.95 (ISBN 0-8423-6694-6). Tyndale.
HIGH SCHOOL TEACHERS
Belting, Paul E. & Clevenger, A. W. The High School at Work. 441p. 1982. Repr. of 1939 ed. lib. bdg. 30.00 (ISBN 0-89760-093-2). Telegraph Bks.
Rudman, Jack. Senior High School. (Teachers Lesson Plan Bk.: S-I). (gr. 9-12). pap. 3.95 (ISBN 0-686-84421-1). Natl Learning.
HIGH SCHOOLS–ADMINISTRATION
Belting, Paul E. & Clevenger, A. W. The High School at Work. 441p. 1982. Repr. of 1939 ed. lib. bdg. 30.00 (ISBN 0-89760-093-2). Telegraph Bks.
HIGH SCHOOLS–ENTRANCE REQUIREMENTS
How to Prepare for TEH High School Entrance Exam. 4th ed. 1983. pap. write for info. (ISBN 0-8120-2671-3). Barron.
HIGH SEAS, JURISDICTION OVER
see Maritime Law
HIGH SOCIETY
see Upper Classes
HIGH-SPEED DATA PROCESSING
see Real-Time Data Processing
HIGH SPEED PHOTOGRAPHY
see Photography, High-Speed
HIGH TEMPERATURE METALLURGY
see Metals at High Temperatures
HIGH TEMPERATURES–PHYSIOLOGICAL EFFECT
see Heat–Physiological Effect
HIGH VACUUM TECHNIQUE
see Vacuum
HIGH VELOCITY FORMING
see High Energy Forming
HIGH-VOLTAGE HIGH-FREQUENCY PHOTOGRAPHY
see Kirlian Photography
HIGHER EDUCATION
see Education, Higher
HIGHER LAW
see Government, Resistance To
HIGHWAY ACCIDENTS
see Traffic Accidents
HIGHWAY COMMUNICATION
see also Traffic Signs and Signals
Rudman, Jack. Administrative Superintendent of Highway Operations. (Career Examination Ser.: C-2608). (Cloth bdg. avail. on request). pap. 12.00 (ISBN 0-8373-2608-7). Natl Learning.
HIGHWAY ENGINEERING
see Roads; Traffic Engineering
HIGHWAY LAW
see Cycling
HIGHWAY SAFETY
see Traffic Safety
HIGHWAY TRANSPORT WORKERS
Rudman, Jack. Motor Equipment Manager. (Career Examination Ser.: C-359). (Cloth bdg. avail. on request). pap. 14.00 (ISBN 0-686-84424-6). Natl Learning.
HIGHWAYS
see Roads
HIKING
see also Backpacking; Mountaineering; Orientation; Trails; Walking
Doan, Daniel. Fifty More Hikes in New Hampshire: Day Hikes & Backpacking Trips from the Coast to Coos County. rev. ed. (Fifty Hikes Ser.). (Illus.). 224p. 1983. pap. 8.95 (ISBN 0-942440-06-4). Backcountry Pubns.
Fuller, Margaret. Trails of Western Idaho. LC 82-5621. (Illus.). 280p. pap. 10.25 (ISBN 0-913140-44-9). Signpost Bk Pub.
Ganci, Dave. Hiking the Southwest: Arizona, New Mexico, & West Texas. LC 82-19418. (A Sierra Club Totebook). (Illus.). 384p. (Orig.). 1983. pap. 8.95 (ISBN 0-87156-338-X). Sierra.
Grodin, Joseph & Grodin, Sharon. High Sierra Hiking Guide to Silver Lake. 3rd ed. Winnett, Thomas, ed. (High Sierra Hiking Guide Ser.: No. 17). (Illus.). 96p. 1983. pap. 4.95 (ISBN 0-89997-027-3). Wilderness Pr.
Houck, Walter & New York-New Jersey Trail Conference Staff. Day Walker: Twenty-Eight Hikes in the New York Metropolitan Area. LC 79-7688. (Illus.). 192p. 1983. pap. 7.95 (ISBN 0-385-14140-8, Anch). Doubleday.
Kemsley, William, ed. The Whole Hiker's Handbook. (Illus.). 1979. pap. 12.95 (ISBN 0-688-08476-1). Quill NY.
Linkhart, Luther. The Trinity Alps: A Hiking & Backpacking Guide. Winnett, Thomas, ed. (Illus.). 192p. 1983. pap. 9.95 (ISBN 0-89997-024-9). Wilderness Pr.
Maughan, Jackie. Hiker's Guide to Idaho. (Illus.). 256p. 1983. pap. 7.95 (ISBN 0-934318-18-2). Falcon Pr MT.
Patterson, Thomas. Wasatch Hiking Map. 1983. pap. 5.00 (ISBN 0-87480-220-2). U of Utah Pr.
Pearson, John R., ed. Hiker's Guide to Trails of Big Bend National Park. 2nd ed. (Illus.). 32p. (Orig.). 1978. pap. 1.00 (ISBN 0-686-38926-3). Big Bend.
Schneider, Bill. Hiker's Guide to Montana. rev. ed. LC 82-84323. (Illus.). 256p. pap. 7.95 (ISBN 0-934318-08-5). Falcon Pr MT.
HILBERT SPACE
Oda, Takayuki. Periods of Hilbert Modular Surfaces. (Progress in Mathematics Ser.: Vol. 19). 1981. text ed. 10.00x (ISBN 3-7643-3084-8). Birkhauser.
HIMALAYA MOUNTAINS
Chorlton, W. Cloud Dwellers of the Himalayas: The Bhotia. (Peoples of the Wild Ser.). 1982. 15.96 (ISBN 0-7054-0705-5, Pub. by Time-Life). Silver.
Harrer, Heinrich. Ladakh: Gods & Mortals Behind the Himalayas. Rickett, Richard, tr. from Ger. (Illus.). 170p. 1980. 27.50x (ISBN 3-524-76002-3). Intl Pubns Serv.
HINDI LANGUAGE
see also Urdu Language
Shah, Kirit N. Learn Hindi: Hindi Sikhiye. Parikh, Bharat, ed. LC 82-99946. (Illus.). 192p. (Orig.). 1983. pap. text ed. 9.95 (ISBN 0-9609614-1-0). K N Shah.
HINDU LAW
Venkatarman, S. A Treatise on Hindu Law. (Orient Longman Law Library). 550p. 1980. pap. text ed. 18.95x (ISBN 0-86131-211-2, Pub. by Orient Longman Ltd India). Apt Bks.

HINDU LITERATURE

Mishra, V. B. From the Vedas to the Manu-Samhita: A Cultural Study. 160p. 1982. text ed. 19.50x (ISBN 0-391-02705-0). Humanities.

HINDU MUSIC

see Music, Indic

HINDU MYTHOLOGY

see Mythology, Hindu

HINDUISM

see also Brahmanism; Caste–India; Dharma; Jains; Karma; Tantrism; Vedas; Yoga

Desai, Santosh N. Hinduism in Thai Life. 163p. 1980. 34.95x (ISBN 0-940500-66-3, Pub by Popular Prakashan India). Asia Bk Corp.

Sarkar, S., ed. Hindustan Year-Book & Who's Who in 1981. 49th ed. 212p. 1981. pap. 12.50x (ISBN 0-8002-3054-X, SA64-762). Intl Pubns Serv.

Vable, D. The Arya Samaj: Hindu without Hinduism. 1983. text ed. write for info. (ISBN 0-7069-2131-3, Pub. by Vikas India). Advent NY.

HIP JOINT

Turner, Roderick & Scheller, Arnold, eds. Revision Total Hip Arthoplasty. 412p. 1982. 59.50 (ISBN 0-8089-1466-9). Grune.

HIPPIES

Kapur, Tribhuwan. Hippies: A Study of Their Drug habits & Sexual Customs. 221p. 1981. 21.00x (ISBN 0-7069-1296-9). Intl Pubns Serv.

HIPPOCAMPUS (BRAIN)

Seifert, Wilfried, ed. Neurobiology of the Hippocampus. Date not set. price not set (ISBN 0-12-634880-4). Acad Pr.

HIPPOLOGY

see Horses

HIROHITO, EMPEROR OF JAPAN, 1901-

Hane, Mikiso, tr. from Japanese. Emperor Hirohito & His Chief Aide de Camp: The Honjo Diary, 1933-36. 250p. 1982. text ed. 22.50 (ISBN 0-686-82128-9, Pub. by U of Tokyo Japan). Columbia U Pr.

HIROSHIGE, 1797-1858

Izzard, Sebastian. Hiroshige: An Exhibition of Selected Prints. (Illus.). 116p. 1983. pap. 20.00 (ISBN 0-9610398-0-9). Ukiyo-e Soc.

HIRSCHSPRUNG'S DISEASE

see Megacolon

HISPANOS

see Mexican Americans

HISTOCHEMISTRY

see also Biological Chemistry; Cytochemistry; Molecular Biology

Cuello, A. C. Immunohistochemistry. (IBRO Handbook Ser.: Methods in the Neurosciences). 500p. 1982. write for info. (ISBN 0-471-10245-8, Pub. by Wiley-Interscience); pap. write for info. (ISBN 0-471-90052-4). Wiley.

HISTOLOGY

see also Botany–Anatomy; Cells; Histochemistry; Microscope and Microscopy; Tissues;

also names of particular tissues or organs, e.g. Muscle, Nerves

Amenta, Peter S. Histology & Embryology Review. LC 82-11322. (Illus.). 172p. 1983. pap. text ed. 10.00 (ISBN 0-668-05486-7, 5486). Arco.

Bacon, R. L. & Niles, N. R. Medical Histology: A Text-Atlas with Introductory Pathology. (Illus.). 368p. 1983. 34.50 (ISBN 0-387-90734-3). Springer-Verlag.

Dodd, E. E. Atlas of Histology. 1979. 38.95 (ISBN 0-07-017230-7). McGraw.

Ratcliffe, N. A. & Llewllyn, P. J. Practical Illustrated Histology. 1982. 70.00x (ISBN 0-333-32653-9, Pub. by Macmillan England). State Mutual Bk.

Roisen, Fred J. & Hsu, Linda. Histology. 2nd ed. (Medical Examination Review Ser.). 1982. pap. text ed. 12.95 (ISBN 0-87488-219-2). Med Exam.

Ross, Michael H. & Reith, Edward J. Histology: A Text & Atlas. 352p. 1983. text ed. 25.50 scp (ISBN 0-06-045602-7, HarpC). Har-Row.

Warren, B. A. & Jeynes, B. J. Basic Histology: A Review with Questions and Explanations. 1983. pap. write for info. (ISBN 0-316-92358-3). Little.

HISTOLOGY–ATLASES

Wismar, Beth L. An Atlas for Histology. (Illus.). 200p. 1983. lib. bdg. 16.95 (ISBN 0-683-09150-6). Williams & Wilkins.

HISTOLOGY, PATHOLOGICAL

Bacon, R. L. & Niles, N. R. Medical Histology: A Text-Atlas with Introductory Pathology. (Illus.). 368p. 1983. 34.50 (ISBN 0-387-90734-3). Springer-Verlag.

HISTOLOGY, VEGETABLE

see Botany–Anatomy

HISTORIANS

see also Archaeologists

Fitzsimons, M. A. The Past Recaptured: Great Historians & the History of History. 1983. price not set. U of Notre Dame Pr.

Joyce, Davis D. History & Historians: Some Essays. LC 82-21865. 116p. (Orig.). 1983. lib. bdg. 18.75 (ISBN 0-8191-2936-4); pap. text ed. 8.25 (ISBN 0-8191-2937-2). U Pr of Amer.

HISTORIANS–GREAT BRITAIN

Sullivan, Harry R. Frederic Harrison. (English Authors Ser.: No. 341). 232p. 1983. lib. bdg. 18.95 (ISBN 0-8057-6827-0, Twayne). G K Hall.

HISTORIANS–UNITED STATES

Wish, Harvey. The American Historian: A Social-Intellectual History of the Writing of the American Past. LC 82-21150. viii, 366p. 1983. Repr. of 1960 ed. lib. bdg. 45.00x (ISBN 0-313-23847-2, WHAM). Greenwood.

HISTORIC BUILDINGS

see also Historic Sites

also specific kinds of historic buildings according to use, e.g. Churches; Hotels, Taverns, etc.; and subdivision Buildings under names of cities, e.g. New York (city)–Buildings

Lowenthal, David & Binney, Marcus, eds. Our Past Before Us: Why Do We Save It? 1981. 33.00x (ISBN 0-85117-219-9, Pub. by M Temple Smith). State Mutual Bk.

McKee, Harley J. Recording Historic Buildings. Rev. ed. (Landmark Reprint Ser.). (Illus.). 176p. 1983. 14.95 (ISBN 0-89133-105-0). Preservation Pr.

Tubesing, Richard. Architectural Preservation & Urban Renovation: An Annotated Bibliography of U. S. Congressional Documents. LC 81-48417. 500p. 1982. lib. bdg. 60.00 (ISBN 0-8240-9386-0). Garland Pub.

HISTORIC HOUSES, ETC.

see Historic Buildings

HISTORIC SITES

see also Historic Buildings

Fenn, Elizabeth A. & Wood, Peter H. Natives & Newcomers: The Way We Lived in North Carolina Before 1770. Nathans, Sydney, ed. LC 82-20128. (The Way We Lived in North Carolina Ser.). (Illus.). viii, 98p. 1983. 11.95 (ISBN 0-8078-1549-7); pap. 6.95 (ISBN 0-8078-4101-3). U of NC Pr.

Lowenthal, David & Binney, Marcus, eds. Our Past Before Us: Why Do We Save It? 1981. 33.00x (ISBN 0-85117-219-9, Pub. by M Temple Smith). State Mutual Bk.

Nathans, Sydney. The Quest for Progress: The Way We Lived in North Carolina, 1870-1920. LC 82-20133. (The Way We Lived in North Carolina Ser.). (Illus.). viii, 108p. 1983. 11.95 (ISBN 0-8078-1552-7); pap. 6.95 (ISBN 0-8078-4104-8). U of NC Pr.

Tubesing, Richard. Architectural Preservation & Urban Renovation: An Annotated Bibliography of U. S. Congressional Documents. LC 81-48417. 500p. 1982. lib. bdg. 60.00 (ISBN 0-8240-9386-0). Garland Pub.

Watson, Harry L. An Independent People: The Way We Lived in North Carolina, 1770-1820. Nathans, Sydney, ed. LC 82-20098. (The Way We Lived in North Carolina Ser.). (Illus.). viii, 118p. 1983. 11.95 (ISBN 0-8078-1550-0); pap. 6.95 (ISBN 0-8078-4102-1). U of NC Pr.

HISTORIC WATERS (INTERNATIONAL LAW)

see Territorial Waters

HISTORICAL ART

see History in Art

HISTORICAL ATLASES

see Classical Geography

HISTORICAL CRITICISM

see Historiography

HISTORICAL DICTIONARIES

see History–Dictionaries

HISTORICAL FICTION

see also subdivision Fiction under names of countries, cities, etc., and under names of historical events and characters

Landry, Monica & Olivier, Julien. Tantine: l'Histoire de Lucille Landry Augustine Gabrielle. Anderson, Penny & Granger, Mary, trs. (Oral History Ser.). (Illus.). 45p. (Fr.). (gr. 9). 1981. pap. 2.00x (ISBN 0-911409-05-X). Natl Mat Dev.

HISTORICAL RECORD PRESERVATION

see Archives

HISTORICAL RESEARCH

see also Historiography

Henderson, Harold. Seizing the Day: How to Take the Day Off & Change Your Life. 172p. 1983. pap. 7.95 (ISBN 0-87243-120-7). Templegate.

HISTORICAL SITES

see Historic Sites

HISTORICAL SOCIETIES

Schwalm, N. Daniel, Jr., ed. Journal of the Johannes Schwalm Historical Association, Vol. 2, No. 2. (Illus.). 62p. (Orig.). 1982. pap. 7.50 (ISBN 0-939016-06-0). Johannes Schwalm Hist.

HISTORIOGRAPHY

see also Historians; Historical Research; Local History; Psychohistory

also subdivision Historiography under names of countries, e.g. United States–History–Historiography

Bloch, M. The Historian's Craft. 1954. pap. 7.00 (ISBN 0-7190-0664-3). Manchester.

Breisach, Ernst. Historiography: Ancient, Medieval, & Modern. LC 82-20246. 416p. 1983. pap. 12.50 (ISBN 0-226-07275-4). U of Chicago Pr.

Geyl, Pieter. Use & Abuse of History. 1955. text ed. 14.50x (ISBN 0-686-83843-2). Elliots Bks.

Graham, G., ed. Historical Explanation Reconsidered. (Scots Philosophical Monographs: No. 4). 96p. 1983. pap. 12.00 (ISBN 0-08-028478-7). Pergamon.

Henige, David. Oral Historiography. LC 82-168. 208p. 1982. text ed. 28.00x (ISBN 0-582-64364-3); pap. text ed. 9.95x (ISBN 0-582-64363-5). Longman.

Rotenstreich, Nathan. Between Past & Present: An Essay On History. 1958. text ed. 13.50x (ISBN 0-686-83489-5). Elliots Bks.

HISTORIOGRAPHY–ADDRESSES, ESSAYS, LECTURES

Oakeshott, Michael. On History & Other Essays. LC 82-22617. 224p. 1983. text ed. 25.75x (ISBN 0-389-20355-6). B&N Imports.

Tuchman, Barbara. Practicing History: Selected Essays. 1982. pap. 7.95 (ISBN 0-345-30363-6). Ballantine.

HISTORY

Here are entered general works about history, its methods, philosophy, etc. For works on the history of specific places or periods, see World History; History, Ancient; History, modern, etc.

see also Anthropo-Geography; Archaeology; Biography; Boundaries; Church History; Constitutional History; Culture; Diplomacy; Discoveries (In Geography); Ethnology; Genealogy; Heraldry; Heroes; Historians; Historic Sites; Historical Fiction; Historical Research; Kings and Rulers; Medals; Military History; Naval History; Numismatics; Political Science; Revolutions; Riots; Seals (Numismatics); Social History; Treaties

also subdivisions Antiquities, Foreign Relations, History and Politics and Government under names of countries, states, cities, etc.

Beringer, Richard E. Historical Analysis: Contemporary Approaches to Clio's Craft. LC 77-10589. 317p. 1978. pap. text ed. 18.95x (ISBN 0-471-06996-5). Wiley.

Breisach, Ernst. Historiography: Ancient, Medieval, & Modern. LC 82-20246. 416p. 1983. pap. 12.50 (ISBN 0-226-07275-4). U of Chicago Pr.

Chartier, Armand. Litterature Historique: Populaire Franco-Amercaine. 108p. (Fr.). 1981. pap. text ed. 3.00x (ISBN 0-911409-40-8). Natl Mat Dev.

Fitzsimons, M. A. The Past Recaptured: Great Historians & the History of History. 1983. price not set. U of Notre Dame Pr.

Guedalla, Philip. The Hundredth Year. 312p. 1982. Repr. of 1939 ed. lib. bdg. 35.00 (ISBN 0-89987-315-4). Darby Bks.

Gunn, Fenja. The Artificial Face: A History of Cosmetics. (Illus.). 220p. (gr. 6 up). 1983. pap. 9.95 (ISBN 0-88254-795-X). Hippocrene Bks.

Johnson, Richard & McLennan, Gregor, eds. Making Histories: Studies in History Writing & Politics. 384p. 1982. 35.00x (ISBN 0-8166-1164-5); pap. 15.95 (ISBN 0-8166-1165-3). U of Minn Pr.

Ossa, Helen. They Saved Our Birds. (Illus.). 288p. (gr. 6 up). 1983. pap. 5.95 (ISBN 0-88254-714-3). Hippocrene Bks.

Walter, Fogg. One Thousand Sayings of History: Presented as Pictures in Prose. 915p. 1982. Repr. of 1929 ed. lib. bdg. 50.00 (ISBN 0-89984-208-9). Century Bookbindery.

Whiting, J. R. A Handful of History. 112p. 1982. pap. text ed. 9.00x (ISBN 0-86299-000-9, 61269, Pub. by Sutton England). Humanities.

HISTORY–ADDRESSES, ESSAYS, LECTURES

Joyce, Davis D. History & Historians: Some Essays. LC 82-21865. 116p. (Orig.). 1983. lib. bdg. 18.75 (ISBN 0-8191-2936-4); pap. text ed. 8.25 (ISBN 0-8191-2937-2). U Pr of Amer.

Kant, Immanuel. Perpetual Peace & Other Essays on Politics, History, & Morals. Humphrey, Ted, ed. & tr. from Ger. LC 82-11748. (HPC Philosophical Classics Ser.). 152p. 1982. lib. bdg. 13.50 (ISBN 0-915145-48-0); pap. text ed. 2.95 (ISBN 0-915145-47-2). Hackett Pub.

Labriola, Antonio. Essays on the Materialistic Conception of History. Kerr, Charles H., tr. LC 82-73433. 246p. Repr. of 1908 ed. lib. bdg. 18.50x (ISBN 0-88116-006-7). Brenner Bks.

Lloyd-Jones, Hugh & Pearl, Valerie, eds. History & Imagination: Essays in Honor of H. R. Trevor-Roper. 386p. 1982. 45.00 (ISBN 0-8419-0782-X). Holmes & Meier.

HISTORY–ANECDOTES

see History–Curiosa and Miscellany

HISTORY–ATLASES

see Classical Geography

HISTORY–BIBLIOGRAPHY

Francois, Michal & Keul, Michael, eds. International Bibliography of Historical Sciences, Vol. 47-48. 458p. (Ital.). 1982. 90.00x (ISBN 0-686-82086-X, Pub. by K G Saur). Gale.

HISTORY–CRITICISM

see Historiography

HISTORY–CURIOSA AND MISCELLANY

Barraclough, Geoffrey. Main Trends in History. 259p. 1979. 10.95 (ISBN 0-8419-0505-3). Holmes & Meier.

HISTORY–DICTIONARIES

Wetterau, Bruce. The Macmillan Concise Dictionary of World History. 672p. 1983. 39.95 (ISBN 0-02-626110-3). Macmillan.

HISTORY–HISTORIOGRAPHY

see Historiography

HISTORY–JUVENILE LITERATURE

Chisholm. First Guide to History. 1983. 10.95 (ISBN 0-86020-625-4, 21151). EDC.

HISTORY–PERIODICALS

Great Events: Four as Reported in the New York Times. 91p. (gr. 9-12). 1982. pap. text ed. 7.95 (ISBN 0-667-00692-3). Microfilming Corp.

The New York Times File: Critical Issues, 1982. 76p. (gr. 9-12). 1982. write for info. Microfilming Corp.

HISTORY–PHILOSOPHY

see also History (Theology)

also subdivision History–Philosophy under names of countries, e.g. United States–History–Philosophy

McAllister, David W. The Reconstruction of Gianbattista Vico's Theory of the Cycles of History with Applications to Contemporary Historical Experience. (The Essential Library of the Great Philosophers). (Illus.). 149p. 1983. 47.75 (ISBN 0-89266-396-0). Am Classical Coll Pr.

Meinecke, Friedrich. Historism: The Rise of a New Historical Outlook. 524p. 1972. 32.00 (ISBN 0-7100-7045-4). Routledge & Kegan.

Shils, Edward. Tradition. LC 80-21643. viii, 334p. 1981. pap. 10.95 (ISBN 0-226-75326-3). U of Chicago Pr.

HISTORY–RESEARCH

see Historical Research

HISTORY–STUDY AND TEACHING

Stephens, W. B. Teaching Local History. 1977. 16.50 (ISBN 0-7190-0660-0). Manchester.

HISTORY–STUDY AND TEACHING (HIGHER)

Bajaj, Satish K. Secondary Social Science Workbook. (Illus.). 236p. 1981. pap. text ed. 7.95x (ISBN 0-86131-271-6, Pub. by Orient Longman Ltd India). Apt Bks.

HISTORY–THEOLOGY

see History (Theology)

HISTORY–YEARBOOKS

The New York Times File: Critical Issues, 1982. 76p. (gr. 9-12). 1982. write for info. Microfilming Corp.

HISTORY (THEOLOGY)

Trimingham, J. Spencer. History in Two Dimensions: A Christian Interpretation of History as Being an Equation Between Time & Eternity. 1983. 11.95 (ISBN 0-533-05395-1). Vantage.

HISTORY, ANCIENT

see also Archaeology; Civilization, Ancient; Numismatics

also names of ancient races and peoples, e.g. Indo-Europeans; hittites; Mediterranean Race; and names of countries of antiquity

Aubry, M. P. Handbook of Cenozoic Calcareous Nannoplankton, 7 vols. Date not set. 50.00 ea. Am Mus Natl Hist.

Fornara, Charles W., ed. Archaic Times to the End of the Peloponnesian War: Translated Documents of Greece & Rome, No. 1. LC 79-54018. 232p. Date not set. price not set (ISBN 0-521-25019-6); pap. price not set (ISBN 0-521-29946-2). Cambridge U Pr.

Ormerod. Piracy in the Ancient World. 286p. 1982. pap. 40.00x (ISBN 0-85323-044-7, Pub. by Liverpool Univ England). State Mutual Bk.

Williams, Hector. The Lamps, Pt. V. (Kenchreai Estern Port of Corinth Ser.). (Illus.). xvi, 104p. 1981. write for info. (ISBN 90-04-06198-3). E J Brill.

HISTORY, BIBLICAL

see Bible–History of Biblical Events

HISTORY, CHURCH

see Church History

HISTORY, CONSTITUTIONAL

see Constitutional History

HISTORY, ECCLESIASTICAL

see Church History

HISTORY, ECONOMIC

see Economic History

HISTORY, LOCAL

see Local History

HISTORY, MEDIEVAL

see Middle Ages–History

HISTORY, MILITARY

see Military History

HISTORY, MODERN

see also Reformation; Renaissance

Mckay & Hill. A History of Western Society, 2 vols. 2d ed. 1982. text ed. 23.95 (ISBN 0-686-84597-8, HS1976); write for info. HM.

HISTORY, MODERN–PERIODICALS

see History–Periodicals

HISTORY, MODERN–PHILOSOPHY

see History–Philosophy

HISTORY, MODERN–20TH CENTURY

see also European War, 1914-1918; Twentieth Century; World War, 1939-1945

Douglas, Roy. Nineteen Thirty-Nine: A Retrospect Forty Years After. 101p. 1983. 19.50 (ISBN 0-208-02020-9, Archon Bks). Shoe String.

Simpson, Amos, et al. Death of an Old World: 1914-1945. LC 78-67276. 1979. pap. text ed. 2.95x (ISBN 0-88273-326-5). Forum Pr IL.

Simpson, Amos E., et al. Genesis of a New World: Nineteen Forty-five to Present. LC 78-67276. 1979. pap. text ed. 2.95x (ISBN 0-88273-327-3). Forum Pr IL.

HISTORY, NATURAL

see Natural History

HISTORY, NAVAL

see Naval History

HISTORY, PHILOSOPHY OF

see History–Philosophy

HISTORY, UNIVERSAL

see World History

HISTORY AND SCIENCE

see Science and Civilization

HISTORY IN ART

Powell, Eustace G. The Dutch School of Historical & Portrait Painting, 2 vols. (The Art Library of the Great Masters of the World). (Illus.). 147p. 1983. Set. 137.50 (ISBN 0-86650-043-X). Gloucester Art.

HISTORY, MODERN-YEARBOOKS

see History-Yearbooks

HISTRIONICS

see Acting; Theater

HITCHCOCK, ALFRED JOSEPH, 1899-1980

Spoto, Donald. The Dark Side of Genius: The Life of Alfred Hitchcock. 576p. 1983. 21.50i (ISBN 0-316-80723-0). Little.

HITLER, ADOLF, 1889-1945

Haffner, Sebastian. The Meaning of Hitler. Osers, Ewald, tr. from Ger. 180p. 1983. pap. text ed. 5.95x (ISBN 0-674-55776-X). Harvard U Pr.

Hauner, Milan. Hitler: A Chronology of His Life & Time. LC 82-16718. 250p. 1982. 25.00x (ISBN 0-312-38816-0). St Martin.

Irving, David. The Secret Diaries of Hitler's Doctor. 320p. 1983. 15.95 (ISBN 0-02-558250-X). Macmillan.

Walther, Herbert, ed. Hitler. (Illus.). 256p. 1982. 12.98 (ISBN 0-8119-0518-7, Pub. by Bison Bks). Fell.

HOBBIES

Ewing, George M. Living on a Shoestring: A Scrounge Manuel for the Hobbyist. Heid, Jim, ed. (Illus.). 1983. write for info. Green.

Yates, Raymond F. & Yates, Marguerite W. Early American Crafts & Hobbies. LC 82-48834. (Illus.). 224p. 1983. pap. 5.72i (ISBN 0-06-463575-9, EH 575). B&N NY.

HOBOES

see Tramps

HOCKEY

see also Field Hockey

Aaseng, Nate. Hockey: You Are the Coach. LC 82-17170. (You Are the Coach Ser.). (Illus.). 104p. (gr. 4up). 1983. PLB 8.95g (ISBN 0-8225-1554-7). Lerner Pubns.

Croce, Pat & Cooper, Bruce C. Conditioning for Ice Hockey Year-Round. LC 82-83917. (Illus.). 176p. (Orig.). 1983. pap. 7.95 (ISBN 0-88011-090-2). Leisure Pr.

Hollander, Zander. The Complete Handbook of Pro-Hockey: 1983 Edition. 1982. pap. 3.95 (ISBN 0-451-11845-6, AE1845, Sig). NAL.

Ice Hockey Rules 1980-81. 5.95 (ISBN 0-88314-158-2). AAHPERD.

Schultz, Dave & Fischler, Stan. The Hammer: Confessions of a Hockey Enforcer. 224p. 1983. pap. 2.95 (ISBN 0-425-05887-5). Berkley Pub.

Sloman, Larry. Thin Ice: A Season in Hell with the New York Rangers. 1983. pap. 3.95 (ISBN 0-440-18571-8). Dell.

HOCKEY-BIOGRAPHY

Wolff, Craig T. Wayne Gretzky: Portrait of a Hockey Player. 64p. (gr. 3-7). 1983. pap. 1.95 (ISBN 0-380-82420-5, 82420-5, Camelot). Avon.

Zola, Meguido. Gretzky! Gretzky! Gretzky! (Picture Life Ser.). (Illus.). 48p. (gr. k-3). 1983. PLB 7.90 (ISBN 0-531-04597-8). Watts.

HOCKNEY, DAVID

Hockney, David. David Hockney Photographs. 1982. 30.00 (ISBN 0-902825-15-1). Petersburg Pr.

HOFMANN, HANS, 1880-

Brewer, Donald J. Hans Hofmann Paintings. (Illus.). 16p. 1968. 7.00x (ISBN 0-686-99836-7). La Jolla Mus Contemp Art.

HOFMANNSTHAL, HUGO HOFMANN, EDLER VON, 1874-1929

Hammelmann, H. A. Hugo von Hofmannsthal. 1957. text ed. 29.50x (ISBN 0-686-83571-9). Elliots Bks.

HOGS

see Swine

HOKKU

see Haiku

HOLDEN, WILLIAM, 1918-

Thomas, Bob. Golden Boy: The Untold Story of William Holden. (Illus.). 1983. 16.95 (ISBN 0-312-33697-7). St Martin.

HOLDING COMPANIES

Finney, H. A. Consolidated Statements. LC 82-48362. (Accountancy in Transition Ser.). 242p. 1982. lib. bdg. 25.00 (ISBN 0-8240-5313-3). Garland Pub.

Garnsey, Gilbert. Holding Companies & Their Published Accounts Bound with Limitations of A Balance Sheet. LC 82-48364. (Accountancy in Transition Ser.). 232p. 1982. lib. bdg. 25.00 (ISBN 0-8240-5315-X). Garland Pub.

Robson, T. B. Consolidated & Other Group Accounts. 2nd ed. LC 82-48381. (Accountancy in Transition Ser.). 156p. 1982. lib. bdg. 20.00 (ISBN 0-8240-5326-5). Garland Pub.

HOLIDAYS

see also Anniversaries; Christmas; Fourth of July; Schools-Exercises and Recreations; Thanksgiving Day; Vacations

Gregory, Ruth W. Anniversaries & Holidays. 4th ed. 1983. pap. text ed. price not set (ISBN 0-8389-0389-4). ALA.

McMasters, Dale. American Holidays & Special Occasions. (Social Studies). 14p. (gr. 3-6). 1980. wkbk. 5.00 (ISBN 0-8209-0266-7, AH-1). ESP.

McSpadden, J. W. The Book of Holidays. 346p. 1983. Repr. of 1917 ed. lib. bdg. 35.00 (ISBN 0-89984-823-0). Century Bookbindery.

Mills. Design for Holidays & Tourism. 1983. text ed. price not set (ISBN 0-408-00534-3). Butterworth.

Polon, Linda & Cantwell, Aileen. The Whole Earth Holiday Book. 1983. pap. text ed. 12.95 (ISBN 0-673-16585-X). Scott F.

Tietjen, Mary L. Holy Days & Holidays: Activities, Crafts & Stories for Children. LC 82-62416. 1983. pap. 2.95 (ISBN 0-8091-2531-5). Paulist Pr.

HOLIDAYS-JUVENILE LITERATURE

Bild, Ian & Humphries, Stephen. Finding Out about Seaside Holidays. (Finding Out about Ser.). (Illus.). 48p. (gr. 5-8). 1983. 12.50 (ISBN 0-7134-4439-8, Pub. by Batsford England). David & Charles.

HOLISM

Association for Holistic Health Staff. The National Directory of Holistic Health Professionals. 269p. 1982. pap. 7.95 (ISBN 0-686-38102-5). Assn Holistic.

Diamond, John. The Collected Papers of John Diamond, M.D, 2 vols. 1983. pap. 19.95 ea. Vol. 1, 88p. (ISBN 0-911238-75-1). Vol. 2, 170p (ISBN 0-911238-76-X). Regent House.

--Holistic Therapy: Lectures on a Spiritual Basis of Holistic Therapy. 67p. 1983. pap. 19.95x (ISBN 0-911238-79-4). Regent House.

Howells, John G. Integral Clinical Investigation: As Aspect of Panathropic Medicine. 272p. 1982. 65.00x (ISBN 0-333-29446-7, Pub. by Macmillan England). State Mutual Bk.

King, Serge. Kahuna Healing. LC 82-42704. 212p. (Orig.). 1983. pap. 6.75 (ISBN 0-8356-0572-8, Quest). Theos Pub Hse.

Legere, Thomas E. Thoughts on the Run: Glimpses of Wholistic Spirituality. 144p. 1983. pap. 7.95 (ISBN 0-86683-698-5). Winston Pr.

Moore, Michael C. & Moore, Lynda J. A Complete Handbook of Holistic Health. 253p. 1983. 17.95 (ISBN 0-13-168914-2); pap. 8.95 (ISBN 0-13-168906-1). P-H.

Ryan, Tim & Jappinen, Rae. The Whole Again Resources Guide. LC 82-61917. (Illus.). 315p. 1982. pap. 12.95 (ISBN 0-88496-193-1). SourceNet.

Starck, Marcia. Astrology: Key to Holistic Health. Robertson, Arlene, ed. 220p. (Orig.). 1982. pap. 9.95 (ISBN 0-930706-11-0). Seek-It Pubns.

West, Patricia E. Astrology Handbook for Therapists & Holistic Health Practitioners. (Orig.). 1983. pap. 5.50 (ISBN 0-942384-02-4). Red Dragon.

Wigmore, Ann. Be Your Own Doctor: A Positive Guide to Natural Living. 2nd ed. 194p. 1983. pap. 3.95 (ISBN 0-686-43188-X). Avery Pub.

HOLLAND

see Netherlands

HOLLAND HOUSE

The Holland House Diaries 1831-1840: The Diary of Henry R. V. Fox, Third Lord Holland with Extracts from the Diary of Dr. John Allen. 578p. 1977. 42.50 (ISBN 0-7100-8406-4). Routledge & Kegan.

HOLLAR, WENCESLAUS, 1607-1677

Pennington, Richard. A Descriptive Catalogue of the Etched Works of Wenceslaus Hollar, 1607-1677. LC 81-51828. 452p. 1982. 150.00 (ISBN 0-521-22408-X). Cambridge U Pr.

HOLLYWOOD, CALIFORNIA

Taylor, John R. Strangers in Paradise: The Hollywood Emigres, 1933-1950. LC 82-21312. 256p. 1983. 16.45 (ISBN 0-03-061944-0). HR&W.

HOLOCAUST, JEWISH (1939-1945)

Braham, Randolph L. Perspectives on the Holocaust. (Holocaust Studies). 1983. lib. bdg. 20.00 (ISBN 0-89838-124-X). Kluwer Nijhoff.

Breitowicz, Jakob. Through Hell to Life. LC 82-61793. (Illus.). 1983. 10.00 (ISBN 0-88400-091-5). Shengold.

Costanza, Mary S. The Living Witness: Art in the Concentration Camps & Ghettos. 1982. 19.95 (ISBN 0-02-906660-3). Free Pr.

Dimsdale, Joel E., ed. Survivors, Victims & Perpetrators: Essays on the Nazi Holocaust. LC 79-24834. (Illus.). 474p. (Orig.). 1982. pap. text ed. 22.00 (ISBN 0-89116-351-4). Hemisphere Pub.

Druks, Herbert. Jewish Resistance to the Holocaust. 132p. 1983. text ed. 14.95x (ISBN 0-8290-1295-8). Irvington.

Eisenberg, Azriel. Witness to the Holocaust. 672p. 1983. pap. 12.95 (ISBN 0-8298-0614-8). Pilgrim NY.

Eliach, Yaffa & Gurewitsch, Brana. The Liberators: Eyewitness Accounts of the Liberation of Concentration Camps, Liberation Day Vol. 1. LC 81-70261. (The Liberators Ser.). (Illus.). 59p. (Orig.). 1981. pap. 8.95 (ISBN 0-9609970-1-6). Ctr For Holo.

Gurewitsch, Bonnie. Bibliography. (Bibliography Ser.). 27p. (Orig.). Date not set. pap. 3.00 (ISBN 0-9609970-0-8). Ctr For Holo.

Haas, Gerda S. These I Do Remember: Fragments from the Holocaust. LC 82-71674. 300p. 1983. 16.95 (ISBN 0-87027-203-9). Cumberland pr.

Insdorf, Annett. Indelible Shadows: Film & the Holocaust. LC 82-48892. (Illus.). 256p. 1983. pap. 8.95 (ISBN 0-394-71464-4, Vin). Random.

Jackson, Livia. Elli: Coming of Age in the Holocaust. 1983. pap. 6.95 (ISBN 0-8129-6327-X). Times Bks.

Laska, Vera. Women in the Resistance & in the Holocaust: The Voices of Eyewitnesses. LC 82-12018. (Contributions in Women Studies: No. 37). 352p. 1983. lib. bdg. 29.95 (ISBN 0-313-23457-4, LWH/). Greenwood.

Mendelsohn, J. The Final Solution in the Extermination Camps & the Aftermath. LC 81-80320. (The Holocaust Ser.). 250p. 1982. lib. bdg. 50.00 (ISBN 0-8240-4886-5). Garland Pub.

--The Judicial System & the Jews in Nazi Germany. LC 81-80321. (The Holocaust Ser.). 245p. 1982. lib. bdg. 50.00 (ISBN 0-8240-4887-3). Garland Pub.

--Legalizing the Holocaust: The Later Phase, 1939-1943. LC 81-80310. 265p. 1982. lib. bdg. 50.00 (ISBN 0-8240-4876-8). Garland Pub.

--Punishing the Perpetrators of the Holocaust: The Brandt, Pohl & Ohlendorf Cases. LC 81-80325. 269p. 1982. lib. bdg. 50.00 (ISBN 0-8240-4891-1). Garland Pub.

--Punishing the Perpetrators of the Holocaust: The Ohlendorf & the Von Weizsaecker Cases. LC 81-80326. (The Holocaust Ser.). 310p. 1982. lib. bdg. 50.00 (ISBN 0-8240-4892-X). Garland Pub.

--Relief & Rescue of Jews from Nazi Oppression, 1943-1945. LC 81-80322. (The Holocaust Ser.). 264p. 1982. lib. bdg. 50.00 (ISBN 0-8240-4888-1). Garland Pub.

--Relief in Hungary & the Failure of the Joel Brand Mission. LC 81-80323. (The Holocaust Ser.). 256p. 1982. lib. bdg. 50.00 (ISBN 0-8240-4889-X). Garland Pub.

--Rescue to Switzerland: The Mussy & Saly Mayer Affair. LC 81-80324. (The Holocaust Ser.). 280p. 1982. lib. bdg. 50.00 (ISBN 0-8240-4890-3). Garland Pub.

--The Wannsee Protocol & a 1944 Report on Auschwitz by the Office of Strategic Services. LC 81-80319. (The Holocaust Ser.). 264p. 1982. lib. bdg. 50.00 (ISBN 0-8240-4885-7). Garland Pub.

Mendelsohn, John. Deportation of the Jews to the East: Settin, 1940 to Hungary 1944. LC 81-80316. (The Holocaust Ser.). 256p. 1982. lib. bdg. 50.00 (ISBN 0-8240-4882-2). Garland Pub.

--The Einsatzgruppen or Murder Commandos. LC 81-80318. (The Holocaust Ser.). 256p. 1982. lib. bdg. 50.00 (ISBN 0-8240-4884-9). Garland Pub.

--Jewish Emigration from 1933 to the Evian Conference of 1938. LC 81-80313. (The Holocaust Ser.). 260p. 1982. lib. bdg. 50.00 (ISBN 0-8240-4879-2). Garland Pub.

--Jewish Emigration: The SS St. Louis Affair & Other Cases. LC 81-80315. (The Holocaust Ser.). 274p. 1982. lib. bdg. 50.00 (ISBN 0-8240-4881-4). Garland Pub.

--Jewish Emigration 1938-1940, Rublee Negotations & Intergovernmental Committee. LC 81-80314. (The Holocaust Ser.). 250p. 1982. lib. bdg. 50.00 (ISBN 0-8240-4880-6). Garland Pub.

--Medical Experiments on Jewish Inmates of Concentration Camps. LC 81-80317. (The Holocaust Ser.). 282p. 1982. lib. bdg. 50.00 (ISBN 0-8240-4883-0). Garland Pub.

--Propaganda & Aryanization, 1938-1944. LC 81-80312. (The Holocaust Ser.). 255p. 1982. lib. bdg. 50.00 (ISBN 0-8240-4878-4). Garland Pub.

Morse, Arthur D. While Six Million Died: A Chronicle of American Apathy. LC 82-22291. 432p. 1983. Repr. of 1966 ed. 18.95 (ISBN 0-87951-174-5). Overlook Pr.

Rothchild, Sylvia, ed. Voices from the Holocaust. 1982. pap. 7.95 (ISBN 0-452-00603-1, Mer). NAL.

Seventy First Infantry Division, U.S. Army. The Seventy-First Came to Gunskirchen Lager. 2nd ed. Blumenthal, David R., intro. by. (Witness to the Holocaust Ser.: No. 1). (Illus.). 28p. 1983. pap. 1.50 (ISBN 0-89937-036-5). Witness Holocaust.

Strom, Margot S. & Parsons, William S. Facing History & Ourselves: Holocaust & Human Behavior. (Illus.). 400p. (gr. 9-12). 1982. pap. text ed. 15.00 (ISBN 0-9607970-1-7). Intentional Ed.

HOLOGRAPHY

Jeong, Tung Hon. International Exhibition of Holography. Croydon, Michael, compiled by. LC 82-83046. 26p. (Orig.). 1982. pap. text ed. 7.00 (ISBN 0-910535-00-0). Lake Forest.

HOLY GHOST

see Holy Spirit

HOLY GRAIL

see Grail

HOLY ORDERS

see Clergy-Office

HOLY ORTHODOX EASTERN CATHOLIC AND APOSTOLIC CHURCH

see Orthodox Eastern Church

HOLY ROMAN EMPIRE

Vann, James Allen. The Swabian Kreis: Institutional Growth in the Holy Roman Empire, 1648-1715. write for info. P Lang Pubs.

HOLY SEE

see Papacy; Popes

HOLY SHROUD

Tribbe, Frank C. Portrait of Jesus? The Illustrated Story of the Shroud of Turin. 176p. 1983. 17.95 (ISBN 0-8128-2904-2). Stein & Day.

HOLY SPIRIT

see also Gifts, Spiritual; Pentecost; Trinity

Congar, Yves. I Believe in the Holy Spirit, 3 Vols. Incl. The Experience of the Spirit. 300p. Vol. 1 (ISBN 0-8164-0518-2); Vol. 2. Lord & Giver of Life. 300p (ISBN 0-8164-0535-2); Vol. 3. The River of Life Flows in the East & in the West. 300p (ISBN 0-8164-0537-9). 300p. 1983. 24.95 ea.; Set. 70.00 (ISBN 0-8164-0540-9). Seabury.

DeWelt, Don. Nine Lessons on the Holy Spirit. 187p. 1978. 3.95 (ISBN 0-89900-116-5). College Pr Pub.

Hagin, Kenneth E. The Holy Spirit & his Gifts. 1974. pap. 5.00 (ISBN 0-89276-082-6). Hagin Ministry.

Kidd, Sunnie D. & Kidd, James W. Brother Jerry's Stories: Following the Inspiration of the Holy Spirit. 34p. 1982. pap. text ed. 2.50 (ISBN 0-910727-00-7). Golden Phoenix.

Koren, Henry J. To the Ends of the Earth: A General History of the Congregation of the Holy Ghost. 656p. 1982. text ed. 18.50x (ISBN 0-8207-0157-2). Duquesne.

Pegram, Don R. Sinning Against the Holy Spirit. 1982. pap. 1.00 (ISBN 0-89265-085-0). Randall Hse.

Religous Education Staff. The Spirit Alive in Liturgy: Spirit Masters. 1981. 9.95 (ISBN 0-686-84105-0). Wm C Brown.

--The Spirit Alive in You: Spirit Masters. 1982. 9.95 (ISBN 0-697-01805-9). Wm C Brown.

Yandian, Bob. The Holy Spirit: Oil & Wine. 32p. (Orig.). 1982. pap. 1.50x (ISBN 0-943436-00-1). Grace Fellow.

HOLY SPIRIT ASSOCIATON FOR THE UNIFICATION OF WORLD CHRISTIANITY

James, Gene, ed. The Unification Church & The Family. (Conference Ser.: No. 17). 1983. pap. text ed. price not set (ISBN 0-932894-17-8). Unif Theol Seminary.

Quebedeaux, Richard, ed. Lifestyle: Conversations with Members of the Unification Church. LC 82-50799. (Conference Ser.: No. 13). (Orig.). 1982. 12.95 (ISBN 0-932894-18-6); pap. 9.95 (ISBN 0-932894-13-5). Unif Theol Seminary.

HOME AND SCHOOL

see also Parent-Teacher Relationships

Asheim, Lester, et al. Reading & Successful Living: The Family-School Partnership. 150p. 1983. write for info. (ISBN 0-208-02003-9, Lib Prof Pubns); pap. 11.50x (ISBN 0-208-02004-7, Lib Prof Pubns). Shoe String.

Quisenberry, James D., ed. & intro. by. Changing Family Lifestyles: Their Effect on Children. (Illus.). 64p. 1982. pap. 5.75 (ISBN 0-87173-100-2). ACEI.

HOME APPLIANCES

see Household Appliances

HOME BUYING

see House Buying

HOME CARE SERVICES

see also Home Nursing

Perlman, Robert, ed. Family Home Care: Critical Issues for Services & Policies. (Home Health Care Services Quarterly, Vol. 3, No. 3-4). 328p. 1983. text ed. 29.95 (ISBN 0-86656-220-6); pap. text ed. 14.95 (ISBN 0-86656-221-4). Haworth Pr.

HOME CONSTRUCTION

see House Construction

HOME DECORATION

see Interior Decoration

HOME DESIGN

see Architecture, Domestic

HOME ECONOMICS

see also Consumer Education; Cookery; Cost and Standard of Living; Dairying; Entertaining; Food; Food Service; Fuel; Furniture; Heating; House Cleaning; Housewives; Interior Decoration; Marketing (Home Economics); Mobile Home Living; Needlework; Recipes; Servants; Sewing; Ventilation

Allred, Tamera S. From Deadlines to Diapers: A Career Guide for Successful Homemaking. 174p. 1982. pap. 6.95 (ISBN 0-936860-10-3). Liberty Pr.

Anderson, E. P. & Ley, C. J. Projecting a Picture of Home Economics: Public Relations in Secondary Programs. 1982. 4.00 (ISBN 0-686-38743-0). Home Econ Educ.

Beeton, Isabella M. Mrs. Beeton's Cookery & Household Management. Rev. ed. LC 64-3849. (Illus.). 1606p. 1982. Repr. of 1980 ed. 37.50x (ISBN 0-7063-5743-4). Intl Pubns Serv.

Brown, Philomena. A Basic Dictionary of Home Economics. 64p. 1982. 25.00x (ISBN 0-7135-1317-9, Pub. by Bell & Hyman England). State Mutual Bk.

Douglas, Erika, ed. The Family Circle Hints Book. 1982. 12.95 (ISBN 0-8129-1016-8). Times Bks.

Doyle, Alfreda C. Suggestions for Thrifty Ways to Legally Obtain Cashoffs Or Cents Off Coupons. 26p. 1983. pap. text ed. 6.95 (ISBN 0-910811-22-9). Center Self.

Faulkner, Chuck. Seven Hundred & Fifty Helpful Household Hints. Friedman, Robert S., ed. LC 82-19820. 160p. (Orig.). 1983. pap. 6.95 (ISBN 0-89865-262-6). Donning Co.

Parker, Frances J. Home Economics: An Introduction to a Dynamic Profession. 2nd ed. 224p. 1983. text ed. 19.95 (ISBN 0-02-391710-5). Macmillan.

Young, Pam & Jones, Peggy. The Sidetracked Sisters Catch Up on the Kitchen. 224p. 1983. pap. 6.95 (ISBN 0-446-37526-8). Warner Bks.

HOME ECONOMICS–JUVENILE LITERATURE
Allen, Sarah. A Cleaner World. (Cambridge Dinosaur Information Ser.). (Illus.). 26p. (gr. 7-10). 1983. pap. 1.50 (ISBN 0-521-27200-9). Cambridge U Pr.
Kyte, Kathy S. In Charge: A Complete Handbook for Kids with Working Parents. LC 82-17927. (Illus.). 96p. (gr. 4 up). 1983. 5.95 (ISBN 0-394-85408-X); lib. bdg. 8.99 (ISBN 0-394-95408-4). Knopf.
HOME EDUCATION
see Self-Culture
HOME GAMES
see Indoor Games
HOME HEALTH AGENCIES
see Home Care Services
HOME LABOR
see also Cottage Industries
Goldschmidt-Clermont, Luisella. Unpaid Work in the Household: A Review of Economic Evaluation Methods. (Women, Work & Development: No. 1). xi, 137p. 1982. 10.00 (ISBN 92-2-103085-7). Intl Labour Office.
HOME LIBRARIES
see Libraries, Private
HOME NURSING
see also Practical Nursing
Accreditation of Home Health Agencies: Criteria & Standards Manual for NLN-APHA Accreditation of Home Health Agencies & Community Nursing Services. 48p. 1980. 3.95 (ISBN 0-686-38201-3, 21-1306). Natl League Nurse.
Administrator's Handbook for the Structure, Operation, & Expansion of Home Health Agencies. 550p. 1977. 30.00 (ISBN 0-686-38137-8, 21-1653). Natl League Nurse.
Expansion of Home Health Services & the Community Health System. 34p. 1977. 3.95 (ISBN 0-686-38207-2, 21-1699). Natl League Nurse.
State Organization Planning for Home Health Care. 56p. 1976. 4.95 (ISBN 0-686-38172-6, 21-1629). Natl League Nurse.
Visiting Nurse Association, Inc., of Burlington, VT. The Problem-Oriented System in a Home Health Agency: A Training Manual. (League Exchange Ser.: No. 103). 127p. 1974. 5.95 (ISBN 0-686-38191-2, 21-1554). Natl League Nurse.
Weston, Trevor. A Doctor's Guide to Home Medical Care. (Illus.). 224p. 1983. pap. 6.95 (ISBN 0-8092-5970-2). Contemp Bks.
HOME PURCHASE
see House Buying
HOME REMODELING
see Dwellings–Remodeling
HOME REPAIRS
see Dwellings–Maintenance and Repair
HOME RULE (IRELAND)
see also Irish Question
Rea, Desmond, ed. Northern Ireland, the Republic of Ireland & Great Britain: Problems of Political Co-Operation. 300p. 1982. 50.00x (Pub. by Macmillan England). State Mutual Bk.
HOME STORAGE
see Storage in the Home
HOME STUDY COURSES
see Self-Culture
HOME WORKSHOPS
see Workshops
HOMELESSNESS
see also Migrant Labor; Poor; Refugees; Rogues and Vagabonds; Tramps
Baxter, Ellen & Hopper, Kim. Private Lives-Public Spaces: Homeless Adults on the Streets of New York City. 129p. (Orig.). 1981. pap. 6.50 (ISBN 0-88156-002-2). Comm Serv Soc NY.
Hopper, Kim, et al. One Year Later: The Homeless Poor in New York City. LC 82-200214. 92p. (Orig.). 1982. pap. 6.50 (ISBN 0-88156-000-6). Comm Serv Soc NY.
HOMEMAKERS
see Housewives
HOMEOPATHY
Borland, Douglas. Homeopathy in Practice. reprint ed. LC 82-84366. 1983. pap. 9.95 (ISBN 0-87983-326-2). Keats.
Boyd, Hamish. Introduction to Homeopathic Medicine. LC 82-84367. 1983. pap. 12.95 (ISBN 0-87983-324-6). Keats.
Pratt, Noel. Homeopathic Prescribing. reprint ed. LC 82-84324. 1983. pap. 8.95 (ISBN 0-87983-325-4). Keats.
Whitmont, Edward C. Psyche & Substance: Essays on Homoeopathy in the Light of Jungian Psychology. 222p. 1983. pap. 9.95 (ISBN 0-913028-66-5). North Atlantic.
HOMER
MacCary, W. T. Childlike Achilles: Ontogeny & Phylogeny in the Iliad. LC 82-4458. 304p. 1982. text ed. 25.00 (ISBN 0-686-82113-0). Columbia U Pr.
Vivante, Paolo. The Homeric Imagination: A Study of Homer's Poetic Perception of Reality. 215p. 1983. Repr. of 1970 ed. text ed. 22.50x (ISBN 0-8290-1296-6). Irvington.
HOMES
see Dwellings
HOMES (INSTITUTIONS)
see Charities; Children–Institutional Care
HOMESTEAD LAW
Thear, Katie. The Family Smallholding. (Illus.). 168p. 1983. 22.50 (ISBN 0-7134-1935-0, Pub. by Batsford England); pap. 14.95 (ISBN 0-7134-1936-9, Pub. by Batsford England). David & Charles.
HOMESTEADING
see Agriculture–Handbooks, Manuals, etc.; Frontier and Pioneer Life; Homestead Law
HOMICIDE
see also Assassination; Euthanasia; Infanticide; Murder; Suicide
Danto, Bruce L., et al, eds. The Human Side of Homicide. 336p. 1982. 24.00 (ISBN 0-231-04964-1). Columbia U Pr.
Dietz, Mary L. Killing for Profit: The Social Organization of Felony Homicide. (Illus.). 232p. 1983. text ed. 22.95X (ISBN 0-8304-1008-2). Nelson-Hall.
MacDowell, D. M. Athenian Homicide Law in the Age of the Orators. 1963. 14.50 (ISBN 0-7190-1212-0). Manchester.
HOMILETICS
see Preaching
HOMILIES
see Sermons
HOMING PIGEONS
see Pigeons
HOMOEOPATHY
see Homeopathy
HOMOLOGY THEORY
see also K-Theory
Franks, John M. Homology & Dynamical Systems. LC 82-8897. (Conference Board of the Mathematical Sciences Ser.: Vol. 49). 14.00 (ISBN 0-8218-1700-0). Am Math.
Kleinerman, Samuel N. The Cohomology of Chevalley Groups of Exceptional Lie Type. LC 82-11545. (Memoirs of the American Mathematical Society Ser.: No. 268). 5.00 (ISBN 0-8218-2268-3). Am Math.
HOMOSEXUALITY
see also Gay Liberation Movement; Lesbianism
Altman, Dennis. The Homosexualization of America. LC 82-73959. 256p. 1983. pap. 9.13 (ISBN 0-8070-4143-2, BP-654). Beacon Pr.
Brown, Hudson. The First Official Gay Handbook. (Illus.). 160p. (Orig.). 1983. pap. 5.95 (ISBN 0-943084-03-2). Print Mat.
Galloway, David & Sabisch, Christian, eds. Calamus: Male Homosexuality in Twentieth Century Literature: An International Anthology. 480p. 1982. pap. 9.50 (ISBN 0-688-00606-X). Quill NY.
Gide, Andre. Corydon. Howard, Richard, tr. from French. 1982. 15.50 (ISBN 0-374-13012-4); pap. 8.25 (ISBN 0-374-51777-0). FS&G.
Heron, Ann, ed. One Teenager in Ten: Writings by Gay & Lesbian Youth. 120p. (gr. 7-12). 1983. pap. 3.95 (ISBN 0-932870-26-0). Alyson Pubns.
Human Rights Foundation. Demystifying Homosexuality: A Teacher's Sourcebook about Lesbians & Gay Men. 150p. 1983. pap. 12.95x (ISBN 0-8290-1273-7). Irvington.
Katz, Jonathan N. Gay-Lesbian Almanac. LC 81-48237. (Illus.). 812p. 1983. write for info. (ISBN 0-06-014968-X, HarpT); pap. write for info. (ISBN 0-06-090966-8, CN-0966, HarpT). Har-Row.
Kellog, Stuart, ed. Literary Visions of Homosexuality: Homosexuality in Literature. (Journal of Homosexuality Ser.: Vol. 8, no. 3-4). 200p. 1983. text ed. 18.95 (ISBN 0-686-83516-6). Haworth Pr.
McDonald, Boyd & Leyland, Winston, eds. Sex: True Homosexual Experiences from STH Writers, Vol.3. (Illus.). 192p. (Orig.). 1982. pap. 12.00 (ISBN 0-917342-98-4). Gay Sunshine.
Richardson, Frank M. Mars Without Venus: Study of Some Homosexual Generals. 188p. 1982. 14.95 (ISBN 0-85158-148-X, Pub. by Salem Hse Ltd.). Merrimack Bk Serv.
Weinberg, George. Society & the Healthy Homosexual. 160p. 1983. pap. 5.95 (ISBN 0-312-73851-X). St Martin.
Weinberg, Thomas S. Gay Men, Gay Selves: The Social Construction of Homosexual Identities. 225p. 1983. text ed. 19.95x (ISBN 0-8290-1275-3). Irvington.
HOMOSEXUALITY–LAW AND LEGISLATION
Works on the criminal aspects of homosexuality are entered under the heading sodomy.
Johnson, Paul R. & Eaves, Thomas F. Gays & the New Right: A Debate. Garrison, Clay, ed. (Illus.). 145p. (Orig.). 1983. 4.95x (ISBN 0-910097-03-8); pap. 4.95. Marco & Johnson.
Lesbian & Gay Media Advocates. Talk Back: The Gay Person's Guide to Media Action. 120p. 1982. pap. 3.95 (ISBN 0-932870-10-4). Alyson Pubns.
HOMOSEXUALITY AND CHRISTIANITY
Damian, Peter. Book of Gomorrah: An Eleventh-Century Treaties Against Clerical Homosexual Practices. Payer, Pierre J., tr. 120p. 1982. pap. text ed. 7.50x (ISBN 0-88920-123-4, 40794, Pub. by Wilfred Laurier U Pr Canada). Humanities.
DiMaria-Kuiper, Johannes W. Hot Under the Collar: Self-Portrait of a Gay Pastor. 1983. pap. 8.95 (ISBN 0-686-38773-2). Mercury Pr.
Flatt, Bill & Flatt, Dowell. Counseling the Homosexual. 9.95 (ISBN 0-934916-49-7). Natl Christian Pr.
Ways, New. Homosexuality & the Catholic Church. 1983. write for info. (ISBN 0-88347-149-3). Thomas More.
Wright, Ezekiel & Inesse, Daniel. God Is Gay: An Evolutionary Spiritual Work. 2nd, rev. ed. 1982. pap. 4.95 (ISBN 0-934350-01-9). Tayu Pr.
HOMOSEXUALS
Shilts, Randy. The Mayor of Castro Street: The Life & Times of Harvey Milk. (Illus.). 388p. 1983. pap. 9.95 (ISBN 0-312-52331-9). St Martin.
HOMOTOPY THEORY
Nicas, Andrew J. Induction Theorems for Groups of Homotopy Manifold Structures. LC 82-11546. (Memoirs of the American Mathematical Society Ser.: No. 267). 6.00 (ISBN 0-8218-2267-5, MEMO/267). Am Math.
HONDA MOTORCYCLE
Scott, Ed. Honda XL-XR125-200 Singles 1979-1982. Wauson, Sydnie A., ed. (Illus.). 352p. (Orig.). 1982. pap. text ed. 10.95 (ISBN 0-89287-355-8, M318). Clymer Pubns.
HONDURAS–POLITICS AND GOVERNMENT
MacCameron, Robert. Bananas, Labor, & Politics in Honduras: 1954-1963. (Foreign & Comparative Studies Program, Latin American Ser.: No. 5). (Orig.). 1982. pap. text ed. write for info. (ISBN 0-915984-96-2). Syracuse U Foreign Comp.
HONEY
see also Bee Culture; Bees; Cookery (Honey)
Michaels, Fern. Wild Honey. 1982. pap. 2.95 (ISBN 0-686-82569-1). PB.
HONEYBEES
see Bees
HONGKONG–DESCRIPTION AND TRAVEL
Boschman, Roger. Hong Kong by Night. (Asia by Night Ser.). (Illus.). 64p. (Orig.). 1981. pap. 4.95 (ISBN 962-7031-07-0, Pub. by CFW Pubns Hong Kong). C E Tuttle.
Hong Kong Travel Guide. (Berlitz Travel Guides). (Illus.). 1982. pap. 4.95 (ISBN 0-02-969790-5, Berlitz). Macmillan.
Insight Guides. Hong Kong. (Illus.). 460p. 1983. 18.95 (ISBN 0-13-394643-6); pap. 14.95 (ISBN 0-13-394635-5). P-H.
Maitland, Derek, ed. Hong Kong in Focus. (The "In Focus" Ser.). (Illus.). 64p. (Orig.). 1981. pap. 5.95 (ISBN 962-7031-14-3). C E Tuttle.
Williams, Charles F. The Complete Guide to Hong Kong. (The Complete Guide to Asia Ser.). (Illus.). 112p. 1981. pap. 6.95 (ISBN 962-7031-02-X, Pub. by CFW Pubns Hong Kong). C E Tuttle.
HONOLULU
Singletary, Milly. Three Days in Downtown Honolulu. (Illus.). 48p. (Orig.). 1982. pap. 4.95 (ISBN 0-941244-02-4). Sunset Pubns.
HONOR, DECORATIONS OF
see Decorations of Honor
HONOR SYSTEM
see Self-Government (In Education)
HONORARY DEGREES
see Degrees, Academic
HOOVER, HERBERT CLARK, PRES. U. S., 1874-1964
West Branch & Herbert Hoover. 48p. pap. 1.00 (ISBN 0-686-43255-X). Penfield.
HOOVER, JOHN EDGAR, 1895-1972
O'Reilly, Kenneth. Hoover & the Un-Americans: The FBI, HUAC & the Red Menace. write for info. (ISBN 0-87722-301-7). Temple U Pr.
HOPI INDIANS
see Indians of North America–Southwest, New
HOPKINS, MARK, 1802-1887
Rudolph, Frederick. Mark Hopkins & the Log: Williams College, 1836-1872. 1956. text ed. 39.50x (ISBN 0-686-83618-9). Elliots Bks.
HORACE (QUINTUS HORATIUS FLACCUS)
Minadeo, Richard. The Golden Plectrum: Sexual Symbolism in Horace's Odes. (Studies in Classical Antiquity: Band 4). 247p. 1982. pap. text ed. 23.00x (ISBN 90-6203-664-3, Pub. by Rodopi Holland). Humanities.
HORDE
see Nomads
HORIZONTAL PROPERTY
see Condominium (Housing)
HORMONES
see also Endocrine Glands; Endocrinology; Peptide Hormones
also names of hormones
Albertini, A. & Ekins, R. P., eds. Free Hormones in Blood: Proceedings of the Advanced Course on Free Hormone Assays & Neuropeptides, Venice, Italy, June 15-17, 1982. (Symposia of the Giovanni Lorenzini Foundation Ser.: Vol. 14). 392p. 1982. 70.25 (ISBN 0-444-80463-3, Biomedical Pr). Elsevier.
Choh Hao Li, ed. Hormonal Proteins & Peptides, Vol. 1. LC 82-22770. Date not set. price not set (ISBN 0-12-447211-7). Acad Pr.
Gray, C. H. & James, V. H., eds. Hormones in Blood, Vol. 4. 3rd ed. Date not set. price not set (ISBN 0-12-296204-4). price not set (ISBN 0-12-296205-2). Acad Pr.
Litwack, Gerald, ed. Biochemical Actions of Hormones, Vol. 10. LC 70-107567. 374p. 1982. 42.00 (ISBN 0-12-452809-0). Acad Pr.
Sowers, J. R., ed. Hypothalmic Hormones. LC 79-19856. (Benchmark Papers in Human Physiology Ser.: Vol. 14). 368p. 1980. 46.00 (ISBN 0-87933-358-8). Hutchinson Ross.
Van Der Molen, H. J. & Klopper, A., eds. Hormonal Factors in Fertility, Infertility & Contraception: Proceedings of the Tenth Meeting of the International Study Group for Steroid Hormones, Rome, December 2-4, 1981. (International Congress Ser.: No. 580). 318p. 1982. 86.00 (ISBN 0-444-90258-9, Excerpta Medica). Elsevier.
HOROLOGY
see also Clocks and Watches; Days; Time
Gerschler, Malcolm C. The Clock & Watch Pronunciary. LC 82-91052. (Illus.). 256p. 1983. 16.95 (ISBN 0-9609628-1-6); pap. 11.95 (ISBN 0-9609628-2-4). Wag on Wall.
HOROSCOPES
Huber, Bruno & Huber, Louise. Life Clock: Age Progression in the Horoscope, Vol. 1. 224p. 1982. 8.95 (ISBN 0-87728-554-3). Weiser.
Super Horoscope Nineteen Eighty-Three: Aries. (Super Horoscope Ser.). (Illus.). 256p. 1982. pap. 3.25 (ISBN 0-448-14243-0, G&D). Putnam Pub Group.
Super Horoscope Nineteen Eighty-Three: Capricorn. (Super Horoscope Ser.). (Illus.). 256p. 1982. pap. 3.25 (ISBN 0-448-14252-X, G&D). Putnam Pub Group.
Super Horoscope Nineteen Eighty-Three: Cancer. (Super Horoscope Ser.). (Illus.). 256p. 1982. pap. 3.25 (ISBN 0-448-14246-5, G&D). Putnam Pub Group.
Super Horoscope Nineteen Eighty-Three: Gemini. (Super Horoscope Ser.). (Illus.). 256p. 1982. pap. 3.25 (ISBN 0-448-14245-7, G&D). Putnam Pub Group.
Super Horoscope Nineteen Eighty-Three: Leo. (Super Horoscope Ser.). (Illus.). 256p. 1982. pap. 3.25 (ISBN 0-448-14247-3, G&D). Putnam Pub Group.
Super Horoscope Nineteen-Eighty Three: Libra. (Super Horoscope Ser.). (Illus.). 256p. 1982. pap. 3.25 (ISBN 0-448-14249-X, G&D). Putnam Pub Group.
Super Horoscope Nineteen-Eighty Three: Pisces. (Super Horoscope Ser.). (Illus.). 256p. 1982. pap. 3.25 (ISBN 0-448-14254-6, G&D). Putnam Pub Group.
Super Horoscope Nineteen-Eighty Three: Sagittarius. (Super Horoscope Ser.). (Illus.). 256p. 1982. pap. 3.25 (ISBN 0-448-14251-1, G&D). Putnam Pub Group.
Super Horoscope Nineteen-Eighty Three: Scorpio. (Super Horoscope Ser.). (Illus.). 256p. 1982. pap. 3.25 (ISBN 0-448-14250-3, G&D). Putnam Pub Group.
Super Horoscope Nineteen-Eighty Three: Taurus. (Super Horoscope Ser.). (Illus.). 256p. 1982. pap. 3.25 (ISBN 0-448-14244-9, G&D). Putnam Pub Group.
Super Horoscope Nineteen Eighty Three: Virgo. (Super Horoscope Ser.). (Illus.). 256p. 1982. pap. 3.25 (ISBN 0-448-14248-1, G&D). Putnam Pub Group.
Super Horoscopes Nineteen Eighty-Three: Aquarius. (Super Horoscope Ser.). (Illus.). 256p. 1982. pap. 3.25 (ISBN 0-448-14253-8, G&D). Putnam Pub Group.
HOROSCOPY
see Astrology
HORROR FILMS
Daniels, Les. Living in Fear: A History of Horror in the Mass Media. (Quality Paperbacks Ser.). (Illus.). 256p. 1983. pap. 12.95 (ISBN 0-306-80193-0). Da Capo.
HORROR TALES
see also Ghost Stories
Hoke, Helen, ed. Ghastly, Ghoulish, Gripping Tales. (Terrific Triple Titles Ser.). 176p. (gr. 7 up). 1983. PLB 8.60 (ISBN 0-531-04593-5). Watts.
HORS D'OEUVRES
see Cookery (Appetizers); Cookery (Relishes)
HORSE
see Horses
HORSE-BREAKING
see Horse-Training
HORSE BREEDING
see also Horse Breeds
Baker, Frank H., ed. Stud Manager's Handbook: International Stockmen's School Handbooks, Vol. 18. 500p. 1982. lib. bdg. 30.00 (ISBN 0-86531-507-8, Pub. with Winrock International). Westview.
Blood-Horse, ed. Stake Winners of 1982. (Annual Supplement to the Blood-Horse). 900p. 1983. 30.00 (ISBN 0-936032-61-8); pap. 20.00 (ISBN 0-936032-62-6). Blood-Horse.
Blood-Horse-Thoroughbred Owners & Breeders Assn. The Breeder's Guide of 1982, 1 vol. (Bound Supplements of the Blood-Horse). 1983. 47.50 (ISBN 0-936032-58-8). Blood-Horse.
Hislop, John. Breeding for Racing. 1976. 14.95 (ISBN 0-686-83969-2, Pub by Secker & Warburg). David & Charles.
HORSE BREEDS
see also names of specific breeds
Horse Identifier: A Field Guide to Horse Breeds. LC 80-50439. (Illus.). 128p. 1983. pap. 7.95 (ISBN 0-8069-7728-0). Sterling.
HORSE RACE BETTING
Davidowitz, Steve. Betting Thoroughbreds: A Professional's Guide for the Horseplayer. Rev. ed. (Illus.). 232p. 1983. pap. 7.25 (ISBN 0-525-48046-3, 0772-230). Dutton.

Hughes, Wayne C., Jr. Thoroughbred Wagering: How to Win Before You Play, Pt. II. 1983. pap. 24.00 (ISBN 0-686-38884-4). Write A Book.

Quinn, James. The Literature of Thoroughbred Handicapping 1965-1982: A Selective Review for the Practioner. LC 82-84680. (Illus.). 176p. 1983. pap. 9.95 (ISBN 0-89650-794-7). Gamblers.

Zolotow, Maurice. Confessions of a Racetrack Fiend: Or, How to Pick the Six, & My Other Secrets for the Weekend Horseplayer. 180p. 1983. 10.95 (ISBN 0-312-16220-0). St Martin.

HORSE-RACING

see also Horse Race Betting; Race Horses; Steeplechasing

Blood-Horse, ed. Stake Winners of 1982. (Annual Supplement to the Blood-Horse). 900p. 1983. 30.00 (ISBN 0-936032-61-8); pap. 20.00 (ISBN 0-936032-62-6). Blood-Horse.

Craig, Dennis. Horse Racing. 250p. 30.00 (ISBN 0-87556-059-8). Saifer.

Danion, Boots. Handcapping in the Winner's Circle: How to Win at the Track. Pollack, Martin, ed. LC 82-73261. 192p. (Orig.). 1982. pap. 9.95 (ISBN 0-936836-05-9). Alliance Pubs.

Hislop, John. Breeding for Racing. 1976. 14.95 (ISBN 0-686-83969-2, Pub by Secker & Warburg). David & Charles.

Quinn, James. The Literature of Thoroughbred Handicapping 1965-1982: A Selective Review for the Practioner. LC 82-84680. (Illus.). 176p. 1983. pap. 9.95 (ISBN 0-89650-794-7). Gamblers.

Rickman, John. Eight Flat-Racing Stables. (Illus.). 1979. 14.95 (ISBN 0-434-63710-6, Pub. by Heinemann). David & Charles.

Welcome, John. Irish Horse-Racing. 1983. 18.95 (ISBN 0-686-38872-0, Pub. by Salem Hse Ltd). Merrimack Bk Serv.

--Irish Horse-Racing: An Illustrated History. 1982. 60.00x (ISBN 0-7171-1046-X, Pub. by Gill & Macmillan Ireland). State Mutual Bk.

Zolotow, Maurice. Confessions of a Racetrack Fiend: Or, How to Pick the Six, & My Other Secrets for the Weekend Horseplayer. 180p. 1983. 10.95 (ISBN 0-312-16220-0). St Martin.

HORSE SENSE

see Common Sense

HORSE TRAILS

see Trails

HORSE-TRAINING

Katcha Goodwon. The Complete Thinking Man's Guide to Handicapping & Training. 232p. (Orig.). 1983. 19.95 (ISBN 0-932896-05-7). Westcliff Pub.

Knox-Thompson, Elaine & Dickens, Susanne. The Young Horse. (Illus.). 160p. 1979. 12.95 (ISBN 0-00-195081-9, Pub. by W Collins Australia). Intl Schol Bk Serv.

HORSEMANSHIP

see also Coaching; Horsemen; Rodeos

Condax, Kate D. Riding: An Illustrated Guide. LC 82-16460. (Illus.). 208p. 1983. 14.95 (ISBN 0-668-05424-7, 5424). Arco.

Kidd, Jane. A Festival of Dressage. LC 82-8780. (Illus.). 144p. 1983. 16.95 (ISBN 0-668-05654-1, 5654). Arco.

Kust, Matthew. Man & Horse in History. (Illus.). 159p. 1983. 15.95x (ISBN 0-89891-005-6, Plutarch Pr). Advent NY.

O'Connor, Sally, ed. The Uscia Book of Evening: The Official Handbook of the United States Combined Training Association. (Illus.). 288p. 1982. 16.95 (ISBN 0-201-05447-7). A-W.

HORSEMANSHIP–JUVENILE LITERATURE

Haney, Lynn. Show Rider. (Illus.). 96p. 1982. 11.95 (ISBN 0-399-20908-5); pap. 5.95 (ISBN 0-399-20909-3). Putnam Pub Group.

HORSEMEN

see also Cowboys

Kust, Matthew. Man & Horse in History. (Illus.). 159p. 1983. 15.95x (ISBN 0-89891-005-6, Plutarch Pr). Advent NY.

HORSES

see also Draft Horses; Horse Breeds; Horsemen; Quarter Horse; Race Horses

Gurney, Eric. How to Live with a Headstrong Horse. (Illus.). 192p. 1982. 6.95 (ISBN 0-13-415406-1). P-H.

Price, Steven D. All the King's Horses: The Story of the Budweiser Clydesdales. (Illus.). 200p. 1983. 26.00 (ISBN 0-670-22588-6). Viking Pr.

Saunders, Ray. Horsekeeping: Management, Ailments & Injuries. (Illus.). 116p. 1983. 12.95 (ISBN 0-8069-3750-5); pap. 6.95 (ISBN 0-8069-7626-8). Sterling.

Stoneridge, M. A. Practical Horseman's Book of Horsekeeping. LC 82-45150. (Illus.). 352p. 1983. 24.95 (ISBN 0-385-17788-7). Doubleday.

HORSES–BREEDING

see Horse Breeding

HORSES–BREEDS

see Horse Breeds

HORSES–HISTORY

Kust, Matthew. Man & Horse in History. (Illus.). 159p. 1983. 15.95x (ISBN 0-89891-005-6, Plutarch Pr). Advent NY.

HORSES–JUVENILE LITERATURE

Greydanus, Rose. Horses. LC 82-20296. (Now I Know Ser.). (Illus.). 32p. (gr. k-2). 1982. lib. bdg. 8.89 (ISBN 0-89375-900-7). Troll Assocs.

Morris, Dean. Horses. LC 77-8243. (Read About Ser.). (Illus.). 40p. (gr. k-3). 1983. PLB 13.30 (ISBN 0-8393-0008-5). Raintree Pubs.

Popescu, Charlotte. Horses at Work. (History in Focus Ser.). (Illus.). 72p. (gr. 7-12). 1983. 14.95 (ISBN 0-7134-4451-7, Pub. by Batsford England). David & Charles.

Ventura, Piero. Man & the Horse. (Illus.). 80p. 1982. 11.95 (ISBN 0-399-20842-9). Putnam Pub Group.

HORSES–TRAINING

see Horse-Training

HORSESHOE PITCHING

see Quoits

HORSEWOMEN

see Horsemen

HORTICULTURE

see also Agricultural Pests; Bulbs; Grafting; Greenhouses; Hydroponics; Insects, Injurious and Beneficial; Landscape Gardening; Mushroom Culture; Plant Propagation; Pruning; Vegetable Gardening

Ingels, Jack E. Landscaping: Principles & Practices. 2nd ed. (Illus.). 1983. text ed. 16.00 (ISBN 0-8273-2157-0); instrs.' guide 3.25 (ISBN 0-8273-2158-9). Delmar.

Kaden, Vera. The Illustration of Plants & Gardens, 1500-1850. (Illus.). 113p. 1982. pap. 15.00 (ISBN 0-686-43333-5). Intl Pubns Serv.

Reiley, H. Edward & Shry, Carroll L., Jr. Introductory Horticulture. 2nd ed. 640p. 1983. text ed. write for info. (ISBN 0-8273-2198-8); instr's guide 3.75 (ISBN 0-8273-2199-6). Delmar.

Riotte, Louise. Roses Love Garlic: Secrets of Companion Planting with Flowers. (Illus.). 224p. (Orig.). 1982. pap. 6.95 (ISBN 0-88266-331-3). Garden Way Pub.

Unsworth. Effects of Gaseous Air Pollution in Agriculture & Horticulture. 1982. text ed. 89.95 (ISBN 0-686-37584-X). Butterworth.

Walls, Ian. Modern Greenhouse Methods: Flowers & Plants. 220p. 1982. 31.00x (ISBN 0-584-10386-7, Pub. by Muller Ltd). State Mutual Bk.

--Modern Greenhouse Methods: Vegetables. 220p. 1982. 31.00x (ISBN 0-584-10388-3, Pub. by Muller Ltd). State Mutual Bk.

HOSPICES (TERMINAL CARE)

see Terminal Care Facilities

HOSPITAL ADMINISTRATION

see Hospitals–Administration

HOSPITAL ATTENDANTS

see Hospitals–Staff

HOSPITAL CARE

see also Coronary Care Units; Intensive Care Units; Monitoring (Hospital Care)

Allaire, Barbara & McNeil, Robert. Teaching Patient Relations in Hospitals: The Hows & Whys. LC 82-22765. (Illus.). 200p. 1983. 75.00 (ISBN 0-87258-377-5, AHA-049150). Am Hospital.

Carroll, Jean G. Patient Care Audit Criteria: Standards for Hospital Quality Assurance. LC 82-72867. 250p. 1983. 49.50 (ISBN 0-87094-392-8). Dow Jones-Irwin.

Meshenberg, Kathryn & Burns, Linda, eds. Hospital Ambulatory Care: Making It Work. 200p. 1983. 37.50 (ISBN 0-87258-402-X, AHA-016620). Am Hospital.

HOSPITAL CARE, COST OF

see Hospitals–Rates

HOSPITAL CHARGES

see Hospitals–Rates

HOSPITAL EMPLOYEES

see Hospitals–Staff

HOSPITAL ENDOWMENTS

see Endowments

HOSPITAL HOUSE STAFF

see Interns (Medicine)

HOSPITAL INTERNS

see Interns (Medicine)

HOSPITAL MANAGEMENT

see Hospitals–Administration

HOSPITAL MEDICAL RECORDS

see Medical Records

HOSPITAL PERSONNEL

see Hospitals–Staff

HOSPITAL RATES

see Hospitals–Rates

HOSPITAL SOCIAL WORK

see Medical Social Work

HOSPITAL SUPPLIES

see Medical Supplies

HOSPITAL TRAINING SCHOOLS

see Nursing Schools

HOSPITAL WORKERS

see Hospitals–Staff

HOSPITALS

see also Children–Hospitals; Hospital Care; Medicine, Clinical; Nurses and Nursing; Nursing Homes; Psychiatric Hospitals; Terminal Care Facilities

also subdivision Hospitals under names of cities, e.g. New York (City)–Hospitals

Alperin, Stanley, ed. The Federal Hospital Phone Book: 1983-84. pap. 24.95 (ISBN 0-916524-19-1). US Direct Serv.

--The Hospital Phone: 1983-84. pap. 29.95 (ISBN 0-916524-18-3). US Direct Serv.

American Hospital Association. Hospital Statistics: Data from the American Hospital Association Annual Survey, 1981. 240p. 1982. pap. text ed. 40.00 (ISBN 0-87258-364-3, AHA-082082). Am Hospital.

--Introduction to Discharge Planning for Hospitals, 1982. LC 82-22644. 32p. 1982. pap. 9.50 (ISBN 0-87258-381-3, AHA-004160). Am Hospital.

Ayliffe, G. A. & Taylor, L. J. Hospital-Acquired Infection: Principles & Prevention. (Illus.). 144p. 1982. pap. text ed. 15.00 (ISBN 0-7236-0608-0). Wright-PSG.

Bennett, Addison C. Productivity & the Quality of Work Life in Hospitals. Dwight, Beryl M., ed. (Illus.). 96p. 1983. 30.00 (ISBN 0-87258-405-4). Am Hospital.

Crittenden, Faith J. Discharge Planning for Health Care Facilities. 224p. 1983. pap. text ed. 17.95 (ISBN 0-89303-210-7). R J Brady.

Directory of Multihospital Systems, 1983. 80p. 1983. write for info. (ISBN 0-87258-403-8, 103147). Am Hospital.

Lang, Regine. A Century of Health Care Ministry: A History of St. Francis Medical Center. (Illus.). 224p. 1982. text ed. 24.95 (ISBN 0-88136-011-2). Jostens.

Mullner, Ross & Killingsworth, Cleve. Surveys of the American Hospital Association Hospital Data Center. 214p. (Orig.). 1982. 48.75 (ISBN 0-87258-387-2, AH-097100). Am Hospital.

HOSPITALS–ACCOUNTING

American Hospital Association. Estimated Useful Lives of Depreciable Hospital Assets. 1978. pap. 5.00 (ISBN 0-87258-247-7, AHA-061107). Am Hospital.

Linklater, R. Bruce. Internal Control of Hospital Finances: A Guide for Management. (Financial Management Ser.). (Illus.). 96p. 1983. 32.50 (ISBN 0-87258-398-8, AHA-061150). Am Hospital.

Touche Ross & Co. Controlling Assets & Transactions in Hospitals: How to Improve Internal Accounting Control. Rev. ed. (Illus.). 108p. 1982. pap. 9.95 (ISBN 0-930228-17-0). Healthcare Fin Man Assn.

HOSPITALS–ADMINISTRATION

American Hospital Association. Planning Hospital Health Promotion Services for Business & Industry. 140p. 1982. pap. 33.75 (ISBN 0-87258-378-3, AHA-070175). Am Hospital.

Benjamin, Robert C. & Kemppainen, Rudolph C. Hospital Administrator's Desk Book. 270p. 1983. 41.50 (ISBN 0-13-394890-0, Busn). P-H.

Engstrom, Karen M. Consent Manual: Policies, Laws, Procedures, 2nd ed. 115p. pap. write for info (ISBN 0-87125-078-0). Catholic Health.

Housley, Charles E. Strategies in Hospital Material Management: Case Analysis & Masterplanning. LC 82-20620. 602p. 1982. 42.50 (ISBN 0-89443-668-6). Aspen Systems.

Hunter, B. Administration of Hospital Wards. 1972. 11.00 (ISBN 0-7190-0525-6). Manchester.

James B. & Peters, Joseph P. Strategic Thinking: New Frontier for Hospital Management. 1983. pap. write for info. (ISBN 0-87258-404-6). Am Hospital.

Schulz, Rockwell & Johnson, Alton C. Management of Hospitals. 2nd ed. 352p. 1983. 20.95x (ISBN 0-07-055652-0). McGraw.

HOSPITALS–ATTENDANTS

see Hospitals–Staff

HOSPITALS–CHARGES

see Hospitals–Rates

HOSPITALS–DESIGN AND CONSTRUCTION

Architectural Record Magazine Staff. Hospitals & Health Care Facilities. 1978. 41.95 (ISBN 0-07-002338-7). McGraw.

HOSPITALS–EMPLOYEES

see Hospitals–Staff

HOSPITALS–HOUSE STAFF

see Interns (Medicine)

HOSPITALS–JUVENILE LITERATURE

Claypool, Jane. Career Prep: Working In A Hospital. (Jem High Interest-Low Reading Level Ser.). (Illus.). 64p. (gr. 7-9). 1983. PLB 9.29 (ISBN 0-671-44889-7). Messner.

HOSPITALS–MANAGEMENT AND REGULATION

see Hospitals–Administration

HOSPITALS–NURSES

see Hospitals–Staff; Nurses and Nursing

HOSPITALS–PSYCHIATRIC SERVICES

see Psychiatric Hospitals

HOSPITALS–RATES

Billing Systems for Health Professionals. 7.95 (ISBN 0-910085-05-6). Info Res MI.

HOSPITALS–SAFETY MEASURES

American Hospital Association & National Safety Council. Safety Guide for Health Care Institutions. (Illus.). 1983. write for info. (ISBN 0-87258-302-3, AHA-181136). Am Hospital.

HOSPITALS–STAFF

AHA Clearinghouse for Hospital Management Engineering, ed. Medical Staffing Based on Patient Classification: An Examination of Cases Studies. 176p. 1983. pap. 18.75 (ISBN 0-87258-384-8). Am Hospital.

Institute for the Study of Labor & Economic Crisis. Worker's Report on the Conditions of Labor & Their Effect on Patient Care at San Francisco General Hospital. 42p. (Orig.). 1979. pap. 2.00 (ISBN 0-89935-006-2). Synthesis Pubns.

Rudman, Jack. Hospital Safety Officer. (Career Examination Ser.: C-118). (Cloth bdg. avail. on request). pap. 10.00 (ISBN 0-8373-0118-1). Natl Learning.

--Hospital Safety Officer Trainee. (Career Examination Ser.: C-119). (Cloth bdg. avail. on request). pap. 10.00 (ISBN 0-8373-0119-X). Natl Learning.

HOSPITALS, INSANE

see Psychiatric Hospitals

HOSPITALS, PSYCHIATRIC

see Psychiatric Hospitals

HOST-PARASITE RELATIONSHIPS

Eickenberg, H. U., ed. The Influence of Antibiotics on the Host-Parasite Relationship. (Illus.). 270p. 1982. pap. 25.00 (ISBN 0-387-11680-X). Springer-Verlag.

Misaghi, I. J. Physiology & Biochemistry of Plant-Pathogen Interactions. 275p. 1982. 32.50x (ISBN 0-306-41059-1, Plenum Pr). Plenum Pub.

HOSTILITIES

see War; War (International Law)

HOT-HOUSES

see Greenhouses

HOT-WATER HEATERS

see Water Heaters

HOTEL ADMINISTRATION

see Hotel Management

HOTEL MANAGEMENT

Berman, Susan. Your Career in Hotel Management. (Arco's Career Guidance Ser.). (Illus.). 128p. 1983. lib. bdg. 7.95 (ISBN 0-668-05501-4); pap. 4.50 (ISBN 0-668-05513-8). Arco.

Borsenik, Frank D. The Management of Maintenance & Engineering Systems in Hospitality Industries. LC 78-13677. (Service Management Ser.). 494p. 1979. text ed. 27.95 (ISBN 0-471-03213-1). Wiley.

Bull, Jean & Bull, Gordon. Questions in Hotel Reception. 96p. 1981. 25.00x (ISBN 0-85950-310-0, Pub. by Thornes England). State Mutual Bk.

Dix, Colin. Accomodation Operations. 176p. 1979. 20.00x (ISBN 0-7121-0174-8, Pub. by Macdonald & Evans). State Mutual Bk.

Motel-Hotel Management Directory: 1982-1983 Edition. 1982. 30.00 (ISBN 0-915260-10-7). Atcom.

Ninemeier, Jack D. Purchasing, Receiving & Storage: Operational Manual for Restaurants, Hotels & Institutions. 360p. 1983. 3 ring binder 64.95 (ISBN 0-8436-2261-X). CBI Pub.

Paige, Grace & Paige, Jane. The Hotel Receptionist. 1982. pap. 30.00x (ISBN 0-304-29757-7, Pub. by Cassell England). State Mutual Bk.

Sutton, D. F. Financial Management in Hotel & Catering Operations. 252p. 1983. pap. 17.50 (ISBN 0-434-91887-3, Pub. by Heinemann England). David & Charles.

Taylor, D. & Thomason, R. Profitable Hotel Reception. (International Series in Hospitality Management). (Illus.). 236p. 1982. 30.00 (ISBN 0-08-026769-6); pap. 14.95 (ISBN 0-08-026768-8). Pergamon.

HOTELS, TAVERNS, ETC.

see also Coffee Houses; Hotel Management; Restaurants, Lunchrooms, etc.; Tourist Camps, Hostels, etc.

also names of individual hotels and restaurants

Berger, Terry. Country Inns: The Rocky Mountains. 96p. 1983. pap. 10.95 (ISBN 0-03-062211-5). HR&W.

Cudworth, Marsha & Michaels, Howard. Victorian Holidays: A Guide to Guesthouses, Bed & Breakfast Inns & Restaurants of Cape May, N. J. 2nd rev. & enlarged ed. LC 82-83816. 125p. (Orig.). pap. 6.95 (ISBN 0-9608554-1-6). Lady Raspberry.

Edinger, Claudio. Chelsea Hotel. (Illus.). 160p. (Orig.). 1983. 29.95 (ISBN 0-89659-368-1); pap. 14.95 (ISBN 0-89659-338-X). Abbeville Pr.

Lawliss, Chuck. Country Inns: The Mississippi. 96p. 1983. pap. 10.95 (ISBN 0-03-062212-3). HR&W.

Lecler, Rene. The Three Hundred Best Hotels in the World. LC 82-10778. (Illus.). 240p. 1983. pap. 9.95 (ISBN 0-89919-160-6). Ticknor & Fields.

McCullum, Anne, ed. World Hotel Directory 1981-1982. 7th ed. 887p. 1981. 47.50x (ISBN 0-582-90308-4). Intl Pubns Serv.

McGinty, Brian. Palace Inns. LC 78-73. (Illus.). 192p. 1978. pap. 9.95 (ISBN 0-686-81982-9). Stackpole.

Medlik, S. Business of Hotels. 1980. pap. 12.50 (ISBN 0-434-91249-2, Pub. by Heinemann). David & Charles.

Rankin, Jake & Rankin, Marni. The Getaway Guide IV: Short Vacations in Southern California. LC 82-19060. (Illus.). 248p. (Orig.). 1983. pap. 9.95 (ISBN 0-686-43071-9). Pacific Search.

--The Getaway Guide 0778997xx: Short Vacations in the Pacific Northwest. revised ed. LC 82-18784. (2nd). 223p. 1983. pap. 9.95 (ISBN 0-686-43073-5). Pacific Search.

Rice, Kym. Early American Taverns: For the Entertainment of Friends & Strangers. LC 82-42786. 1983. pap. 12.95. Regnery-Gateway.

Schuhholz, Annaliese & Diekmann, Jens. Romantik Hotels & Restaurants: Multilingual Guide. Rev. ed. (Illus.). 170p. 1983. pap. 5.95 (ISBN 0-912944-73-0). Berkshire Traveller.

Welles, Sigourney. The Best Bed & Breakfast in the World. LC 82-83265. 348p. 1983. pap. 9.95 (ISBN 0-914788-65-5). East Woods.

HOTELS, TAVERNS, ETC.–ACCOUNTING

Ryan, Chris. An Introduction to Hotel & Catering Economics. 288p. 1980. 35.00x (ISBN 0-85950-424-7, Pub. by Thornes England). State Mutual Bk.

HOTELS, TAVERNS, ETC.–MANAGEMENT
see Hotel Management

HOTELS, TAVERNS, ETC.–VOCATIONAL GUIDANCE

Morton, Alexander C. The Official Career Guide to Food Service & Hospitality Management. (Illus.). 128p. 1983. pap. 7.95 (ISBN 0-686-82173-4). Arco.

HOTELS, TAVERNS, ETC.–EUROPE

Guesthouses, Farmhouses & Inns in Europe. 256p. 1983. pap. 8.95 (ISBN 0-86145-088-4, Pub. by Auto Assn-British Tourist Authority England). Merrimack Bk SErv.

HOTELS, TAVERNS, ETC.–GREAT BRITAIN

British Hotels, Restaurants & Caterers Association. Hotels & Restaurants in Britain 1983. (Illus.). 550p. 1983. pap. 12.95 (ISBN 0-13-394916-8). P-H.

British Tourist Authority. Hotels & Restaurants in Britain, 1982-3. LC 52-21171. (Illus.). 600p. 1982. pap. 10.00x (ISBN 0-7095-0897-2). Intl Pubns Serv.

Eason, Helena. Bristol's Historic Inns. 80p. 1982. 30.00x (ISBN 0-905459-30-X, Pub. by Redcliffe England). State Mutual Bk.

Guesthouses, Farmhouses & Inns in Britain. 280p. 1983. pap. 8.95 (ISBN 0-86145-137-6, Pub. by Auto Assn-British Tourist Authority England). Merrimack Bk Serv.

A Guide to London's Best Pubs. 224p. 1983. pap. 6.95 (ISBN 0-907080-47-2, Pub. by Auto Assn-British Tourist Authority England). Merrimack Bk Serv.

Hotels & Restaurants in Britain. 608p. 1983. pap. 12.95 (ISBN 0-686-38449-0, Pub. by Auto Assn-British Tourist Authority England). Merrimack Bk Serv.

Ronay, Egon. Egon Ronay's Lucas Guide to Hotels, Restaurants & Inns in Great Britain & Ireland, 1983. LC 74-644899. (Illus.). 862p. 1983. pap. 13.95 (ISBN 0-03-063331-1). HR&W.

Watkins, Paul. Historic English Inns. (Golden Hart Guides Ser.). (Illus.). 96p. 1983. pap. 3.95 (ISBN 0-283-98915-7, Pub by Sidgwick & Jackson). Merrimack Bk Serv.

HOTELS, TAVERNS, ETC.–IRELAND

Taylor, Sybil. Ireland's Pubs. (Illus., Orig.). 1983. pap. 6.95 (ISBN 0-14-006488-5). Penguin.

HOTLINES (PSYCHIATRY)
see Crisis Intervention (Psychiatry)

HOURS (TIME)
see Days; Time

HOURS OF LABOR
see also Holidays

Nitsch, Susan L. How to Become a Freelance Secretary. Pasich, William, ed. (Illus.). 53p. 1983. pap. 3.95 (ISBN 0-943544-01-7). Secretarial Pubns.

Rosow, Jerome M. & Zager, Robert. New Work Schedules for A Changing Society. 128p. 10.95 (ISBN 0-686-84774-1); softcover summary 4.95 (ISBN 0-686-84775-X). Work in Amer.

HOUSE BUYING

Adkins, Jan. How a House Happens. (Illus.). 30p. 1983. pap. 3.95 (ISBN 0-8027-7206-4). Walker & Co.

Bell, William W. Secrets of a Professional Home Buyer. LC 82-21980. 160p. 1983. softcover 12.95 (ISBN 0-930294-00-9). World Wide OR.

Boroson, Warren. How to Buy or Sell Your Home in a Changing Market. 250p. 1983. softcover 15.95 (ISBN 0-87489-278-3). Med Economics.

Dawson, Joseph C. Seeking Shelter: How to Find & Finance an Energy-Efficient Home. (Illus.). 256p. 1983. pap. 9.95 (ISBN 0-688-00903-4). Quill NY.

Dooley, Thomas W. Buy Now! How Alternative Financing Can Work For You. 48p. (Orig.). 1982. pap. 2.95 (ISBN 0-88462-444-7). Real Estate Ed Co.

Goetze, Rolf. Rescuing the American Dream: Public & the Crisis in Housing. 128p. 1983. text ed. 22.50x (ISBN 0-8419-0855-9); pap. text ed. 10.50x (ISBN 0-8419-0862-1). Holmes & Meier.

HOUSE CLEANING

Cleaning. LC 82-5717. (Home Repair & Improvement Ser.). lib. bdg. 15.96 (ISBN 0-8094-3491-1, Pub. by Time-Life). Silver.

HOUSE CONSTRUCTION
see also Drainage, House; Dwellings–Maintenance and Repair; Dwellings–Remodeling

Adkins, Jan. How a House Happens. (Illus.). 30p. 1983. pap. 3.95 (ISBN 0-8027-7206-4). Walker & Co.

Brann, Donald R. How to Build a Two Bedroom Ranch House. LC 82-90748. 224p. 1983. pap. 6.95 (ISBN 0-87733-831-0). Easi-Bild.

Briggs Amasco Ltd. Flat Roofing: A Guide to Good Practice. (Illus.). 216p. 1982. pap. 33.95 (ISBN 0-9507919-0-3, Pub. by RIBA). Intl Schol Bk Serv.

Chapman, Keeler C. & Traister, John E. Homes for the Nineteen-Eighties: An Energy & Construction Design Aid. LC 82-5929. (Illus.). 256p. pap. 16.95 (ISBN 0-8306-1425-7). TAB Bks.

Kern, Barbara & Kern, Ken. The Earth Sheltered: Owner-Built Home. LC 82-99912. (Illus.). 272p. (Orig.). 1982. pap. 9.95 (ISBN 0-910225-00-1). Owner-Builder.

Landis, Michael & Moholt, Ray. Patios & Decks: How to Plan, Build & Enjoy. (Illus.). 193p. 1983. pap. 9.95 (ISBN 0-89586-162-3). H P Bks.

National Association of Home Builders. Construction Cost Control. Rev. ed. (Illus.). 64p. 1982. pap. text ed. 13.00 (ISBN 0-86718-153-2). Natl Assn Home.

--Cost Effective Site Planning. Rev. ed. (Illus.). 142p. 1982. pap. text ed. 20.00 (ISBN 0-86718-156-7). Natl Assn Home.

One Twenty Early American Plans. 96p. Date not set. 2.25 (ISBN 0-918894-23-9). Home Planners.

One Twenty-Five Contemporary Home Plans. 112p. Date not set. 2.25 (ISBN 0-918894-24-7). Home Planners.

Three Fifty-One Story Home Plans. 256p. Date not set. 4.95 (ISBN 0-918894-28-X). Home Planners.

Two Hundred-Five Multi-Level Home Plans. 192p. Date not set. 3.95 (ISBN 0-918894-29-8). Home Planners.

Two Hundred-Ten One-Story Home Plans. 192p. Date not set. 3.95 (ISBN 0-918894-27-1). Home Planners.

Wade, Herb. Building Underground: The Design & Construction Handbook for Earth-Sheltered Houses. Balitas, Maggie, ed. (Illus.). 320p. (Orig.). 1983. 19.95 (ISBN 0-87857-421-2, 04-000-0); pap. 14.95 (ISBN 0-87857-422-0, 04-000-1). Rodale Pr Inc.

HOUSE DECORATION
see Interior Decoration

HOUSE DRAINAGE
see Drainage, House; Plumbing; Sanitation; Sewerage

HOUSE-FLIES
see Flies

HOUSE MOVING
see Moving of Buildings, Bridges, etc.

HOUSE PLANS
see Architecture, Domestic–Designs and Plans

HOUSE PURCHASING
see House Buying

HOUSE SELLING

Andreassi, Michael W. & MacRae, C. Duncan. Homeowner Income Tax Provisions & Metropolitan Housing Markets: A Simulation Study. LC 81-51624. 78p. 1981. pap. 9.00 (ISBN 0-87766-297-5, URI 29900). Urban Inst.

Boroson, Warren. How to Buy or Sell Your Home in a Changing Market. 250p. 1983. softcover 15.95 (ISBN 0-87489-278-3). Med Economics.

HOUSEHOLD APPLIANCES

Godfrey, Robert S. Means Systems Costs, 1983. 8th ed. LC 76-17689. 425p. 1983. pap. 37.50 (ISBN 0-911950-51-6). Means.

HOUSEHOLD EXPENSES
see Cost and Standard of Living

HOUSEHOLD GOODS
see Household Appliances; Kitchen Utensils

HOUSEHOLD MANAGEMENT
see Home Economics

HOUSEHOLD MOVING
see Moving, Household

HOUSEHOLD UTENSILS
see Implements, Utensils, etc.; Kitchen Utensils

HOUSEHOLD WORKERS
see Servants

HOUSEKEEPING
see Home Economics

HOUSEMAIDS
see Servants

HOUSES
see Architecture, Domestic; Dwellings

HOUSES, APARTMENT
see Apartment Houses

HOUSEWIVES
see also Mothers; Wives

Angus, Fay. How to Do Everything Right & Live to Regret It: Confessions of a Harried Housewife. LC 82-48425. 192p. 1983. 10.95 (ISBN 0-686-82600-0, HarpR). Har-Row.

Davidson, Caroline. A Woman's Work Is Never Done: A History of Housework in the British Isles 1650-1950. (Illus.). 256p. 1983. 19.95 (ISBN 0-7011-3901-3, Pub. by Chatto & Windus). Merrimack Bk Serv.

Morgan, Marie. Breaking Through: How to Overcome Housewives' Depression. 204p. 1983. pap. 9.95 (ISBN 0-86683-697-7). Winston Pr.

Segalla, Rosemary A. Departure from Traditional Roles: Mid-LIfe Women Break the Daisy Chains. Nathan, Peter E., ed. LC 82-20089. (Research in Clinical Psychology Ser.: No. 5). 164p. 1982. 34.95 (ISBN 0-8357-1386-5). Univ Microfilms.

Young, Pam & Jones, Peggy. The Sidetracked Sisters Catch Up on the Kitchen. 224p. 1983. pap. 6.95 (ISBN 0-446-37526-8). Warner Bks.

HOUSING
see also Aged–Dwellings; Homelessness; Public Housing; Real Estate Management; Relocation (Housing); Second Homes

Batley, Richard. Power Through Bureaucracy: Urban Political Analysis in Brazil. LC 82-16872. 240p. 1982. 27.50x (ISBN 0-312-63437-4). St Martin.

Beer, William R. Language Policy & National Unity. LC 81-67475. 256p. 1983. text ed. 30.00x (ISBN 0-86598-058-6). Allanheld.

Belliveou, Jim & Belliveou, Mary. Riches Under Your Roof. LC 82-15420. 288p. 1983. 17.95 (ISBN 0-03-053016-4); pap. 9.95 (ISBN 0-03-053301-5). HR&W.

Bradbury, Katharine L. & Downs, Anthony. Housing & Energy in the Nineteen Eighties. new ed. 320p. 1983. 28.95 (ISBN 0-8157-1050-X); pap. 10.95 (ISBN 0-8157-1049-6). Brookings.

Downs, Anthony. No Vacancy: Rental Housing in the 1980's. 225p. 1983. 24.95 (ISBN 0-8157-1922-1); pap. 9.95 (ISBN 0-8157-1921-3). Brookings.

Goetze, Rolf. Rescuing the American Dream: Public & the Crisis in Housing. 128p. 1983. text ed. 22.50x (ISBN 0-8419-0855-9); pap. text ed. 10.50x (ISBN 0-8419-0862-1). Holmes & Meier.

Hamburger, Robert. All the Lonely People: Life in a Single Room Occupancy Hotel. LC 82-19128. 352p. 1983. 15.95 (ISBN 0-89919-159-2). Ticknor & Fields.

MacLennan, Duncan. The Economics of Housing. (Illus.). 300p. (Orig.). 1982. pap. text ed. 17.50x (ISBN 0-582-44381-4). Longman.

Nutt-Powell, Thomas E. & Furlong, Michael. The States & Manufactured Housing. (Illus.). 231p. 1980. pap. 10.00 (ISBN 0-943142-02-4). Joint Cen Urban.

Porter, Douglas R. & Cole, Susan. Affordable Housing: Twenty Examples from the Private Sector. LC 82-83409. (Illus.). 106p. 1982. pap. text ed. 18.00 (ISBN 0-87420-616-2, A13). Urban Land.

Purkis, Andrew & Hodson, Paul. Housing & Community Care. 58p. 1982. pap. text ed. 9.75x (ISBN 0-7199-1076-5, Pub. by Bedford England). Renouf.

Rudman, Jack. Administrative Housing Inspector. (Career Examination Ser.: C-2604). (Cloth bdg. avail. on request). pap. 12.00 (ISBN 0-8373-2604-4). Natl Learning.

Stevens, Robert W., ed. Community Self-Help Housing Manual: Partnership in Action. (Illus.). 72p. (Orig.). 1982. pap. 4.75x (ISBN 0-942850-00-9). Intermediate Tech.

Weicher, John, et al. Rental Housing: Is There a Crisis? LC 81-53063. 113p. 1981. text ed. 16.50 (ISBN 0-87766-307-6, URI 33400). Urban Inst.

HOUSING–FINANCE
see also Mortgages

Eastgate, Robert J. Master Guide to Creative Financing of Real Estate Investments. LC 82-9313. 246p. 1982. text ed. 89.50 (ISBN 0-87624-366-9). Inst Busn Plan.

Follain, James, et al. Place to Place Indexes of the Price of Housing. 98p. 1979. pap. text ed. 5.50 (ISBN 0-87766-265-7). Urban Inst.

Peterson, George E. Tax Exempt Financing of Housing Investment. 45p. 1980. pap. text ed. 11.00 (ISBN 0-87766-251-7). Urban Inst.

HOUSING–LAW AND LEGISLATION

Grieson, Ronald E., ed. The Urban Economy & Housing. LC 81-48269. 256p. 1982. 27.95X (ISBN 0-669-05331-7). Lexington Bks.

National Housing Law Project. The Subsidized Housing Handbook: How to Provide, Preserve, & Manage Housing for Lower-Income People. 500p. (Orig.). 1982. pap. 40.00 (ISBN 0-9606098-3-0). Natl Housing Law.

Nicholas, James C. State Regulation: Housing Prices. 140p. 1982. pap. text ed. 10.95 (ISBN 0-88285-075-X, Dist. by Transaction Bks). Ctr Urban Pol Res.

Wendt, Paul F. Housing Policy-the Search for Solutions: A Comparison of the United Kingdom, Sweden, West Germany & the United States since World War II. LC 82-20942. (Publications of the Institute of Business & Economic Research, University of California). xii, 283p. 1983. Repr. of 1962 ed. lib. bdg. 35.00x (ISBN 0-313-23695-X, WEHO). Greenwood.

HOUSING–GREAT BRITAIN

Historic Houses, Castles & Gardens in Great Britain & Ireland, 1982. LC 57-35834. (Illus.). 179p. 1982. pap. 4.50x (ISBN 0-900486-31-7). Intl Pubns Serv.

HOUSING FOR THE AGED
see Aged–Dwellings

HOUSING PROJECTS, GOVERNMENT
see Public Housing

HOUSING SECURITY
see Burglary Protection

HOUSTON, TEXAS

Brown, Stanley H. A Tale of Two Cities: Houston & Detroit. (Illus.). 1983. 16.95 (ISBN 0-87795-486-0). Arbor Hse.

The Complete Houston Area Directory: A Comprehensive Guide to Over 130,000 Businesses, Manufacturers, Retailers, Social & Professional Services, Institutions, Organizations in Houston & Nearby Towns, 2 Vols. 2000p. 1983. pap. 95.00 per set (ISBN 0-87436-043-9). ABC Clio.

Fauntleroy, Fran, ed. Houston Epicure 1982-83. (Epicure Ser.). 160p. 1982. pap. 5.95 (ISBN 0-89716-114-9). Peanut Butter.

Young, Dale. Marmac Guide to Houston. Nicholson, Diana M., ed. (Guidebook Ser.). 296p. (Orig.). 1983. pap. 6.95 (ISBN 0-939944-03-0). Marmac Pub.

HOWARD, OLIVER OTIS, 1830-1909

McFeely, William s. Yankee Stepfather: General O. O. Howard & the Freedmen. 368p. 1983. pap. 6.25x (ISBN 0-393-00537-2). Norton.

HOWELLS, WILLIAM DEAN, 1837-1920

Eble, Kenneth. William Dean Howells. 2nd ed. (United States Authors Ser.). 1982. lib. bdg. 13.95 (ISBN 0-8057-7372-X, Twayne). G K Hall.

Fischer, William C. & Lohmann, Christopher K. Selected Letters of W. D. Howells: Vol. 5, 1902-1911. (Critical Editions Program). 494p. 1983. lib. bdg. 40.00 (ISBN 0-8057-8531-0, Twayne). G K Hall.

Simpson, James W. The Editor's Study: A Comprehensive Edition of W. D. Howell's Column. LC 81-50049. 464p. 1983. 38.50X (ISBN 0-87875-213-7). Whitston Pub.

HUALAPAI INDIANS
see Indians of North America–Southwest, New

HUDSON RIVER AND VALLEY

Goodwin, Maude W. Dutch & English on the Hudson. 1919. text ed. 8.50x (ISBN 0-686-83529-8). Elliots Bks.

Rachlin, Joseph W. & Tauber, Gilbert, eds. Papers of the Fifth Symposium on Hudson River Ecology 1980. 107p. (Orig.). 1981. pap. 15.00x (ISBN 0-89062-131-4, Pub. by HRES). Pub Ctr Cult Res.

HUGHES, TED

Sagar, Keith & Tabor, Stephen. Ted Hughes: A Bibliography, 1945-1980. 300p. 1982. 32.00 (ISBN 0-7201-1654-6, Pub. by Mansell England). Wilson.

Sager, Keith, ed. The Achievement of Ted Hughes. LC 82-13522. 240p. 1983. text ed. 25.00x (ISBN 0-8203-0650-9). U of Ga Pr.

HUGO, VICTOR MARIE, COMTE, 1802-1885

Josephson, Matthew. Victor Hugo: A Realistic Biography of the Great Romantic. 514p. 1982. Repr. of 1942 ed. lib. bdg. 45.00 (ISBN 0-89760-415-6). Telegraph Bks.

HULME, THOMAS ERNEST, 1883-1917

Roberts, Michael. T. E. Hulme. 356p. 1982. Repr. of 1938 ed. text ed. 21.00x (ISBN 0-85635-411-2, 61258, Pub. by Carcanet New Pr England). Humanities.

HUMAN ABNORMALITIES
see Abnormalities, Human

HUMAN ANATOMY
see Anatomy, Human

HUMAN BEHAVIOR
see also Behavior Modification; Psychobiology; Psychology, Comparative

Abraham, Ralph & Shaw, Chris. Dynamics: The Geometry of Behavior: Pt. 2, Stable & Chaotic Behavior. (Visual Mathematics Ser.). 1983. price not set. Aerial Pr.

Beck, Alan & Katcher, Aaron, eds. New Perspectives on Our Lives with Companion Animals. LC 82-40484. 640p. 1983. 25.00x (ISBN 0-8122-7877-1). U of Pa Pr.

Edwards, R. G. & Purdy, J. M. Human Conception In Vitro. LC 82-71006. 1982. 37.00 (ISBN 0-12-232740-3). Acad Pr.

Elorza. Matematicas para Ciencias del Comportamiento. 300p. (Span.). 1983. pap. text ed. write for info. (ISBN 0-06-310700-7, Pub. by HarLA Mexico). Har-Row.

Ford, Jill. Human Behavior: Towards a Practical Understanding Library of Social Work. 160p. 1983. pap. 7.95 (ISBN 0-7100-9218-0). Routledge & Kegan.

Fulton. The Frontal Lobes & Human Behaviour. 30p. 1982. 50.00x (ISBN 0-85323-311-X, Pub. by LIverpool Univ England). State Mutual Bk.

Gale, Anthony & Edwards, John A., eds. Physiological Correlates of Human Behaviour, Vol. 1. Date not set. Vol. 1. price not set (ISBN 0-12-273901-9); Vol. 2. price not set (ISBN 0-12-273902-7); Vol. 3. price not set (ISBN 0-12-273903-5). Acad pr.

Grover, Sonja C. The Analysis of Human Behavior: A Psychological Laboratory Manual. 130p. 1982. pap. text ed. 12.95x (ISBN 0-8290-1256-7). Irvington.

Heslin, Richard & Patterson, Miles. Nonverbal Behavior & Social Psychology. (Perspectives in Social Psychology Ser.). 196p. 1982. 24.50x (ISBN 0-306-40952-6, Plenum Pr). Plenum Pub.

Jackins, Harvey, ed. Human Side of Human Beings: Chinese Translation. Sung See Whai, tr. (Chinese.). pap. 3.00 (ISBN 0-911214-84-4). Rational Isl.

Kantowitz, Barry H. & Sorkin, Robert D. Human Factors: Understanding People-System Relationships. 600p. 1983. text ed. 30.95x (ISBN 0-471-09594-X); tchr's. manual avail. (ISBN 0-471-87201-6); lab. manual avail. (ISBN 0-471-87200-8). Wiley.

Kendall, Philip C., ed. Advances in Cognitive Behavioral Research & Therapy, Vol. 2. (Serial Publication). Date not set. price not set (ISBN 0-12-010602-7). Acad Pr.

Kerr, Mary M. & Nelson, C. Michael. Strategies for Managing Behavior Problems. 448p. 1983. text ed. 14.95 (ISBN 0-675-20032-6). Merrill.

Krantz, David S. & Baum, Andrew. Handbook of Psychology & Health: Cardiovascular Disorders & Behavior, No.3. 400p. 1983. text ed. write for info. (ISBN 0-89859-185-6). L Erlbaum Assocs.

Lopez, Jesus. Of Human Dignity, Literary Services Agency, Inc., ed. 485p. 1982. pap. 3.95 (ISBN 0-917188-20-9). Nationwide Pr.

Maze, J. R. The Meaning of Behavior. 216p. 1983. text ed. 29.50x (ISBN 0-04-150081-4). Allen Unwin.

Ortiz. The Psychology of Human Behavior: A Study Guide for Psychology One-Hundred. 178p. 1982. write for info. West Pub.

Rosenblatt, Jay, et al, eds. Advances in the Study of Behavior, Vol. 13. (Serial Publication). Date not set. price not set (ISBN 0-12-004513-3). Acad Pr.

Rowe, John R. & Pasch, Marvin. The New Model Me. (gr. 8-12). 1983. price not set (ISBN 0-8077-2733-4). Tchrs Coll.

Schwartz, Barry. Psychology of Learning & Behavior: Essays on Behavior Theory. 500p. 1982. pap. text ed. 14.95x (ISBN 0-393-95305-X). Norton.

Semin, Gun R. & Manstead, S. R., eds. The Accountability of Conduct. (European Monograph Soc.: No. 33). Date not set. price not set (ISBN 0-12-636650-0). Acad Pr.
Siebold. Attitudes & Behavior. 256p. 1983. 22.95 (ISBN 0-03-060293-9). Praeger.

HUMAN BEINGS ON OTHER PLANETS
see Life on Other Planets

HUMAN BIOLOGY
see also Physical Anthropology
Rowlinson, Pat & Jenkins, Morton. Human Biology: An Activity Approach. (Illus.). 304p. 1982. pap. text ed. 9.95 (ISBN 0-521-28200-4). Cambridge U Pr.

HUMAN BODY
see Body, Human

HUMAN CHROMOSOMES
Boyce, A. J. Chromosome Variation in Human Evolution: Symposia of the Institute of Biology Ser, Vol. 14. 131p. 1975. 29.95 (ISBN 0-470-09330-7). Wiley.

HUMAN ECOLOGY
see also Anthropo-Geography; Community Life; Environmental Policy; Man-Influence of Environment; Man-Influence on Nature; Population; Social Psychology; Sociology
Curtis, R. K. Evolution or Extinction: The Choice Before Us-A Systems Approach to the Study of the Future. 420p. 1982. 50.00 (ISBN 0-08-027933-3); pap. 25.00 (ISBN 0-08-027932-5). Pergamon.
Dasgupta, Partha. The Control of Resources. (Illus.). 240p. 1983. text ed. 22.50x (ISBN 0-674-16980-8). Harvard U Pr.
Howden, P. Ecologistics. 1982. 30.00x (ISBN 0-9507230-0-2, Pub. by Element Bks). State Mutual Bk.
Hughes, J. Donald. American Indian Ecology. (Illus.). 200p. 1983. 20.00 (ISBN 0-87404-070-1). Tex Western.
Jamison, P. L. & Seguras, S. L., eds. The Eskimo of Northwestern Alaska: A Biological Perspective. LC 77-18941. (US-IBP Synthesis Ser.: Vol. 8). 319p. 1978. 46.00 (ISBN 0-87933-319-7). Hutchinson Ross.
LaConte, P. & Gibson, J. E. Human & Energy Factors: Factors in Urban Planning; A Systems Approach. 1982. 50.00 (ISBN 90-247-2688-3, Pub. by Martinus Nijhoff Netherlands). Kluwer Boston.
Mitchell, Henry. The Essential Earthman. 1983. pap. 6.25 (ISBN 0-374-51765-7). FS&G.
ReVelle, Charles & ReVelle, Penny. The Environment: Issues & Choices. 762p. 1981. text ed. write for info (ISBN 0-87150-758-7). Grant Pr.
Ritterbush, Philip C. The Built Environment: Ideas in Engineering for Human Adaptive Potential. (Illus.). 150p. (Orig.). 1983. pap. 27.00x (ISBN 0-942776-04-6). Inst Cult Prog.
Turnbull, Colin M. The Human Cycle. 320p. (Orig.). 1983. 14.95 (ISBN 0-671-22620-7). S&S.
Unispace International Round Table, New York, 8-10 March 1982. Alternative Space Futures & the Human Condition: Proceedings. Karnik, K., ed. 180p. 1982. 20.00 (ISBN 0-08-029969-5). Pergamon.
Wadden, Richard A. Energy Utilization & Environmental Health: Methods for Prediction & Evaluation of Impact on Human Health. LC 78-9688. 216p. Repr. of 1978 ed. text ed. 29.50 (ISBN 0-686-84496-3). Krieger.
Wicker, Allan W. An Introduction to Ecological Psychology. 300p. 1983. pap. text ed. 12.95x (ISBN 0-8290-1291-5). Irvington.
Woodward, Herbert N. Human Survival in a Crowded World. LC 82-23921. 158p. 1983. pap. 9.95x (ISBN 0-89950-068-4). McFarland & Co.

HUMAN EMBRYOLOGY
see Embryology, Human

HUMAN ENGINEERING
see also Human Information Processing; Man-Machine Systems
Bailey, Robert W. Human Error in Computer Systems. (Illus.). 160p. 1983. pap. 15.95 (ISBN 0-13-445056-6). P-H.
Berchem-Simon, Odette, ed. Ergonomics Glossary: Terms Commonly Used in Ergonomics. 264p. (Eng., Fr. & Ger.). 1982. 47.50x (ISBN 90-313-0500-6). Intl Pubns Serv.
Bull, Alan T. & Holt, Geoffrey. Biotechnology: International Trends & Perspectives. 86p. 1982. 5.50 (ISBN 92-64-12362-8). OECD.
Hollaender, Alexander & Laskin, Allen I., eds. Basic Biology of New Developments in Biotechnology. (Basic Life Sciences Ser.: Vol. 25). 579p. 1983. 69.50x (ISBN 0-306-41244-6, Plenum Pr). Plenum Pub.
IFAC. Modelling & Control of Biotechnical Processes: Proceedings of the First IFAC Workshop, Helsinki, 17-19 August 1982. Halme, A., ed. (IFAC Proceedings Ser.). 350p. 1983. 85.00 (ISBN 0-08-029978-4). Pergamon.
Kvalseth. Ergonomics in Action. 1983. text ed. write for info. (ISBN 0-86103-061-3). Butterworth.
Organisation for Economic Co-Operation & Development. Biotechnology-International Trends & Perspectives. 84p. (Orig.). 1982. pap. 11.00x (ISBN 92-64-12362-8). OECD.
Siemens Teams of Authors. Video Workstation Ergonomics. (Siemens Teams of Authors Ser.). 1981. text ed. 14.95x (ISBN 0-471-26126-2, Pub. by Wiley Heyden). Wiley.

HUMAN ENVIRONMENT
see Human Ecology

HUMAN EVOLUTION
see also Fossil Man; Sociobiology
Boyce, A. J. Chromosome Variation in Human Evolution: Symposia of the Institute of Biology Ser, Vol. 14. 131p. 1975. 29.95 (ISBN 0-470-09330-7). Wiley.
Eldredge, Niles & Tattersall, Ian. The Myths of Human Evolution. LC 82-1118. 192p. 1982. 16.95 (ISBN 0-231-05144-1). Columbia U Pr.
Morris Wu, Eleanor B. Human Efflorescence: A Study in Man's Evolutionary & Historical Development. 352p. 1983. write for info. (ISBN 0-87527-323-8). Green.
Swanson, Carl P. Ever-Expanding Horizons: The Dual Informational Sources of Human Evolution. LC 82-21750. (Illus.). 132p. 1983. lib. bdg. 13.50x (ISBN 0-87023-391-2); pap. 7.50 (ISBN 0-87023-392-0). U of Mass Pr.
Wilber, Ken. Up from Eden: A Transpersonal View of Human Evolution. LC 82-42678. (Illus.). 384p. 1983. pap. 8.95 (ISBN 0-394-71424-5). Shambhala Pubns.

HUMAN EXPERIMENTATION IN MEDICINE
Jones, James H. Bad Blood: The Tuskegee Syphilis Experiment. 1982. 7.95 (ISBN 0-686-81884-9). Free Pr.

HUMAN FERTILIZATION IN VITRO
see Fertilization in Vitro, Human

HUMAN GENETICS
see also Genetic Counseling; Genetic Psychology; Genetics; Human Chromosomes
Bonne-Tamir, Batsheva & Cohen, Tirza, eds. Human Genetics, Part A: The Unfolding Genome. LC 82-17230. (Progress in Clinical & Biological Research Ser.: Vol. 103A). 531p. 1982. 88.00 (ISBN 0-8451-0168-4). A R Liss.
--Human Genetics, Part B: Medical Aspects. LC 82-17230. (Progress in Clinical & Biological Research Ser.: Vol. 103B). 619p. 1982. 98.00 (ISBN 0-8451-0169-2). A R Liss.
Schull, W. J. & Chakraborty, R., eds. Human Genetics: A Selection of Insights. LC 78-13701. (Benchmark Papers in Genetics: Vol. 10). 359p. 1979. 43.50 (ISBN 0-87933-321-9). Hutchinson Ross.
Winchester, A. M. & Mertens, Thomas R. Human Genetics. 1982. text ed. 16.95 (ISBN 0-675-20008-3). Merrill.

HUMAN GENETICS-SOCIAL ASPECTS
Nagle, James J. Heredity & Human Affairs. 3rd ed. (Illus.). 448p. 1983. text ed. 18.95 (ISBN 0-8016-3626-4). Mosby.

HUMAN GEOGRAPHY
see Anthropo-Geography

HUMAN IN VITRO FERTILIZATION
see Fertilization in Vitro, Human

HUMAN INFORMATION PROCESSING
Berg, Lee. Acusto-Optic Signal Processing. (Optical Engineering Ser.). 472p. 1983. 65.00 (ISBN 0-8247-1667-1). Dekker.

HUMAN INTERACTION
see Social Interaction

HUMAN LOCOMOTION
see also Running; Swimming; Walking
Denny-Brown. The Cerebral Control of Movement. 222p. 1982. 50.00x (ISBN 0-85323-001-3, Pub. by Liverpool Univ England). State Mutual Bk.
Northrip, John W., et al. Analysis of Sport Motion: Anatomic & Biomechanic Perspectives. 3rd ed. 365p. 1983. pap. text ed. write for info. (ISBN 0-697-07206-1). Wm C Brown.

HUMAN MECHANICS
see also Human Locomotion; Kinesiology
Barrow, Harold M. Man & Movement: Principles of Physical Education. 3rd ed. LC 82-20398. 410p. 1983. text ed. write for info. (ISBN 0-8121-0861-2). Lea & Febiger.
Stockholm, Alan J. A Biomechanics Manual for Coaches & Physical Educators. (Illus.). 125p. 1983. pap. 7.50 (ISBN 0-935496-03-3). AC Pubns.

HUMAN OPERATORS (SYSTEMS ENGINEERING)
see Man-Machine Systems

HUMAN PALEONTOLOGY
see Fossil Man

HUMAN PARASITOLOGY
see Medical Parasitology

HUMAN RELATIONS
see Interpersonal Relations

HUMAN RESOURCE DEVELOPMENT
see Manpower Policy

HUMAN RIGHTS
see Civil Rights; Civil Rights (International Law)

HUMAN SCIENCE
see Anthroposophy

HUMAN SUBSYSTEMS (SYSTEMS ENGINEERING)
see Man-Machine Systems

HUMANE SOCIETIES
see Animals, Treatment Of; Child Welfare

HUMANE TREATMENT OF ANIMALS
see Animals, Treatment of

HUMANISM
see also Culture; Hellenism; Humanistic Ethics; Humanities; Philosophical Anthropology; Renaissance
Bernstein, Eckhard. German Humanism. (World Authors Ser.). 176p. 1983. lib. bdg. 18.95 (ISBN 0-8057-6537-9, Twayne). G K Hall.
Einstein, Albert. Essays in Humanism. 130p. 1983. pap. 4.95 (ISBN 0-8022-2417-2). Philos Lib.
Grassi, Ernesto. Heidegger & the Question of Renaissance Humanism: Four Studies, Vol. 24. Krois, John M., tr. 110p. 1983. 11.00 (ISBN 0-86698-062-8). Medieval & Renaissance NY.
Hitchcock, James. What Is Secular Humanism? Why Humanism Became Secular & How It Is Changing Our World. (Illus.). 180p. 1982. pap. 6.95 (ISBN 0-89283-163-4). Servant.
Johnson, Earl S. The Humanistic Teaching of Earl S. Johnson. Haas, John, ed. (The Academy of Independent Scholars Retrospections Ser.). 210p. 1983. lib. bdg. 20.00X (ISBN 0-86531-542-6). Westview.
Plummer, Ken. Documents of Life: An Introduction to the Problems & Literature of a Humanistic Method. (Contemporary Social Research Ser.: No. 7). 208p. 1983. text ed. 28.50x (ISBN 0-04-321029-5); pap. text ed. 12.50x. Allen Unwin.
Pollard, T. E. Fullness of Humanity: Christ's Humanness & Ours. 128p. 1982. text ed. 19.95x (ISBN 0-907459-10-2, Pub. by Almond Pr England); pap. text ed. 9.95x (ISBN 0-907459-11-0, Pub. by Almond Pr England). Eisenbrauns.
Rubenstein, Richard L., ed. Modernization: The Humanist Response to Its Promise & Problems. LC 82-83241. 400p. 1982. 24.95 (ISBN 0-89226-015-7). ICF Pr.
Westerlund, Stuart R. Humane Education & Realms of Humaneness: Readings. LC 82-15936. (Illus.). 286p. 1983. lib. bdg. 23.00 (ISBN 0-8191-2724-8); pap. text ed. 11.50 (ISBN 0-8191-2725-6). U Pr of Amer.

HUMANISM-20TH CENTURY
Geisler, Norman L. Is Man the Measure? An Evaluation of Contemporary. 160p. (Orig.). 1982. pap. 6.95 (ISBN 0-8010-3787-5). Baker Bk.

HUMANIST ETHICS
see Humanistic Ethics

HUMANISTIC EDUCATION
see Education, Humanistic

HUMANISTIC ETHICS
Harron, Frank & Burnside, John. Health & Human Values: A Guide to Making Your Own Decisions. 24.95 (ISBN 0-686-42812-9); pap. 6.95 (ISBN 0-686-42813-7, Y-448). Yale U Pr.
Harron, Frank, et al. Health & Human Values: Making Your Own Decisions. 185p. 1983. 24.95 (ISBN 0-686-83922-6); pap. 6.95 (ISBN 0-686-83923-4). Yale U Pr.
Hume, David. An Enquiry Concerning the Principles of Morals. Schneewind, J. B., ed. LC 82-11679. (HPC Philosophical Classics Ser.). 132p. lib. bdg. 13.50 (ISBN 0-915145-46-4); pap. text ed. 2.95 (ISBN 0-915145-45-6). Hackett Pub.
Rist, John M. Human Value: A Study in Ancient Philosophical Ethics. (Philosophia Antiqua Ser.: Vol. 40). v, 175p. 1982. pap. write for info. (ISBN 90-04-06757-4). E J Brill.

HUMANISTIC PSYCHOLOGY
Davis, Bruce & Davis, Genny W. The Magical Child Within You. LC 82-84601. (Illus.). 112p. 1983. pap. 5.95 (ISBN 0-911717-00-5). Inner Light Pub.
Maul, Gail & Maul, Terry. Beyond Limit: Ways to Growth & Freedom. 1982. pap. text ed. 9.95x (ISBN 0-673-15422-X). Scott F.

HUMANITARIANISM (RELIGION)
see Humanism-20th Century; Jesus Christ-Divinity; Positivism; Trinity; Unitarianism

HUMANITIES
see also Education, Humanistic; Science and the Humanities
Martin, F. David & Jacobus, Lee A. The Humanities Through the Arts. 3rd ed. (Illus.). 520p. 1983. pap. text ed. 19.95 (ISBN 0-07-040639-1, C). McGraw.
Post, Gaines, Jr. The Humanities: What is Their Place in American Education & Culture? (Vital Issues Ser.: Vol. XXXI, No. 9). 0.80 (ISBN 0-686-84149-2). Ctr Info Am.

HUMANITIES-STUDY AND TEACHING
Coast Community Colleges. Study Guide for the Televised Course Humanities Through the Arts. (Illus.). 288p. 1983. 12.95x (ISBN 0-07-011474-9, C). McGraw.
Conley, Diane, ed. Peterson's Guides to Graduate Study: Humanities & Social Sciences, 1983. 1200p. 1982. pap. 18.95 (ISBN 0-87866-186-7). Petersons Guides.
Ronning, Ronald H. & Reedy, Jeremiah, eds. Articulating the Ineffable: Approaches to the Teaching of Humanities. LC 81-43697. 130p. 1983. pap. text ed. 8.25 (ISBN 0-8191-2702-7). U Pr of Amer.

HUMANITIES AND SCIENCE
see Science and the Humanities

HUME, DAVID, 1711-1776
Berry, Christopher J. Hume, Hegel & Human Nature. 1983. lib. bdg. 41.50 (ISBN 90-247-2682-4, Pub. by Martinus Nijhoff Netherlands). Kluwer Boston.
Wright, John P. The Sceptical Realism of David Hume. ix, 256p. 1983. 29.50x (ISBN 0-8166-1223-4); pap. 13.95x (ISBN 0-8166-1224-2). U of Minn Pr.

HUMMING-BIRDS
Mobbs, A. J. Hummingbirds. 176p. 1982. 80.00x (ISBN 0-86230-049-5, Pub. by Saiga Pub). State Mutual Bk.

HUMOR
see Wit and Humor

HUMORISTS
see also Satirists
Armour, Richard. Drug Store Days: My Youth Among the Pills & Potions. rev. ed. LC 82-23762. (Illus.). 192p. 1983. pap. 5.95 (ISBN 0-88007-125-7). Woodbridge Pr.
Fowler, Douglas. S. J. Perelman. (United States Authors Ser.). 192p. 1983. lib. bdg. 12.95 (ISBN 0-8057-7376-2, Twayne). G K Hall.

HUMOROUS ILLUSTRATIONS
see Caricatures and Cartoons; Wit and Humor, Pictorial

HUMUS
Christman, Russell F. & Gjessing, Egil, eds. Aquatic & Terrestrial Humic Materials. LC 82-71526. (Illus.). 525p. 1982. 39.95 (ISBN 0-250-40550-4). Ann Arbor Science.
Darwin, Charles R. The Formation of Vegetable Mould, Through the Action of Worms, with Observations on Their Habits. LC 72-3903. (Illus.). vii, 326p. 1972. write for info. (ISBN 0-404-08416-8). AMS Pr.

HUNGARIAN LANGUAGE
Berlitz Editors. Hungarian for Travellers. 1981. 4.95 (ISBN 0-02-964270-1, Berlitz). Macmillan.
Victor-Rood, Juliette. Say It in Hungarian. (Say It In Ser.). (Illus.). 224p. (Orig.). 1983. pap. 2.95 (ISBN 0-486-24423-7). Dover.

HUNGARIAN LANGUAGE-DICTIONARIES
Hungarian Pocket Dictionary: English-Hungarian, Vol. I. 13th ed. 606p. 1982. pap. 7.50x (ISBN 963-05-0546-0). Humanities.
Orszagh, Laszlo, ed. English-Hungarian Dictionary. 13th ed. 608p. 1982. 6.25x (ISBN 963-05-2975-0). Intl Pubns Serv.

HUNGARIAN LITERATURE (COLLECTIONS)
Kolumban, Nicholas, ed. Turmoil in Hungary: An Anthology of Twentieth Century Hungarian Poetry. LC 82-81365. (Illus.). 186p. 1982. pap. 6.00 (ISBN 0-89823-039-X). New Rivers Pr.

HUNGARIAN LITERATURE-BIO-BIBLIOGRAPHY
Csapodi, Csaba. Bibliotheca Corviniana: The Library of King Matthias Corvinus of Hungary. 2nd, Rev. ed. Horn, Z., tr. LC 82-187248. (Illus.). 334p. (Hungarian.). 1981. 50.00x (ISBN 963-207-617-6). Intl Pubns Serv.

HUNGARIANS IN FOREIGN COUNTRIES
Janics, Kalman. Czechoslovak Policy & the Hungarian Minority: 1945-1948. Borsody, Stephen, tr. from Hungarian. & intro. by. LC 80-67487. (Brooklyn College Studies on Society in Change). 288p. 1982. 25.00x (ISBN 0-914710-99-0). East Eur Quarterly.
--Czechoslovak Policy & the Hungarian Minority, 1945-1948. 288p. 1982. 25.00 (ISBN 0-686-82241-2). Columbia U Pr.

HUNGARY-ANTIQUITIES
Gero, Gyozo. Turkish Monuments in Hungary. Horn, Zsuzsanna, tr. (Illus.). 92p. (Orig., Hungarian.). 1976. pap. 5.00x (ISBN 963-13-4704-4). Intl Pubns Serv.

HUNGARY-DESCRIPTION AND TRAVEL
Detshy, Mihaly. Sarosptak (Hungary) Boros, Laszlo, tr. from Hungarian. (Illus.). 118p. 1979. pap. 5.00x (ISBN 963-13-0389-6). Intl Pubns Serv.

HUNGARY-ECONOMIC CONDITIONS
Roman, Zoltan. Productivity & Economic Growth. Lukacs, Laszlo, tr. from Hungarian. LC 82-173070. (Illus.). 276p. 1982. 30.00x (ISBN 963-05-2786-3). Intl Pubns Serv.

HUNGARY-FOREIGN RELATIONS
Lukacs, Lajos. The Vatican & Hungary 1846-1878: Reports & Correspondence on Hungary of the Apostolic Nuncios in Vienna. Kormos, Zsofia, tr. 795p. 1981. text ed. 55.00x (ISBN 963-05-2446-5, 41422, Pub. by Kultura Pr Hungary). Humanities.

HUNGARY-HISTORY
Detshy, Mihaly. Sarosptak (Hungary) Boros, Laszlo, tr. from Hungarian. (Illus.). 118p. 1979. pap. 5.00x (ISBN 963-13-0389-6). Intl Pubns Serv.
Evans, S. The Slow Rapprochement: Britain & Turkey in the Age of Kemal Ataturk, 1919-38. 123p. 1982. pap. text ed. 8.00x (ISBN 0-906719-04-6, Pub. by Eothen Pr England). Humanities.
Gero, Gyozo. Turkish Monuments in Hungary. Horn, Zsuzsanna, tr. (Illus.). 92p. (Orig., Hungarian.). 1976. pap. 5.00x (ISBN 963-13-4704-4). Intl Pubns Serv.
Katzburg, Nathaniel. Hungary & the Jews: Policy & Legislation 1920-1943. 299p. 1981. 18.00 (ISBN 965-226-020-7). Hermon.
Lorinczy, Gyorgy. Sopron. (Illus.). 116p. 1971. 7.50x (ISBN 0-686-43339-4). Intl Pubns Serv.

HUNGARY-POLITICS AND GOVERNMENT
Kemeny, Gabor. Hungarista: Ways of Hungarian Foreign Politics. 40p. pap. 3.50 (ISBN 0-935484-07-8). Universe Pub Co.

HUNGARY-SOCIAL CONDITIONS
Domotor, Tekla. Hungarian Folk Beliefs. LC 82-48163. (Illus.). 324p. 1983. 17.50x (ISBN 0-253-32876-4). Ind U Pr.

HUNGER
see also Appetite
Byron, William, ed. The Causes of World Hunger. LC 82-60591. 1983. pap. 8.95 (ISBN 0-8091-2483-1). Paulist Pr.

HUNTING
see also Camping; Decoys (Hunting); Fowling; Game and Game-Birds; Dogs

also headings beginning with names of animals and birds hunted, e.g. Deer Hunting, Duck Shooting, Fox Hunting, Moose Hunting

Harbour, Dave. Advanced Wild Turkey Hunting & World Records. (Illus.). 264p. 1983. 19.95 (ISBN 0-8329-0286-1, Pub. by Winchester Pr.). New Century.

Shelsby, Earl & Gilford, James, eds. Basic Hunter's Guide. rev. ed. (Illus.). 280p. (Orig.). 1982. pap. text ed. 14.95 (ISBN 0-935998-46-2). Natl Rifle Assn.

HUNTING–HISTORY

Speth, John D. Bison Kills & Bone Counts: Decision Making by Ancient Hunters. LC 82-21976. (Prehistoric Archaeology & Ecology Ser.). (Illus.). 272p. 1983. pap. 9.00 (ISBN 0-226-76949-6). U of Chicago Pr.

HUNTING–AFRICA

Capstick, Peter H. Death in the Dark Continent. (Illus.). 1983. 14.95 (ISBN 0-312-18615-0). St Martin.

HUNTING–UNITED STATES

Roosevelt, Theodore. Ranch Life & the Hunting Trail. LC 82-20091. (Illus.). 196p. 1983. 19.95x (ISBN 0-8032-3865-7, BB 833); pap. 8.95 (ISBN 0-8032-8913-8, Bison). U of Nebr Pr.

HUNTING DOGS

see also Retrievers

also particular breeds of hunting dogs

Grissom, Ken. Buckskind & Black Powder. (Illus.). 224p. 1983. 14.95 (ISBN 0-8329-0285-3, Pub. by Winchester Pr.). New Century.

HURRICANE (FIGHTER PLANES)

Stewart, Adrian. Hurricane: The War Exploits of the Fighter Air-Craft. 1982. 60.00x (ISBN 0-686-82343-5, Pub. by W Kimber). State Mutual Bk.

HURRICANES

Here are entered mainly works on storms in the neighborhood of the West Indies.

see also Disaster Relief; Storms

McNulty, Faith. Hurricane. LC 79-2672. (Illus.). 64p. (gr. 3-5). 1983. 8.61i (ISBN 0-06-024142-X, HarpJ); PLB 8.89g (ISBN 0-06-024143-8). Har-Row.

HUSAIN, ZAKIR

Siddiqui, M. I. Martyrdom of Husain. 3.95 (ISBN 0-686-83883-1). Kazi Pubns.

HUSBAND AND WIFE

see also Divorce; Support (Domestic Relations)

Beer. Househusbands. LC 82-12079. 176p. 1983. 23.95 (ISBN 0-03-059978-4). Praeger.

HUSBANDRY

see Agriculture

HUSSERL, EDMUND, 1859-1938

Miller, J. Philip. Numbers in Presence & Absence: A Study of Husserl's Philosophy of Mathematics. 1982. lib. bdg. 29.50 (ISBN 0-686-37593-9, Pub. by Martinus Nijhoff). Kluwer Boston.

HUTTERITE BRETHREN

Hostetler, John A. Hutterite Life. 2nd ed. LC 82-83962. (Illus., Orig.). 1983. pap. 4.95 (ISBN 0-8361-3329-3). Herald Pr.

HUXLEY, ALDOUS LEONARD, 1894-1963

Wood, Douglas K. Men Against Time: Nicolas Berdyaev, T. S. Eliot, Aldous Huxley, & C. G. Jung. LC 82-526. x, 254p. 1982. text ed. 22.50x (ISBN 0-7006-0222-4). Univ Pr KS.

HUZVARESH

see Pahlavi Language

HYBRID VIGOR

see Heterosis

HYBRIDITY OF RACES

see Miscegenation

HYBRIDIZATION

see also Genetics; Heterosis

Levin, Donald A., ed. Hybridization: An Evolutionary Perspective. LC 78-10947. (Benchmark Papers in Genetics: Vol. 11). 321p. 1979. 36.50 (ISBN 0-87933-341-3). Hutchinson Ross.

HYDATID DISEASE

see Echinococcosis

HYDE, EDWARD, 1ST EARL OF CLARENDON, 1609-1674

Miller, George E. Edward Hyde, Earl of Clarendon. (English Authors Ser.: No. 337). 192p. 1983. lib. bdg. 18.95 (ISBN 0-8057-6823-8, Twayne). G K Hall.

HYDRAULIC CEMENT

see Cement

HYDRAULIC ENGINEERING

see also Boring; Channels (Hydraulic Engineering); Drainage; Flood Control; Hydraulic Machinery; Hydraulics; Hydrodynamics; Irrigation; Offshore Structures; Pumping Machinery; Reclamation of Land; Rivers; Shore Protection; Stream Measurements; Water-Supply Engineering; Wells

Australasian Conference on Hydraulics & Fluid Mechanic, 1977: Sixth Conference. 627p. (Orig.). 1977. pap. text ed. 67.50x (ISBN 0-85825-088-8, Pub. by Inst Engineering Australia). Renouf.

Australasian Conference on Hydraulics & Fluid Mechanics, 1980: Seventh Conference. 575p. (Orig.). 1980. pap. text ed. 67.50x (ISBN 0-85825-136-1, Pub. by Inst Engineering Australia). Renouf.

Bartlett, R. E. & Madill, W. Hydraulics for Public Health Engineers. (Illus.). 198p. 1982. 33.00 (ISBN 0-85334-148-6, Pub. by Applied Sci England). Elsevier.

Coastal Discharges: Engineering Aspects & Experience. 224p. 1981. 99.00x (ISBN 0-7277-0124-X, Pub. by Telford England). State Mutual Bk.

Severn Barrage. 164p. 1982. 99.00x (ISBN 0-7277-0156-8, Pub. by Telford England). State Mutual Bk.

Smith, P. E., ed. Applying Research to Hydraulic Engineering. LC 82-72777. 752p. 1982. pap. text ed. 53.00 (ISBN 0-87262-316-5). Am Soc Civil Eng.

HYDRAULIC ENGINEERING–PROBLEMS, EXERCISES, ETC.

Anders, James E., Sr. Industrial Hydraulics Troubleshooting. (Illus.). 192p. 1983. 28.00 (ISBN 0-07-001592-9, P&RB). McGraw.

HYDRAULIC MACHINERY

see also Pumping Machinery

Lambeck. Hydraulic Pumps & Motors. (Mechanical Engineering Ser.). 240p. 1983. price not set. Dekker.

HYDRAULICS

see also Channels (Hydraulic Engineering); Fire Extinction; Fluids; Hydraulic Engineering

American Society of Civil Engineers, ed. Classic Papers in Hydraulics. 672p. 1982. pap. text ed. 49.00 (ISBN 0-87262-310-6). Am Soc Civil Eng.

Brebbia. Computational Hydraulics. 1982. text ed. 39.95. Butterworth.

Smith. Basic Hydraulics. 1982. text ed. 19.95 (ISBN 0-408-01112-2). Butterworth.

Waddington, D. & Herlevich, F. Ann. Evaluation of Pumps & Motors for PV Water Pumping Systems. (Progress in Solar Energy Supplements SERI Ser.). 150p. 1983. pap. text ed. 13.50x (ISBN 0-89553-081-3). Am Solar Energy.

HYDROBIOLOGY

see Fresh-Water Biology; Marine Biology

HYDROCARBONS

see also Alkylation

Cooke, Marcus & Dennis, Anthony J., eds. Polynuclear Aromatic Hydrocarbons: Physical & Biological Chemistry. (International Symposium on Polynuclear Aromatic Hydrocarbons, Sixth). 1982. 65.00 (ISBN 0-935470-13-1). Battelle.

International Workshop, World Hydrocarbon Markets. World Hydrocarbon Markets-Current Status, Projected Prospects & Future Trends: Proceedings of the International Workshop, Mexico City, April 1982. Wionczek, M. S., ed. (Illus.). 225p. 1982. 40.00 (ISBN 0-08-029962-8). Pergamon.

Matar, Sami. Synfuels: Hydrocarbons of the Future. 293p. 1982. 39.95x (ISBN 0-87814-189-8). Pennwell Pub.

HYDRODYNAMICS

see also Cavitation; Channels (Hydraulic Engineering); Hydraulics; Magnetohydrodynamics; Turbulence; Waves

AIP Conference, 88th, La Jolla Institute, 1981. Mathematical Methods in Hydrodynamics & Integrability in Dynamical Systems: Proceedings. Tabor, Michael & Treves, Yvain M., eds. LC 82-72462. 352p. 1982. lib. bdg. 34.00 (ISBN 0-88318-187-8). Am Inst Physics.

HYDROFOIL BOATS

McLeavy, Roy, ed. Jane's Surface Skimmers, 1982. (Jane's Yearbooks). (Illus.). 400p. 1982. 99.50 (ISBN 0-86720-614-4). Sci Bks Intl.

HYDROFOILS (VESSELS)

see Hydrofoil Boats

HYDROGEN

Van Kranendonk, Jan. Solid Hydrogen: Theory of the Properties of Solid H2, HD, & D2. 300p. 1982. 39.50x (ISBN 0-306-41080-X, Plenum Pr). Plenum Pub.

World Hydrogen Energy Conference, Fourth. Hydrogen Energy Process IV: Proceedings of the World Hydrogen Energy Conference, Fourth, Pasadena, CA 13-17 June, 1982. Veziroglu, T. N. & Van Vorst, W. D., eds. Kelley, J. H. (Advances in Hydrogen Energy Ser.: No. 3). 2000p. 1982. 350.00 (ISBN 0-08-028699-2). Pergamon.

HYDROGEN NUCLEUS

see Protons

HYDROGENATION

Harriman, A. & West, M. A., eds. Photogeneration of Hydrogen. Date not set. price not set (ISBN 0-12-326380-8). Acad Pr.

HYDROGEOLOGY

Back, William, ed. Chemical Hydrogeology. Freeze, Allan. LC 81-11853. (Benchmark Papers in Geology Ser.: Vol. 73). 423p. 1983. 49.00 (ISBN 0-87933-440-1). Hutchinson Ross.

Bogomolov, Yu. G. & Zhabin, V. F., eds. Effect of Reclamation on Hydrogeological Conditions. Erastov, Konstantin, tr. from Rus. 300p. 1983. 97.00 (ISBN 0-677-06070-X). Gordon.

Freeze, R. A. & Back, W., eds. Physical Hydrogeology. LC 82-2976. (Benchmark Papers in Geology: Vol. 72). 448p. 1983. 48.00 (ISBN 0-87933-431-2). Hutchinson Ross.

Narasimhan, T. N. & Freeze, R. Allan, eds. Recent Trends in Hydrogeology. (Special Papers: No. 189). 1982. 32.00x (ISBN 0-8137-2189-X). Geol Soc.

Rona, P. A. & Lowell, R. P. Seafloor Spreading Centers: Hydrothermal Systems. LC 79-18265. (Bench Papers in Geology: Vol. 56). 424p. 1980. 51.50 (ISBN 0-87933-363-4). Hutchinson Ross.

HYDROLOGY

see also Hydrogeology; Oceanography; Radioisotopes in Hydrology; Water

also headings beginning with the word Water

El-Shaarawi, A. H., ed. Time Series Methods in Hydrosciences: Proceedings of the International Conference, Burlington, Ontario, Canada, October 6-8, 1981. (Developments in Water Science Ser.: No. 17). 614p. 1982. 85.00 (ISBN 0-444-42102-5). Elsevier.

Fritz, Jack. Small & Mini Hydropower Systems: Resource Assessment & Project Feasibility. Allen-Browne, Patricia, ed. (Illus.). 448p. 1983. 31.95 (ISBN 0-07-022470-6, P&RB). McGraw.

Hydrology & Water Resources, 1982. 215p. (Orig.). 1982. pap. text ed. 37.50x (ISBN 0-85825-165-5, Pub. by Inst Engineering Australia). Renouf.

Hydrology Symposium. 189p. (Orig.). 1978. pap. text ed. 36.00x (ISBN 0-85825-096-9, Pub. by Inst Engineering Australia). Renouf.

Methods of Hydrological Computations for Water Projects. (Studies & Reports in Hydrology: No. 38). 122p. 1982. pap. 17.00 (ISBN 92-3-102005-6, U1236, UNESCO). Unipub.

Research on Urban Hydrology, Vol. 3. (Technical Papers in Hydrology: No. 21). 144p. 1981. pap. 14.50 (ISBN 92-3-101984-8, U1230, UNESCO). Unipub.

HYDROMAGNETIC WAVES

see Magnetohydrodynamics

HYDROMECHANICS

see Fluid Mechanics

HYDROPATHY

see Hydrotherapy

HYDROPHYTES

see Algae; Fresh-Water Biology; Marine Flora

HYDROPLANES

McLeavy, Roy, ed. Jane's Surface Skimmers 1983. 16th ed. (Jane's Yearbooks). (Illus.). 1983. 99.50x (ISBN 0-86720-644-6). Sci Bks Intl.

HYDROPONICS

Rotter, Hans-August. Growing Plants Without Soil. (Illus.). 120p. 1983. 15.95 (ISBN 0-7158-0797-8, Pub. by EP Publishing England). Sterling.

Seifert, Anne & Hoyt, Fred. Hydroponic Home Gardening: Made Easy! (Illus.). 120p. (Orig.). 1983. pap. 4.50 (ISBN 0-943584-00-0). Varnes Pubs.

HYDROTHERAPY

see also Baths; Health Resorts, Watering-Places, etc.

Szekely, Edmond B. Healing Waters. (Illus.). 64p. 1976. pap. 3.50 (ISBN 0-89564-049-X). IBS Intl.

HYGIENE, DENTAL

see Teeth–Care and Hygiene

HYGIENE, PUBLIC

see Public Health

HYGIENE, RURAL

see Health, Rural

HYGIENE, SOCIAL

see Prostitution; Public Health; Venereal Diseases

HYGIENE, TROPICAL

see Tropical Medicine

HYMENOPTERA

see also Ants; Bees

Riegel, Garland T. The American Species of Dacnusinae Hymenoptera-Braconidae. (Novitates Arthropodae Ser.). (Illus.). 200p. (Orig.). 1982. pap. 12.00x (ISBN 0-916170-19-5). J-B Pubs.

HYMN PLAYING

see Hymns–Accompaniment

HYMNOLOGY

see Hymns

HYMNS

see also Carols; Church Music; Psalmody; Religious Poetry

Hymns from the Four Winds: A Collection of Asian American Hymns. 240p. (Orig.). 1983. pap. 6.95 (ISBN 0-687-18126-7). Abingdon.

Milosz, Czeslaw. Hymn O Perle: Hymn to the Pearl. 1982. 10.00 (ISBN 0-930042-45-X). Mich Slavic Pubns.

HYMNS–ACCOMPANIMENT

Schilling, S. Paul. The Faith We Sing. LC 82-21749. 240p. 1983. pap. write for info. (ISBN 0-664-24434-3). Westminster.

HYPERACTIVITY

see Hyperkinesia

HYPERBARIC OXYGENATION

Burakovsky, V. I. & Bockeria, L. A. Hyperbaric Oxygenation & Its Value in Cardiovascular Surgery. 343p. 1981. 11.50 (ISBN 0-8285-2282-0, Pub. by Mir Pubs USSR). Imported Pubns.

HYPERCINESIA

see Hyperkinesia

HYPERDULIA

see Mary, Virgin–Cultus

HYPERGLYCEMIA

Zack, Jinny. Sugar Isn't Always Sweet. Tanner, Don, ed. (Illus.). 204p. (Orig.). 1983. pap. 5.95 (ISBN 0-88005-002-0). Uplift Bks.

HYPERGLYCOSEMIA

see Hyperglycemia

HYPERKINESIA

Cragg, Shelia. A Whirldwind Named Tim. 2nd, Rev. ed. 192p. 1982. pap. text ed. 3.50 (ISBN 0-88449-099-8, A324572). Vision Hse.

Fontenelle, Don H. Understanding & Managing Overactive Children: A Guide for Parents & Teachers. 200p. 1983. 13.95 (ISBN 0-13-936765-9); pap. 6.95 (ISBN 0-13-936757-8). P-H.

Morley, John, ed. Bronchial Hyperactivity. 1982. 22.95 (ISBN 0-12-506450-0). Acad Pr.

HYPERTENSION

see also Renal Hypertension

An Abstract Compendium from the World Literature on the Use of Atenolol in the Management of Hypertension. (Illus.). 96p. 1982. write for info. (ISBN 0-88137-001-0). TransMedica.

Caplan, Robert D., et al. Social Support & Patient Adherence: Experimental Survey Findings. 284p. 1980. pap. 16.00x (ISBN 0-87944-260-3). Inst Soc Res.

Genest, Jacques & Kuchel, Otto. Hypertension: Physiopathology & Treatment. 2nd ed. (Illus.). 1376p. 1983. 89.00 (ISBN 0-07-023061-7). McGraw.

Goodfriend, Theodore, ed. Hypertension Essentials: Concepts, Causes, Consequences & Control. Date not set. price not set (ISBN 0-8089-1534-7). Grune.

Kahn, Ada P. High Blood Pressure. (Help Yourself to Health Ser.). 96p. (Orig.). 1983. pap. 3.95 (ISBN 0-8092-5599-5). Contemp Bks.

Kincaid-Smith, P. S. & Whitworth, J. A., eds. Hypertension: Mechanisms & Management. 200p. 1982. text ed. 15.00 (ISBN 0-86792-005-X, Pub by Adis Pr Australia). Wright-PSG.

Kotchen, Theodore A. & Kotchen, Jane M. High Blood Pressure in the Young. 1983. text ed. 34.50 (ISBN 0-7236-7032-3). Wright-PSG.

Magnani, Bruno & Hansson, Lennart, eds. Potassium, the Heart & Hypertension: A Symposium Sponsored by the Italian Society of Cardiology. LC 82-51013. (Illus.). 200p. 1982. write for info. (ISBN 0-88137-000-2). TransMedica.

Perry & Smith. Mild Hypertension: To Lease of Not to Treat, Vol. 304. 1978. 57.00 (ISBN 0-89072-059-2). NY Acad Sci.

Sleight, Peter & Freis, Edward. Hypertension: Cardiology, Vol. I. (BIMR Ser.). 320p. 1982. text ed. 39.95 (ISBN 0-686-37992-6). Butterworth.

Velasco, Manuel. Arterial Hypertension. (International Congress Ser.: No. 410). 1978. 33.50 (ISBN 0-444-15260-1). Elsevier.

Wollam, Gary L. & Hall, W. Dallas, eds. Hypertension Management. 350p. 1983. text ed. write for info. (ISBN 0-86792-009-2). Wright-PSG.

HYPERTHERMIA

see Heat–Physiological Effect

HYPHOMYCETES

see Moniliales

HYPNOSIS

see Hypnotism

HYPNOTISM

see also Mental Suggestion; Mind and Body; Personality, Disorders of; Psychoanalysis; Subconsciousness

Araoz, Daniel L. & Bleck, Robert T. Hypnosex: Sexual Joy Through Self-Hypnosis. 1983. 5.95 (ISBN 0-87795-466-6, Pub. by Priam). Arbor Hse.

Rossi, Sheila I. & Pam, Leslie. Hypnotic Experiences: A Medley of Inductions (includes 60-mintue audiotape) 400p. 1983. text ed. 29.50x (ISBN 0-8290-1314-8). Irvington.

HYPNOTISM–THERAPEUTIC USE

Boyne, Gil, ed. Hypnosis; New Tool in Nursing Practice. 197p. 1982. 20.00 (ISBN 0-930298-12-8). Westwood Pub Co.

Clarke, J. Christopher & Jackson, Arthur. Hypnosis & Behavior Therapy: The Treatment of Anxiety & Phobias. 1983. text ed. price not set (ISBN 0-8261-3450-5). Springer Pub.

Duke, Robert E. How to Lose Weight & Stop Smoking Through Self-Hypnosis (includes audio cassette) 140p. 1983. text ed. 18.95x (ISBN 0-8290-1276-1). Irvington.

Francuch, Peter D. & Jones, Arthur E. Intensive Spiritual Hypnotherapy. LC 82-62015. 450p. 1983. 25.00 (ISBN 0-939386-04-6). Spiritual Advisory.

Lankton, Stephen R. & Lankton, Carol H. The Answer Within: A Clinical Framework of Ericksonian Hypnotherapy. 400p. 1983. 35.00 (ISBN 0-87630-320-3). Brunner-Mazel.

HYPOACOUSTIC CHILDREN

see Children, Deaf

HYPOPHYSIS CEREBRI

see Pituitary Body

HYPOTHALAMUS

Sowers, J. R., ed. Hypothalmic Hormones. LC 79-19856. (Benchmark Papers in Human Physiology Ser.: Vol. 14). 368p. 1980. 46.00 (ISBN 0-87933-358-8). Hutchinson Ross.

HYPOTHECATION

see Mortgages

HYPOTHERMIA

Pozos, Robert S. & Wittmers, Lorentz E., Jr., eds. The Nature & Treatment of Hypothermia. LC 82-23909. (University of Minnesota Continuing Medical Education Ser.: Vol. 2). (Illus.). 288p. 1983. 35.00x (ISBN 0-8166-1154-8). U of Minn Pr.

HYPOXIA

see Anoxemia

HYSTERECTOMY

Dennerstein, Lorraine, et al. Hysterectomy: A Book to Help You Deal with the Physical & Emotional Aspects. (Illus.). 160p. 1982. 11.95x (ISBN 0-19-554371-8); pap. 6.95x (ISBN 0-19-554366-1). Oxford U Pr.

HYSTERIA
see also Witchcraft
Levi, Steven C. The Committee of Vigilance of Nineteen Sixteen: A Case Study in Official Hysteria. (Illus.). 128p. 1983. lib. bdg. 15.95x (ISBN 0-89950-058-7). McFarland & Co.
Weintraub, Michael I. Hysterical Conversion Reaction: A Guide to Diagnosis & Treatment. (Illus.). 185p. 1983. text ed. 25.00 (ISBN 0-89335-178-4). SP Med & Sci Bks.

I

I CHING
Anthony, Carol K. Guide to the I Ching. 2nd ed. 184p. 1982. pap. 5.95 (ISBN 0-9603832-3-9). Anthony Pub Co.
KeGan, Frank R. Intro to the Xray I, Links the Objective Patterns of Astrology & the Process Symbolism of the I Ching. (Illus.). 1982. pap. 5.00 (ISBN 0-933646-20-8). Aries Pr.
IATROGENIC DISEASES
Herman, P. G., ed. Iatrogenic Thoracic Complications. (Radiology of Iatrogenic Disorders Ser.). (Illus.). 243p. 1983. 54.90 (ISBN 0-387-90729-7). Springer-Verlag.
IBIZA–DESCRIPTION AND TRAVEL
Ibiza Travel Guide. (Berlitz Travel Guides). (Illus.). 1982. pap. 4.95 (ISBN 0-02-969240-7, Berlitz). Macmillan.
IBO LANGUAGE
Penfield, Joyce. Communicating with Quotes: The Igbo Case. LC 82-15626. (Contributions in Intercultural & Comparative Studies Ser.: No. 8). (Illus.). 152p. 1983. lib. bdg. 29.95 (ISBN 0-313-23767-0, PEN/). Greenwood.
IBSEN, HENRIK, 1828-1906
Chamberlain, John. Ibsen: The Open Vision. 208p. 1982. text ed. 31.50x (ISBN 0-485-11227-2, Athlone Pr). Humanities.
Muir. Last Periods of Shakespeare, Racine, & Ibsen. 128p. 1982. 40.00x (ISBN 0-85323-012-9, Pub. by Liverpool Univ England). State Mutual Bk.
ICE–MANUFACTURE
see Refrigeration and Refrigerating Machinery
ICE AGE
see Glacial Epoch
ICE CREAM, ICES, ETC.
see also Confectionery; Desserts
Arum, Nancy. Ice Cream & Ices. LC 82-48653. (Great American Cooking School Ser.). (Illus.). 80p. 1983. 8.61i (ISBN 0-06-015148-X, HarpT). Har-Row.
Quinn, Thomas R. Old-Fashioned Homemade Ice Cream: With 58 Original Recipes. (Illus.). 48p. (Orig.). 1983. pap. 2.95 (ISBN 0-486-24495-4). Dover.
Robbins, Carol T. & Wolff, Herbert. The Very Best: Ice Cream & Where to Find It. LC 82-91069. (Illus.). 252p. (Orig.). 1982. pap. 8.95 (ISBN 0-911729-00-3). Very Best.
ICE HOCKEY
see Hockey
ICE SKATING
see Skating
ICEBERGS
Schultz, Gwen. Icebergs & Their Voyages. LC 75-9958. 95p. 1975. 6.00 (ISBN 0-688-32047-3). Reading Gems.
ICELAND–DESCRIPTION AND TRAVEL
Burton, Richard. Ultima Thule. LC 82-73425. 788p. Repr. of 1875 ed. lib. bdg. 65.00 (ISBN 0-88116-001-6). Brenner Bks.
ICELAND–HISTORY
Burton, Richard. Ultima Thule. LC 82-73425. 788p. Repr. of 1875 ed. lib. bdg. 65.00 (ISBN 0-88116-001-6). Brenner Bks.
ICES
see Ice Cream, Ices, etc.
ICHTHYOLOGY
see Fishes
ICONOGRAPHY
see Art; Christian Art and Symbolism; Idols and Images; Portraits
ICONS
Dancu, Juliana & Dancu, Dumitru. Romanian Icons on Glass. (Illus.). 179p. 1983. 13.50x (ISBN 0-8143-1711-1). Wayne St U Pr.
Weitzmann, Kurt & Alibegasvili, Gaiane. Icons. 422p. 1982. 175.00x (ISBN 0-237-45645-1, Pub. by Evans Bros). State Mutual Bk.
ICOSAHEDRA
Coxeter, H. S., et al. The Fifty-Nine Icosahedra. (Illus.). 30p. 1982. pap. 12.00 (ISBN 0-387-90770-X). Springer-Verlag.
IDAHO–DESCRIPTION AND TRAVEL
Delucia, Alan A. Compact Atlas of Idaho. (Illus.). 110p. (Orig.). Date not set. pap. 20.95x (ISBN 0-940982-02-1). Ctr Bus Devel & Res.
Derig, Betty & Sharp, Flo. The Idaho Rambler: For Gadabouts & Stay-at-Homes. rev. ed. LC 82-80104. 266p. (Orig.). 1982. pap. 7.95 (ISBN 0-686-38094-0). Rambler Pr.
Fuller, Margaret. Trails of Western Idaho. LC 82-5621. (Illus.). 280p. pap. 10.25 (ISBN 0-913140-44-9). Signpost Bk Pub.
Maughan, Jackie. Hiker's Guide to Idaho. (Illus.). 256p. 1983. pap. 7.95 (ISBN 0-934318-18-2). Falcon Pr MT.
IDAHO–HISTORY
Gittins, H. Leigh. Pocatello Portrait: The Early Years, Eighteen Seventy-Eight to Nineteen Twenty-Eight. LC 82-50896. (Illus.). 1982. 19.95 (ISBN 0-89301-089-8). U Pr of Idaho.
Hart, Newell, ed. The Trail Blazer: History of S.E. Idaho, Daughters of Pioneers. Rev., 1930 ed. 1976. 11.00 (ISBN 0-941462-02-1). Cache Valley.
Welch, Julia C. Gold Town to Ghost Town: The Story of Silver City, Idaho. LC 82-60053. (Illus.). 1982. 7.95 (ISBN 0-89301-087-1). U Pr of Idaho.
IDEAL STATES
see Utopias
IDEALISM
see also Form (Philosophy); Materialism; Pragmatism; Transcendentalism
Dupain, Max & Johnson, Peter. Leslie Wilkinson: A Practical Idealist. (Illus.). 128p. 1983. 50.00 (ISBN 0-9594202-1-5). Allen Unwin.
Weigle, Luther A. American Idealism. 1928. text ed. 22.50x (ISBN 0-686-83462-3). Elliots Bks.
IDEALS (PSYCHOLOGY)
Shepherd, J. W. & Ellis, H. D. Identification Evidence: A Psychological Evaluation. 164p. 1982. 23.50 (ISBN 0-08-028441-8). Pergamon.
IDENTIFICATION OF CRIMINALS
see Crime and Criminals–Identification
IDENTIFICATION OF DOCUMENTS
see Legal Documents
IDENTIFICATION OF FIREARMS
see Firearms–Identification
IDENTIFICATION OF PLANTS
see Plants–Identification
IDENTITY
Debus, Michael. The Search for Identity, Conscience & Rebirth. 1982. pap. 2.50 (ISBN 0-903540-59-2). St George Bk Serv.
IDENTITY (PSYCHOLOGY)
Breakwell, Glynis M. Threatened Identities. 270p. 1983. 34.95x (ISBN 0-471-10233-4, Pub. by Wiley-Interscience). Wiley.
Epstein, A. L. Ethos & Identity. 1982. pap. 6.50x (ISBN 0-422-76370-5, Pub. by Tavistock England). Methuen Inc.
Identity, Modernity & the Claim to Know Better. 22p. 1982. pap. 5.00 (ISBN 92-808-0441-3, TUNU 203, UNU). Unipub.
Krieger, Susan. The Mirror Dance: Identity in a Women's Community. 1983. write for info. (ISBN 0-87722-304-1). Temple U Pr.
Sarbin, Theodore R. & Scheibe, Karl. Studies in Social Identity. 416p. 1983. 15.00 (ISBN 0-03-059542-8). Praeger.
IDENTITY, PERSONAL
see Personality
IDEOGRAPHY
see Chinese Language–Writing
IDEOLOGY
Hanley, Sarah. The Lit De Justice of the Kings of Francs: Constitutional Ideology in Legend, Ritual, & Discourse. LC 82-61374. (Illus.). 440p. 1983. 45.00x (ISBN 0-691-05382-0). Princeton U Pr.
Ideology & Social Psychology: Extremism, Moderation & Contradiction. LC 82-10719. 243p. 1982. 22.50 (ISBN 0-312-40457-3). St Martin.
Kelley, Donald R. The Beginning of Ideology: Consciousness & Society in the French Reformation. LC 80-41237. 366p. Date not set. pap. 14.95 (ISBN 0-521-27483-4). Cambridge U Pr.
Lloyd, Christopher, ed. Social Theory & Political Practice. (Wolfson College Lectures Ser.). 190p. 1983. 24.95 (ISBN 0-19-827447-5); pap. 12.95 (ISBN 0-19-827448-3). Oxford U Pr.
Phillips, Kevin P. Post-Conservative America: People, Politics, & Ideology in a Time of Crisis. LC 82-48898. 288p. 1983. pap. 6.95 (ISBN 0-394-71438-5, Vin). Random.
IDOLATRY
see Idols and Images
IDOLS AND IMAGES
Baines, J. Fecundity Figures: Egyptian Personification & the Iconology of a Genre. 200p. 1982. text ed. 75.00x (ISBN 0-85668-087-7, 40651, Pub. by Aris & Phillips England). Humanities.
Egenter, Nold. Gottersitze Aus Schilf und Bambus. (Illus.). 152p. (Ger.). 1982. write for info. (ISBN 3-261-04821-2). P Lang Pubs.
--Sacred Symbols of Reed & Bamboo. (Illus.). 152p. 1982. write for info. (ISBN 3-261-04821-2). P Lang Pubs.
IGBO LANGUAGE
see Ibo Language
IGNATIUS OF LOYOLA, SAINT
see Loyola, Ignacio De, Saint, 1491-1556
IGUANAS
see Lizards
IKEBANA
see Flower Arrangement, Japanese
IKONS
see Icons
ILLINOIS
see also names of cities, counties, etc. in Illinois
McDonald, Julie J. Pathways to the Present in Fifty Iowa & Illinois Communities. LC 77-153937. (Illus.). 310p. 1981. pap. 15.50x (ISBN 0-9608464-0-9). Boyar.
ILLINOIS–ANTIQUITIES
Lopinot, Neal H. & Hutto, M. Denise. Archaeological Investigations at the Kingfish Site, St. Clair County, Illinois. LC 82-50285. (Research Paper Ser.: No. 25). Date not set. price not set (ISBN 0-88104-001-0). S Ill U Pr.
ILLINOIS–HISTORY
Bial, Raymond. Ivesdale: A Photographic Essay. LC 82-73325. (Champaign County Historical Archives Historical Publications Ser.: No. 5). (Illus.). 1982. 12.00 (ISBN 0-9609646-0-6). Champaign County.
Logan County Heritage Foundation, ed. History of Logan County, Illinois, Nineteen Eighty-Two. (Illus.). 700p. 1982. write for info. Logan County.
May, George W. History of Massac County, Illinois. (Illus.). 232p. 1983. Repr. of 1955 ed. 6.00x (ISBN 0-9605566-4-8). G W May.
--Massac County Nineteen Fifty-Five to Nineteen Eighty-Two: Accompanies History of Massac County. 1983. 1.00 (ISBN 0-686-42830-7). G W May.
Pichaske, David R. Salem-Peoria, Eighteen Eighty-Three to Nineteen Eighty-Two. (Illus.). 256p. (Orig.). 1982. pap. 6.95 (ISBN 0-933180-40-3). Ellis Pr.
ILLINOIS–POLITICS AND GOVERNMENT
Garber, Lee O. & Hubbard, Ben C. Law, Finance, & the Teacher in Illinois. 1983. write for info. (ISBN 0-8134-2252-3). Interstate.
Harmon, Robert B. Government & Politics in Illinois: An Information Source Survey. 32p. 1978. pap. 3.00 (ISBN 0-686-37407-X). Vance Biblios.
ILLITERACY
Gilmore, William J. Elementary Literacy on the Eve of the Industrial Revolution: Trends in Rural New England. (Illus.). 91p. 1982. pap. 5.95 (ISBN 0-912296-57-7, Dist. by U Pr of VA). Am Antiquarian.
Literacy & Illiteracy. (Educational Studies & Documents: No. 42). 31p. 1982. pap. 5.00 (ISBN 92-3-101854-X, U1233, UNESCO). Unipub.
Planning, Administration & Monitoring in Literacy: Portfolio of Literacy Materials, 3 Vols. 66p. 1981. pap. 17.50 set (ISBN 0-686-81857-1, UB101, UNESCO). Unipub.
Stevenson, Colin. A Quick March to Literacy: A Study of Reading & Writing Disability in the British Army. 1983. price not set (ISBN 0-8077-2737-7). Tchrs Coll.
ILLUMINATION
see Lighting
ILLUMINATION OF BOOKS AND MANUSCRIPTS
see also Alphabets
Beach, Milo C. The Adventures of Rama. (Illus.). 64p. (Orig.). 1983. 13.00 (ISBN 0-934686-51-3). Freer.
ILLUMINATION OF BOOKS AND MANUSCRIPTS–EXHIBITIONS
Harthan, John. Illuminated Manuscripts: The Victoria & Albert Museum Introductions to the Decorative Arts. (Illus.). 48p. 9.95 (ISBN 0-88045-019-3). Stemmer Hse.
ILLUSIONS, OPTICAL
see Optical Illusions
ILLUSTRATED BOOKS, CHILDREN'S
see also Picture-Books for Children
Children's Book Illustration III. (Illus.). 140p. 1975. 21.50 (ISBN 0-89192-352-7). Transbooks.
ILLUSTRATED CHILDREN'S BOOKS
see Illustrated Books, Children's
ILLUSTRATION, BIOLOGICAL
see Biological Illustration
ILLUSTRATION, SCIENTIFIC
see Scientific Illustration
ILLUSTRATION, TECHNICAL
see Technical Illustration
ILLUSTRATION OF BOOKS
see also Caricature; Drawing; Illumination of Books and Manuscripts; Scientific Illustration; Technical Illustration
also subdivisions illustrations or pictures, illustrations, etc. under specific subjects, e.g. Bible–Pictures, eillustrations, etc.; Shakespeare, William–Illustrations
British Association of Illustrators Staff. Images: The British Association of Illustrators Sixth Annual 1981-82. (Illus.). 1983. 35.00 (ISBN 0-393-50001-2). Norton.
Children's Book Illustration III. (Illus.). 140p. 1975. 21.50 (ISBN 0-89192-352-7). Transbooks.
Tanaka, Ikko, ed. Illustration in Japan, Vol. 3. (Illus.). 180p. 1983. 59.50 (ISBN 0-87011-550-2). Kodansha.
ILLUSTRATIONS, HUMOROUS
see Caricatures and Cartoons; Wit and Humor, Pictorial
ILLUSTRATORS
Art Director's Index to Photographers & Illustrators, No. 9. (Orig.). 1983. pap. 24.95 (ISBN 0-686-82534-9, Pub. by Roto-Vision Switzerland). Norton.
ILLYRIAN LANGUAGE (SLAVIC)
see Serbo-Croatian Language
IMAGE CONVERTERS
Electronic Image Processing. (IEE Conference Publications: No. 214). 251p. 1982. pap. 51.00 (ISBN 0-85296-262-2). Inst Elect Eng.
Green, William B. Digital Image Processing: A Systems Approach. (Van Nostrand Reinhold Electrical-Computer Science & Engineering Ser.). 203p. 1982. text ed. 34.50 (ISBN 0-442-28801-8). Van Nos Reinhold.
IMAGE TUBES
see Image Converters
IMAGERY (PSYCHOLOGY)
Sheikh, Anees A. Imagery: Current Theory, Research, & Application. (Personality Processes Ser.). 450p. 1983. 39.95 (ISBN 0-471-09225-8, Pub. by Wiley-Interscience). Wiley.
IMAGES AND IDOLS
see Idols and Images
IMAGINATION
see also Creative Ability; Fantasy; Imagery (Psychology)
Fleming, Spencer. How to Develop the Creative Powers of your Imagination. (Human Development Library Book). (Illus.). 63p. (Orig.). 1983. pap. 6.95 (ISBN 0-89266-388-X). Am Classical Coll Pr.
Hohler, Thomas P. Imagination & Reflection: Intersubjectivity. 1983. lib. bdg. 29.50 (ISBN 90-247-2732-4, Pub. by Martinus Nijhoff Netherlands). Kluwer Boston.
LaCroix, Flora. Concepts of Imagination Development. 1983. lib. bdg. price not set (ISBN 0-89874-594-2). Krieger.
Neuberger, Phyllis J. Suppose You Were a Kitten. LC 82-91105. (Illus.). (gr. 1-3). 1982. pap. 2.95 (ISBN 0-9610050-0-9). P J Neuberger.
IMAGING SYSTEMS
Kazan, Benjamin, ed. Advances in Image Pickup & Display, Vol. 6. (Serial Publication). Date not set. price not set (ISBN 0-12-022106-3). Acad Pr.
Leach, K. G. The Physical Aspects of Radioisotopic Organ Imaging. 1976. 25.00x (ISBN 0-686-99803-0, Pub. by Brit Inst Radiology England). State Mutual Bk.
Reba, Richard & Goodenough, David J. Diagnostic Imaging Medicine. 1983. 87.00 (ISBN 90-247-2798-7, Pub. by Martinus Nijhoff Netherlands). Kluwer Boston.
Sklansky, J. & Bisconte, J. C., eds. Biomedical Images & Computers: St. Pierre de Chartreuse, France 1980, Proceedings. (Lecture Notes in Medical Informatics: Vol. 17). 332p. 1982. pap. 21.00 (ISBN 0-387-11579-X). Springer-Verlag.
IMBECILITY
see Mentally Handicapped
IMMERSION, BAPTISMAL
see Baptism
IMMIGRATION
see Emigration and Immigration
IMMIGRATION LAW
see Emigration and Immigration Law
IMMORAL LITERATURE
see Literature, Immoral
IMMORTALISM
Here are entered works on the concept of living indefinitely in the flesh. For works on the concept of the survival of the soul after death, see Immortality.
see also Immortality
Drummond, Henry. The Doctrine of Immortality & the Conquest of Eternal Life. (An Essential Knowledge Library Bk.). (Illus.). 137p. 1983. Repr. of 1886 ed. 67.75 (ISBN 0-89901-102-0). Found Class Reprints.
IMMORTALITY
Here are entered works on the concept of the survival of the soul after death. For works on the concept of living indefinitely in the flesh, see Immortalism.
see also Future Life; Soul
Clarke, William N. Immortality. 1920. text ed. 24.50x (ISBN 0-686-83578-6). Elliots Bks.
Immortality. 20p. Date not set. pap. 0.95 (ISBN 0-911336-81-8). Sci of Mind.
Reichenbach, Bruce. Is Man the Phoenix? A Study of Immortality. LC 82-21905. 198p. 1983. pap. text ed. 9.50 (ISBN 0-8191-2672-1). U Pr of Amer.
IMMUNE COMPLEX DISEASES
Espinoza, Luis R. & Osterland, C. Kirk, eds. Circulating Immune Complexes. LC 82-83042. (Illus.). 1983. pap. 37.50 (ISBN 0-87993-188-4). Futura Pub.
IMMUNE SERUM GLOBULIN
see Immunoglobulins
IMMUNITIES AND PRIVILEGES
see Privileges and Immunities
IMMUNITIES OF FOREIGN STATES
Materials on Jurisdictional Immunities of States & their Property. 657p. 1983. pap. 32.00 (ISBN 0-686-84902-7, UN81/5/10, UN). Unipub.
IMMUNITY
see also Allergy; Antigens; Communicable Diseases; Immunochemistry; Toxins and Antitoxins; Vaccination also subdivision Preventive Innoculations under certain diseases, e.g. Tuberculosis–Preventive Innoculations
Koch, William. Immunity & Oxidative Therapy. 6.00x (ISBN 0-943080-15-0). Cancer Control Soc.
Locke, Steven & Hornig-Rohan, Mady. Mind & Immunity: Behavioral Immunology (1976-1982)--an Annotated Bibliography. 240p. (Orig.). 1983. 35.00 (ISBN 0-910903-01-8); pap. 22.50 (ISBN 0-910903-02-6). Elliot Pr.
Thomson, D. M., ed. Assessment of Immune Status by the Leukocyte Adherence Inhibition Test. LC 82-3984. 380p. 1982. 45.00 (ISBN 0-12-689750-6). Acad Pr.

IMMUNITY (EXEMPTION)
see Privileges and Immunities
IMMUNOCHEMISTRY
Colowick, Sidney P. & Kaplan, Nathan O., eds. Methods in Enzymology: Vol. 93, Pt. F: Immunochemical Techniques, Conventional Antibodies, FC Receptors & Cytotoxicity. 393p. 1983. price not set (ISBN 0-12-181993-0). Acad Pr.
Colowick, Sidney P. & Kaplan, Nathan O., eds. Methods in Enzymology: Vol. 92, Pt. E: Immunochemical Techniques. Date not set. 65.00 (ISBN 0-12-181992-2). Acad Pr.
Cuello, A. C. Immunohistochemistry. (IBRO Handbook Ser.: Methods in the Neurosciences). 500p. 1982. write for info. (ISBN 0-471-10245-8, Pub. by Wiley-Interscience); pap. write for info. (ISBN 0-471-90052-4). Wiley.
Glynn, L. E. & Steward, M. W. Immunochemistry: An Advanced Textbook. LC 77-1630. 628p. 1977. 121.00x (ISBN 0-471-99508-8, Pub. by Wiley-Interscience). Wiley.
IMMUNOGLOBULINS
see also Antigens
August, J. T., ed. Monoclonal Antibodies in Drug Development. (Illus.). 237p. (Orig.). 1982. lexitone 24.00 (ISBN 0-9609094-0-0). Am Phar & Ex.
Colowick, Sidney P. & Kaplan, Nathan O., eds. Methods in Enzymology: Vol. 93, Pt. F: Immunochemical Techniques, Conventional Antibodies, FC Receptors & Cytotoxicity. 393p. 1983. price not set (ISBN 0-12-181993-0). Acad Pr.
Ritzmann, Stephan E., ed. Pathology of Immunoglobulins: Diagnostic & Clinical Aspects. LC 82-18021. (Protein Abnormalities Ser.: Vol. 2). 396p. 1982. 38.00 (ISBN 0-8451-2801-9). A R Liss.
Ritzmann, Stephen E., ed. Physiology of Immunoglobulins: Diagnostic & Clinical Aspects. LC 82-13101. (Protein Abornormalities Ser.: Vol. 1). 372p. 1982. 38.00 (ISBN 0-686-43002-6). A R Liss.
Schmidt, R. E. & Stroehmann, I., eds. Immunglobulintherapie. (Beitraege zu Infusionstherapie und klinische Ernaehrung: Vol. 11). viii, 160p. 1983. pap. 36.00 (ISBN 3-8055-3660-7). S Karger.
Seiler, F. R. & Geursen, R. G., eds. Seven S-Immunglobulin zur intravenoesen Anwendung. (Beitraege zu Infusionstherapie und klinische Ernaehrung: Vol. 9). (Illus.). viii, 176p. 1982. pap. 36.00 (ISBN 3-8055-3632-1). S Karger.
IMMUNOLOGY
see also Immunity; Veterinary Immunology
Atassi, M. Z. & Benjamini, E., eds. Immunobiology of Proteins & Peptides-II, Vol.150. (Advances in Experimental Medicine & Biology). 238p. 1982. 35.00x (ISBN 0-306-41110-5, Plenum Pr). Plenum Pub.
Beall, Gildon N. Allergy & Clinical Immunology. (UCLA Internal Medicine Today Ser.). 352p. 1983. 29.50 (ISBN 0-471-09568-0, Pub. by Wiley Med). Wiley.
Eickenberg, H. U., ed. The Influence of Antibiotics on the Host-Parasite Relationship. (Illus.). 270p. 1982. pap. 25.00 (ISBN 0-387-11680-X). Springer-Verlag.
Gergely, J., et al, eds. Antibody Structure & Molecular Immunology. 1975p. (Proceedings). 17.75 (ISBN 0-444-10936-6). Elsevier.
Graf, T. & Jaenisch, R., eds. Tumorviruses, Neoplastic Transformation & Differentiation. (Current Topics in Microbiology & Immunology Ser.: Vol. 101). (Illus.). 198p. 1983. 40.00 (ISBN 0-387-11665-6). Springer-Verlag.
Inchley, Christopher. Immunobiology. (Studies in Biology: No. 128). 88p. 1981. pap. text ed. 8.95 (ISBN 0-7131-2808-9). E Arnold.
International Immunodiagnostic Testing Markets. 1983. 995.00 (ISBN 0-686-37714-1, 290). Predicasts.
Klaustermeyer, William B. Practical Allergy & Immunology: Family Practice Today-A Comprehensive Postgraduate Library. 216p. 1983. 14.95 (ISBN 0-471-09564-8, Pub. by Wiley Med). Wiley.
Lichtenstein, Lawrence M. & Fauci, Anthony S. Current Therapy in Allergy & Immunology. 400p. 1983. 44.00 (ISBN 0-941158-07-1, D3002-9). Mosby.
Miler, I. The Immunity of the Foetus & Newborn Infant. 1983. 41.50 (ISBN 90-247-2610-7, Pub. by Martinus Nijhoff Netherlands). Kluwer Boston.
New York Academy of Sciences Annals of, October 19-21, 1981. Immunological Tolerance to Self & Non-Self: Proceedings, Vol. 392. Battisto, Jack R. & Claman, Henry N., eds. 436p. 1982. 80.00 (ISBN 0-89766-174-5). NY Acad Sci.
Ogra, P. L. & Jacobs, D., eds. Regulation of the Immune Response: Eighth Annual Convocation on Immunology, Amherst, June 1982. (Illus.). x, 390p. 1983. 130.00 (ISBN 3-8055-3574-0). S Karger.
Paul, W. E., et al, eds. Annual Review of Immunology, Vol. 1. 1983. text ed. 27.00 (ISBN 0-8243-3001-3). Annual Reviews.
Ricci, M. & Marone, G., eds. Progress in Clinical Immunology. (Monographs in Allergy: Vol. 18). (Illus.). viii, 222p. 1983. 90.00 (ISBN 3-8055-3697-6). S Karger.
Schell, Musher. Pathogenesis & Immunology of Treponemal Infections. (Immunology Ser.). 424p. 1983. 65.00 (ISBN 0-8247-1384-2). Dekker.
Serrou, B. & Rosenfeld, S., eds. New Immunomodulating Agents & Biological Response Modifiers. (Human Cancer Immunology Ser.: Vol. 3). 400p. 1982. 106.50 (ISBN 0-444-80401-3, Biomedical Pr). Elsevier.
Strickland. Immunoparasitology. 304p. 1982. 39.95 (ISBN 0-03-061499-6). Praeger.
Webb, David R., ed. Immunopharmacology & the Regulation of Leukocyte Function. (Immunology Ser.: Vol. 19). (Illus.). 312p. 1982. 45.00 (ISBN 0-8247-1707-4). Dekker.
Zaleski, Marek B., et al. Immunogenetics. 512p. 1983. text ed. 34.95 (ISBN 0-273-01925-2). Pitman Pub MA.
IMPACT PHENOMENA (NUCLEAR PHYSICS)
see Collisions (Nuclear Physics)
IMPEACHMENTS
see also Privileges and Immunities
Ehrlich, Walter. Presidential Impeachment. 1974. pap. text ed. 2.95x. Forum Pr IL.
IMPERIALISM
see also Militarism
also subdivision Foreign Relations under names of countries
Fish, Carl R. Path of Empire. 1919. text ed. 8.50x (ISBN 0-686-83685-5). Elliots Bks.
Marcy, Sam. Imperialism & the Crisis in the Socialist Camp. 57p. 1979. pap. 1.50 (ISBN 0-89567-030-5). WV PUbs.
Offiong, Daniel O. Imperialism & Dependency: Obstacles in African Development. 304p. 1983. 12.95 (ISBN 0-88258-126-0); pap. 6.95 (ISBN 0-88258-127-9). Howard U Pr.
IMPLANTATION, ION
see Ion Implantation
IMPLEMENTS, UTENSILS, ETC.
see also Agricultural Implements; Agricultural Machinery; Kitchen Utensils; Tools
also subdivision Implements under Indians, Mound-builders and similar headings; names of particular implements, e.g. Knives, Scythes
The Official 1983 Price Guide to Kitchen Collectibles. 1st ed. LC 82-84636. 544p. 1983. 9.95 (ISBN 0-87637-371-6). Hse of Collectibles.
IMPORT AND EXPORT CONTROLS
see Foreign Trade Regulation
IMPORT RESTRICTIONS
see Foreign Trade Regulation
IMPORTS
see Commerce
IMPRESSIONISM (ART)
Kean, Beverly W. All the Empty Palaces: The Great Merchant Patrons of Modern Art in Pre-Revolutionary Russia. LC 82-8536. (Illus.). 336p. 1983. 29.50 (ISBN 0-87663-412-9). Universe.
Lee, Ellen W. & Smith, Tracy E. The Aura of Neo-Impressionism: The W. J. Holliday Collection of the Indianapolis Museum of Art. LC 82-84036. (Centennial Catalogue Series). (Illus.). 296p. (Orig.). 1983. 45.00x (ISBN 0-936260-04-1); pap. 25.00x (ISBN 0-936260-05-X). Ind Mus Art.
IMPRINTING (PSYCHOLOGY)
Scott, J. P., ed. Critical Periods. LC 78-632. (Benchmark Papers in Animal Behavior: Vol. 12). 381p. 1978. 48.50 (ISBN 0-87933-119-4). Hutchinson Ross.
IMPRINTS (IN BOOKS)
Nicholson, Margaret. Catalogue of Pre-Nineteen Hundred Imprints Relating to America in the Royal Library, Brussels. LC 82-48979. (Orig.). 1983. lib. bdg. write for info. (ISBN 0-527-67200-9). Kraus Intl.
IMPRISONMENT
see also Juvenile Detention Homes; Prisons
Malloy, Edward A. The Ethics of Law Enforcement & Criminal Punishment. LC 82-20015. 102p. (Orig.). 1983. lib. bdg. 16.75 (ISBN 0-8191-2842-2); pap. 6.75 (ISBN 0-8191-2843-0). U Pr of Amer.
IMPROVISATION (MUSIC)
Bailey, Derek. Musical Improvisation. 154p. 1983. 14.95 (ISBN 0-686-82656-6); pap. 6.95 (ISBN 0-686-82657-4). P-H.
IMPULSE
Zuckerman, Marvin, ed. Biological Bases for Sensation Seeking, Impulsivity & Anxiety. 320p. 1983. text ed. write for info. (ISBN 0-89859-255-0). L Erlbaum Assocs.
IN-LINE DATA PROCESSING
see on-Line Data Processing
IN-SERVICE TRAINING
see Employees, Training Of
INAUDIBLE SOUND
see Ultrasonics
INBORN ERRORS OF METABOLISM
see Metabolism, Inborn Errors of
INCAPACITY, ESTIMATION OF
see Disability Evaluation
INCARNATION
Kennedy, D. G. Incarnational Elements in Hilton's Spirituality. (Salzburg-Elizabethan Studies: Vol. 92, No. 3). 312p. 1982. pap. text ed. 25.00x (ISBN 0-391-02732-8, 41225, Pub. by Salzburg Austria). Humanities.
INCENDIARISM
see Arson
INCENTIVES IN INDUSTRY
see also Employee Ownership; Profit-Sharing; Rewards (Prizes, etc.); Wages
Robert Morris Associates. Incentive Compensation Systems for Commercial Loan Officers: State of the Art. LC 82-25913. (Illus.). 48p. (Orig.). 1983. pap. text ed. 19.50 (ISBN 0-936742-07-0). Robt Morris Assocs.
INCEST
De Young, Mary. The Sexual Victimization of Children. LC 82-17197. 190p. 1982. lib. bdg. 18.95x (ISBN 0-89950-063-3). McFarland & Co.
Incest: A Biosocial View. (Studies in Anthropology). 184p. 1983. price not set. Acad Pr.
Mayer, Adele. Incest: A Treatment Manual for Therapy with Victims, Spouses & Offenders. LC 82-83779. 275p. 1982. lib. bdg. 24.95x (ISBN 0-918452-36-8). Learning Pubns.
Renshaw, Domeena C. Incest: Understanding & Treatment. 1982. text ed. 17.95 (ISBN 0-316-74031-4). Little.
Renvoize, Jean. Incest: A Family Pattern. 224p. 1983. 15.95 (ISBN 0-7100-9073-0). Routledge & Kegan.
INCINERATORS
Brunner, Calvin. Incineration Systems Course Notebook. 411p. 1982. Wkbk. 85.00 (ISBN 0-86587-111-6). Gov Insts.
Rudman, Jack. Incinerator Stationary Engineer. (Career Examination Ser.: C-2636). (Cloth bdg. avail. on request). pap. 10.00 (ISBN 0-8373-2636-2). Natl Learning.
--Senior Incinerator Stationary Engineer. (Career Examination Ser.: C-2637). (Cloth bdg. avail. on request). pap. 10.00 (ISBN 0-8373-2637-0). Natl Learning.
--Supervising Incinerator Stationary Engineer. (Career Examination Ser.: C-2638). pap. 12.00 (ISBN 0-8373-2638-9). Natl Learning.
INCOME
see also Capital; Consumption (Economics); Gross National Product; Profit; Retirement Income
Ben-Porath, Yoram. Income Distribution & the Family. LC 82-61326. 248p. (Orig.). 1982. pap. 6.95 (ISBN 0-686-43273-8). Population Coun.
Field, Frank, ed. The Wealth Report Two. (Inequality in Society Ser.). 200p. (Orig.). 1983. pap. price not set (ISBN 0-7100-9452-3). Routledge & Kegan.
Kinsey, Thomas D. Learn to Double Your Income Legitimately in Four Years or Less. 64p. 1983. pap. text ed. 10.00 (ISBN 0-941046-06-0). ERGO Business Bks.
Nygard, F. & Sandstrom, A. Measuring Income Inequality. (Stockholm Studies in Statistics: Vol. 1). 436p. 1982. pap. text ed. 30.00x (ISBN 91-22-00439-4, Pub. by Almqvist & Wiksell Sweden). Humanities.
Ozawa, Martha N. Income Maintenance & Work Incentives: Toward a Synthesis. 300p. 1982. 29.95 (ISBN 0-03-058647-X). Praeger.
Page, Benjamin I. Who Gets What From Government. LC 82-13454. 288p. 1983. 15.95 (ISBN 0-520-04702-8). U of Cal Pr.
Piachaud, David. The Distribution & Redistribution of Incomes. 140p. 1982. pap. text ed. 11.00x (ISBN 0-7199-1086-2, Pub. by Bedford England). Renouf.
Willman, Paul. Fairness, Collective Bargaining, & Income Policy. (Illus.). 208p. 1982. 34.95x (ISBN 0-19-827252-9). Oxford U Pr.
INCOME DISTRIBUTION
see Income
INCOME STATEMENTS
see Financial Statements
INCOME TAX
see also Capital Gains Tax; Real Property and Taxation
Andreassi, Michael W. & MacRae, C. Duncan. Homeowner Income Tax Provisions & Metropolitan Housing Markets: A Simulation Study. LC 81-51624. 78p. 1981. pap. 9.00 (ISBN 0-87766-297-5, URI 29900). Urban Inst.
Armstrong, R. Personal Income Tax Practice Set: 1983 Edition. 1983. 6.50x (ISBN 0-07-002525-8, G). McGraw.
Bandy, Dale & Swad, Randy. Federal Income Tax Procedures, 1983. 320p. 1983. pap. text ed. 19.00 (ISBN 0-13-309104-X). P-H.
Ellentuck, Albert B. Year End Tax Planning Manual 1982. 384p. 1982. perfect bd. 46.50 (ISBN 0-88262-807-0). Warren.
H & R Block. H & R Block Income Tax Workbook. 1982. 5.95 (ISBN 0-02-079200-X). Macmillan.
Harmon, Susan M., ed. Readings in Income Taxation. (Huebner School Ser.). (Orig.). 1982. pap. text ed. 12.00 (ISBN 0-943590-04-3). Amer College.
Hulten, Charles R., ed. Depreciation, Inflation, & the Taxation of Income from Capital. LC 81-533061. 319p. 1981. text ed. 32.00 (ISBN 0-87766-311-4, URI 33800). Urban Inst.
Tucker, Stefan F. & Cowan, Martin B., eds. Real Estate Income Taxation 1982. 816p. 1982. 48.00 (ISBN 0-88262-829-1). Warren.
INCOME TAX-DEDUCTIONS
Holzman, Robert S. Take It Off: Two Thousand Three Hundred Sixty-Three Deductions Most People Overlook. rev. & expanded ed. 1983. 16.30i (ISBN 0-06-015036-X, HarpT); pap. 8.61 (ISBN 0-06-464053-1, BN-4053). Har-Row.
INCOME TAX-LAW
Hoffman, William H. & Willis, Eugene. West Federal Taxation: Individual Income Taxes, 1983 Annual Edition. 1068p. 1982. text ed. 24.95 (ISBN 0-314-67113-7); write for info. instr's manual (ISBN 0-314-67322-9). West Pub.
INCOME TAX-UNITED STATES
Porter, Sylvia. Sylvia Porter's Income Tax Book, 1983. 176p. 1982. pap. 3.95 (ISBN 0-380-81687-3, 81687). Avon.
Singer, Penny. The Underground Economy: Earnings That Go Undeclared on Income Tax Forms. (Vital Issues, Vol. XXX 1980-81: No. 8). 0.60 (ISBN 0-686-81603-X). Ctr Info Am.
INCOME TAX-UNITED STATES-LAW
Gaffney, D. J. & Skadden, D. H. Principles of Federal Income Taxation, 1983-84. 608p. 1983. 25.00 (ISBN 0-07-022631-8, C); price not set instr's manual (ISBN 0-07-022632-6); 10.00 (ISBN 0-07-022633-4). McGraw.
Muhammad, S. A. How to Prepare Your Own Income Tax Return. LC 82-91051. 192p. 1982. pap. 5.00 (ISBN 0-9609996-0-4). TPA Pub.
INCOME TAX, MUNICIPAL
Hulten, Charles R., ed. Depreciation, Inflation, & the Taxation of Income from Capital. LC 81-533061. 319p. 1981. text ed. 32.00 (ISBN 0-87766-311-4, URI 33800). Urban Inst.
INCORPORATION
Hayden, John L. How to Incorporate in Tax Free Nevada for Only 50 Dollars. LC 80-85433. 88p. (Orig.). pap. 8.97 (ISBN 0-940008-00-9). Entrepreneurs.
Heisler, Roland C. Federal Incorporation: Constitutional Questions Involved. LC 13-8920. (University of Pennsylvania Law School Ser.: No. 3). viii, 231p. 1982. Repr. of 1913 ed. lib. bdg. 28.50 (ISBN 0-89941-179-7). W S Hein.
Jander, Klaus H. & Mertin, Dietz. Zur Gruendung und Fuehrung von Tochtergesellschaften in den U. S. A. German American Chamber of Commerce, Inc., ed. 200p. (Ger.). 1982. text ed. 29.00 (ISBN 0-86640-008-7). German Am Chamber.
Williams, Phillip G. How to Form Your Own Illinois Corporation Before the Inc. Dries: A Step-by-Step Guide, with Forms. 136p. (Orig.). 1983. lib. bdg. 9.95 (ISBN 0-936284-25-0); pap. 9.95 (ISBN 0-936284-26-9). P Gaines Co.
INCUNABULA
see also Bibliography–Rare Books; Printing–History
King, Dorothy, ed. Check List of the Incunabula in the William Allan Neilson Library. (Illus.). 20p. 1975. pap. 1.50 (ISBN 0-87391-026-5). Smith Coll.
INDEMNITY INSURANCE
see Insurance, Liability
INDEPENDENCE DAY (U. S.)
see Fourth of July
INDEPENDENT ADMINISTRATIVE AGENCIES
see Independent Regulatory Commissions
INDEPENDENT CONTRACTORS
see Employers' Liability; Labor Contract; Liability (Law)
INDEPENDENT REGULATORY COMMISSIONS
Congressional Quarterly Inc. Staff. Federal Regulatory Directory: 1983-1984. LC 79-644368. 900p. 1983. 29.95 (ISBN 0-87187-257-9). Congr Quarterly.
--Regulations: Process & Politics. LC 82-14292. 192p. 1982. pap. 9.25 (ISBN 0-87187-243-9). Congr Quarterly.
Davis, Glenn & Helfand, Gary. The Uncertain Balance: Federal Regulators in a Changing Political Economy. 224p. (Orig.). 1983. pap. text ed. 8.95x (ISBN 0-89529-184-3). Avery Pub.
INDEPENDENT SCHOOLS
see Private Schools
INDETERMINISM
see Free Will and Determinism
INDEXES
see also Abstracting and Indexing Services; Periodicals–Indexes; Subject Headings;
also subdivision Indexes or Dictionaries, Indexes, etc. under specific subjects, e.g. Biography–Dictionaries, Indexes, etc.
Brewer, Annie M. Indexes, Abstracts & Digests. 801p. 1982. 150.00x (ISBN 0-8103-1686-2). Gale.
INDEXES, CARD
see Files and Filing (Documents)
INDEXING
see also Cataloging; Files and Filing (Documents)
Rowley, Jennifer E. Abstracting & Indexing. 155p. 1982. 15.00 (ISBN 0-85157-336-3, Pub. by Bingley England). Shoe String.
INDEXING AND ABSTRACTING SERVICES
see Abstracting and Indexing Services
INDEXING VOCABULARIES
see Subject-Headings
INDIA
see also names of cities, villages and geographic areas in India
Ali, Shanti S. & Ramchandani, R. R., eds. India & the Western Indian Ocean States: Towards Regional Cooperation in Development. 310p. 1981. 27.50x (ISBN 0-940500-85-X, Pub by Allied Pubs India). Asia Bk Corp.
Bhardwaj, Surinder M. Hindu Places of Pilgrimage in India: A Study in Cultural Geography. (Illus.). 278p. 1983. pap. 7.95 (ISBN 0-520-04951-9, CAL 621). U of Cal Pr.
Hopkins, E. Wasburn. Ethics of India. 1924. text ed. 10.50x (ISBN 0-686-83539-5). Elliots Bks.

Mehrotra, Raja R. Names of India. (International Library of Names). 250p. 1983. text ed. 24.50x (ISBN 0-8290-1293-1). Irvington.

Rothermund, Dietmar. India. 224p. 1982. 75.00x (ISBN 0-584-11021-9, Pub. by Muller Ltd). State Mutual Bk.

Sharma, Jagdish S. Encyclopedia India, 2 Vols. 2nd & rev. ed. 1407p. 1981. Set. 195.00 (ISBN 0-940500-78-7, Pub by S Chand India). Asia Bk Corp.

INDIA–BIBLIOGRAPHY

The Times of India Directory & Yearbook, Including Who's Who, 1982. 58th ed. (Illus.). 984p. 1982. 50.00 (ISBN 0-8002-3056-6, A19-14). Intl Pubns Serv.

INDIA–BIOGRAPHY

Chakravorty, Basuda. Jyotindra Nath Mukherjee: The Humanist Revolutionary. 1982. 8.00 (ISBN 0-8364-0919-1, Pub. by Minerva India). South Asia Bks.

Coburn, Thomas. Devi Mahatmya. 1983. 17.50x (ISBN 0-686-42973-7). South Asia Bks.

Concept-Research & Reference Division, ed. Who's Who of Indian Geographers. 139p. 1982. text ed. 15.25x (ISBN 0-391-02808-1, Pub. by Concept India). Humanities.

Maharaja Ranjit Singh as Patron of the Arts. 1982. 29.00x (ISBN 0-8364-0865-9, Pub. by Marg). South Asia Bks.

Natu, Bal. Glimpses of the God-Man, Meher Baba: Vol. III, February 1952 - February 1953. LC 79-913293. (Illus.). 344p. (Orig.). 1982. pap. 7.95 (ISBN 0-913078-44-1). Sheriar Pr.

Swami Shraddhananda. The Story of an Epoch: Swami Virajananda & His Times. Swami Shraddhananda, tr. from Bengali. 298p. 1982. pap. text ed. write for info. (ISBN 0-87481-511-8, Pub. by Ramakrishna Math Madras India). Vedanta Pr.

INDIA–CIVILIZATION

Basham, A. L. The Wonder That Was India. (Illus.). 568p. 1983. 34.95 (ISBN 0-283-35457-7, Pub by Sidgwick & Jackson). Merrimack Bk Serv.

Gokhale, B. G. Bharatavarsha: A Political & Cultural History of India. 360p. 1982. text ed. 21.50x (ISBN 0-391-02792-1, 41075, Pub. by Sterling India). Humanities.

Maity, S. K. Cultural History of Ancient India. 120p. 1982. text ed. 12.00x (ISBN 0-391-02809-X). Humanities.

Singh, K. S. Economies of the Tribes & Their Transformation. 400p. 1982. text ed. 41.00x (ISBN 0-391-02786-7, 40956, Pub. by Concept India). Humanities.

INDIA–ECONOMIC CONDITIONS

Goldsmith, Raymond W. The Financial Development of India, Japan, & the United States. LC 82-8541. 136p. 1983. text ed. 12.95x (ISBN 0-300-02934-9). Yale U Pr.

McAlpin, Michelle B. Subject to Famine: Food Crisis & Economic Change in Western India, 1860-1920. LC 82-61376. 320p. 1983. 35.00x (ISBN 0-691-05385-5). Princeton U Pr.

Mascarenhas, R. C. Technology Transfer & Development: India's Hindustan Machine Tools Company. 235p. 1982. softcover 19.50 (ISBN 0-86531-934-0). Westview.

INDIA–ECONOMIC POLICY

Dandekar, V. M. Peasant Worker Alliance. (R. C. Dutt Lectures on Political Economy: 1979). 104p. 1981. pap. text ed. 8.95 (ISBN 0-86131-274-0, Pub. by Orient Longman Ltd India). Apt Bks.

INDIA–EMIGRATION AND IMMIGRATION

Bahadur Singh, I., ed. Inidans in Southeast Asia. 232p. 1982. 34.95 (ISBN 0-940500-53-1, Pub. by Sterling India). Asia Bk Corp.

INDIA–FOREIGN RELATIONS

Bhatia, H. L., ed. Does Foreign Aid Help? 120p. 1981. 14.95x (ISBN 0-940500-84-1, Pub by Allied Pubs India). Asia Bk Corp.

Kaul, T. N. Reminiscences: Discreet & Indiscreet. (Illus.). 312p. 1982. 42.50 (ISBN 0-686-42809-9, Pub by Lancer India). Asia Bk Corp.

Naik, J. A. India & the Communist Countries. 224p. 1982. text ed. 31.00x (ISBN 0-391-02573-2, 90404). Humanities.

--India & the West-Documents: 1979. 231p. 1982. text ed. 31.00x (ISBN 0-391-02572-4, 90402). Humanities.

INDIA–FOREIGN RELATIONS–GREAT BRITAIN

Banerji, Arun. Aspects of Indo-British Economic Relations, 1858-98. (Illus.). 272p. 1981. text ed. 24.95 (ISBN 0-19-561341-4). Oxford U Pr.

Copland, Ian. The British Raj & the Indian Princes. 1982. 18.50x (ISBN 0-8364-0893-4, Pub. by Macmillan India). South Asia Bks.

Kamerkar, Mani. British Paramountcy: British-Baroda Relations, 1818-1848. 253p. 1980. 34.50 (ISBN 0-940500-75-2, Pub by Popular Prakashan India). Asia Bk Corp.

INDIA–FOREIGN RELATIONS–UNITED STATES

Sultan, Tanvir. INDO-US Relations: A Study of Foreign Policies. 260p. 1982. 29.95 (ISBN 0-940500-82-5, Pub by Depp & Deep India). Asia Bk Corp.

INDIA–HISTORY

Dandekar, R. N. The Age of Guptas & Other Essays. 1982. 30.00 (ISBN 0-8364-0916-7, Pub. by Ajanta). South Asia Bks.

Desai, Sudha V. Social Life in Maharashtra Under the Peshwas. 220p. 1980. 29.95 (ISBN 0-940500-72-8). Asia Bk Corp.

Gokhale, B. G. Bharatavarsha: A Political & Cultural History of India. 360p. 1982. text ed. 21.50x (ISBN 0-391-02792-1, 41075, Pub. by Sterling India). Humanities.

Guha, Ranajit. A Rule of Property for Benga: An Essay on the Idea of Permanent Settlement. 2nd ed. 22p. 1982. text ed. 17.95x (ISBN 0-86131-289-9, Pub. by orient Longman Ltd India). Apt Bks.

Namboodiripad, E. M. Crisis Into Chaos: Political India 1981. 172p. 1981. pap. text ed. 4.25 (ISBN 0-86131-279-1, Pub. by Orient Longman Ltd India). Apt Bks.

Ray, David & Singh, Amritjit, eds. India: A New Letters Book. 277p. 1983. pap. 10.95 (ISBN 0-8214-0736-8, 82-85058). Ohio U Pr.

Scholberg, Henry. Bibliography of Goa & the Portuguese in India. 413p. 1982. text ed. 64.50x (ISBN 0-391-02762-X, Pub. by Promilla & Co India). Humanities.

Shah, Giri Raj. Indian Heritage. 187p. 1982. text ed. 12.00x (ISBN 0-391-02806-5, Pub. by Abhinav India). Humanities.

Sharma, Rama & Gopal. The History of Vijayanagar Empire. 1980. Vols. 1 & 2. 74.95 (ISBN 0-940500-93-0); Vol. 1 Beginnings & Expansion, 247p. Vol. 2 Decline & Disappearance, 611p. Asia Bk Corp.

Vatsal, Tulsi. Indian Political History: From the Marathas to Modern Times. (Illus.). v, 225p. 1982. pap. text ed. 7.95x (ISBN 0-686-42712-2, Pub. by Orient Longman Ltd India). Apt Bks.

INDIA–HISTORY–EARLY TO 1000 A.D

Smith, Bardwell, ed. Essays on Gupta Culture. 1983. 34.00x (ISBN 0-8364-0871-3); text ed. 20.00x (ISBN 0-686-42974-5). South Asia Bks.

INDIA–HISTORY–BRITISH OCCUPATION, 1765-1947

Bayly, C. A. Rulers, Merchants & Bazaars: North Indian Society in the Age of British Expansion, 1780-1880. LC 82-4420. (South Asian Studies: No. 28). (Illus.). 488p. Date not set. price not set (ISBN 0-521-22932-4). Cambridge U Pr.

Mill, James. History of British India, 3 vols. 2nd ed. 1972. Repr. of 1820 ed. Set. 65.00x (ISBN 0-8002-2629-1). Intl Pubns Serv.

Moorhouse, Geoffrey. India Britannica. LC 82-48127. (Illus.). 272p. 1983. 22.07i (ISBN 0-06-015115-3, HarpT). Har-Row.

Penner, Peter & MacLean, Richard. The Rebel Bureaucrat: Frederick John Shore 1799-1837 as Critic of William Bentinick's India. 1982. 24.00x (ISBN 0-8364-0920-5, Pub. by Chanakya). South Asia Bks.

Renford, Raymond K. The Non-Official British in India to 1920. 400p. 1982. 34.00x (ISBN 0-19-561388-0). Oxford U Pr.

INDIA–HISTORY–1947-

Chandra, Bipan. Nationalism & Colonialism in Modern India. 408p. 1981. text ed. 32.50x (ISBN 0-86131-194-9, Pub. by Orient Longman Ltd India). Apt Bks.

Collins, Larry & Lapierre, Dominique. Mountbatten & the Partition of India. viii, 191p. 1982. text ed. 20.00x (ISBN 0-7069-1787-1, Pub. by Vikas India). Advent NY.

Pandit, H. N. Fragments of History: India's Freedom Movement & after. 299p. 1982. 34.99x (ISBN 0-940500-55-8, Pub. by Sterling India). Asia Bk Corp.

Rajan, Mohan S. Atoms of Hope. 155p. 1980. 14.95x (ISBN 0-940500-39-6, Pub by Allied Pubs India). Asia Bk Corp.

Thapar, Romesh. An Indian Future. 164p. 1981. 16.95 (ISBN 0-940500-89-2, Pub by Pubs Allied India). Asia Bk Corp.

INDIA–INDUSTRIES

Nadkarni, M. V. Marketable Surplus & Market Dependence: A Study of a Millet Region. 176p. 1980. 23.50x (ISBN 0-940500-80-9, Pub by Allied Pubs India). Asia Bk Corp.

INDIA–POLITICS AND GOVERNMENT

Char, S. V. Readings in the Constitutional History of India. 720p. 1982. 49.00x (ISBN 0-19-561264-7). Oxford U Pr.

Dandekar, V. M. Peasant Worker Alliance. (R. C. Dutt Lectures on Political Economy; 1979). 104p. 1981. pap. text ed. 8.95 (ISBN 0-86131-274-0, Pub. by Orient Longman Ltd India). Apt Bks.

Fadia, Babu L. State Politics in India, 2 Vols. 1125p. 1983. Set. text ed. 55.00x (ISBN 0-391-02827-8, Pub. by Radiant Pub India). Humanities.

Gokhale, B. G. Bharatavarsha: A Political & Cultural History of India. 360p. 1982. text ed. 21.50x (ISBN 0-391-02792-1, 41075, Pub. by Sterling India). Humanities.

Haq, Ehsanul. Education & Political Culture in India. 176p. 1981. 22.50x (ISBN 0-940500-54-X, Pub. by Sterling India). Asia Bk Corp.

Khilnani, N. M. Panorama of Indian Diplomacy. 314p. 1981. 27.50x (ISBN 0-940500-74-4, Pub by S Chand India). Asia Bk Corp.

Kumar, Ravinder & Panigrahi, D. N., eds. Selected Works of Motilal Nehru, Vol. 1. 400p. 1983. text ed. 45.00x (ISBN 0-7069-1885-1, Pub. by Vikas India). Advent NY.

Namboodiripad, E. M. Crisis Into Chaos: Political India 1981. 172p. 1981. pap. text ed. 4.25 (ISBN 0-86131-279-1, Pub. by Orient Longman Ltd India). Apt Bks.

Noorani, A. G., ed. Public Law in India. 340p. 1982. text ed. 40.00x (ISBN 0-7069-1390-6, Pub. by Vikas India). Advent NY.

Philip, A. T. & Sivaji Rao, K. H. Indian Government & Politics. 299p. 1981. 19.95x (ISBN 0-940500-45-0, Pub. by Sterling India). Asia Bk Corp.

Prasad, Nageshwar. Ideology & Organization in Indian Politics. 304p. 1980. 29.95x (ISBN 0-940500-77-9, Pub by Allied Pubs India). Asia Bk Corp.

Puri, Balraj. Jammu & Kasmir: Triumph & Tragedy of Indian Federalisation. 280p. 1981. 32.95x (ISBN 0-940500-47-7, Pub. by Sterling India). Asia Bk Corp.

Ray, Syamal K. Indian Bureaucracy at the Crossroads. 407p. 1979. 34.95 (ISBN 0-686-42714-9, Pub. by Sterling India). Asia Bk Corp.

Roy, M. N. New Orientation. 1982. 18.00 (ISBN 0-8364-0910-8, Pub. by Ajanta). South Asia Bks.

Suntharalingam, R. Indian Nationalism: An Historical Analysis. 1983. text ed. write for info. (ISBN 0-7069-2106-2, Pub. by Vikas India). Advent NY.

Varma, S. P. Modern Political Theory. 2nd ed. xvii, 426p. 1982. text ed. 27.50 (ISBN 0-7069-1380-9, Pub. by Vikas India). Advent NY.

Vatsal, Tulsi. Indian Political History: From the Marathas to Modern Times. (Illus.). v, 225p. 1982. pap. text ed. 7.95x (ISBN 0-686-42712-2, Pub. by Orient Longman Ltd India). Apt Bks.

INDIA–POLITICS AND GOVERNMENT–1947-

Chandra, Bipan. Nationalism & Colonialism in Modern India. 408p. 1981. text ed. 32.50x (ISBN 0-86131-194-9, Pub. by Orient Longman Ltd India). Apt Bks.

Naik, J. A., ed. Indian Politics Documents, Events & Figures 1979. 360p. 1982. text ed. 46.00x (ISBN 0-391-02831-6, Pub. by Avinash India). Humanities.

INDIA–POPULATION

Desai, A. R. Urban Family & Family Planning in India. 224p. 1980. Repr. 22.95x (ISBN 0-940500-70-1). Asia Bk Corp.

Mohan, Rakesh. The Effects of Population Growth, of the Pattern of Demand, & of Technology on the Process of Urbanization: An Application to India. LC 82-8600. (World Bank Staff Working Papers: No. 520). (Orig.). 1982. pap. 3.00 (ISBN 0-8213-0008-3). World Bank.

Rele, J. R. & Kanitkar, Tara. Fertility & Family Planning in Greater Bombay. 217p. 1980. 22.95x (ISBN 0-940500-87-6, Pub by Popular Prakashan India). Asia Bk Corp.

Singh, K. S., ed. Tribal Movements in India, Vol. 1. 1982. 25.00X (ISBN 0-8364-0901-9, Pub. by Manohar India). South Asia Bks.

INDIA–RACE QUESTION

Sivakumar, Chitra. Education, Social Inequality & Social Change in Karnataka. (Studies in Sociology & Social Anthropology). 160p. 1982. text ed. 12.00x (ISBN 0-391-02797-2, Pub. by Hindustan India). Humanities.

INDIA–RELIGION

Barth, A. Religions of India. 6th ed. Wood, J., tr. from Fr. 309p. 1980. Repr. of 1880 ed. 23.95x (ISBN 0-940500-64-7). Asia Bk Corp.

Chopra, P. N., ed. Religions & Communities of India. 316p. 1982. text ed. 32.25x (ISBN 0-391-02748-4). Humanities.

--Religions & Communities of India. 324p. 1982. 65.00x (ISBN 0-85692-081-9, Pub. by J M Dent). State Mutual Bk.

Deloria, Vine, Jr. God Is Red. 1983. pap. 3.95 (ISBN 0-440-33044-0, LE). Dell.

Varadpande, M. L. Religion & Theatre in India. 100p. 1982. text ed. 10.00x (ISBN 0-391-02794-8). Humanities.

INDIA–RURAL CONDITIONS

Ramachandran, H. Behaviour in Space: Rural Marketing in an Underdeveloped Economy. 121p. 1982. text ed. 14.50x (ISBN 0-391-02784-0, 40855, Pub. by Concept India). Humanities.

INDIA–SOCIAL CONDITIONS

Sivakumar, Chitra. Education, Social Inequality & Social Change in Karnataka. (Studies in Sociology & Social Anthropology). 160p. 1982. text ed. 12.00x (ISBN 0-391-02797-2, Pub. by Hindustan India). Humanities.

INDIA–SOCIAL LIFE AND CUSTOMS

Desai, Sudha V. Social Life in Maharashtra Under the Peshwas. 220p. 1980. 29.95 (ISBN 0-940500-72-8). Asia Bk Corp.

Rajan, V. N. Victimology in India. 176p. 1981. 14.95x (ISBN 0-940500-86-8, Pub by Allied Pubs India). Asia Bk Corp.

Sivakumar, Chitra. Education, Social Inequality & Social Change in Karnataka. (Studies in Sociology & Social Anthropology). 160p. 1982. text ed. 12.00x (ISBN 0-391-02797-2, Pub. by Hindustan India). Humanities.

Welbon, Guy & Yocum, Glenn, eds. Festivals in South India & Sri Lanka. 1982. 25.00X (ISBN 0-8364-0900-0, Pub.by Manohar India). South Asia Bks.

Yadava, Ganga P. Dhanapala & His Times: A Socio-Cultural Study Based Upon His Works. 276p. 1982. text ed. 16.00x (ISBN 0-391-02785-9, 40902, Pub. by Concept India). Humanities.

INDIA–SOCIAL POLICY

Sivakumar, Chitra. Education, Social Inequality & Social Change in Karnataka. (Studies in Sociology & Social Anthropology). 160p. 1982. text ed. 12.00x (ISBN 0-391-02797-2, Pub. by Hindustan India). Humanities.

INDIA–RUBBER

see Rubber

INDIA–RUBBER INDUSTRY

see Rubber Industry and Trade

INDIAN BLANKETS

see Indians of North America–Textile Industry and Fabrics

INDIAN CORN

see Corn

INDIAN FOLK-LORE

see Folk-Lore, Indian

INDIAN LITERATURE

Swann, Brian. Smoothing the Ground: Essays on the Native American Oral Literature. 416p. 1983. 12.95x (ISBN 0-520-04902-0); pap. 9.95 (ISBN 0-520-04913-6). U of Cal Pr.

INDIAN LITERATURE (AMERICAN INDIAN)

see Indian Literature

INDIAN MUTINY, 1857-1858

see India–History–British Occupation, 1765-1947

INDIAN OCEAN

Kapur. The Indian Ocean: Regional & International Power Politics. 256p. 1983. 29.95 (ISBN 0-03-058641-0). Praeger.

Nairn, Alan E. & Stehli, Francis G., eds. The Ocean Basins & Margins, Vol. 6: The Indian Ocean. 750p. 1982. 85.00x (ISBN 0-306-37776-4, Plenum Pr). PLenum Pub.

INDIAN OCEAN REGION

Ali, Shanti S. & Ramchandani, R. R., eds. India & the Western Indian Ocean States: Towards Regional Cooperation in Development. 310p. 1981. 27.50x (ISBN 0-940500-85-X, Pub by Allied Pubs India). Asia Bk Corp.

Namboodiri, P. K. & Anand, J. P. Intervention in the Indian Ocean. 361p. 1982. 34.95x (ISBN 0-940500-81-7, Pub by ABC Pub Hse India). Asia Bk Corp.

INDIAN POETRY (AMERICAN INDIAN)

see Indian Poetry

INDIAN POETRY

Naravane, V. S. Sarojini Naidu: An Introduction to Her Life, Work & Poetry. 160p. 1980. 20.00x (ISBN 0-86131-253-8, Pub. by Orient Longman Ltd India). Apt Bks.

INDIANA–DESCRIPTION AND TRAVEL

Jerse, Dorothy W. & Stedman, Judith, eds. On the Banks of the Wabash: A Photograph Album of Greater Terre Haute, 1900-1950. LC 82-47955. (Illus.). 128p. (Orig.). 1983. 20.00x (ISBN 0-253-19035-5); pap. 12.95 (ISBN 0-253-20309-0). Ind U Pr.

INDIANA–HISTORY

Jerse, Dorothy W. & Stedman, Judith, eds. On the Banks of the Wabash: A Photograph Album of Greater Terre Haute, 1900-1950. LC 82-47955. (Illus.). 128p. (Orig.). 1983. 20.00x (ISBN 0-253-19035-5); pap. 12.95 (ISBN 0-253-20309-0). Ind U Pr.

INDIANAPOLIS

Curtis, Donald R., ed. Indianapolis Dining Guide, 1983. (Illus.). 272p. (Orig.). 1982. pap. 6.95 (ISBN 0-9607968-1-9). Indytype.

INDIANAPOLIS SPEEDWAY RACE

Fox, Jack & Hungness, Carl, eds. Indianapolis Five Hundred Yearbook, 1982. 224p. 1982. 16.95 (ISBN 0-915088-32-0); pap. 10.95 (ISBN 0-915088-31-2). C Hungness.

INDIANS–ETHNOLOGY

see Indians of North America

also indians of South America and similar headings

INDIANS–FOLK-LORE

see Folk-Lore, Indian

INDIANS–LITERATURE

see Indian Literature

INDIANS–ORIGIN

Shutler, Richard, Jr., ed. Early Man in the New World. (Illus.). 200p. 1983. 29.95 (ISBN 0-8039-1958-1); pap. 14.95 (ISBN 0-8039-1959-X). Sage.

INDIANS IN ART

see subdivision Pictorial Works under Indians; Indians Of North America and similar headings

INDIANS OF CENTRAL AMERICA

Barreiro, Jose & Wright, Robin M., eds. Native Peoples in Struggle: Russell Tribunal & Other International Forums. LC 82-72533. (Illus.). 166p. 1982. pap. 12.00 (ISBN 0-932978-07-X). Anthropology Res.

Steltzer, Ulli. Health in the Highlands: The Chimaltenango Development Program of Guatemala. LC 82-48872. (Illus.). 128p. 1983. 30.00 (ISBN 0-295-95994-0); pap. 0.00 (ISBN 0-295-96024-8). U of Wash Pr.

INDIANS OF CENTRAL AMERICA–ANTIQUITIES

see also Guatemala–Antiquities

Magee, Susan F. MesoAmerican Archaeology: A Guide to the Literature & Other Information Sources. (Guides & Bibliographics Ser.: No. 12). 81p. 1981. pap. text ed. 5.95x (ISBN 0-292-75053-6). U of Tex Pr.

INDIANS OF CENTRAL AMERICA-ART

Strecker, Matthias. Rock Art of East Mexico & Central America: An Annotated Bibliography. 2nd ed. (Monograph X). 86p. pap. 7.00 (ISBN 0-917956-36-2). UCLA Arch.

INDIANS OF CENTRAL AMERICA-ETHNOLOGY

see Indians of Central America

INDIANS OF CENTRAL AMERICA-FOLK-LORE

see Folk-Lore, Indian

INDIANS OF CENTRAL AMERICA-LANGUAGES

Sherzer, Joel. Kuna Ways of Speaking: An Ethnographic Perspective. (Texas Linguistic Ser.). 288p. 1983. 22.50 (ISBN 0-292-74305-X). U of Tex Pr.

INDIANS OF CENTRAL AMERICA-ORIGIN

see Indians-Origin

INDIANS OF MEXICO

see also Nahuas

Parmenter, Ross. Four Lienzos of the Coixtlahuaca Valley. (Studies in Pre-Columbian Art & Archaeology: No. 26). (Illus.). 88p. 1982. pap. 12.00x (ISBN 0-88402-109-2). Dumbarton Oaks.

Steininger, G. Russell & Van de Velde, Paul. Three Dollars a Year, Being the Story of San Pablo Cuatro Venados, a Typical Zapotecan Indian Village that Hangs on a Slope of the Sierras in Southwestern Mexico: Being the Story of San Pablo Cuatro Venados, a Typical Zapotecan Indian Village that Hangs on a Slope of the Sierras in Southwestern Mexico. LC 71-165660. Repr. of 1935 ed. 12.00 (ISBN 0-87917-016-6). Ethridge.

INDIANS OF MEXICO-ANTIQUITIES

Magee, Susan F. MesoAmerican Archaeology: A Guide to the Literature & Other Information Sources. (Guides & Bibliographics Ser.: No. 12). 81p. 1981. pap. text ed. 5.95x (ISBN 0-292-75053-6). U of Tex Pr.

INDIANS OF MEXICO-ART

The God-Kings of Mexico. (Treasures of the World Ser.). 1982. lib. bdg. 26.60 (ISBN 0-86706-069-7, Pub. by Stonehenge). Silver.

INDIANS OF MEXICO-ETHNOLOGY

see Indians of Mexico

INDIANS OF MEXICO-FOLK-LORE

see Folk-Lore, Indian

INDIANS OF MEXICO-ORIGIN

see Indians-Origin

INDIANS OF MEXICO-RELIGION AND MYTHOLOGY

Taggart, James M. Nahuat Myth & Social Structure. (Texas Pan American Ser.). (Illus.). 272p. 1983. text ed. 25.00x (ISBN 0-292-75524-4). U of Tex Pr.

INDIANS OF NORTH AMERICA

Here are entered works on the Indians of North America in general. For works of specific tribes or groups of tribes see subdivisions-Eastern States,-Northwest, Pacific,-Southwest, New,-Southwest, Old,-The West.

see also Aleuts; Eskimos

Barreiro, Jose & Wright, Robin M., eds. Native Peoples in Struggle: Russell Tribunal & Other International Forums. LC 82-72533. (Illus.). 166p. 1982. pap. 12.00 (ISBN 0-932978-07-X). Anthropology Res.

Brooks, Bearl. American Indians. (Social Studies). 24p. (gr. 4-6). 1977. wkbk. 5.00 (ISBN 0-8209-0239-X, SS-6). ESP.

Chepesiuk, Ronald & Shankman, Arnold, eds. American Indian Archival Material: A Guide to Holdings in the Southeast. LC 82-15447. xiii, 323p. 1982. lib. bdg. 39.95 (ISBN 0-313-23731-X, CAI/). Greenwood.

Gilliland, Hap. Bill Red Coyote is a Nut. (Beginning Reading for All Ages Ser.). 1981. 1.95 (ISBN 0-89992-101-9). MT Coun Indian.

--We Live on an Indian Reservation. (Beginning Reading for All Ages Ser.). 1981. 1.95 (ISBN 0-89992-100-0). MT Coun Indian.

Hooton, Ernest A. Indians of Pecos Pueblo. 1930. text ed. 175.00x (ISBN 0-686-83582-4). Elliots Bks.

Hughes, J. Donald. American Indian Ecology. (Illus.). 200p. 1983. 20.00 (ISBN 0-87404-070-1). Tex Western.

Hulsizer, Allan. The Indian Boy's Day's: The Indian Then & Now-His Presence & Influence on Our Culture. 64p. 1983. 5.50 (ISBN 0-682-49959-5). Exposition.

Johnston, Patricia C. Eastman Johnson's Lake Superior Indians. (Illus., Orig.). 1983. price not set (ISBN 0-942934-30-X); pap. price not set (ISBN 0-942934-29-6). Johnston Pub.

McBeth, Sally J. Ethnic Identity & the Boarding School Experience of West-Central Oklahoma American Indians. LC 82-21983. (Illus.). 184p. (Orig.). 1983. lib. bdg. 21.75 (ISBN 0-8191-2895-3); pap. text ed. 10.00 (ISBN 0-8191-2896-1). U Pr of Amer.

Myres, Sandra L. Native Americans of Texas. Rosenbaum, Robert J., ed. (Texas History Ser.). (Illus.). 45p. 1981. pap. text ed. 1.95x (ISBN 0-89641-083-8). American Pr.

Reece, Colleen. Mark of Our Moccasins. (Indian Culture Ser.). 1982. 2.95 (ISBN 0-686-81747-8). MT Coun Indian.

Swenson, Sally, ed. Native Resource Control & the Multinational Corporate Challenge -- Background Documents. (Illus.). 40p. 1982. pap. 3.50 (ISBN 0-932978-08-8). Anthropology Res.

Tahlequah Indian Writer's Group. Echoes of Our Being. Conley, Robert J., ed. (Illus.). 76p. 1982. pap. 5.00 (ISBN 0-940392-00-3). Indian U Pr.

Taylor, Ralph & Brooks, Bearl. No American Indians. (Social Studies Ser.). 24p. (gr. 4-6). 1979. wkbk. 5.00 (ISBN 0-8209-0240-3, SS-7). ESP.

Wheeler, M. J. First Came the Indians. LC 82-13916. (Illus.). 32p. (gr. 1-5). 1983. 9.95 (ISBN 0-689-50258-3, McElderry Bk). Atheneum.

INDIANS OF NORTH AMERICA-AMUSEMENTS

see Indians of North America-Social Life and Customs

INDIANS OF NORTH AMERICA-ANTIQUITIES

Swanson, James & Kollenborn, Tom. Superstition Mountain: A Ride Through Time. (Illus.). 210p. 1982. Repr. of 1981 ed. 12.95 (ISBN 0-910973-00-8). Arrowhead Pr.

Swigart, Edmund K. The Prehistory of the Indians of Western Connecticut. (Occasional Paper Ser.: No. One). 49p. pap. text ed. write for info. (ISBN 0-936322-02-0). Am Indian Arch.

INDIANS OF NORTH AMERICA-ARMS AND ARMOR

White, Loring. Frontier Patrol: The Army & the Indians in Northeastern California, 1861. (ANCRR Research Paper: No. 2). 28p. 1974. 4.00 (ISBN 0-686-38943-3). Assn NC Records.

INDIANS OF NORTH AMERICA-ART

Halpin, Marjorie M. Totem Poles: An Illustrated Guide. (Illus.). 64p. (Orig.). 1983. pap. 8.95 (ISBN 0-295-96026-4). U of Wash Pr.

Sheehan, Carol. Pipes That Won't Smoke; Coal That Won't Burn: Haida Sculpture in Argillite. (Illus.). 214p. 1982. pap. 19.95 (ISBN 0-686-84107-7, 28739-4). U of Chicago Pr.

Thompson, Robert & Cornet, Joseph. The Four Moments of the Sun. LC 81-14033. (Illus.). pap. 19.95 (ISBN 0-89468-003-X). Natl Gallery Art.

Wade, Edwin L. & Strickland, Rennard. As in a Vision: Masterworks of American Indian Art. LC 82-40456. (Illus.). 144p. (Orig.). 1983. pap. 19.95 (ISBN 0-8061-1841-5). U of Okla Pr.

INDIANS OF NORTH AMERICA-BEADWORK

see Beadwork; Indians of North America-Textile Industry and Fabrics

INDIANS OF NORTH AMERICA-BIOGRAPHY

see also names of individual Indians, e.g. Geronimo

Brooks, Bearl. Famous American Indian Leaders. (Social Studies). 24p. (gr. 4-6). 1979. wkbk. 5.00 (ISBN 0-8209-0243-8, SS-10). ESP.

Canfield, Gae W. Sarah Winnemucca of the Northern Paiutes. LC 82-40448. (Illus.). 336p. 1983. 19.95 (ISBN 0-8061-1814-8). U of Okla Pr.

Little Pigeon, pseud. Children of the Ancient Ones. 1982. pap. 12.00 (ISBN 0-8309-0344-5). Herald Hse.

Wilson, Raymond. Ohiyesa: Charles Eastman, Santee Sioux. LC 82-4937. (Illus.). 1983. 15.95 (ISBN 0-252-00978-9). U of Ill Pr.

INDIANS OF NORTH AMERICA-BLANKETS

see Indians of North America-Textile Industry and Fabrics

INDIANS OF NORTH AMERICA-BOATS

Adney, Edwin T. & Chapelle, Howard I. The Bark Canoes & Skin Boats of North America. 2nd ed. (Illus.). 260p. 1983. Repr. of 1964 ed. text ed. 19.95 (ISBN 0-87474-204-8). Smithsonian.

INDIANS OF NORTH AMERICA-CIVILIZATION

see Indians of North America-Culture

INDIANS OF NORTH AMERICA-CULTURAL ASSIMILATION

Zucker, Jeff & Hummel, Kay. Oregon Indians: Culture, History & Current Affairs; an Atlas & Introduction. (Illus.). 192p. (Orig.). 1983. write for info. (ISBN 0-87595-094-9, Western Imprints); pap. write for info. (ISBN 0-87595-109-0, Western Imprints). Oreg Hist Soc.

INDIANS OF NORTH AMERICA-CULTURE

Here is entered literature dealing with the cultural condition (i.e. arts, industries, religion and mythology, etc.) of the Indian at a given time or period.

Bingham, Sam & Bingham, Janet, eds. Between Sacred Mountains: Stories & Lessons from the Land. 296p. 1982. 30.00 (ISBN 0-910675-00-7); pap. 20.00 (ISBN 0-910675-01-5). Rock Point.

Grinnell, George B. The Fighting Cheyennes. LC 56-10392. (The Civilization of the American Indian Ser.: Vol. 44). (Illus.). 450p. 1983. pap. 14.95 (ISBN 0-8061-1839-3). U of Okla Pr.

Marriott, Alice. The Ten Grandmothers. LC 45-1584. (The Civilization of the American Indians Ser.: Vol. 26). 306p. 1983. pap. 10.95 (ISBN 0-8061-1825-3). U of Okla Pr.

Underhill, Ruth M. The Navajos. LC 59-5996. (The Civilization of the American Indian Ser.: Vol. 43). (Illus.). 288p. 1983. pap. 9.95 (ISBN 0-8061-1816-4). U of Okla Pr.

INDIANS OF NORTH AMERICA-CUSTOMS

see Indians of North America-Social Life and Customs

INDIANS OF NORTH AMERICA-DRAMA

Sears, Priscilla F. A Pillar of Fire to Follow: American Indian Dramas 1808-1859. LC 81-85523. 149p. 1982. 11.95 (ISBN 0-87972-193-6); pap. 5.95 (ISBN 0-87972-194-4). Bowling Green Univ.

INDIANS OF NORTH AMERICA-ECONOMIC CONDITIONS

White, Richard. The Roots of Dependency: Subsistence, Environment, & Social Change among the Choctaws, Pawnees, & Navajos. LC 82-11146. (Illus.). 500p. 1983. 26.50x (ISBN 0-8032-4722-2). U of Nebr Pr.

INDIANS OF NORTH AMERICA-EDUCATION

see also particular schools, e.g. Carlisle, Pennsylvania. United States Indian School

McBeth, Sally J. Ethnic Identity & the Boarding School Experience of West-Central Oklahoma American Indians. LC 82-21983. (Illus.). 184p. (Orig.). 1983. lib. bdg. 21.75 (ISBN 0-8191-2895-3); pap. text ed. 10.00 (ISBN 0-8191-2896-1). U Pr of Amer.

INDIANS OF NORTH AMERICA-ETHNOLOGY

see Indians of North America

INDIANS OF NORTH AMERICA-FICTION, JUVENILE

Wheeler, M. J. First Came the Indians. LC 82-13916. (Illus.). 32p. (gr. 1-5). 1983. 9.95 (ISBN 0-689-50258-3, McElderry Bk). Atheneum.

INDIANS OF NORTH AMERICA-FOLK-LORE

see Folk-Lore, Indian

INDIANS OF NORTH AMERICA-GOVERNMENT RELATIONS

see also Indians of North America-Cultural Assimilation

Bleyhl, Norris A., compiled by. Indian-White Relationships in Northern California 1849-1920 in the Congressional Set of U.S. Public Documents. 109p. 1978. 12.00 (ISBN 0-686-38930-1). Assn NC Records.

--Some Newspaper References Concerning Indian-White Relationships in Northeastern California 1850-1920. 209p. 1979. 9.00 (ISBN 0-686-38929-8). Assn NC Records.

Hecht, Robert A. Occupation of Wounded Knee. Rahmas, Sigurd C., ed. (Events of Our Times Ser.: No. 22). 32p. (Orig.). 1982. 2.95x (ISBN 0-87157-723-2); pap. text ed. 1.95 (ISBN 0-87157-223-0). SamHar Pr.

Keller, Robert H., Jr. American Prostestantism & United States Indian Policy, 1869-82. LC 82-8514. (Illus.). xiv, 354p. 1983. 27.95x (ISBN 0-8032-2706-X). U of Nebr Pr.

Matthiessen, Peter. In the Spirit of Crazy Horse. (Illus.). 704p. 1983. 20.95 (ISBN 0-670-39702-4). Viking Pr.

Rosenstiel, Annette, ed. Red & White: Indian Views of the White Man, 1492-1982. LC 82-23901. (Illus.). 192p. 1983. 14.95 (ISBN 0-87663-373-4). Universe.

Tiller, Veronica E. The Jicarilla Apache Tribe: A History, 1846-1970. LC 82-6973. (Illus.). 265p. 1983. 23.95x (ISBN 0-8032-4409-6). U of Nebr Pr.

INDIANS OF NORTH AMERICA-HISTORY

see also Indians of North America-Wars

American Indian Archaeological Institute, Inc. Ten Thousand Years of Indian Lifeways in Connecticut & Southern New England. 1983. pap. price not set (ISBN 0-936322-01-2). Am Indian Arch.

Bingham, Sam & Bingham, Janet, eds. Between Sacred Mountains: Stories & Lessons from the Land. 296p. 1982. 30.00 (ISBN 0-910675-00-7); pap. 20.00 (ISBN 0-910675-01-5). Rock Point.

Cremony, John C. Life among the Apaches. LC 82-16106. 322p. 1983. pap. 6.50e not set (ISBN 0-8032-6312-0, BB 828, Bison). U of Nebr Pr.

Daniels, Arthur M. A Journal of Sibley's Indian Expedition During the Summer of 1863 & Record of the Troops Employed. (Illus.). 154p. 1980. Repr. 30.00 (ISBN 0-911506-13-6). Thueson.

Danky, James P. & Hady, Maureen B. Native American Press in Wisconsin & the Nation: Proceedings of the Conference on the Native American Press in Wisconsin & the Nation, April 22-23, 1982. LC 82-17634. 197p. 1982. pap. 6.50. U Wis Lib Sch.

Dewing, Rolland. Wounded Knee: The Impact & Signifigance of the Second Incident. 225p. 1983. 18.95x (ISBN 0-8290-1290-7). Irvington.

Floyd, Dale R. Actions With Indians. 1983. pap. 4.95 (ISBN 0-88342-248-4). Old Army.

Gray, John S. Centennial Campaign: The Sioux War of 1876. LC 76-47160. (Source Custeriana Ser.: Vol. 8). (Illus.). 1983. pap. 10.95 (ISBN 0-686-43313-0). Old Army.

Harris-Salomon, Julian. Indians of the Lower Hudson Region: The Munsee. (Illus.). 95p. 1982. 18.95 (ISBN 0-686-38723-6); pap. 14.95 (ISBN 0-89062-134-9). Hist Soc Rockland.

Malakoff, Anna & Powdrrell, Fances D. Minkapee. LC 81-86202. (Illus.). 88p. 1983. 11.95 (ISBN 0-86666-072-0). GWP.

Riley, Carroll L. The Frontier People: The Greater Southwest in the Protohistoric Period. LC 82-50284. (Occasional Paper Ser.: No. 1). Date not set. price not set (ISBN 0-88104-000-2). S Ill U Pr.

Roberts, Helen H. Concow-Maidu Indians of Round Valley. Mill, Dorothy, ed. (ANCRR Occasional Publication Ser.: No. 5). 1980. 6.00 (ISBN 0-686-38939-5). Assn NC Records.

Stallard, Patricia Y. Glittering Misery: Dependents of the Indian Fighting Army. LC 77-94535. (Illus.). 1983. pap. 6.95 (ISBN 0-88342-239-5). Old Army.

Vaughan, Alden T. Narratives of North American Indian Captivity: A Selective Bibliography. LC 82-48771. 100p. 1983. lib. bdg. 18.00 (ISBN 0-8240-9222-8). Garland Pub.

INDIANS OF NORTH AMERICA-HISTORY-SOURCES

Rosenstiel, Annette, ed. Red & White: Indian Views of the White Man, 1492-1982. LC 82-23901. (Illus.). 192p. 1983. 14.95 (ISBN 0-87663-373-4). Universe.

INDIANS OF NORTH AMERICA-JUVENILE LITERATURE

see also Indians of North America-Fiction, Juvenile also Juvenile works, identified by grade key, may be found in other subdivisions

Lyons, Grant. Pacific Coast Indians of North America. (Illus.). 96p. (gr. 4-6). 1983. PLB 8.29 (ISBN 0-671-45801-9). Messner.

Miner, Jane Claypool. Navajo Victory-Being a Native American. Schroeder, Howard, ed. LC 82-1422. (Crisis Ser.). (Illus.). 64p. (gr. 4-5). 1982. lib. bdg. 7.95 (ISBN 0-89686-175-9). Crestwood Hse.

INDIANS OF NORTH AMERICA-LAND TRANSFERS

see also Indians of North America-Government Relations; Indians of North America-Treaties

Kammer, Jerry. The Second Long Walk: The Navajo-Hopi Land Dispute. 1982. pap. 9.95 (ISBN 0-8263-0642-X, S-70P). U of NM Pr.

INDIANS OF NORTH AMERICA-LANGUAGES-DICTIONARIES

Dawson, Ralph E., III & Dawson, Shirley. Cherokee-English Interliner, First Epistle of John of the New Testament. 25p. 1982. pap. 2.50 spiral bdg. (ISBN 0-940392-11-9). Indian U Pr.

INDIANS OF NORTH AMERICA-LEGAL STATUS, LAWS, ETC.

see also Indians of North America-Treaties

Strickland, Bernard F. & Wilkinson, Charles F., eds. Felix S. Cohen's Handbook of Federal Indian Law. 950p. 1982. 80.00 (ISBN 0-87215-413-0). Michie-Bobbs.

INDIANS OF NORTH AMERICA-MEDICINE

see also Medicine-Man

Wilson, Raymond. Ohiyesa: Charles Eastman, Santee Sioux. LC 82-4937. (Illus.). 1983. 15.95 (ISBN 0-252-00978-9). U of Ill Pr.

INDIANS OF NORTH AMERICA-MISSIONS

Barton, Winifred W. John P. Williamson: A Brother to the Sioux. LC 80-53176. (Illus.). 308p. 1980. Repr. of 1919 ed. 16.00 (ISBN 0-9610012-0-8). Sunnycrest Pub.

INDIANS OF NORTH AMERICA-MUSIC

Vennum, Thomas, Jr. The Ojibwa Dance Drum: Its History & Construction. (Folklife Ser.: Vol. 2). (Illus.). 320p. (Orig.). 1983. pap. 12.50x (ISBN 0-87474-941-7). Smithsonian.

INDIANS OF NORTH AMERICA-MYTHOLOGY

see Folk-Lore, Indian; Indians of North America-Religion and Mythology

INDIANS OF NORTH AMERICA-ORIGIN

see Indians-Origin

INDIANS OF NORTH AMERICA-PHILOSOPHY

Highwater, Jamake, ed. The Primal Mind: Vision & Reality in Indian America. 1982. pap. 6.95 (ISBN 0-452-00602-3, Mer). NAL.

INDIANS OF NORTH AMERICA-PICTORIAL WORKS

Masayesva, Victor & Younger, Erin, eds. Hopi Photographers-Hopi Images. (Sun Tracks Ser.). 1983. 25.00 (ISBN 0-8165-0809-7); pap. 14.95 (ISBN 0-8165-0804-6). U of Ariz Pr.

Momaday, N. Scott, intro. by. With Eagle Glance: American Indian Photographic Images, 1868-1931. (Illus.). 63p. 1982. pap. 6.95 (ISBN 0-934490-39-2). Mus Am Ind.

INDIANS OF NORTH AMERICA-PORTRAITS

see Indians of North America-Pictorial Works

INDIANS OF NORTH AMERICA-RELIGION AND MYTHOLOGY

see also Katcinas

Chupco, Lee & Coachman, Ward. Creek (Muscogee) New Testament Concordance. 167p. 1982. pap. 15.00 spiral bdg. (ISBN 0-940392-10-0). Indian U Pr.

Marriott, Alice. The Ten Grandmothers. LC 45-1584. (The Civilization of the American Indians Ser.: Vol. 26). 306p. 1983. pap. 10.95 (ISBN 0-8061-1825-3). U of Okla Pr.

Walker, Deward E., Jr. Myths of Idaho Indians. 1979. 10.95 (ISBN 0-89301-066-9). U Pr of Idaho.

INDIANS OF NORTH AMERICA-RESERVATIONS

Hislop, Donald L. The Nome Lackee Indian Reservation, 1854-1870. (ANCRR Occasional Publication Ser.: No. 4). 99p. 1978. 7.00 (ISBN 0-686-38935-2). Assn NC Records.

INDIANS OF NORTH AMERICA-SCHOOLS

see Indians of North America-Education

INDIANS OF NORTH AMERICA-SOCIAL CONDITIONS

Churchill, Ward, ed. Marxism & Native Americans. 250p. Date not set. 20.00 (ISBN 0-89608-178-8); pap. 7.50 (ISBN 0-89608-177-X). South End Pr.

White, Richard. The Roots of Dependency: Subsistence, Environment, & Social Change among the Choctaws, Pawnees, & Navajos. LC 82-11146. (Illus.). 500p. 1983. 26.50x (ISBN 0-8032-4722-2). U of Nebr Pr.

INDIANS OF NORTH AMERICA-SOCIAL LIFE AND CUSTOMS

American Indian Archaeological Institute, Inc. Ten Thousand Years of Indian Lifeways in Connecticut & Southern New England. 1983. pap. price not set (ISBN 0-936322-01-2). Am Indian Arch.

Bia, Fred & Lynch, R. Nihit Hahoodzoodoo-Diijjidi doo Adaadaa: Our Community-Today & Yesterday, Bk. 1. (Illus.). 98p. 1982. 10.00x (ISBN 0-936008-04-0). Navajo Curr.

Bingham, Sam & Bingham, Janet, eds. Between Sacred Mountains: Stories & Lessons from the Land. 296p. 1982. 30.00 (ISBN 0-910675-00-7); pap. 20.00 (ISBN 0-910675-01-5). Rock Point.

INDIANS OF NORTH AMERICA-SPORTS

see Indians of North America-Social Life and Customs

INDIANS OF NORTH AMERICA-TEXTILE INDUSTRY AND FABRICS

Kent, Kate P. Puelo Indian Textiles: A Living Tradition. (Studies in American Indian Art). (Illus.). 136p. 1983. write for info. (ISBN 0-933452-07-1); pap. write for info. (ISBN 0-933452-08-X). Schol Am Res.

INDIANS OF NORTH AMERICA-TREATIES

see also Indians of North America-Government Relations; Indians of North America-Land Transfers; also names of specific treaties

Richter, Daniel K. Rediscovered Links in the Covenant Chain: Previously Unpublished Transcripts of New York Indian Treaty Minutes, 1677-1691. 40p. 1982. pap. 4.50 (ISBN 0-912296-56-9, Dist. by U Pr of VA). Am Antiquarian.

INDIANS OF NORTH AMERICA-WARS

Bevier, Abraham G. The Indians: Or Narratives of Massacres & Depredations on the Frontier in Wawasink & Its Vicinity During the American Revolution. 1975. pap. 2.95 (ISBN 0-686-82641-8). Lib Res.

Gray, John S. Centennial Campaign: The Sioux War of 1876. LC 76-47160. (Source Custeriana Ser.: Vol. 8). (Illus.). 1983. pap. 10.95 (ISBN 0-686-43313-0). Old Army.

Stallard, Patricia Y. Glittering Misery: Dependents of the Indian Fighting Army. LC 77-94535. (Illus.). 1983. pap. 6.95 (ISBN 0-88342-239-5). Old Army.

INDIANS OF NORTH AMERICA-WARS-1866-1895

Butterworth, F. Edward. Secrets of the Mighty Sioux. 1982. pap. 11.00 (ISBN 0-8309-0352-6). Ind Pr MO.

INDIANS OF NORTH AMERICA-WEAVING

see Indians of North America-Textile Industry and Fabrics

INDIANS OF NORTH AMERICA-WOMEN

Albers, Patricia & Medicine, Beatrice. The Hidden Half: Studies of Plains Indian Women. LC 82-23906. 286p. (Orig.). 1983. lib. bdg. 22.50 (ISBN 0-8191-2956-9); pap. text ed. 11.75 (ISBN 0-8191-2957-7). U Pr of Amer.

Blady, Michael. Children at Risk: Making a Difference Through the Court Appointed Special Advocate Project. (Illus.). 318p. 1982. wkbk 7.50 (ISBN 0-686-84113-1). NCJW.

Green, Rayna. Native American Women: A Contextual Bibliography. LC 82-48571. 160p. 1983. 19.50x (ISBN 0-253-33976-6). Ind U Pr.

Roessel, Ruth. Women in Navajo Society. LC 81-1293. (Illus.). 184p. 1981. 15.00x (ISBN 0-936008-01-6). Navajo Curr.

INDIANS OF NORTH AMERICA-CANADA

Sheehan, Carol. Pipes That Won't Smoke; Coal That Won't Burn: Haida Sculpture in Argillite. (Illus.). 214p. 1982. pap. 19.95 (ISBN 0-686-84107-7, 28739-4). U of Chicago Pr.

INDIANS OF NORTH AMERICA-EASTERN STATES

Francke, Arthur E. Coacoochee, Made from the Sands of Florida: An Account of a Once Free Seminole Chief Presented in Free Verse. LC 82-62492. (Historic Byways of Florida Ser.: Vol. XI). (Illus.). 60p. (Orig.). 1982. pap. 5.95 (ISBN 0-686-38771-6, 32). St Johns Oklawaha.

Russell, Howard S. Indian New England Before the Mayflower. LC 79-63082. (Illus.). 296p. 1983. pap. 11.50 (ISBN 0-87451-255-7). U Pr of New Eng.

Swigart, Edmund K. The Prehistory of the Indians of Western Connecticut. (Occasional Paper Ser.: No. One). 49p. pap. text ed. write for info. (ISBN 0-936322-02-0). Am Indian Arch.

INDIANS OF NORTH AMERICA-SOUTHWEST, NEW

Berry, Michael S. Time: Space & Transition in Anasazi Prehistory. 112p. 1982. 20.00x (ISBN 0-87480-212-1). U of Utah Pr.

Bia, Fred & Lynch, R. Nihit Hahoodzoodoo-Diijjidi doo Adaadaa: Our Community-Today & Yesterday, Bk. 1. (Illus.). 98p. 1982. 10.00x (ISBN 0-936008-04-0). Navajo Curr.

Bingham, Sam & Bingham, Janet, eds. Between Sacred Mountains: Stories & Lessons from the Land. 296p. 1982. 30.00 (ISBN 0-910675-00-7); pap. 20.00 (ISBN 0-910675-01-5). Rock Point.

Cremony, John C. Life among the Apaches. LC 82-16106. 322p. 1983. pap. 6.50e not set (ISBN 0-8032-6312-0, BB 828, Bison). U of Nebr Pr.

Kabotie, Michael, et al, eds. Hopi Voices & Visions. 80p. (Orig.). 1983. pap. 7.50 (ISBN 0-935252-32-0). Street Pr.

LeBlanc, Steven A. The Mimbres People: Ancient Pueblo Painters of the American Southwest. (New Aspects of Antiquity Ser.). (Illus.). 1983. 29.95 (ISBN 0-500-39017-7). Thames Hudson.

Longacre, William A. & Holbrook, Sally J., eds. Multidisciplinary Research at Grasshopper Pueblo, Arizona. (Anthropological Papers: No. 40). 150p. 1982. pap. 12.95x monograph (ISBN 0-8165-0425-3). U of Ariz Pr.

Masayesva, Victor & Younger, Erin, eds. Hopi Photographers-Hopi Images. (Sun Tracks Ser.). 1983. 25.00 (ISBN 0-8165-0809-7); pap. 14.95 (ISBN 0-8165-0804-6). U of Ariz Pr.

Page, Susanne & Page, Jake. Hopi. LC 81-19037. (Illus.). 240p. 1982. 50.00 (ISBN 0-8109-1082-9). Abrams.

Powell, Shirley. Mobility & Adaptation: The Anasazi of Black Mesa, Arizona. (Publications in Archaeology Ser.). 1983. price not set (ISBN 0-8093-1107-0). S Ill U Pr.

Roessel, Ruth. Women in Navajo Society. LC 81-1293. (Illus.). 184p. 1981. 15.00x (ISBN 0-936008-01-6). Navajo Curr.

Sayles, E. B., et al. The Cochise Cultural Sequence in Southeastern Arizona. (Anthropological Papers: No. 42). 1983. pap. 12.95x (ISBN 0-8165-0806-2). U of Ariz Pr.

Southwest: Handbook of North American Indians, Vol. 10. LC 77-17162. (Handbook of North American Indians Ser.). (Illus.). 868p. 1983. 27.50 (ISBN 0-87474-190-4). Smithsonian.

Underhill, Ruth M. The Navajos. LC 59-5996. (The Civilization of the American Indian Ser.: Vol. 43). (Illus.). 288p. 1983. pap. 9.95 (ISBN 0-8061-1816-4). U of Okla Pr.

INDIANS OF NORTH AMERICA-THE WEST

Grinnell, George B. The Fighting Cheyennes. LC 56-10392. (The Civilization of the American Indian Ser.: Vol. 44). (Illus.). 450p. 1983. pap. 14.95 (ISBN 0-8061-1839-3). U of Okla Pr.

Lowie, Robert H. The Crow Indians. (Illus.). xxii, 350p. 1983. pap. 8.95 (ISBN 0-8032-7909-4, BB836, Bison). U of Nebr Pr.

Marriott, Alice. The Ten Grandmothers. LC 45-1584. (The Civilization of the American Indians Ser.: Vol. 26). 306p. 1983. pap. 10.95 (ISBN 0-8061-1825-3). U of Okla Pr.

Mixco, Mauricio J. Kiliwa Texts: "When I Have Donned My Crest of Stars". (Anthropological Papers: No. 107). (Illus.). xvi, 307p. (Orig.). 1983. pap. 20.00x (ISBN 0-87480-219-9). U of Utah Pr.

INDIANS OF NORTH AMERICA-UNITED STATES

see Indians of North America

INDIANS OF NORTH AMERICA, CIVILIZATION OF

see Indians of North America-Cultural Assimilation

INDIANS OF SOUTH AMERICA

Barreiro, Jose & Wright, Robin M., eds. Native Peoples in Struggle: Russell Tribunal & Other International Forums. LC 82-72533. (Illus.). 166p. 1982. pap. 12.00 (ISBN 0-932978-07-X). Anthropology Res.

Hanbury-Tenison, R. Aborigines of the Amazon Rain Forest. (Peoples of the Wild Ser.). 1983. 15.96 (ISBN 0-7054-0707-1, Pub. by Time-Life). Silver.

INDIANS OF SOUTH AMERICA-ETHNOLOGY

see Indians of South America

INDIANS OF SOUTH AMERICA-FOLK-LORE

see Folk-Lore, Indian

INDIANS OF SOUTH AMERICA-JUVENILE LITERATURE

Beck, Barbara L. The Incas. rev. ed. (First Bks.). (Illus.). 72p. (gr. 4 up). 1983. PLB 8.90 (ISBN 0-531-04528-5). Watts.

INDIANS OF SOUTH AMERICA-LEGENDS

see also Folk-Lore, Indian

Urioste, George L., ed. Hijos de Pariya Qaqa: La tradicion oral de Waru Chiri (Mitologia, ritual y costumbres) (Foreign & Comparative Studies Program, Latin American Ser.: No. 6). (Orig.). 1983. pap. write for info. (ISBN 0-915984-97-0). Syracuse U Foreign Comp.

Wilbert, Johannes & Simoneau, Karin, eds. Folk Literature of the Toba Indians. LC 82-620030. (Latin American Studies: No. 54). 1983. text ed. write for info. (ISBN 0-87903-054-2). UCLA Lat Am Ctr.

INDIANS OF SOUTH AMERICA-ORIGIN

see Indians-Origin

INDIANS OF SOUTH AMERICA-RELIGION AND MYTHOLOGY

Chapman, Anne. Drama & Power in a Hunting Society: The Selk'nam of Tierra del Fuego. LC 82-4286. (Illus.). 240p. 1982. 39.50 (ISBN 0-521-23884-6). Cambridge U Pr.

INDIANS OF SOUTH AMERICA-SOCIAL CONDITIONS

Kroeger, Axel & Barbira-Freedman, Francois. Cultural Change & Health: The Case of South American Rainforest Indians. 73p. 1982. write for info. (ISBN 3-8204-6277-5). P Lang Pubs.

INDIANS OF THE UNITED STATES

see Indians of North America

INDIANS OF THE WEST INDIES-ORIGIN

see Indians-Origin

INDIC ARCHITECTURE

see Architecture-India

INDIC ART

see Art, Indic

INDIC DRAMA-HISTORY AND CRITICISM

Vatsyayan, Kapila. Traditional Indian Theatre: Multiple Stream. (Illus.). 230p. 1980. 16.95 (ISBN 0-940500-28-0, Pub. by National Bk India). Asia Bk Corp.

Wade, Bonnie C., ed. Performing Arts in India: Essays on Music, Dance & Drama. LC 82-20141. (Monograph Ser.: No. 21). (Illus.). 270p. 1983. lib. bdg. 21.75 (ISBN 0-8191-2872-4); pap. text ed. 11.00 (ISBN 0-8191-2873-2). U Pr of Amer.

INDIC FICTION

Bald, Suresht R. Novelists & Political Consciousness: Literary Expression of Indian Nationalism, 1919-1947. 1982. 17.50x (ISBN 0-8364-0921-3, Pub. by Chanakya). South Asia Bks.

INDIC LITERATURE-HISTORY AND CRITICISM

Franda, Marcus. Punjabis, War & Women: The Short Stories of Gulzar Singh Sandhu. 1983. 17.00x (ISBN 0-8364-0936-1, Pub. by Heritage India). South Asia Bks.

INDIC MUSIC

see Music, Indic

INDIC PAINTING

see Painting, Indic

INDIC PAINTINGS

see Paintings, Indic

INDIC PERIODICALS

Shaw, Graham W. & Quraishi, Salim, eds. The Bibliography of South Asian Periodicals: A Union List of Periodicals in South Asian Languages. LC 82-16454. 148p. 1983. text ed. 26.50x (ISBN 0-389-20338-6). B&N Imports.

INDIC PHILOSOPHY

see Philosophy, Indic

INDICATING INSTRUMENTS

see Recording Instruments

INDICES

see Indexes

INDIGESTION

see Dyspepsia

INDIGNATION

see Anger

INDIRECT TAXATION

see Taxation

INDIVIDUALISM

see also Communism; Laissez-Faire; Personalism; Self-Interest; Socialism

Evans, Christopher. Understanding Yourself. (Illus.). 160p. 1983. pap. 6.95 (ISBN 0-89104-084-6, A & W Visual Library). A & W Pubs.

INDOCHINA

Here are entered works on the area comprising Laos, Cambodia and Vietnam.

Tahir-Keli. U. S. Strategic Interests in Southwest Asia. 236p. 1982. 27.95 (ISBN 0-03-062043-0). Praeger.

INDOCHINA-POLITICS AND GOVERNMENT

King, Peter, ed. Australia's Vietnam: Australia in the Second Indo-China War. 288p. 1983. text ed. 28.50x (ISBN 0-86861-037-2). Allen Unwin.

INDO-EUROPEAN LANGUAGES

see also Armenian Language; Celtic Languages; Germanic Languages; Greek Language

Baldi, Philip. An Introduction to the Indo-European Languages. 208p. 1983. price not set (ISBN 0-8093-1090-2); pap. price not set (ISBN 0-8093-1091-0). S Ill U Pr.

INDO-EUROPEAN MYTHOLOGY

see Mythology, Indo-European

INDO-GERMANIC LANGUAGES

see Indo-European Languages

INDONESIA

Indonesia: Implementation of a Large-Scale Nonformal Education Project. (Illus.). 208p. (Orig.). 1982. pap. 9.00 (ISBN 0-932288-64-2). Ctr Intl Ed U of MA.

INDONESIA-DESCRIPTION AND TRAVEL

Dalton, Bill. Indonesia Handbook. (Illus.). 492p. Date not set. write for info. Moon Pubns CA.

Indonesia Handbook. 2nd ed. (Illus.). 486p. 1980. 9.95 (ISBN 0-686-43405-6). Bradt Ent.

Smith, Datus C, Jr. The Land & People of Indonesia. Rev. ed. LC 82-48964. (Portraits of the Nations Ser.). (Illus.). 160p. (gr. 4 up). 1983. 10.53i (ISBN 0-397-32048-5, JBL J); PLB 10.89g (ISBN 0-397-32049-3). Har-Row.

INDONESIA-ECONOMIC CONDITIONS

Booth, Anne & McCawley, Peter, eds. The Indonesian Economy During the Soeharto Era. (East Asian Social Science Monographs). (Illus.). 356p. 1981. text ed. 42.00x (ISBN 0-19-580477-5). Oxford U Pr.

Thorburn, Craig. Teknologi Kampungan: A Compendium of Indonesian Indigenous Technologies. Darrow, Ken & Stanley, Bill, eds. (Illus.). 154p. 1982. pap. 5.00 (ISBN 0-917704-16-9). Volunteers Asia.

INDONESIA-FOREIGN RELATIONS

Reinhardt, Jon M. Foreign Policy & National Integration: The Case of Indonesia. (Illus.). 230p. 1971. 8.50 (ISBN 0-686-38048-7). Yale U SE Asia.

INDONESIA-POLITICS AND GOVERNMENT

Anderson, Benedict & Kahin, Audrey, eds. Interpreting Indonesian Politics: Thirteen Contributions to the Debate, 1964-1981. (Interim Report Ser.). 180p. (Orig.). 1982. monograph 9.00 (ISBN 0-87763-028-3). Cornell Mod Indo.

King, Dwight Y. Interest Groups & Political Linkage in Indonesia. (Special Report Ser.: No. 20). 176p. (Orig.). 1982. pap. 12.50 (ISBN 0-686-37563-7, Pub. by U Cal Ctr S&SE Asian Stud). Cellar.

Liddle, R. William, et al, eds. Political Participation in Modern Indonesia. (Illus.). x, 206p. pap. 9.50 (ISBN 0-686-38046-0). Yale U SE Asia.

INDONESIA-SOCIAL CONDITIONS

Smith, Datus C, Jr. The Land & People of Indonesia. Rev. ed. LC 82-48964. (Portraits of the Nations Ser.). (Illus.). 160p. (gr. 4 up). 1983. 10.53i (ISBN 0-397-32048-5, JBL J); PLB 10.89g (ISBN 0-397-32049-3). Har-Row.

INDOOR GAMES

see also Amusements

Home Entertainment in the 1980s. (Reports Ser.: No. 511). 206p. 1982. 985.00 (ISBN 0-686-38952-2). Intl Res Dev.

INDUCTION (LOGIC)

see also Induction (Mathematics)

Goodman, Nelson. Fact, Fiction & Forecast. 4th ed. 176p. 1983. text ed. 10.00x (ISBN 0-674-29070-4); pap. text ed. 4.95x (ISBN 0-674-29071-2). Harvard U Pr.

INDUCTION (MATHEMATICS)

Nicas, Andrew J. Induction Theorems for Groups of Homotopy Manifold Structures. LC 82-11546. (Memoirs of the American Mathematical Society Ser.: No. 267). 6.00 (ISBN 0-8218-2267-5, MEMO/267). Am Math.

INDUCTION HEATING

Davies, E. J. & Simpson, P. G. Induction Heating Handbook. 460p. 1979. 39.95 (ISBN 0-07-084515-8). McGraw.

INDUSTRIAL ACCIDENTS

see also Disability Evaluation; Employers' Liability; Workmen'S Compensation;

also subdivision Accidents, Safety Appliances, and Safety Measures under particular industries or occupations, e.g. Railroads-Accidents

Lagadec, P. Major Technological Risk: An Assessment of Industrial Disasters. (Illus.). 536p. 1982. 60.00 (ISBN 0-08-028913-4). Pergamon.

INDUSTRIAL ACCIDENTS-PREVENTION

see Industrial Safety

INDUSTRIAL ADMINISTRATION

see Industrial Management

INDUSTRIAL ARBITRATION

see Arbitration, Industrial

INDUSTRIAL ARCHAEOLOGY

Here are entered works on the organized study of the physical remains of industries of the 18th and 19th centuries.

Ashmore, Owen. The Industrial Archaeology of North-West England. (Illus.). 272p. Date not set. 25.00 (ISBN 0-7190-0820-4). Manchester.

Trinder, Barrie. The Making of the Industrial Landscape. (Illus.). 288p. 1982. text ed. 24.95x (ISBN 0-460-04427-3, Pub. by J. M. Dent England). Biblio Dist.

INDUSTRIAL ARTS

see also Agriculture; Art Industries and Trade; Artisans; Bookbinding; Engineering; Inventions; Machinery; Machinery in Industry; Manufactures; Mechanical Engineering; Mills and Mill-Work; Patents; Research, Industrial; Technical Education; Technology

also names of specific industries, arts, trades, etc., e.g. Bookbinding; Printing; Ship-building

Scott, William R. & Cunnison, J. Industries of the Clyde Valley During the War. (Economic & Social History of the World War Ser.). 1924. text ed. 49.50x (ISBN 0-686-83583-2). Elliots Bks.

INDUSTRIAL ARTS-EXAMINATIONS, QUESTIONS, ETC.

Rudman, Jack. General Industrial Training Supervisor. (Career Examination Ser.: C-2893). (Cloth bdg. avail. on request). pap. 14.00 (ISBN 0-8373-2893-4). Natl Learning.

--General Mechanic (USPS) (Career Examination Ser.: C-835). (Cloth bdg. avail. on request). pap. 10.00 (ISBN 0-8373-0835-6). Natl Learning.

INDUSTRIAL ARTS-EXHIBITIONS

see Exhibitions

INDUSTRIAL BUYING

see Industrial Procurement

INDUSTRIAL CAPACITY

Kaplan, Carol, ed. Capacity Management Case Studies: Technical Notes. 200p. 1982. Repr. 250.00 (ISBN 0-931900-04-2). Inst Software Eng.

Rao, Ashok. Capacity Management Training Aid. LC 82-72090. 39p. 1982. tchr's. ed 27.00 (ISBN 0-935406-18-2). Am Prod & Inventory.

INDUSTRIAL CHEMISTRY

see Chemical Engineering; Chemistry, Technical

INDUSTRIAL COMMUNICATION

see Communication in Management

INDUSTRIAL COUNSELING

see Employee Counseling

INDUSTRIAL DESIGN

see Design, Industrial

INDUSTRIAL DISCIPLINE

see Labor Discipline

INDUSTRIAL DISEASES
see Occupational Diseases
INDUSTRIAL DISTRICTS
Here are entered works on self-contained industrial areas within which utilities, transportation, and other general services are offered to a group of companies.
Industrial Real Estate: An Annotated Bibliography. 34p. 10.00 (ISBN 0-686-38199-8). Soc Industrial Realtors.
INDUSTRIAL DISTRICTS-WATER SUPPLY
see Water-Supply, Industrial
INDUSTRIAL DRAWING
see Mechanical Drawing
INDUSTRIAL EDUCATION
see Technical Education
INDUSTRIAL ELECTRONICS
see also Electronic Control
Humphries, James T. & Sheets, Leslie P. Industrial Electronics. 1983. text ed. 28.95 (ISBN 0-534-01415-1, Breton). Wadsworth Pub.
INDUSTRIAL ENGINEERING
see also Automation; Engineering Economy; Human Engineering; Industrial Relations; Industrial Statistics; Production Engineering; Psychology, Industrial; Quality Control; Standardization; Systems Engineering
Bennett, S. & Linkens, D. A., eds. Computer Control of Industrial Processes. (IEE Control Engineering Ser.: No. 21). 220p. 1982. pap. 40.00 (ISBN 0-906048-80-X). Inst Elect Eng.
Canadian Government. Winning Low Energy Building Designs. 651p. 1980. text ed. 35.00x (ISBN 0-660-50675-0, Pub. by Inst Engineering Australia). Renouf.
Coates, D. F. Rock Mechanics Principles. 442p. 1981. pap. text ed. 26.40 (ISBN 0-660-10933-6, Pub. by Inst Engineering Australia). Renouf.
Connolly, Terence. Engineers & Organizations. LC 82-22703. (Industrial Engineering Ser.). 384p. 1983. pap. text ed. 18.95 (ISBN 0-534-01409-7). Brooks-Cole.
Filley, Richard D. & Szoka, Kathryn. Communicating with Graphics: A Series from Industrial Engineering. 1982. pap. text ed. 19.50 (ISBN 0-89806-036-2); pap. text ed. 15.00 members. Inst Indus Eng.
Langer, Steven, ed. Compensation of Industrial Engineers. 7th ed. 1982. pap. 75.00 (ISBN 0-916506-75-4). Abbott Langer Assocs.
Nyvlt, Jaroslav. Industrial Crystallisation: The Present State of the Art. 2nd ed. 1983. pap. write for info. (ISBN 0-89573-069-3). Verlag-Chemie.
INDUSTRIAL EQUIPMENT
see also Industrial Archaeology; Industrial Equipment Leases; Office Equipment and Supplies; Replacement of Industrial Equipment
Jane's Airport Equiptment 1982-1983. (Jane's Yearbooks). (Illus.). 400p. 120.00 (ISBN 0-86720-610-1). Sci Bks Intl.
Paruit, Bernard. Illustrated Glossary of Process Equipment. (Illus.). 1983. text ed. 40.00x (ISBN 0-87201-692-7). Gulf Pub.
Rudman, Jack. Assistant Procurement Coordinator. (Career Examination Ser.: C-916). (Cloth bdg. avail. on request). pap. 12.00 (ISBN 0-8373-0916-6). Natl Learning.
--Principal Purchasing Agent. (Career Examination Ser.: C-912). (Cloth bdg. avail. on request). pap. 12.00 (ISBN 0-8373-0912-3). Natl Learning.
Workholding. LC 82-61237. (Productivity Equipment Ser.). 640p. 1982. 44.50 (ISBN 0-87263-090-0). SME.
INDUSTRIAL EQUIPMENT-MAINTENANCE AND REPAIR
see Plant Maintenance
INDUSTRIAL EQUIPMENT LEASES
Ferrara, William L. The Lease Purchase Decision: How Some Companies Make It. 49p. pap. 4.95 (ISBN 0-86641-038-4, 7899). Natl Assn Accts.
Ferrara, William L. & Thies, James B. The Lease-Purchase Decision. 126p. pap. 12.95 (ISBN 0-86641-011-2, 80117). Natl Assn Accts.
INDUSTRIAL ESPIONAGE
see Business Intelligence
INDUSTRIAL ESTATES
see Industrial Districts
INDUSTRIAL EXHIBITIONS
see Exhibitions
INDUSTRIAL HEALTH
see also Factory Laws and Legislation; Industrial Accidents; Occupational Diseases
American Health Research Institute, Ltd. Accidents in Occupations & Industry: A Medical Subject Analysis & Research Index with Bibliography. Bartone, John C., ed. 120p. 1983. 29.95 (ISBN 0-88164-012-3); pap. 21.95 (ISBN 0-88164-013-1). ABBE Pubs Assn.
American Welding Society. Effects of Welding on Health, No. II: Evaluation of the Literature from Jan. 1978 to May 1979. 45p. 1981. 32.00 (ISBN 0-686-43369-6). Am Welding.
Brennan, Andrew, ed. Worksite Health Promotion. 96p. 1982. pap. text ed. 9.95 (ISBN 0-89885-142-4). Human Sci Pr.
Cralley, Lester V. & Cralley, Lewis J., eds. Industrial Hygiene Aspects of Plant Operations, Vol. 1. 774p. 1982. 47.50 (ISBN 0-02-949350-1). Free Pr.
Cuplan, Robert D., et al. Job Demands & Worker Health. 358p. 1980. pap. 17.00x (ISBN 0-87944-265-4). Inst Soc Res.
Egdaul, Richard H. & Walsh, Diana C., eds. Corporate Medical Departments: A Changing Agenda. (Industry & Health Care Ser.: Vol. 1). 272p. 1983. prof ref 35.00x. Ballinger Pub.
Erfurt, John C. & Foote, Andrea. Blood Pressure Control Programs in Industrial Settings. 83p. 1979. pap. 5.00 (ISBN 0-87736-334-X). U of Mich Inst Labor.
Gardner, A. Ward, ed. Current Approaches to Occupational Health, Vol. 2. (Illus.). 414p. 1982. text ed. 37.50 (ISBN 0-7236-0618-8). Wright-PSG.
House, James S. Occupational Stress & the Mental & Physical Health of Factory Workers. 356p. 1980. pap. 16.00x (ISBN 0-87944-254-9). Inst Soc Res.
International Labour Office. Education & Training Policies in Occupational Safety & Health & Ergonomics: International Symposium. (Occupational Safety & Health Ser.: No. 47). viii, 389p. (Orig., Eng., Fr., & Span.). 1982. pap. 19.95 (ISBN 92-2-003002-0). Intl Labour Office.
Lauwerys, Roberts R. Industrial Chemical Exposure: Guidelines for Biological Monitoring. LC 82-70668. (Illus.). 150p. 1983. text ed. 22.50 (ISBN 0-931890-10-1). Biomed Pubns.
Legator & Hollaender. Occupational Monitoring for Genetic Hazards, Vol. 269. 1975. 17.00 (ISBN 0-89072-023-1). NY Acad Sci.
Occupational Safety & Health Library. Date not set. member 180.00 (ISBN 0-686-95622-2); non-member 225.00 (ISBN 0-686-99865-0). Natl Safety Coun.
Safety & Health in the Construction of Fixed Offshore Installations in the Petroleum Industry. 129p. 1981. pap. 11.50 (ISBN 92-2-102900-X, ILO 200, ILO). Unipub.
Safety & Health of Migrant Workers: International Symposium. 337p. 1982. 14.95 (ISBN 92-2-001906-X). Intl Labour Office.
Teresinski, Michael F. & Cheremisinoff, Paul N. Industrial Respiratory Protection. LC 82-72859. (Illus.). 200p. 1983. 27.50 (ISBN 0-250-40587-3). Ann Arbor Science.
INDUSTRIAL HEALTH ENGINEERING
see Industrial Health
INDUSTRIAL LAWS AND LEGISLATION
Here are entered works of a comprehensive character which deal with laws and legislation regulating industry. Works on the theory of state regulation of industry are entered under Industry and State; Laissez-Faire.
see also Factory Laws and Legislation; Labor Laws and Legislation; Trade-Marks; Trade Regulation
Contemporary Legal Environment of Employee Benefit Plans: Answers to the Questions on Subject Matter, CEBS Course 5. 4th ed. 113p. 1982. pap. text ed. 15.00 (ISBN 0-89154-175-6). Intl Found Employ.
Contemporary Legal Environment of Employee Benefit Plans: Learning Guide, CEBS Course 5. 4th ed. 1982. spiral binding 18.00 (ISBN 0-89154-176-4). Intl Found Employ.
INDUSTRIAL LOCATION
see Industries, Location of
INDUSTRIAL MAINTENANCE
see Plant Maintenance
INDUSTRIAL MANAGEMENT
see also Assembly-Line Methods; Big Business; Business; Business Consultants; Business Intelligence; Communication in Management; Controllership; Corporate Planning; Executives; Executives, Training of; Factory Management; Industries, Location of; Industrial Health; Industrial Organization; Industrial Procurement; Industrial Relations; Industrial Sociology; Labor Productivity; Management Audit; Managerial Economics; Marketing; Marketing Management; Materials Management; New Business Enterprises; Office Management; Personnel Management; Production Control; Production Management; Sales Management; Small Business-Management; Technological Innovations; Welfare Work in Industry
Ackoff, R. L. Concept of Corporate Planning. LC 74-100318. 158p. 1969. 19.95 (ISBN 0-471-00290-9, Pub. by Wiley-Interscience). Wiley.
Antoni, Manfred. Arbeit Als Betriebswirtschaftlicher Grundbegriff. vii, 286p. (Ger.). 1982. write for info. (ISBN 3-8204-5798-4). P Lang Pubs.
Asian Regional Team for Employment Promotion, Bangkok. Employment Expansion Through Local Resource Mobilisation: Papers & Poceedings of a Workshop, Comilla, Bangladesh, 1-3 July 1981. iv, 45p. 1981. 5.00 (ISBN 92-2-102696-5). Intl Labour Office.
Bedworth, David D. Industrial Systems: Planning, Analysis, Control. 504p. 1973. 32.95x (ISBN 0-471-06654-0); avail. tchrs. manual (ISBN 0-471-07495-0). Wiley.
Fassnacht, Karl. Unternehmungsplanung und Mitbestimmung Nach Dem Betriebsverfassungsgesetz. 248p. (Ger.). 1982. write for info. (ISBN 3-8204-5846-8). P Lang Pubs.
Gitman, Lawrence J., ed. Business World. McDaniel, Carl. 600p. 1982. 23.95 (ISBN 0-471-08165-5); tchr's. manual avail. (ISBN 0-471-87095-1). Wiley.
Harris, Philip R. New World, New Ways, New Management. 320p. 1983. 22.95 (ISBN 0-8144-5755-X). Am Mgmt.
Jackson, E. B. & Jackson, R. L. Industrial Information Systems: A Manual for Higher Managements & Their Information-Librarian Associates. LC 78-15890. (The Information Sciences Ser.). 314p. 1979. 45.00 (ISBN 0-87933-328-6). Hutchinson Ross.
Labour Management elations in Public Enterprises in Africa. (Labour-Management Ser.: No. 60). 175p. 7.15 (ISBN 92-2-103009-1). Intl Labour Office.
Nunlist, Robert A. & Seibert, Joseph C. Industrial & Consumer Credit Management. 320p. 1983. text ed. 25.95 (ISBN 0-88244-258-9). Grid Pub.
O'Brien, Richard & Dickinson, Alyce M., eds. Industrial Behavior Modification: A Management Handbook. 480p. 35.00 (ISBN 0-686-84781-4). Work in Amer.
Paul, Samuel. Strategic Management of Development Programmes: Guidelines for Action. International Labour Office, ed. (Management Development Ser.: No. 19). vii, 137p. (Orig.). 1982. pap. 10.00 (ISBN 92-2-103252-3). Intl Labour Office.
Schlosstein, Karl-Hans. Die Westfalischen Fabrikengerichtsdeputationen: Vorbilder, Werdegang und Scheitern. 219p. (Ger.). 1982. write for info. (ISBN 3-8204-7111-1). P Lang Pubs.
Supply Management. 163p. 1981. 20.00 (ISBN 92-2-102365-6). Intl Labour Office.
White, Lawrence J. Corporate Governance in the 1980s: New Roles & Images for Directors & Executives. (Seven Springs Studies). 1981. pap. 3.00 (ISBN 0-943006-04-X). Seven Springs.
INDUSTRIAL MANAGEMENT-CASE STUDIES
Lawrence, Paul R. & Dyer, Davis. Renewing American Industry. LC 82-72096. 400p. 1983. 25.00 (ISBN 0-02-918170-4). Free Pr.
INDUSTRIAL MANAGEMENT-GREAT BRITAIN
Marsh, Arthur. Employee Relations Policy & Decision Making. 248p. 1982. text ed. 41.50x (ISBN 0-566-00540-9). Gower Pub Ltd.
INDUSTRIAL MANAGEMENT-RUSSIA
Guroff, Gregory & Carstensen, Fred V. Entrepreneurship in Imperial Russia & the Soviet Union. LC 82-15056. 384p. 1983. 40.00x (ISBN 0-691-05376-6); pap. 12.95 (ISBN 0-691-10141-8). Princeton U Pr.
INDUSTRIAL MATERIALS
see Materials
INDUSTRIAL MEDICINE
see Medicine, Industrial
INDUSTRIAL MOBILIZATION
see also Military Supplies; Munitions
Leitenberg, Milton & Ball, Nicole, eds. The Structure of the Defense Industry: An International Survey. LC 82-42565. 1982. 27.50x (ISBN 0-312-76757-9). St Martin.
Scott, William R. & Cunnison, J. Industries of the Clyde Valley During the War. (Economic & Social History of the World War Ser.). 1924. text ed. 49.50x (ISBN 0-686-83583-2). Elliots Bks.
INDUSTRIAL NOISE
Miller, Richard. Noise Control Solutions for the Stone Industry. (Illus.). 90p. pap. text ed. 45.00 (ISBN 0-89671-028-9). Southeast Acoustics.
Miller, Richard K. Industrial Noise Update. (Illus.). 87p. 1981. pap. text ed. 30.00 (ISBN 0-89671-025-4). Southeast Acoustics.
--Noise Control for Construction. (Illus.). 140p. text ed. 55.00 (ISBN 0-89671-023-8). Southeast Acoustics.
--Noise Control Solutions for Printing & Publishing. (Illus.). 77p. 1981. pap. text ed. 45.00 (ISBN 0-89671-026-2). Southeast Acoustics.
--Noise Control Solutions for the Food Industry. (Illus.). 110p. text ed. 45.00 (ISBN 0-89671-034-3). Southeast Acoustics.
--Noise Control Solutions for the Food Industry, Vol. II. (Illus.). 120p. 1981. pap. text ed. 45.00 (ISBN 0-89671-024-6). Southeast Acoustics.
--Noise Control Solutions for the Footwear Industry. 90p. pap. text ed. 45.00 (ISBN 0-89671-027-0). Southeast Acoustics.
--Noise Control Solutions for the Glass Industry. 120p. pap. text ed. 90.00 (ISBN 0-89671-016-5). Southeast Acoustics.
--Noise Control Solutions for the Metal Products Industry. (Illus.). 120p. text ed. 45.00 (ISBN 0-89671-031-9). Southeast Acoustics.
--Noise Control Solutions for the Metal Products Industry, Vol. II. (Illus.). 120p. pap. text ed. 45.00 (ISBN 0-89671-021-1). Southeast Acoustics.
--Noise Control Solutions for the Paper Industry. (Illus.). 80p. text ed. 45.00 (ISBN 0-89671-033-5). Southeast Acoustics.
--Noise Control Solutions for the Textile Industry. (Illus.). 90p. text ed. 45.00 (ISBN 0-89671-035-1). Southeast Acoustics.
--Noise Control Solutions for the Wood Products Industry. 80p. text ed. 45.00 (ISBN 0-89671-032-7). Southeast Acoustics.
--Power Plant Noise Control. (Illus.). 130p. pap. text ed. 65.00 (ISBN 0-89671-019-X). Southeast Acoustics.
INDUSTRIAL ORGANIZATION
see also Industrial Management; Industrial Sociology
Craven, John V. Industrial Organization, Anti-Trust & Public Policy. (Middlebury College Conference Series in Economic Issues). 1982. lib. bdg. 25.00 (ISBN 0-89838-103-7). Kluwer-Nijhoff.
Lenz, Martin. Aussensteurrecht und Organisationsstruktur. 502p. (Ger.). 1982. write for info. (ISBN 3-8204-5829-8). P Lang Pubs.
Stigler, George. The Organization of Industry. LC 82-20013. viii, 328p. 1968. pap. 10.95 (ISBN 0-226-77432-5). U of Chicago Pr.
INDUSTRIAL PAINTING
see Painting, Industrial
INDUSTRIAL PARKS
see Industrial Districts
INDUSTRIAL PLANTS
see Factories
INDUSTRIAL PROCESS CONTROL
see Process Control
INDUSTRIAL PROCESSING
see Manufacturing Processes
INDUSTRIAL PROCUREMENT
Gambino, Anthony J. The Make-or-Buy Decision. 128p. pap. 12.95 (ISBN 0-86641-000-7, 80120). Natl Assn Accts.
Moriarty, Rowland T. Industrial Buying Behavior: Concepts, Issues, & Applications. 208p. 1982. 28.95x (ISBN 0-669-06212-X). Lexington Bks.
Rudman, Jack. Procurement Clerk. (Career Examination Ser.: C-2623). (Cloth bdg. avail. on request). pap. 8.00 (ISBN 0-8373-2623-0). Natl Learning.
--Purchasing Technician. (Career Examination Ser.: C-913). (Cloth bdg. avail. on request). pap. 10.00 (ISBN 0-8373-0913-1). Natl Learning.
INDUSTRIAL PRODUCTION
see Industry; Supply and Demand
INDUSTRIAL PROJECT MANAGEMENT
see also Network Analysis (Planning)
Cleland, D. I. & King, W. R. Systems Analysis & Project Management. 3rd ed. 512p. 1983. 24.95 (ISBN 0-07-011311-4). McGraw.
INDUSTRIAL PROPERTY
see also Trade-Marks
Angell, Joseph K. A Treatise on the Right of Property in Tide Waters & in the Soil & Shores Thereof. 1983. Repr. of 1826 ed. lib. bdg. 37.50x (ISBN 0-8377-0214-3). Rothman.
INDUSTRIAL PSYCHOLOGY
see Psychology, Industrial
INDUSTRIAL PURCHASING
see Industrial Procurement
INDUSTRIAL RELATIONS
see also Arbitration, Industrial; Collective Bargaining; Employee Counseling; Employees' Magazines, Handbooks, etc.; Employees' Representation in Management; Grievance Procedures; Industrial Sociology; Labor Contract; Labor Laws and Legislation; Personnel Management; Strikes and Lockouts; Trade-Unions
also local subdivisions of countries other than United States, and names of cities, e.g. Industrial Relations-India; Industrial Relations-New York (City)
Action Taken on the Resolution Adopted by the International Labour Conference at its 59th to 64th Sessions. 63p. 1979. 7.15 (ISBN 92-2-101952-7). Intl Labour Office.
Allen, Robert E. & Keaveny, Timothy J. Contemporary Labor Relations. 672p. 1983. text ed. 24.95 (ISBN 0-686-82182-3). A-W.
Blanpain, Roger, ed. Comparative Labour Law & Industrial Relations. 416p. 1983. text ed. 30.00 (ISBN 0-87179-396-2). BNA.
Bloch, Richard I. & Zack, Arnold. The Labor Agreement in Negotiation & Arbitration. 200p. 1983. text ed. 20.00 (ISBN 0-87179-398-9). BNA.
Bowey, Angela M., ed. Handbook of Salary & Wage Systems. 2nd ed. 446p. 1982. text ed. 47.50 (ISBN 0-566-02261-3). Gower Pub Ltd.
Cox & Johnston. Conflict, Politics & the Urban Scene. LC 81-16620. 288p. 1983. 25.00x (ISBN 0-312-16233-2). St Martin.
Gaswirth, Marc, et al. Teachers' Strikes in New Jersey. LC 81-23489. (Studies in Industrial Relations & Human Resources Ser.: No. 1). 179p. 1982. pap. 10.00 (ISBN 0-8108-1569-9). Scarecrow.
Getman, Julius G. & Blackburn, John D. Labor Relations: Law, Practice & Policy. 2nd ed. LC 82-21042. 749p. 1982. text ed. write for info. (ISBN 0-88277-102-7). Foundation Pr.
Justice, Betty W. Unions, Workers, & the Law. (George Meany Center for Labor Studies Ser.: No. 2). 280p. 1983. text ed. 17.50 (ISBN 0-87179-393-8); pap. text ed. 12.50 (ISBN 0-87179-400-4). BNA.

Labor Law Group, ed. Labor Relations & Social Problems: A Course Book. Incl. Unit 1: Collective Bargaining in Private Employment. Atleson, James B., et al, eds. 820p. with 1982 Suppl. 24.00 (ISBN 0-87179-281-8); Unit 2: Legislation Protecting the Individual Employee. Covington, Robert N. & Goldman, Alvin L., eds. 814p. 1982. 22.50 (ISBN 0-87179-377-6); Unit 3: Discrimination in Employment. 4th ed. Getman, Julius, et al, eds. 870p. 1979. with 1982 Suppl. 24.00 (ISBN 0-87179-397-0); Unit 4: Collective Bargaining in Public Employment. 3rd ed. Grodin, Joseph R., et al, eds. 430p. 1979. 15.00 (ISBN 0-87179-310-5); Unit 5: Cases & Materials on Negotiation. 2nd ed. 280p. 1980. 12.00 (ISBN 0-87179-335-0); Unit 6: Arbitration & Conflict Resolution. Teple, Edwin R. & Moberly, Robert B., eds. 614p. 1979. 20.00 (ISBN 0-87179-308-3); Unit Reference Supplement. 5th ed. Aaron, Benjamin, ed. 210p. 1981. 6.00 (ISBN 0-87179-345-8); Unit R-2: Reference Supplement -- Discrimination in Employment. Jones, James E., Jr., ed. 304p. 1979. 6.00 (ISBN 0-87179-311-3). BNA.

Marchington, M. Managing Industrial Relations. 208p. 1982. 19.00 (ISBN 0-07-084580-8). McGraw.

Mario, D. Adapting Working Hours to Modern Needs: The Time Factor in the New Approach to Working Conditions. viii, 50p. 1980. 14.95 (ISBN 92-2-101659-5); pap. 8.55 (ISBN 92-2-101658-7). Intl Labour Office.

Pearlman, Kenneth & Schmidt, Frank L. Contemporary Problems in Personnel. 3rd ed. 400p. 1983. text ed. 18.95 (ISBN 0-471-87376-4). Wiley.

Simmons, John & Mares, William J. Working Together. LC 82-47826. (Illus.). 320p. 1983. 15.00 (ISBN 0-394-51343-6). Knopf.

Tawney. American Labor Movement. 1980. 26.00 (ISBN 0-312-02503-3). St Martin.

Torrington, Derek & Hitner, Trevor. Management & the Multi-Racial Work Force. 117p. 1982. text ed. 34.00x (ISBN 0-566-00585-9). Gower Pub Ltd.

Wallerstein, Immanuel, ed. Labor in the World Social Structure. (Explorations in the World Economy Ser.: Vol. 2). (Illus.). 272p. 1983. 25.00 (ISBN 0-8039-1922-0). Sage.

Witte, John F. Democracy, Authority, & Alienation in Work: Worker's Participation in an American Corporation. LC 80-16241. 216p. 1982. pap. 5.95 (ISBN 0-226-90421-0). U of Chicago Pr.

Yudelman, David. The Emergence of Modern South Africa: State, Capital, & the Incorporation of Organized Labor on the South African Gold Fields, 1902-1939. LC 82-9375. (Contributions in Comparative Colonial Studies: No. 13). (Illus.). 288p. 1983. lib. bdg. 35.00 (ISBN 0-313-23170-2, YMS/). Greenwood.

INDUSTRIAL RELATIONS–AFRICA

Labour Management elations in Public Enterprises in Africa. (Labour-Management Ser.: No. 60). 175p. 7.15 (ISBN 92-2-103009-1). Intl Labour Office.

Yudelman, David. The Emergence of Modern South Africa: State, Capital, & the Incorporation of Organized Labor on the South African Gold Fields, 1902-1939. LC 82-9375. (Contributions in Comparative Colonial Studies: No. 13). (Illus.). 288p. 1983. lib. bdg. 35.00 (ISBN 0-313-23170-2, YMS/). Greenwood.

INDUSTRIAL RELATIONS–ASIA

An Account of an Asian Bipartite Study Tour on Labour-Management Relations to the United Kingdom & Federal Republic of Germany: 6 September- 8 November 1958. (Labour-Management Relations Ser.: No. 6). 205p. 8.55 (ISBN 0-686-84658-3). Intl Labour Office.

International Labour Office. Labour Relations & Development: Country Studies on Japan, the Philippines, Singapore & Sri Lanka. (Labour Management Relations Ser.). 153p. 1982. pap. 11.40 (ISBN 92-2-102964-6). Intl Labour Office.

Seventh Asian Regional Conference, Teheran, 1971. Agenda for Asia: The Social Perplexities of the Second Development Decade. 48p. 1971. write for info. (ISBN 92-2-100103-2). Intl Labour Office.

INDUSTRIAL RELATIONS–AUSTRALIA

Hill, John. From Subservience to Strike: Industrial Relations in the Banking Industry. LC 82-2684. (Illus.). 296p. 1983. text ed. 32.50x (ISBN 0-7022-1830-8). U of Queensland Pr.

INDUSTRIAL RELATIONS–GERMANY

Maitland, Ian. The Causes of Industrial Disorder: A Comparison of a British & a German Factory. (Routledge Direct Edition Ser.). 192p. 1983. pap. 12.95 (ISBN 0-7100-9207-5). Routledge & Kegan.

INDUSTRIAL RELATIONS–GREAT BRITAIN

Bowers, John & Deaton, David. Labour Hoarding in British Industry. (Warwick Studies in Industrial Relations). (Illus.). 176p. 1982. text ed. 29.50x (ISBN 0-631-13128-0, Pub. by Basil Blackwell England). Biblio Dist.

Maitland, Ian. The Causes of Industrial Disorder: A Comparison of a British & a German Factory. (Routledge Direct Edition Ser.). 192p. 1983. pap. 12.95 (ISBN 0-7100-9207-5). Routledge & Kegan.

Marsh, Arthur. Employee Relations Policy & Decision Making. 248p. 1982. text ed. 41.50x (ISBN 0-566-00540-9). Gower Pub Ltd.

INDUSTRIAL RELATIONS–JAPAN

Ozawa, Terutomo. People & Productivity in Japan. (Work in America Institute Studies in Productivity). 1982. 35.00 (ISBN 0-08-029506-1). Pergamon.

INDUSTRIAL RELATIONS–LATIN AMERICA

Nash, June. We Eat the Mines & the Mines Eat Us: Dependence & Exploitation in Bolivian Tin Mines. 363p. 1982. pap. 13.00 (ISBN 0-231-04711-8). Columbia U Pr.

Vivo, G. Hugo. El Crecimiento de las Empresas en los Estados Unidos y en la America Latina: Un Estudio Comparativo. LC 81-70693. 121p. (Orig., Span.). 1982. pap. 9.95 (ISBN 0-89729-306-1). Ediciones.

INDUSTRIAL RESEARCH

see Research, Industrial

INDUSTRIAL REVOLUTION

see Industry–History

INDUSTRIAL SAFETY

see also Factory Laws and Legislation; Industrial Accidents

also subdivisions Safety Appliances and Safety Measures under subjects, e.g. Factories–Safety Appliances

Beaumont, P. B. Safety at Work & the Unions. 208p. 1983. text ed. 25.25x (ISBN 0-7099-0097-X, Pub. by Croom Helm Ltd England). Biblio Dist.

Deterrence & Compensation: Legal Liability in Occupational Safety & Health. 76p. 1982. pap. 10.00 (ISBN 92-2-103010-5, ILO 194, ILO). Unipub.

Institute of Petroleum. Model Code of Safe Practices for the Petroleum Industry: The Petroleum Pipeline, Pt. 6. 1982. write for info. (ISBN 0-471-26139-4, Pub. by Wiley Interscience). Wiley.

International Labour Office. Education & Training Policies in Occupational Safety & Health & Ergonomics: International Symposium. (Occupational Safety & Health Ser.: No. 47). viii, 389p. (Orig., Eng., Fr., & Span.). 1982. pap. 19.95 (ISBN 92-2-003002-0). Intl Labour Office.

--Sixth International Report on the Prevention & Suppression of Dust in Mining, Tunnelling, & Quarrying, 1973-1977. International Labour Office, ed. (Occupational Safety & Health Ser.: No. 48). viii, 152p. 1982. pap. 10.00 (ISBN 92-2-103006-7). Intl Labour Office.

Levy, Barry S. & Wegman, David H., eds. Occupational Health: Recognizing & Preventing Work-Related Diseases. 1982. pap. text ed. 19.95 (ISBN 0-316-52234-1). Little.

Occupational Safety & Health Library. Date not set. member 180.00 (ISBN 0-686-95622-2); non-member 225.00 (ISBN 0-686-99865-0). Natl Safety Coun.

Rom, William N., ed. Environmental & Occupational Medicine. 1982. text ed. 68.50 (ISBN 0-316-75560-5). Little.

Rudman, Jack. Principal Safety Coordinator. (Career Examination Ser.: C-2669). (Cloth bdg. avail. on request). pap. 12.00 (ISBN 0-8373-2669-9). Natl Learning.

--Safety Consultant. (Career Examination Ser.: C-2540). (Cloth bdg. avail. on request). pap. 10.00 (ISBN 0-8373-2640-0). Natl Learning.

Safety & Health in the Construction of Fixed Offshore Installations in the Petroleum Industry. 129p. 1981. pap. 11.50 (ISBN 92-2-102900-X, ILO 200, ILO). Unipub.

Safety & Health of Migrant Workers: International Symposium. 337p. 1982. 14.95 (ISBN 92-2-001906-X). Intl Labour Office.

Teaching Occupational Health & Safety at the Secondary & College Level. 144p. 10.95 (ISBN 0-88314-187-6). AAHPERD.

Viscusi, W. Kip. Risk by Choice: Regulating Health & Safety in the Workplace. (Illus.). 216p. 1983. text ed. 18.50x (ISBN 0-674-77302-0). Harvard U Pr.

INDUSTRIAL SALVAGE

see Salvage (Waste, etc.)

INDUSTRIAL SECURITY MEASURES

see Industry-Security Measures

INDUSTRIAL SITES

see also Industrial Districts

Brown, Walter C. Blueprint Reading for Industry. Rev. ed. LC 82-20949. 345p. 1983. spiral bdg. 14.00 (ISBN 0-87006-429-0). Goodheart.

INDUSTRIAL SOCIOLOGY

Here are entered works on social relations within industry, as distinguished from labor-management relations. Works about the impact of industry on culture and social changes, and works about the social responsibilities of businessmen are entered under Industry-Social Aspects.

see also Industrial Organization; Industry–Social Aspects

Benjamin, Roger. The Limits of Politics: Collective Goods & Political Change in Post-Industrial Societies. LC 79-19473. 148p. 1982. pap. text ed. 5.00x (ISBN 0-226-04234-0). U of Chicago Pr.

DeBrizzi, John A. Ideology & the Rise of Labor Theory in America. LC 82-12024. (Contributions in Labor History Ser.: No. 14). 224p. 1983. lib. bdg. 29.95 (ISBN 0-313-23614-3, DID/). Greenwood.

Epstein, Marc J. & Flamholtz, Eric G. Corporate Social Performance: The Measurement of Product & Service Contributions. 133p. pap. 12.95 (ISBN 0-86641-050-3, 7792). Natl Assn Accts.

Hirszowicz, Maria. Industrial Sociology. 280p. 1982. 27.50x (ISBN 0-312-41559-1). St Martin.

INDUSTRIAL STATISTICS

see also subdivision Industries under names of countries, cities, etc

Handbook of Industrial Statistics. 22.00 (ISBN 0-686-43223-1, E.82.II.B.2). UN.

United Nations. Yearbook of Industrial Statistics 1980. 14th ed. Incl. Vol. I. General Industrial Statistics. 613p. 45.00x (ISBN 0-8002-1142-1); Vol. II. Commodity Production Data, 1971-1980. 750p. 45.00x (ISBN 0-8002-1143-X). LC 76-646970. (Illus.). 1982. Intl Pubns Serv.

Yearbook of Industrial Statistics 1980, 2 vols. Incl. Vol. 1, General Industrial Statistics. 612p; Vol. 2, Commodity Production Data 1971-80. 750p. 1983. pap. 45.00 set (ISBN 0-686-43290-8, UN 82/17/11, UN). Unipub.

INDUSTRIAL TECHNICIANS

see Technicians in Industry

INDUSTRIAL UNIONS

see Trade-Unions

INDUSTRIAL VACUUM

see Vacuum Technology

INDUSTRIAL WASTES

see Factory and Trade Waste

INDUSTRIAL WATER SUPPLY

see Water-Supply, Industrial

INDUSTRIAL WELFARE WORK

see Welfare Work in Industry

INDUSTRIALIZATION

see also Technical Assistance; Underdeveloped Areas

Agro-Industrialization of Urban-Based Small Industries. 76p. 1982. pap. 5.00 (ISBN 92-808-0092-2, TUNU 205, UNU). Unipub.

Business Week Team. The Reindustrialization of America. 1983. pap. 5.95 (ISBN 0-671-45617-2). WSP.

Kemp, Tom. Industrialisation of the Non Western World. 206p. (Orig.). 1983. pap. text ed. 11.95 (ISBN 0-582-49234-3). Longman.

INDUSTRIES

see Industrial Arts; Industrial Mobilization; Industry; also subdivision Industries under names of countries, etc. e.g. United States–Industries; names of particular industries

INDUSTRIES, CHEMICAL

see Chemical Industries

INDUSTRIES, HOME

see Home Labor

INDUSTRIES, LOCATION OF

see also Store Location

Kundell, James E. & White, Fred C. Prime Farmland in Georgia. 49p. 1982. pap. 6.50 (ISBN 0-89854-081-X). U of GA Inst Govt.

Townroe, Peter M. Location Factors for Industry Decentralizing from Metropolitan Sao Paulo, Brazil. LC 82-8664. (World Bank Staff Working Papers: No. 517). (Orig.). 1982. pap. write for info. (ISBN 0-8213-0005-9). World Bank.

INDUSTRIES, SERVICE

see Service Industries

INDUSTRY

see also Big Business; Businessmen; Employees' Representation in Management; Entrepreneur; Industrial Capacity; Industrial Equipment; Industrial Management; Industrial Organization; Industrial Relations; Industrialization; Interindustry Economics; Machinery in Industry; New Business Enterprises; Research, Industrial; Small Business; Water-Supply, Industrial

Joglekar, Rajani & Clerman, Robert J. Biotechnology in Industry: Selected Applications & Unit Operations. LC 82-48642. (Illus.). 200p. 1983. 27.50 (ISBN 0-250-40605-5). Ann Arbor Science.

Ouellette, Robert P. & Thomas, L. W. Automation Impacts on Industry. LC 82-48646. (Illus.). 200p. 1983. 27.50 (ISBN 0-250-40609-8). Ann Arbor Science.

Roman, Zoltan. Productivity & Economic Growth. Lukacs, Laszlo, tr. from Hungarian. LC 82-173070. (Illus.). 276p. 1982. 30.00x (ISBN 963-05-2786-3). Intl Pubns Serv.

Scott, William R. & Cunnison, J. Industries of the Clyde Valley During the War. (Economic & Social History of the World War Ser.). 1924. text ed. 49.50x (ISBN 0-686-83583-2). Elliots Bks.

Stigler, George. The Organization of Industry. LC 82-20013. viii, 328p. 1968. pap. 10.95 (ISBN 0-226-77432-5). U of Chicago Pr.

INDUSTRY–HISTORY

see also Commerce–History; Home Labor; Machinery in Industry

Toynbee, Arnold. Lectures on the Industrial Revolution of the Eighteenth Century in England: Popular Addresses, Notes & Other Fragments. 282p. 1982. Repr. of 1908 ed. lib. bdg. 40.00 (ISBN 0-89984-470-7). Century Bookbindery.

INDUSTRY–ORGANIZATION

see Industrial Organization

INDUSTRY–PERIODICALS–INDEXES

Sicignano, Robert & Prichard, Doris. Special Issues Index: Specialized Contents of Business, Industrial, & Consumer Journals. LC 82-11725. 315p. 1982. lib. bdg. 35.00 (ISBN 0-313-23278-4, SII/). Greenwood.

INDUSTRY–SECURITY MEASURES

Hughes, Denis & Bowler, Peter. The Security Survey. 154p. 1982. text ed. 34.25x (ISBN 0-566-02291-5). Gower Pub Ltd.

INDUSTRY–SOCIAL ASPECTS

Here are entered works about the impact of industry on culture and societal changes, and works about the social responsibilities of businessmen. Works on social relations within industry, as distinguished from labor-management relations, are entered under Industrial Sociology.

see also Industrial Sociology

Barwise, Jon & Perry, John. Situations & Attitudes. 256p. 1983. 17.50x (ISBN 0-262-02189-7). MIT Pr.

Cassedy & Nussbaum. Nine to Five Survival Guide. 1983. pap. 5.95 (ISBN 0-14-006751-5). Penguin.

Hysom, John L. Business & Its Environment. Bolce, William J., ed. (Illus.). 450p. 1982. text ed. 19.95 (ISBN 0-314-63259-X); tchrs.' manual avail. (ISBN 0-314-63260-3). West Pub.

Johnson. The Social Evolution of Industrial Britain. 188p. 1982. 49.00x (ISBN 0-85323-073-0, Pub. by Liverpool Univ England). State Mutual Bk.

Magaziner, Ira C. & Reich, Robert B. Minding America's Business: The Decline & Rise of the American Economy. LC 81-13663. (Illus.). 400p. 1983. pap. 5.95 (ISBN 0-394-71538-1, Vin). Random.

INDUSTRY–STATISTICS

see Industrial Statistics

INDUSTRY (PSYCHOLOGY)

see Work

INDUSTRY AND STATE

Here are entered works on the relation of Industry and State in general as well as those concerned with the United States. For works on Industry and State in other countries, see local subdivisions below.

see also Agriculture and State; Commercial Policy; Economic Policy; Full Employment Policies; Government Business Enterprises; Government Ownership; Industrial Laws and Legislation; Labor Laws and Legislation; Laissez-Faire; Price Regulation; Public Interest; Subsidies; Trade Regulation; Transportation and State

also specific industries or commercial products

Brozen, Yale. Concentration, Mergers & Public Policy. (Illus.). 496p. 1982. text ed. 29.95 (ISBN 0-02-904270-4). Free Pr.

Hysom, John L. Business & Its Environment. Bolce, William J., ed. (Illus.). 450p. 1982. text ed. 19.95 (ISBN 0-314-63259-X); tchrs.' manual avail. (ISBN 0-314-63260-3). West Pub.

Macavoy, Paul W., ed. Unsettled Questions on Regulatory Reform. 1978. pap. 3.25 (ISBN 0-8447-3328-8). Am Enterprise.

Machan, Tibor R. & Johnson, M. Bruce. Regulation & Deregulation: Economic Policy & Justice. (Pacific Institute). 1983. price not set prof ref (ISBN 0-88410-928-3). Ballinger Pub.

Wachter, Michael L. & Wachter, Susan M. Toward a New U. S. Industrial Policy? LC 81-16060. 536p. 1983. pap. 12.95x (ISBN 0-8122-1142-1). U of Pa Pr.

INDUSTRY AND STATE–EUROPE

Franzmeyer, Fritz. Approaches to Industrial Policy Within the EC & Its Impact on European Integration. 167p. 1982. text ed. 40.00x (ISBN 0-566-00358-9). Gower Pub Ltd.

INDUSTRY AND STATE–GREAT BRITAIN

Utton, M. A. The Political Economy of Big Business. LC 82-10739. 272p. 1982. 32.50x (ISBN 0-312-62255-4). St Martin.

INDUSTRY AND WAR

see War–Economic Aspects

INEBRIATES

see Alcoholics

INEBRIETY

see Alcoholism

INEFFICIENCY, INTELLECTUAL

see also Intelligence Tests; Mentally Handicapped Children

Heron, Alastair & Myers, Mary, eds. Intellectual Impairment. Date not set. price not set (ISBN 0-12-342680-4). Acad Pr.

INEQUALITY

see Equality

INFALLIBILITY OF THE CHURCH

see Catholic Church–Infallibility

INFALLIBILITY OF THE POPE

see Popes–Infallibility

INFANCY OF ANIMALS

see Animals, Infancy of.

INFANT EDUCATION

see Education, Preschool

INFANT MORTALITY

see Infants–Mortality

INFANT PSYCHOLOGY

Hanson, Marci J., ed. Atypical Infant Development. (Illus.). 1983. pap. text ed. price not set (ISBN 0-8391-1788-4, 18414). Univ Park.

Lichtenberg, Joseph D. Psychoanalysis & Infant Research. 176p. 1983. text ed. price not set (ISBN 0-88163-002-0). L Erlbaum Assocs.

Lipsitt, Lewis P., ed. Developmental Psychobiology: The Significance of Infancy. LC 76-14775. 160p. 1976. text ed. 14.95 (ISBN 0-89859-134-1). L Erlbaum Assocs.

McClowry, Dan P., et al, eds. Infant Communication: Development Assessment & Intervention. Date not set. price not set (ISBN 0-8089-1533-9). Grune.

Tronick, Edward Z., ed. Social Interchange in Infancy: Affect, Cognition & Communication. (Illus.). 240p. 1982. 29.95 (ISBN 0-8391-1510-5, 17493). Univ Park.

INFANT SUDDEN DEATH
see Sudden Death in Infants

INFANT WELFARE
see Maternal and Infant Welfare

INFANTICIDE
see also Abortion

Quay, Effie A. And Now Infanticide. 2nd ed. 1980. pap. 1.00 (ISBN 0-937930-01-6). Sun Life.

INFANTS
see also Children; Infant Psychology

Bibliotheca Press Research Division, compiled by. The Baby Index. 300p. 1983. pap. 16.95 (ISBN 0-939476-66-5). Biblio Pr GA.

Cheldelin, Larry V. Your Baby's Secret World: Four Phases for Effective Parenting (A Professional & Practical Guide) Brown, J., ed. (Illus., Orig.). 1983. pap. 9.50 (ISBN 0-8283-1850-6). Branden.

Divas, Mireille. I'm a Year Old Now. (Illus.). 176p. 1983. 15.95 (ISBN 0-13-451344-4); pap. 7.95 (ISBN 0-13-451336-3). P-H.

Leach, Penelope. Babyhood. 2nd, Enl. ed. LC 82-48881. 1983. 17.95 (ISBN 0-394-53092-6); pap. 9.95 (ISBN 0-394-71436-9). Knopf.

Miler, I. The Immunity of the Foetus & Newborn Infant. 1983. 41.50 (ISBN 90-247-2610-7, Pub. by Martinus Nijhoff Netherlands). Kluwer Boston.

Stoutt, Glenn R., Jr. The First Month of Life. 2nd ed. 175p. 1983. pap. 9.95 (ISBN 0-87489-312-7). Med Economics.

Time-Life Books, ed. A Commonsense Guide to Sex, Birth, & Babies. (Library of Health Ser.). 1983. lib. bdg. 18.60 (ISBN 0-8094-3827-5). Silver.

Withall, Sabrina. The Baby's Book of Babies. LC 82-48238. (Illus.). 48p. (Orig.). (ps). 1983. pap. 3.80i (ISBN 0-06-091015-1, CN 1015, CN). Har-Row.

INFANTS–CARE AND HYGIENE
see also Baby Sitters; Prenatal Care

Cataldo, Christine Z. Infant & Toddler Programs: A Guide to Very Early Childhood Education. LC 82-11418. (Illus.). 240p. Date not set. pap. text ed. 9.95 (ISBN 0-201-11020-2). A-W.

Clulow, C. F. To Have & to Hold: Marriage, the First Baby, & Preparing Couples for Parenthood. 168p. 1982. 16.50 (ISBN 0-08-028470-1); pap. 9.50 (ISBN 0-08-028471-X). Pergamon.

Cohen, Jean L. & Goirand, Roger. Your Baby. (Illus.). 216p. 1982. 17.95; pap. 8.95. P-H.

Eheart, Brenda & Martan, Susan. The Fourth Trimester: On Becoming a Mother. 1983. 13.95 (ISBN 0-686-43210-X); pap. 7.50 (ISBN 0-686-43211-8). ACC.

Getting in Touch with Yourself-And Your Parents. 1982. pap. 4.25 (ISBN 0-686-82559-4). St Anthony Mess Pr.

Gibson, Dennis L. Live, Grow & Be Free: A Guide to Self-Parenting. 136p. 1982. pap. 4.95 (ISBN 0-89840-031-7). Here's Life.

Heinl, Tina. The Baby Massage Book: Using Touch for Better Bonding & Happier Babies. (Illus.). 144p. 1983. 15.95 (ISBN 0-13-056226-2); pap. 7.95 (ISBN 0-13-056218-1). P-H.

Lurie, Robert & Neugebauer, Roger, eds. Caring for Infants & Toddlers: What Works, What Doesn't, Vol. II. 182p. (Orig.). pap. 10.00 (ISBN 0-942702-01-8). Child Care.

Madden, Chris C. Baby Hints Handbook. Date not set. pap. 3.95 (ISBN 0-449-90078-9, Columbine). Fawcett.

Salk, Lee. Your Child's First Year. (Orig.). 1983. pap. 7.95 (ISBN 0-346-12581-2). Cornerstone.

Schneider, Vimala. Infant Massage: A Handbook for Loving Parents. 128p. 1982. pap. 4.95 (ISBN 0-553-01409-9). Bantam.

Turtle, William J. Dr. Turtle's Babies. 336p. 1983. pap. 3.95 (ISBN 0-446-31065-4). Warner Bks.

INFANTS–CLOTHING

Boyles, Margaret. Margaret Boyles' Craft Designs for Babies. 1983. write for info (ISBN 0-671-43902-2). S&S.

INFANTS–DISEASES

Field, Tiffany & Sostek, Anita, eds. High Risk Infants: Perceptual & Physiological Processes. write for info (ISBN 0-8089-1563-0). Grune.

INFANTS–GROWTH
see Children–Growth

INFANTS–LAW
see Children–Law

INFANTS–MORTALITY
see also Sudden Death in Infants

Stinson, Peggy & Robert. The Long Dying of Baby Andrew. (Atlantic Monthly Press Book Ser.). 384p. 1983. 16.50 (ISBN 0-316-81635-3). Little.

INFANTS–NUTRITION
see also Breast Feeding; Milk

Cameron, Margaret & Hofvander, Tngve. Manual on Feeding Infants & Young Children. 3rd ed. (Illus.). 240p. 1983. pap. 9.95 (ISBN 0-19-261403-7). Oxford U Pr.

Hull, Sylvia. Cooking for a Baby. 1983. pap. 3.95 (ISBN 0-14-046367-4). Penguin.

Schmidt, E. H. & Hildebrandt, A., eds. Health Evaluation of Heavy Metals in Infant Formula & Junior Food, Berlin: 1981, Proceedings. (Illus.). 192p. 1983. 16.00 (ISBN 0-387-11823-3). Springer-Verlag.

INFANTS–PSYCHOLOGY
see Infant Psychology

INFANTS (NEWBORN)
see also Infants (Premature);
also names of special diseases of new-born infants, e.g. Erythroblastosis Fetalis

Lipsitt, Lewis P. & Field, Tiffany M., eds. Perinatal Risk & Newborn Behavior. 208p. 1982. text ed. 19.95x (ISBN 0-89391-123-2). Ablex Pub.

McCracken, George H. & Nelson, John D., eds. Antimicrobial Therapy for Newborns: Practical Application. write for info (ISBN 0-8089-1565-7). Grune.

Robertson, James & Robertson, Joyce. A Baby in the Family. 1983. pap. 6.95 (ISBN 0-14-046499-9). Penguin.

Thompson, Theodore R. Intensive Care of Newborn Infants: A Practical Manual. (Illus.). 414p. spiral bdg. 29.50 (ISBN 0-8166-1090-8). U of Minn Pr.

Warshaw, Joseph B. & Hobbins, John. Perinatal Medicine in Primary Practice. 1982. 34.95 (ISBN 0-201-08294-2, Med-Nurse). A-W.

INFANTS (NEWBORN)–BIBLIOGRAPHY

Craig Norback & Co. The Gerber Baby Encyclopedia. (Orig.). 1983. pap. price not set (ISBN 0-440-53292-2). Dell.

INFANTS (NEWBORN)–DISEASES

McCracken, George H. & Nelson, John D., eds. Antimicrobial Therapy for Newborns: Practical Application. write for info (ISBN 0-8089-1565-7). Grune.

INFANTS (NEWBORN)–MORTALITY
see Infants–Mortality

INFANTS (PREMATURE)

Avery, Mary E. & Litwack, Georgia. Born Early: The Story of a Premature Baby. (Illus.). 160p. 1983. 15.00i (ISBN 0-686-84515-3). Little.

Nance, Sherri. Premature Babies: A Handbook for Parents. 1983. 8.95 (ISBN 0-87795-502-6, Pub. by Priam). Arbor Hse.

INFANTS, FOOD FOR
see Infants–Nutrition

INFECTION
see also Communicable Diseases

Bailey, Ross R., ed. Single Dose Treatment of Urinary Tract Infection. 1982. text ed. write for info. (ISBN 0-86792-007-6, Pub by Adis Pr Australia). Wright-PSG.

Breese, Burtis B. & Hall, Caroline. Beta Hemolytic Streptococcal Diseases. (Illus.). 287p. 1978. 50.00 (ISBN 0-471-09476-5, Pub. by Wiley Med). Wiley.

Eckhart, J., ed. Sepsis unter besonderer Beruecksichtigung der Ernaehrungsprobleme. (Beitraege zu Infusionstherapie und klinische Ernaehrung: Vol. 10). (Illus.). viii, 200p. 1983. pap. 30.00 (ISBN 3-8055-3677-1). S Karger.

Infection Control. 52p. 1975. 3.95 (ISBN 0-686-38334-6, 20-1582). Natl League Nurse.

Mardh, P. A. & Holmes, K. K., eds. Chlamydial Infections: Proceedings, 5th International Symposium, Lund, Sweden, June 15-19, 1982. (Fernstrom Foundation Ser.: Vol. 2). 454p. 1982. 62.75 (ISBN 0-444-80431-5, Biomedical Pr). Elsevier.

Ruettgers, H., ed. Trichomoniasis. (Journal: Gynaekologische Rundschau: Vol. 22, Supplement 2). (Illus.). iv, 88p. 1983. pap. 17.00 (ISBN 3-8055-3646-1). S Karger.

Schaad, U. B., ed. Paediatrische Infektionskrankheiten III. (Paediatrische Fortbildungskurse fuer die Praxis: Vol. 58). (Illus.). viii, 120p. 1983. pap. 54.00 (ISBN 3-8055-3680-1). S Karger.

Schell, Musher. Pathogenesis & Immunology of Treponemal Infections. (Immunology Ser.). 424p. 1983. 65.00 (ISBN 0-8247-1384-2). Dekker.

INFECTIOUS DISEASES
see Communicable Diseases

INFECTIOUS HEPATITIS
see Hepatitis, Infectious

INFECTIOUS JAUNDICE
see Hepatitis, Infectious

INFERTILITY
see Sterility

INFINITESIMAL CALCULUS
see Calculus

INFIRMARIES
see Hospitals

INFLAMMATION

Bekemeier, H., ed. Trends in Inflammation Research Two. Hirschelmann, R. (Agents & Actions Supplements: Vol. 10). 315p. 1982. text ed. 37.95 (ISBN 3-7643-1344-7). Birkhauser.

Velo, G. P., ed. Trends in Inflammation Research One. (Agents & Actions Supplement Ser.: Vol. 7). 362p. 1980. text ed. 98.10x (ISBN 3-7643-1177-0). Birkhauser.

INFLATION (FINANCE)
see also Currency Question; Paper Money; Price Regulation; Wage-Price Policy

Booz & Allen. Coping with Inflation: Experiences of Financial Executives in the U. K., West Germany & Brazil. LC 81-706. 1982. 4.00. Finan Exec.

Bovet, Eric D. Stagflation: The Penalty of Speculative Production in a Multi-Stage Economy. LC 82-48021. 1983. price not set (ISBN 0-669-05883-1). Lexington Bks.

Bruck. Capital Markets under Inflation. 456p. 1982. 29.95 (ISBN 0-03-063249-8). Praeger.

Bruck, Nicholas, ed. Mercados de Capitales Bajo Inflacion. (Illus.). 496p. 1982. 24.95 (ISBN 0-910365-00-8). Decade Media.

Clarke, F. L. The Tangled Web of Price Variation Accounting: The Development of Ideas Underlying Professional Prescriptions in Six Counties. LC 82-82485. (Accountancy in Transition Ser.). 466p. 1982. lib. bdg. 55.00 (ISBN 0-8240-5300-1). Garland Pub.

DiPrima, Richard. Perspective On... Inflation. LC 80-70424. 181p. (Orig.). 1980. pap. text ed. 4.95 (ISBN 0-86652-005-8). Educ Indus.

Feldstein, Martin. Inflation: Tax Rules & Capital Formation. LC 82-10854. (National Bureau of Economic Research-Monograph). 304p. 1983. lib. bdg. 31.00x (ISBN 0-226-24085-1). U of Chicago Pr.

Goldschmidt, Y. & Admon, K. Profit Measurement During Inflation: Accounting, Economic & Financial Aspects. LC 77-4500. (Operations Managment Ser.). 1977. 39.95x (ISBN 0-471-01983-6, Pub. by Wiley-Interscience). Wiley.

Hahn, Frank. Money & Inflation. 136p. 1983. 12.50x (ISBN 0-262-08129-6). MIT Pr.

Hudson, John. Inflation: A Theoretical Survey & Synthesis. 171p. 1983. pap. text ed. 9.95x (ISBN 0-04-339034-X). Allen Unwin.

Illustrations of Disclosure of Inflation Accounting Information. (Financial Report Survey Ser.: No. 23). 1982. pap. 30.00 (ISBN 0-686-84295-2). Am Inst CPA.

Investing to Beat Inflation. 1979. 4.95 (ISBN 0-686-42902-8). Harian.

Kiewiet, D. Roderick. Macroeconomics & Micropolitics: The Electoral Effects of Economic Issues. LC 82-21985. (Illus.). 160p. 1983. lib. bdg. 16.00x (ISBN 0-226-43532-6). U of Chicago Pr.

Matthiessen, Lars. The Impact of Rising Oil Prices on the World Economy. 211p. 1982. text ed. 37.00x (ISBN 0-333-33185-0, Pub. by Macmillan England). Humanities.

Moore, Geoffrey. Business Cycles, Inflation, & Forecasting. 2nd ed. 488p. 42.50 (ISBN 0-88410-284-X); pap. 19.95 (ISBN 0-88410-285-8). Ballinger Pub.

O'Driscoll, Gerald P. Inflation or Deflation? Prospects for Capital Formation, Employment, & Economic Recovery. (Pacific Institute). 1983. write for info. (ISBN 0-88410-930-5). Ballinger Pub.

OECD Staff. International Aspects of Inflation. The Hidden Economy. (OECD Occasional Studies). (Orig.). 1982. pap. 14.50x (ISBN 92-64-12330-X). OECD.

Peretz, Paul. The Political Economy of Inflation in the United States. 264p. 1983. 28.00 (ISBN 0-226-65671-3); pap. 14.00 (ISBN 0-226-65672-1). U of Chicago Pr.

Seed, Allen H., IV. The Impact of Inflation on Internal Planning & Control. 239p. pap. 17.95 (ISBN 0-86641-010-4, 81131). Natl Assn Accts.

Shilling, A. G. & Sokoloff, Kiril. Is Inflation Ending? Are You Ready? LC 82-23962. (Illus.). 288p. 1983. 17.95 (ISBN 0-07-056879-0, P&RB). McGraw.

Tuccillo, John. Housing & Investment in an Inflationary World: Theory & Evidence. (Illus.). 55p. (Orig.). 1980. pap. text ed. 5.50 (ISBN 0-87766-281-9). Urban Inst.

Weiner, Seymoure. How to Stop Inflation Without A Recession. 64p. 1982. 7.95 (ISBN 0-89962-300-X). Todd & Honeywell.

Whitney. Inflation Since Nineteen Forty-Five. 368p. 1982. 32.95 (ISBN 0-03-061352-3). Praeger.

INFLUENZA

Neustadt, Richard & Fineberg, Harvey. The Epidemic that Never Was: Policy-Making & the Swine Flu Scare. LC 82-40023. 288p. (Orig.). 1983. pap. 7.95 (ISBN 0-394-71147-5, Vin). Random.

INFORMATION, FREEDOM OF
see Freedom of Information

INFORMATION, GOVERNMENT
see Government Information

INFORMATION CENTERS
see Information Services

INFORMATION DISPLAY SYSTEMS

Leondes, C. T., ed. Advances in Control & Dynamic Systems, Vol. 19. (Serial Publication). Date not set. price not set (ISBN 0-12-012719-9). Acad Pr.

--Advances in Control & Dynamic Systems: Series Publication, Vol. 20. Date not set. price not set (ISBN 0-12-012720-2). Acad Pr.

Weston, G. F. & Bittleston, R. Alphanumeric Displays: Devices, Drive Circuits & Applications. 208p. 1983. 32.50i (ISBN 0-07-069468-0, P&RB). McGraw.

INFORMATION MEASUREMENT

Mancall, Jacqueline C. & Drott, M. Carl. Measuring Student Information Use: A Guide for School Library Media Specialists. 175p. 1983. lib. bdg. 19.50 (ISBN 0-87287-366-8). Libs Unl.

INFORMATION NETWORKS, LIBRARY
see Library Information Networks

INFORMATION PROCESSING, HUMAN
see Human Information Processing

INFORMATION SCIENCE
see also Documentation; Electronic Data Processing; Information Services; Information Storage and Retrieval Systems; Library Science

Childers, Thomas. Information & Referral: Libraries & Information Science. Davis, Charles H., ed. (Libraries & Information Science Ser.). 384p. (Orig.). 1983. text ed. 37.50. Ablex Pub.

Dretske, Fred I. Knowledge & the Flow of Information. 288p. 1983. pap. 8.95x (ISBN 0-262-54038-X). MIT Pr.

Kasschau. Information Technology & Psychology. 272p. 1982. 29.95 (ISBN 0-03-061771-5). Praeger.

Kenney, Brigitte L., ed. Cable for Information Delivery: A Guide for Librarians, Educators & Cable Professionals. 175p. 1983. 34.50 (ISBN 0-86729-056-0); pap. 27.50 (ISBN 0-86729-055-2). Knowledge Indus.

Kent & Lancour. Encyclopedia of Library & Information Science, Vol. 37, (Suppl. 1) 1983. price not set (ISBN 0-8247-2037-7). Dekker.

Kent, Allen & Galvin, Thomas J., eds. Information Technology: Critical Choices for Library Decision-Makers. (Bks in Library & Informtion Science: Vol. 40). 504p. 1982. 57.50 (ISBN 0-686-82222-6). Dekker.

King, Donald W., et al, eds. Key Papers in the Economics of Information. 380p. 1982. 29.95 (ISBN 0-86729-040-4). Knowledge Indus.

Longley, Dennis & Shain, Michael. Dictionary of Information Technology. 450p. 1983. 34.95 (ISBN 0-471-89574-1, Pub. by Wiley-Interscience). Wiley.

Riley, Tom & Relyea, Harold C., eds. Freedom of Information Trends in the Information Age. 180p. 1983. text ed. 27.50x (ISBN 0-7146-3221-X, F Cass Co). Biblio Dist.

Rowley, J. E. & Turner, C. M. D. The Dissemination of Information. (Grafton Library of Information Science). 353p. 1978. lib. bdg. 32.50x (ISBN 0-89158-830-2). Westview.

Rudman, Jack. Administrative Public Information Specialist. (Career Examination Ser.: C-2607). (Cloth bdg. avail. on request). pap. 12.00 (ISBN 0-8373-2607-9). Natl Learning.

--Public Information Assistant. (Career Examination Ser.: C-2956). (Cloth bdg. avail. on request). pap. 10.00 (ISBN 0-8373-2956-6). Natl Learning.

--Public Information Officer. (Career Examination Ser.: C-2950). (Cloth bdg. avail. on request). pap. 12.00 (ISBN 0-8373-2950-7). Natl Learning.

Shain, M. & Longley, D. A Dictionary of Information Technology. 1982. 75.00x (ISBN 0-686-42940-0, Pub. by Macmillan England). State Mutual Bk.

Sharp, J. R. & Mann, M., eds. A Select List of Newsletters in the Field of Librarianship & Information Science. 63p. 1981. pap. 40.00x (ISBN 0-905984-72-2, Pub. by Brit Lib England). State Mutual Bk.

Stokes, Adrian. Concise Encyclopedia of Information Technology. 272p. 1983. 17.95 (ISBN 0-13-167205-3); pap. 9.95 (ISBN 0-13-167213-4). P-H.

Sweeney, G. P., ed. Information & the Transformation of Society: Papers from the First Joint International Conference of the Institute of Information Scientists & the American Society for Information Science, St. Patrick's College, Dublin, Ireland, 28-30 June, 1982. (Contemporary Topics in Information Transfer Ser.: Vol. 2). 368p. 1982. 51.00 (ISBN 0-444-86505-5, North Holland). Elsevier.

Varlejs, Jana & DeProspo, Ernest, eds. The Economics of Information. LC 82-14842. 92p. 1982. pap. 9.95x (ISBN 0-89950-059-5). McFarland & Co.

Williams, M. B., ed. Pathways to the Information Society: Proceedings of the Sixth International Conference on Computer Communication, London, 1982. 1018p. 1982. 55.00 (ISBN 0-444-86464-4, North Holland). Elsevier.

Williams, Martha E., ed. The Annual Review of Information Science & Technology, Vol. 18. LC 66-25096. 400p. 1983. 45.00 (ISBN 0-86729-050-1). Knowledge Indus.

Zorkoczy, Peter. Information Technology: An Introduction. LC 82-10115. (Illus.). 137p. 1983. 29.95 (ISBN 0-86729-037-4). Knowledge Indus.

INFORMATION SERVICES
see also Archives; Documentation; Information Storage and Retrieval Systems; Libraries; Reference Services (Libraries); Research

Blackmarr, Brian, et al. Syntopican X, Papers & Proceedings June 21 to 24, 1982 "The Informatio Manager in Focus". A Key Role Takes Shape". 340p. 1982. 40.00 (ISBN 0-935220-07-0). IIWPA.

Contemporary Problems in Technical Library & Information Center Management: A State-of the-Art. 1974. 18.50 (ISBN 0-686-42904-4). Knowledge Indus.

Continuing Library Education As Viewed in Relation to Other Continuing Professional Movements. 1974. 25.00 (ISBN 0-686-42905-2). Knowledge Indus.

Cost Reduction for Special Libraries & Information Centers. 1974. 12.50 (ISBN 0-686-42908-7). Knowledge Indus.

Directory of Educational Documentation & Information Services. 4th ed. 106p. 1983. pap. 7.50 (ISBN 92-3-002026-5, U 1245, UNESCO). Unipub.

Dodd, James B. Free-Based Information Centers in Libraries. 150p. 1983. 36.50 (ISBN 0-86729-049-8); pap. 27.50 (ISBN 0-86729-048-X). Knowledge Indus.

Duke, Judith S., ed. The Knowledge Industry Two Hundred: America's Two Hundred Largest Media Companies, 1983. 400p. 1983. pap. 88.00 (ISBN 0-86729-034-X). Knowledge Indus.
The El-Hi Market: 1982-87. 1982. spiral bdg. 750.00 (ISBN 0-686-42873-0). Knowledge Indus.
Hofacker, Winfried & Floegel, Ekkehard. The Custom Apple & Other Mysteries, Vol. I. Trap, Charles, ed. (Apple Information Ser.). 192p. (Orig.). 1982. pap. 24.95 (ISBN 0-936200-05-7). IJG Inc.
Horton, Forest W., Jr. Five Easy Steps to IRM. 75p. 1983. 29.95 (ISBN 0-9606408-2-7). Info Mgmt Pr.
Information Roundup: Microfilm & Data Processing for the Library & Information Center. (Proceedings of the 4th ASIS Mid-Year Meeting, 1975) 1975. 14.00 (ISBN 0-686-42891-9). Knowledge Indus.
Jennings, Margaret, compiled by. Library & Reference Facilities in the Area of the District of Columbia. 11th ed. 285p. 1983. pap. 39.50 (ISBN 0-86729-021-8). Knowledge Indus.
Key Papers on the Use of Computer-Based Bibliographic Services. 1973. 10.00 (ISBN 0-686-42911-7). Knowledge Indus.
King, Donald W., et al, eds. Key Papers in the Economics of Information. 380p. 1982. 29.95 (ISBN 0-86729-040-4). Knowledge Indus.
Lesko, Matthew. Information U. S. A. 1224p. 1983. pap. 19.95 (ISBN 0-14-046564-2). Penguin.
--Information U. S. A. 1983. 41.75 (ISBN 0-670-39823-3). Viking Pr.
The Marketing of Information Analysis Center Products & Services. 1971. 6.50 (ISBN 0-686-42912-5). Knowledge Indus.
Mason, Marilyn G. The Federal Role in Library & Information Services. 150p. 1983. 34.50 (ISBN 0-86729-010-2); pap. 27.50 (ISBN 0-86729-009-9). Knowledge Indus.
Microcomputer Hardware & Software in the El-Hi Market: 1983-87. 1983. spiral 950.00 (ISBN 0-686-42882-X). Knowledge Indus.
Penniman, Howard R., ed. Canada at the Polls, 1979 & 1980. 1982. 17.25 (ISBN 0-8447-3474-8); pap. 9.25 (ISBN 0-8447-3472-1). Am Enterprise.
Rees, Alan M., ed. Consumer Health Information Service, 1982. 125p. reference bk. 25.00 (ISBN 0-686-84112-3). Microfilming Corp.
Rosenau, Fred. S. & Chase, Leslie, eds. Business Realities in the Information Industry. 100p. 1983. 39.95 (ISBN 0-942774-10-8). Info Indus.
Rudman, Jack. Associate Information & Referral Coordinator. (Career Examination Ser.: C-2926). (Cloth bdg. avail. on request). pap. 12.00 (ISBN 0-8373-2926-4). Natl Learning.
--Information & Referral Aide. (Career Examination Ser.: C-2892). (Cloth bdg. avail. on request). pap. 10.00 (ISBN 0-8373-2892-6). Natl Learning.
--Information & Referral Coordinator. (Career Examination Ser.: C-2927). (Cloth bdg. avail. on request). pap. 12.00 (ISBN 0-8373-2927-2). Natl Learning.
--Magnetic Tape Librarian. (Career Examination Ser.: C-2872). (Cloth bdg. avail. on request). pap. 10.00 (ISBN 0-8373-2872-1). Natl Learning.
Stern, B. T., ed. Information & Innovation: Proceedings of a Seminar of ICSU-AB on the Role of Information in the Innovative Process, Amsterdam, The Netherlands, 1982. (Contemporary Topics in Information Transfer Ser.: Vol. 1). 192p. 1982. 38.50 (ISBN 0-444-86496-2, North Holland). Elsevier.
Washington Information Workbook. 6th ed. 65.00 (ISBN 0-934940-12-6). Wash Res.
Woods, Lawrence A. & Pope, Nolan F. The Librarian's Guide to Microcomputer Technology & Applications. 150p. 1983. 34.50 (ISBN 0-86729-045-5); pap. 27.50 (ISBN 0-86729-044-7). Knowledge Indus.

INFORMATION STORAGE AND RETRIEVAL SYSTEMS

see also Computers; Data Base Management; Electronic Data Processing; Libraries–Automation

Accounting & Information Systems: Answers to Questions on Subject Matter for the Learning Guide, CEBS Course 6. 1982. pap. text ed. 15.00 (ISBN 0-89154-186-1). Intl Found Employ.
Accounting & Information Systems: Learning Guide, CEBS Course 6. 1982. spiral binding 18.00 (ISBN 0-89154-185-3). Intl Found Employ.
Alkins, Arthur C. Fundamentals of Data Processing. (Plaid Ser.). 200p. 1983. pap. 8.95 (ISBN 0-87094-389-8). Dow Jones-Irwin.
Batty, C. D. The Electronic Library. 160p. 1983. price not set (Pub. by Bingley England). Shoe String.
Brackett, Michael H. Developing Data Structured Information Systems. (Illus.). 250p. (Orig.). 1983. pap. 20.00 (ISBN 0-9605884-1-8). Orr & Assocs.
Brookes, Cyril & Grouse, Phil. Information Systems Design & Analysis. 488p. 1983. 24.00 (ISBN 0-13-464685-1). P-H.
Burch, J. G., et al. Information Systems: Theory & Practice. 3rd ed. 1983. 29.95 (ISBN 0-471-06211-1). Wiley.
Changing Patterns in Information Retrieval: Proceedings of the 10th Annual National Information Retrieval Colloquium. 1973. 15.00 (ISBN 0-686-42900-1). Knowledge Indus.
Consumer Media Expenditures, 1982-87: The Competition Between Print & Electronic Media. 1983. spiral 995.00 (ISBN 0-686-42874-9). Knowledge Indus.
Donovan, J. & Madnick, S. Information Systems: Data Base, Telecommunications, Transaction Manager & Performance Education. Date not set. text ed. price not set (ISBN 0-07-039457-1); price not set instr's manual (ISBN 0-07-039458-X). McGraw.
Hagler, Ronald. Bibliographic Record & Information Technology. 1982. text ed. 25.00 (ISBN 0-8389-0367-3). ALA.
Hart, Jack & Mahan, Don. Cross Reference Utility: A Programming Aid for the IBM Personal Computer. (Illus.). 192p. 1983. pap. 29.95 (ISBN 0-13-194746-X). P-H.
Information Sources, Inc. The Small Systems Software & Services Sourcebook. Koolish, Ruth K., ed. 504p. 1982. pap. 125.00 (ISBN 0-943906-00-8). Info Sources.
Jackson, E. B. & Jackson, R. L. Industrial Information Systems: A Manual for Higher Managements & Their Information-Librarian Associates. LC 78-15890. (The Information Sciences Ser.). 314p. 1979. 45.00 (ISBN 0-87933-328-6). Hutchinson Ross.
Lane, J. E. Microprocessors & Information Handling. (Computing in the Eighties Ser.). 67p. 1981. pap. 15.00x (ISBN 0-85012-334-8). Intl Pubns Serv.
Norman, Adrian. Electronic Document Delivery: The Artemis Concept. 226p. 1982. 45.00 (ISBN 0-686-82554-3). Knowledge Indus.
Popyk, M. K. Word Processing & Information Systems: A Practical Approach. 352p. 1983. 15.50 (ISBN 0-07-050574-8, G). McGraw.
Salton, G. & Schneider, H. J., eds. Research & Development in Information Retrieval: Proceedings, Berlin, 1982. (Lecture Notes in Computer Science Ser.: Vol. 146). 311p. 1983. pap. 14.50 (ISBN 0-387-11978-7). Springer-Verlag.
Schmidt, J. W. & Brodie, M. L., eds. Relational Database Systems: Analysis & Comparison. 618p. 1983. 19.80 (ISBN 0-387-12032-7). Springer-Verlag.
Stokes, Adrian. Concise Encyclopedia of Information Technology. 272p. 1983. 17.95 (ISBN 0-13-167205-3); pap. 9.95 (ISBN 0-13-167213-4). P-H.
Xerox Rank (UK) Ltd, Uxbridge, UK, ed. Brave New World? Living with Information Technology. 188p. 1983. 15.90 (ISBN 0-08-025847-6). Pergamon.
Zmud, Robert W. Information Systems In Organizations. 1983. text ed. 25.95x (ISBN 0-673-15438-6). Scott F.

INFORMATION STORAGE AND RETRIEVAL SYSTEMS–BUSINESS

Aschner, Katherine, ed. Taking Control of Your Office Records. 150p. 1983. 32.95 (ISBN 0-86729-057-9); pap. 22.95 (ISBN 0-86729-058-7). Knowledge Indus.
The Business Information Markets: 1982-1987. 1982. spiral 850.00 (ISBN 0-686-42871-4). Knowledge Indus.
Campbell, Malcolm J. Case Studies in Business Information Provision. 204p. 1983. price not set (ISBN 0-85157-353-3, Pub. by Bingley England). Shoe String.
Chapman, E. N. & Martin, William. Self-Paced Guide for SSK: With Applications for the Hospitality Industry. 3rd ed. 96p. 1982. pap. text ed. 5.95 (ISBN 0-574-20638-8, 13-3638). SRA.
Christy, Ron & Jones, Billy M. The Complete Information Bank for Entrepreneurs & Small Business Managers. LC 81-70750. (Illus.). 300p. 19.50 (ISBN 0-941958-00-0, Wichita Ctr Entrep SBM). WSU Hist Resources.
Dickson, G. W. & Wetherbe, J. Management Information Systems Management. 576p. 1982. 26.95x (ISBN 0-07-016825-3); write for info. instr's manual (ISBN 0-07-016826-1). McGraw.
--Management Information Systems Management Cases. 224p. 1982. 12.95x (ISBN 0-07-016827-X). McGraw.
Hergert, Richard & Hergert, Douglas. Doing Business with Pascal. 380p. 1982. pap. text ed. 16.95 (ISBN 0-89588-091-1). Sybex.
Houghton, B. & Wisdom, J. C. Non-Bibliographic On-Line Databases: An Investigation into Their Uses Within the Fields of Economics & Business Studies. 34p. 1981. pap. 30.00x (ISBN 0-905984-70-6, Pub. by Brit Lib England). State Mutual Bk.
Leitch, Robert A. & Davis, K. Roscoe. Accounting Information Systems. (Illus.). 720p. 1983. 29.95 (ISBN 0-13-002949-1). P-H.
McLeod, Raymond, Jr. Management Information Systems. 2nd ed. 160p. 1983. price not set (ISBN 0-574-21410-0, 13-4410); write for info. casebook (ISBN 0-574-21412-7, 13-4412); write for info. tchr's. guide (ISBN 0-574-21411-9, 13-4411). SRA.
Manual for the Preparation of Records in Development-Information Systems: Recommended Methods for Development-Information Systems. 272p. 1983. pap. 20.00 (ISBN 0-88936-354-4, IDRC TS40, IDRC). Unipub.
Strauss, Lawrence. Electronic Marketing: Emerging TV & Computer Channels for Interactive Home Shopping. 160p. 1983. 34.95 (ISBN 0-86729-023-4). Knowledge Indus.
Wu, Frederick H. Accounting Information Systems: Theory & Practice. (Illus.). 608p. 1983. text ed. 23.00 (ISBN 0-07-072121-1, C). Supplementary materials available from publisher. write for info. instr's manual (ISBN 0-07-072122-X). McGraw.

INFORMATION STORAGE AND RETRIEVAL SYSTEMS–CHEMISTRY

Grayson, Martin. Information Retrieval in Chemistry & Chemical Patent Law. (Encylopedia Reprint Ser.). 125p. 1983. 17.95 (ISBN 0-471-89057-X, Pub. by Wiley-Interscience). Wiley.

INFORMATION STORAGE AND RETRIEVAL SYSTEMS–EDUCATION

The College Market: 1981-86. 1981. spiral 550.00 (ISBN 0-686-42876-5). Knowledge Indus.
Corporate Monitor, Inc. Educational Software Directory. 1982. pap. text ed. 22.50 (ISBN 0-87287-352-8). Libs Unl.
Directory of Educational Documentation & Information Services. 4th ed. 106p. 1983. pap. 7.50 (ISBN 92-3-002026-5, U 1245, UNESCO). Unipub.
The El-Hi Market: 1982-87. 1982. spiral bdg. 750.00 (ISBN 0-686-42873-0). Knowledge Indus.

INFORMATION STORAGE AND RETRIEVAL SYSTEMS–ENGINEERING

Technical Documentation Standards: For Computer Programmes & Computer Based Systems Used in Engineering. 133p. 1981. 165.00x (ISBN 0-85012-247-3, Pub. by Telford England). State Mutual Bk.

INFORMATION STORAGE AND RETRIEVAL SYSTEMS–HUMANITIES

Cok, Mary V., et al. All in Order: Information Systems for the Arts. LC 81-9506. (Illus.). 191p. 1981. pap. 7.95 (ISBN 0-89062-132-2, Pub by National Assembly State Arts Agencies). Pub Ctr Cult Res.
Hartner, Elizabeth P. An Introduction to Automated Literature Searching. (Bks in Library & Information Science: Vol. 36). (Illus.). 168p. 1981. 23.50 (ISBN 0-8247-1293-5). Dekker.
The Invisible Medium: The State of the Art of Microform & a Guide to the Literature. 1973. 6.50 (ISBN 0-686-42910-9). Knowledge Indus.

INFORMATION STORAGE AND RETRIEVAL SYSTEMS–LAW

Marcus, Michael & Brown, Leroy. The Computer in Your Legal Practice. (Illus.). 240p. 1983. 24.95 (ISBN 0-13-164400-9); pap. 19.95 (ISBN 0-13-164392-4). P-H.
Miskin, C. Library & Information Services for the Legal Profession. 1981. 45.00x (ISBN 0-905984-73-0, Pub. by Brit Lib England). State Mutual Bk.

INFORMATION STORAGE AND RETRIEVAL SYSTEMS–MEDICINE

Chapman, E. N. & Williams, Catherine. A Self-Paced Guide to the Health Care Industry to Accompany SSK. 3rd ed. 96p. 1983. pap. text ed. write for info. (ISBN 0-574-20567-5). SRA.
Manell, P. & Johansson, S. G., eds. The Impact of Computer Technology on Drug Information: Proceedings of the IFIP-IMIA Working Conference, Uppsala, Sweden, October 26-28, 1981. 262p. 1982. 34.00 (ISBN 0-444-86451-2, North Holland). Elsevier.

INFORMATION STORAGE AND RETRIEVAL SYSTEMS–SCIENCE

Adkinson, B. W. Two Centuries of Federal Information. LC 78-7294. (Publications in the Information Science Ser.). 235p. 1978. 43.50 (ISBN 0-87933-269-7). Hutchinson Ross.
Ahl, David H., ed. Computers in Science & Social Studies. 192p. 1983. pap. 14.95 (ISBN 0-916688-44-5). Creative Comp.
Burgess, Eric. Celestial Basic: Astronomy on Your Computer. LC 82-60187. (Illus.). 300p. 1982. pap. text ed. 13.95 (ISBN 0-89588-087-3). Sybex.

INFORMATION STORAGE AND RETRIEVAL SYSTEMS–SOCIAL SCIENCES

Ahl, David H., ed. Computers in Science & Social Studies. 192p. 1983. pap. 14.95 (ISBN 0-916688-44-5). Creative Comp.
Geyer, R. F. & Zouwen, J. van der, eds. Dependence & Inequality: A Systems Approach to the Problems of Mexico & Other Developing Countries. (Systems Science & World Order Library: Innovations in Systems Science). (Illus.). 336p. 1982. 35.00 (ISBN 0-08-027952-X). Pergamon.

INFORMATION THEORY

see also Automatic Control; Coding Theory; Data Transmission Systems; Error-Correcting Codes (Information Theory); Information Measurement; Language and Languages; Semantics; Signal Theory (Telecommunication); Speech Processing Systems; Telecommunication

Gallager, R. G. Information Theory & Reliable Communication. LC 68-26850. 588p. 1968. 41.95x (ISBN 0-471-29048-3). Wiley.
Rubin, Michael R. Information Economics & Policy in the United States. 1983. lib. bdg. price not set. Libs Unl.
Thomas, Sari. Communication Theory & Interpersonal Interaction. 308p. 1983. text ed. 29.50 (ISBN 0-89391-134-8). Ablex Pub.

INFRA-RED PHOTOGRAPHY

see Photography, Infra-Red

INFRA-RED SPECTROMETRY

The Infrared Spectra Handbook of Surfactants. 1982. 275.00 (ISBN 0-8456-0086-9). Sadtler Res.
Paternite, Stephen & Paternite, David, eds. American Infrared Survey. LC 82-6160. (Illus.). 88p. 1982. 21.95 (ISBN 0-9609812-0-9). Photo Survey.
Person. Vibrational Intensities in Infrared & Raman Spectroscopy. (Studies in Physical & Theoretical Chemistry). 1982. 95.75 (ISBN 0-444-42115-7). Elsevier.
Siesler, H. W. & Holland-Moritz, K. Infared & Raman Spectroscopy of Polymers. (Practical Spectroscopy Ser.: Vol. 4). (Illus.). 400p. 1980. 55.00 (ISBN 0-8247-6935-X). Dekker.
Van der Marel, R. & Beutelspacher, H. Atlas of Infrared Spectroscopy of Clay Minerals & Their Admixtures. 1976. 106.50 (ISBN 0-444-41187-9). Elsevier.

INFRA-RED SPECTRUM

see Spectrum, Infra-Red

INFRA-RED TECHNOLOGY

see also Photography, Infra-Red

Hudson, R. D. & Hudson, J. W., eds. Infrared Detectors. LC 75-4923. (Benchmark Papers in Optics: Vol. 2). 392p. 1975. 51.50 (ISBN 0-87933-135-6). Hutchinson Ross.

INHALATION THERAPY

Shoup, Cynthia A. Laboratory Exercises in Respiratory Therapy. 2nd ed. (Illus.). 266p. 1983. pap. text ed. 15.95 (ISBN 0-8016-4594-8). Mosby.

INHERITANCE (BIOLOGY)

see Heredity

INHERITANCE AND TRANSFER TAX

see also Gifts–Taxation; Real Property and Taxation

Crumbley, D. L. & Milam, Edward E. Estate Planning in the '80s. 224p. 1983. 15.95 (ISBN 0-8144-5758-4). Am Mgmt.
Kahn, Waggoner. Provisions of the Internal Revenue Code & Treasury Regulations Pertaining to the Federal Taxation of Gifts, Trusts, & Estates 1983. 1983. pap. write for info. Little.
McNulty, John K. Federal Estate & Gift Taxation in a Nutshell. 3rd ed. LC 82-24726. (Nutshell Ser.). 493p. 1983. pap. text ed. 7.95 (ISBN 0-314-71766-8). West Pub.

INHERITANCE TAX

see Inheritance and Transfer Tax

INITIALISMS

see Acronyms

INITIATIONS (IN RELIGION, FOLK-LORE, ETC.)

see also Baptism

Archdiocese of Dubuque, R.C.I.A. Foundations of Christian Initiation. 96p. 1982. wire coil 7.95 (ISBN 0-697-01781-8). Wm C Brown.
Steiner, Rudolf. Initiation & Its Results. 134p. 7.00 (ISBN 0-686-38222-6). Sun Bks.

INJECTIONS

see also Parenteral Therapy

Trissel, L. A. Pocket Guide to Injectable Drugs. 159p. 1981. pap. text ed. 13.50 (ISBN 0-471-09131-6, Pub. by Wiley Med). Wiley.

INJURIES

see Accidents; First Aid in Illness and Injury; Sports–Accidents and Injuries; Traumatism; Wounds

INJURIES (LAW)

see Accident Law; Employers' Liability; Medical Jurisprudence; Personal Injuries; Torts

INJURIOUS INSECTS

see Insects, Injurious and Beneficial

INKBLOT TEST, RORSCHACH

see Rorschach Test

INLAND NAVIGATION

see also Canals; Lakes; Rivers

Curry, Jane. The River's in My Blood: Riverboat Pilots Tell Their Stories. LC 82-11068. xx, 279p. 1983. 17.50 (ISBN 0-8032-1416-2). U of Nebr Pr.

INLAND RULES OF THE ROAD

see Inland Navigation

INNOVATIONS, AGRICULTURAL

see Agricultural Innovations

INNOVATIONS, TECHNOLOGICAL

see Technological Innovations

INNOVATIONS IN EDUCATION

see Educational Innovations

INNS

see Hotels, Taverns, etc.

INNS OF COURT, LONDON

Green, A. Wigfall. Inns of Court & Early English Drama. 1931. text ed. 39.50x (ISBN 0-686-83590-5). Elliots Bks.

INNUIT

see Eskimos

INNUIT LANGUAGE

see Eskimo Language

INORGANIC CHEMISTRY

see Chemistry, Inorganic

INPUT EQUIPMENT (COMPUTERS)

see Computer Input-Output Equipment

INPUT-OUTPUT ANALYSIS

see Interindustry Economics

INPUT-OUTPUT EQUIPMENT (COMPUTERS)

see Computer Input-Output Equipment

INQUISITIVENESS

see Curiosity

INSANE–LEGAL STATUS, LAWS, ETC.

see Insanity–Jurisprudence; Mental Health Laws

INSANE HOSPITALS

see Psychiatric Hospitals

INSANITY
Here are entered works on the legal aspects of mental disorders. Popular works and works on regional or social aspects of mental disorders are entered under Mental Illness. Systematic descriptions of mental disorders are entered under Psychology, pathological. Works on clinical aspects of mental disorders, including therapy, are entered under Psychiatry.
see also Depression, Mental; Genius; Hysteria; Manic-Depressive Psychoses; Mental Illness; Neuroses; Personality, Disorders Of; Psychiatry; Psychology, Pathological; Schizophrenia; Suicide
Kirchhoff, Theodore. Handbook of Insanity for Practitioners & Students. 362p. 1982. Repr. of 1895 ed. lib. bdg. 85.00 (ISBN 0-8495-3138-1). Arden Lib.

INSANITY-JURISPRUDENCE
Here are entered works on the legal status of persons of unsound mind. Works on the law affecting the welfare of the insane are entered under the heading Mental Health Laws. Works on psychiatry as applied in courts of law are entered under the heading Forensic Psychiatry.
see also Criminal Liability; Forensic Psychiatry; Liability (Law)
Cook, Earleen H. The Insane or Mentally Impaired Defendant: A Selected Bibliography. (Public Administration Ser.). 57p. 1983. pap. 8.25 (ISBN 0-88066-355-3). Vance Biblios.
Herr, Stanley S. & Arons, Stephen. Legal Rights & Mental-Health Care. Talbot, J., frwd. by. LC 81-47823. 1983. write for info. (ISBN 0-669-04910-7). Lexington Bks.
Winslade, William J. & Ross, Judith W. The Insanity Plea. 256p. 1983. 14.95 (ISBN 0-686-83836-X, ScribT). Scribner.
--The Insanity Plea. 240p. 1983. 14.95 (ISBN 0-684-17897-4). Scribner.

INSANITY, HYSTERICAL
see Hysteria

INSANITY AND GENIUS
see Genius

INSCRIPTIONS-ITALY
Bodel, John. Roman Brick Stamps in the Kelsey Museum. (Kelsey Museum Ser.). (Illus.). 1983. pap. text ed. 22.50 (ISBN 0-472-08039-3). U of Mich Pr.

INSCRIPTIONS, ASSYRIAN
see Cuneiform Inscriptions

INSCRIPTIONS, BABYLONIAN
see Cuneiform Inscriptions

INSCRIPTIONS, BEHISTUN
see Cuneiform Inscriptions

INSCRIPTIONS, CUNEIFORM
see Cuneiform Inscriptions

INSCRIPTIONS, DEMOTIC
see Egyptian Language-Inscriptions

INSCRIPTIONS, EGYPTIAN
see Egyptian Language-Inscriptions

INSCRIPTIONS, HIERATIC
see Egyptian Language-Inscriptions

INSCRIPTIONS, ITALIC
Lucas, Elizabeth H., ed. Calligraphy, An Affair of the Heart: Italic Letterforms. 1982. write for info. E H Lucas.

INSCRIPTIONS, JEWISH
Brooten, Bernadette J. Women Leaders in the Ancient Synagogue: Inscriptional Evidence & Background Issues. LC 82-10658. (Brown Judaic Studies). 292p. 1982. pap. 20.00 (ISBN 0-89130-587-4, 14 00 36). Scholars Pr CA.

INSCRIPTIONS, LATIN
Goodburn, Roger. The Roman Inscriptions of Britain: Index. 96p. 1982. text ed. 15.75x (ISBN 0-86299-026-2, Pub. by Sutton England). Humanities.

INSCRIPTIONS, MAYA
see Picture-Writing, Maya

INSECT BEHAVIOR
see Insects-Behavior

INSECT CONTROL
Bennett, F. V. & Symmons, P. M. A Review of Estimates of the Effectiveness of Certain Control Techniques & Insecticides Against the Desert Locust. 1972. 35.00x (ISBN 0-85135-060-7, Pub. by Centre Overseas Research). State Mutual Bk.
Carr, Anna. Rodale's Color Handbook of Garden Insects. (Illus.). 256p. 1983. pap. 10.95 (ISBN 0-87857-460-3, 01-637-1). Rodale Pr Inc.
Croft, B. A. & Hoyt, S. C. Integrated Management of Insect Pests of Pome & Stone Fruit. (Environemental Science & Technology Texts & Monographs). 464p. 1983. 52.50 (ISBN 0-471-05334-1, Pub. by Wiley-Interscience). Wiley.
Field Observations of the Behavior of Hoppers of the Red Locust (Nomadacris Septemfasciata Serville) 1959. 35.00x (ISBN 0-85135-043-7, Pub. by Centre Overseas Research). State Mutual Bk.
Frishman, Austin M. & Schwartz, Arthur P. The Cockroach Combat Manual. (Illus.). 1980. pap. 4.95 (ISBN 0-688-03613-9). Quill NY.
Harriss, E. G. & Williams, N. G. Mixtures of Insecticides for Tsetse Fly Control: Potentiation Between a-Endosulfan & Deltalmethrin Applied to Glossina Austeni Newst. 1981. 35.00x (ISBN 0-85135-122-0, Pub. by Centre Overseas Research). State Mutual Bk.
Hemming, C. F. & Taylor, T. H., eds. Proceedings of the International Study Conference on the Current & Future Problems of Acridology, London, 1970. 1972. 50.00x (ISBN 0-686-82422-9, Pub. by Centre Overseas Research). State Mutual BK.
Johnston, D. R., ed. Factors Affecting Aerial Application of Microencapsulated Pheromone Formulation for Control of Pectinophora Gossypiella (Saunders) by Communication Disruption on Cotton in Egypt. 1982. 35.00x (ISBN 0-686-82424-5, Pub. by Centre Overseas Research). State Mutual Bk.
Johnston, H. B. & Buxton, D. R. Field Observations on Locusts in Eastern Africa. 1949. 35.00x (ISBN 0-85135-008-9, Pub. by Centre Overseas Research). State Mutual Bk.
Lloyd, J. H. Operational Research on Preventive Control of the Red Locust (Nomadacris Septemfasciata Serville) 1959. 35.00x (ISBN 0-85135-020-8, Pub. by Centre Overseas Research). State Mutual Bk.
Maccuaig, R. D. & Yeates, M. N. Theoretical Studies on the Efficiency of Insecticidal Sprays for the Control of Flying Locust Swarms. 35.00x (ISBN 0-85135-057-7, Pub. by Centre Overseas Research). State Mutual Bk.
Rainey, R. C. Meteorology & the Migration of Desert Locusts: Applications of Synoptic Meteorology in Locust Control. 1963. 35.00 (ISBN 0-686-82414-8, Pub. by Centre Overseas Research). State Mutual Bk.
Rowell, C. Fraser. Environmental Control of Colouration in an Acridid, Gastrimargus Africanus (Saussure) 1970. 35.00x (ISBN 0-85135-000-3, Pub. by Centre Overseas Research). State Mutual Bk.
Service, M. W. Methods for Sampling Adult Simulidae, with Special Reference to the Simulium Damnosum Complex. 1977. 35.00x (ISBN 0-85135-087-9, Pub. by Centre Overseas Research). State Mutual Bk.
Sully, Langdon. How to Get Rid of Fleas...Now & Forever. LC 82-99950. (Illus.). 64p. 1982. write for info. (ISBN 0-910877-00-9). Langdon Assocs.
Waloff, Z. & Rainey, R. C. Field Studies on Factors Affecting the Displacement of Desert Locust Swarms in Eastern Africa. 1951. 35.00x (ISBN 0-85135-042-9, Pub. by Centre Overseas Research). State Mutual Bk.

INSECT CONTROL-BIOLOGICAL CONTROL
Steiner, Walter & Tabachnick, WAlter, eds. Recent Development in the Genetics of Insect Disease Vectors. (Illus.). 665p. text ed. 26.00 (ISBN 0-87563-224-6). Stipes.

INSECT METAMORPHOSIS
see Insects-Metamorphosis

INSECT POPULATIONS
Ashall, C. & Ellis, P. E. Studies on Numbers & Mortality in Field Populations of the Desert Locust (Schistocerca Gregaria Forskal) 1962. 35.00x (ISBN 0-85135-004-6, Pub. by Centre Overseas Research). State Mutual Bk.
Dempster, J. P. The Population Dynamics of the Moroccan Locust (Dociostaurus Maroccanus Thunb) in Cyprus. 1957. 35.00x (ISBN 0-85135-011-9, Pub. by Centre Overseas Research). State Mutual Bk.
Richards, O. W. & Waloff, N. Studies on the Biology & Population Dynamics of British Grasshoppers. 1954. 35.00x (ISBN 0-85135-034-8, Pub. by Centre Overseas Research). State Mutual Bk.
Waloff, Z. The Upsurges & Recessions of the Desert Locust Plague: An Historical Survey. 1968. 35.00x (ISBN 0-85135-041-0, Pub. by Centre Overseas Research). State Mutual Bk.

INSECTICIDES
see also Insects, Injurious and Beneficial; Spraying; also names of insecticides
Bennett, F. V. & Symmons, P. M. A Review of Estimates of the Effectiveness of Certain Control Techniques & Insecticides Against the Desert Locust. 1972. 35.00x (ISBN 0-85135-060-7, Pub. by Centre Overseas Research). State Mutual Bk.
Insecticide Evaluation 1981. 141p. 1983. pap. 9.00 (ISBN 0-686-42854-4, R174, IRRI). Unipub.
Maccuaig, R. D. & Yeates, M. N. Theoretical Studies on the Efficiency of Insecticidal Sprays for the Control of Flying Locust Swarms. 35.00x (ISBN 0-85135-057-7, Pub. by Centre Overseas Research). State Mutual Bk.
Page, B. G. & Thomson, W. T. Insecticide, Herbicide Fungicide Quick Guide, 1983. 140p. Date not set. pap. 12.00 (ISBN 0-913702-20-X). Thomson Pub CA.

INSECTIVOROUS PLANTS
Darwin, Charles R. Insectivorous Plants, Vol. 12. LC 72-3897. (Illus.). x, 462p. 1972. write for info. AMS Pr.

INSECTS
see also Diptera; Entomology; Hymenoptera; Lepidoptera; Orthoptera
also Ants; Butterflies; Moths; Wasps; and similar headings
Doncaster, John P. Francis Walker's Aphids. (Illus.). viii, 165p. 1961. 16.50 (ISBN 0-565-00074-8). Sabbot-Natural Hist Bks.

INSECTS-ANATOMY
Albrecht, F. O. The Anatomy of the Red Locust (Nomadacris Septemfasciate Serville) 1956. 35.00x (ISBN 0-85135-067-4, Pub. by Centre Overseas Research). State Mutual Bk.

INSECTS-BEHAVIOR
Ahmad, Sami, ed. Herbivorous Insects: Host-Seeking Behavior & Mechanisms. LC 82-20717. Date not set. price not set (ISBN 0-12-045580-3). Acad Pr.
Bassler, U. Neural Basis of Elementary Behavior in Stick Insects. Strausfeld, C., tr. (Studies in Brain Function: Vol.10). (Illus.). 180p. 1983. 32.60 (ISBN 0-387-11918-3). Springer-Verlag.
Chapman, R. F. A Laboratory Study of Roosting Behavior in Hoppers of the African Migratory Locust (Locusta Migratoria Migratorioides R & F) 1955. 35.00x (ISBN 0-85135-007-0, Pub. by Centre Overseas Research). State Mutual Bk.
Hunter-Jones, P. Laboratory Studies on the Inheritance of Phase Characters in Locusts. 1958. 35.00x (ISBN 0-85135-018-6, Pub. by Centre Overseas Research). State Mutual Bk.
Pringle, W. S. Insect Flight. Head, J. J., ed. LC 78-53327. (Carolina Biology Readers Ser.). 16p. 1983. pap. text ed. 1.60 (ISBN 0-19-914167-3, 45-9652). Carolina Biological.
Rainey, R. C. & Waloff, Z. The Behavior of the Red Locust (Normadacris Septemfasciata Serville) in Relation to the Topography, Meteorology & Vegetatation of the Rukwa Rift Valley, Tanganyika. 1957. 35.00x (ISBN 0-85135-031-3, Pub. by Centre Overseas Research). State Mutual Bk.
Stokes, Donald W. A Guide to Observing Insect Lives. (Stokes Nature Guides). 1983. 15.00i (ISBN 0-316-81724-4). Little.
Stower, W. J. & Popov, G. B. Oviposition Behavior & Egg Mortality of the Desert Locust (Schistocerca Gregaria Forskal) on the Coast of Eritrea. 1958. 35.00x (ISBN 0-85135-037-2, Pub. by Centre Overseas Research). State Mutual Bk.

INSECTS-BIOLOGICAL CONTROL
see Insect Control-Biological Control

INSECTS-COLLECTION AND PRESERVATION
Hopkins, G. H. & Rothschild, M. An Illustrated Catalogue of the Rothschild Collection of Fleas, Vol. V: Leptopsyllidae & Ancistropsyllidae. 530p. 1971. 180.00x (ISBN 0-686-82366-4, Pub. by Brit Mus England). State Mutual Bk.
--An Illustrated Catalogue of the Rothschild Collection of Fleas, Vol. IV: Hystrichopsyllidae (Tenophthalminae, Dinopsyllinae & Listropsyllinae) 594p. 1966. 175.00x (ISBN 0-686-82367-2, Pub. by Brit Mus England). State Mutual Bk.
--An Illustrated Catalogue of the Rothschild Collection of Fleas, Vol. III: Hystrichopsyllidae (Acedestiinae, Anamiopsyllinae, Histrichopsyllinae, Neopsyllinae, Rhadinopsyllinae & Stenoponiinae) 559p. 1962. 125.00x (ISBN 0-686-82369-9, Pub. by Brit Mus England). State Mutual Bk.
--An Illustrated Catalogue of the Rothschild Collection of Fleas, Vol. II: Coptopsyllidae, Verminpsyllidae, Sephanociridae, Tschnopsyllidae, Hypsophthalmidae & Xiphiopsyllidae. 446p. 1956. 110.00x (ISBN 0-686-82370-2, Pu b. by Brit Mus England). State Mutual Bk.
--An Illustrated Catalogue of the Rothschild Collection of Fleas, Vol. I: Tungidae & Pulicidae. 362p. 1953. 90.00x (ISBN 0-686-82372-9, Pub. by Brit Mus England). State Mutual Bk.
Mardon, D. K. An Illustrated Catalogue of the Rothschild Collection of Fleas, Vol. VI: Pygiopsyllidae. 298p. 1981. 200.00x (ISBN 0-686-82365-6, Pub. by Brit Mus England). State Mutual Bk.

INSECTS-CONTROL
see Insect Control

INSECTS-DEVELOPMENT
see also Insects-Metamorphosis
Norris, M. J. Factors Affecting the Rate of Sexual Maturation of the Desert Locust (Schistocerca Gregaria Forskal) in the Laboratory. 1957. 35.00x (ISBN 0-85135-024-0, Pub. by Centre Overseas Research). State Mutual Bk.

INSECTS-EMBRYOLOGY
see Embryology-Insects

INSECTS-EXTERMINATION
see Insect Control

INSECTS-JUVENILE LITERATURE
Graham, Ada & Graham, Frank. Busy Bugs. LC 82-22085. (Illus.). 64p. (gr. 5 up). 1983. PLB 9.95 (ISBN 0-396-08126-6). Dodd.
Penn, Linda. Young Scientists Explore Insects, Bk. 1. (gr. 1-3). 1982. 3.95 (ISBN 0-86653-070-3, GA 403). Good Apple.

INSECTS-METAMORPHOSIS
Tata, J. R. Metamorphosis. Head, J. J., ed. (Carolina Biology Readers Ser.). (Illus.). 16p. 1983. pap. text ed. 1.60 (ISBN 0-89278-246-3). Carolina Biological.

INSECTS-MIGRATION
Davey, J. T. & Johnston, H. B. The African Migratory Locust (Locusta Migratoria Migratorioides) R & FO in Nigeria. 91p. 1956. 35.00x (ISBN 0-85135-009-7, Pub. by Centre Overseas Research). State Mutual Bk.
Davies, D. E. Seasonal Breeding & Migrations of the Desert Locust (Schistocerca Gregaria Forskal) in North-Eastern Africa & the Middle East. 1952. 35.00x (ISBN 0-85135-010-0, Pub. by Centre Overseas Research). State Mutual Bk.
Fortescue-Foulkes, J. Seasonal Breeding & Migrations of the Desert Locust (Schistocerca Gregaria Forskal) in South-Western Asia. 1953. 35.00x (ISBN 0-85135-015-1, Pub. by Centre Overseas Research). State Mutual Bk.

INSECTS-PHYSIOLOGY
Bassler, U. Neural Basis of Elementary Behavior in Stick Insects. Strausfeld, C., tr. (Studies in Brain Function: Vol.10). (Illus.). 180p. 1983. 32.60 (ISBN 0-387-11918-3). Springer-Verlag.
Leonbardt, Barbara A. & Berzoa, Morton, eds. Insect Pheromone Technology: Chemistry & Applications. (ACS Symposium Ser.: No. 190). 1982. write for info. (ISBN 0-8412-0724-0). Am Chemical.
Treherne, J. E., et al, eds. Advances in Insect Physiology, Vol. 16. (Serial Publication). 368p. 1982. 55.00 (ISBN 0-12-024216-8). Acad Pr.

INSECTS-PICTORIAL WORKS
Oxender, Jean J. Kinder-Fun More Insects Series, 6 bks. (Kinder-Fun Ser.). (Illus.). 96p. (Orig.). (gr. k-3). Set. pap. text ed. 18.00 (ISBN 0-89039-224-2); 64 flash cards incl. Ann Arbor Pubs.

INSECTS-RESEARCH
see Entomological Research

INSECTS-AFRICA
Chapman, R. F. A Laboratory Study of Roosting Behavior in Hoppers of the African Migratory Locust (Locusta Migratoria Migratorioides R & F) 1955. 35.00x (ISBN 0-85135-007-0, Pub. by Centre Overseas Research). State Mutual Bk.
Davey, J. T. & Johnston, H. B. The African Migratory Locust (Locusta Migratoria Migratorioides) R & FO in Nigeria. 91p. 1956. 35.00x (ISBN 0-85135-009-7, Pub. by Centre Overseas Research). State Mutual Bk.
Dempster, J. P. The Population Dynamics of the Moroccan Locust (Dociostaurus Maroccanus Thunb) in Cyprus. 1957. 35.00x (ISBN 0-85135-011-9, Pub. by Centre Overseas Research). State Mutual Bk.
Johnston, H. B. Annotated Catalogue of African Grasshoppers: Supplement. 1968. 45.00x (ISBN 0-521-05443-5, Pub. by Centre Overseas Research). State Mutual Bk.
Johnston, H. B. & Buxton, D. R. Field Observations on Locusts in Eastern Africa. 1949. 35.00x (ISBN 0-85135-008-9, Pub. by Centre Overseas Research). State Mutual Bk.
Joyce, R. J. The Ecology of Grasshoppers in Cast Central Sudan. 1952. 35.00x (ISBN 0-85135-019-4, Pub. by Centre Overseas Research). State Mutual Bk.
Merton, L. F. The Moroccan Locust (Dociostaurus Maroccanus Thunberg) 1961. 35.00X (ISBN 0-85135-021-6, Pub. by Centre Overseas Research). State Mutual Bk.
Riley, J. R. & Reynolds, D. R. Radar Observations of Spodoptera Exempta Kenya: March-April 1979. 1981. 35.00x (ISBN 0-85135-115-8, Pub. by Centre Overseas Research). State Mutual Bk.
Waloff, Z. & Rainey, R. C. Field Studies on Factors Affecting the Displacement of Desert Locust Swarms in Eastern Africa. 1951. 35.00x (ISBN 0-85135-042-9, Pub. by Centre Overseas Research). State Mutual Bk.

INSECTS-AUSTRALIA
Buckley, R. Ant-Plant Interactions in Australia. 1982. text ed. 54.50 (ISBN 90-6193-684-5, Pub. by Junk Pubs Netherlands). Kluwer Boston.

INSECTS-EUROPE
Chinery. A Field Guide to the Insects of Britain & Northern Europe. 29.95 (ISBN 0-686-42784-X, Collins Pub England). Greene.
Richards, O. W. & Waloff, N. Studies on the Biology & Population Dynamics of British Grasshoppers. 1954. 35.00x (ISBN 0-85135-034-8, Pub. by Centre Overseas Research). State Mutual Bk.

INSECTS-NORTH AMERICA
Larew, Hiram & Capizzi, Joseph. Common Insect & Mite Galls of the Pacific Northwest. (Oregon State Monographs; Studies in Entomology: No. 5). (Illus.). 80p. (Orig.). 1983. pap. 4.95 (ISBN 0-87071-055-9). Oreg St U Pr.
Stone, Alan, et al, eds. A Catalog of the Diptera of America North of Mexico. 2nd printing ed. 1700p. 1983. Repr. of 1965 ed. text ed. 37.50x (ISBN 0-87474-890-9). Smithsonian.

INSECTS, DESTRUCTIVE AND USEFUL
see Insects, Injurious and Beneficial

INSECTS, INJURIOUS AND BENEFICIAL
see also Agricultural Pests; Garden Pests; Insect Control; Insecticides
also subdivision Diseases and Pests under names of Crops, Plants, Trees, etc. e.g. Fruit-Diseases and Pests; also specific names of insect pests
Anderson, Roger F. Forest & Shade Tree Entomology. LC 60-11714. 428p. 1960. 28.95x (ISBN 0-471-02739-1). Wiley.
Wilson, M. C. & Schuder, D. L. Insects of Ornamental Plants. 2nd ed. LC 85-50792. (Practical Insect Pest Management Ser.). (Illus.). 150p. 1982. pap. text ed. 6.95x (ISBN 0-917974-93-X). Waveland Pr.

INSECTS, INJURIOUS AND BENEFICIAL–BIOLOGICAL CONTROL
see Insect Control–Biological Control
INSECTS, INJURIOUS AND BENEFICIAL–CONTROL
see Insect Control
INSECTS, INJURIOUS AND BENEFICIAL–EXTERMINATION
see Insect Control
INSECTS AS CARRIERS OF DISEASE–CONTROL
see Insect Control
INSIGNIA
see also Decorations of Honor; Emblems
Campbell, Burt L. Marine Badges & Insignia of the World: Including Marines, Commandos & Navel Infantrymen. (Illus.). 160p. 1983. 16.95 (ISBN 0-7137-1138-8, Pub. by Blandford Pr England). Sterling.
Davis, Brian L. Badges & Insignia of the Third Reich 1933-1945. (Illus.). 160p. 1983. 16.95 (ISBN 0-7137-1130-2, Pub. by Blandford Pr England). Sterling.
Olson, David V. Badges & Distinctive Insignia of the Kingdom of Saudi Arabia, Vol. I. (Illus.). 192p. (Orig.). Date not set. pap. 10.00 (ISBN 0-9609690-0-4). Olson QMD.
--Badges & Distinctive Insignia of the Kingdom of Saudi Arabia. 186p. 1981. pap. 10.00 (ISBN 0-686-84348-7). Olson QMD.
Royal Saudi Air Force: Badges & Distinctive Insignia of the Kingdom of Saudi Arabia, Vol. II. 1982. 10.00 (ISBN 0-686-83747-9). Olson QMD.
INSOLVENCY
see Bankruptcy
INSOLATION
see Solar Radiation
INSPECTION OF BUILDINGS
see Building Inspection
INSPECTION OF FOOD
see Food Adulteration and Inspection
INSPECTION OF SCHOOLS
see School Management and Organization
INSPIRATION
see also Bible–Inspiration; Creation (Literary, Artistic, etc.); Creative Ability; Enthusiasm; Revelation
Hagin, Kenneth E. Casting Your Cares Upon the Lord. 1981. pap. 1.00 (ISBN 0-89276-023-0). Hagin Ministry.
Hagin, Kenneth, Jr. How to Make the Dream God Gave You Come True. 1981. pap. 1.00 (ISBN 0-89276-708-1). Hagin Ministry.
Kauffman, Karen, compiled by. Mighty Fortress Is Our God. 1982. 3.95 (ISBN 0-8378-2031-6). Gibson.
Kidd, Sunnie D. & Kidd, James W. The Dynamic Aspects of Inspiration. 38p. (Orig.). 1982. pap. 2.50 (ISBN 0-910727-02-3). Golden Phoenix.
Petty, Jo, compiled by. Pathways of Gold. 1983. 5.50 (ISBN 0-8378-1709-9). Gibson.
Stanley, Gary S. The Garimus File. (Illus., Orig.). 1983. pap. 7.95 (ISBN 0-86605-107-4). Heres Life.
Swami Rama. Inspired Thoughts. 250p. (Orig.). 1983. pap. 6.95 (ISBN 0-89389-086-3). Himalayan Intl Inst.
White, Ruthe. Touch Me Again, Lord. 144p. (Orig.). 1983. pap. 5.95 (ISBN 0-89840-038-4). Heres Life.
INSTALLATION SERVICE (CHURCH OFFICERS)
Mall, E. Jane. Abingdon Manual of Installation Services. 80p. (Orig.). 1983. pap. 4.95 (ISBN 0-687-00367-9). Abingdon.
INSTINCT
see also Habit; Psychology, Comparative
Wilm, Emil C. Theories of Instinct. 1925. text ed. 39.50x (ISBN 0-686-83818-1). Elliots Bks.
INSTITUTIONAL CHURCH
see Church Work
INSTITUTIONS, ASSOCIATIONS, ETC.
see Associations, Institutions, etc.
INSTITUTIONS, CHARITABLE AND PHILANTHROPIC
see Charities
INSTITUTIONS, INTERNATIONAL
see International Agencies; International Cooperation
INSTRUCTION
see Education; Teaching;
also subdivision Instruction and Study under Music and under names of musical instruments
INSTRUCTIONAL MATERIALS
see Teaching–Aids and Devices
INSTRUCTIONAL MATERIALS CENTERS
AASL School Media Centers. Instructional Design & the Library Media Specialist. (Focus on Trends & Issues Ser.: No. 5). 44p. (Orig.). 1979. pap. text ed. 5.00 (ISBN 0-8389-3234-7). ALA.
Bennett, Linda L. Volunteers in the School Media Center. 350p. 1983. pap. text ed. 23.50 (ISBN 0-87287-351-X). Libs Unl.
Gothberg, Helen. Impact: Television-Video in Libraries & Schools. 1983. 22.50 (ISBN 0-208-01859-X, Lib Prof Pubns); pap. price not set (ISBN 0-208-01860-3, Lib Prof Pubns). Shoe String.
Jay, Hilda L. Stimulating Student Search: Library Media Classroom Teacher Techniques. 160p. 1983. 18.50 (ISBN 0-208-01936-7, Lib Prof Pubns); pap. 14.50 (ISBN 0-208-01926-X). Shoe String.
Martin, Betty. The School Library Media Specialist's Survival Handbook. 1983. price not set (ISBN 0-208-01997-9, Lib Prof Pubns); pap. price not set (ISBN 0-208-01998-7). Shoe String.
Sive, Mary R. Media Selection Handbook. 230p. 1982. lib. bdg. 22.50 (ISBN 0-87287-350-1). Libs Unl.
INSTRUCTIONAL OBJECTIVES
see Education–Aims and Objectives
INSTRUCTIONAL SYSTEMS ANALYSIS
see Educational Statistics
INSTRUCTIONAL TECHNOLOGY
see Educational Technology
INSTRUCTIONS TO JURIES
Douthwaite, Graham. Jury Instructions on Damages in Tort Actions. 1981. text ed. 37.50 (ISBN 0-87473-137-2). A Smith Co.
INSTRUCTIVE GAMES
see Educational Games
INSTRUCTORS
see College Teachers
INSTRUMENTAL MUSIC
see also Band Music; Dance Music; Military Music also Piano Music, Organ Music and similar headings
Baehr, Tom. A Pleasant Addiction. (Illus.). 48p. (Orig.). 1982. 5.95 (ISBN 0-9608842-1-1). Hogfiddle Pr.
The Keyboard Works of Felix Maximo Lopez: An Anthology. Espinosa, Alma, ed. LC 82-24767. (Illus.). 216p. (Orig.). 1983. lib. bdg. 23.50 (ISBN 0-8191-3038-9); pap. text ed. 12.25 (ISBN 0-8191-3039-7). U Pr of Amer.
INSTRUMENTAL MUSIC–INSTRUCTION AND STUDY
see also names of specific musical instruments with or without the subdivision Instruction and Study
Sheet Music Magazine & Keyboard Classics Magazine, ed. The Do-it Yourself Handbook for Keyboard Playing. Date not set. price not set (ISBN 0-943748-00-3). Shacor Inc.
INSTRUMENTATION AND ORCHESTRATION
see also Musical Instruments
Kennan, Kent W. Cassette Supplement for "The Technique of Orchestration". 1981. cassette 8.95x (ISBN 0-292-71070-4). U of Tex Pr.
INSTRUMENTS, AERONAUTICAL
see Aeronautical Instruments
INSTRUMENTS, ASTRONOMICAL
see Astronomical Instruments
INSTRUMENTS, ELECTRIC
see Electric Apparatus and Appliances
INSTRUMENTS, ELECTRONIC
see Electronic Instruments
INSTRUMENTS, MEDICAL
see Medical Instruments and Apparatus
INSTRUMENTS, MUSICAL
see Musical Instruments
INSTRUMENTS, NEGOTIABLE
see Negotiable Instruments
INSTRUMENTS, OPTICAL
see Optical Instruments
INSTRUMENTS, SCIENTIFIC
see Scientific Apparatus and Instruments
INSTRUMENTS OF WAR
see Munitions
INSULAR FLORA AND FAUNA
see Island Flora and Fauna
INSULATION (HEAT)
Makram-Ebeid, S. & Tuck, B., eds. Semi-Insulating Three-Four Materials: Evian 1982. 420p. 1982. text ed. 62.95x (ISBN 0-906812-22-4). Birkhauser.
Turner, W. C. & Malloy, J. F. Thermal Insulation Handbook. 1981. 64.50 (ISBN 0-07-039805-4). McGraw.
INSULTS
see Invective
INSURANCE
see also Insurance Companies; Risk (Insurance); Self-Insurance
Benjamin, Bernard. General Insurance. 1977. 18.95 (ISBN 0-434-90136-9, Pub. by Heinemann). David & Charles.
Chasen, Nancy H. Policy Wise: The Practical Guide to Insurance Decisions for Older Consumers. (American Association of Retired Persons Publications). 148p. 1983. pap. 5.95 (ISBN 0-673-24806-2). Scott F.
Enforcing Secured Claims: A Course Handbook. 1983. 30.00 (ISBN 0-686-43271-1). PLI.
Gaines, Price, ed. Who Writes What, 1983. 432p. 1982. spirial bdg. 12.60 (ISBN 0-87218-027-1). Natl Underwriter.
Glendenning, G. Williams & Holtom, Robert B. Personal Lines Underwriting. 2nd ed. LC 77-81989. 582p. 1982. text ed. 18.00 (ISBN 0-89462-003-7). IIA.
Horn, Ronald C. Code of Professional Ethics of the American Institute for Property & Liability Underwriters. American Institute, ed. LC 79-50832. 86p. 1979. pap. 3.00 (ISBN 0-89463-021-0). Am Inst Property.
Hughes, Charles. Guide to Texas Title Insurance. 1983. 11.95 (ISBN 0-87201-777-X). Gulf Pub.
Long, John D., ed. Issues in Insurance, 2 vols. 2nd ed. LC 81-66116. 852p. 1981. text ed. 18.00 ea. Vol. (ISBN 0-89463-034-2). Am Inst Property.
Milling-Stanley, Jeanne, ed. World Insurance Yearbook 1981. 5th ed. 467p. 1980. 82.50x (ISBN 0-582-90305-X). Intl Pubns Serv.
Smith, Robert S. & Kensicki, Peter R. Principles of Insurance Protection. LC 80-84218. 752p. 1981. pap. text ed. 17.00 (ISBN 0-89462-006-1). IIA.
Wood, Glenn L. & Lilly, Claude C. III. Personal Risk Management & Insurance, 2 Vols. 2nd ed. LC 80-69852. 935p. 1980. text ed. 18.00 ea. vol. Am Inst Property.
INSURANCE–AGENTS
Anderson, Ronald T. Automating Your Agency Book. LC 82-60877. 288p. 1982. text ed. 16.35 (ISBN 0-87218-321-1). Natl Underwriter.
Horn, Ronald C. On Professions, Professionals, & Professional Ethics. LC 78-67501. 114p. 1978. pap. 3.00 (ISBN 0-89463-020-2). Am Inst Property.
INSURANCE–BIBLIOGRAPHY
Gaines, Price, ed. Life Financial Reports. 1982 ed. 784p. 1982. pap. 29.00 (ISBN 0-87218-023-9). Natl Underwriter.
--Life Rates & Data. 1982 ed. LC 76-7124. 730p. 1982. pap. 13.50 (ISBN 0-87218-022-0). Natl Underwriter.
INSURANCE–DATA PROCESSING
Anderson, Ronald T. Automating Your Agency Book. LC 82-60877. 288p. 1982. text ed. 16.35 (ISBN 0-87218-321-1). Natl Underwriter.
Gantt, Michael D. & Gatza, James. Computers in Insurance. LC 80-67525. 150p. 1981. pap. 7.00 (ISBN 0-89463-029-6). Am Inst Property.
INSURANCE–EXAMINATIONS, QUESTIONS, ETC.
Rudman, Jack. Insurance Examiner. (Career Examination Ser.: C-2694). (Cloth bdg. avail. on request). pap. 10.00 (ISBN 0-8373-2694-X). Natl Learning.
--Insurance Fund Hearing Representative Trainee. (Career Examination Ser.: C-880). (Cloth bdg. avail. on request). pap. 10.00 (ISBN 0-8373-0880-1). Natl Learning.
--Principal Insurance Examiner. (Career Examination Ser.: C-2696). (Cloth bdg. avail. on request). pap. 12.00 (ISBN 0-8373-2696-6). Natl Learning.
--Senior Insurance Examiner. (Career Examination Ser.: C-2685). (Cloth bdg. avail. on request). pap. 12.00 (ISBN 0-8373-2685-0). Natl Learning.
INSURANCE–FINANCE
Breslin, Cormick & Troxel, Terrie E. Property-Liability Insurance Accounting & Finance. LC 78-67500. 349p. 1980. text ed. 16.00 (ISBN 0-89463-015-6). Am Inst Property.
INSURANCE–RISK
see Risk (Insurance)
INSURANCE–SALESMANSHIP
see Insurance–Agents
INSURANCE–SELF-ASSURANCE
see Self-Insurance
INSURANCE–STATISTICS
Hossack, I. B. & Pollard, J. H. Introductory Statistics with Applications in General Insurance. LC 82-4421. 250p. Date not set. price not set (ISBN 0-521-24781-0); pap. price not set (ISBN 0-521-28957-2). Cambridge U Pr.
INSURANCE, AUTOMOBILE
Automobile Insurance. 60p. 1982. 12.00 (ISBN 0-686-81761-3). Ctr Analysis Public Issues.
INSURANCE, BUSINESS
Church, Frederic C., Jr. Avoiding Surprises: Eight Steps to an Efficient, Low-Cost Corporate Risk Management & Insurance Program. LC 81-71318. (Illus.). 286p. 1982. 17.95 (ISBN 0-9607398-0-7). Boston Risk Magmt.
Gaunt, Larry D. & Williams, Numan A. Commercial Liability Underwriting. 2nd ed. LC 82-82396. 672p. 1982. text ed. 18.00 (ISBN 0-89462-013-4). IIA.
Hickmott, G. J. Principles & Practice of Interruption Insurance. 937p. 1981. 125.00 (ISBN 0-900886-56-0, Pub. By Witherby & Co England). State Mutual Bk.
McGinn, Daniel F. Actuarial Fundamentals for Multiemployer Plans. 122p. (Orig.). 1982. pap. text ed. 10.00 (ISBN 0-89154-191-8). Intl Found Employ.
Malecki, Donald S. & Donaldson, James H. Commercial Liability Risk Management & Insurance, 2 Vols. LC 78-67497. 978p. Date not set. text ed. 18.00 (ISBN 0-686-82665-5). Am Inst Property.
INSURANCE, CORPORATE
see Insurance, Business
INSURANCE, DISABILITY
Greenston, Peter & Hagan, Michael. Insuring the Disabled: A Study of the Impact of Changes to the Social Security Disability Insurance Program. LC 81-50055. (Illus.). 69p. (Orig.). 1981. pap. text ed. 5.75 (ISBN 0-87766-292-4, URI 31700). Urban Inst.
Rudman, Jack. Senior Services Disability Analyst. (Career Examination Ser.: C-859). (Cloth bdg. avail. on request). pap. 10.00 (ISBN 0-8373-0859-3). Natl Learning.
INSURANCE, GROUP
Here are entered works on group insurance in general and on group life insurance. Works on group insurance in other specific fields are entered under Insurance, Casualty; Insurance, Hospitalization etc.
Beam, Burton T., Jr. Group Insurance: Basic Concepts & Alternatives. Date not set. price not set (ISBN 0-943590-00-0). Amer College.
INSURANCE, HEALTH
see also Health Maintenance Organizations; Medical Care; Workmen's Compensation
Blendon, Robert J. & Moloney, Thomas W., eds. New Approaches to the Medicaid Crisis. (Health Care Economics & Technology Ser.). 480p. 1983. 33.95 (ISBN 0-86621-007-5). F&S Pr.
Greenfield, Margaret. Medicare & Medicaid: The 1965 & 1967 Social Security Amendments. LC 82-25157. x, 143p. 1983. Repr. of 1968 ed. lib. bdg. 25.00x (ISBN 0-313-23841-3, GRME). Greenwood.
Jehle, Faustin F. Complete & Easy Guide to Social Security & Medicare. 1982. pap. 6.95 (ISBN 0-440-01129-9, Dell Trade Pbks). Dell.
Numbers, Ronald L., ed. Compulsory Health Insurance: The Continuing American Debate. LC 82-6145. (Contributions in Medical History Ser.: No. 11). 184p. 1982. 27.50 (ISBN 0-313-23436-1). Greenwood.
Prudential Insurance Company of America. Health Insurance Fundamentals: To Prepare for the Health Insurance License Examination. LC 76-17650. 170p. pap. text ed. 4.95 (ISBN 0-471-01937-2). Krieger.
Rudman, Jack. Assistant Health Insurance Administrator. (Career Examination Ser.: C-358). (Cloth bdg. avail. on request). pap. 12.00 (ISBN 0-686-84412-2). Natl Learning.
--Health Insurance Administrator. (Career Examination Ser.: C-2687). (Cloth bdg. avail. on request). pap. 12.00 (ISBN 0-8373-2687-7). Natl Learning.
Sigerist, Henry E. Medicine & Human Welfare. 1941. text ed. 29.50x (ISBN 0-686-83623-5). Elliots Bks.
INSURANCE, INDEMNITY
see Insurance, Liability
INSURANCE, LIABILITY
see also Insurance, Automobile
Gaunt, Larry D. & Williams, Numan A. Commercial Liability Underwriting. 2nd ed. LC 82-82396. 672p. 1982. text ed. 18.00 (ISBN 0-89462-013-4). IIA.
Johns, Corydon T. An Introduction to Liability Claims Adjusting Book. 3rd, rev. ed. LC 82-61231. 672p. 1982. text ed. 25.00 (ISBN 0-87218-320-3). Natl Underwriter.
Launie, J. J. & Lee, J. Finley. Principles of Property & Liability Underwriting. 2nd ed. LC 77-81988. 562p. 1981. text ed. 18.00 (ISBN 0-89462-002-9). IIA.
Malecki, Donald S. & Donaldson, James H. Commercial Liability Risk Management & Insurance, 2 Vols. LC 78-67497. 978p. Date not set. text ed. 18.00 (ISBN 0-686-82665-5). Am Inst Property.
INSURANCE, LIFE
see also Annuities; Insurance, Group; Probabilities
Advanced Sales Reference Service Editorial Staff. Tax Facts on Life Insurance. 1982 ed. 470p. 1982. pap. 6.00 (ISBN 0-87218-414-5). Natl Underwriter.
Cummins, J. David & Smith, Barry D. Risk Classification in Life Insurance. 1982. lib. bdg. 45.00 (ISBN 0-89838-114-2). Kluwer-Nijhoff.
Life Office Management Association, ed. Life Insurance Investments: Readings. (FLMI Insurance Education Program Ser.). 186p. 1982. pap. text ed. 10.00 (ISBN 0-915322-48-X). LOMA.
Prudential Insurance Company of America. Life Insurance Fundamentals: To Prepare for the Life Insurance Agents' License Examination. LC 76-17652. 314p. Repr. of 1976 ed. pap. text ed. 8.95 (ISBN 0-471-01938-0). Krieger.
Zelizer, Viviana A. Morals & Markets: The Development of Life Insurance in the United States. 210p. 1983. pap. text ed. 12.95x (ISBN 0-87855-929-9). Transaction Bks.
INSURANCE, LIFE–ACCOUNTING
Zucconi, Paul J. Generally Accepted Accounting Principles for Life Insurance Companies. Crane, John R., ed. (FLMI Insurance Education Program Ser.). 28p. 1982. pap. text ed. 3.00 (ISBN 0-915322-51-X). LOMA.
INSURANCE, LIFE–EXAMINATIONS, QUESTIONS, ETC.
see Insurance–Examinations, Questions, etc.
INSURANCE, LIFE–MATHEMATICS
see also Probabilities
Workman, Lewis C. Mathematical Foundations of Life Insurance: Instructor's Manual. (FLMI Insurance Education Program Ser.). 314p. 1982. pap. 13.00 tchrs ed. (ISBN 0-915322-54-4). LOMA.
--Mathematical Foundations of Life Insurance: Student Guide. (FLMI Insurance Education Program Ser.). 257p. 1982. pap. 7.00 workbook (ISBN 0-915322-53-6). LOMA.
--Mathematical Foundations of Life Insurance. LC 82-80669. (Insurance Education Program Ser.). 467p. 1982. text ed. 12.50 (ISBN 0-915322-52-8). LOMA.
INSURANCE, MARINE
Goodacre, J. Kenneth. Marine Insurance Claims. 1050p. 1981. 125.00 (ISBN 0-900886-53-6, Pub. By Witherby & Co England). State Mutual Bk.
Greenacre, C. T. Templeman on Marine Insurance. 600p. 1981. 70.00x (ISBN 0-7121-1395-9, Pub. by Macdonald & Evans). State Mutual Bk.

INSURANCE, MULTIPLE LINE
Turner, Richard D. & Waranch, Seeman. Multiple-Lines Insurance Protection. LC 81-80772. 704p. 1981. pap. text ed. 17.00 (ISBN 0-89462-007-X). IIA.
INSURANCE, MUTUAL
see Insurance
INSURANCE, POSTAL LIFE
see Insurance, Life
INSURANCE, PROPERTY
see also Insurance, Marine
Launie, J. J. & Lee, J. Finley. Principles of Property & Liability Underwriting. 2nd ed. LC 77-81988. 562p. 1981. text ed. 18.00 (ISBN 0-89462-002-9). IIA.
Rodda, Williams H. & Trieschmann, James S. Commercial Property Risk Management & Insurance, 2 Vols. LC 78-52690. 1982. Vol. 1. text ed. 18.00 (ISBN 0-89463-004-0); Vol. 2. text ed. 18.00 (ISBN 0-89463-005-9). Am Inst Property.
INSURANCE, SELF
see Self-Insurance
INSURANCE, SICKNESS
see Insurance, Health
INSURANCE, SOCIAL
see Social Security
INSURANCE, STATE AND COMPULSORY
see Social Security
INSURANCE, TRANSPORTATION
see Insurance, Marine
INSURANCE, UNEMPLOYMENT
Rudman, Jack. Unemployment Insurance Referee. (Career Examination Ser.: C-917). (Cloth bdg. avail. on request). pap. 14.00 (ISBN 0-8373-0917-4). Natl Learning.
Tax Foundation, Incorporated. Unemployment Insurance: Trends & Issues. (Research Publication Ser.: No. 35). 88p. (Orig.). 1982. pap. 5.00 (ISBN 0-686-37951-9). Tax Found.
INSURANCE, WORKING-MEN'S
see Social Security
INSURANCE AGENTS
see Insurance-Agents
INSURANCE COMPANIES
Dolin, Armin. Buy-Sell-Merge-Affiliate: Insurance Agency Manual & Workbook, 2 vols. LC 82-81856. 626p. 1982. Set. 75.00 (ISBN 0-87218-319-X). Vol. I, 490p. Vol. II, 136p. Natl Underwriter.
Hammes, Carol A. & Anderson, Ronald T. Agency Operations & Sales Management. LC 82-82395. 653p. 1982. pap. text ed. 17.00 (ISBN 0-89462-037-1). IIA.
Webb, Bernard L. & Launie, J. J. Insurance Company Operations, 2 Vols. 2nd ed. LC 81-66113. 935p. 1981. Vol. 1. text ed. 18.00 (ISBN 0-89463-024-5); Vol. 2. text ed. 18.00 (ISBN 0-89463-025-3). Am Inst Property.
INSURANCE LAW
Lorimer, James J. & Perlet, Harry F., Jr. The Legal Environment of Insurance, 2 Vols. LC 81-66114. 823p. 1981. Vol. 1. text ed. 18.00 (ISBN 0-89463-026-1); Vol. 2. text ed. 18.00 (ISBN 0-686-82668-X). Am Inst Property.
INSURRECTIONS
see Revolutions
INTANGIBLE PROPERTY
see Copyright; Intellectual Property; Licenses; Patents; Trade-Marks
INTEGER PROGRAMMING
see also Programming (Electronic Computers)
Garfinkel, Robert & Nemhauser, George L. Integer Programming. LC 72-3881. (Decision & Control Ser.). 528p. 1972. 39.95x (ISBN 0-471-29195-1, Pub. by Wiley-Interscience). Wiley.
INTEGRAL EQUATIONS
see also Functional Analysis
Mikhlin & Smolitskii. Approximate Methods for Solution of Differential & Integral Equations. 1967. 20.00 (ISBN 0-444-00022-4). Elsevier.
INTEGRALS
Baker, Christopher T. & Miller, Geoffrey F. Treatment of Integral Equations by Numerical Methods. Date not set. 37.00 (ISBN 0-12-074120-2). Acad Pr.
McShane, E. J., ed. Unified Integration. LC 82-16266. (Pure & Applied Mathematics Ser.). Date not set. price not set (ISBN 0-12-486260-8). Acad Pr.
INTEGRALS, ELLIPTIC
see Functions, Elliptic
INTEGRALS, GENERALIZED
see also Measure Theory
Bartle, Robert G. Elements of Integration. LC 75-15979. 129p. 1966. 22.95x (ISBN 0-471-05457-7). Wiley.
INTEGRATED CIRCUITS
Electronics Magazine. Large Scale Integration. 1976. 28.50 (ISBN 0-07-019187-5). McGraw.
Kasper, Joseph & Feller, Steven. Digital Integrated Circuits. 197p. 1983. 19.95 (ISBN 0-13-213587-6); pap. 12.95 (ISBN 0-13-213579-5). P-H.
Mavor, J. & Jack, M. A. Introduction to MOS LSI Design. 350p. 1982. 35.00 (ISBN 0-201-11440-2, Adv Bk Prog). A-W.
Williams, Arthur B. Designer's Handbook of Integrated Circuits. 944p. 1983. 59.50 (ISBN 0-686-82175-0, C). McGraw.
INTEGRATED DATA PROCESSING
see Electronic Data Processing
INTEGRATION, NUMERICAL
see Numerical Integration
INTEGRATION, RACIAL
see Race Relations
INTEGRATION IN EDUCATION
see Articulation (Education); School Integration
INTEGRITY
see Self-Respect
INTEGUMENT (SKIN)
see Skin
INTELLECT
see also Creation (Literary, Artistic, etc.); Imagination; Inefficiency, Intellectual; Intelligence Tests; Knowledge, Theory of; Logic; Memory; Perception; Reason; Senses and Sensation; Thought and Thinking; Wisdom
Asimov, Isaac. The Roving Mind. 348p. 1983. 17.95 (ISBN 0-87975-201-7). Prometheus Bks.
Chomsky, Noam. Modular Approaches to the Study of the Mind. (SDSU Distinguished Research Lecture Ser.). 120p. 1983. 12.00 (ISBN 0-916304-56-6); pap. 6.00 (ISBN 0-916304-55-8). Campanile.
Discovering the Human Mind. LC 81-52417. (Discovering Science Ser.). lib. bdg. 15.96 (ISBN 0-86706-060-3, Pub. by Stonehenge). Silver.
Ehrenberg, Miriam & Ehrenberg, Otto. Brain Power: A Total Program for Increasing Your Intelligence. 256p. 1983. 15.95 (ISBN 0-89479-121-4, A & W Visual Library). A & W Pubs.
Hollander, Bernard. Brain, Mind, & the External Signs of Intelligence. LC 78-72802. 1931. 32.50 (ISBN 0-404-60864-7). AMS Pr.
Meirowitz, Marcus & Jacobs, Paul I. Brain Muscle Builders: Games to Increase Your Natural Intelligence. 288p. 1983. 13.95 (ISBN 0-13-080986-1); pap. 6.95 (ISBN 0-13-080978-0). P-H.
Osborne, R. Travis & McGork, Frank C., eds. The Testing of Negro Intelligence. 402p. 1982. 18.50 (ISBN 0-936396-02-4). Foun Human GA.
Premack, David. Intelligence in Ape & Man. LC 76-26470. 370p. 1976. text ed. 24.95 (ISBN 0-89859-136-8). L Erlbaum Assocs.
Schwanauer, Francis. The Flesh of Thought is Pleasure or Pain. LC 82-17674. 136p. (Orig.). 1983. pap. text ed. 8.75 (ISBN 0-8191-2765-5). U Pr of Amer.
Witt, Scott. How to be Twice as Smart: Boosting Your Brainpower & Unleashing the Miracles of Your Mind. LC 82-14358. 262p. 1983. pap. 4.95 (ISBN 0-13-402339-0, Reward). P-H.
INTELLECTRONICS
see Artificial Intelligence; Bionics
INTELLECTUAL COOPERATION
see also Congresses and Conventions; Cultural Relations; Educational Exchanges; Exchange of Persons Programs; Library Cooperation
also subdivision Relations (General) Under names of countries, e.g. United States-Relations (General) with Latin America
Price, Paxton P., ed. International Book & Library Activities: The History of a U. S. Foreign Policy. LC 82-3297. 264p. 1982. 15.00 (ISBN 0-8108-1545-1). Scarecrow.
INTELLECTUAL FREEDOM
see Censorship; Freedom of Information; Liberty of Speech
INTELLECTUAL INEFFICIENCY
see Inefficiency, Intellectual
INTELLECTUAL PROPERTY
see also Copyright; Industrial Property
Goldstein, Paul. Copyright, Patent, Trademark & Related State Doctrines: Cases & Materials on the Law of Intellectual Property. 2nd ed. (University Casebook Ser.). 183p. 1982. write for info. tchrs. manual (ISBN 0-88277-105-1). Foundation Pr.
INTELLECTUALS
see also Professions;
also subdivision Intellectual Life under names of countries, cities, etc., e.g. France-Intellectual Life
Kamenkay, Eugene & Smith, F. B. Intellectuals & Revolution. 22.50 (ISBN 0-312-41893-0). St Martin.
INTELLIGENCE
see Intellect
INTELLIGENCE, ARTIFICIAL
see Artificial Intelligence
INTELLIGENCE, BUSINESS
see Business Intelligence
INTELLIGENCE LEVELS
see also Intelligence Tests
Godson, Roy, ed. Analysis & Estimates. (Intelligence Requirements for the 1980's: Vol. 2). 224p. 1980. pap. 7.50 (ISBN 0-87855-827-6). Transaction Bks.
--Elements of Intelligence. (Intelligence Requirements for the 1980's: Vol. I). 124p. (Orig.). 1979. pap. 4.95 (ISBN 0-87855-826-8). Transaction Bks.
INTELLIGENCE LEVELS-TESTING
see Intelligence Tests
INTELLIGENCE OF ANIMALS
see Instinct; Psychology, Comparative
INTELLIGENCE SERVICE
see also Espionage; Secret Service
Deacon, Richard. A History of the Japanese Secret Service. 320p. 1982. 40.00x (ISBN 0-584-10383-2, Pub. by Muller Ltd). State Mutual Bk.
Mathams, R. J. Sub Rosa: Memoirs of an Australian Intelligence Analyst. 200p. 1983. text ed. 19.95x (ISBN 0-86861-380-0). Allen Unwin.
Smith, Bradley F. The Shacow Warriors: O.S.S. & the Origins of the C.I.A. 400p. 1983. 14.95 (ISBN 0-465-07756-0). Basic.
INTELLIGENCE TESTING
see Intelligence Tests
INTELLIGENCE TESTS
see also Stanford-Binet Test; Wechsler Intelligence Scale for Children
Munzert, Alfred. Test Your Computer IQ. Levy, Valerie, ed. (Test Yourself Ser.). (Orig.). 1983. pap. 4.95 (ISBN 0-671-47171-6). Monarch Pr.
Pictoral Test of Intelligence. write for info. (RivEd). HM.
INTELLIGENT MACHINES
see Artificial Intelligence; Conscious Automata
INTEMPERANCE
see Alcoholism; Temperance
INTENSIVE CARE UNITS
see also Coronary Care Units
Abels, Linda F., et al. Critical Care Nursing: Process & Practice. (Illus.). 825p. 1983. pap. text ed. 25.95 (ISBN 0-8016-0083-9). Mosby.
Dillard, Jack. Heart Stop: No Death at All. (Illus.). 42p. (Orig.). 1982. pap. write for info. (ISBN 0-940588-08-0). Hazlett Print.
Joyce, Joan M. Handbook of Critical Care Nursing. Gardner, Alvin f., ed. (Allied Professions Monograph Ser.). 1983. 35.00 (ISBN 0-87527-318-1). Green.
Kirchhoff, Karin T. Coronary Precautions: A Diffusion Survey. Kalisch, Philip & Kalisch, Beatrice, eds. LC 82-17613. (Studies in Nursing Management: No. 8). 128p. 1982. 34.95 (ISBN 0-8357-1377-6). Univ Microfilms.
Langfitt, Dot E. Critical Care: Certification Practice Exams. (Illus.). 224p. 1983. pap. text ed. 12.95 (ISBN 0-89303-246-8). R J Brady.
--Critical Care: Certification Preparation & Review. (Illus.). 640p. 1983. text ed. 27.95 (ISBN 0-89303-245-X). R J Brady.
Meador, Billie. Critical Care Nursing Review & Self-Test. 250p. 1983. softcover 16.95 (ISBN 0-87489-300-3). Med Economics.
Sibbald, William J. Synopsis of Critical Care. (Illus.). 274p. 1983. lib. bdg. price not set (ISBN 0-683-07710-4). Williams & Wilkins.
Thompson, Theodore R. Intensive Care of Newborn Infants: A Practical Manual. (Illus.). 414p. spiral bdg. 29.50 (ISBN 0-8166-1090-8). U of Minn Pr.
Tinker, J. & Rapin, M., eds. Care of the Critically Ill Patient. (Illus.). 1150p. 1983. 124.00 (ISBN 0-387-11289-8). Springer-Verlag.
Walton, Douglas N. Ethics of Withdrawal of Life-Support Systems: Case Studies on Decision Making in Intensive Care. LC 82-15662. (Contributions in Philosophy: No. 23). 288p. 1983. lib. bdg. 29.95x (ISBN 0-313-23752-2, R726). Greenwood.
Wills, Sheryle L. & Tremblay, Sharyn F. Critical Care Review for Nurses. LC 82-42829. 475p. (Orig.). 1983. pap. write for info. (ISBN 0-940122-06-5). Multi Media CO.
INTERACTION, SOCIAL
see Social Interaction
INTERACTION ANALYSIS IN EDUCATION
Turner, Glen. The Social World of the Comprehensive School: How Pupils Adapt. 160p. 1983. text ed. 23.50x (ISBN 0-7099-2424-0, Pub. by Croom Helm Ltd England). Biblio Dist.
INTERCHANGE OF PERSONS
see Exchange of Persons Programs
INTERCHANGE OF POPULATION
see Population Transfers
INTERCONNECTED ELECTRIC UTILITY SYSTEMS
see Electric Utilities
INTERCULTURAL COMMUNICATION
Fuglesang, Andreas, ed. About Understanding: Ideas & Observations on Cross Cultural Communication. 232p. 1983. pap. text ed. 10.95 (ISBN 0-910365-01-6). Decade Media.
INTERCULTURAL EDUCATION
see also Race Awareness
Baker, Gwendolyn C. Planning & Organizing for Multicultural Instruction. LC 82-8910. (Illus.). 288p. 1983. pap. text ed. 10.95 (ISBN 0-201-10188-2). A-W.
Landis, Dan & Brislin, Richard W., eds. Handbook of Intercultural Training: Area Studies in Intercultural Training, Vol. III. (General Psychology Ser.: No. 116). 325p. 1983. 40.00 (ISBN 0-08-027535-4); Set. before 4/83 85.00 (ISBN 0-08-027537-0). Pergamon.
Lynch, James. Multicultural Curriculum. 160p. 1983. pap. 17.50 (ISBN 0-7134-4510-6, Pub. by Batsford England). David & Charles.
INTERCULTURAL RELATIONS
see Cultural Relations
INTEREST AND USURY
Donald, D. W. Compound Interest & Annuities--Certain. 1975. 21.50 (ISBN 0-434-90366-3, Pub. by Heinemann). David & Charles.
Fisher, Irving. The Rate of Interest: With a New Introduction by Donald Dewey. LC 82-48363. (Accountancy in Transition Ser.). 472p. 1982. lib. bdg. 50.00 (ISBN 0-8240-5314-1). Garland Pub.
Reynolds, Mack. Compounded Interests. (Boskone Bks.). (Illus.). xii, 164p. 1983. 13.00 (ISBN 0-915368-20-X); deluxe ed. 25.00 (ISBN 0-915368-82-X). NESFA Pr.
INTEREST AND USURY-TABLES, ETC.
see also Investments-Tables, etc.
Thorndike's Compound Interest & Annuity Tables. 1982. 60.00 (ISBN 0-88262-836-4). Warren.
INTERFACES, CHEMISTRY OF
see Surface Chemistry
INTERFEROMETER
Jones, R. & Wykes, C. M. Holographic & Speckle Interferometry. LC 82-1338. 250p. Date not set. price not set (ISBN 0-521-23268-6). Cambridge U Pr.
INTERFERONS
Gresser, I., ed. Interferon 3, 1981. LC 79-4142. 164p. 1982. 19.00 (ISBN 0-12-302252-5). Acad Pr.
Merigan, Thomas C. & Friedman, Robert M., eds. Interferons: Symposium. 481p. 1982. 42.00 (ISBN 0-12-491220-6). Acad Pr.
INTERGOVERNMENTAL FISCAL RELATIONS
see also Grants-In-Aid; Intergovernmental Tax Relations
Davey, Kenneth. Financing Regional Government: International Practices & Their Relevance to the Third World. (Public Administration in Developing Countries Ser.). 220p. 1983. 24.95 (ISBN 0-471-10356-X, Pub. by Wiley-Interscience). Wiley.
Rose, Richard & Page, Edward C., eds. Fiscal Stress in Cities. LC 82-9500. (Illus.). 256p. Date not set. 29.95 (ISBN 0-521-24607-5). Cambridge U Pr.
Wallich, Christine. State Finances in India. LC 82-11087. (World Bank Staff Working Papers: No. 523). (Orig.). 1982. pap. 3.00 (ISBN 0-8213-0013-X). World Bank.
INTERGOVERNMENTAL TAX RELATIONS
Burchell, Robert W. & Carr, James H. The Rise & Fall of the Intergovernmental City. 480p. 1983. pap. text ed. 27.50x (ISBN 0-88285-091-1, Dist. by Transaction Bks). Ctr Urban Pol Res.
INTERINDUSTRY ECONOMICS
see also Diversification in Industry
Skolka, J. V., ed. Compilation of Input-Output Tables, Gouvieux, France, 1981: Proceedings. (Lecture Notes in Economics & Mathematical Sciences Ser.: Vol. 203). 307p. 1983. pap. 21.00 (ISBN 0-387-11553-6). Springer-Verlag.
INTERIOR DECORATION
see also Church Decoration and Ornament; Coverlets; Drapery; Floor Coverings; Furniture; Lighting; Lighting, Architectural and Decorative; Mural Painting and Decoration; Paper-Hanging; Upholstery; Wall-Paper
Andersen, Georg & Dean, Edith. Interior Decorating. 192p. 1983. 12.95 (ISBN 0-87123-288-X). Bethany Hse.
Architectural Record Magazine. Record Interiors. 1983. pap. write for info. (ISBN 0-07-002391-3). McGraw.
Belloli, Jay. Innovations: Contemporary Home Environments. (Illus.). 38p. 1973. 6.00x (ISBN 0-686-99821-9). La Jolla Mus Contemp Art.
Corbin, Patricia. Summer Cottages & Castles: Scenes from the Good Life. (Illus.). 144p. 1983. 29.95 (ISBN 0-525-93279-8, 02908-870). Dutton.
Douglas, Peter. The Ideal Home Book of Interiors. 128p. 1983. pap. 9.95 (ISBN 0-7137-1327-5, Pub. by Blandford Pr England). Sterling.
Forge, Suzanne. Victorian Splendour: Australian Interior Decoration, 1837-1901. (Illus.). 162p. 1981. 65.00x (ISBN 0-19-554299-1). Oxford U Pr.
Giralt-Miracle, Daniel. New Interiors, No. 1. 246p. 1982. 9.95 (ISBN 84-7031-213-8, Pub. by Editorial Blume Spain). Intl Schol Bk Serv.
Leach, Sid D. Techniques of Interior Rendering & Design Presentation. (Illus.). 200p. 1983. 29.95 (ISBN 0-07-036806-6, P&RB). McGraw.
Loewer, H. Peter. Bringing the Outdoors In. Date not set. pap. 4.95 (ISBN 0-449-08464-7, Columbine). Fawcett.
Murray, Carolyn S., ed. The Los Angeles Times California Home Book. (Illus.). 216p. 1982. 35.00 (ISBN 0-8109-1276-7). Abrams.
Ribalta, Marta. New Interiors, No. 2. (Illus.). 300p. 1982. 9.95 (ISBN 84-7031-226-X, Pub. by Editorial Blume Spain). Intl Schol Bk Serv.
--New Interiors, No. 3. (Illus.). 262p. 1982. 9.95 (ISBN 84-7031-227-8, Pub. by Editorial Blume Spain). Intl Schol Bk Serv.
INTERIOR DECORATION-ENCYCLOPEDIAS, YEARBOOKS
Pegler, Martin M. Dictionary of Interior Design. (Illus.). 250p. 1983. 25.00 (ISBN 0-87005-447-3). Fairchild.
INTERIOR DECORATION-HANDBOOKS, MANUALS, ETC.
Diekman, Norman & Pile, John. Drawing Interior Architecture: A Guide to Rendering & Presentation. 176p. 1983. 32.50 (ISBN 0-8230-7159-6, Whitney Lib). Watson-Guptill.
Gilliatt, Mary. Decorating on the Cheap. LC 82-40499. (Illus.). 192p. 1983. pap. 10.95 (ISBN 0-89480-353-0). Workman Pub.
Kent, Kathryn. The Good Housekeeping Complete Guide to Traditional American Decorating. (Illus.). 1982. 27.45 (ISBN 0-87851-212-8). Hearst Bks.
INTERIOR DECORATION-HISTORY
Lynes, Russell. The Tastemakers. LC 82-25116. (Illus.). xiv, 362p. 1983. Repr. of 1955 ed. lib. bdg. 45.00x (ISBN 0-313-23843-X, LYTA). Greenwood.
Peirce, Donald & Alswang, Hope. American Interiors: New England & the South. LC 82-74299. (Illus.). 64p. 1983. pap. 7.95 (ISBN 0-87663-583-4). Universe.

INTERIOR DECORATION–VOCATIONAL GUIDANCE
Gordon, Susan. Your Career in Interior Design. (Arco's Career Guidance Ser.). (Illus.). 128p. 1983. lib. bdg. 7.95 (ISBN 0-668-05508-1); pap. 4.50 (ISBN 0-668-05516-2). Arco.
INTERMENT
see Burial
INTERMUNICIPAL LAW
see Conflict of Laws
INTERNAL COMBUSTION ENGINES
see Gas and Oil Engines
INTERNAL MEDICINE
see also Cardiology; Endocrinology; Gastroenterology; Hematology; Nephrology
Bollet, A. J. Harrison's Principles of Internal Medicine Patient Management Problems: PreTest Self-Assessment & Review, Vol. 2. 276p. 1983. 32.00 (ISBN 0-07-051929-3). McGraw-Pretest.
Frick, P., et al, eds. Advances in Internal Medicine & Pediatrics, Vol. 50. (Illus.). 190p. 1983. 39.00 (ISBN 0-387-11445-9). Springer-Verlag.
Isselbacher, K. J., et al. Harrison's Principles of Internal Medicine. 9th ed. 1979. 2 vol. ed. 80.00 (ISBN 0-07-032069-1); 1 vol. ed. 65.00 (ISBN 0-07-032068-3). McGraw.
Kammerer, William & Gross, Richard. Medical Consultation: Role of Internist on Surgical, Obstetrical & Psychiatric Services. 582p. 1983. lib. bdg. price not set (ISBN 0-683-04507-5). Williams & Wilkins.
Kaye, Donald & Rose, Louis F. Fundamentals of Internal Medicine. LC 82-3600. (Illus.). 1434p. 1983. text ed. 34.95 (ISBN 0-8016-2622-6). Mosby.
Petersdorf, Robert G. & Adams, Raymond D. Harrison's Principles of Internal Medicine. 10th ed. (Illus.). 2240p. 1983. 70.00x (ISBN 0-07-049603-X); Set of 2 vols. 90.00x (ISBN 0-07-079309-3). McGraw.
Sodeman, William, ed. Self-Assessment of Current Knowledge in Internal Medicine. 6th ed. 1982. pap. text ed. 26.00 (ISBN 0-87488-257-5). Med Exam.
Stein, Jay H., ed. Internal Medicine. 1983. single vol. 65.00 (ISBN 0-316-81231-5); 2 vols. 80.00 (ISBN 0-316-81232-3) (ISBN 0-316-81233-1). Little.
Weatherall, D. J., et al, eds. The Oxford Textbook of Medicine, 2 vols. (Illus.). 2700p. 1983. Set. 85.00 (ISBN 0-19-261159-3). Oxford U Pr.
INTERNAL MIGRATION
see Migration, Internal
INTERNAL REVENUE
see also Income Tax; Inheritance and Transfer Tax; Licenses
Flynn, David H. & Pancheri, Michael. The IRA Handbook. (Illus.). 224p. 1983. 12.95 (ISBN 0-8329-0263-2). New Century.
Wade, Jack W., Jr. When You Owe the IRS. (Illus.). 192p. 1983. 12.95 (ISBN 0-02-622230-2, Collier). Macmillan.
INTERNAL REVENUE LAW
Gates, Bryan. How to Represent Your Client Before the IRS. 256p. 1982. 24.95 (ISBN 0-07-022993-7, P&RB). McGraw.
Internal Revenue Code of Nineteen Hundred Fifty-Four: Congressional Commitee Reports, 83rd Congress, 2nd Session, 3 Reports: H.R. 1337; S.R. 1622; H.R. 2543. 1182p. 1982. Repr. of 1954 ed. lib. bdg. 40.00x (ISBN 0-89941-169-X). W S Hein.
Larson, Martin A. IRS vs. Middle Class. 1983. 12.95 (ISBN 0-8159-5824-2); pap. 5.95 (ISBN 0-8159-5827-7). Devin.
Reams, Bernard D., Jr., ed. Internal Revenue Acts of the United States: The Revenue Act of 1954 with Legislative Histories & Congressional Documents, 11. LC 82-83005. 8000p. 1982. lib. bdg. 440.00 (ISBN 0-89941-168-1). W S Hein.
--Internal Revenue Acts of the United States: 1950-1951 Legislative Histories, Laws & Administrative Documents, 7 vols. in 9. LC 82-81278. 1982. lib. bdg. 360.00 (ISBN 0-89941-155-X). W S Hein.
INTERNATIONAL ADMINISTRATION
see International Agencies; International Organization
INTERNATIONAL AGENCIES
Here are entered works on public international organizations and agencies of international government. Particular organizations are entered under their respective names.
see also International Organization
Acronyms & Abbreviations Covering the United Nations System & Other International Organizations. 26.00 (ISBN 0-686-84918-3, A/C/E/F/R/S.81.I.26). UN.
Armstrong, David. The Rise of International Organization. LC 82-16767. (Making of the 20th Century Ser.). 180p. 1982. 22.50x (ISBN 0-312-68427-4). St Martin.
Robertson, Arthur H. The Law of International Institutions in Europe. LC 61-13627. (Melland Schill Lecture Ser.). 140p. 1961. 10.00 (ISBN 0-379-11901-3). Oceana.
INTERNATIONAL AGENCIES–DIRECTORIES
Hodson, Henry V., ed. International Foundation Directory. 2nd ed. LC 73-90303. 378p. 1979. 65.00 (ISBN 0-905118-41-3). Intl Pubns Serv.
INTERNATIONAL AGREEMENTS
see Treaties
INTERNATIONAL ARBITRATION
see Arbitration, International
INTERNATIONAL BANK FOR RECONSTRUCTION AND DEVELOPMENT
Ayres, Robert L. Banking on the Poor: The World Bank & World Poverty. 296p. 1983. 17.50x (ISBN 0-262-01070-4). MIT Pr.
INTERNATIONAL BANKING
see Banks and Banking, International
INTERNATIONAL BOUNDARIES
see Boundaries
INTERNATIONAL BUSINESS ENTERPRISES
see also Investments, Foreign
Berkman, Harold W. & Vernan, Ivan R. Contemporary Perspectives in International Business. 1979. 15.95 (ISBN 0-395-30562-4). HM.
Campbell, Duncan C. & Rowan, Richard L. Multinational Corporations & the OECD Industrial Relations Guidelines. (Multinational Industrial Relations Ser.: No. 11). (Illus.). 250p. (Orig.). 1983. pap. 22.00 (ISBN 0-89546-039-4). Indus Res Unit-Wharton.
Casson, Mark, ed. The Growth of International Business. 288p. 1983. text ed. 28.50x (ISBN 0-04-330333-1). Allen Unwin.
Daniels, John D. & Ogram, Ernest W., Jr. International Business: Environments & Operations. 3rd ed. (Illus.). 252p. Date not set. pap. price not set Instrs' Manual (ISBN 0-201-10224-2). A-W.
Davis, Stanley M., ed. Managing & Organizing Multinational Corporations. 516p. 59.00 (ISBN 0-686-84794-6). Work in Amer.
Eiteman, David K. & Stonehill, Arthur I. Multinational Business Finance. 108p. Date not set. pap. text ed. price not set Instrs' Manual (ISBN 0-201-03835-8). A-W.
Fennema, M. International Networks of Banks & Industry. 1982. lib. bdg. 34.50 (ISBN 90-247-2620-4, Pub. by Martinus Nijhoff Netherlands). Kluwer Boston.
Frame, J. Davidson. International Business & Global Technology. LC 82-48480. 224p. 1982. 24.95 (ISBN 0-669-06156-5). Lexington Bks.
Garcia, Connie & Medina, Arthur. Businessman's Guide to the Caribbean. 624p. 1983. text ed. 45.00 (ISBN 0-934642-05-2); pap. 35.00 (ISBN 0-934642-08-7). Puerto Rico Almanacs.
Gladwin, Thomas N. & Walter, Ingo. Multinationals Under Fire: Lessons in the Management of Conflict. LC 79-21741. 689p. 1980. 39.50x (ISBN 0-471-01969-0, Pub. by Wiley-Interscience). Wiley.
Hawk, Barry E. United States Antitrust Laws & Multinational Business. (Seven Springs Studies). 1982. pap. 3.00 (ISBN 0-943006-06-6). Seven Springs.
Hermann, A. H. Conflicts of National Laws with International Business Activity: Issues of Extraterritoriality. (British-North America Committee Ser.). 104p. 1982. pap. 6.00 (ISBN 0-902594-41-9, BN30-NPA195). Natl Planning.
Kowalewski. Transnational Corporations & Caribbean Inequalities. 252p. 1982. 27.95 (ISBN 0-03-062001-5). Praeger.
Maxwell, Stephen, ed. Scotland, Multinationals & the Third World. 160p. 1982. text ed. 13.75 (ISBN 0-906391-28-8, 40980, Pub. by Mainstream Scotland). Humanities.
Murphy, Kathleen J. Macroproject Development in the Third World: An Analysis of Transnational Partnerships. (Replica Edition). 150p. 1982. softcover 17.00x (ISBN 0-86531-939-1). Westview.
Rosenthal, Douglas E. & Knighton, William M. National Laws & International Commerce: The Problem of Extraterritoriality. (Chatham House Papers Ser.: No. 17). 96p. (Orig.). 1982. pap. 10.00 (ISBN 0-7100-9338-1). Routledge & Kegan.
Rugman, Alan M., ed. New Theories of the Multinational Enterprise. LC 82-6003. 1982. 27.50x (ISBN 0-312-57245-X). St Martin.
Sauvant, Karl P. & Lavipour, Farid G., eds. Controlling Multinational Enterprises: Problems, Strategies, Counterstrategies. (Special Studies in International Economics). 335p. 1982. softcover 25.00x (ISBN 0-89158-020-4). Westview.
Shepard. International Corporation Taxation. 1980. 70.00 (ISBN 0-07-050537-3). McGraw.
Stopford, John M. & Dunning, John H., eds. World Directory of Multinational Enterprises, 3 Vols. 2nd ed. 1700p. 1982. Set. 365.00x (ISBN 0-8103-0521-6, Pub. by Macmillan England). Gale.
Taylor, Michael & Thrift, Nigel, eds. The Geography of the Multinationals: Studies in the Spatial Development & Economic Consequences of Multinational Corporations. LC 82-6002. 352p. 1982. 35.00x (ISBN 0-312-32176-7). St Martin.
Transnational Corporations in the Fertilizer Industry. 8.00 (ISBN 0-686-43222-3, E.82.II.A.10). UN.
Wallace, Cynthia D. Legal Control of the Multinational Enterprise. 1982. lib. bdg. 58.50 (ISBN 90-247-2668-9, Pub. by Martinus Nijhoff Netherlands). Kluwer Boston.
Wentworth, Felix & Christopher, Martin, eds. Managing International Distribution. 296p. 1979. text ed. 37.00x (ISBN 0-566-02108-0). Gower Pub Ltd.
INTERNATIONAL BUSINESS ENTERPRISES–ACCOUNTING
Arpan, Jeffrey S. & Radebaugh, Lee H. International Accounting & Multinational Enterprises. LC 80-26070. 400p. 1982. text ed. 27.95 (ISBN 0-471-87746-8); tchr's manual avail. (ISBN 0-471-89512-1). Wiley.
Bindon, Kathleen R. Inventories & Foreign Currency Translation Requirements. Farmer, Richard N., ed. LC 82-21729. (Research for Business Decisions Ser.). 1983. write for info. (ISBN 0-8357-1391-1). Univ Microfilms.
INTERNATIONAL CLAIMS
see Claims
INTERNATIONAL COMPETITION
see Competition, International
INTERNATIONAL CONFERENCES, CONGRESSES AND CONVENTIONS
see Congresses and Conventions
INTERNATIONAL COOKERY
see Cookery, International
INTERNATIONAL COOPERATION
Here are entered general works on international cooperative activities with or without the participation of governments.
see also Agriculture, Cooperative; Arbitration, International; Congresses and Conventions; Economic Assistance; European Cooperation; Intellectual Cooperation; International Agencies; International Organization; Reconstruction (1939-1951); Technical Assistance
Burke, Edmund. A Vindication of Natural Society. LC 81-84826. (Illus.). 130p. 1982. 8.50 (ISBN 0-86597-009-2); pap. text ed. 4.50 (ISBN 0-86597-010-6). Liberty Fund.
Coate. Global Issue Regimes. 238p. 1982. 28.95 (ISBN 0-03-059276-3). Praeger.
Foell, Wesley K. Management of Energy-Environment Systems: Methods & Case Studies. LC 78-13617. (International Institute Series on Applied Systems Analysis). 487p. 1979. 49.95x (ISBN 0-471-99721-8, Pub. by Wiley-Interscience). Wiley.
Kapteyn & Kooijmans. International Organisation & Integration, Vol. 1A. 1982. lib. bdg. 195.00 (ISBN 90-247-2579-8, Pub. by Martinus Nijhoff Netherlands). Kluwer Boston.
Kapteyn & Koomans. International Organisation & Integration, Vol. 1B. 1982. lib. bdg. 99.00 (ISBN 90-247-2657-3, Pub. by Martinus Nijhoff Netherlands). Kluwer Boston.
Kapteyn & Kooymans. International Organisation & Integration, Vol. IIA. 1982. lib. bdg. 99.00 (ISBN 90-247-2587-9, Pub. by Martinus Nijhoff Netherlands). Kluwer Boston.
Khan, K. R. The Law & Organisation of International Community Agreements. 1982. lib. bdg. 74.00 (ISBN 90-247-2554-2, Pub. by Martinus Nijhoff Netherlands). Kluwer Boston.
Knight, Frank H. Freedom & Reform. LC 81-83237. 502p. 1982. 14.00 (ISBN 0-86597-004-1); pap. 6.50 (ISBN 0-86597-005-X). Liberty Fund.
Pavlic, Breda & Uranga, Raul R. The Challenges of South-South Cooperation. 450p. 1983. lib. bdg. 25.00x (ISBN 0-686-42948-6). Westview.
World Economic Recovery: The Priority of International Monetary & Financial Co-operation. 25p. 1983. pap. 5.00 (ISBN 0-686-43289-4, UN 82/2C3, UN). Unipub.
INTERNATIONAL COOPERATION IN EDUCATION
see Educational Exchanges
INTERNATIONAL ECONOMIC INTEGRATION
World Economic Recovery: The Priority of International Monetary & Financial Co-operation. 25p. 1983. pap. 5.00 (ISBN 0-686-43289-4, UN 82/2C3, UN). Unipub.
INTERNATIONAL ECONOMIC RELATIONS
see also Balance of Payments; Commercial Policy; Economic Assistance; International Business Enterprises; International Economic Integration; International Finance; Investments, Foreign; Technical Assistance;
also subdivision Foreign Economic Relations under names of countries, e.g. United States–Foreign Economic Relations
Batten, David F. Spatial Analysis of Interacting Economies. 1982. lib. bdg. 26.00 (ISBN 0-89838-109-6). Kluwer-Nijhoff.
Bergesen, Albert, ed. Crises in the World-System. (Political Economy of the World-System Annuals: Vol. 6). (Illus.). 288p. 1983. 25.00 (ISBN 0-8039-1936-0); pap. 12.50 (ISBN 0-8039-1937-9). Sage.
Bergsten, C. Fred & Cline, William R. Trade Policy in the 1980's. (Policy Analyses in International Economics Ser.: No. 3). 88p. 1982. 6.00 (ISBN 0-88132-002-1). Inst Intl Eco.
Bergsten, Fred & Cline, William R. Trade Policy in the 1980's. 600p. 1983. 35.00 (ISBN 0-88132-008-0). Inst Intl Eco.
Carroll, John E. Acid Rain: An Issue in Canadian-American Relations. LC 82-82205. (Canadian-American Committee). 98p. (Orig.). 1982. pap. 6.00 (ISBN 0-89068-064-7). Natl Planning.
Cassen, Robert & Jolly, Richard, eds. Rich Country Interests & Third World Development. LC 82-42561. 1982. 32.50x (ISBN 0-312-68101-1). St Martin.
Connolly. The International Monetary System. 352p. 1982. 33.95 (ISBN 0-03-061794-4). Praeger.
Ethier, Wilfred J. Modern International Economics. 550p. 1982. text ed. 22.95x. Norton.
Foreman-Peck, James. A History of the World Economy: Economic Relations Since 1850. LC 82-24295. 320p. 1983. text ed. 27.50 (ISBN 0-389-20337-8). B&N Imports.
Hanreider, Wolfram F. Economic Issues & the Atlantic Community. 192p. 1982. 22.95 (ISBN 0-03-060584-9). Praeger.
Hodgson, John S. & Herander, Mark G. International Economic Relations. (Illus.). 496p. 1982. text ed. 24.95 (ISBN 0-13-472753-3). P-H.
Hoskins, Linus A. The New International Economic Order: A Bibliographic Handbook. LC 82-17640. 122p. (Orig.). 1983. lib. bdg. 17.75 (ISBN 0-8191-2789-2); pap. text ed. 7.75 (ISBN 0-8191-2790-6). U Pr of Amer.
International Committee for Social Sciences Information & Documentation (UNESCO), ed. International Bibliography of Economics - Bibliographie Internationale de Science Economique, Vol. 28. LC 55-2317. (International Bibliography of the Social Sciences - Bibliographie Internationale des Sciences Sociales). 502p. 1981. 90.00x (ISBN 0-422-80900-4). Intl Pubns Serv.
Jha, L. K. North South Debate. 153p. 1982. text ed. 10.75x (ISBN 0-391-02769-7, 41257). Humanities.
--North South Debate. 1982. 14.00x (ISBN 0-8364-0907-8, Pub. by Heritage India). South Asia Bks.
Kenwood, A. G. & Lougheed, A. L. The Growth of the International Economy, 1820-1980: An Introductory Text. 320p. 1983. pap. text ed. 12.95x (ISBN 0-04-330332-3). Allen Unwin.
Levine, Herbert M. World Politics Debated. 1st ed. 384p. 1983. pap. text ed. 14.95x (ISBN 0-07-037433-3, C). McGraw.
Matthiessen, Lars. The Impact of Rising Oil Prices on the World Economy. 211p. 1982. text ed. 37.00x (ISBN 0-333-33185-0, Pub. by Macmillan England). Humanities.
Myrdal, Gunnar. Beyond the Welfare State: Economic Planning & Its International Implications. LC 82-15819. xiii, 287p. 1982. Repr. of 1960 ed. lib. bdg. 35.00x (ISBN 0-313-23697-6, MYBW). Greenwood.
Promoting World Recovery: A Statement on Global Economic Strategy by Twenty-Six Economists from Fourteen Countries. 1982. 3.00 (ISBN 0-88132-013-7). Inst Intl Eco.
Rosenthal, Douglas E. & Knighton, William M. National Laws & International Commerce: The Problem of Extraterritoriality. (Chatham House Papers Ser.: No. 17). 96p. (Orig.). 1982. pap. 10.00 (ISBN 0-7100-9338-1). Routledge & Kegan.
United Nations, ed. World Economic Survey, 1981-82. LC 48-1401. (Illus.). 97p. (Orig.). 1981. pap. 9.00x (ISBN 0-8002-1110-3). Intl Pubns Serv.
U. S. Department of Commerce. Foreign Business Practices: Materials on Practical Aspects of Exporting, International Licensing & Investing. 1981. 50.00 (ISBN 0-686-37967-5). Info Gatekeepers.
Weintraub, Sidney & Purvis, Hoyt, eds. Foreign Economic Decisionmaking: Case Studies from the Johnson Administration & Their Implications. (Policy Research Project Report Ser.: No. 54). 300p. 1983. 9.00 (ISBN 0-89940-656-4). LBJ Sch Pub Aff.
Weiss, Thomas G. & Jennings, Anthony. More for the Least? Prospects for Poorest Countries in the Eighties. LC 82-48170. 208p. 1982. 24.95x (ISBN 0-669-06009-7). Lexington Bks.
Widman, Lisle. The Making of International Monetary Policy. 272p. 1982. 30.00 (ISBN 0-935328-14-9). Intl Law Inst.
Williams, A. O. International Trade & Investment: A Managerial Approach. 461p. 1982. text ed. 29.95x (ISBN 0-471-03293-X). Ronald Pr.
INTERNATIONAL EDUCATIONAL EXCHANGES
see Educational Exchanges
INTERNATIONAL EXCHANGE
see Foreign Exchange
INTERNATIONAL EXCHANGE OF PERSONS PROGRAMS
see Exchange of Persons Programs
INTERNATIONAL EXHIBITIONS
see Exhibitions
INTERNATIONAL FEDERATION
see International Organization
INTERNATIONAL FINANCE
see also Balance of Payments; Banks and Banking, International; Foreign Exchange; Loans, Foreign
Bair, Frank E., ed. International Marketing Handbook: Supplement. 1232p. 1982. 75.00x (ISBN 0-8103-0546-1). Gale.
Davis, L. J. Bad Money. 224p. 1982. 12.95 (ISBN 0-312-06524-8). St Martin.
Fekete, Janos. Back to the Realities: Reflections of a Hungarian Banker. 359p. 1982. text ed. 42.00x (ISBN 963-05-2987-4, 41219, Pub. by Kultura Pr Hungary). Humanities.
Geisst, Charles R. A Guide to the Financial Markets. 160p. 1981. 55.00x (ISBN 0-333-30919-7, Pub. by Macmillan England). State Mutual Bk.
Havrilesky, Thomas M. & Schweitzer, Robert, eds. Contemporary Developments in Financial Institutions & Markets. LC 82-19901. (Illus.). 450p. 1983. pap. 18.95 (ISBN 0-88295-409-1). Harlan Davidson.

King, Kenneth. U. S. Monetary Policy & European Responses in the 1980's. (Chatham House Papers in Foreign Policy Ser.). 128p. (Orig.). 1982. pap. 10.00 (ISBN 0-7100-9337-3). Routledge & Kegan.

Lessard, Donald R. International Financial Management: Theory & Application. LC 79-501. 626p. 1982. text ed. 18.95 (ISBN 0-471-87747-6). Wiley.

Report of the Ad Hoc Intergovermental High-Level Group of Experts on the Evolution of the International Monetary System. 13p. 1983. pap. 2.50 (ISBN 0-686-84912-4, UN82/2D2, UN). Unipub.

Rogers, James H. America Weighs Her Gold. 1931. text ed. 29.50x (ISBN 0-686-83460-7). Elliots Bks.

Tew, Brian. The Evolution of the International Monetary System, 1945-81. 2nd ed. 250p. 1982. pap. text ed. 15.00 (ISBN 0-686-84477-7). Sheridan.

Wharton School of Finance & Commerce, University of Pennsylvania. A Study of Mutual Funds: Report of the Committee on Interstate & Foreign Commerce-(87th Congress, 2nd Session, House Report No. 2274) LC 62-62400. xxxiii, 595p. 1982. Repr. of 1962 ed. lib. bdg. 38.50 (ISBN 0-89941-181-9). W. S. Hein.

INTERNATIONAL FISCAL RELATIONS
see Intergovernmental Fiscal Relations

INTERNATIONAL GRANTS-IN-AID
see Economic Assistance

INTERNATIONAL INSTITUTIONS
see International Cooperation

INTERNATIONAL JURISDICTION
see Jurisdiction (International Law)

INTERNATIONAL LABOR ACTIVITIES
see also names of individual labor organizations, e.g. International Labor Organization

Gaspar, Sandor. The International Trade Union Movement. 382p. 1981. 45.00x (ISBN 0-569-08699-X, Pub. by Collets). State Mutual Bk.

Moulaert, Frank & Salinas, Wilson. Regional Analysis & the New International Division of Labor. (Studies in Applied Regional Science). 1982. lib. bdg. 24.00 (ISBN 0-89838-107-X). Kluwer-Nijhoff.

INTERNATIONAL LABOR LAWS AND LEGISLATION
see Labor Laws and Legislation, International

INTERNATIONAL LABOR ORGANIZATION

Trade Unions & the ILO: A Workers' Education Manual. vii, 96p. 1982. 5.70 (ISBN 92-2-102003-7). Intl Labour Office.

INTERNATIONAL LAW
see also Aliens; Arbitration, International; Boundaries; Civil Rights (International Law); Claims; Diplomatic and Consular Service; Diplomats; Equality of States; Extradition; Fishery Law and Legislation; International Cooperation; International Organization; Labor Laws and Legislation, International; Maritime Law; Natural Law; Neutrality; Pirates; Refugees, Political; Territorial Waters; Treaties; War (International Law)
also subdivisions Laws and Legislation and Laws and Regulations under topics of international concern

Ferencz, Ben. Enforcement of International Law, 2 vols. 1983. lib. bdg. 90.00 set (ISBN 0-379-12147-6); Vol. 1, 500p. lib. bdg. 45.00 (ISBN 0-379-12148-4); Vol. 2, 500p. lib. bdg. 45.00 (ISBN 0-379-12149-2). Oceana.

Hingorani, R. C. Studies in International Law. 115p. 1981. 30.00 (ISBN 0-379-20719-2). Oceana.

Kirgis, Frederic L. Prior Consultation in International Law. LC 82-17354. (Procedural Aspects of International Law Ser.: Vol. 16). 736p. 1983. write for info. (ISBN 0-8139-0971-6). U Pr of Va.

Lachs, Manfred. The Teacher in International Law. 1982. lib. bdg. 47.50 (ISBN 90-247-2566-6, Pub. by Martinus Nijhoff Netherlands). Kluwer Boston.

Lillich, Richard B., ed. The Family in International Law: Some Emerging Problems. 160p. 1981. 17.50 (ISBN 0-87215-355-X). Michie-Bobbs.

Matthews, James N., ed. Kime's International Law Directory for 1982. 90th ed. LC 9-19874. 810p. 1982. 60.00x (ISBN 0-900503-15-7). Intl Pubns Serv.

Perl, Raphael. The Falkalan Island Dispute in International Law & Politics: A Documentary Sourcebook. 600p. 1983. lib. bdg. 45.00 (ISBN 0-379-11251-5). Oceana.

Shepard. Guide to International Law. 1983. 75.00 (ISBN 0-07-067513-9). McGraw.

The Futures Group. Handbook for U. S. Participation in Multilateral Diplomacy. 350p. 1983. lib. bdg. 40.00x (ISBN 0-379-12146-8). Oceana.

U. N. Law Reports: Sept. 1982 to Aug. 1983, Vol. 17. 60.00 (ISBN 0-8027-2983-5). Walker & Co.

Westlake, John. Chapters on the Principles of International Law. xix, 275p. 1982. Repr. of 1894 ed. lib. bdg. 27.50x (ISBN 0-8377-1328-5). Rothman.

INTERNATIONAL LAW-ADDRESSES, ESSAYS, LECTURES

Institut de Droit International, ed. Session de Zagreb 1971. (Institut de Droit international Annuaire: Vol. 54, 1-2). xciv, 1392p. 1971. pap. 450.00 (ISBN 3-8055-1537-5). S Karger.

--Session d'Edimbourg 1969. (Institut de Droit international Annuaire: Vol. 53, 1-2). xcii, 1238p. 1969. pap. 179.75 (ISBN 3-8055-1534-0). S Karger.

--Session d'Oslo 1977. (Institut de Droit international Annuaire: Vol. 57, 1-2). lx, 416p. 1978. pap. 320.50 (ISBN 3-8055-2956-2). S Karger.

--Session du Centenaire, Rome 1973. (Institut de Droit international Annuaire: Vol. 55). xcviii, 916p. 1973. pap. 296.50 (ISBN 3-8055-2175-8). S Karger.

INTERNATIONAL LAW-CASES

Francis, Deak. American International Law Cases: 1971-1978, Vols. 1-20. Incl. Vols. 21- Ruddy, F. 1980. LC 78-140621. 50.00 ea. (ISBN 0-379-20075-9). Oceana.

White, Bertha R. Index to American International Law Cases. 1982. write for info. (ISBN 0-379-20097-X). Oceana.

INTERNATIONAL LAW-HISTORY

Hosack, John. On the Rise & Growth of the Law of Nations, as Established by General Usage & by Treaties, from the Earliest Time to the Treaty of Utrecht. xii, 394p. 1982. Repr. of 1882 ed. lib. bdg. 35.00x (ISBN 0-8377-0647-5). Rothman.

INTERNATIONAL LAW-SOURCES
see also Treaties

Hosack, John. On the Rise & Growth of the Law of Nations, as Established by General Usage & by Treaties, from the Earliest Time to the Treaty of Utrecht. xii, 394p. 1982. Repr. of 1882 ed. lib. bdg. 35.00x (ISBN 0-8377-0647-5). Rothman.

INTERNATIONAL LAW, PRIVATE
see Conflict of Laws

INTERNATIONAL LOANS
see Loans, Foreign

INTERNATIONAL MONETARY FUND

Bergsten, C. Fred. From Rambouillet to Versailles: A Symposium. (Princeton Studies in International Finance: No. 51). 1982. pap. text ed. 2.50x (ISBN 0-88165-056-0). Princeton U Int Finan Econ.

Gilbert, Milton. Quest for World Monetary System: Gold-Dollar System & It's Aftermath. LC 80-17865. 255p. 1980. 26.95x (ISBN 0-471-07998-7, Pub. by Wiley-Interscience). Wiley.

Williamson, John. The Lending Policies of the International Monetary Fund. (Policy Analyses in International Economics Ser.: No. 1). 80p. (Orig.). 1982. pap. 6.00x (ISBN 0-88132-000-5). Inst Intl Eco.

Williamson, John, ed. IMF Conditionality. (Series: No. 5). 700p. 1983. 30.00 (ISBN 0-88132-006-4). Inst Intl Eco.

INTERNATIONAL ORGANIZATION
Here are entered works on theories and efforts leading toward worldwide or regional political organization of nations.
see also Concert of Europe; International Agencies; International Cooperation; International Law; Reconstruction (1939-1951); Regionalism (International Organization); Security, International; World Politics
also names of specific organizations, e.g. United Nations, Pan American Union

Brodie, Bernard & Intriligator, Michael D., eds. National Security & International Stability. LC 82-18913. 368p. 1983. text ed. 27.50 (ISBN 0-89946-172-7). Oelgeschlager.

Krasner, Stephen D., ed. International Regimes. (Political Economy Ser.). 384p. 1983. text ed. 29.95x (ISBN 0-8014-1550-0); pap. text ed. 9.95x (ISBN 0-8014-9250-5). Cornell U Pr.

INTERNATIONAL ORGANIZATIONS
see International Agencies

INTERNATIONAL PAYMENTS, BALANCE OF
see Balance of Payments

INTERNATIONAL POLICE

Reader's Digest Editors. Great Cases of Interpol. LC 81-50533. (Illus.). 560p. 1982. 16.50 (ISBN 0-89577-101-2, Pub. by RD Assn). Random.

INTERNATIONAL POLITICS
see World Politics

INTERNATIONAL PRIVATE LAW
see Conflict of Laws

INTERNATIONAL RELATIONS
Here are entered works dealing with the theory of international intercourse. Historical accounts are entered under the headings World Politics; United States-Politics and Government; etc. Works dealing with foreign relations from the point of view of an individual state are entered under the name of the state with subdivision Foreign Relations.
see also Ambassadors; Arbitration, International; Balance of Power; Boundaries; Catholic Church-Relations (Diplomatic); Competition, International; Congresses and Conventions; Cultural Relations; Detente; Diplomacy; Diplomatic and Consular Service; Diplomatic Negotiations in International Disputes; Diplomats; Disarmament; Geography, Political; Geopolitics; Intergovernmental Fiscal Relations; International Cooperation; International Economic Relations; International Law; International Organization; Munitions; Nationalism; Peace; Reconstruction (1939-1951); Refugees, Political; Security, International; Treaties; World Politics
also subdivision Foreign Relations under names of countries, e.g. France-Foreign Relations; also names of international alliances, congresses, treaties, etc. e.g. Holy Alliance; Versailles, Treaty of, 1918

Abdallah. Abdallah Dictionary of International Relations & Conference Terminology in English-Arabic. 1982. 40.00x (ISBN 0-86685-289-1). Intl Bk Ctr.

Aberbach, Joel D. & Putnam, Robert D. Bureaucrats & Politicians in Western Democracies. 324p. 1982. pap. text ed. 9.95x (ISBN 0-674-08627-9). Harvard U Pr.

Bagby, Wesley M. Contemporary International Problem. 248p. 1983. 19.95 (ISBN 0-88229-774-0); pap. text ed. 9.95 (ISBN 0-88229-775-9). Nelson-Hall.

Bandopadhyaya, J. North Over South: A NonWestern Perspective of International Relations. 1982. 26.00x (ISBN 0-8364-0894-2). South Asia Bks.

Bergesen, Albert, ed. Crises in the World-System. (Political Economy of the World-System Annuals: Vol. 6). (Illus.). 288p. 1983. 25.00 (ISBN 0-8039-1936-0); pap. 12.50 (ISBN 0-8039-1937-9). Sage.

Borisov, C. B. & Dubinin, Y. V. Modern Diplomacy of Capitalist Powers. (World Leaders Speeches & Writings Ser.). 396p. 1983. 50.00 (ISBN 0-08-028173-7). Pergamon.

Burke, Edmund. A Vindication of Natural Society. LC 81-84826. (Illus.). 130p. 1982. 8.50 (ISBN 0-86597-009-2); pap. text ed. 4.50 (ISBN 0-86597-010-6). Liberty Fund.

Butler, William E., ed. International Commercial Arbitration: Soviet Commercial & Maritime Arbitration. LC 80-10606. 1980. 75.00 (ISBN 0-686-84383-5). Oceana.

Duke, David C. Distant Obligations: Modern Writers & Foreign Causes. 320p. 1983. 27.50 (ISBN 0-19-503221-7). Oxford U Pr.

Frei, Daniel. Managing International Crisis. (Advances in Political Science: An International Ser.: Vol. 2). 1982. 22.50 (ISBN 0-8039-1849-6). Sage.

Gordon, L. Growth Policies & the International Order. 1979. pap. 6.95 (ISBN 0-07-023813-8). McGraw.

Hartmann, Frederick N. The Relations of Nations. 6th ed. 736p. 1983. text ed. 23.95 (ISBN 0-02-351350-0). Macmillan.

International Committee for Social Science Information & Documentation (UNESCO), ed. International Bibliography of Political Science - Bibliographie Internation ale de Science Politique, Vol. 28. LC 54-14355. (International Bibliogarphy of the Social Science Ser.). 451p. 1981. 90.00x (ISBN 0-422-80920-9). Intl Pubns Serv.

Isard, Walter, ed. International & Regional Conflict: Analytic Approaches. Nagao, Yoshimi. (Peace Science Studies Sers.). 240p. 1983. prof ref 36.00x (ISBN 0-88410-030-8). Ballinger Pub.

Knight, Frank H. Freedom & Reform. LC 81-83237. 502p. 1982. 14.00 (ISBN 0-86597-004-1); pap. 6.50 (ISBN 0-86597-005-X). Liberty Fund.

The Logical Consistency & Soundness of the Balance of Power Theory. (Monograph Series in World Affairs: Vol. 19 Bk. 3). 1983. pap. 5.00 (ISBN 0-87940-070-6). U of Denver Intl.

Mansbach, Richard W. & Vasquez, John A. In Search of Theory: A New Paradigm for Global Politics. 1983. pap. 12.50 (ISBN 0-231-05061-5). Columbia U Pr.

Maoz, Zeev. Paths to Conflict: International Dispute Initiation, 1816-1976. 270p. 1982. softco ver 21.50 (ISBN 0-86531-933-2). Westview.

Mattis, Ann, ed. The Emerging Global Village: Society for International Development World Conference, 25th. 250p. Date not set. text ed. 25.00 (ISBN 0-8223-0561-5); pap. text ed. 11.00 (ISBN 0-8223-0562-3). Duke.

Nordlinger, Eric A. On the Autonomy of the Democratic State. (Center for International Affairs Ser.). 247p. 1982. pap. text ed. 7.95x (ISBN 0-674-63409-8). Harvard U Pr.

OECD. The Search of Consensus: The Role of Institutional Dialogue Between Governments, Labour & Employers. 77p. 1982. pap. 7.50x (ISBN 92-64-12373-3). OECD.

Osgood, Robert E. The Successor Generation: Its Challenges & Responsibilities. 45p. pap. 6.00 (ISBN 0-87855-874-8). Transaction Bks.

Rystad, G., ed. Congress & American Foreign Policy. (Lund Studies in International History: No. 13). 156p. 1982. text ed. 18.00x (ISBN 91-24-31480-3, Pub. by Almquist & Wiksell Sweden). Humanities.

Sanders, Ralph. International Dynamics of Technology. LC 82-9220. (Contributions in Political Science Ser.: No. 87). 352p. 1983. lib. bdg. 35.00 (ISBN 0-313-23401-9, SAD/). Greenwood.

Schiavone, Guiseppe, ed. East-West Relations: Prospects for the 1980s. LC 81-21433. 315p. 1982. 32.50x (ISBN 0-312-22496-6). St Martin.

Turner, Robert F. The War Powers Resolution: Its Implementation in Theory & Practice. (Philadelphia Policy Papers). (Orig.). 1983. pap. 3.95 (ISBN 0-910191-06-9). For Policy Res.

Uri, Pierre. North-South: Developing a New Relationship. (The Atlantic Papers: No. 75/6). 58p. (Orig.). 1976. pap. text ed. 4.75x (ISBN 0-686-83679-0). Allanheld.

Zhou Guo, ed. China & the World, No. 2. (China & the World Ser.). 123p. 1982. pap. 1.95 (ISBN 0-8351-1115-6). China Bks.

INTERNATIONAL RELATIONS-ADDRESSES, ESSAYS, LECTURES

Frieddrich Ebert Foundation, ed. Towards One World? International Responses to the Brandt Report. 1981. 33.00x (ISBN 0-85117-218-0, Pub. by M Temple Smith). State Mutual Bk.

INTERNATIONAL RELATIONS-DICTIONARIES

Pereznieto. Derecho Internacional Privado. 2nd ed. 332p. (Span.). 1981. pap. text ed. write for info. (ISBN 0-06-316703-4, Pub. by HarLA Mexico). Har-Row.

INTERNATIONAL RELATIONS-YEARBOOKS

Foreign Policy & the Modern World-System. (Sage International Yearbook of Foreign Policy Studies: Vol. 8). (Illus.). 320p. 1983. 25.00 (ISBN 0-8039-1927-1); pap. 12.50 (ISBN 0-8039-1928-X). Sage.

INTERNATIONAL SECURITY
see Security, International

INTERNATIONAL SYSTEM OF UNITS
see Metric System

INTERNATIONAL TRADE
see Commerce

INTERNATIONAL TRADE REGULATION
see Foreign Trade Regulation

INTERNMENT CAMPS
see Concentration Camps

INTERNS (MEDICINE)

The Internship Experience. Date not set. 5.00 (ISBN 0-686-83877-7). Am Assn Coll Pharm.

INTEROCEANIC CANALS
see Canals

INTERPERSONAL COMMUNICATION

Bittner, John R. Each Other: An Introduction to Interpersonal Communication. (Illus.). 368p. 1983. text ed. 16.95 (ISBN 0-13-222190-X). P-H.

Branden, Nathaniel. If You Could Hear What I Cannot Say: Learning to Communicate with the Ones You Love. 1983. pap. 8.95 (ISBN 0-686-82126-2). Bantam.

Gurian, Anita & Formanek, Ruth. The Socially Competent Child: A Parent's Guide to Social Development from Infancy to Early Adolescence. 206p. 1983. 12.95 (ISBN 0-395-32205-7). HM.

Hopper, Robert. Interpersonal Communication for Professionals. (Procom Ser.). 1983. pap. text ed. 8.95 (ISBN 0-673-15551-X). Scott F.

Kennedy, Andrew K. Dramatic Dialogue: The Dialogue of Personal Encounter. LC 82-4257. 304p. 45.00 (ISBN 0-521-24620-2); pap. 13.95 (ISBN 0-521-28845-2). Cambridge U Pr.

McCroskey, James C. & Richmond, Virginia P. The Quiet Ones: Communication Apprehension & Shyness. (Comm Comp Ser.). 39p. 1982. pap. text ed. 2.95x (ISBN 0-89787-313-0). Gorsuch Scarisbrick.

Samovar, Larry A. & King, Stephen W. Communication & Discussion in Small Groups. (Comm Comp Ser.). (Illus.). 48p. 1981. pap. text ed. 2.95 (ISBN 0-89787-308-4). Gorsuch Scarisbrick.

Shedd, Charlie W. Talk to Me. rev. ed. LC 82-45455. 120p. 1983. pap. 5.95 (ISBN 0-385-18328-3, Galilee). Doubleday.

Weber, Eric & Simring, Steven S. How to Win Back the One You Love. 192p. 1983. 11.95 (ISBN 0-02-624700-3). Macmillan.

Weisinger, Hendrie & Lobsenz, Norman. Nobody's Perfect. 288p. 1983. pap. 3.50 (ISBN 0-446-30575-8). Warner Bks.

INTERPERSONAL PERCEPTION
see Social Perception

INTERPERSONAL RELATIONS
see also Dependency (Psychology); Group Relations Training; Interpersonal Communication; Intimacy (Psychology); Personal Space; Social Participation; Teacher-Student Relationships

Atwater, Eastwood. Psychology of Adjustment: Personal Growth in a Changing World. 2nd ed. (Illus.). 448p. 1983. pap. 19.95 (ISBN 0-13-734855-X). P-H.

Benton, Joanna. Keeping Close. (Orig.). 1983. pap. 10.00 (ISBN 0-8065-0839-6). Citadel Pr.

Berger, Charles R. & Bradac, James J. Language & Social Knowledge Uncertainty in Interpersonal Relations. 208p. 1982. pap. text ed. 14.95 (ISBN 0-7131-6196-5). E Arnold.

Blau, Peter M. Exchange & Power in Social Life. LC 64-23827. 352p. 1964. 29.95x (ISBN 0-471-08030-6). Wiley.

Breton, Myron. Lasting Relationships: How to Recognize the Man or Woman Who's Right for You. 204p. 1983. pap. 5.95 (ISBN 0-89104-333-0, A & W Visual Library). A & W Pubs.

Broadbent, W. W. How to be Loved. 208p. 1977. pap. 2.95 (ISBN 0-446-30024-1). Warner Bks.

Brothers, Joyce. What Every Woman Should Know About Men. 288p. 1983. pap. 2.95 (ISBN 0-345-30848-4). Ballantine.

Buehler, Janice A. Nurses & Physicians in Transition. Kalisch, Philip & Kalisch, Beatrice, eds. LC 82-10940. (Studies in Nursing Management: No. 10). 164p. 1982. 39.95 (ISBN 0-8357-1379-2). Univ Microfilms.

Buscaglia, Leo. Living, Loving & Learning. 264p. 1982. 13.50 (ISBN 0-686-84812-8). Slack Inc.

Casey, W. W. How to Meet Men (For Ladies Only) 16p. pap. 3.00x (ISBN 0-943462-01-0). CaseCo.

Christopher, Beth. Love for the Taking. (Finding Mr. Right Ser.). 208p. 1983. pap. 2.75 (ISBN 0-380-83311-5). Avon.

Colman, Carol. Love & Money: What Your Finances Say About Your Personal Relationships. 300p. 1983. 15.95 (ISBN 0-698-11189-3, Coward). Putnam Pub Group.

Davis, A. Jann. Please See My Need. (Illus.). pap. 5.95x (ISBN 0-9609184-0-X). Satellite Cont.

DeVito, Joseph A. The Interpersonal Communication Book. 3rd ed. 508p. 1983. pap. text ed. 14.95 scp (ISBN 0-06-041651-3, HarpC); instr's. manual avail. (ISBN 0-06-361631-9). Har-Row.
Evatt, Cris & Feld, Bruce. The Givers & the Takers. (Illus.). 256p. 1983. 12.95 (ISBN 0-02-536690-4). Macmillan.
Fields, Uriah J. How Lovers Can Become Friends. 26p. 1982. pap. 2.95 (ISBN 0-938844-04-0). Am Mutuality.
Flake-Hobson, Carol & Robinson, Bryan E. Child Development & Relationships. (Illus.). 608p. 1983. text ed. 15.95 (ISBN 0-201-04092-1). A-W.
Fruehling. Relacciones Humanas. 141p. 6.32 (ISBN 0-07-022540-0). McGraw.
Guisewite, Cathy. Eat Your Way to a Better Relationship. LC 82-72420. 60p. (Orig.). 1983. pap. 2.95 (ISBN 0-8362-1987-2). Andrews & McMeel.
Hagstrom, Dick. Getting along with Yourself & Others. 1982. pap. 6.95 (ISBN 0-8423-0998-5). Tyndale.
Halloran, Jack. Activity Giude for Applied Human Relations. 2nd ed. (Illus.). 192p. 1983. Workbook 8.95 (ISBN 0-686-38835-6). P H.
Halpern, James & Halpern, Ilsa. Projections: Our World of Imaginary Relationships. 192p. 1983. 13.95 (ISBN 0-399-31017-7). Seaview Bks.
Hauer, Gerhard. Longing for Tenderness. 160p. (Orig.). 1983. pap. 4.95 (ISBN 0-87784-835-1). Inter-Varsity.
Heider, Fritz. The Psychology of Interpersonal Relations. reprint ed. Krauss, Robert M., intro. by. 336p. 1982. Repr. of 1958 ed. write for info. (ISBN 0-89859-282-8). L Erlbaum Assocs.
Hercules, Costas. Selfishians, Otherishites & Fairishers: A Guide to Harmonious Relationships. (Illus.). 96p. 1982. 10.00 (ISBN 0-943900-01-8); pap. 5.95 (ISBN 0-943900-00-X). Fairisher Pr.
Johnson, Ward. Caring Is What Counts. (Illus.). 40p. (ps-3). Date not set. 5.95 (ISBN 0-910313-05-9). Parker Bro.
Klerman, Gerald & Weissman, Myrna. Interpersonal Psychotherapy of Depression. 1983. text ed. 20.95x (ISBN 0-465-03396-2). Basic.
Kopf, Ebs Dumm. How to Seduce Married Women. Fonyam, John, ed. (Illus.). 415p. 1983. 25.00 (ISBN 0-910253-00-5). Backwards & Backwards.
Lasswell, Marcia & Lobsenz, Norman. Equal Time: The New Way of Living, Loving, & Working Together. LC 82-45254. 240p. 1983. 15.95 (ISBN 0-385-17473-X). Doubleday.
Lein, Laura & Sussman, Marvin B., eds. The Ties That Bind: Men's & Women's Social Networks. LC 82-23230. (Marriage & Family Review Ser.: Vol. 5, No. 4). 128p. 1983. text ed. 19.95 (ISBN 0-86656-161-7, B161). Haworth Pr.
Lewis, Phillip V. Managing Human Relations. 512p. 1983. text ed. 22.95x (ISBN 0-534-01428-3). Kent Pub Co.
Masello, Robert. What Do Men Want from Women? 160p. (Orig.). 1983. pap. 4.95 (ISBN 0-345-30822-0). Ballantine.
Merser, Cheryl. Honorable Intentions. LC 82-45180. 256p. 1983. 13.95 (ISBN 0-689-11311-0). Atheneum. .
Miller, Keith. A Second Touch. 1982. 7.95 (ISBN 0-8499-0338-6). Word Pub.
Minshull, Ruth. How to Choose Your People. 280p. 1972. write for info. (ISBN 0-937922-02-1). SAA Pub.
Moracco, John & Higgins, Earl. Comprensive Approach to Human Relations Development. 360p. 1983. pap. text ed. price not set (ISBN 0-915202-38-7). Accel Devel.
Morganstern, Michael. How to Make Love to a Woman. 144p. 1983. pap. 2.95 (ISBN 0-345-30962-6). Ballantine.
Oakeshott, Michael. On History & Other Essays. LC 82-22617. 224p. 1983. text ed. 25.75x (ISBN 0-389-20355-6). B&N Imports.
Palnik, Paul. Couples: How Two Worlds Become One. (Orig.). 1983. pap. 3.95 (ISBN 0-440-51303-0, Dell Trade Pbks). Dell.
Parelman, Allison. Emotional Intimacy in Marriage: A Sex-Roles Perspective. Nathan, Peter E., ed. LC 82-20218. (Research in Clinical Psychology Ser.: No. 4). 150p. 1983. 34.95 (ISBN 0-8357-1387-3, Pub. by UMI Res Pr). Univ Microfilms.
Perlman, Helen H. Relationship: The Heart of Helping People. LC 78-19064. x, 236p. 1979. pap. 7.95 (ISBN 0-226-66036-2). U of Chicago Pr.
Peterson, James R. The Playboy Advisor on Love & Sex. (Illus.). 350p. 1983. 16.95 (ISBN 0-399-50742-6, Perigee); pap. 7.95 (ISBN 0-399-50741-8). Putnam Pub Group.
Phillips, Gerald M. & Goodall, H. Lloyd, Jr. Loving & Living: Improve Your Friendships & Marriage. 218p. 1983. 13.95 (ISBN 0-13-541136-X); pap. 6.95 (ISBN 0-13-541128-9). P-H.
Rubin, Theodore I. One to One: Understanding Human Relationships. Orig. Title: Locks. 256p. 1983. 15.75 (ISBN 0-670-43596-1). Viking Pr.
Rush, Myron D. Richer Relationships. 180p. 1983. pap. 4.95 (ISBN 0-88207-399-0). Victor Bks.
Ryan, Kevin & Ryan, Marilyn. Making a Marriage: A Personal Book of Love, Marriage & Family. 224p. 1983. pap. 5.95 (ISBN 0-312-50663-5). St Martin.
Satir, Virginia M. Peoplemaking. LC 73-188143. 1972. 9.95 (ISBN 0-8314-0031-5); pap. 7.95. Sci & Behavior.
Shaw, Diana & Berry, Caroline F. Options: The Female Teen's Guide to Coping with the Problems of Today's World. LC 80-2871. 168p. 1983. pap. 4.95 (ISBN 0-385-17057-2, Anch). Doubleday.
Solomon, Charles R. The Rejection Syndrome. 144p. 1982. pap. 4.95 (ISBN 0-8423-5417-4). Tyndale.
Sueltz, Arthur F. Life at Close Quarters. 1982. 6.95 (ISBN 0-8499-0285-1). Word Pub.
Thomas, Sari. Communication Theory & Interpersonal Interaction. 308p. 1983. text ed. 29.50 (ISBN 0-89391-134-8). Ablex Pub.
Tuson, Jacqueline. Links-Personal Relationships. 96p. 1978. 26.00x (ISBN 0-85950-078-0, Pub. by Thornes England). State Mutual Bk.
Valletutti, J. & Bender, Michael. Teaching Interpersonal & Community Living Skills: A Curriculum Model for Handicapped Adolescents & Adults. 288p. 1982. pap. text ed. 19.95 (ISBN 0-8391-1748-5, 18341). Univ Park.
Weber, Eric. Meeting People: 101 Best Opening Lines. 1983. pap. 2.95 (ISBN 0-517-54954-9, Harmony). Crown.
Weber, Eric & Cochran, Molly. How to Pick Up Women. 1980. text ed. 12.95 (ISBN 0-914094-14-9). Symphony.
Weber, Eric & Miller, Judi. Shy Persons Guide to a Happier Love Life. Repr. of 1979 ed. text ed. 11.95 (ISBN 0-914094-17-3). Symphony.
What Men Know About Women. (Blank Books Ser.). 128p. 1982. cancelled 0.00 (ISBN 0-939944-15-4). Marmac Pub.
What Women Know About Men. (Blank Books Ser.). 128p. 1982. cancelled 0.00 (ISBN 0-939944-16-2). Marmac Pub.
Wild, Victor. The Complete Book of How to Succeed with Women. (Illus.). 208p. (Orig.). 1981. pap. 11.95 (ISBN 0-938444-01-8). Wildfire Pub.
Wilde, Mary P. & Davis, Gevevieve. How to Tell if He's Cheating: And What to Do About It. 112p. (Orig.). 1983. pap. 3.95 (ISBN 0-936750-05-7). Wetherall.

INTERPLANETARY PROPULSION
see Space Vehicles–Propulsion Systems

INTERPLANETARY VOYAGES
Here are entered early, imaginary and descriptive accounts of travel beyond the earth.
McCarty, James A. & Elkins, Don. The RA Material: An Ancient Astronaut Speaks. Stine, Hank, ed. LC 82-12967. 192p. (Orig.). 1983. pap. 6.95 (ISBN 0-89865-260-X). Donning Co.

INTERPLEADER
see Actions and Defenses

INTERPRETATION
see Hermeneutics

INTERPRETATION, BIBLICAL
see Bible–Criticism, Interpretation, etc.

INTERPRETATION AND CONSTRUCTION (LAW)
see Law–Interpretation and Construction

INTERPRETATIVE SPEECH
see Oral Interpretation

INTERPRETERS
see Translators

INTERPRETIVE DANCING
see Modern Dance

INTERSCHOLASTIC ATHLETICS
see School Sports

INTERSTATE AGREEMENTS
Rorer, David. American Inter-State Law. Mayer, Levy, ed. lvii, 400p. 1983. Repr. of 1879 ed. lib. bdg. 35.00x (ISBN 0-8377-1038-3). Rothman.

INTERSTATE COMPACTS
see Interstate Agreements

INTERSTATE COOPERATION
see Interstate Agreements

INTERSTELLAR VOYAGES
see Interplanetary Voyages

INTERVALS (MUSIC)
see Musical Intervals and Scales

INTERVERTEBRAL DISK
Cauthen, Joseph C. Lumbar Spine Surgery: Indications, Techniques, Failures & Alternatives. (Illus.). 234p. 1983. lib. bdg. 45.00 (ISBN 0-683-01500-1). Williams & Wilkins.

INTERVIEWING
see also Employment Interviewing; Interviews; Social Case Work
Cannell, Charles F. Experiments in Interviewing Techniques: Field Experiments in Health Reporting, 1971-1977. 446p. 1979. pap. 18.00x (ISBN 0-87944-247-6). Inst Soc Res.
Pascal, Gerald R. The Practical Art of Diagnostic Interviewing. (Dorsey Professional Ser.). 275p. 1983. 17.95 (ISBN 0-87094-367-7). Dow Jones-Irwin.

INTERVIEWING, MEDICAL
see Medical History Taking

INTERVIEWS
see also Interviewing
Christenson, Boyd & Hanson, Nancy E. Boyd Christenson Interviews. (Illus.). 212p. 1983. 15.95 (ISBN 0-911007-00-8). Prairie Hse.
Medley, H. Anthony. Sweaty Palms: The Neglected Art of Being Interviewed. (Illus.). 191p. 1978. 6.95 (ISBN 0-534-97999-8). Lifetime Learn.

INTESTINES
see also Colon (Anatomy)
Alexander-Williams, J. Large Intestine. new ed. (BIMR Gastroenterolgy Ser.: vol. 3). 1983. text ed. price not set (ISBN 0-407-02289-9). Butterworth.
Liebermann-Meffert, D., et al, eds. Greater Omentum: Anatomy, Physiology, Pathology, Surgery. (Illus.). 361p. 1983. 166.00 (ISBN 0-387-11882-9). Springer-Verlag.
Robinson, J. W. & Dowling, R. H. Intestinal Adaptation & Its Mechanisms. (Illus.). 646p. 1982. text ed. 75.00 (ISBN 0-85200-442-7, Pub. by MTP Pr England). Kluwer Boston.
Shiner, Margot. Ultrastructure of the Small Intestinal Mucosa: Normal & Disease-Related Appearances. (Illus.). 175p. 1982. 70.00 (ISBN 0-387-11732-6). Springer-Verlag.

INTESTINES–DISEASES
see also Diarrhea; Digestive Organs–Diseases; Intestines–Radiography
Liebermann-Meffert, D., et al, eds. Greater Omentum: Anatomy, Physiology, Pathology, Surgery. (Illus.). 361p. 1983. 166.00 (ISBN 0-387-11882-9). Springer-Verlag.
Shiner, Margot. Ultrastructure of the Small Intestinal Mucosa: Normal & Disease-Related Appearances. (Illus.). 175p. 1982. 70.00 (ISBN 0-387-11732-6). Springer-Verlag.

INTESTINES–RADIOGRAPHY
Sellink, J. L. & Miller, R. E. Radiology of the Small Bowel, Modern Enteroclysis Technique & Atlas. 1982. text ed. 98.00 (ISBN 90-247-2460-0, Pub. by Martinus Nijhoff Netherlands). Kluwer Boston.

INTESTINES–SURGERY
Liebermann-Meffert, D., et al, eds. Greater Omentum: Anatomy, Physiology, Pathology, Surgery. (Illus.). 361p. 1983. 166.00 (ISBN 0-387-11882-9). Springer-Verlag.

INTIMACY (PSYCHOLOGY)
Craig, James R. Intimacy Training. 200p. (Orig.). 1983. pap. 12.95 (ISBN 0-686-38457-1). J R Craig.
Holub, Alex. Escape from Intimacy. LC 82-83495. 144p. 1983. pap. 5.95 (ISBN 0-86666-064-X). GWP.
Krieger, Susan. The Mirror Dance: Identity in a Women's Community. 1983. write for info. (ISBN 0-87722-304-1). Temple U Pr.
Merser, Cheryl. Honorable Intentions. LC 82-45180. 256p. 1983. 13.95 (ISBN 0-689-11311-0). Atheneum.

INTOLERANCE
see Religious Liberty; Toleration

INTOXICANTS
see Alcohol; Alcoholic Beverages

INTOXICATION
see Alcoholism; Narcotic Habit; Temperance

INTRAMURAL SPORTS
Intramural Ideas. 32p. 3.95 (ISBN 0-88314-107-8). AAHPERD.

INTRAOCULAR PRESSURE, HIGH
see Glaucoma

INTRAUTERINE CONTRACEPTIVES
see also Birth Control; Contraception
Newton, John R. Managing Patients with Intrauterine Devices. 1980. pap. 7.95 (ISBN 0-686-42718-1). Creative Infomatics.

INTRAVENOUS THERAPY
McGill, Shirley L. & Smith, Jean R. IV Therapy. (Illus.). 166p. 1983. pap. 11.95 (ISBN 0-89303-277-8). R J Brady.

INTROSPECTION (THEORY OF KNOWLEDGE)
see Self-Knowledge, Theory of

INTUITION OF DURATION
see Time Perception

INVALID COOKERY
see Cookery for the Sick

INVALIDS–RECREATION
see Handicapped–Recreation

INVASION OF PRIVACY
see Privacy, Right of

INVECTIVE
McPhee, Nancy. The Second Book of Insults. 1983. pap. 3.95 (ISBN 0-14-006474-5). Penguin.

INVENTIONS
see also Creation (Literary, Artistic, etc.); Inventors; Patents; Research, Industrial; Technological Innovations; Technology Transfer
MacCracken, Calvin D. A Handbook for Inventors. (Illus.). 224p. 1983. 14.95 (ISBN 0-686-83660-X, ScribT). Scribner.
Meinhardt, Peter. Inventions, Patents & Trade Marks in Great Britain. 1971 ed. 397p. 25.00 (ISBN 0-686-37380-4). Beekman Pubs.
Thompson, Holland. Age of Invention. 1921. text ed. 8.50x (ISBN 0-686-83456-9). Elliots Bks.

INVENTORS
see also Engineers
Leslie, Stuart W. Boss Kettering. (Illus.). 416p. 1983. 19.95 (ISBN 0-231-05600-1). Columbia U Pr.

INVENTORY CONTROL
see also Materials Management; Stores or Stock-Room Keeping
APICS, ed. Capacity Planning & Control Reprints. 110p. 1975. pap. 10.50 (ISBN 0-935406-16-6). Am Prod Inventory.
Bekiroglu, Haluk, ed. Simulation in Inventory & Production Control. 1983. softbound 20.00 (ISBN 0-686-42972-9). Soc Computer Sim.
Bindon, Kathleen R. Inventories & Foreign Currency Translation Requirements. Farmer, Richard N., ed. LC 82-21729. (Research for Business Decisions Ser.). 1983. write for info. (ISBN 0-8357-1391-1). Univ Microfilms.
Davis, David C., et al, eds. Service Parts Management Reprints. LC 82-72118. 123p. 1982. pap. 10.50 (ISBN 0-935406-19-0). Am Prod & Inventory.
Jones, E. R. Simplified Inventory System: For Collectors, Investors & Dealers. (Illus.). 68p. 1982. 6.75 (ISBN 0-9600934-3-5). E R Jones.
Rudman, Jack. Inventory Control Clerk. (Career Examination Ser.: C-2616). (Cloth bdg. avail. on request). pap. 8.00 (ISBN 0-8373-2616-8). Natl Learning.

INVENTORY MANAGEMENT
see Inventory Control

INVERTEBRATES
see also Arthropoda; Crustacea; Insects; Mollusks; Protozoa
Harrison, Frederick W. & Cowden, Ronald R., eds. Developmental Biology or Freshwater Invertebrates. LC 82-14964. 588p. 1982. 72.00 (ISBN 0-8451-0222-2). A R Liss.
Highnam, K. & Hill, L. Comparative Endocrinology of the Invertebrates. 2nd ed. 1977. 36.00 (ISBN 0-444-19497-5). Elsevier.

INVESTIGATIONS
see also Criminal Investigation; Governmental Investigations
Donaghy, William C. Our Silent Language: An Introduction to Nonverbal Communication. (Comm Comp). (Illus.). 54p. 1980. pap. text ed. 2.95x (ISBN 0-89787-304-1). Gorsuch Scarisbrick.

INVESTIGATIONS, GOVERNMENTAL
see Governmental Investigations

INVESTMENT ADVISERS
Mittre, Sid & Gassen, Chris. Investment Analysis & Portfolio Management. 857p. text ed. 25.95 (ISBN 0-15-546882-0); tchr's. manual 2.95 (ISBN 0-15-546883-9). HarBraceJ.

INVESTMENT AND SAVING
see Saving and Investment

INVESTMENT BANKING
Hayes, Samuel L., III & Spence, A. Michael. Competition in the Investment Banking Industry. (Illus.). 176p. 1983. text ed. 20.00x (ISBN 0-674-15415-0). Harvard U Pr.

INVESTMENT COMPANIES
see Investment Trusts

INVESTMENT IN REAL ESTATE
see Real Estate Investment

INVESTMENT TRUSTS
Donoghue, William E. & Tilling, Thomas. William E. Donoghue's No-Load Mutual Fund Guide: How to Take Advantage of the Investment Opportunity of the '80s. LC 82-48116. (Illus.). 224p. 1983. write for info. (ISBN 0-06-015096-3, HarpT). Har-Row.
Fitzgerald, T. H. Money Market Directory of Pension Funds & Their Investment Managers: 1983. 1982. 385.00 (ISBN 0-939712-02-4). Money Mkt.

INVESTMENTS
see also Annuities; Bonds; Brokers; Capital Investments; Investment Advisers; Investment Banking; Investment Trusts; Loans; Mortgages; Real Estate Investment; Securities; Stock-Exchange; Stocks
Altman, Edward I. Financial Handbook. 5th ed. LC 81-10473. 1344p. 1981. 55.00x (ISBN 0-471-07727-5, Pub. by Ronald Pr). Wiley.
Amling, Frederick. Investments. 5th ed. (Illus.). 704p. 1984. 25.95 (ISBN 0-13-504324-7). P-H.
--Principles of Investment. 3rd ed. (Plaid Ser.). 198p. 1983. pap. 12.95 (ISBN 0-87094-336-7). Dow Jones-Irwin.
Birdwell, Roger W. High-Tech Investing. 257p. 1983. 17.95 (ISBN 0-686-43181-2). Times Bks.
Branch, Ben. Fundamentals of Investing. LC 75-26703. 301p. 1976. 29.95x (ISBN 0-471-09650-4). Wiley.
Brown, Brendon. A Theory of Hedge Investment. LC 82-5651. 240p. 1982. 25.00 (ISBN 0-312-79783-4). St Martin.
Burme, Marshall E. & Friend, Irwin. The Changing Role of the Individual Investor: A Twentieth Century Fund Report. LC 78-18303. 256p. Repr. of 1978 ed. pap. text ed. 15.95 (ISBN 0-471-04547-0). Krieger.
Casey, Douglas R. Crisis Investing. 2nd ed. LC 79-64112. 1980. 12.50 (ISBN 0-936906-00-6). Stratford Pr.
Dreman, David. The New Contrarian Investment Strategy: The Psychology of Stock Market Sucess. LC 78-21820. Date not set. 16.95 (ISBN 0-394-52364-4). Random.
Elton, Edwin J. & Gruber, Martin J. Modern Portfolio Theory & Investment Analysis. LC 80-19517. (Illus.). 553p. 1981. 26.50 (ISBN 0-471-04690-6). Wiley.
Financial Times Business Publishing Ltd., ed. Offshore Financial Centres. 1982. 159.00x (ISBN 0-902998-41-2, Pub. by Finan Times England). State Mutual Bk.
Fong, H. G. Bond Portfolio Analysis & Management. LC 82-73626. 225p. 1983. 32.50 (ISBN 0-87094-245-X). Dow Jones-Irwin.
Francis, J. C. Readings in Investments. 1980. 17.95 (ISBN 0-07-019963-9). McGraw.

Green, Alex, pseud. Money Magic: Incredible Low-Risk Way to Build your Fortune. LC 82-82535. (Illus.). 112p. (Orig.). 1983. pap. 5.95 (ISBN 0-910067-00-7). G K Pr.
Hardy, C. Colburn. Dun & Bradstreet's Guide to Your Investments: 1983. 28th ed. LC 73-18050. (Illus.). 224p. 1983. write for info. (ISBN 0-06-015098-X, HarpT); pap. 9.57 (ISBN 0-06-091037-2, CN-1037). Har-Row.
Harper, Victor L. Handbook of Investment Products & Services. rev. ed. LC 75-26986. (Illus.). 429p. 1977. 17.95 (ISBN 0-13-378737-0). NY Inst Finance.
Heatter, Justin W. The Small Investor's Guide to Large Profits in the Stock Market. 192p. 1983. 14.95 (ISBN 0-686-83838-6, ScribT). Scribner.
Hopkins & Mergers, Thomas H. Acquisitions & Divestitures: A Guide to Their Impact for Investors & Directors. LC 82-71347. 125p. 1982. 17.95 (ISBN 0-87094-200-X). Dow Jones-Irwin.
Hume, John F. Get-Rich-Quick Schemes in the Stock Market & Sound Investment Practices. (A New Stock Market Library Bk.). (Illus.). 133p. 1983. 47.75 (ISBN 0-86654-056-3). Inst Econ Finan.
Kuklin, R. Learn to Invest & Trade on Wall Street. 2nd ed. LC 79-64472. 240p. 1982. pap. 7.95 (ISBN 0-9606504-5-8). Dill Ent.
Lynch, Ransom V. & Ostberg, Donald R. Calculus: A First Course. 704p. 1983. Repr. of 1970 ed. text ed. 32.50 (ISBN 0-89874-597-7). Krieger.
Maddi, Salvatore R. & Kobasa, Suzanne. The Hardy Executive: Health Under Stress. LC 82-73631. (Dorsey Professional Ser.). 325p. 1983. 22.50 (ISBN 0-87094-381-2). Dow Jones-Irwin.
Maginn, John & Tuttle, Donald, eds. Managing Investment Portfolios. 47.50 (ISBN 0-686-84714-8); student ed. 23.75 (ISBN 0-88262-874-7). Warren.
Pessin, Allan H. & Ross, Joseph A. Words of Wall Street: 2,000 Investment Terms Defined. 225p. 1983. 15.95 (ISBN 0-87094-382-0); pap. 9.95 (ISBN 0-87094-417-7). Dow Jones-Irwin.
Pierce, Phyllis. The Dow Jones Investor's Handbook, 1983. LC 66-17630. 136p. 1983. 11.95 (ISBN 0-87094-397-9). Dow Jones-Irwin.
Reed, Dick A. The Complete Investor's Guide to Silver Dollar Investing. 1982. 18.95 (ISBN 0-911349-00-6). English Fact.
Snyder, Julian. The Way of the Hunter Warrior: How to Make a Killing in Any Market. LC 82-61459. 190p. 1982. 12.95 (ISBN 0-943940-00-1). Dutton.
Stark, Brian J. Special Situation Investing: Hedging, Arbitrage & Liquidation. LC 82-73635. 250p. 1983. 27.50 (ISBN 0-87094-384-7). Dow Jones-Irwin.
Toney, Albert & Tilling, Thomas. Winning Investments in High-Tech. 1983. 14.95 (ISBN 0-671-46235-0). S&S.
Tuccillo, John. Housing & Investment in an Inflationary World: Theory & Evidence. (Illus.). 55p. (Orig.). 1980. pap. text ed. 5.50 (ISBN 0-87766-281-9). Urban Inst.
Udell, Gerald G. & Baker, Kenneth G. How to Assess Before You Invest: Pies IV-Preliminary Innovation (self) Evaluation System. rev. ed. LC 82-88234. Orig. Title: Pies II-Manual for Innovation Evaluation. (Illus.). 242p. 1982. pap. 16.50 (ISBN 0-943812-00-3). Locus.
United Business Service, ed. Successful Investing. rev. ed. 1983. pap. 14.95 (ISBN 0-671-46734-4). S&S.
Warfield, Gerald. The Investor's Guide to Stock Quotations: And Other Financial Listings. LC 82-47539. (Illus.). 416p. 1983. pap. 10.53i (ISBN 0-06-091036-4, CN 1036, CN). Har-Row.
Woodwell, Donald R. Automating Your Financial Portfolio: An Investor's Guide to Personal Computers. LC 82-73637. 220p. 1983. 17.50 (ISBN 0-87094-399-5). Dow Jones-Irwin.

INVESTMENTS–TABLES, ETC.

Thorndike's Compound Interest & Annuity Tables. 1982. 60.00 (ISBN 0-88262-836-4). Warren.

INVESTMENTS–AFRICA

Page, John, Jr. Shadow Prices for Trade Strategy & Investment Planning in Egypt. LC 82-8594. (World Bank Staff Working Papers: No. 521). (Orig.). 1982. pap. 5.00 (ISBN 0-8213-0009-1). World Bank.

INVESTMENTS–EUROPE

Buckley, Peter J. & Roberts, Brian R. European Direct Investment in the U. S. A. Before World War I. 200p. 1981. 49.00x (ISBN 0-333-29079-8, Pub. by Macmillan England). State Mutual Bk.

INVESTMENTS–RUSSIA

Dyker, David A. The Process of Investment in the Soviet Union. LC 82-14600. (Soviet & East European Studies). (Illus.). 240p. Date not set. 39.50 (ISBN 0-521-24831-0). Cambridge U Pr.

INVESTMENTS, AMERICAN

Williamson, J. Peter. Foundation Investment Strategies: New Possibilities in the 1981 Tax Law. (Seven Springs Studies). 18p. 1982. pap. 3.00 (ISBN 0-943006-05-8). Seven Springs.

INVESTMENTS, FOREIGN

see also Loans, Foreign; Technical Assistance

Buckley, Peter J. & Roberts, Brian R. European Direct Investment in the U. S. A. Before World War I. 200p. 1981. 49.00x (ISBN 0-333-29079-8, Pub. by Macmillan England). State Mutual Bk.
Fry, Earl H. The Politics of International Investment. 224p. 1983. 24.95 (ISBN 0-07-022610-5, P&RB). McGraw.
Gupta, Kanhaya L. & Islam, M Anisul. Foreign Capital, Savings & Growth. 1983. lib. bdg. 34.50 (ISBN 90-277-1449-5, Pub. by Reidel Holland). Kluwer Boston.
Lombard, Francois J. The Foreign Investment Screening Process in L.D.C.'s: The Case of Columbia, 1967-1975. (Replica Edition Ser.). 171p. 1979. softcover 25.00x (ISBN 0-89158-399-8). Westview.
Mikesell, Raymond F. Foreign Investment in Mining Projects: Case Studies of Recent Experiences. LC 82-14113. 320p. 1983. text ed. 30.00 (ISBN 0-89946-170-0). Oelgeschlager.
OECD Staff. International Investment & Multinational Enterprises: Mid-Term Report on the 1976 Declaration & Decisions. 80p. (Orig.). 1982. pap. 6.00 (ISBN 92-64-12349-0). OECD.
Wells, Louis T., Jr. Third World Multinationals: The Rise of Foreign Investment from Developing Countries. 272p. 1983. 25.00 (ISBN 0-262-23113-1). MIT Pr.
Williams, A. O. International Trade & Investment: A Managerial Approach. 461p. 1982. text ed. 29.95x (ISBN 0-471-03293-X). Ronald Pr.

INVESTMENTS, FOREIGN–LAW AND LEGISLATION

Forry, John I. A Practical Guide to Foreign Investment in the United States, Suppl. 2nd ed. 350p. 1983. text ed. 80.00 (ISBN 0-906524-05-9); pap. text ed. 30.00 (ISBN 0-906524-06-7). BNA.

ION EXCHANGE

Brouillard, F., ed. Physics of Ion-Ion & Electron-Ion Collisions. (NATO ASI Series B, Physics: Vol. 83). 535p. 1983. 69.50x (ISBN 0-306-41105-9, Plenum Pr). Plenum Pub.

ION FLOW DYNAMICS

see also Magnetohydrodynamics; Plasma (Ionized Gases)

Bonnemann, K. H., et al, eds. Ionic Liquids, Molten Salts, & Polyelectrolytes: Berlin (West), 1982 Proceedings. (Lecture Notes in Physics Ser.: Vol. 172). 253p. 1983. pap. 14.50 (ISBN 0-387-11952-3). Springer-Verlag.

ION IMPLANTATION

Ryssel, H. & Glawischnig, H. Ion Implantation Techniques, Berchtesgaden, FRG, 1982. (Springer Series in Electrophysics: Vol. 10). (Illus.). 372p. 1983. 30.00 (ISBN 0-387-11878-0). Springer-Verlag.

IONIC FLOWS

see Ion Flow Dynamics

IONIZATION

see also Collisions (Nuclear Physics); Ion Exchange

Ahrens, L. H. Ionization Potentials: Some Variations, Implications & Applications. (Illus.). 100p. 1983. 30.00 (ISBN 0-08-025274-5). Pergamon.
Smirnov, B. M. Physics of Weakly Ionized Gas. 428p. 1981. 12.00 (ISBN 0-8285-2197-2, Pub. by Mir Pubs USSR). Imported Pubns.

IONIZING RADIATION

see also X-Rays

Sowby, F. D. & International Commission on Radiological Protection, eds. Protection Against Ionizing Radiation in the Teaching of Science: ICRP Publication, No. 36. 14p. 1982. pap. 10.00 (ISBN 0-08-029818-4). Pergamon.

IOWA

see also names of cities, counties, towns, etc. in Iowa

Bauer, Douglas. Prairie City, Iowa: Three Seasons at Home. 330p. 1982. pap. 8.95 (ISBN 0-8138-1329-8). Iowa St U Pr.
McDonald, Julie J. Pathways to the Present in Fifty Iowa & Illinois Communities. LC 77-153937. (Illus.). 310p. 1981. pap. 15.50x (ISBN 0-9608464-0-9). Boyar.

IOWA–DESCRIPTION AND TRAVEL

Liffring-Zug, Joan, compiled by. This is Grant Wood Country. 2nd ed. (Illus.). 64p. pap. 9.00 (ISBN 0-9603858-2-7). Penfield.
Pyle, Donna M. Sioux City. (Illus.). 32p. (Orig.). 1981. pap. 1.00 (ISBN 0-9606944-0-4). Pyle.

IOWA–HISTORY

Hanft, Ethel W. Outstanding Iowa Women: Past & Present, Vol. 2. 1983. price not set. River Bend.
Leland Centennial Committee. Milestones Along the Way: Leland, Iowa. 227p. 1982. pap. 20.00 (ISBN 0-89279-047-4). Graphic Pub.
Troeger, Jack. From Rift to Drift: Iowa's Story in Stone. (Illus.). 120p. 1983. 12.50 (ISBN 0-8138-1521-5). Iowa St U Pr.
Wolf, Robert C. Fossils of Iowa: Field Guide to Paleozois Deposits. (Illus.). 203p. 1983. pap. 10.50 (ISBN 0-8138-1334-4). Iowa St U Pr.

IRAN

Hickman, William F. Ravaged & Reborn: The Iranian Military, 1979-1982. LC 82-73900. 75p. 1983. pap. 5.95 (ISBN 0-8157-3611-8). Brookings.

IRAN–BIBLIOGRAPHY

Elwell-Sutton, L. P., ed. Bibliographical Guide to Iran. LC 82-22748. 300p. 1983. text ed. 35.00x (ISBN 0-389-20339-4). B&N Imports.

IRAN–BIOGRAPHY

Sayyed Mohammad Ali Jamalzadeh & Heston, W. L. Isfahan Is Half the World: Memories of a Persian Boyhood. LC 82-61370. (Princeton Library of Asian Translations). (Illus.). 384p. 1983. 37.50 (ISBN 0-691-06563-2). Princeton U Pr.

IRAN–FOREIGN RELATIONS

Ahmad, Jalal Al-e. Gharbzadegi: Weststruckness. Green, John & Alizadeh, Ahmad, trs. from Persian. LC 82-61280. (Illus.). 204p. (Orig.). 1982. text ed. 16.95 (ISBN 0-939214-08-3); pap. text ed. 9.95 (ISBN 0-939214-07-5). Mazda Pubs.
Ismael, Tareq Y. Iraq & Iran: Roots of Conflict. LC 82-1562. (Contemporary Issues in the Middle East Ser.). (Illus.). 280p. 1982. 24.00x (ISBN 0-8156-2279-1); pap. 12.95x (ISBN 0-8156-2280-5). Syracuse U Pr.
Ramazani, R. K. The United States & Iran: The Patterns of Influence. 204p. 1982. 23.95 (ISBN 0-03-049001-4); pap. 11.95 (ISBN 0-03-048996-2). Praeger.
Tahir-Kheli. The Iran-Iraq War. 224p. 1983. 25.95 (ISBN 0-03-062906-3). Praeger.

IRAN–HISTORY

Chase, Joan. During the Reign of the Queen of Persia. LC 82-48680. 288p. 1983. 14.37i (ISBN 0-06-015136-6, HarpT). Har-Row.
Keddie, Nikki R. & Hooglund, Eric, eds. The Iranian Revolution & the Islamic Republic: Proceedings of a Conference Held at the Woodrow Wilson International Center for Scholars, May 21-22, 1982. LC 82-62038. 210p. (Orig.). 1982. pap. 7.50 (ISBN 0-916808-19-X). Mid East Inst.
Reid, James J. Trebalism & Society in Islamic Iran 1500-1629. (Studies in Near Eastern Culture & Society Ser.: Vol. 4). 220p. 1983. pap. write for info. (82-50984); write for info. (ISBN 0-89003-125-8). Undena Pubns.
A View from Tehran: A Diplomatist Looks at the Shah's Regime in 1964. 12p. 1979. 1.50 (ISBN 0-686-83451-8, Inst Study Diplomacy). Geo U Sch For Serv.

IRAN–HISTORY–TO 640

Stern, Ephraim. The Material Culture of the Land of the Bible in the Persian Period 538-331 B.C. (Illus.). 304p. 1982. pap. text ed. 65.00x (ISBN 0-85668-137-7, 40917, Pub. by Aris & Phillips England). Humanities.

IRAN–POLITICS AND GOVERNMENT

Bakhash, Shaul. The Politics of Oil & Revolution in Iran. LC 82-72116. 61p. 1982. pap. 5.95 (ISBN 0-8157-0781-9). Brookings.
Behn, Wolfgang, ed. The Iranian Opposition in Exile: An Annotated Bibliography of Publications from 1962-1979. 249p. (Orig.). 1979. pap. text ed. 32.50x (ISBN 3-447-02064-4). Intl Pubns Serv.
Green, Jerold. Revolution in Iran. 218p. 1982. 24.95 (ISBN 0-03-062409-6). Praeger.
Keddie, Nikki R. Religion & Politics in Iran: Shi'ism from Quiestism to Revolution. LC 82-17351. 288p. 1983. text ed. 22.50x (ISBN 0-300-02874-1). Yale U Pr.
Yadegari, Mohammad. Ideological Revolution in the Muslim World. Quinlan, Hamid, ed. LC 82-74123. (Illus.). 95p. 1983. pap. 3.50 (ISBN 0-89259-040-8). Am Trust Pubns.

IRAN–RELIGION

Keddie, Nikki R. Religion & Politics in Iran: Shi'ism from Quiestism to Revolution. LC 82-17351. 288p. 1983. text ed. 22.50x (ISBN 0-300-02874-1). Yale U Pr.

IRAN–SOCIAL CONDITIONS

Youth & New Ways of Life in Iran. 14p. 1982. pap. 5.00 (ISBN 0-686-81841-5, TUNU 197, UNU). Unipub.

IRAN–SOCIAL LIFE AND CUSTOMS

Ahmad, Jalal Al-e. Gharbzadegi: Weststruckness. Green, John & Alizadeh, Ahmad, trs. from Persian. LC 82-61280. (Illus.). 204p. (Orig.). 1982. text ed. 16.95 (ISBN 0-939214-08-3); pap. text ed. 9.95 (ISBN 0-939214-07-5). Mazda Pubs.

IRANIAN LANGUAGES

see Kurdish Language; Persian Language

IRANIAN POTTERY

see Pottery, Iranian

IRAQ

Niblock, Tim, ed. Iraq: The Contemporary State. LC 82-42566. 304p. 1982. 27.50 (ISBN 0-312-43585-1). St Martin.

IRAQ–FOREIGN RELATIONS

Ismael, Tareq Y. Iraq & Iran: Roots of Conflict. LC 82-1562. (Contemporary Issues in the Middle East Ser.). (Illus.). 280p. 1982. 24.00x (ISBN 0-8156-2279-1); pap. 12.95x (ISBN 0-8156-2280-5). Syracuse U Pr.

IRAQ–HISTORY

Marr, Phebe. The Modern History of Iraq. 275p. 1983. lib. bdg. 25.00x (ISBN 0-86531-119-6). Westview.

IRELAND

see also Northern Ireland;
also names of cities, towns and counties in Ireland, e.g. Dublin; Kerry

Murphy, Michael. Names of Ireland. (International Library of Names). 250p. 1983. text ed. 24.50x (ISBN 0-8290-1286-9). Irvington.
O'Connell, James & Gallagher, Tom, eds. Contemporary Irish Studies. 200p. 1982. 20.00 (ISBN 0-7190-0919-7). Manchester.

IRELAND–BIBLIOGRAPHY

Shannon, Michael O. Modern Ireland: A Bibliography for Research, Planning & Development. 760p. 1982. 65.00 (ISBN 0-85365-914-1, Pub. by Lib Assn England). Oryx Pr.

IRELAND–BIOGRAPHY

Levinson, Leah. With Wooden Sword. (Illus.). 350p. 1983. 22.95X (ISBN 0-930350-42-1). NE U Pr.
O'Hara, Mary. A Song for Ireland. (Illus.). 208p. 1983. 19.95 (ISBN 0-7181-2161-9, Pub by Michael Joseph). Merrimack Bk Serv.
--A Song for Ireland. 1983. 19.95 (ISBN 0-686-38871-2, Pub. by Michael Joseph). Merrimack Bk Serv.
Wallace, Martin. One Hundred Irish Lives. (Illus.). 168p. (Orig.). 1983. cancelled (ISBN 0-7153-8331-0). David & Charles.
--One Hundred Irish Lives. LC 82-24289. (Illus.). 168p. 1983. text ed. 17.50x (ISBN 0-389-20364-5). B&N Imports.

IRELAND–CIVILIZATION

O'Connell, James & Gallagher, Tom, eds. Contemporary Irish Studies. 200p. 1982. 20.00 (ISBN 0-7190-0919-7). Manchester.

IRELAND–DESCRIPTION AND TRAVEL

Clarke, Harold. The Splendour of Ireland. (Illus.). 64p. 1982. 15.95 (ISBN 0-900346-36-1, Pub. by Salem Hse Ltd.). Merrimack Bk Serv.
Department of Foreign Affairs. Facts about Ireland. 2nd ed. (Illus.). 258p. Date not set. 14.50 (ISBN 0-906404-10-X, Pub. by Dept Foreign Ireland); pap. 9.95 (ISBN 0-906404-12-6). Irish Bks Media.
Haughton, Joseph P. & Gillmoor, Desmond A. The Geography of Ireland. (Aspects of Ireland Ser.: Vol. 5). (Illus.). 59p. 1979. pap. 5.95 (ISBN 0-906404-05-3, Pub. by Dept Foreign Ireland). Irish Bks Media.

IRELAND–DESCRIPTION AND TRAVEL–GUIDEBOOKS

Birnbaum, Stephen. Great Britain & Ireland 1983. (Get 'em & Go Travel Guide Ser.). 1982. 11.95 (ISBN 0-395-32871-3). HM.
Harvard Student Agencies. Let's Go Britain & Ireland. (The Let's Go Ser.). (Illus.). 450p. 1983. pap. 7.95 (ISBN 0-312-48210-8). St Martin.
Watney, John. Cruising in British & Irish Waters. (Illus.). 224p. 1983. 23.95 (ISBN 0-7153-8402-3). David & Charles.

IRELAND–GENEALOGY

De Breffny, Brian. Irish Family Names: Arms, Origins, & Locations. 50.00x (ISBN 0-7171-1225-X). State Mutual Bk.
Fairbairn, James. Fairbairn's Crests of the Families of Great Britain & Ireland. LC 68-25887. (Illus.). 800p. 1968. 32.30 (ISBN 0-8048-0177-0). C E Tuttle.
O'Laughlin, Michael C. The Flaherty Book. (Irish Family History Ser.). (Illus.). 50p. 1983. saddle stitch 9.95 (ISBN 0-940134-22-5). Irish Genealog.

IRELAND–HISTORIC HOUSES, ETC.

Scheaff, Nicholas. Iveagh House. (Aspects of Ireland Ser.: Vol. 2). (Illus.). 65p. (Orig.). 1978. pap. 5.95 (ISBN 0-906404-02-9, Pub. by Dept Foreign Ireland). Irish Bks Media.

IRELAND–HISTORY

Bew, P. & Gibbon, P. The State in Northern Ireland, 1921-72. 224p. 1982. pap. 8.50 (ISBN 0-7190-0814-X). Manchester.
Elton, G., ed. Annual Bibliography of British & Irish History 1981. 196p. 1982. text ed. 37.50x (ISBN 0-391-02728-X, Pub. by Harvester England). Humanities.
Gerald of Wales. History & Topography of Ireland. O'Meara, John, tr. 1983. pap. 5.95 (ISBN 0-14-044423-8). Penguin.
Johnson, Paul. Ireland: Land of Troubles. (Illus.). 224p. 1982. 14.50 (ISBN 0-8419-0758-7). Holmes & Meier.
Johnston, M., ed. Ireland Under the Ascendancy, 1688-1800. 280p. 1982. 49.00x (ISBN 0-7171-0896-1, Pub. by Macmillan England). State Mutual Bk.
Maltby, Arthur. The Government of Northern Ireland Nineteen Twenty-Two to Seventy-Two: A Catalogue & Breviate of Parliamentary Papers. 258p. 1974. text ed. 30.00x (ISBN 0-7165-2151-2, Pub by Irish Academic Pr). Biblio Dist.
Silke. Kinsale. 224p. 1982. 49.00x (ISBN 0-85323-090-0, Pub. by Liverpool Univ England). State Mutual Bk.
Spenser, Edmund & Davies, John. Ireland under Elizabeth & James the First. Morley, Henry, ed. 445p. 1982. Repr. of 1890 ed. lib. bdg. 50.00 (ISBN 0-89987-647-1). Darby Bks.

IRELAND–HISTORY–FICTION

Dearle, Norman B. Economic Chronicle of the Great War For Great Britain & Ireland: 1914-1919. (Economic & Social History of the World War Ser.). 1929. text ed. 65.00x (ISBN 0-686-83531-X). Elliots Bks.

IRELAND–POLITICS AND GOVERNMENT

Bew, Paul & Patterson, Henry. Sean Lemass & the Making of Modern Ireland, 1945-66. 1982. 70.00x (ISBN 0-7171-1260-8, Pub. by Gill & Macmillan Ireland). State Mutual Bk.
Bowman, John. De Valera & the Ulster Question, Nineteen Seventeen to Nineteen Seventy-three. 384p. 1983. 39.00 (ISBN 0-19-822681-0). Oxford U Pr.
Gallagher, Michael. The Irish Labor Party in Transition, 1957-82. 1982. 79.00x (ISBN 0-7171-1250-0, Pub. by Gill & Macmillan Ireland). State Mutual Bk.

Maltby, Arthur. The Government of Northern Ireland Nineteen Twenty-Two to Seventy-Two: A Catalogue & Breviate of Parliamentary Papers. 258p. 1974. text ed. 30.00x (ISBN 0-7165-2151-2, Pub by Irish Academic Pr). Biblio Dist.

Rea, Desmond. Political Co-operation in Divided Societies: A Series of Papers Relevant to the Conflict in Northern Ireland. 1982. 79.00x (ISBN 0-7171-1162-8, Pub. by Gill & Macmillan Ireland). State Mutual Bk.

Rea, Desmond, ed. Northern Ireland, the Republic of Ireland & Great Britain: Problems of Political Co-Operation. 300p. 1982. 50.00x (Pub. by Macmillan England). State Mutual Bk.

IRELAND–SOCIAL CONDITIONS

Peillon, Michael. Contemporary Irish Society: An Introduction. 231p. 1982. pap. text ed. 10.00x (ISBN 0-7171-1141-5, 90243, Pub. by Gill & Mac Ireland). Humanities.

IRELAND–SOCIAL LIFE AND CUSTOMS

Carroll, Noel. Sport in Ireland. (Aspects of Ireland Ser.: Vol. 6). (Illus.). 105p. Date not set. pap. 5.95 (ISBN 0-906404-06-1, Pub. by Dept Foreign Ireland). Irish Bks Media.

Peillon, Michael. Contemporary Irish Society: An Introduction. 231p. 1982. pap. text ed. 10.00x (ISBN 0-7171-1141-5, 90243, Pub. by Gill & Mac Ireland). Humanities.

--Irish Society: An Introduction. 1982. 39.00x (ISBN 0-7171-1141-5, Pub. by Gill & Macmillan Ireland). State Mutual Bk.

Shannon, Elizabeth. Up in the Dark. LC 82-73037. (Illus.). 384p. 1983. 14.95 (ISBN 0-689-11364-1). Atheneum.

IRIS (PLANT)

Cassidy, G. E. & Linnegar, S. Growing Irises. (Illus.). 160p. 1982. 16.50 (ISBN 0-7099-0706-0). Timber.

Mathew, Brian. Crocus. (Illus.). 224p. 1982. 50.00 (ISBN 0-917304-23-3). Timber.

IRISH AMERICANS

Dolan, Jay P. The Immigrant Church: New York's Irish & German Catholics, 1815-1865. LC 82-23827. (Illus.). xiv, 221p. 1983. pap. text ed. 7.95x (ISBN 0-268-01151-6, 85-11511). U of Notre Dame Pr.

Griffin, William D. A Portrait of the Irish in America. (Illus.). 272p. 1982. pap. 14.95 (ISBN 0-686-83722-3, ScribT). Scribner.

IRISH ARCHITECTURE

see Architecture–Ireland

IRISH ART

see Art, Irish

IRISH AUTHORS

see Authors, Irish

IRISH BULLS

see Irish Wit and Humor

IRISH DRAMA (ENGLISH)–HISTORY AND CRITICISM

Hogan, Robert. Since O'Casey: And Other Essays on Irish Drama. LC 82-22813. (Irish Literary Studies: No. 15). 166p. 1983. text ed. 28.50x (ISBN 0-389-20346-7). B&N Imports.

IRISH FOLK-LORE

see Folk-Lore, Irish

IRISH HARP

see Harp

IRISH LEGENDS

see Legends, Irish

IRISH LITERATURE (ENGLISH)–HISTORY AND CRITICISM

Mac Cana, Proinsias. Literature in Irish. (Aspects of Ireland Ser.: Vol. 8). (Illus.). 69p. 1981. pap. 6.95 (ISBN 0-906404-08-8, Pub. by Dept Foreign Ireland). Irish Bks Media.

Martin, Augustine. Anglo-Irish Literature. (Aspects of Ireland Ser.: Vol. 7). (Illus.). 71p. 1981. pap. 6.95 (ISBN 0-906404-07-X, Pub. by Dept Foreign Ireland). Irish Bks Media.

Ure. Yeats & Anglo-Irish Literature. 216p. 1982. 50.00x (ISBN 0-85323-322-5, Pub. by Liverpool Univ England). State Mutual Bk.

IRISH POETRY (COLLECTIONS)

Comprises poetry in Irish language and poetry written by Irish authors in English or other languages.

A Golden Treasury of Irish Verses. 364p. 1982. Repr. of 1930 ed. lib. bdg. 35.00 (ISBN 0-89760-753-8). Telegraph Bks.

O'Levenson, Jordan, ed. Irish In Memoriam Poetry: The Books of Tears. LC 82-90968. (Orig.). 1983. pap. 15.95 (ISBN 0-914442-10-4). Levenson Pr.

IRISH POETRY–HISTORY AND CRITICISM

Freyer, Grattan. W. B. Yeats & the Anti-Democratic Tradition. 1982. 45.00x (ISBN 0-686-99819-7, Pub. by Gill & Macmillan Ireland). State Mutual Bk.

Wolfe, Humbert. The Poems from the Irish. 1982. lib. bdg. 34.50 (ISBN 0-686-81928-4). Porter.

IRISH QUESTION

see also Home Rule (Ireland)

Rea, Desmond, ed. Northern Ireland, the Republic of Ireland & Great Britain: Problems of Political Co-Operation. 300p. 1982. 50.00x (Pub. by Macmillan England). State Mutual Bk.

IRISH REPUBLICAN ARMY

Inside the Irish Republican Army. 47p. 1975. 2.00 (ISBN 0-686-43097-2). Recon Pubns.

IRISH TALES

see Tales, Irish

IRISH WIT AND HUMOR

Spalding, Henry D. Irish Laffs. (Illus.). 96p. 1982. pap. 3.95 (ISBN 0-8246-0289-7). Jonathan David.

IRON

see also Building, Iron and Steel; Cast Iron; Steel

Dunford, H. B. & Dolphin, D. The Biological Chemistry of Iron. 1982. 59.50 (ISBN 90-277-1444-4, Pub. by Reidel Holland). Kluwer Boston.

IRON–METALLURGY

Transactions of the Iron & Steel Society, Vol. II. 130p. 1983. 52.00 (ISBN 0-911277-01-3). Iron & Steel.

Twenty-Fourth Mechanical Working & Steel Processing Conference Proceedings. 570p. 52.00 (ISBN 0-89520-153-4). Iron & Steel.

IRON AND STEEL BUILDING

see Building, Iron and Steel

IRON AND STEEL WORKERS

Iron & Steel Committee, Tenth Session, Geneva, 13-22 October 1981: Note on the Proceedings. iii, 71p. 1982. 7.15 (ISBN 92-2-102937-9). Intl Labour Office.

IRON INDUSTRY AND TRADE

see also Cast Iron; Enameled Ware; Iron and Steel Workers; Steel Industry and Trade

Transactions of the Iron & Steel Society, Vol. I. 130p. 1982. 52.00 (ISBN 0-911277-00-5). Iron & Steel.

IRON INDUSTRY AND TRADE–VOCATIONAL GUIDANCE

Rudman, Jack. Foreman (Structures - Group C) (Iron Work) (Career Examination Ser.: C-1324). (Cloth bdg. avail. on request). pap. 12.00 (ISBN 0-8373-1324-4). Natl Learning.

IRON INDUSTRY AND TRADE–JAPAN

Japan's Iron & Steel Industry 1981. 30th ed. LC 55-33803. 227p. (Orig.). 1981. pap. 35.00 (ISBN 0-8002-3005-1). Intl Pubns Serv.

IRON WORKERS

see Iron and Steel Workers

IRON-WORKS

Badger, Carl B. Badger's Illustrated Catalogue of Cast-Iron Architecture. 1982. pap. 8.95 (ISBN 0-486-24223-4). Dover.

IRONWORK

see Architectural Ironwork; Welding

IROQUOIS INDIANS

see Indians of North America–Eastern States

IRRADIATION

see also Radioactivation Analysis

Ganmaster. Food Irradiation Now. 1982. 22.00 (ISBN 90-247-2763-4, Pub. by Martinus Nijhoff Netherlands). Kluwer Boston.

Training Manual on Food Irradiation: Technology & Techniques. (Technical Reports Ser.: No. 114). 205p. 1982. pap. 26.75 (ISBN 92-0-115082-2, IDC114/2, IAEA). Unipub.

IRRIGATION

see also Arid Regions; Dams; Reservoirs; Windmills

Bumli, George R., ed. Principles of Project Formulation for Irrigation & Drainage Projects. LC 82-73505. 132p. 1982. pap. text ed. 15.75 (ISBN 0-87262-345-9). Am Soc Civil Eng.

Hillel, Daniel, ed. Advances in Irrigation, Vol. II. Date not set. price not set (ISBN 0-12-024302-4). Acad Pr.

Huston, Harvey. The Right of Appropriation & the Colorado System of Laws in Regard to Irrigation. 334p. 1983. Repr. of 1893 ed. lib. bdg. 27.50x (ISBN 0-8377-0649-1). Rothman.

Lysimeters. (FAO Irrigation & Drainage Paper: No. 39). 68p. 1982. pap. 7.50 (ISBN 92-5-101186-9, F2330, FAO). Unipub.

Majumdar, S. K. Irrigation Engineering. 350p. Date not set. 4.00x (ISBN 0-07-451756-2). McGraw.

O'Brien, Michael & Mason, Roger D. A Late Formative Irrigation Settlement below Monte Alban: Survey & Excavation on the Xoxocotlan Piedmont, Oaxaca, Mexico. (Institute of Latin American Studies Special Publications). (Illus.). 254p. 1982. text ed. 25.00x (ISBN 0-292-74628-8). U of Tex Pr.

Organization, Operation & Maintenance of Irrigation Schemes. (FAO Irrigation & Drainage Paper: No. 40). 166p. 1983. pap. 12.75 (ISBN 92-5-101245-8, F2356, FAO). Unipub.

IRRIGATION–MEXICO

O'Brien, Michael & Mason, Roger D. A Late Formative Irrigation Settlement below Monte Alban: Survey & Excavation on the Xoxocotlan Piedmont, Oaxaca, Mexico. (Institute of Latin American Studies Special Publications). (Illus.). 254p. 1982. text ed. 25.00x (ISBN 0-292-74628-8). U of Tex Pr.

IRVING, HENRY, SIR, 1838-1905

Mayer, David, ed. Henry Irving & The Bells. (Illus.). 160p. 1982. 20.00 (ISBN 0-7190-0798-4). Manchester.

ISAIAH, THE PROPHET

Cothen, Joe H. The Preacher's Notebook on Isaiah. 1983. pap. 6.95 (ISBN 0-88289-365-3). Pelican.

ISCHEMIC HEART DISEASE

see Coronary Heart Disease

ISLAM

see also Civilization, Islamic; Koran; Muslims also special headings with Islam added in parentheses; subdivision Islam under special topics, e.g. Marriage–Islam; headings beginning with the words Islamic and Muslim

Boisard, Marcel. The Humanism of Islam. Quinlan, Hamid, ed. Al-Jarrahi, Abdussamad, tr. from Fr. LC 82-70456. 200p. (Orig.). 1983. pap. 8.00 (ISBN 0-89259-035-1). Am Trust Pubns.

Dermenghem, Emile. Muhammad & the Islamic Tradition. Watt, Jean M., tr. LC 81-47412. 192p. Date not set. 10.95 (ISBN 0-87951-073-0); pap. 6.95 (ISBN 0-87951-170-2). Overlook Pr.

Dobbins, Frank A. The Contributions of Mohammedanism to the Historical Growth of Mankind & Its Future Prospects. (Illus.). 103p. Repr. of 1883 ed. 97.75 (ISBN 0-89901-111-X). Found Class Reprints.

Gilsenan, Michael. Recognizing Islam: An Anthropologist's Introduction. 287p. 1983. 16.50 (ISBN 0-686-37688-9); pap. 7.95 (ISBN 0-686-37689-7). Pantheon.

Nabi, Malik B. The Quranic Phenomenon. Kirkari, Abu B., tr. from Fr. LC 82-70460. 150p. (Orig.). 1982. pap. 8.00 (ISBN 0-89259-023-8). Am Trust Pubns.

Quasem, M. A. Salvation of the Soul & Islamic Devotions. 200p. (Orig.). 1983. pap. 8.95 (ISBN 0-7103-0033-6, Kegan Paul). Routledge & Kegan.

Roboz, Steven & Steiner, Rudolf. Islam: Study Notes. Roboz, Steven, ed. 33p. 1980. pap. 2.95 (ISBN 0-88010-050-8, Pub. by Steiner Book Centre Canada). Anthroposophic.

Sabiq, Sayyed. Figh Al Sunnah. Quilan, Hamid, ed. Izzidien, Movel Y., tr. from Arabic. LC 82-70450. 1700p. (Orig.). 1983. text ed. 30.00 (ISBN 0-89259-033-5); pap. 20.00 (ISBN 0-686-81828-8). Am Trust Pubns.

Shariati, Ali. Man & Islam. Marjani, Fatollah, tr. from Farsi. 150p. (Orig.). 1982. pap. 4.95 (ISBN 0-941722-00-7, Pub. by Handami Found Iran). Book Dist Ctr.

Siddique, Kaukab. Islam-the Wave of the Future. LC 82-83624. 75p. (Orig.). 1983. pap. 2.00 (ISBN 0-942978-04-8). Am Soc Ed & Rel.

Swarup, Ram. Islam Through Sahih Muslim. 224p. 1983. 12.00 (ISBN 0-682-49948-X). Exposition.

ISLAM–BIBLIOGRAPHY

Encyclopaedia of Islam Supplement, fasc. 5-6: Djawhar-al-Irake. 167p. 1982. pap. write for info. (ISBN 90-04-06712-4). E J Brill.

Encyclopedie de l'Islam. Supplement, livr. 5-6: Djawhar-al-Iraki. 168p. 1982. pap. write for info. (ISBN 90-04-06711-6). E J Brill.

ISLAM–HISTORY

Engineer, Asghar A. The Origin & Development of Islam: An Essay on Its Socio-Economic Growth. 248p. 1980. text ed. 18.95 (ISBN 0-86131-174-4, Pub. by Orient Longman Ltd India). Apt Bks.

Keddie, Nikki R. & Hooglund, Eric, eds. The Iranian Revolution & the Islamic Republic: Proceedings of a Conference Held at the Woodrow Wilson International Center for Scholars, May 21-22, 1982. LC 82-62038. 210p. (Orig.). 1982. pap. 7.50 (ISBN 0-916808-19-X). Mid East Inst.

Siddiqui, A. H. Philosophical Interpretation of History. 9.95 (ISBN 0-686-83884-X). Kazi Pubns.

Sluglett, Peter, compiled by. Theses on Islam, Middle East, & Northwest Africa, 1880-1978. 200p. 1982. 28.00 (ISBN 0-7201-1651-1, Pub. by Mansell England). Wilson.

ISLAM–RELATIONS

Malik, Z. I. Democracy in Islam. 1.95 (ISBN 0-686-83891-2). Kazi Pubns.

Siddiqui, A. H. The Cracy & the Islamic State. 2.50 (ISBN 0-686-83892-0). Kazi Pubns.

ISLAM–AFRICA

Clarke, Peter. West Africa & Islam. 280p. 1982. pap. text ed. 19.95 (ISBN 0-7131-8029-3). E Arnold.

ISLAM–EGYPT

Hussain, Asaf. Islamic Movements in Egypt, Pakistan & Iran: An Annotated Bibliography. 192p. 1982. 32.00 (ISBN 0-7201-1648-1, Pub. by Mansell England). Wilson.

ISLAM–INDIA

Izzidien, Mouel Y. Nisab Al Ihtisab. Quinlan, Hamid, ed. LC 82-70458. 230p. (Orig.). 1982. pap. 5.00 (ISBN 0-89259-031-9). Am Trust Pubns.

Schimmel, Annermarie. Islam in India & Pakistan. (Iconography of Religions Ser.: XXII/9). (Illus.). x, 34p. 1982. pap. write for info. (ISBN 90-04-06479-6). E J Brill.

Troll, Christian W., ed. Islam in India-Studies & Commentaries: Vol. 1, The Akbar Mission & Miscellaneous Studies. 240p. 1982. text ed. 32.50x (ISBN 0-7069-1889-4, Pub. by Vikas India). Advent NY.

ISLAM–IRAN

Hussain, Asaf. Islamic Movements in Egypt, Pakistan & Iran: An Annotated Bibliography. 192p. 1982. 32.00 (ISBN 0-7201-1648-1, Pub. by Mansell England). Wilson.

ISLAM–PAKISTAN

Akbar, Ahmed. Religion & Politics in Muslim Society: Order & Conflict in Pakistan. LC 82-14774. (Illus.). 225p. Date not set. price not set (ISBN 0-521-24635-0). Cambridge U Pr.

Hussain, Asaf. Islamic Movements in Egypt, Pakistan & Iran: An Annotated Bibliography. 192p. 1982. 32.00 (ISBN 0-7201-1648-1, Pub. by Mansell England). Wilson.

Schimmel, Annermarie. Islam in India & Pakistan. (Iconography of Religions Ser.: XXII/9). (Illus.). x, 34p. 1982. pap. write for info. (ISBN 90-04-06479-6). E J Brill.

ISLAM–TURKEY

Dankoff, Robert, tr. Wisdom of Royal Glory-Kutadgu Bilig: A Turko-Islamic Mirror for Princes. LC 82-20159. (Publications of The Center for Middle Eastern Studies: No. 16). 320p. 1983. 25.00 (ISBN 0-226-97179-1). U of Chicago Pr.

ISLAM AND CHRISTIANITY

see Christianity and Other Religions–Islam

ISLAM AND ECONOMICS

Choudhury, Masudul A. An Islamic Social Welfare Function. Quinlan, Hamid, ed. LC 82-74125. (Illus.). 60p. 1983. pap. 2.00 (ISBN 0-89259-041-6). Am Trust Pubns.

ISLAM AND STATE

Siddique, Kankab. Islamic Revolution: The Iranian Experiment. Naeem, Nadrat, ed. (Illus.). 100p. (Orig.). pap. 3.50 (ISBN 0-942978-03-X). Am Soc Ed & Rel.

ISLAMIC ARCHITECTURE

see Architecture, Islamic

ISLAMIC ART

see Art, Islamic

ISLAMIC CIVILIZATION

see Civilization, Islamic

ISLAMIC COUNTRIES–HISTORY

Bennigsen, Alexandre & Broxup, Marie. The Islamic Threat to the Soviet State. LC 82-16826. 224p. 1983. 27.50x (ISBN 0-312-43739-0). St Martin.

ISLAMIC COUNTRIES–POLITICS

Bassiouni, M. C., ed. The Islamic Criminal Justice System. LC 81-22370. 255p. 1982. lib. bdg. 30.00 (ISBN 0-379-20745-1); pap. 8.00 (ISBN 0-379-20749-4). Oceana.

ISLAMIC LAW

Hazm, Imam Ibn. Al Muhalla. Quinlan, Hamid, ed. Ayad, Foaud, tr. LC 82-70454. (Illus.). 125p. 1983. pap. 4.50 (ISBN 0-89259-037-8). Am Trust Pubns.

ISLAMIC LITERATURE

see also Koran

Chejne, A. G. Ibn Hazm. 19.95 (ISBN 0-686-83558-1); pap. 14.95 (ISBN 0-686-83558-1). Kazi Pubns.

Daryabadi, A. M. Holy Quaran Arabic-English. 19.95 (ISBN 0-686-83591-3). Kazi Pubns.

El Liwaru, Saidi J. & El Liwaru, Maisha Z. The Muslim Family Reader. Quinlan, Hamid, ed. LC 82-74126. 130p. 1983. pap. 4.00 (ISBN 0-89259-028-9). Am Trust Pubns.

Feroz-ul-Lughat (Urdu) Dictionary. 29.95 (ISBN 0-686-83586-7). Kazi Pubns.

Ha, Ta. Al-Dhabh. 2.50 (ISBN 0-686-83897-1). Kazi Pubns.

Holy Quran. (Arabic.). 14.95 (ISBN 0-686-83880-7). Kazi Pubns.

Holy Quran: Deluxe Arabic Only. 29.95 (ISBN 0-686-83596-4). Kazi Pubns.

Qazi, M. A. ABC Islamic Reader. pap. 2.00 (ISBN 0-686-83566-2). Kazi Pubns.

--Alif Ba Ta Islamic Reader. pap. 2.00 (ISBN 0-686-83570-0). Kazi Pubns.

Siddiqui, M. I. Excellent Qualities of Holy Quran. 2.50 (ISBN 0-686-83882-3). Kazi Pubns.

ThanWi, A. A. Holy Quran: Arabic-Urdu. 14.95 (ISBN 0-686-83593-X). Kazi Pubns.

Yousuf Ali, A. Al-Quran-Al-Karim. pap. 14.95 soft cover (ISBN 0-686-83568-9). Kazi Pubns.

ISLAMIC PHILOSOPHY

see Philosophy, Islamic

ISLAMIC WOMEN

see Women, Muslim

ISLAND FLORA AND FAUNA

Sauer, Jonathan D. Cayman Islands Seashore Vegetation: A Study in Comparative Biogeography. LC 82-2608. (Publications in Geographical Sciences: Vol. 25). 166p. 1983. pap. 16.00x (ISBN 0-520-09656-8). U of Cal Pr.

ISLANDS

see also Coral Reefs and Islands; Island Flora and Fauna; United States–Territories and Possessions

Carreira, Antonio. The People of the Cape Verde Islands. 1982. 21.50 (ISBN 0-208-01988-X, Archon Bks). Shoe String.

ISLANDS–JUVENILE LITERATURE

Braymer, Marjorie. Atlantis: The Biography of a Legend. LC 82-16727. (Illus.). 256p. (gr. 7 up). 1983. 12.95 (ISBN 0-689-50264-8, McElderry Bk). Atheneum.

ISLANDS OF LANGERHANS

see Pancreas

ISLANDS OF THE INDIAN OCEAN

Newitt, Malyn. The Comoro Islands. (Nations of Contemporary Africa Ser.). 135p. 1983. 17.50x (ISBN 0-86531-292-3). Westview.

ISLANDS OF THE PACIFIC

Dalton & Stanley. South Pacific Handbook. (Illus.). 578p. 1982. 12.95 (ISBN 0-686-43406-4). Bradt Ent.

McDermott, John W. How to Get Lost & Found in the Cook Islands. 1979. 9.95 (ISBN 0-686-37619-6). Orafa Pub Co.

Pacific Islands Business & Trade Directory, 1982: With a Special Australian & New Zealand Exporters Section. 27th ed. LC 72-622889. (Illus.). 724p. (Orig.). 1982. pap. 45.00x (ISBN 0-8002-3106-6). Intl Pubns Serv.

Stanley, David. South Pacific Handbook. 2nd ed. 574p. Date not set. price not set (ISBN 0-9603322-3-5). Moon Pubns CA.

ISLE OF MAN

Kinvig. A History of the Isle of Man. 208p. 1982. 49.00x (ISBN 0-85323-483-3, Pub. by Liverpool Univ England). State Mutual Bk.

ISLE OF WIGHT

Arnold, C. J. The Anglo-Saxon Cemeteries of the Isle of Wight. 208p. 1982. 99.00x (ISBN 0-7141-1359-X, Pub. by Brit Mus Pubns England). State Mutual Bk.

ISOENZYMES

Rattazzi, Mario C. & Scandalios, John G., eds. Isozymes. LC 77-12288. (Current Topics in Biological & Medical Research Ser.: Vol. 6). 297p. 1982. 58.00 (ISBN 0-8451-0255-9). A R Liss.

ISOLATION, SOCIAL

see Social Isolation

ISOMETRIC EXERCISE

LeWitt, Joe. Isometric Drawings. 1981. pap. 10.00 (ISBN 0-686-43403-X). J Weber Gall.

ISOPERIMETRICAL PROBLEMS

see Calculus of Variations

ISOPTERA

see Termites

ISOSTASY

Andrews, John T., ed. Glacial Isostasy. LC 73-12624. (Benchmark Papers in Geology: Vol. 10). 491p. 1974. text ed. 54.00 (ISBN 0-87933-051-1). Hutchinson Ross.

ISOTOPE SEPARATION

see also Nuclear Fuels

Ehrfeld, W. Elements of Flow & Diffusion Processes in Separation Nozzles. (Springer Tracts in Modern Physics Ser.: Vol. 97). (Illus.). 160p. 1983. 26.00 (ISBN 0-387-11924-8). Springer-Verlag.

ISOTOPES

see also Isotope Separation; Radioactive Tracers; Radioisotopes

also subdivision Isotopes under names of elements, e.g. Carbon-Isotopes

Faure, Gunter. Principles of Isotope Geology. LC 77-4479. (Intermediate Geology Ser.). 464p. 1977. text ed. 36.95 (ISBN 0-471-25665-X). Wiley.

ISOTOPIC INDICATORS

see Radioactive Tracers

ISOZYMES

see Isoenzymes

ISRAEL

Alpert, Carl. Technion: The Story of Israel's Institute of Technology. LC 82-11556. (Illus.). 439p. 1983. 25.00x (ISBN 0-87203-102-0). Hermon.

The Israel Yearbook, 1982. 38th ed. LC 51-36641. (Illus.). 335p. 1982. 35.00x (ISBN 0-8002-3023-X). Intl Pubns Serv.

Wainright, Aristides. The Curse of the Arabs & the Ethical Deterioration of the State of Israel. (Illus.). 117p. 1983. 77.85 (ISBN 0-86722-036-8). Inst Econ Pol.

ISRAEL-ANTIQUITIES

Levine, Lee I., ed. The Jerusalem Cathedral, Vol. 2. (Studies in the History, Archaeology, Geography & Ethnography of the Land of Israel). 300p. 1983. 25.00x (ISBN 0-8143-1715-4). Wayne St U Pr.

ISRAEL-ARMED FORCES

Gunston, Bill. An Illustrated Guide to the Israeli Air Force. LC 81-71938. (Illustrated Military Guides Ser.). (Illus.). 160p. 1983. 9.95 (ISBN 0-668-05506-5, 5506). Arco.

Luttwak, Edward N. & Horowitz, Daniel. The Israeli Army; 1948 to 1973, Vol. 1. 1983. text ed. 25.00 (ISBN 0-686-84857-8). Abt Bks.

ISRAEL-BIOGRAPHY

Shamir, Ruth. All Our Vows. LC 82-61795. 1983. 11.95 (ISBN 0-88400-090-7). Shengold.

ISRAEL-DESCRIPTION AND TRAVEL

Bazak Guide to Israel, 1983-1984. LC 66-1422. (Illus.). 500p. (Orig.). 1983. pap. 11.49i (ISBN 0-06-091021-6, CN 1021, CN). Har-Row.

ISRAEL-DESCRIPTION AND TRAVEL-GUIDEBOOKS

Baedeker. Baedeker's Israel. (Baedeker Ser.). (Illus.). 250p. 1983. pap. 12.95 (ISBN 0-13-056176-2). P-H.

Fodor's Israel 1983. (Illus.). 368p. 1983. traveltex 12.95 (ISBN 0-679-00929-9). McKay.

Harvard Student Agencies. Let's Go Greece, Israel, & Egypt. (The Let's Go Ser.). (Illus.). 474p. 1983. pap. 7.95 (ISBN 0-312-48213-2). St Martin.

ISRAEL-DIRECTORIES

Directory of Israel 1982. 27th ed. LC 66-1345. 444p. 1982. 70.00 (ISBN 0-8002-3047-7). Intl Pubns Serv.

ISRAEL-FOREIGN RELATIONS

Timerman, Jacobo. The Longest War: Israel in Lebanon. LC 82-20208. 192p. 1983. pap. 2.95 (Vin). Random.

Waterman, Isaac. The Ultimate Goals of Israel's World Policies. (Illus.). 117p. 1983. 87.85 (ISBN 0-86722-017-1). Inst Econ Pol.

ISRAEL-HISTORY

Jagersma, Henk. A History of Israel in the Old Testament Period. Bowden, John, tr. LC 82-48548. 320p. 1983. pap. text ed. 13.95 (ISBN 0-8006-1692-8). Fortress.

Lods, Adolphe. Israel, from Its Beginning to the Middle of the Eighth Century. Hooke, S. H., tr. LC 75-41180. 1948. 24.75 (ISBN 0-404-14569-8). AMS PR.

Torrey, Charles C. Chronicler's History of Israel: Chronicles-Ezra-Nehemiah Restored to It's Original Form. 1954. text ed. 11.50x (ISBN 0-686-37866-0). Elliots Bks.

ISRAEL-POLITICS AND GOVERNMENT

Almogi, Yosef. Total Commitment. LC 81-70146. (Illus.). 320p. 1982. 20.00 (ISBN 0-8453-4749-7). Cornwall Bks.

Brubeck, William H. Israelis & Palestinians: The Need for an Alliance of Moderates. (Seven Springs Studies). 43p. 1982. pap. 3.00 (ISBN 0-943006-14-7). Seven Springs.

Elon, Amos. Israelis: Founders & Sons. 1983. pap. 5.95 (ISBN 0-14-022476-9, Pelican). Penguin.

Freedman. Israel in the Begin Era. 288p. 1982. 29.95 (ISBN 0-03-059376-X). Praeger.

Kieval, Gershon R. Party Politics in Israel & the Occupied Terrorities. LC 82-12000. (Contributions in Political Science Ser.: No. 95). 288p. 1983. lib. bdg. 35.00 (ISBN 0-313-23325-X, KIP/). Greenwood.

Liebman, Charles S. & Don-Yehiya, Eliezer. Civil Religion in Israel: Traditional Judaism & Political Culture in the Jewish State. LC 82-17427. 270p. 1983. 19.95x (ISBN 0-520-04817-2). U of Cal Pr.

Peri, Yoram. Between Battles & Ballots: Israeli Military in Politics. 368p. p.n.s. (ISBN 0-521-24414-5). Cambridge U Pr.

Schenker, Hillel, ed. After Lebanon: The Israeli-Palestinian Connection. 320p. 1983. 15.95 (ISBN 0-8298-0654-7). Pilgrim NY.

Shimshoni, Daniel. Israeli Democracy. 1982. text ed. 34.95 (ISBN 0-02-928620-4). Free Pr.

Spatial Distribution of Political Power & Regional Disparities in the Israeli Case. (UNCRD Working Paper: No. 82-4). 34p. 1982. pap. 6.00 (ISBN 0-686-82541-1, CRD 138, UNCRD). Unipub.

Timerman, Jacobo. The Longest War: Israel in Lebanon. Acoca, Miguel, tr. from Span. LC 82-48584. 167p. 1982. 11.95 (ISBN 0-394-53022-5). Knopf.

--The Longest War: Israel in Lebanon. LC 82-20208. 192p. 1983. pap. 2.95 (Vin). Random.

ISRAEL-RELIGION

Aviad, Janet. Return to Judaism: Religious Renewal in Israel. LC 82-17663. 208p. 1983. lib. bdg. 20.00x (ISBN 0-226-03236-1). U of Chicago Pr.

ISRAEL-SOCIAL LIFE AND CUSTOMS

Oliphant, Laurence & Zeevy, Rechavam. Life in the Holy Land. (Illus.). 475p. 1982. text ed. 16.00 (ISBN 0-86628-042-1). Ridgefield Pub.

ISRAEL-ARAB BORDER CONFLICTS, 1949-

Caplan, Neil. Futile Diplomacy: Early Arab-Zionist Negotiation Attempts, 1913-1931, Vol. 1. 250p. 1983. text ed. 32.00x (ISBN 0-7146-3214-7, F Cass Co). Biblio Dist.

Grose, Peter. The Next Steps Toward Peace Between Israel & Its Neighbors. (Seven Springs Reports). 45p. 1980. pap. 2.00 (ISBN 0-943006-09-0). Seven Springs.

Jansen, Michael. The Battle of Beirut: Why Israel Invaded Lebanon. 160p. 1983. 17.50 (ISBN 0-89608-174-5); pap. 6.50 (ISBN 0-89608-173-7). South End Pr.

Lilienthal, Alfred M. The Zionist Connection II: What Price Peace? Rev. ed. 904p. 1982. Repr. of 1978 ed. 11.95 (ISBN 0-686-43256-8); pap. 9.95. North American Inc.

Timerman, Jacobo. The Longest War: Israel in Lebanon. Acoca, Miguel, tr. from Span. LC 82-48584. 167p. 1982. 11.95 (ISBN 0-394-53022-5). Knopf.

--The Longest War: Israel in Lebanon. LC 82-20208. 192p. 1983. pap. 2.95 (Vin). Random.

ISRAEL-ARAB WAR, 1967

Brubeck, William H. Reflections on the Path to Middle East Peace. (Seven Springs Studies). 1982. pap. 3.00 (ISBN 0-943006-00-7). Seven Springs.

Greene, Joseph N., Jr. & Klutznick, Philip M. The Path to Peace: Arab-Israeli Peace & the United States. 50p. 1981. pap. 3.00 (ISBN 0-943006-13-9). Seven Springs.

Grose, Peter. The Next Steps Toward Peace Between Israel & Its Neighbors. (Seven Springs Reports). 45p. 1980. pap. 2.00 (ISBN 0-943006-09-0). Seven Springs.

--The United States, NATO & Israeli-Arab Peace. (Seven Springs Reports). 1980. pap. 2.00 (ISBN 0-943006-11-2). Seven Springs.

Mroz, John E. Influence in Conflict: The Impact of Third Parties on the Arab-Israeli Dispute Since 1973. 400p. 1983. 40.00 (ISBN 0-08-028797-2); pap. 14.95 (ISBN 0-08-028796-4). Pergamon.

ISRAELI NATIONAL CHARACTERISTICS

see National Characteristics, Israeli

ISTANBUL-HISTORY

Hohlfelder, Robert L. City, Town & Countryside in the Early Byzantine Era. (Brooklyn College Studies on Society in Change). 280p. 1982. 22.50x (ISBN 0-88033-013-9). East Eur Quarterly.

ITALIAN AMERICANS

see also Italians in the United States

Nelli, Humbert S. From Immigrants to Ethnics: The Italian Americans. 228p. 1983. 24.95 (ISBN 0-19-503200-4). Oxford U Pr.

ITALIAN ARCHITECTURE

see Architecture-Italy

ITALIAN ART

see Art, Italian

ITALIAN AUTHORS

see Authors, Italian

ITALIAN DRAMA (COLLECTIONS)

Pirandello, Luigi. Sicilian Comedies. LC 82-62097. 1983. 18.95 (ISBN 0-933826-50-8); pap. 6.95 (ISBN 0-933826-51-6). Performing Arts.

ITALIAN DRAWINGS

see Drawings, Italian

ITALIAN FOLK-LORE

see Folk-Lore, Italian

ITALIAN LANGUAGE

Lebano, Edoardo A. & Baldini, Pier R. Buon Giorno a Tutti: First-Year Italian. 512p. 1983. text ed. 20.95 (ISBN 0-471-04308-7); tchrs.' avail. (ISBN 0-471-05793-2); wkbk. avail. (ISBN 0-471-04309-5). Wiley.

ITALIAN LANGUAGE-CONVERSATION AND PHRASE BOOKS

see also Italian Language-Self-Instruction; Italian Language-Text-Books for Children

Lexus. The Italian Travelmate. LC 82-83994. (Illus.). 128p. 1983. pap. 1.95 (ISBN 0-307-46604-3, Golden Pr). Western Pub.

Traveler's Italian. (EH Ser.). (Ital.). 1980. pap. 17.95 (ISBN 0-686-37988-8, 612). B&N NY.

ITALIAN LANGUAGE-DICTIONARIES-ENGLISH

Reynolds, Barbara. The Concise Cambridge Italian Dictionary. 792p. 1975. pap. 8.95 (ISBN 0-14-051064-8). Penguin.

ITALIAN LANGUAGE-EXAMINATIONS, QUESTIONS, ETC.

Rudman, Jack. Foreign Language: Italian. (Regents External Degree Ser.: REDP-29). 17.95 (ISBN 0-8373-5679-2); pap. 9.95 (ISBN 0-8373-5629-6). Natl Learning.

ITALIAN LANGUAGE-READERS

see also Italian Language-Text-Books for Children

Foglio, Frank. Ehi, Dio! Arcangeli, Gianfranco, ed. (Ital.). 1972. pap. 1.90 (ISBN 0-8297-0753-0). Life Pubs Intl.

Keller, W. Philip. Il Buon Pastore E Le Sue Pecore. Arcangeli, Gianfranco, ed. (Ital.). 1980. pap. 1.60 (ISBN 0-8297-0970-3). Life Pubs Intl.

Richardson, Don. Il Figlio Della Pace. Arcangeli, Gianfranco, ed. 230p. (Ital.). 1981. pap. 2.00 (ISBN 0-8297-0940-1). Life Pubs Intl.

ITALIAN LANGUAGE-SELF-INSTRUCTION

see also Italian Language-Conversation and Phrase Books

Berlitz Italian for Your Trip. 192p. 1982. 8.95 (ISBN 0-02-965180-8, Berlitz). Macmillan.

ITALIAN LANGUAGE-STUDY AND TEACHING

Rudman, Jack. Italian: Senior High School. (Teachers License Examination Ser.: T-32B). (Cloth bdg. avail. on request). pap. 13.95 (ISBN 0-686-84417-3). Natl Learning.

ITALIAN LANGUAGE-TEXT-BOOKS FOR CHILDREN

see also Italian Language-Conversation and Phrase Books

Colyer, Penrose. I Can Read Italian: My First English Italian Word Book. (I Can Read Bks.). (Illus.). 116p. (gr. 2 up). 1983. PLB 9.40 (ISBN 0-531-04601-X). Watts.

ITALIAN LETTERS

Marchione, Margherita, ed. Lettere Di Clemente Rebora 1897-1930, Vol. I. 680p. 1976. 20.00 (ISBN 0-686-84877-2). Am Inst Ital Stud.

Marchione, Margherita & Scalia, S. Eugene, eds. Carteggio Di Giovanni Boine, Vol. I_IV. Incl. Vol. I. Bione-Prezzolini, 1908-1915. Prezzolini, Giuseppe, pref. by. 264p. 1971. 10.00 (ISBN 0-686-84878-0); Vol. II. Boine-Emilio Cecchi 1911-1917. Martini, Carlo, pref. by. 252p. 1972. 10.00 (ISBN 0-686-84879-9); Vol. III. Boine-Amici Del Rinnovamento, 1905-1917. Vigorelli, Giancarlo, pref. by. 1132p. 1977. 25.00 (ISBN 0-686-84880-2); Boine-Amici De La Voce Ed Altri, 1900-1917. Amoretti, Giovanni, pref. by. 15.00 (ISBN 0-686-84881-0). Date not set. Am Inst Ital Stud.

ITALIAN LITERATURE-HISTORY AND CRITICISM

Bainbrigge, Marion S. A Walk in Other Worlds with Dante. 253p. 1982. Repr. of 1914 ed. lib. bdg. 40.00 (ISBN 0-89760-092-4). Telegraph Bks.

Treves, Giuliana A. The Golden Ring: The Anglo-Florentines, 1847-1862. Sprigge, Sylvia, tr. from Ital. 221p. 1982. Repr. of 1956 ed. lib. bdg. 45.00 (ISBN 0-89760-897-6). Telegraph Bks.

Whitfield, J. H. A Short History of Italian Literature. 1980. pap. 6.50 (ISBN 0-7190-0782-8). Manchester.

ITALIAN MUSIC

see Music, Italian

ITALIAN PAINTING

see Painting, Italian

ITALIAN PAINTINGS

see Paintings, Italian

ITALIAN POETRY (COLLECTIONS)

Here are entered collections by various authors. For English translations see subdivision Translations into English.

Marchione, Margherita, tr. Twentieth Century Italian Poetry: A Bilingual Anthology. 302p. 1974. 10.00 (ISBN 0-686-84882-9). Am Inst Ital Stud.

ITALIAN POETRY-HISTORY AND CRITICISM

Bernardo, Aldo S. & Pellegrini, Anthony L., eds. Dante, Petrarch & Others: Studies in the Italian Trecento. 1983. write for info. (ISBN 0-86698-061-X). Medieval & Renaissance NY.

Marchione, Margherita, ed. Lettere Di Clemente Rebora 1897-1930, Vol. I. 680p. 1976. 20.00 (ISBN 0-686-84877-2). Am Inst Ital Stud.

ITALIAN SCULPTURE

see Sculpture-Italy

ITALIAN SONGS

see Songs, Italian

ITALIAN TALES

see Tales, Italian

ITALIANS IN THE UNITED STATES

see also Italian Americans

Hall, Jacqueline & Hall, Jo E. Italian-Swiss Settlement of Plumas County, 1860-1920. (ANCRR Occasional Paper: No. 1). 55p. 1973. 4.00 (ISBN 0-686-38934-4). Assn NC Records.

ITALIC INSCRIPTIONS

see Inscriptions, Italic

ITALY-ANTIQUITIES

MacKendrick, Paul. The Mute Stones Speak: The Story of Archaeology in Italy. 2nd ed. 1983. 25.50 (ISBN 0-393-01678-1). Norton.

Tomlinson, R. A. Epidauros. (Illus.). 96p. 1982. pap. text ed. 21.00x (ISBN 0-246-11404-5, Pub. by Granada England). Humanities.

ITALY-BIOGRAPHY

Marchione, Margherita. L' Imagine Tesa: The Life & Works of Clemente Rebora. enl. ed. 410p. 1974. 10.00 (ISBN 0-686-84873-X). Am Inst Ital Stud.

Marchione, Margherita, ed. Lettere Di Clemente Rebora 1897-1930, Vol. I. 680p. 1976. 20.00 (ISBN 0-686-84877-2). Am Inst Ital Stud.

Marchione, Margherita & Scalia, S. Eugene, eds. Carteggio Di Giovanni Boine, Vol. I_IV. Incl. Vol. I. Bione-Prezzolini, 1908-1915. Prezzolini, Giuseppe, pref. by. 264p. 1971. 10.00 (ISBN 0-686-84878-0); Vol. II. Boine-Emilio Cecchi 1911-1917. Martini, Carlo, pref. by. 252p. 1972. 10.00 (ISBN 0-686-84879-9); Vol. III. Boine-Amici Del Rinnovamento, 1905-1917. Vigorelli, Giancarlo, pref. by. 1132p. 1977. 25.00 (ISBN 0-686-84880-2); Boine-Amici De La Voce Ed Altri, 1900-1917. Amoretti, Giovanni, pref. by. 15.00 (ISBN 0-686-84881-0). Date not set. Am Inst Ital Stud.

Margherita, Marchione. Clemente Rebora: A Man's Quest for the Absolute. (Twayne's World Authors Ser.). 180p. 1979. 12.50 (ISBN 0-686-84874-8). Am Inst Ital Stud.

ITALY-CIVILIZATION

Burckhardt, Jacob. The Civilization of the Renaissance in Italy. (Illus.). 486p. 1983. 13.95 (ISBN 0-7148-2140-3, Pub by Salem Hse Ltd). Merrimack Bk Serv.

ITALY-DESCRIPTION AND TRAVEL

Bethemont, Jacques & Pelletier, Jean. Italy: A Geographical Introduction. King, Russel, ed. (Illus.). 224p. 1982. text ed. 28.00x (ISBN 0-582-30073-8). Longman.

Sartogo, Piero. Italian Re-Evolution: Design in Italian Society in the Eighties. LC 82-82515. (Illus.). 208p. (Orig.). 1982. pap. text ed. 29.50 (ISBN 0-934418-14-4). La Jolla Mus Contemp Art.

ITALY-DESCRIPTION AND TRAVEL-GUIDEBOOKS

Fodor's Budget Italy '83. (Illus.). 192p. 1983. pap. 6.95 (ISBN 0-679-00883-7). McKay.

Harvard Student Agencies. Let's Go Italy. (The Let's Go Ser.). (Illus.). 416p. 1983. pap. 7.95 (ISBN 0-312-48214-0). St Martin.

Italian Riviera Travel Guide. (Berlitz Travel Guides). (Illus.). 1982. pap. 4.95 (ISBN 0-02-969280-6, Berlitz). Macmillan.

Michelin Green Guide: Italia. (Green Guide Ser.). (Ital.). 1983. pap. write for info. (ISBN 2-06-035391-2). Michelin.

Michelin Green Guide: Italie. (Green Guide Ser.). 1983. pap. write for info. (ISBN 2-0600-5300-5). Michelin.

Michelin Green Guide: Italien. (Green Guide Ser.). (Ger.). 1983. pap. write for info. (ISBN 2-06-025360-8). Michelin.

ITALY-ECONOMIC CONDITIONS

Chubb, Judith. Patronage, Power & Poverty in Southern Italy: A Tale of Two Cities. LC 82-1325. (Cambridge Studies in Modern Political Economies). (Illus.). 320p. 1983. 39.50 (ISBN 0-521-23637-1). Cambridge U Pr.

ITALY-HISTORY

Hughes, Serge. The Fall & Rise of Modern Italy. LC 82-18387. xiv, 322p. 1983. Repr. of 1967 ed. lib. bdg. 39.75x (ISBN 0-313-23737-9, HUFR). Greenwood.

Sprigge, Cecil. Development of Modern Italy. 1943. text ed. 18.50x (ISBN 0-686-83525-5). Elliots Bks.

Stephens, J. N. The Fall of the Florentine Republic 1512-1530. (Oxford-Warburg Studies). 300p. 1983. 39.50 (ISBN 0-19-822599-7). Oxford U Pr.

ITALY-SOCIAL LIFE AND CUSTOMS

Sartogo, Piero. Italian Re-Evolution: Design in Italian Society in the Eighties. LC 82-82515. (Illus.). 208p. (Orig.). 1982. pap. text ed. 29.50 (ISBN 0-934418-14-4). La Jolla Mus Contemp Art.

ITASCA STATE PARK, MINNESOTA
Hall, Steve. Itasca: Source of America's Greatest River. LC 82-12598. (Minnesota Historic Sites Pamphlet Ser.: No. 19). 32p. 1982. pap. 4.95 (ISBN 0-87351-157-3). Minn Hist.
ITERATIVE METHODS (MATHEMATICS)
Ansorge, R., et al, eds. Iterative Solution of Nonlinear Systems of Equations, Oberwolfach,*FRG, 1982: Proceedings. (Lecture Notes in Mathematics: Vol. 953). 202p. 1983. pap. 12.00 (ISBN 0-387-11602-8). Springer-Verlag.
IVORIES
see also Netsukes
Beckwith, John. Ivory Carvings in Early Medieval England. (Illus.). 168p. 1972. 49.00x (ISBN 0-19-921007-1). Oxford U Pr.
Maskell, Alfred. Ivories. LC 66-20572. (Illus.). 551p. 1966. 57.50 (ISBN 0-8048-0269-6). C E Tuttle.
IVORY CARVING
see Ivories

J

JACK-RABBITS
see Hares; Rabbits
JACKSON, ANDREW, PRES. U. S., 1767-1845
Ogg, Frederic A. Reign of Andrew Jackson. 1919. text ed. 8.50x (ISBN 0-686-83729-0). Elliots Bks.
JACKSONVILLE, FLORIDA–HISTORY
Jacksonville & Company. 365p. 1982. 12.00 (ISBN 0-686-38784-8). Jr. League FL.
JACOBITE CHURCH
Cruickshanks, Eveline, ed. Ideology & Conspiracy: Aspects of Jacobitism 1689-1759. 231p. 1982. text ed. 31.50x (ISBN 0-85976-084-7, 40740, Pub. by John Donald Scotland). Humanities.
JAGGER, MICK, 1943-
Dowley, Tim. Mick Jagger & the Stones. (Illus.). 128p. (gr. 6 up). 1983. pap. 9.95 (ISBN 0-88254-734-8). Hippocrene Bks.
Miles. Mick Jagger in His Own Words. (Illus.). 128p. (Orig.). 1983. pap. 6.95 (ISBN 0-399-41011-2). Delilah Bks.
JAI ALAI
see Pelota (Game)
JAILS
see Prisons
JAINAS
see Jains
JAINS
Caillat, Collette. Jain Cosmology. (Illus.). 192p. 1982. 55.00 (ISBN 0-517-54662-0, Harmony). Crown.
JAMAICA–DESCRIPTION AND TRAVEL
Insight Guides. Jamaica. (Illus.). 320p. 1983. pap. 14.95 (ISBN 0-13-509000-8). P-H.
LaBrucherie, Roger A. A Jamaica Journey. (Illus.). 112p. 1983. 16.95 (ISBN 0-939302-08-X, Pub. by Imagenes Pr). C E Tuttle.
JAMAICA–SOCIAL CONDITIONS
Manley, Michael. Jamaica: Struggle in the Periphery. (Illus.). 259p. 1982. 15.95 (ISBN 0-906495-97-0); pap. 7.95 (ISBN 0-906495-98-9). Writers & Readers.
JAMES, ALICE, 1848-1892
Yeazell, Ruth B., ed. The Death & Letters of Alice James: Selected Correspondence. (Illus.). 224p. 1983. pap. 6.95 (ISBN 0-520-04963-2, CAL 632). U of Cal Pr.
JAMES, HENRY, 1843-1916
Blackmur, R. P. Studies in Henry James. Makowsky, Veronica A., ed. LC 82-18911. 256p. 1983. 19.50 (ISBN 0-8112-0863-X); pap. 9.25 (ISBN 0-8112-0864-8, NDP 552). New Directions.
Budd, John, compiled by. Henry James: A Bibliography of Criticism, 1975-1981. LC 82-21463. 216p. 1983. lib. bdg. 35.00 (ISBN 0-313-23515-5, BHJ/). Greenwood.
Flower, Dean. Henry James in Northhampton: Vision & Revision. 28p. 1971. pap. 3.00 (ISBN 0-87391-027-3). Smith Coll.
Hirsch, Marianne. Beyond the Single Version: Henry James, Michael Butor, Uwe Johnson. 18.00 (ISBN 0-917786-21-1). French Lit.
Hutchinson, Stuart. Henry James: An American As Modernist. (Critical Studies). 136p. 1983. text ed. 27.00 (ISBN 0-389-20344-0). B&N Imports.
Long, Robert E. Henry James: The Early Novels. (United States Authors Ser.). 225p. 1983. lib. bdg. 13.95 (ISBN 0-8057-7379-7, Twayne). G K Hall.
Stone, William W. Balzac, James & the Realistic Novel. LC 82-61388. 224p. 1983. 19.50x (ISBN 0-691-06567-5). Princeton U Pr.
JAMES, PRINCE OF WALES, THE OLD PRETENDER, 1688-1766
Macdougall, Norman. James III: A Political Study. 323p. 1982. text ed. 38.00x (ISBN 0-85976-078-2, Pub. by Donald Scotland). Humanities.
JAMES, WILLIAM, 1842-1910
Barzun, Jacques. A Stroll with William James. LC 82-48108. 288p. 1983. 16.50 (ISBN 0-06-015090-4, HarpT). Har-Row.
Bjork, Daniel W. The Compromised Scientist: William James in the Development of American Psychology. (Illus.). 224p. 1983. text ed. 25.00 (ISBN 0-231-05500-5); pap. 12.00 (ISBN 0-231-05501-3). Columbia U Pr.

JANITORS
ASBO's Maintenance & Operations Research Committee. Custodial Methods & Procedures Manual. 1981. 12.95 (ISBN 0-910170-19-3). Assn Sch Busn.
Rudman, Jack. Assistant Custodial Work Supervisor. (Career Examination Ser.: C-2916). (Cloth bdg. avail. on request). pap. 10.00 (ISBN 0-8373-2916-7). Natl Learning.
--Institution Steward. (Career Examination Ser.: C-2626). (Cloth bdg. avail. on request). pap. 10.00 (ISBN 0-8373-2626-5). Natl Learning.
JAPAN–BIOGRAPHY
Danly, Robert L. In the Shade of Spring Leaves: The Life & Writings of Higuchi Ichiyo, a Woman of Letters in Meiji Japan. LC 81-50434. (Illus.). 355p. 1983. pap. text ed. 10.95 (ISBN 0-300-02981-0). Yale U Pr.
--In the Shade of Spring Leaves: The Life & Writings of Higuchi Ichiyo, a Woman of Letters in Meiji Japan. pap. 10.95 (ISBN 0-686-42821-8, Y-456). Yale U Pr.
JAPAN–CIVILIZATION
Christopher, Robert. Japan Explained: The Mind of the New Goliath. 1983. price not set (ISBN 0-671-44947-8, Linden). S&S.
Japan Culture Institute Staff. Discover Japan: Words, Customs & Concepts, Vol. 1. LC 82-48294. (Discover Japan Ser.). (Illus.). 208p. 1983. Repr. of 1975 ed. 17.95 (ISBN 0-87011-546-4). Kodansha.
--Discover Japan: Words, Customs, & Concepts, Vol.2. LC 82-48294. (Discover Japan Ser.). (Illus.). 216p. 1983. 17.95 (ISBN 0-686-84483-1). Kodansha.
JAPAN–COMMERCE
American Chamber of Commerce in Japan. Exporting to Japan. 1982. 10.00 (ISBN 0-686-37954-3). A M Newman.
Japan External Trade Organization. White Paper on International Trade: Japan, 1981. 33rd ed. LC 52-36099. (Illus.). 419p. 1981. pap. 45.00 (ISBN 4-8224-0113-8). Intl Pubns Serv.
JAPAN–DESCRIPTION AND TRAVEL
Nagasawa, Kimiko & Condon, Camy. Eating Cheap in Japan. (Illus.). 104p. (Orig.). 1972. pap. 7.50 (ISBN 0-8048-1401-5, Pub. by Shufunotomo Co Ltd Japan). C E Tuttle.
Popham, Peter. The Complete Guide to Japan. (The Complete Asian Guide Ser.). (Illus.). 144p. (Orig.). 1982. pap. 9.95 (ISBN 962-7031-17-8). C E Tuttle.
--Japan in Focus. (The "In Focus" Ser.). (Illus.). 64p. (Orig.). 1982. pap. 5.95 (ISBN 962-7031-20-8). C E Tuttle.
JAPAN–DESCRIPTION AND TRAVEL–GUIDEBOOKS
Brown, Jan & Kmetz, Yoko Sakakibara. Exploring Tohoku: A Guide to Japan's Back Country. LC 82-17467. (Illus.). 312p. (Orig.). 1983. pap. 9.95 (ISBN 0-8348-0177-9). Weatherhill.
Wharton, John. Jobs in Japan: Complete Guide to Living & Working in Japan. LC 82-84053. (Illus.). 220p. 1983. pap. 9.95 (ISBN 0-911285-00-8). Global Pr Co.
JAPAN–ECONOMIC CONDITIONS
Akao, Nobutoshi, ed. Japan's Economic Security. LC 82-10257. 1982. 27.50x (ISBN 0-312-44064-2). St Martin.
Diamond's Japan Business Directory 1982. 16th ed. LC 74-84890. (Illus.). 1500p. 1982. 335.00x (ISBN 0-8002-3017-5). Intl Pubns Serv.
Economic & Foreign Affairs Research Association (Tokyo), ed. Statistical Survey of Japan's Economy, 1982. LC 54-43626. (Illus.). 83p. (Orig.). 1982. pap. 20.00x (ISBN 0-8002-3040-X). Intl Pubns Serv.
The Economic Survey of Japan, 1980-81. 30th ed. LC 51-61351. (Illus.). 272p. 1981. pap. 50.00x (ISBN 4-7890-0167-9). Intl Pubns Serv.
Gibney, Frank. Miracle by Design: The Real Reasons Behind Japan's Economic Success. 256p. 1982. 16.82 (ISBN 0-8129-1024-9). Times Bks.
Goldsmith, Raymond W. The Financial Development of India, Japan, & the United States. LC 82-8541. 136p. 1983. text ed. 12.95x (ISBN 0-300-02934-9). Yale U Pr.
Japan: A Compendium-Facts & Figures on Development, Administration & Planning. 55p. pap. 6.00 (ISBN 0-686-82538-1, CRD 137, UNCRD). Unipub.
Japan Chamber of Commerce & Industry. Standard Trade Index of Japan, 1983-84. 27th ed. LC 55-36368. 1500p. 1983. 135.00x (ISBN 0-8002-3006-X). Intl Pubns Serv.
Kunio, Yoshihara. Sogo Shosha: The Vanguard of Japanese Economy. (Illus.). 376p. 1982. 24.95x (ISBN 0-19-582534-9). Oxford U Pr.
Takezawa, S., et al. Improvements in the Quality of Working Life in Three Japanese Industries. International Labour Office, ed. vi, 175p. 1982. pap. 12.85 (ISBN 92-2-103051-2). Intl Labour Office.
Tsuru, Shigego. The Mainsprings of Japanese Growth: A Turning Point. (Atlantic Papers: No. 76/3). (Orig.). 1977. pap. text ed. 4.75x (ISBN 0-686-83621-9). Allanheld.
Vernon, Raymond. Two Hungry Giants: The United States & Japan in the Quest for Oil & Ores. (Center for International Affairs). (Illus.). 192p. 1983. text ed. 16.00x (ISBN 0-674-91470-8). Harvard U Pr.

JAPAN–FOREIGN RELATIONS
Chapman, J. W. & Drifte, R., eds. Japan's Quest for Comprehensive Security: Defense, Diplomacy & Dependence. LC 81-48263. 272p. 1982. 25.00x (ISBN 0-312-44070-7). St Martin.
Japan Institute of International Affairs, Tokyo. White Papers of Japan, 1980-81: Annual Abstract of Official Reports & Statistics of the Japanese Government. LC 72-620531. (Illus.). 232p. 1982. pap. 40.00x (ISBN 0-8002-3058-2). Intl Pubns Ser.
Sigur, Gastonz & Kim, Young C. Japanese & U. S. Policy in Asia. 208p. 1982. 22.95 (ISBN 0-03-061849-5). Praeger.
Tsoukalis, Loukas & White, Maureen. Japan & Western Europe: Conflict & Cooperation. LC 82-6031. 1982. 25.00 (ISBN 0-686-81980-2). St Martin.
JAPAN–FOREIGN RELATIONS–CHINA
Bedeski, Robert E. The Fragile Entente: The Nineteen Seventy-Eight Japan-China Peace Treaty in a Global Context. (Replica Edition Ser.). 235p. 1983. softcover 18.50x (ISBN 0-86531-944-8). Westview.
Toshihiko, Shimada, et al. Japan's Road to the Pacific War: The China Quagmire. Morley, James W., ed. Crowley, James B., tr. from Japanese. (Studies of the East Asian Institute). 508p. 1983. 30.00x (ISBN 0-231-05522-6). Columbia U Pr.
JAPAN–HISTORY
Beck, Clark L. & Burks, Ardath W. Aspects of Meiji Modernization: The Japan Helpers & the Helped. 45p. 1983. pap. text ed. 4.95x (ISBN 0-87855-936-1). Transaction Bks.
Borton, Hugh. Japan's Modern Century--from Perry to 1970. 2nd ed. 610p. 1970. 25.50x (ISBN 0-471-07032-7). Wiley.
The Economic Survey of Japan, 1980-81. 30th ed. LC 51-61351. (Illus.). 272p. 1981. pap. 50.00x (ISBN 4-7890-0167-9). Intl Pubns Serv.
Fukutake, Tadashi. Japanese Social Structure, 1870-1980. Dore, Ronald P., tr. 180p. 1982. text ed. 14.50x (ISBN 0-86008-316-0, Pub. by U of Tokyo Japan). Columbia U Pr.
Jansen, Mariuse, et al. Japan in the Nineteen Thirtys. Waldner, George, ed. LC 82-80791. (Papers on International Issues: No.3). 1982. free. Southern Ctr Intl Stud.
Lehmann, Jean-Pierre. The Roots of Modern Japan. LC 82-743. 372p. 1982. 26.00x (ISBN 0-312-69310-9). St Martin.
Lewin, Roland. The American Magic: Codes, Ciphers & the Defeat of Japan. 1983. pap. 5.95 (ISBN 0-14-006471-0). Penguin.
Rohlich, Thomas H., tr. A Tale of Eleventh-Century Japan: Hamamatsu Chunagon Monogatari. LC 82-61380. (Princeton Library of Asian Translations). 256p. 1983. 30.00x (ISBN 0-691-05377-4). Princeton U Pr.
Statler, Oliver. Japanese Pilgrimage. (Illus.). 288p. 1983. 17.95 (ISBN 0-688-01890-4). Morrow.
Warner, Denis & Warner, Peggy. The Sacred Warriors. 272p. 1982. 24.95 (ISBN 0-442-25418-0). Van Nos Reinhold.
Wray, Harry & Conroy, Hilary, eds. Japan Examined: Perspectives on Modern Japanese History. LC 82-15926. 421p. 1983. lib. bdg. 22.50x (ISBN 0-8248-0806-1); pap. text ed. 12.95x (ISBN 0-8248-0839-8). UH Pr.
Young, A. Morgan. Japan in Recent Times, 1912-1926. LC 76-136554. 347p. 1973. Repr. of 1929 ed. lib. bdg. 18.75x (ISBN 0-8371-5480-4, YOJR). Greenwood.
JAPAN–INDUSTRIES
Current Electronic Components Industry in Japan. (Japanese Industry Studies: No. J77). 155p. 1980. 310.00. Intl Res Dev.
Current Machine Tools Industry in Japan. (Japanese Industry Studies: No. J75). 103p. 1981. 394.00 (ISBN 0-686-38961-1). Intl Res Dev.
Dodwell Marketing Consultants. Industrial Groupings in Japan, 1982-83. rev. ed. LC 78-324735. (Illus.). 529p. 1982. pap. 335.00x (ISBN 0-8002-3032-9). Intl Pubns Serv.
Industrial Robots Industry in Japan. (Japanese Industry Studies: No. J76). 228p. 1980. 310.00 (ISBN 0-686-38962-X). Intl Res Dev.
Japan Motor Industrial Federation. Guide to the Motor Industry of Japan, 1982. 22nd ed. LC 73-648715. (Illus.). 263p. (Orig.). 1982. pap. 45.00x (ISBN 0-8002-3101-5). Intl Pubns Serv.
Lee. Japanese Management. 318p. 1982. 30.95 (ISBN 0-03-061773-1). Praeger.
McLean, Mick. The Japanese Electronics Challenge. LC 82-42710. 170p. 1982. 27.50x (ISBN 0-312-44066-9). St Martin.
Profile of Electronic Components Manufacturers in Japan. (Japanese Industry Studies: No. J78). 172p. 1981. 280.00 (ISBN 0-686-38963-8). Intl Res Dev.
Sasaki, Naoto. Management & Industrial Structure in Japan. 142p. 24.00 (ISBN 0-686-84796-2). Work in Amer.
Schonberger, Richard J. Japanese Manufacturing Techniques: Nine Hidden Lessons in Simplicity. LC 82-48495. 1982. 14.95 (ISBN 0-02-929100-3). Free Pr.
Semiconductor-Microelectronics Industry in Japan. (Japanese Industry Studies: No. J79). 207p. 1982. 495.00 (ISBN 0-686-38964-6). Intl Res Dev.
JAPAN–MILITARY POLICY
Blaker. Japan's National Security. 128p. 1983. 6.96 (ISBN 0-03-062003-1). Praeger.

Johnson, U. Alexis & Packard, George R. The Common Security Interests of Japan, The United States & NATO. 38p. pap. 6.00x (ISBN 0-87855-873-X). Transaction Bks.
JAPAN–POLITICS AND GOVERNMENT
Morss, Elliott R. & Gow, David D., eds. Implementing Rural Development Projects: Nine Critical Problems. 325p. 1983. softcover 23.50x (ISBN 0-86531-942-1). Westview.
White, James W. Migration in Metropolitan Japan: Social Change & Political Behavior. (Japan Research Monographs: No. 2). 364p. (Orig.). 1982. pap. 12.00x (ISBN 0-912966-53-X). IEAS.
JAPAN–POPULATION
Mosk, Carl, ed. Patriarchy & Fertility: The Evolution of Natality in Japan & Sweden 1880-1960. (Population & Social Structure: Advances in Historical Demography). Date not set. price not set (ISBN 0-12-508480-3). Acad Pr.
JAPAN–RELATIONS (GENERAL) WITH FOREIGN COUNTRIES
Pringsheim, Klaus H. Neighbors Across the Pacific: The Development of Economic & Political Relations Between Canada & Japan. LC 82-11713. (Contributions in Political Science Ser.: No. 90). 256p. 1983. lib. bdg. 29.95 (ISBN 0-313-23507-4, PRN/). Greenwood.
JAPAN–SOCIAL CONDITIONS
Passin, Herbert. Society & Education in Japan. LC 82-48167. 347p. 1982. pap. 6.25 (ISBN 0-87011-554-5). Kodansha.
Powell, Irena. Writers & Society in Modern Japan. LC 82-48432. 230p. 1983. 24.95 (ISBN 0-87011-558-8). Kodansha.
White, James W. Migration in Metropolitan Japan: Social Change & Political Behavior. (Japan Research Monographs: No. 2). 364p. (Orig.). 1982. pap. 12.00x (ISBN 0-912966-53-X). IEAS.
JAPAN–SOCIAL LIFE AND CUSTOMS
Bernstein, Gail L. Haruko's World: A Japanese Farm Woman & Her Community. LC 82-61783. (Illus.). 192p. 1983. text ed. 19.50x (ISBN 0-8047-1174-7). Stanford U Pr.
Fukutake, Tadashi. Japanese Social Structure, 1870-1980. Dore, Ronald P., tr. 180p. 1982. text ed. 14.50x (ISBN 0-86008-316-0, Pub. by U of Tokyo Japan). Columbia U Pr.
Japan Culture Institute Staff. Discover Japan: Words, Customs, & Concepts, Vol.2. LC 82-48294. (Discover Japan Ser.). (Illus.). 216p. 1983. 17.95 (ISBN 0-686-84483-1). Kodansha.
Lancaster, Clay. The Japanese Influence in America. LC 82-22650. (Illus.). 314p. 1983. Repr. of 1963 ed. 39.95 (ISBN 0-89659-342-8). Abbeville Pr.
Plath, David W. Long Engagements: Maturity in Modern Japan. xii, 235p. 1983. pap. 6.95 (ISBN 0-8047-1176-3). Stanford U Pr.
JAPANESE ARCHITECTURE
see Architecture–Japan
JAPANESE ART
see Art, Japanese
JAPANESE FLOWER ARRANGEMENT
see Flower Arrangement, Japanese
JAPANESE IN THE UNITED STATES
Burgess, James Z. Burgess History: The Tennessee Pioneer. 300p. 1982. lib. bdg. 49.95x (ISBN 0-89370-740-6). Borgo Pr.
Oda, James. Heroic Struggles of Japanese Americans: Partisans Fighters from American's Concentration Camps. 3rd ed. LC 25-3182. 1982. 12.95 (ISBN 0-686-38079-7); pap. 8.00 (ISBN 0-686-38080-0). ODA.
Okubo, Mine. Citizen 13660. LC 82-20221. (Illus.). 226p. (Orig.). 1983. pap. 8.95 (ISBN 0-295-95989-4). U of Wash Pr.
JAPANESE LANGUAGE
Passin, Herbert. Encounter with Japan: The American Army Language School. LC 82-48166. Orig. Title: Beirkugun Nihongo-Nihon to No Deai. 220p. 1983. 15.00 (ISBN 0-87011-544-8). Kodansha.
JAPANESE LANGUAGE–CONVERSATION AND PHRASE BOOKS
Berlitz Editors. Japanese for Travel Cassettepack. 1983. 14.95 (ISBN 0-02-962850-4, Berlitz); cassette incl. Macmillan.
Getting By in English for Japanese. 90p. 1983. pap. price not set (ISBN 0-8120-2659-4). Barron.
Getting By in Japanese. 90p. 1983. pap. 2.95 (ISBN 0-8120-2664-0). Barron.
Hart, Babe. Speedy Japanese: To Get You There & Back. (Speedy Language Ser.). (Illus.). 24p. (Orig., Japanese.). 1979. pap. 1.75 (ISBN 0-9602838-4-6). Baja Bks.
Miura, Akira. Japanese Words & Their Uses. LC 82-51099. 240p. 1983. 14.00 (ISBN 0-8048-1386-8). C E Tuttle.
JAPANESE LANGUAGE–DICTIONARIES–ENGLISH
Getting By in English for Japanese. 90p. 1983. pap. price not set (ISBN 0-8120-2659-4). Barron.
Getting By in Japanese. 90p. 1983. pap. 2.95 (ISBN 0-8120-2664-0). Barron.
JAPANESE LANGUAGE–READERS
Jorden, Eleanor H. Reading Japanese. 607p. Date not set. includes 17 cassettes 185.00x (ISBN 0-88432-096-0, J450). J Norton Pubs.
Watabe, Masakazu & Gilbert, Kent S. Japanese: A Graded Approach to Reading, Writing & Vocabulary Building. 336p. 1983. 18.50 (ISBN 0-8048-1448-1). C E Tuttle.

JAPANESE LANGUAGE–TEXTBOOKS FOR FOREIGNERS
Sato, Esther M., et al. Japanese Now: Text, Vol. 2. 208p. 1983. text ed. 20.00x (ISBN 0-8248-0795-2); tchrs. ed. 15.00x (ISBN 0-8248-0796-0); wkbk. 4.00x (ISBN 0-8248-0797-9). UH Pr.
JAPANESE LANGUAGE–VOCABULARY
Watabe, Masakazu & Gilbert, Kent S. Japanese: A Graded Approach to Reading, Writing & Vocabulary Building. 336p. 1983. 18.50 (ISBN 0-8048-1448-1). C E Tuttle.
JAPANESE LANGUAGE–WRITING
Watabe, Masakazu & Gilbert, Kent S. Japanese: A Graded Approach to Reading, Writing & Vocabulary Building. 336p. 1983. 18.50 (ISBN 0-8048-1448-1). C E Tuttle.
JAPANESE LITERATURE–HISTORY AND CRITICISM
LaFleur, William R. The Karma of Words: Buddhism & the Literary Arts in Medieval Japan. LC 82-45909. 232p. 1983. text ed. 25.00x (ISBN 0-520-04600-5). U of Cal Pr.
JAPANESE LITERATURE–TRANSLATIONS INTO ENGLISH
Kara Monogatari. Geddes, Ward, tr. from Japanese. & intro. by. (Occasional Paper Arizona State Univ., Center for Asian Studies Ser.: No.16). 150p. 1983. pap. 4.00. ASU Ctr Asian.
JAPANESE NATIONAL CHARACTERISTICS
see National Characteristics, Japanese
JAPANESE PAINTING
see Painting, Japanese
JAPANESE PAINTINGS
see Paintings, Japanese
JAPANESE POETRY–HISTORY AND CRITICISM
Ueda, Makoto. Modern Japanese Poets & the Nature of Literature. LC 82-60487. 432p. 1983. 28.50x (ISBN 0-8047-1166-6). Stanford U Pr.
JAPANESE POETRY–TRANSLATIONS INTO ENGLISH
Levy, Howard S., tr. Fujiwara No Teika: One Hundred Selections. (East Asian Poetry in Translation Ser.: No. 19). 1981. pap. 8.00 (ISBN 0-686-37539-4). Oriental Bk Store.
--Minamoto No Sanetomo (1192-1219) As a Love Poet (Japanese Love Poems 501-600) (East Asian Poetry in Translation Ser.: No. 14). 1980. pap. 8.00 (ISBN 0-686-37536-X). Oriental Bk Store.
--Saigyo: More Love Poems (101-200) (East Asian Poetry in Translation Ser.: No. 15). 1981. pap. 8.00 (ISBN 0-686-37537-8). Oriental Bk Store.
--Saigyo (1112-1190) As a Love Poet: One Hundred More Selections (210-300), Japanese Love Poems (1001-1100) (East Asian Poetry in Translation Ser.: No. 20). 1981. pap. 8.00 (ISBN 0-686-37540-8). Oriental Bk Store.
Levy, Howard S. & Ohsawa, Junko, trs. Japanese Love Poems (301-400) (East Asian Poetry in Translation Ser.: No. 11). 1980. pap. 8.00 (ISBN 0-686-37533-5). Oriental Bk Store.
Sato, Hirosaki. One Hundred Frogs: From Renga to Haiku to English. LC 82-17505. (Illus.). 300p. 1983. pap. 14.95 (ISBN 0-8348-0176-0). Weatherhill.
JAPANESE POTTERY
see Pottery, Japanese
JAPANESE SWORDS
see Swords
JAPANESE TEA CEREMONY
Levy, Howard S., tr. Saigyo (1118-1190) As a Love Poet (Japanese Love Poems, 401-500) (East Asian Poetry in Translation Ser.: No. 12). 1980. pap. 8.00 (ISBN 0-686-37534-3). Oriental Bk Store.
--Saigyo (1118-1190) the Poet of Reflective Being & Natural Scene. (East Asian Poetry in Translation Ser.: No. 13). 1980. pap. 8.00 (ISBN 0-686-37535-1). Oriental Bk Store.
Levy, Howard S. & Ohsawa, Junko, trs. Senryu Selections. (East Asian Poetry in Translation Ser.: No. 10). 1979. pap. 8.00 (ISBN 0-686-37532-7). Oriental Bk Store.
Tanaka, Sen'o. The Tea Ceremony. LC 73-79766. (Illus.). 214p. 1983. pap. 12.95 (ISBN 0-87011-578-2). Kodansha.
JARRELL, RANDALL, 1914-1965
Ferguson, Suzanne. Critical Essays on Randall Jarrell. (Critical Essays in American Literature Ser.). 313p. 1983. lib. bdg. 35.00 (ISBN 0-8161-8486-0). G K Hall.
JARRY, ALFRED, 1873-1907
Stillman, Linda K. Alfred Jarry. (World Authors ser.). 184p. 1983. lib. bdg. 16.95 (ISBN 0-8057-6528-X, Twayne). G K Hall.
--La Theatralite dans l'Oeuvre d'Alfred Jarry. (Fr.). 16.00 (ISBN 0-917786-12-2). French Lit.
JAVA
Insight Guides. Java. (Illus.). 300p. 1983. 18.95 (ISBN 0-686-84573-0); pap. 14.95 (ISBN 0-13-509976-5). P-H.
JAVANESE LANGUAGE
Wolff, John U. & Poedjosoedarmo, Soepomo. Communicative Codes in Central Java. (Linguistics Ser.: VIII). 207p. 1982. 7.50 (ISBN 0-87727-116-X). Cornell SE Asia.
JAWBONING
see Wage-Price Policy
JAYS
see also Blue Jay
Bancroft, G. Thomas & Woolfenden, Glen E. Molt of Scrub Jays & Blue Jays in Florida. 51p. 1982. write for info. (ISBN 0-943610-29-X). Am Ornithologists.
JAZZ DANCE
Andreu, Helene C. Jazz Dance: An Adult Beginner's Guide. 192p. 1983. 15.95 (ISBN 0-13-509968-4); pap. 7.95 (ISBN 0-13-509950-1). P-H.
Frich, Elisabeth. Matt Mattox Book of Jazz Dance. (Illus.). 128p. 1983. 19.95 (ISBN 0-8069-7048-0); pap. 12.95 (ISBN 0-8069-7662-4). Sterling.
Goodman, Kraines M. & Kan, Esther J. Jump into Jazz: A Primer for the Beginning Jazz Dance Student. (Illus.). 127p. 1983. pap. 6.59 (ISBN 0-87484-571-8). Mayfield Pub.
Lane, Christy. All That Jazz & More: The Complete Book of Jazz Dancing. LC 82-83944. (Illus.). 400p. (Orig.). 1983. pap. 19.95 (ISBN 0-88011-124-0). Leisure Pr.
JAZZ MUSIC
see also Blues (Songs, etc.); Instrumentation and Orchestration
Balliett, Whitney. Jelly Roll, Jabbo & Fats: Nineteen Portraits in Jazz. 224p. 1983. 19.95 (ISBN 0-19-503275-6). Oxford U Pr.
Brooks, Edward. The Bessie Smith Companion. (Roots of Jazz Ser.). xx, 250p. 1983. lib. bdg. 22.50 (ISBN 0-306-76202-1). Da Capo.
Driggs, Frank & Lewine, Harris. Black Beauty, White Heat: A Pictorial History of Classic Jazz, 1920-1950. LC 82-60449. 360p. 1982. 39.95 (ISBN 0-688-03771-2). Morrow.
Ferris, William. Blues from the Delta. (Roots of Jazz Ser.). (Illus.). 226p. 1983. Repr. of 1979 ed. lib. bdg. 25.00 (ISBN 0-306-76215-3). Da Capo.
Goldblatt, Burt. Burt Goldblatt's Jazz Gallery One. Schlamm, Rhoda, ed. LC 82-61418. (Illus.). 200p. 1982. pap. 18.95 (ISBN 0-910945-00-4). Newbold Pub.
The Jazz Tradition. rev. ed. 256p. 1983. pap. 5.95 (ISBN 0-19-503291-8, GB 688, GB). Oxford U Pr.
Lyons, Len. The One Hundred One Best Jazz Albums: A History of Jazz on Records. 1980. pap. 9.95 (ISBN 0-688-08720-5). Quill NY.
Lyttleton, Humphrey. The Best of Jazz II: Enter the Giants, 1931-1944. LC 81-21418. (Illus.). 239p. 1983. pap. 6.95 (ISBN 0-8008-0731-6, Crescendo). Taplinger.
Miller, Paul E., ed. Esquire's Jazz Book: 1944-1946, 3 Vols. (Roots of Jazz Ser.). 1979. Repr. Set. lib. bdg. 65.00 (ISBN 0-306-79528-0); lib. bdg. 22.50 ea.; 1944 vol. (ISBN 0-306-79525-6); 1945 vol. (ISBN 0-306-79526-4); 1946 vol. (ISBN 0-306-79527-2). Da Capo.
Morgenstern, Dan & Nanry, Charles. Annual Review of Jazz Studies Two. (Illus.). 192p. 1983. pap. text ed. 15.00 (ISBN 0-87855-906-X). Transaction Bks.
Starr, S. Frederick. Red & Hot: The Fate of Jazz in the Soviet Union. (Illus.). 300p. 1983. 16.95 (ISBN 0-19-503163-6). Oxford U Pr.
Taylor, Bob. Sight-Reading Jazz: Melody, Bass Clef Version, Bk. 1. Taylor, Jennifer J., ed. (Illus., Orig.). 1982. pap. text ed. 12.95x (ISBN 0-943950-02-3). Taylor James.
Williams, Edward. The Jazz Traditions. rev. ed. 256p. 1983. 18.95 (ISBN 0-19-503290-X). Oxford U Pr.
Williams, Martin. Where's the Melody? A Listener's Introduction to Jazz. (Quality Paperbacks Ser.). 224p. 1983. pap. 7.95 (ISBN 0-306-80183-3). Da Capo.
Williams, Martin, ed. The Art of Jazz: Essays on the Development & Nature of Jazz. LC 79-10083. (Roots of Jazz Ser.). 248p. 1979. Repr. of 1959 ed. lib. bdg. 25.00 (ISBN 0-306-79556-6). Da Capo.
JAZZ MUSIC–BIBLIOGRAPHY
Levey, Joseph. The Jazz Experience: A Guide to Appreciation. (Illus.). 144p. 1983. 13.95 (ISBN 0-13-510248-0); pap. 6.95 (ISBN 0-13-510230-8). P-H.
JAZZ MUSIC–DISCOGRAPHY
Laubich, Arnold & Spencer, Ray. Art Tatum: A Guide to His Recorded Music. LC 82-10752. (Studies in Jazz: No. 2). 359p. 1982. 17.50 (ISBN 0-8108-1582-6). Scarecrow.
JAZZ MUSICIANS
Claghorn, Charles E. Biographical Dictionary of Jazz. 377p. 1983. 25.00 (ISBN 0-13-077966-0, Busn). P-H.
Dance, Stanley. The World of Earl Hines. (Da Capo Quality Paperbacks). (Illus.). 334p. 1983. pap. 10.95 (ISBN 0-306-80182-5). Da Capo.
Laubich, Arnold & Spencer, Ray. Art Tatum: A Guide to His Recorded Music. LC 82-10752. (Studies in Jazz: No. 2). 359p. 1982. 17.50 (ISBN 0-8108-1582-6). Scarecrow.
Lyons, Len. The Great Jazz Pianists: Speaking of Their Lives & Music. (Illus.). 224p. 1983. 12.95 (ISBN 0-688-01920-X). Morrow.
--The Great Jazz Pianists: Speaking of Their Lives & Music. (Illus.). 224p. 1983. pap. 6.95 (ISBN 0-688-01921-8). Quill NY.
JAZZ MUSICIANS–CORRESPONDENCE, REMINISCENCES, ETC.
see Musicians–Correspondence, Reminiscences, etc.
JAZZ MUSICIANS–PORTRAITS
see Musicians–Portraits
JEANNERET-GRIS, CHARLES EDOUARD, 1887-1965
Fondation Le Corbusier & Architectural History Foundation, eds. Le Corbusier Sketchbooks: Volume 4, 1957-1964. (Illus.). 520p. (Fr. & Eng.). 1982. 150.00x (ISBN 0-262-12093-3). MIT Pr.
JEEP VEHICLE
see Automobiles–Types–Jeep
JEFFERIES, RICHARD, 1848-1887
Salt, H. S. Richard Jefferies: A Study. 128p. 1982. Repr. of 1894 ed. lib. bdg. 25.00 (ISBN 0-89984-610-6). Century Bookbindery.
--Richard Jefferies: A Study. 128p. 1982. Repr. of 1894 ed. lib. bdg. 25.00 (ISBN 0-89760-851-8). Telegraph Bks.
JEFFERSON, THOMAS, PRES. U. S., 1743-1826
Adams, Dickinson W., ed. Jefferson's Extracts from the Gospels: "The Philosophy of Jesus" & "The Life & Morals of Jesus". LC 82-61371. (The Papers of Thomas Jefferson, Second Ser.). 384p. 1983. 30.00x (ISBN 0-691-04699-9). Princeton U Pr.
Bowers, Claude G. & Browder, Earl. The Heritage of Jefferson. Franklin, Francis, ed. LC 82-24251. 48p. 1983. Repr. of 1944 ed. lib. bdg. 19.75x (ISBN 0-313-23839-1, BOHE). Greenwood.
James, Marquis. They Had Their Hour: Benjamin Franklin, Thomas Jefferson. 324p. 1982. Repr. of 1926 ed. lib. bdg. 40.00 (ISBN 0-8495-2802-X). Arden Lib.
Johnson, Allen. Jefferson & His Colleagues. 1921. text ed. 8.50x (ISBN 0-686-83595-6). Elliots Bks.
Muzzey, David S. Thomas Jefferson. 319p. 1982. Repr. of 1918 ed. lib. bdg. 45.00 (ISBN 0-89987-590-4). Darby Bks.
Padover, Saul K. Jefferson. 459p. 1982. Repr. of 1942 ed. lib. bdg. 50.00 (ISBN 0-8495-4415-7). Arden Lib.
JEHOVAH'S WITNESSES
Grieshaber, Erich & Grieshaber, Jean. Expose of Jehovah's Witnesses. 128p. 1983. pap. text ed. 2.95 (ISBN 0-936728-08-6). Word for Today.
JEREMIAH THE PROPHET
Fettke, Steven M. Messages to a Nation in Crisis: An Introduction to the Prophecy of Jeremiah. LC 82-19997. (Illus.). 72p. (Orig.). 1983. pap. text ed. 6.75 (ISBN 0-8191-2839-2). U Pr of Amer.
JEROME, SAINT (HIERONYMUS, SAINT)
Hornblower, Jane. Hieronymus of Cardia. (Classical & Philosophical Monographs). 314p. 1981. text ed. 44.00x (ISBN 0-19-814717-1). Oxford U Pr.
JERUSALEM–DESCRIPTION
Walker, Shoshana. Haggadah. 104p. 1982. 24.95 (ISBN 965-220-017-4, Carta Maps & Guides Pub Isreal). Hippocrene Bks.
JERUSALEM–DESCRIPTION–GUIDEBOOKS
Dudman, Helge. Street People. (Illus.). 263p. 1982. 14.95 (ISBN 965-220-039-5, Carta Maps & Guides Pub Isreal). Hippocrene Bks.
Isaacs, Marty. Marty's Walking Tours of Biblical Jerusalem. (Illus.). 128p. 1982. pap. 4.95 (ISBN 0-686-43008-5, Carta Maps & Guides Pub Isreal). Hippocrene Bks.
JERUSALEM–HISTORY
Har-El, Menashe & Zeevy, Rechavam. This Is Jerusalem. 2nd ed. (The Har-El Ser.). (Illus.). 1982. text ed. 16.00 (ISBN 0-86628-041-3). Ridgefield Pub.
Miskin, J. Robert. Among Lions: The Battle for Jerusalem, June 5-7, 1967. (War Library). 432p. 1983. pap. 4.95 (ISBN 0-345-29673-7). Ballantine.
JESTERS
see Fools and Jesters
JESTS
see Wit and Humor
JESUITS
Winterborn, Benjamin. Changing Scenes. Thompson, Marie K. & Roth, Beth N., eds. (Illus., Orig.). 1980. 17.95 (ISBN 0-19-213226-1). Oxford U Pr.
JESUS, SOCIETY OF
see Jesuits
JESUS CHRIST
see also Antichrist; Atonement; Christianity; Incarnation; Lord's Supper; Millennium; Salvation; Second Advent; Trinity
Bruce, F. F. Jesus & Paul: Places They Knew. 128p. 1983. Repr. of 1981 ed. 12.95 (ISBN 0-8407-5281-4). Nelson.
Campbell, Alexander. Stories of Jesus, Stories of Now. 80p. (Orig.). (gr. 1-6). 1980. pap. 12.95 (ISBN 0-940754-04-5). Ed Ministries.
Dooley, Kate C. The Jesus Book. LC 82-61422. 48p. (Orig.). 1983. pap. 2.95 (ISBN 0-8091-2514-5). Paulist Pr.
Drew, George. The Original Ideas of Jesus That Are Changing the World. 45p. (Orig.). 1980. pap. 5.45 (ISBN 0-940754-05-3). Ed Ministries.
Failing, George E. Did Christ Die for All? 1.25 (ISBN 0-937296-02-3, 222-B). Presence Inc.
Gunn, James. Christ: The Fullness of the Godhead, a Study in New Testament Christology. 256p. 1983. pap. 5.50 (ISBN 0-87213-283-8). Loizeaux.
Jesus. 23p. 1982. pap. 7.55 (ISBN 0-88479-034-7). Arena Lettres.
Knight, G. Wilson. Christ & Nietzsche: An Essay in Poetic Wisdom. 1982. 25.00 (ISBN 0-8495-3135-7). Arden Lib.
Lockyer, Herbert. Portraits of the Savior. 144p. 1983. 9.95 (ISBN 0-8407-5288-1); pap. 4.95 (ISBN 0-8407-5838-3). Nelson.
Murray, Andrew. Jesus Himself. 27p. 1966. pap. 0.85 (ISBN 0-87509-096-6). Chr Pubns.
O'Collins, Gerald. What Are They Saying about Jesus. rev. ed. (WATSA Ser.). 96p. 1983. pap. 3.95 (ISBN 0-686-84554-4). Paulist Pr.
Pannenberg, Wolfhart. Jesus: God & Man. 2nd ed. Wilkens, Lewis L. & Priebe, Duane A., trs. LC 76-26478. 432p. 1982. pap. 12.95 (ISBN 0-664-24468-8). Westminster.
Rowden, Harold H., ed. Christ the Lord: Studies in Christology Presented to Donald Guthrie. LC 82-171. 1982. 19.95 (ISBN 0-87784-955-2). Inter-Varsity.
Simons, Frans. Man kann wieder Christ sein: Eine Abrechnung mit der Theologie und der "kritischen" Bibelwissenschaft. 231p. 1978. write for info. (ISBN 3-261-03011-9). P Lang Pubs.
Steiner, Rudolf. Jesus & Christ. Bledsoe, John, tr. from Ger. 23p. 1976. pap. 1.50 (ISBN 0-88010-042-7). Anthroposophic.
Stroup, George W. Jesus Christ for Today, Vol. 7. LC 82-13494. (Library of Living Faith). 120p. 1982. pap. 5.95 (ISBN 0-664-24450-5). Westminster.
Suh, Chul Won. The Creation-Mediatorship of Jesus Christ. (Amsterdam Studies in Theology: Vol. IV). 325p. 1982. pap. text ed. 27.75x (ISBN 90-6203-624-4, Pub. by Rodopi Holland). Humanities.
Talmage, James E. Jesus the Christ. (Classics in Mormon Literature Ser.). 804p. 1982. 10.95 (ISBN 0-87747-903-8). Deseret Bk.
Tozer, A. W. Christ, the Eternal Son. Smith, G. B., ed. 136p. 1982. pap. 3.50 mm (ISBN 0-87509-230-6). Chr Pubns.
Tyrrell, Bernard J. Christotherapy II: A New Horizon for Counselors, Spiritual Directors & Seekers of Healing & Growth in Christ. (Orig.). 1982. 12.95 (ISBN 0-8091-0332-X); pap. 8.95 (ISBN 0-8091-2482-3). Paulist Pr.
Zahl, Paul. Who Will Deliver Us? 96p. (Orig.). 1983. pap. price not set (ISBN 0-8164-2468-3). Seabury.
JESUS CHRIST–ART
see also Bible–Pictures, Illustrations, etc.; Christian Art and Symbolism; Icons
Emerson, James C., ed. The Life of Christ in the Conception & Expression of Chinese & Oriental Artists. (The Great Art Masters of the World Ser.). (Illus.). 117p. 1983. 61.75 (ISBN 0-86650-054-5). Gloucester Art.
Sledge, Linda C. Shivering Babe, Victorious Lord: The Nativity in Poetry & Art. 1981. 24.95 (ISBN 0-8028-3553-8). Eerdmans.
JESUS CHRIST–ATONEMENT
see Atonement
JESUS CHRIST–BEATITUDES
see Beatitudes
JESUS CHRIST–BIOGRAPHY
Bull, Norman. The Story of Jesus. 160p. 1983. 13.95 (ISBN 0-687-39659-X). Abingdon.
Demarest, Bruce A. Who Is Jesus? 132p. 1983. pap. 4.50 (ISBN 0-88207-103-3). SP Pubns.
Flusser, David. Die Rabbinischen Gleichnisse und der Gleichniserzahler Jesus. 322p. (Ger.). 1981. write for info. (ISBN 3-261-04778-X). P Lang Pubs.
Modras, Ronald. Jesus of Nazareth: A Life Worth Living. (Nazareth Bks). 120p. 1983. pap. 3.95 (ISBN 0-86683-713-2). Winston Pr.
Murry, J. Middleton. The Life of Jesus. 1982. Repr. of 1927 ed. lib. bdg. 35.00 (ISBN 0-8495-3939-0). Arden Lib.
Ness, Gladys M. Jesus & the Twelve in 30 A. D. 64p. 1983. 6.95 (ISBN 0-8059-2863-4). Dorrance.
Olson, Chet, ed. Jesus One: The Life & Wisdom of Jesus in Scripture. 2nd ed. (Life & Wisdom of Jesus Ser.). 216p. 9.95 (ISBN 0-940298-07-4); pap. 6.95 (ISBN 0-940298-06-6). Spiritwarrior Pub.
Stevens, Clifford. The Life of Christ. 196p. (Orig.). 1983. pap. 5.95 (ISBN 0-87973-617-8, 617). Our Sunday Visitor.
JESUS CHRIST–BIOGRAPHY–APOCRYPHAL AND LEGENDARY LITERATURE
Beskow, Per. Strange Tales About Jesus: A Survey of Unfamiliar Gospels. LC 82-16001. 144p. 1983. pap. 6.95 (ISBN 0-8006-1686-3, 1-1686). Fortress.
JESUS CHRIST–BIOGRAPHY–HISTORY AND CRITICISM
Coscia, Louis W., pseud. The Promised One. 192p. Date not set. price not set. Todd & Honeywell.
Foote, G. W. & Wheeler, J. M., eds. Sepher Toldoth Jeshu: The Jewish Life of Christ. (Illus.). 49p. 1982. pap. 3.00 (ISBN 0-910309-02-7). Am Atheist.
JESUS CHRIST–BIOGRAPHY–JUVENILE LITERATURE
see also Jesus Christ–Nativity–Juvenile Literature
Sherlock, Connie. Life of Jesus. Beegle, Shirley, ed. (Think 'N Check Quizzes Ser.). (Illus.). 16p. (Orig.). (gr. 4-8). 1983. pap. 1.50 (ISBN 0-87239-689-4, 2793). Standard Pub.
JESUS CHRIST–CHARACTER
Bangley, Bernard. Growing in His Image. 160p. 1983. pap. 2.95 (ISBN 0-87788-328-9). Shaw Pubs.
JESUS CHRIST–CRUCIFIXION
Jackman, Stuart. The Davidson File. LC 82-13443. 128p. 1983. pap. 7.95 (ISBN 0-664-24459-9). Westminster.
Pio, Padre. The Agony of Jesus. 40p. 1954. pap. 0.75 (ISBN 0-686-81635-8). TAN Bks Pubs.
JESUS CHRIST–DEVOTIONAL LITERATURE
Ashton, Marvin J. Ye Are My Friends. 151p. 1982. 6.95 (ISBN 0-87747-934-8). Deseret Bk.

Bailey, Keith M. Aprender a Vivir: Learning to Live. Bucher, Dorothy, tr. 125p. (Spanish.). 1980. 1.50 (ISBN 0-87509-299-3). Chr Pubns.
Bickimer, David A. Christ the Placenta. LC 82-24097. 230p. (Orig.). 1983. pap. 12.95x (ISBN 0-89135-034-9). Religious Educ.
Bixler, Russell. Learning To Know God As Provider. 96p. 1982. pap. 2.50 (ISBN 0-88368-120-X). Whitaker Hse.
Bloch, Carl, illus. Jesus, the Son of Man. (Illus.). 80p. 1983. pap. 12.95 (ISBN 0-87973-652-6, 652). Our Sunday Visitor.
Christ in You. 224p. 1983. pap. 5.00 (ISBN 0-87516-506-0). De Vorss.
Edwards, Ruth. Answer Me. (Illus., Orig.). 1983. pap. 5.56 (ISBN 0-89390-042-7); pap. text ed. 6.95. Resource Pubns.
Fearon, Mary & Hirstein, Sandra J. Celebrating the Gift of Jesus. 64p. 1982. pap. 2.75 (ISBN 0-697-01794-X); program manual 6.95 (ISBN 0-697-01795-8). Wm C Brown.
Heijkoop, H. L. Unto Christ. 47p. pap. 0.60 (ISBN 0-88172-087-9). Believers Bkshelf.
Hybels, Bill. Christians in the Marketplace. 144p. 1982. pap. 4.95 (ISBN 0-88207-314-1). Victor Bks.
Maxwell, Neal A. Even as I Am. 128p. 1982. 6.95 (ISBN 0-87747-943-7). Deseret Bk.
Mosqueda, John. Jesus, Emotions & You. 128p. 1983. pap. 5.95 (ISBN 0-686-82090-8). Good News.
Murray, Andrew. The Master's Indwelling. 144p. 1983. pap. text ed. 2.95 (ISBN 0-88368-121-8). Whitaker Hse.
--The True Vine. 128p. 1983. pap. text ed. 2.50 (ISBN 0-88368-118-8). Whitaker Hse.
Ogilvie, Lloyd J. You've Got Charisma. 176p. 1983. pap. 3.50 (ISBN 0-687-47268-7). Abingdon.
Palms, Roger C. The Pleasure of His Company. 1982. pap. 5.95 (ISBN 0-8423-4847-6). Tyndale.
Reynolds, R. Gene. Assurance. 128p. 1982. pap. 3.95 (ISBN 0-8423-0088-0). Tyndale.
Savelle, Jerry. Sharing Jesus Effectively. (Orig.). 1982. pap. 3.95 (ISBN 0-89274-251-8). Harrison Hse.
Vogl, Carl. Begone Satan. 1935p. 1954. pap. 1.75 (ISBN 0-686-81636-6). TAN Bks Pubs.
Watchman Nee. The Messenger of the Cross. Kaung, Stephen, tr. (Orig.). 1980. pap. text ed. 3.10 (ISBN 0-935008-50-0). Christian Fellow Pubs.
Weischedel, Randall. The Joy of Ascension. LC 82-7349. (Illus.). 160p. 1983. 8.95 (ISBN 0-87516-499-4). De Vorss.
Wickens, Paul A. Christ Denied. 49p. 1982. pap. 1.25 (ISBN 0-686-81637-4). TAN Bks Pubs.
Zanzig, Thomas. Jesus is Lord! (Illus.). 208p. pap. 7.95 (ISBN 0-88489-149-6). St Marys.

JESUS CHRIST-DIVINITY
see also Trinity; Unitarianism
Menendez, Josefa. The Way of Devine Love. 506p. pap. 3.50 (ISBN 0-686-81632-3). TAN Bks Pubs.

JESUS CHRIST-EXAMPLE
Porter, Mark. The Time of Your Life. 1983. pap. 4.95 (ISBN 0-88207-387-7). Victor Bks.

JESUS CHRIST-FAMILY-ART
see Jesus Christ-Art

JESUS CHRIST-HISTORICITY
Mead, G. R. Pistis Sophia. 216p. 1982. pap. 22.95 (ISBN 0-7224-0214-7). Robinson & Watkins.
Robinson, James M. A New Quest of the Historical Jesus & Other Essays. LC 82-48586. 224p. 1983. pap. text ed. 11.95 (ISBN 0-8006-1698-7). Fortress.

JESUS CHRIST-HISTORY OF DOCTRINES
Carmody, John. The Heart of the Christian Matter: An Ecumenical Approach. 304p. (Orig.). 1983. pap. 11.95 (ISBN 0-687-16765-5). Abingdon.
Fuller, Reginald & Perkins, Pheme. Who Is This Christ? Gospel Christology & Contemporary Faith. LC 82-48590. 176p. 1983. pap. 8.95 (ISBN 0-8006-1706-1, 1-1706). Fortress.

JESUS CHRIST-HOLY SHROUD
see Holy Shroud

JESUS CHRIST-ICONOGRAPHY
see Jesus Christ-Art

JESUS CHRIST-INCARNATION
see Incarnation

JESUS CHRIST-JEWISH INTERPRETATIONS
Schonle, Volker. Johannes, Jesus und die Juden. 288p. (Ger.). 1982. write for info. (ISBN 3-8204-5877-8). P Lang Pubs.

JESUS CHRIST-JUVENILE LITERATURE
see also Jesus Christ-Biography-Juvenile Literature; Jesus Christ-Nativity-Juvenile Literature
Bennett, Marian. Baby Jesus ABC's. (Little Happy Day Bks.). (Illus.). 24p. (Orig.). (gr. k-3). 1983. pap. 0.45 (ISBN 0-87239-651-7, 2121). Standard Pub.
Heide, F. P. Jesus Says I Am. (gr. 2-5). 1983. 6.95 (ISBN 0-570-04077-9). Concordia.
Klug, Ron & Lyn, Klug. Jesus Lives. LC 82-72848. 32p. (Orig.). (ps). 1983. pap. 3.50 (ISBN 0-8066-1952-X, 10-3527). Augsburg.
Nystrom, Carolyn. Jesus Is No Secret. (Children's Bible Basics Ser.). (Illus.). (gr. 2 up). 1983. 4.50 (ISBN 0-8024-0193-7). Moody.
Richards, Jean H. Jesus Went About Doing Good. LC 80-70475. (gr. 1-4). 1983. 5.95 (ISBN 0-8054-4289-8). Broadman.
St. Clair, Barry. Hey, Who Is That Man? (YA) (gr. 9-12). pap. 3.50 (ISBN 0-88207-583-7). Victor Bks.
Tiner, John H. They Followed Jesus: Word Search Puzzles. 48p. pap. 1.50 (ISBN 0-87239-586-3). Standard Pub.
Yasuda, Chizuko, illus. Children Praise Jesus. (Baby's First Fabric Bks.). (Illus.). (ps). 1983. fabric 1.95 (ISBN 0-8307-0878-2). Regal.
--Jesus & the Children. (Baby's First Fabric Bks.). (Illus.). 6p. (ps). 1983. fabric 1.95 (ISBN 0-8307-0877-4). Regal.
--Jesus Tells About the Kind Shepherd. (Baby's First Fabric Bks.). (Illus.). 6p. (ps). 1983. 1.95 (ISBN 0-8307-0875-8). Regal.

JESUS CHRIST-LIFE
see Jesus Christ-Biography

JESUS CHRIST-LORD'S SUPPER
see Lord's Supper

JESUS CHRIST-MEDITATIONS
see Jesus Christ-Devotional Literature

JESUS CHRIST-MIRACLES
Allen, Ronald J. Our Eyes Can Be Opened: Preaching the Miracle Stories of the Synoptic Gospels Today. LC 81-43679. 146p. 1983. pap. text ed. 8.25 (ISBN 0-8191-2671-3). U Pr of Amer.
Storr, Catherine & Bennett, Russell, eds. Miracles By the Sea. LC 82-23022. (People of the Bible Ser.). (Illus.). 32p. (gr. 1-2). 1983. PLB 11.55 (ISBN 0-8172-1983-8). Raintree Pubs.

JESUS CHRIST-MYSTICAL BODY
see also Mystical Union
Reader, J. The Divine Mystery. 79p. pap. 3.95 (ISBN 0-88172-117-4). Believers Bkshelf.

JESUS CHRIST-NAME
Raya, Joseph. Acathist Hymn to the Name of Jesus. De Vinck, Jose M., ed. 40p. 1983. 5.00x (ISBN 0-911726-45-4); pap. 3.50x (ISBN 0-911726-46-2). Alleluia Pr.

JESUS CHRIST-NATIVITY-ART
see Jesus Christ-Art

JESUS CHRIST-NATIVITY-JUVENILE LITERATURE
Bennett, Marian. The Story of Baby Jesus. (Illus.). 24p. (Orig.). (ps-k). 1983. pap. 0.45 (ISBN 0-87239-654-1, 2124). Standard Pub.

JESUS CHRIST-NATIVITY-SERMONS
see Christmas Sermons

JESUS CHRIST-PARABLES
Storr, Catherine & Bennett, Russell, eds. The Prodigal Son. LC 82-23011. (People of the Bible Ser.). (Illus.). 32p. (gr. 1-2). 1983. PLB 11.55 (ISBN 0-8172-1982-X). Raintree Pubs.

JESUS CHRIST-PARABLES-SERMONS
Boice, James M. The Parables of Jesus. 1983. pap. 6.95 (ISBN 0-8024-0163-5). Moody.

JESUS CHRIST-PASSION-ART
see Jesus Christ-Art

JESUS CHRIST-PERSON AND OFFICES
Rahner, Karl. The Love of Jesus & the Love of Neighbor. 96p. 1983. pap. 5.95 (ISBN 0-8245-0570-0). Crossroad NY.
Talec, Pierre. Christ & the Sacrament Church. 144p. 1983. pap. 9.95 (ISBN 0-8164-2455-1). Seabury.

JESUS CHRIST-PERSONALITY
see Jesus Christ-Character

JESUS CHRIST-PICTURES, ILLUSTRATIONS, ETC.
see Jesus Christ-Art

JESUS CHRIST-PROPHETIC OFFICE
Howes, Fred. This Is the Prophet Jesus. LC 82-72741. 256p. 1983. pap. 8.95 (ISBN 0-87516-497-8). De Vorss.

JESUS CHRIST-RESURRECTION
see also Easter
Price, Nelson L. The Destruction of Death. 1983. 3.25 (ISBN 0-8054-1528-9). Broadman.
Stevenson, Kenneth & Habermas, Gary B. Verdict on the Shroud: Evidence for the Death & Resurrection of Jesus Christ. (Illus.). 220p. 1981. pap. 6.95 (ISBN 0-89283-174-X). Servant.

JESUS CHRIST-SAYINGS
see Jesus Christ-Words

JESUS CHRIST-SECOND ADVENT
see Second Advent

JESUS CHRIST-SERMON ON THE MOUNT
see Sermon on the Mount

JESUS CHRIST-TEACHINGS
Abernathy, David & Perrin, Norman. Understanding the Teaching of Jesus. 288p. (Orig.). 1983. pap. 13.95 (ISBN 0-8164-2438-1). Seabury.
Hayes, Norvel. Jesus Taught Me to Cast out Devils. 89p. 1982. pap. 2.50 (ISBN 0-89274-272-0). Harrison Hse.
Lawson, LeRoy. Lord of Promises: Adult Course. LC 82-17034. 112p. 1983. pap. 2.50 (ISBN 0-87239-611-8). Standard Pub.
--Lord of Promises (Student) Adult Course. 96p. 1983. pap. 2.25 (ISBN 0-87239-612-6). SRA.
Lierman, Deonna. Pocketful of Promises. (Illus.). 24p. 1983. pap. 0.45 (ISBN 0-87239-650-9, 2120). Standard Pub.
Maschke, Ruby. Promises of Jesus From the Gospel: Puzzle Book. (Illus.). 48p. 1983. pap. 1.50 (ISBN 0-87239-591-X, 2789). Standard Pub.
Niwano, Nichiko. My Father My Teacher: A Spiritual Journey. Gage, Richard L., tr. from Jap. 143p. (Orig.). 1982. pap. 3.50 (ISBN 4-333-01095-0, Pub. by Kosei Pub Co Japan). C E Tuttle.
Szekely, Edmond B. The Essene Gospel of Peace, Bk. 1. (Illus.). 72p. 1981. pap. 1.00 (ISBN 0-89564-000-7). IBS Intl.
--The Essene Gospel of Peace, Bk. 2. (Illus.). 132p. 1981. pap. 5.80 (ISBN 0-89564-001-5). IBS Intl.
--The Essene Gospel of Peace, Bk. 3: Lost Scrolls of the Essene Brotherhood. (Illus.). 144p. 1981. pap. 5.60 (ISBN 0-89564-002-3). IBS Intl.
--The Essene Gospel of Peace, Bk. 4: Teachings of the Elect. (Illus.). 40p. 1981. pap. 4.50 (ISBN 0-89564-003-1). IBS Intl.
--The Essene Jesus. (Illus.). 72p. 1977. pap. 4.50 (ISBN 0-89564-007-4). IBS Intl.
--The Essene Origins of Christianity. (Illus.). 184p. 1981. pap. 8.50 (ISBN 0-89564-015-5). IBS Intl.

JESUS CHRIST-THEOSOPHICAL INTERPRETATIONS
Jakubowsky, Frank. The Psychological Patterns of Jesus Christ. 342p. (Orig.). 1982. pap. 14.95 (ISBN 0-932588-02-6). Jakubowsky.
Ruether, Rosemary R. To Change the World: Christology & Cultural Criticism. 96p. 1983. pap. 5.95 (ISBN 0-8245-0573-5). Crossroad NY.
Thomas Aguinas. The Grace of Christ. (Summa Theologial Ser.: Vol. 49). 1974. 16.95 (ISBN 0-07-002024-8). McGraw.

JESUS CHRIST-WORDS
Failing, George E. Did Christ Die for All? 1.25 (ISBN 0-937296-02-3, 222-B). Presence Inc.
Jakubowsky, Frank. The Psychological Patterns of Jesus Christ. 342p. (Orig.). 1982. pap. 14.95 (ISBN 0-932588-02-6). Jakubowsky.

JESUS CHRIST IN ART
see Jesus Christ-Art

JESUS CHRIST IN FICTION, DRAMA, POETRY, ETC.
Adams, Dickinson W., ed. Jefferson's Extracts from the Gospels: "The Philosophy of Jesus" & "The Life & Morals of Jesus". LC 82-61371. (The Papers of Thomas Jefferson, Second Ser.). 384p. 1983. 30.00x (ISBN 0-691-04699-9). Princeton U Pr.

JESUS CHRIST IN LITERATURE
see Jesus Christ in Fiction, Drama, Poetry, etc.

JESUS MOVEMENT
see Jesus People

JESUS PEOPLE
Wilkerson, David. Jesus Person: Pocket Promise Book. LC 72-86208. 96p. 1979. pap. 1.95 (ISBN 0-8307-0191-5). Regal.

JET PLANES
Ethell, Jeffrey & Price, Alfred. The German Jets in Combat. (Illus.). 160p. 1980. 17.95 (ISBN 0-86720-582-2). Sci Bks Intl.
Masters, David. German Jet Genesis. (Illus.). 160p. 1982. 19.95 (ISBN 0-86720-622-5). Sci Bks Intl.
Serling, Robert J. The Jet Age. (Epic of Flight Ser.). 1982. lib. bdg. 19.96 (ISBN 0-8094-3301-X, Pub. by Time-Life). Silver.

JET PROPELLED AIRPLANES
see Jet Planes

JEWELRY
see also Crown Jewels; Gems
Goldemberg, Rose L. All About Jewelry: The One Indispensable Guide for Buyers, Wearers, Lovers, Investors. (Illus.). 1983. 15.95 (ISBN 0-87795-419-4, Pub. by Priam); pap. 6.95 (ISBN 0-87795-453-4). Arbor Hse.
--All About Jewelry: The One Indispensible Guide for Jewelry Buyers, Wearers, Lovers, & Investors. LC 82-72057. (Illus.). 165p. 1983. 15.95 (ISBN 0-686-84342-8); pap. 6.95. Arbor Hse.
The Official 1983 Price Guide to Antique Jewelry. 1st ed. LC 82-84641. 240p. 1983. pap. 2.95 (ISBN 0-87637-373-2). Hse of Collectibles.
Ross, Heather C. The Art of Bedouin Jewellery. 1982. 59.00x (ISBN 0-907513-01-8, Pub. by Cave Pubns England). State Mutual Bk.
--The Art of Bedouin Jewellery: A Saudi Arabian Profile. (Illus.). 132p. 1982. 45.00 (ISBN 0-7103-0032-8, Kegan Paul). Routledge & Kegan.

JEWELRY, ANCIENT
Ogden, Jack. Jewellery of the Ancient World. LC 82-60069. (Illus.). 250p. 1982. 45.00 (ISBN 0-8478-0444-5). Rizzoli Intl.

JEWELRY MAKING
see also Enamel and Enameling; Silverwork
Bagley, Peter. Making Silver Jewellery. (Illus.). 144p. 1983. 29.95 (ISBN 0-7134-2580-6, Pub. by Batsford England). David & Charles.

JEWELS
see Crown Jewels; Gems; Jewelry

JEWISH-ARAB RELATIONS
see also Israel-Arab Border Conflicts, 1949-
Carroll, Raymond. The Palestine Question. (Impact Ser.). 96p. (gr. 7 up). 1983. PLB 8.90 (ISBN 0-531-04549-8). Watts.
Elon, Amos. Israelis: Founders & Sons. 1983. pap. 5.95 (ISBN 0-14-022476-9, Pelican). Penguin.
Worth, Richard. Israel & the Arab States. (Impact Ser.). 96p. (gr. 7 up). 1983. PLB 8.90 (ISBN 0-531-04545-5). Watts.

JEWISH ART
see Art, Jewish

JEWISH CHILDREN
Syme, Daniel & Bogot, Howard. I'm Growing. (Illus.). 32p. (ps-1). 1982. pap. 4.00 (ISBN 0-8074-0167-6, 101095). UAHC.

JEWISH CHRONOLOGY
see Chronology, Jewish

JEWISH COURTS
see Courts, Jewish

JEWISH DRAMA
see also Yiddish Drama
Cohen, Sarah B., ed. From Hester Street to Hollywood: The Jewish-American Stage & Screen. LC 82-47924. (Jewish Literature & Culture Ser.). 288p. 1983. 22.50x (ISBN 0-253-32500-5). Ind U Pr.

JEWISH FOLK-LORE
see Folk-Lore, Jewish

JEWISH HOLOCAUST (1939-1945)
see Holocaust, Jewish (1939-1945)

JEWISH INSCRIPTIONS
see Inscriptions, Jewish

JEWISH LANGUAGE
see Hebrew Language; Yiddish Language

JEWISH LAW
see also Commandments, Ten; Courts, Jewish
Sheinkopf, David I. Gelatin & Jewish Law. 1982. pap. 7.95 (ISBN 0-8197-0488-1). Bloch.

JEWISH LITERATURE (COLLECTIONS)
see also Apocalyptic Literature; Cabala; Hebrew Literature; Talmud
Lieberman, Leo & Beringause, Arthur. Classics of Jewish Literature. 1983. 20.00 (ISBN 0-8022-2092-4). Philos Lib.
Lubetski, Edith & Lubetski, Meir. Building a Judaica Library Collection. 260p. Date not set. lib. bdg. 27.50 (ISBN 0-87287-375-7). Libs Unl.

JEWISH LITERATURE-HISTORY AND CRITICISM
Trenchard, Warren C. Ben Sira's View of Women: A Literary Analysis. LC 82-16755. (Brown Judaic Studies: No. 38). 352p. 1982. pap. 15.75 (ISBN 0-89130-593-9, 14-00-38). Scholars Pr CA.
Yudkin, Leon I. Jewish Writing & Identity in the Twentieth Century. LC 82-827. 180p. 1982. 22.50x (ISBN 0-312-44234-3). St Martin.

JEWISH MIGRATION
see Jews-Migrations

JEWISH PORTRAITS
see Portraits

JEWISH SECTS
see also Essenes; Orthodox Judaism; Qumran Community; Reform Judaism
Grad, Eli & Roth, Bette. Congregation Shaarey Zedek: 5622-5742 1861-1981. 198p. 1982. 25.00 (ISBN 0-8143-1713-8). Wayne St U Pr.

JEWISH SONGS
see Songs, Jewish

JEWISH TALES
see Tales, Jewish

JEWISH THEOLOGY
see also Judaism
Joseph, Howard, et al, eds. Truth & Compassion: Essays on Judaism & Religion for Rabbi Dr. Solomon Frank at Eighty. 250p. 1982. text ed. 11.50x (ISBN 0-919812-17-1, 40948, Pub. by Laurier U Pr). Humanities.
Kellerman, Eli. Jewish Ceremonial: A Guide to Jewish Prayer & Ritual. 69p. 1983. pap. 9.95 (ISBN 965-220-038-7, Carta Maps & Guides Pub Isreal). Hippocrene Bks.

JEWISH WAY OF LIFE
see also Women, Jewish
Bubis, Gerald B. & Wasserman, Harry. Synagogue Havurot: A Comparative Study. LC 82-23912. 160p. (Orig.). 1983. lib. bdg. 21.50 (ISBN 0-8191-2969-0, Co-pub. by Ctr Jewish Comm Studies); pap. text ed. 10.00 (ISBN 0-8191-2970-4). U Pr of Amer.
Cohen, Steven M. & Hyman, Paula, eds. The Evolving Jewish Family. 256p. 1983. text ed. 30.00x (ISBN 0-8419-0860-5). Holmes & Meier.
Fabric of My Life. 4.95 (ISBN 0-686-81719-2); pap. 1.25. NCJW.
Gittelsohn, Roland B. The Extra Dimension. 228p. 1983. pap. 7.95 (ISBN 0-8074-0170-6, 168500). UAHC.
Heilman, Samuel C. The People of the Book: Drama, Fellowship, & Religion. LC 82-13369. 264p. 1983. lib. bdg. 22.50x (ISBN 0-226-32492-3). U of Chicago Pr.
Herzog, Yaacov D. The Mishnah. 15.00 (ISBN 0-686-84235-9). Bloch.
Kasher, Menachem M. Israel Passover Haggadah. LC 64-17316. (Illus.). 1983. Repr. of 1964 ed. 13.95 (ISBN 0-88400-018-4). Shengold.
Schachter-Shalomi, Zalman & Gropman, Donald. The First Step: A Guide to the New Jewish Spirit. 144p. 1983. pap. 5.95 (ISBN 0-553-01418-8). Bantam.
Shaanan, Alexander. Dear God, is Justice Still With You? (Illus.). 144p. 1983. 8.95 (ISBN 0-89962-306-9). Todd & Honeywell.

JEWISH WIT AND HUMOR
Fuchs, Esther. Encounters with Israeli Authors. LC 82-62086. (Illus.). 104p. 1983. pap. 7.50 (ISBN 0-916288-14-5). Micah Pubns.
Kruger, Mollee. Daughters of Chutzpah: Humorous Verse on the Jewish Woman. LC 82-71394. (Illus.). 110p. (Orig.). 1983. pap. 5.50x (ISBN 0-9602036-7-2). Biblio NY.
Nero, pseud. By My Laugh Its Jewish. 110p. 1983. text ed. 12.50x (ISBN 0-85303-197-5, Pub. by Vallentine Mitchell England); pap. text ed. 6.50x (ISBN 0-85303-198-3). Biblio Dist.
Spalding, Henry D. Jewish Laffs. LC 82-9990. (Illus.). 96p. 1982. pap. 3.95 (ISBN 0-8246-0290-0). Jonathan David.

JEWISH WOMEN
see Women, Jewish
JEWISH YOUTH
see Youth, Jewish
JEWS
see also Prophets; Youth, Jewish
Valensi, Lucette & Udovitch, Abraham L. The Last Arab Jews: The Communities of Jerba. (Social Orders: A Series of Tracts & Monographs). 1983. write for info. (ISBN 3-7186-0135-4). Harwood Academic.
JEWS–BIBLIOGRAPHY
Cutter, Charles & Oppenheim, Micha F. Jewish Reference Sources: A Select, Annotated Bibliographic Guide. LC 82-15434. (Reference Library of Social Science: Vol. 126). 180p. 1983. lib. bdg. 19.95 (ISBN 0-8240-9347-X). Garland Pub.
Stuhlman, Daniel D. Library of Congress Headings for Judaica. LC 82-73398. (Orig.). 1982. pap. 5.00 (ISBN 0-934402-13-2). BYLS Pr.
JEWS–BIOGRAPHY
see also Women, Jewish
also Jews in Germany; Jews in the United States and similar headings
Golan, Matti. Shimon Peres: A Biography. Friedman, Ina, tr. LC 82-7354. (Illus.). 275p. (Hebrew.). 1982. 22.50 (ISBN 0-312-71736-9). St Martin.
Shaanan, Alexander. Dear God, is Justice Still With You? (Illus.). 144p. 1983. 8.95 (ISBN 0-89962-306-9). Todd & Honeywell.
Shamir, Ruth. All Our Vows. LC 82-61795. 1983. 11.95 (ISBN 0-88400-090-7). Shengold.
Whitney, George G. Born to Survive, 1936-1946. (Illus.). 200p. Date not set. pap. 12.95 (ISBN 0-686-84299-5). Banyan Bks.
JEWS–CABALA
see Cabala
JEWS–CHILDREN
see Jewish Children
JEWS–COURTS
see Courts, Jewish
JEWS–CUSTOMS
see Jews–Social Life and Customs
JEWS–DIASPORA
see also Jews–Migrations
Jones, G. Lloyd. The Discovery of Hebrew in Tudor England: A Third Language. 300p. 1982. 35.00 (ISBN 0-7190-0875-1). Manchester.
JEWS–DISPERSION
see Jews–Diaspora
JEWS–EMIGRATION AND IMMIGRATION
see Jews–Migrations
JEWS–EXODUS
see Exodus, the
JEWS–FOLK-LORE
see Folk-Lore, Jewish
JEWS–HISTORY
see also Chronology, Jewish
Brooten, Bernadette J. Women Leaders in the Ancient Synagogue: Inscriptional Evidence & Background Issues. LC 82-10658. (Brown Judaic Studies). 292p. 1982. pap. 20.00 (ISBN 0-89130-587-4, 14 00 36). Scholars Pr CA.
Grad, Eli & Roth, Bette. Congregation Shaarey Zedek: 5622-5742 1861-1981. 198p. 1982. 25.00 (ISBN 0-8143-1713-8). Wayne St U Pr.
Hughley, Ella J. The Truth About Black Biblical Hebrew Israelites (Jews) (Orig.). 1982. pap. 5.00 (ISBN 0-9605150-1-1). Hughley Pubns.
Katzburg, Nathaniel. Hungary & the Jews: Policy & Legislation 1920-1943. 299p. 1981. 18.00 (ISBN 965-226-020-7). Hermon.
Leo Baeck Institute Yearbooks Index: Volumes I-XX, 1956-1975. 224p. 1982. 37.50 (ISBN 0-436-25541-3, Pub. by Secker & Warburg). David & Charles.
McCalden, David. Exiles from History. (Illus.). 40p. (Orig.). 1982. pap. 5.00 (ISBN 0-910607-00-1). D McCalden.
Paul, Louis. The Chosen Race. (Illus.). 111p. 1982. 6.95 (ISBN 0-9608890-1-9); pap. 4.96 (ISBN 0-9608890-0-0). L Paul Pub.
Rossel, Seymour. Journey Through Jewish History, Vol. II. (Illus.). 128p. (gr. 6). 1983. pap. text ed. 4.95 (ISBN 0-87441-366-4). Behrman.
Simonsohn, Shlomo. A History of the Jews in the Duchy of Mantua. (Illus.). 902p. 1977. text ed. 22.00 (ISBN 0-686-42970-2). K Sefer.
Wollman-Tsamir, Pinchas. The Graphic History of the Jewish Heritage. 224p. 1982. 22.50. Shengold.
JEWS–HISTORY–586 B.C.-70 A.D.
Reinhold, Meyer. Diaspora: The Jews Among the Greeks & Romans. (Illus.). 192p. 1983. 24.95 (ISBN 0-88866-619-5). Samuel Stevens.
JEWS–HISTORY–70-1789
Metzger, Therese & Metzger, Mendel. Jewish Life in the Middle Ages: Illuminated Hebrew Manuscripts of the Thirteenth to the Sixteenth Centuries. (Illus.). 316p. 85.00 (ISBN 0-933516-57-6). Alpine Fine Arts.
JEWS–INTELLECTUAL LIFE
Schwartz, Leo W., ed. Great Ages & Ideas of the Jewish People. 6.95 (ISBN 0-394-60413-X). Modern Lib.
JEWS–LAW
see Jewish Law
JEWS–LITERATURE
see Hebrew Literature
JEWS–LITURGY AND RITUAL
Fredman, Ruth G. The Passover Seder. 1982. pap. 5.95 (ISBN 0-452-00606-6, Mer). NAL.
JEWS–MARRIAGE
see Marriage–Jews
JEWS–MIGRATIONS
see also Jews–Diaspora
Mendelsohn, John. Jewish Emigration: The SS St. Louis Affair & Other Cases. LC 81-80315. (The Holocaust Ser.). 274p. 1982. lib. bdg. 50.00 (ISBN 0-8240-4881-4). Garland Pub.
--Jewish Emigration 1938-1940, Rublee Negotations & Intergovernmental Committee. LC 81-80314. (The Holocaust Ser.). 250p. 1982. lib. bdg. 50.00 (ISBN 0-8240-4880-6). Garland Pub.
Sachar, Abram. The Redemption of the Unwanted. 1983. 19.95 (ISBN 0-312-66729-9, Pub. by Marek). St Martin.
JEWS–POLITICAL AND SOCIAL CONDITIONS
see also Jews–Diaspora; Zionism
Elazar, Daniel J. Kinship & Consent: The Jewish Political Tradition & Its Contemporary Uses. LC 82-21851. 412p. 1983. lib. bdg. 24.75 (ISBN 0-8191-2800-7, Co-pub. by Ctr Jewish Comm Studies); pap. text ed. 13.75 (ISBN 0-8191-2801-5). U Pr of Amer.
JEWS–RELIGION
see Judaism
JEWS–RITUAL
see Jews–Liturgy and Ritual; Jews–Social Life and Customs
JEWS–SECTS
see Jewish Sects
JEWS–SOCIAL CONDITIONS
see Jews–Political and Social Conditions
JEWS–SOCIAL LIFE AND CUSTOMS
see also Jewish Way of Life
Cohen, Steven M. & Hyman, Paula, eds. The Evolving Jewish Family. 256p. 1983. text ed. 30.00x (ISBN 0-8419-0860-5). Holmes & Meier.
Heilman, Samuel C. The People of the Book: Drama, Fellowship, & Religion. LC 82-13369. 264p. 1983. lib. bdg. 22.50x (ISBN 0-226-32492-3). U of Chicago Pr.
JEWS–WOMEN
see Women, Jewish
JEWS–ZIONISM
see Zionism
JEWS IN ENGLAND
see Jews in Great Britain
JEWS IN EUROPE
Mendelsohn, Ezra. The Jews of East Central Europe Between the World Wars. LC 81-48676. (Illus.). 320p. 1983. 27.50x (ISBN 0-253-33160-9). Ind U Pr.
JEWS IN FOLK-LORE
see Folk-Lore, Jewish
JEWS IN FOREIGN COUNTRIES
see Jews–Diaspora
JEWS IN FRANCE
Marrus, Michael R. & Paxton, Robert O. Vichy France & the Jews. LC 82-16869. 432p. (Orig.). 1983. pap. 12.95 (ISBN 0-8052-0741-4). Schocken.
Schnapper, Dominique. Jewish Identities in France: An Analysis of Contmporary French Jewry. Goldhammer, Arthur, tr. LC 82-17495. (Illus.). 224p. 1983. lib. bdg. 25.00x (ISBN 0-226-73910-4). U of Chicago Pr.
JEWS IN GREAT BRITAIN
Kokosalakis, N. Ethnic Identity & Religion: Tradition & Change in Liverpool Jewry. LC 82-13609. (Illus.). 276p. 1983. lib. bdg. 23.50 (ISBN 0-8191-2732-9); pap. text ed. 11.50 (ISBN 0-8191-2733-7). U Pr of Amer.
JEWS IN ITALY
Hughes, H. Stuart. Prisoners of Hope: The Silver Age of the Italian Jews, 1924-1974. 184p. 1983. text ed. 15.00x (ISBN 0-674-70727-3). Harvard U Pr.
JEWS IN LITERATURE
Stern, Menahem, ed. Greek & Latin Authors on Jews & Judaism: From Herodotus to Plutarch, Vol. 1. 576p. 1981. Repr. text ed. 43.75x (ISBN 965-208-035-7, Pub. by Brill Holland). Humanities.
JEWS IN LITHUANIA
Levin, Dov. Lithuanian Jewry's Armed Resistance to the Nazis. 224p. 1983. text ed. 35.00x (ISBN 0-8419-0831-1). Holmes & Meier.
JEWS IN MEXICO
Liebman, Seymour. The Enlightened. 1967. pap. 6.95 (ISBN 0-87024-311-X). U of Miami Pr.
JEWS IN POLAND
Krakowski, Shmuel. The War of the Doomed: Jewish Armed Resistance in Poland, 1942-1944. 250p. 1983. text ed. 35.00x (ISBN 0-8419-0851-6); pap. text ed. 18.50x (ISBN 0-8419-0852-4). Holmes & Meier.
JEWS IN RUSSIA
Goldberg, Ben Z. The Jewish Problem in the Soviet Union: Analysis & Solution. LC 82-15842. (Illus.). x, 374p. 1982. Repr. of 1961 ed. lib. bdg. 45.00x (ISBN 0-313-23692-5, GOJE). Greenwood.
Stanislawski, Michael. Tsar Nicholas I & the Jews: The Transformation of Jewish Society in Russia, 1825-1855. (Illus.). 320p. 1983. 17.95 (ISBN 0-8276-0216-2). Jewish Pubn.
JEWS IN THE NETHERLANDS
Gans, Mozes Heiman. Memorbook: Pictorial History of Dutch Jewry from the Renaissance to 1940. (Illus.). 852p. 1983. 75.00. Wayne St U Pr.
JEWS IN THE UNITED STATES
Farb, Milton H. & Singer, David, eds. American Jewish Year Book, Vol. 83. 450p. 1982. 23.50 (ISBN 0-8276-0221-9). Jewish Pubn.
Halpern, Ben. The American Jew: A Zionistic Analysis. LC 82-16875. 192p. 1983. pap. 6.95 (ISBN 0-8052-0742-2). Schocken.
Moore, Deborah D. At Home in America: Second Generation New York Jews. (Illus.). 320p. 1983. pap. 10.00 (ISBN 0-231-05063-1). Columbia U Pr.
JEWS IN THE UNITED STATES - BIBLIOGRAPHY
The Jewish Experience in America: A Historical Bibliography. 190p. 1982. lib. bdg. 23.50 (ISBN 0-87436-034-X). ABC-Clio.
JEWS IN THE UNITED STATES–HISTORY
Friedman, Murray, ed. Jewish Life in Philadelphia, 1830-1940. (Illus.). 320p. 1983. 19.95 (ISBN 0-89727-050-9). Inst Study Human.
The Jewish Experience in America: A Historical Bibliography. 190p. 1982. lib. bdg. 23.50 (ISBN 0-87436-034-X). ABC-Clio.
Turitz, Leo & Turitz, Evelyn. Jews in Early Mississippi. LC 82-25093. (Illus.). 144p. (Orig.). 1983. 20.00x (ISBN 0-87805-178-3). U Pr of Miss.
JEWS IN THE UNITED STATES–POLITICAL AND SOCIAL CONDITIONS
Zweigenhaft. Jews in Protestant Establishment. 144p. 1982. 23.95 (ISBN 0-03-062607-2); pap. 10.95 (ISBN 0-03-062606-4). Praeger.
JEWS IN THE UNITED STATES–SOCIAL LIFE AND CUSTOMS
Shepard, Ricahrd F. & Levi, Vicki G. Live & Be Well: A Celebration of Yiddish Culture in America from the First Immigrants to the Second World War. (Illus.). 192p. Date not set. price not set (ISBN 0-345-30752-6); pap. 9.95 (ISBN 0-345-29435-1). Ballantine.
JIG (MECHANICAL DEVICE)
see Jigs and Fixtures
JIGS AND FIXTURES
U. S. Plumbing Fixtures & Fittings. 1982. 995.00 (ISBN 0-686-37719-2, 286). Predicasts.
JITNEY BUSES
see Motor Buses
JIU-JITSU
see also Judo
Kirby, George. Jujitsu: Basic Techniques of the Gentle Art. (Illus., Orig.). 1983. pap. 6.95 (ISBN 0-89750-088-1, 425). Ohara Pubns.
JOACHIM, JOSEPH, 1831-1907
Bickley, Nora. Letters from & to Joseph Joachim. Bickley, Nora, tr. LC 70-183496. 470p. Date not set. Repr. of 1914 ed. price not set. Vienna Hse.
JOB, A SLAVE
Vawter, Bruce. Job & Jonah: Questioning the Hidden God. LC 82-62413. 1983. pap. 5.95 (ISBN 0-8091-2524-2). Paulist Pr.
JOB APPLICATIONS
see Applications for Positions
JOB ANALYSIS
see also Job Evaluation
Gael, Sidney. Job Analysis: A Guide to Assessing Work Activities. LC 82-49036. (Management & Social & Behavioral Science Ser.). 1983. text ed. price not set (ISBN 0-87589-564-6). Jossey-Bass.
Zemke, Ron & Kramlinger, Thomas. Figuring Things Out: A Trainer's Guide to Needs & Tasks Analysis. LC 81-12805. (Illus.). 352p. Date not set. text ed. 27.50 (ISBN 0-201-09098-8). A-w.
JOB DISCRIMINATION
see Discrimination in Employment
JOB EVALUATION
see also Job Analysis
House, Ernest R. & Mathison, Sandra, eds. Evaluation Studies Review Annual, 1982, Vol. 7. LC 76-15865. 736p. 1982. 37.50 (ISBN 0-8039-0386-3). Sage.
Olmstead, Barney & Smith, Suzanne. Job Sharing Handbook. 1983. pap. 6.95 (ISBN 0-14-046544-8). Penguin.
JOB OPENINGS
see Job Vacancies
JOB PERFORMANCE STANDARDS
see Performance Standards
JOB RATING
see Job Evaluation
JOB RESUMES
see Applications for Positions; Resumes (Employment)
JOB SATISFACTION
Hegarty, Christopher & Goldberg, Philip. How to Manage Your Boss. 312p. 1982. pap. 9.95 (ISBN 0-931432-15-4). Whatever Pub.
Hopkins, Anne E. Work & Job Satisfaction in the Public Sector. 160p. 1983. text ed. 25.00x (ISBN 0-86598-111-6). Allanheld.
Sell, R. G. & Shipley, Patricia, eds. Satisfactions in Work Design: Ergonomics & Other Approaches. LC 79-311845. 202p. 1979. 25.00x (ISBN 0-85066-180-3). Intl Pubns Serv.
Toch, Hans & Grant, J. Douglas. Change Through Participation: Humanizing Human Service Settings. (Library of Social Research). (Illus.). 240p. 1982. 22.00 (ISBN 0-8039-1886-0); pap. 10.95 (ISBN 0-8039-1887-9). Sage.
JOB TRAINING
see Occupational Training
JOB VACANCIES
Aves, Diane K. & Anderson, Debra. Planning Your Job Search: Making the Right Moves. 84p. 1982. 9.75 (ISBN 0-88440-036-0). Sis Kenny Inst.
How to Steal a Job. 11.95 (ISBN 0-930566-03-3). FMA Bus.
Marcon, Mike. The TNT Job Getting System. Taylor, Margot W., ed. 128p. (Orig.). 1983. 9.95 (ISBN 0-911529-00-4). Worthington Co.
JOBS
see Occupations; Professions
JOHN, SAINT, APOSTLE
Dine, Jim, illus. Apocalypse: The Revelation of Saint John, the Divine. (Illus.). 64p. 1982. 1500.00 (ISBN 0-910457-00-X). Arion Pr.
Meinardus, Otto F. St. John of Patmos & the Seven Churches of the Apocalypse. (In the Footsteps of the Saints Ser.). 160p. 15.00 (ISBN 0-89241-070-1); pap. 5.95 (ISBN 0-89241-043-4). Caratzas Bros.
Schonle, Volker. Johannes, Jesus und die Juden. 288p. (Ger.). 1982. write for info. (ISBN 3-8204-5877-8). P Lang Pubs.
JOHN HENRY
Williams, Brett. John Henry: A Bio-Bibliography. LC 82-12056. (Popular Culture Bio-Bibliographies Ser.). 192p. 1983. lib. bdg. 29.95 (ISBN 0-313-22250-9, WJH/). Greenwood.
JOHN PAUL 2ND, POPE
DiFranco, Anthony. Pope John Paul II: Bringing Love to a Troubled World. Schneider, Thomas, ed. (Taking Part Ser.). (Illus.). 48p. (gr. 3 up). 1983. PLB 7.95 (ISBN 0-87518-241-0). Dillon Pr.
Hebblethwaite, P. & Kaufmann, L. Juan Pablo II: Una Biografia Ilustrada. 1980. pap. 7.95 (ISBN 0-07-033422-6). McGraw.
JOHN THE BAPTIST, SAINT, ca. 5 B.C.-ca. 30 A.D.
Dallison, Dennis. Reflections of My Life: The Apology of John the Baptist. Norman, Ruth, ed. 77p. (Orig.). 1982. pap. text ed. 2.50 (ISBN 0-932642-75-6). Unarius.
St. John Chrysostom. Sermon on the Decollation of St. John the Baptist, & on Herodias, & on Good & Evil Women. (Early Slavic Literatures, Studies, Texts, & Seminar Materials: Vol. 3). Orig. Title: V 29 den' mesiatsa avgusta slovo Ioanna Zlatoustogo na useknovenie glavy. 45p. (Church Slavic & Gr.). 1982. pap. 4.00 (ISBN 0-933884-23-0). Berkeley Slavic.
JOHNSON, BEN CAMPBELL
Brock, D. Heyward. A Ben Jonson Companion. LC 81-48383. 320p. 1983. 25.00x (ISBN 0-253-31159-4). Ind U Pr.
JOHNSON, JACK
Roberts, Randy. Papa Jack: Jack Johnson & the Era of White Hopes. LC 82-49017. 288p. 1983. 14.95 (ISBN 0-686-84093-3). Free Pr.
JOHNSON, LYNDON BAINES, PRES. U. S., 1908-1973
Casoni, Jennifer. Sincerely, Lyndon: The Handwriting of Lyndon Baines Johnson. 100p. (Orig.). 1983. pap. 14.95 (ISBN 0-9608816-1-1). Univ Autograph.
JOHNSON, UWE, 1934-
Hirsch, Marianne. Beyond the Single Version: Henry James, Michael Butor, Uwe Johnson. 18.00 (ISBN 0-917786-21-1). French Lit.
JOINTS
Beighton, P., et al. Hypermobility of Joints. (Illus.). 105p. 1983. 44.00 (ISBN 0-387-12113-7). Springer-Verlag.
Gooch. Behavior of Joints in High Temperature Materials. Date not set. 53.30 (ISBN 0-85334-187-7). Elsevier.
Himalayan International Institute. Joints & Glands Exercises. 2nd ed. Ballentine, Rudolph M., ed. (Illus.). 90p. (Orig.). 1982. pap. 3.95 (ISBN 0-89389-083-9). Himalayan Intl Inst.
Jones, Peter. Fasteners, Joints & Adhesives: A Guide to Engineering Solid Constructions. 416p. 1983. 24.95 (ISBN 0-13-307694-6); pap. 14.95 (ISBN 0-13-307686-5). P-H.
JOINTS–RADIOGRAPHY
Goldman, Amy Beth & Dines, David M. Shoulder Arthrography. Goldman, Amy Beth, ed. (Little, Brown Library in Radiology). 1982. text ed. 42.50 (ISBN 0-316-31931-7). Little.
JOKES
see Wit and Humor
JONAH, THE PROPHET
Briscoe, Jill. Jonah & Little Worm. 120p. 1983. 6.95 (ISBN 0-8407-5289-X). Nelson.
Champion, Vici. Yet Forty Days. 1982. 6.95 (ISBN 0-533-05443-5). Vantage.
Couchman, Bob & Couchman, Win. Ruth & Jonah: People in Process. (Carpenter Studyguides Ser.). 64p. 1983. saddle-stiched members' handbk. 1.95 (ISBN 0-87788-736-5); leader's handbook 2.95 (ISBN 0-87788-737-3). Shaw Pubs.
Ferguson, Sinclair. Man Overboard. 1982. pap. 3.95 (ISBN 0-8423-4015-7). Tyndale.
Vawter, Bruce. Job & Jonah: Questioning the Hidden God. LC 82-62413. 1983. pap. 5.95 (ISBN 0-8091-2524-2). Paulist Pr.
JONAH, THE PROPHET–JUVENILE LITERATURE
Storr, Catherine & Bennett, Russell, eds. Jonah & the Whale. LC 82-23023. (People of the Bible Ser.). (Illus.). 32p. (gr. 1-2). 1983. PLB 11.55 (ISBN 0-8172-1984-6). Raintree Pubs.

JONES, JOHN PAUL, 1747-1792
Urquhart, James. John Paul Jones: Bicentennial Salute & Souvenir from Great Britain. (Illus.). 140p. (Orig.). 1982. pap. 18.00x (ISBN 0-9507033-4-6). J Russell.

JONES, JOHN PAUL, 1747-1792–JUVENILE LITERATURE
Brandt, Keith. John Paul Jones: Hero of the Seas. LC 82-16045. (Illus.). 48p. (gr. 4-6). 1983. PLB 6.89 (ISBN 0-89375-849-3); pap. text ed. 1.95 (ISBN 0-89375-850-7). Troll Assocs.

JORDAN
Mostyn, Trevor, ed. Jordan: A Middle East Economic Digest Guide. 240p. (Orig.). 1983. pap. write for info. (ISBN 0-7103-0029-8, Kegan Paul). Routledge & Kegan.

JORN, ASGER OLUF, 1914-
Anderson, Troels & Atkins, Guy. Asger Jorn. LC 82-60792. (Illus.). 98p. 1982. pap. 9.00 (ISBN 0-89207-034-X). S R Guggenheim.

JOSEPH, THE PATRIARCH
Getz, Gene A. Joseph: From Prison to Palace. LC 82-18571. 1983. pap. 4.95 (ISBN 0-8307-0870-7, 5417907). Regal.

JOSEPH BONAPARTE, KING OF SPAIN, 1768-1844
Abbott, John S. History of Joseph Bonaparte: King of Naples & Italy. 391p. Repr. of 1869 ed. lib. bdg. 30.00 (ISBN 0-686-82064-9). Darby Bks.

JOSHUA, SON OF NUN
Girzone, Joseph F. Joshua. 320p. 1983. 11.95 (ISBN 0-911519-03-3). Richelieu Court.

JOURNALISM
see also College and School Journalism; Government and the Press; Journalism, Medical; Journalism, Pictorial; Liberty of the Press; News-Letters; Newspaper Publishing; Newspapers; Periodicals; Press; Radio Journalism; Reporters and Reporting; Sports Journalism; Television Broadcasting of News
Chancellor, John & Mears, Walter R. The News Business: Getting & Writing the News as Two Top Journalists Do It. LC 82-48126. 224p. 1983. 12.95 (ISBN 0-06-015104-8, HarpT). Har-Row.
Copperud, Roy H. & Nelson, Roy P. Editing the News. 300p. 1983. pap. text ed. write for info. (ISBN 0-697-04353-3). Wm C Brown.
Douglass, Frederick. Frederick Douglass: The Narrative & Selected Writings. 1981. pap. 4.95 (ISBN 0-686-38904-2, Mod LibC). Modern Lib.
Edward R. Murrow Papers, 1927-1965. 38p. 1982. reference bk. 25.00 (ISBN 0-667-00669-9). Microfilming Corp.
Jacobi, Peter. Writing with Style: The News Story & the Feature. LC 82-62576. (Communications Library). 111p. (Orig.). 1982. pap. 15.00 (ISBN 0-931368-12-X). Ragan Comm.
Mencher, Melvin. Basic News Writing. 350p. 1983. pap. text ed. write for info. (ISBN 0-697-04354-1); instr's. manual avail. (ISBN 0-697-04358-4); student wkbk. avail. (ISBN 0-697-04357-6). Wm C Brown.
Murray, Donald. Writing for Readers: Notes on the Writer's Craft from the Boston Globe. (Illus.). 160p. (Orig.). 1983. pap. 8.95 (ISBN 0-87106-975-X). Globe Pequot.
Porter, William E. The Italian Journalist. 256p. 1983. text ed. 18.00 (ISBN 0-472-10028-9). U of Mich Pr.
The Press: Free & Responsible? (Symposia Ser.). 114p. 1982. 7.95 (ISBN 0-89940-411-1). LBJ Sch Pub Aff.
Saling, Ann. Article Writing: A Creative Challenge. 208p. 1982. pap. 7.50 (ISBN 0-910455-00-7). ANSAL Pr.
Smeyak, Paul. Broadcast News Writing. 2nd ed. LC 82-9293. (Grid Series in Advertising & Journalism). 300p. 1983. pap. text ed. 11.95 (ISBN 0-686-42906-0). Grid Pub.
Syndicated Columnists Directory. 30.00 (ISBN 0-913046-14-0). Public Relations.
Weaver, David H. Videotex Journalism: Teletext, Viewdata, & the News. 160p. 1983. text ed. write for info. (ISBN 0-89859-263-1). L Erlbaum Assocs.

JOURNALISM–BIOGRAPHY
see Journalists

JOURNALISM–HANDBOOKS, MANUALS, ETC.
Cappon, Rene J & Associated Press. The Associated Press Guide to Newswriting. 196p. 1982. pap. 7.95 (ISBN 0-201-10320-6). A-W.
Schraeger, Sam. Breaking In: A Beginner's Guide to News Writing for Print & Radio. 72p. (Orig.). pap. text ed. 6.95 (ISBN 0-9609268-0-1). H & S Pub Co.

JOURNALISM–POLITICAL ASPECTS
Clarke, Peter & Evans, Susan H. Covering Campaigns: Journalism in Congressional Elections. LC 82-60738. 168p. 1983. 17.95x (ISBN 0-8047-1159-3). Stanford U Pr.

JOURNALISM–VOCATIONAL GUIDANCE
Teel, Leonard R. & Taylor, Ron. Into the Newsroom: An Introduction to Journalism. (Illus.). 224p. 1983. 14.95 (ISBN 0-13-477133-8); pap. 7.95 (ISBN 0-13-477125-7). P-H.

JOURNALISM–UNITED STATES
Rubin, Richard L. Press, Party, & Presidency. 1981. pap. text ed. 6.95x (ISBN 0-393-95206-1). Norton.
--Press, Party, & Presidency. (Illus.). 1982. 18.95 (ISBN 0-393-01497-5). Norton.

JOURNALISM, MEDICAL
Publishing a Professional Journal: An Editor's Guide. 15.00 (ISBN 0-934510-21-0, K022). Am Dental.

JOURNALISM, PICTORIAL
see also Photography, Journalistic
Photojournalism. LC 82-19149. (Life Library of Photography). lib. bdg. 22.60 (ISBN 0-8094-4429-1, Pub. by Time-Life). Silver.

JOURNALISTIC PHOTOGRAPHY
see Photography, Journalistic

JOURNALISTS
see also Journalism–Vocational Guidance; Women Journalists
Cavett, Dick & Porterfield, Christopher. Eye on Cavett. (Illus.). 1983. 15.95 (ISBN 0-87795-463-1). Arbor Hse.
Directory of the American Society of Journalists & Authors, 1981-82. 1982. 40.00 (ISBN 0-686-82230-7). Educ Indus.
Phelan, James. Scandals, Scamps, & Scoundrels: The Casebook of An Investigative Reporter. 1982. 13.95 (ISBN 0-394-48196-8). Random.
Straight, Michael. After Long Silence. (Illus.). 1983. 17.50 (ISBN 0-393-01729-X). Norton.
Thomas, Norman & Wilson, Edmund. Who Killed Carlo Tresca? Mope, Warren, ed. 36p. 1983. pap. 3.95x (ISBN 0-911687-00-9). Mountain Laurel.
Wallraff, Gunter. Wallraff: The Undesirable Journalist. Gooch, Steve & Knight, Paul, trs. LC 78-70935. 192p. pap. 6.95 (ISBN 0-87951-169-9). Overlook Pr.

JOURNALISTS–CORRESPONDENCE, REMINISCENCES, ETC.
see also subdivision Personal Narratives under names of Wars, e.g. World War, 1939-1945–Personal Narratives
Blishen, Edward. A Back-Handed War. 224p. 1983. pap. 14.95 (ISBN 0-241-10919-1, Pub. by Hamish Hamilton England). David & Charles.
--Uncommon Entrance. 192p. 1983. pap. 14.95 (ISBN 0-241-10920-5, Pub. by Hamish Hamilton England). David & Charles.
Brady, James. The Press Lord. 1983. pap. 3.95 (ISBN 0-440-17080-X). Dell.
Broun, Heywood H. Whose Little Boy Are You? A Memoir of the Broun Family. (Illus.). 1983. 13.95 (ISBN 0-312-87765-X, Pub. by Marek). St Martin.
Campbell, Tom. The Contemplative Stroller. (Illus.). 96p. 1982. pap. 4.95 (ISBN 0-9607506-1-4). News Rev Pub.
China: An Uncensored Look. LC 79-63789. 254p. 1983. pap. 4.95 (ISBN 0-933256-41-8). Second Chance.
Chorley, Henry F. Thirty Years' Musical Recollections. Newman, Ernest, ed. LC 77-183330. 411p. Date not set. Repr. of 1926 ed. price not set. Vienna Hse.
Hall, Bill, ed. Bill Hall & the Killer Chicken. (Illus.). 102p. 1981. pap. 4.95 (ISBN 0-9607506-0-6). News Rev Pub.
Hollis, Daniel W., III. An Alabama Newspaper Tradition: Grover C. Hall & the Hall Family. (Illus.). 224p. 1983. text ed. 19.95 (ISBN 0-8173-0136-4). U of Ala Pr.
Perreault, Robert B. La Presse Franco-Americaine et la Politique: L'Oeuvre de Charles-Roger Daoust. (Illus., Fr.). pap. text ed. 3.50 (ISBN 0-911409-39-4). Natl Mat Dev.
Reasoner, Harry. Before the Colors Fade. LC 82-16685. 206p. 1983. pap. 5.95 (ISBN 0-688-01544-1). Quill NY.
Salisbury, Harrison. Journey for Our Times: A Memoir. LC 81-47904. (Bessie Bks.). 416p. 1983. 18.75i (ISBN 0-06-039006-9, HarpT). Har-Row.
Solomon, Barbara P. Short Flights. 348p. 1983. 18.75 (ISBN 0-670-33053-1). Viking Pr.

JOURNALS (MACHINERY)
see Bearings (Machinery)

JOURNEYS
see Voyages and Travels

JOY AND SORROW
see also Happiness
Draper, James T., Jr. Discover Joy: Studies in Philippians. 1983. pap. 4.95 (ISBN 0-8423-0606-4); leader's guide 2.95 (ISBN 0-8423-0607-2). Tyndale.
Moncure, Jane B. Joy. (What is It? Ser.). (Illus.). 32p. (gr. k-3). 1982. PLB 6.50 (ISBN 0-89565-224-2). Communication Skill.

JOYCE, JAMES, 1882-1941
Benstock, B., ed. Poems for James Joyce. 47p. 1981. pap. text ed. 4.25x (ISBN 0-905261-04-6, 51407, Pub. by Malton Pr Ireland). Humanities.
O'Brien, Darcy. The Conscience of James Joyce. 274p. 1983. Repr. of 1968 ed. 13.50 (ISBN 0-87752-221-9). Gordian.
Peterson, Richard F., et al, eds. Work in Progress: Joyce Centenary Essays. 192p. 1983. 15.95x (ISBN 0-8093-1094-5). S Ill U Pr.
White, David A. The Grand Continuum: Reflections on Joyce & Metaphysics. LC 82-4740. (Critical Essays in Modern Literature). 208p. 1983. text ed. 19.95x (ISBN 0-8229-3803-0). U of Pittsburgh Pr.

JUAN, DON
Perl, William R. Operation Action: Rescue from the Holocaust. 1983. 16.95 (ISBN 0-8044-1725-3); pap. 9.95 (ISBN 0-8044-6645-9). Ungar.

JUDAEO-GERMAN
see Yiddish Language

JUDAICA
see Jews

JUDAISM
Here are entered works on Jewish faith and practice in which the main stream of orthodox Judaism is treated and no cleavage is stressed.
see also Cabala; Commandments, Ten; Jesus Christ–Jewish Interpretations; Jewish Theology; Jews; Reform Judaism
Aviad, Janet. Return to Judaism: Religious Renewal in Israel. LC 82-17663. 208p. 1983. lib. bdg. 20.00x (ISBN 0-226-03236-1). U of Chicago Pr.
Greenstein, Howard R. Judaism: An Eternal Covenant. LC 82-17601. 208p. 1983. pap. 9.95 (ISBN 0-8006-1690-1, 1-1690). Fortress.
Joy, Donald M., ed. Moral Development Foundations: Judeo-Christian Alternatives to Piaget-Kohlberg. 240p. (Orig.). 1983. pap. 12.95 (ISBN 0-687-27177-0). Abingdon.
Porton, Gary G. The Traditions of Rabbi Ishmael, Pt. IV: The Material as a Whole. (Studies in Judaism in Late Antiquity: Vol. 19). xiv, 261p. 1982. write for info. (ISBN 90-04-06414-1). E J Brill.
Segal, Abraham. One People: A Study in Comparative Judaism. Zlotowitz, Bernard M., ed. 160p. (Orig.). (gr. 7-9). 1983. pap. text ed. 6.95 (ISBN 0-8074-0169-2, 140025). UAHC.
Wyschogrod, Michael. The Body of Faith: The Corporeal Election of Israel. 320p. (Orig.). 1983. pap. price not set (ISBN 0-8164-2479-9). Seabury.

JUDAISM–HISTORY
Davies, W. D. Jewish & Pauline Studies. LC 82-48620. 432p. 1983. text ed. 29.95 (ISBN 0-8006-0694-9). Fortress.
Joseph, Howard, et al, eds. Truth & Compassion: Essays on Judaism & Religion for Rabbi Dr. Solomon Frank at Eighty. 250p. 1982. text ed. 11.50x (ISBN 0-919812-17-1, 40948, Pub. by Laurier U Pr). Humanities.
Lilker, Shalom. Kibbutz Judaism: A New Tradition in the Making. (Kibbutz, Cooperative Society, & Alternative Social Policy Ser.: Vol. 7). 264p. 1982. lib. bdg. 14.95 (ISBN 0-8482-4876-7). Norwood Edns.
Neusner, Jacob. Ancient Israel after Catastrophe: The Religious World View of the Mishnah. LC 82-15972. 1983. write for info. (ISBN 0-8139-0980-5). U Pr of Va.
--Formative Judaism. LC 82-16746. (Brown Judaic Studies). 182p. 1982. pap. 13.50 (ISBN 0-89130-594-7, 14 00 37). Scholars Pr CA.
Nickelsburg, George W. & Stone, Michael E. Faith & Piety in Early Judaism: Texts & Documents. LC 82-71830. 272p. 1983. 19.95 (ISBN 0-8006-0679-5). Fortress.
Rausch, David A. Messianic Judaism: Its History, Theology, & Polity. (Texts & Studies in Religion: Vol. 14). 304p. 1983. 39.95x (ISBN 0-88946-802-8). E Mellen.
Sanders, E. P. Paul, the Law & the Jewish People. LC 82-17487. 240p. 1983. 19.95 (ISBN 0-8006-0698-1, 1-698). Fortress.

JUDAISM–JUVENILE LITERATURE
Bogot, Howard. Yoni. 1982. pap. 4.00 (ISBN 0-686-82564-0). UAHC.
Saypol, Judyth & Wikler, Madeline. My Very Own Haggadah. Rev. ed. (Illus.). 32p. (ps-4). pap. text ed. 2.50 (ISBN 0-930494-23-7). Kar Ben.

JUDAISM–LITURGY AND RITUAL
see Jews–Liturgy and Ritual

JUDAISM–REFORM MOVEMENT
see Reform Judaism

JUDAISM–RELATIONS–CHRISTIANITY
Friedman, Jerome. The Most Ancient Testimony: Sixteenth-Century Christian-Hebraica in the Age of Renaissance Nostalgia. LC 82-18830. x, 279p. 1983. text ed. 24.95 (ISBN 0-8214-0700-7, 82-84697). Ohio U Pr.

JUDAISM, ORTHODOX
see Orthodox Judaism

JUDAISM, REFORM
see Reform Judaism

JUDAISM AND CHRISTIANITY
see Christianity and Other Religions–Judaism

JUDGES
see also Courts; Judicial Process; Justice, Administration of; Women Lawyers
Brooks, Terrance V. & Stewart, Tamara A., eds. Judicial Discipline & Disability Digest: 1980 Supplement. LC 81-65601. 256p. 1983. 95.00 (ISBN 0-938870-29-7); lib. bdg. 50.00. Am Judicature.
Browne, Irving. Short Studies of Great Lawyers. iv, 382p. 1982. Repr. of 1878 ed. lib. bdg. 30.00x (ISBN 0-8377-0330-1). Rothman.

JUDGMENT DAY
see also Second Advent
Brown, Vinson, et al. Prevent Doomsday! new ed. (Illus.). 96p. 1983. pap. 4.95 (ISBN 0-8283-1875-1). Branden.
Campbell, Roger F. A Place to Hide. 108p. 1983. pap. 3.95 (ISBN 0-88207-383-4). Victor Bks.

JUDGMENTS BY PEERS
see Jury

JUDICIAL BEHAVIOR
see Judicial Process

JUDICIAL DECISION-MAKING
see Judicial Process

JUDICIAL INVESTIGATIONS
see Governmental Investigations

JUDICIAL PROCESS
see also Evidence (Law); Law–Interpretation and Construction
Carp, Robert A. & Rowland, C. K. Policymaking & Politics in the Federal District Courts. LC 82-13462. (Illus.). 256p. 1983. text ed. 17.95x (ISBN 0-87049-369-8). U of Tenn Pr.
Dubois, Philip, ed. Judicial Reform. (Orig.). 1982. pap. 6.00 (ISBN 0-918592-56-9). Policy Studies.
Lauffer, Armand. Assessment Tools: For Practitioners, Managers & Trainers. (Sage Human Services Guides: Vol. 30). 172p. 1982. pap. 8.50 (ISBN 0-8039-1007-X). Sage.
Levin, A. Leo, ed. The American Judiciary: Critical Issues. Wheeler, Russell R. (The Annals of the American Academy of Political & Social Science: Vol. 462). 224p. 1982. 15.00 (ISBN 0-8039-1852-6); pap. 7.95 (ISBN 0-8039-1853-4). Sage.
Mooney, Christopher F. Inequality & the American Conscience: Justice Through the Judicial System. (Woodstock Studies). 144p. 1983. pap. 5.95 (ISBN 0-8091-2500-5). Paulist Pr.

JUDICIAL REVIEW
see also Legislative Power
Redish, Martin H. Federal Courts: Cases, Comments & Questions. LC 82-24763. 871p. 1983. text ed. 24.95 (ISBN 0-314-71146-5). West Pub.

JUDICIARY
see Courts

JUDO
see also Karate
Glass, George. Your Book of Judo. (Your Book Of...Ser.). (Illus.). 80p. (gr. 3-6). 1977. 8.95 (ISBN 0-571-11054-1). Faber & Faber.
Judo Rulebook, 1978-1980. Date not set. 3.50 (ISBN 0-686-43035-2). AAU Pubns.

JUGENDSTIL
see Art Nouveau

JUJITSU
see Jiu-Jitsu

JULY FOURTH
see Fourth of July

JUMPING
Martin, David E., et al. The High Jump Book. (Illus.). 158p. Date not set. pap. 8.95 (ISBN 0-911521-09-7). Tafnews.

JUNG, CARL GUSTAV, 1875-1961
Babcock, Winifred. Jung, Hesse, Harold: Contributions of C. G. Jung, Hermann Hesse, and Preston Harold to Spiritual Psychology. LC 83-12945. 1983. 14.95 (ISBN 0-396-08082-0); pap. 8.95 (ISBN 0-396-08113-4). Dodd.
Clift, Wallace B. Jung & Christianity: The Challenge of Reconciliation. 192p. 1983. pap. 6.95 (ISBN 0-8245-0552-2). Crossroad NY.
Kafka, Franz. The Basic Writings of C. G. Jung. Muir, Willa & Muir, Edwin, trs. LC 52-9771. 6.95 (ISBN 0-394-60422-9). Modern Lib.
Martin, P. W. Experiment in Depth: A Study of the Work of Jung, Eliot & Toynbee. 275p. 1982. Repr. of 1955 ed. lib. bdg. 40.00 (ISBN 0-89987-649-8). Darby Bks.
Rollins, Wayne G. Jung & The Bible. LC 82-48091. 156p. 1983. pap. 9.50 (ISBN 0-8042-1117-5). John Knox.
Stein, Murray, ed. Jungian Analysis. 1982. 19.95 (ISBN 0-87548-350-X). Open Court.
Storr, Anthony, ed. The Essential Jung. LC 82-61441. 375p. Date not set. 35.00x (ISBN 0-691-08615-X); pap. 9.95 (ISBN 0-691-02455-3). Princeton U Pr.
Wood, Douglas K. Men Against Time: Nicolas Berdyaev, T. S. Eliot, Aldous Huxley, & C. G. Jung. LC 82-526. x, 254p. 1982. text ed. 22.50x (ISBN 0-7006-0222-4). Univ Pr KS.

JUNIOR COLLEGES
see also Community Colleges
Ward, Phebe. Terminal Education in the Junior College. 282p. 1982. Repr. of 1947 ed. lib. bdg. 30.00 (ISBN 0-8495-5662-7). Arden Lib.

JUNIPERO, FRAY
see Serra, Junipero, Father, 1713-1784

JUNK
see Waste Products

JUNK MAIL
see Advertising–Direct-Mail

JUPITER (PLANET)
Munro, Alice. The Moons of Jupiter. LC 82-48734. 233p. 1983. 12.95 (ISBN 0-394-52952-9). Knopf.

JURIDICAL PSYCHOLOGY
see Psychology, Forensic

JURISDICTION (INTERNATIONAL LAW)
see also Arbitration, International
Institute for the Study of Conflict, London. Annual of Power & Conflict, 1981-82. 11th ed. LC 77-370326. 485p. 1982. 77.50x (ISBN 0-8002-3061-2). Intl Pubns Serv.

JURISPRUDENCE
see also Law; Law–Philosophy; Law and Politics; Public Law; Sociological Jurisprudence
Lightwood, John M. The Nature of Positive Law. xiv, 419p. 1982. Repr. of 1883 ed. lib. bdg. 35.00x (ISBN 0-8377-0814-1). Rothman.
Wortley, Ben A. Jurisprudence. LC 66-29259. 473p. 1967. 19.00 (ISBN 0-379-00323-6). Oceana.

JURISPRUDENCE, COMPARATIVE
see Comparative Law

JURISPRUDENCE, DENTAL
see Dental Jurisprudence

JURISPRUDENCE, MEDICAL
see Medical Jurisprudence

JURISTIC PSYCHOLOGY
see Psychology, Forensic
JURISTS
see Lawyers
JURY
see also Instructions to Juries
Committee on Jury Standards & American Bar Association. Standards Relating to Juror Use & Management. 196p. 1982. 10.00 (ISBN 0-89656-063-5). Natl Ctr St Courts.
Elwork, Amiram & Sales, Bruce D. Making Jury Instructions Understandable. 300p. 1982. 35.00 (ISBN 0-87215-450-5). Michie-Bobbs.
JUSTICE
see also Due Process of Law
Abel, Alan. Don't Get Mad...Get Even! A Manual for Retaliation. (Illus.). 1983. 10.95 (ISBN 0-393-01614-5); pap. 4.95 (ISBN 0-393-30118-4). Norton.
Atkinson, A. B. Social Justice & Public Policy. 480p. 1982. 37.50x (ISBN 0-262-01067-4). MIT Pr.
Fishkin, James S. Justice, Equal Opportunity & the Family. LC 82-10939. 208p. 1983. text ed. 18.95x (ISBN 0-300-02865-2). Yale U Pr.
Gray, John N. Mill on Liberty: A Defence. (International Library of Philosophy). 120p. 1983. 17.95 (ISBN 0-7100-9270-9). Routledge & Kegan.
Machan, Tibor R. & Johnson, M. Bruce. Regulation & Deregulation: Economic Policy & Justice. (Pacific Institute). 1983. price not set prof ref (ISBN 0-88410-928-3). Ballinger Pub.
Neilson, Francis. In Quest of Justice. 135p. 1944. pap. 1.00 (ISBN 0-911312-31-5). Schalkenbach.
Walzer, Michael. The Spheres of Justice: A Defense of Pluralism & Equality. LC 82-72409. 356p. 1983. 19.95 (ISBN 0-465-08190-8). Basic.
JUSTICE, ADMINISTRATION OF
see also Courts; Criminal Justice, Administration of; Due Process of Law; Governmental Investigations; Judges
Hyman, Harold M. & Wiecek, William M. Equal Justice Under Law. LC 81-47658. (New American Nation Ser.). (Illus.). 572p. 1983. pap. 7.64i (ISBN 0-06-090929-3, CN 929, CN). Har-Row.
JUSTICE IN LITERATURE
Parker, M. D. The Slave of Life: A Study of Shakespeare & the Idea of Justice. 264p. 1983. Repr. of 1955 ed. lib. bdg. 35.00 (ISBN 0-89984-830-3). Century Bookbindery.
JUSTICES' CLERKS
see Clerks of Court
JUSTINIANUS 1ST, EMPEROR OF THE EAST, 483-565
Justinian the Great: The Emperor & Saint. LC 82-82095. (Illus.). 1982. 14.50 (ISBN 0-914744-58-5); pap. 9.50 (ISBN 0-914744-59-3). Inst Byzantine.
JUVENILE AUTOMOBILE DRIVERS
see Automobile Drivers
JUVENILE COURTS
see also Probation
Bortner, M. A. Inside a Juvenile Court: The Tarnished Ideal of Individualized Justice. 328p. 1982. 42.50 (ISBN 0-8147-1041-7). NYU Pr.
Fabricant, Michael. Juvenile Injustice: Dilemmas of the Family Court System. 198p. (Orig.). 1981. pap. 7.00 (ISBN 0-88156-003-0). Comm Serv Soc NY.
Fisher, Stanley. Standards Relating to Pretrial Court Proceedings. (Juvenile Justice Standards Project Ser.). 160p. Date not set. 20.00x (ISBN 0-88410-227-0); pap. 10.00x (ISBN 0-88410-811-2). Ballinger Pub.
Juvenile Justice in New Jersey. 124p. 1982. 17.00 (ISBN 0-686-81767-2). Ctr Analysis Public Issues.
Kaldate, S. V. Society, Deinquent & Juvenile Court. 1982. 18.00x (ISBN 0-8364-0911-6, Pub. by Ajanta). South Asia Bks.
Manak, James P. Standards Relating to Prosecution. (Juvenile Justice Standards Project Ser.). 112p. 1980. 20.00x (ISBN 0-88410-238-6); pap. 10.00x (ISBN 0-88410-814-7). Ballinger Pub.
Teitelbaum, Lee. Standards Relating to Counsel for Private Parties. (Juvenile Justice Standards Project Ser.). 240p. 1980. 20.00x (ISBN 0-88410-215-7); pap. 10.00x (ISBN 0-88410-817-1). Ballinger Pub.
JUVENILE DELINQUENCY
see also Child Welfare; Gangs; Juvenile Courts; Juvenile Detention Homes; Narcotics and Youth; Rehabilitation of Juvenile Delinquents
American Correctional Association Staff. Issues in Juvenile Corrections. (Series 2: No. 2). 29p. (Orig.). 1981. pap. 3.50 (ISBN 0-942974-24-7). Am Correctional.
American Health Research Institute, Ltd. Juvenile Delinquency: A Medical & Psychological Subject Analysis & Research Index With Bibliog. Bartone, John C., ed. 1983. 29.95 (ISBN 0-88164-002-6); pap. 21.95 (ISBN 0-88164-003-4). ABBE Pubs Assn.
Arnold, William & Brungardt, Terrence. Juvenile Misconduct & Delinquency. LC 82-82284. 512p. 1983. pap. text ed. 16.95 (ISBN 0-395-32562-5); instrs.' manual avail. (ISBN 0-395-32563-3). HM.
Eldefonso, Edward. Law Enforcement & the Youthful Offender. 3rd ed. LC 77-13331. 363p. 1978. 22.95 (ISBN 0-471-03234-4); tchrs.' manual 5.00 (ISBN 0-471-03769-9). Wiley.
Giallombardo, Rose, ed. Juvenile Delinquency: A Book of Readings. 3rd ed. LC 75-35887. 1976. pap. text ed. 17.95x (ISBN 0-471-29726-7). Text ed. 14.25 o.p. Wiley.
Hyde, Margaret O. Juvenile Justice & Injustice. rev. ed. (Single Title Ser.). 128p. (gr. 7 up). 1983. PLB 9.90 (ISBN 0-531-04594-3). Watts.
Journalism Reseach Fellows of 1982. Juvenile Justice: Myths & Realities. Farkas, Susan, ed. 96p. (Orig.). 1983. pap. 7.50 (ISBN 0-937846-96-1). Inst Educ Lead.
Kaldate, S. V. Society, Deinquent & Juvenile Court. 1982. 18.00x (ISBN 0-8364-0911-6, Pub. by Ajanta). South Asia Bks.
Rosenberg, Bernard & Silverstein, Harry. The Varieties of Delinquent Experience. LC 82-10576. 192p. pap. 6.95 (ISBN 0-8052-0736-8). Schocken.
Wynn, Bobby C., ed. Crime & Juvenile Delinquency 1980. 40p. 1982. reference bk. 25.00 (ISBN 0-667-00647-8). Microfilming Corp.
JUVENILE DETENTION HOMES
American Correctional Association Staff. Standards for Juvenile Community Residential Services. 52p. (Orig.). 1978. pap. 7.50 (ISBN 0-942974-37-9). Am Correctional.
--Standards for Juvenile Detention Facilities & Services. 94p. (Orig.). 1979. pap. 10.00 (ISBN 0-942974-34-4). Am Correctional.
--Standards for Juvenile Probation & Aftercare Services. 62p. (Orig.). 1979. pap. 7.50 (ISBN 0-942974-36-0). Am Correctional.
--Standards for Juvenile Training Schools & Services. 109p. (Orig.). 1979. pap. 10.00 (ISBN 0-942974-35-2). Am Correctional.
JUVENILE DRINKING
see Alcohol and Youth
JUVENILE ENCYCLOPEDIAS
see Children's Encyclopedias and Dictionaries
JUVENILE LITERATURE
see Children's Literature (Collections); also subdivisions under Children's Literature

K

K-THEORY
Dennis, R. K., ed. Algebraic K-Theory: Proceedings, Oberwolfach, FRG, 1980, Vol. II. (Lecture Notes in Mathematics Ser.: Vol. 967). 409p. 1983. pap. 20.00 (ISBN 0-387-11966-3). Springer-Verlag.
Draxl, Peter K. Skew Fields. LC 82-22036. (London Mathematical Society Lecture Note Ser.: No. 81). 194p. Date not set. pap. 19.95 (ISBN 0-521-27274-2). Cambridge U Pr.
KABBALA
see Cabala
KABUKI
Kabuki: The Program Book of Japan's Grand Kabuki on it's 1982 Tour. (Illus.). 1982. pap. 5.00 (ISBN 0-87830-579-3). Theatre Arts.
KACHINAS
see Katcinas
KAFIR WARS
see South Africa–History
KAFKA, FRANZ, 1883-1924
Grusa, Jiri. Kafka from Prague. (Illus.). 128p. (Orig.). pap. 12.50. Schocken.
Hayman, Ronald. Kafka: A Biography. 380p. 1983. pap. 8.95 (ISBN 0-19-520411-5, GB 722, GB). Oxford U Pr.
KAMIKAZE AIRPLANES
Hoyt, Edwin P. The Kamikazes. (Illus.). 1983. 16.50 (ISBN 0-87795-496-8). Arbor Hse.
KAMPUCHEA
Pradhan, Prakash C. Foreign Policy of Kampuchea. 400p. 1983. text ed. 30.00x (ISBN 0-391-02799-9, Pub. by Radiant Pub India). Humanities.
KAMUTI
see Bonsai
KANSAS–DESCRIPTION AND TRAVEL
Barkley, T. M. Field Guide to the Common Weeds of Kansas. LC 82-21914. (Illus.). 160p. 1983. text ed. 17.95x (ISBN 0-7006-0233-X); pap. 7.95 (ISBN 0-7006-0224-0). Univ Pr KS.
KANSAS–HISTORY
Communications (Telephone, Telegraph, Radio, Newspaper) 130p. 1982. 5.50 (ISBN 0-686-84757-1). Shawnee County Hist.
Manely, Robert N. Kansas: Our Pioneer Heritage. (Illus.). 88p. 1982. pap. 6.75 tchr's. guide (ISBN 0-939644-05-3). Media Prods & Mktg.
Manley, Robert N. Kansas, Our Pioneer Heritage. (Illus.). 215p. 1982. 12.50 (ISBN 0-939644-03-7). Media Prods & Mktg.
KANSAS CITY, MISSOURI
Stein, Shifra. Day Trips: Gas-Saving Getaways Less Than Two Hours from Greater Kansas City. (Illus.). 96p. 1980. pap. 4.50 (ISBN 0-9609752-0-9). S Stein Prods.
--Discover Kansas City: A Guide to Unique Shops, Services & Businesses. (Illus.). 1981. pap. 7.95 (ISBN 0-9609752-1-7). S Stein Prods.
KANT, IMMANUEL, 1724-1804
Cassirer, Ernst. Kant's Life & Thought. Haden, James, tr. LC 81-3354. 429p. 1983. pap. text ed. 11.95x (ISBN 0-300-02982-9). Yale U Pr.
--Kant's Life & Thought. Haden, James, tr. pap. 11.95 (ISBN 0-686-42819-6, Y-451). Yale U Pr.
Grayeff, F. Kant's Theoretical Philosophy. 240p. 1970. pap. 7.50 (ISBN 0-7190-0441-1). Manchester.
Hoffman, Piotr. The Anatomy of Idealism: Passivity & Activity in Kant, Hegel & Marx. 1982. lib. bdg. 24.00 (ISBN 0-686-37433-9, Pub. by Martinus Nijhoff Netherlands). Kluwer Boston.
Kant, Immanuel. Kant's Theory of the Summum Bonum. (The Essential Library of the Great Philosophers). (Illus.). 103p. 1983. Repr. of 1888 ed. 81.75 (ISBN 0-89901-084-9). Found Class Reprints.
Rescher, Nicholas. Kant's Theory of Knowledge & Reality: A Group of Essays. LC 82-21817. (Nicholas Rescher Ser.). 160p. (Orig.). 1983. lib. bdg. 20.75 (ISBN 0-8191-2960-7); pap. text ed. 9.75 (ISBN 0-8191-2961-5). U Pr of Amer.
Wilm, Emil C. Immanuel Kant: Seventeen Twenty-Four to Nineteen Twenty-Four. 1925. text ed. 18.50x (ISBN 0-686-83577-8). Elliots Bks.
KARATE
Chinese Martial Arts. (Illus., Orig.). 1982. pap. 2.95 (ISBN 0-8351-1101-6). China Bks.
Chun, Richard. Advancing in Tae Kwon Do. LC 82-47519. (Illus.). 352p. 1983. 34.62i (ISBN 0-06-015029-7, HarpT). Har-Row.
--Moo Duk Kwan, Vol. II. LC 81-186107. (Illus.). 220p. (Orig.). 1983. pap. 8.95 (ISBN 0-89750-085-7, 422). Ohara Pubns.
Karate Rulebook, 1982. Date not set. 9.50 (ISBN 0-686-43036-0). AAU Pubns.
Kim, Daeshik & Leland, Tom W. Karate. 3rd ed. (Exploring Sports Ser.). 1983. pap. write for info. (ISBN 0-697-09976-8). Wm C Brown.
Kozuki, Russell. Power Karate. LC 82-19321. (Illus.). 144p. (Orig.). 1983. pap. 5.95 (ISBN 0-8069-7720-5). Sterling.
Lee, Chong. Kicks for Competition. LC 82-61733. (Illus.). 124p. (Orig.). 1982. pap. 6.50 (ISBN 0-89750-083-0, 420). Ohara Pubns.
Logan, William & Petras, Herman. Handbook of the Martial Arts. LC 82-48832. (Illus.). 284p. 1983. pap. 7.95 (ISBN 0-06-464064-7, BN 4064). B&N NY.
Long, Harold & Wheeler, Allen. Dynamics of Isshinryu Karate Orange Belt, Bk. 1. Condry, Steve, ed. (Isshinryu Karate Ser.). (Illus.). 1978. pap. 3.95 (ISBN 0-89826-002-7). Natl Paperback.
--Who's Who in Karate. 110p. (Orig.). 1981. pap. 3.95 (ISBN 0-89826-007-8). Natl Paperback.
Schlesinger, Tom. Fighting Strategy: Winning Combinations. LC 82-70680. (Illus.). 101p. (Orig.). 1982. pap. 5.95 (ISBN 0-86568-035-3, 306). Unique Pubns.
Tackett, Tim. Hsing-I Kung-Fu, Vol. II. LC 75-24802. (Illus.). 224p. (Orig.). 1983. pap. 7.95 (ISBN 0-89750-084-9, 421). Ohara Pubns.
Taekwondo Handbook, 1977-1980. Date not set. 3.00 (ISBN 0-686-43038-7). AAU Pubns.
Theriault, Jean Y. & Jennings, Joseph. Full-Contact Karate. (Illus.). 192p. (Orig.). 1983. pap. 7.95 (ISBN 0-8092-5597-9). Contemp Bks.
KARMA
see also Anthroposophy
Anand, Kewal K. Indian Philosophy: The Concept of Karma. 396p. 1982. 34.95 (ISBN 0-940500-91-4, Pub by Bharatiya Vidya India). Asia Bk Corp.
Baker, Douglas, ed. Karmic Laws: The Esoteric Philosophy of Disease & Rebirth. 96p. 1983. pap. 6.95 (ISBN 0-85030-299-4). Newcastle Pub.
Keyes, Charles F. & Daniel, E. Valentine. Karma: An Anthropological Inquiry. LC 81-19719. 328p. 1983. text ed. 27.50x (ISBN 0-520-04429-0). U of Cal Pr.
LaFleur, William R. The Karma of Words: Buddhism & the Literary Arts in Medieval Japan. LC 82-45909. 232p. 1983. text ed. 25.00x (ISBN 0-520-04600-5). U of Cal Pr.
Steiner, Rudolf. Karmic Relationships: Esoteric Studies, Vol. I. Adams, George, tr. from Ger. 205p. 1981. 14.50 (ISBN 0-85440-260-8, Pub. by Steinerbooks). Anthroposophic.
--Karmic Relationships: Esoteric Studies, Vol. 7. Osmond, D. S., tr. from Ger. 140p. 1973. 9.95 (ISBN 0-85440-276-4, Pub. by Steinerbooks). Anthroposophic.
--Karmic Relationships: Esoteric Studies, Vol. 8. Osmond, D. S., tr. from Ger. Orig. Title: Cosmic Christianity & the Impulse of Michael. 102p. 1975. 9.95 (ISBN 0-85440-018-4, Pub. by Steinerbooks). Anthroposophic.
--Karmic Relationships: Esoteric Studies (The Karmic Relationships of the Anthroposophics Movement, Vol. 3. 3rd ed. Adams, George, tr. 179p. 1977. 12.95 (ISBN 0-85440-313-2, Pub. by Steinerbooks). Anthroposophic.
--Karmic Relationships: Esteric Studies, Vol. 2. Adams, George & Cotterell, M., trs. from Ger. Davy, C. & Osmond, D. S. 1974. 14.50 (ISBN 0-85440-281-0, Pub. by Steinerbooks). Anthroposophic.
Szekely, Edmond B. Creative Work: Karma Yoga. (Illus.). 32p. 1973. pap. 2.95 (ISBN 0-89564-066-X). IBS Intl.
KATCINAS
Bunzel, Ruth L. Suni Katcinas. LC 72-13917. Repr. of 1932 ed. lib. bdg. 27.50 (ISBN 0-686-84607-9). Rio Grande.
KAWASAKI MOTORCYCLE
Vesely, Anton. Kawasaki KZ500 & 550 Fours 1979-1981 Service Repair Performance. Wauson, Sydnie A., ed. (Illus.). 268p. (Orig.). 1982. pap. 10.95 (ISBN 0-89287-363-9). Clymer Pubns.
Vesely, Anton & Wauson, Sydnie. Kawasaki Jet Ski 1976-1981 Service-Repair-Maintenance. (Illus.). 164p. (Orig.). 1982. pap. 10.95 (ISBN 0-89287-354-X, X956). Clymer Pubns.
KAYAKS
see Canoes and Canoeing
KEATS, JOHN, 1795-1821
Van Ghent, Dorothy. Keats: The Myth of the Hero. Robinson, Jeffrey C., ed. LC 82-61391. 328p. 1983. 25.00x (ISBN 0-691-06569-1). Princeton U Pr.
KEELEY CURE
see Alcoholism–Treatment
KELLER, HELEN ADAMS, 1880-1968
Wilkie, Katherine. Helen Keller. new ed. (Childhood of Famous Americans Ser.). (Illus.). 204p. (Orig.). (gr. 2 up). 1983. pap. 3.95 (ISBN 0-672-52749-9). Bobbs.
KELLY, GRACE
see Grace, Princess of Monaco, 1929-
KENNEDY, JOHN FITZGERALD, PRES. U. S., 1917-1963
Parmet, Herbert S. J.F.K. The Presidency of John F. Kennedy. (Illus.). 608p. 1983. 24.95 (ISBN 0-385-27419-X). Dial.
Seaborg, Glenn T. & Loeb, Benjamin S. Kennedy, Khrushchev, & the Test Ban. (Illus.). 336p. 1983. pap. 7.95 (ISBN 0-520-04961-6, CAL 629). U of Cal Pr.
KENNEDY, JOHN FITZGERALD, PRES. U. S., 1917-1963–JUVENILE LITERATURE
Frolick, S. J. Once There Was a President. rev. ed. LC 80-69972. (Once There Was... Ser.). 64p. (gr. 3-7). 1980. pap. 6.95 (ISBN 0-9605426-0-4). Black Star Pub.
KENNEDY FAMILY
Wills, Garry. The Kennedy Imprisonment. 1983. pap. 3.95 (ISBN 0-686-43232-0). PB.
KENOSIS (THEOLOGY)
see Incarnation
KENSINGTON, ENGLAND
Stearn, W. T. The Natural History Museum at South Kensington: A History of the British Museum (Natural History) 1753-1980. (Illus.). 350p. 1981. 37.50x (ISBN 0-434-73600-7). Sabbot-Natural Hist Bks.
KENT, ENGLAND–DESCRIPTION AND TRAVEL
West, Jenny. The Windmills of Kent. 128p. 1982. 29.00x (ISBN 0-7050-0065-6, Pub. by C Skilton Scotland). State Mutual Bk.
KENTUCKY–HISTORY
Arnow, Harriette S. Seedtime on the Cumberland. LC 82-40464. (Illus.). 480p. 1983. 28.00x (ISBN 0-8131-1487-X); pap. 13.00x (ISBN 0-8131-0146-8). U Pr of Ky.
KENYA
Fox, James. White Mischief. LC 82-42800. (Illus.). 299p. 1983. 15.95 (ISBN 0-394-50918-8). Random.
KENYA–DESCRIPTION AND TRAVEL
Kenya Travel Guide. (Berlitz Travel Guides). (Illus.). 1982. pap. 4.95 (ISBN 0-02-969290-3, Berlitz). Macmillan.
KENYA–ECONOMIC CONDITIONS
Kenya & Zimbabwe. 375.00x (ISBN 0-686-99851-0, Pub. by Metra England). State Mutual Bk.
KENYA–POLITICS AND GOVERNMENT
Kim, Chong Lim & Barkan, Joel D. The Legislative Connection: The Politics of Representation in Kenya, Korea, & Turkey. (Duke Press Policy Studies). (Illus.). 400p. Date not set. prepub. 35.00 (ISBN 0-8223-0534-8). Duke.
KERAMICS
see Ceramics
KERESAN INDIANS
see Indians of North America–Southwest, New
KEROUAC, JOHN, 1922-1969
Kerouac, Jack. Dear Carolyn: (Letters to Carolyn Cassady) Knight, Arthur & Knight, Kit, eds. 1983. pap. 5.00 ltd. ed. (ISBN 0-934660-06-9). TUVOTI.
McNally, D. Desolate Angel: Jack Kerouac, the Beat Generation & America. 1980. pap. 6.95 (ISBN 0-07-045670-4). McGraw.
Nicosia, Gerald. Memory Babe: A Critical Biography of Jack Kerouac. Jordan, Fred, ed. (Illus.). 760p. 1983. 22.50 (ISBN 0-394-52270-2, GP865). Grove.
KERTESZ, ANDRE
Johnson, Brooks. Andre Kertesz, Master of Photography. LC 82-72323. (Illus.). 64p. 1982. pap. 7.50 (ISBN 0-940744-38-4). Chrysler Museum.
Kertesz, Andre. Andre Kertesz: A Lifetime of Perception. LC 82-70745. 260p. 1982. 45.00 (ISBN 0-8109-1207-4). Abrams.
KESEY, KEN
Tanner, Stephen L. Ken Kesey. (United States Authors Ser.). 180p. 1983. lib. bdg. 13.95 (ISBN 0-8057-7385-1, Twayne). G K Hall.
KETTERING, CHARLES FRANKLIN, 1876-1958
Leslie, Stuart W. Boss Kettering. (Illus.). 416p. 1983. 19.95 (ISBN 0-231-05600-1). Columbia U Pr.
Piety, Patricia & Kettering, Charles F. The Kettering Digest. (Illus.). 94p. 1982. pap. 3.95 (ISBN 0-913428-45-0). Landfall Pr.
KEW–ROYAL GARDENS
Rosbotham, Lyle. Kew, The Royal Botanic Gardens. (Illus.). 52p. 1982. pap. 30.00 (ISBN 0-917796-02-0). Press Four Fifty One.

KEY WEST, FLORIDA
Cox, Christopher. A Key West Companion. (Illus.). 208p. 1983. 19.95 (ISBN 0-312-45182-2). St Martin.
Langley, Joan & Langley, Wright. Key West Images of the Past. LC 81-71478. (Illus.). 132p. 1982. 19.95 (ISBN 0-9609272-1-2); pap. 9.95 (ISBN 0-9609272-0-4). Images Key.
Sherrill, Chris & Aiello, Roger. Key West, the Last Resort. (Illus.). 171p. Date not set. pap. 6.95 (ISBN 0-686-84261-8). Banyan Bks.
Stevenson, George B. Keyguide to Key West & the Florida Keys. (Illus.). 64p. Date not set. pap. 3.50 (ISBN 0-686-84251-0). Banyan Bks.
Windhorn, Stan & Langley, Wright. Yesterday's Florida Keys. (Seemann's Historic Cities Ser.: No. 12). (Illus.). 128p. 1982. pap. 9.95 (ISBN 0-911607-00-5). Langley Pr.
--Yesterday's Key West: Seemann's Historic Cities Ser. LC 73-80596. (No. 4). (Illus.). 144p. 1983. Repr. of 1973 ed. pap. price not set (ISBN 0-911607-01-3). Langley Pr.
KEYNES, JOHN MAYNARD, 1883-1946
Wood, John C., ed. John Maynard Keynes: Critical Assessments. (Assessments of Leading Economists Ser.). 2096p. 1983. Set of 4 vols. text ed. 495.00x (ISBN 0-7099-2729-0, Pub. by Croom Helm Ltd England). Biblio Dist.
KEYNESIAN ECONOMICS
Coddington, Alan. Keynesian Economics: The Search for First Principles. 144p. 1983. text ed. 18.50x (ISBN 0-04-330334-X). Allen Unwin.
Parker, Glen L. The Economic Consequences of Keynesian Policy: Aspects of a Crisis. 1982. 7.50 (ISBN 0-533-05411-7). Vantage.
KHMERS
Foreign Service Institute. Khmer Basic Course, 2 vols. Date not set. Vol. 1. with 19 cassettes 185.00x (ISBN 0-88432-097-9, KH1); Vol. 2. with 29 cassettes 175.00x (ISBN 0-88432-098-7, KH50). J Norton Pubs.
KHRUSHCHEV, NIKITA SERGEEVICH, 1894-1971
Medvedev, Roy. Khruschev. LC 82-45545. (Illus.). 350p. 1983. 17.95 (ISBN 0-385-18387-9, Anchor Pr). Doubleday.
Seaborg, Glenn T. & Loeb, Benjamin S. Kennedy, Khrushchev, & the Test Ban. (Illus.). 336p. 1983. pap. 7.95 (ISBN 0-520-04961-6, CAL 629). U of Cal Pr.
KIANGSI, CHINA (PROVINCE)
Ocko, Jonathan K. Bureaucratic Reform in Provincial China: Ting Jih-ch'ang in Restoration Kiangsu, 1867-1870. (Harvard East Asian Monographs: No. 103). 316p. 1983. text ed. 20.00x (ISBN 0-674-08617-1). Harvard U Pr.
KIBBUTZ
see Collective Settlements
KICKAPOO INDIANS
see Indians of North America–The West
KIDNAPPING
Abrahms, Sally. Children in the Crossfire: The Tragedy of Parental Kidnapping. LC 82-73030. 320p. 1983. 12.95 (ISBN 0-689-11339-0). Atheneum.
KIDNEY FAILURE
see Renal Insufficiency
KIDNEYS
see also Nephrology; Urinary Organs; Urine
also headings beginning with the word Renal
Bricker, Neal S. & Kirschenbaum, Michael. The Kidney: Diagnosis & Management. 525p. 1983. 29.95 (ISBN 0-471-09572-9, Pub. by Wiley Med). Wiley.
Dunn, Michael J. & Patrono, Carlo, eds. Prostaglandins & the Kidney: Biochemistry, Physiology, Pharmacology, & Clinical Applications. 406p. 1982. 49.50 (ISBN 0-306-41054-0, Plenum Med Bk). Plenum Pub.
Fang, L. S. Manual of Clinical Nephrology. 231p. 1982. 13.95 (ISBN 0-07-019901-9). McGraw-Pretest.
Harvey, R. J. Kidneys & the Internal Environment. 1974. 10.95x (ISBN 0-412-12260-X, Pub. by Chapman & Hall England). Methuen Inc.
Kjellstrand, C. M., ed. The Belding H. Scribner Festschrift. (Journal: Nephron: Vol. 33, No. 2). (Illus.). 96p. 1983. pap. 48.00 (ISBN 3-8055-3675-5). S Karger.
Kurokawa, K. & Tanner, R., eds. Recent Advances in Renal Metabolism. (Mineral Electrolyte Metabolism Ser.: Vol. 9: No. 4-5). (Illus.). 140p. 1983. pap. price not set (ISBN 3-8055-3652-6). S Karger.
Mallick. Case Presentations: In Renal Medicine. 1982. text ed. write for info (ISBN 0-407-00234-0). Butterworth.
O'Connor, W. J. Normal Renal Function: The Excretion of Water & Electrolytes Derived from Food & Drink. (Illus.). 442p. 1982. text ed. 27.50 (ISBN 0-19-520400-X). Oxford U Pr.
Porter, George, ed. Nephrotoxic Mechanisms of Drugs & Environmental Toxins. LC 82-13156. 486p. 1982. 49.50x (ISBN 0-306-40977-1, Plenum Med Bk). Plenum Pub.
KIDNEYS–DISEASES
see also Calculi, Urinary; Renal Hypertension; Renal Insufficiency
Avram, M. M., ed. Prevention of Kidney Disease & Long-Term Survival. 304p. 1982. 35.00x (ISBN 0-306-40965-8, Plenum Med Bk). Plenum Pub.
Brater, Craig. Drug Use in Renal Disease. (Illus.). 250p. 1982. text ed. write for info. (ISBN 0-86792-005-X, Pub by Adis Pr Australia). Wright-PSG.
Cummings, Nancy B. & Michael, Alfred F., eds. Immune Mechanisms in Renal Disease. 550p. 1982. 65.00x (ISBN 0-306-40948-8, Plenum Pr). Plenum Pub.
Haensel, Phyllis C. Certain Choices. Hoff, Marshall G. & Bock, Glenn H., eds. (Illus.). 32p. (Orig.). (gr. 7-9). Date not set. pap. text ed. price not set (ISBN 0-940210-01-0). U Minn Pediatric.
Klahr, Saulo, ed. The Kidney & Body Fluids in Health & Disease. 616p. 1982. 9.50x (ISBN 0-306-41062-1, Plenum Med Bk). Plenum Pub.
Kuss, Rene & Murphy, Gerald P., eds. Renal Tumors: Proceedings of the International Symposium on Kidney Tumors, 1st. LC 82-14008. (Progress in Clinical & Biological Research Ser.: Vol. 100). 692p. 1982. 72.00 (ISBN 0-8451-0100-5). A R Liss.
Stone, William J. & Rabin, Pauline L., eds. Chronic End-Stage Renal Diseases. Date not set. price not set (ISBN 0-12-672280-3). Acad Pr.
KIDNEYS–TRANSPLANTATION
Brynger, Hans. Clinical Kidney Transplant. 240p. 1982. 44.50 (ISBN 0-8089-1523-1). Grune.
Marberger, Michael & Dreikorn, Kurt. Renal Preservation. (International Perspectives In Urology: Vol. 8). (Illus.). 352p. 1983. lib. bdg. price not set (ISBN 0-683-05585-2). Williams & Wilkins.
KIERKEGAARD, SOREN AABYE, 1813-1855
Brandt, Frithiof. Soren Kierkegaard His Life - His Works. Born, Ann R., tr. (Danes of the Present & Past). (Illus.). 117p. (Danish.). 1983. pap. text ed. 7.95 (ISBN 0-933748-05-1). Nordic Bks.
Fletcher, David B. Social & Political Perspectives in the Thought of Soren Kierkegaard. LC 81-43716. 88p. 1983. lib. bdg. 18.00 (ISBN 0-8191-2689-6); pap. text ed. 7.00 (ISBN 0-8191-2690-X). U Pr of Amer.
KILLING, MERCY
see Euthanasia
KINDERGARTEN–METHODS AND MANUALS
Laforteza, Purificacion G. Creative Kindergarten Teaching. 127p. (Orig.). 1982. pap. 8.00 (ISBN 0-686-37576-9, Pub. by New Day Philippines). Cellar.
KINDNESS TO ANIMALS
see Animals, Treatment Of
KINEMATICS
see also Mechanical Movements; Mechanics; Motion
Beggs, Joseph S. Kinematics. LC 82-15835. (Illus.). 1983. text ed. 24.50 (ISBN 0-89116-355-7). Hemisphere Pub.
KINESICS
see Nonverbal Communication
KINESIOLOGY
see also Human Locomotion; Human Mechanics; Motor Ability
Dowell, Linus. Principles of Mechanical Kinesiology. 506p. 1982. pap. text ed. 20.95x (ISBN 0-89641-109-5). American Pr.
Jensen, Clayne & Schultz, Gordon. Applied Kinesiology. 3rd ed. (Illus.). 352p. text ed. 24.95x (ISBN 0-07-032469-7, C). McGraw.
KINESIOTHERAPY
see Exercise Therapy
KINETIC ART
Diamond, John. Some Contributions of Behavioral Kineseology to Art. (Behavioral Kinesiology Ser.). 73p. 1983. pap. 29.95 (ISBN 0-915628-14-7). Zeppelin.
KINETIC THEORY OF GASES
see Gases, Kinetic Theory of
KINETIC THEORY OF LIQUIDS
see Liquids, Kinetic Theory of
KINETICS
see Dynamics; Mechanics, Analytic; Motion
KINETICS, CHEMICAL
see Chemical Reaction, Rate Of
KING, HENRY, BP. OF CHICHESTER, 1592-1669
Keynes, Geoffrey. A Bibliography of Henry King. (Illus.). 117p. 1977. 30.00 (ISBN 0-906795-18-4, Pub. by St Pauls Biblios England). U Pr of Va.
KING, MARTIN LUTHER, 1929-1968
An Explanation of Dr. Martin Luther's Small Catechism. 265p. 1982. write for info. (ISBN 0-89279-043-1). Board Pub Evang.
Garrow, David J. The FBI & Martin Luther King, Jr. 1983. pap. 5.95 (ISBN 0-14-006486-9). Penguin.
KING, MARTIN LUTHER, 1929-1968–JUVENILE LITERATURE
Richardson, Nigel. Martin Luther King. (Profiles Ser.). (Illus.). 64p. (gr. 4-6). 1983. 7.95 (ISBN 0-241-10931-0, Pub. by Hamish Hamilton England). David & Charles.
Thompson, Marguerite. Martin Luther King Jr. A Story For Children. 24p. 1983. 3.00 (ISBN 0-912444-25-8). Gaus.
KING, STEPHEN, 1947-
Winter, Douglas B. Stephen King. (Starmont Reader's Guide Ser.: No. 16). 128p. 1982. Repr. lib. bdg. 11.95x (ISBN 0-89370-023-1). Borgo Pr.
KINGS AND RULERS
see also Courts and Courtiers; Despotism; Dictators also subdivision Kings and Rulers under names of countries, e.g. Great Britain–Kings and Rulers
The Barbarian Kings. (Treasures of the World Ser.). 1982. lib. bdg. 22.60 (ISBN 0-86706-071-9, Pub. by Stonehenge). Silver.
Fleure, H. F. & Peake, Harold. Priests & Kings. (Corridors of Time Ser.: No. 4). 1927. text ed. 24.50x (ISBN 0-686-83710-X). Elliots Bks.
KININS
Back, Nathan & Dietze, Gunther, eds. Kinins III. (Advances in Experimental Medicine & Biology: Vol. 156). 1190p. 1983. 145.00x (ISBN 0-306-41167-9, Plenum Pr). Plenum Pub.
KINSHIP
see also Family; Tribes and Tribal System
Chao, Paul. Chinese Kinship. 220p. 1983. 30.00 (ISBN 0-7103-0020-4). Routledge & Kegan.
Dumont, Louis. Affinity As a Value: Marriage Alliance in South India with Comparative Essays on Austrailia. LC 82-13468. (Illus.). 248p. 1983. lib. bdg. 22.00x (ISBN 0-226-16964-2). U of Chicago Pr.
KIOWA INDIANS
see Indians of North America–The West
KIPLING, RUDYARD, 1865-1936
Cornell, Luis L. Kipling in India. 224p. 1982. Repr. of 1966 ed. lib. bdg. 35.00 (ISBN 0-89760-165-3). Telegraph Bks.
KIRLIAN PHOTOGRAPHY
Gennaro, L. & Guzzon, F. Kirlian Photography: Research & Prospects. (Illus.). 152p. 1982. 14.95 (ISBN 0-85692-045-2, Pub. by Salem Hse Ltd.). Merrimack Bk Serv.
Oldfield, Harry & Durie, Bruce. New Discoveries in Kirlian Photography. 1982. 32.00x (ISBN 0-906540-21-6, Pub. by Element Bks). State Mutual Bk.
KISSINGER, HENRY ALFRED, 1923-
Hersh, Seymour, ed. The Price of Power: Kissinger in the Nixon White House. 480p. 1983. 16.95 (ISBN 0-671-44760-2). Summit Bks.
KISWAHILI LANGUAGE
see Swahili Language
KITCHEN CABINETS
Better Homes & Gardens Books editors, ed. Better Homes & Gardens Step-by-Step Cabinets & Shelves. (Illus.). 1983. pap. 5.95 (ISBN 0-696-01065-8). Meredith Corp.
Cary, Jere. Building Your Own Kitchen Cabinets. (Illus.). 1983. pap. 11.95 (ISBN 0-918804-15-9). Taunton.
KITCHEN-GARDENS
see Vegetable Gardening
KITCHEN UTENSILS
see also Food Processor Cookery
Franklin, Linda C. Three Hundred Years of Kitchen Collectables: Identification & Value Guide. 2nd ed. 340p. 1983. pap. 10.95 (ISBN 0-89689-041-4). Bks Americana.
Saks, Mark. The Calculator Cookbook: Maximizing the Computational Power of Your Hand-Held Calculator. 320p. 1983. 22.95 (ISBN 0-13-110395-4); pap. 10.95 (ISBN 0-13-110387-3). P-H.
KITCHENS
see also Kitchen Cabinets
Better Homes & Gardens Books editors, ed. Better Homes & Gardens All About Your House: Your Kitchen. (All About your House Ser.). 160p. 1983. 9.95 (ISBN 0-696-02161-7). Meredith Corp.
Cadwallader, Sharon. The Living Kitchen. (Tools for Today Ser.). 1983. pap. 6.95 (ISBN 0-686-84928-0). Sierra.
Data Notes Publishing Staff. Kitchen Recycling: Data Notes. 35p. 1983. pap. text ed. 9.95 (ISBN 0-911569-51-0). Data Notes Pub.
Young, Pam & Jones, Peggy. The Sidetracked Sisters Catch Up on the Kitchen. 224p. 1983. pap. 6.95 (ISBN 0-446-37526-8). Warner Bks.
KITES
Ito, Toshio & Komura, Hirotsugu. Kites: The Science & the Wonder. (Illus.). 176p. (Orig.). 1983. pap. 11.95 (ISBN 0-87040-526-8). Kodansha.
Newnham, Jack. Kites to Make & Fly. 1982. pap. 2.50 (ISBN 0-14-049139-2, Puffin). Penguin.
KLEIST, HEINRICH VON, 1777-1811
McGlathery, James M. Desire's Sway: The Plays & Stories of Heinrich von Kleist. 272p. 1983. 17.95x (ISBN 0-8143-1734-0). Wayne St U Pr.
KLOSSOWSKI, BALTHASAR, 1910-
Klossowski de Rola, Stanislas. Balthus. LC 82-48579. (Icon Editions Ser.). (Illus.). 1983. 24.04i (ISBN 0-06-431275-5, HarpT). Har-Row.
KNEE
Cailliet, Rene. Knee Pain & Disability. 2nd ed. LC 82-17296. (Pain Ser.). (Illus.). 220p. 1983. pap. text ed. 11.95 (ISBN 0-8036-1621-X, 1621-X). Davis Co.
Mueller, W. The Knee: Form, Function, & Ligament Reconstruction. (Illus.). 314p. 1983. 110.00 (ISBN 0-387-11716-4). Springer-Verlag.
KNEE JERK
see Reflexes
KNEIPP CURE
see Hydrotherapy
KNIGHTS AND KNIGHTHOOD–JUVENILE LITERATURE
Gibson, Michael & Pike, Trisha. All About Knights. (Full Color Fact Books). (Illus.). 32p. (gr. 4-12). 1982. PLB 7.95 (ISBN 0-8219-0016-1, 35547). EMC.
KNIGHTS TEMPLARS (MONASTIC AND MILITARY ORDER)
see Templars
KNITTING
see also Beadwork
Chilton Staff, ed. McCall's Big Book of Christmas Knit & Crochet. LC 82-70537. 304p. (Orig.). 1982. pap. 12.95 (ISBN 0-8019-7252-3). Chilton.
--McCall's Big Book of Knit Crochet. LC 82-70538. (Illus.). 304p. (Orig.). 1982. pap. 12.95 (ISBN 0-8019-7253-1). Chilton.
Compton, Rae. Complete Book of Traditional Knitting. (Illus.). 240p. 1983. 19.95 (ISBN 0-686-83844-0, ScribT). Scribner.
Hollingworth, Shelagh. Traditional Knitting. (Illus.). 64p. 1983. pap. 4.95 (ISBN 0-7134-4336-7, Pub. by Batsford England). David & Charles.
Taylor, Gertrude. The Complete Book of Knitting. 304p. 1983. pap. 9.95 (ISBN 0-686-83773-8, ScribT). Scribner.
KNITTING–PATTERNS
Starmore, Alice. Scandinavian Knitwear: Thirty Original Designs from Traditional Patterns. 128p. 1982. 39.00x (ISBN 0-686-82320-6, Pub. by Bell & Hyman England). State Mutual Bk.
KNIVES
Goins, John E. Pocketknives-Markings, Manufacturers & Dealers. 2nd ed. LC 82-83511. (Illus.). 280p. (Orig.). 1982. pap. 8.95 (ISBN 0-940362-06-6). Knife World.
The Official 1983 Price Guide to Pocket Knives. 1st ed. LC 82-84635. 240p. 1983. pap. 2.95 (ISBN 0-87637-372-4). Hse of Collectibles.
Sanchez, John. Blade Master: Advanced Survival Skills for Knife Fighters. (Illus.). 96p. 1982. pap. 10.00 (ISBN 0-87364-259-7). Paladin Ent.
KNOTS AND SPLICES
see also Macrame
Fry, Eric C. The Book of Knots & Ropework: Practical & Decorative. (Illus.). 176p. 1983. 10.95 (ISBN 0-517-54885-2); pap. 4.95 (ISBN 0-517-54886-0). Crown.
Hin, Floris. This is Knotting & Splicing. (This Is Ser.). (Illus.). 127p. 1983. 17.95 (ISBN 0-914814-35-4). Sail Bks.
Spencer, Chas. L. Knots, Splices, & Fancy Work. 1981. 25.00x (ISBN 0-85174-157-6, Pub. by Brown, Son & Ferguson). State Mutual Bk.
KNOWABLENESS OF GOD
see God–Knowableness
KNOWLEDGE, BOOKS OF
see Encyclopedias and Dictionaries
KNOWLEDGE, REFLEXIVE
see Self-Knowledge, Theory of
KNOWLEDGE, THEORY OF
see also Belief and Doubt; Cognition; Common Sense; Experience; Gestalt Psychology; Identity; Ideology; Intellect; Perception; Pragmatism; Rationalism; Reality; Self-Knowledge, Theory of; Senses and Sensation; Truth; Values
Adorno, Theodor. Against Epistemology: Studies in Husserl & the Phenomenological Antimonies. Domingo, Willis, tr. from Ger. (Studies in Contemporary German Social Thought). 256p. 1983. 27.50x (ISBN 0-262-01073-9). MIT Pr.
Brownhill, R. J. Education & the Nature of Knowledge. (New Patterns of Learning Ser.). 144p. 1983. text ed. 27.25x (ISBN 0-7099-0654-4, Pub. by Croom Helm Ltd England). Biblio Dist.
Cohen, Robert S. & Wartofsky, Marx. Epistemology, Methodology, & the Social Sciences. 1983. lib. bdg. 48.00 (ISBN 90-277-1454-1, Pub. by Reidel Holland). Kluwer Boston.
Collingwood, Robin G. Speculum Mentis: The Map of Knowledge. LC 82-15552. 327p. 1982. Repr. of 1924 ed. lib. bdg. 39.75x (ISBN 0-313-23701-8, COSM). Greenwood.
Harbert, David L. Existence, Knowing, & Philosophical Systems. LC 82-17565. 226p. (Orig.). 1983. lib. bdg. 21.75 (ISBN 0-8191-2804-X); pap. text ed. 10.25 (ISBN 0-8191-2805-8). U Pr of Amer.
Johari, Harish. Leela: Game of Knowledge. (Illus.). 170p. (Orig.). 1983. pap. 14.95 (ISBN 0-7100-0689-6). Routledge & Kegan.
Powell, Ralph A. Freely Chosen Reality. LC 82-21943. 194p. (Orig.). 1983. lib. bdg. 21.50 (ISBN 0-8191-2924-0); pap. text ed. 10.25 (ISBN 0-8191-2925-9). U Pr of Amer.
Rescher, Nicholas. Kant's Theory of Knowledge & Reality: A Group of Essays. LC 82-21817. (Nicholas Rescher Ser.). 160p. (Orig.). 1983. lib. bdg. 20.75 (ISBN 0-8191-2960-7); pap. text ed. 9.75 (ISBN 0-8191-2961-5). U Pr of Amer.
Schank, Roger & Abelson, Robert. Scripts, Plans, Goals, & Understanding: An Inquiry into Human Knowledge Structures. 256p. 1977. text ed. 14.95 (ISBN 0-89859-138-4). L Erlbaum Assocs.
Schwanauer, Francis. The Flesh of Thought is Pleasure or Pain. LC 82-17674. 136p. (Orig.). 1983. pap. text ed. 8.75 (ISBN 0-8191-2765-5). U Pr of Amer.
Shapiro, Barbara J. Probability & Certainty in Seventeenth Century England: A Study of the Relationships Between Natural Science, Religion, History, Law, Literature. LC 82-61385. 368p. 1983. 35.00x (ISBN 0-691-05379-0). Princeton U Pr.

Shope, Robert K. The Analysis of Knowing. LC 82-15099. 377p. 1983. 25.00x (ISBN 0-691-07275-2); pap. 8.95x (ISBN 0-691-02025-6). Princeton U Pr.

Willard, Charles A. Argumentation & the Social Grounds of Knowledge. LC 81-16199. 322p. 1983. text ed. 20.00 (ISBN 0-8173-0096-1). U of Ala Pr.

KNOWLEDGE OF GOD

see God-Knowableness

KNOWLEDGE OF SELF, THEORY OF

see Self-Knowledge, Theory of

KNOX, JOHN, 1505-1572

Smith, G. Barnett & Martin, Dorothy. John Knox: Apostle of the Scottish Reformation. LC 82-12608. 128p. 1982. pap. 3.95 (ISBN 0-8024-4354-0). Moody.

KOASATI INDIANS

see Indians of North America-Eastern States

KOLBE, MAXIMILLAN

Forristal, Desmond. Kolbe: A Saint in Auschwitz. (Patron Bk.). Orig. Title: Maximillian of Auschwitz. 191p. (Orig.). Date not set. pap. 2.95 (ISBN 0-89944-066-5, P066-5). D Bosco Multimedia.

KOMMUNISTICHESKAIA PARTIIA SOVETSKOGO SOIUZA

see Communist Party of Russia

KONGO

see Congo

KORAN

Khalifa, R. A. Quran Times Hadith Equals Zero. 85p. (Orig.). 1983. 9.50 (ISBN 0-934894-35-3). Islamic Prods.

Majul, Cesar A. The Names of God in Relation to the Mathematical Structure of Quran. 35p. (Orig.). 1983. 1.50 (ISBN 0-934894-04-3). Islamic Prods.

Quasem, M. A. Jewels of the Qur'an: Al-Ghazali's Theory. 240p. (Orig.). 1983. pap. 8.95 (ISBN 0-7103-0034-4). Routledge & Kegan.

KORAN-LAW

see Islamic Law

KOREA

Dong, Wonmo & Sunoo, Harold H., eds. Whither Korea? Views of Korean Christian Scholars in North America. viii, 166p. 1975. 4.00 (ISBN 0-932014-01-1). AKCS.

KOREA-DESCRIPTION AND TRAVEL

Fodor's Korea. (Illus.). 160p. 1983. traveltex 8.95 (ISBN 0-679-00968-X). McKay.

Insight Guides. Korea. (Illus.). 378p. 1983. 18.95 (ISBN 0-13-516633-0); pap. 14.95 (ISBN 0-13-516641-1). P-H.

Reid, Daniel P. The Complete Guide to Korea. (The Complete Asian Guide Ser.). (Illus.). 128p. (Orig.). 1982. pap. 9.95 (ISBN 962-7031-18-6). C E Tuttle.

--Korea in Focus. (The "In Focus" Ser.). (Illus.). 64p. (Orig.). 1982. pap. 5.95 (ISBN 962-7031-21-6). C E Tuttle.

KOREA-ECONOMIC CONDITIONS

Cole, David C. & Park, Yung C. Financial Development in Korea, 1945-1978. (Harvard East Asian Monographs: No. 106). 340p. 1983. text ed. 15.00x (ISBN 0-674-30147-1). Harvard U Pr.

Korean Traders Association. Korean Trade Directory, 1982-83. 23rd ed. LC 60-45910. 905p. 1982. 35.00x (ISBN 0-8002-3039-6). Intl Pubns Serv.

National Bureau of Statistics, Economic Planning Board, ed. Korea Statistical Yearbook 1981. 28th ed. LC 59-23483. 615p. 1981. 35.00x (ISBN 0-8002-3004-3). Intl Pubns Serv.

South Korea, 1980. 375.00x (ISBN 0-686-99849-9, Pub. by Metra England). State Mutual Bk.

Turner, John E., et al. Community Development & Rational Choice: A Korean Study, Vol. 20, Bk. 1. (Monograph Series in World Affairs). 120p. (Orig.). 1983. pap. 5.00 (ISBN 0-87940-072-2). U of Denver Intl.

Wijnbergen, S. Van. Short-Run Macro-Economic Adjustment Policies in South Korea: A Quantitative Analysis. LC 82-8408. (World Bank Staff Working Papers: No. 510). (Orig.). 1982. pap. 5.00 (ISBN 0-8213-0000-8). World Bank.

KOREA-FOREIGN RELATIONS

Dong, Wonmo, ed. Korean-American Relations at Crossroads. xiv, 178p. 1982. 8.00 (ISBN 0-932014-07-0). AKCS.

Kwak, Tai-Hwan & Chay, John, eds. U. S. - Korean Relations, 1882-1982. 433p. 1983. lib. bdg. 25.00x (ISBN 0-86531-608-2). Westview.

KOREA-HISTORY

see also Korean War, 1950-1953

Cumings, Bruce. Child of Conflict: The Korean-American Relationship 1943-1953. LC 82-48871. (Publications on Asia of the School of International Studies: No. 37). 350p. 1983. 22.50 (ISBN 0-295-95995-9). U of Wash Pr.

Lee, Ki-Baik. A New History of Korea. Wagner, Edward W. & Schultz, Edward J., trs. from Korean. (Harvard-Yenching Institute Ser.). (Illus.). 472p. 1983. text ed. 25.00x (ISBN 0-674-61575-1). Harvard U Pr.

Tai Sung An. North Korea in Transition: From Dictatorship to Dynasty. LC 82-15866. (Contributions in Political Science Ser.: No. 95). 216p. 1983. lib. bdg. 29.95 (ISBN 0-313-23638-0, ANK/). Greenwood.

KOREA-POLITICS AND GOVERNMENT

Kim, Chong Lim & Barkan, Joel D. The Legislative Connection: The Politics of Representation in Kenya, Korea, & Turkey. (Duke Press Policy Studies). (Illus.). 400p. Date not set. prepub. 35.00 (ISBN 0-8223-0534-8). Duke.

McCune, George M. Korea Today. LC 82-20290. xxi, 372p. 1982. Repr. of 1950 ed. lib. bdg. 45.00x (ISBN 0-313-23446-9, MCKT). Greenwood.

KOREAN LANGUAGE

Jones, B. J. Let's Learn Korean. LC 82-82601. (Illus.). 62p. 1982. 14.50 (ISBN 0-930878-27-2); cassette incl. Hollym Intl.

KOREAN LITERATURE-BIBLIOGRAPHY

Zong, In-sob. A Guide to Korean Literature. LC 82-84416. 296p. 1983. 20.00 (ISBN 0-930878-29-9). Hollym Intl.

KOREAN WAR, 1950-1953

Cumings, Bruce. Child of Conflict: The Korean-American Relationship 1943-1953. LC 82-48871. (Publications on Asia of the School of International Studies: No. 37). 350p. 1983. 22.50 (ISBN 0-295-95995-9). U of Wash Pr.

Goulden, J. C. Korea: The Untold Story of the War. 736p. 1983. pap. 12.95 (ISBN 0-07-023580-5, GB). McGraw.

KOREANS IN FOREIGN COUNTRIES

Kim, Byong-suh & Lee, Sang Hyun, eds. The Korean Immigrant in America. x, 175p. 1980. 7.00 (ISBN 0-932014-05-4). AKCS.

Sunoo, Harold H., ed. Koreans in America. 210p. 1977. 4.00 (ISBN 0-932014-02-X). AKCS.

KRIEGSSPIEL

see War Games

KRISHNA

Johnson, Una, et al. Krishna Reddy: A Retrospective. (Illus.). 78p. (Orig.). 1981. pap. 10.00 (ISBN 0-89062-138-1, Pub by Bronx Museum Arts). Pub Ctr Cult Res.

KRISHNAMURTI, JIDDU, 1895-

Lutyens, Mary. Krishnamurti: The Years of Fulfillment. 1983. 15.50 (ISBN 0-374-18224-8). FS&G.

KRONSTADT, RUSSIA-HISTORY-REVOLT, 1921

Getzler, Israel. Kronstadt Nineteen Seventeen-Nineteen Twenty-One: The Fate of a Soviet Democracy. LC 82-9575. (Soviet & East European Studies). 296p. 1983. 44.50 (ISBN 0-521-24479-X). Cambridge U Pr.

KUBO-FUTURISM

see Futurism

KUMRAN COMMUNITY

see Qumran Community

KUNDALI YOGA

see Yoga, Hatha

KUNG-FU

see Karate

KURDISH LANGUAGE

Krotkoff, Georg. A Neo-Aramaic Dialect of Kurdistan. (American Oriental Ser.: Vol. 64). 1982. 21.00 (ISBN 0-940490-64-1). Am Orient Soc.

KURMANJI LANGUAGE

see Kurdish Language

L

LABOR (OBSTETRICS)

see also Childbirth; Natural Childbirth; Obstetrics

Cohen, Wayne R. & Friedman, Emanuel A., eds. Management of Labor. 1983. price not set (ISBN 0-8391-1816-3, 17884). Univ Park.

Malinowski, Janet S. & DeLoach, Carolyn P. Nursing Care of the Labor Patient. (Illus.). 350p. 1983. pap. text ed. 12.95 (ISBN 0-8036-5802-8, 5802-8). Davis Co.

Worth. Labor & Delivery. 1983. write for info. (ISBN 0-07-071818-0); pap. write for info. McGraw.

Worth, C. Labor & Birth: A Coaching Guide for Fathers & Friends. (Having a Baby Ser.). 160p. 1983. 14.95 (ISBN 0-07-071818-0, GB); pap. 6.95. McGraw.

LABOR, COOLIE

see Chinese in Foreign Countries

LABOR, DIVISION OF

see Division of Labor

LABOR, HOURS OF

see Hours of Labor

LABOR, MIGRANT

see Migrant Labor

LABOR, ORGANIZED

see Trade-Unions

LABOR, PAINLESS (OBSTETRICS)

see Natural Childbirth

LABOR AND CAPITAL

see Industrial Relations

LABOR AND LABORING CLASSES

see also Apprentices; Arbitration, Industrial; Artisans; Capital; Church and Labor; Collective Bargaining; Cost and Standard of Living; Discrimination in Employment; Division of Labor; Employees, Dismissal of; Employees, Rating of; Employees' Representation in Management; Employment Agencies; Friendly Societies; Home Labor; Hours of Labor; Industrial Relations; International Labor Activities; Job Satisfaction; Machinery in Industry; Middle Classes; Migrant Labor; Occupations; Old Age Pensions; Part-Time Employment; Peasantry; Pension Trusts; Poor; Professions; Proletariat; Servants; Slavery; Socialism; Strikes and Lockouts; Supplementary Employment; Trade-Unions; Unemployed; Wages; Welfare Work in Industry; Youth-Employment

also classes of laborers, e.g. Coal-Miners, Railroads-Employees; subdivisions Economic Conditions and Social Conditions under names of countries, cities, etc., e.g. U. S.-Economic Conditions

Brennan, Mary E., ed. Canadian Conference, 14th Annual Nov. 23-27, 1981 Proceedings. 280p. (Orig.). 1982. pap. 14.00 (ISBN 0-89154-177-2). Intl Found Employ.

Burawoy, Michael & Shocpol, Theda, eds. Marxian Inquiries: Studies of Labor, Class, & States (Supplement to the American Journal of Sociology) 1983. lib. bdg. 25.00x (08039-0); pap. 12.50 (08040-4). U of Chicago Pr.

Day, Graham & Caldwell, Lisley, eds. Diversity & Decomposition in the Labour Market. 211p. 1982. text ed. 36.50x (ISBN 0-566-00556-5). Gower Pub Ltd.

Frisch, Michael H. & Walkowitz, Daniel J., eds. Working-Class America: Essays on Labor, Community, & American Society. LC 81-23971. (Working Class in American History Ser.). 368p. 1983. 29.50 (ISBN 0-252-00953-3); pap. 8.95 (ISBN 0-252-00954-1). U of Ill Pr.

Gorz, Andre. Beyond the Proletariat. 250p. 1982. 20.00 (ISBN 0-89608-168-0); pap. 7.50 (ISBN 0-89608-167-2). South End Pr.

Harris, Herbert. American Labor. 1938. text ed. 39.50x (ISBN 0-686-83463-1). Elliots Bks.

International Labour Office staff. Year Book of Labour Statistics, 1982. 42nd ed. xv, 760p. 1983. text ed. 63.00 (ISBN 92-2-003262-7). Intl Labour Office.

International Labour Organisation (Geneva), ed. Yearbook of Labor Statistics, 1981. 41st ed. LC 36-130. (Illus.). 704p. 1982. 75.00 (ISBN 92-2-002850-6). Intl Pubns Serv.

International Labour Organisation, 5th Conference of American States Members,Petropolis. Application & Supervision of Labour Legislation in Agriculture: Report I. 56p. 1952. 3.40 (ISBN 0-686-84712-1, CRA 1952/5/1). Intl Labour Office.

Keil, Hartmut & Jentz, John B., eds. German Workers in Industrial Chicago, 1850-1910: A Comparative Perspective. (Illus.). 300p. 1983. text ed. price not set (ISBN 0-87580-089-0). N Ill U Pr.

Langford, D. A. Direct Labour Organizations in the Construction Industry. 135p. 1982. text ed. 35.50x (ISBN 0-566-00542-5). Gower Pub Ltd.

Mother Jones. Mother Jones Speaks: Collected Writings & Speeches. Foner, Philip S., ed. 650p. 1983. lib. bdg. 35.00 (ISBN 0-913460-88-5); pap. 14.95 (ISBN 0-913460-89-3). Monad Pr.

New Forms of Work Organisation, Vol. 1. ix, 174p. 1982. 17.45 (ISBN 92-2-102005-3); pap. 12.45 (ISBN 92-2-101991-8). Intl Labour Office.

Paradis, Adrian A. The Labor Almanac. 230p. 1983. lib. bdg. 22.50 (ISBN 0-87287-374-9). Libs Unl.

Ponomarev, B. N., ed. International Working-Class Movement, Vol. 2. 654p. 1981. 11.50 (ISBN 0-8285-2295-2, Pub. by Progress Pubs USSR). Imported Pubns.

Rural Workers' Organisations in Fiji. 50p. 1982. 6.85 (ISBN 92-2-103004-0). Intl Labour Office.

Second Tripartite Technical Meeting for the Printing & Allied Tra des, Geneva, 22 September-1 October 1981: Note on the Proceedings. iii, 82p. 1982. 8.55 (ISBN 92-2-102936-0). Intl Labour Office.

Tomorrow's Workers. LC 82-17154. 1982. 25.95 (ISBN 0-669-06090-9). Heath.

Wallerstein, Immanuel, ed. Labor in the World Social Structure. (Explorations in the World Economy Ser.: Vol. 2). (Illus.). 272p. 1983. 25.00 (ISBN 0-8039-1922-0). Sage.

Wright, Becky A., ed. EDP Institute Proceedings, Dec. 13-16, 1981. 111p. (Orig.). 1982. pap. 10.00 (ISBN 0-89154-178-0). Intl Found Employ.

LABOR AND LABORING CLASSES-ACCIDENTS

see Industrial Accidents

LABOR AND LABORING CLASSES-DISCIPLINE

see Labor Discipline

LABOR AND LABORING CLASSES-HISTORY

Here are entered general works and works dealing with the United States in particular. Works dealing with the history of labor and laboring classes in other specific areas will be found in the geographical subdivisions which follow.

Cronin, James E. & Sirianni, Carmen, eds. Work, Community & Power: The Experience of Labor in Europe & America, 1900-1925. 1983. write for info. (ISBN 0-87722-308-4); pap. write for info. (ISBN 0-87722-309-2). Temple U Pr.

Green, James R., ed. Workers' Struggles, Past & Present: A "Radical America" Reader. 1983. write for info. (ISBN 0-87722-293-2). Temple U Pr.

Jones, Mike H. Supremacy & Subordination of Labour: The Hierarchy of Work in the Early Labour Movement. xi, 220p. 1982. text ed. 27.00x (ISBN 0-435-82417-1). Heinemann Ed.

Orth, Samuel P. Armies of Labor. 1919. text ed. 8.50x (ISBN 0-686-83479-8). Elliots Bks.

LABOR AND LABORING CLASSES-INSURANCE

see Insurance, Health; Old Age Pensions; Insurance, Unemployment

LABOR AND LABORING CLASSES-JUVENILE LITERATURE

Claypool, Jane. Unemployment. (Impact Ser.). 96p. (gr. 7 up). 1983. PLB 8.90 (ISBN 0-531-04586-2). Watts.

LABOR AND LABORING CLASSES-WAGES

see Wages

LABOR AND LABORING CLASSES-AFRICA

Magubane, Bernard & Nzongola-Ntalaja, eds. Proletarianization & Class Struggle in Africa. (Contemporary Marxism Ser.). (Illus., Orig.). 1983. pap. 6.50 (ISBN 0-89935-019-4). Synthesis Pubns.

LABOR AND LABORING CLASSES-ASIA

Seventh Asian Regional Conference, Teheran, 1971. Agenda for Asia: The Social Perplexities of the Second Development Decade. 48p. 1971. write for info. (ISBN 92-2-100103-2). Intl Labour Office.

LABOR AND LABORING CLASSES-CANADA

Struthers, James. No Fault of Their Own: Unemployment & the Canadian Welfare State, 1914-1941. (State & Economic Life Ser.). 264p. 1983. 31.00 (ISBN 0-8020-2480-7); pap. 12.50 (ISBN 0-8020-6502-3). U of Toronto Pr.

LABOR AND LABORING CLASSES-CHILE

DeShazo, Peter. Urban Workers & Labor Unions in Chile, 1902-1927. LC 82-70557. (Illus.). 384p. 1983. 30.00 (ISBN 0-299-09220-8). U of Wis Pr.

LABOR AND LABORING CLASSES-EUROPE

Cronin, James E. & Sirianni, Carmen, eds. Work, Community & Power: The Experience of Labor in Europe & America, 1900-1925. 1983. write for info. (ISBN 0-87722-308-4); pap. write for info. (ISBN 0-87722-309-2). Temple U Pr.

Hoxa, Enver. Party of Labor of Albania, Report Submitted to the 8th Congress. 82p. 1981. pap. 2.00 (ISBN 0-86714-021-6). Marxist-Leninist.

Immigrant Workers in Europe: Their Legal Status. 245p. 1982. pap. 18.75 (ISBN 92-3-101867-1, U1221, UNESCO). Unipub.

Pasic, N. & Grozdanic, S., eds. Workers' Management in Yugoslavia: Recent Developments & Trends. viii, 198p. 1982. 19.95 (ISBN 92-2-103034-2); pap. 14.25 (ISBN 92-2-103035-0). Intl Labour Office.

Sturmthal, Adolf. Left of Center: European Labor since World War II. LC 82-11022. 296p. 1983. 21.95 (ISBN 0-252-01008-6). U of Ill Pr.

Washington, Booker T. & Park, Robert E. The Man Farthest Down: A Record of Observation & Study in Europe. (Social Science Classics, Black Classics). 1983. pap. 19.95 (ISBN 0-87855-933-7). Transaction Bks.

LABOR AND LABORING CLASSES-FRANCE

Cross, Gary S. Immigrant Workers in Industrial France: The Making of a New Laboring Class. 1983. write for info. (ISBN 0-87722-300-9). Temple U Pr.

LABOR AND LABORING CLASSES-GREAT BRITAIN

Brown, Kenneth D. The English Labour Movement, 1700-1951. 280p. 1982. 45.00x (ISBN 0-7171-0870-8, Pub. by Macmillan England). State Mutual Bk.

Gorny, Joseph. The British Labour Movement & Zionism 1917-1948. 200p. 1983. text ed. 32.00x (ISBN 0-7146-3162-0, F Cass Co). Biblio Dist.

Hinton, James. Labour & Socialism: A History of the British Labour Movement, 1870-1970. LC 82-21798. 230p. 1983. lib. bdg. 22.00x (ISBN 0-87023-393-9). U of Mass Pr.

Kingsford, Peter. The Hunger Marchers in Britain, 1920-1940. 230p. 1982. text ed. 26.50x (ISBN 0-85315-555-0, Pub. by Lawrence & Wishart Ltd England). Humanities.

Redford, A. & Chaloner, W. H., eds. Labour Migration in England, 1800-50. 1976. pap. 9.00 (ISBN 0-7190-0636-8). Manchester.

Winter, Jay, ed. The Working Class in Modern British History. LC 82-9424. 336p. Date not set. price not set (ISBN 0-521-23444-1). Cambridge U Pr.

LABOR AND LABORING CLASSES-ISRAEL

Almogi, Yosef. Total Commitment. LC 81-70146. (Illus.). 320p. 1982. 20.00 (ISBN 0-8453-4749-7). Cornwall Bks.

LABOR AND LABORING CLASSES-JAPAN

Moore, Joe. Japanese Workers & the Struggle for Power, 1945-1947. LC 82-70552. (Illus.). 304p. 1983. 22.50 (ISBN 0-299-09320-4). U of Wis Pr.

LABOR AND LABORING CLASSES-LATIN AMERICA

MacCameron, Robert. Bananas, Labor, & Politics in Honduras: 1954-1963. (Foreign & Comparative Studies Program, Latin American Ser.: No. 5). (Orig.). 1982. pap. text ed. write for info. (ISBN 0-915984-96-2). Syracuse U Foreign Comp.

LABOR AND THE CHURCH

see Church and Labor

LABOR ARBITRATION
see Arbitration, Industrial
LABOR CONTRACT
see also Collective Bargaining; Employees, Dismissal Of; Grievance Procedures; Temporary Employment; Discrimination in Employment–Law and Legislation; Wages
Contracting Out. 19.95 (ISBN 0-930566-10-6). FMA Bus.
Rudman, Jack. Principal Labor Specialist. (Career Examination Ser.: C-2670). (Cloth bdg. avail. on request). pap. 12.00 (ISBN 0-8373-2670-2). Natl Learning.
LABOR COSTS
see also Non-Wage Payments; Wages
Simler, Norman J. The Impact of Unionism on Wage-Income Ratios in the Manufacturing Sector of the Economy. LC 82-21141. (University of Minnesota Studies in Economics & Business: No. 22). iii, 71p. 1983. Repr. of 1961 ed. lib. bdg. 22.50x (ISBN 0-313-23700-X, SIIM). Greenwood.
LABOR DISCIPLINE
Redeker, James R. Discipline: Policies & Procedures. 250p. 1983. text ed. 20.00 (ISBN 0-87179-394-6); pap. text ed. 15.00 (ISBN 0-87179-399-7). BNA.
LABOR DISPUTES
see also Arbitration, Industrial; Collective Bargaining; Strikes and Lockouts
Institute for the Study of Labor & Economic Crisis. Worker's Report on the Conditions of Labor & Their Effect on Patient Care at San Francisco General Hospital. 42p. (Orig.). 1979. pap. 2.00 (ISBN 0-89935-006-2). Synthesis Pubns.
LABOR ECONOMICS
see also Industrial Relations; Labor and Laboring Classes
Appleton, J. D. Labour Economics. 3rd ed. 250p. 1982. pap. text ed. 15.95 (ISBN 0-7121-2703-8). Intl Ideas.
Creedy, Thomas. Economics of Labor. 1982. text ed. 19.95 (ISBN 0-408-10826-6). Butterworth.
DeBrizzi, John A. Ideology & the Rise of Labor Theory in America. LC 82-12024. (Contributions in Labor History Ser.: No. 14). 224p. 1983. lib. bdg. 29.95 (ISBN 0-313-23614-3, DID/). Greenwood.
Joll, Caroline & McKenna, Chris. Developments in Labour Market Analysis. (Illus.). 40p. 1983. text ed. 29.95x (ISBN 0-04-331089-3); pap. text ed. 16.50x (ISBN 0-04-331090-7). Allen Unwin.
LABOR EXCHANGES
see Employment Agencies
LABOR FORCE
see Labor Supply
LABOR GRIEVANCES
see Grievance Procedures
LABOR LAWS AND LEGISLATION
see also Employees, Dismissal Of; Factory Laws and Legislation; Hours of Labor; Labor Contract; Strikes and Lockouts; Trade-Unions; Workmen's Compensation
also subdivision Legal Status, Laws, etc. under names of professions, e.g. Teachers–Legal Status, Laws, etc.
Atleson, James B. Values & Assumptions in American Labor Law. LC 82-21993. 240p. 1983. lib. bdg. 25.00x (ISBN 0-87023-389-0). U of Mass Pr.
Barbash, Joseph & Feerick, John D. Unjust Dismissal & At Will Employment. (Litigation & Administrative Practice Course Handbook Ser.). 343p. 1982. pap. 30.00 (H4-4885). PLI.
Blanpain, Roger, ed. Comparative Labour Law & Industrial Relations. 416p. 1983. text ed. 30.00 (ISBN 0-87179-396-2). BNA.
Brena. La Ley Federal del Trabajo. 250p. (Span.). 1983. pap. text ed. write for info. (ISBN 0-06-310067-3, Pub. by HarLA Mexico). Har-Row.
Cox, Archibald. Law & the National Labor Policy. LC 82-20930. 111p. 1983. Repr. of 1960 ed. lib. bdg. 27.50x (ISBN 0-313-23794-8, COLN). Greenwood.
Deterrence & Compensation: Legal Liability in Occupational Safety & Health. 76p. 1982. pap. 10.00 (ISBN 92-2-103010-5, ILO 194, ILO). Unipub.
Karatnycky, Adrian & Motyl, Alexander. Workers Rights, East & West. 130p. 1980. pap. 4.59 (ISBN 0-87855-867-5). Transaction Bks.
Labor Laws of Korea. Date not set. 10.00. A M Newman.
Mother Jones. Mother Jones Speaks: Collected Writings & Speeches. Foner, Philip S., ed. 650p. 1983. lib. bdg. 35.00 (ISBN 0-913460-88-5); pap. 14.95 (ISBN 0-913460-89-3). Monad Pr.
Summers, Clyde W., et al. Statutory Supplement to Cases & Materials on Labor Law. 2nd ed. (University Casebook Ser.). 104p. 1982. pap. text ed. write for info. (ISBN 0-88277-084-5). Foundation Pr.
Working Conditions & Enviornment: A Wokers' Education Manual. viii, 84p. 7.15 (ISBN 92-2-103189-6). Intl Labour Office.
LABOR LAWS AND LEGISLATION–ASIA
Amjad, Rashid, ed. The Development of Labou-Intensive Industry in ASEAN Countries. 337p. 1981. 15.00 (ISBN 92-2-102750-3); pap. 10.00 (ISBN 92-2-102751-1). Intl Labour Office.
LABOR LAWS AND LEGISLATION–LATIN AMERICA
Nash, June. We Eat the Mines & the Mines Eat Us: Dependence & Exploitation in Bolivian Tin Mines. 363p. 1982. pap. 13.00 (ISBN 0-231-04711-8). Columbia U Pr.
LABOR LAWS AND LEGISLATION, INTERNATIONAL
International Labour Conference, 67th Session: Record of Proceedings. ciii, 1254p. 1981. 42.00 (ISBN 92-2-102415-6). Intl Labour Office.
LABOR-MANAGEMENT RELATIONS
see Industrial Relations
LABOR MARKET
see Labor Supply
LABOR NEGOTIATIONS
see Arbitration, Industrial; Collective Bargaining
LABOR ORGANIZATIONS
see Trade-Unions
LABOR OUTPUT
see Labor Productivity
LABOR PARTY (GREAT BRITAIN)
see Labour Party (Great Britain)
LABOR POLICY
see also Labor Laws and Legislation; Manpower Policy
Allen, Robert E. & Keaveny, Timothy J. Contemporary Labor Relations. 672p. 1983. text ed. 24.95 (ISBN 0-686-82182-3). A-W.
LABOR PRODUCTIVITY
see also Machinery in Industry
Gibson, Price. Quality Circles: One Approach to Productivity Improvement. (Work in America Institute Studies in Productivity). 1982. 35.00 (ISBN 0-08-029507-X). Pergamon.
Gruneberg, Michael M. & Oborne, David J. Industrial Productivity: A Psychological Perspective. 232p. 1982. 60.00 (ISBN 0-333-28160-8, Pub. by Macmillan England). State Mutual Bk.
Guggenheim, Gus N. Protocol for Productivity. Guggenheim, Alan, ed. (Textile Industry Management Ser.: No. 1). 132p. 1982. 17.95x (ISBN 0-910377-03-0); pap. 13.95x (ISBN 0-910377-00-6). Guggenheim.
Guzzo, Richard A. & Bondy, Jeffrey S. A Guide to Worker Productivity Experiments in the U. S., 1976-1981. 125p. 14.50 (ISBN 0-686-84782-2). Work in Amer.
Justus, Fred. Products of America. (Social Studies Ser.). 24p. (gr. 3-6). 1979. wkbk. 5.00 (ISBN 0-8209-0267-5, POA-1). ESP.
Kanter, Rosabeth M. The Changemasters: Innovation for Productivity in the American Corporation. 1983. 16.50 (ISBN 0-671-42802-0). S&S.
Moses, Joseph L. & Byham, William C., eds. Applying the Assessment Center Method. 322p. 26.00 (ISBN 0-686-84783-0). Work in Amer.
Rosow, Jerome M. & Zager, Robert. Productivity Through Work Innovations. 176p. 1982. 15.00 (ISBN 0-686-84772-5); softcover summary 6.50 (ISBN 0-686-84773-3). Work in Amer.
Zager, Robert, ed. The Innovative Organization: Productivity Programs in Action. Rosow, Michael P. 300p. 27.50 (ISBN 0-686-84779-2). Work in Amer.
LABOR PRODUCTIVITY–ACCOUNTING
see Productivity Accounting
LABOR RELATIONS
see Industrial Relations
LABOR REPRESENTATION IN REGULATION OF INDUSTRY
see Employees' Representation in Management
LABOR SUPPLY
see also Employment Agencies; Job Vacancies; Manpower; Manpower Policy; Unemployed; Youth–Employment
Cooper, C. A. & Clark, J. A., eds. Employment, Economics & Technology: The Impact of Technological Change on the Labor Market. LC 82-42543. 180p. 1982. 25.00x (ISBN 0-312-24459-2). St Martin.
Dixon, Marlene & Jonas, Susanne, eds. The New Nomads: From Immigrant Labor to Transnational Working Class. LC 82-10356. (Contemporary Marxism Ser.). (Illus.). 165p. (Orig.). 1982. pap. 6.50 (ISBN 0-89935-018-6). Synthesis Pubns.
Joll, Caroline & McKenna, Chris. Developments in Labour Market Analysis. (Illus.). 40p. 1983. text ed. 29.95x (ISBN 0-04-331089-3); pap. text ed. 16.50x (ISBN 0-04-331090-7). Allen Unwin.
Krueger, Anne O. Trade & Employment in Developing Countries: Synthesis & Conclusions, Vol. 3. LC 80-15826. (National Bureau of Economic Research - Monograph). 232p. 1983. 25.00x (ISBN 0-226-45494-0). U of Chicago Pr.
Labour Market Inforrmation Through Key Informants. 90p. 5.70 (ISBN 92-2-103082-2). Intl Labour Office.
Leary, Virginia. International Labour & National Law. 1981. lib. bdg. 52.50 (ISBN 90-247-2551-8, Pub. by Martinus Nijhoff Netherlands). Kluwer Boston.
OECD Staff. Labour Force Statistics, 1969-1980. (Orig., English-French.). 1982. pap. 22.00x (ISBN 92-64-02327-5). OECD.
LABOR TURNOVER
see also Employment Agencies
Vogt, Judith F. & Cox, John L. Retaining Professional Nurses: A Planned Process. 03/1983 ed. (Illus.). 256p. text ed. 19.95 (ISBN 0-8016-5226-X). Mosby.
LABOR-UNIONS
see Trade-Unions
LABORATORIES
see also Chemical Laboratories; Medical Laboratories
Hawkins, M. D. Technician Safety & Laboratory Practice. 256p. 1980. 30.00x (ISBN 0-304-30550-2, Pub. by Cassell England). State Mutual Bk.
LABORATORIES–APPARATUS AND SUPPLIES
Carelse, Xavier. Making Science Laboratory Equipment: A Manual for Students & Teachers in Developing Countries. 240p. 1983. pap. price not set (ISBN 0-471-10353-5, Pub. by Wiley-Interscience). Wiley.
LABORATORIES, CHEMICAL
see Chemical Laboratories
LABORATORIES, MEDICAL
see Medical Laboratories
LABORATORY TECHNICIANS
see also Dental Technicians; Medical Technologists
Hawkins, M. D. Technician Safety & Laboratory Practice. 256p. 1980. 30.00x (ISBN 0-304-30550-2, Pub. by Cassell England). State Mutual Bk.
Rudman, Jack. Laboratory Technician Trainee. (Career Examination Ser.: C-2909). (Cloth bdg. avail on request). pap. 10.00 (ISBN 0-8373-2909-4). Natl Learning.
LABORERS
see Labor and Laboring Classes
LABOUR PARTY (GREAT BRITAIN)
Bealey, Frank & Pelling, Henry. Labour & Politics, 1900-1906: A History of the Labour Representation Committee. LC 82-15828. xi, 317p. 1982. lib. bdg. 45.00x (ISBN 0-313-23693-3, BELAP). Greenwood.
Gallagher, Michael. The Irish Labour Party in Transition, 1957-81. 351p. 1983. 25.00 (ISBN 0-7190-0866-2). Manchester.
Hinton, James. Labour & Socialism: A History of the British Labour Movement, 1870-1970. LC 82-21798. 230p. 1983. lib. bdg. 22.00x (ISBN 0-87023-393-9). U of Mass Pr.
Kogan, David & Kogan, Maurice. The Battle for the Labour Party. 160p. 1982. 20.00x (ISBN 0-312-06958-8). St Martin.
Minkin, Lewis. The Labour Party Conference: A Study in the Politics of Intra-Party Democracy. 464p. 1982. pap. 12.50 (ISBN 0-7190-0800-X). Manchester.
Warde, Alan. Consensus & Beyond: The Development of Labour Party Strategy since the Second World War. 240p. 1982. 25.00 (ISBN 0-7190-0849-2). Manchester.
LACE AND LACE MAKING
see also Macrame
Lorant, Tessa. The Batsford Book of Hand & Machine Knitted Laces. (Illus.). 144p. 1982. 27.50 (ISBN 0-7134-3920-3, Pub. by Batsford England). David & Charles.
Maidens, Ena. The Techniques of Crocheted & Openwork Lace. (Illus.). 144p. 1982. 22.50 (ISBN 0-7134-2568-7, Pub. by Batsford England). David & Charles.
Stott, Geraldine & Cook, Bridget. One Hundred Traditional Bobbin Lace Patterns. LC 82-82932. (Illus.). 144p. (Orig.). 1983. pap. 12.95 (ISBN 0-88332-290-0, 8250). Larousse.
Wardle, Patricia. Victorian Lace. Date not set. 21.95 (ISBN 0-903585-13-8). Robin & Russ.
Wright, Thomas. The Romance of the Lace Pillow. Date not set. 21.95 (ISBN 0-903585-12-X). Robin & Russ.
LACERTILIA
see Lizards
LADYFISH
see Bonefish
LAFAYETTE, MARIE JOSEPH PAUL YVES ROCH GILBERT DU MOTIER, MARQUIS DE, 1757-1834
Bernier, Olivier. Lafayette: Hero of Two Worlds. (Illus.). 320p. 1983. 17.50 (ISBN 0-525-24181-7, 01699-510). Dutton.
LAFOLLETTE, PHILIP FOX, 1897-
Miller, John E. Governor Philip F. LaFollette: The Wisconsin Progressives & the New Deal. 256p. 1982. 21.00. U of MO Pr.
LAGUARDIA, FIORELLO HENRY, 1882-1947
Elliott, Lawrence. Little Flower: The Life & Times of Fiorello La Guardia. (Illus.). 256p. 1983. 13.95 (ISBN 0-688-02057-7). Morrow.
LAISSEZ-FAIRE
see also Competition; Industry and State
Hodgetts, R. & Smart, T. Essentials of Economics & Free Enterprise. (gr. 9-12). 1982. pap. text ed. 19.60 (ISBN 0-201-03958-3); manual 21.20 (ISBN 0-201-03959-1). A-W.
Lindsell, Harold. Free Enterprise: A Judeo-Christian Defense. 1982. pap. 5.95 (ISBN 0-8423-0922-5). Tyndale.
LAITY
Henrichsen, Walter A. & Garrison, William N. Layman, Look Up! God Has a Place for You. 128p. 1983. pap. 4.95 (ISBN 0-310-37721-8). Zondervan.
LAKE CHAMPLAIN
see Champlain, Lake
LAKE DISTRICT, ENGLAND
Acland, C. H. D. The Country Life Picture Book of the Lake District. (Illus.). 1983. 19.95 (ISBN 0-393-01733-8, Country Life). Norton.
Marshall, J. D. & Walton, J. K. The Lake Counties from Nineteen-Thirty to the Mid Twentieth Century. 320p. 1982. 30.00 (ISBN 0-7190-0824-7). Manchester.
Presences of Nature: Words & Images of the Lake District. 224p. 1982. pap. 50.00x (ISBN 0-907852-00-9, Pub. by Travelling Light). State Mutual Bk.
LAKE-DWELLERS AND LAKE-DWELLINGS
Fuller, Frank. Engineering of Pile Installations. (Illus.). 320p. 1983. 37.50 (ISBN 0-07-022618-0, P&RB). McGraw.
LAKES
see also Limnology
also names of lakes e.g. Superior Lake
Dussart, Bernard H. Man-Made Lakes As Modified Ecosystems: Scope Report 2. (Scientific Committee on Problems of the Environment Ser.). 76p. 1972. pap. 8.00x (ISBN 0-471-99595-9, Pub. by Wiley-Interscience). Wiley.
Ilmavirta, V. & Jones, R. I. Lakes & Water Management. 1982. 54.50 (ISBN 90-6193-758-2, Pub. by Junk Pubs Netherlands). Kluwer Boston.
Kabisch, Klaus & Hemmerling, Joachim. Small Ponds, Lakes & Pools. (Illus.). 261p. 1983. 14.95 (ISBN 0-668-05674-6, 5674). Arco.
Sebestyen, Tibor. Lake Balaton: A Comprehensive Guide. Halapy, Lilli, tr. from Hungarian. (Illus.). 206p. 1982. 10.00x (ISBN 963-13-1234-8). Intl Pubns Serv.
Thorton, J. A. Lake McIlwaine: The Eutrophication & Recovery of a Tropical African Man-Made Lake. 1982. text ed. 49.50 (ISBN 90-6193-102-9, Pub. by Junk Pubs Netherlands). Kluwer Boston.
Updegraffe, Imelda & Updegraffe, Robert. Rivers & Lakes. (Turning Points Ser.). (Illus.). 24p. 1983. pap. 3.50 (ISBN 0-14-049192-9, Puffin). Penguin.
LAMAZE METHOD OF CHILDBIRTH
see Natural Childbirth
LAMB, CHARLES, 1775-1834
Bakalla, Muhammad H. Arabic Linguistics: An Introduction & Bibliography. 600p. 1982. 44.00 (ISBN 0-7201-1583-3, Pub. by Mansell England). Wilson.
Talfourd, T. N. The Letters & Life of Charles Lamb. 370p. 1982. Repr. of 1911 ed. lib. bdg. 40.00 (ISBN 0-89984-466-9). Century Bookbindery.
LAMBETH CONFERENCE
Smyth, Norman. Story of Church Unity: The Lambeth Conference of Anglican Bishops & the Congregational-Episcopal Approaches. 1923. text ed. 29.50x (ISBN 0-686-83788-6). Elliots Bks.
LAMPREYS
Hardisty, M. W. & Potter, I. G., eds. Biology of Lampreys. Vol. 4A. write for info.; Vol. 4B. write for info. (ISBN 0-12-324824-8). Acad Pr.
LAMPS
Smith, Ruth E. & Feltner, Helen A. Price Guide to Miniature Lamps Book I & II. 48p. 1982. pap. 10.00 (ISBN 0-916838-72-2). Schiffer.
Sussman, Varda. Decorated Jewish Oil Lamps. (Illus.). 144p. 1982. text ed. 50.00x (ISBN 0-85668-164-4, 40455, Pub. by Aris & Phillips England). Humanities.
LANCELOT
Newman, Sharan. The Chessboard Queen. 320p. 1983. 13.95 (ISBN 0-312-13176-3). St Martin.
LAND
see Land Use
LAND–VALUATION
see Farms–Valuation; Real Property–Valuation
LAND, CONDEMNATION OF
see Eminent Domain
LAND, RECLAMATION OF
see Reclamation of Land
LAND CREDIT
see Agricultural Credit
LAND DRAINAGE
see Drainage
LAND FORMS
see Landforms
LAND-GRANT COLLEGES
see State Universities and Colleges
LAND RECLAMATION
see Reclamation of Land
LAND REFORM
Here are entered works on land distribution combined with the socio-economic policy relating to the population of that area of distribution.
see also Agriculture and State
Geisler, Charles & Popper, Frank. Land Reform, American Style. 256p. Date not set. text ed. 28.00x (ISBN 0-86598-016-0). Allanheld.
Herring, Ronald J. Land to the Tiller: The Political Economy of Agrarian Reform in South Asia. LC 82-48903. (Illus.). 336p. 1983. text ed. 30.00x (ISBN 0-300-02725-7). Yale U Pr.
Moise, Edwin E. Land Reform in China & North Vietnam: Consolidating the Revolution at the Village Level. LC 82-15900. 330p. 1983. 18.95x (ISBN 0-8078-1547-0). U of NC Pr.
Simon, Laurence R. El Salvador Land Reform: Nineteen Eighty to Nineteen Eighty-One. Stephens, James C., Jr., ed. (Impact Audit Ser.: No. 2). 55p. (Orig.). 1981. pap. 5.00 (ISBN 0-910281-01-7). Oxfam Am.
LAND SLIDES
see Landslides
LAND SURVEYING
see Surveying

LAND TAX
see Land Value Taxation; Real Property Tax
LAND TENURE-LAW
see also Homestead Law; Land Titles; Landlord and Tenant; Leases; Real Property
Scurlock, John. Retroactive Legislation Affecting Interests in Land. LC 54-62006. (Michigan Legal Studies). xv, 390p. 1982. Repr. of 1953 ed. lib. bdg. 30.00 (ISBN 0-89941-175-4). W S Hein.
LAND TENURE-GERMANY
Dilcher, Gerhard & Hoke, Rudolf. Grundrechte Im 19, Jahrhundert. 283p. (Ger.). 1982. write for info. (ISBN 3-8204-7100-6). P Lang Pubs.
LAND TITLES
see also Leases; Mortgages; Possession (Law); Real Property; Vendors and Purchasers
Crow, Judson O. McDowell County, North Carolina, Land Entry Abstracts 1843-1869, Vol. 1. LC 82-20499. 504p. 1983. pap. 25.00 (ISBN 0-87152-365-5). Reprint.
LAND TRUSTS
Goldstein, Herb, compiled by. Compendium of Land Trust Documents. pap. 3.00 (ISBN 0-686-84741-5). Comm Serv.
LAND USE
see also Agriculture; Eminent Domain; Feudalism; Real Estate Business; Real Property; Reclamation of Land; Rent
Black, Peter E. Conservation of Water & Related Resources. 234p. 1982. 25.95 (ISBN 0-03-060419-2). Praeger.
Everhart, Marion E. Land Classification for Rural & Urban Uses, Management & Valuation. LC 82-74565. (Illus.). 190p. 1983. 23.50 (ISBN 0-935988-23-8). Todd Pub.
Foth, Henry & Schafer, John. Soil Geography & Land Use. LC 79-27731. 484p. 1980. text ed. 32.95 (ISBN 0-471-01710-8). Wiley.
Kundell, James E. & White, Fred C. Prime Farmland in Georgia. 49p. 1982. pap. 6.50 (ISBN 0-89854-081-X). U of GA Inst Govt.
LaConte, P. & Haines, Y. Y. Water Resources & Land-Use Planning: A Systems Approach. 1982. lib. bdg. 57.50 (ISBN 90-247-2726-X, Pub. by Martinus Nijhoff Netherlands). Kluwer Boston.
Mandelker, Daniel R. Land Use Law. 400p. 1982. 35.00 (ISBN 0-87215-525-0). Michie-Bobbs.
Peterson, Craig A. & McCarthy, Claire. Handling Zoning & Land Use Litigation: A Practical Guide. 769p. 1982. 40.00 (ISBN 0-87215-451-3). Michie-Bobbs.
Pooley, Beverly J. Planning & Zoning in the United States. LC 61-63301. (Michigan Legal Publications Ser.). 123p. 1982. Repr. of 1961 ed. lib. bdg. 26.00 (ISBN 0-89941-173-8). W S Hein.
Real Estate Research Corporation. Infill Development Strategies. LC 82-50809. (Illus.). 132p. 1982. pap. 24.95 (ISBN 0-87420-613-8, 127). Urban Land.
Roberts, E. F. The Law & the Preservation of Agricultural Land. LC 82-12616. 145p. 1982. pap. 6.95 (ISBN 0-9609010-0-0). NE Regional Ctr.
Rudman, Jack. Land Management Specialist. (Career Examination Ser.: C-2618). (Cloth bdg. avail. on request). pap. 10.00 (ISBN 0-8373-2618-4). Natl Learning.
--Principal Land Management Specialist. (Career Examination Ser.: C-2620). (Cloth bdg. avail. on request). pap. 12.00 (ISBN 0-8373-2620-6). Natl Learning.
--Senior Juvenile Counselor. (Career Examination Ser.: C-421). (Cloth bdg. avail. on request). pap. 12.00 (ISBN 0-8373-0421-0). Natl Learning.
--Senior Land Management Specialist. (Career Examination Ser.: C-2619). (Cloth bdg. avail. on request). pap. 12.00 (ISBN 0-8373-2619-2). Natl Learning.
Woodward, Robert G., ed. Advanced Land Management. 1982. 20.00 (ISBN 0-89419-243-4). Inst Energy.
LAND USE-TAXATION
see Land Value Taxation; Real Property Tax
LAND USE-UNITED STATES
Jackson, R. H. Land Use In America. (Scripta Geography Ser.). 226p. 1982. 22.95x (ISBN 0-470-27363-1). Halsted Pr.
Platt, Rutherford H. & Macinko, George, eds. Beyond the Urban Fringe: Land-Use Issues of Nonmetropolitan America. (Illus.). 384p. 1983. 39.50x (ISBN 0-8166-1099-1). U of Minn Pr.
LAND USE, URBAN-PLANNING
see City Planning
LAND VALUATION
see Farms-Valuation; Real Property-Valuation
LAND VALUE TAXATION
McLure, Charles E., Jr. & Mieszkowski, Peter, eds. Fiscal Federalism & the Taxation of Natural Resources: Nineteen Eighty One Tred Conference. LC 81-48561. (A Lincoln Institute of Land Policy Bk.). 272p. 1982. 35.95 (ISBN 0-669-05436-4). Lexington Bks.
Pittsburgh's Land Value Tax. 16p. 1981. pap. 0.25 (ISBN 0-911312-61-7). Schalkenbach.
Prest, A. R. The Taxation of Urban Land. 208p. 1982. 25.00 (ISBN 0-7190-0817-4). Manchester.
LAND-WARRANTS
see Land Titles

LANDFORMS
see also names of topographical features e.g. Mountains; Plains
Twidale, C. R. Granite Landforms. 372p. 1982. 115.00 (ISBN 0-444-42116-5). Elsevier.
LANDLORD AND TENANT
see also Apartment Houses; Leases; Rent
Baranov, Alvin B. How to Evict a Tenant. 11th ed. (Illus.). 147p. 1982. Repr. of 1978 ed. 9.95 (ISBN 0-910531-04-8). Wolcotts.
Bierbrier, Doreen. Living with Tenants: How to Happily Share Your House with Renters for Profit & Security. 128p. (Orig.). 1983. pap. 7.00 (ISBN 0-9609586-0-6). Housing Connect.
Kane, Andy. Tenant's Revenge: How to Tame Your Landlord. (Illus.). 96p. 1982. pap. 6.95 (ISBN 0-87364-258-9). Paladin Ent.
Nelken, D., ed. The Limits of the Legal Process: A Study of Landlords, Law & Crime. Date not set. price not set (ISBN 0-12-515280-9). Acad Pr.
Rudman, Jack. Senior Tenant Supervisor. (Career Examination Ser.: C-544). (Cloth bdg. avail. on request). pap. 12.00 (ISBN 0-8373-0544-6). Natl Learning.
--Tenant Supervisor. (Career Examination Ser.: C-543). (Cloth bdg. avail. on request). pap. 10.00 (ISBN 0-8373-0543-8). Natl Learning.
LANDMARKS, PRESERVATION OF
see Natural Monuments
LANDSCAPE ARCHITECTURE
see also Landscape Gardening; Parks; Perennials; Plants, Ornamental; Shrubs; Trees; Urban Beautification; Woody Plants
Bye, A. E. Art into Landscape, Landscape into Art. LC 82-22406. (Illus.). 178p. 1983. 26.00 (ISBN 0-914886-19-3); pap. 19.75 (ISBN 0-914886-20-7). PDA Pubs.
Kerr, Kathleen W. & Kerr, Francis K., eds. Cost Data for Landscape Construction, 1982. 4th ed. (Illus.). 264p. 1983. pap. 27.50 (ISBN 0-937890-03-0). Kerr Assoc.
Michel, Tim. Homeowner's Guide to Landscape Design. (Illus.). 176p. (Orig.). 1983. pap. 10.95 (ISBN 0-914378-94-5). Countryman.
Moffat, Anne & Schiller, Marc. Landscape Design that Saves Energy. (Illus.). 224p. 1981. pap. 9.95 (ISBN 0-688-00395-8). Quill NY.
Wikesr, Kathleen, ed. Lafile. 2000p. 1983. 34.95 (ISBN 0-911241-03-5). Am Soc Landscape.
LANDSCAPE ARCHITECTURE-JAPAN
Higuchi, Tadahiko. The Visual & Spatial Structure of Landscapes. Terry, Charles, tr. from Japanese. (Illus.). 232p. 1983. 20.00x (ISBN 0-262-08120-2). MIT Pr.
LANDSCAPE GARDENING
see also Landscape Architecture
Flint, Harrison. The Country Journal Book of Hardy Trees & Shrubs. (Illus.). 176p. (Orig.). 1983. pap. 8.95 (ISBN 0-918678-02-1). Country Journ.
Landscaping. LC 82-19374. (Home Repairs & Improvement Ser.). lib. bdg. 15.96 (ISBN 0-8094-3515-2, Pub. by Time-Life). Silver.
Michel, Tim. Homeowner's Guide to Landscape Design. (Illus.). 176p. (Orig.). 1983. pap. 10.95 (ISBN 0-914378-94-5). Countryman.
Ribalta, Marta, ed. Habitat: Lanscape Gardening, No. 7. (Illus.). 94p. 1982. pap. 14.95 (ISBN 84-7031-089-5, Pub. by Editorial Blume Spain). Intl Schol Bk Serv.
Smith, Ken. Southern Home Landscaping. (Illus.). 192p. (Orig.). 1982. pap. 7.95 (ISBN 0-89586-063-5). H P Bks.
LANDSCAPE PAINTING
Finley, Gerald. George Heriot: Postmaster Painter of the Canadas. 288p. 1983. 35.00 (ISBN 0-8020-5584-2). U of Toronto Pr.
Proby, Kathryn H. Mario Sanchez-Painter of Key West Memories. LC 81-50557. (Illus.). 64p. Date not set. pap. 14.95 (ISBN 0-686-84313-4). Banyan Bks.
Rosenthal, Michael. Constable: The East Anglian Landscapes. LC 82-48908. (Illus.). 240p. 1983. 29.95 (ISBN 0-300-03014-2). Yale U Pr.
LANDSCAPE PHOTOGRAPHY
see Photography-Landscapes
LANDSLIDES
Reeves, R. B., ed. Application of Walls to Landslide Control Problems. LC 82-70668. 144p. 1982. pap. text ed. 14.00 (ISBN 0-87262-302-5). Am SOc Civil Eng.
LANGERHANS, ISLANDS OF
see Pancreas
LANGUAGE, LEGAL
see Law-Language
LANGUAGE, PHILOSOPHY OF
see Languages-Philosophy
LANGUAGE, PSYCHOLOGY OF
see Psycholinguistics
LANGUAGE ACQUISITION
see Children-Language

LANGUAGE AND LANGUAGES
Here are entered works on language in general, works on the origin and history of language, and surveys of languages; Works dealing with the scientific study of human speech, including phonetics, phonemics, morphology and syntax, are entered under Linguistics. Works on the philosophy and psychology of language are entered under Languages-Philosophy, and Languages-Psychology, respectively.
see also Bilingualism; Children-Language; Communication; Conversation; Languages-Philosophy; Linguistics; Multilingualism; Programming Languages (Electronic Computers); Psycholinguistics; Rhetoric; Semantics; Sociolinguistics; Speech; Writing
also names of particular languages or groups of cognate languages, e.g. English Language, Semitic Languages
Andersen, Roger W., ed. Pidginization & Creolization & Language Acquisition. 320p. 1983. pap. text ed. 20.95 (ISBN 0-88377-266-3). Newbury Hse.
Bailey, Charles-James N. On the Yin & Yang Nature of Language. viii, 120p. 1982. pap. 10.95 (ISBN 0-89720-060-8). Karoma.
Balakian, A. A., ed. The Symbolist Movement in the Literature of European Languages. (Comparative History of Literatures in European Language Ser.: Vol. 2). 732p. 1982. text ed. 53.00x (ISBN 963-05-2694-8, Pub. by Kultura Pr Hungary). Humanities.
Bloom, Lois, ed. Readings in Language Development. LC 77-10717. (Communications Disorders Ser.). 506p. 1978. text ed. 26.50x (ISBN 0-471-08221-X). Wiley.
Borg, Albert J. & De Waard, Jan. A Study of Aspect in Maltese. xvi, 188p. 1981. 15.50 (ISBN 0-89720-042-X); pap. 10.50 (ISBN 0-89720-043-8). Karoma.
Claussen, Paulette M. Speech-Language-Hearing Update: The Standard Reference Guide, Vol. 5, No. 2. 790p. 1982. 40.00 (ISBN 0-686-84041-0). Update Pubns AZ.
--Speech-Language-Hearing Update: The Standard Reference Guide, Vol. 6, No. 1. 80p. 1982. 40.00 (ISBN 0-943002-02-8). Update Pubns AZ.
Gollasch, Frederick, ed. Language & Literacy: The Selected Writings of Kenneth S. Goodman: Reading, Language & the Classroom Teacher, Vol. II. 200p. 1982. 30.00 (ISBN 0-7100-9005-6). Routledge & Kegan.
Kodij, J. Ambiguity in Natural Language. 1973. pap. 17.00 (ISBN 0-444-10508-5). Elsevier.
Kugler, Paul. The Alchemy of Discourse: An Archetypal Approach to Language. 144p. 1982. 21.50 (ISBN 0-8387-5020-6). Bucknell U Pr.
Lass, Norman J., ed. Speech & Language: Advances in Basic Research & Practice, Vol. 6. (Serial Publication). 496p. 1982. 55.00 (ISBN 0-12-608606-0). Acad Pr.
Lefebvre, Claire. Syntaxe de l'Haitien. Magloire-Holly, Helene & Piou, Nanie, eds. xiv, 251p. (Fr.). 1982. pap. 15.00 (ISBN 0-89720-055-1). Karoma.
Lewis, Michael & Rosenblum, Leonard A. Interaction, Conversation & the Development of Language. LC 82-21225. 344p. 1983. Repr. of 1977 ed. lib. bdg. write for info. (ISBN 0-89874-588-8). Krieger.
Miller, John W. The Definition of the Thing: With Some Notes on Language. 192p. 1983. pap. 6.25x (ISBN 0-393-30059-5). Norton.
Moorhouse, A. C. The Syntax of Sophocles. (Mnemosyne: Suppl. 75). xiii, 353p. 1982. pap. write for info. (ISBN 90-04-06599-7). E J Brill.
Pelligrini, Anthony D. & Yawkey, Thomas D. The Development of Oral & Written Language in Social Contexts. Freedle, Roy O., ed. (Advances in Discourse Processes Ser.: Vol. 13). 320p. (Orig.). 1983. text ed. 32.50 (ISBN 0-89391-171-2); pap. text ed. 16.50 (ISBN 0-89391-172-0). Ablex Pub.
Pope, M. K. From Latin to Modern French. 600p. 1934. 20.00 (ISBN 0-7190-0176-5). Manchester.
Rauch, Irmangard & Carr, Gerald F., eds. Language Change. LC 82-48626. 288p. 1983. 20.00x (ISBN 0-253-33196-X). Ind U Pr.
Revesz, G. E. Introduction to Formal Languages. 256p. 1983. 25.95x (ISBN 0-07-051916-1). McGraw.
Richards, Jack. Error Analysis: Perspectives on Second Language Acquisition. (Applied Linguistics & Language Study). 1974. pap. text ed. 10.75 (ISBN 0-582-55044-0). Longman.
Ryan, Ellen B. & Giles, Howard. Attitudes Towards Language Variation Social & Applied Contexts. 304p. 1982. pap. text ed. 18.95 (ISBN 0-7131-6195-7). E Arnold.
LANGUAGE AND LANGUAGES-ADDRESSES, ESSAYS, LECTURES
Byrnes, Heidi, ed. Georgetown University Round Table on Languages & Linguistics 1982: Contemporary Perceptions of Language: Interdisciplinary Dimensions. LC 58-31607. (Georgetown University Round Table on Languages and Linguistics (GURT) Ser.). 262p. (Orig.). 1983. pap. text ed. 8.95 (ISBN 0-87840-117-2). Georgetown U Pr.
Oller, John W., Jr., ed. Issues in Language Testing Research. 512p. 1983. pap. text ed. 21.95 (ISBN 0-88377-217-5). Newbury Hse.
LANGUAGE AND LANGUAGES-PHILOSOPHY
see Languages-Philosophy
LANGUAGE AND LANGUAGES-POLITICAL ASPECTS
see Languages-Political Aspects

LANGUAGE AND LANGUAGES-PRINTING
see Printing-Style Manuals
LANGUAGE AND LANGUAGES-PROGRAMMED INSTRUCTION
Darvall, Lixi. How to Get What You Want in Nine Languages (incl. Hebrew) 160p. 1982. pap. 4.95 (ISBN 0-686-43007-7, Carta Maps & Guides Pub Isreal). Hippocrene Bks.
LANGUAGE AND LANGUAGES-PSYCHOLOGY
see Psycholinguistics
LANGUAGE AND LANGUAGES-STUDY AND TEACHING
Blair, Robert W., ed. Innovative Approaches to Language Teaching & Language Learning. 328p. 1982. pap. text ed. 19.95 (ISBN 0-88377-247-7). Newbury Hse.
Carter, Ronald & Burton, Deirdre. Literary Text & Language Study. 128p. 1982. pap. text ed. 9.95 (ISBN 0-7131-6263-5). E Arnold.
Cimorell-Strong, Jacqueline M. Language Facilitation: A Cognitive Approach. 1983. pap. text ed. price not set (ISBN 0-8391-1799-X, 18449). Univ Park.
Corder, S. Pit. Error Analysis & Interlanguage. 128p. 1981. pap. text ed. 11.95x (ISBN 0-19-437073-9). Oxford U Pr.
Gillham, Bill. Two Worlds Together: A First Sentences Language Programme. 64p. 1983. text ed. 19.50x (ISBN 0-04-371091-3); pap. text ed. 8.95x (ISBN 0-04-371092-1). Allen Unwin.
Griffee, Dale. Listen & Act: Scenes for Language Learning. Rost, Michael, ed. (Illus.). 96p. 1982. pap. text ed. 5.50 (ISBN 0-940264-18-8); of two 20.00 set (ISBN 0-940264-21-8); of 20 cards 4.00 set (ISBN 0-940264-20-X). Lingual Hse Pub.
Healey, F. G. Foreign Language Teaching in the Universities. 1967. 23.50 (ISBN 0-7190-0291-5). Manchester.
Kinsella, Valerie, ed. Surveys 1: Eight State-of-the Art Articles on Key Areas in Language Teaching. LC 82-4332. (Cambridge Language Teaching Surveys 1 Ser.). 168p. 1983. 19.95 (ISBN 0-521-24886-8); pap. 8.95 (ISBN 0-521-27046-4). Cambridge U Pr.
--Surveys 2: Eight State-of-the Art Articles on Key Areas in Language Teaching. LC 82-45961. (Cambridge Language Teaching Surveys 2 Ser.). 168p. Date not set. 19.95 (ISBN 0-521-24887-6); pap. 8.95 (ISBN 0-521-27047-2). Cambridge U Pr.
La Forge, P. G. Counseling & Culture in Second Language Acquisition. (Language Teaching Methodology Ser.). 128p. 1983. pap. 111.90 (ISBN 0-08-029477-4). Pergamon.
Richmond, Edmun B. New Directions in Language Teaching in Sub-Saharan Africa: A Seven-Country Study of Current Policies & Programs for Teaching Official & National Languages & Adult Functional Literacy. LC 82-23831. (Illus.). 74p. (Orig.). 1983. pap. text ed. 6.50 (ISBN 0-8191-2980-1, Co-pub. by Ctr Applied Ling). U Pr of Amer.
Rogers-Warren, Ann & Warren, Steven F., eds. Teaching Functional Language. (Language Intervention Ser.). (Illus.). 1983. price not set (ISBN 0-8391-1798-1, 15660). Univ Park.
Seliger, Herbert W. & Long, Michael H., eds. Classroom Oriented Research in Second Language Acquisition. 364p. 1983. pap. text ed. 15.95 (ISBN 0-88377-267-1). Newbury Hse.
Synthesis in Second Language Teaching: An Introduction to Languistics. (Illus.). 693p. 1982. text ed. 19.95 (ISBN 0-919950-01-9). Second Lang.
LANGUAGE AND SOCIETY
see Sociolinguistics
LANGUAGE ARTS
see also Communication; English Language; Literature-Study and Teaching; Reading; Speech
Calin, Andrei & Calabro, John J. Sulindac - A Five-Year Perspective: Proceedings of an International Symposium. Language Center, Inc., tr. 128p. 1982. write for info. (ISBN 0-911910-20-4). Merck.
Chapman, Raymond. The Language of English Literature. 160p. 1982. pap. text ed. 9.95 (ISBN 0-7131-6371-2). E Arnold.
Elliot, F. Language Is You, Bk. 2. rev. ed. (gr. 7-8). 1982. pap. text ed. 5.83 (ISBN 0-201-20173-9, Sch Div); tchr's. ed. 6.19 (ISBN 0-201-20174-7). A-W.
Elliott, F. Language is You, Bk. 1. rev. ed. 1982. pap. text ed. 5.83 (ISBN 0-201-20148-8, Sch Div); tchr's ed. 6.19 (ISBN 0-201-20149-6). A-W.
Greenberg, Joanne C., et al. The Language Arts Handbook: A Total Communication Approach. 1982. text ed. 19.95x (ISBN 0-673-15808-X). Scott F.
Jenkins, Carol & Savage, John. Activities for Integrating the Language Arts. (Illus.). 224p. 1983. 16.95 (ISBN 0-13-003699-4); pap. 12.95 (ISBN 0-13-003681-1). P-H.
Justus, Fred. Auditory Discrimination. (Language Arts Ser.). (gr. 1-2). 1977. wkbk. 5.00 (LA-6). ESP.
--Basic Skills Auditory Discrimination Workbook. (Basic Skills Workbooks). 32p. (gr. 1-2). 1983. 0.99 (ISBN 0-8209-0545-3). ESP.
--Basic Skills Look, Hear, & Make Words Workbook. (Basic Skills Workbooks). 32p. (gr. k-1). 1983. 0.99 (ISBN 0-8209-0578-X, EEW-8). ESP.
McMasters, Dale. Basic Study & Research. (Language Arts Ser.). 24p. (gr. 5-9). 1979. wkbk. 5.00 (ISBN 0-8209-0304-3, BSR-1). ESP.
Moffett & Wagner. Student Centered Language Arts & Reading: K-13. 3rd ed. 1982. text ed. 24.50 (ISBN 0-686-84556-0, EA98). HM.

Patty, Catherine. Comprehension Development. (Language Arts). 24p. (gr. 3-5). 1980. wkbk. 5.00 (ISBN 0-8209-0318-3, LA-4). ESP.
Richmond, John. Resources of Classroom Language. 224p. 1982. pap. text ed. 14.95 (ISBN 0-7131-6234-1). E Arnold.
Shafer, Robert E. & Staab, Claire. Language Functions & School Success. 1983. text ed. 8.95x (ISBN 0-673-15834-9). Scott F.
Vaughn, James E. Basic Skills Vocabulary Workbook: Junior High. (Basic Skills Workbooks). 32p. (gr. 7-9). 1982. wkbk. 0.99 (ISBN 0-8209-0383-3, VW-H). ESP.
--Basic Skills Vocabulary Workbook: Senior High. (Basic Skills Workbooks). 32p. (gr. 9-12). 1982. wkbk. 0.99 (ISBN 0-8209-0384-1, VW-I). ESP.

LANGUAGE ARTS-STUDY AND TEACHING
see Language Arts

LANGUAGE ARTS (ELEMENTARY)
Bruno, Angela & Jessie, Karen. Hands-On Activities for Children's Writing. (Illus.). 256p. 1983. pap. 14.95 (ISBN 0-13-383596-0). P-H.

LANGUAGES-PHILOSOPHY
see also Analysis (Philosophy)
Cohen, Robert & Wartofsky, Marx. Language, Logic, & Method. 1983. 69.50 (ISBN 90-277-0725-1, Pub. by Reidel Holland). Kluwer Boston.
Leinfellner, Werner & Kraemer, Eric. Language & Ontology. (Sprachen und Ontologie.). 1982. lib. bdg. 78.00 (ISBN 90-277-9080-9, Pub. by Reidel Holland). Kluwer Boston.
Warnock, G. J. Morality & Language. LC 82-18171. 240p. 1983. text ed. 35.00x (ISBN 0-389-20349-1). B&N Imports.

LANGUAGES-POLITICAL ASPECTS
Beer, William R. Language Policy & National Unity. LC 81-67475. 256p. 1983. text ed. 30.00x (ISBN 0-86598-058-6). Allanheld.

LANGUAGES-PSYCHOANALYSIS
see Psycholinguistics

LANGUAGES-PSYCHOLOGY
see Psycholinguistics

LANGUAGES-SOCIOLOGICAL ASPECTS
see Sociolinguistics

LANGUAGES, MODERN-GLOSSARIES, VOCABULARIES, ETC.
see Polyglot Glossaries, Phrase Books, etc.

LANGUAGES, MODERN-STUDY AND TEACHING
Burling, Robbins. Sounding Right. 160p. 1982. pap. text ed. 12.95 (ISBN 0-88377-216-7). Newbury Hse.

LANGUES, OFFICIAL
see Languages-Political Aspects

LANGUE D'OIL
see French Language

LAOS-HISTORY
Stuart-Fox, Martin, ed. Contemporary Laos: Studies in the Politics and Society of the Lao People's Republic. 345p. 27.50 (ISBN 0-312-16676-1). St Martin.

LAPAROTOMY
see Abdomen-Surgery

LAPIDARY ART
see Gem Cutting

LAPLACE'S EQUATIONS
see Harmonic Functions

LARAMIE FORMATION
see Geology, Stratigraphic-Cretaceous

LARGE PRINT BOOKS
see Large Type Books

LARGE TYPE BOOKS
Aiken, Joan. The Girl from Paris. (General Ser.). 1983. lib. bdg. 17.50 (ISBN 0-8161-3497-9, Large Print Bks). G K Hall.
Alsop, Joseph. FDR. large type ed. LC 82-5870. (Illus.). 303p. 1982. Repr. of 1982 ed. 11.95 (ISBN 0-89621-369-2). Thorndike Pr.
--FDR: A Centenary Remembrance 1882-1945. (Illus.). 1982. pap. 3.50 (ISBN 0-671-45891-4). WSP.
Andrews, V. C. Flowers in the Attic. (Readers Request Ser.). 1983. lib. bdg. 18.95 (ISBN 0-8161-3429-4, Large Print Bks). G K Hall.
--If There Be Thorns. (Readers Request Ser.). 1983. lib. bdg. 18.95 (ISBN 0-8161-3429-4, Large Print Bks). G K Hall.
--Petals on the Wind. (Readers Request Ser.). 1982. lib. bdg. 19.95 (ISBN 0-8161-3427-8, Large Print Bks). G K Hall.
Archer, Jeffrey. The Prodigal Daughter. (General Ser.). 1983. lib. bdg. 21.50 (ISBN 0-8161-3499-5, Large Print Bks). G K Hall.
Barnard, Robert. Death by Sheer Torture. 1983. pap. 2.95 (ISBN 0-440-11976-6). Dell.
Battle, Lois. War Brides. large type ed. LC 82-7347. 693p. 1982. Repr. of 1982 ed. 13.95 (ISBN 0-89621-374-9). Thorndike Pr.
Benchley, Peter. The Girl of the Sea of Cortez. (General Ser.). 1983. lib. bdg. 14.95 (ISBN 0-8161-3487-1, Large Print Bks). G K Hall.
Bernard, Robert. Death & the Princess. (Nightingale Series Paperbacks). 1983. pap. 9.95 (ISBN 0-8161-3520-7, Large Print Bks). G K Hall.
Birmingham, Stephen. The Grandes Dames. (General Ser.). 1983. lib. bdg. 18.95 (ISBN 0-8161-3498-7, Large Print Bks). G K Hall.
Bloomingdale, Teresa. Murphy Must Have Been a Mother. (General Ser.). 1983. lib. bdg. 13.95 (ISBN 0-8161-3505-3, Large Print Bks). G K Hall.
Brand, Max. Ride the Wild Trail. (General Ser.). 1983. lib. bdg. 13.95 (ISBN 0-8161-3435-9, Large Print Bks). G K Hall.
--Steve Train's Ordeal. large print ed. LC 82-859. 341p. 1982. Repr. of 1924 ed. 10.95 (ISBN 0-89621-351-X). Thorndike Pr.
--Wild Freedom. 240p. 1983. pap. 2.25 (ISBN 0-446-30230-9). Warner Bks.
Buckley, William F., Jr. Marco Polo, If You Can. 1983. pap. 3.50 (ISBN 0-380-61424-3, 61424-3). Avon.
--Marco Polo, If You Can. large print ed. LC 82-5470. 414p. 1982. Repr. of 1982 ed. 13.95 (ISBN 0-89621-361-7). Thorndike Pr.
Carroll, James. Family Trade. (General Ser.). 1983. lib. bdg. 18.95 (ISBN 0-8161-3483-9, Large Print Bks). G K Hall.
Clark, Mary H. A Cry in the Night. (General Ser.). 1983. lib. bdg. 15.95 (ISBN 0-8161-3486-3, Large Print Bks). G K Hall.
Condon, Richard. Prizzi's Honor. 320p. 1983. pap. 3.50 (ISBN 0-425-05778-X). Berkley Pub.
Cross, Amanda. The James Joyce Murder. large type ed. LC 82-6027. 275p. 1982. Repr. of 1982 ed. 9.95 (ISBN 0-89621-373-0). Thorndike Pr.
--The Theban Mysteries. large print ed. LC 82-5469. 275p. 1982. Repr. of 1979 ed. 9.95x (ISBN 0-89621-362-5). Thorndike Pr.
Cunningham, E. V. The Case of the Kidnapped Angel. (Nightingale Series Paperbacks). 1983. pap. 7.95 (ISBN 0-8161-3471-5, Large Print Bks). G K Hall.
Dailey, Janet. Foxfire Light. (Nightingale Series Paperbacks). 1983. pap. 8.95 (ISBN 0-8161-3494-4, Large Print Bks). G K Hall.
--The Second Time. (Nightingale Series Paperbacks). 1983. pap. 7.95 (ISBN 0-8161-3517-7, Large Print Bks). G K Hall.
David-Neel, Alexandra. The Power of Nothingness. large type ed. LC 82-10387. 217p. 1982. Repr. of 1982 ed. 9.95 (ISBN 0-89621-382-X). Thorndike Pr.
Davis, Lester & Davis, Irene. Ike & Mamie. large type ed. LC 82-5869. (Illus.). 410p. 1982. Repr. of 1981 ed. 12.95 (ISBN 0-686-82639-6). Thorndike Pr.
Dowdell, Dorothy. Hibiscus Lagoon. large type ed. LC 82-10336. 267p. 1982. Repr. of 1981 ed. 9.95 (ISBN 0-89621-379-X). Thorndike Pr.
--The Impossible Dream. LC 82-16751. 286p. 1982. Repr. of 1981 ed. 9.95 (ISBN 0-89621-390-0). Thorndike Pr.
Eden, Dorothy. An Important Family. 352p. 1983. pap. 3.50 (ISBN 0-380-63297-7). Avon.
Fast, Howard. Max. (General Ser.). 1983. lib. bdg. 18.95 (ISBN 0-8161-3495-2, Large Print Bks). G K Hall.
Francis, Dick. Twice Shy. (General Ser.). 1982. lib. bdg. 14.95 (ISBN 0-8161-3445-6, Large Print Bks). G K Hall.
--Twice Shy. 320p. 1983. pap. 3.50 (ISBN 0-449-20053-1, Crest). Fawcett.
Fraser, Antonia. Quiet as a Nun. 1982. pap. 3.95 (ISBN 0-393-30120-6). Norton.
Gardner, John. For Special Services. (General Ser.). 355p. 1982. lib. bdg. 13.95 (ISBN 0-8161-3477-4, Large Print Bks). G K Hall.
Gilbert, Michael. Mr. Calder & Mr. Behrens. 1983. pap. 2.95 (ISBN 0-14-006637-3). Penguin.
Gilman, Dorothy. The Elusive Mrs. Pollifax. (Nightingale Series Paperbacks). 1983. pap. 8.95 (ISBN 0-8161-3370-0, Large Print Bks). G K Hall.
--A Palm for Mrs. Pollifax. (Nightingale Series Paperbacks). 1983. pap. 10.95 (ISBN 0-8161-3369-7, Large Print Bks). G K Hall.
Grey, Zane. The Call of the Canyon. large type ed. LC 82-10448. 355p. 1982. Repr. of 1921 ed. 11.95 (ISBN 0-89621-386-2). Thorndike Pr.
--Majesty's Rancho. Large Print ed. LC 82-709. 501p. 1982. Repr. of 1937 ed. 11.95x (ISBN 0-89621-347-1). Thorndike Pr.
Hager, Jean. Captured By Love. Large Print ed. LC 82-10667. 299p. 1982. 10.95 (ISBN 0-89621-389-7). Thorndike Pr.
Hailey, Elizabeth F. Life Sentences. (General Ser.). 1983. lib. bdg. 16.95 (ISBN 0-8161-3473-1, Large Print Bks). G K Hall.
Hale, Arlene. In the Name of Love. LC 82-10666. 285p. 1982. 10.95 (ISBN 0-89621-388-9). Thorndike Pr.
Hastings, Brooke. Rough Diamond. (Nightingale Series Paperbacks). 1983. pap. 10.95 (ISBN 0-8161-3523-1, Large Print Bks). G K Hall.
Haycox, Ernest. Sundown Jim. (General Ser.). 1982. lib. bdg. 13.95 (ISBN 0-8161-3357-3, Large Print Bks). G K Hall.
--The Wild Brunch. (General Ser.). 1983. lib. bdg. 14.95 (ISBN 0-8161-3443-X, Large Print Bks). G K Hall.
Higgins, Jack. Touch the Devil. (General Ser.). 1983. lib. bdg. 16.95 (ISBN 0-8161-3484-7, Large Print Bks). G K Hall.
Hills, Ida. A Love to Remember. large print ed. LC 82-5478. 222p. 1982. Repr. of 1980 ed. 9.95x (ISBN 0-89621-363-3). Thorndike Pr.
Hogan, Ray. The Doomsday Posse. (General Ser.). 1982. lib. bdg. 10.95 (ISBN 0-8161-3364-6, Large Print Bks). G K Hall.
--R the Doomsday Bullet. (General Ser.). 1983. lib. bdg. 11.95 (ISBN 0-8161-3432-4, Large Print Bks). G K Hall.
Holland, Isabelle. The Lost Madonna. 272p. 1983. pap. 2.95 (ISBN 0-449-20020-5, Crest). Fawcett.
--Moncrief. large type ed. LC 82-10362. 431p. 1982. Repr. of 1975 ed. 10.95 (ISBN 0-89621-381-1). Thorndike Pr.
Holland, Isabelled. The Lost Madonna. large print ed. LC 82-4873. 419p. 1982. Repr. of 1982 ed. 11.95 (ISBN 0-89621-364-1). Thorndike Pr.
Holt, Victoria. The Judas Kiss. (General Ser.). 1982. lib. bdg. 15.95 (ISBN 0-8161-3342-5, Large Print Bks). G K Hall.
Huffaker, Clair. The Cowboy & the Cossack. large type ed. LC 82-10540. 560p. 1982. Repr. of 1973 ed. 11.95 (ISBN 0-89621-385-4). Thorndike Pr.
--Seven Ways from Sundown. large print ed. LC 82-838. 212p. 1982. Repr. of 1960 ed. 9.95x (ISBN 0-89621-350-1). Thorndike Pr.
Jenkins, Peter. A Walk Across America. (General Ser.). 1982. lib. bdg. 15.95 (ISBN 0-8161-3459-6, Large Print Bks). G K Hall.
Jenkins, Peter & Jenkins, Barbara. The Walk West: A Walk Across America II. (General Ser.). 1983. lib. bdg. 18.95 (ISBN 0-8161-3460-X, Large Print Bks). G K Hall.
Kushner, Harold S. When Bad Things Happen to Good People. (General Ser.). 1982. lib. bdg. 11.95 (ISBN 0-8161-3465-0, Large Print Bks). G K Hall.
Laker, Rosalind. Gilded Splendour. (General Ser.). 1982. lib. bdg. 17.95 (ISBN 0-8161-3476-6, Large Print Bks). G K Hall.
L'Amour, Louis. The Cherokee Trail. (General Ser.). 1983. lib. bdg. 12.95 (ISBN 0-8161-3464-2, Large Print Bks). G K Hall.
Loring, Emilie. There is Always Love. (General Ser.). 1983. lib. bdg. 14.50 (ISBN 0-8161-3518-5, Large Print Bks). G K Hall.
Lovesey, Peter. The False Inspector Dew. (Nightingale Series Paperbacks). 1983. pap. 9.95 (ISBN 0-8161-3481-2, Large Print Bks). G K Hall.
--The False Inspector Dew. 1983. pap. 2.95 (ISBN 0-394-71338-9). Pantheon.
Ludlum, Robert. The Road to Gandolfo. (General Ser.). 1983. lib. bdg. 15.95 (ISBN 0-8161-3506-1, Large Print Bks). G K Hall.
MacDonald, John D. Cinnamon Skin. (General Ser.). 1983. lib. bdg. 14.95 (ISBN 0-8161-3504-5, Large Print Bks). G K Hall.
McElroy, Lee. Eyes of the Hawk. large type ed. LC 82-10542. 299p. 1982. Repr. of 1982 ed. 9.95 (ISBN 0-89621-384-6). Thorndike Pr.
MacInnes, Helen. Cloak of Darkness. (General Ser.). 1983. lib. bdg. 18.95 (ISBN 0-8161-3486-3, Large Print Bks). G K Hall.
Marsh, Ngaio. Light Thickens. (General Ser.). 1983. lib. bdg. 16.95 (ISBN 0-8161-3509-6, Large Print Bks). G K Hall.
Michaels, Barbara. The Dark on the Other Side. (General Ser.). 1983. lib. bdg. 14.95 (ISBN 0-8161-3414-6, Large Print Bks). G K Hall.
Murray, Rachel. Design for Enchantment. (Nightingale Series Paperbacks). 1983. pap. 8.95 (ISBN 0-8161-3501-0, Large Print Bks). G K Hall.
Nye, Nelson. The Long Run. (General Ser.). 1983. lib. bdg. 11.95 (ISBN 0-8161-3454-5, Large Print Bks). G K Hall.
Patrick, Maxine. Snowbound Heart. Bd. with Captive Kisses. 1982. pap. 2.50 (ISBN 0-451-11748-4, AE1748, Sig). NAL.
Patten, Lewis B. The Angry Horseman. large type ed. LC 82-10534. 233p. 1982. Repr. of 1960 ed. 9.95 (ISBN 0-89621-383-8). Thorndike Pr.
Pentecost, High. Death Mask. (Nightingale Series Paperbacks). 1983. pap. 9.95 (ISBN 0-8161-3500-2, Large Print Bks). G K Hall.
Perry, Thomas. The Butcher's Boy. 1983. pap. 2.95 (ISBN 0-441-08950-X, Pub. by Charter Bks). Ace Bks.
Persico, Joseph E. The Imperial Rockefeller. large type ed. LC 82-5994. 523p. 1982. Repr. of 1982 ed. 13.95 (ISBN 0-89621-371-4). Thorndike Pr.
Peters, Elizabeth. The Copenhagen Connection. (General Ser.). 1982. lib. bdg. 13.95 (ISBN 0-8161-3467-7, Large Print Bks). G K Hall.
Pilcher, Rosamunde. The Carousel. (Nightingale Series Paperbacks). 1983. pap. 7.95 (ISBN 0-8161-3488-X, Large Print Bks). G K Hall.
Plain, Belva. Eden Burning. (General Ser.). 1982. lib. bdg. 16.95 (ISBN 0-8161-3424-3, Large Print Bks). G K Hall.
Pocketpac Bks. Promises for the Golden Years. 96p. 1983. pap. 1.95 (ISBN 0-87788-320-3). Shaw Pubs.
Porter, Donald C. The Renegade. (Readers Request Ser.). 1983. lib. bdg. 19.95 (ISBN 0-8161-3447-2, Large Print Bks). G K Hall.
--Renno. (Readers Request Ser.). 1983. lib. bdg. 17.95 (ISBN 0-8161-3450-2, Large Print Bks). G K Hall.
--Tomahawk. (Readers Request Ser.). 1983. lib. bdg. 18.95 (ISBN 0-8161-3451-0, Large Print Bks). G K Hall.
--War Chief. (Readers Request Ser.). 1983. lib. bdg. 19.95 (ISBN 0-8161-3448-0, Large Print Bks). G K Hall.
--White Indian. (Readers Request Ser.). 1983. lib. bdg. 19.95 (ISBN 0-8161-3446-4, Large Print Bks). G K Hall.
Porter, Donald P. The Sachem. (Readers Request Ser.). 1983. lib. bdg. 19.95 (ISBN 0-8161-3449-9, Large Print Bks). G K Hall.
Potok, Chaim. The Book of Lights. large print ed. LC 82-3277. 660p. 1982. Repr. of 1981 ed. 13.95 (ISBN 0-89621-358-7). Thorndike Pr.
Reiser, Virginia, ed. Favorite Short Stories in Large Print. 720p. 1982. lib. bdg. 17.95 (ISBN 0-8161-3434-0, Large Print Bks). G K Hall.
Rendell, Ruth. Master of the Moor. (General Ser.). 1982. lib. bdg. 13.95 (ISBN 0-8161-3437-5, Large Print Bks). G K Hall.
Robey, Harriet. There's a Dance in the Old Dame Yet. (General Ser.). 1982. lib. bdg. 14.95 (ISBN 0-8161-3478-2, Large Print Bks). G K Hall.
Ross, Dana F. Washington. (General Ser.). 1983. price not set (Large Print Bks). G K Hall.
Schell, Jonathan. The Fate of the Earth. 1982. pap. 2.50 (ISBN 0-380-61325-5, 61325, Discus). Avon.
--The Fate of the Earth. large type ed. LC 82-10299. 405p. 1982. Repr. of 1982 ed. 10.95 (ISBN 0-89621-380-3). Thorndike Pr.
Seifert, Elizabeth. Two Doctors, Two Loves. (General Ser.). 1983. lib. bdg. 13.50 (ISBN 0-8161-3496-0, Large Print Bks). G K Hall.
Sheed, Wilfred. Clare Booth Luce. large type ed. LC 82-5871. 378p. 1982. Repr. of 1982 ed. 11.95 (ISBN 0-89621-366-8). Thorndike Pr.
Shore, anne. The Searching Heart. (Nightingale Series Paperbacks). 1983. pap. 7.95 (ISBN 0-8161-3472-3, Large Print Bks). G K Hall.
Slaughter, Frank G. Doctor's Daughters. large type ed. LC 82-3362. 446p. 1982. Repr. of 1981 ed. 13.95 (ISBN 0-89621-355-2). Thorndike Pr.
Steel, Danielle. Now & Forever. (General Ser.). 1982. lib. bdg. 16.95 (ISBN 0-8161-3330-1, Large Print Bks). G K Hall.
Steele, Danielle. Once in a Lifetime. (General Ser.). 1983. lib. bdg. 14.95 (ISBN 0-8161-3407-3, Large Print Bks). G K Hall.
Taylor, Elizabeth A. The Cable Car Murder. large print ed. LC 82-5468. 412p. 1982. Repr. of 1980 ed. 11.95x (ISBN 0-89621-360-9). Thorndike Pr.
Teichmann, Howard. Fonda: My Life. large type ed. LC 82-5983. (Illus.). 697p. 1982. Repr. of 1981 ed. 13.95 (ISBN 0-89621-370-6). Thorndike Pr.
Truman, Margaret. Murder in the Supreme Court. (General Ser.). 1983. lib. bdg. 15.50 (ISBN 0-8161-3516-9, Large Print Bks). G K Hall.
Turnbull, Agnes S. Gown of Glory. (General Ser.). 1982. lib. bdg. 15.95 (ISBN 0-8161-3475-8, Large Print Bks). G K Hall.
Tyler, Anne. Dinner at the Homesick Restaurant. (General Ser.). 1982. lib. bdg. 15.95 (ISBN 0-8161-3438-3, Large Print Bks). G K Hall.
--Dinner at the Homesick Restaurant. 320p. 1983. pap. 3.50 (ISBN 0-425-05999-5). Berkley Pub.
Van Loon, Antonia. Sunshine & Shadow. large print ed. LC 82-3278. 568p. 1982. Repr. of 1981 ed. 12.95 (ISBN 0-89621-359-5). Thorndike Pr.
Van Slyke, Helen. Always is Not Forever. 480p. 1982. pap. 3.50 (ISBN 0-446-31009-3). Warner Bks.
--Public Smiles, Private Tears. large type ed. LC 82-10341. 540p. 1982. Repr. of 1982 ed. 13.95 (ISBN 0-89621-376-5). Thorndike Pr.
Van Slyke, Helen & Ashton, Sharon. The Santa Ana Wind. 256p. 1982. pap. 3.50 (ISBN 0-446-31017-4). Warner Bks.
Wakefield, Dan. Under the Apple Tree. (General Ser.). 1983. lib. bdg. 16.50 (ISBN 0-8161-3474-X, Large Print Bks). G K Hall.
Young, Carter T. Winter Drift. large print ed. LC 82-839. 275p. 1982. Repr. of 1980 ed. 9.95x (ISBN 0-89621-352-8). Thorndike Pr.

LARTIGUE, JACQUES-HENRI
Guibert, Herve. Bonjour Monsieur Lartigue. Walker, Janet M., ed. Grasselli, Margaret M., tr. LC 82-83899. (Illus.). 68p. (Orig.). 1982. pap. 11.25 (ISBN 0-88397-044-9). Intl Exhibit Foun.

LARYNGECTOMY
Keith, Robert I. Handbook for the Laryngectomee. 2nd ed. 1983p. 1983. pap. text ed. write for info. (ISBN 0-8134-2290-6). Interstate.

LAS VEGAS, NEVADA
Karlins, Marvin. Psyching Out Vegas. (Illus.). 280p. 1983. 12.00 (ISBN 0-914314-03-3). Lyle Stuart.

LAS VEGAS, NEVADA-DESCRIPTION
Anderson, John A. Las Vegas Survival Guide. LC 81-71218. 200p. (Orig.). 1982. pap. 5.95 (ISBN 0-9607626-0-4). Anderson Comm.

LASER PHOTOGRAPHY
see Holography

LASER SPECTROSCOPY
Advances in Laser Spectroscopy, Vol. I. 245p. 1982. 47.95 (ISBN 0-471-26185-8, Pub. by Wiley Heyden). Wiley.
Demtroeder, W. Laser Spectroscopy: Basic Concepts & Instrumentation. (Springer Series in Chemical Physics: Vol. 5). (Illus.). 694p. 1983. 29.00 (ISBN 0-387-10343-0). Springer-Verlag.
Eisenthal, K. B., et al, eds. Picosecond Phenomena III, Garmisch Partenkirchen, FRG, 1982: Proceedings. (Springer Series in Chemical Physics: Vol. 23). (Illus.). 401p. 1983. 30.00 (ISBN 0-387-11912-4). Springer-Verlag.

LASERS
AIP Conference, 90th, Boulder, 1982. Laser Techniques for Extreme Ultraviolet Spectroscopy: Proceedings. McIlrath, T. J. & Freeman, R. R., eds. LC 82-73205. 497p. 1982. lib. bdg. 37.00 (ISBN 0-88318-189-4). Am Inst Physics.

AIP Conference, 91st, Los Alamos, 1982. Laser Acceleration of Particles: Proceedings. Channell, Paul J., ed. LC 82-73361. 276p. 1982. lib. bdg. 32.00 (ISBN 0-88318-190-8). Am Inst Physics.
Bertolotti, M., ed. Physical Processes in Laser-Materials Interactions. (NATO ASI Series B, Physics: Vol. 84). 535p. 1983. 69.50x (ISBN 0-306-41107-5, Plenum Pr). Plenum Pub.
Brederlow, G., et al. The High-Power Iodine Laser. (Springer Ser. in Optical Sciences: Vol. 34). (Illus.). 182p. 1983. 35.00 (ISBN 0-387-11792-X). Springer-Verlag.
Coleman, H. W. & Pfund, P. A., eds. Engineering Applications of Laser Velocimetry. 1982. 40.00 (H00230). ASME.
Demokan, M. S. Mode-Locking in Solid-State & Semiconductor Lasers. 227p. 1982. 39.95 (ISBN 0-471-10498-1). Res Stud Pr.
Duley, W. W. Laser Processing & Analysis of Materials. 450p. 1982. 59.59x (ISBN 0-306-41067-2, Plenum Pr). Plenum Pub.
International Conference, Brighton, United Kingsom, March 1982 & Jerrard. Electro-Optics Laser International, 82: Proceedings. 1982. text ed. write for info. (ISBN 0-408-01235-8). Butterworth.
Marconi's International Register. 83rd ed. 1982. 70.00 (ISBN 0-916446-08-5). Tele Cable.
Megawatt Infrared Laser Chemistry. LC 78-6721. 122p. Repr. of 1978 ed. text ed. 11.50 (ISBN 0-471-03074-0). Krieger.
Mooradian, A. & Killinger, D. K. Optical & Laser Remote Sensing. (Springer Ser. in Optical Sciences: Vol. 39). (Illus.). 400p. 1983. 30.00 (ISBN 0-387-12170-6). Springer-Verlag.
Payne, Keith B., ed. Laser Weapons in Space: Policy Issues. (Replica). 150p. 1982. softcover 17.00 (ISBN 0-86531-937-5). Westview.
Pellegrini, C. Developments in High Power Lasers & Their Applications. 1982. 89.50 (ISBN 0-444-85459-2, Pub. by Applied Sci England). Elsevier.
Schneider, H. Laser Light. 1978. 8.95 (ISBN 0-07-055451-X). McGraw.
Tillman, Dick & Powlison, Dave. The New Laser Sailing. (Illus.). 160p. 1983. 14.95 (ISBN 0-914814-32-X). Sail Bks.
Velikhov, E. P. Molecular Gas Lasers. 266p. 1981. pap. 8.00 (ISBN 0-8285-2280-4, Pub. by Mir Pubs USSR). Imported Pubns.

LASERS IN MEDICINE

Dixon. Surgical Application of Lasers. (Illus.). 1983. 39.50 (ISBN 0-8151-2514-3). Year Bk Med.
Satelle, D. B. & Lee, W. I., eds. Biomedical Applications of Laser Light Scattering: Proceedings, Workshop Meeting, Cambridge, U. K., 1981. 428p. 1982. 85.00 (ISBN 0-444-80456-0, Biomedical Pr). Elsevier.

LAST JUDGMENT

see Judgment Day

LASTS (SHOES)

see Boots and Shoes

LATIN AMERICA

see also names of Latin-American countries and geographic areas of Latin America, e.g. Brazil; Caribbean Area; South America; names of cities, towns, and geographic areas in specific countries

Baden, Nancy T., ed. Social Responsibility & Latin America. (Proceedings of the Pacific Coast Council on Latin American Studies: Vol. 8). (Illus.). 190p. (Orig.). 1981. pap. 12.00 (ISBN 0-916304-53-1). Campanile.
Black, Jan K. Latin America: An Introduction. 450p. 1983. lib. bdg. price not set (ISBN 0-86531-212-5); pap. text ed. price not set (ISBN 0-86531-213-3). Westview.
Carim, Enver, ed. Latin America & Caribbean: 1982-83. (World of Information Ser.). 256p. pap. 24.95 (ISBN 0-911818-32-4). World Almanac.
Cine Cubano. (Illus.). 174p. Date not set. 7.00 (ISBN 0-686-38852-6). Symrna.

LATIN AMERICA-CIVILIZATION

Demaree, Kristyna P., ed. Continuity & Change in Latin America. (Proceedings of the Pacific Coast Council on Latin American Studies: Vol. 9). (Illus.). 130p. (Orig.). 1982. pap. 12.00 (ISBN 0-916304-54-X). Campanile.

LATIN AMERICA-COMMERCE

Syrquin, Moshe, ed. Trade, Stability, Technology & Equity in Latin America. LC 82-13890. write for info. (ISBN 0-12-680050-2). Acad Pr.

LATIN AMERICA-DISCOVERY AND EXPLORATION

see America-Discovery and Exploration

LATIN AMERICA-ECONOMIC CONDITIONS

Altimir, Oscar. The Extent of Poverty in Latin American. rev. ed. LC 82-8533. (World Bank Staff Working Papers: No. 522). (Orig.). 1982. pap. text ed. 3.00 (ISBN 0-8213-0012-1). World Bank.
CEPAL Review. 1981. 3.00 (ISBN 0-686-84899-3, E. 81.II.G.4.). UN.
Cortes-Conde, Roberto & Hunt, Shane J., eds. Latin American Economies: Growth & the Export Sector, 1880-1930. 260p. 1983. write for info. (ISBN 0-8419-0771-4). Holmes & Meier.
Hammergren, Linn. Development & the Politics of Administrative Reform: Lessons from Latin America. (Replica Edition Ser.). 220p. 1983. softcover 19.00x (ISBN 0-86531-956-1). Westview.
Syrquin, Moshe, ed. Trade, Stability, Technology & Equity in Latin America. LC 82-13890. write for info. (ISBN 0-12-680050-2). Acad Pr.
Tussie, Diana. Latin America in the World Economy. LC 82-47501. 213p. 1982. 25.00x (ISBN 0-312-47333-8). St Martin.

LATIN AMERICA-HISTORY

Shepherd, William R. Hispanic Nations of a New World. 1921. text ed. 8.50x (ISBN 0-686-83565-4). Elliots Bks.

LATIN AMERICA-POLITICS AND GOVERNMENT

Bruck & Corke, eds. Who's Who in Latin America: Government & Politics. 300p. (Span. & Eng.). 1983. 65.00 (ISBN 0-910365-02-4). Decade Media.
Bucheli, Fausto & Maxson, Robin. Hostage. 208p. (Orig.). 1982. pap. 6.95 (ISBN 0-310-45631-2). Zondervan.
Hammergren, Linn. Development & the Politics of Administrative Reform: Lessons from Latin America. (Replica Edition Ser.). 220p. 1983. softcover 19.00x (ISBN 0-86531-956-1). Westview.
Morris, Michael A. & Millan, Victor, eds. Controlling Latin American Conflicts: Ten Approaches. Replica ed. 300p. 1982. softcover 21.50 (ISBN 0-86531-938-3). Westview.
Wesson, Robert. Democracy in Latin America: Promise & Problems. (Political Science Ser.). 220p. 1982. 26.95 (ISBN 0-03-061641-7). Praeger.

LATIN AMERICA-RELIGION

Das Goswami, Satsvarupa. Srila Prbhupada in Latin America. Dasa, Mandalesvara & Dasi, Bimala, eds. (Prabhupada-lila). (Orig.). Vol. 7. pap. text ed. 2.00 (ISBN 0-911233-05-9). Gita-Nagari.
Esquivel, Adolfo P. Christ in a Poncho: Witnesses to the Nonviolent Struggle in Latin America. Barr, Robert R., tr. from Span. LC 82-28760. 160p. (Orig.). 1983. pap. 6.95 (ISBN 0-88344-104-7). Orbis Bks.

LATIN AMERICA-SOCIAL CONDITIONS

Altimir, Oscar. The Extent of Poverty in Latin American. rev. ed. LC 82-8533. (World Bank Staff Working Papers: No. 522). (Orig.). 1982. pap. text ed. 3.00 (ISBN 0-8213-0012-1). World Bank.
Graham, Richard & Goldston, Angela. Social Studies: History. (Latin American Curriculum Units for Junior & Community Colleges Ser.). v, 46p. 1981. pap. text ed. 3.95 (ISBN 0-86728-008-5). U TX Inst Lat Am Stud.
Ritter, Archibald R. & Pollock, David H., eds. Latin American Prospects for the 1980's: Equity, Democratization & Development. 344p. 1983. 29.95 (ISBN 0-03-061363-9). Praeger.

LATIN AMERICA-SOCIAL LIFE AND CUSTOMS

Hinds, Harold E., Jr. & Tatum, Charles M., eds. Studies in Latin American Popular Culture, Vol. 2. 1983. pap. 25.00 (ISBN 0-9608664-1-8). New Mexico St Univ.

LATIN-AMERICAN ART

see Art, Latin-American

LATIN-AMERICAN LITERATURE-BIBLIOGRAPHY

Woodbridge, Hensley C. Spanish & Spanish-American Literature: An Annotated Guide to Selected Bibliographies. (Selected Bibliographies in Language & Literature: 4). 74p. 1983. 10.50x (ISBN 0-87352-954-5); pap. 5.75x (ISBN 0-87352-955-3). Modern Lang.

LATIN-AMERICAN LITERATURE-HISTORY AND CRITICISM

Torres-Rioseco, Arturo. New World Literature: Tradition & Revolt in Latin America. LC 82-20961. 250p. 1983. Repr. of 1949 ed. lib. bdg. 29.75x (ISBN 0-313-23444-2, TRNW). Greenwood.

LATIN-AMERICAN MUSIC

see Music, Latin-American

LATIN AMERICAN STUDIES

Glab, Edward, Jr., ed. Latin American Culture Studies: Information & Materials for Teaching about Latin America. 3rd ed. (Latin American Culture Studies Project Ser.). xi, 466p. 1981. pap. text ed. 9.95x (ISBN 0-86728-001-8). U TX Inst Lat Am Stud.
Graham, Richard & Goldston, Angela. Social Studies: History. (Latin American Curriculum Units for Junior & Community Colleges Ser.). v, 46p. 1981. pap. text ed. 3.95 (ISBN 0-86728-008-5). U TX Inst Lat Am Stud.
Higgins, Susan. A Latin Filmography. (Latin American Culture Studies Project Ser.). ix, 1978p. 1978. pap. text ed. 5.00x (ISBN 0-86728-011-5). U TX Inst Lat Am Stud.
Research Libraries of the New York Public Libraries & Library of Congress. Bibliographic Guide to Latin American Studies: 1982. 1983. lib. bdg. 350.00 (ISBN 0-8161-6974-8, Biblio Guides). G K Hall.

LATIN DRAMA-TRANSLATIONS INTO ENGLISH

Seneca, L. Thyestes: A Tragedy. Elder, Jane, tr. from Latin. 58p. 1982. pap. text ed. 6.25x (ISBN 0-85635-434-1, 80730, Pub. by Carcanet Pr England). Humanities.

LATIN INSCRIPTIONS

see Inscriptions, Latin

LATIN LANGUAGE

see also Inscriptions, Latin; Romance Languages

Cambridge School Classics Project: Cambridge Latin Course. 2nd ed. 1982. Unit 1-Stages 1-12. 8.95 (ISBN 0-521-28740-5); Language Information. 1.25 (ISBN 0-521-28792-8); Unit 11A. 4.50 (ISBN 0-521-28743-X). Cambridge U Pr.
Conway, R. S. The Making of Latin: An Introduction to Latin, Greek & English Etymology. 1983. 20.00 (ISBN 0-89241-335-2); pap. 12.50 (ISBN 0-89241-341-7). Caratzas Bros.
An Etymology of Latin & Greek. xix, 252p. 1983. 25.00 (ISBN 0-89241-334-4); pap. 12.50 (ISBN 0-89241-340-9). Caratzas Bros.
Knudsvig, Glenn M., et al. Latin for Reading: A Beginner's Textbook with Exercises. LC 82-51023. 376p. 1982. pap. text ed. 12.95x (ISBN 0-472-08038-5). U of Mich Pr.
Marsh, Carole. Of All the Gaul: Latin for Kids. (Tomorrow's Books). (Illus.). 62p. 1983. 5.95 (ISBN 0-935326-17-0). Gallopade Pub Group.

LATIN LANGUAGE-ABBREVIATIONS

see Abbreviations

LATIN LANGUAGE-DICTIONARIES-ENGLISH

Glare, P. G., ed. Oxford Latin Dictionary. 2150p. 1982. 145.00x (ISBN 0-19-864224-5). Oxford U Pr.
Woodhouse, S. C., ed. Latin-English & English-Latin Dictionary. (Routledge Pocket Dictionaries Ser.). 496p. (Orig.). 1982. pap. 8.95 (ISBN 0-7100-9267-9). Routledge & Kegan.

LATIN LANGUAGE-GRAMMAR

Daly, Lloyd W. Iohannis Philoponi: De Vocabulis Quae Diversum Signification Exhibent Secundum Differentiam Accentus. LC 81-72156. (Memoirs Ser.: Vol. 151). 1983. 20.00 (ISBN 0-87169-151-5). Am Philos.

LATIN LANGUAGE, MEDIEVAL AND MODERN

see also Christian Literature, Early

Brooks, Nicholas, ed. Latin & the Vernacular Languages in Early Medieval Britain. (Studies in the Early History of Britain Ser.: Vol. 1). 200p. 1982. text ed. 52.50x (ISBN 0-7185-1209-X, Leicester). Humanities.

LATIN LITERATURE (COLLECTIONS)

see also Classical Literature (Collections)

Colker, Marvin L., ed. Analecta Dublinensia: Three Medieval Latin Texts in the Library of Trinity College Dublin. LC 75-1954. 1975. 22.00X (ISBN 0-910956-56-1). Medieval Acad.

LATIN LITERATURE (SELECTIONS: EXTRACTS, ETC.)

Wheelock, Frederic M. Latin Literature: A Book of Readings. (COS Ser.). 331p. (Latin.). (gr. 10-12). 1967. pap. 3.95 (ISBN 0-06-460080-7, 80). B&N NY.

LATIN POETRY-GENERAL-TRANSLATIONS INTO ENGLISH

Isbell, Harold. Last Poets of Imperial Rome. 1983. pap. 5.95 (ISBN 0-14-044246-4). Penguin.

LATIN POETRY-TRANSLATIONS INTO ENGLISH

Virgil. The Georgics. Wells, Robert, ed. 95p. 1982. text ed. 12.50x (ISBN 0-85635-338-8, 60776, Pub. by Carcanet New Pr England). Humanities.

LATIN RHETORIC

see Rhetoric, Ancient

LATTER-DAY SAINTS

see Mormons and Mormonism

LATTICE THEORY

Chu-Kia Wang & Salmon, Charles G. Introductory Structural Analysis. (Illus.). 656p. 1983. 29.95 (ISBN 0-13-501569-3). P-H.
Devreese, J. T. & Van Doren, V. E., eds. Ab Initio Calculation of Phonon Spectra. 275p. 1983. 42.50x (ISBN 0-306-41119-9, Plenum Pr). Plenum Pub.
Pandit, G. S. & Gupta, S. P. Structural Analysis: A Matrix Approach. 592p. Date not set. 11.00x (ISBN 0-07-096554-4). McGraw.
Smolira, M. Analysis of Structures by the Force-Displacement Method. 1980. 61.50 (ISBN 0-85334-814-6, Pub. by applied Sci England). Elsevier.

LATVIAN TALES

see Tales, Latvian

LAUGHING GAS

see Nitrous Oxide

LAUREATES

see Poets Laureate

LAUREL, STANLEY

Scagnetti, Jack. The Laurel & Hardy Scrapbook. 1982. pap. 8.95 (ISBN 0-8246-0278-1). Jonathan David.

LAVOISIER, ANTOINE LAURENT, 1743-1794

Grey, Vivian. The Chemist Who Lost His Head: The Story of Antoine Lavoisier. (Illus.). 112p. 1982. 9.95 (ISBN 0-698-20559-6, Coward). Putnam Pub Group.

LAW, JOHN, 1671-1729

Hough, Emerson. The Mississippi Bubble: How the Star of Good Fortune Rose & Set & Rose Again, by a Woman's Grace, for one John Law of Lauriston. 452p. 1982. Repr. of 1902 ed. lib. bdg. 25.00 (ISBN 0-8495-2435-0). Arden Lib.

LAW

see also Courts; Jurisprudence; Justice; Justice, Administration Of; Lawyers; Legal Ethics; Legislation; Natural Law; Statutes

also names of legal systems, e.g. Canon Law, Common Law, Roman Law; special branches of law, e.g. Constitutional Law, Criminal Law, Maritime Law; specific legal topics, e.g. Contracts, Mortgages, Sanctions (Law); subdivision Laws and Legislation under subjects, e.g. Postal Service-Law

American Law Institute. Restatement of the Law: Second Property, Donative Transfers, Vol. 1. Casner, A. James, ed. 552p. 1983. text ed. write for info. (ISBN 0-314-73635-2). Am Law Inst.
Aubert, Vilhelm. In Search of Law. 220p. 1983. text ed. 26.50x (ISBN 0-389-20385-8). B&N Imports.
Brown, Brendan F., ed. The Natural Law Reader. LC 59-8601. (Docket Ser.: Vol. 13). 230p. 1960. pap. 2.50 (ISBN 0-379-11313-9). Oceana.
Brown, Gordon W. & Rosenberg, R. Robert. Understanding Business & Personal Law: Performance Guide. 7th ed. (Illus.). 144p. Date not set. pap. text ed. 5.80 (ISBN 0-07-053636-8, G). McGraw.
Collins, Hugh. Marxism & Law. (Marxist Introductions Ser.). (Illus.). 200p. 1982. 22.00 (ISBN 0-19-876093-0). Oxford U Pr.
Grilliot. Introduction to Law & the Legal System. 3d ed. 1983. text ed. 23.95 (ISBN 0-686-84528-5, BS13); instr's manual avail.; study guide 7.95 (ISBN 0-686-84529-3, BS15). HM.
Grilliot, Harold J. Introduction to Law & the Legal System. 3rd ed. 672p. 1983. text ed. 24.95 (ISBN 0-395-32701-6); write for info. supplementary materials. HM.
Heard, Franklin F. Oddities of the Law. 192p. 1983. Repr. of 1885 ed. lib. bdg. 20.00x (ISBN 0-8377-0648-3). Rothman.
Hempstead, Walter E., Jr. Y.O.L. (Your Own Law) A Complete Guide for the Layman. 240p. Date not set. 9.95 (ISBN 0-686-37904-7). Hempstead House.
Hodlering, Michael F., et al, eds. Arbitration & the Law, 1982. (Arbitration & the Law Ser.). 472p. (Orig.). 1983. text ed. 75.00 (ISBN 0-686-37920-9). Am Arbitration.
Nelson, Ted & Ames, Margery E., eds. Legal & Regulatory Affairs Manual. 1982. pap. 10.00 (ISBN 0-686-37426-6). Coun NY Law.
Parkinson, C. Northcote. Parkinson: The Law, Complete. 224p. 1983. pap. 2.95 (ISBN 0-345-30064-5). Ballantine.
Stern, Arlene L., ed. Law Librarian's Professional Desk Reference & Diary, 1983. v, 569p. 1982. text ed. 20.00x (ISBN 0-8377-1128-2). Rothman.
Summers, Dennis. HGV Law Guide. 1981. text ed. 15.95 (ISBN 0-408-00569-6). Butterworth.

LAW-ADDRESSES, ESSAYS, LECTURES

see also Forensic Orations

Tearle, Barbara, ed. Index to Legal Essays. 352p. 1982. 40.00 (ISBN 0-7201-1653-8, Pub. by Mansell England). Wilson.

LAW-BIBLIOGRAPHY

see also Information Storage and Retrieval Systems-Law

Research Libraries of the New York Public Library & Library of Congress. Bibliographic Guide to Law: 1982. 1983. lib. bdg. 225.00 (ISBN 0-8161-6975-6, Biblio Guides). G K Hall.

LAW-BIOGRAPHY

see also Judges; Lawyers

Gellinek, Christian. Hugo Grotius. (World Authors Ser.: No. 680). 176p. 1983. lib. bdg. 19.95 (ISBN 0-8057-6525-5, Twayne). G K Hall.

LAW-CONSTRUCTION

see Law-Interpretation and Construction

LAW-DATA PROCESSING

Congressional Information Service, Inc. Staff, ed. CIS Online User Guide & Thesaurus. 400p. 1982. loose-leaf 75.00 (ISBN 0-686-43131-6). Cong Info.
Congressional Information Service, Inc. Staff. CIS U. S. Congressional Committee Hearings Index: Part VI, 1953-1958. 3600p. 1982. 1625.00 (ISBN 0-686-43134-0). Cong Info.
Kelman, Alistair & Sizer, Richard. The Computer in Court. 104p. 1982. text ed. 33.50x (ISBN 0-566-03419-0). Gower Pub Ltd.

LAW-DICTIONARIES

Becker, U. Dictionary of Commercial Law. 992p. 1980. 175.00x (ISBN 0-7121-5489-2, Pub. by Macdonald & Evans). State Mutual Bk.
Burton, William C. Legal Thesaurus. 1983. 19.95 (ISBN 0-02-691020-9). Macmillan.
West Publishing Company. Everyone's Law Encyclopedia: A Guide to American Law. (Illus.). 3000p. 1983. text ed. 660.00 (set) (ISBN 0-314-73224-1). West Pub.

LAW-DIRECTORIES

see Lawyers-Directories

LAW-EXAMINATIONS

see Law Examinations

LAW-HISTORY AND CRITICISM

see also Comparative Law

Andrews, William. Legal Lore: Curiosities of Law & Lawyers. xii, 117p. 1982. Repr. of 1897 ed. lib. bdg. 22.50x (ISBN 0-686-81666-8). Rothman.
Forsyth, William. Hortensius the Advocate: An Historical Essay on the Office & Duties of an Advocate. xvii, 404p. 1982. Repr. of 1882 ed. lib. bdg. 35.00x (ISBN 0-8377-0617-3). Rothman.
Goodwin, John. High Points of Legal History: The Development of Business Law. LC 82-15127. 138p. (Orig.). 1982. pap. text ed. 9.95 (ISBN 0-942280-01-6). Pub Horizons.
Polson, Archer. Law & Lawyers or: Sketches & Illustrations of Legal History & Biography, 2 Vols. (Illus.). 1982. Repr. of 1840 ed. lib. bdg. 57.50x (ISBN 0-8377-1013-8). Rothman.
Scott, Henry W. The Evolution of Law: A Historical Review. 165p. 1982. Repr. of 1908 ed. lib. bdg. 22.50x (ISBN 0-8377-1127-4). Rothman.

Spanoghe & Feenstra. Honderdvijftig jaar Rechtsleven in Belgie en Nederland, 1830-1980: Praeadviezen Uitgebracht Vooreen Colloquium Georganiseerd door de Juridische Faculteiten van de Universiteiten van Gent en Leiden. Gent, 1980. (Leidse Juridische Reeks Ser.: Vol. 15). (Illus.). xvii, 534p. 1981. pap. write for info. E J Brill.

LAW-INTERPRETATION AND CONSTRUCTION

see also Judicial Process; Statutes

Ducat, Craig R. & Chase, Harold W. Constitutional Interpretation. 3rd ed. 1550p. 1983. text ed. 27.95 (ISBN 0-314-69640-7). West Pub.

Mitchell, W. J., ed. The Politics of Interpretation. 1983. pap. price not set (ISBN 0-226-53220-8). U of Chicago Pr.

Polyviou, Polynos G. Equal Protection of the Laws. 759p. 1980. text ed. 55.00x (ISBN 0-7156-1399-5, Pub. by Duckworth England). Sheridan.

LAW-JEWS

see Jewish Law

LAW-LANGUAGE

Goldfarb, Ronald & Raymond, James. Clear Understandings: A Guide to Legal Writing. 174p. 1983. pap. 8.95 (ISBN 0-394-70634-X). Random.

LAW-PHILOSOPHY

see also Free Will and Determinism; Jurisprudence; Law and Ethics

Boukema, H. J. Good Law: Toward a Rational Lawmaking Process. 156p. 1982. write for info. (ISBN 3-8204-7020-4). P Lang Pubs.

Ladenson, Robert F. A Philosophy of Free Expression & Its Constitutional Applications. LC 82-18106. (Philosophy & Society Ser.). 224p. 1983. text ed. 34.50x (ISBN 0-8476-6761-8). Rowman.

LAW-POPULAR WORKS

Crowley, Aleister. The Law Is for All. 2nd ed. Regardie, Israel, ed. 368p. 1983. pap. 10.95 (ISBN 0-941404-25-0). Falcon Pr AZ.

Lasson, Kenneth & Public Citizen Litigation Group. Representing Yourself: What You Can do Without a Lawyer. 1983. 16.50 (ISBN 0-374-24943-1); pap. text ed. 8.25 (ISBN 0-374-51726-6). FS&G.

Reader's Digest Editors. You & the Law. 3rd., rev. ed. LC 82-61749. 864p. 1983. 20.50 (ISBN 0-89577-164-0, Pub. by RD Assn). Random.

LAW-PRACTICE

see Procedure (Law)

LAW-RELIGIOUS ASPECTS

see Religion and Law

LAW-SOCIOLOGY

see Sociological Jurisprudence

LAW-STUDY AND TEACHING

see also Law Examinations

Grilliot. Introduction to Law & the Legal System. 3d ed. 1983. text ed. 23.95 (ISBN 0-686-84528-5, BS13); instr's manual avail.; study guide 7.95 (ISBN 0-686-84529-3, BS15). HM.

Lewis, Alfred J. Using American Law Books. 136p. 1983. pap. text ed. 7.95 (ISBN 0-8403-2869-9). Kendall-Hunt.

Schwartz, Alan & Scott, Robert E. Commercial Transactions Principles & Policies. (University Casebook Ser.). 1104p. 1982. text ed. write for info. tchr's manual (ISBN 0-88277-121-3); pap. write for info. Foundation Pr.

Stevens, Robert. Law School: Legal Education in America from the 1850s to the 1980s. LC 82-11148. (Studies in Legal History Ser.). xvi, 334p. 1983. 19.95x (ISBN 0-8078-1537-3). U of NC Pr.

Warner, Ralph & Ihara, Toni. Twenty-Nine Reasons Not to Go to Law School. LC 82-99889. 128p. 1982. pap. 4.95 (ISBN 0-917316-49-5). Nolo Pr.

LAW-ASIA

Kim, Chin. Selected Writings on Asian Law. LC 82-21490. xiii, 573p. 1982. lib. bdg. 37.50x (ISBN 0-8377-0741-2). Rothman.

LAW-EUROPE

Jacobs, F. G., ed. Yearbook of European Law 1981. 1982. 89.00x (ISBN 0-19-825384-2). Oxford U Pr.

Raeff, Marc. The Well-Ordered Police State: Social & Institutional Change Through Law in the Germanies & Russia, 1660-1800. LC 82-19980. 304p. 1983. text ed. 23.50x (ISBN 0-300-02869-5). Yale U Pr.

LAW-FRANCE

Centre National de la Recherce Scientifique, ed. Annuaire Francais de Droit International, Vol. XXVII (1981) LC 57-28515. 1206p. (Fr.). 1982. 125.00x (ISBN 2-222-03121-4). Intl Pubns Serv.

LAW-GERMANY

Silberberg, H. The German Standard Contracts Act. 124p. 1979. 75.00 (ISBN 0-7121-5485-X, Pub. by Macdonald & Evans). State Mutual Bk.

LAW-GREAT BRITAIN

Andrews, William. The Lawyer, in History, Literature & Humour. 276p. 1982. Repr. of 1896 ed. lib. bdg. 27.50x (ISBN 0-8377-0211-9). Rothman.

Atiyah, P. S. Law & Modern Society. 240p. 1983. 22.00 (ISBN 0-19-219166-7). Oxford U Pr.

Marsh, S. B. & Soulsby, J. Outlines of English Law. 304p. 1982. write for info. (ISBN 0-07-084655-3). McGraw.

Redmond, P. W. General Principles of English Law. 416p. 1979. 35.00x (ISBN 0-7121-0725-8, Pub. by Macdonald & Evans). State Mutual Bk.

LAW-GREAT BRITAIN-HISTORY AND CRITICISM

Duman, Daniel. The English & Colonial Bars in the Nineteenth Century. 256p. 1983. text ed. 30.00x (ISBN 0-85664-468-4, Pub. by Croom Helm Ltd England). Biblio Dist.

Tanner, Joseph R. English Constitutional Conflicts of the Seventeenth Century, 1603-1689. LC 82-25122. x, 315p. 1983. Repr. of 1928 ed. lib. bdg. 49.75x (ISBN 0-313-23855-3, TAEN). Greenwood.

Treharne, R. F. The Baronial Plan of Reform, 1258-1263. 1932. 31.00 (ISBN 0-7190-0397-0). Manchester.

LAW-GREECE (ANCIENT)

see Law, Greek

LAW-IRELAND

Comyn, James. Irish at Law. 1981. 21.50 (ISBN 0-436-10580-2, Pub. by Secker & Warburg). David & Charles.

LAW-MONGOLIA (MONGOLIAN PEOPLE'S REPUBLIC)

Butler, William E. The Mongolian Legal System. 1982. lib. bdg. 195.00 (ISBN 90-247-2685-9, Pub. by Martinus Nijhoff Netherlands). Kluwer Boston.

LAW-RUSSIA

Butler, W. E. Collected Legislation of the U. S. S. R, 7 binders. Incl. Union Republic Legislation, 1 binder; Constitutions, 2 binders; U. S. S. R, 4 binders. LC 78-24391. 1980. Set. 680.00 (ISBN 0-379-20450-9). Oceana.

LAW-UNITED STATES

Arbetman, Lee P. & Mcmahon, Edward T. New York State Supplement to Street Law: A Course in Practical Law. 2d ed. 75p. (gr. 9-12). 1983. pap. text ed. 4.95 (ISBN 0-314-73470-8). West Pub.

Caron, Denis R. Connecticut Foreclosures: An Attorney's Manual of Practice & Procedure. 2nd ed. 229p. 1982. 35.00 (ISBN 0-910051-00-3). CT Law Trib.

Congressional Quarterly Inc. Staff. Supreme Court, Justice & the Law. 1983. pap. 9.25 (ISBN 0-87187-253-6). Congr Quarterly.

League of Woman Voters of New York State. The Judicial System in New York State. rev. ed. Anderson, Claire, ed. (Illus.). 39p. 1982. pap. 2.75 (ISBN 0-938588-04-4). LWV NYS.

Pruyn, John V. Catalogue of Books Relating to the Literature of the Law. 300p. 1982. Repr. of 1901 ed. lib. bdg. 32.50x (ISBN 0-8377-1015-4). Rothman.

Sloan, Irving J., ed. Protection of Abused Victims: State Laws & Decisions. 1982. 35.00 (ISBN 0-379-10237-4). Oceana.

Wright, Charles A. Handbook of the Law of Federal Courts. 4th ed. (Hornbook Ser.). 773p. 1983. text ed. write for info. (ISBN 0-314-71354-9). West Pub.

--Handbook on the Law of Federal Courts. 4th ed. (Hornbook Ser.). 900p. 1983. write for info (ISBN 0-314-74293-X). West Pub.

LAW-UNITED STATES-BIBLIOGRAPHY

Hall, Kermit L. A Comprehensive Bibliography of American Constitutional & Legal History, 1896-1979, 2 vols. (Orig.). 1983. Set. lib. bdg. 320.00 (ISBN 0-527-37408-3). Kraus Intl.

LAW-UNITED STATES-HISTORY AND CRITICISM

Bakken, Gordon M. The Development of Law on the Rocky Mountain Frontier: Civil Law & Society, 1850-1912. LC 82-10984. (Contributions in Legal Studies: No. 27). 208p. 1983. lib. bdg. 29.95 (ISBN 0-313-23285-7, BDL/). Greenwood.

Biemer, Linda B. Women & Property in Colonial New York: The Transition from Dutch to English Law, 1643-1727. Berkhofer, Robert, ed. LC 82-23701. (Studies in American History & Culture: No. 38). 1983. write for info. (ISBN 0-8357-1392-X). Univ Microfilms.

Ericson, Joe E. Judges of the Republic of Texas, Eighteen Thirty-Six through Eighteen Forty-Six. (Illus.). 350p. 1980. 20.00 (ISBN 0-911317-04-X). Ericson Bks.

Gardner, Linda. The Texas Supreme Court: An Index of Selected Sources on the Court & Its Members, 1836 to 1981. (Tarlton Law Library Legal Bibliography Ser.: No. 25). 142p. 1982. pap. 15.00 (ISBN 0-935630-08-2). U of Tex Tarlton Law Lib.

Nordham, George W. George Washington & the Law. (Illus.). 156p. 12.75 (ISBN 0-686-38396-6). Adams Pr.

LAW-UNITED STATES-POPULAR WORKS

Arbetman, Lee P. & McMahon, Edward T. Street Law: New York Supplement. 2nd ed. (Illus.). (gr. 9-12). 1982. write for info. (ISBN 0-314-72084-7). West Pub.

Bailey, F. Lee. How to Protect Yourself Against Cops In California & Other Strange Places. LC 82-48516. 96p. 1983. 9.95 (ISBN 0-8128-2891-7). Stein & Day.

Steingold, Fred S. The Practical Guide to Michigan Law. LC 82-10965. (Illus.). 184p. 1983. pap. 8.95 (ISBN 0-472-06341-3). U of Mich Pr.

LAW-WALES

Duman, Daniel. The English & Colonial Bars in the Nineteenth Century. 256p. 1983. text ed. 30.00x (ISBN 0-85664-468-4, Pub. by Croom Helm Ltd England). Biblio Dist.

LAW (THEOLOGY)

Coppenger, Mark T. A Christian View of Justice. Date not set. pap. 6.95 (ISBN 0-8054-6126-4). Broadman.

Sanders, E. P. Paul, the Law & the Jewish People. LC 82-17487. 240p. 1983. 19.95 (ISBN 0-8006-0698-1, 1-698). Fortress.

LAW, ACCIDENT

see Accident Law

LAW, ADMINISTRATIVE

see Administrative Law

LAW, ADVERTISING

see Advertising Laws

LAW, AGRICULTURAL

see Agricultural Laws and Legislation

LAW, ANCIENT

see Law, Greek

LAW, ANGLO-AMERICAN

see Law-Great Britain; Law-United States

LAW, ARAB

see Islamic Law

LAW, BANKING

see Banking Law

LAW, BUILDING

see Building Laws

LAW, BUSINESS

see Business Law

LAW, CIVIL

see Civil Law

LAW, COMMERCIAL

see Commercial Law

LAW, COMPARATIVE

see Comparative Law

LAW, CONSTITUTIONAL

see Constitutional Law

LAW, CORPORATION

see Corporation Law

LAW, CRIMINAL

see Criminal Law

LAW, EDUCATIONAL

see Educational Law and Legislation

LAW, EMIGRATION

see Emigration and Immigration Law

LAW, ENGINEERING

see Engineering Law

LAW, FACTORY

see Factory Laws and Legislation

LAW, FISHERY

see Fishery Law and Legislation

LAW, GREEK

Here are entered works on Ancient Greek law. Works on modern Greek Law would be entered under the heading Law-Greece, Modern.

MacDowell, D. M. Athenian Homicide Law in the Age of the Orators. 1963. 14.50 (ISBN 0-7190-1212-0). Manchester.

LAW, HEBREW

see Jewish Law

LAW, HINDU

see Hindu Law

LAW, HOMESTEAD

see Homestead Law

LAW, IMMIGRATION

see Emigration and Immigration Law

LAW, INDUSTRIAL

see Factory Laws and Legislation; Industrial Laws and Legislation; Industry and State; Labor Laws and Legislation

LAW, INSURANCE

see Insurance Law

LAW, INTERNAL REVENUE

see Internal Revenue Law

LAW, INTERNATIONAL

see International Law

LAW, ISLAMIC

see Islamic Law

LAW, JEWISH

see Jewish Law

LAW, LABOR

see Labor Laws and Legislation

LAW, MARITIME

see Maritime Law

LAW, MEDICAL

see Medical Laws and Legislation

LAW, MERCHANT

see Commercial Law

LAW, MOSAIC

see Jewish Law

LAW, NATURAL

see Natural Law

LAW, PRACTICE OF

see Practice of Law

LAW, PROBATE

see Probate Law and Practice

LAW, PUBLIC

see Public Law

LAW, ROMAN

see Roman Law

LAW, SCROLL OF THE

see Torah Scrolls

LAW, SEMITIC

see Islamic Law; Jewish Law

LAW, WATER

see Water-Laws and Legislation

LAW AND ART

Art & the Law. LC 82-51091. 1982. pap. text ed. write for info. (ISBN 0-314-71294-1). West Pub.

Leland, Caryn. The Art Law Primer. 32p. 1981. pap. 5.00x (ISBN 0-933032-03-X). FCA Bks.

Weil, Stephen E. Beauty & the Beasts: On Museums, Art, the Law, & the Market. 304p. 1983. text ed. 17.50x (ISBN 0-87474-958-1); pap. text ed. 9.95x (ISBN 0-87474-957-3). Smithsonian.

LAW AND CHRISTIANITY

see Religion and Law

LAW AND ETHICS

see also Legal Ethics

Maru, Olavi, ed. Supplement to the Digest of Bar Association Ethics Opinions, 1980: Including 1970 & 1975 Supplements & Index. ix, 835p. Date not set. 50.00 (ISBN 0-910059-01-2). Am Bar Foun.

LAW AND MENTAL ILLNESS

see Insanity-Jurisprudence; Mental Health Laws

LAW AND MORALS

see Law and Ethics

LAW AND POLITICS

MacCormick, Neil. Legal Right & Social Democracy: Essays in Legal & Political Philosophy. 1982. 39.95 (ISBN 0-19-825385-0). Oxford U Pr.

LAW AND RELIGION

see Religion and Law

LAW AND SCIENCE

see Science and Law

LAW AND SOCIETY

see Sociological Jurisprudence

LAW AND TECHNOLOGY

see Technology and Law

LAW BOOKS

see Law-Bibliography

LAW ENFORCEMENT

see also Peace Officers

Bailey, F. Lee. How to Protect Yourself Against Cops In California & Other Strange Places. LC 82-48516. 96p. 1983. 9.95 (ISBN 0-8128-2891-7). Stein & Day.

Cheatham, T. Richard. Communication & Law Enforcement. (Procom Ser.). 1983. pap. text ed. 7.95 (ISBN 0-673-15556-0). Scott F.

Eldefonso, Edward. Law Enforcement & the Youthful Offender. 3rd ed. LC 77-13331. 363p. 1978. 22.95 (ISBN 0-471-03234-4); tchrs.' manual 5.00 (ISBN 0-471-03769-9). Wiley.

Eldefonso, Edward, et al. Principles of Law Enforcement: Overview of the Justice System. 3rd ed. LC 80-70901. 383p. 1982. text ed. 19.95x (ISBN 0-471-05509-3); tchr's manual (law) avail. (ISBN 0-471-86651-2). Wiley.

Malloy, Edward A. The Ethics of Law Enforcement & Criminal Punishment. LC 82-20015. 102p. (Orig.). 1983. lib. bdg. 16.75 (ISBN 0-8191-2842-2); pap. 6.75 (ISBN 0-8191-2843-0). U Pr of Amer.

Myers, Don A. Sole Prints: A Reference Guide for Law Enforcement Personnel. (Illus.). 180p. 1982. ref. manual 24.95 (ISBN 0-9608626-0-9). S O L E Pubns.

Pace, Denny F. & Styles, Jimmie C. Organized Crime: Concepts & Control. 2nd ed. (Illus.). 304p. 1983. 20.95 (ISBN 0-13-640946-6). P-H.

Rudman, Jack. Law Department Investigator. (Career Examination Ser.: C-849). (Cloth bdg. avail. on request). pap. 10.00 (ISBN 0-8373-0849-6). Natl Learning.

LAW EXAMINATIONS

Rudman, Jack. Law Library Clerk. (Career Examination Ser.: C-2888). (Cloth bdg. avail. on request). pap. 10.00 (ISBN 0-8373-2888-8). Natl Learning.

--Legal Coordinator. (Career Examination Ser.: C-2651). (Cloth bdg. avail. on request). pap. 12.00 (ISBN 0-8373-2651-6). Natl Learning.

Walder, Loretta. Pass This Bar: A Readiness Guide for Bar Examination Preparation. 1982. pap. 9.95 (ISBN 0-471-89877-5). Wiley.

LAW IN THE BIBLE

see Jewish Law

LAW IN THE KORAN

see Islamic Law

LAW LIBRARIES

see also Information Storage and Retrieval Systems-Law

Marke, Julius J. A Catalogue of the Law Collection at New York University: Published by the Law Center of N.Y.U. LC 53-6439. 1372p. 1953. 85.00 (ISBN 0-379-00125-X). Oceana.

Miskin, C. Library & Information Services for the Legal Profession. 1981. 45.00x (ISBN 0-905984-73-0, Pub. by Brit Lib England). State Mutual Bk.

LAW LISTS

see Lawyers-Directories

LAW OF NATIONS

see International Law

LAW OF NATURE

see Natural Law

LAW OF SUPPLY AND DEMAND

see Supply and Demand

LAW OF THE SEA

see Maritime Law

LAW OFFICES

see also Legal Secretaries

Brill, Steven. The American Lawyer Guide to Leading Law Firms, 1983-1984, 2 vols. Kenyon, Joan, ed. 1000p. 1983. 475.00 ea. Vol. 1 (ISBN 0-9606682-2-5). Vol. 2 (ISBN 0-9606682-3-3). Set. write for info. (ISBN 0-9606682-1-7). Am Law Pub.

Nieland, Robert G. & Doan, Rachel N. State Court Administrative Offices. 2nd ed. LC 82-82912. 1982. pap. 6.95 (ISBN 0-938870-28-9). Am Judicature.

LAW REPORTS, DIGESTS, ETC.
see also Advisory Opinions
also subdivision Cases under legal subjects
Massachusetts Board of Bar Overseers, compiled by. Massachusetts Attorney Discipline Reports, Vol. II. 250p. Date not set. price not set (ISBN 0-88063-026-4). Butterworth Legal Pubs.

LAW SCHOOLS
Stevens, Robert. Law School: Legal Education in America from the 1850s to the 1980s. LC 82-11148. (Studies in Legal History Ser.). xvi, 334p. 1983. 19.95x (ISBN 0-8078-1537-3). U of NC Pr.

LAWBOOKS
see Law-Bibliography

LAWN TENNIS
see Tennis

LAWNS
see also Grasses; Ground Cover Plants
Mac Perry's Florida Lawn & Garden Care. LC 77-9038. (Illus.). 160p. 1982. pap. 7.95 (ISBN 0-686-84278-2). Banyan Bks.
MacCasKey, Michael. Lawns & Ground Covers: How to Select, Grow & Enjoy. 160p. (Orig.). 1982. pap. 7.95 (ISBN 0-89586-099-6). H P Bks.
Vengris, Jonas. Lawns. Rev. ed. LC 82-82822. (Illus.). 250p. 1982. pap. 15.50 (ISBN 0-913702-19-6). Thomson Pub CA.

LAWRENCE, DAVID HERBERT, 1885-1930
Herzinger, Kim A. D. H. Lawrence in His Time. LC 81-65863. 240p. 1982. 28.50 (ISBN 0-8387-5028-1). Bucknell U Pr.
Holderness, Graham. D. H. Lawrence: History, Ideology & Fiction. 1982. 75.00x (ISBN 0-7171-1197-0, Pub. by Gill & Macmillan Ireland). State Mutual Bk.
Lawrence, D. H. Collected Letters, 2 vols. 1962. Set. 40.00 (ISBN 0-670-22773-0). Viking Pr.
Simpson, Hilary. D. H. Lawrence & Feminism. 174p. 1982. text ed. write for info (ISBN 0-87580-090-4). N Ill U Pr.

LAWYERS
see also Bar Associations; Judges; Law Offices; Legal Ethics; Practice of Law; Tax Consultants; Women Lawyers
Andrews, William. Legal Lore: Curiosities of Law & Lawyers. xii, 117p. 1982. Repr. of 1897 ed. lib. bdg. 22.50x (ISBN 0-686-81666-8). Rothman.
Brill, Steven. The American Lawyer Guide to Leading Law Firms, 1983-1984, 2 vols. Kenyon, Joan, ed. 1000p. 1983. 475.00 ea. Vol. 1 (ISBN 0-9606682-2-5). Vol. 2 (ISBN 0-9606682-3-3). Set. write for info. (ISBN 0-9606682-1-7). Am Law Pub.
Browne, Irving. Short Studies of Great Lawyers. iv, 382p. 1982. Repr. of 1878 ed. lib. bdg. 30.00x (ISBN 0-8377-0330-1). Rothman.
Forsyth, William. Hortensius the Advocate: An Historical Essay on the Office & Duties of an Advocate. xvii, 404p. 1982. Repr. of 1882 ed. lib. bdg. 35.00x (ISBN 0-8377-0617-3). Rothman.
Langer, Steven, ed. Compensation of Attorneys: Non-Law Firms. 4th ed. 1982. pap. 110.00 (ISBN 0-686-84834-9). Abbott Langer Assocs.
Polson, Archer. Law & Lawyers or: Sketches & Illustrations of Legal History & Biography, 2 Vols. (Illus.). 1982. Repr. of 1840 ed. lib. bdg. 57.50x (ISBN 0-8377-1013-8). Rothman.
Rothblatt, Henry B. That Damned Lawyer. 1983. 14.95 (ISBN 0-89696-198-2). Dodd.
Rudman, Jack. Adminstrative Attorney. (Career Examination Ser.: C-2597). (Cloth bdg. avail. on request). pap. 12.00 (ISBN 0-8373-2597-8). Natl Learning.
Stewart, James A. The Partners: Inside Americ's Most Powerful Law Firms. 384p. 1983. 16.95 (ISBN 0-671-42023-2). S&S.

LAWYERS-DIRECTORIES
Maine Bar Directory 1983. 350p. 1983. write for info. Tower Pub Co.
Wasserman, Paul. Law & Legal Information Directory. 2nd ed. 580p. 1982. 148.00x (ISBN 0-8103-0172-5). Gale.

LAWYERS-FEES
Nice Work (Local Attorneys' Fees) 50p. 1982. 9.00 (ISBN 0-686-81771-0). Ctr Analysis Public Issues.

LAWYERS-GREAT BRITAIN
Andrews, William. The Lawyer, in History, Literature & Humour. 276p. 1982. Repr. of 1896 ed. lib. bdg. 27.50x (ISBN 0-8377-0211-9). Rothman.
Browne, Irving. Short Studies of Great Lawyers. iv, 382p. 1982. Repr. of 1878 ed. lib. bdg. 30.00x (ISBN 0-8377-0330-1). Rothman.
Ives, E. W. The Common Lawyers of Pre-Reformation England: Thomas Kebell, A Case Study. LC 82-1297. (Cambridge Studies in English Legal History). (Illus.). 512p. Date not set. 79.50 (ISBN 0-521-24011-5). Cambridge U Pr.
Roscoe, Henry. Lives of Eminent British Lawyers. 428p. 1982. Repr. of 1830 ed. lib. bdg. 35.00x (ISBN 0-8377-1037-5). Rothman.

LAY LEADERSHIP
see Christian Leadership

LAYMEN
see Laity

LAYOUT
see Printing-Layout and Typography

LAYOUT, FACTORY
see Factories-Design and Construction

LAYOUT AND TYPOGRAPHY, ADVERTISING
see Advertising Layout and Typography

LEAD
Nriagu, Jerome O. Lead & Lead Poisoning in Antiquity. (Environmental Science & Technology Texts & Monographs). 456p. 1983. 49.95 (ISBN 0-471-08767-X, Pub. by Wiley-Interscience). Wiley.

LEAD-POISONING
Nriagu, Jerome O. Lead & Lead Poisoning in Antiquity. (Environmental Science & Technology Texts & Monographs). 456p. 1983. 49.95 (ISBN 0-471-08767-X, Pub. by Wiley-Interscience). Wiley.

LEADERSHIP
see also Christian Leadership; Elite (Social Sciences); Meetings; Recreation Leadership; Small Groups
Avakian, Bob. Leadership. Incl. If There is to be Revolution, There Must be a Revolutionary Party. 74p. 1982. 2.00 (ISBN 0-686-82470-9); Anarchism. Avakian, Bob. 1982. 1.00 (ISBN 0-686-82471-7); Bob Avakian Speaks on the Mao Defendants' Railroad & the Historic Battles Ahead. 69p. 1981. 1.50 (ISBN 0-686-82472-5); Summing Up the Black Panther Party. 1980. 0.60 (ISBN 0-686-82473-3); Communists are Rebels. 1980. 0.50 (ISBN 0-686-82474-1); Important Struggles in Building the RCP. 55p. 1978. 1.00 (ISBN 0-686-82475-X); New Constitution of the RCP, U. S. A. 1981. 0.75 (ISBN 0-686-82476-8). 5.00 (ISBN 0-686-82469-5). RCP Pubns.
Barber, Cyril J. & Strauss, Gary H. Leadership: The Dynamics of Success. 126p. pap. 4.95 (ISBN 0-87921-068-0). Attic Pr.
Bass, Bernard M. Stogdill's Handbook of Leadership. 2nd ed. (Illus.). 1057p. 1981. text ed. 39.95. Free Pr.
Bothwell, Lin K. The Art of Leadership: Skill-Building Techniques that Produce Results. (Illus.). 272p. 1983. 18.95 (ISBN 0-13-047100-3); pap. 9.95 (ISBN 0-13-047092-9). P-H.
Czudnowski, Moshe M., ed. Does Who Governs Matter? (International Yearbook for Studies of Leaders & Leadership Ser.). 300p. 1982. 25.00x (ISBN 0-87580-085-8); pap. 12.50 (ISBN 0-87580-529-9). N Ill U Pr.
Fiedler, Fred E., et al. Improving Leadership Effectiveness: The Leader Match Concept. LC 76-20632. (Self-Teaching Guides). 229p. 1976. pap. text ed. 9.95 (ISBN 0-471-25811-3). Wiley.
Fiore, M. V. & Strauss, P. S. How to Develop Dynamic Leadership: A Short Course for Professionals. (Wiley Professional Development Programs). 274p. 1977. 24.95x (ISBN 0-471-02314-0). Wiley.
Johnson, David W. & Johnson, Frank P. Joining Together: Group Theory & Group Skills. 2nd ed. LC 74-23698. 480p. 1982. 17.95 (ISBN 0-13-510396-7). P-H.
Kriyananda, Swami. The Art of Creative Leadership. 16p. 1980. pap. 2.95 (ISBN 0-916124-20-7). Ananda.
Lutzenkirchen, Hans P. Optimale Fuhrparkbestandsplanung. 316p. (Ger.). 1982. write for info. (ISBN 3-8204-5802-6). P Lang Pubs.
Reed, Harold W. The Dynamics of Leadership. 263p. 1982. pap. text ed. 12.95x (ISBN 0-8134-2261-2). Interstate.

LEAFLETS
see Pamphlets

LEAL, VALDES
Du Gue Trapier, E. Valdes Leal: Baroque Concept of Death & Suffering in his Paintings. (Illus.). 1956. pap. 1.50 (ISBN 0-87535-090-9). Hispanic Soc.

LEAR, EDWARD, 1812-1888
Jackson, Holbrook. The Complete Nonsense of Edward Lear. 288p. 1982. Repr. of 1947 ed. lib. bdg. 30.00 (ISBN 0-8495-3400-3). Arden Lib.
Van Thal, Herbert, ed. Edward Lear's Journals: A Selection. 260p. 1982. Repr. of 1952 ed. lib. bdg. 35.00 (ISBN 0-8495-3401-1). Arden Lib.

LEARNED INSTITUTIONS AND SOCIETIES
see also Societies
Benedict, Stephen. Cultural Institutions Across America: Functions & Funding. 28p. 1982. pap. 3.00 (ISBN 0-943006-15-5). Seven Springs.

LEARNING, ART OF
see Study, Method of

LEARNING, PSYCHOLOGY OF
see also Conditioned Response; Learning Ability; Learning Disabilities
Bridgeman, Bruce & Bridgeman, Dinae, eds. Readings on Fundamental Issues on Learning & Memory. 343p. 1977. pap. text ed. 14.95x (ISBN 0-8422-0548-9). Irvington.
Estes. Models of Learning, Memory & Choice. 410p. 1982. 29.95 (ISBN 0-03-059266-6). Praeger.
Gallahue, David L. Motor Development & Movement Experiences for Young Children. LC 75-37676. 413p. 1976. text ed. 25.50x (ISBN 0-471-29042-4). Wiley.
Gallahue, David L., et al. A Conceptual Approach to Moving & Learning. LC 75-2369. 423p. 1975. text ed. 25.95x (ISBN 0-471-29043-2); tchrs.' resource bk. 6.00x (ISBN 0-471-29039-4). Wiley.
Helton, George, et al. Psychoeducational Assessment: Contexts, Concepts & Measures. Date not set. price not set (ISBN 0-8089-1482-0). Grune.
Juch, Bert. Personal Development: The Roundabout Climb. 200p. 1983. 29.95 (ISBN 0-471-10458-2, Pub. by Wiley-Interscience). Wiley.
Monroe, Walter S. Directing Learning in the Elementary School. 480p. 1982. Repr. of 1932 ed. lib. bdg. 45.00 (ISBN 0-89987-648-X). Darby Bks.
Rogers, Carl R. Freedom to Learn. 448p. 1982. text ed. 9.95 (ISBN 0-675-20012-1). Merrill.
Schwartz, Barry. Psychology of Learning & Behavior: Essays on Behavior Theory. 500p. 1982. pap. text ed. 14.95x (ISBN 0-393-95305-X). Norton.
Senesh, Lawrence. The Optimum of Knowledge Academy of Independent. Boulding, Kenneth E., ed. (Academy of Independent Scholars Forum Ser.). 1983. lib. bdg. 20.00 (ISBN 0-86531-544-2). Westview.
Tsukada, Y. & Agranoff, B. W. Neurobiological Basis of Learning & Memory. 260p. 1980. text ed. 39.95 (ISBN 0-471-05148-9, Pub. by Wiley Med). Wiley.
Waterhouse, Philip. Managing the Learning Process. (Illus.). 191p. 1983. pap. 13.50 (ISBN 0-686-84664-8). Nichols Pub.
Wise, Francis H. Who's Boss? Training Your Baby or Child in Self-Management. Wise, Joyce M., ed. (Illus.). 235p. (Orig.). 1982. pap. 8.25 (ISBN 0-915766-58-2). Wise Pub.
Worell, Judith, ed. Psychological Development in the Elementary Years. (Educational Psychology Ser.). 504p. 39.50 (ISBN 0-12-764050-9). Acad Pr.

LEARNING ABILITY
see also Learning, Psychology Of; Learning Disabilities
Hart, Leslie A. Human Brain & Human Learning. 256p. 1983. text ed. 22.50x (ISBN 0-686-37692-7); pap. text ed. 12.50x (ISBN 0-582-28379-5). Longman.
Narrol, Harvey G. & Giblon, Shirley T. Your Child's Hidden Learning Potential: An Essay on Teaching the Fourth "R"-Reasoning. 1983. pap. text ed. write for info. (ISBN 0-8391-1745-0, 18228). Univ Park.
Senesh, Lawrence. The Optimum of Knowledge Academy of Independent. Boulding, Kenneth E., ed. (Academy of Independent Scholars Forum Ser.). 1983. lib. bdg. 20.00 (ISBN 0-86531-544-2). Westview.

LEARNING CENTER APPROACH TO TEACHING
see Open Plan Schools

LEARNING DISABILITIES
see also Reading Disability
Alternatives for Children With Learning Problems. 1975. pap. 5.75 (ISBN 0-934338-09-4). NAIS.
Carnine, Douglas & Elkind, David. Interdisciplinary Voices in Learning Disabilities & Remedial Education. (Illus.). 196p. (Orig.). 1982. pap. text ed. 15.00x (ISBN 0-936104-27-9). Pro-Ed.
Cherne, J. The Learning Disabled Child in Your Church School. (09). 1983. pap. 3.50 (ISBN 0-570-03883-9). Concordia.
Chicorel, Marietta, ed. Chicorel Abstracts to Reading & Learning Disabilities, 1981, Vol. 19. (Chicorel Index Ser.). 380p. 1983. 95.00x (ISBN 0-934598-83-5). Am Lib Pub Co.
Clifton, Merritt. Learning Disabilities: What the Publicity Doesn't Tell. 24p. 1982. pap. 3.00 (ISBN 0-686-37937-3). Samisdat.
Das, J. P. & Mulcaby, R., eds. Theory & Research in Learning Disabilities. LC 82-112219. 300p. 1982. 37.50x (ISBN 0-306-41112-1, Plenum Pr). Plenum Pub.
Duke, Robert E. Why Children Fail & How You Can Help Them: Meditation-Therapy. 130p. 1983. 16.95x (ISBN 0-686-84047-X). Irvington.
Evans, James S. An Uncommon Gift. LC 82-25930. (A Bridgebooks Publication). 180p. 1983. write for info. (ISBN 0-664-27009-3). Westminster.
Hampshire, Susan. Susan's Story: An Autobiographical Account of My Struggle with Words. (Illus.). 168p. 1982. 11.95 (ISBN 0-312-77966-6). St Martin.
Kloep, Marion. Zur Psychologie der Aufgabenschwierigkeit. vi, 355p. (Ger.). 1982. write for info. (ISBN 3-8204-5833-6). P Lang Pubs.
Lerner, J. W. & List, L. K. Reading & Learning Disabilities. Date not set. price not set (ISBN 0-07-037220-9). McGraw.
Mercer, Cecil D. Students with Learning Disabilities. 544p. 1983. text ed. 23.95 (ISBN 0-675-20042-3). Additional supplements may be obtained from publishter. Merrill.
Myklebust, Helmer, ed. Progress in Learning Disabilities, Vol. 5. Date not set. price not set (ISBN 0-8089-1500-2). Grune.
Painting, Donald H. Helping Children with Specific Learning Disabilities: A Practical Guide for Parents & Teachers. 196p. 1983. 12.92 (ISBN 0-13-387258-0); pap. 6.95 (ISBN 0-13-387241-6). P-H.
Philp, M. & Duckworth, D. Children with Disabilities & Their Families: A Review of Research. (NFER Research Publications Ser.). 131p. 1982. pap. text ed. 14.75x (ISBN 0-7005-0491-5, NFER). Humanities.
Ridenour, Dian M. & Johnston, Jane. A Guide to Post-Secondary Educational Opportunities for the Learning Disabled. 183p. 1981. pap. 12.00 (ISBN 0-9608010-0-6). Time Out.
Sheppard, Anne. BivaD (David) For Parents of Learning Disabled Children. 24p. (Orig.). 1983. pap. 1.25 (ISBN 0-8298-0650-4). Pilgrim NY.
Sleeman, Phillip J., et al. Designing Learning Programs & Environments for Students with Special Learning Needs. (Illus.). 304p. 1983. pap. text ed. 24.75x (ISBN 0-398-04770-7). C C Thomas.
Wise, Bernice Kemmler. Teaching Materials for the Learning Disabled. LC 80-18114. 70p. 1980. pap. text ed. 5.00 (ISBN 0-8389-0311-8). ALA.
Woodward, Delores M. The Learning Disabled Adolescent. 200p. 1983. price not set (ISBN 0-89443-875-1). Aspen Systems.
Wren, Carol T., et al, eds. Language Learning Disabilities: Diagnosis & Remediation. 1983. price not set (ISBN 0-89443-935-9). Aspen Systems.

LEARNING DISORDERS
see Learning Disabilities

LEASES
see also Landlord and Tenant
Anderson, Kenneth R. Lease Escalators & Other Pass-Through Clauses: 1983. 2nd rev. ed. 35p. 1983. pap. 13.50 (ISBN 0-912104-70-8). Inst Real Estate.

LEASES, INDUSTRIAL EQUIPMENT
see Industrial Equipment Leases

LEATHER
Genfan, Herb & Taetzch, Lyn. Latigo Leather. (Illus.). 160p. 1976. pap. 7.95 (ISBN 0-8230-2651-5). Watson-Guptill.

LEATHER, CORDOVAN
see Leather Work

LEATHER WORK
see also Saddlery
Hamilton-Head, Ian. Leatherwork. 134p. 1983. pap. 7.50 (ISBN 0-7137-1342-9, Pub. by Blandford Pr England). Sterling.

LEAVES
Dale, John E. & Milthorpe, Frederick L. The Growth & Functioning of Leaves. LC 82-4377. (Illus.). 550p. Date not set. price not set (ISBN 0-521-23761-0). Cambridge U Pr.

LEBANON
Randal, Jonathan. Book on Lebanon. 256p. 1983. 16.75 (ISBN 0-670-55186-4). Viking Pr.

LEBANON-HISTORY
Timerman, Jacobo. The Longest War: Israel in Lebanon. Acoca, Miguel, tr. from Span. LC 82-48584. 167p. 1982. 11.95 (ISBN 0-394-53022-5). Knopf.

LEBANON-POLITICS AND GOVERNMENT
Gordon, David C. The Republic of Lebanon: A Nation in Jeopardy. (Profiles-Nations of the Contemporary Middle East). 175p. 1983. price not set (ISBN 0-86531-450-0). Westview.
Randal, Jonthan. The Tragedy of Lebanon. 1983. pap. 16.75 (ISBN 0-670-42259-2). Viking Pr.

LEBESGUE MEASURE
see Measure Theory

LEBRUN, MARIE LOUISE ELISABETH (VIGEE) 1755-1842-JUVENILE LITERATURE
Baillio, Joseph. Elisabeth Louise Vigee Le Brun 1755-1842. LC 82-81554. 148p. 1982. 29.95 (ISBN 0-912804-06-8, Dist. by U of Wash Pr). Kimbell Art.

LE CORBUSIER
see Jeanneret-Gris, Charles Edouard, 1887-1965

LECTIONARIES
Johnson, Sherman E. The Year of the Lord's Favor: Preaching the Three-Year Lectionary. 300p. 1983. pap. 13.95 (ISBN 0-8164-2359-8). Seabury.
A Word in Season, Monastic Lectionary for the Divine Office, Advent to Christmastide. 1981. pap. 16.50 (ISBN 0-686-81962-4). St Bedes Pubns.

LEE, JOSEPH BRACKEN, 1899-
Lythgoe, Dennis L. Let'em Holler: A Political Biography of J. Bracken Lee. LC 82-60039. (Illus.). xii, 343p. 1982. 17.50 (ISBN 0-913738-33-6). Utah St Hist Soc.

LEE, ROBERT EDWARD, 1807-1870
Frassanito, William A. Grant & Lee: The Virginia Campaigns, 1864-1865. (Illus.). 448p. 1983. 19.95 (ISBN 0-686-83857-2, ScribT). Scribner.

LEE, ROBERT EDWARD, 1807-1870-JUVENILE LITERATURE
Monsell, Helen A. Robert E. Lee. new ed. (Childhood of Famous Americans Ser.). (Illus.). 204p. (Orig.). (gr. 2 up). 1983. pap. 3.95 (ISBN 0-672-52750-2). Bobbs.

LEEDS, ENGLAND
Fraser, Derek, ed. A History of Modern Leeds. 488p. 1982. 25.00 (ISBN 0-7190-0747-X); pap. 8.50 (ISBN 0-7190-0781-X). Manchester.

LEG
Kennedy, William. Legs. 1983. pap. 5.95 (ISBN 0-14-006484-2). Penguin.
Olinekova, Gayle. Legs! Super Legs in Six Weeks. (Illus.). 128p. 1983. pap. 7.95 (ISBN 0-671-47241-0, Fireside). S&S.

LEGACIES, TAXATION OF
see Inheritance and Transfer Tax

LEGAL AID SOCIETIES
Maguire, John M. The Lance of Justice: A Semi-Centennial History of the Legal Aid Society 1876-1926. xi, 305p. 1982. Repr. of 1928 ed. lib. bdg. 30.00x (ISBN 0-8377-0847-8). Rothman.

LEGAL ARGUMENTS
see Forensic Orations

LEGAL ASSISTANTS
Berkey, Rachel L. New Career Opportunities in the Paralegal Profession. LC 82-13929. (Illus.). 160p. 1983. 10.95 (ISBN 0-668-05478-6); pap. 5.95 (ISBN 0-668-05482-4). Arco.

LEGAL BIBLIOGRAPHY
see Law-Bibliography; Legal Research
LEGAL CERTAINTY
see Law-Interpretation and Construction
LEGAL CITATION
see Citation of Legal Authorities
LEGAL COMPOSITION
see also Forms (Law)
Block, Gertrude. Effective Legal Writing: A Style Book for Law Students & Lawyers. 2nd ed. 205p. 1983. pap. text ed. write for info. (ISBN 0-88277-109-4). Foundation Pr.
LEGAL DIRECTORIES
see Lawyers-Directories
LEGAL DOCUMENTS
Gibson, J. S., compiled by. Bishops Transcripts & Marriage Licences, Bonds & Allegations: A Guide to Their Location & Indexes. 2nd ed. 52p. 1982. pap. 5.00x (ISBN 0-906428-11-4). Intl Pubns Serv.
LEGAL EDUCATION
see Law-Study and Teaching
LEGAL ESSAYS
see Law-Addresses, Essays, Lectures
LEGAL ETHICS
Digest of Bar Association Ethics Opinions: 1980 Supplement. ix, 835p. 1982. 50.00 (ISBN 0-686-83920-X). Am Bar Foun.
LEGAL FEES
see Lawyers-Fees
LEGAL FORMS
see Forms (Law)
LEGAL HISTORY
see Law-History and Criticism
LEGAL HOLIDAYS
see Holidays
LEGAL LANGUAGE
see Law-Language
LEGAL LITERATURE SEARCHING
see Information Storage and Retrieval Systems-Law
LEGAL MEDICINE
see Medical Jurisprudence
LEGAL OFFICES
see Law Offices
LEGAL PROCEDURE
see Procedure (Law)
LEGAL PROFESSION
see Lawyers
LEGAL PSYCHOLOGY
see Psychology, Forensic
LEGAL RESEARCH
see also Citation of Legal Authorities
Teply, Larry L. Legal Research & Citation: Programmed Materials. 326p. 1982. 9.95 (ISBN 0-314-65784-3). West Pub.
LEGAL RESPONSIBILITY
see Liability (Law)
LEGAL SECRETARIES
see also Law Offices
California Legal Secretary's Resource. 4th ed. 362p. 1981. looseleaf 19.00 (ISBN 0-911110-32-1); 1983 suppl. incl. Parker & Son.
Rudman, Jack. Principal Court Clerk. (Career Examination Ser.: C-2588). (Cloth bdg. avail. on request). pap. 12.00 (ISBN 0-8373-2588-9). Natl Learning.
--Senior Legal Stenographer. (Career Examination ser.: C-2634). (Cloth bdg. avail. on request). pap. 10.00 (ISBN 0-8373-2634-6). Natl Learning.
LEGAL STATUS OF WOMEN
see Women-Legal Status, Laws, etc.
LEGAL STYLE
see Law-Language
LEGATIONS
see Diplomatic and Consular Service
LEGENDS
see also Fables; Fairy Tales; Folk-Lore; Mythology; Romances; Saints
also subdivisions Legends under special subjects, e.g. Mary, Virgin-Legends
Grant, Charles L. The Dodd, Mead Gallery of Horror. 1983. 15.95 (ISBN 0-396-08160-6). Dodd.
LEGENDS-JUVENILE LITERATURE
see also Legends, American, French, etc. for other juvenile works
Wann, Brian. The Fox & the Buffalo. 12p. (Orig.). pap. 2.50 (ISBN 0-88138-003-2, Pub. by Envelope Bks). Green Tiger Pr.
LEGENDS, AMERICAN
Dobie, J. Frank. Coronado's Children: Tales of Lost & Buried Treasures of the Southwest. 367p. 1982. Repr. of 1931 ed. lib. bdg. 50.00 (ISBN 0-89987-170-4). Darby Bks.
Williams, Stanley T. American Spirit in Letters. 1926. text ed. 22.50x (ISBN 0-686-83468-2). Elliots Bks.
LEGENDS, BRITISH
Cooke, Michael. The Ancient Curse of the Baskervilles. LC 82-83499. 96p. pap. 4.95 (ISBN 0-934468-14-1). Gaslight.
LEGENDS, CHINESE
Clifton, Lucille. Everett Anderson's Goodbye. (Illus.). 32p. (gr. k-3). 1983. 9.95 (ISBN 0-03-063518-7). HR&W.
Lee, Jeanne. Legend of the Li River. (Illus.). 32p. (gr. k-3). 1983. 11.95 (ISBN 0-03-063523-3). HR&W.
McNaughton, Colin. Crazy Bear. (Illus.). 32p. (gr. k-2). 1983. 10.95 (ISBN 0-03-063043-6). HR&W.
Williams, Margery. The Velveteen Rabbit. LC 82-15606. (Illus.). 48p. (gr. k-4). 1983. 11.95 (ISBN 0-03-063517-9); ltd. ed. 100.00 (ISBN 0-03-063612-4). HR&W.
LEGENDS, CHRISTIAN
Metford, J. C. A Dictionary of Christian Lore & Legend. (Illus.). 1983. 24.95 (ISBN 0-500-01262-8). Thames Hudson.
LEGENDS, EGYPTIAN
MacKenzie, Donald A. Egyptian Myth & Legend. 404p. 1983. pap. 8.25 (ISBN 0-88072-016-6). Tanager Bks.
LEGENDS, GERMANIC
Ratcliff, Ruth. German Tales & Legends. 144p. 1982. 29.00x (ISBN 0-584-62059-4, Pub. by Muller Ltd). State Mutual Bk.
LEGENDS, IRISH
Croker, Thomas C. Fairy Legends & Tradition of the South Ireland. LC 82-5885. 1983. 50.00 (ISBN 0-8201-1380-8). Schol Facsimiles.
LEGENDS AND STORIES OF ANIMALS
see Animals, Legends and Stories Of
LEGERDEMAIN
see Conjuring; Magic
LEGISLATION
see also Bills, Legislative; Governmental Investigations; Judicial Review; Law; Legislative Bodies; Legislative Power; Parliamentary Practice also legislation on particular subjects; e.g. Factory Laws and Legislation
Harris, Fred R. & Hain, Paul L. America's Legislative Process. 1983. 21.95x (ISBN 0-673-15357-6). Scott F.
Purcell, L. Edward, ed. Suggested State Legislation, 1983, Vol. 42. 395p. (Orig.). 1982. pap. 15.00 (ISBN 0-87292-032-1). Coun State Govts.
LEGISLATION, COMPARATIVE
see Comparative Law
LEGISLATIVE BILLS
see Bills, Legislative
LEGISLATIVE BODIES
see also Legislative Power; Legislators; Parliamentary Practice; Right and Left (Political Science)
Brownson, Charles & Brownson, Anna L. Advance Locator for Capitol Hill. 19th ed. 520p. 1983. 10.00 (ISBN 0-87289-054-6). Congr Staff.
Brownson, Charles B. & Brownson, Anna L. Congressional Staff Directory: 1983. 24th ed. 1064p. 1983. 30.00 (ISBN 0-87289-055-4). Congr Staff.
Keeler, Mary F. & Cole, Maija J., eds. Proceedings in Parliament Sixteen Twenty-Eight. LC 75-43321. (Proceedings in Parliament 1628 Ser.). 700p. 1983. Vol. V: Lords Proceedings Sixteen Twenty-Eight. text ed. 85.00x (ISBN 0-300-02051-1); Vol. VI: Appendixes & Indexes. text ed. 55.00x (ISBN 0-300-02467-3). Yale U Pr.
Muir, William K., Jr. Legislature: California's School of Politics. LC 82-16128. 197p. 1983. 19.00x (ISBN 0-226-54627-6). U of Chicago Pr.
LEGISLATIVE BODIES-COMMITTEES
see also Governmental Investigations; United States-Congress-Committees
Harris, Fred R. & Hain, Paul L. America's Legislative Process. 1983. 21.95x (ISBN 0-673-15357-6). Scott F.
LEGISLATIVE BODIES-RULES AND PRACTICE
see Parliamentary Practice
LEGISLATIVE DISTRICTS
see Election Districts
LEGISLATIVE HISTORIES
Nabors, Eugene. Legislative Reference Checklist: The Key to Legislative Histories from 1789-1903. LC 82-18074. xv, 440p. 1982. text ed. 39.50x (ISBN 0-8377-0908-3). Rothman.
LEGISLATIVE INVESTIGATIONS
see Governmental Investigations
LEGISLATIVE POWER
see also Federal Government; Judicial Review; Legislative Bodies; Legislation; State Governments; War and Emergency Powers
Cheney, Richard B. & Cheney, Lynne V. Kings of the Hill: Power & Personality in the House of Representatives. (Illus.). 224p. 1983. 14.95 (ISBN 0-8264-0230-5). Crossroad NY.
LEGISLATORS
Cheney, Richard B. & Cheney, Lynne V. Kings of the Hill: Power & Personality in the House of Representatives. (Illus.). 224p. 1983. 14.95 (ISBN 0-8264-0230-5). Crossroad NY.
Muir, William K., Jr. Legislature: California's School of Politics. LC 82-16128. 197p. 1983. 19.00x (ISBN 0-226-54627-6). U of Chicago Pr.
LEGUMES
Here are entered works on those plants belonging to the family Leguminosae, the pods or seeds of which are edible for man or domestic animals, e.g. peas, beans, lentils, etc., treated collectively.
see also names of luguminous plants
Arora, S. K. Chemistry & Biochemistry of Legumes. 400p. 1982. text ed. 49.50 (ISBN 0-7131-2854-2). E Arnold.
Hunter, Peter J. Peter Hunter's Guide to Grasses, Clovers, & Weeds. (Illus.). 80p. pap. 5.95 (ISBN 0-938670-02-6). By Hand & Foot.
Legumes in Human Nutrition. (FAO Food & Nutrition Paper: No. 20). 152p. 1982. pap. 11.75 (ISBN 92-5-101181-8, F2329, FAO). Unipub.
LEISURE
see also Hobbies; Recreation; Retirement; Time Allocation
Coping with Stress Through Leisure. (Leisure Today Ser.). 32p. 1.50 (ISBN 0-88314-218-X). AAHPERD.
Dowd, E. Thomas. Leisure Counseling: Concepts & Applications. (Illus.). 392p. 1983. text ed. price not set (ISBN 0-398-04824-X). C C Thomas.
Edginton, C. R. & Williams, J. G. Productive Management of Leisure Service Organizations: A Behavioral Approach. 530p. 1978. 22.95x (ISBN 0-471-01574-1). Wiley.
Education for Leisure. (Leisure Today Ser.). 32p. 1.50 (ISBN 0-88314-113-2). AAHPERD.
Evaluation of Leisure Programs. (Leisure Today Ser.). 24p. 1.50 (ISBN 0-88314-114-0). AAHPERD.
Goodale, Thomas & Witt, Peter A., eds. Recreation & Leisure: Issues in an Era of Change. LC 79-92646. 394p. (Orig.). 1980. pap. text ed. 14.95x (ISBN 0-910251-00-2). Venture Pub PA.
High Adventure Leisure Pusuits & Risk Recreation. 32p. 1.50 (ISBN 0-88314-115-9). AAHPERD.
Leisure & Aging. (Leisure Today Ser.). 32p. 1.50 (ISBN 0-88314-119-1). AAHPERD.
Leisure & Popular Culture. (Leisure Today Ser.). 32p. 1.50 (ISBN 0-88314-118-3). AAHPERD.
Leisure Counseling. (Leisure Today Ser.). 32p. 1.50 (ISBN 0-88314-120-5). AAHPERD.
The Leisure Revolution: Its Impact on Culture. (Leisure Today Ser.). 32p. 1.50 (ISBN 0-88314-117-5). AAHPERD.
Leisure Today: Selected Readings, Vol. II. 160p. 10.95 (ISBN 0-88314-123-X). AAHPERD.
Managing Leisure Services. (Leirure Today Ser.). 32p. 1.50 (ISBN 0-88314-124-8). AAHPERD.
Opportunities in Recreation & Leisure. (Leisure Today Ser.). 123p. 7.95 (ISBN 0-686-84055-0). AAHPERD.
Play. (Leisure Today Ser.). 32p. 1.50 (ISBN 0-88314-121-3). AAHPERD.
Population Dynamics. (Leirsure Today Ser.). 32p. 1.50 (ISBN 0-88314-126-4). AAHPERD.
LENDING
see Loans
LENIN, VLADIMIR ILICH, 1870-1924
Egan, David R. & Egan, Melinda A. V. I. Lenin: An Annotated Bibliography of English-Language Sources to 1980. LC 82-659. 516p. 1982. 32.50 (ISBN 0-8108-1526-5). Scarecrow.
Harding, Neil. Lenin's Political Thought, Vols. 1 & 2. 550p. 1982. pap. text ed. 19.95x (ISBN 0-391-02698-4). Humanities.
Topalian, Elyse. V. I. Lenin. (Impact Biography Ser.). (Illus.). 128p. (gr. 7 up). 1983. PLB 8.90 (ISBN 0-531-04589-7). Watts.
Tumarkin, Nina. Lenin Lives! The Lenin Cult in Soviet Russia. (Illus.). 384p. 1983. 20.00 (ISBN 0-674-52430-6). Harvard U Pr.
LENINGRAD
Kelly, Laurence, intro. by. St. Petersburg: A Traveller's Companion. LC 82-20575. (Illus.). 304p. (Orig.). 1983. pap. 7.95 (ISBN 0-689-70645-6, 294). Atheneum.
LENNON, JOHN, 1940-1980
Green, John. Dakota Days: The Untold Story of John Lennon's Final Years. 1983. 15.95 (ISBN 0-312-18176-0). St Martin.
Shotton, Peter & Schaffner, Nicholas. John Lennon in My Life. LC 82-42853. (Illus.). 224p. 1983. 22.50 (ISBN 0-8128-2916-6); deluxe signed edition 200.00 (ISBN 0-8128-2915-8); pap. 14.95 (ISBN 0-8128-6185-X). Stein & Day.
LENSES
see also Contact Lenses
Clayman, Henry M. & Jaffe, Norman S. Intraocular Lens Implantation: Techniques & Complications. LC 82-8267. (Illus.). 300p. 1983. text ed. 59.50 (ISBN 0-8016-1080-X). Mosby.
LENSES, PHOTOGRAPHIC
Reynolds, Clyde. Lenses. (Photographer's Library). (Illus.). 1983. pap. 12.95x (ISBN 0-240-51120-4). Focal Pr.
LENSLESS PHOTOGRAPHY
see Holography
LENT
see also Easter
Cole, Joan. A Lenten Journey with Jesus. 48p. 1982. pap. 1.50 (ISBN 0-89243-172-5). Liguori Pubns.
Ellebracht, Mary P. Easter Passage: The RCIA Experience. 204p. 1983. pap. 11.95 (ISBN 0-86683-693-4). Winston Pr.
Steinke, Peter L. Preaching the Theology of the Cross: Sermons & Worship Ideas for Lent & Easter. LC 82-72638. 128p. (Orig.). 1983. pap. 5.95 (ISBN 0-8066-1944-9, 10-5144). Augsburg.
LENT-PRAYER BOOKS AND DEVOTIONS
Sullivan, Barbara. A Page a Day for Lent Nineteen Eighty-Three. LC 82-60607. 56p. 1983. pap. 2.50. Paulist Pr.
LENTEN SERMONS
Here are entered sermons preached during the season of Lent. If they are limited in their scope to the passion of Jesus Christ, entry is made under Jesus Christ-Passion-Sermons.
Currin, Beverly M. The Hope That Never Disappoints. 128p. (Orig.). 1983. pap. 6.95 (ISBN 0-687-17415-5). Abingdon.
Dunnam, Maxie. The Sanctuary for Lent, 1983. 48p. 1983. pap. 22.00 per 100 (ISBN 0-687-36845-6). Abingdon.
Shelby, Donald J. Bold Expectations of the Gospel. 96p. (Orig.). 1983. pap. 3.95 (ISBN 0-8358-0454-2). Upper Room.
LENTICULAR DEGENERATION
see Hepatolenticular Degeneration
LEONARDO DA VINCI, 1452-1519
Keele, Kenneth D. Leonardo da Vinci's Elements of the Science of Man: monograph. Date not set. price not set (ISBN 0-12-403980-4). Acad Pr.
Leonardo Da Vinci. (Famous People Ser.). 1983. 6.50 (ISBN 0-8120-5512-8). Barron.
LEPANTO, BATTLE OF, 1571
Beeching, Jack. The Galleys at Lepanto. (Illus.). 272p. 1983. 15.95 (ISBN 0-686-83833-5, ScribT). Scribner.
LEPIDOPTERA
E. W. Classey Ltd., ed. The Leipodoptera of America North of Mexico. 1982. 135.00x (ISBN 0-86096-016-1, Pub. by E W Classey England). State Mutual Bk.
Odiyo, P. O. Seasonal Distribution & Migrations of Agrotis Ipsilon (Hufnagel) Leipidoptera, Noctuidae. 1975. 35.00x (ISBN 0-85135-070-4, Pub. by Centre Overseas Research). State Mutual Bk.
LEPROSY
International Labour Office. Vocational Rehabilitation of Leprosy Patients Report on the ILO-DANIDA Asian Seminar Bombay, India (26 October-6 November, 1981) iii, 126p. 1982. pap. 8.55 (ISBN 92-2-103047-4). Intl Labour Office.
LEPTONS (NUCLEAR PHYSICS)
see also Electrons
Atwood, W. B. & Bjorken, J. D. Lectures on Lepton Nucleon Scattering & Quantum Chromo-Dynamics. (Progress in Physics Ser.: Vol. 4). 1982. 34.95 (ISBN 3-7643-3079-1). Birkhauser.
LERMONTOV, MIKHAIL IUREVICH, 1814-1841
Garrard, John. Mikhail Lermontov. (World Authors Ser.). 1982. lib. bdg. 15.95 (ISBN 0-8057-6514-X, Twayne). G K Hall.
LESBIANISM
Krieger, Susan. The Mirror Dance: Identity in a Women's Community. 1983. write for info. (ISBN 0-87722-304-1). Temple U Pr.
Samois. Coming to Power: Writings & Graphics on Lesbian S/M. rev. ed. (Illus.). 288p. 1983. pap. 7.95 (ISBN 0-932870-28-7). Alyson Pubns.
LESOTHO
Hailey, William M. The Republic of South Africa & the High Commission Territories. LC 82-11865. vii, 136p. 1982. Repr. of 1963 ed. lib. bdg. 25.00x (ISBN 0-313-23625-9, HARS). Greenwood.
LESS DEVELOPED COUNTRIES
see Underdeveloped Areas
LESSING, DORIS MAY, 1919-
Draine, Betsy. Substance under Pressure: Artistic Coherence & Evolving Form in the Novels of Doris Lessing. LC 82-70556. 240p. 1983. 18.95 (ISBN 0-299-09230-5). U of Wis Pr.
Kessler, Heilgard. Individuum und Gesellschaft In Den Romanen der Doris Lessing. 188p. (Ger.). 1982. write for info. (ISBN 3-8204-6272-4). P Lang Pubs.
LESSING, GOTTHOLD EPHRAIM, 1729-1781
Harris, Edward P. & Wucherpfennig, Wolf, eds. Lessing Yearbook XIV 1982. 308p. 1983. 25.00 (ISBN 0-8143-1733-2). Wayne St U Pr.
LETTER PICTURES
Lambert, Yvon & Barthes, Roland. Cy Twombly: A Catologue Raisome. (Illus.). 222p. 1983. 95.00 (ISBN 0-8390-0305-6). Allanheld & Schram.
LETTER-WRITING
see also Commercial Correspondence
Meyer, Harold E. Lifetime Encyclopedia of Letters. LC 82-13343. 403p. 1983. 25.00 (ISBN 0-13-536383-7, Busn). P-H.
LETTERING
see also Alphabets; Illumination of Books and Manuscripts; Sign Painting
Lancaster, John. Lettering Techniques. LC 82-82920. (Illus.). 120p. 1983. pap. 7.95 (ISBN 0-668-05716-5, 5716). Arco.
Tarr, John C. The History of Written & Printed Letters. 160p. 1982. 70.00x (ISBN 0-284-39192-1, Pub. by C Skilton Scotland). State Mutual Bk.
LETTERS
see also English Letters; French Letters
Colvin, Sidney, ed. The Letters of Robert Louis Stevenson to His Family & Friends, 2 Vols. 389p. 1982. Repr. of 1910 ed. Set. lib. bdg. 65.00 (ISBN 0-8495-5054-8). Arden Lib.
Powell, William S., ed. Correspondence of William Tryon & Other Selected Papers, Vol. II: 1768-1818. (Illus.). xxxiii, 958p. 1981. 28.00 (ISBN 0-86526-147-4). NC Archives.
LETTERS IN MANUSCRIPT
see Autographs
LETTERS OF THE ALPHABET
see Alphabet
LEUCEMIA
see Leukemia
LEUCOCYTES
Bagge, U. & Born, G. V. White Blood Cells. 1982. 34.50 (ISBN 90-247-2681-6, Pub. by Martinus Nijhoff Netherlands). Kluwer Boston.
Boggs, Dane R. & Winkelstein, Alan. White Cell Manual. 4th ed. (Illus.). 130p. 1983. pap. text ed. 6.95 (ISBN 0-8036-0961-2, 0961-2). Davis Co.
Webb, David R., ed. Immunopharmacology & the Regulation of Leukocyte Function. (Immunology Ser.: Vol. 19). (Illus.). 312p. 1982. 45.00 (ISBN 0-8247-1707-4). Dekker.

LEUKEMIA

Bloomfield, C. D. Adult Leukemias. 1982. 69.50 (ISBN 90-247-2478-3, Pub. by Martinus Nijhoff Netherlands). Kluwer Boston.

Miner, Jane Claypool. This Day is Mine: Living With Leukemia. Schroeder, Howard, ed. LC 82-1423. (Crisis Ser.). (Illus.). 64p. (gr. 4-5). 1982. lib. bdg. 7.95 (ISBN 0-89686-173-2). Crestwood Hse.

Neth, R., et al, eds. Modern Trends in Human Leukemia V: New Results in Clinical & Biological Research Including Pediatric Oncology; Proceedings, Wilsede, FRG, June 1982. (Haematology & Blood Transfusion Ser.: Vol. 28). 600p. 1983. pap. 84.00 (ISBN 0-387-11858-6). Springer-Verlag.

LEVANT-ANTIQUITIES

Gerstenblith, Patty. The Levant at the Beginning of the Middle Bronze Age. (American Schools of Oriental Research Dissertation Ser.: No. 5). 1983. pap. text ed. price not set (ISBN 0-89757-105-3, Pub. by Am Sch Orient Res). Eisenbrauns.

LEVELLERS

Winstanley, Gerrard. The Law of Freedom & Other Writings. Hill, Christopher, ed. LC 82-14604. (Past & Present Publications Ser.). 395p. Date not set. price not set (ISBN 0-521-25299-7). Cambridge U Pr.

LEVI-STRAUSS, CLAUDE

Pace, David. Claude Levi-Strauss: The Bearer of Ashes. 330p. (Orig.). 1983. 19.95 (ISBN 0-7100-9297-0). Routledge & Kegan.

LEVY ON CAPITAL

see Capital Levy

LEWIS, CLARENCE IRVING, 1883-1964

Harbert, David L. Existence, Knowing, & Philosophical Systems. LC 82-17565. 226p. (Orig.). 1983. lib. bdg. 21.75 (ISBN 0-8191-2804-X); pap. text ed. 10.25 (ISBN 0-8191-2805-8). U Pr of Amer.

LEWIS, CLIVE STAPLES, 1898-1963

Ford, Paul F. Companion to Narnia: A Complete, Illustrated Guide to the Themes, Characters, & Events of C. S. Lewis's Imaginary World. LC 80-7734. (Illus.). 512p. 1983. pap. 6.68 (ISBN 0-06-250341-3, HarpR). Har-Row.

Murphy, Brian. C. S. Lewis. (Starmont Reader's Guide Ser.: No. 14). 96p. 1983. Repr. lib. bdg. 10.95x (ISBN 0-89370-045-2). Borgo Pr.

--Reader's Guide to C. S. Lewis. Schlobin, Roger C., ed. (Reader's Guides to Contemporary Science Fiction & Fantasy Authors Ser.: Vol. 14). (Illus., Orig.). 1983. 10.95x (ISBN 0-916732-38-X); pap. text ed. 4.95x (ISBN 0-916732-37-1). Starmont Hse.

LEWIS AND CLARK EXPEDITION

Betts, Robert B. In Search of York: The Black Member of the Lewis & Clark Expedition. 1982. 10.00 (ISBN 0-87081-144-4). Colo Assoc.

Moulton, Gary E. Atlas of the Lewis & Clark Expedition. LC 82-675167. (Journals of the Lewis & Clark Expedition Ser.). 132p. 1982. 80.00x (ISBN 0-8032-2861-9). U of Nebr Pr.

LEXICOLOGY

see also Semantics; Vocabulary

Johnstone, T. M., ed. Jibbale Lexicon. 366p. 1981. text ed. 65.00x (ISBN 0-19-713602-8). Oxford U Pr.

LIABILITY (LAW)

see also Criminal Liability; Employers' Liability; Insurance, Liability; Negligence; Products Liability; Torts

Edwards, Mary F., ed. How to Recognize & Handle Recreational Liability Cases: Sports Torts. 271p. 1980. pap. 25.00 (ISBN 0-941916-04-9). Assn Trial Ed.

LIABILITY, CRIMINAL

see Criminal Liability

LIABILITY, EMPLOYERS'

see Employers' Liability

LIABILITY FOR PERSONAL INJURIES

see Personal Injuries

LIABILITY INSURANCE

see Insurance, Liability

LIBEL AND SLANDER

see also Liberty of Speech; Liberty of the Press; Privacy, Right Of

Kinzer, Mark. Taming the Tongue: Why Christians Should Care about What They Say. (Living as a Christian Ser.). 1982. pap. 2.50 (ISBN 0-89283-165-0). Servant.

LIBERAL EDUCATION

see Education, Humanistic

LIBERAL JUDAISM

see Reform Judaism

LIBERAL THEOLOGY

see Liberalism (Religion)

LIBERALISM

see also Laissez-Faire

Breines, Wini. Community & Organization in the New Left 1962-1968: The Great Refusal. 224p. 1982. 26.95 (ISBN 0-03-060099-5). Praeger.

Logue, William. From Philosophy to Sociology: The Evolution of French Liberalism, 1870-1914. 270p. 1983. write for info (ISBN 0-87580-088-2). N Ill U Pr.

Wilcox, Laird. Directory of the American Left: Supplement. 1983. pap. 5.95 (ISBN 0-933592-28-0). Edit Res Serv.

LIBERALISM (RELIGION)

Orton, William A. Liberal Tradition. 1945. text ed. 12.50x (ISBN 0-686-83606-5). Elliots Bks.

LIBERTY

see also Anarchism and Anarchists; Civil Rights; Conformity; Equality; Liberalism; Religious Liberty

Benoyendranath, Banerjea. The Practice of Freedom. 1983. 9.00x (ISBN 0-8364-0918-3, Pub. by Minerva India). South Asia Bks.

Gray, John N. Mill on Liberty: A Defence. (International Library of Philosophy). 120p. 1983. 17.95 (ISBN 0-7100-9270-9). Routledge & Kegan.

McClosky, Herbert & Brill, Alida. Dimensions of Tolerance: What Americans Believe about Civil Liberties. LC 82-72959. 450p. 1983. 27.50x (ISBN 0-87154-591-8). Russell Sage.

Mill, John S. On Liberty. 1983. pap. 2.95 (ISBN 0-14-043207-8). Penguin.

Phillips, Michael J. The Dilemma of Individualism: Status, Liberty, & American Constitutional Law. LC 82-15580. (Contributions in American Studies: No. 67). 240p. 1983. lib. bdg. 29.95 (ISBN 0-313-23690-9, KF4749). Greenwood.

Phillips, Wendell. Wendell Phillips on Civil Rights & Freedom. 2nd ed. Filler, Louis, ed. LC 82-17343. 252p. 1983. pap. text ed. 10.25 (ISBN 0-8191-2793-0). U Pr of Amer.

Stevens, I. N. & Yardley, D. C. The Protection of Liberty. (Mainstream Ser.). 200p. 1982. text ed. 18.50x (ISBN 0-631-12944-8, Pub. by Basil Blackwell England). Biblio Dist.

Wood, William. In Defense of Liberty. 1928. text ed. 22.50x (ISBN 0-686-83580-8). Elliots Bks.

LIBERTY (THEOLOGY)

see Freedom (Theology)

LIBERTY OF INFORMATION

see Freedom of Information

LIBERTY OF RELIGION

see Religious Liberty

LIBERTY OF SPEECH

see also Freedom of Information; Libel and Slander; Liberty of the Press

Bosmajian, Haig A. The Principles & Practice of Freedom of Speech. 2nd ed. LC 82-23739. 424p. 1983. pap. text ed. 15.75 (ISBN 0-8191-2962-3). U Pr of Amer.

DiPrima, Richard. The First Amendment. LC 81-65895. (Orig.). (gr. 6-12). 1982. pap. text ed. 3.95 (ISBN 0-86652-012-0). Educ Indus.

Stevens, John D. Shaping the First Amendment: The Development of Free Expression. (CommText Ser.: Vol. 11). 160p. 1982. 15.00 (ISBN 0-8039-1876-3); pap. 7.95 (ISBN 0-8039-1877-1). Sage.

LIBERTY OF THE PRESS

see also Censorship; Condemned Books; Freedom of Information; Libel and Slander; Press; Public Opinion

Curry. Press Control Around the World. 304p. 1982. 29.95 (ISBN 0-03-059869-9). Praeger.

LIBERTY OF THE WILL

see Free Will and Determinism

LIBRARIANS

see also Library Science–Vocational Guidance

Asheim, Lester, ed. Persistent Issues in American Librarianship. LC 61-15050. vi, 114p. 1961. lib. bdg. 7.00 (ISBN 0-226-02960-3). U of Chicago Pr.

Berkner, Dimity S. & Sellen, Betty-Carol, eds. New Options for Librarians. 1983. pap. 19.95 (ISBN 0-918212-73-1). Neal-Schuman.

Compton, Charles H. Memories of a Librarian. 1954. 5.00 (ISBN 0-937322-06-7). St Louis Public Library.

Durrance, Joan. Armed for Action: The Power of an Informed Citizenry. 250p. lib. bdg. 24.95 (ISBN 0-918212-71-5). Neal-Schuman.

Lancaster, F. W. Libraries & Librarians in on Age of Electronics. LC 82-81403. (Illus.). ix, 229p. 1982. text ed. 22.50 (ISBN 0-87815-040-4). Info Resources.

Lichtenwanger, William, ed. Oscar Sonneck & American Music. LC 82-13670. 280p. 1983. 22.50 (ISBN 0-252-01021-3). U of Ill Pr.

LIBRARIANS-CONGRESSES

see Library Science-Congresses

LIBRARIANS-SALARIES, PENSIONS, ETC.

Lynch, Mary Jo & Myers, Margaret. ALA Survey of Librarian Salaries. LC 82-11537. 112p. 1982. pap. text ed. 40.00 (ISBN 0-8389-3275-4). ALA.

LIBRARIANS, TRAINING OF

see Library Schools and Training

LIBRARIANSHIP

see Library Science

LIBRARIES

see also Archives; Information Services; Public Libraries

Doyle, Alfreda C. Survival Suggestions for Libraries (Continued...) 25p. 1983. pap. 9.95 (ISBN 0-939476-93-2). Biblio Pr GA.

McMasters, Dale. Basic Skills Library Workbook. (Basic Skills Workbooks). 32p. (gr. 4-7). 1983. 0.99 (ISBN 0-686-42990-7, LW-1). ESP.

--Using the Library. (Language Arts Ser.). 24p. (gr. 4-8). 1979. wkbk. 5.00 (ISBN 0-8209-0307-8, LIB-1). ESP.

O'Hare, Joanne. Bowker Annual of Library & Book Trade Information, 1983. 55.00 (ISBN 0-686-83430-5). Bowker.

LIBRARIES-ACCESSION DEPARTMENTS

see Acquisitions (Libraries)

LIBRARIES-ACCOUNTING

see Library Finance

LIBRARIES-ADMINISTRATION

see Library Administration; Library Science

LIBRARIES-ARRANGEMENT OF BOOKS ON SHELVES

see Classification-Books

LIBRARIES-AUTOMATION

see also Information Storage and Retrieval Systems

Batty, C. D. The Electronic Library. 160p. 1983. price not set (Pub. by Bingley England). Shoe String.

Boss, Richard W. The Library Manager's Guide to Automation. 165p. 1983. 36.50 (ISBN 0-86729-052-8); pap. 27.50 (ISBN 0-86729-051-X). Knowledge Indus.

Chen, Ching-chih & Bressler, Stacey E. Microcomputers in Libraries. (Applications in Information Management & Technology Ser.). (Illus.). 259p. (Orig.). 1982. pap. text ed. 22.95 (ISBN 0-918212-61-8). Neal-Schuman.

Dodd, Sue. Cataloging Machine: Readable Data Files. 268p. 1982. text ed. 35.00 (ISBN 0-8389-0365-7). ALA.

Dowlin, Kenneth E. The Electronic Library: The Promise & the Process. (Applications in Information Management & Technology Ser.). (Illus.). 225p. lib. bdg. 24.95 (ISBN 0-918212-75-8). Neal-Schuman.

Fisher, P. S. & Slonim, Jacob. Advances in Distributed Processing Management, Vol. 2. (Advances in Library EDP Management Ser.). 200p. 1983. price not set (ISBN 0-471-26232-3, Pub. by Wiley Heyden). Wiley.

Hartner, Elizabeth P. An Introduction to Automated Literature Searching. (Bks in Library & Information Science: Vol. 36). (Illus.). 168p. 1981. 23.50 (ISBN 0-8247-1293-5). Dekker.

Kent, Allen & Galvin, Thomas J., eds. Information Technology: Critical Choices for Library Decision-Makers. (Bks in Library & Informtion Science: Vol. 40). 504p. 1982. 57.50 (ISBN 0-686-82222-6). Dekker.

Lancaster, F. W. Libraries & Librarians in on Age of Electronics. LC 82-81403. (Illus.). ix, 229p. 1982. text ed. 22.50 (ISBN 0-87815-040-4). Info Resources.

Oulton, A. J. & Bishop, E. The Teaching of Computer Appreciation & Library Automation. 136p. 1981. pap. 40.00x (ISBN 0-905984-75-7, Pub. by Brit Lib Engalnd). State Mutual Bk.

Plaister, Jean M. Computing in Laser: Regional Library Cooperation. 64p. 1982. pap. 15.00 (ISBN 0-85365-954-0). Oryx Pr.

Potter, William G. & Faber, Arlene. Serials Automation for Acquisition & Inventory Control. 192p. 1982. pap. text ed. 15.00 (ISBN 0-8389-3267-3). ALA.

Tedd, Lucy A. The Teaching of On-Line Cataloguing & Searching & the Use of New Technology in UK Schools of Librarianship & Information Science. 126p. 1981. pap. 40.00x (ISBN 0-905984-67-6, Pub. by Brit Lib England). State Mutual Bk.

Woods, Lawrence A. & Pope, Nolan F. The Librarian's Guide to Microcomputer Technology & Applications. 150p. 1983. 34.50 (ISBN 0-86729-045-5); pap. 27.50 (ISBN 0-86729-044-7). Knowledge Indus.

LIBRARIES-BIBLIOGRAPHY

Vervliet, H. D. Annual Bibliography of the History of the Printed Book & Libraries. 1983. lib. bdg. 85.00 (ISBN 0-686-37696-X, Pub. by Martinus Nijhoff Netherlands). Kluwer Boston.

LIBRARIES-BIBLIOGRAPHICAL SEARCHING

see Searching, Bibliographical

LIBRARIES-CATALOGS

see Library Catalogs

LIBRARIES-CLASSIFICATION

see Classification-Books

LIBRARIES-CONGRESSES

see Library Science-Congresses

LIBRARIES-HANDBOOKS, MANUALS, ETC.

Bulick, Stephen. Structure & Subject Interaction: Toward a Sociology of Knowledge in the Social Sciences. (Bks in Library & Information Science: Vol. 41). (Illus.). 256p. 1982. 35.00 (ISBN 0-8247-1847-X). Dekker.

Harvey, John F. & Dickinson, Elizabeth M., eds. Librarians' Affirmative Action Handbook. LC 82-10644. 316p. 1983. 18.50 (ISBN 0-8108-1581-8). Scarecrow.

Mallery, Mary S. & DeVore, Ralph E. Sign System for Libraries. LC 82-11612. 40p. 1982. pap. text ed. 5.00 (ISBN 0-8389-0377-0). ALA.

LIBRARIES-INFORMATION NETWORKS

see Library Information Networks

LIBRARIES-ORDER DEPARTMENT

see Acquisitions (Libraries)

LIBRARIES-ORGANIZATION

see Libraries; Library Administration; Library Science

LIBRARIES-REFERENCE BOOKS

see Reference Books

LIBRARIES-REFERENCE DEPARTMENT

see also Reference Services (Libraries)

Walford, A. J., compiled by. Walford's Guide to Reference Material: Vol. 1, Science & Technology. 4th ed. 712p. 1980. 60.00 (ISBN 0-85365-611-8, Pub. by Lib Assn England). Oryx Pr.

--Walford's Guide to Reference Material: Vol. 3, Generalities, Languages, the Arts & Literature. 3rd ed. 720p. 1977. 67.50 (ISBN 0-85365-409-3, Pub. by Lib Assn England). Oryx Pr.

LIBRARIES-SECURITY MEASURES

Fennelly, Lawrence J. Museum, Archive, & Library Security. new ed. 866p. 1982. text ed. 55.00 (ISBN 0-409-95058-0). Butterworth.

LIBRARIES-SUPPLIES

see Library Fittings and Supplies

LIBRARIES-ASIA

Bowden, Russell, ed. Library Education Programmes in Developing Countries with Special Reference to Asia. (IFLA Publications: No. 20). 208p. 1983. price not set (ISBN 3-598-20383-7, Pub. by K G Saur). Shoe String.

LIBRARIES-AUSTRALIA

Library Association of Australia, Special Libraries Section. Directory of Special Libraries in Australia. 5th ed. 425p. 1982. 65.00x (ISBN 0-909915-93-8). Intl Pubns Serv.

Wood, Fiona. Use & Perception of an Academic Library. (ANUP Library: Occassional Paper No. 3). 80p. (Orig.). 1982. pap. text ed. 13.95 (ISBN 0-7081-1958-1, 1151, Pub. by ANUP Australia). Bks Australia.

LIBRARIES-CHINA

Renyong, Wu & Enguang, Wang, eds. Directory of Chinese Libraries. (World Books Reference Guide: No. 3). 500p. (Chinese & Eng.). 1982. 48.00x (ISBN 0-686-81685-4). Gale.

LIBRARIES-EGYPT

King, David A. Catalogue of the Scientific Manuscripts in the Egyptian National Library, Pt. 1. (Catalogs Ser.: Vol. 2). (Arabic.). 1981. pap. 40.00 (ISBN 0-686-84036-4, Pub. by Am Res Ctr Egypt). Undena Pubns.

LIBRARIES-GERMANY

Foundations of the German Academic Library. LC 82-3879. 234p. 1982. pap. text ed. 15.00 (ISBN 0-8389-0352-5). ALA.

LIBRARIES-GREAT BRITAIN

Moore, Nick, ed. On-Line Information in Public Libraries: A Review of Recent British Research. 69p. 1981. 35.00x (ISBN 0-905984-76-5, Pub. by Brit Lib England). State Mutual Bk.

Plaister, Jean M. Computing in Laser: Regional Library Cooperation. 64p. 1982. pap. 15.00 (ISBN 0-85365-954-0). Oryx Pr.

LIBRARIES-INDIA

Sharma, R. N., ed. Indian Librarianship. 1982. 20.00x (ISBN 0-8364-0890-X, Pub. by Kalyani). South Asia Bks.

LIBRARIES-ITALY

Paredi, Angelo. A History of the Ambrosiana. McInerny, Constance & McInerny, Ralph, trs. 112p. (Orig.). 1983. pap. text ed. 9.95x (ISBN 0-268-01078-1). U of Notre Dame Pr.

LIBRARIES-LATIN AMERICA

Hannesdottir, Sigrun K., ed. Education of School Librarian for Central America & Panama. (IFLA Publications: No. 22). 120p. 1983. 20.00 (ISBN 3-598-20384-5, Pub. by K G Saur). Shoe String.

LIBRARIES-SCOTLAND

Ballantyne, G. H. The Signet Library Edinburgh & Its Librarians. 191p. 1982. 55.00x (ISBN 0-900649-18-6, Pub. by Scot Lib Scotland). State Mutual Bk.

LIBRARIES, ARCHITECTURAL

see Architectural Libraries

LIBRARIES, BUSINESS

see Business Libraries

LIBRARIES, CHURCH

Smith, Ruth S. Getting the Books Off the Shelves: Making the Most of Your Congregation's Library. 126p. (Orig.). 1975. pap. 4.95 (ISBN 0-8164-1236-7). Seabury.

LIBRARIES, COLLEGE

see Libraries, University and College

LIBRARIES, LAW

see Law Libraries

LIBRARIES, MEDICAL

see Medical Libraries

LIBRARIES, MUSIC

see Music Libraries

LIBRARIES, PARISH

see Libraries, Church

LIBRARIES, PRIVATE

see also Book Collecting

Doyle, Alfreda. Starting a Self Sufficiency Library; Suggested Places to Look for Used & Inexpensive Books. 25p. 1983. pap. text ed. 4.00 (ISBN 0-910811-32-6). Center Self.

Wise, Thomas J. Introduction to the Ashley Library Catalog 1922-30. 64p. Date not set. pap. 10.00. Saifer.

LIBRARIES, PUBLIC

see Public Libraries

LIBRARIES, SCHOOL

see School Libraries

LIBRARIES, SCIENTIFIC

see Scientific Libraries

LIBRARIES, SPECIAL

see also Business Libraries

also types of special libraries, e.g. Music Libraries

Coplen, Ron, compiled by. Special Libraries: A Cumulative Index. 94p. 1982. 18.75 (ISBN 0-686-81712-5). SLA.

Cost Reduction for Special Libraries & Information Centers. 1974. 12.50 (ISBN 0-686-42908-7). Knowledge Indus.

LIBRARIES, TECHNICAL

see Technical Libraries

LIBRARIES, UNIVERSITY AND COLLEGE
Foundations of the German Academic Library. LC 82-3879. 234p. 1982. pap. text ed. 15.00 (ISBN 0-8389-0352-5). ALA.
Malthus, Thomas R., et al. The Malthus Library Catalogue: The Personal Collection of Thomas Robert Malthus at Jesus College, Cambridge University. 150p. 1983. 19.50 (ISBN 0-08-029386-7). Pergamon.
Myers, Marcia J. & Jirjees, Jassim M. The Accuracy of Telephone Reference-Information Services in Academic Libraries: Two Studies. LC 82-10785. 1983. 17.50 (ISBN 0-8108-1584-2). Scarecrow.
LIBRARIES, YOUNG PEOPLE'S
Katz, Bill, ed. Reference Services for Children & Young Adults. (The Reference Librarian Ser.: Nos. 7 & 8). 168p. 1983. text ed. 14.95 (ISBN 0-86656-201-X, B201). Haworth Pr.
LiBrotto, Ellen V., ed. New Directions for Young Adult Services. 256p. 1983. 24.95 (ISBN 0-8352-1684-5). Bowker.
LIBRARIES AND PUBLISHING
Line, Maurice B. & Vickers, Stephen. Universal Availability of Publications. (IFLA Publications: No. 25). 200p. 1983. price not set (ISBN 3-598-20387-X, Pub. by K G Saur). Shoe String.
LIBRARIES AND READERS
Mallett, Jerry J. Library Skills Activity Puzzles Series, 5 bks. Incl. Book Bafflers (ISBN 0-87628-188-9); Dictionary Puzzlers (ISBN 0-87628-273-7); Lively Locators (ISBN 0-87628-539-6); Reading Incentives (ISBN 0-87628-719-4); Resource Rousers (ISBN 0-87628-741-0). 64p. (gr. 2-6). 1982. pap. 6.95 ea. (ISBN 0-686-81680-3). Ctr Appl Res.
LIBRARIES AND STATE
Mason, Marilyn G. The Federal Role in Library & Information Services. 150p. 1983. 34.50 (ISBN 0-86729-010-2); pap. 27.50 (ISBN 0-86729-009-9). Knowledge Indus.
Price, Paxton P., ed. International Book & Library Activities: The History of a U. S. Foreign Policy. LC 82-3297. 264p. 1982. 15.00 (ISBN 0-8108-1545-1). Scarecrow.
LIBRARIES AND STUDENTS
Lindberg, John. Routines for Research: A Handbook of Basic Library Skills. LC 82-15962. 172p. 1983. lib. bdg. 20.75 (ISBN 0-8191-2750-7); pap. text ed. 10.00 (ISBN 0-8191-2751-5). U Pr of Amer.
LIBRARIES AND THE PHYSICALLY HANDICAPPED
Dequin, Henry C. Librarians Serving Disabled Children & Young People. 306p. 1983. lib. bdg. 22.50 (ISBN 0-87287-364-1). Libs Unl.
Lucas, Linda & Karrenbrock, Marilyn H. The Disabled Child in the Library. 1983. lib. bdg. 22.50 (ISBN 0-87287-355-2). Libs Unl.
Massis, Bruce E. & Cylke, Kurt, eds. Library Service for the Blind & Physically Handicapped: An International Approach, Vol. 2. (IFLA Publications: No. 23). 100p. 1983. 18.00 (ISBN 3-598-20385-3, Pub. by K G Saur). Shoe String.
Needham, William L. & Jahoda, Gerald. Improving Library Service to Physically Disabled Persons: A Self-Evaluation Checklist. 135p. 1983. lib. bdg. 18.50 (ISBN 0-686-82503-9). Libs Unl.
LIBRARIES FOR THE BLIND
see Blind, Libraries for the
LIBRARY ACQUISITIONS
see Acquisitions (Libraries)
LIBRARY ADMINISTRATION
Blazek, Ron, ed. Achieving Accountability. 280p. 1982. pap. text ed. 14.50 (ISBN 0-8389-0349-5). ALA.
Cost Reduction for Special Libraries & Information Centers. 1974. 12.50 (ISBN 0-686-42908-7). Knowledge Indus.
Dougherty, Richard M. & Heinritz, Fred J. Scientific Management of Library Operations. 2nd ed. LC 81-18200. 286p. 1982. 15.00 (ISBN 0-8108-1485-4). Scarecrow.
Overton, David. Planning the Administrative Library. (IFLA Publications: No. 26). 1983. price not set (ISBN 3-598-20388-8, Pub. by K G Saur). Shoe String.
Parker, J. S., ed. Aspects of Library Development Planning. 200p. 1982. 26.00 (Pub. by Mansell England). Wilson.
Riggs, Donald E. Strategic Planning for Library Managers. 1983. write for info. (ISBN 0-89774-049-1). Oryx Pr.
Sager, Donald J. Participatory Management in Libraries. LC 82-783. (Library Administration Ser.: No. 3). 216p. 1982. 14.50 (ISBN 0-8108-1530-3). Scarecrow.
Stevens, Norman D. Communication Throughout Libraries. LC 82-10502. (Scarecrow Library Administration Ser.: No. 6). 195p. 1983. 14.50 (ISBN 0-686-84523-4). Scarecrow.
LIBRARY ARCHITECTURE
Fuhlrott, Rolf, ed. Library Interior Layout & Design. (IFLA Publications: No. 24). 1983. price not set (ISBN 3-598-20386-1, Pub. by K G Saur). Shoe String.
LIBRARY AUTOMATION
see Libraries–Automation
LIBRARY BUILDINGS
see Library Architecture
LIBRARY CATALOGS
see also Catalogs, Subject; Catalogs, Union
Matthews, Joseph R. Public Access to Online Catalogs: A Planning Guide for Managers. 345p. 1982. pap. text ed. 28.50 (ISBN 0-910965-00-5). Online.
LIBRARY CATALOGS–UNION CATALOGS
see Catalogs, Union
LIBRARY CLASSIFICATION
see Classification–Books
LIBRARY CONFERENCES
see Library Science–Congresses
LIBRARY CONSORTIA
see Library Cooperation
LIBRARY COOPERATION
see also Catalogs, Union; Intellectual Cooperation; Library Information Networks
Plaister, Jean M. Computing in Laser: Regional Library Cooperation. 64p. 1982. pap. 15.00 (ISBN 0-85365-954-0). Oryx Pr.
Price, Paxton P., ed. International Book & Library Activities: The History of a U. S. Foreign Policy. LC 82-3297. 264p. 1982. 15.00 (ISBN 0-8108-1545-1). Scarecrow.
LIBRARY EDUCATION
Bowden, Russell, ed. Library Education Programmes in Developing Countries with Special Reference to Asia. (IFLA Publications: No. 20). 208p. 1983. price not set (ISBN 3-598-20383-7, Pub. by K G Saur). Shoe String.
Hannesdottir, Sigrun K., ed. Education of School Librarian for Central America & Panama. (IFLA Publications: No. 22). 120p. 1983. 20.00 (ISBN 3-598-20384-5, Pub. by K G Saur). Shoe String.
Herzog, David A. Science & Social Studies Workbook for the GED Test. (Arco's Preparation for the GED Examination Ser.). 256p. 1983. pap. 5.95 (ISBN 0-668-05541-3, 5541). Arco.
LIBRARY FINANCE
see also Taxation, Exemption From
Prentice, Ann E. Financial Planning for Libraries. LC 82-7330. 236p. 1983. 14.50 (ISBN 0-8108-1565-6). Scarecrow.
Van House, Nancy A. Public Library User Fees: The Use & Finance of Public Libraries. LC 82-11741. (Contributions in Librarianship & Information Science Ser.: No. 43). (Illus.). 160p. 1983. lib. bdg. 27.50 (ISBN 0-313-22753-5, DPU/). Greenwood.
LIBRARY FITTINGS AND SUPPLIES
see also Bookmobiles
Futas, Elizabeth. The Library Forms Illustrated Handbook. (Illus.). 550p. 1983. lib. bdg. 49.95 (ISBN 0-918212-69-3). Neal-Schuman.
LIBRARY INFORMATION NETWORKS
Costa, Betty & Costa, Marie. A Practical Guide to Microcomputers in Small Libraries & Media Centers. 175p. 1983. lib. bdg. 19.50 (ISBN 0-87287-354-4). Libs Unl.
LIBRARY NETWORKS
see Library Information Networks
LIBRARY OF CONGRESS CLASSIFICATION
see Classification, Library of Congress
LIBRARY RESEARCH
see Library Science–Research
LIBRARY RESOURCES
Here are entered works describing the resources and special collections in libraries which are available for research in various fields. Works describing the resources and special collections in a particular field are entered under the subject with subdivision Library Resources, e.g. Africa–Library Resources. Works on the methods used to acquire, process, and maintain special collections in libraries are entered under Libraries–Special Collections.
Downs, Robert B., ed. American Library Resources: A Bibliographical Guide Supplement, 1971-1980. 224p. 1981. text ed. 30.00 (ISBN 0-8389-0342-8). ALA.
Gates, Jean K. Guide to the Use of Libraries & Information Sources. 5th ed. (Illus.). 288p. 1983. text ed. 19.95x (ISBN 0-07-022990-2, C); pap. text ed. 13.50x (ISBN 0-07-022989-9). McGraw.
Josey, E. J. & DeLoach, Marva L., eds. Ethnic Collections in Libraries. 1983. 24.95 (ISBN 0-918212-63-4). Neal-Schuman.
Keller, Clara. American Library Resources Cumulative Index, 1870-1970. 96p. 1981. text ed. 25.00 (ISBN 0-8389-0341-X). ALA.
LIBRARY SCHOOL EDUCATION
see Library Education
LIBRARY SCHOOLS AND TRAINING
Oulton, A. J. & Bishop, E. The Teaching of Computer Appreciation & Library Automation. 136p. 1981. pap. 40.00x (ISBN 0-905984-75-7, Pub. by Brit Lib Engalnd). State Mutual Bk.
Tedd, Lucy A. The Teaching of On-Line Cataloguing & Searching & the Use of New Technology in UK Schools of Librarianship & Information Science. 126p. 1981. pap. 40.00x (ISBN 0-905984-67-6, Pub. by Brit Lib England). State Mutual Bk.
LIBRARY SCIENCE
see also Bibliography; Cataloging; Classification–Books; Information Storage and Retrieval Systems also headings beginning with the word Library
Baskin, Barbara & Harris, Karen. Mainstreamed Library. 324p. 1983. text ed. 35.00. ALA.
Birge, Lynn. Serving Adult Learners. (ALA Ser. in Librarianship). 230p. 1981. pap. text ed. 18.00 (ISBN 0-8389-0346-0). ALA.
Bisaillon, Blaise. The Public Library: What Is Its Place & Function in the United States? (Vital Issues, Vol. XXIX 1979-80: No. 3). 0.60 (ISBN 0-686-81608-0). Ctr Info Am.
Fang. Modern Publishing & Librarianship. 1983. write for info. (Pub. by K G Saur). Shoe String.
Harrison, Alice W. & Collister, Edward A. The Conservation of Archival & Library Materials: A Resource Guide to Audiovisual Aids. LC 82-652. 202p. 1982. 13.50 (ISBN 0-8108-1523-0). Scarecrow.
Harvey, Richard. Genealogy for Librarians. 200p. 1983. 19.50 (Pub. by Bingley England). Shoe String.
Kumar, Krishan. Library Manual. 300p. 1982. text ed. 32.50x (ISBN 0-7069-1751-0, Pub. by Vikas India). Advent NY.
Mackee, Monique M. Handbook of Comparative Librarianship. 3rd ed. 550p. 1983. price not set (ISBN 0-85157-348-7, Pub. by Bingley England). Shoe String.
Merrill-Oldham, Jan. Conservation & Preservation of Library Materials. LC 82-1875. 1982. pap. text ed. 10.00 (ISBN 0-917590-07-4). Univ Conn Lib.
Miskin, C. Library & Information Services for the Legal Profession. 1981. 45.00x (ISBN 0-905984-73-0, Pub. by Brit Lib England). State Mutual Bk.
Nickerson, Sheila B. Writer's in the Public Library. 1983. price not set (ISBN 0-208-01872-7, Lib Prof Pubns); pap. price not set (ISBN 0-208-01873-5). Shoe String.
Parker, J. S., ed. Library Science & Education. 200p. 1982. 26.00 (ISBN 0-7201-1661-9, Pub. by Mansell England). Wilson.
Scroggie, W. Graham. W. Graham Scroggie Library Series, 7 Vols. 1982. pap. 18.00 (ISBN 0-8254-3740-7). Kregel.
Toor, Ruth & Weisburg, Hilda K. Library Media Specialist's Daily Plan Book. 256p. 1982. spiral wire 16.50X (ISBN 0-87628-534-5). Ctr Appl Res.
Wehmeyer, Lillian B. The School Librarian As Educator. 2nd ed. 320p. 1983. lib. bdg. 22.50 (ISBN 0-87287-372-2). Libs Unl.
LIBRARY SCIENCE–BIBLIOGRAPHY
Kent & Lancour. Encyclopedia of Library & Information Science, Vol. 37, (Suppl. 1) 1983. price not set (ISBN 0-8247-2037-7). Dekker.
Sharp, J. R. & Mann, M., eds. A Select List of Newsletters in the Field of Librarianship & Information Science. 63p. 1981. pap. 40.00x (ISBN 0-905984-72-2, Pub. by Brit Lib England). State Mutual Bk.
LIBRARY SCIENCE–CONGRESSES
Library Association, London. Conference Proceedings: Nottingham 1979. (Orig.). 1979. pap. text ed. 10.35 (ISBN 0-85365-503-0, Pub. by Lib Assn England). Oryx Pr.
LIBRARY SCIENCE–DATA PROCESSING
Chen, Ching-chih & Bressler, Stacey E. Microcomputers in Libraries. (Applications in Information Management & Technology Ser.). (Illus.). 259p. (Orig.). 1982. pap. text ed. 22.95 (ISBN 0-918212-61-8). Neal-Schuman.
Information Roundup: Microfilm & Data Processing for the Library & Information Center. (Proceedings of the 4th ASIS Mid-Year Meeting, 1975) 1975. 14.00 (ISBN 0-686-42891-9). Knowledge Indus.
Woods, Lawrence A. & Pope, Nolan F. The Librarian's Guide to Microcomputer Technology & Applications. 150p. 1983. 34.50 (ISBN 0-86729-045-5); pap. 27.50 (ISBN 0-86729-044-7). Knowledge Indus.
LIBRARY SCIENCE–DICTIONARIES
Harrod, L. M. The Librarians' Glossary & Reference Book: Of Terms Used in Librarianship Documentation & the Book Trade. (Grafton Library Ser.). 904p. 1982. Repr. of 1977 ed. 49.95x (ISBN 0-233-96744-3). Lexington Bks.
Young, Hartsell. ALA Glossary of Library & Information Science. 1983. text ed. price not set (ISBN 0-8389-0371-1). ALA.
LIBRARY SCIENCE–EXAMINATIONS, QUESTIONS ETC.
Rudman, Jack. Library Technician. (Career Examination Ser.: C-2544). (Cloth bdg. avail. on request). pap. 10.00 (ISBN 0-8373-2544-7). Natl Learning.
--Principal Librarian. (Career Examination Ser.: C-2915). (Cloth bdg. avail. on request). pap. 14.00 (ISBN 0-8373-2915-9). Natl Learning.
LIBRARY SCIENCE–PERIODICALS
Aaron, Shirley L. & Scales, Part R., eds. School Library Media Annual, 1983, Vol. 1. 350p. 1983. lib. bdg. 23.50 (ISBN 0-87287-353-6). Libs Unl.
LIBRARY SCIENCE–PERIODICALS–INDEXES
McMullen, Haynes & Barr, Larry. Library Articles in Periodicals Before 1876: Bibliography & Abstracts. 600p. 1983. lib. bdg. 65.00x (ISBN 0-89950-066-8). McFarland & Co.
LIBRARY SCIENCE–PROGRAMMED INSTRUCTION
Library & Reference Skills, 4 Bks, Bks. C-F. pap. 1.47 ea.; ea tchr's eds. 1.47. Bowmar-Noble.
LIBRARY SCIENCE–RESEARCH
Barber, Peggy, ed. Sixty-Eight Great Ideas. LC 82-11518. 72p. Date not set. pap. 5.00 (ISBN 0-8389-0376-2). ALA.
Brickford, Maynard. National Catalog of Sources for the History of Librarianship. 12p. 1982. pap. text ed. 10.00 (ISBN 0-686-37932-2); write for info. Microfiche. ALA.
Daly, Richard R. After Day One. 32p. (Orig.). Date not set. pap. text ed. 4.00 (ISBN 0-686-83760-6). ALA.
Rowley, Jenny E. & Rowley, Peter J. Operations Research. 152p. (Orig.). Date not set. pap. text ed. 10.00 (ISBN 0-8389-0337-1). ALA.
LIBRARY SCIENCE–STUDY AND TEACHING
see Library Education
LIBRARY SCIENCE–VOCATIONAL GUIDANCE
Breivik, Patricia S. Planning the Library Instruction Program. 156p. (Orig.). 1982. pap. text ed. 10.00 (ISBN 0-8389-0358-4). ALA.
Heim, Kathleen M., ed. The Status of Women in Librarianship: Historical, Sociological, & Economic Issues. 350p. 1983. 29.95 (ISBN 0-918212-62-6). Neal-Schuman.
Ireland, LaVerne H. The Teacher's & Librarian's Alternative Job Hunt Helper: An Annotated List of Transferable Job Skills & Alternative Career Possibilities. Date not set. 3.00 (ISBN 0-686-37851-2). Petervin Pr.
LIBRARY SERVICE TO THE PHYSICALLY HANDICAPPED
see Libraries and the Physically Handicapped
LIBRARY SKILLS
see Libraries–Handbooks, Manuals, etc.; Libraries and Readers
LIBRARY SUPPLIES
see Library Fittings and Supplies
LIBRARY SURVEYS
Here are entered works on the technique employed, and reports, etc., of individual surveys.
Carter, Virginia L., compiled by. How to Survey Your Readers. 48p. 1981. 10.50 (ISBN 0-89964-189-X). CASE.
Lynch, Mary Jo & Myers, Margaret. ALA Survey of Librarian Salaries. LC 82-11537. 112p. 1982. pap. text ed. 40.00 (ISBN 0-8389-3275-4). ALA.
LIBYA
Allan, J. A., ed. Libya Since Independence: Economic & Social Development. LC 82-42564. 1982. 22.50x (ISBN 0-312-48363-5). St Martin.
LICENSED PRACTICAL NURSES
see Practical Nursing
LICENSES
see also Business Tax
Morehead, John W. Finding & Licensing New Products & Technology from the U. S. A. 500p. 1982. 495.00 (ISBN 0-943420-00-8). Tech Search Intl.
LICHENS
Misra, A. & Agrawal, R. P. Lichens. 103p. 1978. 30.00 (ISBN 0-686-84458-0, Pub. by Oxford & I B H India). State Mutual Bk.
LICHTENSTEIN, ROY, 1923-
Alloway, Lawrence. Roy Lichtenstein. (Modern Masters Ser.). (Illus.). 128p. 1983. 24.95 (ISBN 0-89659-330-4); pap. 16.95 (ISBN 0-89659-331-2). Abbeville Pr.
LIE ALGEBRAS
see also Lie Groups
Gilmore, Robert. Lie Groups, Lie Algebras & Some of Their Applications. LC 73-10030. 587p. 1974. 52.95x (ISBN 0-471-30179-5, Pub. by Wiley-Interscience). Wiley.
Winter, D., ed. Lie Algebras & Related Topics, New Brunswick, New Jersey 1981: Proceedings. (Lecture Notes in Mathematics: Vol. 933). 236p. 1983. pap. 11.00 (ISBN 0-387-11563-3). Springer-Verlag.
LIE GROUPS
see also Lie Algebras
Gilmore, Robert. Lie Groups, Lie Algebras & Some of Their Applications. LC 73-10030. 587p. 1974. 52.95x (ISBN 0-471-30179-5, Pub. by Wiley-Interscience). Wiley.
LIECHTENSTEIN
Larke, T. A. Index to Liechtenstein, 1 Vol. 1982. pap. text ed. 14.95 (ISBN 0-9608460-4-2, FL1). Answer-Bk.
LIFE
see also Conduct of Life; Death; Ethics; Ontology; Philosophical Anthropology
Basu, Romen. Your Life to Live. 180p. 1972. write for info. (Pub. by Filma K L Mukhopadhyay India). R Basu.
Jones-Lee, M. W., ed. The Value of Life & Safety: Proceedings of a Conference Held by the Geneva Association. 310p. 1982. 55.50 (ISBN 0-444-86439-3, North Holland). Elsevier.
Lenoir, Timothy. The Strategy of Life. 1982. 59.00 (ISBN 90-277-1363-4, Pub. by Reidel Holland). Kluwer Boston.
Llamzon, Benjamin S. The Self Beyond: Toward Life's Meaning. LC 82-16073. 198p. 1983. pap. text ed. 10.75 (ISBN 0-8191-2741-8). U Pr of Amer.
Tributsch, Helmut. How Life Learned to Live: Adaptation in Nature. Varon, Miriam, tr. from Ger. (Illus.). 264p. 1983. 13.95 (ISBN 0-262-20045-7). MIT Pr.
LIFE–ORIGIN
see also Man–Origin
Price, Charles C., ed. Synthesis of Life. LC 74-3026. (Benchmark Papers in Organic Chemistry: Vol. 1). 391p. 1974. text ed. 52.50 (ISBN 0-87933-131-3). Hutchinson Ross.

Szekely, Edmond B. The Cosmotherapy of the Essenes. (Illus.). 64p. 1975. pap. 3.50 (ISBN 0-89564-012-0). IBS Intl.
--The Discovery of the Essene Gospel of Peace: The Essenes & the Vatican. (Illus.). 96p. 1977. pap. 4.80 (ISBN 0-89564-004-X). IBS Intl.
--The Essene Communions with the Infinite. (Illus.). 64p. 1979. pap. 3.95 (ISBN 0-89564-009-0). IBS Intl.
--The Essene Science of Life. (Illus.). 64p. 1976. pap. 3.50 (ISBN 0-89564-010-4). IBS Intl.
--The Essene Way: Biogenic Living. (Illus.). 200p. 1981. pap. 8.80 (ISBN 0-89564-019-8). IBS Intl.
--The Essene Way: World Pictures & Cosmic Symbols. (Illus.). 40p. 1978. pap. 1.80 (ISBN 0-89564-050-3). IBS Intl.
--The First Essene. (Illus.). 240p. 1981. pap. 9.50 (ISBN 0-89564-018-X). IBS Intl.
--The Teachings of the Essenes from Enoch to the Dead Sea Scrolls. (Illus.). 112p. 1981. pap. 4.80 (ISBN 0-89564-006-6). IBS Intl.
--The Tender Touch: Biogenic Fulfillment. (Illus.). 120p. 1977. text ed. 5.50 (ISBN 0-89564-020-1). IBS Intl.

LIFE (BIOLOGY)
see also Biology; Genetics; Longevity; Protoplasm; Reproduction
Price, Charles C., ed. Synthesis of Life. LC 74-3026. (Benchmark Papers in Organic Chemistry: Vol. 1). 391p. 1974. text ed. 52.50 (ISBN 0-87933-131-3). Hutchinson Ross.
Scientists for Life. The Position of Modern Science on the Beginning of Human Life. 47p. (Orig.). 1975. pap. 1.00 (ISBN 0-937930-02-4). Sun Life.

LIFE, FUTURE
see Future Life

LIFE, JEWISH WAY OF
see Jewish Way of Life

LIFE, ORIGIN OF
see Life–Origin

LIFE, SPIRITUAL
see Spiritual Life

LIFE AFTER DEATH
see Future Life; Immortality

LIFE INSURANCE
see Insurance, Life

LIFE-LONG EDUCATION
see Adult Education

LIFE ON OTHER PLANETS
Here are entered works on the question of life in outer space. Works on the biology of man or other earth life while in outer space are entered under Space Biology.
Asimov, Isaac. Extraterrestrial Civilizations. Date not set. pap. 5.95 (ISBN 0-449-90020-7, Columbine). Fawcett.
Feinberg, Gerald & Schapiro, Robert. Life Beyond Earth: The Intelligent Earthling's Guide to Extraterrestrial Life. (Illus.). 480p. 1980. pap. 9.95 (ISBN 0-688-08642-X). Quill NY.
Fox, Frederick & Miller, Richard. Earthman Come Home. LC 81-85707. 273p. 1983. pap. 6.95 (ISBN 0-86666-054-2). GWP.
Krupp, E. C. Echoes of the Ancient Skies: The Astronomy of Lost Civilization. LC 82-48121. (Illus.). 352p. 1983. 19.18i (ISBN 0-06-015101-3, HarpT). Har-Row.
Rood, Robert T. & Trefil, James S. Are We Alone? (Illus.). 272p. 1983. pap. 6.95 (ISBN 0-686-83774-6, ScribT). Scribner.

LIFE ON OTHER PLANETS–JUVENILE LITERATURE
Marsh, Carole. The Backyard Searcher's Extra Terrestrial Log Book. (Tomorrow's Books). (Illus.). 28p. 1983. 2.95 (ISBN 0-935326-27-8). Gallopade Pub Group.
--How to Find An Extra Terrestrial in Your Own Backyard. (Tomorrow's Books). (Illus.). 74p. 1983. 2.95 (ISBN 0-935326-09-X). Gallopade Pub Group.

LIFE-SAVING APPARATUS
Nukols, M. L. & Smith, K. A., eds. The Characterization of Carbon Dioxide Absorbing Agents for Life Support Equipment. (OED Ser.: Vol. 10). 1982. 40.00 (H00239). ASME.

LIFE SCIENCE ENGINEERING
see Bioengineering

LIFE SCIENCES
see also Agriculture; Biology; Medicine
Milton, J. S. & Tsokos, J. O. Statistical Methods in the Biological & Health Sciences. 512p. 1983. 29.95x (ISBN 0-07-042359-8, C); instr's. manual 5.95 (ISBN 0-07-042360-1). McGraw.

LIFE SPAN PROLONGATION
see Longevity

LIFTS
see Elevators

LIGHT
see also Color; Lasers; Optics; Photobiology; Photometry; Radiation; Spectrum Analysis; X-Rays
Adorno, Theodor W. Prisms. Weber, Samuel & Weber, Shierry, trs. from Ger. 272p. 1983. pap. 6.95x (ISBN 0-262-51025-1). MIT Pr.
Bohren, Craig F. & Huffman, Donald R. Absorption & Scattering of Light by Small Particles. 550p. 1983. 44.95 (ISBN 0-471-05772-X, Pub. by Wiley-Interscience). Wiley.

LIGHT–CHEMICAL ACTION
see Photochemistry

LIGHT–JUVENILE LITERATURE
Watson, Philip. Light Fantastic. LC 82-80989. (Science Club Ser.). (Illus.). 48p. (gr. 3-6). 1983. PLB 8.16 (ISBN 0-688-00969-7); pap. 5.25 (ISBN 0-688-00975-1). Lothrop.

LIGHT–SCATTERING
Barron, L. D. Molecular Light Scattering & Optical Activity. 425p. Date not set. price not set (ISBN 0-521-24602-4). Cambridge U Pr.
Bohren, Craig F. & Huffman, Donald R. Absorption & Scattering of Light by Small Particles. 550p. 1983. 44.95 (ISBN 0-471-05772-X, Pub. by Wiley-Interscience). Wiley.
Cantow, H. J., et al. Light Scattering from Polymers. (Advances in Polymer Science: Vol. 48). (Illus.). 167p. 1983. 39.50 (ISBN 0-387-12030-0). Springer-Verlag.
Dahneke, Barton E. Measurement of Suspended Particles By Quasi-Elastic Light Scattering. 400p. 1982. 39.95 (ISBN 0-471-87289-X, Pub. by Wiley-Interscience). Wiley.

LIGHT, ELECTRIC
see Photometry

LIGHT, ELECTROMAGNETIC THEORY OF
see Electromagnetic Theory

LIGHT, INVISIBLE
see Spectrum, Infra-Red

LIGHT AMPLIFICATION BY STIMULATED EMISSION OF RADIATION
see Lasers

LIGHTER THAN AIR CRAFT
see Air-Ships

LIGHTING
see also Daylight; Lamps; Lighting, Architectural and Decorative
IES Office Lighting Committee. Proposed American National Standard Practice for Office Lighting. (Illus.). 44p. 1982. Repr. 9.00 (ISBN 0-87995-011-0); 13.50 (ISBN 0-686-82676-0). Illum Eng.
Kaufman, John E., ed. IES Lighting Handbook: Student Reference. abr. ed. (Illus.). 125p. 1982. pap. 15.00 (ISBN 0-87995-010-2). Illum Eng.
Lynes, J. A. & Pritchard, D. C., eds. Developments in Lighting, Vols. 1 & 2. Vol. 1, 1978. 47.25 (ISBN 0-85334-774-3, Pub. by Applied Sci England); Vol. 2, 1982. 51.25 (ISBN 0-85334-985-1). Elsevier.
Lyone, Stanley. Management Guide to Modern Industrial Lighting. 2nd ed. 176p. 1983. text ed. write for info. (ISBN 0-408-01147-5). Butterworth.
Natural Lighting. (Illus.). 1982. pap. 9.95 (ISBN 0-918984-05-X). SolarVision.

LIGHTING, ARCHITECTURAL AND DECORATIVE
Egan, M. David & Klas, Rodger H. Concepts in Lighting for Architecture. (Illus.). 224p. 1983. 23.95 (ISBN 0-07-019054-2, C). McGraw.
Godfrey, Robert S. Residential-Light Commercial Cost Data, 1983. 2nd ed. 275p. 1983. pap. 33.25 (ISBN 0-911950-52-4). Means.
Sunset Books & Sunset Magazine, ed. Home Lighting. LC 82-81371. (Illus.). 96p. (Orig.). 1982. pap. 4.95 (ISBN 0-376-01312-5). Sunset-Lane.

LIGHTING, DECORATIVE
see Lighting, Architectural and Decorative

LIGHTS, LITURGICAL
see Candles and Lights

LIGHTS AND CANDLES
see Candles and Lights

LIGNITE
see also Coal
Tewalt, Susan J., et al. Geological Circular 82-2: Detailed Evaluation of Two Texas Lignite Deposits of Fluvial & Deltaic Origins. (Illus.). 12p. 1982. Repr. 1.00 (ISBN 0-686-37546-7). U of Tex Econ Geology.

LILIES
Harrison, Richmond E. Know Your Lilies. (Illus.). 84p. 1982. 12.50 (ISBN 0-589-00430-1, Pub. by H Timmins S Africa). Intl Schol Bk Serv.
Jekyll, Gertrude. Lilies for English Gardens. (Illus.). 156p. 1982. 29.50 (ISBN 0-907462-28-6). Antique Collect.

LILIUOKALANI, QUEEN OF HAWAII, 1838-1917
Allen, Helena G. The Betrayal of Liliukalani: Last Queen of Hawaii, 1838-1917. LC 82-71912. (Illus.). 420p. 1983. 19.95 (ISBN 0-87062-144-0). A H Clark.

LIMBS (ANATOMY)
see Extremities (Anatomy)

LIMBS, ARTIFICIAL
see Artificial Limbs

LIMERICKS
see also Nonsense-Verses
Goldstein, Sam. A Printer's Limericks: Limericklets Ser. (No. 6). (Illus.). 1982. pap. 1.00 (ISBN 0-938338-18-8). Winds World Pr.
Gosset, Melinda Lu. Doggerelimericks I. (Limericklets Ser.: No. 12). (Illus.). 1982. pap. 1.00 (ISBN 0-938338-23-4). Winds World Pr.
--Doggerelimericks II. (Limericklets Ser.: No. 13). (Illus.). 1982. pap. 1.00 (ISBN 0-938338-24-2). Winds World Pr.
--Doggerelimericks III. (Limericklets Ser.: No. 14). (Illus.). pap. 1.00 (ISBN 0-938338-25-0). Winds World Pr.
Tusselman, Goldie. Bazoomericks. (Limericklets Ser.: No. 9). (Illus.). 1982. pap. 1.25 (ISBN 0-938338-20-X). Winds World Pr.
--Bazoomericks II. (Illus.). 1982. pap. 1.25 (ISBN 0-938338-21-8). Winds World Pr.
--Bazoomericks III. (Limericklets Ser.: No. 11). pap. 1.25 (ISBN 0-938338-22-6). Winds World Pr.
1.00. More Printer's Limericks. (Limericklets Ser.: No. 7). 1982. pap. 1.00 (ISBN 0-938338-19-6). Winds World Pr.

LIMITATION OF ARMAMENT
see Disarmament

LIMITATIONS (LAW)
see Estates (Law); Real Property

LIMITATIONS, CONSTITUTIONAL
see Constitutional Law

LIMITATIONS, CONTRACTUAL
see Contracts

LIMITED ACCESS HIGHWAYS
see Express Highways

LIMITED COMPANIES
see Corporations

LIMITED PARTNERSHIP
Burdick, Francis M. The Law of Partnership, Including Limited Partnerships. lii, 422p. 1983. Repr. of 1899 ed. lib. bdg. 37.50x (ISBN 0-8377-0333-6). Rothman.

LIMITS (MATHEMATICS)
see Calculus

LIMNOLOGY
see also Fresh-Water Biology; Water Chemistry
Cole, Gerald A. Textbook of Limnology. 3rd ed. (Illus.). 434p. 1983. text ed. 24.95 (ISBN 0-8016-1004-4). Mosby.
Hobbie, J. E., ed. Limnology of Tundra Ponds: Barrow, Alaska. LC 80-26373. (US-IBP Synthesis Ser.: Vol. 13). 514p. 1980. 34.00 (ISBN 0-87933-386-3). Hutchinson Ross.

LIMU
see Algae

LINCOLN, ABRAHAM, PRES. U. S., 1809-1865
Herndon, William H. Life of Lincoln. LC 82-73435. 511p. Repr. of 1942 ed. lib. bdg. 37.50x (ISBN 0-88116-005-9). Brenner Bks.
Stephenson, Nathaniel W. Abraham Lincoln & the Union. 1918. text ed. 8.50x (ISBN 0-686-83453-4). Elliots Bks.

LINCOLN-DOUGLAS DEBATES, 1858
Corrigan, B. C. Tailgating-The Lincoln-Douglas Debates: A Tour of the Seven Original Debate Sites on the Eve of Their 125th Anniversary. LC 82-73684. 60p. 1982. pap. write for info. ADS Pr.

LINEAR ALGEBRAS
see Algebras, Linear

LINEAR COMPLEXES
see Complexes

LINEAR DIFFERENTIAL EQUATIONS
see Differential Equations, Linear

LINEAR DIGITAL FILTERS (MATHEMATICS)
see Digital Filters (Mathematics)

LINEAR ELLIPTIC DIFFERENTIAL EQUATIONS
see Differential Equations, Elliptic

LINEAR MAPS
see Linear Operators

LINEAR OPERATORS
Chatelin, Francoise. Special Approximation of Linear Operators. (Computer Science & Applied Mathematics Ser.). Date not set. price not set (ISBN 0-12-170620-6). Acad Pr.
Hoermander, L. The Analysis of Linear Partial Differential Operators II: Differential Operators with Constant Coefficients. (Illus.). 380p. 1983. 49.50 (ISBN 0-387-12139-0). Springer-Verlag.
--The Analysis of Linear Partial Differential Operators I: Distribution Theory & Fourier Analysis. (Grundlehren der Mathematischen Wissenschaften: Vol. 256). (Illus.). 380p. 1983. 39.00 (ISBN 0-387-12104-8). Springer-Verlag.
Naylor, A. W. & Sell, G. R. Linear Operator Theory in Engineering & Science. (Applied Mathematical Sciences Ser.: Vol. 40). (Illus.). 624p. 1982. 28.00 (ISBN 0-387-90748-3). Springer-Verlag.

LINEAR PERSPECTIVE
see Perspective

LINEAR SPACES
see Vector Spaces

LINEAR SYSTEM THEORY
see System Analysis

LINEAR TOPOLOGICAL SPACES
see also Distributions, Theory of (Functional Analysis); Topological Algebras
Gierz, G. Bundles of Topological Vector Spaces & Their Duality. (Lecture Notes in Mathematics: Vol. 955). 296p. 1983. pap. 13.50 (ISBN 0-387-11610-9). Springer-Verlag.

LINEAR VECTOR SPACES
see Vector Spaces

LINEN
Messenger, Betty. Picking Up the Linen Threads. 1982. 40.00x (ISBN 0-85640-210-9, Pub. by Blackstaff Pr). State Mutual Bk.

LINERS
see Ocean Liners

LINGUISTIC ANALYSIS
see Analysis (Philosophy)

LINGUISTICS
Here are entered works dealing with the scientific study of human speech, including phonetics, phonemics, morphology, and syntax. Works dealing with language in general, the origin and history of language and surveys of languages, are entered under the heading Language and Languages.
see also Phonetics; Sociolinguistics
Barentsen, A., ed. Studies in Slavic & General Linguistics, Vol. 1. 472p. 1980. pap. text ed. 46.00x (ISBN 90-6203-523-X, Pub. by Rodopi Holland). Humanities.
Burke, Carol, ed. Plain Talk. LC 82-81678. (Illus.). 160p. (Orig.). 1983. pap. 3.50 (ISBN 0-911198-67-9). Purdue.
Carling & Moore. Language Understanding. LC 82-10568. 240p. 1982. 22.50x (ISBN 0-312-46922-5). St Martin.
Coates, Jennifer. The Semantics of the Modal Auxiliaries. (Linguistics Ser.). 260p. 1983. text ed. 33.00x (ISBN 0-7099-0735-4, Pub. by Croom Helm Ltd England). Biblio Dist.
Crystal, David, ed. Linguistic Controversies. 256p. 1982. text ed. 44.95 (ISBN 0-7131-6349-6). E Arnold.
Frawley, William, ed. Linguistics & Literacy. (Topics in Language & Linguistics). 495p. 1982. 55.00x (ISBN 0-306-41174-1, Plenum Pr). Plenum Pub.
Gannon, Peter & Czerniewska, Pam. Using Linguistics: An Educational Focus. 224p. 1980. pap. text ed. 16.95 (ISBN 0-7131-6294-5). E Arnold.
Golinkoff, Roberta M., ed. The Transition from Prelinguistic to Linguistic Communication: Issues & Implications. 1983. text ed. price not set (ISBN 0-89859-257-7). L Erlbaum Assocs.
Hartley. Linguistics for Language Learners. 1982. 50.00x (ISBN 0-333-26683-8, Pub. by Macmillan England). State Mutual Bk.
Kerkhof, J. Studies in the Language of Geoffrey Chaucer. 2nd, rev. enl. ed. (Leidse Germanistische en Anglistische Reeks Ser.: Vol. 5). xii, 503p. 1982. pap. write for info. (ISBN 90-04-06789-2). E J Brill.
Lehrmann, Winfred P. Linguistische Theorien der Moderne. 173p. (Ger.). 1981. write for info. (ISBN 3-261-04889-1). P Lang Pubs.
Martinet, Andre. Elements of General Linguistics. Palmer, Elisabeth, tr. LC 64-19845. (Midway Reprint Ser.). 206p. 1982. pap. 8.00x (ISBN 0-226-50875-7). U of Chicago Pr.
Noam Chomsky on the Generative Enterprise: A Discussion with Riny Huybregts & Henk van Riemsdijk. 136p. 1982. pap. 18.00x (ISBN 90-70176-70-X). Foris Pubns.
Problems in General Linguistics. (Miami Linguistic Ser.: No. 8). 317p. 1973. 15.00 (ISBN 0-87024-310-1). U of Miami Pr.
What Is Linguistics? 1980. pap. 0.50 (ISBN 0-917496-13-2). Hornbeam Pr.

LINGUISTICS–ADDRESSES, ESSAYS, LECTURES
Linguistic Association of Canada & the U. S. Eighth LACUS Forum: Proceedings. Gutwinski, Waldemar & Jolly, Grace, eds. 1981. pap. text ed. 10.95 (ISBN 0-917496-22-1). Hornbeam Pr.
Linguistic Association of Canada & the U.S. Seventh Lacus Forum: Proceedings. Copeland, J. E. & Davis, P. W., eds. 1980. pap. text ed. 10.95 (ISBN 0-917496-19-1). Hornbeam Pr.

LINGUISTICS–BIBLIOGRAPHY
Kaplan, Robert, et al, eds. Annual Review of Applied Linguistics, 1981. 280p. 1982. pap. text ed. 17.95 (ISBN 0-88377-258-2). Newbury Hse.

LINGUISTICS–PROGRAMMED INSTRUCTION
Marvell-Mell, Linnaea. NLP Skillbuilders: Advanced Techniques in Neuro-Linguistic Programming, Book II. (NLP Skillbuilders Ser.). (gr. 9-12). 1982. 34.95 (ISBN 0-686-38220-X); write for info. Metamorphous Pr.
--NLP Skillbuilders: Basic Techniques in Neuro-Linguistic Programming, Book I. (NLP Skillbuilders Ser.). (Illus.). (gr. 9-12). 1982. 34.95 (ISBN 0-686-38226-9); write for info. Metamorphous Pr.

LINGVO INTERNACIA (ARTIFICIAL LANGUAGE)
see Esperanto (Artificial Language)

LINKAGE (GENETICS)
see also Chromosomes
Mueller, D. Sister Chromatid Exchange Test. (Illus.). 120p. 1983. 16.50 (ISBN 0-86577-069-7). Thieme-Stratton.

LINNE, CARL VON, 1707-1778
Lindroth, Stan, et al. Linnaeus: The Man & His Work. Frangsmyr, Tore, ed. Srigley, Michael & Vowles, Bernard, trs. from Swedish. LC 82-2044. (Illus.). 288p. 1983. text ed. 25.00x (ISBN 0-520-04568-8). U of Cal Pr.

LIONS
Schaller, George B. Golden Shadows, Flying Hooves: With a New Afterword. LC 82-23731. (Illus.). 344p. 1983. pap. 9.95 (ISBN 0-226-73632-6). U of Chicago Pr.

LIPAN INDIANS
see Indians of North America–Southwest, New

LIPID METABOLISM
Kritchevsky, David & Gibney, Michael J., eds. Animal & Vegetable Proteins in Lipid Metabolism & Atherosclerosis. LC 82-23961. (Current Topics in Nutrition & Disease Ser.: Vol. 8). 200p. 1983. write for info. (ISBN 0-8451-1607-X). A R Liss.

LIPIDOSIS
Desnick, Robert J. & Gatt, Shimon, eds. Gaucher Disease: A Century of Delineation & Research. LC 82-4611. (Progress in Clinical & Biological Research Ser.: Vol. 95). 764p. 1982. 76.00 (ISBN 0-8451-0095-5). A R Liss.

LIPIDS
see also Lipid Metabolism; Lipoproteins; Steroids
Christie, W. W. Lipid Analysis: Isolation, Separation, Identification & Structural Analysis of Lipids. 2nd ed. LC 82-491. (Illus.). 220p. 1982. 50.00 (ISBN 0-08-023791-6); 18.00 (ISBN 0-08-023792-4). Pergamon.
Gunstone, F. D. & Norris, F. D. Lipids in Foods: Chemistry, Biochemistry & Application Technology. 175p. 1983. 40.01 (ISBN 0-08-025499-3); pap. 18.01 (ISBN 0-08-025498-5). Pergamon.
Makita, Akira & Handa, Shizuo, eds. New Vistas in Glycolipid Research. (Advances in Experimental Medicine & Biology Ser.: Vol. 152). 504p. 1982. 62.50x (ISBN 0-306-41108-3, Plenum Pr). Plenum Pub.
Mangold, H. K. & Paltavy, F., eds. Ether Lipids: Biomedical Aspects. LC 82-11619. Date not set. price not set (ISBN 0-12-468780-6). Acad Pr.
Yagi, Kunio, ed. Lipid Peroxides in Biology & Medicine: Symposium. LC 82-16430. 1982. 29.50 (ISBN 0-12-768050-0). Acad Pr.
LIPOIDOSIS
see Lipidosis
LIPOPROTEINS
Ostro. Liposomes. (Immunology Ser.). 408p. 1983. price not set (ISBN 0-8247-1717-1). Dekker.
Schneider, J. & Kaffarnick, H. Lipoproteins & Age. 74p. 17.00 (ISBN 0-86577-068-9). Thieme-Stratton.
LIP-READING
see Deaf-Means of Communication
LIPSIUS, JUSTUS, 1547-1606
Oestreich, Gerhard. Neostoicism & the Early Modern State. Oestreich, B. & Koenigsberger, H. G., eds. LC 81-12285. (Cambridge Studies in Early Modern History Ser.). 272p. 1982. 49.50 (ISBN 0-521-24202-9). Cambridge U Pr.
LIQUEFACTION OF GASES
see Gases-Liquefaction
LIQUEURS
Hallgarten, Peter A. Spirits & Liqueurs. 2nd ed. (Books on Wine). 192p. 1983. pap. 7.95 (ISBN 0-571-13057-7). Faber & Faber.
LIQUID CHROMATOGRAPHY
Simpson, C. F. Techniques of Liquid Chromatography. 400p. 1982. 54.95x (ISBN 0-471-26220-X, Pub. by Wiley Heyden). Wiley.
LIQUID CRYSTALS
Brown, Glenn H., ed. Advances in Liquid Crystals, Vol. 5. Date not set. price not set (ISBN 0-12-025005-5); price not set lib. ed. (ISBN 0-12-025082-9); price not set microfiche (ISBN 0-12-025083-7). Acad Pr.
Cognard, Jacques. Alignment of Nematic Liquid Crystals & Their Mixtures. (Molecular Crystals & Liquid Crystals Supplement Ser.). 78p. 1982. 27.00 (ISBN 0-677-05905-1). Gordon.
Siemens Teams of Authors. Optoelectronics: Liquid-Crystal Display. (Siemens Team of Authors Ser.). 1981. text ed. 57.00x (ISBN 0-471-26125-4, Pub. by Wiley Heyden). Wiley.
LIQUID FUELS
see also Petroleum As Fuel
Black, J. Liquid Fuels in Australia: A Social Science Research Perspective. 280p. 1983. 37.50 (ISBN 0-08-024834-9); 21.00 (ISBN 0-08-024833-0). Pergamon.
LIQUID-VAPOR EQUILIBRIUM
see Vapor-Liquid Equilibrium
LIQUIDATION
Here are entered works on the winding up of companies or of the affairs of an individual.
Stark, Brian J. Special Situation Investing: Hedging, Arbitrage & Liquidation. LC 82-73635. 250p. 1983. 27.50 (ISBN 0-87094-384-7). Dow Jones-Irwin.
LIQUIDS
see also Brownian Movements; Hydraulics; Hydrodynamics
Cho, Chun H. Measurement & Control of Liquid Level: An Independent Learning Module of the Instrument Society of America. LC 82-48156. 288p. 1982. text ed. 39.95x (ISBN 0-87664-625-9). Instru Soc.
Reintjes, John F., ed. Nonlinear Optical Parametric Processes in Liquids & Gases. LC 82-11603. Date not set. price not set (ISBN 0-12-585980-5). Acad Pr.
Rowlinson, J. & Swinton, F. L. Liquids & Liquid Mixtures. 3rd ed. 320p. 1982. text ed. 69.95 (ISBN 0-408-24192-6); pap. text ed. 34.95 (ISBN 0-408-24193-4). Butterworth.
Vargaftik, N. B. Handbook of Physical Properties of Liquids & Gases: Pure Substances & Mixtures. 2nd ed. LC 82-25857. 1983. text ed. 59.95 (ISBN 0-89116-356-5). Hemisphere Pub.
Watson, Philip. Liquid Magic. LC 82-80988. (Science Club Ser.). (Illus.). 48p. (gr. 3-6). 1983. PLB 8.16 (ISBN 0-688-00967-0); pap. 5.25 (ISBN 0-688-00974-3). Lothrop.
LIQUIDS-DIFFUSION
see Diffusion
LIQUIDS, KINETIC THEORY OF
Dyer, A. Liquid Scintillation Counting Practice. 122p. 1980. 29.95 (ISBN 0-471-25664-1, Pub. by Wiley Heyden). Wiley.

LISP (COMPUTER PROGRAM LANGUAGE)
Shapiro, Stuart. Lisp: An Interactive Approach. 1983. text ed. p.n.s. (ISBN 0-914894-44-7). Computer Sci.
LISTENING
Battaglia, J. & Fisher, M., eds. Yoshi Goes To New York: Authentic Discourse for Listening Comprehension. (Materials for Language Practice Ser.). (Illus.). 64p. 1982. 3.95 (ISBN 0-08-028648-8). Pergamon.
Benward, Bruce. Ear Training: A Technique for Listening. 2nd ed. 220p. 1983. write for info. (ISBN 0-697-03547-6); instr's dictation manual avail. (ISBN 0-697-03548-4); 14 tapes avail. Wm C Brown.
Brooks, Bearl. Basic Skills Listening for Sounds Workbook. (Basic Skills Workbooks). 32p. (gr. 2-3). 1983. 0.99 (ISBN 0-8209-0546-1, PW-6). ESP.
Devine, Thomas G. Listening Skills Schoolwide: Activities & Programs. (Orig.). 1982. pap. 6.50 (ISBN 0-8141-2956-0). NCTE.
Drakeford, John W. The Awesome Power of the Listening Heart. 192p. 1982. pap. 5.95 (ISBN 0-310-70261-5). Zondervan.
Erway, E. A. Listening: A Programmed Approach. 1979. pap. 13.95 (ISBN 0-07-019660-5); instr's manual avail. McGraw.
Geeting, Baxter & Geeting, Corinne. How to Listen Assertively. 1983. 8.50 (ISBN 0-686-84062-3). Intl Gen Semantics.
Glatthorn, Allan A. & Adams, Herbert R. Listening Your Way to Management Success. (Goals Ser.). 1983. pap. text ed. 7.95 (ISBN 0-673-15802-0). Scott F.
Hirsh, Robert O. Listening: A Way To Process Information Aurally. (Comm Comp Ser.). (Illus.). 45p. 1979. pap. text ed. 2.95 (ISBN 0-89787-316-5). Gorsuch Scarisbrick.
Mumford, S. Conversation Pieces: Exercises in Elementary Listening Comprehension, Teacher's Book. (Materials for Language Practice Ser.). pap. 3.95 tchr's wkbk. (ISBN 0-08-029443-X). Pergamon.
Patty, Catherine. Learning to Listen. (Language Arts Ser.). 24p. (gr. 4-7). 1980. wkbk. 5.00 (ISBN 0-8209-0317-5, LA-3). ESP.
Rost, Michael & Stratton, Robert. Listening Transitions: From Listening to Speaking. 2d ed. 72p. pap. text ed. 5.00 (ISBN 0-940264-16-1); 3 cassettes 25.00 (ISBN 0-940264-17-X); transcripts 3.50 (ISBN 0-940264-28-5). Lingual Hse Pub.
Steil, Lyman K. & Barker, Larry L. Effective Listening: Key to Your Success. LC 82-11512. (Illus.). Date not set. pap. text ed. 7.95 (ISBN 0-201-16425-6). A-W.
Steil, Lyman K. & DeMare, George. Listening-It Can Change Your Life: A Handbook for Scientists & Engineers. 170p. 1983. 18.95x (ISBN 0-471-86165-0). Ronald Pr.
Wicks, Robert J. Helping Others: Ways of Listening, Sharing & Counseling. 1982. 14.95 (ISBN 0-89876-040-2). Gardner Pr.
LISTENING-PROGRAMMED INSTRUCTIONS
Liddle. Ears. (gr. k-3). pap. 2.28 response bk. (ISBN 0-8372-4235-5); tchr's handbk. 2.28 (ISBN 0-8372-4236-3); tape set avail. Bowmar-Noble.
Wehrli, Kitty. Listening Experiences (Primary) (Illus.). 60p. (gr. 1). 1981. 4.00 (ISBN 0-686-84636-2); tchr's script 1.00. Ann Arbor Pubs.
LITERACY
see Illiteracy
LITERARY AGENTS
see also Authors and Publishers
Author Aid-Research Associates International, ed. Literary Agents of North America: Marketplace 1983-84. 128p. (Orig.). 1983. pap. 14.95 (ISBN 0-911085-00-9, 0082-1). Author Aid.
Curtis, Richard. How to Be Your Own Literary Agent. 1983. 12.95 (ISBN 0-395-33123-4). HM.
LITERARY CALENDARS
Espy, Willard. Children's Almanac of Words at Play. (Illus.). 256p. 1982. 15.95 (C N Potter Bks); pap. 8.95. Crown.
LITERARY CHARACTERS
see Characters and Characteristics in Literature
LITERARY CRITICISM
see Criticism
LITERARY CURIOSA
Grosse, Lloyd T. & Lyster, Alan F. Fifteen Hundred Literary References Everyone Should Know. LC 82-18444. 256p. (Orig.). 1983. pap. 3.95 (ISBN 0-668-05596-0, 5596). Arco.
LITERARY PRIZES
Porter, Peter & Sergeant, Howard. Gregory Awards. 1981. 11.50 (ISBN 0-436-37812-4, Pub. by Secker & Warburg). David & Charles.
Weiss, Jacqueline S. Prizewinning Books for Children: Themes & Stereotypes in U.S. Prizewinning Prose Fiction for Children. LC 82-48624. (Libraries & Librarianship Special Ser.). 1983. write for info. (ISBN 0-669-06352-5). Lexington Bks.
LITERARY PROPERTY
see Copyright
LITERARY RESEARCH
Cooke, Thomas D., ed. The Present State of Scholarship in Fourteen Century Literature. (Illus.). 304p. 1983. 23.80 (ISBN 0-8262-0379-5). U of MO Pr.

LITERATURE-ADDRESSES, ESSAYS, LECTURES
see also Literature-History and Criticism
Weigand, Hermann J. Critical Probings: Essays in European Literature. Goldsmith, Ulrich K., ed. 310p. Date not set. price not set. P Lang Pubs.
LITERATURE-ANTHOLOGIES
see Anthologies
LITERATURE-BIOGRAPHY
see Authors
LITERATURE-COLLECTIONS
Here are entered general collections. For collections limited to specific periods see subdivisions below, e.g. Literature, Medieval; Literature, Modern.
Abrahams, William, ed. Prize Stories 1983: The O. Henry Awards. 360p. 1983. 16.95 (ISBN 0-385-18115-9). Doubleday.
Kennerly, Karen, ed. Hesitant Wolf, Scrupulous Fox: Fables Selected from World Literature. LC 82-3328. (Illus.). 352p. 1983. pap. 9.95 (ISBN 0-8052-0717-1). Schocken.
Morrow, Bradford, ed. Conjunctions: 4. (Conjunctions Bi-Annual Volumes of New Writing). (Illus.). 240p. 1983. 22.50 (ISBN 0-941964-06-X); pap. 7.50 (ISBN 0-941964-05-1). Conjunctions.
Wepsiec, Jan. Sociology: An/International Bibliography of Serial Literature 1880-1980. 176p. 1982. 37.00 (ISBN 0-7201-1652-X, Pub. by Mansell England). Wilson.
LITERATURE-ESTHETICS
Jauss, Hans R. Aesthetic Experience & Literary Hermeneutics. Shaw, Michael, tr. LC 82-4786. (Theory & History of Literature Ser.: Vol. 3). 384p. 1982. 29.50x (ISBN 0-8166-1003-7); pap. 12.95 (ISBN 0-8166-1006-1). U of Minn Pr.
LITERATURE-EVALUATION
see Bibliography-Best Books; Books and Reading; Criticism; Literature-History and Criticism
LITERATURE-EXAMINATIONS, QUESTIONS, ETC.
Veitch, Carol & Boklage, Cecilia. Literature Puzzles for Elementary & Middle Schools. 120p. 1983. pap. text ed. 12.50 (ISBN 0-87287-363-3). Libs Unl.
LITERATURE-HISTORY AND CRITICISM
see also Authors; Literature-Addresses, Essays, Lectures
Bristol, Evelyn, ed. & intro. by. East European Literature: Papers from the Second World Congress for Soviet & East European Studies. 106p. 1982. pap. 8.00 (ISBN 0-933884-26-5). Berkeley Slavic.
Chasse, Paul. Les Arts et La Litterature Ches la Franco-Americains de la nouvelle-angleterre. (Fr.). (gr. 9-10). 1975. pap. text ed. 1.25 (ISBN 0-911409-10-6). Natl Mat Dev.
Chekhov, Anton. Letters on the Short Story, the Drama & Other Literary Topics. Friedland, Louis S., ed. 346p. 1982. Repr. of 1924 ed. lib. bdg. 35.00 (ISBN 0-686-81845-8). Darby Bks.
Cooke, Thomas D., ed. The Present State of Scholarship in Fourteen Century Literature. (Illus.). 304p. 1983. 23.80 (ISBN 0-8262-0379-5). U of MO Pr.
Davies & Beatty. Literature of the Romantic Period, 1750-1850. 228p. 1982. 40.00x (ISBN 0-85323-353-5, Pub. by Liverpool Univ England). State Mutual Bk.
Greene, Myles. Adventures in Philosophical Poetry & Literature. 48p. 1983. 1.95 (ISBN 0-9606994-2-2). Greenview Pubns.
Hochman, Baruch. The Test of Character: On the Victorian Novel & the Modern. LC 81-71793. 224p. 1983. 27.50 (ISBN 0-8386-3122-3). Fairleigh Dickinson.
Hurst, H. Norman. Four Elements in Literature. 192p. 1982. Repr. of 1936 ed. lib. bdg. 35.00 (ISBN 0-89984-917-2). Century Bookbindery.
King, James R. The Literary Moment as a Lens on Reality. LC 82-17319. 224p. 1983. text ed. 20.00x (ISBN 0-8262-0393-0). U of Mo Pr.
Leslie, A. & Willson, Jeanne, eds. A Tribute to Hermann Weigand. 144p. 1982. pap. 9.95 (ISBN 0-911173-00-5). Dimension Pr.
Lethbridge, T. C. The Power of the Pendulum. (Illus.). 160p. 1983. pap. 5.95 (ISBN 0-7100-9499-X). Routledge & Kegan.
McKeague, Patricia M. Writing about Literature: Step by Step. 144p. 1982. pap. text ed. 8.95 (ISBN 0-8403-2712-9). Kendall-Hunt.
Meijer, Reinder P. Literature of the Low Countries. 416p. 1978. 40.00x (ISBN 0-85950-099-3, Pub. by Thornes England). State Mutual Bk.
Oates, Joyce Carol. The Profane Art: Essays & Reviews. 224p. 1983. 13.95 (ISBN 0-525-24166-3, 01354-410). Dutton.
Partridge, Colin. The Making of New Cultures: A Literary Perspective. (Costerus New Series: Vol. 34). 131p. 1982. pap. text ed. 14.00x (ISBN 90-6203-644-9, Pub. by Rodopi Holland). Humanities.
Rockwell, Joan. Fact in Fiction: The Use of Literature in the Systematic Study of Society. 211p. 1974. 18.95 (ISBN 0-7100-7877-3). Routledge & Kegan.
Said, Edward W. The World, the Text, & the Critic. 352p. 1983. 20.00x (ISBN 0-674-96186-2). Harvard U Pr.
Smith, Barbara H. On the Margins of Discourse: The Relation of Literature to Language. LC 78-18274. xviii, 226p. 1978. pap. 7.50 (ISBN 0-226-76453-2). U of Chicago Pr.

Streika, Joseph P., ed. Literary Theory & Criticism: Essays in Honor of Rene Wellek at the Occasion of His 80th Birthday. 1983. 95.00 (ISBN 0-686-37581-5); pre-pub. 80.00 (ISBN 0-686-37582-3). P Lang Pubs.
Walsh, Chad. From Utopia to Nightmare. 191p. 1962. 10.00 (ISBN 0-89366-131-7). Ultramarine Pub.
Weigand, Hermann J. Critical Probings: Essays in European Literature. Goldsmith, Ulrich K., ed. 310p. Date not set. price not set. P Lang Pubs.
Whipple, Edwin P. Outlooks on Society, Literature & Politics. 345p. 1982. Repr. of 1888 ed. lib. bdg. 50.00 (ISBN 0-89987-890-3). Darby Bks.
Woolf, Virginia. Letter to a Young Poet. 1982. lib. bdg. 34.50 (ISBN 0-686-81936-5). Porter.
LITERATURE-INFLUENCE
see Literature and Morals
LITERATURE-MORAL AND RELIGIOUS ASPECTS
see Literature and Morals
LITERATURE-PHILOSOPHY
Dube, Anthony & Franson, J. Earl. Structure & Meaning: An Introduction to Literature. LC 82-83173. 1296p. 1983. text ed. 18.95 (ISBN 0-395-32570-6); write for info. instr's manual (ISBN 0-395-32571-4). HM.
Leavis, F. R. The Critic as Anti-Philosopher. Singh, G., ed. Bd. with Essays & Papers. LC 82-13580. 208p. 1983. text ed. 16.00x (ISBN 0-8203-0656-8). U of Ga Pr.
Rogers, William Elford. The Three Genres & the Interpertation of Lyric. LC 82-12293. 280p. 1983. pap. 23.50 (ISBN 0-691-06554-3). Princeton U Pr.
Trimpi, Wesley. Muses of One Mind: The Literary Analysis of Experience & Its Continuity. LC 82-61389. 450p. 1983. 40.00x (ISBN 0-691-06568-3). Princeton U Pr.
LITERATURE-PRIZES
see Literary Prizes
LITERATURE-PSYCHOLOGY
see also Esthetics; Literature-Philosophy
Van Kamm, Adrian & Healy, Kathleen. The Demon & the Dove: Personality Growth Through Literature. LC 82-20173. 308p. 1983. pap. text ed. 11.50 (ISBN 0-8191-2897-X). U Pr of Amer.
LITERATURE-QUESTIONS
see Literature-Examinations, Questions, etc.
LITERATURE-RESEARCH
see Literary Research
LITERATURE-SELECTIONS
see Literature-Collections
LITERATURE-STUDY AND TEACHING
Austin, Mary & Jenkins, Esther. Promoting World Understanding Through Literature, K-8. 300p. 1983. lib. bdg. 22.50 (ISBN 0-87287-356-0). Libs Unl.
Boas, Ralph P. & Smith, Edwin. An Introduction to the Study of Literature. 454p. 1982. Repr. of 1933 ed. lib. bdg. 30.00 (ISBN 0-89760-097-5). Telegraph Bks.
Dube. Structure & Meaning. 2d ed. 1982. text ed. 19.95 (ISBN 0-686-84579-X, LT26); instr's. manual avail. (LT27). HM.
Mallik, David & Moss, Peter, eds. New Essays in the Teaching of Literature. 1982p. (Orig.). pap. text ed. 10.25 (ISBN 0-909955-38-7). Boynton Cook Pubs.
LITERATURE, APOCALYPTIC
see Apocalyptic Literature
LITERATURE, CLASSICAL
see Classical Literature (Collections)
LITERATURE, COMIC
see Comedy
LITERATURE, COMPARATIVE
Maurer, Walter. Englische und Anglo-Deutsche Lehnubersetzungen Im Russichen. 192p. (Ger.). 1982. write for info. (ISBN 3-261-05033-0). P Lang Pubs.
LITERATURE, COMPARATIVE-AMERICAN AND ENGLISH
Habict, Werner, ed. English & American Studies in German: Summaries of Theses & Monographs, 1981. 168p. (Orig.). 1982. pap. 42.50x (ISBN 3-484-43081-8). Intl Pubns Serv.
LITERATURE, COMPARATIVE-GERMAN AND RUSSIAN
Maurer, Walter. Englische und Anglo-Deutsche Lehnubersetzungen Im Russichen. 192p. (Ger.). 1982. write for info. (ISBN 3-261-05033-0). P Lang Pubs.
LITERATURE, EPIC
see Epic Literature
LITERATURE, EROTIC
see Erotic Literature
LITERATURE, IMMORAL
see also Censorship; Erotic Literature; Literature and Morals; Sex in Literature
Jackson, Holbrook. The Fear of Books. LC 82-15785. x, 199p. 1982. Repr. of 1932 ed. lib. bdg. 29.75x (ISBN 0-313-23738-7, JAFB). Greenwood.
LITERATURE, MEDIEVAL
see also Christian Literature, Early; Romances; also subdivisions referring to Medieval Literature under specific national literatures, e.g. English Literature-Middle English; French Literature-Old French
Blake, N. F. The Canterbury Tales. 720p. 1980. text ed. 98.50 (ISBN 0-7131-6217-1). E Arnold.

Fischer, Steven R. The Complete Medieval Dreambook: A Multilingual, Alphabetical "Somnia Danielis" Collation. 172p. 1982. write for info. (ISBN 3-261-05001-2). P Lang Pubs.
Ford, Boris, ed. Medieval Literature, Pt. 2. 1983. pap. 5.95 (ISBN 0-14-022272-3, Pelican). Penguin.
Robbins, Paul. Medieval Romance. 1983. pap. 4.95 (ISBN 0-8283-1881-6). Branden.
Rothwell, W. & Barron, W. R. Studies in Medieval Literature & Languages. Blamires, D. M. & Thorpe, L., eds. 404p. 1973. 29.00 (ISBN 0-7190-0550-7). Manchester.
Van Buuren, Catherine. The Buke of the Sevyne Sagis: A Middle Scots Version of the Seven Sages of Rome. (Germanic & Anglistic Studies of the University of Leiden: Vol. 20). (Illus.). xii, 463p. 1982. pap. write for info. (ISBN 90-04-06753-1). E J Brill.

LITERATURE, MEDIEVAL–HISTORY AND CRITICISM

Beranek, Bernard. Annuale Mediavele, Vol. 21. 138p. 1982. 13.50x (ISBN 0-686-82238-2). Humanities.
Best, Thomas W. Reynard the Fox. (World Authors Ser.: No. 673). 170p. 1983. lib. bdg. 18.95 (ISBN 0-8057-6520-4, Twayne). G K Hall.
Cummins, Patricia W. Literary & Historical Perspectives of the Middle Ages. 232p. 1982. 8.00 (ISBN 0-937058-15-7). West Va U Pr.
Fischer, Steven R. The Complete Medieval Dreambook: A Multilingual, Alphabetical "Somnia Danielis" Collation. 172p. 1982. write for info. (ISBN 3-261-05001-2). P Lang Pubs.
Morris, Rosemary. The Character of King Arthur in Medieval Literature. LC 82-3712. (Arthurian Studies IV). 224p. 1982. text ed. 47.50x (ISBN 0-8476-7118-6). Rowman.
Niedzielski, Henri & Runte, Hans, eds. Jean Misrahi Memorial Volume: Studies in Medieval Literature. 20.00 (ISBN 0-917786-00-9). French Lit.

LITERATURE, MEDIEVAL–TRANSLATIONS

see Translations–Literature, Medieval

LITERATURE, MODERN (COLLECTIONS)–20TH CENTURY

Galloway, David & Sabisch, Christian, eds. Calamus: Male Homosexuality in Twentieth Century Literature: An International Anthology. 480p. 1982. pap. 9.50 (ISBN 0-688-00606-X). Quill NY.
Le Guin, Ursula K. The Altered I: Ursula K. Le Guin's Science Fiction Writing Workshop. Harding, Lee, ed. 1978. pap. 7.50 (ISBN 0-425-03849-1). Ultramarine Pub.

LITERATURE, MODERN–HISTORY AND CRITICISM

Habict, Werner, ed. English & American Studies in German: Summaries of Theses & Monographs, 1981. 168p. (Orig.). 1982. pap. 42.50x (ISBN 3-484-43081-8). Intl Pubns Serv.
Kurzawa, Werner. Analytische Aspekte der Literarischen Wertung. 254p. (Ger.). 1982. write for info. P Lang Pubs.
Roberts, Edgar. Writing Themes About Literature. 5th ed. 352p. 1983. pap. 9.95 (ISBN 0-13-971655-6). P H.
Thomas, R. H. & Bullivant, K. Literature in Upheaval. 1974. 17.00 (ISBN 0-7190-0576-0). Manchester.

LITERATURE, MODERN–HISTORY AND CRITICISM–20TH CENTURY

see also Dadaism

Segal, Naomi. The Banal Object: Theme & Thematics in Proust, Rilke, Hofmannsthal & Sartre. 147p. 1981. 49.00x (ISBN 0-85457-099-3, Pub. by Inst Germanic Stud England). State Mutual Bk.
Woll, Josephine & Treml, Vladimir. Soviet Dissident Literature: A Critical Guide. 1983. lib. bdg. 25.00 (ISBN 0-8161-8626-X, Hall Reference). G K Hall.

LITERATURE AND MORALS

see also Censorship; Literature, Immoral

Price, Martin. Forms of Life: Character & Moral Imagination in the Novel. LC 82-16064. 400p. 1983. text ed. 27.50x (ISBN 0-300-02867-9). Yale U Pr.
Timm, Joan S. & Timm, Henry C. Athena's Mirror: Moral Reasoning in Poetry, Short Story & Drama. 1983. write for info. (ISBN 0-915744-34-1). Character Res.

LITERATURE AND MUSIC

see Music and Literature

LITERATURE AND SCIENCE

see also Science Fiction (Collections)

Cosslett, Tess. The Scientific Movement & Victorian Literature. LC 82-10284. 1982. 22.50x (ISBN 0-312-70298-1). St Martin.
White, Kenneth S. Einstein & Modern French Drama: An Analogy. LC 82-21789. 132p. (Orig.). 1983. lib. bdg. 17.75 (ISBN 0-8191-2942-9); pap. text ed. 7.75 (ISBN 0-8191-2943-7). U Pr of Amer.

LITERATURE AND SOCIETY

Bryan, T. Avril. Censorship & Social Conflict in the Spanish Theatre: The Case of Alfonso Sastre. LC 82-17445. 156p. (Orig.). 1983. lib. bdg. 19.25 (ISBN 0-8191-2829-5); pap. text ed. 8.75 (ISBN 0-8191-2830-9). U Pr of Amer.

LITERATURE AND STATE

see also State Encouragement of Science, Literature, and Art

Bald, Suresht R. Novelists & Political Consciousness: Literary Expression of Indian Nationalism, 1919-1947. 1982. 17.50x (ISBN 0-8364-0921-3, Pub. by Chanakya). South Asia Bks.
Woll, Josephine & Treml, Vladimir. Soviet Dissident Literature: A Critical Guide. 1983. lib. bdg. 25.00 (ISBN 0-8161-8626-X, Hall Reference). G K Hall.

LITERATURE AND WAR

see War and Literature

LITERATURE AS A PROFESSION

see Authors; Authorship; Journalism; Journalists

LITHIUM

Gabano, J. B., ed. Lithium Batteries. Date not set. price not set (ISBN 0-12-271180-7). Acad Pr.
Jefferson, James W. & Greist, John H. Lithium Encyclopedia for Clinical Practice. (Illus.). 185p. 1983. spiral bdg. 17.00x (ISBN 0-88048-011-4). Am Psychiatric.
Lux, H. D. & Aldenhoff, J. B., eds. Basic Mechanisms in the Action of Lithium: Proceedings of a Symposium at Schloss Ringberg, Bavaria, Germany, October 4-6,1981. (International Congress Ser.: No. 572). 272p. 1982. 74.50 (ISBN 0-444-90249-X, Excerpta Medica). Elsevier.
Schou, M. Lithium Treatment of Manic-Depressive Illness. 2nd, rev. ed. (Illus.). x, 70p. 1983. pap. 11.50 (ISBN 3-8055-3678-X). S Karger.

LITHOGRAPHS

Miro, Joan. Miro Lithographs. (Art Library). (Illus.). 48p. (Orig.). 1983. pap. 2.50 (ISBN 0-486-24437-7). Dover.

LITHOGRAPHY

Muench, John. The Painter's Guide to Lithography. 125p. 1982. 22.50 (ISBN 0-89134-057-2); pap. 14.95 (ISBN 0-89134-058-0). North Light Pub.

LITHOLOGY

see Petrology

LITHUANIA

Dembrowski, Harry E. The Union of Lublin: Polish Federalism in the Golden Age. (East European Monographs: No. 116). 384p. 1982. 27.50x (ISBN 0-88033-009-0). East Eur Quarterly.

LITIGATION, GOVERNMENT

see Government Litigation

LITTLE, MALCOLM, 1925-1965

Goodman, Benjamin, intro. by. Malcolm X: The End of White World Supremacy. 160p. 1983. pap. 6.95 (ISBN 0-394-62469-6). Seaver Bks.

LITTLE PRESSES

Bibliotheca Press Educational Division. Small Press Publishers Workbook. 50p. 1983. wkbk. 19.95 (ISBN 0-939476-77-0). Biblio Pr GA.
Henderson, Bill, ed. Pushcart Prize VIII: Best of the Small Presses, 1983-84 Edition. 500p. 1983. 24.00 (ISBN 0-916366-18-9). Pushcart Pr.
Update Publicare Staff. Small Press Update: Notebook of Back Issues. 35p. 1983. pap. text ed. 8.00 (ISBN 0-686-38898-4). Update Pub Co.

LITTLE'S DISEASE

see Cerebral Palsy

LITURGICAL CANDLES

see Candles and Lights

LITURGICAL LIGHTS

see Candles and Lights

LITURGICAL YEAR

see Church Year

LITURGICS

see also Christian Art and Symbolism; Church Music; Church Year; Sacraments (Liturgy)

Collins, Mary & Power, David, eds. A Creative Tradition. (Concilium 1983: Vol. 162). 128p. (Orig.). 1983. pap. 6.95 (ISBN 0-8164-2442-X). Seabury.
International Committee on English in the Liturgy. Documents on the Liturgy, 1963-1979: Conciliar, Papal & Curial Texts. O'Brien, Thomas C., ed. LC 82-83580. 1496p. 1983. text ed. 45.00 (ISBN 0-8146-1281-4). Liturgical Pr.
Neophitos, Angelo. The Seasons Sing of God. (Illus.). 145p. 1979. pap. 4.95 (ISBN 0-686-81994-2). St Thomas Seminary.
Neville, Gwen K. & Westerhoff, John H., III. Learning Through Liturgy. 189p. 1983. pap. 6.95 (ISBN 0-8164-2423-3). Seabury.
Reeder, Rachel, ed. Liturgy: One Church, Many Churches. (Quarterly Journal of The Liturgical Conference: Vol. 3, No. 2). (Illus.). 80p. (Orig.). 1983. pap. text ed. 7.95 (ISBN 0-918208-30-0). Liturgical Conf.

LITURGICS–CATHOLIC CHURCH

St. Maximus the Confessor. The Church, the Liturgy & the Soul of Man. Stead, Dom J., tr. from Gr. LC 82-10545. 1982. pap. 6.95 (ISBN 0-932506-23-2). St Bedes Pubns.

LITURGIES

see also Hymns; Installation Service (Church Officers); Liturgies; Mass; Ritual

also subdivision Liturgy and Ritual, or name of ritual, under names of churches, e.g. Catholic Church–Liturgy and Ritual; Church of England–Book of Common Prayer

David, Katalin. Treasures in Hungarian Ecclesiastical Collections. Hoch, Elizabeth, tr. from Hungarian. (Illus.). 150p. 1982. 27.50x (ISBN 963-13-1460-X). Intl Pubns Serv.
Gilsdorf, Helen M., ed. Modern Liturgy Index. 2nd ed. 1983. pap. 5.56 (ISBN 0-89390-040-0); pap. text ed. 6.95. Resource Pubns.
McBride, Alfred. Year of the Lord: Reflections on the Sunday Readings. cycle A 6.95 (ISBN 0-697-01847-4); cycle B 6.95 (ISBN 0-697-01848-2). Wm C Brown.
Reeder, Rachel, ed. Liturgy: Diakonia. (Journal of The Liturgical Conference: Vol. 2, No. 4). (Illus.). 84p. (Orig.). 1982. pap. 7.95 (ISBN 0-918208-28-9). Liturgical Conf.
--Liturgy: With Lyre & Harp. (Quarterly Journal of The Liturgical Conference: Vol. 3, No. 3). (Illus.). 80p. (Orig.). 1983. pap. text ed. 7.95 (ISBN 0-918208-31-9). Liturgical Conf.
Religous Education Staff. The Spirit Alive in Liturgy: Spirit Masters. 1981. 9.95 (ISBN 0-686-84105-0). Wm C Brown.
Sloyan, Virginia, ed. Signs, Songs & Stories. (Illus.). 160p. 1982. pap. 8.50 (ISBN 0-8146-1285-7). Liturgical Pr.

LITURGY

see Liturgics

LIVER

Csomos, G. Clinical Hepatology: History-Present State-Outlook. (Illus.). 430p. 1982. 42.00 (ISBN 0-387-11838-1). Springer-Verlag.

LIVER–DISEASES

see also Hepatolenticular Degeneration

Colon, A. R. Pediatric Hepatology. (Medical Outline Ser.). 1982. pap. text ed. 25.00 (ISBN 0-87488-407-1). Med Exam.
Epstein. Kidney in Liver Disease. 1982. 75.00 (ISBN 0-444-00655-9). Elsevier.
Gitnick, Gary L., ed. Current Hepatology, Vol. 1. (Current Ser). (Illus.). 384p. 1980. 50.00 (ISBN 0-471-09518-4, Pub. by Wiley Med). Wiley.
Lapis, K. & Johannessen, J. V. Liver Carcinogenesis. 1979. 35.00 (ISBN 0-07-036368-4). McGraw.
Patrick, R. S. Color Atlas of Liver Pathology. (Color Atlases of Pathology Ser.). (Illus.). 192p. 1982. 75.00 (ISBN 0-19-921033-0). Oxford U Pr.
Popper, Hans & Schaffner, Fenton, eds. Progress in Liver Diseases, Vol. 7. 1982. 59.00 (ISBN 0-8089-1467-7). Grune.

LIVER–SURGERY

Calne, Roy Y., ed. Liver Transplant. write for info. (ISBN 0-12-790767-X). Grune.

LIVESTOCK

see also Cattle; Goats; Horses; Range Management; Sheep

also headings beginning with the word Livestock

Acker, Duane. Animal Science & Industry. (Illus.). 720p. 1983. 27.95 (ISBN 0-13-037416-4). P-H.
Brown, T. Freeze Branding. (Orig.). 1982. pap. 3.50 (ISBN 0-911217-00-2). SW Amer Pub Co.
Camels & Camel Milk. (FAO Animal Production & Health Papers: No. 26). 69p. 1982. pap. 7.50 (ISBN 92-5-101169-9, F2310, FAO). Unipub.
Development & Economic Comparison of Selection Criteria for Cows & Bulls with a Dairy Herd Simulation Model. 196p. 1983. pap. 29.00 (ISBN 90-220-0813-4, PDC253, Pudoc). Unipub.
Gillespie, James. Modern Livestock & Poultry Production. 2nd ed. (Illus.). 662p. 1983. text ed. 23.80 (ISBN 0-8273-2200-3); write for info. instr's guide (ISBN 0-8273-2201-1). Delmar.
Hormones in Animal Production. (FAO Animal Production & Health Paper: No. 31). 53p. 1982. pap. 7.50 (ISBN 92-5-101213-X, F2342, FAO). Unipub.
Kempster, A. J. & Cuthbertson, A., eds. Carcase Evaluation in Livestone Breeding, Production & Marketing. 250p. 1982. lib. bdg. 40.00 (ISBN 0-86531-531-0). Westview.
Livestock Environment II. LC 82-72456. 624p. 1982. text ed. 36.50 (ISBN 0-916150-45-3). Am Soc Ag Eng.
Livestock in Asia: Issues & Policies. 192p. 1983. pap. 12.00 (ISBN 0-88936-353-6, IDRC 202, IDRC). Unipub.
Politiek, R. D. & Bakker, J. J., eds. Livestock Production in Europe: Perspectives & Prospects. (Developments in Animal & Veterinary Sciences Ser.: No. 8). 354p. 1982. 58.25 (ISBN 0-444-42105-X). Elsevier.
Ward, Gerald M. Energy Impacts Upon Future Livestock Production. (Special Study in Agriculture-Aquaculture Science & Policy). 250p. 1982. lib. bdg. 30.00 (ISBN 0-86531-286-9). Westview.

LIVESTOCK–DISEASES

see Veterinary Medicine

LIVESTOCK–HOUSING

see also Farm Buildings

Midwest Plan Service. Solar Livestock Housing Handbook. 1st ed. (Illus., Orig.). 1983. pap. 4.00 (ISBN 0-89373-056-4, MWPS-23). Midwest Plan Serv.

LIVESTOCK BUILDINGS

see Livestock–Housing

LIVING, COST OF

see Cost and Standard of Living

LIZARDS

Burghardt, Gordon M., ed. Iguanas of the World: Their Behavior, Ecology & Conservation. Rand, A. Stanley. LC 82-7932. (Animal Behavior, Ecology, Conservation & Management Ser.). (Illus.). 472p. 1983. 55.00 (ISBN 0-8155-0917-0). Noyes.
Huey, Raymond B. & Pianka, Eric R., eds. Lizard Ecology: Studies of a Model Organism. (Illus.). 720p. 1983. text ed. 35.00x (ISBN 0-674-53673-8). Harvard U Pr.
Storr, G. M. & Smith, L. A. Lizards of Western Astralia: Skinks, Vol. 1. (Illus.). xii, 200p. 1982. pap. 23.00 (ISBN 0-85564-195-9, Pub. by U of W Austral Pr). Intl Schol Bk Serv.

LLOYD, HAROLD CLAYTON, 1894-1971

Dardis, Tom. Harold Lloyd. 1983. write for info. (ISBN 0-670-45227-0). Viking Pr.

LLOYDS BANK, LIMITED

Winton, J. R. Lloyds Bank, Nineteen Eighteen to Nineteen Sixty-Nine. (Illus.). 222p. 1982. 37.50x (ISBN 0-19-920125-0). Oxford U Pr.

LOAN SHARKING

see Interest and Usury

LOANS

see also Debts, Public; Interest and Usury; Investments; Loans, Foreign; Mortgage Loans

Behrens, Robert H. Commercial Problem Loans: How to Identify, Supervise, & Collect the Problem Loan. 2nd ed. LC 82-16416. 226p. 1983. 35.00 (ISBN 0-87267-039-2). Bankers.
Donaldson. The Medium-Term Loan Market. LC 82-42619. 176p. 1982. 25.00x (ISBN 0-312-52820-5). St Martin.
Reisman, Albert F., ed. Business Loan Workouts: A Course Handbook. 699p. 1981. 30.00 (ISBN 0-686-43272-X, A4-4039). PLI.
Rudman, Jack. Loan Advisor. (Career Examination Ser.: C-1321). (Cloth bdg. avail. on request). pap. 12.00 (ISBN 0-8373-1321-X). Natl Learning.

LOANS, FOREIGN

Williamson, John, ed. IMF Conditionality. (Series: No. 5). 700p. 1983. 30.00 (ISBN 0-88132-006-4). Inst Intl Eco.

LOBBYING

Moe, Terry M. The Organization of Interests: Incentives & the Internal Dynamics of Political Interest Groups. LC 79-13238. (Illus.). x, 282p. 1982. pap. text ed. 9.00x (ISBN 0-226-53352-2). U of Chicago Pr.
Nader, Ralph. Ralph Nader Presents a Citizens' Guide to Lobbying. 1983. 12.95 (ISBN 0-934878-26-9); pap. 6.95 (ISBN 0-934878-27-7). Dembner Bks.

LOCAL ADMINISTRATION

see Local Government

LOCAL COLOR IN LITERATURE

see also Poetry of Places; France in Literature; Italy in Literature

Donavan, Josephine. New England Local Color Literature: A Women's Tradition. LC 82-40252. 250p. 1982. 12.95 (ISBN 0-8044-2138-2). Ungar.

LOCAL ELECTIONS

see Elections

LOCAL FINANCE

see also Local Taxation; Municipal Finance; Finance

Davey, Kenneth. Financing Regional Government: International Practices & Their Relevance to the Third World. (Public Administration in Developing Countries Ser.). 220p. 1983. 24.95 (ISBN 0-471-10356-X, Pub. by Wiley-Interscience). Wiley.
Drebin, Allan R. & Chan, James L. Objectives of Accounting & Financial Reporting by Governmental Units: A Research Study, 2 vols. Incl. Vol. I. (Illus.). 128p. pap. no charge; Vol. II. (Illus.). 200p. pap. 7.50 (ISBN 0-686-84260-X). 1981. Municipal.
Hayes, Frederick O., et al. Linkages: Improving Financial Management in Local Government. LC 82-60180. 184p. (Orig.). 1982. pap. text ed. 12.00 (ISBN 0-87766-313-0, 33700). Urban Inst.

LOCAL GOVERNMENT

Here are entered works which deal with local government of districts, counties, townships, etc. Works dealing with government of municipalities only are entered under Municipal Government; those dealing with government of counties only are entered under County Government.

see also Cities and Towns; County Government; Decentralization in Government; Elections; Municipal Government; Public Administration; Villages

Bennett, R. J. Central Grants to Local Governments: The Politics & Economic Impact of the Rate Support Grant in England & Wales. LC 82-4378. (Cambridge Geographical Studies: No. 17). (Illus.). 300p. 1982. 49.50 (ISBN 0-521-24908-2). Cambridge U Pr.
Burrus, Bernie R. Administrative Law & Local Government. LC 63-63661. (Michigan Legal Publications Ser.). 139p. 1982. Repr. of 1963 ed. lib. bdg. 30.00 (ISBN 0-89941-170-3). W S Hein.
Hatry, Harry, et al. Efficiency Measurement for Local Government Services: Some Initial Suggestions. 204p. pap. text ed. 6.50 (ISBN 0-87766-266-5). Urban Inst.
Jacobs, Everett M., ed. Soviet Local Politics & Government. (Illus.). 224p. 1983. text ed. 28.50x (ISBN 0-04-329042-6). Allen Unwin.
Knight, Fred, et al, eds. Telecommunications for Local Government. LC 82-15617. (Practical Management Ser.). (Illus.). 224p. (Orig.). 1982. 19.50 (ISBN 0-87326-036-8). Intl City Mgt.
Lockard, Dunne. The Politics of State & Local Government. 3rd ed. 288p. 1983. pap. text ed. 20.95 (ISBN 0-02-371530-8). Macmillan.
Morris, David J. The New City-States. LC 82-82572. (Illus.). 76p. Date not set. pap. 4.95 (ISBN 0-917582-49-7). Inst Local Self Re.
Siena, James V., ed. Antitrust & Local Government. LC 82-16825. 224p. 1982. text ed. 32.95 (ISBN 0-932020-16-X); pap. text ed. 19.95 (ISBN 0-932020-17-8). Seven Locks Pr.
Zuckerman, Michael. Peaceable Kingdoms: New England Towns in the Eighteenth Century. LC 82-18365. ix, 329p. 1983. Repr. of 1970 ed. lib. bdg. 39.75x (ISBN 0-313-22634-2, ZUPK). Greenwood.

LOCAL GOVERNMENT–AFRICA

Mawhood, Philip. Local Government for Development: The Experience of Tropical Africa. (Public Administration in Developing Countries Ser.). 250p. 1983. price not set (ISBN 0-471-10510-4, Pub. by Wiley-Interscience). Wiley.

LOCAL GOVERNMENT–CANADA

Brownstone, Meyer & Plunkett, T. J. Politics & the Reform of Local Government in Metropolitan Winnipeg. LC 81-19658. (Lane Ser. in Regional Government). 240p. 1983. 35.00x (ISBN 0-520-04197-6). U of Cal Pr.

LOCAL GOVERNMENT–GREAT BRITAIN

Stewart, John. Local Government: The Conditions of Local Choice. (Institute of Local Government Studies). 216p. 1983. text ed. 28.50x (ISBN 0-04-352102-9); pap. text ed. 12.95x (ISBN 0-04-352103-7). Allen Unwin.

LOCAL HISTORY

Here are entered works on the writing and compiling of local histories. Works concerned with local history of specific areas are entered under names of countries, states, etc. with subdivision History, Local, or under names of places with or without the subdivision History.

Ericson, Jack T. Genealogy & Local History: Title List, Parts 2 & 3. 85p. 1981. write for info. Microfilming Corp.

Stephens, W. B. Teaching Local History. 1977. 16.50 (ISBN 0-7190-0660-0). Manchester.

LOCAL JUNIOR COLLEGES

see Community Colleges

LOCAL TAXATION

see also Income Tax, Municipal

Hulten, Charles R., ed. Depreciation, Inflation, & the Taxation of Income from Capital. LC 81-533061. 319p. 1981. text ed. 32.00 (ISBN 0-87766-311-4, URI 33800). Urban Inst.

LOCAL TRANSIT

Black, J. Thomas & Morina, Michael. Downtown Office Growth & the Role of Public Transit. LC 82-50921. (Illus.). 122p. (Orig.). 1982. pap. text ed. 26.00 (ISBN 0-87420-615-4, D31). Urban Land.

De Silva, Clarence W. & Wormley, David N. Automated Guideway Transit Analysis & Design. LC 80-8927. 304p. 1983. 37.95x (ISBN 0-669-04407-5). Lexington Bks.

Kirby, Ronald, et al. An Assessment of Short-Range Transit Planning in Selected U. S. Cities. 82p. (Orig.). 1979. pap. text ed. 4.00 (ISBN 0-87766-274-6). Urban Inst.

Levett, John, ed. Jane's Urban Transport Systems, 1982. (Jane's Yearbooks). (Illus.). 500p. 1982. 110.00 (ISBN 0-86720-612-8). Sci Bks Intl.

--Jane's Urban Transport Systems 1983. 2nd ed. (Jane's Yearbooks). (Illus.). 500p. 1983. 125.00 (ISBN 0-86720-645-4). Sci Bks Intl.

LOCALIZATION OF CEREBRAL FUNCTIONS

see Brain–Localization of Functions

LOCATION OF INDUSTRIES

see Industries, Location Of

LOCATION OF STORES

see Store Location

LOCH NESS

see Ness, Loch

LOCKE, JOHN, 1632-1704

Colman, John. John Locke's Moral Philosophy. 280p. 1982. text ed. 27.50 (ISBN 0-686-82135-1, Pub. by Edinburgh U Pr Scotland). Columbia U Pr.

Dunn, John. The Political Thought of John Locke: An Historical Account of the Argument of the 'Two Treatises of Government' 306p. 1983. pap. 12.95 (ISBN 0-521-27139-8). Cambridge U Pr.

Locke, John. The Correspondence of John Locke, Vol. 6: Letters 2199 to 2664. De Beer, E. S., ed. 806p. 1981. text ed. 119.00x (ISBN 0-19-824563-7). Oxford U Pr.

--A Letter Concerning Toleration. Tully, James, ed. (HPC Philosophical Classics Ser.). 96p. 1983. pap. text ed. 3.95 (ISBN 0-915145-60-X). Hackett Pub.

LOCKOUTS

see Strikes and Lockouts

LOCOMOTIVE DIESELS

see Diesel Locomotives

LOCOMOTIVES

see also Diesel Locomotives; Electric Locomotives

Eatwell, David. Steam Locomotives. (Illus.). 64p. 1983. pap. 4.95 (ISBN 0-7134-1835-4, Pub. by Batsford England). David & Charles.

LOCOMOTIVES–HISTORY

Cooke, Brian. The Fall & Rise of Steam. (Illus.). 128p. 1982. 22.95 (ISBN 0-86720-623-3). Sci Bks Intl.

Hewison, C. H. Locomotive Boiler Explosions. (Illus.). 144p. 1982. 16.50 (ISBN 0-7153-8305-1). David & Charles.

Westwood, J. N. Soviet Locomotive Technology During Industrilization 1928-1952. 1982. 80.00 (ISBN 0-686-42925-7, Pub. by Macmillan England). State Mutual Bk.

LOCOMOTIVES–PICTORIAL WORKS

Cooke, Brian. The Fall & Rise of Steam. (Illus.). 128p. 1982. 22.95 (ISBN 0-86720-623-3). Sci Bks Intl.

LOCUSTS

Albrecht, F. O. The Anatomy of the Red Locust (Nomadacris Septemfasciate Serville) 1956. 35.00x (ISBN 0-85135-067-4, Pub. by Centre Overseas Research). State Mutual Bk.

Ashall, C. & Ellis, P. E. Studies on Numbers & Mortality in Field Populations of the Desert Locust (Schistocerca Gregaria Forskal) 1962. 35.00x (ISBN 0-85135-004-6, Pub. by Centre Overseas Research). State Mutual Bk.

Bennett, F. V. & Symmons, P. M. A Review of Estimates of the Effectiveness of Certain Control Techniques & Insecticides Against the Desert Locust. 1972. 35.00x (ISBN 0-85135-060-7, Pub. by Centre Overseas Research). State Mutual Bk.

Betts, E. Outbreaks of the African Migratory Locust (Locusta Migratoria Migratoriodes R & F) Since 1871. 1961. 35.00x (ISBN 0-85135-005-4, Pub. by Centre Overseas Research). State Mutual Bk.

Bullen, F. T. The Distribution of the Damage Potential of the Desert Locust (Schistocerca Gregaria Forskal) 1969. 35.00x (ISBN 0-85135-045-3, Pub. by Centre Overseas Research). State Mutual Bk.

Burnett, G. F. Field Observations on the Behavior of the Red Locust (Nomadacris Septemfasciata Serville) in the Solitary Phase. 1951. 35.00x (ISBN 0-85135-006-2, Pub. by Centre Overseas Research). State Mutual Bk.

Casimir, M. & Bament, R. C. An Outbreak of the Australian Plague Locust, (Hortoicetes Terminiferal Walk.), During 1966-67 & the Influence of Weather on Swarm Flight. 1974. 35.00x (ISBN 0-85135-062-3, Pub. by Centre Overseas Research). State Mutual Bk.

Chapman, R. F. A Laboratory Study of Roosting Behavior in Hoppers of the African Migratory Locust (Locusta Migratoria Migratorioides R & F) 1955. 35.00x (ISBN 0-85135-007-0, Pub. by Centre Overseas Research). State Mutual Bk.

Davey, J. T. & Johnston, H. B. The African Migratory Locust (Locusta Migratoria Migratorioides) R & FO in Nigeria. 91p. 1956. 35.00x (ISBN 0-85135-009-7, Pub. by Centre Overseas Research). State Mutual Bk.

Davies, D. E. Seasonal Breeding & Migrations of the Desert Locust (Schistocerca Gregaria Forskal) in North-Eastern Africa & the Middle East. 1952. 35.00x (ISBN 0-85135-010-0, Pub. by Centre Overseas Research). State Mutual Bk.

Dempster, J. P. The Population Dynamics of the Moroccan Locust (Dociostaurus Maroccanus Thunb) in Cyprus. 1957. 35.00x (ISBN 0-85135-011-9, Pub. by Centre Overseas Research). State Mutual Bk.

The Desert Locust Pocket Book. 1978p. 37.00x (ISBN 0-85135-083-6, Pub. by Centre Overseas Research). State Mutual Bk.

Dirsh, V. A. Morphometrical Studies on Phases of the Desert Locust (Schistocerca Gregaria Forskal) 1953. 35.00x (ISBN 0-85135-066-6, Pub. by Centre Overseas Research). State Mutual Bk.

Field Observations of the Behavior of Hoppers of the Red Locust (Nomadacris Septemfasciata Serville) 1959. 35.00x (ISBN 0-85135-043-7, Pub. by Centre Overseas Research). State Mutual Bk.

Fortescue-Foulkes, J. Seasonal Breeding & Migrations of the Desert Locust (Schistocerca Gregaria Forskal) in South-Western Asia. 1953. 35.00x (ISBN 0-85135-015-1, Pub. by Centre Overseas Research). State Mutual Bk.

Hemming, C. F. & Symmons, P. M. The Germination & Growth of Schouwia Purpurea (Forskal) Schweinf & Its Role as a Habitat of the Desert Locust. 1969. 35.00x (ISBN 0-85135-054-2, Pub. by Centre Overseas Research). State Mutual Bk.

Hemming, C. F. & Taylor, T. H., eds. Proceedings of the International Study Conference on the Current & Future Problems of Acridology, London, 1970. 1972. 50.00x (ISBN 0-686-82422-9, Pub. by Centre Overseas Research). State Mutual Bk.

Hunter-Jones, P. Laboratory Studies on the Inheritance of Phase Characters in Locusts. 1958. 35.00x (ISBN 0-85135-018-6, Pub. by Centre Overseas Research). State Mutual Bk.

Johnston, D. R., ed. Factors Affecting Aerial Application of Microencapsulated Pheromone Formulation for Control of Pectinophora Gossypiella (Saunders) by Communication Disruption on Cotton in Egypt. 1982. 35.00x (ISBN 0-686-82424-5, Pub. by Centre Overseas Research). State Mutual Bk.

Johnston, H. B. Annotated Catalogue of African Grasshoppers: Supplement. 1968. 45.00x (ISBN 0-521-05443-5, Pub. by Centre Overseas Research). State Mutual Bk.

Johnston, H. B. & Buxton, D. R. Field Observations on Locusts in Eastern Africa. 1949. 35.00x (ISBN 0-85135-008-9, Pub. by Centre Overseas Research). State Mutual Bk.

Joyce, R. J. The Ecology of Grasshoppers in Cast Central Sudan. 1952. 35.00x (ISBN 0-85135-019-4, Pub. by Centre Overseas Research). State Mutual Bk.

Lloyd, J. H. Operational Research on Preventive Control of the Red Locust (Nomadacris Septemfasciata Serville) 1959. 35.00x (ISBN 0-85135-020-8, Pub. by Centre Overseas Research). State Mutual Bk.

Locust & Grasshopper Agricultural Manual. 1982. 195.00 (ISBN 0-85135-120-4, Pub. by Centre Overseas Research). State Mutual Bk.

The Locust Handbook. 1966. 35.00 (ISBN 0-85135-053-4, Pub. by Centre Overseas Research). State Mutual Bk.

Maccuaig, R. D. & Yeates, M. N. Theoretical Studies on the Efficiency of Insecticidal Sprays for the Control of Flying Locust Swarms. 35.00x (ISBN 0-85135-057-7, Pub. by Centre Overseas Research). State Mutual Bk.

Magor, J. T. Outbreaks of the Australian Plague Locust (Hortoicetes Terminifera Walk.) During the Seasons 1937 to 1962, with Particular Reference to Rainfall. 1970. 35.00x (ISBN 0-85135-002-X, Pub. by Centre Overseas Research). State Mutual Bk.

Magor, J. T. & Ward, P. Illustrated Descriptions, Distribution Maps & Bibliography of the Species of Quelea (Weaverbirds; Ploceidae) (Illus.). 1972. 35.00x (ISBN 0-85135-058-5, Pub. by Centre Overseas Research). State Mutual Bk.

Merton, L. F. The Moroccan Locust (Dociostaurus Maroccanus Thunberg) 1961. 35.00X (ISBN 0-85135-021-6, Pub. by Centre Overseas Research). State Mutual Bk.

Nickerson, N. Pigmentation of Hoppers of the Desert Locust (Schistocerca Gregaria Forskal) in Relation to Phase Coloration. 1956. 35.00x (ISBN 0-85135-023-2, Pub. by Centre Overseas Research). State Mutual Bk.

Norris, M. J. Factors Affecting the Rate of Sexual Maturation of the Desert Locust (Schistocerca Gregaria Forskal) in the Laboratory. 1957. 35.00x (ISBN 0-85135-024-0, Pub. by Centre Overseas Research). State Mutual Bk.

--Laboratory Experiments on Aviposition Responses of the Desert Locust (Schistocerca Gregaria Forskal) 1968. 35.00x (ISBN 0-686-82420-2, Pub. by Centre Overseas Research). State Mutual Bk.

--Reproduction in the Red Locust (Nomadacris Septemfasciata Serville) in the Laboratory. 1959. 35.00x (ISBN 0-85135-027-5, Pub. by Centre Overseas Research). State Mutual Bk.

--Reproduction in the Sert Locust (Schistocerca Gregaria Forskal) 1952. 35.00x (ISBN 0-85135-026-7, Pub. by Centre Overseas Research). State Mutual Bk.

Odiyo, P. O. Seasonal Distribution & Migrations of Agrotis Ipsilon (Hufnagel) Leipidoptera, Noctuidae. 1975. 35.00x (ISBN 0-85135-070-4, Pub. by Centre Overseas Research). State Mutual Bk.

Popov, G. & Ratcliffe, M. The Sahelian Tree Locust Anacridium Melanorhodon Walker. 1968. 35.00x (ISBN 0-85135-044-5, Pub. by Centre Overseas Research). State Mutual Bk.

Popov, G. B. Ecological Studies on Oviposition by Swarms of the Desert Locust (Schistocerca Gregaria Forskal) in Eastern Africa. 1958. 35.00x (ISBN 0-85135-029-1, Pub. by Centre Overseas Research). State Mutual Bk.

--Studies on Oviposition, Egg Development & Mortality in Oedaleus Senegalenis: Krauss, Orthoptera, Acridoidea in the Sahel. 1980. 35.00x (ISBN 0-85135-111-5, Pub. by Centre Overseas Research). State Mutual Bk.

Rainey, R. C. Meteorology & the Migration of Desert Locusts: Applications of Synoptic Meteorology in Locust Control. 1963. 35.00 (ISBN 0-686-82414-8, Pub. by Centre Overseas Research). State Mutual Bk.

Rainey, R. C. & Waloff, Z. The Behavior of the Red Locust (Normadacris Septemfasciata Serville) in Relation to the Topography, Meteorology & Vegetatation of the Rukwa Rift Valley, Tanganyika. 1957. 35.00x (ISBN 0-85135-031-3, Pub. by Centre Overseas Research). State Mutual Bk.

Richards, O. W. The Study of the Numbers of the Red Locust (Nomadacris Septemfasciata Serville) 1953. 35.00x (ISBN 0-85135-032-1, Pub. by Centre Overseas Research). State Mutual Bk.

Richards, O. W. & Waloff, N. Studies on the Biology & Population Dynamics of British Grasshoppers. 1954. 35.00x (ISBN 0-85135-034-8, Pub. by Centre Overseas Research). State Mutual Bk.

Riley, J. R. & Reynolds, D. R. Radar Observations of Spodoptera Exempta Kenya: March-April 1979. 1981. 35.00x (ISBN 0-85135-115-8, Pub. by Centre Overseas Research). State Mutual Bk.

Roffey, J. Locusts & Grasshoppers of Economic Importance in Thailand. 1979. 75.00x (ISBN 0-686-82431-8, Pub. by Centre Overseas Research). State Mutual Bk.

--Observations on Night Flight on the Desert Locust (Schistocerca Gregaria Forskal) 1963. 35.00x (ISBN 0-85135-033-X, Pub. by Centre Overseas Research). State Mutual Bk.

Shulov, A. The Development of Eggs of the Red Locust, Nomandacris Septemfasciata (Serville) & the African Migratory Locust, Locusta Migratoria Migratoria Migratorioides (R&F), & Its Interruption under Particular Conditions of Humidity. 1970. 35.00x (ISBN 0-85135-001-1, Pub. by Centre Overseas Research). State Mutual Bk.

Shulov, A. & Pener, M. P. Studies on the Development of Eggs of the Desert Locust (Schistocerca Gregaria Forskal) & Its Interruption under Particular Conditions of Humidity. 1963. 35.00x (ISBN 0-85135-035-6, Pub. by Centre Overseas Research). State Mutual Bk.

Stower, W. J. The Colour Patterns of Hoppers of the Desert Locust (Schistocerca Gregaria Forskal) 1959. 35.00x (ISBN 0-85135-036-4, Pub. by Centre Overseas Research). State Mutual Bk.

Stower, W. J. & Popov, G. B. Oviposition Behavior & Egg Mortality of the Desert Locust (Schistocerca Gregaria Forskal) on the Coast of Eritrea. 1958. 35.00x (ISBN 0-85135-037-2, Pub. by Centre Overseas Research). State Mutual Bk.

Uvarov, B. P. Grasshoppers & Locusts: A Handbook of General Acridology, 2 Vols. Vol. 1, 1966. 50.00x (ISBN 0-521-06669-7, Pub. by Centre Overseas Research); Vol. 2, 1977. 70.00x (ISBN 0-85135-072-0, Pub. by Centre Overseas Research). State Mutual Bk.

Uvarov, B. P. & Chapman, E. Observations on the Moroccan Locust (Dociostaurus Maroccanus Thunberg) in Cyprus, 1950. 1951. 35.00x (ISBN 0-85135-039-9, Pub. by Centre Overseas Research). State Mutual Bk.

Versey-Fitzgerald, D. F. The Vegetation of the Outbreak Areas of the Red Locust (Nomadacris Septemfasciata Serville in Tanganyika & Northern Rhodesia) 1955. 35.00x (ISBN 0-85135-014-3, Pub by Centre Overseas Research). State Mutual Bk.

Waloff, Z. Some Temporal Characteristics of Desert Locust Plagues. 1976. 35.00x (ISBN 0-85135-075-5, Pub. by Centre Overseas Research). State Mutual Bk.

--The Upsurges & Recessions of the Desert Locust Plague: An Historical Survey. 1968. 35.00x (ISBN 0-85135-041-0, Pub. by Centre Overseas Research). State Mutual Bk.

Waloff, Z. & Rainey, R. C. Field Studies on Factors Affecting the Displacement of Desert Locust Swarms in Eastern Africa. 1951. 35.00x (ISBN 0-85135-042-9, Pub. by Centre Overseas Research). State Mutual Bk.

Wardhaugh, K. & Ashour, Y. Experiments on the Incubation & Hopper Development Periods of the Desert Locust (Schistocerca) Gregaria Forskal) in Saudi Arabia. 1969. 35.00x (ISBN 0-85135-048-8, Pub. by Centre Overseas Research). State Mutual Bk.

LODGE, HENRY CABOT, 1850-1924

Widenor, William C. Henry Cabot Lodge & the Search for an American Foreign Policy. (Illus.). 402p. 1983. pap. 8.95 (ISBN 0-520-04962-4, CAL 631). U of Cal Pr.

LOESS

Pesci, M., ed. Studies on Loess. 555p. 1980. pap. text ed. 46.50x (ISBN 963-05-2871-1, 41212, Pub. by Kultura Pr Hungary). Humanities.

LOGGING

see Lumbering

LOGIC

see also Abstraction; Fallacies (Logic); Identity; Induction (Logic); Knowledge, Theory Of; Probabilities; Reasoning; Thought and Thinking

Annemann, Theodore. Practical Mental Logic. (Illus.). 310p. (Orig.). 1983. pap. 5.95 (ISBN 0-486-24426-1). Dover.

Carlsen-Jones, M. Introduction to Logic. 624p. 1983. 22.95 (ISBN 0-07-032890-0). McGraw.

Carroll, Lewis. The Philosopher's Alice: Alice's Adventures in Wonderland & Through the Looking-Glass. (Illus.). 256p. 1983. pap. 7.95 (ISBN 0-312-60518-8). St Martin.

Chadwick, Henry, ed. Boethius: The Consolations of Music, Logic, Theology, & Philosophy. 330p. 1981. text ed. 39.00 (ISBN 0-19-826447-X). Oxford U Pr.

Edgar, William J. The Problem Solver's Guide to Logic. LC 82-20285. 106p. (Orig.). 1983. pap. text ed. 6.50 (ISBN 0-8191-2876-7). U Pr of Amer.

Jech, T. Axiom of Choice. (Studies in Logic: Vol. 75). 1973. 19.50 (ISBN 0-444-10484-4). Elsevier.

Warren, Thomas B. Logic & the Bible. 1983. write for info (ISBN 0-934916-01-2). Natl Christian Pr.

LOGIC–ADDRESSES, ESSAYS, LECTURES

Cohen, Robert & Wartofsky, Marx. Language, Logic, & Method. 1983. 69.50 (ISBN 90-277-0725-1, Pub. by Reidel Holland). Kluwer Boston.

LOGIC–HISTORY

Giuberti, F. Materials for a Study on Twelfth Century Scholasticism. (History of Logic Ser.: Vol. II). 158p. 1982. 34.95x (ISBN 0-686-42759-9, Pub. by Bibliopolis Italy); pap. text ed. 19.95x (ISBN 88-7088-056-7). Humanities.

Maieru, A., ed. English Logic in Italy in the 14th & 15th Centuries. (History of Logic Ser.: Vol. I). 388p. 1982. 45.00x (ISBN 88-7088-054-0, Pub. by Bibliopolis Italy); pap. text ed. 24.95x (ISBN 88-7088-057-5). Humanities.

LOGIC, DEDUCTIVE

see Logic

LOGIC, INDUCTIVE

see Induction (Logic)

LOGIC, MEDIEVAL

Gallais, Pierre. Dialectique du Recit Medieval. (Faux Titre Ser.: Band 9). 322p. (Fr.). 1982. pap. text ed. 30.00x (ISBN 90-6203-744-5, Pub. by Rodopi Holland). Humanities.

LOGIC, SYMBOLIC AND MATHEMATICAL

see also Algebra, Abstract; Algebra, Boolean; Categories (Mathematics); Goedel's Theorem; Machine Theory; Model Theory; Probabilities; Reasoning; Science–Methodology; Set Theory

Fitch, Frederick B. Symbolic Logic: An Introduction. 238p. 1952. 15.95x (ISBN 0-471-07001-7). Wiley.

Florens, J. P., et al, eds. Specifying Statistical Models, From Parametric to Non-Parametric, Using Bayesian or Non-Bayesian Approaches: Proceedings, Louvain-la-Neuve, Belgium, 1981. (Lecture Notes in Statistics Ser.: Vol. 16). (Illus.). 204p. 1983. pap. 14.00 (ISBN 0-387-90809-9). Springer-Verlag.

Klenk, Virginia. Understanding Symbolic Logic. (Illus.). 480p. 1983. 21.95 (ISBN 0-13-936468-4). P-H.

Marek, Wiktor. Elements of Logic & Foundations of Mathematics in Problems. 1982. 39.50 (ISBN 90-277-1084-8, Pub. by Reidel Holland). Kluwer Boston.

Van Dalen, D. & Lascar, D., eds. Logic Colloquium 1980: Papers Intended for the European Meeting of the Association for Symbolic Logic. (Studies in Logic & the Foundations of Mathematics: Vol. 108). 342p. 1982. 51.00 (ISBN 0-444-86465-2, North Holland). Elsevier.

LOGIC AND FAITH

see Faith and Reason

LOGIC OF MATHEMATICS

see Mathematics-Philosophy

LOGICAL ANALYSIS

see Analysis (Philosophy)

LOIRE RIVER AND VALLEY-DESCRIPTION AND TRAVEL

Michelin Green Guide: Schlosser Loire. (Green Guide Ser.). (Ger.). 1983. pap. write for info. (ISBN 2-06-023241-4). Michelin.

Wade, Richard. Companion Guide to the Loire. (Illus.). 333p. 1983. 15.95 (ISBN 0-13-154526-4); pap. 7.95 (ISBN 0-13-154518-3). P-H.

LOLIGO

see Squids

LONDON, JACK, 1876-1916

Beauchamp, Gorman. Jack London. (Starmont Reader's Guide Ser.: No. 15). 96p. 1983. Repr. lib. bdg. 10.95x. Borgo Pr.

--Reader's Guide to Jack London. Schlobin, Roger C., ed. (Reader's Guides to Contemporary Science Fiction & Fantasy Authors Ser.: Vol. 15). (Illus., Orig.). 1983. 10.95x (ISBN 0-916732-40-1); pap. text ed. 4.95x (ISBN 0-916732-39-8). Starmont Hse.

Tavernier-Courbin, Jacqueline. Critical Essays on Jack London. (Critical Essays in American Literature Ser.). 308p. 1983. lib. bdg. 30.00 (ISBN 0-8161-8465-8). G K Hall.

Umland, Samuel J. Call of the Wild & White Fang Notes. 70p. (Orig.). 1982. pap. text ed. 2.50 (ISBN 0-8220-0279-5). Cliffs.

Watson, Charles N., Jr. The Novels of Jack London: A Reappraisal. LC 82-70548. 324p. 1983. 19.95 (ISBN 0-299-09300-X). U of Wis Pr.

LONDON

Timbs, John. The Romance of London: Historic Sketches, Remarkable Duels, Notorious Highwaymen, Rogueries, Crimes, & Punishments, & Love & Marriage. 509p. 1982. Repr. lib. bdg. 50.00 (ISBN 0-89984-469-3). Century Bookbindery.

LONDON-DESCRIPTION

Greenwood, James. The Seven Curses of London. LC 82-195528. xxvi, 293p. 1982. Repr. of 1869 ed. 27.50x (ISBN 0-686-84020-8, Pub. by B Blackwell England). Porcupine Pr.

Skilton, Charles. Old London Postcard Album. 146p. 1982. 35.00x (ISBN 0-686-81688-9, Pub. by C Skilton Scotland). State Mutual Bk.

LONDON-DESCRIPTION-GUIDEBOOKS

Baedeker's City Guide: London. 192p. 1983. pap. 9.95 (ISBN 0-86145-120-1, Pub. by Auto Assn-British Tourist Authority England). Merrimack Bk Serv.

Dalzell, W. R. The Shell Guide to the History of London. (Illus.). 1982. 29.95 (ISBN 0-393-01593-9). Norton.

Hatts, Leigh. Country Walks Around London. (Illus.). 160p. 1983. 18.95 (ISBN 0-7153-8439-2). David & Charles.

Nicholson, Robert. Nicholson's London Guide. (Illus.). 1983. pap. 4.95 (ISBN 0-686-38865-8). Merrimack Bk Serv.

Piper, David. Companion Guide to London. (Illus.). 520p. 1983. 16.95 (ISBN 0-13-154542-6); pap. 8.95 (ISBN 0-13-154534-5). P-H.

Rothman's Concise Guide to London. 320p. 1983. pap. 8.95 (ISBN 0-907574-21-1, Pub. by Auto Assn-British Tourist Authority England). Merrimack Bk Serv.

This Is Your London. 128p. 1983. pap. 3.95 (ISBN 0-7095-1325-9, Pub. by Auto Assn-British Tourist Authority England). Merrimack Bk Serv.

LONDON-HISTORY

Barker, Felix & Hyde, Ralph. London: As It Might Have Been. 224p. 1982. 55.00x (ISBN 0-7195-3857-2, Pub. by Murray England). State Mutual Bk.

Dalzell, W. R. The Shell Guide to the History of London. (Illus.). 1982. 29.95 (ISBN 0-393-01593-9). Norton.

LONDON-HOTELS, TAVERNS, ETC.

London Hotels & Restaurants. 154p. 1983. pap. 3.95 (ISBN 0-7095-1292-9, Pub. by Auto Assn-British Tourist Authority England). Merrimack Bk Serv.

LONDON-INDUSTRIES

Flanders, Dennis. The Great Livery Companies of the City of London. 120p. 1982. 75.00x (ISBN 0-284-98512-0, Pub. by C Skilton Scotland). State Mutual Bk.

LONDON-INTELLECTUAL LIFE

Woolf, Virginia. The London Scene. 1982. 10.00 (ISBN 0-394-52866-2). Random.

LONDON-MARKETS

A Guide to London's Best Shops. 224p. 1983. pap. 6.96 (ISBN 0-907080-36-7, Pub. by Auto Assn-British Tourist Authority England). Merrimack Bk Serv.

LONDON-SUBURBS

Aldous, Tony. Illustrated London News Book of London's Villages. 1981. 29.95 (ISBN 0-436-01150-6, Pub. by Secker & Warburg); pap. 12.50 (ISBN 0-436-01151-4). David & Charles.

Reid, Kenneth C. Watermills of London Countryside: Their Place in English Landscape & Life, 2 vols. 1982. Vol. I. 50.00 ea. (ISBN 0-284-39165-4, Pub. by C Skilton Scotland). Vol. II (ISBN 0-284-98584-8). State Mutual Bk.

LONDON-TOWER OF LONDON

Abbott, G. Ghosts of the Tower of London. (Illus.). 85p. pap. 4.95 (ISBN 0-434-00595-9, Pub. by Heinemann). David & Charles.

LONELINESS

Buntain, Ruth J. Children in the Shadows. 78p. pap. 4.95 (ISBN 0-686-82632-9). Review & Herald.

Fritz, Jean. Homesick: My Own Story. (Illus.). 176p. 1982. 9.95 (ISBN 0-399-20933-6). Putnam Pub Group.

Hauer, Gerhard. Longing for Tenderness. 160p. (Orig.). 1983. pap. 4.95 (ISBN 0-87784-835-1). Inter-Varsity.

LONG ISLAND

Gish, Noel J. & Yockstick, Elizabeth. Long Island Studies Program: Activity Manual. (Illus.). 111p. (gr. 4). 1981. 49.00 (ISBN 0-943068-10-X). Graphic Learning.

LONG ISLAND-DESCRIPTION AND TRAVEL

Penny, Larry. Walking the Hamptons: A Guide to the Natural Heritage of the South Fork. 1983. 18.95 (ISBN 0-916366-20-0). Pushcart Pr.

LONG ISLAND-HISTORY

Pisano, Ronald G. The Long Island Landscape, Eighteen Sixty-Five through Nineteen Fourteen: The Halcyon Years. (Illus.). 44p. (Orig.). 1981. write for info. catalogue (ISBN 0-943526-03-5). Parrish Art.

LONGEVITY

see also Aging; Immortalism; Middle Age

Barasch, Marc, ed. Breaking One Hundred: Americans Who Have Lived Over a Century. (Illus.). 64p. 1983. pap. 4.95 (ISBN 0-688-01926-9). Quill NY.

Callahan, Edward J. & McCluskey, Kathleen, eds. Life-Span Development Psychology: Non-Normative-Life Events. LC 82-22784. Date not set. price not set (ISBN 0-12-155140-7). Acad Pr.

Chee Soo. The Tao of Long Life: The Chinese Art of Ch'ang Ming. 176p. 1983. pap. 7.95 (ISBN 0-85030-320-6). Newcastle Pub.

Dhillon, Sukhraj S. Health, Happiness & Longevity Eastern & Western Approach. (Illus.). 224p. (Orig.). 1983. pap. 12.95 (ISBN 0-87040-527-6). Kodansha.

Kent, Saul. The Life-Extension Revolution: The Source Book for Optimum Health & Maximum Lifespan. (Illus.). 480p. 1983. pap. 7.95 (ISBN 0-688-01952-8). Quill NY.

Kieffer, Jarold A. Gaining the Dividends of Longer Life: A New Strategy. 250p. 1983. lib. bdg. 22.50 (ISBN 0-86531-083-1); pap. text ed. 11.50X (ISBN 0-86531-174-9). Westview.

Morgan, Robert F. & Wilson, Jane. Growing Younger: How to Add Years to Your Life By Measuring & Controlling Your Body Age. LC 82-42854. 264p. 1983. 19.95 (ISBN 0-8128-2918-2). Stein & Day.

Santrock, John W. Life-Span Development. 864p. 1983. text ed. write for info. (ISBN 0-697-06556-1); pap. text ed. avail.; instr's manual avail. (ISBN 0-697-06558-8); study guide avail. (ISBN 0-697-06559-6). Wm C Brown.

Segerberg, Osborn. Living to be a One Hundred: 1,200 Who Did & How They Did It. (Illus.). 416p. 1983. pap. 9.95 (ISBN 0-686-83778-9, ScribT). Scribner.

LOOKING-GLASSES

see Mirrors

LOOMS

Hoffmann, Marta. The Warp Weighted Loom. pap. 16.95 (ISBN 82-00-08094-3). Robin & Russ.

LORD'S PRAYER

Boff, Leonardo. The Lord's Prayer: The Prayer of Integral Liberation. Morrow, Theodore, tr. LC 82-18811. Orig. Title: Portugese. 144p. (Orig.). 1983. pap. 6.95 (ISBN 0-88344-299-X). Orbis Bks.

LaVerdiere, Eugene. When We Pray: Meditation on the Lord's Prayer. LC 82-73512. 176p. 1983. pap. 4.95 (ISBN 0-87793-263-8). Ave Maria.

LORD'S PRAYER-JUVENILE LITERATURE

Hutson, Joan. The Lord's Prayer. Mahany, Patricia, ed. (Happy Day Bks.). (Illus.). 24p. (ps-2). 1983. 1.29 (ISBN 0-87239-640-1, 3560). Standard Pub.

LORD'S SUPPER

see also Mass; Sacraments

Barclay, William. The Lord's Supper. LC 82-2774. 1982. pap. 5.95 (ISBN 0-664-24432-7). Westminster.

Bridge, Donald & Phypers, David. Communion: The Meal That Unites? 192p. 1983. pap. 5.95 (ISBN 0-87788-160-X). Shaw Pubs.

Rogness, Alvin N. Table of the Lord: Holy Communion in the Life of the Church. LC 82-72640. 96p. (Orig.). 1983. pap. 4.50 (ISBN 0-8066-1946-5, 10-6182). Augsburg.

LORD'S SUPPER-MEDITATIONS

Fearon, Mary & Hirstein, Sandra J. The Eucharist Makes Us One. box set 79.95 (ISBN 0-697-01843-1); program dir. manual 4.50 (ISBN 0-697-01844-X); write for info. study leaflets; write for info. tchr's. manual. Wm C Brown.

LORIES

see Parrots

LORRAIN, CLAUDE

see Gelee, Claude, Called Claude Lorrain, 1600-1682

LORRIES (MOTOR VEHICLES)

see Motor-Trucks

LOS ANGELES-DESCRIPTION

Brodsly, David. L. A. Freeway: An Appreciative Essay. (Illus.). 188p. 1983. pap. 8.95 (ISBN 0-520-04546-7, CAL 535). U of Cal Pr.

Irvin, Judith L. & Downey, Joan M. Los Angeles Studies Program: Activity Manual. Yockstick, Elizabeth, ed. Martinez-Miller, Orlando, tr. (Illus.). 73p. (Spanish.). (gr. 3). 1981. 49.00 (ISBN 0-943068-41-X). Graphic Learning.

LOS ANGELES-DESCRIPTION-GUIDEBOOKS

Advocate Gay Visitors Guide to Los Angeles, 1982-1983. LC 82-80355. 1982. pap. 4.95 (ISBN 0-917076-04-4). Liberation Pubns.

Chapman, Marvey. Marmac Guide to Los Angeles: 1984 Olympic Games Edition. Nicholson, Diana, ed. (Marmac Guide Ser.). (Illus.). 304p. (Orig.). 1983. pap. 6.95 (ISBN 0-939944-14-6). Marmac Pub.

Grad, Laurie B. Dining In--Los Angeles. (Dining In--Ser.). (Illus.). 190p. 1982. pap. 8.95 (ISBN 0-89716-121-1). Peanut Butter.

Wurman, Richard S., ed. Los Angles-Access. rev. ed. (Access Guidebook Ser.). (Illus.). 1982. pap. 9.95 (ISBN 0-9604858-2-1). Access Pr.

LOS ANGELES-HISTORY

Elias, Judith. Los Angeles: Dream to Reality, Eighteen Eighty-Five to Nineteen Fifteen. (Santa Susana Pr California Masters Ser.: No. 5). (Illus.). 112p. 1983. 70.00 (ISBN 0-937048-33-X). CSUN.

Hylen, Arnold. Los Angeles Before the Freeways: 1850-1950, Images of a Era. (Illus.). 162p. 1981. 30.00 (ISBN 0-686-84000-3). Dawsons.

LOS ANGELES BASEBALL CLUB (NATIONAL LEAGUE)

Honig, Donald. The Los Angeles Dodgers: An Illustrated Tribute. (Illus.). 192p. 1983. 19.95 (ISBN 0-312-49880-2). St Martin.

LOUIS 14TH, KING OF FRANCE, 1638-1715

Hatton, H. William III & Luis XIV. 342p. 1982. 49.00x (ISBN 0-85323-253-9, Pub. by Liverpool Univ England). State Mutual Bk.

LOUIS PHILIPPE, KING OF FRANCE, 1773-1850

Lucas-Dubreton, J. Louis XVIII. Lyon, F. H., tr. 303p. 1982. Repr. of 1927 ed. lib. bdg. 40.00 (ISBN 0-8495-3268-X). Arden Lib.

LOUISIANA-GENEALOGY

Evans, Norma P., compiled by. Pontiff Paths: Two Hundred Years in Louisiana. LC 82-82598. (Illus.). 300p. (Orig.). 1982. write for info. (ISBN 0-686-81969-1); pap. 30.00. N P Evans.

LOUISIANA-HISTORY

Comite des Archives de la Louisiane, ed. History of Pointe Coupee Parish, Louisiana. (Illus.). 370p. 1983. 35.00 (ISBN 0-88107-005-X). Natl ShareGraphics.

Conrad, Glenn R. & Brasseaux, Carl A. A Selected Bibliography of Scholarly Literature on Colonial Louisiana & New France. 150p. 10.00 (ISBN 0-940984-06-7). U of SW LA Ctr LA Studies.

De Villiers du Terrage, Marc. The Last Years of French Louisiana. Brasseaux, Carl A. & Conrad, Glenn R., eds. Phillips, Hosea, tr. LC 82-73751. 525p. 20.00x (ISBN 0-940984-05-9). U of SW LA Ctr LA Studies.

Ericson, Carolyn & Ingmire, Frances, eds. First Settlers of the Louisiana Territory, 2 vols, Vol. 1. LC 82-84532. 235p. (Orig.). pap. 19.50 (ISBN 0-911317-09-0). Ericson Bks.

Evans, Norma P., compiled by. Pontiff Paths: Two Hundred Years in Louisiana. LC 82-82598. (Illus.). 300p. (Orig.). 1982. write for info. (ISBN 0-686-81969-1); pap. 30.00. N P Evans.

LOUISVILLE, KENTUCKY

Ryan, Bruce, ed. Program Abstracts 1980: AAG Louisville Meeting. 248p. (Orig.). 1980. pap. 3.00 (ISBN 0-89291-150-6). Assn Am Geographers.

LOUVRE, PARIS

Laclotte-Cuzin. The Louvre. 29.95 (ISBN 0-935748-49-0). ScalaBooks.

LOVE

see also Courtly Love; Friendship; Marriage

Agrippa, Cornelius. The Ladies' Oracle. 1982. pap. 5.95 (ISBN 0-374-18263-9). FS&G.

Amen, Carol V. Love Goes 'Round the Circle. (Better Living Ser.). pap. 0.95 (ISBN 0-8280-1268-7). Review & Herald.

Buscaglia, Leo. Living, Loving & Learning. 264p. 1982. 13.50 (ISBN 0-686-84812-8). Slack Inc.

Canfield, Muriel. I Wish I Could Say, "I Love You". 224p. (Orig.). 1983. pap. 4.95 (ISBN 0-87123-265-0). Bethany Hse.

Couer de Jesus d' Elbee, Jean du. I Believe In Love. Teichert, Marilyn & Stebbins, Madeline, trs. LC 82-24134. (Fr.). 1983. pap. 3.95 (ISBN 0-932506-21-6). St Bedes Pubns.

Ford, Edward E. Choosing to Love: A New Way to Respond. 192p. 1983. pap. 7.95 (ISBN 0-86683-695-0). Wilton Pr.

Gallagher, Chuck. Love is a Couple. 1980. 3.95 (ISBN 0-8215-6464-1). Sadlier.

--Love Takes Greatness. 1980. 3.95 (ISBN 0-8215-6465-X). Sadlier.

--Parents are Lovers. 1980. 3.95 (ISBN 0-8215-6466-8). Sadlier.

Hecke, Roswitha. Love Life. (Illus.). 144p. 1982. 17.95 (ISBN 0-394-52894-8, CP860, BC); pap. 9.95 (ISBN 0-394-62425-4, E832). Grove.

Hirsch, Abby & Dooley, Susan. The Lessons of Love. 224p. 1983. 13.95 (ISBN 0-688-01916-1). Morrow.

Jayne, Sears R., tr. Commentary on Plato's Symposium on Love by Marsilio Ficino. 2nd rev. ed. 300p. (Latin.). Date not set. pap. price not set (ISBN 0-88214-600-9). Spring Pubns.

LaVelle, Mike. Crazy for Love. (Illus., Orig.). 1983. pap. 4.95 (ISBN 0-440-50926-2, Dell Trade Pbks). Dell.

Liebowitz, Michael R. The Chemistry of Love. 1983. 15.50i (ISBN 0-316-52430-1). Little.

Love. LC 72-92810. 160p. Date not set. 9.95 (ISBN 0-03-063201-3); boxed leatherbound gift ed. 15.00 (ISBN 0-03-063293-5). HR&W.

Love Victorian Style II, 4 vols. (Victorian Library). 1394p. 1982. pap. 15.00 boxed set (ISBN 0-394-62426-2, B480, BC). Grove.

McCarty, Michele. Loving. 256p. (Orig.). (gr. 11-12). 1982. pap. text ed. 6.50 (ISBN 0-697-01808-3); tchrs. manual 7.00 (ISBN 0-697-01809-1). Wm C Brown.

Madow, Leo. Love: How to Understand & Enjoy It. 192p. 1982. pap. 4.95 (ISBN 0-686-37895-4, ScribT). Scribner.

Price, Eugenia. Make Love Your Aim. 192p. 1983. pap. 5.59 (ISBN 0-310-31311-2). Zondervan.

Sweeting, George. Catch the Spirit of Love. 120p. 1983. pap. 3.95 (ISBN 0-88207-108-4). Victor Bks.

Weber, Eric & Miller, Judi. Shy Persons Guide to a Happier Love Life. Repr. of 1979 ed. text ed. 11.95 (ISBN 0-914094-17-3). Symphony.

LOVE (THEOLOGY)

see also God-Love; God-Worship and Love; Self-Love (Theology)

Chapian, Marie. Love & Be Loved. 192p. 1983. pap. 5.95 (ISBN 0-8007-5092-6, Power Bks). Revell.

Rahner, Karl. The Love of Jesus & the Love of Neighbor. 96p. 1983. pap. 5.95 (ISBN 0-8245-0570-0). Crossroad NY.

LOVE (THEOLOGY)-MEDITATIONS

Welch, Reuben. We Really Do Need Each Other. 112p. 1982. pap. 5.95 (ISBN 0-310-70221-6). Zondervan.

LOVE, COURTLY

see Courtly Love

LOVE OF SELF (THEOLOGY)

see Self-Love (Theology)

LOVE POETRY

Bellamy, Joe D. & Weingarten, Roger, eds. Love Stories-Love Poems. 300p. (Orig.). 1982. pap. 12.95 (ISBN 0-931362-07-5). Fiction Intl.

Grigson. The Gambit Book of Love Poems. 1983. 10.95 (ISBN 0-87645-088-5); pap. 6.95 (ISBN 0-87645-115-6). Gambit.

LOVECRAFT, HOWARD PHILLIPS, 1890-1937

Joshi, S. T. H. P. Lovecraft. (Starmont Reader's Guide Ser.: No. 13). 84p. 1982. Repr. lib. bdg. 11.95x (ISBN 0-89370-044-4). Borgo Pr.

--Reader's Guide to H. P. Lovecraft. Schlobin, Roger C., ed. (Reader's Guides to Contemporary Science Fiction & Fantasy Authors Ser.: Vol. 13). (Illus., Orig.). 1982. 11.95x (ISBN 0-916732-36-3); pap. text ed. 5.95x (ISBN 0-916732-35-5). Starmont Hse.

LOW BODY TEMPERATURE

see Hypothermia

LOW-CALORIE DIET

see also Cookery-Reducing Recipes; Sugar-Free Diet

Calorie-Trimmed Recipes. pap. 5.95 (ISBN 0-696-01110-7). Meredith Corp.

Imfeld, T. N. Identification of Low Caries Risk Dietary Components. (Monographs in Oral Science: Vol. 11). (Illus.). viii, 172p. 1983. 76.25 (ISBN 3-8055-3634-8). S Karger.

Wurtman, Judith J. The Carbohydrate Craver's Diet. 214p. 1983. 12.95 (ISBN 0-395-33160-9). HM.

LOW-CHOLESTEROL DIET

Stern, Ellen & Michaels, Jonathan. The Good Heart Diet Cookbook. 256p. 1983. pap. 6.95 (ISBN 0-446-37547-0). Warner Bks.

LOW-FAT DIET

see also Cookery-Reducing Recipes

Williams, Jacqueline B. & Silverman, Goldie. No Salt No Sugar No Fat Cookbook. LC 81-83793. (Illus.). 150p. (Orig.). 1982. pap. 5.95 (ISBN 0-911954-65-1). Nitty Gritty.

LOW GERMAN LANGUAGE

Witte, Ulrich. Die Bezeichnungen Fur Den Bottcher Im Niederdeutschen Sprachbereich. xii, 489p. (Ger.). 1982. write for info. (ISBN 3-8204-6288-0). P Lang Pubs.

LOW INCOME HOUSING

see Housing; Public Housing

LOW SODIUM DIET
see Salt-Free Diet
LOW SUGAR DIET
see Sugar-Free Diet
LOW TEMPERATURE ENGINEERING
see also Gases-Liquefaction; Refrigeration and Refrigerating Machinery
Fast, R. W. Advances in Cryogenic Engineering, Vol.27. 1252p. 1982. 95.00 (ISBN 0-306-41103-2, Plenum Pr). Plenum Pub.
LOWELL, ROBERT, 1917-1977
Bell, Vereen M. Robert Lowell: Nihilist as Hero. 272p. 1983. text ed. 17.50x (ISBN 0-674-77585-6). Harvard U Pr.
LOWELL, MASSACHUSETTS-HISTORY
Bender, Thomas. Toward an Urban Vision: Ideas & Institutions in Nineteenth-Century America. LC 82-47980. 296p. (Orig.). 1982. pap. text ed. 7.50x (ISBN 0-8018-2925-9). Johns Hopkins.
LOWRY, MALCOLM, 1909-1957
Woolmer, J. Howard. Malcolm Lowry, A Bibliography. LC 82-50810. (Illus.). 162p. 1983. 30.00 (ISBN 0-913506-12-5). Woolmer-Brotherson.
LOYOLA, IGNACIO DE, SAINT, 1491-1556
Proterra, Michael. Homo Spiritualis Nititur Fide: Martin Luther & Ignatius of Loyola, an Analytical & Comparative Study of a Hermeneutic Based on the Heuristic Structure of Discretio. LC 82-21837. 92p. (Orig.). 1983. lib. bdg. 17.50 (ISBN 0-8191-2938-0); pap. text ed. 7.25 (ISBN 0-8191-2939-9). U Pr of Amer.
LUBRICATION AND LUBRICANTS
see also Bearings (Machinery); Oils and Fats
also names of lubricants
Lubrication, Friction & Wear. 332p. (Orig.). 1980. pap. text ed. 60.00x (ISBN 0-85825-148-5, Pub. by Inst Engineering Australia). Renouf.
LUCE, CLARE BOOTHE, 1903-
see Boothe, Clare, 1903-
LUDICROUS, THE
see Wit and Humor
LUDWIG 2ND, KING OF BAVARIA, 1845-1886
Peters, Robert. The Picnic in the Snow: Ludwig of Bavaria. LC 82-81364. (Illus.). 103p. 1982. pap. 5.00 (ISBN 0-89823-037-3). New Rivers Pr.
LUKACS, GEORG, 1885-1971
Congdon, Lee. The Young Lukacs. LC 82-11162. xiii, 235p. 1983. 21.00x (ISBN 0-8078-1538-1). U of NC Pr.
LUKE, SAINT
Keyes, Sharrel. Luke: Following Jesus. (Fisherman Bible Studyguides Ser.). 80p. 1983. pap. 2.50 (ISBN 0-87788-539-7). Shaw Pubs.
LULLABIES
see Children'S Songs
LUMBER TRADE
see also Lumbering; Timber; Woodwork
Maxwell, Robert S. & Baker, Robert D. Sawdust Empire: The Texas Lumber Industry 1830-1940. LC 82-40442. (Illus.). 256p. 1983. 24.95 (ISBN 0-89096-148-4). Tex A&M Univ Pr.
Morgan, Murray. The Mill on the Boot: The Story of the St. Paul & Tacoma Lumber Company. LC 82-16107. (Illus.). 296p. 1982. 19.95 (ISBN 0-295-95949-5). U of Wash Pr.
LUMBER TRADE-TABLES AND READY-RECKONERS
Forest Industries Commission on Timber Valuation & Taxation. Timber Tax Journal, Vol. 18. 335p. 1982. 30.00 (ISBN 0-686-43165-0, Pub. by FICTVT). Intl Schol Bk Serv.
LUMBERING
see also Lumber Trade
Macklin, Ronald R. The Logging Business Management Handbook. LC 82-83344. (Illus.). 176p. 1983. pap. 48.50 (ISBN 0-87930-146-5). Miller Freeman.
Rosholt, Malcolm. The Wisconsin Logging Book Eighteen Thirty-Nine to Nineteen Thirty-Nine. 3rd. ed. LC 80-53389. (Illus.). 304p. 1983. Repr. of 1980 ed. lib. bdg. 24.95 (ISBN 0-910417-01-6). Rosholt Hse.
LUNATIC ASYLUMS
see Psychiatric Hospitals
LUNCH ROOMS
see Restaurants, Lunchrooms, etc.
LUNCHEONS
Ewalt, Norma & Huth, Tom. Decadent Dinners & Lascivious Lunches. LC 82-71880. (Illus.). 320p. 1982. 10.95 (ISBN 0-686-82435-0). Clear Creek.
Williams, Christie. Brunch. LC 80-85004. (Illus.). 177p. (Orig.). 1981. pap. 5.95 (ISBN 0-911954-59-7). Nitty Gritty.
LUNG FUNCTION TESTS
see Pulmonary Function Tests
LUNGS
see also Respiration
Abramson, Joan. Practical Application of the Gas Laws to Pulmonary Physiology. 97p. (Orig.). 1981. pap. text ed. 5.95 (ISBN 0-89787-107-3). Gorsuch Scarisbrick.
LUNGS-CANCER
Straus, Marc. Lung Cancer: Clinical Diagnosis & Treatment. Date not set. price not set (ISBN 0-8089-1487-1). Grune.
LUNGS-CIRCULATION
see Pulmonary Circulation
LUNGS-DISEASES
see also Cystic Fibrosis; Pneumonia; Respiratory Insufficiency
Bone, Roger C. Pulmonary Disease Review, Vol. 1. (Pulmonary Disease Review Ser.). 581p. 1980. 45.00 (ISBN 0-471-05736-3, Pub. by Wiley Med). Wiley.
Fanburg. Sacoidosis & Other Granulatons Diseases of the Lung. (Lung & Biology in Health & Disease Ser.: Vol. 19). 544p. 1983. 59.75 (ISBN 0-8247-1866-6). Dekker.
Gebbers, J. O. & Burkhardt, A. Hair-Spray Induced Lung Lesion. (Illus.). 1982. 60.00 (ISBN 0-08-029788-9). Pergamon.
Newball. Immunopharmacology of the Lung. (Lung Biology in Health & Disease Ser.: Vol. 20). 536p. 1983. 65.00 (ISBN 0-8247-1827-5). Dekker.
Petty, Thomas L. Prescribing Home Oxygen for COPD. 128p. 9.95 (ISBN 0-86577-078-6). Thieme-Stratton.
Ziment, I. Practical Pulmonary Disease. (Family Practice Today: A Comprehensive Post Graduate Library). 226p. 1982. text ed. 14.85 (ISBN 0-471-09560-5, Pub. by Wiley Med.). Wiley.
LUNGS-RADIOGRAPHY
see Chest-Radiography
LUNGS-SURGERY
Humphrey, E. W. Manual of Pulmonary Surgery. (Comprehensive Manuals of Surgical Specialities). (Illus.). 259p. 1983. 149.50 (ISBN 0-387-90732-7). Springer-Verlag.
LUPUS ERYTHEMATOSUS
Bell, Linda. The Red Butterfly: Coping with Lupus Disease. 1983. pap. 4.95 (ISBN 0-8283-1880-8). Branden.
Hayslett, John P. & Hardin, John A. Advances in Systematic Lupus Erythematosis. Repr. write for info (ISBN 0-8089-1560-6). Grune.
Schur, Peter H., ed. The Clinical Management of Systemic Lupus Erythematosus. Date not set. price not set (ISBN 0-8089-1543-6). Grune.
LUTHER, MARTIN, 1483-1546
Bornkamm, Heinrich. Luther in Mid-Career 1521-1530. Bachmann, E. Theodore, tr. from German. LC 82-48591. 736p. 1983. 36.95 (ISBN 0-8006-0692-2, 1-692). Fortress.
Brokering, Herb & Bainton, Roland. Pilgrimage to Luther's Germany. 80p. 1983. 14.95 (ISBN 0-86683-629-2). Winston Pr.
Curts, Paul. Luther's Variations in Sentence Arrangement From the Modern Literary Usage With Primary Reference to the Position of the Verb. 1910. pap. text ed. 29.50x (ISBN 0-686-83611-1). Elliots Bks.
Edwards, Mark U., Jr. Luther's Last Battles: Politics & Polemics, 1531-46. 272p. 1983. 19.95x (ISBN 0-8014-1564-0). Cornell U Pr.
Kolb, R. & Lumpp, D. Martin Luther: Companion of the Contemporary Christian. LC 12-2959. 1982. pap. 8.95 (ISBN 0-686-99857-X). Concordia.
Manns, Peter. Martin Luther: An Illustrated Biography. (Illus.). 128p. 1983. 14.95 (ISBN 0-8245-0563-8). Crossroad NY.
Olin, John C. & Smart, James D., eds. Luther, Erasmus, & the Reformation: A Catholic-Protestant Reappraisal. LC 82-15500. x, 150p. 1982. Repr. of 1969 ed. lib. bdg. 22.50x (ISBN 0-313-23652-6, 0LLE). Greenwood.
Olivier, D. Luther's Faith: The Cause of the Gospel in the Church. LC 12-2961. 1982. pap. 12.95 (ISBN 0-570-03868-5). Concordia.
Proterra, Michael. Homo Spiritualis Nititur Fide: Martin Luther & Ignatius of Loyola, an Analytical & Comparative Study of a Hermeneutic Based on the Heuristic Structure of Discretio. LC 82-21837. 92p. (Orig.). 1983. lib. bdg. 17.50 (ISBN 0-8191-2938-0); pap. text ed. 7.25 (ISBN 0-8191-2939-9). U Pr of Amer.
Robbert, G. S. Luther as Interpreter of Scripture. LC 12-2960. 1982. pap. 8.95 (ISBN 0-570-03867-7). Concordia.
LUTHERAN CHURCH-ADDRESSES, ESSAYS, LECTURES
Pasolini, Pier P. Lutheran Letters. Hood, Stuart, tr. from Ital. 192p. 1983. text ed. 14.75x (ISBN 0-85635-410-4, Pub. by Carcanet New Pr England). Humanities.
LUTHERAN CHURCH-DOCTRINAL AND CONTROVERSIAL WORKS
Braaten, Carl E. Principles of Lutheran Theology. LC 82-16542. 160p. 1983. pap. 8.95 (ISBN 0-8006-1689-8). Fortress.
LUTHERAN CHURCH-MISSOURI SYNOD
see Evangelical Lutheran Synod of Missouri, Ohio and other states
LUTHERANS IN NORTH AMERICA
Jones, George F. & Savalle, Don, eds. Detailed Reports on the Salzburger Emigrants Who Settled in America, Vol. 7, 1740. (Wormsloe Foundation Ser.). 328p. 1983. 25.00x (ISBN 0-8203-0664-9). U of Ga Pr.
LUXEMBURG, ROSA, 1870-1919
Dunayavskaya, Raya. Rosa Luxemburg, Women's Liberation & Marx's Philosophy of Revolution. 260p. 1982. text ed. 19.95x (ISBN 0-391-02569-4, Pub. by Harvester England); pap. text ed. 10.95x (ISBN 0-391-02793-X). Humanities.
LUXEMBURG-DESCRIPTION AND TRAVEL-GUIDEBOOKS
Fodor's Belgium & Luxembourg: 1983. 336p. 1983. traveltex 12.95 (ISBN 0-679-00898-5). McKay.
Michelin Green Guide: Beilgie-Luxemburg. (Green Guide Ser.). (Dutch.). 1983. pap. write for info. (ISBN 2-06-055131-5). Michelin.
Tomes, John. Belgium & Luxembourg. 6th ed. (Blue Guides Ser.). (Illus.). 1983. 25.50 (ISBN 0-393-01656-0); pap. 14.95 (ISBN 0-393-30063-3). Norton.
LYCANTHROPY
see Werewolves
LYMPHATIC SYSTEM
see Lymphatics
LYMPHATICS
see also Sarcoidosis
Kinmonth, J. B. The Lymphatics: Surgery, Lymphography & Diseases of the Chyle & Lymph Systems. 432p. 1982. text ed. 14.95 (ISBN 0-7131-4410-6). E Arnold.
Nieuwenhuis, Paul & Van den Brock, A. A., eds. In Vivo Immunology: Histophysiology of the Lymphoid System. (Advances in Experimental Medicine & Biology). 900p. 1982. 95.00x (ISBN 0-306-41039-7, Plenum Pr). Plenum Pub.
LYMPHOMA
Burg, G. & Braun-Falco, O. Cutaneous Lymphomas, Pseudolymphomas, & Related Disorders. (Illus.). 550p. 1983. 135.00 (ISBN 0-387-10467-4). Springer-Verlag.
LYMPHOID TISSUE
Reynolds, G. J. Lymphoid Tissue: Institute of Medical Laboratory Sciences Monographs. (Illus.). 128p. 1982. pap. 10.00 (ISBN 0-7236-0645-5). Wright-PSG.
LYRIC DRAMA
see Opera
LYRIC POETRY
see Poetry
LYTLE, ANDREW NELSON, 1902-
Kramer, Victor A. & Bailey, Patricia A. Andrew Lytle, Walker Percy, Peter Taylor: A Reference Guide. 1983. lib. bdg. 39.00 (ISBN 0-8161-8399-6, Hall Reference). G K Hall.

M

M. G. AUTOMOBILE
see Automobiles, Foreign-Types-M. G.
MACARONI WHEAT
see Wheat
MACARTHUR, DOUGLAS, 1880-1964
Cortesi, Lawrence. The Deadly Skies. 1983. pap. 3.25 (ISBN 0-8217-1132-6). Zebra.
MCCARTHY, JOSEPH RAYMOND, 1909-1957
Oshinsky, David M. Conspiracy So Immense: The World of Joe McCarthy. (Illus.). 288p. 1983. 19.95 (ISBN 0-02-923490-5). Free Pr.
MACHINE DATA STORAGE AND RETRIEVAL SYSTEMS
see Information Storage and Retrieval Systems
MACHINE DESIGN
see Machinery-Design
MACHINE EMBROIDERY
see Embroidery
MACHINE INTELLIGENCE
see Artificial Intelligence
MACHINE LANGUAGE
see Programming Languages (Electronic Computers)
MACHINE QUILTING
see Quilting
MACHINE-SHOP MATHEMATICS
see Shop Mathematics
MACHINE SHOPS-AUTOMATION
Blythe, Hal T., et al. Competencies in Materials Development & Machine Operation, Self Directive Activities: A Functional Approach. 2nd ed. (Illus.). 173p. 1982. pap. text ed. 6.95x (ISBN 0-686-43235-5). American Pr.
MACHINE SHORTHAND
see Stenotypy
MACHINE THEORY
see also Artificial Intelligence; Automata; Coding Theory; Control Theory; Computers
Mayr, D. & Sussmann, G. Space, Time, & Mechanics. 1983. lib. bdg. 34.95 (ISBN 90-277-1525-4, Pub. by Reidel Holland). Kluwer Boston.
Wilson, Charles E., et al. Kinematics & Dynamics of Machinery. 752p. 1983. text ed. 33.50 scp (ISBN 0-06-044437-1, HarpC); solutions manual avail. (ISBN 0-06-364577-7). Har-Row.
MACHINE-TOOLS
see also Jigs and Fixtures; Manufacturing Processes
also specific machine tools, e.g. Planning Machines
American Machinist Magazine. Tools of Our Trade. LC 82-7773. 1982. 33.95 (ISBN 0-07-001547-3, P&RB). McGraw.
Oliver, C. Operations Manual for Machine Tool Technology. 272p. 1982. pap. 15.95 (ISBN 0-471-04744-9). Wiley.
MACHINE-TOOLS, AUTOMATIC
see Machine-Tools
MACHINERY
see also Bearings (Machinery); Construction Equipment; Electric Engineering; Electric Machinery; Engines; Friction; Gearing; Hydraulic Machinery; Inventions; Locomotives; Lubrication and Lubricants; Machine-Tools; Mechanical Drawing; Mechanical Engineering; Mechanics; Patents; Replacement of Industrial Equipment; Sealing (Technology); Shafting; Windmills
also machinery used in particular industries or for special purposes, e.g. Agricultural Machinery; Calculating Machines
Barron, D. Assemblers & Loaders. 3rd ed. 1978. 22.00 (ISBN 0-444-19462-2). Elsevier.
Iliffe, J. Basic Machine Principles. 2nd ed. 1972. 10.50 (ISBN 0-444-19582-3). Elsevier.
International Conference on Mining Machinery: 1979, 2 vols. 581p. (Orig.). 1979. pap. text ed. 67.50x (ISBN 0-85825-113-2, Pub. by Inst Engineering Australia). Renouf.
Ormerod, Allan. Modern Preparation & Weaving Machinery. new ed. 296p. text ed. 49.95 (ISBN 0-408-01212-9). Butterworth.
Orth, Samuel P. Boss & the Machine. 1919. text ed. 8.50x (ISBN 0-686-83493-3). Elliots Bks.
Reliability of Large Machines. 116p. (Orig.). 1982. pap. text ed. 37.50x (ISBN 0-85825-170-1, Pub. by Inst Engineering Australia). Renouf.
Rexford, Kenneth. Electrical Control for Machines. 2nd ed. 384p. 1983. pap. text ed. 24.00 (ISBN 0-8273-2175-9); lab manual 8.00 (ISBN 0-8273-2177-5); write for info. instr's guide (ISBN 0-8273-2176-7). Delmar.
Ritter, Collett. Men of the Machine. (Illus.). 254p. 1977. 8.95 (ISBN 0-913428-28-0). Landfall Pr.
Sethi, G. S. & Kakkar, K. C. Workshop Calculations. 150p. Date not set. 2.00x (ISBN 0-07-451903-4). McGraw.
Stoss, John. Machines Always Existed. 1983. 8.95 (ISBN 0-916620-57-3). Portals Pr.
Who Makes Machinery? West Germany, 1982. 44th ed. LC 53-30391. 884p. 1982. pap. 15.00x (ISBN 3-87362-019-7). Intl Pubns serv.
MACHINERY-DESIGN
see also Human Engineering
Juvinall, Robert C. Fundamentals of Machine Component Design. 700p. 1983. text ed. 29.95 (ISBN 0-471-06485-8); tchr's. manual avail. (ISBN 0-471-89556-3). Wiley.
MACHINERY-VIBRATION
Applied Mechanics Workshop: Machinery, Vibration & Noise. 75p. (Orig.). 1978. pap. text ed. 24.00x (ISBN 0-85825-091-8, Pub. by Inst Engineering Australia). Renouf.
Bramer, T. C., et al. Basic Vibration Control. 1978. pap. 19.95x (ISBN 0-419-11440-8, Pub. by E & FN Spon England). Methuen Inc.
Srinivasan, R. Mechanical Vibration Analysis. 480p. Date not set. 9.00x (ISBN 0-07-451932-8). McGraw.
MACHINERY AND CIVILIZATION
see Technology and Civilization
MACHINERY IN INDUSTRY
see also Automation; Division of Labor; Labor Productivity; Technological Innovations
Cooper, C. A. & Clark, J. A., eds. Employment, Economics & Technology: The Impact of Technological Change on the Labor Market. LC 82-42543. 180p. 1982. 25.00x (ISBN 0-312-24459-2). St Martin.
MACHINES
see Machinery
MACHINING OF METALS
see Metal-Work
MACKINAC-HISTORY
Gringhuis, Dirk, et al. Mackinac History, Vol. 2. (Illus.). 76p. (Orig.). 1982. pap. 5.00 (ISBN 0-911872-34-5). Mackinac Island.
MACNEICE, LOUIS
Marsack, Robyn. The Cave of Making: The Poetry of Louis MacNeice. 140p. 1982. 17.95 (ISBN 0-19-811718-3). Oxford U Pr.
MACRAME
Spencer, Chas. L. Knots, Splices, & Fancy Work. 1981. 25.00x (ISBN 0-85174-157-6, Pub. by Brown, Son & Ferguson). State Mutual Bk.
MACROBIOTIC DIET
Kushi, Michio. The Macrobiotic Diet & Exercise Book. 176p. 1983. pap. 7.95 (ISBN 0-686-43184-7). Avery Pub.
MACROBIOTICS
see Macrobiotic Diet
MACROECONOMICS
Anderson, W. H. & Putallaz, Ann. Macroeconomics. (Illus.). 480p. 1983. pap. text ed. 16.95 (ISBN 0-13-542811-4). P-H.
Branson. Macroeconomica. 2nd ed. 436p. (Span.). 1981. pap. text ed. write for info. (Pub. by HarLA Mexico). Har-Row.
Dadayan, V. S. Macroeconomic Models. 208p. 1981. 7.00 (ISBN 0-8285-2271-5, Pub. by Progress Pubs USSR). Imported Pubns.
Fischer, S. & Dornbusch, R. Introduction to Macroeconomics. 608p. 1983. 15.95 (ISBN 0-07-021005-5). McGraw.
Laidler, David. Monetarist Perspectives. 224p. 1983. text ed. 20.00x (ISBN 0-674-58240-3). Harvard U Pr.

Mansfield, Edwin. Principles of Macroeconomics. 4th ed. 600p. 1982. text ed. 14.95x (ISBN 0-393-95266-5). Norton.
--Principles of Macroeconomics: Reading Issues & Cases. 4th ed. 1982. text ed. write for info (ISBN 0-393-95340-8); write for info study guide. Norton.
Miller. Macroeconomics. 1983. text ed. 23.95 (ISBN 0-686-84543-9, EC56); instr's manual avail. (EC58); study guide 8.95 (ISBN 0-686-84544-7, EC58). HM.
Mishkin, Frederic S. A Rational Expectations Approach to Macroeconomics: Testing Policy Ineffectiveness & Efficient-Markets Models. LC 82-20049. (National Bureau of Economic Research-Monograph). 192p. 1983. lib. bdg. 20.00x (ISBN 0-226-53186-4). U of Chicago Pr.
Peston, Maurice. Whatever Happened to Macro-Economics? 96p. 1982. pap. 4.95 (ISBN 0-7190-0796-8). Manchester.
Salant, Michael A. Post Keynesian Macrodynamics: A More General Theory. LC 82-99901. (Illus.). 170p. 1982. write for info. (ISBN 0-9609288-1-2); pap. write for info. (ISBN 0-9609288-0-4). M A Salant.
Sayer, Staurt. Introduction to Macroeconomic Policy. 320p. 1982. text ed. 17.95 (ISBN 0-408-10779-0). Butterworth.
Taylor, Lance. Structuralist Macroeconomics: Applicable Models for the Third World. 1983. text ed. 18.95x (ISBN 0-465-08239-4). Basic.
Vane, H. & Thompson, J. An Introduction to Macroeconomic Policy. 317p. 1982. text ed. 27.50x (ISBN 0-7108-0130-0, Pub. by Harvester England). Humanities.

MACROMOLECULES

Bovey, F. A. & Winslow, F. H., eds. Macromolecules: Student Edition. 576p. 1982. pap. 23.00 (ISBN 0-12-119756-5). Acad Pr.
Bovey, Frank A. & Jelinski, Lynn W., eds. Chain Structure & Conformation of Macromolecules. LC 82-20779. (Monograph). 1982. 19.50 (ISBN 0-12-119780-8). Acad Pr.
Dixon, W. G. Special Relativity: The Foundation of Macroscopic Physics. LC 77-83991. (Illus.). 261p. 1982. pap. 19.95 (ISBN 0-521-27241-6). Cambridge U Pr.
Die Makronomolekulare Chemise: Supplements 2 & 3, 2 vols. 589p. 1979. pap. 55.00 set (ISBN 0-686-83931-5). Transbooks.

MACROPHAGES

Koren. Macrophage-Mediated Antibody... (Immunology Ser.). 384p. 1983. price not set (ISBN 0-8247-7011-0). Dekker.
Normann, Sigurd J. & Sorkin, Ernst, eds. Macrophages & Natural Killer Cells. (Advances in Experimental Medicine & Biology: Vol. 155). 849p. 1982. 95.00x (ISBN 0-306-41180-6, Plenum Pr). PLenum Pub.

MACROPHOTOGRAPHY

see also Photomicrography
White, William. Photomacrography. 1983. 49.95x (ISBN 0-240-51189-1). Focal Pr.

MACY, ANNE (SULLIVAN)-1866-1936

Keller, Helen. Teacher: Anne Sullivan Macy, a Tribute by the Foster-Child of Her Mind. 1982. Repr. of 1955 ed. 17.00 (ISBN 0-89783-025-3). Larlin Corp.

MADONNA

see Mary, Virgin

MADRID-DESCRIPTION-GUIDEBOOKS

Fodor's Madrid. (Illus.). 128p. 1983. pap. 4.95 (ISBN 0-679-00965-5). McKay.

MAECENATISM

see Art Patronage

MAFIA

Reuter, Peter. Monopoly & the Mafia. 228p. 1983. 17.50 (ISBN 0-262-18107-X). MIT Pr.

MAGAZINE ADVERTISING

see Advertising, Magazine

MAGAZINES

see Periodicals

MAGIC

Here are entered works dealing with occult science (supernatural arts). Works on modern parlor magic, legerdemain, prestidigitation, etc. are entered under the heading Conjuring.
see also Alchemy; Cabala; Conjuring; Idols and Images; Medicine, Magic, Mystic, and Spagiric; Occult Sciences; Symbolism of Numbers; Tantrism; Witchcraft
Adrion. Art of Magic. Date not set. pap. 3.95 (ISBN 0-8120-2086-3). Barron.
Crowley, Aleister & Regardie, Israel. Magick Without Tears. 3rd ed. 560p. 1982. 49.94 (ISBN 0-941404-16-1); pap. 13.95 (ISBN 0-941404-17-X). Falcon Pr Az.
Junior League of Birmingham, Alabama, et al, eds. Magic. 348p. 1982. 9.95 (ISBN 0-686-43391-2). Magic.
Lamb, Geoffrey. Magic, Witchcraft & the Occult. (Illus.). 176p. 1982. Repr. of 1977 ed. pap. 9.95 (ISBN 0-88254-705-4). Hippocrene Bks.
Regardie, Israel. The Complete Golden Dawn System of Magic, 2 vols. 1200p. 1983. Vol. 1. 59.54 (ISBN 0-941404-12-9); Vol. 1. collector's ed. 150.00 (ISBN 0-941404-11-0); Vol. 2. 59.95 (ISBN 0-941404-14-5); Vol. 2. collector's ed. 150.00 (ISBN 0-941404-13-7). Falcon Pr Az.
--Eye in the Triangle. 523p. 1982. 49.95 (ISBN 0-941404-07-2); pap. 12.95 (ISBN 0-941404-08-0). Falcon Pr Az.
--Foundations of Practical Magic. 160p. 1983. pap. 6.95 (ISBN 0-85030-315-X). Newcastle Pub.
--Gems from the Equinox. 1100p. 1982. Repr. of 1974 ed. 39.95 (ISBN 0-941404-10-2). Falcon Pr Az.
--What You Should Know About the Golden Dawn. 3rd, rev. ed. 220p. 1983. pap. 10.95 (ISBN 0-941404-15-3). Falcon Pr Az.
Riva, Anna. Candle Burning Magic. 96p. 1980. pap. 3.50 (ISBN 0-943832-06-3). Intl Imports.
--Devotions to the Saints. 112p. 1982. pap. 3.50 (ISBN 0-943832-08-X). Intl Imports.
--Golden Secrets of Mystic Oils. 64p. 1978. pap. 3.50 (ISBN 0-943832-05-5). Intl Imports.
--Modern Herbal Spellbook. (Illus.). 1974. pap. 3.00 (ISBN 0-943832-03-9). Intl Imports.
--Secrets of Magical Seals. (Illus.). 64p. 1975. pap. 3.50 (ISBN 0-943832-04-7). Intl Imports.
Zarathustra, Frater, pseud. The What & Why of Magick. LC 82-91047. 48p. 1982. pap. 4.00 (ISBN 0-939856-30-1). Tech Group.

MAGIC-JUVENILE LITERATURE

Hammond, Bernice. Hokus-Pokus the Goodwill Pixie. Davis, Audrey, ed. (Illus.). 110p. 1981. text ed. 10.50 (ISBN 0-9609398-0-6). Assn Preserv.
White, Nelson & White, Anne. Secret Magic Revealed. 2nd ed ed. LC 82-50720. (Illus.). 120p. (Orig.). 1982. pap. 25.00 (ISBN 0-939856-29-8). Tech Group.

MAGISTRATES

see Judges

MAGNESIUM

Bennett, W. A. Character & Tonnage of the Turk Magnesite Deposit. (Reports of Investigations Ser.: No. 7). (Illus.). 1943. 0.25 (ISBN 0-686-38465-2). Geologic Pubns.

MAGNESIUM METABOLISM

Altura, B. M. & Altura, Bella T., eds. Dietary Minerals & Cardiovascular Disease. (Journal: Magnesium: Vol. 1, No. 3-6). (Illus.). vi, 178p. 1983. pap. 78.00 (ISBN 3-8055-3682-8). S Karger.

MAGNETIC FIELDS

see also Magnetic Resonance
Howard, Robert & Bumba, V. Atlas of Solar Magnetic Fields. 1967. 10.00 (ISBN 0-87279-637-X). Carnegie Inst.
Loewinsohn, Ron. Magnetic Field(s) LC 82-48879. 1983. 12.95 (ISBN 0-394-53105-1). Knopf.

MAGNETIC RECORDERS AND RECORDING

see also Video Tape Recorders and Recording
Gardner. Master Creative Tape Recording. (Illus.). 1977. pap. 9.95 (ISBN 0-408-00244-1). Focal Pr.
Sinclair. Beginner's Guide to Tape Recording. (Illus.). 1978. pap. 9.95 (ISBN 0-408-00330-8). Focal Pr.
--Master Stereo Cassette Recording. (Illus.). 1976. pap. 9.95 (ISBN 0-408-00238-7). Focal Pr.

MAGNETIC RESONANCE

see also Electron Paramagnetic Resonance; Nuclear Magnetic Resonance
Cohen, Jack S. Magnetic Resonance in Biology, Vol. 2. (Magnetic Resonance in Biology Ser.). 280p. 1983. price not set (ISBN 0-471-05175-6, Pub. by Wiley-Interscience). Wiley.
Waugh, J. S., ed. Advances in Magnetic Resonance, Vol. 11. Date not set. price not set (ISBN 0-12-025511-1); price not set lib. ed. (ISBN 0-12-025580-4); price not set microfiche (ISBN 0-12-025581-2). Acad Pr.

MAGNETIC RESONANCE, NUCLEAR

see Nuclear Magnetic Resonance

MAGNETISM

see also Electricity; Electromagnetic Theory; Electromagnetism
also headings beginning with the word Magnetic
Marson, Ron. Magnetism. (Science with Simple Things Ser.: No. 33). (Illus.). 80p. 1983. pap. 12.95 (ISBN 0-941008-33-9). Tops Learning.

MAGNETOHYDRODYNAMICS

see also Ion Flow Dynamics; Plasma Dynamics
Priest, E. Solar Magnetohydrodynamics. 1982. lib. bdg. 99.00 (ISBN 90-277-1374-X, Pub. by Reidel Holland). Kluwer Boston.

MAGNETS-JUVENILE LITERATURE

Adler, David. Amazing Magnets. LC 82-17377. (Question & Answer Bks.). (Illus.). 32p. (gr. 3-6). 1983. PLB 8.59 (ISBN 0-89375-894-9); pap. text ed. 1.95 (ISBN 0-89375-895-7). Troll Assocs.

MAGNOLIA

Biggs, Margaret K. Magnolias & Such. (Illus.). 1982. 2.00 (ISBN 0-943696-00-3). Red Key Pr.

MAGRITTE, RENE, 1898-1967

Lanchner, Carolyn & Rosenstock, Laura. Four Modern Masters: De Chirico, Ernst, Magritte, & Miro. (Illus.). 122p. 1982. pap. 14.95 (ISBN 0-686-83914-5, 28738-6). U of Chicago Pr.

MAGYAR LANGUAGE

see Hungarian Language

MAGYAR LITERATURE

see Hungarian Literature (Collections)

MAH JONG

Walters, Derek, ed. Your Future Revealed by the Maj Jongg. 192p. 1983. pap. 9.95 (ISBN 0-85030-290-0). Newcastle Pub.

MAHAKA

see Tobacco

MAHAYANA BUDDHISM

Chang, Garma C., ed. A Treasury of Mahayana Sutras: Selections from the Maharatnakuta Sutra. Buddhist Association of the United States, tr. from Chinese. LC 82-42776. (Institute for Advanced Study of World Religion (IASWR) Ser.). 640p. 1983. 22.50x (ISBN 0-271-00341-3). Pa St U Pr.

MAHOMET THE PROPHET

see Mohammed, the Prophet, 570-632

MAIDEN AUNTS

see Single Women

MAIL-ORDER BUSINESS

see also Advertising-Direct-Mail
Brumbaugh, J. Frank. Mail Order Make Easy. Date not set. pap. 10.00 (ISBN 0-87980-394-0). Wilshire.
Farlow, George. How to Successfully Sell Information by Mail. 120p. 1982. pap. 10.00 (ISBN 0-936300-05-1). Pr Arden Park.
Goldstein, Sue. The Underground Shopper: A Guide to Discount Mail-Order Shopping. 260p. 1983. pap. 5.95 (ISBN 0-8362-7915-8). Andrews & McMeel.
Hoge, Cecil C., Sr. Mail Order Know-How. LC 82-50903. 472p. 1982. 19.95 (ISBN 0-89815-016-7); pap. 16.95 (ISBN 0-89815-015-9). Ten Speed Pr.
Jones, E. R. The Business Guide to Selling Information by Mail. (Illus.). 110p. 1982. 15.00 (ISBN 0-9600934-4-3). E R Jones.
Schwartz, Eugene M. Mail Order: How to Get Your Share of the Hidden Profits That Exist in Your Business. 288p. 1982. 50.00 (ISBN 0-932648-33-9). Boardroom.

MAIL PLANES

see Transport Planes

MAIL SERVICE

see Postal Service

MAIMONIDES

see Moses ben Maimon, 1135-1204

MAINE

Chase, Virginia. Speaking of Maine: A Selection from the Writings of Virginia Chase. Shea, Margaret, ed. (Illus.). 128p. (Orig.). 1983. pap. price not set (ISBN 0-89272-164-2). Down East.

MAINE-DESCRIPTION AND TRAVEL

Calvert, Mary. Maine Captured in Color. (Illus.). 120p. 1982. 12.95 (ISBN 0-9609914-0-9). M Calvert.
Cayford, John E. Fort Knox-Fortress of Maine. 120p. 1983. write for info. Cay Bel.
Gibson, John. Fifty Hikes in Maine: Day Hikes & Backpacking Trips from the Coast to Katahdin. 2nd, rev. ed. LC 82-25276. (Fifty Hikes Ser.). (Illus.). 192p. (Orig.). 1983. pap. 8.95 (ISBN 0-942440-13-7). Backcountry Pubns.
Wheelwright, Thea. Along the Maine Coast. 128p. 1981. 9.98 (ISBN 0-517-14160-4). Crown.

MAINE-GENEALOGY

Ames, Agnes. Ames Ancestry-Europe to Maine. enl. ed. LC 79-91192. 210p. 1982. pap. 20.00 (ISBN 0-941216-05-5). Cay Bel.
Hoffman, Donna. Bucksport Vital Records. LC 82-73244. 125p. 1982. pap. 14.95 (ISBN 0-941216-03-9). Cay-Bel.

MAINE-HISTORY

Agger, Lee. Women of Maine. (Illus.). 250p. 1982. pap. 10.95 (ISBN 0-930096-21-5). G Gannett.
Caldwell, Bill. Islands of Maine: Where America Really Began. LC 81-81541. (Illus.). 240p. 1981. 12.95 (ISBN 0-930096-17-7). G Gannett.
Cayford, John E. Fort Knox-Fortress of Maine. 120p. 1983. write for info. Cay Bel.
--Maine's Hall of Fame, Vol. 1. 300p. 1983. write for info. Cay Bel.
Clifford, Harold B. The Boothbay Region, 1906-1960. LC 61-14423. (Illus.). 368p. 1982. Repr. of 1961 ed. 15.95 (ISBN 0-87027-204-7). Cumberland Pr.
Merrill, Daphne W. A Salute to Maine. 1983. 12.95 (ISBN 0-533-05534-2). Vantage.
Niss, Bob. Faces of Maine. (Illus., Orig.). 1982. pap. 8.95 (ISBN 0-930096-20-7). G Gannett.
Williamson, Joseph. The History of the City of Belfast, Maine. Belfast Free Library, ed. LC 82-60448. (Illus.). 956p. 1982. Repr. of 1877 ed. 50.00 (ISBN 0-89725-035-4). NE History.

MAINSTREAMING IN EDUCATION

Roffman, Arlyn J. The Classroom Teacher's Guide to Mainstreaming. (Illus.). 112p. 1983. 14.75x (ISBN 0-398-04786-3). C C Thomas.

MAINTENANCE

see also Plant Maintenance
Bullock, James H. Maintenance Planning & Control. 146p. pap. 12.95 (ISBN 0-86641-026-0, 79113). Natl Assn Accts.

MAINTENANCE (DOMESTIC RELATIONS)

see Support (Domestic Relations)

MAIZE

see Corn

MAJOR ORDERS

see Clergy

MAJORCA-DESCRIPTION AND TRAVEL-GUIDEBOOKS

Magorca & Minorca Travel Guide. (Berlitz Travel Guides). (Illus.). 1982. pap. 4.95 (ISBN 0-02-969350-0, Berlitz). Macmillan.

MAKE-UP (COSMETICS)

see Cosmetics

MAKE-UP, THEATRICAL

Savini, Tom. Grande Illusions: The Art & Technique of Special Make-up Effects. (Illus.). 136p. 1983. pap. 12.95 (ISBN 0-911137-00-9). Imagine.

MAKHORKA

see Tobacco

MALACOLOGY

see Mollusks

MALAYA-HISTORY

Barr, Pat. Taming the Jungle in British Malaya. 1977. 12.50 (ISBN 0-436-03365-8, Pub. by Secker & Warburg). David & Charles.
Yeo Kim Wah. The Politics of Decentralization: Colonial Controversy in Malaya, 1920-1929. 395p. 1982. 34.95 (ISBN 0-19-582524-1). Oxford U Pr.

MALAYSIA

Insight Guides. Malaysia. (Illus.). 304p. 1983. 18.95 (ISBN 0-13-548040-X); pap. 14.95 (ISBN 0-13-547992-4). P-H.

MALAYSIA-HISTORY

Andaya, Leonard & Andaya, Barbara. A History of Malaysia. LC 82-42612. 372p. 1982. 30.00x (ISBN 0-312-38120-4). St Martin.
Chin, Kin Wah. The Defence of Malaysia & Singapore: The Transformation of a Security System 1957-1971. LC 82-4330. (International Studies). 200p. 1983. 39.50 (ISBN 0-521-24325-4). Cambridge U Pr.

MALCOLM X

see Little, Malcolm, 1925-1965

MALDIVE ISLANDS

Maloney, Clarence. People of the Maldive Islands. (Illus.). 432p. 1980. text ed. 27.95x (ISBN 0-86131-158-2, Pub. by Orient Longman Ltd India). Apt Bks.

MALE PHOTOGRAPHY

see Photography of Men

MALEBRANCHE, NICOLAS, 1638-1715

McCracken, Charles J. Malebranche & British Philosophy. (Illus.). 1982. 58.00x (ISBN 0-19-824664-1). Oxford U Pr.

MALESHERBES, CHRETIEN GUILLAUME DE LAMOIGNON DE, 1721-1794

Allison, John M. Lamoignon de Malesherbes: Defender & Reformer of the French Monarchy, 1721-1794. 1938. text ed. 42.50x (ISBN 0-686-83605-7). Elliots Bks.

MALFORMATIONS, CONGENITAL

see Abnormalities, Human

MALI

Mondot-Bernard, J. & Labonne, M. Satisfaction of Food Requirements in Mali to 2000 A. D. 214p. (Orig.). 1982. pap. 15.00x (ISBN 92-64-12300-8). OECD.

MALLARME, STEPHANE, 1842-1898

Cohn, Robert G. Mallarme's un Coup de Des: An Exegesis. 1949. text ed. 24.50x (ISBN 0-686-83613-8). Elliots Bks.

MALLEA, EDVARDO

Mallea, Eduardo. History of an Argentine Passion. Miller, Yvette E., ed. Litchblau, Myron, tr. 184p. 1982. pap. 10.95 (ISBN 0-935480-10-2). Lat Am Lit Rev Pr.

MALNUTRITION

Chen, Lincoln C. & Scrimshaw, Nevin S., eds. Diarrhea & Malnutrition: Interactions, Mechanisms & Interventions. 310p. 1983. 39.50x (ISBN 0-306-41046-X, Plenum Pr). Plenum Pub.

MALORY, THOMAS, SIR, 15TH CENTURY

Ihle, Sandra N. Malory's Grail Quest: Invention & Adaptation in Medieval Prose Romance. LC 82-70554. (Illus.). 224p. 1983. text ed. 22.50 (ISBN 0-299-09240-2). U of Wis Pr.
Wilson, Robert H. Characterization in Malory. 1982. lib. bdg. 34.50 (ISBN 0-686-81923-3). Porter.

MALPRACTICE

Camp, John. One Hundred Years of Medical Murder. 224p. 1983. 12.95 (ISBN 0-370-30354-7, Pub by The Bodley Head). Merrimack Bk Serv.
Dickerson, R. W. Accountants & the Law of Negligence. LC 82-48361. (Accountancy in Transition Ser.). 668p. 1982. lib. bdg. 65.00 (ISBN 0-8240-5312-5). Garland Pub.
Flaster, Donald J. Malpractice: A Guide to the Legal Rights of Doctors & Patients. 256p. 1983. 15.95 (ISBN 0-686-83840-8, ScribT). Scribner.
Kahapea, Alexander. Statute of Limitations on Malpractice. (Illus.). 320p. 1983. 25.00 (ISBN 0-89962-295-X). Todd & Honeywell.

MALTA

Malta Travel Guide. (Berlitz Travel Guides). (Illus.). 1982. pap. 4.95 (ISBN 0-02-969360-8, Berlitz). Macmillan.

MAMMALS

see also Fur-Bearing Animals; Marine Mammals; Primates; Rodentia
also names of families, genera, species, etc.
Baker, Rollin H. Michigan Mammals. (Illus.). 700p. 1982. 60.00 (ISBN 0-686-43260-6). Mich St U Pr.
Conisbee, L. R. A List of Names Proposed for Genera & Subgenera of Recent Mammals from the Publication of T. S. Palmer's Index Generum Mammalium 1904 to the End of 1951. 110p. 1953. 11.00 (ISBN 0-565-00210-4). Sabbot-Natural Hist Bks.
Corbett & Ovenden. The Mammals of Britain & Europe. pap. 15.95 (ISBN 0-686-42745-9, Collins Pub England). Greene.

Eisenberg, J. F. & Kleiman, D. G., eds. Advances in the Study of Mammalian Behavior. (American Society of Mammalogists Special Publication Ser.: No.7). 753p. 1983. 45.00, 36.00 members (ISBN 0-943612-06-3). Am Soc Mammalogists.
Kemp, T. S., ed. Mammal-Like Reptiles & the Origins of Mammals. 384p. 1982. 44.50 (ISBN 0-12-404120-5). Acad Pr.
Kunz, Thomas H., ed. Ecology of Bats. 450p. 1982. 49.50x (ISBN 0-306-40950-X, Plenum Pr). Plenum Pub.
Lawrence, R. D. The Ghost Walker. LC 82-12111. 264p. 1982. 15.95 (ISBN 0-03-061594-1). HR&W.
McFerron, Martha. Mammals. (Science Ser.). 24p. (gr. 3-6). 1982. wkbk. 5.00 (ISBN 0-8209-0161-X, S-23). ESP.
Vandenbergh, John G., ed. Pheromones & Reproduction in Mammals. LC 82-22776. Date not set. price not set (ISBN 0-12-710780-0). Acad Pr.

MAMMALS–JUVENILE LITERATURE
Board, Tessa. Mammals. (Insight Ser.). (Illus.). 40p. (gr. 4 up). 1983. PLB 8.90 (ISBN 0-531-03473-9). Watts.
Crump, Donald J., ed. Giants from the Past. LC 81-47893. (Books for World Explorers: No. IV). 104p. (gr. 3-8). 1983. 6.95 (ISBN 0-87044-424-7); PLB 8.50 (ISBN 0-87044-429-8). Natl Geog.

MAMMALS–AFRICA
Dorst & Dandelot. A Field Guide to the Larger Mammals of Africa. 34.95 (ISBN 0-686-42779-3, Collins Pub England). Greene.
Haltenorth & Diller. A Field Guide to the Mammals of Africa. 34.95 (ISBN 0-686-42780-7, Collins Pub England). Greene.
Schaller, George B. Golden Shadows, Flying Hooves: With a New Afterword. LC 82-23731. (Illus.). 344p. 1983. pap. 9.95 (ISBN 0-226-73632-6). U of Chicago Pr.

MAMMALS–EUROPE
Corbett & Ovenden. The Mammals of Britain & Europe. pap. 15.95 (ISBN 0-686-42745-9, Collins Pub England). Greene.

MAMMALS–GREAT BRITAIN
Corbett & Ovenden. The Mammals of Britain & Europe. pap. 15.95 (ISBN 0-686-42745-9, Collins Pub England). Greene.

MAMMALS–NORTH AMERICA
Baker, Rollin H. Michigan Mammals. (Illus.). 700p. 1982. 60.00 (ISBN 0-87013-234-2). Wayne St U Pr.
Christensen, James R. & Larrison, Earl J. Mammals of the Pacific Northwest. LC 82-60054. (Illus.). 1982. 17.95 (ISBN 0-89301-085-5). U Pr of Idaho.
Jones, J. Knox, Jr., et al. Mammals of the Northern Great Plains. LC 82-2693. (Illus.). 422p. 1983. 32.50x (ISBN 0-8032-2557-1). U of Nebr Pr.
Leopold, A. Starker & Gutierrez, Ralph J. North American Game Birds & Mammals. (Illus.). 208p. 1983. pap. 10.95 (ISBN 0-686-83783-5, ScribT). Scribner.
Olin, George. Mammals of the Southwest Desert. Rev. ed. Houk, Rose, et al, eds. LC 81-86094. (Illus.). 104p. 1982. pap. 5.95 (ISBN 0-911408-60-6). SW Pks Mnmts.
Southard, Doris. North American Game Birds & Mammals. (Illus.). 224p. 1983. pap. 10.95 (ISBN 0-686-83781-9, ScribT). Scribner.

MAMMARY GLANDS
see also Breast
Georgiade, Nicholas G. Aesthetic Breast Surgery. (Illus.). 378p. 1983. lib. bdg. price not set (ISBN 0-683-03450-2). Williams & Wilkins.

MAN
see also Anthropology; Color of Man; Creation; Ethnology; Heredity; Human Biology; Men; Philosophical Anthropology; Women
Hickey, Denis. Home from Exile: An Approach to Post-Existentialist Philosophizing. LC 82-20059. 504p. (Orig.). (gr. 2-5). 1983. lib. bdg. 29.50 (ISBN 0-8191-2848-1); pap. text ed. 17.75 (ISBN 0-8191-2849-X). U Pr of Amer.
Hocking, William E. Man & the State. 1926. text ed. 19.50x (ISBN 0-686-83615-4). Elliots Bks.
Trigg, Roger. The Shaping of Man: Philosophical Aspects of Sociobiology. LC 82-16868. 208p. 1983. 14.95 (ISBN 0-8052-3840-9). Schocken.

MAN–FOOD HABITS
see Food Habits

MAN–INFLUENCE OF ENVIRONMENT
see also Anthropo-Geography; Color of Man; Environmental Health; Genetic Psychology; Regionalism
Barnes, Bernard. Man & the Changing Landscape. (Work Notes 3). (Illus.). 144p. pap. text ed. 14.00x (ISBN 0-906367-12-3, Merseyside County Mus of Liverpool England). Smithsonian.
Fedoseyev, P. & Timofeyev, T. Social Problems of Man's Enviornment: Where We Live & Work. 334p. 1981. 8.50 (ISBN 0-8285-2273-1, Pub. by Progress Pubs USSR). Imported Pubns.
Griffiths, John F. Climate & the Environment: The Atmospheric Impact on Man. LC 76-5801. (Westview Environmental Studies Ser.: Vol. 2). 1976. pap. text ed. 11.00 (ISBN 0-236-40022-3). Westview.
Hanley, W. S. & Cooper, M. J. Man & the Australian Environment. 362p. 1981. 22.00x (ISBN 0-07-072952-2). McGraw.
Kaplan. Cognition & Environment. 304p. 1982. 29.95 (ISBN 0-03-062344-8); pap. 13.95 (ISBN 0-03-062346-4). Praeger.
McClanahan, Ed. The Natural Man. 1983. 11.95 (ISBN 0-374-21969-9). FS&G.

MAN–INFLUENCE ON NATURE
see also Environmental Policy; Pollution
Barnes, Bernard. Man & the Changing Landscape. (Work Notes 3). (Illus.). 144p. pap. text ed. 14.00x (ISBN 0-906367-12-3, Merseyside County Mus of Liverpool England). Smithsonian.
Bennett, Charles F., Jr. Man & Earth's Ecosystems: An Introduction to the Geography of Human Modification of the Earth. LC 75-22330. 331p. 1976. text ed. 27.50x (ISBN 0-471-06638-9). Wiley.
Drew, David. Man-Environment Processes. (Processes in Physical Geography Ser.: No. 6). (Illus.). 152p. 1983. pap. text ed. 9.95x (ISBN 0-04-551063-6). Allen Unwin.
Holzner, W. & Werger, M. J. Man's Impact on Vegetation. 1983. 98.00 (ISBN 90-6193-685-3, Pub. by Junk Pubs Netherlands). Kluwer Boston.
Keith, David. Man & the Natural World. LC 82-14384. (Illus.). 432p. 1983. 19.95 (ISBN 0-394-49945-X). Pantheon.
Straub, Calvin C. The Man-Made Environment. 248p. 1982. pap. text ed. 14.95 (ISBN 0-8403-2903-2). Kendall-Hunt.

MAN–JUVENILE LITERATURE
Lambert, Mark. Rainbow Encyclopedia of Prehistoric Life. (Illus.). 144p. (gr. 4 up). 1982. 9.95 (ISBN 0-528-82388-4). Rand.

MAN–ORIGIN
see also Evolution; Human Evolution; Life–Origin
Discovering the Origins of Man. (Discovering Science Ser.). 1982. lib. bdg. 15.96 (ISBN 0-86706-058-1, Pub. by Stonehenge). Silver.

MAN–PARASITES
see Medical Parasitology

MAN (PHILOSOPHY)
see Philosophical Anthropology

MAN (THEOLOGY)
see also Sex (Theology); Sin; Soul; Work (Theology)
Buck, Peter H. Anthropology & Religion. 1939. text ed. 11.50x (ISBN 0-686-83471-2). Elliots Bks.
Felins, Yehuda. Nature & Man in the Bible: Chapters in Biblical Ecology. 1982. 25.00x (ISBN 0-900689-19-6). Bloch.
Macquarrie, John. In Search of Humanity: A Theological & Philosophical Approach. 288p. 1983. 16.95 (ISBN 0-8245-0564-6). Crossroad NY.
Sanrilippo, Leonardo. The Philosophical Essence of Man. (Illus.). 104p. 1983. 29.95 (ISBN 0-89266-400-2). Am Classical Coll Pr.
Steiner, Rudolf. Man as a Being of Sense & Perception. Lenn, Dorothy, tr. from Ger. 53p. 1981. pap. 6.00 (ISBN 0-919924-11-5, Pub. by Steiner Book Centre Canada). Anthroposophic.
--Man as a Picture of the Living Spirit. Adams, George, tr. from Ger. 31p. (Orig.). 1972. pap. 1.95 (ISBN 0-85440-253-5, Pub. by Steinerbooks). Anthroposophic.
--Man as Symphony of the Creative Word. 3rd ed. Compton-Burnett, Judith, tr. from Ger. 223p. 1978. pap. 10.95 (ISBN 0-85440-324-8, Pub. by Steinerbooks). Anthroposophic.
--Man-Hieroglyph of the Universe. Adams, George & Adams, Mary, trs. from Ger. 221p. 1972. 16.00 (Pub. by Steinerbooks). Anthroposophic.
Tymieniecka, A. T. The Phenomenology of Man & the Human Condition. 1983. lib. bdg. 69.50 (ISBN 90-277-1447-9, Pub. by Reidel Holland). Kluwer Boston.

MAN (THEOLOGY)–BIBLICAL TEACHING
Flynn, Leslie B. What Is Man? 132p. 1983. pap. 4.50 (ISBN 0-88207-104-1). Victor Bks.

MAN, ANTIQUITY OF
see Man–Origin

MAN, DOCTRINE OF
see Man (Theology)

MAN, ERECT POSITION OF
see Posture

MAN, FOSSIL
see Fossil Man

MAN, PREHISTORIC
see also Fossil Man; Glacial Epoch; Lake-Dwellers and Lake-Dwellings; Man–Origin; Paleo-Indians also subdivision Antiquities under names of countries, cities, etc., e.g. Rome (City)–Antiquities
Kennedy, G. E. Paleoanthropology. 1980. 24.95 (ISBN 0-07-034046-3). McGraw.
Skinner, Mark F. & Sperber, Geoffrey H., eds. Atlas of Radiographs of Early Man. LC 82-13989. 346p. 1982. 70.00 (ISBN 0-8451-0218-4). A R Liss.
Trinkaus, Erick, ed. The Sanidar Neandertals. (Monograph). Date not set. price not set (ISBN 0-12-700550-1). Acad Pr.

MAN, PREHISTORIC–JUVENILE LITERATURE
Hart, Angela. Prehistoric Man. (Easy-Read Fact Bk.). (Illus.). 32p. (gr. 2-4). 1983. PLB 8.60 (ISBN 0-531-04511-0). Watts.

MAN, PREHISTORIC–EUROPE
Clark, Geoffrey A. The Asturian of Cantabria: Early Holocene Hunter-Gatherers in Northern Spain. (Anthropological Papers Ser.: No. 41). 160p. 1983. pap. 18.95x monograph (ISBN 0-8165-0800-3). U of Ariz Pr.

MAN AND WIFE
see Husband and Wife

MAN-MACHINE CONTROL SYSTEMS
see Man-Machine Systems

MAN-MACHINE SYSTEMS
Badre, Albert & Shneiderman, Ben, eds. Directions in Human-Computer Interaction. 240p. 1982. text ed. 27.50 (ISBN 0-89391-144-5). Ablex Pub.
Man-Machine Systems. (IEE Conference Publications: No. 212). 280p. 1982. pap. 56.00 (ISBN 0-85296-264-9). Inst Elect Eng.
Wiefels, H., ed. Analysis, Design, & Evaluation of Man-Machine Systems: Proceedings of the IFAC-IFIP-IEA-IFORS Symposium, Baden-Baden, FR Germany, 27-29 September 1982. (IFAC Proceedings Ser.). 550p. 1983. 137.00 (ISBN 0-08-029348-4). Pergamon.

MAN-MADE LAKES
see Reservoirs

MAN ON OTHER PLANETS
see Life on Other Planets

MAN POWER
see Manpower

MAN-TO-MAN COMBAT
see Hand-To-Hand Fighting

MANAGEMENT
see also Business; Campaign Management; Computer Programming Management; Executive Ability; Executives; Factory Management; Farm Management; Hospitals–Administration; Industrial Management; Office Management; Organization; Organizational Change; Personnel Management; Planning; Scheduling (Management); School Management and Organization also subdivision management under specific subjects, e.g. Railroads–Management
Advanced Management Programme: An Indian Example. (Management Development Manual Ser.: No. 32). (Illus.). 124p. 1969. 5.70 (ISBN 0-686-84662-1). Intl Labour Office.
Anderson, R. G. Management, Planning & Control. 400p. 1981. 35.00x (ISBN 0-7121-1277-4, Pub. by Macdonald & Evans). State Mutual Bk.
Awani, Alfred O. Project Management Techniques. (Illus.). 192p. 19.95 (ISBN 0-89433-197-3). Petrocelli.
Beck, John & Cox, Charles. Advances in Management Education. LC 80-40117. 360p. 1980. 48.00x (ISBN 0-471-27775-4, Pub. by Wiley-Interscience). Wiley.
Belasco, James A. & Hampton, David R. Management Today. 2nd ed. LC 80-28981. 460p. 1981. text ed. 22.95 (ISBN 0-471-08579-0); avail. tchrs. manual. Wiley.
Bettencourt, Vladimir. New Discoveries in the Psychology of Management. (Research Center for Economic Psychology Library). (Illus.). 148p. 1983. 59.75 (ISBN 0-86654-061-X). Inst Econ Finan.
Bloomfield, Horace R. Female Executives & the Degeneration of Management. (Illus.). 129p. 1983. 59.85 (ISBN 0-86654-063-6). Inst Econ Finan.
Bourland, Gary N. An Executive Primer: The Management Club. 15p. 1983. spiral 5.95x (ISBN 0-9609350-0-2). Management Club.
Bowling, W Kerby & Loving, Waldon. Management Fumbles & Union Recoveries. 232p. 1982. pap. text ed. 12.95 (ISBN 0-8403-2775-7). Kendall-Hunt.
Boyle, Denis & Bradick, Bill. The Challenge of Change: Developing Business Leaders for the 1980s. 45p. 1961. pap. text ed. 10.00x (ISBN 0-566-02283-4). Gower Pub Ltd.
Brown, Warren B. & Moberg, Dennis G. Organization & Management. LC 79-18709. (Management Ser.). 685p. 1980. text ed. 27.95 (ISBN 0-471-02023-0). Wiley.
Burack, Elmer H. Managing Careers in Organizations: A Managerial Summary. 150p. (Orig.). 1983. pap. 13.00 (ISBN 0-942560-07-8); pap. text ed. 10.95 (ISBN 0-686-38251-X). Brace-Park.
Burkett, David. Very Good Management: A Guide to Managing-by-Communication. 146p. 1983. 12.95 (ISBN 0-13-941377-4); pap. 6.95 (ISBN 0-13-941369-3). P-H.
Caplan, Edwin H. & Champoux, Joseph E. Cases in Management Accounting: Context & Behavior. 88p. pap. 12.95 (ISBN 0-686-37886-5, 78101). Natl Assn Accts.
Carroll, Stephen J., Jr. & Schuler, Randall S. Human Resources Management in the 1980s. 250p. 1983. pap. text ed. 15.00 (ISBN 0-87179-401-2). BNA.
Chapman, E. N. & Martin, William. Self-Paced Guide for SSK: With Applications for the Hospitality Industry. 3rd ed. 96p. 1982. pap. text ed. 5.95 (ISBN 0-574-20638-8, 13-3638). SRA.
Chapman, E. N. & Williams, Catherine. A Self-Paced Guide to the Health Care Industry to Accompany SSK. 3rd ed. 96p. 1983. pap. text ed. write for info. (ISBN 0-574-20567-5). SRA.
Chua, J. E. & Ling, S. C. The Management of Business. 2nd ed. 1982. 10.00x (ISBN 0-07-099026-3). McGraw.
Cooper, Cary. Psychology & Management. (Psychology for Professional Groups Ser.). 275p. 1981. text ed. 25.00x (ISBN 0-333-31856-0, Pub. by Macmillan England); pap. text ed. 10.95x (ISBN 0-333-31875-7). Humanities.
Cope, Robert E. Successful Participative Management in Smaller Companies. 125p. (Orig.). 1982. pap. text ed. 18.00 (ISBN 0-9610044-0-1). QDP Inc.
Copeman, George. The Managing Director. 2nd ed. 283p. 1982. text ed. 36.75x (ISBN 0-09-147280-6, Pub. by Busn Bks England). Renouf.
Davis, Stanley M., ed. Managing & Organizing Multinational Corporations. 516p. 59.00 (ISBN 0-686-84794-6). Work in Amer.
Fallon, William K. AMA Management Handbook. 2nd ed. 1872p. 1983. 69.95 (ISBN 0-8144-0100-7). Am Mgmt.
Fein, Mitchell. Improshare: An Alternative to Traditional Managing. 1981. pap. text ed. 15.00 (ISBN 0-89806-031-1); pap. text ed. 7.50 members. Inst Indus Eng.
Finch, Frank. Concise Encyclopedia of Management Techniques. 1976. 18.95 (ISBN 0-434-90240-3, Pub. by Heinemann). David & Charles.
Fleming, Quentin W. How to Put "Earned Value" into Your Management Control System: A Special Edition Describing the Government's Cost-Schedule Control System Criteria. (Illus.). 350p. (Orig.). 1983. 29.95x (ISBN 0-942280-04-0); pap. 15.95x (ISBN 0-942280-03-2). Pub Horizons.
Ford, Charles H. The Super Executive's Guide to Getting Things Done. 272p. 1983. 14.95 (ISBN 0-8144-5724-X). Am Mgmt.
Franks, J. R. & Broyles, J. E. Modern Managerial Finance. LC 79-83955. 376p. 1979. 45.95 (ISBN 0-471-99751-X); pap. 21.00x (ISBN 0-471-27563-8, Pub. by Wiley-Interscience). Wiley.
Fulmer, Robert M. The New Management. 3rd ed. 544p. 1983. text ed. 20.95 (ISBN 0-02-339740-3). Macmillan.
Gautschi, Theodore. Management Forum, Vol.1. 2nd ed. 1982. pap. 12.95 (ISBN 0-686-83908-0). Lord Pub.
--Management Forum, Vol. 2. pap. 12.95 (ISBN 0-686-83907-2). Lord Pub.
Gee, Edwin A. & Tyler, Chaplin. Managing Innovation. LC 76-7056. 284p. Repr. of 1976 ed. text ed. 21.00 (ISBN 0-471-29503-5). Krieger.
Glassman, Alan M. The Challenge of Management: A Behavioral Orientation. LC 77-16095. 304p. 1978. text ed. 14.95 (ISBN 0-471-02767-7); tchrs. manual o.p. avail. Wiley.
Godiwalla, Yezdi H. Strategic Management: Broadening Business Policy. 320p. 1983. 38.95 (ISBN 0-03-059388-3). Praeger.
Greenland, David. Guidelines for Modern Resource Management. 224p. 1983. pap. text ed. 11.95 (ISBN 0-675-20004-0). Merrill.
Hall, Jay. Ponderables. LC 82-83907. 93p. 1982. pap. text ed. 9.95 (ISBN 0-937932-02-7). Teleometrics.
Harmon, Paul. Successful Management. 224p. 1982. pap. text ed. 14.95 (ISBN 0-8403-2833-8). Kendall-Hunt.
Harper, W. M. & Lim, H. C. Operational Research. (Illus.). 310p. 1982. pap. text ed. 13.50x (ISBN 0-7121-1539-0). Intl Ideas.
Harvey, Don. Business Policy & Strategic Management. 640p. 1982. text ed. 20.95 (ISBN 0-686-84128-X). Additional supplements may be obtained from publisher. Merrill.
Hellriegel, Don & Slocum, John. Organizational Behavior. 3rd ed. (Management Ser.). (Illus.). 700p. 1983. 19.95 (ISBN 0-314-69653-9); tchrs.' manual avail. (ISBN 0-314-71096-5); study guide avail. (ISBN 0-314-71097-3). West Pub.
Hitt, Michael A. & Middlemist, R. Dennis. Management: Concepts & Effective Practices. (Illus.). 650p. 1983. text ed. 21.95 (ISBN 0-314-69654-7); instrs.' manual avail. (ISBN 0-314-71098-1); study guide avail. (ISBN 0-314-71099-X). West Pub.
Horn, R. E. Writing Management Reports. 1979. 375.00 (ISBN 0-686-83947-1). Info Res Inc.
How Japan Absorbed American Management Methods. 37p. pap. 8.25 (ISBN 92-833-1484-0, APO). Unipub.
How to Prepare for the Graduate Management Test (GMAT) 5th ed. 1982. pap. 7.95 (ISBN 0-8120-2553-9). Barron.
Japanese-Style Management: Its Foundations & Prospects. 132p. 1982. pap. 11.75 (ISBN 92-833-1068-3, APO). Unipub.
Johns, Gary. Organizational Behavior: Understanding Life at Work. 1983. text ed. 24.95 (ISBN 0-673-15366-5). Scott F.
Kempin, Frederick G., Jr. & Wiesen, Jeremy L. Legal Aspects of the Management. 3rd ed. (Illus.). 850p. 1983. text ed. 23.95 (ISBN 0-314-69658-X); instrs.' manual avail. (ISBN 0-314-71103-1). West Pub.
Kepner, Charles H. & Tregoe, Benjamin. The Rational Manager. LC 65-21586. 240p. 1976. Repr. of 1965 ed. 14.95 (ISBN 0-686-38777-5). Kepner-Tregoe.
Kepner, Charles H. & Tregoe, Benjamin B. The New Rational Manager. 220p. Date not set. 14.95 (ISBN 0-686-82623-X). Princeton Res Inst.
Kosecoff, Jacqueline & Fink, Arlene. Do-It-Yourself Evaluation: A Practitioner's Guide. (Illus.). 280p. 1982. 29.95 (ISBN 0-8039-1896-8); pap. 14.95 (ISBN 0-8039-1897-6). Sage.
Kowalski, Casimir & Cangemi, Joseph P. Participative Management: A Practical Approach. 1983. 12.50 (ISBN 0-8022-2422-9). Philos Lib.
Kreitner, Robert. Management. 2nd ed. LC 82-83364. 656p. 1982. text ed. 24.94 (ISBN 0-395-32620-6). HM.
Lee. Japanese Management. 318p. 1982. 30.95 (ISBN 0-03-061773-1). Praeger.

--Management by Japanese Systems. 576p. 1982. 31.95 (ISBN 0-03-062051-1). Praeger.

Lee, Sang M. Introduction to Management Science. 736p. 1983. text ed. 28.95 (ISBN 0-686-38856-9). Dryden Pr.

Levin, Dick. Buy Low, Sell High, Collect Early & Pay Late: The Manager's Guide to Financial Survival. (Illus.). 224p. 1983. 15.95 (ISBN 0-13-109439-4). P-H.

Levinson, Robert E. The Decentralized Company: Making the Most of Entrepreneurial Management. 192p. 1982. 15.95 (ISBN 0-8144-5674-X). Am Mgmt.

Lundstedt, Sven B. & Colglazier, E. William, eds. Managing Innovation: The Social Dimensions of Creativity, Invention & Technology. 260p. 29.50 (ISBN 0-686-84788-1). Work in Amer.

McGuire, Joseph W. Theories of Business Behavior. LC 82-15550. xix, 268p. 1982. Repr. of 1964 ed. lib. bdg. 35.00x (ISBN 0-313-23567-8, MCTH). Greenwood.

Machiavelli, Niccolo. Machiavelli's Thoughts on the Management of Men. (A Human Development Library Bk.). (Illus.). 112p. 1983. 49.85 (ISBN 0-86654-053-9). Inst Econ Finan.

McLeod, Raymond, Jr. Management Information Systems. 2nd ed. 160p. 1983. price not set (ISBN 0-574-21410-0, 13-4410); write for info. casebook (ISBN 0-574-21412-7, 13-4412); write for info. tchr's. guide (ISBN 0-574-21411-9, 13-4411). SRA.

Maitland, Ian. The Causes of Industrial Disorder: A Comparison of a British & a German Factory. (Routledge Direct Edition Ser.). 192p. 1983. pap. 12.95 (ISBN 0-7100-9207-5). Routledge & Kegan.

Management Principles: Answers to Questions on Subject Matter, CEBS Course 4. 1982. pap. 15.00 (ISBN 0-89154-172-1). Intl Found Employ.

Management Principles: Learning Guide CEBS Course 4. 1982. spiral binding 18.00 (ISBN 0-89154-171-3). Intl Found Employ.

Martin, Shan. Managing Without Managers: Alternative Work Arrangements in Public Organizations. (Sage Library of Social Research). (Illus.). 176p. 1983. 22.00 (ISBN 0-8039-1960-3); pap. 10.95 (ISBN 0-8039-1961-1). Sage.

Massarik, Fred. Participative Management. 1983. 35.00 (ISBN 0-08-029509-6). Pergamon.

Matthies, Leslie H. Documents to Manage By. LC 82-81937. (Illus.). 1982. 14.00x (ISBN 0-911054-06-5). Office Pubns.

Mayo-Smith, Ian. Managing People: Three International Case Studies. 12p. (Orig.). 1981. pap. 3.95x (ISBN 0-931816-12-2). Kumarian Pr.

Mills, P. Managing for Profit. 160p. 1982. 22.00 (ISBN 0-07-084575-1). McGraw.

Nash, Michael. Managing Organizational Performance. LC 82-49040. (Management & Social & Behavioral Science Ser.). 1983. text ed. price not set (ISBN 0-87589-561-1). Jossey-Bass.

Newman, William H. & Warren, E. Kirby. The Process of Management: Strategy, Action, Results (CPCU Edition) 5th ed. LC 81-11985. 578p. 1982. Repr. of 1982 ed. text ed. 23.00 (ISBN 0-89463-036-9). Am Inst Property.

Novosad, John P. A Management Reference & Guide. 160p. 1982. pap. text ed. 9.95 (ISBN 0-8403-2918-0). Kendall-Hunt.

O'Connor, Dennis J. & Bueso, Alberto T. Personal Financial Management: A Forecasting & Control Approach. (Illus.). 560p. 1983. text ed. 21.95 (ISBN 0-13-657940-X). P-H.

Paine, Frank T. & Anderson, Carl R. Strategic Management. 368p. 1983. text ed. 26.95 (ISBN 0-03-061828-2). Dryden Pr.

Peters, Thomas J. & Waterman, Robert H., Jr. In Search of Excellence: Lessons from America's Best Run Companies. LC 82-47530. (Illus.). 384p. 1982. 19.18i (ISBN 0-06-015042-4, HarpT). Har-Row.

Plunkett, W. Richard. Supervision: The Direction of People at Work. 3rd ed. 400p. 1983. text ed. write for info. (ISBN 0-697-08087-0); instrs.' manual avail. (ISBN 0-697-08095-1). Wm C Brown.

Proctor, Tony. Management: Theory & Principles. 250p. 1982. pap. text ed. 15.95 (ISBN 0-7121-1389-4). Intl Ideas.

Ramey, Ardella & Mrozek, Ronald. A Company Policy & Personnel Workbook. (Successful Business Library). 300p. 1982. 33.95 (ISBN 0-916378-19-5). Pub Serv Inc.

Rao, K. V. Management Science. 552p. Date not set. 8.00x (ISBN 0-07-451975-1). McGraw.

Rosenberg, Jerry M. Dictionary of Business & Management. 2nd. ed. 600p. 1983. 29.95 (ISBN 0-471-86730-6, Pub. by Wiley-Interscience). Wiley.

Rudman, Jack. Program Administrator. (Career Examination Ser.: C-2868). (Cloth bdg. avail. on request). pap. 14.00 (ISBN 0-8373-2868-3). Natl Learning.

--Special Projects Coordinator. (Career Examination Ser.: C-2933). (Cloth bdg. avail. on request). pap. 12.00 (ISBN 0-8373-2933-7). Natl Learning.

Rush, Myron D. Management: A Biblical Approach. 1983. pap. 7.95 (ISBN 0-88207-607-8). Victor Bks.

Sasaki, Naoto. Management & Industrial Structure in Japan. 142p. 24.00 (ISBN 0-686-84796-2). Work in Amer.

Schellenberger, R. & Boseman, G. MANSYM III: A Dynamic Management Simulator with Decision Support System. (Management Ser.). 94p. 1982. pap. text ed. 12.95 (ISBN 0-471-08581-2); tchrs. manual 6.00 (ISBN 0-471-86815-9). Wiley.

Schlesinger, Leonard & Eccles, Robert G. Managing Behavior in Organizations: Texts, Cases, Readings Led. (Illus.). 704p. 1983. text ed. 24.95x (ISBN 0-07-055332-7, C); instructor's manual 13.95 (ISBN 0-07-055333-5). McGraw.

Schuler, Randall S. Effective Personal Management. (Illus.). 600p. 1983. text ed. 19.95 (ISBN 0-314-69676-8); instrs.' manual avail. (ISBN 0-314-71144-9); study guide avail. (ISBN 0-314-71122-8). West Pub.

Scott, C. Principles of Management Information Systems. 1983. write for info. (ISBN 0-07-056103-6). McGraw.

Sherwood, John J., et al. Management Development Strategies. 34p. 1983. 35.00 (ISBN 0-08-029510-X). Pergamon.

Sperber, Nathaniel N. & Lerbinger, Otto. Manager's Public Relations Handbook. LC 81-22896. 256p. 1982. text ed. 25.00 (ISBN 0-201-14199-X). A-W.

Staff Management. 133p. 1981. 20.00 (ISBN 92-2-102939-5). Intl Labour Office.

Stewart & Garson. Organizational Behavior & Public Management. 312p. 1983. price not set. Dekker.

Storey, John. Managerial Prerogative & the Question of Control. (Direct Edition Ser.). 180p. (Orig.). 1983. pap. 18.50 (ISBN 0-7100-9203-2). Routledge & Kegan.

Szilagyi, Andrew D., Jr. & Wallace, Marc J. Organizational Behavior & Performance. 3rd ed. 1983. text ed. 24.95x (ISBN 0-673-16572-8). Scott F.

Taylor, M. Coverdale on Management. 1982. 19.00 (ISBN 0-434-90275-6, Pub. by Heinemann). David & Charles.

Terry & Rue. Principles of Management. 4th ed. (Plaid Ser.). 1982. pap. 8.95 (ISBN 0-87094-338-3). Dow Jones-Irwin.

Tregoe, Benjamin B. & Zimmerman, John W. Top Management Strategy. 1983. pap. price not set (ISBN 0-671-25402-2, Touchstone Bks). S&S.

Turner, Steve & Weed, Frank. Conflict in Organizations: Practical Guidelines Any Manager Can Use. (Illus.). 192p. 1983. 14.95 (ISBN 0-13-167395-5); pap. 6.95 (ISBN 0-13-167387-4). P-H.

Unit Management. 112p. 1980. 7.95 (ISBN 0-686-84494-7, 20-1783). Natl Learning Nurse.

Varney, Glenn H. Management by Objectives Workbook. 1974. pap. 6.50 (ISBN 0-686-38067-3). Mgmt Advisory.

Vernon-Harcourt, Tony. Rewarding Management 1982. 4th ed. 148p. (Orig.). 1981. pap. text ed. 38.50x (ISBN 0-566-02327-X). Gower Pub Ltd.

Vineyard, Sue. Finding Your Way Through the Maze of Volunteer Management. (Illus.). 68p. (Orig.). 1981. pap. text ed. 4.95 (ISBN 0-911029-00-1). Heritage Arts.

Wheelen, Thomas L. & Hunger, J. David. Strategic Management & Business Policy. LC 82-13886. 944p. 1983. text ed. 23.95 (ISBN 0-201-09011-2); instrs' manual 400 pg. avail. (ISBN 0-201-09012-0). A-W.

Williams, Frederick. Executive Communication Power: Basic Skills for Management Success. 170p. 1983. 12.95 (ISBN 0-13-294157-0); pap. 6.95 (ISBN 0-13-294116-3). P-H.

MANAGEMENT–CASE STUDIES

Hartley, Robert F. Management Mistakes. LC 82-12102. (Grid Series in Management). 220p. 1983. text ed. 11.95 (ISBN 0-88244-256-2). Grid Pub.

Mautz, R. K. & Winjum, James. Criteria for Management Control Systems. LC 81-67794. 1981. 5.50 (ISBN 0-910586-41-1). Finan Exec.

Schuler, Randall S. & Dalton, Dan R. Case Problems in Management. 2nd ed. (Management Ser.). (Illus.). 315p. 1983. pap. text ed. 11.95 (ISBN 0-314-69677-6). West Pub.

MANAGEMENT–PROGRAMMED INSTRUCTION

Material & Techniques for Co-Operative Management Training: Project Preparation & Appraisal. 130p. 1981. 20.00 (ISBN 92-2-102446-6). Intl Labour Office.

MANAGEMENT–STUDY AND TEACHING

Nyman, Tore. A Guide to the Teaching of Collective Bargaining. 91p. 1981. 2.85 (ISBN 0-686-84631-1). Intl Labour Office.

Owens, James. Management Training. LC 82-51057. 104p. 1982. Instrs' Handbook 29.95 (ISBN 0-943170-03-6). Management Ed.

Tjosvold, Dean & Johnson, David W. Productive Conflict Management: Perspectives for Organizations. 224p. 1983. 18.95x (ISBN 0-8290-1266-4). Irvington.

MANAGEMENT, EMPLOYEES' REPRESENTATION IN

see Employees' Representation in Management

MANAGEMENT, GAME

see Wildlife Management

MANAGEMENT, INDUSTRIAL

see Industrial Management

MANAGEMENT, MARKETING

see Marketing Management

MANAGEMENT, PRODUCT

see Product Management

MANAGEMENT, SALES

see Sales Management

MANAGEMENT, WILDLIFE

see Wildlife Management

MANAGEMENT ACCOUNTING

see Managerial Accounting

MANAGEMENT AUDIT

Contracting for Audit & Management Advisory Services with the Federal Government. 1981. pap. 21.00 (ISBN 0-686-84277-4). Am Inst CPA.

MANAGEMENT AUDITING

see Management Audit

MANAGEMENT CONSULTANTS

see Business Consultants

MANAGEMENT INFORMATION SYSTEMS

Leitch, Robert A. & Davis, K. Roscoe. Accounting Information Systems. (Illus.). 720p. 1983. 29.95 (ISBN 0-13-002949-1). P-H.

MANAGEMENT MARKETING

see Marketing Management

MANAGEMENT OF FACTORIES

see Factory Management

MANAGERIAL ACCOUNTING

see also Cost Accounting

Anderson, Donald L. & Raun, Donald L. Information Analysis in Management Accounting. LC 77-14938. (Wiley Ser. in Accounting & Information Systems). 706p. 1978. pap. text ed. 30.95x (ISBN 0-471-02815-0). Wiley.

Bartlett, Roger W. Power Base Attribution & the Perceived Legitimacy of Managerial Accounting. Farmer, Richard N., ed. LC 82-23697. (Research for Business Decisions Ser.: No. 57). 1983. write for info. (ISBN 0-8357-1393-8). Univ Microfilms.

Batty, J. Management Accountancy. 5th ed. 896p. 1982. pap. text ed. 29.95x (ISBN 0-7121-1272-3). Intl Ideas.

Brown, J. Lewis & Howard, Leslie R. Managerial Accounting & Finance. 4th ed. 896p. 1982. pap. text ed. 29.95x (ISBN 0-7121-1751-2). Intl Ideas.

Dougherty, Frank P. & Jopling, Samuel H. Managerial Accounting in Canada. LC 82-73436. 651p. 1983. text ed. 24.95x (ISBN 0-931920-47-7). Dame Pubns.

Francia, Arthur J. & Strawser, Robert H. Accounting for Managers. LC 82-71152. 1982. text ed. 24.95x (ISBN 0-931920-38-8). Dame Pubns.

Gambino, Anthony J. & Palmer, John R. Management Accounting in Colonial America. 40p. pap. 4.95 (ISBN 0-86641-052-X, 7685). Natl Assn Accts.

Harper, W. M. Cost Accounting. (Cost & Management Accounting Ser.: Vol. 1). 250p. 1982. pap. text ed. 13.95 (ISBN 0-7121-0468-2). Intl Ideas.

--Management Accounting (Cost & Management Accounting, Vol. 2. 250p. 1982. pap. text ed. 13.95x (ISBN 0-7121-0469-0). Intl Ideas.

Holmes, James R. & Lander, Gerald H. Profile of the Management Accountant. 140p. pap. 12.95 (ISBN 0-686-37887-3, 82139). Natl Assn Accts.

Rossell, James H. & Frasure, William W. Managerial Accounting: An Introduction. 3rd ed. Date not set. text ed. 22.95 (ISBN 0-675-08420-2); wkbk. 7.95 (ISBN 0-675-08107-6). Additional supplements may be obtained from publisher. Merrill.

Seiler, Robert E. & Collins, Frank. Accounting Principles for Management: An Introduction. 3rd ed. Date not set. text ed. 22.95 (ISBN 0-675-08267-6); wkbk. 8.95 (ISBN 0-675-08106-8). Additional supplements may be obtained from publisher. Merrill.

Shim, J. K. & Siegel, J. G. Schaum's Outline of Managerial Accounting. (Schaum Outline Ser.). 320p. 1983. 7.95x (ISBN 0-07-057305-0, GB). McGraw.

Titard, Pierre L. Managerial Accounting: An Introduction. 704p. 1983. text ed. 26.95 (ISBN 0-03-061556-9). Dryden Pr.

MANAGERIAL ECONOMICS

Brown, J. Lewis & Howard, Leslie R. Managerial Accounting & Finance. 4th ed. 896p. 1982. pap. text ed. 29.95x (ISBN 0-7121-1751-2). Intl Ideas.

Ullman, John E., ed. Social Costs in Modern Society: A Qualitative & Quantitative Assessment. LC 82-18590. (Illus.). 272p. 1983. lib. bdg. 29.95 (ISBN 0-89930-019-7, USC/, Quorum). Greenwood.

Wynne, George G. Cutback Management. (Learning from Abroad Ser.: Vol. 6). 84p. 1983. pap. text ed. 5.95x (ISBN 0-87855-930-2). Transaction Bks.

MANAGERS

see Executives

MANCHESTER, ENGLAND

Willan, T. S. Elizabethan Manchester. 1980. 19.00 (ISBN 0-7190-1336-4). Manchester.

MANDAN INDIANS

see Indians of North America–The West

MANET, EDOUARD, 1832-1883

Reff, Theodore. Manet & Modern Paris. 1982. pap. 17.50 (ISBN 0-89468-060-9). Natl Gallery Art.

--Manet & Modern Paris: One Hundred Paintings, Drawings, Prints, & Photographs by Manet & His Contemporaries. LC 82-18965. (Illus.). 280p. 1983. 39.95 (ISBN 0-226-70720-2); pap. write for info. U of Chicago Pr.

Richardson, John. Manet. (Phaidon Color Library). (Illus.). 1983. 27.50 (ISBN 0-7148-2233-7, Pub. by Salem Hse Ltd); pap. 18.95 (ISBN 0-7148-2243-4). Merrimack Bk Serv.

MANGANESE ORES

Bashkin, S. & Stoner, J. O., Jr. Atomic Energy-Level & Grotrian Diagrams, Vol. 4: Manganese I-XXV. 354p. 1983. 72.50 (ISBN 0-444-86463-6, North Holland). Elsevier.

MANGROVE

Clough, B. F., ed. Mangrove Ecosystems in Australia. LC 81-68098. 302p. 1982. text ed. 24.95 (ISBN 0-7081-1170-X, 1222). Bks Australia.

MANHATTAN PROJECT

see United States–Army–Manhattan Engineering District

MANIC-DEPRESSIVE PSYCHOSES

see also Depression, Mental; Psychology, Pathological

Schou, M. Lithium Treatment of Manic-Depressive Illness. 2nd, rev. ed. (Illus.). x, 70p. 1983. pap. 11.50 (ISBN 3-8055-3678-X). S Karger.

MANICHAEISM

Klimkeit, Hans-Joachim. Manichaean Art & Calligraphy. (Iconography of Religion: Vol. XX). (Illus.). xii, 50p. 1982. pap. write for info. (ISBN 90-04-06478-8). E J Brill.

MANIFEST DESTINY (U. S.)

see Messianism, American; United States–Territories and Possessions

MANIFOLDS (MATHEMATICS)

Aubin, T. Nonlinear Analysis on Manifolds: Monge-Ampere Equations. (Grundlehren der mathematischen Wiszenschaften Ser.: Vol. 252). 204p. 1983. 29.50 (ISBN 0-387-90704-1). Springer-Verlag.

Bombieri, Enrico. Seminar on Minimal Submanifolds. LC 82-61356. (Annals of Mathematics Studies, 103). 500p. 1983. 45.00 (ISBN 0-686-38855-0); pap. 15.00 (ISBN 0-691-08319-3). Princeton U Pr.

Elworthy, K. D. Stochastic Differential Equations on Manifolds. LC 82-4426. (London Mathematical Society Lecture Note Ser.: No. 70). 326p. 1982. pap. 27.50 (ISBN 0-521-28767-7). Cambridge U Pr.

Nottrot, R. Optimal Processes on Manifolds: An Application of Stokes' Theorem. (Lecture Notes on Mathematics Ser.: Vol. 963). 124p. 1983. pap. 8.00 (ISBN 0-387-11963-9). Springer-Verlag.

MANIKINS

see Models, Fashion

MANILA ROPE

see Rope

MANIPULATION (THERAPEUTICS)

Michelle, Arthur A. You Don't Have to Ache: Orthotherapy. 224p. 1983. pap. 5.95 (ISBN 0-87131-411-8). M Evans.

MANNEQUINS

see Models, Fashion

MANNERS AND CUSTOMS

see also Bohemianism; Caste; Chivalry; Clothing and Dress; Costume; Courts and Courtiers; Fairs; Festivals; Funeral Rites and Ceremonies; Gifts; Halloween; Holidays; Marriage Customs and Rites; Popular Culture; Rites and Ceremonies; Sports; Students; Tipping; Toasts; Tournaments; Travel; Women–History

Wiseman, Bernard. Don't Make Fun. (Illus.). (gr. 4-8). 8.95 (ISBN 0-686-43089-1). HM.

MANNHEIM SLIDE RULE

see Slide-Rule

MANPOWER

see also Labor Supply; Military Service, Compulsory; also such headings as Agricultural Laborers, Chemists, etc.

Margiotta, Franklin D. & Brown, James. Changing U. S. Military Manpower Realities. (Special Studies in Military Affairs). 290p. 1983. lib. bdg. 25.00 (ISBN 0-89158-935-X). Westview.

MANPOWER DEVELOPMENT AND TRAINING

see Occupational Training

MANPOWER POLICY

see also Full Employment Policies; Labor Supply

Burack, Elmer H. Human Resource Planning Approaches: A Managerial Summary. 150p. (Orig.). 1983. pap. 13.00 (ISBN 0-942560-09-4); pap. text ed. 10.95 (ISBN 0-686-38254-4). Brace-Park.

Carroll, Stephen J., Jr. & Schuler, Randall S. Human Resources Management in the 1980s. 250p. 1983. pap. text ed. 15.00 (ISBN 0-87179-401-2). BNA.

Fulton, O. & Gordon, A. Higher Education & Manpower Planning: A Comparative Study of Planned & Market Economies. 127p. 1982. 11.40 (ISBN 92-2-102973-5). Intl Labour Office.

Graham, H. T. Human Resources Management. 288p. 1981. 29.00X (ISBN 0-7121-0817-3, Pub. by Macdonald & Evans). State Mutual Bk.

Rossi, Robert J. & Gilmartin, Kevin J. Agencies Working Together: A Guide to Interagency Coordination & Planning. (Sage Human Service Guides: Vol. 28). 120p. 1982. pap. 7.50 (ISBN 0-8039-0973-X). Sage.

Schram, Barbara & Mandell, Betty. Human Services: Strategies of Intervention. 450p. 1983. text ed. 17.95 (ISBN 0-471-87068-4). Wiley.

Segal, Morley, ed. Foundations of Human Resource Development. 175p. 1983. pap. text ed. 399.00 (ISBN 0-934698-18-X). New Comm Pr.

Singleton, W. T. & Spurgeon, P., eds. Measurement of Human Resources. LC 74-14848. 370p. 1975. 32.50x (ISBN 0-85066-068-8). Intl Pubns Serv.

Workforce Reductions in Undertakings. 214p. 1982. pap. 15.75 (ISBN 92-2-102911-5, ILO 199, ILO). Unipub.

MANPOWER TRAINING PROGRAMS
see Occupational Training
MANPOWER UTILIZATION
see Manpower Policy
MANSFIELD, KATHERINE, 1888-1923
Hankin, C. A. Katherine Mansfield & Her Confessional Stories. LC 81-21340. 320p. 1982. 22.50x (ISBN 0-312-45095-8). St Martin.
Hormasji, Nariman. Katherine Mansfield: An Appraisal. 160p. 1982. Repr. of 1967 ed. lib. bdg. 35.00 (ISBN 0-89984-703-X). Century Bookbindery.
Mansfield, Katherine. Journal of Katherine Mansfield. LC 82-11541. (Illus.). 255p. 1983. pap. 6.95 (ISBN 0-88001-023-1). Ecco Pr.
MANSLAUGHTER
see Assassination; Homicide; Murder
MANTEGNA, ANDREA, 1431-1506
Martindale, Andrew. The Triumphs of Caesar by Andrea Mantegna in the Collection of Her Majesty the Queen at Hampton Court. (Illus.). 342p. 1982. 74.00x (ISBN 0-19-921025-X). Oxford U Pr.
MANUAL ALPHABETS
see Deaf-Means of Communication
MANUAL SKILL
see Motor Ability
MANUFACTURES
see also Catalogs, Commercial; Commerce; Home Labor; Industrial Arts; Industrial Capacity; Machinery; Manufacturing Processes; Mills and Mill-Work; Patents; Production Engineering; Trade-Marks; Workshops
also names of articles manufactured, e.g. Boots and Shoes, Hosiery, Knit Goods; and names of industries, e.g. Automobile Industry and Trade, Paper Making and Trade; also subdivision Manufactures under names of countries, cities, etc. e.g. United States-Manufactures
Abernathey, William J. & Clark, Kim B. Industrial Renaissance: Producing a Competitive Future in America. 1983. 19.00 (ISBN 0-465-03254-0). Basic.
Manufacturing in Australia, 2 vols. 263p. (Orig.). 1980. pap. text ed. 12.00x (ISBN 0-85825-131-0, Pub. by Inst Engineering Australia). Renouf.
MANUFACTURES-ACCOUNTING
Parris, John. Retention of Title on the Sale of Goods. 184p. 1982. text ed. 36.75x (ISBN 0-246-11612-9, Pub. by Granada England). Renouf.
MANUFACTURES-DIRECTORIES
Diaz. Derecho Mercantil. 300p. (Span.). 1983. pap. text ed. write for info. (ISBN 0-06-310500-4, Pub. by HarLA Mexico). Har-Row.
Hendricks, N. S., ed. Michigan Manufacturers Directory. 1983. 118.36 (ISBN 0-936526-01-7). Pick Pub MI.
Lambeth, Ida M., ed. Directory of Texas Manufacturers, 1983, 2 Vols. LC 34-27861. 1200p. Date not set. Set. pap. 85.00 (ISBN 0-686-83437-2). U of Tex Busn Res.
Newman, Phyllis E., et al, eds. California Manufacturers Register 1983. 36th ed. LC 48-3418. 896p. 1983. text ed. 125.00 (ISBN 0-911510-87-7). Times-M Pr.
MANUFACTURING ENGINEERING
see Production Engineering
MANUFACTURING MANAGEMENT
see Production Management
MANUFACTURING PROCESSES
see also Assembly-Line Methods; Fasteners; Machine-Tools; Manufactures; Materials; Metal-Work; Mills and Mill-Work; Process Control; Woodwork
Besant, C. B. Computer-Aided Design & Manufacture. 2nd ed. LC 79-40971. (Engineering Science Ser.). 228p. 1983. 54.95 (ISBN 0-470-27372-0); pap. 24.95 (ISBN 0-470-27373-9). Halsted Pr.
Bloch, H. P. & Geitner, F. K. Failure Analysis & Troubleshooting. (Practical Machinery Management for Process Plants Ser.). 1983. text ed. 59.95x (ISBN 0-87201-872-5). Gulf Pub.
De Renzo, D. J., ed. Cogeneration Technology & Economics for the Process Industries. LC 82-22279. (Energy Technology Review: No. 81). (Illus.). 395p. 1983. 42.00 (ISBN 0-8155-0932-4). Noyes.
Flexible Manufacturing Systems: Proceedings of the 1st International Conference, Brighton, England, October 1982. (Illus.). 519p. 1982. pap. text ed. 98.00x (ISBN 0-903608-30-8, Pub. by IFSPUBS). Scholium Intl.
Heyer, H. Einfuehrung in die Theorie Markoffacher Prozesse. 253p. 1979. pap. text ed. 14.95x. (ISBN 3-411-01564-0). Birkhauser.
Ingersoll Engineers. The FMS Report. Mortimer, John, ed. (Illus.). 180p. 1983. pap. text ed. 89.00x (ISBN 0-903608-31-6, Pub. by IFSPUBS). Scholium Intl.
Kazanas, H., et al. Manufacturing Processes. 1981. 18.95 (ISBN 0-07-033465-X); instr's manual avail. McGraw.
Kuhn, Sarah. Computer Manufacturing in New England. (Illus.). 187p. 1982. pap. 12.00 (ISBN 0-943142-03-2). Joint Cen Urban.
Langer, Steven, ed. Compensation in Manufacturing: Engineers & Managers. 4th ed. 1982. pap. 95.00 (ISBN 0-916506-74-6). Abbott Langer Assocs.
Meade, L. E., intro. by. Material & Process Advances '82. (National SAMPE Technical Conference Ser.). (Illus.). 1982. 60.00 (ISBN 0-938994-21-2). Soc Adv Material.
Morrow, John, intro. by. Materials Overview for 1982. (The Science of Advanced Materials & Process Engineering Ser.). (Illus.). 1982. 60.00 (ISBN 0-686-37996-9). Soc Adv Material.
MANURES
see Fertilizers and Manures
MANUSCRIPT DEPOSITORIES
see Archives
MANUSCRIPTS
see also Autographs; Illumination of Books and Manuscripts; Music-Manuscripts
Ann Arbor Publishers Editorial Staff. Manuscript Writing, 2 levels. (Manuscript Writing Ser.). (gr. 1-3). 1978. Level one. 4.00 (ISBN 0-89039-235-8); Level two. 4.00 (ISBN 0-89039-212-9). Ann Arbor Pubs.
--Manuscript Writing: Words Book 1 & 2. (Manuscript Writing Words Ser.). (gr. 3-6). Book 1. 5.00 (ISBN 0-89039-214-5); Book 2. 5.00 (ISBN 0-89039-216-1). Ann Arbor Pubs.
Codex Alimentarius Commission: Procedural Manual. 120p. 1982. pap. 9.00 (ISBN 92-5-101141-9, F2299, FAO). Unipub.
Gallager, Nancy E. & Wilson, Dunning S. Haudlist of Arabic Medical Manuscripts at UCLA. LC 82-50985. 28p. 1983. price not set (ISBN 0-89003-128-2). Undena Pubns.
Marks, Richard & Morgan, Nigel. Golden Age of English Manuscript Painting, 1200-1500. (Illus.). 1981. 27.75x (ISBN 0-686-82197-1). Intl Pubns Serv.
Plummer, John. The Last Flowering: French Painting in Manuscripts, 1420-1530. (Illus.). 252p. 1982. 89.00 (ISBN 0-19-503262-4). Oxford U Pr.
Vizetelly, Frank H. The Preparation of Manuscripts for the Printer. 148p. 1982. Repr. of 1905 ed. lib. bdg. 25.00 (ISBN 0-8495-5531-0). Arden Lib.
MANUSCRIPTS-BIBLIOGRAPHY
Carpenter, Kenneth E. Books & Society in History. 300p. 1983. 29.95 (ISBN 0-8352-1675-6). Bowker.
MANUSCRIPTS-CONSERVATION AND RESTORATION
see also Books-Conservation and Restoration
Baker, John B. & Soroka, Marguerite C., eds. Library Conservation: Preservation in Perspective. LC 78-16133. (Publications in the Informtion Sciences Ser.). 459p. 1978. 50.00 (ISBN 0-87933-332-4). Hutchinson Ross.
MANUSCRIPTS-RESTORATION
see Manuscripts-Copservation and Restoration
MANUSCRIPTS, ILLUMINATED
see Illumination of Books and Manuscripts
MAOISM
see Communism
MAORI WARS, 1843-1870
see New Zealand-History
MAP READING
see Maps
MAPS
see also Atlases; Automobile Touring-Road Guides
Barnette, David W. Map Coloring, Polyhedra & the Four-Color Problem. (Dolciani Mathematical Expositions Ser.: Vol. 8). Date not set. pap. price not set (ISBN 0-88385-309-4). Math Assn.
Cheyney, Arnold & Capone, Donald. The Map Corner. 1983. pap. text ed. 12.95 (ISBN 0-673-16615-5). Scott F.
Gatty, Harold. How to Find Your Way on Land & Sea: Reading Nature's Maps. (Illus.). 272p. 1983. 8.95 (ISBN 0-8289-0502-9). Greene.
Map Master. 1980. 7.95 (ISBN 0-933162-01-4). Creative Sales.
Martinet, Jean. Singularities of Smooth Functions & Maps. Simon, C. P., tr. LC 81-18034. (London Mathematical Society Lecture Note Ser.: No. 58). 180p. 1982. pap. 19.95 (ISBN 0-521-23398-4). Cambridge U Pr.
Minton, Janis. Basic Skills Map Workbook. (Basic Skills Workbooks). 32p. (gr. 4-7). 1983. 0.99 (ISBN 0-8209-0540-2, SSW-4). ESP.
--Learning to Read Maps. (Social Studies Ser.). 24p. (gr. 4-7). 1978. wkbk. 5.00 (ISBN 0-8209-0256-X, SS-23). ESP.
--Understanding Maps. (Social Studies Ser.). 24p. (gr. 4-7). 1979. wkbk. 5.00 (ISBN 0-8209-0257-8, SS-24). ESP.
Petersen, Grant. Roads of Alameda, Contra Costa & Marin Counties: A Topographic Guide for Bicylists. 200p. Date not set. pap. 5.95 (ISBN 0-930588-07-X). Heyday Bks.
MAPS-BIBLIOGRAPHY
Research Libraries of the New York Public Library & Library of Congress. Bibliographic Guide to Maps & Atlases: 1982. 1983. lib. bdg. 150.00 (ISBN 0-8161-6976-4, Biblio Guides). G K Hall.
Zogner, Redaktion L., ed. Bibliographia Cartographica, Vol. 8. xii, 223p. 1983. 28.00 (ISBN 3-598-20624-0, Pub. by K G Saur). Shoe String.
MAPS-JUVENILE LITERATURE
Aten, Jerry. Maptime... U. S. A. (gr. 4-8). 1982. 5.95 (ISBN 0-86653-093-2, GA 422). Good Apple.
MAPS, GEOLOGICAL
see Geology-Maps
MAPS, HISTORICAL
see Classical Geography
MAPS, LINEAR
see Linear Operators
MARATHON RUNNING
Benyo, Richard. The Masters of the Marathon. LC 82-73028. 256p. 1983. 12.95 (ISBN 0-689-11340-4). Atheneum.
Johnson, Bob & Bragg, Patricia. The Complete Triathlon Swim-Bike-Run: Distance Training Manual. (Illus.). 600p. 1982. 24.95 (ISBN 0-87790-029-9). Health Sci.
Taylor, William N. Marathon Running: A Medical Science Handbook. (Illus.). 112p. 1982. pap. 12.95x (ISBN 0-89950-054-4). McFarland & Co.
MARBLEHEAD, MASSACHUSETTS-DESCRIPTION
Randall, Peter E. Salem & Marblehead. (Illus.). 88p. 1983. pap. 8.95t (ISBN 0-89272-163-4). Down East.
MARCOS, FERDINAND EDRALIN, PRES. PHILIPPINE REPUBLIC, 1917-
Manila, Gabriel J. Marcos: Wild Child of the Sierra Morena. Bonner, Deborah, tr. 167p. 1982. text ed. 17.50x (ISBN 0-285-64924-8, Pub. by Condor Bk England). Humanities.
MARCUSE, HERBERT, 1898-
Katz, Barry. Herbert Marcuse & The Art of Liberation: An Intellectual Biography. 240p. 1982. 22.50 (ISBN 0-8052-7126-0, Pub by NLB England); pap. 8.50 (ISBN 0-8052-7127-9). Nichols Pub.
MARGARINE
see Oleomargarine
MARIA THERESA, EMPRESS OF AUSTRIA, 1717-1780
Duffy, Christopher. Royal Adversaries: The Armies of Frederick the Great & Maria Theresa. (Illus.). 572p. boxed set 32.00 (ISBN 0-88254-713-5). Hippocrene Bks.
MARICOPA INDIANS
see Indians of North America-Southwest, New
MARIHUANA
Abel, E. L. Marihuana: The First Twelve Thousand Years. 1982. pap. 6.95 (ISBN 0-07-000047-6). McGraw.
Himmelstein, Jerome L. The Strange Career of Marihuana: Politics & Ideology of Drug Control in America. LC 82-12181. (Contributions in Political Science Ser.: No. 94). (Illus.). 208p. 1983. lib. bdg. 27.95 (ISBN 0-313-23517-1, HSC/). Greenwood.
Mann. Marijuana Alert. 1983. write for info. (ISBN 0-07-039907-7); pap. write for info. (ISBN 0-07-039906-9). McGraw.
Sloman, Larry. Reefer Madness: A of Marijuana in America. (Illus.). 360p. 1983. pap. 8.95 (ISBN 0-394-62446-7, Ever). Grove.
Wilkerson, Don. Marijuana: Revised & Updated. 160p. 1983. pap. 4.95 (ISBN 0-8007-5107-8, Power Bks.). Revell.
MARIIA, MOTHER, 1891-1945
Hackel, Sergei. Pearl of Great Price: The Life of Mother Maria Skobtsova 1891-1945. rev. ed. LC 81-21356. 160p. 1982. pap. 5.95 (ISBN 0-913836-85-0). St Vladimirs.
MARIJUANA
see Marihuana
MARINE ARCHAEOLOGY
see Underwater Archaeology
MARINE ARCHITECTURE
see Naval Architecture; Ship-Building
MARINE BIOLOGY
see also Marine Ecology; Marine Fauna; Marine Flora; Marine Resources; Marine Sediments; Ocean Bottom; Photography, Submarine; Seashore Biology; Sedimentation and Deposition; Shells
Abbott, David, ed. The Biographical Encyclopedias of Science: The Chemists. 1982. 30.00x (ISBN 0-584-10854-0, Pub. by Muller Ltd). State Mutual Bk.
Albert, Donna. Beautiful American Marine. LC 82-90348. (Illus., Orig.). 1982. pap. 5.95 (ISBN 0-9608924-0-0). DJA Writ Circle.
Barnes, M. Oceanography & Marine Biology: An Annual Review, Vol. 20. (Illus.). 778p. 1982. 82.80 (ISBN 0-08-028460-4). Pergamon.
Blaxter, J. H., et al. Advances in Marine Biology, Vol. 20. (Serial Publication). 65.00 (ISBN 0-12-026120-0). Acad Pr.
McConnaughey, Bayard H. & Zottoli, Robert. Introduction to Marine Biology. 4th ed. 660p. 1983. text ed. 27.95 (ISBN 0-8016-3259-5). Mosby.
Rowe, Gilbert T. The Sea: Deep-Sea Biology. (Ideas & Observations on Progress in the Study of the Seas: Vol. 8). 525p. 1983. 65.00x (ISBN 0-471-04402-4, Pub. by Wiley-Interscience). Wiley.
Taylor, D. A. Introduction to Marine Biology. 336p. 1983. text ed. 49.95 (ISBN 0-408-00586-6); pap. text ed. 29.95 (ISBN 0-408-00585-8). Butterworth.
Tolbert, N. E. & Osmond, C. B., eds. Photorespiration in Marine Plants. (Illus.). 139p. 1976. 7.50 (ISBN 0-686-37454-1). Sabbot-Natural Hist Bks.
MARINE BIOLOGY-JUVENILE LITERATURE
Blumberg, Rhoda. The First Travel Guide to the Bottom of the Sea. LC 82-17938. (Illus.). 96p. (gr. 4 up). 1983. 9.00 (ISBN 0-688-01692-8). Lothrop.
Conway, Lorraine. Marine Biology. (gr. 5-8). 1982. 5.95 (ISBN 0-86653-056-8, GA 400). Good Apple.
MARINE BIOLOGY-RESEARCH
MacDonald, A. G. & Priede, J. G., eds. Experimental Biology at Sea. Date not set. price not set (ISBN 0-12-464160-1). Acad Pr.
MARINE CHEMISTRY
see Chemical Oceanography
MARINE DEPOSITION
see Sedimentation and Deposition
MARINE DISASTERS
see Shipwrecks
MARINE ECOLOGY
Burrell, D. C. Marine Environmental Studies in Boca de Quadra & Smeaton Bay: Chemical & Geochemical. (IMS Report Ser.: No. R82-2). 1980. write for info. (ISBN 0-914500-16-3). U of AK Inst Marine.
Clark, R. B., intro. by. The Long-Term Effects of Oil Pollution on Marine Populations, Communities & Ecosystems: Proceedings. (RSL Philosophies. Transactions Series B, Vol. 297: No. 1087). (Illus.). 260p. 1982. text ed. 80.00x (ISBN 0-85403-188-X). Scholium Intl.
Hynes. The Ecology of Running Waters. 580p. 1982. 60.00x (ISBN 0-85323-100-1, Pub. by Liverpool Univ England). State Mutual Bk.
MARINE ENGINEERING
see also Electricity on Ships
Blakey, T. N., ed. English for Maritime Studies Book. (Materials for Language Practice (ESP)). 192p. 1982. pap. 9.95 (ISBN 0-08-028636-4). Pergamon.
Bolger, Philip C. Thirty-Odd Boats. LC 82-80403. (Illus.). 224p. 1982. 22.50 (ISBN 0-87742-152-8). Intl Marine.
Goodman, A. W. Univalent Functions, 2 vols. 47.50 ea. Vol. I (ISBN 0-936166-10-X). Vol. II (ISBN 0-936166-12-6). Mariner Pub.
Grayson, Stan. Old Marine Engines: The World of the One Longer. LC 82-80402. (Illus.). 224p. 1982. 22.50 (ISBN 0-87742-155-2). Intl Marine.
Prescott, John. Directory of Shipowners, Shipbuilders & Marine Engineers, 1982. 80th ed. LC 35-4199. 1534p. 1982. 70.00x (ISBN 0-617-00277-0). Intl Pubns Serv.
Rose, Pat R. The Solar Boat Book. rev. ed. 266p. 1983. 14.95 (ISBN 0-89815-089-2); pap. 8.95 (ISBN 0-89815-086-8). Ten Speed Pr.
Souchotte, E. Marine Auxiliary Machinery. 6th ed. 512p. 1983. text ed. 49.95 (ISBN 0-408-01123-8). Butterworth.
MARINE ENGINEERING-BIBLIOGRAPHY
Bernardi, S. D. Bibliography of Schlicht Functions. 1983. 32.50 (ISBN 0-936166-09-6). Mariner Pub.
MARINE FAUNA
see also Fishes; Marine Mammals
Gotshall, Daniel W. Marine Animals of Baja California. LC 82-50492. (Illus.). 112p. 1982. ltd. ed. 29.95 (ISBN 0-930118-08-1, Dist. by Western Marine Enterprises); pap. 17.95 (ISBN 0-930030-24-9). Sea Chall.
MARINE FAUNA-GREAT BRITAIN
Hopkins, A. & Brassley, P. The Wildlife of Rivers & Canals. 192p. 1982. 50.00x (ISBN 0-86190-061-8, Pub. by Moorland). State Mutual Bk.
MARINE FLORA
see also Primary Productivity (Biology)
Tolbert, N. E. & Osmond, C. B., eds. Photorespiration in Marine Plants. (Illus.). 139p. 1976. 7.50 (ISBN 0-686-37454-1). Sabbot-Natural Hist Bks.
MARINE GEOLOGY
see Submarine Geology
MARINE INSURANCE
see Insurance, Marine
MARINE INVERTEBRATES
Walls, Jerry G., ed. The Encyclopedia of Marine Invertebrates. (Illus.). 736p. 1982. 49.95 (ISBN 0-87666-495-8, H-951). TFH Pubns.
MARINE LAW
see Maritime Law
MARINE MAMMALS
Katona, Steve & Richardson, David. A Field Guide to the Whales, Porpoises, & Seals of the Gulf of Maine & Eastern Canada: Cape Cod to Labrador. (Illus.). 224p. 1983. 17.95 (ISBN 0-686-83664-2, ScribT); pap. 9.95 (ISBN 0-686-83665-0). Scribner.
Mammals in the Seas: Vol. III, General Papers & Large Cetaceans. 504p. 1982. 80.50 (ISBN 92-5-100513-3, F2319, FAO). Unipub.
MARINE METEOROLOGY
see Meteorology, Maritime
MARINE POLLUTION
see also Oil Pollution of Rivers, Harbors, etc.
Champ, Michael A. & Park, P. K. Global Marine Pollution Bibliography: For Ocean Dumping of Municipal & Industrial Wastes. 424p. 1982. 69.50x (ISBN 0-306-65205-6, Plenum Pr). Plenum Pub.
Dawson, James. Superspill. (Illus.). 128p. 1981. 18.95 (ISBN 0-86720-588-1). Sci Bks Intl.
Ellis, Derek V., ed. Marine Tailings Disposal. LC 82-73416. (Illus.). 368p. 1982. 37.50 (ISBN 0-250-40614-4). Ann Arbor Science.
Palmer, H. D. & Gross, M. G., eds. Ocean Dumping & Marine Pollution: Geological Aspects of Waste Disposal at Sea. LC 78-10436. 268p. 1979. 31.50 (ISBN 0-87933-343-X). Hutchinson Ross.
Park, Kilho P. & Duedall, Iver W. Wastes in the Ocean: Radioactive Wastes in the Ocean, Vol. 3. (Environmental Science & Technology Texts & Monographs). 870p. 1983. 33.45 (ISBN 0-471-09770-5, Pub. by Wiley Interscience). Wiley.
Vernberg, Winona B., et al, eds. Physiological Mechanisms of Marine Pollutant Toxicity. 1982. 45.00 (ISBN 0-12-718460-0). Acad Pr.
MARINE RESOURCES
see also Fisheries; Fishery Products; Salt; Sea-Water

Brown, Gardner M., Jr. & Crutchfield, James, eds. Economics of Ocean Resources: A Research Agenda. LC 82-17471. 242p. (Orig.). 1983. pap. 12.00 (ISBN 0-295-95982-7, Pub. by Wash Sea Grant). U of Wash Pr.

Finn, Daniel P. Managing the Ocean Resources of the United States: The Role of the Federal Marine Sanctuary Program. (Lecture Notes in Coastal & Estuarine Studies: Vol. 2). (Illus.). 193p. 1982. pap. 16.00 (ISBN 0-387-11583-8). Springer-Verlag.

Henry, Charlier H. & Justus, John R. Handbook of Ocean Energy. (Illus.). 1983. 34.95 (ISBN 0-8311-1133-X). Indus Pr.

MARINE SEDIMENTS

Palmer, H. D. & Gross, M. G., eds. Ocean Dumping & Marine Pollution: Geological Aspects of Waste Disposal at Sea. LC 78-10436. 268p. 1979. 31.50 (ISBN 0-87933-343-X). Hutchinson Ross.

Perkins, Bob F. Deltaic Sedimentation on the Louisiana Coast. 1982. 10.00. SEPM.

Riedel, W. R. & Saito, T., eds. Marine Plankton & Sediments: Kiel Symposium. (Micropaleontology Special Publications Ser.: No. 3). 235p. 1980. 20.00 (ISBN 0-686-84254-5). Am Mus Natl Hist.

MARINE SHIPPING

see Shipping

MARINE STRUCTURES

see Offshore Structures

MARINE TECHNOLOGY

see Marine Engineering

MARINE TRANSPORTATION

see Shipping

MARINE ZOOLOGY

see Marine Fauna

MARINERS

see Seamen

MARIOLATRY

see Mary, Virgin-Cultus

MARIOLOGY

see Mary, Virgin-Theology

MARIONETTES

see Puppets and Puppet-Plays

MARITAL COUNSELING

see Marriage Counseling

MARITIME DISCOVERIES

see Discoveries (In Geography)

MARITIME HISTORY

see subdivisions Navy or History, Naval under names of countries, e.g. United States-History, Naval and Great Britain-Navy

MARITIME LAW

see also Commercial Law; Freight and Freightage; Insurance, Marine; Neutrality; Pirates; Territorial Waters

Angell, Joseph K. A Treatise on the Right of Property in Tide Waters & in the Soil & Shores Thereof. 1983. Repr. of 1826 ed. lib. bdg. 37.50x (ISBN 0-8377-0214-3). Rothman.

Canfield, George L. & Dalzell, George W. The Law of the Sea: A Manual of the Principles of Admiralty Law for Students, Mariners & Ship Operators. xvi, 315p. 1983. Repr. of 1926 ed. lib. bdg. 35.00x (ISBN 0-8377-0442-1). Rothman.

Carlson, Kurt. The Law of the Sea Treaty: Current Choices. 64p. 1981. 2.50 (ISBN 0-686-81729-X). World Without War.

Hopkins, F. N. Business & Law for the Shipmaster. 6th ed. 908p. 1982. text ed. 65.00x (ISBN 0-85174-434-6). Sheridan.

Karatzas, Theodoros & Ready, Nigel. The Greek Code of Private Maritime Law. 1982. lib. bdg. 32.50 (ISBN 90-247-2586-0, Pub. by Martinus Nijhoff Netherlands). Kluwer Boston.

Laursen, Finn. Toward a New International Marine Order. 1982. lib. bdg. 39.00 (ISBN 90-247-2597-6, Pub. by Martinus Nijhoff Netherlands). Kluwer Boston.

Markow, Herbert L. Small Boat Law. LC 77-154289. 435p. Date not set. pap. 36.00 (ISBN 0-686-84262-6). Banyan Bks.

--Small Boat Law 1978 Supplement. 144p. Date not set. pap. 18.00 (ISBN 0-686-84270-7). Banyan Bks.

--Small Boat Law 1979-1980 Supplement. 174p. Date not set. pap. 21.00 (ISBN 0-686-84271-5). Banyan Bks.

O'Connell, D. P. The International Law of the Sea, Vol. I. Shearer, I. A., ed. (Illus.). 664p. 1982. 74.00 (ISBN 0-19-825346-X). Oxford U Pr.

OECD Staff. Maritime Transport, 1981. 162p. (Orig.). 1982. pap. 10.00x (ISBN 92-64-12347-4). OECD.

Oxman, Bernard, ed. The Law of the Sea: A U. S. Policy Dilemma. 250p. 1983. text ed. 22.95 (ISBN 0-917616-59-6); pap. text ed. 7.95 (ISBN 0-917616-53-7). ICS Pr.

MARITIME METEOROLOGY

see Meteorology, Maritime

MARITIME SHIPPING

see Shipping

MARKET SURVEYS

see also Advertising Research; Public Opinion Polls; Store Location

Roca, Ruben A., ed. Market Research for Shopping Centers. 1980. 35.00 (ISBN 0-913598-11-9). Intl Coun Shop.

MARKETING

see also Commodity Exchanges; Customer Service; Export Marketing; Merchandising; New Products; Physical Distribution of Goods; Price Policy; Retail Trade; Sales Management; Sales Promotion

also Subdivision Marketing under Names of Commodities, E.g. Farm Produce-Marketing; Fruit-Marketing

Bagozzi, Richard P. Casual Models in Marketing. LC 79-11622. (Theories in Marketing Ser.). 303p. 1980. text ed. 30.50 (ISBN 0-471-01516-4). Wiley.

Bernard, Edward, pseud. The Name Changers. (Illus.). 528p. (Orig.). 1982. pap. 3.95 (ISBN 0-910797-00-5). Marketing Effect.

Burgett, Gordon L. How To Produce & Market Your Own Audio Cassettes. 100p. 1983. pap. 7.95 (ISBN 0-9605078-3-3). Successful Sem.

Cornelius, Hal & Lewis, William. Career Guide for Sales & Marketing. Levy, Valerie, ed. (Career Blazers Guides). 1983. pap. 7.95 (ISBN 0-671-47169-4). Monarch Pr.

Eastman, Susan Tyler & Klein, Robert. Strategies in Broadcast & Cable Promotion: Commercial Television, Radio, Cable, Pay Television, Public Television. 352p. 1982. pap. text ed. 13.95x (ISBN 0-534-01156-X). Wadsworth Pub.

Frye, Tom. Scratching on the Eight Ball. 351p. 1982. pap. 4.95 (ISBN 0-939644-04-5). Media Prods & Mktg.

Gaedeke, Ralph M. & Tootelian, Dennis H. Marketing: Principles & Applications. (Illus.). 700p. 1983. text ed. 19.95 (ISBN 0-314-69649-0); tchrs.' manual avail. (ISBN 0-314-71091-4); student guide avail. (ISBN 0-314-71142-2). West Pub.

Giles, G. D. Marketing. 256p. 1981. 19.00x (ISBN 0-7121-1290-1, Pub. by Macdonald & Evans). State Mutual Bk.

Harris, Beatrice & Lange, Debbie, eds. Harris Indian Marketers Industrial Directory, 1983. (Illus.). 700p. 1982. 52.50 (ISBN 0-916512-29-0). Harris Pub.

Hathaway-Bates, John. How to Organize your Marketing. 162p. (Orig.). 1981. pap. 9.25 (ISBN 0-910333-01-7). Asigan Ltd.

Hobson, Grant D. Marketing Books to Consumers: Trends in Trade, Paperback, Book Club & Mail Order Publishing. 1980. spiral 750.00 (ISBN 0-686-42879-X). Knowledge Indus.

Kaynak. Marketing in the Third World. 320p. 1982. 29.95 (ISBN 0-03-062179-8). Praeger.

Lace, Vivian & Carlsen, Fran, eds. Harris Ohio Marketers Industrial Directory, 1983. (Illus.). 1000p. 1982. 78.00 (ISBN 0-916512-58-4). Harris Pub.

Lamb, Charles W., Jr. Marketing: Cases for Analysis. LC 82-81740. 512p. 1982. pap. 13.95 (ISBN 0-395-32636-2); write for info. instr's manual (ISBN 0-395-32637-0). HM.

Lovelock, Christopher H. Services Marketing: Texts, Cases & Readings. (Illus.). 624p. 1983. 27.95 (ISBN 0-13-806786-4). P-H.

Lovelock, Christopher H. & Weinberg, Charles B. Marketing for Public & Non-Profit Managers. 400p. 1983. text ed. write for info. (ISBN 0-471-03722-2). Wiley.

Maresca, Carmela C. Careers in Marketing: A Woman's Guide. 240p. 1982. 16.95 (ISBN 0-13-115139-8); pap. 8.95 (ISBN 0-13-115121-5). P-H.

The Marketing of Information Analysis Center Products & Services. 1971. 6.50 (ISBN 0-686-42912-5). Knowledge Indus.

Michman, Ronald D. Marketing to Changing Consumer Markets: Environmental Scanning. 188p. 1983. 27.95 (ISBN 0-03-059429-4). Praeger.

Microcomputer Hardware & Software in the El-Hi Market: 1983-87. 1983. spiral 950.00 (ISBN 0-686-42882-X). Knowledge Indus.

Pride & Ferrell. Marketing. 3rd ed. 1982. text ed. 27.95 (ISBN 0-686-84538-2, BS36); write for info. supplementary materials. HM.

Pride, William M. & Ferrell, O. C. Marketing: Basic Concepts & Decisions. 3rd ed. LC 82-83363. 784p. 25.95 (ISBN 0-395-32816-0); write for info. supplementary materials. HM.

PROMODATA (Promotion, Marketing & Advertising Data), 1982. 2nd ed. 336p. 1982. 87.50x (ISBN 0-8002-3071-X). Intl Pubns Serv.

Ries. Marketing Warfare. 1983. write for info. (ISBN 0-07-052730-X). McGraw.

Robicheaux, Robert. Marketing: Contemporary Dimensions. 3rd ed. LC 82-82470. 432p. 1982. pap. text ed. 13.95 (ISBN 0-395-33166-8). HM.

Schewe, Charles & Smith, Reuben. Marketing: Concepts & Applications. 2nd ed. 736p. 1983. 25.95 (ISBN 0-07-055251-7, C); write for info. instr's manual (ISBN 0-07-055252-5); study guide 8.95 (ISBN 0-07-055253-3); write for info. test book (ISBN 0-07-055254-1). McGraw.

Silver, Morris. Prophets & Markets. 1982. lib. bdg. 35.00 (ISBN 0-89838-112-6). Kluwer-Nijhoff.

Skurski, Roger. Soviet Marketing & Economic Development. LC 82-792. 256p. 1983. 27.50x (ISBN 0-312-74842-6). St Martin.

Stern, Edward L., ed. Direct Marketing Market Place 1983. 4th ed. LC 79-649244. 480p. 1983. pap. 48.00 (ISBN 0-934464-04-9). Hilary Hse Pub.

Strauss, Lawrence. Electronic Marketing: Emerging TV & Computer Channels for Interactive Home Shopping. 160p. 1983. 34.95 (ISBN 0-86729-023-4). Knowledge Indus.

The United Kingdom Marketing Handbook 1982-83. 460p. 1982. 42.50x (ISBN 0-903617-14-5). Intl Pubns Serv.

Walsh, L. S. International Marketing. 272p. 1981. 30.00x (ISBN 0-7121-0968-4, Pub. by Macdonald & Evans). State Mutual Bk.

Williams, Joe B. & Williams, Joan. U. S. Statistical Rankings. 138p. 1981. pap. 25.00 (ISBN 0-939644-02-9). Media Prods & Mktg.

Williams, Keith C. Behavioral Aspects of Marketing. 1981. pap. 17.50 (ISBN 0-434-92300-1, Pub. by Heinemann). David & Charles.

Witt, Robert E. Marketing Doctoral Dissertation Abstracts, 1981. (Bibliography Ser.). 138p. 1982. pap. 11.00 (ISBN 0-686-83902-1). Am Mktg.

Witt, Robt. E., ed. Marketing Doctoral Dissertation Abstracts. 135p. 1982. 11.00 (ISBN 0-686-84358-4). Am Mktg.

MARKETING-BIBLIOGRAPHY

Bush, Ronald F. & Hunt, Shelby D., eds. Marketing Theory: Philosophy of Science Perspectives Proceedings. LC 82-6747. (Illus.). 315p. (Orig.). 1982. pap. text ed. 24.00 (ISBN 0-87757-159-7). Am Mktg.

Carter, Robert A., ed. Trade Marketing Handbook. 320p. 1983. 29.95 (ISBN 0-8352-1692-6); pap. 19.95 (ISBN 0-8352-1693-4). Bowker.

Spekman, Robert E. & Wilson, David T., eds. Issues in Industrial Marketing: A View to the Future Proceedings. LC 81-8054. (Illus.). 99p. (Orig.). 1982. pap. text ed. 10.00 (ISBN 0-87757-154-6). Am Mktg.

Walker, Bruce J., et al, eds. An Assessment of Marketing Thought & Practice: Proceedings of the Educators' Conference, 1982. LC 82-6693. (Illus.). 465p. (Orig.). 1982. pap. text ed. 30.00 (ISBN 0-87757-158-9). Am Mktg.

MARKETING-RESEARCH

see Marketing Research

MARKETING (HOME ECONOMICS)

see also Consumers; Consumer Education; Shopping

Bingham, Joan & Riccio, Dolores. The Smart Shopper's Guide to Food Buying & Preparation. 320p. 1983. pap. 6.95 (ISBN 0-686-83711-8, ScribT). Scribner.

Nash, M. J. How to Save a Fortune Using Refunds & Coupons. (Orig.). 1982. pap. 5.95x (ISBN 0-934650-03-9). Sunnyside.

MARKETING MANAGEMENT

see also Product Management

Britt, Steuart H. & Boyd, Harper W. Marketing Management & Administrative Action. 5th ed. (Illus.). 496p. 1983. text ed. 16.95 (ISBN 0-07-006949-2, C). McGraw.

Kinnear, Thomas C. & Taylor, James R. Marketing Research: An Applied Approach. 2nd ed. (McGraw-Hill Ser. in Marketing). (Illus.). 720p. 1983. text ed. 24.95x (ISBN 0-07-034745-X, C); exercises 12.95x (ISBN 0-07-034747-6); write for info. instr's manual (ISBN 0-07-034746-8). McGraw.

Langer, Steven, ed. Income in Sales-Marketing Management. 3rd ed. 1982. pap. 95.00 (ISBN 0-686-84835-7). Abbott Langer Assocs.

Lazer & Culley. Marketing Management: Foundations & Practices. 1983. text ed. 28.95 (ISBN 0-686-84533-1, BS28); instr's. manual avail. HM.

Lazer, William & Culley, James. Marketing Management: Foundations & Practices. LC 82-84160. 820p. 1983. 26.95 (ISBN 0-395-32716-4); write for info. instr's. manual (ISBN 0-395-33178-1). HM.

Schwartz, David J. Marketing Today: A Basic Approach. 3rd ed. 630p. 1981. text ed. 22.95 (ISBN 0-15-555089-6); tchr's. manual with tests 2.95 (ISBN 0-15-555090-X); wkbk. 7.95 (ISBN 0-15-555092-6). HarBraceJ.

MARKETING OF FARM PRODUCE

see Farm Produce-Marketing

MARKETING RESEARCH

see also Market Surveys

Aaker, David A. & Day, George S. Marketing Research: Private & Public Sector Decisions. LC 79-18532. (Marketing Ser.). 628p. 1980. text ed. 26.95 (ISBN 0-471-00059-0). Wiley.

Douglas, Susan P. & Craig, C. Samuel. International Marketing Research. 384p. 1983. 24.95 (ISBN 0-13-473132-8). P-H.

Doyle, Alfreda C. Suggestions for Telemarketing Operations. 26p. 1983. pap. text ed. 6.95 (ISBN 0-910811-27-X). Center Self.

Greensted, C. S. & Jardine, A. K. Essentials of Statistics in Marketing. 1978. pap. 13.95 (ISBN 0-686-84209-X, Pub. by W Heinemann). David & Charles.

Haller, Terry. Danger: Marketing Researcher at Work. LC 82-13261. (Illus.). 312p. 1983. lib. bdg. 35.00 (ISBN 0-89930-026-X, HMK/, Quorum). Greenwood.

Kinnear, Thomas C. & Taylor, James R. Marketing Research: An Applied Approach. 2nd ed. (McGraw-Hill Ser. in Marketing). (Illus.). 720p. 1983. text ed. 24.95x (ISBN 0-07-034745-X, C); exercises 12.95x (ISBN 0-07-034747-6); write for info. instr's manual (ISBN 0-07-034746-8). McGraw.

Marketing Trends in the Asia Pacific Region: Economic Forecasts & Consumer Developments, the Asia Pacific Centre. 221p. 1982. text ed. 144.00x (ISBN 0-566-02361-X). Gower Pub Ltd.

Marks, Stanley J. & Marks, Ethel M. The Blue Book of the U. S. Consumer Market, 1983. 1983. pap. 50.00 (ISBN 0-686-38795-3). Bur Intl Aff.

MARKETS

see also Commodity Exchanges; Fairs;

also Retail Trade; Grocery Trade, and similar headings

McCree, Marcia. Flea Market America: The Bargain Hunter's Passport to Fleadom. (Illus.). 128p. 1983. pap. 7.50 (ISBN 0-912528-31-1). John Muir.

Quertermous, Steve, ed. Flea Market Trader. 4th, rev. ed. 288p. Date not set. pap. 7.95 (ISBN 0-89145-212-5). Collector Bks.

MARKING (STUDENTS)

see Grading and Marking (Students)

MARKOFF PROCESSES

see Markov Processes

MARKOV CHAINS

see Markov Processes

MARKOV PROCESSES

Dynkin, E. B. Markov Processes & Related Problems of Analysis. LC 81-38438. (London Mathematical Society Lecture Note Ser.: No. 54). 300p. 1982. pap. 24.95 (ISBN 0-521-28512-7). Cambridge U Pr.

Freedman, B. Markov Chains. (Illus.). 382p. 1983. Repr. of 1971 ed. 28.00 (ISBN 0-387-90808-0). Springer-Verlag.

Freedman, D. Approximating Countable Markov Chains. (Illus.). 140p. 1983. Repr. of 1972 ed. 20.00 (ISBN 0-387-90804-8). Springer-Verlag.

Rozanov, Y. A. Markov Random Fields. Elson, C. M., tr. from Rus. (Illus.). 201p. 1983. 42.00 (ISBN 0-387-90708-4). Springer-Verlag.

MARKS, ARTISTS'

see Artists' Marks

MARKS, POTTERS'

see Pottery-Marks

MARLOWE, CHRISTOPHER, 1564-1593

Malz, Wilfried. Studien Zum Problem des Metaphorischen Redens Am Beispiel Von Texten Aus Shakeskpeares "Richard II" und Marlowes "Edward II". 251p. (Ger.). 1982. write for info. (ISBN 3-8204-5824-7). P Lang Pubs.

MARMION, COLUMBA, ABBOT, 1858-1923

Alexander, J. H. Marmion: Studies in Interpretation & Composition. (Salzburg-Romantic Reassessment Ser.: No. 30). 257p. 1981. pap. text ed. 25.00x (ISBN 0-391-02768-9, 40662, Pub. by Salzburg Austria). Humanities.

MARPRELATE CONTROVERSY

Wilson, John D. Martin Marprelate & Shakespeares Fluellen. 1982. lib. bdg. 34.50 (ISBN 0-686-81921-7). Porter.

MARRIAGE

see also Divorce; Domestic Relations; Family; Family Life Education; Marriage Counseling; Remarriage; Sex; Sexual Ethics; Weddings; Wives

Aldous, Joan. Two Paychecks: Life in Dual Earner Families. (Sage Focus Editions). (Illus.). 232p. 1982. 22.00 (ISBN 0-8039-1882-8); pap. 10.95 (ISBN 0-8039-1883-6). Sage.

Alex, Marlee & Alex, Ben. I Love You. 60p. 1983. 10.95 (ISBN 0-87123-262-6). Bethany Hse.

Allbritton, Cliff. How to Get Married: And Stay That Way. LC 82-71219. (Orig.). 1983. pap. 4.95 (ISBN 0-8054-5653-8). Broadman.

Carroll, Anne Kristin. Together Forever: For Healthy Marriages, or for Strained, or Broken Ones. 256p. (Orig.). 1982. pap. 7.95 (ISBN 0-310-45021-7). Zondervan.

Clinefelter, Dennis & Clinefelter, Terry. Premarital Planning. 1982. pap. 5.00 (ISBN 0-8309-0356-9). Herald Hse.

Clulow, C. F. To Have & to Hold: Marriage, the First Baby, & Preparing Couples for Parenthood. 168p. 1982. 16.50 (ISBN 0-08-028470-1); pap. 9.50 (ISBN 0-08-028471-X). Pergamon.

Crabb, Lawrence J., Jr. The Marriage Builder: A Blueprint for Couples & Counselors. 176p. 1982. 8.95 (ISBN 0-310-22580-9). Zondervan.

Davis, Julie & Weiss, Herman. How to Get Married: A Proven Plan for Finding the Right Mate. 64p. (Orig.). 1983. pap. 2.95 (ISBN 0-345-31102-7). Ballantine.

Davis, Oscar, Jr. Save Your Marriage. 1982. 4.95 (ISBN 0-686-84101-8). Carlton.

Denham, Hardy R., Jr. After You've Said I Do. 80p. (Orig.). 1983. pap. 5.95 (ISBN 0-939298-18-X). J M Prods.

Denton, Wallace & Denton, Juanita H. Creative Couples: The Growth Factor in Marriage. LC 82-17439. 156p. 1983. pap. 8.95 (ISBN 0-664-24453-X). Westminster.

Drakeford, John W. Marriage: How to Keep a Good Thing Growing. 192p. 1982. pap. 5.95 (ISBN 0-310-70081-7). Zondervan.

Elliot, Elisabeth. What God Has Joined. 32p. 1983. Repr. 1.50 (ISBN 0-89107-276-4). Good News.

Ember, Melvin. Marriage, Family, & Kinship: Comparative Studies of Social Organization. LC 82-83702. 425p. 1983. 30.00 (ISBN 0-87536-113-7); pap. 15.00 (ISBN 0-87536-114-5). HRAFP.

George, Denise. The Student Marriage. (Orig.). 1983. pap. 4.25 (ISBN 0-8054-6939-7). Broadman.

Getting in Touch with Yourself-And Your Parents. 1982. pap. 4.25 (ISBN 0-686-82559-4). St Anthony Mess Pr.

Getz, Gene A. Les Dimension du Mariage. Cosson, Annie, ed. Cousin, Elvire, tr. from Eng. Orig. Title: The Measure of a Marriage. 128p. (Fr.). 1982. pap. 1.75 (ISBN 0-8297-1246-1). Life Pubs Intl.

Gibson, Dennis L. Live, Grow & Be Free: A Guide to Self-Parenting. 136p. 1982. pap. 4.95 (ISBN 0-89840-031-7). Here's Life.
Groth, Jeanette. Thank You for My Spouse. 1983. pap. 2.25 (ISBN 0-570-03885-5). Concordia.
Hess, Bartlett & Hess, Margaret. How Does Your Marriage Grow? 180p. 1983. pap. 4.95 (ISBN 0-88207-529-2). Victor Bks.
Kasper, Walter. Theology of Christian Marriage. 112p. 1983. pap. 5.95 (ISBN 0-8245-0559-X). Crossroad NY.
Kramer, Rita W. Marriage Happens to the Nicest People. (Illus.). 128p. 1983. 6.00 (ISBN 0-682-49949-8). Exposition.
Lasswell, Marcia & Lobsenz, Norman. Equal Time: The New Way of Living, Loving, & Working Together. LC 82-45254. 240p. 1983. 15.95 (ISBN 0-385-17473-X). Doubleday.
Levande & Koch. Marriage & the Family. 1983. 19.95 (ISBN 0-686-84655-9); supplementary materials avail. HM.
Levande, Diane I. & Koch, Joanne B. Marriage & the Family. LC 82-81562. 496p. 1982. pap. text ed. 20.95 (ISBN 0-395-32577-3); instrs.' manual avail. (ISBN 0-395-32578-1). HM.
Olson, David H. & Miller, Brent C., eds. Family Study Review Yearbook. (Family Study Review Yearbooks). (Illus.). 768p. 1983. 37.50 (ISBN 0-8039-1924-7). Sage.
Parelman, Allison. Emotional Intimacy in Marriage: A Sex-Roles Perspective. Nathan, Peter E., ed. LC 82-20218. (Research in Clinical Psychology Ser.: No. 4). 150p. 1983. 34.95 (ISBN 0-8357-1387-3, Pub. by UMI Res Pr). Univ Microfilms.
Perkins, Patt & Hootman, Marcia. How to Forgive Your Ex-Husband. (Illus.). 150p. (Orig.). 1982. pap. 6.95 (ISBN 0-943172-01-2). New Wave.
Petersen, William J. Harriet Beecher Stowe had a Husband. 1983. pap. 2.95 r (ISBN 0-686-82689-2, 07-1329-X). Tyndale.
--Martin Luther Had a Wife. 1983. pap. 2.95 (ISBN 0-8423-4104-8). Tyndale.
Raphael, Levine & Healy, Rett. The Ten Commandments of Marriage. (Illus.). 96p. 1983. pap. 7.95 (ISBN 0-914842-96-X). Madrona Pubs.
Ryan, Kevin & Ryan, Marilyn. Making a Marriage: A Personal Book of Love, Marriage & Family. 224p. 1983. pap. 5.95 (ISBN 0-312-50663-5). St Martin.
Sangrey, Dawn. Wifestyles: Women Talk about Marriage. 1983. 16.95 (ISBN 0-440-09721-5). Delacorte.
Saxton, Lloyd. The Individual, Marriage, & the Family. 5th ed. 512p. 1982. text ed. 22.95x (ISBN 0-534-01003-2). Wadsworth Pub.
Strong, Bryan & DeVault, Christine. The Marriage & Family Experience. 2nd ed. (Illus.). 600p. 1983. text ed. 20.95 (ISBN 0-314-69682-2). West Pub.
Timmons, Tim. Maximum Marriage. rev. & updated ed. 160p. pap. 5.95 (ISBN 0-8007-5106-X, Power Bks). Revell.
Weber, Eric & Simring, Steven S. How to Win Back the One You Love. 192p. 1983. 11.95 (ISBN 0-02-624700-3). Macmillan.
Weitzman, Leonore. The Marriage Contract. LC 80-69645. 536p. 1982. pap. 8.95 (ISBN 0-02-934610-X). Free Pr.
Whiston, Lionel A. For Those in Love: Making Your Marriage Last a Lifetime. 128p. 1983. 9.95 (ISBN 0-687-13285-1). Abingdon.
White, Jerry. The Uneasy Marriage. (Critical Concern Ser.). 1983. write for info. (ISBN 0-88070-018-1). Multnomah.
Wright, Norm. Celebration of Marriage. LC 82-83835. (Illus.). 160p. (Orig.). 1983. pap. 4.95 (ISBN 0-89081-327-2). Harvest Hse.

MARRIAGE–BIBLICAL TEACHING
Anderson, Ann K. I Gave God Time. 1982. 7.95 (ISBN 0-8423-1560-8). Tyndale.
Gillham, Anabel. Friends & Lovers for Life. 1982. pap. 5.95 (ISBN 0-8423-0931-4). Tyndale.
Gundry, Paricia. Heirs Together. 192p. 1982. pap. 5.95 (ISBN 0-310-25371-3). Zondervan.
Robertson, John M. Together: Prayers & Promises for Newlyweds. 64p. 1982. pap. 2.50 (ISBN 0-8423-7282-2). Tyndale.

MARRIAGE–JEWS
see also Marriage, Mixed
Gittelsohn, Roland B. The Extra Dimension. 228p. 1983. pap. 7.95 (ISBN 0-8074-0170-6, 168500). UAHC.

MARRIAGE–INDIA
Dumont, Louis. Affinity As a Value: Marriage Alliance in South India with Comparative Essays on Austrailia. LC 82-13468. (Illus.). 248p. 1983. lib. bdg. 22.00x (ISBN 0-226-16964-2). U of Chicago Pr.

MARRIAGE–JAPAN
Plath, David W. Long Engagements: Maturity in Modern Japan. xii, 235p. 1983. pap. 6.95 (ISBN 0-8047-1176-3). Stanford U Pr.

MARRIAGE–UNITED STATES
Bell, Donald. Being a Man: The Paradox of Masculinity. 1982. 12.95 (ISBN 0-86616-013-2). Lewis Pub Co.

MARRIAGE (JEWISH LAW)
see Marriage–Jews

MARRIAGE, MIXED
Here are entered works on marriage between persons of different religions, or person of different denominations within christianity. Works on marriage between persons of different races are entered under the heading Miscegenation.
Beauchamp, Gary & Beauchamp, Deanna. Religiously Mixed Marriage. 4.75 (ISBN 0-89137-528-7). Quality Pubns.

MARRIAGE COUNSELING
Broderick, Carlfred B. The Theraputic Triangle: A Sourcebook on Marital Therapy. (Illus.). 200p. 1983. 20.00 (ISBN 0-8039-1943-3). Sage.
L'Abate, Luciano & McHenry, Sherry, eds. Methods of Marital Intervention. Date not set. price not set (ISBN 0-8089-1502-9). Grune.
Segraves, R. T. Marital Therapy: A Combined Psychodynamic-Behavioral Approach. (Critical Issues in Psychiatry Ser.). 295p. 1982. 24.50x (ISBN 0-306-40936-4, Plenum Pr). Plenum Pub.
White, Henry E., Jr. Making Marriage Successful. 420p. 1983. text ed. 18.95x (ISBN 0-8290-1261-3). Irvington.

MARRIAGE CUSTOMS AND RITES
see also Wedding Etiquette
Bride's Magazine Editors. The Bride's Wedding Planner. Date not set. pap. 6.95 (ISBN 0-449-90005-3, Columbine). Fawcett.

MARRIAGE GUIDANCE
see Marriage Counseling

MARRIAGE LICENSES
see Registers of Births, Deaths, Marriages, etc.

MARRIAGE REGISTERS
see Registers of Births, Deaths, Marriages, Etc.

MARRIED WOMEN
Here are entered works on the legal status of women during marriage, especially on the effect of marriage on their legal capacity. Works on legal relations between husband and wife are entered under Husband and wife. For works on the legal conditions of women in general, see the heading Women-Legal Status, Laws, etc.
Institute for Advanced Study of Human Sexuality. Sex & the Married Woman. 224p. 1983. pap. 8.95 (ISBN 0-671-47283-6, Wallaby). S&S.
Sangrey, Dawn. Wifestyles: Women Talk about Marriage. 1983. 16.95 (ISBN 0-440-09721-5). Delacorte.

MARS (PLANET)
Van Nostrand, Frederic. Mars Through the Signs. 64p. 1982. pap. 4.95 (ISBN 0-940058-05-7). Clancy Pubns.

MARSH ECOLOGY
Furtado, J. I. & Mori, S. Tasek Bera: The Ecology of a Freshwater Swamp. 1982. text ed. 79.00 (ISBN 90-6193-100-2, Pub. by Junk Pubs Netherlands). Kluwer Boston.
Siry, Joseph V. Marshes of the Ocean Shore: Development of an Ecological Ethic. LC 82-45899. (Environmental History Ser.: No. 6). 264p. 1983. 22.50x (ISBN 0-89096-150-6). Tex A&M Univ Pr.

MARSHALL, JOHN, 1755-1835
Corwin, Edward S. John Marshall & the Constitution. 1919. text ed. 8.50x (ISBN 0-686-83597-2). Elliots Bks.

MARSHES
see also Drainage; Marsh Ecology; Moors and Heaths; Reclamation of Land
Wilson, Ron & Lee, Pat. Marshland World. (Illus.). 160p. 1983. 16.95 (ISBN 0-7137-1199-X, Pub. by Blandford Pr England). Sterling.

MARTHA'S VINEYARD, MASSACHUSETTS
Allen, Everett S. Martha's Vineyard: An Elegy. 1982. 15.95 (ISBN 0-316-03257-3). Little.

MARTI, JOSE, 1853-1895
Kirk, John M. Jose Marti: Mentor of the Cuban Nation. LC 82-15920. 1983. 17.95 (ISBN 0-8130-0736-4). U Presses Fla.
Lubian, Rafael & Arias, M. M. Marti en los Campos de Cuba Libre. (Illus.). 186p. (Span.). 1982. pap. 9.95 (ISBN 0-89729-319-3). Ediciones.

MARX, KARL, 1818-1883
Carver, Terrel. Marx's Social Theory. 128p. 1983. 17.95 (ISBN 0-19-219170-5); pap. 6.95 (ISBN 0-19-289158-8). Oxford U Pr.
Cernuschi, Alberto. The Constructive Manifesto. LC 82-18903. 1983. 8.50 (ISBN 0-8022-2411-3). Philos Lib.
Clarke, Simon. Marx, Marginalism & Modern Sociology. (Contemporary Social Theory Ser.). 272p. 1982. text ed. 29.95x (ISBN 0-333-29252-9, Pub. by Macmillan England); pap. text ed. 11.95x (ISBN 0-333-29253-7). Humanities.
Felix, David. Marx as Politician. 288p. 1983. write for info (ISBN 0-8093-1073-2). S Ill U Pr.
Fischer, N. & Georgopoulos, N., eds. Continuity & Change in Marxism. 249p. 1982. text ed. 19.95x (ISBN 0-391-02564-3, Pub. by Macmillan England). Humanities.
Foner, Phillip S., ed. Karl Marx Remembered: Comments at the Time of His Death. 2nd. rev. ed. 282p. (Orig.). 1983. pap. 6.95 (ISBN 0-89935-020-8). Synthesis Pubns.
Kamenka, Eugene. The Portable Karl Marx. 1983. 18.75 (ISBN 0-670-41173-6). Viking Pr.
Lefevre, Henri. The Sociology of Marx. 218p. 1982. 25.00 (ISBN 0-231-05580-3, Pub. by Morningside); pap. 7.95 (ISBN 0-231-05581-1). Columbia U Pr.
Mehring, Franz. Karl Marx. 1981. pap. text ed. 11.95x (ISBN 0-391-02305-5). Humanities.
Norhausberber, Rudolph C. The Historical-Philosophical Significance of Comte, Darwin, Marx & Freud. (Human Development Library Book). (Illus.). 139p. 1983. 59.85 (ISBN 0-89266-392-8). Am Classical Coll Pr.
O'Neill, John. For Marx Against Althusser: And Other Essays. LC 82-17353. (Current Continental Research Ser.). (Illus.). 192p. (Orig.). 1983. lib. bdg. 20.50 (ISBN 0-8191-2815-5); pap. text ed. 9.50 (ISBN 0-8191-2816-3). U Pr of Amer.
Parkinson, G. H., ed. Marx & Marxisms: Royal Institute of Philosophy Lectures, 1979-1980. LC 82-4424. 240p. 1982. pap. 12.95 (ISBN 0-521-28904-1). Cambridge U Pr.

MARXIAN ECONOMICS
Burawoy, Michael & Shocpol, Theda, eds. Marxian Inquiries: Studies of Labor, Class, & States (Supplement to the American Journal of Sociology) 1983. lib. bdg. 25.00x (08039-0); pap. 12.50 (08040-4). U of Chicago Pr.
Lichthein, George. Marxism: A Historical & Critical Study. rev. ed. 432p. 1964. pap. 10.00 (ISBN 0-7100-4645-6). Routledge & Kegan.
Nove, Alec. The Economics of Feasible Socialism. 272p. 1983. text ed. 29.50x (ISBN 0-04-335048-8); pap. text ed. 9.95x (ISBN 0-04-335049-6). Allen Unwin.

MARXISM
see Communism; Socialism

MARY, VIRGIN
Breen, Eileen, compiled by. Mary the Second Eve. 40p. 1977. pap. 1.25 (ISBN 0-686-81627-7). TAN Bks Pubs.
Liguori, Alphonse. The Blessed Virgin Mary. 96p. pap. 3.00 (ISBN 0-686-81623-4). TAN Bks Pubs.

MARY, VIRGIN–CULTUS
see also Mary, Virgin–Feasts
Smith, Jody B. The Image of Guadalupe: Myth or Miracle? LC 80-2066. (Illus.). 192p. 1983. 14.95 (ISBN 0-385-15971-4). Doubleday.
Warner, Marina. Alone of All Her Sex: The Myth & the Cult of the Virgin Mary. LC 82-40051. (Illus.). 488p. 1983. pap. 9.95 (ISBN 0-394-71155-6, Vin). Random.

MARY, VIRGIN–FEASTS
Von Krusenstierna, Sten, ed. Services of Our Lady. 70p. 1982. pap. text ed. write for info. St Alban Pr.

MARY, VIRGIN–MEDITATIONS
Pio, Padre. Meditation Prayer on Mary Immaculate. (Illus.). 28p. pap. 0.50 (ISBN 0-686-81640-4). Tan Bks Pubs.

MARY, VIRGIN–PRAYER-BOOKS AND DEVOTIONS
Hart, John. Regard the Lilies, Regard the Blood: Poems to the Blessed Virgin. 80p. 1983. 6.00 (ISBN 0-682-49941-2). Exposition.
Moran, Patrick R., ed. Day by Day with Mary. 204p. 1983. pap. 6.95 (ISBN 0-87973-613-5, 613). Our Sunday Visitor.
Von Krusenstierna, Sten, ed. Services of Our Lady. 70p. 1982. pap. text ed. write for info. St Alban Pr.

MARY, VIRGIN–THEOLOGY
Kung, Hans & Moltmann, Jurgen. Mary in the Churches. (Concilium 1983: Vol. 168). 128p. (Orig.). 1983. pap. 6.95 (ISBN 0-8164-2448-9). Seabury.

MARY MAGDALENE, SAINT
Saba, Bonaventure. The Sinful, Intimate & Mysterious Life of Mary Magdalene, 2 vols. (A Significant Historical Personalities Library Bk.). (Illus.). 316p. 1983. 98.75 (ISBN 0-89266-397-9). Am Classical Coll Pr.

MARY STUART, QUEEN OF THE SCOTS, 1542-1587
Bregy, Katherine. Queen of Paradox: A Stuart Tragedy (Mary Stuart, Queen of Scots) 221p. 1982. Repr. of 1950 ed. lib. bdg. 35.00 (ISBN 0-8495-0612-3). Arden Lib.
Kurlbaum-Siebert, Margarete. Mary Queen of Scots. Hamilton, Mary A., tr. 504p. 1982. Repr. of 1929 ed. lib. bdg. 40.00 (ISBN 0-8495-3137-3). Arden Lib.
Laing, Malcolm. Preliminary Dissertation on the Participation of Mary, Queen of Scots, in the Murder of Darnley, 2 Vols. 371p. 1982. Repr. of 1804 ed. Set. lib. bdg. 200.00 (ISBN 0-89987-549-1). Darby Bks.

MARYLAND
Fisher, Charles O. & Murray, Richard C. Guide to Maryland Negligence Cases. 200p. 1982. 25.00 (ISBN 0-87215-472-6). Michie-Bobbs.

MARYLAND–DESCRIPTION AND TRAVEL
Dilisio, James E. Maryland: A Geography. (Geographies of the United States Ser.). 256p. 1983. lib. bdg. 35.00 (ISBN 0-86531-092-0); pap. text ed. 18.00 (ISBN 0-86531-474-8). Westview.
Jones, Carleton. Lost Baltimore Landmarks. LC 82-60385. (Illus.). 64p. (Orig.). 1982. pap. 7.95 (ISBN 0-940776-04-9). Maclay Assoc.

MARYLAND–GENEALOGY
Donnelly, Mary L. Willett Family of Maryland, Colonial Pewters, Kentucky Pioneers. LC 82-74006. (Illus.). 712p. 1983. 40.00 (ISBN 0-939142-07-4). Private Pub.

MARYLAND–HISTORIC BUILDINGS
Farquhar, Roger B. Old Homes & History of Montgomery County, Maryland. (Illus.). 1981. 35.00 (ISBN 0-910086-06-0). Am Hist Res.

MARYLAND–HISTORY
Farquhar, Roger B. Old Homes & History of Montgomery County, Maryland. (Illus.). 1981. 35.00 (ISBN 0-910086-06-0). Am Hist Res.

MARYLAND–JUVENILE LITERATURE
Seiden, Art. Michael Shows Off Baltimore. (Show Off Ser.). (Illus.). 32p. (gr. 1-5). 1982. 4.95 (ISBN 0-942806-01-8). Outdoor Bks.

MASCULINITY (PSYCHOLOGY)
Murray, Meg M., ed. Face to Face: Fathers, Mothers, Masters, Monsters--Essays for a Nonsexist Future. LC 82-11708. (Contributions in Women's Studies: No. 36). 360p. 1983. lib. bdg. 29.95 (ISBN 0-313-23044-7, MFF/). Greenwood.
Pleck, Joseph H. The Myth of Masculinity. 240p. 1983. pap. 6.95 (ISBN 0-262-66050-4). MIT Pr.
Schmidt, Jerry & Brock, Raymond. The Emotions of a Man. LC 82-84070. 192p. (Orig.). 1983. pap. 4.95 (ISBN 0-89081-330-2). Harvest Hse.
Smith, David W. The Friendless American Male. LC 82-21518. 1983. pap. 4.95 (ISBN 0-8307-0863-4, 5417309). Regal.

MASERS, OPTICAL
see Lasers

MASKS (PLAYS)
see Masques

MASKS (SCULPTURE)
Brice, Donna. Step-by-Step Guide For: Making Busts & Masks (Cold-Cast Bronze or Plaster Hydrocal) LC 82-15703. (Illus.). 52p. 1983. 18.95 (ISBN 0-910733-00-7); pap. 10.95 (ISBN 0-910733-01-5). ICTL Pubns.

MASONIC ORDERS
see Freemasons

MASONRY
see also Cement; Concrete; Foundations; Grouting; Plastering; Walls
Rudman, Jack. Foreman (Structures - Group B) (Masonry) (Career Examination Ser.: C-1323). (Cloth bdg. avail. on request). pap. 12.00 (ISBN 0-8373-1323-6). Natl Learning.

MASONS (SECRET ORDER)
see Freemasons

MASQUES
Sutherland, Sarah P. Masques in Jacobean Tragedy. LC 81-69122. 1982. 24.50 (ISBN 0-404-62279-8). AMS Pr.

MASS
see also Altar Boys; Lord's Supper
Loret, Pierre. The Story of the Mass: From the Last Supper to the Present Day. 144p. 1982. pap. 3.50 (ISBN 0-89243-171-7). Liguori Pubns.

MASS (PHYSICS)
see also Mass Spectrometry; Mass Transfer
Soldano, B. A. Mass, Measurement & Motion Sequel Two: A New Look at Maxwell's Equations & the Permittivity of Free Space. Brantley, William H., ed. (Illus.). 50p. (Orig.). 1982. pap. 7.00x (ISBN 0-943410-00-2). Grenridge Pub.

MASS CASUALTIES–TREATMENT
see Emergency Medical Services

MASS COMMUNICATION
see Communication; Mass Media; Telecommunication

MASS CULTURE
see Popular Culture

MASS FEEDING
see Food Service

MASS MEDIA
see also Moving-Pictures; Newspapers; Radio Broadcasting; Television Broadcasting; Violence in Mass Media
Bagdikian, Ben H. The Media Monopoly. LC 82-72503. 320p. 1983. 14.18 (ISBN 0-8070-6162-X). Beacon Pr.
Black, Jay & Whitney, Frederick C. Introduction to Mass Communications. 445p. 1983. pap. text ed. write for info (ISBN 0-697-04355-X); instrs.' manual avail. (ISBN 0-697-04360-6). Wm C Brown.
Charren, Peggy & Sandler, Martin W. Changing Channels: Living (Sensibly) with Television. LC 82-16243. (Illus.). 320p. 1982. 24.95 (ISBN 0-201-07253-X); pap. 11.95 (ISBN 0-201-07254-8). A-W.
DeFleur, Melvin & Lowery, Shearon. Milestones in Mass Communication Research. (Illus.). 448p. 1983. text ed. 22.50x (ISBN 0-582-28352-3); pap. text ed. 10.95x (ISBN 0-582-28353-1). Longman.
Glattbach, Jack. Media & the Developing World: Pluralism or Polarization? (Seven Springs Studies). 1982. pap. 3.00 (ISBN 0-943006-08-2). Seven Springs.
Greenberg, Bradley S., et al. Mexican Americans & the Mass Media. (Communication & Information Science Ser.). 304p. 1983. text ed. 35.00 (ISBN 0-89391-126-7). Ablex Pub.
Letheby, Sam. Moving Along. (Illus.). 100p. 1983. 9.95 (ISBN 0-939644-06-1). Media Prods & Mktg.
Mitchell, Craig. Media Promotion. LC 82-71765. 192p. 1983. pap. price not set (ISBN 0-87251-076-X). Crain Bks.
Monaco, James. Media: The Compleat Guide. (Illus.). 300p. 1982. 24.95 (ISBN 0-918432-40-5); pap. 9.95 (ISBN 0-918432-41-3). NY Zoetrope.
Pember, Don R. Mass Media In America. 4th ed. 448p. 1983. pap. text ed. write for info. (ISBN 0-574-22725-3); write for info. instr's. guide (ISBN 0-574-22726-1). SRA.
Rudman, Jack. Media Specialist. (Career Examination Ser.: C-2894). (Cloth bdg. avail. on request). pap. 12.00 (ISBN 0-8373-2894-2). Natl Learning.

Schrank, Jeffrey. Understanding Mass Media. (Illus.). 260p. 1981. pap. 11.95 (ISBN 0-8174-6334-8, Amphoto). Watson-Guptill.
Sissors, Jack & Goodrich, William. Media Planning Workbook. 240p. 1983. pap. text ed. write for info. (ISBN 0-87251-080-8, CB063). Crain Bks.
Thomas, Sari. Studies in Mass Communication. (Studies in Mass Communication & Technology). 308p. 1983. text ed. 29.50 (ISBN 0-89391-133-X). Ablex Pub.

MASS MEDIA–LAW AND LEGISLATION
Gordon, David. Problems in the Law of Mass Communications: Programmed Instruction. 1982 ed. 183p. 1982. write for info. problems bk. (ISBN 0-88277-104-3); pap. text ed. write for info. Foundation Pr.
Jamieson, Kathleen H. & Campbell, Karlyn K. The Interplay of Influence: Mass Media & Their Public in News, Advertising, Politics. 304p. 1982. pap. text ed. 11.95x (ISBN 0-534-01267-1). Wadsworth Pub.

MASS MEDIA–SOCIAL ASPECTS
Jamieson, Kathleen H. & Campbell, Karlyn K. The Interplay of Influence: Mass Media & Their Public in News, Advertising, Politics. 304p. 1982. pap. text ed. 11.95x (ISBN 0-534-01267-1). Wadsworth Pub.
Mayer, Henry & Garde, Pauline. The Media: Questions & Answers Australian Surveys, 1940 to 1980. 224p. 1983. text ed. 37.50x (ISBN 0-86861-348-7). Allen Unwin.
Ulloth, Dana R. & Klinge, Peter L. Mass Media: Past, Present, & Future. (Illus.). 400p. 1983. pap. text ed. 12.95 (ISBN 0-314-69683-0). West Pub.
Wood, Donald N. & Leps, A. Arvo. Mass Media & the Individual. (Illus.). 550p. 1983. text ed. 15.95 (ISBN 0-314-69687-3); instrs.' manual avail. (ISBN 0-314-71139-2). West Pub.

MASS MEDIA–STUDY AND TEACHING
Wimmer, Roger D. & Dominick, Joseph R. Mass Media Research: An Introduction. 416p. 1982. text ed. 22.95x (ISBN 0-534-01228-0). Wadsworth Pub.
Zuckman, Harvey L. & Gaynes, Martin J. Mass Communications in a Nutshell. 2nd ed. LC 82-20029. 473p. 1982. pap. text ed. 6.95 (ISBN 0-314-69869-8). West Pub.

MASS MEDIA–AUSTRALIA
Western, J. S. & Hughes, Colin A. The Mass Media in Australia: Second Edition. 2nd ed. LC 82-2685. (Illus.). 209p. 1983. text ed. 22.50x (ISBN 0-7022-1682-8); pap. text ed. 12.50x (ISBN 0-7022-1692-5). U of Queensland Pr.

MASS PSYCHOLOGY
see Social Psychology

MASS SPECTROMETRY
Meuzelaar, H. L. & Haverkamp, J. Pyrolysis Mass Spectrometry of Recent & Fossil Biomaterials. (Techniques & Instrumentation in Analytical Chemistry Ser.: Vol. 3). 294p. 1982. 61.75 (ISBN 0-444-42099-1). Elsevier.

MASS TRANSFER
Lydersen, Aksel L. Mass Transfer in Engineering Practice. 300p. 1983. 39.95 (ISBN 0-471-10437-X, Pub. by Wiley-Interscience). Wiley.
Wakao, N. & Kaguei, S. Heat & Mass Transfer in Packed Beds. (Topics in Chemical Engineering Ser.: Vol. 1). 360p. 1982. write for info. Gordon.
Zaric, Z. Structure of Turbulence in Heat & Mass Transfer. 1982. 90.00 (ISBN 0-07-072731-7). McGraw.

MASS TRANSIT
see Local Transit

MASSACHUSETTS–DESCRIPTION AND TRAVEL
Clayton, Barbara & Whitley, Kathleen. Exploring Coastal Massachusetts. (Illus.). 1983. pap. 12.95 (ISBN 0-686-84716-4). Dodd.

MASSACHUSETTS–ECONOMIC CONDITIONS
Massachusetts Bar Association Staff & Massachusetts Society of Certified Public Accountants Staff. Massachusetts Corporate Tax Manual with 1982 Supplement. 300p. 1983. write for info. looseleaf binder (ISBN 0-88063-021-3). Butterworth Legal Pubs.
Reschovsky, Andrew, et al. The Massachusetts State Tax System: Options for Reform. (Illus.). 300p. 1983. pap. write for info. (ISBN 0-943142-04-0). Joint Cen Urban.
Riley, Michael. Massachusetts Legal Forms-Probate. 175p. 1983. write for info. looseleaf binder (ISBN 0-88063-013-2). Butterworth Legal Pubs.
Walsh, Joseph. Massachusetts Legal Forms-Corporations. 175p. 1983. write for info. looseleaf binder (ISBN 0-88063-015-9). Butterworth Legal Pubs.

MASSACHUSETTS–GENEALOGY
Kelley, Louise H. & Straw, Dorothy, eds. Vital Records, Town of Harwich Masschusetts, 1694 to 1850. 616p. 1982. write for info. (ISBN 0-88492-040-2). W S Sullwold.
Oliver, Andrew & Peabody, James B. The Records of Trinity Chruch, Boston: Vol. II-1728-1830. LC 80-68230. 1094p. 1982. 25.00x (ISBN 0-8139-0982-1, Colonial Soc MA). U Pr of Va.
Stickney, Matthew. A Genealogical Memoir of the Descendants of Philip & Mary Fowler of Ipswich, Massachusetts, Ten Generations 1590-1882. 247p. 18.00 (ISBN 0-88389-003-8). Essex Inst.
Wyman, Thomas B. The Genealogies & Estates of Charlestown, Massachusetts, 1629-1818. Dearborn, David C., frwd. by. LC 82-60408. 1060p. 1982. Repr. of 1879 ed. 65.00x (ISBN 0-89725-031-1). NE History.

MASSACHUSETTS–HISTORY
Massachusettes Historical Society. Proceedings of the Massachusettes Historical Society, Vol. 93. 1982. 25.00 (ISBN 0-686-37595-5); pap. 20.00 (ISBN 0-686-37596-3). Mass Hist Soc.

MASSACHUSETTS–HISTORY–COLONIAL PERIOD, ca. 1600-1775
Abbot, W. W. The Colonial Origins of the United States, 1607-1763. LC 74-28127. (American Republic Ser). 160p. 1975. pap. text ed. 11.50 (ISBN 0-471-00140-6). Wiley.
Potter, Janice. The Liberty We Seek: Loyalist Ideology in Colonial New York & Massachusetts. 256p. 1983. text ed. 22.50x (ISBN 0-674-53026-8). Harvard U Pr.

MASSACHUSETTS–HISTORY, LOCAL
Kelley, Louise H. & Straw, Dorothy, eds. Vital Records, Town of Harwich Masschusetts, 1694 to 1850. 616p. 1982. write for info. (ISBN 0-88492-040-2). W S Sullwold.

MASSACHUSETTS–POLITICS AND GOVERNMENT
Formisano, Ronald P. The Transformation of Political Culture: Massachusetts Parties, 1790s-1840s. (Illus.). 599p. 1983. 35.00 (ISBN 0-19-503124-5). Oxford U Pr.

MASSAGE
see also Chiropractic; Electrotherapeutics; Mechanotherapy
Anhui Medical School Hospital. Chinese Massage Therapy. Lee, Hor M. & Whincup, Gregory, trs. from Chinese. LC 82-42677. (Illus.). 192p. (Orig.). 1983. pap. 6.95 (ISBN 0-394-71423-7). Shambhala Pubns.
Fox, Michael W. The Healing Touch. Orig. Title: Dr. Michael Fox's Massage Program for Cats & Dogs. 152p. 1983. pap. 6.95X (ISBN 0-937858-18-8). Newmarket.
Goldberg, Audrey G. Body Massage for the Beauty Therapist. (Illus.). 1972. pap. 11.50 (ISBN 0-686-84218-9, Pub. by W Heinemann). David & Charles.
Heinl, Tina. The Baby Massage Book: Using Touch for Better Bonding & Happier Babies. (Illus.). 144p. 1983. 15.95 (ISBN 0-13-056226-2); pap. 7.95 (ISBN 0-13-056218-1). P-H.
Lavier, J. Chinese Micro-Massage: Acupuncture Without Needles. (Illus.). 96p. (Orig.). 1983. pap. 5.95 (ISBN 0-7225-0362-8, Pub. by Thorsons Pubs England). Sterling.
Malouf, Pyrrha. Metamassage: How to Massage Your Way to a Beautiful Complexion - All Over. (Illus.). 1983. 6.95 (ISBN 0-87795-472-0, Pub. by Priam). Arbor Hse.
West, Ouida. The Magic of Massage: Your Health is in your Hands. (Illus.). 192p. (Orig.). 1983. pap. 12.95 (ISBN 0-933328-60-5). Delilah Bks.

MASTABAS
see Tombs

MATCHBOXES
Schiffer, Nancy, compiled by. Matchbox Toys. (Illus.). 204p. (Orig.). 1983. pap. 14.95 (ISBN 0-916838-74-9). Schiffer.

MATCHES
see also Matchboxes
Finch, Christopher & Ramachandran, Srinivasa. Matchmaking: Science Technology & Manufacturing. 220p. 1983. 65.00x (ISBN 0-470-27371-2). Halsted Pr.

MATERIA MEDICA
see also Aphrodisiacs; Drugs; Drugs–Dosage; Materia Medica, Vegetable; Medicine–Formulae, Receipts, Prescriptions; Pharmacology; Pharmacy; Therapeutics also names of drugs
Austin, Phylis A. & Thrash, Agatha M. Natural Remedies: A Manual. 283p. (Orig.). 1983. pap. price not set (ISBN 0-942658-05-1). Yuchi Pines.

MATERIA MEDICA, ARABIC
see Medicine, Arabic

MATERIA MEDICA, VEGETABLE
see also Botany, Medical; Herbs; Medicine, Medieval
Badmajew, Peter, Jr. & Badmajew, Vladimir, Jr. Healing Herbs: The Heart of Tibetan Medicine. LC 82-81022. (Illus.). 96p. 1982. pap. 2.95 (ISBN 0-943014-00-X, 607). Red Lotus Pr.
Boulos, Loutfy. Medicinal Plants of North Africa. Ayensu, Edward S., ed. LC 82-20412. (Medicinal Plants of the World Ser.: No. 3). (Illus.). 300p. 1983. 29.95 (ISBN 0-917256-16-6). Ref Pubns.
Jackson, Betty P. Powdered Vegetable Drugs. Snowdon, Derek, ed. 216p. 1974. 40.00x (ISBN 0-85950-005-5, Pub. by Thornes England). State Mutual Bk.
Pahlow, Manfried. Living Medicine: The Healing Properties of Plants. (Illus.). 96p. (Orig.). 1983. pap. 6.95 (ISBN 0-7225-0592-2, Pub. by Thorsons Pubs England). Sterling.

MATERIAL HANDLING
see Materials Handling

MATERIAL SCIENCE
see Materials

MATERIALISM
see also Idealism; Naturalism
Mukerji, Chandra. From Graven Images: Patterns of Modern Materialism. (Illus.). 368p. 1983. 30.00x (ISBN 0-231-05166-2); pap. 10.00 (ISBN 0-231-05167-0). Columbia U Pr.
Roy, M. N. Materialism. 1982. Repr. of 1951 ed. 18.50 (ISBN 0-8364-0914-0, Pub. by Ajanta). South Asia Bks.

MATERIALS
see also Biomedical Materials; Composite Materials; Manufacturing Processes; Materials at High Temperatures; Materials Management; Raw Materials
Brady, G. S. & Clauser, H. Materials Handbook. 11th ed. 1977. 46.75 (ISBN 0-07-007069-5). McGraw.
Creyke, W. E. & Sainsbury, I. E. Design with Non-Ductile Materials. (Illus.). xix, 290p. 1982. 57.50 (ISBN 0-85334-149-4, Pub. by Applied Sci England). Elsevier.
Feldman, Leonard, et al. Materials Analysis by Channeling: Submicron Crystallography. 1982. 42.00 (ISBN 0-12-252680-5). Acad Pr.
Handbook of Industrial Materials. 1983. text ed. 65.00 (ISBN 0-87201-523-8). Gulf Pub.
Herman, Herbert, ed. Treatise on Materials Science & Technology: Embrittlement of Engineering Alloys, Vol. 25. (Serial Publication). Date not set. price not set (ISBN 0-12-341825-9). Acad Pr.
Jowett, C. E. Materials & Process in Electronics. 329p. 1982. text ed. 43.50x (ISBN 0-09-145100-0). Sheridan.
Kaldis, E., ed. Current Topics in Material Science, Vol. 9. 520p. 1982. 109.25 (ISBN 0-444-86274-9, North Holland). Elsevier.
Materials & Processes: Continuing Innovations. (Illus.). 1983. 60.00 (ISBN 0-938994-22-0). Soc Adv Material.
Meade, L. E., intro. by. Material & Process Advances '82. (National SAMPE Technical Conference Ser.). (Illus.). 1982. 60.00 (ISBN 0-938994-21-2). Soc Adv Material.
Morrow, John, intro. by. Materials Overview for 1982. (The Science of Advanced Materials & Process Engineering Ser.). (Illus.). 1982. 60.00 (ISBN 0-686-37996-9). Soc Adv Material.
Pollack, ed. Material Science & Metallurgy. 3rd ed. 1980. text ed. 22.95 (ISBN 0-8359-4280-5); solutions manual avail. (ISBN 0-8359-4282-1). Reston.
Radford, Don. The Materials We Use. (Science in Today's World). (Illus.). 72p. (gr. 7-12). 1983. 14.95 (ISBN 0-7134-4073-2, Pub. by Batsford England). David & Charles.
Tottle, C. R. Encyclopedia of Metallurgy & Materials. (Illus.). 800p. 1983. text ed. 85.00x (ISBN 0-911378-45-6). Sheridan.
Van der Beist. Analysis of High Temperature Materials. Date not set. 53.50 (ISBN 0-85334-172-9). Elsevier.
Walters, A. H., et al, eds. Biodeterioration of Materials, Vols. 1 & 2. 1968-72. Vol. 1: Microbiological & Allied Aspects. 96.50 (ISBN 0-85334-623-2); Vol.2: Biodynamic Effects of Messinian Salinity. 96.50 (ISBN 0-85334-538-4). Elsevier.

MATERIALS–CREEP
Mukherjee, S. Boundary Element Methods in Creep & Fracture. (Illus.). 224p. 1983. 35.00 (ISBN 0-85334-163-X, Pub. by Applied Sci England). Elsevier.
Rueesck, H., et al. Creep & Shrinkage: Their Effect on the Behavior of Concrete Structures. (Illus.). 304p. 1983. 60.00 (ISBN 0-387-90669-X). Springer-Verlag.

MATERIALS–DYNAMIC TESTING
see also Structural Dynamics
Mader, Charles L., et al, eds. Los Alamos Explosives Performance Data. LC 82-40391. (Los Alamos Series on Dynamic Material Properties: Vol. 7). 824p. 1983. 45.00x (ISBN 0-520-04014-7). U of Cal Pr.

MATERIALS–FATIGUE
see also Fracture Mechanics; also subdivision Fatigue under specific subjects, e.g. Metals–Fatigue
American Welding Society. Fatigue Fractures in Welded Contructions. 1967. 25.00. Am Welding.
Hertzberg, Richard W. Deformation & Fracture Mechanics of Engineering Materials. 2d ed. 725p. 1983. 36.95 (ISBN 0-686-84628-1). Wiley.

MATERIALS–HANDLING AND TRANSPORTATION
see Materials Handling

MATERIALS–TESTING
see also Materials–Fatigue
Krautkraemer, J. & Krautkraemer, H. Ultrasonic Testing of Materials. 3rd, rev. ed. Zenzinger, B. W., tr. from Ger. (Illus.). 79.50 (ISBN 0-387-11733-4). Springer-Verlag.

MATERIALS, STRENGTH OF
see Strength of Materials

MATERIALS AT HIGH TEMPERATURES
see also Metals at High Temperatures
Baylac, G., ed. Inelastic Analysis & Life Prediction In Elevated Temperature Design. (PVP Ser.: Vol. 59). 250p. 1982. 44.00 (H00216). ASME.
Cole, James L. & Stwalley, William C., eds. High Temperature Chemistry. (ACS Symposium Ser.: No. 179). 1982. write for info. (ISBN 0-8412-0689-9). Am Chemical.
Jortner, J., ed. Thermomechanical Behavior of High Temperature Composites. (AD-04 Ser.). 1982. 30.00 (H00248). ASME.
Yamada, Y. & Roche, R. L., eds. An International Dialogue of Experiences In Elevated Temperature Design: Benchmark Problem Studies & Piping System At Elevated Temperatures. (PVP Ser.: Vol. 66). 204p. 1982. 30.00 (H00223). ASME.
Yamada, Y & Roche, R. L., eds. An International Dialogue of Experiences In Elevated Temperature Design: Material Behavior at Elevated Temperatures & Components Analysis. (PVP Ser.: Vol. 60). 178p. 1982. 34.00 (H00217). ASME.

MATERIALS HANDLING
see also Cargo Handling; Conveying Machinery; Freight and Freightage; Motor-Trucks
Apple, J. M. Plant Layout & Materials Handling. 3rd ed. LC 77-75127. (Illus.). 600p. 1977. 27.95x (ISBN 0-471-07171-4). Wiley.
Boresi, Arthur P., et al. Advanced Mechanics of Materials. 3rd ed. LC 77-28283. 696p. 1978. text ed. 38.95x (ISBN 0-471-08892-7). Wiley.

MATERIALS MANAGEMENT
see also Purchasing
Bailey, Peter & Farmer, David. Materials Management Handbook. 300p. 1982. text ed. 47.50x (ISBN 0-566-02272-9). Gower Pub Ltd.

MATERNAL AND INFANT WELFARE
see also Unmarried Mothers
Eheart, Brenda & Martan, Susan. The Fourth Trimester: On Becoming a Mother. 1983. 13.95 (ISBN 0-686-43210-X); pap. 7.50 (ISBN 0-686-43211-8). ACC.
Parker, Gordon. Maternal Overprotection: A Defined Risk Factor to Psychiatric Disorders. write for info. Grune.

MATERNITY NURSING
see Obstetrical Nursing

MATHEMATICAL ABILITY–TESTING
The Three-R's Test. write for info. (RivEd). HM.

MATHEMATICAL ANALYSIS
see also Algebra; Algebras, Linear; Calculus; Combinatorial Analysis; Engineering Mathematics; Fourier Analysis; Functions; Harmonic Analysis; Mathematical Optimization; Nonlinear Theories; Numerical Analysis; Programming (Electronic Computers)
Apostol, T. M. Calculus: One-Variable Calculus with an Introduction to Linear Algebra, Vol. 1. 2nd ed. LC 73-20899. 666p. 1967. text ed. 30.95x (ISBN 0-471-00005-1). Wiley.
Bartle, Robert G. The Elements of Real Analysis. 2nd ed. LC 75-15979. 480p. 1976. text ed. 30.50x (ISBN 0-471-05464-X); arabic translation avail. (ISBN 0-471-06391-6). Wiley.
Blair, Karin. Cubal Analysis. 220p. Date not set. price not set (ISBN 0-913660-17-5); pap. price not set (ISBN 0-913660-18-3). Magic Circle Pr.
Eells, J., ed. Complex Analysis Trieste: Proceedings, 1981. (Lecture Notes in Mathematics Ser.: Vol. 950). 428p. 1983. pap. 20.50 (ISBN 0-387-11596-X). Springer-Verlag.
Fischer, E. Intermediate Real Analysis. (Undergraduate Texts in Mathematics Ser.). (Illus.). 770p. 1983. 28.00 (ISBN 0-387-90721-1). Springer-Verlag.
Goldberg, Richard R. Methods of Real Analysis. 2nd ed. LC 75-30615. 1976. text ed. 31.95x (ISBN 0-471-31065-4). Wiley.
Malik, S. C. Principles of Real Analysis. LC 82-20051. 1982. 19.95x (ISBN 0-470-27369-0). Halsted Pr.
Perry, P. Scattering Theory by the Enss Method. (Mathematical Reports: Vol. 1, No. 1). 150p. 1982. write for info. (ISBN 3-7186-0093-5). Harwood Academic.
Singh, S. P. & Burry, J. H., eds. Nonlinear Analysis & Applications. (Lecture Notes in Pure & Applied Mathematics: Vol. 80). (Illus.). 488p. 49.75 (ISBN 0-8247-1790-2). Dekker.
Smith, K. T. Primer of Modern Analysis. 2nd ed. (Undergraduate Texts in Mathematics Ser.). 482p. 1983. 28.00 (ISBN 0-387-90797-1). Springer-Verlag.
Stewart, I. & Tall, D. O. Complex Analysis. LC 82-4351. (Illus.). 250p. Date not set. price not set (ISBN 0-521-24513-3); pap. price not set (ISBN 0-521-28763-4). Cambridge U Pr.

MATHEMATICAL DRAWING
see Mechanical Drawing

MATHEMATICAL ECONOMICS
see Economics, Mathematical

MATHEMATICAL INDUCTION
see Induction (Mathematics)

MATHEMATICAL LOGIC
see Logic, Symbolic and Mathematical

MATHEMATICAL MACHINE THEORY
see Machine Theory

MATHEMATICAL MODELS
see also Digital Computer Simulation; Game Theory; Machine Theory; Programming (Electronic Computers); System Analysis also subdivision Mathematical Models under specific subjects, e.g. Human Behavior–Mathematical Models
Gilchrist, R., ed. GLIM 82: Proceedings of the International Conference on Generalized Linear Models, 1982. (Lecture Notes in Statistics: Vol. 14). (Illus.). 188p. 1983. pap. 12.50 (ISBN 0-387-90777-7). Springer-Verlag.

Nicholson, H., ed. Modelling of Dynamical Systems, Vol. I. (IEE Control Engineering Ser.: No. 12). (Illus.). 256p. 1980. casebound 68.00 (ISBN 0-906048-38-9). Inst Elect Eng.

Whiteman, Charles H. Linear Rational Expaectations Models: A User's Guide. 130p. 1983. 19.50 (ISBN 0-8166-1181-5); pap. 9.95 (ISBN 0-8166-1179-3). U of Minn Pr.

Yaglom, I. M. Mathematical Structures & Mathematical Modeling. 296p. 1983. write for info. (ISBN 0-677-06110-2). Gordon.

MATHEMATICAL OPTIMIZATION

see also Decision-Making-Mathematical Models; Dynamic Programming; Experimental Design; Programming (Mathematics); System Analysis

Dennis, John E. & Schnabel, Robert B. Numerical Methods for Unconstrained Optimization & Nonlinear Equations. (Illus.). 272p. 1983. text ed. 27.00 (ISBN 0-13-627216-9). P-H.

Fletcher, R. Practical Methods of Optimization: Unconstrained Optimization, Vol. 1. LC 79-41486. 120p. 1980. 26.95x (ISBN 0-471-27711-8, Pub. by Wiley-Interscience). Wiley.

Ryan, E. P. Optimal Relay & Saturating Control Systems Synthesis. (IEE Control Engineering Ser.: No. 14). 352p. 1982. casebound 94.00 (ISBN 0-906048-56-7). Inst Elect Eng.

MATHEMATICAL PHYSICS

see also Elasticity; Electricity; Engineering Mathematics; Ergodic Theory; Gases, Kinetic Theory of; Hydrodynamics; Magnetism; Nonlinear Theories; Perturbation (Mathematics); Sound; System Analysis; Thermodynamics; Transport Theory

Arsenin, E. Basic Equations & Special Functions of Mathematical Physics. 1968. 13.50 (ISBN 0-444-19778-8). Elsevier.

Kreyszig, Erwin. Advanced Engineering Mathematics. 5th ed. 1100p. 1983. text ed. 36.95 (ISBN 0-471-86251-7); tchrs.' manual avail. (ISBN 0-471-89855-4). Wiley.

Novikov, S. P., ed. Mathematical Physics Reviews. Hamermesh, Morton, tr. from Russian. (Soviet Scientific Reviews, Section C: Vol. 4). 240p. 1982. 72.50 (ISBN 0-686-84002-X). Harwood Academic.

Rao, Bhaskara K., ed. Theories of Charges: A Study of Finitely Additive Measures. (Pure & Applied Mathmatics Ser.). Date not set. price not set (ISBN 0-12-095780-9). Acad Pr.

MATHEMATICAL PROGRAMMING (MANAGEMENT)

see Scheduling (Management)

MATHEMATICAL RECREATIONS

see also Chess

Ainley, Stephen. Mathematical Puzzles. 168p. 1983. 12.95 (ISBN 0-13-561845-2); pap. 4.95 (ISBN 0-13-561837-1). P-H.

--Mathemtical Puzzles. 156p. 1982. 30.00x (ISBN 0-7135-1327-6, Pub. by Bell & Hyman England). State Mutual Bk.

Heafford, Philip. The Math Entertainer. LC 82-40420. (Illus.). 176p. 1983. pap. 3.95 (ISBN 0-394-71374-5, Vin). Random.

Steinhaus, H. Mathematical Snapshots. 3rd, rev., & enl. ed. (Illus.). 320p. 1983. pap. 7.95 (ISBN 0-19-503267-5, GB 726, GB). Oxford U Pr.

The, Diagram Group. Number Puzzles. 96p. (Orig.). 1983. pap. 1.75 (ISBN 0-345-30479-9). Ballantine.

MATHEMATICAL SEQUENCES

see Sequences (Mathematics)

MATHEMATICAL SETS

see Set Theory

MATHEMATICAL STATISTICS

see also Biometry; Errors, Theory Of; Estimation Theory; Multivariate Analysis; Probabilities; Regression Analysis; Sampling (Statistics); Sequential Analysis; Statistical Astronomy; Statistics; Time-Series Analysis

Anderson, Theodore W. Introduction to Multivariate Statistical Analysis. LC 58-6068. (Probability & Mathematical Statistics Ser.). 374p. 1958. 36.95x (ISBN 0-471-02640-9). Wiley.

Arthanari, Subramanyam & Dodge, Yadolah. Mathematical Programming in Statistics. LC 80-21637. (Probability & Math Statistics Ser.: Applied Probability & Statistics). 413p. 1981. 34.95x (ISBN 0-471-08073-X, Pub. by Wiley-Interscience). Wiley.

Bashaw, W. L. Mathematics for Statistics. LC 69-16123. 326p. 1969. pap. 18.50x (ISBN 0-471-05531-X). Wiley.

Bennett, Carl A. & Franklin, N. L. Statistical Analysis in Chemistry & the Chemical Industry. (Probability & Mathematical Statistics: Applied Probability & Statistics Section). 1954. 50.50 (ISBN 0-471-06633-8, Pub by Wiley-Interscience). Wiley.

Bickel, Peter J. & Doksum, Kjell, eds. A Festschrift for Erich L. Lehmann. (Wadsworth Statistics-Probability Ser.). 461p. 1982. 39.95 (ISBN 0-534-98044-9). Wadsworth Pub.

Brownlee, Kenneth A. Statistical Theory & Methodology in Science & Engineering. 2nd ed. 590p. 1965. 39.95x (ISBN 0-471-11355-7). Wiley.

Brunk, H. D. Introduction to Mathematical Statistics. 3rd ed. LC 74-82348. 400p. 1975. text ed. 27.50 (ISBN 0-471-00834-6). Wiley.

Davison, Mark L. Multidimensional Scaling. (Probability & Mathematical Statistics: Applied Probability & Statistic Section Ser.). 300p. 1983. 25.25 (ISBN 0-471-86417-X, Pub. by Wiley-Interscience). Wiley.

Galambos, Janos. The Asymptotic Theory of Extreme Order Statistics. LC 78-1916. (Probability & Mathematical Staistics Ser.). 352p. 1978. 47.95x (ISBN 0-471-02148-2, Pub. by Wiley-Interscience). Wiley.

Gilchrist, R., ed. GLIM 82: Proceedings of the International Conference on Generalized Linear Models, 1982. (Lecture Notes in Statistics: Vol. 14). (Illus.). 188p. 1983. pap. 12.50 (ISBN 0-387-90777-7). Springer-Verlag.

Heyer, H. Theory of Statistical Experiments. (Springer Series in Statistics). (Illus.). 289p. 1983. 19.80 (ISBN 0-387-90785-8). Springer-Verlag.

Hogg, Robert V. & Tanis, Elliot A. Probability & Statistical Inference. 2nd ed. 500p. 1983. text ed. 22.95 (ISBN 0-02-355730-3). Macmillan.

Kendall, Maurice & Stuart, Allan. Advanced Theory of Statistics, Vol. 4. 700p. 1983. 65.00 (ISBN 0-02-847860-6). Free Pr.

Kshirsagar. A Course in Linear Models. (Statistics: Textbooks & Monographs). 488p. 1983. write for info. (ISBN 0-8247-1585-3). Dekker.

Pfanzagl, J. Contributions to a General Asymptotic Statistical Theory. (Lecture Notes in Statistics Ser.: Vol. 13). (Illus.). 315p. 1983. pap. 16.80 (ISBN 0-387-90776-9). Springer-Verlag.

MATHEMATICAL SYMBOLS

see Abbreviations

MATHEMATICIANS

Ashurst, F. Gareth. Founders of Modern Mathematics. 128p. 1982. 39.00x (ISBN 0-584-10380-8, Pub. by Muller Ltd). State Mutual Bk.

Reid, Constance. Jerzy Neyman-From Life. (Illus.). 320p. 1982. 19.80 (ISBN 0-387-90747-5). Springer-Verlag.

MATHEMATICS

see also Algebra; Arithmetic; Axioms; Biomathematics; Business Mathematics; Calculus; Dynamics; Economics, Mathematical; Engineering Mathematics; Equations; Errors, Theory of; Fourth Dimension; Fractions; Functions; Game Theory; Geometry; Graphic Methods; Groups, Theory of; Harmonic Analysis; Induction (Mathematics); Kinematics; Logic, Symbolic and Mathematical; Maxima and Minima; Mensuration; Metric System; Numbers, Theory of; Numerals; Numeration; Probabilities; Sequences (Mathematics); Set Theory; Shop Mathematics; Statics; Transformations (Mathematics); Trigonometry; Vector Analysis

also headings beginning with the word Mathematical

Alefeld, Gotz & Herzberger, Jurgen. Introduction to Interval Computations. Rockne, Jon, tr. from Ger. (Computer Science & Applied Mathematics Ser.). Date not set. price not set (ISBN 0-12-049820-0). Acad Pr.

Anton, Howard & Kolman, B., eds. Mathematics with Applications for the Management, Life & Social Sciences. 2nd ed. LC 81-66947. 851p. 1982. text ed. 20.00 (ISBN 0-12-059561-3). Acad Pr.

Baker, Vernoon C. & Aufmann, Richard N. Essential Mathematics with Applications. LC 82-82928. 288p. 1982. pap. text ed. 20.95 (ISBN 0-395-33195-1); write for info. answer booklet (ISBN 0-395-33196-X). HM.

Barker & Aufmann. Essential Mathematics with Applications. 1982. 9.95 (ISBN 0-686-84648-6); supplementary materials avail. HM.

Bashaw, W. L. Mathematics for Statistics. LC 69-16123. 326p. 1969. pap. 18.50x (ISBN 0-471-05531-X). Wiley.

Berge, C. & Bresson, D., eds. Combinatorial Mathematics: Proceedings of the International Colloquium on Graph Theory & Combinatorics, Marseille-Luminy, June, 1981. (North-Holland Mathematics Studies: Vol. 75). 660p. 1983. 106.50 (ISBN 0-444-86512-8, North Holland). Elsevier.

Berger, Marc A. & Sloan, Alan D. A Method of Generalized Characteristics. LC 82-8741. (Memoirs of the American Mathematical Society Ser.: No. 266). 4.00 (ISBN 0-8218-2266-7, MEMO/266). Am Math.

Bitter, et al. McGraw-Hill Mathematics, 8 levels. Incl. Level 1. text ed. 7.40 (ISBN 0-07-005761-3); tchr's ed. 21.40 (ISBN 0-07-005771-0); wkbk. 3.68 (ISBN 0-07-005781-8); Level 2. text ed. 7.40 (ISBN 0-07-005762-1); tchr's ed. 21.40 (ISBN 0-07-005772-9); wkbk 3.68 (ISBN 0-07-005782-6); Level 3. text ed. 12.08 (ISBN 0-07-005763-X); tchr's ed. 22.44 (ISBN 0-07-005773-7); wkbk. 4.08 (ISBN 0-07-005783-4); Level 4. text ed. 12.08 (ISBN 0-07-005764-8); tchr's ed. 22.44 (ISBN 0-07-005774-5); wkbk. 4.08 (ISBN 0-07-005784-2); Level 5. text ed. 12.08 (ISBN 0-07-005765-6); tchr's ed. 22.44 (ISBN 0-07-005775-3); wkbk. 4.08 (ISBN 0-07-005785-0); Level 6. text ed. 12.08 (ISBN 0-07-005766-4); tchr's ed. 22.44 (ISBN 0-07-005776-1); wkbk. 4.08 (ISBN 0-07-005786-9); Level 7. text ed. 14.56 (ISBN 0-07-005767-2); tchr's ed. 23.84 (ISBN 0-07-005777-X); wkbk. 4.08 (ISBN 0-07-005787-7); Level 8. text ed. 14.56 (ISBN 0-07-005768-0); tchr's ed. 23.84 (ISBN 0-07-005778-8); wkbk. 4.08 (ISBN 0-07-005788-5). 1981. write for info. supplementary materials. McGraw.

Boas, Mary L. Mathematical Methods in Physical Sciences. LC 66-17646. 778p. 1966. 29.95x (ISBN 0-471-08417-4). Wiley.

Brooks, Bearl. Bilingual Mathematics: Grade Four. (Math Ser.). 24p. 1977. wkbk. 5.00 (ISBN 0-8209-0137-7, BLM-3). ESP.

--Bilingual Mathematics: Grade Three. (Math Ser.). 24p. 1977. wkbk. 5.00 (ISBN 0-8209-0136-9, BLM-2). ESP.

--Bilingual Mathematics: Grade Two. (Math Ser.). 24p. 1977. wkbk. 5.00 (ISBN 0-8209-0135-0, BLM-1). ESP.

Burton, T. A., ed. Volterra Integral & Differential Equations. LC 82-18932. (Mathematics in Science & Engineering Ser.). Date not set. price not set (ISBN 0-12-147380-5). Acad Pr.

Coombs, Clyde H. Psychology & Mathematics: An Essay on Theory. 104p. 1983. text ed. 12.50 (ISBN 0-472-10034-3). U of Mich Pr.

Curtis, Alan R. Practical Math for Business. 3d ed. LC 82-84521. 368p. 1983. pap. text ed. 16.95 (ISBN 0-395-32698-2); instr's. annotated ed. 17.95 (ISBN 0-395-32699-0). HM.

DAvenport, H. The Higher Arithmetic: An Introduction to the Theory of Numbers. 172p. 1983. pap. 4.00 (ISBN 0-486-24452-0). Dover.

Findley, W., et al. Creep & Relaxation of Nonlinear Viscoelastic Materials. 1976. 72.50 (ISBN 0-444-10775-4). Elsevier.

Forman, William & Gavurin, Lester L. Elements of Arithmetic, Algebra & Geometry. LC 78-159159. 318p. 1972. text ed. 20.95x (ISBN 0-471-00654-8). Wiley.

Fowler, Frank P. & Sandberg, E. W. Basic Mathematics for Administration. LC 62-15189. 339p. 1962. text ed. 26.95x (ISBN 0-471-26976-X); supp. mat. avail. (ISBN 0-471-26978-6); test avail. (ISBN 0-471-26985-9). Wiley.

Graham, Ronald, et al. Ramsey Theory. LC 80-14110. (Interscience in Discrete Mathematics Ser.). 174p. 1980. 26.95x (ISBN 0-471-05997-8, Pub. by Wiley Interscience). Wiley.

Guillemin, Victor, ed. Studies in Applied Mathematics: Volume Dedicated to Irving Segal. (Advances in Mathematics: Supplementary Studies: Vol. 8). Date not set. 36.00 (ISBN 0-12-305480-X). Acad Pr.

Harper, W. M. & Stafford, L. W. Basic Mathematics. 176p. 1981. 29.00x (ISBN 0-7121-0287-6, Pub. by Macdonald & Evans). State Mutual Bk.

An Introduction to Infinitely Many Variates. 132p. 1959. 20.00 (ISBN 0-686-42733-5). Goose Pond Pr.

Justus, Fred. Algebra. (Math Ser.). 24p. (gr. 7-11). 1979. wkbk. 5.00 (ISBN 0-8209-0101-6, A-11). ESP.

--Applied Mathematics for Business & Home. (Math Ser.). 24p. (gr. 6 up). 1979. wkbk. 5.00 (ISBN 0-8209-0117-2, A-27). ESP.

--Arithmetic Exercises: Grade Eight. (Math Ser.). 24p. (gr. 8). 1978. wkbk. 5.00 (ISBN 0-8209-0098-2, A-8). ESP.

--Arithmetic Exercises: Grade Five. (Math Ser.). 24p. (gr. 5). 1979. wkbk. 5.00 (ISBN 0-8209-0095-8, A-5). ESP.

--Arithmetic Exercises: Grade Four. (Math Ser.). 24p. (gr. 4). 1979. wkbk. 5.00 (ISBN 0-8209-0094-X, A-4). ESP.

--Arithmetic Exercises: Grade Seven. (Math Ser.). 24p. (gr. 7). 1979. wkbk. 5.00 (ISBN 0-8209-0097-4, A-7). ESP.

--Arithmetic Exercises: Grade Six. (Math Ser.). 24p. (gr. 6). 1977. wkbk. 5.00 (ISBN 0-8209-0096-6, A-6). ESP.

--Basic Arithmetic Fundamentals. (Math Ser.). 24p. (gr. 3-6). 1977. wkbk. 5.00 (ISBN 0-8209-0116-4, A-26). ESP.

--Basic Skills Counting Money Workbook. (Basic Skills Workbooks). 32p. (gr. 2-4). 1983. 0.99 (ISBN 0-8209-0569-0, MW-2). ESP.

--Basic Skills Counting Workbook. (Basic Skills Workbooks). 32p. (gr. k-1). 1983. 0.99 (ISBN 0-8209-0564-X, EEW-5). ESP.

--Clock & Time Related Problems. (Math Ser.). 24p. (gr. 4-8). 1976. wkbk. 5.00 (ISBN 0-8209-0115-6, A-25). ESP.

--Counting Money. (Math Ser.). 24p. (gr. 2-4). 1979. wkbk. 5.00 (ISBN 0-8209-0113-X, A-23). ESP.

--Drills & Tests: Grades Seven to Ten. (Math Ser.). 24p. 1979. wkbk. 5.00 (ISBN 0-8209-0100-8, A-10). ESP.

--Drills & Tests: Grades Six to Nine. (Math Ser.). 24p. 1979. wkbk. 5.00 (ISBN 0-8209-0099-0, A-9). ESP.

--Geometric Figures & Concepts. (Math Ser.). 24p. (gr. 4-9). 1976. wkbk. 5.00 (ISBN 0-8209-0114-8, A-24). ESP.

--Geometry. (Math Ser.). 24p. (gr. 7-11). 1979. wkbk. 5.00 (ISBN 0-8209-0102-4, A-12). ESP.

--Graphic Mathematics. (Math Ser.). 24p. (gr. 5-9). 1976. wkbk. 5.00 (ISBN 0-8209-0119-9, A-29). ESP.

--Measuring Devices & Instruments. (Math Ser.). 24p. (gr. 4-6). 1976. wkbk. 5.00 (ISBN 0-8209-0118-0, A-28). ESP.

--My First Number Book. (Early Education Ser.). 24p. (gr. 1). 1981. wkbk. 5.00 (ISBN 0-8209-0216-0, K-18). ESP.

--Number Exercises: Grade 1. (Math Ser.). 24p. 1980. wkbk. 5.00 (ISBN 0-8209-0091-5, A-1). ESP.

--Number Exercises: Grade 2. (Math Ser.). 24p. 1977. wkbk. 5.00 (ISBN 0-8209-0092-3, A-2). ESP.

--Number Exercises: Grade 3. (Math Ser.). 24p. 1976. wkbk. 5.00 (ISBN 0-8209-0093-1, A-3). ESP.

--One & One More. (Math Ser.). 24p. (gr. 1). 1980. wkbk. 5.00 (ISBN 0-8209-0088-5, A-0). ESP.

--Programmed Math: Grade 1. (Math Ser.). 24p. 1976. wkbk. 5.00 (ISBN 0-8209-0127-X, PM-1). ESP.

--Programmed Math: Grade 2. (Math Ser.). 24p. 1976. wkbk. 5.00 (ISBN 0-8209-0128-8, PM-2). ESP.

--Programmed Math: Grade 3. (Math Ser.). 24p. 1980. wkbk. 5.00 (ISBN 0-8209-0129-6, PM-3). ESP.

--Programmed Math: Grade 4. (Math Ser.). 24p. wkbk. 5.00 (ISBN 0-8209-0130-X, PM-4). ESP.

--Programmed Math: Grade 5. (Math Ser.). 24p. 1977. wkbk. 5.00 (ISBN 0-8209-0131-8, PM-5). ESP.

--Programmed Math: Grade 6. (Math Ser.). 24p. 1979. wkbk. 5.00 (ISBN 0-8209-0132-6, PM-6). ESP.

--Programmed Math: Grade 7. (Math Ser.). 24p. 1977. 5.00 (ISBN 0-8209-0133-4, PM-7). ESP.

--Programmed Math: Grade 8. (Math Ser.). 24p. 1977. wkbk. 5.00 (ISBN 0-8209-0134-2, PM-8). ESP.

--Programmed Math: Kindergarten. (Math Ser.). 24p. 1977. wkbk. 5.00 (ISBN 0-8209-0126-1, PM-R). ESP.

--Remedial Arithmetic. (Math Ser.). 24p. (gr. 3-5). 1979. wkbk. 5.00 (ISBN 0-8209-0112-1, A-22). ESP.

--Remedial Arithmetic 1A. (Math Ser.). 24p. (gr. 2-3). 1978. wkbk. 5.00 (ISBN 0-8209-0109-1, A-19). ESP.

--Remedial Arithmetic 1B. (Math Ser.). 24p. (gr. 2-4). 1978. wkbk. 5.00 (ISBN 0-8209-0110-5, A-20). ESP.

--Remedial Arithmetic 1C. (Math Ser.). 24p. (gr. 3-5). 1978. wkbk. 5.00 (ISBN 0-8209-0111-3, A-21). ESP.

--Secret Messages: Add.-Subt. (Puzzles Ser.). 24p. (gr. 3-5). 1980. wkbk. 5.00 (ISBN 0-8209-0301-9, PU-15). ESP.

--Secret Messages: Mult.-Div. (Puzzles Ser.). 24p. (gr. 3-5). 1980. wkbk. 5.00 (ISBN 0-8209-0302-7, PU-16). ESP.

--Simple Additon & Subtraction. (Math Ser.). 24p. (gr. k-1). 1982. wkbk. 5.00 (ISBN 0-8209-0089-3, A-K). ESP.

--Units of Measure. (Math Ser.). 24p. (gr. 3-5). 1979. wkbk. 5.00 (ISBN 0-8209-0120-2, A-30). ESP.

--Written Problems in Math: Grade 2. (Math Ser.). 24p. 1980. wkbk. 5.00 (ISBN 0-8209-0122-9, A-32). ESP.

Kadison, Richard V. & Ringrose, John R., eds. Fundamentals of the Theory of Operator Algebras, Vol. 1. LC 82-13768. Date not set. price not set (ISBN 0-12-393301-3). Acad Pr.

Keedy, M. & Smith, S. Applying Mathematics. (gr. 10-12). 1983. 16.20 (ISBN 0-201-05072-2, Sch Div); 18.50 (ISBN 0-201-05073-0) (ISBN 0-201-05075-7). Skills Bk. write for info. (ISBN 0-201-05074-9). A-W.

Kockman, Stanely D. The Symplectic Corbordism Ring II. LC 79-27872. (Memoirs of thr American Mathematical Society Ser.: No. 271). 10.00 (ISBN 0-8218-2271-3, MEMO/271). Am Math.

Kulikowski, J. L., ed. Discrete Mathematics. (Banach Center Publications: Vol. 7). (Illus.). 224p. 1982. 40.00x (ISBN 83-01-01494-6). Intl Pubns Serv.

Lacret-Subirat, Fabian. Lacret Mathematics Basic Concepts & Skills: Grade 9-12. 2nd ed. (Illus.). 518p. 1983. 12.85 (ISBN 0-686-43020-4); s.p. 8.00 (ISBN 0-686-43021-2). Lacret Pub.

McMasters, Dale. Basic Skills Written Problems in Math Workbook. (Basic Skills Workbooks). 32p. (gr. 3-4). 1983. 0.99 (ISBN 0-8209-0574-7, MW-7). ESP.

--Written Problems in Math: Grade 4. (Math Ser.). 24p. 1981. wkbk. 5.00 (ISBN 0-8209-0124-5, A-34). ESP.

Manoukian, Edward B. Remoralization. (Pure & Applied Mathematics Ser.). Date not set. price not set (ISBN 0-12-468450-5). Acad Pr.

Nustad, Harry L. & Wesner, Terry H. Essentials of Technical Mathematics. 600p. 1983. text ed. write for info. (ISBN 0-697-08551-1); instrs' manual avail. (ISBN 0-697-08553-8); wkbk. avail. (ISBN 0-697-08552-X). Wm C Brown.

Peake, Jim. Basic Mathematics, Vol. II. 560p. 1982. pap. text ed. 19.95 (ISBN 0-8403-2787-0). Kendall-Hunt.

--Basic Mathematics, Vol. I. 288p. 1982. pap. text ed. 12.95 (ISBN 0-8403-2786-2). Kendall-Hunt.

Pshenichny, B. & Danikin, Y. Numerical Methods in Extremal Problems. 276p. 1978. 8.95 (ISBN 0-8285-0732-5, Pub. by MIR Pubs USSR). Imported Pubns.

Raedmacher, H. Higher Mathematics from an Elementary Point of View. Goldfeld, L., ed. 160p. Date not set. text ed. price not set (ISBN 3-7643-3064-3). Birkhauser.

Rosenberg, Richard. Competence in Mathematics, Bk. I. (Mathematic Ser.). 96p. 1981. wkbk. 4.50 (ISBN 0-9602800-4-9). Comp Pr.

--Competence in Mathematics, Bk. II. (Mathematics Ser.). 90p. 1981. wkbk. 4.50 (ISBN 0-9602800-5-7). Comp Pr.

Shaw, Marie-Jose. Written Problems in Math: Grade 3. (Math Ser.). 24p. 1982. wkbk. 5.00 (ISBN 0-8209-0123-7, A-33). ESP.

Smith, Douglas, et al. A Transition in Advanced Mathematics. LC 82-20737. 200p. 1983. text ed. 21.95 (ISBN 0-534-01249-3). Brooks-Cole.

Speiser, D., ed. Daniel Bernoulli: Werke Band 2: Mathematische Schriften. 403p. 1982. text ed. 60.00x (ISBN 3-7643-1084-7). Birkhauser.

Stancl, Donald L. & Stancl, Mildred L. Applications of College Mathematics: Management, Life, & Social Sciences. 736p. Date not set. 26.95 (ISBN 0-669-03860-1); instr's guide 1.95 (ISBN 0-669-03861-X); price not set computer supplement (ISBN 0-669-03881-4). Heath.

Strelich, Thomas, Sr. & Strelich, Virginia. The New Basics. (gr. 3-6). 1982. pap. text ed. write for info. (Sch Div). A-W.

Symposian Applied Mathematics. Computed Tomography. Shepp, Lawrence A., ed. LC 82-18508. 20.00 (ISBN 0-8218-0033-7, PSAPM-27); pap. 14.00 (ISBN 0-686-84532-3). Am Math.

Van der Houwen, P. Construction of Integrated Formulas for Initial Value Problems. 1976. 64.00 (ISBN 0-444-10903-X). Elsevier.

Vermeersch, LaVonne F. & Southwick, Charles E. Practical Problems in Mathematics for Graphic Arts. Rev. ed. LC 82-72128. (Illus.). 176p. 1983. pap. text ed. 7.00 (ISBN 0-8273-2100-7); Instr's Guide avail. (ISBN 0-8273-2101-5). Delmar.

Walker, Mary Lou. Rhythm, Time, & Value. (Music Ser.). 24p. (gr. 3 up). 1980. wkbk. 5.00 (ISBN 0-8209-0278-0, MU-7). ESP.

MATHEMATICS–ADDRESSES, ESSAYS, LECTURES

Cantor, D., et al, eds. Selected Papers of Theodore S. Motzkin. Date not set. text ed. price not set (ISBN 3-7643-3087-2). Birkhauser.

Halmos, P. R. Selecta Volume One: Research Contributions. (Illus.). 458p. 1983. 32.00 (ISBN 0-387-90755-6). Springer-Verlag.

--Selecta Volume Two: Expository Writing. (Illus.). 256p. 1983. 19.80 (ISBN 0-387-90756-4). Springer-Verlag.

Hsu, P. L. Collected Papers. (Illus.). 589p. 1983. 48.00 (ISBN 0-387-90725-4). Springer-Verlag.

Hua, L. K. Selected Papers. (Illus.). 888p. 1983. 42.00 (ISBN 0-387-90744-0). Springer-Verlag.

Obata, M., ed. Selected Papers of Yano Kentaro. (North-Holland Mathematics Studies: No. 70). 366p. 1982. 53.25 (ISBN 0-444-86495-4, North Holland). Elsevier.

Troelstra, A. S. & Van Dalen, D., eds. The L. E. J. Brouwer Centenary Symposium: Proceedings of the Conference Held at Noordwijkerhout, June 1981. (Studies in Logic & the Foundations of Mathematics: Vol. 110). 456p. 1982. 68.00 (ISBN 0-444-86494-6, North Holland). Elsevier.

MATHEMATICS–CURIOSA AND MISCELLANY

Jenkins, Gerald & Wild, Anne. Mathematical Curiosities, Vol. III. 28p. 1983. pap. 3.95 (ISBN 0-13-561225-X). P-H.

MATHEMATICS–DATA PROCESSING

Ashley, R. Background Math for a Computer World. 2nd ed. LC 80-11562. (Wiley Self-Teaching Guides). 308p. 1980. pap. text ed. 8.95 (ISBN 0-471-08086-1). Wiley.

Bundy, Alan. The Computer Modelling of Mathematical Reasoning. Date not set. price not set (ISBN 0-12-141252-0). Acad Pr.

MATHEMATICS–DICTIONARIES

International Mathematic Union, ed. World Dictionary of Mathematics 1982. 7th ed. 728p. 23.00 (ISBN 0-686-84619-2, WRLDIR/7). Am Math.

MATHEMATICS–EARLY WORKS TO 1800

see also Mathematics, Greek

Sesiano, J. Diophantus' Arithmetica: Books IV to VI in the Arabic Translation of Qusta ibn Luqa. (Sources in the History of Mathematics & Physical Sciences Ser.: Vol. 3). (Illus.). 502p. 1983. 72.00 (ISBN 0-387-90690-8). Springer-Verlag.

MATHEMATICS–EXAMINATIONS, QUESTIONS, ETC.

Allasio, John. Practice RCT Math Exam, No. 12. (gr. 9-12). 1982. of 20 5.50 set (ISBN 0-937820-44-X). Westsea Pub.

Allasio, John, et al. Practice RCT Math Exam, No. 10. (gr. 9-12). of 20 5.50 set (ISBN 0-937820-40-7). Westsea Pub.

--Practice RCT Math Exam, No. 11. (gr. 9-12). 1982. of 20 5.50 set (ISBN 0-937820-42-3). Westsea Pub.

Artino, Ralph A. & Gaglione, Anthony M. Contest Problem Book IV: Annual High School Examinations 1973-1982. LC 82-51076. (New Mathematical Library Ser.: No. 29). 200p. 1982. write for info. (ISBN 0-88385-629-8). Math Assn.

Black, Richard L., et al. Ninth Year Mathematics. (Arco's Regents Review Ser.). 288p. (Orig.). 1983. pap. 3.95 (ISBN 0-686-82195-5, 5701). Arco.

Herzog, David A. Mathematics Workbook for the GED Test. LC 82-20571. (Arco's Preparation for the GED Examination Ser.). 256p. 1983. pap. 5.95 (ISBN 0-668-05542-1). Arco.

Rosenberg, Richard. Lovejoy's Math Review for the SAT. Levy, Valerie, ed. (Exam Preparation Guides). (Orig.). 1983. pap. 7.95 (ISBN 0-671-47150-3). Monarch Pr.

Scholastic Testing Service Editors. Practice for High School Competency Tests in Mathematics. 160p. 1983. pap. 4.95 (ISBN 0-668-05548-0, 5548). Arco.

MATHEMATICS–HANDBOOKS, MANUALS, ETC.

Ashlock, Robert B. & Johnson, Martin L. Guide Each Child's Learning of Mathematics: A Diagnostic Approach to Instruction. 612p. 1983. text ed. 21.95 (ISBN 0-675-20023-7). Additional supplements may be obtained from publisher. Merrill.

Mathfile: User's Guide. 350p. 1982. 50.00 (ISBN 0-8218-0216-X). Am Math.

MATHEMATICS–HISTORY

see also Mathematics, Chinese; Mathematics, Greek, and similar headings

Ashurst, F. Gareth. Founders of Modern Mathematics. 128p. 1982. 39.00x (ISBN 0-584-10380-8, Pub. by Muller Ltd). State Mutual Bk.

Boyer, Carl B. History of Mathematics. LC 68-16506. 717p. 1968. 29.95x (ISBN 0-471-09374-2). Wiley.

Calinger, Ronald, ed. Classics of Mathematics. LC 80-15567. (Classics Ser.). (Orig.). 1982. pap. 18.00x (ISBN 0-935610-13-8). Moore Pub IL.

Reid, Constance. Jerzy Neyman-From Life. (Illus.). 320p. 1982. 19.80 (ISBN 0-387-90747-5). Springer-Verlag.

MATHEMATICS–JUVENILE LITERATURE

Crary, Elizabeth. My Name Is Not Dummy. (Children's Problem Solving Bks.). (Illus.). 32p. (Orig.). (ps-2). 1983. PLB 8.95 (ISBN 0-9602862-9-2); pap. 3.95 (ISBN 0-9602862-8-4). Parenting Pr.

Dittmar, Mark. Math Montana & Friends. (gr. 4-6). 1982. 5.95 (ISBN 0-86653-084-3, GA 430). Good Apple.

Eicholz, Robert & O'Daffer, Phares. Mathematics In Our World. rev. ed. (gr. 1). 1982. 18.75 (ISBN 0-201-18111-8, Sch Div); team package, with tchr's. ed. 56.25 (ISBN 0-201-18112-6, Sch Div). A-W.

Smart, Margaret A. Focus on Pre-Algebra. (Illus.). 48p. (Orig.). (gr. 6-9). 1983. pap. text ed. 4.94 (ISBN 0-918932-81-5). Activity Resources.

MATHEMATICS–LABORATORIES

see Computation Laboratories

MATHEMATICS–OUTLINES, SYLLABI, ETC.

Bitter, et al. McGraw-Hill Mathematics, 8 levels. Incl. Level 1. text ed. 7.40 (ISBN 0-07-005761-3); tchr's ed. 21.40 (ISBN 0-07-005771-0); wkbk. 3.68 (ISBN 0-07-005781-8); Level 2. text ed. 7.40 (ISBN 0-07-005762-1); tchr's ed. 21.40 (ISBN 0-07-005772-9); wkbk 3.68 (ISBN 0-07-005782-6); Level 3. text ed. 12.08 (ISBN 0-07-005763-X); tchr's ed. 22.44 (ISBN 0-07-005773-7); wkbk. 4.08 (ISBN 0-07-005783-4); Level 4. text ed. 12.08 (ISBN 0-07-005764-8); tchr's ed. 22.44 (ISBN 0-07-005774-5); wkbk. 4.08 (ISBN 0-07-005784-2); Level 5. text ed. 12.08 (ISBN 0-07-005765-6); tchr's ed. 22.44 (ISBN 0-07-005775-3); wkbk. 4.08 (ISBN 0-07-005785-0); Level 6. text ed. 12.08 (ISBN 0-07-005766-4); tchr's ed. 22.44 (ISBN 0-07-005776-1); wkbk. 4.08 (ISBN 0-07-005786-9); Level 7. text ed. 14.56 (ISBN 0-07-005767-2); tchr's ed. 23.84 (ISBN 0-07-005777-X); wkbk. 4.08 (ISBN 0-07-005787-7); Level 8. text ed. 14.56 (ISBN 0-07-005768-0); tchr's ed. 23.84 (ISBN 0-07-005778-8); wkbk. 4.08 (ISBN 0-07-005788-5). 1981. write for info. supplementary materials. McGraw.

Blitzer, Robert & Gill, Jack C. College Mathematics Review. (Illus.). 238p. (Orig.). 1982. pap. text ed. 12.95x (ISBN 0-943202-03-5). H & H Pub.

MATHEMATICS–PHILOSOPHY

Descartes, Rene. Discours de la Methode. Gadoffre, G., ed. (Modern French Text Ser.). 1961. pap. write for info. (ISBN 0-7190-0144-7). Manchester.

Kitcher, Phillip. The Nature of Mathematical Knowledge. 273p. 1983. 18.95 (ISBN 0-19-503149-0). Oxford U Pr.

McCoy, N. H. Rings & Ideals. (Carus Monograph: No. 8). 216p. 1948. 16.50 (ISBN 0-88385-008-7). Math Assn.

Miller, J. Philip. Numbers in Presence & Absence: A Study of Husserl's Philosophy of Mathematics. 1982. lib. bdg. 29.50 (ISBN 0-686-37593-9, Pub. by Martinus Nijhoff). Kluwer Boston.

MATHEMATICS–POPULAR WORKS

Steinhaus, H. Mathematical Snapshots. 3rd, rev., & enl. ed. (Illus.). 320p. 1983. pap. 7.95 (ISBN 0-19-503267-5, GB 726, GB). Oxford U Pr.

MATHEMATICS–PROBLEMS, EXERCISES, ETC.

Berrondo, Marie. Mathematical Games. Dax, Peter & Fitzpatrick, Mariana, trs. (Illus.). 192p. 1983. 15.95 (ISBN 0-13-561399-X); pap. 6.95 (ISBN 0-13-561381-7). P-H.

Newman, D. J. A Problem Seminar. (Problem Books in Mathematics). 113p. 1983. 12.95 (ISBN 0-387-90765-3). Springer-Verlag.

Wells, David. Can You Solve These? 77p. 1983. pap. 3.95 (ISBN 0-13-114074-4). P-H.

MATHEMATICS–PROGRAMMED INSTRUCTION

Aitken, Alexander C. Determinants & Matrices. LC 82-24168. (University Mathematical Texts Ser.). 144p. 1983. Repr. of 1956 ed. lib. bdg. 27.50x (ISBN 0-313-23294-6, AIDE). Greenwood.

Baggaley, Andrew R. Mathematics for Introductory Statistics: A Programmed Review. 203p. 1969. pap. 15.95x (ISBN 0-471-04008-8). Wiley.

Bitter, et al. McGraw-Hill Mathematics, 8 levels. Incl. Level 1. text ed. 7.40 (ISBN 0-07-005761-3); tchr's ed. 21.40 (ISBN 0-07-005771-0); wkbk. 3.68 (ISBN 0-07-005781-8); Level 2. text ed. 7.40 (ISBN 0-07-005762-1); tchr's ed. 21.40 (ISBN 0-07-005772-9); wkbk 3.68 (ISBN 0-07-005782-6); Level 3. text ed. 12.08 (ISBN 0-07-005763-X); tchr's ed. 22.44 (ISBN 0-07-005773-7); wkbk. 4.08 (ISBN 0-07-005783-4); Level 4. text ed. 12.08 (ISBN 0-07-005764-8); tchr's ed. 22.44 (ISBN 0-07-005774-5); wkbk. 4.08 (ISBN 0-07-005784-2); Level 5. text ed. 12.08 (ISBN 0-07-005765-6); tchr's ed. 22.44 (ISBN 0-07-005775-3); wkbk. 4.08 (ISBN 0-07-005785-0); Level 6. text ed. 12.08 (ISBN 0-07-005766-4); tchr's ed. 22.44 (ISBN 0-07-005776-1); wkbk. 4.08 (ISBN 0-07-005786-9); Level 7. text ed. 14.56 (ISBN 0-07-005767-2); tchr's ed. 23.84 (ISBN 0-07-005777-X); wkbk. 4.08 (ISBN 0-07-005787-7); Level 8. text ed. 14.56 (ISBN 0-07-005768-0); tchr's ed. 23.84 (ISBN 0-07-005778-8); wkbk. 4.08 (ISBN 0-07-005788-5). 1981. write for info. supplementary materials. McGraw.

Guidebook to Mathematics. (gr. 7-12). pap. 2.37 (ISBN 0-8372-4376-9); tchr's handbk. 2.37 (ISBN 0-8372-4377-7). Bowmar-Noble.

Sackheim & Robbins. Programmed Mathematics for Nurses. 1983. 14.95 (ISBN 0-02-405170-5). Macmillan.

Wehrli, Kitty. Math Readiness Workbook: Math Readiness Pretest Manual. (Michigan Arithmetic Program Ser.). (Illus.). (gr. k-3). 1978. 1.00 (ISBN 0-89039-241-2); 1.00 (ISBN 0-89039-238-2). Ann Arbor Pubs.

MATHEMATICS–STATISTICAL METHODS

see Mathematical Statistics

MATHEMATICS–STUDY AND TEACHING

see also Mathematical Models

Hackworth, Robert D. Math Anxiety Reduction: A Workbook. (Illus.). 210p. (Orig.). 1982. pap. text ed. 12.95x (ISBN 0-943202-04-3). H & H Pub.

Howson, A. G. A History of Mathematics Education in England. LC 82-4175. (Illus.). 300p. 1982. 49.50 (ISBN 0-521-24206-1). Cambridge U Pr.

International Congress on Mathematical Education Staff, Fourth. C. I. M. E Lectures: Proceedings. Zweng, M., ed. 700p. Date not set. text ed. price not set (ISBN 3-7643-3082-1). Birkhauser.

Ready, Barbara C., ed. Peterson's Guides to Graduate Study: Physical Sciences & Mathematics, 1983. 650p. (Orig.). 1982. pap. 17.95 (ISBN 0-87866-188-3). Petersons Guides.

Shufelt, Gwen, ed. The Agenda in Action: Yearbook, 1983. LC 82-22367. (Illus.). 256p. 1983. 14.50 (ISBN 0-87353-201-5). NCTM.

MATHEMATICS–STUDY AND TEACHING (ELEMENTARY)

Justus, Fred. Basic Skills Mathematics Workbook: Grade 1. (Basic Skills Workbooks). 32p. (gr. 1). 1982. tchrs' ed. 0.99 (ISBN 0-8209-0388-4, MW-B). ESP.

--JUmbo Math Yearbook: Grade 1. (Jumbo Math Ser.). 96p. (gr. 1). 1980. 14.00 (ISBN 0-8209-0030-3, JMY 1). ESP.

Reys, Barbara. Elementary School Mathematics: What Parents Should Know About Estimation. (Illus.). 16p. 1982. pap. 2.50 (ISBN 0-87353-202-3). NCTM.

--Elementary School Mathematics: What Parents Should Know About Problem Solving. (Illus.). 16p. 1982. pap. 2.50 (ISBN 0-87353-203-1). NCTM.

Vaughn, Jim. Basic Skills Mathematics Workbook: Grade 2. (Basic Skills Workbooks). 32p. (gr. 2). 1982. tchrs' ed. 0.99 (ISBN 0-8209-0389-2, MW-C). ESP.

--Basic Skills Mathematics Workbook: Grade 3. (Basic Skills Workbooks). 32p. 1982. tchrs' ed. 0.99 (ISBN 0-8209-0390-6, MW-D). ESP.

--Basic Skills Mathematics Workbook: Grade 4. (Basic Skills Workbooks). 32p. (gr. 4). tchrs' ed. 0.99 (ISBN 0-8209-0391-4, MW-E). ESP.

--Basic Skills Mathematics Workbook: Grade 5. (Basic Skills Worrkbooks). 32p. (gr. 5). 1982. tchrs' ed. 0.99 (ISBN 0-8209-0392-2, MW-F). ESP.

--Basic Skills Mathematics Workbook: Grade 6. (Basic Skills Workbooks). 32p. (gr. 6). tchrs' ed. 0.99 (ISBN 0-8209-0393-0, MW-G). ESP.

--Basic Skills Mathematics Workbook: Grade 7. (Basic Skills Workbooks). 32p. (gr. 7). 1982. tchrs' ed. 0.99 (ISBN 0-8209-0394-9, MW-H). ESP.

--Basic Skills Mathematics Workbook: Grade 8. (Basic Skills Workbooks). 32p. (gr. 8). 1982. tchrs' ed. 0.99 (ISBN 0-8209-0395-7, MW-I). ESP.

--Jumbo Math Yearbook: Grade 2. (Jumbo Math Ser.). 96p. (gr. 2). 1980. 14.00 (ISBN 0-8209-0031-1, JMY 2). ESP.

--Jumbo Math Yearbook: Grade 3. (Jumbo Math Ser.). 96p. (gr. 3). 1978. 14.00 (ISBN 0-8209-0032-X, JMY 3). ESP.

--Jumbo Math Yearbook: Grade 4. (Jumbo Math Ser.). 96p. (gr. 4). 1978. 14.00 (ISBN 0-8209-0033-8, JMY 4). ESP.

--Jumbo Math Yearbook: Grade 5. (Jumbo Math Ser.). 96p. (gr. 5). 1978. 14.00 (ISBN 0-8209-0034-6, JMY 5). ESP.

--Jumbo Math Yearbook: Grade 6. (Jumbo Math Ser.). 96p. (gr. 6). 1978. 14.00 (ISBN 0-8209-0035-4, JMY 6). ESP.

--Jumbo Math Yearbook: Grade 7. (Jumbo Math Ser.). 96p. (gr. 7). 1978. 14.00 (ISBN 0-8209-0036-2, JMY 7). ESP.

--Jumbo Math Yearbook: Grade 8. (Jumbo Math Ser.). 96p. (gr. 8). 1979. 14.00 (ISBN 0-8209-0037-0, JMY 8). ESP.

MATHEMATICS–STUDY AND TEACHING (SECONDARY)

Breslich, Ernest R. The Technique of Teaching Secondary School Mathematics. 239p. 1982. Repr. of 1930 ed. lib. bdg. 45.00 (ISBN 0-89984-089-2). Century Bookbindery.

Gill, Jack C. & Blitzer, Robert. Competency in College Mathematics. 2nd ed. Hackworth, Robert D., intro. by. 488p. 1982. write for info. (ISBN 0-943202-07-8). H & H Pub.

Justus, Fred. Programmed Math: Grade 1. (Math Ser.). 24p. 1976. wkbk. 5.00 (ISBN 0-8209-0127-X, PM-1). ESP.

--Programmed Math: Grade 2. (Math Ser.). 24p. 1976. wkbk. 5.00 (ISBN 0-8209-0128-8, PM-2). ESP.

--Programmed Math: Grade 3. (Math Ser.). 24p. 1980. wkbk. 5.00 (ISBN 0-8209-0129-6, PM-3). ESP.

--Programmed Math: Grade 4. (Math Ser.). 24p. wkbk. 5.00 (ISBN 0-8209-0130-X, PM-4). ESP.

--Programmed Math: Grade 6. (Math Ser.). 24p. 1979. wkbk. 5.00 (ISBN 0-8209-0132-6, PM-6). ESP.

--Programmed Math: Grade 7. (Math Ser.). 24p. 1977. 5.00 (ISBN 0-8209-0133-4, PM-7). ESP.

--Remedial Arithmetic 1A. (Math Ser.). 24p. (gr. 2-3). 1978. wkbk. 5.00 (ISBN 0-8209-0109-1, A-19). ESP.

--Remedial Arithmetic 1C. (Math Ser.). 24p. (gr. 3-5). 1978. wkbk. 5.00 (ISBN 0-8209-0111-3, A-21). ESP.

--Secret Messages: Mult.-Div. (Puzzles Ser.). 24p. (gr. 3-5). 1980. wkbk. 5.00 (ISBN 0-8209-0302-7, PU-16). ESP.

--Simple Additon & Subtraction. (Math Ser.). 24p. (gr. k-1). 1982. wkbk. 5.00 (ISBN 0-8209-0089-3, A-K). ESP.

--Units of Measure. (Math Ser.). 24p. (gr. 3-5). 1979. wkbk. 5.00 (ISBN 0-8209-0120-2, A-30). ESP.

--Written Problems in Math: Grade 2. (Math Ser.). 24p. 1980. wkbk. 5.00 (ISBN 0-8209-0122-9, A-32). ESP.

McMasters, Dale. Written Problems in Math: Grade 4. (Math Ser.). 24p. 1981. wkbk. 5.00 (ISBN 0-8209-0124-5, A-34). ESP.

Nuffield Foundation. Nuffield Maths Four: Math 5-11. rev. ed. Albany, Eric A., ed. 96p. 1981. tchrs.' ed 15.95 (ISBN 0-582-19174-2); pupils' book 5.50 (ISBN 0-582-19178-5); spiritmasters 39.95 (ISBN 0-582-17017-6). Longman.

--Nuffield Maths Three: Maths 5-11. rev. ed. Albany, Eric A., ed. 112p. 1980. tchrs.' manual 10.95 (ISBN 0-582-19177-7); pupils' book 3.95 (ISBN 0-582-19173-4); spiritmasters avail. (ISBN 0-582-17016-8). Longman.

--Nuffield Maths Two. rev. ed. Albany, Eric A., ed. (Maths 5-11). 50p. 1980. worksheets K-L 35.00 (ISBN 0-582-17015-X); worksheets pack J 23.95 (ISBN 0-582-17014-1); worksheets pack G 29.95 (ISBN 0-582-17011-7); worksheets pack H 29.95 (ISBN 0-582-17012-5); worksheets pack I 23.95 (ISBN 0-582-17013-3). Longman.

Shaw, Marie-Jose. Written Problems in Math: Grade 3. (Math Ser.). 24p. 1982. wkbk. 5.00 (ISBN 0-8209-0123-7, A-33). ESP.

Vaughn, J. Basic Skills Mathematics Workbook: Grade 9. (Basic Skills Workbooks). 32p. (gr. 9). 1982. tchrs' ed. 0.99 (ISBN 0-8209-0396-5, MW-J). ESP.

MATHEMATICS–1961-

Barnett, Raymond A. & Burke, Charles J. Applied Mathematics for Business & Economics, Life Sciences & Social Sciences. (Illus.). 1983. text ed. 27.95 (ISBN 0-89517-049-3). Dellen Pub.

Cleaves, Cheryl & Hobbs, Margie. Basic Mathematics for Trades & Technologies. (Illus.). 640p. 1983. text ed. 21.95 (ISBN 0-686-81986-1). P-H.

Cochran, James A. Applied Mathematics: Principles, Techniques, & Applications. LC 82-7055. (Mathematics Ser.). 399p. 1982. text ed. 34.95 (ISBN 0-534-98026-0). Wadsworth Pub.

Ewen, Dale & Topper, Michael A. Mathematics for Technical Education. 2nd ed. (Illus.). 496p. 1983. text ed. 23.95 (ISBN 0-13-565168-9). P-H.

Hashisaki, Joseph. Theory & Applications of Mathematics for Elementary School Teachers. 450p. 1984. text ed. 23.95 (ISBN 0-471-09637-7); tchr's. manual avail. (ISBN 0-471-87234-2). Wiley.

Herzog, David A. Mathematics Workbook for the GED Test. LC 82-20571. (Arco's Preparation for the GED Examination Ser.). 256p. 1983. pap. 5.95 (ISBN 0-668-05542-1). Arco.

MATHEMATICS, ANCIENT

Sesiano, J. Diophantus' Arithmetica: Books IV to VI in the Arabic Translation of Qusta ibn Luqa. (Sources in the History of Mathematics & Physical Sciences Ser.: Vol. 3). (Illus.). 502p. 1983. 72.00 (ISBN 0-387-90690-8). Springer-Verlag.

MATHEMATICS, BUSINESS

see Business Mathematics

MATHEMATICS, GREEK
Sesiano, J. Diophantus' Arithmetica: Books IV to VI in the Arabic Translation of Qusta ibn Luqa. (Sources in the History of Mathematics & Physical Sciences Ser.: Vol. 3). (Illus.). 502p. 1983. 72.00 (ISBN 0-387-90690-8). Springer-Verlag.
MATHEMATICS, LOGIC OF
see Mathematics–Philosophy
MATHEMATICS OF FINANCE
see Business Mathematics
MATRICES
see also Eigenvalues; Multivariate Analysis
Barnett, Stephen. Matrices in Control Theory. rev. ed. 236p. 1984. lib. bdg. price not set (ISBN 0-89874-590-X). Krieger.
Gourlay, A. R. & Watson, G. A. Computational Methods for Matrix Eigenproblems. LC 73-2783. 1979. pap. text ed. 14.95x (ISBN 0-471-27586-7, Pub. by Wiley-Interscience). Wiley.
Graybill, Franklin A. Matrices with Applications in Statistics. 2nd ed. LC 82-8485. (Wadsworth Statistics-Probability Ser.). 461p. 1983. 31.95 (ISBN 0-534-98038-4). Wadsworth Pub.
Knittel, Patricia, ed. Selected Bibliography: Quality Control, Vol. II. (Orig.). 1982. pap. 15.00 (ISBN 0-89938-009-3). Tech & Ed Ctr Graph Arts RIT.
MATRICES–PROGRAMMED INSTRUCTION
Dorf, Richard C. Matrix Algebra: A Programmed Introduction. 260p. 1969. pap. 19.95x (ISBN 0-471-21909-6). Wiley.
MATRIMONIAL REGIME
see Husband and Wife
MATRIMONY
see Marriage
MATRIX MECHANICS
see also Quantum Statistics; Quantum Theory; Wave Mechanics
Hawkes, Susan & Wang, John L., eds. Extracellular Matrix: Symposium. LC 82-22631. 1982. 34.00 (ISBN 0-12-333320-2). Acad Pr.
Masterson, Keith & Solar Energy Research Institute. Matrix Approach for Testing Mirrors, Pt. 2. (Progress in Solar Energy Ser.: Suppl.). 125p. 1983. pap. 13.00x (ISBN 0-89553-133-X). Am Solar Energy.
MATSUO, BASHO, 1664-1694
see Basho, Matsuo, 1644-1694
MATTER–PROPERTIES
see also Brownian Movements; Capillarity; Chemistry, Physical and Theoretical; Colloids; Diffusion; Elasticity; Gases; Mass (Physics)
Brophy, J. H., et al. Thermodynamics of Structure. (Structure & Properties of Materials Ser: Vol. 2). 216p. 1964. pap. text ed. 17.50x (ISBN 0-471-10610-0). Wiley.
Walton, Alan J. Three Phases of Matter. 2nd ed. (Illus.). 1982. 41.00x (ISBN 0-19-851957-5); pap. 18.95x (ISBN 0-19-851953-2). Oxford U Pr.
MAUSOLEUMS
see Sepulchral Monuments; Tombs
MAXIMA AND MINIMA
see also Calculus of Variations; Mathematical Optimization
Pincus-Witten, Robert. Entries (Maximalism) (Illus.). 250p. 1983. pap. 14.95 (ISBN 0-915570-20-3). Oolp Pr.
MAXIMILIAN, EMPEROR OF MEXICO, 1832-1867
Blasio, Jose L. Maximilian, Emperor of Mexico. 1934. text ed. 42.50x (ISBN 0-686-83620-0). Elliots Bks.
MAY-FLIES
O'Donnell, Kevin, Jr. Mayflies. 304p. 1982. pap. 2.50 (ISBN 0-425-05776-3). Berkley Pub.
MAYA HIEROGLYPHICS
see Picture-Writing, Maya
MAYAN LANGUAGES
England, Nora C. A Gammar of Mam Mayan Language: A Mayan Language. (Texas Linguistics Ser.). 365p. 1983. text ed. 25.00x (ISBN 0-292-72726-7). U of Tex Pr.
MAYAS–ANTIQUITIES
see also Guatemala–Antiquities
Carlson, Loraine. The TraveLeer Guide to Yucatan. rev. ed. LC 82-17449. (Illus.). 208p. (Orig.). 1982. pap. 6.95 (ISBN 0-932554-04-0). Upland Pr.
Turner, B. L., II & Harrison, Peter D., eds. Pulltrouser Swamp: Ancient Maya Habitat, Agriculture, & Settlement in Northern Belize. (Texas Pan American Ser.). (Illus.). 296p. text ed. 22.50x (ISBN 0-292-75067-6). U of Tex Pr.
MAYAS–JUVENILE LITERATURE
Beck, Barbara L. The Ancient Maya. rev. ed. (First Bks.). (Illus.). 72p. (gr. 4 up). 1983. PLB 8.90 (ISBN 0-531-04529-3). Watts.
MAYFLIES
see May-Flies
MAZDAISM
see Zoroastrianism
MAZE PUZZLES
Diagram Group. Maze Puzzles. 96p. (Orig.). 1983. pap. 1.75 (ISBN 0-345-30477-2). Ballantine.
Kishida, K. Mazeland. 100p. 1983. 9.95 (ISBN 0-13-566612-0); pap. 3.95 (ISBN 0-13-566604-X). P-H.
Koziakin, Vladimir. Mazewarps. 1983. pap. 2.50 (ISBN 0-517-54965-4, C N Potter Bks). Crown.
MAZUT
see Petroleum As Fuel
MAZZEI, FILIPPO, 1730-1816
Marchione, Margherita, tr. Philip Mazzei: Jefferson's "Zealous Whig". 352p. 1975. 9.95 (ISBN 0-686-84875-6); pap. 5.95 (ISBN 0-686-84876-4). Am Inst Ital Stud.
MEAD, MARGARET, 1901-1978
Freeman, Derek. Margaret Mead & Samoa: The Making & Unmaking of an Anthropological Byth. (Illus.). 416p. 1983. 25.00 (ISBN 0-674-54830-2). Harvard U Pr.
Ludle, Jacqueline. Margaret Mead. (Impact Biography Ser.). (Illus.). (gr. 7 up). 1983. PLB 8.90 (ISBN 0-531-04590-0). Watts.
MEALS FOR SCHOOL CHILDREN
see School Children–Food
MEANING (PSYCHOLOGY)
see also Language and Languages; Semantics; Thought and Thinking
Rapoport, Amos. The Meaning of the Built Environment: A Non-Verbal Communication Approach. 200p. 1982. 25.00 (ISBN 0-8039-1892-5); pap. 12.50 (ISBN 0-8039-1893-3). Sage.
MEASURABLE SETS
see Measure Theory
MEASURE OF INFORMATION
see Information Measurement
MEASURE THEORY
see also Ergodic Theory; Spectral Theory (Mathematics)
Bartle, Robert G. Elements of Integration. LC 75-15979. 129p. 1966. 22.95x (ISBN 0-471-05457-7). Wiley.
Berka, Karel. Measurement: Its Concepts, Theories & Problems. 1983. 49.50 (ISBN 90-277-1416-9, Pub. by Reidel Holland). Kluwer Boston.
Koelzow, D. & Maharam-Stone, D., eds. Measure Theory, Oberwolfach FRG Nineteen Eighty-One: Proceedings. (Lecture Notes in Mathematics: No. 943). 945p. 1983. pap. 20.50 (ISBN 0-387-11580-3). Springer-Verlag.
Soldano, B. A. Mass, Measurement & Motion Sequel Two: A New Look at Maxwell's Equations & the Permittivity of Free Space. Brantley, William H., ed. (Illus.). 50p. (Orig.). 1982. pap. 7.00x (ISBN 0-943410-00-2). Grenridge Pub.
MEASUREMENT OF AREA
see Area Measurement
MEASUREMENT OF STREAMS
see Stream Measurements
MEASUREMENTS, ELECTRONIC
see Electronic Measurements
MEASUREMENTS, OPTICAL
see Optical Measurements
MEASUREMENTS, PHYSICAL
see Physical Measurements
MEASURING
see Mensuration
MEAT
see also Cookery (Meat)
Graves, Will. Raising Your Own Meat for Pennies a Day. Stetson, Fred, ed. (Illus.). 160p. (Orig.). 1983. pap. 6.95 (ISBN 0-88266-330-5). Garden Way Pub.
Laurie, R. Developments in Meat Science, Vols. 1 & 2. 1980-81. Vol. 1. 43.00 (ISBN 0-85334-866-9, Pub. by Applied Sci England); Vol. 2. 65.75 (ISBN 0-85334-986-X). Elsevier.
MEAT CONSUMPTION
see Meat Industry and Trade
MEAT CUTTING
Macgregor, Roderick. The Structure of the Meat Animals. 272p. 1981. 35.00x (ISBN 0-291-39625-9, Pub. by Tech Pr). State Mutual Bk.
MEAT INDUSTRY AND TRADE
see also Cattle Trade
OECD Staff. Meat Balances in OECD Member Countries, 1975-1980. 85p. (Orig., English-French.). 1982. pap. text ed. 8.50x (ISBN 92-64-02323-2). OECD.
MEAT PACKING INDUSTRY
see Meat Industry and Trade
MEATLESS MEALS
see Vegetarianism
MECCA
Guelloz, Ezzedine. Pilgrimage to Mecca. (Illus.). 208p. 1982. 60.00 (ISBN 0-85692-059-2, Pub. By Salem Hse Ltd.). Merrimack Bk Serv.
MECHANIC ARTS
see Industrial Arts
MECHANICAL ARITHMETIC
see Calculating-Machines
MECHANICAL BRAINS
see Conscious Automata; Cybernetics
MECHANICAL DRAWING
see also Architectural Drawing; Blue-Prints; Design, Industrial; Electronic Drafting; Engineering Graphics; Graphic Methods; Lettering; Technical Illustration
Australian Engineering Drawing Handbook: Basic Principles & Techniques, Pt. 1. 122p. (Orig.). 1977. pap. text ed. 13.50x (ISBN 0-85825-068-3, Pub. by Inst Engineering Australia). Renouf.
Australian Engineering Drawing Handbook: Structural Drawing, Pt. 2. 76p. (Orig.). 1977. pap. text ed. 13.50x (ISBN 0-85825-069-1, Pub. by Inst Engineering Australia). Renouf.
Gorbea. Tecnicas Mecanograficas Modernas. 3rd ed. 240p. 12.20 (ISBN 0-07-023791-3). McGraw.
Greening. Construction Drawing. 1982. text ed. 19.95 (ISBN 0-408-00672-2); pap. text ed. 9.95 (ISBN 0-408-00646-3). Butterworth.
Hardman, William E. How To Read Shop Prints & Drawings With Blueprints. 236p. 1982. pap. text ed. 19.95 (ISBN 0-910399-01-8). Natl Tool & Mach.
Jeary. Engineering Drawing Two Checkbook Limp. 1982. text ed. 19.95 (ISBN 0-408-00683-8); pap. text ed. 9.95. Butterworth.
Levens. Problems in Mechanical Drawing. 5th ed. 1980. text ed. 14.25 (ISBN 0-07-037440-6). McGraw.
Lieblich, Jerome H. Drawing Requirements Manual. 5th ed. 719p. 1983. perfect bdg. 29.95 (ISBN 0-912702-18-4); loose leaf 44.95 (ISBN 0-912702-17-6). Global Eng.
Madsen, David A. & Shumaker, Terence M. Civil Drafting Technology. (Illus.). 144p. 1983. 17.95 (ISBN 0-13-134890-6, 402-403). P-H.
Rudman, Jack. Senior Drafting Technician. (Career Examination Ser.: C-2679). (Cloth bdg. avail. on request). pap. 10.00 (ISBN 0-8373-2679-6). Natl Learning.
Thomas, M. A Guide to the Preparation of Civil Engineering Drawings. 1982. 65.00x (ISBN 0-333-28081-4, Pub. by Macmillan England). State Mutual Bk.
Wirshing, J. R. & Wirshing, R. H. Civil Engineering Drafting. 352p. 1983. pap. 14.95x (ISBN 0-07-071127-5, G). McGraw.
MECHANICAL DRAWING–EXAMINATIONS, QUESTIONS ETC.
Donaldson, Stanley S. Test Papers on Technical Drawing. 104p. 1981. 37.00x (ISBN 0-291-39488-4, Pub. by Tech Pr). State Mutual Bk.
Rudman, Jack. Drafting Technician. (Career Examination Ser.: C-2678). (Cloth bdg. avail. on request). pap. 10.00 (ISBN 0-8373-2678-8). Natl Learning.
--Principal Drafting Technician. (Career Examination Ser.: C-2680). (Cloth bdg. avail. on request). pap. 12.00 (ISBN 0-8373-2680-X). Natl Learning.
MECHANICAL DRAWINGS
see Engineering Drawings
MECHANICAL ENGINEERING
Here are entered works relating to the application of the principles of mechanics to the design construction and operation of machinery.
see also Chemical Engineering; Electric Engineering; Machinery; Marine Engineering; Mechanical Movements; Mechanics, Applied; Power (Mechanics); Production Engineering
Beer, F. P. & Johnston, E. R. Mechanics for Engineers, 2 vols. 3rd ed. 1976. Vol. 1: Statistics. 26.95 (ISBN 0-07-004271-3); solns. manual 18.50 (ISBN 0-07-004272-1); Vol. 2: Dynamics. 26.95 (ISBN 0-07-004273-X); solns. manual 25.00 (ISBN 0-07-004270-5); Combined ed. 35.50 (ISBN 0-686-84863-2). McGraw.
Berger & Associates Cost Consultants, Inc. The Berger Building & Design Cost File, 1983: Mechanical, Electrical Trades, Vol. 2. LC 83-70008. 207p. 1983. pap. 26.45 (ISBN 0-942564-04-9). Building Cost File.
Boresi, Arthur P., et al. Advanced Mechanics of Materials. 3rd ed. LC 77-28283. 696p. 1978. text ed. 38.95x (ISBN 0-471-08892-7). Wiley.
Constance, J. D. Mechanical Engineering for Professional Engineers' Examination. 3rd ed. 1981. 18.95 (ISBN 0-07-012457-4). McGraw.
Fletcher, L. S., ed. ASME Conference on Mechanical Engineering Education-1980: Proceedings. 181p. 1982. 15.00 (I00145). ASME.
Hibbeler, R. C. Engineering Mechanics: Dynamics. 3rd ed. 512p. 1983. text ed. 25.95 (ISBN 0-02-354260-8). Macmillan.
Jensen, A. & Chenoweth, H. H. Applied Engineering Mechanics. 4th ed. 464p. 23.95x (ISBN 0-07-032492-1). McGraw.
Mechanical Engineering Education in America: It's First Century. 101p. 1982. 20.00 (I00146). ASME.
Merrick, Charles M., ed. Management Division History, 1886-1980: American Society of Mechanical Engineers. (Hive Management History Ser.: No. 84). 200p. 1983. lib. bdg. 23.75 (ISBN 0-87960-118-3). Hive Pub.
Radiation Curing: Conference Proceedings, Vol. VI. LC 82-60954. 430p. 1982. 40.00 (ISBN 0-87263-088-9). SME.
MECHANICAL ENGINEERING–HANDBOOKS, MANUALS, ETC.
Nelson, Carl A. Millwrights & Mechanics Guide. new ed. (Audel Ser.). 1983. 19.95 (ISBN 0-672-23373-8). Bobbs.
MECHANICAL ENGINEERING–TABLES, CALCULATIONS, ETC.
Kamal, M. H. & Wolf, J. A., Jr. Computational Methods In Ground Transportation Systems. (AMD Ser.: Vol. 50). 1982. 40.00 (H00234). ASME.
MECHANICAL HANDLING
see Materials Handling
MECHANICAL MOVEMENTS
see also Automata; Gearing
Hiscox, Gardner D. Mechanical Movements, Powers & Devices. 405p. 1983. pap. 8.50 (ISBN 0-88072-018-2). Tanager Bks.
MECHANICAL PAINTING
see Painting, Industrial
MECHANICAL PERSPECTIVE
see Perspective
MECHANICAL QUADRATURE
see Numerical Integration
MECHANICAL SPEECH RECOGNIZER
see Automatic Speech Recognition
MECHANICS
see also Biomechanics; Deformations (Mechanics); Dynamics; Elasticity; Engineering; Fluids; Force and Energy; Friction; Gases; Hydraulics; Hydrodynamics; Kinematics; Liquids; Machinery; Mass (Physics); Mathematical Physics; Matter–Properties; Mechanical Movements; Motion; Power (Mechanics); Rock Mechanics; Soil Mechanics; Statics; Statistical Mechanics; Strains and Stresses; Strength of Materials; Thermodynamics; Vibration; Wave Mechanics
Findley, W., et al. Creep & Relaxation of Nonlinear Viscoelastic Materials. 1976. 72.50 (ISBN 0-444-10775-4). Elsevier.
Gallavotti, G. The Elements of Mechanics. (Texts & Monographs in Physics). (Illus.). 528p. 1983. 48.00 (ISBN 0-387-11753-9). Springer-Verlag.
Leech, J. W. Classical Mechanics. 1965. pap. 5.95x (ISBN 0-412-20070-8, Pub. by Chapman & Hall England). Methuen Inc.
Mura, T. Micromechanics of Defects in Solids. 1982. lib. bdg. 98.00 (ISBN 90-247-2560-7, Pub. by Martinus Nijhoff Netherlands). Kluwer Boston.
Oden, J. T. & Reddy, J. N. Variational Methods in Theoretical Mechanics. 2nd, rev. ed. (Universitext Ser.). 308p. 1983. pap. 20.00 (ISBN 0-387-11917-5). Springer-Verlag.
Reddy, J. N., ed. Penalty-Finite Elements Mehtods In Mechanics. (AMD Ser.: Vol. 51). 1982. 40.00 (H00235). ASME.
Santilli, R. M. Foundations of Theoretical Mechanics II: Birkhoffian Generalization of Hamiltonian Mechanics. (Texts & Monographs in Physics). 370p. 1983. 66.00 (ISBN 0-387-09482-2). Springer-Verlag.
Ziegler, H. An Introduction to Thermomechanics. 2nd rev. ed. (North-Holland Ser. in Applied Mathematics & Mechanics: Vol. 21). 340p. 1983. 53.25 (ISBN 0-444-86503-9, North Holland). Elsevier.
MECHANICS, ANALYTIC
see also Continuum Mechanics; Dynamics; Elasticity; Hydrodynamics; Kinematics; Statics; Statistical Mechanics
Curry, Stephen H. & Whelpton, Robin. Manual of Laboratory Pharmcokinetics: Experiments in Biopharmaceutics, Biochemical Pharmacology & Pharmacokinetics with a Consideration of Relevant Instrumental & Chromatographic Techniques. 250p. 1983. write for info. (ISBN 0-471-10247-4, Pub. by Wiley-Interscience). Wiley.
MECHANICS, APPLIED
see also Mechanical Engineering
Bruch, Charles D. Mechanics for Technology. LC 75-31719. 386p. 1976. text ed. 24.95x (ISBN 0-471-11369-7). Wiley.
Byars, Edward F. Engineering Mechanics of Deformable Bodies. 4th ed. 528p. 1983. text ed. 29.50 scp (ISBN 0-06-041109-0, HarpC); solution manual avail. (ISBN 0-06-361100-7). Har-Row.
Ginsberg, Jerry H. & Genin, Joseph. Statics & Dynamics Combined Edition. LC 76-30664. 1016p. 1977. text ed. 35.95x (ISBN 0-471-01795-7). Wiley.
Harrison, H. R. & Nettleton, T. Principles of Engineering Mechanics. 264p. 1978. pap. text ed. 18.95 (ISBN 0-7131-3378-3). E Arnold.
Smith, C. E. Applied Mechanics-Dynamics. 2nd ed. 518p. 1982. text ed. 27.95x (ISBN 0-471-02966-1). Wiley.
Titherington, D. & Rimmer, J. G. Applied Mechanics. 2nd ed. 192p. Date not set. 9.00 (ISBN 0-07-084659-6). McGraw.
U. S. National Congress of Applied Mechanics, 9th. Proceedings. 480p. 1982. 75.00 (H00228). ASME.
Wu, Theodore Y. & Hutchinson, John W., eds. Advances in Applied Mechanics: Serial Publication, Vol. 23. Date not set. price not set (ISBN 0-12-002023-8); price not set Lib. ed. (ISBN 0-12-002057-2); price not set Microfiche (ISBN 0-12-002058-0). Acad Pr.
MECHANICS, CELESTIAL
Chebotarev, G. Analytical & Numerical Methods of Celestial Mechanics. 1967. 22.50 (ISBN 0-444-00023-2). Elsevier.
MECHANICS, FRACTURE
see Fracture Mechanics
MECHANICS, NONLINEAR
see Nonlinear Mechanics
MECHANICS OF CONTINUA
see Continuum Mechanics
MECHANISMS (MACHINERY)
see Mechanical Movements
MECHANIZATION OF LIBRARY PROCESSES
see Libraries–Automation
MECHANIZED INFORMATION STORAGE AND RETRIEVAL SYSTEMS
see Information Storage and Retrieval Systems
MECHANOTHERAPY
see also Exercise Therapy; Massage
Lowe, Carl & Nechas, Jim. Body Healing. (Illus.). 440p. 1983. 21.95 (ISBN 0-87857-441-7, 05-024-0). Rodale Pr Inc.
MEDALS
Gaylor, John. Military Badge Collecting. (Illus.). 176p. 1983. 31.50 (ISBN 0-436-37705-5, Pub. by Secker & Warburg). David & Charles.

Jones, Mark. A Catalogue of the French Medals in the British Museum: Vol. 1, AD 1402-1610. 288p. 1982. 129.00x (ISBN 0-7141-0855-3, Pub. by Brit Mus Pubns England). State Mutual Bk.

MEDIA CENTERS (EDUCATION)
see Instructional Materials Centers

MEDIATION, INTERNATIONAL
see also Arbitration, International

McMullen, Christopher J. Resolution of the Yemen Crisis, 1963: A Case Study in Mediation. LC 80-25944. 56p. 1980. 3.00 (ISBN 0-934742-07-3, Inst Study Diplomacy). Geo U Sch For Serv.

MEDICAID

Bovbjerg, Randall R. & Holahan, John. Medicaid in the Reagan Era: Federal Policy & State Choices. LC 82-83893. (Changing Domestic Priorities Ser.). 72p. (Orig.). 1982. pap. 7.95 (ISBN 0-87766-319-X, 34500). Urban Inst.

Grimaldi, Paul L. Medicaid Reimbursement of Nursing-Home Care. 1982. 15.95 (ISBN 0-8447-3456-X); pap. 7.95 (ISBN 0-8447-3457-8). Am Enterprise.

Rudman, Jack. Senior Medicaid Claims Examiner. (Career Examination Ser.: C-2692). (Cloth bdg. avail. on request). pap. 10.00 (ISBN 0-8373-2692-3). Natl Learning.

--Supervising Medicaid Claims Examiner. (Career Examination Ser.: C-2693). (Cloth bdg. avail. on request). pap. 12.00 (ISBN 0-8373-2693-1). Natl Learning.

Spitz, Bruce. Medicaid Nursing Home Reimbursment in New York. (Illus.). 65p. (Orig.). 1981. pap. text ed. 7.00 (ISBN 0-87766-289-4). Urban Inst.

Spitz, Bruce & Weeks, Jane. Medicaid Nursing Home Reimbursement in Minnesota. LC 80-54798. (Illus.). 64p. (Orig.). 1981. pap. text ed. 6.00. Urban Inst.

--Medicaid Nursing Home Reimbursment in Illinois. LC 80-54797. (Illus.). 55p. (Orig.). 1981. pap. text ed. 6.00 (ISBN 0-87766-287-8). Urban Inst.

MEDICAL ANTHROPOLOGY
see also Folk Medicine

Foster, George M. & Anderson, Barbara G. Medical Anthropology. LC 78-18449. 354p. 1978. text ed. 23.95 (ISBN 0-471-04342-7). Wiley.

MEDICAL APPARATUS
see Medical Instruments and Apparatus

MEDICAL ASSISTANTS
see Medical Technologists

MEDICAL BOTANY
see Botany, Medical

MEDICAL CARE
see also Dental Care; Health Maintenance Organizations; Home Care Services; Hospital Care; Insurance, Health; Medical Social Work

AHA Clearinghouse for Hospital Management Engineering, compiled by. In-House Training Programs on Quantitative Techniques: A Collection of Case Studies. LC 82-11654. 148p. 1982. pap. text ed. 18.75 (ISBN 0-87258-369-4, AHA-133200). Am Hospital.

American Hospital Association. American Hospital Association Guide to the Health Care Field. 584p. 1982. pap. 60.00 (ISBN 0-87258-363-5, AHA-010082). Am Hospital.

--ICD-9-CM Coding Handbook for Entry-Level Coders, with Answers. LC 79-18639. 348p. 1979. pap. text ed. 23.75 (ISBN 0-87258-264-7, AHA-148165). Am Hospital.

Chapman, Jane & Chapman, Harry. Psychology of Health Care: A Humanistic Perspective. LC 82-21873. 250p. 1983. pap. text ed. 12.95 (ISBN 0-534-01291-4). Brooks-Cole.

Clare, A. W. & Corney, R. H., eds. Social Work & Primary Health Care. Date not set. 35.00 (ISBN 0-12-174740-9). Acad Pr.

Cornacchia, Harold J. & Barrett, Stephen. Shopping for Health Care: The Essential Guide to Products & Services. 1982. pap. 9.95 (ISBN 0-452-25366-7, Plume). NAL.

Correa, Hector & El Torky, Mohamed A. The Biological & Social Determinants of the Demographic Transition. LC 82-16042. (Illus.). 298p. (Orig.). 1983. lib. bdg. 24.25 (ISBN 0-8191-2754-X); pap. text ed. 12.75 (ISBN 0-8191-2755-8). U Pr of Amer.

Diagram Group. The Healthy Body: A Maintenance Manual. (Medical Library). (Illus.). 192p. 1982. pap. 8.95 (ISBN 0-452-25352-7, 1293-4). Mosby.

Greene, Ralph C. Medical Overkill. (Illus.). 320p. 1983. 14.50. G F Stickley.

Hadley, Jack. More Medical Care, Better Health? An Economic Analysis of Mortality Rates. LC 82-70898. 235p. 1982. 20.00 (ISBN 0-87766-303-3, 32900). Urban Inst.

Hafen, Brent Q. Medical Self Care & Assessment. (Illus.). 400p. 1983. pap. text ed. 11.95X (ISBN 0-89582-095-1). Morton Pub.

Health Care in the 1980s: Who Provides? Who Plans? Who Pays? 98p. 1978. 5.50 (ISBN 0-686-38323-0, 52-1755). Natl League Nurse.

Jain, Sagar C., ed. Policy Issues in Personal Health Services: Current Perspectives. 500p. 1983. price not set (ISBN 0-89443-672-4). Aspen Systems.

Kent, P. W., ed. International Aspects of the Provision of Medical Care. 224p. 1976. 25.00 (ISBN 0-85362-160-8, Oriel). Routledge & Kegan.

Lewis, Charles E. & Fein, Rashi. A Right to Health: The Problem of Access to Primary Medical Care. LC 76-181829. 380p. Repr. of 1976 ed. text ed. 29.50 (ISBN 0-471-01494-X). Krieger.

Luke, Roice D. & Krueger, Janelle. Quality Assurance. 400p. 1983. write for info. (ISBN 0-89443-930-8). Aspen Systems.

Milio, Nancy. Primary Care & the Public Health: Judging Impacts, Goals, & Polices Public's. LC 81-47275. 272p. 1983. 27.95x (ISBN 0-669-04571-3). Lexington Bks.

Priest, R. G. Psychiatry in Medical Practice. 500p. 1982. text ed. 58.00x (ISBN 0-7121-1672-9). Intl Ideas.

Rodwin, Victor G. The Health Planning Predicament: France, Quebec, England, & the United States. Leslie, Charles, ed. LC 82-45910. (Comparative Studies of Health Systems & Medical Care Ser.). 160p. 1983. 16.50x (ISBN 0-520-04446-0). U of Cal Pr.

Rudman, Jack. Medical Claims Examiner. (Career Examination Ser.: C-2691). (Cloth bdg. avail. on request). pap. 10.00 (ISBN 0-8373-2691-5). Natl Learning.

St. Vincent Hospital Staff & Peck, Theresa. Wellness: Extending the Health Care Mission. Date not set. pap. price not set (ISBN 0-87125-079-9). Cath Health.

Schnurrenger. Principles of Health Maintenance. 272p. 1983. 32.00 (ISBN 0-03-062828-8). Praeger.

Waitzkin, Howard. The Second Sickness: Contradictions of Capitalist Health Care. (Illus.). 320p. 1982. text ed. 19.95 (ISBN 0-02-933750-X). Free Pr.

Wilson, Florence A. & Neuhauser, Duncan. Health Services in the United States. 2nd ed. 368p. 1982. text ed. 17.50x (ISBN 0-88410-713-2). Ballinger Pub.

MEDICAL CARE–ADMINISTRATION
see Public Health Administration

MEDICAL CARE–BIBLIOGRAPHY

Disease Control Centers, Atlanta, Georgia. Author-Title & Subject Catalogs of the Centers for Disease Control Library. 1983. lib. bdg. 750.00 (ISBN 0-8161-0395-X, Hall Library). G K Hall.

MEDICAL CARE–DIRECTORIES

Cornacchia, Harold J. & Barrett, Stephen. Shopping for Health Care: The Essential Guide to Products & Services. LC 82-6405. (Medical Library). 381p. 1982. pap. 9.95 (ISBN 0-686-84856-X, 1140-7). Mosby.

MEDICAL CARE–RESEARCH
see Medical Research

MEDICAL CARE, AMBULATORY
see Ambulatory Medical Care

MEDICAL CARE, COST OF
see also Hospitals–Rates

Arthur D. Little, Inc. Health Care Cost Containment: Challenge to Industry. LC 80-6830. 1980. 5.20 (ISBN 0-910586-34-9). Finan Exec.

Billing Systems for Health Professionals. 7.95 (ISBN 0-910085-05-6). Info Res MI.

Fuchs, Victors R. Who Shall Live? 1983. pap. 8.25 (ISBN 0-465-09186-5). Basic.

Olson, Mancur, ed. New Approach to the Economics of Health Care. 1982. 18.25 (ISBN 0-8447-2212-X); pap. 10.25 (ISBN 0-8447-2213-8). Am Enterprise.

Silvers, J. B., et al, eds. Health Care Financial Management in the 1980's: Time of Transition. (Illus.). 275p. (Orig.). 1983. pap. text ed. price not set (ISBN 0-914904-86-8). Health Admin Pr.

MEDICAL CARE FOR THE AGED
see Aged–Medical Care

MEDICAL CHEMISTRY
see Chemistry, Medical and Pharmaceutical

MEDICAL COLLEGES
see also Medicine–Study and Teaching

American Law Association. Medic Programs: District & School. 136p. Date not set. pap. text ed. 4.00 (ISBN 0-8389-3159-6). ALA.

Brown, Sanford J. Getting into Medical School. 6th ed. 256p. 1983. pap. price not set (ISBN 0-8120-2542-3). Barron.

Fry, John & Hunt. The Royal College of General Practitioners: The First 25 Years. (Illus.). 350p. 1982. text ed. 29.00 (ISBN 0-85200-360-9, Pub. by MTP Pr England). Kluwer Boston.

Morrison, James W. Veterianary College Admission Test. 384p. 1983. pap. 10.95 (ISBN 0-668-05545-6, 5545). Arco.

Norback & Company, ed. Arco's Guide to Hospital Schools. (Arco's Occupational Guides Ser.). 144p. 1983. lib. bdg. 11.95 (ISBN 0-668-05527-8); pap. 6.95 (ISBN 0-668-05534-0). Arco.

Wechsler, Henry & Gale, Barbara. Medical School Admissions: A Strategy for Success. 1983. pap. 12.95 prof ref (ISBN 0-88410-915-1). Ballinger Pub.

MEDICAL COMMUNICATION
see Communication in Medicine

MEDICAL COOPERATION
see Group Medical Practice; Medical Social Work

MEDICAL COSTS
see Medical Care, Cost of

MEDICAL DEVICES
see Medical Instruments and Apparatus

MEDICAL DIAGNOSIS
see Diagnosis

MEDICAL EDUCATION
see also Medical Colleges; Medical Research; Medical Students; Medicine–Study and Teaching

Friedman, Charles P. & Purcell, Elizabeth, eds. The New Biology & Medical Education: Merging the Biological, Information, & Cognitive Sciences. (Illus.). 300p. 1983. pap. 15.00 (ISBN 0-914362-40-2). J Macy Foun.

Purcell, Elizabeth F., ed. The Role of the University Teaching Hospital: An International Perspective. (Illus.). 258p. 1982. pap. 10.00 (ISBN 0-914362-39-9). J Macy Foun.

MEDICAL ELECTRICITY
see Electrotherapeutics

MEDICAL ELECTRONICS
see also Radiotherapy

Geddes, L. A. & Baker, L. E. Principles of Applied Biomedical Instrumentation. 2nd ed. LC 74-34390. (Biomedical Engineering & Health Systems Ser.). 616p. 1975. 42.50x (ISBN 0-471-29496-9, Pub. by Wiley-Interscience). Wiley.

MEDICAL EMERGENCIES
see also Accidents; Emergency Medical Services; Emergency Nursing; First Aid in Illness and Injury

Arnold, Peter & Pendagast, Edward, Jr. Emergency Handbook: A First Aid Manual for Home & Travel. (Medical Library). 272p. 1982. pap. 5.95 (ISBN 0-452-25372-1). Mosby.

Swartz, Morris A. & Moore, Mary E. Medical Emergency Manual. 3rd ed. (Illus.). 195p. 1983. text ed. price not set (ISBN 0-683-07597-7). Williams & Wilkins.

Wilkins, Earle W., Jr. MGH Textbook of Emergency Medicine. 2nd ed. (Illus.). 1056p. 1983. text ed. price not set (ISBN 0-683-09084-4). Williams & Wilkins.

MEDICAL ENGINEERING
see Biomedical Engineering

MEDICAL ETHICS
see also Euthanasia; Human Experimentation in Medicine; Malpractice; Medicine and Religion; Pastoral Medicine; Social Medicine

Abrams, Natalie & Buckner, Michael D. Medical Ethics: A Clinical Textbook & Reference for the Health Care Professions. 848p. 1982. text ed. 45.00 (ISBN 0-262-01068-2, Pub. by Bradford); pap. text ed. 25.00 (ISBN 0-262-51024-3). MIT Pr.

Arras, John & Hunt, Robert. Ethical Issues in Modern Medicine. 2nd ed. 574p. 1983. pap. 18.95 (ISBN 0-87484-574-2). Mayfield Pub.

Ferman, Edward L., ed. The Best from Fantasy & Science Fiction. 24th ed. 2.95 (ISBN 0-441-05485-4, Pub. by Ace Science Fiction). Ace Bks.

Gorovitz, Sam & Maklin, Ruth. Moral Problems in Medicine. 2nd ed. (Illus.). 640p. 1983. text ed. 23.95 (ISBN 0-13-600742-2). P-H.

Harron, Frank & Burnside, John. Health & Human Values: A Guide to Making Your Own Decisions. LC 82-13394. 212p. 1983. text ed. 24.95x (ISBN 0-300-02898-9); pap. 6.95 (ISBN 0-300-03026-6). Yale U Pr.

Levine, Carol & Veatch, Robert M., eds. Cases in Bioethics from the Hastings Center Report. LC 82-81217. 124p. 1982. pap. 7.95 (ISBN 0-916558-17-7). Inst Soc Ethics.

Simmons, Paul D. Birth & Death: Bioethical Decision-Making. LC 82-20160. (Biblical Perspectives on Current Issues). 276p. 1983. pap. price not set (ISBN 0-664-24463-7). Westminster.

MEDICAL EXAMINATIONS
see Diagnosis

Bates, Barbara. A Guide to Physical Examination. 3rd ed. (Illus.). 580p. 1983. text ed. 32.50 (ISBN 0-397-54399-9, Lippincott Medical). Lippincott.

MEDICAL EXPERIMENTS ON HUMANS
see Human Experimentation in Medicine

MEDICAL FEES
see also Physicians–Salaries, Pensions, etc.

Ostow, Miriam & Brecher, Charles. Dollars & Service Delivery in Health Care. (Conservation of Human Resources: Vol. 19). Date not set. text ed. 27.50x (ISBN 0-916672-59-X). Allanheld.

MEDICAL FOLK-LORE
see Folk Medicine

MEDICAL FORMULARIES
see Medicine–Formulae, Receipts, Prescriptions

MEDICAL GROUP PRACTICE
see Group Medical Practice

MEDICAL GYMNASTICS
see Exercise Therapy

MEDICAL HISTORY TAKING

Bocchicchio, Lucille & Castle, Sue. Our Child's Medical History. LC 82-71745. 288p. 1982. 14.95 (ISBN 0-8119-0472-5). Fell.

Kraytman, M. The Complete Patient History. 1979. 16.95 (ISBN 0-07-035421-9). McGraw.

MEDICAL INSPECTION IN SCHOOLS
see School Health

MEDICAL INSTRUMENTS AND APPARATUS
see also Lasers in Medicine

Critser, James R. Radiological Equipment. 115p. 1982. 80.00 (ISBN 0-914428-97-7, 10R-81). Lexington Data.

Critser, James R., Jr. Medical Therapeutic Apparatus Systems. 131p. 1982. 80.00 (ISBN 0-914428-98-5, 10TAS-81). Lexington Data.

Swit, David & Hadley, Richard. The Practical Guide to GMP's. 60p. (Orig.). 1982. pap. 38.00 (ISBN 0-914176-17-X). Wash Busn Info.

Whelan, P. E., ed. Medical Device Register, 1983. LC 81-645923. 1400p. 1983. 75.00x (ISBN 0-942036-03-4). Directory Systems Inc.

MEDICAL INTERNS
see Interns (Medicine)

MEDICAL INTERVIEWING
see Medical History Taking

MEDICAL JOURNALISM
see Journalism, Medical

MEDICAL JURISPRUDENCE
see also Dental Jurisprudence; Forensic Psychiatry; Medical Laws and Legislation; Psychology, Forensic also subdivision Jurisprudence under subjects to which medical jurisprudence is applicable, e.g. Insanity–Jurisprudence

American Health Research Institute, Ltd. Medical Jurisprudence & Criminal Law: A Medical Subject Analysis with Research Index & Bibliography. Bartone, John C., ed. 120p. 1983. 29.95 (ISBN 0-88164-008-5); pap. 21.95 (ISBN 0-88164-009-3). ABBE Pubs Assn.

Champagne, Anthony & Dawes, Rosemary N. Courts & Modern Medicine. 320p. 1983. text ed. price not set (ISBN 0-398-04834-7). C C Thomas.

DeForest, P. R. & Gaenssien, R. E. Forensic Science: An Introduction to Criminalistics. 544p. 1983. 23.95 (ISBN 0-07-016267-0). McGraw.

Engstrom, Karen M. Consent Manual: Policies, Laws, Procedures, 2nd ed. 115p. pap. write for info (ISBN 0-87125-078-0). Catholic Health.

Harron, Frank & United Ministries in Education Health & Human Values Program. Biomedical Ethical Issues: A Digest of Law & Policy Development. LC 82-13394. 112p. 1983. pap. text ed. 4.95x (ISBN 0-300-02974-8). Yale U Pr.

Lipscher, Betty S., ed. Forensic Services Directory, 1982-1983: The National Register of Forensic Experts,Litigation Consultants & Legal Support Specialists. 3rd ed. 1982. 69.50 (ISBN 0-9602962-1-2). Natl Forensic.

Mason. Forensic Medicine for Lawyers. 2nd ed. 1983. text ed. write for info. (ISBN 0-407-00244-8). Butterworth.

Metzger, Norman. The Arbitration & Grievance Process: A Guide for Health Care Supervisors. LC 82-20654. 254p. 1983. 26.50 (ISBN 0-89443-671-6). Aspen Systems.

Montgomery, Carol F. Medical Desk Manual for Law Offices. LC 82-71194. (Illus.). 167p. 1967. pap. 15.00 (ISBN 0-941916-01-4). Assn Trial Ed.

Rudman, Jack. Forensic Medicine Investigator. (Career Examination Ser.: C-2936). (Cloth bdg. avail. on request). pap. 12.00 (ISBN 0-8373-2936-1). Natl Learning.

--Forensic Scientist I (Toxicology) (Career Examination Ser.: C-2937). (Cloth bdg. avail. on request). pap. 14.00 (ISBN 0-8373-2937-X). Natl Learning.

--Forensic Scientist II (Toxicology) (Career Examination Ser.: C-2938). (Cloth bdg. avail. on request). pap. 14.00 (ISBN 0-8373-2938-8). Natl Learning.

--Senior Medical Conduct Investigator. (Career Examination Ser.: X-2610). (Cloth bdg. avail. on request). pap. 10.00 (ISBN 0-8373-2610-9). Natl Learning.

Shapiro, Louis. Clinical Trials. (Statistics, Textbook & Monographs). 280p. 1983. price not set (ISBN 0-8247-1741-4). Dekker.

Spaulding, Edith R. An Experimental Study of Psychopathic Delinquent Women. (Historical Foundations of Forensic Psychiatry & Psychology Ser.). (Illus.). xviii, 368p. 1983. Repr. of 1923 ed. lib. bdg. 45.00 (ISBN 0-306-76185-8). Da Capo.

MEDICAL LABORATORIES

Karni, Karen & Viskochil, Karen, eds. Clinical Laboratory Management: A Guide for Clinical Laboratory Scientists. 1982. text ed. 24.95 (ISBN 0-316-48275-7). Little.

Lee, Leslie W. & Schmidt, L. M. Elementary Principles of Laboratory Instruments. 5th ed. (Illus.). 416p. 1983. text ed. 19.95 (ISBN 0-8016-2918-7). Mosby.

MEDICAL LABORATORY TECHNICIANS
see Medical Technologists

MEDICAL LABORATORY TECHNOLOGY
see Medical Technology

MEDICAL LAWS AND LEGISLATION
see also Medical Jurisprudence; Public Health Laws

American Hospital Association. Taking Part in the Legislative Process: A Guide for the Hospital's Chief Executive Officer. LC 78-15750. 32p. 1978. pap. 6.25 (ISBN 0-87258-245-0, AHA-118527). Am Hospital.

Bureaucratic Malpractice: Hospital Regulations in N. J. 120p. 1982. 17.00 (ISBN 0-686-81762-1). Ctr Analysis Public Issues.

Christoffel, Tom. Health & the Law: A Handbook for Health Professionals. 464p. 1982. text ed. 29.95 (ISBN 0-02-905370-6). Free Pr.

Ficarra. Medicolegal Handbook: A Guide for Winning. 328p. 1983. price not set (ISBN 0-8247-7005-6). Dekker.

Michaels, Joel L. Legal Issues in a Fee-for-Service-Prepaid Medical Group. (Going Prepaid Ser.). 75p. (Orig.). 1982. pap. 15.00 (ISBN 0-933948-75-1). Ctr Res Ambulatory.

Walton, Douglas N. Ethics of Withdrawal of Life-Support Systems: Case Studies on Decision Making in Intensive Care. LC 82-15662. (Contributions in Philosophy: No. 23). 288p. 1983. lib. bdg. 29.95x (ISBN 0-313-23752-2, R726). Greenwood.

MEDICAL LIBRARIES

see also Information Storage and Retrieval Systems–Medicine

Willeford, George, Jr. Medical Word Finder. 3rd ed. 464p. 1983. 19.95 (ISBN 0-13-573527-0, Busn). P-H.

MEDICAL LITERATURE SEARCHING

see Information Storage and Retrieval Systems–Medicine

MEDICAL MANPOWER

see Medical Personnel

MEDICAL MATHEMATICS

see Medicine–Mathematics

MEDICAL MICROBIOLOGY

see also Medical Mycology; Micro-Organisms, Pathogenic

Cooke, E. M. Clinical Microbiology for Medical Students. Gibson, G. L., ed. 1983. 18.95 (ISBN 0-471-90017-6, Pub. by Wiley Med). Wiley.

McCracken, Alexander W. & Cawson, Broderick A. Clinical & Oral Microbiology. (Illus.). 1982. text ed. 32.00 (ISBN 0-07-010296-1, C). McGraw.

Shanson, D. C. Microbiology in Clinical Practice. (Illus.). 600p. 1982. 32.50 (ISBN 0-7236-0636-6). Wright-PSG.

MEDICAL MICROSCOPY

see Microscopy, Medical

MEDICAL MYCOLOGY

English, Mary P. Medical Mycology. (Studies in Biology: No. 119). 64p. 1980. pap. text ed. 8.95 (ISBN 0-7131-2795-3). E Arnold.

MEDICAL PARASITOLOGY

Katz, M., et al. Parasitic Diseases. (Illus.). 264p. 1983. 27.75 (ISBN 0-387-90689-4). Springer-Verlag.

Nuclear Techniques in the Study of Parasitic Infections. (Proceedings Ser.). 631p. 1983. pap. 73.50 (ISBN 92-0-010282-4, ISP 596, IAEA). Unipub.

Zaman, V. Handbook of Medical Parasitology. 200p. 1982. pap. text ed. 27.50 (ISBN 0-86792-000-9, Pub by Adis Pr Australia). Wright-PSG.

MEDICAL PERSONNEL

see also Dental Personnel; Dentists; Physicians

also similar headings

Chenevert, Melodie. STAT: Special Techiques in Assertiveness Training for Women in the Health Professions. (Illus.). 144p. 1983. text ed. 10.95 (ISBN 0-8016-1135-0). Mosby.

Consumer Guide Editors. Health Careers: Where the Jobs Are & How to Get Them. Date not set. pap. 6.95 (ISBN 0-449-90075-4, Columbine). Fawcett.

Lawrence, Kenneth. Health Care Executive's Appointment Book, 1983. 256p. 1982. 28.50 (ISBN 0-89443-848-4). Aspen Systems.

Perrin, Linda. Your Career in Health Care. (Arco's Career Guidance Ser.). (Illus.). 128p. 1983. lib. bdg. 7.95 (ISBN 0-668-05503-0); pap. 4.50 (ISBN 0-668-05514-6). Arco.

Pressman, Robert M. & Siegler, Rodie. The Independent Practitioner: Practice Management for the Allied Health Profess onal. LC 82-73633. (Dorsey Professional Ser.). 250p. 1983. 19.95 (ISBN 0-87094-315-4). Dow Jones-Irwin.

Rothman, William A. Interviewing for a Career in Health Care. 148p. 1983. pap. 6.95 (ISBN 0-938352-51-2). Hampton Pr MI.

Rudman, Jack. Treatment Unit Clerk. (Career Examination Ser.: C-319). (Cloth bdg. avail. on request). pap. 10.00 (ISBN 0-8373-0319-2). Natl Learning.

MEDICAL PERSONNEL–EDUCATION

see Medical Education

MEDICAL PHYSICS

Damask, A. C. & Swenberg, C. E., eds. Medical Physics, Vol. 3. Date not set. price not set (ISBN 0-12-201203-8). Acad Pr.

Ghista, D. N. & Yang, W. J., eds. Cardiovascular Engineering, Part III: Diagnosis. (Advances in Cardiovascular Physics: Vol. 5). (Illus.). x, 158p. 1983. 68.50 (ISBN 3-8055-3611-9). S Karger.

MEDICAL POLICY

see also Medical Laws and Legislation

Lewis, Irving J. & Sheps, Cecil G. The Sick Citadel: The American Academic Medical Center & the Public Interest. 224p. 1983. text ed. 25.00 (ISBN 0-89946-173-5). Oelgeschlager.

Mechanic, David, ed. Handbook of Health, Health Care & the Health Services. (Illus.). 832p. 1983. text ed. 49.95 (ISBN 0-02-920690-1). Free Pr.

Neustadt, Richard & Fineberg, Harvey. The Epidemic that Never Was: Policy-Making & the Swine Flu Scare. LC 82-40023. 288p. (Orig.). 1983. pap. 7.95 (ISBN 0-394-71147-5, Vin). Random.

MEDICAL PROFESSION

see Medicine; Physicians

MEDICAL RADIOGRAPHY

see Radiography, Medical

MEDICAL RADIOLOGY

see Radiology, Medical

MEDICAL RECORDS

see also Medical History Taking

Rudman, Jack. Medical Records Assistant. (Career Examination Ser.: C-2952). (Cloth bdg. avail. on request). pap. 10.00 (ISBN 0-8373-2952-3). Natl Learning.

MEDICAL REGISTRATION AND EXAMINATION

see Medical Laws and Legislation

MEDICAL RESEARCH

see also Cancer Research; Dental Research; Human Experimentation in Medicine; Pharmaceutical Research

Mechanic, David, ed. Handbook of Health, Health Care & the Health Services. (Illus.). 832p. 1983. text ed. 49.95 (ISBN 0-02-920690-1). Free Pr.

Newell, D. G., ed. Campylobacter: Progress in Research. (Illus.). 400p. 1982. text ed. 69.00 (ISBN 0-85200-455-9, Pub. by MTP Pr England). Kluwer Boston.

Van Keep, Pieter A. & Utian, Wulf H., eds. The Controversial Climacteric. (Illus.). 200p. 1982. text ed. 25.00 (ISBN 0-85200-410-9, Pub. by MTP Pr England). Kluwer Boston.

Worth, H. G. & Curnow, D. H. Metabolic Pathways in Medicine. 192p. 1980. text ed. 29.50 (ISBN 0-7131-4336-3). E Arnold.

MEDICAL RESEARCH ETHICS

see Medical Ethics

MEDICAL SCHOOLS

see Medical Colleges

MEDICAL SECRETARIES

Rudman, Jack. Senior Medical Stenographer. (Career Examination Ser.: C-2940). (Cloth bdg. avail. on request). pap. 12.00 (ISBN 0-8373-2940-X). Natl Learning.

MEDICAL SERVICES

see Medical Care

MEDICAL SOCIAL WORK

see also Psychiatric Social Work

Hubschman, Lynn. Hospital Social Work Practice. 196p. 1983. 29.95 (ISBN 0-03-061926-2). Praeger.

Lurie, Abraham & Rosenberg, Gary, eds. Social Work With Groups in Health Settings. LC 82-18151. 124p. 1982. pap. 7.95 (ISBN 0-88202-137-0). N Watson.

Orque, Modesta S. & Bloch, Bobbie. Ethnic Nursing Care: A Multi-Cultural Approach. (Illus.). 414p. 1983. pap. text ed. 14.95 (ISBN 0-8016-3742-2). Mosby.

Rudman, Jack. Senior Medical Social Worker. (Career Examination Ser.: C-2629). (Cloth bdg. avail. on request). pap. 12.00 (ISBN 0-8373-2629-X). Natl Learning.

--Supervising Medical Social Worker. (Career Examination Ser.: C-2630). (Cloth bdg. avail. on request). pap. 12.00 (ISBN 0-8373-2630-3). Natl Learning.

Turner, Francis J., ed. Differential Diagnosis & Treatment in Social Work. 3rd, rev. ed. LC 82-48390. 1983. 24.95 (ISBN 0-02-932990-6). Free Pr.

MEDICAL SOCIOLOGY

see Social Medicine

MEDICAL STATISTICS

Duncan, Robert C., et al. Introductory Biostatistics for the Health Sciences. LC 76-44291. 163p. 1977. 12.50 (ISBN 0-471-01604-7, Pub. by Wiley Medical); avail. solutions (ISBN 0-471-03944-6). Wiley.

MEDICAL STUDENTS

Broadhead, Robert S. The Private Lives of Medical Students. 200p. 1983. 24.95 (ISBN 0-87855-478-5). Transaction Bks.

Gusky, Jeff, et al. Medical Student Ward Survival Manual. LC 82-60882. (Illus.). 22p. (Orig.). 1982. pap. text ed. 13.95 (ISBN 0-910015-00-7). Med Student Pubs.

MEDICAL SUPPLIES

see also Medical Instruments and Apparatus

Swit, David & Hadley, Richard. The Practical Guide to GMP's. 60p. (Orig.). 1982. pap. 38.00 (ISBN 0-914176-17-X). Wash Busn Info.

MEDICAL TECHNOLOGISTS

Rudman, Jack. Medical Equipment Technician. (Career Examination Ser.: C-2654). (Cloth bdg. avail. on request). pap. 10.00 (ISBN 0-8373-2654-0). Natl Learning.

MEDICAL TECHNOLOGY

see also Medicine, Clinical

Gay, James & Jacobs, Barbara S., eds. The Technolgy Explosion in Medical Science: Implications for the Health Care Industry & the Public (1981-2001) (Health Care Administration Monographs: Vol. 2). 128p. 1983. text ed. 14.95 (ISBN 0-89335-181-4). SP Med & Sci Bks.

MEDICAL ULTRASONICS

see Ultrasonics in Medicine

MEDICAL VIROLOGY

see Virus Diseases

MEDICARE

see Insurance, Health

MEDICI, HOUSE OF

Tracy, Mark. Secrets of the Great Italian Dames at the Court of the De'Medicis. (The Memoirs Collections of Significant Historical Personalities Ser.). (Illus.). 119p. 1983. Repr. of 1916 ed. 89.75 (ISBN 0-89901-085-7). Found Class Reprints.

MEDICINAL PLANTS

see Botany, Medical

MEDICINE

see also Abnormalities, Human; Anatomy; Aviation Medicine; Bacteriology; Biomedical Engineering; Botany, Medical; Chemistry, Medical and Pharmaceutical; Chiropractic; Dentistry; Diseases–Causes and Theories of Causation; Family Medicine; Folk Medicine; Health; Health Resorts, Watering-Places, etc.; Histology; Homeopathy; Hospitals; Hypnotism; Materia Medica; Mind and Body; Nurses and Nursing; Pathology; Pharmacology; Pharmacy; Physiology; Surgery; Tropical Medicine; Women in Medicine

also headings beginning with the word Medical

Aherne, William & Dunnill, Michael. Morphometry. 176p. 1982. text ed. 49.50 (ISBN 0-7131-4403-3). E Arnold.

Darvill, Fred T., Jr. Mountaineering Medicine: A Wilderness Medical Guide. 10th ed. Winnett, Thomas, ed. (Illus.). 60p. 1983. pap. 1.95 (ISBN 0-89997-021-4). Wilderness Pr.

Griffiths, David. Psychology & Medicine. (Psychology for Professional Groups Ser.). 320p. 1981. text ed. 25.00x (ISBN 0-333-31862-5, Pub. by Macmillan England); pap. text ed. 10.95x (ISBN 0-333-31877-3). Humanities.

Houston, J. C., et al. A Short Textbook of Medicine. LC 82-73298. (Illus.). 772p. 1983. pap. text ed. 19.95x (ISBN 0-668-05739-4, 5739). Arco.

International Medical Imaging Markets. 1983. 995.00 (ISBN 0-686-37715-X, 289). Predicasts.

Macovski, Albert. Medical Imaging Systems. (Illus.). 256p. 1983. 29.95 (ISBN 0-13-572685-9). P-H.

Marinero, Hazel. Arzneimittelhaftung In Den USA und Deutschland. xxvii, 292p. (Ger.). 1982. write for info. (ISBN 3-8204-7121-9). P Lang Pubs.

Morgan, John P. & Kagan, Doreen V., eds. Society & Medication: Conflicting Signals for Prescribers & Patients. LC 81-48145. 1983. write for info. (ISBN 0-669-05290-6). Lexington Bks.

Vilazon. Critical Care Medicine. (International Congress Ser.: No. 499). 1979. 21.50 (ISBN 0-444-90107-8). Elsevier.

Winters, Robert W. & Bell, Ralph B. Acid-Base Physiology in Medicine: A Self-Instruction Program. 3rd ed. 1982. text ed. 19.95 (ISBN 0-316-94739-3). Little.

MEDICINE–ABBREVIATIONS

Patient Care Magazine Editors. Medical Abbreviations Handbook. 200p. 1982. softcover 7.95 (ISBN 0-87489-309-7). Med Economics.

Schertel, A. Abkuerzungen in der Medizin: Abbreviations in Medicine - Abreviations en Medecine. 3rd ed. 200p. 1983. pap. 12.00 (ISBN 3-8055-3669-0). S Karger.

MEDICINE–ADDRESSES, ESSAYS, LECTURES

Leffkowitz, M. & Steinitz, H., eds. Ninth Congress of Life Assurance Medicine, Tel Aviv, March 1967: Proceedings. vi, 368p. 1968. pap. 68.50 (ISBN 3-8055-0910-3). S Karger.

MEDICINE–APPARATUS

see Medical Instruments and Apparatus

MEDICINE–BIBLIOGRAPHY

see also Information Storage and Retrieval Systems–Medicine

Medical Books & Serials in Print, 1983: An Index to Literature in the Health Sciences, 2 vol. set. 2055p. 1983. 75.00x (ISBN 0-8352-1617-9). Bowker.

Parkinson, E. M. Catalogue of Medical Books in the Manchester University Library, 1480-1700. 1972. 56.50 (ISBN 0-7190-1246-5). Manchester.

MEDICINE–COST OF MEDICAL CARE

see Medical Care, Cost Of

MEDICINE–DATA PROCESSING

Abramson, J. H. & Peritz, E. Calculator Programs for the Health Sciences. (Illus.). 326p. 1983. text ed. 37.50x (ISBN 0-19-503187-3); pap. text ed. 18.95x (ISBN 0-19-503188-1). Oxford U Pr.

American Hospital Association Clearinghouse for Hospital Management Engineering, ed. Computer-Assisted Medical Record Systems: An Examination of Case Studies. 148p. 1982. pap. 18.75 (ISBN 0-87258-375-9, AHA-148200). Am Hospital.

Blum, R. L. Discovery & Representation of Causal Relationships from a Large Time-Oriented Clinical Database: The RX Project. (Lecture Notes in Medical Informatics Ser.: Vol. 19). 242p. 1983. pap. 18.00 (ISBN 0-387-11962-0). Springer-Verlag.

Cornell, Joseph A. Computers in Hospital Pharmacy Management: Fundamentals & Applications. 225p. 1983. write for info. (ISBN 0-89443-673-2). Aspen Systems.

Ehrlich, Ann. Role of Computers on Medical Practice Management. LC 81-69069. (Illus.). 8.95. Colwell Co.

Gonzalez, Carlos F., et al. Computed Brain & Orbital Tomography: Technique & Interpretation. LC 76-28530. (Diagnostic & Therapeutic Radiology Ser.). 1976. 70.00x (ISBN 0-471-01692-6, Pub. by Wiley-Med). Wiley.

Kember, N. F. Introduction to Computer Applications in Medicine. 176p. 1982. pap. text ed. 17.95 (ISBN 0-7131-4414-9). E Arnold.

Sklansky, J. & Bisconte, J. C., eds. Biomedical Images & Computers: St. Pierre de Chartreuse, France 1980, Proceedings. (Lecture Notes in Medical Informatics: Vol. 17). 332p. 1982. pap. 21.00 (ISBN 0-387-11579-X). Springer-Verlag.

MEDICINE–DICTIONARIES

Austrin, Miriam G. Young's Learning Medical Terminology Step by Step: Textbook & Workbook. (Illus.). 416p. 1983. pap. 18.95 (ISBN 0-8016-5662-1). Mosby.

DiLorenzo-Kearon, Maria. Medical Spanish. 256p. Date not set. with 12 cassettes 145.00x (ISBN 0-88432-079-0, MS20). J Norton Pubs.

English-Chinese Dictionary of Medicine. 1675p. 1979. text ed. 24.95 (ISBN 0-8351-1048-6). China Bks.

Guidos, Barbara & Hamilton, Betty. MASA: Medical Acronyms, Symbols, & Abbreviations. 300p. 1983. lib. bdg. 49.95 (ISBN 0-918212-72-3). Neal-Schuman.

Hart, T. L. Speedy Spanish for Medical Personnel. Hart, T. L. & Hart, Babe, eds. Hart, Babe, tr. (Speedy Language Ser.). (Illus.). 24p. (Orig., Span.). 1980. pap. 1.95 (ISBN 0-9602838-6-2). Baja Bks.

Lillis, Carol. Brady's Introduction to Medical Terminology. 2nd ed. (Illus.). 224p. 1983. pap. text ed. 10.95 (ISBN 0-89303-234-4). R J Brady.

Ordang, Laurence. The Bantam Medical Dictionary. 464p. 1982. pap. 4.95 (ISBN 0-553-22673-8). Bantam.

Unseld, Dieter. Medical Dictionary of the English & German Languages: Medizinisches Worterbuch der Deutschen und Englischen Sprache. 8th ed. 593p. 1982. 30.00x (ISBN 0-686-43337-8). Intl Pubns Serv.

MEDICINE–EXAMINATIONS, QUESTIONS, ETC.

Anderson, Fred A. Scoring High on Medical & Health Sciences Exams. 24p. (Orig.). 1983. pap. 1.75 (ISBN 0-939570-02-5). Skills Improvement.

Yurdhuck, Ruth. C. G. F. N. S. Examination Review. 1983. pap. text ed. price not set. (ISBN 0-87488-512-4). Med Exam.

MEDICINE–FEES

see Medical Fees

MEDICINE–FORMULAE, RECEIPTS, PRESCRIPTIONS

see also Pharmacopoeias; Pharmacy

Koch, Hugh. Drug Utilization in Office-Based Practice: A Summary of Findings National Ambulatory Medical Care United States, 1980, Ser.13-72. Shipp, Audrey, ed. 55p. 1982. pap. text ed. 1.95 (ISBN 0-8406-0270-7). Natl Ctr Health Stats.

United States Pharmacopeia & National Formulary. 1980. USP XX-NF XV. 75.00 (ISBN 0-686-37677-3); with annual supplements 100.00 (ISBN 0-686-37678-1); third supplement 9.00 (ISBN 0-686-37679-X); third supplement plus all future supplements 27.00 (ISBN 0-686-37680-3); with annual supplements 100.00. USPC.

MEDICINE–HANDBOOKS, MANUALS, ETC.

Husak, Glen. How to Buy & Use Medicine. (The Health Ser.). (Illus.). 45p. (gr. 7-12). 1981. pap. text ed. 3.00 (ISBN 0-910839-24-7). Hopewell.

Reader's Digest Editors. Family Health Guide & Medical Encyclopedia. rev ed. LC 76-23541. (Illus.). 640p. 1976. 16.98 (ISBN 0-89577-032-6). RD Assn.

Walraven & Harding. Manual of Advanced Prehospital Care. 2nd ed. (Illus.). 416p. 1983. pap. text ed. 19.95 (ISBN 0-89303-252-2). R J Brady.

Wingate, Martin B. Management for Physicians. 1983. pap. text ed. write for info. (ISBN 0-87488-246-X). Med Exam.

MEDICINE–HISTORY

see also Medicine, Arabic; Medicine, Medieval

also similar headings

Armour, R. It All Started with Hippocrates: A Mercifully Brief History of Medicine. 1972. pap. 2.95 (ISBN 0-07-002284-4). McGraw.

Armstrong, David. Political Anatomy of the Body: Medical Knowledge in Britain in the Twentieth Century. LC 82-9546. 176p. Date not set. 29.95 (ISBN 0-521-24746-2). Cambridge U Pr.

Emmerson, Joan S., compiled by. Catalogue of the Pybus Collection of Medical Books, Letters & Engravings from the 15th-20th Centuries Held in the University Library, Newcastle upon Tyne. 280p. 1982. 60.00. Manchester.

Gordon, Richard. Great Medical Disasters. 256p. 1983. 16.95 (ISBN 0-8128-2911-5). Stein & Day.

Haldane, John S. Organisms & Enviorment as Illustrated by the Physiology of Breathing. 1917. text ed. 32.50x (ISBN 0-686-83659-6). Elliots Bks.

Hudson, Robert P. Disease & It's Control: The Shaping of Modern Thought. LC 82-21135. (Contributions in Medical History: No. 12). 288p. 1983. lib. bdg. 29.95 (ISBN 0-313-23806-5, HHD/). Greenwood.

New Jersey Medicine in the Revolutionary Era, 1763-1767: An Exhibition. (Illus.). 36p. 1976. pap. 2.00 (ISBN 0-686-81827-X). NJ Hist Soc.

Pritchet, C. D. Iohannis Alexandrini Commentaria in Librum de Sectis Galeni. xxi, 108p. 1982. write for info. (ISBN 90-04-06566-0). E J Brill.

Underhill, Frank P. Physiology of the Amino Acids. 1915. text ed. 32.50x. Elliots Bks.

Withington, Edward. Medical History from Earliest Times: A Popular History of the Healing Art 1894. 430p. pap. 25.00 (ISBN 0-87556-415-1). Saifer.

MEDICINE–INSTRUMENTS

see Medical Instruments and Apparatus

MEDICINE–LAWS AND LEGISLATION

see Medical Laws and Legislation

MEDICINE–MATHEMATICS

Paul, J. P. Computing in Medicine. 1982. 120.00x (ISBN 0-333-31886-2, Pub. by Macmillan England). State Mutual Bk.

Pretschner, D. P. Engymetry & Personal Computing in Nuclear Medicine. (Lecture Notes in Medical Informatics: Vol. 18). 133p. 1983. pap. 11.50 (ISBN 0-387-11598-6). Springer-Verlag.

MEDICINE–MISCELLANEA

Gordon, Richard. Great Medical Disasters. 256p. 1983. 16.95 (ISBN 0-8128-2911-5). Stein & Day.

MEDICINE–MORAL AND RELIGIOUS ASPECTS

see Medical Ethics; Medicine and Religion

MEDICINE–PHILOSOPHY

Armstrong, David. Political Anatomy of the Body: Medical Knowledge in Britain in the Twentieth Century. LC 82-9546. 176p. Date not set. 29.95 (ISBN 0-521-24746-2). Cambridge U Pr.

Clark, Mason A., ed. The Healing Wisdom of Doctor P. P. Quimby. (Illus.). 128p. (Orig.). 1982. pap. text ed. 8.95 (ISBN 0-931400-02-3). Frontal Lobe.

Ziegler, Alfred J. Archetypal Medicine. Hartman, Gary V., tr. from Ger. Orig. Title: Morbismus: von der Besten aller Gesundheiten. 175p. (Orig.). 1983. pap. 13.50 (ISBN 0-88214-322-0). Spring Pubns.

MEDICINE–POPULAR WORKS

see Medicine, Popular

MEDICINE–PRACTICE

see also Children–Diseases; Communicable Diseases; Diagnosis; Electrotherapeutics; Group Medical Practice; Gynecology; Hydrotherapy; Infants–Diseases; Malpractice; Massage; Mechanotherapy; Nurses and Nursing; Obstetrics; Therapeutics

also names of diseases and groups of diseases, e.g. Bronchitis, Fever, Nervous System–Diseases

Hurst, J. Willis. Medicine for Practicing Physian. new ed. 2000p. 1983. text ed. 40.00 (ISBN 0-409-95031-9). Butterworth.

Kramer, Dean C. Medical Practice Management. 288p. 1982. pap. 15.95 (ISBN 0-316-50322-3). Little.

Monteiro, E. S. Anecdota Medica. (Illus.). 112p. 1983. pap. 6.95 (ISBN 0-686-42982-6). Hippocrene Bks.

Willard, Mervyn. Nutritional Management for the Practicing Physician. 1982. 26.95 (ISBN 0-201-08320-5, 08320, Med-Nurse). A-W.

MEDICINE–RESEARCH

see Medical Research

MEDICINE–SOCIAL ASPECTS

see Social Medicine

MEDICINE–STUDY AND TEACHING

Anspaugh, David & Ezell, Gene. Teaching Today's Health. 512p. 1983. text ed. 18.95 (ISBN 0-675-20025-3). Additional supplements may be obtained from publisher. Merrill.

Dyche, June. Educational Program Development for Employees in Health Care Agencies. 384p. (Orig.). 1982. pap. text ed. 23.50 (ISBN 0-9609732-0-6). Tri-Oak.

Gray, D. Pereira. Training for General Practice. 352p. 1981. 49.00x (ISBN 0-7121-2004-1, Pub. by Macdonald & Evans). State Mutual Bk.

Harron, Frank & United Ministries in Education Health & Human Values Program. Human Values in Medicine & Health Care: Audio-Visual Resources. LC 82-13394. 96p. 1983. pap. text ed. 3.95x (ISBN 0-300-02975-6). Yale U Pr.

MEDICINE–TERMINOLOGY

Fisher, J. Patrick. Basic Medical Terminology. 2nd ed. 288p. 1983. pap. text ed. 14.95 (ISBN 0-672-61573-8); cassettes 150.00 (ISBN 0-672-61575-4); instr's guide 3.33 (ISBN 0-672-61574-6). Bobbs.

Noricks, Michael. Spanish for Medical Personnel: A Short Course. 64p. (Orig.). 1983. pap. price not set (ISBN 0-910669-00-7); write for info. 2 cassettes (ISBN 0-910669-01-5). Pacific Lang.

Willeford, George, Jr. Medical Word Finder. 3rd ed. 464p. 1983. 19.95 (ISBN 0-13-573527-0, Busn). P-H.

MEDICINE–TROPICS

see Tropical Medicine

MEDICINE–YEAR BOOKS

Brinkhous, Kenneth M., ed. Year Book of Pathology & Clinical Pathology, 1983. 1983. 44.00 (ISBN 0-8151-1238-6). Year Bk Med.

Freedman, Daniel X., ed. Year Book of Psychiatry & Applied Mental Health 1983. 1983. 45.00 (ISBN 0-686-83776-2). Year Bk Med.

Hamburger, Jean. Advances in Nephrology, Vol. 7. 1978. 55.00 (ISBN 0-8151-4116-5). Year Bk Med.

--Advances in Nephrology, Vol. 8. 1979. 55.00 (ISBN 0-8151-4117-3). Year Bk Med.

--Advances in Nephrology, Vol. 9. 1980. 55.00 (ISBN 0-8151-4118-1). Year Bk Med.

--Advances in Nephrology, Vol. 10. 1981. 55.00 (ISBN 0-8151-4119-X). Year Bk Med.

Hoffer. Year Book of Nuclear Medicine 1983. 1983. 45.00 (ISBN 0-8151-4527-6). Year Bk Med.

Hollister, Leo E. Year Book of Drug Therapy 1983. 1983. 42.00 (ISBN 0-8151-4621-3). Year Bk Med.

McCoy, Frederick J., ed. Year Book of Plastic & Reconstructive Surgery 1983. 1983. 45.00 (ISBN 0-686-83767-3). Year Bk Med.

Oski, Frank A. Year Book of Pediatrics 1983. 1983. 35.00 (ISBN 0-8151-6566-8). Year Bk Med.

Pitkin, Roy M., ed. Year Book of Obstetrics & Gynecology 1983. 1983. 35.00 (ISBN 0-8151-6692-3). Year Bk Med.

Rakel, Robert E., ed. Year Book of Family Practice 1983. 1983. 41.00 (ISBN 0-8151-7024-6). Year Bk Med.

Scott, Ronald B. & Fraser, James, eds. The Medical Annual 1982-83. (Illus.). 408p. 1982. pap. text ed. 29.50 (ISBN 0-7236-0655-2). Wright-PSG.

Wagner, David K., et al, eds. Year Book of Emergency Medicine 1983. 1983. 40.00 (ISBN 0-686-83756-8). Year Bk Med.

MEDICINE–AFRICA

American Health Research Institute, Ltd. Developing Countries: Status & Progress by Medical Subject Analysis & Research Index with Bibliography. Bartone, John C., ed. 120p. 1983. 29.95 (ISBN 0-941864-93-6); pap. 21.95 (ISBN 0-941864-92-8). ABBE Pubs Assn.

Boulos, Loutfy. Medicinal Plants of North Africa. Ayensu, Edward S., ed. LC 82-20412. (Medicinal Plants of the World Ser.: No. 3). (Illus.). 300p. 1983. 29.95 (ISBN 0-917256-16-6). Ref Pubns.

Buschkens, W. & Slikkerveer, L. Health Care in East Africa. (Studies in Developing Countries: No. 28). 144p. 1982. text ed. 10.50x (ISBN 0-686-82311-7, 41379, Pub. by Van Gorcum Holland). Humanities.

Janzen, J. M., ed. Causality & Classification in African Medicine & Health. 280p. 1983. 22.50 (ISBN 0-08-028134-6). Pergamon.

MEDICINE–ASIA

American Health Research Institute, Ltd. Developing Countries: Status & Progress by Medical Subject Analysis & Research Index with Bibliography. Bartone, John C., ed. 120p. 1983. 29.95 (ISBN 0-941864-93-6); pap. 21.95 (ISBN 0-941864-92-8). ABBE Pubs Assn.

MEDICINE–CHINA

Hillier, Sheila & Jewell, John. Health Care & Traditonal Medicine in China, 1800-1982. 600p. 1983. price not set (ISBN 0-7100-9425-6). Routledge & Kegan.

Kaptchuk, Ted J. The Web That Has No Weaver: Understanding Chinese Medicine. LC 82-2511. 1983. pap. 19.95 (ISBN 0-312-92932-3). Congdon & Weed.

MEDICINE–CHINA–1949-

Lucas, Elissa. Chinese Medical Modernization: Comparative Policy Continuity from 1930-1980. 190p. 1982. 25.95 (ISBN 0-03-059454-5). Praeger.

MEDICINE–GREAT BRITAIN

Armstrong, David. Political Anatomy of the Body: Medical Knowledge in Britain in the Twentieth Century. LC 82-9546. 176p. Date not set. 29.95 (ISBN 0-521-24746-2). Cambridge U Pr.

Taylor, Rex & Gilmore, Anne, eds. Current Trends in British Gerontology. 230p. 1982. text ed. 35.00x (ISBN 0-566-00495-X). Gower Pub Ltd.

MEDICINE–LATIN AMERICA

American Health Research Institute, Ltd. Developing Countries: Status & Progress by Medical Subject Analysis & Research Index with Bibliography. Bartone, John C., ed. 120p. 1983. 29.95 (ISBN 0-941864-93-6); pap. 21.95 (ISBN 0-941864-92-8). ABBE Pubs Assn.

MEDICINE–TIBET

Badmajew, Peter, Jr. & Badmajew, Vladimir, Jr. Healing Herbs: The Heart of Tibetan Medicine. LC 82-81022. (Illus.). 96p. 1982. pap. 2.95 (ISBN 0-943014-00-X, 607). Red Lotus Pr.

MEDICINE–UNITED STATES

New Jersey Medicine in the Revolutionary Era, 1763-1767: An Exhibition. (Illus.). 36p. 1976. pap. 2.00 (ISBN 0-686-81827-X). NJ Hist Soc.

MEDICINE, ARABIC

Gallager, Nancy E. & Wilson, Dunning S. Haudlist of Arabic Medical Manuscripts at UCLA. LC 82-50985. 28p. 1983. price not set (ISBN 0-89003-128-2). Undena Pubns.

MEDICINE, BOTANIC

LaArta, Moulton. Nature's Medicine Chest, Set 4. 96p. 1975. 5.50 (ISBN 0-935596-07-0). Gluten Co.

LeArta, Moulton. Nature's Medicine Chest, 6 bks. Set. 32.00 (ISBN 0-935596-10-0). Gluten Co.

--Nature's Medicine Chest, Set 2. 96p. 1975. 5.00 (ISBN 0-935596-05-4). Gluten Co.

--Nature's Medicine Chest, Set 3. 96p. 1976. 5.50 (ISBN 0-935596-06-2). Gluten Co.

--Nature's Medicine Chest, Set 5. 96p. 1976. 5.50 (ISBN 0-935596-08-9). Gluten Co.

--Nature's Medicine Chest, Set 6. 96p. 1977. 5.50 (ISBN 0-935596-09-7). Gluten Co.

Moulton, LeArta. Nature's Medicine Chest, Set 1. 96p. 1974. 5.00 (ISBN 0-935596-04-6). Gluten Co.

MEDICINE, CLERICAL

see Pastoral Medicine

MEDICINE, CLINICAL

see also Clinical Enzymology; Diagnosis; Medical Laboratories; Medical Technologists; Medical Technology; Pathology; Radioactivation Analysis

Astaldi, G., et al, eds. Current Studies on Standardization Problems in Clinical Pathology, Haematology & Radiation Therapy for Hodgkins' Disease. (International Congress Ser.: No. 400). (Proceedings). 1975. pap. 72.00 (ISBN 0-444-15162-1). Elsevier.

Creger, W. P., et al, eds. Annual Review of Medicine: Selected Topics in the Clinical Sciences, Vol. 34. LC 51-1659. (Illus.). 1983. text ed. 27.00 (ISBN 0-8243-0534-5). Annual Reviews.

Epstein, Jerome & Gaines, John. Clinical Respiratory Care of the Adult Patient. (Illus.). 448p. 1983. pap. text ed. 21.95 (ISBN 0-89303-209-3). R J Brady.

Galen, P. S. & Gambino, S. R. Beyond Normality: The Predictive Value & Efficiency of Medical Diagnosis. LC 75-25915. 237p. 1975. 32.95x (ISBN 0-471-29047-5, Pub. by Wiley Medical). Wiley.

Halsted, Charles H. & Halsted, James A. The Laboratory in Clinical Medicine. (Illus.). 1083p. 1981. text ed. 72.00 (ISBN 0-7216-4479-1). Saunders.

Hart, Gordon M., Jr. The Process of Clinical Supervision. (Illus.). 288p. 1982. pap. text ed. 25.95 (ISBN 0-8391-1700-0, 14257). Univ Park.

Howells, John G. Integral Clinical Investigation: As Aspect of Panathropic Medicine. 272p. 1982. 65.00x (ISBN 0-333-29446-7, Pub. by Macmillan England). State Mutual Bk.

Judge, Richard D. & Zuidema, George D. Clinical Diagnosis: A Physiologic Approach. 4th ed. 1982. text ed. 29.95 (ISBN 0-316-47589-0). Little.

Kissel, Stanley. Private Practice for the Mental Health Clinician. 1983. write for info. (ISBN 0-89443-849-2). Aspen Systems.

Lundberg, George D. Using the Clinical Laboratory in Medical Decision Making. 1983. text ed. 30.00 (ISBN 0-89189-164-1, 45-9-013-00). Am Soc Clinical.

Tunbridge, David, ed. Notes on Clinical Methods. 120p. pap. 5.95 (ISBN 0-7190-0851-4). Manchester.

MEDICINE, COMMUNICATION IN

see Communication in Medicine

MEDICINE, DENTAL

see Teeth–Diseases

MEDICINE, FORENSIC

see Medical Jurisprudence

MEDICINE, INDUSTRIAL

see also Disability Evaluation; Industrial Health; Occupational Diseases

American Health Research Institute, Ltd. Occupational Medicine: International Survey with Medical Subject Directory & Bibliography. LC 82-72030. 120p. 1983. 29.95 (ISBN 0-941864-77-4); pap. 21.95 (ISBN 0-941864-76-6). ABBE Pubs Assn.

Navarro, Vicente & Berman, Daniel, eds. Health & Work under Capitalism: An International Perspective, Vol. 5. (Policy, Politics, Health & Medicine). 312p. 1983. pap. text ed. 16.50 (ISBN 0-89503-035-7). Baywood Pub.

MEDICINE, INTERNAL

see Internal Medicine; Medicine–Practice

MEDICINE, LEGAL

see Medical Jurisprudence

MEDICINE, MAGIC, MYSTIC, AND SPAGIRIC

see also Aphrodisiacs; Folk Medicine

Fenner, Edward T. Rasayana Siddhi: Medicine & Alchemy in the Buddhist Tantras. (Traditional Healing Ser.). 300p. 1983. 39.95 (ISBN 0-932426-28-X). Trado-Medic.

MEDICINE, MEDIEVAL

see also Herbs; Medicine, Arabic

Stevenson, Robert K. The Golden Era of Preventive Medicine. LC 82-99906. 120p. (Orig.). 1982. pap. 8.95 (ISBN 0-9606252-2-4). Stevenson Intl.

MEDICINE, OCCULT

see Medicine, Magic, Mystic, and Spagiric

MEDICINE, OCCUPATIONAL

see Medicine, Industrial

MEDICINE, ORTHOMOLECULAR

see Orthomolecular Medicine

MEDICINE, PASTORAL

see Pastoral Medicine

MEDICINE, POPULAR

see also Folk Medicine; Medicine–Dictionaries

Benson, Ragnar. Survivalist's Medicine Chest. (Illus.). 80p. 1982. pap. 5.95 (ISBN 0-87364-256-2). Paladin Ent.

Culbert, Michael L. What the Medical Establishment Won't Tell You That Could SAVE YOUR LIFE! Friedman, Robert S., ed. LC 82-9607. 280p. (Orig.). 1983. pap. 7.95 (ISBN 0-89865-256-1). Donning Co.

Howden, P. Smallternatives Too. 1982. 25.00x (ISBN 0-686-99812-X, Pub. by Element Bks). State Mutual Bk.

Saint-Pierre, Gaston & Boater, Debbie. The Metamorphic Technique. 1982. 25.00x (ISBN 0-686-99809-X, Pub. by Element Bks). State Mutual Bk.

Thompson & Cox. Steps to Better Health: Common Problems & What to Do About Them. 1983. pap. 9.95 (ISBN 0-8359-7077-9). Reston.

MEDICINE, PREVENTIVE

see also Bacteriology; Immunity; Pathology; Public Health

American Health Research Institute, Ltd. Preventive Medicine: Current Medical Subject Analysis & Research Directory with Bibliography. Bartone, John C., ed. LC 81-71811. 120p. 1982. 29.95 (ISBN 0-941864-36-7); pap. 21.95 (ISBN 0-941864-37-5). ABBE Pubs Assn.

Carr, Rachel. Arthritis: Relief Beyond Drugs. (Illus.). 160p. 1983. pap. 6.68i (ISBN 0-06-464054-X, BN 4054). B&N NY.

Douglass, William C. & Walker, Morton. DMSO: The New Healing Power. (Illus.). 1983. 14.95 (ISBN 0-8159-5315-1). Devin.

Marshall, Daniel P. & Rabold, J. Gregory. Staying Healthy Without Medicine: A Manual of Home Prevention & Treatment. (Illus.). 336p. 1983. lib. bdg. 27.95x (ISBN 0-88229-635-3). Nelson-Hall.

Rondle, C. J., ed. Disease Eradication. 270p. 1981. 60.00x (ISBN 0-333-31188-4, Pub. by Macmillan England). State Mutual Bk.

Stevenson, Robert K. The Golden Era of Preventive Medicine. LC 82-99906. 120p. (Orig.). 1982. pap. 8.95 (ISBN 0-9606252-2-4). Stevenson Intl.

MEDICINE, PSYCHOSOMATIC

see also Iatrogenic Diseases; Pediatrics–Psychosomatic Aspects

also subdivision Diseases–Psychosomatic Aspects under names of organs and regions of the body, e.g. Skin–Diseases–Psychosomatic Aspects

Blackmore, Richard. A Treatise of the Spleen & Vapours: Or, Hypocondriacal & Hysterical Affections. 320p. 1976. 40.00 (ISBN 0-686-84923-X, Oriel). Routledge & Kegan.

Millon, Theodore & Green, Catherine J., eds. Handbook of Clinical Health Psychology. 632p. 1982. 50.00x (ISBN 0-306-40932-1, Plenum Pr). Plenum Pub.

Pennebaker, James W. The Psychology of Physical Symptoms. (Illus.). 192p. 1982. 19.95 (ISBN 0-387-90730-0). Springer-Verlag.

Reres, Mary E. Stress in Patient Care. 1983. pap. price not set (ISBN 0-8391-1815-5, 16608). Univ Park.

Turk, Dennis & Meichenbaum, Donald. Pain & Behavioral Medicine. LC 82-11695. (Clinical & Psychology & Psychotherapy Ser.). 422p. 1983. 25.00x (ISBN 0-89862-002-3). Guilford Pr.

Ursin, H. & Murison, R., eds. Biological & Physical Basis of Psychosomatic Disease: Based on Papers Presented at a Conference on Psychological Load & Stress in the Work Environment, Bergen, Norway, 1980. (Illus.). 304p. 1982. 60.00 (ISBN 0-08-029774-9). Pergamon.

Wentworth-Rohr, Ivan. Symptom Reduction Through Clinical Biofeedback. 256p. 1983. text ed. 26.95x (ISBN 0-89885-135-1). Human Sci Pr.

Wise, T. N. & Freyberger, H., eds. Consultation Liaison Throughout the World. (Advances in Psychosomatic Medicine: Vol. 11). (Illus.). xii, 250p. 1983. 112.75 (ISBN 3-8055-3667-4). S Karger.

MEDICINE, RURAL

see also Health, Rural

Dammann, Nancy. A Social History of the Frontier Nursing Service. (Illus.). 179p. (Orig.). 1982. pap. 5.95 (ISBN 0-9609376-0-9). Soc Change Pr.

Rosenblatt, R. A. & Moscovice, I. S. Rural Health Care. (Health Services Ser.). 301p. 1982. text ed. 19.95 (ISBN 0-471-05419-4, Pub. by Wiley Med). Wiley.

MEDICINE, SOCIAL

see Social Medicine

MEDICINE, TROPICAL

see Tropical Medicine

MEDICINE, VETERINARY

see Veterinary Medicine

MEDICINE AND ART

see also Anatomy, Artistic

Berg, Geri, ed. The Visual Arts & Medical Education. (Medical Humanities Ser.). 160p. 1983. price not set (ISBN 0-8093-1038-4). S Ill U Pr.

MEDICINE AND CHRISTIANITY

see Medicine and Religion

MEDICINE AND PSYCHOLOGY

see also Medicine, Psychosomatic; Psychiatry

Hine, F. R., et al. Introduction to Behavioral Science in Medicine. (Illus.). 350p. 1983. pap. 22.00 (ISBN 0-387-90736-X). Springer-Verlag.

Korn, Errol R. & Johnson, Karen. Visualization: The Uses of Imagery in the Health Professions. LC 82-73617. (The Dorsey Professional Ser.). 300p. 1983. 27.95 (ISBN 0-87094-403-7). Dow Jones-Irwin.

Lipkin. Psychosocial Factors Affecting Health. 396p. 1982. 37.95 (ISBN 0-03-061964-5). Praeger.

MEDICINE AND RELIGION

see also Faith-Cure; Mental Healing; Pastoral Medicine

American Health Research Institute, Ltd. Religion & Medicine: A Medical Subject Analysis & Research Index with Bibliography. Bartone, John C., ed. 120p. 1983. 29.95 (ISBN 0-88164-032-8); pap. 21.95 (ISBN 0-88164-033-6). ABBE Pubs Assn.

Fenner, Edward T. Rasayana Siddhi: Medicine & Alchemy in the Buddhist Tantras. (Traditional Healing Ser.). 300p. 1983. 39.95 (ISBN 0-932426-28-X). Trado-Medic.

Larlham, Hattie. Dear Children. 152p. 1983. 9.95 (ISBN 0-8361-3325-0). Herald Pr.

MEDICINE AND SPORTS

see Sports Medicine

MEDICINE IN ART

see Medicine and Art

MEDICINE-MAN

Bourke, John G. The Medicine Men of the Apache. LC 77-135517. (A Paper from the Nineteh Annual Report (1887, 1888) of the Bureau of American Ethnology). (Illus.). 196p. 1983. Repr. of 1892 ed. casebound 20.00 (ISBN 0-87380-050-8). Rio Grande.

MEDICINES, PHYSIOLOGICAL EFFECT OF

see Pharmacology

MEDIEVAL ARCHITECTURE

see Architecture, Medieval

MEDIEVAL ART
see Art, Medieval
MEDIEVAL CIVILIZATION
see Civilization, Medieval
MEDIEVAL HISTORY
see Middle Ages–History
MEDIEVAL LITERATURE
see Literature, Medieval
MEDIEVAL PHILOSOPHY
see Philosophy, Medieval
MEDITATION
Here are entered works on meditation or mental prayer as a method of promoting the spiritual life. Works that contain collections of meditations are entered under the heading Meditations.
see also Retreats; Transcendental Meditation

Ashcroft-Nowicki, Dolores. First Steps in Ritual: Safe, Effective Techniques for Experiencing the Inner Worlds. 96p. 1983. pap. 6.95 (ISBN 0-85030-314-1). Newcastle Pub.
Dhiravamsa. The Dynamic Way of Meditation. 160p. 1983. pap. 8.95 (ISBN 0-85500-163-1). Newcastle Pub.
--The Dynamic Way of Meditation: The Release & Cure of Pain & Suffering Through Vipassana Meditative Techniques. 160p. (Orig.). 1983. pap. 7.95 (ISBN 0-85500-163-1, Pub. by Thorsons Pubs England). Sterling.
Hall, Manly. Meditation Disciplines. pap. 3.50 (ISBN 0-89314-800-8). Philos Res.
Herzog, Stephanie. Joy in the Classroom. Ray, Ann, ed. (Illus.). 1982. text ed. 6.95 (ISBN 0-916438-46-5). Univ of Trees.
Himalayan Institute. Meditation in Christianity. rev. ed. LC 79-92042. 150p. 1983. pap. 3.95 (ISBN 0-89389-085-5). Himalayan Intl Inst.
Howard, Colin. Slowmotional Meditation. 540p. 1983. 45.00 (ISBN 0-686-84355-X). Olam.
Hyatt, Christopher S. Undoing Yourself with Energized Meditation & Other Devices. 114p. 1982. pap. 9.95 (ISBN 0-941404-06-4). Falcon Pr Az.
Lehodey, Dom V. The Ways of Mental Prayer. 408p. 1924. pap. 6.00 (ISBN 0-686-81633-1). TAN Bks Pubs.
McCormick, Thomas & Fish, Sharon. Meditation: A Practical Guide to a Spiritual Discipline. 132p. (Orig.). 1983. pap. 3.95 (ISBN 0-87784-844-0). Inter-Varsity.
Regardie, Israel & Hyatt, Christopher S. The Regardie Tapes. 1982. pap. 49.95 set of 6 (ISBN 0-941404-05-6); pap. 11.95 each. Falcon Pr Az.
Reynolds, David K. Naikin Psychotherapy: Meditation for Self-Development. LC 82-21862. 184p. 1983. 15.00x (ISBN 0-226-71029-7). U of Chicago Pr.
Rhoades, Gale R. Waybill to Lost Spanish Signs & Symbols. (Illus., Orig.). 1982. pap. 6.00 (ISBN 0-942688-02-3). Dream Garden.
Steinbrecher, Edwin. Inner Guide Meditation. 200p. 1983. pap. 9.95 (ISBN 0-85030-300-1). Newcastle Pub.
Steiner, Rudolf. Knowledge of the Higher Worlds & Its Attainment. Metaxa, George & Monges, Henry B., trs. from Ger. LC 79-101595. 224p. 1983. 14.00 (ISBN 0-88010-045-1); pap. 6.95 (ISBN 0-88010-046-X). Anthroposophic.
Szekely, Edmond B. Biogenic Meditation: Biogenic Self-Analysis, Creative Microcosmos. (Illus.). 40p. 1978. pap. 1.80 (ISBN 0-89564-051-1). IBS Intl.

MEDITATIONS
Here are entered works containing thoughts or reflections on spiritual truths. Works on the nature of meditation are entered under the heading Meditation.
see also Devotional Calendars; Devotional Literature; Jesus Christ–Devotional Literature; Spiritual Exercises; also subdivisions Meditations under Bible, Jesus Christ, Lord's Supper, and similar headings

Ackland, Donald F. Broadman Comments, October-December, 1983. 1983. pap. 2.35 (ISBN 0-8054-1480-0). Broadman.
Adams, George. The Lemniscatory Ruled Surface in Space & Counterspace. Eberhart, Stephen, tr. from Ger. & Eng. (Illus.). 83p. 1979. pap. 9.95 (ISBN 0-686-43395-5, Pub. by Steinerbooks). Anthroposophic.
Allen, Charles L. Joyful Living in the Fourth Dimension. 160p. 1983. 8.95 (ISBN 0-8007-1351-6). Revell.
Allen, James. Morning & Evening Thoughts. 80p. 3.50 (ISBN 0-686-38228-5). Sun Bks.
Allen, Milton H. Why Do Good People Suffer? 1983. pap. 4.95 (ISBN 0-8054-5208-7). Broadman.
Allen, Ronald B. When Song is New. 1983. 5.95 (ISBN 0-8407-5825-1). Nelson.
Armstrong, William H. Through Troubled Waters: A Young Father's Struggles with Grief. 96p. (Orig.). 1983. pap. 2.50 (ISBN 0-687-41895-X, Festival). Abingdon.
Arnold, Katrin. Anna Joins in. 28p. Date not set. text ed. 9.95 (ISBN 0-687-01530-8). Abingdon.
Atkinson, David. The Wings of Refuge: The Message of Ruth. (Bible Speaks Today Ser.). 128p. 1983. pap. 4.95 (ISBN 0-87784-820-3). Inter-Varsity.
Auer, Jim. Sorting it Out with God. 64p. 1982. pap. 1.95 (ISBN 0-89243-163-6). Liguori Pubns.
Baker, Don & Nester, Emery. Depression: Finding Hope & Meaning in Life's Darkest Shadow. (Critical Concern Ser.). 1983. write for info. (ISBN 0-88070-011-4). Multnomah.
Bakker, Jim & Bakker, Tammy. You Can Make It. 128p. (Orig.). Date not set. pap. 2.95 (ISBN 0-89221-098-2). New Leaf.
Barber, Cyril J. Ruth: An Expositional Commentary. 1983. pap. 6.95 (ISBN 0-8024-0184-8). Moody.
Barkman, Alma. Days Remembered. (Illus.). 96p. 1983. pap. price not set (ISBN 0-8024-0188-0). Moody.
Barrs, Jerram. Shepherds & Sheep. 96p. (Orig.). 1983. pap. 2.95 (ISBN 0-87784-395-3). Inter-Varsity.
Bednar, Zdenek F. Keep Your Chin Up. LC 82-73984. 144p. (Orig.). 1983. pap. write for info. (ISBN 0-89272-165-0). Down East.
Bell, Martin. Way of the Wolf. (Epiphany Ser.). 144p. 1983. pap. 2.95 (ISBN 0-345-30522-1). Ballantine.
Benet, Juan. A Meditation. Rabassa, Gregory, tr. from Span. 372p. 1983. pap. 8.95 (ISBN 0-89255-065-1). Persea Bks.
Biggs, Mouzon, Jr. Moments to Hold Close. 144p. 1983. 8.95 (ISBN 0-687-27147-9). Abingdon.
Bishop, Joseph P. The Eye of the Storm. 128p. (Orig.). 1983. pap. 3.95 (ISBN 0-87123-263-4). Bethany Hse.
Blackwood, Cheryl P. A Bright-Shining Place. (Epiphany Ser.). 240p. 1983. pap. 2.75 (ISBN 0-345-30698-8). Ballantine.
Boardman, Peter. Sacred Summits. (Illus.). 264p. 1983. 20.00 (ISBN 0-89886-045-8). Mountaineers.
Bonhoeffer, Dietrich. The Martyred Christian: 160 Readings. Brown, Joan W., ed. 256p. 1983. 14.95 (ISBN 0-02-513120-6). Macmillan.
Boulding, Maria. The Coming of God. 224p. 1982. pap. text ed. 9.00 (ISBN 0-8146-1278-4). Liturgical Pr.
Brandt, L. Meditations on a Loving God. 1983. 9.95 (ISBN 0-570-03858-8). Concordia.
Brandt, R. L. Charasmatics: Are We Missing Something? 1981. pap. 4.95 (ISBN 0-686-38055-X). Bridge Pub.
Buhler, Walther. Living with Your Body. Maloney, L., tr. from Ger. 117p. (Orig.). 1979. pap. 9.95 (ISBN 0-85440-345-0, Pub. by Steinerbooks). Anthroposophic.
Bunyan, John. Christiana's Journey. Rev. ed. Wright, Christopher, ed. 1982. pap. 4.95 (ISBN 0-88270-533-4). Bridge Pub.
Caldwell, Louis O. Cogradulations: A Graduation Remembrance. (Ultra Books). 64p. 1983. 4.95 (ISBN 0-8010-2485-4). Baker Bk.
Calhoun, Don. The Oceanic Quest: Toward a Religion Beyond Illusion. 1983. 10.95 (ISBN 0-533-05591-1). Vantage.
Cardwell, Julia C. The Moonshine Special. (Illus.). 1983. 5.75 (ISBN 0-8062-1908-4). Carlton.
Carretto, Carlo. Blessed Are You Who Believed. Wall, Barbara, tr. from Ital. LC 82-22504. (Illus.). 96p. (Orig.). 1983. 8.95 (ISBN 0-88344-040-7); pap. 4.95 (ISBN 0-88344-038-5). Orbis Bks.
Chadbourne, Mary. Reflection & Recollections. 24p. (Orig.). 1982. pap. 3.50 (ISBN 0-9607370-1-4). Morel Bks.
Clark, Olivene. Heirloom of Memories. 1983. 8.50 (ISBN 0-8062-2137-2). Carlton.
Coleman, Jean. Chapter Twenty-Nine. 1979. pap. 2.50 (ISBN 0-686-38054-1). Bridge Pub.
Coleman, William V. Prayer-Talk: Casual Conversations with God. LC 82-74085. 112p. (Orig.). 1983. pap. 3.95 (ISBN 0-87793-265-4). Ave Maria.
Cornwall, Judson. Give Me-Make Me. 1979. 1.25 (ISBN 0-88270-387-0). Bridge Pub.
Correu, Larry M., ed. The Best of These Days. LC 82-13415. 132p. 1983. 8.95 (ISBN 0-664-21391-X). Westminster.
Crossman, Eileen. Mountain Rain. 1982. pap. 5.95 (ISBN 0-85363-146-8). OMF Bks.
Custodio, Sidney & Dudley, Cliff. Love Hungry Priest. 144p. (Orig.). 1983. pap. 2.95 (ISBN 0-89221-099-0). New Leaf.
D'Angelo, Louise. Too Busy for God? Think Again! 120p. 1975. pap. 2.50 (ISBN 0-686-81631-5). TAN Bks Pubs.
Dao, Wong Ming. Stone Made Smooth. 1982. pap. 6.95 (ISBN 0-907821-00-6). OMF Bks.
Deal, William S. The Other Shepherd. 1982. 2.95 (ISBN 0-686-38053-3). Crusade Pubs.
Delaney, Sue. The Lord, the Lion & Mutn. pap. 0.95 (ISBN 0-89985-995-X). Christ Nations.
--Mutu Finds the Way to Heaven. pap. 0.95 (ISBN 0-89985-996-8). Christ Nations.
Dennett, E. The Step I Have Taken. Daniel, R. P., ed. 53p. pap. 2.75 (ISBN 0-88172-140-9). Believers Bkshelf.
Dertinger, Charles J. Reflections. 1983. write for info. (ISBN 0-8062-2043-0). Carlton.
Doering, Jeanne. The Power of Encouragement. 176p. (Orig.). 1983. pap. 4.95 (ISBN 0-686-82020-7). Moody.
Doyle, Brendan & Fox, Matt. Meditations with TM Julian of Norwich. LC 82-73955. (Meditations with TM). (Illus.). 128p. (Orig.). 1982. pap. 6.95 (ISBN 0-939680-11-4). Bear & Co.
Elmo, Francis, tr. from Span. I in Christ Arisen. LC 81-85745. Orig. Title: Yo en Cristo Resucitado. 100p. Date not set. pap. price not set (ISBN 0-9607590-0-X). F Elmo.
Evans, C. S. Preserving the Person: A Look at the Human Sciences. 178p. 1982. pap. 5.95 (ISBN 0-8010-3385-3). Baker Bk.
Failing, George E. Secure & Rejoicing. 0.95 (ISBN 0-937296-03-1, 223-A). Presence Inc.
Fair, Harold L. Class Devotions. 128p. (Orig.). 1983. pap. 4.95 (ISBN 0-687-08623-X). Abingdon.
Fator, Sue. The Adventures of Tomoteo. pap. 1.25 (ISBN 0-89985-992-5). Christ Nations.
Featherstone, Vaughn G. Purity of Heart. LC 82-72728. 103p. 1982. 5.95 (ISBN 0-87747-914-3). Deseret Bk.
Fenocketti, Mary. Coping with Pain. 80p. 1982. pap. 1.95 (ISBN 0-89243-166-0). Liguori Pubns.
Fischer, John. Dark Horse. 100p. 1983. price not set (ISBN 0-88070-016-5). Multnomah.
Fitzgerald, Ernest A. Diamonds Everywhere: Appreciating God's Gifts. 112p. (Orig.). 1983. pap. 5.95 (ISBN 0-687-10734-2). Abingdon.
Forch, Carolyn. Undetermined. Wright, C. D. & Gander, Forrest, eds. (Lost Roads Ser.: No. 24). 55p. (Orig.). 1982. pap. 5.95 (ISBN 0-686-83488-7). Lost Roads.
Foreman, Max L. Rx from the Pulpit. 1982. 20.00 (ISBN 0-8197-0490-3). Bloch.
Fox, Matt & Swimme, Brian. Manifesto for a Global Civilization. LC 82-71450. 64p. (Orig.). 1982. pap. 3.50 (ISBN 0-939680-05-X). Bear & Co.
Fox, Matthew. Meditations with TM Meister Eckhart. LC 82-71451. (Meditations with TM Ser.). (Illus.). 128p. (Orig.). 1982. pap. 6.95 (ISBN 0-939680-04-1). Bear & Co.
--Western Spirituality: Historical Roots, Ecumenical Routes. 440p. pap. 10.95 (ISBN 0-939680-01-7). Bear & Co.
Fox, Matthew, frwd. by. Whee! We, Wee All the Way Home: A Guide to a Sensual Prophetic Spirituality. 264p. pap. 8.95 (ISBN 0-686-42950-8). Bear & Co.
Fullman, Everett L. Living the Lord's Prayer. (Epiphany Ser.). 128p. 1983. pap. 2.50 (ISBN 0-345-30432-2). Ballantine.
Gardner, Hope & Gunnell, Sally. Teach Me in My Way. 5.95 (ISBN 0-686-84351-7). Olympus Pub Co.
Gibb, C. C. More Than Enough. 83p. pap. 3.95 (ISBN 0-88172-071-2). Believers Bkshelf.
Harakas, Emily. Daily Lenten Meditations for Orthodox Christians. 1983. pap. 2.95 (ISBN 0-937032-27-1). Light&Life Pub Co MN.
Harless, Dan. Discoveries. 1982. pap. 4.95 (ISBN 0-89225-207-3). Gospel Advocate.
Hayhurst, Emma L. I Will. 2nd ed. 1982. pap. 4.95 (ISBN 0-938736-09-4). Life Enrich.
Haynes-Klassen, Joanne. Learning to Live, Learning to Love: A Book About You, A Book About Everyone. (Illus.). 150p. 1983. pap. 7.95 (ISBN 0-915190-38-9). Jalmar Pr.
Hennessee, Leona. Liberty or Bondage? 1982. pap. 4.95 (ISBN 0-88270-531-8). Bridge Pub.
Hifler, Joyce S. Put your Mind at Ease. 128p. (Orig.). 1983. pap. 5.95 (ISBN 0-687-34929-X). Abingdon.
Howard, J. Grant. Balancing Life's Demands: A New Perpective on Priorities. 1983. pap. write for info. (ISBN 0-88070-012-2). Multnomah.
Hughes, John J. Proclaiming the Good News: Homilies for a Cycle. 156p. 1983. pap. 14.95 (ISBN 0-87973-722-0, 722). Our Sunday Visitor.
Irwin, James B. More Than Earthlings. 1983. 5.95 (ISBN 0-8054-5255-9). Broadman.
Jenkins, Jerry. Janell. (Margo Mystery Ser.). 128p. 1983. pap. 2.95 (ISBN 0-8024-4322-2). Moody.
Jones, Alex. Seven Mansions of Color. LC 82-73248. 160p. 1983. pap. 7.50 (ISBN 0-87516-500-1). De Vorss.
Keller, W. Phillip. Wonder O' the Wind. 1982. 9.95 (ISBN 0-8499-0337-8). Word Pub.
Kennedy, D. J. Pourquoi Je Crois. Cosson, Annie, ed. Schneider, Michele, tr. from Eng. Orig. Title: Why I Believe. 173p. (Fr.). 1982. pap. 2.00 (ISBN 0-8297-1238-0). Life Pubs Intl.
Kuhn, Isobel. Second-Mile People. 1982. pap. 3.50 (ISBN 0-85363-145-X). OMF Bks.
Laney, J. Carl. Marching Orders. 168p. 1983. pap. 4.95 (ISBN 0-88207-398-2). Victor Bks.
Lawrence, Emeric. Jesus Present & Coming: Daily Meditations on the Advent & Christmas Masses. LC 82-20380. 128p. 1982. pap. 7.95 (ISBN 0-8146-1284-9). Liturgical Pr.
L'Engle, Madeleine. The Love Letters. (Epiphany Ser.). 384p. 1983. pap. 2.95 (ISBN 0-345-30617-1). Ballantine.
Lewis, C. S. The Grand Miracle. (Epiphany Ser.). 176p. 1983. pap. 2.95 (ISBN 0-345-30539-6). Ballantine.
A Light to the Nations. 201p. 1983. pap. 3.95 (ISBN 0-88479-036-3). Arena Lettres.
Lindsay, Gordon. One Body, One Spirit, One Lord. pap. 3.95 (ISBN 0-89985-991-7). Christ Nations.
Livingston, Elizabeth J. The Hideout. 100p. (Orig.). 1983. pap. 2.95 (ISBN 0-8024-3532-7). Moody.
Lowery, Daniel. Following Christ: A Handbook of Catholic Moral Teaching. 160p. 1983. pap. 3.50 (ISBN 0-89243-173-3). Liguori Pubns.
Lowery, Fred. Whistling in the Dark. McDonnell, John, as told to. 416p. 1983. 15.95 (ISBN 0-88289-298-3). Pelican.
Lund, Candida. Coming of Age. 1982. 12.95 (ISBN 0-88347-146-9). Thomas More.
MacArthur, John, Jr. The Ultimate Priority. 1983. pap. 4.95 (ISBN 0-8024-0186-4). Moody.
McConnell, William T. The Gift of Time. 132p. (Orig.). 1983. pap. 3.95 (ISBN 0-87784-838-6). Inter-Varsity.
McCumber, W. E. The Good News. 184p. 1982. pap. 4.95 (ISBN 0-8341-0699-X). Beacon Hill.
McNamara, William. Earthy Mysticism: Contemplation & the Life of Passionate Presence. 128p. 1983. pap. 5.95 (ISBN 0-8245-0562-X). Crossroad NY.
Marshall, Catherine & Le Sourd, Leonard. My Personal Prayer Diary. (Epiphany Bks.). 1983. pap. 3.95 (ISBN 0-345-30612-0). Ballantine.
Martin, Alfred & Martin, John A. Isaiah: The Glory of the Messiah. (Orig.). 1983. pap. 7.95 (ISBN 0-8024-0168-6). Moody.
Martin, Dorothy. The Story of Billy Carrell. 160p. (Orig.). 1983. pap. 3.95 (ISBN 0-8024-0519-3). Moody.
Martin, Jeff. Thou Shalt Meditate. 40p. 1980. pap. 1.50 (ISBN 0-686-83199-3). Harrison Hse.
Molnar, Paul J. Quotes & Notes to Share. Goebel, Patrice, ed. (Orig.). 1982. pap. 4.95 (ISBN 0-938736-06-X). Life Enrich.
Moore, Barry & Hefley, Marti. In Spite of Myself. 1982. 9.95 (ISBN 0-8423-1584-5); pap. 5.95 (ISBN 0-8423-1581-0). Tyndale.
Morton, Craig & Burger, Robert. The Courage to Believe. (Epiphany Bks.). (Illus.). 1983. pap. 2.75 (ISBN 0-345-30564-7). Ballantine.
Murray, Andrew. God's Will: Our Dwelling Place. Orig. Title: Thy Will Be Done. 144p. 1983. pap. text ed. 2.95 (ISBN 0-88368-119-6). Whitaker Hse.
Nee, T. S. El Mensajero de la Cruz. Carrodeguas, Andy & Marosi, Esteban, eds. Silva, Jose D., tr. from Eng. Orig. Title: The Messenger of the Cross. 168p. (Span.). 1982. pap. 2.00 (ISBN 0-8297-1230-5). Life Pubs Intl.
Nordvedt, Matilda & Steinkueler, Pearl. Ideas for Junior High Leaders. (Orig.). 1983. pap. 4.95 (ISBN 0-8024-0187-2). Moody.
Nouwen, Henri J. The Way of the Heart. (Epiphany Bks.). 1983. pap. 2.50 (ISBN 0-345-30530-2). Ballantine.
O'Donnell, Edward. Priestly People. 64p. 1982. pap. 1.50 (ISBN 0-89243-168-7). Liguori Pubns.
O'Driscoll, Herbert. Crossroads: Times of Decision for People of God. 96p. 1983. pap. 5.95 (ISBN 0-8164-2432-2). Seabury.
Oke, Janette. When Calls the Heart. 240p. (Orig.). 1983. pap. 4.95 (ISBN 0-87123-611-7). Bethany Hse.
Owen, John. Sin & Temptation: Insight into the Workings & Motives of the Human Heart. Houston, James M., ed. (Classics of Faith & Devotion). 1983. 9.95 (ISBN 0-88070-013-0). Multnomah.
Parks, Helen J. Holding the Ropes. 156p. 1983. 5.95 (ISBN 0-8054-5194-3). Broadman.
Partridge, Bonnie & Stock, Susan. Someone Cares. 1.50 (ISBN 0-686-84354-1). Olympus Pub Co.
Perry, Lloyd & Sell, Charles. Speaking to Life's Problems. 1983. pap. price not set (ISBN 0-8024-0170-8). Moody.
Pollard, Frank. Keeping Face. 1983. 3.25 (ISBN 0-8054-5216-8). Broadman.
Ponder, Catherine. Dare to Prosper. 80p. 1983. pap. 3.00 (ISBN 0-87516-511-7). De Vorss.
--Open your Mind to Receive. 128p. 1983. pap. 3.95 (ISBN 0-87516-507-9). De Vorss.
Pope, Dorothy. He Wanted to Die. 1972. pap. 1.50 (ISBN 0-85363-086-0). OMF Bks.
Popejoy, Bill & Arcangeli, Gianfranco. Beni E Benignita. (Italian.). 1980. pap. 1.75 (ISBN 0-8297-0664-X). Life Pubs Intl.
Popoff, Peter. Set Free from Satan's Slavery. Tanner, Don, ed. LC 82-83455. 64p. 1982. pap. 2.00 (ISBN 0-938544-17-9). Faith Messenger.
Porch, James M. Daybreak: Faith for Ordinary Days. 1983. 3.25 (ISBN 0-8054-5206-0). Broadman.
Quoist, Michel. With Open Heart. 264p. (Orig.). 1983. pap. 8.95 (ISBN 0-8245-0569-7). Crossroad NY.
Rao, Shanto R. The Children's Mahabharata. (Illus.). 350p. 1980. pap. text ed. 7.50x (ISBN 0-86131-266-X, Pub by Orient Longman Ltd India). Apt Bks.
Redemptorist Pastoral Publication. Jesus Loves You. 80p. (gr. 1-3). 1983. 4.95 (ISBN 0-89243-175-X). Liguori Pubns.
Reeve, Pamela. La Fe Es. Orig. Title: Faith Is. 50p. (Span.). 1983. spiral bd 4.95 (ISBN 0-930014-96-0). Multnomah.
Reichel, Jocelyn. I Seen a Million Sparrows. (Illus.). 144p. 1983. pap. 5.95 (ISBN 0-8024-0185-6). Moody.
Rifkin, Jeremy & Howard, Ted. The Emerging Order: God in the Age of Scarcity. (Epiphany Bks.). 1983. pap. 2.95 (ISBN 0-345-30464-0). Ballantine.
Rodriguez, Cookie. Larmes de Delivrance. Cosson, Annie, ed. Luc-Barbier, Jean, tr. from Eng. Orig. Title: Please Make Me Cry. 234p. (Fr.). 1982. pap. 2.50 (ISBN 0-8297-1109-0). Life Pubs Intl.
Ross, Skip & Carlson, Carole. Say Yes to Your Potential. 1983. 8.95 (ISBN 0-8499-0309-2). Word Pub.
Rynberg, Elbert. God's New Job: An Exploration of the Roads of Love. limited ed. 160p. 1983. 8.50 (ISBN 0-682-49970-6). Exposition.
St. Cyr, Albert N. And Cross the Rivers of My Mind. 1983. 6.95 (ISBN 0-533-05603-9). Vantage.

Sander, J. Oswald. Satan Is No Myth. 141p. 1983. pap. 5.95 (ISBN 0-686-84263-4). Moody.
Sanderson, Joyce. Why Are You Here Now? 83p. (Orig.). 1981. pap. 6.95 (ISBN 0-942494-10-5). Coleman Graphics.
Sandford, John & Sandford, Paula. Transformation of the Inner Man. 1982. pap. 5.95 (ISBN 0-88270-539-3). Bridge Pub.
Sanford, Agnes. The Healing Touch of God. (Epiphany Ser.). 224p. 1983. pap. 2.50 (ISBN 0-345-30661-9). Ballantine.
Schroeder, David. Solid Ground: Facts on the Faith for Young Christians. Bubna, Paul, frwd. by. 255p. 1982. pap. 5.95 (ISBN 0-87509-323-X); Leader's guide 3.50 (ISBN 0-87509-326-4). Chr Pubns.
Schuller, Robert H. Living Powerfully One Day at a Time. 400p. 1983. pap. 6.95 (ISBN 0-8007-5113-2, Power Bks). Revell.
Shankaranarayanan, S. Glory of the Divine Mother: Devi Mahatmyam. 330p. (Eng. & Sanskrit.). 1983. 12.95 (ISBN 0-941524-08-6). Lotus Light.
Simpson, A. B. Wholly Sanctified: Legacy Edition. Rev. ed. King, L. L., intro. by. 136p. 1982. pap. 5.95 (ISBN 0-87509-306-X). Chr Pubns.
Skains, Margo F. Change Your Mind. (Orig.). (YA) 1983. pap. write for info. (ISBN 0-911197-01-X). Miracle Pub Co.
Smith, Katherine V. Chickens, Cookies, & Cozzin George. 144p. (Orig.). 1983. pap. text ed. 6.95 (ISBN 0-687-06485-6). Abingdon.
Snyder, Bernadette. Graham Crackers, Galoshes & God. 96p. 1982. pap. 2.95 (ISBN 0-89243-164-4). Liguori Pubns.
Spangler, David, ed. Cooperation with Spirit: Further Conversations with John. 32p. 1982. pap. 3.00 (ISBN 0-936878-07-X). Lorian Pr.
Spindle, Richard. They Never Stopped Teaching. 96p. 1982. pap. 2.50 (ISBN 0-8341-0735-X). Beacon Hill.
Sproul, R. C. In Search of Dignity. LC 82-18576. (In Search Of Ser.). 1983. 10.95 (ISBN 0-8307-0869-3, 5110407). Regal.
Steer, John L. & Dudley, Cliff. Vietnam, Curse or Blessing. (Illus.). 192p. (Orig.). 1982. pap. 2.95 (ISBN 0-89221-091-5). New Leaf.
Stein, Shifra. I Love You. 1982. 5.50 (ISBN 0-8378-1711-0). Gibson.
Swindoll, Charles R. Standing Out: Being Real in a Phony World. Orig. Title: Home: Where Life Makes Up Its Mind. 105p. 1983. pap. write for info. (ISBN 0-88070-014-9). Multnomah.
Szekely, Edmond B. Father, Give Us Another Chance. (Illus.). 62p. 1969. pap. 6.80 (ISBN 0-89564-071-6). IBS Intl.
--Man in the Cosmic Ocean. (Illus.). 56p. 1970. pap. 3.50 (ISBN 0-89564-054-6). IBS Intl.
--Toward the Conquest of the Inner Cosmos. (Illus.). 64p. 1969. pap. 6.80 (ISBN 0-89564-053-8). IBS Intl.
Teegarden, Keneth L. We Call Ourselves Disciples. 2nd ed. 116p. 1983. pap. 5.95 (ISBN 0-8272-4215-8). Bethany Pr.
Thompson, Phyllis. Each to Her Post. 1982. pap. 3.95 (ISBN 0-340-26933-2). OMF Bks.
Timmerman, John J. Markings on a Long Journey: Selections from the writing of John J. Timmerman. Mulder, Rodney J. & Timmerman, John J., eds. 320p. (Orig.). 1982. pap. 9.95 (ISBN 0-8010-8867-4). Baker Bk.
Timmons, Tim. Loneliness Is Not a Disease. (Epiphany Bks.). 1983. pap. 2.25 (ISBN 0-345-30509-4). Ballantine.
Tozer, A. W. That Incredible Christian. 135p. 1964. 4.95 (ISBN 0-87509-196-2); pap. 3.25 (ISBN 0-87509-197-0); 2.50 (ISBN 0-87509-250-0). Chr Pubns.
Tsai, Christiana. Jewels from the Queen of the Dark Chamber. LC 82-12544. 128p. 1982. pap. 3.95 (ISBN 0-8024-4336-2). Moody.
Uhlein, Gabriele. Meditations with TM Hildegrade of Bingen. LC 82-73363. (Meditations with TM). 128p. (Orig.). 1982. pap. 6.95 (ISBN 0-939680-12-2). Bear & Co.
Vander Shrier, Nettie. The Golden Thread. 169p. 1983. pap. 2.95 (ISBN 0-8024-0173-2). Moody.
VON Keitzell, F. By Many Infallible Proofs. 76p. pap. 3.95 (ISBN 0-88172-137-9). Believers Bkshelf.
Vuilleumier, Marion R. Meditations in the Mountains. 128p. (Orig.). 1983. pap. 6.95 (ISBN 0-687-24260-6). Abingdon.
Walsh, Vincent M. The Kingdom at Hand. 340p. pap. 6.00 (ISBN 0-943374-00-6). Key of David.
Weir, William & Abata, Russell M. Dealing with Depression. 144p. 1982. pap. 3.50 (ISBN 0-89243-170-9). Liguori Pubns.
Whitaker, Robert C. Hang in There. 1974. 1.25 (ISBN 0-88270-106-1). Bridge Pub.
White, Etson. Revelation of God. 1983. 8.95 (ISBN 0-533-05567-9). Vantage.
Wilson, Bob. The Good that Lives After Them. Kings, John, ed. (Illus.). 170p. 1982. 14.50 (ISBN 0-9608192-0-7). B Wilson.
Woodruff, Sue. Meditations with TM Mechtild of Magdeburg. LC 82-73366. (Meditations with TM Ser.). (Illus.). 128p. (Orig.). 1982. pap. 6.95 (ISBN 0-939680-06-8). Bear & Co.
Woods, Richard. Symbion. LC 82-73365. 264p. (Orig.). 1982. pap. 8.95 (ISBN 0-939680-08-4). Bear & Co.

MEDITERRANEAN DISEASE
see Thalassemia
MEDITERRANEAN REGION
Pinkele, Carl F. & Pollis, Adamantis. The Contemporary Mediterranean World. 394p. 1983. 32.95 (ISBN 0-03-060091-X). Praeger.
Rosenthal, Glenda G. The Mediterranean Basin. new ed. 224p. 1982. text ed. 39.95 (ISBN 0-408-10711-1). Butterworth.
MEDITERRANEAN REGION-ANTIQUITIES
Buchthal, Hugo. Art of the Mediterranean World: 100-1400 A. D. Folda, Jaroslav, et al, eds. (Art History Ser.: No. V.). (Illus.). 207p. 1983. 75.00 (ISBN 0-916276-11-2). Decatur Hse.
Foster, K. Minoan Ceramic Relief. (Studies in Mediterranean Archaeology: No. LXIV). 196p. 1982. pap. text ed. 69.00x (ISBN 91-86098-08-X, Pub. by Astroms Sweden). Humanities.
MEDITERRANEAN REGION-DESCRIPTION AND TRAVEL
Schillebeeckx, Edward. Paul the Apostle. (Illus.). 128p. 1983. 14.95 (ISBN 0-8245-0574-3). Crossroad NY.
MEDITERRANEAN REGION-HISTORY
Borowiec, Andrew. The Mediterranean Feud. 206p. 1983. 28.95 (ISBN 0-03-061847-9). Praeger.
MEDIUMS
see Spiritualism
MEETINGS
see also Forums (Discussion and Debate); Leadership; Parliamentary Practice
Carnes, William T. Effective Meetings for Busy People: Let's Decide It & Go Home. 368p. 1983. pap. 9.95 (ISBN 0-07-010118-3, P&RB). McGraw.
Murray, Sheila L. How to Organize & Manage a Seminar: What to Do & When to Do It. 204p. 1983. 13.95 (ISBN 0-13-425199-7); pap. 6.95 (ISBN 0-13-425181-4). P-H.
Newman, Pamela & Lynch, Alfred F. Behind Closed Doors: A Guide to Successful Meetings. (Illus.). 192p. 1983. pap. 9.95 (ISBN 0-13-072025-9). P-H.
Ward, John R. Meetings by Telephone. (Illus.). 57p. 1980. pap. 3.75x (ISBN 0-910195-00-5). Genesis Pubns.
MEETINGS, CORPORATE
see Corporate Meetings
MEGACOLON
Holschneider, Alexander M. Hirschsprung's Disease. (Illus.). 124p. 1982. 59.00 (ISBN 0-86577-050-6). Thieme-Stratton.
MEGAVITAMIN THERAPY
see Orthomolecular Medicine
MEIOSIS
John, Bernard & Lewis, Kenneth. The Meiotic Mechanism. Head, J. J., ed. LC 76-29381. (Carolina Biology Readers Ser.). (Illus.). 32p. 1983. pap. text ed. 2.00 (ISBN 0-89278-265-X, 45-9665). Carolina Biological.
MEIR, GOLDA (MABOVITZ), 1898-
Keller, Mollie. Golda Meir. (Impact Biography Ser.). (Illus.). 128p. (gr. 7 up). 1983. PLB 8.90 (ISBN 0-531-04591-9). Watts.
MEISSEN PORCELAIN
Miller, J. Jefferson. Eighteenth-Century Meissen Porcelain from the Margaret M. & Arthur J. Mourot Collection in the Virgina Museum. 1983. pap. write for info. (ISBN 0-917046-13-7). Va Mus Fine Arts.
MELANOMA
Mackie, Rona M., ed. Malignant Melanoma. (Pigment Cell Ser.: Vol. 6). (Illus.). vi, 220p. 1983. 88.25 (ISBN 3-8055-3690-9). S Karger.
Ortonne, Jean-Paul & Mosher, David B. Vitiligo & Other Hypomelanoses of Hair & Skin. (Topics in Dermatology Ser.). 680p. 1983. 79.50x (ISBN 0-306-40974-7, Plenum Med Bk). Plenum Pub.
MELVILLE, HERMAN, 1819-1891
Duban, James. Melville's Major Fiction: Politics, Theology, & Imagination. (Illus.). 250p. 1982. 22.00 (ISBN 0-87580-086-6). N Ill U Pr.
Melville, Herman. Redburn, White-Jacket, Moby-Dick. Tanselle, Thomas G., ed. LC 82-18677. 1500p. 1983. 27.50 (ISBN 0-940450-09-7). Literary Classics.
Moore, Richard. That Cunning Alphabet: Melville's Aesthetics of Nature. (Costerus New Ser.: No. 35). 232p. 1982. pap. text ed. 18.50x (ISBN 90-6203-734-8, Pub. by Rodopi Holland). Humanities.
Rogin, Michael P. Subversive Genealogy: Politics & Art in Herman Melville. LC 82-48743. 363p. 1983. 20.00 (ISBN 0-394-50609-X). Knopf.
Stern, Milton R. Critical Essays on Herman Melville's "Typee". (Critical Essays on American Literature Ser.). 1982. lib. bdg. 32.00 (ISBN 0-8161-8445-3). G K Hall.
MEMBERSHIP CORPORATIONS
see Corporations, Nonprofit
MEMBRANES (BIOLOGY)
see also Plasma Membranes
Aloia, Roland C., ed. Membrane Fluidity in Biology: Vol. 1: Concepts of Membrane Structure. 1982. 43.00 (ISBN 0-12-053001-5). Acad Pr.
Beck, J. S. Biomembranes: Fundamentals in Relation to Human Biology. 1979. 24.95 (ISBN 0-07-004263-2). McGraw.
Brock, Thomas D. Membrane Filtration: A User's Guide & Reference Manual. (Illus.). 1983. 29.95 (ISBN 0-910239-00-2). Sci Tech Inc.
Critser, James R., Jr. Membrane Separation Processes. (Ser.5-82). 1983. 135.00 (ISBN 0-88178-002-2). Lexington Data.
Eisenberg, Adi & Yeager, Howard L., eds. Perfluorinated Ionomer Membranes. (ACS Symposium Ser.: No. 180). 1982. write for info. (ISBN 0-8412-0698-8). Am Chemical.
Hoffman, Joseph F & Giebisch, Gerhard H., eds. Membranes in Growth & Development. LC 82-7178. (Progress in Clinical & Biological Research Ser.: Vol. 91). 644p. 1982. 94.00 (ISBN 0-8451-0091-2). A R Liss.
Nowotny, Alois, ed. Pathological Membranes. (Biomembranes Ser.: Vol. 11). 494p. 1983. 55.00x (ISBN 0-306-41065-6, Plenum Pr). Plenum Pub.
Sato, Ryo & Kagawa, Yasuo, eds. Transport & Bioenergetics in Bimembranes. 261p. 1983. 45.00x (ISBN 0-306-41282-9, Plenum Pr). Plenum Pub.
Sato, Ryo & Shun-Ichi Ohnishi, eds. Structure, Dynamics & Biogenesis of Biomembranes. 187p. 1983. 39.50x (ISBN 0-306-41283-7, Plenum Pr). Plenum Pub.
Sheppard, John R. & Anderson, V. Elving, eds. Membranes & Genetic Disease. LC 82-12672. (Progress in Clinical & Biological Research Ser.: Vol. 97). 422p. 1982. 68.00 (ISBN 0-8451-0097-1). A R Liss.
MEMBRANES (TECHNOLOGY)
Bronner, Felix & Kleinzeller, Arnost, eds. Current Topics in Membranes & Transport, Vol. 18. (Serial Publication). Date not set. price not set (ISBN 0-12-153318-2). Acad Pr.
MEMOIRS
see Autobiography; Biography;
also subdivision Correspondence, Reminiscences, etc. under classes of people, e.g. Actors-Correspondence, reminiscenses, etc.; subdivision History-Sources under names of countries; subdivision Personal Narratives under names of wars, diseases, etc. e.g. World War, 1939-1945-Personal Narratives
Sassoon, Siegfried. Memoirs of a Fox-Hunting Man. 320p. 1960. pap. 6.95 (ISBN 0-571-06454-X). Faber & Faber.
MEMORIAL TABLETS
see Sepulchral Monuments
MEMORY
Chi, M. T., ed. Trends in Memory Development. (Contributions to Human Development: Vol. 9). (Illus.). xiv, 160p. 1983. pap. 76.75 (ISBN 3-8055-3661-5). S Karger.
Ellis, Henry C. & Hunt, R. Reed. Fundamentals of Human Memory & Cognition. 3rd ed. 350p. 1983. pap. text ed. write for info. (ISBN 0-697-06554-5); instr's. manual avail. (ISBN 0-697-06555-3). Wm C Brown.
Estes. Models of Learning, Memory & Choice. 410p. 1982. 29.95 (ISBN 0-03-059266-6). Praeger.
Herold, Mort. You Can Have a Near-Perfect Memory. (Illus.). 272p. 1983. pap. 7.95 (ISBN 0-8092-5942-7). Contemp Bks.
Howe, Michael J. Introduction to the Psychology of Memory. 160p. 1983. pap. text ed. 9.50 scp (ISBN 0-06-042925-9, HarpC). Har-Row.
Linderman, Charles R. See it Now. LC 82-73246. 210p. 1982. pap. 12.50 (ISBN 0-941216-02-0). Cay-Bel.
Loftus, Geoffrey R. & Loftus, Elizabeth F. Human Memory: The/Processing of Information. 192p. 1976. pap. text ed. 6.95 (ISBN 0-89859-135-X). L Erlbaum Assocs.
Misenheimer, Luther, III. Basic Skills Memory Development Workbook. (Basic Skills Workbooks). 32p. (gr. 5-9). 1983. 0.99 (ISBN 0-8209-0582-8, MDW-1). ESP.
--Memory Development. (Language Arts Ser.). wkbk. 5.00 (ISBN 0-8209-0325-6, LA-11). ESP.
Tsukada, Y. & Agranoff, B. W. Neurobiological Basis of Learning & Memory. 260p. 1980. text ed. 39.95 (ISBN 0-471-05148-9, Pub. by Wiley Med). Wiley.
Tulving, Endel. Elements of Episodic Memory. (Oxford Psychology Ser.). 400p. 1982. 29.95 (ISBN 0-19-852102-2). Oxford U Pr.
Underwood, Benton J. Attributes of Memory. 1983. 21.95x (ISBN 0-673-15798-9). Scott F.
Woody, Charles D. Memory, Learning, & Higher Function: A Cellular View. (Illus.). 512p. 1982. 65.00 (ISBN 0-387-90525-1). Springer-Verlag.
MEMPHIS, TENNESSEE
Crawford, Charles W., ed. Memphis Memories: Thirty-Two Historic Postcards. (Illus.). 16p. 1983. pap. 3.95 (ISBN 0-87049-382-5). U of Tenn Pr.
MEN
see also Masculinity (Psychology)
Beer. Househusbands. LC 82-12079. 176p. 1983. 23.95 (ISBN 0-03-059978-4). Praeger.
Doyle, James A. The Male Experience. 320p. 1983. pap. text ed. write for info. (ISBN 0-697-06553-7). Wm C Brown.
Gothard, Bill. Men's Manual, Vol. 8. LC 79-88994. (Illus.). 270p. 1983. 20.00 (ISBN 0-916888-09-6). Inst Basic Youth.
Solomon, Kenneth & Levy, Norman B., eds. Men in Transition: Theory & Therapy. 500p. 1982. 39.50x (ISBN 0-306-40976-3, Plenum Pr). Plenum Pub.
Yale University Division of Student Mental Hygiene Staff. Psychosocial Problems of College Men. Wedge, Bryant M., ed. 1958. text ed. 13.50x (ISBN 0-686-83715-0). Elliots Bks.
MEN-PHOTOGRAPHY
see Photography of Men
MEN-PRAYER-BOOKS AND DEVOTIONS
Conway, Jim. Los Hombres En Su Crisis De Media Vida. Orig. Title: Men in Mid-Life Crisis. 256p. 1982. pap. 4.95 (ISBN 0-311-46088-7). Casa Bautista.
MENDELSSOHN-BARTHOLDY, FELIX, 1809-1847
Devrient, Edward. My Recollections of Felix Mendelssohn-Bartholdy & His Letters to Me. Macfarren, Natalia, tr. LC 72-163799. 307p. Date not set. Repr. of 1869 ed. price not set. Vienna Hse.
Hiller, Ferdinand. Mendelsshon: Letters & Recollections. Von Glehn, M. E., tr. LC 70-163790. 234p. Date not set. Repr. of 1874 ed. price not set. Vienna Hse.
MENDING
see Sewing
MENNONITE COOKERY
see Cookery, American
MENNONITES
see also Amish
Hostetler, John A. Mennonite Life. 2nd ed. LC 82-83963. (Illus.). 48p. 1983. pap. 4.95 (ISBN 0-8361-1995-9). Herald Pr.
Jacobs, Donald R. Pilgrimage in Mission. 168p. (Orig.). 1983. pap. 6.50 (ISBN 0-8361-3324-2). Herald Pr.
Miller, Levi. Our People: The Amish & Mennonites of Ohio. (Illus.). 56p. (Orig.). 1982. pap. 2.50 (ISBN 0-8361-3331-5). Herald Pr.
Rindzinsky, Milka, tr. from English. Confesion de fe las Iglesias Menonitas. 32p. (Orig.). 1983. pap. 0.60x (ISBN 0-8361-1258-X). Herald Pr.
Toews, John B. Czars, Soviets & Mennonites. LC 81-71490. 221p. 1982. pap. 10.95 (ISBN 0-87303-064-8). Faith & Life.
MENNONITES-CATECHISM AND CREEDS
Gallardo, Jose. The Way of Biblical Justice. LC 82-83386. (Mennonite Faith Ser.: Vol. 11). 80p. (Orig.). 1983. pap. 0.95 (ISBN 0-8361-3321-8). Herald Pr.
MENNONITES-HISTORY
Kroeker, N. J. First Mennonite Villages in Russia 1789-1943: Khortistsa-Rosental. LC 82-167271. (Illus.). 279p. 1981. 20.00 (ISBN 0-88925-294-7). N J Kroeker.
MENNONITES IN RUSSIA
Kroeker, N. J. First Mennonite Villages in Russia 1789-1943: Khortistsa-Rosental. LC 82-167271. (Illus.). 279p. 1981. 20.00 (ISBN 0-88925-294-7). N J Kroeker.
MEN'S CLOTHING
see also individual articles of apparel
Dolce, Donald & Devellard, Jean-Paul. The Consumer's Guide to Menswear. pap. 11.95 (ISBN 0-89696-188-5). Dodd.
MENSTRUAL CYCLE
see Menstruation
MENSTRUATION
Golub, Sharon, ed. Menarche: The Physiological, Psychological, & Social Effects of the Onset of Menstruation. LC 82-48105. 352p. 1983. 29.95x (ISBN 0-669-05982-X). Lexington Bks.
Kingston, Beryl. You Can Relieve Menstrual Problems. 126p. 1982. 10.95 (ISBN 0-13-976795-9); pap. 4.95 (ISBN 0-13-976787-8). P-H.
Witt, Reni L. PMS: What Every Woman Should Know About Premenstrual Syndrome. LC 82-42724. 200p. 1983. 14.95 (ISBN 0-8128-2903-4). Stein & Day.
MENSURATION
see also Area Measurement; Gaging; Geodesy; Physical Measurements; Surveying; Tolerance (Engineering)
also subdivision Measurement under special subjects, e.g. Altitudes-Measurement
Birke, Lynda & Gardner, Katy. Why Suffer? Periods & their Problems. 76p. 1983. pap. 3.95 (ISBN 0-86068-284-6, Virago Pr). Merrimack Bk Serv.
MENTAL CHRONOMETRY
see Time Perception
MENTAL CULTURE
see Mental Discipline
MENTAL DEFICIENCY
see also Inefficiency, Intellectual; Mentally Handicapped
Bioler, I. & Sternlicht, M. The Psychology of Mental Retardation. LC 77-4137. 800p. 1977. 39.95 (ISBN 0-88437-013-5). Psych Dimensions.
Menolascino, Frank J., et al. Curative Aspects of Mental Retardation: Biomedical & Behavioral Advances. LC 82-17787. 356p. 1983. text ed. 25.95 (ISBN 0-933716-29-X). P H Brookes.
MENTAL DEPRESSION
see Depression, Mental
MENTAL DISCIPLINE
see also Education; Memory; Self-Culture
Gibson, Janice T. Discipline Is Not a Dirty Word. 176p. 1983. 12.95 (ISBN 0-86616-027-2); pap. 7.95 (ISBN 0-86616-023-X). Lewis Pub Co.
Hubbard, L. Ron. Self Analysis. Date not set. 8.95 (ISBN 0-88404-109-3). Bridge Pub.
MENTAL DISEASES
see Mental Illness; Psychology, Pathological
MENTAL HEALING
see also Faith-Cure; Medicine, Magic, Mystic, and Spagiric; Mental Suggestion; Mind and Body; Psychotherapy; Subconsciousness

Dhiravamsa. The Dynamic Way of Meditation: The Release & Cure of Pain & Suffering Through Vipassana Meditative Techniques. 160p. (Orig.). 1983. pap. 7.95 (ISBN 0-85500-163-1, Pub. by Thorsons Pubs England). Sterling.
Drury, Nevill. The Healing Power: A Handbook of Alternative Medicine & Natural Health in Australia & New Zealand. (Illus.). 235p. 1982. pap. 12.95 (ISBN 0-938190-10-5). North Atlantic.
Fine, Reuben. The Healing of the Mind. 416p. 1982. text ed. 39.95. Free Pr.
Hicks, Roy. Healing Your Insecurities. (Orig.). 1982. pap. 2.25 (ISBN 0-89274-249-6). Harrison Hse.
Jaffe, Dennis T. Healing from Within. 288p. 1982. pap. 3.50 (ISBN 0-553-22537-5). Bantam.
King, Serge. Kahuna Healing. LC 82-42704. 212p. (Orig.). 1983. pap. 6.75 (ISBN 0-8356-0572-8, Quest). Theos Pub Hse.
Ray, Barbara W. The Reiki Factor: A Guide to Physical & Spiritual Healing. 144p. 1983. 8.00 (ISBN 0-682-49935-8). Exposition.
Spiegelman. The Knight: The Theory & Method of Jung's Active Imagination Techique. (Illus.). 1982. pap. 6.95 (ISBN 0-941404-23-4). Falcon Pr Az.
Spiegelman, J. Marvin. The Tree. 2nd ed. 464p. 1982. pap. 12.95 (ISBN 0-941404-04-8). Falcon Pr Az.

MENTAL HEALTH
see also Community Mental Health Services; Emotions; Happiness; Mental Health Personnel; Mental Health Services; Mental Illness; Personality; Psychiatry; Psychology; Psychology, Pathological; Relaxation; Self-Actualization (Psychology); Stress (Psychology); Success
Baer, Louis S. Better Health with Fewer Pills. LC 82-8394. 132p. 1982. pap. 5.95 (ISBN 0-664-24425-4). Westminster.
Callan, John P. Your Guide to Mental Help. (People's Health Library). 200p. 1982. 12.50 (ISBN 0-89313-059-1). G F Stickley.
Freedman, Daniel X., ed. Year Book of Psychiatry & Applied Mental Health 1983. 1983. 45.00 (ISBN 0-686-83776-2). Year Bk Med.
Greenspan, M. A New Approach to Women & Therapy. 384p. 1983. 19.95 (ISBN 0-07-024349-2, GB). McGraw.
Guidano, V. F. & Liotti, G. Cognitive Processes of Emotional Disorders. LC 83-13188. (Psychology & Psychotherapy Ser.). 347p. 1983. text ed. 24.50x (ISBN 0-89862-006-6). Guilford Pr.
Hafen, Brent Q. & Brog, Molly J. Emotional Survival. 114p. 1983. 11.95 (ISBN 0-13-274480-5); pap. 5.95 (ISBN 0-13-274472-4). P-H.
Petrie, Sidney & Stone, Robert B. Helping Yourself with Autogenics. LC 82-14488. 205p. 1983. 14.95 (ISBN 0-13-387407-9, Parker); pap. 4.95 (ISBN 0-13-387399-4). P-H.
Solomon, Kenneth & Levy, Norman B., eds. Men in Transition: Theory & Therapy. 500p. 1982. 39.50x (ISBN 0-306-40976-3, Plenum Pr). Plenum Pub.
Taylor, Christine M. Returning to Mental Health. 160p. 1981. 29.00x (ISBN 0-85950-307-0, Pub. by Thornes England). State Mutual Bk.
Veroff, Joseph & Dawan, Elizabeth. Americans View Their Mental Health, 1976. LC 82-80684. 1982. write for info. (ISBN 0-89138-939-3). ICPSR.

MENTAL HEALTH CONSULTATION
see Psychiatric Consultation

MENTAL HEALTH LAWS
see also Insanity-Jurisprudence
Herr, Stanley S. Rights & Advocacy for Retarded People. LC 81-47573. 1983. write for info. (ISBN 0-669-04682-5). Lexington Bks.
Herr, Stanley S. & Arons, Stephen. Legal Rights & Mental-Health Care. Talbot, J., frwd. by. LC 81-47823. 1983. write for info. (ISBN 0-669-04910-7). Lexington Bks.
Ziegenfuss, James T., Jr. Patients' Rights & Organizational Models: Sociotechnical Systems Research on Mental Health Programs. LC 82-21786. (Illus.). 364p. (Orig.). 1983. lib. bdg. 25.75 (ISBN 0-8191-2950-X); pap. text ed. 14.00 (ISBN 0-8191-2951-8). U Pr of Amer.

MENTAL HEALTH PERSONNEL
see also Clinical Psychology; Psychiatric Nursing; Psychiatric Social Work; Psychiatrists
McCaslin, Rosemary W. The Older Person as a Mental Health Worker. (Adult & Aging Ser.: Vol. 12). 1983. text ed. 21.95 (ISBN 0-8261-4290-7). Springer Pub.
Rudman, Jack. Chemical Specialist in Adult Psychiatric & Mental Health Nursing. (Certified Nurse Examination Ser.: CN-14). 21.95 (ISBN 0-8373-6164-8); pap. 13.95 (ISBN 0-8373-6114-1). Natl Learning.

MENTAL HEALTH RESEARCH
see Psychiatric Research

MENTAL HEALTH SERVICES
see also Community Mental Health Services; Psychiatric Hospitals
Cooper, Saul & Hodges, William F., eds. The Mental Health Construction Field, Vol. XI. 224p. 1983. text ed. 24.95x (ISBN 0-89885-130-0). Human Sci Pr.
Heilveil, Ira. Video in Mental Health Practice: An Activities Handbook. 1983. pap. text ed. price not set (ISBN 0-8261-4331-8). Springer Pub.
Menolascino, Frank J. & McCann, Brian, eds. Mental Health & Mental Retardation: Bridging the Gap. (Illus.). 272p. 1983. pap. text ed. 27.50 (ISBN 0-8391-1784-1, 19593). Univ Park.
Schainblatt, Al & Hatry, Harry. Mental Health Services: What Happens To the Client? (Illus.). 119p. (Orig.). 1980. pap. text ed. 5.50 (ISBN 0-87766-275-4). Urban Inst.
Snowden, Lonnie, ed. Reaching the Underserved: Mental Health Needs of Neglected Populations. (Sage Annual Review of Community Mental Health: Vol. 3). (Illus.). 1982. pap. 25.00 (ISBN 0-8039-1856-9); pap. 12.50 (ISBN 0-8039-1857-7). Sage.
Talbott, John A. & Kaplan, Seymour R., eds. Psychiatric Administration: A Comprehensive Text for the Clinician-Executive. Date not set. price not set (ISBN 0-8089-1529-0). Grune.
Ziegenfuss, James T., Jr. Patients' Rights & Organizational Models: Sociotechnical Systems Research on Mental Health Programs. LC 82-21786. (Illus.). 364p. (Orig.). 1983. lib. bdg. 25.75 (ISBN 0-8191-2950-X); pap. text ed. 14.00 (ISBN 0-8191-2951-8). U Pr of Amer.

MENTAL HOSPITALS
see Psychiatric Hospitals

MENTAL HYGIENE
see Mental Health

MENTAL ILLNESS
Here are entered popular works and works on regional or social aspects of mental disorders. Works on the legal aspects of mental illness are entered under Insanity. Systematic descriptions of mental disorders are entered under Psychology, Pathological. Works on clinical aspects of mental disorders, including therapy, are entered under Psychiatry.
see also Mental Deficiency; Mental Health; Mentally Ill; Psychiatry; Psychology, Pathological
Aguilera, Donna C. & Messick, Janice M. Crisis Intervention: Therapy for Psychological Emergencies. LC 81-9470. (Medical Library). 146p. 1982. pap. 6.95 (ISBN 0-686-84855-1, 0086-3). Mosby.
Bean, Philip. Mental Illness: Changes & Trends. 500p. 1983. 64.95 (ISBN 0-471-10240-7, Pub. by Wiley-Interscience). Wiley.
Glasscote, R. M., et al. Preventing Mental Illness: Efforts & Attitudes. LC 80-65220. 138p. 1980. 10.00x (ISBN 0-89042-503-5). Am Psychiatric.
McCulloch, Jock. Black Soul White Artifact: Fanon's Clinical Psychology & Social Theory. LC 82-14605. 240p. Date not set. price not set (ISBN 0-521-24700-4). Cambridge U Pr.
MacDonald, Michael. Mystical Bedlam: Madness, Anxiety, & Healing in Seventeenth Century England. LC 80-25787. (Cambridge Monographs on the History of Medicine). (Illus.). 323p. Date not set. pap. 14.95 (ISBN 0-521-27382-X). Cambridge U Pr.
Taylor, Christine M. Returning to Mental Health. 160p. 1981. 29.00x (ISBN 0-85950-307-0, Pub. by Thornes England). State Mutual Bk.

MENTAL ILLNESS-DIAGNOSIS
American Psychiatric Association. Diagnostic & Statistical Manual of Mental Disorders (DSM-III) LC 79-55868. (Illus.). 506p. 1980. Casebound. 29.95x (ISBN 0-89042-041-6, 42-041-6); pap. 23.95x (ISBN 0-89042-042-4, 42-042-4). Am Psychiatric.
--Quick Reference to the Diagnostic Criteria from (DSM-III) (Illus.). 267p. 1980. 12.00x (ISBN 0-89042-043-2, 42-043-2). Am Psychiatric.
APA Task Force on Nomenclature & Statistics. Desk Reference to the Diagnostic Criteria from (DSM-III) (Illus.). 300p. 1983. spiral bound 15.00 (ISBN 0-89042-046-7, 42-046-7). Am Psychiatric.

MENTAL ILLNESS-PERSONAL NARRATIVES
Parker, Marjorie F. Return to Reality. 144p. 1983. 10.50 (ISBN 0-89962-304-2). Todd & Honeywell.

MENTAL ILLNESS-RESEARCH
see Psychiatric Research

MENTAL ILLNESS AND LAW
see Insanity-Jurisprudence

MENTAL INSTITUTIONS
see Psychiatric Hospitals

MENTAL PRAYER
see Meditation

MENTAL RETARDATION
see Mental Deficiency

MENTAL STEREOTYPE
see Stereotype (Psychology)

MENTAL SUGGESTION
see also Autogenic Training; Hypnotism; Mental Healing
Vienne', Augustus. The Power of Auto-Suggestion & How to Master it for the Energizing of One's Life. (Illus.). 121p. 1983. 39.75 (ISBN 0-89920-053-2). Am Inst Psych.

MENTAL TESTS
see Educational Tests and Measurements; Intelligence Tests; Psychological Tests

MENTALLY HANDICAPPED
see also Inefficiency, Intellectual; Mental Deficiency
Blatt, Burton. Revolt of the Idiots. 1976. 10.95 (ISBN 0-686-84868-3). Exceptional Pr Inc.
Dudley, James R. Living with Stigma: The Plight of Being Mentally Retarded. 110p. 1983. text ed. price not set (ISBN 0-398-04831-2). C C Thomas.
Hallas, Charles H. & Fraser, William I. The Care & Training of the Mentally Handicapped: A Manual for the Caring Professionals. 7th ed. (Illus.). 424p. 1982. pap. text ed. 15.00 (ISBN 0-7236-0624-2). Wright-PSG.
Harris, Sandra L. Families of the Developmentally Disabled: A Guide to Behavioral Interventions. (General Psychology Ser.: No. 119). 170p. 1983. 16.50 (ISBN 0-08-030125-8). Pergamon.
Heaton-Ward, W. A. Left Behind: A Study of Mental Handicap. 256p. 1977. 29.00x (ISBN 0-7121-1236-7, Pub. by Macdonald & Evans). State Mutual Bk.
Herr, Stanley S. Rights & Advocacy for Retarded People. LC 81-47573. 1983. write for info. (ISBN 0-669-04682-5). Lexington Bks.
McCormack, Michael K., ed. Prevention of Mental Retardation & Other Developlmental Disabilities. (Pediatric Habilitation Ser.: Vol. 1). (Illus.). 680p. 1980. 49.75 (ISBN 0-8247-6950-3). Dekker.
Matson, Johnny L. & Barrett, Rowland P., eds. Psychopathology in the Mentally Retarded. Date not set. price not set (ISBN 0-8089-1511-8). Grune.
Matson, Johnny L. & Mulick, James A., eds. Handbook of Mental Retardation. 650p. 1983. 75.00 (ISBN 0-08-028060-9); before 7/83 55.00 (ISBN 0-08-029421-9). Pergamon.
Menolascino, Frank J. & McCann, Brian, eds. Mental Health & Mental Retardation: Bridging the Gap. (Illus.). 272p. 1983. pap. text ed. 27.50 (ISBN 0-8391-1784-1, 19593). Univ Park.
Miner, Jane Claypool. She's My Sister: Having a Retarded Sister. Schroeder, Howard, ed. LC 82-1424. (Crisis Ser.). (Illus.). 64p. (gr. 4-5). 1982. lib. bdg. 7.95 (ISBN 0-89686-171-6). Crestwood Hse.
Motor Fitness Testing Manual for the Moderately Mental Retarded. 80p. 1975. 6.50 (ISBN 0-88314-135-3). AAHPERD.
Tjosvold, Dean & Tjosvold, Mary. Working with the Mentally Handicapped in Their Residences. (Illus.). 256p. 1981. text ed. 19.95 (ISBN 0-02-932490-4). Free Pr.
Whitman, Thomas L. & Scibak, John W., eds. Behavior Modification with the Severely & Profoundly Retarded: Research & Application. LC 82-22720. (Monograph). Date not set. write for info. (ISBN 0-12-747280-0). Acad Pr.
Woods, Grace E. Care of the Mentally Handicapped: Past & Future. 1983. text ed. write for info. (ISBN 0-7236-0674-9). Wright-PSG.

MENTALLY HANDICAPPED-EDUCATION
Noar, Gertrude. Individualized Instruction for the Mentally Retarded. 1974. pap. 4.95 (ISBN 0-914420-50-X). Exceptional Pr Inc.

MENTALLY HANDICAPPED-LAWS AND LEGISLATION
see Mental Health Laws

MENTALLY HANDICAPPED-REHABILITATION
Craft, Ann & Craft, Michael. Sex & The Mentally Handicapped. Rev. ed. 1982. pap. 7.95 (ISBN 0-7100-9293-8). Routledge & Kegan.
Vocational Rehabilitation of the Mentally Retarded: Proceedings, Conclusions & Recommendations of a Seminar on Vocational Rehabilitation of the Mentally Retarded, Held in Kingston, Jamaica, from 4 to 15 September, 1978. ii, 200p. 1982. 5.70 (ISBN 92-2-102018-5). Intl Labour Office.

MENTALLY HANDICAPPED CHILDREN
see also Mentally Ill Children
also names of particular institutions
Biswas, Manju. Mentally Retarded & Normal Children: A Comparative Study of Their Family Conditions. 157p. 1980. 19.95x (ISBN 0-940500-50-7, Pub. by Sterling India). Asia Bk Corp.
Jacobs, Jerry. The Search for Help: A Study of the Retarded Child in the Community. LC 82-13535. 150p. 1983. pap. text ed. 8.25 (ISBN 0-8191-2680-2). U Pr of Amer.

MENTALLY HANDICAPPED CHILDREN-EDUCATION
Jacobs, Jerry. The Search for Help: A Study of the Retarded Child in the Community. LC 82-13535. 150p. 1983. pap. text ed. 8.25 (ISBN 0-8191-2680-2). U Pr of Amer.
Knoblock, Peter. Teaching Emotionally Disturbed Children. LC 82-83370. 448p. 1982. text ed. 24.95 (ISBN 0-395-29708-7); write for info. instr's. manual (ISBN 0-395-29709-5). HM.

MENTALLY HANDICAPPED CHILDREN-PERSONAL NARRATIVES
Dougan, Terrell & Isbell, Lyn. We Have Been There: Families Share the Joys & Struggles of Living with Mental Retardation. 208p. (Orig.). 1983. pap. 9.95 (ISBN 0-687-44306-7). Abingdon.

MENTALLY ILL
see also Mental Illness; Mentally Handicapped
Ahlem, Lloyd. Help for Families of the Mentally Ill. (Trauma Bks.: Ser. 2). 1983. pap. 2.50 (ISBN 0-570-08257-9). Concordia.

MENTALLY ILL-HOSPITALS
see Psychiatric Hospitals

MENTALLY ILL-LEGAL STATUS, LAWS, ETC.
see Insanity-Jurisprudence; Mental Health Laws

MENTALLY ILL-PERSONAL NARRATIVES
see Mental Illness-Personal Narratives

MENTALLY ILL CHILDREN
Shafii, Mohammad & Shafii, Sharon L., eds. Pathways of Human Development; Treatment of Emotional Disorders in Infancy, Childhood & Adolescence. LC 82-80780. (Orig.). 1982. pap. text ed. 24.95 (ISBN 0-686-81689-7). Thieme-Stratton.

MENTALLY ILL CHILDREN-EDUCATION
Epanchin, Betty C. & Paul, James L. Casebook for Educating the Emotionally Disturbed. 288p. 1982. pap. text ed. 9.95 (ISBN 0-675-20018-0). Merrill.

MENTALLY RETARDED
see Mentally Handicapped

MENTALLY RETARDED CHILDREN
see Mentally Handicapped Children

MENUS
see also Buffets (Cookery); Breakfasts; Caterers and Catering; Dinners and Dining; Luncheons
Sunset Books & Sunset Magazine, ed. Picnics & Tailgate Parties. LC 81-82868. (Illus.). 96p. 1982. pap. 4.95 (ISBN 0-376-02536-0). Sunset-Lane.
Virgil M. Hancher Auditorium, The University of Iowa. Entertaining Arts: Menus & Recipes from Performers & Patrons. LC 82-81567. (Illus.). 258p. 1982. spiral bdg. 14.70 (ISBN 0-941016-06-4). Penfield.

MERCANTILE LAW
see Commercial Law

MERCHANDISE
see Commercial Products

MERCHANDISE, DISPLAY OF
see Display of Merchandise

MERCHANDISING
Hamilton, Robert. An Introduction to Merchandise, Parts IV & V: Italian Bookkeeping & Practical Bookkeeping, with a Note by B. S. Yamey. LC 82-48366. (Accountancy in Transition Ser.). 247p. 1982. lib. bdg. 25.00 (ISBN 0-8240-5317-6). Garland Pub.
Packard, Sidney & Winters, Arthur. Fashion Buying & Merchandising. 2nd ed. (Illus.). 390p. 1983. text ed. 16.50 (ISBN 0-87005-445-7). Fairchild.

MERCHANT MARINE
see also Harbors; Insurance, Marine; Merchant Seamen; Merchant Ships; Shipping; Steamboats and Steamboat Lines
Paine, Ralph D. Old Merchant Marine. 1919. text ed. 8.50x (ISBN 0-686-83653-7). Elliots Bks.

MERCHANT MARINE-LAW
see Maritime Law

MERCHANT MARKS
see Trade-Marks

MERCHANT SEAMEN
Brookesmith, Frank. I Remember the Tall Ships. (Illus.). 270p. Repr. 20.00 (ISBN 0-87556-543-3). Saifer.
Hope, Ronald. The Seaman's World: Merchant Seamen's Reminiscences. 1982. 32.00x (ISBN 0-245-53893-3, Pub. by Ian Harrap England). State Mutual Bk.

MERCHANT SEAMEN'S SONGS
see Sea Songs

MERCHANT SHIPS
see also Ocean Liners; Steamboats and Steamboat Lines; Tankers; Work Boats
Jarvis, R. C. & Craig, R. Liverpool Registry of Merchant Ships. 278p. 1967. 22.50 (ISBN 0-7190-1114-0). Manchester.
Streater, R. A. & Greenman, D., eds. Jane's Merchant Ships, 1982-1983. (Jane's Yearbooks). (Illus.). 1000p. 1982. 140.00 (ISBN 0-86720-589-X). Sci Bks Intl.

MERCHANTMEN
see Merchant Ships

MERCURY (PLANET)
Roseveare, N. T. Mercury's Perihelion from Le Verrier to Einstein. (Illus.). 216p. 1982. 49.00x (ISBN 0-19-858174-2). Oxford U Pr.

MERCURY COMPOUNDS
D'itri, P. A. & D'itri, F. M. Mercury Contamination: A Human Tragedy. 311p. Repr. of 1977 ed. text ed. 28.95 (ISBN 0-471-02654-9). Krieger.

MERCY DEATH
see Euthanasia

MEREDITH, GEORGE, 1828-1909
Woods, Alice. George Meredith's Poems. 1982. lib. bdg. 34.50 (ISBN 0-686-81934-9). Porter.

MERGER OF CORPORATIONS
see Consolidation and Merger of Corporations

MERISTEM
see Plant Cells and Tissues; Growth (Plants)

MERIT (CHRISTIANITY)
Cooper, A. A. An Inquiry Concerning Virtue, or Merit. Walford, D. E., ed. 152p. 1977. 15.50 (ISBN 0-7190-0657-0). Manchester.

MERIT SYSTEM
see Civil Service Reform

MERMAIDS
Green Tiger Press, ed. Mermaids. (Illus.). 12p. (Orig.). 1982. pap. 2.50 (ISBN 0-88138-001-6, Pub. by Envelope Bks). Green Tiger Pr.

MESOPOTAMIA
see Iraq

MESOPOTAMIAN POTTERY
see Pottery, Ancient

MESSIANISM, AMERICAN
Merk, Federick & Merrk, Lois B. Manifest Destiny & Mission in American History: A Reinterpretation. LC 82-25146. ix, 265p. 1983. Repr. lib. bdg. 35.00x (ISBN 0-313-23844-8, MERM). Greenwood.

METABOLIC DISORDERS
see Metabolism, Disorders of

METABOLISM
see also Bioenergetics; Calcium Metabolism; Carbohydrate Metabolism; Carbohydrates in the Body; Drug Metabolism; Fat Metabolism; Fatty Acid Metabolism; Lipid Metabolism; Nutrition; Protein Metabolism; Urea

Cohen, Margo P. & Foa, Piero P., eds. Special Topics in Endocrinology & Metabolism, Vol. 4. (Special Topics in Endocrinology & Metabolism). 251p. 1982. 38.00 (ISBN 0-8451-0703-8). A R Liss.
Denton, R. M. & Pogson, C. I. Metabolic Regulation. 1976. pap. 6.50x (ISBN 0-412-13150-1, Pub. by Chapman & Hall England). Methuen Inc.
Kurokawa, K. & Tanner, R., eds. Recent Advances in Renal Metabolism. (Mineral Electrolyte Metabolism Ser.: Vol. 9: No. 4-5). (Illus.). 140p. 1983. pap. price not set (ISBN 3-8055-3652-6). S Karger.
Martini, Luciano & James, V. H., eds. Current Topics in Experimental Endocrinology: Vol. 5: Fetal Endocrinology & Metabolism. (Serial Publication). Date not set. price not set (ISBN 0-12-153205-4). Acad Pr.
Miller, Peter M. The Hilton Head Metabolism Diet. 256p. 1983. 14.50 (ISBN 0-446-51266-4). Warner Bks.
Rohe, Fred. Metabolic Ecology. 1982. 5.95x (ISBN 0-686-37598-X). Cancer Control Soc.

METABOLISM, DISORDERS OF
see also Diabetes; Metabolism, Inborn Errors of; Obesity
Desnick, Robert J. & Patterson, Donald F., eds. Animal Models of Inherited Metabolic Diseases. LC 82-8961. (Progress in Clinical & Biological Research Ser.: Vol. 94). 544p. 1982. 54.00 (ISBN 0-8451-0094-7). A R Liss.

METABOLISM, INBORN ERRORS OF
Cockburn, Forrester & Gitzelmann, Richard, eds. Inborn Errors of Metabolism in Humans. LC 82-12709. 308p. 1982. 54.00 (ISBN 0-8451-3008-0). A R Liss.

METAL CORROSION
see Corrosion and Anti-Corrosives

METAL CURTAIN WALLS
see Walls

METAL-CUTTING
see also Cutting Machines; Metal-Cutting Tools
American Machinist Magazine Staff. Metalcutting: Today's Techniques for Engineers & Shop Personnel. 1979. 24.50 (ISBN 0-07-001545-7). McGraw.
Kops, L. & Ramalingham, R., eds. On the Art of Cutting Metals: Seventy Five Years Later. (PED Ser.: Vol. 7). 1982. 40.00 (H00251). ASME.

METAL-CUTTING TOOLS
American Welding Society. Specification for Metal Cutting Machine Tool Weldments. (incl. 1975 Revision). 1971. 8.00 (ISBN 0-686-43353-X). Am Welding.

METAL ENGRAVERS
see Engravers

METAL INDUSTRIES
see Metal Trade; Metal-Work; Mineral Industries

METAL IONS
Sigel. Metal Ions in Biological Systems, Vol. 15. 520p. 1983. 75.00 (ISBN 0-8247-1750-3). Dekker.

METAL OXIDES
see Metallic Oxides

METAL POWDERS
Wendon, G. W. Aluminium & Bronze Flake Powders. 1982. 159.00x (ISBN 0-686-81701-X, Pub. by Electrochemical Scotland). State Mutual Bk.

METAL-ROLLING
see Rolling (Metal-Work)

METAL TRADE
Jones, L. & Vaughan, J. Scientific & Technical Information on the Metals Industry: Report of the Metals Information Review Committee. 1982. 50.00x (ISBN 0-7123-3008-9, Pub. by Brit Lib England). State Mutual Bk.

METAL-WORK
see also Founding; Silverwork; Welding
Miller, Richard K. Noise Control Solutions for the Metal Products Industry. (Illus.). 120p. text ed. 45.00 (ISBN 0-89671-031-9). Southeast Acoustics.
--Noise Control Solutions for the Metal Products Industry, Vol. II. (Illus.). 120p. pap. text ed. 45.00 (ISBN 0-89671-021-1). Southeast Acoustics.
Robinson, B. W. Japanese Sword-Fittings & Associated Metalwork. (Baur Collection Geneva: Vol. 7). (Illus.). 448p. 1981. 250.00 (ISBN 2-88031-003-2, Pub. by Baur Foundation Switzerland). Routledge & Kegan.
Van der Voort, G. F. Metallurgy. 608p. 1983. 28.95x (ISBN 0-07-066970-8). McGraw.
Working with Metal. (Home Repair & Improvement Ser.). 1981. lib. bdg. 15.96 (ISBN 0-8094-3471-7, Pub. by Time-Life). Silver.

METAL-WORK-HISTORY
Waldbaum, Jane C. Metalwork from Sardis: The Finds Through 1974. (Archaeological Exploration of Sardis Monographs: No. 8). (Illus.). 280p. 1983. text ed. 40.00x (ISBN 0-674-57070-7). Harvard U Pr.

METAL-WORKING MACHINERY
see also Machine-Tools
Strasser, Federico. Metal Stamping Plant Productivity Handbook. (Illus.). 300p. 1983. 29.95 (ISBN 0-8311-1147-X). Indus Pr.

METALLIC ALLOYS
see Alloys

METALLIC FILMS
Tellier. Size Effects of Thin Films. (Thin Films Science & Technology Ser.: Vol. 2). 1982. 68.00 (ISBN 0-444-42106-8). Elsevier.

METALLIC OXIDES
Hellwege, K. H., ed. Magnetic & Other Properties of Xides & Related Compounds: Hexagonal Ferrites. Special Lanthanide & Actinide Compounds. (Landolt-Boernstein Ser.: Group III, Vol. 12, Pt. C). (Illus.). 650p. 1983. 408.00 (ISBN 0-387-10137-3). Springer-Verlag.
Kofstad, Per. Nonstoichiometry, Diffusion & Electrical Conductivity in Binary Metal Oxides. LC 82-20336. 394p. 1983. Repr. of 1972 ed. lib. bdg. write for info. (ISBN 0-89874-569-1). Krieger.
Mavor, J. & Jack, M. A. Introduction to MOS LSI Design. 350p. 1982. 35.00 (ISBN 0-201-11440-2, Adv Bk Prog). A-W.

METALLOGRAPHY
Mount, Ellis, ed. Micrographs in Sci-Tech Libraries. LC 82-23435. (Science & Technology Libraries, Vol. 3, No. 3). 73p. 1983. text ed. 20.00 (ISBN 0-86656-218-4, B218). Haworth Pr.

METALLOORGANIC COMPOUNDS
see Organometallic Compounds

METALLURGICAL ANALYSIS
see also Alloys; Chemistry, Analytic
Westwood, W. & Cooper, B. S. Analytical Methods in Use in Non-Ferrous Mining & Metallurgy: A Selective Review. 54p. (Orig.). 1973. 14.50 (ISBN 0-900488-17-4). IMM North Am.

METALLURGY
see also Alloys; Chemical Engineering; Chemistry, Technical; Electrometallurgy; Metals; Metals at High Temperatures; Physical Metallurgy; Powder Metallurgy; Smelting
also names of metals, with or without the subdivision Metallurgy
Atherton, M. P. & Gribble, C. J., eds. Migmatitxes, Melting & Metamorphism. 200p. Date not set. text ed. 24.95 (ISBN 0-906812-26-7). Birkhauser.
Bulk-Mineable Metal Deposits. 1983. write for info. Minobras.
Devereux, Owen F. Topics in Metallurgical Thermodynamics. 416p. 1983. write for info. (ISBN 0-471-86963-5, Pub. by Wiley-Interscience). Wiley.
Higgins, Raymond A. Engineering Metallurgy, 2 Vols. Incl. Vol. 1. Applied Physical Metallurgy. 576p. lib. bdg. price not set (ISBN 0-89874-567-5); Vol. 2. Metallurgical Process Technology. 480p. lib. bdg. price not set (ISBN 0-89874-568-3). LC 82-19292. 1983. lib. bdg. write for info. Krieger.
Hoyle, G. Electroslag Processes: Principles & Practice. (Illus.). 228p. 1982. 51.25 (ISBN 0-85334-164-8). Elsevier.
Jones, L. & Vaughan, J. Scientific & Technical Information on the Metals Industry: Report of the Metals Information Review Committee. 1982. 50.00x (ISBN 0-7123-3008-9, Pub. by Brit Lib England). State Mutual Bk.
Kaye & Street. Die Casting Metallurgy. 1982. text ed. 49.95 (ISBN 0-408-10717-0). Butterworth.
Linchevsky, B. Methods of Metallurgical Experiment. 296p. 1982. 7.00 (ISBN 0-8285-2283-9, Pub. by Mir Pubs USSR). Imported Pubns.
Nicoll, A. R. Acustic Emission. (Illus.). 385p. (Eng.). 1980. 63.00 (ISBN 0-686-37418-5, Pub. by DGM Metallurgy Germany). IR Pubns.
Pollack, ed. Material Science & Metallurgy. 3rd ed. 1980. text ed. 22.95 (ISBN 0-8359-4280-5); solutions manual avail. (ISBN 0-8359-4282-1). Reston.
Rosenqvist, T. Principles of Extractive Metallurgy. 2nd ed. 608p. 1983. 42.95x (ISBN 0-07-053910-3, C). McGraw.
Van der Voort, G. F. Metallurgy. 608p. 1983. 28.95x (ISBN 0-07-066970-8). McGraw.

METALLURGY-DICTIONARIES
Tottle, C. R. Encyclopedia of Metallurgy & Materials. (Illus.). 800p. 1983. text ed. 85.00x (ISBN 0-911378-45-6). Sheridan.

METALLURGY, PHYSICAL
see Physical Metallurgy

METALLURGY, POWDER
see Powder Metallurgy

METALORGANIC COMPOUNDS
see Organometallic Compounds

METALS
see also Alloys; Earths, Rare; Metallic Films; Metallic Oxides; Metallography; Mineralogy; Nonferrous Metals; Precious Metals; Transition Metals
also particular metals and metal groups, e.g. Iron
American Society for Hospital Engineering & American Society for Hospital Purchasing & Materials Management. Silver Recovery for Hospitals. LC 80-19943. 36p. 1980. pap. 10.00 (ISBN 0-87258-331-7, AHA-172100). Am Hospital.
Bass, J. & Fischer, K. H. Metals: Electronic Transport Phenomena. (Landolt Boernstein Ser.: Group III, Vol. 15, Subvol. A). (Illus.). 400p. 1983. 271.10 (ISBN 0-387-11082-8). Springer-Verlag.
Collie, M. J., ed. Etching Compositions & Processes. LC 82-7894. (Chemical Technology Rev. 210). (Illus.). 308p. 1983. 42.00 (ISBN 0-8155-0913-8). Noyes.

METALS-CORROSION
see Corrosion and Anti-Corrosives

METALS-HIGH ENERGY FORMING
see High Energy Forming

METALS-MICROSCOPIC STRUCTURE
see Metallography

METALS-RECYCLING
Data Notes Publishing Staff. Metal Recycling: Data Notes. 30p. 1983. pap. text ed. 9.95 (ISBN 0-911569-44-8). Data Notes Pub.
National Association of Recycling Industries Inc. Recycled Metals in the Nineteen Eighties. (Illus.). 188p. 1982. 40.00 (ISBN 0-686-81901-2). Natl Recycling.

METALS, NONFERROUS
see Nonferrous Metals

METALS, POWDERED
see Metal Powders

METALS, TRANSMUTATION OF
see Alchemy

METALS AT HIGH TEMPERATURES
Freyhardt, H. C. Analytical Methods: High-Melting Metals. (Crystals, Growth, Properties, & Applications Ser.: Vol. 7). (Illus.). 150p. 1982. 42.00 (ISBN 0-387-11790-3). Springer-Verlag.

METALS IN THE BODY
Schmidt, E. H. & Hildebrandt, A., eds. Health Evaluation of Heavy Metals in Infant Formula & Junior Food, Berlin: 1981, Proceedings. (Illus.). 192p. 1983. 16.00 (ISBN 0-387-11823-3). Springer-Verlag.

METALWORK
see Metal-Work

METAMORPHOSIS
see also Insects-Metamorphosis
Tata, J. R. Metamorphosis. Head, J. J., ed. (Carolina Biology Readers Ser.). (Illus.). 16p. 1983. pap. text ed. 1.60 (ISBN 0-89278-246-3). Carolina Biological.

METAMORPHOSIS (IN RELIGION, FOLK-LORE, ETC.)
see also Witchcraft; Werewolves
Tomlinson, Charles. Poetry & Metamorphosis. LC 82-19893. 112p. Date not set. 19.95 (ISBN 0-521-24848-5). Cambridge U Pr.

METAMORPHOSIS (INSECTS)
see Insects-Development

METAPHOR
Blessington, Francis C. & Rotella, Guy, eds. Motive for Metaphor. 192p. 1983. 18.95x (ISBN 0-930350-38-3). NE U Pr.

METAPHYSICS
see also Causation; Cosmology; Form (Philosophy); God; Knowledge, Theory Of; Ontology; Space and Time; Values
Beasley-Murray, Stephen. Towards a Metaphysics of the Sacred. LC 82-8288. (Special Studies: No. 8). 1982. pap. 7.95 (ISBN 0-86554-038-1). Assn Baptist P.
Chaney, Earlyne. The Masters & Astara. 2nd ed. (Illus.). 100p. 1982. pap. 8.50 (ISBN 0-918936-13-6). Astara.
Eddington, Thomas. Contemporary Artistic & the Metaphysics of the Art Expression. (An Essential Knowledge Library Bk.). (Illus.). 137p. 1983. 43.55 (ISBN 0-86650-051-0). Gloucester Art.
Faulkenstein, Dezmon A. Faulkenstein's Theories are Loose on the Earth. 1982. 7.95. Vantage.
Harth, Erich. Windows on the Mind: Reflections on the Physical Basis of Consciousness. LC 81-11158. (Illus.). 272p. 1983. Repr. pap. 7.95 (ISBN 0-688-01596-4). Quill NY.
Malebranche, Nicolas. Entretiens sur la Metaphysique: Dialogues on Metaphysics. Doney, Willis, tr. from Fr. (Janus Ser.). 359p. 1980. 20.00 (ISBN 0-913870-57-9). Abaris Bks.
Schlesinger, George N. Metaphysics: Issues & Techniques. LC 82-24408. 288p. 1983. text ed. 28.50x (ISBN 0-389-20380-7); pap. text ed. 16.50x (ISBN 0-389-20381-5). B&N Imports.
Taylor, Richard. Metaphysics. 3rd ed. 160p. 1983. pap. 8.50 (ISBN 0-686-82032-0). P-H.
Voltaire. Traite de Metaphysique. (Modern French Text Ser.). 1937. pap. write for info. (ISBN 0-7190-0166-8). Manchester.
Weyl, Hermann. Open World: Three Lectures on the Metaphysical Implications of Science. 1932. text ed. 24.50x (ISBN 0-686-83658-8). Elliots Bks.
White, Alan. Absolute Knowledge: Hegel & the Problem of Metaphysics. 190p. 1983. text ed. 22.95x (ISBN 0-8214-0717-1, 82-84861); pap. 11.95 (ISBN 0-8214-0718-X, 82-84879). Ohio U Pr.
Wood, Lorraine. I Am Jeremiah. Pena, Lilian M., ed. 290p. 1982. pap. 3.95 (ISBN 0-942128-00-1). Desert Light.

METAPSYCHOLOGY
see Psychical Research; Spiritualism

METEORITES
Hey, M. H., et al. Catalogue of Meteorites with Special Reference to Those Represented in the Collection of the British Museum (Natural History) 3rd ed. 1966. 62.50 set (ISBN 0-686-37455-X). Catalog (ISBN 0-565-00464-6). Appendix to the Catalogue of Meteorites 1977 (ISBN 0-565-00789-0). Sabbot-Natural Hist Bks.
Pejovic, Brian. Man & Meteorites. Stewart, T. H. & Stewart, S. M., eds. (Illus.). 120p. 1982. 14.95 (ISBN 0-907733-01-8). Sheridan.

METEOROLOGICAL OBSERVATIONS
see Meteorology-Observations

METEOROLOGY
see also Atmosphere; Climatology; Evaporation; Floods; Hurricanes; Rainbow; Solar Radiation; Storms; Thunderstorms; Tornadoes; Weather; Weathering; Winds
also headings beginning with the word Meteorological
Annual Report of the World Meteorological Organization 1981. 195p. 1982. pap. 25.00 (ISBN 92-63-10592-8, W 536, WMO). Unipub.
Commission for Instruments & Methods of Observation: Abridged Final Report of the Eighth Session. 89p. 1982. pap. 20.00 (ISBN 92-63-10590-1, W 534, WMO). Unipub.
Discovering the Weather. LC 81-52418. (Discovering Science Ser.). lib. bdg. 15.96 (ISBN 0-86706-059-X, Pub. by Stonehenge). Silver.
Meteorological Services of the World. 180p. 1982. pap. 24.00 (ISBN 0-686-83881-5, W539, WMO). Unipub.
Miller, Albert & Thompson, Jack C. Elements of Meteorology. 4th ed. 448p. 1983. text ed. 23.95 (ISBN 0-675-20005-9). Additional supplements may be obtained from publisher. Merrill.
Plate, E., ed. Engineering Methodology. (Studies in Wind Engineering & Industrial Aerodynamics: No. 1). 740p. 1982. 149.00 (ISBN 0-444-41972-1). Elsevier.
Regional Association Three, South America: Abridged Final Report of the Eighth Session. 144p. 1983. pap. 20.00 (ISBN 92-63-10594-4, W543, WMO). Unipub.
Spiegel, Herbert J. & Gruber, Arnold. From Weather Vanes to Satellites: An Introduction to Meteorology. LC 82-8349. 241p. 1983. text ed. 16.95 (ISBN 0-471-86401-3). Wiley.
Thirty-Fourth Session of the Executive Committee: Abridged Report with Resolutions. 209p. 1982. pap. 25.00 (ISBN 92-63-10599-5, W541, WMO). Unipub.

METEOROLOGY-OBSERVATIONS
Fitch, A. A., ed. Developments in Geophysical Exploration Methods, Vol. 3. (Illus.). 320p. 1982. 57.50 (ISBN 0-85334-126-5, Pub. by Applied Sci England). Elsevier.

METEOROLOGY, MARITIME
see also Hurricanes
Burgess, C. R. Meteorology for Seamen. 4th ed. 251p. 1982. text ed. 25.00x (ISBN 0-85174-315-3). Sheridan.
Stommel, Henry & Stommel, Elizabeth. Volcano Weather. 1983. 15.00 (ISBN 0-915160-71-4). Seven Seas.

METER
see Versification

METER (STANDARD OF LENGTH)
see Metric System

METERS, FLOW
see Flow Meters

METERS, PARKING
see Parking Meters

METHANE
Durbin, Enoch & McGeer, Patrick L., eds. Methane: Fuel for the Future. 350p. 1982. 42.50x (ISBN 0-306-41122-9, Plenum Pr). Plenum Pub.

METHOD OF STUDY
see Study, Method Of

METHOD OF WORK
see Work

METHODIST CHURCH
Gowland, D. A. Methodist Secessions. 192p. 1979. 24.00 (ISBN 0-7190-1335-6). Manchester.
Langford, Thomas A. Practical Divinity: Theology in the Wesleyan Tradition. 304p. (Orig.). 1983. pap. 9.95 (ISBN 0-687-33326-1). Abingdon.
Schwartz, Charles D. & Schwartz, Ouida D. A Flame of Fire: The Story of Troy Annual Conference. LC 82-70624. (Illus.). 376p. (Orig.). 1982. pap. text ed. 15.00x (ISBN 0-914960-38-5). Academy Bks.

METHODIST CHURCH-BIOGRAPHY
Miller, Barbara & Miller, Kathy. We're Gonna Win! (Illus.). 192p. 1983. 9.95 (ISBN 0-8007-1340-0). Revell.

METHODIST CHURCH-EDUCATION
Williams, Colbert V. The Methodist Contribution to Education in the Bahamas. 256p. 1982. text ed. 34.00x (ISBN 0-86299-027-0, Pub. by Sutton England). Humanities.

METHODOLOGY
see also Analysis (Philosophy); Problem Solving; Research
also subdivision Methodology under special subjects, e.g. Science-methodology; Theology-Methodology
Groner, Rudolph & Groner, Marina, eds. Methods of Heuristics. 488p. 1983. text ed. write for info. (ISBN 0-89859-251-8). L Erlbaum Assocs.
Methodology in Human Fatigue Assessment: Symposium on Methodology in Human Fatigue Assessment, Kyoto, Japan, 1969. LC 72-304858. 200p. 1971. 22.50x (ISBN 0-85066-049-1). Intl Pubns Serv.

METHYL GROUPS
Usdin, E. Biochemistry of S Adenosylmethionine & Related Compounds. 1982. 195.00x (ISBN 0-686-42937-0, Pub. by Macmillan England). State Mutual Bk.

METOPOSCOPY
see Physiognomy

METRIC SPACES
Lingenberg, Rolf. Metric Planes & Metric Vector Spaces. LC 78-21906. 274p. Repr. of 1979 ed. text ed. 28.50 (ISBN 0-686-84493-9). Krieger.

METRIC SYSTEM
American Welding Society. Metric Practice Guide for the Welding Industry: A1.1. 1980. 8.00 (ISBN 0-686-43367-X). Am Welding.

Horowitz, Ruth. Honor & the American Dream: Culture & Social Identity in a Chicano Community. LC 82-7642. (Crime, Law & Deviance Ser.). 300p. 1983. 32.50 (ISBN 0-8135-0966-1); pap. 12.95 (ISBN 0-8135-0991-2). Rutgers U Pr.

--Z-80 Microcomputer Design Projects. 1980. pap. 13.95 (ISBN 0-672-21682-5). Sams.
Barnett, Nancy B. & Baker, John T. Texas Instruments Compact Computer Forty User's Guide. 336p. (Orig.). 1983. pap. 14.95 (ISBN 0-89512-057-7). Tex Instr Inc.
Barrette, Pierre, ed. Microcomputers in K-Twelve Education, Second Annual Congerence Proceedings. 1983. pap. write for info. (ISBN 0-914894-87-0). Computer Sci.
Berenson, Howard. Mostly BASIC Applications for Apple II, Bk. 2. Date not set. pap. 12.95 (ISBN 0-672-21864-X). Sams.
--Mostly BASIC Applications for your TRS-80, Bk.2. Date not set. pap. 12.95 (ISBN 0-672-21865-8). Sams.
Blank, Hannah I. Mastering Micros. (Illus.). 250p. 1983. 24.95x (ISBN 0-89433-207-4). Petrocelli.
Blumenthal, Susan. Understanding & Buying a Small Business Computer. Date not set. pap. 8.95 (ISBN 0-672-21890-9). Sams.
Bocchino, William A. Simplified Guide to Microcomputers with Practical Programs & Applications. LC 82-3671. 256p. 1982. 19.95 (ISBN 0-13-810085-3, Busn). P-H.
Bradbeer, Robin & Allason, Julian. Choosing & Using a Business Microcomputer. 172p. 1982. text ed. 32.50x (ISBN 0-566-03405-0). Gower Pub Ltd.
Brandon, Peter S. & Moore, Geoffrey. Microcomputers in Building Appraisal. 320p. 1983. pap. 25.95 (ISBN 0-89397-147-2). Nichols Pub.
Brooner, Ernie. Microcomputer Data-Base Management. Date not set. pap. 12.95 (ISBN 0-672-21875-5). Sams.
Brown, Jerald R. & Finkel, LeRoy. BASIC for the Apple II. LC 82-10962. (Self-Teaching Guide). 410p. 1982. pap. 12.95 (ISBN 0-471-86596-6). Wiley.
CES Industries, Inc. Staff. Microcomputer Technology, Unit 2. (Ed-Lab Experiment Manual Ser.). (Illus.). (gr. 9-12). 1981. lab manual 11.50 (ISBN 0-86711-023-6). CES Industries.
Chen, Ching-chih & Bressler, Stacey E. Microcomputers in Libraries. (Applications in Information Management & Technology Ser.). (Illus.). 259p. (Orig.). 1982. pap. text ed. 22.95 (ISBN 0-918212-61-8). Neal-Schuman.
Christie, Linda & Curry, Jess, Jr. The ABC's of Microcomputers: A Computer Literacy Primer. (Illus.). 218p. 1983. 15.95 (ISBN 0-13-000620-3); pap. 7.95 (ISBN 0-13-000612-2). P-H.
Coan. Basic Apple BASIC. Date not set. 10.95 (ISBN 0-686-82001-0, 5626). Hayden.
Cole, Jim. Ninety-Nine Tips & Tricks for the New Pocket Computers. 128p. (Orig.). 1982. pap. 7.95 (ISBN 0-86668-019-5). ARCsoft.
Cusmano, Anthony J. How to Use the Microcomputer in Your Small Business. LC 82-60723. (Orig.). 1982. pap. 12.95 (ISBN 0-943214-01-7). Media Pubns.
Daniels, Shirley. All You Need to Know About Microcomputers: The Small Business Manager's Advisory. LC 79-64577. (Illus.). 144p. 1979. pap. text ed. 7.95 (ISBN 0-89914-003-3). Third Party Pub.
Desautels, Edouard J. Advanced Uses of Visicalc R, for the IBM Personal Computer. (Microcomputer Power Ser.). 256p. 1983. pap. write for info. (ISBN 0-697-09973-3); write for info. diskette (ISBN 0-697-09974-1). Wm C Brown.
DeVoney, Chris & Summe, Richard. IBM's Personal Computer. Noble, David F. & Noble, Virginia D., eds. 303p. 1982. 23.95 (ISBN 0-88022-101-1); pap. 14.95 (ISBN 0-88022-100-3). Que Corp.
Dictionary of Japanese Microcomputer. 30p. 1983. 30.00x (ISBN 0-686-38826-7). Sci & Tech Pr.
Directory of Japanese Computers. 400p. 1983. 250.00x (ISBN 0-686-38825-9). Sci & Tech Pr.
Edwards, Chris. Developing Microcomputer-Based Business Systems. (Illus.). 224p. 1983. pap. 14.95 (ISBN 0-13-204552-4). P-H.
Fernandes, Judi N. & Ashley, Ruth. CP-M Eighty-Six for the IBM Personal Computer. (A Self-Teaching & Wiley IBM PC Ser.). 331p. 1983. pap. text ed. 14.95 (ISBN 0-471-89719-1). Wiley.
Freedman, M. David & Evans, Lansing B. Designing Systems with Microcomputers: A Systematic Approach. (Illus.). 320p. 1983. text ed. 26.00 (ISBN 0-13-201350-9). P-H.
Froehlich, John P. TRS-80 More than BASIC. 1981. pap. 10.95 (ISBN 0-672-21813-5). Sams.
Fudge, Don. Hi-Res Secrets Graphics Applications System. (Illus.). 240p. 1982. binder 50.00 (ISBN 0-930182-33-2). Avant Garde CR.
Gagliardi, Gary. How to Make Your Microcomputer Pay Off. (Data Processing Ser.). (Illus.). 300p. 1983. 21.95 (ISBN 0-534-97926-2). Lifetime Learn.
Galanter, Eugene. Kids & Computers: The Parent's Microcomputer Handbook; How to Write & Run Your Own BASIC Programs. LC 82-82310. 192p. 1983. pap. 7.95 (ISBN 0-399-50749-3, Perigee). Putnam Pub Group.
Genet, Russell M. & Wolpert, Robert C., eds. Microcomputers in Astronomy. LC 82-84769. 200p. (Orig.). 1983. pap. 18.95 (ISBN 0-911351-03-5). Fairborn Observ.
Glossbrenner, Alfred. The Complete Handbook of Personal Computer Communications. 1983. pap. 14.95 (ISBN 0-312-15718-5). St Martin.
Goldberg, Kenneth P. & Sherwood, Robert D. Microcomputers & Parents. (Education Ser.). 224p. 1983. pap. text ed. 8.50 (ISBN 0-471-87278-4). Wiley.
Grillo, John P. & Robertson, J. D. Data & File Management for the IBM Personal Computer. (Microcomputer Power Ser.). 240p. 1983. pap. write for info. (ISBN 0-697-09987-3); diskette avail. (ISBN 0-697-09988-1). Wm C Brown.
--Users Guide with Applications for the IBM Personal Computer. (Microcomputer Power Ser.). 330p. 1983. pap. write for info. (ISBN 0-697-09985-7); diskette avail. (ISBN 0-697-09986-5). Wm C Brown.
Grogono, Peter. Mouse: A Language for Microcomputers. (Illus.). 200p. 1983. text ed. 17.50 (ISBN 0-89433-201-5). Petrocelli.
Grosjean, Paul, ed. The Best of SYNC. 170p. 1983. pap. 9.95 (ISBN 0-916688-43-7). Creative Comp.
Hartley, Michael G. & Buckley, Anne, eds. Microelectronics & Microcomputer Applications. 200p. 1983. 15.00 (ISBN 0-7190-0905-7). Manchester.
Hartnell, Tim. The Timex Sinclair Two Thousand Explored. 218p. 1983. text ed. 14.95 (ISBN 0-471-89099-5). Wiley.
Hearn, D. Donald & Baker, M. Pauline. Microcomputer Graphics: Techniques & Applications. (Illus.). 272p. 1983. text ed. 24.95 (ISBN 0-13-580670-4); pap. text ed. 18.95 (ISBN 0-13-580662-3). P-H.
Henderson, Thomas. The Osborne Portable Computer. Cardona, Elizabeth & Noble, David, eds. LC 82-42766. 1983. pap. 12.95 (ISBN 0-88022-015-5). Que Corp.
Hergert, Douglas. Your Timex Sinclair 1000 & ZX81. 176p. 1982. pap. 6.95 (ISBN 0-89588-099-7). Sybex.
Hughes, Lawrence E. Data Communications for CP-M Based Micro-Computers. 1983. text ed. 21.95 (ISBN 0-8359-1229-9); pap. text ed. 15.95 (ISBN 0-8359-1228-0). Reston.
Introduction to Microcrocomputers: PET Set. 1982. 47.49 (ISBN 0-07-079225-9). McGraw.
Lamoitier, J. P. Basic Exercises for the IBM Personal Computer. LC 82-60234. (Illus.). 252p. (Orig.). 1982. pap. text ed. 13.95 (ISBN 0-89588-088-1). Sybex.
Leventhal, Lance. Microcomputer Experimentation with the Synertek SYM-1. (Illus.). 512p. 1983. text ed. 19.95 (ISBN 0-13-580910-X). P-H.
Lewis, R., ed. Involving Micros in Education: Proceedings of the IFIP TC 3 & University of Lancaster Joint Working Conference, Lancaster, England, March 24-26, 1982. 240p. 1982. 36.25 (ISBN 0-444-86459-8). Elsevier.
McGlynn, Daniel R. McGlynn's Simplified Guide to Small Computers for Business. 250p. 1983. 14.95 (ISBN 0-471-86853-1, Pub. by Wiley Interscience). Wiley.
McWilliams, Peter A. The Personal Computer Book. (Illus.). 289p. 1982. pap. 9.95 (ISBN 0-931580-90-0). Prelude Press.
Mau. Create Word Puzzles with Your Microcomputer. 14.95 (ISBN 0-686-82004-5, 6251). Hayden.
Microcomputer Aftermarkets. (Reports Ser.: No. 519). 191p. 1982. 985.00 (ISBN 0-686-38959-X). Intl Res Dev.
Miller, Inabeth, intro. by. Microcomputer Directory: Applications in Educational Settings. 2nd ed. 316p. 1982. 15.00 (ISBN 0-943484-00-6). Gutman Lib.
Modeling & Simulation on Microcomputers: 1983. 1983. softbound 20.00 (ISBN 0-686-38790-2). Soc Computer Sim.
Money, S. A. Microprocessor Data Book. (Illus.). 272p. 1982. 38.00 (ISBN 0-07-042706-2, P&RB). McGraw.
Mosher, Doug. Your Color Computer. 350p. 1983. pap. text ed. 12.95 (ISBN 0-89588-097-0). Sybex.
Muscat, E. & Lorton, P. Microcomputer Applications for the Data Processing Work Kit TRS-80 Diskette. 1982. 99.00 (ISBN 0-07-044107-3, G); wkkit 50.00 (ISBN 0-07-044108-1); user's guide 3.90 (ISBN 0-07-044109-X). McGraw.
Needleman, Theodore. Microcomputers for Accountants. (Illus.). 186p. 1983. 24.95 (ISBN 0-13-580696-8); pap. 14.95 (ISBN 0-13-580688-7). P-H.
North, Alan. Thirty-One New Atari Computer Programs for Home, School & Office. new ed. (Illus.). 96p. (Orig.). 1982. pap. 8.95 (ISBN 0-86668-018-7). ARCsoft.
Page, Edward. One Hundred Timex 1000-Sinclair ZX-81 Programming Tips & Tricks. new ed. 128p. (Orig.). (gr. 7-12). 1982. pap. 7.95 (ISBN 0-86668-020-9). ARCsoft.
--Thirty Seven Timex 1000-Sinclair ZX-81 Computer Programs for Home, School & Office. (Illus.). 96p. (Orig.). 1982. pap. 8.95 (ISBN 0-86668-021-7). ARCsoft.
Pasahow, E. J. Microcomputer Interfacing for Electronics Technicians. 1981. text ed. 13.95 (ISBN 0-07-048718-9); instr's manual avail. McGraw.
Pasakow, E. J. Microprocessors & Microcomputers for Electronics Technicians. 1981. text ed. 13.95 (ISBN 0-07-048713-8); instr's manual avail. McGraw.
Personal & Other Microcomputers. 1982. 1095.00 (E72). Predicasts.
Presley, Bruce. A Guide to Programming IBM Personal Computer. 173p. 1982. pap. 16.95 (ISBN 0-442-26015-6). Van Nos Reinhold.
Rafiquzzaman, Mohamed. Microprocessors & Microcomputer Development Systems: Designing Microprocessor-Based Systems. 640p. 1983. text ed. 26.50 scp (ISBN 0-06-045312-5, HarpC); instr's. manual avail. (ISBN 0-06-365303-6). Harper-Row.
Randall, Robert. Microcomputers in Small Business: How to Select & Implement Microcomputer Hardware in Your Small Business. (Illus.). 134p. 1983. 16.95 (ISBN 0-13-580753-0); pap. 8.95 (ISBN 0-13-580746-8). P-H.
Rony, Peter. Microcomputer Interfacing & Programming. 2nd ed. Date not set. pap. 17.95 (ISBN 0-672-21933-6). Sams.
Schofield, J. Microcumputer-Based Aids for the Disabled. 1981. pap. text ed. 29.95x (ISBN 0-471-87721-2, Pub. by Wiley Heyden). Wiley.
Sorger, T. J. Buying a Computer Micro-Mini or Main Frame. (Illus.). pap. 12.95 (ISBN 0-9604072-1-9). Sorger Assocs.
Spencer, Donald D. BASIC Workbook for Microcomputers. 1983. 7.95x (ISBN 0-89218-040-4). Camelot Pub.
Stewart, Ian & Jones, Robin. Timex Sinclair One-Thousand: Programs, Games, & Graphics. 100p. 1982. pap. 10.95 (ISBN 3-7643-3080-5). Birkhauser.
Swaay, Maarten V. & Lenhert, Donald H. Fundamentals of Microcomputers. 238p. 1982. looseleaf bound 49.95 (ISBN 0-935506-04-7). Carnegie Pr.
Titus, Jonathan & Larsen, David. Eighty Eighty A Cookbook. 1980. pap. 15.95 (ISBN 0-672-21697-3). Sams.
Troutner, Joanne J. The Media Specialist, The Microcomputer, & the Curriculum. 175p. 1983. lib. bdg. 19.50 (ISBN 0-87287-367-6). Libs Unl.
Trueblood, Mark & Genet, Russell M. Microcomputer Control of Telescopes. LC 82-84768. 220p. (Orig.). 1983. pap. 24.95 (ISBN 0-911351-02-7). Fairborn Observ.
Weber, Jeffrey R. User's Guide to the Timex-Sinclair ZX-81. (WSI's How to Use Your Microcomputer Ser.). 280p. (Orig.). 1983. pap. cancelled (ISBN 0-938862-27-8). Weber Systems.
Webster, Tony. Microcomputer Buyer's Guide. 2nd ed. (Illus.). 352p. 1983. pap. text ed. 19.95 (ISBN 0-07-068959-8, P&RB). McGraw.
White, Fred. One Hundred & One Apple Computer Programming Tips & Tricks. new ed. 128p. (Orig.). 1982. pap. 8.95 (ISBN 0-86668-015-2). ARCsoft.
--Thirty-Three New Apple Computer Programs for Home, School & Office. new ed. (Illus.). 96p. (Orig.). 1982. pap. 8.95 (ISBN 0-86668-016-0). ARCsoft.
Whitehouse, Gary, et al. IIE Microsoftware: Economic Analysis. 1981. 140.00, 175.00 non-members (ISBN 0-89806-013-3). Inst Indus Eng.
--IIE Microsoftware: Production Control. 1981. 140.00, 175.00 non-members (ISBN 0-89806-012-5). Inst Indus Eng.
--IIE Microsoftware: Project Management. 1981. 140.00, 175.00 non-members (ISBN 0-89806-030-3). Inst Indus Eng.
--IIE Microsoftware: Work Measurement. 1982. 140.00, 175.00 non-members (ISBN 0-89806-035-4). Inst Indus Eng.
Wild, Victor. Your Fortune in the Microcomputer Business: Getting Started, Vol. I. (Illus.). 304p. 1982. pap. 15.95 (ISBN 0-938444-04-2). Wildfire Pub.
--Your Fortune in the Microcomputer Business: Growth, Survival, Success, Vol. II. (Illus.). 256p. 1982. pap. 15.95 (ISBN 0-938444-05-0). Wildfire Pub.
Zimmerman, Steven & Conrad, Leo. Business Applications for the IBM Personal Computer. (Illus.). 224p. 1983. 16.95 (ISBN 0-89303-243-3). R J Brady.
--Osborne User's Guide: Applications & Programming. (Illus.). 264p. 1982. text ed. 19.95 (ISBN 0-89303-207-7); pap. 14.95 (ISBN 0-89303-206-9). R J Brady.
--Pocket Computer Users Guide for the TRS-80TM, PC-1, & Sharp 1211. (Microcomputer Power Ser.). 192p. 1983. pap. write for info. (ISBN 0-697-09980-6). Wm C Brown.
Zumchak, Eugene. Microcomputer Design & Troubleshooting. Date not set. pap. 17.95 (ISBN 0-672-21819-4). Sams.

MICROECONOMICS

see also Managerial Economics

Awh, Robert Y. Microeconomics: Theory & Applications. LC 75-38643. 492p. 1976. text ed. 30.95x (ISBN 0-471-03849-0); wkbk., micro 11.95x (ISBN 0-471-03853-9); tchrs. manual avail. (ISBN 0-471-03854-7). Wiley.
Champsaur, Paul & Milleron, Jean-Claude. Advanced Exercises in Microeconomics. Bonin, John P. & Bonin, Helene, trs. from Fr. (Illus.). 272p. 1983. text ed. 27.50x (ISBN 0-674-00525-2). Harvard U Pr.
Fischer, S. & Dornbusch, R. Introduction to Microeconomics. 640p. 1983. 15.95 (ISBN 0-07-021006-3). McGraw.
Jhigan, M. L. Micro Economic Theory. 2nd ed. 775p. 1982. text ed. 45.00x (ISBN 0-7069-1803-7, Pub. by Vikas India). Advent NY.
Mansfield, Edwin. Principles of Microeconomics: Readings, Issues & Cases. 4th ed. 1982. text ed. write for info. (ISBN 0-393-95331-9); write for info. tchr's manual (ISBN 0-393-95273-8); write for info. study guide (ISBN 0-393-95334-3); write for info. test item file. Norton.
Miller, Norman C. Microeconomics. 750p. 1983. text ed. 23.95 (ISBN 0-395-32579-X); write for info. instr's manual (ISBN 0-395-32580-3); study guide 8.95 (ISBN 0-395-32581-1). HM.
Salvatore, D. Schaum's Outline of Microeconomic Theory. 2nd ed. 336p. 1983. 7.95 (ISBN 0-07-054514-6). McGraw.
Scott, Robert H. & Nigro, Nic. Principles of Microeconomics. 516p. 1982. pap. text ed. 18.95 (ISBN 0-02-408370-4). Macmillan.
--Principles of Microeconomics. 516p. 1982. pap. 18.95 (ISBN 0-02-408370-4). Macmillan.

MICROELECTRONICS

see also Integrated Circuits; Printed Circuits

Hartley, Michael G. & Buckley, Anne, eds. Microelectronics & Microcomputer Applications. 200p. 1983. 15.00 (ISBN 0-7190-0905-7). Manchester.
Microelectronics Eighty Two: First Microelectronics Conference. 143p. (Orig.). 1982. pap. text ed. 37.50x (ISBN 0-85825-166-3, Pub. by Inst Engineering Australia). Renouf.

MICROELEMENTS

see Trace Elements

MICROENCAPSULATION

Ferguson, Mary H. Microencapsulation: Selected Papers from the Fourth Internation Symposium on Microencapsulation. 44p. 1981. pap. text ed. 13.50 (ISBN 0-917330-42-0). Am Pharm Assn.

MICROFILM

Information Roundup: Microfilm & Data Processing for the Library & Information Center. (Proceedings of the 4th ASIS Mid-Year Meeting, 1975) 1975. 14.00 (ISBN 0-686-42891-9). Knowledge Indus.
Thomas Register Guide to the Microfilm Collection: 1905-1938. 30p. 1982. 25.00 (ISBN 0-89235-072-5). Res Pubns Conn.

MICROGRAPHIC ANALYSIS

see Metallography; Microscope and Microscopy

MICROMINIATURIZATION (ELECTRONICS)

see Microelectronics

MICRO-ORGANISMS

see also Bacteria; Fungi; Microbiology; Microscope and Microscopy; Protozoa; Soil Micro-Organisms; Viruses

Austin, C. R. & Short, R. V., eds. Germ Cells & Fertilization. 2nd ed. LC 81-18060. (Reproduction in Mammals Ser.: No. 1). (Illus.). 180p. 1982. 24.50 (ISBN 0-521-24628-8); pap. 11.95 (ISBN 0-521-28861-4). Cambridge U Pr.
Marshall, K. C. Advances in Microbial Ecology, Vol. 6. 252p. 1982. 39.50x (ISBN 0-306-41064-8, Plenum Pr). Plenum Pub.

MICRO-ORGANISMS, PATHOGENIC

see also Medical Microbiology

Roberts, T. A., et al, eds. Psychrotrophic Microorganisms in Spoilage & Pathogenicity. LC 81-67902. 552p. 1982. 49.50 (ISBN 0-12-589720-0). Acad Pr.

MICROPALEONTOLOGY

Saito, T. & Burckle, L. H., eds. Late Neogene Epoch Boundaries. (Micropaleontology Special Publications Ser.: No. 1). 224p. 1975. 20.00 (ISBN 0-686-84248-0). Am Mus Natl Hist.

MICROPROCESSORS

Alexandridis, Nikitas. Microprocessor Systems Architecture & Engineering. 1983. text ed. p.n.s. (ISBN 0-914894-66-8). Computer Sci.
Buchbaum, W. H. & Mauro, R. Microprocessor-Based Electronic Games. 304p. 1983. 9.95 (ISBN 0-07-008722-9). McGraw.
Byers, T. J. Microprocessor Support Chips: Theory, Design, & Applications. (Illus.). 300p. 1983. 38.00 (ISBN 0-07-009518-3, P&RB). McGraw.
CES Industries, Inc. Staff. Microprocessor: Student Guide. (Ed-Lab Experiment Manual Ser.). (Illus.). (gr. 9-12). 1981. write for info. lab manual (ISBN 0-86711-018-X). CES Industries.
--Microprocessors. (ED-Lab Experiment Manual Ser.). (Illus.). (gr. 9-12). write for info. lab manual (ISBN 0-86711-022-8). CES Industries.
--Microprocessors Concepts, Unit 1. (Ed-Lab Experiment Manual Ser.). (Illus.). (gr. 9-12). 1981. lab manual 9.50 (ISBN 0-86711-021-X). CES Industries.
Coffron, James W. & Long, William E. Practical Interfacing Techniques for Microprocessor Systems. (Illus.). 432p. 1983. 26.95 (ISBN 0-13-691394-6). P-H.
Foulger, R. J. Programming Embedded Microprocessors: A High-Level Language Solution. (Illus.). 240p. (Orig.). 1982. pap. 28.00x (ISBN 0-85012-336-4). Intl Pubns Serv.
Hall, D. V. Microprocessors & Digital Systems. 1980. text ed. 24.50 (ISBN 0-07-025571-7); instr's. manual & key avail. McGraw.
Hall, Douglas V. Microprocessors & Digital Systems. 2nd ed. (Illus.). 480p. 1983. 22.05 (ISBN 0-07-025552-0, G). McGraw.

Hall, Douglas V. & Hall, Marybelle B. Experiments in Microprocessors & Digital Systems. 2nd ed. (Illus.). 192p. 1983. 10.95x (ISBN 0-07-025553-9, Gregg). McGraw.
Hartley, M. G. & Buckley, A., eds. Challenge of Microprocessors. 208p. 1979. 18.50 (ISBN 0-7190-0757-7). Manchester.
Hayes, J. P. Digital System Design Using Microprocessors. 656p. 1982. 24.95x (ISBN 0-07-027367-7). McGraw.
Heathkit-Zenith Educational Systems. Microprocessors. 407p. 1983. 21.95 (ISBN 0-13-581074-4); pap. 14.95 (ISBN 0-13-581082-5). P-H.
Lane, J. E. Microprocessors & Information Handling. (Computing in the Eighties Ser.). 67p. 1981. pap. 15.00x (ISBN 0-85012-334-8). Intl Pubns Serv.
Leahy, William F. Microprocesor Architecture & Programming. LC 77-1552. 252p. Repr. of 1977 ed. text ed. 29.95 (ISBN 0-471-01889-9). Krieger.
Microprocessor Systems, 1980. 107p. (Orig.). 1980. pap. text ed. 37.50x (ISBN 0-85825-147-7, Pub. by Inst Engineering Australia). Renouf.
Microprocessor Systems, 1981. 120p. (Orig.). 1981. pap. text ed. 37.50x (ISBN 0-85825-160-4, Pub. by Inst Engineering Australia). Renouf.
Money, S. A. Microprocessor Data Book. (Illus.). 272p. 1982. 38.00 (ISBN 0-07-042706-2, P&RB). McGraw.
Morse. The Eighty Eighty-Six to Eighty Eighty-Eight Primer: An Introduction to Their Architecture, System Design, & Programming. 2nd ed. Date not set. 10.95 (ISBN 0-686-82002-9, 6255). Hayden.
Paker, Yacup, ed. Multi-Microprocessor Systems. Date not set. price not set (ISBN 0-12-543980-6). Acad Pr.
Parr. Beginners Guide to Microprocessors. 1982. text ed. 9.95 (ISBN 0-408-00579-3). Butterworth.
Pasakow, E. J. Microprocessors & Microcomputers for Electronics Technicians. 1981. text ed. 13.95 (ISBN 0-07-048713-8); instr's manual avail. McGraw.
Rafiquzzaman, Mohamed. Microprocessors & Microcomputer Development Systems: Designing Microprocessor-Based Systems. 640p. 1983. text ed. 26.50 scp (ISBN 0-06-045312-5, HarpC); instr's. manual avail. (ISBN 0-06-365303-6). Har-Row.
Texas Instruments Engineering Staff. Sixteen Bit Microprocessor Systems. (Illus.). 592p. 1982. 45.00 (ISBN 0-07-063760-1, P&RB). McGraw.
Zarrella, John. Designing with the 8088 Microprocessor. 180p. (Orig.). 1983. pap. write for info. (ISBN 0-935230-07-6). Microcomputer Appns.
Zissos, ed. System Design with Microprocessors. 2nd ed. Date not set. price not set; pap. price not set (ISBN 0-12-781740-9). Acad Pr.

MICROSCOPE AND MICROSCOPY
see also Electron Microscope; Histology; Microbiology; Micropaleontology; Microscopy, Medical; Photomicrography; Stains and Staining (Microscopy)
Ayres, Ronald F. VLSI Design: Silicon Compilation & the Art of Automatic Microchip Design. (Illus.). 496p. 1983. text ed. 39.95 (ISBN 0-13-942680-9). P-H.
International Micrographics Source Book: A Worldwide Source for Every Important Service & Equipment Category. 350p. 1982. 59.50 (ISBN 0-686-82571-3). Knowledge Indus.
Parson. Short Wave Length Microscopy, Vol. 306. 1978. 45.00 (ISBN 0-89072-062-2). NY Acad Sci.

MICROSCOPIC ANALYSIS
see Metallography; Microscope and Microscopy

MICROSCOPIC ANATOMY
see Histology

MICROSCOPIC ORGANISMS
see Micro-Organisms

MICROSCOPY, MEDICAL
Locquin. Handbook of Microscopy. 1982. text ed. 119.95 (ISBN 0-408-10679-4). Butterworth.
Trump, B. F. & Jones, R. T. Diagnostic Electron Microscopy, Vol. 1. (Diagnostic Electron Microscopy Ser.). 346p. 1978. text ed. 65.00 (ISBN 0-471-89196-7, Pub. by Wiley Med). Wiley.

MICROWAVE COMMUNICATION SYSTEMS
see also Radiotelephone
EUROMICRO Symposium on Microprocessing & Microprogramming, 8th, 1982. Microsystems: Architecture, Integration & Use. Van Spronsen, C. J. & Richter, L., eds. 375p. 1982. 59.75 (ISBN 0-444-86470-9, North Holland). Elsevier.

MICROWAVE COOKERY
Better Homes & Gardens Books editors, ed. Better Homes & Gardens Microwave Plus Cook Book. (Illus.). 96p. 1983. 5.95 (ISBN 0-696-00850-5). Meredith Corp.
Caloric Microwave Cookbook. 1982. write for info (ISBN 0-87502-105-0). Benjamin Co.
Durkee, Jean K. Tout de Suite: A la Microwave, 2 vols. Incl. Vol. I. French, Acadian & Creole Recipes, Delicious, Nutrious & Colorful. (Illus.). 224p. 1977. write for info; Mexican, Italian & French Recipes Tested & Tasted by the Author. (Illus.). 232p. 1982. write for info.. (Illus.): 224p. 1977. Tout de Suite.
--Tout de Suite a la Microwave I. LC 77-93096. (Illus.). 224p. 1977. plastic comb bdg. 9.95 (ISBN 0-9605362-0-5). Tout de Suite.
--Tout de Suite a la Microwave II. LC 80-53827. (Illus.). 236p. 1980. plastic comb bdg. 9.95 (ISBN 0-9605362-1-3). Tout de Suite.
Farm Journal's Food Editors. Farm Journal's Country-Style Microwave Cookbook 2. LC 82-12025. 128p. (Orig.). 1982. pap. 3.95 (ISBN 0-89795-014-3). Farm Journal.
Microwave Cook Book. pap. 5.95 (ISBN 0-696-01035-6). Meredith Corp.
More from Your Microwave. pap. 5.95 (ISBN 0-686-43159-6). Meredith Corp.
Vahey, Esther J. Micro Wave the Easy Way Vol. II. (Audio Cassette Cooking School Library). 16p. 1982. pap. text ed. 12.95x. Cuisine Con.
Weale, Margaret. The Slimmer's Microwave Cookbook. (Illus.). 120p. (Orig.). 1983. 17.50 (ISBN 0-7153-8392-2). David & Charles.

MICROWAVE DEVICES
see also Microwave Communication Systems
Allan, Thomas D. Satellite Microwave Remote Sensing. (Marine Science Ser.). 450p. 1983. 110.00 (ISBN 0-470-27397-6). Halsted Pr.
Gordy, W. & Cook, L., eds. Microwave Molecular Spectra. (Technique of Organic Chemistry Ser.: Vol.9, Pt.2). 747p. Repr. of 1970 ed. text ed. 67.50 (ISBN 0-471-93161-6). Krieger.
Helszajn, J. Nonreciprocal Microwave Junctions & Circulators. LC 75-5588. 370p. Repr. of 1975 ed. text ed. 34.95 (ISBN 0-471-36935-7). Krieger.
Steneck, N. H., ed. Risk-Benefit Analysis: The Microwave Case. LC 82-50313. (Illus.). 1982. 15.00 (ISBN 0-911302-44-1). San Francisco Pr.

MIDDLE AGE
see also Aging; Climacteric; Longevity
Conway, Sally. You & Your Husband's Mid-Life Crisis. 1982. pap. 2.50 (ISBN 0-451-11560-0, AE1560, Sig). NAL.
How To Avoid Mid-Life Crisis. (Blank Books Ser.). 128p. 1982. cancelled (ISBN 0-939944-10-3). Marmac Pub.
Maitland, David. Against the Grain: Coming through Mid-Life Crises. 208p. 1981. pap. 8.95 (ISBN 0-8298-0675-X). Pilgrim NY.
Middle & Late Life Transitions. LC 82-61685. (The Annals of the American Academy of Political & Social Science: Vol. 464). 1982. 15.00 (ISBN 0-8039-1932-8); pap. 10.00 (ISBN 0-8039-1933-6). Sage.
Natow, A. B. & Heslin, J. Nutrition for the Prime of Your Life. 352p. 1983. 17.95 (ISBN 0-07-028414-8, GB). McGraw.

MIDDLE AGE AND EMPLOYMENT
see Age and Employment

MIDDLE AGES-HISTORIOGRAPHY
Sterns, Indrikis, ed. The Greater Medieval Historians: A Reader. LC 82-15919. 472p. (Orig.). 1983. lib. bdg. 30.50 (ISBN 0-8191-2752-3); pap. text ed. 17.25 (ISBN 0-8191-2753-1). U Pr of Amer.

MIDDLE AGES-HISTORY
see also Chivalry; Civilization, Medieval; Europe-History-476-1492; Feudalism; Fifteenth Century; Fourteenth Century; Holy Roman Empire; Monasticism and Religious Orders; Twelfth Century
Allmand. War, Literature, & Politics in the Late Middle Ages. 216p. 1982. 50.00x (ISBN 0-85323-273-3, Pub. by Liverpool Univ England). State Mutual Bk.
Cummins, Patricia W. Literary & Historical Perspectives of the Middle Ages. 232p. 1982. 8.00 (ISBN 0-937058-15-7). West Va U Pr.
Heyworth, P. L., ed. Medieval Studies for J. A. W. Bennett: Aetatis suae LXX. (Illus.). 438p. 1981. 65.00x (ISBN 0-19-812628-X). Oxford U Pr.
Shatzmiller, Maya. L'Historiographie Merinde: Ibn Khaldun et ses Contemporains. (Illus.). xii, 163p. 1982. write for info. (ISBN 90-04-06759-0). E J Brill.
Shulvass, Moses A. The History of the Middle Ages, 2 Vols. Incl. Vol. 1. The Antiquity (ISBN 0-89526-660-1); Vol. 2. The Early Middle Ages (ISBN 0-89526-842-6). LC 81-85564. 19.95 ea. Regnery-Gateway.
Wood, Charles T. The Quest for Eternity: Medieval Manners & Morals. LC 82-40476. (Illus.). 176p. 1983. pap. 8.95 (ISBN 0-87451-259-X). U Pr of New Eng.

MIDDLE ATLANTIC STATES
Weiner, Neal O. & Schwartz, David M. The Interstate Gourmet: Mid-Atlantic States, Vol. 2. (Illus.). 256p. 1983. pap. 5.95 (ISBN 0-671-44993-1). Summit Bks.

MIDDLE CLASSES
see also Proletariat
Confidence Men & Painted Women: A Study of Middle-Class Culture in America, 1830-1870. (Yale Historical Publications Misc.: No. 129). 19.95 (ISBN 0-686-42811-0). Yale U Pr.
Halttunen, Karen. Confidence Men & Painted Women: A Study of Middle-Class Culture in America, 1830-1870. LC 82-8336. (Yale Historical Publications Misc.: No. 129). (Illus.). 280p. 1983. text ed. 19.95x (ISBN 0-300-02835-0). Yale U Pr.
Lowe, Donald M. History of Bourgeois Perception. LC 81-7529. (Illus.). x, 226p. 1982. pap. 6.95 (ISBN 0-226-49429-2). U of Chicago Pr.

MIDDLE EAST
see Near East

MIDDLE ENGLISH
see English Language-Middle English, 1100-1500; English Literature (Collections)-Middle English (1100-1500)

MIDGES
see Diptera

MIDRASH-FOLK-LORE
see Folk-Lore, Jewish

MIDWAY, BATTLE OF, 1942
Prange, G. W. Miracle at Midway. Goldstein, D. M. & Dillon, K. V., eds. (New Press Ser.). 416p. 1982. 24.95 (ISBN 0-07-050672-8). McGraw.

MIDWIFERY
see Obstetrics

MIDWIVES
Butler, Barbara M. The Evolution of the Black Nurse Midwife. 64p. 1983. 5.50 (ISBN 0-682-49966-8). Exposition.
Dammann, Nancy. A Social History of the Frontier Nursing Service. (Illus.). 179p. (Orig.). 1982. pap. 5.95 (ISBN 0-9609376-0-9). Soc Change Pr.
Ojo, O. A. & Briggs, Enang. Textbook for Midwives in the Tropics. 480p. 1982. pap. text ed. 18.95 (ISBN 0-7131-4413-0). E Arnold.

MIGRAINE
Geist, Harold. Migraine: Psychological, Psychiatric & Physiological Aspects. LC 82-26856. 1983. text ed. 11.50 (ISBN 0-89874-601-9). Krieger.
Kohlenberg, Robert J. Migraine Relief: A Personal Treatment Program. 1983. pap. write for info. (ISBN 0-06-091026-7, CN-1026). Har-Row.
Wentworth, Josie A. Migraine Prevention Cookbook. LC 82-45277. (Illus.). 216p. 1983. 13.95 (ISBN 0-385-18052-7). Doubleday.

MIGRANT LABOR
see also Migration, Internal
Safety & Health of Migrant Workers: International Symposium. 337p. 1982. 14.95 (ISBN 92-2-001906-X). Intl Labour Office.

MIGRATION, INTERNAL
see also Cities and Towns-Growth; Emigration and Immigration
Webb, John N. & Brown, Malcolm. Migrant Families. LC 76-165605. (Research Monograph Ser.: Vol. 18). (Illus.). xxx, 192p. 1971. Repr. of 1938 ed. lib. bdg. 25.00 (ISBN 0-306-70350-5). Da Capo.

MIGRATION, JEWISH
see Jews-Migrations

MIGRATION OF INSECTS
see Insects-Migration

MIGRATORY WORKERS
see Migrant Labor

MILITARISM
see also Disarmament; Imperialism; Military Service, Compulsory
Carlton, David & Schaerf, Carlo, eds. The Arms Race in the Nineteen Eighties. LC 81-21303. 256p. 1982. 27.50x (ISBN 0-312-04946-3). St Martin.
Soelle, Dorothee. The Arms Race Kills Even Without War. LC 82-48543. 128p. 1983. pap. 6.95 (ISBN 0-8006-1701-0). Fortress.

MILITARY AIRPLANES
see Airplanes, Military

MILITARY ART AND SCIENCE
see also Air Warfare; Armaments; Armed Forces; Armies; Arms and Armor; Atomic Warfare; Attack and Defense (Military Science); Biological Warfare; Civil Defense; Disarmament; Fortification; Industrial Mobilization; Naval Art and Science; Psychological Warfare; Scouts and Scouting; Signals and Signaling; Soldiers; Spies; Strategy; Tank Warfare; Veterans; War; War Games
also headings beginning with the word Military
Bothe, M. & Partsch, K. J. New Rules for Victims of Armed Conflict. 1982. lib. bdg. 145.00 (ISBN 90-247-2537-2, Pub. by Martinus Nijhoff Netherlands). Kluwer Boston.
Dunnigan, James F. How to Make War: A Comprehensive Guide to Modern Warfare. rev., upd. ed. (Illus.). 444p. 1983. pap. 7.95 (ISBN 0-688-01975-7). Quill NY.
Hogg, Ian & Weeks, John, eds. Jane's 1982-83 Military Annual. (Illus.). 158p. 1982. 15.95 (ISBN 0-86720-633-0). Sci Bks Intl.
Johnson, Sandee S. Cadences: The Jody Call Book, No. 1. 180p. (Orig.). 1983. lib. bdg. 10.95 (ISBN 0-938936-13-1). Daring Pr.
Kaplan, Larry. Infantry: Cumulative Index by Author, Title, & Subject. 30.00 (ISBN 0-89126-111-7). MA AH Pub.
Keegan, John. The Face of Battle. 1983. pap. 5.95 (ISBN 0-14-004897-9). Penguin.
Langford, David. War in Two Thousand Eighty: The Future of Military Technology. (Illus.). 232p. 1983. Repr. of 1979 ed. 16.50 (ISBN 0-7153-7661-6). David & Charles.
Lider, Julien. Military Theory: Concept, Structure, Problems. LC 82-734. 426p. 1982. 35.00x (ISBN 0-312-53240-7). St Martin.
Malone, Dandridge M. Small Unit Leadership. (Illus.). 160p. (Orig.). 1983. pap. 8.95 (ISBN 0-89141-173-9). Presidio Pr.
Mitre Corp. Military Communications System Control Symposium. 1980. 60.00 (ISBN 0-686-38472-5). Info Gatekeepers.
Nunn, Frederick M. Yesterday's Soldiers: European Military Professionalism in South America, 1890-1940. LC 82-6961. xiv, 358p. 1983. 26.95x (ISBN 0-8032-3305-1). U of Nebr Pr.
Yarmolinsky, Adam & Foster, Gregory D. Paradoxes of Power: The Military Establishment in the Eighties. LC 82-48523. 160p. 1983. 15.00x (ISBN 0-253-34291-0). Ind U Pr.

MILITARY ART AND SCIENCE-DICTIONARIES
Pretz, Bernhard. Dictionary of Military Technological Abbreviations & Acronyms. 450p. 1983. price not set. Routledge & Kegan.

MILITARY ART AND SCIENCE-EARLY WORKS TO 1800
Caesar, Julius. The Conquest of Gaul. rev. ed. Handford, S. A., tr. 1983. pap. 3.95 (ISBN 0-14-044433-5). Penguin.

MILITARY ART AND SCIENCE-HISTORY
Childs, John. Armies & Warfare in Europe, 1648-1789. 208p. 1982. text ed. 22.50x (ISBN 0-8419-0820-6). Holmes & Meier.
The History of Army Command & General Staff. write for info. Sunflower U Pr.

MILITARY BIOGRAPHY
see also Generals
Reed, Thomas S. A Profile of Brigadire General Alfred N. A. Duffie. 1982. 11.00 (ISBN 0-89126-109-5). MA AH Pub.

MILITARY CAREER
see Military Service As a Profession

MILITARY-CIVIL RELATIONS
see Militarism; Military Policy

MILITARY COMPENSATION
see Pensions, Military

MILITARY COSTUME
see Uniforms, Military

MILITARY DRAFT
see Military Service, Compulsory

MILITARY EDUCATION
Anderson, Fred A. The Complete PFE Study Reference. 96p. (Orig.). 1983. pap. 15.95 (ISBN 0-939570-01-7). Skills Improvement.

MILITARY EQUIPMENT, SUPPLIES, ETC.
see Military Supplies; Uniforms, Military
The Official 1984 Price Guide to Military Collectibles. 1st ed. LC 82-84650. 240p. 1983. pap. 2.95 (ISBN 0-87637-378-3). Hse of Collectibles.

MILITARY HEALTH
McNeil, John S. & Wright, Roosevelt, Jr. Military Retirement: Socio-Economic & Mental Health Dilemmas. 220p. 1983. text ed. 24.95x (ISBN 0-86598-078-0). Allanheld.

MILITARY HISTORY
see also Military Art and Science-History; Military Biography; Military Policy; Naval History
also subdivisions History, or History, military under names of countries, e.g. United States-History, Military; particuliar wars, battles, sieges, etc.; also France-Army; United States-Army, and similar headings
Jendricke, Bernhard. Die Nachkriegszeit Im Spiegel der Satire. 388p. (Ger.). 1982. write for info. (ISBN 3-8204-6268-6). P Lang Pubs.
Knox, Donald. Death March: The Survivors of Bataan. (Illus.). 512p. pap. 8.95 (ISBN 0-15-625224-4, Harv). HarBraceJ.
Militaria. (What's It Worth Ser.). Date not set. pap. 2.95 (ISBN 0-686-82601-9). Dell.

MILITARY LIFE
see Soldiers

MILITARY MUSIC
see also Band Music
also subdivision Songs and Music under names of wars, e.g. United States-History-Civil War, 1861-1865-Songs and Music
Johnson, Sandee S. Cadences: The Jody Call Book, No. 1. 180p. (Orig.). 1983. lib. bdg. 10.95 (ISBN 0-938936-13-1). Daring Pr.

MILITARY PENSIONS
see Pensions, Military

MILITARY PERSONNEL
see Soldiers

MILITARY POLICY
see also Deterrence (Strategy); Militarism
also subdivision Military Policy under names of countries, e.g. United States-Military Policy
Arlingaus, Bruce E. Military Development in Africa: Political & Economic Risks of Arms Transfers. (Special Studies on Africa). 175p. 1983. lib. bdg. 23.50 (ISBN 0-86531-434-9). Westview.
Gooch, John & Perlmutter, Amos, eds. Military Deception & Strategic Surprise. 200p. 1982. text ed. 30.00x (ISBN 0-7146-3202-3, F Cass Co). Biblio Dist.
Harries-Jenkins, Gwyn. Armed Forces & the Welfare Societies: Challenges in the 1980's. LC 82-10500. 256p. 1982. 27.50x (ISBN 0-312-04926-9). St Martin.
Quade, E. Analysis for Military Decisions. 1970. 34.25 (ISBN 0-444-10014-8). Elsevier.

MILITARY POWER
see Air Power; Armies; Disarmament; Military Art and Science; Navies

MILITARY RECONNAISSANCE
see also Scouts and Scouting
Drendel, Lou. SR-Seventy-One Blackbird in Action. (Illus.). 50p. 1982. 4.95 (ISBN 0-89747-136-9, 1055). Squad Sig Pubns.

MILITARY RESEARCH
see also Research; Research and Development Contracts

Sanders, Ralph. International Dynamics of Technology. LC 82-9220. (Contributions in Political Science Ser.: No. 87). 352p. 1983. lib. bdg. 35.00 (ISBN 0-313-23401-9, SAD/). Greenwood.

MILITARY SCHOOLS
see Military Education

MILITARY SCIENCE
see Military Art and Science

MILITARY SERVICE, COMPULSORY
see also Conscientious Objectors; also subdivisions Recruiting, etc. under armies, e.g. United States–Army–Recruiting, etc.

Goodpoaster, Andrew J. & Elliott, Lloyd H. Toward a Consensus on Military Service. 70p. 1982. pap. 6.00x (ISBN 0-686-43306-8). Transaction Bks.

Ward, R. E. May I Kill You? Draft-Dodging & Military Escape Stories, A Collection. (Illus.). 156p. (Orig.). 1982. pap. 5.00 (ISBN 0-9610280-1-7). Reward Pub.

MILITARY SERVICE, VOLUNTARY
see also subdivision Recruting, enlistment, etc. under armies, navies, etc., e.g. United States-Army-Recruiting, enlistment, etc.

Goodpoaster, Andrew J. & Elliott, Lloyd H. Toward a Consensus on Military Service. 70p. 1982. pap. 6.00x (ISBN 0-686-43306-8). Transaction Bks.

MILITARY SERVICE AS A PROFESSION

Bradley, Jeff. A Young Person's Guide to Military Service. 160p. 1983. 11.95 (ISBN 0-916782-31-X); pap. 5.95 (ISBN 0-916782-32-8). Harvard Common Pr.

Gordon, Susan. Your Career in the Military. (Arco's Career Guidance Ser.). (Illus.). 128p. 1983. lib. bdg. 7.95 (ISBN 0-668-05502-2); pap. 4.50 (ISBN 0-668-05511-1). Arco.

Meiers, Steve, ed. Basic Training: A Consumer's Guide to the Military. 52p. 1982. pap. 2.95 (ISBN 0-942046-00-5). Prog Found.

MILITARY SIGNALING
see Signals and Signaling

MILITARY SOCIOLOGY
see Sociology, Military

MILITARY STAFFS
see Armies–Staffs

MILITARY STRATEGY
see Military Art and Science; Strategy

MILITARY SUPPLIES

Foss, Christopher, ed. Jane's Military Vehicles & Ground Support Equipment, 1983. (Jane's Yearbooks Ser.). (Illus.). 700p. 1983. 140.00x (ISBN 0-86720-647-0). Sci Bks Intl.

Jane's Military Vehicles & Ground Support Equipment, 1982. (Jane's Yearbooks). (Illus.). 600p. 140.00 (ISBN 0-86720-600-4). Sci Bks Intl.

Kemp, Anthony & Haythornthwaite, Philip. Weapons & Equipment Series, 3 vols. (Illus.). 525p. 1982. boxed set 50.00 (ISBN 0-7137-1296-1, Pub. by Blandford Pr England). Sterling.

MILITARY TRAINING
see Military Education

MILITARY TRAINING, UNIVERSAL
see Military Service, Compulsory

MILITARY UNIFORMS
see Uniforms, Military

MILITARY VEHICLES
see Vehicles, Military

MILK
see also Cheese; Cookery (Dairy Products)

Robinson, R. K. Dairy Microbiology, Vol. 1: The Microbiology of Milk. 1981. 43.00 (ISBN 0-85334-948-7, Pub. by Applied Sci England). Elsevier.

--Dairy Microbiology, Vol. 2: The Microbiology of Milk Products. 1981. 51.25 (ISBN 0-85334-961-4, Pub. by Applied Sci England). Elsevier.

MILK GLASS
see Glassware

MILK PRODUCTS
see Dairy Products

MILK SUBSTITUTES
see Food Substitutes

MILLAY, EDNA ST. VINCENT, 1892-1950

Brittin, Norman A. Edna St. Vincent Millay. Rev. ed. (United States Authors Ser.). 1982. lib. bdg. 12.95 (ISBN 0-8057-7362-2, Twayne). G K Hall.

MacDougall, Allan R., ed. Letters of Edna St. Vincent Millay. 384p. pap. 7.95 (ISBN 0-89272-152-9). Down East.

MILLENNIUM
see also Second Advent

Bryant, M. Darrol & Dayton, Donald, eds. The Coming Kingdom: Essays in American Millennialism & Eschatology. (Conference Ser.: No. 16). 1983. pap. text ed. write for info. (ISBN 0-932894-16-X). Unif Theol Seminary.

MILLING MACHINERY
Here are entered works on machinery used in the process of grinding, etc.
see also Flour Mills; Mills and Mill-Work

Milling: Methods & Machines. LC 82-61032. 254p. 1982. 32.00 (ISBN 0-87263-110-9). SME.

MILLS (BUILDINGS)
see Factories; Flour Mills

MILLS AND MILL-WORK
see also Windmills

Weiss, Norman. Memoirs of a Millman, Vol. 1. 245p. 1982. text ed. 12.00 (ISBN 0-686-43344-0). Maywood Pub.

MILTON, JOHN, 1563-1647?

Corns, Thomas N. The Development of Milton's Prose Style. (English Monographs). 132p. 1982. 19.95x (ISBN 0-19-811717-5). Oxford U Pr.

Foot, Isaac. John Milton, Selections from His Works & Tributes to His Genius. 151p. 1982. Repr. of 1935 ed. lib. bdg. 65.00 (ISBN 0-89987-279-4). Darby Bks.

MILTON, JOHN, 1608-1674

Martz, Louis. The Paradise Within: Studies in Vaughan, Traherne, & Milton. 236p. 1983. pap. 7.95x (ISBN 0-300-00164-9). Yale U Pr.

Wilson, A. N. The Life of John Milton. 320p. 1983. 19.95 (ISBN 0-19-211776-9). Oxford U Pr.

MILTON, JOHN, 1608-1674–CRITICISM AND INTERPRETATION

Ide, Richard S. & Wittreich, Joseph, eds. Milton Studies, Vol. XVII: Composite Orders: The Genres of Milton's Last Poems. LC 69-12335. 340p. 1983. 29.95x (ISBN 0-8229-3473-6). U of Pittsburgh Pr.

Simmonds, James D., ed. Milton Studies, Vol. 16. LC 69-12335. (Illus.). vi, 199p. 1983. 17.95x (ISBN 0-8229-3465-5). U of Pittsburgh Pr.

Woodhouse, A. S. Milton: The Poet. 1982. lib. bdg. 34.50 (ISBN 0-686-81933-0). Porter.

MILTON, JOHN, 1608-1674–PARADISE LOST

Davies, Stevie. Images of Kinship in "Pardise Lost". Milton's Politics & Christian Liberty. LC 82-17485. 256p. 1983. text ed. 21.00x. U of Mo Pr.

McColley, Diane K. Milton's Eve. (Illus.). 1983. 17.50 (ISBN 0-252-00980-0). U of Ill Pr.

MIND
see Intellect; Psychology

MIND AND BODY
see also Body, Human; Consciousness; Dreams; Faith-Cure; Hypnotism; Medicine, Psychosomatic; Mental Healing; Mental Suggestion; Nervous System; Personality, Disorders of; Psychoanalysis; Psychology, Pathological; Self; Sleep; Subconsciousness; Temperament

Genzlinger, Anna L. The Jessup Dimension. 164p. 1981. pap. 9.95 (ISBN 0-911306-28-5). G Barker Bks.

Holmes, Ernest & Holmes, Fenwicke. Voice Celestial. (Illus.). 352p. Date not set. pap. 11.95 (ISBN 0-911336-70-2). Sci of Mind.

Holmes, Ernest & Smith, Alberta. Questions & Answers on the Science of Mind. 192p. 1981. pap. write for info. (ISBN 0-911336-88-5). Sci of Mind.

Shirly, Hunter B. Mapping the Mind. (Illus.). 376p. 1983. text ed. 27.95 (ISBN 0-911012-19-2). Nelson-Hall.

Stortz, Margaret R. Start Living Every Day of Your Life: How to Use the Science of Mind. 96p. 1981. pap. 2.95 (ISBN 0-911336-87-7). Sci of Mind.

MIND-CURE
see Faith-Cure; Mental Healing; Mind and Body

MIND-DISTORTING DRUGS
see Hallucinogenic Drugs

MINE VENTILATION

Hartman, Howard L., ed. Proceedings, First Mine Ventilation Symposium. LC 82-71996. (Illus.). 312p. 1982. 22.00x (ISBN 0-89520-298-0). Soc Mining Eng.

MINERAL COLLECTING
see Mineralogy–Collectors and Collecting

MINERAL INDUSTRIES
see also Ceramics; Metallurgy; Mines and Mineral Resources; Mining Engineering also specific types of mines and mining, e.g. Coal Mines and Mining

Banks, Ferdinand E. Resources & Energy: An Economic Analysis. LC 81-47967. 368p. 1983. 34.95x (ISBN 0-669-05203-5). Lexington Bks.

Gorton, Richard K. Underground Mine Accounting. 57p. (Orig.). 1982. pap. 19.95 (ISBN 0-686-37986-1). Advance Pr.

Guidebook to Finland Tour, 1977 Prospecting Symposium. 48p. 1977. 14.50 (ISBN 0-686-38290-0). IMM North Am.

Johnson, T. B. & Barnes, R. J., eds. Application of Computers & Operations in the Mineral Industry: 17th International Symposium. LC 82-70016. (Illus.). 806p. 1982. text ed. 35.00x (ISBN 0-89520-293-X). Soc Mining Eng.

Jones, M. J. & Oblatt, R., eds. Tours Guidebook, Eleventh CMMC. 76p. (Orig.). 1978. pap. text ed. 21.75x (ISBN 0-900488-40-9). IMM North Am.

Report of IMM Mission to China. 1980. 72.00 (ISBN 0-686-38294-3). IMM North Am.

MINERAL LANDS
see Mines and Mineral Resources

MINERAL OILS–LAW AND LEGISLATION
see Petroleum Law and Legislation

MINERAL RESOURCES
see Mines and Mineral Resources

MINERALOGICAL CHEMISTRY

Seyferth, D. & King, R., eds. Annual Surveys of Organometallic Chemistry, Vols. 1-3. 1965-68. 38.50 ea. Vol. 1, 1964 (ISBN 0-444-40527-5). Vol. 2, 1965 (ISBN 0-444-40528-3). Vol. 3, 1966 (ISBN 0-444-40529-1). Elsevier.

MINERALOGY
see also Crystallography; Gems; Meteorites; Mineralogical Chemistry; Petrology; Rocks also names of minerals, e.g. Feldspar, Quartz

Dietrich, R. V. & Wicander, E. Reed. Rocks, Minerals & Fossils. (Self-Teaching Guides Ser.). 288p. 1983. pap. text ed. 9.95 (ISBN 0-471-89883-X). Wiley.

Hey, M. H. & Embry, P. G. An Index of Mineral Species & Varieties Arranged Chemically with an Alphabetical Index of Accepted Mineral Names & Synonyms. 2nd ed. 1975. 62.50x set (ISBN 0-686-37456-8). Index (ISBN 0-565-00097-7) (ISBN 0-565-00578-2) (ISBN 0-565-00725-4). Sabbot-Natural Hist Bks.

O'Donoghue. Beginners Guide to Minerals. 1983. text ed. 9.95. Butterworth.

Picot, P. & Johan, Z. Atlas of Ore Minerals. (Illus.). 406p. Date not set. 170.25 (ISBN 0-444-99684-2). Elsevier.

Szekely, Edmond B. The Book of Minerals. (Illus.). 40p. 1978. pap. 2.95 (ISBN 0-89564-046-5). IBS Intl.

MINERALOGY–COLLECTING OF SPECIMENS
see Mineralogy–Collectors and Collecting

MINERALOGY–COLLECTORS AND COLLECTING

Brocardo, G. Minerals & Gemstones: An Identification Guide. (Illus.). 220p. (gr. 6 up). 1983. 12.95 (ISBN 0-88254-756-9). Hippocrene Bks.

MINERALOGY–JUVENILE LITERATURE

Marcus, Elizabeth. Rocks & Minerals. LC 82-17424. (Question & Answer Bks.). (Illus.). 32p. (gr. 3-6). 1983. PLB 8.59 (ISBN 0-89375-876-0); pap. text ed. 1.95 (ISBN 0-89375-877-9). Troll Assocs.

MINERALS
see Mineralogy; Mines and Mineral Resources

MINERALS IN PLANTS
see Plants–Assimilation

MINERALS IN THE BODY

Altura, B. M. & Altura, Bella T., eds. Dietary Minerals & Cardiovascular Disease. (Journal: Magnesium: Vol. 1, No. 3-6). (Illus.). vi, 178p. 1983. pap. 78.00 (ISBN 3-8055-3682-8). S Karger.

MINERS

Cullins, Warren & Cullins, Laura. Zeballos, Its Gold Its People Yesterday & Today: An Historical Documentation. (Orig.). 1982. pap. 9.75 (ISBN 0-9608386-0-0). Cullins.

MINERS' NYSTAGMUS
see Nystagmus

MINES AND MINERAL RESOURCES
see also Mineralogy; Mining Engineering; Mining Geology; Precious Metals; Prospecting; Raw Materials also specific types of mines and mining, e.g. Coal Mines and Mining, Gold Mines and Mining

Brooks, R. R. Biological Methods of Prospecting for Minerals. 325p. 1983. price not set (ISBN 0-471-87400-0, Pub. by Wiley-Interscience). Wiley.

Concise World Atlas of Geology & Mineral Deposits. 110p. 1982. 52.00x (ISBN 0-900117-28-1, Pub. by Mining Journal England). State Mutual Bk.

The Infrared Spectra Handbook of Minerals & Clays. 1982. 225.00 (ISBN 0-686-84522-6). Sadtler Res.

Jobson's Mining Year Book, 1982. 25th ed. LC 66-2200. (Illus.). 491p. 1982. 105.00x (ISBN 0-8002-3052-3). Intl Pubns Serv.

Kuhner, David & Rizzo, Tania, eds. Biblioteca De Re Metallica: The Herbert Clark Hoover Collection of Mining & Metallurgy. LC 80-82055. (Illus.). 219p. 1980. 125.00 (ISBN 0-937368-00-8). Honnold Lib.

Li, Ta M., intro. by. Mineral Resources of the Pacific Rim. LC 82-71990. (Illus.). 229p. (Orig.). 1982. pap. 30.00x (ISBN 0-89520-299-9, 299-9). Soc Mining Eng.

Nightingale, William G., ed. Mining International Yearbook 1982. 95th ed. LC 50-18583. 687p. 1982. 92.50 (ISBN 0-582-90311-4). Intl Pubns Serv.

Proceedings of the Working Group Meeting on Enviornmental Management in Mineral Resource Development. (Mineral Resources Development Ser.: No. 49). 141p. 1983. pap. 12.00 (ISBN 0-686-43283-5, UN 82/2F9, UN). Unipub.

Van der Marel, R. & Beutelspacher, H. Atlas of Infrared Spectroscopy of Clay Minerals & Their Admixtures. 1976. 106.50 (ISBN 0-444-41187-9). Elsevier.

Vokes, F. M., ed. Mineral Deposits of Europe: Vol. 1-Northwest Europe. 362p. 1979. 86.25x (ISBN 0-900488-44-1). IMM North Am.

Westwood, W. & Cooper, B. S. Analytical Methods in Use in Non-Ferrous Mining & Metallurgy: A Selective Review. 54p. (Orig.). 1973. 14.50 (ISBN 0-900488-17-4). IMM North Am.

Wolle, Muriel S. Montana Pay Dirt: A Guide to the Mining Camps of the Treasure State. LC 63-14650. (Illus.). 436p. 1983. Repr. of 1963 ed. 29.95 (ISBN 0-8040-0210-X, 82-71421). Ohio U Pr.

MINES AND MINERAL RESOURCES–DICTIONARIES

Verbic, S. Yugoslavin Mining Dictionary: English-Serbo-English. 527p. 1981. pap. text ed. 25.00x (ISBN 0-89918-783-8). Vanous.

MINES AND MINERAL RESOURCES–ASIA

Report of IMM Mission to China. 1980. 72.00 (ISBN 0-686-38294-3). IMM North Am.

MINES AND MINERAL RESOURCES–AUSTRALIA

Birrell, Robert & Hill, Douglas, eds. Quarry Australia? Social & Environmental Perspectives on Managing the Nations Resources. (Illus.). 384p. 1982. text ed. 44.00x (ISBN 0-686-84066-6). Oxford U Pr.

Jones, M. J. & Oblatt, R., eds. Tours Guidebook, Eleventh CMMC. 76p. (Orig.). 1978. pap. text ed. 21.75x (ISBN 0-900488-40-9). IMM North Am.

MINES AND MINERAL RESOURCES–CANADA

MacDowell, Laurel S. Remember Kirkland Lake: The Gold-Miners' Strike of 1941-42. (The State & Economic Life Ser.). 308p. 1983. 30.00x (ISBN 0-8020-5585-0); pap. 12.50 (ISBN 0-8020-6457-4). U of Toronto Pr.

MINES AND MINERAL RESOURCES–EUROPE

Dunning, F. W. & Mykura, W., eds. Mineral Deposits of Europe: Vol. 2-Southeast Europe. 304p. 1981. text ed. 100.00x (ISBN 0-900488-63-8). IMM North Am.

MINES AND MINERAL RESOURCES–SOUTH AMERICA

Becker, David G. The New Bourgeoisie & the Limits of Dependency: Mining, Class, & Power in "Revolutionary" Peru. LC 82-61352. 368p. 1983. 35.00x (ISBN 0-691-07645-6); pap. 9.95 (ISBN 0-691-02213-5). Princeton U Pr.

MINES AND MINERAL RESOURCES–UNITED STATES

Collins, Edward W. Geological Circular 82-3: Surficial Evidence of Tectonic Activity & Erosion Rates, Palestine, Keechi, & Oakwood Salt Domes, East Texas. (Illus.). 39p. 1982. 1.75 (ISBN 0-686-37547-5). U of Tex Econ Geology.

Digerness, David S. The Mineral Belt: Georgetown, Mining, Colorado Central Railroad, Vol. III. (Illus.). 416p. 49.00 (ISBN 0-686-84503-X). Sundance.

Dobie, J. Frank. Coronado's Children: Tales of Lost & Buried Treasures of the Southwest. 367p. 1982. Repr. of 1931 ed. lib. bdg. 50.00 (ISBN 0-89987-170-4). Darby Bks.

Galloway, William E. & Henry, Christopher D. Report of Investigations No. 113: Depositional Framework, Hydrostratigraphy, & Uranium Mineralization of the Oakville Sandstone (Miocene), Texas Coastal Plain. (Illus.). 51p. 1982. 2.50 (ISBN 0-686-37542-4). U of Tex Econ Geology.

Levine, Brian. Cities of Gold: History of the Victor-Cripple Creek Mining District. (Illus.). pap. 6.95 (ISBN 0-937080-09-8). Century One.

Smith, Duane A. Song of the Hammer & Drill: The Colorado San Juans, 1860-1914. Raese, Jon W. & Goldberg, J. H., eds. (Illus.). 194p. 1982. 28.95 (ISBN 0-918062-49-7). Colo Sch Mines.

Tewalt, Susan J., et al. Geological Circular 82-2: Detailed Evaluation of Two Texas Lignite Deposits of Fluvial & Deltaic Origins. (Illus.). 12p. 1982. Repr. 1.00 (ISBN 0-686-37546-7). U of Tex Econ Geology.

MINES AND MINING
see Mineral Industries; Mines and Mineral Resources; Mining Engineering

MINI COMPUTERS
see Minicomputers

MINIATURE CAR RACING
see Model Car Racing

MINIATURE COMPUTERS
see Minicomputers

MINIATURE HOUSES
see Doll-Houses

MINIATURE TREES
see Bonsai

MINIATURES (ILLUMINATION OF BOOKS AND MANUSCRIPTS)
see Illumination of Books and Manuscripts

MINICOMPUTERS
see also Microcomputers; Microprocessors

Behrendt, Bill. Pocket Magic. 96p. 1982. 17.95 (ISBN 0-13-683847-2); pap. 9.95 (ISBN 0-13-683839-1). P-H.

Krutch, John. Experiments in Artificial Intelligence for Small Computers. 1981. pap. 8.95 (ISBN 0-672-21785-6). Sams.

Librach, Hank. Pocket Computer Primer. 96p. 1982. 17.95 (ISBN 0-13-683862-6); pap. 9.95 (ISBN 0-13-683854-5). P-H.

Porochnia, Leonard. The Minicomputer: To Buy or Not to Buy. 122p. pap. 12.95 (ISBN 0-86641-085-6, 82134). Natl Assn Accts.

Sorger, T. J. Buying a Computer Micro-Mini or Main Frame. (Illus.). pap. 12.95 (ISBN 0-9604072-1-9). Sorger Assocs.

MINIMA
see Maxima and Minima

MINIMUM WAGE
see Wages–Minimum Wage

MINING
see Mineral Industries; Mines and Mineral Resources; Mining Engineering

MINING, ELECTRIC
see Electricity in Mining

MINING ENGINEERING
see also Boring; Electricity in Mining; Mine Ventilation; Petroleum Engineering; Strip Mining; Tunnels and Tunneling

Chugh, Y. P., intro. by. State-of-the-Art of Ground Control in Longwall Mining & Mining Subsidence. LC 82-71991. (Illus.). 271p. (Orig.). 1982. pap. text ed. 38.00x (ISBN 0-89520-400-2, 400-2). Soc Mining Eng.

Gomez, Manuel, ed. Radiation Hazards in Mining: Control, Measurement, & Medical Aspects. LC 81-70691. (Illus.). 1105p. 1982. 58.00x (ISBN 0-89520-290-5). Soc Mining Eng.

Hustrulid, William H., ed. Underground Mining Methods Handbook. LC 80-70416. (Illus.). 1754p. 1982. 120.00x (ISBN 0-89520-049-X). Soc Mining Eng.
Kratzsch, H. Mining Subsidence Engineering. Fleming, R. F., tr. from Ger. (Illus.). 580p. 1983. 59.00 (ISBN 0-387-11930-2). Springer-Verlag.
Marple, V. A. & Liu, B. Y. H., eds. Aerosol In the Mining & Industrial Work Environments: Fundamentals & Status, 3 vol. set, Vol. 1. LC 82-70701. (Illus.). 360p. 1983. 37.50 (ISBN 0-250-40531-8); Set. 93.75 (ISBN 0-250-40533-4). Ann Arbor Science.
--Aerosols In the Mining & Industrial Work Environments: Characterization, 3 vol. set, Vol. 2. LC 82-70701. (Illus.). 283p. 1983. 18.75 (ISBN 0-250-40532-6); Set. 93.75 (ISBN 0-250-40533-4). Ann Arbor Science.
--Aerosols In the Mining & Industrial Work Environment: Instrumentation, 3 Vols, Vol. 3. LC 82-70701. (Illus.). 500p. 1983. 37.50 (ISBN 0-250-40597-0). Ann Arbor Science.
Metal Structures in the Mining, Gas & Oil Industries: Metal Stuctures Conferences, 1978. 114p. (Orig.). 1978. pap. text ed. 31.50 (ISBN 0-85825-104-3, Pub. by Inst Engineering Australia). Renouf.
Mular, Andrew L. & Jergensen, Gerald V., III, eds. Design & Installation of Communication Circuits. LC 82-71992. (Illus.). 1022p. 1982. 40.00x (ISBN 0-89520-401-0). Soc Mining Eng.
North, Oliver S. Mineral Exploration, Mining, & Processing Patents, 1980. (Illus.). 135p. 1982. 35.00x (ISBN 0-89520-294-8). Soc Mining Eng.
Proceedings, Annual Uranium Seminar, No.5. LC 81-71601. (Illus.). 187p. 1982. pap. text ed. 20.00x (ISBN 0-89520-291-3). Soc Mining Eng.
Schlitt, W. J., intro. by. Interfacing Technologies in Solution Mining. LC 82-71423. (Illus.). 370p. (Orig.). 1982. pap. 30.00 (ISBN 0-89520-295-6, 295-6). Soc Mining Eng.
Schlitt, W. J. & Larson, W. C., eds. Gold & Silver Leaching, Recovery & Economics. LC 81-68558. (Illus.). 148p. 1981. pap. text ed. 20.00x (ISBN 0-89520-289-1). Soc Mining Eng.

MINING GEOLOGY

Baumgardner, Robert W., et al. Report of Investigations No. 114: The Wink Sink, a Salt Dissolution & Collapse Feature, Winker County, Texas. (Illus.). 38p. 1982. 1.50 (ISBN 0-686-37544-0). U of Tex Econ Geology.
Galloway, William E. & Henry, Christopher D. Report of Investigations No. 113: Depositional Framework, Hydrostratigraphy, & Uranium Mineralization of the Oakville Sandstone (Miocene), Texas Coastal Plain. (Illus.). 51p. 1982. 2.50 (ISBN 0-686-37542-4). U of Tex Econ Geology.
Lacy, Willard C., ed. Mining Geology. LC 82-968. (Benchmark Papers in Geology: Vol. 69). 480p. 1983. 58.00 (ISBN 0-87933-426-6). Hutchinson Ross.
Riordon, P. H. & Hollister, V. F., eds. Geology of Asbestos Deposits. LC 80-52898. (Illus.). 118p. (Orig.). 1981. pap. 32.00x (ISBN 0-89520-277-8, 277-8). Soc Mining Eng.
Silver, Burr A. Exploration Geology. 1982. 43.00 (ISBN 0-89419-253-1). Inst Energy.

MINING MACHINERY

see also Electricity in Mining
Clark, J., et al. Thin Seam Coal Mining Technology. LC 82-7968. (Energy Tech. Rev. 80). (Illus.). 385p. 1983. 36.00 (ISBN 0-8155-0909-X). Noyes.
Martin, James W. & Martin, Thomas J. Surface Mining Equipment. LC 82-81951. (Illus.). 450p. 1982. 77.00 (ISBN 0-9609060-0-2). Martin Consult.

MINISTERS (DIPLOMATIC AGENTS)

see Ambassadors; Diplomatic and Consular Service

MINISTERS OF RELIGIOUS EDUCATION

see Directors of Religious Education

MINISTERS OF THE GOSPEL

see Clergy

MINISTRY

see Church Work; Clergy–Office; Pastoral Theology

MINISTRY, URBAN

see City Clergy

MINNEAPOLIS

Martin, Judith A. & Lanegran, David. Where We Live: The Residential Districts of Minneapolis & St. Paul. LC 82-11064. (Illus.). 144p. 1983. 29.50x (ISBN 0-8166-1093-2); pap. 14.95 (ISBN 0-8166-1094-0). U of Minn Pr.
Waldemar, Carla. Dining In--Minneapolis-St. Paul, Vol. II. (Dining In--Ser.). 210p. 1982. pap. 8.95 (ISBN 0-89716-120-3). Peanut Butter.

MINNESOTA–DESCRIPTION AND TRAVEL

Johnston, Patricia C. Pretty Red Wing, Minnesota Rivertown. (Illus.). 96p. (Orig.). 1983. price not set (ISBN 0-942934-28-8); pap. price not set (ISBN 0-942934-27-X). Johnston Pub.
Spadaccini, Victor M. & Whiting, Karen L. Minnesota Pocket Data Book 1983-1984. 300p. (Orig.). 1983. pap. 24.95 (ISBN 0-911493-00-X). Blue Sky.

MINNESOTA–DESCRIPTION AND TRAVEL–GUIDEBOOK

Blakely, Roger. North From Duluth: Tourist & Hiking Guide for Minnesota's North Shore. LC 81-83882. (Illus.). 96p. 1981. pap. 10.00. New Rivers Pr.
Buchanan, James W. Minnesota Walk Book: A Guide to Hiking & Cross-Country Skiing In the Viking-Land Region, Vol. VI. (Walk Book Ser.). (Illus.). 64p. 1982. pap. 4.50 (ISBN 0-931714-19-2). Nodin Pr.
Bufhanan, James W. Minnesota Walk Book: A Guide to Backpacking & Hiking in the Arrowhead & Isle Royale, Vol. 1. Reprint ed. 105p. 1982. pap. 4.50 (ISBN 0-931714-02-8). Nodin Pr.

MINOR PROPHETS

see Prophets

MINOR SURGERY

see Surgery, Minor

MINORITES

see Franciscans

MINORITIES

see also Discrimination; Jews–Diaspora; Nationalism; Population Transfers; Race Discrimination; Race Relations; Segregation; Self-Determination, National also names of individual races of peoples, e.g. Chinese in Foreign Countries; Germans in the United States; also subdivisions Foreign Population and Race relations under names of countries, cities, etc.
Coyle, Dominick J. Minorities in Revolt. LC 81-65866. (Illus.). 256p. 1982. 28.50 (ISBN 0-8386-3120-7). Fairleigh Dickinson.
Hapgood, Hutchins. The Spirit of the Ghetto. Rischin, Moses, ed. (Illus.). 360p. 1983. pap. 7.95x (ISBN 0-674-83266-3, Belknap Pr). Harvard U Pr.
Johnston, Jerom, et al. An Evaluation of Freestyle: A Television Series to Reduce Sex-Role Stereotypes. 308p. 1980. pap. 16.00 (ISBN 0-87944-256-5). Inst Soc Res.
Josey, E. J. & DeLoach, Marva L., eds. Ethnic Collections in Libraries. 1983. 24.95 (ISBN 0-918212-63-4). Neal-Schuman.
Siegel, Mark A. & Jacobs, Nancy R., eds. Minorities: A Changing Role in American Society. rev. ed. (Instructional Aides Ser.). 88p. 1982. pap. text ed. 11.95 (ISBN 0-936474-25-4). Instruct Aides TX.
Stanford, E. P. & Lockery, Shirley, eds. Trends & Status of Minority Aging, Vol. 8. (Proceedings of the Institute on Minority Aging). 150p. (Orig.). 1982. pap. 10.00 (ISBN 0-916304-57-4). Campanile.

MINORITIES–EDUCATION

Appleton, Nicholas & Benevento, Nicole. Cultural Pluralism in Education: Theoretical Foundations. (Illus.). 288p. (Orig.). 1983. pap. text ed. 12.95 (ISBN 0-582-28233-0). Longman.
Clements, Zacharie J. & Burrell, Leon F. I Want to Make It: A Primer for Minority Students & Others Who Want to be Successful in College. LC 82-50564. 125p. (Orig.). (gr. 7-12). 1983. pap. 5.95 (ISBN 0-88247-686-6). R & E Res Assoc.
Ortiz, Flora I. Career Patterns in Education: Women, Men & Minorities in Public School Administration. (Illus.). 224p. 1981. 22.95x (ISBN 0-686-84384-3). J F Bergin.
Weinberg, Meyer. The Search for Quality Integrated Education: Policy & Research on Minority Students in School & College. LC 82-12016. (Contributions to the Study of Education: No. 7). (Illus.). 320p. 1983. lib. bdg. 35.00 (ISBN 0-313-23714-X, LC214). Greenwood.

MINORITIES–EMPLOYMENT

see also Affirmative Action Programs
Hill, Robert B. Occupational Attainment: Minorities & Women in Selected Industries, 1969-1979. 150p. 1983. pap. 6.95 (ISBN 0-87855-606-0). Transaction Bks.
Johnson, Willis L., ed. Directory of Special Programs for Minority Group Members: Career Information, Service, Employment Skills Banks, Financial Aid Services. 612p. 1980. 19.95. Impact VA.

MINORITIES–SOCIAL CONDITIONS

Burgest, David R. Social Work Practice with Minorities. LC 81-14461. 322p. 1982. text ed. 16.50 (ISBN 0-8108-1476-5). Scarecrow.
Chunn, Jay, II & Dunston, Patricia, eds. Mental Health & People of Color: Curriculum Development & Change. (Illus.). 688p. 1983. 24.95 (ISBN 0-88258-097-3). Howard U Pr.
Fair, Martha H. Tools for Survival: A Positive Action Plan for Minorities & Women. (Illus.). 160p. (Orig.). Date not set. pap. 12.95 (ISBN 0-911181-00-8). Harris Learning.
Orque, Modesta S. & Bloch, Bobbie. Ethnic Nursing Care: A Multi-Cultural Approach. (Illus.). 414p. 1983. pap. text ed. 14.95 (ISBN 0-8016-3742-2). Mosby.

MINORITIES–GREAT BRITAIN

British Family Research Committee. Families in Britain. 350p. 1983. pap. 25.00 (ISBN 0-7100-9236-9). Routledge & Kegan.

MINORS (LAW)

see Children–Law

MINSTREL SHOWS

see Musical Revues, Comedies, etc.

MIRACLE-PLAYS

see Mysteries and Miracle-Plays

MIRACLES

see also Jesus Christ–Miracles; Supernatural
Galloway, Dale E. Expect a Miracle. 1982. pap. 4.95 (ISBN 0-8423-0822-9). Tyndale.
Rogo, Scott D. Miracles: A Parascientific Inquiry into Wondrous Phenomena. (Illus.). 352p. 1982. pap. 9.95 (ISBN 0-8092-5596-0). Contemp Bks.
Theissen, Gerd. The Miracle Stories of the Early Christian Tradition. Riches, John, ed. McDonagh, Francis, tr. LC 82-48546. 416p. 1983. text ed. 27.95 (ISBN 0-8006-0700-7). Fortress.

MIRO, JOAN, 1893-

Lanchner, Carolyn & Rosenstock, Laura. Four Modern Masters: De Chirico, Ernst, Magritte, & Miro. (Illus.). 122p. 1982. pap. 14.95 (ISBN 0-686-83914-5, 28738-6). U of Chicago Pr.

MIRRORS

Masterson, Keith & Solar Energy Research Institute. Matrix Approach for Testing Mirrors, Pt. 2. (Progress in Solar Energy Ser.: Suppl.). 125p. 1983. pap. 13.00x (ISBN 0-89553-133-X). Am Solar Energy.

MISCARRIAGE

see Abortion

MISCEGENATION

Here are entered works on marriage between persons of different races, especially between whites and Afro-Americans, and on the resulting mixture or hybridity of races.
see also Marriage, Mixed
Sundquist, Eric J. Faulkner: The House Divided. LC 82-8923. 256p. 1983. 16.95q (ISBN 0-8018-2898-8). Johns Hopkins.

MISDEMEANORS (LAW)

see Criminal Law

MISHNAH

Neusner, Jacob. Ancient Israel after Catastrophe: The Religious World View of the Mishnah. LC 82-15972. 1983. write for info. (ISBN 0-8139-0980-5). U Pr of Va.

MISREPRESENTATION (LAW)

see Fraud

MISSILES, GUIDED

see Guided Missiles

MISSING PERSONS

Jaeger, Marietta. The Lost Child. 128p. 1983. pap. 4.95 (ISBN 0-310-45811-0). Zondervan.

MISSIOLOGY

see Missions–Theory

MISSION OF THE CHURCH

Here are entered works on the chief objective and responsibility of the church as viewed in its entirety. Works on missionary work are entered under Missions.
see also Church and the World; Missions
Glasser, Arthur F. & McGavran, Donald A. Contemporary Theologies of Mission. 320p. (Orig.). 1983. pap. 12.95 (ISBN 0-8010-3790-5). Baker Bk.

MISSIONARIES

Bennett, Adrian A. Missionary Journalist in China: Young J. Allen & His Magazines, 1860-1883. LC 81-19761. (Illus.). 336p. text ed. 28.00x (ISBN 0-8203-0615-0). U of Ga Pr.
Koll, Elsie. The Golden Thread: Diary of Mrs. Elsie Koll, Missionary to China. SCales, John L., ed. (Illus.). 180p. (Orig.). 1982. pap. 4.95 (ISBN 0-942504-00-3). Overcomer Pr.
Neely, Lois. Fire in His Bones. 1982. pap. 6.95 (ISBN 0-8423-0869-5). Tyndale.
Shenk, Wilbert R. Henry Venn: Missionary Statesman. LC 82-18779. 192p. (Orig.). 1983. pap. 9.95 (ISBN 0-88344-181-0). Orbis Bks.

MISSIONARIES–CORRESPONDENCE, REMINISCENCES, ETC.

Fitch, Janet. Foreign Devil: Reminiscences of a China Missionary Daughter, 1909-1935. (Asian Library Ser.: No. 39). 1982. 28.75x (ISBN 0-686-37543-2). Oriental Bk Store.
Smith, John C. From Colonialism to World Community: The Church's Pilgrimage. LC 82-12138. 1982. pap. 8.95 (ISBN 0-664-24452-1). Westminster.
Taylor, Norman. God-Given Promises: Meet Every Need. LC 82-61861. 152p. pap. 3.95 (ISBN 0-87808-192-5). William Carey Lib.

MISSIONARY EDUCATION

see Missions–Study and Teaching

MISSIONS

see also Communication (Theology); Evangelistic Work; Missionaries; Salvation Army also subdivision Missions under names of churches, denominations, religious orders, etc. e.g. Church of England–Missions; Jesuits–Missions; Lutheran Church–Missions; Spanish Missions of California
Bennett, Gordon H. & Vedder, Eugene P., Jr. Missions Guidebook. (Illus.). 284p. 1983. write for info. (ISBN 0-942504-12-7); pap. write for info. (ISBN 0-942504-13-5). Overcomer Pr.
Episcopal Church Center. The Work You Give Us to Do: A Mission Study. 179p. (Orig.). 1982. pap. 4.95 (ISBN 0-8164-7116-9); study guide 1.25 (ISBN 0-8164-7117-7). Seabury.
Gilliland, Dean S. Pauline Theology & Mission Practice. 304p. 1983. pap. 12.95 (ISBN 0-8010-3788-3). Baker Bk.
Smith, John C. From Colonialism to World Community: The Church's Pilgrimage. LC 82-12138. 1982. pap. 8.95 (ISBN 0-664-24452-1). Westminster.

MISSIONS–BIBLICAL TEACHING

Senior, Donald & Stuhlmueller, Carroll. The Biblical Foundations for Mission. LC 82-22430. 368p. (Orig.). 1983. 25.00 (ISBN 0-88344-046-6); pap. 14.95 (ISBN 0-88344-047-4). Orbis Bks.

MISSIONS–STUDY AND TEACHING

Kauffman, Richard A. Pilgrimage in Mission Study Guide. 60p. 1983. pap. 4.95 (ISBN 0-8361-1260-1). Herald Pr.

MISSIONS–THEORY

DuBose, Francis M. God Who Sends. 1983. 9.95 (ISBN 0-8054-6331-3). Broadman.

MISSIONS–AFRICA

Keim, Curtis A. & Brown, Howard. Missions in Africa: Relevant or Relic? A Conference. (African Humanities Ser.). 89p. (Orig.). 1980. pap. text ed. 5.00 (ISBN 0-941934-30-6). Ind U Afro-Amer Arts.
Kenya Mission Team. Church Planting, Watering & Increasing in Kenya. Humble, B. J., ed. (Illus.). 130p. 1981. pap. 2.95 (ISBN 0-88027-002-0). Firm Foun Pub.

MISSIONS–CHINA

Koll, Elsie. The Golden Thread: Diary of Mrs. Elsie Koll, Missionary to China. SCales, John L., ed. (Illus.). 180p. (Orig.). 1982. pap. 4.95 (ISBN 0-942504-00-3). Overcomer Pr.
Taylor, Alice H. Rescued from the Dragon. 199p. (Orig.). 1982. pap. 5.25 (ISBN 0-89367-078-2). Light & Life.

MISSIONS–JAPAN

Bollinger, Edward E. The Cross & the Floating Dragon: The Gospel in Ryukyu. (Illus.). 368p. 1983. pap. 10.95 (ISBN 0-87808-190-9). William Carey Lib.

MISSIONS–RUSSIA

Jackson, J. H. The Eternal Flame: The Story of a Preaching Mission in Russia. 1956. 2.50 (ISBN 0-686-42985-0). Townsend Pr.
--Many But One: The Ecumenics of Charity. LC 64-19899. 1964. 4.50 (ISBN 0-686-42984-2). Townsend Pr.

MISSIONS, CITY

see City Missions

MISSIONS, INDIAN

see Indians of North America–Missions

MISSIONS TO JEWS

Cohen, Martin A. & Croner, Helga, eds. Christian Mission-Jewish Mission. 224p. pap. 7.95 (ISBN 0-8091-2475-0). Paulist Pr.

MISSISSIPPI–HISTORY

Ericson, Carolyn & Ingmire, Frances, eds. First Settlers of the Mississippi Territory, 2 vols. LC 82-83848. 110p. (Orig.). pap. 19.50 (ISBN 0-911317-07-4). Ericson Bks.
McCarthy, Kenneth G., Jr., ed. Hattiesburg: A Pictorial History. LC 82-10868. (Illus.). 240p. 1982. 25.00 (ISBN 0-87805-169-4). U Pr of Miss.

MISSISSIPPI–POLITICS AND GOVERNMENT

Hudlin, Richard A. & Brimah, K. Farouk. State of Mississippi's Procurement Policies & Minority Business Enterprises. 1981. 1.00 (ISBN 0-686-38010-X). Voter Ed Proj.

MISSISSIPPI VALLEY–ANTIQUITIES

Morse, Dan F. & Morse, Phyllis A., eds. Archaeology of the Central Mississippi Valley. LC 82-22734. (New World Archaeological Record). Date not set. price not set (ISBN 0-12-508180-4). Acad Pr.

MISSISSIPPI VALLEY–DESCRIPTION AND TRAVEL

Galloway, Patricia K., ed. La Salle & His Legacy: Frenchmen & Indians in the Lower Mississippi Valley. LC 82-17498. 274p. 1982. 20.00x (ISBN 0-87805-171-6). U Pr of Miss.

MISSOURI–DESCRIPTION AND TRAVEL

Stein, Shifra. Day Trips: Gas-Saving Getaways Less Than Two Hours from Greater Kansas City. (Illus.). 96p. 1980. pap. 4.50 (ISBN 0-9609752-0-9). S Stein Prods.
--Discover Kansas City: A Guide to Unique Shops, Services & Businesses. (Illus.). 1981. pap. 7.95 (ISBN 0-9609752-1-7). S Stein Prods.

MISTAKES

see Errors

MITCHELL, MARGARET, 1900-1949

Edwards, Anne. The Road to Tara: The Life of Margaret Mitchell. LC 82-19520. (Illus.). 384p. 1983. 15.95 (ISBN 0-89919-169-X). Ticknor & Fields.
Harwell, Richard, ed. Gone With the Wind as Book & Film. (Illus.). 300p. 1983. 19.95 (ISBN 0-686-82616-7). U of SC Pr.

MITES

Hoy, Marjorie. Recent Advances in Knowledge of the Phytoseiidae. (Illus.). 100p. (Orig.). 1983. pap. 7.00x (ISBN 0-931876-62-1). Ag Sci Pubns.

MITOSIS

Sakai, Hikoichi & Mohri, Hideo, eds. Biological Functions of Microtubules & Related Structure: Proceedings, 13th Oji International Seminar, Tokyo, Japan, December, 1981. LC 82-11609. 1982. 32.00 (ISBN 0-12-615080-X). Acad Pr.

MITRAL VALVE–DISEASES

see Heart–Diseases

MITTENS

see Gloves

MIXED CYCLOIDS (CHEMISTRY)

see Heterocyclic Compounds

MIXED MARRIAGE

see Marriage, Mixed

MIXTEC LITERATURE–HISTORY AND CRITICISM
Parmenter, Ross. Four Lienzos of the Coixtlahuaca Valley. (Studies in Pre-Columbian Art & Archaeology: No. 26). (Illus.). 88p. 1982. pap. 12.00x (ISBN 0-88402-109-2). Dumbarton Oaks.

MO-PEDS
see Mopeds

MOBILE, ALABAMA
Langley, Michael. Protection of Minority Political Participation Abadoned in Supreme Court's Ruling on Mobile Elections. 1980. 1.00 (ISBN 0-686-38004-5). Voter Ed Proj.

MOBILE HOME LIVING
Buchanan, J. Consumers Guide to Mobile Home Living. 1982. pap. 3.50 (ISBN 0-918734-32-0). Reymont.
Peterson, Kay. Home is Where You Park It. Rev. ed. (Illus.). 200p. 1982. pap. 7.95 (ISBN 0-910449-00-7). Roving Pr Pub.

MOBILITY
see Migration, Internal; Occupational Mobility

MOBILIZATION, INDUSTRIAL
see Industrial Mobilization

MODEL AIRPLANES
see Airplanes–Models

MODEL CAR RACING
Preston, Geoff. Race Aurora AFX: A Guide to HO Model Racing Cars. (Illus.). 100p. (Orig.). 1982. pap. 12.50x (ISBN 0-85242-727-1). Intl Pubns Serv.

MODEL CARS
see Automobiles–Models

MODEL CITIES
see City Planning

MODEL-MAKING
see Models and Modelmaking

MODEL RAILROADS
see Railroads–Models

MODEL THEORY
Shelah, S. Proper Forcing. (Lecture Notes in Mathematics: Vol. 940). 496p. 1983. pap. 25.00 (ISBN 0-387-11593-5). Springer-Verlag.
Vogt, William G. & Mickle, Marlin H., eds. Modeling & Simulation: Proceedings of the 13th Annual Pittsburgh Conference on Modeling & Simulation, 4 pts, Vol. 13. LC 73-85004. 1744p. 1982. pap. text ed. 40.00 ea. Pt. 1; 512p (ISBN 0-87664-712-3). Pt. 2; 546p (ISBN 0-87664-713-1). Pt. 3; 408p (ISBN 0-87664-714-X). Pt. 4; 368p (ISBN 0-87664-715-8). Set. pap. text ed. 149.00 (ISBN 0-87664-716-6). Instru Soc.

MODELS, ARCHITECTURAL
see Architectural Models

MODELS, CHEMICAL
see Chemical Models

MODELS, FASHION
Hardy, Karen. Not Just Another Pretty Face: An Intimate Look at America's Top Male Models. 1984. 11.95 (ISBN 0-452-25395-0, Plume). NAL.
Stafford, Marilyn. The Inside Secrets to a Modeling Career! Terschluse, Marilyn, ed. LC 82-60444. (Illus.). 75p. (Orig.). (gr. 12 up). pap. 7.95 (ISBN 0-910025-00-2). MidCoast Pubns.
Weinstein, Bob. Breaking Into Modeling: A Guide for Beginners. LC 82-20630. (Illus.). 160p. (gr. 10-12). 1983. PLB 12.95 (ISBN 0-668-05597-9); pap. 7.95 (ISBN 0-668-05600-2). Arco.

MODELS AND MODELMAKING
see also Architectural Models; Pattern-Making; Simulation Methods
also subdivision Models under names of objects, e.g. Automobiles–Models; and Machinery–Models; Surfaces, Models of
Mowll, William. S.S. Great Britian: The Model Ship. LC 82-60766. 1982. 22.95 (ISBN 0-87021-866-2). Naval Inst Pr.
Polk's Bluebook of Model Ships. (Blue Book of Hobbies Ser.). (Illus.). 135p. write for info. Polk.

MODERN ART
see Art, Modern–20th Century

MODERN DANCE
Raffe, Marjorie & Harwood, Cecil. Eurthmy & the Impulse of Dance. 63p. 1974. pap. 5.00 (ISBN 0-85440-278-0, Pub. by Steinerbooks). Anthroposophic.

MODERN GEOMETRY
see Geometry, Modern

MODERN HISTORY
see History, Modern

MODERN MUSIC
see Music–History and Criticism–20th Century

MODERN PHILOSOPHY
see Philosophy, Modern

MODERN POETRY
see Poetry, Modern (Collections)

MODES, MUSICAL
see Musical Intervals and Scales

MODULATION (ELECTRONICS)
see also Carrier Control Systems
Connor, F. R. Modulation. (Introductory Topics in Electronics & Telecommunication). 144p. 1982. pap. text ed. 9.95 (ISBN 0-7131-3457-7). E Arnold.

MODULES (ALGEBRA)
Baltes, H. P. & Hilf, E. R. Spectra of Finite Systems: A Review of Weyl's Problem--The Eigenvalue Distribution of the Wave Equation for Finite Domains & It Applications on the Physics of Small Systems. 116p. 1976. pap. 11.95x (ISBN 3-411-01491-1). Birkhauser.
Lucas, W. F., ed. Modules in Applied Mathematics: Differential Equation Models, Vol. 1. (Illus.). 400p. 1982. 28.00 (ISBN 0-387-90695-9). Springer-Verlag.
--Modules in Applied Mathematics, Vol. 2: Political & Related Models. (Illus.). 396p. 1983. 28.00 (ISBN 0-387-90696-7). Springer-Verlag.
--Modules in Applied Mathematics, Vol. 4: Life Science Models. (Illus.). 416p. 1983. 28.00 (ISBN 0-387-90739-4). Springer-Verlag.
UMAP Modules Nineteen Eighty-One: Tools for Teaching. 746p. 1982. text ed. 39.95 (ISBN 3-7643-3085-6). Birkhauser.

MOGOLLON INDIANS
see Indians of North America–Southwest, New

MOHAMMED, THE PROPHET, 570-632
Nadwi, Abul H. Muhammad Rasulullah: The Life of the Prophet Muhammad. rev. ed. 225p. 1983. pap. 7.00 (ISBN 0-89259-034-3). Am Trust Pubns.

MOHAMMEDAN
see headings beginning with the word Islamic or Muslim

MOHAMMEDANISM
see Islam

MOHAMMEDANS
see Muslims

MOHAVE DESERT, CALIFORNIA
Bagley, Helen G. Sand in My Shoe: Homestead Days in Twentynine Palms. 2nd ed. Weight, Harold & Weight, Lucile, eds. LC 77-94990. (Illus.). 269p. 1980. Repr. of 1978 ed. 11.95 (ISBN 0-912714-08-5). Homestead Pub.

MOHAVE INDIANS
see Indians of North America–Southwest, New

MOHEGAN INDIANS
see Indians of North America–Eastern States

MOLD, VEGETABLE
see Humus; Soils

MOLDING (CLAY, PLASTER, ETC.)
see Prosthesis

MOLECULAR ASYMMETRY
see Stereochemistry

MOLECULAR BIOLOGY
Edelman, M. & Hallick, R. B., eds. Methods in Chloroplast Molecular Biology. 1152p. 1982. 183.00 (ISBN 0-444-80368-8, Biomedical Pr). Elsevier.
Feifelder, David. Molecular Biology: A Comprehensive Introduction to Prokaryotes & Eukaryotes. (Illus.). 876p. 1983. text ed. 33.50 (ISBN 0-86720-012-X). Sci Bks Intl.
Frazier, William A. & Glaser, Luis, eds. Cellular Recognition. LC 82-6555. (UCLA Symposia on Molecular & Cellular Biology Ser.: Vol. 3). 966p. 1982. 152.00 (ISBN 0-8451-2602-4). A R Liss.
Freifelder, David. Problems in Molecular Biology. 272p. 1982. pap. text ed. 8.95 (ISBN 0-86720-013-8). Sci Bks Intl.
Kaplan, Nathan O. & Robinson, Arthur, eds. From Cyclotrons to Cytochromes: Essays in Molecular Biology & Chemistry. LC 82-1785. 1982. 64.00 (ISBN 0-12-397580-8). Acad Pr.
Noble, D. & Blundell, T. L., eds. Progress in Biophysics & Molecular Biology, Vol. 38. (Illus.). 210p. 1982. 77.00 (ISBN 0-08-029683-1). Pergamon.
--Progress in Biophysics & Molecular Biology, Vol. 39. (Illus.). 230p. 1983. 78.00 (ISBN 0-08-030015-4). Pergamon.
Work, T. S. & Work, E., eds. Laboratory Techniques in Biochemistry & Molecular Biology, Vols. 1-7. (Illus.). 1969-1979. Vol. 1. 70.75 (ISBN 0-444-10036-9); Vol. 2. 63.00 (ISBN 0-444-10055-5); Vol. 3. 89.00 (ISBN 0-444-10386-4); Vol. 4. 98.25 (ISBN 0-444-10985-4); Vol. 5. 107.75 (ISBN 0-444-11216-2); Vol. 6. 84.25 (ISBN 0-7204-4221-4); Vol. 7. 84.25 (ISBN 0-7204-4224-9). Elsevier.

MOLECULAR DYNAMICS
see also Gases, Kinetic Theory Of; Quantum Theory; Wave Mechanics
Fieck, G. Symmetry of Polycentric Systems: The Polycentric Tensor Algebra for Molecules. (Lecture Notes in Physics: Vol. 167). 137p. 1983. pap. 7.50 (ISBN 0-387-11589-7). Springer-Verlag.
Workshop Conference Hoechst Schloss Reisenburg, 11th, October 11-15, 1981 & Bartmann, W. Structure of Complexes Between Biopolymers & Low Molecular Weight Molecules: Proceeding. 1982. 42.95x (ISBN 0-471-26144-0, Pub. by Wiley Heyden). Wiley.

MOLECULAR ORBITALS
Fleming, I. Frontier Orbitals & Organic Chemical Reactions. LC 76-3800. 249p. 1976. 43.50x (ISBN 0-471-01820-1); pap. 17.50 (ISBN 0-471-01819-8, Pub. by Wiley-Interscience). Wiley.
Richards, W. Graham & Cooper, David L. Ab Initio Molecular Orbital Calculations for Chemists. 2nd ed. (Illus.). 1982. pap. 17.95 (ISBN 0-19-855369-2). Oxford U Pr.

MOLECULAR PHYSIOLOGY
see Biological Physics

MOLECULAR THEORY
see also Gases, Kinetic Theory Of
Kueppers, B. O. Molecular Theory of Evolution: Outline of a Physico-Chemical Theory of the Origin of Life. (Illus.). 321p. 1983. 32.00 (ISBN 0-387-12080-7). Springer-Verlag.

MOLECULES
see also Macromolecules; Molecular Orbitals
Counting Molecules-Approaching the Limit of Chemical Analysis. 1982. 5.00 (ISBN 0-910362-20-3). Chem Educ.
Hellwege, K. H., ed. Molecular Constants. (Landolt-Boerstein Ser.: Group II, Vol. 14, Subvol. A). 790p. 1983. 542.00 (ISBN 0-387-11365-7). Springer-Verlag.

MOLIERE, JEAN BAPTISTE POQUELIN, 1622-1673
Wadsworth, Philip A. Moliere & the Italian Theatrical Tradition. 15.00 (ISBN 0-686-38458-X). French Lit.

MOLLUSKS
see also Shells; Snails; Squids
Boyle, P. R. Molluscs & Man. (Studies in Biology: No. 134). 64p. 1981. pap. text ed. 8.95 (ISBN 0-7131-2824-0). E Arnold.
Carstarphen, Dee. The Conch Book. LC 81-9632. (Illus.). 80p. Date not set. pap. 6.95 (ISBN 0-686-84296-0). Banyan Bks.
Sharabati, Doreen. Saudi Arabian Seashells. 1982. 50.00x (ISBN 0-9507641-0-8, Pub. by Cave Pubns England). State Mutual Bk.
Wilbur, Karl M., ed. The Mollusca: Metabolic Biochem & Molecular Biomechanics, Vol. 1. Incl. The Mollusca: Biochemistry of Mollusca Environmental Biochemistry. price not set (ISBN 0-12-751402-3). Date not set. price not set (ISBN 0-12-751401-5). Acad Pr.
--The Mollusca: Vol. 3: Development. Date not set. write for info. (ISBN 0-12-751403-1). Acad Pr.

MOLLUSKS–NEW ZEALAND
Powell, A. W. B. New Zealand Mollusca. (Illus.). 532p. 1983. 60.00 (ISBN 0-00-216906-1, Pub. by W Collins Australia). Intl Schol Bk Serv.

MOLTEN SALTS
see Fused Salts

MONACHISM
see Monasticism and Religious Orders

MONARCHS
see Kings and Rulers

MONASTIC VOCATION
see Vocation (In Religious Orders, Congregations, etc.)

MONASTICISM AND RELIGIOUS ORDERS
see also Benedictines; Franciscans; Jesuits; Retreats; Vocation (In Religious Orders, Congregations, etc.)
Faricy, Robert. The End of the Religious Life. 96p. 1983. pap. 6.96 (ISBN 0-86683-690-X). Winston Pr.

MONASTICISM AND RELIGIOUS ORDERS–MIDDLE AGES, 600-1500
Costumes of Religious Orders of the Middle Ages. 300p. Date not set. pap. 35.00 (ISBN 0-87556-491-7). Saifer.

MONASTICISM AND RELIGIOUS ORDERS, TAOIST
Wong, Bruce M. TSFR: The Taoist Way to Total Sexual Fitness, For Men. 80p. 1982. pap. 9.95 (ISBN 0-910295-00-X). Golden Dragon Pub.

MONET, CLAUDE, 1840-1926
House, John. Monet. (Phaidon Color Library). (Illus.). 84p. 1983. 25.00 (ISBN 0-7148-2162-4, Pub. by Salem Hse Ltd); pap. 17.95 (ISBN 0-7148-2160-8). Merrimack Bk Serv.

MONETARY POLICY
see also Credit; Fiscal Policy
Basagni, Fabio. International Monetary Relations After Jamaica. (The Atlantic Papers: No. 76/4). (Orig.). 1977. pap. text ed. 4.75x (ISBN 0-686-83641-3). Allanheld.
Batchelor, Roy A. & Wood, Geoffrey E., eds. Exchange Rate Policy. LC 81-23262. 265p. 1982. 27.50x (ISBN 0-312-27389-4). St Martin.
Bryant, Ralph C. Controlling Money: The Federal Reserve & Its Critics. LC 82-45983. 150p. 1983. 18.95 (ISBN 0-8157-1136-0); pap. 7.95 (ISBN 0-8157-1135-2). Brookings.
Cochran, John A. Money, Banking, & the Economy. 528p. 1983. text ed. 23.95 (ISBN 0-02-323050-9). Macmillan.
Desai, Meghnad. Testing Monetarism. 250p. 1983. pap. 13.50 (ISBN 0-86187-225-8). F Pinter Pubs.
Dreyer, Jacob S., et al, eds. International Monetary System: A Time of Turbulence. 1982. 29.95 (ISBN 0-8447-2228-6); pap. 14.95 (ISBN 0-8447-2227-8). Am Enterprise.
Gulati, I. S. International Monetary Development & the Third World: A Proposal to Readress the Balance. (R. C. Dutt Lectures on Political Economy Ser.: 1978). 48p. 1980. pap. text ed. 2.95x (ISBN 0-686-42711-4, Pub. by Orient Longman Ltd India). Apt Bks.
Hansen, Alvin. Monetary Theory & Fiscal Policy. LC 82-20924. ix, 236p. 1983. Repr. of 1949 ed. lib. bdg. 29.75x (ISBN 0-313-23736-0, HAMT). Greenwood.
Laidler, David. Monetarist Perspectives. 224p. 1983. text ed. 20.00x (ISBN 0-674-58240-3). Harvard U Pr.
Lee, S. Y. Financial Structures & Monetary Policy. 300p. 1982. 49.00x (ISBN 0-333-28617-0, Pub. by Macmillan England). State Mutual Bk.
Merk, Gerard, ed. Acta Monetaria. 128p. 1980. 59.00x (ISBN 0-686-81993-4, Pub. by Macdonald & Evans). State Mutual Bk.
Wrightsman, Dwayne. An Introduction to Monetary Theory & Policy. 3rd, rev. ed. LC 82-48746. 384p. 1982. 14.95 (ISBN 0-02-935910-4); pap. text ed. 9.95 (ISBN 0-02-935920-1). Free Pr.

MONETARY POLICY–GREAT BRITAIN
Congdon, Tim. Monetary Control in Britain. 150p. 1982. 50.00x (ISBN 0-333-26831-8, Pub. by Macmillan England). State Mutual Bk.

MONETARY QUESTION
see Currency Question; Money

MONEY
see also Banks and Banking; Banks and Banking, Central; Barter; Capital; Coinage; Coins; Credit; Currency Question; Finance; Finance, Public; Foreign Exchange; Gold; Inflation (Finance); Paper Money; Precious Metals; Silver; Silver Question; Wealth also names of coins, e.g. Dollar
Auernheimer, Leonardo & Ekelund, Robert B. The Essential of Money & Banking. LC 81-11466. 445p. 1982. 23.95 (ISBN 0-471-02103-2); avail. instrs' manual (ISBN 0-471-87633-X). Wiley.
Bryant, Ralph C. Controlling Money: The Federal Reserve & Its Critics. LC 82-45983. 150p. 1983. 18.95 (ISBN 0-8157-1136-0); pap. 7.95 (ISBN 0-8157-1135-2). Brookings.
Cochran, John A. Money, Banking, & the Economy. 528p. 1983. text ed. 23.95 (ISBN 0-02-323050-9). Macmillan.
Gould, Bruce G. The Most Dangerous Money Book Ever Written. 444p. (Orig.). 1983. pap. 100.00 (ISBN 0-918706-13-0). B Gould Pubns.
Gruber, Barbara. Barbara Jean's Household Money Tips: Hundreds of Ideas for Saving Money on Food, Clothing, Decorating. 256p. 1983. pap. 7.95 (ISBN 0-525-93294-1, 0772-230). Dutton.
Hansen, Alvin. Monetary Theory & Fiscal Policy. LC 82-20924. ix, 236p. 1983. Repr. of 1949 ed. lib. bdg. 29.75x (ISBN 0-313-23736-0, HAMT). Greenwood.
Harris, L. Monetary Theory. 1980. 26.95 (ISBN 0-07-026840-1). McGraw.
Hickman, John & Oakes, Dean. Standard Catalog of National Bank Notes. (Illus.). 1982. text ed. 75.00 (ISBN 0-87341-026-2). Krause Pubns.
Husak, G. & Pahre, P. The Money Series, 11 bks. Incl. Banking. 25p. pap. text ed. 2.00 (ISBN 0-910839-18-2); Buying a House. 32p. pap. text ed. 2.00 (ISBN 0-910839-20-4); Buying Furniture for Your Home. 46p. pap. text ed. 3.00 (ISBN 0-910839-13-1); Finding a Place to Live. 28p. pap. text ed. 2.50 (ISBN 0-910839-14-X); How to Borrow Money. 39p. pap. text ed. 2.50 (ISBN 0-910839-17-4); How to Budget Your Money. 23p. pap. text ed. 2.50 (ISBN 0-910839-16-6); How to Buy Clothes. 44p. pap. text ed. 3.00 (ISBN 0-910839-12-3); How to Buy Food. 40p. pap. text ed. 3.00 (ISBN 0-910839-11-5); Insurance. 40p. pap. text ed. 2.00 (ISBN 0-910839-19-0); Where to Get Medical Help. 33p. pap. text ed. 2.50 (ISBN 0-910839-15-8). (Illus.). 28p. (gr. 7-12). 1977. tchrs' ed. 2.00 (ISBN 0-910839-21-2). Hopewell.
McCulloch, J. H. Money & Inflation: A Monetarist Approach. 2nd ed. 1981. 8.00 (ISBN 0-686-83746-0). Acad Pr.
Meyer, Laurence H., ed. Improving Money Stock Control: Problems, Solutions & Consequences. 1982. lib. bdg. 25.00 (ISBN 0-89838-115-0). Kluwer-Nijhoff.
Pappas, Duane R. The Romance of Money. (The Library of Business Psychology). (Illus.). 119p. 1983. 57.15 (ISBN 0-86722-024-4). Inst Econ Pol.
Rogers, James H. America Weighs Her Gold. 1931. text ed. 29.50x (ISBN 0-686-83460-7). Elliots Bks.
Smith, Sharon. Money Management. (Math Ser.). 24p. (gr. 7 up). 1982. wkbk. 5.00 (ISBN 0-8209-0121-0, A-31). ESP.
Wisely, William. A Tool of Power: The Political History of Money. LC 76-57701. 416p. Repr. of 1977 ed. text ed. 33.95 (ISBN 0-471-02235-7). Krieger.
Wrightsman, Dwayne. An Introduction to Monetary Theory & Policy. 3rd, rev. ed. LC 82-48746. 384p. 1982. 14.95 (ISBN 0-02-935910-4); pap. text ed. 9.95 (ISBN 0-02-935920-1). Free Pr.

MONEY–JUVENILE LITERATURE
Byers, Patricia & Preston, Julia. The Kid's Money Book. LC 82-184275. (Illus.). 120p. 1983. pap. 4.95 (ISBN 0-89709-041-1). Liberty Pub.
Derry, Ruth. Scholar Dollars. (gr. 3-6). 1982. 5.95 (ISBN 0-86653-057-6, GA 415). Good Apple.
Tuttle, Wainwright. There's Something Wrong with Our Money. (Illus.). 139p. (Orig.). (gr. 11-12). 1982. pap. 3.57 (ISBN 0-9609494-0-2). Jebco Bks.

MONEY–TABLES, ETC.
Fielding's World Currency & Metric Converter. 2.95 (ISBN 0-686-38816-X). Fielding.

MONEY–EUROPE
Johnston, R. B. The Economics of the Euro-Market: History, Theory & Policy. LC 82-10300. 296p. 1982. 27.50x (ISBN 0-312-23295-0). St Martin.
Kane, Daniel. The Eurodollar Market & the Years of Crisis. LC 82-16828. 224p. 1983. 25.00x (ISBN 0-312-26735-5). St Martin.

MONEY–GREAT BRITAIN
Congdon, Tim. Monetary Control in Britain. 150p. 1982. 50.00x (ISBN 0-333-26831-8, Pub. by Macmillan England). State Mutual Bk.

MONEY RAISING
see Fund Raising
MONEY SUPPLY
see Money
MONGOLIAN LANGUAGE
Lessing, F. D. Mongolian-English Dictionary. LC 60-14517. 1220p. 1982. Repr. of 1960 ed. 55.00x (ISBN 0-910980-40-3). Mongolia.
MONGOLIAN LITERATURE
Gronbech, Kaare & Krueger, John R., eds. An Introduction to Classical (Literary) Mongolian. 2nd, Rev. ed. 91p. (Orig.). 1976. pap. 22.50x (ISBN 3-447-01661-2). Intl Pubns Serv.
MONILIALES
Subramanian, C. V., ed. Hyphomycetes. 496p. 65.00 (ISBN 0-12-675620-1). Acad Pr.
MONITORING (HOSPITAL CARE)
see also Hospital Care
Daily, Elaine K. & Schroeder, John S. Hemodynamic Waveforms: Exercises in Identification & Analysis. 1st ed. (Illus.). 308p. 1983. pap. text ed. 15.95 (ISBN 0-8016-1212-8). Mosby.
MONKS
see Monasticism and Religious Orders
MONOCOTYLEDONS
Tomlinson, P. B. Anatomy of the Monocotyledons, Vol. 7: Helobiae (Alismatidae) (Including the Seagrasses) (Illus.). 576p. 1982. text ed. 98.00x (ISBN 0-19-854502-9). Oxford U Pr.
MONOPOLIES-UNITED STATES
Agar, Herbert & Tate, Allen, eds. Who Owns America? A New Declaration of Independence. LC 82-24752. 352p. 1983. pap. text ed. 12.75 (ISBN 0-8191-2767-1). U Pr of Amer.
MONOPOLIES, PARTIAL
see Oligopolies
MONROE, MARILYN, 1926-1962
Speriglio, Milo A. Marilyn Monroe: Murder Cover-Up. LC 82-51319. (Illus.). 276p. (Orig.). 1983. pap. 7.95 (ISBN 0-930990-77-3). Seville Pub.
MONSTERS
see also Abnormalities, Human
Grant, Charles L. The Dodd, Mead Gallery of Horror. 1983. 15.95 (ISBN 0-396-08160-6). Dodd.
Thaler, Mike. Scared Silly. (Illus.). 1982. pap. 1.95 (ISBN 0-380-80291-0, 80291, Camelot). Avon.
MONSTERS-JUVENILE LITERATURE
Bendick, Jeanne. Scare a Ghost, Tame a Monster. LC 82-23696. (Illus.). 120p. (gr. 3-6). 1983. price not set (ISBN 0-664-32701-X). Westminster.
Brett, Bernard. Monsters. (Chiller Ser.). 128p. 1983. PLB 8.79 (ISBN 0-671-46745-X). Messner.
MONTAIGNE, MICHEL EYQUEM DE, 1533-1592
Collins, W. Lucas. Montagne. 192p. 1982. Repr. of 1879 ed. lib. bdg. 25.00 (ISBN 0-89760-166-1). Telegraph Bks.
Jean, B. & Mouret, F. Montaigne, Descartes et Pascal. 1971. pap. 10.00 (ISBN 0-7190-0422-5). Manchester.
Lowenthal, Marvin. The Autobiography of Michel De Montaigne. 348p. 1982. Repr. of 1935 ed. lib. bdg. 25.00 (ISBN 0-89760-516-0). Telegraph Bks.
McFarlane, I. D. & Maclean, Ian. Montaigne: Essays in Memory of Richard Sayce. (Illus.). 1982. 41.00x (ISBN 0-19-815769-X). Oxford U Pr.
MONTALE, EUGENIO, 1896-
Cambon, Glauco. Eugenio Montale's Poetry: A Dream in Reason's Presence. 270p. 1982. 22.50 (ISBN 0-691-06520-9). Princeton U Pr.
De C. L. Huffman, Claire. Montale & the Occasions of Poetry. LC 82-61368. 356p. 1983. 25.00x (ISBN 0-691-06562-4). Princeton U Pr.
MONTANA
see also cities, counties, towns, etc. in montana
Alwin, John A. Eastern Montana: A Portrait of the Land & its People. (Montana Geographic Ser.: No. 2). (Illus.). 128p. 1982. pap. 12.95 (ISBN 0-938314-02-5). MT Mag.
Cunningham, Carolyn, compiled by. Montana Weather. (Illus.). 156p. 1982. pap. 6.95 (ISBN 0-938314-03-3). MT Mag.
Sample, Mike. Angler's Guide to Montana. (Illus.). 256p. (Orig.). 1983. pap. 8.95 (ISBN 0-934318-13-1). Falcon Pr MT.
Schneider, Bill. Hiker's Guide to Montana. rev. ed. LC 82-84323. (Illus.). 256p. pap. 7.95 (ISBN 0-934318-08-5). Falcon Pr MT.
Toole, K. Ross. Twentieth-Century Montana: A State of Extremes. LC 75-177348. (Illus.). 278p. (Orig.). 1983. pap. 12.95 (ISBN 0-8061-1826-1). U of Okla Pr.
Turbak, Gary. Traveler's Guide to Montana. (Illus.). 256p. 1983. pap. 7.95 (ISBN 0-934318-14-X). Falcon Pr MT.
MONTANA-HISTORY
Dimsdale, Thomas. Vigilantes of Montana. LC 80-29395. (Classics of the Old West Ser.). lib. bdg. 17.28 (ISBN 0-8094-3959-X). Silver.
Howard, Joseph K. Montana: High, Wide & Handsome. LC 82-17667. xiv, 350p. 1983. pap. 7.50 (ISBN 0-8032-7214-6, BB 820, Bison). U of Nebr Pr.
MONTANA-SOCIAL LIFE AND CUSTOMS
Lopach, James, et al. We the People of Montana. 320p. 1983. 19.95 (ISBN 0-87842-154-8); pap. 10.95 (ISBN 0-87842-159-9). Mountain Pr.
MONTANA FORMATION
see Geology, Stratigraphic-Cretaceous
MONTESQUIEU, CHARLES LOUIS DE SECONDAT, BARON DE LA BREDE ET DE, 1689-1755
Hampson, Norman. Will & Circumstance: Montesquieu, Rousseau, & the French Revolution. LC 82-40455. 208p. 1983. 17.50x (ISBN 0-8061-1843-1). U of Okla Pr.
MONTEVERDI, CLAUDIO, 1567-1643
Arnold, Denis. Monteverdi Church Music. LC 81-71298. (BBC Music Guides Ser.). 64p. (Orig.). 1983. pap. 4.95 (ISBN 0-295-95923-1). U of Wash Pr.
MONTGOLFIER, JACQUES ETIENNE, 1745-1799
Gillispie, Charles C. The Montgolfier Brothers & the Invention of Aviation, 1783-1784: With a Word on the Importance of Ballooning for the Science of Heat & for the Art of Building Railroads. LC 82-61363. (Illus.). 272p. 1983. 35.00 (ISBN 0-691-08321-5). Princeton U Pr.
MONTGOLFIER, JOSEPH MITCHELL, 1740-1810
Gillispie, Charles C. The Montgolfier Brothers & the Invention of Aviation, 1783-1784: With a Word on the Importance of Ballooning for the Science of Heat & for the Art of Building Railroads. LC 82-61363. (Illus.). 272p. 1983. 35.00 (ISBN 0-691-08321-5). Princeton U Pr.
MONTGOMERY COUNTY, MARYLAND
Farquhar, Roger B. Old Homes & History of Montgomery County, Maryland. (Illus.). 1981. 35.00 (ISBN 0-910086-06-0). Am Hist Res.
MONTREAL-DESCRIPTION-GUIDEBOOKS
Arthur Frommer's Guide to Montreal-Quebec, 1983-84. Date not set. pap. 3.95 (ISBN 0-671-45296-7). Frommer-Pasmantier.
Montreal Travel Guide. (Berlitz Travel Guides). (Illus.). 1982. pap. 4.95 (ISBN 0-02-969590-2, Berlitz). Macmillan.
Scheller, William G. Randonnees aux Environs de Montreal. Booth, Janine, tr. from English. (AMC Country Walks Bks.). Orig. Title: Country Walks Near Montreal. (Illus.). 200p. (Orig., French.). 1983. pap. 6.95 (ISBN 0-910146-46-2). Appalach Mtn.
MONUMENTAL THEOLOGY
see Bible-Antiquities
MONUMENTS, NATURAL
see Natural Monuments
MONUMENTS, SEPULCHRAL
see Sepulchral Monuments
MOON
see also Tides
British Astronomical Association. Observing the Moon. (Illus.). 64p. 1983. pap. text ed. 10.95 (ISBN 0-89490-085-4). Enslow Pubs.
Cherrington, Ernest H. Exploring the Moon Through Binoculars & Small Telescopes. (Illus.). 224p. 1983. pap. 10.00 (ISBN 0-486-24491-1). Dover.
MOON-JUVENILE LITERATURE
Adler, David. All About the Moon. LC 82-17422. (Question & Answer Bks.). (Illus.). 32p. (gr. 3-6). 1983. PLB 8.59 (ISBN 0-89375-886-8); pap. text ed. 1.95 (ISBN 0-89375-887-6). Troll Assocs.
DeBruin, Jerry. Young Scientists Explore the Moon, Bk. 3. (gr. 4-7). 1982. 3.95 (ISBN 0-86653-074-6, GA 407). Good Apple.
MOON SYSTEM
see Blind-Printing and Writing Systems
MOONLIGHTING
see Supplementary Employment
MOON'S TYPE FOR THE BLIND
see Blind-Printing and Writing Systems
MOORE, BRIAN, 1921-
McSweeney, Kerry. Four Contemporary Novelists: Angus Wilson, Brian Moore, John Fowles, V. S. Naipaul. 232p. 1983. 24.95 (ISBN 0-7735-0399-4). McGill-Queens U Pr.
MOORE, GEORGE, 1852-1933
Wolfe, Humbert. George Moore. 1982. lib. bdg. 34.50 (ISBN 0-686-81926-8). Porter.
MOORISH ARCHITECTURE
see Architecture, Islamic
MOORISH ART
see Art, Islamic
MOORISH LANGUAGE (INDIA)
see Urdu Language
MOORS AND HEATHS
see also Marshes
Thackrah, J. R. Making of the Yorkshire Dales. 160p. 1982. 50.00x (ISBN 0-86190-070-7, Pub. by Moorland). State Mutual Bk.
MOPEDS
Reeves, Lawrence. Mopeds: A Guide to Models, Maintenance, & Safety. (Illus.). 96p. (gr. 8-11). 1983. PLB 8.79 (ISBN 0-671-46100-1). Messner.
MORAL CONDITIONS
see also Sex Customs
also subdivision Moral Conditions under names of countries, cities, etc., e.g. United States-Moral Conditions
Galliher, John & Cross, John. Morals Legislation Without Morality: The Case of Nevada. (Crime, Law & Deviance Ser.). 140p. 1983. 16.00 (ISBN 0-8135-0983-1). Rutgers U Pr.
Scott, Walter. Old Mortality. Calder, Angus, ed. 1975. pap. 4.95 (ISBN 0-14-043098-9). Penguin.
MORAL EDUCATION
see also Christian Education; Religious Education
Demaray, Kathleen. Instruye al Nino. Orig. Title: Train up a Child. (Illus.). 24p. (Span.). 1982. Spiral Wire Bound 4.95 (ISBN 0-89367-085-5). Light & Life.
Wilson, John & Cowell, Barbara. Dialogues on Moral Education. 180p. (Orig.). 1983. pap. price not set (ISBN 0-89135-035-7). Religious Educ.
Woodside, Alexander & Wyatt, David K., eds. Moral Order & the Question of Change: Essays on Southeast Asian Thought. LC 82-51022. (Yale University Southeast Asia Studies Monograph: No. 24). 413p. 1982. pap. 16.00x (ISBN 0-938692-02-X). Yale U SE Asia.
MORAL PHILOSOPHY
see Ethics
MORAL THEOLOGY
see Christian Ethics
MORAL VIRTUES
see Virtue and Virtues
MORALS
see Conduct of Life; Ethics; Moral Conditions
MORALS AND LAW
see Law and Ethics
MORALS AND LITERATURE
see Literature and Morals
MORAVIAN INDIANS
see Indians of North America-Eastern States
MORE, THOMAS, SIR, SAINT, 1478-1535
Fox, Alistair. Thomas More: History & Providence. LC 82-11178. 288p. 1983. text ed. 19.95x (ISBN 0-300-02951-9). Yale U Pr.
Gogan, Brian. The Commom Corps of Christendom: Ecclesiological Themes in the Writing of Sir Thomas More. (Studies in the History of Christian Thought Ser.: Vol. 26). xii, 404p. 1982. write for info. (ISBN 90-04-06508-3). E J Brill.
Logan, George M. The Meaning of More's Utopia. LC 82-16147. (Illus.). 320p. 1983. 27.50x (ISBN 0-691-06557-8). Princeton U Pr.
Roper, William. A Life of Sir Thomas More. (Illus.). 128p. (Orig.). 1983. pap. 6.95 (ISBN 0-87243-118-5). Templegate.
MORGAN, JOHN PIERPONT, 1867-1943
Jackson, Stanley. J. P. Morgan. LC 81-40333. 464p. 1983. 22.95 (ISBN 0-8128-2824-0). Stein & Day.
MORGAN HORSE
Sheally, John H., II. Morgans in the Colonies & Across the Pond. LC 78-54664. (Illus.). 143p. 1978. write for info. JCP Corp VA.
MORGAN'S CALVARY DIVISION (C.S.A.)
Holter, Wayne V. & Phillips, James M. Morgan Fire & Steel. LC 82-90180. (Illus.). 140p. 18.95 (ISBN 0-932572-10-3). Phillips Holter.
MORMONS AND MORMONISM
Bunker, Gary L. & Bitton, Davis. The Mormon Graphic Image, Eighteen Thirty-Four to Nineteen Fourteen: Cartoons, Caricatures, & Illustrations. (Publications in the American West: Vol. 16). (Illus.). 140p. 1983. 20.00 (ISBN 0-87480-218-0). U of Utah Pr.
Hacken, Sara. Games & Puzzles for Mormon Youth. 64p. 1982. 4.95 (ISBN 0-87747-932-1). Deseret Bk.
Johnson, Sonia. From Housewife to Heretic. LC 80-2964. 408p. 1983. pap. 8.95 (ISBN 0-385-17494-2, Anch). Doubleday.
Morey, Robert A. How to Answer a Mormon. 128p. (Orig.). 1983. pap. 3.95 (ISBN 0-87123-260-X). Bethany Hse.
Talmage, James E. Jesus the Christ. (Classics in Mormon Literature Ser.). 804p. 1982. 10.95 (ISBN 0-87747-903-8). Deseret Bk.
Utah & the Mormons: Index in the Microfilm Collection. 13p. Date not set. 15.00 (ISBN 0-89235-059-8). Res Pubns Conn.
MORMONS AND MORMONISM-HISTORY
Cannon, Donald Q. & Cook, Lyndon W., eds. Far West Record. LC 82-23476. 318p. 1983. 10.95 (ISBN 0-87747-901-1). Deseret Bk.
Hafen, Mary A. Recollections of a Handcart Pioneer of 1860: A Woman's Life on the Mormon Frontier. (Illus.). 117p. 1983. 10.95x (ISBN 0-8032-2325-0); pap. 4.50 (ISBN 0-8032-7219-7, BB 841, Bison). U of Nebr Pr.
Paul, Louis. The Chosen Race. (Illus.). 111p. 1982. 6.95 (ISBN 0-9608890-1-9); pap. 4.96 (ISBN 0-9608890-0-0). L Paul Pub.
Sonne, Conway B. Saints on the Seas: A Maritime History of Mormon Migration, 1830-1890. (Publications in the American West: Vol. 17). (Illus.). 240p. 1983. 20.00 (ISBN 0-87480-221-0). U of Utah Pr.
MOROCCO-DESCRIPTION AND TRAVEL
Morocco Travel Guide. (Berlitz Travel Guides). (Illus.). 1982. pap. 4.95 (ISBN 0-02-969370-5, Berlitz). Macmillan.
MORONS
see Mentally Handicapped
MORPHOGENESIS
see also Botany-Morphology; Cell Differentiation; Morphology
Jaenicke, L., ed. Biochemistry of Differentiation & Morphogenesis. (Collequium Mosbach Ser.: Vol. 33). (Illus.). 301p. 1983. 37.00 (ISBN 0-387-12010-6). Springer-Verlag.
MORPHOLOGY
see also Abnormalities, Human; Morphogenesis
Dodge, J. Atlas of Biological Ultrastructures. 1968. 10.50 (ISBN 0-444-19949-7). Elsevier.
Krammer, Kurt. Valve Morphology in the Genus Cymbella: C. A. Agardh. Helmcke, J. G. & Krammer, Kurt, eds. (Micromorphology of Datom Valves Ser.). (Illus.). 300p. (Orig.). 1982. lib. bdg. 67.50x (ISBN 3-7682-1333-1). Lubrecht & Cramer.
MORPHOLOGY (PLANTS)
see Botany-Morphology
MORRIS, WILLIAM, 1834-1896
Forman, H. B. The Books of William Morris. 45.00x (ISBN 0-87556-290-6). Saifer.
MORSE, JEDIDIAH, 1761-1826
Phillips, Joseph W. Jedidiah Morse & New England Congregationalism. 305p. 1983. 30.00 (ISBN 0-8135-0982-3). Rutgers U Pr.
MORTALITY
see also Infants-Mortality; Insurance, Life-Mathematics
Benjamin, B. & Pollard, J. H. Analysis of Mortality & Other Actuarial Statistics. 212p. 1980. 31.50 (ISBN 0-434-90137-7, Pub. by Heinemann). David & Charles.
Chiang, Chin L. Life Table & Its Applications. LC 82-20331. 1983. lib. bdg. 29.50 (ISBN 0-89874-570-5). Krieger.
National Center for Health Statistics. Mortality Detail Files, 1972-1977. LC 82-80686. 1982. write for info. (ISBN 0-89138-940-7). ICPSR.
MORTGAGE LENDING
see Mortgage Loans
MORTGAGE LOANS
see also Mortgages
Eastgate, Robert J. Master Guide to Creative Financing of Real Estate Investments. LC 82-9313. 246p. 1982. text ed. 89.50 (ISBN 0-87624-366-9). Inst Busn Plan.
FHA Level Payment Home Loan Tables. 224p. (Orig.). 1983. pap. 4.95 (ISBN 0-89471-209-8). Running Pr.
Woodruff, Archibald, Jr. Farm Mortgage Loans of Life Insurance Companies. 1937. text ed. 39.50x (ISBN 0-686-83543-3). Elliots Bks.
MORTGAGES
see also Agricultural Credit; Housing-Finance; Mortgage Loans
Cooper-Hill, James & Greenberg, Martin J. Cases & Material on Mortgages & Real Estate Finance. (Contemporary Legal Education Ser.). 632p. 1982. 27.50 (ISBN 0-87215-499-8). Michie-Bobbs.
Mettling, Stephen R. Assumptions & Purchase Money Mortgages (A & PMM) (Creative Financing Skill Development Ser.). 49p. 1982. pap. 10.95 (ISBN 0-88462-137-5). Real Estate Ed Co.
--Graduated Payment Adjustable Mortage Loan (GPAML) (Creative Financing Skill Developing Ser.). 40p. 1982. pap. 9.95 (ISBN 0-88462-136-7). Real Estate Ed Co.
--The Graduated Payment Mortgage (GPM) Bd. with The Pledged Account Mortgage (PAM; The Flip Mortgage. (Creative Financing Skill Development Ser.). 47p. (Orig.). 1982. pap. 10.95 (ISBN 0-88462-135-9). Real Estate Ed Co.
Protzman, John M. Confounded Interest. (Illus.). 44p. (Orig.). 1982. pap. 11.95 (ISBN 0-9608898-0-9, 2-EJD). JMP Mfg.
Rudman, Jack. Mortgage Analyst. (Career Examination Ser.: C-2653). (Cloth bdg. avail. on request). pap. 10.00 (ISBN 0-8373-2653-2). Natl Learning.
Tuccillo, John & Weicher, John. Local Mortgage Revenue Bonds: Economic & Financial Impacts. (Illus.). 46p. (Orig.). 1979. pap. text ed. 4.00 (ISBN 0-87766-252-5). Urban Inst.
Vance, Mary. Mortgage & Construction Finance: A Bibliography. (Architecture Ser.: Bibliography A-778). 57p. 1982. pap. 8.25 (ISBN 0-88066-202-6). Vance Biblios.
MORTGAGES-TAXATION
Rudman, Jack. Mortgage Tax Clerk. (Career Examination Ser.: C-929). (Cloth bdg. avail. on request). pap. 10.00 (ISBN 0-8373-0929-8). Natl Learning.
MORTUARY CUSTOMS
see Burial; Funeral Rites and Ceremonies; Undertakers and Undertaking
MORTUARY STATISTICS
see Infants-Mortality; Mortality
MOSAIC LAW
see Jewish Law
MOSAICS
see also Mural Painting and Decoration
Rottgen, Steffi, et al. The Art of Mosaics: Selections from the Gilbert Collection. rev. ed. Hall, Alla T., tr. from German. (Illus.). 224p. (Orig.). 1982. 27.50 (ISBN 0-87587-109-7); pap. 17.50. LA Co Art Mus.
MOSCOW-DESCRIPTION
Moscow Travel Guide. (Berlitz Travel Guides). (Illus.). 1982. pap. 4.95 (ISBN 0-02-969380-2, Berlitz). Macmillan.
MOSES
Berg, Jean H. Moses: Leader & Lawgiver. (Illus.). 40p. (Fr.). (gr. k-4). 1982. 4.95 (ISBN 0-87510-163-1). Chr Science.
Campbell, Alexander. Live with Moses. 90p. (Orig.). 1982. pap. 12.95 (ISBN 0-940754-13-4). Ed Ministries.
MOSES-JUVENILE LITERATURE
Barrett, Ethel. Moses: Mission Impossible! (Bible Biographies Ser.). 1982. pap. text ed. 2.50 (ISBN 0-8307-0772-7, 5811201). Regal.

Berg, Jean H. Moses: Leader & Lawgiver. (Illus.). 40p. (Ger.). (gr. k-4). 1982. 4.95 (ISBN 0-87510-164-X). Chr Science.

--Moses: Leader & Lawgiver. (Illus.). 40p. (Span.). (gr. k-4). 4.95 (ISBN 0-87510-166-6). Chr Science.

MOSES BEN MAIMON, 1135-1204

Heschel, Abraham J. Maimonides. Newgroschel, Joachim, tr. from German. 1983. text ed. 8.25 (ISBN 0-374-51759-2). FS&G.

MOSLEM

see headings beginning with the word Islamic or Muslim

MOSLEMS

see Muslims

MOSQUITOES-EXTERMINATION

Larid, Marshall & Miles, James W., eds. Integrated Mosquito Control Methodologies, Vol. 1. Date not set. price not set (ISBN 0-12-434001-6). Acad Pr.

Rudman, Jack. Mosquito Control Inspector. (Career Examination Ser.: C-2912). (Cloth bdg. avail. on request). pap. 10.00 (ISBN 0-8373-2912-4). Natl Learning.

MOTET

Here are entered works on the motet as a musical form.

Tischler, Hans. The Earliest Motets (to ca. 1270) A Complete Comparative Edition, 3 vols. LC 78-15005. 1982. Set. 425.00 (ISBN 0-300-01534-8); Vol. 1, 856 pp. write for info. (ISBN 0-300-02918-7); Vol. 2, 636 pp. write for info. (ISBN 0-300-02919-5); Vol. 3, 256 pp. write for info. (ISBN 0-300-02920-9). Yale U Pr.

MOTHER AND CHILD

Allen, Elizabeth C. Mother, Can you Hear Me? 1983. 13.95 (ISBN 0-89696-194-X). Dodd.

Brazelton, T. Berry. Infants & Mothers: Differences in Development. rev. ed. 1983. pap. 9.95 (ISBN 0-440-54010-0, Delta). Dell.

--Infants & Mothers: Differences in Development. rev. ed. 1983. 16.95 (ISBN 0-440-04259-3, Sey Lawr). Delacorte.

Diamond, John. Re-Mothering Experience: How to Totally Love. Orig. Title: How to Totally Love. 90p. 1983. pap. 15.95x (ISBN 0-915628-13-9). Zeppelin.

Eheart, Brenda & Martan, Susan. The Fourth Trimester: On Becoming a Mother. 1983. 13.95 (ISBN 0-686-43210-X); pap. 7.50 (ISBN 0-686-43211-8). ACC.

Hunter, Brenda. Where Have All the Mothers Gone? 176p. 1982. 8.95 (ISBN 0-310-45550-2). Zondervan.

Radl, Shirley L. Money, Morals, & Motherhood: The Hidden Agenda of the Religious New Right. 1983. pap. 7.95 (ISBN 0-686-43193-6, Delta). Dell.

--Money, Morals, & Motherhood: The Hidden Agenda of the Religious New Right. 1983. 15.95 (ISBN 0-686-38881-X, Sey Lawr). Delacorte.

Vaughn, Ruth. What's a Mother to Say? 1982. pap. 2.95 (ISBN 0-87162-241-6, D8824). Warner Pr.

MOTHER-GODDESSES

Olson, Carl, ed. The Book of the Goddess, Past & Present: An Introduction to Her Religion. 275p. 1983. 14.95 (ISBN 0-8245-0566-2). Crossroad NY.

MOTHER THERESA

Craig, Mary. Mother Teresa. (Profiles Ser.). (Illus.). 64p. (gr. 4-6). 1983. 7.95 (ISBN 0-241-10933-7, Pub. by Hamish Hamilton England). David & Charles.

MOTHERS

see also Grandparents; Housewives; Maternal and Infant Welfare; Prenatal Care; Stepmothers

Arcana, Judith. Every Mother's Son. LC 82-12912. 336p. 1983. 16.95 (ISBN 0-385-15640-5, Anchor Pr). Doubleday.

Arndt, Elise. A Mother's Touch. 156p. 1983. pap. 4.95 (ISBN 0-88207-101-7). Victor Bks.

Badinter, Elisabeth. Mother Love: Myth & Reality. Gray, Francine, frwd. by. 384p. 1982. pap. 8.95 (ISBN 0-02-048350-3). Macmillan.

Boyce, Jean. What Every Mother Knows. 1982. 5.50 (ISBN 0-686-84484-X). Gibson.

Dally, Ann. Inventing Motherhood: The Consequences of an Ideal. LC 82-10517. 360p. 1983. 19.95 (ISBN 0-8052-3830-1). Schocken.

Deledda, Grazia. The Mother. LC 23-16660. 1974. 12.95 (ISBN 0-910220-57-3). Berg.

Doumanis, Mariella, ed. Mothering in Greece: Behavioral Development. Date not set. price not set. Acad Pr.

Falcon Press Staff. Hi Mom. 64p. 1982. pap. 3.95 (ISBN 0-941404-24-2). Falcon Pr Az.

Gordon, Adele. Somebody's Mother. 48p. 1983. 6.95 (ISBN 0-89962-325-5). Todd & Honeywell.

Hunter, Brenda. Where Have All the Mothers Gone? 176p. 1982. 8.95 (ISBN 0-310-45550-2). Zondervan.

Inoue, Yasushi. Chronicle of My Mother. Moy, Jean O., tr. LC 82-48168. Orig. Title: Waga Haha No Ki. 113p. (Japanese.). 1983. 14.95 (ISBN 0-87011-533-2). Kodansha.

Satprem. Mother's Agenda Nineteen Seventy-one, Vol. 12. LC 80-472990. (Mother's Agenda Ser.). Orig. Title: L'Agenda De Mere, Vol. 12. 400p. (Orig.). 1983. pap. text ed. 12.50 (ISBN 0-938710-05-2). Inst Evolutionary.

MOTHERS-EMPLOYMENT

Aldous, Joan. Her & His Paychecks: Life in Dual Earner Families. (Sage Focus Editions). (Illus.). 232p. 1982. 22.00 (ISBN 0-8039-1882-8); pap. 10.95 (ISBN 0-8039-1883-6). Sage.

Behrman, Debra L. Family and-or Career: Plans of First-Time Mothers. Nathan, Peter, ed. LC 82-17572. (Studies in Clinical Psychology: No. 2). 176p. 1982. 34.95 (ISBN 0-8357-1381-4). Univ Microfilms.

Bodin, Jeanne & Mitelman, Bonnie. Mothers Who Work: Strategies for Coping. 320p. (Orig.). 1983. pap. 5.95 (ISBN 0-345-30140-4). Ballantine.

Copeland, Tom, ed. Parents in the Workplace: A Management Resource for Employers. (Illus.). 30p. folder 16.50 (ISBN 0-934140-17-0). Toys N Things.

Hunter, Brenda. Where Have All the Mothers Gone? 176p. 1982. 8.95 (ISBN 0-310-45550-2). Zondervan.

Kuzma, Kay, ed. Working Mothers. 2nd ed. LC 81-51822. 1981. 14.95 (ISBN 0-936906-08-1). Stratford Pr.

MOTHERS-RELIGIOUS LIFE

Hanes, Mari. The Child Within. 1983. pap. 2.50 (ISBN 0-8423-0219-0). Tyndale.

MOTHERS (IN RELIGION, FOLKLORE, ETC.)

see Mother-Goddesses

MOTHERS, UNMARRIED

see Unmarried Mothers

MOTHS

Fletcher, D. S. & Nye, I. W. The Generic Names of Moths of the World, Vol. IV: Bombycoidea, Castnioidea, Cossoidea, Mimallonoidea, Sesioidea, Sphingoidea, Zygaenoidea, Vol. IV. (Illus.). xiv, 192p. 1982. 56.50 (ISBN 0-565-00848-X). Sabbot-Natural Hist Bks.

Tweedie & Wilkinson. The Butterflies & Moths of Britain & Europe. pap. 8.95 (ISBN 0-686-42746-7, Collins Pub England). Greene.

MOTILITY OF CELLS

see Cells-Motility

MOTION

see also Force and Energy; Kinematics; Mechanical Movements; Mechanics; Movement, Psychology Of; Rotational Motion

Soldano, B. A. Mass, Measurement & Motion Sequel Two: A New Look at Maxwell's Equations & the Permittivity of Free Space. Brantley, William H., ed. (Illus.). 50p. (Orig.). 1982. pap. 7.00x (ISBN 0-943410-00-2). Grenridge Pub.

Watson, Philip. Super Motion. LC 82-80990. (Science Club Ser.). (Illus.). 48p. (gr. 3-6). 1983. PLB 8.16 (ISBN 0-688-00971-9); pap. 5.25 (ISBN 0-688-00976-X). Lothrop.

MOTION PERCEPTION (VISION)

Epstein, W. Stability & Constancy in Visual Perception: Mechanisms & Processes. 463p. 1977. 39.50x (ISBN 0-471-24355-8). Wiley.

Wertheim, Alexander H. & Wagennar, Willem A., eds. Tutorials on Motion Perception. LC 82-16554. (NATO Conference Ser. III, Human Factors: Vol. 20). 280p. 1982. 39.50 (ISBN 0-306-41126-1, Plenum Pr). Plenum Pub.

MOTION-PICTURE CAMERAS

see Moving-Picture Cameras

MOTION PICTURES

see Moving-Pictures

MOTION STUDY

see Time and Motion Study

MOTIVATION (PSYCHOLOGY)

see also Achievement Motivation; Conflict (Psychology); Self-Actualization (Psychology); Threat (Psychology)

Apter, Michael, ed. The Experience of Motivation: The Theory of Psychological Reversals. LC 81-66676. 392p. 1982. 31.50 (ISBN 0-12-058920-6). Acad Pr.

Beck, Robert C. Motivation: Theories & Principles. (Illus.). 480p. 1983. text ed. 23.95 (ISBN 0-13-603910-3). P-H.

Brody, Nathan, ed. Motivation. LC 82-22654. Date not set. price not set (ISBN 0-12-134840-7). Acad Pr.

Buck, Ross W. Human Motivation & Emotion. LC 75-37893. 529p. 1976. text ed. 26.95x (ISBN 0-471-11570-3). Wiley.

Hamilton, Vernon. The Cognitive Structures & Processes of Human Motivation & Personality. 575p. 1983. price not set (ISBN 0-471-10526-0, Pub. by Wiley Interscience). Wiley.

Page, Monte M., ed. Nebraska Symposium on Motivation, 1982: Personality--Current Theory & Research. LC 53-11655. (Nebraska Symposium on Motivation Ser.: Vol. 30). xv, 270p. 1983. 22.95x (ISBN 0-8032-3667-0); pap. 12.95x (ISBN 0-8032-8708-9). U of Nebr Pr.

MOTIVATION IN EDUCATION

Hawley, Robert C. Ten Steps for Motivating Reluctant Learners. 42p. (Orig.). pap. 3.95 (ISBN 0-913636-14-2). Educ Res MA.

MOTONEURON TRANSMISSION

see Neuromuscular Transmission

MOTOR ABILITY

see also Kinesiology

Dixon, John P. The Spatial Child. (Illus.). 288p. 1983. text ed. price not set (ISBN 0-398-04821-5). C C Thomas.

Kawamura, Yojiro, ed. Oral-Facial Sensory & Motor Functions. Dubner, Ronald. (Illus.). 354p. 1981. 72.00 (ISBN 4-87417-077-3). Quint Pub Co.

Lippert, Frederick G., III & Farmer, James. Psychomotor Skills in Orthopaedic Surgery. (Illus.). 171p. Date not set. lib. bdg. price not set (ISBN 0-683-05051-6). Williams & Wilkins.

Wickstrom, Ralph L. Fundamental Motor Patterns. 3rd ed. LC 82-21659. (Illus.). 250p. 1983. text ed. price not set (ISBN 0-8121-0879-5). Lea & Febiger.

MOTOR ABILITY-TESTING

Motor Fitness Testing Manual for the Moderately Mental Retarded. 80p. 1975. 6.50 (ISBN 0-88314-135-3). AAHPERD.

Testing for Impaired, Disabled, & Handicapped Individuals. 112p. 1975. 5.25 (ISBN 0-88314-190-6). AAHPERD.

MOTOR BUS DRIVERS

Rudman, Jack. School Bus Executive. (Career Examination Ser.: C-2887). (Cloth bdg. avail. on request). pap. 14.00 (ISBN 0-8373-2887-X). Natl Learning.

MOTOR BUSES

Creighton, John. British Buses Since 1945. (Illus.). 144p. 1983. 16.95 (ISBN 0-7137-1258-9, Pub. by Blandford Pr England). Sterling.

MOTOR-CARS

see Automobiles

MOTOR CYCLES

see Motorcycles

MOTOR DEXTERITY

see Motor Ability

MOTOR LEARNING

Barrow, Harold M. Man & Movement: Principles of Physical Education. 3rd ed. LC 82-20398. 410p. 1983. text ed. write for info. (ISBN 0-8121-0861-2). Lea & Febiger.

Carr, Janet H. & Shepherd, Roberta B. A Motor Relearning Programme for Stroke. 175p. 1983. 24.50 (ISBN 0-89443-931-6). Aspen Systems.

Espenschade, Anna S. & Eckert, Helen M. Motor Development. 2nd ed. (Special Education Ser.). 368p. 1980. pap. text ed. 9.95 (ISBN 0-675-08142-4). Merrill.

Gallahue, David L. Motor Development & Movement Experiences for Young Children. LC 75-37676. 413p. 1976. text ed. 25.50x (ISBN 0-471-29042-4). Wiley.

MOTOR PSYCHOLOGY

see Movement, Psychology Of

MOTOR SKILL

see Motor Ability

MOTOR-TRUCK DRIVERS

see Highway Transport Workers

MOTOR-TRUCKS

see also Materials Handling; Vans

Burness, Taqd. Pickup & Van Spotter's Guide, 1945-1982. (Illus.). 160p. 1982. pap. 9.95 (ISBN 0-87938-156-6). Motorbooks Intl.

Chek-Chart. Truck Lubrication Guide, 1983. 80p. 1983. pap. text ed. 31.80x (ISBN 0-88098-024-9). H M Gousha.

Edmund's Vans, Pickups, Offroad Buyer's Guide, 1983. (Illus.). 1983. pap. 2.50 (ISBN 0-440-02304-1). Dell.

Hollander Publishing Co., Inc. Auto-Truck Interchange Manual, 3 vols. 48th ed. (Auto-Truck Interchange Ser.). (Illus.). 2166p. Set. 112.00 (ISBN 0-943032-22-9). Hollander Co.

--Auto-Truck Interchange Manual: Wheel Cover Supplement. 48th ed. (Auto-Truck Interchange Ser.). (Illus.). 88p. 1982. 16.00 (ISBN 0-943032-23-7). Hollander Co.

--Auto-Truck Manual: Special Wheel Supplement. 48th ed. (Auto-Truck Interchange Ser.). (Illus.). 16p. 1982. 6.00 (ISBN 0-943032-24-5). Hollander Co.

Trucker's Atlas. 1982. 9.95 (ISBN 0-933162-04-9). Creative Sales.

MOTOR-TRUCKS-JUVENILE LITERATURE

Scarry, Richard. Richard Scarry's Lowly Worm Car & Truck Book. LC 82-61012. (Illus.). 16p. (ps-2). 1983. pap. 2.95 (ISBN 0-394-85760-7). Random.

Sheffer, H. R. Trucks. Schroeder, Howard, ed. (Movin' On Ser.). (Illus.). 48p. (Orig.). (gr. 5-6). 1983. lib. bdg. 7.95 (ISBN 0-89686-197-X). Crestwood Hse.

MOTOR VEHICLE DRIVERS

see Highway Transport Workers; Motor Bus Drivers

MOTOR VEHICLE OPERATORS

see Automobile Drivers

MOTOR VEHICLES

see also Automobiles; Motorcycles; Tracklaying Vehicles

Rudman, Jack. Motor Vehicle Program Manager. (Career Examination Ser.: C-311). (Cloth bdg. avail. on request). pap. 12.00 (ISBN 0-8373-0311-7). Natl Learning.

--Motor Vehicle Program Manager I. (Career Examination Ser.: C-312). (Cloth bdg. avail. on request). pap. 12.00 (ISBN 0-8373-0312-5). Natl Learning.

--Motor Vehicle Program Manager II. (Career Examination Ser.: C-313). (Cloth bdg. avail. on request). pap. 14.00 (ISBN 0-8373-0313-3). Natl Learning.

--Motor Vehicle Program Manager III. (Career Examination Ser.: C-314). (Cloth bdg. avail. on request). pap. 14.00 (ISBN 0-8373-0314-1). Natl Learning.

--Senior Motor Vehicle License Clerk. (Career Examination Ser.: C-2611). (Cloth bdg. avail. on request). pap. 10.00 (ISBN 0-8373-2611-7). Natl Learning.

Wallace, Angelo. Automotive Literature Index: 1977-1981. 327p. pap. 24.95 (ISBN 0-9606804-4-6). Wallace Pub.

MOTOR VEHICLES-EMISSION CONTROL DEVICES

see Motor Vehicles-Pollution Control Devices

MOTOR VEHICLES-EXHAUST CONTROL DEVICES

see Motor Vehicles-Pollution Control Devices

MOTOR VEHICLES-POLLUTION CONTROL DEVICES

Crouse, W. H. & Anglin, D. L. Automotive Emission Control. 3rd ed. 1983. text ed. write for info. (ISBN 0-07-014816-3); write for info. instr's planning guide; write for info wkbk. (ISBN 0-07-014817-1). McGraw.

MOTOR VEHICLES-RECREATIONAL USE

Peterson, Kay. Directory of Informational Sources for RVers. 34p. 1983. pap. 1.95 bklet (ISBN 0-910449-03-1). Roving Pr Pub.

--Home is Where You Park It. Rev. ed. (Illus.). 200p. 1982. pap. 7.95 (ISBN 0-910449-00-7). Roving Pr Pub.

--Is Full-Time RVing for You? (Illus.). 24p. 1983. pap. 1.95 bklet (ISBN 0-910449-04-X). Roving Pr Pub.

--The Rainbow Chasers. (Illus.). 216p. 1982. pap. 6.75 (ISBN 0-910449-01-5). Roving Pr Pub.

--Survival of the Snowbirds. (Illus.). 222p. 1982. pap. 7.95 (ISBN 0-910449-02-3). Roving Pr Pub.

Sheffer, H. R. R.V.'s. Schroeder, Howard, ed. (Movin' On Ser.). (Illus.). 48p. (Orig.). (gr. 5-6). 1983. lib. bdg. 7.95 (ISBN 0-89686-198-8). Crestwood Hse.

Woodall's RV Buyer's Guide, 1983. pap. 2.95 (ISBN 0-671-46094-3). Woodall.

MOTOR VEHICLES-SMOG CONTROL DEVICES

see Motor Vehicles-Pollution Control Devices

MOTOR VEHICLES IN WAR

see Tanks (Military Science)

MOTORCYCLE RACING

Code, Keith. A Twist of the Wrist: The Motorcycle Road Racers Handbook. LC 82-73771. (Illus.). 120p. 1983. 14.95 (ISBN 0-918226-08-2). Acrobat.

MOTORCYCLES

see also Mopeds; Motorcycling

also names of motorcycles, e.g. B.S.A. motorcycle, Honda motorcycle

Wallach, Theresa. Easy Motorcycle Riding. LC 82-19322. (Illus.). 160p. 1983. pap. 4.95 (ISBN 0-8069-7712-4). Sterling.

MOTORCYCLES-JUVENILE LITERATURE

Sheffer, H. R. Cycles. Schroeder, Howard, ed. (Movin' On Ser.). (Illus.). 48p. (Orig.). (gr. 5-6). 1983. lib. bdg. 7.95 (ISBN 0-89686-199-6). Crestwood Hse.

MOTORCYCLING

Stermer, Bill. Motorcycle Touring. LC 82-82675. 160p. 1982. pap. 7.95 (ISBN 0-89586-170-4). H P Bks.

MOTORS

see also Automobiles-Motors; Diesel Motor; Electric Motors; Gas and Oil Engines; Machinery

also subdivision Motors under subjects, e.g. Automobiles-Motors

Britain's Top Five Hundred Motor Distributors. 70p. 1982. 195.00x (ISBN 0-85938-165-X, Pub. by Jordan & Sons England). State Mutual Bk.

Livesey, W. A. Motor Trade Handbook. new ed. 256p. Date not set. pap. text ed. price not set (ISBN 0-408-01135-1). Butterworth.

Rudman, Jack. Motor Equipment Mechanic. (Career Examination Ser.: C-459). (Cloth bdg. avail. on request). pap. 12.00 (ISBN 0-8373-0459-8). Natl Learning.

MOTTOES

Pine, L. G. A Dictionary of Mottoes. 150p. 1983. price not set (ISBN 0-7100-9339-X). Routledge & Kegan.

MOULAGE

see Prosthesis

MOULD, VEGETABLE

see Humus

MOUNT, WILLIAM SYDNEY, 1807-1868

Cassedy, David & Shrott, Gail. William Sidney Mount: Annotated Bibliography & Listings of Archival Holdings of the Museums at Stony Brook. (Illus., Orig.). 1983. pap. write for info. (ISBN 0-943924-05-7). Mus Stony.

MOUNTAIN CLIMBING

see Mountaineering

MOUNTAIN LIONS

see Pumas

MOUNTAINEERING

see also Rock Climbing; Trails

Schneider, Bill. Where the Grizzly Walks. 1982. pap. 8.95 (ISBN 0-87842-153-X). Mountain Pr.

Shaw, Robin. The Climber's Bible: A Complete Basic Guide to Rock & Ice Climbing & an Introduction to Mountaineering. LC 78-20097. (Outdoor Bible Ser.). (Illus.). 144p. 1983. pap. 5.95 (ISBN 0-385-14075-4). Doubleday.

Tasker, Joe. Savage Arena. (Illus.). 288p. 1982. 18.95 (ISBN 0-312-69984-0). St Martin.

MOUNTAINEERING-BIBLIOGRAPHY
Jones, J. Emlyn, intro. by. Alpine Club Library Catalogue: Books & Periodicals. vii, 580p. (Orig.). 1982. pap. 95.00x (ISBN 0-686-82671-X). Heinemann Ed.
MOUNTAINS
see also Geology, Structural; Mountaineering; Volcanoes
Ferriss, Lloyd. Secrets of a Mountain. Jack, Susan, ed. (Secrets of Ser.). (Illus.). 76p. (Orig.). 1982. pap. 5.95 (ISBN 0-930096-18-5). G Gannett.
Jinhai, He. Mount Taishan. (Illus.). 120p. (Orig.). 1982. pap. 7.95 (ISBN 0-8351-0978-X). China Bks.
Lyttleton, R. A. The Earth & Its Mountains. 206p. 1982. 38.95 (ISBN 0-471-10530-9, Pub. by Wiley-Interscience). Wiley.
Updegraffe, Imelda & Updegraffe, Robert. Mountains & Valleys. (Turning Points Ser.). (Illus.). 24p. 1983. pap. 3.50 (ISBN 0-14-049189-9, Puffin). Penguin.
Vaughan, Thomas, et al. Mount St. Helens Remembered. (Illus.). 224p. (Orig.). 1983. price not set (ISBN 0-87595-110-4, Western Imprints); pap. price not set (ISBN 0-87595-111-2, Western Imprints). Oreg Hist Soc.
MOUNTAINS-JUVENILE LITERATURE
George, Jean C. One Day in the Alpine Tundra. LC 82-45590. (Illus.). 48p. (gr. 5-7). 1983. 9.57i (ISBN 0-690-04325-2, TYC-J); PLB 9.89g (ISBN 0-690-04326-0). Har-Row.
MOUNTAINS IN LITERATURE
Tobias, Charles & Drasdo, Harold, eds. The Mountain Spirit. 264p. 1983. pap. 25.00 (ISBN 0-87951-168-0). Overlook Pr.
MOUNTBATTEN, LOUIS MOUNTBATTEN, EARL, 1900-1979
Collins, Larry & Lapierre, Dominique. Mountbatten & the Partition of India. viii, 191p. 1982. text ed. 20.00x (ISBN 0-7069-1787-1, Pub. by Vikas India). Advent NY.
MOUTH
see also Salivary Glands; Teeth
Cimasoni, G. Crevicular Fluid Updated. (Monographs in Oral Science: Vol. 12). (Illus.). viii, 142p. 1983. 60.00 (ISBN 3-8055-3705-0). S Karger.
Gartner, Leslie P. Essentials of Oral Histology & Embryology. LC 82-90755. (Illus.). 120p. 1982. pap. text ed. 8.75 (ISBN 0-910841-00-4). Jen Hse Pub Co.
Learning about Your Oral Health, 5 levels. 7.50 ea. Level I (ISBN 0-934510-16-4, W017). Level II (ISBN 0-934510-17-2, W018). Level III (ISBN 0-934510-18-0, W019). Level IV (ISBN 0-934510-19-9, W020). Pre-school (ISBN 0-934510-20-2, W021). Am Dental.
Oral Health Care for the Geriatric Patient in a Long Term Care Facility. 5.25 (ISBN 0-934510-13-X, J010). Am Dental.
MOUTH-BACTERIOLOGY
see Mouth-Microbiology
MOUTH-DISEASES
Schroeder, H. E. Pathobiologie oraler Strukturen. (Illus.). x, 198p. 1983. pap. 23.50 (ISBN 3-8055-3692-5). S Karger.
MOUTH-DISEASES-DIAGNOSIS
Cohn, Ellen R. & McWilliams, Betty J. Clinical Orofacial Assessment. 200p. 1983. text ed. 20.00 (ISBN 0-941158-13-6, D1078-8). Mosby.
MOUTH-MICROBIOLOGY
McCracken, Alexander W. & Cawson, Broderick A. Clinical & Oral Microbiology. (Illus.). 1982. text ed. 32.00 (ISBN 0-07-010296-1, C). McGraw.
MOUTH-SURGERY
see also Teeth-Extraction
Messing, J. J. Operative Dental Surgery. 2nd ed. 1982. 79.00x (ISBN 0-333-31040-3, Pub. by Macmillan England). State Mutual Bk.
Moore, J. R. & Gillbe, G. V., eds. Principles of Oral Surgery. 3rd ed. 254p. pap. 12.50 (ISBN 0-7190-0801-8). Manchester.
MOUTH-ORGAN
Gindick, Jon. Rock N' Blurs Harmonica. 2nd ed. (Illus.). 1982. 7.95 (ISBN 0-930948-02-5). J Gindick.
MOVEMENT, DISORDERS OF
see Movement Disorders
MOVEMENT, ECUMENICAL
see Ecumenical Movement
MOVEMENT, PSYCHOLOGY OF
see also Motion Perception (Vision); Motor Ability; Time and Motion Study
Laban, Rudolph & Lawrence, F. C. Effort. 112p. 1979. 30.00x (ISBN 0-7121-0534-4, Pub. by Macdonald & Evans). State Mutual Bk.
MOVEMENT CURE
see Mechanotherapy
MOVEMENT DISORDERS
DeVeaugh-Geiss, Joseph. Tardive Dyskinesia & Related Involuntary Movement Disorders. (Illus.). 222p. 1982. text ed. 35.00 (ISBN 0-7236-7006-4). Wright-PSG.
MOVEMENTS OF PLANTS
see Plants-Irritability and Movements
MOVIE CAMERAS
see Moving-Picture Cameras
MOVING, HOUSEHOLD
Mathews, Betty W. How to get the Nittie Gritties Out of that Move. 64p. 1983. pap. 3.50 (ISBN 0-86666-087-9). GWP.
MOVING OF BUILDINGS, BRIDGES, ETC.
Finsand, Mary J. The Town that Moved. LC 82-9703. (Carolrhoda on my Own Bks). (Illus.). 48p. (gr. 1-4). 1983. PLB 6.95g (ISBN 0-87614-200-5). Carolrhoda Bks.
MOVING-PICTURE ACTORS AND ACTRESSES
Daniel, John. Ava Gardner. (Illus.). 224p. 1983. 10.95 (ISBN 0-312-06240-0). St Martin.
Hampshire, Susan. Susan's Story: An Autobiographical Account of My Struggle with Words. (Illus.). 168p. 1982. 11.95 (ISBN 0-312-77966-6). St Martin.
Herman, Gary. Burt Reynolds: Flesh & Blood Fantasy. (Illus.). 144p. (Orig.). 1983. pap. 9.95 (ISBN 0-933328-64-8). Delilah Bks.
Lenburg, Len. Dustin Hoffman: Hollywood's Anti-Hero. (Illus.). 192p. 1983. 10.95 (ISBN 0-312-22268-8). St Martin.
Pohle, Robert W., Jr. & Hart, Douglas C. The Films of Christopher Lee. LC 82-10424. (Illus.). 249p. 1983. 32.50 (ISBN 0-8108-1573-7). Scarecrow.
Robinson, Jay & Hardiman, Jim. The Comeback. 1983. pap. 2.95 (ISBN 0-8423-0401-0). Tyndale.
Thomas, Bob. Golden Boy: The Untold Story of William Holden. (Illus.). 1983. 16.95 (ISBN 0-312-33697-7). St Martin.
Thomas, Tony. The Films of Olivia de Havilland. (Illus.). 256p. 1983. 18.95 (ISBN 0-8065-0805-1). Citadel Pr.
Wilding, Michael. The Wilding Way: The Story of My Life. (Illus.). 240p. 1982. 10.95 (ISBN 0-312-87954-7). St Martin.
MOVING-PICTURE ADAPTATIONS
see Film Adaptations
MOVING-PICTURE AUTHORSHIP
Haun, Harry. The Movie Quote Book. LC 82-48799. (Illus.). 432p. (Orig.). 1983. pap. 8.61i (ISBN 0-06-091045-3, CN 1045, CN). Har-Row.
Pauly, Thomas H. An American Odyssey: Elia Kazan & American Culture. 1983. write for info. (ISBN 0-87722-296-7). Temple U Pr.
Schwartz, N. L. & Schwartz, S. The Hollywood Writers' Wars. 352p. 1983. pap. 8.95 (ISBN 0-07-055791-8, GB). McGraw.
MOVING-PICTURE CAMERAS
Gleasner, Diana. The Movies. (Inventions That Changed Our Lives Ser.). (Illus.). (gr. 4-6). 1983. 7.95 (ISBN 0-8027-6482-7); lib. bdg. 8.85 (ISBN 0-8027-6483-5). Walker & Co.
MOVING-PICTURE CARTOONS
Lenburg, Jeff. The Encyclopedia of Animated Cartoon Series. (Quality Paperbacks Ser.). (Illus.). 192p. 1983. pap. 14.95 (ISBN 0-306-80191-4). Da Capo.
--The Great Cartoon Directors. LC 82-23923. (Illus.). 1983. lib. bdg. price not set (ISBN 0-89950-036-6). McFarland & Co.
MOVING-PICTURE CRITICISM
Here are entered works dealing with the concept and technique of moving-picture reviews.
see also Moving-Picture Plays-History and Criticism
Geduld, Harry M. Dr. Jekyll & Mr. Hyde: An Anthology of Commentary, Including the Text. LC 82-48271. 175p. 1983. lib. bdg. 25.00 (ISBN 0-8240-9469-7). Garland Pub.
Mintz, Marilyn D. The Martial Arts Films. LC 82-74498. (Illus.). 243p. 1983. Repr. of 1978 ed. 12.95 (ISBN 0-8048-1408-2). C E Tuttle.
MOVING-PICTURE DIRECTION
see Moving-Pictures-Production and Direction
MOVING-PICTURE EDITING
see Moving-Pictures-Editing
MOVING-PICTURE FILM EDITING
see Moving-Pictures-Editing
MOVING-PICTURE INDUSTRY
see also Moving-Pictures-Production and Direction
Fell, John L. Film Before Griffith. 352p. 1983. pap. 12.95 (ISBN 0-520-04758-3, CAL 578). U of Cal Pr.
Goldman, William. Adventures in the Screen Trade: A Personal View of Hollywood & Screenwriting. 416p. 1983. pap. 17.50 (ISBN 0-446-51273-7). Warner Bks.
Hurst, Walter E. The Movie Industry Book, Part II. Rico, Don & Kargodorian, Annette, eds. (The Entertainment Industry Ser.: Vol. 23). (Illus.). 112p. (Orig.). 1982. 20.00 (ISBN 0-911370-56-0); pap. 10.00 (ISBN 0-911370-55-2). Seven Arts.
Kaplan, Mike, ed. Variety: International Motion Picture Marketplace, 1982-1983. LC 82-9182. 430p. 1982. 50.00 (ISBN 0-8240-9378-X). Garland Pub.
Locke, Robert, ed. Hollywood Reporter Studio Blu-Book. 280p. 1983. pap. 25.00 (ISBN 0-941140-01-6). Verdugo Pr.
Maltby, Richard. Harmless Entertainmnet: Hollywood & the Ideology of Concensus. LC 82-10344. 425p. 1983. 26.50 (ISBN 0-8108-1548-6). Scarecrow.
Mast, Gerald. Movies in Our Midst: Documents in the Cultural History of Film in America. LC 81-16223. (Illus.). xxiv, 766p. 1983. pap. 12.50 (ISBN 0-226-50981-8). U of Chicago Pr.
Novak, Don. Screenplay Sales Directory the Complete How, Who & Where of Selling your Film-Tv Script. rev. ed. 100p. 1983. pap. 12.95 (ISBN 0-910665-00-1); pap. text ed. 10.35. Joshua Pub Co.
Perry, George. Movies From the Mansion: A History of Pinewood Studios. (Illus.). 192p. 1982. 19.95 (ISBN 0-241-10799-7). NY Zoetrope.
Squire, Jason E. The Movie Business Book. (Illus.). 448p. 1983. 24.95 (ISBN 0-13-604603-7); pap. 13.95 (ISBN 0-13-604595-2). P-H.
Stuart, Jerome. Those Crazy Wonderful Years: When We Ran Warner Brothers. (Illus.). 256p. 1983. 14.95 (ISBN 0-686-82522-5). Lyle Stuart.
MOVING-PICTURE INDUSTRY-BIOGRAPHY
see Moving-Pictures-Biography
MOVING-PICTURE MUSIC
Arnell & Groucutt. Music for TV & Films. (Illus.). 1983. 31.95x (ISBN 0-240-51196-4). Focal Pr.
Atkins, Irene K. Source Music in Motion Pictures. LC 81-65338. (Illus.). 192p. 1983. 22.50 (ISBN 0-8386-3076-6). Fairleigh Dickinson.
MOVING-PICTURE PLAYS
see also Film Adaptations; Moving-Pictures-Plots, Themes, etc.
Briley, John. Gandhi: Screenplay for the Film by Richard Attenborough. 192p. 1983. 6.95 (ISBN 0-394-62471-8, E856, Ever). Grove.
Cowie, Peter, ed. International Film Guide 1983. (International Film Guide Ser.). (Illus.). 496p. 1982. pap. 10.95 (ISBN 0-900730-00-5). NY Zoetrope.
Goldman, William. Adventures in the Screen Trade: A Personal View of Hollywood & Screenwriting. 416p. 1983. pap. 17.50 (ISBN 0-446-51273-7). Warner Bks.
Mazursky, Paul & Capetanos, Leon. Tempest: A Screenplay. LC 82-81975. (Illus.). 1982. 11.95 (ISBN 0-933826-40-0); pap. 4.95 (ISBN 0-933826-41-9). Performing Arts.
Mordden, Ethan. The Hollywood Musical. (Illus.). 264p. 1982. pap. 8.95 (ISBN 0-312-38838-1). St Martin.
Novak, Don. Screenplay Sales Directory the Complete How, Who & Where of Selling your Film-Tv Script. rev. ed. 100p. 1983. pap. 12.95 (ISBN 0-910665-00-1); pap. text ed. 10.35. Joshua Pub Co.
Pickard, Roy. Movies on Video. 1982. 20.00x (ISBN 0-584-11029-4, Pub. by Muller Ltd). State Mutual Bk.
MOVING-PICTURE PLAYS-HISTORY AND CRITICISM
Fell, John L. Film Before Griffith. 352p. 1983. pap. 12.95 (ISBN 0-520-04758-3, CAL 578). U of Cal Pr.
Halliwell, Leslie. Halliwell's Hundred: A Nostalgic Choice of Films from the Golden Age. LC 81-84272. 403p. 1982. 25.00 (ISBN 0-684-17447-2). Scribner.
Hoberman, J. & Rosenbaum, Jonathan. Midnight Movies. LC 82-47526. (Illus.). 224p. 1983. 14.95 (ISBN 0-06-015052-1, HarpT); pap. 7.95i (ISBN 0-06-090990-0, CN-990). Har-Row.
Munn, Michael. Great Film Epics: The Stories Behind the Scenes. (Ungar Film Library). (Illus.). 191p. 1983. pap. 11.95 (ISBN 0-8044-6532-0). Ungar.
MOVING-PICTURE PLOTS
see Moving-Pictures-Plots, Themes, etc.
MOVING-PICTURE PRODUCERS AND DIRECTORS
Coursodon, J. P. & Sauvage, Pierre. American Directors, 2 Vols. 1983. Vol. I, 448p. 21.95 (ISBN 0-07-013263-1, GB); pap. 11.95 (ISBN 0-07-013261-5); Vol. II, 432p. 21.95 (ISBN 0-07-013264-X); pap. 11.95 (ISBN 0-07-013262-3). McGraw.
Curtis, James. James Whale. LC 82-5965. (Filmmakers Ser.: No. 1). 267p. 1982. 16.50 (ISBN 0-8108-1561-3). Scarecrow.
Krogh, Daniel & McCarty, John. The Amazing Herschell Gordon Lewis & His World of Exploitation Films. (Illus.). 240p. (Orig.). 1983. pap. 14.95x (ISBN 0-938782-03-7). Fantaco.
Kurosawa, Akira. Something Like an Autobiography. Bock, Audie E., tr. from Japanese. LC 82-48900. 240p. 1983. pap. 6.95 (ISBN 0-394-71439-3, Vin). Random.
Leki, Ilona. Alain Robbe-Grillet. (World Authors Ser.). 200p. 1983. lib. bdg. 16.95 (ISBN 0-8057-6529-8, Twayne). G K Hall.
Lenburg, Jeff. The Great Cartoon Directors. LC 82-23923. (Illus.). 1983. lib. bdg. price not set (ISBN 0-89950-036-6). McFarland & Co.
Lev, Peter. Claude Lelouch, Film Director. LC 81-72036. (Illus.). 184p. 1982. 24.50 (ISBN 0-8386-3114-2). Fairleigh Dickinson.
Nowell-Smith, Geoffrey. Visconti. 1967. pap. 8.95 (ISBN 0-436-09853-9, Pub by Secker & Warburg). David & Charles.
Schelly, William. Harry Langdon. LC 82-6035. (Filmmakers Ser.: No. 3). 249p. 1982. 16.00 (ISBN 0-8108-1567-2). Scarecrow.
Shores, Edward. George Roy Hill. (Filmmakers Ser.). 208p. 1983. lib. bdg. 19.95 (ISBN 0-8057-9290-2, Twayne). G K Hall.
Thompson, Frank T. William A. Wellman. (Filmmakers Ser.: No. 4). 339p. 1983. 22.50 (ISBN 0-8108-1594-X). Scarecrow.
Tonetti, Claretta. Luchino Visconti. (Filmmakers Ser.). 219p. 1983. lib. bdg. 24.00 (ISBN 0-8057-9289-9, Twayne). G K Hall.
MOVING-PICTURE PRODUCTION
see Moving-Pictures-Production and Direction
MOVING-PICTURE PROJECTION
see also Moving-Picture Projectors
Kloepfel, Don V., frwd. by. Motion Picture Projection & Theatre Presentation Manual. (Illus.). 166p. 1982. pap. text ed. 20.00 (ISBN 0-940690-01-2). Soc Motion Pic & TV Engrs.
MOVING-PICTURE PROJECTORS
Gleasner, Diana. The Movies. (Inventions That Changed Our Lives Ser.). (Illus.). (gr. 4-6). 1983. 7.95 (ISBN 0-8027-6482-7); lib. bdg. 8.85 (ISBN 0-8027-6483-5). Walker & Co.
MOVING-PICTURE STARS
see Moving-Picture Actors and Actresses
MOVING-PICTURE THEATERS
see also Moving-Picture Projection
Kloepfel, Don V., frwd. by. Motion Picture Projection & Theatre Presentation Manual. (Illus.). 166p. 1982. pap. text ed. 20.00 (ISBN 0-940690-01-2). Soc Motion Pic & TV Engrs.
Kobal, John. Foyer Pleasure: Fifty Colourful Years of Cinema Lobby Cards. 160p. 1982. 32.00x (ISBN 0-906053-33-1, Pub. by Cave Pubns England). State Mutual Bk.
MOVING-PICTURE WRITING
see Moving-Picture Authorship
MOVING-PICTURES
Here are entered general works on moving-pictures. Works on organization and management in the motion picture field are entered under Moving-Picture Industry. Works on photographic processes are entered under Cinematography.
see also Afro-Americans in Motion Pictures; Cinematography; Horror Films; Moving-Picture Projection; Women in Moving-Pictures
Belton, John. Cinema Stylists. LC 82-10793. (Filmmakers Ser.: No. 2). (Illus.). 384p. 1983. 19.50 (ISBN 0-8108-1585-0). Scarecrow.
Essoe, Gabe. The Book of Movielists. (Illus.). 256p. 1982. pap. 8.95 (ISBN 0-517-54802-X, Arlington Hse). Crown.
Finch, Christopher. Making of the Dark Crystal. (Illus.). 96p. 1983. pap. 10.95 (ISBN 0-686-84850-0). HR&W.
Harmetz, Aljean. Rolling Breaks: And other Movie Business. LC 82-49191. 1983. 13.95 (ISBN 0-394-52886-7). Knopf.
Horrocho, Roger & Tremewan, Phillip. On Film. (Illus.). 72p. 1980. pap. 6.95 (ISBN 0-86863-356-9, Pub. by Heinemann Pubs New Zealands). Intl Schol Bk Serv.
Roud, Richard. A Passion for Films. 1983. pap. 15.75 (ISBN 0-670-36687-0). Viking Pr.
Rovin, Jeff. The Second Signet Book of Movie Lists. 1982. pap. 1.95 (ISBN 0-451-11516-3, AJ1516, Sig). NAL.
Stoddard, Karen M. Saints & Shrews: Women & Aging in American Popular Film. LC 82-15821. (Contributions in Women's Studies: No. 39). 192p. 1983. lib. bdg. 27.95 (ISBN 0-313-23391-8, STS/). Greenwood.
Thomas, Sari, ed. Film-Culture: Explorations of Cinema in Its Social Context. LC 81-23254. 281p. 1982. 17.50 (ISBN 0-8108-1519-2); pap. 8.50 (ISBN 0-8108-1520-6). Scarecrow.
Withers, Robert S. Introduction to Film. (Illus.). 304p. (Orig.). 1983. pap. 5.72i (ISBN 0-686-37885-7, COS CO 202). B&N NY.
Young, Robert, Jr. Movie Memo. (Illus.). 64p. 1982. 24.00 (ISBN 0-88014-058-5). Mosaic Pr OH.
MOVING-PICTURES-BIBLIOGRAPHY
International Film Bibliography, 1981, Vol. II. 165p. 1982. 29.95 (ISBN 3-88690-056-8). NY Zoetrope.
MOVING-PICTURES-BIOGRAPHY
see also Moving-Picture Actors and Actresses; Moving-Picture Producers and Directors
Finch, Christopher. Making of the Dark Crystal. (Illus.). 96p. 1983. pap. 10.95 (ISBN 0-686-84850-0). HR&W.
Goldman, William. Adventures in the Screen Trade: A Personal View of Hollywood & Screenwriting. 416p. 1983. pap. 17.50 (ISBN 0-446-51273-7). Warner Bks.
Jacques Cattell Press. Who Was Who on Screen. 3rd ed. 1983. 65.00 (ISBN 0-8352-1578-4). Bowker.
Kurosawa, Akira. Something Like an Autobiography. Bock, Audie E., tr. from Japanese. LC 82-48900. 240p. 1983. pap. 6.95 (ISBN 0-394-71439-3, Vin). Random.
Pollock, Dale. Skywalking: The Life & Films of George Lucas. 1983. 14.95 (ISBN 0-517-54677-9, Harmony). Crown.
MOVING-PICTURES-CENSORSHIP
Inglis, Ruth, ed. Freedom of the Movies: A Report of Self-Regulation from the Commission on Freedom of the Press. LC 74-3391. x, 240p. 1974. Repr. of 1947 ed. lib. bdg. 32.50 (ISBN 0-306-70591-5). Da Capo.
MOVING-PICTURES-COSTUME
see Costume
MOVING-PICTURES-CRITICISM
see Moving-Picture Criticism
MOVING-PICTURES-DIRECTION
see Moving-Pictures-Production and Direction
MOVING-PICTURES-DIRECTORIES
Maltin, Leonard, ed. The Whole Film Sourcebook. 1982. pap. 8.95 (ISBN 0-452-25361-6, Z5361, Plume). NAL.
--The Whole Film Sourcebook. LC 82-84314. 476p. 1983. 14.95 (ISBN 0-87663-416-1). Universe.
Media Referral Service. The Film File: 1982-83 Edition. 341p. (Orig.). 1982. pap. 30.00 (ISBN 0-911125-01-9). Media Ref.
Pickard, Roy. Movies on Video. 1982. 20.00x (ISBN 0-584-11029-4, Pub. by Muller Ltd). State Mutual Bk.

Samuels, Stuart. Midnight Movies. 224p. 1983. 9.95 (ISBN 0-02-081450-X). Macmillan.

MOVING-PICTURES–EDITING

Academy of Motion Picture Arts & Science. Annual Index to Motion Picture Credits, 1981. LC 79-644761. 469p. 1982. lib. bdg. 150.00 (ISBN 0-686-82498-9, AN81). Greenwood.

MOVING-PICTURES–FILM EDITING

see Moving-Pictures–Editing

MOVING-PICTURES–HISTORY

Altomara, Rita E. Hollywood on the Palisades: A Filmography of Silent Feaures Made in Fort Lee, New Jersey 1903-1927. 120p. 1983. lib. bdg. 20.00 (ISBN 0-8240-9225-2). Garland Pub.

Beaver, Frank. On Film: A History of the Motion Picture. 544p. 1982. 21.50 (ISBN 0-07-004219-5, C). McGraw.

D. W. Griffith Papers, 1897-1954. 190p. 1982. reference bk. 9.95 (ISBN 0-667-00673-7). Microfilming Corp.

Eaton, Mick, ed. Screen Reader Two: Cinema & Semiotics. Neale, Stephen. 197p. 1982. 17.95 (ISBN 0-900676-08-6). NY Zoetrope.

Geist, Kenneth. Pictures Will Talk: The Life & Films of Joseph L. Mankiewicz. (Quality Paperbacks Ser.). (Illus.). 458p. 1983. pap. 9.95 (ISBN 0-306-80188-4). Da Capo.

Insdorf, Annett. Indelible Shadows: Film & the Holocaust. LC 82-48892. (Illus.). 256p. 1983. pap. 8.95 (ISBN 0-394-71464-4, Vin). Random.

Koszarski, Richard. The Astoria Studio & Its Fabulous Films: A Picture History with 225 Stills & Photographs. (Illus.). 144p. (Orig.). (gr. 7 up). 1983. pap. 9.95 (ISBN 0-486-24475-X). Dover.

McCarty, John. Splatter Movies Two: Breaking the Last Taboo. rev. ed. (Illus.). 250p. 1983. pap. 14.95x (ISBN 0-938782-04-5). Fantaco.

McClure, Arthur F. Research Guide to Film History. LC 81-86010. 125p. (Orig.). 1983. pap. 15.95 (ISBN 0-88247-689-0). R & E Res Assoc.

Mast, Gerald. Movies in Our Midst: Documents in the Cultural History of Film in America. LC 81-16223. (Illus.). xxiv, 766p. 1983. pap. 12.50 (ISBN 0-226-50981-8). U of Chicago Pr.

Perry, George. Movies From the Mansion: A History of Pinewood Studios. (Illus.). 192p. 1982. 19.95 (ISBN 0-241-10799-7). NY Zoetrope.

Rollins, Peter C., ed. Hollywood as Historian: American Film in a Cultural Context. LC 82-49118. 288p. 1983. 26.00 (ISBN 0-8131-1486-1); pap. 10.00 (ISBN 0-8131-0154-9). U Pr of Ky.

Sarris, Andrew. The John Ford Movie Mystery. LC 75-37286. (Illus.). 192p. 1983. pap. 6.95 (ISBN 0-253-28515-1). Ind U Pr.

Short, K. R. Film & Propaganda in World War II. LC 82-23838. 300p. 1983. text ed. 23.95x (ISBN 0-87049-386-8). U of Tenn Pr.

Simon, John. Something to Declare: Twelve Years of Films from Abroad. LC 82-16534. 422p. 1983. 19.95 (ISBN 0-686-42946-X, C N Potter). Crown.

MOVING-PICTURES–MONTAGE

see Moving-Pictures–Editing

MOVING-PICTURES–MORAL AND RELIGIOUS ASPECTS

Short, Robert. The Gospel from Outer Space. 1983. pap. 5.95 (ISBN 0-686-43269-X, HarpR). Harper Row.

MOVING-PICTURES–MUSICAL ACCOMPANIMENT

see Moving-Picture Music

MOVING-PICTURES–PLAY-WRITING

see Moving-Picture Authorship

MOVING-PICTURES–PLOTS, THEMES, ETC.

Films on specific topics are entered under specific headings, e.g. Horror Films; War Films; Children in Motion Pictures; Death in Motion Pictures.

see also Film Adaptations

Garbicz, Adam & Klinowski, Jacek. Cinema, the Magic Vehicle: A Guide to It's Achievement. LC 82-10405. (Illus.). 560p. 1983. pap. 12.50 (ISBN 0-686-84572-2). Schocken.

Horner, William R. Bad at the Bijou. (Illus.). 168p. 1982. lib. bdg. 17.95x (ISBN 0-89950-060-9). McFarland & Co.

MOVING-PICTURES–PRODUCTION AND DIRECTION

see also Moving-Picture Producers and Directors

Association of Independent Producers. Independent Production Handbook. (Illus.). 1982. 25.95 (ISBN 0-240-51204-9). Focal Pr.

Dworkin, Susan. Making Tootsie: A Film Study With Dustin Hoffman & Sydney Pollack. 192p. 1983. pap. 6.95 (ISBN 0-937858-19-6). Newmarket.

Geist, Kenneth. Pictures Will Talk: The Life & Films of Joseph L. Mankiewicz. (Quality Paperbacks Ser.). (Illus.). 458p. 1983. pap. 9.95 (ISBN 0-306-80188-4). Da Capo.

Howkins, John. New Technologies, New Policies? 74p. 1982. pap. 9.95 (ISBN 0-85170-128-0). NY Zoetrope.

Munn, Michael. Great Film Epics: The Stories Behind the Scenes. (Ungar Film Library). (Illus.). 191p. 1983. pap. 11.95 (ISBN 0-8044-6532-0). Ungar.

Silver, Alain & Ward, Elizabeth. The Film Director's Team: A Practical Guide to Organizing & Managing Film Production. LC 82-18181. (Illus.). 224p. 1983. 12.95 (ISBN 0-668-05466-2). Arco.

Singer, Michael & Flying Armadillo Staff, eds. Directors: A Complete Guide. 300p. 1982. pap. text ed. 30.00 (ISBN 0-943728-00-2). Lone Eagle Prods.

Thompson, David. Overexposures: The Crisis in American Filmmaking. 333p. 1981. pap. 8.95 (ISBN 0-688-00489-X). Quill NY.

Wiese, Michael. Film & Video Budgets. 1983. pap. 14.95 (ISBN 0-941188-02-7). M Wiese Film Prod.

MOVING-PICTURES–REVIEWS

Alvarez, Max J. Index to Motion Pictures Reviewed by Variety, 1907-1980. LC 81-23236. 520p. 1982. 32.50 (ISBN 0-8108-1515-X). Scarecrow.

Slide, Anthony, ed. Selected Film Criticism: 1896-1911. LC 82-10623. 134p. 1982. 11.00 (ISBN 0-8108-1575-3). Scarecrow.

--Selected Film Criticism, 1931-1940. LC 82-10642. 292p. 1982. 16.00 (ISBN 0-8108-1570-2). Scarecrow.

--Selected Film Criticism, 1941-1950. LC 81-23344. 280p. 1983. 17.50 (ISBN 0-8108-1593-1). Scarecrow.

MOVING-PICTURES–SOCIAL ASPECTS

Rollins, Peter C., ed. Hollywood as Historian: American Film in a Cultural Context. LC 82-49118. 288p. 1983. 26.00 (ISBN 0-8131-1486-1); pap. 10.00 (ISBN 0-8131-0154-9). U Pr of Ky.

MOVING-PICTURES–SPECIAL EFFECTS

see Cinematography, Trick

MOVING-PICTURES–STUDY AND TEACHING

McDonald, Bruce & Orsinsi, Leslie. Basic Language Skills Through Film: An Instructional Program for Secondary Students. 300p. 1983. lib. bdg. 22.50 (ISBN 0-87287-368-4). Libs Unl.

MOVING-PICTURES–TITLING

see Moving-Pictures–Editing

MOVING-PICTURES–VOCATIONAL GUIDANCE

see Moving-Pictures As a Profession

MOVING-PICTURES–YEARBOOKS

Clark, Al. The Film Yearbook 1983. (Illus.). 192p. (Orig.). 1983. pap. 12.95 (ISBN 0-394-62465-3, Ever). Grove.

Cowie, Peter, ed. International Film Guide 1983. (International Film Guide Ser.). (Illus.). 496p. 1982. pap. 10.95 (ISBN 0-900730-00-5). NY Zoetrope.

Kemps International Film & Television Yearbook, 1981-82. 26th ed. LC 59-47486. 1074p. 1981. 65.00x (ISBN 0-905255-99-2). Intl Pubns Serv.

Kemps International Film & Television Yearbook, 1982-83. 27th ed. LC 59-47486. 1216p. 1982. 65.00x (ISBN 0-86259-019-1). Intl Pubns Serv.

MOVING-PICTURES–FRANCE

Bandy, Mary Lea, ed. Rediscovering French Film. (Illus.). 240p. 1982. pap. 14.95 (ISBN 0-87070-335-8, Pub. by Museum Mod Art). NYGS.

Paris, James R. The Great French Films. (Illus.). 288p. 1983. 18.95 (ISBN 0-8065-0806-X). Citadel Pr.

MOVING-PICTURES–GERMANY

Franklin, James. New German Cinema. (Filmmakers Ser.). 248p. 1983. lib. bdg. 19.95 (ISBN 0-8057-9288-0, Twayne). G K Hall.

Welch, David. Propaganda & the German Cinema, 1933-1945. (Illus.). 420p. 1983. 34.00 (ISBN 0-19-822598-9). Oxford U Pr.

MOVING-PICTURES–GREAT BRITAIN

McArthur, Colin, ed. Scotch Reels. (Illus.). 96p. 1982. pap. 9.95 (ISBN 0-85170-121-3). NY Zoetrope.

Wilson, David, ed. Projecting Britain: Ealing Studios Film Posters. (Illus.). 96p. 1982. 19.95 (ISBN 0-85170-122-1). NY Zoetrope.

MOVING-PICTURES–JAPAN

Silver, Alain. The Samurai Film. LC 82-22288. (Illus.). 242p. 1983. 17.95 (ISBN 0-87951-175-3). Overlook Pr.

MOVING-PICTURES–RUSSIA

Dulmatovskaya, G. & Shilova, I. Who's Who in Soviet Cinema. 685p. 1982. 12.50 (ISBN 0-8285-1553-0, Pub. by Progress Pubs USSR). Imported Pubns.

MOVING-PICTURES, DOCUMENTARY

Barnouw, Erik. Documentary: A History of the Non-Fiction Film. rev. ed. (Illus.). 368p. 1983. pap. 8.95 (ISBN 0-19-503301-9, GB 451, GB). Oxford U Pr.

MOVING-PICTURES, TALKING

see also Video Tapes

Booth, Wayne C. The Rhetoric of Film. Rev. ed. 576p. 1982. pap. 9.95 (ISBN 0-226-06558-8). U of Chicago Pr.

MOVING-PICTURES AND RELIGION

see Moving-Pictures–Moral and Religious Aspects

MOVING-PICTURES AS A PROFESSION

see also Acting As a Profession

Bell, Rivian & Koenig, Teresa. Careers at a Movie Studio. LC 82-20865. (Early Career Bks.). (Illus.). 36p. (gr. 2-5). 1983. PLB 5.95g (ISBN 0-8225-0347-6). Lerner Pubns.

MOVING-PICTURES IN EDUCATION

National Information Center for Educational Media. Index to 16mm Educational Film. LC 82-60348. 1983. pap. 164.00 (ISBN 0-89320-052-2). Univ SC Natl Info.

--Index to 35mm Educational Filmstrips. 1983. pap. 124.00 (ISBN 0-89320-054-9). Univ SC Natl Info.

MOVING-PICTURES ON TELEVISION

see Television Broadcasting of Films

MOZAMBIQUE

Isaacman, Allen & Isaacman, Barbara. Mozambique: Sowing the Seeds of Revolution. 160p. 1983. lib. bdg. price not set (ISBN 0-86531-210-9). Westview.

MOZART, JOHANN CHRYSOSTOM WOLFGANG AMADEUS, 1756-1791

Osborne, Charles. The Complete Operas of Mozart. (Quality Paperbacks Ser.). (Illus.). 349p. 1983. pap. 9.95 (ISBN 0-306-80190-6). Da Capo.

Sadie, Stanley. The New Grove Mozart. (New Grove Composer Biography Ser.). (Illus.). 1983. 16.50 (ISBN 0-393-01680-3); pap. 7.95 (ISBN 0-393-30084-6). Norton.

Smith, Erik. Mozart Serenades, Divertimenti, & Dances. LC 81-71300. (BBC Music Guides Ser.). (Orig.). 1983. pap. 4.95 (ISBN 0-686-43217-7). U of Wash Pr.

MOZART, JOHANN CHRYSOSTOM WOLFGANG AMADEUS, 1756-1791–JUVENILE LITERATURE

McLeish, Kenneth & McLeish, Valerie. Mozart. (Composers & their World Ser.). (Illus.). 90p. (gr. 9-12). 1983. 5.95 (ISBN 0-434-95125-0, Pub. by Heinemann England). David & Charles.

MUCK

see Humus

MUCOVISCIDOSIS

see Cystic Fibrosis

MUD-LADEN FLUIDS

see Drilling Muds

MUDS, DRILLING

see Drilling Muds

MUHAMMAD 'ABD ALLAH, CALLED THE MAD MULLAH, d. 1920

Ismail, V. Muhammad: The Last Prophet. 4.95 (ISBN 0-686-83579-4). Kazi Pubns.

MUHAMMAD THE PROPHET

see Mohammed, the Prophet, 570-632

MUHAMMADANISM

see Islam

MUHAMMADANS

see Muslims

MUI TSAI

see Slavery

MULTICOMPONENT FLOW

see Multiphase Flow

MULTI-FAMILY HOUSING

see Apartment Houses

MULTILINGUALISM

see also Bilingualism

Lourie, Margaret & Conklin, Nancy. A Host of Tongues. 272p. 1983. write for info. (ISBN 0-02-906390-6); pap. text ed. write for info. (ISBN 0-02-906500-3). Free Pr.

MULTINATIONAL CORPORATIONS

see International Business Enterprises

MULTIPHASE FLOW

see also Two-Phase Flow

Greenkorn. Flow Phenomena. (Energy, Power & Environment Ser.). 520p. 1983. 75.00 (ISBN 0-8247-1861-5). Dekker.

Heidrick, T. R., ed. Measurement in Polyphase Flows-Nineteen Eighty-Two. 129p. 30.00 (G00209). ASME.

Holland, C. D. Fundamentals of Multicomponent Distillation. 1981. text ed. 39.95 (ISBN 0-07-029567-0); solutions manual avail. McGraw.

Meyer, Richard E., ed. Theory of Dispersed Multiphase Flow. (Symposium). Date not set. 28.00 (ISBN 0-12-493120-0). Acad Pr.

MULTI-PHASE MATERIALS

see Composite Materials

MULTIPLE EMPLOYMENT

see Supplementary Employment

MULTIPLE LINE INSURANCE

see Insurance, Multiple Line

MULTIPLE SCLEROSIS

Kuroiwa, Y. & Kurland, L. T., eds. Multiple Sclerosis East & West. (Illus.). vi, 398p. 1983. 118.75 (ISBN 3-8055-3674-7). S Karger.

Multiple Sclerosis: A Self-Help Guide. 1982. 7.95x (ISBN 0-7225-0804-2). Cancer Control Soc.

MULTIPLICATION

Frank Schaffer Publications. Kindergarten Skills. (Getting Ready for Kindergarten Ser.). (Illus.). 24p. (ps-k). 1980. workbook 1.29 (ISBN 0-86734-012-6, FS 3025). Schaffer Pubns.

Mock, Valerie E. Mulitiplication & Division Riddles. (Learning Workbooks Mathematics). (gr. 3-5). pap. 1.50 (ISBN 0-686-38851-8). Pitman.

--Multiplication Drill. (Learning Workbooks Mathematics). (gr. 3-5). pap. 1.50 (ISBN 0-8224-4186-1). Pitman.

MULTIVARIATE ANALYSIS

Arnold, Steven F. The Theory of Linear Models & Multivariate Analysis. LC 80-23017. (Probability & Math Statistics Ser.). 475p. 1981. 39.95x (ISBN 0-471-05065-2). Wiley.

Bloomberg, Hans & Ylinen, R., eds. Algebraic Theory for Multivariable Linear Systems. (Math Science Engineering Ser.). Date not set. price not set (ISBN 0-12-107150-2). Acad Pr.

Callier, F. M. & Desoer, C. A. Multivariable Feedback Systems. (Springer Texts in Electrical Engineering). (Illus.). 275p. 1983. 36.00 (ISBN 0-387-90768-8); pap. 19.50 (ISBN 0-387-90759-9). Springer-Verlag.

Fornell. A Second Generation of Multivariate Analysis, 2 Vols. 444p. 1982. 44.50 ea. Vol. 1 (ISBN 0-03-062632-3). Vol. 2 (ISBN 0-03-062627-7). 79.50 set. Praeger.

Gnanadesikan, Ramanathan. Methods for Statistical Data Analysis of Multivariate Observations. LC 76-14994. (Probability & Mathematical Statics Ser.). 1977. 35.95x (ISBN 0-471-30845-5, Pub. by Wiley-Interscience). Wiley.

Jacobson, M. Statistical Analysis of Counting Processes. (Lecture Notes in Statistics Ser.: Vol. 12). 226p. 1983. pap. 14.80 (ISBN 0-387-90769-6). Springer-Verlag.

Layton, J. M. Multivariable Control Theory. (IEE Control Engineering Ser.: No. 1). (Illus.). 247p. 1976. casebound 39.00 (ISBN 0-901223-89-1). Inst Elect Eng.

Leininger, G., ed. Computer Aided Design of Multivariate Technological Systems: Proceedings of the IFAC Symposium, Indiana, USA, 15-17 September 1982. (IFAC Proceedings Ser.). 600p. 1983. 150.00 (ISBN 0-08-029357-3). Pergamon.

Meek & Turner. Statistical Analysis for Business Decisions. 1983. text ed. 27.95 (ISBN 0-686-84537-4, BS31); instrs' manual avail. HM.

Meek, Gary E. & Turner, Stephen J. Statistical Analysis for Business Decisions. 768p. 1983. text ed. 27.95 (ISBN 0-395-32274-X); write for info. instr's. manual (ISBN 0-395-32825-X). HM.

Morrison, Donald F. Applied Linear Statistical Methods. 544p. 1983. 30.95 (ISBN 0-13-041020-9). P-H.

Norcliffe, G. B. Inferential Statistics for Geographers. (Illus.). 272p. 1983. text ed. 15.00x (ISBN 0-686-84478-5). Sheridan.

Owens, D. H. Feedback & Multivariable Systems. (IEE Control Engineering Ser.). (Illus.). 320p. 1978. casebound 47.75 (ISBN 0-906048-03-6). Inst Elect Eng.

Schempp, Walter & Zeller, Karl, eds. Multivariate Approximation Theory Two. (International Series of Numerical Mathematics Ser.: Vol. 61). Date not set. text ed. 34.95 (ISBN 3-7643-1373-0). Birkhauser.

MUMMIES

Cockburn, Eve & Cockburn, Aiden. Mummies, Diseases & Ancient Cultures. Abridged ed. LC 79-25682. (Illus.). 256p. Date not set. price not set (ISBN 0-521-27237-8). Cambridge U Pr.

David, A. R., ed. The Manchester Museum Mummy Project. 1979. 25.50 (ISBN 0-7190-1293-7). Manchester.

Thompson, David L. Mummy Portraits in the J. Paul Getty Museum. LC 82-81303. 70p. 1982. pap. 16.95 (ISBN 0-89236-038-0). J P Getty Mus.

MUNCH, EDVARD, 1863-1944

Selz, J. Edvard Munch. (Q.A.P. Art Ser.). (Illus.). pap. 4.95 (ISBN 0-517-51837-6). Crown.

MUNICIPAL ADMINISTRATION

see Municipal Government

MUNICIPAL BUDGETS

Golembiewski & Rabin. Public Budgeting & Finance. (Public Adminstration & Public Policy Ser.). 400p. 1983. price not set (ISBN 0-8247-1668-X). Dekker.

Schick, Allen, ed. Perspective On Budgeting (Par Classics II) LC 80-81208. 1980. 10.95 (ISBN 0-936678-01-1). Am Soc Pub Admin.

Wagner, Richard E. & Tollison, Robert D. Balanced Budgets, Fiscal Responsibility & the Constitution. 109p. 1982. pap. 6.00 (ISBN 0-932790-36-4). Cato Inst.

MUNICIPAL CIVIL SERVICE

see Municipal Officials and Employees

MUNICIPAL CONTRACTS

see Public Contracts

MUNICIPAL ELECTIONS

see Elections

MUNICIPAL EMPLOYEES

see Municipal Officials and Employees

MUNICIPAL ENGINEERING

see also Bridges; City Planning; Drainage; Housing; Parks; Refuse and Refuse Disposal; Sanitary Engineering; Sewerage; Shore Protection; Water-Supply

Foster, W. S. Handbook of Municipal Administration & Engineering. 1977. 34.95 (ISBN 0-07-021630-4). McGraw.

MUNICIPAL FINANCE

see also Finance, Public; Licenses; Local Finance; Local Taxation; Municipal Budgets

Agranoff, Robert, ed. Human Services on a Limited Budget. (Practical Management Ser.). (Illus.). 224p. (Orig.). 1983. pap. 19.50 (ISBN 0-87326-038-4). Intl City Mgt.

Carr, James H. Crisis & Constraints in Municipal Finance: Local Fiscal Prospects in a Period of Uncertainty. 256p. 1983. pap. text ed. 12.95x (ISBN 0-88285-092-X, Dist. by Transaction Bks). Ctr Urban Pol Res.

David, Irwin T. & Sturgeon, C. Eugene. How to Evaluate & Improve Internal Controls in Government Units. LC 81-83910. (Illus.). 111p. 1981. pap. 18.00 Nonmember (ISBN 0-686-84336-3); pap. 16.00 Member (ISBN 0-686-84337-1). Municipal.

Directory of Financial Services for State & Local Governments. 210p. 1982. pap. 15.00 Nonmember (ISBN 0-686-84359-2); pap. 9.00 Member (ISBN 0-686-84360-6). Municipal.

Disclosure Guidelines for State & Local Governments. LC 79-88879. 76p. 6.00 (ISBN 0-686-84333-9). Municipal.

Fisher, Glen W. Financing Local Improvements by Special Assessment. LC 74-18143. (Illus.). 59p. 1974. pap. 6.00 (ISBN 0-686-84375-4). Municipal.

Harrell, Rhett D. Developing a Financial Management Information System for Local Govcernments: The Key Systems. LC 80-84383. (Illus.). 42p. 1980. pap. 8.00 Nonmember (ISBN 0-686-84364-9); pap. 7.00 Member (ISBN 0-686-84365-7). Municipal.

Hayes, Frederick O., et al. Linkages: Improving Financial Management in Local Government. LC 82-60180. 184p. (Orig.). 1982. pap. text ed. 12.00 (ISBN 0-87766-313-0, 33700). Urban Inst.

Hirsch, Werner Z., ed. The Economics of the Municipal Labor Market. (Monograph & Research Ser.: No. 33). 400p. 1983. write for info. (ISBN 0-89215-117-X). U Cal LA Indus Rel.

Holder, William W. A Study of Selected Concepts for Government Financial Accounting & Reporting. LC 85-50315. 69p. 1980. pap. 5.00 (ISBN 0-686-84264-2). Municipal.

Hulten, Charles R., ed. Depreciation, Inflation, & the Taxation of Income from Capital. LC 81-533061. 319p. 1981. text ed. 32.00 (ISBN 0-87766-311-4, URI 33800). Urban Inst.

Lehan, Edward A. Simplified Governmental Budgeting. LC 81-82463. (Illus.). 86p. 1981. nonmemeber 30.00 (ISBN 0-686-84272-3); member 25.00 (ISBN 0-686-84273-1). Municipal.

Lenz, Gary L. Fixed Asset Accounting & Reporting. (Illus.). 432p. 1980. pap. 27.50 nonmember (ISBN 0-686-84265-0); pap. 25.00 member (ISBN 0-686-84266-9). Municipal.

Matzer, John F., Jr., ed. Capital Financing Strategies. (Practical Management Ser.). (Illus.). 224p. (Orig.). 1983. pap. 19.50 (ISBN 0-87326-037-6). Intl City Mgt.

Miller, Girard. Effective Budgetary Presentations: The Cutting Edge. LC 82-81886. (Illus.). 230p. 1982. pap. 23.50 nonmember (ISBN 0-686-84268-5); pap. 18.50 (ISBN 0-686-84269-3). Municipal.

--A Public Investor's Guide to Money Market Instruments. LC 82-80937. (Illus.). 111p. 1982. pap. 13.00 Nonmember (ISBN 0-686-84370-3); pap. 11.00 Member (ISBN 0-686-84371-1). Municipal.

Moak, Lennox L. Municipal Bonds: Planning, Sale, & Administration. (Debt Administration Ser.). (Illus.). 400p. nonmember 37.00 (ISBN 0-686-84287-1); member 32.00 (ISBN 0-686-84288-X). Municipal.

Moak, Lennox L. & Killian, Kathryn W. Operating Budget Manual. LC 64-12365. (Illus.). 347p. 1963. 12.00 (ISBN 0-686-84284-7). Municipal.

Municipal Finance Officers Association. A Capital Improvement Programming Handbook for Small Cities & Other Governmental Units. LC 78-71712. (Illus.). 80p. 1978. 15.00 (ISBN 0-686-84280-4). Municipal.

--Community Development Block Grant Budgetary & Financial Management. 134p. 1978. 14.95 (ISBN 0-686-84366-5). Municipal.

--A Debt Management Handbook for Small Cities & Other Governmental Units. LC 78-71726. (Debt Administration Ser.). (Illus.). 69p. 1978. 15.00 (ISBN 0-686-84294-4). Municipal.

--Governmental Accounting, Auditing, & Financial Reporting. LC 80-84747. (Illus.). 314p. 1980. nonmember 35.00 (ISBN 0-686-84252-9); member 27.50 (ISBN 0-686-84253-7). Municipal.

--A Guidebook to Improved Financial Management for Small Cities & Other Governmental Units. LC 78-71709. (Illus.). 115p. 1978. 9.00 (ISBN 0-686-84362-2). Municipal.

--Guidelines for the Preparation pf a Public Employee Retirement System Comprehensive Annual Financial Report. (Illus.). 66p. 1980. pap. 10.00 Nonmember (ISBN 0-686-84368-1); pap. 10.00 Member (ISBN 0-686-84369-X). Municipal.

--Is Your City Heading For Financial Difficulty? A Guidebook for Small Cities & Other Governmental Units. (Illus.). 43p. 1978. 6.00 (ISBN 0-686-84361-4). Municipal.

--Official Statements for Offerings of Securities by Local Governments-Examples & Guidlines. 64p. 1981. Nonmember Price 12.00 (ISBN 0-686-84334-7); Member Price 10.00 (ISBN 0-686-84335-5). Municipal.

--An Operating Budget Handbook for Small Cities & Other Governmental Units. LC 78-71727. (Illus.). 148p. 1978. 15.00 (ISBN 0-686-84276-6). Municipal.

Municipal Finance Officers Association Government Finance Research Center. State & Local Government Finance & Financial Management: A Compendium of Current Research. LC 78-70328. 690p. 1978. 18.00 (ISBN 0-686-84363-0). Municipal.

Municipal Finance Officers Association. State & Local Government Fiscal Almanac 1982-MFOA Membership Directory. 400p. 1982. pap. 50.00 Nonmemmber (ISBN 0-686-84339-8); pap. 35.00 Member (ISBN 0-686-84340-1). Municipal.

--A Treasury Management Handbook for Small Cities & Other Governmental Units. LC 78-71725. (Illus.). 93p. 1978. 15.00 (ISBN 0-686-84374-6). Municipal.

National Council on Governmental Accounting. Governmental Accounting & Financial Reporting Principles. (NCGA Statement 1). (Illus.). 49p. 1979. pap. 10.00 (ISBN 0-686-84258-8). Municipal.

Peterson, George. The Economic & Fiscal Accompaniments of Population Change. 44p. pap. text ed. 2.75 (ISBN 0-686-84408-4). Urban Inst.

Rose, Richard & Page, Edward C., eds. Fiscal Stress in Cities. LC 82-9500. (Illus.). 256p. Date not set. 29.95 (ISBN 0-521-24607-5). Cambridge U Pr.

MUNICIPAL FINANCE–ACCOUNTING

see Finance, Public–Accounting

MUNICIPAL GOVERNMENT

see also Elections; Local Government; Municipal Finance; Municipal Officials and Employees; Municipal Research; Public Administration also subdivision Politics and Government under names of cities, e.g. San Francisco–Politics and Government

Brcher, Charles & Horton, Raymond, eds. Setting Municipal Priorities 1983. 200p. 1982. 25.00 (ISBN 0-8147-1042-5). Columbia U Pr.

Briggs, Steven. The Municipal Grievance Process. (Monograph & Research Ser.: No. 34). 350p. 1983. price not set (ISBN 0-89215-118-8). U Cal LA Indus Rel.

Forrest, Ray & Henderson, Jeff. Urban Political Economy & Social Theory. 220p. 1982. text ed. 32.00x (ISBN 0-566-00493-3). Gower Pub Ltd.

Foster, W. S. Handbook of Municipal Administration & Engineering. 1977. 34.95 (ISBN 0-07-021630-4). McGraw.

Griffith, Ernest S. A History of American City Government: The Conspicuous Failure, 1870-1900. LC 82-23872. 320p. 1983. lib. bdg. 26.50 (ISBN 0-8191-3001-X, Co-pub. by Natl Municipal League); pap. text ed. 14.50 (ISBN 0-8191-3002-8). U Pr of Amer.

--A History of American City Government: The Progressive Years & Their Aftermath, 1900-1920. 364p. 1983. lib. bdg. 27.50 (ISBN 0-8191-3003-6, Co-pub. by Natl Municipal League); pap. text ed. 15.50 (ISBN 0-8191-3004-4). U Pr of Amer.

Griffith, Ernest S. & Adrian, Charles R. A History of American City Government: The Formation of Traditions, 1775-1870. LC 82-23877. 240p. 1983. lib. bdg. 24.75 (ISBN 0-8191-2999-2, Co-pub. by Natl Municipal League); pap. text ed. 13.50 (ISBN 0-8191-3000-1). U Pr of Amer.

MUNICIPAL INCOME TAX

see Income Tax, Municipal

MUNICIPAL JUNIOR COLLEGES

see Community Colleges

MUNICIPAL OFFICIALS AND EMPLOYEES

Hirsch, Werner Z., ed. The Economics of the Municipal Labor Market. (Monograph & Research Ser.: No. 33). 400p. 1983. write for info. (ISBN 0-89215-117-X). U Cal LA Indus Rel.

MFOA Committee on Public Employee Retirement Administration. Public Employee Retirement Administration. 134p. 1977. 15.00 (ISBN 0-686-84367-3). Municipal.

MUNICIPAL RESEARCH

Gappert, Gary & Knight, Richard V. Cities of the Twenty First Century. (Urban Affairs Annual Reviews: Vol. 23). (Illus.). 320p. 1982. 25.00 (ISBN 0-8039-1910-7); pap. 12.50 (ISBN 0-8039-1911-5). Sage.

MUNICIPAL SERVICES WITHIN CORPORATE LIMITS

see Municipal Government

MUNICIPAL TAXATION

see Local Taxation

MUNICIPAL TRANSIT

see Local Transit

MUNICIPAL TRANSPORTATION

see Urban Transportation

MUNICIPAL UTILITIES

see Public Utilities

MUNICIPALITIES

see Cities and Towns; Municipal Government

MUNITIONS

see also Armaments; Weapons Systems

Arlinghaus, Bruce E., ed. Arms for Africa: Military Assistance & Foreign Policy in the Developing World. LC 81-48668. 256p. 1982. 26.95x (ISBN 0-669-05527-1). Lexington Bks.

Hartley, Keith. NATO Arms Co-Operation: A Study in Economics & Politics. 240p. 1983. text ed. 35.00x (ISBN 0-04-341022-7). Allen Unwin.

Trade Unionism & Munitions. (Economic & Social History of the World War Ser.). 1924. text ed. 49.50x (ISBN 0-686-83830-0). Elliots Bks.

Tuomi & Vayrynen. Militarization & Arms Production. LC 82-16882. 320p. 1983. 30.00x (ISBN 0-312-53255-5). St Martin.

MURAL PAINTING AND DECORATION

see also Mosaics

Barnett, Alan W. Community Murals. LC 79-21552. (Illus.). 520p. 1983. 60.00. Art Alliance.

--Community Murals. LC 79-21552. (Illus.). 520p. 1983. 60.00 (ISBN 0-8453-4731-4). Cornwall Bks.

Davey, Norman & Ling, Roger. Wall-Painting in Roman Britain. (Illus.). 232p. 1982. pap. text ed. 25.25x (ISBN 0-904387-96-8, Pub. by Alan Sutton England). Humanities.

MURDER

see also Assassination; Homicide; Infanticide; Trials (Murder)

Briggs, L. Vernon. The Manner of Man that Kills. (Historical Foundations of Forensic Psychiatry & Psychology Ser.). (Illus.). 444p. 1983. Repr. of 1921 ed. lib. bdg. 45.00 (ISBN 0-306-76182-3). Da Capo.

Hoole, William S. The Birmingham Horrors. (Illus.). 272p. (Orig.). 1980. pap. 4.95 (ISBN 0-87397-151-5). Strode.

Hughes, Jon C. The Tanyard Murder: On the Case with Lafcadio Hearn. LC 82-20280. (Illus.). 138p. (Orig.). 1983. lib. bdg. 19.50 (ISBN 0-8191-2833-3); pap. text ed. 8.25 (ISBN 0-8191-2834-1). U Pr of Amer.

Meyer, Peter. The Yale Murder: The Fatal Romance of Bonnie Garland & Richard Herrin. 1983. pap. 3.50 (ISBN 0-425-05940-5). Berkley Pub.

Michaud, Stephen G. & Aynesworth, Hugh. The Only Living Witness. (Illus.). 464p. 1983. 16.95 (ISBN 0-671-44961-3, Linden). S&S.

Miller, Marilee. Landis: Pillar of the Church, Hypocrite, & Murderer. LC 82-84678. (Illus.). 192p. 1982. pap. 9.95 (ISBN 0-911141-00-6). Kindred Joy.

Schreiber, Flora R. The Shoemaker. 1983. write for info. (ISBN 0-671-22652-5). S&S.

Stout, Steve. The Starved Rock Murders. (Illus.). 210p. 1982. pap. 6.95 (ISBN 0-686-43142-1). Utica Hse.

Williamson, Audrey. The Mystery of the Princes: An Investigation into a Supposed Murder. 216p. 1981. pap. text ed. 8.25x (ISBN 0-904387-58-5, Pub. by Sutton England). Humanities.

MURDER TRIALS

see Trials (Murder)

MURROW, EDWARD R.

Edward R. Murrow Papers, 1927-1965. 38p. 1982. reference bk. 25.00 (ISBN 0-667-00669-9). Microfilming Corp.

MUSCLE

see also Contractility (Biology); Neuromuscular Transmission

Sjodin, R. A. Ion Transport in Skeletal Muscle. (Transport in the Life Sciences Ser.). 157p. 1982. text ed. 35.00x (ISBN 0-471-05265-5, Pub. by Wiley-Interscience). Wiley.

Stracher, Alfred, ed. Muscle & Non-Muscle Motility, Vol. 1. LC 82-11567. (Molecular Biology Ser.). Date not set. price not set (ISBN 0-12-673001-6); price not set Vol. 2 (ISBN 0-12-673002-4). Acad Pr.

MUSCLE STRENGTH

Bass, Clarence. Ripped: The Sensible Way to Achieve Ultimate Muscularity. (Illus.). 104p. 1980. pap. 9.95 (ISBN 0-9609714-0-8). Bear & Co.

--Ripped Two. (Illus.). 179p. 1982. pap. 12.95 (ISBN 0-9609714-1-6). Clarence Bass.

Columbu, Franco. Franco Columbu's Complete Book of Bodybuilding. (Illus.). 160p. 1983. pap. 8.95 (ISBN 0-8092-5983-4). Contemp Bks.

Combes, Laura. Winning Women's Bodybuilding. Reynolds, Bill, ed. (Illus.). 176p. (Orig.). 1983. pap. 7.95 (ISBN 0-8092-5616-9). Contemp Bks.

Heidenstam, Oscar. The New Muscle Building for Beginners. (Illus.). 96p. 1983. pap. 3.95 (ISBN 0-668-05731-9, 5731). Arco.

Leen, Edie & Bertling, Ed. The Bodybuilder's Training Diary. 160p. 1983. spiral bdg. 6.95 (ISBN 0-89037-258-6). Anderson World.

Physique Handbook, 1977-1978. Date not set. 5.00 (ISBN 0-686-43037-9). AAU Pubns.

Sprague, Ken & Reynolds, Bill. The Gold's Gym Book of Bodybuilding. (Illus.). 288p. (Orig.). 1983. 17.95 (ISBN 0-8092-5694-0); pap. 10.95 (ISBN 0-8092-5693-2). Contemp Bks.

Weider, Joe. The Weider System of Bodybuilding. Reynolds, Bill, ed. (Illus.). 224p. (Orig.). 1983. 17.95 (ISBN 0-8092-5561-8); pap. 8.95 (ISBN 0-8092-5559-6). Contemp Bks.

Weightlifting Handbook, 1979-1980. Date not set. 4.50 (ISBN 0-686-43041-7). AAU Pubns.

MUSCLE TISSUE

see Muscle

MUSCLES

Here are entered works on the gross anatomy and movements of muscles. Works on the histology and physiological properties of muscular tissue are entered under the heading Muscle.

see also Muscle Strength; Neuromuscular Transmission also names of muscles

Dowben, Robert M. & Shay, Jerry W., eds. Cell & Muscle Motility, Vol. 3. 295p. 1983. 39.50x (ISBN 0-306-41157-1, Plenum Pr). Plenum Pub.

Kendall, Florence P. & Wadsworth, Gladys. Muscles: Testing & Function. (Illus.). 329p. 1983. lib. bdg. price not set (ISBN 0-683-04575-X). Williams & Wilkins.

McMahon, Thomas A. Muscles, Reflexes, & Locomotion. LC 82-61378. (Illus.). 384p. 1983. 50.00 (ISBN 0-686-43259-2); pap. 15.00. Princeton U Pr.

MUSCLES–DISEASES

see also Neuromuscular Diseases

Bulcke, J. A. & Baert, A. L. Clinical & Radiological Aspects of Myopathies: CT Scanning-EMG-Radio-Isotopes. (Illus.). 187p. 1983. 56.00 (ISBN 0-387-11443-2). Springer-Verlag.

Janda. Diagnosis of Dysfunction in Normal Muscles. Date not set. text ed. price not set (ISBN 0-407-00201-4). Butterworth.

MUSCULAR COORDINATION

see Motor Ability

MUSCULOSKELETAL SYSTEM–DISEASES

Textbook of Disorders & Injuries of Musculoskeletal Structure. 2nd ed. (Illus.). 688p. 1983. text ed. price not set (ISBN 0-683-07500-4). Williams & Wilkins.

MUSEUM CURATORSHIP AS A PROFESSION

see Museum Work As a Profession

MUSEUM OF FINE ARTS, BOSTON

Museum of Fine Arts, Boston. Illustrated Handbook, Museum of Fine Arts. (Illus.). 438p. 1975. pap. 3.50 (ISBN 0-686-83419-4). Mus Fine Arts Boston.

MUSEUM WORK AS A PROFESSION

Rudman, Jack. Museum Supervisor. (Career Examination Ser.: C-2941). (Cloth bdg. avail. on request). pap. 10.00 (ISBN 0-8373-2941-8). Natl Learning.

MUSEUMS

see also Art Museums; Museum Work As a Profession also subdivision Galleries and Museums under names of cities, e.g. new york (City)–Galleries and Museums; names of individual museums; and subdivision Collection and Preservation under Insect, Zoological Specimens and similar headings

Adams, G. Donald. Museum Public Relations. (AASLH Management Ser.: Vol. 2). Date not set. text ed. price not set (ISBN 0-910050-65-1). AASLH.

Alexander, Edward P. Museum Masters. Date not set. text ed. price not set (ISBN 0-910050-68-6). AASLH.

Brewington, M. V. Check List of the Paintings, Drawings & Prints at the Kendall Whaling Museum. (Illus.). 74p. 1957. pap. 2.00 (ISBN 0-686-83951-X). Kendall Whaling.

Brewington, M. V. & Brewington, Dorothy. Kendall Whaling Museum Paintings. LC 65-28071. (Illus.). 137p. 1965. 23.50 (ISBN 0-686-83944-7). Kendall Whaling.

--Kendall Whaling Museum Prints. LC 70-107611. (Illus.). 209p. 1969. 37.50 (ISBN 0-686-83946-3). Kendall Whaling.

Fennelly, Lawrence J. Museum, Archive, & Library Security. new ed. 866p. 1982. text ed. 55.00 (ISBN 0-409-95058-0). Butterworth.

Frank, Stuart M. & Webb, Robert L. M. V. Brewington: A Bibliography & Catalogue of the Brewington Press. 36p. 1982. commemorative & numbered ed. 6.00 (ISBN 0-686-83948-X); pap. 4.00 (ISBN 0-686-83949-8). Kendall Whaling.

Kimbell Art Museum. Kimbell Art Museum: A Catalogue of the Collection. LC 73-177945. (Illus.). 336p. 1972. 25.00 (ISBN 0-912804-00-9). Kimbell Art.

Rosenwald & Rosenbach: The Birth of a Collection. 1983. pap. write for info. (ISBN 0-939084-15-5). Rosenbach Mus & Lib.

Serrell, Beverly. Making Exhibit Labels: A Step-by-Step Guide. (Illus.). 128p. 1983. pap. text ed. 11.95 (ISBN 0-910050-64-3). AASLH.

MUSEUMS–DIRECTORIES

McLanathan, Richard. World Art in American Museums: A Personal Guide. 384p. 1983. 15.95 (ISBN 0-385-18515-4, Anchor Pr). Doubleday.

MUSEUMS–JUVENILE LITERATURE

Althea. Visiting a Museum. (Cambridge Dinosaur Information Ser.). 26p. (gr. 7-10). 1983. pap. 1.50 (ISBN 0-521-27160-6). Cambridge U Pr.

Stan, Susan. Careers in an Art Museum. LC 82-18654. (Early Career Bks.). (Illus.). 36p. (gr. 2-5). 1983. PLB 5.95g (ISBN 0-8225-0337-9). Lerner Pubns.

MUSEUMS–GREAT BRITAIN

Hudson, Kenneth, ed. The Good Museums Guide: The Best Museums & Art Galleries in the British Isles. 320p. 1982. 30.00x (ISBN 0-333-32763-2, Pub. by Macmillan England). State Mutual Bk.

Potterton, Homan, intro. by. The National Gallery of Ireland Illustrated Summary Catalogue of Paintings. 1982. 125.00x (ISBN 0-7171-1144-X, Pub. by Gill & Macmillan Ireland). State Mutual Bk.

MUSHROOM CULTURE

Lange & Hora. Collins Guide to Mushrooms & Toadstools. 29.95 (ISBN 0-686-42766-1, Collins Pub England). Greene.

Nonis, V. Mushrooms & Toadstools: A Colour Field Guide. (Illus.). 230p. (gr. 6 up). 1983. 12.95 (ISBN 0-88254-755-0). Hippocrene Bks.

MUSHROOMS

see also Fungi; Mushroom Culture

Lange & Hora. Collins Guide to Mushrooms & Toadstools. 29.95 (ISBN 0-686-42766-1, Collins Pub England). Greene.

MUSHROOMS–CULTURE

see Mushroom Culture

MUSIC

see also Choral Music; Christmas Music; Church Music; Composition (Music); Dance Music; Electronic Music; Folk Music; Folk-Songs; Improvisation (Music); Instrumental Music; Instrumentation and Orchestration; Jazz Music; Military Music; Moving-Picture Music; National Songs; Opera; Romanticism in Music; School Music; Singing; Songs; Sound; Symphony Orchestras; Television Music also subdivision Songs and Music under specific subjects, classes of persons, names of individuals, institutions, societies, etc; also other headings beginning with the words Music and Musical

Bent, Ian, ed. Source Materials & the Interpretation of Music: A Memorial Volume to Thurston Dart. (Illus.). 474p. 1981. text ed. 70.00x (ISBN 0-8476-4785-4). Rowman.

Chadwick, Henry, ed. Boethius: The Consolations of Music, Logic, Theology, & Philosophy. 330p. 1981. text ed. 39.00 (ISBN 0-19-826447-X). Oxford U Pr.

Chorley, Henry F. Thirty Years of Musical Recollections, 2 Vols. 1983. Repr. of 1862 ed. Set. lib. bdg. 59.50 (ISBN 0-306-76216-1). Da Capo.

Gargan, William & Sharma, Sue. Find that Tune: An Index to Rock, Folk-Rock, Disco & Soul in Collections. 400p. 1983. lib. bdg. 39.95 (ISBN 0-918212-70-7). Neal-Schuman.

Hobson, Libby. Basic Skills Music Workbook. (Basic Skills Workbooks). 32p. (gr. 4-7). 1983. 0.99 (ISBN 0-8209-0542-9, MUW-1). ESP.

--What's Music All About? (Music Ser.). 24p. (gr. 3-6). 1977. wkbk. 5.00 (ISBN 0-8209-0272-1, MU-1). ESP.

Holler, Kathy. Seasons. (Science Ser.). 24p. (gr. 3-6). 1982. wkbk. 5.00 (ISBN 0-8209-0163-6, S-25). ESP.

Johnston, T. H. & Greig, C. Music with Your Project. 1982. pap. 8.50 (ISBN 0-08-025761-5). Pergamon.

Justus, Fred. Science Adventures. (Science Ser.). 24p. (gr. 4). 1977. wkbk. 5.00 (ISBN 0-8209-0142-3, S-4). ESP.

--Science Facts. (Science Ser.). 24p. (gr. 6). 1978. wkbk. 5.00 (ISBN 0-8209-0144-X, S-6). ESP.

--Science Goals. (Science Ser.). 24p. (gr. 5). 1980. wkbk. 5.00 (ISBN 0-8209-0143-1, S-5). ESP.

--The Science World. (Science Ser.). 24p. (gr. 4-7). 1978. wkbk. 5.00 (ISBN 0-8209-0156-3, S-18). ESP.

Patty, Catherine. The Orchestra. (Music Ser.). 24p. (gr. 5-9). 1977. wkbk. 5.00 (ISBN 0-8209-0273-X, MU-2). ESP.

Roes, Carol. Hula Book, No. 10. 1982. pap. 4.50 (ISBN 0-930932-23-4); record incl. M Loke.

--Hula Book: The Governor's Waltz & The Steersman, No. 9. 1982. pap. 4.50 (ISBN 0-686-43079-4); record incl. M Loke.

--Hula Book: Twelve Little Letters & Plus & Minus, No. 8. 1982. pap. 4.50 (ISBN 0-930932-21-8); record incl. M Loke.

Schiff, David. The Music of Elliott Carter. (Illus.). 370p. 1983. lib. bdg. 39.50 (ISBN 0-903873-06-0). Da Capo.

Short, Michael. Your Book of Music. LC 82-9377. (Your Book Of...Ser.). (Illus.). 96p. (gr. 3-6). 1983. 8.95 (ISBN 0-571-18031-0). Faber & Faber.

Walker, Mary Lou. Basic Skills Music Workbook. (Basic Skills Workbooks). 32p. (gr. 3-5). 1983. 0.99 (ISBN 0-8209-0543-7, MUW-2). ESP.

--Exercises in Bass Clef. (Music Ser.). 24p. (gr. 4 up). 1980. wkbk. 5.00 (ISBN 0-8209-0282-9, MU-11). ESP.

--Exercises in Treble Clef. (Music Ser.). 24p. (gr. 2-6). 1980. wkbk. 5.00 (ISBN 0-8209-0275-6, MU-4). ESP.

--Harmony, Chords, & Scales. (Music Ser.). 24p. (gr. 3 up). 1980. wkbk. 5.00 (ISBN 0-8209-0279-9, MU-8). ESP.

--Introduction to Bass Clef. (Music Ser.). 24p. (gr. 3 up). 1980. wkbk. 5.00 (ISBN 0-8209-0281-0, MU-10). ESP.

--Music Notation. (Music Ser.). 24p. (gr. 1 up). 1980. wkbk. 5.00 (ISBN 0-8209-0277-2, MU-6). ESP.

--Music Signs. (Music Ser.). 24p. (gr. 1 up). 1980. wkbk. 5.00 (ISBN 0-8209-0276-4, MU-5). ESP.

--Musical Puzzles. (Music Ser.). 24p. (gr. 3 up). 1980. wkbk. 5.00 (ISBN 0-8209-0280-2, MU-9). ESP.

--Treble Clef & Notes. (Music Ser.). 24p. (gr. 1 up). 1980. wkbk. 5.00 (ISBN 0-8209-0274-8, MU-3). ESP.

MUSIC-ADDRESSES, ESSAYS, LECTURES

Gordon, Roderick D. Doctoral Dissertations in Music & Music Education, 1972-1977. 296p. 1978. 3.00 (ISBN 0-686-37912-8). Music Ed.

Stanford, Charles V. Studies & Memories. 224p. 1983. pap. 6.25 (ISBN 0-88072-009-3). Tanager Bks.

MUSIC-ANALYSIS, APPRECIATION

Dickinson, Edward. The Spirit of Music: How to Find It & How to Share It. 218p. 1982. Repr. of 1927 ed. lib. bdg. 25.00 (ISBN 0-8495-1142-9). Arden Lib.

Hopkins, Antony. Understanding Music. 256p. 1982. 30.00x (ISBN 0-460-02234-2, Pub. by J M Dent). State Mutual Bk.

Kamien, R. Music: An Appreciation. 2nd ed. 1979. text ed. 23.50 (ISBN 0-07-033279-7); supplementary material avail. McGraw.

Kaufmann, Helen L. The Home Book of Music Appreciation. 324p. 1983. Repr. of 1940 ed. lib. bdg. 30.00 (ISBN 0-8495-3140-3). Arden Lib.

King, Alec H. A Wealth of Music. 250p. 1983. price not set (ISBN 0-85157-330-4, Pub. by Bingley England). Shoe String.

Rossi, Nicki. Hearing Music: An Introduction. 428p. (Orig.). pap. text ed. 16.95 (ISBN 0-15-535597-X); instructors manual 1.95 (ISBN 0-15-535598-8); records 20.95 (ISBN 0-15-535599-6). HarBraceJ.

Tovey, Donald F. Essays in Musical Analysis: Concertos & Choral Works. 448p. 1981. 22.50x (ISBN 0-19-315148-0); pap. 12.50x (ISBN 0-19-315149-9). Oxford U Pr.

MUSIC-APPRECIATION

see Music-Analysis, Appreciation

MUSIC-BIBLIOGRAPHY

see also Music-Discography; Music-Manuscripts; Music Libraries

Music Books: World's Greatest Hits from 1900 to 1919. pap. 5.00 (ISBN 0-517-50566-5). Crown.

Research Libraries of the New York Public Library & Library of Congress. Bibliographic Guide to Music: 1982. 1983. lib. bdg. 125.00 (ISBN 0-8161-6977-2, Biblio Guides). G K Hall.

Research Libraries of the New York Public Library. Dictionary Catalog of the Music Collection. 2nd ed. 1983. lib. bdg. 6000.00 (ISBN 0-8161-0374-7, Hall Library). G K Hall.

Selective Music Lists-1978: Full Orchestra, String Orchestra. 32p. 2.00 (ISBN 0-686-37918-7). Music Ed.

Wilson, Bernard E. The Newberry Library Catalog of Early American Printed Sheet Music. 1983. lib. bdg. 330.00 (ISBN 0-8161-0389-5, Hall Library). G K Hall.

MUSIC-BIO-BIBLIOGRAPHY

Ensor, Wendy-Ann. More Heroes & Heroines in Music. (Illus.). 48p. 1983. pap. 5.00 laminated (ISBN 0-19-321106-8); cassette 18.00 (ISBN 0-19-321107-6). Oxford U Pr.

MUSIC-BIOGRAPHY

see Composers; Conductors (Music); Music-Bio-Bibliography; Musicians; Pianists; Singers

MUSIC-CATALOGING

see Cataloging of Music

MUSIC-COMPOSITION

see Composition (Music)

MUSIC-DISCOGRAPHY

Fagan, Ted & Moran, William, eds. The Encyclopedic Discography of Victor Recordings. LC 82-9343. (Discographies Ser.: No. 7). (Illus.). 488p. 1982. lib. bdg. 49.95 (ISBN 0-313-23003-X, FPM/). Greenwood.

Goggin, Jim. Turk Murphy: Just for the Record. LC 82-62235. (Illus.). 360p. 1983. 20.00 (ISBN 0-916870-57-X); pap. text ed. 12.95 (ISBN 0-916870-58-8). Creative Arts Bk.

Gray, Michael H. & Gibson, Gerald D. Bibliography of Discographies: Vol. 3: Popular Music. 200p. 1983. 37.50 (ISBN 0-8352-1683-7). Bowker.

Tinnell, Roger D. An Annotated Discography of Music in Spain before 1650. xvi, 146p. 1980. 12.00 (ISBN 0-942260-09-0). Hispanic Seminary.

MUSIC-ESTHETICS

see Music-Philosophy and Esthetics

MUSIC-HISTORY AND CRITICISM

Bernard Shaw: Collected Music Criticism, 4 vols. LC 77-183507. Date not set. One vol. of London Music in 1888-89. price not set; Three vols. of Music in London, 1890-94, in a slipcase. price not set. Vienna Hse.

Chorley, Henry F. Thirty Years' Musical Recollections. Newman, Ernest, ed. LC 77-183330. 411p. Date not set. Repr. of 1926 ed. price not set. Vienna Hse.

Lebrecht, Norman. Discord. LC 82-21872. (Illus.). 272p. 1983. 25.00 (ISBN 0-87663-389-0). Universe.

McLeish, Kenneth & McLeish, Valerie. The Story of Music. (Illus.). 32p. pap. 4.75 laminated (ISBN 0-19-321437-7). Oxford U Pr.

Mitchell, Donald & Keller, Hans, eds. Music Survey: New Series, 1949-1952. (Illus.). 817p. 1983. 59.95 (ISBN 0-571-10040-6). Faber & Faber.

Murphy, Judith. Conflict, Consensus, & Communication. 32p. 1980. 1.00 (ISBN 0-686-37911-X). Music Ed.

Poultney, David. Studying Music History: Learning, Reasoning & Writing About Music History & Literature. 256p. 1983. pap. text ed. 9.95 (ISBN 0-13-858860-0). P-H.

Prunieres, Henry. A New History of Music: The Middle Ages to Mozart. Lockspeiser, Edward, tr. & ed. LC 75-183327. 413p. Date not set. Repr. of 1943 ed. price not set. Vienna Hse.

Rosenfeld, Paul. Discoveries of a Music Critic. LC 79-183510. 402p. Date not set. Repr. of 1936 ed. price not set. Vienna Hse.

White, J. Perry. Twentieth Century Choral Music: An Annotated Bibliography of Music Suitable for Use by High School Choirs. LC 82-10239. x, 153p. 1982. 17.50 (ISBN 0-8108-1568-0). Scarecrow.

MUSIC-HISTORY AND CRITICISM-400-1500

see also Motet

Tischler, Hans. The Earliest Motets (to ca. 1270) A Complete Comparative Edition, 3 vols. LC 78-15005. 1982. Set. 425.00 (ISBN 0-300-01534-8); Vol. 1, 856 pp. write for info. (ISBN 0-300-02918-7); Vol. 2, 636 pp. write for info. (ISBN 0-300-02919-5); Vol. 3, 256 pp. write for info. (ISBN 0-300-02920-9). Yale U Pr.

MUSIC-HISTORY AND CRITICISM-18TH CENTURY

Abraham, Gerald, ed. The New Oxford History of Music, Vol. VIII: The Age of Beethoven, 1790-1830. (Illus.). 778p. 1983. 49.95 (ISBN 0-19-316308-X). Oxford U Pr.

Krehbiel, Henry E. Music & Manners in the Classical Period. 286p. 1983. pap. 6.75 (ISBN 0-686-38399-0). Tanager Bks.

Schneider-Cuvay, M. Michaela & Rainer, Werner, eds. Salzburg, Pt. 2. (The Symphony 1720-1840 Series B: Vol. 8). lib. bdg. 90.00 (ISBN 0-8240-3818-5). Garland Pub.

MUSIC-HISTORY AND CRITICISM-19TH CENTURY

see also Romanticism in Music

Abraham, Gerald, ed. The New Oxford History of Music, Vol. VIII: The Age of Beethoven, 1790-1830. (Illus.). 778p. 1983. 49.95 (ISBN 0-19-316308-X). Oxford U Pr.

Cooke, Deryck. Vindications: Essays on Romantic Music. LC 82-4295. 160p. 1982. 24.95 (ISBN 0-521-24765-9); pap. 7.95 (ISBN 0-521-28947-5). Cambridge U Pr.

Fuller-Maitland, J. A. English Music in the 19th Century. rev. ed. 328p. 1983. pap. 6.95 (ISBN 0-88072-003-4). Tanager Bks.

Schneider-Cuvay, M. Michaela & Rainer, Werner, eds. Salzburg, Pt. 2. (The Symphony 1720-1840 Series B: Vol. 8). lib. bdg. 90.00 (ISBN 0-8240-3818-5). Garland Pub.

MUSIC-HISTORY AND CRITICISM-20TH CENTURY

see also Jazz Music

Brett, Philip. Benjamin Britten: Peter Grimes. LC 82-14627. (Cambridge Opera Handbooks). (Illus.). 180p. Date not set. price not set (ISBN 0-521-22916-2); pap. price not set (ISBN 0-521-29716-8). Cambridge U Pr.

Levy, Alan H. Musical Nationalism: American Composers' Search for Identity. LC 82-12168. (Contributions in American Studies: No. 66). 208p. 1983. lib. bdg. 27.95 (ISBN 0-313-23709-3, LMN/). Greenwood.

MUSIC-INSTRUCTION AND STUDY

see also Composition (Music); Conducting; Instrumental Music-Instruction and Study; Instrumentation and Orchestration; Sight-Reading (Music)

also subdivision Instruction and Study under names of musical instruments, e.g. Piano-Instruction and Study

Andress, Barbara L. Music in Early Childhood: Prepared by the National Commission on Instruction. 54p. 1973. 3.50 (ISBN 0-686-37917-9). Music Ed.

Birge, Edward B. History of Public School Music in the United States. 323p. Repr. of 1937 ed. 5.50 (ISBN 0-686-37916-0). Music Ed.

Brookhart, C. E., ed. Graduate Music Teacher Education Report: A Final Report by the MENC Commission on Graduate Music Teacher Education. 25p. 6.00 (ISBN 0-686-37915-2). Music Ed.

Colwell, Richard, ed. Symposium in Music Education: A Festschrift for Charles Leonhard. LC 81-71592. 329p. 15.00 (ISBN 0-686-38473-3). U IL Sch Music.

Dickinson, Edward. The Spirit of Music: How to Find It & How to Share It. 218p. 1982. Repr. of 1927 ed. lib. bdg. 25.00 (ISBN 0-8495-1142-9). Arden Lib.

Gagne, Danai A. & Thomas, Judith. Dramas in Elemental Scales: A Collection of Mini-Dramas for Voice & Orff Instruments. 1982. pap. 7.50 (ISBN 0-918812-19-4). Magnamusic.

Gordon, Roderick D. Doctoral Dissertations in Music & Music Education, 1972-1977. 296p. 1978. 3.00 (ISBN 0-686-37912-8). Music Ed.

Hazard, William R. Tort Liability & the Music Educator. 32p. 1979. 2.00 (ISBN 0-686-37919-5). Music Ed.

Hicks, Charles E. & Standifer, James A., eds. Methods & Perspectives in Urban Music Education. LC 82-16105. (Illus.). 524p. (Orig.). 1983. lib. bdg. 28.75 (ISBN 0-8191-2760-4); pap. text ed. 16.75 (ISBN 0-8191-2761-2). U Pr of Amer.

Hobson, Libby. What's Music All About? (Music Ser.). 24p. (gr. 3-6). 1977. wkbk. 5.00 (ISBN 0-8209-0272-1, MU-1). ESP.

Holt, Dennis M. & Thompson, Keith P. Developing Competencies to Teach Music in the Elementary Classroom. (Elementary Education Ser.). 360p. 1980. spiral 12.95 (ISBN 0-675-08135-1); instr's. manual 3.95. Merrill.

Lamb, Norman. Guide to Teaching Strings. 4th ed. (College Instrumental Technique Ser.). 190p. 1983. text ed. write for info. (ISBN 0-697-03539-5). Wm C Brown.

Landon, Joseph W. How to Write Learning Activity Packages for Music Education. (Contemporary Music Education Ser.). 109p. 1973. pap. 6.95x (ISBN 0-930424-01-8). Music Educ Pubns.

--Leadership for Learning in Music Education. LC 75-305303. (Contemporary Music Eduction Ser.). 306p. (Orig.). 1975. pap. 9.95x (ISBN 0-943988-02-0). Music Educ Pubns.

Livingston, James A. & Poland, Michael D. Accountability & Objectives for Music Education. (Contemporary Music Education Ser.). (Orig.). 1972. pap. 4.95x (ISBN 0-930424-00-X). Music Educ Pubns.

Livingston, Robert A. The Music Information & Education Guide. 1983. 10.00 (ISBN 0-9607558-2-9). GLGLC Music.

McGuire, David C. Evaluation of Music Faculty in Higher Education. 24p. 1979. 2.00 (ISBN 0-686-37914-4). Music Ed.

Mark, Michael L. Source Readings in Music Education. 1982. text ed. 16.95x (ISBN 0-02-871910-7). Schirmer Bks.

Murphy, Judith. Conflict, Consensus, & Communication. 32p. 1980. 1.00 (ISBN 0-686-37911-X). Music Ed.

Mursell, James L. Human Values in Music Education. 388p. 1982. Repr. of 1934 ed. lib. bdg. 35.00 (ISBN 0-89987-646-3). Darby Bks.

Nordoff & Robbins. Music Therapy in Special Education. 1983. 13.50 (ISBN 0-918812-22-4). Magnamusic.

Nye, Vernice T. Music for Young Children. 3rd ed. 240p. 1983. pap. text ed. write for info. (ISBN 0-697-03562-X). Wm C Brown.

Poultney, David. Studying Music History: Learning, Reasoning & Writing About Music History & Literature. 256p. 1983. pap. text ed. 9.95 (ISBN 0-13-858860-0). P-H.

Simons, Gene M. Early Childhood Musical Development: A Bibliography of Research Abstracts, 1960-1975. 136p. 1978. 3.00 (ISBN 0-686-37913-6). Music Ed.

Vahey, Esther J. Micro Wave the Easy Way Vol. II. (Audio Cassette Cooking School Library). 16p. 1982. pap. text ed. 12.95x. Cuisine Con.

Walker, Mary Lou. Rhythm, Time, & Value. (Music Ser.). 24p. (gr. 3 up). 1980. wkbk. 5.00 (ISBN 0-8209-0278-0, MU-7). ESP.

--Treble Clef & Notes. (Music Ser.). 24p. (gr. 1 up). 1980. wkbk. 5.00 (ISBN 0-8209-0274-8, MU-3). ESP.

MUSIC-JEWS

see Jews-Liturgy and Ritual

MUSIC-JUVENILE LITERATURE

Braithewaite, Walter. A Book of Songs. Vaughan, Michael, ed. 29p. (gr. 5-7). 1978. pap. 4.00 (ISBN 0-88010-036-2, Pub. by Steinerbooks). Anthroposophic.

Ensor, Wendy-Ann. Heroes & Heroines in Music. (Illus.). 1982. pap. 5.00 (ISBN 0-19-321105-X); cassette 18.00. Oxford U Pr.

Kaplan, Don. See with Your Ears: The Creative Music Book. LC 82-81463. (Illus.). 128p. (Orig.). (gr. 1-7). 1982. pap. 6.95 (ISBN 0-938530-09-7, 09-7); tchr's guide 2.00 (ISBN 0-938530-20-8, 20-8). Lexikos.

MUSIC-MANUSCRIPTS

Fenlon, Iain, ed. Cambridge Music Manuscripts 900-1700. LC 81-17059. 174p. 1982. 54.50 (ISBN 0-521-24452-8). Cambridge U Pr.

Lewis, Nigel. Paperchase: Mozart, Beethoven, Bach...The Search for their Lost Music. 246p. 1982. 19.95 (ISBN 0-241-10235-9, Pub. by Hamish Hamilton England). David & Charles.

A Wealth of Music in the Collections of the British Library & the British Museum. 250p. 1983. 25.00 (ISBN 0-686-84759-8, Pub. by Bingley England). Shoe String.

Wilson, Bernard E. The Newberry Library Catalog of Early American Printed Sheet Music. 1983. lib. bdg. 330.00 (ISBN 0-8161-0389-5, Hall Library). G K Hall.

MUSIC-MISCELLANEA

McLeish, Kenneth & McLeish, Valerie. Music Round the World. (Illus.). 32p. pap. 4.75 laminated (ISBN 0-19-321434-2). Oxford U Pr.

Rees, Dafydd & Lazell, Barry. Chart File, Vol. 2. 192p. (Orig.). 1983. pap. 2.95 (ISBN 0-933328-68-0). Delilah Bks.

MUSIC-MODES

see Musical Intervals and Scales

MUSIC-PERFORMANCE

see also Conducting; Improvisation (Music)

Bloom, Ken. American Song: The Complete Stage Musical, Vol. I. (Illus.). 500p. 1983. 24.95 (ISBN 0-918432-48-0). NY Zoetrope.

MUSIC-PHILOSOPHY AND ESTHETICS

see also Romanticism in Music

Ballantine, Christopher. Music, Society & Ideology. (Monographs on Musicology: Vol. 2). 1982. write for info. (ISBN 0-677-06050-5). Gordon.

Clifton, Thomas. Music as Heard: A Study in Applied Phenomenology. LC 82-10944. (Illus.). 336p. 1983. text ed. 32.50x (ISBN 0-300-02091-0). Yale U Pr.

Mark, Michael L. Source Readings in Music Education. 1982. text ed. 16.95x (ISBN 0-02-871910-7). Schirmer Bks.

Mursell, James L. Human Values in Music Education. 388p. 1982. Repr. of 1934 ed. lib. bdg. 35.00 (ISBN 0-89987-646-3). Darby Bks.

Rowell, Lewis. Thinking about Music: An Introduction to the Philosophy of Music. LC 82-21979. 308p. 1983. lib. bdg. 25.00x (ISBN 0-87023-386-6). U of Mass Pr.

MUSIC-STUDY AND TEACHING

see Music-Instruction and Study

MUSIC-TERMINOLOGY

Levarie, Siegmund & Levy, Ernst. Musical Morphology: A Discourse & a Dictionary. LC 82-21274. (Illus.). 376p. 1983. 29.50X (ISBN 0-87338-286-2). Kent St U Pr.

MUSIC-THEORY

see also Composition (Music); Instrumentation and Orchestration; Music-Philosophy and Esthetics; Musical Intervals and Scales

Brye, Joseph. Basic Principles of Music Theory. (Illus.). 278p. 1965. 25.50x (ISBN 0-8260-1460-7). Wiley.

Lerdahl, Fred & Jackendoff, Ray. A Generative Theory of Tonal Music. (Cognitive Theory & Mental Representation Ser.). (Illus.). 434p. 1983. write for info. MIT Pr.

Rahn, Jay. A Theory for All Music: Problems & Solutions in the Analysis of Non-Western Forms. 288p. 1983. 35.00x (ISBN 0-8020-5538-9). U of Toronto Pr.

MUSIC-THERAPEUTIC USE

see Music Therapy

MUSIC-VOCATIONAL GUIDANCE

Seigel, Alan H. Breakin' In...to the Music Business. (Illus.). 272p. (Orig.). 1983. text ed. 14.95 (ISBN 0-89524-171-4, 8609); pap. 8.95 (ISBN 0-89524-156-0, 8604). Cherry Lane.

MUSIC-YEARBOOKS

Dudman, Jane. International Music Guide 1983. (International Music Guide Ser.). (Illus.). 304p. 1982. pap. 10.95 (ISBN 0-900730-05-6). NY Zoetrope.

MUSIC, AFRICAN

Besmer, Fremont E. Kidan Daran Salla: Music for the Eve of the Muslim Festivals of Id Al-Fitr & Id Al-Kabir in Kano, Nigeria. (African Humanities Ser.). (Illus.). 84p. (Orig.). 1974. pap. text ed. 4.00 (ISBN 0-941934-10-1). Ind U Afro-Amer Arts.

MUSIC, AFRO-AMERICAN

see Afro-American Music

MUSIC, AMERICAN

Jones, Charles K. & Greenwich, Lorenzo K. A Choice Collection of the Works of Francis Johnson: America's First Native-Born Master of Music, Vol. 1. LC 82-62078. (Illus.). 150p. 1983. 24.95 (ISBN 0-911073-00-0). Point Two.

Rockwell, John. All American Music: Composition in the Late Twentieth Century. LC 82-48885. 288p. 1983. 15.95 (ISBN 0-394-51163-8). Knopf.

MUSIC, APPRECIATION OF

see Music-Analysis, Appreciation

MUSIC, ASIAN

Sakata, Hiromi L. Music in the Mind: The Concepts of Music & Musician in Afghanistan. LC 82-23296. (Illus.). 250p. 1983. 32.50 (ISBN 0-87338-287-0). Kent St U Pr.

MUSIC, AUSTRALIAN

Balough, Teresa. A Musical Genius from Australia. (Illus.). 161p. 1982. pap. 13.50 (ISBN 0-686-84841-1, Pub. by CSIRO Australia). Intl Schol Bk Serv.

MUSIC, BRITISH

see also Music, English

Crowest, Frederick J. The Story of British Music From the Earliest Times to the Tudor Period. 404p. 1983. pap. 6.95 (ISBN 0-88072-002-6). Tanager Bks.

MUSIC, CHINESE

Riddle, Ronald. Flying Dragons, Flowing Streams: Music in the Life of San Fancisco's Chinese. LC 82-12005. (Contributions in Intercultural & Comparative Studies: No. 7). xiv, 249p. 1983. lib. bdg. 29.95 (ISBN 0-313-23682-8, RIF/). Greenwood.

MUSIC, CHORAL

see Choral Music

MUSIC, DRAMATIC

see Musical Revue, Comedy, Etc.; Opera

MUSIC, EFFECT OF

see Music, Influence of; Music Therapy

MUSIC, ELECTRONIC

see Electronic Music

MUSIC, ENGLISH

see also Music, British

Crowest, Frederick J. The Story of British Music From the Earliest Times to the Tudor Period. 404p. 1983. pap. 6.95 (ISBN 0-88072-002-6). Tanager Bks.

Fuller-Maitland, J. A. English Music in the 19th Century. rev. ed. 328p. 1983. pap. 6.95 (ISBN 0-88072-003-4). Tanager Bks.

MUSIC, EUROPEAN

Chorley, Henry F. Music & Manners in France & Germany, 3 Vols. 1983. Repr. of 1844 ed. Set. lib. bdg. 89.50 (ISBN 0-306-76217-X). Da Capo.

MUSIC, INDIC

Kuppuswamy, Gowri & Hariharan, H. Teaching of Music. 88p. 1980. 9.95 (ISBN 0-940500-57-4, Pub. by Sterling India). Asia Bk Corp.

Kuppuswamy, Gowry. Indian Dance & Music Literature: A Select Bibliography. 1982. 12.00x (ISBN 0-8364-0903-5, Pub. by Biblia Impex). South Asia Bks.

Saxena, S. K. Aesthetical Essays: Studies in Aesthetics; Hindustani Music & Kathak Dance. 1982. 18.00x (ISBN 0-8364-0898-5, Pub. by Chanakya). South Asia Bks.

Wade, Bonnie C., ed. Performing Arts in India: Essays on Music, Dance & Drama. LC 82-20141. (Monograph Ser.: No. 21). (Illus.). 270p. 1983. lib. bdg. 21.75 (ISBN 0-8191-2872-4); pap. text ed. 11.00 (ISBN 0-8191-2873-2). U Pr of Amer.

MUSIC, INFLUENCE OF

see also Music Therapy

Mursell, James L. Human Values in Music Education. 388p. 1982. Repr. of 1934 ed. lib. bdg. 35.00 (ISBN 0-89987-646-3). Darby Bks.

MUSIC, INSTRUMENTAL

see Instrumental Music

MUSIC, ITALIAN

McCrickard, Eleanor F., ed. Alessandro Stradella's "Esule dalle sfere". Cantata for the Souls of Purgatory. Scaglione, Aldo, tr. from Ital. LC 82-17544. (Early Musical Masterworks). 152p. 1983. 27.00x (ISBN 0-8078-1536-5). U of NC Pr.

MUSIC, LATIN-AMERICAN

Appleby, David P. The Music of Brazil. (Illus.). 248p. 1983. text ed. 22.50x (ISBN 0-292-75068-4). U of Tex Pr.

MUSIC, MEDIEVAL

see Music-History and Criticism-400-1500

MUSIC, MEXICAN

Parker, Robert. Carlos Chavez: Mexico's Modern-Day Orpheus. (Music Ser.). 192p. 1983. lib. bdg. 21.95 (ISBN 0-8057-9455-7, Twayne). G K Hall.

MUSIC, MILITARY

see Military Music

MUSIC, PHYSICAL EFFECT OF

see Music Therapy

MUSIC, POLYNESIAN

McLean, Mervyn. Supplement: An Annotated Bibliography of Oceanic Music & Dance. 74p. 1982. pap. text ed. 8.00x (ISBN 0-8248-0862-2). UH Pr.

MUSIC, POPULAR (SONGS, ETC.)

see also Country Music; Rock Music

Diamond, Neil, ed. The Neil Diamond Songbook. (Illus.). 376p. 1982. 29.95 (ISBN 0-933328-46-X). Delilah Bks.

Reader's Digest Editors. Popular Songs That Will Live Forever. LC 81-8447. (Illus.). 252p. 1982. 20.50 (ISBN 0-89577-104-7, Pub. by RD Assn). Random.

Savage, William W., Jr. Singing Cowboys & All That Jazz: A Short History of Popular Music in Oklahoma. LC 82-17560. (Illus.). 200p. 1983. 14.95 (ISBN 0-8061-1648-X). U of Okla Pr.

Waters, Roger. Pink Floyd Lyric Book. (Illus.). 96p. (Orig.). 1983. pap. 6.95 (ISBN 0-7137-1280-5, Pub. by Blandford Pr England). Sterling.

MUSIC, POPULAR (SONGS, ETC.)-DISCOGRAPHY

Whitburn, Joel. The Billboard Book of Top Forty Hits: 1955-1982. (Illus.). 512p. 1983. pap. 15.00 (ISBN 0-8230-7511-7, Billboard Pub). Watson-Guptill.

MUSIC, POPULAR (SONGS, ETC.)-HISTORY AND CRITICISM

Tobler, John & Grundy, Stuart. The Record Producers. (Illus.). 256p. 1983. 19.95 (ISBN 0-312-66593-8); pap. 10.95 (ISBN 0-312-66594-6). St Martin.

MUSIC, POPULAR (SONGS, ETC.)-WRITING AND PUBLISHING

Bennett, Roy C. The Songwriter's Guide to Writing & Selling Hit Songs. 160p. 1983. 12.95 (ISBN 0-13-822783-7); pap. 6.95 (ISBN 0-13-822775-6). P-H.

George, Nelson. Top of the Charts. (Illus.). 448p. (Orig.). 1983. pap. 14.95 (ISBN 0-8329-0260-8). New Century.

MUSIC, RELIGIOUS

see Church Music

MUSIC, RUSSIAN

Schwarz, Boris. Music & Musical Life in Soviet Russia: Enlarged Edition, 1917-1981. LC 82-48267. 736p. 1983. write for info. (ISBN 0-253-33956-1). Ind U Pr.

Van den Toorn, Pieter C. The Music of Igor Stravinsky. LC 82-2560. (Composers of the Twentieth Century Ser.). 536p. 1983. text ed. 35.00x (ISBN 0-300-02693-5). Yale U Pr.

MUSIC, SACRED

see Church Music

MUSIC, SPANISH

Tinnell, Roger D. An Annotated Discography of Music in Spain before 1650. xvi, 146p. 1980. 12.00 (ISBN 0-942260-09-0). Hispanic Seminary.

MUSIC, THEATRICAL

see Musical Revue, Comedy, etc.; Opera

MUSIC AND LITERATURE

List, George. Music & Poetry in a Colombian Village: A Tri-Cultural Heritage. LC 82-48534. (Illus.). 640p. 1983. 35.00x (ISBN 0-253-33951-0). Ind U Pr.

MUSIC AND ROMANTICISM

see Romanticism in Music

MUSIC AND SOCIETY

Ballantine, Christopher. Music, Society & Ideology. (Monographs on Musicology: Vol. 2). 1982. write for info. (ISBN 0-677-06050-5). Gordon.

Krehbiel, Henry E. Music & Manners in the Classical Period. 286p. 1983. pap. 6.75 (ISBN 0-686-38399-0). Tanager Bks.

Lebrecht, Norman. Discord. LC 82-21872. (Illus.). 272p. 1983. 25.00 (ISBN 0-87663-389-0). Universe.

MUSIC BOX

Jacobson, James A. Woodturning Music Boxes. (Illus.). 192p. (Orig.). 1983. pap. 10.95 (ISBN 0-8069-7726-4). Sterling.

MUSIC CONDUCTORS

see Conductors (Music)

MUSIC FESTIVALS

Rabin, Carol P. Music Festivals in America. Rev. ed. LC 78-73844. (Illus.). 286p. 1983. pap. 8.95 (ISBN 0-912944-74-9). Berkshire Traveller.

MUSIC LIBRARIES

Lichtenwanger, William, ed. Oscar Sonneck & American Music. LC 82-13670. 280p. 1983. 22.50 (ISBN 0-252-01021-3). U of Ill Pr.

MUSIC OF THE SPHERES

see Harmony of the Spheres

MUSIC PUBLISHERS

see Publishers and Publishing

MUSIC READING

see Sight-Reading (Music)

MUSIC THERAPY

Beal, Mary R. & Gilbert, Janet P. Music Curriculum Guidelines For Moderately Retarded Adolescents. 122p. 1982. spiral 14.75x (ISBN 0-398-04757-X). C C Thomas.

Diamond, John. Life Energy in Music: Notes on Music & Sound. 140p. 1983. pap. 19.95 (ISBN 0-915628-20-1). Zeppelin.

Lingerman, Hal A. Healing Energies of Music. LC 82-42706. 198p. (Orig.). 1983. pap. 6.50 (ISBN 0-8356-0570-1, Quest). Theos Pub Hse.

MUSIC TRADE

Tobler, John & Grundy, Stuart. The Record Producers. (Illus.). 256p. 1983. 19.95 (ISBN 0-312-66593-8); pap. 10.95 (ISBN 0-312-66594-6). St Martin.

Wainwright, David. Broadwood by Appointment: A History. (Illus.). 360p. 1983. text ed. 30.00x (ISBN 0-87663-419-6). Universe.

MUSICAL ABILITY-TESTING

Music Aptitude Test. write for info. (RivEd). HM.

MUSICAL BOX

see Music Box

MUSICAL COMEDIES

see Musical Revues, Comedies, etc.

MUSICAL COMEDY

see Musical Revue, Comedy, Etc.

MUSICAL COMPOSITION

see Composition (Music)

MUSICAL EDUCATION

see Music-Instruction and Study

MUSICAL FESTIVALS

see Music Festivals

MUSICAL INSTRUCTION

see Music-Instruction and Study

MUSICAL INSTRUMENTS

see also Instrumentation and Orchestration; Orchestra also groups of instruments, e.g. Stringed Instruments; also names of individual musical instruments, e.g. Piano, Violin

Buck, Peter. Arts & Crafts of Hawaii: Musical Instruments, Sec. IX. (Special Publication Ser.: No. 45). 39p. 1957. pap. 3.00 (ISBN 0-910240-42-6). Bishop Mus.

Irwin, John R. Musical Instruments of the Southern Appalachian Mountains. (Illus.). 108p. 1983. pap. 8.50 (ISBN 0-916838-80-3). Schiffer.

McLeish, Kenneth & McLeish, Valerie. Instruments & Orchestras. (Illus.). 32p. pap. 4.75 laminated (ISBN 0-19-321435-0). Oxford U Pr.

MUSICAL INSTRUMENTS-INDUSTRY AND TRADE

see Music Trade

MUSICAL INSTRUMENTS-INSTRUCTION AND STUDY

see Instrumental Music-Instruction and Study

MUSICAL INTERVALS AND SCALES

Smith-Glendenning, Ruby. All about Scales, Step by Step. 1983. 7.95 (ISBN 0-533-05472-9). Vantage.

MUSICAL MODES

see Musical Intervals and Scales

MUSICAL PERFORMANCE

see Music-Performance

MUSICAL RESEARCH

see Musicology

MUSICAL REVUE, COMEDY, ETC.

For descriptive or historical material. Scores are entered under the heading Musical, Revues, Comedies, etc.

Mordden, Ethan. The Hollywood Musical. (Illus.). 264p. 1982. pap. 8.95 (ISBN 0-312-38838-1). St Martin.

MUSICAL REVUES, COMEDIES, ETC.

Bradley, Ian. Annotated Gilbert & Sullivan. 1983. pap. 7.95 (ISBN 0-14-070848-0). Penguin.

MUSICAL REVUES, COMEDIES, ETC.-STORIES, PLOTS, ETC.

Bacharach, A. L. & Pearce, J. R., eds. The Musical Companion. (Illus.). 800p. 1982. Repr. of 1977 ed. 24.95 (ISBN 0-575-02263-9, Pub by Gollancz England). David & Charles.

MUSICAL THERAPY

see Music Therapy

MUSICIANS

see also Composers; Conductors (Music); Jazz Musicians; Music-Bio-Bibliography; Pianists; Rock Musicians; Singers; Women Musicians

Berger, Morroe, et al. Benny Carter: A Life in American Music, 2 vols. LC 82-10634. (Studies in Jazz: No. 1). 877p. 1982. Set. 45.00 (ISBN 0-8108-1580-X). Vol. I, Biography, 456p. Vol. II, Discography, Filmography, & Bibliography, iv, 417p. Scarecrow.

Bierley, Paul E. Hallelujah Trombone! The Story of Henry Fillmore. LC 82-90686. 1982. pap. 14.95 (ISBN 0-918048-03-6). Integrity.

Blancq, Charles. Sonny Rollins: The Journey of a Jazzman. (Music Ser.). 160p. (gr. 10-12). 1982. pap. 18.95 (ISBN 0-8057-9460-3, Twayne). G K Hall.

Butler, Dougal & Tengrove, Chris. Full Moon: The Amazing Rock & Roll Life of the Late Keith Moon. 269p. 1981. pap. 6.95 (ISBN 0-688-00759-7). Quill NY.

Clarke, F. R. Healey William: Life & Music. 480p. 1983. 37.50x (ISBN 0-8020-5549-4). U of Toronto Pr.

Cooke, Deryck. Vindications: Essays on Romantic Music. LC 82-4295. 160p. 1982. 24.95 (ISBN 0-521-24765-9); pap. 7.95 (ISBN 0-521-28947-5). Cambridge U Pr.

Ensor, Wendy-Ann. More Heroes & Heroines in Music. (Illus.). 48p. 1983. pap. 5.00 laminated (ISBN 0-19-321106-8); cassette 18.00 (ISBN 0-19-321107-6). Oxford U Pr.

An Evening With John Denver. 7.95 (ISBN 0-89524-052-1). Cherry Lane.

Peters, Richard. Barry Manilow: An Illustrative Biography. (Illus.). 104p. (Orig.). 1983. pap. 8.95 (ISBN 0-933328-65-6). Delilah Bks.

MUSICIANS-CORRESPONDENCE, REMINISCENCES, ETC.

Camden, Archie. Blow by Blow: The Memories of a Musical Rogue & Vagabond. (Illus.). 208p. 1983. text ed. 15.00x (ISBN 0-87663-421-8). Universe.

Clooney, Rosemary & Strait, Raymond. This for Remembrance. 352p. 1982. pap. 2.95 (ISBN 0-425-05968-5). Berkley Pub.

Heifetz, Josefa. From Bach to Verse: Comic Mnemonics for Famous Musical Themes. (Orig.). 1983. pap. 4.95 (ISBN 0-14-006691-8). Penguin.

Jones, Bessie. For the Ancestors: Autobiographical Memories. Stewart, John, ed. LC 82-8593. (Illus.). 211p. 1983. 14.95 (ISBN 0-252-00959-2). U of Ill Pr.

Pepper, Art & Pepper, Laurie. Straight Life. 1983. pap. 9.95 (ISBN 0-02-872010-5). Schirmer Bks.

Schone, Alfred & Hiller, Ferdinand, eds. The Letters of a Leipzig Cantor: Being the Letters of Moritz Hauptmann to Franz Hauser, Ludwig Spohr, & Other Musicians, 2 vols. Coleridge, A. D., tr. LC 75-163789. Date not set. Repr. of 1892 ed. price not set. Vienna Hse.

MUSICIANS-PORTRAITS

Marchbank, Pearce, ed. With the Beatles: The Historic Photographs of Dezo Hoffmann. (Illus.). 96p. (Orig.). 1983. pap. 12.95 (ISBN 0-399-41009-0). Delilah Bks.

Smith, David & Neal, Peters. Peter Allen: Between the Moon & New York City. (Illus.). 160p. (Orig.). 1983. pap. 9.95 (ISBN 0-933328-57-5). Delilah Bks.

MUSICIANS, WOMEN

see Women Musicians

MUSICOLOGY

see also Ethnomusicology

Lichtenwanger, William, ed. Oscar Sonneck & American Music. LC 82-13670. 280p. 1983. 22.50 (ISBN 0-252-01021-3). U of Ill Pr.

MUSLIM ARCHITECTURE

see Architecture, Islamic

MUSLIM ART

see Art, Islamic

MUSLIM CIVILIZATION

see Civilization, Islamic

MUSLIM LITERATURE

see Islamic Literature

MUSLIM PHILOSOPHY

see Philosophy, Islamic

MUSLIM WOMEN

see Women, Muslim

MUSLIMISM

see Islam

MUSLIMS

Siddiqui, Zeba. Kareem & Fatimah. Quinlan, Hamid, ed. LC 82-70452. 50p. 1982. pap. 3.50 (ISBN 0-89259-032-7). Am Trust Pubns.

MUSLIMS-WOMEN

see Women, Muslim

MUSLIMS IN ASIA

Bennigsen, Alexandre & Broxup, Marie. The Islamic Threat to the Soviet State. LC 82-16826. 224p. 1983. 27.50x (ISBN 0-312-43739-0). St Martin.

MUSLIMS IN INDIA

Page, David. Prelude to Partition: The Indian Muslims & the Imperia; System of Control; 1920-32. 300p. 1982. 18.95x (ISBN 0-19-561303-1). Oxford U Pr.

MUSSELMEN

see Muslims

MUSSOLINI, BENITO, 1883-1945

Creighton, Warren S. The Contributions of Mussolini to the Civilization of Mankind. (Illus.). 115p. 1983. 75.45 (ISBN 0-86722-038-4). Inst Econ Pol.

MUSSULMANISM

see Islam

MUSTANG (FIGHTER PLANES)

Ethell, Jeffrey. Mustang: A Documentary History. (Illus.). 160p. 1981. 18.95 (ISBN 0-86720-561-X). Sci Bks Intl.

MUTAGENESIS

see also Radiogenetics

Heddle, John A., ed. Mutagenicity: New Horizons in Genetic Toxicology. LC 81-22940. (Cell Biology Ser.). 1982. 55.00 (ISBN 0-12-336180-X). Acad Pr.

Lawrence, Christopher W. Induced Mutagenesis: Molecular Mechanisms & Thier Implications for Enviornmental Protection. (Basic Life Sciences Ser.). 434p. 1982. 55.00x (ISBN 0-306-41163-6, Plenum Pr). Plenum Pub.

Murray, Randall, ed. Mutagens & Carcinogens. 147p. 1977. 18.50x (ISBN 0-8422-4119-1). Irvington.

Sorsa, Marja & Vainio, Harri, eds. Mutagens in Our Enviroment. LC 82-20320. (Progress in Clinical & Biological Research Ser.: V0l. 109). 502p. 1982. 50.00 (ISBN 0-8451-0109-9). A R Liss.
Sugimura, Takashi & Kondo, Sohei, eds. Environmental Mutagens & Carcinogens. LC 82-15231. 784p. 1982. 80.00 (ISBN 0-8451-3007-2). A R Liss.

MUTATION (BIOLOGY)
see also Evolution; Origin of Species; Variation (Biology)
McMahan, Forrest R. Human Mutation. LC 82-99887. (Illus.). 72p. (Orig.). 1982. pap. 3.95 (ISBN 0-910217-00-9). Synergetics WV.

MUTUAL BENEFIT ASSOCIATIONS
see Friendly Societies

MUTUAL FUNDS
see Investment Trusts

MUTUAL INSURANCE
see Insurance

MUTUAL SECURITY PROGRAMS, 1951-
Chichester, Michael & Wilkinson, John. The Uncertain Ally. 264p. 1982. text ed. 38.00x (ISBN 0-566-00534-4). Gower Pub Ltd.
Churchill, Winston S. Defending the West. 1981. 40.00x (ISBN 0-85117-210-5, Pub. by M Temple Smith). State Mutual Bk.
Tucker, Gardiner. Toward Rationalizing Allied Weapons Production. (The Atlantic Papers: No. 76/1). 54p. (Orig.). 1976. pap. text ed. 4.75 (ISBN 0-686-83681-2). Allanheld.

MYCENAE
Taylour, William. The Myceneans. rev. ed. (Ancient Peoples & Places Ser.). (Illus.). 1983. 19.95 (ISBN 0-500-02103-1). Thames Hudson.

MYCENAEAN CIVILIZATION
see Civilization, Mycenaean

MYCOBACTERIUM
Chadwick, Maureen V. Mycobacteria. (Institute of Medical Laboratory Sciences Monographs). 128p. 1982. pap. text ed. write for info. (ISBN 0-7236-0595-5). Wright-PSG.

MYCOLOGY
see also Fungi; Medical Mycology
De Sole, S. Entwicklung der Drelipore von Coprinus Radiatus (Bolt.) Fr. (Bibliotheca Mycologica 88). (Illus.). 148p. 1982. pap. 20.00 (ISBN 3-7682-1343-9). Lubrecht & Cramer.
Halling, Roy E. The Genus Collybia (Agaricales) in the Northeastern U. S. & Adjacent Canada. (Mycologia Memoirs 8). (Illus.). 150p. 1983. 27.00 (ISBN 3-7682-1345-5). Lubrecht & Cramer.
Koske, R. E. Cookbook Statistics for Plant Pathology & Mycology. 65p. (Orig.). 1982. pap. text ed. 7.50x (ISBN 0-934454-94-9). Lubrecht & Cramer.
Razin, Shmuel, ed. Methods in Mycoplasmology: Diagnostic Mycoplasmology, Vol. 2. Date not set. price not set (ISBN 0-12-583802-6). Acad Pr.

MYCOSIS
International Symposium on Vaginal Mycoses Vienna, September 1981. (Journal: Chemotherapy: Suppl. 1, Vol. 28). (Illus.). 112p. 1983. pap. 21.75 (ISBN 3-8055-3638-0). S Karger.

MYCOTOXINS
see also Aflatoxins
Mycotoxin Surveillance. (FAO Food & Nutrition Papers: No. 21). 68p. 1982. pap. 7.50 (ISBN 92-5-101180-X, F2306, FAO). Unipub.

MYNAHS
Low, Rosemary. Mynah Birds. (Illus.). 93p. 3.95 (ISBN 0-7028-1002-9). Avian Pubns.

MYODYNAMICS
see Muscles

MYOLOGY
see Muscles

MYOPATHY
see Muscles-Diseases

MYSIDAE
Morgan, Mark D. Ecology of Mysidacea. 1982. text ed. 54.50 (ISBN 90-6193-761-2, Pub. by Junk Pubs Netherlands). Kluwer Boston.

MYSTERIES (DRAMATIC)
see Mysteries and Miracle-Plays

MYSTERIES, RELIGIOUS
see also Mother-Goddesses; Rites and Ceremonies
Raguin, Yves. Attention to the Mystery: Entry into the Spiritual Life. LC 82-60595. 1983. pap. 5.95 (ISBN 0-8091-2494-7). Paulist Pr.

MYSTERIES AND MIRACLE-PLAYS
Craig, Barbara. The Evolution of a Mystery Play: Le Sacrifice d'Abraham. 20.00 (ISBN 0-917786-30-0). French Lit.

MYSTERIES AND MIRACLE-PLAYS-HISTORY AND CRITICISM
Lumiansky, R. M. & Mills, David. The Chester Mystery Cycle: Essays & Documents. LC 82-1838. vii, 321p. 1982. 40.00x (ISBN 0-8078-1522-5). U of NC Pr.

MYSTERY STORIES
see Adventure and Adventurers; Detective and Mystery Stories

MYSTICAL BODY OF CHRIST
see Jesus Christ-Mystical Body

MYSTICAL THEOLOGY
see Mysticism

MYSTICAL UNION
Here are entered works dealing with the indwelling of the Triune God, or of any person of the trinity, in the hearts of believers and conversely, works dealing with the union between man and the Triune God, especially between man and Jesus Christ. Works dealing with the church as the mystical body of Christ are entered under the heading Jesus Christ-Mystical Body.
Duckworth, Marion. The Strong Place. 1983. pap. 4.95 (ISBN 0-8423-6663-6). Tyndale.
Huelsman, Richard J. Intimacy with Jesus: An Introduction. LC 82-60587. 1983. pap. 4.95 (ISBN 0-8091-2492-0). Paulist Pr.

MYSTICISM
see also Cabala; Christian Art and Symbolism; Enthusiasm; Private Revelations; Symbolism of Numbers; Tantrism
Bird, Christopher. The Divining Hand: The 500-Year-Old Mystery of Dowsing. (Illus.). 353p. 1983. pap. 13.50 (ISBN 0-525-48038-2, 01311-390). Dutton.
Childs, Michael. An Introduction to Mastery. (Orig.). 1982. pap. 10.00 (ISBN 0-910247-00-5). Source Unlimited.
Crowley, Aleister & Regardie, Israel. Magick Without Tears. 3rd ed. 560p. 1982. 49.94 (ISBN 0-941404-16-1); pap. 13.95 (ISBN 0-941404-17-X). Falcon Pr Az.
Curtiss, H. A. & Curtiss, F. H. Gems of Mysticism. 83p. 3.50 (ISBN 0-686-38219-6). Sun Bks.
Fortune, Dion, ed. The Esoteric Orders & Their Work. 144p. 1983. pap. 7.95 (ISBN 0-85030-310-9). Newcastle Pub.
McNamara, William. Earthy Mysticism: Contemplation & the Life of Passionate Presence. 128p. 1983. pap. 5.95 (ISBN 0-8245-0562-X). Crossroad NY.
Regardie, Israel. Eye in the Triangle. 523p. 1982. 49.95 (ISBN 0-941404-07-2); pap. 12.95 (ISBN 0-941404-08-0). Falcon Pr Az.
Richmond, Olney H. The Mystic Test Book. (Orig.). 1983. pap. 9.95 (ISBN 0-87877-064-X). Newcastle Pub.
--The Mystic Test Book. 1983. lib. bdg. 17.95x (ISBN 0-89370-664-7). Borgo Pr.

MYTH
see also Mythology
Giraroot, N. J. Myth & Meaning in Early Taoism: The Themes of Chaos (hun-tun) LC 81-21964. (Hermeneutics Ser.). (Illus.). 430p. 1983. 27.50x (ISBN 0-520-04330-8). U of Cal Pr.

MYTHOLOGY
see also Art and Mythology; Folk-Lore; Gods; Heroes; Mother-Goddesses; Myth
also Bull (Cats, Death, Kings and Rulers, Moon) (In Religion, Folk-Lore, etc.); and similar headings as listed in references under Religion, Primitive; also subdivision Religion, Primitive; also subdivision Religion and Mythology under Indians, Indians of North America (South America, etc.)
Beltz, Walter. God & the Gods: Myths. 1983. pap. 5.95 (ISBN 0-14-022192-1, Pelican). Penguin.
Keightley, Thomas. The Fairy Mythology. 560p. 1982. 30.00x (Pub. by Wildwood House). State Mutual Bk.
Lethbridge, T. C. The Legend of the Sons of God: A Fantasy? (Illus.). 128p. 1983. pap. 5.95 (ISBN 0-7100-9500-7). Routledge & Kegan.
Levi-Strauss, Claude. From Honey to Ashes: Introduction to a Science of Mythology, Vol. 2. Weightman, John & Weightman, Doreen, trs. LC 82-15965. 512p. 1973. pap. 10.95 (ISBN 0-226-47489-5). U of Chicago Pr.
--The Raw & the Cooked: Introduction to a Science of Mythology, Vol. 1. Weightman, John & Weightman, Doreen, trs. LC 82-15895. (Illus.). xiv, 388p. 1969. pap. 8.95 (ISBN 0-226-47487-9). U of Chicago Pr.
Mitchell, Meredith. Heroes & Victims. Sternback-Scott, Sisa & Smith, Lindsay, eds. 1983. 16.95 (ISBN 0-938434-18-7); pap. 11.95 (ISBN 0-938434-15-2). Sigo Pr.
Peter, Lily. In the Beginning: Great Myths of the Western World. (Illus.). 1983. 19.00 (ISBN 0-938626-15-9); pap. 9.95 (ISBN 0-938626-18-3). U of Ark Pr.

MYTHOLOGY-BIBLIOGRAPHY
Zamora, Lois P., ed. The Apocalyptic Vision in America: Interdisciplinary Essays on Myth & Culture. LC 81-85524. 272p. 1982. 19.95 (ISBN 0-686-82270-6). Bowling Green Univ.

MYTHOLOGY-DICTIONARIES
Room, Adrian. Dictionary of the Origins of Names in Classical Mythology: Mythonoma. 320p. 1983. 18.95 (ISBN 0-7100-9262-8). Routledge & Kegan.

MYTHOLOGY-JUVENILE LITERATURE
see also subdivision Juvenile Literature under Mythology, Classical, Mythology, Greek, and similar headings.
Vrooman, Christine W. Willowby's World of Unicorns. Kane, Sandy & Ogden, Peggy, eds. (Willowby's World Ser.). (Illus.). 32p. (gr. 2-6). 1982. pap. 1.75 (ISBN 0-910349-00-2). Cloud Ten.

MYTHOLOGY, BRAHMAN
see Mythology, Hindu; Vedas

MYTHOLOGY, CLASSICAL
see also Gods; Heroes
also names of mythological persons and objects
Bulfinch, Thomas. Bulfinch's Mythology. 7.95 (ISBN 0-394-60437-7). Modern Lib.
Godolphin, F. R., ed. & intro. by. Great Classical Myths. LC 64-10293. 6.95 (ISBN 0-394-60417-2). Modern Lib.
Sienkewicz, Thomas J. Classical Gods & Heroes in the National Gallery of Art. LC 82-23818. (Illus.). 50p. (Orig.). 1983. pap. text ed. 8.75 (ISBN 0-8191-2967-4). U Pr of Amer.

MYTHOLOGY, CLASSICAL-DICTIONARIES
see Mythology-Dictionaries

MYTHOLOGY, EGYPTIAN
MacKenzie, Donald A. Egyptian Myth & Legend. 404p. 1983. pap. 8.25 (ISBN 0-88072-016-6). Tanager Bks.

MYTHOLOGY, GREEK-JUVENILE LITERATURE
Richardson, I. M. Prometheus & the Story of Fire. LC 82-15979. (Illus.). 32p. (gr. 4-8). 1983. PLB 8.79 (ISBN 0-89375-859-0); pap. text ed. 2.50 (ISBN 0-89375-860-4). Troll Assocs.

MYTHOLOGY, HINDU
see also Symbolism of Numbers
Dandekar, R. N. The Age of Guptas & Other Essays. 1982. 30.00 (ISBN 0-8364-0916-7, Pub. by Ajanta). South Asia Bks.

MYTHOLOGY, INDIAN (AMERICAN INDIAN)
see Indians of Mexico-Religion and Mythology; Indians of North America-Religion and Mythology; Indians of South America-Religion and Mythology

MYTHOLOGY, INDO-EUROPEAN
Dumezil, Georges. The Stakes of the Warrior. Puhvel, Jaan, ed. Weeks, David, tr. from Fr. LC 82-13384. 128p. 1983. text ed. 14.95 (ISBN 0-520-04834-2). U of Cal Pr.

MYTHOLOGY, VEDIC
see Mythology, Hindu; Vedas

MYTHOLOGY IN ART
see Art and Mythology

MYTHOLOGY IN LITERATURE
Gould, Karen L. Claude Simon's Mythic Muse. 16.00. French Lit.

MYTHS
see Mythology

N

NABOKOV, VLADIMIR VLADIMIROVICH, 1899-1977
Fowler, Douglas. Reading Nabokov. LC 82-17342. 224p. 1983. pap. text ed. 10.25 (ISBN 0-8191-2721-3). U Pr of Amer.

NAHUAS
Taggart, James M. Nahuat Myth & Social Structure. (Texas Pan American Ser.). (Illus.). 272p. 1983. text ed. 25.00x (ISBN 0-292-75524-4). U of Tex Pr.

NAHUATL LANGUAGE
see Aztec Language

NAHUATLECAS
see Nahuas

NAIDU, SAROJINI, 1879-1949
Naravane, V. S. Sarojini Naidu: An Introduction to Her Life, Work & Poetry. 160p. 1980. 20.00x (ISBN 0-86131-253-8, Pub. by Orient Longman Ltd India). Apt Bks.

NAIPAUL, VIDIADHAR SURAJPRASAD, 1932-
McSweeney, Kerry. Four Contemporary Novelists: Angus Wilson, Brian Moore, John Fowles, V. S. Naipaul. 232p. 1983. 24.95 (ISBN 0-7735-0399-4). McGill-Queens U Pr.

NAMES
see also Names, Geographical; Names, Personal
Case, Paul F. The Name of Names. 1981. 2.00 (ISBN 0-686-38082-7). Builders of Adytum.
Dunkling, Leslie. The Guinness Book of Names. (Illus.). 192p. (Orig.). 1982. pap. 9.95 (ISBN 0-85112-293-0, Pub. by Guinness Superlatives England). Sterling.
Koss, Gerhard. Names of Germany. (International Library of Names). 250p. 1983. text ed. 24.50x (ISBN 0-8290-1285-0). Irvington.
Mehrotra, Raja R. Names of India. (International Library of Names). 250p. 1983. text ed. 24.50x (ISBN 0-8290-1293-1). Irvington.
Murphy, Michael. Names of Ireland. (International Library of Names). 250p. 1983. text ed. 24.50x (ISBN 0-8290-1286-9). Irvington.
Schlueter, Paul. Names & American Literature. (International Library of Names). 250p. 1983. text ed. 24.50x (ISBN 0-8290-1284-2). Irvington.

NAMES, CHRISTIAN
see Names, Personal

NAMES, FICTICIOUS
see Anonyms and Pseudonyms

NAMES, GEOGRAPHICAL
Brasch, Walter M. Columbia County Place Names. (Illus.). 232p. (Orig.). 1982. 15.00 (ISBN 0-88023-028-2). Columbia County Hist Soc.
Names of Countries. (FAO Terminology Bulletin Ser.: No. 20, Rev. 6). 59p. 1983. pap. 7.50 (ISBN 92-5-001242-X, F2357, FAO). Unipub.

NAMES, GEOGRAPHICAL-UNITED STATES
Coulet du Gard, Rene. Dictionary of Spanish Place Names of the Northwest Coast of America: California, Vol. I. 190p. 1982. 24.00 (ISBN 0-939586-01-0). Edns Des Deux Mondes.
--Dictionary of Spanish Place Names of the Northwest Coast of America: Oregon, Washington State, British Columbia, Alaska, Vol. II. 190p. 1983. 24.00 (ISBN 0-939586-02-9). Edns Des Deux Mondes.
McArthur, Lewis A. Oregon Geographic Names. 5th, rev. ed. McArthur, Lewis L., rev. by. 864p. 1982. 21.95 (ISBN 0-87595-113-9, Western Imprints); pap. 14.95 (ISBN 0-87595-114-7, Western Imprints). Oreg Hist Soc.
Stewart, George R. Names on the Land: A Historical Account of Placenaming in the United States. 4th ed. LC 82-6578. 560p. 1982. pap. 10.00 (ISBN 0-938530-02-X, 02-X). Lexikos.

NAMES, PERSONAL
see also Anonyms and Pseudonyms
also Name under names of persons, Jesus Christ-Name
Bailey, Sandra B. Big Book of Baby Names. 160p. 1982. pap. 5.95 (ISBN 0-89586-191-7). H P Bks.
Cameron, Catherine. The Name Givers: How They Influence Your Life. 230p. 1983. 13.95 (ISBN 0-13-609495-3); pap. 6.95 (ISBN 0-13-609487-2). P-H.
Dunkling, Leslie A. First Names First. 290p. 1982. Repr. of 1977 ed. 40.00x (ISBN 0-686-82089-4). Gale.
Francis, Linda & Hartzel, John. What's in a Name? (Orig.). 1982. pap. write for info. (ISBN 0-8423-7935-5). Tyndale.
Franks, Ray. What's in a Nickname? LC 82-90195. (Illus.). 208p. (Orig.). 1982. pap. 12.95 (ISBN 0-943976-00-6). R Franks Ranch.
Mapes, Lola R. Name Games. 80p. (gr. 3-5). 1983. pap. text ed. 5.95 (ISBN 0-86530-077-1, IP 77-1). Incentive Pubs.

NAMIBIA
Namibia. 1981. 1.50 (ISBN 0-910082-05-7). Am Pr Serv Comm.

NAMIBIA-POLITICS AND GOVERNMENT
Hovey, Gail. Namibia's Stolen Wealth: North American Investment & South African Occupation. (Illus.). 52p. (Orig.). 1982. pap. 2.50 (ISBN 0-943428-04-1). Africa Fund.
Rotberg, Robert I., ed. Namibia: Political & Economic Prospects. LC 81-48672. 144p. 1982. 18.95 (ISBN 0-669-05531-X). Lexington Bks.

NANTUCKET, MASSACHUSETTS-HISTORY
Duprey, Kenneth. Old Houses on Nantucket. (Illus.). 256p. 1983. 16.95 (ISBN 0-8038-5399-8). Hastings.

NAPOLEON 1ST, EMPEROR OF THE FRENCH, 1769-1821
Glover, Michael. The Napoleonic Wars: An Illustrated History 1792-1815. (Illus.). 240p. 1982. pap. 14.95 (ISBN 0-88254-710-0). Hippocrene Bks.
Hazen, Charles D. The French Revolution & Napoleon. 385p. 1982. Repr. of 1917 ed. lib. bdg. 50.00 (ISBN 0-89987-390-1). Darby Bks.
Napoleon's Book of Fate. 192p. 1983. pap. 2.50 (ISBN 0-668-05734-3, 5734). Arco.
Nofi, Albert A., ed. Napoleon at War: Selected Writings from F. Lorraine Petre. (Illus.). 300p. (gr. 6 up). 1983. 19.95 (ISBN 0-88254-805-0). Hippocrene Bks.
Rogers, H. C. Napoleon's Army. (Illus.). 192p. 1982. pap. 8.95 (ISBN 0-88254-709-7). Hippocrene Bks.

NAPOLEON 3RD, EMPEROR OF THE FRENCH, 1808-1873
Echard, William E. Napoleon III & the Concert of Europe. LC 82-12660. 325p. 1983. text ed. 32.50x (ISBN 0-8071-1056-6). La State U Pr.

NAPOLEONIC WARS
see France-History-Revolution, 1789-1799; Peninsular War, 1807-1814

NARCISSISM
Steingart, Irving. Cognition as Pathological Play in Borderline-Narcissistic Personalities. 256p. 1983. text ed. 25.00 (ISBN 0-89335-179-2). SP Med & Sci Bks.

NARCOTIC ADDICTION
see Narcotic Habit

NARCOTIC HABIT
see also Narcotics and Youth
American Health Research Institute, Ltd. Drug Withdrawal Symptoms: A Medical Subject Analysis & Research Index with Bibliography. Bartone, John C., ed. 120p. 1983. 29.95 (ISBN 0-941864-88-X); pap. 21.95 (ISBN 0-941864-89-8). ABBE Pubs Assn.

NARCOTIC TRADE
see Narcotics, Control of

NARCOTICS
see also Heroin
Demand & Supply of Opiates for Medical & Scientific Needs. 15.00 (ISBN 0-686-84922-1, E.82.XI.4). UN.
Estimated World Requirements of Narcotic Drugs in 1982: Supplement 6. 8p. 1983. pap. 1.00 (ISBN 0-686-84909-4, UN82/11/2S6, UN). Unipub.
Woods, Arthur. Dangerous Drugs. 1931. text ed. 29.50x (ISBN 0-686-83520-4). Elliots Bks.

NARCOTICS, CONTROL OF
see also Narcotic Habit
American Health Research Institute, Ltd. World Survey of Drug & Narcotic Control: A Medical Subject Analysis & Research Index with Bibliography. Bartone, John C., ed. 120p. 1983. 29.95 (ISBN 0-88164-014-X); pap. 21.95 (ISBN 0-88164-015-8). ABBE Pubs Assn.

Himmelstein, Jerome L. The Strange Career of Marihuana: Politics & Ideology of Drug Control in America. LC 82-12181. (Contributions in Political Science Ser.: No. 94). (Illus.). 208p. 1983. lib. bdg. 27.95 (ISBN 0-313-23517-1, HSC/). Greenwood.

NARCOTICS AND YOUTH

Baker, Joe. Coping with Drug Abuse: A Lifeline for Parents. LC 82-12723. (Illus.). 60p. 1982. pap. 9.95 (ISBN 0-943690-00-5). DARE.

NARRATION (RHETORIC)

Meisel, Martin. Realizations: Narrative, Pictorial, & Theatrical Arts of the Nineteenth Century. LC 82-12292. (Illus.). 416p. 1983. 45.00x (ISBN 0-691-06553-5). Princeton U Pr.

Morrison, Kristin. Cantors & Chronicles: The Use of Narrative in the Plays of Samuel Beckett & Harold Pinter. LC 82-16086. 240p. 1983. lib. bdg. 20.00x (ISBN 0-226-54130-4). U of Chicago Pr.

NARRATIVE PAINTING

Meisel, Martin. Realizations: Narrative, Pictorial, & Theatrical Arts of the Nineteenth Century. LC 82-12292. (Illus.). 416p. 1983. 45.00x (ISBN 0-691-06553-5). Princeton U Pr.

NARRATIVE WRITING

see Narration (Rhetoric)

NATAL-HISTORY

Brain, Joy. Christian Indians in Natal, 1860-1911. (Illus.). 272p. 1982. 18.95x (ISBN 0-19-570297-2). Oxford U Pr.

NATCHEZ, MISSISSIPPI

Eidt, Mary B. & Gandy, Joan W., eds. The Complete Guide to Natchez. LC 76-56980. (Illus.). 111p. 1982. pap. text ed. 5.00 (ISBN 0-9609728-0-3). Myrtle Bank.

NATCHEZ INDIANS

see Indians of North America-Eastern States

NATIONAL ACCOUNTING

see National Income-Accounting

NATIONAL ANTHEMS

see National Songs

NATIONAL BANK NOTES

Hickman, John & Oakes, Dean. Standard Catalog of National Bank Notes. (Illus.). 1982. text ed. 75.00 (ISBN 0-87341-026-2). Krause Pubns.

NATIONAL CHARACTERISTICS, ARGENTINE

Mallea, Eduardo. History of an Argentine Passion. Miller, Yvette E., ed. Litchblau, Myron, tr. 184p. 1982. pap. 10.95 (ISBN 0-935480-10-2). Lat Am Lit Rev Pr.

NATIONAL CHARACTERISTICS, AUSTRALIAN

Environmental Engineering Conference, Canberra Australia, 1979. The Status of the National Environment. 110p. (Orig.). 1979. pap. text ed. 24.00x (ISBN 0-85825-115-9, Pub. by Inst Engineering Australia). Renouf.

NATIONAL CHARACTERISTICS, FRENCH

Zeldin, Theodore. The French. (Illus.). 512p. 1983. 22.50 (ISBN 0-394-52947-2). Pantheon.

NATIONAL CHARACTERISTICS, GERMAN

Dundes, Alan. German National Character: An Anthropological Study, or Life Is Like a Chicken Coop Ladder. (Illus.). 176p. 1983. 16.00x (ISBN 0-231-05494-7). Columbia U Pr.

NATIONAL CHARACTERISTICS, ISRAELI

Elon, Amos. Israelis: Founders & Sons. 1983. pap. 5.95 (ISBN 0-14-022476-9, Pelican). Penguin.

NATIONAL CHARACTERISTICS, JAPANESE

Christopher, Robert. Japan Explained: The Mind of the New Goliath. 1983. price not set (ISBN 0-671-44947-8, Linden). S&S.

NATIONAL DEBTS

see Debts, Public

NATIONAL EMBLEMS

see Emblems

NATIONAL FORESTS

see Forest Reserves

NATIONAL GUARD (U. S.)

see United States-National Guard

NATIONAL HEALTH SERVICE, GREAT BRITAIN

see Great Britain-National Health Service

NATIONAL HOCKEY LEAGUE

Gilbert, John. NHL Shooters. (Illus.). 96p. 1982. pap. 9.95 (ISBN 0-943392-03-9). Tribeca Comm.

NATIONAL HOLIDAYS

see Holidays

NATIONAL INCOME

see also Gross National Product

Modigliani & Hemming. The Determinants of National Savings & Wealth: Proceedings of a Conference Held by International Economic Association in Bergamo, Italy. LC 82-10377. 305p. 1982. 35.00x (ISBN 0-312-19590-7). St Martin.

NATIONAL INCOME-ACCOUNTING

Fabricant, Solomon. Studies in Social & Private Accounting. LC 82-82488. (Accountancy in Transition Ser.). 300p. 1982. lib. bdg. 40.00 (ISBN 0-8240-5337-0). Garland Pub.

NATIONAL INCOME-INDIA

Rao, V. K. India's National Income 1950-1980: An Analysis of Economic Growth & Change. LC 82-22972. (Illus.). 224p. 1983. 20.00 (ISBN 0-8039-1950-6). Sage.

NATIONAL PARKS AND RESERVES

see also Forest Reserves; Natural Monuments; Wilderness Areas

also names of national parks, e.g. Yellowstone National Park

Lister, Robert H. & Lister, Florence C. Those Who Came Before: Southwestern Archeology in the National Park System. Houk, Rose & Priehs, T. J., eds. 1983. pap. price not set (ISBN 0-911408-62-2). SW Pks Mnmts.

Melius, Kenneth W. National Forest Campground Guide. LC 82-51299. (Illus.). 310p. 1983. pap. 8.95 (ISBN 0-9610130-0-1). Tensleep.

Rowe, Robert D & Chestnut, Lauraline G., eds. Managing Air Quality & Scenic Resources at National Parks & Wilderness Areas. (Replica Edition). 310p. 1982. softcover 20.00x (ISBN 0-86531-941-3). Westview.

NATIONAL PARKS AND RESERVES-AFRICA

Williams. A Field Guide to the National Parks of East Africa. 29.95 (ISBN 0-686-42781-5, Collins Pub England). Greene.

NATIONAL PLANNING

see Economic Policy; Social Policy

NATIONAL PRODUCT, GROSS

see Gross National Product

NATIONAL PSYCHOLOGY

see Ethnopsychology

NATIONAL SELF-DETERMINATION

see Self-Determination, National

NATIONAL SOCIALISM

see also Fascism; Socialism

Angolia, John R. On the Field of Honor: A History of the Knight's Cross Bearers, Vol. 1. (Illus.). 288p. 1979. 17.95 (ISBN 0-912138-19-X). Bender Pub CA.

Kater, Michael H. The Nazi Party: A Social Profile of Members & Leaders, 1919-1945. (Illus.). 400p. 1983. text ed. 25.00x (ISBN 0-674-60655-8). Harvard U Pr.

Littlejohn, David. Foreign Legions of the Third Reich, Vol. 1. (Illus.). 208p. 1979. 17.95 (ISBN 0-912138-17-3). Bender Pub CA.

Overy, R. The Nazi Economic Recovery Nineteen Thirty-two to Nineteen Thirty-eight. (Studies in Economic & Social History). 80p. 1982. pap. text ed. 4.75x (ISBN 0-333-31119-1, Pub. by Macmillan England). Humanities.

Stachura, Peter D. Gregor Strasser & the Rise of Nazism. 208p. 1983. text ed. 19.50x (ISBN 0-04-943027-0). Allen Unwin.

Stachura, Peter D., ed. The Nazi Machdtergreifung. 208p. 1983. text ed. 19.50x (ISBN 0-04-943026-2). Allen Unwin.

Tenenbaum, Edward A. National Socialism vs. International Capitalism. 1942. text ed. 39.50x (ISBN 0-686-83630-8). Elliots Bks.

NATIONAL SOCIALIST WORKERS PARTY

see Nationalsozialistische Deutsche Arbeiter-Partei

NATIONAL SONGS

see also Folk-Songs

also names of national songs, e.g. Star Spangled Banner

Shaw, Martin & Coleman, Henry. National Anthems of the World. 5th, rev. & enl. ed. Cartledge, T. M. & Reed, W. L., eds. 511p. 1983. 19.95 (ISBN 0-7137-0888-3, Pub. by Blandford Pr England). Sterling.

NATIONAL TRAINING LABORATORIES

Bradford, Leland P., et al, eds. T-Group Theory & Laboratory Method: Innovation in Re-Education. LC 64-11499. 498p. 1964. 32.95x (ISBN 0-471-09510-9). Wiley.

NATIONALISM

see also Languages-Political Aspects; Minorities; Nationalism and Socialism; Patriotism; Regionalism; Self-Determination, National

Breuilly, John. Nationalism & the State. 366p. 1982. 25.00x (ISBN 0-312-56005-2). St Martin.

Groth, Alexander J. Major Ideologies: An Interpretative of Democracy, Socialism & Nationalism. LC 82-18755. 256p. 1983. Repr. of 1971 ed. text ed. write for info. (ISBN 0-89874-579-9). Krieger.

Sathyamurthy, T. V. Sociology of Nationalism: Contemporary Perspectives. 224p. 1983. text ed. 25.00 (ISBN 0-86598-117-5). Allanheld.

Smith, Anthony D. Theories of Nationalism. 2nd ed. 392p. 1983. text ed. 36.00x (ISBN 0-8419-0846-X); pap. text ed. 16.00x (ISBN 0-8419-0845-1). Holmes & Meier.

NATIONALISM-IRELAND

Boyce, D. George. Nationalism in Ireland. 1982. 70.00x (ISBN 0-7171-1219-5, Pub. by Gill & Macmillan Ireland). State Mutual Bk.

Hepburn. Nationalism & Socialism in Twentieth-Century Ireland. 268p. 1982. 55.00x (ISBN 0-85323-343-8, Pub. by Liverpool Univ England). State Mutual Bk.

NATIONALISM AND RELIGION

see also Church and State; Islam and State; Religion and State; War and Religion

Liebman, Charles S. & Don-Yehiya, Eliezer. Civil Religion in Israel: Traditional Judaism & Political Culture in the Jewish State. LC 82-17427. 270p. 1983. 19.95x (ISBN 0-520-04817-2). U of Cal Pr.

NATIONALISM AND SOCIALISM

Hepburn. Nationalism & Socialism in Twentieth-Century Ireland. 268p. 1982. 55.00x (ISBN 0-85323-343-8, Pub. by Liverpool Univ England). State Mutual Bk.

Zwick, Peter. National Communism. 270p. 1982. lib. bdg. 28.50 (ISBN 0-86531-427-6); pap. text ed. 12.00 (ISBN 0-86531-428-4). Westview.

NATIONALISM IN LITERATURE

Haberly, David T. Three Sad Races: Racial Identity & National Consciousness in Brazilian Literature. LC 82-4467. (Illus.). 198p. p.n.s. (ISBN 0-521-24722-5). Cambridge U Pr.

NATIONALITY (CITIZENSHIP)

see Citizenship

NATIONALIZATION

see Government Ownership

NATIONALSOZIALISTISCHE DEUTSCHE ARBEITER-PARTEI

Kater, Michael H. The Nazi Party: A Social Profile of Members & Leaders, 1919-1945. (Illus.). 400p. 1983. text ed. 25.00x (ISBN 0-674-60655-8). Harvard U Pr.

NATIONALSOZIALISTISCHE DEUTSCHE ARBEITER-PARTEI, WAFFENSCHUTZSTAFFEL

Koehl, Robert L. The Black Corps: The Structure & Power Struggles of the Nazi SS. LC 81-69824. (Illus.). 448p. 1983. 27.50 (ISBN 0-299-09190-2). U of Wis Pr.

NATIONS, LAW OF

see International Law

NATIVE RACES

see also Ethnology; Indians of North America-Government Relations;

also subdivision Native Races under names of continents, countries, etc. e.g. Africa-Native Races

McCulloh, James H. Researches on America: Being an Attempt to Settle Some Points Relative to the Aboriginess of America. 220p. 1982. pap. 7.95 (ISBN 0-912526-32-7). Lib Res.

NATO

see North Atlantic Treaty Organization

NATURAL BOUNDARIES

see Boundaries

NATURAL CALAMITIES

see Natural Disasters

NATURAL CHILDBIRTH

Childbirth God's Way. 1982. 1.25 (ISBN 0-89858-027-7). Fill the Gap.

Derricotte, Toi. Natural Birth. 80p. (Orig.). 1983. 11.95 (ISBN 0-89594-102-3); pap. 4.95 (ISBN 0-89594-101-5). Crossing Pr.

Green, Mimi & Naab, Maxine. Lamaze is for Chickens: A Manual for Prepared Childbirth. 2nd ed. (Avery's Childbirth Education Ser.). (Illus.). 128p. 1983. pap. 6.95 (ISBN 0-89529-181-9). Avery Pub.

Karmel, Marjorie. Thank You, Dr. Lamaze. LC 80-8372. 192p. 1983. pap. 4.76i (ISBN 0-06-090996-X, CN 996, CN). Har-Row.

Matteson, Peggy, ed. Handbook in Prepared Childbirth. (Avery's Childbirth Education Ser.). (Illus.). 112p. 1982. pap. 5.50 (ISBN 0-89529-204-1). Avery Pub.

Schuman, Tamara. The Parent Manual: Handbook for a Prepared Childbirth. 3rd ed. (Avery's Childbirth Education Ser.). (Illus.). 128p. 1983. pap. 5.50 (ISBN 0-89529-203-3). Avery Pub.

Sumner, Philip E. & Phillips, Celeste R. Shared Childbirth: A Guide to Family Birth Centers. 1982. pap. 6.95 (ISBN 0-452-25368-3, Z5368, Plume). NAL.

--Shared Childbirth: A Guide to Family Birth Centers. LC 82-6467. (Medical Library). (Illus.). 136p. 1982. pap. 6.95 (ISBN 0-452-25368-3, 4757-0). Mosby.

Tarr, Katherine. Herbs, Helps, & Pressure Points For Pregnancy & Childbirth. (Illus.). 69p. 1981. pap. 3.95 (ISBN 0-9609514-0-7). Sunbeam.

NATURAL DISASTERS

see also Floods; Forest Fires; Storms

School Buildings & Natural Disasters. (Education, Buildings & Equipment Ser.: No. 4). 85p. 1982. pap. 9.50 (ISBN 0-686-84622-2, U1237, UNESCO). Unipub.

NATURAL FOOD

see Food, Natural

NATURAL FOOD COOKERY

see Cookery (Natural Foods)

NATURAL GARDENING

see Organic Gardening

NATURAL GAS

see Gas, Natural

NATURAL HISTORY

see also Aquariums; Biology; Botany; Geographical Distribution of Animals and Plants; Geology; Marine Biology; Mineralogy; Paleontology; Zoology

Brown, Vinson. The Amateur Naturalist's Diary. (Illus.). 192p. 1983. 15.95 (ISBN 0-13-023689-6); pap. 8.95 (ISBN 0-13-023671-3). P-H.

Gould, Stephen J. Hen's Teeth & Horse's Toes: Further Reflections in Natural History. (Illus.). 1983. 15.50 (ISBN 0-393-01716-8). Norton.

Grainger, Margaret, ed. The Natural History Prose Writings of John Clare. (Illus.). 472p. 1982. 69.00 (ISBN 0-19-818517-0). Oxford U Pr.

Kopper, Philip. The National Museum of Natural History. 496p. 1982. 60.00 (ISBN 0-8109-1359-3). Abrams.

Simon, Claude. The World About Us. Weissbort, Daniel, tr. from Fr. 120p. 1983. 13.95 (ISBN 0-86538-033-3); pap. 6.95 (ISBN 0-86538-034-1). Ontario Rev NJ.

Steiner, Rudolf. The Boundaries of Natural Science. Amrine, Frederick, tr. from Ger. 190p. 1983. 14.00 (ISBN 0-88010-018-4). Anthroposophic.

A Tree of Memories Nature Essays. 6.00 (ISBN 0-9608926-0-5). McClain.

NATURAL HISTORY-BIBLIOGRAPHY

American Museum of Natural History, New York. The New Catalog of the American Museum of Natural History. 1983. lib. bdg. 1300.00 (ISBN 0-8161-0274-0, Hall Library). G K Hall.

NATURAL HISTORY-JUVENILE LITERATURE

see also Geology-Juvenile Literature

also Animals-Juvenile Literature; birds-Juvenile Literature, and similar headings; also names of individual animals, birds, etc.

Baskin, Leonard. Leonard Baskin's Miniature Natural History, 4 vols. LC 82-12612. (Illus., Each vol. 32 pages). 1983. Set. slipcased 9.95 (ISBN 0-394-85567-1). Pantheon.

Sanger, Marjory B. Forest in the Sand. LC 82-4076. (Illus.). 160p. (gr. 7 up). 1983. 10.95 (ISBN 0-689-50248-6, McElderry Bk). Atheneum.

NATURAL HISTORY-AFRICA

Schaller, George B. Golden Shadows, Flying Hooves: With a New Afterword. LC 82-23731. (Illus.). 344p. 1983. pap. 9.95 (ISBN 0-226-73632-6). U of Chicago Pr.

NATURAL HISTORY-ALASKA

Nelson, Richard K. Make Prayers to the Raven: A Koyukon View of the Northern Forest. LC 82-8441. 300p. 1983. 25.00 (ISBN 0-226-57162-9). U of Chicago Pr.

NATURAL HISTORY-EUROPE

Brusewitz, Gunnar. Wings & Seasons. Wheeler, Walston, tr. from Swedish. (Illus.). 119p. 1983. 20.00 (ISBN 0-88072-029-8). Tanager Bks.

NATURAL HISTORY-NEPAL

Lancaster, Roy. Plant Hunting in Nepal. (Illus.). 194p. 1982. 19.95 (ISBN 0-7099-1606-X). Timber.

NATURAL HISTORY-NEW ZEALAND

Powell, A. W. Shells of New Zealand. 154p. 1982. pap. 42.00x (ISBN 0-7233-0470-X, Pub. by Whitcoulls New Zealand). State Mutual Bk.

NATURAL HISTORY-UNITED STATES

Black, Charles T. & Worden, Diane D., eds. Michigan Nature Centers & Other Environmental Education Facilities. 64p. 1982. pap. 6.50 (ISBN 0-939294-06-0, LB 1047). Beech Leaf.

Pace, Antonio, ed. Luigi Castiglioni's Viaggio: Travels in the Unites States of America, 1785-1787. (Illus.). 560p. 1983. text ed. 39.00 (ISBN 0-8156-2264-3). Syracuse U Pr.

Schneider, Richard C. The Natural History of the Minocki of the Lakeland Region of Wisconsin. (Illus.). 255p. 1980. 9.95 (ISBN 0-936984-03-1). Schneider Pubs.

NATURAL HISTORY, BIBLICAL

see Bible-Natural History

NATURAL LAW

see also Ethics; International Law; Jurisprudence; Law-Philosophy; Liberty; Political Ethics

Reader's Digest Editors. You & Your Rights. LC 81-84665. 448p. 1982. 20.50 (ISBN 0-89577-137-3, Pub. by RD Assn). Random.

NATURAL MONUMENTS

see also Forest Reserves; National Parks and Reserves; Wilderness Areas; Wildlife Refuges

Lowenthal, David & Binney, Marcus, eds. Our Past Before Us: Why Do We Save It? 1981. 33.00x (ISBN 0-85117-219-9, Pub. by M Temple Smith). State Mutual Bk.

Trimble, Stephen. Timpanogos Cave: A Window into the Earth. Priehs, T. J. & Dodson, Carolyn, eds. LC 82-61192. 1983. pap. price not set (ISBN 0-911408-64-9). SW Pks Mnmts.

NATURAL RESOURCES

see also Aquatic Resources; Commercial Products; Conservation of Natural Resources; Fisheries; Forests and Forestry; Geothermal Resources; Marine Resources; Mines and Mineral Resources; Power Resources; Reclamation of Land; Water Resources Development; Water-Supply; Wind Power

Conn, W. David, ed. Energy & Material Resources: Attitudes, Values, & Public Policy. (AAAS Selected Symposium 75). 200p. 1982. lib. bdg. 22.00 (ISBN 0-86531-521-3). Westview.

Eichorn, W. & Henn, R., eds. Economic Theory of Natural Resources. 592p. 1982. pap. text ed. 42.50 (ISBN 3-7908-0274-3). Birkhauser.

Institution of Chemical Engineers. Management & Conservation of Resources: Proceedings of the Conference Organised by the Institution of Chemical Engineers at the University of Salford, UK, April 1982. (Institution of Chemical Engineers Symposium Ser.: No. 72). 206p. 1982. 45.00 (ISBN 0-08-028769-7). Pergamon.

Marks, Robert. Non-Renewable Resources & Disequilibrium Macrodynamics. LC 78-75018. write for info. (ISBN 0-8240-4053-8). Garland Pub.

Proceedings of the Seventh Session of the Committee on Natural Resources. (Water Resources Ser.: No. 53). 146p. 1981. pap. 12.00 (ISBN 0-686-82549-7, UN 81/2F10, UN). Unipub.

Youngguist, Walter. Investing in Natural Resources. 269p. 1983. pap. 8.95 (ISBN 0-87094-415-0). Dow Jones-Irwin.

NATURAL RESOURCES–LAW AND LEGISLATION
see also Water–Laws and Legislation; Wildlife Conservation–Law and Legislation
Harman, Elizabeth J. & Head, Brian W., eds. State Capital & Resources in the North & West of Australia. (Illus.). 388p. 1982. pap. text ed. 18.00 (ISBN 0-686-83952-8, Pub. by U of W Austral Pr). Intl Schol Bk Serv.
McLure, Charles E., Jr. & Mieszkowski, Peter, eds. Fiscal Federalism & the Taxation of Natural Resources: Nineteen Eighty One Tred Conference. LC 81-48561. (A Lincoln Institute of Land Policy Bk.). 272p. 1982. 35.95 (ISBN 0-669-05436-4). Lexington Bks.
Portney, Paul R., ed. Current Issues in Natural Resource Policy. LC 82-47982. 272p. 1982. 27.50 (ISBN 0-8018-2916-X); pap. 9.50 (ISBN 0-8018-2917-8). Resources Future.
NATURAL RESOURCES–AFRICA
Remote Sensing & Development. 24p. 1982. pap. 7.50 (ISBN 0-88936-302-1, IDRC 174, IRDC). Unipub.
NATURAL RESOURCES–ALASKA
Morehouse, Thomas A., ed. Alaskan Resources Development: Issues of the 1980's. 350p. 1983. lib. bdg. 25.00x (ISBN 0-86531-512-4). Westview.
NATURAL RESOURCES–ASIA
Remote Sensing & Development. 24p. 1982. pap. 7.50 (ISBN 0-88936-302-1, IDRC 174, IRDC). Unipub.
NATURAL RESOURCES–LATIN AMERICA
Remote Sensing & Development. 24p. 1982. pap. 7.50 (ISBN 0-88936-302-1, IDRC 174, IRDC). Unipub.
NATURAL RESOURCES–UNITED STATES
Bennett, Charles F. Conservation & Management of Natural Sources in the United States. 375p. 1983. text ed. 19.95 (ISBN 0-471-04652-3). Wiley.
NATURAL RIGHTS
see Natural Law
NATURAL SCIENCE
see Natural History; Physics; Science
NATURAL SELECTION
see also Evolution; Heredity; Origin of Species
Bajema, Carl J., ed. Natural Selection Theory: From the Speculations of the Greeks to the Quantitative Measurements of the Biometricians. LC 82-15633. (Benchmark Papers in Systematic and Evolutionary Biology: Vol. 5). 400p. 1983. 42.00 (ISBN 0-87933-412-6). Hutchinson Ross.
Darwin, Charles R. The Origin of Species by Means of Natural Selection. LC 72-3891. (Illus.). write for info. (ISBN 0-404-08404-4). AMS Pr.
NATURAL WATER CHEMISTRY
see Water Chemistry
NATURALISM
Boardman, Peter. Sacred Summits. (Illus.). 264p. 1983. 20.00 (ISBN 0-89886-045-8). Mountaineers.
NATURALISTS
see also Biologists; Scientists
Hudson, W. H. The Book of a Naturalist. 360p. 1982. 30.00x (ISBN 0-7045-0408-1, Pub. by Wildwood House). State Mutual Bk.
Pace, Antonio, ed. Luigi Castiglioni's Viaggio: Travels in the Unites States of America, 1785-1787. (Illus.). 560p. 1983. text ed. 39.00 (ISBN 0-8156-2264-3). Syracuse U Pr.
NATURE
see also Man–Influence on Nature
Adams, Raymond J., Jr. Avian Research at the Kalamazoo Nature Center 1970 to 1978. (Illus.). 86p. 1982. pap. 5.00 (ISBN 0-939294-11-7). Beech Leaf.
Bush, Elsie. The Big Creek Album: Yesterday & Today. (Illus.). 132p. 1982. 25.00 (ISBN 0-9609440-0-1). D & E Bush.
Fisher, Muriel. A Touch of Nature. (Illus.). 91p. 1982. 29.95 (ISBN 0-00-216979-7, Pub. by W Collins Australia). Intl Schol Bk Serv.
Manning, S. A. Nature in the West Country. 1979. 6.50 (ISBN 0-437-09502-9, Pub. by World's Work). David & Charles.
Moore, Richard. That Cunning Alphabet: Melville's Aesthetics of Nature. (Costerus New Ser.: No. 35). 232p. 1982. pap. text ed. 18.50x (ISBN 90-6203-734-8, Pub. by Rodopi Holland). Humanities.
Penn, Linda. Young Scientists Explore the World of Nature, Bk. 1. (gr. 1-3). 1982. 3.95 (ISBN 0-86653-069-X, GA 402). Good Apple.
Simpson, James Y. Nature: Cosmic, Human & Divine. 1929. text ed. 29.50x (ISBN 0-686-83632-4). Elliots Bks.
Trefil, James S. The Unexpected Vista: A Physicist's View of Nature. (Illus.). 256p. 14.95 (ISBN 0-684-17869-9, ScribT). Scribner.
NATURE–PHILOSOPHY
see Philosophy of Nature
NATURE, EFFECT OF MAN ON
see Man–Influence on Nature
NATURE, LAW OF
see Natural Law
NATURE, PHILOSOPHY OF
see Philosophy of Nature
NATURE CONSERVATION
see also Natural Monuments; Wildlife Conservation
Cahn, Robert. The Fight to Save Wild Alaska. (Illus.). 34p. 1982. pap. write for info. (ISBN 0-930698-14-2). Natl Audubon.
NATURE IN ORNAMENT
see Decoration and Ornament; Design, Decorative–Plant Forms
NATURE IN THE BIBLE
Felins, Yehuda. Nature & Man in the Bible: Chapters in Biblical Ecology. 1982. 25.00x (ISBN 0-900689-19-6). Bloch.
NATURE PHOTOGRAPHY
Angeloglou, Christopher & Schofield, Jack, eds. Successful Nature Photography: How to Take Beautiful Pictures of the Living World. 240p. 1983. 24.95 (ISBN 0-8174-5925-1, Amphoto). Watson-Guptill.
Kinne, Russ. Complete Book of Nature Photography. rev ed. (Illus.). 1980. 16.95 (ISBN 0-8174-2470-9, Amphoto). Watson-Guptill.
Launchbury. Nature Photography. (Photographer's Library). (Illus.). 1983. pap. 12.95x (ISBN 0-240-51193-X). Focal Pr.
Norton, B. Wilderness Photography. 1977. pap. 6.95 (ISBN 0-07-047464-8). McGraw.
Patterson, Freeman. Photography of Natural Things. 164p. 1982. 26.95 (ISBN 0-7706-0020-4); pap. 15.95 (ISBN 0-7706-0022-0). Van Nos Reinhold.
Thompson, Gerald & Oxford Scientific Films Members. Focus on Nature. (Illus.). 184p. 1983. cancelled (ISBN 0-87663-423-4). Universe.
NATURE PROTECTION
see Nature Conservation
NATURE STUDY
see also Animals, Habits and Behavior of; Animals, Legends and Stories Of; Biology; Botany; Nature Photography; Zoology
Bryant, Christopher R. The City's Countryside. 1983. pap. 15.95x (ISBN 0-582-30045-2). Longman.
Hudson, W. H. The Book of a Naturalist. 360p. 1982. 30.00x (ISBN 0-7045-0408-1, Pub. by Wildwood House). State Mutual Bk.
Reader's Digest Editors. Joy of Nature: How to Observe & Appreciate the Great Outdoors. LC 76-29320. (Illus.). 352p. 1977. 15.99 (ISBN 0-89577-036-9). RD Assn.
NATURE STUDY–JUVENILE LITERATURE
Paton, John & Dell, Catherine. Rainbow Encyclopedia of Nature. (Illus.). 144p. (gr. 4-6). 1982. 9.95 (ISBN 0-528-82387-6). Rand.
NAUTICAL ALMANACS
Reed's Nautical Almanac & Coast Pilot: East Coast Edition, 1983. 800p. 1983. pap. 19.95 (ISBN 0-900335-74-2, Better Boating Assoc). Norton.
NAUTICAL ASTRONOMY
see also Navigation; Time
Schlereth, Hewitt. Celestial Navigation by Sun Lines. (The Cruising Navigator Ser.: Vol. 2). (Illus.). 352p. 1983. 25.00 (ISBN 0-915160-53-6). Seven Seas.
NAUTICAL TERMS
see Naval Art and Science–Dictionaries; Naval Art and Science–Terminology
NAVAHO INDIANS
see Indians of North America–Southwest, New
NAVAL ADMINISTRATION
see Naval Art and Science; United States–Navy
NAVAL ARCHITECTURE
see also Boat-Building; Electricity on Ships; Marine Engineering; Ship-Building; Warships
also types of vessels, e.g. Motor-Boats
Munro-Smith. Applied Naval Architecture. 1967. 17.50 (ISBN 0-444-19850-4). Elsevier.
Transactions, Vol. 88. 450p. 1981. 25.00 (ISBN 0-9603048-2-7). Soc Naval Arch.
Transactions, Vol.89. (Illus.). 455p. 1982. 25.00 (ISBN 0-9603048-3-5). Soc Naval Arch.
NAVAL ART AND SCIENCE
see also Marine Engineering; Military Art and Science; Naval Strategy; Navies; Navigation; Seamanship; Seamen; Ship-Building; Signals and Signaling; Warships
Moore, John E., ed. Jane's 1982-83 Naval Annual. (Illus.). 158p. 1982. 15.95 (ISBN 0-86720-634-9). Sci Bks Intl.
Richardson, Doug. Naval Armament. (Illus.). 160p. 1982. 19.95 (ISBN 0-86720-553-9). Sci Bks Intl.
NAVAL ART AND SCIENCE–DICTIONARIES
Layton, C. W. Dictionary of Nautical Words & Terms. 2nd, rev. ed. 395p. 1982. text ed. 32.50x (ISBN 0-85174-422-2). Sheridan.
NAVAL ART AND SCIENCE–TERMINOLOGY
Layton, C. W. Dictionary of Nautical Words & Terms. 2nd, rev. ed. 395p. 1982. text ed. 32.50x (ISBN 0-85174-422-2). Sheridan.
NAVAL ARTILLERY
see Artillery
NAVAL BATTLES
see also Naval History
also subdivision History, Naval under names of countries, e.g. Great Britain–History, Naval; also names of naval battles
Perkins, Roger & Douglas-Morris, K. J. Gunfire in Barbary: Admiral Lord Exmouth's Battle with the Corsairs of Algiers in 1816. (Illus.). 200p. 1982. text ed. 24.50x (ISBN 0-85937-271-5). Sheridan.
NAVAL BIOGRAPHY
see Seamen; Naval History
also subdivision Biography under Navies e.g. United States–Navy–Biography
NAVAL CONSTRUCTION
see Naval Architecture; Ship-Building
NAVAL ENGINEERING
see Marine Engineering
NAVAL HISTORY
Paine, Ralph D. Fight For a Free Sea. 1920. text ed. 8.50x (ISBN 0-686-83550-6). Elliots Bks.
Rudolph, Wolfgang. Harbor & Town: A Maritime Cultural History. Feininger, T. Lux, tr. from Ger. (Illus.). 231p. 1983. 22.50 (ISBN 0-686-84698-2). Hippocrene Bks.
Wood, William. Elizabethan Sea-Dogs. 1918. text ed. 8.50x (ISBN 0-686-83535-2). Elliots Bks.
NAVAL PENSIONS
see Pensions, Military
NAVAL SCIENCE
see Naval Art and Science
NAVAL SHIPS
see Warships
NAVAL SIGNALING
see Signals and Signaling
NAVAL STRATEGY
Till, Geoffrey. Maritime Strategy & the Nuclear Age. 220p. 1982. 60.00x (ISBN 0-333-26109-7, Pub. by Macmillan England). State Mutual Bk.
NAVAL WARFARE
see Naval Art and Science; Naval Battles
NAVIES
see also Armies; Disarmament; Naval Art and Science; Seamen; Warships
also Great Britain–Navy; United States–Navy; and similar headings
Spencer, Warren F. The Confederate Navy in Europe. LC 81-23283. 288p. 1983. text ed. 19.95 (ISBN 0-8173-0115-1). U of Ala Pr.
NAVIGATION
see also Electronics in Navigation; Harbors; Inland Navigation; Knots and Splices; Nautical Almanacs; Nautical Astronomy; Naval Art and Science; Navigation (Astronautics); Pilots and Pilotage; Seamanship; Ship-Building; Shipwrecks; Signals and Signaling; Steam-Navigation; Submarines; Tides; Winds; Yachts and Yachting
also names of nautical instruments, e.g. Compass, Gyroscope
Keys, Gerry. Practical Navigation by Calculator. (Illus.). 176p. 1982. pap. text ed. 14.95x (ISBN 0-540-07410-1). Sheridan.
Noer, H. Rolf. Navigator's Pocket Calculator Handbook. LC 82-74136. (Illus.). 176p. (Orig.). 1983. pap. 16.00 (ISBN 0-87033-295-3). Cornell Maritime.
Schlereth, Hewitt. Celestial Navigation by Sun Lines. (The Cruising Navigator Ser.: Vol. 2). (Illus.). 352p. 1983. 25.00 (ISBN 0-915160-53-6). Seven Seas.
NAVIGATION–DICTIONARIES
see Naval Art and Science–Dictionaries
NAVIGATION–TABLES
Schlereth, Hewitt. Sight Reduction Tables for Small Boat Navigation. LC 82-19210. (The Cruising Navigator Ser.: Vol. 00). 196p. 1983. 25.00 (ISBN 0-915160-54-4). Seven Seas.
NAVIGATION, AERIAL
see Navigation (Aeronautics)
NAVIGATION (AERONAUTICS)
see also Electronics in Aeronautics
Etkin, Bernard. Dynamics of Flight Stability & Control. 2nd ed. LC 81-13058. 370p. 1982. text ed. 29.95x (ISBN 0-471-08936-2). Wiley.
NAVIGATION (ASTRONAUTICS)
see also Space Flight
Mills, H. R. Positional Astronomy & Astro-Navigation Made Easy: A New Approach Using the Pocket Calculator. 284p. 1978. 65.00x (ISBN 0-85950-062-4, Pub. by Thornes England). State Mutual Bk.
NAVIGATION, ELECTRONICS IN
see Electronics in Navigation
NAVIGATION, INLAND
see Inland Navigation
NAVIGATION, RADAR IN
see Radar in Navigation
NAVIGATION LAWS
see Inland Navigation; Maritime Law
NAVIGATORS
see Discoveries (In Geography); Explorers; Seamen
NAVY
see Naval Art and Science; Navies
also subdivision Navy under names of countries, e.g. United States–Navy
NAZI MOVEMENT
see Germany–Politics and Government–1933-1945
NAZI PARTY
see Nationalsozialistische Deutsche Arbeiter-Partei
NAZISM
see National Socialism
NEAR EAST
see also Arab Countries
also names of specific countries, cities, geographic areas, etc. in the Near East, e.g. Iraq; Mesopotamia; Jerusalem
Bender, David L., ed. The Middle East: Opposing Views. (Opposing Views Ser.). 1982. lib. bdg. 10.95 (ISBN 0-89908-340-4); pap. 5.95 (ISBN 0-89908-315-3). Greenhaven.
Carim, Enver, ed. Middle East Review: 1983. (World of Information Ser.). 350p. 1983. pap. 24.95 (ISBN 0-911818-33-2). World Almanac.
Clay, Albert T. Neo-Babylonian Letters From Erech. 1920. text ed. 26.50x (ISBN 0-686-83634-0). Elliots Bks.
Goetze, Albrecht. Old Babylonian Omen Texts. 1947. text ed. 29.50x (ISBN 0-686-83651-0). Elliots Bks.
Gotlieb, Yousef. Self-Determination in the Middle East. 190p. 1982. 22.95 (ISBN 0-03-062408-8). Praeger.
Hackman, George G., ed. Temple Documents of the Third Dynasty of Ur From Umma. 1937. text ed. 27.50x (ISBN 0-686-83806-8). Elliots Bks.
Mendes-Flohr, Paul R., ed. A Land of Two Peoples: Martin Buber on Jews & Arabs. 350p. 1983. 29.95 (ISBN 0-19-503165-2). Oxford U Pr.
Partington, David H., ed. The Middle East Annual: Issues & Events, Vol. 1. 1982. lib. bdg. 45.00 (ISBN 0-8161-8571-9, Hall Reference). G K Hall.
Roberts, David. Yesterday the Holy Land. Van der Mass, Ed, tr. from Dutch. (Illus.). 144p. (Eng.). 1982. 16.95 (ISBN 0-310-45620-7). Zondervan.
Tremayne, Archibald. Records From Erech, Time of Cyrus & Cambyses. 1926. text ed. 29.50x (ISBN 0-686-83726-6). Elliots Bks.
Venn-Brown, Janet, ed. For a Palestinian: A Memorial to Wael Zuaiter. (Illus.). 200p. 1983. write for info. (ISBN 0-7103-0039-5, Kegan Paul). Routledge & Kegan.
NEAR EAST–BIBLIOGRAPHY
Catalog of the Arabic Collection, Harvard University. 1983. lib. bdg. 1450.00 (ISBN 0-8161-0398-4, Hall Library). G K Hall.
NEAR EAST–CIVILIZATION
Dandamayev, M. A., ed. Societies & Languages of the Ancient Near East: Studies in Honour of I. M. Diakonoff. 380p. 1982. pap. 48.00x (ISBN 0-686-82295-1, 51309, Pub. by Aris & Phillips England) (ISBN 0-85668-205-5). Humanities.
Garsoian, Nina & Mathews, Thomas, eds. East of Byzantium: Syria & Armenia in the Formative Period. LC 82-9665. (Dumbarton Oaks Symposium). (Illus.). 266p. 1982. 35.00x (ISBN 0-88402-104-1). Dumbarton Oaks.
NEAR EAST–DESCRIPTION AND TRAVEL
Griffith, Susan. Traveller's Survival Kit to the East: Turkey, Iraq, Iran, Afghanistan, India, Nepal, Sri Lanka, Burma. 2nd ed. 176p. 1982. pap. 9.95 (ISBN 0-907638-03-1, Pub. by Vacation Wk). Bradt Ent.
Littell, Franklin H. A Pilgrim's Interfaith Guide to the Holy Land. (Illus.). 84p. 1982. 7.95 (ISBN 0-686-43011-5, Carta Maps & Guides Pub Isreal). Hippocrene Bks.
NEAR EAST–ECONOMIC CONDITIONS
Grandin, Nicole. Le Soudan Nilotique et L'Administration Britannique (1898-1956) Elements D'Interpretation Sociohistorique d'une Experience Coloniale. (Social, Economic, & Political Studies of the Middle East: Vol. 29). (Illus.). xiv, 348p. 1982. pap. write for info. (ISBN 90-04-06404-4). E J Brill.
The Gulf States, 1981. 375.00x (ISBN 0-686-99852-9, Pub. by Metra England). State Mutual Bk.
Hiro, D. Inside the Middle East. 1983. 19.95 (ISBN 0-07-029055-5); pap. 8.95 (ISBN 0-07-029056-3). McGraw.
Mostyn, Trevor, ed. Bahrain: A Middle East Economic Digest Guide. (Illus.). 240p. 1983. pap. write for info. (ISBN 0-7103-0030-1, Kegan Paul). Routledge & Kegan.
--United Arab Emirates: A Middle East Economic Digest Guide. 324p. (Orig.). 1982. pap. 15.00 (ISBN 0-7103-0014-X, Kegan Paul). Routledge & Kegan.
NEAR EAST–FOREIGN RELATIONS
Andrews, F. David, ed. Lost Peoples of the Middle East: Documents on the Struggle for Survival & Independence of the Kurds, Assyrians, & other Minority Races of the Middle East. Ltd. 350 Copies 34.95. Documentary Pubns.
McLaurin. Middle East Foreign Policy. 336p. 1982. 34.95 (ISBN 0-03-057753-5); student ed. avail. (ISBN 0-03-057754-3). Praeger.
The Middle East & North Africa 1982-83. 1013p. 1983. 105.00 (ISBN 0-905118-75-8, EUR 35). Europa.
NEAR EAST–FOREIGN RELATIONS–FRANCE
Benson, Vladimir. The Failure of the American Dream & the Moral Responsibility of the United States for the Crisis in the Middle East & for the Collapse of the World Order. (The Great Currents of History Library Bk.). (Illus.). 141p. 1983. 57.85 (ISBN 0-86722-025-2). Inst Econ Pol.
NEAR EAST–FOREIGN RELATIONS–UNITED STATES
Benson, Vladimir. The Failure of the American Dream & the Moral Responsibility of the United States for the Crisis in the Middle East & for the Collapse of the World Order. (The Great Currents of History Library Bk.). (Illus.). 141p. 1983. 57.85 (ISBN 0-86722-025-2). Inst Econ Pol.
Brubeck, William H. The American National Interest & Middle East Peace. (Seven Springs Studies). 1981. pap. 3.00 (ISBN 0-943006-03-1). Seven Springs.
Garfinkle, Adam M. Western Europe's Middle East Diplomacy & the United States. LC 82-21111. (Philadelphia Policy Papers). 116p. 1983. pap. 3.95 (ISBN 0-910191-05-0). For Policy Res.
NEAR EAST–HISTORY
Ahlstrom, G. W. Royal Administration & National Religion in Ancient Palestine. (Studies in the History of Ancient Near East Ser.: Vol. 1). xiv, 112p. 1982. pap. write for info. (ISBN 90-04-06562-8). E J Brill.

Dandamayev, M. A., ed. Societies & Languages of the Ancient Near East: Studies in Honour of I. M. Diakonoff. 380p. 1982. pap. 48.00x (ISBN 0-686-82295-1, 51309, Pub. by Aris & Phillips England) (ISBN 0-85668-205-5). Humanities.

Goldschmidt, Arthur, Jr. A Concise History of the Middle East. 2nd rev. ed. 450p. 1983. lib. bdg. 30.00x (ISBN 0-86531-598-1); pap. text ed. 11.50x (ISBN 0-86531-599-X). Westview.

Legum, Colin & Shaked, Haim, eds. Middle East Contemporary Survey 1980-81, Vol. V. 1000p. 1983. text ed. 140.00x (ISBN 0-8419-0825-7). Holmes & Meier.

Perry, Glenn E. The Middle East: Fourteen Islamic Centuries. (Illus.). 336p. 1983. pap. 14.95 (ISBN 0-13-581603-3). P-H.

Stern, Ephraim. The Material Culture of the Land of the Bible in the Persian Period 538-331 B.C. (Illus.). 304p. 1982. pap. text ed. 65.00x (ISBN 0-85668-137-7, 40917, Pub. by Aris & Phillips England). Humanities.

NEAR EAST–JUVENILE LITERATURE

Ferrara, Peter. East vs West in the Middle East. (Impact Ser.). 96p. (gr. 7 up). 1983. PLB 8.90 (ISBN 0-531-04543-9). Watts.

Spencer, William. The Islamic States in Conflict. (Impact Ser.). 96p. (gr. 7 up). 1983. PLB 8.90 (ISBN 0-531-04544-7). Watts.

NEAR EAST–LANGUAGES

Dandamayev, M. A., ed. Societies & Languages of the Ancient Near East: Studies in Honour of I. M. Diakonoff. 380p. 1982. pap. 48.00x (ISBN 0-686-82295-1, 51309, Pub. by Aris & Phillips England) (ISBN 0-85668-205-5). Humanities.

NEAR EAST–POLITICS AND GOVERNMENT

Ben-Dor, Gabriel. State & Conflict in the Middle East. 200p. 1983. text ed. 30.00x (ISBN 0-7146-3224-4, F Cass Co). Biblio Dist.

Doumergu, Emil. Saudi Arabia & the Explosion of Terrorism in the Middle East. (The Great Currents of History Library Book). (Illus.). 137p. 1983. 77.85 (ISBN 0-86722-016-3). Inst Econ Pol.

Grandin, Nicole. Le Soudan Nilotique et L'Administration Britannique (1898-1956) Elements D'Interpretation Sociohistorique d'une Experience Coloniale. (Social, Economic, & Political Studies of the Middle East: Vol. 29). (Illus.). xiv, 348p. 1982. pap. write for info. (ISBN 90-04-06404-4). E J Brill.

Haskins, James. Leaders of the Middle East. (Illus.). 192p. (gr. 5-12). 1983. 10.95 (ISBN 0-89490-086-2). Enslow Pubs.

Hiro, D. Inside the Middle East. 1983. 19.95 (ISBN 0-07-029055-5); pap. 8.95 (ISBN 0-07-029056-3). McGraw.

Hurewitz, J. C. Middle East Politics: The Military Dimension. (Encore Edition Ser.). 550p. 1983. softcover 32.50x (ISBN 0-86531-546-9). Westview.

NEAR EAST–RELIGION

Layish, Ahoron. Marriage, Divorce & Succession in the Druz Family: A Study Based on Decisions of Druz Arbitrators & Religious Courts in Israel & the Golan Heights. (Social, Economic & Political Studies of the Middle East Ser.: Vol. 31). (Illus.). xxv, 474p. 1982. pap. write for info. (ISBN 90-04-06412-5). E J Brill.

NEAR EAST–SOCIAL CONDITIONS

Grandin, Nicole. Le Soudan Nilotique et L'Administration Britannique (1898-1956) Elements D'Interpretation Sociohistorique d'une Experience Coloniale. (Social, Economic, & Political Studies of the Middle East: Vol. 29). (Illus.). xiv, 348p. 1982. pap. write for info. (ISBN 90-04-06404-4). E J Brill.

NEAR EAST–SOCIAL LIFE AND CUSTOMS

Bates, Daniel & Rassam, Amal. Peoples & Cultures of the Middle East. (Illus.). 288p. 1983. pap. 12.95 (ISBN 0-13-656793-2). P-H.

Layish, Ahoron. Marriage, Divorce & Succession in the Druz Family: A Study Based on Decisions of Druz Arbitrators & Religious Courts in Israel & the Golan Heights. (Social, Economic & Political Studies of the Middle East Ser.: Vol. 31). (Illus.). xxv, 474p. 1982. pap. write for info. (ISBN 90-04-06412-5). E J Brill.

NEAR EASTERN ARCHITECTURE

see Architecture–Near East

NEBRASKA

see also names of cities, counties, towns, etc. in Nebraska

Perkey, Elton. Perkey's Nebraska Place-Names, Vol. XXVIII. LC 82-80300. 1982. write for info. Nebraska Hist.

NEBRASKA–HISTORY

Reisdorff, James J. & Bartels, Michael M. Railroad Stations in Nebraska: An Era of Use & Reuse. LC 82-61823. (Illus.). 112p. 1982. text ed. 23.50 (ISBN 0-9609568-0-8). South Platte.

NEBULAE

see also Galaxies

Orion Nebula to Honor Henry Draper Symposium, Dec 4-5, 1981. Proceedings. Glassgold, A. E. & Huggins, P. J., eds. 338p. 1982. 65.00 (ISBN 0-89766-180-X). NY Acad Sci.

NECHAEV, SERGEI GENNADIEVICH, 1847-1882

Avrich, Paul. Bakunin & Nechaev. 32p. 1974. pap. 1.00 (ISBN 0-900384-09-3). Left Bank.

NECK–RADIOGRAPHY

Lasjaunias, Pierre. Craniofacial & Upper Cervical Arteries: Collateral Circulation & Angiographic Protocols. 300p. 1983. lib. bdg. write for info. (ISBN 0-683-04898-8). Williams & Wilkins.

NECROMANCY

see Magic

NEEDLEPOINT CANVAS WORK

see Canvas Embroidery

NEEDLEPOINT EMBROIDERY

see Canvas Embroidery

NEEDLEWORK

see also Applique; Dressmaking; Embroidery; Lace and Lace Making; Patchwork; Quilting; Samplers; Sewing

Davis, Mary Kay. The Needlework Doctor: How to Solve Every Kind of Needlework Problem. (Illus.). 320p. 1983. 24.95 (ISBN 0-13-611087-8); pap. 13.95 (ISBN 0-13-611079-7). P-H.

Pakula, Marion B. & Goldberg, Rhoda O. Needlecraft Sports Designs. (Illus.). 1983. 19.95 (ISBN 0-517-54968-9); pap. 10.95 (ISBN 0-517-54969-7). Crown.

Sestay, Catherine J. Needlework: A Selected Bibliography with Special Reference to Embroidery & Needlepoint. LC 82-5806. 162p. 1982. 12.00 (ISBN 0-8108-1554-0). Scarecrow.

NEGATIVE IONS

see Anions

NEGEB

Hillel, Daniel. The Negev: Land, Water & Life in a Desert Environment. LC 82-5218. 288p. 1982. 29.95 (ISBN 0-03-062067-8); pap. 12.95 (ISBN 0-03-062068-6). Praeger.

NEGLIGENCE

see also Accident Law; Employers' Liability; Products Liability; Tort Liability of Municipal Corporations; Torts

Fisher, Charles O. & Murray, Richard C. Guide to Maryland Negligence Cases. 200p. 1982. 25.00 (ISBN 0-87215-472-6). Michie-Bobbs.

NEGOTIABLE INSTRUMENTS

see also Bonds

Scottish Banknotes. 15.00. StanGib Ltd.

NEGOTIATION

see also Arbitration, Industrial; Arbitration, International; Collective Bargaining; Treaties

Fisher, Roger & Ury, William. Getting to Yes: Negotiating Agreement Without Giving In. 1983. pap. 4.95 (ISBN 0-14-006534-2). Penguin.

Huyler, Jean W. Crisis Communications & Communicating About Negotiations. rev., 2nd ed. Orig. Title: Crisis Communications. 92p. pap. 8.95x (ISBN 0-941554-03-1). EdCom.

Levin, Edward. Negotiating Tactics: Bargain Your Way to Winning. Date not set. pap. 6.95 (ISBN 0-449-90074-6, Columbine). Fawcett.

Pye, Lucien W. Chinese Commercial Negotiating Style. LC 82-14228. (Rand Corporation Research Studies). 112p. 1982. text ed. 17.50 (ISBN 0-89946-168-9); pap. text ed. 6.95 (ISBN 0-89946-171-9). Oelgeschlager.

Shea, Gordon F. Creative Negotiating: Productive Tools & Techniques for Solving Problems, Resolving Conflicts & Settling Differences. 1983. 17.95 (ISBN 0-8436-0885-4). CBI Pub.

Williams, Gerald R. Legal Negotiation & Settlement. LC 82-19975. 207p. 1983. pap. text ed. write for info. (ISBN 0-314-68093-4); tchrs.' manual avail. (ISBN 0-314-73521-6). West Pub.

NEGOTIATIONS IN INTERNATIONAL DISPUTES

see Diplomatic Negotiations in International Disputes

NEGRO RACE

see Black Race

NEGRO SPIRTUALS

see Spirituals (Songs)

NEHRU, JAWAHARLAL, 1889-1964

Gopal, S. The Mind of Jawaharlal Nehru. 50p. 1980. pap. text ed. 3.95x (ISBN 0-86131-205-8, Pub. by Orient Longman Ltd India). Apt Bks.

--Selected Works of Jawaharlal Nehru, Vol. 14. 1982. 36.00x (ISBN 0-8364-0904-3, Orient Longman). South Asia Bks.

NEILL, ALEXANDER SUTHERLAND, 1883-1973

Placzek, Beverly, ed. Record of a Friendship: The Correspondence of Wilhelm Reich & A. S. Neill. 1983. pap. 11.95 (ISBN 0-374-51770-3). FS&G.

NEMATODA

Dropkin, Victor H. Introduction to Plant Nematology. LC 80-13556. 293p. 1980. 31.50x (ISBN 0-471-05578-6, Pub. by Wiley Interscience). Wiley.

Stone, A. R. & Platt, H. M., eds. Concepts in Nematode Systematics. (Systematics Symposium Special Ser.: Vol. 22). write for info. (ISBN 0-12-672680-9). Acad Pr.

NEMATOSPORA

see Yeast

NEMEROV, HOWARD

Wyllie, Diana E. Elizabeth Bishop & Howard Nemerov: A Reference Guide. 1983. lib. bdg. 33.00 (ISBN 0-8161-8527-1, Hall Reference). G K Hall.

NEO-FACISM

see Fascism

NEO-IMPRESSIONISM (ART)

see Impressionism (Art)

NEO-LATIN LANGUAGES

see Romance Languages

NEONATAL DEATH

see Infants–Mortality

NEONATES

see Infants (Newborn)

NEONATOLOGY

Bossi, E., ed. Praktische Neonatologie. (Paediatrische Fortbildungskurse fuer die Praxis Ser.: Vol. 57). (Illus.). viii, 150p. 1983. pap. 72.00 (ISBN 3-8055-3657-7). S Karger.

NEOPLASMS

see Tumors

NEPAL

Gibbons, Robert & Ashford, Bob. The KIngdoms of the Himalayas: Nepal, Sikkim, & Bhutan. (Illus.). 250p. 1983. 17.50 (ISBN 0-88254-802-6). Hippocrene Bks.

NEPAL–DESCRIPTION AND TRAVEL

Hayes, J. L. Nepal Trail Guide Series. Incl. No. 1: Everest & Solu-Khumbu. 75p; No. 2: North of Pokhara. 75p; No. 3: North of Kathmandu. 75p. (Illus.). price 9.95 set (ISBN 0-686-43407-2). Bradt Ent.

Hoefer, Hans. Nepal. (Illus.). 368p. 1982. pap. 17.50 (ISBN 9971-925-10-9). Lee Pubs Group.

Insight Guides. Nepal. (Illus.). 384p. 1983. pap. 14.95 (ISBN 0-13-611038-X). P-H.

NEPAL–ECONOMIC CONDITIONS

Poudyal, Sriram. Planned Development in Nepal. 1982. 14.00 (ISBN 0-8364-0917-5, Pub. by Sterling). South Asia Bks.

NEPAL–SOCIAL LIFE AND CUSTOMS

Majupuria, Trilok C. & Gupta, S. P. Nepal: The Land of Festivals (Religious, Cultural, Social & Historical Festivals) (Illus.). 152p. 1981. 14.95x (ISBN 0-940500-83-3, Pub by S Chand India). Asia Bk Corp.

NEPHRITIS

see Kidneys–Diseases

NEPHROLOGY

see also Kidneys

Cohen, J. J., et al, eds. Nephrology Forum. (Illus.). 376p. 1983. pap. 34.50 (ISBN 0-387-90764-5). Springer-Verlag.

Gonick, Harvey C. Current Nephrology. (Current Nephrology Ser.: Vol. 6). 376p. 1983. 55.00 (ISBN 0-471-09559-1, Pub. by Wiley Med). Wiley.

Gonick, Harvey C., ed. Current Nephrology, Vol. 4. (Current Ser.). (Illus.). 500p. 1980. text ed. 55.00x (ISBN 0-471-09519-2, Pub. by Wiley Med). Wiley.

Hamburger. Advances in Nephrology, Vol. 12. 1983. 55.00 (ISBN 0-8151-4135-1). Year Bk Med.

Hamburger, Jean. Advances in Nephrology, Vol. 7. 1978. 55.00 (ISBN 0-8151-4116-5). Year Bk Med.

--Advances in Nephrology, Vol. 8. 1979. 55.00 (ISBN 0-8151-4117-3). Year Bk Med.

--Advances in Nephrology, Vol. 9. 1980. 55.00 (ISBN 0-8151-4118-1). Year Bk Med.

--Advances in Nephrology, Vol. 10. 1981. 55.00 (ISBN 0-8151-4119-X). Year Bk Med.

Kjellstrand, C. M., ed. The Belding H. Scribner Festschrift. (Journal: Nephron: Vol. 33, No. 2). (Illus.). 96p. 1983. pap. 48.00 (ISBN 3-8055-3675-5). S Karger.

Urizar, Rodrigo E. & Largent, Jill A. Pediatric Nephrology. (New Directions in Therapy Ser.). 1982. text ed. 50.00 (ISBN 0-87488-846-8). Med Exam.

NERVE-CELLS

see Nerves; Neurons

NERVE TRANSMISSION

see Neural Transmission

NERVES

see also Nervous System; Neuromuscular Transmission; Synapses

also particular nerves, e.g. Olfactory Nerve, Optic Nerve

Liveson, Jay A. & Ma, Dong M. Nerve Conduction Handbook. (Illus.). 380p. 1983. pap. text ed. 22.50 (ISBN 0-8036-5646-7, 5646-7). Davis Co.

NERVES–ANATOMY

see Neuroanatomy

NERVES–DISEASES

see Nervous System–Diseases

NERVES–SURGERY

see Nervous System–Surgery

NERVES–WOUNDS AND INJURIES

see Nervous System–Wounds and Injuries

NERVOUS SYSTEM

see also Biological Control Systems; Brain; Central Nervous System; Nerves; Neuroanatomy; Neurologic Examination; Shock; Spinal Cord

Ottoson, D. Physiology of the Nervous System. 1982. 125.00x (ISBN 0-333-30819-0, Pub. by Macmillan England). State Mutual Bk.

NERVOUS SYSTEM–DEGENERATION AND REGENERATION

Bergen, Adrienne F. & Colangelo, Cheryl. Positioning the Client with Central Nervous System Deficits: The Wheelchair & Other Adapted Equiptment. (Illus.). 191p. (Orig.). 1982. pap. text ed. 19.95 (ISBN 0-686-38095-9). Valhalla Rehab.

NERVOUS SYSTEM–DISEASES

see also Fear; Nervous System–Radiography; Neurological Nursing; Pediatric Neurology

also specific diseases, e.g. Insanity, Neurasthenia, Neuritis

Adams, J. H. & Murray, Margaret F. Atlas of Post-Mortem Techniques in Neuropathology. LC 82-4313. (Illus.). 120p. 1982. 29.95 (ISBN 0-521-24121-9). Cambridge U Pr.

Kautzky, R. Neuroradiology: A Neuropathological Approach. Boehm, W. M. & Kellet, V. B., trs. from Ger. 400p. 1982. 98.00 (ISBN 0-387-10934-X). Springer-Verlag.

Massey, E. Wayne & Lashner, Robert T., eds. Mononeuropathies. (Illus.). 1983. price not set (ISBN 0-8391-1817-1, 18066). Univ Park.

Refsum, S. & Bolis, C. L., eds. International Conference on Peripheral Neuropathies: Proceedings, International Conference, Madrid, June, 1981. (International Congress Ser.: No. 592). 210p. 1982. 62.75 (ISBN 0-444-90277-5, Excerpta Medica). Elsevier.

Weisberg, Leon A. & Strub, Richard L. Essentials of Clinical Neurology. 1983. pap. text ed. 14.95 (ISBN 0-8391-1778-7, 17817). Univ Park.

Weller, R. O., et al. Clinical Neuropathology. (Illus.). 350p. 1982. 45.00 (ISBN 0-686-82305-2). Springer-Verlag.

NERVOUS SYSTEM–RADIOGRAPHY

Kautzky, R. Neuroradiology: A Neuropathological Approach. Boehm, W. M. & Kellet, V. B., trs. from Ger. 400p. 1982. 98.00 (ISBN 0-387-10934-X). Springer-Verlag.

NERVOUS SYSTEM–SURGERY

see also Brain–Surgery

DeJong, Russell N. Year Book of Neurology & Neurosurgery, 1983. 1983. 35.00 (ISBN 0-8151-2424-4). Year Bk Med.

Krayenbuehl, H., et al, eds. Advances & Technical Standards in Neurosurgery, Vol.9. (Illus.). 177p. 1983. 37.00 (ISBN 0-387-81718-2). Springer-Verlag.

Landolt, A. M., ed. Complications in Neurosurgery I. (Progress in Neurological Surgery Ser.: Vol. 11). (Illus.). viii, 130p. 1983. 58.75 (ISBN 3-8055-3691-7). S Karger.

Merrem, G. & Goldhahn, W. E. Neurosurgical Operations. (Illus.). 560p. 1983. 92.00 (ISBN 0-387-11374-6). Springer-Verlag.

Pfeiffer, Steven. Neuroscience Approached Through Cell Culture. 248p. 1982. 75.00 (ISBN 0-8493-6340-3). CRC Pr.

NERVOUS SYSTEM–WOUNDS AND INJURIES

European Organization for Research & Treatment of Cancer. Treatment of Neoplastic Lesions of the Nervous System: Proceedings of a Symposium Sponsored by the European Organization for Research & Treatment of Cancer (EORTC), Brussels, April, 1980. Hildebrand, J. & Gangji, D., eds. (Illus.). 178p. 1982. 50.00 (ISBN 0-08-027989-9). Pergamon.

NERVOUS SYSTEM, AUTONOMIC

Diamond, John. Behavioral Kinesiology & the Autonomic Nervous System. (Behavioral Kinesiology Ser.). 85p. 1983. pap. 47.50 (ISBN 0-911238-78-6). Regent House.

Nilsson, S. Autonomic Nerve Function in the Vertebrates. (Zoophysiology Ser.: Vol. 13). (Illus.). 280p. 1983. 47.50 (ISBN 0-387-12124-2). Springer-Verlag.

NERVOUS SYSTEM, VEGETATIVE

see Nervous System, Autonomic

NERVOUS TRANSMISSION

see Neural Transmission

NESS, LOCH

Dinsdale, Tim. Loch Ness Monster. 4th ed. (Illus.). 208p. (Orig.). 1982. pap. 9.50 (ISBN 0-7100-9022-6). Routledge & Kegan.

NESTS OF BIRDS

see Birds–Eggs and Nests

NET NATIONAL PRODUCT

see National Income

NETHERLANDIC LANGUAGE

see Dutch Language

NETHERLANDS

see also names of cities, towns, geographic areas, etc. in the Netherlands

Gupta, M. M. & Sanchez, E., eds. Fuzzy Information & Decision Processes. 480p. 1982. 74.50 (ISBN 0-686-83998-6, North Holland). Elsevier.

NETHERLANDS–DESCRIPTION AND TRAVEL

Gulati, R. D. & Parma, S. Studies on Lake Vechten & Tjeukemeer: The Netherlands. 1982. 87.00 (ISBN 90-6193-762-0, Pub. by Junk Pubs Netherlands). Kluwer Boston.

NETHERLANDS–DESCRIPTION AND TRAVEL–GUIDEBOOKS

Fodor's Holland 1983. 336p. 1983. 12.95 (ISBN 0-679-00924-8). McKay.

Michelin Green Guide: Nederland. (Green Guide Ser.). (Dutch.). 1983. pap. write for info. (ISBN 2-06-055460-8). Michelin.

NETHERLANDS–ECONOMIC CONDITIONS

Holland Exports: Trade Information Directories, 1982, 4 vols. Incl. Vol. 1-Cosumer Goods: Food; Vol. 2-Consumer Goods: Non-Food; Vol. 3-Commercial Gardening & Farming; Vol. 4-Industrial Products. 1982. Set. pap. 60.00x (ISBN 0-8002-3035-3). Intl Pubns Serv.

NETHERLANDS–EMIGRATION AND IMMIGRATION

Swierenga, Robert P. Dutch Emigrants to the United States, South Africa, South America, & Southeast Asia, 1835-1880: An Alphabetical Listing by Household Heads & Independent Persons. LC 82-23056. 368p. 1983. lib. bdg. 50.00 (ISBN 0-8420-2207-4). Scholarly Res Inc.

--Dutch Immigrants in U.S. Ship Passenger Manifests, 1820-1880: An Alphabetical Listing by Household Heads & Independent Persons, 2 Vols. LC 82-23078. 1328p. 1983. lib. bdg. 125.00 set (ISBN 0-8420-2206-6). Scholarly Res Inc.

NETHERLANDS–HISTORY

Bordewyk, H. W., et al. Netherlands & the World War: Studies in the War History of a Neutral: Volume 4-Effect of the War upon Banking & Currency-War Finances in the Netherlands, 1918-1922-Costs of the War. (Economic & Social History of the World War Ser.). 1928. text ed. 75.00x (ISBN 0-686-83642-1). Elliots Bks.

Buning, W. De Cock & Alting, J. H. Netherlands & the World War: Studies in the War HIstory of a Neutral: Volume 3-Effect of the War Upon the Colonies. (Economic & Social History of the World War Ser.). 1928. text ed. 49.50x (ISBN 0-686-83636-7). Elliots Bks.

Burnchurch, Richard de. An Outline of Dutch History. (Illus.). 128p. (Orig.). 1980. pap. 10.00 (ISBN 0-686-43014-X, Wouter Wagner Netherlands). Heinman.

NETHERLANDS–SOCIAL LIFE AND CUSTOMS

Bing, Valetyn & Braet Von Uberfeldt, Jan. Regional Costumes of the Netherlands. Wardle, Patricia, tr. from Dutch. (Illus.). 142p. 1978. 75.00 (ISBN 0-686-43013-1, Terra Netherlands). Heinman.

NETSUKES

Okada, Barbara T. Netsuke: Masterpieces from the Metropolitan Museum of Art. Howand, Kathleen, ed. LC 81-38344. (Illus.). 219p. 1982. 24.50 (ISBN 0-87099-273-2). Abrams.

NETWORK ANALYSIS (PLANNING)

Knoke, David & Kuklinski, James H. Network Analysis. (Sage University Papers: Quantitative Applications in the Social Sciences: Vol. 28). 88p. pap. 4.50 (ISBN 0-8039-1914-X). Sage.

NETWORK THEORY

see Electric Networks; System Analysis

NETWORKS, ELECTRIC

see Electric Networks

NETWORKS OF LIBRARIES

see Library Information Networks

NEURAL TRANSMISSION

Cuello, A., ed. Co-Transmission. 224p. 1982. 85.00x (ISBN 0-333-32592-3, Pub. by Macmillan England). State Mutual Bk.

Hodgkin. The Conduction of the Nervous Impulse. 108p. 1982. 50.00x (ISBN 0-85323-061-7, Pub. by Liverpool Univ England). State Mutual Bk.

Katz. The Release of Neural Transmitter Substances. 70p. 1982. 50.00x (ISBN 0-85323-060-9, Pub. by Liverpool Univ England). State Mutual Bk.

NEUROANATOMY

Becker, R. Frederick & Fix, James A. Outline of Functional Neuroanatomy. (Illus.). 1983. pap. text ed. price not set (ISBN 0-8391-1707-8, 16896). Univ Park.

Haines, Duane E. Neuroanatomy: An Atlas of Structures, Sections & Systems. (Illus.). 184p. 1983. text ed. write for info. (ISBN 0-8067-0851-4). Urban & S.

Lang, J. Clinical Anatomy of the Head: Neurocranium, Orbita, Craniocervical Regions. (Illus.). 489p. 1983. 490.00 (ISBN 0-387-11014-3). Springer-Verlag.

Matzke, Howard A. & Foltz, Floyd M. Synopsis of Neuroanatomy. 4th ed. (Illus.). 185p. 1983. pap. 7.95 (ISBN 0-19-503244-6). Oxford U Pr.

NEUROBIOLOGY

Eadis, M. J. & Tyrer, J. H., eds. Biochemical Neourology. LC 82-22859. 278p. 1983. 48.00 (ISBN 0-8451-3009-9). A R Liss.

Federoff, S. & Hertz, L., eds. Advances in Cellular Neurobiology, Vol. 3. (Serial Publication). 448p. 1982. 56.00 (ISBN 0-12-008303-5). Acad Pr.

Fedoroff, S. & Hertz, L., eds. Advances in Cellular Neurobiology, Vol. 4. (Serial Publication). 420p. 1983. price not set (ISBN 0-12-008304-3). Acad Pr.

Kernut, G. A. & Phillus, J. W., eds. Progress in Neurobiology, Vol. 17. 289p. 1983. 115.00 (ISBN 0-08-029697-1). Pergamon.

Mill, P. J. Comparative Neurobiology. 200p. 1982. pap. text ed. 19.95 (ISBN 0-7131-2810-0). E Arnold.

Pfeiffer, Carl C. & Smythies, John R., eds. International Review of Neurobiology, Vol. 24. (Serial Publication). Date not set. price not set (ISBN 0-12-366824-7). Acad Pr.

Seifert, Wilfried, ed. Neurobiology of the Hippocampus. Date not set. price not set (ISBN 0-12-634880-4). Acad Pr.

Shepherd, Gordon M. Neurobiology. 1982. 35.00x (ISBN 0-19-503054-0); pap. 21.95x (ISBN 0-19-503055-9). Oxford U Pr.

Tsukada, Y. & Agranoff, B. W. Neurobiological Basis of Learning & Memory. 260p. 1980. text ed. 39.95 (ISBN 0-471-05148-9, Pub. by Wiley Med). Wiley.

Tsukada, Y., ed. Genetic Approaches to Development Neurobiology. 269p. 1983. 43.00 (ISBN 0-387-11872-1). Springer-Verlag.

NEUROCHEMISTRY

Eadis, M. J. & Tyrer, J. H., eds. Biochemical Neourology. LC 82-22859. 278p. 1983. 48.00 (ISBN 0-8451-3009-9). A R Liss.

Frolkis, V. V. Aging & Life-Prolonging Processes. (Illus.). 380p. 1983. 39.20 (ISBN 0-387-81685-2), Springer-Verlag.

Stastny, F. Glucocorticoids & Brain Development. (Monographs in Neural Sciences: Vol. 9). (Illus.). viii, 200p. 1983. 54.00 (ISBN 3-8055-3626-7). S Karger.

NEUROCYTE

see Neurons

NEUROENDOCRINOLOGY

Baertschi, A. J. & Dreifus, J. J., eds. Neuroendocrinology of Vasopressin Carticolberin & Optimelanocortins. 1982. 33.00 (ISBN 0-12-072440-5). Acad Pr.

Magee, Michael C. Basic Science for the Practicing Urologist. LC 82-4561. (Illus.). 250p. Date not set. price not set (ISBN 0-521-24567-2). Cambridge U Pr.

NEUROLOGIC EXAMINATION

Samuels, Martin A. Manual of Neurologic Therapeutics: With Essentials of Diagnosis. (Spiral Manual Ser.). 1982. spiralbound 15.95 (ISBN 0-316-76991-6). Little.

NEUROLOGICAL NURSING

Robertson, Caroline E. Neurological-Neurosurgical Nursing Handbook. Gardner, Alvin F., ed. (Allied Health Professions Monograph Ser.). 434p. 1983. 40.00 (ISBN 0-87527-322-X). Green.

Snyder, Mariah. A Guide to Neurological & Neurosurgical Nursing. 768p. 1983. 25.95 (ISBN 0-471-09835-3, Pub. by Wiley Med). Wiley.

Swift-Bandini, Nancy. Manual of Neurological Nursing. (Spiral Manual Ser.). 1982. spiralbound 12.95 (ISBN 0-316-82541-7). Little.

NEUROLOGY

see also Electrophysiology; Nervous System; Neurobiology; Neurochemistry; Neuroendocrinology; Neuro-Psychopharmacology; Pediatric Neurology; Psychology, Pathological

Atrens, D. M. & Curthoys, J. S., eds. Neuroscience & Behavior: An Introduction. 2nd ed. 214p. 1982. 8.00 (ISBN 0-686-81705-2); subscription 9.95. Acad Pr.

Banna, M. Clinical Neuroradiology. (Illus.). 1983. text ed. price not set (ISBN 0-8391-1809-0, 17523). Univ Park.

Bishop, Beverly & Craik, Rebecca L. Neural Plasticity. 1982. pap. 5.00 (ISBN 0-912452-38-2). Am Phys Therapy Assn.

Broughton, R. J., ed. Henri Gastaut & the Marseilles School's Contribution to the Neurosciences: Proceedings of the 25th & Final Colloque de Marseille. (Electroencephalography & Clinical Neurophysiology Ser.: Suppl. No. 35). 448p. 1982. 130.25 (ISBN 0-444-80363-7, Biomedical Pr). Elsevier.

Bures, Jan & Krekule, Ivan. Practical Guide to Computer Applications in Neurosciences. 1983. 42.95 (ISBN 0-471-10012-9, Pub. by Wiley-Interscience). Wiley.

Cowan, W. M., et al, eds. Annual Review of Neuroscience, Vol 6. (Illus.). 1983. text ed. 27.00 (ISBN 0-8243-2406-4). Annual Reviews.

DeJong, Russell N. Year Book of Neurology & Neurosurgery, 1983. 1983. 35.00 (ISBN 0-8151-2424-4). Year Bk Med.

Heiss, W. D. & Phelps, M. F., eds. Positron Emission Tomography of the Brain. (Illus.). 300p. 1983. 51.50 (ISBN 0-387-12130-7). Springer-Verlag.

Liveson, Jay A. & Ma, Dong M. Nerve Conduction Handbook. (Illus.). 380p. 1983. pap. text ed. 22.50 (ISBN 0-8036-5646-7, 5646-7). Davis Co.

Lowenthal, A. Agar Gel Electrophoresis in Neurology. 1964. 18.00 (ISBN 0-444-40377-9). Elsevier.

Romand, R., ed. Development of Auditory & Vestibular Systems. Date not set. price not set (ISBN 0-12-594450-0). Acad Pr.

Scheinberg, Labe C. & Giesser, Barbara. Neurology Handbook. 2nd ed. 1982. pap. text ed. 11.95 (ISBN 0-87488-604-X). Med Exam.

Schlaefke, M. E., et al, eds. Central Neurone Environment & the Control Systems of Breathing & Circulation. (Proceedings in Life Sciences Ser.). 275p. 1982. 35.00 (ISBN 0-387-11671-0). Springer-Verlag.

Sever, John L. & Madden, David, eds. Polyomaviruses & Human Neurological Disease. LC 82-22945. (Progress in Clinical & Biological Research Ser.: Vol. 105). 376p. 1983. 66.00 (ISBN 0-8451-0105-6). A R Liss.

Sun, Grace Y. & Bazan, Nicolas, eds. Neural Membranes. (Experimental & Clinical Neuroscience Ser.). (Illus.). 544p. 1983. 59.50 (ISBN 0-89603-052-0). Humana.

Todorov. Clinical Neurology. 1983. price not set (ISBN 0-86577-084-0). Thieme-Stratton.

Tyrer, John H. & Eadie, Mervyn J. Clinical & Experimental Neurology, Vol. 18. 248p. text ed. 57.00 (ISBN 0-686-37437-1). Wright-PSG.

Wolman, Benjamin B., ed. Progress: Vol. I of the International Encyclppedia of Psychiatry, Psychology, Psychoanalysis & Neurology. 1983. 89.00 (ISBN 0-918228-28-X). Aesculapius Pubs.

NEUROMUSCULAR DISEASES

Goodgold, Joseph & Eberstein, Arthur. Electrodiagnosis of Neuromuscular Diseases. 3rd ed. (Illus.). 358p. 1983. lib. bdg. 34.00 (ISBN 0-683-03686-6). Williams & Wilkins.

NEUROMUSCULAR TRANSMISSION

see also Muscle; Nerves

Granits. Mechanisms Regulating the Discharge of Motoneurons. 92p. 1982. 50.00x (ISBN 0-85323-340-3, Pub. by Liverpool Univ England). State Mutual Bk.

NEURONS

AIP Conference, 89th, Argonne National Laboratory, 1981. Neutron Scattering: Proceedings. Faber, John, Jr., ed. LC 82-73094. 397p. 1982. lib. bdg. 35.50 (ISBN 0-88318-188-6). Am Inst Physics.

Malmfors, T. & Thoenen, T. Six-Hydroxydopamine & Catecholamine Neurons. 1971. 30.00 (ISBN 0-444-10087-3). Elsevier.

NEUROPATHOLOGY

see Nervous System–Diseases

NEUROPHARMACOLOGY

see also Neuro-Psychopharmacology

Breggin, Peter R. Psychiatric Drugs: Hazards to the Brain. 352p. 1983. text ed. 24.95 (ISBN 0-8261-2930-7). Springer Pub.

Schlumpf, M. & Lichtensteiger, W., eds. Drugs & Hormones in Brain Development. (Monographs in Neural Sciences: Vol. 10). (Illus.). iv, 180p. 1983. 75.50 (ISBN 3-8055-3514-7). S Karger.

Testing Drugs for the Aging Brain. (Journal: Gerontology: Vol. 28, Suppl. 2). (Illus.). vi, 58p. 1983. pap. 33.00 (ISBN 3-8055-3659-3). S Karger.

Yetiv, Jack & Bianchine, Joseph R. Recent Advances in Clinical Therapeutics: Psychopharmacology, Neuropharmacology, Gastrointestinal Therapeutics. (Vol. 2). write for info (ISBN 0-8089-1542-8). Grune.

NEUROPHYSIOLOGY

see also Neural Transmission; Reflexes

Bassler, U. Neural Basis of Elementary Behavior in Stick Insects. Strausfeld, C., tr. (Studies in Brain Function: Vol.10). (Illus.). 180p. 1983. 32.60 (ISBN 0-387-11918-3). Springer-Verlag.

Lavine, Robert A. Neurophysiology: The Fundamentals. LC 80-2611. 192p. 1982. 13.95 (ISBN 0-669-04343-5). Heath.

Ottoson, D. Physiology of the Nervous System. 1982. 125.00x (ISBN 0-333-30819-0, Pub. by Macmillan England). State Mutual Bk.

Ottoson, David. Physiology of the Nervous System. (Illus.). 584p. 1983. 45.00 (ISBN 0-19-520410-7); pap. 27.95 (ISBN 0-19-520409-3). Oxford U Pr.

Pfaltz, C. R., ed. Neurophysiological & Clinical Aspects of Vestibular Disorders. (Advances in Oto-Rhino-Laryngology: Vol. 30). (Illus.). viii, 250p. 1983. 90.00 (ISBN 3-8055-3607-0). S Karger.

Somjen, George G. Neurophysiology: The Essentials. 400p. 1983. text ed. price not set (ISBN 0-683-07856-9). Williams & Wilkins.

Zrenner, E. Neurophysiological Aspects of Color Vision in Primates. (Studies of Brain Function: Vol. 9). (Illus.). 218p. 1983. 37.00 (ISBN 0-387-11653-2). Springer-Verlag.

NEUROPSYCHOLOGY

Benton, Arthur L., et al. Contributions to Neuropsychological Assessment: A Clinical Manual. (Illus.). 145p. 1983. text ed. 28.95x (ISBN 0-19-503192-X); pap. text ed. 18.95x (ISBN 0-19-503193-8). Oxford U Pr.

Boddy, John. Brain Systems & Psychological Concepts. LC 77-21203. 461p. 1978. 48.00 (ISBN 0-471-99601-7); pap. 21.95x (ISBN 0-471-99600-9, Pub. by Wiley-Interscience). Wiley.

Broadbent, D. E. & Weiskrantz, L., eds. The Neuropsychology of Cognitive Function: Proceedings of a Royal Society Discussion Meeting, November 18-19, 1981. (RSL Philosophical Transcriptions of the Royal Society of London, Ser. B: Vol. 298, No. 1089). (Illus.). 230p. 1982. text ed. 68.00x (ISBN 0-85403-190-1, Pub. by Royal Soc London). Scholium Intl.

Ferguson, Norman B. Neuropsychology Laboratory Manual. rev. ed. 1982. 5.95 (ISBN 0-87735-630-0). Freeman C.

Filskov, Susan B. & Boll, Thomas J. Handbook of Clinical Neuropsychology. LC 80-15392. (Personality Processes Ser.). 806p. 1981. 39.95x (ISBN 0-471-04802-X, Pub. by Wiley-Interscience). Wiley.

Goldern, Charles J., et al, eds. Clinical Neuropsychology: Interface with Neurological & Psychiatric Disorders. Date not set. price not set (ISBN 0-8089-1541-X). Grune.

Isaccson, Robert L. & Spear, Norman, eds. The Expression of Knowledge: Neurobehavioral Transformation into Action. LC 82-13253. 442p. 1982. 39.50 (ISBN 0-306-40927-5, Plenum Pr). Plenum Pub.

Malatesha, Rattihalli N. Neuropsychology & Cognition. 1982. lib. bdg. 135.00 (ISBN 90-247-2752-9, Pub. by Martinus Nijhoff Netherlands). Kluwer Boston.

Moses, James A., Jr. & Golden, Charles, eds. Interpretation of the Luria-Nebraska Neuropsychological Battery, Vol. 2. Date not set. text ed. price not set (ISBN 0-8089-1537-1). Grune.

Moses, James A., Jr., et al, eds. Interpretation of the Luria-Nebraska, Vol. 1. Date not set. price not set (ISBN 0-8089-1532-0). Grune.

Pribram, Karl H. Languages of the Brain: Experimental Paradoxes & Principles in Neuropsychology. 5th ed. 432p. 1982. Repr. of 1971 ed. text ed. 19.95x (ISBN 0-913412-22-8). Brandon Hse.

Reinis, Stanislav & Goldman, Jerome M. The Chemistry of Behavior: A Molecular Approach to Neuronal Plasticity. LC 82-13294. 622p. 1982. 55.00 (ISBN 0-306-41161-X, Plenum Pr). Plenum Pub.

NEURO-PSYCHOPHARMACOLOGY

Breggin, Peter R. Psychiatric Drugs: Hazards to the Brain. 352p. 1983. text ed. 24.95 (ISBN 0-8261-2930-7). Springer Pub.

Feldman, Robert S. & Quenzer, Linda F. Fundamentals of Neuropsychopharmacology. (Illus.). 650p. 1983. price not set (ISBN 0-87893-178-3). Sinauer Assoc.

Kornetsky, Conan. Pharmacology: Drugs Affecting Behavior. LC 76-6062. 288p. Repr. of 1976 ed. text ed. 28.95 (ISBN 0-471-50410-6). Krieger.

NEUROSES

see also Depression, Mental; Medicine, Psychosomatic; Mentally Ill; Obsessive-Compulsive Neuroses; Phobias

also particular neuroses, e.g. Anxiety, Hysteria

Bovill, Diana. Tutorial Therapy: Teaching Neurotics to Treat Themselves. (Illus.). 200p. 1982. text ed. 25.00 (ISBN 0-85200-451-6, Pub. by MTP Pr England). Kluwer Boston.

Rivers, W. H. Instinct & the Unconscious: A Contribution to a Biological Theory of the Psycho-Neuroses. 252p. 1982. Repr. of 1920 ed. lib. bdg. 50.00 (ISBN 0-89984-849-4). Century Bookbindery.

Straus, Erwin. Man, Time & World: The Anthropological Psychology of Erwin Straus. Moss, Donald, tr. from Ger. 185p. 1982. text ed. 15.50x (ISBN 0-8207-0159-9, 90007). Duquesne.

NEUROSURGERY

see Nervous System–Surgery

NEUROSURGICAL NURSING

see Neurological Nursing

NEUROTROPIC DRUGS

see Neuropharmacology

NEUTRALITY

see also War (International Law)

American Neutrality, 1914-1917: Essays on the Causes of American Intervention in the World War. 1935. text ed. 13.50 (ISBN 0-686-83464-X). Elliots Bks.

Bordewyk, H. W., et al. Netherlands & the World War: Studies in the War History of a Neutral: Volume 4-Effect of the War upon Banking & Currency-War Finances in the Netherlands, 1918-1922-Costs of the War. (Economic & Social History of the World War Ser.). 1928. text ed. 75.00x (ISBN 0-686-83642-1). Elliots Bks.

Buning, W. De Cock & Alting, J. H. Netherlands & the World War: Studies in the War HIstory of a Neutral: Volume 3-Effect of the War Upon the Colonies. (Economic & Social History of the World War Ser.). 1928. text ed. 49.50x (ISBN 0-686-83636-7). Elliots Bks.

Kalin, Walter. Das Prinzip des Non-Refoulement. 393p. (Ger.). 1982. write for info. (ISBN 3-261-05041-1). P Lang Pubs.

Whiteman, Harold B., Jr. Neutrality, 1941. 1941. text ed. 29.50x (ISBN 0-686-83645-6). Elliots Bks.

NEUTRON ACTIVATION ANALYSIS

see Radioactivation Analysis

NEUTRONS

see also Atoms; Electrons; Protons

Cierjacks, S., ed. Neutron Sources: For Applied & Pure Nuclear Research. (Neutron Physics & Nuclear Data in Science & Technology Ser.: Vol. 2). 370p. 1982. 65.00 (ISBN 0-08-029351-4). Pergamon.

NEVADA

see also names of cities, counties, etc. in Nevada

Hayden, John L. How to Incorporate in Tax Free Nevada for Only 50 Dollars. LC 80-85433. 88p. (Orig.). pap. 8.97 (ISBN 0-940008-00-9). Entrepreneurs.

NEVADA–HISTORY

Davis, Samuel P. History of Nevada, 2 Vols. (Illus.). 1983. 75.00 (ISBN 0-686-42715-7). Nevada Pubns.

Reproduction of Thompson & West: History of Nevada 1881. (Illus.). 1958. 60.00 (ISBN 0-913814-52-0). Nevada Pubns.

NEW BUSINESS ENTERPRISES

Handy, Jim. How to Uncover Hidden Business Opportunities that Make Money. LC 82-12574. 216p. 1983. 14.95 (ISBN 0-13-436071-0, Parker); pap. 4.95 (ISBN 0-13-436063-X). P-H.

Shilling, Dana. Be Your Own Boss: A Step-by-Step Guide to Financial Independence Through Your Own Small Business. 490p. 1983. 14.95 (ISBN 0-688-01572-7). Morrow.

Toncre, Emery. The Action Step Plan to Owning & Operating a Successful Business. (Illus.). 228p. 1983. 15.95 (ISBN 0-13-003327-8); pap. 6.95 (ISBN 0-13-003319-7). P-H.

Welsh, John & White, Jerry. The Entrepreneur's Master Planning Guide: How to Launch A Successful New Business. (Illus.). 408p. 1983. 24.95 (ISBN 0-13-282814-6); pap. 11.95 (ISBN 0-13-282806-5). P-H.

NEW CHURCH

see New Jerusalem Church

NEW ENGLAND

Theodore Thornton Munger: New England Minister. 1913. text ed. 65.00x (ISBN 0-686-83814-9). Elliots Bks.

NEW ENGLAND–DESCRIPTION AND TRAVEL
Dwight, Theodore. Sketches of Scenery & Manners in the United States. LC 82-10258. 1983. 30.00x (ISBN 0-8201-1383-2). Schol Facsimiles.
Hoy, John C. & Bernstein, Melvin H., eds. New England's Vital Resource: The Labor Force. LC 82-3902. 149p. 1982. 12.00. NE Board Higher Ed.
NEW ENGLAND–DESCRIPTION AND TRAVEL–GUIDEBOOKS
Delaney, Edmund. The Conneticut River: New England's Historic Waterway. (Illus.). 224p. 1983. pap. 9.95 (ISBN 0-87106-980-6). Globe Pequot.
Duncan, Roger F. & Ware, John P. A Cruising Guide to the New England Coast. Rev. ed. (Illus.). 1983. 24.95 (ISBN 0-396-08166-5). Dodd.
Faulke, Robert & Faulke, Patricia. Budget Vacations & Daytrips in New England. 224p. 1983. pap. 8.95 (ISBN 0-87106-978-4). Globe Pequot.
Smith, Sharon. Yankee Magazine's Travel Guide to New England: Summer-Fall 1983. (Illus.). 200p. 1983. pap. 2.50 (ISBN 0-89909-004-4). Yankee Bks.
Squier, Elizabeth. Guide to Recommended Country Inns of New England. 8th ed. 304p. 1983. pap. 7.95 (ISBN 0-87106-976-8). Globe Pequot.
Weiner, Neal O. & Schwartz, David M. The Interstate Gourmet: New England, Vol. 1. 1982. pap. write for info. (ISBN 0-671-44992-3). Summit Bks.
NEW ENGLAND–GENEALOGY
Jordan, Tristram F. The Jordan Memorial. Jordan, William B., Jr., frwd. by. LC 82-81274. (Illus.). 488p. 1982. Repr. of 1882 ed. 35.00x (ISBN 0-89725-030-3). NE History.
NEW ENGLAND–HISTORY
Andrews, Charles M. Fathers of New England. 1919. text ed. 8.50x (ISBN 0-686-83545-X). Elliots Bks.
Cronon, William. Changes in the Land. (Illus.). 1982. 14.50 (ISBN 0-8090-3405-0); pap. 6.75 (ISBN 0-8090-0158-6). Hill & Wang.
Harding, R. Brewster. Roadside New England, 1900-1955. 80p. pap. 9.95 (ISBN 0-89272-158-8). Down East.
Russell, Howard S. Indian New England Before the Mayflower. LC 79-63082. (Illus.). 296p. 1983. pap. 11.50 (ISBN 0-87451-255-7). U Pr of New Eng.
NEW ENGLAND–HISTORY–ANECDOTES
Gilmore, William J. Elementary Literacy on the Eve of the Industrial Revolution: Trends in Rural New England. (Illus.). 91p. 1982. pap. 5.95 (ISBN 0-912296-57-7, Dist. by U Pr of VA). Am Antiquarian.
NEW ENGLAND–HISTORY–COLONIAL PERIOD, ca. 1600-1775
Clark, Charles E. The Eastern Frontier: The Settlement of Northern New England, 1610-1763. LC 82-40477. 460p. 1983. pap. 16.50 (ISBN 0-87451-252-2). U Pr of New Eng.
Miller, Perry. The New England Mind: From Colony to Province. 528p. 1983. pap. text ed. 8.95x (ISBN 0-674-61301-5, Belknap). Harvard U Pr.
--The New England Mind: The Seventeenth Century. 540p. 1983. pap. text ed. 8.95x (ISBN 0-674-61306-6, Belknap). Harvard U Pr.
Zuckerman, Michael. Peaceable Kingdoms: New England Towns in the Eighteenth Century. LC 82-18365. ix, 329p. 1983. Repr. of 1970 ed. lib. bdg. 39.75x (ISBN 0-313-22634-2, ZUPK). Greenwood.
NEW ENGLAND–JUVENILE LITERATURE
Anctil, Pierre. A Franco-American Bibliography: New England. 137p. 1979. pap. 5.25x (ISBN 0-911409-36-X). Natl Mat Dev.
Costabel, Eva D. A New England Village. LC 82-13738. (Illus.). 64p. (gr. 4 up). 1983. 11.95 (ISBN 0-689-30972-4). Atheneum.
NEW ENGLAND–POLITICS
White, John K. The Fractured Electorate: Political Parties & Social Change in Southern New England. LC 82-40471. (Illus.). 196p. 1983. 16.00 (ISBN 0-87451-258-1); pap. 8.00 (ISBN 0-87451-260-3). U Pr of New Eng.
NEW ENGLAND–SOCIAL LIFE AND CUSTOMS
Dwight, Theodore. Sketches of Scenery & Manners in the United States. LC 82-10258. 1983. 30.00x (ISBN 0-8201-1383-2). Schol Facsimiles.
NEW FRANCE–HISTORY
see Canada–History–To 1763 (New France)
NEW GUINEA–HISTORY
White, J. P. & O'Connell, J. F., eds. A Prehistory of Australia, New Guinea & Sahul: International Edition. LC 81-71781. Date not set. 29.50 (ISBN 0-12-746730-0). Acad Pr.
NEW GUINEA–SOCIAL LIFE AND CUSTOMS
Williams, Francis E. Orokaiva Society. LC 82-25129. (Illus.). xxiii, 355p. 1983. Repr. of 1930 ed. lib. bdg. 59.50x (ISBN 0-313-23846-4, WIOR). Greenwood.
NEW HAMPSHIRE–DESCRIPTION AND TRAVEL
Doan, Daniel. Fifty More Hikes in New Hampshire: Day Hikes & Backpacking Trips from the Coast to Coos County. rev. ed. (Fifty Hikes Ser.). (Illus.). 224p. 1983. pap. 8.95 (ISBN 0-942440-06-4). Backcountry Pubns.
NEW HAMPSHIRE–HISTORY
Carter, N. F. History of Pembroke, 2 Vols. 1976. Repr. of 1895 ed. 45.00X (ISBN 0-89725-032-X). NH Pub Co.
Cogswell, Leander W. History of the Town of Henniker. 1973. Repr. of 1880 ed. 45.00X (ISBN 0-912274-29-8). NH Pub Co.
Flanagan, Martin J. The Passing Parade: The Story of Somersworth, NH, 1910-1981. LC 82-62138. (Illus.). 285p. 1983. 10.00 (ISBN 0-89725-036-2). NE History.
Turner, Lynn W. The Ninth State: New Hampshire's Formative Years. LC 82-13386. (Illus.). 530p. 1983. 19.95x (ISBN 0-8078-1541-1). U of NC Pr.
NEW HAMPSHIRE–POLITICS AND GOVERNMENT
Turner, Lynn W. The Ninth State: New Hampshire's Formative Years. LC 82-13386. (Illus.). 530p. 1983. 19.95x (ISBN 0-8078-1541-1). U of NC Pr.
The William Plumer Papers: A Guide to the Microform Edition. 87p. 1982. 25.00 (ISBN 0-667-00663-X). Microfilming Corp.
NEW JERSEY
see also names of individual cities, counties, towns, etc. in New Jersey
Garwood, Alfred N., ed. New Jersey Economic Almanac. 300p. Date not set. pap. 29.95 (ISBN 0-686-38088-6). NJ Assocs.
NEW JERSEY–DESCRIPTION AND TRAVEL
Cudworth, Marsha & Michaels, Howard. Victorian Holidays: A Guide to Guesthouses, Bed & Breakfast Inns & Restaurants of Cape May, N. J. 2nd rev. & enlarged ed. LC 82-83816. 125p. (Orig.). pap. 6.95 (ISBN 0-9608554-1-6). Lady Raspberry.
Ludlum, David M. The New Jersey Weather Book. 250p. Date not set. 24.95 (ISBN 0-8135-0915-7); pap. 14.95 (ISBN 0-8135-0940-8). Rutgers U Pr.
Nixdorf, Bert. Hikes & Bike Rides for the Delaware Valley & Southern New Jersey: With Emphasis on the Pine Barrens, No. 1. (Illus.). 140p. (Orig.). pap. 5.50 (ISBN 0-9610474-0-2). B Nixdorf.
Schwartz, Helen. The New Jersey House. (Illus.). 238p. 1983. 25.00 (ISBN 0-8135-0965-3); pap. 14.95 (ISBN 0-8135-0990-4). Rutgers U Pr.
Stansfield, Charles A., Jr. New Jersey: A Geography. 240p. 1983. lib. bdg. 35.00x (ISBN 0-89158-957-0); pap. text ed. 20.00x (ISBN 0-86531-491-8). Westview.
NEW JERSEY–HISTORICAL GEOGRAPHY
Juet, Robert. Juet's Journal, The Voyage of the Half Moon from 4 April to 7 November 1609, Vol. 12. 37p. 1959. pap. 4.00 (ISBN 0-686-81823-7). NJ Hist Soc.
Niemcewicz, Julian U., ed. Under Their Vine & Fig Tree: Travels Through America in 1797-1799, 1805 with Some Further Account of Life in New Jersey, Vol. 14. (Illus.). 398p. 20.00 (ISBN 0-686-81808-3). NJ Hist Soc.
NEW JERSEY–GENEALOGY
Nelson, William. New Jersey Biographical & Genealogical Notes, Vol. 9. 222p. 1916. 6.95 (ISBN 0-686-81825-3). NJ Hist Soc.
Pack, Charles P. Thomas Hatch of Barnstable & Some of His Descendants. 356p. boxed 15.00 (ISBN 0-686-81805-9). NJ Hist Soc.
NEW JERSEY–HISTORY
Bassett, William B. Historic American Buildings Survey of New Jersey. (Illus.). 210p. 1977. 13.95 (ISBN 0-686-81818-0); pap. 9.95 (ISBN 0-686-81819-9). NJ Hist Soc.
Congar, Samuel H., ed. Records of the Town of Newark, New Jersey, from its Settlement in 1666 to its Incorporation as a City in 1836, Vol. 6. 308p. 1966. pap. 8.50 (ISBN 0-686-81799-0). NJ Hist Soc.
Doane, George W. The Goodly Heritage of Jerseymen: The First Annual Address before the New Jersey Historical Society at Their Meeting in Trenton, on Thursday, January 15, 1846. 2nd ed. 32p. 1971. pap. 2.00 (ISBN 0-686-81822-9). NJ Hist Soc.
Levitt, James H. For Want of Trade: Shipping & the New Jersey Ports, 1680-1783, Vol. 17. 224p. 1981. 19.95 (ISBN 0-911020-03-9). NJ Hist Soc.
The New Jersey Historical Society Collection of World War I Posters. (Illus.). 87p. 1976. pap. 10.00 (ISBN 0-686-81826-1). NJ Hist Soc.
Semi-Centennial Celebration of the Foundation of the New Jersey Historical Society, at Newark, N.J., May 16, 1895, Vol. 8. 223p. pap. 6.95 (ISBN 0-686-81802-4). NJ Hist Soc.
Skemer, Don C. & Morris, Robert C. Guide to the Manuscript Collections of the New Jersey Historical Society, Vol. 15. 245p. 1979. 20.00 (ISBN 0-911020-00-4). NJ Hist Soc.
Thayer, Theodore. As We Were: The Story of Old Elizabethtown, Vol. 13. (Illus.). 280p. 1964. 17.95 (ISBN 0-686-81820-2). NJ Hist Soc.
NEW JERSEY–HISTORY–REVOLUTION, 1775-1783
Jones, E. Alfred. The Loyalists of New Jersey: Their Memorials, Petitions, Claims, etc., from English Records, Vol. 10. 346p. 1927. 12.50 (ISBN 0-686-81824-5). NJ Hist Soc.
NEW JERSEY–POLITICS AND GOVERNMENT
Ershkowitz, Herbert. The Origin of the Whig & Democratic Parties, New Jersey Politics, 1820-1837. LC 82-17652. (Illus.). 300p. (Orig.). 1983. lib. bdg. 23.00 (ISBN 0-8191-2769-8); pap. text ed. 11.50 (ISBN 0-8191-2770-1). U Pr of Amer.
Garwood, Alfred N., ed. The New Jersey Municipal Data Book. 3rd ed. 608p. 1983. pap. 59.95 (ISBN 0-686-38090-8). NJ Assocs.
New Jersey Political Almanac, 1982-83. 1982. 10.00 (ISBN 0-686-81770-2). Ctr Analysis Public Issues.
NEW JERUSALEM CHURCH
Meyers, Mary A. A New World Jerusalem: The Swedenborgian Experience in Community Cinstruction. LC 82-11997. (Contributions in American Studies: No. 65). (Illus.). 256p. 1983. lib. bdg. 29.95 (ISBN 0-313-23602-X, MNJ/). Greenwood.
NEW LEFT
see College Students–Political Activity; Radicalism; Right and Left (Political Science)
NEW MARKET, BATTLE OF, 1864
Davis, William C. The Battle of New Market. LC 82-18705. (Illus.). 280p. 1983. pap. 7.95 (ISBN 0-8071-1078-7). La State U Pr.
Zucker, Jeff & Hummel, Kay. Oregon Indians: Culture, History & Current Affairs; an Atlas & Introduction. (Illus.). 192p. (Orig.). 1983. write for info. (ISBN 0-87595-094-9, Western Imprints); pap. write for info. (ISBN 0-87595-109-0, Western Imprints). Oreg Hist Soc.
NEW ORLEANS–DESCRIPTION
Reeves, Sally K. & Reeves, William D. Historic City Park: New Orleans. (Illus.). 256p. 1982. 24.95 (ISBN 0-9610062-0-X). Friends City Park.
Transitour, Inc. The Streetcar Guide to Uptown New Orleans. Raarup, Peter, ed. (Illus.). 128p. pap. 5.95 (ISBN 0-686-82700-7). Pelican.
White, Gene. The New Orleans Guide. 2nd ed. (Illus.). 84p. 1982. pap. 3.95x (ISBN 0-9607056-0-0). Monticello Pr.
NEW ORLEANS–HISTORY
Cruise, Boyd & Harton, Merle. Signor Faranta's Iron Theatre. LC 82-83592. (Illus.). 150p. 1982. 15.95x (ISBN 0-917860-13-6). Historic New Orleans.
Historic New Orleans Collection. Orleans Gallery: The Founders. (Illus.). 48p. (Orig.). 1982. pap. 5.00x (ISBN 0-917860-10-1). Historic New Orleans.
NEW PRODUCTS
see also Design, Industrial
Grant, Donald P. Design by Objectives: Multiple Objective Design Analysis & Evaluation in Architectural, Environmental & Product Design. LC 82-73290. 50p. (Orig.). 1982. pap. text ed. 4.00 (ISBN 0-910821-00-3). Design Meth.
Morehead, John W. Finding & Licensing New Products & Technology from the U. S. A. 500p. 1982. 495.00 (ISBN 0-943420-00-8). Tech Search Intl.
Sell's Directory of Products & Services, 1982. 97th ed. LC 73-640793. 938p. (Orig.). 1981. pap. 60.00x (ISBN 0-85499-509-9). Intl Pubns Serv.
NEW YORK (CITY)–BIOGRAPHY
Schermerhorn, Gene. Letters to Phil, Memories of a New York Boyhood, 1848-1856. Gill, Brendan, frwd. by. (Illus.). 96p. 1982. 10.95 (ISBN 0-9608788-0-7); Ltd. Ed 35.00 (ISBN 0-9608788-1-5). NY Bound.
NEW YORK (CITY)–DESCRIPTION
Gosen, Patricia E. New York City Metropolitan Area, Studies Program, Work-A-Text. Irvin, J. L., ed. (Illus.). 76p. (Orig.). (gr. 4). 1981. wkbk. 3.50 (ISBN 0-943068-01-0). Graphic Learning.
NEW YORK (CITY)–DESCRIPTION–GUIDEBOOKS
Baedeker's City Guide: New York. 192p. 1983. pap. 9.95 (ISBN 0-86145-118-X, Pub. by Auto Assn-British Tourist Authority England). Merrimack Bk Serv.
Edinger, Claudio. Chelsea Hotel. (Illus.). 160p. (Orig.). 1983. 29.95 (ISBN 0-89659-368-1); pap. 14.95 (ISBN 0-89659-338-X). Abbeville Pr.
Hauser, Joan, ed. Manhattan Epicure. (Epicure Ser.). 160p. 1983. pap. 8.95 (ISBN 0-89716-123-8). Peanut Butter.
Lawrence, Peter. A Kid's New York. 1982. pap. 6.95 (ISBN 0-380-81315-7, 81315). Avon.
Leapman, Michael. Companion Guide to New York. (Illus.). 352p. 1983. 15.95 (ISBN 0-13-154682-1); pap. 7.95 (ISBN 0-13-154674-0). P-H.
Moss, Lydia & Conway, Madeleine. Gourmet to Go: The New York Guide to Dining out at Home. 290p. (Orig.). 1982. pap. 5.95 (ISBN 0-9609862-0-0). MC Prods.
Nicholson, Robert. Guide to England & Wales. (Illus.). 1983. pap. 9.95 (ISBN 0-686-38863-1). Merrimack Bk Serv.
--Nicholson's New York Guide. 1983. pap. 4.95 (ISBN 0-686-38867-4). Merrimack Bk Serv.
--Streetfinder. rev. ed. 1983. pap. 4.95 (ISBN 0-686-38864-X). Merrimack Bk Serv.
Shins, Susan. Food by Phone: Manhattan's Best Meals & Munchies Delivered to Your Door. 256p. 1983. pap. 8.95 (ISBN 0-517-54923-9). Crown.
Thomas, Bill & Thomas, Phyllis. Natural New York. 320p. 1983. 17.95 (ISBN 0-03-057554-0); pap. 10.95 (ISBN 0-03-057553-2). HR&W.
Thomas Cook, Inc. & Norback & Co., Inc. Thomas Cook Travel Guide to New York. (Orig.). Date not set. pap. 3.95 (ISBN 0-440-18889-X). Dell.
Where to Go in Britain. (Illus.). 1983. pap. 12.95 (ISBN 0-686-38868-2, Pub. by Auto Assn-British Tourist Authority England). Merrimack Bk Serv.
Zuesse, Eric, ed. Bargain Finder: The Encyclopedic Money Saving Guide to New York City, for Residents & Tourists. 352p. 1983. pap. 4.95 (ISBN 0-9608950-0-0). Consumers All.
NEW YORK (CITY)–ECONOMIC CONDITIONS
Douglas, Eileen. Eileen Douglas's New York Inflation Fighters' Guide. LC 82-20378. (Illus.). 256p. (Orig.). 1983. pap. 5.95 (ISBN 0-688-01851-3). Quill NY.
NEW YORK (CITY)–GALLERIES AND MUSEUMS
Cultural Assistance Center Staff. A Guide to New York City Museums. 2nd ed. (Illus.). 64p. Date not set. pap. 1.50 (ISBN 0-486-24454-7). Dover.
NEW YORK (CITY)–HISTORY
Block, Alan. East Side - West Side: Organizing Crime in New York, 1930-1950. 280p. 1983. pap. 9.95 (ISBN 0-87855-931-0). Transaction Bks.
Dolan, Jay P. The Immigrant Church: New York's Irish & German Catholics, 1815-1865. LC 82-23827. (Illus.). xiv, 221p. 1983. pap. text ed. 7.95x (ISBN 0-268-01151-6, 85-11511). U of Notre Dame Pr.
Gold, Joyce. From Windmills to the World Trade Center. (Illus.). 96p. (Orig.). 1983. pap. 1.95 (ISBN 0-686-38105-X). Old Warren.
Spann, Edward K. The New Metropolis: New York City, 1840-1857. (Illus.). 546p. 1983. pap. 12.50 (ISBN 0-231-05085-2). Columbia U Pr.
NEW YORK (CITY)–METROPOLITAN OPERA
Strauss, Richard. The Metropolitan Opera Classics Library: Der Rosenkavalier. 16.95 (ISBN 0-316-56834-1); 75.00 (ISBN 0-316-56837-6). Little.
NEW YORK (CITY)–POLICE
Hauser, Thomas. The Trail of Patrolman Thomas Shea. 288p. pap. 3.50 (ISBN 0-380-62778-7, Discus). Avon.
NEW YORK (CITY)–POOR
Baxter, Ellen & Hopper, Kim. Private Lives-Public Spaces: Homeless Adults on the Streets of New York City. 129p. (Orig.). 1981. pap. 6.50 (ISBN 0-88156-002-2). Comm Serv Soc NY.
Hopper, Kim, et al. One Year Later: The Homeless Poor in New York City. LC 82-200214. 92p. (Orig.). 1982. pap. 6.50 (ISBN 0-88156-000-6). Comm Serv Soc NY.
NEW YORK (CITY)–SOCIAL CONDITIONS
Gosen, Patricia E. New York City Metropolitan Area, Studies Program, Work-A-Text. Irvin, J. L., ed. (Illus.). 76p. (Orig.). (gr. 4). 1981. wkbk. 3.50 (ISBN 0-943068-01-0). Graphic Learning.
NEW YORK (STATE)–BIOGRAPHY
Rose, Elizabeth A. & Carson, Robert R. Lizzie's Own Journal: La Vie Heureuse. 1983. 10.00 (ISBN 0-533-05628-4). Vantage.
NEW YORK (STATE)–DESCRIPTION AND TRAVEL
Jones, Louis C. Three Eyes on the Past: Exploring New York State Folk Life. LC 82-7334. (York State Bks.). (Illus.). 240p. (Orig.). 1982. pap. 12.95 (ISBN 0-8156-0179-4). Syracuse U Pr.
NEW YORK (STATE)–DESCRIPTION AND TRAVEL–GUIDEBOOKS
Leight, Warren D. The I Hate New York Guidebook. (Orig.). 1983. pap. price not set (ISBN 0-440-53609-X, Dell Trade Pbks). Dell.
Michelin Green Guide: New York. (Green Guide Ser.). (Fr.). 1983. pap. write for info. (ISBN 2-06-005480-X). Michelin.
NEW YORK (STATE)–ECONOMIC CONDITIONS
Douglas, Eileen. Eileen Douglas's New York Inflation Fighters' Guide. LC 82-20378. (Illus.). 256p. (Orig.). 1983. pap. 5.95 (ISBN 0-688-01851-3). Quill NY.
NEW YORK (STATE)–GENEALOGY
Fay, Loren V. Broome County, N. Y. Genealogical Research Secrets. 25p. 1982. pap. 5.00 (ISBN 0-942238-04-4). L V Fay.
--Delaware County, N. Y. Genealogical Research Secrets. 30p. 1982. pap. 5.00 (ISBN 0-942238-13-3). L V Fay.
--Fulton County, N. Y. Genealogical Research Secrets. (Illus.). 25p. 1982. pap. 5.00 (ISBN 0-942238-18-4). L V Fay.
--Genesee County, N. Y. Genealogical Research Secrets. 25p. 1982. pap. 5.00 (ISBN 0-942238-19-2). L V Fay.
--Montgomery County, N. Y. Genealogical Research Secrets. 25p. 1982. pap. 5.00 (ISBN 0-942238-29-X). L V Fay.
--New York State Area Key. Bd. with New York State Area Key Corrections. 1p. 1982 (ISBN 0-942238-99-0). 200p. 1979. pap. 12.00 (ISBN 0-942238-98-2). L V Fay.
--Rensselaer County, N. Y. Genealogical Research Secrets. 30p. 1982. pap. 5.00 (ISBN 0-942238-42-7). L V Fay.
--Saratoga County, N. Y. Genealogical Research Secrets. 25p. 1982. pap. 5.00 (ISBN 0-942238-46-X). L V Fay.
--Schenectady County, N. Y. Genealogical Research Secrets. 25p. 1982. pap. 5.00 (ISBN 0-942238-47-8). L V Fay.
--Schoharie County, N. Y. Genealogical Research Secrets. 25p. 1982. pap. 5.00 (ISBN 0-942238-48-6). L V Fay.
--Tioga County, N. Y. Genealogical Research Secrets. 25p. 1982. pap. 5.00 (ISBN 0-942238-54-0). L V Fay.
--Wayne County, N. Y. Genealogical Research Secrets. 30p. 1982. pap. 5.00 (ISBN 0-942238-59-1). L V Fay.

--Yates County, N. Y. Genealogical Research Secrets. 25p. 1982. pap. 5.00 (ISBN 0-942238-62-1). L V Fay.

Smith, Evelyn R. Name Index to Arad Thomas' 1871: Pioneer History of Orleans County, New York. 32p. 1982. lib. bdg. 12.00x (ISBN 0-932334-55-5); pap. text ed. 8.00x (ISBN 0-932334-56-3). Heart of the Lakes.

Stewart, Lois. The Ancestors & Descendants of James Montaney (1799-1857) of Oppenheim, Fulton County, N.Y. LC 82-82521. (Illus.). 448p. 1982. 25.00 (ISBN 0-9609512-0-2). L Stewart.

NEW YORK (STATE)–HISTORY

Fitch, Asa. Their Own Voices: Oral Accounts of Early Settlers in Washington County, New York. Adler, Winston, ed. 135p. 1983. 12.95 (ISBN 0-932334-59-8); pap. 8.95 (ISBN 0-932334-60-1). Heart of the Lakes.

Flynn, Edward J. You're the Boss. LC 82-24156. x, 244p. 1983. Repr. of 1947 ed. lib. bdg. 29.75x (ISBN 0-313-23627-5, FLYB). Greenwood.

NEW YORK (STATE)–HISTORY–COLONIAL PERIOD, ca. 1600-1775

Potter, Janice. The Liberty We Seek: Loyalist Ideology in Colonial New York & Massachusetts. 256p. 1983. text ed. 22.50x (ISBN 0-674-53026-8). Harvard U Pr.

NEW YORK (STATE)–HISTORY, LOCAL

Ellis, Franklin. History of Columbia County, New York 1878. (Illus.). 550p. 1983. Repr. of 1878 ed. deluxe ed. price not set (ISBN 0-932334-57-1). Heart of the Lakes.

Hoew, Abba L., et al. Brewster through the Years, 1848-1948. LC 82-15405. (Illus.). 192p. Repr. of 1948 ed. 12.00 (ISBN 0-916346-46-3). Harbor Hill Bks.

NEW YORK (STATE)–POLITICS AND GOVERNMENT

Flynn, Edward J. You're the Boss. LC 82-24156. x, 244p. 1983. Repr. of 1947 ed. lib. bdg. 29.75x (ISBN 0-313-23627-5, FLYB). Greenwood.

NEW YORK (STATE)–SOCIAL LIFE AND CUSTOMS

Jones, Louis C. Three Eyes on the Past: Exploring New York State Folk Life. LC 82-7334. (York State Bks.). (Illus.). 240p. (Orig.). 1982. pap. 12.95 (ISBN 0-8156-0179-4). Syracuse U Pr.

NEW YORK TIMES

Falk, Byron A. & Falk, Valerie R. Personal Name Index to the New York Times Index: Eighteen Fifty-One to Nineteen Seventy-Four, Vol. 21. 421p. 1982. lib. bdg. 61.00 (ISBN 0-89902-121-2). Roxbury Data.

NEW ZEALAND–DESCRIPTION AND TRAVEL

King, Michael. New Zealand in Color. (Illus.). 112p. 1983. 19.95 (ISBN 0-312-57169-0). St Martin.

McDermott, John W. How to Get Lost & Found in New Zealand. 4th ed. 1981. 9.95 (ISBN 0-686-37617-X). Orafa Pub Co.

New Zealand National Bibliography, 1981. 16th ed. LC 73-640530. 547p. 1981. pap. 35.00x (ISBN 0-8002-3049-3). Intl Pubns Serv.

Reid, J. C. & Cape, Peter. A Book of New Zealand. Rev. ed. (Illus.). 291p. 1979. 15.95 (ISBN 0-00-216942-8, Pub. by W Collins Australia). Intl Schol Bk Serv.

Temple, Philip. Ways to the Wilderness: Great New Zealand Walking Tracks. (Illus.). 168p. 1977. 25.00x (ISBN 0-7233-0537-4). Intl Pubns Serv.

NEW ZEALAND–DISCOVERY AND EXPLORATION

New Zealand National Bibliography, 1981. 16th ed. LC 73-640530. 547p. 1981. pap. 35.00x (ISBN 0-8002-3049-3). Intl Pubns Serv.

NEW ZEALAND–ECONOMIC CONDITIONS

Easton, Brian & Thomson, Norman. An Introduction to the New Zealand Economy. LC 81-19737. (Illus.). 339p. 1983. text ed. 25.00x (ISBN 0-7022-1920-7); pap. 13.50x (ISBN 0-7022-1940-1). U of Queensland Pr.

NEW ZEALAND–HISTORY

Begg, A. Charles & Begg, Neil C. The World of John Boultbee. 329p. 1982. 39.00x (ISBN 0-7233-0604-4, Pub. by Whitcoulls New Zealand). State Mutual Bk.

King, Michael. New Zealanders at War. (Illus.). 307p. 1982. 19.95 (ISBN 0-86863-399-2, Pub. by Heinemann Pubs New Zealand). Intl Schol Bk Serv.

McIntyre, W. David, ed. Journal of Henry Sewell, 1853-57: Volume 1, Feb. 1853-May 1854. 510p. 1982. 90.00x (ISBN 0-7233-0624-9, Pub. by Whitcoulls New Zealand). State Mutual Bk.

--The Journal of Henry Sewell, 1853-57: Volume 2-May 1854-May 1857. 371p. 1982. 75.00x (ISBN 0-7233-0625-7, Pub. by Whitcoulls New Zealand). State Mutual Bk.

Miller, Harold G. New Zealand. LC 82-24157. (British Empire History Ser.). 156p. 1983. Repr. lib. bdg. 27.50x (ISBN 0-313-22997-X, MINZ). Greenwood.

NEW ZEALAND–MAPS

New Zealand National Bibliography, 1981. 16th ed. LC 73-640530. 547p. 1981. pap. 35.00x (ISBN 0-8002-3049-3). Intl Pubns Serv.

NEW ZEALAND–POLITICS AND GOVERNMENT

New Zealand National Bibliography, 1981. 16th ed. LC 73-640530. 547p. 1981. pap. 35.00x (ISBN 0-8002-3049-3). Intl Pubns Serv.

NEW ZEALAND LITERATURE (COLLECTIONS)

Maddock, Shirley & Easther, Michael. A Christmas Garland: A New Zealand Christmas Album, 1642-1900, In Twelve Parts. (Illus.). 96p. 1983. 15.95 (ISBN 0-00-216981-9, Pub. by W Collins Australia). Intl Schol Bk Serv.

NEW ZEALAND LITERATURE–HISTORY AND CRITICISM

National Library of New Zealand, ed. New Zealand National Bibliography 1980. 15th ed. LC 73-640530. 565p. (Orig.). 1981. pap. 35.00x (ISBN 0-8002-3003-5). Intl Pubns Serv.

NEW ZEALAND PAINTING

see Painting, New Zealand

NEWBORN INFANTS

see Infants (Newborn)

NEWFOUNDLAND–DESCRIPTION AND TRAVEL

South, R. Biogeography & Ecology of the Island of Newfoundland. 1983. 120.00 (ISBN 90-6193-101-0, Pub. by Junk Pubs Netherlands). Kluwer Boston.

NEWMAN, JOHN HENRY, CARDINAL, 1801-1890

Siebenschuh, William R. Fictional Techniques & Factual Works. LC 82-8373. 200p. 1983. text ed. 18.00x (ISBN 0-8203-0636-3). U of Ga Pr.

Sugg, Joyce, ed. A Packet of Letters: A Selection from the Correspondence of John Henry Newman. (Illus.). 194p. 1983. 19.95 (ISBN 0-19-826442-9). Oxford U Pr.

NEWS BROADCASTS

see Radio Journalism; Television Broadcasting of News

NEWS-LETTERS

Arth, Marvin & Ashmore, Helen. The Newsletter Editor's Desk Book. 3rd ed. 136p. 1982. softcover 10.00 (ISBN 0-938270-03-6). Parkway Pr.

Evanson, Roy. Illustrating Your Newsletter. (Illus.). 1982. pap. 3.95 (ISBN 0-916068-19-6). Groupwork Today.

Hagood, Patricia, ed. Oxbridge Directory of Newsletters 1983-84. 3rd rev. ed. 400p. 1983. pap. 60.00 (ISBN 0-917460-11-1). Oxbridge Comm.

Helmken, Charles M. Creative Newsletter Graphics. 3rd ed. 280p. 1981. 40.00 (ISBN 0-89964-195-4). CASE.

Update Publishing Staff. The Update Directory of Updating Newsletters. 25p. 1983. pap. text ed. 8.95 (ISBN 0-686-38859-3). Update Pub Co.

NEWS PHOTOGRAPHY

see Photography, Journalistic

NEWSPAPER ADVERTISING

see Advertising, Newspaper

NEWSPAPER PUBLISHING

Brendon, Piers. The Life & Death of the Press Barons. LC 82-73017. 288p. 1983. 14.95 (ISBN 0-689-11341-2). Atheneum.

Cushman, Kathleen & Miller, Edward, eds. How to Produce a Small Newspaper: A Guide for Independent Journalists. 2nd, Rev. ed. (Illus.). 192p. (Orig.). 1983. pap. 8.95 (ISBN 0-916782-39-5). Harvard Common Pr.

NEWSPAPER STYLE

see Journalism–Handbooks, Manuals, Etc.

NEWSPAPERS

see also Advertising, Newspaper; Liberty of the Press; Newspaper Publishing; Periodicals; Press; Reporters and Reporting

also names of individual newspapers, e.g. New York Times; Washington Post; American Newspapers, English, etc.

Bond, Serena K. Basic Skills School Newspaper Workbook. (Basic Skills Workbooks). 32p. (gr. 8-12). 1983. 0.99 (ISBN 0-8209-0553-4, SNW-1). ESP.

--The School Newspaper. (Language Arts Ser.). 24p. (gr. 8-12). 1982. wkbk. 5.00 (ISBN 0-8209-0328-0, J-1). ESP.

Kelly, Tom. The Imperial Post: The Meyers, the Grahams & the Paper that Rules Washington. (Illus.). 304p. 1983. 14.95 (ISBN 0-688-01919-6). Morrow.

Oppenheim, S. Chesterfield & Shields, Carrington. Newspapers & the Antitrust Laws. 531p. 1982. 35.00 (ISBN 0-87215-476-9). Michie-Bobbs.

Sibley, Marilyn M. Lone Stars & State Gazettes: Texas Newspapers Before the Civil War. LC 82-45898. (Illus.). 408p. 1983. 21.50 (ISBN 0-89096-149-2). Tex A&M Univ Pr.

Walker, Martin. Powers of the Press: Twelve of the World's Influential Newspapers. 416p. 1983. 20.00 (ISBN 0-8298-0659-8). Pilgrim NY.

NEWSPAPERS–BIBLIOGRAPHY

Early English Newspapers, Bibliography & Guide to the Microfilm Collection. Date not set. price not set (ISBN 0-89235-076-8). Res Pubns Conn.

NEWSPAPERS–DIRECTORIES

Syndicated Columnists Directory. 30.00 (ISBN 0-913046-14-0). Public Relations.

Weaver, Maureen. Viewpoints: A Directory of Major Newspapers & Their Op-Ed Pollicies. 32p. 1983. pap. 2.00 (ISBN 0-910175-03-9). Campaign Political.

NEWSPAPERS–SECTIONS, COLUMNS, ETC.

Campbell, Tom. The Contemplative Stroller. (Illus.). 96p. 1982. pap. 4.95 (ISBN 0-9607506-1-4). News Rev Pub.

Hall, Bill, ed. Bill Hall & the Killer Chicken. (Illus.). 102p. 1981. pap. 4.95 (ISBN 0-9607506-0-6). News Rev Pub.

NEWSPAPERS, PUBLISHING OF

see Newspaper Publishing

NEWTON, ISAAC, SIR, 1642-1727

Cohen, I. Bernard. The Newtonian Revolution: With Illustrations of the Transformation of Scientific Ideas. LC 79-18637. (Illus.). 404p. Date not set. pap. 16.95 (ISBN 0-521-27380-3). Cambridge U Pr.

Dobbs, B. J. The Foundations of Newton's Alchemy: Or "The Hunting of the Greene Lyon". LC 74-31795. (Cambridge Paperback Library). (Illus.). 300p. Date not set. pap. 16.95 (ISBN 0-521-27381-1). Cambridge U Pr.

Ipsen, David C. Issac Newton: Reluctant Genius. (Illus.). 96p. 1983. 9.95 (ISBN 0-89490-090-0). Enslow Pubs.

NEWTON, JOHN, 1725-1807

Newton, John. John Newton. (Golden Oldies Ser.). 128p. (Orig.). 1983. pap. 2.95 (ISBN 0-8024-0158-9). Moody.

NEZ PERCE INDIANS

see Indians of North America–The West

NICARAGUA

Booth, John A. The End & the Beginning: The Nicaraguan Revolution. LC 82-2690. (Latin America & the Caribbean Special Studies). 277p. 1982. 25.00 (ISBN 0-89158-939-2); pap. 11.50 (ISBN 0-86531-148-X). Westview.

Skarmeta, Antonio. La Insurreccion. 240p. (Span.). 1982. pap. 8.00 (ISBN 0-910061-05-X). Ediciones Norte.

NICARAGUA–HISTORY

Campaign for Political Rights. U.S. Covert Operations Against Nicaragua: A Public Forum. (Illus.). 95p. pap. 5.00 (ISBN 0-910175-02-0). Campaign Political.

NICHOLAS OF CUSA

see Nicolaus Cusanus, Cardinal, 1401-1464

NICKEL

Betteridge, W. Nickel & its Alloys. 160p. 1977. 29.00x (ISBN 0-686-81991-8, Pub. by Macdonald & Evans). State Mutual Bk.

NICKEL INDUSTRY

Betteridge, W. Nickel & its Alloys. 160p. 1977. 29.00x (ISBN 0-686-81991-8, Pub. by Macdonald & Evans). State Mutual Bk.

NICOLAUS CUSANUS, CARDINAL, 1401-1464

Hopkins, Jasper. Nicholas of Cusa on God As Not-Other: Translation & an Appraisal of De Li Non Aliud. 2nd ed. LC 82-73976. Date not set. Repr. of 1979 ed. text ed. 20.00 (ISBN 0-938060-26-0). Banning Pr.

NIDOLOGY

see Birds–Eggs and Nests

NIETZSCHE, FRIEDRICH WILHELM, 1844-1900

Bohlmann, Otto. Yeats & Nietzsche: An Exploration of Major Nietzschean Echoes in the Writings of William Butler Yeats. 240p. 1981. 39.00x (ISBN 0-333-27601-9, Pub. by Macmillan England). State Mutual Bk.

Deleuze, Gilles & Tomlinson, Hugh. Nietzsche & Philosophy. (European Perspectives Ser.). 275p. 1983. text ed. 25.00. Columbia U Pr.

Knight, G. Wilson. Christ & Nietzsche: An Essay in Poetic Wisdom. 1982. 25.00 (ISBN 0-8495-3135-7). Arden Lib.

Mencken, Henry L. The Philosophy of Friedrich Nietzsche. 325p. 1982. pap. 7.00 (ISBN 0-939482-05-3). Noontide.

Nietzsche, Friedrich. Basic Writings of Nietzsche. Kaufmann, Walter, ed. & tr. 9.95 (ISBN 0-394-60406-7). Modern Lib.

NIGERIA–BIBLIOGRAPHY

Jegede, Oluremi. Bibliography on the Constitutions of Nigeria. LC 81-83448. 72p. 1981. pap. 15.00 (ISBN 0-379-20739-7). Oceana.

Jegede, Oluremi, compiled by. Nigerian Legal Bibliography. 320p. Date not set. lib. bdg. 50.00 (ISBN 0-379-20801-6). Oceana.

NIGERIA–ECONOMIC CONDITIONS

Nafziger, E. Wayne. The Economics of Political Instability: The Nigerian-Biafran War. 210p. 1982. 19.50 (ISBN 0-86531-932-4). Westview.

Nigeria: Business Opportunities in the Nineteen Eighties. 288p. 425.00x (ISBN 0-686-99847-2, Pub. by Metra England). State Mutual Bk.

Political Processes & Regional Development Planning in Nigeria. (UNCRD Working Paper: No. 82-7). 1983. pap. 6.00 (ISBN 0-686-43301-7, CRD 144, UNCRD). Unipub.

Zartman, I. William, ed. The Political Economy of Nigeria. 304p. 1983. 30.95 (ISBN 0-03-061476-7); pap. 13.95 (ISBN 0-03-061827-4). Praeger.

NIGERIA–HISTORY

Isichei, Elizabeth. A History of Nigeria. LC 81-12342. (Illus., Orig.). 1983. text ed. 35.00x (ISBN 0-582-64331-7); pap. text ed. 10.95x (ISBN 0-582-64330-9). Longman.

Isichel, Elizabeth, ed. Studies in the History of the Plateau State, Nigeria. 224p. 1981. 75.00x (ISBN 0-333-26931-4, Pub. by Macmillan England). State Mutual Bk.

NIGERIA–HISTORY–CIVIL WAR, 1967-1969

Nafziger, E. Wayne. The Economics of Political Instability: The Nigerian-Biafran War. 210p. 1982. 19.50 (ISBN 0-86531-932-4). Westview.

NIGERIA–JUVENILE LITERATURE

Emecheta, Buchi. The Wrestling Match. LC 82-177750. 74p. (gr. 6-10). 7.95 (ISBN 0-8076-1060-7); pap. 4.95 (ISBN 0-8076-1061-5). Braziller.

NIGERIA–POLITICS AND GOVERNMENT

Dent, Martin. Nigeria: The Politics of Military Rule. 200p. 1983. text ed. 30.00x (ISBN 0-7146-3138-8, F Cass Co). Biblio Dist.

Mba, Nina E. Nigerian Women Mobilized: Women's Political Activity in Southern Nigeria, 1900-1965. LC 82-15477. (Illus.). xii, 348p. 1982. pap. 12.95x (ISBN 0-87725-148-7). UCB Intl Studies.

Nafziger, E. Wayne. The Economics of Political Instability: The Nigerian-Biafran War. 210p. 1982. 19.50 (ISBN 0-86531-932-4). Westview.

Niven, Rex. Nigerian Kaleidoscope: Memoirs of a Colonial Servant. 1982. 25.00 (ISBN 0-208-02008-X, Archon Bks). Shoe String.

Nwabueze, B. O. The Presidential Constitution of Nigeria. LC 82-47637. 558p. 1982. 45.00x (ISBN 0-312-64032-3). St Martin.

Political Processes & Regional Development Planning in Nigeria. (UNCRD Working Paper: No. 82-7). 1983. pap. 6.00 (ISBN 0-686-43301-7, CRD 144, UNCRD). Unipub.

Zartman, I. William, ed. The Political Economy of Nigeria. 304p. 1983. 30.95 (ISBN 0-03-061476-7); pap. 13.95 (ISBN 0-03-061827-4). Praeger.

NIGERIA–SOCIAL CONDITIONS

Amadi, Elechi. Ethics in Nigerian Culture. 128p. (Orig.). 1982. pap. text ed. 7.50 (ISBN 0-435-89030-1). Heinemann Ed.

Kirk-Greene, Anthony H. Mutumin Kirkii: The Concept of the Good Man in Hausa. (Hans Wolff Memorial Lecture Ser.). (Orig.). 1974. pap. text ed. 3.00 (ISBN 0-941934-08-X). Ind U Afro-Amer Arts.

Watts, Michael J. Silent Violence: Food, Famine, & Peasantry in Northern Nigeria. LC 82-13384. (Illus.). 500p. 1983. text ed. 38.50x (ISBN 0-520-04323-5). U of Cal Pr.

NIGHT IN LITERATURE

Hamilton, Morse. Who's Afraid of the Dark? 32p. pap. 2.25 (ISBN 0-380-82883-9, Camelot). Avon.

NIGHT STICKS

see Truncheons

NIHILISM

see also Anarchism and Anarchists; Russia–History–19th Century; Terrorism

Fandozzi, Phillip R. Nihilism & Technology: A Heideggerian Investigation. LC 82-17337. 158p. (Orig.). 1983. lib. bdg. 19.25 (ISBN 0-8191-2825-2); pap. text ed. 8.75 (ISBN 0-8191-2826-0). U Pr of Amer.

NIKON CAMERA

see Cameras–Types–Nikon

NILE RIVER AND VALLEY

Moorehead, Alan. The White Nile. LC 82-48896. (Illus.). 254p. 1983. pap. 12.95 (ISBN 0-394-71445-8, Vin). Random.

NIMITZ, CHESTER WILLIAM, 1885-1966

Driskill, Frank A. & Casad, Dede. Admiral of the Hills: Biography of Chester W. Nimitz. 1983. 11.95 (ISBN 0-89015-364-7). Eakin Pubns.

NIN, ANAIS, 1903-

Deduck, Patricia A. Realism, Reality & the Fictional Theory of Alain Robbe-Grillet & Anais Nin. LC 82-13549. 118p. 1982. lib. bdg. 19.00 (ISBN 0-8191-2719-1); pap. text ed. 8.25 (ISBN 0-8191-2720-5). U Pr of Amer.

NINETEENTH CENTURY

Pinkney, David H. Nineteenth Century, Eighteen Fifteen to Nineteen Fourteen. 1979p. 1979. pap. text ed. 2.95x (ISBN 0-88273-325-7). Forum Pr IL.

NISEI

see Japanese in the United States

NITRATES

Breimer, T. Environmental Factors & Cultural Measures Affecting the Nitrate of Spinach. 1982. pap. text ed. 22.00 (ISBN 90-247-3053-8, Pub. by Martinus Nijhoff Netherlands). Kluwer Boston.

NITROGEN

West, N. E. & Skujins, J., eds. Nitrogen in Desert Ecosystems. LC 78-17672. (US-IBP Synthesis Ser.: Vol. 9). 307p. 1978. 31.50 (ISBN 0-87933-333-2). Hutchinson Ross.

NITROGEN–FIXATION

Postgate, J. R. Fundamentals of Nitrogen Fixation. LC 82-4182. (Illus.). 200p. Date not set. price not set (ISBN 0-521-24169-3); pap. price not set (ISBN 0-521-28494-5). Cambridge U Pr.

NITROGEN COMPOUNDS

see also Alkaloids

Robertson, C. P. & Herrera, R. Nitrogen Cycling in Ecosystems of Latin America & the Caribbean. 1982. 65.00 (ISBN 0-686-38400-8, Pub. by Martinus Nijhoff Netherlands). Kluwer Boston.

NITROGEN FIXATION

see Nitrogen–Fixation

NITROSO COMPOUNDS

see also Chemical Reactions

Scanlan, Richard A. & Tannenbaum, Steven R., eds. N-Nitroso Compounds. (ACS Symposium Ser.: No. 174). 1981. write for info. (ISBN 0-8412-0667-8). Am Chemical.

NITROUS OXIDE

Smith, W. D. Under the Influence: A History of Nitrous Oxide & Oxygen Anaesthesia. 208p. 1982. 40.00 (ISBN 0-333-31681-9, Pub. by Macmillan England). State Mutual Bk.

NIXON, RICHARD MILHOUS, PRES. U. S., 1913-

Ehrlichman, John. Witness to Power: The Nixon Years. 1982. pap. 3.95 (ISBN 0-671-45995-3). PB.

NO PLAYS

Tsukui, Nobuko. Ezra Pound & Japanese Noh Plays. LC 82-23833. 132p. (Orig.). 1983. lib. bdg. 18.75 (ISBN 0-8191-2987-9); pap. text ed. 8.25 (ISBN 0-8191-2988-7). U Pr of Amer.

NOAH

Petersen, Mark E. Noah & the Flood. 97p. 1982. 6.95 (ISBN 0-87747-935-6). Deseret Bk.

NOBILITY

see also Heraldry

also subdivision Nobility under names of countries, e.g. France-Nobility

Ruvigny & Raineval, Melville, eds. Ruvigny's Titled Nobility of Europe: An International Peerage, or "Who's Who" of the Sovereigns, Princes & Nobles of Europe. 1605p. 1980. Repr. of 1914 ed. 112.50x (ISBN 0-85011-028-9). Intl Pubns Serv.

NOISE

see also Industrial Noise; Noise Control

Miller, Richard K. Noise & Energy. (Illus.). 134p. text ed. 45.00 (ISBN 0-89671-022-X). Southeast Acoustics.

Stephens, Irving E. & Barnes, Dorothy L. A Bibliography of Noise for 1977-1981. LC 72-87107. (Bibliography of Noise Ser.). 177p. 1983. 22.50x (ISBN 0-686-83742-8). Whitston Pub.

White, R. G., et al. Noise & Vibration. 866p. 1982. 122.95x (ISBN 0-470-27553-7). Halsted Pr.

Yang, S. J. Low-Noise Electrical Motors. (Monographs in Electrical & Electronic Engineering). (Illus.). 112p. 1981. 34.50x (ISBN 0-19-859332-5). Oxford U Pr.

NOISE, ELECTRONIC

see Electronic Noise

NOISE, RANDOM

see Random Noise Theory

NOISE CONTROL

Bragdon, Clifford R. Municipal Noise Legislation. text ed. 45.00 (ISBN 0-89671-018-1). Southeast Acoustics.

Hickling, Robert & Kamal, Mounir M. Engine Noise: Excitation, Vibration, & Radiation. (General Motors Research Symposia Ser.). 490p. 1982. 62.50x (ISBN 0-306-41168-7, Plenum Pr). PLenum Pub.

International Conference on Noise Control Engineering. The Inter-Noise Eighty-Two: Proceedings, 2 Vol. set. 55.00 (ISBN 0-686-37431-2). Noise Control.

Miller, Richard. Noise Control Solutions for the Stone Industry. (Illus.). 90p. pap. text ed. 45.00 (ISBN 0-89671-028-9). Southeast Acoustics.

Miller, Richard K. Corporate Noise Impast Assessment Manual. 1981. pap. text ed. 55.00 (ISBN 0-89671-029-7). Southeast Acoustics.

--Noise Control for Construction. (Illus.). 140p. text ed. 55.00 (ISBN 0-89671-023-8). Southeast Acoustics.

--Noise Control Solutions for Printing & Publishing. (Illus.). 77p. 1981. pap. text ed. 45.00 (ISBN 0-89671-026-2). Southeast Acoustics.

--Noise Control Solutions for the Food Industry. (Illus.). 110p. text ed. 45.00 (ISBN 0-89671-034-3). Southeast Acoustics.

--Noise Control Solutions for the Food Industry, Vol. II. (Illus.). 120p. 1981. pap. text ed. 45.00 (ISBN 0-89671-024-6). Southeast Acoustics.

--Noise Control Solutions for the Footwear Industry. 90p. pap. text ed. 45.00 (ISBN 0-89671-027-0). Southeast Acoustics.

--Noise Control Solutions for the Glass Industry. 120p. pap. text ed. 90.00 (ISBN 0-89671-016-5). Southeast Acoustics.

--Noise Control Solutions for the Metal Products Industry. (Illus.). 120p. text ed. 45.00 (ISBN 0-89671-031-9). Southeast Acoustics.

--Noise Control Solutions for the Metal Products Industry, Vol. II. (Illus.). 120p. pap. text ed. 45.00 (ISBN 0-89671-021-1). Southeast Acoustics.

--Noise Control Solutions for the Paper Industry. (Illus.). 80p. text ed. 45.00 (ISBN 0-89671-033-5). Southeast Acoustics.

--Noise Control Solutions for the Textile Industry. (Illus.). 90p. text ed. 45.00 (ISBN 0-89671-035-1). Southeast Acoustics.

--Noise Control Solutions for the Wood Products Industry. 80p. text ed. 45.00 (ISBN 0-89671-032-7). Southeast Acoustics.

--Power Plant Noise Control. (Illus.). 130p. pap. text ed. 65.00 (ISBN 0-89671-019-X). Southeast Acoustics.

Smith, Timothy J. Combustion Noise Control. (Illus.). 180p. pap. text ed. 45.00 (ISBN 0-89671-042-4). Southeast Acoustics.

NOISE POLLUTION

Bragdon, Clifford R. Municipal Noise Legislation. text ed. 45.00 (ISBN 0-89671-018-1). Southeast Acoustics.

Hill, Gladwin. Noise-The Most Ubiquitous of All Pollutions: What's Being Done to Tone It Down? (Vital Issues, Vol. XXVIII 1978-79: No. 3). 0.50. Ctr Info Am.

Miller, Richard K. Industrial Noise Update. (Illus.). 87p. 1981. pap. text ed. 30.00 (ISBN 0-89671-025-4). Southeast Acoustics.

NOMADS

Galaty, John G. & Salzman, Philip C., eds. Change & Development in Nomadic & Pastoral Societies. (International Studies in Sociology & Social Anthropology: Vol. 33). v, 173p. 1982. pap. write for info. (ISBN 90-04-06587-3). E J Brill.

Man, J. Jungle Nomads of Equador: The Waorani. (Peoples of the Wild Ser.). 1982. write for info. (ISBN 0-7054-0704-7, Pub. by Time-Life). Silver.

NOMENCLATURE

see Names

NOMS DE PLUME

see Anonyms and Pseudonyms

NON-ALIGNMENT

see Neutrality

NONCONFORMITY

see Conformity

NON-EUCLIDEAN GEOMETRY

see Geometry, Non-Euclidean

NONFERROUS METAL INDUSTRIES

Gill, C. B. Non-Ferrous Extractive Metallurgy. LC 79-28696. 346p. 1980. 49.95x (ISBN 0-471-05980-3, Pub. by Wiley-Interscience). Wiley.

NONFERROUS METALS

see also Nonferrous Metal Industries

Maple, M. B. & Fischer, O., eds. Superconductivity in Ternary Compounds II: Superconductivity & Magnetism. (Topics in Current Physics: Vol. 34). (Illus.). 335p. 1982. 32.00 (ISBN 0-387-11814-4). Springer-Verlag.

NON-FORMAL EDUCATION

Population Education in Non-Formal Education & Development Programmes. 260p. 1981. pap. 12.25 (ISBN 0-686-82543-8, UB107, UNESCO Regional Office). Unipub.

NONFOSSIL FUELS

see Synthetic Fuels

NONLINEAR DIFFERENTIAL EQUATIONS

see Differential Equations, Nonlinear

NONLINEAR MECHANICS

Hagedorn, Peter. Non-Linear Oscillations. (Engineering Science Ser.). (Illus.). 308p. 1982. pap. 19.95 (ISBN 0-19-856156-3). Oxford U Pr.

Morawetz, C. S. Lectures on Nonlinear Waves & Shocks. (Tata Institute Lectures on Mathematics). 137p. 1982. pap. 6.70 (ISBN 0-387-10830-0). Springer-Verlag.

NONLINEAR PROGRAMMING

Ben-Israel, Adi, et al. Optimality in Nonlinear Programming: A Feasible Directions Approach. LC 80-36746. (Pure & Applied Mathematics Ser.). 144p. 1981. 24.95 (ISBN 0-471-08057-8, Pub. by Wiley-Interscience). Wiley.

NONLINEAR THEORIES

see also Differential Equations, Nonlinear; System Analysis

Ansorge, R., et al, eds. Iterative Solution of Nonlinear Systems of Equations, Oberwolfach, FRG, 1982: Proceedings. (Lecture Notes in Mathematics: Vol. 953). 202p. 1983. pap. 12.00 (ISBN 0-387-11602-8). Springer-Verlag.

Aubin, T. Nonlinear Analysis on Manifolds: Monge-Ampere Equations. (Grundlehren der mathematischen Wiszenschaften Ser.: Vol. 252). 204p. 1983. 29.50 (ISBN 0-387-90704-1). Springer-Verlag.

Doebner, H. D. & Palev, T. D., eds. Twistor Geometry & Non-Linear Systems: Proceedings, Primorsko, Bulgaria, 1980. (Lecture Notes in Mathematics Ser.: Vol. 970). 216p. 1983. pap. 11.50 (ISBN 0-387-11972-8). Springer-Verlag.

Goessel, M. Nonlinear Time-Discrete Systems: A General Approach by Nonlinear Superposition. (Lecture Notes in Control & Information Science: Vol. 41). 112p. 1983. pap. 8.00 (ISBN 0-387-11914-0). Springer-Verlag.

Lakshmikantham, V., ed. Nonlinear Phenomena in Mathematical Science: (Symposium) LC 82-20734. 1982. 94.50 (ISBN 0-12-434170-5). Acad Pr.

Reintjes, John F., ed. Nonlinear Optical Parametric Processes in Liquids & Gases. LC 82-11603. Date not set. price not set (ISBN 0-12-585980-5). Acad Pr.

Singh, S. P. & Burry, J. H., eds. Nonlinear Analysis & Applications. (Lecture Notes in Pure & Applied Mathematics: Vol. 80). (Illus.). 488p. 49.75 (ISBN 0-8247-1790-2). Dekker.

Woodroofe, M. Nonlinear Renewal Theory in Sequential Analysis. LC 81-84856. (CBMS-NSF Regional Conference Ser.: No. 39). v, 119p. 1982. 14.50 (ISBN 0-89871-180-0). Soc Indus Appl Math.

NONNUTRITIVE SWEETNERS

see also Sugar Substitutes

Business Communications Staff. Sugar, Sweeteners & Substitutes. 1982. 1250.00 (ISBN 0-89336-091-0, C-005). BCC.

The U. S. Sweetener Industry. 1981. 475.00 (ISBN 0-686-38423-7, 140). Busn Trend.

NONPROFIT CORPORATIONS

see Corporations, Nonprofit

NON-RESISTANCE TO GOVERNMENT

see Government, Resistance to

NONSELFGOVERNING TERRITORIES

see Colonies

NONSENSE-VERSES

Lear, Edward. An Edward Lear Alphabet. LC 82-10037. (Illus.). 32p. (gr. k-3). 1983. 9.50 (ISBN 0-688-00964-6); PLB 9.12 (ISBN 0-688-00965-4). Lothrop.

NON-SUPPORT

see Support (Domestic Relations)

NONVERBAL COMMUNICATION

see also Personal Space

Bellak & Baker. Reading Faces. 1983. pap. 3.50 (ISBN 0-553-22851-X). Bantam.

Caro, Mike. Caro's Book of Tells: Poker Body Language. 275p. 1983. 16.95 (ISBN 0-914314-04-1). Gambling Times.

Donaghy, William C. Our Silent Language: An Introduction to Nonverbal Communication. (Comm Comp). (Illus.). 54p. 1980. pap. text ed. 2.95x (ISBN 0-89787-304-1). Gorsuch Scarisbrick.

Feldman, Robert S., ed. Development of Nonverbal Behavior in Children. (Illus.). 315p. 1983. 27.50 (ISBN 0-387-90716-5). Springer-Verlag.

Katz, Albert M. & Katz, Virginia T. Foundations of Nonverbal Communication: Readings, Exercises, & Commentary. LC 82-10729. (Orig.). 1983. pap. price not set (ISBN 0-8093-1070-8). S Ill U Pr.

Malandro, Loretta A. & Barker, Larry L. Nonverbal Communication. 400p. Date not set. pap. text ed. 13.95 (ISBN 0-201-05336-5). A-W.

Rapoport, Amos. The Meaning of the Built Environment: A Non-Verbal Communication Approach. 200p. 1982. 25.00 (ISBN 0-8039-1892-5); pap. 12.50 (ISBN 0-8039-1893-3). Sage.

Wiemann, John M. & Harrison, Randall P., eds. Nonverbal Interaction. (Sage Annual Reviews of Communication Research: Vol. 11). (Illus.). 320p. 1983. 25.00 (ISBN 0-8039-1930-1); pap. 12.50 (ISBN 0-8039-1931-X). Sage.

NONVIOLENCE

see also Passive Resistance

Culliton, Joseph. Non-Violence-Central to Christian Spirituality: Perspectives from Scriptures to the Present. LC 82-7964. (Toronto Studies in Theology: Vol. 8). 312p. 1982. 39.95x (ISBN 0-88946-964-4). E Mellen.

Nakhre, A. Social Psychology of Non-Violent Action: A Study of Three Satyagrahas. 207p. 1982. text ed. 15.50x (ISBN 0-391-02761-1, Pub. by Chanakya India). Humanities.

Nakhre, Amrot. Social Psychology of Nonviolent Action: A Study of Three Satyagrahas. 1982. 15.00x (ISBN 0-8364-0897-7, Pub. by Chanakya). South Asia Bks.

NON-VIOLENT NON-COOPERATION

see Passive Resistance

NON-WAGE PAYMENTS

see also Old Age Pensions; Profit-Sharing; Social Security; Welfare Work in Industry

American Institute of Certified Public Accountants. Audit & Accounting Guide: Audits of Employee Benefit Plans. 1983. write for info. Am Inst CPA.

Contemporary Benefit Issues & Administration: Answers to Questions on Subject Matter, CEBS Course 10. 4th ed. 123p. 1982. pap. 15.00 (ISBN 0-89154-189-6). Intl Found Employ.

Contemporary Benefit Issues & Administration: Learning Guide, CEBS Course 10. 4th ed. 1982. spiral binding 18.00 (ISBN 0-89154-188-8). Intl Found Employ.

Contemporary Benefit Issues & Administration: Readings, CEBS Course 10, 2 Vols. 4th ed. 1982. spiral binding 20.00 (ISBN 0-89154-190-X). Intl Found Employ.

Contemporary Legal Environment of Employee Benefit Plans: Answers to the Questions on Subject Matter, CEBS Course 5. 4th ed. 113p. 1982. pap. text ed. 15.00 (ISBN 0-89154-175-6). Intl Found Employ.

Contemporary Legal Environment of Employee Benefit Plans: Learning Guide, CEBS Course 5. 4th ed. 1982. spiral binding 18.00 (ISBN 0-89154-176-4). Intl Found Employ.

Doyle, Alfreda C. Creative Suggestions on Obtaining Company Benefits for a Small Business. 26p. 1983. pap. text ed. 6.95 (ISBN 0-910811-21-0). Center Self.

Foote, Andrea & Erfurt, John C. Cost Effectiveness of Occupational Employee Assistance Programs: Test of an Evaluation Method. 110p. 1978. 6.00 (ISBN 0-87736-328-5). U of Mich Inst Labor.

Griffes, Ernest J., ed. Employee Benefits Programs: Management, Planning & Control. 250p. 1983. 30.00 (ISBN 0-686-83835-1). Dow Jones-Irwin.

Hieb, Elizabeth A., ed. Textbook for Employee Benefit Plan Trustees, Administrators & Advisors 1981: Proceedings, Vol. 23. 322p. 1982. text ed. 30.00 (ISBN 0-89154-187-X). Intl Found Employ.

McCaffery, Robert M. Managing the Employee Benefits Program. rev. ed. 256p. 1983. 29.95 (ISBN 0-8144-5760-6). Am Mgmt Assns.

Matthews, Joseph & Berman, Dorothy. Your Rights & Benefits over Fifty-Five. 224p. 1983. pap. 11.95 (ISBN 0-201-05539-2). A-W.

Nektarios, Miltiadis. Public Pensions, Capital Formation, & Economic Growth. Replica ed. 175p. 1982. softcover 20.00 (ISBN 0-86531-936-7). Westview.

OECD. Marginal Employment Subsidies. 98p. pap. 8.50 (ISBN 92-64-12374-1). OECD.

Rudman, Jack. Compensation Claims Clerk. (Career Examination Ser.: C-866). (Cloth bdg. avail. on request). pap. 8.00 (ISBN 0-8373-0866-6). Natl Learning.

--Compensation Claims Examiner Trainee. (Career Examination Ser.: C-879). (Cloth bdg. avail. on request). pap. 10.00 (ISBN 0-8373-0879-8). Natl Learning.

--Principal Worker's Compensation Review Analyst. (Career Examination Ser.: C-310). (Cloth bdg. avail. on request). pap. 14.00 (ISBN 0-8373-0310-9). Natl Learning.

Soltow, Martha J. & Gravelle, Susan. Worker Benefits: Industrial Welfare in America 1900-1935. LC 82-25494. 242p. 1983. 16.50 (ISBN 0-8108-1614-8). Scarecrow.

Wallace, Marc J., Jr. & Fay, Charles H. Compensation Theory & Practice. 304p. 1982. pap. text ed. 11.95x (ISBN 0-534-01399-6). Kent Pub Co.

Wright, Becky A. Collection of Employer Contributions: Institute Proceedings, May 10-13, 1982, Las Vegas. 103p. (Orig.). 1982. pap. 10.00 (ISBN 0-89154-196-9). Intl Found Employ.

Wright, Becky A., ed. Benefit Plan Professionals Institute: Proceedings, June 20-23, 1982, Lake Tahoe, Nev. 82p. (Orig.). 1982. pap. 10.00 (ISBN 0-89154-199-3). Intl Found Employ.

NORFOLK, ENGLAND

Robinson, John M. The Dukes of Norfolk. (Illus.). 288p. 1983. 29.95 (ISBN 0-19-215869-4). Oxford U Pr.

NORFOLK ISLAND

Hoare, Merval. Norfolk Island: An Outline of Its History, 1774-1981. 3rd ed. LC 82-4719. (Illus.). 188p. 1983. pap. 8.95 (ISBN 0-7022-1941-X). U of Queensland Pr.

NORMANDY

Keegan, John. Six Armies in Normandy: From D-Day to the Liberation of Paris. 1983. pap. 6.95 (ISBN 0-14-005293-3). Penguin.

NORMANDY-DESCRIPTION AND TRAVEL

Michelin Green Guide: Normandie. (Green Guide Ser.). (Fr.). 1983. pap. write for info. (ISBN 2-06-003451-5). Michelin.

Roberts, Nesta. Companion Guide to Normandy. (Illus.). 317p. 1983. 15.95 (ISBN 0-13-154583-3); pap. 7.95 (ISBN 0-13-154575-2). P-H.

NORSE LANGUAGES

see Scandinavian Languages

NORTH AFRICA

see Africa, North

NORTH AMERICA-DESCRIPTION AND TRAVEL-GUIDEBOOKS

Leon, Vicki & Haag, Michael. The Moneywise Guide to North America. (Illus.). 400p. (Orig.). 1983. pap. 9.95 (ISBN 0-89141-172-0). Presidio Pr.

Simpson, Norman T. Country Inns & Back Roads: North America. 18th ed. LC 70-615664. (Illus.). 486p. (Orig.). 1983. pap. 8.95 (ISBN 0-912944-75-7). Berkshire Traveller.

NORTH AMERICA-DISCOVERY AND EXPLORATION

see America-Discovery and Exploration

NORTH AMERICA-HISTORY

Lunny, Robert M. Early Maps of North America. (Illus.). 48p. 1961. pap. 4.00 (ISBN 0-686-81821-0). NJ Hist Soc.

NORTH AMERICA-HISTORY-BIBLIOGRAPHY

Research Libraries of the New York Public Library & Library of Congress. Bibliographic Guide to North American History: 1982. 1983. lib. bdg. 150.00 (ISBN 0-8161-6978-0, Biblio Guides). G K Hall.

NORTH AMERICA-MAPS

Lunny, Robert M. Early Maps of North America. (Illus.). 48p. 1961. pap. 4.00 (ISBN 0-686-81821-0). NJ Hist Soc.

Martin, Robert S. & Martin, James C. Contours of Discovery: Pointed Maps Delineating the Texas & Southern Chapters in the Cartographic History of North America, 1513-1930. LC 82-83547. 35.00 (ISBN 0-87611-058-8). Tex St Hist Assn.

NORTH AMERICAN INDIANS

see Indians of North America

NORTH ATLANTIC REGION

Reader's Digest Editors. North American Wildlife. LC 81-50919. (Illus.). 576p. 1982. 20.50 (ISBN 0-89577-102-0). RD Assn.

NORTH ATLANTIC TREATY ORGANIZATION

Buteaux, Paul. Strategy, Doctrine, & the Politcs of Alliance: Theatre Nuclear Force Modernization in NATO. Replica ed. 150p. 1982. softcover 17.00 (ISBN 0-86531-940-5). Westview.

Chichester, Michael & Wilkinson, John. The Uncertain Ally. 264p. 1982. text ed. 38.00x (ISBN 0-566-00534-4). Gower Pub Ltd.

Foreign Policy Research Institute Staff. The Three Percent Solution & the Future of NATO. 118p. (Orig.). 1981. pap. 6.95 (ISBN 0-910191-02-6). For Policy Res.

Golden, James R. NATO Burden-Sharing. (Washington Papers: No. 96). 120p. 6.95 (ISBN 0-03-062769-9). Praeger.

Grose, Peter. The United States, NATO & Israeli-Arab Peace. (Seven Springs Reports). 1980. pap. 2.00 (ISBN 0-943006-11-2). Seven Springs.

Hartley, Keith. NATO Arms Co-Operation: A Study in Economics & Politics. 240p. 1983. text ed. 35.00x (ISBN 0-04-341022-7). Allen Unwin.

Henderson, Nicholas. The Birth of NATO. 135p. 1983. lib. bdg. 17.50 (ISBN 0-86531-466-7). Westview.
Johnson, U. Alexis & Packard, George R. The Common Security Interests of Japan, The United States & NATO. 38p. pap. 6.00x (ISBN 0-87855-873-X). Transaction Bks.
Kissinger, Henry A. The Troubled Partnership: A Re-appraisal of the Atlantic Alliance. LC 82-15533. xii, 266p. 1982. Repr. of 1965 ed. lib. bdg. 25.00x (ISBN 0-313-23219-9, KIPA). Greenwood.
Taylor, Trevor. Defense, Technology & International Integration. 290p. 1982. 30.00x (ISBN 0-312-19115-4). St Martin.
Tucker. Atlantic Alliance & Its Critics. 204p. 1983. 24.95 (ISBN 0-03-062888-1); pap. 12.75 (ISBN 0-03-063352-4). Praeger.
Vigor, P. H. Soviet Blitzkrieg Theory. LC 82-10421. 200p. 1983. 22.50x (ISBN 0-312-74755-1). St Martin.
Vogt, John W. Improving the NATO Force Capabilities. 12p. pap. 1.00 (ISBN 0-87855-742-3). Transaction Bks.

NORTH CAROLINA

Clayton, Thomas H. Close to the Land: The Way We Lived in North Carolina, 1820-1870. Nathans, Sydney, ed. LC 82-20143. (The Way We Lived in North Carolina Ser.). (Illus.). viii, 98p. 1983. 11.95 (ISBN 0-8078-1551-9); pap. 6.95 (ISBN 0-8078-4103-X). U of NC Pr.

NORTH CAROLINA-DESCRIPTION AND TRAVEL

Fenn, Elizabeth A. & Wood, Peter H. Natives & Newcomers: The Way We Lived in North Carolina Before 1770. Nathans, Sydney, ed. LC 82-20128. (The Way We Lived in North Carolina Ser.). (Illus.). viii, 98p. 1983. 11.95 (ISBN 0-8078-1549-7); pap. 6.95 (ISBN 0-8078-4101-3). U of NC Pr.
Nathans, Sydney. The Quest for Progress: The Way We Lived in North Carolina, 1870-1920. LC 82-20133. (The Way We Lived in North Carolina Ser.). (Illus.). viii, 108p. 1983. 11.95 (ISBN 0-8078-1552-7); pap. 6.95 (ISBN 0-8078-4104-8). U of NC Pr.
Watson, Harry L. An Independent People: The Way We Lived in North Carolina, 1770-1820. Nathans, Sydney, ed. LC 82-20098. (The Way We Lived in North Carolina Ser.). (Illus.). viii, 118p. 1983. 11.95 (ISBN 0-8078-1550-0); pap. 6.95 (ISBN 0-8078-4102-1). U of NC Pr.

NORTH CAROLINA-GENEALOGY

Crow, Judson O. McDowell County, North Carolina, Land Entry Abstracts 1843-1869, Vol. 1. LC 82-20499. 504p. 1983. pap. 25.00 (ISBN 0-87152-365-5). Reprint.
Fleming, John K. History of the Third Creek Presbyterian Church. 1967. 8.00 (ISBN 0-686-37869-5). Synod NC Church.
Kerr, Mary H. Warren County, North Carolina, Records: Abstracted Records of Colonial Bute County, North Carolina, 1764-1779, & Bute County Marriages, Vol. I. LC 82-20498. 104p. 1983. Repr. of 1967 ed. 25.00 (ISBN 0-87152-366-3). Reprint.
Topkins, Robert M. Marriage & Death Notices from the Western Carolinian (Salisbury, North Carolina) 1820-1842: An Indexed Abstract. LC 82-20495. 264p. 1983. Repr. of 1975 ed. 22.50 (ISBN 0-87152-367-1). Reprint.

NORTH CAROLINA-HISTORY

Bell, John L., Jr. Hard Times: Beginnings of the Great Depression in North Carolina, 1929-1933. (Illus.). xi, 87p. 1982. pap. 3.00 (ISBN 0-86526-196-2). NC Archives.
Butler, Lindley S. Rockingham County: A Brief History. 92p. 1982. pap. 2.00 (ISBN 0-86526-198-9). NC Archives.
Fenn, Elizabeth A. & Wood, Peter H. Natives & Newcomers: The Way We Lived in North Carolina Before 1770. Nathans, Sydney, ed. LC 82-20128. (The Way We Lived in North Carolina Ser.). (Illus.). viii, 98p. 1983. 11.95 (ISBN 0-8078-1549-7); pap. 6.95 (ISBN 0-8078-4101-3). U of NC Pr.
Morgan, David T., ed. The John Gray Blount Papers, Vol. IV: 1803-1833. (Illus.). xxxiv, 662p. 1982. 28.00 (ISBN 0-86526-189-X). NC Archives.
Nathans, Sydney. The Quest for Progress: The Way We Lived in North Carolina, 1870-1920. LC 82-20133. (The Way We Lived in North Carolina Ser.). (Illus.). viii, 108p. 1983. 11.95 (ISBN 0-8078-1552-7); pap. 6.95 (ISBN 0-8078-4104-8). U of NC Pr.
Schumann, Marguerite. Tar Heel Sights: Guide to North Carolina's Heritage. LC 82-49030. (Illus.). 192p. 1983. pap. 8.95 (ISBN 0-914788-64-7). East Woods.
Watson, Harry L. An Independent People: The Way We Lived in North Carolina, 1770-1820. Nathans, Sydney, ed. LC 82-20098. (The Way We Lived in North Carolina Ser.). (Illus.). viii, 118p. 1983. 11.95 (ISBN 0-8078-1550-0); pap. 6.95 (ISBN 0-8078-4102-1). U of NC Pr.

NORTH CAROLINA-POLITICS AND GOVERNMENT

Hudlin, Richard A. & Farouk, Brimah K. State of North Carolina's Procurement Policies & Minority Business Enterprises. 1981. 1.00 (ISBN 0-686-38011-8). Voter Ed Proj.
Langley, Michael. State of North Carolina's Procurement Policies & Minority Business Enterprises. 1980. 1.00 (ISBN 0-686-38008-8). Voter Ed Proj.
League of Women Voters Staff. North Carolina: Our State Government. (Illus.). 116p. 1982. lib. bdg. 12.95 (ISBN 0-89089-029-3). Carolina Acad.
Towe, William H. Barriers to Black Political Participation in North Carolina. 1972. 3.00 (ISBN 0-686-37999-3). Voter Ed Proj.

NORTH CAROLINA-POLITICS AND GOVERNMENT-1775-1865

Kruman, Marc W. Parties & Politics in North Carolina, 1836 to 1865. LC 82-20364. 384p. 1983. text ed. 37.50x (ISBN 0-8071-1041-8); pap. text ed. 14.95x (ISBN 0-8071-1061-2). La State U Pr.

NORTH CAROLINA-SOCIAL CONDITIONS

Parramore, Thomas C. Express Lanes & Country Roads: The Way We Lived in North Carolina, 1920-1970. Nathans, Sydney, ed. LC 82-21747. (The Way We Lived in North Carolina Ser.). (Illus.). 120p. 11.95 (ISBN 0-8078-1553-5); pap. 6.95 (ISBN 0-8078-4105-6). U of NC Pr.
Wilson, Emily H. Hope & Dignity: Older Black Women of the South. 1983. write for info. (ISBN 0-87722-302-5). Temple U Pr.

NORTH CAROLINA-SOCIAL LIFE AND CUSTOMS

Fenn, Elizabeth A. & Wood, Peter H. Natives & Newcomers: The Way We Lived in North Carolina Before 1770. Nathans, Sydney, ed. LC 82-20128. (The Way We Lived in North Carolina Ser.). (Illus.). viii, 98p. 1983. 11.95 (ISBN 0-8078-1549-7); pap. 6.95 (ISBN 0-8078-4101-3). U of NC Pr.
Nathans, Sydney. The Quest for Progress: The Way We Lived in North Carolina, 1870-1920. LC 82-20133. (The Way We Lived in North Carolina Ser.). (Illus.). viii, 108p. 1983. 11.95 (ISBN 0-8078-1552-7); pap. 6.95 (ISBN 0-8078-4104-8). U of NC Pr.
Watson, Harry L. An Independent People: The Way We Lived in North Carolina, 1770-1820. Nathans, Sydney, ed. LC 82-20098. (The Way We Lived in North Carolina Ser.). (Illus.). viii, 118p. 1983. 11.95 (ISBN 0-8078-1550-0); pap. 6.95 (ISBN 0-8078-4102-1). U of NC Pr.

NORTH SEA

Suendermann, J. & Lenz, W., eds. North Sea Dynamics. (Illus.). 670p. 1983. 41.00 (ISBN 0-387-12013-0). Springer-Verlag.

NORTHERN BUDDHISM

see Mahayana Buddhism

NORTHERN IRELAND

Barroitt, Denis P. & Carter, Charles F. The Northern Ireland Problem: A Study in Group Relations. LC 82-15568. 163p. 1982. Repr. of 1962 ed. lib. bdg. 22.50x (ISBN 0-313-23262-8, BANI). Greenwood.
Maltby, Arthur. The Government of Northern Ireland Nineteen Twenty-Two to Seventy-Two: A Catalogue & Breviate of Parliamentary Papers. 258p. 1974. text ed. 30.00x (ISBN 0-7165-2151-2, Pub by Irish Academic Pr). Biblio Dist.
Rea, Desmond. Political Co-operation in Divided Societies: A Series of Papers Relevant to the Conflict in Northern Ireland. 1982. 79.00x (ISBN 0-7171-1162-8, Pub. by Gill & Macmillan Ireland). State Mutual Bk.
Rea, Desmond, ed. Northern Ireland, the Republic of Ireland & Great Britain: Problems of Political Co-Operation. 300p. 1982. 50.00x (Pub. by Macmillan England). State Mutual Bk.

NORTHMEN IN AMERICA

see America-Discovery and Exploration

NORTHWEST, NEW

see Northwestern States

NORTHWEST, OLD-DESCRIPTION AND TRAVEL

Golovin, Pavel N. Civil & Savage Encounters: The Worldly Travel Letters of an Imperial Russian Navy Officer, 1860-61. Dmytryshyn, Basil & Crownhart-Vaughan, E. A., trs. from Rus. (North Pacific Studies Ser.). (Illus.). 208p. (Orig.). 1982. 21.95 (ISBN 0-87595-067-1, Western Imprints); pap. 14.95 (ISBN 0-87595-095-7, Western Imprints). Oreg Hist Soc.

NORTHWEST, OLD-HISTORY

Holm, Bill, annotations by. Soft Gold: The Fur Trade & Cultural Exchange on the Northwest Coast of America. LC 82-81739. (Illus.). 312p. (Orig.). 1982. 29.95 (ISBN 0-87595-107-4, Western Imprints); pap. 19.95 (ISBN 0-87595-108-2, Western Imprints). Oreg Hist Soc.
Ogg, Frederic A. Old Northwest. 1919. text ed. 8.50x (ISBN 0-686-83654-5). Elliots Bks.

NORTHWEST, PACIFIC-DESCRIPTION AND TRAVEL

Ford, Phyllis. Provocative Facts. 120p. 1982. 7.00 (ISBN 0-686-84025-9). U OR Ctr Leisure.
Plumb, Gregory A. Waterfalls of the Pacific Northwest. (Illus.). 224p. 1983. pap. 9.95 (ISBN 0-916076-60-1). Writing.

NORTHWEST, PACIFIC-DESCRIPTION AND TRAVEL-GUIDEBOOKS

Martin, Wanda J. & MaClean, Jelorma. Car Free Connexions: Discover the Northwest by Boat, Plane, Train, & Bus. (Illus.). 112p. (Orig.). 1983. pap. 6.95 (ISBN 0-940546-00-0). Connexions.
Rankin, Jake & Rankin, Marni. The Getaway Guide 0778997xx: Short Vacations in the Pacific Northwest. revised ed. LC 82-18784. (2nd). 223p. 1983. pap. 9.95 (ISBN 0-686-43073-5). Pacific Search.

NORTHWEST, PACIFIC-HISTORY

Davenport, Marge. Northwest Glory Days. (Illus.). 208p. (Orig.). 1983. pap. 6.95 (ISBN 0-938274-02-3). Paddlewheel.
Karamanski, Theodore J. Fur Trade & Exploration: Opening the Far Northwest, Eighteen Twenty-One to Eighteen Fifty-Two. LC 82-40453. (Illus.). 360p. 1983. 22.95 (ISBN 0-8061-1833-4). U of Okla Pr.

NORWAY-POLITICS AND GOVERNMENT

Olsen, Johan P., ed. Organized Democracy: Political Institutions in a Welfare State-the Case of Norway. 272p. 1983. pap. 26.00x (ISBN 82-00-06442-5, Universitet). Columbia U Pr.

NORWEGIAN LANGUAGE

see also Danish Language

Berlitz Editors. Norwegian for Travel Cassettepack. 1983. 14.95 (ISBN 0-02-962870-9, Berlitz); cassette incl. Macmillan.

NOSE, ACCESSORY SINUSES OF

Draf, W. Endoscopy of the Paranasal Sinuses: Technique-Typical Findings-Theraputic Possibilities. Pohl, W. E., tr. from Ger. (Illus.). 112p. 1983. 27.50 (ISBN 0-387-11258-8). Springer-Verlag.

NOSTRADAMUS (MICHEL DE NOTRE DAME), 1503-1566

Erickstad, H. G. The Prophecies of Nostradamus in Historical Sequence from A.D. 1550-2005. LC 80-53660. 218p. 1982. 10.00 (ISBN 0-533-04862-1). Vantage.
Leoni, Edgar. Nostradamus: Life & Literature. 1982. 16.00 (ISBN 0-517-38809-X). Nosbooks.
Roberts, Henry C., tr. The Complete Prophecies of Nostradamus. (Illus.). 352p. 1983. 10.95 (ISBN 0-517-54956-5). Crown.

NOTARIES

Pennsylvania Association of Notaries. Practical Guide for Notaries Public in Pennsylvania. 18th ed. LC 63-11110. 1982. pap. write for info. Penn Assoc Not.
Wolcotts-Legal Forms. California Notary's Journal. 202p. 1982. 11.95 (ISBN 0-910531-00-5); pap. 7.95 (ISBN 0-910531-01-3). Wolcotts.

NOTE-TAKING

Dochterman, Delores. The Art of Taking Minutes. LC 82-42639. 208p. 1982. 12.95 (ISBN 0-9609526-0-8). Snyder Pub Co.

NOTICE OF DISMISSAL

see Employees, Dismissal of

NOTRE DAME, MICHEL DE, 1503-1566

see Nostradamus (Michel de Notre Dame), 1503-1566

NOVELISTS

see Authors

NOVELS

see Fiction; Plots (Drama, Novel, etc.)

NUCLEAR CHEMISTRY

Here are entered works on the application of chemical techniques to the study of the structure and properties of atomic nuclei, their transformations and reactions. Works on the chemical effects of high energy radiation on matter are entered under Radiation chemistry. Works on the chemical properties of radioactive substances and their use in chemical studies are entered under Radiochemistry.

see also Nuclear Physics; Radiation Chemistry; Radiochemistry

Analytical Chemistry in Energy Technology. Analytical Chemistry in Nuclear Technology: Proceedings of the 25th ORNL Conference. Lyon, W. S., ed. LC 81-70867. (Illus.). 402p. 1982. 29.95 (ISBN 0-250-40469-9). Ann Arbor Science.

NUCLEAR ENERGY

see Atomic Energy

NUCLEAR ENGINEERING

see also Atomic Power; Nuclear Fuels; Nuclear Reactors; Radioisotopes

Cadwell, Jerry J. Nuclear Facility Threat Analysis & Tactical Response Procedures. (Illus.). 120p. 1983. 22.50x (ISBN 0-398-04778-2). C C Thomas.
Harms, A. A. & Heindler, M. Nuclear Energy Synergetics: An Introduction to Conceptual Models of Integrated Nuclear Energy Systems. 252p. 1982. 35.00x (ISBN 0-306-40951-8, Plenum Pr). Plenum Pub.
King, J. R., Jr., ed. Engineering & Business-Converting Engineers to Businessmen. LC 82-83563. 1982. pap. text ed. 11.00 (ISBN 0-87262-342-4). Am Soc Civil Eng.
Lamarsh, John R. Introduction to Nuclear Engineering. 2nd ed. LC 82-8678. (AW-Nuclear Science & Engineering Ser.). (Illus.). 652p. Date not set. text ed. price not set (ISBN 0-201-14200-7). A-W.

NUCLEAR ENGINEERING-SAFETY MEASURES

see also Radioactive Waste Disposal

OECD. Critical Flow Modeling in Nuclear Safety. 102p. 1982. pap. 13.00 (ISBN 92-64-12366-0). OECD.

NUCLEAR EXCITATION

Demas, J. N., ed. Excited State Lifetime Measurements: Monograph. LC 82-16253. 288p. 1983. price not set (ISBN 0-12-208920-0). Acad Pr.

NUCLEAR FUEL ELEMENTS

OECD. Dry Storage of Spent Fuel Elements. 272p. 1982. pap. 17.00 (ISBN 92-64-02351-8). OECD.

NUCLEAR FUELS

see also Nuclear Fuel Elements; Reactor Fuel Reprocessing; Thorium; Uranium

Graves, Harvey W. Nuclear Fuel Management. LC 78-19119. 1979. text ed. 37.95x (ISBN 0-471-03136-4). Wiley.
Kessler, G. Nuclear Fission Reactors: Potential Role & Risk of Converters & Breeders. (Topics in Energy Ser.). (Illus.). 257p. 1983. 37.00 (ISBN 0-387-81713-1). Springer-Verlag.
OECD Staff. Nuclear Energy & Its Fuel Cycle: Prospects to 2025. 262p. 1982. pap. 24.00 (ISBN 92-64-12306-7). OECD.
Silvennoinen, P. Nuclear Fuel Cycle Optimization: Methods & Modelling Techniques. (Illus.). 138p. 1982. 25.00 (ISBN 0-08-027310-6). Pergamon.

NUCLEAR MAGNETIC RESONANCE

Mooney, E. F. & Webb, G. A., eds. Annual Reports on NMR Spectroscopy, 2 Vols. Date not set. Vol. 13. 99.50 (ISBN 0-12-505313-4); Vol. 14. price not set (ISBN 0-12-505314-2). Acad Pr.
Webb, G. A. Nuclear Magnetic Resonance, Vol. 10. 372p. 1982. 199.00x (ISBN 0-85186-332-9, Pub. by Royal Soc Chem England). State Mutual Bk.

NUCLEAR MEDICINE

see also Radioactivity-Physiological Effect; Radioisotopes in Pharmacology

Bulcke, J. A. & Baert, A. L. Clinical & Radiological Aspects of Myopathies: CT Scanning-EMG-Radio-Isotopes. (Illus.). 187p. 1983. 56.00 (ISBN 0-387-11443-2). Springer-Verlag.
Ell, P. J. & Walton, S. Radionuclide Ventricular Function Studies: Correlation with ECG, Echo & X-ray Data. 1982. text ed. 99.50 (ISBN 90-247-2639-5, Pub. by Martinus Nijhoff Netherlands). Kluwer Boston.
Hoffer. Year Book of Nuclear Medicine 1983. 1983. 45.00 (ISBN 0-8151-4527-6). Year Bk Med.
Leach, K. G. The Physical Aspects of Radioisotopic Organ Imaging. 1976. 25.00x (ISBN 0-686-99803-0, Pub. by Brit Inst Radiology England). State Mutual Bk.
Mettler, Fred A. & Guiberteau, Milton J., eds. Essentials of Nuclear Medicine Imaging. Date not set. price not set (ISBN 0-8089-1538-X). Grune.
Nuclear Medicine-Factors Influencing the Choice & Use of Radionuclides in Diagnosis & Therapy: NCRP Report 70. 1982. 12.00 (ISBN 0-913392-57-X). NCRP Pubns.
Nuclear Techniques in the Study of Parasitic Infections. (Proceedings Ser.). 631p. 1983. pap. 73.50 (ISBN 92-0-010282-4, ISP 596, IAEA). Unipub.
Osbakken, Mary D., et al. Techniques, Diagnostics & Advances in Nuclear Cardiology. (Illus.). 344p. 1983. text ed. 53.50x (ISBN 0-398-04772-3). C C Thomas.
Pretschner, D. P. Engymetry & Personal Computing in Nuclear Medicine. (Lecture Notes in Medical Informatics: Vol. 18). 133p. 1983. pap. 11.50 (ISBN 0-387-11598-6). Springer-Verlag.
Raynaud, C., ed. Nuclear Medicine & Biology Advances: Proceedings of the Third World Congress on Nuclear Medicine & Biology, August 29 - September 2, 1982, Paris, France, 7 Vols. 3685p. 1982. Set. 300.00 (ISBN 0-08-029814-1). Pergamon.
Sorenson, James A., ed. Physics in Nuclear Medicine: The Slide Set. 1982. slide set 295.00 (ISBN 0-8089-1530-4). Grune.

NUCLEAR PARTICLES

see Particles (Nuclear Physics)

NUCLEAR PHYSICS

see also Atomic Energy; Chemistry, Physical and Theoretical; Collisions (Nuclear Physics); Nuclear Chemistry; Nuclear Engineering; Nuclear Excitation; Nuclear Reactors; Particle Accelerators; Particles (Nuclear Physics); Radiobiology; Scattering (Physics)

Bates, David & Bederson, Benjamin. Advances in Atomic & Molecular Physics, Vol. 18. (Serial Publication). 1982. 83.50 (ISBN 0-12-003818-8); Lib. ed. 64.00 (ISBN 0-12-003888-9); Microfiche 44.80 (ISBN 0-12-003889-7). Acad Pr.
Crasemann, Bernd, ed. Xray & Atomic Inner-Shell Physics, 1982. LC 82-74075. (AIP Conf. Proc. Ser.: No. 94). 802p. 1982. lib. bdg. 44.50 (ISBN 0-88318-193-2). Am Inst Physics.
Harms, A. A. & Heindler, M. Nuclear Energy Synergetics: An Introduction to Conceptual Models of Integrated Nuclear Energy Systems. 252p. 1982. 35.00x (ISBN 0-306-40951-8, Plenum Pr). Plenum Pub.
Hellwege, K. H., ed. Molecular Constants. (Landolt-Boerstein Ser.: Group II, Vol. 14, Subvol. A). 790p. 1983. 542.00 (ISBN 0-387-11365-7). Springer-Verlag.
Satchler, George R. Direct Nuclear Reactions. (International Ser. of Monographs on Physics). (Illus.). 750p. 1982. 89.00x (ISBN 0-19-851269-4). Oxford U Pr.
Shirokov, Y. M. & Yudin, N. P. Nuclear Physics, 2 vols. 749p. 1982. Set. 16.95 (ISBN 0-8285-2451-3, Pub. by Mir Pubs USSR). Imported Pubns.

NUCLEAR POLARIZATION

see Polarization (Nuclear Physics)

NUCLEAR POWER

see Atomic Power

NUCLEAR PRESSURE VESSELS

Nichols, R. W., ed. Advances in Non-Destructive Examination for Structural Integrity: Proceedings of the International Seminar on Non-Destructive Examination in Relation to Structural Integrity, 2nd, Paris, Aug. 24-25, 1981. (Illus.). 464p. 1982. 90.25 (ISBN 0-85334-158-3, Pub. by Applied Sci England). Elsevier.

NUCLEAR REACTORS

see also Breeder Reactors; Reactor Fuel Reprocessing

Bender, F. Underground Siting of Nuclear Power Plants: Internationales Symposium, 1981. (Illus.). 409p. (Ger. & Eng.). 1982. pap. text ed. 63.25 (ISBN 3-510-65108-1). Lubrecht & Cramer.

Cameron, I. R. Nuclear Fission Reactors. 410p. 1982. 42.50x (ISBN 0-306-41073-7, Plenum Pr). PLenum Pub.

Jaeger, T. A. & Roley, B. A., eds. International Conference on Structural Mechanics in Reactor Technology: Third Proceedings, London, 1975, 8 pts. in 5 vols. 1976. Set. pap. 213.00 (ISBN 0-444-10974-9). Elsevier.

Jaeger, T. A. & Roleyr, B. A., eds. International Conference on Structural Mechanics in Reactor Technology: Proceedings, Fourth, San Francisco, 1977, 13 Vols. (SMIRT 1977). 1978. Set. pap. 298.00 (ISBN 0-686-43416-1). Elsevier.

Kessler, G. Nuclear Fission Reactors: Potential Role & Risk of Converters & Breeders. (Topics in Energy Ser.). (Illus.). 257p. 1983. 37.00 (ISBN 0-387-81713-1). Springer-Verlag.

Nuclear Negotiations: Reassesing Arms Control Goals in U. S.-Soviet Relations. LC 82-83390. (Symposia Ser.). 204p. 1982. 7.95 (ISBN 0-89940-004-3). L B J Sch Pub Aff.

Steele, L. E. Assuring Structural Integrity of Steel Reactor Pressure Vessels. 1980. 41.00 (ISBN 0-85334-906-1, Pub. by Applied Sci England). Elsevier.

Steele, L. E. & Stahlkopf, K. E. Structural Integrity of Light Water Reactor Components. (Illus.). 405p. 1982. 82.00 (ISBN 0-85334-157-5, Pub. by Applied Sci England). Elsevier.

Watts, Richard J. Elementary Principles of Diffusion: Theory & the Chain Reaction. (Illus.). 307p. (Orig.). 1982. pap. 25.00x (ISBN 0-9609112-0-0). Desperation Pr.

Weisman, Joel, ed. Elements of Nuclear Reactor Design. 526p. 1983. text ed. 34.50 (ISBN 0-89874-518-7). Krieger.

NUCLEAR REACTORS–ACCIDENTS

Glendenning, Norman R., ed. Direct Nuclear Reactions: Monograph. LC 82-24365. Date not set. price not set (ISBN 0-12-286320-8). Acad Pr.

Gray, Mike & Rosen, Ira. The Warning: Accident at Three Mile Island. 288p. 1983. pap. 7.95 (ISBN 0-8092-5547-2). Contemp Bks.

Mueller, U. & Guenther, C., eds. Post Accident Debris Cooling: Proceedings of the Fifth Post Accident Heat Removal Information Exchange Meeting, 1982, Nuclear Research Center Karlsrube. (Illus.). 364p. (Orig.). 1983. pap. text ed. 30.00x (ISBN 3-7650-2034-6). Sheridan.

Smith, Robert C. How to Survive a Nuclear Disaster. 1983. pap. 3.95 (ISBN 0-8217-1131-8). Zebra.

NUCLEAR REACTORS–COOLING

Mueller, U. & Guenther, C., eds. Post Accident Debris Cooling: Proceedings of the Fifth Post Accident Heat Removal Information Exchange Meeting, 1982, Nuclear Research Center Karlsrube. (Illus.). 364p. (Orig.). 1983. pap. text ed. 30.00x (ISBN 3-7650-2034-6). Sheridan.

NUCLEAR REACTORS–FUEL

see Nuclear Fuels

NUCLEAR REACTORS–FUEL ELEMENTS

see Nuclear Fuel Elements

NUCLEAR REACTORS–SAFETY MEASURES

Dhillon, Balbir S. Power System Reliability, Safety & Management. LC 82-72852. (Illus.). 350p. 1983. 39.95 (ISBN 0-250-40548-2). Ann Arbor Science.

Smeathers, Bryan K. Prepare for & Survive a Nuclear Attack! LC 82-73105. (Illus.). 120p. (Orig.). 1983. pap. write for info. (ISBN 0-910629-00-5). Audubon Pub Co.

NUCLEAR REACTOR FUEL REPROCESSING

see Reactor Fuel Reprocessing

NUCLEAR SCATTERING

see Scattering (Physics)

NUCLEAR SPECTROSCOPY

Dawson, J. B. & Sharp, B. L., eds. Annual Reports on Analytical Atomic Spectroscopy, Vol. 10. 342p. 1982. 165.00x (ISBN 0-85186-717-0, Pub. by Royal Soc Chem England). State Mutual Bk.

NUCLEAR WARFARE

see Atomic Warfare

NUCLEAR WASTES

see Radioactive Wastes

NUCLEAR WEAPONS

see Atomic Weapons

NUCLEIC ACIDS

see also Nucleotides

Cohn, Waldo, ed. Progress in Nucleic Acid Research & Molecular Biology, Vol. 27. (Serial Publication). 320p. 1982. 37.00 (ISBN 0-12-540027-6); Lib. ed. 48.50 (ISBN 0-686-81656-0); Microfische 26.00 (ISBN 0-12-540099-3). Acad Pr.

Parthier, B. & Boulter, D., eds. Nucleic Acids & Proteins in Plants II: Structure, Biochemistry, & Physiology of Nucleic Acids. (Encyclopedia of Plant Physiology: Vol. 14 B). (Illus.). 774p. 1983. 125.00 (ISBN 0-387-11140-9). Springer-Verlag.

Progress in Nucleic Acid Research, Vol. 28. (Serial Publication). Date not set. price not set (ISBN 0-12-540028-4); price not set Lib. ed. (ISBN 0-12-540100-0). Acad Pr.

NUCLEONS

see Particles (Nuclear Physics)

NUCLEOSIDES

Nass, G., ed. Modified Nucleosides & Cancer: Workshop, Freiburg, FRG, 1981. (Recent Results in Cancer Research Ser.: Vol. 84). (Illus.). 440p. 1983. 50.50 (ISBN 0-387-12024-6). Springer-Verlag.

NUCLEOTIDES

see also Nucleosides

Everse, Johannes, et al, eds. The Pyridine Nucleotide Coenzymes. 416p. 1982. 46.00 (ISBN 0-12-244750-6). Acad Pr.

NUCLEUS (CELLS)

see Cells

NUCLEUS OF THE ATOM

see Nuclear Physics

NUDE IN ART

see also Anatomy, Artistic; Photography of the Nude

Fraser, Gordon. Bill Brandt: Nudes 1945-1980. 132p. 1982. 55.00x (ISBN 0-86092-064-X, Pub. by Fraser Bks). State Mutual Bk.

NUMBER CONCEPT- JUVENILE LITERATURE

Frank Schaffer Publications. Beginning Activities with Numbers. (Getting Ready for Kindergarten Ser.). (Illus.). 24p. (ps-k). 1980. workbook 1.29 (ISBN 0-86734-014-2, FS 3027). Schaffer Pubns.

Frank Schaffer Publications, Inc. Numbers. (Help Your Child Learn Ser.). (Illus.). 24p. (ps-2). 1978. workbook 1.29 (ISBN 0-86734-002-9, FS 3003). Schaffer Pubns.

NUMBER GAMES

see Arithmetic-Study and Teaching; Mathematical Recreations

NUMBER STUDY

see Arithmetic-Study and Teaching

NUMBER SYMBOLISM

see Symbolism of Numbers

NUMBER THEORY

see Numbers, Theory of

NUMBERS, THEORY OF

see also Algebraic Number Theory; Forms, Quadratic; Goedel's Theorem; Groups, Theory of; Numeration

Bertin, M. J., ed. Seminaire de Theorie des Nombres: Paris 1980-1982. (Progress in Mathematics Ser.: Vol. 22). 360p. 1982. text ed. 20.00 (ISBN 3-7643-3066-X). Birkhauser.

Christine, Lois. The Secret Life of Numbers. 208p. (Orig.). 1983. pap. 8.00 (ISBN 0-936878-06-1). Lorian Pr.

Koblitz, Neal, ed. Modern Trends in Number Theory Related to Fermat's Last Theorem. (Progress in Mathematics Ser.: Vol. 26). 470p. 1982. text ed. 30.00 (ISBN 3-7643-3104-6). Birkhauser.

Pogorzelski, Henry A. & Ryan, William J. Foundations of Semiological Theory of Numbers. 590p. (Orig.). 1982. pap. text ed. 29.95 (ISBN 0-89101-053-X). U Maine Orono.

Sierpinski, W. Two Hundred & Fifty Problems in Elementary Number Theory. 1970. 21.50 (ISBN 0-444-00071-2). Elsevier.

NUMERALS

see also Numeration; Symbolism of Numbers

Flegg, Graham. Numbers: Their History & Meaning. LC 82-19134. (Illus.). 288p. 1983. 14.95 (ISBN 0-8052-3847-6). Schocken.

NUMERATION

see also Numerals

Marzollo, Jean & Savage, Beth. Number & Number Values. (gr. k-2). pap. 1.50 (ISBN 0-8224-4183-7). Pitman.

NUMERATION–JUVENILE LITERATURE

Hillman, Priscilla. The Merry Mouse Counting & Colors Book. LC 81-43652. (Illus.). 14p. (gr. k-3). 1983. 3.95 (ISBN 0-385-17916-2). Doubleday.

Miller, Jane. Farm Counting Book. (Illus.). 32p. (ps-3). 1983. 6.95 (ISBN 0-13-304790-3). P-H.

Walt Disney Productions. Mickey's Counting Book. LC 82-18554. (Disney's Wonderful World of Reading: No. 51). (Illus.). 32p. (ps-1). 1983. 4.95 (ISBN 0-394-85735-6); PLB 4.99 (ISBN 0-394-95735-0). Random.

NUMERICAL ANALYSIS

see also Digital Filters (Mathematics); Finite Element Method; Iterative Methods (Mathematics); Numerical Calculations; Numerical Integration

Brebbia, C. A., ed. Boundary Element Methods in Engineering, Southampton, England 1982: Proceedings. (Illus.). 649p. 1982. 59.00 (ISBN 0-387-11819-5). Springer-Verlag.

Calmet, J., ed. Computer Algebra: EUROCAM 82, Marseille, France 1982. (Lecture Notes in Computer Science: Vol. 144). 301p. 1983. pap. 14.00 (ISBN 0-387-11607-9). Springer-Verlag.

Cavanagh, J. Digital Computer Arithmetic. 352p. 1983. 31.95 (ISBN 0-686-84225-1, C). McGraw.

Cavanaugh, Joseph. Digital Computer Arithmetic. (Computer Science Ser.). (Illus.). 352p. 1983. 31.95 (ISBN 0-07-010282-1). McGraw.

Chess Skill in Men & Medicine. 2nd ed. (Texts & Monographs in Computer Science). (Illus.). 280p. 1983. 14.00 (ISBN 0-387-90790-4); pap. write for info. (ISBN 0-387-90815-3). Springer-Verlag.

Cryer, Colin W. Numerical Functional Analysis. (Monographs on Numerical Analysis). 592p. 1982. 39.00 (ISBN 0-19-853410-8). Oxford U Pr.

Hackbusch, W. & Trottenberg, U., eds. Multigrid Methods, Koeln-Porz, FRG, 1981: Proceedings. (Lecture Notes in Mathematics Ser.: Vol. 960). 652p. 1983. pap. 28.80 (ISBN 0-387-11955-8). Springer-Verlag.

Pachner, J. Handbook of Numerical Analysis Applications: Programs for Engineers & Scientists. 672p. 1983. 65.00 (ISBN 0-07-048057-5, P&RB). McGraw.

Swartzlander, E. E., Jr., ed. Computer Arithmetic. LC 78-14397. (Benchmark Papers in Electrical Engineering & Computer Science: Vol. 21). 400p. 1979. 56.50 (ISBN 0-87933-350-2). Hutchinson Ross.

Thompson, Thomas M. From Error-Correcting Codes Through Spere Packing to Simple Groups. (Carus Monograph: No. 21). Date not set. text ed. price not set (ISBN 0-88385-023-0). Math Assn.

Turner, P. R., ed. Topics in Numerical Analysis: Proceedings, S.E.R.C. Summer School, Lancaster, 1981. (Lecture Notes in Mathematics Ser.: Vol. 965). 202p. 1983. pap. 11.00 (ISBN 0-387-11967-1). Springer-Verlag.

Vandergraft, James S., ed. Introduction to Numerical Computations. LC 82-16252. (Computer Science & Applied Mathematics Ser.). 369p. 1983. price not set (ISBN 0-12-711356-8). Acad Pr.

Watson, W. A. Numerical Analysis. 240p. 1981. pap. text ed. 13.95 (ISBN 0-7131-2817-8). E Arnold.

NUMERICAL ANALYSIS LABORATORIES

see Computation Laboratories

NUMERICAL CALCULATIONS

see also Computation Laboratories; Digital Filters (Mathematics)

Thompson, J. F., ed. Numerical Grid Generation: Proceedings of the Symposium on the Numerical Generation of Curvilinear Coordinate Systems & Use in the Numerical Solution of Partial Differential Equations, Nashville, Tennessee, April 13-16, 1982. 944p. 1982. 95.00 (ISBN 0-444-00757-1, North Holland). Elsevier.

NUMERICAL FILTERS

see Digital Filters (Mathematics)

NUMERICAL INTEGRATION

Hammerlin, G., ed. Numerical Integration. (International Series of Numerical Mathematics: Vol. 57). 275p. text ed. 29.95x (ISBN 3-7643-1254-8). Birkhauser.

Hinze, J., ed. Numerical Integration of Differential Equations & Large Linear Systems: Proceedings, Bielfeld, FRG, 1980. (Lecture Notes in Mathematics Ser.: Vol. 968). 412p. 1983. pap. 20.00 (ISBN 0-387-11970-1). Springer-Verlag.

NUMERICAL SEQUENCES

see Sequences (Mathematics)

NUMEROLOGY

see Symbolism of Numbers

NUMISMATICS

see also Medals; Seals (Numismatics)

Kosambi, Damodar D. Indian Numismatics. (Illus.). 159p. 1981. text ed. 25.00x (ISBN 0-86131-018-7, Pub. by Orient Longman Ltd India). Apt Bks.

Mackay, James. Numismatics. 144p. 1982. 25.00x (ISBN 0-584-11017-0, Pub. by Muller Ltd). State Mutual Bk.

NUNS

Hackel, Sergei. Pearl of Great Price: The Life of Mother Maria Skobtsova 1891-1945. rev. ed. LC 81-21356. 160p. 1982. pap. 5.95 (ISBN 0-913836-85-0). St Vladimirs.

Murphy, Paul I. & Arlington, R. Rene. La Popessa. 296p. 1983. 16.50 (ISBN 0-446-51258-3). Warner Bks.

NUREMBERG TRIAL OF MAJOR GERMAN WAR CRIMINALS, 1945-1946

Conot, Robert E. Justice at Nuremberg: The First Comprehensive, Dramatic Account of the Trial of the Leaders. LC 82-48395. (Illus.). 640p. 1983. 19.18i (ISBN 0-06-015117-X, HarpT). Har-Row.

NUREYEV, RUDOLF, 1939-

Barnes, Clive. Nureyev. (Illus.). 272p. 1982. 35.00 (ISBN 0-9609736-2-1). Helene Obolensky Ent.

NURSE AND PATIENT

Luckraft, Dorothy, ed. Black Awareness: Implications for Black Patient Care. LC 75-25301. 43p. 1976. pap. text ed. write for info. (ISBN 0-937126-78-0). Am Journal Nur.

Minnick, Ann. Patient Teaching by Registered Nurses. Kalisch, Philip & Kalisch, Beatrice, eds. LC 82-17623. (Studies in Nursing Management: No. 9). 100p. 1982. 34.95 (ISBN 0-8357-1378-4). Univ Microfilms.

NURSE-PATIENT RELATIONSHIP

see Nurse and Patient

NURSERY RHYMES

see also Children's Poetry

Justus, Fred. Nursery Rhymes. (Early Education Ser.). 24p. (gr. k-1). 1979. wkbk. 5.00 (ISBN 0-686-42865-X, K-2). ESP.

Llimona, Mercedes, illus. Strawberry Shortcake's Favorite Mother Goose Rhymes. LC 82-5204. (Illus.). 48p. (ps-1). 1983. PLB 6.99 (ISBN 0-394-95431-9); pap. 5.95 (ISBN 0-394-85431-4). Random.

Marshak, Samuil & Harms, David. The Merry Starlings. Rottenberg, Dorian, tr. from Rus. LC 82-47725. (Illus.). 24p. (ps-3). 1983. 9.57i (ISBN 0-06-024089-X, HarpJ); PLB 9.89g (ISBN 0-06-024090-3). Har-Row.

Marshall, Ray & Paul, Korky. Jack & Jill. Klimo, Kate, ed. (Illus.). 10p. 1983. 3.95 (ISBN 0-671-46238-5, Little). S&S.

--Sing a Song of Sixpence. Klimo, Kate, ed. (Chubby Pop-Ups Ser.). (Illus.). 10p. (ps-k). 1983. 3.95 (ISBN 0-671-46237-7, Little). S&S.

Nelson, Carolyn. Basic Skills Nursery Rhymes Workbook. (Basic Skills Workbooks). 32p. (gr. k-1). 1983. 0.99 (ISBN 0-8209-0565-8, EEW-6). ESP.

Patz, Nancy. Moses Supposes His Toeses Are Roses: And Seven Other Silly Old Rhymes. LC 82-3099. (Illus.). 32p. (gr. 4-8). 12.95 (ISBN 0-15-255690-7, HJ). HarBraceJ.

Zokeisha. Mother Goose. Klimo, Kate, ed. (Chubby Shape Bks.). (Illus.). 16p. (ps-k). 1983. 2.95 (ISBN 0-671-46127-3, Little). S&S.

NURSERY SCHOOLS

see also Day Care Centers; Education, Preschool

Dwight, Theodore. Sketches of Scenery & Manners in the United States. LC 82-10258. 1983. 30.00x (ISBN 0-8201-1383-2). Schol Facsimiles.

Lombardo, Victor S. & Lombardo, Edith F. Developing & Administering Early Childhood Programs. (Illus.). 224p. 1983. 23.50x (ISBN 0-398-04773-1). C C Thomas.

NURSES–CORRESPONDENCE, REMINISCENCES, ETC.

Van Devanter, Lynda & Morgan, Christopher. Home Before Morning: The Story of an Army Nurse in Vietnam. 1983. 16.95 (ISBN 0-8253-0132-7). Beaufort Bks NY.

NURSES AND NURSING

see also Cancer Nursing; Cardiovascular Disease Nursing; Children-Care and Hygiene; Cookery for the Sick; Diet in Disease; Dieticians; Emergency Nursing; First Aid in Illness and Injury; Geriatric Nursing; Gynecologic Nursing; Home Nursing; Hospitals; Infants-Care and Hygiene; Neurological Nursing; Nurse and Patient; Obstetrical Nursing; Orthopedic Nursing; Pediatric Nursing; Practical Nursing; Psychiatric Nursing; Public Health Nursing; School Nursing; Sick; Surgical Nursing; Tuberculosis Nursing also subdivisions Hospitals, Charities, etc. and Medical and Sanitary Affairs under names of wars, e.g. United States-History-Civil War, 1861-1865-Hospitals, Charities, etc.; World War, 1939-1945-Medical and Sanitary Affairs

Accountability & the Open Curriculum in Baccalaureate Nursing Education. 48p. 1976. 4.50 (ISBN 0-686-38180-7, 15-1628). Natl League Nurse.

AD Graduates: Can They Fit Your System's Needs? 40p. 1978. 4.50 (ISBN 0-686-38360-5, 23-1736). Natl League Nurse.

Aiding Ambulatory Patients. LC 82-21253. (Nursing Photobook Ser.). (Illus.). 160p. 13.95 (ISBN 0-916730-49-2). Intermed Comm.

Anderson, Edith H. & Reed, Suellen B. Innovative Approaches to Baccalaureate Programs in Nursing. 50p. 1979. 4.50 (ISBN 0-686-38271-4, 15-1804). Natl League Nurse.

Ashkenas, Thais L. Aids & Deterrents to the Performance of Associate Degree Graduates in Nursing. (League Exchange Ser.: No. 99). 168p. 1973. 6.95 (ISBN 0-686-38359-1, 23-1465). Natl League Nurse.

Attending Ob-Gyn Patients. LC 82-15627. (Nursing Photobook Ser.). (Illus.). 160p. 13.95 (ISBN 0-916730-48-4). Intermed Comm.

Author Index to NLN Publications. 47p. 1981. 5.95 (ISBN 0-686-38351-6, 41-1849). Natl League Nurse.

Baccalaureate Nursing Education for Registered Nurses: Issues & Approaches. 63p. 1980. 5.50 (ISBN 0-686-38361-3, 15-1812). Natl League Nurse.

Baloff, Marsha. Crosswords for Nurses. Paquet, Judith B., ed. 120p. 1982. 9.95 (ISBN 0-913590-94-0). Slack Inc.

Benedikter, Helen. From Nursing Audit to Multidisciplinary Audit. 45p. 1977. 4.95 (ISBN 0-686-38333-8, 20-1673). Natl League Nurse.

The Board Member in the Community Agency. 32p. 1972. 2.95 (ISBN 0-686-38139-4, 21-1453). Natl League Nurse.

Bonaparte, T. H. & Franzen, William L. Instructional Innovations: Ideals, Issues, Impediments. 165p. 1977. 7.50 (ISBN 0-686-38272-2, 16-1687). Natl League Nurse.

Booth. Nurses Handbook of Investigations. 224p. 1982. pap. text ed. 10.50 (ISBN 0-06-318235-1, Pub. by Har-Row Ltd England). Har-Row.

Bower, F. L. Nursing & the Concept of Loss. (Nursing Concept Modules Ser.). 214p. 1980. 15.95 (ISBN 0-471-04790-2). Wiley.

Boyne, Gil, ed. Hypnosis; New Tool in Nursing Practice. 197p. 1982. 20.00 (ISBN 0-930298-12-8). Westwood Pub Co.

Bristow, Opal & Stickney, Carol. Discharge Planning for Continuity of Care. (League Exchange Ser.: No. 112). 144p. 1976. 5.95 (ISBN 0-686-38206-4, 21-1604). Natl League Nurse.
Budget Management in Baccalaureate Nursing Programs. 59p. 1981. 4.95 (ISBN 0-686-38140-8, 15-1848). Natl League Nurse.
Buehler, Janice A. Nurses & Physicians in Transition. Kalisch, Philip & Kalisch, Beatrice, eds. LC 82-10940. (Studies in Nursing Management: No. 10). 164p. 1982. 39.95 (ISBN 0-8357-1379-2). Univ Microfilms.
Bullough, Bonnie & Bullough, Vern. Nursing Issues & Nursing Strategies for the Eighties. 1983. pap. 17.95 (ISBN 0-8261-4441-1). Springer Pub.
Burns, Kathryn A. Managing the Burn Patient: A Guide for Nurses. LC 82-62402. 1983. write for info. (ISBN 0-913590-97-5). Slack Inc.
Carl, Mary K. & Kramer, Marlene. Curriculum in Graduate Education in Nursing: Part I-Factors Influencing Curriculum in Graduate Education in Nursing. 61p. 1975. 4.95 (ISBN 0-686-38253-6, 15-1596). Natl League Nurse.
Carnegie, Mary E. Disadvantaged Students in R.N. Programs. (League Exchange Ser.: No. 100). 118p. 1974. 6.95 (ISBN 0-686-38365-6, 14-1471). Natl League Nurse.
Carrying Out Special Procedures. (Nursing Photobook Ser.). (Illus.). 160p. 13.95 (ISBN 0-916730-45-X). Intermed Comm.
Challenges: Stepping Stones to Success. 49p. 1981. 4.50 (ISBN 0-686-38141-6, 52-1861). Natl League Nurse.
The Changing Student Population in Diploma Programs. 90p. 1980. 6.50 (ISBN 0-686-38362-1, 16-1811). Natl League Nurse.
Charting a Course for Future Action: For Diploma Programs in Nursing. 46p. 1978. 4.95 (ISBN 0-686-38318-4, 16-1741). Natl League Nurse.
Chater, Shirley. Operation Update: The Search for Rhyme & Reason. 32p. 1976. 3.50 (ISBN 0-686-38326-5, 14-1608). Natl League Nurse.
Child. Organization. 2nd ed. 1983. text ed. 21.00 (ISBN 0-06-318221-1, Pub. by Har-Row Ltd England); pap. text ed. 10.50 (ISBN 0-06-318222-X, Pub. by Har-Row Ltd England). Har-Row.
Chinn, Peggy L. & Jacobs, Maeona K. Theory & Nursing: A Systematic Approach. LC 82-7912. (Illus.). 222p. 1983. pap. text ed. 13.95 (ISBN 0-8016-0961-5). Mosby.
Clark, N. & Peters, M. Scorable Self-Care Evaluation (SSCE) LC 82-61594. 64p. 1983. pap. 16.00 (ISBN 0-913590-95-9). Slack Inc.
Cognitive Dissonance: Interpreting & Implementing Faculty Practice Roles in Nursing Education. 48p. 1980. 4.95 (ISBN 0-686-38310-9, 15-1831). Natl League Nurse.
Collaboration for Quality Health Care: Education of Beginning Practitioners of Nursing & Utilization of Graduates. 111p. 1977. 5.95 (ISBN 0-686-38363-X, 14-1654). Natl League Nurse.
Community Health Nursing: Education & Practice. 97p. 1980. 6.95 (ISBN 0-686-38203-X, 52-1834). Natl League Nurse.
Conflict Management: Flight, Fight, or Negotiate? 41p. 1977. 4.95 (ISBN 0-686-38143-2, 52-1677). Natl League Nurse.
Connolly, Arlene F. & Kelley, Jean. Curriculum in Graduate Education in Nursing: Part III-Development & Improvement of Graduate Education in Nursing. 46p. 1977. 4.50 (ISBN 0-686-38256-0, 15-1679). Natl League Nurse.
Creason, Nancy S. Effects of External Funding: On Instructional Components of Baccalaureate & Higher Degree Nursing Programs. (League Exchange Ser.: No. 119). 74p. 1978. 5.95 (ISBN 0-686-38147-5, 15-1732). Natl League Nurse.
Creating a Positive Work Environment. 106p. 1980. 5.95 (ISBN 0-686-38144-0, 16-1817). Natl League Nurse.
Credentialing in Nursing: Design for a Workshop. 48p. 1980. 4.95 (ISBN 0-686-38319-2, 52-1832). Natl League Nurse.
Criteria & Standards Manual for NLN-APHA Accreditation: Home Health Agencies & Community Nursing Services. 48p. 1980. 3.95 (ISBN 0-686-38131-9). Natl League Nurse.
Curren, Anna M. Clinical Nursing Skills. (Illus.). 370p. 1983. pap. text ed. 21.95 (ISBN 0-918082-02-1). Wallcur Inc.
Current Issues Affecting Nursing as a Part of Higher Education. 58p. 1976. 4.95 (ISBN 0-686-38320-6, 15-1639). Natl League Nurse.
Decade Assessment: Accentuating the Positive. 39p. 1980. 4.95 (ISBN 0-686-38321-4, 52-1841). Natl League Nurse.
DeChow, Georgeen H. & Rines, Alice R. Preparing the Associate Degree Graduate. 71p. 1977. 5.50 (ISBN 0-686-38275-7, 23-1661). Natl League Nurse.
Decision Making Within the Academic Environment. 63p. 1978. 4.95 (ISBN 0-686-38145-9, 15-1719). Natl League Nurse.
The Department Chairperson: Leader & Manager. 36p. 1981. 4.50 (ISBN 0-686-38146-7, 23-1875). Natl League Nurse.
Dickerson, Thelma M. & Dyer, Marilyn. Designing & Building a Curriculum. 98p. 1979. 5.95 (ISBN 0-686-38259-5, 16-1776). Natl League Nurse.
Directory of Career Mobility Programs in Nursing Education: 1975. 263p. 1976. 9.95 (ISBN 0-686-38178-5, 19-1605). Natl League Nurse.
Donnelly, G. F., et al. The Nursing System: Issues, Ethics & Politics. LC 80-12402. 224p. 1980. 13.50 (ISBN 0-471-04441-5). Wiley.
The Emergence of Nursing As a Political Force. 95p. 1979. 5.95 (ISBN 0-686-38345-1, 41-1760). Natl League Nurse.
Epstein, Rhoda & Conley, Virginia. Developing a Master's Program in Nursing. 37p. 1978. 3.95 (ISBN 0-686-38262-5, 15-1747). Natl League Nurse.
Epstein, Rhoda B. & Millsap, Margaret. Coping with Change through Assessment & Evaluation. 102p. 1976. 5.50 (ISBN 0-686-38248-X, 23-1618). Natl League Nurse.
Ercolano, N. Review of Medical Nursing. 1978. text ed. 12.50 (ISBN 0-07-019541-2). McGraw.
Erickson, Helen & Tomlin, Evelyn. Modeling & Role Modeling: A Theory & Paradigm for Nursing. (Illus.). 240p. 1983. text ed. 17.95 (ISBN 0-13-586198-5); pap. 13.95 (ISBN 0-13-586180-2). P-H.
Ethical Issues in Nursing & Nursing Education. 72p. 1980. 5.50 (ISBN 0-686-38322-2, 16-1822). Natl League Nurse.
The Faculty's Role in Policy Development. 88p. 1981. 5.95 (ISBN 0-686-38312-5, 16-1850). Natl League Nurse.
Farley, Venner M. An Evaluative Study of an Open Curriculum: Career Ladder Nursing Program. (League Exchange Ser.: No. 118). 65p. 1978. 5.95 (ISBN 0-686-38181-5, 19-1728). Natl League Nurse.
Financial Management for Schools of Nursing. 113p. 1974. 5.50 (ISBN 0-686-38148-3, 16-1549). Natl League Nurse.
Financial Management of Department of Nursing Services. 32p. 1979. 3.95 (ISBN 0-686-38149-1, 20-1798). Natl League Nurse.
Fitzpatrick, Joyce & Whall, Ann. Conceptual Models of Nursing & Analysis Evaluation: Applications. (Illus.). 352p. 1982. pap. text ed. 21.95 (ISBN 0-89303-233-6). R J Brady.
Fleischman, Marjorie R. Dosage Calculation: Method & Workbook. (League Exchange Ser.: No. 106). 106p. 1975. 5.95 (ISBN 0-686-38188-2, 20-1560). Natl League Nurse.
Focus on Educational Mobility in Nursing: Compilation of 10 Papers. 91p. 1982. pap. 43.95 (ISBN 0-87258-368-6, AHA-154165). Am Hospital.
Forrest, Jane & Watson, Margaret. Practical Nursing & Anatomy for Pupil Nurses. 272p. 1981. pap. text ed. 12.95 (ISBN 0-7131-4392-4). E Arnold.
Franklin, Doris R. Selective & Nonselective Admissions Criteria in Junior College Nursing Programs. (League Exchange Ser.: No. 104). 68p. 1975. 5.50 (ISBN 0-686-38369-9, 23-1561). Natl League Nurse.
French, Peter. Social Skills for Nursing Practice. 260p. 1983. pap. text ed. 17.50x (ISBN 0-7099-1009-6, Pub. by Croom Helm Ltd England). Biblio Dist.
From Student to Worker: The Process & Product. 43p. 1976. 3.95 (ISBN 0-686-38366-4, 23-1657). Natl League Nurse.
Ganong, Joan M. & Ganong, Walter L. Help for the Licensed Practical Nurse. 2nd ed. (Help Series of Management Guides). 71p. 1981. pap. 9.85 (ISBN 0-933036-11-6). Ganong W L Co.
Ganong, Joan M. & Ganong, Warren L. Help with Career Ladders in Nursing. (Help Series of Management Guides). 142p. 1977. pap. 13.75 (ISBN 0-933036-06-X). Ganong W L Co.
--Help with Primary Nursing: Accountability through the Nursing Process. 2nd ed. (Help Series of Management Guides). 90p. 1980. pap. 9.95 (ISBN 0-933036-13-2). Ganong W L Co.
Garfinkel, Robin & Rubens, Yvonne A. The NLN Pre-Nursing & Guidance Examination: A Validation Study. 46p. 1979. 3.95 (ISBN 0-686-38305-2, 17-1788). Natl League Nurse.
Generating Effective Teaching. 81p. 1978. 5.95 (ISBN 0-686-38301-X, 16-1749). Natl League Nurse.
Getting Our Act Together. 74p. 1979. 5.95 (ISBN 0-686-38150-5, 52-1805). Natl League Nurse.
Hamilton, Helen K., ed. Procedures. LC 82-15643. (Nurse's Reference Library). (Illus.). 1000p. 1982. text ed. 23.95 (ISBN 0-916730-40-9). Intermed Comm.
Hamric, Ann B. & Sprose, Judith. The Clinical Nurse Specialist in Theory & Practice. Date not set. price not set (ISBN 0-8089-1519-3). Grune.
Hector, Winifred. Modern Nursing. 7th ed. (Illus.). 596p. 1982. pap. text ed. 32.50x (ISBN 0-433-14218-9). Intl Ideas.
Hoexter, Joan C. & Hayes, Janice E. Curriculum in Graduate Education in Nursing: Part II-Components in the Curriculum Development Process. 64p. 1976. 4.95 (ISBN 0-686-38255-2, 15-1632). Natl League Nurse.
Holmquist, Emily & Sloan, Marjorie. Depth & Scope, Guides for Curriculum in a Technical Nursing Program: A Study for the Determination & Application of Unlimited Depth & Limited Scope in a Technical Nursing Program. (League Exchange Ser.: No. 117). 89p. 1978. 6.95 (ISBN 0-686-38258-7, 23-1697). Natl League Nurse.
Hyman, Ronald T. & Thomson, Robert P. Strategies for Effective Teaching: A Basis for Creativity. 195p. 1975. 6.95 (ISBN 0-686-38277-3, 16-1538). Natl League Nurse.
Instructor Accountability: Issues, Facts, Impact. 208p. 1976. 7.95 (ISBN 0-686-38313-3, 16-1626). Natl League Nurse.
The Issue is Leadership. 128p. 1975. 5.95 (ISBN 0-686-38152-1, 21-1570). Natl League Nurse.
Issues in Diploma Nursing Education in the Eighties. 31p. 1980. 4.95 (ISBN 0-686-38324-9, 14-1599). Natl League Nurse.
Jacobson, Sharol F. & McCrath, H. Marie. Nurses Under Stress. 320p. 1983. 14.95 (ISBN 0-471-07899-9, Pub. by Wiley Med). Wiley.
Johnson, Dorothy E. & King, Imogene M. Theory Development: What, Why, How? 86p. 1978. 5.95 (ISBN 0-686-38281-1, 15-1708). Natl League Nurse.
Jones, D. A. & Lepley, M. Nursing Assessment Across the Life Span. 600p. 1983. 28.95x (ISBN 0-07-032805-6). McGraw.
Joyce, Joan M. Handbook of Critical Care Nursing. Gardner, Alvin f., ed. (Allied Professions Monograph Ser.). 1983. 35.00 (ISBN 0-87527-318-1). Green.
A Judgement of Merit-Evaluation of Programs in Nursing: Applications. 57p. 1979. 4.95 (ISBN 0-686-38302-8, 16-1773). Natl League Nurse.
A Judgement of Merit-Evaluation of Programs in Nursing: Methodology. 75p. 1979. 4.95 (ISBN 0-686-38303-6, 16-1765). Natl League Nurse.
Kaiser, Joan E. A Comparison of Students: Practical Nursing Programs & Students in Associate Degree Nursing Programs. (League Exchange Ser.: No. 109). 78p. 1976. 5.50 (ISBN 0-686-38364-8, 23-1592). Natl League Nurse.
Kemp, Jerrold E. Determining the Plus & Minus Outcomes of Innovation in Nursing Education. 47p. 1977. 4.50 (ISBN 0-686-38261-7, 23-1682). Natl League Nurse.
Kirchhoff, Karin T. Coronary Precautions: A Diffusion Survey. Kalisch, Philip & Kalisch, Beatrice, eds. LC 82-17613. (Studies in Nursing Management: No. 8). 128p. 1982. 34.95 (ISBN 0-8357-1377-6). Univ Microfilms.
Knopf, Lucille. RNs One & Five Years after Graduation. 113p. 1975. 6.95 (ISBN 0-686-38368-0, 19-1535). Natl League Nurse.
Kozier, Barbara & Erb, Glenora. Fundamentals of Nursing. 2nd ed. 1983. 22.95 (ISBN 0-201-11711-8, Med-Nurse); instr's guide avail. (ISBN 0-201-11712-6); wkbk 10.95 (ISBN 0-201-11714-2). A-W.
Lange, Crystal M. Identification of Learning Styles. 32p. 1979. 3.50 (ISBN 0-686-38264-1, 23-1793). Natl League Nurse.
Lewis, Eloise R. & Maszkiewicz, Ruth C. Developing the Functional Role in Master's Education in Nursing. 63p. 1980. 5.50 (ISBN 0-686-38263-3, 15-1840). Natl League Nurse.
Licensure & Credentialing. 47p. 1978. 4.95 (ISBN 0-686-38325-7, 52-1706). Natl League Nurse.
Litwack, Lawrence L. & Forbes, Elizabeth. The Challenge of Clinical Evaluation. 42p. 1979. 4.50 (ISBN 0-686-38284-6, 16-1763). Natl League Nurse.
Lynch, Eleanor A. Evaluation: Principles & Processes. 32p. 1978. 3.50 (ISBN 0-686-38295-1, 23-1721). Natl League Nurse.
Lynch, Eleanor A. & Torres, Gertrude J. Curriculum Evaluation. (Faculty-Curriculum Development Ser.: Pt. II). 52p. 1974. 4.50 (ISBN 0-686-38266-8, 15-1530). Natl League Nurse.
Lyons, John M. & Brown, Elsa L. Analyzing the Cost of Baccalaureate Nursing Education. 32p. 1982. 4.95 (ISBN 0-686-38138-6, 15-1880). Natl League Nurse.
McCaffery. Nursing Management of the Patient with Pain. 1983. pap. text ed. 15.50 (ISBN 0-06-318239-4, Pub. by Har-Row Ltd England). Har-Row.
McGriff, Erline P. & Cooper, Signe. Accountability to the Consumer through Continuing Education in Nursing. 32p. 1974. 3.00 (ISBN 0-686-38242-0, 14-1507). Natl League Nurse.
Maggs, Chistopher. The Origins of General Nursing. 176p. 1983. text ed. 25.25x (ISBN 0-7099-1734-1, Pub. by Croom Helm Ltd England). Biblio Dist.
Management of Conflict. 58p. 1981. 4.95 (ISBN 0-686-38158-0, 16-1859). Natl League Nurse.
Messer, Sandra S. Politics for Nursing: Threat or Opportunity? 31p. 1980. 3.95 (ISBN 0-686-38348-6, 41-1816). Natl League Nurse.
Moseley, H. Jewel & Clift, Virgil A. Cultural Dimensions in the Baccalaureate Nursing Curriculum. 108p. 1977. 5.95 (ISBN 0-686-38249-8, 15-1662). Natl League Nurse.
National League for Nursing. Criteria for Departments of Nursing in Acute Care Settings: A Guide for Self-Appraisal. 2nd, rev. ed. 85p. 1980. 5.95 (ISBN 0-686-38289-7, 20-1714). Natl League Nurse.
--Criteria for Departments of Nursing in Long-Term Care Settings: A Guide for Self-Appraisal. 2nd, rev. ed. 85p. 1980. 5.95 (ISBN 0-686-38291-9, 20-1830). Natl League Nurse.
--Toward Excellence in Nursing Education: A Guide for Diploma School Improvement. 3rd ed. 58p. 1977. cancelled (ISBN 0-686-38282-X, 16-1656). Natl League Nurse.
NLN Nursing Data Book: 1981. 188p. 1981. 12.95 (ISBN 0-686-38354-0, 19-1882). Natl League Nurse.
Nursing Drug Handbook 83. 1000p. 1983. 17.95 (ISBN 0-916730-54-9). Intermed Comm.
The Open Curriculum in Nursing Education: Final Report of the NLN Open Curriculum Study. 465p. 1979. 12.95 (ISBN 0-686-38186-6, 19-1799). Natl League Nurse.
Orque, Modesta S. & Bloch, Bobbie. Ethnic Nursing Care: A Multi-Cultural Approach. (Illus.). 414p. 1983. pap. text ed. 14.95 (ISBN 0-8016-3742-2). Mosby.
Pathways to Quality Care. 42p. 1976. 3.95 (ISBN 0-686-38336-2, 20-1636). Natl League Nurse.
Patient Education. 38p. 1976. 3.95 (ISBN 0-686-38338-9, 20-1633). Natl League Nurse.
Pennington, Elisabeth A. Interdisciplinary Education in Nursing. (League Exchange Ser.: No. 130). 40p. 1981. 4.95 (ISBN 0-686-38273-0, 15-1877). Natl League Nursing.
Personnel Management for Schools of Nursing. 58p. 1975. 4.50 (ISBN 0-686-38162-9, 16-1575). Natl League Nurse.
Peterson, Carol J. & Broderick, Mary E. Competency-Based Curriculum & Instruction. (League Exchange Ser.: No. 22). 59p. 1979. 4.50 (ISBN 0-686-38246-3). Natl League Nurse.
Peterson, Carol J. & Waters, Verle. Partners in Educational Preparation for Nursing Practice. 32p. 1982. 6.50 (ISBN 0-686-38274-9, 14-1884). Natl League Nurse.
Peterson, Carol J. & Williams, Pat E. Curriculum Development & Its Implementation Through a Conceptual Framework. 64p. 1978. 5.95 (ISBN 0-686-38250-1, 23-1723). Natl League Nurse.
Peterson, Carol W. & Connelly, Shirley. Teaching & Evaluating Synthesis in an Associate Degree Nursing Program: A Developmental Experience. (League Exchange Ser.: No.107). 79p. 1975. 5.50 (ISBN 0-686-38279-X, 23-1573). Natl League Nurse.
A Plan for Nurse Staffing in Hospital Emergency Services. (League Exchange Ser.: No. 116). 58p. 1978. 5.95 (ISBN 0-686-38339-7, 20-1696). Natl League Nurse.
Policies & Procedures of Accreditation for Programs in Nursing Education. 3rd ed. 31p. 1979. 3.50 (ISBN 0-686-38133-5, 14-1437). Natl League Nurse.
The Political Challenges for Associate Degree Nursing: Issues of the Present, Direction for the Future. 45p. 1980. 4.50 (ISBN 0-686-38328-1, 23-1813). Natl League Nurse.
Political, Social, & Educational Forces on Nursing: Impact of Social Forces. 32p. 1979. 3.95 (ISBN 0-686-38327-3, 15-1774). Natl League Nurse.
Poshek, Neila & De Tornya, Rheba. Teaching-Learning Strategies in Baccalaureate Nursing Education. 34p. 1976. 3.50 (ISBN 0-686-38280-3, 15-1622). Natl League Nurse.
Price, Pamela A. & Moore, Anne J. Strategies in Administration& Teaching in Associate Degree Nursing Education. 66p. 1976. 4.95 (ISBN 0-686-38278-1, 23-1630). Natl League Nurse.
Primary Nursing: One Nurse-One Client, Planning Care Together. 72p. 1977. 5.95 (ISBN 0-686-38340-0, 52-1695). Natl League Nurse.
Problem-Oriented Systems of Patient Care. 227p. 1974. 8.95 (ISBN 0-686-38208-0, 21-1522). Natl League Nurse.
Proceedings of the NLN Open Curriculum Conferences. Incl. Conference I. 154p. 1974. 6.95 (ISBN 0-686-38182-3, 19-1534); Conference II. 113p. 1975. 5.95 (ISBN 0-686-38183-1, 19-1559); Conference III. 250p. 1975. 7.50 (ISBN 0-686-38184-X, 19-1586); Conference IV. 122p. 1976. 5.95 (ISBN 0-686-38185-8, 19-1627). Natl League Nurse.
Program Evaluation. 71p. 1978. 5.95 (15-1738). Natl League Nurse.
Providing a Climate for the Utilization of Nursing Personnel. 136p. 1975. 5.95 (ISBN 0-686-38165-3, 20-1566). Natl League Nurse.
Puetz, Belinda E. Networking for Nurses: Intra & Interprofessional Relations. LC 82-20669. 206p. 1982. 22.50 (ISBN 0-89443-670-8). Aspen Systems.
Quality Assurance: Models for Nursing Education. 65p. 1976. 5.95 (ISBN 0-686-38367-2, 15-1611). Natl League Nurse.
Raff, Beverly & Boyle, Rena F. Evaluation of Teaching Effectiveness. 42p. 1977. 4.50 (ISBN 0-686-38298-6, 15-1680). Natl League Nurse.
Ranzou, Marie-Louise & Applegate, Margaret. The Communtiy College & Continuing Education of Health Care Personnel. 66p. 1978. 5.50 (ISBN 0-686-38243-9, 23-1710). Natl League Nurse.
The Realities of Primary Nursing Care: Risk, Roles, Research. 89p. 1978. 5.95 (ISBN 0-686-38342-7, 52-1716). Natl League Nurse.
Redmond, Gertrude T. & Ouellette, Frances. Concept & Case Studies in Physical & Mental Health Nursing: A Life Cycle Approach. 1982. pap. 12.95 (ISBN 0-201-06207-0, Med-Nurse). A-W.

Rehabilitative Aspects of Nursing: A Programmed Instruction Series, 2 pts. Incl. Unit 1. Physical Therapeutic Measures: Concepts & Goals. 51p. 1966. 3.95 (ISBN 0-686-38193-9, 19-1220); Unit 2. Range of Joint Motion. 172p. 1967. 4.50 (ISBN 0-686-38194-7, 19-1277). Natl League Nurse.

Richardson, Joseph A. & Matheny, Kenneth B. Concepts & Components of Effective Teaching. 94p. 1978. 5.95 (ISBN 0-686-38285-4, 16-1750). Natl League Nurse.

Robischon, Paulette & Lange, Crystal M. Utilization of the Clinical Laboratory in Baccalaureate Nursing Programs. 33p. 1978. 3.95 (ISBN 0-686-38283-8, 15-1726). Natl League Nurse.

Roles, Rights, & Resposibilities: The Educational Administrator's 3 R's. 41p. 1978. 4.50 (ISBN 0-686-38171-8, 16-1712). Natl League Nurse.

Rudman, Jack. Commission on Graduates of Foreign Nursing Schools Qualifying Examinations (CGFNS) (Admission Test Ser.: ATS-90). 25.95 (ISBN 0-8373-5190-1); pap. 17.95 (ISBN 0-8373-5090-5). Natl Learning.

Ryan, W. & Pedder, M. Basic Science for Nurses. 2nd ed. 256p. 1981. 17.50 (ISBN 0-07-072939-5). McGraw.

Sachs, Lorraine P. & Kane, Michael T. Measurement & Evaluation in Nursing Education. 106p. 1980. 5.50 (ISBN 0-686-38304-4, 17-1807). Natl League Nurse.

Santora, Dolores. Conceptual Frameworks Used in Baccalaureate & Master's Degree Curricula. (League Exchange Ser.: No. 126). 49p. 1980. 4.95 (ISBN 0-686-38247-1, 15-1828). Natl League Nurse.

Schwartz, Doris R. Faculty Research Development Grants: A Follow-up Report. (League Exchange Ser.: No. 125). 52p. 1981. 5.95 (ISBN 0-686-38311-7, 14-1835). Natl League Nurse.

Selected Readings from Open Curriculum Literature. 2nd ed. 32p. 1977. 3.95 (19-1676). Natl League Nurse.

Shields, Mary R. The Construction & Use of Teacher-Made Tests. 2nd ed. 116p. 1965. 4.95 (ISBN 0-686-38287-0, 14-136). Natl League Nurse.

Spencer, Roberta T. & Nichols, Lynn W. Clinical Pharmacology & Nursing Management. (Illus.). 1056p. 1983. text ed. 29.50 (ISBN 0-397-54304-2, Lippincott Medical). Lippincott.

Stanton, Marjorie & Carlson, Sylvia. The Changing Role of the Professional Nurse: Implications for Nursing Education. (Faculty-Curriculum Development Ser.: Pt. V). 49p. 1975. 4.25 (ISBN 0-686-38269-2, 15-1574). Natl League Nurse.

Stevens, Barbara J. & Kelley, Jean A. Cognitive Dissonance: An Examination of CBHDP Stated Beliefs & Their Effect on Education Programs. 49p. 1981. 4.95 (ISBN 0-686-38244-7, 15-1851). Natl League Nurse.

Strong, Jo Ann & Egoville, Barbara B. Considerations in Clinical Evaluation: Instructors, Students, Legal Issues, Data. 55p. 1979. 4.95 (ISBN 0-686-38286-2, 16-1764). Natl League Nurse.

Stuart-Burchardt, Sandra. Perceptorships in Nursing. 150p. 1983. price not set (ISBN 0-89443-936-7). Aspen Systems.

A Study of the NLN Accreditation Program. 150p. 1982. 25.00 (19-1885). Natl League Nurse.

Tanner, Christine A. & Schneider, Harriet. Developing Tests to Evaluate Student Achievement in Baccalaureate Nursing Programs. 64p. 1979. 5.50 (ISBN 0-686-38293-5, 15-1761). Natl League Nurse.

Tier, Lynne L. & Roberts, Barbara D. Teaching & Evaluation in the Classroom. 73p. 1980. 5.95 (ISBN 0-686-38252-8, 23-1826). Natl League Nurse.

Tippett-Neilson, Terry E. & Behler, Donna M. Adult Nurse Practitioner Certification Review. 352p. 1983. 17.95 (ISBN 0-471-86410-2, Pub. by Wiley Med.). Wiley.

Today's Issues: Tomorrow's Achievement. 43p. 1976. 4.50 (ISBN 0-686-38331-1, 16-1635). Natl League Nurse.

Torres, Gertrude & Kelley, Jean. Curriculum Revision in Baccalaureate Nursing Education. (Faculty-Curriculum Development Ser.: Pt. VI). 49p. 1975. 4.25 (ISBN 0-686-38270-6, 15-1576). Natl League Nurse.

Torres, Gertrude & Lynch, Eleanor A. Unifying the Curriculum: The Integrated Approach. (Faculty-Curriculum Development Ser.: Pt. IV). 46p. 1974. 3.95 (ISBN 0-686-38268-4, 15-1552). Natl League Nurse.

Torres, Gertrude & Yura, Helen. Conceptual Framework-Its Meaning & Function. (Faculty-Curriculum Development Ser.: Pt. III). 56p. 1975. 4.50 (ISBN 0-686-38267-6, 15-1558). Natl League Nurse.

Valasek, V. F. Diagnostic Tests & Nursing Implications. 704p. 1983. 13.95x (ISBN 0-07-066805-1). McGraw.

Visiting Nurse Assoc. of New Haven, CT. Child Health Conference: Nurses' Resource Manual. (League Exchange Ser.: No. 101). 127p. 1975. 6.50 (ISBN 0-686-38202-1, 21-1502). Natl League Nurse.

Watchorn, G. W. Medical Calculations for Nurses. 2nd ed. 84p. 1976. pap. 2.95 (ISBN 0-571-04915-X). Faber & Faber.

Whelan, Wayne L. Academic Litigation as Educational Consumerism. 32p. 1979. 3.50 (ISBN 0-686-38136-X, 23-1791). Natl League Nurse.

Will, Connie A. & Eighmy, Judith B. Being a Long-Term Care Nursing Assistant. (Illus.). 1983. pap. text ed. 10.95 (ISBN 0-89303-232-8). R J Brady.

Wilson, Richard E. & Drage, Martha O. Collaboration in Health Care Education. LC 23-1617. 65p. 1976. 4.95 (ISBN 0-686-38245-5). Natl League Nurse.

Wolf, Margaret S. & Duffy, Mary E. Simulations-Games: A Teaching Strategy for Nursing Education. 39p. 1978. 3.95 (ISBN 0-686-38276-5, 23-1756). Natl League Nurse.

Wooldridge, Powhatan & Leonard, Robert C. Behavioral Science & Nursing Theory. 240p. 1983. pap. text ed. 14.95 (ISBN 0-8016-5623-0). Mosby.

Yura, Helen & Friesner, Arlyne. Curriculum Process for Developing or Revising Baccalaureate Nursing Programs. 65p. 1978. 4.95 (ISBN 0-686-38257-9, 15-1700). Natl League Nurse.

Yura, Helen & Torres, Gertrude J. The Process of Curriculum Development. (Faculty-Curriculum Development Ser.: Pt. I). 102p. 1974. 5.50 (ISBN 0-686-38265-X, 15-1521). Natl League Nurse.

NURSES AND NURSING–ADMINISTRATION

see Nursing Service Administration

NURSES AND NURSING–BIBLIOGRAPHY

Lockwood, DeLauna, ed. Cumulative Index to Nursing & Allied Health Literature, Vol. 27. LC 78-643434. 110p. 1982. write for info. (ISBN 0-910478-18-X). Glendale Advent Med.

NURSES AND NURSING–EXAMINATIONS, QUESTIONS, ETC.

Bergeron, Dave. First Responder: Self-Instructional Workbook. (Illus.). 166p. 1982. 5.95 (ISBN 0-89303-227-1). R J Brady.

Kane, Michael T. & Laskevich, Leonarda A. From Concept to Standardized Test. 48p. 1979. 3.95 (ISBN 0-686-38300-1, 17-1796). Natl League Nurse.

Kirby, Sandra. On Your Mark: Self-Assessment for General Nurses. (Illus.). 300p. 1982. text ed. 24.00 (ISBN 0-86792-002-5, Pub by Adis Pr Australia). Wright-PSG.

Lynch, Eleanor A. A Historical Survey of the Test Services of the NLN. 76p. 1980. 4.95 (ISBN 0-686-38314-1, 17-1777). Natl League Nurse.

Martinell, Patricia & Seaman, Patricia. National Certification Examinations: For Nurse Practitioners & Other primary Health Care Providers Study Guide & Manual. 125p. 1983. pap. text ed. 9.95x (ISBN 0-8290-1279-6). Irvington.

Meador, Billie. Critical Care Nursing Review & Self-Test. 250p. 1983. softcover 16.95 (ISBN 0-87489-300-3). Med Economics.

Medical-Surgical Nurse. (Certified Nurse Examination Ser.: CN-11). 21.95 (ISBN 0-8373-6161-3); pap. 13.95 (ISBN 0-8373-6111-7). Natl Learning.

Rudman, Jack. Adult Nurse Practitioner. (Certified Nurse Examination Ser.: CN-1). 21.95 (ISBN 0-8373-6151-6); pap. 13.95 (ISBN 0-8373-6101-X). Natl Learning.

--Chemical Specialist in Medical-Surgical Nursery. (Certified Nurse Examination Ser.: CN-13). 21.95 (ISBN 0-8373-6163-X); pap. 13.95 (ISBN 0-8373-6113-3). Natl Learning.

--Family Nurse Practitioner. (Certified Nurse Examination Ser.: CN-2). 21.95 (ISBN 0-8373-6152-4); pap. 13.95 (ISBN 0-8373-6102-8). Natl Learning.

--Gerontological Nurse. (Certified Nurse Examination Ser.: CN-5). 21.95 (ISBN 0-8373-6155-9); pap. 13.95 (ISBN 0-8373-6105-2). Natl Learning.

--Gerontological Nurse Practitioner. (Certified Nurse Examination Ser.: CN-6). 21.95 (ISBN 0-8373-6156-7); pap. 13.95 (ISBN 0-8373-6106-0). Natl Learning.

--High Risk Perinatal Nurse. (Certified Nurse Examination Ser.: CN-10). 21.95 (ISBN 0-8373-6160-5); pap. 13.95 (ISBN 0-8373-6110-9). Natl Learning.

--Maternal & Child Health Nurse. (Certified Nurse Examination Ser.: CN-9). 21.95 (ISBN 0-8373-6159-1); pap. 13.95 (ISBN 0-8373-6109-5). Natl Learning.

--Mental Hygiene Nursing Program Coordinator. (Career Examination Ser.: C-2665). (Cloth bdg. avail. on request). pap. 12.00 (ISBN 0-8373-2665-6). Natl Learning.

--National Certifying Examination for Physician's Assistants (PA) (Admission Test Ser.: ATS-91). 25.95 (ISBN 0-8373-5191-X); pap. 17.95 (ISBN 0-8373-5091-3). Natl Learning.

--Nurse Administrator. (Career Examination Ser.: C-2913). (Cloth bdg. avail. on request). pap. 12.00 (ISBN 0-8373-2913-2). Natl Learning.

--Nursing Administration. (Certified Nurse Examination Ser.: CN-16). 21.95 (ISBN 0-8373-6166-4); pap. 13.95 (ISBN 0-8373-6116-8). Natl Learning.

--Nursing Administration (Advanced) (Certified Nurse Examination Ser.: CN-17). 21.95 (ISBN 0-8373-6167-2); pap. 13.95 (ISBN 0-8373-6117-6). Natl Learning.

--Nursing School Entrance Examinations for Registered and Graduate Nurses (RN) (Admission Test Ser.: ATS-19). 21.95 (ISBN 0-8373-5119-7); pap. 13.95 (ISBN 0-8373-5019-0). Natl Learning.

Shields, Mary R. The Construction & Use of Teacher-Made Tests. 2nd ed. 116p. 1965. 4.95 (ISBN 0-686-38287-0, 14-136). Natl League Nurse.

The Use of Tests in Schools of Nursing: The NLN Achievement Tests. 3rd ed. 41p. 1964. 1.95 (ISBN 0-686-38309-5, 14-51). Natl League Nurse.

Walton, Peggy J. The Nursing Curriculum Outline Study Guide. pap. text ed. 27.50 (ISBN 0-911067-00-0). Health Ed Train.

NURSES AND NURSING–HISTORY

Dammann, Nancy. A Social History of the Frontier Nursing Service. (Illus.). 179p. (Orig.). 1982. pap. 5.95 (ISBN 0-9609376-0-9). Soc Change Pr.

NURSES AND NURSING–LEGAL STATUS, LAWS, ETC.

Accountability: Accepting the Challenge. 90p. 1976. 5.95 (ISBN 0-686-38316-8, 16-1621). Natl League Nurse.

Chem Sources-USA. 24th ed. 1983. 150.00 (ISBN 0-937020-03-6). Directories Pub.

Raising Your Political Blood Pressure. 41p. 1980. 4.95 (ISBN 0-686-38349-4, 52-1827). Natl League Nurse.

Regulatory Agencies: The Effect on Health Care Institutions. 35p. 1974. 3.95 (ISBN 0-686-38329-X, 20-1514). Natl League Nurse.

NURSES AND NURSING–PROGRAMMED INSTRUCTION

Lachman, Vicki D. Stress Management: A Manual for Nurses. write for info (ISBN 0-8089-1554-1). Grune.

NURSES AND NURSING–PSYCHOLOGICAL ASPECTS

Donnelly, Gloria F. RN's Survival Sourcebook: Coping with Stress. (Illus.). 225p. 1983. softcover 10.95 (ISBN 0-87489-299-6). Med Economics.

Eisenberg, M. G. Psychological Aspects of Physical Disability: A Guide for the Health Care Educator. (League Exchange Ser.: No. 114). 38p. 1977. 3.95 (ISBN 0-686-38192-0, 20-1692). Natl League Nurse.

Foley, Theresa S. & Davies, Marilyn A. Rape: Nursing Care of Victims. (Illus.). 512p. 1983. pap. text ed. 12.95 (ISBN 0-8016-1620-4). Mosby.

Hall, John. Psychology for Nurses & Health Visitors. Chapman, Antony & Gale, Anthony, eds. (Psychology for Professional Groups Ser.). 320p. 1982. 49.00x (ISBN 0-333-31863-5, Pub. by Macmillan England). State Mutual Bk.

--Psychology for Nurses & Health Visitors. (Psychology for Professional Groups Ser.). 320p. 1982. text ed. 25.00x (ISBN 0-333-31863-3, Pub. by Macmillan England); pap. text ed. 10.95x (ISBN 0-333-31876-5). Humanities.

Mosley, Doris Y. Nursing Students' Perceptions of the Urban Poor. (League Exchange Ser.: No. 115). 56p. 1977. 5.50 (ISBN 0-686-38344-3, 23-1694). Natl League Nurse.

Socialization & Resocializaton of Nurses for Professional Nursing Practice. 41p. 1977. 4.50 (ISBN 0-686-38370-2, 15-1659). Natl League Nurse.

NURSES AND NURSING–RESEARCH

see Nursing Research

NURSES AND NURSING–STUDY AND TEACHING

see also Nursing Schools

Allen, Hazel O. & Murrell, John, eds. Nurse Training. 224p. 1978. 30.00x (ISBN 0-7121-1405-X, Pub. by Macdonald & Evans). State Mutual Bk.

Angel, Gerry & Petronko, Diane. Developing the New Assertive Nurse. 1983. pap. text ed. 17.95 (ISBN 0-8261-3511-0). Springer Pub.

Betts. Patient Centred Multiple Choice Questions, Vol. 1. 96p. 1982. pap. text ed. 6.50 (ISBN 0-06-318231-9, Pub. by Har-Row Ltd England). Har-Row.

Blenkin & Kelly. Primary Curriculum in Action. 1983. text ed. 21.00 (ISBN 0-06-318223-8, Pub. by Har-Row Ltd England); pap. text ed. 10.50 (Pub. by Har-Row Ltd England). Har-Row.

Conley, Virginia & Friesner, Arlyne. Evaluation of Students in Baccalaureate Nursing Programs. 98p. 1977. 5.95 (ISBN 0-686-38296-X, 15-1684). Natl League Nurse.

Hiraki, Akemi & Parlocha, Pamela Kees. Returning to School: The RN to BSN Handbook. 1983. pap. text ed. write for info. (ISBN 0-316-36460-6). Little.

White, Marguerite B. Curriculum Development from a Nursing Model: The Crisis Theory Framework. (Springer Series on the Teaching of Nursing: Vol. 8). 1983. pap. text ed. price not set (ISBN 0-8261-3281-2). Springer Pub.

NURSING (INFANT FEEDING)

see Breast Feeding

NURSING ADMINISTRATION

see Nursing Service Administration

NURSING HOMES

see also Geriatric Nursing

Accreditation Manual for Long Term Care Facilities 1983. 86p. 1983. pap. 15.00 (ISBN 0-86688-059-3). Joint Comm Hosp.

Boling, Edwin T. & Vrooman, David M. Nursing Home Management: A Humanistic Approach. (Illus.). 403p. 1983. text ed. price not set (ISBN 0-398-04823-1). C C Thomas.

Durman, E. C. & Dunlop, Burton. Volunteers in Social Services: Consumer Assessment of Nursing Homes. 48p. 1979. pap. text ed. 7.00 (ISBN 0-87766-261-4). Urban Inst.

Ernst, Nora S. & West, Helen L. Nursing Home Staff Development. 1983. text ed. 15.95 (ISBN 0-8261-3860-8). Springer Pub.

Grimaldi, Paul L. Medicaid Reimbursement of Nursing-Home Care. 1982. 15.95 (ISBN 0-8447-3456-X); pap. 7.95 (ISBN 0-8447-3457-8). Am Enterprise.

Halbur, Bernice T. Turnover Among Nursing Personnel in Nursing Homes. Kalisch, Philip & Kalisch, Beatrice, eds. LC 82-8353. (Studies in Nursing Management: No. 2). 116p. 1982. 34.95 (ISBN 0-8357-1354-7). Univ Microfilms.

Moirashine. Long Term Care of the Aging. LC 82-62399. 176p. 1982. pap. 14.50 (ISBN 0-943432-00-6). Slack Inc.

Spitz, Bruce. Medicaid Nursing Home Reimbursment in New York. (Illus.). 65p. (Orig.). 1981. pap. text ed. 7.00 (ISBN 0-87766-289-4). Urban Inst.

Spitz, Bruce & Weeks, Jane. Medicaid Nursing Home Reimbursement in Minnesota. LC 80-54798. (Illus.). 64p. (Orig.). 1981. pap. text ed. 6.00. Urban Inst.

--Medicaid Nursing Home Reimbursment in Illinois. LC 80-54797. (Illus.). 55p. (Orig.). 1981. pap. text ed. 6.00 (ISBN 0-87766-287-8). Urban Inst.

NURSING LAW

see Nurses and Nursing–Legal Status, Laws, etc.

NURSING PSYCHOLOGY

see Nurses and Nursing–Psychological Aspects

NURSING RESEARCH

Brink, Pamela J. & Wood, Marilynn T. Basic Steps in Planning Nursing Research. 2nd ed. LC 82-17426. 304p. 1983. pap. text ed. 15.95 (ISBN 0-534-01241-8). Brooks-Cole.

Guide for the Development of Nursing Libraries. 4th rev. ed. 50p. 1981. 4.50 (ISBN 0-686-38352-4, 41-1857). Natl League Nurse.

Horsley, Jo Anne. Using Research to Improve Nursing Practice: A Guide. (Monographs in Applied Nursing Ser.). Date not set. pap. price not set (ISBN 0-8089-1510-X). Grune.

Notter, Lucille. Essentials of Nursing Research. 3rd ed. 192p. 1983. pap. 9.95 (ISBN 0-8261-1595-0). Springer Pub.

Sherwen, Laurie N. & Weingarten, Carol-Grace. Analysis & Application of Nursing Research: Parent-Neonate Issues Studies. LC 82-20201. 300p. 1983. pap. text ed. 13.95 (ISBN 0-534-01292-2). Brooks-Cole.

NURSING SCHOOLS

Personnel Management for Schools of Nursing. 58p. 1975. 4.50 (ISBN 0-686-38162-9, 16-1575). Natl League Nurse.

Shane, Donea L. Returning to School: A Guide for Nurses. 320p. 1983. text ed. 18.95 (ISBN 0-13-779165-8); pap. 14.95 (ISBN 0-13-779157-7). P-H.

State-Approved Schools of Nursing: L.P.N. - L.V.N. 1981. 81p. 1981. 5.50 (ISBN 0-686-38358-3, 19-1854). Natl League Nurse.

State Approved Schools of Nursing: R. N. 1981. 96p. 1981. 6.50 (ISBN 0-686-38357-5, 19-1853). Natl League Nurse.

NURSING SERVICE ADMINISTRATION

Concerns in the Acquisition & Allocation of Nursing Personnel. 49p. 1978. 4.95 (ISBN 0-686-38142-4, 20-1709). Natl League Nurse.

Ganong, Joan M. & Ganong, Warren L. Help with Managerial Leadership in Nursing: 101 Tremendous Trifles. (Help Series of Management Guides). 160p. 1980. pap. 13.95 (ISBN 0-933036-35-3). Ganong W L Co.

--One Hundred One Exciting Exercise: HELP Worksheets for Nurse Managers & Educators. (Help Series of Management Guides). 109p. 1978. pap. 10.95 (ISBN 0-933036-16-7). Ganong W L Co.

Hein, Eleanor C. & Nicholson, M. Jean. Contemporary Leadership Behavior: Selected Readings. 1982. pap. 14.95 (ISBN 0-316-35447-3). Little.

Huckabay, Loucine M. Patient Classification: A Basis for Staffing. (League Exchange Ser.: No. 131). 40p. 1981. 4.50 (ISBN 0-686-38337-0, 20-1864). Natl League Nurse.

Identifying Problems in the Motivation, Performance, & Retention of Nursing Staff. 58p. 1979. 4.95 (ISBN 0-686-38151-3). Natl League Nurse.

La Monica, Elaine. Nursing Leadership & Management: An Experiential Approach. 300p. 1983. text ed. 22.95 (ISBN 0-534-01337-6). Brooks-Cole.

Levenson, Goldie. Use of Patient Statistics for Program Planning. 33p. 1979. 3.95 (ISBN 0-686-38176-9, 21-1794). Natl League Nurse.

Management Perspectives. 32p. 1979. 3.95 (ISBN 0-686-38159-9, 52-1767). Natl League Nurse.

Nursing Administration: A Selected Annotated Bibliography of Current Periodical Literature in Nursing Administration & Management. (League Exchange Ser.: No. 120). 36p. 1979. 3.95 (ISBN 0-686-38355-9, 20-1745). Natl League Nurse.

Nursing Service in a Specialty, a Rural, & an Urban Hospital. 57p. 1978. 4.95 (ISBN 0-686-38335-4, 20-1720). Natl League Nurse.

People Power: Pressures, Problems, Persuasion, Patients, Perspectives. 58p. 1976. 5.50 (ISBN 0-686-38347-8, 20-1623). Natl League Nurse.

The Problem-Oriented System: A Multidisciplinary Approach. 91p. 1974. 5.95 (ISBN 0-686-38341-9, 20-1546). Natl League Nurse.

Role Expectations: Nurse Administrators, Governing Boards, Chief Executive Officers. 48p. 1977. 4.95 (ISBN 0-686-38167-X, 20-1693). Natl League Nurse.

The Role of the Director of Nursing Service. 35p. 1977. 3.95 (ISBN 0-686-38169-6, 20-1646). Natl League Nurse.

Vogt, Judith F. & Cox, John L. Retaining Professional Nurses: A Planned Process. 03/1983 ed. (Illus.). 256p. text ed. 19.95 (ISBN 0-8016-5226-X). Mosby.

NUT CULTURE

see Nuts

NUTRITION

see also Animal Nutrition; Diet; Digestion; Feeds; Food; Food Habits; Malnutrition; Metabolism; Minerals in the Body; Trace Elements in Nutrition; Vitamins

also subdivision Nutrition under subjects, e.g. Children–Nutrition

Abravanel, Eliott D. & King, Elizabeth A. Dr. Abravanel's Body Type Diet & Lifetime Nutrition Plan. (Illus.). 256p. 1983. 12.95 (ISBN 0-553-05036-2). Bantam.

Beal, Virginia A. Nutrition in the Life Span. LC 79-24610. 467p. 1980. text ed. 26.95 (ISBN 0-471-03664-1). Wiley.

Bender. Dictionary of Nutrition. 5th ed. 1983. text ed. write for info. Butterworth.

Bland, Jeffrey, ed. Medical Applications of Clinical Nutrition. LC 82-84365. 250p. 1983. 25.00 (ISBN 0-87983-327-0). Keats.

Bourne, G. H., ed. Aspects of Human & National Nutrition. (World Review of Nutrition & Dietetics Ser.: Vol. 41). (Illus.). xii, 260p. 1982. 140.75 (ISBN 3-8055-3591-0). S Karger.

Brody, Jane. Jane Brody's Nutrition Book. 1982. pap. 8.95 (ISBN 0-686-82120-3). Bantam.

Brown, Judith E. Nutrition for Your Pregnancy: The University of Minnesota Guide. LC 82-21852. (Illus.). 140p. 1983. 12.95 (ISBN 0-8166-1151-3). U of Minn Pr.

Cohen, Leslie. Nourishing a Happy Affair: Nutrition Alternatives for Individual & Family Needs. (Illus.). 150p. (Orig.). 1983. pap. 5.95 (ISBN 0-943914-02-7, Dist by Kampmann & Co.). Larson Pubns Inc.

Correa, Hector & El Torky, Mohamed A. The Biological & Social Determinants of the Demographic Transition. LC 82-16042. (Illus.). 298p. (Orig.). 1983. lib. bdg. 24.25 (ISBN 0-8191-2754-X); pap. text ed. 12.75 (ISBN 0-8191-2755-8). U Pr of Amer.

Cunningham, John J. Introduction to Nutritional Physiology. (Illus.). 400p. 19.95 (ISBN 0-89313-031-1); text ed. 19.95 (ISBN 0-686-38084-3). G F Stickley.

Darby, W. J., et al, eds. Annual Review of Nutrition, Vol. 3. 330p. 1983. 27.00 (ISBN 0-8243-2803-5). Annual Reviews.

Dennison, Darwin. The Dine System: The Nutrition Plan for Better Health. 1982. pap. 8.95 (ISBN 0-452-25367-5, Plume). NAL.

--The Dine System: The Nutritional Plan for Better Health. LC 82-8254. (Medical Library). (Illus.). 196p. 1982. pap. 8.95 (ISBN 0-686-84854-3, 1258-6). Mosby.

Evaluations of Nutrition Interventions, No. 24. (FAO Food & Nutrition Paper). 194p. 1983. pap. 14.50 (ISBN 92-5-101228-8, F2360, FAO). Unipub.

Food & Nutrition Group. Feed, Need, Greed. Tafler, Sue & Phillips, Connie, eds. (Illus.). 108p. (Orig.). 1980. pap. 5.00 (ISBN 0-9607314-0-7); tchr's. ed. 5.00 (ISBN 0-686-84488-2). Sci People.

Frederick, Carlton. Carlton Frederick's Nutrition Guide for the Prevention & Cure of Common Ailments & Diseses. LC 82-10705. (Illus.). 194p. Date not set. pap. 8.95 (ISBN 0-671-44509-X, Fireside). S&S.

Fulwood, Robinson & Johnson, Clifford L. Hematological & Nutritional Biochemistries References Data of Persons 6 Months-74 Years of Age: United States, 1976-1980. Cox, Klaudia, tr. (Ser. 11: No. 232). 60p. 1982. pap. 1.95 (ISBN 0-8406-0267-7). Natl Ctr Health Stats.

Garrison, Robert. Nutrition Desk Reference Book. 1983. 25.00 (ISBN 0-87983-328-9). Keats.

Goldfarb, I. William & Yates, Anthony P. Total Parenteral Nutrition: Concepts & Methods. 96p. pap. text ed. write for info. (ISBN 0-935170-07-3). Synapse Pubns.

Guthrie, Helen. Introductory Nutrition. 5th ed. 692p. 1983. pap. text ed. 23.95 (ISBN 0-8016-1997-1). Mosby.

Harbert, Lloyd & Scandizzo, Pasquale L. Food Distribution & Nutrition Intervention: The Case of Chile. LC 82-8370. (World Bank Staff Working Papers: No. 512). (Orig.). 1982. pap. text ed. 5.00 (ISBN 0-8213-0001-6). World Bank.

Hostage, Jacqueline. Jackie's Diet & Nutrition Charts. 128p. 1982. pap. 5.95 (ISBN 0-932620-10-8, Pub. by Betterway Pubns). Berkshire Traveller.

Hui, Yiu H. Human Nutrition & Diet Therapy. LC 82-20136. 900p. 1983. text ed. 25.00 (ISBN 0-534-01336-8). Brooks-Cole.

Improvement of Nutritional Quality of Food Crops. (FAO Plant Production & Protection Paper: No. 34). 92p. 1981. pap. 7.50 (ISBN 92-5-101166-4, F2298, FAO). Unipub.

Johnson, I. D. Advances in Clinical Nutrition. 500p. 1982. text ed. 49.00 (ISBN 0-85200-496-6, Pub. by MTP Pr England). Kluwer Boston.

Kasper, W. & Goebell, H., eds. Colon & Nutrition. (Illus.). 350p. 1982. text ed. 75.00 (ISBN 0-85200-444-3, Pub. by MTP Pr England). Kluwer Boston.

Kerschner, Velma L. Nutrition & Diet Therapy. 3rd ed. LC 82-22120. 350p. 1983. pap. text ed. 11.95 (ISBN 0-8036-5302-6). Davis Co.

Ketcham, Katherine & Mueller, Ann. Eating Right to Stay Sober. 260p. 1983. 14.95 (ISBN 0-914842-97-8). Madrona Pubs.

Klein, Diane & Badalamenti, Rosalyn T. Eating Right for Two: The Complete Nutrition Guide & Cookbook for a Healthy Pregnancy. 320p. (Orig.). 1983. pap. 7.95 (ISBN 0-345-30915-4). Ballantine.

Kleinberger, G. & Deutsch, E., eds. New Aspects of Clinical Nutrition. (Illus.). x, 662p. 1983. pap. 74.25 (ISBN 3-8055-3683-6). S Karger.

Kunin. Mega Nutrition. 1980. 12.95 (ISBN 0-07-035639-4). McGraw.

Kunin, Richard A. Mega-Nutrition: The New Prescription for Maximum Health, Energy & Longevity. LC 81-220. (Medical Library). 312p. 1982. pap. 6.95 (ISBN 0-686-84853-5, 2808-3). Mosby.

Lehman, S. C. Nutrition & Food Preparation & Preventive Care & Maintenance. (Lifeworks Ser.). 1981. text ed. 5.80 (ISBN 0-07-037094-X). McGraw.

Long, Patricia J. & Shannon, Barbara. Focus on Nutrition. (Illus.). 336p. 1983. pap. 13.95 (ISBN 0-13-322800-2). P H.

--Nutrition: An Inquiry into the Issues. (Illus.). 608p. 1983. pap. text ed. 23.95 (ISBN 0-13-627802-7). P-H.

Minor, Lewis J. L. J. Minor Foodservice Standards Series: Nutritional Standards, Vol. 1. (Illus.). 1983. text ed. 20.00 (ISBN 0-87055-425-5). AVI.

--L. J. Minor Foodservice Standards Series: Sanitation, Safety, Environmental Standards, Vol. 2. (Illus.). 1983. text ed. 20.00 (ISBN 0-87055-428-X). AVI.

Natow, A. B. & Heslin, J. Nutrition for the Prime of Your Life. 352p. 1983. 17.95 (ISBN 0-07-028414-8, GB). McGraw.

OECD Staff. Meat Balances in OECD Member Countries, 1975-1980. 85p. (Orig., English-French.). 1982. pap. text ed. 8.50x (ISBN 92-64-02323-2). OECD.

Parker, Merren. For Goodness Sake. 169p. 1982. pap. 4.95 (ISBN 0-00-216929-0, Pub. by W Collins Australia). Intl Schol Bk Serv.

Partee, Phillip E. The Layman's Guide to Buying & Eating a Natural Balanced Diet. 130p. (Orig.). 1983. pap. 3.95x (ISBN 0-686-84761-X). Sprout Pubns.

Pearson, Durk & Shaw, Sandy. Life Extension. 896p. 1983. pap. 12.95 (ISBN 0-446-87990-8). Warner Bks.

Perez-Polo, J. Regino & De Vellis, Jean, eds. Growth & Trophic Factors. LC 83-954. (Progress in Clinical & Biological Research Ser.: Vol. 118). 472p. 1983. 45.00 (ISBN 0-8451-0118-8). A R Liss.

Pfeiffer, Carl. Mental & Elemental Nutrients. 1975. 11.95x (ISBN 0-87983-114-6). Cancer Control Soc.

Reader's Digest Editors. Eat Better, Live Better. LC 82-60100. (Illus.). 416p. 1982. 21.50 (ISBN 0-89577-141-1, Pub. by RD Assn). Random.

Reed, Barbara. Nutritional Guidelines For the Counselor. 1982. pap. 10.00 (ISBN 0-686-83743-6). Natural Pr.

Relman, Arnold S., intro. by. Current Concepts in Nutrition. (Illus.). 131p. (Orig.). 1979. pap. text ed. 6.00 (ISBN 0-910133-01-8). MA Med Soc.

Ridgeway, Donald G. The Healthy Peasant Gourmet. LC 82-90747. (Illus.). 220p. 1983. 12.95 (ISBN 0-910361-01-0); pap. 7.95 (ISBN 0-910361-00-2). Earth Basics.

Rohe, Fred. Fred Rohe's Complete Book of Natural Foods. LC 82-50282. (Illus.). 448p. (Orig.). 1983. pap. 10.95 (ISBN 0-394-71240-4). Shambhala Pubns.

Sourcebook on Food & Nutrition. 3rd ed. LC 82-82014. 549p. 1982. 49.50 (ISBN 0-8379-4503-8). Marquis.

Taylor, Keith B. & Anthony, Luean E. Clinical Nutrition. (Illus.). 640p. 1983. pap. text ed. 21.95x (ISBN 0-07-063185-9, HP). McGraw.

Taylor, T Geoffrey. Nutrition & Health. (Studies in Biology: No. 141). 64p. 1982. pap. text ed. 8.95 (ISBN 0-7131-2840-2). E Arnold.

Thrash, Agatha & Thrash, Calvin. Nutrition for Vegetarians. (Illus.). 155p. 1982. pap. 8.95 (ISBN 0-942658-03-5). Yuchi Pines.

Towards Better Health & Nutrition. 83p. 1981. pap. 7.00 (ISBN 0-686-81852-0, UB97, UNESCO). Unipub.

Walker, Norman W. Pure & Simple Natural Weight Control. LC 81-11080. 1981. pap. 4.95 (ISBN 0-89019-078-X). O'Sullivan Woodside.

Whitney, Eleanor N. & Cataldo, Corrine. Understanding Normal & Clinical Nutrition. (Illus.). 1000p. 1983. text ed. 26.95 (ISBN 0-314-69685-7); tchrs.' manual avail. (ISBN 0-314-71137-6). West Pub.

Wines, W. F. Foods, Fads & Foolishness. rev. ed. 165p. 1982. pap. 5.95 (ISBN 0-911579-00-1). Fleur-Di-Lee.

Winick, M. Nutrition in Health & Disease. 261p. 1980. text ed. 24.95x (ISBN 0-471-05713-4, Pub. by Wiley-Interscience). Wiley.

Winters, R. W. & Greene, H. L., eds. Nutritional Support of the Seriously Ill Patient, Vol. 1. LC 82-18426. (Bristol-Myers Nutrition Symposia Ser.). Date not set. price not set (ISBN 0-12-759801-4). Acad Pr.

Wurtman, Judith J. The American Eater: Some Nutritional Problems & Some Solutions. (Vital Issues, Vol. XXIX 1979-80: No. 2). 0.60 (ISBN 0-686-81607-2). Ctr Info Am.

NUTRITION–JUVENILE LITERATURE

Moncure, Jane B. The Healthkin Food Train. LC 82-14710. (Healthkins Ser.). (Illus.). 32p. (ps-2). 1982. lib. bdg. 6.95 (ISBN 0-89565-240-4). Childs World.

Rhodes, Janis. Nutrition Mission. (ps-2). 1982. 4.95 (ISBN 0-86653-092-4, GA 443). Good Apple.

NUTRITION–RESEARCH

Carroll, Margaret D. & Abraham, Sidney. Dietary Intake Source Data: United States, 1976-80. Olmstead, Mary, ed. (Ser. 11: No. 231). 50p. 1982. pap. text ed. 1.75 (ISBN 0-8406-0265-0). Natl Ctr Health Stats.

Daperr, H. H., ed. Advances in Nutritional Research, Vol. 5. 270p. 1983. 39.50x (ISBN 0-306-41095-8, Plenum Pr). Plenum Pub.

Directory of Food & Nutrition Information Services & Resources. Date not set. price not set. Oryx Pr.

Joy, Leonard, ed. Nutrition Planning. new ed. 154p. Date not set. text ed. price not set (ISBN 0-86103-007-9). Butterworth.

Lusk, Graham. The Elements of the Science of Nutrition. (Nutrition Foundations Reprint Ser.). 844p. 1982. 38.50 (ISBN 0-12-460460-9). Acad Pr.

NUTRITION–STUDY AND TEACHING

Society for Nutrition Education. A Brief Guide to Becoming a Nutrition Advocate. 19p. (Orig.). 1982. pap. 3.75 (ISBN 0-910869-15-4). Soc Nutrition Ed.

Van Camp, Diana. Jumbo Nutrition Yearbook: Grade 2. (Jumbo Nutrition Ser.). 96p. (gr. 2). 1981. 14.00 (ISBN 0-8209-0041-9, JNY 2). ESP.

NUTRITION DISORDERS

Feldman. Nutrition in the Middle & Later Years. (Illus.). 352p. 1982. text ed. 29.50 (ISBN 0-7236-7046-3). Wright-PSG.

Willard, Mervyn. Nutritional Management for the Practicing Physician. 1982. 26.95 (ISBN 0-201-08320-5, 08320, Med-Nurse). A-W.

NUTRITION OF CHILDREN

see Children–Nutrition; Infants–Nutrition

NUTRITION OF PLANTS

see Plants–Nutrition

NUTRITION RESEARCH

see Nutrition–Research

NUTS

see also Cookery (Nuts);

also names of nuts, e.g. Walnut

Buyers, Rebecca. The Marvelous Macadamia Nut. LC 82-73616. (Illus.). 84p. (Orig.). 1982. pap. write for info. (ISBN 0-941034-74-7). I Chalmers.

Stebbins, Robert L. & Walheim, Lance. Western Fruit, Berries & Nuts: How to Select, Grow & Enjoy. (Illus.). 192p. (Orig.). pap. 7.95 (ISBN 0-89586-078-3). H P Bks.

Thomson, Paul H. Macadamia Handbook. 60p. 1983. pap. 5.00 (ISBN 0-9602066-3-9). Bonsall Pub.

NYSTAGMUS

see also Electronystagmography

Honrubia, Vicente & Brazier, Mary, eds. Nystagmus & Vertigo: Clinical Approach to the Patient with Dizziness. LC 82-3906. (UCLA Forum in Medical Sciences Ser.: No. 24). 320p. 1982. 26.00 (ISBN 0-12-355080-7). Acad Pr.

O

O. HENRY

see Porter, William Sydney, 1862-1910

OAK

Miller, Howard & Lamb, Samuel. Oaks of North America. 1983. price not set. Naturegraph.

OAKLAND, CALIFORNIA

Peterson, George, et al. The Future of Oakland's Capital Plant. LC 80-54776. 80p. (Orig.). 1981. pap. text ed. 6.00 (ISBN 0-87766-290-8). Urban Inst.

OAKLEY, ANNIE, 1860-1926

Heidish, Marcy. The Secret Annie Oakley. (Illus.). 205p. 1983. 14.95 (ISBN 0-453-00437-7). NAL.

OBEDIENCE

Beecher, Willard & Beecher, Marguerite. The Sin of Obedience. 88p. (Orig.). 1982. pap. 4.75 (ISBN 0-942350-00-6). Beecher Found.

OBESITY

Addanki, Sam & Kindrick, Shirley A. Renewed Health for Diabetics & Obese People. Brennan, R. O., ed. (Orig.). 1982. pap. 3.50 (ISBN 0-9609896-0-9). Nu-Diet.

Claypool, Jane. Why Do Some People Get Fat? (Creative's Little Question Books). (Illus.). 32p. (gr. 3-4). 1982. lib. bdg. 5.95 (ISBN 0-87191-898-6). Creative Ed.

Lamb, Howard. The Fatbook. 133p. 1982. loose-leaf 39.95 (ISBN 0-9609150-0-1). H Lamb.

OBLIGATION

see Responsibility

OBSCENE LITERATURE

see Literature, Immoral

OBSEQUIES

see Funeral Rites and Ceremonies

OBSERVATIONS, METEOROLOGICAL

see Meteorology–Observations

OBSERVATORIES, METEOROLOGICAL

see Meteorology–Observations

OBSESSIVE-COMPULSIVE NEUROSES

Hodgson, Ray & Miller, Peter. Self-Watching: Addictions, Habits, Compulsions: What to do About Them. 1983. 17.95 (ISBN 0-87196-726-X). Facts on File.

OBSTETRICAL NURSING

Ingalls, A. Joy & Salerno, M. Constance. Maternal & Child Health Nursing. (Illus.). 800p. 1983. pap. text ed. 23.95 (ISBN 0-8016-2324-3); study guide 10.95 (ISBN 0-8016-2323-5). Mosby.

Malinowski, Janet S. & DeLoach, Carolyn P. Nursing Care of the Labor Patient. (Illus.). 350p. 1983. pap. text ed. 12.95 (ISBN 0-8036-5802-8, 5802-8). Davis Co.

Reeder, Sharon R. & Mastroianni, Luigi, Jr. Maternity Nursing. 15th ed. (Illus.). 1200p. 1983. text ed. 29.95 (ISBN 0-397-54369-7, Lippincott Medical). Lippincott.

OBSTETRICS

see also Abortion; Cesarean Section; Childbirth; Labor (Obstetrics); Midwives; Obstetrical Nursing; Pregnancy; Women–Diseases

Benson, Ralph C., ed. Current Obstetric & Gynecologic Diagnosis & Treatment. 4th ed. 1050p. 1982. 25.00 (ISBN 0-87041-213-2). Lange.

Clayton, Stanley & Lewis, T. L. Obstetrics by Ten Teachers. 552p. 1980. text ed. 26.50 (ISBN 0-7131-4365-7). E Arnold.

Cohen, Wayne R. & Friedman, Emanuel A., eds. Management of Labor. 1983. price not set (ISBN 0-8391-1816-3, 17884). Univ Park.

Friedman, Emanuel A. Obstetrical Decision Making. 222p. 1982. 34.00 (ISBN 0-941158-01-2, D1680-8). Mosby.

Gibbs, R. S. & Gibbs, C. E. Ambulatory Obstetrics: A Clinical Guide. LC 79-18554. 1979. pap. text ed. 15.95x (ISBN 0-471-05227-2, Pub. by Wiley Medical). Wiley.

Huang, C. L. & Daniels, V. G., eds. Companion to Obstetrics. (Companion Ser.). 1982. text ed. write for info. (ISBN 0-85200-378-1, Pub. by MTP Pr England). Kluwer Boston.

Pitkin, Roy M., ed. Year Book of Obstetrics & Gynecology 1983. 1983. 35.00 (ISBN 0-8151-6692-3). Year Bk Med.

Symonds & Zuspan. Clinical Procedures in Obstetrics. (Reproductive Medicine Ser.). 528p. 1983. price not set (ISBN 0-8247-1778-3). Dekker.

Vontver, Louis A. Obstetrics & Gynecology Review. 3rd ed. LC 82-8773. (Illus.). 320p. 1983. pap. text ed. 10.00 (ISBN 0-668-05484-0, 5484). Arco.

Warshaw, Joseph B. & Hobbins, John. Perinatal Medicine in Primary Practice. 1982. 34.95 (ISBN 0-201-08294-2, Med-Nurse). A-W.

Willson, J. Robert & Carrington, Elsie R. Obstetrics & Gynecology. 7th ed. (Illus.). 800p. 1983. text ed. 39.95 (ISBN 0-8016-5597-8). Mosby.

Wynn, Ralpf M. Obstetrics & Gynecology. 3rd ed. LC 82-20879. (Illus.). 310p. 1982. text ed. write for info. (ISBN 0-8121-0875-2). Lea & Febiger.

Yiu-Chiu, Victoria S. & Chiu, Lee C. Atlas of Obstetrical Ultrasonography. (Illus.). 312p. 1982. 49.50 (ISBN 0-8391-1765-5, 18074). Univ Park.

OBSTETRICS–POPULAR WORKS

Sheppard, Bruce D. & Sheppard, Carroll A. The Complete Guide to Women's Health. LC 82-14802. (Illus.). 421p. 1982. 19.95 (ISBN 0-936166-07-X). Mariner Pub.

OBSTETRICS–SURGERY

see also Cesarean Section

Cohen, Nancy Wainer & Estner, Lois J. Silent Knife: Cesarean Prevention & Vaginal Birth after Cesarean (VBAC) (Illus.). 480p. 1983. 29.95x (ISBN 0-89789-026-4); pap. 14.95x. J F Bergin.

OBSTETRICS, OPERATIVE

see Obstetrics–Surgery

O'CASEY, SEAN, 1884-1964

Lowery, Robert, ed. O'Casey Annual. (Literary Annuals: No. 2). 240p. 1983. text ed. 42.00x (ISBN 0-333-32458-7, 40972, Pub. by Macmillan England). Humanities.

OCCIDENTAL ART

see Art

OCCULT MEDICINE

see Medicine, Magic, Mystic, and Spagiric

OCCULT SCIENCES
see also Alchemy; Astrology; Cabala; Clairvoyance; Conjuring; Demonology; Initiations (In Religion, Folk-Lore, etc.); Magic; Palmistry; Spiritualism; Superstition; Witchcraft
Abell, George & Singer, Barry. Science & the Paranormal. (Illus.). 432p. 1983. pap. 8.95 (ISBN 0-686-83708-8, ScribT). Scribner.
Cavendish, Richard, ed. Man, Myth & Magic: The Illustrated Encyclopedia of Mythology, Religion & the Unknown. 2nd ed. (Illus.). 3268p. 1983. lib. bdg. 399.95 (ISBN 0-86307-041-8). M Cavendish Corp.
Crowley, Aleister. The Magical Record of the Beast 666. Symonds, John & Grant, Kenneth, eds. 326p. 1972. 16.95 (ISBN 0-7156-0636-0). US Games Syst.
Dean, Malcolm, ed. Ephemeris of Chiron. rev. 2nd ed. 1982. 6.95 (ISBN 0-686-82682-5). Weiser.
Gauld, Alan. Mediumship & Survival: A Century of Investigations. 288p. 1982. 40.00x (ISBN 0-434-28320-7, Pub. by Heinemann England). State Mutual Bk.
Gray, William G. Western Inner Workings. (The Sangreal Sodality Ser.: Vol. 1). 188p. Date not set. pap. price not set (ISBN 0-87728-560-8). Weiser.
Kerr, Howard & Crow, Charles L., eds. The Occult in America. LC 82-24770. (Illus.). 234p. 1983. 16.95 (ISBN 0-252-00983-5). U of Ill Pr.
Lamb, Geoffrey. Magic, Witchcraft & the Occult. (Illus.). 176p. 1982. Repr. of 1977 ed. pap. 9.95 (ISBN 0-88254-705-4). Hippocrene Bks.
Montgomery, Ruth. Threshold to Tomorrow. 256p. 1983. 13.95 (ISBN 0-399-12759-3). Putnam Pub Group.
Steiger, Brad. The Seed. 192p. 1983. pap. 2.75 (ISBN 0-425-05845-X). Berkley Pub.
Steiner, Rudolf. Occult Science: An Outline. Adams, George & Adams, Mary, trs. from Ger. 352p. 1969. 14.50 (ISBN 0-85440-207-1, Pub. by Steinerbooks). Anthroposophic.
--The Occult Significance of the Blood. 3rd ed. Barfield, Owen, tr. from Ger. 32p. 1978. pap. 1.95 (ISBN 0-85440-186-5, Pub. by Steinerbooks). Anthroposophic.
White, Nelson H. Magick & the Law: Vol. 5, or How to Set-Up & Operate Your Own Occult Shop. LC 80-50273. (Illus.). 75p. (Orig.). 1982. pap. 10.00 (ISBN 0-939856-31-X). Tech Group.
Wilcox, Laird M. Directory of the Occult & Paranormal: Supplement, 1983. 1983. pap. 5.95 (ISBN 0-933592-29-9). Edit Res Serv.
OCCULTISM
see Occult Sciences
OCCUPATION, CHOICE OF
see Vocational Guidance
OCCUPATION TAX
see Business Tax
OCCUPATION THERAPY
see Occupational Therapy
OCCUPATIONAL ACCIDENTS
see Industrial Accidents
OCCUPATIONAL CRIMES
see White Collar Crimes
OCCUPATIONAL DISEASES
see also Fatigue; Lead-Poisoning; Medicine, Industrial; Nystagmus; Skin-Diseases; Workmen's Compensation
Vainio, H., et al. Occupational Cancer & Carcinogenesis. 1981. 49.50 (ISBN 0-07-066798-5). McGraw.
OCCUPATIONAL HEALTH AND SAFETY
see Industrial Safety
OCCUPATIONAL MEDICINE
see Medicine, Industrial
OCCUPATIONAL MOBILITY
Metcalf, David. Low Pay, Occupational Mobility, & Minimum Wage Policy in Britain. 1981. pap. 4.25 (ISBN 0-8447-3450-0). Am Enterprise.
OCCUPATIONAL THERAPY
see also Art Therapy; Handicraft; Music Therapy; Recreational Therapy
Briggs, Anne K. & Agrin, Alice R., eds. Crossroads: A Reader for Psychosocial Occupational Therapy. 2nd ed. 215p. 1982. pap. text ed. 15.00 (ISBN 0-910317-04-6). Am Occupe Therapy.
Fransella, Fay. Psychology for Occupational Therapists. Chapman, Antony & Gale, Anthony, eds. (Psychology for Professional Groups Ser.). 300p. 1982. 49.00x (ISBN 0-333-31859-5, Pub. by Macmillan England). State Mutual Bk.
--Psychology for Occupational Therapists. (Psychology for Professional Groups Ser.). 320p. 1982. text ed. 25.00x (ISBN 0-333-31859-5, Pub. by Macmillan England); pap. text ed. 10.95x (ISBN 0-333-31883-8). Humanities.
Hopkins, Helen L. & Smith, Helen D. Willard & Spackman's Occupational Therapy. 6th ed. (Illus.). 950p. 1983. text ed. write for info. (ISBN 0-397-54361-1, Lippincott Medical). Lippincott.
Langdon, Lawrence & Langdon, Helen J. Initiating Occupational Therapy Programs Within the Public School System: A Guide for Occupational Therapists & Public School Administrators. LC 82-60925. 112p. Date not set. 14.50 (ISBN 0-913590-91-6). Slack Inc.
Reed, Kathlyn & Sanderson, Sharon. OTR Concepts of Occupational Therapy. 2nd ed. (Illus.). 312p. 1983. text ed. price not set (ISBN 0-683-07205-6). Williams & Wilkins.
Williams, John W. & Ostrow, Patricia C. Health Accounting for Quality Assurance: A Manual for Assessing & Improving Outcomes of Care. rev. ed. 116p. 1982. pap. text ed. 25.00 (ISBN 0-910317-08-9). Am Occup Therapy.
OCCUPATIONAL TRAINING
Here are entered works on the vocationally oriented process of endowing people with a skill after either completion or termination of their formal education. Works on vocational instruction within the standard educational system are entered under Vocational Education. Works on retraining persons with obsolete vocational skills are entered under Occupational Retraining. Works on training of employees on the job are entered under Employees, Training Of.
see also Non-Formal Education
Borus, Michael E., ed. Tomorrow's Workers. 208p. 1982. 25.95 (ISBN 0-669-06090-9). Lexington Bks.
Connor, John J. On-the-Job-Training. (Illus.). 112p. 1983. pap. text ed. 14.95 (ISBN 0-934634-56-4). Intl Human Res.
Mann, Dale, et al. Chasing the American Dream: Jobs, Schools, & Employment Training Programs in New York State: Technical Report. 47p. (Orig.). 1980. 10.00 (ISBN 0-88156-006-5); pap. 2.00 (ISBN 0-88156-005-7). Comm Serv Soc NY.
Rudman, Jack. Manpower Development Specialist. (Career Examination Ser.: C-2688). (Cloth bdg. avail. on request). pap. 12.00 (ISBN 0-8373-2688-5). Natl Learning.
--Manpower Program Administrator. (Career Examination Ser.: C-2671). (Cloth bdg. avail. on request). pap. 12.00 (ISBN 0-8373-2671-0). Natl Learning.
--Vocational Training Supervisor. (Career Examination Ser.: C-2673). (Cloth bdg. avail. on request). pap. 12.00 (ISBN 0-8373-2673-7). Natl Learning.
OCCUPATIONS
see also Civil Service Positions; Handicraft; Job Evaluation; Occupational Mobility; Professions; Vocational Guidance
also individual occupations and industries; also subdivision Vocational Guidance under appropriate subjects, e.g. Agriculture–Vocational Guidance
Norris, Willa. The Career Information Service. 4th ed. 1979. 24.50 (ISBN 0-395-30685-X). HM.
Weinstein, Robert V. Jobs for the Twenty-First Century. (Illus.). 192p. 1983. pap. 6.95 (ISBN 0-02-082560-9, Collier). Macmillan.
OCCUPATIONS–CLASSIFICATION
Gottfredson, Gary D. & Holland, John L. Dictionary of Holland Occupational Codes. 520p. (Orig.). 1982. pap. 17.75 (ISBN 0-89106-020-0, 7889). Consulting Psychol.
OCCUPATIONS–DISEASES
see Occupational Diseases
OCCUPATIONS–HYGIENIC ASPECTS
see Industrial Health
OCCUPATIONS–JUVENILE LITERATURE
Bell, Rivian & Koenig, Teresa. Careers with a Record Company. LC 82-20840. (Early Career Bks.). (Illus.). 36p. (gr. 2-5). 1983. PLB 5.95g (ISBN 0-8225-0348-4). Lerner Pubns.
Florian, Doug. People Working. LC 82-45188. (Illus.). 32p. (ps-3). 1983. 9.57i (ISBN 0-690-04263-9, TYC-J); PLB 9.89g (ISBN 0-690-04264-7). Har-Row.
OCCUPATIONS AND BUSY WORK
see Creative Activities and Seatwork
OCEAN
see also Underwater Exploration; Oceanography
also names of oceans, e.g. Pacific Ocean
Chia, L. S. & MacAndrews, C. Southeast Asian Seas: Frontiers for Development. 1982. 36.50x (ISBN 0-07-099247-9). McGraw.
Couper, Alstair, ed. The Times Atlas of the Oceans. (Illus.). 256p. 1983. 75.00 (ISBN 0-686-82708-2). Sci Bks Intl.
Discovering the Sea. LC 81-50814. (Discovering Science Ser.). lib. bdg. 15.96 (ISBN 0-86706-053-0, Pub. by Stonehenge). Silver.
Finn, Daniel P. Managing the Ocean Resources of the United States: The Role of the Federal Marine Sanctuary Program. (Lecture Notes in Coastal & Estuarine Studies: Vol. 2). (Illus.). 193p. 1982. pap. 16.00 (ISBN 0-387-11583-8). Springer-Verlag.
Kester, Dana R. & Ketchum, Bostwick H. Wastes in the Ocean: Dredged Material Disposal in the Ocean, Vol. 2. (Environmental Science & Technology Ser.). 320p. 1983. 39.95x (ISBN 0-471-09771-3, Pub. by Wiley-Interscience). Wiley.
Reader's Digest Editors. Secrets of the Seas. LC 72-80582. (Illus.). 384p. 1972. 13.96 (ISBN 0-89577-051-2). RD Assn.
Updegraffe, Imelda & Updegraffe, Robert. Seas & Oceans. (Turning Points Ser.). (Illus.). 24p. 1983. pap. 3.50 (ISBN 0-14-049193-7, Puffin). Penguin.
OCEAN–ECONOMIC ASPECTS
see Marine Resources; Shipping
OCEAN–JUVENILE LITERATURE
Adler, David. Our Amazing Ocean. LC 82-17373. (Question & Answer Bks.). (Illus.). 32p. (gr. 3-6). 1983. PLB 8.59 (ISBN 0-89375-882-5); pap. text ed. 1.95 (ISBN 0-89375-883-3). Troll Assocs.
Althea. Signposts of the Sea. (Cambridge Dinosaur Wingate Ser.). (Illus.). 32p. (gr. 10-12). 1983. pap. 1.95 (ISBN 0-521-27171-1). Cambridge U Pr.
OCEAN–RESEARCH
see Oceanographic Research
OCEAN (IN RELIGION, FOLK-LORE, ETC.)
see Folk-Lore of the Sea
OCEAN BIRDS
see Sea Birds
OCEAN BOTTOM
see also Marine Sediments; Sedimentation and Deposition; Submarine Geology
Rona, P. A. & Lowell, R. P. Seafloor Spreading Centers: Hydrothermal Systems. LC 79-18265. (Bench Papers in Geology: Vol. 56). 424p. 1980. 51.50 (ISBN 0-87933-363-4). Hutchinson Ross.
OCEAN FISHING
see Salt-Water Fishing
OCEAN FLOOR
see Ocean Bottom
OCEAN LIFE
see Marine Biology
OCEAN LINERS
Plowman, Peter. Passenger Ships of Australia & New Zealand: 1913-1981, Vol. II. 224p. 1982. 40.00x (ISBN 0-85177-247-1, Pub. by Conway Maritime England). State Mutual Bk.
--Passenger Ships of Australia & New Zealand: 1876-1912, Vol. I. 224p. 1982. 40.00x (ISBN 0-85177-246-3, Pub. by Conway Maritime England). State Mutual Bk.
OCEAN RESOURCES
see Marine Resources
OCEAN ROUTES
see Trade Routes
OCEAN TRANSPORTATION
see Shipping
OCEAN TRAVEL
see also Steamboats and Steamboat Lines; Yachts and Yachting
Blum, Ethel. The Total Traveller by Ship. rev. ed. 400p. 1983. pap. 12.95 (ISBN 0-88254-738-0). Hippocrene Bks.
Kane, Robert B. & Kane, Barbara W. Frieghter Voyaging. LC 82-51070. (Illus.). 120p. (Orig.). 1982. pap. 7.95 (ISBN 0-910711-00-3). Voyaging Pr.
Spiess, Gerry & Bree, Marlin. Alone Against the Atlantic. (Illus.). 208p. 1983. pap. 2.95 (ISBN 0-425-05844-1). Berkley Pub.
OCEAN WAVES
Lorch, Carlos. Lopez: Hawaiian Surf Legend. (Illus.). 84p. 1982. pap. 8.95 (ISBN 0-911449-01-9). Mntn & Sea.
OCEANICA
see also Geographic Areas, and names of islands or groups of islands, e.g. Islands of the Pacific, Polynesia, Samoan Islands, Tahiti
McArthur, Norma. Island Populations of the Pacific. LC 82-24169. (Illus.). xvi, 381p. 1983. Repr. of 1967 ed. lib. bdg. 45.00x (ISBN 0-313-22914-7, MCIPP). Greenwood.
OCEANICA–DESCRIPTION AND TRAVEL–GUIDEBOOKS
McDermott, John W. How to Get Lost & Found in the Cook Islands. 1979. 9.95 (ISBN 0-686-37619-6). Orafa Pub Co.
OCEANICA–HISTORY
Spate, O. H. The Pacific Since Magellan, Vol. II: Monopolists & Freebooters. (Illus.). xxiii, 426p. 1983. 59.50x (ISBN 0-686-43209-6). U of Minn Pr.
OCEANOGRAPHIC RESEARCH
see also Underwater Exploration
Marchuk, G. I. & Kagan, B. A. Ocean Tides: Mathematical Models & Numerical Experiments. Cartwright, D. E., tr. LC 82-18898. (Illus.). 240p. 1983. 65.00 (ISBN 0-08-026236-8). Pergamon.
OCEANOGRAPHY
see also Chemical Oceanography; Coasts; Diving; Marine Biology; Meteorology, Maritime; Navigation; Ocean; Ocean Bottom; Ocean Waves; Oceanographic Research; Sea-Water; Submarine Geology; Tides; Underwater Exploration
Barnes, M. Oceanography & Marine Biology: An Annual Review, Vol. 20. (Illus.). 778p. 1982. 82.80 (ISBN 0-08-028460-4). Pergamon.
Beer, T. Environmental Oceanography: An Introduction to the Behaviour of Coastal Waters. (PIL Ser.). (Illus.). 109p. 1983. 40.00 (ISBN 0-08-026291-0); pap. 14.00 (ISBN 0-08-026290-2). Pergamon.
Brewer, P. G. Oceanography: The Present & the Future. (Illus.). 392p. 1983. 39.80 (ISBN 0-387-90720-3). Springer-Verlag.
Conway, Lorraine. Oceanography. (gr. 5-8). 1982. 5.95 (ISBN 0-86653-066-5, GA401). Good Apple.
Csanady, G. T. Circulation in the Coastal Ocean. 1982. 52.50 (ISBN 90-277-1400-2, Pub. by Reidel Holland). Kluwer Boston.
Goldberg, Edward D., et al, eds. The Sea: Marine Modeling. LC 62-18366. (Ideas & Observations on Progress in the Study on the Seas Ser.: Vol. 6). 992p. 1977. 87.95x (ISBN 0-471-31091-3, Pub. by Wiley-Interscience). Wiley.
Poynter, Margaret & Collins, Donald. Under the High Seas: New Frontiers in Oceanography. LC 82-16338. (Illus.). 160p. (gr. 5-9). 1983. 10.95 (ISBN 0-689-30977-5). Atheneum.
Thurman, Harold V. Essentials of Oceanography. 512p. 1983. text ed. 19.95 (ISBN 0-675-20031-8). Merrill.
OCEANOGRAPHY–RESEARCH
see Oceanographic Research
OCEANOGRAPHY, PHYSICAL
see Oceanography
OCEANOLOGY
see Oceanography
O'CONNOR, FLANNERY
O'Connor, Flannery. The Presence of Grace & Other Book Reviews. Martin, Carter W., ed. LC 82-20064. 200p. 1983. 16.00 (ISBN 0-8203-0663-0). U of Ga Pr.
OCULOMOTOR SYSTEM
see Eye–Movements
ODONTOLOGY
see Teeth
ODORS
Arnould-Taylor, W. E. Aromatherapy for the Whole Person. 96p. 1981. 32.00 (ISBN 0-85950-337-2, Pub. by Thornes England). State Mutual Bk.
ODSCHI LANGUAGE
see Twi Language
OFF-BROADWAY THEATER
Auerbach, Doris. Sam Shepard, Arthur Kopit, & the Off-Broadway Theater. (United States Authors Ser.). 1982. lib. bdg. 13.95 (ISBN 0-8057-7371-1, Twayne). G K Hall.
OFF-TRACK BETTING
see Horse Race Betting
OFFENDERS, FEMALE
see Female Offenders
OFFICE, ECCLESIASTICAL
see Clergy–Office
OFFICE, TENURE OF
see Civil Service
OFFICE ADMINISTRATION
see Office Management
OFFICE EMPLOYEES
see Clerks
OFFICE EQUIPMENT AND SUPPLIES
see also Calculating-Machines; Electronic Office Machines; Typewriters; Writing–Materials and Instruments
Condon, M. A. Office Printers: A Practical Evaluation Guide. (Office Technology in the Eighties Ser.: No. 5). 57p. 1982. pap. 17.50x (ISBN 0-85012-371-2). Intl Pubns Serv.
Firth, R. J. Viewdata Systems: A Practical Evaluation Guide. (Office Technology in the Eighties Ser.). (Illus.). 114p. (Orig.). 1982. pap. 15.00x (ISBN 0-85012-370-4). Intl Pubns Serv.
IES Office Lighting Committee. Proposed American National Standard Practice for Office Lighting. (Illus.). 44p. 1982. Repr. 9.00 (ISBN 0-87995-011-0); 13.50 (ISBN 0-686-82676-0). Illum Eng.
OFFICE ETIQUETTE
see Business Etiquette
OFFICE MACHINES
see Electronic Office Machines; Office Equipment and Supplies
OFFICE MANAGEMENT
see also Business Etiquette; Business Records; Office Equipment and Supplies; Office Practice; Personnel Management; Public Records; Receptionists; School Secretaries; Secretaries
Denyer, J. C. Office Administration. 4th ed. Mugridge, A. L., rev. by. 214p. 1982. pap. 9.95 (ISBN 0-7121-1540-4). Intl Ideas.
Tedesco, Eleanor & Mitchell, Robert. Administrative Office Management: Systems & Services. 752p. 1983. text ed. write for info. (ISBN 0-471-09062-X). Wiley.
Walley, B. H. Handbook of Office Management. 2nd ed. 297p. 1982. text ed. 35.75x (Pub. by Busn Bks England). Renouf.
OFFICE PRACTICE
see also Calculating-Machines; Clerks; Commercial Correspondence; Electronic Data Processing; Electronic Office Machines; Files and Filing (Documents); Office Equipment and Supplies; Secretaries; Shorthand; Typewriting
Austin, Evelyn. Secretarial Services. 208p. 1982. pap. text ed. 11.00 (ISBN 0-7121-1984-1). Intl Ideas.
Charneco. Competencias para la Oficina Moderna. 360p. 9.50 (ISBN 0-07-010649-5). McGraw.
Dochterman, Delores. The Art of Taking Minutes. LC 82-42639. 208p. 1982. 12.95 (ISBN 0-9609526-0-8). Snyder Pub Co.
Duenas. Curso Basico de Practicas Secretariales. 120p. 1982. 4.56 (ISBN 0-07-017992-1, G). McGraw.
Gregg's Office Job Training Program: Supervisor's Handbook. 1981. 11.70 (ISBN 0-07-000958-9). McGraw.
Hammer, Hy. Practice for Clerical, Typing & Stenographic Tests. 6th ed. LC 82-13912. 208p. (Orig.). 1983. pap. 8.00 (ISBN 0-668-05616-9, 5616). Arco.
Krevolin, Nathan. Communication Systems & Procedures for the Modern Office. (Illus.). 464p. 1983. 21.95 (ISBN 0-13-153668-0). P-H.
Mitchell, Carol A. Machine Transcription: A Comprehensive Approach for Today's Office Specialist. 176p. (Orig.). 1983. pap. text ed. 10.95 (ISBN 0-672-97986-1); instr's. guide 6.67 (ISBN 0-672-97987-X); working papers 3.95 (ISBN 0-672-97988-8); tapes 266.00 (ISBN 0-672-97989-6). Bobbs.
Spencer, Anne. On the Edge of the Organization: The Role of the Outside Director. 120p. 1983. 24.95 (ISBN 0-471-90018-4, Pub. by Wiley-Interscience). Wiley.

Wolff, Nancy. Tempo: An Office-Procedures Simulation. 1983. write for info. client co. manual (ISBN 0-574-20708-2, 13-3708); write for info. employee handbook (ISBN 0-574-20705-8, 13-3705); write for info. working papers (ISBN 0-574-20707-4, 13-3707); write for info. model answers (ISBN 0-574-20674-4, 13-3674); write for info. office manager handbook (ISBN 0-574-20706-6, 13-3706). SRA.

OFFICE PRACTICE–AUTOMATION

Cohen, Aaron & Cohen, Elaine. Planning the Electronic Office. (Illus.). 288p. Date not set. 29.95 (ISBN 0-07-011583-4, P&RB). McGraw.

Condon, M. A. Office Printers: A Practical Evaluation Guide. (Office Technology in the Eighties Ser.: No. 5). 57p. 1982. pap. 17.50x (ISBN 0-85012-371-2). Intl Pubns Serv.

Derfler, Frank, Jr. & Stallings, Frank. A Manager's Guide to Local Networks. (Illus.). 154p. 1983. 21.95 (ISBN 0-13-549766-3); pap. 14.95 (ISBN 0-13-549758-2). P-H.

Doswell, Andrew. Office Automation. (Information Processing). 280p. 1983. 33.95 (ISBN 0-471-10457-4, Pub. by Wiley-Interscience). Wiley.

Field, R. M. A Glossary of Office Automation Terms. 32p. 1982. pap. text ed. 15.00 (ISBN 0-914548-42-5). Soc Tech Comm.

Finn, Nancy B. The Electronic Office. (Illus.). 144p. 1983. pap. 12.95 (ISBN 0-13-251819-8). P-H.

Popyk, M. K. Word Processing & Information Systems: A Practical Approach. 352p. 1983. 15.50 (ISBN 0-07-050574-8, G). McGraw.

Simpson, Alan, ed. The Office of the Future, No. 1: Planning for the Office of the Future. 140p. 1981. pap. text ed. 23.50x (ISBN 0-566-03404-2). Gower Pub Ltd.

--The Office of the Future, No. 2: Planning for the Electronic Mail. 133p. 1982. pap. text ed. 23.50x (ISBN 0-566-03406-9). Gower Pub Ltd.

--The Office of the Future, No. 3: Planning for Word Processing. 150p. 1982. pap. text ed. 23.50x (ISBN 0-566-03414-X). Gower Pub Ltd.

Tapscott, Don. Office Automation: A User-Driven Method. 264p. 1982. 27.50 (ISBN 0-306-41071-0, Plenum Pr). Plenum Pub.

OFFICE RECORDS

see Business Records

OFFICE SUPPLIES

see Office Equipment and Supplies

OFFICIAL PUBLICATIONS

see Government Publications

OFFICIAL SECRETS

Robertson, K. G. Public Secrets: A Study in the Development of Government Secrets. 224p. 1982. 50.00x (ISBN 0-333-32008-5, Pub. by Macmillan England). State Mutual Bk.

OFFSHORE INSTALLATIONS

see Offshore Structures

OFFSHORE STRUCTURES

Chung, J. S. Offshore Mechanics-Artic Engineering-Deepsea Systems Symposium, First: Proceedings, 2 Vols, Vol. 1. 1982. 45.00 (I00148). ASME.

Chung, J. S., ed. Offshore Mechanics-Artic Engineering-Deepsea Systems Symposium, First: Proceedings, 2 Vols, Vol. 2. 289p. 1982. 45.00 (I00148). ASME.

Dawson, Thomas H. Offshore Structural Engineering. (Illus.). 352p. 1982. text ed. 34.95 (ISBN 0-13-633206-4). P-H.

Fatigue in Offshore Structural Steels. 136p. 1981. 90.00x (ISBN 0-7277-0108-8, Pub. by Telford England). State Mutual Bk.

Goldstein. The Politics of Offshore Oil. 208p. 1982. 21.95 (ISBN 0-03-059813-3). Praeger.

Safety & Health in the Construction of Fixed Offshore Installations in the Petroleum Industry. 129p. 1981. pap. 11.50 (ISBN 92-2-102900-X, ILO 200, ILO). Unipub.

Wave & Wind Directionality: Applications to the Design of Offshore Structures. 1983. text ed. 79.95 (ISBN 0-87201-906-3). Gulf Pub.

Whitehead, Harry. An A-Z of Offshore Oil & Gas. text ed. 39.95x (ISBN 0-87201-052-X). Gulf Pub.

OGLALA INDIANS

see Indians of North America–The West

OHIO–ANTIQUITIES

Ormerod, Dana E. White Rocks: A Woodland Rockshelter in Monroe County, Ohio. LC 82-21378. (Research Papers in Archaeology). 100p. 1983. pap. 6.00 (ISBN 0-87338-285-4). Kent St U Pr.

OHIO–DESCRIPTION AND TRAVEL

Hauck, John W. The C, L & N: The Narrow Gauge in Ohio. (Illus.). 1983. price not set (ISBN 0-87108-629-8). Pruett.

Zimmermann, George. Ohio: Off the Beaten Path. (Illus.). 160p. 1983. pap. 5.95 (ISBN 0-914788-67-1). East Woods.

OHIO RIVER AND VALLEY

Laycock, George & Laycock, Ellen. The Ohio Valley Guide to America's Heartland. LC 81-43579. (Illus.). 400p. 1983. pap. 10.95 (ISBN 0-385-17591-4, Dolp). Doubleday.

OHM'S LAW

CES Industries, Inc. Staff. Programming for Ohms Law, Unit 1. (Ed-Lab Experiment Manual Ser.). (Illus.). (gr. 9-12). 1982. write for info. lab manual (ISBN 0-86711-029-5). CES Industries.

OIL

see Oils and Fats; Petroleum

OIL AND GAS LAW

see Gas, Natural–Law and Legislation; Petroleum Law and Legislation

OIL AND GAS LEASES

Livingston, Virginia. Office Administration of Oil & Gas Leases. 1982. 30.00 (ISBN 0-89419-208-6). Inst Energy.

Lowe, John, ed. Fundamentals of Petroleum Land Titles. 1982. 46.00 (ISBN 0-89931-034-6). Inst Energy.

Lowe, John S., ed. Fundamentals of Oil & Gas Leasing. 1982. 48.00 (ISBN 0-89931-030-3). Inst Energy.

--Oil & Gas of the Williston Basin. 1982. 55.00 (ISBN 0-89419-224-8). Inst Energy.

Mosburg, Lewis G. Leveraged Oil & Gas Programs. 1982. 50.00 (ISBN 0-89419-209-4). Inst Energy.

OIL ENGINES

see Gas and Oil Engines

OIL FIELDS

see also Oil Well Drilling; Petroleum; Petroleum–Pipe Lines

Hunt, A. Lee. Pocket Guide to Supervising in the Oilfield. 1983. pap. text ed. 6.95 (ISBN 0-87201-714-1). Gulf Pub.

U. S. Oilfield Equipment. 1982. 995.00 (285). Predicasts.

OIL INDUSTRIES

see also Oils and Fats; Petroleum Industry and Trade

Barrett, M. Edgar & Cormack, Mary P. Management Strategy in the Oil & Gas Industries: Cases & Readings. 1982. text ed. 34.95 (ISBN 0-87201-506-8). Gulf Pub.

Jackson, Elaine. Lufkin: From Sawdust to Oil. 1982. 24.95 (ISBN 0-87201-437-1). Gulf Pub.

Jones, M. E. Logistic Support: Subsea Oil Production. 1983. text ed. 35.95 (ISBN 0-87201-434-7). Gulf Pub.

U. S. Oilfield Equipment. 1982. 995.00 (285). Predicasts.

OIL LANDS

see Oil Fields

OIL LEASES

see Oil and Gas Leases

OIL-PAINTING

see Painting

OIL POLLUTION OF RIVERS, HARBORS, ETC.

Clark, R. B., intro. by. The Long-Term Effects of Oil Pollution on Marine Populations, Communities & Ecosystems: Proceedings. (RSL Philosophies. Transactions Series B, Vol. 297: No. 1087). (Illus.). 260p. 1982. text ed. 80.00x (ISBN 0-85403-188-X). Scholium Intl.

OECD. Combatting Oil Spills: Some Economic Aspects. 140p. (Orig.). 1982. pap. 9.50X (ISBN 92-64-12341-5). OECD.

--The Cost of Oil Spills: Expert Studies Presented to OECD Seminar. 252p. (Orig.). 1982. pap. 15.00x (ISBN 92-64-12339-3). OECD.

Wardley-Smith, J. The Control of Oil Pollution. 272p. 1983. 40.00x (ISBN 0-8448-1439-3). Crane-Russak.

OIL POLLUTION OF WATER

see also Oil Pollution of Rivers, Harbors, Etc.

Clark, R. B., intro. by. The Long-Term Effects of Oil Pollution on Marine Populations, Communities & Ecosystems: Proceedings. (RSL Philosophies. Transactions Series B, Vol. 297: No. 1087). (Illus.). 260p. 1982. text ed. 80.00x (ISBN 0-85403-188-X). Scholium Intl.

Wardley-Smith, J. The Control of Oil Pollution. 272p. 1983. 40.00x (ISBN 0-8448-1439-3). Crane-Russak.

OIL RESERVOIR ENGINEERING

Cranmer, John L., Jr. BASIC Reservoir Engineering Manual. 240p. 1982. 49.95x (ISBN 0-87814-196-0). Pennwell Pub.

OIL ROYALITIES

see Oil and Gas Leases

OIL SEEDS

see Oilseeds

OIL-SHALES

see also Petroleum

Gary, James H., ed. Proceedings of the Fifteenth Oil Shale Symposium: Proceedings of the Fifteenth Symposium. (Illus.). 606p. 1982. pap. 23.00 (ISBN 0-918062-50-0). Colo Sch Mines.

Peterson, Kathy K., ed. Oil Shale: The Environmental Challenges II. 2nd ed. (Illus.). 402p. 1982. 20.00 (ISBN 0-918062-51-9). Colo Sch Mines.

Raese, Jon W. & Baughman, Gary L., eds. Oil Shale Symposium Proceedings Index 1964-82. 100p. 1982. pap. text ed. 30.00 (ISBN 0-918062-52-7). Colo Sch Mines.

Robl, Tom & Koppenaal, Dave. The Chemical & Engineering Properties of Eastern Oil Shale. Pettit, Rhonda, ed. 303p. (Orig.). 1982. pap. text ed. 10.00 (ISBN 0-86607-014-1). Inst Mining & Minerals.

OIL TANKERS

see Tankers

OIL WELL DRILLING

see also Drilling Muds

Canadian Association of Oilwell Drillling Contractors. Drilling Rig Task Details & Performance Standards for the Driller. (Drilling-Servicing Rig Task Details & Performance Standards Ser.). 1982. pap. text ed. 9.95x (ISBN 0-87201-930-6). Gulf Pub.

Canadian Association of Oilwell Drilling Contractors. Drilling Rig Task Details & Performance Standards for the Derrickhand. (Drilling-Servicing Rig Task Details & Performance Standards Ser.). 1982. pap. 9.95 (ISBN 0-87201-931-4). Gulf Pub.

--Drilling Rig Task Manual & Performance Standards for the Floorhand. (Drilling-Servicing Rig Details & Performance Standards Ser.). 1982. pap. text ed. 9.95x (ISBN 0-87201-933-0). Gulf Pub.

--Drilling Task Details & Performance Standards for the Motorhand. (Drilling-Servicing Rig Task Details & Performance Standards Ser.). 1982. pap. 9.95x (ISBN 0-87201-932-2). Gulf Pub.

--Drilling Task Details for the Rig Manager. (Drilling-Servicing Rig Task Details & Performance Standards Ser.). 1982. pap. 9.95x (ISBN 0-87201-929-2). Gulf Pub.

--An Introduction to Oilwell Drilling & Servicing. 1982. pap. 6.95x (ISBN 0-87201-202-6). Gulf Pub.

--Servicing Rig Task Details & Performance Standards for the Derrickhand. (Drilling-Servicing Rig Task Details & Performance Standards Ser.). 1982. pap. text ed. 9.95x (ISBN 0-87201-936-5). Gulf Pub.

--Servicing Rig Task Details & Performance Standards for the Floorhand. (Drilling-Servicing Rig Task Details & Performance Standards Ser.). 1982. pap. text ed. 9.95x (ISBN 0-87201-937-3). Gulf Pub.

--Servicing Rig Task Details & Performance Standards for the Rig Operator. (Drilling-Servicing Rig Task Details & Performance Standards Ser.). 1982. pap. 9.95x (ISBN 0-87201-935-7). Gulf Pub.

Canadian Association of Oilwell Drilling Contractor. SI Drilling Manual. 1983. text ed. 175.00 (ISBN 0-87201-211-5). Gulf Pub.

Canadian Association of Oilwell Performance Standards Ser. Servicing Rig Task Details & Performance Standards for the Rig Manager. (Drilling-Servicing Rig Task Details & Performance Standards Ser.). 1982. pap. text ed. 9.95x (ISBN 0-87201-934-9). Gulf Pub.

Cranmer, John L. Basic Drilling Engineering Manual. 168p. 1982. 49.95x (ISBN 0-87814-199-5). Pennwell Pub.

Geological & Mud Logging in Drilling Control. 1982. text ed. 19.95x (ISBN 0-87201-433-9). Gulf Pub.

Love, W. W. Disposal Systems. (Mud Equipment Manual Ser.: No. 11). 1982. pap. 10.75x (ISBN 0-87201-623-4). Gulf Pub.

Love, W. W. & Brandt, Louis. Shale Shakers. (Mud Equipment Manual Ser.: No. 3). 1982. pap. text ed. 10.75 (ISBN 0-87201-615-3). Gulf Pub.

Ormsby, George. Hydrocyclones. (Mud Equipment Manual Ser.: No. 6). 1982. pap. text ed. 10.75 (ISBN 0-87201-618-8). Gulf Pub.

Phillips, Jack J. Handbook of Training Evaluation & Measurement Methods. 1982. 19.95 (ISBN 0-87201-877-6). Gulf Pub.

Warring, R. H. Handbook of Valves, Piping & Pipelines. 1982. 65.00x (ISBN 0-87201-885-7). Gulf Pub.

White, Doug. Agitation & Addition. (Mud Pump Manual Ser.: No. 9). 1982. pap. 10.75x (ISBN 0-87201-621-8). Gulf Pub.

OILS AND FATS

see also Lubrication and Lubricants; Oil Industries; Oilseeds; Petroleum

also names of fats and oils

Report of the Sixteenth Session of the Intergovernmental Group on Oilseeds, Oils & Fats: Committee on Commodity Problems, Fifty-Fourth Session. 11p. 1982. pap. 7.50 (ISBN 0-686-83876-9, F2322, FAO). Unipub.

OILS AND FATS, EDIBLE

Torrey, S., ed. Edible Oils & Fats: Developments Since 1978. LC 82-19091. (Food Technology Review: No. 57). (Illus.). 402p. 1983. 44.00 (ISBN 0-8155-0923-5). Noyes.

Weiss, Theodore J. Foods Oils & Their Uses. 2nd ed. (Illus.). 1983. text ed. 27.50 (ISBN 0-87055-420-4). AVI.

OILSEED INDUSTRY

see Oil Industries

OILSEEDS

see also Oils and Fats; Seeds

Induced Mutations: A Tool in Plant Research. 538p. 1981. pap. 55.00 (ISBN 0-686-82544-6, ISP 591, IAEA). Unipub.

Kramer, J. K. & Saver, F. D., eds. High & Low Erucic Acid Rapeseed Oils: Production, Usage, Chemistry & Toxilogical Evaluation. LC 82-13805. Date not set. price not set (ISBN 0-12-425080-7). Acad Pr.

Report of the Sixteenth Session of the Intergovernmental Group on Oilseeds, Oils & Fats: Committee on Commodity Problems, Fifty-Fourth Session. 11p. 1982. pap. 7.50 (ISBN 0-686-83876-9, F2322, FAO). Unipub.

OJI LANGUAGE

see Twi Language

OKLAHOMA–DESCRIPTION AND TRAVEL

Ottaway, Hal N. & Edwards, Jim L. The Vanished Splendor: Postcard Views of Early Oklahoma City. LC 82-72945. (Illus.). 64p. Date not set. 15.95 (ISBN 0-910453-00-4). Abalache Bkshop.

Vaughn-Roberson, Courtney & Vaughn-Roberson, Glen. City in the Osage Hills: A History of Tulsa, Oklahoma. (Illus.). 1983. price not set (ISBN 0-87108-644-1). Pruett.

OKLAHOMA–JUVENILE LITERATURE

Newsom, D. Earl. The Birth of Oklahoma. (Illus.). 278p. (gr. 5-12). 1983. 14.95 (ISBN 0-934188-08-4); PLB 14.95 (ISBN 0-686-38034-7). Evans Pubns.

OLD AGE–DISEASES

see Geriatrics

OLD AGE, SURVIVORS AND DISABILITY INSURANCE

see Insurance, Disability; Old Age Pensions; Social Security

OLD AGE AND EMPLOYMENT

see Age and Employment

OLD AGE PENSIONS

see also Disability Evaluation; Pension Trusts

also subdivisions Pensions, and Salaries, Pensions, etc. under names of industries, professions, etc. e.g. Teachers–Salaries, Pensions, etc.

Hartman, Robert W. Pay & Pensions for Federal Employees. 150p. 1983. 18.95 (ISBN 0-8157-3496-4); pap. 7.95 (ISBN 0-8157-3495-6). Brookings.

OLD AGE, SURVIVORS AND DISABILITY INSURANCE

see Social Security

OLD ENGLISH LANGUAGE

see Anglo-Saxon Language; English Language–Middle English, 1100-1500

OLD ENGLISH LITERATURE

see English Literature (Collections)–Middle English (1100-1500)

OLD FRENCH LITERATURE

see French Literature (Collections)–To 1500

OLD INDIC LANGUAGE

see Vedic Language

OLD MILLS

see Flour Mills; Mills and Mill-Work

OLD ORDER AMISH

see Amish

OLD RED SANDSTONE (GEOLOGY)

see Geology, Stratigraphic–Devonian

OLDER WORKERS

see Age and Employment

OLDSMOBILE AUTOMOBILE

see Automobiles–Types–Oldsmobile

O'LEARY, JOHN, 1830-1907

O'Leary, John. The Running Game: The Campaign Journals of John O'Leary. (Illus.). 96p. 1983. 9.95 (ISBN 0-686-43254-1). NY Zoetrope.

OLEFINS

Henman, T. J. World Index of Polyolefin Stabilizers. 1983. text ed. 135.00 (ISBN 0-87201-920-9). Gulf Pub.

OLEOMARGARINE

Van Stuyvenberg. Margarine: An Economic, Social & Scientific History, 1869-1969. 366p. 1982. 49.00x (ISBN 0-85323-130-3, Pub. by Liverpool Univ England). State Mutual Bk.

OLIGOPHRENIA

see Mental Deficiency

OLIGOPOLIES

Nicholson, N. Oligopoly & Conflict. 244p. 1982. 39.00x (ISBN 0-85323-220-2, Pub. by Liverpool Univ England). State Mutual Bk.

OLYMPIC GAMES

Gordon, Barclay F. Olympic Architecture: Building for the Summer Games. 160p. 1983. 16.00 (ISBN 0-471-06069-0, Pub. by Wiley-Interscience). Wiley.

Petillon, Mary & Newman, Sharon. Olympics Made Easy. (Illus.). 202p. (gr. 5-9). 1982. pap. text ed. 8.95 (ISBN 0-910935-00-9); wkbk. 8.95. Vista Graphics.

Vital Issues Editor & Bradley, Bill. The Olympic Games: What's to Become of Them? (Vital Issues, Vol. XXIX 1979-80: No. 7). 0.50 (ISBN 0-686-81612-9). Ctr Info Am.

OMAHA INDIANS

see Indians of North America–The West

OMAI, SOUTH SEA ISLANDER

McCormick, E. H. Omai, Pacific Envoy. (Illus.). 382p. 1977. 33.00x (ISBN 0-19-647952-5). Oxford U Pr.

OMAN

Graz, Liesl. The Omanis: Sentinels of the Gulf. (Illus.). 216p. 1982. text ed. 25.00x (ISBN 0-582-78348-8). Longman.

Whelan, John, ed. Oman: A Middle East Economic Digest Guide. (MEED Practical Guide Ser.). (Illus.). 198p. (Orig.). 1982. pap. 15.00 (ISBN 0-7103-0013-1, Kegan Paul). Routledge & Kegan.

OMAR KHAYYAM

Shahid, Irfan. Omar Khayyam, the Philosopher-Poet of Medieval Islam. LC 82-12023. 32p. 1982. lib. bdg. 5.95 (ISBN 0-87840-022-2). Georgetown U Pr.

OMELETS

see Cookery (Eggs)

OMENS

see also Dreams; Signs and Symbols

Signs & Wonders Today. 1983. Repr. write for info. Creation Hse.

ON-LINE BIBLIOGRAPHIC SEARCHING

Gilreath, Charles L. Computer Literature Searching: Research Strategies & Databases. 108p. 1983. lib. bdg. 18.50x (ISBN 0-86531-526-4). Westview.

Key Papers on the Use of Computer-Based Bibliographic Services. 1973. 10.00 (ISBN 0-686-42911-7). Knowledge Indus.

Matthews, Joseph R. Public Access to Online Catalogs: A Planning Guide for Managers. 345p. 1982. pap. text ed. 28.50 (ISBN 0-910965-00-5). Online.

Moore, Nick, ed. On-Line Information in Public Libraries: A Review of Recent British Research. 69p. 1981. 35.00x (ISBN 0-905984-76-5, Pub. by Brit Lib England). State Mutual Bk.

Tedd, Lucy A. The Teaching of On-Line Cataloguing & Searching & the Use of New Technology in UK Schools of Librarianship & Information Science. 126p. 1981. pap. 40.00x (ISBN 0-905984-67-6, Pub. by Brit Lib England). State Mutual Bk.

ON-LINE DATA PROCESSING
see also On-Line Bibliographic Searching; Real-Time Data Processing; Time-Sharing Computer Systems

Fayen, Emily G. The Era of Online Public Access Catalogs. 150p. 1983. 34.50 (ISBN 0-86729-054-4); pap. 27.50 (ISBN 0-86729-053-6). Knowledge Indus.

Hiltz, S. R. Online Communities. Shneiderman, Ben, ed. (Human-Computer Interaction Ser.). 272p. 1983. text ed. 29.50 (ISBN 0-89391-145-3). Ablex Pub.

Trends in On-Line Computer Control Systems. (IEE Conference Publications: No. 208). 124p. 1982. pap. 44.00 (ISBN 0-85296-256-8). Inst Elect Eng.

ONCOLOGY
see also Cancer; Tumors

Brade, W., ed. Tegafur-Ftorafur. (Beitraege zur Onkologie-Contributions to Oncology Ser.: Vol. 14). viii, 200p. 1983. pap. 39.00 (ISBN 3-8055-3653-4). S Karger.

Brain, Michael C. & McCulloch, Peter B. Current Therapy in Hematology-Oncology. 400p. 1983. text ed. 44.00 (ISBN 0-941158-05-5, D07809). Mosby.

Deeley, Thomas J., ed. Topical Reviews in Radiotherapy & Oncology, Vol. 2. (Illus.). 264p. 1982. text ed. 37.50 (ISBN 0-7236-0616-1). Wright-PSG.

Deftos, L. J. Medullary Thyroid Carcinoma. (Beitraege zur Onkologie. Contributions to Oncology Ser.: Vol. 17). (Illus.). viii, 144p. 1983. pap. 60.00 (ISBN 3-8055-3703-4). S Karger.

Krisch, K., ed. Schilddruesentumoren. (Beitraege zur Onkologie. Contributions to Oncology Ser.: Vol. 16). (Illus.). vi, 74p. 1983. pap. 24.95 (ISBN 3-8055-3695-X). S Karger.

Mammakarzinom. (Journal: Onkologie: Vol. 5, Suppl. 1). (Illus.). 68p. 1982. pap. 14.50 (ISBN 3-8055-3643-7). S Karger.

Weber-Stadelmann, W., ed. Adriamycin & Derivatives in Gastrointestinal Cancer. (Beitraege zur Onkologie. Contributions to Oncology Ser.: Vol. 15). (Illus.). vi, 144p. 1983. pap. 58.75 (ISBN 3-8055-3689-5). S Karger.

ONE-PARENT FAMILY
see Single-Parent Family

ONEIDA COMMUNITY

Rich, Jane K. & Blake, Nelson M., eds. A Lasting Spring: Jessie Catherine Kinsley, Daughter of the Oneida Community. LC 82-19200. (York State Bks.). (Illus.). 300p. (Orig.). 1983. 32.00x (ISBN 0-8156-0183-2); pap. 14.95 (ISBN 0-8156-0176-X). Syracuse U Pr.

ONEIDA INDIANS
see Indians of North America–Eastern States

ONEIROMANCY
see Dreams

ONTARIO

Arnopoulos, Sheila M. Voices from French Ontario. 216p. 1982. 17.50 (ISBN 0-7735-0405-2); pap. 6.95 (ISBN 0-7735-0406-0). McGill-Queens U Pr.

ONTOGENY
see also Evolution

Bateson, P. P. & Klopfer, Peter H., eds. Perspectives in Ethology, Vol. 5: Ontogeny. 500p. 1982. 39.50x (ISBN 0-306-41063-X, Plenum Pr). Plenum Pub.

ONTOLOGY
see also Change; Existentialism; Identity; Metaphysics; Philosophical Anthropology; Philosophy

Barukinamwo, Matthieu. Edith Stein: Pour une Ontologie Dynamique, Ouverte a la Transcendance Totale. 184p. (Fr.). 1982. write for info. (ISBN 3-8204-5974-X). P Lang Pubs.

Harbert, David L. Existence, Knowing, & Philosophical Systems. LC 82-17565. 226p. (Orig.). 1983. lib. bdg. 21.75 (ISBN 0-8191-2804-X); pap. text ed. 10.25 (ISBN 0-8191-2805-8). U Pr of Amer.

Leinfellner, Werner & Kraemer, Eric. Language & Ontology. (Sprachen und Ontologie.). 1982. lib. bdg. 78.00 (ISBN 90-277-9080-9, Pub. by Reidel Holland). Kluwer Boston.

Sayre, Kenneth M. Plato's Late Ontology: A Riddle Resolved. LC 82-61382. 370p. 1983. 25.00 (ISBN 0-691-07277-9). Princeton U Pr.

Siegel, James E. Comeuppance. 96p. 1983. 13.95 (ISBN 0-8022-2413-X). Philos Lib.

OOLOGY
see Birds–Eggs and Nests

OPALS

Bingham, Rebecca. Opals. (Illus.). 48p. 1982. 30.00 (ISBN 0-88014-042-9). Mosaic Pr OH.

OPEL (AUTOMOBILE)
see Automobiles, Foreign–Types–Opel

OPEN CLASSROOM APPROACH TO TEACHING
see Open Plan Schools

OPEN-CUT MINING
see Strip Mining

OPEN EDUCATION
see Open Plan Schools

OPEN FORUM
see Forums (Discussion and Debate)

OPEN-PIT MINING
see Strip Mining

OPEN PLAN SCHOOLS

The National Slide Collection on Learning Resources. LC 79-720353. 1982. 179.50 (ISBN 0-686-84122-0); members 159.50 (ISBN 0-686-84123-9). Assn Ed Comm Tech.

OPEN-SPACE PLAN SCHOOLS
see Open Plan Schools

OPERA
see also Ballet
also names of specific opera companies, e.g. New York (City)–Metropolitan Opera

Chatfield-Taylor, Joan. Backstage at the Opera. LC 82-12877. (Illus.). 132p. (Orig.). 1982. pap. 12.95 (ISBN 0-87701-271-7). Chronicle Bks.

De Ockham, Guillelmi. Opera Politica, Vol. 1. 2nd ed. Offler, H. S., ed. 378p. 1974. 37.50 (ISBN 0-7190-0548-5). Manchester.

--Opera Politica, Vol. 2. Offler, H. S., ed. 504p. 1963. 44.00 (ISBN 0-7190-0081-5). Manchester.

Puccini, Giacomo. Puccini's Madama Butterfly. (Opera Libretto Ser.). 64p. (Orig.). 1983. pap. 1.95 (ISBN 0-486-24465-2). Dover.

Rosenthal, Harold. My Mad World of Opera: The Autobiography of the Editor of Opera Magazine. (Illus.). 234p. 1982. text ed. 29.75x (ISBN 0-8419-6305-3). Holmes & Meier.

Verdi, Giuseppe. Verdi's Aida. 96p. (Orig.). 1983. pap. 1.95 (ISBN 0-486-24459-8). Dover.

--Verdi's Rigoletto. (Opera Libretto Ser.). 64p. (Orig.). 1983. pap. 1.95 (ISBN 0-486-24497-0). Dover.

Virga, Patricia H. The American Opera to 1790. Buelow, George, ed. LC 82-15950. (Studies in Musicology: No. 61). 414p. 1982. 49.95 (ISBN 0-8357-1374-1). Univ Microfilms.

OPERA-BIBLIOGRAPHY

Combined Catalog of the Opera Collections in the Music Libraries at the University of California at Berkeley & the University of California, Los Angeles. 1983. lib. bdg. 125.00 (ISBN 0-8161-0392-5, Hall Library). G K Hall.

OPERA-HISTORY AND CRITICISM

Goodman, Andrew. Gilbert & Sullivan at Law. LC 82-12175. (Illus.). 264p. 1982. 25.00 (ISBN 0-8386-3179-7). Fairleigh Dickinson.

Porges, Heinrich. Wagner Rehearsing the Ring: An Eye-Witness Account of the Stage Rehearsals of the First Bayeuth Festival. Jacobs, Robert L., tr. (Illus.). 145p. 1983. 19.95 (ISBN 0-521-23722-X). Cambridge U Pr.

OPERA-STORIES, PLOTS, ETC.
see Operas–Stories, Plots, etc.

Kerr, Caroline V., tr. & ed. The Story of Bayreuth As Told in "The Bayreuth Letters of Richard Wagner". LC 78-163795. 364p. Date not set. Repr. of 1912 ed. price not set. Vienna Hse.

OPERA-ENGLAND

White, Eric W. Benjamin Britten: His Life & Operas. rev. ed. Evans, John, ed. LC 82-10882. (Illus.). 320p. 1983. text ed. 30.00x (ISBN 0-520-04893-8); pap. text ed. 12.95x (ISBN 0-520-04894-6). U of Cal Pr.

OPERA, COMIC
see Opera

OPERAS
see also Musical Revues, Comedies, etc.

Cord, William O. An Introduction to Richard Wagner's Der Ring Des Nibelungen: A Handbook. LC 82-14417. (Illus.). 175p. 1983. text ed. 19.95x (ISBN 0-8214-0648-5, 82-84176); pap. 11.95 (ISBN 0-8214-0708-2, 82-84770). Ohio U Pr.

OPERAS-SCORES

Osborne, Charles. The Complete Operas of Mozart. (Quality Paperbacks Ser.). (Illus.). 349p. 1983. pap. 9.95 (ISBN 0-306-80190-6). Da Capo.

OPERAS-STORIES, PLOTS, ETC.

Giacomo, Giuseppe & Illica, Luigi, eds. La Boheme. (Metropolitan Opera Classics Library). 224p. 1983. 17.45i (ISBN 0-316-56838-4); deluxe ed. 75.00 (ISBN 0-316-56840-6); pap. 9.70i (ISBN 0-316-56839-2). Little.

OPERATING STATEMENTS
see Financial Statements

OPERATIONAL AMPLIFIERS

Faulkenberry, Luces M. An Introduction to Operational Amplifiers with Linear Applications. 2nd ed. LC 81-13043. (Electronic Technology Ser.). 560p. 1982. text ed. 22.95x (ISBN 0-471-05790-8); solutions manual 5.00 (ISBN 0-471-86319-X). Wiley.

OPERATIONAL ANALYSIS
see Operations Research

OPERATIONAL AUDITING
see Management Audit

OPERATIONAL RESEARCH
see Operations Research

OPERATIONS AUDITING
see Management Audit

OPERATIONS RESEARCH
see also Mathematical Optimization; Network Analysis (Planning); Queuing Theory; Research, Industrial; Scheduling (Management); Simulation Methods; Statistical Decision; Systems Engineering

Feichtinger, Gustav & Kall, Peter. Operations Research in Progress. 1982. 56.50 (ISBN 90-277-1464-9, Pub. by Reidel Holland). Kluwer Boston.

Greenberg, H. J. & Murphy, F. H. Advanced Techniques in the Practice of Operations Research. (Publications in Operations Research Ser.: Vol. 4). 470p. 1982. 47.50 (ISBN 0-444-00750-4, North Holland). Elsevier.

Mjelde, K. M. Methods of the Allocation of Limited Resources. 100p. 1983. price not set (ISBN 0-471-10439-6, Pub. by Wiley-Interscience). Wiley.

OPERATIVE DENTISTRY
see Dentistry, Operative

OPERATIVE OBSTETRICS
see Obstetrics–Surgery

OPERATIVE SURGERY
see Surgery, Operative

OPERATORS, DIFFERENTIAL
see Differential Operators

OPERATORS, LINEAR
see Linear Operators

OPERETTA-STORIES, PLOTS, ETC.
see Operas–Stories, Plots, etc.

OPERETTAS
see Musical Revues, Comedies, etc.; Operas

OPHIDIA
see Snakes

OPHIOLOGY
see Snakes

OPHTHALMOLOGY
see also Eye; Pediatric Ophthalmology

Current Concepts in Ophthalmology. (Illus.). 81p. (Orig.). 1980. pap. text ed. 6.00 (ISBN 0-910133-00-X). MA Med Soc.

Ernest, J. T., ed. Year Book of Ophthalmology, 1983. 1983. 40.00 (ISBN 0-8151-3137-2). Year Bk Med.

Gorin, George. History of Opthalmology. LC 82-61325. xvi, 630p. 1982. text ed. 40.00 (ISBN 0-914098-25-X). Publish or Perish.

OPHTHALMOLOGY, VETERINARY
see Veterinary Ophthalmology

OPHTHALMOMETRY
see Eye–Examination

OPIATES
see Narcotics

OPINION, PUBLIC
see Public Opinion

OPINION POLLS
see Public Opinion Polls

OPPOSITION, THEORY OF

Dezso, Laszlo, ed. Contrastive Studies Hungarian-English. 122p. (Orig.). 1982. pap. 7.50x (ISBN 963-05-2719-7). Intl Pubns Serv.

OPTICAL COMPUTING
see Optical Data Processing

OPTICAL DATA PROCESSING
see also Computers–Optical Equipment; Information Display Systems

Biotechnology Equipment & Supplies. (Reports Ser.: No. 513). 179p. 1982. 985.00 (ISBN 0-686-38954-9). Intl Res Dev.

Rogers, G. L. Noncoherent Optical Processing. LC 77-5453. 192p. Repr. of 1977 ed. text ed. 33.95 (ISBN 0-471-73055-6). Krieger.

OPTICAL ILLUSIONS

Pappas, Theoni. What Do You See? An Optical Illusion Study. (Illus.). 36p. 1982. pap. 14.95 (ISBN 0-933174-18-7). Wide World-Tetra.

OPTICAL INSTRUMENTS
see also Astronomical Instruments; Computers–Optical Equipment; Glass; Lenses; Microscope and Microscopy; Mirrors; Telescope
also names of specific instruments, e.g. Spectroscope

Eccles, M. J. & Sim, M. E. Low Light Level Detectors in Astronomy. LC 82-12881. (Cambridge Astrophysics Ser.: No. 3). (Illus.). 200p. Date not set. price not set (ISBN 0-521-24088-3). Cambridge U Pr.

OPTICAL MASERS
see Lasers

OPTICAL MEASUREMENTS

Dahneke, Barton E. Measurement of Suspended Particles By Quasi-Elastic Light Scattering. 400p. 1982. 39.95 (ISBN 0-471-87289-X, Pub. by Wiley-Interscience). Wiley.

OPTICAL ROTATION

Barron, L. D. Molecular Light Scattering & Optical Activity. 425p. Date not set. price not set (ISBN 0-521-24602-4). Cambridge U Pr.

Mason, S. F. Molecular Optical Activity & the Chiral Discriminations. LC 82-1125. (Illus.). 250p. 1982. 39.50 (ISBN 0-521-24702-0). Cambridge U Pr.

OPTICAL SCANNERS

Gottlieb & Ireland. Electro-Optical & Acoustic-Optical Scanning & Deflection. (Optical Engineering Ser.). 216p. 1983. price not set (ISBN 0-8247-1811-9). Dekker.

OPTICS
see also Color; Dispersion; Electron Optics; Electrooptics; Light; Optical Measurements; Perspective; Photochemistry; Photometry; Radiation; Spectrum Analysis
also headings beginning with the word Optical; also Optics, Geometrical; Optics, Physiological; and similar headings

Frieden, B. R. Probability, Statistical Optics, & Data Analysis. (Springer Series in Information Sciences: Vol. 10). (Illus.). 404p. 1983. 39.00 (ISBN 0-387-11769-5). Springer-Verlag.

Gagliardi, Robert M. & Karp, Sherman. Optical Communications. LC 75-26509. 432p. 1976. 54.50x (ISBN 0-471-28915-9, Pub. by Wiley-Interscience). Wiley.

Gaskill, Jack D. Linear Systems, Fourier Transforms & Optics. LC 78-1118. (Pure & Applied Optics Ser.). 1978. 39.95x (ISBN 0-471-29288-5, Pub. by Wiley-Interscience). Wiley.

Gerrard, A. & Burch, J. Introduction to Matrix Methods in Optics. LC 72-21192. (Pure & Applied Optics Ser.). 1975. 68.95x (ISBN 0-471-29685-6, Pub. by Wiley-Interscience). Wiley.

Hudson, R. D. & Hudson, J. W., eds. Infrared Detectors. LC 75-4923. (Benchmark Papers in Optics: Vol. 2). 392p. 1975. 51.50 (ISBN 0-87933-135-6). Hutchinson Ross.

Mehring, M. Principles of High Resolution NMR in Solids. (Illus.). 342p. 1983. 38.00 (ISBN 0-387-11852-7). Springer-Verlag.

Obstfeld, Henri. Optics in Vision. 2nd ed. 1982. text ed. 49.95 (ISBN 0-407-00240-5). Butterworth.

Progress in Optics, Vols. 1-8. Vol. 1, 1961. 35.75 (ISBN 0-444-10318-X); Vol. 2, 1963. 32.75 (ISBN 0-444-10319-8); Vol. 4, 1965. 24.95 (ISBN 0-444-10321-X); Vol. 5, 1966. 21.20 (ISBN 0-444-10322-8); Vol. 6, 1967. 39.75 (ISBN 0-444-10323-6); Vol. 7, 1969. 42.25 (ISBN 0-444-10324-4); Vol. 8, 1971. 44.50 (ISBN 0-444-10020-2). Elsevier.

Progress in Optics, Vols. 9-17. Vol. 9, 1971. 42.25 (ISBN 0-444-10111-X); Vol. 10, 1972. 49.00 (ISBN 0-444-10394-5); Vol. 11, 1973. 59.75 (ISBN 0-444-10497-6); Vol. 12, 1975. 59.75 (ISBN 0-7204-1512-8); Vol. 13, 1976. 51.00 (ISBN 0-444-10806-8); Vol. 14, 1977. 70.25 (ISBN 0-444-10914-5); Vol. 15, 1978. 64.00 (ISBN 0-7204-1515-2); Vol. 16, 1979. 76.75 (ISBN 0-444-85087-2); Vol. 17, 1980. 64.00 (ISBN 0-444-85309-X). Elsevier.

Ruben, M. & Woodward, E. G. Revision Clinical Optics. 1982. 60.00x (ISBN 0-333-26107-0, Pub. by Macmillan England). State Mutual Bk.

Williams, Charles S. & Becklund, Orville A. Optics: A Short Course for Engineers & Scientists. 414p. 1983. text ed. write for info. (ISBN 0-89874-617-5). Krieger.

OPTICS, ELECTRONIC
see Electron Optics

OPTICS, FIBER
see Fiber Optics

OPTIMISM

Fisher, Lillian E. Violet Richardson Ward: Founder-President of Soroptimist. 1983. 10.95 (ISBN 0-533-05563-6). Vantage.

OPTIMIZATION (MATHEMATICS)
see Mathematical Optimization

OPTIMIZATION THEORY
see Mathematical Optimization

ORAL COMMUNICATION
Here are entered works on speaking as a means of communication. Works on the oral production of meaningful sounds in language are entered under Speech.
see also Conversation; Oral Interpretation; Speech; Speech Processing Systems

Aitchison, June. The Articulate Mammal. 2nd., rev., & enl. ed. LC 82-49138. (Illus.). 288p. 1983. text ed. 15.50x (ISBN 0-87663-422-6). Universe.

Ambrester, Marcus L. & Julian, Faye D. Speech Communication Reader. 217p. (Orig.). 1983. pap. text ed. 8.95x (ISBN 0-88133-013-2). Waveland Pr.

Skopec, Eric W. Business & Professional Speaking. (Illus.). 288p. 1983. pap. 16.95 (ISBN 0-13-107532-2). P-H.

ORAL CONTRACEPTIVES

Dickey, Richard P. Managing Contraceptive Pill Patients. 3rd ed. (Illus.). 8.65 (ISBN 0-686-42717-3). Creative Infomatics.

Fairweather, D., ed. Some Metabolic Considerations of Oral Contraceptive Usage: Proceedings of the 2nd International Norgestral Symposium. (International Congress Ser.: No. 34). 1975. pap. 18.75 (ISBN 0-444-15159-1). Elsevier.

Jeffcoate, S. L. & Sandler, M. Progress Towards a Male Contraceptive. (Current Topics in Reproductive Endocrinology Ser.). 220p. 1983. 45.00 (ISBN 0-471-10417-5, Pub. by Wiley Med). Wiley.

ORAL HISTORY

Cook, Patsy A., ed. Directory of Oral History Programs in the United States. 138p. 59.95 (ISBN 0-667-00680-X). Microfilming Corp.

Henige, David. Oral Historiography. LC 82-168. 208p. 1982. text ed. 28.00x (ISBN 0-582-64364-3); pap. text ed. 9.95x (ISBN 0-582-64363-5). Longman.

Russell, Bert. Swiftwater People. 1st ed. (Oral History Ser.: No. 2). 1979. pap. 7.95 (ISBN 0-930344-02-2); 10.95 (ISBN 0-930344-05-7). Lacon Pubs.

ORAL INTERPRETATION
see also Story-Telling

Doll, Howard D. Oral Interpretation of Literature: An Annotated Bibliography with Multimedia Listings. LC 82-3344. 505p. 1982. 32.50 (ISBN 0-8108-1538-9). Scarecrow.

Tedlock, Dennis. The Spoken Word & the Work of Interpretation. LC 82-40489. (Illus.). 400p. 1983. 35.00x (ISBN 0-8122-7880-1); pap. 14.95x (ISBN 0-8122-1143-X). U of Pa Pr.

ORAL MICROBIOLOGY
see Mouth–Microbiology

ORAL SURGERY
see Mouth–Surgery

ORATORS, AFRO-AMERICAN
see Afro-American Orators

ORATORY

see also Debates and Debating; Public Speaking

Bennett, Charles E., ed. Dialogus de Oratoribus. 1983. pap. 10.00 (ISBN 0-89241-226-7). Caratzas Bros.

Braden, Waldo W. The Oral Tradition in the South. LC 82-20827. 152p. 1983. text ed. 17.50x (ISBN 0-8071-1093-0). La State U Pr.

ORBITALS, MOLECULAR

see Molecular Orbitals

ORCHESTRA

see also Conducting; Conductors (Music); Instrumentation and Orchestration; Symphony Orchestras

Kennedy, Michael. The Halle: A History of the Orchestra from 1858-1983. 1983. write for info. (ISBN 0-7190-0921-9). Manchester.

McLeish, Kenneth & McLeish, Valerie. Instruments & Orchestras. (Illus.). 32p. pap. 4.75 laminated (ISBN 0-19-321435-0). Oxford U Pr.

ORCHESTRA–JUVENILE LITERATURE

Storms, Laura. Careers with an Orchestra. LC 82-17284. (Early Career Bks.). (Illus.). 36p. (gr. 2-5). 1983. PLB 5.95g (ISBN 0-8225-0344-1). Lerner Pubns.

ORCHESTRATION

see Instrumentation and Orchestration

ORCHID CULTURE

Darwin, Charles R. The Various Contrivances by Which Orchids are Fertilised by Insects. 2nd ed. LC 72-3892. (Illus.). xvi, 300p. 1972. write for info. (ISBN 0-404-08406-0). AMS Pr.

Rentoul, J. N. Growing Orchids. (Illus.). 218p. 1982. 14.95 (ISBN 0-85091-147-8). Timber.

--Growing Orchids Book Three: Vandas, Denrobiums & Others. (Illus.). 241p. 1983. 26.95 (ISBN 0-917304-22-5); pap. 19.95 (ISBN 0-917304-32-2). Timber.

Rittershausen, Brian & Rittershausen, Wilma. Orchids As Indoor Plants. (Illus.). 90p. 1983. pap. 7.95 (ISBN 0-7137-1303-8, Pub. by Blandford Pr England). Sterling.

ORCHIDS

see also Orchid Culture

Banerji, M. L. Orchids of Nepal. (Illus.). 135p. (Orig.). 1982. text ed. 12.50 (ISBN 0-934454-95-7). Lubrecht & Cramer.

Williams & Arlott. A Field Guide to the Orchids of Britain & Europe. 29.95 (ISBN 0-686-42774-2, Collins Pub England). Greene.

Williams, John G. & Williams, Andrew E. Field Guide to Orchids of North America. (Illus.). 144p. 1983. flexi-cover 10.95 (ISBN 0-87663-415-3). Universe.

ORDER STATISTICS

Gibbons, Jean D., et al. Selecting & Ordering Populations: A New Statistical Methodology. LC 77-3700. (Probability & Mathematical Statistics). 1977. 51.50x (ISBN 0-471-02670-0, Pub. by Wiley-Interscience). Wiley.

ORDERS, MAJOR

see Clergy

ORDERS, MONASTIC

see Monasticism and Religious Orders

ORDINAL POSITION OF CHILDREN

see Birth Order

ORDINARY'S COURTS

see Probate Law and Practice

ORDINATION OF WOMEN

Maitland, Sara. A Map of the New Country: Women & Christianity. LC 82-13142. 218p. 1983. 12.95 (ISBN 0-7100-9326-8). Routledge & Kegan.

OREGON

see also names of cities, counties and towns in Oregon

Bell, Mimi. Offbeat Oregon. (Orig.). 1983. pap. 6.95 (ISBN 0-87701-274-1). Chronicle Bks.

Skinner, Constance L. Adventures of Oregon. 1920. text ed. 8.50x (ISBN 0-686-83454-2). Elliots Bks.

OREGON–DESCRIPTION AND TRAVEL

Holden, Ronald & Holden, Glenda. Touring the Wine Country of Oregon. (Touring the Wine Country of.....Ser.). (Illus.). 208p. (Orig.). pap. 6.95 (ISBN 0-910571-00-7). Holden Travel Res.

Loring, J. M. & Loring, Louise. Pictographs & Petroglyphs of the Oregon Country: Columbia River & Northern Oregon, Pt. 1. (Monograph XXI). (Illus.). pap. 18.50 (ISBN 0-917956-35-4). UCLA Arch.

Park, Chung I. Best Sellers & Best Choices, 1982. LC 81-640911. (Orig.). pap. 4.75x (ISBN 0-939670-02-X). Ad Digest.

Smith, Kathy. A Rainy Day Guide to Portland. (Orig.). 1983. pap. 6.95 (ISBN 0-87701-288-1). Chronicle Bks.

Thompson, Philip. Stranger In Town: A Guide to Taverns in Oregon & Southwest Washington. 1983. pap. 4.95 (ISBN 0-932576-14-1). Breitenbush Pubns.

OREGON–GENEOLOGY

Rees, Helen G. Shaniko People. (Illus.). 1982. 10.95 (ISBN 0-8323-0414-X); pap. 7.95 (ISBN 0-8323-0415-8). Binford.

OREGON–HISTORY

Duniway, David. Glimpses of Historic South Salem. 56p. (Orig.). 1982. pap. 3.95 (ISBN 0-686-42960-5). S Salem News.

Engeman, Richard H. The Jacksonville Story. (Illus.). 1980. 10.00x (ISBN 0-943388-01-5); pap. 2.95 (ISBN 0-943388-02-3). South Oregon.

--Preliminary Guide to Local History Materials: Jacksonville Museum Library. (Illus.). 86p. 1978. 5.00x (ISBN 0-943388-00-7). South Oregon.

McArthur, Lewis A. Oregon Geographic Names. 5th, rev. ed. McArthur, Lewis L., rev. by. 864p. 1982. 21.95 (ISBN 0-87595-113-9, Western Imprints); pap. 14.95 (ISBN 0-87595-114-7, Western Imprints). Oreg Hist Soc.

Nelson, P. N. & Nelson, L. N., eds. Oregon Gold. 1983. pap. 5.95 (ISBN 0-942652-00-2). Windriver Scribes.

O'Harra, Marjorie. Ashland: The First 130 Years. (Illus.). 200p. pap. 8.95 (ISBN 0-943388-03-1). South Oregon.

Reed, Ione. Pioneering in Oregon's Coast Range: Surviving the Depression Years. (Illus.). 140p. (Orig.). 1983. pap. 7.95 (ISBN 0-934784-31-0). Calapooia Pubns.

Rees, Helen G. Shaniko People. (Illus.). 1982. 10.95 (ISBN 0-8323-0414-X); pap. 7.95 (ISBN 0-8323-0415-8). Binford.

Wallin, Cheryl W. The Lane County Kid's Book: Stories to 1900. (Illus.). 96p. 1982. pap. write for info. (ISBN 0-9607040-0-0). Silver Pennies.

OREGON, UNIVERSITY OF

Belknap, George N. The Blue Ribbon University. 1976. pap. 1.25 (ISBN 0-87114-082-9). U of Oreg Bks.

--Henry Villard & the University of Oregon. 1976. pap. 2.00 (ISBN 0-87114-083-7). U of Oreg Bks.

--The University of Oregon Charter. 1976. pap. 1.25 (ISBN 0-87114-081-0). U of Oreg Bks.

OREGON TRAIL

Barton, Lois. Spencer Butte Pioneers: One Hundred Years on the Sunny Side of the Butte 1850-1950. Mills, Charlotte & Northwest Matrix, eds. LC 82-61837. (Illus.). 144p. 1982. pap. write for info. (ISBN 0-9609420-0-9). S Butte Pr.

ORESTES–DRAMA

Prag, A. J. The Oresteia: Iconographic & Narrative Tradition. (Illus.). 210p. 1983. pap. text ed. 65.00x (ISBN 0-85668-134-2, 41065, Pub. by Aris & Phillips England). Humanities.

ORGAN

Irwin, Stevens. Dictionary of Pipe Organ Stops. 2nd ed. 1983. 20.00 (ISBN 0-02-871150-5). Schirmer Bks.

Ogasapian, John. Church Organs: A Guide to Selection & Purchase. 128p. (Orig.). 1983. pap. 5.95 (ISBN 0-8010-6706-5). Baker Bk.

ORGAN TRADE

see Music Trade

ORGAN TRANSPLANTATION

see Transplantation of Organs, Tissues, Etc.

ORGANIC CHEMISTRY

see Chemistry, Organic

ORGANIC GARDENING

Frey, Deborah A., ed. The Organic Gardening 1984 Planning Guide & Country Calendar. (Illus.). 96p. pap. 5.95 (ISBN 0-87857-459-X, 01-171-1). Rodale Pr Inc.

ORGANIC MATTER IN SOIL

see Humus

ORGANICALLY GROWN FOOD

see Food, Natural

ORGANICULTURE

see Organic Gardening

ORGANIZATION

see also Industrial Management; Industrial Organization; Management; Planning

Beardshaw, John & Palfreman, David. The Organization in It's Environment. 2nd ed. 625p. 1982. pap. text ed. 21.95 (ISBN 0-7121-1541-2). Intl Ideas.

Brown, Warren B. & Moberg, Dennis G. Organization & Management. LC 79-18709. (Management Ser.). 685p. 1980. text ed. 27.95 (ISBN 0-471-02023-0). Wiley.

Perkins, Dennis N., et al. Managing Creation: The Challenge of Building a New Organization. (Organizational Assessment & Change Ser.). 225p. 1983. 24.95 (ISBN 0-471-05204-3, Pub. by Wiley-Interscience). Wiley.

Shafritz, Jay M. & Whitbeck, Philip H., eds. Classics of Organization Theory. (Classics Ser.). (Orig.). 1978. pap. 10.00x (ISBN 0-935610-02-2). Moore Pub IL.

ORGANIZATION–RESEARCH

see Organizational Research

ORGANIZATION, INDUSTRIAL

see Industrial Organization

ORGANIZATION, INTERNATIONAL

see International Organization

ORGANIZATION DEVELOPMENT

see Organizational Change

ORGANIZATION FOR ECONOMIC COOPERATION AND DEVELOPMENT

Annual Reports on Competition Policy in OECD Member Countries, 1981. 94p. 1982. pap. 9.00 (ISBN 92-64-12271-0). OECD.

Camps, Miriam. First World Relationships: The Role of the OECD. 56p. (Orig.). 1975. pap. text ed. 4.75x (ISBN 0-686-83638-3). Allanheld.

OCED Staff. Controls & Impediments Affecting Inward Direct Investment in OECD Member Countries. 36p. 1982. pap. 6.00 (ISBN 92-64-12344-X). OECD.

OECD. Annual Reports on Competion Policy in OECD Member Countries 1982-1. 85p. 1982. pap. 8.00x (ISBN 92-64-12363-6). OECD.

OECD Staff. Activities of OECD in 1981. 119p. 1982. pap. 8.00 (ISBN 92-64-12310-5). OECD.

--Annual Reports on Consumer Policy in OECD Member Countries, 1981. 125p. 1982. pap. 13.00x (ISBN 92-64-12301-6). OECD.

--Economic & Ecological Interdependence. 86p. (Orig.). 1982. pap. 6.50 (ISBN 92-64-12311-3). OECD.

--Employment in the Public Sector. 79p. (Orig.). 1982. pap. 7.25 (ISBN 92-64-12319-9). OECD.

--Energy Policies & Programmes of IEA Countries, 1981 Review. 300p. 1982. pap. 20.00x (ISBN 92-64-12335-0). OECD.

--The Engineering Industries in OECD Member Countries, 1976-1979. 93p. 1982. pap. 10.00 (ISBN 92-64-02283-X). OECD.

--Export Credit Financing Systems in OECD Member Countries. 252p. (Orig.). 1982. pap. 12.50x (ISBN 92-64-12291-5). OECD.

--OECD Economic Outlook, No. 31. 150p. 1982. pap. 11.00 (ISBN 0-686-37445-2). OECD.

--OECD Economic Outlook Historical Statistics, 1960-1980. 150p. (Orig.). 1982. pap. 11.00x (ISBN 92-64-02325-9). OECD.

ORGANIZATION OF PETROLEUM EXPORTING COUNTRIES

Al-Chalabi, Fadhil J. OPEC & the International Oil Industry: A Changing Structure. (Illus.). 176p. 1980. pap. 9.95 (ISBN 0-19-877155-X). Oxford U Pr.

Fesharaki, Fereidum & Isaak, David T. OPEC, The Gulf & the World Petroleum Market: A Study in Government Policy & Downstream Operations. (Special Studies in International Economics & Business). 250p. 1983. lib. bdg. 27.50x (ISBN 0-86531-305-9). Westview.

Ghosh, Arabinda. OPEC, The Petroleum Industry, & United States Energy Policy. LC 82-13245. (Illus.). 296p. 1983. lib. bdg. 35.00 (ISBN 0-89930-010-3, HD9566, Quorum). Greenwood.

Mossavar-Rahmani, Bijan & Mossavar-Rahmani, Sharmir B. OPEC & Natural Gas Trade: Prospects & Problems. (Special Study in International Economics & Business). 175p. 1983. lib. bdg. 22.50X (ISBN 0-86531-354-7). Westview.

OPEC. Annual Statistical Bulletin, 1981. 16th ed. LC 74-640556. (Illus.). 236p. (Orig.). 1982. pap. 30.00 (ISBN 0-8002-3107-4). Intl Pubns Serv.

Quandt, William B. Saudi Arabia's Oil Policy. LC 82-73524. 65p. 1982. pap. 5.95 (ISBN 0-8157-7287-4). Brookings.

Sampson, Martin W., III. International Policy Coordination: Issues in OPEC & EACM. (Monograph Series in World Affairs: Vol. 19, Bk. 4). 100p. (Orig.). 1983. pap. 5.00 (ISBN 0-87940-071-4). U of Denver Intl.

ORGANIZATIONAL BEHAVIOR

Armandi, Barry R. & Barbera, John J. Organizational Behavior: Classical & Contemporary Readings. 368p. 1982. pap. text ed. 17.95 (ISBN 0-8403-2807-9). Kendall-Hunt.

Breton, Albert & Breton, Raymond. Why Disunity? 83p. 1980. pap. text ed. 6.95x (ISBN 0-920380-70-0, Inst Res Pub Canada). Renouf.

Campbell, John P. & Daft, Richard L. What to Study: Generating & Developing Research Questions. (Studying Organizations: Innovations in Methodology). 168p. 1982. 17.95 (ISBN 0-8039-1871-2); pap. 7.95 (ISBN 0-8039-1872-0). Sage.

Costley, Dan L. & Todd, Ralph. Human Relations in Organizations. 2d ed. (Illus.). 570p. 1983. text ed. 17.95 (ISBN 0-314-69643-1); write for info. instr's. manual (ISBN 0-314-71087-6). West Pub.

Hellriegel, Don & Slocum, John. Organizational Behavior. 3rd ed. (Management Ser.). (Illus.). 700p. 1983. 19.95 (ISBN 0-314-69653-9); tchrs. manual avail. (ISBN 0-314-71096-5); study guide avail. (ISBN 0-314-71097-3). West Pub.

Johns, Gary. Organizational Behavior: Understanding Life at Work. 1983. text ed. 24.95 (ISBN 0-673-15366-5). Scott F.

Kakabadse, Andrew. People & Organisations. 143p. 1982. text ed. 32.00x (ISBN 0-566-00373-2). Gower Pub Ltd.

McGuire, Joseph W. Theories of Business Behavior. LC 82-15550. xix, 268p. 1982. Repr. of 1964 ed. lib. bdg. 35.00x (ISBN 0-313-23567-8, MCTH). Greenwood.

Marsh, Carole. A Kid's Book of Smarts: How to Think, Make Decisions, Figure Things Out, Budget your Time, Money, Plan your Day, Week, Life & Other Things Adults Wish They'd Learned When They Were Kids! (Tomorrow's Books). (Illus.). 68p. 1983. 7.95 (ISBN 0-935326-18-9). Gallopade Pub Group.

Nash, Michael. Managing Organizational Performance. LC 82-49040. (Management & Social & Behavioral Science Ser.). 1983. text ed. price not set (ISBN 0-87589-561-1). Jossey-Bass.

Natemeyer, Walter E., ed. Classics of Organizational Behavior. LC 78-26983. (Classics Ser.). (Orig.). 1978. pap. 10.00x (ISBN 0-935610-03-0). Moore Pub IL.

Neugarten, Dail A. & Shafritz, Jay M., eds. Sexuality in Organizations: Romantic & Coercive Behaviors at Work. (Orig.). 1980. pap. 10.00x (ISBN 0-935610-14-6). Moore Pub IL.

Oshry, Barry. Middle Power. (Notes on Power Ser.). (Orig.). 1980. pap. 4.95 (ISBN 0-910411-08-5). Power & Sys.

--Middles of the World, Integrate! (Orig.). 1982. pap. 5.95 (ISBN 0-910411-09-3). Power & Sys.

--Organic Power. LC 80-4780. (Notes on Power Ser.). (Orig.). 1976. pap. text ed. 3.25 (ISBN 0-910411-03-4). Power & Sys.

--Organization Spasms. (Notes on Power Ser.). (Orig.). 1978. pap. 3.75 (ISBN 0-910411-06-9). Power & Sys.

--Power & Position. LC 88-8848. (Notes on Power Ser.). (Orig.). 1977. pap. text ed. 7.50 (ISBN 0-910411-04-2). Power & Sys.

--Take a Look at Yourself: Self-in-System Sensitizers. (Notes on Power Ser.). (Orig.). 1978. pap. text ed. 5.00 (ISBN 0-910411-05-0). Power & Sys.

Punch, Maurice, ed. Control in the Police Organization. (Organization Studies: No. 4). 368p. 1983. 30.00x (ISBN 0-262-16090-0). MIT Pr.

Staw, Barry. Psychological Foundations of Organizational Behavior. 2nd ed. 1983. pap. text ed. 15.95x (ISBN 0-673-16005-X). Scott F.

Stewart & Garson. Organizational Behavior & Public Management. 312p. 1983. price not set. Dekker.

Szilagyi, Andrew D., Jr. & Wallace, Marc J. Organizational Behavior & Performance. 3rd ed. 1983. text ed. 24.95x (ISBN 0-673-16572-8). Scott F.

Szilagyi, Andrew D., Jr. & Wallace, Marc J., Jr. Reader for Organizational Behavior & Performance. 1983. pap. text ed. 12.95x (ISBN 0-673-16573-6). Scott F.

Young, Dennis R. If Not for Profit, for What? A Behavioral Theory of the Nonprofit Sector Based on Entrepreneurship. Simon, John, frwd. by. LC 82-48482. 192p. 1983. 20.95x (ISBN 0-669-06154-9). Lexington Bks.

ORGANIZATIONAL CHANGE

Carnall, C. A. The Evaluation of Organisational Change. 130p. 1982. text ed. 31.00x (ISBN 0-566-00519-0). Gower Pub Ltd.

Dunphy, D. C. & Dick, B. Organizational Change by Choice. 312p. Date not set. 21.00x (ISBN 0-07-072947-6). McGraw.

Dyer, William G. Contemporary Issues in Management & Organization Development. LC 82-8732. 224p. 1982. text ed. 15.95 (ISBN 0-201-10348-6). A-W.

Goodman, Paul S. Assessing Organizational Change: Rushton Quality of Work Experiment. LC 78-31857. (Organizational Behavior Assessment & Change Ser.). 1979. 32.50x (ISBN 0-471-04782-1, Pub. by Wiley-Interscience). Wiley.

Harris, Philip R. New World, New Ways, New Management. 320p. 1983. 22.95 (ISBN 0-8144-5755-X). Am Mgmt.

Lawrence, Paul R. & Dyer, Davis. Renewing American Industry. LC 82-72096. 400p. 1983. 25.00 (ISBN 0-02-918170-4). Free Pr.

Seashore, Stanley E. & Lawler, Edward. Assessing Organization Change: A Guide to Methods, Measures & Practices. (Organizational Assessment & Change Ser.). 500p. 1983. price not set (ISBN 0-471-89484-2, Pub. by Wiley-Interscience). Wiley.

Trebesch, Karsten. Organisation Development in Europe, 2 vols. 1628p. 1981. Set. 150.00 (ISBN 0-7121-5612-7, Pub. by Macdonald & Evans). State Mutual Bk.

ORGANIZATIONAL RESEARCH

Campbell, John P. & Daft, Richard L. What to Study: Generating & Developing Research Questions. (Studying Organizations: Innovations in Methodology). 168p. 1982. 17.95 (ISBN 0-8039-1871-2); pap. 7.95 (ISBN 0-8039-1872-0). Sage.

Evan, W. M. Organization Theory: Structures, Systems, & Environments. LC 76-22742. 312p. 1976. 31.95x (ISBN 0-471-01512-1). Wiley.

Hakel, Milton D. & Sorcher, Melvin. Making it Happen: Designing Research with Implementation in Mind. (Studying Organizations: Innovations in Methodology). (Illus.). 144p. 1982. 17.95 (ISBN 0-8039-1865-8); pap. 7.95 (ISBN 0-8039-1866-6). Sage.

Hunter, John E. & Schmidt, Frank L. Meta-Analysis: Cumulating Research Findings Across Studies. (Studing Organizations in Methodology). 144p. 1982. 17.95 (ISBN 0-8039-1863-1); pap. 7.95 (ISBN 0-8039-1864-X). Sage.

James, Lawrence R. & Mulaik, Stanley A. Causal Analysis: Assumptions, Models, & Data: Studying Organizations: Innovations in Methodology. 144p. 1982. 17.95 (ISBN 0-8039-1867-4); pap. 7.95 (ISBN 0-8039-1868-2). Sage.

McGrath, Joseph E. & Martin, Joanne. Judgement Calls in Research. (Studying Organizations: Innovations in Methodology Ser.). (Illus.). 128p. 1982. 17.95 (ISBN 0-8039-1873-9); pap. 7.95 (ISBN 0-8039-1874-7). Sage.

Van Maanen, John. Varieties of Qualitative Research. (Studying Organization: Innovations in Methodology Ser.). 168p. 1982. 17.95 (ISBN 0-8039-1869-0); pap. 7.95 (ISBN 0-8039-1870-4). Sage.

ORGANIZATIONS

see Associations, Institutions, etc.

ORGANIZATIONS, INTERNATIONAL

see International Agencies

ORGANIZED CAMPS

see Camps

ORGANIZED CRIME

see also Gambling; Mafia; Narcotics, Control of; Prostitution

Block, Alan. East Side - West Side: Organizing Crime in New York, 1930-1950. 280p. 1983. pap. 9.95 (ISBN 0-87855-931-0). Transaction Bks.
Dietz, Mary L. Killing for Profit: The Social Organization of Felony Homicide. (Illus.). 232p. 1983. text ed. 22.95X (ISBN 0-8304-1008-2). Nelson-Hall.
Pace, Denny F. & Styles, Jimmie C. Organized Crime: Concepts & Control. 2nd ed. (Illus.). 304p. 1983. 20.95 (ISBN 0-13-640946-6). P-H.

ORGANOBORON COMPOUNDS
Mikhailov, B. M. & Bubnov, Yu N. Organoboron Compounds in Organic Synthesis. (Soviet Scientific Reviews Supplement Ser.). Date not set. price not set (ISBN 3-7186-0113-3). Harwood Academic.

ORGANOMETALLIC COMPOUNDS
see also particular organometallic compounds, e.g. Organomagnesium Compounds
Abel, E. W. & Stone, F. G. Organometallic Chemistry, Vol. 9. 557p. 1982. 290.00x (ISBN 0-85186-571-2, Pub. by Royal Soc Chem England). State Mutual Bk.
Carraher, Charles E., Jr. & Sheats, John E., eds. Advances in Organometallic & Inorganic Polymer Science. (Illus.). 472p. 1982. 67.50 (ISBN 0-686-82220-X). Dekker.
Davies, S. G., ed. Organotransition Metal Chemistry: Applications to Organic Synthesis. (Organic Chemistry Ser.: Vol. 2). (Illus.). 428p. 1982. 85.00 (ISBN 0-08-026202-3). Pergamon.
Organometallic Chemistry Reviews: Annual Surveys: Silicon-Germanium-Tin-Lead. (Journal of Organometallic Chemistry Library: Vol. 13). 700p. 1982. 149.00 (ISBN 0-444-42121-1). Elsevier.
Pope, M. T. Heteropoly & Isopoly Oxometalates. (Inorganic Chemistry Concepts Ser.: Vol. 8). (Illus.). 190p. 1983. 52.00 (ISBN 0-387-11889-6). Springer-Verlag.
Stone, F. G. & West, Robert, eds. Advances in Organomettalic Chemistry, Vol. 20. (Serial Publication). 384p. 1982. 56.00 (ISBN 0-12-031120-8); lib. ed. 73.00 (ISBN 0-12-031185-2); microfiche 39.50 (ISBN 0-12-031186-0). Acad Pr.
Wilkinson, Geoffrey & Stone, F. G., eds. Comprehensive Organometallic Chemistry: The Synthesis, Reactions & Structures of Organometallic Compounds. LC 82-7595. 9000p. 1982. 2150.00 (ISBN 0-08-025269-9). Pergamon.

ORGANOPHOSPHORUS COMPOUNDS
Hutchinson, D. W. & Miller, J. A. Organophosphorous Chemistry, Vol. 12. 288p. 1982. 215.00x (ISBN 0-85186-106-7, Pub. by Royal Soc Chem England). State Mutual Bk.
Mulder & Caldwell, eds. Sulfate Metabolism & Sulfate Conjugation: Proceedings of an International Workshop held at Noordwijkerhout, Netherlands, Sept. 20-23, 1981. (Illus.). 323p. 1982. text ed. 37.00 (ISBN 0-85066-233-8, Pub. by Taylor & Francis England). J K Burgess.

ORGANOSULPHUR COMPOUNDS
Ando, W. Photoxidation of Organosulfur Compounds. (Sulfur Reports Ser.). 80p. 1981. pap. 17.00 (ISBN 3-7186-0073-0). Harwood Academic.
Drozd, V. N. & Zefirov, N. S. Sigmatropic Additions & Cyclosubstitutions in Five-Membered Heterocyclic Compounds Containing Exocyclic Double Bonds. (Sulfur Reports Ser.). 45p. 1981. pap. 15.00 (ISBN 3-7186-0081-1). Harwood Academic.
McFarland, J. W. Sulfonyl Isocyanates & Sulfonyl Isothiocyanates. (Sulfur Reports Ser.). 54p. 1981. pap. 15.00 (ISBN 3-7186-0082-X). Harwood Academic.
Maw, G. A. Biochemistry of S-Methyl-L-Systeine & its Principal Derivatives. (Sulfur Reports Ser.). 31p. (Orig.). 1982. pap. text ed. 23.00 (ISBN 3-7186-0112-5). Harwood Academic.

ORGANS
see Organ

ORGANS, ARTIFICIAL
see Artificial Organs

ORGASM
Brauer, Alan P., et al. ESO: How You & Your Lover Can Give Each Other Hours of Extended Sexual Orgasm. (Illus.). 192p. 1983. pap. 13.50 (ISBN 0-446-51270-2). Warner Bks.
Kline-Graber, Georgia & Graber, Benjamin. Woman's Orgasm: A Guide to Sexual Satisfaction. 240p. 1983. pap. 3.50 (ISBN 0-446-31123-5). Warner Bks.

ORGONOMY
Sharaf, Myron. Fury on Earth: A Biography of Wilhelm Reich. LC 82-5707. (Illus.). 560p. 1983. 24.95 (ISBN 0-312-31370-5). St Martin.

ORIENTAL ART
see Art, Oriental

ORIENTAL PHILOSOPHY
see Philosophy, Oriental

ORIENTAL POTTERY
see Pottery, Oriental

ORIENTAL RUGS
see Rugs, Oriental

ORIENTAL STUDIES
see also Egyptology; Orientalists
Dolezal, Ivan. Asian & African Studies, Vol. 18. 323p. 1982. text ed. 13.75x (ISBN 0-7007-0156-7, 41190, Pub. by Curzon Pr England). Humanities.
Lindell, K., et al. The Kammu Year: Its Lore & Music. (Studies on Asian Topics: No. 4). 191p. 1982. pap. text ed. 10.50x (ISBN 0-7007-0151-6, Pub by Curzon Pr England). Humanities.
Mayerchak, Patrick M., ed. Scholars' Guide to Washington DC for Southeast Asian Studies. (Scholars' Guides to Washington, D.C. Series: Vol. 9). 350p. 1983. text ed. 29.95x (ISBN 0-87474-626-4); pap. text ed. 12.50x (ISBN 0-87474-625-6). Smithsonian.
Papanek, Hanna & Minnault, Gail. Separate Worlds: Studies of Purdah in South Asia. 1982. 24.00 (ISBN 0-8364-0895-0). South Asia Bks.
Rocher, Rosane. Orientalism, Poetry & Millenium. 1983. 34.00x (ISBN 0-8364-0870-5). South Asia Bks.

ORIENTALISTS
Rocher, Rosane. Orientalism, Poetry & Millenium. 1983. 34.00x (ISBN 0-8364-0870-5). South Asia Bks.
Wickremaratne, L. A. Genesis of an Orientalist. 1983. 17.50x (ISBN 0-8364-0867-5). South Asia Bks.

ORIENTALS
see Asians

ORIENTATION
Kals, W. S. Land Navigation Handbook: The Sierra Club Guide to Map & Compass. LC 82-16917. (Outdoor Activities Guide Ser.). (Illus.). 288p. 1983. pap. 8.95 (ISBN 0-87156-331-2). Sierra.
Smith, Roger. The Penguin Book of Orienteering. 1983. pap. 4.95 (ISBN 0-14-046438-7). Penguin.

ORIENTATION (COLLEGE STUDENTS)
see College Student Orientation

ORIENTATION (STUDENTS)
see Students

ORIENTATION (TEACHERS)
see Teachers, Training of

ORIGIN OF LIFE
see Life-Origin

ORIGIN OF MAN
see Man-Origin

ORIGIN OF SPECIES
see also Hybridization; Natural Selection; Variation (Biology)
Ehrlich, Paul R. & Ehrlich, Anne H. Extinction: The Causes & Consequences of the Disappearance of Species. 400p. 1983. pap. 4.50 (ISBN 0-345-28895-5). Ballantine.

ORIGINAL SIN
see Sin, Original

ORISKANY FORMATION
see Geology, Stratigraphic-Devonian

ORNAMENT
see Decoration and Ornament

ORNAMENTAL ALPHABETS
see Alphabets; Illumination of Books and Manuscripts

ORNAMENTAL DESIGN
see Design, Decorative

ORNAMENTAL PLANTS
see Plants, Ornamental

ORNAMENTAL SHRUBS
Flint, Harrison. The Country Journal Book of Hardy Trees & Shrubs. (Illus.). 176p. (Orig.). 1983. pap. 8.95 (ISBN 0-918678-02-1). Country Journ.

ORNAMENTAL TREES
Flint, Harrison. The Country Journal Book of Hardy Trees & Shrubs. (Illus.). 176p. (Orig.). 1983. pap. 8.95 (ISBN 0-918678-02-1). Country Journ.

ORNITHOLOGY
Brusewitz, Gunnar. Wings & Seasons. Wheeler, Walston, tr. from Swedish. (Illus.). 119p. 1983. 20.00 (ISBN 0-88072-029-8). Tanager Bks.
Career Opportunities in Ornithology. 1974. write for info. (ISBN 0-943610-34-6). Am Ornithologists.
Cramp, Stanley, ed. Handbook of the Birds of Europe, the Middle East, & North Africa: The Birds of the Western Paleartic, Vol. III: Waders to Gulls. (Illus.). 920p. 1983. 89.00 (ISBN 0-19-857506-8). Oxford U Pr.
Paynter, Raymond A., Jr. Ornithological Gazetteer of Venezuela. (Illus.). iii, 245p. 1982. 12.50 (ISBN 0-686-38914-X). Nutall Ornithological.
Report of the American Ornithologists' Union ad hoc Committee on Scientific & Educational Use of Wild Birds. 1975. 1.00 (ISBN 0-943610-35-4). Am Ornithologists.
Sibley, Charles G. & American Ornithologists' Union, eds. Proceedings: International Ornithological Congress, 13th, 2 vols. 1250p. 1963. 10.00 (ISBN 0-943610-00-1). Am Ornithologists.

OROGRAPHY
see Mountains

ORPHANS' COURTS
see Probate Law and Practice

ORTEGA Y GASSET, JOSE, 1883-1955
Weigert, Andrew J. Life & Society: A meditation on the Social Thought of Jose Ortega y Gassett. 250p. 1983. text ed. 19.95x (ISBN 0-8290-1278-8). Irvington.

ORTHODONTIA
see Orthodontics

ORTHODONTICS
Holt, Robert L. Straight Teeth: Orthodontics for Everyone. LC 80-10562. (Illus.). 283p. 1980. pap. 7.95 (ISBN 0-930926-07-2). Calif Health.

ORTHODOX EASTERN CHURCH
Coniaris, A. M. Introducing the Orthodox Church. 1982. pap. 6.95. Light&Life Pub Co MN.
Cronk, George. The Message of the Bible: An Orthodox Christian Perspective. LC 82-7355. 293p. (Orig.). 1982. pap. 8.95 (ISBN 0-913836-94-X). St Vladimirs.
Hopko, Thomas. All the Fulness of God: Essays on Orthodoxy, Ecumenism & Modern Society. LC 82-5454. 188p. (Orig.). 1982. pap. 6.95 (ISBN 0-913836-96-6). St Vladimirs.
Meyendorff, John. The Byzantine Legacy in the Orthodox Church. LC 82-797. 268p. (Orig.). 1982. pap. 8.95 (ISBN 0-913836-90-7). St Vladimirs.

ORTHODOX EASTERN CHURCH-ASCETICISM
see Asceticism

ORTHODOX EASTERN CHURCH-HISTORY
Polyzoides, G. History & Teachings of the Eastern Greek Orthodox Church. (Illus.). 96p. 3.20 (ISBN 0-686-83964-1). Divry.

ORTHODOX EASTERN CHURCH-LITURGY AND RITUAL
Chrysostom, John. The Divine Liturgy of Our Father Among the Saints, John Chrysostom, Archbishop of Constantinople. Holy Transfiguration Monastery, tr. from Greek. 94p. 1982. plastic covers, comb. binding 10.00x (ISBN 0-913026-54-9). St Nectarios.
Coniaris, A. M. The Stewardship Challange for the Orthodox Christian. 1883. pap. 6.95 (ISBN 0-937032-30-1). Light&Life Pub Co MN.
Drillock, David & Drickson, John, eds. The Divine Liturgy. 368p. 1982. text ed. 30.00 (ISBN 0-913836-95-8); pap. 20.00 (ISBN 0-913836-93-1). St Vladimirs.
Polyzoides, G. What We See & Hear in a Greek Eastern Orthodox Church. 92p. 3.20 (ISBN 0-686-83965-X). Divry.

ORTHODOX EASTERN CHURCH-RELATIONS-CATHOLIC CHURCH
Chrysostomos, Archimandrite. Orthodoxy & Papism. Williams, Theodore M., ed. 70p. 1982. pap. 4.00 (ISBN 0-911165-00-2). Ctr Trad Orthodox.

ORTHODOX EASTERN CHURCH, GREEK
Batalden, Stephen K. Catherine II's Greek Prelate: Eugenios Voulgaris in Russia, 1771-1806. (East European Monographs: No. 115). 288p. 1982. 25.00x (ISBN 0-88033-006-6). East Eur Quarterly.
Moskos, C. C., Jr. & Papajohn, J. C. Greek Orthodox Youth Today. Vaporis, N. M., intro. by. (Saints Peter & Paul Youth Ministry Lectures Ser.). 56p. (Orig.). 1983. pap. 3.00 (ISBN 0-916586-56-1). Holy Cross Orthodox.
Palmer, G. E. & Sherrard, Philip, trs. The Philokalia, Vol. 1: The Complete Text Compiled By St. Nikodimos of the Holy Mountain & St. Markarios of Corinth, Vol. 1. 384p. 1983. pap. 9.95 (ISBN 0-571-13013-5). Faber & Faber.

ORTHODOX EASTERN CHURCH, RUSSIAN-HISTORY
Batalden, Stephen K. Catherine II's Greek Prelate: Eugenios Voulgaris in Russia, 1771-1806. (East European Monographs: No. 115). 288p. 1982. 25.00x (ISBN 0-88033-006-6). East Eur Quarterly.
Freeze, Gregory. The Parish Clergy in Nineteenth-Century Russia: Crisis, Reform, Counter-Reform. LC 82-61361. 552p. 1983. 50.00x (ISBN 0-691-05381-2). Princeton U Pr.

ORTHODOX JUDAISM
see also Jewish Sects
Heilman, Samuel C. The People of the Book: Drama, Fellowship, & Religion. LC 82-13369. 264p. 1983. lib. bdg. 22.50x (ISBN 0-226-32492-3). U of Chicago Pr.

ORTHOEPY
see Phonetics

ORTHOMOLECULAR MEDICINE
see also Chemotherapy; Nutrition
Baum, H. & Gergely, J., eds. Molecular Aspects of Medicine, Vol. 4. (Illus.). 452p. 1982. 150.00 (ISBN 0-08-030007-3). Pergamon.

ORTHOMOLECULAR THERAPY
see Orthomolecular Medicine

ORTHOPEDIA
see also Orthodontics; Orthopedic Nursing; Orthopedic Surgery; Osteotomy
also special conditions to which orthopedic methods are applicable, e.g. Hip Joints-Diseases; Spine-Abnormities and Deformities
Bucholz, Robert W. & Wenger, Dennis R. Orthopaedic Decision Making. 300p. 1983. text ed. 36.00 (ISBN 0-941158-10-1, D0798-1). Mosby.
Coventry, Mark B., ed. Year Book of Orthopedics, 1983. 1983. 40.00 (ISBN 0-8151-1884-8). Year Bk Med.

ORTHOPEDIC MANIPULATION
see Manipulation (Therapeutics)

ORTHOPEDIC NURSING
Brunner, Nancy A. Orthopedic Nursing: A Programmed Approach. 4th ed. (Illus.). 288p. 1983. spiral 14.95 (ISBN 0-8016-0839-2). Mosby.

ORTHOPEDIC SURGERY
American Academy of Orthopaedic Surgeons. Symposium on the Foot & Ankle. Kiene, Richard H. & Johnson, Kenneth A., eds. (Illus.). 240p. 1983. text ed. 47.50 (ISBN 0-8016-0133-9). Mosby.
Demos, T. Radiologic Case Studies: A Study Guide for the Orthopedic Surgeon. LC 82-62398. 299p. 1983. 39.50 (ISBN 0-943432-02-2). Slack Inc.
Duthie, R. B. & Bentley, George, eds. Mercer's Orthopaedic Surgery. (Illus.). 1200p. 1983. 150.00 (ISBN 0-8391-1806-6, 19828). Univ Park.
Lippert, Frederick G., III & Farmer, James. Psychomotor Skills in Orthopaedic Surgery. (Illus.). 171p. Date not set. lib. bdg. price not set (ISBN 0-683-05051-6). Williams & Wilkins.

ORTHOPTERA
see also Locusts
Herrera, L. Catalogue of the Orthoptera of Spain. 1982. 37.00 (ISBN 90-6193-131-2, Pub. by Junk Pubs Netherlands). Kluwer Boston.

ORWELL, GEORGE, 1903-1950
Hammond. A George Orwell Companion. LC 82-875. 304p. 1982. 28.50x (ISBN 0-312-32452-9). St Martin.
Howe, Irving. Orwell's 1984: Text, Source, Criticism. 2nd ed. 450p. 1982. pap. text ed. 9.95 (ISBN 0-15-565811-5). HarBraceJ.

OSAGE INDIANS
see Indians of North America-The West

OSCILLATIONS
Gardner, Floyd M. Phaselock Techniques. 2nd ed. LC 78-20777. 285p. 1979. 24.95x (ISBN 0-471-04294-3, Pub by Wiley-Interscience). Wiley.

OSCILLATORS, CRYSTAL
Matthys, Robert J. Crystal Oscillator Circuits. 240p. 1983. write for info. (ISBN 0-471-87401-9, Pub. by Wiley-Interscience). Wiley.

OSMANIC LANGUAGE
see Turkish Language

OSMANLI LANGUAGE
see Turkish Language

OSMOREGULATION
Gilles, R. Mechanisms of Osmoregulation in Animals: Maintenance of Cell Volume. LC 78-4608. 667p. 1979. 114.75x (ISBN 0-471-99648-3, Pub. by Wiley-Interscience). Wiley.

OSTEOARTHRITIS
see Arthritis

OSTEOGENESIS
see Bone-Growth

OSTEOLOGY
see Bones; Skeleton

OSTEOPOROSIS
Avioli, Louis V. The Osteoporatic Syndrome: Detection & Prevention. write for info (ISBN 0-8089-1548-7). Grune.
Notelowitz, Morris & Ware, Marsha. Stand Tall! The Informed Woman's Guide to Preventing Osteoporosis. (Illus.). 200p. 1982. 12.95 (ISBN 0-937404-12-8); pap. 6.95 (ISBN 0-937404-14-4). Triad Pub FL.

OSTEOTOMY
Bombelli, R. Osteoarthritis of the Hip: Classification & Pathogenesis-The Role of Osteotomy as Consequent Therapy. 2nd, rev. & enl ed. (Illus.). 386p. 1983. 165.00 (ISBN 0-387-11422-X). Springer-Verlag.

OSTRACODA
Hanai, Tetsuro. Studies on Japanese Ostracoda. (Illus.). 320p. 1982. text ed. 60.00 (ISBN 0-86008-314-4, Pub. by U of Tokyo Japan). Columbia U Pr.

OSTREA
see Oysters

OSWIECIM (CONCENTRATION CAMP)
Hart, Kitty. Return to Auschwitz. LC 81-69155. 200p. 1983. pap. 7.95 (ISBN 0-689-70637-5, 283). Atheneum.
Mendelsohn, J. The Wannsee Protocol & a 1944 Report on Auschwitz by the Office of Strategic Services. LC 81-80319. (The Holocaust Ser.). 264p. 1982. lib. bdg. 50.00 (ISBN 0-8240-4885-7). Garland Pub.

OTARIA
see Seals (Animals)

OTJI LANGUAGE
see Twi Language

OTO INDIANS
see Indians of North America-The West

OTOLARYNGOLOGY
Calderelli, David D. Pediatric Otolaryngology. (New Directions in Therapy Ser.). 1982. 32.50 (ISBN 0-87488-695-3). Med Exam.
Farb, Stanley N. Otolaryngology. 5th ed. (Medical Exam Review Bks.: Vol. 16). 1982. pap. text ed. 22.00 (ISBN 0-87488-116-1). Med Exam.
Gates, George A. Current Therapy in Otolaryngology: Head & Neck Surgery 1982-1983. 391p. 1982. text ed. 44.00 (ISBN 0-941158-00-4, D1770-7). Mosby.
Holt, G. Richard & Mattox, Douglas E. Decision Making in Otolaryngology: Head & Neck Surgery. 256p. 1983. text ed. 32.00 (ISBN 0-941158-09-8, D2250-6). Mosby.
Lee, K. J. Essential Otolaryngology. 3rd ed. 1982. pap. 23.50 (ISBN 0-87488-313-X). Med Exam.
Parella, Michael M., ed. Year Book of Otolaryngology 1983. 1983. 40.00 (ISBN 0-8151-6640-0). Year Bk Med.
Pfaltz, C. R., ed. Follows. (Advances in Oto-Rhino-Laryngology Ser.: Vol. 32). (Illus.). viii, 192p. 1983. 78.00 (ISBN 3-8055-3701-8). S Karger.
Surjan, L. & Bodo, G., eds. Borderline Problems in Otorhinolaryngology: Proceedings, 12th World Congress, Budapest, Hungary, June 12-27, 1981. 724p. 1982. 121.00 (ISBN 0-444-90261-9, Excerpta Medica). Elsevier.

OTOLOGY
see Ear

OTOMI INDIANS
see Indians of Mexico

OTORHINOLARYNGOLOGY
see Otolaryngology

OUT OF THE BODY EXPERIENCES
see Astral Projection

OUTDOOR COOKERY
see Cookery, Outdoor

OUTDOOR EDUCATION
see also Camping; Physical Education and Training; School Excursions

Ford, Phyllis M. Principles & Practices of Outdoor-Environment Education. LC 80-23200. 348p. 1981. text ed. 20.95 (ISBN 0-471-04768-6). Wiley.

Research in Outdoor Education: Summaries of Doctoral Studies. 8.95 (ISBN 0-88314-220-1). AAHPERD.

OUTDOOR LIFE
see also Camping; Country Life; Hiking; Mountaineering; Picnicking; Sports

Green, Paul. The Outdoor Leadership Handbook. 42p. 1982. pap. write for info. (ISBN 0-913724-32-7). Survival Ed Assoc.

Lawrence, R. D. The Ghost Walker. LC 82-12111. 264p. 1982. 15.95 (ISBN 0-03-061594-1). HR&W.

Lund, Duane R. Nature's Bounty for Your Take. 1982. 6.95 (ISBN 0-934860-20-3). Adventure Pubns.

Risk, Paul H. Outdoor Safety & Survival. 300p. 1983. write for info. (ISBN 0-471-03891-1). Wiley.

Rockswold, E. P., ed. Pre-Immigrant & Pioneer. 1982. pap. 5.95 (ISBN 0-934860-22-X). Adventure Pubns.

Wood, Dave. Wisconsin Life Trip. 1982. 4.95 (ISBN 0-934860-21-1). Adventure Pubns.

OUTDOOR RECREATION
see also Camping; Parks; Picnicking; Recreation Areas; Wildlife Conservation

Arnold, Caroline. How Do We Have Fun? (Easy-Read Community Bks.). (Illus.). 32p. (gr. k-3). 1983. PLB 7.90 (ISBN 0-531-04506-4). Watts.

Ford, Phyllis. Eco-Acts. rev. 2nd ed. 200p. 1982. 10.00 (ISBN 0-686-84023-2). U OR Ctr Leisure.

Ford, Phyllis M. Principles & Practices of Outdoor-Environment Education. LC 80-23200. 348p. 1981. text ed. 20.95 (ISBN 0-471-04768-6). Wiley.

Perry, John & Perry, Jane G. The Sierra Club Guide to the Natural Areas of California. LC 82-16936. (Sierra Club Books Guides to the Natural Areas of the United States). (Illus.). 380p. (Orig.). 1983. pap. 9.95 (ISBN 0-87156-333-9). Sierra.

--The Sierra Club Guide to the Natural Areas of Oregon & Washington. LC 82-16937. (The Sierra Club Books Guides to the Natural Areas of the United States). (Illus.). 380p. (Orig.). 1983. pap. 9.95 (ISBN 0-87156-334-7). Sierra.

OUTDOOR RELIEF
see Charities; Public Welfare

OUTER SPACE
see also Space Environment

Mirabito, Michael M. The Exploration of Outer Space with Cameras: A History of the NASA Unmanned Spacecraft Missions. (Illus.). 225p. 1983. lib. bdg. 19.95x (ISBN 0-89950-061-7). McFarland & Co.

OUTER SPACE–EXPLORATION

Discovering Space Exploration. (Discovering Science Ser.). 1983. lib. bdg. 15.96 (ISBN 0-86706-111-1, Pub. by Stonehenge). Silver.

Our Need for New Worlds. 58p. 1976. 2.50 (ISBN 0-686-83933-1). Transbooks.

OUTER SPACE–JUVENILE LITERATURE

Couper, Heather & Henbest, Nigel. All About Space. (Full Color Fact Books). (Illus.). 32p. (gr. 4-12). 1982. PLB 7.95 (ISBN 0-8219-0014-5, 35545). EMC.

Isaaman. Spacegames. 1983. pap. 4.95 (ISBN 0-86020-683-1, 24062). EDC.

Lambert, Mark. Fifty Facts About Space. (Fifty Facts About Ser.). (Illus.). 32p. (gr. 4-6). 1983. PLB 8.90 (ISBN 0-531-09210-0). Watts.

Taylor, L. B., Jr. Space: Battleground of the Future? (Impact Ser.). 128p. (gr. 7 up). 1983. PLB 8.90 (ISBN 0-531-04546-3). Watts.

OUTLAWS

Keen, Maurice. The Outlaws of Medieval Legend. (Studies in Social History). 235p. 1977. 25.00 (ISBN 0-7100-8682-2). Routledge & Kegan.

Steckmesser, Kent L. Western Outlaws: The "Good Badman" in Fact, Film & Folklore. 170p. Date not set. 17.95 (ISBN 0-941690-07-5); pap. 10.95 (ISBN 0-941690-08-3). Regina Bks.

OUTPUT EQUIPMENT (COMPUTERS)
see Computer Input-Output Equipment

OUTSIDE BROKERS
see Brokers

OVENS
see Stoves

OVER-THE-COUNTER MARKETS

Standard's & Poor's. OTC Handbook. 1982. 39.50 (ISBN 0-07-051885-8). McGraw.

OVERACTIVITY
see Hyperkinesia

OVERLAND JOURNEYS TO THE PACIFIC

Oliver, Susan. Odyssey: A Daring Transatlantic Journey. 256p. 1983. 14.75 (ISBN 0-02-592920-8). Macmillan.

OVERSEAS EMPLOYEES
see Americans in Foreign Countries–Employment

OVERSIGHT, CONGRESSIONAL (UNITED STATES)
see United States–Congress–Powers and Duties

OVERTIME
see Hours of Labor

OVERWEIGHT
see Obesity

OVID (PUBLIUS OVIDIUS NASO)

Booth, Joan, tr. Ovid: Amores, Bk. II. 220p. 1983. text ed. 14.50x (ISBN 0-85668-174-1, 41067, Pub. by Aris & Phillips England). Humanities.

OWLS

Storms, Laura. The Owl Book. (Early Nature Picture Bks.). (Illus.). 32p. (gr. k-3). 1983. PLB 4.95g (ISBN 0-8225-1117-7). Lerner Pubns.

OWNERSHIP
see Property

OXFORD–DESCRIPTION AND TRAVEL–GUIDEBOOKS

Oxford Travel Guide. (Berlitz Travel Guides). (Illus.). 1982. pap. 4.95 (ISBN 0-02-969500-7, Berlitz). Macmillan.

Watkins, Paul. Oxford. (Golden Hart Guides Ser.). (Illus.). 96p. 1983. pap. 3.95 (ISBN 0-283-98907-6, Pub by Sidgwick & Jackson). Merrimack Bk Serv.

OXFORD AND ASQUITH, HERBERT HENRY ASQUITH, 1ST EARL OF, 1852-1928

Brock, Michael & Brock, Eleanor, eds. H. H. Asquith: Letters to Venetia Stanley. (Illus.). 672p. 1983. 35.00 (ISBN 0-19-212200-2). Oxford U Pr.

Cregier, Don M. Chiefs Without Indians: Asquith, Lloyd George, & the Liberal Remnant, 1916-1935. LC 82-17546. (Illus.). 330p. (Orig.). 1983. lib. bdg. 23.50 (ISBN 0-8191-2806-6); pap. text ed. 12.50 (ISBN 0-8191-2807-4). U Pr of Amer.

OXFORD UNIVERSITY

Oxford University. Statutes, Decrees & Regulations of the University of Oxford: 1981 Vol. 726p. (Orig.). 1981. pap. text ed. 29.95x (ISBN 0-19-920128-5). Oxford U Pr.

OXFORD UNIVERSITY–HISTORY

Engel, A. J. From Clergyman to Don: The Rise of the Academic Profession in Nineteenth-Century Oxford. 336p. 1983. 55.00 (ISBN 0-19-822606-3). Oxford U Pr.

OXIDATION
see also Peroxides

Mandt, Mikkel G. & Bell, Bruce A. Oxidation Ditches in Wastewater Treatment. LC 82-70700. (Illus.). 169p. 1982. 29.95 (ISBN 0-250-40430-3). Ann Arbor Science.

Wieland, Heinrich. On the Mechanism of Oxidation. 1932. text ed. 42.50x (ISBN 0-686-83656-1). Elliots Bks.

OXIDATION, PHYSIOLOGICAL

Koch, William. Immunity & Oxidative Therapy. 6.00x (ISBN 0-943080-15-0). Cancer Control Soc.

OXIDES
see also Metallic Oxides

Ochiai, E. Aromatic Amine Oxides. 1967. 61.00 (ISBN 0-444-40429-5). Elsevier.

OXYGEN
see also Ozone

Oxygen & Life: Second BOC Priestley Conference. 236p. 1982. 69.00x (ISBN 0-85186-825-8, Pub. by Royal Soc Chem England). State Mutual Bk.

Semenza, G. Of Oxygen, Fuels & Living Matter, Vol. 2, Pt. 2. (Evolving Life Sciences: Recollections on Scientific Ideas & Events Ser.). 508p. 1982. text ed. 65.00x (ISBN 0-471-27924-2, Pub. by Wiley-Interscience). Wiley.

OXYGEN DEFICIENCY IN THE BLOOD
see Anoxemia

OXYGEN STEELMAKING
see Steel–Metallurgy

OXYGEN THERAPY
see also Hyperbaric Oxygenation

Petty, Thomas L. Prescribing Home Oxygen for COPD. 128p. 9.95 (ISBN 0-86577-078-6). Thieme-Stratton.

OXYGENASES

American Welding Society. Operator's Manual for Oxyfuel Gas Cutting: C4.2. 1978. 8.00 (ISBN 0-686-43371-8). Am Welding.

OXYGENATION, HYPERBARIC
see Hyperbaric Oxygenation

OYSTERS

Qualman, Al. Blood on the Half Shell. (Illus.). 1982. pap. 6.50 (ISBN 0-8323-0411-5). Binford.

OZONE

Rice, Rip G. & Netzer, Aharon, eds. Handbook of Ozone Technology & Applications, Vol. 2. LC 81-70869. (Illus.). 325p. 1983. 49.95 (ISBN 0-250-40577-6). Ann Arbor Science.

--Handbook of Ozone Technology & Applications, Vol. 3. LC 81-70869. (Illus.). 325p. 1983. 49.95 (ISBN 0-250-40578-4). Ann Arbor Science.

--Handbook of Ozone Technology & Applications, Vol. 4. LC 81-70869. (Illus.). 325p. 1983. 49.95 (ISBN 0-250-40579-2). Ann Arbor Science.

P

P-FIFTY-ONE (FIGHTER PLANES)
see Mustang (Fighter Planes)

P L-ONE (COMPUTER PROGRAM LANGUAGE)

Brown, Gary D. FORTRAN to PL-I Dictionary: PL-I to FORTRAN Dictionary. LC 82-21283. 218p. 1983. Repr. of 1975 ed. lib. bdg. write for info. (ISBN 0-89874-587-X). Krieger.

PACEMAKER, ARTIFICIAL (HEART)

Sonnenburg, David & Birnbaum, Michael. Understanding Pacemakers. (Illus.). 192p. 1982. pap. 12.95 (ISBN 0-686-83697-9, ScribT). Scribner.

PACIFIC AREA
see also Islands of the Pacific; Oceanica

Graebner, Norman A. Empire On the Pacific. c, 280p. (gr. 12). 1983. lib. bdg. 22.50 (ISBN 0-87436-033-1). ABC Clio.

Marketing Trends in the Asia Pacific Region: Economic Forecasts & Consumer Developments, the Asia Pacific Centre. 221p. 1982. text ed. 144.00x (ISBN 0-566-02361-X). Gower Pub Ltd.

Quo, F. Q., ed. Politics of the Pacific Nations. (Replica Edition Ser.). 275p. 1983. softcover 20.00x (ISBN 0-86531-951-0). Westview.

PACIFIC COAST

California Coastal Commission. The California Coastal Access Guide: Anniversary Ed. LC 82-45905. (Illus.). 285p. 25.00 (ISBN 0-520-04984-5). U of Cal Pr.

PACIFIC SETTLEMENT OF INTERNATIONAL DISPUTES
see Arbitration, International; Diplomatic Negotiations in International Disputes

PACIFIC STATES–DESCRIPTION AND TRAVEL–GUIDEBOOKS

Weiner, Neal O. & Schwartz, David M. The Interstate Gourmet: California & the Pacific Northwest, Vol. 3. (Illus.). 288p. 1983. pap. 5.95 (ISBN 0-671-44994-X). Summit Bks.

PACKAGING
see also Aerosols; Microencapsulation

Business Communications Staff. Tamperproof Packaging. 1983. 1500.00 (ISBN 0-89336-355-3, GB-067). BCC.

Hanlon, Joseph F. Handbook of Package Engineering. 2nd ed. 576p. 1983. 63.00 (ISBN 0-07-025994-1, P&RB). McGraw.

PACKING (TRANSPORTATION)
see Backpacking

PACKING INDUSTRY
see Meat Industry and Trade

PADDY FIELD CULTURE
see Irrigation

PAEDOPHILIA
see Pedophilia

PAGANINI, NICCOLO, 1782-1840

Kendall, Alan. Paganini. (Illus.). 160p. 1982. 24.95 (ISBN 0-241-10845-4, Pub. by Hamish Hamilton England). David & Charles.

PAGANISM

MacMullen, Ramsay. Paganism in the Roman Empire. pap. 7.95 (ISBN 0-686-42822-6, Y-454). Yale U Pr.

Wind, Edgar. Pagan Mysteries in the Renaissance. (Illus.). 1958. text ed. 49.50x (ISBN 0-686-83672-3). Elliots Bks.

PAHLAVI LANGUAGE
see also Persian Language

King, M., ed. Parsing Natural Language. Date not set. price not set (ISBN 0-12-408280-7). Acad Pr.

PAIN
see also Suffering

American Health Research Institute, Ltd. Pain: Medical Subject Analysis & Research Index With Bibliography. Bartone, John C., ed. LC 82-72028. 120p. 1983. 29.95 (ISBN 0-941864-72-3); pap. 21.95 (ISBN 0-941864-73-1). ABBE Pubs Assn.

Benjamin, Ben. Listen to Your Pain. 1983. write for info. (ISBN 0-670-43017-X). Viking Pr.

--Listen to Your Pain. 1983. pap. 7.95 (ISBN 0-14-006687-X). Penguin.

Berry, Hedley, ed. Contemporary Topics in Pain Management: An Update on Zomepirac, No. 52. 1982. write for info. (ISBN 0-8089-1536-3). Grune.

Brena, Steven & Chapman, Stanley, eds. Management of Chronic Pain. 326p. 1983. text ed. 40.00 (ISBN 0-89335-165-2). SP Med & Sci Bks.

Cailliet, Rene. Knee Pain & Disability. 2nd ed. LC 82-17296. (Pain Ser.). (Illus.). 220p. 1983. pap. text ed. 11.95 (ISBN 0-8036-1621-X, 1621-X). Davis Co.

Florence, D. & Hegedus, Frank. Coping with Chronic Pain: A Patient's Guide to Wellness. 1982. 5.25 (ISBN 0-686-84598-6). Sis Kenny Inst.

Korst, J. K. Pirprofen in the Treatment of Pain & Inflammation. (Illus.). 92p. (Orig.). 1982. pap. text ed. 14.00 (ISBN 3-456-81207-8, Pub by Hans Huber Switzerland). J K Burgess.

Kotarba, Joseph A. Chronic Pain. (Sociological Observations Ser.: Vol. 13). 256p. 1982. 25.00 (ISBN 0-8039-1880-1); pap. 12.50 (ISBN 0-8039-1881-X). Sage.

Matthews, B. & Hill, R. G., eds. Anatomical, Physiological, & Pharmacological Aspects of Trigeminal Pain: Proceedings of the Third World Congress on Pain; International Association for the Study of Pain, Dunblane, Perthshire, U.K., September 11-12, 1981. (International Congress Ser.: No. 588). 312p. 1982. 78.75 (ISBN 0-444-90269-4, Excerpta Medica). Elsevier.

Natural Ways to Relieve Pain. 1980. 4.95 (ISBN 0-686-42903-6). Harian.

PAINE, THOMAS, 1737-1809

Fast, Howard. Citizen Tom Paine. 2nd ed. 360p. 1983. pap. 6.95 (ISBN 0-394-62464-5, Ever). Grove.

PAINLESS LABOR (OBSTETRICS)
see Natural Childbirth

PAINT
see also Corrosion and Anti-Corrosives; Fillers (In Paper, Paint, etc.); Pigments

Ash, M. & Ash, I. Formulary of Paints & Other Coatings Vol. 2. 1982. 35.00 (ISBN 0-8206-0292-2). Chem Pub.

Paint & Painting. 1983. pap. 26.95 (ISBN 0-8120-2654-3). Barron.

PAINT-SCREEN PROCESS
see Screen Process Printing

PAINTED GLASS
see Glass Painting and Staining

PAINTERS–AUSTRALIA

Woollaston, Toss. Sage Tea. 268p. 1982. 17.95 (ISBN 0-00-216982-7, Pub. by W Collins Australia). Intl Schol Bk Serv.

PAINTERS–CANADA

Finley, Gerald. George Heriot: Postmaster Painter of the Canadas. 288p. 1983. 35.00 (ISBN 0-8020-5584-2). U of Toronto Pr.

Harper. Early Painters & Engravers in Canada. 1981. 75.00 (ISBN 0-686-43128-6). Apollo.

PAINTERS–FRANCE

Opperman, Hal. Jean-Baptiste Oudry Sixteen Eighty-Six to Seventeen Fifty-Five. 250p. (Orig.). 1983. 50.00 (ISBN 0-912804-11-4); pap. 24.95 (ISBN 0-912804-12-2). Kimbell Art.

PAINTERS–UNITED STATES

Albright, Thomas & Butterfield, Jan. Oliver Jackson. LC 82-61511. (Illus.). 32p. (Orig.). 1982. pap. 10.00 (ISBN 0-932216-10-2). Seattle Art.

Chew, Paul A., ed. Southwestern Pennsylvania Painters, 1800-1945. LC 81-52933. (Illus.). 178p. (Orig.). 1983. pap. 12.95 (ISBN 0-686-38092-4). Westmoreland.

--Southwestern Pennsylvania Painters, 1800-1945. LC 81-52933. (Illus.). xii, 166p. 1983. pap. 12.95 (ISBN 0-686-43201-0). U of Pittsburgh Pr.

Fielding, Mantle. Dictionary of American Painters, Sculptors & Engravers. 1974. 30.00 (ISBN 0-913274-03-8). Apollo.

Gaugh, Harry. William de Kooning. (Modern Masters Ser.). (Illus.). 128p. 1983. 24.95 (ISBN 0-89659-332-0); pap. 16.95 (ISBN 0-89659-333-9). Abbeville Pr.

Noble, John. The Legendary Wichita Bill: A Retrospective Exhibition of Paintings. LC 82-61985. (Illus.). 44p. 1982. pap. 5.00 (ISBN 0-939324-06-7). Wichita Art Mus.

Paul Cadmus. (Illus.). 128p. Date not set. 24.95 (ISBN 0-89659-334-7); pap. 16.95 (ISBN 0-89659-335-5). Abbeville Pr.

Proby, Kathryn H. Mario Sanchez-Painter of Key West Memories. LC 81-50557. (Illus.). 64p. Date not set. pap. 14.95 (ISBN 0-686-84313-4). Banyan Bks.

Westphal, Ruth. Plein Air Painters of California: The Southland. LC 82-90314. (Illus.). 228p. 1982. 75.00 (ISBN 0-9610520-0-7). Westphal Pub.

Wooden, Howard E. Edward Laning: American Realist (1906-1981) - A Retrospective Exhibition. LC 82-61463. (Illus.). 56p. 1982. pap. 6.00 (ISBN 0-939324-05-9). Wichita Art Mus.

--Lily Harmon, Fifty Years of Painting: A Retrospective Exhibition. LC 82-62680. 56p. 1982. pap. 6.00 (ISBN 0-939324-07-5). Wichita Art Mus.

Young. Dictionary of American Artists, Sculptors, & Engravers. 1968. 60.00 (ISBN 0-686-43150-2). Apollo.

PAINTERS' MARKS
see Artists' Marks

PAINTERS' MATERIALS
see Artists' Materials

PAINTING
see also Animal Painting and Illustration; China Painting; Color; Expressionism (Art); Glass Painting and Staining; Illumination of Books and Manuscripts; Impressionism (Art); Landscape Painting; Mural Painting and Decoration; Narrative Painting; Paintings; Perspective; Portrait Painting; Preraphaelitism; Stencil Work; Still-Life Painting; Textile Painting; Trompe L'Oeil Painting; Water-Color Painting

Basu, Romen. Canvas & the Brush. 116p. 1970. write for info. (Pub. by Filma K L Mukhopadhyay India). R Basu.

Boos-Hamberger, Hilde. The Nine Training Sketches for the Painter (Nature's Moods) by Rudolf Steiner. Fletcher, John, ed. Frommer, E., tr. from Ger. 23p. 1982. pap. 1.95 (ISBN 0-88010-058-3, Pub. by Steinerbooks). Anthroposophic.

Cikovsky, Nicolai, Jr., intro. by. & Lectures on the Affinity of Painting with the Other Fine Arts by Samuel F. B. Morse. LC 82-13551. (Illus.). 144p. 1983. text ed. 20.00x (ISBN 0-8262-0389-2). U of Mo Pr.

Groddeck, Marie. The Seven Training Sketches for the Painter by Rudolf Steiner. Fletcher, John, ed. Martin, Inge, tr. from Ger. 23p. 1982. pap. 1.95 (ISBN 0-88010-059-1, Pub. by Steinerbooks). Anthroposophic.

Havlice, Patricia P. World Painting Index: First Supplement 1973-1980, 2 vols. Incl. Vol. I. Bibliography, Paintings by Unknown Artists, Painters & Their Works; Vol. II. Titles of Works & Their Painters. LC 82-3355. 1233p. 1982. 62.50 (ISBN 0-8108-1531-1). Scarecrow.

Paint & Painting. 1983. pap. 26.95 (ISBN 0-8120-2654-3). Barron.

Wilson, Simon. Surrealist Painting. (Phaidon Color Library). (Illus.). 84p. 1983. 27.50 (ISBN 0-7148-2234-5, Pub. by Salem Hse Ltd); pap. 18.95 (ISBN 0-7148-2244-2). Merrimack Bk Serv.

PAINTING–HISTORY

see also Painting, French; Painting, Italian, and similar headings

Chaitanya, Krishna. A History of Indian Painting: The Rajasthani Traditions, Vol. 3. 134p. 1982. text ed. 50.00x (ISBN 0-391-02413-2, Pub. by Abhinav India). Humanities.

Kallir, Jane. Grandma Moses: The Artist Behind the Myth. (Illus.). 160p. (Orig.). pap. 15.00 (ISBN 0-910810-21-4). Johannes.

Mingay, Gordon. Mrs. Hurst Dancing & Other Scenes from Regency Life 1812-1823. (Illus.). 158p. 1982. 25.00 (ISBN 0-312-55129-0). St Martin.

Venable, Frank R., ed. Full Colour Reproductions of Some of the Greatest Paintings of Profane & Divine Love. (A Promotion of the Arts Library Bk.). 98p. 1983. 68.45 (ISBN 0-86650-052-9). Gloucester Art.

PAINTING–TECHNIQUE

see also Airbrush Art

Crawshaw, Alwyn. How To Paint with Acrylics. 64p. 1982. pap. 5.95 (ISBN 0-89586-158-5). H P Bks.

Garrard, Peter J. How To Paint with Oils. 64p. 1982. pap. 5.95 (ISBN 0-89586-160-7). H P Bks.

Kay, Reed. Painter's Guide to Studio Methods & Materials. (Illus.). 352p. 1982. 19.95 (ISBN 0-13-647958-8); pap. 12.95 (ISBN 0-13-647941-3). P-H.

Long, Jean. How to Paint the Chinese Way. (Illus.). 128p. 1983. pap. 7.50 (ISBN 0-7137-1343-7, Pub. by Blandford Pr England). Sterling.

Purwin, Sig. The Roller Book. 128p. 1983. pap. 11.95 (ISBN 0-89134-056-4). North Light Pub.

Reid, Charles. Painting What You Want to See: Forty-Six Lessons, Assignments, & Painting Critiques on Watercolor & Oil. (Illus.). 144p. 1983. 22.50 (ISBN 0-8230-3878-5). Watson-Guptill.

Salemme, Lucia A. The Complete Book of Painting Techniques. 1982. 35.00 (ISBN 0-02-927910-0). Free Pr.

Shaw, Jackie. Painting in the Pantry with Jackie. (Illus.). 32p. (Orig.). 1982. pap. 5.50 (ISBN 0-941284-15-8). Deco Design Studio.

--There's a Rainbow in my Paintbox. (Orig.). 1977. pap. 5.95 (ISBN 0-941284-05-0). Deco Design Studio.

Swann, Edward. Prelude to Painting Improvement. 64p. 1982. 25.00x (ISBN 0-284-98560-0, Pub. by C Skilton Scotland). State Mutual Bk.

--Sketches for Painting Practice. 48p. 1982. 20.00x (ISBN 0-284-98563-5, Pub. by C Skilton Scotland). State Mutual Bk.

Wilson, David A. The Finer Art of Painting. 40p. (Orig.). 1983. pap. 3.00 (ISBN 0-934852-26-X). Lorien Hse.

PAINTING–TECHNIQUE–JUVENILE LITERATURE

DeMuth, Vivienne. All Kinds of Things. (Paint by Number: No. 1482). (Illus.). 32p. (gr. 1 up). 1983. pap. 1.99 (ISBN 0-307-21482-6). Western Pub.

Ehlert, Lois. Designs. (Paint by Number: No. 1481). (Illus.). 32p. (gr. 1 up). 1983. pap. 1.99 (ISBN 0-307-21481-8). Western Pub.

Testa, Fulvio. If You Take a Paintbrush: A Book of Colors. LC 82-45512. (Illus.). 32p. (ps-2). 1983. 10.95 (ISBN 0-8037-3829-3, 01063-320). Dial Bks Young.

Ziegler, Bill. On the Move. (Paint by Number: No. 1483). (Illus.). 32p. (gr. 1 up). 1983. pap. 1.99 (ISBN 0-307-21483-4). Western Pub.

PAINTING, AMERICAN

Fawcett, David M. & Callander, Lee A. Native American Painting: Selections from the Museum of the American Indian. 96p. 1982. pap. 15.95x (ISBN 0-934490-40-6). Mus Am Ind.

A New World: American Painting, 1760-1900. (Illus.). 240p. 1983. write for info. Mus Fine Arts Boston.

Perry, Lilla C., illus. Lilla Cabot Perry: Impressionists. (Illus., Orig.). 1982. pap. 6.00 (ISBN 0-941430-06-5). Santa Fe E Gallery.

PAINTING, BRITISH

Rose, Andrew. The Pre-Raphaelites. (Phaidon Color Library). (Illus.). 84p. 1983. 25.00 (ISBN 0-7148-2180-2, Pub. by Salem Hse Ltd); pap. 17.95 (ISBN 0-7148-2166-7). Merrimack Bk Serv.

PAINTING, CHINESE

Lai, T. C. Understanding Chinese Painting. (Illus.). 240p. 16.95 (ISBN 0-86519-021-6). Lee Pubs Group.

Long, Jean. How to Paint the Chinese Way. (Illus.). 128p. 1983. pap. 7.50 (ISBN 0-7137-1343-7, Pub. by Blandford Pr England). Sterling.

PAINTING, DECORATIVE

see Art, Decorative; Decoration and Ornament; Mural Painting and Decoration

PAINTING, ENGLISH

see Painting, British

PAINTING, FRENCH

Kean, Beverly W. All the Empty Palaces: The Great Merchant Patrons of Modern Art in Pre-Revolutionary Russia. LC 82-8536. (Illus.). 336p. 1983. 29.50 (ISBN 0-87663-412-9). Universe.

Rust, David E. Small French Paintings from the Bequest of Ailsa Mellon Bruce. LC 78-606019. (Illus.). pap. 2.00 (ISBN 0-89468-048-X). Natl Gallery Art.

PAINTING, GOTHIC

Meiss, Millard. Francesco Traini. Maginnis, Hayden B., ed. (Art History Ser.: No. VI). (Illus.). 124p. 1983. 40.00 (ISBN 0-916276-12-0). Decatur Hse.

PAINTING, INDIC

Chaitanya, Krishna. A History of Indian Painting: The Rajasthani Traditions, Vol. 3. 134p. 1982. text ed. 50.00x (ISBN 0-391-02413-2, Pub. by Abhinav India). Humanities.

Six Indian Painters. 1983. pap. 13.50 (ISBN 0-8120-2651-9). Barron.

PAINTING, INDUSTRIAL

see also Lettering; Paint; Sign Painting; Wood Finishing

also subdivision Painting under particular subjects, e.g. Automobiles–Painting

Rudman, Jack. Foreman (Structures - Group F) (Painting) (Career Examination Ser.: C-1325). (Cloth bdg. avail. on request). pap. 12.00 (ISBN 0-8373-1325-2). Natl Learning.

PAINTING, ITALIAN

Meiss, Millard. Francesco Traini. Maginnis, Hayden B., ed. (Art History Ser.: No. VI). (Illus.). 124p. 1983. 40.00 (ISBN 0-916276-12-0). Decatur Hse.

PAINTING, JAPANESE

Cahill, James. Sakaki Hyakusen & Early Nanga Painting. (Japan Research Monograph: No. 3). (Illus.). 100p. (Orig.). 1983. pap. 8.00x (ISBN 0-912966-58-0). IEAS.

PAINTING, MECHANICAL

see Painting, Industrial

PAINTING, MODERN–20TH CENTURY

Baier, Lesley K. & Shestack, Alan. The Katherine Ordway Collection, Yale University Art Gallery. (Illus.). 128p. 1983. pap. write for info. (ISBN 0-89467-025-5). Yale Art Gallery.

Matthews, J. H. Eight Painters: The Surrealist Context. LC 82-10801. (Illus.). 288p. 1982. text ed. 24.00x (ISBN 0-8156-2274-0). Syracuse U Pr.

PAINTING, NARRATIVE

see Narrative Painting

PAINTING, NEW ZEALAND

Brown, Gordon H. & Hamish, Keith. An Introduction to New Zealand Painting, 1839-1930. (Illus.). 256p. 1982. 29.95 (ISBN 0-00-216989-4, Pub. by W Collins Australia). Intl Schol Bk Serv.

PAINTING, RELIGIOUS

see Christian Art and Symbolism

PAINTING, ROMANIAN

Florea, Vasile. Romanian Painting. (Illus.). 176p. 1983. 13.50x (ISBN 0-8143-1731-6). Wayne St U Pr.

PAINTING, TROMPE L'OEIL

see Trompe L'Oeil Painting

PAINTINGS

see also Portraits; Water Colors

Bryans Dictionary of Painters & Engravers, 5 Vols. Date not set. 200.00 (ISBN 0-686-43124-3). Apollo.

Chernow, Burt. Gabor Peterdi: Paitings. LC 82-50989. (Illus.). 120p. 1983. 29.95 (ISBN 0-8008-3121-7). Taplinger.

Havlice, Patricia P. World Painting Index: First Supplement 1973-1980, 2 vols. Incl. Vol. I. Bibliography, Paintings by Unknown Artists, Painters & Their Works; Vol. II. Titles of Works & Their Painters. LC 82-3355. 1233p. 1982. 62.50 (ISBN 0-8108-1531-1). Scarecrow.

Klarwein, Mati. Inscapes: Real Estate Paintings by Mati Klarwein. 1983. pap. 8.95 (ISBN 0-517-54955-7, Harmony). Crown.

Nunn, Ancel E., illus. Dreamscapes. 1982. 49.95 (ISBN 0-940672-06-5). Shearer Pub.

Thakurx, Upendra. Madhubani Paintings. 158p. 1982. text ed. 37.50x (ISBN 0-391-02411-6, Pub. by Macmillan England). Humanities.

PAINTINGS–CATALOGS

Here are entered dealers' and general catalogs. Catalogs of private collections are entered under Paintings–Private Collections. Catalogs of exhibitions are entered under Painting–Exhibitions.

McDonald, Robert. A Contemporary Collection on Loan from the Rothschild Bank AG, Zurich. (Illus.). 1983. write for info. (ISBN 0-934418-16-0). La Jolla Mus Contemp Art.

Smithsonian Institution, Washington D.C. Descriptive Catalog of Painting & Sculpture in the National Museum of American Art. 1983. lib. bdg. 125.00 (ISBN 0-8161-0408-5, Hall Library). G K Hall.

PAINTINGS–COLLECTORS AND COLLECTING

Mucsi, Andras. Catalogue of the Old Masters Gallery at the Christian Museum in Esztergom. Halapy, Lili, tr. from Hungarian. (Illus.). 136p. 1975. pap. 7.50x (ISBN 963-13-4290-5). Intl Pubns Serv.

PAINTINGS–EXHIBITIONS

see also Art–Exhibitions; Art Museums; also names of individual museums or subdivision galleries and museums under names of cities, e.g. Metropolitan Museum of Art, New York City; Paris-Museums and Galleries

Albright, Thomas & Butterfield, Jan. Oliver Jackson. LC 82-61511. (Illus.). 32p. (Orig.). 1982. pap. 10.00 (ISBN 0-932216-10-2). Seattle Art.

King, Alma S. An Exhibition of Paintings by American Impressionists. (Illus.). 64p. (Orig.). 1982. pap. 5.00 (ISBN 0-941430-04-9). Santa Fe E Gallery.

--Max Weber: An Exhibition of Works. (Illus.). 24p. (Orig.). 1982. pap. 7.50 (ISBN 0-941430-05-7). Santa Fe E Gallery.

Perry, Lilla C., illus. Lilla Cabot Perry: Impressionists. (Illus., Orig.). 1982. pap. 6.00 (ISBN 0-941430-06-5). Santa Fe E Gallery.

Potterton, Homan, intro. by. The National Gallery of Ireland Illustrated Summary Catalogue of Paintings. 1982. 125.00x (ISBN 0-7171-1144-X, Pub. by Gill & Macmillan Ireland). State Mutual Bk.

Wilmerding, John. Important Information Inside: The Art of John F. Peto & the Idea of Still Life Painting in Nineteenth Century America. write for info. Natl Gallery Art.

--Important Information Inside: The Art of John F. Peto & the Idea of Still-Life Painting in 19th Century America. LC 82-48489. (Icon Editions). (Illus.). 1983. 33.65i (ISBN 0-06-438941-3, HarpT). Har-Row.

PAINTINGS–JUVENILE LITERATURE

Green Tiger Press, ed. Flying Horse. 12p. (Orig.). 1982. pap. 2.50 (ISBN 0-88138-005-9, Pub. by Envelope Bks). Green Tiger Pr.

--Mermaids. (Illus.). 12p. (Orig.). 1982. pap. 2.50 (ISBN 0-88138-001-6, Pub. by Envelope Bks). Green Tiger Pr.

--Women with Long Hair. (Illus.). 12p. (Orig.). 1982. pap. 2.50 (ISBN 0-88138-006-7, Pub. by Envelope Bks). Green Tiger Pr.

Nigg, Joe. Gryphons. (Illus.). 12p. (Orig.). 1982. pap. 2.50 (ISBN 0-88138-004-0, Pub. by Envelope Bks). Green Tiger Pr.

PAINTINGS–PRIVATE COLLECTIONS

Bowen, Robert G., Jr. My Philosophy: Why My Paintings are Signed "A Friend of Civilization". LC 81-69045. (Orig.). 1982. black & white ed. 30.00 (ISBN 0-9607512-1-1); color ed. 30.00 (ISBN 0-9607512-3-8); pap. 4.00 black & white ed. (ISBN 0-9607512-0-3); pap. 6.00 color ed. (ISBN 0-9607512-2-X). R G Bowen.

Carlson, Victor. Hubert Robert: Drawings & Watercolors. LC 78-22022. (Illus.). pap. 5.00 (ISBN 0-89468-040-4). Natl Gallery Art.

Chapel, Jeannie. Victorian Taste: The Complete Catalogue of Paintings at the Royal Holloway College. (Illus.). 144p. 1983. pap. 25.00 (ISBN 0-8390-0302-1). Allanheld & Schram.

Fine, Ruth E. Lessing J. Rosenwald: Tribute to a Collector. LC 81-14133. (Illus.). pap. 19.95 (ISBN 0-89468-004-8). Natl Gallery Art.

Joseph Wright of Derby: A Selection of Paintings from the Collection of Mr. & Mrs. Paul Mellon. LC 78-101454. (Illus.). pap. 2.25 (ISBN 0-89468-041-2). Natl Gallery Art.

PAINTINGS, ABSTRACT

see Art, Modern–20th Century

PAINTINGS, AMERICAN

Albright, Thomas & Butterfield, Jan. Oliver Jackson. LC 82-61511. (Illus.). 32p. (Orig.). 1982. pap. 10.00 (ISBN 0-932216-10-2). Seattle Art.

Berreth, David, ed. American Paintings: 1830-1915. LC 82-61415. (Illus.). 40p. (Orig.). 1982. pap. 3.00 (ISBN 0-940784-03-3). Miami Univ Art.

Downing, Thomas. Thomas Downing Paintings Nineteen Sixty-Two to Nineteen Sixty-Seven. (Illus.). 24p. 1968. 3.00x (ISBN 0-686-99834-0). La Jolla Mus Contemp Art.

Frankenstein, Alfred. The Reminiscent Object: Paintings by William Michael Harnett, John Frederick Peto & John Haberle. (Illus.). 68p. 1965. 3.00x (ISBN 0-686-99840-5). La Jolla Mus Contemp Art.

King, Alma S. An Exhibition of Paintings by American Impressionists. (Illus.). 64p. (Orig.). 1982. pap. 5.00 (ISBN 0-941430-04-9). Santa Fe E Gallery.

Krane, Susan. The Paintings of Joe Zucker Nineteen Sixty-Nine to Nineteen Eighty-Two. LC 82-72220. (Illus.). 1982. pap. 12.00 (ISBN 0-914782-45-2). Buffalo Acad.

Miller, Henry. The Paintings of Henry Miller. (Illus.). 132p. (Orig.). 1982. text ed. 35.00 (ISBN 0-87701-280-6); pap. 16.95 (ISBN 0-87701-276-8). Chronicle Bks.

Nelson-Rees, A. Paintings by Selden Connor Gile, 1877-1947. LC 82-83509. (Illus.). 72p. 1982. 20.00 (ISBN 0-938842-02-1). WIM Oakland.

Pisano, Ronald G. American Paintings from The Parrish Art Museum. LC 82-61450. (Illus.). 52p. pap. write for info (ISBN 0-943526-07-8). Pachyderm Pr.

--American Realist & Impressionist: Paintings From the Collection of Mr. & Mrs. Haig Tashjian. (Illus., Orig.). 1982. write for info. catalogue. Parrish Art.

Post-Impressionism: Cross-Currents in European & American Painting, 1880-1906. LC 80-13795. (Illus.). pap. 2.00 (ISBN 0-89468-046-3). Natl Gallery Art.

Price, Bren. Inside the Wind. Hausman, Gerald, ed. LC 82-19302. (Illus.). 64p. 1983. 37.95 (ISBN 0-86534-016-1). Sunstone Pr.

Wilson, William. Joyce Treiman: Paintings 1961-1972. (Illus.). 28p. 1972. 3.00x (ISBN 0-686-99823-5). La Jolla Mus Contemp Art.

PAINTINGS, BRITISH

Fletcher, Hans. Paintings from the Royal Academy. Walker, Janet M., ed. LC 82-82937. (Illus.). 52p. (Orig.). 1982. pap. 13.00 (ISBN 0-88397-043-0). Intl Exhibit Foun.

PAINTINGS, CHINESE

Whitfield, Roderick. The Art of Paintings from Dunhuang: The Art of Central Asia, the Stein Collection in the British Museum, Vol. II. LC 81-80657. (Illus.). 340p. 1983. through April 30, 1983 375.00 (ISBN 0-87011-555-3); after April 30, 1983 425.00 (ISBN 0-686-81735-4). Kodansha.

PAINTINGS, DUTCH

Blankert, Albert, et al. Gods, Saints & Heroes: Dutch Painting in the Age of Rembrandt. LC 80-20371. (Illus.). pap. 14.00 (ISBN 0-89468-039-0). Natl Gallery Art.

Bruyn, J. A Corpus of Rembrandt Paintings, Vol. 1. 1983. lib. bdg. 325.00 (ISBN 90-247-2614-X, Pub. by Martinus Nijhoff). Kluwer Boston.

Kuznetsov, Yury & Linnik, Irene. Dutch Painting in Soviet Museums. LC 80-66702. (Illus.). 523p. 1982. 45.00 (ISBN 0-8109-0803-4). Abrams.

PAINTINGS, ENGLISH

see Paintings, British

PAINTINGS, EUROPEAN

Department of Paintings Museum of Fine Arts. Summary Catalogue of European Paintings. (Illus.). 368p. 1983. price not set (ISBN 0-87846-230-9). Mus Fine Arts Boston.

European Paintings: An Illustrated Summary Catalog. LC 74-16421. (Illus.). pap. 6.50 (ISBN 0-89468-038-2). Natl Gallery Art.

Post-Impressionism: Cross-Currents in European & American Painting, 1880-1906. LC 80-13795. (Illus.). pap. 2.00 (ISBN 0-89468-046-3). Natl Gallery Art.

PAINTINGS, FRENCH

Plummer, John. The Last Flowering: French Painting in Manuscripts, 1420-1530. (Illus.). 252p. 1982. 89.00 (ISBN 0-19-503262-4). Oxford U Pr.

PAINTINGS, GERMAN

Vegh, Janos. Sixteenth Century German Panel Paintings. 2nd, Rev. ed. Horn, Susanna, tr. from Hungarian. LC 77-357632. 133p. 1972. 13.50x (ISBN 963-13-1280-1). Intl Pubns Serv.

PAINTINGS, INDIC

Singh, Chandramani. Centres of Pahari Paintings. 174p. 1981. text ed. 62.00x (ISBN 0-391-02412-4, Pub. by Abhinav India). Humanities.

Zebrowski, Mark. Deccani Paintings. LC 82-45907. (Illus.). 256p. 1983. 85.00 (ISBN 0-520-04878-4). U of Cal Pr.

PAINTINGS, ITALIAN

Cass, David B. & Wetenhall, John. Italian Paintings, 1859-1910: From Collections in the Northeastern Unites States. (Illus.). 82p. 1982. pap. 6.95 (ISBN 0-686-38389-3). S & F Clark.

Shapley, Fern R. Catalog of the Italian Paintings, 2 vols. LC 79-4410. pap. 10.00 set (ISBN 0-89468-053-6). Vol. 1 (ISBN 0-89468-054-4). Vol. 2 (ISBN 0-89468-055-2). Natl Gallery Art.

Tomory, Peter. Catalog of the Italian Paintings Before 1800. LC 76-730. (Illus.). 198p. 1976. 19.50 (ISBN 0-916758-01-X). Ringling Mus Art.

PAINTINGS, JAPANESE

Addiss, Stephen. Samurai Painters. LC 82-48781. (Great Japanese Art Ser.). (Illus.). 48p. 1982. 18.95 (ISBN 0-87011-563-4). Kodansha.

Zolbrod, Leon M. Haiku Painting. LC 82-48792. (Great Japanese Art Ser.). (Illus.). 48p. 1983. 18.95 (ISBN 0-87011-560-X). Kodansha.

PAINTINGS, MODERN

see Art, Modern–20th Century

PAINTINGS, POLISH

Terlecki, Tymon. Stanislaw Wyspianski. (World Authors Ser.). 166p. 1983. lib. bdg. 18.95 (ISBN 0-8057-6521-2, Twayne). G K Hall.

PAINTINGS, ROMANESQUE

Oakeshott, Walter. Sigena: Romanesque Paintings in Spain & the Winchester Bible Artists. (Illus.). 227p. 1972. 49.00x (ISBN 0-19-921006-3). Oxford U Pr.

PAINTS

see Paint

PAIUTE INDIANS

see Indians of North America–Southwest, New

PAKISTAN

Burki, Shahid J. Pakistan: A Nation in the Making. (Nations of Contemporary Asia). 128p. 1983. lib. bdg. 16.00 (ISBN 0-86531-353-9). Westview.

PAKISTAN–ECONOMIC CONDITIONS

Adams, John & Igbal, Sabiha. Exports, Politics, & Economic Development: Pakiston, 1970-1982. (Replica Edition Ser.). 185p. 1983. softcover 18.50x (ISBN 0-86531-959-6). Westview.

Rural Development & Local Level Planning in Pakistan. (UNCRD Working Paper: No. 82-9). 36p. 1983. pap. 6.00 (ISBN 0-686-43303-3, CRD 147, UNCRD). Unipub.

PAKISTAN–FOREIGN RELATIONS

Venkataramani, M. S. The American Role in Pakistan. 480p. 1982. text ed. 36.75x (ISBN 0-391-02764-6, 40389, Pub. by Radiant Pub India). Humanities.

PAKISTAN–POLITICS AND GOVERNMENT

Adams, John & Igbal, Sabiha. Exports, Politics, & Economic Development: Pakiston, 1970-1982. (Replica Edition Ser.). 185p. 1983. softcover 18.50x (ISBN 0-86531-959-6). Westview.

Maniruzzaman, Talukder. Group Interests & Political Changes: Studies of Pakistan & Bangladesh. 1982. 24.00x (ISBN 0-8364-0892-6). South Asia Bks.

PAKISTAN-RELATIONS (GENERAL) WITH FOREIGN COUNTRIES

Ahmad, Akhtaruddin. Nationalism or Islam: Indo-Pakistan Episode. LC 80-52050. 338p. 1982. 10.95 (ISBN 0-533-04737-4). Vantage.

Venkataramani, M. S. The American Role in Pakistan. 480p. 1982. text ed. 36.75x (ISBN 0-391-02764-6, 40389, Pub. by Radiant Pub India). Humanities.

PAKISTAN LITERATURE

see also Urdu Literature

Hasan, Khalid, ed. Versions of Truth: Urdu Short Stories from Pakistan. 1983. text ed. write for info. (ISBN 0-7069-2128-3, Pub. by Vikas India). Advent NY.

PALATE, CLEFT

see Cleft Palate

PALEO-AMERICANS

see Paleo-Indians

PALEO-AMERINDS

see Paleo-Indians

PALEOANTHROPOLOGY

see Man, Prehistoric

PALEOBIOLOGY

see Paleobotany; Paleoecology; Paleontology

PALEOBOTANY

Dilcher, D. L. & Taylor, T. N., eds. Biostratigraphy of Fossil Plants: Sucessional & Paleoecological Analyses. LC 79-27418. 259p. 1980. 31.50. Hutchinson Ross.

Pandey, S. N., et al. Textbook of Botany: Vol. II: Bryophyta, Pteridophyta, Gymnosperms & Paleobotany. 2nd ed. viii, 531p. 1981. text ed. 25.00x (ISBN 0-7069-1355-8, Pub. by Vikas India). Advent NY.

Shukla, A. C. & Misra, S. P. Essentials of Paleobotany. 2nd ed. (Illus.). 1982. text ed. 20.00 (ISBN 0-7069-1450-3, Pub. by Vikas India). Advent NY.

Streel, M., et al, eds. Advances in Paleozoic Botany. 1972. Repr. 27.75 (ISBN 0-444-41080-5). Elsevier.

PALEOCLIMATOLOGY

see also Dendrochronology

Libby, Leona M. Past Climates: Tree Thermometers, Commodities & People. 157p. 1983. text ed. 25.00x (ISBN 0-292-73019-5). U of Tex Pr.

PALEOECOLOGY

Gall, J. C. Ancient Sedimentary Environments & the Habitats of Living Organisms: Introduction to Paleoecology. Wallace, P., tr. from Fr. (Illus.). 230p. 1983. 24.00 (ISBN 0-387-12137-4). Springer-Verlag.

PALEOETHNOGRAPHY

see Archaeology; Man, Prehistoric

PALEOGEOGRAPHY

Zambrano, E. & Vasquez, E. Paleogeographic & Petroleum Synthesis of Western Venezuela. 70p. 1972. 60.00x (ISBN 2-7108-0194-9, Pub. by Graham & Trotman England). State Mutual Bk.

PALEO-INDIANS

Shutler, Richard, Jr., ed. Early Man in the New World. (Illus.). 200p. 1983. 29.95 (ISBN 0-8039-1958-1); pap. 14.95 (ISBN 0-8039-1959-X). Sage.

PALEONTOLOGY

see also Extinct Animals; Micropaleontology; Paleobotany; Sedimentary Structures

also mollusks, Fossil; Vertebrates, Fossil, and similar headings

Babin, Claude. Elements of Palaeontology. LC 79-1323. 446p. 1980. 57.00 (ISBN 0-471-27577-8, Pub. by Wiley-Interscience); pap. 24.00x (ISBN 0-471-27576-X). Wiley.

Bolliger, Markus. Die Gattung Pulmonaria in Westeuropa. (Phanerogamarum Monographiae VIII). 250p. (Orig., Ger.). 1982. text ed. 54.00x (ISBN 3-7682-1338-2). Lubrecht & Cramer.

Cleevely, R. J. World Palaeontological Collections. 450p. 1982. 80.00 (ISBN 0-7201-1655-4, Pub. by Mansell England). Wilson.

Dietrich, R. V. & Wicander, E. Reed. Rocks, Minerals & Fossils. (Self-Teaching Guides Ser.). 288p. 1983. pap. text ed. 9.95 (ISBN 0-471-89883-X). Wiley.

Dunbar, Carl O. & Waage, Karl M. Historical Geology. 3rd ed. LC 72-89681. (Illus.). 556p. 1969. text ed. 28.95x (ISBN 0-471-22507-X). Wiley.

Fairbridge, R. W. & Jablonski, D., eds. The Encyclopedia of Paleontology. LC 79-11468. (Encyclopedia of Earth Sciences Ser.: Vol. VII). 886p. 1979. 98.00 (ISBN 0-87933-185-2). Hutchinson Ross.

Hakansson, H. & Gerloff, J., eds. Diatomaceae III: Festschrift Niels Foged on the Occassion of his 75th Birthday. (Nova Hedwigia Beiheft: 73.). (Illus.). 386p. (Orig., Eng. & Ger.). 1982. lib. bdg. 67.50x (ISBN 3-7682-5473-9). Lubrecht & Cramer.

Hilber, Oswald. Die Gattung Pleurotus (Fr.) Kummer Unter Besonderer Beruecksichtigung des Pleurotus-Eryngii-Komplexes. (Bibliotheca Mycologica Ser.: Vol. 87). (Illus.). 447p. (Orig., Ger.). 1982. text ed. 80.00x (ISBN 3-7682-1335-8). Lubrecht & Cramer.

Honjo, S., ed. Ocean Biocoenosis: Microfossil Counterparts in Sediment Traps. (Micropaleontology Special Publications Ser.: No. 5). 1982. 50.00 (ISBN 0-686-84259-6). Am Mus Natl Hist.

Hurzeler, Johannes. Contribution a L'odontologie et a la Phylogenese du Genre Pliopithecus Gervais. Bd. with Die Primatenfunde aus der miozanen Spaltenfullung von neudorf an der March, Devin ska Nova Ves, Tschechoslowakei. Zapfe, Helmuth. 1961. LC 78-72721. 1954. 79.50 (ISBN 0-404-18296-8). AMS Pr.

Kloidt, M. & Lysek, G. Die Epiphylle Pilzfora von Acer Platanoides L. (Bibliotheca Mycologica 86 Ser.). 144p. (Orig.). 1982. pap. text ed. 22.50 (ISBN 3-7682-1332-3). Lubrecht & Cramer.

Renzglia, Karen S. Comparative Developmental Investigation of the Gametophyte Generation in the Metzgeriales (Hepatophyta) (Bryophytorum Bibliotheca Ser.: 24). (Illus.). 253p. (Orig.). 1982. text ed. 54.00x (ISBN 3-7682-1336-6). Lubrecht & Cramer.

Simpson, George G. Attending Marvels: A Patagonian Journal. LC 82-13438. (Phoenix Ser.). 296p. 1982. pap. 9.50 (ISBN 0-226-75935-0). U of Chicago Pr.

Takayanagi, T. & Saito, T., eds. Progress in Micropaleontology: Papers in Honor of Professor Kiyoshi Asano. (Micropaleontology Special Publications Ser.). 422p. 1976. 35.00 (ISBN 0-686-84247-2). Am Mus Natl Hist.

Van Landingham, S. L. Catalogue of the Fossil & Recent Genera & Species of Diatoms & Their Syhonyms: Navicula, Pt. 5. 2963p. 1975. text ed. 40.00x (ISBN 3-7682-0475-8). Lubrecht & Cramer.

--Catalogue of the Fossil & Recent Genera & Species of Diatoms & Their Synonyms: Neidium-Rhocicosigma, Pt. 6. 3605p. 1978. text ed. 40.00x (ISBN 3-7682-0476-6). Lubrecht & Cramer.

Watson, D. M. Paleontology & Modern Biology. 1951. text ed. 39.50x (ISBN 0-686-83673-1). Elliots Bks.

Yen, T. F. & Kawahara, F. K., eds. Chemical & Geochemical Aspects of Fossil Energy Extraction. LC 82-72858. (Illus.). 266p. 1983. 37.50 (ISBN 0-250-40462-1). Ann Arbor Science.

PALEONTOLOGY-MEXICO

Maudslay, A. P. Archaeology: Biologia Centrali-America or, Contibutions to the Knowledge of the Fauna & Flora of Mexico & Central America. Godman, F. Ducane & Salvin, Osbert, eds. LC 74-30688. (Illus.). 907p. 1983. 250.00x (ISBN 0-8061-9919-9, Pub. by Milpatron Publishing Corp). U of Okla Pr.

PALEONTOLOGY-UNITED STATES

Wolf, Robert C. Fossils of Iowa: Field Guide to Paleozois Deposits. (Illus.). 203p. 1983. pap. 10.50 (ISBN 0-8138-1334-4). Iowa St U Pr.

PALEONTOLOGY, BOTANICAL

see Paleobotany

PALEONTOLOGY, STRATIGRAPHIC

Dilcher, D. L. & Taylor, T. N., eds. Biostratigraphy of Fossil Plants: Sucessional & Paleoecological Analyses. LC 79-27418. 259p. 1980. 31.50. Hutchinson Ross.

PALEONTOLOGY, ZOOLOGICAL

see Paleontology

PALEOZOOLOGY

see Paleontology

PALESTINE-ANTIQUITIES

see also Bible-Antiquities; Dead Sea Scrolls

Moorey, Roger. Excavation in Palestine. 1982. 35.00x (ISBN 0-7188-2432-6, Pub. by Lutterworth Pr England). State Mutual Bk.

PALESTINE-DESCRIPTION AND TRAVEL

Kaganoff. Guide to America Holy Land Studies, 1620-1948, Vol. 2. 234p. 1982. 26.95 (ISBN 0-03-062812-1). Praeger.

PALESTINE-HISTORY

see also Bible-History of Biblical Events; Judaism-History

Hunt, Edward D. Holy Land Pilgramage in the Later Roman Empire, AD 312-460. 280p. 1982. 39.95x (ISBN 0-19-826438-0). Oxford U Pr.

Ma'Oz, Moshe, ed. Studies on Palestine During the Ottoman Period. 582p. 1975. text ed. 34.50x (ISBN 0-686-74322-9, Pub. by Magnes Israel). Humanities.

Stern, Ephraim. The Material Culture of the Land of the Bible in the Persian Period 538-331 B.C. (Illus.). 304p. 1982. pap. text ed. 65.00x (ISBN 0-85668-137-7, 40917, Pub. by Aris & Phillips England). Humanities.

PALESTINE-POLITICS AND GOVERNMENT

Brubeck, William H. Israelis & Palestinians: The Need for an Alliance of Moderates. (Seven Springs Studies). 43p. 1982. pap. 3.00 (ISBN 0-943006-14-7). Seven Springs.

PALESTINE-RELIGION

De Boer, P. A. H. Religieuze Aspecten van het Palestijnse Vraagstuk. x, 39p. 1982. pap. write for info. (ISBN 90-04-06727-2). E J Brill.

PALESTINIAN ARABS

see also Jewish-Arab Relations

Heller, Mark A. A Palestinian State. 192p. 1983. text ed. 16.00x (ISBN 0-674-65221-5). Harvard U Pr.

Paolucci, Henry. Zionism, the Superpowers, & the P.L.O. LC 82-15728. 80p. 1982. 6.95 (ISBN 0-918680-18-2, GHGP 708). Griffon Hse.

PALESTINIANS

see Palestinian Arabs

PALMER, SAMUEL, 1805-1881

Brown, D. B. Samuel Palmer: Paintings, Drawings & Prints in the Ashmolean Museum, Oxford. 50.00x (ISBN 0-900090-95-2, Pub. by Ashmolean Mus Oxford). State Mutual Bk.

PALMERSTON, HENRY JOHN, 3RD VISCOUNT, 1784-1865

Guedalla, Philip. Gladstone & Palmerston: Being the Correspondence of Lord Palmerston with Mr. Gladstone, 1851-1865. 367p. 1982. Repr. of 1928 ed. lib. bdg. 40.00 (ISBN 0-89987-314-6). Darby Bks.

PALMISTRY

Count de St. Germain. The Theory of the Mounts of the Hand & the Message They Convey to the Future of Man. (Illus.). 131p. 1983. Repr. of 1898 ed. 115.45 (ISBN 0-89901-110-1). Found Class Reprints.

PALSY, SHAKING

see Paralysis Agitans

PAMPHLETS

Clark, Sandra. Elizabethan Pamphleteers: Popular Moralistic Pamphlets, 1580-1640. LC 81-72064. (Illus.). 320p. 1982. 30.00 (ISBN 0-8386-3173-8). Fairleigh Dickinson.

PAN-AFRICANISM

Amaral, David. Lusophone African Liberators: The University Years. (Graduate Student Paper Competition Ser.). 20p. (Orig.). 1979. pap. text ed. 2.00 (ISBN 0-941934-27-6). Ind U Afro-Amer Arts.

Esedebe, P. Olisanwuche. Pan-Africanism. 271p. 1983. 12.95 (ISBN 0-88258-124-4); pap. 6.95 (ISBN 0-88258-125-2). Howard U Pr.

PANAMA CANAL

Mahan, Alfred T. The Panama Canal & the Sea Power in the Pacific. (The Great Issues of History Library). (Illus.). 107p. 1983. Repr. of 1913 ed. 79.85 (ISBN 0-86722-027-9). Inst Econ Pol.

Taft, William H. The Physical, Political & International Value of the Panama Canal. (The Great Issues of History Library). (Illus.). 111p. 1983. Repr. of 1914 ed. 75.85 (ISBN 0-86722-028-7). Inst Econ Pol.

PANCREAS

see also Enzymes

Federlin, Konrad & Pfeifeer, Ernst F. Islet Pancreas Transplantation & Artificial Pancreas. 315p. 39.95 (ISBN 0-86577-062-X). Thieme-Stratton.

Goebell, H., ed. European Pancreatic Club: EPC XIV Meeting, Essen Sept.-Oct. 1982, Abstracts. (Journal: Digestion: Vol. 25, No. 1). 80p. 1982. pap. 34.75 (ISBN 3-8055-3633-X). S Karger.

PANCREAS-DISEASES

see also Cystic Fibrosis

Kovac, Alexander & Kozarek, Richard. Guide to Diagnostic Imaging: Vol. III - The Pancreas. 1983. write for info. (ISBN 0-87488-415-2). Med Exam.

PANCREAS-SURGERY

Paloyan, Daniel. Pancreatitis. 1983. text ed. price not set (ISBN 0-87488-570-1). Med Exam.

PANCREATIC CYSTIC FIBROSIS

see Cystic Fibrosis

PANGENESIS

see Heredity; Reproduction

PAPACY

see also Catholic Church; Popes

Miller, Michael. What Are They Saying About Papal Primacy? (WATSA Ser.). 128p. 1983. pap. 3.95 (ISBN 0-8091-2501-3). Paulist Pr.

PAPACY-HISTORY

Abdel-Massih, Ernest. The Life & Miracles of Pope Kirillos VI. 139p. (Orig.). 1982. pap. text ed. 3.00 (ISBN 0-932098-20-7). St Mark Coptic Orthodox.

Abdel-Massih, Ernest T. The Life & Miracles of Pope Kirillos VI. 1982. pap. text ed. 3.00 (ISBN 0-686-84212-X). Ctr for NE & North African Stud.

Barstow, Anne L. Married Priests & the Reforming Papacy: The 11th Century Debates. LC 82-7914. (Texts & Studies in Religion: Vol. 12). 344p. 1982. 39.95x (ISBN 0-88946-987-3). E Mellen.

Cheetham, Nicolas. Keepers of the Keys: A History of the Popes from St. Peter to John Paul II. LC 82-16950. (Illus.). 352p. 1983. 17.95 (ISBN 0-684-17863-X, ScribT). Scribner.

Lunt, W. E. Financial Relations of the Papacy with England to 1327. 1967. Repr. of 1939 ed. 20.00X (ISBN 0-910956-13-8). Medieval Acad.

--Financial Relations of the Papacy with England, 1327-1534. 1962. 25.00X (ISBN 0-910956-48-0). Medieval Acad.

PAPAGO INDIANS

see Indians of North America-Southwest, New

PAPAGO LANGUAGE

Zepeda, Ofelia. A Papago Grammar. 175p. 1983. pap. text ed. 8.95x (ISBN 0-8165-0792-9). U of Ariz Pr.

PAPAL INFALLIBILITY

see Popes-Infallibility

PAPER

see also Fillers (In Paper, Paint, etc.); Paper Coatings

Mark. Handbook of Physical & Mechanical Testing of Paper & Paperboard, Vol. 1. 821p. 1983. price not set (ISBN 0-8247-1871-2). Dekker.

Rance, H. F. Structure & Physical Properties of Paper. (Handbook of Paper Science: Vol. 2). 1982. 85.00 (ISBN 0-444-41974-8). Elsevier.

Webb, Shelia. Paper: The Continuous Thread. LC 82-12840. (Themes in Art Ser.). (Illus.). 72p. (Orig.). 1983. pap. 6.95x (ISBN 0-910386-69-2, Pub. by Cleveland Mus Art). Ind U Pr.

PAPER BOARD

see Paperboard

PAPER-BOUND EDITIONS

see Bibliography-Paperback Editions

PAPER BOX INDUSTRY

Rosa, Manuel A., ed. Corrugating Defect Terminology: Fabrication Manuel for Corrugated Box Plants. 4th, rev. ed. (Illus.). 236p. 1982. pap. 49.95 (ISBN 0-89852-403-2, 01 01R 103). TAPPI.

PAPER COATINGS

Coating Conference: Proceedings. 179p. 1981. pap. 44.95 (ISBN 0-686-43238-X, 01 05 0482). TAPPI.

Heiser, Edward J. & Allswede, Jerry L., eds. Blade Coating Defect Terminology. (Illus.). 53p. 1982. pap. 24.95 (ISBN 0-686-43234-7, 01 01 R094). TAPPI.

Yin, Robert I., ed. Paper Coating Additives: Description of Functional Properties & List of Available Products. 4th ed. 72p. 1982. pap. 34.95 (ISBN 0-89852-401-6, 01 01 R101). TAPPI.

PAPER-CUTTING

see Paper Work

PAPER DOLLS

see Paper Work

PAPER FOLDING

see Paper Work

PAPER-HANGING

see also Wall-Paper

Sunset Books & Sunset Magazine, ed. Wallcoverings. LC 82-81370. (Illus.). 96p. (Orig.). 1982. pap. 4.95 (ISBN 0-376-01673-6). Sunset-Lane.

PAPER INDUSTRY

see Paper Making and Trade

PAPER MAKING AND TRADE

see also Book Industries and Trade; Wood Pulp Industry

Annual Meeting: Proceedings. 449p. 1982. pap. 44.95 (ISBN 0-686-43236-3, 01050182). TAPPI.

Annual Meeting: Proceedings. 416p. 1980. pap. 19.95 (ISBN 0-686-43237-1, 01 05 0180). TAPPI.

Atchinson, Joseph E. Nonwood Plant Fiber Pulping Progress Report. (No. 13). 148p. 1983. pap. 48.95 (ISBN 0-89852-404-0, 01 01 R104). TAPPI.

Bosar, Gary J. Mechanical End Face Seals-Guidelines for the Pulp & Paper Industry. (Illus.). 21p. 1981. 24.95 (ISBN 0-89852-392-3, 01-01-R092). TAPPI.

Casey, James P. Pulp & Paper: Chemistry & Technology, Vol. 4. 3rd ed. 600p. 1983. price not set (ISBN 0-471-03178-X, Pub. by Wiley-Interscience). Wiley.

Engineering Conference: Proceedings, 3 bks. 577p. 1982. Set. pap. 104.95 (ISBN 0-686-43239-8, 01 05 0582); 44.95 ea. TAPPI.

Envirmental Conference: Proceedings. 298p. 1982. pap. 44.95 (ISBN 0-686-43240-1, 01 05 0382). TAPPI.

Estimated Production of Pulp, Paper & Paperboard in Certain Countries in 1981. 30p. 1982. pap. 7.50 (ISBN 0-686-84613-3, F2327, FAO). Unipub.

Heiser, Edward J. & Allswede, Jerry L., eds. Blade Coating Defect Terminology. (Illus.). 53p. 1982. pap. 24.95 (ISBN 0-686-43234-7, 01 01 R094). TAPPI.

Hyzer, Donald V., ed. Project Implementation: Project Case Histories, Vol. 2. (Illus.). 242p. 1982. pap. 44.95 (ISBN 0-89852-402-4, 01 01 R102). TAPPI.

International Pulp Bleaching Conference: Proceedings. 223p. 1982. pap. 44.95 (ISBN 0-686-43244-4, 01 05 1282). TAPPI.

International Sulfite Pulping Conference: Proceedings. 223p. 1982. pap. 44.95 (ISBN 0-686-43245-2, 01 05 1782). TAPPI.

Miller, Richard K. Noise Control Solutions for the Paper Industry. (Illus.). 80p. text ed. 45.00 (ISBN 0-89671-033-5). Southeast Acoustics.

OECD Staff. Pulp & Paper Industry 1980. 129p. (Orig.). 1982. pap. 12.50x (ISBN 92-64-02322-4). OECD.

Paper Synthetic Conference: Proceedings. 364p. 1982. pap. 44.95 (ISBN 0-686-43243-6, 01 05 0782). TAPPI.

Papermakers Conference: Proceedings. 304p. 1982. pap. 44.95 (01 05 0282). TAPPI.

Papermakers: Proceedings. 270p. 1981. pap. 34.95 (ISBN 0-686-43242-8, 01 05 0281). TAPPI.

Parham, Russell A. & Gray, Richard L. The Practical Identification of Wood Pulp Fibers. 212p. 1982. 34.95 (ISBN 0-89852-400-8, 01 01R0100). TAPPI.

Projected Pulp & Paper Mills in the World, 1981-1991. 126p. 1982. pap. 9.00 (ISBN 92-5-101204-0, F2308, FAO). Unipub.

Pulp & Paper Capacities Nineteen Eighty-One to Nineteen Eighty-Six. 248p. 1982. pap. 16.00 (ISBN 92-5-001214-4, F2321, FAO). Unipub.

Pulp & Paper Capacities Survey 1981-1986: Supplement. 13p. 1982. pap. 7.50 (ISBN 92-5-001233-0, F2335, FAO). Unipub.

Pulp & Paper Week Staff. Pulp & Paper North American Industry Factbook, 1982-83. (Illus.). 392p. 1982. 145.00 (ISBN 0-87930-090-6). Miller Freeman.

The Pulping & Paper Making Potential of Tropical Hardwoods: Mixed Species from the Gogol Timber Area, Papua New Guinea, Vol. VI. 32p. 1979. 6.00 (ISBN 0-643-00339-8, CO64, CSIRO). Unipub.

Pulping Conference: Proceedings. 514p. 1982. pap. 44.95 (ISBN 0-686-43246-0, 01 05 0682). TAPPI.

Research & Development Division Conference: Proceedings. 341p. 1982. pap. 44.95 (ISBN 0-686-43247-9, 01 05 1682). TAPPI.

Rosa, Manuel A., ed. Corrugating Defect Terminology: Fabrication Manuel for Corrugated Box Plants. 4th, rev. ed. (Illus.). 236p. 1982. pap. 49.95 (ISBN 0-89852-403-2, 01 01R 103). TAPPI.

Testing Conference (Joint with Corrugated) Proceedings. 34p. 1982. pap. 34.95 (ISBN 0-686-43248-7, 01 05 0982). TAPPI.
Testing Conference (Joint with Printing & Reprography) Proceedings. 196p. 1979. pap. 4.95 (ISBN 0-686-43249-5, 01 05 1079). TAPPI.
Testing Conference (Joint with Printing & Reprography) Proceeding. 225p. 1977. pap. 4.95 (ISBN 0-686-43250-9, 01 05 1077). TAPPI.
Watt, Alexander. The Art of Papermaking. (Illus.). 240p. Date not set. pap. 20.00 (ISBN 0-87556-581-6). Saifer.
Yin, Robert I., ed. Paper Coating Additives: Description of Functional Properties & List of Available Products. 4th ed. 72p. 1982. pap. 34.95 (ISBN 0-89852-401-6, 01 01 R101). TAPPI.

PAPER MAKING AND TRADE–JUVENILE LITERATURE
Gibbons, Gail. Paper, Paper Everywhere. LC 82-3109. (Illus.). 32p. (gr. 6-10). 10.95 (ISBN 0-15-259488-4, HJ). HarBraceJ.

PAPER MONEY
Englsh Paper MOney. 18.00. StanGib Ltd.
Krause, Chester L. & Lemke, Robert F. Standard Catalog of United States Paper Money. 2nd ed. LC 81-81976. (Illus.). 1982. pap. 14.50 (ISBN 0-87341-074-2). Krause Pubns.
Pick, Albert. Standard Catalog of World Paper Money, Vol. 2. 4th ed. Bruce, Colin & Shafer, Neil, eds. (Illus.). 960p. 1982. 35.00. Krause Pubns.
Wilhite, Bob & Lemke, Bob. Standard Guide to U. S. Coin & Paper Money Valuations. 9th ed. LC 79-67100. (Illus.). 1982. pap. 2.25 (ISBN 0-87341-025-4). Krause Pubns.

PAPER WORK
see also Decoupage
Bottomley, Jim. Paper Projects for Creative Kids of All Ages. 160p. 1983. 12.45i (ISBN 0-316-10348-9); pap. 8.70i (ISBN 0-316-10349-7). Little.
Drayton, Grace G. More Dolly Dingle Paper Dolls. 32p. 1979. pap. 2.75 (ISBN 0-486-23848-2). Dover.
Grater, Michael. Make It in Paper: Creative Three-Dimensional Paper Projects. (Illus.). 96p. (gr. 5 up). 1983. pap. 2.50 (ISBN 0-486-24468-7). Dover.
Menten, Ted. Fish & Sea Life Cut & Use Stencils. (Illus.). 64p. (Orig.). 1983. pap. 3.50 (ISBN 0-486-24436-9). Dover.
Paper Tearing With Surprise Climax, No. 11. Date not set. price not set (ISBN 0-915398-21-4). Visual Evangels.
Temko, Florence. Chinese Papercuts: Their Story & How to Make & Use Them. LC 82-12854. (Illus.). 168p. (Orig.). 1982. pap. 10.95 (ISBN 0-8351-0999-2). China Bks.
Tierney, Tom. Cut & Assemble a Toy Theater: The Nutcracker Ballet. 32p. 1981. pap. 3.95 (ISBN 0-486-24194-7). Dover.
--Great Empresses & Queens Paper Dolls in Full Color. 32p. 1982. pap. 3.00 (ISBN 0-486-24268-4). Dover.
--Isadora Duncan, Martha Graham & Other Stars of the Modern Dance Paper Dolls in Full Color. (Illus.). 32p. (Orig.). (gr. 9 up). 1983. pap. 3.50 (ISBN 0-486-24490-3). Dover.
--Marilyn Monroe Paper Dolls. 32p. 1979. pap. 2.75 (ISBN 0-486-23769-9). Dover.
--Vivien Leigh Paper Dolls in Full Cover. 32p. 1981. pap. 3.00 (ISBN 0-486-24207-2). Dover.

PAPER WORK–JUVENILE LITERATURE
Grater, Michael. Cut & Fold Extraterrestrial Invaders That Fly: Twenty-Two Full-Color Spaceships. (Illus.). 36p. (Orig.). 1983. pap. 4.95 (ISBN 0-486-24473-3). Dover.
Smith, Albert G., Jr. Cut & Assemble Main Street: Nine Easy-to-Make Full-Color Buildings in H-C Scale. (Illus.). 48p. (Orig.). (gr. 4 up). 1983. pap. 4.95 (ISBN 0-486-24473-3). Dover.
Tierney, Tom. American Family of the Colonial Era: Paper Dolls in Full Color. (Illus.). 32p. (Orig.). (gr. 3 up). 1983. pap. 3.00 (ISBN 0-486-24394-X). Dover.
--Great Fashion Designs of the Belle Epoque: Paper Dolls in Full Color. (Illus.). 32p. (gr. 5 up). Date not set. pap. 3.50 (ISBN 0-486-24425-3). Dover.
--Judy Garland Paper Dolls in Full Color. (Illus.). 32p. (Orig.). pap. 3.50 (ISBN 0-486-24404-0). Dover.
Young, Sheila. Betty Bonnet Paper Dolls in Full Color. (Toy Bks., Paper Dolls). (Illus.). 32p. (Orig.). (gr. 3 up). 1982. pap. 3.50 (ISBN 0-486-24415-6). Dover.

PAPERBACKS
see Bibliography–Paperback Editions

PAPERBOARD
Mark. Handbook of Physical & Mechanical Testing of Paper & Paperboard, Vol. 1. 821p. 1983. price not set (ISBN 0-8247-1871-2). Dekker.

PAPUA NEW GUINEA
Annan, Bill & Hinchcliffe, Keith. Planning Policy Analysis & Public Spending: Theory & the Papua New Guinea Practice. 168p. 1982. text ed. 35.00x (ISBN 0-566-00496-8). Gower Pub Ltd.
Beier, Ulli. Voices of Independence. 1980. 20.00 (ISBN 0-686-42889-7). St Martin.
Gewertz, Deborah B. Sepik River Societies: A Historical of the Chambri & Their Neighbors. LC 82-48902. 256p. 1983. text ed. 25.50x (ISBN 0-300-02872-5). Yale U Pr.
Stanner, W. E. The South Seas in Transition: A Study of Post-War Rehabilitation & Reconstruction in Three British Pacific Dependencies. LC 82-15534. xiv, 448p. 1982. Repr. of 1953 ed. lib. bdg. 39.75x (ISBN 0-313-23661-5, STSOS). Greenwood.

PARABLES
see also Bible–Parables; Fables; Jesus Christ–Parables
Castagnola, Lawrence. Parables for Little People. (Illus.). 101p. (Orig.). (gr. 4 up). 1982. pap. 5.56 (ISBN 0-89390-034-6); pap. text ed. 6.95. Resource Pubns.

PARABOLE
see Metaphor

PARACELSUS, 1493-1541
Webster, Charles. From Paracelsus to Newton: Magic & the Making of Modern Science. LC 82-4586. (Illus.). 120p. Date not set. price not set (ISBN 0-521-24919-8). Cambridge U Pr.

PARACLETE
see Holy Spirit

PARAGUAY
Roett, Riordan. Paraguay. 135p. 1983. lib. bdg. 16.50x (ISBN 0-86531-272-9). Westview.
Warren, Harris G. Paraguay: An Informal History. LC 82-15519. (Illus.). xii, 393p. 1982. Repr. of 1949 ed. lib. bdg. 45.00x (ISBN 0-313-23651-8, WARP). Greenwood.

PARAGUAYAN WAR, 1865-1870
Lindenov, Christopher. First Triple Alliance: Letters of Christopher Lindenov, Danish Envoy to London, 1668-1672. Westergaard, Waldemar, ed. 1947. text ed. 49.50x (ISBN 0-686-83551-4). Elliots Bks.

PARAKEET
see Budgerigars; Parrots

PARALINGUISTICS
see Nonverbal Communication

PARALYSIS, CEREBRAL
see Cerebral Palsy

PARALYSIS AGITANS
Birkmayer, W. & Riederer, P. Parkinson's Disease: Biochemistry, Clinical Pathology, & Treatment. Reynolds, G., tr. from Ger. (Illus.). 240p. 1983. 39.00 (ISBN 0-387-81722-0). Springer-Verlag.

PARAMAGNETIC RESONANCE, ELECTRONIC
see Electron Paramagnetic Resonance

PARAMEDICAL PERSONNEL
see Allied Health Personnel

PARAPLEGIA
Eareckson, Joni & Estes, Steve. A Step Further. 192p. 1982. mass market pb 3.95 (ISBN 0-310-23972-9). Zondervan.

PARAPSYCHOLOGY
see Psychical Research

PARASITE-HOST RELATIONSHIPS
see Host-Parasite Relationships

PARASITES–MAN
see Medical Parasitology

PARASITIC DISEASES
see Medical Parasitology

PARASITOLOGY
see also Medical Parasitology; Veterinary Medicine
Baker, J. R. & Muller, R. Advances in Parasitology, Vol. 21. (Serial Publication). 336p. 1982. 52.00 (ISBN 0-12-031721-4). Acad Pr.
Lumsden, W. H., et al, eds. Advances in Parasitology, Vol. 20. (Serial Publication). 1982. 58.50 (ISBN 0-12-031720-6). Acad Pr.
Mettrick, D. F. & Desser, S. S., eds. Parasites-Their World & Ours: Proceedings of the Fifth International Congress of Parasitology, Toronto, Canada, August 7-14, 1982. 465p. 1982. 64.00 (ISBN 0-444-80433-1, Biomedical Pr). Elsevier.
Owen, Dawn, ed. Animal Models in Parasitology. 250p. 1982. 70.00x (ISBN 0-333-32182-0, Pub. by Macmillan England). State Mutual Bk.
Schultz, Myron G., intro. by. Current Concepts in Parasitology. (Illus.). 137p. (Orig.). 1979. pap. text ed. 6.00 (ISBN 0-910133-04-2). MA Med Soc.
Strickland. Immunoparasitology. 304p. 1982. 39.95 (ISBN 0-03-061499-6). Praeger.

PARENT AND CHILD
see also Adolescence; Adolescent Parents; Boys; Child Abuse; Children–Management; Fathers; Girls; Mother and Child; Mothers; Single-Parent Family; Stepchildren; Stepfathers; Stepmothers; Youth
Abrahms, Sally. Children in the Crossfire: The Tragedy of Parental Kidnapping. LC 82-73030. 320p. 1983. 12.95 (ISBN 0-689-11339-0). Atheneum.
Ahrens, Herman C., Jr. Life with Your Parents. 24p. 1983. pap. 1.25 (ISBN 0-8298-0667-9). Pilgrim NY.
Baker, Pat. I Now Pronounce You Parent: What Other Books Don't Tell You About Babies. 96p. (Orig.). 1983. pap. 4.95 (ISBN 0-8010-0850-6). Baker Bk.
Behrstock, Barry & Turbo, Richard. The Parent's When-Not-To-Worry Book. LC 80-7894. 272p. 1983. pap. 4.76i (ISBN 0-686-82652-3, CN 1043, CN). Har-Row.
Berends, Polly B. Whole Child-Whole Parent: A Spiritual & Practical Guide to Parenthood. rev. ed. LC 81-48029. (Illus.). 1983. write for info. (ISBN 0-06-014971-X, HarpT). Har-Row.
Berger, Stuart. Divorce Without Victims. 200p. 1983. 12.95 (ISBN 0-395-33115-3). HM.
Biegert, John E. Mirando Hacia Arriba en Medio de la Enfermedad. 24p. (Orig., Span.). 1983. pap. 1.25 (ISBN 0-8298-0663-6). Pilgrim NY.
Bodenhamer, Greg. Back in Control: How to Get Your Children to Behave. 144p. 1983. 9.95 (ISBN 0-13-055871-0). P-H.
Bradley, Fred O. & Stone, Lloyd A. Parenting Without Hassles: Children as Partners. LC 82-62365. 170p. 1983. 8.95 (ISBN 0-913420-14-X). Olympus Pub Co.
Buntain, Ruth J. Children in the Shadows. 78p. pap. 4.95 (ISBN 0-686-82632-9). Review & Herald.
Campbell, Ross. How to Really Love Your Child. 1982. pap. 2.75 (ISBN 0-451-11871-5, AE1871, Sig). NAL.
Canter, Lee & Canter, Marlene. Assertive Discipline for Parents. LC 82-74174. 206p. 1982. 12.95 (ISBN 0-06-859835-1). Canter & Assoc.
Collins, Glenn. How to Be a Guilty Parent. (Illus.). 1983. 8.95 (ISBN 0-8129-1034-6). Times Bks.
Copeland, Tom, ed. Parents in the Workplace: A Management Resource for Employers. (Illus.). 30p. folder 16.50 (ISBN 0-934140-17-0). Toys N Things.
Coplen, Dotty. Parenting A Path Through Childhood. 1982. pap. 7.25 (ISBN 0-903540-61-4, Pub. by Floris Books). St George Bk Serv.
Divas, Mireille. I'm a Year Old Now. (Illus.). 176p. 1983. 15.95 (ISBN 0-13-451344-4); pap. 7.95 (ISBN 0-13-451336-3). P-H.
Gallagher, Chuck. Hurrah for Parents. 1980. 3.95 (ISBN 0-8215-6467-6). Sadlier.
--Parents are Lovers. 1980. 3.95 (ISBN 0-8215-6466-8). Sadlier.
Heinl, Tina. The Baby Massage Book: Using Touch for Better Bonding & Happier Babies. (Illus.). 144p. 1983. 15.95 (ISBN 0-13-056226-2); pap. 7.95 (ISBN 0-13-056218-1). P-H.
Kiley, Dan. Dr. Dan's Prescriptions: 1001 Nonmedical Hints for Solving Parenting Problems. 256p. 1982. 12.95 (ISBN 0-698-11175-3, Coward). Putnam Pub Group.
Klaus, Marshall H. & Kennell, John H. Bonding: The Beginnings of Parent to Infant Attachment. (Medical Attachment Ser.). (Illus.). 256p. 1983. pap. price not set (ISBN 0-452-25402-7, 2696-X). Mosby.
Krause, Engelbert. Die Gegenseitigen Unterhalltsanspruche Zwichen Eltern und Kindern In der Deutschen Privatrechtsgeschichte. vi, 237p. (Ger.). 1982. write for info. (ISBN 3-8204-7123-5). P Lang Pubs.
Kroes, Carolyn M. Roses & Thorns: View from the Other Side of the Mountain. 1982. 8.95 (ISBN 0-533-05479-6). Vantage.
Lutzer, Erwin & Orr, Bill. If I Could Change My Mom & Dad. 128p. 1983. pap. 3.50 (ISBN 0-8024-0174-0). Moody.
Marsh, Carole. Meet in the Middle: The Parents Test - The Kids Test. (Tomorrow's Books). (Illus.). 48p. 1983. 3.95 (ISBN 0-935326-24-3). Gallopade Pub Group.
Master, Roy. How to Survive Your Parents. LC 82-71162. 182p. 1982. pap. 6.50 (ISBN 0-933900-10-4). Foun Human Under.
Noyes, Joan & Macneill, Norma. Your Child Can Win: Strategies, Activities & Games for Parents of Children with Learning Disabilities. 258p. 1983. 11.95 (ISBN 0-688-01942-0). Morrow.
Pizzo, Peggy. Parent to Parent: Working Together for Ourselves & Our Children. LC 85-73875. 320p. 1983. 13.41 (ISBN 0-8070-2300-0). Beacon Pr.
Richards, Lawrence O. The Word Parents Handbook. 1983. 8.95 (ISBN 0-8499-0328-9). Word Bks.
Rogers, Fred & Head, Barry. Mister Rogers Talks with Parents. (Illus.). 1983. pap. 5.95 (ISBN 0-425-05883-2). Berkley Pub.
Roth, Eugene. Children & Their Fathers. Reich, Hanns, ed. (Illus.). 1983. pap. 4.95 (ISBN 0-8090-1505-6, Terra Magica). Hill & Wang.
Sala, Harold J. The Power of Persuasive Parenting. 111p. (Orig.). 1982. pap. 5.75x (ISBN 0-686-37686-2, Pub. by New Day Philippines). Cellar.
Satir, Virginia M. Peoplemaking. LC 73-188143. 1972. 9.95 (ISBN 0-8314-0031-5); pap. 7.95. Sci & Behavior.
Sayers, Robert. Fathering: It's Not the Same. (Illus.). 95p. 1983. pap. 10.95 (ISBN 0-686-38770-8). Nurtury Fam.
Schultz, Jerelyn. Contemporary Parenting Choices. 260p. 1983. pap. text ed. 14.95 (ISBN 0-8138-0358-6). Iowa St U Pr.

PARENT AND CHILD (LAW)
see also Adoption; Children–Law; Custody of Children; Stepchildren; Support (Domestic Relations)
Cassetty, Judith, ed. The Parental Child-Support Obligation: Research, Practice, & Social Policy. LC 81-48464. 320p. 1982. 28.95x (ISBN 0-669-05376-7). Lexington Bks.

PARENT EDUCATION
Kliman, Gilbert W. & Rosenfeld, Albert. Responsible Parenthood. LC 79-3437. 360p. 1983. pap. 8.95 (ISBN 0-03-063537-3). HR&W.

PARENT-TEACHER RELATIONSHIPS
see also Home and School
Wolf, Joan S. & Stephens, Thomas M. Effective Skills in Parent & Teacher Conferencing the Parent's Perpective. pap. 4.95 (ISBN 0-936882-81-6). NCEMMH.

PARENTAL CUSTODY
see Custody of Children

PARENTERAL THERAPY
Goldfarb, I. William & Yates, Anthony P. Total Parenteral Nutrition: Concepts & Methods. 96p. pap. text ed. write for info. (ISBN 0-935170-07-3). Synapse Pubns.

PARENTS, ADOLESCENT
see Adolescent Parents

PARENTS AND TEACHERS
see Parent-Teacher Relationships

PARENTS WITHOUT PARTNERS
see Single-Parent Family

PAREXIC ANALYSIS
see Numerical Analysis

PARGETTING
see Plastering

PARI-MUTUEL BETTING
see Horse Race Betting

PARIS–DESCRIPTION–GUIDEBOOKS
Baedeker's City Guide: Paris. 176p. 1983. pap. 9.95 (ISBN 0-86145-115-5, Pub. by Auto Assn-British Tourist Authority England). Merrimack Bk Serv.
Michelin Green Guide: Paris. (Green Guide Ser.). (Fr.). 1983. pap. write for info. (ISBN 2-06-003511-2). Michelin.
Michelin Green Guide: Paris. (Green Guide Ser.). (Ger.). 1983. pap. write for info. (ISBN 2-06-023570-7). Michelin.

PARIS–HISTORY
Rose, R. B. The Making of the Sans-Culottes: Democratic Ideas & Institutions in Paris 1789-92. 224p. 1982. 22.50 (ISBN 0-7190-0879-4). Manchester.

PARIS–INTELLECTUAL LIFE
Fitch, Noel R. Sylvia Beach & the Lost Generation: A History of Literary Paris in the Twenties & Thirties. (Illus.). 1983. 25.00 (ISBN 0-393-01713-3). Norton.

PARIS–MONTPARNASSE
Huddleston, Sisley. Back to Montparnasse: Glimpses of Broadway in Bohemia. (Illus.). 313p. 1982. Repr. of 1931 ed. lib. bdg. 40.00 (ISBN 0-89984-916-4). Century Bookbindery.

PARISH LIBRARIES
see Libraries, Church

PARISH MANAGEMENT
see Church Management

PARISH REGISTERS
see Registers of Births, Deaths, Marriages, etc.

PARISH SCHOOLS
see Church Schools

PARISHES
see also Pastoral Theology
Sweetser, Thomas P. Successful Parishes: How They Meet the Challenge of Change. 204p. 1983. pap. 9.95 (ISBN 0-686-43057-3). Winston Pr.

PARKING, AUTOMOBILE
see Automobile Parking

PARKING METERS
Rudman, Jack. Parking Meter Supervisor. (Career Examination Ser.: C-2592). (Cloth bdg. avail. on request). pap. 10.00 (ISBN 0-8373-2592-7). Natl Learning.

PARKINSON'S DISEASE
see Paralysis Agitans

PARKMAN, FRANCIS, 1823-1893
Doughty, Howard. Francis Parkman. 420p. 1983. pap. text ed. 9.95x (ISBN 0-674-31775-0). Harvard U Pr.

PARKS
see also Amusement Parks; Landscape Gardening; National Parks and Reserves; Playgrounds
Directory of Professional Preparation Programs in Recreation, Parks, & Related Areas. 1983. price not set. AAHPERD.

PARKS–VOCATIONAL GUIDANCE
Rudman, Jack. Administrative Park & Recreation Manager. (Career Examination Ser.: C-2606). (Cloth bdg. avail. on request). pap. 12.00 (ISBN 0-8373-2606-0). Natl Learning.
--Associate Park Service Worker. (Career Examination Ser.). (Cloth bdg. avail. on request). pap. 10.00 (ISBN 0-8373-2469-6). Natl Learning.
--General Park Manager. (Career Examination Ser.: C-386). (Cloth bdg. avail. on request). pap. 14.00 (ISBN 0-8373-0386-9). Natl Learning.
--Greenskeeper. (Career Examination Ser.: C-2656). (Cloth bdg. avail. on request). pap. 10.00 (ISBN 0-8373-2656-7). Natl Learning.
--Park Maintenance Supervisor. (Career Examination Ser.: C-2942). (Cloth bdg. avail. on request). pap. 12.00 (ISBN 0-8373-2942-6). Natl Learning.
--Park Manager I. (Career Examination Ser.: C-383). (Cloth bdg. avail. on request). pap. 12.00 (ISBN 0-8373-0383-4). Natl Learning.
--Park Manager II. (Career Examination Ser.: C-384). (Cloth bdg. avail. on request). pap. 12.00 (ISBN 0-8373-0384-2). Natl Learning.
--Park Manager III. (Career Examination Ser.: C-385). (Cloth bdg. avail. on request). pap. 14.00 (ISBN 0-8373-0385-0). Natl Learning.

PARKWAYS
see Express Highways

PARLIAMENTARY GOVERNMENT
see Representative Government and Representation

PARLIAMENTARY PRACTICE
Dod's Parlimentary Companion 1982. 163rd ed. LC 6-7438. 729p. 1982. 60.00x (ISBN 0-905702-07-7). Intl Pubns Serv.

Ericson, Jon. Motion by Motion: A Commentary on Parlimentary Procedure. 130p. 1983. pap. text ed. 9.95x (ISBN 0-8290-1272-9). Irvington.
Hardcastle, Lena L. Parliamentary Law Rules & Procedures for Conducting Conventions. LC 81-85392. 272p. 1982. 17.95 (ISBN 0-9608716-0-8). Stuart Bks.
Twining, William & Miers, David. How to Do Things with Rules: A Primer of Interpretation. 2nd ed. xx, 387p. 1982. text ed. 37.50x (ISBN 0-297-78083-2). Rothman.

PARLIAMENTS
see Legislative Bodies

PAROCHIAL LIBRARIES
see Libraries, Church

PAROCHIAL SCHOOLS
see Church Schools

PAROLE
see also Probation

American Correctional Association Staff. Guidelines for Adult Parole Authorities-Adult Probation & Parole Field Services. 281p. (Orig.). 1981. pap. 15.00 (ISBN 0-942974-33-6). Am Correctional.
--Probation & Parole Directory. 480p. (Orig.). 1981. pap. 25.00 (ISBN 0-942974-05-0). Am Correctional.
--Standards for Adult Parole Authorities. 2nd ed. 53p. 1980. pap. 7.50 (ISBN 0-942974-28-X). Am Correctional.
--Standards for Adult Probation & Parole Field Services. 2nd ed. 65p. 1981. pap. 7.50 (ISBN 0-942974-29-8). Am Correctional.
--The Status of Probation & Parole. (Series 2: No. 3). 30p. (Orig.). 1981. pap. 3.50 (ISBN 0-942974-23-9). Am Correctional.
Whitehouse, Jack E. How & Where to Find the Facts: Researching Corrections Including Probation & Parole. LC 82-61337. 125p. (Orig.). 1983. pap. 6.95 (ISBN 0-88247-694-7). R & E Res Assoc.

PAROLE EVIDENCE
see Evidence (Law)

PARROTS
see also Budgerigars; Cockateels

Lendon, Alan. Australian Parrots in Field & Aviary. (Illus.). 344p. 1979. 32.95 (ISBN 0-207-12424-8). Avian Pubns.
Low, Rosemary. How to Keep Parrots, Cockatiels & Macaws in Cage or Aviary. (Illus.). 96p. 1980. 3.95 (ISBN 0-7028-1029-0). Avian Pubns.
Starika, W. A. & Richardson, E. L., eds. The T.F.H. Book of Parrots: With a Special Illustrated Section on Surgical Sexing William C. Satterfield. (Illus.). 80p. 1982. 6.95 (ISBN 0-87666-806-6, HP-015). TFH Pubns.

PARSI LANGUAGE
see Pahlavi Language

PART-SONGS
see also Motet

Hillier, Paul, ed. Three Hundred Years of English Partsongs. 96p. (Orig.). 1983. pap. 5.95 (ISBN 0-571-10045-7). Faber & Faber.

PART-TIME EMPLOYMENT
see also Supplementary Employment

Davidson, P. Moonlighting: A Complete Guide to Over 200 Exciting Part-Time Jobs. 288p. 1983. 7.95 (ISBN 0-07-049607-2, GB). McGraw.

PARTIAL DIFFERENTIAL EQUATIONS
see Differential Equations, Partial

PARTIAL MONOPOLIES
see Oligopolies

PARTIALLY-SEEING CHILDREN
see Visually Handicapped Children

PARTICIPATION, SOCIAL
see Social Participation

PARTICLE ACCELERATORS

Carrigan, R. A., Jr. & Huson, F. R., eds. The State of Particle Accelerators & High Energy (Fermilab Summer School, 1981) LC 82-73861. (AIP Conference Proceedings Ser.: No.92). 337p. 1982. lib. bdg. 33.75 (ISBN 0-88318-191-6). Am Inst Physics.

PARTICLES
see also Colloids; Dust; Light-Scattering

AIP Conference, 87th, Fermilab School, 1981. Physics of High Energy Particle Accelerators: Proceedings. Carrigan, R. A., et al, eds. LC 82-72421. 960p. 1982. lib. bdg. 48.00 (ISBN 0-88318-186-X). Am Inst Physics.
AIP Conference, 91st, Los Alamos, 1982. Laser Acceleration of Particles: Proceedings. Channell, Paul J., ed. LC 82-73361. 276p. 1982. lib. bdg. 32.00 (ISBN 0-88318-190-8). Am Inst Physics.
Dahneke, Barton E. Measurement of Suspended Particles By Quasi-Elastic Light Scattering. 400p. 1982. 39.95 (ISBN 0-471-87289-X, Pub. by Wiley-Interscience). Wiley.
Flamm, D. & Schoberl, F. Introduction to the Quark Model of Elementary Particles. (Quantum Numbers, Gauge Theories & Hadron Spectroscopy Ser.: Vol. 1). 384p. 1982. 73.50 (ISBN 0-677-16270-7). Gordon.
Honerkamp, J. & Pohlmeyer, J., eds. Structural Elements in Particle Physics & Statistical Mechanics. (NATO ASI Series B, Physics: Vol. 82). 470p. 1983. 65.00x (ISBN 0-306-41038-9, Plenum Pr). Plenum Pub.
Stanley-Wood, N. & Allen, T. Particle Size Analysis. 459p. 1983. text ed. 74.95x (ISBN 0-471-26221-8, Pub. by Wiley-Interscience). Wiley.
Symposium on Inhaled Particles & Vapours. Inhaled Particles: Proceedings, Vol. V. Walton, W. H., ed. (Illus.). 900p. 1982. 150.00 (ISBN 0-08-026838-2). Pergamon.

PARTICLES (NUCLEAR PHYSICS)
see also Collisions (Nuclear Physics); Particle Accelerators; Polarization (Nuclear Physics); Transport Theory
also names of particles–e.g. Electrons, Neutrons, Protons

Mitter, H., ed. Electroweak Interactions, Schladming (Graz), Austria 1982: Proceedings. (Acta Physia Austriaca Supplementum: Vol. 24). (Illus.). 474p. 1983. 38.00 (ISBN 0-387-81729-8). Springer-Verlag.
Panvini, R. S. & Alam, M. S., eds. Novel Results in Particle Physics. LC 82-73954. (AID Conf. Proc.: No. 93). 384p. 1982. lib. bdg. 35.00 (ISBN 0-88318-192-4). Am Inst Physics.

PARTIES
see Entertaining

PARTIES, POLITICAL
see Political Parties

PARTIES FOR CHILDREN
see Children's Parties

PARTNERSHIP
see also Corporation Law; Limited Partnership; Liquidation

Burdick, Francis M. The Law of Partnership, Including Limited Partnerships. lii, 422p. 1983. Repr. of 1899 ed. lib. bdg. 37.50x (ISBN 0-8377-0333-6). Rothman.
Conyngton, Thomas. A Manual of Partnership Relations. LC 6-693. 221p. 1982. Repr. of 1905 ed. lib. bdg. 27.50 (ISBN 0-89941-178-9). W S Hein.
McKnight, Daniel L., Jr. The Complete Partnership Manual & Guide with Tax, Financial & Managerial Strategies. LC 82-5799. 304p. 1982. 39.50 (ISBN 0-13-162230-7, Busn). P-H.
Mechem, Floyd R. Elements of the Law of Partnership. LC 12-36583. xxxviii, 277p. 1982. Repr. of 1896 ed. text ed. 35.00 (ISBN 0-89941-180-0). W S Hein.

PARTNERSHIP, LIMITED
see Limited Partnership

PARTON, DOLLY

Caraeff, Ed. Dolly: Close Up. (Illus.). 96p. (Orig.). 1982. pap. 9.95 (ISBN 0-933328-58-3). Delilah Bks.

PARTURITION
see Childbirth; Labor (Obstetrics)

PASADENA, CALIFORNIA

Sems, Charles. Trolley Days in Pasadena. (Illus.). 196p. Date not set. 34.95 (ISBN 0-87095-086-X). Golden West.

PASCAL (COMPUTER PROGRAM LANGUAGE)

Atkinson, Laurence. PASCAL Programming. LC 80-40126. (Computing Ser.). 428p. 1980. 49.95x (ISBN 0-471-27773-8); pap. 16.95 (ISBN 0-471-27774-6). Wiley.
Belford, G. & Liu, C. L. Structured Pascal. 384p. 1983. 13.95 (ISBN 0-07-038138-0); write for info. instr's manual (ISBN 0-07-038139-9). McGraw.
Cooper, Doug. Standard Pascal Uses Reference Manual. 1983. write for info (ISBN 0-393-95332-7). Norton.
Crandall, Richard E. PASCAL for the Sciences. (Self-Teaching Guides). 224p. 1983. pap. text ed. 12.95 (ISBN 0-471-87242-3). Wiley.
Dale, Nell B. & Orshalick, David W. Introduction to Pascal & Structured Design. 448p. Date not set. pap. 17.95 (ISBN 0-669-04797-X). Heath.
Gear, C. William. Programming in PASCAL. 224p. 1983. text ed. write for info. (ISBN 0-574-21360-0, 13-4360). SRA.
Hergert, Richard & Hergert, Douglas. Doing Business with Pascal: 380p. 1982. pap. text ed. 16.95 (ISBN 0-89588-091-1). Sybex.
Jean, B. & Mouret, F. Montaigne, Descartes et Pascal. 1971. pap. 10.00 (ISBN 0-7190-0422-5). Manchester.
Kemp, R. Pascal for Students. 256p. 1982. pap. text ed. 14.95 (ISBN 0-7131-3447-X). E Arnold.
Luehrmann, A. & Peckham, H. Hands-On Pascal: For the IBM Personal Computer. 448p. 1983. 22.95 (ISBN 0-07-049176-3). McGraw.
Mandell, Steven L. Computers & Data Processing Today with PASCAL. (Illus.). 450p. 1983. pap. text ed. 8.95 (ISBN 0-314-70647-X). West Pub.
Matuszek, D. L. Quick Pascal. 179p. 1982. pap. text ed. 11.95 (ISBN 0-471-86644-X). Wiley.
Moffat, David V. Common Algorithms in Pascal with Programs for Reading. (Software Ser.). 192p. 1983. pap. 8.95 (ISBN 0-13-152637-5). P-H.
Page, E. S. & Wilson, L. B. Information Representation & Manipulation Using PASCAL. LC 82-4505. (Cambridge Computer Science Texts: No. 15). (Illus.). 275p. Date not set. price not set (ISBN 0-521-24954-6); pap. price not set (ISBN 0-521-27096-0). Cambridge U Pr.
Perrott, Ronald & Allison, Donald. PASCAL for FORTRAN Programmers. 1983. text ed. p.n.s. (ISBN 0-914894-09-9). Computer Sci.
Richards, James. PASCAL. 1982. 13.75 (ISBN 0-12-587520-7). Acad Pr.
Rohl, J. S. Writing PASCAL Programs. LC 82-14591. (Cambridge Computer Science Texts Ser.: No. 16). 250p. Date not set. 24.95 (ISBN 0-521-25077-3); pap. 11.95 (ISBN 0-521-27196-7). Cambridge U Pr.
Starkey, J. Denbigh & Ross, Rockford. Fundamental Programming: Pascal. 352p. 1982. pap. text ed. write for info. (ISBN 0-314-71811-7). West Pub.
Underkoffler, Milton. Introduction to Structured Programming with Pascal. 376p. 1983. pap. text ed. write for info. (ISBN 0-87150-394-8, 8040). Prindle.

PASHTOONS
see Pushtuns

PASSIONS
see Emotions

PASSIVE RESISTANCE
see also Nonviolence; War and Religion

Brooks, Svevo & Burkhart, John. A Guide to Political Fasting. LC 82-13008. 56p. (Orig.). 1982. pap. 3.95 (ISBN 0-943726-01-8). Langdon Pubns.

PASSO HOUROSO
see Tournaments

PASSOVER

Bin-Nun, Judy & Cooper, Nancy. Pesach: A Holiday Funtext. (Illus.). 32p. (Orig.). (gr. 1-3). 1983. pap. text ed. 5.00 (ISBN 0-8074-0161-7, 101310). UAHC.

PASTEBOARD
see Paperboard

PASTEL DRAWING

Blockley, John. How To Paint with Pastels. 64p. 1982. pap. 5.95 (ISBN 0-89586-159-3). H P Bks.

PASTEUR, LOUIS, 1822-1895–JUVENILE LITERATURE

Sabin, Francene. Louis Pasteur: Young Scientist. LC 82-15924. (Illus.). 48p. (gr. 4-6). 1983. PLB 6.89 (ISBN 0-89375-853-1); pap. text ed. 1.95 (ISBN 0-89375-854-X). Troll Assocs.

PASTIMES
see Amusements; Games; Sports

PASTON LETTERS

Barber, Richard. The Pastons: A Family. 1983. pap. price not set (ISBN 0-14-006599-7). Penguin.

PASTORAL COUNSELING
Here are entered works on the clergyman as the counselor.
see also Counseling; Pastoral Medicine

Ghezzi, Bert & Kinzer, Mark. Emotions as Resources: A Biblical & Pastorial Approach. 156p. 1983. pap. 3.95 (ISBN 0-89283-158-8). Servant.
Holbrook, D. L. & Holbrook, Becky T. Every Step Along the Way. 3.75 (ISBN 0-89137-418-3). Quality Pubns.
Jones, James A. Counseling Principles for Christian Leaders. 5.95 (ISBN 0-89137-534-1). Quality Pubns.
Loyola College, Pastoral & Counseling Faculty. Pastoral Counseling. (Illus.). 352p. 1982. 21.95 (ISBN 0-13-652867-8). P-H.
Smith, Harold I. Pastoral Care for Single Parents. 158p. 1982. pap. 3.95 (ISBN 0-8341-0782-1). Beacon Hill.
Stone, Howard W. The Caring Church: A Guide for Lay Pastoral Care. LC 82-48415. 144p. (Orig.). 1983. pap. 5.72 (ISBN 0-06-067695-7, HarpR). Har-Row.

PASTORAL MEDICINE

Gibson, Morris. One Man's Medicine. 218p. 1983. 12.95 (ISBN 0-686-84498-X). Beaufort Bks NY.
Kinshita, Louise & Sanderson, Joyce. The Rainbow Path: Healing Ourselves. 78p. 1982. pap. 6.95 (ISBN 0-942494-27-X). Coleman Graphics.
Patterson, Robert. Pastoral Health Care: Understanding the Church's Healing Ministers. 15p. 1983. pap. 0.90 (ISBN 0-87125-080-2). Cath Health.
Weiner, Michael A. The People's Herbal: A Complete Family Guide for All Ages to Safe Home Remedies. LC 82-80371. 227p. 1983. 14.95 (ISBN 0-399-50772-8, Perigee); pap. 7.95 (ISBN 0-399-50756-6). Putnam Pub Group.

PASTORAL OFFICE AND WORK
see Pastoral Theology

PASTORAL PEOPLES
see Nomads

PASTORAL THEOLOGY
see also Church Work; City Clergy; Clergy; Communication (Theology); Pastoral Counseling; Pastoral Medicine

Calian, Carnegie S. Today's Pastor in Tomorrow's World. Rev. ed. LC 82-7114. 1982. pap. 8.95 (ISBN 0-664-24426-2). Westminster.
Malcomson, William L. How to Survive in the Ministry. 88p. 1982. pap. 5.95 (ISBN 0-8170-0964-7). Judson.
Stowe, W. McFerrin. If I were a Pastor. 112p. (Orig.). 1983. pap. 5.95 (ISBN 0-687-18655-2). Abingdon.
Stratman, Gary D. Pastoral Preaching: Timeless Truth for Changing Needs. 112p. (Orig.). 1983. pap. 6.95 (ISBN 0-687-30139-4). Abingdon.
Trotter, W. Five Letters on Worship & Ministry. 39p. pap. 0.60 (ISBN 0-88172-128-X). Believers Bkshelf.
Ver Straten, Charles A. How To Start Lay Shepherding Ministries. 120p. 1983. pap. 5.95 (ISBN 0-8010-9290-6). Baker Bk.

PASTORS
see Clergy; Priests

PASTRY
see also Cake

Arbit, Naomi & Turner, June. Pies & Pastries. (Illus.). 64p. pap. 3.25 (ISBN 0-8249-3011-8). Ideals.
Lambeth, Joseph. Lambeth Method of Cake Decoration & Practical Pastries. (Illus.). 1980. 55.00x (ISBN 0-911202-24-2). Radio City.

PATCHWORK

Bumbalough, Marine. Puppet Pillows. (Illus.). 18p. 1982. pap. 4.00 (ISBN 0-943574-13-7). That Patchwork.
Cassell Ltd., ed. The Patchwork Pattern Book. 1982. 26.00x (ISBN 0-289-70978-4, Pub. by Cassell England). State Mutual Bk.
Farmer, Mary A. Barnyard Beauties. (Illus.). 10p. 1981. pap. 4.00 (ISBN 0-943574-04-8). That Patchwork.
--Be an Angel. (Illus.). 10p. 1981. pap. 4.00 (ISBN 0-943574-07-2). That Patchwork.
--Special Santas. (Illus.). 18p. 1981. pap. 4.00 (ISBN 0-943574-08-0). That Patchwork.
Grosskopf, Susan A. Fabric Frames From Stretch Bars. (Illus.). 40p. 1983. pap. 5.00 (ISBN 0-943574-19-6). That Patchwork.
Johnson, Gail. Fabriscapes. (Illus.). 18p. 1981. pap. 5.00 (ISBN 0-943574-06-4). That Patchwork.
Klein, Mary. A New View of Cathedral Window. (Illus.). 40p. 1983. 5.00 (ISBN 0-943574-20-X). That Patchwork.
McCloskey, Marsha. Wall Quilts. (Illus.). 48p. 1983. 6.00 (ISBN 0-943574-22-6). That Patchwork.
Malone, Maggie. One Hundred-Twenty Patterns for Traditional Patchwork Quilts. LC 82-19671. (Illus.). 240p. 1983. 19.95 (ISBN 0-8069-5488-4); pap. 9.95 (ISBN 0-8069-7716-7). Sterling.
Martin, Nancy J. The Basics of Quilted Clothing. (Illus.). 68p. 1982. pap. 8.00 (ISBN 0-943574-12-9). That Patchwork.
--Nostalgic Noel. (Illus.). 38p. 1982. pap. 6.00 (ISBN 0-943574-14-5). That Patchwork.
Risinger, Hettie. Innovative Patchwork Piecing. (Illus.). 160p. 1983. 16.95 (ISBN 0-8069-5486-8); lib. bdg. 19.99 (ISBN 0-8069-5487-6); pap. 8.95 (ISBN 0-8069-7700-0). Sterling.
Saltkill, Sue. Country Christmas. (Illus.). 48p. 1983. 6.00 (ISBN 0-943574-21-8). That Patchwork.
--Log Cabin Constructions. (Favorite Patchwork Blocks Ser.). (Illus.). 30p. 1982. pap. 6.00 (ISBN 0-943574-11-0). That Patchwork.
Southerland-Holmes, Nancy. Creative Christmas. (Illus.). 18p. 1981. pap. 5.00 (ISBN 0-943574-09-9). That Patchwork.
--Muslin Mummies & Daddies. (Illus.). 10p. 1980. pap. 4.00 (ISBN 0-943574-01-3). That Patchwork.
--Soft Structures. (Illus.). 10p. 1980. pap. 4.00 (ISBN 0-943574-02-1). That Patchwork.
--This Little Pig... (Illus.). 42p. 1982. pap. 6.00 (ISBN 0-943574-10-2). That Patchwork.
Sutherland-Holmes, Nancy. The Calico Collection. (Illus.). 10p. 1980. pap. 4.00 (ISBN 0-943574-03-X). That Patchwork.

PATENTS
see also Inventions; Trade-Marks

Gausewitz, Rilchard L. Patent Pending. 1983. 14.95 (ISBN 0-8159-6522-2). Devin.
Goldstein, Paul. Copyright, Patent, Trademark & Related State Doctrines: Cases & Materials on the Law of Intellectual Property. 2nd ed. (University Casebook Ser.). 183p. 1982. write for info. tchrs. manual (ISBN 0-88277-105-1). Foundation Pr.
Hale, Alan M. Patenting Manual. Rev. ed. (Illus.). 362p. 1982. pap. 58.50 (ISBN 0-943418-01-1). Self Patent.
Meinhardt, Peter. Inventions, Patents & Trade Marks in Great Britain. 1971 ed. 397p. 25.00 (ISBN 0-686-37380-4). Beekman Pubs.

PATHANS
see Pushtuns

PATHOGENIC BACTERIA
see Bacteria, Pathogenic

PATHOGENIC MICRO-ORGANISMS
see Micro-Organisms, Pathogenic

PATHOLOGICAL BOTANY
see Plant Diseases

PATHOLOGICAL CHEMISTRY
see Chemistry, Medical and Pharmaceutical

PATHOLOGICAL HISTOLOGY
see Histology, Pathological

PATHOLOGICAL PHYSIOLOGY
see Physiology, Pathological

PATHOLOGICAL PSYCHOLOGY
see Psychology, Pathological

PATHOLOGY
see also Abnormalities, Human; Bacteriology; Chemistry, Clinical; Diagnosis; Diseases–Causes and Theories of Causation; Histology, Pathological; Immunity; Medicine; Medicine, Preventive; Physiology, Pathological; Therapeutics

Anderson, J. R. Muir's Textbook of Pathology. 1120p. 1980. pap. text ed. 42.50 (ISBN 0-7131-4357-6). E Arnold.
Babson, J. H. Disease Costing. 1973. 11.00 (ISBN 0-7190-0524-8). Manchester.
Beeler, Myrton F. & Catrou, Paul G. Interpretive Chemical Pathology. (Illus.). 272p. 1983. text ed. 35.00 (ISBN 0-89189-165-X, 45-2-040-00). Am Soc Clinical.
Brinkhous, Kenneth M., ed. Year Book of Pathology & Clinical Pathology, 1983. 1983. 44.00 (ISBN 0-8151-1238-6). Year Bk Med.

Brodeur, Armand E. & Silberstein, Michael J. Fundamentals of Radiologic Pathology. (Illus.). 1983. write for info. (ISBN 0-8391-1803-1, 15636). Univ Park.
Cohen, S. I. & Ross, R. N. Handbook of Clinical Psychobiology & Pathology, 2 Vols. Date not set. Vol. 1. 25.00 (ISBN 0-07-011621-0); Vol. 2. 35.00 (ISBN 0-07-011622-9). McGraw.
Crowley, Leonard V. Introduction to Human Disease. 700p. 1983. text ed. 23.95 (ISBN 0-534-01264-7). Brooks-Cole.
Finckh, E. & Clayton-Jones, E., eds. Anatomical & Clinical Pathology. (International Congress Ser.: No. 369). (Abstracts). 1977. pap. 31.25 (ISBN 0-686-43410-2). Elsevier.
Graves, Judy, ed. Directory of Pathology Training Programs, 1984-85. (Illus.). 500p. (Orig.). 1983. pap. 30.00 (ISBN 0-686-42864-1). Intersoc Comm Path Info.
Hill, Rolla B. & Terzian, James A., eds. Environmental Pathology: An Evolving Field. LC 82-14922. 376p. 1982. 60.00 (ISBN 0-8451-0221-4). A R Liss.
Sandblom, Philip. Creativity & Disease. (Illus.). 139p. 1982. 12.50 (ISBN 0-89313-066-4). G F Stickley.
Triennial World Congress World Association of Societies of Pathology (Anatomic & Clinical) Laboratory Medicine, Jerusalem, Israel, XIth, 20-25 Sept. 1981. Advances in Pathology (Anatomic & Clinical) Laboratory Medicine: Proceedings, Vol. I. Levy, E., ed. (Illus.). 542p. 1982. 120.00 (ISBN 0-08-028878-2); 250.00 (ISBN 0-08-029777-3); 200.00 (ISBN 0-08-028859-6). Pergamon.

PATHOLOGY, CELLULAR
see also Cell Culture
Trump, Benjamin F. & Arstila, A. U., eds. Pathobiology of Cell Membranes, Vol. 3. Date not set. price not set (ISBN 0-12-701503-5). Acad Pr.

PATHOLOGY, COMPARATIVE
Peiffer, Robert L., Jr. Comparative Ophthalmic Pathology. (Illus.). 448p. 1983. 60.00x (ISBN 0-398-04780-4). C C Thomas.

PATHOLOGY, DENTAL
see Teeth–Diseases

PATHOLOGY, EXPERIMENTAL
Richter, G. W. & Epstein, M. A., eds. International Review of Experimental Pathology. LC 62-21145. (Serial Publication). 1982. Vol. 23. 34.50 (ISBN 0-12-364923-4); Vol. 24. write for info. (ISBN 0-12-364924-2). Acad Pr.

PATHOLOGY, SURGICAL
Silverberg, Steven G. Principles & Practice of Surgical Pathology, 2 vols. 2048p. 1982. 140.00x (ISBN 0-471-05221-3, Pub. by Wiley Med.). Wiley.

PATHOLOGY, VEGETABLE
see Plant Diseases

PATHS
see Trails

PATIENT AND NURSE
see Nurse and Patient

PATIENT AND PHYSICIAN
see Physician and Patient

PATIENT CARE RECORDS
see Medical Records

PATIENT MONITORING
see Monitoring (Hospital Care)

PATIENTS
see Sick

PATON, ALAN, 1903-
Callan, Edward. Alan Paton. Rev. ed. (Twayne's World Authors Ser.). 1982. lib. bdg. 13.95 (ISBN 0-8057-6512-3, Twayne). G K Hall.

PATRIARCHS AND PATRIARCHATE
Livingstone, E. A., ed. Studia Patristica XVII, 3 Vols. 1520p. 1982. Set. 180.00 (ISBN 0-08-025779-8). Pergamon.

PATRIARCHY
see Family

PATRICK, SAINT, 373?-463?
Hanson, R. P. The Life & Writings of the Historical St. Patrick. 144p. 1983. 11.95 (ISBN 0-8164-0523-9). Seabury.

PATRIOTIC SONGS
see National Songs

PATRIOTISM
see also Nationalism
To Be or Not to Be an American. (Non-Fiction Ser.). Date not set. price not set (ISBN 0-9609008-0-2). C B North.

PATRISTICS
see Fathers of the Church

PATRONAGE, POLITICAL
see also Civil Service Reform
Hutton, John. The Mystery of Wealth: Political Economy, Its Development & Impact on World Events. 416p. 1979. 42.00x (ISBN 0-85950-470-0, Pub. by Thornes England). State Mutual Bk.

PATRONAGE OF ART
see Art Patronage; State Encouragement of Science, Literature, and Art

PATTERN-MAKING
see also Design; Founding; Mechanical Drawing; Wood-Carving
Campbell, Hilary. Designing Patterns: A Fresh Approach to Pattern Cutting. 128p. 1980. 35.00x (ISBN 0-85950-404-2, Pub. by Thornes England). State Mutual Bk.
Kass-Annese, Barbara & Danzer, Hal C. Patterns. 1981. pap. 9.95 (ISBN 0-941304-02-7). Hunter Hse.
Museum of Fine Arts, Boston. A Pattern Book Based on an Applique Quilt by Mrs. Harriet Powers. (Illus.). 32p. 1973. pap. 1.75 (ISBN 0-686-83418-6). Mus Fine Arts Boston.
Rosen, Selma. Children's Clothing: Designing, Selecting Fabrics, Patternmaking, Sewing. LC 82-83319. (Illus.). 150p. 1983. text ed. 15.00. Fairchild.
Waterman, V. Ann. Surface Pattern Design. (Illus.). 104p. (Orig.). 1983. 16.95 (ISBN 0-8038-6779-4). Hastings.

PATTERN PERCEPTION
Knopf, Howard & Dunaway, Kate A. Bragon the Dragon Presents Primary Patterns. (ps-3). 1982. 4.95 (ISBN 0-86653-098-3, GA 439). Good Apple.

PATTON, GEORGE SMITH, 1885-1945
Ayer, Frederick, Jr. Before the Colors Fade; Portrait of a Soldier: George Patton. LC 64-18329. 1971. 14.95 (ISBN 0-910220-61-1). Berg.

PAUL, SAINT, APOSTLE
Bruce, F. F. Jesus & Paul: Places They Knew. 128p. 1983. Repr. of 1981 ed. 12.95 (ISBN 0-8407-5281-4). Nelson.
Davies, W. D. Jewish & Pauline Studies. LC 82-48620. 432p. 1983. text ed. 29.95 (ISBN 0-8006-0694-9). Fortress.
MacDonald, Dennis Ronald. The Legend & the Apostle: The Battle for Paul in Story & Canon. LC 82-21953. 144p. (Orig.). 1983. pap. 9.95 (ISBN 0-664-24464-5). Westminster.
Meeks, Wayne A. The First Urban Christians: The Social World of the Apostle Paul. LC 82-8447. (Illus.). 296p. 1982. 19.95 (ISBN 0-300-02876-8). Yale U Pr.
Meinardus, Otto F. St. Paul in Ephesus & the Cities of Galatia & Cyprus. (In the Footsteps of the Saints). (Illus.). 160p. 15.00 (ISBN 0-89241-071-X); pap. 5.95 (ISBN 0-89241-044-2). Caratzas Bros.
--St. Paul in Greece. (In the Footsteps of the Saints). 160p. 15.00 (ISBN 0-89241-045-0); pap. 5.95 (ISBN 0-89241-072-8). Caratzas Bros.
--St. Paul's Last Journey. (In the Footsteps of the Saints Ser.). 160p. 15.00 (ISBN 0-686-81741-9); pap. 5.95 (ISBN 0-89241-046-9). Caratzas Bros.
Paul the Missionary. 64p. Date not set. pap. 2.95 (ISBN 0-9609302-0-5). L Imperio.
Phipps, William E. Encounter Through Questioning Paul: A Fresh Approach to the Apostle's Life & Letters. LC 82-17580. (Illus.). 114p. (Orig.). 1983. lib. bdg. 19.00 (ISBN 0-8191-2785-X); pap. text ed. 8.25 (ISBN 0-8191-2786-8). U Pr of Amer.
Schillebeeckx, Edward. Paul the Apostle. (Illus.). 128p. 1983. 14.95 (ISBN 0-8245-0574-3). Crossroad NY.

PAULICIANS
Gilliland, Dean S. Pauline Theology & Mission Practice. 304p. 1983. pap. 12.95 (ISBN 0-8010-3788-3). Baker Bk.

PAUPERISM
see Poor

PAVESE, CESARE
Lajolo, Davide. An Absurd Vice: A Biography of Cesare Pavese. Pietralunga, Mario, tr. Pietralunga, Mark. LC 82-14482. 288p. (Ital.). 1983. 18.50 (ISBN 0-8112-0850-8); pap. 9.25 (ISBN 0-8112-0851-6, NDP545). New Directions.

PAW
see Foot

PAWNEE INDIANS
see Indians of North America–The West

PAYMENT
see also Balance of Trade; Debtor and Creditor
Bank for International Settlements, ed. Payment Systems in Eleven Developed Countries. 312p. 1980. 70.00x (ISBN 0-7121-5483-3, Pub. by Macdonald & Evans). State Mutual Bk.
Whiting, D. P. International Trade & Payments. 160p. 1978. 30.00x (ISBN 0-7121-0952-8, Pub. by Macdonald & Evans). State Mutual Bk.

PAZEND
see Pahlavi Language

PEACE
see also Arbitration, International; Disarmament; International Organization; Security, International; Sociology, Military; War
Amos, Sheldon. Political & Legal Remedies for War. 254p. 1982. Repr. of 1880 ed. lib. bdg. 24.00x (ISBN 0-8377-0213-5). Rothman.
Barnes, Harry E. Perpetual War for Perpetual Peace. rev. & enl. ed. 1982. lib. bdg. 79.95 (ISBN 0-87700-454-4). Revisionist Pr.
Chittenden, L. E. Report of the Debates & Proceedings of the Peace Convention Held in Washington, D.C., Feb. 1861. LC 70-158578. 626p. 1971. Repr. of 1864 ed. lib. bdg. 79.50 (ISBN 0-306-70190-1). Da Capo.
Cory, Carol & Lintner, Jay. Peace Futuring. (Orig.). 1983. pap. 1.95 Leader's Bk. (ISBN 0-686-84608-7); pap. 1.95 Student's Bk. (ISBN 0-686-84609-5). Pilgrim NY.
Elizondo, Virgil & Greinacher, Norbert, eds. Church & Peace. (Concilium 1983: Vol. 164). 128p. (Orig.). 1983. pap. 6.95 (ISBN 0-8164-2444-6). Seabury.
Kant, Immanuel. Perpetual Peace. Smith, Campbell, tr. (Most Meaningful Classics in World Culture Ser.). (Illus.). 111p. 1983. 69.85 (ISBN 0-89266-386-3). Am Classical Coll Pr.
Kuhlmann, Caspar. Frieden: Kein Thema Europaischer Schulgeschichtsbucher? 298p. (Ger.). 1982. write for info. (ISBN 3-8204-7028-X). P Lang Pubs.
Miller, Marc, intro. by. Waging Peace. (Southern Exposure Ser.). (Illus.). 120p. (Orig.). 1982. pap. 4.00 (ISBN 0-943810-14-0). Inst Southern Studies.
Morris, Richard B. The Peacemakers: The Great Powers & American Independence. (Illus.). 572p. 1983. 24.95X (ISBN 0-930350-35-9); pap. text ed. 9.95X. NE U Pr.
Mushkat, Marion. The Third World & Peace: Some Aspects of Problems of the Inter-Relationship of Interdevelopment & International Security. LC 82-774. 356p. 1982. 27.50x (ISBN 0-312-80039-8). St Martin.
Schmidt, Stanley, ed. War & Peace: Possible Futures from "Analog". 1983. 12.95 (ISBN 0-385-27916-7). Davis Pubns.
Shannon, Thomas A. What Are They Saying About Peace & War? (WATSA Ser.). 128p. 1983. pap. 3.95 (ISBN 0-8091-2499-8). Paulist Pr.
Shovers, Aaron H. Visions of Peace. LC 81-86206. 352p. 1983. pap. 9.95 (ISBN 0-86666-078-X). GWP.
Soelle, Dorothee. The Arms Race Kills Even Without War. LC 82-48543. 128p. 1983. pap. 6.95 (ISBN 0-8006-1701-0). Fortress.
Wiseman, Henry, ed. Peacekeeping: Appraisals & Proposals. (International Peace Academy Ser.). 400p. 1983. 40.00 (ISBN 0-08-027554-0). Pergamon.

PEACE (THEOLOGY)
Gerlach, Barbara. The Things That Make for Peace: Biblical Meditations. (Illus.). 64p. (Orig.). 1983. pap. 4.95 (ISBN 0-8298-0664-4). Pilgrim NY.
The Non Role of Religion in Peace or How to Convince a Woman to Kill Her Child or Have It Killed by Others. (Analysis Ser.: No. 6). 1982. pap. 10.00 (ISBN 0-686-42841-2). Inst Analysis.
Pollock, Algernon J. La Paz Con Dios. 2nd ed. Mahecha, Alberto, ed. Bautista, SAra, tr. from Eng. (La Serie Diamante). 48p. (Span.). 1982. pap. 0.85 (ISBN 0-942504-09-7). Overcomer Pr.
Sider, Ronald J. & Brubaker, Darrel J., eds. Preaching on Peace. LC 82-10958. 96p. 1982. pap. 3.95. Fortress.

PEACE OFFICERS
see also Police
Egloff, Fred R. El Paso Lawman: G. W. Campbell. (The Early West Ser.). (Illus.). 144p. 1982. 12.95 (ISBN 0-932702-22-8); pap. 7.95 (ISBN 0-932702-24-4); leatherbound collectors ed. 75.00 (ISBN 0-932702-23-6). Creative Texas.

PEACEFUL COEXISTENCE
see United States–Foreign Relations–Russia; World Politics–1945-

PEACEKEEPING FORCES
see International Police

PEAK, ENGLAND
Dodd, A. E. & Dodd, E. M. Peakland Roads & Trackways. 192p. 1982. 40.00x (ISBN 0-86190-066-9, Pub. by Moorland). State Mutual Bk.

PEALE, CHARLES WILLSON, 1741-1827
Richardson, Edgar P. & Hindle, Brooke. Charles Willson Peale & His World. 1983. 40.00 (ISBN 0-8109-1478-6). Abrams.

PEARL HARBOR, ATTACK ON, 1941
Toland, John. Infamy: Pearl Harbor & Its Aftermath. (Illus.). 384p. 1983. pap. 3.95 (ISBN 0-425-05991-X). Berkley Pub.

PEASANT ART
see Art Industries and Trade; Folk Art

PEASANT UPRISINGS
see also names of specific uprisings e.g. Peasants' War
Thaxton, Ralph. China Turned Rightside Up: Revolutionary Legitimacy in the Peasant World. LC 82-40165. (Illus.). 312p. 1983. text ed. 27.50x (ISBN 0-300-02707-9). Yale U Pr.

PEASANTRY
see also Agricultural Laborers; Farmers; Peasant Uprisings; Rural Conditions
Fleure, H. J. & Peake, Harold. Peasants & Potters. (Corridors of Time Ser.: No. 3). 1927. text ed. 24.50x (ISBN 0-686-83689-8). Elliots Bks.
Papousek, D. Peasant-Potters of Los Pueblos. (Studies in Developing Countries: No. 27). 182p. 1981. 15.75 (ISBN 0-686-82313-3, 41327, Pub. by Van Gorcum Holland). Humanities.
Segalen, Martine. Love & Power in the Peasant Family. Matthews, Martine, tr. LC 82-50495. (Illus.). 224p. 1983. 21.00x (ISBN 0-226-74451-5). U of Chicago Pr.
Van Schendel, W. Peasant Mobility. (Studies in Developing Countries: No. 26). 372p. 1981. text ed. 25.75x (41317, Pub. by Van Gorcum Holland). Humanities.

PEASANTRY–CHINA
Thaxton, Ralph. China Turned Rightside Up: Revolutionary Legitimacy in the Peasant World. 27.50 (ISBN 0-686-42817-X). Yale U Pr.

PEASANTRY–VIETNAM (DEMOCRATIC REPUBLIC, 1946-)
Ho Tai, Hue-Tam. Millenarianism & Peasant Politics in Vietnam. (Harvard East Asian Ser.: No. 99). (Illus.). 240p. 1983. text ed. 30.00x (ISBN 0-674-57555-5). Harvard U Pr.

PEASANTS
see Peasantry

PEASANTS' UPRISINGS
see Peasant Uprisings

PEBBLES
see Rocks

PEDAGOGY
see Education; Education–Study and Teaching; Teaching

PEDESTRIANISM
see Walking

PEDIATRIC DENTISTRY
see Pedodontia

PEDIATRIC ENDOCRINOLOGY
Collipp, Platon J. & Castro-Magana, Mariano. Pediatric & Adolescent Endocrinology Case Studies. (Case Studies Ser.). 1982. pap. text ed. write for info. (ISBN 0-87488-054-8). Med Exam.
Hung, Wellington & August, Gilbert P. Advanced Textbook of Pediatric Endocrinology. (Advanced Textbook Ser.). 1982. pap. text ed. 32.50 (ISBN 0-87488-674-0). Med Exam.
Laron, Z. & Butenandt, O., eds. Evaluation of Growth Hormone Secretion. (Pediatric & Adolescent Endocrinology: Vol. 12). 200p. 1983. 58.75 (ISBN 3-8055-3623-2). S Karger.
Pediatric & Adolescent Endocrinology, 2 vols, Vol. 10-11. (Illus.). xxvi, 458p. 1983. 161.75 (ISBN 3-8055-3681-X). S Karger.

PEDIATRIC HEMATOLOGY
Hann, Ian M. & Rankin, Angela, eds. Colour Atlas of Paediatric Haematology. (Illus.). 1983. text ed. 55.00x (ISBN 0-19-261227-1). Oxford U Pr.
Willoughby, M. L. N. Hematology & Oncology: BIMR Pediatrics Ser. (Vol. I). 320p. 1982. text ed. 39.95 (ISBN 0-407-02308-9). Butterworth.

PEDIATRIC NEUROLOGY
see also Child Psychiatry
McLaurin, Robert L., ed. Pediatric Neuropsychology: Surgery of the Developing Nervous System. Date not set. price not set (ISBN 0-8089-1490-1). Grune.

PEDIATRIC NURSING
Association of Pediatric Oncology. Nursing Care of the Child With Cancer. 1982. text ed. write for info. (ISBN 0-316-04884-4). Little.
Ingalls, A. Joy & Salerno, M. Constance. Maternal & Child Health Nursing. (Illus.). 800p. 1983. pap. text ed. 23.95 (ISBN 0-8016-2324-3); study guide 10.95 (ISBN 0-8016-2323-5). Mosby.
Nelson, Nancy P., ed. Nursing Care Plans for the Pediatric Patient. 1982. pap. 25.00 (ISBN 0-295-96019-1, Pub. by Childrens Orthopedic Hosp & Med Ctr). U of Wash Pr.
Rudman, Jack. Child & Adolescent Nurse. (Certified Nurse Examination Ser.: CN-7). 21.95 (ISBN 0-8373-6157-5); pap. 13.95 (ISBN 0-8373-6107-9). Natl Learning.
--Clinical Specialist in Child & Adolescent Psychiatric & Mental Health Nursing. (Certified Nurse Examination Ser.: CN-15). 21.95 (ISBN 0-8373-6165-6); pap. 13.95 (ISBN 0-8373-6115-X). Natl Learning.
--Pediatric Nurse Practitioner. (Certified Nurse Examination Ser.: CN-8). 21.95 (ISBN 0-8373-6158-3); pap. 13.95 (ISBN 0-8373-6108-7). Natl Learning.
Scipien. Comprehensive Pediatric Nursing. 1983. write for info. (ISBN 0-07-055554-0). McGraw.
Tippert-Neilson, Terry E. & Behler, Donna M. Pediatric Nurse Practitioner: Certification Review. 304p. 1983. 17.95 (ISBN 0-471-86411-0, Pub. by Wiley Med.). Wiley.
Whaley, Lucille F. & Wong, Donna L. Nursing Care of Infants & Children. 2nd ed. (Illus.). 1694p. 1983. text ed. 38.95 (ISBN 0-8016-5419-X). Mosby.

PEDIATRIC OPHTHALMOLOGY
Brown, Gary & Tasman, William, eds. Congenital Anomalies of the Optic Disc. Date not set. price not set (ISBN 0-8089-1515-0). Grune.
Crawford, John & Morin, J. Donald, eds. The Eye in Childhood. Date not set. price not set (ISBN 0-8089-1503-7). Grune.
Wybar, Taylor. Pediatric Opthalmology. 632p. 1983. 75.00 (ISBN 0-8247-1841-0). Dekker.

PEDIATRIC PHARMACOLOGY
Carey, Anne. The Children's Pharmacy. new ed. 192p. 1983. 11.95 (ISBN 0-672-52727-8). Bobbs.
Pantell, Robert & Bergman, David. The Parent's Pharmacy. LC 82-13837. (Illus.). 288p. 1982. 16.95 (ISBN 0-201-08153-9); pap. 8.95 (ISBN 0-686-82138-6). A-W.

PEDIATRIC PSYCHIATRY
see Child Psychiatry

PEDIATRIC RADIOLOGY
Radiation Protection in Pediatric Radiology: NCRP Report 68. 1981. 11.00 (ISBN 0-913392-54-5). NCRP Pubns.

PEDIATRICS
see also Children–Care and Hygiene; Children–Diseases; Infants–Diseases
Balkam, Jean & Moran, Cathleen. Pediatric Ambulatory Care Guidelines. 384p. 1983. pap. text ed. 17.95 (ISBN 0-89303-263-8). R J Brady.
Berman, Stephen. Pediatric Decision Making. 300p. 1983. text ed. 36.00 (ISBN 0-941158-17-9, D0640-3). Mosby.
Calderelli, David D. Pediatric Otolaryngology. (New Directions in Therapy Ser.). 1982. 32.50 (ISBN 0-87488-695-3). Med Exam.
Carr, Janet H. & Shepherd, Roberta B. Physiotheraphy in Pediatrics. 2nd ed. 524p. Repr. of 1980 ed. 29.50 (ISBN 0-89443-813-1, Pub. by W Heinemann). Aspen Systems.

Chiarenza, G. A. & Pakakostopoulos, D., eds. Clinical Application of Cerebral Evoked Potentials in Pediatric Medicine: Proceedings of the International Conference, Milan, Italy, January 14-16, 1982. (International Congress Ser.: No. 595). 416p. 1982. 69.25 (ISBN 0-444-90278-3, Excerpta Medica). Elsevier.

Child Abuse. (Clinical Pediatrics Ser.). 1982. text ed. 22.50 (ISBN 0-316-60410-0). Little.

Denhoff, Eric & Feldman, Steven A. Management through Diet & Medication. (Pediatric Habilitation Ser.: Vol. 2). (Illus.). 280p. 1981. 26.50 (ISBN 0-8247-1565-9). Dekker.

Dulcy, Faye & Wilhelm, Irma J., eds. Aquatics: A Revived Approach to Pediatric Management. (Physical & Occupational Therapy in Pediatrics Ser.: Vol. 3, No. 1). 120p. 1983. text ed. 19.95 (ISBN 0-86656-215-X). Haworth Pr.

Fitzgerald, Hiram E. & Lester, Barry M., eds. Theory & Research in Behavioral Pediatrics, Vol. 1. 300p. 1982. 29.50x (ISBN 0-306-40851-1, Plenum Pr). Plenum Pub.

Frick, P., et al, eds. Advances in Internal Medicine & Pediatrics, Vol. 50. (Illus.). 190p. 1983. 39.00 (ISBN 0-387-11445-9). Springer-Verlag.

Gans, Stephen L. Pediatric Edoscopy. write for info (ISBN 0-8089-1547-9). Grune.

Martin, Richard. A Parent's Guide to Childhood Symptoms: Understanding the Signals of Illness from Infancy through Adolescence. 384p. 1982. 14.95 (ISBN 0-312-59658-8). St Martin.

Mellinger, James F. & Stickler, Gunnar B. Critical Problems in Pediatrics. (Illus.). 352p. 1983. text ed. price not set (ISBN 0-397-50545-0, Lippincott Medical). Lippincott.

Modell, Michael & Boyd, Robert. Paediatric Problems in General Practice. (Illus.). 1982. pap. 23.95x (ISBN 0-19-261264-6). Oxford U Pr.

Oski, Frank A. Year Book of Pediatrics 1983. 1983. 35.00 (ISBN 0-8151-6566-8). Year Bk Med.

Rahamimoff, P. & Harell, Moshe. Appetite & Lack of Appetite in Infancy & Early Childhood. 179p. 1979. 15.00x (ISBN 0-87397-146-9). Strode.

Russo, Raymond M., et al. Advanced Textbook of Sexual Development & Disorders in Childhood & Adolescence. (Advances Textbook Ser.). 1983. pap. text ed. price not set (ISBN 0-87488-485-3). Med Exam.

Schaad, U. B., ed. Paediatrische Infektionskrankheiten III. (Paediatrische Fortbildungskurse fuer die Praxis: Vol. 58). (Illus.). viii, 120p. 1983. pap. 54.00 (ISBN 3-8055-3680-1). S Karger.

Silverberg, Mervin. Advanced Textbook of Pediatric Gastroenterology. (Advanced Textbook Ser.). 1982. pap. text ed. 32.50 (ISBN 0-87488-657-0). Med Exam.

Silverman, Arnold & Roy, Claude C. Pediatric Clinical Gastroenterology. 3rd ed. (Illus.). 978p. 1983. text ed. 66.00 (ISBN 0-8016-4623-5). Mosby.

Urizar, Rodrigo E. & Largent, Jill A. Pediatric Nephrology. (New Directions in Therapy Ser.). 1982. text ed. 50.00 (ISBN 0-87488-846-8). Med Exam.

Warshaw, Joseph B. & Hobbins, John. Perinatal Medicine in Primary Practice. 1982. 34.95 (ISBN 0-201-08294-2, Med-Nurse). A-W.

Winters, Robert W. Principles of Pediatric Fluid Therapy. 2nd ed. 1982. pap. text ed. 16.95 (ISBN 0-316-94738-5). Little.

Ziai, Mohsen. Bedside Pediatrics: Diagnostic Evaluation of the Child. 1983. write for info. (ISBN 0-316-98752-2). Little.

PEDIATRICS–PSYCHOSOMATIC ASPECTS

Larlham, Hattie. Dear Children. 152p. 1983. 9.95 (ISBN 0-8361-3325-0). Herald Pr.

PEDIGREES

see Genealogy; Heraldry

PEDODONTIA

Here are entered works on the technical aspects of children's dentistry.

McDonald, Ralph E. & Avery, David R. Dentistry for the Child & Adolescent. 4th ed. (Illus.). 852p. 1983. text ed. 38.50 (ISBN 0-8016-3277-3). Mosby.

PEDOLOGY (CHILD STUDY)

see Children

PEDOLOGY (SOIL SCIENCE)

see Soil Science

PEDOPHILIA

De Young, Mary. The Sexual Victimization of Children. LC 82-17197. 190p. 1982. lib. bdg. 18.95x (ISBN 0-89950-063-3). McFarland & Co.

PEINTURE LETTRISTE

see Letter Pictures

PEKING

Junwen, Liu. Beijing: China's Ancient & Modern Capital. (Illus.). 254p. (Orig.). 1982. pap. 5.95 (ISBN 0-8351-0979-8). China Bks.

PELOTA (GAME)

Hokanson, Joseph D. Your Winning Ticket. (Illus.). 271p. 1982. info. manual 47.50 (ISBN 0-910625-00-X). Ark Val Pubns.

PENAL CODES

see Criminal Law

PENAL INSTITUTIONS

see Prisons

PENAL LAW

see Criminal Law

PENALTIES (CRIMINALS LAW)

see Punishment

PENANCE

see also Church Discipline; Fasting; Forgiveness of Sin

Munoz, Hector. Will You Hear My Confession? Bair, Robert, tr. from Span. LC 82-20597. 174p. 1983. pap. 6.95 (ISBN 0-8189-0439-9). Alba.

PENCIL DRAWING

Borgeson, Bet. The Colored Pencil: Key Concepts for Handling the Medium. (Illus.). 144p. 1983. 22.50 (ISBN 0-8230-0742-1). Watson-Guptill.

PENGUINS

Ainley, David G. & LeResche, Robert E. Breeding Biology of the Adelie Penguin. LC 82-17573. (Illus.). 198p. 1983. text ed. 30.00x (ISBN 0-520-04838-5). U of Cal Pr.

PENINSULAR WAR, 1807-1814

Glover, Michael. Gentleman Volunteer--Letters of George Hennell from the Peninsular War. 1979. 18.95 (ISBN 0-434-29561-2, Pub. by Heinemann). David & Charles.

PENITENTIARIES

see Prisons

PENMANSHIP

see also Alphabets; Calligraphy; Graphology; Lettering; Writing

Ann Arbor Publishers Editorial Staff. Cursive Tracking. 32p. (gr. 2-8). 1973. 4.00 (ISBN 0-89039-015-0). Ann Arbor Pubs.

Barbe, Walter B. & Lucas, Virginia H. Zaner-Bloser Handwriting: Basic Skills & Applications. 1984. write for info pupil texts grade 1-8; write for info tchr's. eds. grade 1-8. Zaner-Bloser.

Brooks, Bearl. Cursive Practice. (Handwriting Ser.). 24p. (gr. 2-3). 1979. wkbk. 5.00 (ISBN 0-8209-0271-3, W-3). ESP.

--Jumbo Cursive Handwriting Yearbook. (Jumbo Handwriting Ser.). 96p. (gr. 3). 1978. wkbk. 14.00 (ISBN 0-8209-0019-2, JHWY-3). ESP.

Brooks, Pearl. Basic Skills Handwriting Workbook: Grade 1. (Basic Skills Workbooks). 32p. 1982. tchrs' ed. 0.99 (ISBN 0-8209-0370-1, CHW-1). ESP.

--Basic Skills Handwriting Workbook: Grade 2. (Basic Skills Workbooks). 32p. 1982. tchr's ed. 0.99 (ISBN 0-8209-0371-X, CHW-2). ESP.

--Basic Skills Handwriting Workbook: Grade 3. (Basic Skills Workbooks). 32p. 1982. tchr's ed. 0.99 (ISBN 0-8209-0372-8, CHW-3). ESP.

Justus, Fred. Basic Skills Writing Capital & Small Letters Workbook. (Basic Skills Workbooks). 32p. (gr. k-1). 1983. 0.99 (ISBN 0-8209-0563-1, EEW-4). ESP.

--Look, Read, & Write. (Early Education Ser.). 24p. (gr. 1). 1982. wkbk. 5.00 (ISBN 0-8209-0219-5, K-21). ESP.

Mayer, Hartwig. Die Althochdeutschen Griffelglossen der Handschrift Ottob. Lat. 3295 (Biblioteca Vaticana) 192p. (Ger.). 1982. write for info. (ISBN 3-261-04965-0). P Lang Pubs.

The New Handwriting Series, 9 Bks. (Bk. C, transition & Bk. D, cursive). (gr. 1-8). Bks. A-I. pap. 2.10 ea.; Bks. A-D. tchr's manual 2.70 (ISBN 0-8372-9455-X); Bks. E-I. tchr's manual 2.70 (ISBN 0-8372-9461-4); suppl. materials avail. Bowmar-Noble.

The Three-R's Test. write for info. (RivEd). HM.

Wiener & Bazerman. Writing Skills Handbook. 1982. pap. text ed. 7.95 (ISBN 0-686-84586-2). HM.

PENMANSHIP–COPY-BOOKS

Brooks, Bearl. Basic Cursive Handwriting. (Handwriting Ser.). 24p. (gr. 2-3). 1979. wkbk. 5.00 (ISBN 0-8209-0270-5, W-2). ESP.

--Basic Manuscript Handwriting. (Handwriting Ser.). 24p. (gr. 1-2). 1978. wkbk. 5.00 (ISBN 0-8209-0269-1, W-1). ESP.

PENNSYLVANIA

see also names of cities, counties, towns, etc. in Pennsylvania

Clint, Florence. Pennsylvania Area Key. 149p. 1976. 12.00 (ISBN 0-686-38096-7). Keyline Pubs.

PENNSYLVANIA–DESCRIPTION AND TRAVEL

Fodor's Pennsylvania. rev. ed. (Illus.). 176p. 1983. traveltex 7.95 (ISBN 0-679-00943-4). McKay.

Gilbert, Dave. Walkers Guide to Harpers Ferry. (Illus.). 80p. 1983. 4.95 (ISBN 0-933126-28-X). Pictorial Hist.

Miller, Dorothy A. Poor Man's Guide to Pittsburgh. 3rd ed. (Illus.). 70p. 1981. pap. 4.95 (ISBN 0-9608484-0-1). New Pittsburgh.

Smith, Myron J., Jr. Keystone Battlewagon, U.S.S. Pennsylvania (BB-38) (Illus.). 48p. 1983. 4.95 (ISBN 0-933126-27-1). Pictorial Hist.

Thwaites, Thomas. Fifty Hikes in Western Pennsylvania: Walks & Day Hikes from the Laurel Highlands to Lake Erie. LC 82-25277. (Fifty Hikes Ser.). (Illus.). 224p. 1983. pap. 8.95 (ISBN 0-942440-10-2). Backcountry Pubns.

PENNSYLVANIA–GENEALOGY

The Account Book of the Clemens Family of Lower Salford Township, Montgomery County, Pennsylvania. LC 75-12149. (Sources & Documents of the Pennsylvania Germans: Vol. I). (Illus.). 1975. 12.50x (ISBN 0-911122-36-2). Penn German Soc.

Cohen, Stan. The Eisenhowers: Gettysburg's First Family. (Illus.). 48p. 1983. 4.95 (ISBN 0-933126-25-5). Pictorial Hist.

Hanlon, LaVonne R. The Marriage of Catherine & David. (Illus.). 68p. (Orig.). 1982. pap. text ed. 7.00 (ISBN 0-9609326-0-7). Fay-West Her.

PENNSYLVANIA–HISTORY

Aoams, Charles J., III. Ghost Stories of Berks County (Pennsylvania) 215p. 1982. pap. 5.95 (ISBN 0-9610008-0-5). C J Adams.

PENNSYLVANIA–SOCIAL LIFE AND CUSTOMS

Glimm, James Y. Flatlanders & Ridgerunners: Folktales from the Mountains of Northern Pennsylvania. LC 82-10895. (Illus.). 240p. 1983. 11.95 (ISBN 0-8229-3471-X); pap. 5.95 (ISBN 0-8229-5345-5). U of Pittsburgh Pr.

PENNSYLVANIA DUTCH

see Pennsylvania Germans

PENNSYLVANIA GERMANS

see also Mennonites;

also names of specific handicrafts for books on Pennsylvania German work in a special field, e.g. Book Plates; Illumination of Books and Manuscripts; Pottery, American

Garvan, Beatrice B. & Hummel, Charles F. The Pennsylvania Germans: A Celebration of Their Arts 1683-1850. LC 82-61416. (Illus.). 200p. 1982. pap. 18.95 (ISBN 0-87633-048-0). Phila Mus Art.

PENOLOGY

see Prisons; Punishment

PENSION TRUSTS

Lynn, Robert J. The Pension Crisis. LC 82-48795. 192p. 1983. 21.95x (ISBN 0-669-06374-6). Lexington Bks.

PENSIONS

see also Annuities; Old Age Pensions; Social Security also names of professions, industries, etc. or subdivision Salaries, Pensions, etc. under names of professions, etc. e.g. Teachers–Salaries, Pensions, etc.

Buechner, Robert W. & Manzler, David L. Accumulating Wealth with Before Tax Dollars (Desk Book) LC 81-86381. (Illus.). 1982. write for info. looseleaf (ISBN 0-87218-417-X); write for info. visual, 48 p. (ISBN 0-87218-416-1). Natl Underwriter.

Coopers & Lybrand. Employer Accounting for Pension Costs & Other Post-Retirement Benefits. LC 81-68568. 1981. 7.10 (ISBN 0-686-83748-7). Finan Exec.

Fitzgerald, T. H. Money Market Directory of Pension Funds & Their Investment Managers: 1983. 1982. 385.00 (ISBN 0-939712-02-4). Money Mkt.

FRS Associates. Pension Asset Management: The Corporate Decision. LC 80-69793. 1980. 6.20 (ISBN 0-910586-36-5). Finan Exec.

Illustrations of Disclosures of Pension Information. (Financial Report Survey Ser.: No. 22). 1982. pap. 14.50 (ISBN 0-686-84297-9). Am Inst CPA.

Levin, Noel A. & Brossman, Mark E. Social Investing for Pension Funds: For Love or Money. 113p. (Orig.). 1982. pap. 16.00 (ISBN 0-89154-183-7). Intl Found Employ.

Life Office Management Association, ed. Pension Planning: Readings. (FLMI Insurance Education Program Ser.). 177p. 1982. pap. text ed. 10.00 (ISBN 0-915322-49-8). LOMA.

Lynn, Robert J. The Pension Crisis. LC 82-48795. 192p. 1983. 21.95x (ISBN 0-669-06374-6). Lexington Bks.

Matthews, Joseph & Berman, Dorothy. Your Rights & Benefits over Fifty-Five. 224p. 1983. pap. 11.95 (ISBN 0-201-05539-2). A-W.

Nektarios, Miltiadis. Public Pensions, Capital Formation, & Economic Growth. Replica ed. 175p. 1982. softcover 20.00 (ISBN 0-86531-936-7). Westview.

Pension Plans: Answers to the Questions on Subject Matter, CEBS Course 2. 5th ed. 82p. 1982. pap. text ed. 15.00 (ISBN 0-89154-179-9). Intl Found Employ.

Pension Plans: Learning Guide, CEBS Course 2. 5th ed. 1982. spiral binding 18.00 (ISBN 0-89154-180-2). Intl Found Employ.

Pritchett, S. Travis & Stinton, John E. Individual Annuities As a Source of Retirement Income. rev. ed. (FLMI Insurance Education Program Ser.). 94p. 1982. pap. text ed. 9.00 (ISBN 0-915322-50-1). LOMA.

Rudman, Jack. Senior Compensation Claims Clerk. (Career Examination Ser.: C-867). (Cloth bdg. avail. on request). pap. 10.00 (ISBN 0-8373-0867-4). Natl Learning.

Wallace, Marc J., Jr. & Fay, Charles H. Compensation Theory & Practice. 304p. 1982. pap. text ed. 11.95x (ISBN 0-534-01399-6). Kent Pub Co.

PENSIONS, MILITARY

see also Disability Evaluation; Veterans

McNeil, John S. & Wright, Roosevelt, Jr. Military Retirement: Socio-Economic & Mental Health Dilemmas. 220p. 1983. text ed. 24.95x (ISBN 0-86598-078-0). Allanheld.

PENTAX CAMERA

see Cameras–Types–Pentax

PENTECOST

Kemper, R. W. The Pentecost Cycle. LC 12-2965. 1982. pap. 7.95 (ISBN 0-570-03872-3). Concordia.

PENTECOSTALISM

see also Jesus People

Dallimore, Arnold. Forerunner of the Charismatic Movement. (Orig.). 1983. pap. 7.95 (ISBN 0-8024-0286-0). Moody.

Lindsell, Harold. The Charismatic Christian. 256p. 1983. 11.95 (ISBN 0-8407-5279-2). Nelson.

Parries, William H. Second Coming Now--With Soul: Babylon the Great Is Fallen. 1983. 8.95 (ISBN 0-533-05570-9). Vantage.

Poloma, Margaret M. The Charismatic Movement: Is There a New Pentecost? (Social Movements: Past & Present Ser.). 1982. lib. bdg. 17.95 (ISBN 0-8057-9701-7, Twayne). G K Hall.

Quebedeaux, Ricahard. The New Charasmatics II: How a Christian Renewal Movement Became a Part of the American Religious Mainstream. LC 82-48417. 228p. 1983. pap. 8.95 (ISBN 0-06-066723-0, HarpR). Har-Row.

PEOPLE, SINGLE

see Single People

PEOPLE'S BANKS

see Banks and Banking, Cooperative

PEPPERELL, WILLIAM, 1646-1734

Rolde, Neil. Sir William Pepperrell of Colonial New England. (Illus.). xi, 221p. 1982. 12.95 (ISBN 0-88448-048-8); pap. 8.95 (ISBN 0-88448-047-X). Harpswell Pr.

PEPPERS

Doeser, Linda & Richardson, Rosamond. The Little Pepper Book. (Illus.). 64p. 1983. 5.95 (ISBN 0-312-48864-5). St Martin.

OECD. Int. Standardisation of Fruit & Vegetables: Sweet Peppers. 48p. 1982. pap. 13.00x (ISBN 92-64-02321-6). OECD.

PEPTIDE HORMONES

Pierce, John G., ed. Proteins & Peptides Hormones. LC 82-6159. (Benchmark Papers in Biochemistry: Vol. 4). 480p. 1982. 58.00 (ISBN 0-87933-417-7). Hutchinson Ross.

PEPTIDES

Atassi, M. Z. & Benjamini, E., eds. Immunobiology of Proteins & Peptides-II, Vol.150. (Advances in Experimental Medicine & Biology). 238p. 1982. 35.00x (ISBN 0-306-41110-5, Plenum Pr). Plenum Pub.

Choh Hao Li, ed. Hormonal Proteins & Peptides, Vol. 1. LC 82-22770. Date not set. price not set (ISBN 0-12-447211-7). Acad Pr.

Devenyi, T. & Gergely, J. Amino Acid Peptides & Proteins. 1974. 56.00 (ISBN 0-444-41127-5). Elsevier.

Gross, Erhard & Meiehnhofer, Hohannes, eds. The Peptides: Analysis, Synthesis, Biology, Vol. 5. (Special Methods in Peptide Synthesis Ser.: Part B). Date not set. price not set (ISBN 0-12-304205-4). Acad Pr.

Satellite Symposium International Congress of Pharmacology, Lucknow, India 8th, July 1981. Current Status of Centrally Acting Peptides: Proceedings, Vol. 38. Dhawan, B. N., ed. LC 82-3825. (Illus.). 288p. 1982. 50.00 (ISBN 0-08-028008-0). Pergamon.

Voelter, W. & Wunsch, E., eds. Chemistry of Peptides & Proteins, Vol. 1. xv, 533p. 1982. 98.00x (ISBN 3-11-008604-2). De Gruyter.

PEPYS, SAMUEL, 1633-1703

Latham, Robert, ed. The Illustrated Pepys: Extracts from the Diary. 240p. 1982. 30.00x (ISBN 0-686-82321-4, Pub. by Bell & Hyman England). State Mutual Bk.

Pepys, Samuel. The Diary of Samuel Pepys, Vol. XI. Latham, Robert & Matthews, William, eds. LC 70-96950. (The Complete Diary of Samuel Pepys). 368p. 1983. 35.00 (ISBN 0-520-02098-7). U of Cal Pr.

--The Diary of Samuel Pepys: The Companion, Vol. X. Latham, Robert, et al, eds. LC 70-96950. (The Complete Diaries of Samuel Pepys). 656p. 1983. 35.00 (ISBN 0-520-02097-9). U of Cal Pr.

--The Diary of Samuel Pepys: Vol. 10, Companion. Latham, Robert, compiled by. LC 70-96950. (Illus.). 626p. 1983. 35.00 (ISBN 0-520-02097-9). U of Cal Pr.

PEQUOT INDIANS

see Indians of North America–Eastern States

PERCENTAGE–PROGRAMMED INSTRUCTION

Loose, Frances F. Decimals & Percentages. (Illus.). 96p. (gr. 4-6). 1977. 7.00 (ISBN 0-89039-200-5); answer key incl. Ann Arbor Pubs.

PERCEPTION

see also Cognition; Consciousness; Gestalt Psychology; Ideology; Motion Perception (Vision); Social Perception

Beck, Jacob. Organizational & Representation in Perception. 400p. 1982. text ed. 39.95 (ISBN 0-89859-175-9). L Erlbaum Assocs.

Tighe, Thomas J., ed. Perception, Cognition & Development: Interactional Analyses. Shepp, Bryan E. 400p. 1983. text ed. 39.95 (ISBN 0-89859-254-2). L Erlbaum Assocs.

PERCEPTION, EXTRASENSORY

see Extrasensory Perception

PERCEPTUAL DEFENSE

see Perception

PERCEPTUAL LEARNING

McCreary, Paul. Perceptual Activities Level 1 Primary: A Multitude of Perceptual Activities. rev. ed. 62p. (gr. 2-4). 1976. 4.00 (ISBN 0-89039-048-7). Ann Arbor Pubs.

--Perceptual Activities Level 2-Advanced: A Multitude of Reusable Perceptual Activities. rev. ed. (Perceptual Activities Ser.). (Illus.). (gr. 2-4). 1976. 5.00 (ISBN 0-89039-047-9). Ann Arbor Pubs.

PERCEVAL (ROMANCES, ETC.)

De Troyes, Chretien. Perceval: Or, the Story of the Holy Grail. 260p. 1983. 35.00 (ISBN 0-08-026296-1); pap. 17.50 (ISBN 0-08-026295-3). Pergamon.

--Perceval: The Story of the Grail. Bryant, Nigel, tr. LC 82-3696. (Arthurian Studies: No. V). 288p. 1982. text ed. 47.50x (ISBN 0-8476-7201-8). Rowman.

PERCOLATION

Kesten, Harry. Percolation Theory for Mathematicians. (Progress in Probability & Statistics Ser.: Vol. 2). 432p. 1982. text ed. 30.00 (ISBN 3-7643-3107-0). Birkhauser.

PERCY, WALKER, 1916-

Kramer, Victor A. & Bailey, Patricia A. Andrew Lytle, Walker Percy, Peter Taylor: A Reference Guide. 1983. lib. bdg. 39.00 (ISBN 0-8161-8399-6, Hall Reference). G K Hall.

PERENNIALS

see also names of individual perennial plants, e.g. Chrysanthemums

Beckett, Kenneth A. Growing Hardy Perennials. (Illus.). 182p. 1982. 14.95 (ISBN 0-7099-0621-8). Timber.

PEREZ, ANTONIO, 1539-1611

Fitzmaurice-Kelly, Julia. Antonio Perez. 1922. pap. 4.00 (ISBN 0-87535-011-9). Hispanic Soc.

PERFECTIONISTS

see Oneida Community

PERFORMANCE ART

Battcock, Gregory & Nickas, Robert, eds. The Art of Performance: A Critical Anthology. LC 79-53323. (Illus.). 256p. 1983. pap. 11.95 (ISBN 0-525-48039-0, 01064-310). Dutton.

Roth, Moira, ed. The Amazing Decade-Women's Performance Art in America 1970-1980. (Illus.). 250p. 1983. pap. 10.00 (ISBN 0-937122-09-2). Astro Artz.

PERFORMANCE BUDGET

see Program Budgeting

PERFORMANCE RATING (OF EMPLOYEES)

see Employees, Rating Of

PERFORMANCE STANDARDS

Fournies, Ferdinand F. Performance Appraisal: Design Manual. (Illus.). 326p. 1983. 96.45 (ISBN 0-917472-09-8). F Fournies.

Rosen, Theodore A. & Daniels, Aubrey C. Performance Management: Improving Quality & Productivity Through Positive Reinforcement. (Illus.). 1982. write for info. (ISBN 0-937100-01-3). Perf Manage.

PERFORMING ARTS

see also Theater; Theatrical Agencies; also other art forms performed on stage or screen, e.g. Ballet, Concerts, Opera

Benamou, Michel & Caramello, Charles, eds. Performance in Postmodern Culture. pap. 7.95 (ISBN 0-930956-00-1). Performing Arts.

Johnson, Claudia D. & Johnson, Vernon E. Nineteenth-Century Theatrical Memoirs. LC 82-15576. 285p. 1982. lib. bdg. 35.00 (ISBN 0-313-23644-5, JNT/). Greenwood.

Wade, Bonnie C., ed. Performing Arts in India: Essays on Music, Dance & Drama. LC 82-20141. (Monograph Ser.: No. 21). (Illus.). 270p. 1983. lib. bdg. 21.75 (ISBN 0-8191-2872-4); pap. text ed. 11.00 (ISBN 0-8191-2873-2). U Pr of Amer.

PERICLES, 499-429 B.C.

Abbott, Evelyn. Pericles & the Golden Age of Athens. 379p. 1982. Repr. of 1891 ed. lib. bdg. 50.00 (ISBN 0-89984-014-0). Century Bookbindery.

PERICOPES

see Lectionaries

PERIODICAL ADVERTISING

see Advertising, Magazine

PERIODICALS

Here are entered works on the periodicals of the world, and on special aspects or sections of periodicals, language, or area, e.g. Latin American Periodicals, French Periodicals.

see also Liberty of the Press; Newspapers; Press also American Periodicals, English Periodicals, and similar headings; also subdivision Periodicals under specific subjects, e.g. Music–Periodicals; also names of specific periodicals

Carter, Virginia L., compiled by. How to Survey Your Readers. 48p. 1981. 10.50 (ISBN 0-89964-189-X). CASE.

Champagne, Lenora, ed. CCLM Catalog of Literary Magazines: 1983. Rev. ed. 64p. 1983. pap. 5.00x (ISBN 0-942332-02-4). Coord Coun Lit Mags.

R. R. Bowker Company, ed. Magazine Industry Market Place, 1983. new ed. 670p. 1983. pap. 39.95 (ISBN 0-8352-1579-2). Bowker.

PERIODICALS–DIRECTORIES

Current British Journals. 1981. 100.00x (ISBN 0-85350-182-3, Pub. by Brit Lib England). State Mutual Bk.

Fulton, Len & Ferber, Ellen, eds. Directory of Small Magazine-Press Editors & Publishers. 200p. 1983. pap. 12.95 (ISBN 0-913218-65-0). Dustbooks.

--International Directory of Little Magazines & Small Presses: 19th Annual. 600p. 1983. 25.95 (ISBN 0-913218-64-2); pap. 17.95 (ISBN 0-913218-63-4). Dustbooks.

PERIODICALS–INDEXES

Here are entered indexes to groups of periodicals and indexes to specific periodicals of such a general nature that they cannot be classified under a specific subject. For periodicals which deal with special subjects see name of subject with or without the subdivisions Indexes or Periodicals.

Hispanic American Periodicals Index, 1980. Valk, Barbara G., ed. LC 75-642408. (Hispanic American Periodicals Index Ser.). 740p. 1983. lib. bdg. 160.00 (ISBN 0-87903-407-6). UCLA Lat Am Ctr.

Lindberg, John. Routines for Research: A Handbook of Basic Library Skills. LC 82-15962. 172p. 1983. lib. bdg. 20.75 (ISBN 0-8191-2750-7); pap. text ed. 10.00 (ISBN 0-8191-2751-5). U Pr of Amer.

Sicignano, Robert & Prichard, Doris. Special Issues Index: Specialized Contents of Business, Industrial, & Consumer Journals. LC 82-11725. 315p. 1982. lib. bdg. 35.00 (ISBN 0-313-23278-4, SII/). Greenwood.

PERIODICALS–SECTIONS, COLUMNS, ETC.

see Newspapers–Sections, Columns, etc.

PERIODICALS, PUBLISHING OF

see also Newspaper Publishing

Manera, Elizabeth S. & Wright, Robert E. Annotated Writer's Guide to Professional Educational Journals. 188p. 1982. pap. 9.95 (ISBN 0-9609782-0-8). Bobets.

PERIODICITY IN ORGANISMS

see Biological Rhythms

PERIPHERAL VASCULAR DISEASES

Van Nouhuys, C. Dominant Exudative Vitreoretinopathy & Other Vascular Disorders of the Peripheral Retina. 1982. 83.00 (ISBN 90-6193-805-8, Pub. by Junk Pubs Netherlands). Kluwer Boston.

PERKINS, MAXWELL

Berg, Scott A. Max Perkins. 1983. pap. 5.95 (ISBN 0-686-37704-4). WSP.

PERLS, FREDERICK S.

Gaines, Jack. Fritz Perls: Here & Now. (Illus.). 1979. 12.95 (ISBN 0-89087-186-8); pap. 8.95. Integrated Pr.

PERMISSIVE WILL OF GOD

see Theodicy

PERON, JUAN DOMINGO, PRES. ARGENTINE REPUBLIC, 1895-1974

Ditella, Guido. Argentina under Peron, 1973-76: The Nation's Experience with a Labor-Based Government. LC 81-23281. 256p. 1982. 25.00x (ISBN 0-312-04871-8). St Martin.

Turner, Frederick C. & Miguens, Jose E., eds. Juan Peron & the Reshaping of Argentina. LC 82-4870. (Pitt Latin American Ser.). (Illus.). 360p. 1983. text ed. 24.95 (ISBN 0-8229-3464-7). U of Pittsburgh Pr.

PEROXIDES

Yagi, Kunio, ed. Lipid Peroxides in Biology & Medicine: Symposium. LC 82-16430. 1982. 29.50 (ISBN 0-12-768050-0). Acad Pr.

PERSIA

see Iran

PERSIAN ART

see Art, Persian

PERSIAN GULF

Nakhleh, Emile A. Persian Gulf & American Policy. 172p. 1982. 22.95 (ISBN 0-03-060594-6). Praeger.

PERSIAN GULF STATES

Porter, J. D., ed. Oman & the Persian Gulf, 1835-1949. 1982. Ltd. to 350 copies 34.95 (ISBN 0-89712-125-2). Documentary Pubns.

PERSIAN LANGUAGE

Jabbari, Ahmad. A Practical Guide to the Persian Alphabet. (Illus.). 66p. (Orig.). 1982. pap. text ed. 7.95 (ISBN 0-939214-12-1). Mazda Pubs.

PERSIAN LANGUAGE–PAHLAVI

see Pahlavi Language

PERSIAN LITERATURE–AVESTAN

see Avesta

PERSIAN POETRY–HISTORY AND CRITICISM

Browne, Edward G. The Press & Poetry of Modern Persia. (Illus.). xi, 357p. 1983. Repr. of 1914 ed. 30.00 (ISBN 0-933770-39-1). Kalimat.

PERSON (PHILOSOPHY)

see Personalism

PERSONAL ACTIONS

see Actions and Defenses

PERSONAL BEAUTY

see Beauty, Personal

PERSONAL COMBAT

see Hand-To-Hand Fighting

PERSONAL DEVELOPMENT

see Personality; Success

PERSONAL EFFICIENCY

see Success

PERSONAL FINANCE

see Finance, Personal

PERSONAL HEALTH

see Health

PERSONAL INCOME TAX

see Income Tax

PERSONAL INJURIES

see also Accident Law; Employers' Liability; Industrial Accidents; Medical Jurisprudence; Sports–Accidents and Injuries; Workmen's Compensation

Hare, Francis H., Jr. & Ricci, Edward M., eds. The Anatomy of a Personal Injury Lawsuit. 2nd ed. LC 81-70743. (Illus.). 508p. 1981. pap. 35.00 (ISBN 0-941916-00-6). Assn Trial Ed.

PERSONAL LIBERTY

see Liberty

PERSONAL NAMES

see Names, Personal

PERSONAL RADIOTELEPHONE

see Citizens Band Radio

PERSONAL SPACE

Pinxten, Rik & Van Dooren, Ingrid. The Anthropology of Space. LC 82-40490. (Illus.). 336p. 1983. 32.50x (ISBN 0-8122-7879-8). U of Pa Pr.

PERSONALISM

see also Idealism; Individualism

Browne, Joseph W. Personal Dignity. LC 82-18944. 1983. 15.00 (ISBN 0-8022-2409-1). Philos Lib.

PERSONALITY

see also Ego (Psychology); Humanistic Psychology; Identity (Psychology); Personalism; Personality Assessment; Rorschach Test; Self; Soul

Barham, Martha. Bridging Two Worlds. Greene, Tom, ed. 246p. (Orig.). 1981. pap. 6.95x (ISBN 0-9609680-0-8). MJB Bks.

Because I Am Human. LC 72-92809. 76p. Date not set. pap. 5.95 (ISBN 0-03-063039-8). HR&W.

Berman. The Glands Regulating Personality: A Study of the Glands of Internal Secretion in Relation to the Types of Human Nature. 341p. 1983. Repr. of 1933 ed. lib. bdg. 40.00 (ISBN 0-89760-051-7). Telegraph Bks.

Buscaglia, Leo. Living, Learning & Loving. 288p. 1983. pap. 5.95 (ISBN 0-449-90024-X, Columbine). Fawcett.

Calero, Henry H. & Nierenberg, Gerald I. How to Read a Person Like a Book. (Illus.). 192p. 1982. pap. 2.95 (ISBN 0-671-45664-4). PB.

Cleckley, Hervey. The Mask of Sanity. LC 82-2124. (Medical Library). 285p. 1982. pap. 8.95 (ISBN 0-452-25341-1, 1158-X). Mosby.

Collins, Pat. How to Be a Really Nice Person: Doing the Right Things - Your Way. 256p. 1983. 11.95 (ISBN 0-87131-406-1). M Evans.

Corsini, Raymond J. & Marsella, Anthony J. Personality Theories, Research & Assessment. LC 82-61261. 620p. 1983. text ed. 21.50 (ISBN 0-87581-288-0). Peacock Pubs.

Ernst, C. & Angst, J. Birth Order: Its Influence on Personality. (Illus.). 370p. 1983. 29.80 (ISBN 0-387-11248-0). Springer-Verlag.

Geis, F. L. Personality Research Manual. 227p. 1978. 13.95 (ISBN 0-471-29519-1); tchr's manual avail. (ISBN 0-471-05236-1). Wiley.

Hubbell, Harold R. Stop It! Quit It! Cut It Out! Or How to Be Painfully Happy. (Orig.). Date not set. pap. price not set (ISBN 0-910093-00-8). J & C Pub.

Lair, Jess. I Don't Know Where I'm Going, but I Sure Ain't Lost. 256p. 1983. pap. 2.75 (ISBN 0-449-20056-6, Crest). Fawcett.

Laufer, William S. & Day, James M, eds. Personality Theory, Moral Development, & Criminal Behavior. LC 82-47684. 1983. write for info. (ISBN 0-669-05556-5). Lexington Bks.

Levin, Bernard. Speaking up. 267p. 1983. 16.95 (ISBN 0-686-38946-8, Pub by Jonathan Cape). Merrimack Bk Serv.

--Taking Sides. 200p. 1983. 16.95 (ISBN 0-686-38945-X, Pub by Jonathan Cape). Merrimack Bk Serv.

Lidz, Theodore. The Person: His & Her Development Throughout the Life Cycle. 615p. 1983. pap. 13.50 (ISBN 0-465-05541-9). Basic.

Personhood. LC 78-66423. 160p. Date not set. 9.95 (ISBN 0-03-063202-1). HR&W.

Rigdon, Robert. Discovering Yourself. 1982. pap. 4.95 (ISBN 0-8423-0617-X). Tyndale.

Schwartz, David J. The Magic of Getting What You Want. 224p. 1983. 11.95 (ISBN 0-688-01824-6). Morrow.

Sheehy, Gail. Pathfinders. 1982. pap. 4.50 (ISBN 0-686-83415-1). Bantam.

Sommer, Bobbe L. Never Ask a Cactus for a Helping Hand! Today is My Time. 80p. 1982. pap. text ed. 3.50 (ISBN 0-8403-2710-2). Kendall-Hunt.

The Way of the Bull. LC 73-83777. 192p. Date not set. 9.95 (ISBN 0-03-062882-2). HR&W.

Wheeler, Ladd, ed. Review of Personality & Social Psychology, No. 3. 3rd ed. (Illus.). 320p. 1982. 25.00 (ISBN 0-8039-1854-2); pap. 12.50 (ISBN 0-8039-1855-0). Sage.

Wilson, Bob. The Art of Goalkeeping. (Illus.). 176p. 1983. 9.95 (ISBN 0-7207-1278-5, Pub by Michael Joseph). Merrimack Bk Serv.

Wirt, Robert D., et al. Multidimensional Description of Child Personality: A Manual for the Personality Inventory for Children. LC 79-57301. 116p. 1977. pap. 10.40 (ISBN 0-87424-152-9). Western Psych.

PERSONALITY, DISORDERS OF

see also Autism; Clinical Psychology; Hypnotism

Steingart, Irving. Cognition as Pathological Play in Borderline-Narcissistic Personalities. 256p. 1983. text ed. 25.00 (ISBN 0-89335-179-2). SP Med & Sci Bks.

PERSONALITY ASSESSMENT

see also Personality Tests

Butcher, James N. & Spielberger, Charles D., eds. Advances in Personality Assesment, Vol. 2. 256p. 1982. text ed. 24.95 (ISBN 0-89859-216-X). L Erlbaum Assocs.

Deinhardt, Carol L. Personality Assessment & Psychological Interpretation. (Illus.). 256p. 1983. 19.75x (ISBN 0-398-04752-9). C C Thomas.

Shirly, Hunter B. Mapping the Mind. (Illus.). 376p. 1983. text ed. 27.95 (ISBN 0-911012-19-2). Nelson-Hall.

PERSONALITY TESTS

Deinhardt, Carol L. Personality Assessment & Psychological Interpretation. (Illus.). 256p. 1983. 19.75x (ISBN 0-398-04752-9). C C Thomas.

PERSONNEL MANAGEMENT

see also Applications for Positions; Communication in Management; Communication in Personnel Management; Discrimination in Employment; Employee Counseling; Employees, Dismissal of; Employees, Rating of; Employees, Training of; Employees' Magazines, Handbooks, Etc.; Employment Agencies; Executives; Executives, Training of; Factory Management; Grievance Procedures; Industrial Sociology; Interviewing; Job Satisfaction; Labor Discipline; Labor Turnover; Psychology, Industrial; Recruiting of Employees; Supervision of Employees; Teachers, Rating of; Time and Motion Study also specific subjects with or without the subdivisions Administration or Personnel Management, e.g. Hospitals–Administration; School Personnel Management

Argyris, Chris. Integrating the Individual & the Organization. LC 64-13209. 330p. 1964. 31.95x (ISBN 0-471-03315-4). Wiley.

Bell, John. An Employee Management Handbook. 384p. 1981. 40.00x (ISBN 0-85950-326-7, Pub. by Thornes England). State Mutual Bk.

Cherrington, David J. Personnel Management: Human Resource Management. 670p. 1983. text ed. write for info. (ISBN 0-697-08085-4); instrs' manual avail. (ISBN 0-697-08192-3); study guide avail. (ISBN 0-697-08094-3). Wm C Brown.

Ellman, Edgar S. Put it in Writing: A Complete Guide for Preparing Employee Personnel Handbooks. 160p. 1982. Comb-bound 59.95 (ISBN 0-8436-0884-6). CBI Pub.

Feldman, Nans A. How to Prepare a Personal Policy Manual. rev. ed. Cobb, Norman B., ed. 252p. 1982. 3-ring looseleaf binder 42.95 (ISBN 0-910053-00-6). Angus Downs.

French, Wendell I., et al. The Personnel Management Process: Cases on Human Resources Administration. 2d ed. (Illus.). 1982. 12.50; instr's. manual 1.00. HM.

Graham, H. T. Human Resources Management. 288p. 1981. 29.00X (ISBN 0-7121-0817-3, Pub. by Macdonald & Evans). State Mutual Bk.

Holley, William H. & Jennings, Kenneth M. Personnel Management: Functions & Issues. 608p. 1983. text ed. 26.95 (ISBN 0-03-062712-5). Dryden Pr.

Institute of Personnel Management, ed. Practical Participation & Involvement: Vol. IV Meeting Education & Training Needs. 144p. 1982. pap. text ed. 44.00x (ISBN 0-85292-292-2, Pub. by Inst Personnel Mgmt England). Renouf.

--Practical Participation & Involvement: Vol. III The Individual & the Job. 197p. 1982. pap. 35.50x (ISBN 0-85292-290-6, Pub. by Inst Personnel Mgmt England). Renouf.

Kakabadse, Andrew. People & Organisations. 143p. 1982. text ed. 32.00x (ISBN 0-566-00373-2). Gower Pub Ltd.

Kuzmits, Frank E. Exercises in Personnel Management. 1982. pap. text ed. 8.95 (ISBN 0-675-09791-6). Additional supplements may be obtained from publisher. Merrill.

McFarland, Walter B. Manpower Cost & Performance Measurement. 109p. pap. 12.95 (7790). Natl Assn Accts.

Moses, Joseph L. & Byham, William C., eds. Applying the Assessment Center Method. 322p. 26.00 (ISBN 0-686-84783-0). Work in Amer.

Patten, Thomas H., Jr., ed. Classics of Personnel Management. LC 79-4233. (Classics Ser.). (Orig.). 1979. pap. 12.50x (ISBN 0-935610-05-7). Moore Pub IL.

Pearlman, Kenneth & Schmidt, Frank L. Contemporary Problems in Personnel. 3rd ed. 400p. 1983. text ed. 18.95 (ISBN 0-471-87376-4). Wiley.

Rosenbloom, David, ed. Public Personnel Policy in a Political Environment: A Symposium. (Orig.). 1982. pap. 6.00 (ISBN 0-918592-59-3). Policy Studies.

Rudman, Jack. Qualifying Examination: Management Service. (Career Examination Ser.: CS-39). (Cloth bdg. avail. on request). pap. 12.00 (ISBN 0-686-84422-X). Natl Learning.

Schafritz, Jay M. Dictionary of Personnel Management & Labor Relations. LC 79-24632. (Orig.). 1980. 29.00 (ISBN 0-935610-09-X). Moore Pub IL.

Schlesinger. Quality of Worklife & the Supervisor. 208p. 1982. 26.95 (ISBN 0-03-061598-4). Praeger.

Thompson, Frank J., ed. Classics of Public Personnel Policy. LC 79-15423. (Classics Ser.). (Orig.). 1979. pap. 11.00x (ISBN 0-935610-07-3). Moore Pub IL.

Vineyard, Sue. Beyond Banquets, Plaques & Pins: Creative Ways to Recognize Volunteers & Staff. 2nd ed. (Illus.). 24p. 1981. pap. text ed. 3.50 (ISBN 0-911029-01-X). Heritage Arts.

PERSONNEL MANAGEMENT–EXAMINATIONS, QUESTIONS, ETC.

Eckles, Robert W. & Carmichael, Ronald L. Supervisory Management. 2nd ed. LC 80-21684. (Management Ser.). 524p. 1981. text ed. 24.95 (ISBN 0-471-05947-1). Wiley.

Employment & Training Coordinator. (Career Examination Ser.: C-2884). (Cloth bdg. avail. on request). pap. 14.00 (ISBN 0-8373-2884-5). Natl Learning.

Rudman, Jack. Eligibility Specialist. (Career Examination Ser.: C-2958). (Cloth bdg. avail. on request). pap. 10.00 (ISBN 0-8373-2958-2). Natl Learning.

--Placement Representative. (Career Examination Ser.: C-869). (Cloth bdg. avail. on request). pap. 12.00 (ISBN 0-8373-0869-0). Natl Learning.

--Placement Representative I. (Career Examination Ser.: C-868). (Cloth bdg. avail. on request). pap. 10.00 (ISBN 0-8373-0868-2). Natl Learning.

--Principal Personnel Clerk. (Career Examination Ser.: C-2944). (Cloth bdg. avail. on request). pap. 12.00 (ISBN 0-8373-2944-2). Natl Learning.

--Senior Personnel Clerk. (Career Examination Ser.: C-2867). (Cloth bdg. avail. on request). pap. 10.00 (ISBN 0-8373-2867-5). Natl Learning.

PERSONNEL SERVICE IN EDUCATION

see also Counseling; Dropouts; Grading and Marking (Students); Group Guidance in Education; Pregnant Schoolgirls; School Psychologists; School Social Work; Vocational Guidance

Gallagher. Handbook of Counseling in Higher Education. 348p. 1983. 37.95 (ISBN 0-03-063216-1). Praeger.

Ireland, LaVerne H. The Teacher's & Librarian's Alternative Job Hunt Helper: An Annotated List of Transferable Job Skills & Alternative Career Possibilities. Date not set. 3.00 (ISBN 0-686-37851-2). Petervin Pr.

Kirrane, Diane E., ed. The School Personnel Management System: 1982. 2nd, Rev. ed. 500p. write for info (ISBN 0-88364-117-8). Natl Sch Boards.

McMaster, John M. Skills in Social & Educational Caring. 148p. 1982. text ed. 32.00x (ISBN 0-566-00385-6). Gower Pub Ltd.

McMaster, John M., ed. Methods in Social & Educational Caring. 140p. 1982. text ed. 32.00x (ISBN 0-566-00386-4). Gower Pub Ltd.

PERSONNEL SERVICE IN HIGHER EDUCATION

Zagoren, Adelaide M., compiled by. Involving Alumni in Career Assistance Programs. 111p. 1982. 14.50 (ISBN 0-89964-192-X). CASE.

PERSONS, SINGLE

see Single People

PERSPECTIVE

see also Drawing

Amandola, Sal, et al. Perspective for the Artist. (Illus.). 64p. (Orig.). 1983. pap. 4.95 (Pentalic). Taplinger.

PERSPECTIVE, TIME

see Time Perspective

PERSUASION (PSYCHOLOGY)

see also Propaganda

Vanderlaan, Roger F. Persuasion. LC 81-71065. 185p. (Orig.). Date not set. pap. 11.95 (ISBN 0-942060-00-8). El Camino.

PERT (MANAGEMENT)

see Critical Path Analysis

PERTURBATION (MATHEMATICS)

Eckhaus, W. & De Jager, E. M., eds. Theory & Applications of Singular Perturbations, Oberwolfach, Germany 1981: Proceedings. (Lecture Note in Mathematics: Vol. 942). 372p. 1982. pap. 18.50 (ISBN 0-387-11584-6). Springer-Verlag.

PERTURBATION THEORY

see Perturbation (Mathematics)

PERU

Gray, Collen. Peru. (World Education Ser.). (Illus., Orig.). 1983. pap. text ed. write for info. (ISBN 0-910054-77-0). Am Assn Coll Registrars.

PERU–ANTIQUITIES

Rivero, Mariano E. & Von-Tschudi, John J. Peruvian Antiquities. Hawks, Francis L., tr. (The Americas Collection Ser.). (Illus.). 306p. 1982. pap. 24.95 (ISBN 0-936332-15-8). Falcon Hill Pr.

Terada, Kazuo, ed. Excavations at Huacaloma in the North Highlands of Peru, 1979: Report No. 2 of the Japanese Scientific Expedition to Nuclear America. (Illus.). 300p. 1982. text ed. 79.50 (ISBN 0-86008-315-2, Pub. by U of Tokyo Japan). Columbia U Pr.

PERU–DESCRIPTION AND TRAVEL–GUIDEBOOKS

Mayer, Anna. El Mundo de Santiago. 22p. (Sp.). (gr. 3-4). 1980. pap. text ed. 5.95 (ISBN 0-933982-18-6). Bradt Ent.

Richter, J. Yurao Janka. (Illus.). 180p. 1982. 15.95 (ISBN 0-930410-05-X). Bradt Ent.

PERU–ECONOMIC CONDITIONS

Becker, David G. The New Bourgeoisie & the Limits of Dependency: Mining, Class, & Power in "Revolutionary" Peru. LC 82-61352. 368p. 1983. 35.00x (ISBN 0-691-07645-6); pap. 9.95 (ISBN 0-691-02213-5). Princeton U Pr.

PERU–POLITICS AND GOVERNMENT

McClintock, Cynthia & Lowenthal, Abraham F., eds. The Peruvian Experiment Reconsidered. LC 82-61377. 484p. 1983. 45.00x (ISBN 0-691-07648-0); pap. 11.95 (ISBN 0-691-02214-3). Princeton U Pr.

PERU–RELIGION

Reville, Albert. The Native Religions of Mexico & Peru: Hibbert Lectures. Wicksteed, Phillip H., tr. LC 77-27167. 224p. 1983. Repr. of 1884 ed. 29.50 (ISBN 0-404-60405-6). Ams Pr.

PERU–SOCIAL CONDITIONS

Becker, David G. The New Bourgeoisie & the Limits of Dependency: Mining, Class, & Power in "Revolutionary" Peru. LC 82-61352. 368p. 1983. 35.00x (ISBN 0-691-07645-6); pap. 9.95 (ISBN 0-691-02213-5). Princeton U Pr.

PERVERSION, SEXUAL

see Sexual Deviation

PEST CONTROL

see also Insect Control; Weed Control; and similar headings; also subdivision Control under names of pests

Akesson, N. B. & Yates, W. E. The Use of Aircraft for Mosquito Control, Oct. 1982. 96p. 10.00 (ISBN 0-686-84357-6). Am Mosquito.

PEST CONTROL–BIOLOGICAL CONTROL

Goden, D. Pest Slugs & Snails: Biology & Control. Gruber, S., tr. from Ger. (Illus.). 470p. 1983. 71.00 (ISBN 0-387-11894-2). Springer-Verlag.

Samways, Michael J. Biological Control of Pests & Weeds. (Studies in Biology: No. 132). 64p. 1981. pap. text ed. 8.95 (ISBN 0-7131-2822-4). E Arnold.

PESTICIDES

see also Fungicides; Herbicides; Insecticides; Spraying and Dusting Residues in Agriculture

Georghiou, G. P. & Saito, Tetsuo, eds. Pest Resistance to Pesticides. 807p. 1983. 89.50x (ISBN 0-306-41246-2, Plenum Pr). Plenum Pub.

Green, M. B. Pesticides: Boon or Bane? LC 76-5881. (Westview Environmental Studies Ser.: Vol. 1). 1976. 18.00 (ISBN 0-89158-610-5). Westview.

Hutson, D. H. & Roberts, T. R. Progress in Pesticide Biochemistry, Vol. 2. 226p. 1982. text ed. 52.00x (ISBN 0-471-10118-4, Pub. by Wiley-Interscience). Wiley.

--Progress in Pesticide Biochemistry, Vol. 3. 500p. 1983. price not set (ISBN 0-471-90053-2, Pub. by Wiley Interscience). Wiley.

Plimmer, Jack R., ed. Pesticides Residues & Exposure. (ACS Symposium Ser.: No. 182). 1982. write for info. (ISBN 0-8412-0701-1). Am Chemical.

PESTICIDES–ENVIRONMENTAL ASPECTS

Vettorazzi, G., ed. International Regulatory Aspects for Pesticide Chemicals, Vol. II. 256p. 1982. 77.00 (ISBN 0-8493-5608-3). CRC Pr.

PESTICIDES–TOXICOLOGY

Fleck, Raymond F. & Hollaender, Alexander, eds. Genetic Toxicology: An/Agricultural Perspective, Vol.21. (Basic Life Sciences). 560p. 1982. 65.00x (ISBN 0-686-83967-6, Plenum Pr.). Plenum Pub.

PESTICIDES AND THE ENVIRONMENT

see Pesticides–Environmental Aspects

PESTS

see also Agricultural Pests; Insects, Injurious and Beneficial

also names of Pests, e.g. Boll-Weevil

The Ecology of Pests: Some Australian Case Histories. 254p. 1981. pap. 15.50 (ISBN 0-686-84865-9, CO 65, CSIRO). Unipub.

PETER, SAINT, APOSTLE–JUVENILE LITERATURE

Johnson, Irene L. The Apostle Peter & His Writing. Sparks, Judith, ed. 48p. (Orig.). (gr. 7 up). 1983. pap. 1.50 (ISBN 0-87239-672-X, 2772). Standard Pub.

PETO, JOHN FREDERICK, 1859-1907

Wilmerding, John. Important Information Inside: The Art of John F. Peto & the Idea of Still Life Painting in Nineteenth Century America. write for info. Natl Gallery Art.

--Important Information Inside: The Art of John F. Peto & the Idea of Still-Life Painting in 19th Century America. LC 82-48489. (Icon Editions). (Illus.). 1983. 33.65i (ISBN 0-06-438941-3, HarpT). Har-Row.

--Still Life Paintings of John F. Peto. (Illus.). 1982. pap. write for info. (ISBN 0-89468-059-5). Natl Gallery Art.

PETROGRAPHY

see Petrology

PETROLEUM

see also Boring; Oil Fields

Crump, G. B. Petroanalysis 81: Proceedings of the Institute of Petroleum London 1982. 416p. 1982. 83.95 (ISBN 0-471-26217-X, Pub. by Wiley Interscience). Wiley.

PETROLEUM–DRILLING FLUIDS

see Drilling Muds

PETROLEUM–GEOLOGY

Evaporite Deposits: Illustration & Interpretation of Some Environmental Sequences. 282p. 1980. 129.00x (ISBN 2-7108-0385-2, Pub. by Graham & Trotman England). State Mutual Bk.

Graham & Trotman Ltd., ed. Nigeria: Its Petroleum Geology, Resources & Potential, Vol. 1. 176p. 1982. 110.00x (ISBN 0-86010-264-5, Pub. by Graham & Trotman England). State Mutual Bk.

Hyne, Norman J. Geology for Petroleum Exploration, Drilling, & Production. (Illus.). 320p. 1983. 31.50 (ISBN 0-07-031659-7, P&RB). McGraw.

Robinson, Joseph E., ed. Computer Applications in Petroleum Geology. LC 82-3113. (Computer Methods in the Geosciences Ser.). 176p. 1982. 26.95 (ISBN 0-87933-432-0); pap. 16.95 (ISBN 0-87933-444-4). Hutchinson Ross.

Whiteman, Arthur. Nigeria: Its Petroleum Geology, Resources & Potential, Vol. 2. 238p. 1982. 110.00x (ISBN 0-86010-265-3, Pub. by Graham & Trotman England). State Mutual Bk.

Zambrano, E. & Vasquez, E. Paleogeographic & Petroleum Synthesis of Western Venezuela. 70p. 1972. 60.00x (ISBN 2-7108-0194-9, Pub. by Graham & Trotman England). State Mutual Bk.

PETROLEUM–LAW

see Petroleum Law and Legislation

PETROLEUM–PIPE LINES

Parker, Marshall. Pipe Line Corrosion & Cathodic Protection. 2nd ed. 1982. text ed. 18.95x (ISBN 0-87201-148-8). Gulf Pub.

Warring, R. H. Handbook of Valves, Piping & Pipelines. 1982. 65.00x (ISBN 0-87201-885-7). Gulf Pub.

PETROLEUM–REFINING

see also Alkylation

Hasselriis, Floyd. Refuse-Derived Feul Processing. LC 82-46061. (Design & Management for Resource Recovery Ser.). 400p. 1983. 29.95 (ISBN 0-250-40314-5). Ann Arbor Science.

Refinery-Petrochemical Plant Construction & Maintenance-Plant Operation & Control-Noise & Pollution Control In Refinery-Petrochemical Plants: A Workbook for Engineers. 148p. 1982. 30.00 (I00154). ASME.

PETROLEUM–TAXATION

see Petroleum Law and Legislation

PETROLEUM–WELL-BORING

see Oil Well Drilling

PETROLEUM AS FUEL

Vegetable Oil Fuels. LC 82-72554. 400p. 1982. pap. 23.50 (ISBN 0-916150-46-1). Am Soc Ag Eng.

PETROLEUM CHEMICALS

Burdick, Donald L. & Leffler, William L. Petrochemicals for the Nontechnical Person. 224p. 1983. 37.50x (ISBN 0-87814-207-X). Pennwell Pub.

Yen, T. F., ed. The Role of Trace Metals in Petroleum. LC 74-77404. (Illus.). 221p. 1982. 39.95 (ISBN 0-250-40061-8). Ann Arbor Science.

PETROLEUM ENGINEERING

see also Oil Reservoir Engineering; Oil Well Drilling; Petroleum Industry and Trade; Prospecting

Abell, J. M. & Sengel, E. W., eds. Petroleum Production Technology. 1981. 36.00 (ISBN 0-89931-027-3). Inst Energy.

Guiliano, Francis A., ed. Introduction to Oil & Gas Technology. 2nd ed. (Short Course Handbooks). (Illus.). 194p. 1981. text ed. 29.00 (ISBN 0-934634-48-3); pap. text ed. 21.00. Intl Human Res.

Kozik, T. J., ed. Risers-Arctic Design Criteria-Equipment Reliability In Hydrocarbon Processing: A Workbook for Engineers. 242p. 1981. 30.00 (I00144). ASME.

Meehan, Nathan D. & Vogel, Eric L. HP-Forty-One Reservior Engineering Manual. 364p. 1982. 59.95x (ISBN 0-87814-186-3). Pennwell Pub.

Silver, Burr A. Subsurface Exploration Stratigraphy. 1982. 45.00 (ISBN 0-89419-254-X). Inst Energy.

--Technique of Using Geologic Data. 1982. 32.00 (ISBN 0-89931-040-0). Inst Energy.

University Course in Digital Seismic Methods Used in Petroleum Exploration. 294p. 1980. 25.00 (ISBN 0-686-42732-7). Goose Pond Pr.

Woodard, Bob, ed. Petroleum Technology for Exploration Support Personnel. 1982. 48.00 (ISBN 0-686-84040-2). Inst Energy.

Young, William J. Organization of Instrumentation Guidelines. 110p. 1982. 29.95x (ISBN 0-87814-187-1). Pennwell Pub.

PETROLEUM ENGINES

see Gas and Oil Engines

PETROLEUM GEOLOGY

see Petroleum–Geology

PETROLEUM INDUSTRY AND TRADE

see also Oil Industries; Petroleum–Refining

Al-Chalabi, Fadhil J. OPEC & the International Oil Industry: A Changing Structure. (Illus.). 176p. 1980. pap. 9.95 (ISBN 0-19-877155-X). Oxford U Pr.

Badger, Daniel & Belgrave, Robert. Oil Supply & Price: What Went Right in 1980? (Atlantic Papers Ser.: No. 47). 70p. 1982. pap. text ed. 6.50x (ISBN 0-86598-110-8). Allanheld.

Banks, Ferdinand E. Resources & Energy: An Economic Analysis. LC 81-47967. 368p. 1983. 34.95x (ISBN 0-669-05203-5). Lexington Bks.

Belgrave, Robert. Oil Supply & Price: Future Crisis Management. (Atlantic Papers: No. 48). 32p. (Orig.). 1982. pap. text ed. 6.50x (ISBN 0-86598-115-9). Allanheld.

Danielson, Albert. The Evolution of OPEC. 304p. (Orig.). 1982. pap. text ed. 8.95 (ISBN 0-15-518795-3). HarBraceJ.

Ghosh, Arabinda. OPEC, The Petroleum Industry, & United States Energy Policy. LC 82-13245. (Illus.). 296p. 1983. lib. bdg. 35.00 (ISBN 0-89930-010-3, HD9566, Quorum). Greenwood.

Goldstein. The Politics of Offshore Oil. 208p. 1982. 21.95 (ISBN 0-03-059813-3). Praeger.

Institute of Petroleum. Model Code of Safe Practices for the Petroleum Industry: The Petroleum Pipeline, Pt. 6. 1982. write for info. (ISBN 0-471-26139-4, Pub. by Wiley Interscience). Wiley.

Kenny, John. Business of Diving. 1972p. text ed. 37.00x (ISBN 0-87201-183-6). Gulf Pub.

Langenkamp, Robert D. Oil Business Fundamentals. 152p. 1982. 25.00x (ISBN 0-87814-198-7). Pennwell Pub.

Lax, Howard L. Political Risk in the International Oil & Gas Industry. LC 82-83329. (Illus.). 212p. 1983. text ed. 28.00 (ISBN 0-934634-20-3). Intl Human Res.

Matthiessen, Lars. The Impact of Rising Oil Prices on the World Economy. 211p. 1982. text ed. 37.00x (ISBN 0-333-33185-0, Pub. by Macmillan England). Humanities.

Mosburg, Lewis G., ed. Raising Money Without Registration. 1982. 45.00 (ISBN 0-89419-230-2). Inst Energy.

--Sample Offering Documents. 1982. 50.00 (ISBN 0-89419-210-8). Inst Energy.

Mosburg, Lewis G., Jr., ed. Petroleum Land Practices. 1981. 49.00 (ISBN 0-89931-024-9). Inst Energy.

Prast, William G. & Lax, Howard L. Oil-Futures Markets: An Introduction. LC 82-48622. 1983. write for info. (ISBN 0-669-06354-1). Lexington Bks.

Riva, Joseph P., Jr. World Petroleum Resources & Reserves. (Special Study). (Illus.). 250p. 1983. lib. bdg. 45.00 (ISBN 0-86531-446-2). Westview.

Roebuck, Field, Jr. Applied Petroleum Resevoir Technology. 1979. 38.00 (ISBN 0-89931-002-8). Inst Energy.

--Economic Analysis of Petroleum Ventures. 1979. 31.00 (ISBN 0-89419-038-5). Inst Energy.

Taher, H. E. Energy: A Global Outlook: The Case for Effective International Cooperation. 2nd ed. (Illus.). 430p. 1983. 46.00 (ISBN 0-08-029972-5); pap. 22.00 (ISBN 0-08-029971-7). Pergamon.

Torrens, Ian. Changing Structures in the World Oil Market. (The Atlantic Papers: No. 41). 43p. (Orig.). 1981. pap. text ed. 6.50 (ISBN 0-86598-049-7). Allanheld.

Transactions Special Issue: Petroleum. 1980. 5.75 (ISBN 0-686-38292-7). IMM North Am.

U. K. Offshore Oil & Gas Directory. 300p. 1982. 99.00x (ISBN 0-7277-0146-0, Pub. by Telford England). State Mutual Bk.

University Course in Digital Seismic Methods Used in Petroleum Exploration. 294p. 1980. 25.00 (ISBN 0-686-42732-7). Goose Pond Pr.

Whitehead, Harry. An A-Z of Offshore Oil & Gas. text ed. 39.95x (ISBN 0-87201-052-X). Gulf Pub.

Willene, Lilly. The Petroleum Secretary's Handbook. 173p. 1982. 25.95x (ISBN 0-87814-195-2). Pennwell Pub.

Zimmermann, Erich W. Conservation in the Production of Petroleum. 1957. text ed. 29.50x (ISBN 0-686-83511-5). Elliots Bks.

PETROLEUM INDUSTRY AND TRADE–ACCOUNTING

Brock, Horace R. & Klingstedt, John P. Accounting for Oil & Gas Producing Companies: Pt. 2: Amortization, Conveyances, Full Costing & Disclosures. LC 81-82890. 384p. 1982. pap. text ed. 22.50 (ISBN 0-940966-02-6). N Texas St U Pro Devel Inst.

Hartman, Don. How to Enter & Profit from American Oil & Gas Lotteries. (Illus.). 192p. 1982. pap. 8.95 (ISBN 0-9609470-0-0). Baja Enter.

Koester, Robert, ed. Oil & Gas Accounting for the Non-Financial Executive. 1982p. 35.00 (ISBN 0-89419-206-X). Inst Energy.

Mosburg, Lewis G. Mosburg Oil Venture Capital from Tax-Oriented Investors, 2 vols. 1982. Vol. I. (ISBN 0-89419-169-1); Vol. II. (ISBN 0-89419-170-5); Set. 90.00 (ISBN 0-89419-172-1). Inst Energy.

Mosburg, Lewis G., Jr. The Economics of Oil & Gas Investment. (Illus.). 23p. (Orig.). 1982. Broker-Dealer Version. pap. text ed. 5.25 (ISBN 0-910649-00-6); Investor Version. pap. text ed. 5.25 (ISBN 0-910649-01-4). Energy Textbks.

PETROLEUM INDUSTRY AND TRADE–AUTOMATION

Aune, A. B. & Vlietstra, J. Automation for Safety in Shipping & Offshore Petroleum Operations. 1980. 89.50 (ISBN 0-444-85498-3). Elsevier.

PETROLEUM INDUSTRY AND TRADE–DICTIONARIES

Glossary of the Petroleum Industry. English-Spanish. 2nd ed. (Glossary of the Petroleum Industry Ser.). 378p. 21.95x (ISBN 0-87814-194-4). Pennwell Pub.

Ketchian, S. & Desbrandes, R. Technical Petroleum Dictionary of Well-Logging, Drilling & Production Terms. 366p. 1965. 99.00x (ISBN 2-7108-0046-2, Pub. by Graham & Trotman England). State Mutual Bk.

Langenkamp, Robert D., ed. Illustrated Petroleum: Reference Dictionary. 2nd ed. (Illus.). 584p. 1982. 45.95x (ISBN 0-87814-160-X). Pennwell Pub.

Palmer, Susan R., ed. Petroleum Industry Glossary. 1982. 32.00 (ISBN 0-89931-032-X). Inst Energy.

PETROLEUM INDUSTRY AND TRADE–ENVIRONMENTAL ASPECTS
Peterson, Kathy K., ed. Oil Shale: The Environmental Challenges II. 2nd ed. (Illus.). 402p. 1982. 20.00 (ISBN 0-918062-51-9). Colo Sch Mines.
PETROLEUM INDUSTRY AND TRADE–HISTORY
Odell, Peter R. & Rosing, Kenneth E. The Future of Oil: World Oil Resources & Use. 2nd ed. 200p. 1983. pap. 23.95 (ISBN 0-89397-146-4). Nichols Pub.
PETROLEUM INDUSTRY AND TRADE–LAW
see Petroleum Law and Legislation
PETROLEUM INDUSTRY AND TRADE–CANADA
Melvin, James R. & Scheffman, David T. An Economic Analysis of the Impact of Rising Oil Prices on Urban Structure. (Ontario Economic Council Research Studies). 160p. (Orig.). 1983. pap. 10.50 (ISBN 0-8020-3395-4). U of Toronto Pr.
PETROLEUM INDUSTRY AND TRADE–INDONESIA
Ooi Jin Bee. The Petroleum Resources of Indonesia. (Natural Resources of South-East Asia Ser.). (Illus.). 256p. 1982. 29.95 (ISBN 0-19-582527-6). Oxford U Pr.
PETROLEUM INDUSTRY AND TRADE–NEAR EAST
Quandt, William B. Saudi Arabia's Oil Policy. LC 82-73524. 65p. 1982. pap. 5.95 (ISBN 0-8157-7287-4). Brookings.
PETROLEUM INDUSTRY AND TRADE–NIGERIA
Graham & Trotman Ltd., ed. Nigeria: Its Petroleum Geology, Resources & Potential, Vol. 1. 176p. 1982. 110.00x (ISBN 0-86010-264-5, Pub. by Graham & Trotman England). State Mutual Bk.
Nigeria: Its Petroleum Geology, Resources & Potential, Vol. 2. 238p. 1983. 59.00x (ISBN 0-8448-1440-7). Crane-Russak.
Whiteman, Arthur. Nigeria: Its Petroleum Geology, Resources & Potential, Vol.1. 176p. 1983. 59.00x (ISBN 0-8448-1426-1). Crane-Russak.
--Nigeria: Its Petroleum Geology, Resources & Potential, Vol. 2. 238p. 1982. 110.00x (ISBN 0-86010-265-3, Pub. by Graham & Trotman England). State Mutual Bk.
PETROLEUM INDUSTRY AND TRADE–UNITED STATES
Chester, Edward W. United States Oil Policy & Diplomacy: A Twentieth Century Overview. LC 82-8379. (Contributions in Economics & Economic History Ser.: No. 52). (Illus.). 384p. 1983. lib. bdg. 35.00 (ISBN 0-313-23174-5, CUO/). Greenwood.
DeVan, Shumway, et al. Oil Industry U. S. A. 1979-80. 1979. 65.00 (ISBN 0-686-84376-2). Oil Daily.
Duerksen, Christopher J. Dow vs California: A Turning Point in the Envirobusiness Struggle. LC 82-19942. (Illus.). 150p. (Orig.). 1982. pap. 10.00 (ISBN 0-89164-076-2). Conservation Foun.
Gordon, Marcy & Jenkins, Anita. Oil Industry U. S. A. 1981-82. 1981. 75.00 (ISBN 0-686-84377-0). Oil Daily.
Hardy, George, ed. Pooling & Unitization in Louisiana. 1982. 39.00 (ISBN 0-89419-229-9). Inst Energy.
--Pooling & Utilization in Texas. 1982. 39.00 (ISBN 0-89419-226-4). Inst Energy.
Horwich, George & Mitchell, Edward J., eds. Policies for Coping with Oil Supply Disruptions. 1982. 16.95 (ISBN 0-8447-2241-3); pap. 8.95 (ISBN 0-8447-2240-5). Am Enterprise.
Knowles, Ruth S. The First Pictorial History of the American Oil & Gas Industry, 1859-1983. (Illus.). 177p. 1983. 15.95 (ISBN 0-8214-0693-0, 82-84622). Ohio U Pr.
Kuntz, Eugene, ed. Pooling & Utilization in Oklahoma. 1982. 39.00 (ISBN 0-89419-219-1). Inst Energy.
Shaffer, Ed. The United States & the Control of World Oil. LC 82-42720. 256p. 1983. 27.50x (ISBN 0-312-83314-8). St Martin.
Tocci, Lisa, et al. Oil Industry U. S. A. 1983. 1982. 75.00 (ISBN 0-686-84378-9). Oil Daily.
Wampler, Ralph L. Forced Pooling! A Guide for Oklahoma Mineral Owners. 1982. pap. write for info. (ISBN 0-943264-01-4). San Anselmo Pub.
PETROLEUM INDUSTRY AND TRADE–VENEZUELA
Zambrano, E. & Vasquez, E. Paleogeographic & Petroleum Synthesis of Western Venezuela. 70p. 1972. 60.00x (ISBN 2-7108-0194-9, Pub. by Graham & Trotman England). State Mutual Bk.
PETROLEUM LAW AND LEGISLATION
see also Oil and Gas Leases
Crumbley, D. Larry. Readings in Selected Tax Problems of the Oil Industry. 280p. 1982. 35.00x (ISBN 0-87814-201-0). Pennwell Pub.
Gary, James H., ed. Proceedings of the Fifteenth Oil Shale Symposium: Proceedings of the Fifteenth Symposium. (Illus.). 606p. 1982. pap. 23.00 (ISBN 0-918062-50-0). Colo Sch Mines.
Hemingway, Richard W. The Law of Oil & Gas. 2nd ed. (Hornbook Ser.). 507p. 1983. text ed. price not set (ISBN 0-314-71558-4). West Pub.
Lowe, John S., ed. Oil & Gas Law for Attorneys. 1982. 58.00 (ISBN 0-89419-199-3). Inst Energy.
Morgenthaler, George J. Oil & Gas Title Examination. 277p. 1982. text ed. 35.00 (ISBN 0-686-82491-1, N1-1342). PLI.
Mosburg, Lewis G., ed. Problems & Pitfalls in Exploration Agreements. 1982p. 50.00 (ISBN 0-89419-225-6). Inst Energy.
PETROLEUM PIPE LINES
see Petroleum–Pipe Lines
PETROLEUM POLLUTION OF WATER
see Oil Pollution of Water
PETROLEUM REFINING
see Petroleum–Refining
PETROLOGY
see also Crystallography; Geochemistry; Geology; Mineralogy; Rocks
also varieties of rock, e.g. Quartz
Le Maitre, R. W. Numerical Petrology. (Developments in Petrology Ser.: No. 8). 282p. 1982. 57.50 (ISBN 0-444-42098-3). Elsevier.
McCall, G. J., ed. Ophiolitic & Related Melanges. LC 81-13490. (Benchmark Papers in Geology Ser.: Vol. 66). 464p. 1983. 56.00 (ISBN 0-87933-421-5, Pub. by Van Nos Reinhold). Hutchinson Ross.
PETROLOGY–JUVENILE LITERATURE
see Rocks–Juvenile Literature
PETROMYZONTIFORMES
see Lampreys
PETS
see also Domestic Animals
also particular species of animals, e.g. Cats, Dogs, etc.
Beck, Alan & Katcher, Aaron, eds. New Perspectives on Our Lives with Companion Animals. LC 82-40484. 640p. 1983. 25.00x (ISBN 0-8122-7877-1). U of Pa Pr.
Palmer, Jean. Small Pets. (Blandford Pet Handbooks Ser.). (Illus.). 96p. 1983. 7.50 (ISBN 0-7137-1202-3, Pub. by Blandford Pr England). Sterling.
The U.S. Pet Food Market. 1982. 495.00 (ISBN 0-686-38413-X, 621). Busn Trend.
Walters, Michelle S. Maryland Pet Profiles. LC 82-61528. (Illus.). 224p. 1982. pap. 10.95 (ISBN 0-686-38107-6). Maryland Pub.
PETS–JUVENILE LITERATURE
Hill. Small Pets. 1983. 5.95 (ISBN 0-86020-649-1, 15121); pap. 2.95 (ISBN 0-86020-648-3, 15122). EDC.
PEWTER
Brett, Vanessa. Phaidon Guide to Pewter. (Illus.). 256p. 1983. 12.95 (ISBN 0-13-662049-3); pap. 6.95 (ISBN 0-13-662031-0). P-H.
PHANEROGAMS
see also Angiosperms
Esau, Katherine. Anatomy of Seed Plants. 2nd ed. LC 76-41191. 550p. 1977. text ed. 29.95 (ISBN 0-471-24520-8). Wiley.
PHANTOMS
see Apparitions; Ghosts
PHARMACEUTICAL ARITHMETIC–PROGRAMMED INSTRUCTION
Sackheim & Robbins. Programmed Mathematics for Nurses. 1983. 14.95 (ISBN 0-02-405170-5). Macmillan.
PHARMACEUTICAL CHEMISTRY
see Chemistry, Medical and Pharmaceutical
PHARMACEUTICAL INDUSTRY
see Drug Trade
PHARMACEUTICAL RESEARCH
August, J. T., ed. Monoclonal Antibodies in Drug Development. (Illus.). 237p. (Orig.). 1982. lexitone 24.00 (ISBN 0-9609094-0-0). Am Phar & Ex.
Bindra, Jasjit S. & Lednicer, Daniel. Chronicles of Drug Discovery, Vol. 2. 300p. 1983. 32.50 (ISBN 0-471-89135-5, Pub. by Wiley-Interscience). Wiley.
Goldberg, Morton E., ed. Pharmacological & Biochemical Properties of Drug Substances, Vol. 2. 257p. 1977. 36.00 (ISBN 0-917330-25-0). Am Pharm Assn.
Johnson, E. M. & Kochhar, D. M., eds. Teratogenesis & Reproductive Toxicology. (Handbook of Experimental Pharmacology Ser.: Vol. 65). (Illus.). 400p. 1983. 116.00 (ISBN 0-387-11906-X). Springer-Verlag.
Jucker, Ernst, ed. Progress in Drug Research, Vol. 26. 412p. 1982. text ed. 98.95 (ISBN 3-7643-1261-0). Birkhauser.
Knoll, Bertha, ed. Symposium on Pharmacology of Learning & Retention, Vol. 4. (Hungarian Pharmacological Society, First Congress Ser.). (Illus.). 103p. 1974. 10.00x (ISBN 963-05-0192-9). Intl Pubns Serv.
Magyar, K., ed. Symposium on Pharmacological Agents & Biogenic Amines in the Central Nervous System. (Hungarian Pharmacological Society, First Congress Ser.: Vol. I). (Illus.). 274p. 1973. 20.00 (ISBN 0-686-43332-7). Intl Pubns Serv.
Vargh, George. Pharmacoangiography in the Diagnosis of Tumours. Kerner, Nora, tr. from Hungarian. (Illus.). 253p. 1981. 35.00x (ISBN 963-05-2912-2). Intl Pubns Serv.
Whitehouse, Jack E. How & Where to Find the Facts: Researching Illegal Drugs. LC 82-61339. 125p. (Orig.). 1983. pap. 6.95 (ISBN 0-88247-696-3). R & E Res Assoc.
PHARMACEUTICALS, DELAYED-ACTION
see Delayed-Action Preparations
PHARMACISTS–LEGAL STATUS, LAWS, ETC.
see Pharmacy–Laws and Legislation
PHARMACODYNAMICS
see Pharmacology
PHARMACOLOGY
see also Chemistry, Medical and Pharmaceutical; Chemotherapy; Drug Metabolism; Drug Resistance in Micro-Organisms; Drugs; Neuropharmacology; Pediatric Pharmacology; Pharmacy; Psychopharmacology; Radioisotopes in Pharmacology
Adrian, R. H., et al, eds. Reviews of Physiology, Biochemistry & Pharmacology, Vol. 96. (Illus.). 194p. 1983. 39.00 (ISBN 0-387-11849-7). Springer-Verlag.
--Reviews of Physiology, Biochemistry, & Pharmacology, Vol. 97. (Illus.). 180p. 1983. 35.50 (ISBN 0-387-12135-8). Springer-Verlag.
Bentley, Peter J. Medical Pharmacology. (Medical Outline Ser.). 1982. pap. text ed. 15.95 (ISBN 0-87488-184-6). Med Exam.
Briggs, Gerald G. Teratogenic Drugs in Clinical Practice. 400p. 1983. price not set (ISBN 0-683-01057-3). Williams & Wilkins.
Caldwell, John & Jakoby, William B., eds. Biological Basis of Detoxification. LC 82-18933. (Biochemical Pharmacology & Toxicology). Date not set. price not set (ISBN 0-12-155060-5). Acad Pr.
Curry, Stephen H. & Whelpton, Robin. Manual of Laboratory Pharmcokinetics: Experiments in Biopharmaceutics, Biochemical Pharmacology & Pharmacokinetics with a Consideration of Relevant Instrumental & Chromatographic Techniques. 250p. 1983. write for info. (ISBN 0-471-10247-4, Pub. by Wiley-Interscience). Wiley.
Dannies, P. & Kozarich, J. W. Pharmacology: Pretest Self-Assessment & Review. 192p. Date not set. 11.95 (ISBN 0-07-051935-8). McGraw.
Fraade, David J., ed. Automation of Pharmaceutical Operations. 400p. 1983. 57.50 (ISBN 0-943330-02-5). Pharm Tech.
George, R., et al, eds. Annual Review of Pharmacology & Toxicology, Vol. 23. LC 61-5649. (Illus.). 1983. text ed. 27.00 (ISBN 0-8243-0423-3). Annual Reviews.
International Congress of Pharmacology. Toward Chronopharmacology: Proceedings of Satellite Symposium to the 8th International Congress of Pharmacology, Nagasaki, Japan, 27-28 July 1981. Takahashi, R. & Halberg, F., eds. (Illus.). 456p. 1982. 80,00 (ISBN 0-08-027977-5). Pergamon.
International Symposium on Quantum Biology & Quantum Pharmacology. Proceedings. Lowdin, Per-Olav & Sabin, John R., eds. 430p. 1982. 64.95 (ISBN 0-471-89123-1, Pub. by Wiley-Interscience). Wiley.
Knoll, Bertha, ed. Symposium on Pharmacology of Learning & Retention, Vol. 4. (Hungarian Pharmacological Society, First Congress Ser.). (Illus.). 103p. 1974. 10.00x (ISBN 963-05-0192-9). Intl Pubns Serv.
Kuemmerle. Clinical Pharmacology in Pregnancy. 1983. price not set (ISBN 0-86577-074-3). Thieme-Stratton.
Lomax, P. & Schoenbaum, E. Enivironment, Drugs & Thermoregulation: International Symposium on the Pharmacology of Thermoregulation, 5th, Saint-Paul-de-Vence, November 1982. (Illus.). xvi, 224p. 1983. 47.50 (ISBN 3-8055-3654-2). S Karger.
Magyar, K., ed. Symposium on Pharmacological Agents & Biogenic Amines in the Central Nervous System. (Hungarian Pharmacological Society, First Congress Ser.: Vol. I). (Illus.). 274p. 1973. 20.00 (ISBN 0-686-43332-7). Intl Pubns Serv.
Neu, H. C. & Sabath, L. D., eds. Ein praktischer Leitfaden fuer die therapeutische Anwendung von Cefotiam. (Pharmanual Ser.: Vol. 3). (Illus.). viii, 192p. 1983. pap. 30.00 (ISBN 3-8055-3694-1). S Karger.
Pharmaceutical Technology Conference, New York, 1982. Proceedings. 700p. 1982. pap. text ed. 75.00 (ISBN 0-943330-01-7). Pharm Tech.
Prescott, L. F. & Gibaldi, M., eds. Handbook of Clinical Pharmacokinetics. 1200p. text ed. write for info. (ISBN 0-86792-004-1, Pub by Adis Pr Australia). Wright-PSG.
Spencer, Roberta T. & Nichols, Lynn W. Clinical Pharmacology & Nursing Management. (Illus.). 1056p. 1983. text ed. 29.50 (ISBN 0-397-54304-2, Lippincott Medical). Lippincott.
Umezawa, H. & Hooper, I. R., eds. Aminoglycoside Antibiotics. (Handbook of Experimental Pharmacology Ser.: Vol. 62). (Illus.). 400p. 1982. 125.00 (ISBN 0-387-11532-3). Springer-Verlag.
Walker, Charles A. Applications of Pharmacokinetics to Patient Care. 192p. 1982. 29.95 (ISBN 0-03-061504-6). Praeger.
Wartak, Joseph. Clinical Pharmacokinetics: A Modern Approach to Individualized Drug Therapy. (Clinical Pharmacology & Therapeutics Ser.: Vol. 2). 232p. 1983. 35.00 (ISBN 0-03-062652-8). Praeger.
Webb, David R., ed. Immunopharmacology & the Regulation of Leukocyte Function. (Immunology Ser.: Vol. 19). (Illus.). 312p. 1982. 45.00 (ISBN 0-8247-1707-4). Dekker.
Wendt, H. & Frosch, P. J. Klinisch-farmakologische modellen voor het testen van Diflucortolonvalerianaat. (Illus.). 64p. (Dutch.). 1982. pap. 24.00 (ISBN 3-8055-3684-4). S Karger.
PHARMACOLOGY–RESEARCH
see Pharmaceutical Research
PHARMACOPOEIAS
see also Drugs; Materia Medica; Medicine–Formulae, Receipts, Prescriptions
United States Pharmacopeia & National Formulary. 1980. USP XX-NF XV. 75.00 (ISBN 0-686-37677-3); with annual supplements 100.00 (ISBN 0-686-37678-1); third supplement 9.00 (ISBN 0-686-37679-X); third supplement plus all future supplements 27.00 (ISBN 0-686-37680-3); with annual supplements 100.00. USPC.
United States Pharmacopeial Convention, 2 vols. 1982. Set. 37.95 (ISBN 0-686-37850-4). USPC.
PHARMACY
see also Botany, Medical; Chemistry, Medical and Pharmaceutical; Drugs; Hospitals; Materia Medica; Medicine–Formulae, Receipts, Prescriptions; Pharmacology; Pharmacopoeias
American Pharmaceutical Association. The Right Drug to the Right Patient. 161p. 1977. three-ring binder 27.00 (ISBN 0-917330-44-7). Am Pharm Assn.
Annotated Bibliography of Pharmacy Practice Contributions in Primary Health Care. Date not set. 5.00 (ISBN 0-686-83879-3). Am Assn Coll Pharm.
Berger, B. A. & Gagnon, J. P. Management Handbook for Pharmacy Practitioners: A Practical Guide for Community Pharmacists. LC 82-48578. (Illus.). x, 204p. (Orig.). 1982. pap. text ed. 14.00x (ISBN 0-938938-08-8, 820-PB-066). Health Sci Consort.
Cyrs, Thomas E., Jr., ed. Handbook for the Design of Instruction in Pharmacy Education. 200p. Date not set. 6.50 (ISBN 0-686-83878-5). Am Assn Coll Pharm.
The Internship Experience. Date not set. 5.00 (ISBN 0-686-83877-7). Am Assn Coll Pharm.
Long Term Care Academy of Pharmacy Practice. Conducting an Inservice Training Program. 34p. 1981. pap. text ed. 12.00 (ISBN 0-917330-45-5); pap. text ed. 21.00 with cassette (ISBN 0-917330-46-3). Am Pharm Assn.
Ostino, G. & Martini, N., eds. Progress in Clinical Pharmacy IV: Proceedings of the European Symposium, Tenth, Stresa, Italy, October 14-17, 1981. (Progress in Clinical Pharmacy: No. IV). 274p. 1982. 59.75 (ISBN 0-444-80437-4, Biomedical Pr). Elsevier.
Report of the AD-HOC Dean Evaluation Committee. Date not set. 5.00 (ISBN 0-686-83874-2). Am Assn Coll Pharm.
Roda, E., ed. Bile Acids in Gastroenterology. 250p. 1983. text ed. 45.00 (ISBN 0-85200-488-5, Pub. by MTP Pr England). Kluwer Boston.
Romano, Joseph A. & Wiener, Matthew B. Mill's Pharmacy State Board Review. 30th ed. 1983. pap. text ed. 16.50 (ISBN 0-87488-430-6). Med Exam.
Rudman, Jack. Pharmacy Assistant II. (Career Examination Ser.: C-2943). (Cloth bdg. avail. on request). pap. 12.00 (ISBN 0-8373-2943-4). Natl Learning.
PHARMACY–BIBLIOGRAPHY
Pasztor, Magda. Bibliography of Pharmaceutical Reference Literature. LC 68-140058. 167p. (Orig.). 1968. pap. 5.00x (ISBN 0-85369-055-3). Intl Pubns Serv.
PHARMACY–HISTORY
Boussel. History of Pharmacy. 1983. 75.00 (ISBN 0-686-43177-4). Thieme-Stratton.
PHARMACY–LAWS AND LEGISLATION
Ainsfeld, Michael H. & Ainsfeld, Evelyn R., eds. International Device GMP's. 200p. 1981. text ed. 165.00 (ISBN 0-935184-01-5). Interpharm.
Anisfeld, Michael H. & Anisfeld, Evelyn R., eds. International Drug GMP's. 2nd ed. 250p. 1983. text ed. 180.00 (ISBN 0-935184-02-3). Interpharm.
PHARMACY–RESEARCH
see Pharmaceutical Research
PHASE CHANGES (STATISTICAL PHYSICS)
see Phase Transformations (Statistical Physics)
PHASE TRANSFORMATIONS (STATISTICAL PHYSICS)
Domb, C. M., ed. Phase Transitions, Vol. 7. Date not set. price not set (ISBN 0-12-220307-0). Acad Pr.
Mutaftschiev, B. Interfacial Aspects of Phase Transformation. 1982. 79.00 (ISBN 90-277-1440-1, Pub. by Reidel Holland). Kluwer Boston.
PHASE TRANSITIONS (STATISTICAL PHYSICS)
see Phase Transformations (Statistical Physics)
PHEASANTS
Holmgren, Virginia. The Pheasant. Schroeder, Howard, ed. (Wildlife Habits & Habitat Ser.). (Illus.). 48p. (gr. 4-5). 1983. lib. bdg. 8.95 (ISBN 0-89686-222-4). Crestwood Hse.
PHENOMENOLOGY
see also Existentialism
Clifton, Thomas. Music as Heard: A Study in Applied Phenomenology. LC 82-10944. (Illus.). 336p. 1983. text ed. 32.50x (ISBN 0-300-02091-0). Yale U Pr.
Darroch, Vivian & Silvers, Ronald J. Interpretive Human Studies: An Introduction to Phenomenological Research. LC 82-13636. 276p. 1983. lib. bdg. 23.50 (ISBN 0-8191-2698-5); pap. text ed. 11.50 (ISBN 0-8191-2699-3). U Pr of Amer.
Harbert, David L. Existence, Knowing, & Philosophical Systems. LC 82-17565. 226p. (Orig.). 1983. lib. bdg. 21.75 (ISBN 0-8191-2804-X); pap. text ed. 10.25 (ISBN 0-8191-2805-8). U Pr of Amer.

International Conference on Collective Phenomena, Fourth: Proceedings, Vol. 373. 233p. 1981. 52.00 (ISBN 0-89766-135-4, Lebowitz Pub); pap. write for info. (ISBN 0-89766-136-2). NY Acad Sci.
Kainz, Howard P. Hegel's Phenomenology: The Evolution of Ethical & Religious Consciousness to the Dialectical Standpoint. 260p. 1983. text ed. 23.95x (ISBN 0-8214-0677-9, 82-84457); pap. 12.95 (ISBN 0-8214-0738-4, 82-85074). Ohio U Pr.
McKenna, William. Husserl's Introduction to Phenomenology. 1982. lib. bdg. 41.50 (ISBN 90-247-2665-4, Pub. by Martinus Nijhoff Netherlands). Kluwer Boston.
O'Neill, John. For Marx Against Althusser: And Other Essays. LC 82-17353. (Current Continental Research Ser.). (Illus.). 192p. (Orig.). 1983. lib. bdg. 20.50 (ISBN 0-8191-2815-5); pap. text ed. 9.50 (ISBN 0-8191-2816-3). U Pr of Amer.
Tymieniecka, A. T. The Phenomenology of Man & the Human Condition. 1983. lib. bdg. 69.50 (ISBN 90-277-1447-9, Pub. by Reidel Holland). Kluwer Boston.

PHEROMONES

Vandenbergh, John G., ed. Pheromones & Reproduction in Mammals. LC 82-22776. Date not set. price not set (ISBN 0-12-710780-0). Acad Pr.

PHILADELPHIA-DESCRIPTION

Fisher, Alan. Country Walks Near Philadelphia. (Country Walks Ser.). (Illus.). 224p. (Orig.). 1983. pap. 6.95 (ISBN 0-910146-47-0). Appalach Mtn.
Hayes, John P. Philadelphia in Color. (Illus., Orig.). 1983. 7.95 (ISBN 0-8038-5898-1). Hastings.
Miller, Fredric M. & Vogel, Morris J. Still Philadelphia: A Photographic History. 1983. write for info. (ISBN 0-87722-306-8). Temple U Pr.

PHILADELPHIA-HISTORY

Driver, Clive E. Passing Through: Letters & Documents Written in Philadelphia by Famous Vistors. (Illus.). 144p. 1983. pap. 10.00 (ISBN 0-939084-14-7). Rosenbach Mus Lib.
Lukacs, John. Philadelphia: Patricians & Philistines, 1900 to 1950. LC 81-15754. (Illus.). 360p. 1982. pap. 9.50 (ISBN 0-89727-044-4). Inst Study Human.
Moore, John M., ed. & intro. by. Friends in the Delaware Valley: Philadelphia Yearly Meeting, 1681-1981. (Illus.). 278p. (Orig.). 1981. 8.95 (ISBN 0-9609122-0-7); pap. 4.95 (ISBN 0-9609122-1-5). Friends Hist Assn.

PHILANTHROPY

see Charities; Endowments; Social Service

PHILATELY AND PHILATELISTS

see Postage-Stamps-Collectors and Collecting

PHILIPPINE FICTION

see also Short Stories, Philippine

Mojares, Resil B. The Origins & Rise of the Filipino Novel: A Generic Study of the Filipino Novel until 1940. 474p. 1983. text ed. 16.50x (ISBN 0-8248-0733-2, Pub. by U of Phillipines Pr); pap. text ed. 13.50x (ISBN 0-8248-0737-5). UH Pr.

PHILIPPINE ISLANDS-DESCRIPTION AND TRAVEL

Barnes, Simon. Philippines in Focus. (The "In Focus" Ser.). (Illus.). 64p. (Orig.). 1981. pap. 5.95 (ISBN 0-686-42860-9). C E Tuttle.
Insight Guides. Philippines. (Illus.). 338p. 1983. 18.95 (ISBN 0-13-662205-4); pap. 14.95 (ISBN 0-13-662197-X). P-H.
Lockhart, Saul. The Complete Guide to Phillippines. (The Complete Asian Guide Ser.). (Illus., Orig.). 1981. pap. 6.95 (ISBN 962-7031-06-2). C E Tuttle.
--Manila by Night. Maitland, Derek, ed. (Asia by Night Ser.). (Illus., Orig.). 1981. pap. 4.95 (ISBN 962-7031-08-9, Pub. by CFW Pubns. Hong Kong). C E Tuttle.

PHILIPPINE ISLANDS-ECONOMIC CONDITIONS

Owen, Norman G. The Philippine Economy & the United States: Studies in Past & Present Interactions. (Michigan Papers on South & Southeast Asia: No. 22). 200p. (Orig.). 1983. text ed. price not set (ISBN 0-89148-024-2); pap. price not set (ISBN 0-89148-025-0). CSSEAS.

PHILIPPINE ISLANDS-FOREIGN RELATIONS

Owen, Norman G. The Philippine Economy & the United States: Studies in Past & Present Interactions. (Michigan Papers on South & Southeast Asia: No. 22). 200p. (Orig.). 1983. text ed. price not set (ISBN 0-89148-024-2); pap. price not set (ISBN 0-89148-025-0). CSSEAS.
Saito, Shiro, ed. Phillipine-American Relations: A Guide to Manuscript Sources in the United States. LC 82-12140. 280p. 1982. lib. bdg. 45.00 (ISBN 0-313-23632-1, SPH/). Greenwood.

PHILIPPINE ISLANDS-HISTORY

Cushner, Nicholas P. Landed Estates in the Colonial Philippines. (Illus.). x, 146p. 1976. pap. 11.50 (ISBN 0-686-38047-9). Yale U SE Asia.
Larkin, John A., ed. Perspectives on Philipine Historigraphy: A Symposium. iv, 74p. 1970. pap. 8.00 (ISBN 0-686-38045-2). Yale U SE Asia.
Scott, William H. Cracks in the Parchment Curtain & Other Essays in Philippine History. (Orig.). 1982. pap. 14.00 (ISBN 0-686-37571-8, Pub. by New Day Philippines). Cellar.
Vance, Lee W. Tracing your Philippine Ancestors, 3 vols. (Illus.). 771p. 1980. 42.50 set (ISBN 0-9608528-0-8); pap. 28.50 set (ISBN 0-9608528-4-0). Philippine Anc.

PHILIPPINE ISLANDS-SOCIAL CONDITIONS

Scaff, Alvin H. Current Social Theory for Philippine Research. 118p. 1982. pap. 7.50 (ISBN 0-686-37570-X, Pub. by New Day Philippines). Cellar.

PHILIPPINE ISLANDS-SOCIAL LIFE AND CUSTOMS

Vance, Lee W. Tracing Your Philippine Ancestors, 3 vols. Set. pap. 28.50 (ISBN 0-9608528-4-0). Vol. 1 (ISBN 0-9608528-1-6). Vol. 2 (ISBN 0-9608528-2-4). Vol. 3 (ISBN 0-9608528-3-2). Philippine Anc.
--Tracing Your Phillippine Ancestors. 42.50 (ISBN 0-9608528-0-8). Philippine Anc.

PHILIPPINE LANGUAGES

see also Tagalog Language

Walrod, Michael R. Discourse Grammar in Ga'dang. Davis, Irvine & Poulter, Virgil, eds. LC 79-66350. (Publications in Linguistics: No. 63). (Illus.). 117p. 1979. pap. text ed. 8.00 (ISBN 0-88312-077-1); microfiche 2.25 (ISBN 0-686-82707-4). Summer Inst Ling.

PHILISTINES

Griffin, Bryan F. Panic Among the Philistines. LC 82-60663. 1983. 12.95 (ISBN 0-89526-633-4). Regnery-Gateway.

PHILOSOPHERS

Broda, Engelbert. Ludwig Boltzmann: Man, Physicist, Philosopher. LC 82-80707. (Illus.). 179p. 1983. 22.50 (ISBN 0-918024-24-2). Ox Bow.
Dutton, Joan P. They Left their Mark. LC 82-83659. (Illus.). 192p. 1983. 15.00 (ISBN 0-937088-05-6); pap. 9.00 (ISBN 0-937088-06-4). Illum Pr.
Friedman, Maurice. Martin Buber's Life & Work: The Middle Years, 1923-1945. (Illus.). 416p. 1983. 29.95 (ISBN 0-525-24176-0, 02908-870). Dutton.
Goodman, Lenn E. Notes on Philosophy & Philosophers. 514p. 1982. pap. 25.95 (ISBN 0-917232-14-3). Gee Tee Bee.

PHILOSOPHERS-CORRESPONDENCES, REMINISCENCES

Rescher, Nicholas. Mid-Journey: An Unfinished Autobiography. LC 82-45083. (Illus.). 204p. (Orig.). 1983. lib. bdg. 21.50 (ISBN 0-8191-2522-9); pap. text ed. 10.25 (ISBN 0-8191-2523-7). U Pr of Amer.

PHILOSOPHERS-FRANCE

Clark, Michael P. Michel Foucault: An Annotated Bibliography Took Kit for A New Age. Cain, William, ed. LC 82-48474. (Modern Critics & Critical Schools Ser.). 600p. 1982. lib. bdg. 60.00 (ISBN 0-8240-9253-8). Garland Pub.

PHILOSOPHERS-GREAT BRITAIN

Burtt, Edwin A., ed. The English Philosophers from Bacon to Mill. 9.95 (ISBN 0-394-60411-3). Modern Lib.

PHILOSOPHERS-GREECE

Henderson, G. P. E. P. Papanoutsos. (World Authors Ser.). 184p. 1983. lib. bdg. 24.95 (ISBN 0-8057-6526-3, Twayne). G K Hall.

PHILOSOPHERS' STONE

see Alchemy

PHILOSOPHICAL ANALYSIS

see Analysis (Philosophy)

PHILOSOPHICAL ANTHROPOLOGY

see also Humanism; Man (Theology); Mind and Body

Gould, Stephen J. The Mismeasure of Man. 352p. 1983. pap. 5.95 (ISBN 0-393-30056-0). Norton.
Macquarrie, John. In Search of Humanity: A Theological & Philosophical Approach. 288p. 1983. 16.95 (ISBN 0-8245-0564-6). Crossroad NY.
Miller, John W. The Philosophy of History: With Reflections & Aphorisms. 192p. 1983. pap. 6.25x (ISBN 0-393-30060-9). Norton.
Sanrilippo, Leonardo. The Philosophical Essence of Man. (Illus.). 104p. 1983. 29.95 (ISBN 0-89266-400-2). Am Classical Coll Pr.

PHILOSOPHY

see also Analysis (Philosophy); Axioms; Belief and Doubt; Causation; Christianity-Philosophy; Consciousness; Cosmology; Creation; Criticism (Philosophy); Esthetics; Ethics; Experience; Free Will and Determinism; Gnosticism; God; Good and Evil; Hedonism; Humanism; Idealism; Ideology; Knowledge, Theory of; Logic; Materialism; Metaphysics; Mind and Body; Mysticism; Naturalism; Ontology; Opposition, Theory of; Optimism; Perception; Personalism; Pluralism; Positivism; Pragmatism; Psychology; Rationalism; Reality; Self (Philosophy); Skepticism; Soul; Space and Time; Structuralism; Teleology; Thought and Thinking; Transcendentalism; Truth; Utilitarianism

Achinstein, Peter. The Nature of Explanation. (Illus.). 320p. 1983. 27.50 (ISBN 0-19-503215-2). Oxford U Pr.
Anyanwu, K. C. The American Experts & the Academic Market: A Comparative Study of Cultural Philosophy. 128p. 1983. 5.00 (ISBN 0-682-49976-5). Exposition.
Banerjee, K. K., ed. Logic, Ontology & Action. (Jadavpur Studies in Philosophy: Vol. 1). 269p. 1982. text ed. 12.50x (ISBN 0-391-02490-6). Humanities.
--Mind, Language & Necessity. (Jadavpur Studies in Philosophy: Vol. 3). 275p. 1982. text ed. 12.50x (ISBN 0-391-02504-X). Humanities.
Barry, Vincent. Philosophy: A Text with Readings. 2nd ed. 544p. 1982. text ed. 21.95x (ISBN 0-534-01216-7). Wadsworth Pub.
Bengesser, Gerhard. Wechselbeziehungen Zwischen Psychiatrie, Psychologie und Philosophie. 178p. (Ger.). 1982. write for info. (ISBN 3-261-05019-5). P Lang Pubs.
Chadwick, Henry, ed. Boethius: The Consolations of Music, Logic, Theology, & Philosophy. 330p. 1981. text ed. 39.00 (ISBN 0-19-826447-X). Oxford U Pr.
DeGrood, David. Haeckel's Theory of the Unity of Nature. (Praxis: Vol.8). 100p. 1982. pap. text ed. 11.50x (ISBN 90-6032-216-9). Humanities.
DeGrood, David H. Radical Currents in Contemporary Philosophy, Vol. II. 1983. 22.50 (ISBN 0-87527-029-8). Green.
Descartes, Rene. Principles of Philosophy. Miller, Reese P. & Miller, Valentine R., trs. 1983. lib. bdg. 59.00 (ISBN 0-686-37924-1, Pub by Reidel Holland). Kluwer Boston.
Dewey, John. Human Nature & Conduct. 5.95 (ISBN 0-394-60439-3). Modern Lib.
Dingoian, George. The Tide is Turning. LC 81-86207. 64p. 1983. pap. 4.95 (ISBN 0-86666-037-2). GWP.
Ewing, A. C. Fundamental Questions of Philosophy. 260p. 1980. pap. 7.95 (ISBN 0-7100-0586-5). Routledge & Kegan.
Goodman, Lenn E. Notes on Philosophy & Philosophers. 514p. 1982. pap. 25.95 (ISBN 0-917232-14-3). Gee Tee Bee.
Haller, R. Grazer Philosophische Studien, Vol. 10. 210p. 1980. pap. text ed. 20.75x (Pub. by Rodopi England). Humanities.
--Grazer Philosophische Studien, Vol. 11. 199p. 1980. pap. text ed. 20.75x (Pub. by Rodopi England). Humanities.
--Grazer Philosophische Studien, Vol. 14. 221p. 1981. pap. text ed. 20.75x (Pub. by Rodopi England). Humanities.
--Grazer Philosphische Studien, Vol. 9. 211p. 1979. pap. text ed. 20.75x (Pub. by Rodopi England). Humanities.
Heyd, Michael. Between Orthodoxy & the Enlightenment. 1983. 65.00 (ISBN 90-247-2508-9, Pub. by Martinus Nijhoff Netherlands). Kluwer Boston.
Huntington, Ellsworth. World Power & Evolution. 1919. text ed. 13.50x (ISBN 0-686-83862-9). Elliots Bks.
Kvart, Igal. A Theory of Counterfactuals. 272p. 1983. text ed. 30.00 (ISBN 0-915145-63-4). Hackett Pub.
Kwancho, C. K. Underground Notebooks on Intellects. 193p. (Orig.). 1982. pap. 8.50x (ISBN 0-9609544-0-6, Aletheia Bks). U Pubns Amer.
Lipman, Matthew. Kio & Gus. LC 79-9315. (Philosophy for Children Ser.). 77p. (gr. k-4). 1982. pap. 6.50 (ISBN 0-916834-19-0). Inst Adv Philo.
Lipman, Matthew & Sharp, A. M. Looking for Meaning: Instructional Manual to Accompany Pixie. 390p. 1982. tchrs. ed. 30.00 (ISBN 0-916834-18-2). Inst Adv Philo.
McLaren, Robert B. The World of Philosophy: An Introduction. LC 82-14214. (Illus.). 272p. 1983. text ed. 23.95x (ISBN 0-8304-1000-7); pap. text ed. 10.95x (ISBN 0-88229-815-1). Nelson-Hall.
Mitcham, Carl & Mackey, Robert, eds. Philosophy & Technology. LC 82-19818. 416p. 1982. pap. text ed. 12.95 (ISBN 0-02-921430-0). Free Pr.
Montague, William P. Belief Unbound. 1930. text ed. 11.50x (ISBN 0-686-83485-2). Elliots Bks.
Nietzsche, Friedrich. Thoughts Out of Season, 2 vols. Levy, Oscar, ed. Collins, Adrian, tr. LC 82-73426. 405p. Repr. of 1909 ed. Set. lib. bdg. 35.00x (ISBN 0-88116-009-1). Brenner Bks.
Nozick, Robert. Philosophical Explanations. 792p. 1983. pap. 9.95 (ISBN 0-674-66479-5, Belknap Pr). Harvard U Pr.
Oizerman, T. I. Dialectical Materialism & the History of Philosophy. 287p. 1982. 7.90 (ISBN 0-8285-2270-7, Pub. by Progress Pubs USSR). Imported Pubns.
Ostenfeld, E. Forms Matter & Mind. 1982. 43.50 (ISBN 90-247-3051-1, Pub. by Martinus Nijhoff Netherlands). Kluwer Boston.
Oxley, William. On Human Consciousness: A Philosophical Discourse. (Salzburg - Poetic Drama Ser.: Vol. 74, No. 2). 114p. 1982. pap. text ed. 25.00x (ISBN 0-391-02802-2, Pub. by Salzburg Austria). Humanities.
Philodemus. On Methods of Inference. De Lacy, Ph. H. & De Lacy, E. A., eds. (The School of Epicurus Ser.). 232p. 1982. text ed. 23.00x (ISBN 88-7088-009-5, 40627, Pub. by Bibliopolis Italy). Humanities.
Rosen, M. & Mitchell, S., eds. The Need for Interpretation: Contemporary Conceptions of the Philospher's Task. 192p. 1982. text ed. 29.50x (ISBN 0-485-11224-8, Althlone Pr). Humanities.
Royce, Josiah. The Spirit of Modern Philosophy. 519p. 1983. pap. 8.95 (ISBN 0-486-24432-6). Dover.
Russell, Henry N. Fate & Freedom. 1927. text ed. 29.50x (ISBN 0-686-83544-1). Elliots Bks.
Schopenhauer, Arthur. The Schopenhauer's Theory of the Essence of Man & of Life. (The Essential Library of the Great Philosophers). (Illus.). 109p. 1983. 71.45 (ISBN 0-89901-094-6). Found Class Reprints.
Sen, P. K. Logic, Induction & Ontology. (Jadavpur Studies in Philosophy: Vol. 2). 241p. 1982. text ed. 16.25x (ISBN 0-391-02491-4). Humanities.
Spencer, W. Wylie. Our Knowledge of Other Minds. 1930. text ed. 29.50x (ISBN 0-686-83671-5). Elliots Bks.
Spiegelberg, H. & Ave-Lallemant, E. Pfander-Studien. 1982. 69.50 (ISBN 90-247-2490-2, Pub. By Martinus Nijhoff Netherlands). Kluwer Boston.
Trias, Eugenio. Philosophy & Its Shadow. Krabbenhoft, Kenneth, tr. LC 82-12803. (European Perspectives Ser.). 160p. 1983. text ed. 20.00x (ISBN 0-231-05288-X). Columbia U Pr.
Van Der Merwe, Alwyn, ed. Old & New Questions in Physics, Cosmology, Philosophy, & Theoretical Biology: Essays in Honor of Wolfgang Yourgrau. 905p. 1983. 95.00x (ISBN 0-306-40962-3, Plenum Pr). Plenum Pub.
Whatever Pub. Inc. Life & Love. 184p. (Orig.). 1982. pap. 4.95 (ISBN 0-9609856-0-3). R Garfield.
Wilson, George A. Reckoning With Life. 1942. text ed. 34.50x (ISBN 0-686-83723-1). Elliots Bks.
Wilson, Robert A. Prometheus Rising. 260p. 1983. pap. 9.95 (ISBN 0-941404-19-6). Falcon Pr Az.
Zedler, Beatrice H. How Philosophy Begins. (Aquinas Lecture Ser.). 55p. 1983. 7.95 (ISBN 0-87462-151-8). Marquette.

PHILOSOPHY-ADDRESSES, ESSAYS, LECTURES

Gregory, Donald R., et al, eds. The Questions Behind the Answers: A Sampler in the Philosophy. LC 80-1373. 164p. 1983. lib. bdg. 20.75 (ISBN 0-8191-2703-5); pap. text ed. 9.25 (ISBN 0-8191-2704-3). U Pr Of Amer.
Hartshorne, Charles. Creative Synthesis & Philosophic Method. LC 82-23780. 358p. 1983. pap. text ed. 13.50 (ISBN 0-8191-2979-8, Co-pub. by Ctr Process Studies). U Pr of Amer.
Lewis, David. Philosophical Papers, Vol. 1. 320p. 1983. 29.95 (ISBN 0-19-503203-9); pap. 9.95 (ISBN 0-19-503204-7). Oxford U Pr.
Neurath, Otto. Philosophical Papers Nineteen Thirteen to Nineteen Forty-Six. Cohen, Robert S. & Neurath, Maria, eds. 1983. lib. bdg. 65.00 (ISBN 90-277-1483-5, Pub. by Reidel Holland). Kluwer Boston.
O'Neill, John. For Marx Against Althusser: And Other Essays. LC 82-17353. (Current Continental Research Ser.). (Illus.). 192p. (Orig.). 1983. lib. bdg. 20.50 (ISBN 0-8191-2815-5); pap. text ed. 9.50 (ISBN 0-8191-2816-3). U Pr of Amer.
Putnam, H. Philosophical Papers: Vol. 3, Realism & Reason. LC 82-12903. 250p. Date not set. price not set (ISBN 0-521-24672-5). Cambridge U Pr.
Schwanauer, Francis. To Make Sure is to Cohere. LC 82-17653. 94p. (Orig.). 1983. pap. text ed. 7.50 (ISBN 0-8191-2766-3). U Pr of Amer.
Szekely, Edmond B. Talks By Edmond Bordeaux Szekely. 48p. 1972. pap. 2.95 (ISBN 0-89564-067-8). IBS Intl.
Tomberlin, James E., ed. Agent, Language, & the Structure of the World: Essays Presented to Hector-Neri Casteneda with His Replies. LC 82-15805. 536p. 1983. lib. bdg. 50.00 (ISBN 0-686-83517-4); pap. text ed. 25.00 (ISBN 0-915145-54-5). Hackett Pub.

PHILOSOPHY-BIOGRAPHY

see Philosophers

PHILOSOPHY-COLLECTED WORKS

Fisch, Max H. & Kloesel, Christian J., eds. Writings of Charles S. Peirce: A Chronological Edition, Vol. 1, 1857-1866. LC 79-1993. 738p. 1982. 32.50 (ISBN 0-253-37201-1). Ind U Pr.
Ridley, Gustave. From Boredom to Bliss. Campbell, Jean, ed. (Illus.). 24p. (Orig.). 1983. pap. 6.95 (ISBN 0-9610544-0-9). Harmonious Pr.

PHILOSOPHY-HISTORY

French, Peter A. & Uehling, Theodore E., Jr., eds. Contemporary Perspectives on the History of Philosophy. (Midwest Studies in Philosophy: Vol. 8). 550p. 1983. 45.00x (ISBN 0-8166-1207-2); pap. 18.95x (ISBN 0-8166-1212-9). U of Minn Pr.
Schopenhauer, Arthur. The Schopenhauer's Interpretation of the History of Philosophy. (The Essential Library of the Great Philosophers). (Illus.). 129p. 1983. 69.85 (ISBN 0-89901-093-8). Found Class Reprints.
Szekely, Edmond B. The Evolution of Human Thought. (Illus.). 44p. 1971. pap. 2.50 (ISBN 0-89564-062-7). IBS Intl.
Wedberg, Anders. A History of Philosophy: Volume 2: The Modern Age to Romanticism. (Illus.). 227p. 1982. 24.50 (ISBN 0-19-824640-4); pap. 9.95 (ISBN 0-19-824692-7). Oxford U Pr.

PHILOSOPHY-INTRODUCTIONS

Hollingdale, R. J. Western Philosophy: An Introduction. LC 79-63624. 158p. 1983. pap. 4.95 (ISBN 0-8008-8130-3). Taplinger.

PHILOSOPHY-METHODOLOGY

see Methodology

PHILOSOPHY-MISCELLANEA

Fisch, Max H. & Kloesel, Christian J., eds. Writings of Charles S. Peirce: A Chronological Edition, Vol. 1, 1857-1866. LC 79-1993. 738p. 1982. 32.50 (ISBN 0-253-37201-1). Ind U Pr.

PHILOSOPHY, AFRICAN

Tort, Patrick & Desalmand, Paul. Sciences Humaines et Philosophie en Afrique: La Difference Culturelle. (Illus.). 399p. (Orig., Fr.). 1978. pap. text ed. 21.00 (ISBN 2-218-04222-3). Intl Pubns Serv.

Zahan, Dominique. The Religion, Spirituality, & Thought of Traditional Africa. Ezra, Kate & Martin, Lawrence M., trs. vi, 180p. 1979. pap. 5.95 (ISBN 0-226-97778-1). U of Chicago Pr.

PHILOSOPHY, ANALYTICAL

see Analysis (Philosophy)

PHILOSOPHY, ANCIENT

see also Gnosticism; Manichaeism

Apostle, H. G. & Gerson, Lloyd P. Aristotle: Selected Works. LC 82-62715. 650p. (Orig.). 1983. text ed. 24.00x (ISBN 0-911589-00-7); pap. 12.00x (ISBN 0-911589-01-5). Peripatetic.

Apuleius, Lucius. The Most Delectable Jests from Lucius Apuleius' the Golden Ass. (Essential Library of the Great Philosophers Ser.). (Illus.). 125p. 1983. 49.75 (ISBN 0-89266-398-7). Am Classical Coll Pr.

Aristotle. An Analysis of the Soul of Man. (The Most Meaningful Classics in World Culture Ser.). (Illus.). 129p. 1983. 57.85 (ISBN 0-89920-052-4). Am Inst Psych.

--The Rhetoric & Poetics. LC 54-9971. 6.95 (ISBN 0-394-60425-3). Modern Lib.

Cicero, Marcus T. The Basic Works. Hadas, Moses, ed. 1964. pap. 3.75 (ISBN 0-686-38908-5, Mod LibC). Modern Lib.

Plato. Philebus. Waterfield, Robin A., tr. from Gr. 1983. pap. 3.95 (ISBN 0-14-044395-9). Penguin.

--The Republic. Jowett, Benjamin, tr. 1982. 7.95 (ISBN 0-394-60813-5). Modern Lib.

--The Works of Plato. Jowett, Benjamin, tr. Date not set. 7.95 (ISBN 0-394-60420-2). Modern Lib.

Plautus. The Amphitruo of Plautus. Sedgwick, W. B., ed. 1960. pap. 11.00 (ISBN 0-7190-0107-2). Manchester.

Plutarch. Plutarch's Lives. Dryden, John, tr. 10.95 (ISBN 0-394-60407-5). Modern Lib.

Rist, John M. Human Value: A Study in Ancient Philosophical Ethics. (Philosophia Antiqua Ser.: Vol. 40). v, 175p. 1982. pap. write for info. (ISBN 90-04-06757-4). E J Brill.

Waley, Arthur. Three Ways of Thought in Ancient China. xv, 216p. 1982. pap. 5.95 (ISBN 0-8047-1169-0, SP-46). Stanford U Pr.

Xenophon. The Respublica Lacedaemoniorum Ascribed to Xenophon. Chrimes, K. M., ed. 1948. pap. 8.50 (ISBN 0-7190-1207-4). Manchester.

PHILOSOPHY, ARAB

see also Philosophy, Islamic

Khawen, Rene R. The Subtle Ruse: The Book of Arabic Wisdom & Guile. 353p. 1982. 17.95 (ISBN 0-85692-035-5, Pub. by Salem Hse Ltd.). Merrimack Bk Serv.

PHILOSOPHY, ASIAN

Dollarhide, Kenneth, tr. Micheren's Senji-sho: An Essay on the Selection of the Proper Time. LC 82-21687. (Studies in Asian Thought & Religion: Vol. 1). 176p. 1983. 29.95x (ISBN 0-88946-051-5). Voter Ed Proj.

PHILOSOPHY, BRITISH

Locke, John. The Correspondence of John Locke, Vol. 6: Letters 2199 to 2664. De Beer, E. S., ed. 806p. 1981. text ed. 119.00x (ISBN 0-19-824563-7). Oxford U Pr.

McCracken, Charles J. Malebranche & British Philosophy. (Illus.). 1982. 58.00x (ISBN 0-19-824664-1). Oxford U Pr.

Manser, Anthony. Bradley's Logic. LC 82-24407. 230p. 1983. text ed. 29.95x (ISBN 0-389-20379-3). B&N Imports.

PHILOSOPHY, BUDDHIST

see also Philosophy, Indic

Hearn, Lafcadio. The Buddhist Writings of Lafcadio Hearn. 304p. 1982. 30.00x (ISBN 0-7045-0421-9, Pub. by Wildwood House). State Mutual Bk.

PHILOSOPHY, CHINESE

Adelmann, F. J. Contemporary Chinese Philosophy. 1983. lib. bdg. 32.50 (ISBN 90-247-3057-0, Pub. by Martinus Nijhoff Netherlands). Kluwer Boston.

Garvy, John W., Jr. Yin & Yang: Using the Traditional Chinese Approach. Liebermann, Jeremiah, ed. (Five Phase Energetics Ser.: No. 2). (Illus.). 1982. pap. 3.00 (ISBN 0-943450-01-2). Wellbeing Bks.

Henricks, Robert C., tr. Philosophy & Argumentation in Third-Century China: The Essays of Hsi K'ang. LC 82-61367. (Princeton Library of Asian Translations). 224p. 1983. 30.00 (ISBN 0-691-05378-2). Princeton U Pr.

Hughes, E. R., ed. & tr. Chinese Philosophy in Classical Times. 382p. 1982. pap. text ed. 4.95 (ISBN 0-460-01973-2, Pub. by Erman). Biblio Dist.

Legge, James. I Ching: Book of Changes. 449p. 1983. pap. 7.95 (ISBN 0-8065-0458-7). Citadel Pr.

Waley, Arthur. Three Ways of Thought in Ancient China. xv, 216p. 1982. pap. 5.95 (ISBN 0-8047-1169-0, SP-46). Stanford U Pr.

PHILOSOPHY, EAST INDIAN

see Philosophy, Indic

PHILOSOPHY, ENGLISH

see Philosophy, British

PHILOSOPHY, FRENCH

Montefiore, Alan, ed. Philosophy in France Today. LC 82-9730. 200p. Date not set. price not set (ISBN 0-521-22838-7); pap. price not set (ISBN 0-521-29673-0). Cambridge U Pr.

Rousseau, Jean J. Les Reveries du Promeneur Solitaire. 2nd ed. Niklaus, R., ed. (Modern French Text Ser.). 1946. pap. write for info. (ISBN 0-7190-0160-9). Manchester.

PHILOSOPHY, GERMAN

Christensen, Darrel E., et al, eds. Contemporary German Philosophy, Vol. 1. 320p. 1982. 17.50x (ISBN 0-271-00336-7). Pa St U Pr.

De Carvalho, Maria C. Karl R. Poppers Philosophie der Wissenschaftlichen und der Vorwissenschaft-Lichen Erfahrung. 203p. (Ger.). 1982. write for info. (ISBN 3-8204-7206-1). P Lang Pubs.

Stepelevich, L., ed. The Young Hegelians: An Anthology. LC 82-9480. (Texts in German Philosophy). 350p. Date not set. 49.50 (ISBN 0-521-24539-7); pap. 15.95 (ISBN 0-521-28772-3). Cambridge U Pr.

PHILOSOPHY, GREEK

see Philosophy, Ancient

PHILOSOPHY, INDIC

see also Philosophy, Buddhist

Anand, Kewal K. Indian Philosophy: The Concept of Karma. 396p. 1982. 34.95 (ISBN 0-940500-91-4, Pub by Bharatiya Vidya India). Asia Bk Corp.

Anand, Mulk R., ed. The Kama Sutra of Vatsyayana. 1982. 175.00x (ISBN 0-85692-093-2, Pub. by J M Dent). State Mutual Bk.

Batchelor, Stephen. Alone with Others. Rosset, Hannelore, ed. (Grove Press Eastern Philosophy & Religion Ser.). 144p. 1983. pap. 5.95 (ISBN 0-394-62457-2, Ever). Grove.

Mahadevan, T. M. P. & Saroja, G. V. Contemporary Indian Philosophy. 282p. 1981. 32.50x (ISBN 0-940500-51-5, Pub. by Sterling India). Asia Bk Corp.

Murty, T. R. Studies in Indian Thought. 1983. 24.00x (ISBN 0-8364-0866-7); text ed. 16.00x (ISBN 0-8364-0631-1). South Asia Bks.

PHILOSOPHY, ISLAMIC

Al-Ghazali. On the Duties of Brotherhood. 6.95 (ISBN 0-686-83895-5). Kazi Pubns.

Attar, Farid Al-Din. Muslim Saints & Mystics. 300p. 1976. pap. 7.95 (ISBN 0-7100-7821-8). Routledge & Kegan.

Fakhry, Majid. A History of Islamic Philosophy. 2nd ed. 450p. 1982. text ed. 27.50x (ISBN 0-231-05532-3). Columbia U Pr.

Malik, Imam & Din, M. R. Muwata. 24.95 (ISBN 0-686-83588-3). Kazi Pubns.

Saqr, A. Islamic Fundamentalism. 5.95 (ISBN 0-686-83888-2). Kazi Pubns.

Shehadi, Fadlou. Metaphysics in Islamic Philosophy. LC 81-18069. 1983. 35.00x (ISBN 0-88206-049-X). Caravan Bks.

Siddiqui, A. H. Islam & Remaking of Humanity. 13.95 (ISBN 0-686-83885-8); pap. 9.95 (ISBN 0-686-83886-6). Kazi Pubns.

--Philosophical Interpretation of History. 9.95 (ISBN 0-686-83884-X). Kazi Pubns.

Siddiqui, M. I. Rights of Allah (God) & Human Rights. 12.50 (ISBN 0-686-83894-7). Kazi Pubns.

--Why Islam Forbids Gambling & Alcohol. 12.50 (ISBN 0-686-83890-4). Kazi Pubns.

PHILOSOPHY, ITALIAN

Malatesta, Errico. Malatesta: Life & Ideas. Richards, Vernon, ed. 309p. 1965. pap. 4.00 (ISBN 0-900384-15-8). Left Bank.

PHILOSOPHY, MEDIEVAL

Boyde, Patrick. Dante Philomythes & Philosopher: Man in the Cosmos. LC 80-40551. (Cambridge Paperback Library). 408p. Date not set. pap. 17.95 (ISBN 0-521-27390-0). Cambridge U Pr.

Wells, Norman J., tr. Francis Suarez: On the Essence of Finite Being as Such, on the Existence of the Essence & Their Distinction. LC 82-81397. (Mediaeval Philosophical Texts in Translation). 312p. Date not set. pap. 24.95 (ISBN 0-87462-224-7). Marquette.

PHILOSOPHY, MODERN

see also Enlightenment; Evolution; Existentialism; Humanism-20th Century; Phenomenology; Positivism; Pragmatism; Transcendentalism

also Philosophy, English; Philosophy, french; and similiar headings

Castell, Alburey. An Introduction to Modern Philosophy: Examining the Human Condition. 4th ed. 656p. 1983. text ed. 21.95 (ISBN 0-02-320080-4). Macmillan.

Matthias, Karl E. Citizen "M" Speaks, Vol. 1. LC 82-74183. (Illus.). 120p. 1982. pap. 6.95 (ISBN 0-9609110-0-6). Creative Lit.

PHILOSOPHY, MODERN-HISTORY

Sallis, John & Silverman, Hugh, eds. Continental Philosophy in America. 272p. 1982. pap. 23.50x (ISBN 0-8207-0160-2). Duquesne.

PHILOSOPHY, MODERN-20TH CENTURY

Ayers, A. J. Philosophy in the Twentieth Century. LC 82-40131. 283p. 1982. 22.50 (ISBN 0-394-50454-2). Random.

PHILOSOPHY, MORAL

see Ethics

PHILOSOPHY, MUSLIM

see Philosophy, Islamic

PHILOSOPHY, ORIENTAL

see also Philosophy, Buddhist; Philosophy, Chinese

Woodside, Alexander & Wyatt, David K., eds. Moral Order & the Question of Change: Essays on Southeast Asian Thought, LC 82-51022. (Yale University Southeast Asia Studies Monograph: No. 24). 413p. 1982. pap. 16.00x (ISBN 0-938692-02-X). Yale U SE Asia.

PHILOSOPHY, PATRISTIC

see Fathers of the Church

PHILOSOPHY, ROMAN

see Philosophy, Ancient

PHILOSOPHY, SCOTTISH

Johnston, G. A., ed. Selections from the Scottish Philosophy of Common Sense. 274p. 17.00 (ISBN 0-87548-365-8). Open Court.

PHILOSOPHY AND RELIGION

see also Christianity-Philosophy; Faith and Reason; Religion-Philosophy

Clift, Wallace B. Jung & Christianity: The Challenge of Reconciliation. 192p. 1983. pap. 6.95 (ISBN 0-8245-0552-2). Crossroad NY.

Cooper, Barry. Michel Foucault: An Introduction to the Study of his Thought. (Studies in Religion & Society: Vol. 2). 176p. 1982. 29.95x (ISBN 0-88946-867-2). E Mellen.

Muccie, Frank J., Jr. I & the Father Are One. 180p. 1982. pap. 9.95 (ISBN 0-938520-01-6). Edenite.

Nakamura, Hajime. Ansatze Modernen Denkens in den Relifionen Japans. (Zeitschrift fur Religions-und geistesgeschichte, Beihefte: 23). viii, 183p. 1982. pap. write for info. (ISBN 90-04-06725-6). E J Brill.

Nielsen, Kai. An Introduction to the Philosophy of Religion. LC 82-16843. 200p. 1982. 20.00x (ISBN 0-312-43310-7). St Martin.

Palmer, G. E. & Sherrard, Philip, trs. The Philokalia, Vol. 1: The Complete Text Compiled By St. Nikodimos of the Holy Mountain & St. Markarios of Corinth, Vol. 1. 384p. 1983. pap. 9.95 (ISBN 0-571-13013-5). Faber & Faber.

PHILOSOPHY AND SCIENCE

see Science-Philosophy

PHILOSOPHY IN LITERATURE

Carroll, Lewis. The Philosopher's Alice: Alice's Adventures in Wonderland & Through the Looking-Glass. (Illus.). 256p. 1983. pap. 7.95 (ISBN 0-312-60518-8). St Martin.

Lang, Berel. F A C E S... & Other Ironies of Writing & Reading. 100p. 1983. 9.75 (ISBN 0-915145-49-9). Hackett Pub.

PHILOSOPHY OF HISTORY

see History-Philosophy

PHILOSOPHY OF LANGUAGE

see Languages-Philosophy

PHILOSOPHY OF LAW

see Law-Philosophy

PHILOSOPHY OF LITERATURE

see Literature-Philosophy

PHILOSOPHY OF MEDICINE

see Medicine-Philosophy

PHILOSOPHY OF NATURE

see also Cosmology

Hastings, R. Nature & Reason in the Decameron. 1975. 22.50 (ISBN 0-7190-1281-3). Manchester.

PHILOSOPHY OF TEACHING

see Education-Philosophy

PHOBIAS

Clarke, J. Christopher & Jackson, Arthur. Hypnosis & Behavior Therapy: The Treatment of Anxiety & Phobias. 1983. text ed. price not set (ISBN 0-8261-3450-5). Springer Pub.

PHOCAENA

see Porpoises

PHOENIX, ARIZONA

Greater Phoenix Street Maps & Street Directory. 96p. 3.00 (ISBN 0-914846-04-3). Golden West Pub.

PHONETICS

see also Speech

also subdivision Phonetics, Phonology, and Pronunciation under names of languages, e.g. English Language-Phonetics

Kohler, K., ed. Pitch Analysis: Journal: Phonetica, Vol. 39, No. 4-5, 1982. (Illus.). 156p. 1982. pap. 56.50 (ISBN 3-8055-3670-4). S Karger.

Singh, Sadanand & Singh, Kala S. Phonetics: Principles & Practices. 2nd ed. (Illus.). 288p. 1983. pap. 14.95 (ISBN 0-8391-1701-9, 16411). Univ Park.

PHONICS

see Reading (Elementary)-Phonetic Method

PHONODISCS

see Phonorecords

PHONOGRAPH

see also Phonorecords; Sound-Recording and Reproducing

Haas, W. Phono-Graphic Translation. 1970. 14.50 (ISBN 0-7190-0394-6). Manchester.

PHONOGRAPH RECORDS

see Phonorecords

PHONOGRAPHY

see Shorthand

PHONOLOGY

see Phonetics

also subdivisions Phonetics, Phonology, and Pronunciation under names of languages, e.g. French Language-Phonetics; English Language-Phonology; Italian Language-Pronunciation

PHONORECORD COLLECTING

Records. (What's It Worth Ser.). Date not set. pap. 2.95 (ISBN 0-686-82603-5). Dell.

PHONORECORDS

see also Music-Discography; Phonotapes

Blaukopf, K., ed. The Phonogram in Cultural Communications. (Illus.). 180p. 1983. pap. 24.00 (ISBN 0-387-81725-5). Springer-Verlag.

Greenfield, Edward, et al. The New Penguin Stereo Record & Cassette Guide. 832p. (Orig.). 1983. pap. 12.95 (ISBN 0-14-046500-6). Penguin.

Mawhinney, Paul C., ed. Musicmaster: The 45 R.P.M. Record Directory, 2 vols. 2500p. (Orig.). 1983. Title directory. pap. write for info. (ISBN 0-910925-01-1); Artist directory. pap. write for info. (ISBN 0-910925-00-3); Set. pap. 150.00 (ISBN 0-910925-02-X). Record-Rama.

Roys, H. E., ed. Disc Recording & Reproduction. LC 77-17927. (Benchmark Papers in Acoustic Ser.: Vol. 12). 416p. 1978. 48.50 (ISBN 0-87933-309-X). Hutchinson Ross.

Rust, Brian. The American Record Label Book: From the Mid-19th Century Through 1942. (Roots of Jazz Ser.). 1983. Repr. of 1978 ed. lib. bdg. 29.50 (ISBN 0-306-76211-0). Da Capo.

PHONORECORDS-BIBLIOGRAPHY

Gray, Michael H. & Gibson, Gerald D. Bibliography of Discographies: Vol. 3: Popular Music. 200p. 1983. 37.50 (ISBN 0-8352-1683-7). Bowker.

Maleady, Antoinette O. Index to Record & Tape Reviews: A Classical Music Buying Guide, 1981. LC 72-3355. 57.50x (ISBN 0-917600-07-X). Chulainn Press.

PHONORECORDS-REVIEWS

Maleady, Antoinette O. Index to Record & Tape Reviews: A Classical Music Buying Guide, 1981. LC 72-3355. 57.50x (ISBN 0-917600-07-X). Chulainn Press.

PHONOTAPES

Burgett, Gordon L. How To Produce & Market Your Own Audio Cassettes. 100p. 1983. pap. 7.95 (ISBN 0-9605078-3-3). Successful Sem.

Greenfield, Edward, et al. The New Penguin Stereo Record & Cassette Guide. 832p. (Orig.). 1983. pap. 12.95 (ISBN 0-14-046500-6). Penguin.

PHONOTAPES-BIBLIOGRAPHY

Maleady, Antoinette O. Index to Record & Tape Reviews: A Classical Music Buying Guide, 1981. LC 72-3355. 57.50x (ISBN 0-917600-07-X). Chulainn Press.

PHONOTYPY

see Stenotypy

PHOSPHATES

Becker. Phosphates & Phosphoric Acid. (Fertilizer Science & Technology Ser.). 592p. 1983. price not set (ISBN 0-8247-1712-0). Dekker.

PHOSPHORIC ACID

Becker. Phosphates & Phosphoric Acid. (Fertilizer Science & Technology Ser.). 592p. 1983. price not set (ISBN 0-8247-1712-0). Dekker.

PHOSPHORUS

see also Organophosphorus Compounds

Grayson, Martin & Griffith, E. J. Topics in Phosphorus Chemistry, Vol. 2. 352p. 1983. 80.00 (ISBN 0-471-89628-4, Pub. by Wiley-Interscience). Wiley.

Quin, Louis D. & Verkade, John G., eds. Phosphorus Chemistry: Proceedings in the 1981 International Conference. (ACS Symposium Ser.: No. 171). 1981. write for info. (ISBN 0-8412-0663-5). Am Chemical.

PHOSPHORUS ORGANIC COMPOUNDS

see Organophosphorus Compounds

PHOTOBIOLOGY

Eisenthal, K. B., et al, eds. Picosecond Phenomena III, Garmisch Partenkirchen, FRG, 1982: Proceedings. (Springer Series in Chemical Physics: Vol. 23). (Illus.). 401p. 1983. 30.00 (ISBN 0-387-11912-4). Springer-Verlag.

PHOTOCELLS

see Photoelectric Cells

PHOTOCHEMISTRY

see also Photobiology

Buchard, O. Photochemistry of Heterocyclic Compounds. LC 75-33855. 622p. 1976. 97.50x (ISBN 0-471-11510-X). Wiley.

Eisenthal, K. B., et al, eds. Picosecond Phenomena III, Garmisch Partenkirchen, FRG, 1982: Proceedings. (Springer Series in Chemical Physics: Vol. 23). (Illus.). 401p. 1983. 30.00 (ISBN 0-387-11912-4). Springer-Verlag.

Photochemical Smog: Contribution of Volatile Organic Compounds. 98p. 1982. pap. 9.50 (ISBN 92-64-12297-4). OECD.

PHOTOELECTRIC CELLS

see also Remote Control

American Institute of Architects. Architect's Handbook of Energy Practice: Photovoltaics. (Illus.). 56p. 1982. pap. 18.00x (ISBN 0-913962-56-2). Am Inst Arch.

Buresch, M. Photovoltaic Energy Systems: Design & Installation. 352p. 1983. 24.50 (ISBN 0-07-008952-3, P&RB). McGraw.

Flavin, Christopher. Electricity from Sunlight: The Future of Photovoltaics. LC 82-62631. (Worldwatch Papers). 1982. pap. 2.00 (ISBN 0-916468-50-X). Worldwatch Inst.

Jacques, J. A. Respiratory Physiology. 1979. text ed. 27.95 (ISBN 0-07-032247-3). McGraw.

Marier, Donald & Winkle, Carl. Alternative Sources of Energy-Wind-Photovoltaics, No. 58. (Orig.). 1982. pap. 3.50 (ISBN 0-917328-48-5). ASEI.

Maycock, Paul D. & Stirewalt, Edward N. Photovoltaics: Sunlight to Electricity in One Step. 1981. 19.95 (ISBN 0-931790-24-7). Brick Hse Pub.

PHOTOELECTRICITY

see also Photoelectronic Devices; Photonuclear Reactions

Anderson, R. T., et al. Reliability Analysis Methodology for Photovoltaic Energy Systems. (Progress in Solar Energy Ser.). 142p. 1983. pap. 13.50 (ISBN 0-89553-132-1). Am Solar Energy.

Palz, W. Photovoltaic Power Generation. 1982. 49.50 (ISBN 90-277-1386-3, Pub. by Reidel Holland). Kluwer Boston.

Photovoltaic System Design. (Illus.). 1982. 59.95 (ISBN 0-918984-04-1). Solarvision.

PHOTOELECTRONIC DEVICES

see also Computers-Optical Equipment; Image Converters; Information Display Systems; Lasers; Photoelectric Cells; Solar Batteries

Carlson, T. A. X-Ray Photoelectron Spectroscopy. LC 77-28499. (Benchmark Papers in Physical Chemistry & Chemical Physics: Vol. 2). 341p. 1978. 51.00 (ISBN 0-87933-325-1). Hutchinson Ross.

Ghosh, P. K. Introduction to Photoelectron Spectroscopy. (Chemical Analysis: A Series of Monographs on Analytical Chemisty & Its Applications). 352p. 1983. 40.00 (ISBN 0-471-06427-0, Pub. by Wiley-Interscience). Wiley.

PHOTOGRAMMETRY

Atkinson, K. B. Developments in Close Range Photogrammetry, Vol. 1. 1982. 45.00 (ISBN 0-85334-882-0, Pub. by Applied Sci England). Elsevier.

Multilingual Dictionary of Remote Sensing & Photogrammetry. 1983. write for info. (ISBN 0-937294-46-2). ASP.

National Symposium. The Profession in Private Practice (Surveying, Photogrammetry) Proceedings of the National Symposium, 1982. 1983. 15.00 (ISBN 0-937294-43-8). ASP.

Survey of the Profession: Photogrammetry, Surveying, Mapping, Remote Sensing. 1982. pap. 150.00 (ISBN 0-937294-40-3). ASP.

PHOTOGRAPHERS

Art Director's Index to Photographers & Illustrators, No. 9. (Orig.). 1983. pap. 24.95 (ISBN 0-686-82534-9, Pub. by Roto-Vision Switzerland). Norton.

Collier, Kathleen W. & Ross, Mary C. Joseph Collier, Pioneer Photographer. (Illus.). 1983. price not set (ISBN 0-87108-633-6). Pruett.

Constantine, Mildred. Tina Modotti: A Fragile Life. (Illus.). 224p. 1983. 30.00. Rizzoli Intl.

Dixon, Penelope & Ryan, Fortune. Photographers of the Farm Security Association: An Annotated Bibliography. LC 81-43333. 250p. 1983. lib. bdg. 30.00. Garland Pub.

Held, Michael & Naylor, Colin. Contemporary Photographers. 1024p. 1982. 70.00x (ISBN 0-312-16791-1). St Martin.

O'Neal, Hank. Berenice Abbott: American Photographer. LC 82-9887. 256p. 1982. 59.95 (ISBN 0-07-047551-2, GB). McGraw.

Rudman, Jack. Senior Photographic Machine Operator. (Career Examination Ser.: C-2882). (Cloth bdg. avail. on request). pap. 10.00 (ISBN 0-8373-2882-9). Natl Learning.

Silverman, Jonathan. For the World to See: The Life of Margaret Bourke-White. (Illus.). 224p. 1983. 46.95 (ISBN 0-686-82650-7). Viking Pr.

PHOTOGRAPHERS-CORRESPONDENCE, REMINISCENCES, ETC.

Niccolini, Binora, ed. Women of Vision: Photographic Statements of 20 Women Photographers. LC 82-81435. (Illus.). 128p. (Orig.). 1982. 39.95 (ISBN 0-88101-002-2); pap. 19.95 (ISBN 0-88101-003-0). Unicorn Pub.

PHOTOGRAPHERS-DIRECTORIES

Goldstein, M. & Waldman, S., eds. The Creative Black Book Photography: North America Vol. II. (Illus.). 565p. 1983. 40.00 (ISBN 0-916098-09-5). Friendly Pubns.

PHOTOGRAPHIC APPARATUS AND SUPPLIES

see Photography-Apparatus and Supplies

PHOTOGRAPHIC COMPOSITION

see Composition (Photography)

PHOTOGRAPHIC DARK ROOMS

see Photography-Studios and Dark Rooms

PHOTOGRAPHIC FILM

see Photography-Films

PHOTOGRAPHIC LENSES

see Lenses, Photographic

PHOTOGRAPHIC MEASUREMENTS

see Photogrammetry

PHOTOGRAPHIC PROCESSING

see Photography-Processing

PHOTOGRAPHIC SCREEN PROCESS PRINTING

see Screen Process Printing

PHOTOGRAPHIC SENSITOMETRY

see also Photography-Films

Eggleston. Applied Sensitometry. 1983. write for info. (ISBN 0-240-51144-1). Focal Pr.

PHOTOGRAPHIC SUPPLIES

see Photography-Apparatus and Supplies

PHOTOGRAPHS

Adams, Ansel, photos by. Ansel Adams: Images Nineteen Twenty-Three to Nineteen Seventy-Four. LC 74-78740. (Illus.). 125.00 (ISBN 0-8212-1132-3). NYGS.

Madigan, Mary Jean & Colgan, Susan, eds. Prints & Photographs: Understanding, Appreciating, Collecting. 160p. 1983. pap. text ed. 25.00 (ISBN 0-8230-8006-4, Art & Antiques). Watson-Guptill.

Page, Susanne & Page, Jake. Hopi. LC 81-19037. (Illus.). 240p. 1982. 50.00 (ISBN 0-8109-1082-9). Abrams.

Spender, Humphrey. Worktown People: Photographs from Northern England, 1937-1938. Mulford, Jeremy, ed. (Illus.). 128p. 1982. 14.95 (ISBN 0-905046-20-X). Falling Wall.

PHOTOGRAPHS-CATALOGS

Cassone, Philip & Cassone, Diane. Hand Jobs. (Illus.). 56p. (Orig.). Date not set. pap. 6.95 (ISBN 0-9610082-0-2). Cassone Pr.

PHOTOGRAPHS-EXHIBITIONS

see Photography-Exhibitions

PHOTOGRAPHY

see also Cameras; Cinematography; Color Photography; Composition (Photography); Kirlian Photography; Lenses, Photographic; Macrophotography; Nature Photography; Photomicrography; Stereoscope; Travel Photography also headings beginning with the word Photographic

Alinder, James. The Contact Print, Nineteen Forty-Six to Nineteen Eighty-Two. LC 82-83985. (Untitled Thirty Ser.). (Illus.). 52p. 1982. pap. 15.00 (ISBN 0-933286-32-5). Friends Photography.

Berger, Paul & Searle, Leroy. Rational Space-Radical Time: Idea Networks in Contemporary Photography. (Illus.). 72p. (Orig.). 1983. pap. 14.95 (ISBN 0-686-42833-1). Henry Art.

Camerart Photo Trade Directory. 20th ed. LC 66-98554. (Illus.). 550p. (Orig.). 1982. pap. 32.50x (ISBN 0-8002-3031-0). Intl Pubns Serv.

Completing the Picture. 1983. pap. 26.95 (ISBN 0-8120-2653-5). Barron.

Depardon, Raymond & Taback, Carol, illus. Aperture, No. 89. (Illus.). 80p. 1983. pap. 12.50 (ISBN 0-89381-112-2). Aperture.

Eastman Kodak Company. Quality Enlarging with Kodak B-W Papers (G-1) (Illus.). 156p. Date not set. pap. 10.95 (ISBN 0-87985-279-8). Eastman Kodak.

Eastman Kodak Company Staff, ed. Images, Images, Images: The Book of Programmed Multi-Image Production (S-12) 3rd ed. (Illus.). 264p. 1983. pap. 19.95 (ISBN 0-87985-327-1). Eastman Kodak.

Eifer, Bert. Developing the Creative Edge in Photography. (Illus.). 160p. (Orig.). 1983. pap. 14.95 (ISBN 0-89879-110-3). Writers Digest.

Gambaccini, Peter. The Photographer's Assistant. (Illus.). 224p. 1982. pap. 12.95 (ISBN 0-399-50684-5, Perige). Putnam Pub Group.

Gordon, Paul L., ed. The Book of Film Care. (H-23 Ser.). (Illus.). 130p. (Orig.). Date not set. pap. text ed. price not set (ISBN 0-87985-321-2). Eastman Kodak.

Hayes, Paul W. & Worton, Scott M. Essentials of Photography. (Illus.). 288p. (Orig.). 1983. pap. text ed. 14.95 (ISBN 0-672-97492-4); instr's. guide 3.33 (ISBN 0-672-97494-0); wkbk. 4.80 (ISBN 0-672-97493-2). Bobbs.

Held, Michael & Naylor, Colin. Contemporary Photographers. 1024p. 1982. 70.00x (ISBN 0-312-16791-1). St Martin.

Holmes, Edward. An Age of Cameras. Rev. ed. LC 75-315789. (Illus.). 160p. 1978. 17.50x (ISBN 0-85242-346-2). Intl Pubns Serv.

Horenstein, Henry. Black & White Photography: A Basic Manual. rev. ed. (Illus.). 256p. 1983. 19.45i (ISBN 0-316-37313-3); pap. 9.70i (ISBN 0-316-37314-1). Little.

Jacobs, Mark & Kokrda, Ken. Photography in Focus. rev ed. LC 75-20872. (Illus.). 181p. 1981. pap. 12.95 (ISBN 0-8174-5405-5, Amphoto). Watson-Guptill.

Lyon, Danny, ed. Pictures from the New World. (Illus.). 144p. 1983. pap. 17.95 (ISBN 0-89381-108-4). Aperture.

Oliphant, Dave & Zigal, Thomas, eds. Perspectives on Photography. (Illus.). 180p. 1982. pap. 14.95 (ISBN 0-87959-098-X). U of Tex Hum Res.

Persson, Richard J. The Stock Photographer's Marketing Guide. (Illus., Orig.). 1982. pap. 9.95 (ISBN 0-9608486-0-6). R J Persson Ent.

Photography as a Tool. LC 82-3174. (Life Library of Photography). lib. bdg. 22.60 (ISBN 0-8094-4409-7, Pub. by Time-Life). Silver.

Polaroid Corporation Staff. Photomicrography with Polaroid Land Films. (Illus.). 54p. (Orig.). 1983. pap. 6.95 (ISBN 0-240-51703-2). Butterworth.

--Polaroid Black & White Land Films. (Illus.). 72p. (Orig.). 1983. pap. 6.95 (ISBN 0-240-51705-9). Butterworth.

Travel Photography. LC 81-21206. (Life Library of Photography). lib. bdg. 22.60 (ISBN 0-8094-4405-4, Pub. by Time-Life). Silver.

Walker, Richard & Walker, Robert. Exploring Photography. LC 82-21006. (Illus.). 1983. text ed. 12.80 (ISBN 0-87006-430-4); write for info. wkbk.; write for info. (ISBN 0-87006-432-0). Goodheart.

PHOTOGRAPHY-ANIMATED PICTURES

see Cinematography; Moving-Pictures

PHOTOGRAPHY-APPARATUS AND SUPPLIES

see also Cameras; Lenses, Photographic; Photographic Sensitometry; Photography-Electronic Equipment; Photography-Films; Photography-Studios and Dark Rooms; Photography, High-Speed

Baczynsky, Mark. Making Custom Cameras & Equipment. (Illus.). 44p. 1982. pap. 9.95 (ISBN 0-89816-008-1). Embee Pr.

Photographic Equipment & Supplies. 1982. 495.00 (ISBN 0-686-38435-0, A556). Busn Trend.

PHOTOGRAPHY-COMPOSITION

see Composition (Photography)

PHOTOGRAPHY-DARKROOM TECHNIQUE

see Photography-Processing

PHOTOGRAPHY-DEVELOPING AND DEVELOPERS

Hoffman. Thermodynamic Theory of Latent Image Formation. 1982. pap. 31.95 (ISBN 0-240-51200-6). Focal Pr.

Maude. Enlarging. (Photographer's Library). (Illus.). 1983. pap. 12.95x (ISBN 0-240-51118-2). Focal Pr.

Polaroid Corporation Staff. Storing, Handling, & Preserving Polaroid Photographs. (Illus.). 64p. (Orig.). 1983. pap. 7.95 (ISBN 0-240-51704-0). Butterworth.

PHOTOGRAPHY-ELECTRONIC EQUIPMENT

Flash. (Photographer's Library). (Illus.). 1983. pap. 12.95x (ISBN 0-240-51119-0). Focal Pr.

PHOTOGRAPHY-ENLARGING

Maude. Enlarging. (Photographer's Library). (Illus.). 1983. pap. 12.95x (ISBN 0-240-51118-2). Focal Pr.

PHOTOGRAPHY-EXHIBITIONS

Adams, Ansel, photos by. Ansel Adams: Images Nineteen Twenty-Three to Nineteen Seventy-Four. LC 74-78740. (Illus.). 125.00 (ISBN 0-8212-1132-3). NYGS.

Lavrentjev, Alexander. Rodchenko Photograph. LC 82-60031. (Illus.). 140p. 1982. 25.00 (ISBN 0-8478-0459-3). Rizzoli Intl.

PHOTOGRAPHY-FILMS

Johnson, Ron & Bone, Jan. Understanding the Film: An Introduction to Film Appreciation. (Illus.). 296p. 1981. pap. 11.95 (ISBN 0-8174-6330-5, Amphoto). Waston-Guptill.

Polaroid Corporation Staff. Polaroid Color Films. (Illus.). 56p. 1983. pap. 6.95 (ISBN 0-240-51706-7). Butterworth.

PHOTOGRAPHY-HANDBOOKS, MANUALS, ETC.

see also Cameras; also types subdivided for specific cameras, e.g. Cameras-Types-Leica

Bailey, David. How to Take Better Pictures. (Illus.). 212p. 1983. 29.50 (ISBN 0-937950-03-3). Xavier-Moreau.

Bodin, Fredrick D. How to Get the Best Travel Photographs. 220p. 1982. pap. 14.95 (ISBN 0-930764-40-4). Van Nos Reinhold.

Carlson, Verne & Carlson, Sylvia. Professional Camerman's Handbook. rev ed. (Illus.). 575p. 1981. 24.95 (ISBN 0-8174-5548-5, Amphoto). Waston-Guptill.

Constantine, John & Wallis, Julia. The Thames & Hudson Maunual of Professional Photography. (Thames & Hudson Manual Ser.). (Illus.). 1983. pap. 10.95 (ISBN 0-500-68025-6). Thames Hudson.

DiSante, Theodore. How to Select & Use Medium-Format Cameras. 192p. 1981. pap. 12.95 (ISBN 0-89586-046-5). H P Bks.

Eastman Kodak. Kodak's Pocket Field Guide to 35mm Photography. 1983. pap. price not set (ISBN 0-671-46833-2). S&S.

Eastman Kodak Company, ed. The Joy of Photography. Bd. with More Joy of Photography. 288p. (Illus.). 312p. 1982. Set. pap. 27.90 (ISBN 0-201-99239-6). A-W.

Eder, Joseph M. Ausführliches Handbuch der Photographie: 1891-93, 4 Vols. (Illus.). 476p. Set. pap. 250.00 (ISBN 0-686-82589-6). Saifer.

Editors of Curtin & London, Inc., ed. The Book of 35mm Photography: A Complete Guide for Creative Photographers. (Illus.). 176p. 1983. pap. 15.95 (ISBN 0-930764-41-2). Curtin & London.

Graves, Carson. The Zone System for 35mm Photographers: A Basic Guide to Exposure Control. 128p. 1982. pap. 13.95 (ISBN 0-930764-39-0). Van Nos Reinhold.

H P Books, ed. How to Take Pictures Like a Pro. 96p. 1982. pap. 5.95 (ISBN 0-89586-198-4). H P Bks.

--SLR Tips & Techniques. 96p. 1982. pap. 5.95 (ISBN 0-89586-187-9). H P Bks.

Kilpatrick, David. Creative Thirty-Five Millimeter Photography: How to Use Equipment & Techniques for More Exciting Pictures. 256p. 1983. 24.95 (ISBN 0-8174-3713-4, Amphoto). Watson-Guptill.

Langford, Michael. Michael Langford's 35 MM Handbook. LC 82-48555. 1983. 16.95 (ISBN 0-394-53129-9); pap. 9.95 (ISBN 0-394-71369-9). Knopf.

Schwartz, Ted. Professional Photographer's Handbook. (Illus.). 320p. 1983. 29.50 (ISBN 0-07-055690-3, P&RB). McGraw.

Special Problems. LC 81-18389. (Life Library of Photography). lib. bdg. 22.60 (ISBN 0-8094-4401-1, Pub. by Time-Life). Silver.

PHOTOGRAPHY-HIGH-SPEED

see Photography, High-Speed

PHOTOGRAPHY-HISTORY

Oliphant, Dave & Zigal, Thomas, eds. Perspectives on Photography. (Illus.). 180p. 1982. pap. 14.95 (ISBN 0-87959-098-X). U of Tex Hum Res.

Research Publications Inc. History of Photography: Bibliography & Reel Guide to the Microfilm Collection. LC 82-15002. 91p. 1982. text ed. 55.00 (ISBN 0-89235-058-X). Res Pubns Conn.

PHOTOGRAPHY-LANDSCAPES

see also Photography, Artistic

Bruck, Axel. Practical Landscape Photography. (Practical Ser.). (Illus.). 1983. write for info. (ISBN 0-240-51080-1). Focal Pr.

Hamaya, Hiroshi, photos by. Landscapes. (Illus.). 178p. 1982. 125.00 (ISBN 0-8109-1278-3). Abrams.

PHOTOGRAPHY-LENSES

see Lenses, Photographic

PHOTOGRAPHY-LIGHTING

see also Photography-Portraits-Lighting and Posing

Kilpatrick. Light & Lighting. (Photographer's Library). (Illus.). 1983. pap. 12.95x (ISBN 0-240-51203-0). Focal Pr.

PHOTOGRAPHY-LIGHT FILTERS

Hayman, Rex. Filters. (Photographer's Library). (Illus.). 1983. pap. 12.95x (ISBN 0-240-51114-X). Focal Pr.

PHOTOGRAPHY-MOVING-PICTURES

see Cinematography; Moving-Pictures

PHOTOGRAPHY-PORTRAITS

see also Photography of Children and Youth; Photography of Women; Wedding Photography

Nixon, Nicholas. Photographs by Nicholas Nixon, No. 31. Alinder, James, ed. LC 82-84610. (Illus.). 52p. (Orig.). 1983. pap. 16.00 (ISBN 0-933286-33-3). Friends Photography.

PHOTOGRAPHY-PORTRAITS-LIGHTING AND POSING

Hart, John. Fifty Portrait Lighting Techniques for Pictures That Sell: Demonstrations of Techniques That Can Put You in Business as a Portrait Photographer. 144p. 1983. 22.50 (ISBN 0-8174-3861-0, Amphoto). Watson-Guptill.

PHOTOGRAPHY-PROCESSING

Baczynsky, Mark. Creative Projects & Processes. (Illus.). 54p. 1982. pap. 9.95 (ISBN 0-89816-007-3). Embee Pr.

Coote, Jack H. Monochrome Darkroom Practice. rev. ed. (Illus.). 320p. 1983. pap. 13.95 (ISBN 0-240-51700-8). Butterworth.

Grill, Tom & Scanlon, Mark. The Essential Darkroom Book: A Complete Guide to Black & White Processing. (Illus.). 176p. 1983. pap. 14.95 (ISBN 0-8174-3838-6, Amphoto). Watson-Guptill.

H P Books, ed. Basic Guide to Black & White Darkroom Techniques. 96p. 1982. pap. 5.95 (ISBN 0-89586-196-8). H P Bks.

--Basic Guide to Creative Darkroom Techniques. 96p. 1982. pap. 5.95 (ISBN 0-89586-197-6). H P Bks.

Jacobson. Focalguide to Home Processing. 2nd ed. (Focalguide Ser.). (Illus.). 1982. pap. 7.95 (ISBN 0-240-51017-8). Focal Pr.

Kerr. Focalguide to the Home Studio. (Focalguide Ser.). (Illus.). 1983. pap. 8.95x (ISBN 0-240-50986-2). Focal Pr.

Stecker, Elinor. How to Create & Use High Contrast Images, Vol. 13. 160p. 1982. pap. 9.95 (ISBN 0-89586-143-7). H P Bks.

PHOTOGRAPHY-SENSITOMETRY

see Photographic Sensitometry

PHOTOGRAPHY-SPECIAL EFFECTS

Wade. Special Effects in the Camera. (Photographer's Library). (Illus.). 1983. pap. 12.95x (ISBN 0-240-51184-0). Focal Pr.

PHOTOGRAPHY-STUDIOS AND DARK ROOMS

Here are entered works on the construction and physical layout of studios and dark rooms.

The Studio. LC 82-6011. (Life Library of Photography). lib. bdg. 22.60 (ISBN 0-8094-4417-8, Pub. by Time-Life). Silver.

PHOTOGRAPHY-SUPPLIES

see Photography-Apparatus and Supplies

PHOTOGRAPHY-YEARBOOKS

Cordy, Peter, ed. Creative Source - Fourth Annual. 4th ed. 442p. 1983. 45.00 (ISBN 0-920986-03-X). Wilcord Pubns.

Crawley, Geoffrey, ed. British Journal of Photography Annual 1983. 123rd ed. (Illus.). 222p. 1983. 24.95 (ISBN 0-900414-28-6, Pub. by Henry Greenwood & Co Ltd England). Writers Digest.

Mason, R. H., ed. Photography Yearbook, 1983. LC 36-13575. (Illus.). 256p. 1982. 35.00x (ISBN 0-85242-806-5). Intl Pubns Serv.

Photography Year-1981. LC 72-91518. (Life Library of Photography). lib. bdg. 22.60 (ISBN 0-8094-1690-5, Pub. by Time-Life). Silver.

Photography-1982. LC 72-91518. (Life Library of Photography). lib. bdg. 22.60 (ISBN 0-8094-1694-8, Pub. by Time-Life). Silver.

PHOTOGRAPHY, AERIAL

see also Remote Sensing

Howard. Aerial Photo Ecology. 1971. 18.00 (ISBN 0-444-19768-0). Elsevier.

PHOTOGRAPHY, ARCHITECTURAL
Here are entered works on the photography of buildings. Works on photography as used in architectural drawings are entered under the heading Photography–Reproduction of plans, drawings, etc.
Llewellyn, Robert, photos by. The Academic Village: Thomas Jefferson University. (Illus.). 80p. 1982. 22.50 (ISBN 0-934738-03-3). Thomasson-Grant.

PHOTOGRAPHY, ARTISTIC
Here are entered works on photography as a fine art, including aesthetic theory, as well as books of artistic photographs.
see also Photography–Landscapes; Photography, Close-Up; Photography of Men; Photography of the Nude; Photography of Women
Ackley, Clifford. Photographs from the Museum Collection. (MFA Bulletin: Vol. 80). (Illus.). 80p. 1983. pap. 4.95 (ISBN 0-686-83421-6). Mus Fine Arts Boston.
Ackley, Clifford S. Exposures: Photographs from the Museum Collection. (MFA Bulletin: Vol. 80). (Illus.). 80p. 1983. pap. 4.95 (ISBN 0-87846-229-5). Mus Fine Arts Boston.
Adams, Robert. Selections from the Strauss Photography Collection. LC 82-71437. 40p. (Orig.). 1982. pap. 7.95 (ISBN 0-914738-29-1). Denver Art Mus.
Boettcher, Jurgen. Coffee Houses of Europe. (Illus.). 1983. 29.95 (ISBN 0-500-54063-2). Thames Hudson.
Booth-Clibborn, Edward, ed. European Photography 1982: European Photography & European Illustration. (Illus.). 240p. 1982. 40.00 (ISBN 0-8109-0866-2). Abrams.
Christenberry, William. William Christenberry: Photographs 1961-1981. (Illus.). 96p. 1983. 30.00 (ISBN 0-89381-110-6). Aperture.
Cohen, Stan B. Missoula County Images. (Illus.). 264p. 1982. 19.95 (ISBN 0-933126-24-7). Pictorial Hist.
Davis, Douglas, intro. by. Photography As Fine Art. (Illus.). 224p. 1983. 50.00 (ISBN 0-525-24184-1, 038-83). Dutton.
Dufair. Woman in the Moon. 1982. pap. 3.50 (ISBN 0-686-83906-4). Merging Media.
Eichling, Jeanne. Dogs, 3 Vols. (Illus.). 48p. 1982. 20.00 ea. (ISBN 0-686-82187-4). Vol. I (ISBN 0-88014-051-8). Vol. II (ISBN 0-686-82187-4). Vol. III (ISBN 0-88014-053-4). Mosaic Pr OH.
Enos, Chris. Gar-baj. LC 81-70289. (Illus.). 54p. (Orig.). 1982. pap. 5.00 (ISBN 0-89822-025-4). Visual Studies.
Faucon, Bernard. Summer Camp. (Illus.). 100p. 1982. 22.50 (ISBN 0-937950-00-9). Xavier-Moreau.
Fayman, Danah. The Photographic Art of Lynn G. Fayman. (Illus.). 22p. 1969. 3.00x (ISBN 0-686-99831-6). La Jolla Mus Contemp Art.
Frank, Robert & Model, Lisette. Charles Pratt: Photographs. LC 82-71396. (Illus.). 88p. Date not set. pap. 25.00 (ISBN 0-89381-111-4). Aperture.
Goude, Jean-Paul & Hayes, Harold. Jungle Fever. (Illus.). 144p. 1982. 32.50 (ISBN 0-937950-01-7). Xavier-Moreau.
The Great Themes. LC 82-5530. (Life Library of Photography). lib. bdg. 22.60 (ISBN 0-8094-4413-5, Pub. by Time-Life). Silver.
Greenough, Sarah & Hamilton, Juan, eds. Alfred Stieglitz: Photographs & Writings. LC 82-7925. (Illus.). 248p. 75.00 (ISBN 0-935112-09-X); pap. write for info. (ISBN 0-89468-027-7). Callaway Edns.
Hales, Peter B. Silver Cities: The Photography of American Urbanization. 1983. write for info. (ISBN 0-87722-299-1). Temple U Pr.
Held, Heinz. Laughing Camera I. Reich, Hanns, ed. (Illus.). 1983. pap. 4.95 (ISBN 0-8090-1506-4, Terra Magica). Hill & Wang.
Herdeg, Walter. Photographis Eighty-Three. (Illus.). 264p. 1983. 59.50 (ISBN 0-8038-5897-3). Hastings.
Hockney, David. David Hockney Photographs. 1982. 30.00 (ISBN 0-902825-15-1). Petersburg Pr.
Masayesva, Victor & Younger, Erin, eds. Hopi Photographers-Hopi Images. (Sun Tracks Ser.). 1983. 25.00 (ISBN 0-8165-0809-7); pap. 14.95 (ISBN 0-8165-0804-6). U of Ariz Pr.
Merlo, Lorenzo. Japanese Photography Today & Its Origin. 192p. 1982. pap. 12.95 (ISBN 0-906333-06-7, Pub. by Salem Hse Ltd). Merrimack Bk Serv.
Newton, Helmut. Big Nudes. (Illus.). 80p. 1982. 27.50 (ISBN 0-937950-02-5). Xavier Moreau.
--Sleepless Nights. (Illus.). 1983. pap. 17.50 (ISBN 0-937950-07-6). Xavier-Moreau.
Plattner, Steven W. Witness to the Forties: Roy Stryker & the Standard Oil (New Jersey) Photography Project. (Illus.). 144p. 1983. 19.95 (ISBN 0-292-77028-6). U of Tex Pr.
Rudiak, Il'ia, ed. Our Age: Photographs. 144p. 1983. 25.00 (ISBN 0-88233-814-5); pap. 10.00 (ISBN 0-88233-815-3). Ardis Pubs.
Russel, John, intro. by. Jennifer Bartlett: In the Garden. (Illus.). 208p. 1982. 35.00 (ISBN 0-8109-0709-7). Abrams.
Selz, Peter & Einstein, Susan. Sam Francis. (Illus.). 296p. 1982. 65.00 (ISBN 0-686-82699-X). Abrams.
Timelapse. 1983. write for info. Merging Media.
Walker, Brian M. Shadows on Glass: A Portfolio of Early Ulster Photography. (Illus.). 140p. 1982. 18.00 (ISBN 0-904651-14-2, Pub. by Salem Hse Ltd). Merrimack Bk Serv.
Wieder, Laurance. Man's Best Friend. (Illus.). 64p. 1982. pap. 12.95 (ISBN 0-8109-2266-5). Abrams.

PHOTOGRAPHY, BIOLOGICAL
see Nature Photography; Photography, Submarine; Photomicrography

PHOTOGRAPHY, CLOSE-UP
see also Macrophotography
Bruck, Axel. Practical Close-Up Photography. (Practical Ser.). (Illus.). write for info. (ISBN 0-240-51190-5). Focal Pr.
Ericksenn, Lief & Sincebaugh, Els. Adventures in Close-Up Photography: Rediscovering Familiar Environments Through Details. 144p. 1983. 22.50 (ISBN 0-8174-3501-8, Amphoto). Watson-Guptill.
Watkins, Derek. Close-Ups. (Photographer's Library). (Illus.). 1983. pap. 12.95x (ISBN 0-240-51188-3). Faber & Faber.

PHOTOGRAPHY, COLOR
see Color Photography

PHOTOGRAPHY, COMMERCIAL
see also Photography, Journalistic; Wedding Photography
Kirby. Glamour Photography. (Photographer's Library). (Illus.). 1983. pap. 12.95x (ISBN 0-240-51116-6). Focal Pr.

PHOTOGRAPHY, DOCUMENTARY
Documentary Photography. (Life Library of Photography). 1983. lib. bdg. 22.60 (ISBN 0-686-42785-8, Pub. by Time-Life). Silver.

PHOTOGRAPHY, FASHION
see Fashion Photography

PHOTOGRAPHY, HIGH-SPEED
Dubovik, Alexander. The Photographic Recording of High-Speed Processes. 2nd ed. Aksenov, Arthur, tr. LC 80-17318. 533p. 1981. 79.95x (ISBN 0-471-04204-8, Pub. by Wiley-Interscience). Wiley.

PHOTOGRAPHY, INFRA-RED
Gibson, H. Lou. Photography by Infrared: Its Principles & Applications. 3rd ed. LC 77-26919. (Photographic Science & Technology & Graphic Arts Ser.). 1978. 54.50x (ISBN 0-471-15895-X, Pub. by Wiley-Interscience). Wiley.

PHOTOGRAPHY, JOURNALISTIC
see also Photography of Sports
Canavor, Natalie. Sell Your Photographs: The Complete Marketing Strategy for the Freelancer. 1982. pap. 6.95 (ISBN 0-452-25362-4, Z5362, Plume). NAL.
Photojournalism. LC 82-19149. (Life Library of Photography). lib. bdg. 22.60 (ISBN 0-8094-4429-1, Pub. by Time-Life). Silver.

PHOTOGRAPHY, KIRLIAN
see Kirlian Photography

PHOTOGRAPHY, LENSLESS
see Holography

PHOTOGRAPHY, NUDE
see Photography of the Nude

PHOTOGRAPHY, PICTORIAL
see Photography, Artistic

PHOTOGRAPHY, SUBMARINE
Hall, Howard & Farley, Lauren. Howard Hall's Guide to Successful Underwater Photography. (Illus.). 192p. (Orig.). 1982. pap. text ed. 15.95 (ISBN 0-932248-03-9). Marcor Pub.
Smith, Paul F., ed. Underwater Photography: Scientific & Engineering Applications. (Illus.). 1983. text ed. write for info. Sci Bks Intl.

PHOTOGRAPHY AND ART
see Art and Photography

PHOTOGRAPHY AS A PROFESSION
Baczynsky, Mark. Making Money with Photography. (Illus.). 86p. 1982. pap. 14.95 (ISBN 0-89816-006-5). Embee Pr.
Brackman, Henrietta. The Perfect Portfolio: Guidelines for Creating a Portfolio That Sells. 192p. 1983. price not set (Amphoto). Watson-Guptill.
Hart, John. Fifty Portrait Lighting Techniques for Pictures That Sell: Demonstrations of Techniques That Can Put You in Business as a Portrait Photographer. 144p. 1983. 22.50 (ISBN 0-8174-3861-0, Amphoto). Watson-Guptill.

PHOTOGRAPHY IN ARCHAEOLOGY
Wilson, David. Air Photo Interpretation For Archaeologists. LC 82-10679. (Illus.). 224p. 1982. 29.95x (ISBN 0-312-01527-5). St Martin.

PHOTOGRAPHY OF ART
Saotome, Mitsugi. Aikido & the Harmony of Nature. (Illus.). 330p. (Orig.). 1983. 25.75 (ISBN 0-8038-0487-3); pap. 17.95 (ISBN 0-8038-0403-2). Hastings.

PHOTOGRAPHY OF CHILDREN AND YOUTH
Franklin, Linda C. Baby Pictures. (Old Fashioned Keepbook Photo Albums Ser.). (Illus.). 32p. 1982. 17.50 (ISBN 0-934504-15-6). Tree Comm.
Photographing Children. LC 82-16733. (Life Library of Photography). lib. bdg. 22.60 (ISBN 0-8094-2976-4, Pub. by Time-Life). Silver.

PHOTOGRAPHY OF MEN
Hardy, Karen. Not Just Another Pretty Face: An Intimate Look at America's Top Male Models. 1984. 11.95 (ISBN 0-452-25395-0, Plume). NAL.

PHOTOGRAPHY OF NATURE
see Nature Photography

PHOTOGRAPHY OF SPORTS
see also Photography, Journalistic; Sports
McQuilkin, Robert. How to Photograph Sports & Action, Vol. 15. 160p. 1982. pap. 9.95 (ISBN 0-89586-145-3). H P Bks.

PHOTOGRAPHY OF THE MALE
see Photography of Men

PHOTOGRAPHY OF THE NUDE
Clergue. Practical Nude Photography. (Practical Ser.). (Illus.). 1983. 22.95x (ISBN 0-240-51202-2). Focal Pr.
Newton, Helmut. Big Nudes. (Illus.). 80p. 1982. 27.50 (ISBN 0-937950-02-5). Xavier Moreau.

PHOTOGRAPHY OF TRAINS
Siviter, R. E. A Handbook of Railway Photography. (Illus.). 128p. 1983. 24.95 (ISBN 0-7153-8265-9). David & Charles.

PHOTOGRAPHY OF WOMEN
Liffring-Zug, Joan, photos by. Women Nineteen Fifty-Seven to Nineteen Seventy-Five. (Illus.). 72p. 20.50 (ISBN 0-9603858-5-1); pap. 10.50 (ISBN 0-9603858-4-3). Penfield.

PHOTOJOURNALISM
see Journalism, Pictorial; Photography, Journalistic

PHOTOLYSIS (CHEMISTRY)
see Photochemistry

PHOTOMACROGRAPHY
see Macrophotography

PHOTOMETRY
see also Color; Flame; Photometry; Light; Optics
Wolpert, Robert C. & Genet, Russell M. Advances in Photoelectric Photometry. LC 82-84767. 200p. (Orig.). 1983. pap. 18.95 (ISBN 0-911351-01-9). Fairborn Observ.

PHOTOMETRY, ASTRONOMICAL
Ghedini, Silvano. Software for Photometric Astronomy. LC 82-8574. (Illus.). 1982. pap. text ed. 26.95 (ISBN 0-943396-00-X). Willman-Bell.

PHOTOMICROGRAPHY
see also Microscope and Microscopy
Gunn. Manual of Document Photomicrography. 1983. 91.95x (ISBN 0-240-51146-8). Focal Pr.
Spitta, Edmund. Photo-Micrography 1899. (Illus.). 163p. pap. 35.00 (ISBN 0-87556-580-8). Saifer.

PHOTONUCLEAR REACTIONS
see also Photoelectricity
Rahman, N. K. & Guidotti, C., eds. Photon-Assisted Collisions & Related Topics. 377p. 1982. 63.50 (ISBN 0-686-84008-9). Harwood Academic.

PHOTOPLAYS
see Moving-Picture Plays

PHOTOPSYCHOGRAPHY
see Kirlian Photography

PHOTOTUBES
see Photoelectric Cells

PHOTOTYPESETTING
Labuz, Ronald. Interfacing in the Eighties: How to Set up Communications Between Word Processors & Phototypesetters. 1983. pap. 3.95 (ISBN 0-86610-125-X). Meridian Pub.

PHOTOGRAPHY
see Phototypesetting

PHOTOVOLTAIC CELLS
see Photoelectric Cells

PHYLOGEOGRAPHY–MAPS
Moore, D. M., ed. Green Planet: The Story of Plant Life on Earth. LC 82-4287. (Illus.). 288p. 1982. 27.50 (ISBN 0-521-24610-5). Cambridge U Pr.

PHYSICAL ANTHROPOLOGY
see also Blood Groups; Children–Growth; Color of Man; Fossil Man; Human Behavior; Human Biology; Human Evolution; Human Genetics; Human Mechanics; Man–Influence of Environment; Primates; Race
Hooton, Ernest A. Indians of Pecos Pueblo. 1930. text ed. 175.00x (ISBN 0-686-83582-4). Elliots Bks.
Iscan, M. Yasar, ed. A Topical Guide to the American Journal of Physical Anthropology. LC 82-21696. 234p. 1983. 24.00 (ISBN 0-8451-0224-9). A R Liss.
Kelemon, Stanley. Somatic Reality. LC 79-88485. 1979. 7.95 (ISBN 0-686-82345-1). Sci & Behavior.
Wolfe, Linda D. Physical Anthropology: A Laboratory Text. (Illus.). 180p. 1983. pap. text ed. 10.95 (ISBN 0-89892-049-3). Contemp Pub Co of Raleigh.

PHYSICAL CHEMISTRY
see Chemistry, Physical and Theoretical

PHYSICAL CULTURE
see Physical Education and Training

PHYSICAL CULTURE PHOTOGRAPHY
see Photography of Men

PHYSICAL DISTRIBUTION OF GOODS
see also Inventory Control; Packaging; Warehouses
Lambert, Douglas M. The Distribution Channels Decision. 197p. pap. 14.95 (ISBN 0-86641-037-6, 78100). Natl Assn Accts.
Ramachandran, H. Behaviour in Space: Rural Marketing in an Underdeveloped Economy. 121p. 1982. text ed. 14.50x (ISBN 0-391-02784-0, 40855, Pub. by Concept India). Humanities.

PHYSICAL EDUCATION AND TRAINING
see also Athletics; Coaching (Athletics); Exercise; Games; Gymnastics; Health Education; Jiu-Jitsu; Physical Education As a Profession; Physical Education for Children; Physical Education for Handicapped Persons; Physical Education for Women; Physical Fitness; Posture; Sports
also names of sports or exercises, e.g. Football; also apparatus used in gymnasiums
Adapted Physical Education Guidelines: Theory & Practices for 70's & 80's. 128p. 1976. 8.95 (ISBN 0-88314-006-3). AAHPERD.
Barrow, Harold M. Man & Movement: Principles of Physical Education. 3rd ed. LC 82-20398. 410p. 1983. text ed. write for info. (ISBN 0-8121-0861-2). Lea & Febiger.
Bass, Clarence. Ripped Two. (Illus.). 179p. 1982. pap. 12.95 (ISBN 0-9609714-1-6). Clarence Bass.
Bucher, Charles A. Foundations of Physical Education & Sport. 9th ed. LC 82-3495. (Illus.). 642p. 1983. pap. text ed. 19.95 (ISBN 0-8016-0868-6). Mosby.
Carnes, Ralph & Carnes, Valerie. Sportspower. (Illus.). 256p. 1982. 14.95 (ISBN 0-312-75344-6). St Martin.
Clayton, Robert D. & Clayton, Joyce A. Concepts & Careers in Physical Education. 3rd ed. 174p. 1982. pap. text ed. 9.95x (ISBN 0-8087-2972-1). Burgess.
Completed Research in Health, Physical Education, Recreation & Dance, Vol. 22. 1980. 9.25 (ISBN 0-686-38058-4). AAHPERD.
Comprehensive Bicyclists Education Program (CBEP) incl. 7 cassettes, 7 filmstrips & 3 modules 99.50 (ISBN 0-88314-225-2); Module I The Bicycling Environment. 40.00 (ISBN 0-88314-226-0); Module II Haxard Awareness. 40.00 (ISBN 0-88314-227-9); Module III Riding with Trafic. 40.00 (ISBN 0-88314-228-7); Basic Bicycling. 4.50 (ISBN 0-686-38062-2). AAHPERD.
Cox, Deborah & Davis, Juliet. Thirty Days to a Beautiful Bottom. 1982. pap. 2.95 (ISBN 0-553-01472-2). Bantam.
Crowder, Vernon & Jolly, Sonny. Concepts of Physical Education. (Illus., Orig.). pap. text ed. 8.95 (ISBN 0-88136-002-3). Jostens.
Fiore, Evely. YWCA Way to Tropical Fitness. LC 82-445639. 192p. 1983. pap. 9.95 (ISBN 0-385-18472-7). Doubleday.
Freidberg, Ardy. Fully Fit in Sixty Minutes a Week: The Complete Shape-Up Program for Men. (Illus.). 64p. 1983. pap. 2.95 (ISBN 0-943392-06-3). Tribeca Comm.
Harrison, Joyce M. Instructional Strategies for Physical Education. 510p. 1983. text ed. write for info. (ISBN 0-697-07205-3). Wm C Brown.
Johnson, Leslie & Schade, Charlene. Rhythmic Aerobex: Workbook. 98p. 1982. 22.95 (ISBN 0-9610234-0-6). Rhythmic Aerobex.
Making Workshops Work in Physical Education & Recreation for Special Populations. 80p. 1976. 3.95 (ISBN 0-88314-128-0). AAHPERD.
Neal, Larry L., ed. The Next Fifty Years: Health, Physical Education, Recreation, Dance. 179p. 1971. pap. 3.50 (ISBN 0-686-84034-8). U OR Ctr Leisure.
Physical Education & Sport for the Secondary School Student. 1983. write for info. AAHPERD.
Physical Education Gold Book: 1982-1984. 448p. 1982. 15.00x (ISBN 0-931250-33-1). Human Kinetics.
Reunification. (Papers of the American Academy of Physical Education: No. 15). 133p. 8.95 (ISBN 0-88314-014-4). AAHPERD.
Rudman, Jack. Director of Physical Development. (Career Examination Ser.: C-914). (Cloth bdg. avail. on request). pap. 14.00 (ISBN 0-8373-0914-X). Natl Learning.
Schmottlach, Neil & Clayton, Irene. Physical Education Handbook. 7th ed. 448p. 1983. 17.95 (ISBN 0-13-667535-2); pap. 14.95 (ISBN 0-13-667527-1). P-H.
Stockholm, Alan J. A Biomechanics Manual for Coaches & Physical Educators. (Illus.). 125p. 1983. pap. 7.50 (ISBN 0-935496-03-3). AC Pubns.
Streicher, M. Reshaping Physical Education. 1970. 20.00 (ISBN 0-7190-0412-8). Manchester.
Sullivan, Molly. Feeling Strong, Feeling Free: Movement Exploration for Young Children. LC 82-61730. 161p. 1982. pap. text ed. 5.50 (ISBN 0-912674-82-2, 100). Natl Assn Child Ed.
What Every Person Should Know about the New Physical Education. 8.95 (ISBN 0-88314-203-1). AAHPERD.

PHYSICAL EDUCATION AND TRAINING–ADMINISTRATION
Assessment Guide for Secondary School Physical Education Programs. 25p. 3.50 (ISBN 0-88314-020-9). AAHPERD.
Bucher, Charles A. Administration of Physical Education & Athletic Programs. 8th ed. LC 82-6479. (Illus.). 632p. 1983. pap. text ed. 21.95 (ISBN 0-8016-0852-X). Mosby.
Complying with Title IX in Physical Education & High School Sports Programs. 20p. 3.50 (ISBN 0-88314-048-9). AAHPERD.
Essentials of a Quality Elementary School Physical Education Program. 16p. 1.95 (ISBN 0-88314-067-5). AAHPERD.
Fuoss, D. E. & Troppman, R. J. Creative Management Techniques in Interscholastic Athletics. LC 76-46500. 494p. 1977. 25.50x (ISBN 0-471-28815-2). Wiley.
Guidelines for Secondary School Physical Education. 12p. 1.50 (ISBN 0-88314-094-2). AAHPERD.
Professional Prepartation in Adapted Physical Education, Therapeutic Recreation & Corrective Therapy. 136p. 1976. 7.95 (ISBN 0-88314-144-2). AAHPERD.
Zeigler, Earle F. Decision Making in Physical Education & Athletics Administration: A Case Method Approach. 181p. 1982. pap. text ed. 10.00x (ISBN 0-87563-221-1). Stipes.

PHYSICAL EDUCATION AND TRAINING–HISTORY
Lee, Mabel. History of Physical Education & Sports in the U. S. A. 384p. 1983. text ed. 16.95 (ISBN 0-471-86315-7). Wiley.

PHYSICAL EDUCATION AND TRAINING–MEDICAL ASPECTS
see Sports Medicine
PHYSICAL EDUCATION AND TRAINING–RESEARCH
Abstracts of Research Papers: Boston. 1981. 4.50 (ISBN 0-88314-003-9). AAHPERD.
Abstracts of Research Papers: Detroit. 1980. 4.25 (ISBN 0-88314-002-0). AAHPERD.
Abstracts of Research Papers: Houston. 1982. 4.50 (ISBN 0-88314-001-2). AAHPERD.
Completed Research in Health, Physical Education, Recreation & Dance, Vol.19. 1977. 9.25 (ISBN 0-88314-044-6). AAHPERD.
Completed Research in Health, Physical Education, Recreation & Dance, Vol. 20. 1978. write for info. (ISBN 0-88314-045-4). AAHPERD.
Completed Research in Health, Physical Education, Recreation & Dance, Vol. 24. 1983. 10.95 (ISBN 0-686-38056-8). AAHPERD.
Research Consortium Symposium Papers 1981. 79p. 4.75 (ISBN 0-88314-150-7). AAHPERD.
Research Consortium Symposium Papers 1980. 96p. 3.95 (ISBN 0-88314-149-3). AAHPERD.
Research on Dance, Vol. III. 176p. 7.95 (ISBN 0-88314-153-1). AAHPERD.
PHYSICAL EDUCATION AND TRAINING–STUDY AND TEACHING
Bucher, Charles A. & Koenig, Constance R. Methods & Materials for Secondary School Physical Education. 6th ed. (Illus.). 454p. 1983. pap. text ed. 20.95 (ISBN 0-8016-0874-0). Mosby.
Directory of Graduate Physical Education Programs 1982. 80p. 11.95 (ISBN 0-88314-058-6). AAHPERD.
Directory of Undergraduate Physical Education Programs 1982. 96p. 11.95 (ISBN 0-88314-059-4). AAHPERD.
PHYSICAL EDUCATION AND TRAINING–TEACHER TRAINING
Bucher, Charles A. & Koenig, Constance R. Methods & Materials for Secondary School Physical Education. 6th ed. (Illus.). 454p. 1983. pap. text ed. 20.95 (ISBN 0-8016-0874-0). Mosby.
PHYSICAL EDUCATION AND TRAINING–AUSTRALIA
Jowitt, Glenn. Race Day. (Illus.). 96p. 1982. 24.95 (ISBN 0-00-216998-3, Pub. by W Collins Australia). Intl Schol Bk Serv.
PHYSICAL EDUCATION AS A PROFESSION
Fordham, Sheldon L. & Leaf, Carol A. Physical Education & Sports: An Introduction to Alternative Careers. LC 77-19115. 385p. 1978. text ed. 25.95x (ISBN 0-471-26622-1). Wiley.
Opportunities in Recreation & Leisure. (Leisure Today Ser.). 123p. 7.95 (ISBN 0-686-84055-0). AAHPERD.
PHYSICAL EDUCATION FOR CHILDREN
see also Physical Education for Handicapped Persons; Physical Education for Mentally Handicapped Children
Essentials of a Quality Elementary School Physical Education Program. 16p. 1.95 (ISBN 0-88314-067-5). AAHPERD.
Humphrey, James H. Child Development Through Physical Education. (Illus.). 200p. 1980. 14.75 (ISBN 0-398-03561-X). C C Thomas.
Wickstrom, Ralph L. Fundamental Motor Patterns. 3rd ed. LC 82-21659. (Illus.). 250p. 1983. text ed. price not set (ISBN 0-8121-0879-5). Lea & Febiger.
PHYSICAL EDUCATION FOR HANDICAPPED PERSONS
Dance for Physically Disabled Persons: A Manual for Teaching Ballroom, Square & Folk Dances to Users of Wheelchairs & Crutches. 128p. 1976. 7.95 (ISBN 0-88314-056-X). AAHPERD.
Physical Education, Recreation, & Related Programs for Autistic & Emotionally Disturbed Children. 128p. 1976. 8.95 (ISBN 0-88314-141-8). AAHPERD.
PHYSICAL EDUCATION FOR MENTALLY HANDICAPPED CHILDREN
Physical Activities for the Mentally Retarded: Ideas for Instruction. 137p. 1968. 4.95 (ISBN 0-88314-221-X). AAHPERD.
Physical Education & Recreation for Impaired, Disabled, & Handicapped Individuals: Past, Present, Future. 432p. 1975. 13.50 (ISBN 0-88314-137-X). AAHPERD.
Practical Guide for Teaching the Mentally Retarded to Swim. 160p. 1969. 5.95 (ISBN 0-88314-174-4). AAHPERD.
Programming for the Mentally Retarded in Physical Education & Recreation. 144p. 1968. 6.95 (ISBN 0-88314-147-7). AAHPERD.
Resource Guide to Team Soccer for the Mentally Handicapped. 80p. 1971. 4.50 (ISBN 0-88314-152-3). AAHPERD.
PHYSICAL EDUCATION FOR THE BLIND
see Blind, Physical Education for The
PHYSICAL EDUCATION FOR WOMEN
see also Gymnastics for Women; Sports for Women
Combes, Laura. Winning Women's Bodybuilding. Reynolds, Bill, ed. (Illus.). 176p. (Orig.). 1983. pap. 7.95 (ISBN 0-8092-5616-9). Contemp Bks.
Friedberg, Ardy. Fully Fit in Sixty Minutes a Week: The Complete Shape-Up Program for Women. (Illus.). 64p. 1983. pap. 2.95 (ISBN 0-943392-07-1). Tribeca Comm.
Madaras, Lynda. What's Happening to My Body? The Growing-Up Book for Mothers & Daughters. (Illus.). 192p. (gr. 4 up). 1983. 14.95 (ISBN 0-937858-25-0); pap. 7.95 (ISBN 0-937858-21-8). Newmarket.
Peterson, Susan L. The Women's Stretching Book. LC 82-83927. (Illus.). 144p. (Orig.). 1983. pap. 6.95 (ISBN 0-88011-095-3). Leisure Pr.
Rosen, Trix. Strong & Sexy: The New Body Beautiful. (Illus.). 144p. (Orig.). 1983. pap. 9.95 (ISBN 0-933328-59-1). Delilah Bks.
Welch, Raquel. Raquel Welch's Health & Beauty Book. (Illus.). Date not set. pap. price not set. NAL.
PHYSICAL ENDURANCE
see Physical Fitness
PHYSICAL FITNESS
see also Muscle Strength
BALPA Medical Study Group. Fit to Fly: A Medical Handbook for Pilots. 80p. 1980. pap. text ed. 5.25x (ISBN 0-246-11401-0, Pub. by Granada England). Renouf.
Bogdonoff, Morton D. Forever Fit: The Exercise Program for Men & Women Over Forty. (Illus.). 224p. 1983. 22.00i (ISBN 0-316-10085-4); pap. 10.45i (ISBN 0-316-10086-2). Little.
Cavnar, Rebecca. Winning at Losing: A Complete Program for Losing Weight & Keeping it off. (Illus.). 150p. 1983. pap. 4.95 (ISBN 0-686-82582-9). Servant.
Chaffee, Suzy & Adler, Bill. The I Love New York Fitness Book. (Illus.). 224p. 1983. 17.95 (ISBN 0-688-02040-2). Morrow.
Columbu, Franco. Franco Columbu's Complete Book of Bodybuilding. (Illus.). 160p. 1983. pap. 8.95 (ISBN 0-8092-5983-4). Contemp Bks.
Delmontegue, Robert. Man's Common Sense Guide to Physical Fitness. (Illus.). 156p. 1982. pap. 5.95 (ISBN 0-88254-707-0). Hippocrene Bks.
DeLyser, Femmy. Jane Fonda's Workout Book for Pregnancy, Birth & Recovery. 1982. 16.95 (ISBN 0-671-43219-2). S&S.
DeVries, Herbert A. & Hales, Dianne. Fitness After 50. (Illus.). 192p. 1983. pap. 5.95 (ISBN 0-686-83789-4, ScribT). Scribner.
Dietrich, John & Waggoner, Susan. The Complete Health Club Handbook. (Orig.). 1983. pap. price not set (ISBN 0-671-47027-2). S&S.
DiGennaro, Joseph. The New Physical Fitness: Exercise for Everybody. (Illus.). 1983. pap. text ed. 6.95X (ISBN 0-89582-097-8). Morton Pub.
Dominguez, Richard H. & Gajda, Robert J. Total Body Training. 288p. 1983. pap. 7.95 (ISBN 0-686-84718-0). Warner Bks.
Edwards, Sally. Triathlon: A Triple Fitness Sport. (Illus.). 224p. (Orig.). 1983. pap. 6.95 (ISBN 0-8092-5555-3). Contemp Bks.
Eschenbach, Vilfred. The Wall Street Maximal Physical Fitness Handbook. (Illus.). 109p. 1983. 55.85 (ISBN 0-86654-065-2). Inst Econ Finan.
Fit Magazine Editors. Breast Care. (Fit Self-Improvement Ser.). 96p. 1983. pap. 7.95 (ISBN 0-89037-259-4). Anderson World.
--Figure Maintenance. (Fit Self-Improvement Ser.). 96p. 1983. pap. 7.95 (ISBN 0-89037-255-1). Anderson World.
--Legs & Thifgs. (Fit Self-Improvement Ser.). 96p. 1983. pap. 7.95 (ISBN 0-89037-260-8). Anderson World.
Getchell, Bud. Physical Fitness: A Way of Life. 2nd ed. LC 78-13094. 1979. pap. text ed. 12.95 (ISBN 0-471-04037-1); avail tchr's manual (ISBN 0-471-04985-9). Wiley.
--Physical Fitness: A Way of Life. 3rd ed. LC 82-17654. 258p. 1983. text ed. 12.95 (ISBN 0-471-09635-0). Wiley.
Good Food & Fitness. pap. 5.95 (ISBN 0-696-01120-4). Meredith Corp.
Gregor, Carol. Working Out Together: A Complete Fitness Program for Partners. (Illus.). 224p. (Orig.). 1983. pap. 9.95 (ISBN 0-425-05878-6). Berkley Pub.
Hix, Charles. Working Out. 1983. 15.95 (ISBN 0-671-45793-4). S&S.
Johnson, Dewayne J. & Riggs, Charles. Conditioning. (Illus.). 77p. 1982. pap. text ed. 2.95 (ISBN 0-89641-090-0). American Pr.
Koch, Susan. Body Dynamics: The Body Shape-Up Book for Women. LC 82-83947. (Illus.). 192p. (Orig.). 1983. pap. 7.95 (ISBN 0-88011-115-1). Leisure Pr.
Leen, Edie & Bertling, Ed. The Bodybuilder's Training Diary. 160p. 1983. spiral bdg. 6.95 (ISBN 0-89037-258-6). Anderson World.
Leighton, Jack R. Fitness, Body Development, & Sports Conditioning Through Weight Training. 2nd ed. (Illus.). 234p. 1983. 24.50x (ISBN 0-398-04761-8). C C Thomas.
Lindsey, Ruth, et al. Fitness for Health, Figure, Physique, Posture. 5th ed. 135p. 1983. pap. text ed. write for info. (ISBN 0-697-07267-3); instr's manual avail. (ISBN 0-697-07268-1). Wm C Brown.
McHugh, Thomas P. The Complete Weight Training Manual. 168p. 1982. pap. text ed. 9.95 (ISBN 0-8403-2751-X). Kendall-Hunt.
Mecca, Stephen J. & Ekin, Cemal A. Invitation to Basic Fitness. (Illus.). 283p. 1983. pap. 15.00 (ISBN 0-89433-211-2). Petrocelli.
Mentzer, Mike & Friedberg, Ardy. The Mentzer Method: Weight Training for Fitness for Men & Women. (Illus., Orig.). 1980. pap. 6.95 (ISBN 0-688-08636-5). Quill NY.
Morgan, Robert F. & Wilson, Jane. Growing Younger: How to Add Years to Your Life By Measuring & Controlling Your Body Age. LC 82-42854. 264p. 1983. 19.95 (ISBN 0-8128-2918-2). Stein & Day.
Olinekova, Gayle. Legs! Super Legs in Six Weeks. (Illus.). 128p. 1983. pap. 7.95 (ISBN 0-671-47241-0, Fireside). S&S.
Personal Fitness Diary: A One-Year Record of Exercise, Diet & Stress Reduction. 128p. (Orig.). 1983. spiral bdg. 7.95 (ISBN 0-8092-5497-2). Contemp Bks.
Phillips, Edgar. The Ultimate in Sports. 32p. 1982. pap. write for info. (ISBN 0-9608576-1-3). Busn Pro Bks.
Physique Handbook, 1977-1978. Date not set. 5.00 (ISBN 0-686-43037-9). AAU Pubns.
Player, Gary & Harris, Norman. Gary Player on Fitness & Success. (Illus.). 1979. pap. 4.95 (ISBN 0-437-12751-6, Pub. by World's Work). David & Charles.
Research Consortium Symposium Papers 1982. 122p. 4.95 (ISBN 0-88314-151-5). AAHPERD.
Rosen, Trix. Strong & Sexy: The New Body Beautiful. (Illus.). 144p. (Orig.). 1983. pap. 9.95 (ISBN 0-933328-59-1). Delilah Bks.
Shapiro, Jacqueline R. & Swaybill, Marion L. Sexibody Diet & Exercise Program. 1982. text ed. 10.95 (ISBN 0-914094-19-X). Symphony.
Sheehan, George. Dr. Sheehan on Fitness. (Illus.). 1983. price not set (ISBN 0-671-45478-1). S&S.
Sorenson, Jacki & Bruns, Bill. Jacki Sorenson's Aerobic Lifestyles. 1983. 15.95 (ISBN 0-671-45616-4, Poseidon). PB.
Sorine, Stephanie. The French Riviera Body Book. (Illus.). 128p. 1983. 12.95 (ISBN 0-312-30527-3). St Martin.
Sprague, Ken & Reynolds, Bill. The Gold's Gym Book of Bodybuilding. (Illus.). 288p. (Orig.). 1983. 17.95 (ISBN 0-8092-5694-0); pap. 10.95 (ISBN 0-8092-5693-2). Contemp Bks.
Springer, Jeanne A. Fitness for You: A Head-to-Toe Stretching Strengthening & Body-Toning Exercise Program for Women. LC 82-90713. (Illus.). 68p. (Orig.). 1982. pap. 3.95 (ISBN 0-9609394-0-7). Kelane Pub.
Stillwell, James & Stockard, Jerry. Fitness Exercises for Elementary School Children: A Guide for Teachers & Parents. LC 82-83926. (Illus.). 176p. (Orig.). 1983. pap. 7.95 (ISBN 0-88011-093-7). Leisure Pr.
Weider, Joe. The Weider System of Bodybuilding. Reynolds, Bill, ed. (Illus.). 224p. (Orig.). 1983. 17.95 (ISBN 0-8092-5561-8); pap. 8.95 (ISBN 0-8092-5559-6). Contemp Bks.
Weightlifting Handbook, 1979-1980. Date not set. 4.50 (ISBN 0-686-43041-7). AAU Pubns.
Weinberg, Robert & Caldwell, Patsy. Health Related Fitness: Theory & Practice. (Illus.). 176p. pap. text ed. 9.95 (ISBN 0-88136-001-5). Jostens.
PHYSICAL GEOGRAPHY
see also Caves; Climatology; Coast Changes; Continents; Earth; Earthquakes; Erosion; Geochemistry; Geophysics; Glaciers; Icebergs; Lakes; Landforms; Landslides; Man-Influence on Nature; Meteorology; Mountains; Ocean; Oceanography; Paleogeography; Rivers; Sedimentation and Deposition; Shore Lines; Tides; Volcanoes; Water, Underground; Winds
also Lakes, Mountains, Ocean, Plains, Rivers, Valleys, and other geographical terms
Fellows, Donald K. Our Environment: An Introduction to Physical Geography. 2nd ed. LC 79-18159. 532p. 1980. text ed. 23.95 (ISBN 0-471-05755-X). Wiley.
PHYSICAL MEASUREMENTS
see also Errors, Theory Of; Mensuration; Physics–Laboratory Manuals; Time Measurements
Asimov, Isaac. The Measure of the Universe. LC 82-48654. (Illus.). 224p. 1983. 13.41i (ISBN 0-06-015129-3, HarpT). Har-Row.
PHYSICAL METALLURGY
see also Metallography
Higgins, Raymond A. Engineering Metallurgy, 2 Vols. Incl. Vol. 1. Applied Physical Metallurgy. 576p. lib. bdg. price not set (ISBN 0-89874-567-5); Vol. 2. Metallurgical Process Technology. 480p. lib. bdg. price not set (ISBN 0-89874-568-3). LC 82-19292. 1983. lib. bdg. write for info. Krieger.
PHYSICAL OCEANOGRAPHY
see Oceanography
PHYSICAL ORGANIC CHEMISTRY
see Chemistry, Physical Organic
PHYSICAL STAMINA
see Physical Fitness
PHYSICAL THERAPY
see also Baths; Electrotherapeutics; Hydrotherapy; Manipulation (Therapeutics); Massage; Occupational Therapy; Recreational Therapy; Ultrasonic Waves–Therapeutic Use
Arnould-Taylor, W. E. The Principles & Practice of Physical Therapy. 196p. 1977. 39.00x (ISBN 0-85950-351-8, Pub. by Thornes England). State Mutual Bk.
Burton, Charles & Nida, Gail. Revised Gravity Lumbar Reduction Therapy Program. 48p. 1982. 6.25 (ISBN 0-88440-026-3). Sis Kenny Inst.
Careers in Activity & Therapy Fields. 36p. 1976. 1.75 (ISBN 0-88314-037-3). AAHPERD.
Carr, Janet H. & Shepherd, Roberta B. Physiotheraphy in Pediatrics. 2nd ed. 524p. Repr. of 1980 ed. 29.50 (ISBN 0-89443-813-1, Pub. by W Heinemann). Aspen Systems.
Fraser, Beverly A. & Hensinger, Robert N. Managing Physical Handicaps: A Practical Guide for Parents, Care Providers, & Educators. LC 82-19716. (Illus.). 256p. 1983. text ed. 17.95 (ISBN 0-933716-30-3). P H Brookes.
Rudman, Jack. Supervising Physical Therapist. (Career Examination Ser.: C-2904). (Cloth bdg. avail. on request). pap. 12.00 (ISBN 0-8373-2904-3). Natl Learning.
--Therapeutic Activities Specialist. (Career Examination Ser.: C-889). (Cloth bdg. avail. on request). pap. 12.00 (ISBN 0-8373-0889-5). Natl Learning.
Veigh, Gretchen. Physical Therapy in the Home: Management, Evaluation & Treatment of Patients. (Illus.). 150p. 1983. 17.50 (ISBN 0-932426-27-1). Trado-Medic.
PHYSICAL TRAINING
see Physical Education and Training
PHYSICALLY HANDICAPPED
see also Architecture and the Physically Handicapped; Blind; Deaf
Bergen, Adrienne F. & Colangelo, Cheryl. Positioning the Client with Central Nervous System Deficits: The Wheelchair & Other Adapted Equipment. (Illus.). 191p. (Orig.). 1982. pap. text ed. 19.95 (ISBN 0-686-37672-2). Valhalla Rehab.
Bilotto, Gerardo & Washam, Veronica. Work Independence & the Severely Disabled: A Bibliography. LC 79-91351. 108p. 1980. 7.50 (ISBN 0-686-38821-6). Human Res Ctr.
Dechesne, B. H. & Pons, C. Sexuality & Handicap: Problems of the Motor Handicapped. (Illus.). 264p. 1983. pap. 29.75x (ISBN 0-398-04746-4). C C Thomas.
Fairweather, Brenda C. & Haun, Donna H. Communication Systems for Severely Handicapped Persons. (Illus.). 110p. 1983. text ed. 15.75x (ISBN 0-398-04809-6). C C Thomas.
Fraser, Beverly A. & Hensinger, Robert N. Managing Physical Handicaps: A Practical Guide for Parents, Care Providers, & Educators. LC 82-19716. (Illus.). 256p. 1983. text ed. 17.95 (ISBN 0-933716-30-3). P H Brookes.
Lam, Rosalind. Getting Together: Study of Members of PHAB Clubs. (NFER General Ser.). 163p. 1982. pap. text ed. 10.50x (ISBN 0-85633-244-5, NFER). Humanities.
Masters, Lowell F. & Mori, Allen A. Adapted Physical Education: A Practitioner's Guide. 350p. 1983. 29.50 (ISBN 0-89443-669-4). Aspen Systems.
Stroman, Duane F. The Awakening Minorities: The Physically Handicapped. LC 82-40235. (Illus.). 268p. 1983. lib. bdg. 23.50 (ISBN 0-8191-2694-2); pap. text ed. 11.50 (ISBN 0-8191-2695-0). U Pr of Amer.
Umbreit, John. Physical Disabilities & Health Conditions: An Introduction. 484p. 1983. text ed. 29.95 (ISBN 0-675-20045-8). Merrill.
Wright, Beatrice A. Physical Disability: A Psychological Approach. 512p. Date not set. text ed. 20.50 scp (ISBN 0-06-047241-3, HarpC). Har-Row.
PHYSICALLY HANDICAPPED–REHABILITATION
Involving Impaired, Disabled & Handicapped Persons in Regular Camp Programs. 128p. 1976. 7.95 (ISBN 0-88314-109-4). AAHPERD.
USTA Education & Research Center. Directory of Tennis Programs for the Disabled. 40p. 1982. 2.00 (ISBN 0-938822-18-7). USTA.
PHYSICALLY HANDICAPPED–TRANSPORTATION
Ashford, Norman & Bell, W. G., eds. Mobility & Transport for Elderly & Handicapped Persons: International Conference Held in Cambridge, England, July, 1981. (Transportation Studies: Vol. 2). Date not set. price not set (ISBN 0-677-16380-0). Gordon.
Garee, Betty, ed. An Accent Guide: Going Places In Your Own Vehicle. (Illus.). 80p. (Orig.). 1982. pap. 6.50 (ISBN 0-915708-13-2). Cheever Pub.
Hopeful Traveler. 256p. 9.95 (ISBN 0-88314-100-0). AAHPERD.
PHYSICALLY HANDICAPPED AND ARCHITECTURE
see Architecture and the Physically Handicapped
PHYSICALLY HANDICAPPED AND LIBRARIES
see Libraries and the Physically Handicapped
PHYSICALLY HANDICAPPED CHILDREN
see also Cerebral Palsy; Children, Deaf; Visually Handicapped Children
Levine, Susan P. & Sharow, Nancy. Recreation Experiences for the Severly Impaired or Nonambulatory Child. (Illus.). 96p. 1983. pap. 11.75x (ISBN 0-398-04783-9). C C Thomas.
Woods, Grace E. Handicapped Children in the Community. 1983. text ed. write for info. (ISBN 0-7236-0675-7). Wright-PSG.

PHYSICIAN AND PATIENT
Barber, Triphy & Langfitt, Dot E. Teaching the Medical-Surgical Patient: Diagnostics & Procedures. (Illus.). 384p. 1983. pap. text ed. 19.95 (ISBN 0-89303-250-6). R J Brady.
Crenshaw. Bedside Manners. 1983. 14.95 (ISBN 0-07-013581-9). McGraw.
Pahre, P. & Stewart, J. Going to the Doctor. (The Health Ser.). (Illus.). 65p. (gr. 7-12). 1981. pap. text ed. 3.00 (ISBN 0-910839-23-9). Hopewell.
Pendleton, David & Hasler, John, eds. Doctor-Patient Communciation. Date not set. price not set (ISBN 0-12-549880-2). Acad Pr.
PHYSICIANS
Browning, Charles H. Private Practice Handbook: The Tools, Tactics & Techniques for Successful Practice Development. 2nd ed. 238p. 1982. 24.95 (ISBN 0-911663-02-9); pap. 21.95 (ISBN 0-911663-01-0). Duncliffs Intl.
Chodoff, Richard. Doctor for the Prosecution: A Fighting Surgeon Takes the Stand. LC 82-20410. 320p. 1983. 15.95 (ISBN 0-399-12767-4). Putnam Pub Group.
Cypress, Beulah K. Medication Therapy in Office Visits for Selected Diagnoses: National Ambulatory Medical Care Survey, United States, 1980. Cox, Klaudia, ed. (Ser. 13: No. 71). 65p. 1982. pap. text ed. 1.85 (ISBN 0-8406-0266-9). Natl Ctr Health Stats.
Doyle, Brian B. & Scheiber, Stephen C., eds. The Impaired Physician. 200p. 1983. 24.50x (ISBN 0-306-41081-8, Plenum Pr). Plenum Pub.
Grey, Seymour. Beyond the Veil: The Adventures of an American Doctor in Saudi Arabia. (Bessie Bks.). 320p. 1983. 17.26i (ISBN 0-06-039014-X, HarpT). Har-Row.
Pahre, P. & Stewart, J. Going to the Doctor. (The Health Ser.). (Illus.). 65p. (gr. 7-12). 1981. pap. text ed. 3.00 (ISBN 0-910839-23-9). Hopewell.
Thomas, Lewis. The Youngest Science: Notes of a Medicine Watcher. (Alfred P. Sloan Foundation Ser.). 300p. 1983. 14.75 (ISBN 0-670-79533-X). Viking Pr.
Zwerski, Abraham J. It Happens to Doctors, Too. 9.95 (ISBN 0-89486-158-1). Hazelden.
PHYSICIANS-BIOGRAPHY
Church, Gene. No Man's Blood. LC 82-83577. 379p. 1983. pap. 7.95 (ISBN 0-86666-155-7). GWP.
Cottman & Blassingame. Out Island Doctor. (Illus.). 288p. 8.95 (ISBN 0-913428-18-3); pap. 4.95 (ISBN 0-686-83953-6). Landfall Pr.
Nordon, Haskell. The Education of a Polish Jew: A Physician's War Memoirs. 314p. 1983. 11.95 (ISBN 0-910563-00-4). D Grossman Pr.
Van-Riper, Charles. My Father, Doctor Van. Carter, James L., ed. LC 81-83254. (Illus.). 9p. 1982. 5.95x. Longyear Res.
Wilson, Raymond. Ohiyesa: Charles Eastman, Santee Sioux. LC 82-4937. (Illus.). 1983. 15.95 (ISBN 0-252-00978-9). U of Ill Pr.
PHYSICIANS-CORRESPONDENCE, REMINISCENCES, ETC.
Croskery, Sidney E. While I Remember. 1982. 27.00x (ISBN 0-85640-260-5, Pub. by Blackstaff Pr). State Mutual Bk.
PHYSICIANS-FEES
see Medical Fees
PHYSICIANS-LEGAL STATUS, LAWS, ETC.
see Medical Laws and Legislation
PHYSICIANS-SALARIES, PENSIONS, ETC.
see also Medical Fees
John R. Zabka Associates, Inc. Compensation Report on Hospital-Based Physicians, 1982-83. (Annual Report Ser.). 230p. 1982. 92.50 (ISBN 0-939326-06-X). Hosp Compensation.
PHYSICIANS-GREAT BRITAIN
Fry, John & Hunt. The Royal College of General Practitioners: The First 25 Years. (Illus.). 350p. 1982. text ed. 29.00 (ISBN 0-85200-360-9, Pub. by MTP Pr England). Kluwer-Boston.
PHYSICIANS IN ART
see Medicine and Art
PHYSICISTS
Aris, Rutherford & Davis, H. Ted, eds. Springs of Scientific Creativity: Essays on Founders of Modern Science. LC 82-23715. (Illus.). 352p. 1983. 32.50x (ISBN 0-8166-1087-8). U of Minn Pr.
Broda, Engelbert. Ludwig Boltzmann: Man, Physicist, Philosopher. LC 82-80707. (Illus.). 179p. 1983. 22.50 (ISBN 0-918024-24-2). Ox Bow.
PHYSICS
see also Astrophysics; Biological Physics; Capillarity; Chemistry, Physical and Theoretical; Diffusion; Dynamics; Elasticity; Electricity; Electrons; Evaporation; Field Theory (Physics); Force and Energy; Friction; Gases; Geophysics; Hydraulics; Kinematics; Light; Liquids; Magnetism; Magnetohydrodynamics; Mathematical Physics; Mechanics; Medical Physics; Meteorology; Molecular Dynamics; Motion; Optics; Physical Metallurgy; Quantum Theory; Radiation; Solid State Physics; Sound; Statics; Thermodynamics
AIP Conference, 84th, APS-AISI, Lehigh University, 1981. Physics in the Steel Industry: Proceedings. Schwerer, Fred C., ed. LC 82-72033. 409p. 1982. lib. bdg. 36.00 (ISBN 0-88318-183-5). Am Inst Physics.
AIP Conference, 85th, Madison, Wisconsin, 1982. Proton-Antiproton Collider Physics: Proceedings. Barger, V., et al, eds. LC 82-72141. 676p. 1982. lib. bdg. 42.00 (ISBN 0-88318-184-3). AM Inst Physics.
Baierlein, Ralph. Newtonian Dynamics. (Illus.). 336p. 1983. text ed. 31.50x (ISBN 0-07-003016-2, C); instructor's manual 16.00 (ISBN 0-07-003017-0). McGraw.
Basdevant, J. L. & Gastmans, R., eds. Fundamental Interactions: Cargese 1981. (NATO Advanced Study Ser. B, Physics: Vol. 85). 712p. 1982. 89.50 (ISBN 0-306-41116-4, Plenum Pr). Plenum Pub.
Billington, E. W. & Tate, A. The Physics of Deformation & Flow. 1981. 59.00 (ISBN 0-07-005285-9). McGraw.
Bologna, G. & Vincelli, M., eds. Data Acquisition in High Physics: Proceedings of the International School of Physics "Enrico Fermi," Course LXXXIV, Varenna, Italy, July 28-Aug. 7, 1981. (Enrico Fermi International Summer School of Physics Ser.: Vol. 84). 400p. 1982. 83.00 (ISBN 0-444-86520-9, North Holland). Elsevier.
Costa, G. & Gatto, R. R., eds. Theory of Fundamental Interactions: Proceedings of the International School of Physics, Enrico Fermi Course LXXXI, Varenna, Italy, July 21 - August 2, 1980. (Enrico Fermi International Summer School of Physics Ser.: Vol. 81). 300p. 1982. 61.75 (ISBN 0-444-86156-4, North Holland). Elsevier.
Cromer, A. Physics in Science & Industry. 1980. text ed. 27.50 (ISBN 0-07-014437-0); supplementary materials avail. McGraw.
Dita, P. & Georgescu, V., eds. Gauge Theories: Fundamentals Interactions & Rigorous Results. (Progress in Physics Ser.: Vol. 5). 389p. Date not set. text ed. 22.50 (ISBN 3-7643-3095-3). Birkhauser.
Duca, Anthony Del. New Visualizations in Elementary Physics. LC 82-60821. (Illus.). 65p. (Orig.). 1982. pap. 11.95x (ISBN 0-9609410-0-2). Magnet Pub.
Edmonds, Dean S., Jr. Cioffari's Experiments in College Physics, 7th ed. 456p. pap. 16.95 (ISBN 0-669-04492-X). Heath.
Euler, Manfred. Physikunterricht: Anspruch und Realitat. 254p. (Ger.). 1982. write for info. (ISBN 3-8204-7103-0). P Lang Pubs.
Ford, Kenneth. Classical & Modern Physics, 3 vols. Incl. Vol. 1. 1972; Vol. 2. text ed. 24.95x (ISBN 0-471-00724-2); answer manual 7.50 (ISBN 0-471-00945-8); Vol. 3. 1974. text ed. 26.95x (ISBN 0-471-00878-8); answer manual o.p. 6.95 (ISBN 0-471-00946-6). LC 76-161385. 1973. combined ed. for vols. 1 & 2 35.95 (ISBN 0-471-00666-1). Wiley.
Frampton, P. H. & Van Dam, H., eds. Third Workshop on Grand Unification. (Progress in Physics Ser.: Vol. 6). 384p. 1982. text ed. 22.50 (ISBN 3-7643-3105-4). Birkhauser.
Gallimore, J. G. Transverse Paraphysics: The New Science of Space, Time & Gravity Control. LC 82-50843. (Illus.). 359p. (Orig.). 1982. pap. text ed. 35.00 (ISBN 0-9603536-4-X). Tesla Bk Co.
Ginzburg, V. L. Waynflete Lectures on Physics: Selected Topics in Contemporary Physics & Astrophysics. (International Series in Natural Philosophy: Vol. 106). (Illus.). 133p. 1983. 25.00 (ISBN 0-08-029147-3). Pergamon.
Goble, Alfred T. & Baker, D. K. Elements of Modern Physics. 2nd ed. (Illus.). 546p. 1971. 27.50x (ISBN 0-471-06755-5). Wiley.
Hybalski, Daniel H. The Flight of Thought. 1983. 6.95 (ISBN 0-533-05576-8). Vantage.
Kane, Joseph W. & Sternheim, Morton M. Physics. 2nd ed. 752p. 1983. text ed. 28.50 (ISBN 0-471-08323-2). Wiley.
Kelly, A. & Mileiko, S. T., eds. Fabrication of Composites, Vol. IV. (Handbook of Composites Ser.). 500p. 1983. 95.75 (ISBN 0-444-86447-4, North Holland). Elsevier.
Marshak, R. E. Perspectives in Modern Physics. 673p. Repr. of 1966 ed. text ed. 25.50 (ISBN 0-470-57295-7). Krieger.
Marton, C. & Septier, A., eds. Advances in Electronics & Electron Physics Supplement, No. 13C. (Serial Publication). 544p. 1983. price not set (ISBN 0-12-014576-6). Acad Pr.
Physics the Easy Way. (gr. 10-12). pap. write for info. (ISBN 0-8120-2658-6). Barron.
Prigogine, I. Advances in Chemical Physics, Vol. 54. Rice, Stuart A., ed. 352p. 1983. price not set (ISBN 0-471-89570-9, Pub. by Wiley-Interscience). Wiley.
Rains, Karen J. & Shugart, Cecil G. The Phenomena of Physics: A Conceptual Laboratory Program. 176p. 1982. pap. text ed. 14.95 (ISBN 0-8403-2771-4). Kendall-Hunt.
Schild, Erich, et al. Environmental Physics in Construction: Its Applications in Architectural Design. 220p. 1982. 95.00x (ISBN 0-246-11224-7, Pub. by Granada England). State Mutual Bk.
Shive, John N. & Weber, Robert L. Similarities in Physics. 277p. 1982. 27.95 (ISBN 0-471-89795-7, Pub. by Wiley-Interscience). Wiley.
Sorenson, James A., ed. Physics in Nuclear Medicine: The Slide Set. 1982. slide set 295.00 (ISBN 0-8089-1530-4). Grune.
Thomson, Joseph J. Electricity & Matter. 1911. text ed. 32.50x (ISBN 0-686-83533-6). Elliots Bks.
Van Der Merwe, Alwyn, ed. Old & New Questions in Physics, Cosmology, Philosophy, & Theoretical Biology: Essays in Honor of Wolfgang Yourgrau. 905p. 1983. 95.00x (ISBN 0-306-40962-3, Plenum Pr). Plenum Pub.
Wess, Julius & Bagger, Jonathan. Supersummetry & Supergravity. (Princeton Series in Physics). 192p. 1983. 40.00 (ISBN 0-691-08327-4); pap. 12.50 (ISBN 0-691-08326-6). Princeton U Pr.
Wolkenstein, V. S. Problems in General Physics. 349p. 1975. 9.45 (ISBN 0-8285-1957-9, Pub. by Mir Pubs USSR). Imported Pubns.
PHYSICS-ADDRESSES, ESSAYS, LECTURES
Goeke, K. & Reinhard, P. G. Time Dependent Hartree-Fock & Beyond, Bad Honnef, FRG, 1982 Proceedings, Vol. 171. (Lecture Notes in Physics). 426p. 1983. pap. 21.00 (ISBN 0-387-11950-7). Springer-Verlag.
Haken, H. Evolution of Order & Chaos in Physics, Chemistry, & Biology: Schloss Elmau, FRG, 1982 Proceedings. (Springer Series in Synergetics: Vol. 17). (Illus.). 287p. 1983. 32.00 (ISBN 0-387-11904-3). Springer-Verlag.
PHYSICS-DICTIONARIES
Parker, Sybil P., ed. Encyclopedia of Physics. 1352p. 1983. 54.50 (ISBN 0-07-045253-9, P&RB). McGraw.
Precis Thesaurus: Physics. 1981. 55.00x (ISBN 0-686-99804-9, Pub. by Brit Lib England). State Mutual Bk.
PHYSICS-EXPERIMENTS
Harris, N. & Hemmerling, E. M. Experiments in Applied Physics. 3rd ed. 1980. text ed. 12.95 (ISBN 0-07-026818-5). McGraw.
PHYSICS-HISTORY
Aris, Rutherford & Davis, H. Ted, eds. Springs of Scientific Creativity: Essays on Founders of Modern Science. LC 82-23715. (Illus.). 352p. 1983. 32.50x (ISBN 0-8166-1087-8). U of Minn Pr.
Casimir, Hendrik B. Haphazard Reality: Half a Century of Science. LC 82-48112. (Sloan Foundation Books). 356p. 1983. 15.00 (ISBN 0-06-015028-9, HarpT). Har-Row.
PHYSICS-LABORATORY MANUALS
Bernard, C. H. & Epp, C. D. Laboratory Experiments in College Physics. 5th ed. 437p. 1980. 14.95 (ISBN 0-471-05441-0). Wiley.
PHYSICS-PROBLEMS, EXERCISES, ETC.
Riley, K. F. Problems for Physics Students: With Hints & Answers. LC 82-4575. 100p. 1982. 24.95 (ISBN 0-521-24921-X); pap. 11.95 (ISBN 0-521-27073-1). Cambridge U Pr.
PHYSICS, ASTRONOMICAL
see Astrophysics
PHYSICS, BIOLOGICAL
see Biological Physics
PHYSICS, NUCLEAR
see Nuclear Physics
PHYSICS, TERRESTRIAL
see Geophysics
PHYSIOGNOMY
see also Face
Lavater, John c. The Science of Physiognomy. (The Most Meaningful Classics in World Culture Ser.). (Illus.). 156p. 1983. Repr. of 1810 ed. 115.00 (ISBN 0-89901-100-4). Found Class Reprints.
PHYSIOGRAPHY
see Geology; Geomorphology; Physical Geography
PHYSIOLOGICAL ACOUSTICS
see Hearing
PHYSIOLOGICAL APPARATUS
Geddes, L. A. & Baker, L. E. Principles of Applied Biomedical Instrumentation. 2nd ed. LC 74-34390. (Biomedical Engineering & Health Systems Ser.). 616p. 1975. 42.50x (ISBN 0-471-29496-9, Pub. by Wiley-Interscience). Wiley.
PHYSIOLOGICAL EFFECT OF CHEMICALS
see Pharmacology
PHYSIOLOGICAL EFFECT OF LIGHT ON PLANTS
see Plants, Effect of Light On
PHYSIOLOGICAL OXIDATION
see Oxidation, Physiological
PHYSIOLOGICAL STRESS
see Stress (Physiology)
PHYSIOLOGICAL THERAPEUTICS
see Therapeutics, Physiological
PHYSIOLOGY
see also Adaptation (Physiology); Anatomy; Body Temperature; Bones; Cells; Climacteric; Digestion; Electrophysiology; Fatigue; Growth; Health; Lymphatics; Metabolism; Muscles; Nervous System; Neurophysiology; Nutrition; Pregnancy; Reproduction; Respiration; Rheology; Secretion; Senses and Sensation
also names of organs and secretions, e.g. Heart, Kidneys, Bile, Gastric Juice
Adrian, R. H., et al, eds. Reviews of Physiology, Biochemistry & Pharmacology, Vol. 96. (Illus.). 194p. 1983. 39.00 (ISBN 0-387-11849-7). Springer-Verlag.
--Reviews of Physiology, Biochemistry, & Pharmacology, Vol. 97. (Illus.). 180p. 1983. 35.50 (ISBN 0-387-12135-8). Springer-Verlag.
Anthony, Catherine P. & Thibodeau, Gary A. Textbook of Anatomy & Physiology. 11th ed. (Illus.). 876p. 1983. text ed. 28.95 (ISBN 0-8016-0289-0). Mosby.
Arnould-Taylor, W. E. A Textbook of Anatomy & Physiology. 112p. 1978. 30.00x (ISBN 0-85950-044-6, Pub. by Thornes England). State Mutual Bk.
Berne, R. M., et al, eds. Annual Review of Physiology, Vol. 45. LC 39-15404. (Illus.). 1983. text ed. 27.00 (ISBN 0-8243-0345-8). Annual Reviews.
Cunningham, John J. Introduction to Nutritional Physiology. (Illus.). 400p. 19.95 (ISBN 0-89313-031-1); text ed. 19.95 (ISBN 0-686-38084-3). G F Stickley.
Greep, Roy O., ed. Reproductive Physiology IV. (International Review of Physiology Ser.: Vol. 27). 1983. text ed. 49.50 (ISBN 0-8391-1555-5, 14206). Univ Park.
Hoar, William S. General & Comparative Physiology. 3rd ed. (Illus.). 928p. 1983. 30.95 (ISBN 0-13-349308-3). P-H.
Holtzmeier, Dawn K. Applied Anatomy & Physiology: A Laboratory Manual & Workbook for Health Careers. 304p. 1983. pap. text ed. 18.50 (ISBN 0-8403-2915-6). Kendall-Hunt.
Larsen, James B. & Billings, Jeffrey D. Laboratory Manual for Human Physiology. 128p. 1982. pap. text ed. 8.95 (ISBN 0-8403-2782-X). Kendall-Hunt.
Neal, Kenneth G. & Kalbus, Barbara H. Anatomy & Physiology: A Laboratory Manual & Study Guide. 4th ed. 448p. 1983. pap. text ed. write for info. (ISBN 0-8087-1449-X). Burgess.
Strand, Fleur L. Physiology: A Regulatory Approach. 2nd ed. 672p. 1983. text ed. 24.95 (ISBN 0-02-417680-X). Macmillan.
Tortora. Principios de Fisiocogia Humana. (Span.). 1983. pap. text ed. price not set (ISBN 0-06-317149-X, Pub. by HarLA Mexico). Har-Row.
Weinreb, Eva L. Anatomy & Physiology. 896p. 1982. text ed. write for info. (ISBN 0-201-08852-5). A-W.
Winters, Robert W. & Bell, Ralph B. Acid-Base Physiology in Medicine: A Self-Instruction Program. 3rd ed. 1982. text ed. 19.95 (ISBN 0-316-94739-3). Little.
Wood, Dennis. Principles of Animal Physiology. 350p. 1982. pap. text ed. 19.95x (ISBN 0-7131-2861-5). E Arnold.
Young, David B., ed. Gastrointestinal Physiology IV. (International Review of Physiology Ser.). (Illus.). 1983. text ed. 34.50 (ISBN 0-8391-1725-6, 14192). Univ Park.
PHYSIOLOGY-APPARATUS
see Physiological Apparatus
PHYSIOLOGY-LABORATORY MANUALS
Benson, Harold J., et al. Anatomy & Physiology Laboratory Textbook: Short & Complete Version, 2 vols. 3rd ed. 350p. 1983. pap. text ed. write for info. wire coil short version (ISBN 0-697-04739-3); instrs' manual avail. (ISBN 0-697-04740-7); pap. text ed. write for info. complete version, 570p. (ISBN 0-697-04737-7); instrs' manual avail. (ISBN 0-697-04738-5). Wm C Brown.
Larsen, James B. & Billings, Jeffrey D. Laboratory Manual for Human Physiology. 128p. 1982. pap. text ed. 8.95 (ISBN 0-8403-2782-X). Kendall-Hunt.
PHYSIOLOGY, COMPARATIVE
see also Veterinary Physiology
also Birds, Animals, and similar headings with or without the subdivision Physiology
Hoar, William S. General & Comparative Physiology. 3rd ed. (Illus.). 928p. 1983. 30.95 (ISBN 0-13-349308-3). P-H.
PHYSIOLOGY, MOLECULAR
see Biological Physics
PHYSIOLOGY, PATHOLOGICAL
Emes, John H. & Nowak, Thomas J. Introduction to Pathophysiology: Basic Principles of the Disease Process. (Illus.). 1983. text ed. 24.95 (ISBN 0-8391-1775-2, 16594). Univ Park.
Utley, Joe R. Pathophysiology & Techniques of Cardiopulmonary Bypass, Vol. II. (Illus.). 274p. 1983. lib. bdg. price not set (ISBN 0-683-08502-6). Williams & Wilkins.
PHYSIOLOGY, VETERINARY
see Veterinary Physiology
PHYSIOLOGY OF PLANTS
see Plant Physiology
PHYSIOPATHOLOGY
see Physiology, Pathological
PHYSIOTHERAPY
see Physical Therapy; Therapeutics, Physiological
PHYSIQUE PHOTOGRAPHY
see Photography of Men
PHYTOCHEMISTRY
see Botanical Chemistry
PHYTOGRAPHY
see Botany
PHYTOLOGY
see Botany
PHYTOPATHOLOGY
see Plant Diseases
PHYTOPHTORA
Erwin, D. C. & Garcia, Bartnicki, eds. Phytophthora: It's Biology, Taxanomy, Ecology & Pathology. 400p. 1983. text ed. 68.00 (ISBN 0-89054-050-0); text ed. 76.00 nonmember (ISBN 0-686-82684-1). Am Phytopathological Soc.
PHYTOSOCIOLOGY
see Plant Communities

PHYTOTHERAPY
see Materia Medica, Vegetable
PIAF, EDITH, 1915-1963
Lange, Monique. Piaf. 252p. 1983. 11.95 (ISBN 0-394-62428-9). Seaver Bks.
PIAGET, JEAN, 1896-
Egan, Kieran. Education & Psychology: Plato, Paiget & Scientific Psychology. (Orig.). 1983. 18.95x. Tchrs Coll.
Liben, Lynn, ed. Piaget & the Foundations of Knowledge. 288p. 1983. text ed. write for info. (ISBN 0-89859-248-8). L Erlbaum Assocs.
Modgil, Sohan & Modgil, Celia, eds. Jean Piaget: An Interdisciplinary Critique. (International Library of Psychology). 200p. 1983. price not set (ISBN 0-7100-9451-5). Routledge & Kegan.
Scholnick, Ellin K. New Trends in Conceptual Representation: Challanges to Piaget's Theory? (Jean Piaget Symposium). 320p. 1983. text ed. write for info. (ISBN 0-89859-260-7). L Erlbaum Assocs.
PIANISTS
Cazort, Jean & Hobson, Constance T. Born to Play: The Life & Career of Hazel Harrison. LC 82-12169. (Contributions to the Study of Music & Dance Ser.: No. 3). (Illus.). 200p. 1983. lib. bdg. 27.95 (ISBN 0-313-23643-7, CBO/). Greenwood.
Moore, Gerald. Furthermoore: Interludes in an Accompanist's Life. 160p. 1983. 22.50 (ISBN 0-241-10909-4, Pub. by Hamish Hamilton England). David & Charles.
Newman, William. The Pianist's Problems. 3rd ed. (Illus.). 208p. 1983. Repr. of 1974 ed. lib. bdg. 22.50 (ISBN 0-306-76213-7). Da Capo.
Plaskin, Glenn. Horowitz: A Biography of Vladimir Horowitz. (Illus.). 640p. 1983. 17.95 (ISBN 0-688-01616-2). Morrow.
PIANISTS–CORRESPONDENCE, REMINISCENCES, ETC.
see Musicians–Correspondence, Reminiscences, Etc.
PIANO
Gaines, James R. The Lives of the Piano. LC 82-48228. (Illus.). 215p. 1983. pap. 10.53i (ISBN 0-06-090997-8, CN 997, CN). Har-Row.
Krehbiel, Henry E. The Pianoforte & It's Music. 324p. 1983. Repr. pap. 6.75x (ISBN 0-88072-007-7). Tanager Bks.
PIANO–HISTORY
Brinsmead, Edgar. History of the Pianoforte. 120p. Date not set. pap. 17.50 (ISBN 0-87556-489-5). Saifer.
Good, Edwin M. Giraffes, Black Dragons & Other Pianos: A Technological History from Christofori to the Modern Concert Grand. LC 81-50787. (Illus.). 328p. 1982. 29.50 (ISBN 0-8047-1120-8). Stanford U Pr.
PIANO–INSTRUCTION AND STUDY
Mitchell, Alice & Szerny, Carl. A Systematic Introduction to Improvisation on the Piano Forte: Opus 200. Anderson, Gordon T., ed. (Longman Music Ser.). 128p. 1983. text ed. 24.95x (ISBN 0-582-28329-9). Longman.
PIANO MUSIC
see also Dance Music
Anderson, Gaylene, ed. Primary Primer: Simplified Piano Duets for Young Latter-day Saints. (Illus.). 32p. (Orig.). 1982. pap. 3.95 (ISBN 0-941214-10-9). Signature Bks.
Krehbiel, Henry E. The Pianoforte & It's Music. 324p. 1983. Repr. pap. 6.75x (ISBN 0-88072-007-7). Tanager Bks.
PIANO TRADE
see Music Trade
PIANOFORTE
see Piano
PICASSO, PABLO, 1881-1973
Becraft, Melvin. Picasso's Guernica: Images within Images. 1983. 6.95 (ISBN 0-533-05440-0). Vantage.
Carmean, E. A., Jr. The Morton G. Neumann Family Collection: Picasso Prints & Drawings, III. LC 81-14151. (Illus.). pap. 2.00 (ISBN 0-89468-042-0). Natl Gallery Art.
PICKLES
Chesman, Andrea. Pickles & Relishes: One Hundred Thirty Recipes, Apple to Zucchini. (Illus.). 160p. (Orig.). 1983. pap. 5.95 (ISBN 0-88266-321-6). Garden Way Pub.
McCrachen, Betsy. Farm Journal's Homemade Pickles & Relishes. LC 76-14048. 128p. (Orig.). 1976. pap. 3.95 (ISBN 0-89795-018-6). Farm Journal.
PICKLING
see Canning and Preserving; Pickles
PICNICKING
see also Cookery, Outdoor
Sunset Books & Sunset Magazine, ed. Picnics & Tailgate Parties. LC 81-82868. (Illus.). 96p. 1982. pap. 4.95 (ISBN 0-376-02536-0). Sunset-Lane.
PICTORIAL DICTIONARIES
see Picture Dictionaries
PICTORIAL JOURNALISM
see Journalism, Pictorial
PICTORIAL PHOTOGRAPHY
see Photography, Artistic
PICTURE BOARDS
see Dummy Board Figures
PICTURE-BOOKS FOR CHILDREN
see also Illustrated Books, Children's
Archer, Peggy. One of the Family. LC 82-82289. (Little Golden Bk.). (Illus.). 24p. 1983. 0.89 (ISBN 0-307-02082-7, Golden Pr). Western Pub.
Beckes, Shirley. Things That Go. (Scribbler Play Bks.). (Illus.). 20p. (ps). 1983. pap. write for info. (ISBN 0-307-20328-X). Western Pub.
Bond, Felicia. Four Valentines in a Rainstorm. (Illus.). (ps-3). 4.95 (ISBN 0-686-43187-1, TYC-J). Har-Row.
Calmenson, Stephanie. Barney's Sandcastle. LC 81-86492. (First Little Golden Bks.). (Illus.). (ps). 1983. 0.69 (ISBN 0-307-11136-9, Golden Pr); PLB price not set (ISBN 0-307-68130-0). Western Pub.
Conklin, Marilyn. Poochie Press-Out Pretties. (Press-Out Bk.: No. 2860). (Illus.). 8p. (ps up). 1983. 1.29 (ISBN 0-307-21186-X). Western Pub.
Crews, Donald. Parade. LC 82-20927. (Illus.). 32p. (gr. k-3). 1983. 10.00 (ISBN 0-688-01995-1); PLB 9.55 (ISBN 0-688-01996-X). Greenwillow.
Doney, Meryl. How I Am Big. (Illus.). 16p. 1983. pap. 0.99 (ISBN 0-86683-705-1). Winston Pr.
--When I Was Little. (Illus.). 16p. 1983. pap. 0.99 (ISBN 0-86683-704-3). Winston Pr.
Egan, Carol B. Body Buddies. (ps-2). 1982. 5.95 (ISBN 0-86653-060-6, GA 420). Good Apple.
Eubank, Mary G. When I Grow Up. (Scribbler Play Bks.). (Illus.). 20p. (ps). 1983. pap. write for info. (ISBN 0-307-20327-1). Western Pub.
Felix, Monique, illus. If I Were a Sheep. (Illus.). 12p. (Orig.). 1982. pap. 2.50 (ISBN 0-914676-67-9, Pub. by Envelope Bks). Green Tiger Pr.
The Friendly Beasts. (First Little Golden Bk.). (Illus.). (ps). 1983. 0.69 (ISBN 0-307-10148-7, Golden Pr); PLB price not set (ISBN 0-307-68148-3). Western Pub.
Gantschev, Ivan. Journey of the Storks. LC 82-61835. (Picture Book Ser.). (Illus.). 32p. (gr. k-5). 1983. 9.95 (ISBN 0-907234-27-5). Neugebauer Pr.
Generowicz, Witold. The Train. (ps-3). Date not set. 5.95 (ISBN 0-8037-8834-7). Dial.
Henry, Lawrence. ABC's. Klimo, Kate, ed. (Learn with E.T. Ser.). (Illus.). 24p. 1982. pap. 1.75 (ISBN 0-671-46439-6, Little). S&S.
--E.T. Counting. Klimo, Kate, ed. (Learn with E.T. Ser.). (Illus.). 24p. 1982. pap. 1.75 (ISBN 0-671-46440-X, Little). S&S.
--What Is This For. Klimo, Kate, ed. (Learn with E.T. Ser.). (Illus.). 24p. 1982. pap. 1.75 (ISBN 0-671-46444-2, Little). S&S.
Herzog, Barbara J. My Own Story & Picture Book. 32p. (Orig.). (gr. 1-4). 1983. pap. 4.98 (ISBN 0-943194-14-8). Childwrite.
I Can Dress Myself. LC 82-82652. (First Little Golden Bk.). (Illus.). (ps). 1983. 0.69 (ISBN 0-307-10140-1, Golden Pr). Western Pub.
Kelley, True. Sunshine & Sculpture. (Scribbler Play Bks.). 20p. (ps). 1983. pap. write for info. (ISBN 0-307-20326-3). Western Pub.
Kenworthy, Catherine. Little Squirt the Fire Engine. LC 82-83382. (First Little Golden Bk.). (Illus.). (ps). 1983. 0.69 (ISBN 0-307-10144-4, Golden Pr); PLB price not set. Western Pub.
Khalsa, Dayal K. Baabee Books, 4 Bks. (Illus.). 1983. Set. 12.95 (ISBN 0-686-43199-5). Bk. 1 (ISBN 0-88776-136-4). Bk. 2 (ISBN 0-88776-137-2). Bk. 3 (ISBN 0-88776-138-0). Bk. 4 (ISBN 0-88776-139-9). Tundra Bks.
King, Heather. Morning to Night. (Scribbler Play Bks.). (Illus.). 20p. (ps). 1983. pap. write for info. (ISBN 0-307-20325-5). Western Pub.
Krahn, Fernando. The Secret in the Dungeon. (Illus.). 32p. (gr. 2). 1983. 9.95 (ISBN 0-89919-148-7, Clarion). HM.
Madigan, Margaret. Good Night, Aunt Lilly. LC 82-84022. (Little Golden Bk.). (Illus.). 24p. (ps-2). 1983. 0.89 (ISBN 0-307-02084-3, Golden Pr); PLB price not set (ISBN 0-307-60218-4). Western Pub.
Marshall, Ray & Paul, Korkey. Hey Diddle Diddle. Klimo, Kate, ed. (Chubby Pop-Ups Ser.). (Illus.). 10p. 1983. 3.95 (ISBN 0-671-46239-3, Little). S&S.
Marshall, Ray & Paul, Korky. Humpty Dumpty. Klimo, Kate, ed. (Chubby Pop-Ups Ser.). (Illus.). 10p. 1983. 3.95 (ISBN 0-671-46236-9, Little). S&S.
Martin, Charles E. Dunkel Takes a Walk. (Illus.). 24p. (gr. k-3). 1983. 10.00 (ISBN 0-688-01815-7); PLB 9.55 (ISBN 0-688-01816-5). Greenwillow.
Mayer, Mercer. All by Myself. (Little Critter Library). (Illus.). 32p. 1983. price not set (ISBN 0-307-10604-7). Western Pub.
--I Was So Bad. LC 82-84109. (Little Critter Library). (Illus.). 32p. 1983. price not set (ISBN 0-307-10603-9, Golden Pr). Western Pub.
--Just Go to Bed. LC 82-84107. (Little Critter Library). (Illus.). 32p. 1983. price not set (Golden Pr). Western Pub.
--Me, Too! LC 82-84106. (Little Critter Library). (Illus.). 32p. 1983. price not set (ISBN 0-307-10606-3, Golden Pr). Western Pub.
--The New Baby. (Little Critter Library). (Illus.). 32p. 1983. price not set (ISBN 0-307-10601-2, Golden Pr). Western Pub.
Morris, Neil & Morris, Ting. Find the Canary. (Mystery Picture Book Ser.). 24p. (gr. k-3). 1983. 5.70i (ISBN 0-316-58375-8). Little.
--Hide & Seek. (Mystery Picture Book Ser.). 24p. (gr. k-3). 1983. 5.70i (ISBN 0-316-58376-6). Little.
--Search for Sam. (Mystery Picture Bk. Ser.). (Illus.). 24p. (gr. k-3). 1983. 5.70 (ISBN 0-316-58378-2). Little.
--Where's My Hat? (Mystery Picture Book Ser.). (Illus.). 24p. (gr. k-3). 1983. 5.70i. Little.
Muntean, Michaela. If You Could Choose a Pet. (First Little Golden Bk.). (Illus.). (ps). 1983. 0.69 (ISBN 0-686-84753-9, Golden Pr); PLB price not set (ISBN 0-307-68143-2). Western Pub.
--Panda Bear's Secret. (First Little Golden Bk.). (Illus.). 24p. (ps). 1983. 0.69 (ISBN 0-307-10136-3, Golden Pr); PLB price not set (ISBN 0-307-68136-X). Western Pub.
Over in the Meadow. LC 82-82642. (First Little Golden Bk.). (Illus.). 24p. (ps). 1983. 0.69 (ISBN 0-307-10141-X, Golden Pr); PLB price not set (ISBN 0-307-68141-6). Western Pub.
Pienkowski, Jan. Home. Klimo, Kate, ed. (Pienkowski Concept Bks.). (Illus.). 32p. (ps-k). 1983. 3.95 (ISBN 0-671-46246-6, Little). S&S.
--Size. Klimo, Kate, ed. (Pienkowski Concept Bks.). (Illus.). 32p. (ps-k). 1983. 3.95 (ISBN 0-671-46244-X, Little). S&S.
--Time. Klimo, Kate, ed. (Pienkowski Concept Bks.). (Illus.). 32p. (ps-k). 1983. 3.95 (ISBN 0-671-46247-4, Little). S&S.
--Weather. Klimo, Kate, ed. (Peinkowski Concept Bks.). (Illus.). 32p. (ps-k). 1983. 3.95 (ISBN 0-671-46245-8, Little). S&S.
Polette, Nancy. E is for Everybody: A Manual for Bringing Fine Picture Books into the Hands & Hearts of Children. 2nd ed. LC 82-10508. 194p. 1982. 12.50 (ISBN 0-8108-1579-6). Scarecrow.
Sanford, Sara L. Jake's Late. (Illus.). 32p. (gr. 1-3). 1983. pap. 1.98 (ISBN 0-943944-01-5). Sneak-A-Peek Bks.
--Smirk Smiles. LC 50-332. (Illus.). 24p. 1983. pap. 1.98 (ISBN 0-943944-00-7, 950-333). Sneak-A-Peek Bks.
Schongut, Emanuel. Catch Kitten. Klimo, Kate, ed. (Kitten Board Bks.). (Illus.). 14p. (ps-k). 1983. 3.95 (ISBN 0-671-46382-9, Little). S&S.
--Hush Kitten. Klimo, Kate, ed. (Kitten Board Bk.). (Illus.). 14p. 1983. 3.95 (ISBN 0-671-46386-1, Little). S&S.
--Look Kitten. Klimo, Kate, ed. (Kitten Board Bks.). (Illus.). 14p. 1983. 3.95 (ISBN 0-671-46388-8, Little). S&S.
--Play Kitten. Klimo, Kate, ed. (Kitten Board Bks.). (Illus.). 14p. 1983. 3.95 (ISBN 0-671-46387-X, Little). S&S.
--Wake Kitten. Klimo, Kate, ed. (Kitten Board Bks.). (Illus.). 14p. 1983. 3.95 (ISBN 0-671-46383-7, Little). S&S.
Spizzirri Publishing Co. Staff. Animal Alphabet: An Educational Coloring Book. Spizzirri, Linda, ed. (Illus.). 32p. (gr. 1-8). 1982. pap. 1.25 (ISBN 0-86545-042-0). Spizzirri.
--Cats of the Wild: An Educational Coloring Book. Spizzirri, Linda, ed. (Illus.). 32p. (gr. 1-8). 1982. pap. 1.25 (ISBN 0-86545-045-5). Spizzirri.
--Counting & Coloring Dinosaurs: An Educational Coloring Book. Spizzirri, Linda, ed. (Illus.). 32p. (gr. 1-8). 1982. pap. 1.25 (ISBN 0-86545-044-7). Spizzirri.
--Endangered Species: An Educational Coloring Book. Spizzirri, Linda, ed. (Illus.). 32p. (gr. 1-8). 1982. pap. 1.25 (ISBN 0-86545-041-2). Spizzirri.
--Kachina Dolls: An Educational Coloring Book. Spizzirri, Linda, ed. (Illus.). 32p. (gr. 1-8). 1982. pap. 1.25 (ISBN 0-86545-046-3). Spizzirri.
--Northeast Indians: An Educational Coloring Book. Spizzirri, Linda, ed. (Illus.). 32p. (gr. 1-8). 1982. pap. 1.25 (ISBN 0-86545-040-4). Spizzirri.
--Northwest Indians: An Educational Coloring Book. Spizzirri, Linda, ed. (Illus.). 32p. (gr. 1-8). 1982. pap. 1.25 (ISBN 0-86545-047-1). Spizzirri.
--Picture Dictionary: An Educational Coloring Book. Spizzirri, Linda, ed. (Illus.). 32p. (gr. 1-8). 1982. pap. 1.25 (ISBN 0-86545-049-8). Spizzirri.
--Planets: An Educational Coloring Book. Spizzirri, Linda, ed. (Illus.). 32p. (gr. 1-8). 1982. pap. 1.95 (ISBN 0-86545-043-9). Spizzirri.
--State Birds: An Educational Coloring Book. Spizzirri, Linda, ed. (Illus.). 32p. (gr. 1-8). 1982. pap. 1.25 (ISBN 0-86545-050-1). Spizzirri.
--Trucks: An Educational Coloring Book. Spizzirri, Linda, ed. (Illus.). 32p. (gr. 1-8). 1982. pap. 1.25 (ISBN 0-86545-051-X). Spizzirri.
--Whales: An Educational Coloring Book. Spizzirri, Linda, ed. (Illus.). 32p. (gr. 1-8). 1982. pap. 1.25 (ISBN 0-86545-039-0). Spizzirri.
Sunshine, Madeline. Puppy Love. LC 82-83330. (Little Golden Bk.). (Illus.). 24p. (ps-2). 1983. 0.89 (ISBN 0-307-01095-3, Golden Pr). Western Pub.
Taylor, Doug. Pac-Baby's ABC. (Illus.). 1983. pap. 1.50 (ISBN 0-686-43029-8). Crown.
--Pac-Baby's Colors. (Illus.). (ps). 1983. pap. 1.50 (ISBN 0-517-55018-0). Crown.
--Pac-Baby's Shapes. (ps). 1983. pap. 1.50 (ISBN 0-517-55020-2). Crown.
--Pac-Baby's 1-2-3. (Illus.). 1983. pap. 1.50 (ISBN 0-517-55019-9). Crown.
Turk, Hanne. A Lesson for Max. LC 82-61833. (Max the Mouse Ser.). (Illus.). 24p. 1983. pap. 2.95 (ISBN 0-907234-23-2). Neugebauer Pr.
--Max the Artlover. LC 82-61832. (Max the Mouse Ser.). (Illus.). 24p. 1983. pap. 2.95 (ISBN 0-907234-25-9). Neugebauer Pr.
--Rainy Day Max. LC 82-61834. (Max the Mouse Ser.). (Illus.). 24p. 1982. pap. 2.95 (ISBN 0-907234-24-0). Neugebauer Pr.
Ward, John & Ward, Joanne. The Wide Mouth Frog. (Illus.). 26p. 1981. pap. 2.50x (ISBN 0-910195-01-3). Genesis Pubns.
Watson, Jean. Sounds, Sounds, All Around. (Illus.). 16p. 1983. Repr. of 1981 ed. pap. 0.99 (ISBN 0-86683-706-X). Winston Pr.
Zokeisha. Mousehouse. Klimo, Kate, ed. (Chubby Shape Bks.). (Illus.). 16p. 1983. 2.95 (ISBN 0-671-46129-X, Little). S&S.
PICTURE DICTIONARIES
see also English Language–Dictionaries, Juvenile
Johnson, Roxanna M. The Picture Communication Symbols. 3rd ed. (Illus.). 118p. 1982. 3 ring bdg. 36.00 (ISBN 0-9609160-0-8). Mayer-Johnson.
PICTURE FRAMES AND FRAMING
Woods, Michael. Mounting & Framing Pictures. LC 82-82919. (Illus.). 96p. 1983. pap. 6.95 (ISBN 0-668-05714-9, 5714). Arco.
PICTURE POST CARDS
see Postal Cards
PICTURE POSTERS
see Posters
PICTURE-WRITING, MAYA
Jones, Christopher & Satterthwaite, Linton. The Monuments & Inscriptions of Tikal, Pt. A: The Carved Monuments. LC 83-1086. (Tikal Reports Ser.: No. 33). (Illus.). 364p. 1982. 55.00 (ISBN 0-934718-07-5). Univ Mus of U PA.
PICTURES
see also Animal Pictures; Caricatures and Cartoons; Paintings; Portraits;
also engravings, Etchings, Paintings, and similar headings; and subdivision Pictorial works under various subjects, e.g. Natural history–Pictorial works
Woodford, Susan. Looking at Pictures. LC 82-14613. (Cambridge Introduction to the History of Art 6 Ser.). (Illus.). 128p. Date not set. 14.95 (ISBN 0-521-24371-8); pap. 1.25 (ISBN 0-521-28647-6). Cambridge U Pr.
PICTURES, HUMOROUS
see Caricatures and Cartoons; Wit and Humor, Pictorial
PIES
see Pastry
PIETISM
see also Evangelicalism
Erb, Peter C., ed. The Pietists. (Classics of Western Spirituality Ser.). 1983. 11.95 (ISBN 0-8091-0334-6); pap. 7.95 (ISBN 0-8091-2509-9). Paulist Pr.
PIEZO-ELECTRIC OSCILLATORS
see Oscillators, Crystal
PIEZO-ELECTRICITY
see Pyro- and Piezo-Electricity
PIG
see Swine
PIG IRON
see Cast Iron
PIGEONS
Allen, William H., Jr. How to Raise & Train Pigeons. LC 58-7602. (Illus.). 160p. 1982. pap. 8.95 (ISBN 0-8069-7652-7). Sterling.
PIGMENTATION
see Color of Man
PIGMENTS
see also Coloring Matter; Dyes and Dyeing; Paint; also names of pigments
Harley. Artists Pigments. 2nd ed. 1982. text ed. 49.95 (ISBN 0-408-70945-6). Butterworth.
Shaw, Jackie. Pigments of your Imagination, Vol. 1 - 3. (Orig.). 1978. Vol. 1. pap. 5.95 (ISBN 0-941284-06-9); Vol. 2. pap. 5.95 (ISBN 0-941284-07-7); Vol. 3. pap. 8.95 (ISBN 0-941284-08-5). Deco Design Studio.
PIGS
see Swine
PILE-DWELLINGS
see Lake-Dwellers and Lake-Dwellings
PILES (CIVIL ENGINEERING)
see Piling (Civil Engineering)
PILES (DISEASE)
see Hemorrhoids
PILGRIMS (NEW PLYMOUTH COLONY)–JUVENILE LITERATURE
Gardner, Allen H. Primer on Planning an Estate. 1981. pap. 15.95 (ISBN 0-686-84884-5). Lerner Law.
PILGRIMS AND PILGRIMAGES
see also Saints
Bevington, Helen. The Journey Is Everything. 250p. Date not set. 14.95 (ISBN 0-8223-0553-4). Duke.
Bhardwaj, Surinder M. Hindu Places of Pilgrimage in India: A Study in Cultural Geography. (Illus.). 278p. 1983. pap. 7.95 (ISBN 0-520-04951-9, CAL 621). U of Cal Pr.
Theertha, Rama. Pilgrimage & Spiritual Advancement. 23p. 1982. write for info. (ISBN 0-937698-02-4). Golden Mean.
PILING (CIVIL ENGINEERING)
Young, F. E., ed. Piles & Foundations. 328p. 1981. 90.00x (ISBN 0-7277-0118-5, Pub. by Telford England). State Mutual Bk.
PILIPINO LANGUAGE
see Tagalog Language
PILOTLESS AIRCRAFT
see Guided Missiles
PILOTS (AERONAUTICS)
see Air Pilots

PILOTS AND PILOTAGE
see also Navigation
Curry, Jane. The River's in My Blood: Riverboat Pilots Tell Their Stories. LC 82-11068. xx, 279p. 1983. 17.50 (ISBN 0-8032-1416-2). U of Nebr Pr.

PIMA INDIANS
see Indians of North America-Southwest, New

PING-PONG
see Table Tennis

PINTER, HAROLD, 1930-
Morrison, Kristin. Cantors & Chronicles: The Use of Narrative in the Plays of Samuel Beckett & Harold Pinter. LC 82-16086. 240p. 1983. lib. bdg. 20.00x (ISBN 0-226-54130-4). U of Chicago Pr.

PIO DA PIETRELCINA, FATHER
St. Albans, Suzanne. Magic of a Mystic: Stories of Padre Pio. 1983. 5.95 (ISBN 0-517-54847-X, C N Potter Bks). Crown.
White, Laura C., tr. Who is Padre Pio? (Illus.). 44p. 1955. pap. 0.75 (ISBN 0-686-81642-0). TAN Bks Pubs.

PIONEERS
see also Frontier and Pioneer Life
Johnston, Mary. Pioneers of the Old South. 1918. text ed. 8.50x (ISBN 0-686-83699-5). Elliots Bks.
Skinner, Constance L. Pioneers of the Old Southwest. 1919. text ed. 8.50x (ISBN 0-686-83700-2). Elliots Bks.

PIPE
see also Heat Pipes; Pipe, Steel; Pipe-Fitting; Pipe Lines
Hartman, W. & Williams, F. Pipe Drafting. 1981. 13.95 (ISBN 0-07-026945-9). McGraw.
Van Stijgeren, E., ed. Recent Advances In Pipe Support Design. (PVP Ser.: Vol. 68). 115p. 1982. 30.00 (H00225). ASME.
--Special Applications in Piping Dynamic Analysis. (PVP Ser.: Vol. 67). 80p. 1982. 20.00 (H00224). ASME.

PIPE, STEEL
American Welding Society. Recommended Practices & Procedures for Welding Plain Carbon Steel Pipe: D10.12. 1979. 8.00 (ISBN 0-686-43365-3). Am Welding.

PIPE-FITTING
see also Plumbing
U. S. Plumbing Fixtures & Fittings. 1982. 995.00 (ISBN 0-686-37719-2, 286). Predicasts.

PIPE LINES
see also Pipe;
also subdivision Pipe Lines under special subjects, e.g. Petroleum-Pipe Lines
Seiders, E. J., ed. Pipline Supervisory & Control Systems Workshop. 90p. 1982. 25.00 (I00149). ASME.
Smoldyrev, A. Ye. Pipeline Transport: Principles of Design. Cooley, W. C., ed. Peaboby, A. L., tr. from Rus. (Illus.). 345p. 1982. 60.00x (ISBN 0-918990-09-2). Terraspace.
Van Stijgeren, E. & Krawzya, L., eds. Practical Considerations In Piping Analysis. (PVP Ser.: Vol. 69). 181p. 1982. 34.00 (H00226). ASME.
Zamrik, S. Y. & Dietrich, D., eds. Pressure Vessels & Piping: Design Technology, 1982-A Decade of Progress. 647p. 1982. 85.00 (G00213). ASME.

PIPE-ORGAN
see Organ

PIPER, JOHN
West, Anthony. John Piper. 1979. 37.50 (ISBN 0-436-56590-0, Pub. by Secker & Warburg). David & Charles.

PIPES, TOBACCO
see Tobacco-Pipes

PIRATES
Ormerod. Piracy in the Ancient World. 286p. 1982. pap. 40.00x (ISBN 0-85323-044-7, Pub. by Liverpool Univ England). State Mutual Bk.
Perkins, Roger & Douglas-Morris, K. J. Gunfire in Barbary: Admiral Lord Exmouth's Battle with the Corsairs of Algiers in 1816. (Illus.). 200p. 1982. text ed. 24.50x (ISBN 0-85937-271-5). Sheridan.

PISCICULTURE
see Fish-Culture

PITT, WILLIAM, 1759-1806
Ehrman, John. The Younger Pitt: The Reluctant Transition. LC 82-42859. (Illus.). 736p. 1983. 49.50x (ISBN 0-8047-1184-4). Stanford U Pr.
--The Younger Pitt: The Years of Acclaim. (Illus.). 650p. 1969. text ed. 45.00x (ISBN 0-8047-1186-0). Stanford U Pr.

PITTSBURGH
Gay, Vernon, photos by. Discovering Pittsburgh's Sculpture. LC 82-50225. (Illus.). 462p. 1982. 21.95 (ISBN 0-8229-3467-1); pap. 12.95 (ISBN 0-8229-5348-X). U of Pittsburgh Pr.
Miller, Dorothy A. Poor Man's Guide to Pittsburgh. 3rd ed. (Illus.). 70p. 1981. pap. 4.95 (ISBN 0-9608484-0-1). New Pittsburgh.

PITUITARY BODY
De Kreter, D. M., et al, eds. The Pituitary & Testis: Clinical & Experimental Studies. (Monographs on Endocrinology: Vol. 25). (Illus.). 200p. 1983. 50.00 (ISBN 0-387-11874-8). Springer-Verlag.
Jefferson. The Invasive Adeomas of the Anterior Pituitary. 76p. 1982. 50.00x (ISBN 0-85323-471-X, Pub. by Liverpool Univ England). State Mutual Bk.

PL-ONE (COMPUTER PROGRAM LANGUAGE)
see P L-One (Computer Program Language)

PLACE-NAMES
see Names, Geographical

PLACENTA
Klopper, A., ed. Immunology of the Human Placenta: Supplement to the Quarterly Journal "Placenta", Vol. 4. 136p. 1982. 35.00 (ISBN 0-03-062117-8). Praeger.
Miller, R. K. The Placenta. Thiede, H., ed. 390p. 1982. 69.50 (ISBN 0-03-063037-1). Praeger.
Ramsey, Elizabeth A. The Placenta: Human & Animal. 204p. 1982. 32.50 (ISBN 0-03-060292-0). Praeger.
Wallenburg. Placental Transfer Primates. 300p. 1982. 56.50 (ISBN 0-03-063036-3). Praeger.

PLACES OF RETIREMENT
see Retirement, Places of

PLAGUE
Gottfried, Robert S. The Black Death. LC 82-48745. 240p. 1983. 14.95 (ISBN 0-02-912630-4). Free Pr.
Magor, J. T. Outbreaks of the Australian Plague Locust (Hortoicetes Terminifera Walk.) During the Seasons 1937 to 1962, with Particular Reference to Rainfall. 1970. 35.00x (ISBN 0-85135-002-X, Pub. by Centre Overseas Research). State Mutual Bk.

PLAINS, THE GREAT
see Great Plains

PLAITING
see Braid

PLANE GEOMETRY
see Geometry, Plane

PLANETS-JUVENILE LITERATURE
Erickson, K. Please, Lord, Untie My Tongue. 1983. pap. 2.25 (ISBN 0-570-03881-2). Concordia.

PLANKTON
see also Fresh-Water Biology
Raymont, J. E. Plankton & Productivity in the Oceans: Zooplankton, Vol. 2. 2nd ed. (Illus.). 700p. 1983. 75.00 (ISBN 0-08-024404-1); pap. 19.00 (ISBN 0-08-024403-3). Pergamon.
Strickland, Richard M. The Fertile Fjord: Plankton in Puget Sound. (A Puget Sound Bk.). (Illus.). 160p. (Orig.). 1983. pap. 8.95 (ISBN 0-295-95979-7, Pub. by Wash Sea Grant). U of Wash Pr.

PLANNED PARENTHOOD
see Birth Control

PLANNING
see also Curriculum Planning; Economic Policy; Educational Planning; Regional Planning; Social Policy
Ackoff, R. L. Concept of Corporate Planning. LC 74-100318. 158p. 1969. 19.95 (ISBN 0-471-00290-9, Pub. by Wiley-Interscience). Wiley.
Anderson, R. G. Management, Planning & Control. 400p. 1981. 35.00x (ISBN 0-7121-1277-4, Pub. by Macdonald & Evans). State Mutual Bk.
Annan, Bill & Hinchcliffe, Keith. Planning Policy Analysis & Public Spending: Theory & the Papua New Guinea Practice. 168p. 1982. text ed. 35.00x (ISBN 0-566-00496-8). Gower Pub Ltd.
Benjamin, Deborah V. A Road Map to Effective Planning & Time Management. rev. ed. 215p. 1982. pap. write for info. (ISBN 0-911347-00-3). Debron.
Branch, Melville C. Comprehensive Planning: General Theory & Principles. LC 83-61680. (Illus.). 1983. text ed. 12.95x (ISBN 0-913530-32-8). Palisades Pub.
Cole, Jacquelyn M. & Cole, Maurice F. Advisory Councils: A Theoretical & Practical Guide for Program Planners. (Illus.). 224p. 1983. text ed. 22.95 (ISBN 0-13-018184-6). P-H.
Killen, James E. Mathematical Programming Methods for Geographers & Planners. LC 82-42839. 384p. 1983. 35.00x (ISBN 0-312-50133-1). St Martin.
Rudman, Jack. Planning & Evaluation Assistant. (Career Examination Ser.: C-549). (Cloth bdg. avail. on request). pap. 12.00 (ISBN 0-8373-0549-7). Natl Learning.
Shrout, Beatrice L. How To: Programs & Skits. LC 82-60776. 240p. (Orig.). 1982. 8.50 (ISBN 0-9609070-0-9). B L Shrout.

PLANNING, CITY
see City Planning

PLANNING, CORPORATE
see Corporate Planning

PLANS
see Architectural Drawing; Maps; Mechanical Drawing

PLANT ANATOMY
see Botany-Anatomy

PLANT AND EQUIPMENT INVESTMENTS
see Capital Investments

PLANT ASSIMILATION
see Plants-Assimilation

PLANT ASSOCIATIONS
see Plant Communities

PLANT-BREEDING
see also Grafting; Grain-Breeding; Plant Genetics; Plant Propagation
Allard, Robert W. Principles of Plant Breeding. LC 60-14240. 485p. 1960. 27.95x (ISBN 0-471-02310-8). Wiley.

PLANT CELLS AND TISSUES
see also Cell Differentiation
Giles, Kenneth L. & Sen, S. K., eds. Plant Cell Culture in Crop Improvement. (Basic Life Sciences Ser.: Vol. 22). 514p. 1983. 65.00x (ISBN 0-306-41160-1, Plenum Pr). Plenum Pub.
Hall, John I. & Moore, Anthony L., eds. Isolation of Membranes & Organelles from Plants Cells. (Biological Techniques Ser.). Date not set. price not set (ISBN 0-12-318820-2). Acad Pr.

PLANT CHEMISTRY
see Botanical Chemistry

PLANT CLASSIFICATION
see Botany-Classification

PLANT COMMUNITIES
see also Botany-Ecology; Halophytes
McIntosh, R. P., ed. Phytosociology. LC 77-20258. (Benchmark Papers in Ecology: Vol. 6). 388p. 1978. 41.50 (ISBN 0-87933-312-X). Hutchinson Ross.

PLANT DESIGN
see Factories-Design and Construction

PLANT DISEASES
see also Garden Pests; Virus Diseases of Plants
also subdivision Diseases and Pests under particular subjects, e.g. Trees-Diseases and Pests
Asada, Y., et al, eds. Plant Infection: The Physiological & Biochemical Basis. 362p. 1983. 56.00 (ISBN 0-387-11873-X). Springer-Verlag.
Baruah, H. K. Textbook of Plant Pathology. 486p. 1979. 50.00 (ISBN 0-686-84470-X, Pub. by Oxford & I B H India). State Mutual Bk.
Buczacki, S. T., ed. Zoosporic Plant Pathogens. Date not set. price not set (ISBN 0-12-139180-9). Acad Pr.
Koske, R. E. Cookbook Statistics for Plant Pathology & Mycology. 65p. (Orig.). 1982. pap. text ed. 7.50x (ISBN 0-934454-94-9). Lubrecht & Cramer.
Misaghi, I. J. Physiology & Biochemistry of Plant-Pathogen Interactions. 275p. 1982. 32.50x (ISBN 0-306-41059-1, Plenum Pr). Plenum Pub.
Pandey, S. N. & Trivedi, P. S. Textbook of Botany: Vol. I: Algae, Fungi, Bacteria, Virus, Lichens, Mycoplasma & Elementary Plant Pathology. 5th ed. viii, 628p. 1982. text ed. 25.00x (ISBN 0-7069-1975-0, Pub. by Vikas India). Advent NY.
Rayechaudhuri, S. P. & Nariani, T. K. Virus & Mycoplasm Diseases of Plants in India. 102p. 1977. 50.00x (ISBN 0-686-84449-1, Pub by Oxford & I B H India). State Mutual Bk.
Rich, Avery E., ed. Potato Diseases. LC 82-24290. (Monograph). Date not set. price not set. Acad Pr.
Schneider, Raymond W., ed. Suppressive Soils & Plant Diseases. LC 82-72591. 96p. 1982. pap. text ed. 9.00 (ISBN 0-89054-048-9). Am Phytopathol Soc.
Singh, R. S. Plant Diseases. 564p. 1978. 62.00x (ISBN 0-686-84464-5, Pub. by Oxford & I B H India). State Mutual Bk.

PLANT ECOLOGY
see Botany-Ecology

PLANT EMBRYOLOGY
see Botany-Embryology

PLANT ENGINEERING
see also Factory and Trade Waste; Industrial Safety; Materials Handling; Plant Maintenance; Stores or Stock-Room Keeping; Water-Supply, Industrial
Elonka, S. M. Standard Basic Math & Applied Plant Calculations. 1977. text ed. 25.95 (ISBN 0-07-019297-9). McGraw.

PLANT FORMS IN DESIGNS
see Design, Decorative-Plant Forms

PLANT GENETICS
Improvement of Oil-Seed & Industrial Crops by Induced Mutations. 353p. 1982. pap. 42.00 (ISBN 92-0-011082-7, ISP 608, IAEA). Unipub.
Induced Mutations: A Tool in Plant Research. 538p. 1981. pap. 55.00 (ISBN 0-686-82544-6, ISP 591, IAEA). Unipub.
Induced Mutations in Vegetatively Propogated Plants II. 310p. 1982. pap. 36.50 (ISBN 92-0-111182-7, ISP 519, IAEA). Unipub.
Moore, D. M. Plant Cytogenetics. 1976. pap. 6.50x (ISBN 0-412-13440-3, Pub. by Chapman & Hall England). Methuen Inc.

PLANT GROWTH
see Growth (Plants)

PLANT INVESTMENTS
see Capital Investments

PLANT LOCATION
see Industries, Location of

PLANT MAINTENANCE
see also Machinery
Cooling, W. Colebrook. Simplified Low-Cost Maintenance Control. rev. ed. 128p. 1983. 24.95 (ISBN 0-8144-5657-X). Am Mgmt Assns.
Mann, Lawrence, Jr. Maintenance Management. LC 81-47628. 384p. 1983. 32.95x (ISBN 0-669-04715-5). Lexington Bks.
Marks, Nolan. On the Spot Repair Manual for Commercial Food Equipment. (Illus.). 80p. 1982. pap. write for info. (ISBN 0-941712-01-X). INtl Pub Corp OH.
Plant Maintenance Program. (Manual of Practice, Operations & Maintenance: No. 3). 112p. (Orig.). 1982. pap. text ed. 10.00 (ISBN 0-943244-38-2). Water Pollution.
Rudman, Jack. Heavy Equipment Repair Supervisor. (Career Examination Ser.: C-2614). (Cloth bdg. avail. on request). pap. 12.00 (ISBN 0-8373-2614-1). Natl Learning.
--Repair Supervisor. (Career Examination Ser.: C-2615). pap. 10.00 (ISBN 0-8373-2615-X); avail. Natl Learning.

PLANT MORPHOLOGY
see Botany-Morphology

PLANT NUTRITION
see Plants-Nutrition

PLANT PATHOLOGY
see Plant Diseases

PLANT PHYSIOLOGY
see also Germination; Growth (Plants); Plants-Assimilation; Plants-Irritability and Movements; Plants-Nutrition; Plants-Reproduction; Plants-Respiration; Plants-Transpiration; Plants, Flowering Of
Asada, Y., et al, eds. Plant Infection: The Physiological & Biochemical Basis. 362p. 1983. 56.00 (ISBN 0-387-11873-X). Springer-Verlag.
Black, C. A. Soil-Plant Relationships. 2nd ed. LC 67-28946. 792p. (Orig.). 1968. 49.95x (ISBN 0-471-07723-2). Wiley.
Devlin, Robert & Witham, Francis. Plant Physiology. 4th ed. 500p. 1983. text ed. write for info. (ISBN 0-87150-765-X). Grant Pr.
Lange, O. L., et al, eds. Physiological Plant Ecology III: Responses to the Chemical & Biological Environment. (Encyclopedia of Plant Physiology Ser.: Vol. 12C). (Illus.). 850p. 1983. 120.00 (ISBN 0-387-10907-2). Springer-Verlag.
Noggle, G. Ray & Fritz, George J. Introductory Plant Physiology. 2nd ed. (Illus.). 704p. 1983. text ed. 30.95 (ISBN 0-13-502096-4). P-H.
Parthier, B. & Boulter, D., eds. Nucleic Acids & Proteins in Plants II: Structure, Biochemistry, & Physiology of Nucleic Acids. (Encyclopedia of Plant Physiology: Vol. 14 B). (Illus.). 774p. 1983. 125.00 (ISBN 0-387-11140-9). Springer-Verlag.
Steward, F. C. & Bidwell, R. G., eds. Plant Physiology: A Treatise: Energy & Carbon Metabolism, Vol. 7. Date not set. 67.50 (ISBN 0-12-668607-6). Acad Pr.
Ting, Irwin P. & Gibbs, Martin, eds. Crassulacean Acid Metobolism. 316p. 1982. pap. 15.00 (ISBN 0-943088-00-3). Am Soc of Plant.
Wintermans, J. F. & Kuiper, P. J., eds. Biochemistry & Metabolism of Plant Lipids: Proceedings of the International Symposium on the Biochemistry & Metabolism of Plant Lipids, Fifth, Groningen, the Netherlands, June 7-10, 1982. (Developments in Plant Biology Ser.: Vol. 8). 600p. 1982. 85.00 (ISBN 0-444-80457-9, Biomedical Pr). Elsevier.

PLANT PROPAGATION
see also Grafting; Plant-Breeding; Seeds
Fitz, Franklin H. A Gardener's Guide to Propagating Food Plants. (Illus.). 160p. 1983. 10.95 (ISBN 0-684-17655-6, ScribT). Scribner.
Hartmann, Hudson T. & Kester, Dale E. Plant Propagation: Principles & Practices. 4th ed. (Illus.). 704p. 1983. text ed. 29.95 (ISBN 0-13-681007-1). P-H.
Improvement of Oil-Seed & Industrial Crops by Induced Mutations. 353p. 1982. pap. 42.00 (ISBN 92-0-011082-7, ISP 608, IAEA). Unipub.
Induced Mutations in Vegetatively Propogated Plants II. 310p. 1982. pap. 36.50 (ISBN 92-0-111182-7, ISP 519, IAEA). Unipub.
Wrights, John I. Plant Propogation for the Amateur Gardener. (Illus.). 1983. 16.95 (ISBN 0-7137-1155-8, Pub. by Blandford Pr England). Sterling.

PLANT REPRODUCTION
see Plants-Reproduction

PLANT RESPIRATION
see Plants-Respiration

PLANT SOCIETIES
see Plant Communities

PLANT TAXONOMY
see Botany-Classification

PLANT-WATER RELATIONSHIPS
Kozlowski, T. T. & Riker, A. J., eds. Water Deficits & Plant Growth: Additional Woody Crop Plants. (Vol. 7). Date not set. price not set (ISBN 0-12-424157-3). Acad Pr.
Kramer, Paul J., ed. Water Relations of Plants. 428p. 1983. price not set (ISBN 0-12-425040-8). Acad Pr.
Turner, N. C. & Kramer, P. J. Adaptation of Plants to Water & High Temperature Stress. 482p. 1980. text ed. 49.95x (ISBN 0-471-05372-4, Pub. by Wiley-Interscience). Wiley.

PLANTATION CROPS
see Tropical Crops

PLANTATION LIFE
Alexander, Donald C. Arkansas Plantation, 1920-1942. 1943. text ed. 32.50x (ISBN 0-686-83477-1). Elliots Bks.

PLANTATIONS
see also Plantation Life
Arrigo, Joseph A. & Batt, Cara M. Plantations: Fourty-Four of Louisiana's Most Beautiful Antebellum Plantation Houses. (Illus.). 96p. (Orig.). Date not set. pap. 5.95 (ISBN 0-938530-19-4, 19-4). Lexikos.
Courtney, P. P. Plantation Agriculture. (Advanced Economic Geographies Ser.). 296p. 1982. 35.00x (ISBN 0-7135-1256-3, Pub. by Bell & Hyman England). State Mutual Bk.
Women's Service League of West Feliciana Parish. Plantation Country. 325p. 1981. 9.95 (ISBN 0-9609422-0-3). Womens Serv.

PLANTING
see Agriculture; Gardening; Landscape Gardening; Trees

PLANTS
see also Botany; Climbing Plants; Flowers; Forage Plants; Gardening; Growth (Plants); Insectivorous Plants; Paleobotany; Phanerogams; Poisonous Plants; Pollen; Succulent Plants; Weeds
also names of individual plants, and headings beginning with the word Plant
Commonwealth Scientific & Industrial Research Institute (CSIRO) A Curious & Diverse Flora. Commonwealth Scientific & Industrial Research Institute (CSIRO) & Australian Academy of Science, eds. 1982. of slides 35.00 set (ISBN 0-686-43170-7, Pub. by CSIRO). Intl Schol Bk Serv.
DeRoo, Sally. Exploring Our Environment: A Resource Guide-Manual-Plants. (Illus.). 168p. 1977. instr.'s manual 6.00 (ISBN 0-89039-208-0). Ann Arbor Pubs.
--Exploring Our Environment: Plants-Student Materials 1. (Illus.). 32p. (gr. 3-6). 1977. wkbk 1.00 (ISBN 0-89039-229-3). Ann Arbor Pubs.
--Exploring Our Environment: Plants-Student Materials 2. 32p. (gr. 3-6). 1977. wkbk 1.00 (ISBN 0-89039-231-5). Ann Arbor Pubs.
Discovering Plant Life. (Discovering Science Ser.). 1983. lib. bdg. 15.96 (ISBN 0-86706-065-4, Pub. by Stonehenge). Silver.
Gleason & Cronquist. Manuel of Vascular Plants. 810p. 1963. text ed. write for info. Grant Pr.
Koedam, A. & Margaris, N. Aromatic Plants. 1982. text ed. 41.50 (ISBN 90-247-2720-0, Pub. by Martinus Nijhoff Netherlands). Kluwer Boston.
Koopowitz, Harold & Kaye, Hilary. Plant Extinction: A Global Crisis. LC 82-62894. 256p. 1983. 16.95 (ISBN 0-913276-44-8). Stone Wall Pr.
The Lives of Plants: Exploring the Wonders of Botany. (Illus.). 256p. 1983. 14.95 (ISBN 0-686-83675-8, ScribT). Scribner.
Moir, May A. The Garden Watcher. LC 82-24728. (Illus.). 96p. 1983. pap. text ed. 12.00x (ISBN 0-8248-0789-8). UH Pr.
Whittaker, Robert H. Ordination of Plant Communities. 1982. 29.50 (ISBN 90-6193-565-2, Pub. by Junk Pubs Netherlands). Kluwer Boston.
PLANTS–ANATOMY
see Botany–Anatomy
PLANTS–ASSIMILATION
Epstein, Emanuel. Mineral Nutrition of Plants: Principles & Perspectives. LC 75-165018. 412p. 1972. 24.95x (ISBN 0-471-24340-X). Wiley.
Sutcliffe, J. F. & Baker, D. A. Plants & Mineral Salts. 1975. 54.00x (ISBN 0-686-84465-3, Pub. by Oxford & I B H India). State Mutual Bk.
PLANTS–CLASSIFICATION
see Botany–Classification
PLANTS–COLLECTION AND PRESERVATION
Kaden, Vera. The Illustration of Plants & Gardens, 1500-1850. (Illus.). 113p. 1982. pap. 15.00 (ISBN 0-686-43333-5). Intl Pubns Serv.
PLANTS–DISEASES
see Plant Diseases
PLANTS–ECOLOGY
see Botany–Ecology
PLANTS–EMBRYOLOGY
see Botany–Embryology
PLANTS–FLOWERING
see Plants, Flowering Of
PLANTS–GENETICS
see Plant Genetics
PLANTS–GROWTH
see Growth (Plants)
PLANTS–IDENTIFICATION
Batson, Wade T. Genera of the Eastern Plants. 3rd ed. LC 77-24339. 203p. 1977. pap. text ed. 11.95x (ISBN 0-471-03497-5). Wiley.
Baumgardt, John P. How to Identify Flowering Plant Families. (Illus.). 269p. 1982. pap. 22.95 (ISBN 0-917304-21-7). Timber.
PLANTS–IRRITABILITY AND MOVEMENTS
see also Insectivorous Plants
Darwin, Charles R. The Power of Movement in Plants. 3rd ed. LC 72-3901. (Illus.). x, 592p. 1972. write for info. (ISBN 0-404-08415-X). AMS Pr.
PLANTS–JUVENILE LITERATURE
Klimo, Kate, ed. Look at Plants with E.T. (Illus.). 14p. 1982. 3.50 (ISBN 0-671-46435-3, Little). S&S.
PLANTS–MORPHOLOGY
see Botany–Morphology
PLANTS–MOVEMENTS
see Plants–Irritability and Movements
PLANTS–NUTRITION
see also Hydroponics
Epstein, Emanuel. Mineral Nutrition of Plants: Principles & Perspectives. LC 75-165018. 412p. 1972. 24.95x (ISBN 0-471-24340-X). Wiley.
Kozma, Pal, ed. Control of the Nutrition of Cultivated Plants-Controle De L'Alimentation Des Plantes Cultivees, 2 Vols. (Third Colloque Europeen et Meditarrneen, Budapest, Universite d'Horticulture, 1972). (Illus.). 1975. 67.50 (ISBN 963-05-0911-3). Intl Pubns Serv.
PLANTS–PATHOLOGY
see Plant Diseases
PLANTS–REPRODUCTION
Willson, Mary F. Plant Reproductive Ecology. 300p. 1983. 40.00 (ISBN 0-471-08362-3, Pub. by Wiley-Interscience). Wiley.
PLANTS–RESPIRATION
Lemon, Edgar R. Co2 & Plants. 350p. 1983. lib. bdg. 25.00x (ISBN 0-86531-597-3). Westview.
Opik, Helgi. Respiration of Higher Plants. (Studies in Biology: No. 120). 64p. 1980. pap. text ed. 8.95 (ISBN 0-7131-2801-1). E Arnold.
PLANTS–SOILLESS CULTURE
see Hydroponics
PLANTS–TRANSPIRATION
Planting & Transplanting. 1982. write for info. Bklyn Botanic.
PLANTS, CULTIVATED
see also Flowers; Gardening; Perennials; Plants, Edible; Plants, Ornamental
Bosel, T. K. & Bhattacharjee, S. K. Garden Plants. 282p. 1980. 50.00x (ISBN 0-686-84453-X, Pub. by Oxford & I B H India). State Mutual Bk.
Denno, Robert F. & McClure, Mark S., eds. Variable Plants & Herbivores in Natureal & Managed Systems. Date not set. price not set (ISBN 0-12-209160-4). Acad Pr.
Foster, Raymond. The Garden in Autumn & Winter. (Illus.). 192p. 1983. 24.95 (ISBN 0-7153-8416-3). David & Charles.
Hawkes, J. G. The Diversity of Crop Plants. (Illus.). 208p. 1983. text ed. 20.00x (ISBN 0-674-21286-X). Harvard U Pr.
Thompson, R. & Casey, R. Perspectives for Peas & Lupins As Protein Crops. 1983. 54.50 (ISBN 90-247-2792-8, Pub. by Martinus Nijhoff Netherlands). Kluwer Boston.
PLANTS, EDIBLE
Crowe, Andrew. A Field Guide to the Native Edible Plants of New Zealand. (Illus.). 196p. 1983. 19.95 (ISBN 0-00-216983-5, Pub. by W Collins Australia). Intl Schol Bk Serv.
PLANTS, EFFECT OF LIGHT ON
Whatley, F. R. & Whatley, J. M. Light & Plant Life. (Studies in Biology: No. 124). 96p. 1980. pap. text ed. 8.95 (ISBN 0-7131-2785-6). E Arnold.
PLANTS, EFFECT OF MINERALS ON
Epstein, Emanuel. Mineral Nutrition of Plants: Principles & Perspectives. LC 75-165018. 412p. 1972. 24.95x (ISBN 0-471-24340-X). Wiley.
PLANTS, FLOWERING OF
Baumgardt, John P. How to Identify Flowering Plant Families. (Illus.). 269p. 1982. pap. 22.95 (ISBN 0-917304-21-7). Timber.
PLANTS, FOSSIL
see Paleobotany
PLANTS, INDUSTRIAL
see Factories
PLANTS, MEDICINAL
see Botany, Medical
PLANTS, ORNAMENTAL
see also Ground Cover Plants;
also names of individual flowers, plants, shrubs, and trees
Krussman, Gerd. A Pocket Guide to Choosing Woody Ornamentals. Epp, Michael, tr. from Ger. Orig. Title: Taschenbuch Der Geholzverwendung. (Illus.). 140p. 1982. pap. 14.95 (ISBN 0-917304-24-1). Timber.
Workman, Richard W. Growing Native: Native Plants for Landscape Use in Coastal South Florida. (Illus.). 64p. pap. 9.95 (ISBN 0-686-84239-1). Banyan Bks.
PLANTS, POISONOUS
see Poisonous Plants
PLANTS, SEX IN
see Plants–Reproduction
PLANTS AND ANIMALS, GEOGRAPHIC DISTRIBUTION OF
see Geographical Distribution of Animals and Plants
PLANTS AND WATER
see Plant-Water Relationships
PLANTS IN LITERATURE
Wait, Minnie W. & Leonard, Merton C. Among Flowers & Trees with the Poets or the Plant Kingdom in Verse: A Practical Cyclopedia for Lovers of Flowers. 415p. 1982. Repr. of 1901 ed. lib. bdg. 45.00 (ISBN 0-89760-020-7). Telegraph Bks.
PLASMA (IONIZED GASES)
see also Plasma Dynamics
Casini, G. Plasma Physics for Thermonuclear Fusion Reactors. (Ispra Courses on Nuclear Engineering & Technology Ser.). 496p. 1982. 74.50 (ISBN 3-7186-0091-9). Harwood Academic.
Golant, V. E., et al. Fundamentals of Plasma Physics. LC 79-19650. (Plasma Physics Ser.). 405p. 1980. 65.95x (ISBN 0-471-04593-4, Pub. by Wiley-Interscience). Wiley.
Klimontovich, Yu L. Kinetic Theory of Nonideal Gases & Nonideal Plasmas, Vol. 105. Bakescu, R., tr. LC 82-9044. (International Series in Natural Philosophy). (Illus.). 328p. 1982. 65.00 (ISBN 0-08-021671-4). Pergamon.
Veprek, S. & Venugopalan, M., eds. Plasma Chemistry, Vol. IV. (Topics in Current Chemistry Ser.: Vol. 107). (Illus.). 186p. 1983. 34.00 (ISBN 0-387-11828-4). Springer-Verlag.
PLASMA DYNAMICS
see also Magnetohydrodynamics
Birdsall. Plasma Physics via Computer. 1983. text ed. write for info. (ISBN 0-07-005371-5). McGraw.
Gormezano, C. & Leotta, G. G., eds. Heating in Toroidal Plasmas III: Proceedings of the 3rd Joint Varenna-Grenoble International Symposium, Grenoble, France, 22-26 March 1982, 3 vols. 1224p. 1982. pap. 150.00 set (ISBN 0-08-029984-9). Pergamon.
PLASMA MEMBRANES
see also Cells–Permeability
Kepner, G. R., ed. Cell Membrane Permeability & Transport. LC 79-11930. (Benchmark Papers in Human Physiology: Vol. 12). 410p. 1979. 50.00 (ISBN 0-87933-352-9). Hutchinson Ross.
Tindall, Richard S. A., ed. Therapeutic Apheresis & Plasma Perfusion. LC 82-17236. (Progress in Clinical & Biological Research Ser.: Vol. 106). 492p. 1982. 48.00 (ISBN 0-8451-0106-4). A R Liss.
PLASMOGENY
see Life–Origin
PLASTERING
Beard, Geoffrey. Stucco & Decorative Plasterwork in Europe. LC 82-49006. (Icon Editions). (Illus.). 165p. 1983. 50.00 (ISBN 0-06-430383-7, HarpT). Har-Row.
PLASTIC COATING
Seymour, R. B. Plastics vs. Corrosives. (Society of Plastics Engineers Monographs). 285p. 1982. text ed. 47.50x (ISBN 0-471-08182-5, Pub. by Wiley-Interscience). Wiley.
PLASTIC INDUSTRIES
see Plastics Industry and Trade
PLASTIC MATERIALS
see Plastics
PLASTIC PRODUCTS
see Plastics
PLASTIC SURGERY
see Surgery, Plastic
PLASTICITY
see also Materials–Creep; Plastics; Rheology
Bishop, Beverly & Craik, Rebecca L. Neural Plasticity. 1982. pap. 5.00 (ISBN 0-912452-38-2). Am Phys Therapy Assn.
Mendelson, Alexander. Plasticity: Theory & Application. LC 82-21231. 368p. 1983. Repr. of 1968 ed. lib. bdg. 21.00 (ISBN 0-89874-582-9). Krieger.
Yong, R. N. & Selig, E. T., eds. Application of Plasticity & Generalized Stress-Strain in Geotechnical Engineering. LC 81-71796. 360p. 1982. pap. text ed. 27.25 (ISBN 0-87262-294-0). Am Soc Civil Eng.
PLASTICS
see also Chemistry, Organic–Synthesis; Gums and Resins; Plasticity; Reinforced Plastics; Thermoplastics
also names of plastics, e.g. Nylon
Ash, M. & Ash, I. Encyclopedia of Plastics, Polymers & Resins Vol. 1, A-G. 1981. 75.00 (ISBN 0-8206-0290-6). Chem Pub.
--Encyclopedia of Plastics, Polymers & Resins Vol. 2, H-P. 1982. 75.00 (ISBN 0-8206-0296-5). Chem Pub.
--Encyclopedia of Plastics, Polymers & Resins Vol. 3, Q-Z. 1983. 75.00 (ISBN 0-8206-0303-1). Chem Pub.
Bikales, Norbert M., ed. Molding of Plastics. LC 78-172950. 230p. pap. text ed. 16.00 (ISBN 0-471-07233-8). Krieger.
Business Communications Staff. Plastics Conference Proceedings, 1982. 1983. 125.00 (ISBN 0-686-84693-1). BCC.
--Plastics in Transportation. 1983. 1000.00 (ISBN 0-686-84702-4, P-069). BCC.
--Plastics Scrap & Regrind. 1983. 1500.00 (ISBN 0-686-84700-8, P-070). BCC.
Green, Andrew, ed. Emerging High Performance Structural Plastic Technology. LC 82-70767. 92p. 1982. pap. text ed. 16.00 (ISBN 0-87262-305-X). Am Soc Civil Eng.
Plastics EMI Shielding: Materials, Equipment, Markets. (Illus.). 170p. 1982. 1500.00 (ISBN 0-686-43331-9). Knowledge Indus.
Whelan, A. & Dunning, D., eds. Developments in Plastics Technology, Vol. 1. (Illus.). 285p. 1983. 57.50 (ISBN 0-85334-155-9, Pub. by Applied Sci England). Elsevier.
Working with Plastics. (Home Repair & Improvement Ser.). 1982. lib. bdg. 15.96 (ISBN 0-8094-3507-1, Pub. by Time-Life). Silver.
PLASTICS–DICTIONARIES
Kaliske, G. Dictionary of Plastics Technology in English, German, French & Russian. 384p. 74.50 (ISBN 0-444-99687-7). Elsevier.
PLASTICS INDUSTRY AND TRADE
Friedel, Robert. Pioneer Plastic: The Making & Selling of Celluloid. LC 81-69818. (Illus.). 176p. 1983. 19.95 (ISBN 0-299-09170-8). U of Wis Pr.
PLATH, SYLVIA, 1932-1963
Novak, Robert. Sleeping with Sylvia Plath. 1983. 3.00 (ISBN 0-686-43216-9). Windless Orchard.
PLATO, 427?-347 B.C.
Allen, R. E. Plato's Parmenides: Translation & Analysis. LC 82-7051. 320p. 1983. 25.00x (ISBN 0-8166-1070-3). U of Minn Pr.
Hare, R. M. Plato. (Past Masters Ser.). 96p. 1982. 13.95 (ISBN 0-19-287586-8). Oxford U Pr.
--Plato. Thomas, Keith, ed. (Past Masters Ser.). 96p. 1983. pap. 3.95 (ISBN 0-19-287585-X, GB). Oxford U Pr.
Harris, W. T. The Mythology of Plato & Dante & the Future Life. (The Essential Library of the Great Philosophers). (Illus.). 107p. 1983. Repr. of 1896 ed. 71.85 (ISBN 0-89901-091-1). Found Class Reprints.
Jayne, Sears R., tr. Commentary on Plato's Symposium on Love by Marsilio Ficino. 2nd rev. ed. 300p. (Latin.). Date not set. pap. price not set (ISBN 0-88214-600-9). Spring Pubns.
PLATTDEUTSCH
see Low German Language
PLATYHELMINTHES
see also Cestoda
Prudhoe, Stephen & Bray, Rodney A. Platyhelminth Parasites of the Amphibia. (Illus.). 218p. 1982. 87.00x (ISBN 0-19-858509-8). Oxford U Pr.
PLAY
see also Amusements; Drama in Education; Games; Hobbies; Recreation; Recreational Therapy; Sports
Manning, Frank E., ed. The World of Play. LC 82-83395. (Annual Proceedings of the American Anthropological Association Study of Play (TAASP)). 240p. (Orig.). 1983. pap. text ed. 14.95 (ISBN 0-88011-059-7). Leisure Pr.
Neuschutz, Karin. The Doll Book. Schneider, Ingun, tr. from Swedish. (Illus.). 184p. (Orig.). 1983. pap. 8.95 (ISBN 0-943914-01-9, Dist. by Kampmann & Co). Larson Pubns Inc.
Play. (Leisure Today Ser.). 32p. 1.50 (ISBN 0-88314-121-3). AAHPERD.
PLAY–THERAPEUTIC USE
see Play Therapy
PLAY CENTERS
see Playgrounds
PLAY DIRECTION (THEATER)
see Theater–Production and Direction
PLAY PRODUCTION (THEATER)
see Theater–Production and Direction
PLAY THERAPY
Weller, B. Helping Sick Children Play. 1982. 25.00x (ISBN 0-7020-0792-7, Pub. by Cassell England). State Mutual Bk.
PLAYBILLS
see also Posters
Playbills: A Guide to the Microfilm Collection. LC 82-5313. 380p. 1982. 65.00 (ISBN 0-89235-037-7). Res Pubns Conn.
PLAYGROUND BALL
see Softball
PLAYGROUNDS
Plantinga, John H. A Creative Alternative to Swingsets: Guidelines for Planning & Designing Creative Playgrounds. 67p. 1977. pap. 4.00 (ISBN 0-686-84035-6). U OR Ctr Leisure.
PLAYING-CARDS
see Cards
PLAYS
see Drama
PLAYS, CHRISTMAS
see Christmas Plays
PLAYS, COLLEGE
see College and School Drama
PLAYS, MEDIEVAL
see Mysteries and Miracle-Plays
PLAYS, TELEVISION
see Television Plays
PLAYS FOR CHILDREN
see Children's Plays
PLAYWRIGHTS
see Dramatists
PLEA BARGAINING
Edwards, Mary F., ed. Settlement & Plea Bargaining. 388p. 1981. pap. 35.00 (ISBN 0-941916-02-2). Assn Trial Ed.
PLEADING
see also Actions and Defenses; Bills of Particulars; Forms (Law)
Givens, R. A. Advocacy: The Art of Pleading a Case. 1980. 60.00 (ISBN 0-07-023355-1); pap. 20.00 (ISBN 0-07-023356-X); suppl. 20.00 (ISBN 0-686-42845-5). McGraw.
PLECTRAL INSTRUMENTS
see Stringed Instruments
PLEISTOCENE PERIOD
see Geology, Stratigraphic–Pleistocene
PLEURA–DISEASES
Light, Richard W. Pleural Diseases. (Illus.). 300p. 1982. text ed. write for info. (ISBN 0-8121-0886-8). Lea & Febiger.
PLINIUS CAECILIUS SECUNDUS, C.
Pliny. Fifty Letters of Pliny, Vol. 3. Sherwin-White, A. N., et al, eds. 350p. 1982. 27.00x (ISBN 0-19-814591-8). Oxford U Pr.
PLIOCENE PERIOS
see Geology, Stratigraphic–Pliocene
PLOTINUS, d. 270 A.D.
Atkinson, M. J., ed. A Commentary on Plotinus: Emnead, Vol. I. (Classical & Philosophical Monographs). 1982. 59.50 (ISBN 0-19-814719-8). Oxford U Pr.
PLOTS (DRAMA, NOVEL, ETC.)
see also Characters and Characteristics in Literature; Film Adaptations; Moving-Pictures–Plots, Themes, etc.; Musical Revues, Comedies, etc.–Stories, Plots, etc.; Operas–Stories, Plots, etc.
Melville, Herman. Redburn, White-Jacket, Moby-Dick. Tanselle, Thomas G., ed. LC 82-18677. 1500p. 1983. 27.50 (ISBN 0-940450-09-7). Literary Classics.
PLUGS (ELECTRICITY)
see Electric Contactors
PLUMBING
see also Drainage, House; Pipe-Fitting; Sanitary Engineering; Sewerage

Blower, G. J. Plumbing. (Illus.). 208p. 1982. pap. text ed. 13.95x (ISBN 0-7121-1750-4). Intl Ideas.
Fredriksson, Don. Plumbing for Dummies: A Guide to the Maintenance & Repair of Everything Including the Kitchen Sink. (Illus.). 256p. 1983. pap. 10.95 (ISBN 0-672-52738-3). Bobbs.
Jones, Peter. The Complete Book of Home Plumbing. (Illus.). 128p. 1983. pap. 10.95 (ISBN 0-686-83787-8, ScribT). Scribner.

PLUMBING-ESTIMATES

The U. S. Plumbing Fixtures Industry. 1982. 475.00 (ISBN 0-686-38428-8, 312). Busn Trend.

PLUMBISM

see Lead-Poisoning

PLUMER, WILLIAM, 1759-1850

The William Plumer Papers: A Guide to the Microform Edition. 87p. 1982. 25.00 (ISBN 0-667-00663-X). Microfilming Corp.

PLURALISM

see also Reality

Clark, Michael D. Coherent Variety: The Idea of Diversity in British & American Conservative Thought. LC 82-9228. (Contributions in Political Science Ser.: No. 86). 248p. 1983. lib. bdg. 35.00 (ISBN 0-313-23284-9, CCV/). Greenwood.
Walzer, Michael. The Spheres of Justice: A Defense of Pluralism & Equality. LC 82-72409. 356p. 1983. 19.95 (ISBN 0-465-08190-8). Basic.

PLURALISM (SOCIAL SCIENCES)

see also Ethnicity

Ehrlich, S. Pluralism on & off Course. (Illus.). 276p. 1982. pap. 40.00 (ISBN 0-08-027936-8); 19.50 (ISBN 0-08-028114-1). Pergamon.

PLURILINGUALISM

see Multilingualism

PLYMOUTH AUTOMOBILE

see Automobiles-Types-Plymouth

PNEUMA

see Soul

PNEUMATIC CONTROL

Wray, Lynn & Meyer, Leo. National Standards for Total System Balance: Air Distribution-Hydronic Systems-Sound. 1982. 45.00 (ISBN 0-910289-00-X). Assoc Air Balance.

PNEUMOMASSAGE

see Massage

PNEUMONIA

Weinstein. Pneumonias. (Seminars in Infections Disease Ser.: Vol. 4). 1983. price not set (ISBN 0-86577-091-3). Thieme-Stratton.

PNEUMONITIS

see Pneumonia

POCKET BATTLESHIPS

see Warships

POCKET COMPANIONS

see Handbooks, Vade-Mecums, etc.

PODAGRA

see Gout

POE, EDGAR ALLAN, 1809-1849

Kush, S. S. The End Befallen Edgar Allen Poe. 28p. 1982. pap. 2.00x (ISBN 0-686-38373-7). Singing Horse.
Montegemery, Marion. Why Poe Drank Liquor: Vol. II in the Trilogy, The Prophetic Poet & the Spirit of the Age. 442p. 1982. 19.95 (ISBN 0-89385-026-8). Sugden.
Robertson, John W. Edgar A. Pe: A Study of a Psychopathic. 331p. 1982. Repr. of 1943 ed. lib. bdg. 45.00 (ISBN 0-89987-728-1). Darby Bks.

POETESSES

see Women Poets

POETICS

Here are entered treatises on the art of poetry (technique and philosophy) Works limited to the philosophy of poetry are entered under the heading Poetry.

see also English Language-Rime-Dictionaries; Poetry-Authorship; Versification

Barnstone, Willis. The Poetics of Ecstasy. 320p. 1983. text ed. cancelled (ISBN 0-8419-0814-1); pap. text ed. 19.50x (ISBN 0-8419-0849-4). Holmes & Meier.
Boulton, Majorie. The Anatomy of Poetry. Rev. ed. 1982. pap. 7.95 (ISBN 0-7100-9087-0). Routledge & Kegan.
Das, Manas M. The Rooted Alien: A Study of Hardy's Poetic Sensibility. 160p. 1982. text ed. 13.75x (ISBN 0-391-02805-7). Humanities.
Deen, Leonard W. Conversing in Paradise: Poetic Genius & Identity-as-Community in Blake's Los. LC 82-20307. 288p. 1983. text ed. 23.00 (ISBN 0-8262-0396-5). U of Mo Pr.
Ferguson, Margaret W. Trials of Desire: Renaissance Defenses of Poetry. LC 82-8525. (Illus.). 280p. 1983. pap. text ed. 22.50x (ISBN 0-300-02787-7). Yale U Pr.
Lamborn, E. A. Poetic Values: A Guide to the Appreciation of the Golden Treasury. 226p. 1982. Repr. of 1928 ed. lib. bdg. 25.00 (ISBN 0-89984-805-2). Century Bookbindery.
Rosenthal, M. L. & Gall, Sally M. The Modern Poetic Sequence: The Genius of Modern Poetry. 544p. 1983. 29.95 (ISBN 0-19-503170-9). Oxford U Pr.

POETRY

see also Children'S Poetry; Hymns; Limericks; Love Poetry; Nursery Rhymes; Poetry of Places; Religious Poetry; Sonnets also English Poetry, French Poetry, etc. and subdivision Poetry under particular subjects and names of famous persons, e.g. Christmas-Poetry, Lincoln, Abraham-Poetry

Cobham, Rosemary. Kaleidoscope Plus. 160p. 1982. 12.95 (ISBN 0-85683-046-1, Pub. by Shepheard-Walwyn). Flatiron Book Dist.
Hollis, Jocelyn. Peace Poems: New Poems on Peace for the 1980s. Topham, J., ed. LC 82-13915. 24p. (Orig.). Date not set. pap. text ed. 3.95 (ISBN 0-933486-40-5). Am Poetry Pr.
Kintgen, Eugene R. The Perception of Poetry. LC 82-48387. 288p. 1983. 22.50x (ISBN 0-253-34345-3). Ind U Pr.
Knott, Bill. Becos: Poems. LC 82-16712. 60p. 1983. 10.00 (ISBN 0-394-52924-3). Random.
Porter, Peter & Sergeant, Howard. Gregory Awards. 1981. 11.50 (ISBN 0-436-37812-4, Pub. by Secker & Warburg). David & Charles.

POETRY-AUTHORSHIP

Hackleman, Wauneta, ed. The Study & Writing of Poetry: American Women Poets Discuss Their Craft. LC 82-50773. 420p. 1983. 27.50X (ISBN 0-87875-259-5); pap. 12.50X (ISBN 0-87875-266-8). Whitston Pub.

POETRY-BIBLIOGRAPHY

Editorial Board, Granger Book Co., ed. Poetry Index Annual 1983. 1983. price not set (ISBN 0-89609-237-2). Granger Bk.
Granger Book Company, Inc., ed. Index to Poetry in Periodicals: 1925 to 1929. LC 81-80120. 230p. 1983. 39.99x (ISBN 0-89609-235-6). Granger Bk.

POETRY-COLLECTIONS

see also the poetry of specific nationalities, e.g. English Poetry, French Poetry

Amanuddin, Syed. World Poetry in English: Essays & Interviews. 179p. 1981. text ed. 12.75x (ISBN 0-391-02790-5, 41054, Pub. by Sterling India). Humanities.
Blessing, Richard. Poems & Stories. 88p. 1983. 13.00 (ISBN 0-937872-12-1); pap. 6.00 (ISBN 0-937872-13-X). Dragon Gate.
Editorial Board, Grange Book Co., ed. The World's Best Poetry: Supplement One: Twentieth Century English & American Verse, 1900-1929. (The Granger Anthology Ser.: No. 1). 400p. 1983. 39.50 (ISBN 0-89609-236-4). Granger Bk.
Findlay, Ted & Beasley, Conger, Jr., eds. Above the Thunder: A Collection of Personal Experiences from Concern Counts. LC 82-72730. (Illus.). 255p. (Orig.). 1982. pap. 6.95 (ISBN 0-686-38089-4). Concern Counts.
Grigson. The Gambit Book of Popular Verse. 1971. pap. 6.95 (ISBN 0-87645-114-8). Gambit.
Grigson, Geoffrey, ed. Country Poems. (Pocket Poet Ser.). 1959. pap. 1.25 (ISBN 0-8023-9046-3). Dufour.
--The Faber Book of Poems & Places. 387p. 1983. pap. 7.95 (ISBN 0-571-13008-9). Faber & Faber.
Lynch, Richard & Rae, Helen, eds. Signal Fire 1982. (Signal Fire Ser.). (Illus.). 104p. (Orig.). 1982. pap. 3.95 (ISBN 0-941588-13-0). Creative Assoc.
Mitchell, Walter & Chenevert, C. Skip, Jr. Unopened Letters & a Virgin Page. limited ed. 64p. 1983. 5.50 (ISBN 0-682-49968-4). Exposition.
Mordecai, Pamela & Morris, Mervyn, eds. Jamaica Woman, No. 29. (Caribbean Writers Ser.). 128p. (Orig.). 1982. pap. text ed. 5.00x (ISBN 0-435-98600-7). Heinemann Ed.
Morris, Joseph & Adams, St. Claire, eds. Facing Forward: Poems of Courage. 257p. 1982. Repr. of 1925 ed. lib. bdg. 30.00 (ISBN 0-89987-645-5). Darby Bks.
Newman, Anne & Suk, Julie, eds. Bear Crossings: An Anthology of North American Poets. 151p. 1983. pap. 6.95 (ISBN 0-917990-08-0). New South Co.
Poetry Series I, Vol. 21. 10.00 (ISBN 0-686-37991-8). Quarterly Rev.
Poetry Series II, Vol. 22. 10.00 (ISBN 0-686-37993-4). Quarterly Rev.
Poetry Series III, Vol. 23. 10.00 (ISBN 0-686-37994-2). Quarterly Rev.
Sargeant, Howard & Fuller, John, eds. Gregory Awards Anthology 1982. 128p. 1982. pap. text ed. 8.50x (ISBN 0-85635-437-6, 51480, Pub. by Carcanet New Pr England). Humanities.
Von Heitlinger, E. I. & Ursus, Thomas O., eds. New Poets Two. (Annual New Poets Anthologies Ser.). 114p. 1983. lib. bdg. 22.95 (ISBN 0-910691-01-0). Ursus Pr.

POETRY-HISTORY AND CRITICISM

Bhattacherje, M. M. Pictorial Poetry. 182p. 1983. Repr. of 1982 ed. lib. bdg. 40.00 (ISBN 0-686-42932-X). Century Bookbindery.
Brink, Charles O. Horace on Poetry: Epistles Book II: The Letters to Augustus & Florus, Vol. 3. LC 63-4908. 656p. 1982. 99.50 (ISBN 0-521-20069-5). Cambridge U Pr.
Cunningham, John. The Poetics of Byron's Comedy in Don Juan. (Salzburg - Romantic Reassessment Ser.: No. 106). 242p. 1982. pap. text ed. 25.00x (ISBN 0-391-02778-6, Pub. by Salzburg Austria). Humanities.
Daydi-Tolson, Santiago. The Post-Civil War Spanish Social Poets. (World Authors Ser.). 192p. 1983. lib. bdg. 19.95 (ISBN 0-8057-6533-6, Twayne). G K Hall.
De C. L. Huffman, Claire. Montale & the Occasions of Poetry. LC 82-61368. 356p. 1983. 25.00x (ISBN 0-691-06562-4). Princeton U Pr.
Ferguson, Margaret W. Trials of Desire: Renaissance Defenses of Poetry. LC 82-8525. (Illus.). 280p. 1983. pap. text ed: 22.50x (ISBN 0-300-02787-7). Yale U Pr.
Greene, Myles. Adventures in Philosophical Poetry & Literature. 48p. 1983. 1.95 (ISBN 0-9606994-2-2). Greenview Pubns.
Grimshaw, James A., Jr., ed. Robert Penn Warren's Brother to Dragons: A Discussion. (Southern Literary Studies). 344p. 1983. text ed. 27.50X (ISBN 0-8071-1065-5). La State U Pr.
Halperin, David M. Before Pastoral: Theocritus & the Ancient Tradition of Bucolic Poetry. LC 82-10879. 296p. 1983. text ed. 26.00x (ISBN 0-300-02582-3). Yale U Pr.
Hogg, James, ed. Stylistic Media of Byron's Satire. (Salzburg - Romantic Reassessment Ser.: Vol. 81, No. 3). 83p. 1982. pap. text ed. 25.00x (ISBN 0-391-02804-9, Pub. by Salzburg Austria). Humanities.
Houston, John P. The Rhetoric of Poetry in the Renaissance & 17th Century. 344p. 1983. text ed. 32.50 (ISBN 0-8071-1066-3). La State U Pr.
Milosz, Czeslaw. The Witness of Poetry. (Charles Eliot Norton Lectures, 1981-1982). 160p. 1983. 8.95 (ISBN 0-674-95382-7). Harvard U Pr.
Moore, Dennis. The Politics of Spenser's Complaints & Sidney's Philsides Poems. (Salzburg - Elizabethean Studies: No. 101). 196p. 1982. pap. text ed. 25.00x (ISBN 0-391-02783-2, Pub. by Salzburg Austria). Humanities.
Ostriker, Alicia. Writing Like a Woman. (Poets on Poetry Ser.). 200p. 1983. pap. 8.95 (ISBN 0-472-06347-2). U of Mich Pr.
Reeves, James. The Critical Sense: Practical Criticism of Prose & of Poetry. 159p. 1982. Repr. of 1956 ed. lib. bdg. 25.00 (ISBN 0-8495-4700-8). Arden Lib.
Rosenthal, M. L. Poetry & the Common Life. LC 82-16913. 176p. 1983. 15.00x (ISBN 0-8052-3851-4); pap. 6.95x (ISBN 0-8052-0738-4). Schocken.
Salmon, Arthur E. Poets of the Apocalypse. (English Authors Ser.). 158p. 1983. lib. bdg. 16.95 (ISBN 0-8057-6846-7, Twayne). G K Hall.
Schomer, Karine. Mahadevi Varma & the Chhayavad Age of Modern Hindi Poetry. LC 81-13002. (Illus.). 368p. 1983. text ed. 30.00 (ISBN 0-520-04255-7). U of Cal Pr.
Steiner, Rudolf & Steiner-von Sivers, Marie. Poetry & the Art of Speech. Wedgwood, Julia & Welburn, Andrew, trs. from Ger. 323p. (Orig.). 1981. pap. 14.00 (ISBN 0-85440-407-4, Pub. by Steinerbooks). Anthroposophic.
Tate, Allen. The Poetry Reviews of Allen Tate, Nineteen Twenty-Four to Nineteen Forty-Four. Brown, Ashley & Cheney, Frances N., eds. LC 82-12687. (Southern Literary Studies). 216p. 1983. 16.95 (ISBN 0-8071-1057-4). La State U Pr.
Tinker, Chauncey B. Good Estate of Poetry. 1929. text ed. 9.50x (ISBN 0-686-83561-1). Elliots Bks.
Vlasopolos, Anca. The Symbolic Method of Coleridge, Baudelaire, & Yeats. 232p. 1983. 17.95x (ISBN 0-8143-1730-8). Wayne St U Pr.
Weinzinger, Anita. Graves As a Critic. (Salzburg - Poetic Drama Ser.: No. 79). 141p. 1982. pap. text ed. 25.00x (ISBN 0-391-02803-0, Pub. by Salzburg Austria). Humanities.
Wright, James. Collected Prose. Wright, Anne, ed. (Poets on Poetry Ser.). 352p. 1982. pap. 8.95 (ISBN 0-472-06344-8). U of Mich Pr.
Zukofsky, Louis. A Test of Poetry. 1981. 12.95 (ISBN 0-393-01446-0, Pub. C Z Pubns); pap. 6.95 (ISBN 0-393-00050-8). Norton.

POETRY-PERIODICALS

Granger Book Company, Inc, ed. Index to Poetry in Periodicals: 1920 to 1924. LC 81-80120. 230p. 1983. 39.99x (ISBN 0-89609-224-0). Granger Bk.

POETRY-PHILOSOPHY

see Poetry

POETRY-SELECTIONS

see Poetry-Collections

POETRY-STUDY AND TEACHING

Marshall, Suzanne R. A Falling Leaf & Other Poetry Activities. LC 82-83777. 92p. 1982. pap. text ed. 10.45 (ISBN 0-918452-41-4). Learning Pubns.

POETRY-TECHNIQUE

see Poetics

POETRY, MODERN (COLLECTIONS)

Price, Melvia, ed. & prologue by. Energy, Beauty & Spirit: An Anthology of Contemporary Poems by Numerous Poets. 1980. pap. 10.95 (ISBN 0-937196-00-2). Sunset Prods.
Seidman, Hugh & Whyatt, Frances, eds. Equal Time. 101p. 1972. pap. 8.00 (ISBN 0-89366-130-9). Ultramarine Pub.
Weissbort, Daniel. Modern Poetry in Translation. 214p. 1983. text ed. 14.75x (ISBN 0-85635-481-3, Pub. by Carcanet New Pr England). Humanities.

POETRY, MODERN-HISTORY AND CRITICISM

Hamburger, Michael. The Truth of Poetry: Tensions in Modern Poetry from Baudelaire to the 1960's. 352p. 1982. text ed. 21.00x (ISBN 0-85635-438-4, 51378, Pub. by Carcanet New Pr England). Humanities.
Verma, Rajendra. Man & Society in Tagore & Eliot. 188p. 1982. text ed. 15.75x (ISBN 0-391-02464-7). Humanities.

POETRY AND MUSIC

see Music and Literature

POETRY AND SCIENCE

see Literature and Science

POETRY FOR CHILDREN

see Children's Poetry; Nursery Rhymes

POETRY OF PLACES

Adcock, Fleur, ed. Contemporary New Zealand Poetry: An Anthology. 160p. 1983. pap. 14.95 (ISBN 0-19-558092-3). Oxford U Pr.

POETRY OF PLACES-HISTORY AND CRITICISM

Hooker, Jeremy. The Poetry of Place. 197p. 1982. text ed. 21.00x (ISBN 0-85635-409-0, 80340, Pub. by Carcanet New Pr England). Humanities.
Johnson, W. R. The Idea of Lyric: Lyric Modes in Ancient & Modern Poetry. Rosenmeyer, Thomas G., ed. LC 81-3384. (Eidos; Studies in Classical Kinds: Vol. 1). 214p. 1983. pap. 7.95 (ISBN 0-520-04821-0). U of Cal Pr.

POETRY OF PLACES-GREAT BRITAIN

Fraser, Antonia, ed. Oxford & Oxfordshire in Verse. 96p. 1983. 13.95 (Pub. by Secker & Warburg). David & Charles.
Godman, Peter, ed. Alcuin: The Bishops, Kings, & Saints of York. (Medieval Texts Ser.). 336p. 1983. 77.00x (ISBN 0-19-822262-9). Oxford U Pr.
Hooker, Jeremy. The Poetry of Place. 197p. 1982. text ed. 21.00x (ISBN 0-85635-409-0, 80340, Pub. by Carcanet New Pr England). Humanities.
Logue, Christopher, ed. London in Verse. 96p. 1983. 13.95 (ISBN 0-436-25675-4, Pub. by Secker & Warburg). David & Charles.
Wilson, Angus, ed. East Anglia in Verse. 112p. 1983. 13.95 (ISBN 0-436-57607-4, Pub. by Secker & Warburg). David & Charles.

POETRY OF PLACES-JAPAN

Heinrich, Amy V. Fragments of Rainbows: The Life & Poetry of Saito Mokichi, 1882-1953. LC 82-12989. (Studies of the East Asian Institute). (Illus.). 224p. 1983. text ed. 22.50x (ISBN 0-231-05428-9). Columbia U Pr.

POETS

see also Dramatists; Poets Laureate; Women Poets

Faas, Ekbert. Young Robert Duncan: Portrait of the Poet as Homosexual in Society. 300p. (Orig.). 1983. 20.00 (ISBN 0-87685-489-7); pap. 10.00 (ISBN 0-87685-488-9); signed cloth 40.00. Black Sparrow.
Hofrichter, Ruth. Three Poets & Reality. 1942. text ed. 11.50x (ISBN 0-686-83821-1). Elliots Bks.
Hogg, James. The Peter Russell Seminar, 1981-82. (Salzburg - Poetic Drama Ser.: No. 72). 143p. 1982. pap. text ed. 25.00x (ISBN 0-391-02776-X, Pub. by Salzburg Austria). Humanities.
Hoole, William S. It's Raining Violets: The Life & Poetry of Robert Loveman. 1981. 8.95 (ISBN 0-916620-55-7). Portals Pr.
Jackson, Richard. Acts of Mind: Conversations with Contemporary Poets. LC 82-4767. 232p. 1983. text ed. 19.95 (ISBN 0-8173-0122-4). U of Ala Pr.
Khristo Botev. 84p. 1982. pap. 5.25 (ISBN 92-3-101489-7, U1228, UNESCO). Unipub.
Myfanwy, Thomas. One of These Fine Days. 164p. 1982. text ed. 14.75x (ISBN 0-85635-387-6, 80253, Pub. by Carcanet New Pr England). Humanities.
Paz, Octavio. On Poets. Schmidt, Michael, tr. from Span. 272p. 1983. text ed. 21.00x (ISBN 0-85635-303-5, Pub. by Carcanet New Pr England). Humanities.
Sharp, Amy. Victorian Poets. 207p. 1982. Repr. of 1891 ed. lib. bdg. 35.00 (ISBN 0-89987-792-3). Darby Bks.
Trakl, Georg. Georg Trakl: A Profile. Graziano, Frank, ed. Mandel, S. & Iverson, R., trs. from Ger. 160p. (Orig.). 1983. 16.00 (ISBN 0-937406-28-7); pap. 6.50 (ISBN 0-937406-27-9). Logbridge-Rhodes.
Wald, Alan M. The Revolutionary Imagination: The Poetry & Politics of John Wheelwright & Sherry Mangan. LC 82-8498. 370p. 1983. 28.00x (ISBN 0-8078-1535-7). U of NC Pr.

POETS-CORRESPONDENCES, REMINISCENCES, ETC.

Gurney, Ivor. The War Letters. Thornton, R. K., ed. 224p. 1982. text ed. 14.75 (ISBN 0-85635-408-2, 80753, Pub. by Carcanet Pr England). Humanities.
Reichel, Norbert. Der Dichter In der Stadt. 205p. (Ger.). 1982. write for info. (ISBN 3-8204-5815-8). P Lang Pubs.
Sassoon, Seigfried. Siegfried Sassoon Diaries, 1920-1922. Hart-Davis, Rupert, ed. Date not set. pap. 18.95 (ISBN 0-571-11685-X). Faber & Faber.
Sassoon, Siegfried. Siegfried Sassoon Diaries, 1915-1918. Hart-Davis, Rupert, ed. 296p. 1983. 19.95 (ISBN 0-571-11997-2). Faber & Faber.
Simpson, Eileen. Poets in their Youth: A Memoir. LC 82-40429. (Illus.). 288p. 1983. pap. 5.95 (ISBN 0-394-71382-6, Vin). Random.

POETS, WOMEN

see Women Poets

POETS LAUREATE

Helgerson, Richard. Self-Crowned Laureates: Spenser, Jonson, Milton, & the Literary System. LC 82-8496. 330p. 1983. text ed. 22.00x (ISBN 0-520-04808-3). U of Cal Pr.

POINT REYES NATIONAL SEASHORE (PROPOSED)
Arnot, Phil & Monroe, Elvira. Exploring Point Reyes: A Trailguide to Point Reyes National Seashore. Rev. ed. LC 82-51259. (Illus.). 144p. 1983. pap. 4.95 (ISBN 0-933174-16-0). Wide World-Tetra.

POISONOUS PLANTS
Leite, Daliel. Don't Scratch! The Book About Poison-Oak. LC 82-70943. (Illus.). 64p. 1982. pap. 3.95 (ISBN 0-943246-01-6). Weathervane CA.
Morton, Julia F. Plants Poisonous to People in Florida & Other Warm Areas. 2nd Rev. ed. (Illus.). 170p. 1982. pap. 19.75 (ISBN 0-9610184-0-2). J F Morton.

POISONOUS SNAKES
Fitch, Henry S. Autecology of the Copperhead, Vol. 13, No. 4. 2nd ed. Hall, Raymond E. & Wilson, Robert W., eds. (Illus.). 203p. 1980. pap. 12.00 (ISBN 0-89338-016-4). U of KS Mus Nat Hist.

POISONS, ECONOMIC
see Pesticides

POISSON'S EQUATIONS
see Harmonic Functions

POKER
Ankeny, Nesmith C. Poker Strategy: Winning With Game Theory. (Illus.). 208p. 1982. pap. 4.95 (ISBN 0-399-50669-1, Perige). Putnam Pub Group.
Sklansky, David & Dionne, Roger. Winning Power. (Illus.). 192p. 1983. 15.95 (ISBN 0-13-961060-X); pap. 7.95 (ISBN 0-13-961052-9). P-H.

POLAND
see also specific cities, areas, etc. in Poland
Marcy, Sam. Poland: Behind the Crisis. 168p. 1982. pap. 3.95 (ISBN 0-89567-076-3). WV Pubs.
Poland Central Statistical Office. Concise Statistical Yearbook of Poland, 1982. 21st ed. LC 49-25078. (Illus.). 304p. (Orig.). 1982. pap. 35.00 (ISBN 0-8002-3025-6). Intl Pubns Serv.
The Transformation in Poland: Some Points of View. 68p. 1982. pap. 5.00 (ISBN 92-808-0343-3, TUNU 198, UNU). Unipub.

POLAND–DESCRIPTION AND TRAVEL
Fodor's Stockholm, Copenhagen, Oslo, Helsinki & Reykjavik. (Illus.). 144p. 1983. pap. 5.95 (ISBN 0-679-00966-3). McKay.

POLAND–ECONOMIC CONDITIONS
Drewnowski, Jan, ed. Crisis in the East European Economy: The Spread of the Polish. LC 82-42560. 1982. 20.00x (ISBN 0-312-17314-8). St Martin.
Hennig, John, et al. New Foundations: The Polish Strike Wave of 1980-81. (Illus.). 85p. (Orig.). pap. 5.00 (ISBN 0-933522-08-8). Kent Popular.
MacDonald, Oliver. Polish August: Documents from the Beginnings of the Polish Workers' Rebellion. (Illus.). 177p. 1982. pap. 6.00 (ISBN 0-939306-02-6). Left Bank.

POLAND–HISTORY
Dembrowski, Harry E. The Union of Lublin: Polish Federalism in the Golden Age. (East European Monographs: No. 116). 384p. 1982. 27.50x (ISBN 0-88033-009-0). East Eur Quarterly.
MacDonald, Oliver. Polish August: Documents from the Beginnings of the Polish Workers' Rebellion. (Illus.). 177p. 1982. pap. 6.00 (ISBN 0-939306-02-6). Left Bank.
Myant, Martin. Poland: A Crisis for Socialism. 253p. 1982. text ed. 21.00x (ISBN 0-85315-557-7, Pub. by Lawrence & Wishart Ltd England). Humanities.

POLAND–INTELLECTUAL LIFE
Konwicki, Tadeusz. The Polish Complex. 1983. pap. 4.95 (ISBN 0-14-006590-3). Penguin.

POLAND–POLITICS AND GOVERNMENT
Drewnowski, Jan, ed. Crisis in the East European Economy: The Spread of the Polish. LC 82-42560. 1982. 20.00x (ISBN 0-312-17314-8). St Martin.
Hennig, John, et al. New Foundations: The Polish Strike Wave of 1980-81. (Illus.). 85p. (Orig.). pap. 5.00 (ISBN 0-933522-08-8). Kent Popular.
Hough, Jerry F. The Polish Crisis: American Policy Options. LC 82-72742. 80p. 1982. pap. 5.95 (ISBN 0-8157-3743-2). Brookings.
MacDonald, Oliver. Polish August: Documents from the Beginnings of the Polish Workers' Rebellion. (Illus.). 177p. 1982. pap. 6.00 (ISBN 0-939306-02-6). Left Bank.
Myant, Martin. Poland: A Crisis for Socialism. 253p. 1982. text ed. 21.00x (ISBN 0-85315-557-7, Pub. by Lawrence & Wishart Ltd England). Humanities.
Staniszkis, Jadwiga. Poland's Self-Limiting Revolution. Gross, Jan T., ed. LC 82-61387. 328p. 1983. 19.50x (ISBN 0-691-09403-9). Princeton U Pr.
Woodall, Jean, ed. Policy & Politics in Contemporary Poland: Reform, Failure & Crisis. 256p. 1982. pap. 14.00 (ISBN 0-86187-222-3). F Pinter Pubs.

POLANSKI, ROMAN
Leaming, Barbara. Polanski. 1983. pap. price not set (ISBN 0-671-24986-X, Touchstone Bks). S&S.

POLAR EXPEDITIONS
see Antarctic Regions; Arctic Regions; Scientific Expeditions
also names of exploring expeditions and explorers

POLARIZATION (NUCLEAR PHYSICS)
Sanderson, R. T., ed. Polar Convalense. Date not set. 19.50 (ISBN 0-12-618080-6). Acad Pr.

POLAROGRAPH AND POLAROGRAPHY
Gnaiger, E. & Forstner, H., eds. Polarographic Oxygen Sensors: Aquatic & Physiological Applications. (Illus.). 370p. 1983. 50.00 (ISBN 0-387-11654-0). Springer-Verlag.

POLEMICS (THEOLOGY)
see Apologetics

POLICE
see also Criminal Investigation; Detectives; Police Communication Systems; Police Questioning; Public Relations–Police; Secret Service
also subdivision Police under names of cities, e.g. Boston–Police
Casey, W. W. You, Too can Beat Police Radar & Avoid Speeding Tickets. 220p. pap. 19.95x (ISBN 0-943462-02-9). CaseCo.
Elliston, Frederick & Feldberg, Michael, eds. Moral Issues in Police Work. 180p. 1983. text ed. 25.00x (ISBN 0-8476-7191-7); pap. 9.95x (ISBN 0-8476-7192-5). Rowman.
Miller, Larry S. & Braswell, Michael C. Human Relations & Police Work. 178p. (Orig.). 1983. pap. text ed. 7.95x (ISBN 0-88133-019-1). Waveland Pr.
Punch, Maurice, ed. Control in the Police Organization. (Organization Studies: No. 4). 368p. 1983. 30.00x (ISBN 0-262-16090-0). MIT Pr.

POLICE–CORRESPONDENCE, REMINISCENCES, ETC.
Putterman, Jaydie & Lesur, Rosalynde. Police. (Illus.). 192p. 1983. 19.95 (ISBN 0-03-062429-0); pap. 11.95 (ISBN 0-03-059597-5). HR&W.

POLICE–EQUIPMENT AND SUPPLIES
see also Truncheons
Downey, Robert J. & Roth, Jordan T. Baton Techniques for Officer Survival. (Illus.). 288p. 1983. pap. 29.75x spiral (ISBN 0-398-04781-2). C C Thomas.

POLICE–EXAMINATIONS, QUESTIONS, ETC.
Rudman, Jack. Border Patrol Agent. (Career Examination Ser.: C-115). (Cloth bdg. avail. on request). pap. 10.00 (ISBN 0-8373-0115-7). Natl Learning.
--Campus Public Safety Officer I. (Career Examination Ser.: C-881). (Cloth bdg. avail. on request). pap. 10.00 (ISBN 0-8373-0881-X). Natl Learning.
--Campus Public Safety Officer II. (Career Examination Ser.: C-882). (Cloth bdg. avail. on request). pap. 12.00 (ISBN 0-8373-0882-8). Natl Learning.
--Campus Security Guard I. (Career Examination Ser.: C-565). (Cloth bdg. avail. on request). pap. 10.00 (ISBN 0-8373-0565-9). Natl Learning.
--Campus Security Guard II. (Career Examination Ser.: C-566). (Cloth bdg. avail. on request). pap. 12.00 (ISBN 0-8373-0566-7). Natl Learning.
--Campus Security Guard III. (Career Examination Ser.: C-567). (Cloth bdg. avail. on request). pap. 12.00 (ISBN 0-8373-0567-5). Natl Learning.
--Senior Training Technician (Police) (Career Examination Ser.: C-418). (Cloth bdg. avail. on request). pap. 14.00 (ISBN 0-8373-0418-0). Natl Learning.
--Training Technician (Police) (Career Examination Ser.: C-417). (Cloth bdg. avail. on request). pap. 12.00 (ISBN 0-8373-0417-2). Natl Learning.

POLICE–HANDBOOKS, MANUALS, ETC.
Brechbuhl, E. Conversation Handbook for Policeman. 128p. 1977. 35.00x (ISBN 0-7121-5619-4, Pub. by Macdonald & Evans). State Mutual Bk.
White, Gregory J. Emergency Childbirth: A Manual. (Illus.). 62p. wire-bound 4.95 (ISBN 0-686-37623-4). Police Train.

POLICE ADMINISTRATION
Bunyard, R. S. Police: Organization & Command. 400p. 1978. 39.00x (ISBN 0-7121-1671-0, Pub. by Macdonald & Evans). State Mutual Bk.
Klockars, C. B. Thinking about Police: Contemporary Readings. (Criminology & Criminal Justice Ser.). 592p. 1983. 15.95 (ISBN 0-07-035054-X, C). McGraw.
Punch, Maurice, ed. Control in the Police Organization. (Organization Studies: No. 4). 368p. 1983. 30.00x (ISBN 0-262-16090-0). MIT Pr.
Whitehouse, Jack E. How & Where to Find the Facts: Researching Police Science. LC 82-50374. 125p. (Orig.). 1983. pap. 6.95 (ISBN 0-88247-691-2). R & E Res Assoc.

POLICE CLUBS
see Truncheons

POLICE COMMUNICATION SYSTEMS
see also Police; Radio; Telecommunication
Dintino, Justin J. & Martens, Frederick T. Police Intelligence Systems in Crime Control: Maintaining a Delicate Balance in a Liberal Democracy. (Illus.). 143p. 1983. text ed. price not set (ISBN 0-398-04830-4). C C Thomas.

POLICE INTERROGATION
see Police Questioning

POLICE MANAGEMENT
see Police Administration
Hernandez, Ernie, Jr. Police Handbook for Applying the Systems Approach & Computer Technology. LC 82-17662. (Illus.). 231p. 1982. 26.95 (ISBN 0-910657-00-9); pap. 19.95 (ISBN 0-910657-01-7). Frontline.

POLICE POWER
see also Eminent Domain; Zoning Law
Campbell, Don. Police: The Exercise of Power. 128p. 1978. 30.00x (ISBN 0-7121-1678-8, Pub. by Macdonald & Evans). State Mutual Bk.

POLICE QUESTIONING
Simpson, Keith. Police: The Investigation of Violence. 240p. 1978. 39.00x (ISBN 0-7121-1689-3, Pub. by Macdonald & Evans). State Mutual Bk.

POLICE RADIO
see Police Communication Systems

POLICY SCIENCES
see also Decision-Making
Baber, Walter F. Organizing the Future: Matrix Models for the Postindustrial Polity. (Illus.). 176p. 1983. text ed. 16.50 (ISBN 0-8173-0123-2). U of Ala Pr.
Browne, William & Hadwiger, Don, eds. Rural Policy. (Orig.). 1982. pap. 6.00 (ISBN 0-918592-55-0). Policy Studies.
Dror, Yehezkel. Public Policymaking Reexamined. (Illus.). 420p. 1983. pap. text ed. 19.95 (ISBN 0-87855-928-0). Transaction Bks.
Dubnick, Mel & Gitelson, Alan, eds. Regulatory Policy Analysis. (Orig.). 1982. pap. 6.00 (ISBN 0-918592-51-8). Policy Studies.
Hogwood, Brian & Peters, Guy. Policy Dynamics. LC 82-10330. 304p. 1982. 27.50x (ISBN 0-312-62014-4). St Martin.
Hoos, Ida R. Systems Analysis in Public Policy: A Critique. rev. ed. LC 82-48766. 320p. 1983. text ed. 30.00x (ISBN 0-520-04953-5); pap. 8.95x (ISBN 0-520-04952-7). U of Cal Pr.
McNichols, Thomas. Policymaking & Executive Action. 6th ed. (Illus.). 832p. 1983. text ed. 27.95x (ISBN 0-07-045680-1); instr's manual 10.95x (ISBN 0-07-045681-X). McGraw.
Mazmanian, Daniel A. & Sebatier, Paul A. Implementation & Public Policy. 1983. 11.95x (ISBN 0-673-16561-2). Scott F.
Paris, David C. & Reynolds, James F. The Logic of Policy Inquiry. Rockwood, Irving, ed. 256p. 1983. text ed. 20.00x (ISBN 0-582-28356-6); pap. text ed. 12.95x (ISBN 0-582-28357-4). Longman.
Trenn, Thaddeus J. America's Golden Bough: Science, Polity, & the Public. LC 82-18873. 196p. 1983. text ed. 25.00 (ISBN 0-89946-160-3). Oelgeschlager.
Wildavsky, Aaron, ed. The Policy Organization. (Managing Information Ser.: Vol. 5). (Illus.). 224p. 1983. 25.00 (ISBN 0-8039-1912-3); pap. 12.50 (ISBN 0-8039-1913-1). Sage.

POLIOMYELITIS–PERSONAL NARRATIVES
Ballardo, Victoria M. Count Me Among the Living: The Story of My Wheelchair Liberation. 160p. 1983. 8.50 (ISBN 0-682-49945-5). Exposition.

POLISH IN THE UNITED STATES
Blejwas, Stanislaus A. & Biskupski, Mieczyslaw B., eds. Pastor of the Poles: Polish American Essays Presented to Right Reverend Monsignor John P. Wodarski. LC 82-72307. (Polish Studies Program Monographs: I). (Illus.). 223p. 1982. 15.00 (ISBN 0-910179-00-X). Polish Stud Prog.

POLISH LANGUAGE
Mazur, B. W. Colloquial Polish. (Colloquial Ser.). 224p. 1983. pap. 12.95 (ISBN 0-7100-9030-7). Routledge & Kegan.
Swan, Oscar E. A Concise Grammar of Polish. 2nd ed. LC 82-24835. 192p. (Orig.). 1983. lib. bdg. 19.75 (ISBN 0-8191-3017-6); pap. text ed. 8.75 (ISBN 0-8191-3018-4). U Pr of Amer.

POLISH LANGUAGE–CONVERSATION AND PHRASE BOOKS
Grala, Maria. Say It in Polish: An Intensive Course for Beginners. 110p. (gr. 6 up). pap. 4.95 (ISBN 83-01-03922-1, Ars Polana Poland). Hippocrene Bks.

POLISH LANGUAGE–SELF INSTRUCTION
Swiecicka-Ziemianek, Maria. Polish: A Beginner's Guide. 327p. Date not set. with 8 cassettes 149.00x (ISBN 0-88432-099-5, P500). J Norton Pubs.

POLISH LITERATURE (COLLECTIONS)
Blejwas, Stanislaus A. & Biskupski, Mieczyslaw B., eds. Pastor of the Poles: Polish American Essays Presented to Right Reverend Monsignor John P. Wodarski. LC 82-72307. (Polish Studies Program Monographs: I). (Illus.). 223p. 1982. 15.00 (ISBN 0-910179-00-X). Polish Stud Prog.

POLISH LITERATURE–HISTORY AND CRITICISM
Milosz, Czeslaw. The History of Polish Literature. rev. ed. LC 82-16084. 570p. 1983. text ed. 28.00x (ISBN 0-520-04465-7); pap. text ed. 8.95x (ISBN 0-520-04477-0). U of Cal Pr.

POLISH PAINTINGS
see Paintings, Polish

POLISH POETRY–HISTORY AND CRITICISM
Terlecki, Tymon. Stanislaw Wyspianski. (World Authors Ser.). 166p. 1983. lib. bdg. 18.95 (ISBN 0-8057-6521-2, Twayne). G K Hall.

POLISH POETRY–TRANSLATIONS INTO ENGLISH
Milosz, Czeslaw. Postwar Polish Poetry: An Anthology. rev. ed. LC 82-16084. 180p. 1983. text ed. 18.00x (ISBN 0-520-04475-4); pap. text ed. 5.95x (ISBN 0-520-04476-2). U of Cal Pr.

POLITENESS
see Courtesy

POLITICAL BEHAVIOR
see Political Psychology

POLITICAL BOUNDARIES
see Boundaries

POLITICAL CLUBS
see also names of individual clubs, e.g. Tammany Hall
Interstate Bureau of Regulations. Political Action Register. Alperin, David S., ed. 2500p. 1982. 249.50 (ISBN 0-911693-02-5). IBR Pub.

POLITICAL CONVENTIONS
see also Political Parties
Davis, James W. National Conventions in an Age of Party Reform. LC 82-9382. (Contributions in Political Science Ser.: No. 91). 384p. 1983. lib. bdg. 35.00 (ISBN 0-313-23048-X, DNC/). Greenwood.

POLITICAL ECONOMY
see Economics

POLITICAL ETHICS
see also Government, Resistance To
Bonino, Jose M. Toward a Christian Political Ethics. LC 82-48541. 144p. 1983. pap. 5.95 (ISBN 0-8006-1697-9, 1-1697). Fortress.
Goodin, Robert E. The Politics of Rational Man. LC 75-35616. 240p. 1976. 38.95x (ISBN 0-471-31360-2, Pub. by Wiley-Interscience). Wiley.
Stockdale, James B. & Hatfield, Mark O. The Ethics of Citizenship. (The Andrew R. Cecil Lectures on Moral Values in a Free Society Ser.: Vol. II). 167p. 1981. 9.95x (ISBN 0-292-72038-6). U of Tex Pr.

POLITICAL GEOGRAPHY
see Geography, Political

POLITICAL MURDER
see Assassination

POLITICAL PARTICIPATION
Hudlin, Richard A. & Farouk, Brimah K. Barriers to Effective Political Participation. 1981. 1.00 (ISBN 0-686-38012-6). Voter Ed Proj.
Langley, Michael. Supreme Court Says Minority Enterprises Must be Given a Piece of the Action. 1980. 1.00 (ISBN 0-686-38005-3). Voter Ed Proj.
Liddle, R. William, et al, eds. Political Participation in Modern Indonesia. (Illus.). x, 206p. pap. 9.50 (ISBN 0-686-38046-0). Yale U SE Asia.
Ritter, Archibald R. & Pollock, David H., eds. Latin American Prospects for the 1980's: Equity, Democratization & Development. 344p. 1983. 29.95 (ISBN 0-03-061363-9). Praeger.
Tannenbaum, Percy H. & Kostrich, Leslie J. Turned-On TV - Turned-Off Voters: Policy Options for Election Projections. (People & Communication Ser.: Vol. 15). 244p. 1983. 25.00 (ISBN 0-8039-1929-8). Sage.

POLITICAL PARTIES
see also Political Clubs; Political Conventions; Politics, Practical; Right and Left (Political Science)
also subvision Politics and Government under names of countries, cities, etc. e.g. United States–Politics and Government; names of political parties, e.g. Democratic Party
Membership Directory, 1983. pap. 15.00 (ISBN 0-915654-54-7). Am Political.

POLITICAL PARTIES–AUSTRALIA
Aitkin, D. Stability & Change in Australian Politics. new ed. 400p. (Orig.). 1982. pap. text ed. 25.95 (ISBN 0-7081-0022-8, 1241, Pub. by ANUP Australia). Bks Australia.

POLITICAL PARTIES–EUROPE
McHale, Vincent & Skowronski, Sharon, eds. Political Parties of Europe, 2 vols. LC 82-15408. (Greenwood Encyclopedia of the World's Political Parties). (Illus.). 1983. Set. lib. bdg. 95.00 (ISBN 0-313-21405-0, MPP/). Greenwood.

POLITICAL PARTIES–FRANCE
Wilson, F. French Political Parties under the Fifth Republic. 256p. 1982. 26.95 (ISBN 0-03-062046-5). Praeger.

POLITICAL PARTIES–GERMANY
Braunthal, Gerard. The West German Social Democrats, 1969-1982: Profile of a Party in Power. (Replica Edition Ser.). 400p. 1983. softcover 25.00x (ISBN 0-86531-958-8). Westview.
Smith, Gordon. Democracy in Western Germany: Parties & Politics in the Federal Republic. 2nd ed. 180p. (Orig.). 1983. pap. text ed. 8.50x (ISBN 0-686-82618-3). Holmes & Meier.

POLITICAL PARTIES–UNITED STATES
Davis, James W. National Conventions in an Age of Party Reform. LC 82-9382. (Contributions in Political Science Ser.: No. 91). 384p. 1983. lib. bdg. 35.00 (ISBN 0-313-23048-X, DNC/). Greenwood.
Formisano, Ronald P. The Transformation of Political Culture: Massachusetts Parties, 1790s-1840s. (Illus.). 599p. 1983. 35.00 (ISBN 0-19-503124-5). Oxford U Pr.
Kruman, Marc W. Parties & Politics in North Carolina, 1836 to 1865. LC 82-20364. 384p. 1983. text ed. 37.50x (ISBN 0-8071-1041-8); pap. text ed. 14.95x (ISBN 0-8071-1061-2). La State U Pr.
Rubin, Richard L. Press, Party, & Presidency. 1981. pap. text ed. 6.95x (ISBN 0-393-95206-1). Norton.
--Press, Party, & Presidency. (Illus.). 1982. 18.95 (ISBN 0-393-01497-5). Norton.
Smallwood, Frank. The Other Candidates: Third Parties in Presidential Elections. LC 82-40478. (Illus.). 312p. 1983. 20.00; pap. 10.95 (ISBN 0-87451-257-3). U Pr of New Eng.

POLITICAL PATRONAGE
see Patronage, Political

POLITICAL PLATFORMS
see Political Parties

POLITICAL PRISONERS–PERSONAL NARRATIVES

Naidoo, Indres & Sachs, Albie. Robben Island: Ten Years as a Political Prisoner in South Africa's Most Notorious Penitentiary. LC 82-49085. Orig. Title: Island in Chains: Ten Years on Robben Island by Prisoner 885-63. 288p. 1983. pap. 6.95 (ISBN 0-394-71514-4, Vin). Random.

Roy, M. N. Fragments of a Prisoner's Diary: India's Message. Repr. of 1950 ed. 18.00 (ISBN 0-8364-0912-4, Pub. by Ajanta). South Asia Bks.

POLITICAL PRISONERS–AFRICA, SOUTH

Naidoo, Indres & Sachs, Albie. Robben Island: Ten Years as a Political Prisoner in South Africa's Most Notorious Penitentiary. LC 82-49085. Orig. Title: Island in Chains: Ten Years on Robben Island by Prisoner 885-63. 288p. 1983. pap. 6.95 (ISBN 0-394-71514-4, Vin). Random.

POLITICAL PRISONERS–RUSSIA

Shifrin, Avraham. U. S. S. R. Labor Camps. 1982. 3.95. Diane Bks.

Solzhenitsyn, Alexander. Prisoners. Rapp, Helen & Thomas, Nancy, trs. from Rus. 1983. 12.50 (ISBN 0-374-23739-5). FS&G.

POLITICAL PSYCHOLOGY

see also Propaganda; Public Opinion

Hollander, Paul. Political Pilgrims. LC 82-48394. 544p. 1983. pap. 8.61i (ISBN 0-06-091029-1, CN 1029, CN). Har-Row.

McCulloch, Jock. Black Soul White Artifact: Fanon's Clinical Psychology & Social Theory. LC 82-14605. 240p. Date not set. price not set (ISBN 0-521-24700-4). Cambridge U Pr.

POLITICAL REFUGEES

see Refugees, Political

POLITICAL REPRESENTATION

see Representative Government and Representation

POLITICAL SCIENCE

see also Administrative Law; Anarchism and Anarchists; Authority; Bureaucracy; Church and State; Citizenship; Civil Rights; Civil Service; Communism; Comparative Government; Conservatism; Constitutional History; Constitutional Law; Constitutions; Decentralization in Government; Democracy; Despotism; Elections; Equality; Federal Government; Geopolitics; Government, Resistance to; Government Ownership; Imperialism; Individualism; International Organization; Jurisprudence; Kings and Rulers; Legislation; Liberalism; Liberty; Local Government; Municipal Government; Nationalism; Natural Law; Police Power; Political Conventions; Political Ethics; Political Parties; Political Psychology; Politics, Practical; Populism; Power (Social Sciences); Pressure Groups; Public Administration; Public Law; Public Opinion; Radicalism; Representative Government and Representation; Revolutions; Right and Left (Political Science); Social Contract; Socialism; State, the; State Governments; Suffrage; Tribes and Tribal System; Taxation; Utopias; World Politics

also subheading Constitution and subdivision Politics and Government under names of countries, states, etc. e.g. United States–Constitution; Massachusetts–Politics and Government

Andrade. Introduccion a la Ciencia Politica. 400p. (Span.). 1982. pap. text ed. write for info. (ISBN 0-06-310030-4, Pub. by HarLA Mexico). Har-Row.

Baber, Walter F. Organizing the Future: Matrix Models for the Postindustrial Polity. (Illus.). 176p. 1983. text ed. 16.50 (ISBN 0-8173-0123-2). U of Ala Pr.

Bentley, Arthur F. Process of Government. (Social Science Classics). 551p. 1983. pap. 19.95 (ISBN 0-87855-934-5). Transaction Bks.

Bertsch, Gary, et al. Comparing Political System: Power & Policy in Three Worlds. 2nd ed. 548p. 1982. text ed. 19.95 (ISBN 0-471-08446-8); avail. tchrs.' manual (ISBN 0-471-86600-8). Wiley.

Blondel, Jean. The Organization of Governments: A Comparative Analysis of Governmental Structures. LC 82-80523. (Political Executives in Comparative Perspective: A Cross-National Empirical Study: Vol. 2). (Illus.). 248p. 1982. 25.00 (ISBN 0-8039-9776-0); pap. 12.50 (ISBN 0-8039-9777-9). Sage.

Bourland, W. George. Who Gets the Antelope's Liver? 12.95 (ISBN 0-686-37633-1). Harp & Thistle.

Boxer, C. Solving Life's Problems: Government & Law, Level 1. 1980. pap. 4.95 (ISBN 0-07-006851-8). McGraw.

Brown, Lawrence D. New Politics, New Policies: Government's Response to Government's Growth. 100p. 1983. pap. 5.95 (ISBN 0-8157-1165-4, 82-45979). Brookings.

Brzezinski, Zbigniew. Power & Principle: Memoirs of the National Security Advisor, 1977-1981. 600p. 1983. 22.50 (ISBN 0-374-23663-1); limited ed. 100.00. FS&G.

Cassirer, Ernst. The Myth of State. LC 82-18392. xii, 303p. 1983. Repr. of 1946 ed. lib. bdg. 29.75x (ISBN 0-313-23790-5, CAMO). Greenwood.

Chapman, B. & Potter, A. M., eds. Wimm: Political Questions. 294p. 1974. 24.00 (ISBN 0-7190-0594-9). Manchester.

Corning, P. A. The Synergism Hypothesis: A Theory of Progressive Evolution. 1983. pap. price not set (ISBN 0-07-013172-4). McGraw.

Dickinson, W. Calvin. James Harrington's Republic. LC 82-24749. 126p. (Orig.). 1983. lib. bdg. 18.50 (ISBN 0-8191-3019-2); pap. text ed. 8.25 (ISBN 0-8191-3020-6). U Pr of Amer.

Elder, Charles D. & Cobb, Roger W. The Political Uses of Symbols. Rockwood, Irving, ed. (Professional Studies in Political Communication). (Illus.). 192p. 1983. text ed. 22.50x (ISBN 0-582-28392-2); pap. text ed. 9.95x (ISBN 0-582-28393-0). Longman.

Etheridge, Lloyd S. Can Governments Learn? 200p. 1983. 22.50 (ISBN 0-08-027218-5). Pergamon.

Goodin, Robert E. The Politics of Rational Man. LC 75-35616. 240p. 1976. 38.95x (ISBN 0-471-31360-2, Pub. by Wiley-Interscience). Wiley.

Grenzke, Janet M. Influence, Change, & the Legislative Process. LC 82-9383. (Contributions in Political Science Ser.: No. 89). (Illus.). 216p. 1983. lib. bdg. 35.00 (ISBN 0-313-23385-3, GRI/). Greenwood.

Groth, Alexander J. Major Ideologies: An Interpretative of Democracy, Socialism & Nationalism. LC 82-18755. 256p. 1983. Repr. of 1971 ed. text ed. write for info. (ISBN 0-89874-579-9). Krieger.

Higgott, Richard A. Political Development Theory: The Contemporary Debate. LC 82-42718. 140p. 1983. 18.95x (ISBN 0-312-62225-2). St Martin.

Holcombe, Randall G. Public Finance & Political Process. LC 82-10803. (Political & Social Economy Ser.). 208p. 1983. price not set (ISBN 0-8093-1082-1). S Ill U Pr.

Kurzweil, Edith & Phillips, William, eds. Writers & Politics: A Partisan Review Reader. 352p. 1983. pap. 11.95 (ISBN 0-7100-9316-0). Routledge & Kegan.

Lane, Charles. A Voluntary Political Government: Letters from Charles Lane. 104p. (Orig.). 1982. pap. 5.95 (ISBN 0-9602574-3-8). M E Coughlin.

Lewellen, Ted C. Political Anthropology: An Introduction. (Illus.). 192p. 1983. text ed. 22.95x (ISBN 0-89789-028-0); pap. text ed. 10.95x (ISBN 0-89789-029-9). J F Bergin.

McCulloch, J. In the Twilight of the Revolution: The Political Theory of Amilcar Cabral. 200p. (Orig.). 1982. pap. write for info. (ISBN 0-7100-9411-6). Routledge & Kegan.

Mansbridge, Jane J. Beyond Adversary Democracy. xiv, 412p. 1980. pap. 10.95 (ISBN 0-226-50355-0). U of Chicago Pr.

Marchetti, Victor & Marks, John D. The CIA & the Cult of Intelligence. 1983. pap. 3.95 (ISBN 0-440-31298-1, LE). Dell.

O'Brien, Mary. The Politics of Reproduction. 1983. pap. 9.95 (ISBN 0-7100-9498-1). Routledge & Kegan.

Paolucci, Henry. A Brief History of Political Thought & Stagecraft. 6.95 (ISBN 0-918680-08-5). Griffon Hse.

Peterson, Merrill D., ed. The Portable Thomas Jefferson. 1975. pap. 14.95 (ISBN 0-670-70359-1). Viking Pr.

Politics & Power Editorial Board. Politics & Power Four: Law, Politics & Justice. (Politics & Power Ser.). 260p. (Orig.). 1982. pap. 17.50 (ISBN 0-7100-0984-4). Routledge & Kegan.

Potel, Jean-Yves. The Promise of Solidarity. 256p. 1982. 26.95 (ISBN 0-03-061776-6); pap. 9.95 (ISBN 0-03-062364-2). Praeger.

Rodee, Carlton C. & Anderson, Totten J. Introduction to Political Science. 4th ed. (Illus.). 544p. 1983. text ed. 24.95x (ISBN 0-07-053386-5, C); write for info. (ISBN 0-07-053387-3). McGraw.

Rosselet-Christ, Claudine. Les Perceptions De Soi, De l'Ideal et D'Autrui Dans les Relations D'Autorite et De Subordination. 183p. (Fr.). 1982. write for info. (ISBN 3-261-04995-2). P Lang Pubs.

Russell, Henry N. Fate & Freedom. 1927. text ed. 29.50x (ISBN 0-686-83544-1). Elliots Bks.

Seers, Dudley, ed. Dependency Theory: A Critical Reassessment. 211p. 1982. 30.00 (ISBN 0-903804-84-0). F Pinter Pubs.

Simon, Roger. Gramsci's Political Thought: An Introduction. 160p. 1982. text ed. 17.00x (ISBN 0-85315-523-2, Pub. by Lawrence & Wishart Ltd England). Humanities.

Sloma, Richard. No-Nonsense Government. LC 82-42727. 248p. 1983. 16.95 (ISBN 0-8128-2901-8). Stein & Day.

Tschirgi, Daniel. Politics of Indecision. 368p. 1983. 24.95 (ISBN 0-03-062361-8). Praeger.

Valsangkar, K, et al. Aspects of Political Theory. (Illus.). 292p. 1981. pap. text ed. 8.95x (ISBN 0-86131-108-6, Pub. by Orient Longman Ltd India). Apt Bks.

Whipple, Edwin P. Outlooks on Society, Literature & Politics. 345p. 1982. Repr. of 1888 ed. lib. bdg. 50.00 (ISBN 0-89987-890-3). Darby Bks.

White, Louise G. & Clark, Robert P. Political Analysis: Technique & Practice. LC 82-22827. (Political Science Ser.). 300p. 1983. pap. text ed. 14.95 (ISBN 0-534-01284-1). Brooks-Cole.

POLITICAL SCIENCE–ADDRESSES, ESSAYS, LECTURES

Andropov, Y. V. Speeches & Writings. (Leaders of the World Ser.). 192p. 1983. 25.00 (ISBN 0-08-028177-X). Pergamon.

Fonvizin, Dennis. Political Writings. Gleason, Walter, tr. from Rus. 170p. Date not set. 22.50 (ISBN 0-88233-799-8). Ardis Pubs.

Gleicher, Jules. The Accidental Revolutionary: Essays on the Political Teaching of Jean-Paul Sartre. LC 82-20067. 216p. (Orig.). 1983. lib. bdg. 18.75 (ISBN 0-8191-2835-X); pap. text ed. 7.75 (ISBN 0-8191-2836-8). U Pr of Amer.

Kant, Immanuel. Perpetual Peace & Other Essays on Politics, History, & Morals. Humphrey, Ted, ed. & tr. from Ger. LC 82-11748. (HPC Philosophical Classics Ser.). 152p. 1982. lib. bdg. 13.50 (ISBN 0-915145-48-0); pap. text ed. 2.95 (ISBN 0-915145-47-2). Hackett Pub.

Miller, David & Siedentop, Larry, eds. The Nature of Political Theory. 262p. 1983. 39.95 (ISBN 0-19-827441-6). Oxford U Pr.

Pearson, Sindey A., Jr. The Constitutional Polity: Essays on the Founding Principles of American Politics. LC 82-15953. 364p. (Orig.). 1983. lib. bdg. 24.25 (ISBN 0-8191-2744-2); pap. text ed. 12.75 (ISBN 0-8191-2745-0). U Pr of Amer.

Young, George. Pendulum of Progress: Essays in Political Science & Scientific Politics. 1931. text ed. 24.50x (ISBN 0-686-83692-8). Elliots Bks.

POLITICAL SCIENCE–BIOGRAPHY

see Political Scientists

POLITICAL SCIENCE–DICTIONARIES

Scruton, Robert. A Dictionary of Political Thought. LC 82-47532. 352p. 1982. write for info. (ISBN 0-06-015044-0, HarpT). Har-Row.

POLITICAL SCIENCE–HISTORY

Bentham, Jeremy. Constitutional Code, Vol. 1. Rosen, F. & Burns, J. H., eds. (The Collected Works of Jeremy Bentham Ser.). 693p. 1983. 98.00 (ISBN 0-19-822608-X). Oxford U Pr.

Finder, Joseph. Red Carpet. (A New Republic Bk.). (Illus.). 336p. Date not set. 16.95 (ISBN 0-03-060484-2). HR&W.

Gunn, J. A. Beyond Liberty & Property: The Process of Self-Recognition in Eighteenth-Century Political Thought. (McGill-Queen's Studies in the History of Ideas). 336p. 1983. 35.00x (ISBN 0-7735-1006-0). McGill-Queens U Pr.

Oestreich, Gerhard. Neostoicism & the Early Modern State. Oestreich, B. & Koenigsberger, H. G., eds. LC 81-12285. (Cambridge Studies in Early Modern History Ser.). 272p. 1982. 49.50 (ISBN 0-521-24202-9). Cambridge U Pr.

POLITICAL SCIENCE–HISTORY–UNITED STATES

Bishirjian, Richard. The Nature of Public Philosophy. LC 82-20170. 62p. 1983. Repr. of 1978 ed. pap. text ed. 3.95 (ISBN 0-8191-2861-9). U Pr of Amer.

Crick, Bernard. The American Science of Politics: Its Origin & Conditions. LC 82-15829. xv, 252p. 1982. lib. bdg. 35.00x (ISBN 0-313-23696-8, CRAS). Greenwood.

Paolucci, Henry. War, Peace & the Presidency. LC 68-8774. 16.95. Griffon Hse.

Sokolow, Asa D. Political Theory of Arthur J. Penty. 1940. pap. text ed. 22.50x (ISBN 0-686-83707-X). Elliots Bks.

POLITICAL SCIENCE–METHODOLOGY

Alker, Hayward R. Dialectical Logics for the Political Sciences. (Ponzan Studies: No. 7). 96p. 1982. pap. text ed. 11.50x (ISBN 90-6203-684-8, Pub. by Rodopi Holland). Humanities.

Falco, Maria J. Truth & Meaning in Political Science: An Introduction to Political Inquiry. 2nd ed. LC 82-25095. 160p. 1983. pap. text ed. 9.75 (ISBN 0-8191-3048-6). U Pr of Amer.

POLITICAL SCIENCE–PERIODICALS

ABC-Clio Staff. Political & Social Science Journals: A Handbook for Writers & Reviewers. LC 82-18455. (Clio Guides to Publishing Opportunities: No. 2). 250p. 1983. lib. bdg. 24.85 (ISBN 0-87436-026-9); pap. 12.85 (ISBN 0-87436-037-4). ABC Clio.

POLITICAL SCIENCE–STUDY AND TEACHING

Justus, Fred. Basic Skills Government Workbook. (Basic Skills Workbooks). 32p. (gr. 7-12). 1983. 0.99 (ISBN 0-8209-0538-0, SSW-2). ESP.

Stevens, Olive. Children Talking Politics: Political Learning in Childhood. (Issues & Ideas in Education Ser.). 206p. 1982. text ed. 24.95x (ISBN 0-85520-489-3, Pub. by Martin Robertson England). Biblio Dist.

POLITICAL SCIENCE–YEARBOOKS

Countries of the World & their Leaders Yearbook, 1982: Supplement. 350p. 1982. 38.00x (ISBN 0-8103-1106-2). Gale.

Paxton, John, ed. The Statesman's Year-Book, 1982-1983. LC 4-3776. 1700p. 1982. 35.00x (ISBN 0-312-76097-3). St Martin.

POLITICAL SCIENCE IN LITERATURE

see Politics in Literature

POLITICAL SCIENTISTS

Stone, Gregory & Lowenstein, Douglas, eds. Lowenstein: Acts of Courage & Belief. 333p. 29.95 (ISBN 0-15-154742-4); pap. 9.95. HarBraceJ.

--Lowenstein: Acts of Courage & Belief. 416p. pap. 9.95 (ISBN 0-15-654302-8, Harv). HarBraceJ.

POLITICAL SOCIETIES

see Political Clubs

POLITICAL SOCIOLOGY

Dowse, R. E. & Hughes, J. A. Political Sociology. LC 76-39229. 457p. 1972. pap. 16.95x (ISBN 0-471-22146-5). Wiley.

Giddens, Anthony. Profiles & Critiques in Social Theory. 230p. 1983. 24.50x (ISBN 0-520-04933-0); pap. 10.95x (ISBN 0-520-04964-0). U of Cal Pr.

Lloyd, Christopher, ed. Social Theory & Political Practice. (Wolfson College Lectures Ser.). 190p. 1983. 24.95 (ISBN 0-19-827447-5); pap. 12.95 (ISBN 0-19-827448-3). Oxford U Pr.

POLITICIANS

see Statesmen

POLITICS, PRACTICAL

Here are entered works dealing with practical political methods in general political machines, electioneering, etc.

see also Business and Politics; Campaign Management; College Students–Political Activity; Elections; Lobbying; Voting

also subdivision Politics and Government under names of countries, states, etc., e.g. Massachusetts–Politics and Government; headings beginning with the word Political

Block, Bob. The Politics of Projects. (Illus.). 160p. 1983. pap. 19.00 (ISBN 0-917072-35-9). Yourdon.

Bourland, W. George. Who Gets the Antelope's Liver? 12.95 (ISBN 0-686-37633-1). Harp & Thistle.

Cannadine, David, ed. Patricians, Power & Politics in Nineteenth Century Towns. LC 82-42544. 240p. 1982. 35.00x (ISBN 0-312-59803-3). St Martin.

Institute for the Study of Labor & Economic Crisis. Grassroots Politics in the Nineteen Eighties: A Case Study. LC 82-7329. (Orig.). 1982. pap. 5.00 (ISBN 0-89935-017-8). Synthesis Pubns.

Johnson, Richard & McLennan, Gregor, eds. Making Histories: Studies in History Writing & Politics. 384p. 1982. 35.00x (ISBN 0-8166-1164-5); pap. 15.95 (ISBN 0-8166-1165-3). U of Minn Pr.

McLean, Iain. Dealing in Votes. LC 82-10421. 1982. 25.00 (ISBN 0-312-18535-9). St Martin.

Phillips, Kevin P. Post-Conservative America: People, Politics, & Ideology in a Time of Crisis. LC 82-48898. 288p. 1983. pap. 6.95 (ISBN 0-394-71438-5, Vin). Random.

Sabato, Larry J. The Rise of Political Consultants: New Ways of Winning Elections. 1983. pap. 9.95 (ISBN 0-465-07041-8). Basic.

POLITICS, PRACTICAL–PERSONAL NARRATIVES

Reagan, Ronald. From California to the Capital. LC 82-12822. 218p. 1983. pap. 7.95 (ISBN 0-8159-6720-9). Devin.

Roosevelt, Elliott. The Conservators. 1983. 16.95 (ISBN 0-87795-456-9). Arbor Hse.

POLITICS, PRACTICAL–PSYCHOLOGICAL ASPECTS

see Political Psychology

POLITICS AND BUSINESS

see Business and Politics

POLITICS AND CHILDREN

see Children and Politics

POLITICS AND CHRISTIANITY

see Christianity and Politics

POLITICS AND LAW

see Law and Politics

POLITICS IN LITERATURE

see also Socialism in Literature

Wald, Alan M. The Revolutionary Imagination: The Poetry & Politics of John Wheelwright & Sherry Mangan. LC 82-8498. 370p. 1983. 28.00x (ISBN 0-8078-1535-7). U of NC Pr.

POLK, JAMES KNOX, PRES. U. S., 1795-1849

Cutler, et al, eds. Correspondence of James Polk, 1842-1843, Vol.6. LC 75-84005. (Polk Project Ser.). 1982. 30.00x (ISBN 0-8265-1211-9). Vanderbilt U Pr.

POLLEN

Huntley, B. & Birks, H. J. An Atlas of Past & Present Pollen Maps for Europe: 0-13000 B. P. LC 82-21613. 650p. Date not set. price not set (ISBN 0-521-23735-1). Cambridge U Pr.

POLLS

see Elections; Public Opinion Polls; Voting

POLLUTION

see also Air–Pollution; Environmental Engineering; Factory and Trade Waste; Refuse and Refuse Disposal; Spraying and Dusting Residues in Agriculture; Water–Pollution

also subdivision Pollution under subjects, e.g. Air–Pollution; Water–Pollution

Bradshaw, A. D. & McNeilly, D. T. Evolution & Pollution. (Studies in Biology: No. 130). 80p. 1981. pap. text ed. 8.95 (ISBN 0-7131-2818-6). E Arnold.

Brown, Richard D. & Ouellette, Robert P. Pollution Control at Electric Power Stations: Comparisons for U. S. & Europe. 110p. 1983. 29.95 (ISBN 0-250-40618-7). Ann Arbor Science.

Chakrabarty, A. M., ed. Biodegradation & Detoxification of Environmental Pollutants. 176p. 1982. 48.50 (ISBN 0-8493-5524-9). CRC Pr.

Commission of the European Communities. Law & Practice Relating to Pollution Control in the Member States of the European Communities: France. 1983. 40.00x (ISBN 0-8448-1442-3). Crane-Russak.

--Law & Practice Relating to Pollution Control in the Member States of the European Communities: Greece. 1983. 40.00x (ISBN 0-8448-1445-8). Crane-Russak.

--Law & Practice Relating to Pollution Control in the Member States of the European Communities: Federal Republic of Germany. 1983. 40.00x (ISBN 0-8448-1443-1). Crane-Russak.

--Law & Practice Relating to Pollution Control in the Member States of the European Communities: Denmark. 1983. 40.00x (ISBN 0-8448-1441-5). Crane-Russak.
--Law & Practice Relating to Pollution Control in the Member States of the European Communities: Italy. 1983. 40.00x (ISBN 0-8448-1447-4). Crane-Russak.
--Law & Practice Relating to Pollution Control in the Member States of the European Communities: Belgium & Luxembourg. 1983. 40.00x (ISBN 0-8448-1435-0). Crane-Russak.
--Law & Practice Relating to Pollution Control in the Member States of the European Communities: Netherlands. 1983. 40.00x (ISBN 0-8448-1448-2). Crane-Russak.
--Law & Practice Relating to Pollution Control in the Member States of the European Communities: Ireland. 1983. 40.00x (ISBN 0-8448-1446-6). Crane-Russak.
--Law & Practice Relating to Pollution Control in the Member States of the European Communities: Comparative Volume. 1983. 40.00x (ISBN 0-8448-1450-4). Crane-Russak.
--Law & Practice Relating to Pollution Control in the Member States of the European Communities: United Kingdom. 1983. 40.00x (ISBN 0-8448-1449-0). Crane-Russak.
Cornaby, Barney, ed. Management of Toxic Substances in Our Ecosystems: Taming the Medusa. LC 81-67257. (Illus.). 186p. 1981. 22.50 (ISBN 0-686-84680-X). Ann Arbor Science.
Environmental Resources Ltd., ed. The Law & Practice Relating to Pollution Control in the Member States of the European Communities, 10 vols. 1982. Set. 850.00 (ISBN 0-686-82384-2, Pub. by Graham & Trotman England); 90.00x ea. State Mutual Bk.
Fleck, Raymond F. & Hollaender, Alexander, eds. Genetic Toxicology: An Agricultural Perspective, Vol.21. (Basic Life Sciences). 560p. 1982. 65.00x (ISBN 0-686-83967-6, Plenum Pr.). Plenum Pub.
Hesketh, Howard E. & Cross, Frank L., Jr. Fugitive Emissions & Controls. LC 82-72348. (The Environment & Energy Handbook Ser.). (Illus.). 150p. 1983. 22.50 (ISBN 0-250-40448-6). Ann Arbor Science.
Huisingh, Donald & Bailey, Vicki, eds. Making Pollution Prevention Pay: Ecology with Economy as Policy. 168p. 1982. 25.00 (ISBN 0-08-029417-0). Pergamon.
The Infrared Spectra Handbook of Priority Pollutants & Toxic Chemicals. 1982. 2.45 (ISBN 0-686-84521-8). Sadtler Res.
Martin, M. H. & Coughtrey, P. J. Biological Monitoring of Heavy Metal Pollution: Land & Air. (Pollution Monitor Ser.: No. 5). (Illus.). x, 468p. 1982. 80.00 (ISBN 0-85334-136-2, Pub. by Applied Sci England). Elsevier.
Moriarty, F., ed. Ecotoxicology: The Study of Pollutants in Exosystems. Date not set. price not set (ISBN 0-12-506760-7). Acad Pr.
Ottaway, J. M. Biochemistry of Pollution. (Studies in Biology: No. 123). 64p. 1980. pap. text ed. 8.95 (ISBN 0-686-43101-4). E Arnold.
Saunders, P. J. Estimation of Pollution Damage. 1976. 21.50 (ISBN 0-7190-0629-5). Manchester.
Vesilind, P. Aarne & Peirce, Jeffrey J. Environmental Pollution & Control. LC 82-48648. (Illus.). 375p. Date not set. pap. 14.95 (ISBN 0-250-40619-5). Ann Arbor Science.
Wood, C. M. & Lee, N. Geography of Pollution. 150p. 1974. pap. 10.50 (ISBN 0-7190-0564-7). Manchester.

POLLUTION–CONTROL
see Pollution

POLLUTION–PREVENTION
see Pollution

POLLUTION CONTROL DEVICES (MOTOR VEHICLES)
see Motor Vehicles–Pollution Control Devices

POLLUTION CONTROL EQUIPMENT
see also Motor Vehicles–Pollution Control Devices
Directory of Pollution Control Equipment Companies in Western Europe. 4th ed. 588p. (Orig.). 1980. pap. 70.00 (ISBN 0-906685-01-X). Intl Pubns Serv.

POLLUTION EQUIPMENT
see Pollution Control Equipment

POLLUTION OF WATER
see Water–Pollution

POLO, MARCO, 1254-1323
Komroff, Manuel. The Travels of Marco Polo. 1983. pap. 4.95 (ISBN 0-87140-132-0). Liveright.
Nitti, John J., ed. Juan Fernandez de Heredia's Aragonese Version of the Libro de Marco Polo. xxxvi, 122p. 1980. 12.00 (ISBN 0-942260-13-9). Hispanic Seminary.
Polo, Marco. The Travels of Marco Polo. Latham, Ronald, tr. from Fr. (Illus.). 318p. 1982. 35.00x (ISBN 0-89835-058-1). Abaris Bks.
--The Travels of Marco Polo. 1982. Repr. lib. bdg. 18.95x (ISBN 0-89967-045-8). Harmony Raine.

POLO, MARCO, 1254-1323–JUVENILE LITERATURE
Thompson, Janice & Lewis, Naomi. Marco Polo & Wellington: Search for Solomon. (Illus.). 32p. (ps-1). 1983. laminated boards 9.95 (ISBN 0-224-02036-6, Pub by Jonathan Cape). Merrimack Bk Serv.

POLTERGEISTS
Steiger, Brad. ETs & Poltergeists: Their True Story. Stine, Hank, ed. LC 82-14671. (Illus.). 152p. (Orig.). 1983. pap. 5.95 (ISBN 0-89865-272-3). Donning Co.

POLYAMINES
Colowick, Sidney P. & Kaplan, Sidney O., eds. Methods in Enzymology: Polyamines, Vol. 94. Date not set. price not set (ISBN 0-12-181994-9). Acad Pr.

POLYCHLORINATED BIPHENYLS
Ackerman, D. G., et al. Destruction & Disposal of PCB'S by Thermal & Non-Thermal Methods. LC 82-22312. (Pollution Technology Review: No. 97). (Illus.). 417p. 1983. 48.00 (ISBN 0-8155-0934-0). Noyes.
MacKay, Donald & Paterson, Sally, eds. Physical Behavior of PCBs In the Great Lakes. LC 82-72347. (Illus.). 442p. 1982. 39.95 (ISBN 0-250-40584-9). Ann Arbor Science.

POLYCYCLIC COMPOUNDS
Segal, Daniel. Polycyclic Groups. LC 82-9476. (Cambridge Tracts in Mathematics Ser.: No. 82). 200p. Date not set. price not set (ISBN 0-521-24146-4). Cambridge U Pr.

POLYGLOT GLOSSARIES, PHRASE BOOKS, ETC.
Jones, Hugh P., ed. Dictionary of Foreign Phrases & Classical Quotations. 552p. 1983. pap. 12.95 (ISBN 0-88072-017-4). Tanager Bks.

POLYGLOTTISM
see Multilingualism

POLYHEDRA
see also Icosahedra; Topology
Barnette, David W. Map Coloring, Polyhedra & the Four-Color Problem. (Dolciani Mathematical Expositions Ser.: Vol. 8). Date not set. pap. price not set (ISBN 0-88385-309-4). Math Assn.
Federico, P. J. Descartes on Polyhedra: A Study of the "De Solidorum Elementis". (Sources in the History of Mathematics & Physical Sciences: Vol. 4). (Illus.). 144p. 1983. 36.00 (ISBN 0-387-90760-2). Springer-Verlag.

POLYMERIZATION
see Polymers and Polymerization

POLYMERS AND POLYMERIZATION
see also Macromolecules; Plastics
Allport, D. C. Block Copolymers. Date not set. price not set (ISBN 0-85334-557-0). Elsevier.
Andrews, E. H., ed. Developments in Polymer Fracture, Vol. 1. 1982. 65.75 (ISBN 0-85334-819-7, Pub. by Applied Sci England). Elsevier.
Ash, M. & Ash, I. Encyclopedia of Plastics, Polymers & Resins Vol. 1, A-G. 1981. 75.00 (ISBN 0-8206-0290-6). Chem Pub.
--Encyclopedia of Plastics, Polymers & Resins Vol. 2, H-P. 1982. 75.00 (ISBN 0-8206-0296-5). Chem Pub.
--Encyclopedia of Plastics, Polymers & Resins Vol. 3, Q-Z. 1983. 75.00 (ISBN 0-8206-0303-1). Chem Pub.
Baijal, S. K. Flow Behavior of Polymers in Porous Media. 116p. 1982. 29.95x (ISBN 0-87814-188-X). Pennwell Pub.
Bark & Allen. Analysis of Polymer Systems. (Applied Science Ser.). 1982. 57.50 (ISBN 0-85334-122-2). Elsevier.
Bassett. Developments in Crystalline Polymers, Vol. 1. 1982. 65.75 (ISBN 0-85334-116-8, Pub. by Applied Sci England). Elsevier.
Bikales, Norbert M., ed. Mechanical Properties of Polymers. LC 78-172950. 280p. pap. text ed. 16.00 (ISBN 0-471-07234-6). Krieger.
Cantow, H. J., et al. Light Scattering from Polymers. (Advances in Polymer Science: Vol. 48). (Illus.). 167p. 1983. 39.50 (ISBN 0-387-12030-0). Springer-Verlag.
--Unusual Properties of New Polymers. (Advances in Polymer Science: Vol. 50). (Illus.). 149p. 1983. 37.00 (ISBN 0-387-12048-3). Springer-Verlag.
Cantow, H. J., et al, eds. Synthesis & Degradation-Rheology & Extrusion. (Advances in Polymer Science: Vol. 47). (Illus.). 170p. 1982. 37.00 (ISBN 0-387-11774-1). Springer-Verlag.
Carraher, Charles E., Jr. & Gebelein, Charles G., eds. Biological Activities of Polymers. (ACS Symposium Ser.: No. 186). 1982. write for info. (ISBN 0-8412-0719-4). Am Chemical.
Carraher, Charles E., Jr. & Sheats, John E., eds. Advances in Organometallic & Inorganic Polymer Science. (Illus.). 472p. 1982. 67.50 (ISBN 0-686-82220-X). Dekker.
Ceausescu, E. Sterospecific Polymerization of Isoprene. (Illus.). 300p. 1982. 60.00 (ISBN 0-08-029987-3). Pergamon.
Dawkins, J. V. Developments in Polymer Characterisation, Vols. 1 & 2. Vol. 1. 45.00 (ISBN 0-85334-789-1, Pub. by Applied Sci England); Vol. 2. 55.50 (ISBN 0-85334-909-6). Elsevier.
Dawkins, J. V., ed. Developments in Polymer Characterisation, Vol. 3. 1982. 61.50 (Pub. by Applied Sci England). Elsevier.
Feit, Eugene D. & Wilkins, Cletus, Jr., eds. Polymer Materials for Electronic Applcations. (ACS Symposium Ser.: No. 184). 1982. write for info. (ISBN 0-8412-0715-1). Am Chemical.
Hermans, J. J. Polymer Solution Properties: Part II, Hydrodynamics & Light Scattering. LC 78-820. (Benchmark Papers in Polymer Chemistry Ser. Vol. 2). 294p. 1978. 52.50 (ISBN 0-87933-323-5); 84.50 set (ISBN 0-87933-094-5). Hutchinson Ross.
Hermans, J. J., ed. Polymer Solution Properties: Part I, Statistics & Thermodynamics. LC 87-820. (Benchmark Papers in Polymer Chemistry: Vol. 1). 234p. 1978. 41.50 (ISBN 0-87933-322-7); 84.50 (ISBN 0-87933-094-5). Hutchinson Ross.
Janeschitz-Kriegl, H. Polymer Melt Rheology & Flow Birefringence. (Polymers-Properties & Applications Ser.: Vol. 6). (Illus.). 524p. 1983. 41.00 (ISBN 0-387-11928-0). Springer-Verlag.
Kresta, Jiri E. Reaction Injection Molding & Fast Polymerization Reactions. (Polymer Science & Technology Ser.: Vol. 18). 310p. 1982. 42.50x (ISBN 0-306-41120-2, Plenum Pr). Plenum Pub.
Matthews, G. A., ed. Polymer Mixing Technology. (Illus.). 280p. 1982. 51.25 (ISBN 0-85334-133-8, Pub. by Applied Sci England). Elsevier.
Mittal, K. L., ed. Physiochemical Aspects of Polymer Surfaces, Vol. 1. 600p. 1983. 75.00x (ISBN 0-306-41189-X, Plenum Pr). Plenum Pub.
--Physiochemical Aspects of Polymer Surfaces, Vol. 2. 675p. 1983. 85.00x (ISBN 0-306-41190-3, Plenum Pr). Plenum Pub.
Morton, Maurice, ed. Anionic Polymerization. LC 82-11627. 268p. 1983. 39.00 (ISBN 0-12-508080-8). Acad Pr.
Pethrick, R. A. & Richards, R. W. Static & Dynamic Properties of the Polymeric Solid State. 1982. 56.50 (ISBN 90-277-1481-9, Pub. by Reidel Holland). Kluwer Boston.
Price, Charles C. & Vandenberg, Edwin J., eds. Coordination Polymerization. (Polymer Science & Technology Ser.). 342p. 1983. 42.50 (ISBN 0-306-41139-3, Plenum Pr). Plenum Pub.
Review: Nineteen Eighty One Session of the Congress. 1982. pap. 3.75 (ISBN 0-8447-0246-3). Am Enterprise.
Saunders, J. H. & Frisch, K. C. High Polymers, Part 2, Vol.16. (Polyurethanes, Chemistry & Technology Ser.). 896p. 1982. Repr. of 1964 ed. lib. bdg. 62.50 (ISBN 0-89874-561-6). Krieger.
Sheldon, R. P. Composite Polymeric Materials. (Applied Science Publications). 228p. 1982. 39.00 (ISBN 0-85334-129-X, Pub. by Applied Sci England). Elsevier.
Siesler, H. W. & Holland-Moritz, K. Infared & Raman Spectroscopy of Polymers. (Practical Spectroscopy Ser.: Vol. 4). (Illus.). 400p. 1980. 55.00 (ISBN 0-8247-6935-X). Dekker.
Stahl, G. Allan, ed. Polymer Science Overview. (ACS Symposium Ser.: No. 175). 1981. write for info. (ISBN 0-8412-0668-6). Am Chemical.
Stepek, J. & Daoust, H. Additives for Plastics. (Polymers: Properties & Applications Ser.: Vol. 5). (Illus.). 256p. 1983. 69.00 (ISBN 0-387-90753-X). Springer-Verlag.
Suh, N. P. & Tucker, C. L., III, eds. Polymer Processing: Analysis & Innovation. (PED Ser.: Vol. 5). 163p. 1982. 30.00 (H00229). ASME.
Swarc, Michael. Living Polymers & Mechanisms of Anionic Polymerization. (Advances in Polymer Science: Vol. 49). (Illus.). 187p. 1983. 45.00 (ISBN 0-387-12047-5). Springer-Verlag.
Tadros, T. F., ed. Effects of Polymers on Dispersion Properties. LC 81-68982. 432p. 1982. 36.00 (ISBN 0-12-682620-X). Acad Pr.
Wilson, A. D. & Prosser, H. J. Developments in Ionic Polymers, Vol. 1. (Illus.). 335p. 1983. 69.75 (ISBN 0-85334-159-1, Pub. by Applied Sci England). Elsevier.
Zachariades, Porter. The Strength & Stiffness of Polymers. (Plastics Engineering Ser.). 368p. 1983. price not set (ISBN 0-8247-1846-1). Dekker.
Zweig, Gunter & Sherma, Joseph, eds. Polymers Vol. I. (CRC Handbook of Chromatography Ser.). 200p. 1982. 56.00 (ISBN 0-8493-3073-4). CRC Pr.

POLYNESIAN ART
see Art, Polynesian

POLYNESIAN MUSIC
see Music, Polynesian

POLYNUCLEOTIDES
see Nucleic Acids

POLYOLEFINES
see Olefins

POLYOMA VIRUS
Sever, John L. & Madden, David, eds. Polyomaviruses & Human Neurological Disease. LC 82-22945. (Progress in Clinical & Biological Research Ser.: Vol. 105). 376p. 1983. 66.00 (ISBN 0-8451-0105-6). A R Liss.

POLYTOPES
Bronosted, A. An Introduction to Convex Polytopes. (Graduate Texts in Mathematics Ser.: Vol. 90). (Illus.). 160p. 1983. 28.00 (ISBN 0-387-90722-X). Springer-Verlag.

POLYURETHANES
see Urethanes

POMO INDIANS
see Indians of North America–Southwest, New

POMOLOGY
see Fruit

POND ECOLOGY
Hobbie, J. E., ed. Limnology of Tundra Ponds: Barrow, Alaska. LC 80-26373. (US-IBP Synthesis Ser.: Vol. 13). 514p. 1980. 34.00 (ISBN 0-87933-386-3). Hutchinson Ross.
Kabisch, Klaus & Hemmerling, Joachim. Small Ponds, Lakes & Pools. (Illus.). 261p. 1983. 14.95 (ISBN 0-668-05674-6, 5674). Arco.

POND LIFE
see Fresh-Water Biology

PONDS, FISH
see Fish Ponds

PONY EXPRESS
Covey, Joan. Pony Express '76' 14.00 (ISBN 0-686-37636-6). Snohomish Pub.

POOL (GAME)
see also Snooker
Byrne, Robert. Byrne's Treasury of Trick Shots in Pool & Billiards. LC 82-47676. (Illus.). 320p. 1982. 19.95 (ISBN 0-15-115224-1). HarBraceJ.
Rafferty, Jean. The Cruel Game: The Inside Story of Snooker. (Illus.). 160p. 1983. 22.50 (ISBN 0-241-10950-7, Pub. by Hamish Hamilton England); pap. 14.95 (ISBN 0-241-10951-5). David & Charles.

POOR
see also Charities; Child Welfare; Cost and Standard of Living; Labor and Laboring Classes; Old Age Pensions; Population; Proletariat; Public Welfare; Tramps; Unemployed
also subdivision Poor under names of cities, e.g. New York (City)–Poor
Goodman, John L., Jr. The Future Poor: Projecting the Population Eligible for Federal Housing Assistance. 15p. pap. text ed. 1.00 (ISBN 0-686-84410-6). Urban Inst.
Goodwin, Leonard. Causes & Cures of Welfare: New Evidence on the Social Psychology of the Poor. LC 82-48634. 224p. 1983. 23.95x (ISBN 0-669-06370-3). Lexington Bks.
Green, Bryan S. Knowing the Poor: A Case Study in Teaxtual Reality Construction. (International Library of Phenomology & Moral Sciences). 224p. 1983. 25.95 (ISBN 0-7100-9282-2). Routledge & Kegan.
Hamburger, Robert. All the Lonely People: Life in a Single Room Occupancy Hotel. LC 82-19128. 352p. 1983. 15.95 (ISBN 0-89919-159-2). Ticknor & Fields.
Korten, David C. & Alfonso, Felipe B., eds. Bureaucracy & the Poor: Closing the Gap. LC 82-83847. (Library of Management for Development). xiv, 258p. (Orig.). 1983. pap. write for info. (ISBN 0-931816-30-0). Kumarian Pr.

POOR–GREAT BRITAIN
Metcalf, David. Low Pay, Occupational Mobility, & Minimum Wage Policy in Britain. 1981. pap. 4.25. (ISBN 0-8447-3450-0). Am Enterprise.

POOR RELIEF
see Charities; Public Welfare

POPE, ALEXANDER, 1688-1744
Jackson, Wallace. Vision & Re-vision in Alexander Pope. 204p. 1983. 17.95x (ISBN 0-8143-1729-4). Wayne St U Pr.
Martin, Peter. Pursuing Innocent Pleasures: The Gardening World of Alexander Pope. 1983. price not set (ISBN 0-208-02011-X, Archon Bks). Shoe String.
Plowden, G. F. C. Pope on Classic Ground. LC 82-14413. 184p. 1983. text ed. 20.95x (ISBN 0-8214-0664-7, 82-84333). Ohio U Pr.
Shankman, Steven. Pope's Iliad: Homer in the Age of Passion. LC 82-61384. 176p. 1983. 19.50x (ISBN 0-691-06566-7). Princeton U Pr.

POPES
see also Papacy
DiFranco, Anthony. Pope John Paul II: Bringing Love to a Troubled World. Schneider, Thomas, ed. (Taking Part Ser.). (Illus.). 48p. (gr. 3 up). 1983. PLB 7.95 (ISBN 0-87518-241-0). Dillon Pr.

POPES–HISTORY
see Papacy–History

POPES–INFALLIBILITY
see also Catholic Church–Infallibility
Tekippe, Terry J., ed. Papal Infallibility: An Application of Lonergan's Theological Method. LC 82-23837. 416p. (Orig.). 1983. lib. bdg. 27.50 (ISBN 0-8191-2995-X); pap. text ed. 15.75 (ISBN 0-8191-2996-8). U Pr of Amer.

POPISH PLOT, 1678
Hibbard, Caroline M. Charles I & the Popish Plot. LC 81-23075. 350p. 1983. 28.00x (ISBN 0-8078-1520-9). U of NC Pr.

POPPER, KARL RAIMUND, SIR, 1902-
Levinson, Paul, ed. In Pursuit of Truth: Essays on the Philosophy of Karl Popper on the Occasion of His 80th Birthday. 304p. 1982. text ed. 25.00x (ISBN 0-391-02609-7, Pub. by Harvester England). Humanities.

POPULAR CULTURE
Hinds, Harold E., Jr. & Tatum, Charles M., eds. Studies in Latin American Popular Culture, Vol. 2. 1983. pap. 25.00 (ISBN 0-9608664-1-8). New Mexico St Univ.
Leisure & Popular Culture. (Leisure Today Ser.). 32p. 1.50 (ISBN 0-88314-118-3). AAHPERD.
The Leisure Revolution: Its Impact on Culture. (Leisure Today Ser.). 32p. 1.50 (ISBN 0-88314-117-5). AAHPERD.
Storch, Robert D., ed. Popular Culture & Custom in Nineteenth-Century England. LC 82-3302. 232p. 1982. 27.50x (ISBN 0-312-63033-6). St Martin.

POPULAR MUSIC
see Music, Popular (Songs, etc.)

POPULATION
see also Animal Populations; Birth Control; Census; Cities and Towns-Growth; Contraception; Demography; Migration, Internal; Mortality
also subdivision Population under names of countries, cities, etc., e.g. United States-Population
Eversley, David & Kollmann, Wolfgang. Population Change & Social Planning. 600p. 1982. text ed. 98.50 (ISBN 0-7131-6345-3). E Arnold.
Graham, Julia B. & Wiedeman, Varley E. Biology of Populations. 136p. 1982. pap. text ed. 8.95 (ISBN 0-8403-2784-6). Kendall-Hunt.
Hakon, H. Concepts & Models of a Quantitative Sociology: The Dynamics of Interacting Populations. (Ser. in Synergetics: Vol. 14). (Illus.). 217p. 1983. 31.50 (ISBN 0-387-11358-4). Springer-Verlag.
McArthur, Norma. Island Populations of the Pacific. LC 82-24169. (Illus.). xvi, 381p. 1983. Repr. of 1967 ed. lib. bdg. 45.00x (ISBN 0-313-22914-7, MCIPP). Greenwood.
Malthus, Thomas R. Essays on Principle of Population. (Penguin English Library). 1983. pap. write for info. (ISBN 0-14-043206-X). Penguin.
Model Life Tables for Developing Countries. (Population Studies: No. 77). 23.00 (ISBN 0-686-84904-3, E.81.XIII.7.). UN.
Model Life Tables for Developing Countries. 351p. 1983. pap. 23.00 (ISBN 0-686-84905-1, UN81/13/7, UN). Unipub.
Osborn, Fairfield, ed. Our Crowded Planet: Essays on the Pressures of Population. LC 82-21145. 240p. 1983. Repr. of 1962 ed. lib. bdg. 29.75x (ISBN 0-313-22639-3). Greenwood.
Overbeck, Johannes. Population: An Introduction. LC 82-81687. 278p. 1982. text ed. 14.95 (ISBN 0-15-543488-8). HarBraceJ.
Population Dynamics. (Leirsure Today Ser.). 32p. 1.50 (ISBN 0-88314-126-4). AAHPERD.
Tamarin, R. H., ed. Population Regulation. LC 77-16178. (Benchmark Papers in Ecology Ser.: Vol. 7). 389p. 1978. 46.00 (ISBN 0-87933-324-3). Hutchinson Ross.
Williamson, Mark. Island Populations. (Illus.). 298p. 1983. pap. 19.95 (ISBN 0-19-854139-2). Oxford U Pr.
Wilson, Yates. Family Planning on A Crowded Planet. LC 82-24160. 96p. 1983. Repr. of 1971 ed. lib. bdg. 22.50x (ISBN 0-313-22680-6, YAFP). Greenwood.

POPULATION-RESEARCH
see Population Research

POPULATION-STATISTICS
Lyons, Daniel S. J. Is There a Population Explosion? 12p. pap. 0.50 (ISBN 0-686-81639-0). TAN Bks Pubs.
Masnick, George & Pitkin, John. The Changing Population of State & Regions: Analysis & Projections, 1970-2000. (Illus.). 250p. (Orig.). 1982. pap. 12.00 (ISBN 0-943142-01-6). Joint Cen Urban.

POPULATION, FOREIGN
see Emigration and Immigration;
also subdivision Emigration and Immigration under names of countries, and subdivision Foreign Population under names of countries, cities, etc.

POPULATION GENETICS
Dawson, Peter S. & King, Charles E. Population Biology: Retrospect & Prospect. 240p. 1983. text ed. 22.00 (ISBN 0-231-05252-9). Columbia U Pr.
Hedrick, Philip W. Genetics of Populations. 600p. 1983. text ed. 29.50 (ISBN 0-86720-011-1). Sci Bks Intl.

POPULATION RESEARCH
Faaland, Just. Population & the World Economy in the 21st Century. LC 82-10579. 272p. 1982. 32.50x (ISBN 0-312-63123-5). St Martin.

POPULATION TRANSFERS
Gruen, Nina & Gruen, Claude. Demographic Changes & Their Effects on Real Estate Markets in the '80s. LC 82-60314. (Development Component Ser.). (Illus.). 27p. 1982. pap. 10.00 (ISBN 0-87420-609-X, D22). Urban Land.
Jones, G. W. & Richter, H. V. Population Resettlement Programs in Southeast Asia. LC 82-73138. (Development Studies Centre Monograph: No. 30). 189p. (Orig.). 1982. pap. text ed. 17.95 (ISBN 0-909150-73-7, 1230). Bks Australia.
Peterson, George. The Economic & Fiscal Accompaniments of Population Change. 44p. pap. text ed. 2.75 (ISBN 0-686-84408-4). Urban Inst.

POPULATIONS, ANIMAL
see Animal Populations

POPULISM
Carto, W. Profiles in Populism. 1982. 12.95 (ISBN 0-8159-6518-4); pap. 7.95 (ISBN 0-8159-6519-2). Devin.
Venturi, Franco. Roots of Revolution: A History of the Populist & Socialist Movements in Nineteenth-Century Russia. Haskell, Francis, tr. xxxviii, 850p. 1960. pap. 14.95 (ISBN 0-226-85270-9). U of Chicago Pr.

PORCELAIN
see also China Painting; Pottery
also names of varieties of porcelain, e.g. Chelsea Porcelain, Dresdan Porcelain
Charles, Bernard H. Pottery & Porcelain: A Glossary of Terms. (Illus.). 320p. 1983. pap. 8.95 (ISBN 0-88254-278-8). Hippocrene Bks.
Detweiler, Susan G. George Washington's Chinaware. LC 81-14993. (Illus.). 240p. 1982. 40.00 (ISBN 0-8109-1779-3). Abrams.
Halle, Antoinette & Mundt, Barbara. Porcelain of the Nineteenth Century. LC 82-50108. (Illus.). 296p. 1983. 85.00 (ISBN 0-8478-0437-2). Rizzoli Intl.
Ketchum, William C., Jr. Pottery & Porcelain. LC 82-48946. 1983. 13.95 (ISBN 0-394-71494-6). Knopf.

PORCELAIN-COLLECTORS AND COLLECTING
The Official 1983 Price Guide to Royal Doulton. 2nd ed. LC 80-81289. 512p. 1983. 9.95 (ISBN 0-87637-355-4). Hse of Collectibles.

PORCELAIN-MARKS
see Pottery-Marks

PORCELAIN, MEISSEN
see Meissen Porcelain

PORCELAIN ENAMELS
see Enamel and Enameling

PORCELAIN PAINTING
see China Painting

PORNOGRAPHY
see also Erotic Art; Literature, Immoral
Davis, Murray S. Smut: Erotic Reality-Obscene Ideology. 161p. 1983. 328p. 1983. 20.00 (ISBN 0-226-13791-0). U of Chicago Pr.
Robinson, James. Pornography: The Polluting of America. Date not set. pap. 2.50 (ISBN 0-8423-4858-1). Tyndale.

PORPHYRIN AND PORPHYRIN COMPOUNDS
Kessel, David & Dougherty, Thomas J., eds. Porphyrin Photosensitization. (Advances in Experimental Medicine & Biology Ser.: Vol. 160). 304p. 1983. 42.50x (ISBN 0-306-41193-8, Plenum Pr). Plenum Pub.

PORPOISES
see also Dolphins
Katona, Steve & Richardson, David. A Field Guide to the Whales, Porpoises, & Seals of the Gulf of Maine & Eastern Canada: Cape Cod to Labrador. (Illus.). 224p. 1983. 17.95 (ISBN 0-686-83664-2, ScribT); pap. 9.95 (ISBN 0-686-83665-0). Scribner.

PORSCHE (AUTOMOBILE)
see Automobiles, Foreign-Types-Porsche

PORT WINE
Howkins, Ben. Rich, Rare & Red: Guide to Port. (Illus.). 224p. 1983. 18.95 (ISBN 0-434-34909-7, Pub. by Heinemann England). David & Charles.

PORTABLE POWER TOOLS
see Power Tools

PORTER, KATHERINE ANNE, 1894-
Demouy, Jane K. Katherin Anne Porter's Women: The Eye of Her Fiction. 248p. 1982. text ed. 22.50x (ISBN 0-292-79018-X). U of Tex Pr.

PORTER, RUFUS, 1792-1884
Lipman, Jean. Rufus Porter Rediscovered. LC 79-28517. 202p. (Orig.). 1980. pap. 10.00 (ISBN 0-517-54116-5, Pub. by Hudson River Mus). Pub Ctr Cult Res.

PORTER, WILLIAM SYDNEY, 1862-1910
Longo, Lucas. O. Henry, Short Story Writer. Rahmas, Sigurd C., ed. (Outstanding Personalities Ser.: No. 88). 32p. (gr. 9-12). 1982. 2.95 (ISBN 0-87157-588-4); pap. text ed. 1.95 (ISBN 0-87157-088-2). SamHar Pr.

PORTFOLIO
see Investments; Securities

PORTER FAMILY
Ferrato, Philip. The Porter Family. (Illus.). 23p. 1980. catalogue 1.00. Parrish Art.

PORTLAND, MAINE
Portland City Directory 1983. 900p. 1983. 160.00 (ISBN 0-89442-034-8). Tower Pub Co.

PORTLAND, OREGON-HISTORY
Vaughan, Thomas & O'Donnell, Terence. Portland: An Informal History & Guide. 2nd, rev. ed. (Illus.). 1983. pap. 6.95 (ISBN 0-87595-101-5, Western Imprints). Oreg Hist Soc.

PORTO RICO
see Puerto Rico

PORTRAIT DRAWING
see also Portrait Painting
Graves, Douglas R. Drawing Portraits. 160p. (Orig.). 1983. pap. 14.95 (ISBN 0-8230-2151-3). Watson-Guptill.

PORTRAIT PAINTING
see also Pastel Drawing; Portrait Drawing
Powell, Eustace G. The Dutch School of Historical & Portrait Painting, 2 vols. (The Art Library of the Great Masters of the World). (Illus.). 147p. 1983. Set. 137.50 (ISBN 0-86650-043-X). Gloucester Art.
Sutton, John. Feature That: A Guide to Painting Features. (Illus.). 36p. (Orig.). 1983. pap. write for info. Scott Pubns MI.

PORTRAITS
see also Caricatures and Cartoons; Photography-Portraits
also subdivision Portraits under local biography, names of wars, and classes of persons, and names of prominent persons
Jacobi, Lotte. Theatre & Dance Photographs. 46p. (Orig.). 1982. pap. 10.95 (ISBN 0-914378-93-7). Countryman.
Ross, Alan. Bill Brandt: Portraits. 120p. 1982. 80.00x (ISBN 0-86092-062-3, Pub. by Fraser Bks). State Mutual Bk.
Schlotterback, Thomas. Five Thousand Years of Faces. (Illus.). 72p. 1983. pap. 9.95 (ISBN 0-942342-02-X). Bellevue Art.

PORTRAITS-CATALOGS
Thompson, David L. Mummy Portraits in the J. Paul Getty Museum. LC 82-81303. 70p. 1982. pap. 16.95 (ISBN 0-89236-038-0). J P Getty Mus.

PORTS
see Harbors

PORTUGAL
see also names of cities, areas, etc. in Portugal
Wohl, H. & Wohl, A. Portugal. 29.95 (ISBN 0-935748-48-2). ScalaBooks.

PORTUGAL-DESCRIPTION AND TRAVEL-GUIDEBOOKS
Baedeker's Portugal. (Illus.). 250p. 1983. pap. 12.95 (ISBN 0-13-056135-5). P-H.
Fodor's Portugal 1983. (Illus.). 320p. 1983. traveltex 11.95 (ISBN 0-679-00945-0). McKay.
Lisbon Travel Guide. (Berlitz Travel Guides). (Illus.). 1982. pap. 4.95 (ISBN 0-02-969200-8, Berlitz). Macmillan.
Michelin Green Guide: Portugal. (Green Guide Ser.). (Fr.). 1983. pap. write for info. (ISBN 2-0600-5542-3). Michelin.
Michelin Red Guide to Espana-Portugal. (Red Guide Ser.). 1983. write for info. (ISBN 2-0600-6333-7). Michelin.
Underwood, Pat. Landscapes of Maderia. 2nd ed. 64p. (gr. 3-4). 1981. pap. 7.95 (ISBN 0-9506942-0-7). Bradt Ent.

PORTUGAL-POLITICS AND GOVERNMENT
Gallagher, Tom. Portugal: A Twentieth Century Interpretation. 256p. 1982. 25.00 (ISBN 0-7190-0876-X). Manchester.

PORTUGUESE IN FOREIGN COUNTRIES
Lopes, Maria Luisa. A Portugese Colonial in America: Belmira Nunes Lopes: The Autobiography of a Cape Verdean-American. Miller, Yvette E., ed. 215p. 1982. pap. 11.95 (ISBN 0-935480-07-2); 25.00 (ISBN 0-935480-08-0). Lat Am Lit Rev Pr.
Scholberg, Henry. Bibliography of Goa & the Portuguese in India. 413p. 1982. text ed. 64.50x (ISBN 0-391-02762-X, Pub. by Promilla & Co India). Humanities.
--Bibliography of Goa & the Portuguese in India. 1982. 55.00x (ISBN 0-8364-0896-9, Pub. by Promilla). South Asia Bks.

PORTUGUESE LANGUAGE-COMPOSITION AND EXERCISES
Foreign Service Institute. Programmatic Portuguese, Vol. II. 600p. Date not set. with 22 cassettes 190.00x (ISBN 0-88432-100-2, P180). J Norton Pubs.

PORTUGUESE LANGUAGE-CONVERSATION AND PHRASE BOOKS
Berlitz Editors. Portuguese for Travel Cassettepack. 1983. 14.95 (ISBN 0-02-962790-7, Berlitz); cassette incl. Macmillan.
Lexus. The Portuguese Travelmate. LC 82-83992. 128p. 1983. pap. 1.95 (ISBN 0-307-46606-X, Golden Pr). Western Pub.
Naar, Maria E. Colloquial Portugese. (Trubner's Colloquial Ser.). 192p. 1972. pap. 7.95 (ISBN 0-7100-7450-6). Routledge & Kegan.

PORTUGUESE LANGUAGE-DICTIONARIES-ENGLISH
Berlitz Editors. Portuguese-English Dictionary. 1982. 4.95 (ISBN 0-02-964440-2, Berlitz). Macmillan.

POSITION ANALYSIS
see Topology

POSITIVE IONS
see Cations

POSITIVISM
see also Agnosticism; Idealism; Materialism; Naturalism; Pragmatism
De La Salle, Vincent A. Positivism & the Degeneration of the Human Mind. (The Great Currents of History Library Books). (Illus.). 121p. 1983. 49.75 (ISBN 0-89266-377-4). Am Classical Coll Pr.
Giddens, Anthony. Profiles & Critiques in Social Theory. 230p. 1983. 24.50x (ISBN 0-520-04933-0); pap. 10.95x (ISBN 0-520-04964-0). U of Cal Pr.
Hayim, Gila J. The Existential Sociology of Jean-Paul Sartre. LC 80-10131. 176p. 1982. pap. text ed. 7.00 (ISBN 0-87023-381-5). U of Mass Pr.
Schopenhauer, Arthur. The Psychological Theory of Positive Thinking. (An Essential Knowledge Library Book). (Illus.). 119p. 1983. 76.85 (ISBN 0-686-82204-8). Am Inst Psych.

POSITRON ANNIHILATION
Coleman, P. G. & Sharma, S. C., eds. Positron Annihilation: Proceedings of the Sixth International Conference on Positron Annihilation, The University of Texas at Arlington, April 3-7, 1982. 1016p. 1983. 123.50 (ISBN 0-444-86534-9, North Holland). Elsevier.

POSOLOGY
see Drugs-Dosage

POSSESSION (LAW)
Menon, Kreshna. The Law of Property. (Orient Longman Law Library). 556p. 1980. pap. text ed. 18.95x (ISBN 0-86125-516-X, Pub. by Orient Longman Ltd India). Apt Bks.

POST CARDS
see Postal Cards

POST-GRADUATE WORK
see Universities and Colleges-Graduate Work

POST-OFFICE
see Postal Service

POST-OPERATIVE CARE
see Postoperative Care

POSTAGE-STAMP COLLECTIONS
see Postage-Stamps-Collectors and Collecting

POSTAGE-STAMPS
Browning, Peter. Fell's International Directory of Stamp-Auction Houses. LC 82-71749. 336p. 1982. 24.95 (ISBN 0-8119-0452-0). Fell.
MacKay, James. The Guinness Book of Stamp Facts & Feats. (Illus.). 256p. 1983. 19.95 (ISBN 0-85112-241-8, Pub. by Guinness Superlatives England); pap. 12.95 (ISBN 0-85112-285-X, Pub. by Guinness Superlatives England). Sterling.
Newport, O. W. Stamps & Postal History of the Channel Islands. 1982. 9.95 (ISBN 0-434-91470-3, Pub. by Heinemann). David & Charles.

POSTAGE-STAMPS-CATALOGS
Africa Since Independence, A-E. (Stanley Gibbons Stamp Catalogues Ser.: Part 12). 1980. 20.00 (ISBN 0-85259-171-3). StanGib Ltd.
Africa Since Independence, F-M. (Stanley Gibbons Stamp Catalogues Ser.: Part 14). 1981. 25.50 (ISBN 0-85259-176-4). StanGib Ltd.
Africa Since Independence, N-Z. (Stanley Gibbons Stamp Catalogues Ser.: Part 14). 1981. 28.50 (ISBN 0-85259-181-0). StanGib Ltd.
Austria & Hungary. (Stanley Gibbons Stamp Catalogue Ser: Part 2). 1982. 17.95 (ISBN 0-85259-121-7). StanGib Ltd.
Balkans. (Stanley Gibbons Stamp Catalogue Ser.: Part 3). 1980. 28.50 (ISBN 0-85259-126-8). StanGib Ltd.
Benelux. (Stanley Gibbons Stamp Catalogue Ser.: Part 4). 1979. 15.00 (ISBN 0-85259-131-4). StanGib Ltd.
Central America. (Stanley Gibbons Stamp Catalogues Ser.: Part 15). 1980. 20.00. StanGib Ltd.
Central Asia. (Stanley Gibbons Stamp Catalogues Ser.: Part 16). 1981. 25.50 (ISBN 0-85259-186-1). StanGib Ltd.
Channel Island Stamp & Postal History. (1st. Ed). (Illus.). 1979. 18.00 (ISBN 0-85259-021-0). StanGib Ltd.
China. (Stanley Gibbons Stamp Catalogue Ser.: Part 17). 1982. 15.95 (ISBN 0-85259-196-9). StanGib Ltd.
Commonwealth Varieties, 1952-1980. 24.00 (ISBN 0-85259-326-0). StanGib Ltd.
Czechoslovakia & Poland. (Stanley Gibbons Stamp Catalogues Ser.: Part 5). 1982. 24.00 (ISBN 0-85259-007-5). StanGib Ltd.
Elizabethan Catalogue, 1983. 1983. 34.50 (ISBN 0-85259-356-2). StanGib Ltd.
Facit Norden Scandinavia Catalogue, 1982. (Illus.). 1982. 15.75. StanGib Ltd.
Facit Postal History, 1982. (Illus.). 1982. 30.00. StanGib Ltd.
Facit Specialized Catalogue. (Illus.). 1983. pns 0.00. StanGib Ltd.
France. (Stanley Gibbons Stamp Catalogues Ser.: Part 6). 1982. 20.00 (ISBN 0-85259-009-1). StanGib Ltd.
Germany. (Stanley Gibbons Stamp Catalogues Ser.: Pt. 7). 1982. 18.00 (ISBN 0-85259-009-1). StanGib Ltd.
Great Britain. 5th ed. (Queen Elizabeth II, Pre-decimal Issues). 1980. 25.00 (ISBN 0-85259-271-X). StanGib Ltd.
Great Britain: Queen Elizabeth Decimal Issues. 3rd. ed. (Vol. 14). (Illus.). 1981. 28.50 (ISBN 0-85259-331-7). StanGib Ltd.
Great Britain: Queen Victoria. 6th ed. (Vol. 1). (Illus.). 1979. 24.00 (ISBN 0-85259-096-2). StanGib Ltd.
Great Britain: The Four Kings. 5th ed. (Vol. 2). (Illus.). 1980. 24.00. StanGib Ltd.
Italy & Switzerland. (Stanley Gibbons Catalogues Ser.: Part 8). 1980. 18.50 (ISBN 0-85259-151-9). StanGib Ltd.
Japan & Korea. (Stanley Gibbons Stamp Catalogues Ser.). 1980. 15.00 (ISBN 0-85259-201-9). StanGib Ltd.
Middle East. (Stanley Gibbons Stamp Catalogues Ser.: Part 19). 1980. 29.50 (ISBN 0-85259-206-X). StanGib Ltd.
Portugal & Spain. (Stanley Gibbons Stamp Catalogues Ser.: Part 9). 1980. 24.00 (ISBN 0-85259-156-X). StanGib Ltd.
Russia. (Stanley Gibbons Stamp Catalogues Ser.: Part 10). 1981. 31.50 (ISBN 0-85259-161-6). StanGib Ltd.
Scandinavia. (Stanley Gibbons Catalogues Ser.: Part 11). 1980. 15.00 (ISBN 0-85259-166-7). StanGib Ltd.
South America. (Stanley Gibbons Stamp Catalogues Ser.: Part 20). 1980. 25.50 (ISBN 0-85259-136-5). StanGib Ltd.
South East Asia. (Stanley Gibbons Stamp Catalogues Ser.: Part 21). 1981. 28.50 (ISBN 0-85259-216-7). StanGib Ltd.
Stamps of the World, 1983: A-J. 1983. 24.00 (ISBN 0-85259-351-1). StanGib Ltd.
Stamps of the World, 1983: K-Z. 1983. 24.00. StanGib Ltd.
Stanley Gibbons. British Commonwealth. (Stanley Gibbons Stamp Catalogue Ser.: Part 1). 1983. 35.00 (ISBN 0-85259-346-5). StanGib Ltd.
United States. (Stanley Gibbons Stamp Catalogues Ser.: Part 22). 1981. 16.50 (ISBN 0-85259-221-3). StanGib Ltd.

Wright, Edmund H., et al, eds. Scott Specialized Catalogue of Canadian Stamps & Covers 1983. (Illus.). 160p. 1982. pap. 3.50 (ISBN 0-89487-050-5). Scott Pub Co.

POSTAGE-STAMPS–COLLECTORS AND COLLECTING

see also Postage-Stamps–Topics

China National Stamp Corp. Staff. Postage Stamp Catalog of PRC (1949-1980) (Illus.). 132p. (Orig.). 1982. pap. 15.00 (ISBN 0-8351-1033-8). China Bks.

Collect Channel Islands Stamps. 10th ed. 4.50 (ISBN 0-85259-004-0). StanGib Ltd.

Collect Isle of Man Stamps. 6th ed. (Illus.). 4.50 (ISBN 0-85259-003-2). StanGib Ltd.

Commonwealth Varieties, 1952-1980. 24.00 (ISBN 0-85259-326-0). StanGib Ltd.

Kindler, Leopard I. Get Top Dollar for Your Stamps. iv, 26p. 1981. pap. 4.95 (ISBN 0-943502-01-2). Kindler.

--Philatelic Agencies, 1982. ii, 20p. (Orig.). 1982. pap. 3.95 (ISBN 0-943502-02-0). Kindler.

Let's Collect British Stamps. 2nd ed. (Illus.). 4.95. StanGib Ltd.

Negus, James. Enjoy Stamp Collecting. 1.00. StanGib Ltd.

Watson, J. Book of Stamps & Collecting. (Illus.). 24.95. StanGib Ltd.

POSTAGE-STAMPS–JUVENILE LITERATURE

Turner, Gladys T. Papa Babe's Stamp Collection. (Illus.). 100p. (gr. 1-8). 1983. 5.50 (ISBN 0-682-49944-7). Exposition.

POSTAGE-STAMPS–TOPICS

Africa Since Independence, A-E. (Stanley Gibbons Stamp Catalogues Ser.: Part 12). 1980. 20.00 (ISBN 0-85259-171-3). StanGib Ltd.

Africa Since Independence, F-M. (Stanley Gibbons Stamp Catalogues Ser.: Part 14). 1981. 25.50 (ISBN 0-85259-176-4). StanGib Ltd.

Africa Since Independence, N-Z. (Stanley Gibbons Stamp Catalogues Ser.: Part 14). 1981. 28.50 (ISBN 0-85259-181-0). StanGib Ltd.

Austria & Hungary. (Stanley Gibbons Stamp Catalogue Ser: Part 2). 1982. 17.95 (ISBN 0-85259-121-7). StanGib Ltd.

Balkans. (Stanley Gibbons Stamp Catalogue Ser.: Part 3). 1980. 28.50 (ISBN 0-85259-126-8). StanGib Ltd.

Benelux. (Stanley Gibbons Stamp Catalogue Ser.: Part 4). 1979. 15.00 (ISBN 0-85259-131-4). StanGib Ltd.

Central America. (Stanley Gibbons Stamp Catalogues Ser.: Part 15). 1980. 20.00. StanGib Ltd.

Central Asia. (Stanley Gibbons Stamp Catalogues Ser.: Part 16). 1981. 25.50 (ISBN 0-85259-186-1). StanGib Ltd.

Channel Island Stamp & Postal History. (1st. Ed). (Illus.). 1979. 18.00 (ISBN 0-85259-021-0). StanGib Ltd.

China. (Stanley Gibbons Stamp Catalogue Ser.: Part 17). 1982. 15.95 (ISBN 0-85259-196-9). StanGib Ltd.

Collect Channel Islands Stamps. 10th ed. 4.50 (ISBN 0-85259-004-0). StanGib Ltd.

Collect Isle of Man Stamps. 6th ed. (Illus.). 4.50 (ISBN 0-85259-003-2). StanGib Ltd.

Commonwealth Varieties, 1952-1980. 24.00 (ISBN 0-85259-326-0). StanGib Ltd.

Czechoslovakia & Poland. (Stanley Gibbons Stamp Catalogues Ser.: Part 5). 1982. 24.00 (ISBN 0-85259-007-5). StanGib Ltd.

DeRighi, R. The Story of the Penny Black. 8.95. StanGib Ltd.

Elizabethan Catalogue, 1983. 1983. 34.50 (ISBN 0-85259-356-2). StanGib Ltd.

Facit Norden Scandinavia Catalogue, 1982. (Illus.). 1982. 15.75. StanGib Ltd.

France. (Stanley Gibbons Stamp Catalogues Ser.: Part 6). 1982. 20.00 (ISBN 0-85259-009-1). StanGib Ltd.

Germany. (Stanley Gibbons Stamp Catalogues Ser.: Pt. 7). 1982. 18.00 (ISBN 0-85259-009-1). StanGib Ltd.

Great Britain. 5th ed. (Queen Elizabeth II, Pre-decimal Issues). 1980. 25.00 (ISBN 0-85259-271-X). StanGib Ltd.

Great Britain: Queen Elizabeth Decimal Issues. 3rd. ed. (Vol. 14). (Illus.). 1981. 28.50 (ISBN 0-85259-331-7). StanGib Ltd.

Great Britain: Queen Victoria. 6th ed. (Vol. 1). (Illus.). 1979. 24.00 (ISBN 0-85259-096-2). StanGib Ltd.

Great Britain: The Four Kings. 5th ed. (Vol. 2). (Illus.). 1980. 24.00. StanGib Ltd.

Italy & Switzerland. (Stanley Gibbons Catalogues Ser.: Part 8). 1980. 18.50 (ISBN 0-85259-151-9). StanGib Ltd.

Japan & Korea. (Stanley Gibbons Stamp Catalogues Ser.). 1980. 15.00 (ISBN 0-85259-201-9). StanGib Ltd.

Kanai, H. Classic Mauritiue. 175.00 (ISBN 0-85259-251-5). StanGib Ltd.

Legge, Dormer H. Penny Kangaroo of Australia, 1913. 11.95 (ISBN 0-85259-071-7). StanGib Ltd.

Let's Collect British Stamps. 2nd ed. (Illus.). 4.95. StanGib Ltd.

Middle East. (Stanley Gibbons Stamp Catalogues Ser.: Part 19). 1980. 29.50 (ISBN 0-85259-206-X). StanGib Ltd.

Portugal & Spain. (Stanley Gibbons Stamp Catalogues Ser.: Part 9). 1980. 24.00 (ISBN 0-85259-156-X). StanGib Ltd.

Richow, Harold E. Encyclopedia of R. F. D. Cancels. (Illus.). 289p. 1983. 26.00 (ISBN 0-916170-21-7). J-B Pubs.

Rose, Stuart. Royal Mail Stamps. 29.95. StanGib Ltd.

Russia. (Stanley Gibbons Stamp Catalogues Ser.: Part 10). 1981. 31.50 (ISBN 0-85259-161-6). StanGib Ltd.

Scandinavia. (Stanley Gibbons Catalogues Ser.: Part 11). 1980. 15.00 (ISBN 0-85259-166-7). StanGib Ltd.

South America. (Stanley Gibbons Stamp Catalogues Ser.: Part 20). 1980. 25.50 (ISBN 0-85259-136-5). StanGib Ltd.

South East Asia. (Stanley Gibbons Stamp Catalogues Ser.: Part 21). 1981. 28.50 (ISBN 0-85259-216-7). StanGib Ltd.

Stanley Gibbons. British Commonwealth. (Stanley Gibbons Stamp Catalogue Ser.: Part 1). 1983. 35.00 (ISBN 0-85259-346-5). StanGib Ltd.

United States. (Stanley Gibbons Stamp Catalogues Ser.: Part 22). 1981. 16.50 (ISBN 0-85259-221-3). StanGib Ltd.

POSTAL CARDS

Album of Old-time Postcards from Houston & Galveston. pap. 3.50 (ISBN 0-931722-01-2). Corona Pub.

Carver, Sally S. American Postcard Guide to Tuck: 1983-84. rev. ed. pap. 8.95 (ISBN 0-686-38919-0). Carves.

Chesney, Allen, ed. Chattanooga Album: Thirty-Two Historic Postcards. LC 82-17330. (Illus.). 16p. 1983. pap. 3.95 (ISBN 0-87049-381-7). U of Tenn Pr.

Crawford, Charles W., ed. Memphis Memories: Thirty-Two Historic Postcards. (Illus.). 16p. 1983. pap. 3.95 (ISBN 0-87049-382-5). U of Tenn Pr.

Hoobler, James A., ed. Nashville Memories: Thirty-Two Historic Postcards. LC 82-23841. (Illus.). 16p. 1983. pap. 3.95 (ISBN 0-87049-385-X). U of Tenn Pr.

Picture Postcards of Old Brooklyn: Twenty-Four Ready-to-Mail Views. (Illus.). 18p. (Orig.). 1983. pap. 2.50 (ISBN 0-486-24489-X). Dover.

Stanley Gibbons Postcard Catalogue. 3rd. ed. 1982. 15.00 (ISBN 0-85259-341-4). StanGib Ltd.

POSTAL LIFE INSURANCE

see Insurance, Life

POSTAL SERVICE

see also Air Mail Service; Pony Express

Fleishman, Joel L. Future of Postal Service. 336p. 1983. 33.95 (ISBN 0-03-059921-0); pap. 4.00 (ISBN 0-03-063562-4). Praeger.

Future Systems, Inc. Electronic Mail: Systems, Developments & Opportunities. (Illus.). 147p. (Orig.). 1982. pap. 385.00x (ISBN 0-940520-49-4). Monegon Ltd.

International Resource Development Inc. Staff, ed. Electronic Mail: Executives Directory. 200p. 1982. 95.00 (ISBN 0-686-82647-7). Knowledge Indus.

J. J. Keller & Associates, Inc. Parcel Shipments Distribution Manual. LC 82-84710. 400p. 1983. loose-leaf 60.00 (ISBN 0-934674-46-9). J J Keller.

Laux, Patricia, ed. Private Fleet Management Guide. LC 82-84709. 350p. 1983. loose-leaf 65.00 (ISBN 0-934674-47-7). J J Keller.

Rudman, Jack. Mail Division Supervisor. (Career Examination Ser.: C-2624). (Cloth bdg. avail. on request). pap. 10.00 (ISBN 0-8373-2624-9). Natl Learning.

POSTAL SERVICE–HISTORY

Newport, O. W. Stamps & Postal History of the Channel Islands. 1982. 9.95 (ISBN 0-434-91470-3, Pub. by Heinemann). David & Charles.

POSTAL SERVICE–JUVENILE LITERATURE

Bolger, William F., intro. by. All about Letters. Rev. ed. LC 82-600601. (Illus.). 64p. (gr. 9-12). 1982. pap. 2.50x (ISBN 0-8141-0113-5, 01135). USPS.

--P. S. Write Soon! All about Letters. LC 82-600641. (Illus.). 64p. (Orig.). (gr. 4-8). 1982. pap. 2.50x (ISBN 0-8141-3796-2, 37962). USPS.

Roth, Harold. First Class! The Postal System in Action. LC 82-14520. (Illus.). 56p. (gr. 3-7). 1983. 10.95 (ISBN 0-394-85384-9); PLB 10.99 (ISBN 0-394-95384-3). Pantheon.

POSTAL SERVICE–GREAT BRITAIN

Farrugia & Gammons. Carrying British Mails. 6.50. StanGib Ltd.

POSTCARDS

see Postal Cards

POSTERS

see also Commercial Art; Playbills; Signs and Signboards

The New Jersey Historical Society Collection of World War I Posters. (Illus.). 87p. 1976. pap. 10.00 (ISBN 0-686-81826-1). NJ Hist Soc.

Sibbett, Ed, Jr. Turn of the Century Posters Coloring Book. 48p. 1978. pap. 2.00 (ISBN 0-486-23705-2). Dover.

POSTOPERATIVE CARE

Women Helping Women: A Guide to Organizing a Post-Mastectomy Program in Your Community. pap. 2.50 (ISBN 0-686-81725-7). NCJW.

POSTURE

see also Physical Education and Training; School Health

Lagerwerff, Ellen B. & Perlroth, Karen A. Mensendieck Your Posture, Encountering Gravity the Correct & Beautiful Way. Rev. ed. LC 72-97093. (Illus.). 1982. pap. 10.00 (ISBN 0-686-84332-0). Aries Pr.

POTASSIUM

Magnani, Bruno & Hansson, Lennart, eds. Potassium, the Heart & Hypertension: A Symposium Sponsored by the Italian Society of Cardiology. LC 82-51013. (Illus.). 200p. 1982. write for info. (ISBN 0-88137-000-2). TransMedica.

POTASSIUM IN THE BODY

Weber, Charles. Arthritis As a Chronic Potassium Deficiency. Rev. ed. 63p. 1981. pap. 8.00 (ISBN 0-9610114-0-8). Kalium.

POTATO STARCH

see Starch

POTATOES

Rich, Avery E., ed. Potato Diseases. LC 82-24290. (Monograph). Date not set. price not set. Acad Pr.

POTAWATOMI INDIANS

see Indians of North America–Eastern States

POTENTIAL FUNCTIONS

see Differential Equations, Partial; Harmonic Analysis

POTTED DWARF TREES

see Bonsai

POTTERS

Fleure, H. J. & Peake, Harold. Peasants & Potters. (Corridors of Time Ser.: No. 3). 1927. text ed. 24.50x (ISBN 0-686-83689-8). Elliots Bks.

POTTERS' MARKS

see Pottery–Marks

POTTERY

see also Porcelain; Transfer Printing

also names of varieties of pottery, e.g. Wedgwood Ware; subdivision Pottery under Indians of North America; Indians of Mexico; and similar headings

Bates, Shirley. Popular Pottery. (Illus.). 128p. 1982. 14.95 (ISBN 0-7134-4168-2, Pub. by Batsford England). David & Charles.

Gillespie, Charles A. Cone Four-Low Fire Pottery. 2nd. Ed ed. (Illus.). 72p. 1983. pap. 9.95 (ISBN 0-9609974-1-5). C A Gillespie.

Ketchum, William C., Jr. Pottery & Porcelain. LC 82-48946. 1983. 13.95 (ISBN 0-394-71494-6). Knopf.

Piche, Thomas. Art Nouveau Glass & Pottery. Meyer, Faith, ed. (Illus.). 16p. (Orig.). 1982. pap. text ed. 4.00 (ISBN 0-932660-06-1). U of NI Dept Art.

POTTERY–COLLECTORS AND COLLECTING

Emerson, Julie. The Collectors: Early European Ceramics & Silver. LC 82-60159. (Illus.). 94p. (Orig.). 1982. pap. 12.95 (ISBN 0-932216-08-0). Seattle Art.

The Official 1983 Price Guide to Hummels. 1st ed. LC 82-84649. 240p. 1983. pap. 2.95 (ISBN 0-87637-318-X). Hse of Collectibles.

POTTERY–DICTIONARIES

Charles, Bernard H. Pottery & Porcelain: A Glossary of Terms. (Illus.). 320p. 1983. pap. 8.95 (ISBN 0-88254-278-8). Hippocrene Bks.

POTTERY–HISTORY

Foster, K. Minoan Ceramic Relief. (Studies in Mediterranean Archaeology: No. LXIV). 196p. 1982. pap. text ed. 69.00x (ISBN 91-86098-08-X, Pub. by Astroms Sweden). Humanities.

Preaud, Tamara & Gauthier, Serge. Ceramics of the Twentieth Century. LC 82-50107. (Illus.). 224p. 1982. 80.00 (ISBN 0-8478-0436-4). Rizzoli Intl.

POTTERY–MARKS

Palissier, Vernon G. The China Collector's Classical Guide of Marks & Monograms. (A Promotion of the Arts Library Bk.). (Illus.). 198p. 1983. Repr. of 1887 ed. 98.75 (ISBN 0-89901-099-7). Found Class Reprints.

POTTERY, AMERICAN

Coysh, A. W. & Stefano, Frank, Jr. Collecting Ceramic Landscapes-British & American Landscapes on Printed Pottery. (Illus.). 80p. 1981. 15.00 (ISBN 0-8048-1407-4, Pub by Lund Humphries England). C E Tuttle.

Henzke, Lucile. Art Pottery of America. LC 82-60328. (Illus.). 480p. 1982. 45.00 (ISBN 0-916838-69-2). Schiffer.

POTTERY, ANCIENT

Frothingham, A. W. Prehistoric Pottery in the Collection from El Acebuchal: site near Carmona, Province of Sevilla. (Illus.). 1953. pap. 0.60 (ISBN 0-87535-075-5). Hispanic Soc.

POTTERY, ASIAN

Southwest Asian Ceramic Society: West Malaysia Chapter. Nonya Ware & Kitchen Ch'ing: Ceremonial & Domestic Pottery of the 19th-20th Centuries Commonly Found in Malaysia. (Illus.). 136p. 39.00x (ISBN 0-19-582516-0). Oxford U Pr.

POTTERY, BRITISH

see also Pottery, English

Coysh, A. W. & Stefano, Frank, Jr. Collecting Ceramic Landscapes-British & American Landscapes on Printed Pottery. (Illus.). 80p. 1981. 15.00 (ISBN 0-8048-1407-4, Pub by Lund Humphries England). C E Tuttle.

POTTERY, CHINESE

Monroe, Betty I. Chinese Ceramics from Chicago Collections. LC 82-18962. (Illus.). 104p. 1982. pap. 12.00 (ISBN 0-941680-01-0). M&L Block.

Williamson, George C. The Book of Famille Rose. LC 72-104208. (Illus.). 231p. 1970. 72.50 (ISBN 0-8048-0880-5). C E Tuttle.

POTTERY, ENGLISH

see also Pottery, British

Oswald, Adrian & Hildyard, R. J. English Brown Stoneware, 1670-1900. (Illus.). 296p. 1983. 60.00 (ISBN 0-571-11905-0). Faber & Faber.

POTTERY, EUROPEAN

Emerson, Julie. The Collectors: Early European Ceramics & Silver. LC 82-60159. (Illus.). 94p. (Orig.). 1982. pap. 12.95 (ISBN 0-932216-08-0). Seattle Art.

Hackenbroch, Yvonne & Hawes, Vivian. The Markus Collection of European Ceramics & Enamels. (Illus.). 220p. 1983. write for info. Mus Fine Arts Boston.

POTTERY, GERMAN

Kirsner, Gary. The Mettlach Book: Illustrated Catalog, Current Prices, & Collector's Information. Gruhl, Jim, ed. (Illus.). 263p. (Orig.). 1983. pap. 25.00 (ISBN 0-911403-18-3). Seven Hills Bks.

Wustrack, Michael K. Die Mechelner Alabaster-Manufaktur Des 16. Und Fruhen 17. Jahrhunderts. 422p. (Ger.). 1982. write for info. (ISBN 3-8204-5713-5). P Lang Pubs.

POTTERY, IRANIAN

Reid, Mehry M. Persian Ceramic Designs. (The International Design Library). (Illus.). 48p. (Orig.). 1983. pap. 2.95 (ISBN 0-88045-024-X). Stemmer Hse.

POTTERY, JAPANESE

Munsterberg, Hugo. The Ceramic Art of Japan: A Handbook for Collectors. LC 63-20586. (Illus.). 272p. 1964. 37.50 (ISBN 0-8048-0083-9). C E Tuttle.

Nakazato, Taroemon. Karatsu. LC 82-48169. (Famous Ceramics of Japan Ser.: Vol. 9). (Illus.). 40p. 1983. 17.75 (ISBN 0-87011-551-0). Kodansha.

Sanders, Herbert H. & Tomimoto, Kenkichi. The World of Japanese Ceramics. LC 67-16771. (Illus.). 267p. 1983. pap. 16.95 (ISBN 0-87011-557-X). Kodansha.

Valenstein, Suzanne & Meech-Pekarik, Julia. Metropolitan Museum of Art, New York. LC 80-82645. (Oriental Ceramics Ser.: Vol. 11). (Illus.). 200p. 1982. 68.00 (ISBN 0-87011-450-6). Kodansha.

POTTERY, MEXICAN

Espejel, Carlos. Mexican Folk Ceramics. (Illus.). 220p. 1982. 35.00 (ISBN 84-7031-222-7, Pub. by Editorial Blume Spain). Intl Schol Bk Serv.

POTTERY, ORIENTAL

Medley, Margaret, ed. Transactions of the Oriental Ceramic Society 1980-1981. (Illus.). 104p. 1982. text ed. 37.50x (ISBN 0-85667-168-1, Pub. by Sotheby Pubns England). Biblio Dist.

POTTERY, PREHISTORIC

see Pottery, Ancient

POTTERY, ROMAN

Peacock, D. P. Pottery in the Roman World: An Ethnoarchaeological Approach. LC 81-12356. (Archaeology Ser.). (Illus.). 192p. 1982. 35.00 (ISBN 0-582-49127-4). Longman.

POTTERY, SPANISH

Artigas, J. Llorens & Corredor-Matheos, J. Spanish Folk Ceramics. (Illus.). 235p. 1982. 35.00 (ISBN 84-7031-362-2, Pub. by Editorial Blume Spain). Intl Schol Bk Serv.

Frothingham, A. W. Prehistoric Pottery in the Collection from El Acebuchal: site near Carmona, Province of Sevilla. (Illus.). 1953. pap. 0.60 (ISBN 0-87535-075-5). Hispanic Soc.

POTTERY CRAFT

Cooper, Emmanuel. Electric Kiln Pottery: The Complete Guide. (Illus.). 144p. 1982. 24.95 (ISBN 0-7134-4037-6, Pub. by Batsford England). David & Charles.

POTTERY MAKING (HANDICRAFT)

see Pottery Craft

POULTRY

see also Cookery (Chicken); Turkeys

also names of specific breeds

Freeman, B. M., ed. Physiology & Biochemistry of the Domestic Fowl, Vol. 4. Date not set. price not set (ISBN 0-12-267104-X). Acad Pr.

Hawksworth. British Poultry: Standards. 4th ed. 1982. text ed. 49.95 (ISBN 0-408-70952-9). Butterworth.

Kay, David. Bantams. (Illus.). 96p. 1983. 12.50 (ISBN 0-7153-8395-7). David & Charles.

Sainsbury, David. Poultry Health & Management. 168p. 1980. text ed. 22.00x (ISBN 0-246-11173-9, Pub. by Granada England); pap. text ed. 12.25x (ISBN 0-246-11350-2). Renouf.

POULTRY–DISEASES

McDougald. Handbook of Poultry Parasites. 250p. 1983. 29.50 (ISBN 0-03-062489-4). Praeger.

POULTRY HATCHERIES

see Poultry Industry

POULTRY INDUSTRY

Gillespie, James. Modern Livestock & Poultry Production. 2nd ed. (Illus.). 662p. 1983. text ed. 23.80 (ISBN 0-8273-2200-3); write for info. instr's guide (ISBN 0-8273-2201-1). Delmar.

Poultry Market. 1982. 445.00 (ISBN 0-686-38418-0, A198). Busn Trend.

POULTRY TRADE

see Poultry Industry

POUND, EZRA LOOMIS, 1885-1972

Froula, Christine. A Guide to Ezra Pound's Selected Poems. LC 82-18776. 256p. 1983. 16.50 (ISBN 0-8112-0856-7); pap. 7.25 (ISBN 0-8112-0857-5, NDP548). New Directions.

Levy, Alan. Ezra Pound: The Voice of Silence. LC 82-83126. 128p. 1982. 9.95 (ISBN 0-932966-25-X). Permanent Pr.

Ruthven, K. K. A Guide to Pound's Personae (1926) 291p. 1983. pap. 7.95 (ISBN 0-520-04960-8, CAL 628). U of Cal Pr.

Saunders, Jeraldine. Cruise Diary. (Illus.). 1982. 9.95 (ISBN 0-686-84160-3). J P Tarcher.

Smith, Paul. Pound Revised. 204p. 1983. text ed. 29.25x (ISBN 0-7099-2346-5, Pub. by Croom Helm Ltd England). Biblio Dist.

Tsukui, Nobuko. Ezra Pound & Japanese Noh Plays. LC 82-23833. 132p. (Orig.). 1983. lib. bdg. 18.75 (ISBN 0-8191-2987-9); pap. text ed. 8.25 (ISBN 0-8191-2988-7). U Pr of Amer.

POUND, EZRA LOOMIS, 1885-1972–BIBLIOGRAPHY

Gallup, Donald. Ezra Pound: A Bibliography. LC 82-15995. 528p. 1983. write for info. U Pr of Va.

POUSSIN, NICOLAS, 1594-1665

Pace, Claire. Felibien's Life of Poussin. 160p. 1980. 60.00x (ISBN 0-302-00542-0, Pub. by Zwemmer England). State Mutual Bk.

POVERTY

see also Charities; Homelessness; Poor; Public Welfare; also subdivisions Economic Conditions and Social Conditions under names of countries, e.g. Great Britain–Economic Conditions; Italy–Social Conditions

Altimir, Oscar. The Extent of Poverty in Latin American. rev. ed. LC 82-8533. (World Bank Staff Working Papers: No. 522). (Orig.). 1982. pap. text ed. 3.00 (ISBN 0-8213-0012-1). World Bank.

Brown, Muriel & Madge, Nicola. Despite the Welfare State. (SSRC-DHSS Studies in Deprivation & Disadvantage). xii, 388p. 1982. text ed. 29.00x (ISBN 0-435-82095-8). Heinemann Ed.

George, Henry. Progress & Poverty. 599p. 1983. pap. 5.00 (ISBN 0-911312-58-7). Schalkenbach.

Goldstein, Richard & Sachs, Stephen, eds. Applied Poverty Research. (Orig.). 1982. pap. 6.00 (ISBN 0-918592-52-6). Policy Studies.

Katz, Michael B., ed. Poverty & Policy in American History: Monograph. (Studies in Social Discontinuity). 226p. 1983. price not set (ISBN 0-12-401760-6); pap. price not set (ISBN 0-12-401762-2). Acad Pr.

Pellegrini, Angelo. Lean Years, Happy Years: The Kitchen, the Garden, & the Cellar. 200p. 1983. 12.95 (ISBN 0-914842-98-6). Madrona Pubs.

Sarveswara Rao. Poverty: An Interdisciplinary Approach. 1982. 24.00x (ISBN 0-8364-0902-7, Pub. by Somaiya). South Asia Bks.

POWDER METALLURGY

see also Metal Powders

Hausner, H. H. & Mal, M. K. Handbook of Powder Metallurgy. 2nd ed. (Illus.). 1982. 85.00 (ISBN 0-8206-0301-5). Chem Pub.

Wendon, G. W. Aluminium & Bronze Flake Powders. 1982. 159.00x (ISBN 0-686-81701-X, Pub. by Electrochemical Scotland). State Mutual Bk.

Who's Who in P-M, 1982. rev. ed. LC 77-14732. 1982. pap. 40.00 (ISBN 0-918404-57-6). Am Powder Metal.

POWELL, ADAM CLAYTON, 1908-1972

Alexander, E. Curtis. Adam Clayton Powell, Jr. A Black Power Political Educator. LC 81-69171. (African American Educator Ser.: Vol. II). (Illus.). 120p. (Orig.). 1982. pap. 6.95 (ISBN 0-938818-03-1). ECA Assoc.

POWELL, ANTHONY, 1905-

Powell, Anthony. The Strangers All Are Gone. (Anthony Powell's Memoirs Ser.). (Illus.). 212p. 1983. 18.50 (ISBN 0-03-063279-X). HR&W.

POWER (MECHANICS)

see also Electric Power; Force and Energy; Machinery; Power Resources; Steam; Wind Power

Bohm & MacDonald. Power: Mechanics of Energy Control. 2nd ed. 1983. 18.64 (ISBN 0-686-38845-3). McKnight.

Coal Fired MHD Power Generation, Vol. 1. 300p. (Orig.). 1981. pap. text ed. 37.50x (ISBN 0-85825-162-0, Pub. by Inst Engineering Australia). Renouf.

Hill, Richard F. Energy Technology Conference Proceedings Series Vols. 1-9, 7 Vols. (Illus.). 1982. pap. 240.00 (ISBN 0-686-38761-9). Gov Insts.

Miller, Robert H. Power System Operation. 2nd ed. (Illus.). 224p. 1983. 34.50 (ISBN 0-07-041975-2, P&RB). McGraw.

Mitchell, J. W. Energy Engineering. 420p. 1983. write for info. (ISBN 0-471-08772-6, Pub. by Wiley-Interscience). Wiley.

Slesser, Malcolm. The Dictionary of Energy. LC 82-10252. 1983. 29.95 (ISBN 0-8052-3816-6). Schocken.

POWER (MECHANICS)–JUVENILE LITERATURE

Berger, Melvin. Energy. (A Reference First Bk.). (Illus.). 96p. (gr. 4 up). 1983. PLB 8.90 (ISBN 0-531-04536-6). Watts.

POWER (PSYCHOLOGY)

see Control (Psychology)

POWER (SOCIAL SCIENCES)

see also Elite (Social Sciences); Law and Politics

Baldwin, W. W. The Price of Power. LC 76-990. 361p. 1976. Repr. of 1948 ed. lib. bdg. 39.50 (ISBN 0-306-70803-5). Da Capo.

Cannadine, David, ed. Patricians, Power & Politics in Nineteenth Century Towns. LC 82-42544. 240p. 1982. 35.00x (ISBN 0-312-59803-3). St Martin.

Giddens, A. & Held, D. Class, Conflict, & Power. 1982. 55.00x (ISBN 0-333-32289-4, Pub. by Macmillan England). State Mutual Bk.

Koch, H. W. President's Guide to People: Power Strategies. 1982. 89.50 (ISBN 0-13-697557-7). Exec Reports.

POWER (THEOLOGY)

see also Authority (Religion)

Migliore, Daniel L. The Power of God, Vol. 8. Mulder, John C., ed. LC 82-20037. (Library of Living Faith). 120p. (Orig.). 1983. pap. 5.95 (ISBN 0-664-24454-8). Westminster.

POWER, BALANCE OF

see Balance of Power

POWER, LEGISLATIVE

see Legislative Power

POWER DISTRIBUTION, ELECTRIC

see Electric Power Distribution

POWER-PLANTS

Miller, Richard K. Power Plant Noise Control. (Illus.). 130p. pap. text ed. 65.00 (ISBN 0-89671-019-X). Southeast Acoustics.

Willenbrock, J. H., ed. Construction of Power Generation Facilities. LC 82-70491. 624p. 1982. pap. text ed. 44.00 (ISBN 0-87262-306-8). Am Soc Civil Eng.

POWER-PLANTS, ATOMIC

see Atomic Power Plants

POWER-PLANTS, STEAM

see Steam Power-Plants

POWER POLITICS

see Balance of Power

POWER PRESSES

see also Metal-Working Machinery

Slesser, Malcolm. The Dictionary of Energy. LC 82-10252. 1983. 29.95 (ISBN 0-8052-3816-6). Schocken.

POWER RESOURCES

Here are entered works on the available sources of mechanical power in general. Works on the physics and engineering aspects of power are entered under Power (Mechanics).

see also Biomass Energy; Electric Power; Energy Conservation; Solar Energy; Wind Power

also specific legal headings related to individual sources of power, e.g. Gas–Law and Legislation; Petroleum Law and Legislation

American Petroleum Institute. Two Energy Futures: A National Choice for the 80's. LC 82-73749. (Illus.). 196p. 1982. pap. write for info. (ISBN 0-89364-048-4). Am Petroleum.

Anderson, Richard J. & Hofman, Peter L. Alternative Energy Sources for the United States. 19p. pap. 2.50x (ISBN 0-87855-743-1). Transaction Bks.

Aronson, Jonathan D., ed. Profit & the Pursuit of Energy: Economic Structures for Energy Transition. Cowhey, Peter F. (Special Studies in Economics). 200p. 1983. lib. bdg. 22.00 (ISBN 0-86531-216-8). Westview.

Axel, Helen, ed. Regional Perspectives on Energy Issues. (Report Ser.: No. 825). (Illus.). vii, 63p. (Orig.). 1982. pap. text ed. 30.00 (ISBN 0-8237-0264-2). Conference Bd.

Banks, Ferdinand E. Resources & Energy: An Economic Analysis. LC 81-47967. 368p. 1983. 34.95x (ISBN 0-669-05203-5). Lexington Bks.

Bickford, J. P. & Mullineux, N. Computation of Power-System Transients. (IEE Monograph Ser.: No. 18). 186p. 1980. pap. 27.50 (ISBN 0-906048-35-4). Inst Elect Eng.

Bisio, Attilio. Encyclopedia of Energy Technology. 4000p. 1983. Set. 350.00 (ISBN 0-471-89039-1, Pub. by Wiley-Interscience). Wiley.

Booth, Don & Booth, Jonathan. Building for Energy Independence with Sun-Earth Buffering & Superinsulation. 1983. pap. 17.95 (ISBN 0-9604422-3-5). Comm Builders.

Bradbury, Katharine L. & Downs, Anthony. Housing & Energy in the Nineteen Eighties. new ed. 320p. 1983. 28.95 (ISBN 0-8157-1050-X); pap. 10.95 (ISBN 0-8157-1049-6). Brookings.

Clerman, Robert J. & Joglekar, Rajani. Biotechnology & Energy Use. LC 77-85093. (Electrotechnology Ser.: Vol. 8). (Illus.). 189p. 1981. 39.95 (ISBN 0-250-40485-0). Ann Arbor Science.

Congressional Quarterly Inc. Staff. Energy Issues: New Directions & Goals. LC 82-2523. (Editorial Research Reports Ser.). 216p. 1982. pap. 7.95 (ISBN 0-87187-234-X). Congr Quarterly.

Craig, Paul P., ed. Energy Decentralization. Levine, Mark D. (AAAS Selected Symposium 72). 175p. 1982. lib. bdg. 18.50 (ISBN 0-86531-407-1). Westview.

Critser, James R., Jr. Energy Systems: Solar, Wind, Water, Geothermal, Ser. 11-82. 1983. 150.00 (ISBN 0-88178-001-4). Lexington Data.

--Energy Systems: Solar, Wind, Water Geothermal, Ser. 11-81. (Ser.11-81). 204p. 1983. 150.00 (ISBN 0-88178-000-6). Lexington Data.

Deudney, Daniel & Flavin, Christopher. Renewable Energy: The Power to Choose. 1983. 18.95 (ISBN 0-393-01710-9). Norton.

Dhillon, Balbir S. Power System Reliability, Safety & Management. LC 82-72852. (Illus.). 350p. 1983. 39.95 (ISBN 0-250-40548-2). Ann Arbor Science.

Discovering Energy. LC 81-51904. (Discovering Science Ser.). lib. bdg. 15.96 (ISBN 0-86706-054-9, Pub. by Stonehenge). Silver.

Dryden. Efficient Use of Energy. 2nd ed. 1982. text ed. 89.95 (ISBN 0-408-01250-1). Butterworth.

El Mallakh, Ragaei & El Mallakh, Dorothea H., eds. New Policy Imperatives for Energy Producers. LC 80-81017. (Illus.). 1980. pap. 16.50x (ISBN 0-918714-06-0). Intl Res Ctr Energy.

Energy Information Resources: An Inventory of Energy Research & Development Information Resources in the Continental United States, Hawaii & Alaska. 1975. 14.00 (ISBN 0-686-42895-1). Knowledge Indus.

Farzin, Yeganeh. The Effect of Discount Rate & Substitute Technology on Depletion of Exhaustible Resources. LC 82-8612. (World Bank Staff Working Papers: No. 516). (Orig.). 1982. pap. 5.00 (ISBN 0-8213-0004-0). World Bank.

Ferguson, R. Comparative Risks of Electricity Generating Fuel Systems in the UK. 216p. 1981. 66.00 (ISBN 0-906048-66-4). Inst Elect Eng.

Franssen, Herman, et al. World Energy Supply & International Security. (Special Reports Ser.). 96p. 1983. 7.50 (ISBN 0-89549-048-X). Inst Foreign Policy Anal.

Future Energy Concepts. (IEE Conference Publication Ser.: No. 192). 360p. 1981. 81.50 (ISBN 0-85296-229-0). Inst Elect Eng.

Hall. Dictionary of Energy. (Energy, Power & Environment Ser.). 360p. 1983. price not set (ISBN 0-8247-1793-7). Dekker.

Healy, Timothy & Houle, Paul. Energy & Society. 2nd ed. 480p. 1983. pap. text ed. 14.95x (ISBN 0-87835-132-9). Boyd & Fraser.

Hellman, Caroline J. C. & Hellman, Richard. The Competitive Economics of Nuclear & Coal Power. LC 82-47500. 208p. 1982. 23.95x (ISBN 0-669-05533-6). Lexington Bks.

Henry, Charlier H. & Justus, John R. Handbook of Ocean Energy. (Illus.). 1983. 34.95 (ISBN 0-8311-1133-X). Indus Pr.

Instrumentation in the Power Industry: Proceedings of the 25th Power Instrumentation Symposium, Vol. 25. LC 62-52679. 292p. 1982. pap. text ed. 25.00x (ISBN 0-87664-703-4). Instru Soc.

International Electric Energy Conference, 1980. 358p. (Orig.). 1980. pap. text ed. 45.00x (ISBN 0-85825-137-X, Pub. by Inst Engineering Australia). Renouf.

Kilpatrick, F. & Matchett, D., eds. Water & Energy: Technical & Policy Issues. LC 82-71351. 672p. 1982. pap. text ed. 52.00 (ISBN 0-87262-308-4). Am Soc Civil Eng.

MacLean, Douglas & Brown, Peter G., eds. Energy & the Future. LC 82-18609. 224p. 1983. text ed. 35.95x (ISBN 0-8476-7149-6); pap. text ed. 18.50x (ISBN 0-8476-7225-5). Rowman.

Meador, Roy. Cogeneration & District Heating. LC 81-67258. (Illus.). 203p. 1981. 19.95 (ISBN 0-250-40420-6). Ann Arbor Science.

Mosburg, Lewis G., Jr., ed. Basics of Structuring Exploration Deals. 1948. 48.00 (ISBN 0-89931-006-0). Inst Energy.

Newcomb, Richard. Future Resources: Their Geostatistical Appraisal. 179p. 1982. 7.50 (ISBN 0-937058-13-0). West Va U Pr.

OECD, IEA. Energy Research, Development & Demonstration in the IEA Countries, 1981 Review of National Programmes. 157p. (Orig.). 1982. pap. 17.00x (ISBN 92-64-12383-0). OECD.

OECD Staff. Employment in the Public Sector. 79p. (Orig.). 1982. pap. 7.25 (ISBN 92-64-12319-9). OECD.

--Energy Policies & Programmes of IEA Countries, 1981 Review. 300p. 1982. pap. 20.00x (ISBN 92-64-12335-0). OECD.

OECD Staff & IEA Staff. World Energy Outlook. (Illus.). 500p. (Orig.). 1982. pap. 45.00 (ISBN 92-64-12360-1). OECD.

Overton, H. P., compiled by. The Alternative Energy Index. 60p. Date not set. pap. text ed. cancelled (ISBN 0-686-82427-X). Center Self.

Patil, P. G. Financial Issues for International Renewable Energy Opportunites: Supplement. (Progress in Solar Energy Ser.). 164p. 1983. pap. text ed. 15.50 (ISBN 0-89553-119-4). Am Solar Energy.

Power System Protection, Vol. II. (Illus.). 344p. 1981. 69.00 (ISBN 0-906048-53-2). Inst Elect Eng.

Power System Protection, Vol. III. (Illus.). 496p. 1981. 69.00 (ISBN 0-906048-54-0). Inst Elect Eng.

Power System Protection Principles & Components, Vol. 1. (Illus.). 544p. 1981. 78.50 (ISBN 0-906048-47-8). Inst Elect Eng.

Rudman, Jack. Supervisor (Power Distributor) (Career Examination Ser.: C-423). (Cloth bdg. avail. on request). pap. 12.00 (ISBN 0-8373-0423-7). Natl Learning.

Sterling, M. J. Power-System Control. (IEE Control Engineering Ser.: No. 6). (Illus.). 250p. 1978. 42.25 (ISBN 0-906048-01-X). Inst Elect Eng.

Telecommunications Energy Conference-Intelec 81. (IEE Conference Publication Ser.: No. 196). 371p. 1981. 81.50 (ISBN 0-85296-236-3). Inst Elect Eng.

Tomain, Joseph P. & Hollis, Shelia S. Energy Decision Making: The Interaction Law & Policy. LC 81-47747. 224p. 1983. 24.95x (ISBN 0-669-04800-3). Lexington Bks.

Veziroglu, T. Nejat, ed. Alternative Energy Sources IV, 8 vols. Incl. Vol. 1. Solar Collectors-Storage. 1982 (ISBN 0-250-40554-7); Vol 2. Solar Heating-Cooling-Desalination. 1982 (ISBN 0-250-40555-5); Vol. 3. Solar Power-Applications-Alcohols. 1982 (ISBN 0-250-40556-3); Vol. 4. Indirect Solar-Wind-Geothermal. 1982 (ISBN 0-250-40557-1); Vol. 5. Nuclear-Hydrogen-Biogas. 1982 (ISBN 0-250-40558-X); Vol. 6. Hydrocarbon Technology-Environment. 1982 (ISBN 0-250-40559-8); Vol. 7. Energy Conservation-Management-Education. 1982 (ISBN 0-250-40560-1); Vol. 8. Energy Programs-Policy-Economics. 1982 (ISBN 0-250-40561-X). LC 82-71533. (Illus.). Set. 510.00 (ISBN 0-250-40553-9); 85.00 ea. Ann Arbor Science.

World Energy Outlook: A Report of the International Energy Agency. 244p. 1982. 60.00x (ISBN 0-584-11028-6, Pub. by Muller Ltd). State Mutual Bk.

Wright, A. & Newberry, P. G. Electric Fuses. (IEE Power Ser.: No. 2). 208p. 1982. pap. 36.00 (ISBN 0-906048-78-8). Inst Elect Eng.

Yearbook of World Energy Statistics 1980. 896p. 1982. 60.00 (ISBN 0-686-81945-4, UN81/17/10, UN). Unipub.

Yearbook of World Energy Supplies 1970-1979. 60.00 (ISBN 0-686-84911-6, E/F.80.XVII.7). UN.

Yearbook of World Energy Supplies 1980. 60.00 (ISBN 0-686-84913-2, E/F.81.XVII.10). UN.

Zimmer, Michael, ed. Cogeneration Handbook II. 310p. 1982. Wkbk. 48.00 (ISBN 0-86587-103-5). Gov Insts.

POWER RESOURCES–AUSTRALIA

Electric Energy, Nineteen Eighty One. 140p. (Orig.). 1981. pap. text ed. 37.50x (ISBN 0-85814-167-1, Pub. by Inst Engineering Australia). Renouf.

Energy Australia. 160p. (Orig.). 1979. pap. text ed. 18.00x (ISBN 0-85825-121-3, Pub. by Inst Engineering Australia). Renouf.

POWER RESOURCES–GREAT BRITAIN

Transport & Energy. 168p. 1981. 90.00x (ISBN 0-7277-0125-8, Pub. by Telford England). State Mutual Bk.

Wailes, Rex. Windmills in England: A Study of Their Origin, Development & Future. 48p. 1982. 25.00x (ISBN 0-284-40007-6, Pub. by C Skilton Scotland). State Mutual Bk.

POWER RESOURCES–INDIA

Hart, David. Nuclear Power in India: A Comparative Analysis. 192p. 1983. text ed. 24.00x (ISBN 0-04-338101-4). Allen Unwin.

POWER SUPPLY

see Power Resources

POWER TOOLS

Hall, Walter. Barnacle Parp's Guide to Garden & Yard Power Tools: Selection, Maintenance & Repair. Wallace, Dan, ed. (Illus.). 200p. 1983. 18.95 (ISBN 0-87857-446-8, 14-012-0); pap. 11.95 (ISBN 0-87857-472-7, 14-012-1). Rodale Pr Inc.

POWER TRANSMISSION, ELECTRIC

see Electric Power Transmission

POWERS (LAW)

see Trusts and Trustees

POWERS, CONGRESSIONAL (UNITED STATES)

see United States–Congress–Powers and Duties

POWYS, LLEWELYN, 1884-1939

Elwin, Malcolm. Life of Llewelyn Powys. 300p. 1982. 39.00x (ISBN 0-686-82400-8, Pub. by Redcliffe England). State Mutual Bk.

Redcliffe Press Ltd., ed. Skin for Skin. 152p. 1982. 25.00x (ISBN 0-686-82401-6, Pub. by Redcliffe England). State Mutual Bk.

POWYS BROTHERS

Graves, Richard P. The Brothers Powys. (Illus.). 384p. 1983. 25.00 (ISBN 0-684-17880-X, ScribT). Scribner.

PRACTICE (LAW)

see Procedure (Law)

PRACTICAL NURSING

see also Home Nursing

Will, Connie A. & Eighmy, Judith B. Being a Long-Term Care Nursing Assistant. (Illus.). 1983. pap. text ed. 10.95 (ISBN 0-89303-232-8). R J Brady.

PRACTICAL POLITICS

see Politics, Practical

PRACTICE OF LAW

see also Law Offices; Legal Composition; Legal Ethics; Legal Secretaries; Trial Practice

Bartlett, Joseph W. The Law Business: A Tired Monopoly. LC 82-11309. vii, 198p. 1982. text ed. 17.50x (ISBN 0-8377-0324-7). Rothman.

PRACTICE TEACHING

see Student Teaching

PRAGMATISM

see also Experience; Reality; Truth; Utilitarianism

Blau, J. L. Pragmatism & Other Essays. 1983. pap. 3.95 (ISBN 0-686-37708-7). WSP.

Durkheim, Emile. Pragmatism & Sociology. Allcock, John B., ed. Whitehouse, J. C., tr. LC 82-14630. 184p. Date not set. price not set (ISBN 0-521-24686-5). Cambridge U Pr.

Lehrer, Adrienne. Wine & Conversation. LC 82-48538. 256p. 1983. 25.00x (ISBN 0-253-36550-3). Ind U Pr.

PRAIRIES

see also Steppes; Tundras

Gravel-Kellogg, Orlentha, ed. Bloom on the Land: A Prairie Pioneer Experience. LC 81-90537. (Illus.). 608p. 1982. 25.00x (ISBN 0-9608684-0-2). Gravel-Kellogg.

Irving, Washington. A Tour of the Praries. (Classics of the Old West Ser.). 1983. lib. bdg. 17.28 (ISBN 0-8094-4034-2). Silver.
Risser, P. G. The True Prairie Ecosystem. LC 79-19857. (The US-IBP Synthesis Ser.: Vol. 16). 544p. 1981. 31.50 (ISBN 0-87933-361-8). Hutchinson Ross.

PRAYER
see also Devotional Exercises; Meditation; Prayers; Retreats
Aglow Staff Editors. Aglow Prayer Diary. 421p. 1982. 9.95 (ISBN 0-930756-70-3). Womens Aglow.
Baelz, Peter. Does God Answer Prayer? (Illus.). 128p. (Orig.). 1983. pap. 6.95 (ISBN 0-87243-117-7). Templegate.
Bedford, Stewart. Prayer Power & Stress Management. Date not set. pap. 8.95 (ISBN 0-935930-05-1). Scott Pubns CA.
Bounds, E. M. Power Through Prayer. 128p. 1983. pap. text ed. 2.50 (ISBN 0-88368-117-X). Whitaker Hse.
Bradshaw, Paul F. Daily Prayer in the Early Church: A Study of the Origins & Early Development of the Divine Office. 202p. 1982. 24.50x (ISBN 0-19-520394-1); pap. 8.85x (ISBN 0-19-520395-X). Oxford U Pr.
Brandt, Catharine. Still Time to Pray. LC 82-72648. 96p. (Orig.). 1983. pap. 4.95 (ISBN 0-8066-1955-4, 10-6007). Augsburg.
Campbell, Will & Campbell, Bonnie. God on Earth: The Lord's Prayer for Our Time. (Illus.). 128p. 1983. 11.95 (ISBN 0-8245-0550-6). Crossroad NY.
Eims, LeRoy. Prayer: More Than Words. LC 82-61301. 1983. pap. 3.95 (ISBN 0-89109-493-8). NavPress.
Faith's Prayer Sequence. 1979. 1.25 (ISBN 0-89858-029-3). Fill the Gap.
Hasler, Richard A. Journal of Prayer. 144p. 1982. 12.95 (ISBN 0-8170-0965-5). Judson.
Hassel, David J. Radical Prayer. 160p. 1983. 6.95 (ISBN 0-8091-0340-0). Paulist Pr.
Hoffman, Marlin A. The Power of Prayer & Fasting. 1.60 (ISBN 0-89137-535-X). Quality Pubns.
Hubbard, David A. The Practice of Prayer. 91p. 1983. pap. 2.95 (ISBN 0-87784-393-7). Inter-Varsity.
Kelman, Stuart. Prayer Transparencies. 32p. (Orig.). 1982. 29.95x (ISBN 0-686-81835-0). Arbit.
Klug, Ronald. My Prayer Journal. LC 12-2964. 1982. pap. 3.95 (ISBN 0-570-03871-5). Concordia.
Kovats, Alexandra. Prayer: A Discovery of Life. (Nazareth Bks). 120p. 1983. pap. 3.95 (ISBN 0-86683-714-0). Winston Pr.
Linn, Matthew & Linn, Dennis. Prayer Course for Healing Life's Hurts. 128p. 1983. pap. 5.95 (ISBN 0-8091-2522-6). Paulist Pr.
Mackintosh, Carlos H. La Oracion y los Cultos de Oracion. 2nd ed. Daniel, Roger P., ed. Bautista, Sara, tr. from Eng. (La Serie Diamante). 40p. (Span.). 1982. pap. 0.85 (ISBN 0-942504-08-9). Overcomer Pr.
Menashe, Abraham. The Face of Prayer. LC 82-48737. 1983. 25.00 (ISBN 0-394-52930-8); pap. 15.00 (ISBN 0-394-71315-X). Knopf.
Murray, Andrew. The Believer's Prayer Life. rev. ed. 128p. Date not set. pap. 3.95 (ISBN 0-87123-277-4). Bethany Hse.
Neel, Peg. How To Pray According to God's Word. 72p. 1982. pap. 2.25 (ISBN 0-88144-004-3, CPS-004). Christian Pub.
Nemeck, Francis K. & Coombs, Marie T. Contemplation. (Ways of Prayer Ser.: Vol. 5). 151p. 1982. 8.95; pap. 4.95 (ISBN 0-686-82184-X). M Glazier.
Parker, William & St. Johns, Elaine. Prayer Can Change Your Life. 288p. 1983. pap. 4.95 (ISBN 0-13-694786-7, Reward). P-H.
Prayer. 20p. 1980. pap. 7.55 (ISBN 0-88479-032-0). Arena Lettres.
Regardie, Israel. Energy, Prayer & Relaxation. 80p. 1982. pap. 6.95 (ISBN 0-941404-02-1). Falcon Pr Az.
Rosage, David E. Follow Me: A Pocket Guide to Daily Scriptural Prayer. 1982. pap. 3.95 (ISBN 0-89283-168-5). Servant.
Rowlett, Martha G. In Spirit & In Truth: A Guide to Praying. 112p. 1983. pap. 4.95 (ISBN 0-8358-0448-8). Upper Room.
Stern, Chaim, ed. Gates of Prayer. 1978. gifted edition 12.50 (ISBN 0-916694-69-0). Central Conf.
Sullivan, Barbara, ed. Daily Prayer: Words & Deeds. 56p. pap. 2.50. Paulist Pr.
Wiersbe, Warren W. Listen! Jesus Is Praying. 1982. pap. 4.95 (ISBN 0-8423-2167-5). Tyndale.

PRAYER-JUVENILE LITERATURE
see also Children-Prayer-Books and Devotions
Groth, J. L. Prayer: Learning How To Talk To God. (Concept Bks.: Ser. 4). 1983. pap. 3.50 ea.; Set. pap. 12.95. Concordia.
Guttschuss, Heather. Growing More Like Jesus. 128p. (ps). Date not set. pap. 5.95 (ISBN 0-8163-0486-6). Pacific Pr Pub Assn.

PRAYER-SERMONS
Wynne, Edward J., Jr. & Thompson, Henry O., eds. Prayer for Today's People: Sermons on Prayer by Carl Michalson (1915-1965) LC 82-17583. 88p. (Orig.). 1983. lib. bdg. 18.50 (ISBN 0-8191-2771-X); pap. text ed. 7.50 (ISBN 0-8191-2772-8). U Pr of Amer.

PRAYER, MENTAL
see Meditation

PRAYER-BOOKS
see also Church of England-Book of Common Prayer; Liturgies
also subdivision Prayer-Books and Devotions under religious denominations, and classes of persons, etc. for whose use the prayers are intended, e.g. Lutheran Church-Prayer-Books and Devotions; family-Prayer-Books and Devotions
Robinson, Ras, ed. Prayer. 48p. (Orig.). 1983. pap. 2.00 (ISBN 0-937778-07-9). Fulness Hse.

PRAYER-MEETINGS
Mackintosh, Carlos H. La Oracion y los Cultos de Oracion. 2nd ed. Daniel, Roger P., ed. Bautista, Sara, tr. from Eng. (La Serie Diamante). 40p. (Span.). 1982. pap. 0.85 (ISBN 0-942504-08-9). Overcomer Pr.

PRAYERS
see also Children-Prayer-Books and Devotions; Lord's Prayer; Meditations; Prayer
also subdivision Prayer-Books and Devotions under religious denominations, classes of persons, etc., e.g. Catholic Church-Prayer-Books and Devotions
Brooke, Avery. Plain Prayers for a Complicated World. 124p. 1983. 5.95 (ISBN 0-8164-0501-8, Vineyard); pap. 2.95 (ISBN 0-8164-2428-4). Seabury.
Coleman, William V. Prayer-Talk: Casual Conversations with God. LC 82-74085. 112p. (Orig.). 1983. pap. 3.95 (ISBN 0-87793-265-4). Ave Maria.
Cumming, John & Burns, Paul, eds. Prayers for Our Times. 144p. 1983. 10.95 (ISBN 0-8245-0071-7); pap. 4.95 (ISBN 0-8245-0107-1). Crossroad NY.
Cummings, J. T. & Moll, H. Prayers for College Students. LC 12-2962. 1982. pap. 4.95 (ISBN 0-570-03869-3). Concordia.
General Conference. My Golden Key Prayer List. pap. 0.50 (ISBN 0-686-82634-5). Review & Herald.
Grant, Gi-Gi. Thirty-Three Prayers. 1983. 6.95 (ISBN 0-533-05468-0). Vantage.
Grenier, M. Special Day Prayers for the Very Young Child. (gr. 1-4). 1983. 7.95 (ISBN 0-570-04076-0). Concordia.
Hagin, Kenneth E. Prevailing Prayer to Peace. 1973. pap. 2.50 (ISBN 0-89276-071-0). Hagin Ministry.
Long, Charles H., ed. Anglican Cycle of Prayer: Partners in Prayer, 1984. (A Cycle of Prayer Ser.). (Illus.). 128p. (Orig.). 1983. pap. price not set (ISBN 0-88028-024-7). Forward Movement.
Noffke, Suzanne. Prayers of Catherine of Siena. LC 82-60746. 288p. 1983. pap. 9.95 (ISBN 0-8091-2508-0). Paulist Pr.
Nouwen, Henri J. Cry for Mercy: Prayers from the Genesee. LC 80-2563. (Illus.). 175p. 1983. pap. 5.95 (ISBN 0-385-17508-6, Im). Doubleday.
Original Publications, tr. from Span. Helping Yourself With Selected Prayers. pap. 3.95 (ISBN 0-942272-01-3). Original Pubns.
Richards, Lawrence O. Believer's Promise Book: Seven Hundred Prayers & Promises from the NIV. 80p. (Orig.). 1982. pap. 1.75 (ISBN 0-310-43462-9). Zondervan.
Savage, Robert C. Pocket Prayers: Seven Hundred & Seventy-Seven Ways to Pray. 1982. pap. 2.95 (ISBN 0-8423-4849-2). Tyndale.
Simons, Thomas G. Blessings for God's People: A Book of Blessings for All Occasions. LC 82-62045. 112p. (Orig.). 1983. pap. 5.95 (ISBN 0-87793-264-6). Ave Maria.

PRAYERS AND INSTRUCTIONS
see Instructions to Juries

PRAYERS FOR CHILDREN
see Children-Prayer-Books and Devotions

PRAYERS FOR YOUTH
see Youth-Prayer-Books and Devotions

PREACHING
see also Bible-Homiletical Use; Communication (Theology); Sermons
Adams, Jay E. Preaching with Purpose. 1983. pap. 5.95 (ISBN 0-87552-078-2). Presby & Reformed.
Allen, Ronald J. Our Eyes Can Be Opened: Preaching the Miracle Stories of the Synoptic Gospels Today. LC 81-43679. 146p. 1983. pap. text ed. 8.25 (ISBN 0-8191-2671-3). U Pr of Amer.
Beatty, David. He That Wins Souls is Wise. 1982. pap. 0.75 (ISBN 0-88144-005-1, CPS-005). Christian Pub.
Burghardt, Walter J. Sir, We Would Like to See Jesus: Homilies from a Hilltop. LC 82-60589. 1983. 12.95 (ISBN 0-8091-0338-9); pap. 8.95 (ISBN 0-8091-2490-4). Paulist Pr.
Champlin, Joseph M. Messengers of God's Word: A Handbook for Lectors. 1983. pap. 3.95 (ISBN 0-8091-2484-X). Paulist Pr.
Edwards, O. C., Jr. Elements of Homiletic. 110p. (Orig.). 1982. pap. 7.95 (ISBN 0-916134-55-5). Pueblo Pub CO.
Horne, Chevis F. Dynamic Preaching. LC 82-70871. (Orig.). 1983. pap. 6.95 (ISBN 0-8054-2110-6). Broadman.
Parkhurst, Charles H. Pulpit & the Pew. 1913. text ed. 29.50x (ISBN 0-686-83717-7). Elliots Bks.
Rothwell, Mel-Thomas. Preaching Holiness Effectively. 160p. 1982. pap. 4.95 (ISBN 0-8341-0784-8). Beacon Hill.

PRECAST CONCRETE CONSTRUCTION
Broms, Bengt B. Precast Piling Practice. 126p. 1981. 65.00x (ISBN 0-7277-0121-5, Pub. by Telford England). State Mutual Bk.

PRECEDENTS (LAW)
see Forms (Law)

PRECIOUS METALS
see also Gold; Silver
El Guindy, M. I., ed. Precious Metals 1982: Proceedings of the 6th International Precious Metals Institute Conference, Newport Beach, California, June 7-11, 1982. 600p. 1983. 125.00 (ISBN 0-08-025396-2). Pergamon.

PRECIPITATION (CHEMISTRY)
Hales, J. P., Jr., ed. Precipitation Chemistry, Vol. 2. 200p. 1982. 35.00 (ISBN 0-08-028782-4). Pergamon.

PRECISIANS
see Puritans

PRECISION OF MEASUREMENT
see Physical Measurements

PRECOCITY
see Gifted Children

PREDICTION THEORY
Gilchrist, Warren. Statistical Forecasting. LC 76-13504. 3058p. 1976. 51.95x (ISBN 0-471-99402-2, Pub. by Wiley-Interscience); pap. 22.95x (ISBN 0-471-99403-0). Wiley.
Whittle, Peter. Prediction & Regulation by Linear Least-Square Methods. 2nd, rev. ed. 224p. 1983. 29.50x (ISBN 0-8166-1147-5); pap. 12.95x (ISBN 0-8166-1148-3). U of Minn Pr.

PREFABRICATED CONCRETE CONSTRUCTION
see Precast Concrete Construction

PREGNANCY
see also Labor (Obstetrics); Obstetrics; Pregnant Schoolgirls; Prenatal Care
Brady, Margaret. Having a Baby Easily. (Illus.). 144p. (Orig.). 1983. pap. 6.95 (ISBN 0-7225-0668-6, Pub. by Thorsons Pubs England). Sterling.
Brown, Judith E. Nutrition for Your Pregnancy: The University of Minnesota Guide. LC 82-21852. (Illus.). 140p. 1983. 12.95 (ISBN 0-8166-1151-3). U of Minn Pr.
Brown, Laverne K. The Year of Birth: A Guide for Expectant Parents. (Illus.). 215p. (Orig.). 1982. pap. 5.95 (ISBN 0-9608446-0-0). Lake Pr.
Cherry, Sheldon. Understanding Pregnancy. rev. ed. 224p. 1983. 11.95 (ISBN 0-672-52758-8). Bobbs.
Darragh, Colleen. The Pregnancy Day-By-Day Book. (Illus.). 192p. 1983. 9.57i (ISBN 0-06-015152-8, HarpT). Har-Row.
DeLyser, Femmy. Jane Fonda's Workout Book for Pregnancy, Birth & Recovery. 1982. 16.95 (ISBN 0-671-43219-2). S&S.
Hess, M. A. & Hunt, A. Pickles & Ice Cream. 1982. 14.95 (ISBN 0-07-028419-9). McGraw.
Jimenez, Sherry L. The Pregnant Woman's Comfort Guide. (Illus.). 192p. 1983. 14.95 (ISBN 0-13-694919-3); pap. 7.95 (ISBN 0-13-694901-0). P-H.
Katz, Jane. Swimming Through Your Pregnancy. LC 82-45296. (Illus.). 224p. 1983. pap. 10.95 (ISBN 0-385-18059-4, Dolp). Doubleday.
Kuemmerle. Clinical Pharmacology in Pregnancy. 1983. price not set (ISBN 0-86577-074-3). Thieme-Stratton.
Linden, Wilhelm Zur. A Child is Born: Pregnancy, Birth, Early Childhood. Collis, J., ed. & tr. from Ger. 223p. 1980. pap. 6.95 (ISBN 0-85440-357-4, Pub.by Steinerbooks). Anthroposophic.
McGuire, Paula. It Won't Happen to Me. LC 82-72754. 224p. 1983. 14.95 (ISBN 0-440-04099-X). Delacorte.
McKay, Susan. Assertive Childbirth: The Future Parent's Guide to a Positive Pregnancy. (Illus.). 256p. 1983. 19.95 (ISBN 0-13-049635-9); pap. 9.95 (ISBN 0-13-049627-8). P-H.
Russell, Keith P. Eastman's Expectant Motherhood. 7th. Rev. ed. 1983. 6.95i (ISBN 0-316-20396-3). Little.
Shapiro, Howard I. The Pregnancy Book for Today's Woman: An Obstetrician Answers all Your Questions About Pregnancy & Childbirth & Some You May Not Have Considered. LC 80-7916. (Illus.). 448p. 1983. 17.26i (ISBN 0-06-181766-X, HarpT). Har-Row.
Simpkin, Diana. The Complete Pregnancy Exercise Program. LC 82-36712. (Medical Library). 176p. 1982. pap. 5.95 (ISBN 0-452-25343-8, 4622-7). Mosby.
Stern, Leo. Drug Use in Pregnancy. 300p. 1983. text ed. write for info. (ISBN 0-86792-011-4, Pub by Adis Pr Australia). Wright-PSG.
Tarr, Katherine. Herbs, Helps, & Pressure Points For Pregnancy & Childbirth. (Illus.). 69p. 1981. pap. 3.95 (ISBN 0-9609514-0-7). Sunbeam.
Woerth, Sheila T., et al, eds. Your Child's Birth: A Comprehensive Guide for Pregnancy, Birth, & Postpartum. (Avery's Childbirth Education Ser.). (Illus.). 96p. (Orig.). 1982. pap. 5.95 (ISBN 0-89529-182-7). Avery Pub.

PREGNANCY, COMPLICATIONS OF
Elkayam, Uri & Gleicher, Norbert, eds. Cardiac Problems in Pregnancy: Diagnosis & Management of Maternal & Fetal Disease. LC 82-9938. 638p. 1982. 85.00 (ISBN 0-8451-0216-8). A R Liss.
Pizer, Hank & O'Brien Palinski, Christine. Coping with Miscarriage. (Medical Library). 192p. 1982. pap. 6.95 (ISBN 0-686-84852-7, 3945-X). Mosby.

PREGNANT GIRLS IN THE SCHOOLS
see Pregnant Schoolgirls

PREGNANT SCHOOLGIRLS
Children As Parents: A Final Report on a Study of Childbearing & Childrearing Among 12 to 15 Year Olds. Date not set. price not set. Child Welfare.
McAnarney, Elizabeth. Premature Adolescent Pregnancy & Parenthood. Date not set. price not set (ISBN 0-8089-1518-5). Grune.
McGuire, Paula. It Won't Happen to Me: Teenagers Talk about Pregnancy. 1983. pap. 6.95 (ISBN 0-440-53845-9, Delta). Dell.
Moore, Kristin A. & Burt, Martha R. Private Crisis, Public Cost: Policy Perspectives on Teenage Childbearing. LC 82-60293. 166p. (Orig.). 1982. pap. text ed. 11.00 (ISBN 0-87766-314-9, 33900). Urban Inst.
O'Brien, Bev. Mom, I'm Pregnant. 125p. 1982. pap. 3.95 (ISBN 0-8423-4495-0). Tyndale.
Richards, Arlene K. & Willis, Irene. What to Do if You or Someone You Know Is under 18 & Pregnant. LC 82-12698. (Illus.). 256p. 1983. 9.55 (ISBN 0-688-51961-X); pap. 7.00 (ISBN 0-688-01044-X). Lothrop.
Teenage Pregnancy: The Kids Next Door. (Youth Elect Ser.). 32p. (Orig.). 1983. pap. 2.75 (ISBN 0-8298-0674-1). Pilgrim NY.

PREHISTORIC ANIMALS
see Extinct Animals; Paleontology

PREHISTORIC ANTIQUITIES
see Archaeology; Man, Prehistoric

PREHISTORIC FAUNA
see Paleontology

PREHISTORIC MAN
see Man, Prehistoric

PREHISTORY
see also Archaeology; Man, Prehistoric
also the earliest period subdivision of specific countries, regions, etc., e.g. Egypt-History-Ancient to 640
Chisholm. Prehistoric Times. 1983. 5.95 (ISBN 0-86020-624-6, 310011); 2.95 (ISBN 0-86020-623-8, 310012). EDC.
Dyer, James. The Penguin Guide to Prehistoric England & Wales. (Illus.). 400p. 1983. pap. 7.95 (ISBN 0-14-046351-8). Penguin.

PREMARITAL COUNSELING
see Marriage Counseling

PREMATURE INFANTS
see Infants (Premature)

PRENATAL CARE
Cedeno & Lazar. The Exercise Plus Pregnancy Program: Exercises for Before, During & After Pregnancy. (Illus.). 192p. 1980. pap. 4.95 (ISBN 0-688-08697-7). Quill NY.
Harris. The Use of Computers in Perinatal Medicine. 416p. 1982. 41.95 (ISBN 0-03-061513-5). Praeger.
Jimenez, Sherry L. The Pregnant Woman's Comfort Guide. (Illus.). 192p. 1983. 14.95 (ISBN 0-13-694919-3); pap. 7.95 (ISBN 0-13-694901-0). P-H.
Klein, Diane & Badalamenti, Rosalyn T. Eating Right for Two: The Complete Nutrition Guide & Cookbook for a Healthy Pregnancy. 320p. (Orig.). 1983. pap. 7.95 (ISBN 0-345-30915-4). Ballantine.
Peterson, Gayle. Holistic Prenatal Care, Vol. I. Mehl, Lewis, ed. (Holistic Approaches to Health & Disease Ser.). 1982. pap. write for info. Mindbody.

PREPAID GROUP MEDICAL PRACTICE
see Health Maintenance Organizations

PRERAPHAELITISM
Rose, Andrew. The Pre-Raphaelites. (Phaidon Color Library). (Illus.). 84p. 1983. 25.00 (ISBN 0-7148-2180-2, Pub. by Salem Hse Ltd); pap. 17.95 (ISBN 0-7148-2166-7). Merrimack Bk Serv.
Ruskin, John. John Ruskin's Critical Vision of the Pre-Raphaellites. (A Promotion of the Arts Library Book). (Illus.). 101p. 1983. 69.85 (ISBN 0-89266-378-2). Am Classical Coll Pr.

PRE-REFORMATION
see Reformation-Early Movements

PRESBYTERIAN CHURCH
see also names of specific branches of the Presbyterian Church, e.g. Presbyterian Church in the U. S.
Ellis, Dorsey D. Look Unto the Rock: A History of the Presbyterian Church, U.S. in West Virginia from 1719 to 1974. LC 82-60889. (Illus.). 372p. (Orig.). 1982. pap. 14.95 (ISBN 0-9609076-0-2). McClain.

PRESBYTERIAN CHURCH-CLERGY-CORRESPONDENCE, REMINISCENCES, ETC.
Barnhouse, Margaret N. That Man Barnhouse. 1983. pap. 7.95 (ISBN 0-8423-7033-1). Tyndale.

PRESBYTERIAN CHURCH-HISTORY
Boyd, Lois A. & Brackenridge, Douglas. Presbyterian Women in America: Two Centuries of a Quest for Status. LC 82-15845. (Contributions to the Study of Religion: No. 9). 416p. 1983. lib. bdg. 35.00 (ISBN 0-313-23678-X, BOY/). Greenwood.
Smith, Toby. Pieces of the Promise. (Illus.). 90p. (Orig.). 1982. pap. 7.95 (ISBN 0-9608762-0-0). T Smith.

PRESBYTERIAN CHURCH IN THE U. S. A.-HISTORY
Fleming, John K. History of the Third Creek Presbyterian Church. 1967. 8.00 (ISBN 0-686-37869-5). Synod NC Church.

PRESCHOOL EDUCATION
see Education, Preschool

PRESCHOOL READERS
see Readers

PRESCRIPTIONS
see Medicine-Formulae, Receipts, Prescriptions

PRESENTS
see Gifts

PRESERVATION OF BOOKS
see Books–Conservation and Restoration

PRESERVATION OF FOOD
see Food–Preservation

PRESERVATION OF HISTORICAL RECORDS
see Archives

PRESERVATION OF MANUSCRIPTS
see Manuscripts–Conservation and Restoration

PRESERVATION OF NATURAL SCENERY
see Natural Monuments

PRESERVATION OF WILDLIFE
see Wildlife Conservation

PRESERVING
see Canning and Preserving

PRESIDENTS–UNITED STATES
see also Elections–United States; War and Emergency Powers
also names of Presidents

Armour, Richard. Our Presidents. rev. ed. LC 82-23762. (Illus.). 96p. 1983. 9.95 (ISBN 0-88007-133-8); pap. 5.95 (ISBN 0-88007-134-6). Woodbridge Pr.

Bailey, Harry A., ed. Classics of the American Presidency. LC 80-61. (Classics Ser.). (Orig.). 1980. pap. 12.50x (ISBN 0-935610-10-3). Moore Pub IL.

Baumgardt, John P. How to Identify Flowering Plant Families. (Illus.). 269p. 1982. pap. 22.95 (ISBN 0-917304-21-7). Timber.

The Cumulated Indexes to the Public Papers of the Presidents of the United States: Jimmy Carter 1977-1981. (Orig.). 1983. lib. bdg. 65.00 (ISBN 0-527-20757-8). Kraus Intl.

Edwards, George C., III & Wayne, Stephen J., eds. Studying the Presidency. LC 82-17472. 320p. 1983. text ed. 19.95x (ISBN 0-87049-378-7); pap. text ed. 9.95 (ISBN 0-87049-379-5). U of Tenn Pr.

Ehrlich, Walter. Presidential Impeachment. 1974. pap. text ed. 2.95x. Forum Pr IL.

Filler, Louis, ed. The President in the Twentieth Century, Vol. I: The Ascendant President: From William McKinley to Lyndon B. Johnson. rev. ed. 424p. 1983. lib. bdg. 22.95 (ISBN 0-89198-127-6); pap. text ed. 10.95 (ISBN 0-89198-128-4). Ozer.

Frantzich, Stephen. Setups: Presidential Popularity in America. 1982. pap. 5.00 (ISBN 0-915654-53-9). Am Political.

Hoxie, R. G. Command Decision & the Presidency. 1977. 15.00 (ISBN 0-07-030605-2). McGraw.

Mann, Nancy W. Tylers & Gardiners on the Village Green: Williamsburg, Va. & East Hampton, Long Island. 1983. 9.50 (ISBN 0-533-05556-3). Vantage.

Page, B. I. & Petracca, M. P. The American Presidency. 496p. 1983. 13.95x (ISBN 0-07-048109-1). McGraw.

Polsby, Nelson. Consequences of Party Reform. (Illus.). 275p. 1983. 24.95 (ISBN 0-19-503234-9, GB736, GB); pap. 8.95 (ISBN 0-19-503315-9). Oxford U Pr.

Rubin, Richard L. Press, Party, & Presidency. 1981. pap. text ed. 6.95x (ISBN 0-393-95206-1). Norton.

--Press, Party, & Presidency. (Illus.). 1982. 18.95 (ISBN 0-393-01497-5). Norton.

Spitzer, Robert J. The Presidency & Public Policy: The Four Arenas of Presidential Power. LC 81-19802. (Illus.). 224p. 1983. text ed. 18.75 (ISBN 0-8173-0109-7). U of Ala Pr.

Thompson, Kenneth W., ed. The Roosevelt Presidency: Four Intimate Perspectives of FDR. LC 82-17479. (Portraits of American Presidents Ser.: Vol. I). 100p. 1983. lib. bdg. 17.25 (ISBN 0-8191-2827-9); pap. text ed. 6.50 (ISBN 0-8191-2828-7). U Pr of Amer.

--Ten Presidents & the Press. LC 82-20293. (American Presidents & the Press Ser.). 128p. (Orig.). 1983. lib. bdg. 17.50 (ISBN 0-8191-2877-5); pap. text ed. 7.25 (ISBN 0-8191-2878-3). U Pr of Amer.

--The Virginia Papers on the Presidency, Vol. X: The White Burkett Miller Center Forums, 1982, Pt. 1. LC 79-66241. 114p. (Orig.). 1983. lib. bdg. 16.50 (ISBN 0-8191-2823-6); pap. text ed. 6.25 (ISBN 0-8191-2824-4). U Pr of Amer.

Young, James S., ed. Problems & Prospects of Presidential Leadership in the Nineteen-Eighties, Vol. 1. LC 82-19981. (Problems & Prospects of the Presidency). (Illus.). 136p. (Orig.). 1982. lib. bdg. 17.25 (ISBN 0-8191-2837-6); pap. text ed. 6.75 (ISBN 0-8191-2838-4). U Pr of Amer.

PRESIDENTS–UNITED STATES–ELECTION

Congressional Quarterly Inc. Staff. Presidential Elections since Seventeen Eighty-Nine. 3rd ed. 200p. 1983. pap. 8.95 (ISBN 0-87187-268-4). Congr Quarterly.

David, Paul T. & Everson, David H., eds. The Presidential Election & Transition, 1980-1981. 304p. 1983. price not set (ISBN 0-8093-1109-7). S Ill U Pr.

Flanigan, William H. & Zingale, Nancy H. American Voting Behavior: Presidential Elections from 1952 to 1980. LC 82-83324. 1982. write for info. (ISBN 0-89138-920-2, ICPSR 7581). ICPSR.

Kagay, Michael. What's Happening to Voter Turnout in American Presidential Elections? (Vital Issues, Vol. XXIX 1979-80: No. 4). 0.60 (ISBN 0-686-81609-9). Ctr Info Am.

Smallwood, Frank. The Other Candidates: Third Parties in Presidential Elections. LC 82-40478. (Illus.). 312p. 1983. 20.00; pap. 10.95 (ISBN 0-87451-257-3). U Pr of New Eng.

Smith, Paul A. Electing a President: Information & Control. Pomper, Gerald M., ed. 256p. 1982. 28.95 (ISBN 0-03-059664-5). Praeger.

White, Theodore H. America in Search of Itself: The Making of the President, 1956-1980. 480p. Date not set. pap. 8.95 (ISBN 0-686-43171-5). Warner Bks.

PRESIDENTS–UNITED STATES–ELECTION–1972

Garza, Hedda, compiled by. The Watergate Investigation Index: Senate Select Committee Hearings & Reports on Presidential Campaign Activities. LC 82-7353. 326p. 1982. lib. bdg. 95.00 (ISBN 0-8420-2175-2). Scholarly Res Inc.

PRESIDENTS–UNITED STATES–ELECTION–1980

Abramson, Paul R. & Aldrich, John H. Change & Continuity in the Nineteen Eighty Elections. LC 82-1359. 279p. 1982. pap. 9.25 (ISBN 0-87187-221-8). Congr Quarterly.

DeMause, Lloyd. Reagan's America. 200p. 1983. 16.95 (ISBN 0-940508-02-8). Creative Roots.

Jaslyn, Richard & Johnson, Janet. Setups: Campaign '80-The Public & the Presidential Selection Process. 1983. pap. 5.00 (ISBN 0-915654-52-0). Am Political.

Sandoz, Ellis & Crabb, Cecil V., eds. A Tide of Discontent: The Nineteen-Eighty Elections & Their Meaning. LC 81-4586. 272p. 1981. pap. 8.95 (ISBN 0-87187-205-6). Congr Quarterly.

PRESIDENTS–UNITED STATES–JUVENILE LITERATURE

Bruce, Preston. From the Door of the White House. LC 81-23672. (Illus.). 160p. (gr. 6 up). 1983. 10.00 (ISBN 0-688-00883-6). Lothrop.

PRESIDENTS–UNITED STATES–MESSAGES

Windt, Theodore O. & Ingold, Beth. Essays in Presidential Rhetoric. 352p. 1982. pap. text ed. 15.95 (ISBN 0-8403-2865-6). Kendall-Hunt.

PRESIDENTS–UNITED STATES–PRESS CONFERENCES

Rubin, Richard L. Press, Party, & Presidency. 1981. pap. text ed. 6.95x (ISBN 0-393-95206-1). Norton.

--Press, Party, & Presidency. (Illus.). 1982. 18.95 (ISBN 0-393-01497-5). Norton.

PRESIDENTS–UNITED STATES–STATE OF THE UNION MESSAGES
see Presidents–United States–Messages

PRESIDENTS–UNITED STATES–WIVES AND CHILDREN

Kimball, Donald L. I Remember Mamie. LC 81-85247. (Illus.). 235p. 1981. 13.95 (ISBN 0-942698-00-2). Trends & Events.

Klapthor, Margaret B. The First Ladies Hall. LC 73-8675. (Illus.). pap. 2.95 (ISBN 0-87474-133-5). Smithsonian.

Quinn, Sandra L. & Kanter, Sanford. America's Royalty: All the President's Children. LC 82-12006. 256p. 1983. lib. bdg. 35.00 (ISBN 0-313-23645-3, QUA/). Greenwood.

PRESLEY, ELVIS ARON, 1935-1977

Elvis: That's the Way It Is. 1983. pap. 3.95 (ISBN 0-440-02195-2). Dell.

PRESS
see also Government and the Press; Liberty of the Press; Newspapers; Periodicals; Public Opinion; Reporters and Reporting

Hollis, Daniel W., III. An Alabama Newspaper Tradition: Grover C. Hall & the Hall Family. (Illus.). 224p. 1983. text ed. 19.95 (ISBN 0-8173-0136-4). U of Ala Pr.

MacDougall, Curtis D. Superstition & the Press. 600p. 1983. 29.95 (ISBN 0-87975-211-4); pap. 12.95 (ISBN 0-87975-212-2). Prometheus Bks.

PRESS–JAPAN

Asano, Osamu & Ishiwata, Mutsuko, eds. The Japanese Press, 1982. 34th ed. Henshu-sha, Century Eibun & Higashi, Shinbu, trs. LC 49-25552. (Illus.). 192p. 1982. pap. 28.50x (ISBN 0-8002-3022-1). Intl Pubns Serv.

PRESS AND GOVERNMENT
see Government and the Press

PRESS CENSORSHIP
see Liberty of the Press

PRESSBOARD
see Paperboard

PRESSED GLASS

Pressed Glass: Eighteen Twenty-Five to Nineteen Twenty-Five. (Illus.). 48p. 1983. 6.00 (ISBN 0-87290-107-6). Corning.

PRESSES, LITTLE
see Little Presses

PRESSES, POWER
see Power Presses

PRESSURE GROUPS
see also Lobbying

Chubb, John E. Interest Groups & the Bureaucracy: The Politics of Energy. LC 82-60106. (Illus.). 336p. 1983. 29.50x (ISBN 0-8047-1158-5). Stanford U Pr.

Moe, Terry M. The Organization of Interests: Incentives & the Internal Dynamics of Political Interest Groups. LC 79-13238. (Illus.). x, 282p. 1982. pap. text ed. 9.00x (ISBN 0-226-53352-2). U of Chicago Pr.

Paige, Connie. The Right-to-Lifers: Who They Are, What They Are, & Where They Get Their Money. 256p. 1983. 13.95. Summit Bks.

Roeder, Edward. PACs Americana: A Directory of Political Action Committees & Their Interests. LC 81-85581. 1982. lib. bdg. 200.00 (ISBN 0-942236-00-9); pap. 200.00. Sunshine Serv.

Sanders, Jerry. Peddlars of Crisis. 340p. 1983. 20.00 (ISBN 0-89608-182-6); pap. 8.00 (ISBN 0-89608-181-8). South End Pr.

Willetts, Peter, ed. Pressure Groups in the Global System. (Global Politics Ser.). 256p. 1982. pap. 14.00 (ISBN 0-86187-224-X). F Pinter Pubs.

PRESSURE GROUTING
see Grouting

PRESSURE PACKAGING
see Aerosols

PRESSURE VESSELS
see also Boilers; Tanks

Berstein, M. D. & Iotti, R. C., eds. Advances In Containment Design & Analysis. 127p. 1982. 30.00 (G00214). ASME.

Chuse, R. Pressure Vessels: The ASME Code Simplified. 1977. 24.50 (ISBN 0-07-010872-2). McGraw.

Palusamy, S. S. & Sampath, S. G., eds. Aspects of Fracture Mechanics In Pressure Vessels & Piping, Vol. 58. (PVP Ser.: Vol. 58). 324p. 1982. 50.00 (H00215). ASME.

Pohto, H. A., ed. High Pressure Engineering & Technology for Pressure Vessels & Piping Systems. (PVP Ser.: Vol. 61). 189p. 1982. 34.00. ASME.

Pugh, C. E. & Wei, B. C., eds. Advances in Design & Analysis Methodology for Pressure Vessels & Piping. (PVP Ser.: Vol. 56). 142p. 1982. 34.00 (H00213). ASME.

Semchyshen, M. Advanced Materials for Pressure Vessel Service with Hydrogen at High Temperature & Pressures. (MPC-18). 288p. 1982. 50.00 (H00227). ASME.

Sundararajan, C., ed. Reliability & Safety of Pressure Components. (PVP Ser.: Vol. 12). 254p. 1982. 50.00 (H00219). ASME.

Widera, G. E. O., ed. Pressure Vessel Design. (PVP: Vol. 57). 217p. 1982. 44.00 (H00214). ASME.

Zamrik, S. Y. & Dietrich, D., eds. Pressure Vessels & Piping: Design Technology, 1982-A Decade of Progress. 647p. 1982. 85.00 (G00213). ASME.

PRESTIDIGITATION
see Conjuring; Magic

PRESTRESSED CONCRETE CONSTRUCTION

Connections for Precast Prestressed Concrete Buildings Including Earthquake Resistance. 1982. ring bd. 30.00 (ISBN 0-937040-20-7, TR2-82). Prestressed Concrete.

Energy-Efficient Accelerated Curing of Concrete. 1982. ring bd. 36.00 (ISBN 0-937040-19-3, TR-1-82). Prestressed Concrete.

Gerwick, Ben C. Construction of Prestressed Concrete Structures. LC 71-140176. (Practical Construction Guides Ser). 1971. 36.95x (ISBN 0-471-29710-0, Pub. by Wiley-Interscience). Wiley.

PCI Journal Twenty-Five Year Index. 1982. pap. 30.00 (ISBN 0-937040-21-5, JR-1-82). Prestressed Concrete.

PRE-TRIAL PROCEDURE
see also Bills of Particulars

Fisher, Stanley. Standards Relating to Pretrial Court Proceedings. (Juvenile Justice Standards Project Ser.). 160p. Date not set. 20.00x (ISBN 0-88410-227-0); pap. 10.00x (ISBN 0-88410-811-2). Ballinger Pub.

PREVENTION OF ACCIDENTS
see Accidents–Prevention

PREVENTION OF CRIME
see Crime Prevention

PREVENTION OF CRUELTY TO ANIMALS
see Animals, Treatment Of

PREVENTION OF DISEASE
see Medicine, Preventive

PREVENTION OF FIRES
see Fire Prevention

PREVENTIVE DENTISTRY
see also Teeth–Care and Hygiene

A Prevention-Oriented School Based Dental Health Program: Guidelines for Implementation. 4 copies 6.00 (ISBN 0-934510-23-7, W014). Am Dental.

PREVENTIVE INOCULATION
see also subdivision Preventive Inoculation under names of diseases, e.g. Tuberculosis–Preventive Inoculation

Neustadt, Richard & Fineberg, Harvey. The Epidemic that Never Was: Policy-Making & the Swine Flu Scare. LC 82-40023. 288p. (Orig.). 1983. pap. 7.95 (ISBN 0-394-71147-5, Vin). Random.

PREVENTIVE MEDICINE
see Medicine, Preventive

PRIBILOF ISLANDS

Alaska Geographic Staff, ed. Island of the Seals: The Pribilofs. (Alaska Geographic Ser.: Vol. 9 No. 3). (Illus., Orig.). 1982. pap. 9.95 (ISBN 0-88240-169-6). Alaska Northwest.

PRICE CONTROL
see Price Regulation

PRICE FIXING
see Price Regulation

PRICE POLICY

Benke, Ralph L., Jr. & Edwards, James Don. Transfer Pricing: Techniques & Uses. 154p. pap. 14.95 (ISBN 0-86641-012-0, 80118). Natl Assn Accts.

Gordon, Lawrence A. & Cooper, Robert. The Pricing Decision. 52p. pap. 4.95 (ISBN 0-86641-001-5, 80123). Natl Assn Accts.

PRICE POLICY, GOVERNMENTAL
see Price Regulation

PRICE REGULATION
see also Wage-Price Policy

Eichorn, W. & Henn, R., eds. Qualitative Studies on Production & Prices. 304p. 1982. text ed. 23.95x (ISBN 3-7908-0275-1). Birkhauser.

Harris, Seymour. Price & Related Controls in the United States. LC 76-10831. 393p. 1976. Repr. of 1945 ed. lib. bdg. 49.50 (ISBN 0-306-70828-0). Da Capo.

PRICE THEORY
see Microeconomics

PRICE-WAGE POLICY
see Wage-Price Policy

PRICES–HISTORY

Weatherman, H. M. Book One, Price Trends. (Illus.). 144p. 1983. pap. 5.50 (ISBN 0-913074-18-7). Weatherman.

Weathermen, Hazel M. Book Two, Price Trends. (Illus.). 304p. 1982. pap. 10.50 (ISBN 0-913074-17-9). Weatherman.

PRICING
see Price Policy

PRIESTESSES
see Priests

PRIESTHOOD
see also Priests

Stockums, Wilhelm. The Priesthood. 242p. 1938. pap. 6.00 (ISBN 0-686-81629-3). TAN Bks Pubs.

PRIESTS
see also Clergy; Priesthood;
also subdivision Clergy under church bodies, e.g. Catholic Church–Clergy; Church of England–Clergy

Barstow, Anne L. Married Priests & the Reforming Papacy: The 11th Century Debates. LC 82-7914. (Texts & Studies in Religion: Vol. 12). 344p. 1982. 39.95x (ISBN 0-88946-987-3). E Mellen.

Custodio, Sidney & Dudley, Cliff. Love Hungry Priest. 144p. (Orig.). 1983. pap. 2.95 (ISBN 0-89221-099-0). New Leaf.

Fleure, H. F. & Peake, Harold. Priests & Kings. (Corridors of Time Ser.: No. 4). 1927. text ed. 24.50x (ISBN 0-686-83710-X). Elliots Bks.

Winterborn, Benjamin. Changing Scenes. Thompson, Marie K. & Roth, Beth N., eds. (Illus., Orig.). 1980. 17.95 (ISBN 0-19-213226-1). Oxford U Pr.

PRIMARY BATTERIES
see Electric Batteries

PRIMARY EDUCATION
see Education, Primary

PRIMARY PRODUCTIVITY (BIOLOGY)

Lieth, Helmut F., ed. Patterns of Primary Production in the Biosphere. LC 78-18691. (Benchmark Papers in Ecology: Vol. 8). 342p. 1978. 46.00 (ISBN 0-87933-327-8). Hutchinson Ross.

PRIMATES
see also Man; Physical Anthropology

Gregory, William K. Studies on the Evolution of the Primates. Bd. with The Dentition of Dryopithecus & the Origin of Man. Gegory, William K. LC 78-72720. 67.50 (ISBN 0-404-18295-X). AMS Pr.

PRIMERS
see also English Language–Dictionaries, Juvenile; Readers

Evelyn & Marie. Pick Your Own Strawberries. (Illus.). 32p. (gr. k-3). 1983. 4.95 (ISBN 0-8062-1892-4). Carlton.

PRIMERS, CHINESE

Chang, Pauline, et al. Beginning Chinese Reader, 2 pts. Pt. 1. 4.95 (ISBN 0-686-38038-X); Pt. 2. 3.95 (ISBN 0-686-38039-8). Far Eastern Pubns.

Liang, James. Pronunciation Exercises for Beginning Chinese. 1.50 (ISBN 0-686-38041-X). Far Eastern Pubns.

PRIMERS, HEBREW
see Hebrew Language–Textbooks for Children

PRIMERS, ITALIAN
see Italian Language–Text-Books for Children

PRIMERS, SPANISH
see Spanish Language–Textbooks for Children

PRIMITIVE ARCHITECTURE
see Architecture, Primitive

PRINCES

Arnold, Sue. Little Princes: From Cradle to Crown. (Illus.). 208p. 1983. 15.95 (ISBN 0-283-98598-4, Pub by Sidgwick & Jackson). Merrimack Bk Serv.

PRINCIPALS, SCHOOL
see School Superintendents and Principals

PRINT MAKERS
see Printmakers

PRINT MAKING
see Prints–Technique

PRINTED CIRCUITS
see also Electronic Circuits

Bishop Graphics, Inc. The Design & Drafting of Printed Circuits. 1979. 40.75 (ISBN 0-07-005430-4). McGraw.

Lindsey, Darry. The Design & Drafting of Printed Circuits. 2nd ed. (Illus.). 400p. 1983. 45.95 (ISBN 0-07-037844-4, P&RB). McGraw.

PRINTERS' IMPRINTS
see Imprints (In Books)

PRINTING

Bodoni, Giambattista. Manuale Typografia, 2 Vols. 20.00x (ISBN 0-87556-035-0). Saifer.

Pierce. Edmund C. Tarbell & The Boston School of Printing, 1889-1980. (Illus.). 1980. 50.00 (ISBN 0-686-43148-0). Apollo.

PRINTING–BIBLIOGRAPHY

Bigmore, F. C. A Bibliography of Printing. 1982. 75.00x (ISBN 0-87556-157-8). Saifer.

PRINTING–COMPOSITION

see Type-Setting

PRINTING–HISTORY

see also Bibliography–Early Printed Books

Hutchings, R. S. The Western Heritage of Type Design. 130p. 1982. 35.00x (ISBN 0-284-39104-2, Pub. by C Skilton Scotland). State Mutual Bk.

Joyce, William L. & Hall, David D., eds. Printing & Society in Early America. 1983. text ed. price not set (ISBN 0-912296-55-0, Dist. by U Pr of VA). Am Antiquarian.

Spencer, Herbert. Pioneers of Modern Typography. (Illus.). 160p. 1983. pap. 15.00 (ISBN 0-262-69081-0). MIT Pr.

PRINTING–JUVENILE LITERATURE

Althea. Making a Book. (Cambridge Dinosaur Information Ser.). (Illus.). 26p. (gr. 7-10). 1983. pap. 1.50 (ISBN 0-521-27159-2). Cambridge U Pr.

PRINTING–LAYOUT AND TYPOGRAPHY

see also Advertising Layout and Typography; Type and Type-Founding

Kleper, Michael L. Illustrated Dictionary of Typographic Communication. (Illus.). 208p. (Orig.). 1983. pap. text ed. 19.00 (ISBN 0-89938-008-5). Tech & Ed Ctr Graph Arts RIT.

PRINTING–LITTLE PRESSES

see Little Presses

PRINTING–STYLE MANUALS

see also Authorship–Handbooks, Manuals, etc.; Proofreading

Black, Ann N. & Smith, Jo R. Ten Tools of Language - Written: Revised Edition II, Form B. rev. ed. 166p. 1983. pap. text ed. 12.60x (ISBN 0-910513-01-5). Mayfield Printing.

Hart's Rules for Compositors & Readers at the University Press, Oxford. 39th ed. 196p. 1982. 11.50 (ISBN 0-19-212983-X). Oxford U Pr.

PRINTING, PRACTICAL

Nievergelt, J. & Coray, G., eds. Document Preparation Systems: A Collection of Survey Articles. 280p. 1982. 42.75 (ISBN 0-444-86493-8, North Holland). Elsevier.

PRINTING, TRANSFER

see Transfer Printing

PRINTING AS A TRADE

Printing Trades Blue Book: 1983 New York Metropolitan Edition. 900p. 1983. pap. 60.00 (ISBN 0-910880-15-8). Lewis.

Second Tripartite Technical Meeting for the Printing & Allied Tra des, Geneva, 22 September-1 October 1981: Note on the Proceedings. iii, 82p. 1982. 8.55 (ISBN 92-2-102936-0). Intl Labour Office.

PRINTING FOR THE BLIND

see Blind–Printing and Writing Systems

PRINTING INDUSTRY

Jordans, ed. Britain's Top Three Hundred Printing Companies. 42p. 1982. 175.00x (ISBN 0-85938-163-3, Pub. by Jordans House England). State Mutual Bk.

Knittel, Patricia, ed. Selected Bibliography: Quality Control, Vol. II. (Orig.). 1982. pap. 15.00 (ISBN 0-89938-009-3). Tech & Ed Ctr Graph Arts RIT.

Miller, Richard K. Noise Control Solutions for Printing & Publishing. (Illus.). 77p. 1981. pap. text ed. 45.00 (ISBN 0-89671-026-2). Southeast Acoustics.

Testing Conference (Joint with Printing & Reprography) Proceedings. 196p. 1979. pap. 4.95 (ISBN 0-686-43249-5, 01 05 1079). TAPPI.

Testing Conference (Joint with Printing & Reprography) Proceeding. 225p. 1977. pap. 4.95 (ISBN 0-686-43250-9, 01 05 1077). TAPPI.

PRINTING INK

Knittel, Patricia, ed. Selected Biliogarphy: Printing Inks, Vol. 1. (Orig.). 1982. pap. 15.00 (ISBN 0-89938-010-7). Tech & Ed Ctr Graph Arts RIT.

PRINTING OF FOREIGN LANGUAGES

see Printing–Style Manuals

PRINTMAKERS

see also Engravers

O'Neill, Barbara T. & Foreman, George C. The Prairie Print Makers. LC 81-86587. (Illus.). 64p. (Orig.). 1982. pap. 6.00 (ISBN 0-9607978-0-7). Kansas Arts Com.

PRINTMAKING

see Prints–Technique

PRINTS

Gordon, Bonnie. The Anatomy of the Image Maps according to Merriam-Webster's Third International Dictionary of the English Language: Unabridged. LC 82-50789. (Artists' Book Ser.). 48p. (Orig.). 1983. pap. 10.00 (ISBN 0-89822-028-9). Visual Studies.

Izzard, Sebastian. Hiroshige: An Exhibition of Selected Prints. (Illus.). 116p. 1983. pap. 20.00 (ISBN 0-9610398-0-9). Ukiyo-e Soc.

Madigan, Mary Jean & Colgan, Susan, eds. Prints & Photographs: Understanding, Appreciating, Collecting. 160p. 1983. pap. text ed. 25.00 (ISBN 0-8230-8006-4, Art & Antiques). Watson-Guptill.

O'Neill, Barbara T. & Foreman, George C. The Prairie Print Makers. LC 81-86587. (Illus.). 64p. (Orig.). 1982. pap. 6.00 (ISBN 0-9607978-0-7). Kansas Arts Com.

Riggs, Timothy A. The Print Council Index to Oeuvre-Catalogues of Prints by European & American Artists. (Orig.). 1983. lib. bdg. 105.00 (ISBN 0-527-75346-7). Kraus Intl.

PRINTS–TECHNIQUE

Hargreaves, Joyce. Techniques of Hand Print-Making. LC 82-74212. (Illus.). 128p. 1983. 12.95 (ISBN 0-8008-7555-9, Pentalic). Taplinger.

PRISON PSYCHOLOGY

Johnson, Robert & Toch, Hans, eds. The Pains of Imprisonment. (Illus.). 352p. 1982. 25.00 (ISBN 0-8039-1902-6); pap. 12.50 (ISBN 0-8039-1903-4). Sage.

PRISON RIOTS

American Correctional Association Staff. Riots & Disturbances in Correctional Institutions. rev. ed. 56p. 1981. pap. 8.00 (ISBN 0-942974-07-7). Am Correctional.

PRISON SCHOOLS

see Prisoners–Education

PRISONERS

American Association of Law Libraries. Providing Legal Services for Prisoners: A Tool for Correctional Administrators. Rev. ed. Orig. Title: Guidelines for Legal Reference Service. 104p. Date not set. pap. 10.00 (ISBN 0-942974-02-6). Am Correctional.

American Bar Association. ABA: Legal Status of Prisoners. 1982. pap. write for info. (ISBN 0-316-03720-6). Little.

Duffee, David E. & Meyer, Peter B. Outcomes & Costs of a Prerelease System. 256p. 1983. text ed. 22.50 (ISBN 0-89946-099-2). Oelgeschlager.

PRISONERS–EDUCATION

Andersen, Svend E. & Holstein, Bjorn E. Ausbildung Im Gefangnis: Lebenshilfe Fur Gefangene der Skadhauge-Plan Im Danischen Strafvolizug. xi, 162p. (Ger.). 1982. write for info. P Lang Pubs.

PRISONERS, EDUCATION OF

see Prisoners–Education

PRISONERS OF WAR

see also Concentration Camps

also subdivision Prisoners and Prisons under individual wars, e.g. United States–History–Revolution, 1775-1783–Prisoners and Prisons

Hubbell, J. G. P.O.W. 1976. 15.00 (ISBN 0-07-030831-4). McGraw.

PRISONS

Berry, Ken. First Offender: Inside A New Zealand Prison. 192p. 1980. 13.95 (ISBN 0-00-222307-4, Pub. by W Collins Australia). Intl Schol Bk Serv.

Esposito, Barbara, et al. Prison Slavery. Bardsley, Kathryn, ed. (Illus., Orig.). pap. 12.95 (ISBN 0-910007-00-4). Comm Abol Prison.

Giallombardo, Rose. Society of Women: A Study of a Women's Prison. LC 66-14132. 1966. pap. text ed. 13.95x (ISBN 0-471-29729-1). Wiley.

Jacobs, James B. New Perspectives on Prisons & Imprisonment. 264p. 1983. text ed. 29.50x (ISBN 0-8014-1586-1); pap. 10.95x (ISBN 0-8014-9248-3). Cornell U Pr.

Pike, Ruth. Penal Servitude in Early Modern Spain. LC 82-70551. (Illus.). 224p. 1983. text ed. 26.00 (ISBN 0-299-09260-7). U of Wis Pr.

PRISONS–EMPLOYEES

American Correctional Association Staff. An Administrator's Guide to Conditions of Confinement Litigation. 22p. (Orig.). 1979. text ed. 3.50 (ISBN 0-942974-12-3). Am Correctional.

PRISONS–COMMONWEALTH OF NATIONS

Berry, Ken. First Offender: Inside A New Zealand Prison. 192p. 1980. 13.95 (ISBN 0-00-222307-4, Pub. by W Collins Australia). Intl Schol Bk Serv.

PRISONS–UNITED STATES

American Correctional Association Staff. Jails. (Series 1: No. 3). 29p. (Orig.). 1981. pap. 3.50 (ISBN 0-942974-19-0). Am Correctional.

--National Jail & Adult Detention Directory. rev. ed. 325p. 1980. pap. 25.00 (ISBN 0-942974-04-2). Am Correctional.

Moore, Herbert L., Jr. South Carolina Prisons. 250p. 1984. 14.95 (ISBN 0-87844-024-0). Sandlapper Pub Co.

Sherman, Michael & Hawkins, Gordon. Imprisonment in America: Choosing the Future. LC 81-10453. xii, 146p. 1981. pap. 5.95 (ISBN 0-226-75280-1). U of Chicago Pr.

PRIVACY, RIGHT OF

Simons, Geoffrey L. Privacy in the Computer Age. 147p. (Orig.). 1982. pap. 22.50x (ISBN 0-85012-348-8). Intl Pubns Serv.

Skousen, Mark. Mark Skousen's Guide to Financial Privacy. 1983. write for info (ISBN 0-671-47060-4). S&S.

Strunk, Orlo, Jr. Privacy: Experience, Understanding, Expression. LC 82-16029. 78p. 1983. lib. bdg. 18.00 (ISBN 0-8191-2687-X); pap. text ed. 7.00 (ISBN 0-8191-2688-8). U Pr of Amer.

PRIVATE CLAIMS

see Claims

PRIVATE HOUSEHOLD WORKERS

see Servants

PRIVATE INTERNATIONAL LAW

see Conflict of Laws

PRIVATE LAW

see Civil Law

PRIVATE LIBRARIES

see Libraries, Private

PRIVATE RADIOTELEPHONE

see Citizens Band Radio

PRIVATE REVELATIONS

Colville, W. J. Ancient Mystery & Modern Revelation. 366p. 15.00 (ISBN 0-686-38210-2). Sun Bks.

PRIVATE SCHOOLS

Berkeley, William D. & Foster, Jerry. Long-Range Planning for Independent Schools. 1979. pap. 13.50 (ISBN 0-934338-36-1). NAIS.

Cibulka, James G. & O'Brien, Timothy J. Inner City Private Elementary Schools: A Study. 225p. 1982. pap. 11.95 (ISBN 0-87462-463-0). Marquette.

Committee on Boarding Schools. International Students in the Independent School: A Handbook. 1981. pap. 7.00 (ISBN 0-686-83733-9). NAIS.

Private Independent Schools: The Bunting & Lyon Blue Book, 1983. 36th ed. LC 72-122324. (Illus.). 45.00 (ISBN 0-913094-36-6). Bunting.

Whalen, Donald J., ed. Handbook for Development Officers at Independent Schools. 2nd ed. 350p. 1982. 30.00 (ISBN 0-89964-194-6). CASE.

PRIVATE SCHOOLS–DIRECTORIES

Shepherd, Rebecca A., ed. Peterson's Annual Guide to Independent Secondary Schools 1983. 924p. 1983. pap. 10.95 (ISBN 0-87866-212-X). Petersons Guides.

PRIVILEGE TAX

see Business Tax

PRIVILEGED DEBTS

see Bankruptcy

PRIVILEGES AND IMMUNITIES

see also Impeachments

Materials on Jurisdictional Immunities of States & their Property. 657p. 1983. pap. 32.00 (ISBN 0-686-84902-7, UN81/5/10, UN). Unipub.

PRIZE-FIGHTING

see Boxing

PRIZES (REWARDS)

see Rewards (Prizes, etc.)

PROBABILITIES

see also Chance; Errors, Theory Of; Mathematical Statistics; Reliability (Engineering); Risk; Sampling (Statistics); Stochastic Processes; Time-Series Analysis

Ang, A. H. & Tang, W. H. Probability Concepts in Engineering Planning & Design, Vol. 1. LC 75-5892. 409p. 1975. text ed. 30.50x (ISBN 0-471-03200-X). Wiley.

--Probability Concepts in Engineering Planning & Design, Vol. 2. 1982. 15.95 (ISBN 0-471-03201-8). Wiley.

Barr, Donald R. & Zehna, Peter W. Probability: Modeling Uncertainty. (Illus.). 480p. Date not set. text ed. price not set (ISBN 0-201-10798-8). A-W.

Bharucha-Reid, A. T., ed. Probabilistic Analysis & Related Topics, Vol. 3. LC 78-106053. 166p. 1983. price not set (ISBN 0-12-095603-9). Acad Pr.

Bickel, Peter J. & Doksum, Kjell, eds. A Festschrift for Erich L. Lehmann. (Wadsworth Statistics-Probability Ser.). 461p. 1982. 39.95 (ISBN 0-534-98044-9). Wadsworth Pub.

Blake, Ian F. Introduction to Applied Probability. LC 78-11360. 528p. 1979. text ed. 33.95x (ISBN 0-471-03210-7). Wiley.

Brewer, K. R. & Hanif, M. Sampling with Unequal Probabilities. (Lecture Notes in Statistics Ser.: Vol. 15). (Illus.). 164p. 1983. pap. 12.80 (ISBN 0-387-90807-2). Springer-Verlag.

Davison, Mark L. Multidimensional Scaling. (Probability & Mathematical Statistics: Applied Probability & Statistic Section Ser.). 300p. 1983. 25.25 (ISBN 0-471-86417-X, Pub. by Wiley-Interscience). Wiley.

Disney, R. & Ott, T., eds. Applied Probability--Computer Science: The Interface, 2 Vols. (Progress in Computer Science). 1982. text ed. 34.00x ea. Vol. 2, 532pp (ISBN 3-7643-3067-8). Vol. 3, 514pp (ISBN 3-7643-3093-7). Birkhauser.

Feller, William. Introduction to Probability Theory & Its Applications, Vol. 1. 3rd ed. LC 68-11708. (Probability & Mathematical Statistics Ser.). 509p. 1968. 29.95x (ISBN 0-471-25708-7). Wiley.

--An Introduction to Probability Theory & Its Applications, Vol. 2. 2nd ed. LC 57-10805. (Probability & Mathematical Statistics Ser). 669p. 1971. 32.95x (ISBN 0-471-25709-5). Wiley.

Frieden, B. R. Probability, Statistical Optics, & Data Analysis. (Springer Series in Information Sciences: Vol. 10). (Illus.). 404p. 1983. 39.00 (ISBN 0-387-11769-5). Springer-Verlag.

Grossman, W. & Pflug, G., eds. Probability & Statistical Inference. 1982. lib. bdg. 49.50 (ISBN 90-277-1427-4, Pub. by Reidel Holland). Kluwer Boston.

Hogg, Robert V. & Tanis, Elliot A. Probability & Statistical Inference. 2nd ed. 500p. 1983. text ed. 22.95 (ISBN 0-02-355730-3). Macmillan.

Hunter, Jeffrey J., ed. Mathematical Techniques of Applied Probability: Vol. 1: Discrete Time Models. 518p. 1983. price not set (ISBN 0-12-361801-0). Acad Pr.

Le Cam, L. & Neyman, J., eds. Probability Models & Cancer: Proceedings of an Interdisciplinary Cancer Study Conference. 310p. 1983. 51.00 (ISBN 0-444-86514-4, North Holland). Elsevier.

Muthu, S. K. Probability & Errors: For the Physical Sciences. 568p. 1982. text ed. 35.00x (ISBN 0-86131-137-X, Pub. by Orient Longman Ltd India). Apt Bks.

Nagel, Ernest. Principles of the Theory of Probability. LC 40-2555. (Midway Reprint Ser.). iv, 80p. 1982. pap. text ed. 7.00x (ISBN 0-226-57581-0). U of Chicago Pr.

Probability & Statistics. 1983. pap. price not set (ISBN 0-8120-2660-8). Barron.

Ripley's Believe It Or Not Staff. Ripley's Believe It Or Not Book of Chance. 352p. 1982. 14.95 (ISBN 0-698-11197-4, Coward). Putnam Pub Group.

PROBATE LAW AND PRACTICE

see also Decedents' Estates; Estates (Law); Inheritance and Transfer Tax; Wills

Mitchell, James E. Maine Probate Manual. 650p. 1983. 65.00 (ISBN 0-89442-036-4). Tower Pub Co.

Saunders, Charles, ed. How to Live & Die with Texas Probate. 4th ed. 1983. pap. 9.95 (ISBN 0-87201-835-0). Gulf Pub.

Stark, Leland A., ed. How to Live & Die with California Probate. pap. 9.95 (ISBN 0-87201-095-3). Gulf Pub.

PROBATION

see also Juvenile Courts; Parole

American Correctional Association Staff. Guidelines for Adult Parole Authorities-Adult Probation & Parole Field Services. 281p. (Orig.). 1981. pap. 15.00 (ISBN 0-942974-33-6). Am Correctional.

--Probation & Parole Directory. 480p. (Orig.). 1981. pap. 25.00 (ISBN 0-942974-05-0). Am Correctional.

--Standards for Adult Probation & Parole Field Services. 2nd ed. 65p. 1981. pap. 7.50 (ISBN 0-942974-29-8). Am Correctional.

--The Status of Probation & Parole. (Series 2: No. 3). 30p. (Orig.). 1981. pap. 3.50 (ISBN 0-942974-23-9). Am Correctional.

Rudman, Jack. Supervising Probation Officer. (Career Examination Ser.: C-2591). (Cloth bdg. avail. on request). pap. 10.00 (ISBN 0-8373-2591-9). Natl Learning.

Whitehouse, Jack E. How & Where to Find the Facts: Researching Corrections Including Probation & Parole. LC 82-61337. 125p. (Orig.). 1983. pap. 6.95 (ISBN 0-88247-694-7). R & E Res Assoc.

PROBLEM CHILDREN–EDUCATION

Quirk, John P. & Worzbyt, John C. The Assessment of Behavior Problem Children: A Systematic Behavioral Approach. (Illus.). 212p. 1983. 19.75x (ISBN 0-398-04790-1). C C Thomas.

Safer, Daniel J. School Programs for Disruptive Adolescents. (Illus.). 384p. 1982. 29.95 (ISBN 0-8391-1698-5). Univ Park.

PROBLEM SOLVING

Albert, Kenneth J. How to Solve Business Problems: The Consultant's Approach to Business Problem Solving. LC 82-14956. 224p. 1983. pap. 9.95 (ISBN 0-07-000753-5, P&RB). McGraw.

Andriole, Stephen J. Handbook of Problem Solving. (Illus.). 327p. 1983. text ed. 25.00 (ISBN 0-89433-186-8). Petrocelli.

Dolan, D. & Williamson, J. Teaching Problem-Solving Strategies. (Resource Bk.). 1982. 16.00 (ISBN 0-201-10231-5). A-W.

Edgar, William J. The Problem Solver's Guide to Logic. LC 82-20285. 106p. (Orig.). 1983. pap. text ed. 6.50 (ISBN 0-8191-2876-7). U Pr of Amer.

Hartling, John. Structured Approach to Problem Solving & Computer Programming. 450p. 1983. 24.00 (ISBN 0-932376-21-5). Digital Pr.

Lewis. Problem-Solving Principles for ADA Programmers: Applied Logic, Psychology, & Grit. Date not set. 9.95 (ISBN 0-686-82005-3, 5211). Hayden.

Newman, D. J. A Problem Seminar. (Problem Books in Mathematics). 113p. 1983. 12.95 (ISBN 0-387-90765-3). Springer-Verlag.

Richardson, Gary L. & Birkin, Stanley J. Problem Solving Using PLIC: An Introduction for Business and the Social Sciences. LC 75-4724. 358p. pap. text ed. 21.95 (ISBN 0-686-84497-1). Krieger.

Segel, Leon. The Problem Solver's Universal Checklist. 17p. (Orig.). 1983. pap. text ed. 5.00 (ISBN 0-9607160-0-9). Ed Acad.

PROCEDURE (LAW)

see also Actions and Defenses; Administrative Procedure; Appellate Procedure; Civil Procedure; Court Rules; Courts; Criminal Procedure; Government Litigation; Judicial Process; Probate Law and Practice

Hempstead, Walter E., Jr. Y.O.L. (Your Own Law) A Complete Guide for the Layman. 240p. Date not set. 9.95 (ISBN 0-686-37904-7). Hempstead House.

Swigert, Victoria L., ed. Law & the Legal Process. (Sage Research Progress Series in Criminology: Vol. 28). (Illus.). 160p. 1982. 18.95 (ISBN 0-8039-1900-X); pap. 8.95 (ISBN 0-8039-1901-8). Sage.

PROCESS CONTROL

De Vries, W. R. & Dornfield, D. A., eds. Inspection & Quality Control in Manufacturing Systems. (PED Ser.: Vol. 6). 1982. 24.00 (H00249). ASME.

Guess, Vincent C. Manufacturing Control System User's Guide. (Illus.). 32p. (Orig.). 1982. pap. 10.00 (ISBN 0-940964-03-1). PSE.

Hardt, D. E., ed. Measurement & Control for Batch Manufacturing. 1982. 40.00 (H00244). ASME.

Manka, Dan, ed. Automated Stream Analysis for Processed Control, Vol. 1. LC 82-8822. 336p. 1982. 39.50 (ISBN 0-12-469001-7). Acad Pr.

Rose, L. M. Application of Mathematical Modelling to Process Development & Design. 1974. 53.50 (ISBN 0-85334-584-8). Elsevier.

Shinskey, F. G. Process Control Systems. 2nd ed. 1979. 34.75 (ISBN 0-07-056891-X). McGraw.

PROCESS CONTROL-DATA PROCESSING

Mellichamp, Duncan A., ed. Real Time Computing: With Applications to Data Acquisition & Control. 464p. 1983. text ed. 39.50 (ISBN 0-442-21372-7). Van Nos Reinhold.

PROCESS ENGINEERING

see Production Engineering

PROCESS ENGINEERING (MANUFACTURES)

see Manufacturing Processes

PROCESSING, INDUSTRIAL

see Manufacturing Processes

PROCESSING, PHOTOGRAPHIC

see Photography-Processing

PROCUREMENT, GOVERNMENT

see Government Purchasing

PROCUREMENT, INDUSTRIAL

see Industrial Procurement

PRODIGAL SON (PARABLE)

see Jesus Christ-Parables

PRODUCER GAS

see Gas and Oil Engines

PRODUCT DIVERSIFICATION

see Diversification in Industry

PRODUCT LIABILITY

see Products Liability

PRODUCT MANAGEMENT

see also New Products

APICS. Management Seminar: Proceedings. 104p. 1982. 6.00 (ISBN 0-935406-15-8). Am Prod & Inventory.

--Master Planning Seminar: Proceedings. 84p. 1982. 6.00 (ISBN 0-935406-13-1). Am Prod & Inventory.

APICS, ed. Capacity Planning & Control Reprints. 110p. 1975. pap. 10.50 (ISBN 0-935406-16-6). Am Prod Inventory.

APICS Annual Conference, 25th. Proceedings. LC 79-640341. 590p. 1982. 30.00 (ISBN 0-686-84381-9). Am Prod & Inventory.

APICS Cirriculum & Certification Program Council Committee, ed. Shop Floor Controls Reprints. 165p. 1973. 13.50 (ISBN 0-935406-17-4). Am Prod & Inventory.

APICS Curriculum & Certification Program Council Planning & Control Committee, ed. Capacity Planning & Control Reprints. 110p. 1975. 10.50 (ISBN 0-686-84380-0). Am Prod & Inventory.

Berry, William, et al. Master Production Scheduling: Principle & Practice. 184p. 1979. 29.00 (ISBN 0-935406-21-2). Am Prod & Inventory.

Data Notes Publishing Staff, compiled by. Generics Data Notes. 75p. Date not set. 10.95 (ISBN 0-686-37653-6). Data Notes Pub.

Swit, David & Hadley, Richard. Product Survival: Lessons of the Tylenol Terrorism. LC 82-62917. 250p. 1982. pap. 45.00 (ISBN 0-914176-18-8). Wash Busn Info.

PRODUCT SAFETY

Swit, David & Hadley, Richard. Product Survival: Lessons of the Tylenol Terrorism. LC 82-62917. 250p. 1982. pap. 45.00 (ISBN 0-914176-18-8). Wash Busn Info.

PRODUCTION, COOPERATIVE

see Cooperation; Cooperative Societies

PRODUCTION CONTROL

see also Inventory Control; Scheduling (Management)

Bekiroglu, Haluk, ed. Simulation in Inventory & Production Control. 1983. softbound 20.00 (ISBN 0-686-42972-9). Soc Computer Sim.

Eckhart, Wolfgang. Der Boden Als Anlargeobjekt und Produktionsfaktor. 173p. (Ger.). 1982. write for info. (ISBN 3-8204-7222-3). P Lang Pubs.

Eichorn, W. & Henn, R., eds. Qualitative Studies on Production & Prices. 304p. 1982. text ed. 23.95x (ISBN 3-7908-0275-1). Birkhauser.

ISA Control Value Standards. LC 81-86095. (ISA Standards Mini-Reference Bks.). 104p. 1982. pap. text ed. 25.00x (ISBN 0-87664-640-2). Instru Soc.

Rosenav, Milton D., Jr. Innovation: Managing the Development of Profitable New Products. (Engineering Ser.). 182p. 1982. 25.00 (ISBN 0-534-97934-3). Lifetime Learn.

PRODUCTION ENGINEERING

see also Assembly-Line Methods; Manufactures; Manufacturing Processes; Materials Handling

Albus, J. S., ed. Information Control Problems in Manufacturing Technology 1982: Proceedings of the 4th IFAC-IFIP Symposium, National Bureau of Standards, Maryland, USA, 26-28 October 1982. (IFAC Proceedings Ser.). 199p. 1983. 50.00 (ISBN 0-08-029946-6). Pergamon.

American Machinist Magazine. Computers in Manufacturing. 300p. 1983. 33.95 (ISBN 0-07-001548-1, P&RB). McGraw.

Bloch, H. P. & Geitner, F. K. Failure Analysis & Troubleshooting. (Practical Machinery Management for Process Plants Ser.). 1983. text ed. 59.95x (ISBN 0-87201-872-5). Gulf Pub.

Brannan, Carl. Process Systems Development. (The Process Engineer's Handbook Ser.). 1938. pap. text ed. 9.95x (ISBN 0-87201-713-3). Gulf Pub.

Institution of Engineering Australia. Manufacturing Engineering International Conference, 1980. 622p. (Orig.). 1980. pap. text ed. 60.00x (ISBN 0-85825-132-9, Pub. by Inst Engineering Australia). Renouf.

Intrumentation Symposium for the Process Industries: Proceedings of the 37th Annual Instrumentation Symposium for the Process Industries, Vol. 37. 122p. 1982. pap. text ed. 35.00x (ISBN 0-87664-717-4). Instru Soc.

Lapina, Ronald P. TI-Fifty-Nine Manual for Estimating Centrifugal Compressor Performance. (Process Compressor Technology Ser.). 1983. text ed. 42.95x (ISBN 0-87201-100-3). Gulf Pub.

Leiberman, Norman P. Process Design in Practice. 1983. text ed. 38.95 (ISBN 0-87201-747-8). Gulf Pub.

Linnhoff, B., et al. Process Integration & Energy Efficiency: A User's Guide. 1983. text ed. 39.95 (ISBN 0-87201-250-6). Gulf Pub.

Manufacturing Engineering: ACME. 280p. (Orig.). 1977. pap. text ed. 36.00x (ISBN 0-85825-083-7, Pub. by Inst Engineering Australia). Renouf.

Materials & Processes: Continuing Innovations. (Illus.). 1983. 60.00 (ISBN 0-938994-22-0). Soc Adv Material.

Taraman, K. CAD-CAM: Meeting Today's Productivity Challenge. 296p. 1982. text ed. 39.00 (ISBN 0-13-110122-6). P-H.

Weinberg, Edgar. Labour-Management Cooperation for Productivity. (Work in America Institute Studies in Productivity). 1983. 35.00 (ISBN 0-08-029511-8). Pergamon.

PRODUCTION-LINE METHODS

see Assembly-Line Methods

PRODUCTION MANAGEMENT

Deis, Paul. Inventory & Production Management in the Nineteen Eighties. (Illus.). 384p. 1983. 25.95 (ISBN 0-13-502559-1). P-H.

Fearon, Harold E. Fundamentals of Production-Operations Management. 2nd ed. (Illus.). 1982. pap. text ed. 9.95 (ISBN 0-314-69647-4); tchrs.' manual avail. (ISBN 0-314-71089-2). West Pub.

Guess, Vincent C. Manufacturing Control System User's Guide. (Illus.). 32p. (Orig.). 1982. pap. 10.00 (ISBN 0-940964-03-1). PSE.

Mabert, Vincent A. & Moodie, Colin L., eds. Production Planning, Scheduling, & Inventory Control: Concepts, Techniques, & Systems. 2nd ed. 1982. 21.00 (ISBN 0-89806-032-X); members 12.00. Inst Indus Eng.

Pantumsinchai, Pricha & Hassan, M. Zia. Basic Programs for Production & Operations Management. (Illus.). 448p. 1983. pap. 14.95 (ISBN 0-686-38834-8). P H.

Riggs, James L. & Felix, Glenn H. Productivity by Objectives. (Illus.). 272p. 1983. text ed. 23.95 (ISBN 0-13-725374-5). P-H.

Spencer, Richard H. Planning Implementation & Control in Product Test Assurance. (Illus.). 240p. 1983. text ed. 27.50 (ISBN 0-13-679506-4). P-H.

Wilburn, James R., ed. Productivity: A National Priority. 79p. (Orig.). 1982. pap. 7.95 (ISBN 0-932612-13-X). Pepperdine U Pr.

PRODUCTIVITY ACCOUNTING

Norbert, Enrick & Mottley, Harry E., Jr. Manufacturing Analysis for Productivity & Quality-Cost Enhancement. 2nd ed. (Illus.). 150p. Repr. of 1968 ed. 22.95 (ISBN 0-8311-1146-1). Indus Pr.

Rosen, Theodore A. & Daniels, Aubrey C. Performance Management: Improving Quality & Productivity Through Positive Reinforcement. (Illus.). 1982. write for info. (ISBN 0-937100-01-3). Perf Manage.

Strasser, Federico. Metal Stamping Plant Productivity Handbook. (Illus.). 300p. 1983. 29.95 (ISBN 0-8311-1147-X). Indus Pr.

PRODUCTIVITY OF LABOR

see Labor Productivity

PRODUCTS, ANIMAL

see Animal Products

PRODUCTS, COMMERCIAL

see Commercial Products

PRODUCTS, DAIRY

see Dairy Products

PRODUCTS, FARINACEOUS

see Starch

PRODUCTS, MANUFACTURED

see Manufactures

PRODUCTS, NEW

see New Products

PRODUCTS, WASTE

see Waste Products

PRODUCTS LIABILITY

see also Product Safety

Stucki, Hans-Ulrich. Product Liability: A Manual of Practice in Selected Nations, 2 vols. LC 80-28894. 1980. 100.00 ea. (ISBN 0-379-20705-2). Oceana.

White, Jeffrey R., ed. Products Liability, 2 vols. 1200p. 1983. Vol. 1. 125.00 set (ISBN 0-941916-07-3); Vol. 2. 0.00 (ISBN 0-941916-08-1). Assn Trial Ed.

PROFESSION OF ARMS

see Military Service As a Profession

PROFESSIONAL BASEBALL CLUBS

see Baseball Clubs

PROFESSIONAL EDUCATION

see also Library Education; Medical Colleges; Technical Education; Universities and Colleges;

also subdivision Study and Teaching under specific professions, e.g. Law-Study and Teaching

Jarvis, Peter. Professional Education. (New Patterns of Learning Ser.). 192p. 1983. text ed. 27.25x (ISBN 0-7099-1409-1, Pub. by Croom Helm Ltd England). Biblio Dist.

PROFESSIONAL ETHICS

see also Business Ethics; Engineering Ethics; Legal Ethics; Medical Ethics

Horn, Ronald C. On Professions, Professionals, & Professional Ethics. LC 78-67501. 114p. 1978. pap. 3.00 (ISBN 0-89463-020-2). Am Inst Property.

PROFESSIONAL LABORATORY EXPERIENCES (EDUCATION)

see Student Teaching

PROFESSIONS

see also College Graduates; Intellectuals; Occupations; Vocational Guidance;

also subdivision Vocational Guidance under specific professions

Dingwall, Robert & Lewis, Philip. The Sociology of the Professions. LC 82-3352. 244p. 1982. 25.00x (ISBN 0-312-74075-1). St Martin.

Phillips, E. Lakin. Stress, Health & Psychological Problems in the Major Professions. LC 82-17556. 478p. (Orig.). 1983. lib. bdg. 30.50 (ISBN 0-8191-2773-6); pap. text ed. 17.50 (ISBN 0-8191-2774-4). U Pr of Amer.

Rona, D. C. Guide to Professional Records. (Illus.). 50p. (Orig.). 1982. pap. 8.50 (ISBN 0-911127-00-3). CRS Con.

PROFESSORS

see College Teachers

PROFIT

see also Capitalism; Entrepreneur; Income; Risk

Obrinsky, Mark. Profit Theory & Capitalism. LC 82-40482. (Illus.). 176p. 1983. 18.00x (ISBN 0-8122-7863-1); pap. 8.95x (ISBN 0-8122-1147-2). U of Pa Pr.

PROFIT-ACCOUNTING

Gilman, Stephen. Accounting Concepts of Profit. LC 82-48365. (Accountancy in Transition Ser.). 656p. 1982. lib. bdg. 65.00 (ISBN 0-8240-5316-8). Garland Pub.

Goldschmidt, Y. & Admon, K. Profit Measurement During Inflation: Accounting, Economic & Financial Aspects. LC 77-4500. (Operations Managment Ser.). 1977. 39.95x (ISBN 0-471-01983-6, Pub. by Wiley-Interscience). Wiley.

Lacey, Kenneth. Profit Measurement & Price Changes. LC 82-48370. (Accountancy in Transition Ser.). 148p. 1982. lib. bdg. 20.00 (ISBN 0-8240-5323-0). Garland Pub.

PROFIT AND LOSS STATEMENTS

see Financial Statements

PROFIT-SHARING

see also Cooperation; Employee Ownership

Buechner, Robert W. & Manzler, David L. Accumulating Wealth with Before Tax Dollars (Desk Book) LC 81-86381. (Illus.). 1982. write for info. looseleaf (ISBN 0-87218-417-X); write for info. visual, 48 p. (ISBN 0-87218-416-1). Natl Underwriter.

PROFIT-SHARING TRUSTS

see Investment Trusts

PROGESTATIONAL HORMONES

see also Oral Contraceptives

Cavalli, F. & McGuire, W. L., eds. Proceedings of the International Symposium on Medroxyprogesterone Acetate: Geneva, Switzerland, February 24-26, 1982. (International Congress Ser.: No. 611). 632p. 1982. 95.75 (ISBN 0-444-90297-X, Excerpta Medica). Elsevier.

PROGRAM BUDGETING

Rudman, Jack. Program Examiner. (Career Examination Ser.: C-2655). (Cloth bdg. avail. on request). pap. 10.00 (ISBN 0-8373-2655-9). Natl Learning.

PROGRAMMABLE CALCULATORS

Abramson, J. H. & Peritz, E. Calculator Programs for the Health Sciences. (Illus.). 326p. 1983. text ed. 37.50x (ISBN 0-19-503187-3); pap. text ed. 18.95x (ISBN 0-19-503188-1). Oxford U Pr.

PROGRAMMING (ELECTRONIC COMPUTERS)

see also Coding Theory; Computer Programming Management; Computer Programs; Electronic Digital Computers; Integer Programming; Programming Languages (Electronic Computers)

also names of specific computers, e.g. IBM 1620

Anbarlian, Harry. Spreadsheeting on the TRS-80 Color Computer. 320p. 1982. text ed. 22.95 (ISBN 0-07-001595-3, C). McGraw.

Aron, Joel D. The Program Development Process: Pt. II: The Programming Team. LC 74-2847. (Illus.). 704p. 1983. text ed. 28.95 (ISBN 0-201-14463-8). A-W.

Atkinson, Laurence. PASCAL Programming. LC 80-40126. (Computing Ser.). 428p. 1980. 49.95x (ISBN 0-471-27773-8); pap. 16.95 (ISBN 0-471-27774-6). Wiley.

Banahan, Mark & Rutter, Andy. The Unix-tm Book. 224p. 1983. pap. 16.95 (ISBN 0-471-89676-4). Wiley.

Brown, Gary D. & Sefton, Donald. Surviving with Packaged Systems. 250p. 1983. 25.00 (ISBN 0-471-87065-X, Pub. by Wiley-Interscience). Wiley.

Burnett, Dale. LOGO: An Introduction. LC 82-73547. (Illus.). 56p. 1983. pap. 7.95 (ISBN 0-916688-39-9). Creative Comp.

Campbell, J. L. & Zimmerman, Lance. Programming the Apple: A Structured Approach. (Illus.). 544p. 1982. pap. 19.95 (ISBN 0-89303-267-0); casebound 24.95 (ISBN 0-89303-269-7). R J Brady.

Cassidy, Pat & Close, Jim. Basic Computer Programming for Kids. (Illus.). 192p. 1983. 17.95 (ISBN 0-13-057927-0); pap. 11.95 (ISBN 0-13-057919-X). P-H.

Chandor, Anthony. Choosing & Keeping Computer Staff. LC 76-357362. (Illus.). 203p. 1976. 17.50 (ISBN 0-04-658217-7). Intl Pubns Serv.

Chase, Leslie. Proven Techniques for Increasing Database Use. 1983. 49.95 (ISBN 0-942774-09-4). Info Indus.

Chaudier, Louann. Leading Consultants in Computer Software & Programming 1983-1984. 300p. (Orig.). 1983. pap. 39.50 (ISBN 0-943692-06-7). J Dick.

Claybrook, Billy G. File Management Techniques. 300p. 1983. text ed. 15.95 (ISBN 0-471-04596-9); solutions bk. avail. (ISBN 0-471-87575-9). Wiley.

Cohen, Ellen M. Auto Calendar Disk. (Professional Software Ser.). 1983. text ed. 65.00 (ISBN 0-471-87459-0). Wiley.

Cole, Jim. Ninety-Nine Tips & Tricks for the New Pocket Computers. 128p. (Orig.). 1982. pap. 7.95 (ISBN 0-86668-019-5). ARCsoft.

DeMarco, Tom. Controlling Software Projects: Management Measurement & Estimation. (Illus.). 296p. 1982. pap. 28.50 (ISBN 0-917072-32-4). Yourdon.

Downing, Douglas. Computer Programming the Easy Way. (Easy Way Ser.). 288p. 1983. pap. 6.95 (ISBN 0-8120-2626-8). Barron.

Friedman, Frank & Koffman, Elliot. Problem Solving & Structured Programming in WATFIV. LC 81-20598. (Illus.). 480p. Date not set. pap. text ed. 15.95 (ISBN 0-201-10482-2). A-W.

Goto, E., ed. RIMS Symposia on Software Science & Engineering: Proceedings, Kyoto, Japan, 1982. (Lecture Notes in Computer Science Ser.: Vol. 147). 232p. 1983. pap. 11.50 (ISBN 0-387-11980-9). Springer-Verlag.

Green, Adam B. D-Base II User's Guide with Applications. 192p. 1983. pap. 29.00 (ISBN 0-13-196519-0). P-H.

Hancock, L. & Krieger, M. The C Primer. 256p. 1983. pap. 14.95 (ISBN 0-07-025981-X, P&RB). McGraw.

Hansen, Per B. Programming a Personal Computer. (Illus.). 400p. 1983. text ed. 18.95 (ISBN 0-13-730267-3). P-H.

Hartling, John. Structured Approach to Problem Solving & Computer Programming. 450p. 1983. 24.00 (ISBN 0-932376-21-5). Digital Pr.

Hu, T. C. & Shing, M. T. A Manual of Computer Program in "Combinatorial Algorithms". 200p. 1983. pap. text ed. 15.00 (ISBN 0-201-11469-0). A-W.

Inman, Don & Inman, Kurt. Assembly Language Graphics for the TRS-80 Color Computer. 1982. text ed. 19.95 (ISBN 0-8359-0318-4); pap. text ed. 14.95 (ISBN 0-8359-0317-6). Reston.

Kamins, S. & Waite, M. Apple Backpack. 208p. 1982. 24.95 (ISBN 0-07-033356-4). McGraw.

Knecht, Ken. Introduction to FORTH. Date not set. pap. 9.95 (ISBN 0-672-21842-9). Sams.

--Using & Programming the Timex Sinclair Computer. Willis, Jerry, ed. 240p. (Orig.). 1983. pap. 9.95 (ISBN 0-88056-107-6). Dilithium Pr.

Leeson, Marjorie M. Programming Logic. 320p. 1983. pap. text ed. write for info. (ISBN 0-574-21420-8, 13-4420); write for info. instr's. guide (ISBN 0-574-21421-6, 13-4421). SRA.

Libes, Sol, ed. Programmer's Guide to CP-MR. 200p. 1983. pap. 12.95 (ISBN 0-916688-37-2). Creative Comp.

Linz, Peter. Programming Concepts & Problem Solving. 1982. 24.95 (ISBN 0-8053-5710-6, 35710). Benjamin-Cummings.

Longworth, G. Standards in Programming. (Illus.). 206p. 1981. text ed. 110.00x (ISBN 0-85012-341-0). Intl Pubns Serv.

Mason, Russell E. Basic, Intermediate Systematic Substitution Training, Set-IS. 1973. Tape 3, t-10, t-11. pap. 25.00x (ISBN 0-89533-017-2). F I Comm.

Mazur, Ken, ed. The Creative TRS-Eighty. (Illus.). 250p. 1983. pap. 15.95 (ISBN 0-916688-36-4). Creative Comp.

Miller, Alan R. The Best of CP-M Software. 250p. 1983. pap. 11.95 (ISBN 0-89588-100-4). Sybex.

Multichannel Time Series Analysis with Digital Computer Programs. 2nd ed. 1982. 25.00 (ISBN 0-686-42735-1). Goose Pond Pr.

Neel, D., ed. Tools & Notions for Program Construction: An Advanced Course. LC 82-4141. 350p. 1982. 29.95 (ISBN 0-521-24801-9). Cambridge U Pr.

North, Alan. One Hundred & One Atari Computer Programming Tips & Tricks. new ed. 128p. (Orig.). 1982. pap. 8.95 (ISBN 0-86668-022-5). ARCsoft.

Organick, E. I. A Programmer's View of the Intel 432 System. 432p. 1983. 29.95 (ISBN 0-07-047719-1, P&RB). McGraw.

Page, Edward. One Hundred Timex 1000-Sinclair ZX-81 Programming Tips & Tricks. new ed. 128p. (Orig.). (gr. 7-12). 1982. pap. 7.95 (ISBN 0-86668-020-9). ARCsoft.

Parker. Computing is Easy. 1982. text ed. 9.95. Butterworth.

Plum, Thomas. Learning to Program in C. (Illus.). 350p. (Orig.). 1983. pap. text ed. 25.00x (ISBN 0-911537-00-7). Plum Hall.

Presley, Bruce. A Guide to Programming IBM Personal Computer. 173p. 1982. pap. 16.95 (ISBN 0-442-26015-6). Van Nos Reinhold.

Purdum, Jack. C Programming Guide. 1983. pap. 17.95 (ISBN 0-88022-022-8). Que Corp.

Random Wavelets & Cybernetic Systems. 136p. 1962. 20.00 (ISBN 0-686-42734-3). Goose Pond Pr.

Rao, P. V. Computer Programming in Fortran & Other Languages. 1982. 3.00x (ISBN 0-07-096569-2). McGraw.

Riley, W. B. Investpak for TRS-80 Model I. 1982. Set. 200.00 (ISBN 0-07-079513-4). McGraw.

Riley, W. B. & Montgomery, A. H. Investpak for Apple II Version. 1982. Set. 200.00 (ISBN 0-07-079512-6). McGraw.

--Investpak for TRS-80 Model III. 1982. 200.00 (ISBN 0-07-079514-2). McGraw.

Siemens Teams of Authors. Software Engineering. (Siemens Team of Authors Ser.). 1980. text ed. 16.95x (ISBN 0-471-26123-8, Pub. by Wiley Heyden). Wiley.

Small, David & Small, Sandy, eds. The Creative Atari. LC 82-71997. (Illus.). 250p. 1983. pap. 15.95 (ISBN 0-916688-34-8). Creative Comp.

Sorger, T. J. Managements Guide to Software Development. (Illus., Orig.). pap. 12.95 (ISBN 0-9604072-2-7). Sorger Assocs.

Starkey, J. Denbigh & Ross, Rockford. Fundamental Programming. 256p. 1982. pap. text ed. write for info. (ISBN 0-314-71810-9). West Pub.

Streitmatter, Gene & Goldstein, Larry J. Pet CBM: An Introduction to Programming & Applications. (Illus.). 320p. 1983. text ed. 19.95 (ISBN 0-89303-205-0); pap. 14.95 (ISBN 0-89303-204-2). R J Brady.

Texas Instruments Learning Center Staff. Programming Discovery in TI LOGO Student Guide. Rev. ed. (Illus.). 32p. (gr. 3-10). 1982. pap. text ed. 5.95 (ISBN 0-89512-067-4). Tex Instr Inc.

Thomas, D. Learn BASIC: A Guide to Programming the Texas Instruments Professional Compact Computer. 256p. 1983. 9.95 (ISBN 0-07-064257-5, GB). McGraw.

Titus, Jonathan & Larsen, David. Eighty Eighty A Cookbook. 1980. pap. 15.95 (ISBN 0-672-21697-3). Sams.

Underkoffler, Milton. Introduction to Structured Programming with Pascal. 376p. 1983. pap. text ed. write for info. (ISBN 0-87150-394-8, 8040). Prindle.

Watts, Harris. The Programme-Maker's Handbook or Goodbye Totter TV. (Illus.). 230p. (Orig.). 1982. text ed. 20.90 (ISBN 0-9507582-1-3); pap. text ed. 12.50 (ISBN 0-9507582-0-5). Kumarian Pr.

White, Fred. One Hundred & One Apple Computer Programming Tips & Tricks. new ed. 128p. (Orig.). 1982. pap. 8.95 (ISBN 0-86668-015-2). ARCsoft.

Wood, Derrick. Paradigms & a Programming Methodology: An Introduction. 1983. text ed. p.n.s. (ISBN 0-914894-45-5). Computer Sci.

Zimmerman, Steven & Conrad, Leo. Osborne User's Guide: Applications & Programming. (Illus.). 264p. 1982. text ed. 19.95 (ISBN 0-89303-207-7); pap. 14.95 (ISBN 0-89303-206-9). R J Brady.

PROGRAMMING (ELECTRONIC COMPUTERS)–VOCATIONAL GUIDANCE

National Computing Centre. Working with Computers: A Guide to Jobs & Careers. 3rd ed. (Illus.). 75p. (Orig.). 1982. pap. 8.50x (ISBN 0-85012-359-3). Intl Pubns Serv.

PROGRAMMING (MATHEMATICS)

see also Dynamic Programming; Scheduling (Management)

Beale, E. Applications of Mathematical Programming Techniques. (Nato Ser.). 1970. 21.50 (ISBN 0-444-19716-8). Elsevier.

Beightler, Charles & Phillips, Donald. Applied Geometric Programming. LC 75-44391. 590p. 1976. 39.95x (ISBN 0-471-06390-8). Wiley.

Broy, M. & Schmidt, G., eds. Theoretical Foundations of Programming Methodology. 1982. lib. bdg. 78.50 (ISBN 90-277-1460-6, Pub. by Reidel Holland); pap. 39.50 (ISBN 90-277-1462-2). Kluwer Boston.

Gallagher, R. H. Optimum Structural Design: Theory & Applications. LC 72-8600. (Numerical Methods in Engineering Ser.). 358p. 1973. 53.95x (ISBN 0-471-29050-5, Pub. by Wiley-Interscience). Wiley.

Goffin. Applications. (Mathematical Programming Studies: Vol. 20). 1982. 27.75 (ISBN 0-444-86478-4). Elsevier.

Messina, P. C. & Murli, A., eds. Problems & Methodolgies in Mathematical Software Production, Sorrento, Italy 1980: Proceedings. (Lecture Notes in Computer Sciences: Vol. 142). 271p. 1983. pap. 12.30 (ISBN 0-387-11603-6). Springer-Verlag.

Nemirovskii, A. S. Problem Complexity & Method Efficiency in Optimization. 350p. 1983. write for info. (ISBN 0-471-10345-4, Pub. by Wiley-Interscience). Wiley.

PROGRAMMING LANGUAGE ONE

see P L-One (Computer Program Language)

PROGRAMMING LANGUAGES (ELECTRONIC COMPUTERS)

see also specific languages, e.g. FORTRAN (Computer Program Language)

Ashley, Ruth & Fernandez, Judi N. Job Control Language. LC 77-27316. (Self-Teaching Guide Ser.). 161p. 1978. pap. text ed. 7.95 (ISBN 0-471-03205-0). Wiley.

Atkinson, Laurence. PASCAL Programming. LC 80-40126. (Computing Ser.). 428p. 1980. 49.95x (ISBN 0-471-27773-8); pap. 16.95 (ISBN 0-471-27774-6). Wiley.

Bailey, T. E. & Lundgaard, Kris. Program Design with Pseudocode. LC 82-17802. (Computer Science Ser.). 160p. 1983. pap. text ed. 13.95 (ISBN 0-534-01361-9). Brooks-Cole.

Beil, Don. The Visicalc Book: IBM PC Edition. 1982. text ed. 21.95 (ISBN 0-8359-8395-1); pap. text ed. 15.95 (ISBN 0-8359-8396-X). Reston.

Cole, A. J. & Morrison, R. An Introduction to Programming with S-Algol. LC 82-14568. 192p. 1983. 15.95 (ISBN 0-521-25001-3). Cambridge U Pr.

Eckols, Steve. Report Writer. Oppliger, Jeannie, ed. LC 80-82868. (Illus.). 106p. (Orig.). 1980. pap. text ed. 13.50 (ISBN 0-911625-07-0). M Murach & Assoc.

Etter, D. M. Structured FORTRAN 77 for Engineers & Scientists. 1982. 19.95 (ISBN 0-8053-2520-4, 32520). Benjamin-Cummings.

Frank, Thomas. Introduction to the PDP11 & its Assembly Language. (P-H Software Ser.). (Illus.). 512p. 1983. text ed. 24.95 (ISBN 0-13-491704-9). P-H.

Griswold, Ralph E. & Griswold, Madge T. The ICON Programming Language. (Illus.). 336p. 1983. pap. text ed. 18.95 (ISBN 0-13-449777-5). P-H.

Grogono, Peter. Mouse: A Language for Microcomputers. (Illus.). 200p. 1983. text ed. 17.50 (ISBN 0-89433-201-5). Petrocelli.

Gruchcow, Jack. The Visicalc Applications Book. 1982. text ed. 21.95 (ISBN 0-8359-8390-0); pap. 16.95. Reston.

Hannawell, Peggy & Sorenson, Marge. Wordstar Training Manual. (Illus.). 100p. 1982. pap. 9.00 (ISBN 0-942728-09-2). Custom Pub Co.

Haskell, Richard. Apple II: Six-Five-Zero-Two Assembly Language Tutor. (Illus.). 240p. 1983. 34.95 (ISBN 0-13-039230-8). P-H.

Lowe, Doug. OS Utilities. Eckols, Steve & Taylor, Judy, eds. LC 80-84103. (Illus.). 185p. (Orig.). 1981. pap. text ed. 15.00 (ISBN 0-911625-11-9). M Murach & Assoc.

McQuillen, Kevin. System 360-370 Assembler Language (DOS) Murach, Mike, ed. LC 74-76436. (Illus.). 407p. (Orig.). 1974. pap. text ed. 22.50 (ISBN 0-911625-01-1). M Murach & Assoc.

--System 360-370 Assembler Language (OS) Murach, Mike, ed. LC 74-29645. (Illus.). 450p. (Orig.). 1975. pap. text ed. 22.50 (ISBN 0-911625-02-X). M Murach & Assoc.

Maurer, Doug. APPLE Assembly Language. write for info (ISBN 0-914894-85-4). Computer Sci.

Mayer, John S. IBM-PC Survivor's Manual: A Primer for the IBM Personal Computer. 35p. (Orig.). 1982. pap. 11.95 (ISBN 0-9609092-0-6). Mayer Assocs.

Nielsen, M. & Schmidt, E. M., eds. Automata, Languages, & Programming: Aarhus, Denmark 1982. (Lecture Notes in Computer Science: Vol. 140). 614p. 1982. pap. 27.60 (ISBN 0-387-11576-5). Springer-Verlag.

Noll, Paul. The Structured Programming Cookbook. Taylor, Judy, ed. LC 77-88256. (Illus.). 221p. 1978. pap. text ed. 15.00 (ISBN 0-911625-04-6). M Murach & Assoc.

Popkin, Gary S. Advanced Structured COBOL. 512p. 1983. pap. text ed. 23.95x (ISBN 0-534-01394-5). Kent Pub Co.

Saxon, James A. & Fritz, Robert E. Beginning Programming with ADA. 240p. 1983. pap. text ed. 16.95 (ISBN 0-686-38833-X). P H.

Scanlon, Leo. IBM PC Assembly Language: A Guide for Programmers. (Illus.). 384p. 1983. 27.95 (ISBN 0-89303-534-3); pap. 19.95 (ISBN 0-89303-241-7). R J Brady.

Stultz, Russell A. The Illustrated CP-M-Wordstar Dictionary. (Illus.). 192p. 1983. pap. 14.95 (ISBN 0-13-450528-X). P-H.

Taylor, John. Atari Four Hundred-Eight Hundred DiskGuide. (DiskGuides Ser.). 32p. (Orig.). 1983. pap. 7.95 (ISBN 0-931988-95-0). Osborne-McGraw.

PROGRAMMING MANAGEMENT (ELECTRONIC COMPUTERS)

see Computer Programming Management

PROGRAMS, COMPUTER

see Computer Programs

PROGRAMS, RADIO

see Radio Programs

PROGRAMS, TELEVISION

see Television Programs

PROGRESS

see also Science and Civilization; Social Change

Bodley, John H. Victims of Progress. 2nd ed. (Illus.). 264p. 1982. pap. 9.95 (ISBN 0-87484-593-9). Mayfield Pub.

Bury, John B. The Idea of Progress: An Inquiry into Its Origin & Growth. LC 82-6261. xl, 357p. 1982. Repr. of 1932 ed. lib. bdg. 39.75x (ISBN 0-313-23374-8, BUIP). Greenwood.

Eldredge, Niles & Tattersall, Ian. The Myths of Human Evolution. LC 82-1118. 192p. 1982. 16.95 (ISBN 0-231-05144-1). Columbia U Pr.

George, Henry. Progress & Poverty. 599p. 1983. pap. 5.00 (ISBN 0-911312-58-7). Schalkenbach.

McPherson, Bruce. Between Two Worlds: Victorian Ambivalence about Progress. LC 82-23814. 92p. (Orig.). 1983. lib. bdg. 17.25 (ISBN 0-8191-2972-0); pap. text ed. 7.25 (ISBN 0-8191-2973-9). U Pr of Amer.

Malik, Rex, ed. Future Imperfect: Science Fact & Science Fiction. 219p. 1982. 25.00 (ISBN 0-686-42971-0). F Pinter Pubs.

Shafer, Robert. Progress & Science. 1922. text ed. 37.50x (ISBN 0-686-83714-2). Elliots Bks.

Shils, Edward. Tradition. LC 80-21643. viii, 334p. 1981. pap. 10.95 (ISBN 0-226-75326-3). U of Chicago Pr.

PROGRESSIVE LENTICULAR DEGENERATION

see Hepatolenticular Degeneration

PROGRESSIVISM (U. S. POLITICS)

Canan, Craig T. Southern Progressive Periodicals Directory. LC 80-644934. 1982. 4.00 (ISBN 0-935396-01-2). Prog Educ.

--U. S. Progressive Periodicals Directory. LC 81-85888. 1982. 8.00 (ISBN 0-935396-02-0). Prog Educ.

Link, Arthur S. & McCormick, Richard L. Progressivism. LC 82-15857. (American History Ser.). 164p. 1983. pap. text ed. 6.95 (ISBN 0-88295-814-3). Harlan Davidson.

Ostrander, Gilman. Ideas of the Progressive Era. 1970. pap. text ed. 1.95x (ISBN 0-88273-226-9). Forum Pr IL.

Watson, Richard L., Jr. The Development of National Power: The United States 1900-1919. LC 82-20175. 380p. 1983. pap. text ed. 13.75 (ISBN 0-8191-2856-2). U Pr of Amer.

PROHIBITED BOOKS–BIBLIOGRAPHY

Speculator Morum. Bibliotheca Arcana: Brief Notices of Books that have been Secretly Printed, Prohibited by Law, Seized, Anathematized, Burnt or Bowdlerized. 189p. 1982. 60.00x (ISBN 0-284-79523-2, Pub. by C Skilton Scotland). State Mutual Bk.

PROHIBITED EXPORTS AND IMPORTS

see Foreign Trade Regulation

PROJECT MANAGEMENT

Rudman, Jack. Assistant Project Coordinator. (Career Examination Ser.). (Cloth bdg. avail. on request). pap. 10.00 (ISBN 0-8373-2590-0). Natl Learning.

--Project Coordinator. (Career Examination Ser.: C-2589). (Cloth bdg. avail. on request). pap. 12.00 (ISBN 0-8373-2589-7). Natl Learning.

--Senior Project Development Coordinator. (Career Examination Ser.: C-2898). (Cloth bdg. avail. on request). pap. 12.00 (ISBN 0-8373-2898-5). Natl Learning.

PROJECT NETWORKS

see Network Analysis (Planning)

PROJECTION (PSYCHOLOGY)

Halpern, James & Halpern, Ilsa. Projections: Our World of Imaginary Relationships. 192p. 1983. 13.95 (ISBN 0-399-31017-7). Seaview Bks.

PROJECTION, MOVING-PICTURE

see Moving-Picture Projection

PROJECTIVE DIFFERENTIAL GEOMETRY

see Geometry, Differential–Projective

PROJECTIVE GEOMETRY

see Geometry, Projective

PROKOFIEV, SERGEI SERGEEVICH, 1891-1953

Gutman, David. Prokofiev: His Life & Times. (Illus.). 150p. (gr. 7 up). 1983. 16.95 (ISBN 0-88254-730-5, Pub. by Midas Bks England). Hippocrene Bks.

PROLETARIAT

see also Labor and Laboring Classes; Poor

Magubane, Bernard & Nzongola-Ntalaja, eds. Proletarianization & Class Struggle in Africa. (Contemporary Marxism Ser.). (Illus., Orig.). 1983. pap. 6.50 (ISBN 0-89935-019-4). Synthesis Pubns.

PROLONGATION OF LIFE SPAN

see Immortalism; Longevity

PROOFREADING

see also Authorship–Handbooks, Manuals, etc.; Printing–Style Manuals

Hart's Rules for Compositors & Readers at the University Press, Oxford. 39th ed. 196p. 1982. 11.50 (ISBN 0-19-212983-X). Oxford U Pr.

PROPAGANDA

see also Advertising; Lobbying; Persuasion (Psychology); Press; Psychological Warfare; Public Opinion; Public Relations; Publicity

also subdivision Propaganda under names of wars, e.g. World War, 1939-1945–Propaganda

Jackson, Ronald. The Power of Progaganda. (Illus.). 224p. 1983. 13.00 (ISBN 0-682-49942-0). Exposition.

Riegel, Oscar W. Mobilizing For Chaos: Story of the New Propaganda. 1934. text ed. 14.50x (ISBN 0-686-83627-8). Elliots Bks.

PROPAGANDA, GERMAN

Welch, David. Propaganda & the German Cinema, 1933-1945. (Illus.). 420p. 1983. 34.00 (ISBN 0-19-822598-9). Oxford U Pr.

PROPAGATION OF PLANTS

see Plant Propagation

PROPER NAMES

see Names

PROPERTIES OF MATTER

see Matter–Properties

PROPERTY

see also Eminent Domain; Income; Possession (Law); Real Property; Wealth

Andreoli, Anthony L. & Shuman, D. R. Guide to Unclaimed Property & Escheat Laws, 2 Vols. LC 82-71985. 2100p. 1982. Vol. I. 249.50 set (ISBN 0-943882-02-8); write for info. (ISBN 0-943882-00-1); Vol. II. write for info. (ISBN 0-943882-02-8). Commonwlth Pub.

Berle, Adolf A., Jr. & Means, Gardiner C. The Modern Corporation & Private Property. xiii, 396p. 1982. Repr. of 1933 ed. lib. bdg. 30.00 (ISBN 0-89941-183-5). W S Hein.

Menon, Kreshna. The Law of Property. (Orient Longman Law Library). 556p. 1980. pap. text ed. 18.95x (ISBN 0-86125-516-X, Pub. by Orient Longman Ltd India). Apt Bks.

Tully, James. A Discourse on Property: John Locke & His Adversaries. 208p. 1983. pap. 9.95 (ISBN 0-521-27140-1). Cambridge U Pr.

PROPERTY–HISTORY

Diosdi, Gyorgy. Ownership in Ancient & Preclassical Roman Law. 1970. 12.50x (ISBN 0-8002-1772-1). Intl Pubns Serv.

PROPERTY–VALUATION

see Valuation

PROPERTY–GREAT BRITAIN

Guide to Commericial Property Development in England, 1974. 1974 ed. (Gower Publications). 550p. 26.95 (ISBN 0-686-37376-6). Beekman Pubs.

Lawson, Frederick H. & Rudden, Bernard. The Law of Property. 2nd ed. (Clarendon Law Ser.). (Illus.). 258p. 1982. text ed. 34.95x (ISBN 0-19-876128-7); pap. text ed. 15.95x (ISBN 0-19-876129-5). Oxford U Pr.

PROPERTY, HORIZONTAL

see Condominium (Housing)

PROPERTY, LITERARY

see Copyright

PROPERTY, REAL

see Real Property

PROPERTY INSURANCE

see Insurance, Property

PROPERTY RIGHTS

see Industrial Property

PROPERTY TAX

Here are entered works on the general property tax, including both real and personal property. Works on the general property tax in individual cities, counties or other local government units are entered under the name of the city, county, etc., with or without the subdivision Taxation.

see also Assessment; Capital Levy; Real Property Tax

Reeves, Clyde H. & Ellsworth, Scott, eds. The Role of the State in Property Taxation. LC 82-48536. (Lincoln Institute of Land Policy Books). 1983. write for info. (ISBN 0-669-06292-8). Lexington Bks.

PROPHECY (CHRISTIANITY)

Aune, David E. Prophecy & Early Christianity. 400p. 1983. 24.95 (ISBN 0-8028-3584-8). Eerdmans.

Hagin, Kenneth E. Seven Steps for Judging Prophecy. 1982. pap. 1.00 (ISBN 0-89276-024-9). Hagin Ministry.

Sutton, Hilton. Questions & Answers on Bible Prophecy. 135p. (Orig.). 1982. pap. 2.95 (ISBN 0-89274-253-4). Harrison Hse.

PROPHETS

Ali-Nadawi, Abul H. Prophet's Stories. Quinlan, Hamid, ed. El-Helbawy, Kamal, tr. from Arabic. LC 82-70453. (Illus.). 200p. (Orig.). 1982. pap. 5.00 (ISBN 0-89259-038-6). Am Trust Pubns.

Coffman, James B. Commentary on the Minor Prophets, Vol. 3. (Firm Foundation Commentary Ser.). 322p. 1983. 10.95 (ISBN 0-88027-107-8). Firm Foun Pub.

Drew, George. The Prophets Speak to Our Time. 62p. (Orig.). 1981. pap. 6.95 (ISBN 0-940754-09-6). Ed Ministries.

Wiesel, Elie. Five Biblical Portraits. LC 81-40458. vii, 157p. 1983. pap. 4.95 (ISBN 0-268-00962-7, 85-09622). U of Notre Dame Pr.

Wolff, Hans W. Confrontations with Prophets. LC 82-48585. 80p. 1983. pap. 3.95 (ISBN 0-8006-1702-9). Fortress.

PROPRIETARY RIGHTS

see Industrial Property; Intellectual Property

PROPULSION OF SPACECRAFT

see Space Vehicles–Propulsion Systems

PROSE LITERATURE

see also Biography (As a Literary Form); Essays; Fiction

Beckett. Worstward Ho. 48p. 1983. 8.95 (ISBN 0-394-53230-9). Grove.

PROSECUTION

Manak, James P. Standards Relating to Prosecution. (Juvenile Justice Standards Project Ser.). 112p. 1980. 20.00x (ISBN 0-88410-238-6); pap. 10.00x (ISBN 0-88410-814-7). Ballinger Pub.

PROSODY

see Versification

PROSPECTING

see also Petroleum–Geology

Lacy, Willard C., ed. Mineral Exploration. LC 82-969. (Benchmark Papers in Geology Ser.: Vol. 70). 448p. 1983. 52.00 (ISBN 0-87933-425-8). Hutchinson Ross.

North, Oliver S. Mineral Exploration, Mining, & Processing Patents, 1980. (Illus.). 135p. 1982. 35.00x (ISBN 0-89520-294-8). Soc Mining Eng.

Underwater Prospecting Techniques: The Gold Divers Handbook. 10th, rev. ed. LC 60-4754. 1977. 3.00 (ISBN 0-686-38066-5). Merlin Engine Wks.

PROSTAGLANDIN

Dunn, Michael J. & Patrono, Carlo, eds. Prostaglandins & the Kidney: Biochemistry, Physiology, Pharmacology, & Clinical Applications. 406p. 1982. 49.50 (ISBN 0-306-41054-0, Plenum Med Bk). Plenum Pub.

Hornstra, G. Dietary Fats, Prostanoids & Arterial Thrombosis. 1983. 48.00 (ISBN 90-247-2667-0, Pub. by Martinus Nijhoff Netherlands). Kluwer Boston.

PROSTATE GLAND–DISEASES

see also Bladder

Greenberger, Monroe E. & Siegel, Mary-Ellen. What Every Man Should Know About His Prostate. (Illus.). Date not set. 12.95 (ISBN 0-8027-0725-4). Walker & Co.

PROSTHESIS

see also Artificial Limbs; Artificial Organs; Pacemaker, Artificial (Heart); Prosthodontics; Vascular Grafts

Chao, Edmund Y. & Ivins, John C. Design & Application for Tumor Prostheses. (Illus.). 375p. 1983. write for info. Thieme-Stratton.

Critser, James R., Jr. Prosthetics & Contact Lens. 126p. 1982. 80.00 (ISBN 0-914428-96-9, 10PC-81). Lexington Data.

Stanley, James C., ed. Biologic & Synthetic Prostheses. 681p. 1982. 79.50 (ISBN 0-8089-1491-X). Grune.

PROSTHODONTICS

Linkow, Leonard I. Dental Implants. (Illus.). 1983. 17.50 (ISBN 0-8315-0162-6). Speller.

PROSTITUTION

see also Sex Crimes; Sexual Ethics; Venereal Diseases

Castle, Charles. La Belle Otero: The Last Great Courtesan. (Illus.). 192p. 1983. 14.95 (ISBN 0-7181-1935-5, Pub by Michael Joseph). Merrimack Bk Serv.

O'Brien, Martin. All the Girls. LC 82-5625. 336p. 1982. 14.95 (ISBN 0-312-02003-1). St Martin.

PROSTITUTION–EUROPE

Wells, Jesse. A History of Prostitution in Western Europe. (Illus.). 104p. 1982. pap. write for info. (ISBN 0-915288-48-6). Shameless Hussy.

PROTECTION AGAINST BURGLARY

see Burglary Protection

PROTECTION OF ANIMALS

see Animals, Treatment of

PROTECTION OF CHILDREN

see Child Welfare

PROTECTION OF ENVIRONMENT

see Environmental Protection

PROTECTION OF NATURAL MONUMENTS

see Natural Monuments

PROTECTION OF NATURE

see Nature Conservation

PROTECTION OF WILDLIFE CONSERVATION

see Wildlife Conservation

PROTECTIVE COATINGS

see also Corrosion and Anti-Corrosives; Gums and Resins; Paint; Paper Coatings

Ash, M. & Ash, I. Formulary of Paints & Other Coatings Vol. 2. 1982. 35.00 (ISBN 0-8206-0292-2). Chem Pub.

PROTEIDS

see Proteins

PROTEIN METABOLISM

Durand, P. & O'Brien, J. S., eds. Genetic Errors of Glycoprotein Metabolism. (Illus.). 220p. 1983. 33.50 (ISBN 0-387-12066-1). Springer-Verlag.

Hermens, W. T. Quantification of Circulating Proteins. 1983. 44.00 (ISBN 90-247-2755-3, Pub. by Martinus Nijhoff Netherlands). Kluwer Boston.

Pierce, John G., ed. Proteins & Peptides Hormones. LC 82-6159. (Benchmark Papers in Biochemistry: Vol. 4). 480p. 1982. 58.00 (ISBN 0-87933-417-7). Hutchinson Ross.

PROTEINS

see also Protein Metabolism

also various protein groups and bodies, e.g. Peptones, Casein

Atassi, M. Z. & Benjamini, E., eds. Immunobiology of Proteins & Peptides-II, Vol.150. (Advances in Experimental Medicine & Biology). 238p. 1982. 35.00x (ISBN 0-306-41110-5, Plenum Pr). Plenum Pub.

Bradshaw, Ralph A., et al, eds. Proteins in Biology & Medicine. 1983. 31.50 (ISBN 0-12-124580-2). Acad Pr.

Choh Hao Li, ed. Hormonal Proteins & Peptides, Vol. 1. LC 82-22770. Date not set. price not set (ISBN 0-12-447211-7). Acad Pr.

Devenyi, T. & Gergely, J. Amino Acid Peptides & Proteins. 1974. 56.00 (ISBN 0-444-41127-5). Elsevier.

Dudley, J. W., ed. Severly Generators of Selection for Oil & Protein in Maize. 1974. 10.00 (ISBN 0-89118-502-X). Crop Sci Soc Am.

Fox, P. F. & Condon, J. J., eds. Food Proteins. (Illus.). xi, 358p. 1982. 78.00 (ISBN 0-85334-143-5, Pub. by Applied Sci England). Elsevier.

Grant, R. A. Applied Protein Chemistry. 1980. 53.50 (ISBN 0-85334-865-0, Pub. by Applied Sci England). Elsevier.

Hudson, B. J., ed. Developments in Food Proteins, Vol. 1. 1982. 71.75 (ISBN 0-85334-987-8, Pub. by Applied Sci England). Elsevier.

Kritchevsky, David & Gibney, Michael J., eds. Animal & Vegetable Proteins in Lipid Metabolism & Atherosclerosis. LC 82-23961. (Current Topics in Nutrition & Disease Ser.: Vol. 8). 200p. 1983. write for info. (ISBN 0-8451-1607-X). A R Liss.

Lapanje, Savo. Physicochemical Aspects of Protein Denaturation. LC 78-1919. 346p. Repr. of 1978 ed. text ed. 40.50 (ISBN 0-471-03409-6). Krieger.

Nei, Masatoshi & Koehn, Richard K., eds. Evolution of Genes & Proteins. (Illus.). 380p. 1983. price not set (ISBN 0-87893-603-3); pap. price not set (ISBN 0-87893-604-1). Sinauer Assoc.

Neurath, Hans & Hill, Robert, eds. The Protein, Vol. 5. 736p. 1982. 78.50 (ISBN 0-12-516305-3); subscription 68.00 (ISBN 0-686-81655-2). Acad Pr.

Peeters, H., ed. Protides of the Biological Fluids: Proceedings of the 30th Colloquium on Protides of the Biological Fluids, May 1982, Brussels, Belguim. LC 58-5908. (Illus.). 760p. 1982. 180.00 (ISBN 0-08-029815-X, H220). Pergamon.

Scopes, R. K. Protein Purifaction: Principles & Practice. (Springer Advanced Texts in Chemistry). (Illus.). 282p. 1983. 29.95 (ISBN 0-387-90726-2). Springer-Verlag.

Voelter, W. & Wunsch, E., eds. Chemistry of Peptides & Proteins, Vol. 1. xv, 533p. 1982. 98.00x (ISBN 3-11-008604-2). De Gruyter.

PROTESTANT EPISCOPAL CHURCH IN THE U. S. A.

Wood, Richard H. A Cyclopedic Dictionary of Ecclesiastical Terms According to the Use of the Episcopal Church. 1983. 10.95 (ISBN 0-8062-2141-0). Carlton.

PROTESTANT REFORMATION

see Reformation

PROTESTANTISM

see also Evangelicalism; Reformation

Bowen, Kurt. Protestants in a Catholic State: Ireland's Privileged Minority. 240p. 1983. 25.00x (ISBN 0-7735-0412-5). McGill-Queens U Pr.

Gollwitzer, Helmut. An Introduction to Protestant Theology. Cairns, David, tr. LC 82-4798. 240p. 1982. pap. 12.95 (ISBN 0-664-24415-7). Westminster.

Roof, Wade C. Community & Commitment: Religious Plausibility in a Liberal Protestant Church. LC 77-16329. 288p. pap. 10.95 (ISBN 0-8298-0669-5). Pilgrim NY.

PROTESTANTISM–HISTORY

Ribuffo, Leo. The Old Christian Right: The Protestant Far Right from the Great Depression to the Cold War. 1983. write for info. (ISBN 0-87722-297-5). Temple U Pr.

PROTESTANTISM, EVANGELICAL

see Evangelicalism

PROTESTS, DIPLOMATIC

see Diplomacy

PROTONS

see also Atoms; Electrons; Neutrons

AIP Conference, 85th, Madison, Wisconsin, 1982. Proton-Antiproton Collider Physics: Proceedings. Barger, V., et al, eds. LC 82-72141. 676p. 1982. lib. bdg. 42.00 (ISBN 0-88318-184-3). AM Inst Physics.

PROTOPLASM

see also Cells; Embryology; Membranes (Biology)

Weiss, D. G. & Gorio, A., eds. Axioplasmic Transport in Physiology & Pathology. (Proceedings in Life Science Ser.). (Illus.). 220p. 1983. 32.00 (ISBN 0-387-11663-X). Springer-Verlag.

PROTOZOA

see also Ciliata; Foraminifera

Baker, John R. The Biology of Protozoa. (Studies in Biology: No. 138). 64p. 1982. pap. text ed. 8.95 (ISBN 0-7131-2837-2). E Arnold.

Curds, C. R., et al. British & Other Freshwater Ciliated Protozoa: Part 2. LC 81-15541. (Synopses of the British Fauna Ser.: No. 23). 400p. Date not set. price not set (ISBN 0-521-25033-1). Cambridge U Pr.

PROUST, MARCEL, 1871-1922

Hughes, Edward. Marcel Proust: A Study in the Quality of Awareness. LC 82-9718. 224p. Date not set. 39.50 (ISBN 0-521-24768-3). Cambridge U Pr.

Murray, Jack. The Proustian Comedy. 17.00 (ISBN 0-917786-13-0). French Lit.

Proust, Marcel. Marcel Proust: Selected Letters, 1880-1903. Kolb, Philip, ed. Manheim, Ralph, tr. LC 81-43567. 456p. 1983. 19.95 (ISBN 0-385-14394-X). Doubleday.

PROVENCE–DESCRIPTION AND TRAVEL

Michelin Green Guide: Provence. (Green Guide Ser.). (Fr.). 1983. pap. write for info. (ISBN 2-06-003631-3). Michelin.

Michelin Green Guide: Provence Franzosische. (Green Guide Ser.). (Ger.). 1983. pap. write for info. Michelin.

PROVERBS

see also Aphorisms and Apothegms; Mottoes

Castle, Tony, ed. The New Book of Christian Quotations. 272p. 1983. pap. 9.95 (ISBN 0-8245-0551-4). Crossroad NY.

Lai, T. C. Chinese Proverbs. (Illus.). 96p. 5.95 (ISBN 0-86519-022-4). Lee Pubs Group.

McLellan, Vern. People Proverbs. LC 82-83841. (Illus.). 1983. pap. 2.95 (ISBN 0-89081-326-4). Harvest Hse.

MLW Publications, ed. The Book of Proverbs from Twenty-One Translations. LC 82-61262. (Illus.). 200p. 1983. pap. 8.95 (ISBN 0-9609348-0-4). MLW Pubns Inc.

Penfield, Joyce. Communicating with Quotes: The Igbo Case. LC 82-15626. (Contributions in Intercultural & Comparative Studies Ser.: No. 8). (Illus.). 152p. 1983. lib. bdg. 29.95 (ISBN 0-313-23767-0, PEN/). Greenwood.

Simpson, J. A., ed. The Concise Oxford Dictionary of Proverbs. 272p. 1983. 16.95 (ISBN 0-19-866131-2). Oxford U Pr.

PROVIDENCE AND GOVERNMENT OF GOD

see also Trust in God

Billheimer, Paul. The Mystery of God's Providence. 1983. pap. 3.95 (ISBN 0-8423-4664-3). Tyndale.

Migliore, Daniel L. The Power of God, Vol. 8. Mulder, John C., ed. LC 82-20037. (Library of Living Faith). 120p. (Orig.). 1983. pap. 5.95 (ISBN 0-664-24454-8). Westminster.

PRUNING

MacCaskey, Michael & Stebbins, Robert L. Pruning: How to Guide for Gardeners. 160p. 1982. pap. 7.95 (ISBN 0-89586-188-7). H P Bks.

PSALMODY

Here are entered works on the singing of Psalms in public worship.

see also Church Music; Hymns

Tully, Mary Jo. Psalms: Faith Songs for the Faith-Filled. 96p. 1982. pap. 3.50 (ISBN 0-697-01824-5). Wm C Brown.

PSALMS (MUSIC)

Hurlow, Janet. Psalms from the Hills of West Virginia. LC 81-68460. (Illus.). 144p. (Orig.). 1982. pap. 7.95 (ISBN 0-939680-02-5). Bear & Co.

PSALTERS

Sandler, Lucy F. The Psalter of Robert de Lisle. (Illus.). 160p. 1982. 98.00x (ISBN 0-19-921028-4). Oxford U Pr.

Wormald, Francis. The Winchester Psalter. (Illus.). 128p. 1973. 49.00x (ISBN 0-19-921004-7). Oxford U Pr.

PSEUDONYMS

see Anonyms and Pseudonyms

PSEUDOROMANTICISMS

see Romanticism

PSYCHAGOGY

see Psychology, Applied; Psychotherapy

PSYCHE (GODDESS) LITERATURE

Richardson, I. M. The Adventures of Eros & Psyche. LC 82-16057. (Illus.). 32p. (gr. 4-8). 1983. PLB 8.79 (ISBN 0-89375-861-2); pap. text ed. 2.50 (ISBN 0-89375-862-0). Troll Assocs.

PSYCHEDELIC DRUGS

see Hallucinogenic Drugs

PSYCHIATRIC CONSULTATION

Alpert, Judith L. & Meyers, Joel. Training in Consultation: Perspectives from Mental Health, Behavioral & Organizational Consultation. (Illus.). 252p. 1983. 21.50x (ISBN 0-398-04801-0). C C Thomas.

Brown, Jeannette A. & Pate, Robert H., Jr. Being a Counselor: Directions & Challenges. LC 82-20764. (Psychology Ser.). 450p. 1983. text ed. 20.95 (ISBN 0-534-01261-2). Brooks-Cole.

Wise, T. N. & Freyberger, H., eds. Consultation Liaison Throughout the World. (Advances in Psychosomatic Medicine: Vol. 11). (Illus.). xii, 250p. 1983. 112.75 (ISBN 3-8055-3667-4). S Karger.

PSYCHIATRIC HOSPITALS

Lion, John R. & Reid, William H. Assalts Within Psychiatric Facilities. write for info (ISBN 0-8089-1559-2). Grune.

PSYCHIATRIC NURSING

Comstock, Betsy, et al, eds. Phenomonology & Treatment of Psychiatric Emergencies. 288p. 1983. text ed. 30.00 (ISBN 0-89335-182-2). SP Med & Sci Bks.

Deyoung, Carol & Glittenberg, Jody. Out of Uniform & Into Trouble Again. LC 82-62400. 120p. 1983. Repr. 16.00 (ISBN 0-913590-98-3). Slack Inc.

Dunlap, L. C. Mental Health Concepts Applied to Nursing. 256p. 1978. 22.50 (ISBN 0-471-04360-5). Wiley.

Perry, Anne G. & Potter, Patricia A. Shock: Comprehensive Nursing Management. (Illus.). 303p. 1983. pap. text ed. 19.95 (ISBN 0-8016-3827-5). Mosby.

Redmond, Gertrude T. & Ouellette, Frances. Concept & Case Studies in Physical & Mental Health Nursing: A Life Cycle Approach. 1982. pap. 12.95 (ISBN 0-201-06207-0, Med-Nurse). A-W.

Rudman, Jack. Psychiatric & Mental Health Nurse. (Certified Nurse Examination Ser.: CN-12). 21.95 (ISBN 0-8373-6162-1); pap. 13.95 (ISBN 0-8373-6112-5). Natl Learning.

Smoyak, Shirley A. & Rouslin, Sheila, eds. A Collection of Classics in Psychiatric Nursing Literature. LC 82-61592. 1982. 30.00 (ISBN 0-913590-96-7). Slack Inc.

Stuart, Gail W. & Sundeen, Sandra J. Principles & Practice of Psychiatric Nursing. 2nd ed. (Illus.). 1052p. 1983. text ed. 27.95 (ISBN 0-8016-4885-8). Mosby.

Wilson, Holly S. & Kneisl, Carol R. Psychiatric Nursing. 2nd ed. 1983. 26.95 (ISBN 0-201-11702-9, Med-Nurse); activity bk 9.95 (ISBN 0-201-11703-7, Med-Nurse); instr's guide 3.95 (ISBN 0-201-08341-8). A-W.

PSYCHIATRIC PERSONNEL

see Mental Health Personnel

PSYCHIATRIC RESEARCH

Barlow, David H. & Hayes, Steven C. The Scientist Practitioner: Research & Accountability in Mental Health & Education. 400p. 1983. 35.00 (ISBN 0-08-027217-7); pap. 14.95 (ISBN 0-08-027216-9). Pergamon.

PSYCHIATRIC SOCIAL WORK

see also Medical Social Work; Pastoral Counseling

Callicutt, James W. & Lecca, Pedro J., eds. Social Work & Mental Health. LC 82-71734. 245p. 1983. 22.95 (ISBN 0-02-905830-9); pap. text ed. write for info. Free Pr.

Hudson, Barbara L. Social Work with Psychiatric Patients. 240p. 1982. 39.00x (ISBN 0-333-26685-4, Pub. by Macmillan England). State Mutual Bk.

Smith, Carole R. Social Work with the Dying & Bereaved. Campling, Jo, ed. (Practical Social Work Ser.). 160p. 1982. 40.00x (ISBN 0-333-30894-8, Pub. by Macmillan England). State Mutual Bk.

Turner, Francis J., ed. Differential Diagnosis & Treatment in Social Work. 3rd, rev. ed. LC 82-48390. 1983. 24.95 (ISBN 0-02-932990-6). Free Pr.

PSYCHIATRISTS

American Psychiatric Association. American Psychiatric Association Biographical Directory, 1983. 1600p. 1983. 89.95x (ISBN 0-89042-182-X); pap. 69.95x (ISBN 0-89042-181-1). Am Psychiatric.

Browning, Charles H. Private Practice Handbook: The Tools, Tactics & Techniques for Successful Practice Development. 2nd ed. 238p. 1982. 24.95 (ISBN 0-911663-02-9); pap. 21.95 (ISBN 0-911663-01-0). Duncliffs Intl.

Schneiderman, Stuart. Jacques Lacan: The Death of an Intellectual Hero. (Illus.). 192p. 1983. 14.95 (ISBN 0-674-47115-6). Harvard U Pr.

PSYCHIATRY

Here are entered works on the clinical and therapeutic aspects of psychology. Works on abnormal psychology in general are entered under the heading Psychology, Pathological.

see also Child Psychiatry; Clinical Psychology; Group Psychotherapy; Mental Health; Mentally Ill; Mental Illness; Neuroses; Psychology, Pathological; Psychotherapy

American Association of Directors of Psychiatric Residency Training & American Medical Student Association. Directory of Psychiatry Residency Training Programs. 610p. 1982. pap. 15.00x (ISBN 0-89042-701-1). Am Psychiatric.

Bengesser, Gerhard. Wechselbeziehungen Zwischen Psychiatrie, Psychologie und Philosophie. 178p. (Ger.). 1982. write for info. (ISBN 3-261-05019-5). P Lang Pubs.

Cavenar, Jesse O., Jr. & Brodie, Keith H., eds. Signs & Symptoms in Psychiatry. (Illus.). 608p. 1983. text ed. 29.50 (ISBN 0-397-50489-6, Lippincott Medical). Lippincott.

Damlouji, Namir F. & Feighner, John. Psychiatry Specialty Board Review. 1983. pap. text ed. price not set. Med Exam.

Dubovsky, Steven L. & Feiger, Allan D. Psychiatric Decision Making. 300p. 1983. text ed. 30.00 (ISBN 0-941158-16-0, D1483-X). Mosby.

Freedman, Daniel X., ed. Year Book of Psychiatry & Applied Mental Health 1983. 1983. 45.00 (ISBN 0-686-83776-2). Year Bk Med.

Glasscote, Raymond M., et al. The Uses of Psychiatry in Smaller General Hospitals. LC 82-22719. 133p. 1983. pap. 12.00x (42-108-0). Am Psychiatric.

Grinspoon, Lester, ed. & intro. by. Psychiatry Update: The American Psychiatric Association Annual Review, Vol. II. (Illus.). 544p. 1983. text ed. 45.00x (ISBN 0-88048-007-6). Am Psychiatric.

Lewis, Jerry M. & Usdin, Gene, eds. Treatment Planning in Psychiatry. LC 82-3985. (Illus.). 433p. 1982. 27.50 (ISBN 0-89042-045-9, 42-045-9). Am Psychiatric.

Masserman, Jules H., ed. Current Psychiatric Therapies, Vol. 21. Date not set. price not set (ISBN 0-8089-1517-7). Grune.

Mathis, James L. Psychiatric Medicine Handbook. Gradner, Alvin F., ed. (Allied Health Professions Monograph Ser.). 1983. price not set (ISBN 0-87527-320-3). Green.

Price, J. Harding. A Synopsis of Psychiatry. (Illus.). 312p. 1982. text ed. 27.50 (ISBN 0-7236-0611-0). Wright-PSG.

Priest, R. G. Psychiatry in Medical Practice. 500p. 1982. text ed. 58.00x (ISBN 0-7121-1672-9). Intl Ideas.

Sainsbury, M. J. Key to Psychiatry: A Textbook for Students. 3rd ed. 426p. 1980. text ed. 22.95 (ISBN 0-471-26009-6, Pub. by Wiley Med). Wiley.

Walker, J. I. Psychiatric Emergencies: Intervention & Resolution. (Illus.). 288p. 1983. pap. text ed. 19.50 (ISBN 0-397-50495-0, Lippincott Medical). Lippincott.

PSYCHIATRY–ADDRESSES, ESSAYS, LECTURES

Favazza, Armando R. & Faheem, Ahmed D. Themes In Cultural Psychiatry: An Annoted Bibliography 1975-1980. LC 82-2738. 208p. 1982. 30.00 (ISBN 0-8262-0377-9). U of MO Pr.

PSYCHIATRY–CASES, CLINICAL REPORTS, STATISTICS

Cumming, Robert G. Case Studies of Psychiatric Emergencies. 1983. 16.95 (ISBN 0-8391-1811-2, 19283). Univ Park.

PSYCHIATRY–COLLECTED WORKS

Dyer, Raymond. Her Father's Daughter: The Work of Anna Freud. LC 82-11334. 332p. 1983. write for info. (ISBN 0-87668-627-7). Aronson.

PSYCHIATRY–DICTIONARIES

Wolman, Benjamin B., ed. Progress: Vol. I of the International Encyclppedia of Psychiatry, Psychology, Psychoanalysis & Neurology. 1983. 89.00 (ISBN 0-918228-28-X). Aesculapius Pubs.

PSYCHIATRY–PHILOSOPHY

Colby, Kenneth M. & Spar, James E. The Fundamental Crisis in Psychiatry: Unreliability of Diagnosis. 236p. 1983. 24.75x (ISBN 0-398-04788-X). C C Thomas.

PSYCHIATRY–RESEARCH

see Psychiatric Research

PSYCHIATRY, CHILD

see Child Psychiatry

PSYCHIATRY, FORENSIC

see Forensic Psychiatry

PSYCHIATRY AND ART

see Art Therapy

PSYCHIATRY IN GENERAL HOSPITALS

see Psychiatric Hospitals

PSYCHIC HEALING

see Mental Healing

PSYCHICAL RESEARCH

see also Apparitions; Astral Projection; Clairvoyance; Dreams; Extrasensory Perception; Ghosts; Hypnotism; Mental Suggestion; Mind and Body; Personality, Disorders Of; Psychology, Religious; Spiritualism; Subconsciousness

Allen, James. All These Things Added. 192p. 6.50 (ISBN 0-686-38209-9). Sun Bks.

--As a Man Thinketh. 88p. 3.50 (ISBN 0-686-38211-0). Sun Bks.

Cavendish, Richard, ed. Man, Myth & Magic: The Illustrated Encyclopedia of Mythology, Religion & the Unknown. 2nd ed. (Illus.). 3268p. 1983. lib. bdg. 399.95 (ISBN 0-86307-041-8). M Cavendish Corp.

Coue, Emile. My Method. 97p. 4.50 (ISBN 0-686-38229-3). Sun Bks.

Curtiss, H. A. & Curtiss, F. H. The Voice of Isis. 472p. 17.50 (ISBN 0-686-38238-2). Sun Bks.

Deigh, Khigh, ed. The Golden Oracle: The Ancient Chinese Way to Prosperity. LC 82-18471. (Illus.). 176p. 1983. 11.95 (ISBN 0-668-05661-4). Arco.

Ebon, M. Psychic Warfare: Threat of Illusion? 304p. 1983. 15.95 (ISBN 0-07-018860-2). McGraw.

Franklin, Lynn & Harrison, Shirley. Psychic Search. 280p. 1981. 12.95 (ISBN 0-930096-22-3). G Gannett.

Giorgi, A., ed. Journal of Phenomenological Psychology. (JPP Ser.: Vol. 13-1). 150p. 1982. pap. text ed. 7.50x. Humanities.

Green, Carolyna. Vagabond Healer. LC 82-90766. 232p. 1983. pap. text ed. 6.95 (ISBN 0-936958-02-2). Emerald Hse.

Harvey, Bill. Mind Magic. 4th ed. Bertisch, Jan & Bragg, Yana, eds. (Illus.). 512p. 1982. pap. 13.00 (ISBN 0-918538-08-4). Ourobourus.

Holmes, Ernest S. Creative Mind. 78p. 4.00 (ISBN 0-686-38214-5). Sun Bks.

Hudesman, Anna. Four Score & Five: Recollections & Reflections. 200p. 1981. 4.95 (ISBN 0-88437-021-6). Psych Dimensions.

Krippner, Stanley. Advances in Parapsychological Research, Vol. 3. 352p. 1982. 32.50x (ISBN 0-306-40944-5, Plenum Pr). Plenum Pub.

McConnell, R. A. Introduction to Parapsychology in the Context of Science. LC 82-99945. (Illus.). 352p. Date not set. pap. 11.00 (ISBN 0-686-37890-3). R A McConnell.

McConnell, R. A., ed. Encounters with Parapsychology. LC 81-90032. (Illus.). ix, 235p. 1982. pap. 9.00 (ISBN 0-686-37892-X). R A McConnell.

--Parapsychology & Self-Deception in Science. LC 81-90464. (Illus.). vii, 150p. Date not set. pap. 7.00 (ISBN 0-686-37891-1). R A McConnell.

Manning, Al G. Helping Yourself with Psycho-Cosmic Power. LC 68-12433. 1983. pap. 5.95 (ISBN 0-941698-06-8). Pan Ishtar.

Mulford, Prentice. Thought Forces. 172p. 7.00 (ISBN 0-686-38235-8). Sun Bks.

Ostrander, Sheila & Schroeder, Lynn. Seventy-Six Psychic Techniques: A Primer in Parapsychology. O'Quinn, John, ed. 8p. 1980. pap. text ed. 2.00 (ISBN 0-9609802-5-3). Life Science.

Puryear, Herbert B. The Edgar Cayce Primer: Discovering the Path to Psychic Power. 240p. 1982. pap. 2.95 (ISBN 0-553-22738-6). Bantam.

Rao, K. Ramakrishna. J. B. Rhine: On the Frontiers of Science. LC 82-17206. (Illus.). 278p. 1982. lib. bdg. 19.95x (ISBN 0-89950-053-6). McFarland & Co.

Roll, William G., et al, eds. Research in Parapsychology 1981: Abstracts & Papers from the Twenty-Fourth Annual Convention of the Parapsychological Association, 1981. LC 66-28580. 252p. 1982. 15.00 (ISBN 0-8108-1550-8). Scarecrow.

Stevenson, Ian. Cases of the Reincarnation Type: Vol. IV-Twelve Cases in Thailand & Burma. LC 74-28263. 1983. price not set (ISBN 0-8139-0960-0). U Pr of Va.

Turnbul, Coulson. Sema-Kanda: Threshold Memories. 254p. 11.50 (ISBN 0-686-38234-X). Sun Bks.

PSYCHOANALYSIS

see also Dreams; Ego (Psychology); Hypnotism; Medicine, Psychosomatic; Mind and Body; Psychohistory; Psychology; Psychology, Pathological; Subconsciousness

Berliner, Arthur K. Psychoanalysis & Society: The Social Thought of Sigmund Freud. LC 82-21932. 216p. (Orig.). 1983. lib. bdg. 20.75 (ISBN 0-8191-2893-7); pap. text ed. 10.50 (ISBN 0-8191-2894-5). U Pr of Amer.

Bettelheim, Bruno. Freud & Man's Soul. LC 82-47809. 112p. 1983. 11.95 (ISBN 0-394-52481-0). Knopf.

Gallop, J. Feminism & Psychoanalysis: The Daughters Seduction. 1982. 55.00x (ISBN 0-333-29471-8, Pub. by Macmillan England). State Mutual Bk.

Miller, Glenn E. Chicago Psychoanalytic Literature Index, 1981. 1982. lib. bdg. 50.00 (ISBN 0-918568-09-9). Chicago Psych.

Peterfreund, Emanuel. The Process of Psychoanalytic Therapy: Models & Strategies. 288p. 1982. text ed. 24.95 (ISBN 0-89859-274-7). L Erlbaum Assocs.

Stein, Murray, ed. Jungian Analysis. 1982. 19.95 (ISBN 0-87548-350-X). Open Court.

PSYCHOANALYSIS–CASES, CLINICAL REPORTS, STATISTICS

Adler, Alfred. The Pattern of Life. 2nd ed. LC 81-71160. pap. 10.00x (ISBN 0-918560-28-4). A Adler Inst.

Freeman, Lucy. Fight Against Fears. 368p. 1983. pap. 3.50 (ISBN 0-446-30329-1). Warner Bks.

PSYCHOANALYSIS–DICTIONARIES

Wolman, Benjamin B., ed. Progress: Vol. I of the International Encyclppedia of Psychiatry, Psychology, Psychoanalysis & Neurology. 1983. 89.00 (ISBN 0-918228-28-X). Aesculapius Pubs.

PSYCHOANALYSIS–HISTORY

Friedlander, Saul. History & Psychoanalysis. Suleiman, Susan, tr. 175p. 1978. 29.50 (ISBN 0-8419-0339-5); pap. 15.50 (ISBN 0-686-43335-1, 0-8419-061). Holmes & Meier.

Schneiderman, Stuart. Jacques Lacan: The Death of an Intellectual Hero. (Illus.). 192p. 1983. 14.95 (ISBN 0-674-47115-6). Harvard U Pr.

PSYCHOANALYSIS AND RELIGION

Rollins, Wayne G. Jung & The Bible. LC 82-48091. 156p. 1983. pap. 9.50 (ISBN 0-8042-1117-5). John Knox.

PSYCHOANALYSIS IN HISTORIOGRAPHY

see Psychohistory

PSYCHOBIOLOGY

Wender, Paul H. & Klein, Donald F. Mind, Mood, & Medicine: A Guide to the New Biopsychiatry. 1982. pap. 7.95 (ISBN 0-452-00601-5, Mer). NAL.

PSYCHOHISTORY

Loewenberg, Peter. Decoding the Past: The Psychohistorical Approach. LC 82-47796. 1983. 20.00 (ISBN 0-394-48152-6). Knopf.

PSYCHOLINGUISTICS

see also Children–Language; Generative Grammar; Speech, Disorders of; Thought and Thinking

Aitchison, June. The Articulate Mammal. 2nd., rev., & enl. ed. LC 82-49138. (Illus.). 288p. 1983. text ed. 15.50x (ISBN 0-87663-422-6). Universe.

Hatch, Evelyn M. Psycholinguistics: A Second Language Perspective. 1983. pap. text ed. 15.95 (ISBN 0-88377-250-7). Newbury Hse.

Le Ny, J. F. & Kintsch, W. Language & Comprehension. Date not set. 51.00 (ISBN 0-444-86538-1). Elsevier.

Martlew, Margaret. The Psychology of Written Language: A Developmental Approach. 432p. 1983. 49.95 (ISBN 0-471-10291-1, Pub. by Wiley-Interscience). Wiley.

Rieber, Robert W., ed. Dialogues on the Psychology of Language & Thought: Conversations with Noam Chomsky, Charles Osgood, Jean Piaget, Ulric Neisser & Marcel Kinsbourne. (Cognition & Language Ser.). 174p. 1983. 19.50x (ISBN 0-306-41185-7, Plenum Pr). Plenum Pub.

PSYCHOLOGICAL ANTHROPOLOGY

see Ethnopsychology

PSYCHOLOGICAL ASPECTS OF DISABILITY

see Handicapped

PSYCHOLOGICAL RESEARCH

Hakel, Milton D. & Sorcher, Melvin. Making it Happen: Designing Research with Implementation in Mind. (Studying Organizations: Innovations in Methodology). (Illus.). 144p. 1982. 17.95 (ISBN 0-8039-1865-8); pap. 7.95 (ISBN 0-8039-1866-6). Sage.

James, Lawrence R. & Mulaik, Stanley A. Causal Analysis: Assumptions, Models, & Data: Studying Organizations: Innovations in Methodology. 144p. 1982. 17.95 (ISBN 0-8039-1867-4); pap. 7.95 (ISBN 0-8039-1868-2). Sage.

McGuigan, F. J. Experimental Psychology: Methods of Research. 4th ed. (Illus.). 416p. 1983. 23.95 (ISBN 0-13-295188-6). P-H.

Need, Jeffrey & Baxter, Pam. Library Use: Handbook for Psychology. 150p. (Orig.). 1983. pap. 15.00x (ISBN 0-912704-76-4). Am Psychol.

Peele, Stanton. The Science of Experience: A Direction for Psychology. LC 81-48555. 1983. price not set (ISBN 0-669-05420-8). Lexington Bks.

Straus, Erwin. Man, Time & World: The Anthropological Psychology of Erwin Straus. Moss, Donald, tr. from Ger. 185p. 1982. text ed. 15.50x (ISBN 0-8207-0159-9, 90007). Duquesne.

Suls, Jerry & Greenwald, Anthony G., eds. Psychological Perspectives on the Self, Vol. 2. 320p. 1983. text ed. write for info. (ISBN 0-89859-276-3). L Erlbaum Assocs.

Van Maanen, John. Varieties of Qualitative Research. (Studying Organization: Innovations in Methodology Ser.). 168p. 1982. 17.95 (ISBN 0-8039-1869-0); pap. 7.95 (ISBN 0-8039-1870-4). Sage.

PSYCHOLOGICAL STRESS

see Stress (Psychology)

PSYCHOLOGICAL TESTS

Here are entered general works on the description of psychological tests and testing, including methods of test construction and applications of testing. Works which discuss testing in a particular field are entered under the appropriate heading with subdivision Testing, e.g. Motivation (Psychology)–Testing.

see also Ability–Testing; Clinical Psychology; Educational Tests and Measurements; Intelligence Tests; Mental Illness–Diagnosis; Personality Assessment; Personality Tests

Slater, Barbara R. & Thomas, John M. Psychodiagnostic Evaluation of Children: A Casebook Approach. 1983. pap. text ed. price not set (ISBN 0-8077-2734-2). Tchrs Coll.

Webb, James T. & McNamara, Kathleen T. Configural Interpretations of the MMPI & CPI. 76p. 1981. pap. write for info. Ohio Psych Pub.

PSYCHOLOGICAL WARFARE

Here are entered general works dealing with methods used to undermine the morale of the civilian population and the military forces of any enemy country.

see also Propaganda;

also subdivision Psychological Aspects under names of wars, e.g. World War, 1939-1945–Psychological Aspects

Barclay, Cyril N. The New Warfare. LC 82-18375. x, 66p. 1983. Repr. of 1953 ed. lib. bdg. 24.50x (ISBN 0-313-23793-X, BANW). Greenwood.

PSYCHOLOGISTS

see also Psychiatrists

Bjork, Daniel W. The Compromised Scientist: William James in the Development of American Psychology. (Illus.). 224p. 1983. text ed. 25.00 (ISBN 0-231-05500-5); pap. 12.00 (ISBN 0-231-05501-3). Columbia U Pr.

Heider, Fritz. The Life of a Psychologist: An Autobiography. LC 82-21803. (Illus.). xii, 196p. 1983. text ed. 12.95x (ISBN 0-7006-0232-1). Univ Pr KS.

Smith, Samuel. Ideas of the Great Psychologists. LC 82-48135. 224p. 1983. pap. 6.68 (ISBN 0-06-463561-9, EH 561, EH). Har-Row.

--Ideas of the Great Psychologists. LC 82-48135. 304p. 1983. 14.34i (ISBN 0-06-015087-4, HarpT). Har-Row.

PSYCHOLOGISTS, SCHOOL

see School Psychologists

PSYCHOLOGY

see also Abstraction; Adjustment (Psychology); Adolescent Psychology; Aggressiveness (Psychology); Assertiveness (Psychology); Attitude (Psychology); Behaviorism (Psychology); Belief and Doubt; Body, Human; Change (Psychology); Child Psychology; Cognition; Consciousness; Control (Psychology); Developmental Psychology; Emotions; Ethnopsychology; Experience; Genetic Psychology; Genius; Gestalt Psychology; Habit; Human Behavior; Humanistic Psychology; Ideology; Imagination; Inefficiency, Intellectual; Instinct; Intellect; Interpersonal Relations; Knowledge, Theory of; Logic; Memory; Mental Health; Motivation (Psychology); Opposition, Theory of; Perception; Personality; Physiognomy; Political Psychology; Problem Solving; Psychical Research; Psychoanalysis; Psychobiology; Psychological Tests; Senses and Sensation; Social Interaction; Social Psychology; Stress (Psychology); Subconsciousness; Temperament; Thought and Thinking; Threat (Psychology); Values

also subdivision Psychology under specific subjects, e.g. Aeronautics–Psychology

Abraham, Ralph & Shaw, Chris. Dynamics: The Geometry of Behavior: Pt. 2, Stable & Chaotic Behavior. (Visual Mathematics Ser.). 1983. price not set. Aerial Pr.

Anderson, Charles & Travis, L. D. Psychology & the Liberal Consensus. 200p. 1982. text ed. 10.50x (ISBN 0-88920-127-7, 40911, Pub. by Wilfrid Laurier U Pr). Humanities.

Bengesser, Gerhard. Wechselbeziehungen Zwischen Psychiatrie, Psychologie und Philosophie. 178p. (Ger.). 1982. write for info. (ISBN 3-261-05019-5). P Lang Pubs.

Blocher, Donald H. & Biggs, Donald A. Counseling Psychology in Community Settings. 304p. 1983. text ed. 23.95 (ISBN 0-8261-3680-X). Springer Pub.

Block, Ned, ed. Readings in Philosophy of Psychology, Vol. I. (Language & Thought Ser.). 320p. 1983. pap. text ed. 8.95x (ISBN 0-674-74876-X). Harvard U Pr.

Bruno, Frank J. Behavior & Life: An Introduction to Psychology. 660p. 1980. text ed. 21.95 (ISBN 0-471-02191-1); study guide 8.95 (ISBN 0-471-06340-1). Wiley.

Childs, Alan W. & Melton, Gary B., eds. Rural Psychology. 455p. 1982. 39.50x (ISBN 0-306-41045-1, Plenum Pr). Plenum Pub.

Chomsky, Noam. Modular Approaches to the Study of the Mind. (SDSU Distinguished Research Lecture Ser.). 120p. 1983. 12.00 (ISBN 0-916304-56-6); pap. 6.00 (ISBN 0-916304-55-8). Campanile.

Coombs, Clyde H. Psychology & Mathematics: An Essay on Theory. 104p. 1983. text ed. 12.50 (ISBN 0-472-10034-3). U of Mich Pr.

Coon, Dennis. Introduction to Psychology. 3rd ed. (Exploration & Application). (Illus.). 700p. 1983. text ed. 22.95 (ISBN 0-314-69642-3); tchrs.' manual avail. (ISBN 0-314-71085-X); study guide avail. (ISBN 0-314-71086-8). West Pub.

De Boer, Theo. Foundations of Critical Psychology. Plantinga, Theodore, tr. 196p. 1982. text ed. 16.50x (ISBN 0-8207-0158-0). Duquesne.

Dember, William N. & Jenkins, James J. General Psychology: The Science of Behavior & Experience. 2nd ed. 700p. 1983. text ed. write for info. (ISBN 0-697-06654-1); write for info. student study guide (ISBN 0-697-06655-X); write for info. instr's manual (ISBN 0-697-06656-8). L Erlbaum Assocs.

Discovering the Human Mind. LC 81-52417. (Discovering Science Ser.). lib. bdg. 15.96 (ISBN 0-86706-060-3, Pub. by Stonehenge). Silver.

Evans, Idella M. & Murdoff, Ron. Psychology for a Changing World. 2nd ed. LC 77-13677. 596p. 1978. text ed. 23.95 (ISBN 0-471-24872-X); tchrs. manual 4.00 (ISBN 0-471-03754-0). Wiley.

Felner, Robert D. & Jason, Leonard A., eds. Preventive Psychology: Theory, Research & Practice. 475p. 1983. 19.50 (ISBN 0-08-026340-2). Pergamon.

Fransella, Fay. Psychology for Occupational Therapists. Chapman, Antony & Gale, Anthony, eds. (Psychology for Professional Groups Ser.). 300p. 1982. 49.00x (ISBN 0-333-31859-5, Pub. by Macmillan England). State Mutual Bk.

Glaros & Coleman, James C. Contemporary Psychology & Effective Behavior. 5th ed. 1983. text ed. 22.95x (ISBN 0-673-15640-0). Scott F.

Gleitman, Henry. Basic Psychology. 500p. 1982. text ed. 21.95x (ISBN 0-393-95254-1); write for info. instr's manual; study guide 8.95x (ISBN 0-393-95261-4); write for info. test item file. Norton.

Goleman, Dan & Freedman, Johnathan. What Psychology Knows That Everyone Should. new paperback ed. (Illus.). 256p. 1983. pap. 8.95 (ISBN 0-86616-011-6). Lewis Pub Co.

Guggenbuehl-Craig, A. Macht als Gefahr beim Helfer. 4th ed. (Psychologische Praxis: Vol. 45). vi, 106p. 1982. pap. 11.50 (ISBN 3-8055-3664-X). S Karger.

Hall, John. Psychology for Nurses & Health Visitors. Chapman, Antony & Gale, Anthony, eds. (Psychology for Professional Groups Ser.). 320p. 1982. 49.00x (ISBN 0-333-31863-3, Pub. by Macmillan England). State Mutual Bk.

Hillman, James. Archetypal Psychology: A Brief Account. 88p. (Orig.). 1983. pap. 7.50 (ISBN 0-88214-321-2). Spring Pubns.

Holdswoth, Ruth. Psychology for Careers Counselling. Chapman, Antony & Gale, Anthony, eds. (Psychology for Professional Groups Ser.). 320p. 1982. 49.00x (ISBN 0-333-31864-1, Pub. by Macmillan England). State Mutual Bk.

James, William. Essays in Psychology. Burkhardt, Frederick & Bowers, Fredson, eds. (The Works of William James: Eleventh Title: Vol. 13). (Illus.). 512p. 1983. text ed. 40.00x (ISBN 0-674-26714-1). Harvard U Pr.

Koteskey, Ronald L. General Psychology for Christian Counselors. 308p. (Orig.). 1983. pap. 10.95 (ISBN 0-687-14044-7). Abingdon.

Lahey, Benjamin B. Psychology: An Introduction. 640p. 1983. text ed. write for info. (ISBN 0-697-06560-X); instrs' manual avail. (ISBN 0-697-06562-6); study guide avail. (ISBN 0-697-06561-8). Wm C Brown.

Lichtenberg, Joseph D. & Kaplan, Samuel, eds. Reflections on Self Psychology. 1983. text ed. write for info. (ISBN 0-88163-001-2). L Erlbaum Assocs.

Linden, W. Psychologishe Perspektiven des Bluthodrucks. (Illus.). vi, 130p. 1983. 47.50 (ISBN 3-8055-3642-9). S Karger.

Lu, Hsien, ed. Major Topics & Issues in Psychology: Scientific Studies in Behavioral Development. 97p. 1972. 14.95x (ISBN 0-8422-0165-3). Irvington.

Mc Curdy, Harold G. Personality of Shakespeare: A Venture in Psychological Method. 1953. text ed. 12.50x (ISBN 0-686-83695-2). Elliots Bks.

McGinn, Colin. The Character of Mind. 144p. 1982. 19.95 (ISBN 0-19-219171-3); pap. 7.50 (ISBN 0-19-289159-6). Oxford U Pr.

Maher, Michael. Psychology. (Stonyhurst Philosophical Ser.). 608p. 1982. pap. text ed. 5.95x (ISBN 0-87343-051-4). Magi Bks.

Malott, Richard W. & Whaley, Donald. Pyschology. 680p. text ed. 19.95 (ISBN 0-918452-43-0). Learning Pubs.

Page, Earle C. Looking at Type. (Illus.). 1983. Comb Bdg. 5.00 (ISBN 0-935652-09-4). Ctr Applications Psych.

Purser, Harry. Psychology for Speech Therapists. Chapman, Antony & Gale, Anthony, eds. (Psychology for Professional Groups Ser.). 300p. 1982. 49.00x (ISBN 0-333-31855-2, Pub. by Macmillan England). State Mutual Bk.

Roberts, Richard. Tales for Jung Folk: Original Fairytales for All Ages Illustrating C. G. Jung's Archetypes of the Collective Unconscious. (Illus.). 175p. (Orig.). 1983. pap. 9.95 (ISBN 0-942380-01-0). Vernal Equinox.

Robinson, Edward S. & Robinson, Florence R. Readings in General Psychology. 812p. 1982. Repr. of 1923 ed. lib. bdg. 85.00 (ISBN 0-89984-848-6). Century Bookbindery.

Rosenzweig, M. R. & Porter, L. W., eds. Annual Review of Psychology, Vol. 34. LC 50-13143. (Illus.). 1983. text ed. 27.00 (ISBN 0-8243-0234-6). Annual Reviews.

Rubin, Zick & McNeil, Elton B. The Psychology of Being Human. 3rd, brief update ed. 544p. 1983. pap. text ed. 18.95 scp (ISBN 0-06-045649-3, HarpC); instr's manual avail. (ISBN 0-06-364212-3); test bank avail. (ISBN 0-06-364213-1); scp study guide 6.00 (ISBN 0-06-044308-1). Har-Row.

Wainer, Howard & Messick, Samuel, eds. Principles of Modern Psychological Measurement: A Festschrift for Frederic M. Lord. 366p. 1983. text ed. price not set (ISBN 0-89859-277-1). L Erlbaum Assocs.

Weaver, Donald B. & Baird, Julia L. How to Do a Literature Search in Psychology. (Illus.). 56p. (Orig.). 1982. pap. text ed. 6.95 (ISBN 0-9609182-0-5). Resource Pr.

Wilm, Emil C. Theories of Instinct. 1925. text ed. 39.50x (ISBN 0-686-83818-1). Elliots Bks.

Worchel, Stephen. Psychology: Principles & Applications. (Illus.). 672p. 1983. text ed. 22.95 (ISBN 0-13-732453-7). P-H.

Zilbergeld, Bernie. The Shrinking of America: Myths of Psychological Change. 1983. 16.50i (ISBN 0-316-98794-8); 16.50. Little.

PSYCHOLOGY–ADDRESSES, ESSAYS, LECTURES

Detloff, Virginia. Index to Spring: An Annual of Archetypal Psychology & Jungian Thought, 1941-1979. 70p. 1983. pap. write for info. (ISBN 0-88214-018-3). Spring Pubns.

Flammer, A. & Kintsch, W., eds. Discourse Processing: An Edited Selection of Papers Presented at the International Symposium, Fribourg, Switzerland. (Advances in Psychology Ser.: Vol. 8). 614p. 1982. 66.00 (ISBN 0-444-86515-2, North Holland). Elsevier.

James, William. Talks to Teachers on Psychology: And to Students on Some of Life's Ideals. Burkhardt, Frederick & Bowers, Redson, eds. (Works of William James: Tenth Title). (Illus.). 384p. 1983. text ed. 25.00x (ISBN 0-674-86785-8). Harvard U Pr.

Sutherland, Norman S. Tutorial Essays in Psychology, Vol. 1. 182p. 1977. text ed. 19.95 (ISBN 0-89859-199-6). L Erlbaum Assocs.

PSYCHOLOGY–BIBLIOGRAPHY

Publication Manual of the American Psychological Association. 3rd ed. 160p. 1983. pap. 15.00 (ISBN 0-912704-57-8). Am Psychol.

Research Libraries of the New York Public Library & Library of Congress. Bibliographic Guide to Psychology: 1982. 1983. lib. bdg. 95.00 (ISBN 0-8161-6979-9, Biblio Guides). G K Hall.

PSYCHOLOGY–DICTIONARIES

Wolman, Benjamin B., ed. Progress: Vol. I of the International Encyclpedia of Psychiatry, Psychology, Psychoanalysis & Neurology. 1983. 89.00 (ISBN 0-918228-28-X). Aesculapius Pubs.

PSYCHOLOGY–EXAMINATIONS, QUESTIONS, ETC.

Rudman, Jack. Psychologist Trainee. (Career Examination Ser.: C-2621). (Cloth bdg. avail. on request). pap. 10.00 (ISBN 0-8373-2621-4). Natl Learning.

--Psychology Assistant I. (Career Examination Ser.: C-919). (Cloth bdg. avail. on request). pap. 10.00 (ISBN 0-8373-0919-0). Natl Learning.

--Psychology Assistant II. (Career Examination Ser.: C-921). (Cloth bdg. avail. on request). pap. 12.00 (ISBN 0-8373-0921-2). Natl Learning.

--Psychology Assistant III. (Career Examination Ser.: C-933). (Cloth bdg. avail. on request). pap. 14.00 (ISBN 0-8373-0922-0). Natl Learning.

PSYCHOLOGY–EXPERIMENTS

see also Psychology, Experimental

Underwood, Benton J. Experimentation in Psychology. corrected ed. 244p. 1983. Repr. of 1975 ed. text ed. price not set (ISBN 0-89874-605-1). Krieger.

PSYCHOLOGY–HISTORY

Bjork, Daniel W. The Compromised Scientist: William James in the Development of American Psychology. (Illus.). 224p. 1983. text ed. 25.00 (ISBN 0-231-05500-5); pap. 12.00 (ISBN 0-231-05501-3). Columbia U Pr.

Dennis, Wayne & Skinner, B. F. Current Trends in Psychology. 225p. 1982. Repr. of 1947 ed. lib. bdg. 45.00 (ISBN 0-8495-1141-0). Arden Lib.

Smith, Samuel. Ideas of the Great Psychologists. LC 82-48135. 224p. 1983. pap. 6.68 (ISBN 0-06-463561-9, EH 561, EH). Har-Row.

--Ideas of the Great Psychologists. LC 82-48135. 304p. 1983. 14.34i (ISBN 0-06-015087-4, HarpT). Har-Row.

PSYCHOLOGY–JUVENILE LITERATURE

Kerr, M. E. Me Me Me Me Me: Not a Novel. LC 82-48521. (A Charlotte Zolotow Bk.). 224p. (YA) (gr. 7 up). 1983. 9.57i (ISBN 0-06-023192-0, HarpJ); PLB 9.89g (ISBN 0-06-023193-9). Har-Row.

PSYCHOLOGY–METHODOLOGY

Fine, Reuben. The Logic of Psychology: A Dynamic Approach. LC 82-21983. 232p. (Orig.). 1983. lib. bdg. 20.50 (ISBN 0-8191-2891-0); pap. text ed. 10.50 (ISBN 0-8191-2892-9). U Pr of Amer.

Peele, Stanton. The Science of Experience: A Direction for Psychology. LC 81-48555. 1983. price not set (ISBN 0-669-05420-8). Lexington Bks.

Runyan, William M. Life Histories & Psychobiography: Explorations in Theory & Method. (Illus.). 304p. 1982. 19.95 (ISBN 0-19-503189-X). Oxford U Pr.

Walker, C. E., ed. The Handbook of Clinical Psychology: Theory, Research & Practice, Vol. I. (The Dorsey Professional Ser.). 425p. 1983. 35.00 (ISBN 0-87094-319-7). Dow Jones-Irwin.

--The Handbook of Clinical Psychology: Theory, Research & Practice, Vol. II. (The Dorsey Professional Ser.). 425p. 1983. 35.00 (ISBN 0-87094-411-8). Dow Jones-Irwin.

PSYCHOLOGY–PERIODICALS

Osier, Donald V. & Wozniak, Robert H. A Century of Serial Publications in Psychology, 1850-1950; An International Bibliography. (Bibliographies in the History of Psychology & Psychiatry Ser.). (Orig.). 1983. lib. bdg. 90.00 (ISBN 0-527-98196-6). Kraus Intl.

PSYCHOLOGY–PROGRAMMED INSTRUCTION

Chapman, A. & Gale, A. Psychology & People. (Psychology for Professional Groups Ser.). 528p. 1982. text ed. 27.75x (ISBN 0-333-33145-1, Pub. by Macmillan England); pap. text ed. 13.00x (ISBN 0-333-33147-8). Humanities.

PSYCHOLOGY–RESEARCH

see Psychological Research

PSYCHOLOGY–STUDY AND TEACHING

Seifert, Kelvin. Educational Psychology. 464p. 1982. pap. text ed. 18.95 (ISBN 0-395-32790-3); write for info. tchr's. manual (ISBN 0-395-32791-1); study guide 6.95 (ISBN 0-395-33183-8). HM.

Tauraso, Nicola M. & Batzler, L. Richard. Manual of Positive Attitude Training Techniques for Children & Young Adults. 1982. 25.00 (ISBN 0-935710-03-5). Hidden Valley.

PSYCHOLOGY, ABNORMAL

see Psychology, Pathological

PSYCHOLOGY, APPLIED

Here are entered general works on the application of psychology in various fields such as industry, advertising, military life. Works on applied psychology intended as guides to successful personal development are entered under such headings as Success and Personality.

see also Behavior Modification; Change (Psychology); Childbirth–Psychology; Clinical Psychology; Counseling; Human Engineering; Interpersonal Relations; Interviewing; Negotiation; Persuasion (Psychology); Psychological Warfare; Psychology, Industrial; School Psychologists

also subdivision Psychological Aspects under specific subjects, e.g. Economics–Psychological Aspects

Cooper, Cary. Psychology & Management. (Psychology for Professional Groups Ser.). 275p. 1981. text ed. 25.00x (ISBN 0-333-31856-0, Pub. by Macmillan England); pap. text ed. 10.95x (ISBN 0-333-31875-7). Humanities.

Dunkin, Naomi. Psychology for Physiotherapists. (Psychology for Professional Groups Ser.). 350p. 1981. text ed. 25.00x (ISBN 0-333-31857-9, Pub. by Macmillan England); pap. text ed. 10.95x (ISBN 0-333-31884-6). Humanities.

Fontana, David. Psychology for Teachers. (Psychology for Professional Groups Ser.). 350p. 1981. text ed. 25.00x (ISBN 0-333-31858-7, Pub. by Macmillan England); pap. text ed. 10.95x (ISBN 0-333-31880-3). Humanities.

Fransella, Fay. Psychology for Occupational Therapists. (Psychology for Professional Groups Ser.). 320p. 1982. text ed. 25.00x (ISBN 0-333-31859-5, Pub. by Macmillan England); pap. text ed. 10.95x (ISBN 0-333-31883-8). Humanities.

Griffiths, David. Psychology & Medicine. (Psychology for Professional Groups Ser.). 320p. 1981. text ed. 25.00x (ISBN 0-333-31862-5, Pub. by Macmillan England); pap. text ed. 10.95x (ISBN 0-333-31877-3). Humanities.

Hall, John. Psychology for Nurses & Health Visitors. (Psychology for Professional Groups Ser.). 320p. 1982. text ed. 25.00x (ISBN 0-333-31863-3, Pub. by Macmillan England); pap. text ed. 10.95x (ISBN 0-333-31876-5). Humanities.

Herbert, Martin. Psychology for Social Workers. (Psychology for Professional Groups Ser.). 350p. 1981. text ed. 25.00x (ISBN 0-333-31866-8, Pub. by Macmillan England); pap. text ed. 10.95x (ISBN 0-333-31878-1). Humanities.

Holdsworth, Ruth. Psychology for Careers Counseling. (Psychology for Professional Groups Ser.). 320p. 1982. text ed. 23.25x (ISBN 0-333-31864-1, Pub. by Macmillan England); pap. text ed. 9.25x (ISBN 0-333-31881-1). Humanities.

Purser, Harry. Psychology for Speech Therapists. (Psychology for Professional Groups Ser.). 300p. 1982. text ed. 22.25x (ISBN 0-333-31855-2, Pub. by Macmillan England); pap. text ed. 19.25x (ISBN 0-333-31885-4). Humanities.

Study Guide & Personal Explorations for Psychology Applied to Modern Life: Adjustment in the 80's. (Psychology Ser.). 182p. 1982. pap. 7.95 (ISBN 0-534-01206-X). Brooks-Cole.

Williams, Robert L. & Long, James D. Toward a Self-Managed Life Style. 3rd ed. LC 82-81112. 288p. 1982. pap. text ed. 12.95 (ISBN 0-395-32590-0); write for info. instr's manual (ISBN 0-395-32591-9). HM.

PSYCHOLOGY, CHILD

see Child Psychology

PSYCHOLOGY, CLINICAL

see Clinical Psychology

PSYCHOLOGY, COMPARATIVE

see also Animals, Habits and Behavior of; Human Behavior; Instinct; Play; Sociobiology

Rajecki, D. W. Comparing Behavior: Studying Man Studying Animals. 304p. 1983. write for info. (ISBN 0-89859-259-3). L Erlbaum Assocs.

PSYCHOLOGY, CRIMINAL

see Criminal Psychology

PSYCHOLOGY, DEVELOPMENTAL

see Developmental Psychology

PSYCHOLOGY, EDUCATIONAL

see Educational Psychology

PSYCHOLOGY, ETHNIC

see Ethnopsychology

PSYCHOLOGY, EXPERIMENTAL

Andreas, Burton G. Experimental Psychology. 2nd ed. LC 78-171910. 608p. 1972. text ed. 29.95 (ISBN 0-471-02905-X). Wiley.

McGuigan, F. J. Experimental Psychology: Methods of Research. 4th ed. (Illus.). 416p. 1983. 23.95 (ISBN 0-13-295188-6). P-H.

PSYCHOLOGY, FORENSIC

see also Criminal Psychology; Evidence (Law); Forensic Psychiatry

Bartol, Curt R. Psychology & American Law. 384p. 1982. text ed. 22.95x (ISBN 0-534-01217-5). Wadsworth Pub.

Wines, Frederick H. Punishment & Reformation. (Historical Foundations of Forensic Psychiatry & Psychology Ser.). xii, 481p. 1983. Repr. of 1919 ed. lib. bdg. 45.00 (ISBN 0-306-76184-X). Da Capo.

PSYCHOLOGY, GENETIC

see Genetic Psychology

PSYCHOLOGY, INDUSTRIAL

see also Industrial Sociology

Argyris, Chris. Integrating the Individual & the Organization. LC 64-13209. 330p. 1964. 31.95x (ISBN 0-471-03315-4). Wiley.

Hill, N. C. Counseling at the Workplace. Date not set. 15.95 (ISBN 0-07-028785-6). McGraw.

Mankin, Don & Ames, Russell E., Jr., eds. Classics of Industrial & Organizational Psychology. LC 80-15699. (Classics Ser.). (Orig.). 1980. pap. 12.50x (ISBN 0-935610-11-1). Moore Pub IL.

Oshry, Barry. Controlling the Contexts of Consciousness: The I, the We, the All of Us. LC 75-9952. (Notes on Power Ser.). (Orig.). 1976. pap. 2.75 (ISBN 0-910411-02-6). Power & Sys.

Toch, Hans & Grant, J. Douglas. Change Through Participation: Humanizing Human Service Settings. (Library of Social Research). (Illus.). 240p. 1982. 22.00 (ISBN 0-8039-1886-0); pap. 10.95 (ISBN 0-8039-1887-9). Sage.

Vance, Charles C. Manager Today, Executive Tomorrow. LC 82-14865. 240p. 1983. Repr. of 1974 ed. lib. bdg. write for info. (ISBN 0-89874-554-3). Krieger.

PSYCHOLOGY, JURISTIC

see Psychology, Forensic

PSYCHOLOGY, LEGAL

see Psychology, Forensic

PSYCHOLOGY, NATIONAL

see Ethnopsychology

PSYCHOLOGY, PATHOLOGICAL

see also Aphasia; Clinical Psychology; Criminal Psychology; Culture Conflict; Depression, Mental; Fantasy; Hysteria; Manic-Depressive Psychoses; Medicine, Psychosomatic; Mental Health; Mental Illness; Narcissism; Neuroses; Personality, Disorders Of; Psychiatric Social Work; Psychiatry; Psychoanalysis; Psychology, Forensic; Rorschach Test; Subconsciousness

Flor-Henry. Cerebral Bases of Psychopathology. 1983. text ed. 40.00 (ISBN 0-7236-7034-X). Wright-PSG.

Halpern, James & Halpern, Ilsa. Projections: Our World of Imaginary Relationships. 192p. 1983. 13.95 (ISBN 0-399-31017-7). Seaview Bks.

Lawton, Susan. Hysterical Fugue. 1983. pap. 5.00 (ISBN 0-937998-07-9). Devin.

Maas, James W., ed. MHPG (3-Methoxy 4-Hydroxyphenethyle Neglycol) Basic Mechansims & Psychopathology. LC 82-11640. (Behavioral Biology Ser.). Date not set. price not set (ISBN 0-12-462920-2). Acad Pr.

Matson, Johnny L. & Barrett, Rowland P., eds. Psychopathology in the Mentally Retarded. Date not set. price not set (ISBN 0-8089-1511-8). Grune.

Maudsley, Henry. The Pathology of Mind. Lewis, Aubrey, ed. (Classics of Psychology & Psychiatry Ser.). 608p. 1983. Repr. of 1867 ed. write for info. (ISBN 0-904014-42-8). F Pinter Pubs.

Miller, John W. In Defense of the Psychological. 1983. 20.00 (ISBN 0-393-01701-X). Norton.

Millon, Therodore. Modern Psychopathology: A Biosocial Approach to Maladaptive Learning & Functioning. (Illus.). 681p. 1983. Repr. of 1969 ed. text ed. 29.95x (ISBN 0-88133-020-5). Waveland Pr.

Schumer, Florence. Abnormal Psychology. 768p. Date not set. 23.95 (ISBN 0-686-82412-1); instr's guide 1.95 (ISBN 0-669-05630-8); 8.95 (ISBN 0-669-05628-6). Heath.

PSYCHOLOGY, PATHOLOGICAL–CASES, CLINICAL REPORTS, STATISTICS

see also Psychiatry–Cases, Clinical Reports, Statistics

Spitzer, Robert L. Psychopathology: A Case Book. (Illus.). 320p. 1983. pap. text ed. 12.95 (ISBN 0-07-060350-2, C). McGraw.

PSYCHOLOGY, POLITICAL

see Political Psychology

PSYCHOLOGY, PRACTICAL

see Psychology, Applied

PSYCHOLOGY, PRISON

see Prison Psychology

PSYCHOLOGY, RACIAL

see Ethnopsychology

PSYCHOLOGY, RELIGIOUS

see also Enthusiasm; Experience (Religion); Miracles; Psychology, Applied

American Health Research Institute, Ltd. Religion & Psychology: A Medical Subject Analysis & Research Index with Bibliography. Bartone, John C., ed. 120p. 1983. 29.95 (ISBN 0-88164-034-4); pap. 21.95 (ISBN 0-88164-035-2). ABBE Pubs Assn.

Malony, H. Newton. Wholeness & Holiness: Readings in the Psychology, Theology of Mental Health. 304p. (Orig.). 1983. pap. 12.95 (ISBN 0-8010-6147-4). Baker Bk.

Markell, Jane & Winn, Jane. Overcoming Stress. 1982. pap. 4.50 (ISBN 0-686-82562-4). Victor Bks.

Paloutzian, Raymond F. Invitation to the Psychology of Religion. 1983. pap. text ed. 11.95x (ISBN 0-673-15343-6). Scott F.

Vande Kempe, Hendrika & Malony, H. Newton. Psychology & Theology: A Bibliography of Historical Bases for the Integration of Psychology & Theology. LC 82-49045. (Bibliographies in the History of Psychology & Psychiatry Ser.). (Orig.). 1983. lib. bdg. 65.00 (ISBN 0-527-92779-1). Kraus Intl.

PSYCHOLOGY, SEXUAL

see Sex (Psychology)

PSYCHOLOGY, SOCIAL

see Social Psychology

PSYCHOLOGY, STRUCTURAL

see Gestalt Psychology

PSYCHOLOGY AND RELIGION

see Psychology, Religious

PSYCHOLOGY OF LANGUAGE

see Psycholinguistics

PSYCHOLOGY OF LEARNING

see Learning, Psychology Of

PSYCHOMOTOR TESTS

see Motor Ability–Testing

PSYCHONEUROSES

see Neuroses

PSYCHOPATHOLOGISTS

see Psychiatrists

PSYCHOPATHOLOGY

see Psychology, Pathological

PSYCHOPHARMACOLOGY

see also Hallucinogenic Drugs; Neuro-Psychopharmacology

Bassuk, Ellen L. & Gelenberg, Alan J., eds. The Practitioner's Guide to Psychoactive Drugs. (Topics in General Psychiatry Ser.). 410p. 1983. 27.50x (ISBN 0-306-41093-1, Plenum Pr). Plenum Pub.

Bobon, D., ed. AMDP System in Psychopharmacology. (Modern Problems of Pharmacopsychiatry: Vol. 20). (Illus.). viii, 240p. 1983. 96.00 (ISBN 3-8055-3637-2). S Karger.

Bowers, Joan S. Psychopharmacology for Non-Medical Therapists: A Manual for Psychologists, Social Workers, Counselors & Nurses. 53p. 1981. pap. write for info. Ohio Psych Pub.

Davis, John M. & Maas, James W., eds. The Affective Disorders: Anthology. (Illus.). 320p. 1983. text ed. 25.00 (ISBN 0-88048-002-5). Am Psychiatric.

Grahame-Smith, D. G. & Hippius, H., eds. Psychopharmacology, Vol. 1. 935p. 1982. Part 1: Basic Preclinical Neuropharmacology. 80.75 (ISBN 0-686-84508-0, Excerpta Medica); Part 2: Clinical Psychopharmacology. 85.00 (ISBN 0-686-84509-9); Set. 153.25 (ISBN 0-444-90294-5). Elsevier.

Greenhill, Maurice & Gralnick, Alexander, eds. Psychopharmacology & Psychotherapy. 1982. text ed. write for info. (ISBN 0-02-912780-7). Free Pr.

Iversen, Leslie & Iversen, Susan, eds. Handbook of Psychopharmacology, New Techniques in Psychopharmacology. (Vol. 15). 440p. 1982. 55.00x (ISBN 0-306-40975-5, Plenum Pr). Plenum Pub.

Iversen, Leslie L. & Iversen, Susan D., eds. Handbook of Psychopharmacology: Neuropeptides, Vol. 16. 594p. 1983. 65.00x (ISBN 0-306-41048-6, Plenum Pr). Plenum Pub.

Iversen, Susan D. & Iversen, Leslie L., eds. Handbook of Psychopharmacology: Biochemical Studies of CNS Receptors, Vol. 17. 420p. 1983. 55.00x (ISBN 0-306-41145-8, Plenum Pr). Plenum Pub.

Janke, W, ed. Response Variability to Psychotropic Drugs. (International Series in Experimental Psychology). (Illus.). 272p. 1983. 37.00 (ISBN 0-08-028907-X). Pergamon.

Tyrer. Drugs in Psychiatric Practice. 1982. text ed. 59.95 (ISBN 0-407-02212-0). Butterworth.

Yetiv, Jack & Bianchine, Joseph R. Recent Advances in Clinical Therapeutics: Psychopharmacology, Neuropharmacology, Gastrointestinal Therapeutics. (Vol. 2). write for info (ISBN 0-8089-1542-8). Grune.

PSYCHOPROPHYLACTIC CHILDBIRTH

see Natural Childbirth

PSYCHOSOMATIC DENTISTRY

see Dentistry–Psychological Aspects

PSYCHOSOMATIC DISEASES IN CHILDREN

see Pediatrics–Psychosomatic Aspects

PSYCHOSOMATIC MEDICINE

see Medicine, Psychosomatic

PSYCHOTECHNICS

see Psychology, Industrial

PSYCHOTHERAPY

see also Art Therapy; Autogenic Training; Behavior Therapy; Child Psychotherapy; Group Psychotherapy; Mental Healing; Psychopharmacology; Recreational Therapy; Sex Therapy

Amada, Gerald. A Guide to Psychothearpy. LC 82-21918. (Illus.). 128p. (Orig.). 1983. lib. bdg. 19.25 (ISBN 0-8191-2928-3); pap. text ed. 8.25 (ISBN 0-8191-2929-1). U Pr of Amer.

Bean, Philip. Mental Illness: Changes & Trends. 500p. 1983. 64.95 (ISBN 0-471-10240-7, Pub. by Wiley-Interscience). Wiley.

Belkin, Gary S. Comntemporary Psychotherapies. 1981. pap. 16.50 (ISBN 0-395-30781-3). HM.

Berry, Patricia. Echo's Subtle Body: Contributions to an Archetypal Psychology. LC 82-19506. 198p. (Orig.). 1982. pap. 9.00 (ISBN 0-88214-313-1). Spring Pubns.

Beutler, Larry E. Eclectic Psychotherapy: A Systematic Approach. (General Psychology Ser.: No. 118). 270p. 1983. 26.00 (ISBN 0-08-028842-1). Pergamon.

Bloch, Sidney. What is Psychotherapy? 208p. 1983. text ed. 18.95x (ISBN 0-19-219154-3). Oxford U Pr.

--What is Psychotherapy? 208p. 1983. pap. 7.95 (ISBN 0-19-289142-1, GB 734, GB). Oxford U Pr.

Cohen, Ronald J. & Maiano, William E. Legal Guidebook in Mental Health. (Illus.). 624p. 1982. text ed. 39.95 (ISBN 0-02-905740-X). Free Pr.

Decker, Robert J. Effective Psychotherapy: The Silent Dialog. 76p. 1982. softcover 5.95 (ISBN 0-932930-51-4). Pilgrimage Inc.

Everstine, Diana S. & Everstine, Louis. People in Crisis: Strategic Therapeutic Interventions. 256p. 1983. 20.00 (ISBN 0-87630-286-X). Brunner-Mazel.

Fensterheim, Herbert & Glazer, Howard I., eds. Behavioral Psychotherapy: Basic Principles & Case Studies in an Integrative Clinical Model. 220p. 1983. 20.00 (ISBN 0-87630-325-4). Brunner-Mazel.

Flefenheimer, Walter V. Techniques of Brief Psychotherapy. LC 82-13891. 224p. 1982. write for info. (ISBN 0-87668-460-6). Aronson.

Ford, Donald H. & Urban, Hugh B. Systems of Psychotherapy: A Comparative Study. LC 63-20630. 712p. 1963. 42.95x (ISBN 0-471-26580-2). Wiley.

Garfield, Sol. L. Psychotherapy: An Eclectic Approach. LC 79-17724. (Personality Processes Ser.). 1980. 25.95x (ISBN 0-471-04490-3, Pub. by Wiley-Interscience). Wiley.

Garfield, Sol L. & Bergin, Allen E. Handbook of Psychotherapy & Behavior Change: An Empirical Analysis. 2nd ed. LC 78-8526. 1978. text ed. 60.95x (ISBN 0-471-29178-1). Wiley.

Gelso, Charles J. & Johnson, Deborah H. Explorations in Time-Limited Counseling & Therapy. (Guidance & Counseling Ser.). 300p. 1983. text ed. 25.95x (ISBN 0-8077-2726-1). Tchrs Coll.

Goleman, Daniel & Speeth, Kathleen. The Essential Psychothempies. 1982. pap. 3.95 (ISBN 0-451-62083-6, ME2083, Ment). NAL.

Greenberg, Harvey. Hanging In: What You Need to Know About Psychotherapy. 1982. 12.95 (ISBN 0-686-38403-2). Four Winds Pr.

Greenhill, Maurice & Gralnick, Alexander, eds. Psychopharmacology & Psychotherapy. 1982. text ed. write for info. (ISBN 0-02-912780-7). Free Pr.

Haldane, J. D. & Alexander, D. A., eds. Models for Psychotherapy: A Primer. 96p. 1982. pap. 9.00 (ISBN 0-08-028446-9). Pergamon.

Hariman, Jusuf. The Therapeutic Efficacy of the Major Psychotherapeutic Techniques. (Illus.). 344p. 1983. 29.50x (ISBN 0-398-04771-5). C C Thomas.

Harper, Frederick D. & Bruce, Gail C. Counseling Techniques: An Outline & Overview. 270p. 1983. pap. text ed. price not set (ISBN 0-935392-04-1). Douglas Pubs.

Kadushin, Phineas. This Is Psychotherapy: For Those Considering It, For Those Involved in It, & for the Curious. LC 82-61943. 320p. 1983. 16.95 (ISBN 0-9610000-0-7). Tip-Top.

Klerman, Gerald & Weissman, Myrna. Interpersonal Psychotherapy of Depression. 1983. text ed. 20.95x (ISBN 0-465-03396-2). Basic.

Lager, Eric & Zwerling, Isreal. Psychotherapy in the Community. Gardner, Alvjn F., ed. (Allied Health Professions Monograph Ser.). 1983. write for info. (ISBN 0-87527-315-7). Green.

Lambert, Michael J. & Christensen, Edwin R. The Assessment of Psychotherapy Outcome. (Personality Processes Ser.). 600p. 1983. 39.95 (ISBN 0-471-08383-6, Pub. by Wiley-Interscience). Wiley.

Mahrer, Alvin R. Experiential Psychotherapy: Basic Practices. 400p. 1983. 27.50 (ISBN 0-87630-318-1). Brunner-Mazel.

Mintz, Elizabeth & Schmeidler, R. The Psychic Thread: Paranormal & Transpersonal Aspects of Psychotherapy. 240p. 1983. 24.95 (ISBN 0-89885-139-4). Human Sci Pr.

Murray, Joan & Abramson, Paul. Bias in Psychotherapy. 412p. 1983. 38.00 (ISBN 0-03-063226-9). Praeger.

Owensby, Lou R. & Covington, Faison. Wonderful Letters to a Therapist. 151p. 1982. pap. 5.95 (ISBN 0-9609462-0-9). Meridian Pr.

Perkins, William. General Principles of Therapy: Current Therapy of Communication Disorders, Vol. 1. (Illus.). 80p. 1982. 10.95 (ISBN 0-86577-077-8). Thieme-Stratton.

Renshaw, Domeena C. Incest: Understanding & Treatment. 1982. text ed. 17.95 (ISBN 0-316-74031-4). Little.

Reynolds, David K. Naikin Psychotherapy: Meditation for Self-Development. LC 82-21862. 184p. 1983. 15.00x (ISBN 0-226-71029-7). U of Chicago Pr.

Rosenbaum, Max, ed. Handbook of Short-Term Therapy Groups. 448p. 1983. 34.95 (ISBN 0-07-053712-7, P&RB). McGraw.

Ryle, Anthony. Psychotherapy: A Cognitive Integration of Theory & Practice. 196p. 1982. 22.00 (ISBN 0-8089-1488-X). Grune.

Shainberg, Diane. Healing in Psychotherapy: The Process of Holistic Change. 170p. 1983. 37.50 (ISBN 0-677-06100-5). Gordon.

Shorr, Joseph E. Psychotherapy Through Imagery. 2nd ed. (Illus.). 216p. 1983. write for info. (ISBN 0-86577-083-2). Thieme-Stratton.

Small, Jacquelyn. Transformers: The Therapists of the Future. 2nd ed. (Illus.). 325p. 1983. pap. 9.95 (ISBN 0-939344-01-7). Eupsychian.

Steere, David A. Bodily Expressions in Psychotherapy. (Illus.). 352p. 1983. 25.00 (ISBN 0-87630-322-X). Brunner-Mazel.

Tapia, Fernando. The Magic Rooster: A Shortcut to Self-Psychotherapy. Martin, Sara H., ed. 1983. 6.95 (ISBN 0-533-05549-0). Vantage.

Weiner, Myron F. The Psychotherapeutic Impasse. 1982. text ed. 19.95 (ISBN 0-02-934620-7). Free Pr.

--Therapist Disclosure: The Use of Self in Psychotherapy. 2nd ed. 1983. 24.95 (ISBN 0-8391-1792-2, 19135). Univ Park.

PSYCHOTHERAPY–RESEARCH

see Psychiatric Research

PSYCHOTIC CHILDREN

see Mentally Ill Children

PSYCHOTROPIC DRUGS

see Psychopharmacology

PTERIDINES

Wachter, H. & Curtius, H. C., eds. Biochemical & Clinical Aspects of Pteridines, Vol. 1. (Illus.). 373p. 1982. 75.00x (ISBN 0-686-82599-3). De Gruyter.

PTERIDOPHYTA

see also Ferns

Page, C. N. The Ferns of Britain & Ireland. LC 82-1126. (Illus.). 450p. Date not set. price not set (ISBN 0-521-23213-9); pap. price not set (ISBN 0-521-29872-5). Cambridge U Pr.

PUBLIC ACCOUNTANTS

see Accountants

PUBLIC ACCOUNTING

see Finance, Public–Accounting

PUBLIC ADMINISTRATION

Here are entered works on the principles and techniques involved in the conduct of public business. Works descriptive of governmental machinery are entered under the area concerned, with the subdivision Politics and Government.

see also Administrative Agencies; Administrative Law; Bureaucracy; Civil Service; Decentralization in Government; Governmental Investigations; Impeachments; Intelligence Service; Personnel Management; Public Records; Trade-Unions–Political Activity

also subdivision Politics and Government under names of countries, cities, etc.

Baber, Walter F. Organizing the Future: Matrix Models for the Postindustrial Polity. (Illus.). 176p. 1983. text ed. 16.50 (ISBN 0-8173-0123-2). U of Ala Pr.

Boes, D., et al, eds. Public Production: International Seminar in Public Economics, Bonn, FRG 1981. (Journal of Economics Supplementum: Vol. 2). (Illus.). 222p. 1983. pap. 62.00 (ISBN 0-387-81726-3). Springer-Verlag.

Chase, Gordon & Reveal, Betsy. How to Manage in the Public Sector. 192p. 1983. pap. text ed. 9.95 (ISBN 0-201-10127-0). A-W.

Cooper, Phillip J. Public Law & Public Administration. 474p. 1983. text ed. 21.95 (ISBN 0-87484-526-2). Mayfield Pub.

Dror, Yehezkel. Public Policymaking Reexamined. (Illus.). 420p. 1983. pap. text ed. 19.95 (ISBN 0-87855-928-0). Transaction Bks.

Fesler, James W., ed. American Public Administration: Pattern of the Past. (PAR Classics Ser.: Vol. IV). 1982. write for info. (ISBN 0-936678-05-4). Am Soc Pub Admin.

Golembiewski & Gibson. Readings in Public Administration: Institutions, Processes, Behavior, Policy. 4th ed. 1982. 17.95 (ISBN 0-686-84649-4). HM.

Golembiewski, Robert T. & Gibson, Frank. Readings in Public Administration: Institutions, Processes, Behavior, Policy. 4th ed. LC 82-81584. 544p. 1982. pap. text ed. 14.50 (ISBN 0-395-32765-2). HM.

Golembiewski, Robert T. & White, Michael. Cases in Public Management. 4th ed. LC 82-81583. 336p. 1982. pap. text ed. 11.50 (ISBN 0-395-32767-9). HM.

Gortner, Harold J. Administration in the Public Sector. 2nd ed. LC 80-19757. 413p. 1981. text ed. 19.95 (ISBN 0-471-06320-7). Wiley.

Hage, George & Dennis, Everette. New Strategies for Public Affairs Reporting: Investigation & Research. 2nd ed. (Illus.). 336p. 1983. text ed. 18.95 (ISBN 0-13-615740-8). P-H.

Hatry, Harry, et al. Efficiency Measurement for Local Government Services: Some Initial Suggestions. 204p. pap. text ed. 6.50 (ISBN 0-87766-266-5). Urban Inst.

Hatry, Harry P., et al. Practical Program Evaluation for State & Local Governments. 2nd ed. LC 81-51346. 124p. 1981. pap. text ed. 7.50 (ISBN 0-87766-296-7, URI 32100). Urban Inst.

Hogwood, Brian & Peters, Guy. Policy Dynamics. LC 82-10330. 304p. 1982. 27.50x (ISBN 0-312-62014-4). St Martin.

Hoos, Ida R. Systems Analysis in Public Policy: A Critique. rev. ed. LC 82-48766. 320p. 1983. text ed. 30.00x (ISBN 0-520-04953-5); pap. 8.95x (ISBN 0-520-04952-7). U of Cal Pr.

Jewell, Don. Public Assembly Facilities: Planning & Management. LC 77-16524. 208p. Repr. of 1978 ed. text ed. 28.95 (ISBN 0-471-02437-6). Krieger.

Klingner. Public Administration: A Management Approach. 1982. 16.95 (ISBN 0-686-84652-4); supplementary materials avail. HM.

Klingner, Donald. Public Administration: A Management Approach. 432p. 1983. text ed. 16.95 (ISBN 0-395-32796-2); instrs.' manual avail. (ISBN 0-395-32797-0). HM.

McKinney, Jerome B. & Howard, Lawrence C. Public Administration: Balancing Power & Accountability. LC 79-12796. (Orig.). 1979. pap. 12.50x (ISBN 0-935610-06-5). Moore Pub IL.

Martin, Shan. Managing Without Managers: Alternative Work Arrangements in Public Organizations. (Sage Library of Social Research). (Illus.). 176p. 1983. 22.00 (ISBN 0-8039-1960-3); pap. 10.95 (ISBN 0-8039-1961-1). Sage.

Mertins, Herman & Hennigan, Patrick J., eds. Applying Professional Standards & Ethics in the Eighties: A Workbook Study Guide for Public Administrators. Date not set. price not set (ISBN 0-936678-04-6). Am Soc Pub Admin.

Neugarten, Dail A. Improving Productivity in Public Organizations. 175p. 1983. 19.50 (ISBN 0-08-028813-8); pap. 8.95 (ISBN 0-08-028812-X). Pergamon.

Nigro, Felix A. & Nigro, Lloyd G. Readings in Public Administration. 512p. 1983. pap. text ed. 11.50 scp (ISBN 0-06-044845-8, HarpC). Har-Row.

Public Agency Communication: Theory & Practice. (Illus.). 256p. 1983. 23.95 (ISBN 0-88229-742-2). Nelson-Hall.

Quinn, T. A. & Salzman, Ed. California Public Administration. 2nd ed. (Illus.). 120p. 1982. pap. 4.95 (ISBN 0-930302-51-6). Cal Journal.

Rosenbloom. Public Adminstration & Law. (Public Adminstration Public Policy Ser.). 280p. 1983. 27.50 (ISBN 0-8247-1791-0). Dekker.

Rudman, Jack. Senior Public Information Assistant. (Career Examination Ser.: C-2957). (Cloth bdg. avail. on reques). pap. 12.00 (ISBN 0-8373-2957-4). Natl Learning.

Shafritz, Jay M. & Hyde, Albert C., eds. Classics of Public Administration. LC 78-6950. (Classics Ser.). (Orig.). 1978. pap. 12.50x (ISBN 0-935610-00-6). Moore Pub IL.

Tummala, Krishna K., ed. Administrative Systems Abroad. LC 82-16130. (Illus.). 386p. 1983. lib. bdg. 25.50 (ISBN 0-8191-2734-5); pap. text ed. 14.00 (ISBN 0-8191-2735-3). U Pr of Amer.

Weeks, J. Devereux. Personal Liability of Public Officials Under Federal Law. LC 80-13271. 17p. 1981. pap. 3.25 (ISBN 0-89854-068-2). U of GA Inst Govt.

White, Anthony G. Basic Texts in Public Administration: A Selected Bibliography. 8p. 1978. pap. 1.50 (ISBN 0-686-37410-X). Vance Biblios.

Wildavsky, Aaron, ed. The Policy Organization. (Managing Information Ser.: Vol. 5). (Illus.). 224p. 1983. 25.00 (ISBN 0-8039-1912-3); pap. 12.50 (ISBN 0-8039-1913-1). Sage.

PUBLIC ADMINISTRATION–BIBLIOGRAPHY

Vance Bibliographies. Index to Public Administration: Bibliography P 877- P 1116 (January 1982-December 1982) (Public Administration Ser.). 78p. 1983. pap. 12.00 (ISBN 0-88066-347-2). Vance Biblios.

Vance Bibliographies Staff. Author Index to Public Administration: Bibliography P1 to P1000 (June 1978-July 1982) (Public Administration Ser.: Bibliography P-1060). 63p. 1982. pap. 9.75 (ISBN 0-88066-210-7). Vance Biblios.

--Subject Index to Public Administration Series: Bibliography P1 to P1000 (June 1978-July 1982) (Public Administration Ser.: Bibliography P1061). 139p. 1982. pap. 18.00 (ISBN 0-88066-211-5). Vance Biblios.

PUBLIC ADMINISTRATION–CASE STUDIES

Vengroff, Richard. Development Administration at the Local Level: The Case of Zaire. (Foreign & Comparative Studies Program, African Ser.: No. 40). (Illus.). 1983. pap. price not set (ISBN 0-915984-63-6). Syracuse U Foreign Comp.

PUBLIC ASSISTANCE

see Public Welfare

PUBLIC COMMUNITY COLLEGES

see Community Colleges

PUBLIC CONTRACTS

see also Government Purchasing; Research and Development Contracts

Hanrahan, John. Government by Contract. 1983. 17.00 (ISBN 0-393-01717-6). Norton.

PUBLIC CORPORATIONS

see Corporations

PUBLIC DEBTS

see Debts, Public

PUBLIC DOCUMENTS

see Government Publications

PUBLIC FINANCE

see Finance, Public

PUBLIC FORUMS

see Forums (Discussion and Debate)

PUBLIC HEALTH

see also Burial; Communicable Diseases; Community Mental Health Services; Disinfection and Disinfectants; Environmental Health; Food Adulteration and Inspection; Hospitals; Industrial Health; Medical Care; Medicine, Preventive; Mental Health; Noise; Occupational Diseases; Pollution; Public Health Nursing; Refuse and Refuse Disposal; Sanitary Engineering; Sanitation; School Health; Sewage Disposal; Social Medicine; Vaccination; Water-Supply

Breslow, Lester, et al, eds. Annual Review of Public Health, Vol. 4. 1983. text ed. 27.00 (ISBN 0-8243-2704-7). Annual Reviews.

Brooks, Stewart M. & Brooks, Natalie A. Turner's Personal & Community Health. 16th ed. (Illus.). 540p. 1983. pap. text ed. 20.95 (ISBN 0-8016-5128-X). Mosby.

Christoffel, Tom. Health & the Law: A Handbook for Health Professionals. 464p. 1982. text ed. 29.95 (ISBN 0-02-905370-6). Free Pr.

Community Health Services in the Health Care Delivery System. 86p. 1974. 3.95 (ISBN 0-686-38204-8, 21-1524). Natl League Nurse.

Community Health: Today & Tomorrow. 130p. 1979. 4.95 (ISBN 0-686-38205-6, 52-1768). Natl League Nurse.

Congressional Quarterly Inc. Staff. National Health Issues. LC 77-12770. (Editorial Research Reports). 207p. 1977. pap. 7.50 (ISBN 0-87187-118-1). Congr Quarterly.

Dundon, Mary L. & Gay, George A. The Nineteen Seventy-Eight Revision of the U. S. Standard Certificates. Olmstead, Mary, tr. (Ser. 4: No. 23). 45p. 1982. pap. 1.75 (ISBN 0-8406-0268-5). Natl Ctr Health Stats.

Faruqee, Rashid. Integrating Family Planning with Health Services: Does it Help? LC 82-8405. (World Bank Staff Working Papers: No. 515). (Orig.). 1982. pap. 3.00 (ISBN 0-8213-0003-2). World Bank.

Frazer, F. W., ed. Rehabilitation Within the Community. 208p. 1983. pap. 7.95 (ISBN 0-571-11901-8). Faber & Faber.

Harron, Frank & United Ministries in Education Health & Human Values Program. Human Values in Medicine & Health Care: Audio-Visual Resources. LC 82-13394. 96p. 1983. pap. text ed. 3.95x (ISBN 0-300-02975-6). Yale U Pr.

Jackson, S. M. & Lane, S. Personal & Community Health. 1982. 25.00x (ISBN 0-7020-0576-2, Pub. by Cas sell England). State Mutual Bk.

Marsteller, Phyllis, ed. Peterson's Guides to Graduate Study: Biological, Agricultural, & Health Sciences, 1983. 1800p. 1982. pap. 21.95 (ISBN 0-87866-187-5). Petersons Guides.

Milio, Nancy. Primary Care & the Public Health: Judging Impacts, Goals, & Polices Public's. LC 81-47275. 272p. 1983. 27.95x (ISBN 0-669-04571-3). Lexington Bks.

Ostrow, Patricia C. & Williamson, John. Quality Assurance Primer: Improving Health Care Outcomes & Productivity. 114p. 1983. 6.00, 8.00 non-members (ISBN 0-910317-10-0). Am Occup Therapy.

Rodwin, Victor G. The Health Planning Predicament: France, Quebec, England, & the United States. Leslie, Charles, ed. LC 82-45910. (Comparative Studies of Health Systems & Medical Care Ser.). 160p. 1983. 16.50x (ISBN 0-520-04446-0). U of Cal Pr.

Spirn, Steven & Benfer, David W. Issues in Health Care Management. LC 82-8842. 498p. 1983. 32.50 (ISBN 0-89443-826-3). Aspen Systems.

Statistical Reporting in Home & Community Health Services. 49p. 1977. 3.95 (ISBN 0-686-38174-2, 21-1652). Natl League Nurse.

Wagenfeld, Morton O. & Lemkau, Paul V., eds. Public Mental Health. (Studies in Community Mental Health). (Illus.). 288p. 1982. 25.00 (ISBN 0-8039-1120-3); pap. 12.50 (ISBN 0-8039-1224-2). Sage.

PUBLIC HEALTH–HISTORY

Winslow, C. E. A. Evolution & Significance of the Modern Public Health Campaign. 1923. text ed. 29.50x (ISBN 0-686-83541-7). Elliots Bks.

PUBLIC HEALTH–LAW AND LEGISLATION

see Public Health Laws

PUBLIC HEALTH–SURVEYS

see Health Surveys

PUBLIC HEALTH–UNDERDEVELOPED AREAS

Dickson, Murray. Where There Is No Dentist. Blake, Michael, ed. LC 82-84067. (Illus.). 192p. (Orig.). 1983. pap. 5.00 (ISBN 0-942364-05-8). Hesperian Found.

Diesfeld, Hans-Jochen. Health Research in Developing Countries. 238p. 1982. write for info. (ISBN 3-8204-7110-3). P Lang Pubs.

PUBLIC HEALTH, RURAL

see Health, Rural

PUBLIC HEALTH, TROPICAL

see Tropical Medicine

PUBLIC HEALTH ADMINISTRATION

Haimann, Theo. Supervisory Management for Health Care Institutions. 3rd ed. 420p. Date not set. text ed. price not set (ISBN 0-87125-081-0). Cath Health.

Harron, Frank & Burnside, John. Health & Human Values: A Guide to Making Your Own Decisions. LC 82-13394. 212p. 1983. text ed. 24.95x (ISBN 0-300-02898-9); pap. 6.95 (ISBN 0-300-03026-6). Yale U Pr.

Harron, Frank & United Ministries in Education Health & Human Values Program. Leader's Manual. LC 82-13394. 48p. 1983. pap. text ed. 2.95x (ISBN 0-300-02972-1). Yale U Pr.

Labor Management Issues in the Health Care Field. 76p. 1976. 4.95 (ISBN 0-686-38153-X, 21-1624). Natl League Nurse.

Lefkowitz, Bonnie. Health Planning: Lessons for the Future. LC 82-18491. 206p. 1982. 23.50 (ISBN 0-89443-927-8). Aspen Systems.

McCaffrey, David P. OSHA & the Politics of Health Regulation. LC 82-11201. 200p. 1982. 24.50x (ISBN 0-306-41050-8, Plenum Pr). Plenum Pub.

McCusker, J. How to Measure & Evaluate Community Health. 2nd ed. 1982. 29.00x (ISBN 0-333-31680-0, Pub. by Macmillan Bk). State Mutual Bk.

Management Information Systems for Public Health-Community Health Agencies: Report of a Conference. 182p. 1974. 5.95 (ISBN 0-686-38155-6, 21-1506). Natl League Nurse.

Management Information Systems for Public Health-Community Health Agencies: Workshop Papers. 69p. 1975. 3.95 (ISBN 0-686-38157-2, 21-1593). Natl League Nurse.

A Manual for Members of Governing Boards of Community & Home Health Agencies: A Prototype. 117p. 1978. 25.00 (ISBN 0-686-38160-2, 21-1753). Natl League Nurse.

Riccardi, Vincent M. & Kurtz, Susanne M. Communication & Counseling in Health Care. 1983. pap. text ed. 14.75x (ISBN 0-398-04825-8). C C Thomas.

Rudman, Jack. Clinic Administrator. (Career Examination Ser.: C-915). (Cloth bdg. avail. on request). pap. 12.00 (ISBN 0-8373-0915-8). Natl Learning.

Selected Management Information Systems for Public Health: Community Health Agencies. 227p. 1978. 8.95 (ISBN 0-686-38154-8, 21-1683). Natl League Nurse.

Skinner, Patricia. Marketing Community Health Services. (League Exchange Ser.: No. 121). 42p. 1978. 3.95 (ISBN 0-686-38161-0, 21-1757). Natl League Nurse.

State of the Art in Management Information Systems for Public Health: Community Health Agencies. 166p. 1976. 5.95 (ISBN 0-686-38156-4, 21-1637). Natl League Nurse.

Stuart, Bruce. State Regulation of Health Service Utilization: Lessons from Michigan. 94p. 1979. pap. text ed. 5.50 (ISBN 0-87766-256-8). Urban Inst.

Thompson, Frank J. Health Policy & the Bureaucracy: Politics & Implementation. 352p. 1983. pap. text ed. 10.95x (ISBN 0-262-70024-7). MIT Pr.

PUBLIC HEALTH LAWS

Health Policy Making in Action: The Passage & Implementation of the National Health Planning & Resources Development Act of 1974. 56p. 1975. 4.50 (ISBN 0-686-38346-X, 41-1600). Natl League Nurse.

Pozgar, George D. Legal Aspects of Health Care Administration. 2nd ed. 250p. 1983. write for info (ISBN 0-89443-810-7). Aspen Systems.

Stuart, Bruce. State Regulation of Health Service Utilization: Lessons from Michigan. 94p. 1979. pap. text ed. 5.50 (ISBN 0-87766-256-8). Urban Inst.

PUBLIC HEALTH NURSING

Elkins, Carolyn. Community Health Nursing in Action. (Illus.). 512p. 1983. text ed. 18.95 (ISBN 0-89303-264-6). R J Brady.

Fitzpatrick, M. Louise. The National Organization for Public Health Nursing 1912-1952: Development of a Practice Field. 226p. 1975. 10.95 (ISBN 0-686-38315-X, 11-1510). Natl League Nurse.

Harish, Yvonne. Patient Care Guides: Practical Information for Public Health Nurses. (League Exchange Ser.: No. 111). 354p. 1976. 12.95 (ISBN 0-686-38189-0, 21-1610). Natl League Nurse.

Index to Public Health Nursing Magazine. 232p. 1974. 35.00 (ISBN 0-686-38353-2, 21-1491). Natl League Nurse.

Rudman, Jack. Community Health Nurse. (Certified Nurse Examination Ser.: CN-4). 21.95 (ISBN 0-8373-6154-0); pap. 13.95 (ISBN 0-8373-6104-4). Natl Learning.

Staff of CHHA-CHS, NLN. Publicity for Your Community Health Agency. rev. ed. 37p. 1978. 3.95 (ISBN 0-686-38166-1, 21-1748). Natl League Nurse.

Who is Taking Care of the Patient? 51p. 1975. 4.95 (ISBN 0-686-38343-5, 20-1557). Natl League Nurse.

Who's Shaping Health Care? 48p. 1982. 5.95 (ISBN 0-686-38350-8, 15-1880). Natl League Nurse.

Why Experiment with Health Care Delivery? 40p. 1976. 4.95 (ISBN 0-686-38177-7, 21-1651). Natl League Nurse.

PUBLIC HEALTH SERVICES

see Public Health

PUBLIC HEALTH SURVEYS

see Health Surveys

PUBLIC HOUSES

see Hotels, Taverns, etc.

PUBLIC HOUSING

Boldy & Heuman. Housing For the Elderly: Planning & Policy Formation in Western Europe & North America. LC 82-10684. 224p. 1982. 25.00x (ISBN 0-312-39349-0). St Martin.

Forman, Rachel Z. Let Us Now Praise Obscure Women: A Comparative Study of Publicly Supported Unmarried Mothers in Government Housing in the United States & Britain. LC 82-17579. 240p. (Orig.). 1983. lib. bdg. 22.00 (ISBN 0-8191-2813-9); pap. text ed. 10.75 (ISBN 0-8191-2814-7). U Pr of Amer.

Goodman, John, Jr. Regional Housing Assistance Allocations & Regional Housing Needs. 40p. 1979. pap. text ed. 4.00 (ISBN 0-87766-263-0). Urban Inst.

Goodman, John L., Jr. The Future Poor: Projecting the Population Eligible for Federal Housing Assistance. 15p. pap. text ed. 1.00 (ISBN 0-686-84410-6). Urban Inst.

Heinberg, et al. Housing Allowances in Kansas City & Wilmington: An Appraisal. (Illus.). 41p. (Orig.). 1976. pap. text ed. 4.00 (ISBN 0-87766-143-X). Urban Inst.

Low-Income Urban Shelter Projects. 61p. 1983. pap. 7.50 (ISBN 0-88936-355-2, IDRC TS41, IDRC). Unipub.

Rasmussen, David W. & Struyk, Raymond J. A Housing Strategy for the City of Detroit: Policy Perspectives Based on Economic Analysis. LC 81-51874. (Illus.). 81p. (Orig.). 1981. pap. text ed. 9.00 (ISBN 0-87766-300-9, URI 32500). Urban Inst.

Struyk, Raymond J. Saving the Housing Assistance Plan: Improving Incentives to Local Governments. 36p. 1980. pap. text ed. 3.50 (ISBN 0-87766-270-3). Urban Inst.

Weicher, John C. & Yap, Lorene. Metropolitan Housing Needs for the 1980's. LC 81-70526. 138p. text ed. 16.50 (ISBN 0-87766-308-4, URI 33500). Urban Inst.

Zais, James P., et al. Housing Assistance for Older Americans: The Reagan Prescription. LC 82-50957. (Changing Domestic Priorities Ser.). 125p. (Orig.). 1982. pap. text ed. 9.95 (ISBN 0-87766-317-3, 34300). Urban Inst.

PUBLIC HYGIENE

see Public Health

PUBLIC INTEREST

Rosenbaum, Robert A. The Public Issues Handbook: A Guide for the Concerned Citizen. LC 82-15812. (Illus.). 416p. 1983. lib. bdg. 35.00 (ISBN 0-313-23504-X, RPI/). Greenwood.

Schubert, Glendon A. The Public Interest: A Critique of the Theory of a Political Concept. LC 82-15509. x, 244p. 1982. Repr. of 1960 ed. lib. bdg. 29.75x (ISBN 0-313-22364-5, SCPU). Greenwood.

PUBLIC JUNIOR COLLEGES

see Community Colleges

PUBLIC LANDS

see Forest Reserves; National Parks and Reserves; United States–Public Lands

PUBLIC LAW

see also Administrative Law; Constitutional Law; Criminal Law; Criminal Procedure; International Law also subdivision Constitutional Law under names of countries

Cooper, Phillip J. Public Law & Public Administration. 474p. 1983. text ed. 21.95 (ISBN 0-87484-526-2). Mayfield Pub.

Simons, Walter. Evolution of International Public Law in Europe Since Grotius. 1931. text ed. 29.50x (ISBN 0-686-83542-5). Elliots Bks.

PUBLIC LAW (CANON LAW)

see Canon Law

PUBLIC LIBRARIES

Bisaillon, Blaise. The Public Library: What Is Its Place & Function in the United States? (Vital Issues, Vol. XXIX 1979-80: No. 3). 0.60 (ISBN 0-686-81608-0). Ctr Info Am.

Van House, Nancy A. Public Library User Fees: The Use & Finance of Public Libraries. LC 82-11741. (Contributions in Librarianship & Information Science Ser.: No. 43). (Illus.). 160p. 1983. lib. bdg. 27.50 (ISBN 0-313-22753-5, DPU/). Greenwood.

White, Lawrence J. The Public Library in the Nineteen Eighties: The Problems of Choice. LC 82-48604. (Lexington Books Special Series in Libraries & Librarianship). 244p. 1983. 22.95x (ISBN 0-669-06342-8). Lexington Bks.

PUBLIC OFFICERS

see also Civil Service; Conflict of Interests (Public Office); Municipal Officials and Employees; Public Administration

Weeks, J. Devereux. Personal Liability of Public Officials Under Federal Law. LC 80-13271. 17p. 1981. pap. 3.25 (ISBN 0-89854-068-2). U of GA Inst Govt.

PUBLIC OPINION

see also Attitude (Psychology); Press; Propaganda; Public Relations; Publicity also subdivision Foreign Opinion, or Foreign Public Opinion, under names of countries or certain wars, e.g. France–History–Revolution, 1789-1799–Foreign Public Opinion

Create Public Opinion, Seize Power. 1979. 0.50 (ISBN 0-686-82481-4). RCP Pubns.

Pater, Alan F. & Pater, Jason R., eds. What They Said in 1982: The Yearbook of Spoken Opinion, Vol. 14. LC 74-111080. 1983. 27.50 (ISBN 0-917734-08-4). Monitor.

PUBLIC OPINION–BIBLIOGRAPHY

Hastings, Elizabeth H. & Hastings, Philip K., eds. Index to International Public Opinion, 1981-1982. LC 80-643917. xviii, 682p. 1983. lib. bdg. 85.00 (ISBN 0-313-23362-4, IN82). Greenwood.

PUBLIC OPINION–RESEARCH

see Public Opinion Polls

PUBLIC OPINION–GREAT BRITAIN

Blackett, R. J. Building an Antislavery Wall: Black Americans in the Atlantic Abolitionist Movement, 1830 to 1860. LC 82-21724. 264p. 1983. text ed. 25.00x (ISBN 0-8071-1082-5). La State U Pr.

PUBLIC OPINION–UNITED STATES

American Correctional Association Staff. Corrections & Public Awareness. (Series 2: No. 1). 25p. (Orig.). 1981. pap. 3.50 (ISBN 0-942974-22-0). Am Correctional.

Apostle, Richard A. & Glock, Charles Y. The Anatomy of Racial Attitudes. LC 82-4867. 277p. 1983. 27.50x (ISBN 0-520-04719-2). U of Cal Pr.

Erikson, Robert S., et al. American Public Opinion: Its Origins, Content, & Impact. 2nd ed. LC 79-17806. 337p. 1980. pap. text ed. 14.95 (ISBN 0-471-03139-9). Wiley.

Kiewiet, D. Roderick. Macroeconomics & Micropolitics: The Electoral Effects of Economic Issues. LC 82-21985. (Illus.). 160p. 1983. lib. bdg. 16.00x (ISBN 0-226-43532-6). U of Chicago Pr.

Yeric, Jerry L. & Todd, John. Public Opinion: The Visible Politics. LC 82-81415. 260p. 1983. pap. text ed. 8.95 (ISBN 0-87581-281-3). Peacock Pubs.

PUBLIC OPINION POLLS

Here are entered works on the technique of public opinion polls or straw votes.

see also Market Surveys

Surveys, Polls, Censuses, & Forcasts Directory. 300p. 1983. 150.00x (ISBN 0-8103-1692-7). Gale.

PUBLIC OWNERSHIP

see Government Ownership

PUBLIC PLAYGROUND

see Playgrounds

PUBLIC POLICY

see Economic Policy; Environmental Policy; Military Policy; Science and State; Social Policy

PUBLIC POLICY (LAW)

Chiswick, Barry, ed. Gateway: U. S. Immigration Issues & Policies. 1982. 22.95 (ISBN 0-8447-2221-9); pap. 12.95 (ISBN 0-8447-2220-0). Am Enterprise.

Wilson, James Q., ed. Crime & Public Policy. 400p. 1983. 22.95 (ISBN 0-917616-52-9); pap. 8.95 (ISBN 0-917616-51-0). ICS Pr.

PUBLIC PROCUREMENT

see Government Purchasing

PUBLIC PURCHASING

see Government Purchasing

PUBLIC RECORDS

see also Archives

Hendricks, Evan. Former Secrets: Government Records Made Public Through the Freedom of Information Act. Shaker, Peggy, ed. 204p. 1982. pap. 15.00 (ISBN 0-910175-01-2). Campaign Political.

PUBLIC RELATIONS

see also Advertising; Customer Relations; Propaganda; Public Opinion; Publicity

Bernstein, Alan B. The Emergency Public Relations Manual. LC 82-80824. 94p. Repr. of 1982 ed. 75.00 (ISBN 0-686-38793-7). PASE.

Black, Sam & Sharpe, Melvin A. Practical Public Relations: Common Sense Guidelines for Business & Professional People. 224p. 1983. 16.95 (ISBN 0-13-693531-1); pap. 8.95 (ISBN 0-13-693523-0). P-H.

Corwen, Leonard. There's a Job for You In: Advertising, Commercial Art, Fashion, Films, Public Relations & Publicity, Publishing, Television & Radio, Travel & Tourism. (Illus.). 192p. (Orig.). 1983. pap. 8.95 (ISBN 0-8329-0273-X). New Century.

Ehrenkranz, Lois B. & Kahn, Gilbert R. Public Relations-Publicity: A Key Link in Communications. (Illus.). 270p. 1983. text ed. 14.50 (ISBN 0-87005-449-X). Fairchild.

Lesly, Philip. Lesly's Public Relations Handbook. 3rd ed. 557p. 1978. 29.95 (ISBN 0-13-530741-4, Busn). P-H.

Londgren, Richard E. Communication by Objectives: A Guide to Productive & Cost-Effective Public Relations & Marketing. (Illus.). 208p. 1983. 16.95 (ISBN 0-13-153650-8); pap. 7.95 (ISBN 0-13-153643-5). P-H.

Rodriguez, Raymond L. Promoters: Structure & Function. Chamberlin, Michael J., ed. 540p. 1982. 41.50 (ISBN 0-03-059919-9). Praeger.

Rudman, Jack. Public Relations Specialist. (Career Examination Ser.: C-2934). (Cloth bdg. avail. on request). pap. 12.00 (ISBN 0-8373-2934-5). Natl Learning.

PUBLIC RELATIONS–BUSINESS

see Public Relations

PUBLIC RELATIONS–CHARITIES

see Public Relations–Social Service

PUBLIC RELATIONS–INDUSTRY

see Public Relations

PUBLIC RELATIONS–POLICE

Varwell, D. W. Police & the Public. 128p. 1978. 30.00x (ISBN 0-7121-1683-4, Pub. by Macdonald & Evans). State Mutual Bk.

PUBLIC RELATIONS–SCHOOLS

see also Parent-Teacher Relationships

Field-Proven Programs for Better Public Relations: Mini Workshops on Public Relations at ASBO's 65th Annual Meeting. 1980. 5.95 (ISBN 0-910170-14-2). Assn Sch Busn.

Hornick, Melvyn. The Successful Marketing of Schools. 90p. 1980. softcover 8.95 (ISBN 0-932930-38-7). Pilgrimage Inc.

Kinder, Jack. School Public Relations: Communicating to the Community. LC 82-60802. (Fastback Ser.: No. 182). 50p. 1982. pap. 0.75 (ISBN 0-87367-182-1). Phi Delta Kappa.

Walling, Donovan R. Complete Book of School Public Relations an Administrator's Manual & Guide. LC 82-12340. 222p. 1982. 17.50 (ISBN 0-13-158337-9, Busn). P-H.

PUBLIC RELATIONS–SOCIAL SERVICE

Leiter, Michael P. & Webb, Mark. Developing Human Service Networks: Community & Organizatonal Relations. 279p. 1983. text ed. 19.50x (ISBN 0-8290-1262-1). Irvington.

PUBLIC RELATIONS–UNIVERSITIES AND COLLEGES

see Public Relations–Schools

PUBLIC RELIEF

see Public Welfare

PUBLIC SCHOOL FACILITIES

see School Facilities

PUBLIC SCHOOL MUSIC

see School Music

PUBLIC SCHOOLS

Here are entered works on primary and secondary schools controlled or supported by state and local government, including, in European countries, the higher schools preparatory to the university (Gymnasiem, Lycees, etc.) Works on the public schools of a particular city are entered under the name of the city with subdivison Public Schools, e.g. New York (City)–Public Schools. Works on British privately endowed schools, known as public schools are entered under Public Schools, Endowed (Great Britain.).

see also Schools; Week-Day Church Schools also headings beginning with the word School

Sommer, Carl. Schools in Crisis: Training for Success or Failure? (Orig.). 1983. write for info. Cahill Pub Co.

PUBLIC SCHOOLS–BUSINESS MANAGEMENT

see also Education–Finance

ASBO Management Techniques Research Committee. Control Points in School Business Management. 1979. 3.00 (ISBN 0-910170-10-X). Assn Sch Busn.

ASBO's Purchasing & Supply Management Research Committee. Cooperative Purchasing Guidelines. 1979. 5.00 (ISBN 0-910170-09-6). Assn Sch Busn.
Hill. The School Business Administrator. 3rd ed. 1982. 6.50 (ISBN 0-910170-26-6). Assn Sch Busn.
McGuffey. Competencies Needed by Chief School Business Administrators. 1980. 11.50 (ISBN 0-910170-17-7). Assn Sch Busn.
Munsterman. Purchasing & Supply Management Handbook for School Business Officials. 1978. 5.00 (ISBN 0-910170-08-8). Assn Sch Busn.
Validated School Business Practices that Work, Vol. III. 1981. 3.25 (ISBN 0-686-84141-7). Assn Sch Busn.

PUBLIC SCHOOLS–FINANCE
see Education–Finance

PUBLIC SCHOOLS–SANITARY AFFAIRS
see School Health

PUBLIC SCHOOLS, ENDOWED (GREAT BRITAIN)
Mervyn, P. Memoirs of a Mis-spent Youth. 1982. 38.00x (ISBN 0-686-99795-6, Pub. by Sycamore Pr England). State Mutual Bk.

PUBLIC SECURITIES
see Securities

PUBLIC SERVICE
see also Public Utilities
Foley, J. & Maneker, M. National Service & the American Future. 1983. pap. 7.95 (ISBN 0-8159-6315-7). Devin.
Leonor, M. D. & Richards, P. J., eds. Target Setting for Basic Needs: The Operation of Selected Government Services. 220p. 1982. 14.25 (ISBN 92-2-102946-8). Intl Labour Office.
Rabin. Handbook of Public Personnel. (Public Administration & Public Policies Ser.). 776p. 1983. write for info. (ISBN 0-8247-1318-4). Dekker.

PUBLIC SERVICE CORPORATIONS
see Public Utilities

PUBLIC SPEAKING
see also Anecdotes; Debates and Debating; Oratory; Preaching; Rhetoric; Speeches, Addresses, etc.; Voice Culture
Andrews, James R. Essentials of Public Communicaton. LC 78-18182. 217p. 1979. text ed. 18.95x (ISBN 0-673-15652-4). Scott F.
Averett, Tanner F. Creative Communication. rev. ed. (Illus.). 379p. 1979. pap. text ed. 8.95 (ISBN 0-931054-09-5). Clark Pub.
Ayres, Joe & Miller, Janice. Effective Public Speaking. 300p. 1983. pap. text ed. write for info. (ISBN 0-697-04229-4); instrs.' manual avail. (ISBN 0-697-04230-8). Wm C Brown.
Britch, Carroll, et al. Speech Acts: Hints & Samples. 112p. (Orig.). 1983. pap. text ed. 6.95x (ISBN 0-88133-016-7). Waveland Pr.
Carlile, Clark S. Thirty Eighty Basic Speech Experiences. 7th ed. 235p. 1982. pap. text ed. 6.75 (ISBN 0-931054-07-9). Clark Pub.
Fletcher, Leon. How to Speak Like a Pro. 272p. (Orig.). 1983. pap. 2.95 (ISBN 0-345-30171-4). Ballantine.
Kebbe, Charles. Profitable Public Speaking. LC 82-45167. 128p. 1983. 8.95 (ISBN 0-689-11309-9). Atheneum.
Linver, Sandy. Speak & Get Results: Complete Guide to Presentations & Speeches That Work in Any Business Situation. 256p. 1983. 13.95 (ISBN 0-671-44204-X). Summit Bks.
Machlin, Evangeline. Teaching Speech for the Stage: A Manual for Classroom Instruction. 1980. pap. 3.95 (ISBN 0-87830-573-4). Theatre Arts.
Minnick. Public Speaking. 2nd ed. 1983. 13.95 (ISBN 0-686-84657-5); supplementary materials avail. HM.
Minnick, Wayne C. Public Speaking. 2d ed. LC 82-83203. 320p. 1983. pap. text ed. 13.95 (ISBN 0-395-32627-3); write for info. instr's. manual (ISBN 0-395-32628-1). HM.
Ryckman, W. G. The Art of Speaking Effectively. (Plaid Ser.). 90p. 1983. pap. 7.95 (ISBN 0-87094-387-1). Dow Jones-Irwin.
Tacey, William S. Business & Professional Speaking. 4th ed. 1983. pap. text ed. write for info. (ISBN 0-697-04235-9). Wm C Brown.
Van Dusen, C. Raymond & Van Smith, Howard. The New Speech-o-Graham: Technique for Persuasive Public Speaking. 264p. 1983. pap. 5.95 (ISBN 0-13-615732-7). P-H.
Wohlmuth, Ed. The Overnight Guide to Public Speaking: The Ed Wohlmuth Method. 128p. 1983. 7.95 (ISBN 0-89471-200-4); lib. bdg. 15.90 (ISBN 0-89471-199-7). Running Pr.

PUBLIC SPEAKING–STUDY AND TEACHING
see Public Speaking

PUBLIC SPENDING POLICY
see Government Spending Policy

PUBLIC TELEVISION
see Television in Education

PUBLIC TRUSTEES
see Trusts and Trustees

PUBLIC TWO-YEAR COLLEGES
see Community Colleges

PUBLIC UTILITIES
Here are entered works on public service or public utility corporation and publications of the commissions controlling them.
see also Corporation Law; Corporations; Electric Utilities; Government Business Enterprises; Public Service; Railroads; Water-Supply
Danielson, Albert L. & Kamerschen, David R., eds. Current Issues in Public-Utility Economics: Essays in Honor of James C. Bonbright. LC 81-48612. 352p. 1983. 34.95x (ISBN 0-669-05440-2). Lexington Bks.
Gormley, William T., Jr. The Politics of Public Utility Regulation. LC 82-42756. 288p. 1983. 22.95 (ISBN 0-8229-3479-5); pap. 8.95x (ISBN 0-8229-5351-X, 195). U of Pittsburgh Pr.
Harak, Charles. The Utility Companies & You: Your Rights & How to Preserve Them. Spriggs, Marshall T., ed. (Orig.). 1983. pap. write for info (ISBN 0-910001-03-0). MA Poverty Law.
Thisse. Locational Analysis of Public Facilities. (Studies in Mathematics & Mangerial Economics: Vol. 31). Date not set. 64.00 (ISBN 0-444-86486-5). Elsevier.

PUBLIC UTILITY REGULATION
see Public Utilities

PUBLIC WELFARE
Here are entered works on tax-supported welfare activities.
see also Charities; Child Welfare; Community Organizations; Day Care Centers; Disaster Relief; Food Relief; Hospitals; Medical Social Work; Poor; Psychiatric Social Work; Social Medicine; Social Service; Social Workers; Unemployed
also subdivision Charities under names of cities, e.g. New York (City)–Charities; also subdivision Civilian Relief under names of wars, e.g. World War, 1939-1945–Civilian Relief
Bean, Philip & MacPherson, Stewart, eds. Approaches to Welfare. 300p. 1983. 27.95 (ISBN 0-7100-9423-X); pap. 14.95 (ISBN 0-7100-9424-8). Routledge & Kegan.
DiNitto, Diana M. & Dye, Thomas R. Social Welfare Politics & Public Policy. (Illus.). 352p. 1983. text ed. 20.95 (ISBN 0-13-819474-2). P-H.
Rein. Dilemmas of Welfare Policy. 190p. 1982. 23.95 (ISBN 0-03-056137-X). Praeger.

PUBLIC WELFARE–UNITED STATES
Conner, Roger. Breaking Down the Barriers: The Changing Relationship Between Illegal Immigration & Welfare. 1982. pap. text ed. 2.50 (ISBN 0-935776-03-6). F A I R.
Ginsberg, Leon H. The Practice of Social Work in Public Welfare. LC 82-71888. 1983. 18.95 (ISBN 0-02-911760-7). Free Pr.
Goodwin, Leonard. Causes & Cures of Welfare: New Evidence on the Social Psychology of the Poor. LC 82-48634. 224p. 1983. 23.95x (ISBN 0-669-06370-3). Lexington Bks.
Hutchinson, Robert. What One Christian Can Do About Hunger in America. LC 82-18199. xii, 115p. (Orig.). 1982. pap. 5.95 (ISBN 0-8190-0651-3, FC 145). Fides Claretian.
Landrum, Roger. National Service & the General Welfare: Has the Time for it Come? (Vital Issues, Vol. XXX 1980-81: No. 9). 0.60 (ISBN 0-686-81604-8). Ctr Info Am.

PUBLIC WORSHIP
see also Liturgics; Prayer-Meetings; Ritual
Ortlund, Anne. Up with Worship. rev. ed. 1982. pap. 4.95 (ISBN 0-8307-0867-7). Regal.
Pegram, Don R. Great Churches-Today's Essentials. 1982. pap. 1.00 (ISBN 0-89265-083-4). Randall Hse.
Webber, Robert. Worship Old & New. 256p. 1982. 11.95 (ISBN 0-310-36650-X). Zondervan.
Willimon, William H. The Service of God. 240p. 1983. 10.95 (ISBN 0-687-38094-4). Abingdon.

PUBLICITY
see also Advertising; Journalism; Press; Propaganda; Public Opinion; Public Relations
Ehrenkranz, Lois B. & Kahn, Gilbert R. Public Relations-Publicity: A Key Link in Communications. (Illus.). 270p. 1983. text ed. 14.50 (ISBN 0-87005-449-X). Fairchild.
Gould, J. Sutherland. How to Publicize Yourself, Your Family, & Your Organization. (Illus.). 176p. 1983. 15.95 (ISBN 0-13-430645-7); pap. 7.95 (ISBN 0-13-430637-6). P-H.
Tedone, David. Practical Publicity: How to Boost Any Cause. (Illus.). 176p. 1983. 12.95 (ISBN 0-916782-36-0); pap. 8.95 (ISBN 0-916782-35-2). Harvard Common Pr.
Yale, David R. The Publicity Handbook. 320p. 1982. pap. 3.50 (ISBN 0-553-20832-2). Bantam.

PUBLISHERS AND AUTHORS
see Authors and Publishers

PUBLISHERS AND PUBLISHING
see also Book Industries and Trade; Books; Booksellers and Bookselling; Catalogs, Publishers'; Copyright; Libraries and Publishing; Little Presses; Newspaper Publishing; Printing
Cassell & the Publishers Association Directory of Publishing in Great Britain, the Commonwealth, Ireland, Pakistan & South Africa, 1983. 10th ed. LC 60-52232. 386p. 1982. pap. 32.50x (ISBN 0-304-30913-3). Intl Pubns Serv.
Cushman, Kathleen & Miller, Edward, eds. How to Produce a Small Newspaper: A Guide for Independent Journalists. 2nd, Rev. ed. (Illus.). 192p. (Orig.). 1983. pap. 8.95 (ISBN 0-916782-39-5). Harvard Common Pr.
Dranov, Paula. The Continuing Education Market, Nineteen Seventy-Nine to Nineteen Eighty-Four: Opportunities & Pitfalls for Publishers & Suppliers. 1979. spiral 450.00 (ISBN 0-686-42872-2). Knowledge Indus.
Duke, Judith S. The Technical, Scientific & Medical Publishing Market. 1981. spiral 850.00 (ISBN 0-686-42881-1). Knowledge Indus.
Falk, Kathryn. How to Write a Romance & Get it Published: With Intimate Advice form the World's Most Popular Romance Writers. 1983. 14.95 (ISBN 0-517-54944-1). Crown.
Fang. Modern Publishing & Librarianship. 1983. write for info. (Pub. by K G Saur). Shoe String.
Geiser, Elizabeth & Dolin, Arnold, eds. The Business of Book Publishing. 360p. 1983. lib. bdg. 30.00x (ISBN 0-89158-998-8). Westview.
Hallewell, L. Books in Brazil: A History of the Publishing Trade. LC 82-10826. 537p. 1982. 27.50 (ISBN 0-8108-1591-5). Scarecrow.
An International Survey of Book Production During the Last Decades. (Statistical Reports & Studies: No. 26). 87p. 1982. pap. 5.25 (ISBN 92-3-102040-4, U1234, UNESCO). Unipub.
McManus, Yvonne. So You Want to Write a Romance. 1983. pap. write for info. PB.
Mann, Jim. Solving Publishing's Toughest Problems. Date not set. 49.95 (ISBN 0-918110-07-6). Folio.
Peabody, Richard, ed. Mavericks: Nine Small Publishers. 90p. (Orig.). 1983. pap. 3.00 (ISBN 0-9602424-9-X). Paycock Pr.
Publishing a Professional Journal: An Editor's Guide. 15.00 (ISBN 0-934510-21-0, K022). Am Dental.
R. R. Bowker Company, ed. Publishers Weekly Yearbook. 1982. 300p. 29.95 (ISBN 0-8352-1689-6); pap. 19.95 (ISBN 0-8352-1691-8). Bowker.
Regnery, Henry. Memoirs of a Dissident Publisher. LC 78-22269. 260p. 1979. 12.95 (ISBN 0-15-173752-5). Regnery-Gateway.
Scherman, William. How to Get the Right Job in Publishing. (Illus.). 256p. (Orig.). 1983. pap. 9.95 (ISBN 0-8092-5683-5). Contemp Bks.
Tattan, L. A. Publish Yourself without Killing Yourself. 191p. (Orig.). 1981. pap. 9.95 (ISBN 0-937362-01-8). InPrint.
The U. S. Book Publishing Industry. 1982. 445.00 (ISBN 0-686-38433-4, 501). Busn Trend.

PUBLISHERS AND PUBLISHING–DATA PROCESSING
Monitor: Online & Electronic Publishing Industry Analytical Review. six-month mini-subscription 100.00 (ISBN 0-686-81699-4). Learned Info.

PUBLISHERS AND PUBLISHING–DIRECTORIES
Archibald, John & Darisse, Alan. A Guide to Multilingual Publishing. 10p. 1982. pap. 6.00 (ISBN 0-914548-36-0). Soc Tech Comm.
Fulton, Len & Ferber, Ellen, eds. Directory of Small Magazine-Press Editors & Publishers. 200p. 1983. pap. 12.95 (ISBN 0-913218-65-0). Dustbooks.
--International Directory of Little Magazines & Small Presses: 19th Annual. 600p. 1983. 25.95 (ISBN 0-913218-64-2); pap. 17.95 (ISBN 0-913218-63-4). Dustbooks.
Holt, Robert L. Publishing: A Complete Guide for Schools, Small Presses, & Entrepreneurs. LC 82-83565. (Calif. Financial Publications Ser.). 1982. 25.95 (ISBN 0-930926-08-0); pap. 19.95 (ISBN 0-930926-09-9). Calif Health.
O'Hara, Deborah A., ed. Publisher's Catalogs Annual 1982-1983. 75p. 1982. write for info (ISBN 0-930466-71-3). Meckler Pub.
Westreich, Budd, ed. Third International Directory of Private Presses (Letterpress) (Illus.). 160p. 1982. 25.00 (ISBN 0-936300-04-3); pap. 15.00 (ISBN 0-936300-03-5). Pr Arden Park.

PUBLISHERS AND PUBLISHING–EUROPE
Amram, David. Makers of Hebrew Books in Italy. 350p. Date not set. 60.00 (ISBN 0-87556-013-X). Saifer.

PUBLISHERS AND PUBLISHING–GREAT BRITAIN
Book Publishing. 95p. 1982. 275.00x (ISBN 0-85938-159-5, Pub. by Jordan & Sons England). State Mutual Bk.
Cassell & the Publishers Association Directory of Publishing in Great Britain, the Commonwealth, Ireland, Pakistan & South Africa, 1983. 10th ed. LC 60-52232. 386p. 1982. pap. 32.50x (ISBN 0-304-30913-3). Intl Pubns Serv.
Robinson, Duncan. William Morris, Edward Burne-Jones & the Kelmscott Chaucer. 160p. 1982. 95.00x (ISBN 0-86092-038-0, Pub. by Fraser Bks). State Mutual Bk.

PUBLISHERS' CATALOGS
see Catalogs, Publishers'

PUBLISHERS' IMPRINTS
see Imprints (In Books)

PUBLISHING AND LIBRARIES
see Libraries and Publishing

PUBLISHING OF NEWSPAPERS
see Newspaper Publishing

PUEBLO INDIANS
see Indians of North America–Southwest, New

PUERTO RICAN LITERATURE
Barradas, Efrain, ed. Apalabramiento: Cuentos puertorriquenos de hoy. (Span.). Date not set. pap. 9.00 (ISBN 0-910061-09-2). Ediciones Norte.

PUERTO RICANS IN THE UNITED STATES
Sanchez Korrol, Virginia E. From Colonia to Community: The History of Puerto Ricans in New York City, 1917-1948. LC 82-18691. (Contributions in Ethnic Studies: No. 9). (Illus.). 256p. 1983. lib. bdg. 29.95 (ISBN 0-313-23458-2, F128). Greenwood.

PUERTO RICO
Carrion, Arturo M., et al. Puerto Rico: A Political & Cultural Odyssey. (Illus.). 1983. 19.50 (ISBN 0-393-01740-0). Norton.

PUERTO RICO–DESCRIPTION AND TRAVEL
Garcia, Connie & Medina, Arthur. Guia Turistica de Puerto Rico. Rivera, Evelyn, tr. from Sp. (Illus.). 192p. (Eng.). 1983. pap. 4.95 (ISBN 0-934642-04-4). Puerto Rico Almanacs.
--The Travel Guide to Puerto Rico: 1982-83. 2nd ed. (Illus.). 340p. 1983. pap. 9.95 (ISBN 0-934642-03-6). Puerto Rico Almanacs.
Puerto Rico Travel Guide. (Berlitz Travel Guides). (Illus.). 1982. pap. 4.95 (ISBN 0-02-969620-8, Berlitz). Macmillan.

PUERTO RICO–POLITICS AND GOVERNMENT
Mathews, Thomas. Puerto Rican Politics & the New Deal. LC 76-1934. 345p. 1976. Repr. of 1960 ed. lib. bdg. 39.50 (ISBN 0-306-70752-7). Da Capo.

PUERTO RICO–SOCIAL CONDITIONS
Ramirez de Arellano, Annette B. & Seipp, Conrad. Colonialism, Catholicism, & Contraception: A History of Birth Control in Puerto Rico. LC 82-13646. 290p. 1983. 24.00x (ISBN 0-8078-1544-6). U of NC Pr.

PUGET SOUND
Cheney, Daniel P. & Mumford, Thomas M., Jr. Shellfish & Seaweed Harvests of Puget Sound. (A Puget Sound Bk.). (Illus.). 144p. (Orig.). 1983. pap. 8.95 (ISBN 0-686-43218-5, Pub. by Wash Sea Grant). U of Wash Pr.

PUGILISM
see Boxing

PULLMAN CARS
see Railroads–Cars

PULMONARY CIRCULATION
Abramson, Joan. Practical Application of the Gas Laws to Pulmonary Physiology. 97p. (Orig.). 1981. pap. text ed. 5.95 (ISBN 0-89787-107-3). Gorsuch Scarisbrick.
Fishman, P. A. Assessment of Pulmonary Function. 1980. text ed. 25.95 (ISBN 0-07-021117-5). McGraw.

PULMONARY DISEASES
see Lungs–Diseases

PULMONARY FUNCTION TESTS
Chusid, E. Leslie, ed. The Selective & Comprehensive Testing of Adult Pulmonary Function. LC 82-84736. 400p. 1983. price not set monograph (ISBN 0-87993-195-7). Futura Pub.

PULMONARY INSUFFICIENCY
see Respiratory Insufficiency

PULPWOOD
Atchinson, Joseph E. Nonwood Plant Fiber Pulping Progress Report. (No. 13). 148p. 1983. pap. 48.95 (ISBN 0-89852-404-0, 01 01 R104). TAPPI.
International Pulp Bleaching Conference: Proceedings. 223p. 1982. pap. 44.95 (ISBN 0-686-43244-4, 01 05 1282). TAPPI.
International Sulfite Pulping Conference: Proceedings. 223p. 1982. pap. 44.95 (ISBN 0-686-43245-2, 01 05 1782). TAPPI.
Projected Pulp & Paper Mills in the World, 1981-1991. 126p. 1982. pap. 9.00 (ISBN 92-5-101204-0, F2308, FAO). Unipub.
Pulp & Paper Capacities Survey 1981-1986: Supplement. 13p. 1982. pap. 7.50 (ISBN 92-5-001233-0, F2335, FAO). Unipub.
Pulping Conference: Proceedings. 514p. 1982. pap. 44.95 (ISBN 0-686-43246-0, 01 05 0682). TAPPI.

PULSE CIRCUITS
CES Industries, Inc. Staff. Pulses & Waveshaping, Bk.IV. (Ed-Lab Experiment Manual). (Illus.). (gr. 9-12). 1982. lab manual 11.50 (ISBN 0-86711-052-X). CES Industries.
Tocci, Ronald J. Fundamentals of Pulse & Digital Circuits. 3rd ed. 1983. text ed. 22.95 (ISBN 0-675-20033-4). Additional supplements may be obtained from publisher. Merrill.

PULSE FAMILY
see Legumes

PULSED CIRCUITS
see Pulse Circuits

PULVERIZERS
see Milling Machinery

PUMAS
Lawrence, R. D. The Ghost Walker. LC 82-12111. 264p. 1982. 15.95 (ISBN 0-03-061594-1). HR&W.

PUMPING MACHINERY
see also Heat Pumps
Chermisinoff, Nicholas P. Fluid Flow: Pumps, Pipes & Channels. LC 81-68034. (Illus.). 702p. 1981. 39.95 (ISBN 0-250-40432-X). Ann Arbor Science.
Mud Circulation Subcommittee of the IADC. Centrifugal Pumps & Piping Systems. 1983. pap. text ed. 24.95 (ISBN 0-87201-616-1). Gulf Pub.
Poynton. Metering Pumps. (Chemical Industries Ser.). 216p. 1983. 29.75 (ISBN 0-8247-1759-7). Dekker.
Pumps & Compressors. 1982. 445.00 (ISBN 0-686-38424-5, A210). Busn Trend.
Rudman, Jack. Senior Pump Operator. (Career Examination Ser.: C-2951). (Cloth bdg. avail. on request). pap. 12.00 (ISBN 0-8373-2951-5). Natl Learning.
Swindell, John G. Rudimentary Treatise on Well-Digging, Boring & Pumpwork, Eighteen Forty-Nine. (Illus.). 88p. pap. 12.50. Saifer.

Waddington, D. & Herlevich, F. Ann. Evaluation of Pumps & Motors for PV Water Pumping Systems. (Progress in Solar Energy Supplements SERI Ser.). 150p. 1983. pap. text ed. 13.50x (ISBN 0-89553-081-3). Am Solar Energy.

PUMPS
see Pumping Machinery

PUNISHMENT
see also Capital Punishment; Corporal Punishment; Criminal Law; Discipline of Children; Parole; Prisons; Probation; Reparation; School Discipline; Sentences (Criminal Procedure)
also particular forms of punishment

Routh, Donald K., ed. Learning, Speech, & the Complex Effects of Punishment: Essays Honoring George J. Wischner. 238p. 1982. 25.00 (ISBN 0-306-40960-7, Plenum Pr). Plenum Pub.

PUNISHMENT OF CHILDREN
see Discipline of Children

PUNS AND PUNNING
Gordon, Harvey C. Punishment: The Art of Punning or How to Lose Friends & Agonize People. 144p. 1983. pap. 1.95 (ISBN 0-446-90263-2). Warner Bks.

PUPIL-TEACHER PLANNING
see Self-Government (In Education)

PUPIL-TEACHER RELATIONSHIPS
see Teacher-Student Relationships

PUPPETS AND PUPPET-PLAYS
Gilbertson, Irvy. Puppet Plays for Missionettes. LC 82-82483. 64p. (Orig.). 1982. pap. 2.95 saddlestitched (ISBN 0-88243-736-4, 02-0736). Gospel Pub.

The Great Muppet Caper. 7.95 (ISBN 0-89524-144-7). Cherry Lane.

Hunt, Tamara & Renfro, Nancy. Pocketful of Puppets: Mother Goose Rhymes. Kelley, Merily H., ed. (Puppetry in Education Ser.). (Illus.). 80p. (Orig.). 1982. pap. 7.50 (ISBN 0-931044-06-5). Renfro Studios.

Jones, Taffy. Whistle-Stop Puppet Theatre. LC 82-23931. (Illus.). 180p. (Orig.). 1983. pap. 13.95x (ISBN 0-89950-072-2). McFarland & Co.

The Muppet Movie. 7.95 (ISBN 0-89524-061-0). Cherry Lane.

Sullivan, Debbie. Pocketful of Puppets: Activities for the Special Child. Keller, Merily H., ed. (Puppetry in Education Ser.). (Illus.). 48p. (Orig.). 1982. pap. 5.50 (ISBN 0-931044-07-3). Renfro Studios.

Sylwester, R. The Puppet & the Word. LC 12-2966. 1982. pap. 4.95 (ISBN 0-570-03873-1). Concordia.

Winez, Yvonne. Pocketful of Puppets: Three Plump Fish & Other Short Stories. Keller, Merily H., ed. (Puppetry in Education Ser.). (Illus.). 48p. (Orig.). 1982. pap. 5.50 (ISBN 0-931044-08-1). Renfro Studios.

PURCELL, HENRY, 1658-1695
Hutchings, Arthur. Purcell. LC 81-71304. (BBC Music Guides Ser.). 87p. (Orig.). 1983. pap. 5.95 (ISBN 0-295-95927-4). U of Wash Pr.

Nelson, Nancy P., ed. Nursing Care Plans for the Pediatric Patient. 1982. pap. 25.00 (ISBN 0-295-96019-1, Pub. by Childrens Orthopedic Hosp & Med Ctr). U of Wash Pr.

Zimmerman, Franklin B. Henry Purcell (Sixteen Fifty-Nine to Sixteen Ninety-Five): His Life & Times. 2nd rev. ed. LC 82-40485. 464p. 1983. 37.50 (ISBN 0-8122-7869-0); pap. 19.95 (ISBN 0-8122-1136-7). U of Pa Pr.

PURCHASERS
see Vendors and Purchasers

PURCHASING
see also Consumer Education; Consumers; Government Purchasing; Industrial Procurement; Marketing (Home Economics); Sales; Shopping

Baily, P. J. Purchasing Supply Management. 1978. pap. 18.50x (ISBN 0-412-15690-3, Pub. by Chapman & Hall England). Methuen Inc.

Bohlinger, Maryanne Smith. Merchandise Buying: A Practical Guide. 2nd ed. 570p. 1982. pap. text ed. write for info. (ISBN 0-697-08086-2). Wm C Brown.

Donohue, Brian. How to Buy an Office Computer or Word Processor. (Illus.). 256p. 1983. 17.95 (ISBN 0-13-403113-X); pap. 8.95 (ISBN 0-13-403105-9). P-H.

Gunderson, Loren. The Gold Book: The Businessman's Guide to the State of Montana's Procedures for the Procurement of Goods & Services. LC 83-80036. (Illus.). 150p. (Orig.). 1983. pap. 30.00 (ISBN 0-934318-12-3). Falcon Pr MT.

Hendricks, N. S. & Pickell, M. R., eds. Michigan Purchasing Directory. 1983. pap. 15.00 (ISBN 0-936526-02-5). Pick Pub MI.

Lysons, C. K. Purchasing. 224p. 1981. 29.00 (ISBN 0-7121-1752-0, Pub. by Macdonald & Evans). State Mutual Bk.

McMasters, Dale. Basic Skills Buying Skills Workbook. (Basic Skills Workbooks). 32p. (gr. 5-8). 1983. 0.99 (ISBN 0-8209-0570-4, MW-3). ESP.

Parsons, W. J. Improving Purchasing Performance. 128p. 1982. text ed. 37.00x (ISBN 0-566-02271-0). Gower Pub Ltd.

Stubblefield, Al. How to Buy Without Cash & Grow Rich. Writer's Service, Inc., ed. 131p. (Orig.). 1982. pap. 14.95 (ISBN 0-911229-00-0). Writers Serv FL.

PURCHASING, AUTOMOBILE
see Automobile Purchasing

PURCHASING, GOVERNMENT
see Government Purchasing

PURCHASING, INDUSTRIAL
see Industrial Procurement

PURDUE UNIVERSITY, LAFAYETTE, INDIANA
Freehafer, Ruth W. R. B. Stewart & Purdue University. 140p. 1983. 10.00 (ISBN 0-931682-14-2). Purdue Univ Bks.

PURE FOOD
see Food Adulteration and Inspection

PURIFICATION OF WATER
see Water-Purification

PURIM (FEAST OF ESTHER)
Chaikin, Miriam. Make Noise, Make Merry: The Story & Meaning of Purim. (Illus.). 96p. (gr. 3-6). 1983. 11.50 (ISBN 0-89919-140-1, Clarion). HM.

PURITANS
see also Church of England; Marprelate Controversy

Breen, T. H. Puritans & Adventurers: Change & Persistence in Early America. 1982. pap. 8.95 (ISBN 0-19-503207-1). Oxford U Pr.

Erikson, K. T. Wayward Puritans: A Study in the Sociology of Deviance. LC 66-16140. 228p. 1966. pap. text ed. 11.95x (ISBN 0-471-24427-9). Wiley.

Hunt, William. The Puritan Movement: The Coming of Revolution in an English County. (Harvard Historical Studies: No. 102). (Illus.). 384p. 1983. text ed. 36.00x (ISBN 0-674-73903-5). Harvard U Pr.

Puritan Personal Writings: Autobiographies & Other Writings, Vol. 8. LC 78-270. (American Puritan Writings Ser.). 240p. 1982. 57.50 (ISBN 0-404-60808-6). AMS Pr.

Puritan Personal Writings: Diaries, Vol. 7. LC 78-269. (American Puritan Writings Ser.). 1982. 57.50 (ISBN 0-404-60807-8). AMS Pr.

PURSUIT PLANES
see Airplanes, Military; Fighter Planes

PUSHKIN, ALEKSANDR SERGEEVICH, 1799-1837
Briggs, A. D. Alexander Pushkin: A Critical Study. LC 82-16242. 258p. 1983. text ed. 26.50x (ISBN 0-389-20340-8). B&N Imports.

Debreczeny, Paul. The Other Pushkin: A Study of Alexander Pushkin's Prose Fiction. LC 81-85449. 392p. 1983. 32.50x (ISBN 0-8047-1143-7). Stanford U Pr.

PUSHTUNS
Singer, A. Guardians of the North-West Frontier: The Pathans. (Peoples of the Wild Ser.). 1982. 15.96 (ISBN 0-7054-0702-0, Pub. by Time-Life). Silver.

PUSINELLI, ANTON, 1815-1878
Lenrow, Elbert, ed. & tr. The Letters of Richard Wagner to Anton Pusinelli. LC 72-93825. 293p. Date not set. Repr. of 1932 ed. price not set. Vienna Hse.

PUT AND CALL TRANSACTIONS
Brenner, Menachem. Option Pricing: Theory & Applications. (Salomon Brothers Center Bks.). 1983. write for info. (ISBN 0-669-05714-2). Lexington Bks.

Standard's & Poor's. Options Handbook. 1982. 29.95 (ISBN 0-07-051884-X). McGraw.

PUZZLES
see also Bible Games and Puzzles; Crossword Puzzles; Educational Games; Mathematical Recreations; Riddles

Ainley, Stephen. Mathemtical Puzzles. 156p. 1982. 30.00x (ISBN 0-7135-1327-6, Pub. by Bell & Hyman England). State Mutual Bk.

Brandreth, Gyles. The Complete Puzzler. 192p. 1983. pap. 6.95 (ISBN 0-312-15839-4). St Martin.

Diagram Group. Logic Puzzles. 96p. 1983. pap. 1.75 (ISBN 0-345-30478-0). Ballantine.

--Picture Puzzles. 96p. (Orig.). 1983. pap. 1.75 (ISBN 0-345-30476-4). Ballantine.

Fixx, James. Games for the Super Intelligent. 128p. 1982. pap. 2.75 (ISBN 0-446-31032-8). Warner Bks.

--More Games for the Super-Intelligent. 144p. 1982. pap. 2.75 (ISBN 0-446-31044-1). Warner Bks.

--Solve It. 128p. 1982. pap. 2.95 (ISBN 0-446-31080-8). Warner Bks.

Hacken, Sara. Games & Puzzles for Mormon Youth. 64p. 1982. 4.95 (ISBN 0-87747-932-1). Deseret Bk.

Heafford, Philip. The Math Entertainer. LC 82-40420. (Illus.). 176p. 1983. pap. 3.95 (ISBN 0-394-71374-5, Vin). Random.

Justus, Fred. Mixty Maxty Puzzles. (Puzzles Ser.). 24p. (gr. 3-5). 1979. wkbk. 5.00 (ISBN 0-8209-0283-7, MMP-1). ESP.

--Mixty Maxty Puzzles. (Puzzles Ser.). 24p. (gr. 5-6). 1979. wkbk. 5.00 (ISBN 0-8209-0284-5, MMP-2). ESP.

--Mixty Maxty Puzzles. (Puzzles Ser.). 24p. (gr. 5-7). 1979. wkbk. 5.00 (ISBN 0-8209-0285-3, MMP-3). ESP.

--Mixty Maxty Puzzles. (Puzzles Ser.). 24p. (gr. 8-12). 1979. wkbk. 5.00 (ISBN 0-8209-0286-1, MMP-4). ESP.

Mason, William. Rubik's Revenge. 154p. 1982. 10.95 (ISBN 0-13-783571-X); pap. 3.95 (ISBN 0-13-783563-9). P-H.

Moore, Rosalind, ed. Dell Pencil Puzzles & Word Games, No. 2. (Orig.). 1983. pap. 3.50 (ISBN 0-440-11718-6). Dell.

Morris, Scot. Omni Games. (Illus.). 192p. 1983. pap. 9.95 (ISBN 0-03-060297-1). HR&W.

Serebriakoff, Victor. A Mensa Puzzle Book. 128p. 1982. 20.00x (ISBN 0-584-11020-0, Pub. by Muller Ltd). State Mutual Bk.

--Puzzles, Problems, & Pastimes for the Superintelligent. 131p. 1983. 9.95 (ISBN 0-13-744664-0); pap. 3.95 (ISBN 0-13-744656-X). P-H.

Smullyan, Raymond. Five Thousand B.C. & Other Philosophical Fantasies. 224p. 1983. 13.95 (ISBN 0-312-29516-2). St Martin.

Stonerod, David. Puzzles in Space. (Illus.). 1982. pap. text ed. 6.50 (ISBN 0-914534-03-3). Stokes.

PUZZLES-JUVENILE LITERATURE
Anderson, Doug. Picture Puzzles for Armchair Detectives. LC 82-19344. (Illus.). 128p. (gr. 6 up). 1983. 9.95 (ISBN 0-8069-4670-9); PLB 9.99 (ISBN 0-8069-4671-7); pap. 3.95 (ISBN 0-8069-7718-3). Sterling.

Hoffman, Phyllis. Play Ball with the New York Yankees. LC 82-20783. (Illus.). 48p. (Orig.). (gr. 4-7). 1983. pap. 2.95 (ISBN 0-689-70759-2, A-135, Aladdin). Atheneum.

Neuman, Jeffrey. Play Ball with the Los Angeles Dodgers. LC 82-20782. (Illus.). 48p. (Orig.). (gr. 4-7). 1983. pap. 2.95 (ISBN 0-689-70760-6, A-136, Aladdin). Atheneum.

Pallas, Nervin. Calculator Puzzles, Tricks & Games. (Illus.). 96p. (gr. 7 up). 1983. pap. 4.95 (ISBN 0-8069-7688-8). Sterling.

PYNCHON, THOMAS, 1937-
Cooper, Peter L. Signs & Symptoms: Thomas Pynchon & the Contemporary World. LC 82-6929. 288p. 1983. 19.95 (ISBN 0-520-04537-8). U of Cal Pr.

Tanner, Tony. Thomas Pynchon. 1982. pap. 4.25 (ISBN 0-416-31670-0). Methuen Inc.

PYRAMID TEXTS
see Egyptian Language-Inscriptions

PYRAMIDS
Gill, Joseph B. The Great Pyramid Speaks to You. 1983. 13.95 (ISBN 0-8022-2405-9). Philos Lib.

PYRIDINE
Everse, Johannes, et al, eds. The Pyridine Nucleotide Coenzymes. 416p. 1982. 46.00 (ISBN 0-12-244750-6). Acad Pr.

PYRO- AND PIEZO-ELECTRICITY
see also Oscillators, Crystal

Gagnepain, J. J. & Meeker, Thrygve R., eds. Piezoelectricity. (Ferroelectrics Ser.: Vols. 40, Nos. 3-4; 41; & 42, Nos. 1-2). 782p. 1982. 300.00 (ISBN 0-677-16415-7). Gordon.

PYROTECHNICS
see Fireworks

PYTHAGORAS, d. 497 B.C.
Hallam, Arthur F. William Lloyd's Life of Pythagoras, with a New Thesis On the Origin of the New Testament. 84p. (Orig.). 1982. pap. 8.50 (ISBN 0-938770-01-2). Capitalist Pr OH.

PYTHAGORAS OF RHEGIUM
Iverson, I. B. Pythagoras & the Quantum World. 1982. 9.75 (ISBN 0-8062-1935-1). Carlton.

PYTHAGOREAN PROPOSITION
Beaulieu, Victor A. The Reconstruction of Pythagoras System on the Vibrational Theory of Number: The Essential Library of the Great Philosophers. (Illus.). 91p. 1983. Repr. of 1905 ed. 97.45 (ISBN 0-89920-050-8). Am Inst Psych.

Taylor, Thomas. Theoretic Arithmetic of the Pythagoreans. pap. 12.50 (ISBN 0-686-43261-4). Philos Res.

Q

QABALAH
see Cabala

QUADRATIC EQUATIONS
see Equations, Quadratic

QUADRATIC FORMS
see Forms, Quadratic

QUADRATURE, MECHANICAL
see Numerical Integration

QUADRUMANA
see Primates

QUAKERS
see Friends, Society Of

QUALITATIVE ANALYSIS
see Chemistry, Analytic-Qualitative

QUALITY CONTROL
see also Process Control;
also names of specific industries, e.g. Food Industry

Caplen, R. H. A Practical Approach to Quality Control. 4th ed. 326p. 1982. pap. text ed. 14.50x (ISBN 0-09-147451-5, Pub. by Busn Bks England). Renouf.

Dewar, Donald L. The Quality Circle: What You Should Know About It. (Illus.). 29p. 1980. pap. 0.75 (ISBN 0-937670-04-9). Quality Circle.

Drury, C. G., ed. Human Reliability in Quality Control. Fox, J. G. LC 75-11695. (Illus.). 315p. 1975. 27.50x (ISBN 0-85066-088-2). Intl Pubns Serv.

Information Sources on Industrial Quality Control. (UNIDO Guides to Information Sources: No. 6). 71p. 1980. pap. 4.00 (ISBN 0-686-82547-0, UNIP256, UN). Unipub.

Knittel, Patricia, ed. Selected Bibliography: Quality Control, Vol. II. (Orig.). 1982. pap. 15.00 (ISBN 0-89938-009-3). Tech & Ed Ctr Graph Arts RIT.

Norbert, Enrick & Mottley, Harry E., Jr. Manufacturing Analysis for Productivity & Quality-Cost Enhancement. 2nd ed. (Illus.). 150p. Repr. of 1968 ed. 22.95 (ISBN 0-8311-1146-1). Indus Pr.

Riordan, John J. & Cotliar, William. How to Develop Your GMP-QC Manual. 96p. 1977. pap. 30.00 (ISBN 0-914176-20-X). Wash Busn Info.

Sample Quality Control Documents. 1981. pap. 3.00 (ISBN 0-686-84314-2). Am Inst CPA.

QUALITY OF AIR
see Air Quality

QUALITY OF WATER
see Water Quality

QUANTITATIVE ANALYSIS
see Chemistry, Analytic-Quantitative

QUANTITY COOKERY
Here are entered works dealing solely with quantity food preparation. Works on quantity preparation and service of food for outside the home are entered under Food Service.
see also Food Service

Cotton, Nathan. Quantity Baking Recipes: Combined Edition, 2 vols. Incl. Vol. I. Cakes, Icings & Cheesecakes. 292p (ISBN 0-8436-2265-2); Vol. II. Breads, Pastries, Pies & Cookies. 284p (ISBN 0-8436-2272-5). 1983. Set. text ed. 39.95 (ISBN 0-8436-2273-3); text ed. 21.95 ea. CBI Pub.

Stowers, Sharon L. Institutional Food Service & Nutritional Care. Stone, Lori J., ed. (Illus.). 151p. 1983. pap. 78.00x (ISBN 0-9609720-0-5). Educ Plan Serv.

QUANTITY SURVEYING
see Building-Estimates

QUANTUM BIOCHEMISTRY
International Symposium on Quantum Biology & Quantum Pharmacology. Proceedings. Lowdin, Per-Olav & Sabin, John R., eds. 430p. 1982. 64.95 (ISBN 0-471-89123-1, Pub. by Wiley-Interscience). Wiley.

QUANTUM CHEMISTRY
see also Chemical Bonds; Molecular Orbitals; Quantum Biochemistry

Eyring, Henry, et al. Quantum Chemistry. 394p. 1944. 26.95x (ISBN 0-471-24981-5). Wiley.

Koetzle, T. F., ed. Structure & Bonding: Relationships Between Quantum Chemistry & Crystallography. Date not set. pap. 7.50 (ISBN 0-937140-25-2). Polycrystal Bk Serv.

McQuarrie, Donald A. Quantum Chemistry. LC 82-51234. (Physical Chemistry Ser.). (Illus.). 1983. text ed. 22.00x (ISBN 0-935702-13-X). Univ Sci Bks.

Quantum Chemistry, International Congress, 3rd & Sabin, J. R. Proceedings, Pts. 1 & 2. 1004p. 1980. pap. text ed. 67.95x (ISBN 0-471-08810-2, Pub. by Wiley-Interscience). Wiley.

Richards, W. Graham & Cooper, David L. Ab Initio Molecular Orbital Calculations for Chemists. 2nd ed. (Illus.). 1982. pap. 17.95 (ISBN 0-19-855369-2). Oxford U Pr.

Sadlej, Joanna. Semi-Empirical Methods of Quantum Chemistry. (Chemical Science Ser.). 416p. 1982. 89.95x (ISBN 0-470-27547-2). Halsted Pr.

Szabo, Attila & Ostlund, Neil S. Modern Quantum Chemistry: Introduction to Advanced Structure Theory. LC 81-71955. 1982. 39.95 (ISBN 0-02-949710-8). Free Pr.

QUANTUM DYNAMICS
see Quantum Theory

QUANTUM MECHANICS
see Quantum Theory

QUANTUM STATISTICS
see also Matrix Mechanics; Quantum Theory; Statistical Mechanics; Wave Mechanics

Fujita, Shigeji. Introduction to Non-Equilibrium Quantum Statistical Mechanics. LC 82-23209. 178p. 1983. Repr. of 1966 ed. lib. bdg. write for info. (ISBN 0-89874-593-4). Krieger.

QUANTUM THEORY
see also Chemistry, Physical and Theoretical; Force and Energy; Molecular Dynamics; Neutrons; Quantum Chemistry; Radiation; Raman Effect; Relativity (Physics); Thermodynamics; Wave Mechanics

Albeverio, S., et al, eds. Stochastic Processes in Quantum Theory & Statistical Physics: Proceedings, Marseille, France, 1981. (Lecture Notes in Physics Ser.: Vol. 173). 337p. 1983. pap. 17.00 (ISBN 0-387-11956-6). Springer-Verlag.

Atwood, W. B. & Bjorken, J. D. Lectures on Lepton Nucleon Scattering & Quantum Chromo-Dynamics. (Progress in Physics Ser.: Vol. 4). 1982. 34.95 (ISBN 3-7643-3079-1). Birkhauser.

Cassels, J. M. Basic Quantum Mechanics. 2nd ed. (Illus.). 206p. Date not set. pap. text ed. 13.50 (ISBN 0-333-31768-8). Scholium Intl.

Duff, M. J. & Isham, C. J., eds. Quantum Structure of Space & Time: Proceedings of the Nuffield Workshop, Imperial College, London, August 3-21, 1981. LC 82-9732. 420p. Date not set. 49.50 (ISBN 0-521-24732-2). Cambridge U Pr.

Eisberg, Robert & Resnick, Robert. Quantum Physics of Atoms, Molecules, Solids, Nuclei & Particles. LC 74-1195. 791p. 1974. text ed. 34.95x (ISBN 0-471-23464-8); avail. solutions (ISBN 0-471-05438-0). Wiley.

Leader, Elliot & Predazzi, Enrico. An Introduction to Gauge Theories & the "New Physics". LC 81-3860. (Illus.). 400p. 1982. 65.00 (ISBN 0-521-23375-5); pap. 27.50 (ISBN 0-521-29937-3). Cambridge U Pr.
Ludwig, G. Foundations of Quantum Mechanics I. (Texts & Monographs in Physics). (Illus.). 426p. 1983. 48.00 (ISBN 0-387-11683-4). Springer-Verlag.
Taylor, John R. Scattering Theory: The Quantum Theory of Nonrelativistic Collisions. 496p. 1983. Repr. of 1972 ed. text ed. price not set (ISBN 0-89874-607-8). Krieger.
Thirring, W. A Course in Mathematical Physics IV: Quantum Mechanics of Large Systems. (Illus.). 290p. 1983. 32.00 (ISBN 0-387-81701-8). Springer-Verlag.

QUARKS
Fritzsch, Harald. Quarks: The Stuff of Matter. (Illus.). 1983. 19.00 (ISBN 0-465-06781-6). Basic.

QUARTER HORSE
Denhardt, Bob. The Quarter Horse. LC 82-45893. (Illus.). 280p. 1983. Repr. of 1941 ed. 14.95 (ISBN 0-89096-144-1). Tex A&M Univ Pr.

QUARTZ OSCILLATORS
see Oscillators, Crystal

QUASI DELICTS
see Torts

QUASI-JUDICIAL AGENCIES
see Independent Regulatory Commissions

QUATERNARY PERIOD
see Geology, Stratigraphic–Quaternary

QUEBEC (PROVINCE)–DESCRIPTION AND TRAVEL
Arthur Frommer's Guide to Montreal-Quebec, 1983-84. Date not set. pap. 3.95 (ISBN 0-671-45296-7). Frommer-Pasmantier.
Warfield, Ronald G. & Juillerat, Lee. Crater Lake. LC 82-82579. (The Story Behind the Scenery Ser.). (Illus.). 48p. (Orig.). 1982. 7.95 (ISBN 0-916122-80-8); pap. 3.00 (ISBN 0-916122-79-4). KC Pubns.

QUEBEC (PROVINCE)–HISTORY
Warfield, Ronald G. & Juillerat, Lee. Crater Lake. LC 82-82579. (The Story Behind the Scenery Ser.). (Illus.). 48p. (Orig.). 1982. 7.95 (ISBN 0-916122-80-8); pap. 3.00 (ISBN 0-916122-79-4). KC Pubns.

QUEBEC (PROVINCE)–HISTORY–TO 1791
see Canada–History–To 1763 (New France)

QUEEN BEES
see Bee Culture

QUEENSLAND, UNIVERSITY OF
Pechey, Susan. Impressions of the University of Queensland. (Illus.). 57p. 1983. text ed. 12.50x (ISBN 0-7022-1853-7). U of Queensland Pr.

QUERCUS
see Oak

QUERIES
see Questions and Answers

QUESTION BOXES
see Questions and Answers

QUESTIONNAIRES
Housden, Theresa & Housden, Jack. How to Design & use Questionnaires. 150p. 1983. pap. 9.95 (ISBN 0-88056-115-7). Dilithium Pr.

QUESTIONS AND ANSWERS
Questions and answers on special subjects are entered under the subject subdivided by Miscellanea, e.g. Theology–Miscellanea. Examination questions on special subjects are entered under the subject subdivided by Examinations, Questions, etc. e.g. Engineering–Examinations, Questions, Etc.
see also Children'S Questions and Answers; Riddles also subdivision Examinations, Questions, Etc. under subjects, e.g. History–Examinations, Questions, Etc
Lechner, Jack. The Ivy League Rock Quiz Book. (Illus.). 144p. (Orig.). 1983. pap. 6.95 (ISBN 0-933328-62-1). Delilah Bks.
Shook, Robert L. The Book of Why. (Illus.). 160p. 1983. 9.95 (ISBN 0-8437-3335-7). Hammond Inc.

QUESTIONS AND ANSWERS, CHILDREN'S
see Children's Questions and Answers

QUEUING THEORY
Chaudhry, M. L. & Templeton, J. G. A First Course in Bulk Queues. 550p. 1983. write for info. (ISBN 0-471-86260-6, Pub. by Wiley-Interscience). Wiley.
Cox, D. R. & Smith, W. L. Queues: Receptors & Recognition Series B. Incl. Vol. 13. Receptor Regulation; Vol. 12. Purinergic Receptors; Vol. 11. Membrane Receptors; Vol. 10. Neurotransmitter Receptors, Part 2: Biogenic Amines; Vol. 9. Neurotransmitter Receptors, Part 1: Amino Acids, Peptides & Benzodiazepines; Vol. 8. Virus Receptors, Part 2: Animal Viruses; Vol. 7. Virus Receptors, Part 1: Bacterial Viruses; Vol. 6. Bacterial Adherence; Vol. 5. Taxis & Behavior; Vol. 4. Specificity of Embryological Interactions; Vol. 3. Microbial Interactions; Vol. 2. Intercellular Junctions & Synapses; Vol. 1. The Specificity & Action of Animal, Bacterial & Plant Toxins. 1971. pap. 11.50x (ISBN 0-412-10930-1, Pub. by Chapman & Hall England). Methuen Inc.
Disney, R. & Ott, T., eds. Applied Probability--Computer Science: The Interface, 2 Vols. (Progress in Computer Science). 1982. text ed. 34.00x ea. Vol. 2, 532pp (ISBN 3-7643-3067-8). Vol. 3, 514pp (ISBN 3-7643-3093-7). Birkhauser.
Stoyan, D. & Daley, D. J. Comparison Methods for Queues & Other Stochastic Models. 1982. text ed. write for info. (ISBN 0-471-10122-2, Pub. by Wiley-Interscience). Wiley.

QUICHES
see Indians of Central America

QUILTING
see also Coverlets
Beyer, Jinny. Medallion Quilts: The Art & Techniques of Creating Medallion Quilts, Including a Rich Collection of Historic & Contemporary Examples. LC 82-13744. 188p. 1982. 29.95 (ISBN 0-914440-57-8). EPM Pubns.
Caraway, Caren. Applique Quilts to Color, 1980. 48p. pap. 2.95 (ISBN 0-686-81961-6). Stemmer Hse.
Center for Self Sufficiency Research Division Staff. Guide to Craft, Quilt, Drapery, Etc. Pattern Sources. 35p. 1983. pap. text ed. 15.95 (ISBN 0-910811-31-8). Center Self.
De Julio, Mary A. Quilts from Montgomery County, New York. (Illus.). 24p. (Orig.). 1981. pap. 3.00 (ISBN 0-9608694-0-9). Montgomery Hist.
Garoutte, Sally, ed. Uncoverings Nineteen Eithty-Two. (Research Papers of American Quilt Study Group: Vol. 3). (Illus.). 1983. pap. write for info. (ISBN 0-9606590-2-1). Am Quilt.
Klein, Mary. A New View of Cathedral Window. (Illus.). 40p. 1983. 5.00 (ISBN 0-943574-20-X). That Patchwork.
McCloskey, Marsha. Wall Quilts. (Illus.). 48p. 1983. 6.00 (ISBN 0-943574-22-6). That Patchwork.
McCloskey, Marsha R. Small Quilts. (Illus.). 48p. 1982. pap. 6.00 (ISBN 0-943574-15-3). That Patchwork.
McDonald, Robert. Artist Quilts. (Illus.). 32p. 1981. 9.50x (ISBN 0-686-99806-5). La Jolla Mus Contemp Art.
Malone, Maggie. One Hundred-Twenty Patterns for Traditional Patchwork Quilts. LC 82-19671. (Illus.). 240p. 1983. 19.95 (ISBN 0-8069-5488-4); pap. 9.95 (ISBN 0-8069-7716-7). Sterling.
Martin, Nancy J. The Basics of Quilted Clothing. (Illus.). 68p. 1982. pap. 8.00 (ISBN 0-943574-12-9). That Patchwork.
--Sew Easy Strip Quilting. (Illus.). 20p. 1980. pap. 5.00 (ISBN 0-943574-00-5). That Patchwork.
Miles, Elaine. Many Hands: Making a Communal Quilt. (Illus.). 75p. (Orig.). 1982. 6.95 (ISBN 0-936810-02-5). R&E Miles.
Murwin, Susan A. & Payne, Suzzy C. The Quick & Easy Giant Dahlia Quilt on the Sewing Machine: Step-By-Step Instructions & Full Size Templates for Three Quilt Sizes. (Illus.). 80p. (Orig.). 1983. pap. 3.95. Dover.
Pottinger, David. Quilts From the Indiana Amish: A Regional Collection. (Illus.). 80p. 1983. 22.95 (ISBN 0-525-93285-2, 02229-660); pap. 12.95 (ISBN 0-525-48043-9, 01258-370). Dutton.
Singletary, Milly. Hawaiian Quilting Made Easy. (Illus.). 48p. pap. 5.00 (ISBN 0-9601256-8-X). Sunset Pubns.
Waugh, Carol W. & LaBelle, Judith L. Quilter's Precises Yardage Guide. (Illus.). 144p. 1983. pap. 4.95 (ISBN 0-8329-0275-6). New Century.
Wright, Sandra L., ed. Quilts from Happy Hands. 192p. 1981. 9.95 (ISBN 0-941468-01-1). Happy Hands.

QUIZ BOOKS
see Questions and Answers

QUMRAN COMMUNITY
see also Dead Sea Scrolls
Davies, Philip. Qumran. 1982. 35.00x (ISBN 0-7188-2458-X, Pub. by Lutterworth Pr England). State Mutual Bk.

QUOITS
Horseshoe Pitching Rules. Date not set. 1.00 (ISBN 0-686-43034-4). AAU Pubns.

QUOTATIONS
see also Aphorisms and Apothegms; Proverbs
Fitzhenry, Robert I., ed. Barnes & Noble Book of Quotations. 340p. 1983. pap. 4.76i (ISBN 0-06-463571-6, EH 571). B&N NY.
Hubbard, L. Ron. When in Doubt, Communicate... Minshull, Ruth & Lefson, Edward, eds. 150p. (Orig.). 1982. pap. cancelled (ISBN 0-937922-08-0). SAA Pub.
Jones, Hugh P., ed. Dictionary of Foreign Phrases & Classical Quotations. 552p. 1983. pap. 12.95 (ISBN 0-88072-017-4). Tanager Bks.
Justus, Fred. Basic Skills Famous Quotations Workbook. (Basic Skills Workbooks). 32p. (gr. 4-7). 1983. 0.99 (ISBN 0-8209-0559-3, SSW-7). ESP.
--Famous Quotes Puzzles. (Puzzles Ser.). 24p. (gr. 6). 1980. wkbk. 5.00 (ISBN 0-8209-0287-X, PU-1). ESP.
Lieberman, Gerald F. Three Thousand Five Hundred Good Quotes for Speakers. LC 81-43552. 480p. 1983. 17.95 (ISBN 0-385-17766-6). Doubleday.
Penfield, Joyce. Communicating with Quotes: The Igbo Case. LC 82-15626. (Contributions in Intercultural & Comparative Studies Ser.: No. 8). (Illus.). 152p. 1983. lib. bdg. 29.95 (ISBN 0-313-23767-0, PEN/). Greenwood.
Prochnow, Herbert V. & Prochnow, Herbert V., Jr. A Treasure Chest of Quotations for All Occasions. LC 82-48130. 480p. 1983. 17.95 (ISBN 0-06-015043-2, HarpT). Har-Row.
Robbins, Maria P., ed. The Cook's Quotation Book. 88p. 1983. 8.95 (ISBN 0-916366-19-7). Pushcart Pr.
Verbatim Diary: MCMLXXXIII. 128p. 1982. 12.50 (ISBN 0-930454-16-2). Verbatim.

R

RABBIT AUTOMOBILE
see Automobiles, Foreign–Types–Rabbit

RABBITS
see also Hares
Bare, Colleen S. Rabbits & Hares. LC 82-45992. (Illus.). 80p. (gr. 4 up). 1983. PLB 9.95 (ISBN 0-396-08127-4). Dodd.
Elementary Science Study: Bones, Rabbit Skeleton. 1982. write for info. (ISBN 0-07-018514-X). McGraw.
Nightengale, Gay. Rabbit Keeping. (Illus.). 94p. 1979. pap. 3.95 (ISBN 0-7028-1099-1). Avian Pubns.
Romney, C. Park. Raising Rabbits at Home. (Illus.). 92p. 1981. pap. 2.95 (ISBN 0-940986-01-9). ValuWrite.

RACE
see also Black Race
Barton, Len & Walker, Stephen. Race, Class & Education. 256p. 1983. text ed. 27.25 (ISBN 0-7099-0683-8, Pub. by Croom Helm Ltd England). Biblio Dist.

RACE AWARENESS
see also Ethnicity; Racism
Gill & Jackson. Adoption & Race. LC 82-42714. 160p. 1983. 22.50x (ISBN 0-686-84407-6). St Martin.
Haberly, David T. Three Sad Races: Racial Identity & National Consciousness in Brazilian Literature. LC 82-4467. (Illus.). 198p. p.n.s. (ISBN 0-521-24722-5). Cambridge U Pr.
Saunders, M. Multicultural Teaching: A Guide for the Classroom. 192p. Date not set. 10.50 (ISBN 0-07-084133-0). McGraw.

RACE DISCRIMINATION
Here are entered works which are limited to overt discriminatory behavior directed against racial or ethnic groups. Works on racism as a attitude as well as works on both attitude and overt discriminatory behavior directed against racial or ethnic groups are entered under Racism. Works on discrimination directed against a particular group are entered under the name of the group with subdivision Social conditions, or similar subdivision, e.g. Civil rights.
see also Discrimination in Employment; Segregation also names of racial or ethnic groups, e.g. Mexicans in the United States
Parcel, Toby L. & Mueller, Charles W., eds. Ascription & Labor Markets: Race & Sex Difference in Earnings. LC 82-22741. (Quantitative Studies Social Relations (Monograph)). Date not set. price not set (ISBN 0-12-545020-6). Acad Pr.
Schofield. Black & White in School. 272p. 1982. 29.95 (ISBN 0-03-056977-X). Praeger.

RACE HORSES
see also Thoroughbred Horse;
also names of individual race horses
Hartigan, Joe. To Own a Racehorse. pap. 7.50x (ISBN 0-87556-601-4). Saifer.
Katcha Goodwon. The Complete Thinking Man's Guide to Handicapping & Training. 232p. (Orig.). 1983. 19.95 (ISBN 0-932896-05-7). Westcliff Pub.
Willett, Peter. The Classic Racehorse. LC 82-11072. (Illus.). 272p. 1983. Repr. of 1981 ed. 23.00 (ISBN 0-8131-1477-2). U Pr of Ky.

RACE PREJUDICE
see Racism

RACE PROBLEMS
see Race Relations

RACE PSYCHOLOGY
see Ethnopsychology

RACE QUESTION
see Race Relations

RACE RELATIONS
see also Culture Conflict; Intercultural Education; Minorities; Miscegenation; Pluralism (Social Sciences); Race Discrimination; Racism; United States–Race Relations
also subdivision Race relations under names of regions, countries, cities, etc., e.g. United States–Race relations; subdivision Native races under names of continents and countries, e.g. South Africa–Native races; and names of individual races and ethnic groups with pertinent topical subdivision, e.g. Afro-Americans–Relations with Jews; Indians of North America–Government relations
Detweiler, Robert & Kornweibel, Theodore. Slave & Citizen: A Critical Annotated Bibliography on Slavery & Race Relations in the Americas. 300p. 1983. pap. 6.00 (ISBN 0-686-84758-X). Campanile.
The Papers of the Congress of Racial Equality: Addendum, 1944-1967. 77p. 1982. reference bk. 25.00 (ISBN 0-667-00664-8). Microfilming Corp.

RACE RELATIONS IN LITERATURE
Sundquist, Eric J. Faulkner: The House Divided. LC 82-8923. 256p. 1983. 16.95q (ISBN 0-8018-2898-8). Johns Hopkins.

RACES OF MAN
see Ethnology

RACIAL IDENTITY OF BLACKS
see Blacks–Race Identity

RACIAL CROSSING
see Miscegenation

RACINE, JEAN BAPTISTE, 1639-1699
Muir. Last Periods of Shakespeare, Racine, & Ibsen. 128p. 1982. 40.00x (ISBN 0-85323-012-9, Pub. by Liverpool Univ England). State Mutual Bk.

RACING PIGEONS
see Pigeons

RACISM
Here are entered works on racism as an attitude as well as works on both attitude and overt discriminatory behavior directed against racial or ethnic groups. Works which are limited to overt discriminatory behavior directed against racial or ethnic groups are entered under Race discrimination. Works on racism directed against a particular group are entered under the name of the group with subdivision Social conditions, or similar subdivision, e.g. Civil rights.
see also Antisemitism; Race Discrimination; Race Relations
Apostle, Richard A. & Glock, Charles Y. The Anatomy of Racial Attitudes. LC 82-4867. 277p. 1983. 27.50x (ISBN 0-520-04719-2). U of Cal Pr.
Stone, Merlin & Women Against Racism. Three Thousand Years of Racism. 32p. 1983. pap. 3.00x (ISBN 0-9603352-2-6). New Sibylline.
Woodward, C. Vann. American Counterpoint: Slavery & Racism in the North-South Dialogue. 320p. 1983. pap. 7.95 (ISBN 0-19-503269-1, GB 727, GB). Oxford U Pr.

RACQUET BALL
see Racquetball

RACQUETBALL
Badminton-Squash-Racquetball 1982-84. (NAGWS Sports Guides Ser.). 3.75 (ISBN 0-88314-079-9). AAHPERD.
Scott, Eugene. Racquetball: The Cult. LC 77-75883. (Illus.). 1979. pap. 6.95 (ISBN 0-385-13006-6, Dolp). Doubleday.

RADAR
Bole, A. G. & Jones, K. D. Automatic Radar Plotting Aids Manual. 160p. 1982. 49.00x (ISBN 0-434-90160-1, Pub. by Heinemann England). State Mutual Bk.
Kassam, S. A. & Thomas, J. B., eds. Nonparametric Detection: Theory & Applications. LC 79-22557. (Benchmark Papers in Electrical Engineering & Computer Science Ser.: Vol. 23). 349p. 1980. 55.00. Hutchinson Ross.
Radar 82. 512p. 1982. pap. 95.00 (ISBN 0-85296-268-1). Inst Elect Eng.
Wiley, Richard G. Electronic Intelligence: An Analysis of Radar Signals. (Artech House Radar Library). (Illus.). 234p. 1982. 40.00 (ISBN 0-89006-124-6). Artech Hse.

RADAR–ANTENNAS
Law, Preston. Shipboard Antennas. (Artech Radar Library). (Illus.). 400p. 1982. 50.00 (ISBN 0-89006-123-8). Artech Hse.

RADAR–DATA PROCESSING
Haykin, S., ed. Array Processing. LC 79-11772. (Benchmark Papers in Electrical Engineering & Computer Science: Vol. 22). 362p. 1979. 56.50 (ISBN 0-87933-351-0). Hutchinson Ross.

RADAR IN NAVIGATION
Law, Preston. Shipboard Antennas. (Artech Radar Library). (Illus.). 400p. 1982. 50.00 (ISBN 0-89006-123-8). Artech Hse.

RADIATION
see also Collisions (Nuclear Physics); Electromagnetic Waves; Food, Effect of Radiation on; Irradiation; Light; Orgonomy; Polarization (Nuclear Physics); Quantum Theory; Radiology; Scattering (Physics); Sound; Spectrum Analysis; Transport Theory; X-Rays
Ecker, Martin. Radiation & All You Need to Know about It. 1981. 4.95x (ISBN 0-394-74650-3). Cancer Control Soc.
Industrial Application of Radioisotopes & Radiation Technology. 595p. 1983. pap. 68.75 (ISBN 92-0-060082-4, ISP 598, IAEA). Unipub.

RADIATION–MEASUREMENT
Here are entered works on the measurement of radiation parameters and values in general. Works on the measurement of the radiation dose are entered under Radiation Dosimetry. Works on the radiation dose in general are entered under Radiation–Dosage.
see also Radiation Dosimetry; Photometry; Radioactivity–Measurement
Grum, Fran & Bartleson, James, eds. Optical Radiation Measurements, Vol. 4. Date not set. price not set (ISBN 0-12-304904-0). Acad Pr.

RADIATION–PHYSIOLOGICAL EFFECT
see also Radioactivity–Physiological Effect; Radiogenetics; Radiotherapy
The Control of Exposure of the Public to Ionizing Radiation in the Event of Accident or Attack. 1982. 20.00 (ISBN 0-913392-58-8). NCRP Pubns.

RADIATION–SAFETY MEASURES
The Dose Limitation System in the Nuclear Fuel Cycle & in Radiation Protection. 675p. 1983. pap. 77.00 (ISBN 92-0-020182-2, ISP 599, IAEA). Unipub.
Sowby, F. D. & International Commission on Radiological Protection, eds. General Principles of Monitoring for Radiation Protection of Workers: ICRP Publication, No. 35. 40p. 1982. pap. 15.00 (ISBN 0-08-029816-8). Pergamon.

RADIATION, SOLAR
see Solar Radiation

RADIATION, STELLAR
see Stars–Radiation

RADIATION BIOLOGY
see Radiobiology
RADIATION CHEMISTRY
Here are entered works on the chemical effects of high energy radiation on matter. Works on the chemical properties of radioactive substances and their use in chemical studies are entered under Radiochemistry. Works on the application of chemical techniques to the study of the structure and properties of atomic nuclei, their transformations and reactions are entered under Nuclear Chemistry.
see also Nuclear Chemistry; Radiochemistry
Baxendale, J. & Busi, F. The Study of Fast Processes & Transient Species by Electron Pulse Radiolysis. 1982. 74.50 (ISBN 90-277-1431-2, Pub. by Reidel Holland). Kluwer Boston.
RADIATION DOSIMETRY
Here are entered works on the measurement of radiation dose. Works on the radiation dose in general are entered under Radiation-Dosage. Works on the measurement of radiation parameters and values in general are entered under Radiation-Measurement.
Biomedical Dosimetry: Physical Aspects of Instrumentation & Calibration. 596p. 1981. pap. 60.25 (ISBN 92-0-010281-6, ISP 567, IAEA). Unipub.
The Dose Limitation System in the Nuclear Fuel Cycle & in Radiation Protection. 675p. 1983. pap. 77.00 (ISBN 92-0-020182-2, ISP 599, IAEA). Unipub.
Dosimetry of X-Ray and Gamma-Ray Beams for Radiation Therapy in the Energy Range 10 KEV to 50 MEV: NCRP Report 69. 1981. 12.00 (ISBN 0-913392-55-3). NCRP Pubns.
McLaughlin, W. L., ed. Trends in Radiation Dosimetry. (Illus.). 320p. 1982. pap. 25.00 (ISBN 0-08-029143-0). Pergamon.
RADIATION ECOLOGY
see Radioecology
RADIATION FIELD PHOTOGRAPHY
see Kirlian Photography
RADIATION GENETICS
see Radiogenetics
RADIATION INDUCED CHEMICAL REACTIONS
see Radiation Chemistry
RADIATION INJURY
see Radiation-Physiological Effect
RADIATION INQUIRY
see Radiation-Physiological Effect
RADIATION MUTAGENESIS
see Radiogenetics
RADIATION PROTECTION
see Radiation-Safety Measures
RADIATION THERAPY
see Radiotherapy
RADICALISM
Epstein, James & Thompson, Dorothy, eds. The Chartist Experience-Studies in Working-Class Radicalism & Culture 1830 to 1860. 416p. 1982. text ed. 28.00x (ISBN 0-333-32971-6, 41403, Pub. by Macmillan England); pap. text ed. 12.50x (ISBN 0-333-32972-4, 41424). Humanities.
Greaves, Richard & Zaller, Robert, eds. Biographical Dictionary of British Radicals in the Seventeenth Century, Vol. 2. 352p. 1982. text ed. 75.00x (ISBN 0-7108-0430-X, Pub. by Harvester England). Humanities.
Hone, J. Ann. For the Cause of Truth: Radicalism in London, 1795-1821. (Historical Monographs). 422p. 1982. 45.00x (ISBN 0-19-821887-7). Oxford U Pr.
Kann. The American Left: Failures & Fortunes. 256p. 1982. 26.95 (ISBN 0-03-061772-3). Praeger.
RADICALS (CHEMISTRY)
Floyd, Robert A., ed. Free Radicals & Cancer. (Illus.). 552p. 1982. 69.75 (ISBN 0-8247-1551-9). Dekker.
RADIO
see also Modulation (Electronics); Police Communication Systems; Radar; Sound-Recording and Reproducing
also subdivision Radio Equipment under subjects, e.g. Automobiles-Radio Equipment; and headings beginning with the word Radio, e.g. Radio Frequency Modulation; Radio In Navigation
Fornatale, Peter & Mills, Joshua E. Radio in the Television Age. LC 79-67675. 240p. 1983. pap. 7.95 (ISBN 0-87951-172-9). Overlook Pr.
RADIO-AMATEURS' MANUALS
see also Amateur Radio Stations
Collins, A. Frederick & Hertzberg, Robert. The Radio Amateur's Handbook. 15th, rev. ed. LC 82-48666. (Illus.). 416p. 1983. 10.53i (ISBN 0-06-181366-4, HarpT). Har-Row.
Rayer. Beginner's Guide to Amateur Radio. (Illus.). 1982. pap. 9.95 (ISBN 0-408-01126-2). Focal Pr.
RADIO-APPARATUS AND SUPPLIES
see also Radio-Transmitters and Transmission; Wave Guides
Stokes, John. Seventy Years of Radio Tubes & Valves. LC 82-15899. (Illus.). 256p. Date not set. 21.95 (ISBN 0-911572-27-9). Vestal.
RADIO-BROADCASTING
see Radio Broadcasting
RADIO-EXAMINATIONS, QUESTIONS, ETC.
Rudman, Jack. Radio Dispatcher. (Career Examination Ser.: C-540). (Cloth bdg. avail. on request). pap. 12.00 (ISBN 0-8373-0540-3). Natl Learning.
RADIO-HANDBOOKS, MANUALS, ETC.
Hellyer & Sinclair. Questions & Answers: Radio & TV. 4th ed. (Illus.). 1976. pap. 4.95 (ISBN 0-408-00249-2). Focal Pr.
King. Beginner's Guide to Radio. 8th ed. (Illus.). 1977. pap. 9.95 (ISBN 0-408-00275-1). Focal Pr.
Orr, William I. Radio Handbook. Date not set. 39.95 (ISBN 0-672-21874-7). Sams.
Woodward, George, ed. Radio Amateur's Handbook. 1983 rev. ed. LC 41-3345. Date not set. price not set (ISBN 0-87259-060-7). Am Radio.
RADIO-REPAIRING
Nineteen Forty-Seven TV & FM Servicing Information. 200p. Date not set. 20.00 (ISBN 0-938630-19-9). Ars Electronics.
Questions & Answers: Radio Repair. (Illus.). pap. 4.95 (ISBN 0-408-00367-7). Focal Pr.
Rider Radio Manuals Index. 258p. Date not set. pap. 20.00 (ISBN 0-938630-23-7). Ars Electronics.
RADIO-TRANSMITTERS AND TRANSMISSION
Barty-King, Hugh. Girdle Round the Earth-Story of Cable & Wireless. 1979. 21.50 (ISBN 0-434-04902-6, Pub. by Heinemann). David & Charles.
RADIO, CITIZENS BAND
see Citizens Band Radio
RADIO ADVERTISING
see also Television Advertising
The One Show: Advertising Best Print, Radio, TV, Vol. 2. 352p. 1981. 32.50 (ISBN 0-9602628-2-2). Am Showcase.
The One Show: Advertising Best Print, Radio, TV, Vol. 3. 336p. 1982. 35.00 (ISBN 0-9602628-3-0). Am Showcase.
RADIO AS A PROFESSION
Lerner, Mark. Careers with a Radio Station. LC 82-20349. (Early Career Bks.). (Illus.). 36p. (gr. 2-5). 1983. PLB 5.95g (ISBN 0-8225-0312-3). Lerner Pubns.
RADIO BROADCASTING
see also Radio-Transmitters and Transmission; Radio Advertising; Radio Journalism; Radio Programs; Television Broadcasting
Eastman, Susan Tyler & Klein, Robert. Strategies in Broadcast & Cable Promotion: Commercial Television, Radio, Cable, Pay Television, Public Television. 352p. 1982. pap. text ed. 13.95x (ISBN 0-534-01156-X). Wadsworth Pub.
Gay, Tim & Hurvitz, David, eds. Radio Contacts. 1982. deluxe ed. 136.00 (ISBN 0-935224-17-3). Larimi Comm.
Hyde, Stuart. Television & Radio Announcing. 4th ed. LC 82-83204. 528p. 1983. text ed. 22.50 (ISBN 0-395-32618-4); write for info. instr's. manual (ISBN 0-395-32619-2). HM.
Parker, Bruce & Farrell, Nigel. TV & Radio: Everybody's Soapbox. (Illus.). 176p. 1983. 13.95 (ISBN 0-7137-1306-2, Pub. by Blandford Pr England); pap. 8.95 (ISBN 0-7137-1337-2, Pub. by Blandford Pr England). Sterling.
RADIO BROADCASTING-MANAGEMENT
Rudman, Jack. Radio Station Manager. (Career Examination Ser.: C-2935). (Cloth bdg. avail. on request). pap. 12.00 (ISBN 0-8373-2935-3). Natl Learning.
RADIO CIRCUITS
Cuthbert, Thomas R. Circuit Design Using Personal Computers. 512p. 1983. 39.95 (ISBN 0-471-87700-X, Pub. by Wiley-Interscience). Wiley.
RADIO COMMERCIALS
see Radio Advertising
RADIO DRAMA
see Radio Plays
RADIO JOURNALISM
Wulfmeyer, K. Tim. Broadcast Newswriting: A Workbook. 118p. 1983. pap. text ed. 8.95 (ISBN 0-8138-0226-1). Iowa St U Pr.
RADIO JOURNALISTS
see Journalists
RADIO MODULATION
see Modulation (Electronics)
RADIO NEWS
see Radio Journalism
RADIO PLAYS
see also Soap Operas
Carr, John D. The Dead Sleep Lightly. LC 82-45870. (Crime Club Ser.). 192p. 1983. 11.95 (ISBN 0-385-18714-9). Doubleday.
RADIO PROGRAMS
see also Radio Plays
Broadcast Information Bureau, Inc. The Radio Programs Source Book. Doris, Liz, ed. 100p. (Orig.). 1982. pap. 62.95 (ISBN 0-943174-01-5). Broadcast Info.
Smith, V. Jackson. Programming for Radio & Television. rev. ed. LC 82-21887. (Illus.). 180p. 1983. lib. bdg. 18.75 (ISBN 0-8191-2887-2); pap. text ed. 8.25 (ISBN 0-8191-2888-0). U Pr of Amer.
RADIO SERVICING
see Radio-Repairing
RADIO STATIONS, AMATEUR
see Amateur Radio Stations
RADIO TRANSMISSION
see Radio-Transmitters and Transmission
RADIOACTIVATION ANALYSIS
Boyd, Robert W. Radiometry & the Detection of Optical Radiation. (Pure & Applied Optics Ser.). 325p. 1983. 34.95x (ISBN 0-471-86188-X, Pub. by Wiley-Interscience). Wiley.
RADIOACTIVE DATING
Currie, Lloyd A., ed. Nuclear & Chemical Dating Techniques. (ACS Symposium Ser.: No. 176). 1982. write for info. (ISBN 0-8412-0669-4). Am Chemical.
RADIOACTIVE INDICATORS
see Radioactive Tracers
RADIOACTIVE ISOTOPES
see Radioisotopes
RADIOACTIVE POLLUTION
see also Radioactive Waste Disposal
Nuclear Power & the Environment. 195p. 1982. pap. 14.00 (ISBN 92-0-129082-9, ISP635, IAEA). Unipub.
RADIOACTIVE TRACERS
see also Carbon-Isotopes; Nuclear Medicine; Radioisotope Scanning; Radioisotopes in Hydrology
Glenn, Howard J., ed. Biologic Applications of Radiotracers. 224p. 1982. 63.50 (ISBN 0-8493-6009-9). CRC Pr.
RADIOACTIVE WASTE DISPOSAL
see also Radioactive Pollution
Blasewitz, A. G. & Davis, John M., eds. Treatment & Handling of Radioactive Wastes. LC 82-22695. 672p. 1983. 65.00 (ISBN 0-935470-14-X). Battelle.
Commission of European Communities, ed. Research & Development on Radioactive Waste Management & Storage: First Annual Progress Report of the European Community Programme 1980-84. (Radioactive Waste Management: A Series of Monographs & Tracts Ser.: Vol. 4). 129p. 1982. write for info. (ISBN 3-7186-0115-X). Harwood Academic.
Duffy, J. I., ed. Treatment, Recovery, & Disposal Processes for Radioactive Wastes: Recent Advances. LC 82-22260. (Pollution Technology Review No.95, Chemical Technology Review No. 216). (Illus.). 287p. 1983. 39.00 (ISBN 0-8155-0922-7). Noyes.
Murdock, Steve H. & Leistritz, F. Larry. Nuclear Waste: Socioeconomic Dimensions. (Special Studies in Science, Technology, & Public Policy-Society). 343p. 1983. price not set. Westview.
Park, Kilho P. & Duedall, Iver W. Wastes in the Ocean: Radioactive Wastes in the Ocean, Vol. 3. (Environmental Science & Technology Texts & Monographs). 870p. 1983. 33.45 (ISBN 0-471-09770-5, Pub. by Wiley Interscience). Wiley.
Site Investigations for Repositories for Solid Radioactive Wastes in Shallow Ground. 89p. 1982. pap. 14.00 (ISBN 0-686-82546-2, IDC 216, IAEA). Unipub.
Walker, Charles A. & Gould, Leroy C., eds. Too Hot to Handle? Social & Policy Issues in the Management of Radioactive Wastes. LC 82-20000. (Yale Fastback Ser.: No. 26). 240p. 1983. text ed. 20.00 (ISBN 0-300-02899-7); pap. 5.95 (ISBN 0-300-02993-4). Yale U Pr.
RADIOACTIVE WASTES
see also Radioactive Waste Disposal
American Society of Civil Engineers, compiled by. Nuclear Facilities Siting. LC 82-73507. 64p. 1982. pap. text ed. 11.75 (ISBN 0-87262-344-0). Am Soc Civil Eng.
--Nuclear Waste Management. LC 82-73506. 52p. 1982. pap. text ed. 11.75 (ISBN 0-87262-343-2). Am Soc Civil Eng.
Jensen, B. S. Migration Phenomena of Radionuclides into the Geosphere: A Critical Review of the Available Information; Radioactive Waste Management. (A Series of Monographs & Tracts: Vol. 5). 200p. 1982. write for info. (ISBN 3-7186-0120-6). Harwood Academic.
Murdock, Steve H. & Leistritz, F. Larry. Nuclear Waste: Socioeconomic Dimensions. (Special Studies in Science, Technology, & Public Policy-Society). 343p. 1983. price not set. Westview.
RADIOACTIVITY-MEASUREMENT
see also Radioactivation Analysis; Radioactive Dating; Radioisotope Scanning
Beeler, J. R. Radiation Effects Computer Experiments. (Defects in Solids Ser.: Vol. 13). 960p. 1982. 168.00 (ISBN 0-444-86315-X, North Holland). Elsevier.
Mitchell, I. V. & Barfoot, K. M. Particle-Induced X-Ray Emission Analysis: Application to Analytical Problems. (Nuclear Science Applications Ser.). 63p. 1981. 14.00 (ISBN 3-7186-0085-4). Harwood Academic.
RADIOACTIVITY-PHYSIOLOGICAL EFFECT
see also Nuclear Medicine
Panati, Charles & Hudson, Michael. The Silent Intruder: Surviving the Radiation Age. 256p. 1983. pap. 3.25 (ISBN 0-425-05828-X). Berkley Pub.
RADIOBIOLOGY
see also Radioactive Tracers; Radioecology; Radiogenetics; Radioisotopes; Radioisotopes in the Body
also subdivision Physiological Effects under radiation subjects, e.g. Radiation-Physiological Effects
Advances in Radiation Biology, Vol. 10. (Serial Publication). Date not set. price not set (ISBN 0-12-035410-1); price not set lib. ed. (ISBN 0-12-035484-5); price not set microfiche (ISBN 0-12-035485-3). Acad Pr.
RADIOCHEMICAL ANALYSIS
see Radioactivation Analysis
RADIOCHEMISTRY
Here are entered works on the chemical properties of radioactive substances and their use in chemical studies. Works on the chemical effects of high energy radiation on matter are entered under Radiation Chemistry. Works on the application of chemical techniques to the study of the structure and properties of atomic nuclei, their transformations and reactions are entered under Nuclear Chemistry.
see also Isotope Separation; Nuclear Chemistry; Radiation Chemistry; Radioactivation Analysis; Radioactive Dating; Radioactive Tracers; Radioisotopes; Reactor Fuel Reprocessing
Sharpe, A. G. & Emeleus, H. J., eds. Advances in Inorganic Chemistry & Radiochemistry, Vol. 26. (Serial Publication). Date not set. price not set (ISBN 0-12-023626-5); price not set lib. ed. (ISBN 0-12-023692-3); price not set microfiche (ISBN 0-12-023693-1). Acad Pr.
RADIODIAGNOSIS
see Diagnosis, Radioscopic
RADIOECOLOGY
see also Radioactive Pollution
Klement, A. W. & Schultz, V., eds. Freshwater & Terrestrial Radioecology: A Selected Bibliography. LC 80-22169. 587p. 1980. 46.00 (ISBN 0-87933-389-8). Hutchinson Ross.
Nuclear Power & the Environment. 195p. 1982. pap. 14.00 (ISBN 92-0-129082-9, ISP635, IAEA). Unipub.
RADIOGENETICS
Crow, James F. How Well Can We Assess Genetic Risk? Not Very. 9.00 (ISBN 0-913392-56-1). NCRP Pubns.
RADIOGRAPHY
see also Radiography, Medical; X-Rays
Ballinger, Philip W. Merrill's Atlas of Radiographic Positions & Radiologic Procedures, 3 Vols. 5th ed. (Illus.). 950p. 1982. text ed. 99.95 (ISBN 0-8016-3408-3). Mosby.
Maurer, Edward L. Practical Applied Roentgenology. 212p. 1983. lib. bdg. 36.00 (ISBN 0-683-05650-6). Williams & Wilkins.
Sweeney, Richard J. Radiographic Artifacts: Their Cause & Control. (Illus.). 263p. 1983. text ed. price not set (ISBN 0-397-50554-X, Lippincott Medical). Lippincott.
RADIOGRAPHY, MEDICAL
see also Angiography; Diagnosis, Radioscopic; Tomography
also subdivision Radiography under names of organs e.g. Brain-Radiography
Chao. Design & Application of Tumor Prostheses. 1983. price not set (ISBN 0-86577-081-6). Thieme-Stratton.
Goldman, Myer & Cope, David. A Radiographic Index. 7th ed. (Illus.). 112p. 1982. pap. text ed. 10.00 (ISBN 0-7236-0660-9). Wright-PSG.
Kelsey, Charles A. Radiation Safety for Laboratory Technicians. Gardner, Alvin F., ed. (Allied Health Professions Monographs). 1983. write for info. (ISBN 0-87527-319-X). Green.
Lauer, Gary. Principles & Practices of the College-Based Radiography Program. Gardner, Alvin F., ed. (Allied Health Professions Monograph). 1983. write for info. (ISBN 0-87527-310-6). Green.
Laws, Priscilla W. & Public Citizen Health Research Group. The X-Ray Information Book: A Consumer's Guide to Avoiding Unnecessary Medical & Dental X-Rays. 1983. 16.50 (ISBN 0-374-29342-2); pap. 7.25 (ISBN 0-374-51730-4). FS&G.
Price, Ronald, et al, eds. Digital Radiography: A Focus on Clinical Utility. 448p. Date not set. 39.50 (ISBN 0-8089-1544-4). Grune.
RADIOISOTOPE SCANNING
Bulcke, J. A. & Baert, A. L. Clinical & Radiological Aspects of Myopathies: CT Scanning-EMG-Radio-Isotopes. (Illus.). 187p. 1983. 56.00 (ISBN 0-387-11443-2). Springer-Verlag.
Kuhl, D. E., ed. Principles of Radionuclide Emission Imaging. 318p. 1983. 25.00 (ISBN 0-08-027093-X). Pergamon.
RADIOISOTOPES
see also Radioactive Tracers; Radioisotope Scanning; Radiotherapy
also subdivision Isotopes under names of elements, e.g. Carbon-Isotopes
Jensen, B. S. Migration Phenomena of Radionuclides into the Geosphere: A Critical Review of the Available Information; Radioactive Waste Management. (A Series of Monographs & Tracts: Vol. 5). 200p. 1982. write for info. (ISBN 3-7186-0120-6). Harwood Academic.
RADIOISOTOPES-INDUSTRIAL APPLICATIONS
see also Radioisotopes in Hydrology
Gardner, Robin P. & Ely, Ralph L., Jr. Radioisotope Measurement Applications in Engineering. LC 82-17126. 496p. 1983. Repr. of 1967 ed. lib. bdg. p.n.s. (ISBN 0-89874-558-6). Krieger.
Industrial Application of Radioisotopes & Radiation Technology. 595p. 1983. pap. 68.75 (ISBN 92-0-060082-4, ISP 598, IAEA). Unipub.
RADIOISOTOPES IN HYDROLOGY
Stable Isotope Hydrology: Deutrium & Oxygen-18 in the Water Cycle. (Technical Report Ser.: No. 210). 337p. 1981. pap. 36.00 (ISBN 92-0-145281-0, IDC 210, IAEA). Unipub.

RADIOISOTOPES IN MEDICINE
see Nuclear Medicine
RADIOISOTOPES IN PHARMACOLOGY
Eckelman, W. C., ed. Technetium Ninety-nine-M: Generators, Chemistry, & Preparation of Radiopharmaceuticals. (Illus.). 168p. 1983. 25.00 (ISBN 0-08-029144-9). Pergamon.
RADIOISOTOPES IN THE BODY
Sowby, F. D., ed. Limits for Intakes of Radionuclides by Workers, 7 vols. ICRD. (ICRP Publications: No. 30). 2500p. 1982. 370.00 (ISBN 0-08-028863-4). Pergamon.
RADIOLARIA, FOSSIL
Catalogue of Planktonic Foraminifera, 6 vols. 1976. Set. 600.00 (ISBN 0-686-84238-3). Am Mus Natl Hist.
RADIOLOGICAL PHYSICS
see Radiology
RADIOLOGY
see also Radiation; Radiography
Armstrong, Peter. Critical Problems in Diagnostic Radiology. (Illus.). 304p. 1983. text ed. 35.00 (ISBN 0-397-50496-9, Lippincott Medical). Lippincott.
Ballinger, Philip W. Merrill's Atlas of Radiographic Positions & Radiologic Procedures, 3 Vols. 5th ed. (Illus.). 950p. 1982. text ed. 99.95 (ISBN 0-8016-3408-3). Mosby.
Bellon, Errol M. Radiologic Interpretation of ERCP: A Clinical Atlas. 1983. pap. text ed. price not set (ISBN 0-87488-707-0). Med Exam.
Bouchard, Eric. Radiology Management: An Introduction. LC 82-22355. (Illus.). 310p. (Orig.). 1983. pap. 18.95X (ISBN 0-940122-04-9). Multi Media CO.
Brogdon, Byron G. Opinions, Comments & Reflections on Radiology. LC 82-82972. (Illus.). 249p. 1982. 27.95 (ISBN 0-939442-01-9). Brentwood Pub.
Gurley, LaVerne T. & Callaway, William J. Introduction to Radiologic Technology. LC 81-82005. (Illus.). 300p. (Orig.). 1982. pap. 14.95x (ISBN 0-940122-02-2). Multi Media CO.
RADIOLOGY, MEDICAL
see also Diagnosis, Radioscopic; Nuclear Medicine; Pediatric Radiology; Radiography, Medical; Radiotherapy
Abrams, Herbert L. Abrams Angiography: Vascular & Interventional Radiology, 3 vols. 2nd ed. 1983. Vol. 1. text ed. (ISBN 0-316-00466-9); Vol. 2. text ed. (ISBN 0-316-00467-7); Vol. 3. text ed. (ISBN 0-316-00468-5); text ed. 275.00 set. Little.
Banna, M. Clinical Neuroradiology. (Illus.). 1983. text ed. price not set (ISBN 0-8391-1809-0, 17523). Univ Park.
Brodeur, Armand E. & Silberstein, Michael J. Fundamentals of Radiologic Pathology. (Illus.). 1983. write for info. (ISBN 0-8391-1803-1, 15636). Univ Park.
Demos, T. Radiologic Case Studies: A Study Guide for the Orthopedic Surgeon. LC 82-62398. 299p. 1983. 39.50 (ISBN 0-943432-02-2). Slack Inc.
Evans & Roberts. Clinical Radiology: For Medical Students. 1982. text ed. 18.50 (ISBN 0-407-00177-8). Butterworth.
Goldman, Amy Beth & Dines, David M. Shoulder Arthrography. Goldman, Amy Beth, ed. (Little, Brown Library in Radiology). 1982. text ed. 42.50 (ISBN 0-316-31931-7). Little.
Lavender, J. Peter, ed. Clinical & Experimental Applications of Krypton-81m. 1978. 50.00x (ISBN 0-686-99802-2, Pub. by Brit Inst Radiology England). State Mutual Bk.
Oliva, L. & Veiga-Pires, J. A., eds. Intervention Radiology: Proceedings, 2nd International Symposium, Venice-Lido, Italy, September 27 - October 1, 1981, No. 2. (International Congress Ser.: No. 575). 366p. 1982. 74.50 (ISBN 0-444-90252-X, Excerpta Medica). Elsevier.
Rose. Invasive Radiology. 1983. 17.50 (ISBN 0-8151-7394-6). Year Bk Med.
Veiga-Pires, J. A. & Grainger, Ronald G., eds. Pioneers in Radiology. 1982. text ed. 19.50 (ISBN 0-686-37440-1, Pub. by MTP Pr England). Kluwer Boston.
RADIOLYSIS
see Radiation Chemistry
RADIOMETRIC ANALYSIS
see Radioactivation Analysis
RADIONUCLIDES
see Radioisotopes
RADIOPHARMACEUTICALS
Cox, P. H. Progress in Radiopharmacology 3. 1983. pap. text ed. 44.00 (ISBN 90-247-2768-5, Pub. by Martinus Nijhoff Netherlands). Kluwer Boston.
RADIOSCOPIC DIAGNOSIS
see Diagnosis, Radioscopic
RADIOTELEPHONE
Rudman, Jack. Radio Telephone Operator. (Career Examination Ser.: C-2883). (Cloth bdg. avail. on request). pap. 10.00 (ISBN 0-8373-2883-7). Natl Learning.
RADIOTHERAPY
see also Ultra-Violet Rays–Therapeutic Use
Deeley, Thomas J., ed. Topical Reviews in Radiotherapy & Oncology, Vol. 2. (Illus.). 264p. 1982. text ed. 37.50 (ISBN 0-7236-0616-1). Wright-PSG.
Wang. Radiation Therapy of Head & Neck Neoplasms. 736p. 1983. text ed. 39.50 (ISBN 0-7236-7049-8). Wright-PSG.
RADIQUET, RAYMOND, 1903-1923
Crosland, Margaret. Raymond Radiquet: A Biographical Study with Selections from His Work. 153p. 1982. 12.95 (ISBN 0-7206-0413-3, Pub. by Peter Owen). Merrimack Bk Serv.
RADON
Deans, Stanley R. The Radon Transform & Some of Its Applications. 350p. 1983. 36.00 (ISBN 0-471-89804-X, Pub. by Wiley-Interscience). Wiley.
RAFFAELO SANZIO D'URBINO
see Raphael (Raffaelo Sanzio D'Urbino), 1483-1520
RAIL TRANSPORTATION
see Railroads
RAILROAD CONSTRUCTION
see Railroad Engineering
RAILROAD ENGINEERING
Moody, John. Railroad Builders. 1919. text ed. 8.50x (ISBN 0-686-83721-5). Elliots Bks.
Rhodes, R. G. & Mulhall, B. E. Magnetic Levitation for Rail Transport. (Monographs on Cryogenics). 114p. 1981. 37.50x (ISBN 0-19-854802-8). Oxford U Pr.
Rudman, Jack. Railroad Equipment Inspector. (Career Examination Ser.: C-210). (Cloth bdg. avail. on request). pap. 12.00 (ISBN 0-8373-0210-2). Natl Learning.
--Railroad Track & Structure Inspector. (Career Examination Ser.: C-209). (Cloth bdg. avail. on request). pap. 12.00 (ISBN 0-8373-0209-9). Natl Learning.
Sperandeo, Andy. Introduction of Model Railroad Wiring. Hayden, Bob, ed. (Illus., Orig.). 1984. pap. price not set (ISBN 0-89024-060-4). Kalmbach.
RAILROAD MERGERS
see Railroads–Consolidation
RAILROAD MODELS
see Railroads–Models
RAILROAD TRAVEL
Norwood, John B. Rio Grande Narrow Gauge. Heimburger, Donald J. & Heimburger, Marilyn M., eds. (Illus.). 312p. 1983. 39.95 (ISBN 0-911581-00-6). Heimburger Hse Pub.
RAILROAD WORKERS
see Railroads–Employees
RAILROADS
see also Eminent Domain; Freight and Freightage; Locomotives
also names of individual railroads
Jane's World Railways, 1982-1983. (Jane's Yearbooks). (Illus.). 550p. 140.00 (ISBN 0-86720-606-3). Sci Bks Intl.
Jones, Wilson E. Next Station Will Be..., Vol. 7. LC 82-62628. (Illus.). 60p. 1982. pap. 8.50 (ISBN 0-941652-00-9). Railroadians.
Norwood, John B. Rio Grande Narrow Gauge. Heimburger, Donald J. & Heimburger, Marilyn M., eds. (Illus.). 312p. 1983. 39.95 (ISBN 0-911581-00-6). Heimburger Hse Pub.
Ransom, P. J. Archaeolgy of Railways. (Illus.). 1981. 31.50 (ISBN 0-437-14401-1, Pub. by Heinemann). David & Charles.
Swanson, Jack W. & Karsh, Jeff. Rail Ventures. 220p. (Orig.). 1982. pap. 14.95 (ISBN 0-9608764-0-5). J W Swanson.
Walthers Fiftieth Anniversary O Scale Railroad Catalog & Craft Train Reference Manual. (Illus.). 336p. 1983. pap. write for info. (ISBN 0-941952-13-4). W K Walthers.
RAILROADS–CARS
see also Electric Railroads–Cars
Morel, Julian. Pullman. (Illus.). 192p. (Orig.). 1983. 19.95 (ISBN 0-7153-8382-5). David & Charles.
RAILROADS–CONSOLIDATION
Conant, Michael. Railroad Mergers & Abandoments. LC 82-15834. (Publications of the Institute of Business & Economic Research, University of California). xiii, 212p. 1982. Repr. of 1964 ed. lib. bdg. 29.75x (ISBN 0-313-23694-1, CORAM). Greenwood.
RAILROADS–EMPLOYEES
Leuthner, Stuart. The Railroaders. LC 81-40236. (Illus.). 160p. 1982. 19.95 (ISBN 0-394-51861-6). Random.
RAILROADS–ENGINEERING
see Railroad Engineering
RAILROADS–FINANCE
see also Railroads–Consolidation
American Railroad Stock Certificates. 28.50. StanGib Ltd.
RAILROADS–FREIGHT
see also Freight and Freightage
Heavy Haul Railways. 428p. 1978. text ed. 60.00x (ISBN 0-909421-11-0, Pub. by Inst Engineering Australia). Renouf.
RAILROADS–FREIGHT CARS
see Railroads–Cars
RAILROADS–HISTORY
Bixler, Herbert E. Railroads: Their Rise & Fall. 115p. (Orig.). 1982. pap. 7.95 (ISBN 0-9610066-0-9). H E Bixler.
Coombs, Gary B. Goleta Depot: The History of a Rural Railroad Station. LC 82-83472. (Illus.). 96p. (Orig.). 1982. 8.00 (ISBN 0-911773-00-2); pap. 5.00 (ISBN 0-911773-01-0). Inst Am Res.
Demoro, Harre W. Electric Railway Pioneer: Commuting on the Northwestern Pacific 1903-1941. (Special Ser.: No. 84). (Illus.). 136p. 1983. price not set (ISBN 0-916374-55-6). Interurban.
Hannah, Perrin K. A Compendium of Burlington Lines Employee Timetables. (Railway History Monograph). 1982. lib. bdg. write for info. (ISBN 0-916170-20-9). J-B Pubs.
Licht, Walter. Working for the Railroad: The Organization of Work in the Nineteenth Century. LC 82-61372. (Illus.). 352p. 1983. 27.50x (ISBN 0-691-04700-6). Princeton U Pr.
Palmer, Lloyd. Steam Towards the Sunset: The Railroads of Lincoln County. (Lincoln County Historical Society Ser.: No. 23). (Illus.). 192p. (Orig.). 1982. pap. 19.95 (ISBN 0-911443-00-2). Lincoln Coun His.
Steinheimer, Richard & Sims, Donald. Growing up with Trains: A Southern California Album. Bradley, Bill, ed. (Special Ser.: No. 83). 1982. 16.95 (ISBN 0-916374-53-X). Interurban.
Vollrath, H. K. Midwest Railroader Remembers: The Frisco & Steam. Carlson, R. W. & Lorenz, R., eds. (Illus.). 106p. 1982. pap. 12.95 (ISBN 0-942322-02-9). Midwest Railroader.
Wood, S. R. & Nichols, H. E. Midwest Railroader Remembers: C&O & Steam. Carlson, R. W. & Lorenz, R., eds. (Illus.). 106p. 1982. pap. 12.95 (ISBN 0-942322-01-0). Midwest Railroader.
RAILROADS–JUVENILE LITERATURE
see also Railroads–Trains–Juvenile Literature
Ransom, P. J. Your Book of Steam Railway Preservation. (Your Book Of...Ser.). (Illus.). 112p. (gr. 5-8). 1983. 10.95 (ISBN 0-571-11931-X). Faber & Faber.
RAILROADS–MERGERS
see Railroads–Consolidation
RAILROADS–MODELS
Freezer, Cyril. Building Model Railways. (Illus.). 122p. (Orig.). 1982. pap. 10.50x (ISBN 0-85242-778-6). Intl Pubns Serv.
Weiss, Harvey. How to Run a Railroad: Everything You Need to Know about Model Trains. LC 76-18128. (Illus.). 96p. (gr. 4-7). 1983. pap. 4.76i (ISBN 0-690-04329-5, TYC-J). Har-Row.
RAILROADS–TRAINS
Behrend, George. Luxury Trains: From the Orient Express to the TGV. LC 81-10366. (Illus.). 1982. 35.00 (ISBN 0-86565-016-0). Vendome.
RAILROADS–TRAINS–JUVENILE LITERATURE
Althea. Going on a Train. (Cambridge Dinosaur Information Ser.). (Illus.). 26p. 1983. pap. 1.50 (ISBN 0-521-27150-9). Cambridge U Pr.
RAILROADS–TRAVEL
see Railroad Travel
RAILROADS–UNIFICATION
see Railroads–Consolidation
RAILROADS–ALASKA
Brovald, Ken C. Alaska's Wilderness Rails: From the Taiga to the Tundra. LC 82-80963. (Illus.). 104p. 1982. pap. text ed. 8.95 (ISBN 0-933126-21-2). Pictorial Hist.
RAILROADS–EUROPE
O'Brien, Patrick. Railways & the Economic Development of Western Europe: 1830-1914. LC 81-23261. 356p. 1982. 30.00x (ISBN 0-312-66277-7). St Martin.
RAILROADS–GREAT BRITAIN
Davies, R. & Grant, M. D. London & Its Railways. (Illus.). 224p. (Orig.). 1983. 23.95 (ISBN 0-7153-8107-5). David & Charles.
Jones, Kenneth W. Railways for Pleasure: The Complete Guide to Steam & Scenic Lines in Great Britain & Ireland. (Illus.). 160p. 1982. pap. 12.95 (ISBN 0-7188-2446-6, Pub. by Salem Hse Ltd.). Merrimack Bk Serv.
Nixon, L. A. British Rail in Colour. (Illus.). 96p. 1983. 14.95 (ISBN 0-686-84472-6). Sci Bks Intl.
Skelton, Peter & Huxtable, Nils. British Steam Revival. (Illus.). 96p. 1983. 14.95 (ISBN 0-86720-640-3). Sci Bks Intl.
RAILROADS–GREAT BRITAIN–HISTORY
Bonavia, Michael R. Railway Policy Between the Wars. 160p. 1982. 15.00 (ISBN 0-7190-0826-3). Manchester.
Christiansen, Rex. A Regional History of the Railways of Great Britain: Vol. 7: The West Midlands. 2nd ed. (Illus.). 305p. 1983. 24.95 (ISBN 0-7153-8468-6). David & Charles.
Hemery, Eric. Walking the Dartmoor Railroads. (Illus.). 152p. (Orig.). 1983. 14.95 (ISBN 0-7153-8348-5). David & Charles.
Snell, J. B. One Man's Railway: J. E. P. Howey & the Romney, Hythe & Dymchurch Railway. (Illus.). 96p. (Orig.). 1983. 17.50 (ISBN 0-7153-8325-6). David & Charles.
RAILROADS–IRELAND
Jones, Kenneth W. Railways for Pleasure: The Complete Guide to Steam & Scenic Lines in Great Britain & Ireland. (Illus.). 160p. 1982. pap. 12.95 (ISBN 0-7188-2446-6, Pub. by Salem Hse Ltd.). Merrimack Bk Serv.
Patterson, E. M. Belfast & County Down Railway. (Illus.). 1982. 12.50 (ISBN 0-7153-8306-X). David & Charles.
RAILROADS–SCOTLAND
Robertson, C. J. The Origins of the Scottish Railway System, 1722-1844. 450p. 1983. text ed. 42.00x (ISBN 0-85976-088-X, Pub. by Donald England). Humanities.
RAILROADS–UNITED STATES
Ehrhardt, Roy. American Railroad Watches: George Townsend 1977. 1982. 8.00 (ISBN 0-913902-40-3). Heart Am Pr.
RAILROADS–UNITED STATES–HISTORY
Digerness, David S. The Mineral Belt: Georgetown, Mining, Colorado Central Railroad, Vol. III. (Illus.). 416p. 49.00 (ISBN 0-686-84503-X). Sundance.
Drury, George. Facts & Figures about North American Railroads: The Unofficial Guide. Hayden, Bob, ed. (Illus., Orig.). 1983. pap. price not set (ISBN 0-89024-061-2). Kalmbach.
Jones, Robert C. The Central Vermont Railway: A Yankee Tradition, Vol. VI. Date not set. 19.50 (ISBN 0-686-82375-3). Sundance.
Lynch, Terry. The Railroads of Kansas City. 1983. price not set (ISBN 0-87108-637-9). Pruett.
McLeod, Robert W. & Lampert, Lyndon J. The Life & Times of the Little Book Cliff Railway. 1983. price not set (ISBN 0-87108-638-7). Pruett.
Reisdorff, James J. & Bartels, Michael M. Railroad Stations in Nebraska: An Era of Use & Reuse. LC 82-61823. (Illus.). 112p. 1982. text ed. 23.50 (ISBN 0-9609568-0-8). South Platte.
RAILWAYS
see Railroads
RAINBOW
Klika, Thom. Ten Thousand Rainbows. (Illus.). 80p. 1983. pap. 6.95 (ISBN 0-312-79096-1); pap. 69.50 prepack of 10 (ISBN 0-312-79098-8). St Martin.
RAINBOW–JUVENILE LITERATURE
Stanish, Bob. Connecting Rainbows. (gr. 3-12). 1982. 7.95 (ISBN 0-86653-081-9, GA 426). Good Apple.
RAINY-DAY GAMES
see Indoor Games
RALEIGH, WALTER, SIR, 1552?-1618
Williams, Norman L. Sir Walter Raleigh. 295p. 1982. Repr. of 1962 ed. lib. bdg. 40.00 (ISBN 0-8495-5821-2). Arden Lib.
RAMAN EFFECT
see also Raman Spectroscopy
Basov, N. G., ed. Stimulated Raman Scattering. Adashko, J. George, tr. (Proceedings (Trudy) of the Lebedev Physics Institute: Vol. 99). 175p. 1982. 45.00x (ISBN 0-306-10968-9, Plenum Pr). Plenum Pub.
Cardona, M., ed. Light Scattering in Solids I. 2nd ed. (Topics in Applied Physics Ser.: Vol. 8). (Illus.). 363p. 1983. pap. 29.00 (ISBN 0-387-11913-2). Springer-Verlag.
RAMAN SPECTROSCOPY
Person. Vibrational Intensities in Infrared & Raman Spectroscopy. (Studies in Physical & Theoretical Chemistry). 1982. 95.75 (ISBN 0-444-42115-7). Elsevier.
Siesler, H. W. & Holland-Moritz, K. Infared & Raman Spectroscopy of Polymers. (Practical Spectroscopy Ser.: Vol. 4). (Illus.). 400p. 1980. 55.00 (ISBN 0-8247-6935-X). Dekker.
Tu, A. T. Raman Spectroscopy in Biology: Principles & Applications. 448p. 1982. text ed. 65.00x (ISBN 0-471-07984-7, Pub. by Wiley-Interscience). Wiley.
RAMAYANA
Raghavan, V., ed. The Ramayana Tradition in Asia. 1982. 18.00x (ISBN 0-8364-0899-3, Pub. by National Sahitya Akademi). South Asia Bks.
RANA
see Frogs
RANCH LIFE
see also Cowboys
Haggerty, Chas. P. Light Flashbacks to a Dark Time. (Illus.). 130p. 1981. pap. 6.95 (ISBN 0-9609936-0-6). Santiam Bks.
Roosevelt, Theodore. Ranch Life & the Hunting Trail. LC 82-20091. (Illus.). 196p. 1983. 19.95x (ISBN 0-8032-3865-7, BB 833); pap. 8.95 (ISBN 0-8032-8913-8, Bison). U of Nebr Pr.
Shepard. Estate Planning for Farmers & Ranchers. 1980. 65.00 (ISBN 0-07-033500-1). McGraw.
Woolston, Bill. Harvest: Wheat Ranching in the Palouse. (Illus.). 128p. 1982. 24.95 (ISBN 0-915664-02-X). Thorn Creek Pr.
RANDOLPH-MACON COLLEGE
Scanlon, James E. Randolph-Macon College: A Southern History, 1825-1967. LC 82-16072. 1983. 15.00x (ISBN 0-8139-0928-7). U Pr of Va.
RANDOM NOISE THEORY
Brown, Robert G. Introduction to Random Signal Analysis & Kalman Filtering. 416p. 1983. text ed. price not set (ISBN 0-471-08732-7). Wiley.
RANDOM PROCESSES
see Stochastic Processes
RANGE MANAGEMENT
see also Livestock
National Academy of Sciences. Developing Strategies for Rangeland Management. 1000p. 1982. lib. bdg. 45.00 (ISBN 0-86531-543-4). Westview.
RANK
see Social Classes
RANSOM, JOHN CROWE, 1888-
Young, Thomas D. John Crowe Ranson: An Annotated Bibliography. Cain, William, ed. LC 82-48279. (Modern Critics & Critical Schools Ser.). 250p. 1982. lib. bdg. 30.00 (ISBN 0-8240-9249-X). Garland Pub.
RAPE
Foley, Theresa S. & Davies, Marilyn A. Rape: Nursing Care of Victims. (Illus.). 512p. 1983. pap. text ed. 12.95 (ISBN 0-8016-1620-4). Mosby.

Holmstrom, Lynda L. & Burgess, Ann W. The Victim of Rape: Institutional Reactions. 1983. pap. 12.95 (ISBN 0-87855-932-9). Transaction Bks.
Holmstrom, Lynda Lytle & Burgess, Ann Wolbert. The Victime of Rape: Institutional Reactions. LC 77-27074. 308p. Repr. of 1978 ed. text ed. 20.95 (ISBN 0-471-40785-2). Krieger.

RAPE (PLANT)
Kramer, J. K. & Saver, F. D., eds. High & Low Erucic Acid Rapeseed Oils: Production, Usage, Chemistry & Toxilogical Evaluation. LC 82-13805. Date not set. price not set (ISBN 0-12-425080-7). Acad Pr.

RAPHAEL (RAFFAELO SANZIO D'URBINO), 1483-1520
Golzio, Vincent. Raphael: His Life, His Art, His Fortunes, 2 vols. (The Great Masters of the World Ser.). (Illus.). 765p. 1982. Repr. of 1968 ed. 237.45 (ISBN 0-89901-089-X). Found Class Reprints.

RAPID READING
Bean, Thomas W. & Bishop, Ashley. Rapid Reading for Professional Success. 176p. 1983. pap. text ed. 10.95 (ISBN 0-8403-2882-6). Kendall-Hunt.

RAPID TRANSIT
see Local Transit

RAPIDS, RUNNING OF
see White-Water Canoeing

RAPPAHANNOCK INDIANS
see Indians of North America–Eastern States

RARE ANIMALS
see also Extinct Animals
Ono, Dane R. & Williams, James D. Vanishing Fishes of North America. (Illus.). 1983. 27.50 (ISBN 0-913276-43-X). Stone Wall Pr.

RARE BOOKS
see Bibliography–Rare Books

RARE EARTH METALS
see Earths, Rare

RARE EARTHS
see Earths, Rare

RARE METALS
see Nonferrous Metals

RAT
see Rats

RATING, JOB
see Job Evaluation

RATING OF EMPLOYEES
see Employees, Rating Of

RATING OF TEACHERS
see Teachers, Rating Of

RATIO ANALYSIS
Van Oosting, James. The Business Report: Writer, Reader & Text. (Illus.). 320p. 1983. pap. 13.95 (ISBN 0-13-107581-0). P-H.

RATIOCINATION
see Reasoning

RATIONALISM
see also Agnosticism; Atheism; Belief and Doubt; Enlightenment; Faith and Reason; Positivism; Reason; Skepticism
Gadol, E. T., ed. Rationality & Sciences: A Memorial Volume for Moritz Schlick. (Illus.). 228p. 1983. 21.00 (ISBN 0-387-81721-2). Springer-Verlag.
Hollis, Martin & Lukes, Steven, eds. Rationality & Relativism. 320p. 1983. 25.00x (ISBN 0-262-08130-X); pap. 12.50x (ISBN 0-262-58061-6). MIT Pr.
Simon, Herbert A. Models of Bounded Rationality, 2 vols. Incl. Vol. 1. Economic Analysis & Public Policy. 392p. 30.00x (ISBN 0-262-19205-5); Vol. 2. Behavioral Economics & Business Organization. 496p. 30.00x (ISBN 0-262-19206-3). 1982. MIT Pr.
Sucha, Peter. Kritischer Rationalismus In Theologischer Prufung. 443p. (Ger.). 1982. write for info. (ISBN 3-8204-5828-X). P Lang Pubs.

RATIONALIZATION OF INDUSTRY
see Industrial Management

RATS
Bohensky, Fred. Photo Manual & Disection Guide of the Rat. (Avery's Anatomy Ser.). (Illus.). 140p. (Orig.). 1983. lab manual 5.95 (ISBN 0-89529-213-0). Avery Pub.
Hendrickson, Robert. More Cunning Than Man: A Social History Of Rats & Men. LC 82-48512. 288p. 1983. 17.95 (ISBN 0-8128-2894-1). Stein & Day.
Nitscheke. Acoustic Behavior in the Rat. 204p. 1982. 24.95 (ISBN 0-03-061973-4). Praeger.

RAW FOOD
see Food, Raw

RAW MATERIALS
see also Commodity Control; Forest Products
Banks, Ferdinand E. Resources & Energy: An Economic Analysis. LC 81-47967. 368p. 1983. 34.95x (ISBN 0-669-05203-5). Lexington Bks.

RAYS, INVISIBLE
see Spectrum, Infra-Red

RAYS, ROENTGEN
see X-Rays

REACTION RATE (CHEMISTRY)
see Chemical Reaction, Rate Of

REACTIONS, CHEMICAL
see Chemical Reactions

REACTOR FUEL ELEMENTS
see Nuclear Fuel Elements

REACTOR FUEL REPROCESSING
Storage of Water Reactor Spent Fuel in Water Pools. (Technical Reports Ser.: No. 218). 140p. 1983. pap. 19.75 (ISBN 92-0-155182-7, IDC 218, IAEA). Unipub.

REACTOR FUELS
see Nuclear Fuels

REACTORS (NUCLEAR PHYSICS)
see Nuclear Reactors

REACTORS, BREEDER
see Breeder Reactors

REACTORS, CHEMICAL
see Chemical Reactors

READERS
see also College Readers; Dialogues; English Language–Dictionaries, Juvenile; Primers; Readers (i.t.a.)
Carr, Pat & Tracey, Steve. Enchantments. (Mindstrechers Level Two). (gr. 4-6). pap. 4.95 (ISBN 0-8224-4508-5). Pitman.
--Great Explorations. (Mindstrechers Level Two). (gr. 4-6). pap. 4.95 (ISBN 0-8224-4507-7). Pitman.
--Star Gazing. (Mindstrechers Level Two). (gr. 4-6). 4.95 (ISBN 0-8224-4505-0). Pitman.
--Who Done It? (Mindstrechers: Level Two). (gr. 4-6). pap. 4.95 (ISBN 0-8224-4506-9). Pitman.
Final Warning. (Doomsday Journal Skillbuilders). write for info. (ISBN 0-8224-1940-8). Pitman.
Fireball. (Doomsday Journal Skillbuilders). write for info. (ISBN 0-8224-1939-4). Pitman.
Glock, Marvin D. & Bender, David S. Probe: College Developmental Reading. 2nd ed. 1980. text ed. 11.95 (ISBN 0-675-08144-0, C57). Additional supplements may be obtained from publisher. Merrill.
Graham, Carolyn. The Electric Elephant & Other Stories. (Illus.). 128p. (Orig.). 1982. pap. text ed. 4.95x (ISBN 0-19-503229-2). Oxford U Pr.
Lost Valley. (Doomsday Journal Skillbuilders). write for info. (ISBN 0-8224-1943-2). Pitman.
Magalnick, B. English Reader. 1979. text ed. 5.62 (ISBN 0-07-039470-9). McGraw.
Rodieck, Jorma. The Little Bitty Snake. Burnett, Yumiko M. & Contreras, Moyra, trs. (Illus.). 24p. 1983. English - Japanese. PLB 9.50 (ISBN 0-940880-06-7); English - Spanish. PLB 9.50 (ISBN 0-940880-02-4); English - French. PLB 9.50 (ISBN 0-940880-04-0); English - Japanese. pap. 4.00 (ISBN 0-940880-07-5); English - Spanish. pap. 4.00 (ISBN 0-940880-03-2); English - French. pap. 4.00 (ISBN 0-940880-05-9). Open Hand.
Ruffner, Tacey. Americana Articles. (Illus.). 138p. 1983. pap. 9.95 (ISBN 0-9610424-0-0). T Ruffner.
The Seep. (Doomsday Journal Skillbuilders). write for info. (ISBN 0-8224-1941-6). Pitman.
Trimmer & Hairston. The Riverside Reader, Vol.II. 1982. pap. text ed. 10.95 (ISBN 0-686-84581-1, EN76); instr's. manual with test items avail. (EN77). HM.
Trimmer, Joseph & Hairston, Maxine. The Riverside Reader, Vol. 2. 576p. 1982. pap. text ed. 9.95 (ISBN 0-395-32639-7); write for info. instr's. manual (ISBN 0-395-32640-0). HM.

READERS–BIBLE
Walvoord, John F. & Zuck, Roy B. The Bib Sac Reader. (Orig.). 1983. pap. 7.95 (ISBN 0-8024-0459-6). Moody.

READERS–HEALTH
Sully, Nina. Health. (Science in Today's World Ser.). (Illus.). 72p. (gr. 7-12). 1983. 14.95 (ISBN 0-7134-4447-9, Pub. by Batsford England). David & Charles.

READERS–SOCIAL STUDIES
Brooks, Bearl. Basic Skills World Neighbors Workbook. (Basic Skills Workbooks). 32p. (gr. 4-7). 1983. 0.99 (ISBN 0-8209-0558-5, SSW-6). ESP.
--Our Community. (Social Studies Ser.). 24p. (gr. 2-3). 1979. wkbk. 5.00 (ISBN 0-8209-0236-5, SS-3). ESP.
--Our Home. (Social Studies Ser.). 24p. (gr. 1). 1979. wkbk. 5.00 (ISBN 0-8209-0234-9, SS-1). ESP.
--Our World Neighbors. (Social Studies Ser.). 24p. (gr. 5-6). 1979. wkbk. 5.00 (ISBN 0-8209-0242-X, SS-9). ESP.
--Shelter & the Family. (Social Studies Ser.). 24p. (gr. 4-6). 1976. wkbk. 5.00 (ISBN 0-8209-0249-7, SS-16). ESP.
Cole, Clara. Basic Needs. (Social Studies). 24p. (gr. 2-3). 1977. wkbk. 5.00 (ISBN 0-8209-0259-4, SS-26). ESP.
Hayes, Marilyn. Social Studies Reading. (Reading Ser.). 24p. (gr. 2). 1980. wkbk. 5.00 (ISBN 0-8209-0195-4, RSS-2). ESP.

READERS (HIGHER EDUCATION)
see College Readers

READERS (I.T.A.)
Frank Schaffer Publications. The Alphabet. (Help Your Child Learn Ser.). (Illus.). 24p. (ps-2). 1978. workbook 1.29 (ISBN 0-86734-001-0, FS 3002). Schaffer Pubns.
--Getting Ready for Reading. (Getting Ready for Kindergarten Ser.). (Illus.). 24p. (ps-k). 1980. workbook 1.29 (ISBN 0-86734-019-3, FS 3032). Schaffer Pubns.
McConnell, Keith. The SeAlphabet Encyclopedia. (The NaturAlphabet Ser.). (Illus.). 48p. (gr. 4 up). 1982. pap. 2.95 (ISBN 0-88045-016-9). Stemmer Hse.
Szekeres, Cyndy. Cyndy Szekeres' ABC. LC 82-839989. (A Golden Sturdy Bk.). (Illus.). 22p. 1983. 3.95 (ISBN 0-307-12120-8, Golden Pr). Western Pub.

READERS, PRESCHOOL
see Primers

READERS AND LIBRARIES
see Libraries and Readers

READERS THEATER
see Oral Interpretation

READINESS FOR SCHOOL
Matthews, Mary. Preparing Your Child for School: A Primer for Parents of Kindergarten & First Grade Students. (Illus.). 16p. (Orig.). 1981. pap. 3.95x. Parents Pointers.

READING
see also Oral Interpretation; Readers; Reading, Psychology Of
Aarons, Trudy & Koelsch, Francine. One Hundred One Reading Activities. 125p. (ps-4). 1982. pap. text ed. 11.95 (ISBN 0-88450-833-1). Communication Skill.
Adams, W. Royce. Reading Skills: A Guide for Better Reading. LC 73-21849. (Self-Teaching Guides Ser). 245p. 1974. 6.95 (ISBN 0-471-00780-3). Wiley.
Aukerman, Robert C. Approaches to Beginning Reading. LC 70-144330. (Illus.). 509p. 1971. pap. text ed. 18.50x (ISBN 0-471-03691-9); avail. tchrs. manual (ISBN 0-471-04850-X). Wiley.
--The Basal Reader Approach to Reading. LC 80-28174. 339p. 1981. text ed. 15.95 (ISBN 0-471-03082-1); pap. text ed. 10.95 (ISBN 0-471-09066-2). Wiley.
Aukerman, Robert C. & Aukerman, Louise R. How Do I Teach Reading. LC 80-23380. 543p. 1981. text ed. 21.95 (ISBN 0-471-03687-0). Wiley.
Awtrey, Amy & Markos, Carol. The Reading Program: Critical Reading, Bk. G. 72p. 1982. pap. 3.50x (ISBN 0-88069-006-2). L A Meyer.
--The Reading Program: Essay Structures, Bk. F. 72p. 1982. pap. 3.50x (ISBN 0-88069-005-4). L A Meyer.
--The Reading Program: Relationships, Bk. E. 58p. 1982. pap. 3.50x (ISBN 0-88069-004-6). L A Meyer.
--The Reading Program: Sentence Structure. 48p. 1982. pap. 3.50x (ISBN 0-88069-002-X). L A Meyer.
--The Reading Program: Signals, Bk. D. 62p. 1982. pap. 3.50x (ISBN 0-88069-003-8). L A Meyer.
--The Reading Program: Vocabulary, Bk. B. 48p. 1982. pap. 3.50x (ISBN 0-88069-001-1). L A Meyer.
--The Reading Program: Word Patterns, Bk. A. 48p. 1982. pap. 3.50 (ISBN 0-88069-000-3). L A Meyer.
Berbrich, Joan D. Reading Today. (Orig.). (gr. 10-12). 1983. pap. write for info. (ISBN 0-87720-449-7). AMSCO Sch.
Bettelheim, Bruno & Zelan, Karen. On Learning to Read: The Child's Fascination with Meaning. 320p. 1983. pap. 5.95 (ISBN 0-394-71194-7, Vin). Random.
Brooks, Bearl. Basic Reading Comprehension: Grade Eight. (Reading Ser.). 24p. 1979. wkbk. 5.00 (ISBN 0-8209-0194-6, R-8). ESP.
--Basic Reading Comprehension: Grade Five. (Reading Ser.). 24p. 1977. wkbk. 5.00 (ISBN 0-8209-0191-1, R-5). ESP.
--Basic Reading Comprehension: Grade Four. (Reading Ser.). 24p. 1980. wkbk. 5.00 (ISBN 0-8209-0190-3, R-4). ESP.
--Basic Reading Comprehension: Grade One. (Reading Ser.). 24p. 1980. wkbk. 5.00 (ISBN 0-8209-0187-3, R-1). ESP.
--Basic Reading Comprehension: Grade Seven. (Reading Ser.). 24p. 1977. wkbk. 5.00 (ISBN 0-8209-0193-8, R-7). ESP.
--Basic Reading Comprehension: Grade Six. (Reading Ser.). 24p. 1979. wkbk. 5.00 (ISBN 0-8209-0192-X, R-6). ESP.
--Basic Reading Comprehension: Grade Three. (Reading Ser.). 24p. 1976. wkbk. 5.00 (ISBN 0-8209-0189-X, R-3). ESP.
--Basic Reading Comprehension: Grade Two. (Reading Ser.). 24p. 1977. wkbk. 5.00 (ISBN 0-8209-0188-1, R-2). ESP.
--Basic Skills Reading Comprehension Workbook. (Basic Skills Workbooks). 32p. (gr. 1-2). 1982. 0.99 (ISBN 0-8209-0554-2, RCW-1). ESP.
--Basic Skills Reading Comprehension Workbooks. (Basic Skills Workbooks). 32p. (gr. 3-4). 1983. 0.99 (ISBN 0-8209-0555-0, RCW-2). ESP.
--Basic Skills Reading Comprehension Workbook. (Basic Skills Workbooks). 32p. (gr. 5-6). 1983. 0.99 (ISBN 0-8209-0556-9, RCW-3). ESP.
--Basic Skills Reading Comprehension Workbook. (Basic Skills Workbooks). 32p. (gr. 7-8). 1983. 0.99 (ISBN 0-8209-0557-7, RCW-4). ESP.
--Bilingual Reading: Level One. (Reading Ser.). 24p. 1979. wkbk. 5.00 (ISBN 0-8209-0196-2, BLR-1). ESP.
--Bilingual Reading: Level Three. (Reading Ser.). 24p. 1981. wkbk. 5.00 (ISBN 0-8209-0198-9, BLR-3). ESP.
--Bilingual Reading: Level Two. (Reading Ser.). 24p. 1981. wkbk. 5.00 (ISBN 0-8209-0197-0, BLR-2). ESP.
Chall, J. S. Learning to Read: The Great Debate. updated ed. 448p. 1983. 18.95 (ISBN 0-07-010382-8, P&RB). McGraw.
Cheek, Earl H., Jr. & Cheek, Martha C. Reading Instruction Through Content Teaching. 1983. text ed. 17.95 (ISBN 0-675-20026-1). Additional supplements may be obtained from publisher. Merrill.
Cowen, John E., ed. Teaching Reading through the Arts. 118p. 1983. pap. 7.00 (ISBN 0-87207-733-0). Intl Reading.
Dzama, Mary Ann. Ready to Read: A Parents Guide. Gilstrap, Robert, ed. (Parent Education Ser.). 287p. 1983. pap. text ed. 8.95 (ISBN 0-471-86637-7). Wiley.
Flemming & Mansbach. Reading for Results. 2d ed. pap. text ed. 11.95 (ISBN 0-686-84576-5, RM98); instr's manual avail. (RM99). HM.
Gentile, Lance M. & Kamil, Michael L. Reading Research Revisited. 1983. text ed. 11.95 (ISBN 0-675-20028-8). Merrill.
Gould. Reading into Writing: A Rhetoric-Reader-Handbook. pap. text ed. 15.95 (ISBN 0-686-84580-3, EN73); instr's. manual avail. (EN74). HM.
Heilman, Arthur W. Improve Your Reading Ability. 4th ed. 176p. 1983. pap. text ed. 11.95 (ISBN 0-675-20040-7). Merrill.
Hodges, Mary Ann. Oral Reading. (Language Arts Ser.). 24p. (gr. 5-8). 1977. wkbk. 5.00 (ISBN 0-8209-0323-X, LA-9). ESP.
Hogins, James B. & Yarber, Robert E. Reading, Writing, & Rhetoric. 5th ed. 576p. 1983. pap. text ed. write for info. (ISBN 0-574-22080-1); write for info. instr's. guide (ISBN 0-574-22081-X). SRA.
Justus, Fred. Look, Read, & Write. (Early Education Ser.). 24p. (gr. 1). 1982. wkbk. 5.00 (ISBN 0-8209-0219-5, K-21). ESP.
--Think & Write. (Early Education Ser.). 24p. (gr. 1). 1982. wkbk. 5.00 (ISBN 0-8209-0220-9, K-22). ESP.
--Unified Reading. (Early Education Ser.). 24p. (gr. 2). 1981. wkbk. 5.00 (ISBN 0-8209-0212-8, K-14). ESP.
--Word Picture Puzzles. (Puzzles Ser.). 24p. (gr. 1). 1980. wkbk. 5.00 (ISBN 0-8209-0296-9, PU-10). ESP.
--Word Scan Puzzles. (Puzzles Ser.). 24p. (gr. 3). 1980. wkbk. 5.00 (ISBN 0-8209-0297-7, PU-11). ESP.
Karn, Joan & Markle, Geraldine. Reading Consultant. (Michigan Learning Module Ser.: No. 33). 1979. write for info. (ISBN 0-914004-36-0). Ulrich.
Kintgen, Eugene R. The Perception of Poetry. LC 82-48387. 288p. 1983. 22.50x (ISBN 0-253-34345-3). Ind U Pr.
LeBlanc, Lanie. Reading Competencies. 1983. pap. text ed. 9.95 (ISBN 0-673-15801-2). Scott F.
McIlwaine, Ia & McIlwaine, John, eds. Bibliography & Reading: A Festschrift in Honour of Ronald Staveley. LC 82-21489. 180p. 1983. 15.00 (ISBN 0-8108-1601-6). Scarecrow.
Misenheimer, Luther, III. Basic Skills Speed Reading Workbook. (Basic Skills Workbooks). 32p. (gr. 5-9). 1983. 0.99 (ISBN 0-8209-0583-6, SRW-1). ESP.
Moffett & Wagner. Student Centered Language Arts & Reading: K-13. 3rd ed. 1982. text ed. 24.50 (ISBN 0-686-84556-0, EA98). HM.
Moffett, James & Wagner, Betty Jane. Student-Centered Language Arts & Reading, K-13: A Handbook for Teachers. 3rd ed. LC 82-83368. 512p. 1983. text ed. 24.95 (ISBN 0-395-32828-4). HM.
Outland, Barbara. Reading! The Success Formula. 432p. 1982. pap. text ed. 21.95 (ISBN 0-8403-2864-8). Kendall-Hunt.
Rakes, Thomas A. & Choate, Joyce S. Individual Evaluation Procedures in Reading. 256p. 1983. 19.95 (ISBN 0-13-457226-2); pap. 14.95 (ISBN 0-13-457218-1). P-H.
Richardson, Ellis & Freeman, Harold, Jr. Reading Progress Feedback System (RFFS) 86p. (Orig.). 1981. pap. 7.00 (ISBN 0-939632-32-2). ILM.
Rupley & Blair. Reading Diagnosis & Direct Instruction: A Guide for the Classroom. pap. text ed. 10.95 (ISBN 0-686-84560-9, ET07). HM.
--Reading Diagnosis & Remediation: Classroom & Clinic. 1982. text ed. 24.95 (ISBN 0-686-84559-5, ET05). HM.
Rye, James. Cloze Procedure & the Teaching of Reading. 144p. (Orig.). 1982. pap. text ed. 6.50x (ISBN 0-435-10781-X). Heinemann Ed.
Scales, Alice M. & Biggs, Shirley A. Reading to Achieve: Strategies for Adult-College Learners. 224p. Date not set. pap. text ed. 8.95 (ISBN 0-675-20034-2). Additional supplements may be obtained from publisher. Merrill.
Sowell, Judith B. & May, Ruth G. Yes, Johnny Can Read. 192p. 1982. pap. text ed. 10.36 (ISBN 0-8403-2874-5). Kendall-Hunt.
Thomas, James L. & Loring, Ruth. Motivating Children & Young Adults to Read. 2nd ed. 1983. price not set (ISBN 0-89774-046-7). Oryx Pr.
Walters, Michael E. Restoring Personal Meaning in Reading Instruction: American Education's Greatest Need. 45p. (Orig.). 1983. pap. text ed. 8.00 (ISBN 0-910609-03-9). Reading Tutor.
Weintraub, Sam & Cowan, Robert J., eds. Vision-Visual Perception. (Annotated Bibliography Ser.). 93p. (Orig.). 1982. pap. text ed. 4.50 (ISBN 0-87207-339-4, 339). Intl Reading.
Wiener, Harvey & Bazerman, Charles. Reading Skills Handbook. 2nd ed. 11.50 (ISBN 0-395-31710-X); 1.00 (ISBN 0-395-31711-8). HM.
Woodington, Cynthia C. & Perry, Leslie A. Teaching the Reading Teachers. (Illus.). 144p. 1983. spiral 14.75x (ISBN 0-398-04762-6). C C Thomas.

READING–ABILITY TESTING
Rinsky, Lee A. & Fossard, Esta de. The Contemporary Classroom Reading Inventory. 166p. (Orig.). 1980. pap. text ed. 8.95 (ISBN 0-89787-510-9). Gorsuch Scarisbrick.

READING–EXAMINATIONS, QUESTIONS, ETC.
Gates-MacGivitie Reading Tests. write for info. (RivEd). HM.
Lackner, Marie & Paterno, Cynthia. Practice RCT Reading Exam, No. 1. 1982. of 10 9.95 set (ISBN 0-937820-34-2). Westsea Pub.
--Practice RCT Reading Exam, No. 2. of 10 9.95 set (ISBN 0-937820-35-0). Westsea Pub.
Nelson Denny Reading Tests. write for info. (RivEd). HM.
The Three-R's Test. write for info. (RivEd). HM.

READING–PROGRAMMED INSTRUCTION
Blumenfeld, Samuel L. Alpha-Phonics: A Primer for Beginning Readers. 160p. (Orig.). 1983. pap. 19.95 (ISBN 0-686-83942-0); 19.95 (ISBN 0-8159-6916-3). Devin.
Brown, James I. Efficient Reading Instructors Manual. 5th ed ed. 75p. 1982. pap. text ed. 19.95 (ISBN 0-943000-07-6). Telstar Inc.
Cebulash. Primary Reading Series. (gr. 1-3). complete set of 6 kits 389.85 (ISBN 0-8372-3871-4) (ISBN 0-686-43195-2). Bowmar-Noble.
Flemming, Laraine. Reading for Results. 2d ed. 468p. 1983. pap. text ed. 12.95 (ISBN 0-395-32605-2); write for info. instr's. manual (ISBN 0-395-32606-0). HM.
Gould, Eric. Reading into Writing: A Rhetoric, Reader, & Handbook. 1982. pap. text ed. 16.95 (ISBN 0-395-32607-9). HM.
Guidebook to Better Reading: Supplementary Readers. Incl. Benchmark (ISBN 0-8372-4219-3); Las Caras de Chico (ISBN 0-8372-4212-6); Explore (ISBN 0-8372-4213-4); Eyebrowse (ISBN 0-8372-4209-6); The Jinx Boat (ISBN 0-8372-4210-X); Junkyard Holiday (ISBN 0-8372-4214-2); Moneywise (ISBN 0-8372-4220-7); On Polecat Mountain (ISBN 0-8372-4216-9); Quest (ISBN 0-8372-4217-7); Snow Bound (ISBN 0-8372-4218-5); Thrust (ISBN 0-8372-4211-8); Venture (ISBN 0-8372-4215-0). pap. 85.95 30-bk. set (ISBN 0-8372-4208-8); pap. 2.97 ea.; tchr's. handbk. 2.97 (ISBN 0-8372-4221-5); dupl. masters avail. Bowmar-Noble.
Hughes & Bond. Reach. (gr. 4-9). pap. 4.59 (ISBN 0-8372-4259-2); tchr's programme 4.59 (ISBN 0-8372-4260-6); tapes avail. Bowmar-Noble.
Loose, Frances F. Bonus Points: Teacher's Handbook. 55p. 1976. 3.50 (ISBN 0-89039-174-2). Ann Arbor Pubs.
Rambeau & Rambeau. Guidebook to Better Reading. (gr. 5-12). pap. 2.97 (ISBN 0-8372-4200-2); tchr's manual 2.97 (ISBN 0-8372-4201-0); West Word Bound Bk. 1.98 (ISBN 0-8372-4202-9); tchr's ed. 1.98 (ISBN 0-8372-4203-7); suppl. reader set & dupl. masters avail. Bowmar-Noble.
Reading Comprehension Series, 8 kits. (gr. 4-8). complete ser. 444.90 (ISBN 0-8372-3725-4); kit 58.59 ea.; tchr's guide 3.48 ea.; posters avail. Bowmar-Noble.
Reading Diagnosis & Direct Instruction: A Guide for the Classroom. 2d ed. LC 82-84609. 1983. pap. text ed. 11.95 (ISBN 0-395-32787-3). HM.
Triple Play Reading Ser, 5 bks. Incl. Kit 1. Falling Star & Other Plays (ISBN 0-8372-2568-X); Kit 2. A Light in the Window & Other Plays (ISBN 0-8372-2569-8); Kit 3. The Motorcross Trial & Other Plays (ISBN 0-8372-2570-1); Kit 4. Purple Power & Other Plays (ISBN 0-8372-2593-0); Kit 5. Second Stringer & Other Plays (ISBN 0-8372-2594-9). (Incl. bks., tchr's. guides, tapes, & dupl. masters). (gr. 4-9). 42.90 ea.; Set. 199.95 (ISBN 0-8372-2595-7). Bowmar-Noble.

READING–REMEDIAL TEACHING
see also Rapid Reading; Reading, Teachers Of
Rupley, William H. & Blair, Timothy R. Reading Diagnosis & Remediation: Classroom & Clinic. 2d ed. LC 82-83365. 496p. 1983. text ed. 23.95 (ISBN 0-395-32785-7); write for info. instr's. manual (ISBN 0-395-32786-5). HM.

READING–STUDY AND TEACHING
see Reading; Reading (Elementary); Reading (Secondary Education)

READING (ELEMENTARY)
see also English Language–Phonetics; Primers; Reading–Remedial Teaching; Reading Readiness
Adams, Anne & Bebensee, Elisabeth L. Success in Reading & Writing: Grade 6. 1983. text ed. 15.95 (ISBN 0-673-16586-8). Scott F.
Banks, Carl. Teach Your Child to Read. LC 81-86350. 64p. 1983. pap. 3.95 (ISBN 0-86666-049-6). GWP.
Blumenfeld, Samuel L. Teach Them to Read: A Step-by-Step Primer. 1982. pap. 19.95 spiral bdg. (ISBN 0-686-81779-6). Devin.
Brooks, Bearl. Basic Skills Reading Workbook: Grade 8. (Basic Skills Workbooks). 32p. (gr. 8). 1982. wkbk. 0.99 (ISBN 0-8209-0362-0, RW-A). ESP.
--Jumbo Reading Yearbook: Kindergarten. (Jumbo Reading Ser.). 96p. (gr. k). 1980. 14.00 (ISBN 0-8209-0011-7, JRY R). ESP.
Cunningham, James & Cunningham, Partricia. Reading in Elementary Classrooms: Strategies & Observations. LC 82-7814. 512p. 1982. text ed. 17.95x (ISBN 0-582-28390-6). Longman.
Evans, A. J. & Palmer, Marilyn. More Writing about Pictures: Using Pictures to Develop Language & Writing Skills. (gr. 1-3). 1982. Bk. 1: Familiar Places. pap. 3.95 (ISBN 0-8077-6037-4); Bk. 2: Action & Activity. pap. 3.95 (ISBN 0-8077-6038-2); Bk. 3: Supplement-Fables. pap. 3.95 (ISBN 0-8077-6039-0); Tchrs' Manual 2.95 (ISBN 0-8077-6040-4). Tchrs Coll.
Gordon, William A. The Reading Curriculum: A Reference Guide to Criterion-Based Skill Development in Grades K-8. 272p. 1982. 29.50 (ISBN 0-03-062128-3). Praeger.
Hittleman, Daniel. Developmental Reading, K-8: Teaching from a Psycholinguistic Perspective. 2d ed. 480p. 1983. text ed. 23.95 (ISBN 0-395-32770-9, EA95); write for info. instr's. manual (ISBN 0-395-32771-7, EA96). HM.
Justus, Fred. Unified Reading. (Early Education Ser.). 24p. (gr. 2). 1981. wkbk. 5.00 (ISBN 0-8209-0212-8, K-14). ESP.
Kusnetz, Len. Your Child Can Be a Super-Reader: A Fun & Easy Approach to Reading Improvement. LC 79-84790. (Illus.). 132p. 1982. 4.95 (ISBN 0-686-84883-7, Dist. by Liberty Pub. Co). Learning Hse.
Roets, Lois. Basic Skills Reading Workbook: Grade 1. (Basic Skills Workbooks). 32p. (gr. 1). 1982. tchrs' ed. 0.99 (ISBN 0-8209-0363-9, RW-B). ESP.
Roets, Lois F. Jumbo Reading Yearbook: Grade 1. (Jumbo Reading Ser.). 96p. (gr. 1). 1979. 14.00 (ISBN 0-8209-0012-5, JRY 1). ESP.
Shaw, Maie-Jose. Basic Skills Reading Workbook: Grade 7. (Basic Skills Workbooks). 32p. (gr. 7). 1982. tchrs' ed. 0.99 (ISBN 0-8209-0369-8, W-H). ESP.
Shaw, Marie-Jose. Basic Skills Reading Workbook: Grade 2. (Basic Skills Workbooks). 32p. (gr. 2). 1982. tchrs' ed. 0.99 (ISBN 0-8209-0364-7, RW-C). ESP.
--Basic Skills Reading Workbook: Grade 4. (Basic Skills Workbooks). 32p. (gr. 4). 1982. tchrs' ed. 0.99 (ISBN 0-8209-0366-3, RW-E). ESP.
--Basic Skills Reading Workbook: Grade 5. (Basic Skills Workbooks). 32p. (gr. 5). 1982. tchrs' ed. 0.99 (ISBN 0-8209-0367-1, W-F). ESP.
--Basic Skills Reading Workbook: Grade 6. (Basic Skills Workbooks). 32p. (gr. 6). 1982. wkbk. 0.99 (ISBN 0-8209-0368-X, RW-G). ESP.
--Basic Skills Reading Workbooks: Grade 3. (Basic Skills Workbooks). 32p. (gr. 3). 1982. wkbk. 0.99 (ISBN 0-8209-0365-5, RW-D). ESP.
--Jumbo Reading Yearbook: Grade 2. (Jumbo Reading Ser.). 96p. (gr. 2). 1978. 14.00 (ISBN 0-8209-0013-3, JRY 2). ESP.
--Jumbo Reading Yearbook: Grade 3. (Jumbo Reading Ser.). 96p. (gr. 3). 1978. 14.00 (ISBN 0-8209-0014-1, JRY 3). ESP.
--Jumbo Reading Yearbook: Grade 4. (Jumbo Reading Ser.). 96p. (gr. 4). 1978. 14.00 (ISBN 0-8209-0015-X, JRY 4). ESP.
--Jumbo Reading Yearbook: Grade 5. (Jumbo Reading Ser.). 96p. (gr. 5). 1978. 14.00 (ISBN 0-8209-0016-8, JRY 5). ESP.
--Jumbo Reading Yearbook: Grade 6. (Jumbo Reading Ser.). 96p. (gr. 6). 1978. 14.00 (ISBN 0-8209-0017-6, JRY 6). ESP.
--Jumbo Reading Yearbook: Grade 7. (Jumbo Reading Ser.). 96p. (gr. 7-12). 1980. 14.00 (ISBN 0-8209-0018-4, JRY 7). ESP.
Taylor, Danny. Family Literacy: Young Children Learning to Read & Write. 176p. (Orig.). 1983. pap. text ed. 9.00x (ISBN 0-435-08204-3). Heinemann Ed.

READING (ELEMENTARY)–PHONETIC METHOD
Alberts, Cecil D. Game Power for Phonics, Computerized. 1981. 28.50 (ISBN 0-686-84762-8). Spin-A-Test Pub.
Brooks, Bearl. Basic Skills Phonics Workbook: Part I. (Basic Skills Workbooks). 32p. (gr. 1-3). 1982. tchrs' ed. 0.99 (ISBN 0-8209-0385-X, PW-1). ESP.
--Basic Skills Phonics Workbook: Part II. (Basic Skills Workbooks). 32p. (gr. 1-3). 1982. tchrs' ed. 0.99 (ISBN 0-8209-0386-8, PW-2). ESP.
--Basic Skills Phonics Workbook: Part III. (Basic Skills Workbooks). 32p. (gr. 1-3). 1982. tchrs' ed. 0.99 (ISBN 0-8209-0387-6, PW-3). ESP.
--Beginning Phonics. (Phonics Ser.). 24p. (gr. 1). 1979. wkbk. 5.00 (ISBN 0-8209-0329-9, P-1). ESP.
--Jumbo Phonics Yearbook. (Jumbo Phonics Ser.). 96p. (gr. 1-3). 1977. 14.00 (ISBN 0-8209-0049-4, JPY 1). ESP.
--Learning Phonics: Grade 1. (Phonics Ser.). 24p. 1979. wkbk. 5.00 (ISBN 0-8209-0330-2, P-2). ESP.
--Learning Phonics: Grade 3. (Phonics Ser.). 24p. 1977. wkbk. 5.00 (ISBN 0-8209-0333-7, P-5). ESP.
--Listening for Sounds. (Phonics Ser.). 24p. (gr. 2). 1977. wkbk. 5.00 (ISBN 0-8209-0332-9, P-4). ESP.
--Phonetic Sounds. (Phonics Ser.). 24p. (gr. 2). 1979. wkbk. 5.00 (ISBN 0-8209-0331-0, P-3). ESP.
--Phonetic Sounds & Symbols: Part 1. (Phonics Ser.). 24p. (gr. 1). 1978. wkbk. 5.00 (ISBN 0-8209-0335-3, P-7). ESP.
--Phonetic Sounds & Symbols: Part 2. (Phonics Ser.). 24p. (gr. 1). 1978. wkbk. 5.00 (ISBN 0-8209-0336-1, P-8). ESP.
--Phonics for Reading & Spelling: Grade 2. (Phonics Ser.). 24p. 1978. wkbk. 5.00 (ISBN 0-8209-0337-X, P-9). ESP.
--Phonics for Reading & Spelling: Grade 3. (Phonics Ser.). 24p. 1978. wkbk. 5.00 (ISBN 0-8209-0338-8, P-10). ESP.
--Phonics for Reading & Spelling: Grade 4. (Phonics Ser.). 24p. 1978. wkbk. 5.00 (ISBN 0-8209-0339-6, P-11). ESP.
--Using Phonics. (Phonics Ser.). 24p. (gr. 1-4). 1978. wkbk. 5.00 (ISBN 0-8209-0334-5, P-6). ESP.
Frank Schaffer Publications. Getting Ready for Phonics. (Getting Ready for Kindergarten Ser.). (Illus.). 24p. (ps-k). 1980. workbook 1.29 (ISBN 0-86734-018-5, FS 3031). Schaffer Pubns.
--Phonics: Consonants. (Help Your Child Learn Ser.). (Illus.). 24p. (ps-2). 1978. workbook 1.29 (ISBN 0-86734-003-7, FS 3004). Schaffer Pubns.
Frank Schaffer Publications, Inc. Phonics: Vowels. (Help Your Child Learn Ser.). (Illus.). 24p. (gr. 1-3). 1978. workbook 1.29 (ISBN 0-86734-004-5, FS 3005). Schaffer Pubns.
Justus, Fred. Phonetic Puzzles: Grade 3. (Puzzles Ser.). 24p. 1980. wkbk. 5.00 (ISBN 0-8209-0289-6, PU-3). ESP.
--Phonetic Puzzles: Grade 4. (Puzzles Ser.). 24p. 1980. 5.00 (ISBN 0-8209-0290-X, PU-4). ESP.
--Phonetic Puzzles: Grade 5. (Puzzles Ser.). 24p. 1980. wkbk. 5.00 (ISBN 0-8209-0291-8, PU-5). ESP.
--Phonetic Puzzles: Grade 6. (Puzzles Ser.). 24p. 1980. 5.00 (ISBN 0-8209-0292-6, PU-6). ESP.
--Phonetic Puzzles: Grade 7. (Puzzles Ser.). 24p. 1980. wkbk. 5.00 (ISBN 0-8209-0293-4, PU-7). ESP.
--Phonetic Puzzles: Grade 8. (Puzzles Ser.). 24p. 1980. wkbk. 5.00 (ISBN 0-8209-0294-2, PU-8). ESP.
Messina, Kathlyn. The Sleeping Giant Reading Program. LC 82-83558. (Illus.). 160p. (Orig.). 1983. pap. 10.95 (ISBN 0-910569-00-2). Hampton Court Pub.
Rinsky, Lee A. Teaching Word Attack Skills. 2nd ed. 174p. 1981. pap. text ed. 9.95 (ISBN 0-89787-511-7). Gorsuch Scarisbrick.
Scott, L. B. A New Time for Phonics, 6 Bks. 1980. Bks. A-C. text ed. 3.16 ea. Bk. A: Consonants (ISBN 0-07-056111-7). Bk. B: Short Vowels (ISBN 0-07-056112-5). Bk. C: Long Vowels (ISBN 0-07-056113-3). Bks. D-F. text ed. 4.72 ea. Bk. D: Consonant Pairs (ISBN 0-07-056114-1). Bk. E: Patterns (ISBN 0-07-056115-X). Bk. F: Sounds & Syllables (ISBN 0-07-056116-8). tchr's manuals for ea. bk. avail. McGraw.

READING (HIGHER EDUCATION)
see also College Readers
Berger, Allen & Robinson, H. Alan, eds. Secondary School Reading: What Research Reveals for Classroom Practice. (Orig.). 1982. pap. 10.75 (ISBN 0-8141-4295-8). NCTE.

READING (PRESCHOOL)
Frank Schaffer Publications. Reading Comprehension. (Help Your Child Learn Ser.). (Illus.). 24p. (gr. 3-5). 1978. workbook 1.29 (ISBN 0-86734-011-8, FS 3012). Schaffer Pubns.
Nail, Simonne & Caillot, Simonne. How to Get Your Child to Read. LC 81-71138. (Illus.). 122p. 1981. pap. 9.00 (ISBN 0-942010-00-0). Famous Pr Pub.

READING (SECONDARY EDUCATION)
Friedman, Carol A. & Meade, Andre T. Reading & Writing Skills Workbook for the GED Test. LC 82-18400. (Arco's Preparation for the GED Examination Ser.). 256p. 1983. pap. 5.95 (ISBN 0-668-05540-5). Arco.
Roe & Stoodt. Secondary School Reading Instruction: The Content Areas. 2d ed. 1983. text ed. 22.95 (ISBN 0-686-84558-7, ET02); instr's manual avail. (ET03). HM.
Roe, Betty D. & Stoodt, Barbara D. Secondary School Reading Instruction: The Content Areas. 2d ed. LC 82-83290. 1983. 21.95 (ISBN 0-395-32783-0); write for info. instr's. manual (ISBN 0-395-32784-9). HM.

READING, CHOICE OF
see Bibliography–Best Books; Books and Reading

READING, INTERPRETATIVE
see Oral Interpretation

READING, PSYCHOLOGY OF
see also Bibliotherapy; Reading–Remedial Teaching; Reading Readiness
Carroll, James & Overton, Barbara. Be Sure Your Child Learns to Read. 160p. 1976. pap. 1.95 (ISBN 0-89826-000-0). Natl Paperback.
Chall, J. S. Stages of Reading Development. 293p. 1983. 18.95 (ISBN 0-07-010380-1, P&RB). McGraw.
Nail, Simonne & Caillot, Simonne. How to Get Your Child to Read. LC 81-71138. (Illus.). 122p. 1981. pap. 9.00 (ISBN 0-942010-00-0). Famous Pr Pub.

READING, TEACHERS OF
Woodington, Cynthia C. & Perry, Leslie A. Teaching the Reading Teachers. (Illus.). 144p. 1983. spiral 14.75x (ISBN 0-398-04762-6). C C Thomas.

READING COMPREHENSION
Adams, L. & Llanas, A. Read It Right It: Materials for Elementary Reading Comprehension. (Materials for Language Practice Ser.). (Illus.). 96p. 1983. pap. 4.95 (ISBN 0-08-029435-9). Pergamon.
Brown, James I. Reading Power. 2nd ed. 400p. 1982. pap. text ed. 10.95 (ISBN 0-669-05318-X). Heath.

READING DISABILITY
see also Dyslexia
Chicorel, Marietta, ed. Chicorel Abstracts to Reading & Learning Disabilities, 1981, Vol. 19. (Chicorel Index Ser.). 380p. 1983. 95.00x (ISBN 0-934598-83-5). Am Lib Pub Co.
Lerner, J. W. & List, L. K. Reading & Learning Disabilities. Date not set. price not set (ISBN 0-07-037220-9). McGraw.

READING INTERESTS OF CHILDREN
see Children–Books and Reading

READING READINESS
Moore, David W. & Readence, John E. Prereading Activities for Content Area Reading & Learning. (Reading Aids Ser.). 72p. (Orig.). 1982. pap. 5.00 (ISBN 0-87207-228-2, 228). Intl Reading.

READING RETARDATION
see Reading Disability

READING TEACHERS
see Reading, Teachers Of

REAGAN, RONALD, PRES. U.S., 1911-
Brownstein, Ronald & Easton, Nina, eds. Reagan's Ruling Class: Portraits of the President's Top 100 Officials. LC 82-60917. 747p. 1982. 24.50 (ISBN 0-936486-03-1). Presidential Acct.
Congressional Quarterly Inc. Staff. Reagan's First Year. LC 82-1386. 184p. 1982. pap. 8.95 (ISBN 0-87187-225-0). Congr Quarterly.
Kimzey, Bruce W. Reaganomics. (Illus.). 118p. 1983. pap. text ed. 4.90 (ISBN 0-314-73187-3). West Pub.
McClelland, Doug. Hollywood on Ronald Reagan: Friends & Enemies Discuss Our President, the Actor. (Illus.). 125p. (Orig.). 1983. pap. 11.95 (ISBN 0-571-12522-0). Faber & Faber.
Reagan, Ronald. Ronald Reagan Talks to America. 1983. 12.95 (ISBN 0-8159-6719-5); pap. 7.95. Devin.

REAGENTS, CHEMICAL
see Chemical Tests and Reagents

REAL ACTIONS
see Actions and Defenses

REAL ESTATE
see Real Property

REAL ESTATE BUSINESS
see also House Buying; House Selling; Industrial Districts; Real Estate Investment; Real Estate Management
Allen, Robert D. & Wolfe, Thomas E. Real Estate Almanac. LC 80-12417. (Real Estate for Professional Practitioners Ser.). 472p. 1980. pap. 22.95 (ISBN 0-471-05854-8). Wiley.
Bell, William W. Secrets of a Professional Home Buyer. LC 82-21980. 160p. 1983. softcover 12.95 (ISBN 0-930294-00-9). World Wide OR.
Bockl, George. Recycling Real Estate: The Number One Way to Make Money in the 80's. LC 82-12244. 237p. 1983. 19.95 (ISBN 0-13-768804-0, Busn). P-H.
Bond, Robert J., et al. California Real Estate Finance. 2nd ed. LC 79-3850. (California Real Estate Ser.). 330p. 1980. text ed. 21.95x (ISBN 0-471-06230-8); avail. questions (ISBN 0-471-86103-0). Wiley.
Bregman, Douglas M. & Miller, Peter G., eds. Model Contingencies for Real Estate Sales. 9.50 (ISBN 0-943954-00-2). Tremont Pr.
Clark, William, ed. Modeling Housing Market Search. LC 82-872. 256p. 1982. 30.00x (ISBN 0-312-53536-8). St Martin.
Cooper-Hill, James & Greenberg, Martin J. Cases & Material on Mortgages & Real Estate Finance. (Contemporary Legal Education Ser.). 632p. 1982. 27.50 (ISBN 0-87215-499-8). Michie-Bobbs.
Covello, Charles J. Real Estate Buying - Selling Guide for Washington. 2nd ed. (Illus.). 83p. 1983. pap. price not set (ISBN 0-88908-723-7). Self Counsel Pr.
De Benedictis, Daniel J. The Complete Real Estate Adviser. Rev. ed. 1983. pap. 6.95 (ISBN 0-346-12578-2). Cornerstone.
Ellis, John T. & Beam, Victoria R. Mastering Real Estate Math in One Day. 1983. pap. 7.95 (ISBN 0-13-559666-1). P-H.
Epley, Donald R. & Millar, James A. Basic Real Estate Finance & Investments. LC 79-19530. 633p. 1980. text ed. 28.50 (ISBN 0-471-03635-8). Wiley.
Follain, James R., Jr. & Malpezzi, S. Dissecting Housing Value & Rent. 132p. (Orig.). pap. text ed. 8.50 (ISBN 0-87766-276-2). Urban Inst.
Gaines, George, Jr. & Coleman, David S. Real Estate Math. 145p. (Orig.). 1980. pap. text ed. 8.95 (ISBN 0-89787-902-3). Gorsuch Scarisbrick.
Graaskamp, James A. Fundamentals of Real Estate Development. LC 81-51563. (Development Component Ser.). (Illus.). 31p. 1980. pap. 10.00 (ISBN 0-87420-601-4, D16). Urban Land.
Greer, Gaylon E. & Farrell, Michael. Contemporary Real Estate: Theory & Practice. 480p. 1983. text ed. 26.95 (ISBN 0-03-056682-7). Dryden Pr.
Griffin, James S. How to Make Money in Commercial Land: A Guide for Investors & Residential Salespersons. Ainsworth, Fay, ed. (Illus., Orig.). 1983. pap. 7.95 (ISBN 0-916682-37-4). Outdoor Empire.
Gruen, Nina & Gruen, Claude. Demographic Changes & Their Effects on Real Estate Markets in the '80s. LC 82-60314. (Development Component Ser.). (Illus.). 27p. 1982. pap. 10.00 (ISBN 0-87420-609-X, D22). Urban Land.
Healy, John E. How to Match Properties, Financing & Prospects for Quick Profitable Real Estate Sales. 1982. 89.50 (ISBN 0-13-423822-2). Exec Reports.

Huges, Patricia & Ochi, Kaz. The Power of Visicalc Real Estate. 166p. 1982. pap. 14.95 (ISBN 0-13-687350-2). P-H.

Industrial Real Estate: An Annotated Bibliography. 34p. 10.00 (ISBN 0-686-38199-8). Soc Industrial Realtors.

Irwin, Robert. Timeshare Properties: What Every Buyer Must Know! LC 82-17185. (Illus.). 224p. 1983. 19.95 (ISBN 0-07-032082-9, P&RB). McGraw.

Kamin, John V. How to Make Money Fast Speculating in Distressed Property. rev. ed. 343p. 1982. Repr. of 1976 ed. 15.00 (ISBN 0-911353-00-3). Forecaster Pub.

Levenkron, David J. Sand & Rubble: The Salton City Story. LC 81-83733. (Illus.). 319p. (Orig.). 1982. pap. 9.95x (ISBN 0-941348-00-8, 825). Justice Pubs.

McIntyre, Alice. Role Playing: A Real Estate Training Tool. Gerth, Dawn M., ed. LC 82-83133. (Illus.). 151p. (Orig.). 1982. pap. text ed. 14.95 (ISBN 0-913652-43-1, 152). Realtors Natl.

Munro, Robert A. & Munro, John A. Real Estate Periodicals Index, 1981, Vol. 1. 118p. (Orig.). 1982. pap. text ed. 60.00x (ISBN 0-911553-00-2). Munro Assocs.

Munro, Robert A & Munro, John A. Real Estate Periodicals Index, 1982, Vol. 2. 135p. (Orig.). 1983. pap. 60.00x (ISBN 0-911553-01-0). Munro Assocs.

Osborne, Thomas. California Real Estate License Manual. 1983. pap. text ed. 17.95x (ISBN 0-673-16579-5). Scott F.

Palmer, Ralph A. Real Estate Principles: The Princeton Real Estate Examination Guide. rev. ed. (Illus.). 348p. 1982. pap. text ed. 16.95 (ISBN 0-89787-905-8). Gorsuch Scarisbrick.

Pivar, William H. Power Real Estate Listing. 170p. 1983. text ed. 12.95 (ISBN 0-88462-480-3). Real Estate Ed Co.

--Power Real Estate Sales. 170p. 1983. text ed. 12.95 (ISBN 0-88462-479-X). Real Estate Ed Co.

The Real Estate Handbook. 256p. 1983. softcover 5.95 (ISBN 0-89471-208-X). Running Pr.

Real Estate Research Corporation. Infill Development Strategies. LC 82-50809. (Illus.). 132p. 1982. pap. 24.95 (ISBN 0-87420-613-8, I27). Urban Land.

Siedel, George J. & Willing, Jean S. Michigan Guide to Real Estate Licensing Examinations for Salespersons & Brokers. LC 81-16394. 160p. 1982. pap. text ed. 12.95 (ISBN 0-471-87760-3). Wiley.

Siemon, Charles L. & Larsen, Wendy U. Vested Rights: Balancing Public & Private Development Expectations. LC 82-50897. 106p. (Orig.). 1982. pap. text ed. 42.00 (ISBN 0-87420-612-X, VO1). Urban Land.

Tracy, Larry J. The Art & Skill of Real Estate & Time Share Selling. 1982. 9.95 (ISBN 0-933984-03-0). Tracy Pub.

Tuccillo, John. Housing & Investment in an Inflationary World: Theory & Evidence. (Illus.). 55p. (Orig.). 1980. pap. text ed. 5.50 (ISBN 0-87766-281-9). Urban Inst.

Tuccillo, John & Villani, Kevin, eds. House Prices & Inflation. LC 81-53062. 175p. 1981. text ed. 21.00 (ISBN 0-87766-306-8, URI 33300). Urban Inst.

Vernor, James D. An Introduction to Risk Management in Property Development. LC 81-51564. (Development Component Ser.). (Illus.). 20p. 1981. pap. 10.00 (ISBN 0-87420-602-2, D18). Urban Land.

Who's Who in Real Estate: The Directory of the Real Estate Professions. 1983. 60.00 (ISBN 0-88262-876-3). Warren.

Wigginton, F. P. The Complete Guide to Profitable Real Estate Listings. 141p. 1983. pap. 6.95 (ISBN 0-87094-413-4). Dow Jones-Irwin.

Wowk, Kathleen. Playing Cards of the World. (Illus.). 160p. 1982. 25.00 (ISBN 0-7188-2408-3). US Games Syst.

REAL ESTATE BUSINESS-EXAMINATIONS, QUESTIONS, ETC.

French, William B. & Martin, Stephen J. Real Estate Review's Guide to Real Estate Licensing Examinations for Salespersons & Brokers. 2nd ed. LC 81-10331. 367p. 1982. text ed. 20.95 (ISBN 0-471-87754-9); write for info. tchr's manual (ISBN 0-471-89519-9). Wiley.

Friedman, Ronald M. Pennsylvania Guide to Real Estate Licensing Examinations for Salespersons & Brokers. LC 79-48053. 124p. 1982. pap. 9.95 (ISBN 0-471-87758-1). Wiley.

How to Prepare for the Real Estate Licensing Exam. 2nd ed. 1983. pap. 7.95 (ISBN 0-8120-2351-X). Barron.

Sigafoos, Robert A. & Oslin, Ronald. Tennessee Guide to Real Estate Licensing Examinations for Salespersons & Brokers. LC 81-11540. 120p. 1982. pap. text ed. 10.95 (ISBN 0-471-87759-X). Wiley.

Wurtzebach, Charles H. & Harvey, Robert O. Texas Guide to Real Estate Licensing Examinations for Salespersons & Brokers. 352p. 1982. text ed. 23.95 (ISBN 0-471-87757-3). Wiley.

REAL ESTATE BUSINESS-LAW AND LEGISLATION

Bernstein, Charles S., ed. Connecticut Real Estate Statutes. 480p. 1983. write for info. looseleaf binder (ISBN 0-88063-007-8). Butterworth Legal Pubs.

Harwood & Jacobus. Texas Real Estate. 3rd ed. 1983. text ed. 21.95 (ISBN 0-8359-7554-1). Reston.

Henszey, Benjamin N. & Friedman, Ronald M. Real Estate Law. LC 78-24808. 383p. 1982. text ed. 24.95 (ISBN 0-471-87753-0); write for info. (ISBN 0-471-89517-2). Wiley.

Hetrick, Patrick K. Webster's Real Estate Law in North Carolina. rev. ed. 1981. 60.00 (ISBN 0-87215-402-5). Michie-Bobbs.

Irvin, Carol K. & Irvin, James D. Ohio Real Estate Law. 2nd ed. (Illus.). 464p. 1982. pap. text ed. 22.95 (ISBN 0-89787-904-X). Gorsuch Scarisbrick.

Jacobus. Texas Real Estate Law. 3rd ed. text ed. 21.95 (ISBN 0-8359-7573-8). Reston.

Kratovil, Robert & Werner, Raymond J. Real Estate Law. 8th ed. 640p. 1983. 31.95 (ISBN 0-13-763292-4); student ed. 24.95 (ISBN 0-686-82022-3). P-H.

Morse, Milton A., Jr. & Taylor, Conway. Modern Real Estate Practice in Texas. 4th rev. ed. 550p. 1982. pap. text ed. 19.95 (ISBN 0-88462-336-X). Real Estate Ed Co.

Rudman, Jack. Senior Attorney (Realty) (Career Examination Ser.: C-568). (Cloth bdg. avail. on request). pap. 14.00 (ISBN 0-8373-0568-3). Natl Learning.

Tucker, Stefan F. & Cowan, Martin B., eds. Real Estate Income Taxation 1982. 816p. 1982. 48.00 (ISBN 0-88262-829-1). Warren.

Weinberg, Norman & Colletti, Paul J. Real Estate Review's New York Guide to Real Estate Licensing Examination for Salespersons. LC 79-56597. 344p. 1982. text ed. 23.95 (ISBN 0-471-87756-5); write for info. tchr's ed. (ISBN 0-471-89518-0). Wiley.

REAL ESTATE BUSINESS-VOCATIONAL GUIDANCE

Handler, Stuart. How to Be a Superstar Selling Commercial & Investment Real Estate. 1983. text ed. 17.95 (ISBN 0-8359-2910-8). Reston.

REAL ESTATE INVESTMENT

see also Real Estate Business

Anderson, Jerry D. Success Strategies for Investment Real Estate: The Professional's Guide to Better Service & Increased Commissions. Berlin, Helene, ed. LC 82-61402. (Illus.). 300p. (Orig.). 1982. pap. text ed. 17.95 (ISBN 0-913652-33-4, BK 153). Realtors Natl.

Arnold, Lee E., Jr. Commercial-Investment Real Estate: Marketing & Management. Gerth, Dawn M., ed. LC 82-62949. (Illus.). 250p. text ed. 19.95 (ISBN 0-913652-53-9, BK 161). Realtors Natl.

Case, Fred E. Professional Real Estate Investing: How to Evaluate Complex Investment Alternatives. 326p. 1983. 22.95 (ISBN 0-13-725861-5); pap. 12.95 (ISBN 0-13-725853-4). P-H.

Collins, Dennis & Boor, Jacklyn. Real Estate Options: How to Score in a Tight Market. 192p. 1983. 13.95 (ISBN 0-13-765123-6); pap. 6.95 (ISBN 0-13-765115-5). P-H.

Eastgate, Robert J. Master Guide to Creative Financing of Real Estate Investments. LC 82-9313. 246p. 1982. text ed. 89.50 (ISBN 0-87624-366-9). Inst Busn Plan.

Epley, Donald R. & Millar, James A. Basic Real Estate Finance & Investments. LC 79-19530. 633p. 1980. text ed. 28.50 (ISBN 0-471-03635-8). Wiley.

Greer, G. E. The Real Estate Investor & the Federal Income Tax. 2nd ed. 267p. 1982. text ed. 29.95x (ISBN 0-471-09738-1). Ronald Pr.

Hall, Robert W. Real Estate Investment Analysis: How to Spot the Top Performers for High Return Real Estate Investing. LC 82-9239. 232p. text ed. 89.50 (ISBN 0-87624-487-8). Inst Busn Plan.

Hughes, Charles. Guide to Texas Title Insurance. 1983. 11.95 (ISBN 0-87201-777-X). Gulf Pub.

Manis, Michael S. Real Estate Investment Analysis. (Real Estate Ser.). 272p. 1983. text ed. 25.95 (ISBN 0-471-86503-6). Wiley.

Marston, Garth & Kelleher, Hugh. Creative Real Estate Financing: A Guide to Buying & Selling Homes in the 1980's. 224p. 1983. 19.95 (ISBN 0-471-86678-4). Ronald Pr.

Pyhrr, Stephen A. & Cooper, James R. Real Estate Investment. LC 81-24130. 798p. 1982. text ed. 28.50 (ISBN 0-471-87752-2). Wiley.

Sofer, Nat. How You Can Build a Fortune Investing in Land. (Illus.). 224p. 1983. 15.95 (ISBN 0-13-444026-9); pap. 7.95 (ISBN 0-13-444018-8). P-H.

Wigginton, F. P. The Complete Guide to Profitable Real Estate Listings. 141p. 1983. pap. 6.95 (ISBN 0-87094-413-4). Dow Jones-Irwin.

REAL ESTATE LOANS

see Mortgage Loans

REAL ESTATE MANAGEMENT

see also Building-Service Employees

Rudman, Jack. Associate Real Property Manager. (Career Examination Ser.: C-2890). (Cloth bdg. avail. on request). pap. 14.00 (ISBN 0-8373-2890-X). Natl Learning.

REAL ESTATE TAX

see Real Property Tax

REAL PROPERTY

Here are entered treatises on real property in the legal sense, i.e. the law of immovable property, and works on real estate in general, or real estate conditions in any particular place. Works on the buying, selling, and management of real estate are entered under the heading Real Estate Business. For land laws use Land Tenure-(country subdivision) e.g. Land Tenure-Sweden.

see also Assessment; Condominium (Housing); Eminent Domain; Estates (Law); Farms; Land Titles; Land Trusts; Landlord and Tenant; Leases; Mortgages; Possession (Law); Real Estate Business-Law and Legislation; Rent; Vendors and Purchasers

Anderson, Kenneth R. & Golden, Dale, eds. Certified Property Manager Profile & Compensation Study. 3rd, rev. ed. 1983. pap. 13.50 (ISBN 0-912104-69-4). Inst Real Estate.

Ficek, Edmund F. & Johnson, Ross H. Real Estate: Principles & Practices. 3rd ed. 1983. 21.95 (ISBN 0-675-20016-4); study guide 8.95 (ISBN 0-675-20064-4). Additional supplements may be obtained from publisher. Merrill.

Gilder, Cornelia B. Preservation for Profit: Ten Case Studies in Commercial Rehabilitation. (Illus.). 27p. (Orig.). 1980. pap. 3.00 (ISBN 0-942000-02-1). Pres League NY.

Haikalis, Peter D. & Freeman, Jean K., eds. Real Estate: A Bibliography of the Monographic Literature. LC 82-23071. 323p. 1983. lib. bdg. 45.00 (ISBN 0-313-23680-1, HAK/). Greenwood.

Harwood & Jacobus. Texas Real Estate. 3rd ed. 1983. text ed. 21.95 (ISBN 0-8359-7554-1). Reston.

McDougal, Myers S. & McDougal, Luther L. Property, Wealth, Land. 2nd ed. 1981. 28.00 (ISBN 0-672-84349-8). Michie-Bobbs.

Rabin, Edward H. Fundamentals of Modern Real Property Law. 2nd ed. (University Casebook Ser.). 1982. write for info. tchrs. manual (ISBN 0-88277-106-X). Foundation Pr.

Waite, Diana S. & Cawley, Frederick D., eds. A Primer: Preservation for the Property Owner. (Illus.). 35p. (Orig.). 1978. pap. 3.00 (ISBN 0-942000-01-3). Pres League NY.

Winokur, James L. American Property Law: Cases, History, Policy & Practice. (Contemporary Legal Education Ser.). 1296p. 1982. text ed. 29.00 (ISBN 0-87215-405-X). Michie-Bobbs.

REAL PROPERTY-TAXATION

see Real Property Tax

REAL PROPERTY-VALUATION

Here are entered works on the general theory and methodology of real property valuation. Works on the valuation of real property for tax purposes are entered under the heading Real Property Tax.

Almy, Richard R., et al. Improving Real Property Assessment: A Reference Manual. LC 78-70575. 1978. 25.00 (ISBN 0-88329-010-3). Intl Assess.

Donne, Robert C. Determinants of Value: An Annotated Bibliography. (Bibliographic Ser.). 48p. 1976. 8.00 (ISBN 0-686-84051-8). Intl Assess.

Everhart, Marion E. Land Classification for Rural & Urban Uses, Management & Valuation. LC 82-74565. (Illus.). 190p. 1983. 23.50 (ISBN 0-935988-23-8). Todd Pub.

Franklin, Douglas & Jankowski, Thaddeus. Understanding Property Revaluation: A Massachusetts Handbook. 176p. (Orig.). 1983. pap. write for info. (ISBN 0-88063-030-2). Butterworth Legal Pubs.

Mason, James J., ed. AIREA Financial Tables. 473p. 1982. 22.50 (ISBN 0-911780-68-8). Am Inst Real Estate Appraisers.

Metrication in Assessment. (Research & Information Ser.). 33p. 1980. 6.50 (ISBN 0-686-84048-8). Intl Assess.

Rudman, Jack. Real Property Appraiser. (Career Examination Ser.: C-841). (Cloth bdg. avail. on request). pap. 10.00 (ISBN 0-8373-0841-0). Natl learning.

--Real Property Appraiser I. (Career Examination Ser.: C-842). (Cloth bdg. avail. on request). pap. 10.00 (ISBN 0-8373-0842-9). Natl Learning.

--Real Property Appraiser II. (Career Examination Ser.: C-843). (Cloth bdg. avail. on request). pap. 10.00 (ISBN 0-8373-0843-7). Natl Learning.

--Real Property Appraiser III. (Career Examination Ser.: C-844). (Cloth bdg. avail. on request). pap. 12.00 (ISBN 0-8373-0844-5). Natl Learning.

--Real Property Appraiser IV. (Career Examination Ser.: C-845). (Cloth bdg. avail. on request). pap. 14.00 (ISBN 0-8373-0845-3). Natl Learning.

--Senior Real Estate Appraiser. (Career Examination Ser.: C-569). (Cloth bdg. avail. on request). pap. 12.00 (ISBN 0-8373-0569-1). Natl Learning.

Zerbst, Robert H. Principles of Real Estate Valuation with Energy Applications. LC 81-70321. (Development Component Ser.). (Illus.). 23p. 1981. pap. 10.00 (ISBN 0-87420-603-0, D19). Urban Land.

REAL PROPERTY-GREAT BRITAIN

Webb, A. N. Edition of the Cartulary of Burscough Priory. 1970. 27.00 (ISBN 0-7190-1152-3). Manchester.

REAL PROPERTY AND TAXATION

Greer, G. E. The Real Estate Investor & the Federal Income Tax. 2nd ed. 267p. 1982. text ed. 29.95x (ISBN 0-471-09738-1). Ronald Pr.

Levine, Mark L. Real Estate Tax Shelter Desk Book. 3rd ed. LC 81-22569. 463p. 1982. text ed. 49.50 (ISBN 0-87624-489-4). Inst Busn Plan.

REAL PROPERTY TAX

see also Land Value Taxation; Real Property and Taxation

International Symposium on the Property Tax, 1980: Proceedings. pap. 10.00 (ISBN 0-686-84045-3). Intl Assess.

Property Tax & the National Income in the U. S., 1929 to 1980. (Research & Information Ser.). 85p. 1982. 11.50 (ISBN 0-686-84050-X). Intl Assess.

Property Tax Legislation in the U. S. 1976, 2 Parts. (Research & Information Ser.). 1977. 10.00 (ISBN 0-686-84046-1). Intl Assess.

REAL-TIME DATA PROCESSING

see also on-Line Data Processing

Mellichamp, Duncan A., ed. Real Time Computing: With Applications to Data Acquisition & Control. 464p. 1983. text ed. 39.50 (ISBN 0-442-21372-7). Van Nos Reinhold.

REALISM IN LITERATURE

see also Romanticism

Ermarth, Elizabeth. Realism & Consensus in the English Novel. LC 82-61360. 304p. 1983. 25.00x (ISBN 0-691-06560-8). Princeton U Pr.

REALITY

see also Experience; Knowledge, Theory Of; Pluralism; Pragmatism; Relativity

Baker, Ralph. Reality. 1982. 7.95 (ISBN 0-533-05434-6). Vantage.

Bell, Michael. The Sentiment of Reality. 224p. 1983. text ed. 22.50x (ISBN 0-04-801023-5). Allen Unwin.

Hintikka, Merrill & Harding, Sandra, eds. Discovering Reality. 1983. lib. bdg. 54.50 (ISBN 90-277-1496-7, Pub. by Reidel Holland). Kluwer Boston.

Nassau, William. The Last Word: Reflections on Reality. LC 82-51052. 160p. 1982. 11.95 (ISBN 0-932966-22-5). Permanent Pr.

Strauch, Ralph E. The Reality Illusion. LC 82-42705. (Illus.). 230p. (Orig.). 1983. pap. 6.95 (ISBN 0-8356-0571-X, Quest). Theos Pub Hse.

REALTY

see Real Property

REAPPORTIONMENT (ELECTION LAW)

see Apportionment (Election Law)

REAPPORTIONMENT OF CONGRESSIONAL DISTRICTS

see Apportionment (Election Law)

REASON

see also Common Sense; Faith and Reason; Reasoning; Wisdom

Hastings, R. Nature & Reason in the Decameron. 1975. 22.50 (ISBN 0-7190-1281-3). Manchester.

Simon, Herbert A. Reason in Human Affairs. LC 82-62448. 128p. 1983. 10.00x (ISBN 0-8047-1179-8). Stanford U Pr.

REASON AND FAITH

see Faith and Reason

REASONING

see also Fallacies (Logic); Induction (Logic); Logic

Bundy, Alan. The Computer Modelling of Mathematical Reasoning. Date not set. price not set (ISBN 0-12-141252-0). Acad Pr.

Willard, Charles A. Argumentation & the Social Grounds of Knowledge. LC 81-16199. 322p. 1983. text ed. 20.00 (ISBN 0-8173-0096-1). U of Ala Pr.

REBELLIONS

see Revolutions

REBELS (SOCIAL PSYCHOLOGY)

see Alienation (Social Psychology); Conformity

REBIRTH

see Reincarnation

RECALL (PSYCHOLOGY)

see Recollection (Psychology)

RECEIPTS

see Recipes

RECEPTIONISTS

see also Secretaries

Twing, J. W. The Receptionist. 160p. 1983. 7.96 (ISBN 0-07-065641-X, G). McGraw.

RECIPES

Here are entered general recipe books. Works containing only cooking recipes are entered under Cookery.

Ashby, Susan. Granny's Muffin House. 1983. pap. 8.95 (ISBN 0-930440-18-8). Royal Pub Co.

Best, Joan & Erikson, Kate. Two Recipe Index, 1982. 250p. 1983. pap. text ed. 9.95 (ISBN 0-686-38724-4). Home Index Pubns.

Darling. With Love from Darling's Kitchen. 1982. pap. 9.95 (ISBN 0-930440-17-X). Royal Pub Co.

Virtue Magazine, ed. Everyday Spice. 2nd ed. LC 82-81674. 142p. 1983. pap. cancelled (ISBN 0-89081-328-0). Harvest Hse.

RECLAMATION OF LAND

see also Drainage; Irrigation; Marshes; Shore Protection

Seymour, John. The Lore of the Land. LC 82-16887. (Illus.). 160p. 1983. 14.95 (ISBN 0-8052-3836-0). Schocken.

RECOLLECTION (PSYCHOLOGY)

Tulving, Endel. Elements of Episodic Memory. (Oxford Psychology Ser.). 400p. 1982. 29.95 (ISBN 0-19-852102-2). Oxford U Pr.

RECONNAISSANCE, MILITARY

see Military Reconnaissance

RECONSTRUCTION (1939-1951)
see also Economic Assistance; International Cooperation
Botting, Douglas. The Aftermath: Europe. (World War II Ser.). 1983. lib. bdg. 19.92 (ISBN 0-8094-3412-1, Pub. by Time-Life). Silver.
Sherrod, Rod. The Aftermath: Asia. (World War II Ser.). 1983. lib. bdg. 19.92 (ISBN 0-8094-3436-9, Pub. by Time-Life). Silver.
RECORD PLAYERS
see Phonograph
RECORDER (PHYSICAL INSTRUMENTS)
see Recording Instruments
RECORDING INSTRUMENTS
see also Information Display Systems
Hoagland, Albert A. Digital Magnetic Recording. LC 82-23203. 164p. 1983. Repr. of 1963 ed. lib. bdg. write for info. (ISBN 0-89874-591-8). Krieger.
RECORDS
see also Archives; Electronic Data Processing; Libraries; Museums;
also specific types of records, e.g. Business Records; Manuscripts, etc.
Brigermann, Chuck. Record Collector's Fact Book, Vol. I. LC 82-73474. (Illus.). 96p. 1983. pap. 7.95 (ISBN 0-89709-037-3). Liberty Pub.
Diamond, Susan Z. Records Management. 192p. 1983. 21.95 (ISBN 0-8144-5729-0). Am Mgmt Assns.
Sanders, Patricia. The Search Consultant's Handbook. 32p. (Orig.). 1983. pap. 3.00 (ISBN 0-942916-02-6). ISC Pubns.
Thomas, Violet S. & Schubert, Dexter R. Records Management: Systems & Administration. 416p. 1983. text ed. 20.95 (ISBN 0-471-09094-8); write for info. (ISBN 0-471-89473-7). Wiley.
RECORDS, BUSINESS
see Business Records
RECORDS, PHONOGRAPH
see Phonorecords
RECORDS OF BIRTHS, ETC.
see Registers of Births, Deaths, Marriages, etc.
RECOVERY OF NATURAL RESOURCES
see Recycling (Waste, etc.)
RECOVERY OF WASTE PRODUCTS
see Salvage (Waste, etc.)
RECREATION
see also Amusements; Community Organizations; Educational Games; Family Recreation; Hobbies; Leisure; Outdoor Recreation; Popular Culture; Recreational Therapy; Vacations
Architectural Record Magazine Staff. Places for People: Hotel, Restaurants, Bars, Clubs, Community Recreation Facilities Camps, Parks, Plazas, Playgrounds. 1976. 36.50 (ISBN 0-07-002201-1). McGraw.
Buck, Peter. Arts & Crafts of Hawaii: Games & Recreation, VIII. (Special Publication Ser.: No. 45). (Illus.). 32p. 1957. pap. 3.00 (ISBN 0-910240-41-8). Bishop Mus.
Completed Research in Health, Physical Education, Recreation & Dance, Vol. 22. 1980. 9.25 (ISBN 0-686-38058-4). AAHPERD.
Coping with Stress Through Leisure. (Leisure Today Ser.). 32p. 1.50 (ISBN 0-88314-218-X). AAHPERD.
Education for Leisure. (Leisure Today Ser.). 32p. 1.50 (ISBN 0-88314-113-2). AAHPERD.
Edwards, Mary F., ed. How to Recognize & Handle Recreational Liability Cases: Sports Torts. 271p. 1980. pap. 25.00 (ISBN 0-941916-04-9). Assn Trial Ed.
Epperson, Arlin. Private & Commercial Recreation: A Text & Reference. LC 76-56453. 385p. 1977. text ed. 23.95 (ISBN 0-471-24335-3). Wiley.
Fimbres, Eric C. Approaching Re-Creation: A Form for Seeing the Delicate Threads. LC 82-90184. (Illus.). 208p. (Orig.). 1982. pap. 5.95 (ISBN 0-9608946-0-8). Life Sustaining.
Neal, Larry L., ed. The Next Fifty Years: Health, Physical Education, Recreation, Dance. 179p. 1971. pap. 3.50 (ISBN 0-686-84034-8). U OR Ctr Leisure.
Rudman, Jack. Activities Director. (Career Examination Ser.: C-2949). (Cloth bdg. avail. on request). pap. 12.00 (ISBN 0-8373-2949-3). Natl Learning.
--Recreation Assistant. (Career Examination Ser.: C-526). (Cloth bdg. avail. on request). pap. 10.00 (ISBN 0-8373-0526-8). Natl Learning.
--Recreation Therapist. (Career Examination Ser.: C-2698). (Cloth bdg. avail. on request). pap. 12.00 (ISBN 0-8373-2698-2). Natl Learning.
--Recreation Worker. (Career Examination Ser.: C-429). (Cloth bdg. avail. on request). pap. 12.00 (ISBN 0-8373-0429-6). Natl Learning.
Schwab, Judith L. Recreation as a Forest Product. (Public Administration Ser.: Bibliography P 1096). 57p. 1982. pap. 8.25 (ISBN 0-88066-286-7). Vance Biblios.
RECREATION-ADMINISTRATION
see also Recreation Leadership
Campus Recreation. (Leisure Today Ser.). 32p. 1.50 (ISBN 0-88314-112-4). AAHPERD.
Conrad, Randy. Your Community Recreation Planning: A Guide for Local Involvement in Comprehensive Recreation Planning. 160p. 1977. pap. 5.00 (ISBN 0-686-84029-1). U OR Ctr Leisure.
Edginton, C. R. & Williams, J. G. Productive Management of Leisure Service Organizations: A Behavioral Approach. 530p. 1978. 22.95x (ISBN 0-471-01574-1). Wiley.
Evaluation of Leisure Programs. (Leisure Today Ser.). 24p. 1.50 (ISBN 0-88314-114-0). AAHPERD.
Farrell, Patricia & Lundegren, Herberta M. The Process of Recreation Programming: Theory & Technique. LC 78-17100. 315p. 1978. text ed. 21.95x (ISBN 0-471-01709-4). Wiley.
High Adventure Leisure Pusuits & Risk Recreation. 32p. 1.50 (ISBN 0-88314-115-9). AAHPERD.
Issues in Correctional Recreation. (Leisure Today Ser.). 32p. 1.50 (ISBN 0-88314-116-7). AAHPERD.
Leisure Counseling. (Leisure Today Ser.). 32p. 1.50 (ISBN 0-88314-120-5). AAHPERD.
Managing Leisure Services. (Leirure Today Ser.). 32p. 1.50 (ISBN 0-88314-124-8). AAHPERD.
Opportunities in Recreation & Leisure. (Leisure Today Ser.). 123p. 7.95 (ISBN 0-686-84055-0). AAHPERD.
Rudman, Jack. Bingo Inspector. (Career Examination Ser.: C-846). (Cloth bdg. avail. on request). pap. 10.00 (ISBN 0-8373-0846-1). Natl Learning.
RECREATION-BIBLIOGRAPHY
Goodale, Thomas & Witt, Peter A., eds. Recreation & Leisure: Issues in an Era of Change. LC 79-92646. 394p. (Orig.). 1980. pap. text ed. 14.95x (ISBN 0-910251-00-2). Venture Pub PA.
RECREATION-STUDY AND TEACHING
see Recreation Leadership
RECREATION ADMINISTRATION
see Recreation-Administration
RECREATION AREAS
see also Outdoor Recreation; Resorts
Directory of Professional Preparation Programs in Recreation, Parks, & Related Areas. 1983. price not set. AAHPERD.
Gold, S. M. Recreation Planning & Design. 1980. 37.50 (ISBN 0-07-023644-5). McGraw.
RECREATION AS A PROFESSION
see Recreation Leadership
RECREATION LEADERSHIP
see also Recreation-Administration
Decker, Larry, ed. Volunteer Coordinator Guide. 61p. 1961. pap. 3.00 (ISBN 0-686-84033-X). U OR Ctr Leisure.
Edginton, C. R. & Williams, J. G. Productive Management of Leisure Service Organizations: A Behavioral Approach. 530p. 1978. 22.95x (ISBN 0-471-01574-1). Wiley.
Farrell, Patricia & Lundegren, Herberta M. The Process of Recreation Programming: Theory & Technique. LC 78-17100. 315p. 1978. text ed. 21.95x (ISBN 0-471-01709-4). Wiley.
Niepath, E. William. Leisure Leadership: Working with People in Recreation & Park Settings. (Illus.). 416p. 1983. 21.95 (ISBN 0-13-530071-1). P-H.
RECREATION MANAGEMENT
see Recreation-Administration
RECREATION RESEARCH
Completed Research in Health, Physical Education, Recreation & Dance, Vol.19. 1977. 9.25 (ISBN 0-88314-044-6). AAHPERD.
Completed Research in Health, Physical Education, Recreation & Dance, Vol. 20. 1978. write for info. (ISBN 0-88314-045-4). AAHPERD.
Completed Research in Health, Physical Education, Recreation & Dance, Vol. 24. 1983. 10.95 (ISBN 0-686-38056-8). AAHPERD.
Smith, Stephen L. Recreation Geography. (Themes in Resource Management Ser.). (Illus.). 240p. 1982. pap. text ed. write for info. (ISBN 0-582-30050-9). Longman.
RECREATIONAL FISHING
see Fishing
RECREATIONAL MOTOR VEHICLES
see Motor Vehicles-Recreational Use
RECREATIONAL THERAPY
Neal, Larry & Edginton, Chris, eds. Exetra Perspectives: Concepts in Therapeutic Recreation. 220p. 1982. 5.95 (ISBN 0-686-84021-6). U OR Ctr Leisure.
Smith, Eugene & Smith, Elaine. Mind Matter Motion: Prescription Running. LC 82-99857. (Illus.). 240p. (Orig.). 1982. pap. 11.95 (ISBN 0-9608910-0-5). Neihardt-Smith.
RECREATIONS
see Amusements; Games; Hobbies; Play; Schools-Exercises and Recreations; Sports
RECREATIONS, MATHEMATICAL
see Mathematical Recreations
RECRUITING OF EMPLOYEES
see also Employment Agencies; Employment Interviewing;
also names of professions with or without subdivision Recruiting
Hodes, Bernard S. The Principles & Practice of Recruitment Advertising. LC 82-71746. 344p. 1982. 29.95 (ISBN 0-8119-0453-9). Fell.
RECTORS
see Clergy
RECUSANTS
see Catholics in England
RECYCLING (WASTE, ETC.)
Here are entered works on the processing of waste paper, cans, bottles, etc. Works on the recycling or reuse of specific materials are entered under Wood Waste, Agricultural wastes, etc. Works on reclaiming and reusing equipment or parts are entered under Salvage (Waste, etc.).
see also Energy Conservation; Salvage (Waste, etc.); Waste Products
Bendersky, David, et al. Resource Recovery Processing Equipment. LC 82-7882. (Pollution Technology Rev. 93). (Illus.). 417p. 1983. 42.00 (ISBN 0-8155-0911-1). Noyes.
Bibliotheca Press Research Project. Selected Topics on Creative Ways to Recycle. (A Recycling Ser.). 1983. text ed. 79.95 (ISBN 0-939476-88-6); pap. text ed. 69.95 (ISBN 0-939476-89-4). Biblio Pr GA.
Brown, Michael D. Resource Recovery Project Studies. (Illus.). 169p. 1983. 29.95 (ISBN 0-250-40611-X). Ann Arbor Science.
Carrol, Frieda. Recycling Suggestions For Home, Business, Associations, Government etc. 60p. Date not set. pap. text ed. 17.95 (ISBN 0-939476-83-5). Biblio Pr GA.
Center for Self Sufficiency Staff. Center for Self Sufficiency Directory of Recycled Cookbooks, Home Remedy Almanacs, How to Books, & Inspirational Books for Library Loan. 100p. 1983. pap. 2.00 (ISBN 0-910811-33-4). Center Self.
Data Notes Publishing Staff. Paper Recycling: Data Notes. 30p. 1983. pap. text ed. 9.95 (ISBN 0-911569-41-3). Data Notes Pub.
Doyle, A. C. Recycling Workbook: Based on Recycling for Living, Fun & Profit. 50p. 1983. 8.95 (ISBN 0-939476-50-9). Biblio Pr GA.
Doyle, Alfreda. Suggestions for Types of Recycling Businesses. 50p. 1983. pap. text ed. 22.95 (ISBN 0-910811-34-2). Center Self.
Doyle, Alfreda C. Business Recycling Suggestions. 26p. 1983. pap. text ed. 6.95 (ISBN 0-910811-24-5). Center Self.
--Suggestions for Hunting Aluminum Cans & Other Aluminum. 26p. 1983. pap. text ed. 6.95 (ISBN 0-910811-26-1). Center Self.
Jabs, Carolyn. Re-Uses: Two Thousand One Hundred Thirty-Three Ways to Recycle & Reuse the Things You Ordinarily Throw Away. 1982. 18.95 (ISBN 0-517-54663-9); pap. 9.95 (ISBN 0-517-54363-X). Crown.
Update Publicare Research Staff. Recycling Update: Notebook of Back Issues. 35p. 1983. pap. text ed. 8.00 (ISBN 0-686-38894-1). Update Pub Co.
RECYCLING OF WASTE PRODUCTS
see Salvage (Waste, etc.)
RED SEA
Lapidoth, R. The Red Sea & the Gulf of Aden. 1982. lib. bdg. 65.00 (ISBN 90-247-2501-1, Pub. by Martinus Nijhoff Netherlands). Kluwer Boston.
REDEVELOPMENT, URBAN
see City Planning
REDFORD, ROBERT
Downing, David. Robert Redford. (Illus.). 224p. 1983. pap. 11.95 (ISBN 0-312-68747-8). St Martin.
REDUCING
see also Low-Calorie Diet
Cavnar, Rebecca. Winning at Losing: A Complete Program for Losing Weight & Keeping it off. (Illus.). 150p. 1983. pap. 4.95 (ISBN 0-686-82582-9). Servant.
Coyle, Neva. Free to Be Thin Daily Planner. 128p. (Orig.). 1983. pap. 5.95 (ISBN 0-87123-284-7). Bethany Hse.
Katch, Frank I. & McArdle, William D. Nutrition, Weight Control, & Exercise. LC 82-25873. (Illus.). 300p. 1983. text ed. price not set (ISBN 0-8121-0867-1). Lea & Febiger.
Pearlman, Barbara. Barbara Pearlman's Four Week Stomach & Waist Shape-up. LC 82-45520. (Illus.). 96p. 1983. pap. 4.95 (ISBN 0-385-18353-4, Dolp). Doubleday.
Polivy, Janet & Herman, Peter. Breaking the Diet Habit: The Natural Weight Alternative. 256p. 1983. 16.50 (ISBN 0-465-00754-6). Basic.
Roman-Lopez, Carmen & Litoff, Carol. Diet Modification. (Illus.). 312p. 1983. pap. 22.95 looseleaf (ISBN 0-89313-030-3). G F Stickley.
Stein, Toby. Getting Thin & Staying Thin. LC 82-48514. 250p. 1983. 14.95 (ISBN 0-8128-2896-8). Stein & Day.
Stuart, Richard B. Act Thin, Stay Thin. 288p. pap. 3.50 (ISBN 0-515-07118-8). Jove Pubns.
Szekely, Edmond B. Biogenic Reducing: The Wonder Week. (Illus.). 56p. 1977. pap. 3.80 (ISBN 0-89564-055-4). IBS Intl.
Williams, Terry. Crossing the Thin Line. 0.95 (ISBN 0-89486-077-1). Hazelden.
REDUCING DIETS
see also Low-Calorie Diet
Bachman, David C. & Noble, H. Bates. The Diet that Lets You Cheat. 1983. pap. 7.95 (ISBN 0-517-54987-5). Crown.
Barbour, Pamela G. & Spivey, Morma G. The Exchange Cookbook for Diabetic & Weight Control Programs. Davidson, Paul C., ed. LC 82-83512. (Illus.). 198p. (Orig.). 1982. pap. 9.95 (ISBN 0-9610028-0-8). G&G Pub.
Breithaupt, S. & Agnew, H. W. The Dallas Doctors' Diet. 208p. 1983. 12.95 (ISBN 0-07-007447-X, GB). McGraw.
Cannizarro, Marilyn. Cooking with Abstinence: An Inspirational Cookbook for the Compulsive Overeater. LC 81-43898. (Illus.). 96p. 1983. pap. 5.95 (ISBN 0-385-18140-X, Dolp). Doubleday.
Cherkasky, Paul. The Rochester Diet. 288p. 1983. 14.95 (ISBN 0-8119-0488-1). Fell.
Costello, Jeanne & Witty, Doreen. Lighten-Up. Neumayer, Lisa, ed. (Illus.). 288p. (Orig.) 1983. pap. write for info. (ISBN 0-9609894-1-2). Costello & Witty.
Crenshaw, Mary A. The Super-Foods Diet Book. 256p. 1983. 12.95 (ISBN 0-02-528820-2). Macmillan.
Eat & Stay Slim. pap. 5.95 (ISBN 0-696-01115-8). Meredith Corp.
Edwards, Ted L., Jr. & Lau, Barbara. Weight Loss to Super Wellness. (Illus.). 176p. (Orig.). 1982. pap. text ed. 7.95 (ISBN 0-686-38849-6). Hills Med.
Eyton, Audrey. The F-Plan Diet. LC 82-17969. 256p. 1983. 12.95 (ISBN 0-517-54934-4). Crown.
George, Phyllis & Adler, Bill. The I Love America Diet. (Illus.). 192p. 1983. 11.95 (ISBN 0-688-01621-9). Morrow.
Jordan, Henry A. & Berland, Theodore. The Doctor's Calories-Plus Diet. 1982. pap. 2.50 (ISBN 0-451-11515-5, AE1515, Sig). NAL.
Katahn, Martin. The Two Hundred Calorie Solution: How to Burn an Extra 200 Calories a Day & Lose Weight. 320p. 1983. pap. 3.50 (ISBN 0-425-06065-9). Berkley Pub.
Mandell, Marshall & Mandell, Fran G. The Mandell's: It's Not Your Fault You're Fat Diet. LC 82-48124. (Illus.). 224p. 1983. 13.41i (ISBN 0-06-015114-5, HarpT). Har-Row.
Marston, Albert R. The Undiet: A Psychological Approach to Permanent Weight Control. (Illus.). 240p. 1983. 13.95 (ISBN 0-13-936815-9); pap. 6.95 (ISBN 0-13-936807-8). P-H.
Mazel, Judy & Schultz, Susan. Beverly Hills Diet Lifetime Plan. 1983. pap. 3.95 (ISBN 0-686-43053-0). Bantam.
Miller, Peter M. The Hilton Head Metabolism Diet. 256p. 1983. 14.50 (ISBN 0-446-51266-4). Warner Bks.
Mirkin, Gabe. Getting Thin: All about Fat-How You Get it, How You Lose It, How You Keep It Off For Good. (Illus.). 320p. 1983. 15.00i (ISBN 0-316-57437-6). Little.
Myerson, Bess & Adler, Bill. The I Love New York Diet. 272p. 1983. pap. 2.95 (ISBN 0-446-30558-8). Warner Bks.
Pinkham, Mary Ellen. Mary Ellen's Help Yourself Diet Plan: The One That Worked for Me! 192p. 1983. 10.95 (ISBN 0-312-51863-3). St Martin.
Price, D. Porter. Intelligent Dieting for Weight Loss & Prevention of Disease. (Illus.). 200p. 1982. 17.95 (ISBN 0-9606246-1-9); pap. 13.95 (ISBN 0-9606246-2-7). SW Sci Pub.
Roman-Lopez, Carmen & Litoff, Carol. Diet Modification. (Illus.). 312p. 1983. pap. 22.95 looseleaf (ISBN 0-89313-030-3). G F Stickley.
Schwartz, Bob. Diets Don't Work. rev. ed. LC 82-70262. (Illus.). 204p. (Orig.). Date not set. 14.95 (ISBN 0-942540-01-8); pap. 9.95 (ISBN 0-942540-02-6). Breakthru Pub.
Showalter, Carol. Three D: The Story of the New Christian Group Diet Program that is Sweeping the Country. 4.95 (ISBN 0-941478-05-X). Paraclete Pr.
The Three D Cookbook. 1982. 9.95 (ISBN 0-941478-01-7). Paraclete Pr.
Walker, Norman W. Pure & Simple Natural Weight Control. LC 81-11080. 1981. pap. 4.95 (ISBN 0-89019-078-X). O'Sullivan Woodside.
Weale, Margaret. The Slimmer's Microwave Cookbook. (Illus.). 120p. (Orig.). 1983. 17.50 (ISBN 0-7153-8392-2). David & Charles.
Wiess, Christine & Hardwick, Ann B. The Complete Calorie-Slim Cookbook. (Illus.). 246p. 1982. pap. 12.00 (ISBN 0-910347-01-8). Chatham Comm Inc.
Wood, Peter. The California Diet & Exercise Program. 280p. 1983. 13.95 (ISBN 0-89037-257-8). Anderson World.
REDUCTION DIVISION (GENETICS)
see Meiosis
REDWOOD
Schrepfer, Susan R. The Fight to Save the Redwoods: A History of Environmental Reform, 1917-1978. LC 81-69828. (Illus.). 352p. 1983. 22.50 (ISBN 0-299-08850-2). U of Wis Pr.
REFERENCE BOOKS
see also Bibliography-Best Books; Encyclopedias and Dictionaries; Reference Services (Libraries)
Elgin, Catherine Z. With Reference to Reference. LC 82-15488. 208p. 1982. lib. bdg. 27.50 (ISBN 0-915145-52-9); pap. text ed. 12.75 (ISBN 0-915145-53-7). Hackett Pub.
Newman, L. M. German Language & Literature: Select Bibliography of Reference Books. 2nd, enl. ed. 175p. 1979. 30.00x (ISBN 0-85457-077-2, Pub. by Inst Germanic Stud England). State Mutual Bk.
RSBR Committee. Reference & Subscription Books Reviews, 1981-1982. (RSBR Ser.). 240p. 1982. pap. text ed. 20.00 (ISBN 0-8389-0380-0). ALA.
Sheehy, Eugene P., ed. Guide to Reference Books: 2nd Supplement. 9th ed. 252p. 1982. pap. text ed. 15.00 (ISBN 0-8389-0361-4). ALA.
Yarbo, Peggy. Reference Materials. (Language Arts Ser.). 24p. (gr. 5-9). 1980. wkbk. 5.00 (ISBN 0-8209-0314-0, RM-1). ESP.

Yarbro, Peggy. Basic Skills Reference Materials Workbook. (Basic Skills Workbooks). 32p. (gr. 4-7). 1983. 0.99 (ISBN 0-8209-0579-8, RMW-1). ESP.

REFERENCE BOOKS–BIBLIOGRAPHY

Data Notes Publishing Staff, compiled by. Data Notes Bibliographical Reference Handbook. 250p. Date not set. pap. text ed. 22.95 (ISBN 0-686-37654-4). Data Notes Pub.

RSBR Committee, ed. Reference & Subscription Book Reviews, 1980-81. 148p. Date not set. pap. text ed. 20.00 (ISBN 0-8389-3269-X). ALA.

Wynar, Bohdan S., ed. American Reference Books Annual 1983, Vol. 14. 900p. 1983. lib. bdg. 47.50 (ISBN 0-87287-383-8). Libs Unl.

REFERENCE BOOKS–JUVENILE LITERATURE

Edwards, Candy. The Reference Point. LC 82-83712. (Illus.). 80p. (gr. 3-6). 1983. pap. text ed. 5.95 (ISBN 0-86530-042-9, IP 42-9). Incentive Pubns.

REFERENCE BOOKS, ENGLISH

see Reference Books

REFERENCE SERVICES (LIBRARIES)

see also Information Services

Evans, Gareth. The Varieties of Reference. McDowell, John, ed. (Illus.). 432p. 1982. 34.95 (ISBN 0-19-824685-4); pap. 10.95x (ISBN 0-19-824686-2). Oxford U Pr.

Katz, Bill, ed. Reference Services for Children & Young Adults. (The Reference Librarian Ser.: Nos. 7 & 8). 168p. 1983. text ed. 14.95 (ISBN 0-86656-201-X, B201). Haworth Pr.

Katz, Bill & Fraley, Ruth A., eds. Video to Online Reference Services & the New Technology. LC 82-232920. (The Reference Librarian: No. 56). 170p. 1983. text ed. 14.95 (ISBN 0-86656-202-8). Haworth Pr.

Library & Reference Skills, 4 Bks, Bks. C-F. pap. 1.47 ea.; ea tchr's eds. 1.47. Bowmar-Noble.

Myers, Marcia J. & Jirjees, Jassim M. The Accuracy of Telephone Reference-Information Services in Academic Libraries: Two Studies. LC 82-10785. 1983. 17.50 (ISBN 0-8108-1584-2). Scarecrow.

REFERENCE WORK (LIBRARIES)

see Reference Services (Libraries)

REFINISHING, FURNITURE

see Furniture Finishing

REFLECTION (THEORY OF KNOWLEDGE)

see Self-Knowledge, Theory of

REFLEXES

see also Conditioned Response

McMahon, Thomas A. Muscles, Reflexes, & Locomotion. LC 82-61378. (Illus.). 384p. 1983. 50.00 (ISBN 0-686-43259-2); pap. 15.00. Princeton U Pr.

REFORM, SOCIAL

see Social Problems

REFORM JUDAISM

Borowitz, Eugene B. Reform Judaism Today. 800p. 1983. pap. text ed. 9.95x (ISBN 0-87441-364-8). Behrman.

REFORM OF CRIMINALS

see Rehabilitation of Criminals

REFORM OF THE CHURCH

see Church Renewal

REFORMATION

see also Counter-Reformation; Europe–History–1492-1648; Protestantism

also names of religious sects, e.g. Huguenots, Hussites, Waldenses

Augustijn, Cornelis & Fraenkel, Pierre, eds. Martini Buceri (Opera Latina) Vol. 1 Opera Omia, Series II. (Studies in Medieval & Reformation Thought Ser.: Vol. 30). viii, 296p. 1982. write for info. (ISBN 90-04-06490-7). E J Brill.

Lacoste, Auguste. Henri Arnaud und die Waldenser. (Basler und Berner Studien zur historischen und systematischen: Vol. 47). 213p. 1982. write for info. (ISBN 3-261-04890-5). P Lang Pubs.

Olin, John C. & Smart, James D., eds. Luther, Erasmus, & the Reformation: A Catholic-Protestant Reappraisal. LC 82-15500. x, 150p. 1982. Repr. of 1969 ed. lib. bdg. 22.50x (ISBN 0-313-23652-6, OLLE). Greenwood.

REFORMATION–BIBLIOGRAPHY

Bibliographie de la Reforme, 1450-1648. 151p. 1982. pap. write for info. (ISBN 90-04-06763-9). E J Brill.

Ozment, Steven E., ed. Reformation Europe: A Guide to Research. 390p. 1982. 18.50x (ISBN 0-910345-01-5); pap. 13.50x (ISBN 0-686-82436-9). Center Reform.

REFORMATION–EARLY MOVEMENTS

Here are entered works descriptive of reform movements preceding the Reformation.

Zimmermann, Gunter. Die Antwort Der Reformatoren Auf Die Zehntenfrage. 175p. 1982. write for info. (ISBN 3-8204-5745-3). P Lang Pubs.

REFORMATION–ENGLAND

Hall, Louis B. The Perilous Vision of John Wyclif. LC 82-18890. 288p. 1983. lib. bdg. 23.95X (ISBN 0-8304-1006-6). Nelson-Hall.

REFORMATION–SCOTLAND

Cowan, Ian B. The Scottish Reformation. LC 82-5834. 256p. 1982. 25.00x (ISBN 0-312-70519-0). St Martin.

REFORMATORIES FOR WOMEN

American Correctional Association Staff. Women in Corrections. (Series 1: No. 1). 85p. (Orig.). 1981. pap. 5.00 (ISBN 0-942974-17-4). Am Correctional.

REFRIGERATION AND REFRIGERATING MACHINERY

see also Air Conditioning; Compressors; Cooling-Towers; Heat Exchangers

Dossat, Roy J. Principles of Refrigeration. 2nd ed. LC 78-2938. 603p. 1978. text ed. 29.95 (ISBN 0-471-03550-5); solutions manual 8.00 (ISBN 0-471-03771-0). Wiley.

Elonka, Stephen M. & Minich, Quaid W. Standard Refrigeration & Air Conditioning Questions & Answers. (Illus.). 416p. 1983. 34.00 (ISBN 0-07-019317-7, P&RB). McGraw.

Gosling, C. T. Applied Air Conditioning & Refrigeration. 2nd ed. 1980. 45.00 (ISBN 0-85334-877-4, Pub. by Applied Sci England). Elsevier.

Heating, Air Conditioning & Refrigeration Equipment. 1981. 695.00 (ISBN 0-686-38426-1, 203). Busn Trend.

REFUGEES

see also Refugees, Political

Kritz, Mary, ed. U. S. Immigration & Refugee Policy. LC 82-47513. 448p. 1982. 23.95xc (ISBN 0-669-05543-3). Lexington Bks.

Spilken, Aron. Escape! The Story the Newspapers Couldn't Print. 1983. 14.95 (ISBN 0-453-00433-4). NAL.

REFUGEES–VIETNAM

Hawthorne, Lesleyanne. Refugee: The Vietnamese Experience. 288p. 1982. 49.00x (ISBN 0-19-554338-6). Oxford U Pr.

REFUGEES, POLITICAL

see also Aliens; Emigration and Immigration Law

also subdivision Refugees under specific wars, e.g. World War, 1939-1945–Refugees

Jackman, Jarrell C. & Borden, Carla M., eds. The Muses Flee Hitler: Cultural Transfer & Adaptation, 1930-1945. (Illus.). 340p. 1983. 17.50 (ISBN 0-87474-554-3); pap. 8.95 (ISBN 0-87474-555-1). Smithsonian.

Pfanner, Helmut F. Exile in New York: German & Austrian Writers After 1933. (Illus.). 272p. 1983. 18.95x (ISBN 0-8143-1727-8). Wayne St U Pr.

Weingarten, Ralph. Die Hilfeleistung der Westlichen Welt bei der Deutschen Judenfrage: Das "Intergovernmental Committee on Political Refugees" 1938-1939. 232p. Date not set. price not set (ISBN 3-261-04939-1). P Lang Pubs.

REFUGES, WILDLIFE

see Wildlife Refuges

REFUSE AND REFUSE DISPOSAL

see also Factory and Trade Waste; Incinerators; Pollution; Radioactive Waste Disposal; Refuse As Fuel; Sewage Disposal; Water–Pollution

Ackerman, D. G., et al. Destruction & Disposal of PCB'S by Thermal & Non-Thermal Methods. LC 82-22312. (Pollution Technology Review: No. 97). (Illus.). 417p. 1983. 48.00 (ISBN 0-8155-0934-0). Noyes.

Francis, Chester & Auerbach, Stanley I., eds. Environment & Solid Wastes: Characterization, Treatment, & Disposal. LC 82-71528. (Illus.). 450p. 1983. 49.95 (ISBN 0-250-40583-0). Ann Arbor Science.

Henstock. Disposal & Recovers of Municipal Solid Waste. 1983. text ed. write for info. (ISBN 0-408-01174-2). Butterworth.

Highland, Joseph H. Hazardous Waste: What is Being Done to Control Its Disposal? (Vital Issues Ser.: Vol. XXXI, No. IV). 0.80 (ISBN 0-686-84137-9). Ctr Info Am.

National Waste Processing Conference-Meeting the Challenge: Proceedings, 1982. 1982. 100.00 (100150). ASME.

Parr, James F., et al, eds. Land Treatment of Hazardous Wastes. LC 82-14402. (Illus.). 422p. 1983. 45.00 (ISBN 0-8155-0926-X). Noyes.

United Nations Environment Programme. Biotechnology & Waste Treatment: Proceedings of a Workshop Sponsored by the United Nations Environment Programme Held at the University of Waterloo, Canada, 27-31 July, 1981. Moo-Young, M., ed. 84p. 1982. 35.00 (ISBN 0-08-028784-0). Pergamon.

REFUSE AS FUEL

see also Biomass Energy

Hasselriis, Floyd. Refuse-Derived Fuel Processing. LC 82-46061. (Design & Management for Resource Recovery Ser.). 400p. 1983. 29.95 (ISBN 0-250-40314-5). Ann Arbor Science.

REFUSE INCINERATORS

see Incinerators

REGIONAL ANATOMY

see Anatomy, Surgical and Topographical

REGIONAL COOPERATION FOR DEVELOPMENT

Chatterji, Manas. Management & Regional Science for Economic Development. 1982. lib. bdg. 30.00 (ISBN 0-89838-108-8). Kluwer-Nijhoff.

REGIONAL PLANNING

see also City Planning; Coastal Zone Management; Social Surveys

Crosby, Robert W., ed. Cities & Regions As Nonlinear Decision Systems. (AAAS Selected Symposium: No. 77). 200p. 1983. lib. bdg. 25.00 (ISBN 0-86531-530-2). Westview.

Goodman, John, Jr. Regional Housing Assistance Allocations & Regional Housing Needs. 40p. 1979. pap. text ed. 4.00 (ISBN 0-87766-263-0). Urban Inst.

Healey, P. & McDougall, G., eds. Planning Theory-Prospects for the Nineteen Eighties: Selected Papers from a Conference Held in Oxford, UK, 2-4 April 1981. (Urban & Regional Planning Ser.). 330p. 1982. 40.00 (ISBN 0-08-027449-8). Pergamon.

LaConte, P. & Haines, Y. Y. Water Resources & Land-Use Planning: A Systems Approach. 1982. lib. bdg. 57.50 (ISBN 90-247-2726-X, Pub. by Martinus Nijhoff Netherlands). Kluwer Boston.

Lim, Gill C., ed. Regional Planning: Evolution, Crisis & Prospects. LC 82-13839. 198p. 1983. text ed. 15.95x (ISBN 0-86598-097-7). Allanheld.

Rabier, Jacques-Rene & Inglehart, Ronald. Euro-Barometer 13: Regional Development & Integration, April 1980. LC 82-81760. 1982. write for info. (ISBN 0-89138-937-7, ICPSR 7957). ICPSR.

Regional Development Dialogue, Vol. 3, No. 1. 242p. 1982. pap. 16.75 (ISBN 0-686-84617-6, CRD139, UNCRD). Unipub.

Regional Studies: The Geneva Programme. (UNCRD Working Paper: No. 82-1). 98p. 1983. pap. 6.00 (ISBN 0-686-43302-5, CRD 146, UNCRD). Unipub.

REGIONAL PLANNING–AFRICA

Political Processes & Regional Development Planning in Nigeria. (UNCRD Working Paper: No. 82-7). 1983. pap. 6.00 (ISBN 0-686-43301-7, CRD 144, UNCRD). Unipub.

REGIONAL PLANNING–GREAT BRITAIN

Munton, Richard. London's Green Belt: Containment in Practice. (London Research Ser. in Geography: No. 3). (Illus.). 184p. 1983. text ed. 24.95x (ISBN 0-04-333020-7). Allen Unwin.

REGIONAL PLANNING–INDIA

Chatterji, Manas. Management & Regional Science for Economic Development. 1982. lib. bdg. 30.00 (ISBN 0-89838-108-8). Kluwer-Nijhoff.

REGIONAL PLANNING–ISRAEL

Spatial Distribution of Political Power & Regional Disparities in the Israeli Case. (UNCRD Working Paper: No. 82-4). 34p. 1982. pap. 6.00 (ISBN 0-686-82541-1, CRD 138, UNCRD). Unipub.

REGIONAL PLANNING–POLAND

Space Economy & Regional Studies in Poland. 145p. 1982. pap. 8.50 (ISBN 0-686-84620-6, CRD140, UNCRD). Unipub.

REGIONALISM

Batteau, Allen, ed. Applachia & America: Autonomy & Regional Dependence. LC 82-40462. (Illus.). 296p. 1983. 26.00x (ISBN 0-8131-1480-2). U Pr of Ky.

Matthews, Ralph. The Creation of Regional Dependency. 336p. 1983. 40.00x (ISBN 0-8020-5617-2); pap. 12.95 (ISBN 0-8020-6510-4). U of Toronto Pr.

The Appalachian Land Ownership Task Force. Who Owns Appalachia? Landownership & Its Impact. LC 82-40173. (Illus.). 272p. 1983. 25.00x (ISBN 0-8131-1476-4). U Pr of Ky.

REGIONALISM (INTERNATIONAL ORGANIZATION)

see also Pan-Africanism

Armstrong, David. The Rise of International Organization. LC 82-16767. (Making of the 20th Century Ser.). 180p. 1982. 22.50x (ISBN 0-312-68427-4). St Martin.

REGISTERS OF BIRTHS, DEATHS, MARRIAGES, ETC.

see also Wills

Genealogical Association of Southwestern Michigan. Cemetery Records of Coloma Township in Berrien County, Michigan. (Orig.). 1983. pap. 8.00 (ISBN 0-686-37858-X). Genealog Assn SW.

A Register of the Marriages Celebrated in Greenbrier County (West) Virginia from 1781-1849. LC 82-82599. 80p. 1983. pap. 15.00 (ISBN 0-937418-07-2). N P Evans.

REGISTRATION OF TRADE-MARKS

see Trade-Marks

REGISTRATION OF VOTERS

see Voters, Registration Of

REGRESSION (PSYCHOLOGY)

Achen, Christopher H. Interpreting & Using Regression. LC 82-42675. (Quantitative Applications in the Social Sciences Ser.: No. 29). 88p. 1982. pap. 4.50 (ISBN 0-8039-1915-8). Sage.

Cohen, Jacob & Cohen, Patricia. Applied Multiple Regression: Correlation Analysis for the Behavioral Sciences. 2nd ed. 512p. 1983. text ed. write for info. (ISBN 0-89859-268-2). L Erlbaum Assocs.

REGRESSION ANALYSIS

Draper, N. R. & Smith, H. Applied Regression Analysis. 2nd ed. LC 80-17951. (Probability & Mathematical Statistics Ser.). 709p. 1981. 28.95x (ISBN 0-471-02995-5, Pub. by Wiley-Interscience). Wiley.

Nicholls, D. F. & Quinn, B. G. Random Coefficient Autoregressive Models: An Introduction. (Lecture Notes in Statistics: Vol. 11). (Illus.). 154p. 1983. pap. 12.00 (ISBN 0-387-90766-1). Springer-Verlag.

REGULATED INDUSTRIES

see Public Utilities

REGULATION OF PRICES

see Price Regulation

REGULATION OF TRADE

see Trade Regulation

REGULATORS (VIGILANTE GROUPS)

see Vigilance Committees

REGULATORY COMMISSIONS

see Independent Regulatory Commissions

REHABILITATION

see also Exercise Therapy; Occupational Therapy; Rehabilitation Centers; Vocational Rehabilitation

Bain, J. Paul, ed. Rehabilitation & Handicapped Literature 1981 Update: A Bibliographic Guide to the Microfiche Collection. 38p. 1982. reference bk. 25.00 (ISBN 0-667-00678-8). Microfilming Corp.

Crewe, Nancy M. & Zola, Irving K. Independent Living for Physically Disabled People: Developing, Implementing & Evaluating Self-Help Rehabilitation Programs. LC 82-48067. (Social & Behavioral Science Ser.). 1983. text ed. 19.95x (ISBN 0-87589-556-5). Jossey-Bass.

Reggio, Kathryn & Davidson, Josephine. Individualized Health Incentive Program Modules For Physically Disabled Students, 5 Vols. Shooltz, Danna, ed. Incl. Vol. 1. Safety & Survival Education. 336p. 1976; Vol. 2. Environmental & Community Health. 62p; Vol. 3. Sociological Health Problems. 56p. 1977; Vol. 4. Mental Health & Family Life Education. (Illus.). 138p. 1977; Vol. 5. Physical Health. (Illus.). 138p. 1977. 4.50 ea.; 17.50 set (ISBN 0-686-38806-2). Human Res Ctr.

Rudman, Jack. Rehabilitation Assistant. (Career Examination Ser.: C-545). (Cloth bdg. available on request). pap. 12.00 (ISBN 0-8373-0545-4). Natl Learning.

--Rehabilitation Inspector. (Career Examination Ser.: C-2639). (Cloth bldg. avail. on request). pap. 10.00 (ISBN 0-8373-2639-7). Natl Learning.

Schofield, J. Microcumputer-Based Aids for the Disabled. 1981. pap. text ed. 29.95x (ISBN 0-471-87721-2, Pub. by Wiley Heyden). Wiley.

Vandergoot, David & Jacobsen, Richard J. New Directions for Placement-Related Research & Practice in the Rehabilitation Process. LC 79-105250. 44p. 1977. 4.75 (ISBN 0-686-38812-7). Human Res Ctr.

REHABILITATION, RURAL

see also Community Development

Leonard, David K. & Marshall, Dale R., eds. Institutions of Rural Development for the Poor: Decentralization & Organizational Linkages. LC 82-15651. (Research Ser.: No. 49). xii, 237p. 1982. pap. 11.50x (ISBN 0-87725-149-5). U of Cal Intl St.

Marsh, Robin R. Development Strategies in Rural Colombia: The Case of Caaueta. LC 82-620032. (Latin American Studies: Vol. 55). 1983. text ed. write for info. (ISBN 0-87903-055-0). UCLA Lat Am Ctr.

REHABILITATION, VOCATIONAL

see Vocational Rehabilitation

REHABILITATION CENTERS

Consolidated Standards Manual for Child, Adolescent, & Adult Psychiatric, Alcoholism, & Drug Abuse Facilities, 1983. 206p. 1983. pap. 30.00 (ISBN 0-86688-058-5). Joint Comm Hosp.

Frazer, F. W., ed. Rehabilitation Within the Community. 208p. 1983. pap. 7.95 (ISBN 0-571-11901-8). Faber & Faber.

REHABILITATION OF CRIMINALS

see also Parole; Probation; Rehabilitation of Juvenile Delinquents

Jarvis, D. C. Institutional Treatment of the Offender. 1977. text ed. 21.95 (ISBN 0-07-032308-9); tchr's. manual & key avail. McGraw.

Pepinsky, Harold E., ed. Rethinking Criminology: New Premises, New Directions. (Research Progress Series in Criminology: Vol. 27). 152p. 1982. 18.95 (ISBN 0-8039-1891-7); pap. 8.95 (ISBN 0-686-82380-X). Sage.

REHABILITATION OF JUVENILE DELINQUENTS

Giallombardo, Rose, ed. Juvenile Delinquency: A Book of Readings. 3rd ed. LC 75-35887. 1976. pap. text ed. 17.95x (ISBN 0-471-29726-7). Text ed 14.25 o.p. Wiley.

REICH, WILHELM, 1897-1957

Placzek, Beverly, ed. Record of a Friendship: The Correspondence of Wilhelm Reich & A. S. Neill. 1983. pap. 11.95 (ISBN 0-374-51770-3). FS&G.

Sharaf, Myron. Fury on Earth: A Biography of Wilhelm Reich. LC 82-5707. (Illus.). 560p. 1983. 24.95 (ISBN 0-312-31370-5). St Martin.

REIGN OF TERROR

see France–History–Revolution, 1789-1799

REINCARNATION

see also Anthroposophy; Karma; Soul

Kostelanetz, Richard. Reincarnations. 1981. pap. 5.00 (ISBN 0-686-84602-8); signed 50.00 (ISBN 0-686-84603-6). Future Pr.

Lodo, Venerable L. Bardo Teachings: The Way of Death & Rebirth. Clark, Nancy & Parke, Caroline M., eds. (Illus.). 76p. 1982. pap. text ed. 5.95 (ISBN 0-910165-00-9). KDK Pubns.

MacGregory, G. Reincarnation as a Christian Hope. 1982. 60.00x (ISBN 0-333-31986-9, Pub. by Macmillan England). State Mutual Bk.

Miles, Eustace. Life After Life: The Theory of Reincarnation. 180p. 8.50 (ISBN 0-686-38223-4). Sun Bks.

Montgomery, Ruth. Threshold to Tomorrow. 256p. 1983. 13.95 (ISBN 0-399-12759-3). Putnam Pub Group.

Schulman, Martin. Karmic Astrology: The Moon's Nodes & Reincarnation. (Vol. 1). 1975. 4.95 (ISBN 0-87728-288-9). Weiser.

Stevenson, Ian. Cases of the Reincarnation Type: Vol. IV-Twelve Cases in Thailand & Burma. LC 74-28263. 1983. price not set (ISBN 0-8139-0960-0). U Pr of Va.

REINFORCED CONCRETE

Schwer, L. E., ed. Nonlinear Numerical Analysis of Reinforced Concrete. 1982. 30.00 (H00242). ASME.

Vance, Mary. Reinforced Concrete: A Bibliography. (Architecture Ser.: Bibliography A 838). 48p. 1982. pap. 7.50 (ISBN 0-88066-248-4). Vance Biblios.

REINFORCED CONCRETE CONSTRUCTION

see also Precast Concrete Construction; Prestressed Concrete Construction

Gioncu, Victor. Thin Reinforced Concrete Shells: Special Analysis Problems. LC 78-10338. 500p. 1980. 63.95x (ISBN 0-471-99735-8, Pub. by Wiley-Interscience). Wiley.

REINFORCED FIBROUS COMPOSITES

see Fibrous Composites

REINFORCED PLASTICS

Pritchard, G., ed. Developments in Reinforced Plastics, No. 2. 196p. 1982. 43.00 (ISBN 0-85334-125-7, Pub. by Applied Sci England). Elsevier.

REINFORCED SOLIDS

see Composite Materials

REJUVENATION

Blauer, Stephen. Rejuvenation: Dr. Ann Wigmore's Complete Diet & Health Program. 280p. (Orig.). 1982. pap. 4.95 (ISBN 0-89529-178-9). Avery Pub.

Hill, Devra. Rejuvenate. 1982. 6.95x (ISBN 0-686-37599-8). Cancer Control Soc.

REKHTA LANGUAGE

see Urdu Language

RELATIONS, RACE

see Race Relations

RELATIVISM, ETHICAL

see Ethical Relativism

RELATIVITY

Adler, R. Introduction to General Relativity. 2nd ed. 1975. 39.95 (ISBN 0-07-000423-4). McGraw.

RELATIVITY (ETHICS)

see Ethical Relativism

RELATIVITY (PHYSICS)

see also Kinematics; Quantum Theory; Space and Time

Epstein, Lewis C. Relativity Visualized. LC 82-84280. (Illus.). 250p. 1983. pap. 12.95 (ISBN 0-935218-03-3). Insight Pr CA.

Sachs, M. General Relativity & Matter. 1982. 39.00 (ISBN 90-277-1381-2, Pub. by Reidel Holland). Kluwer Boston.

Stephani, Hans. General Relativity: An Introduction to the Theory of the Gravitational Field. Stewart, John, ed. LC 81-10115. (Illus.). 300p. 1982. 49.50 (ISBN 0-521-24008-5). Cambridge U Pr.

RELAXATION

Regardie, Israel. Energy, Prayer & Relaxation. 80p. 1982. pap. 6.95 (ISBN 0-941404-02-1). Falcon Pr Az.

RELAYS, ELECTRIC

see Electric Relays

RELEVANCE (PHILOSOPHY)

Schutz, Alfred. Reflections on the Problem of Relevance. Zaner, Richard M., ed. LC 82-11850. xxiv, 186p. 1982. Repr. of 1970 ed. lib. bdg. 25.00x (ISBN 0-313-22820-5, SCRER). Greenwood.

RELIABILITY (ENGINEERING)

see also Quality Control

O'Connor, P. D. Practical Reliability Engineering. 300p. 1981. text ed. 38.00x (ISBN 0-471-25919-5, Pub. by Wiley Heyden). Wiley.

Smith, Charles O. Introduction to Reliability in Design. LC 82-14854. 284p. 1982. Repr. of 1976 ed. lib. bdg. 18.50 (ISBN 0-89874-553-5). Krieger.

RELIEF (AID)

see Charities; Public Welfare

RELIGION

see also Atheism; Agnosticism; Belief and Doubt; Faith; God; Mysteries, Religious; Mysticism; Myth; Mythology; Positivism; Psychology, Religious; Rationalism; Religions; Revelation; Skepticism; Spiritual Life; Supernatural; Superstition; Theology; Theosophy; Worship

also subdivision Religion, or Religion and Mythology, under names of countries, races, peoples, etc., e.g. Egypt-Religion; Indians of North America-Religion and Mythology; also headings beginning with the word Religious

Breaking the Devil's Hold. 1982. 1.25 (ISBN 0-89858-032-3). Fill the Gap.

Buck, Peter H. Anthropology & Religion. 1939. text ed. 11.50x (ISBN 0-686-83471-2). Elliots Bks.

Cabral, J. Religiones, Sectas y Herejias. Carrodeguas, Andy & Marosi, Esteban, eds. Marosi, Antonio, tr. 176p. (Span.). 1982. pap. 3.00 (ISBN 0-8297-1282-8). Life Pubs Intl.

Carmody, John & Carmody, Denise L. Religion: The Great Questions. 160p. 1983. pap. price not set. Seabury.

Childbirth God's Way. 1982. 1.25 (ISBN 0-89858-027-7). Fill the Gap.

Conquest of the Mind. 1982. 3.50 (ISBN 0-89858-037-4). Fill the Gap.

Ellwood, Robert S., Jr. Introducing Religion: From Inside & Outside. (Illus.). 240p. 1983. pap. text ed. 11.95 (ISBN 0-13-477497-3). P-H.

Exposing Demon's Work. 1982. 1.25 (ISBN 0-89858-034-X). Fill the Gap.

Exposing the Devil's Work. 1982. 1.25 (ISBN 0-89858-033-1). Fill the Gap.

Kung, Hans & Schillebeeckx, Edward, eds. Concilium: Religion in the Eighties. (Concilium Ser.: Vols. 151-160). 128p. (Orig.). 1982. pap. 62.55 (ISBN 0-8164-2392-X). Seabury.

Kung, Hans & Schillebeeckz, Edward, eds. Concilium: Religion in the Eighties. (Concilium Ser.: Vols. 131-140). 128p. (Orig.). 1980. pap. 53.55 (ISBN 0-8164-2283-4). Seabury.

Mol, Hans. Meaning & Place: An Introduction to the Social Scientific Study of Religion. (Orig.). 1983. pap. 6.95 (ISBN 0-8298-0638-5). Pilgrim NY.

The Most High God. LC 82-90990. 1982. write for info. (ISBN 0-915540-30-4). Friends Israel.

Parkhurst, Charles H. Pulpit & the Pew. 1913. text ed. 29.50x (ISBN 0-686-83717-7). Elliots Bks.

Promise of Deliverance in Time of Trouble. 1978. 1.25 (ISBN 0-89858-023-4). Fill the Gap.

Promise of Power to Serve. 1978. 1.25 (ISBN 0-89858-024-2). Fill the Gap.

Promise of Total Protection. 1978. 1.25 (ISBN 0-89858-022-6). Fill the Gap.

Protection by Angles. 1982. 3.50 (ISBN 0-89858-041-2). Fill the Gap.

Winden, Hans-Willi. Wie Kam und Wie Kommt Es Zum Osterglauben? 352p. (Ger.). 1982. write for info. (ISBN 3-8204-5820-4). P Lang Pubs.

RELIGION-ADDRESSES, ESSAYS, LECTURES

Marx, Karl & Engels, Friedrich. On Religion. LC 82-17032. (Classics in Religious Studies). 384p. 1982. Repr. of 1964 ed. 10.50x (ISBN 0-89130-599-8, 00 05 03). Scholars Pr CA.

RELIGION-DICTIONARIES

Ferm, Vergilius, ed. Encyclopedia of Religion. LC 62-18535. 1962. 19.95 (ISBN 0-8022-0490-2). Philos Lib.

RELIGION-HISTORY

Bianchi, Ugo & Vermaseren, Maarten J. La Soteriologia dei Culti Orientali Nell' Impero Romano: Atti del Colloquio Internazionale su le Soteriologia dei Culti Orientali Nell' Impero Romano. (Etudes Preliminaires aux Religions Orientales dans l'Empire Romain Ser.: Wol. 92). (Illus.). xxii, 1025p. 1982. write for info. (ISBN 90-04-06501-6). E J Brill.

Cermanovic-Kuzmanovic, A. Monumenta intra fines Iugoslaviae Reperta. (Etudes Preliminaires sux Religions Orientales dan l'Empire Romain: Vol. 74). (Illus.). xi, 76p. 1982. pap. write for info. (ISBN 90-04-06533-4). E J Brill.

Free Religion: An American Faith. 1947. text ed. 39.50x (ISBN 0-686-83554-9). Elliots Bks.

Gaustad, Edwin S. A Documentary History of Religion in America Since 1865. 640p. 1983. pap. 18.95 (ISBN 0-8028-1874-9). Eerdmans.

Hasenfratz, Hans-Peter. Die Toten Lebenden: Eine Religions Phanomenologische Studie zum Sozialen Tod in Archaischen Gasellschaften. Zugleicjh ein Kritischer Beitrag zur Sogenannten Strafopfertheorie. (Zeitschrift fur Religions-und Geistesgeschichte, Beiheft: Vol. 24). xii, 167p. 1982. pap. write for info. (ISBN 90-04-06595-4). E J Brill.

Places, Edouard des. Etudes Plantoniciennes, 1929-1979. (Etudes Preliminaires aux Religions Orientales dans l'Empire Romain Ser.: Vol. 90). (Illus.). xx, 416p. 1981. write for info. (ISBN 90-04-06473-7). E J Brill.

Vermaseren, M. J. Mithriaca III: The Mithraeum at Marino. (Etudes Preliminaires aux Religions Orientales dans l'Empire Romain Ser.: Vol. 16). (Illus.). xiii, 105p. 1982. write for info. (ISBN 90-04-06500-8). E J Brill.

RELIGION-PHILOSOPHY

see also Christianity-Philosophy; Philosophy and Religion

Hall, James. Knowledge, Belief, & Trancedence: Philosophical Problems in Religion. LC 82-21757. 254p. 1983. pap. text ed. 10.75 (ISBN 0-8191-2912-7). U Pr of Amer.

Naropa Institute Journal of Psychology Vol. II. 100p. (Orig.). 1983. pap. 8.00 (ISBN 0-87773-787-8). Great Eastern.

Ormond, Alexander T. The Philosophy of Religion: Lectures Written for the Elliott Lectureship at the Western Theological Seminary. 195p. 1982. Repr. of 1922 ed. lib. bdg. 50.00 (ISBN 0-8495-4219-7). Arden Lib.

Schlink, Basilea. Why Doesn't God Intervene? Evangelical Sisterhood of Mary, tr. from Ger. 32p. 1982. pap. 0.30 (ISBN 3-87209-629-X). Evang Sisterhood Mary.

RELIGION-PSYCHOLOGY

see Psychology, Religious

RELIGION-STUDY AND TEACHING

see also Theology-Study and Teaching

Vermaseren, M. J. Corpus Cultus Cybelae Attidisque CCCA II: Graecia atque Insulae. (Etudes Preliminaires aux Religions Orientales dans l'Empire Romain Ser.: Vol. 50). (Illus.). xxxi, 278p. 1982. write for info. (ISBN 90-04-06499-0). E J Brill.

RELIGION, COMPARATIVE

see Religions

RELIGION, MIXED

see Marriage, Mixed

RELIGION AND ART

see Art and Religion

RELIGION AND LAW

Shepard, William C. The Prosecutor's Reach: Legal Issues & the New Religions. 200p. 1983. 12.95 (ISBN 0-8245-0582-4). Crossroad NY.

RELIGION AND MEDICINE

see Medicine and Religion

RELIGION AND NATIONALISM

see Nationalism and Religion

RELIGION AND PHILOSOPHY

see Philosophy and Religion

RELIGION AND PSYCHOANALYSIS

see Psychoanalysis and Religion

RELIGION AND PSYCHOLOGY

see Psychology, Religious

RELIGION AND SCIENCE

see also Bible and Science; Creation; Evolution; Faith and Reason; Man-Origin

Baker, Ralph. Reality. 1982. 7.95 (ISBN 0-533-05434-6). Vantage.

Burns, J. K. Life Science & Religions. (Illus.). 1983. 25.00 (ISBN 0-8022-2415-6). Philos Lib.

Carty, Charles M. Stigmata & Modern Science. 31p. 1958. pap. 0.65 (ISBN 0-686-81641-2). TAN Bks Pubs.

Chargaff, Erwin. Voices in the Labyrinth: Nature, Man & Science. 190p. 1978. 9.95 (ISBN 0-8164-9322-7). Seabury.

Hare, F. Kenneth. The Experiments of Life: Science & Religion. 192p. 1983. 25.00x (ISBN 0-8020-2486-6); pap. 7.95 (ISBN 0-8020-6506-6). U of Toronto Pr.

Martin, George V. Are There a Beginning & an End to Man's Existence? 1983. 8.95 (ISBN 0-533-05562-8). Vantage.

Talbot, George. Philosophy & Unified Science. 1435p. 1982. Repr. of 1978 ed. 36.50 (ISBN 0-941524-18-3). Lotus Light.

RELIGION AND SCIENCE-HISTORY OF CONTROVERSY

Gorham, Charles T. Religion as a Bar to Progress. 31p. 1981. pap. 3.00 (ISBN 0-686-82051-7). Am Atheist.

RELIGION AND SEX

see Sex and Religion

RELIGION AND SOCIAL PROBLEMS

see Church and Social Problems; Religion and Sociology

RELIGION AND SOCIETY

see Religion and Sociology

RELIGION AND SOCIOLOGY

Works limited to the Christian religion are entered under the heading Sociology, Christian, and related subjects referred to under that heading.

see also Church and Social Problems; Sociology, Christian

Brunkow, Robert, ed. Religion & Society in North America: An Annotated Bibliography. (Clio Bibliography Ser.: No. 12). 514p. 1983. lib. bdg. 60.00 (ISBN 0-87436-042-0). ABC-Clio.

Daly, Lloyd W. Iohannis Philoponi: De Vocabulis Quae Diversum Signification Exhibent Secundum Differentiam Accentus. LC 81-72156. (Memoirs Ser.: Vol. 151). 1983. 20.00 (ISBN 0-87169-151-5). Am Philos.

Debord, Pierre. Aspects Sociaux et economiques de la vie Religieuse dans l'Anatolie Greco-romaine. (Etudes Preliminaires aux Religions Orientale dans l'Empire Romain Ser.: Vol. 88). (Illus.). ix, 476p. 1982. write for info. E J Brill.

Hadden, Jeffrey K. & Long, Theodore E., eds. Religion & Religiosity in America. (Studies in Honor of Joseph H. Fichter). 192p. 1983. 15.95 (ISBN 0-8245-0555-7). Crossroad NY.

Marshall, Gordon. In Search of the Spirit of Capitalism: An Essay on Max Weber's Protestant Ethic Thesis. 233p. 1982. 22.50 (ISBN 0-231-05498-X); pap. 10.00 (ISBN 0-686-82236-6). Columbia U Pr.

Mol, Hans. Meaning & Place: An Introduction to the Social Scientific Study of Religion. (Orig.). 1983. pap. 6.95 (ISBN 0-8298-0638-5). Pilgrim NY.

RELIGION AND STATE

see also Church and State; Islam and State; Nationalism and Religion

Crone, Marie-Luise. Untersuchungen Zur Reichskirchenpolitik Lothars III, 1125-1137: Zwischen Reichskirchlicher Tradition Und Reformkurie. 398p. 1982. write for info (ISBN 3-8204-7019-0). P Lang Pubs.

RELIGION AND WAR

see War and Religion

RELIGION AS A PROFESSION

see Church Work As a Profession

RELIGION IN LITERATURE

see also Bible in Literature; Christianity in Literature; Literature and Morals; Religious Poetry

Anderson, Vincent P. Reaction to Religious Elements in the Poetry of Robert Browning: Introduction & Annotated Bibliography. LC 82-50407. 350p. 1983. 25.00X (ISBN 0-87875-221-8). Whitston Pub.

Davis, James B. La Quete de Paul Gadenne: Une Morale pour Notre Epoque. (Fr.). 12.00 (ISBN 0-917786-18-1). French Lit.

Frietzsche, Arthur H. Disraeli's Religion: The Treatment of Religion in Disraeli's Novels. 62p. 1982. Repr. of 1961 ed. lib. bdg. 10.00 (ISBN 0-8495-1718-4). Arden Lib.

RELIGION IN POETRY

see Religion in Literature

RELIGION OF HUMANITY

see Positivism

RELIGIONS

Here are entered works on the major world religions. Works on religious groups whose adherents recognize special teachings or practices which fall within the normative bounds of the major world religions are entered under Sects. Works on groups or movements whose system of religious beliefs or practices differs significantly from the major world religions and which are often gathered around a specific deity or person are entered under Cults.

see also Babism; Bahaism; Brahmanism; Buddhism; Christianity; Confucius and Confucianism; Cults; Gnosticism; Gods; Hinduism; Islam; Jains; Judaism; Mythology; Paganism; Positivism; Religion; Sects; Shinto; Spiritualism; Taoism; Zoroastrianism

Baum, Gregory & Coleman, John, eds. New Religious Movements. (Concilium 1983: Vol. 161). 128p. (Orig.). 1983. pap. 6.95 (ISBN 0-8164-2441-1); pap. 62.55 10 Volume Subscription (ISBN 0-8164-2453-5). Seabury.

Cain, Sandra E. & Evans, Jack M. Sciencing: An Involvement Approach to Elementary Science Methods. 350p. 1983. pap. text ed. 16.95 (ISBN 0-675-20055-5). Additional supplements may be obtained from publisher. Merrill.

Daly, Lloyd W. Iohannis Philoponi: De Vocabulis Quae Diversum Signification Exhibent Secundum Differentiam Accentus. LC 81-72156. (Memoirs Ser.: Vol. 151). 1983. 20.00 (ISBN 0-87169-151-5). Am Philos.

Hopfe, Lewis M. Religions of the World. 416p. 1983. pap. text ed. 16.95 (ISBN 0-02-474740-8). Macmillan.

McDowell, Josh & Stewart, Don. Understanding Secular Religions: A Handbook of Today's Religions. 160p. 1982. pap. 5.95 (ISBN 0-86605-093-0). Here's Life.

Norbu, Tsampa Yeshe. Rasa Tantra: Blood Marriage-The Sacred Initiation-A Marriage of the Faiths of East & West. (Illus.). 36p. 1980. pap. 6.95 (ISBN 0-9609802-2-9). Life Science.

Platvoet, J. G. Comparing Religions: A Limitative Approach. (Religion & Reason Ser.: No. 24). xiv, 350p. 1982. 49.00x (ISBN 90-279-3170-4). Mouton.

Sethi, A. S. & Pummer, Reinhard, eds. Comparative Religion. LC 79-905771. 200p. 1979. 12.50x (ISBN 0-7069-0810-4). Intl Pubns Serv.

Smart, Ninian. Worldviews: Crosscultural Explorations in Human Beliefs. (Illus.). 224p. 1983. 12.95 (ISBN 0-686-83823-8, ScribT). Scribner.

Thompson, Henry O., ed. The Global Congress of the World's Religions. LC 82-73565. (Conference Ser.: No. 15). (Orig.). 1982. pap. text ed. write for info. (ISBN 0-932894-15-1). Unif Theol Seminary.

Wolfe, Rolland E. The Twelve Religions of the Bible. LC 82-20401. (Studies in the Bible & Early Christianity: Vol. 2). (Illus.). 440p. 1983. 44.95x (ISBN 0-686-84104-2). E Mellen.

RELIGIONS-HISTORY

Sandifer, Kevin W. A Layman's Look at Starting a Religious Archives. Hall, Renee, et al, eds. 48p. (Orig.). 1982. pap. text ed. 7.50 (ISBN 0-910653-00-3). K W Sandifer.

RELIGIONS-JUVENILE LITERATURE

Berger, Gilda. Religion. (A Reference First Bk.). 96p. (gr. 4 up). 1983. PLB 8.90 (ISBN 0-531-04538-2). Watts.

RELIGIONS, COMPARATIVE

see Religions

RELIGIONS, MODERN

see Cults; Sects

RELIGIOUS ART

see Cathedrals; Christian Art and Symbolism; Church Architecture; Idols and Images; Temples

also Art, Buddhist; Art, Gothic; Art, Medieval, and similar headings

RELIGIOUS BELIEF

see Belief and Doubt; Faith

RELIGIOUS BIOGRAPHY

see also Christian Biography

Durham, G. Homer. N. Eldon Tanner: His Life & Service. LC 82-9681. (Illus.). 370p. 1982. 8.95 (ISBN 0-87747-913-5). Deseret Bk.

Hyatt, Lillian. Bonfires at Heaven's Gate: A Biography of Dr. David Hyatt. (Illus.). 160p. (Orig.). 1983. pap. 7.95 (ISBN 0-8164-2354-7). Seabury.

Murphy, Paul I. & Arlington, R. Rene. La Popessa. 296p. 1983. 16.50 (ISBN 0-446-51258-3). Warner Bks.

Vail, Harley W. When Harley Heard from Heaven. LC 82-72633. 84p. 1982. pap. 2.95 (ISBN 0-9609096-0-5). Bethel Pub Or.

RELIGIOUS CEREMONIES

see Rites and Ceremonies

RELIGIOUS DENOMINATIONS

see Religions; Sects;

also particular denominations and sects

RELIGIOUS EDUCATION

Here are entered works dealing with instruction in religion in school and private life, Cf. note under Church and Education.

see also Bible-Study; Christian Education; Moral Education; Sunday-Schools; Theology-Study and Teaching

Arrington, French. Maintaining the Foundations. 1983. pap. 4.95 (ISBN 0-8010-0192-7). Baker Bk.

Barney, Kenneth D. Directions, Please. LC 82-82080. 108p. (Orig.). 1983. pap. 2.50 (ISBN 0-88243-856-5, 02-0856); tchr's. ed. 3.95 (ISBN 0-88243-197-8, 32-0197). Gospel Pub.

Brokering, L. Thirty Six Creative Ideas for Children in the Church School. LC 12-2958. 1982. pap. 4.50 (ISBN 0-570-03865-0). Concordia.

Girzone, Joseph F. Who Will Teach Me? 61p. 1982. 5.00 (ISBN 0-911519-00-9). Richelieu Court.

Mills, Dick. The Four Loves. (Orig.). Date not set. pap. price not set (HH-287). Harrison Hse.

--Hearts & Flowers. (Orig.). Date not set. pap. price not set (ISBN 0-89274-288-7, HH-286). Harrison Hse.

Moran, Gabriel. Religious Education Development. (Images for the Future). 204p. 1983. pap. 9.95 (ISBN 0-86683-692-6). Winston Pr.

Thirty Five Handicraft Projects for Children. LC 12-2957. 1982. pap. 4.50 (ISBN 0-570-03864-2). Concordia.

Willert, Albrecht. Religiose Existenz und Literarische Produktion. 377p. (Ger.). 1982. write for info. (ISBN 3-8204-5994-4). P Lang Pubs.

RELIGIOUS EDUCATION–HOME TRAINING

see also Family–Religious Life

Leonard, Joe, Jr. Planning Family Ministry: A Guide for the Teaching Church. 64p. 1982. pap. 3.95 (ISBN 0-8170-0971-X). Judson.

RELIGIOUS EDUCATION–TEACHING METHODS

Cove, Mary & Regan, Jane. Teaching Religion Effectively Program. 96p. 1982. pap. 3.50 (ISBN 0-697-01825-3); program manual 24.95 (ISBN 0-697-01826-1). Wm C Brown.

RELIGIOUS EDUCATION–TEXT-BOOKS FOR CHILDREN

Burgess, Beverly. Three Bears in the Ministry. 28p. (Orig.). (ps). 1982. pap. 3.50 (ISBN 0-89274-252-6). Harrison Hse.

RELIGIOUS EDUCATION OF ADOLESCENTS

Pipe, Virginia. Explore Together, Vol. 4. 128p. 1982. pap. 11.95 (ISBN 0-8170-0975-2). Judson.

RELIGIOUS EDUCATION OF CHILDREN

Coleman, Bill & Coleman, Patty. God's Own Child. rev. ed. 64p. 1983. Parent's Book. pap. text ed. 3.95 (ISBN 0-89622-188-1); Leader's Guide. wkbk. 1.00 (ISBN 0-89622-187-3). Twenty-Third.

Gale, Elizabeth W. Children Together, Vol. 2. 128p. 1982. pap. 11.95 (ISBN 0-8170-0974-4). Judson.

Hanna, Barbara & Hoover, Janet. Teaching Preschoolers. 3.95 (ISBN 0-89137-608-9). Quality Pubns.

Ivins, Dan. Main Events. LC 82-70869. (Orig.). (gr. 7-12). 1983. pap. 4.50 (ISBN 0-8054-5339-3). Broadman.

Mauck, Diane & Jenkins, Janet. Teaching Primaries. write for info. (ISBN 0-89137-610-0). Quality Pubns.

Moore, Raymond & Moore, Dorothy. Homespun Schools. 1982. 8.95 (ISBN 0-8499-0326-2). Word Pub.

Nyber, D. M. Help for Families With a Problem Child. (Trauma Bks.: Ser. 2). 1983. pap. 2.50 (ISBN 0-570-08259-5). Concordia.

Paul, James L., ed. The Exceptional Child: A Guidebook for Churches & Community Agencies. LC 82-16914. 176p. text ed. 22.00x (ISBN 0-8156-2287-2); pap. text ed. 12.95x (ISBN 0-8156-2288-0). Syracuse U Pr.

Set of Four Trauma Books. (Trauma Bks.: Ser. 2). 1983. Set. pap. 9.15 (ISBN 0-570-08260-9). Concordia.

RELIGIOUS EXPERIENCE

see Experience (Religion)

RELIGIOUS FREEDOM

see Religious Liberty

RELIGIOUS HISTORY

see Church History

RELIGIOUS LIBERTY

see also Church and State; Nationalism and Religion

Clark, Henry B., II. Freedom of Religion in America: Historical Roots, Philosophical Concepts, Contemporary Problems. 143p. 1982. pap. 6.95 (ISBN 0-87855-925-6). Transaction Bks.

RELIGIOUS LIFE

see Christian Life

also subdivision Religious Life under classes of persons, e.g. Family–Religious Life

Allen, Richard. The Life Experience & Gospel Labors of The Rt. Rev. Richard Allen. 96p. (Orig.). 1983. pap. 3.95 (ISBN 0-687-21844-6). Abingdon.

Brown, Marion M. & Leech, Jane K. Dreamcatcher: The Life of John Neihardt. 144p. (Orig.). Date not set. pap. 6.95 (ISBN 0-687-11174-9). Abingdon.

Taylor, A., Jr. The Life of my Years. 160p. (Orig.). 1983. pap. 9.95 (ISBN 0-687-21854-3). Abingdon.

Wallis, Jim. Jim Wallis Revive Us Again: A Sojourner's Story. Raines, Robert A., ed. 192p. 1983. text ed. 9.95 (ISBN 0-687-36173-7). Abingdon.

RELIGIOUS LIFE (JUDAISM)

see Jewish Way of Life

RELIGIOUS LITERATURE

see also Bible As Literature; Christian Literature; Hindu Literature; Islamic Literature; Religious Poetry

The Works of William E. Channing, D.D. 1060p. 1982. Repr. of 1889 ed. lib. bdg. 100.00 (ISBN 0-8495-0959-9). Arden Lib.

RELIGIOUS LITERATURE–BIBLIOGRAPHY

Religious Books, 1876-1982, 3 vol. set. 3650p. 1983. 195.00x (ISBN 0-8352-1602-0). Bowker.

Wilson, John F. & Slavens, Thomas P., eds. Research Guide to Religious Studies. (Sources of Information in the Humanities Ser.). 192p. Date not set. text ed. 20.00 (ISBN 0-8389-0330-4). ALA.

RELIGIOUS MUSIC

see Church Music

RELIGIOUS MYSTERIES

see Mysteries, Religious

RELIGIOUS ORDERS

see Monasticism and Religious Orders

RELIGIOUS PAINTING

see Christian Art and Symbolism

RELIGIOUS POETRY

see also Hymns

Ray, Sondra. Celebration of Breath. 192p. 1983. pap. 6.95 (ISBN 0-89087-355-0). Celestial Arts.

RELIGIOUS PSYCHOLOGY

see Psychology, Religious

RELIGIOUS RITES

see Rites and Ceremonies

RELIGIOUS SCULPTURE

see Christian Art and Symbolism

RELIGIOUS SOCIOLOGY

see Religion and Sociology

RELIGIOUS THOUGHT–GREAT BRITAIN

Pelphrey, Brant. Love Was His Meaning: The Theology & Mysticism of Julain of Norwich. (Salzburg-Elizabethan Studies: Vol. 92, No. 4). 360p. 1982. pap. text ed. 25.00x (ISBN 0-391-02758-1, Pub. by Salzburg Austria). Humanities.

RELIGIOUS VOCATION

see Vocation (In Religious Orders, Congregations, etc.)

RELISHES

see Cookery (Relishes)

RELOCATION (HOUSING)

Newman, Sandra J. & Owen, Michael S. Residential Displacement in the U. S., 1970-1977. 104p. 1982. pap. 12.00x (ISBN 0-87944-281-6). Inst Soc Res.

REMAND HOMES

see Juvenile Detention Homes

REMARRIAGE

Hocking, David. Marrying Again: A Guide for Christians. 160p. 1983. 8.95 (ISBN 0-8007-1338-9). Revell.

McNamara, Lynne & Morrison, Jennifer. Separation, Divorce & After. LC 82-2718. 192p. 1983. pap. 9.95 (ISBN 0-7022-1931-2). U of Queensland Pr.

Ryder, Harriette. How to Get Married Again. (YA) 1978. text ed. 10.95 (ISBN 0-914094-18-1). Symphony.

Sager, Clifford J., et al. Treating the Remarried Family. LC 82-17811. 450p. 1983. 35.00 (ISBN 0-87630-323-8). Brunner-Mazel.

Woodrow, Ralph. Divorce & Remarriage: What Does the Bible Really Say? LC 82-99960. (Illus.). 1982. pap. 3.95 (ISBN 0-916938-06-9). R Woodrow.

REMBRANDT, HARMENSZOON VAN RIJN, 1606-1669

Bruyn, J. A Corpus of Rembrandt Paintings, Vol. 1. 1983. lib. bdg. 325.00 (ISBN 90-247-2614-X, Pub. by Martinus Nijhoff). Kluwer Boston.

Kitson, Michael. Rembrandt. (Phaidon Color Library). (Illus.). 84p. 1983. 27.50 (ISBN 0-7148-2228-0, Pub. by Salem Hse Ltd); pap. 18.95 (ISBN 0-7148-2241-8). Merrimack Bk Serv.

REMEDIAL READING

see Reading–Remedial Teaching

REMEDIAL TEACHING

see also Reading–Remedial Teaching; Speech; Tutors and Tutoring

Carnine, Douglas & Elkind, David. Interdisciplinary Voices in Learning Disabilities & Remedial Education. (Illus.). 196p. (Orig.). 1982. pap. text ed. 15.00x (ISBN 0-936104-27-9). Pro-Ed.

Moore, David P. & Poppino, Mary A. Successful Tutoring: A Practical Guide to Adult Learning Processes. (Illus.). 184p. 1983. 15.75x (ISBN 0-398-04763-4). C C Thomas.

Sewell, Geof. Reshaping Remedial Education. 140p. 1982. text ed. 26.00x (ISBN 0-7099-2348-1, Pub. by Croom Helm Ltd England). Biblio Dist.

REMISSION OF TAXES

see Tax Remission

REMODELING OF BUILDINGS

see Buildings–Repair and Reconstruction

REMODELING OF DWELLINGS

see Dwellings–Remodeling

REMOTE CONTROL

see also Electronic Control; Photoelectric Cells

Young, R. E. Supervisory Remote Control Systems. (IEE Control Engineering Ser.: No. 4). (Illus.). 192p. 1977. casebound 35.75 (ISBN 0-901223-94-8). Inst Elect Eng.

REMOTE SENSING

Allan, Thomas D. Satellite Microwave Remote Sensing. (Marine Science Ser.). 450p. 1983. 110.00 (ISBN 0-470-27397-6). Halsted Pr.

Deepak, Adarsh & Rao, K. R. Remote Sensing Applications for Rice Production. (Illus.). Date not set. price not set (ISBN 0-937194-03-4). Spectrum Pr.

De Loor, G. P., ed. Radar Remote Sensing. (Remote Sensing Reviews: Vol. 1, No. 1). 176p. 1982. 47.50 (ISBN 3-7186-0132-X). Harwood Academic.

Estes, John E. & Senger, Leslie W. Remote Sensing: Techniques for Environmental Analysis. LC 73-8601. 340p. 1974. 24.95x (ISBN 0-471-24595-X). Wiley.

Johannsen, Chris J. & Sanders, James L., eds. Remote Sensing for Resource Management. (Illus.). 688p. 1982. text ed. 45.00 (ISBN 0-935734-08-2). Soil Conservation.

Manual of Remote Sensing, 2 vols. 1983. Set. 99.00 (ISBN 0-686-84867-5). Vol. I (ISBN 0-937294-41-1). Vol. II (ISBN 0-937294-42-X). ASP.

Mooradian, A. & Killinger, D. K. Optical & Laser Remote Sensing. (Springer Ser. in Optical Sciences: Vol. 39). (Illus.). 400p. 1983. 30.00 (ISBN 0-387-12170-6). Springer-Verlag.

Multilingual Dictionary of Remote Sensing & Photogrammetry. 1983. write for info. (ISBN 0-937294-46-2). ASP.

Remote Sensing & Development. 24p. 1982. pap. 7.50 (ISBN 0-88936-302-1, IDRC 174, IRDC). Unipub.

Survey of the Profession: Photogrammetry, Surveying, Mapping, Remote Sensing. 1982. pap. 150.00 (ISBN 0-937294-40-3). ASP.

Zuev, V. E. & Naats, I. E. Inverse Problems of Lidar Sensing of the Atmosphere. (Springer Ser. in Optical Sciences: Vol. 29). (Illus.). 260p. 1983. 41.00 (ISBN 0-387-10913-7). Springer-Verlag.

REMOTE TERRAIN SENSING

see Remote Sensing

RENAISSANCE

see also Civilization, Medieval; Fifteenth Century; Humanism; Literature, Medieval

Friedman, Jerome. The Most Ancient Testimony: Sixteenth-Century Christian-Hebraica in the Age of Renaissance Nostalgia. LC 82-18830. x, 279p. 1983. text ed. 24.95 (ISBN 0-8214-0700-7, 82-84697). Ohio U Pr.

Grassi, Ernesto. Heidegger & the Question of Renaissance Humanism: Four Studies, Vol. 24. Krois, John M., tr. 110p. 1983. 11.00 (ISBN 0-86698-062-8). Medieval & Renaissance NY.

Jensen, DeLamar. Renaissance World. 1979. pap. text ed. 2.95x. Forum Pr IL.

Schmitt, Charles B. Aristotle & the Renaissance. (Martin Classical Lectures: No. XXVII). (Illus.). 208p. 1983. text ed. 18.50x (ISBN 0-674-04525-4). Harvard U Pr.

RENAISSANCE–EUROPE

see Renaissance

RENAISSANCE–FRANCE

Major, James R. Representative Institutions in Renaissance France, 1421-1559. LC 82-25305. ix, 182p. 1983. Repr. of 1960 ed. lib. bdg. 35.00x (ISBN 0-313-23569-4, MAJR). Greenwood.

RENAISSANCE–ITALY

Burckhardt, Jacob. The Civilization of the Renaissance in Italy. LC 54-6894. 6.95 (ISBN 0-394-60497-0). Modern Lib.

Hanning, Robert W. & Rosand, David. Castiglione: The Ideal & the Real in Renaissance Culture. LC 82-6944. (Illus.). 240p. 1983. text ed. 22.50x (ISBN 0-300-02649-8). Yale U Pr.

RENAISSANCE ARCHITECTURE

see Architecture, Renaissance

RENAISSANCE ART

see Art, Renaissance

RENAISSANCE SCULPTURE

see Sculpture, Renaissance

RENAL DISEASES

see Kidneys–Diseases

RENAL FAILURE

see Renal Insufficiency

RENAL HYPERTENSION

Campese, V. M. & Hsueh, W. A., eds. The Kidney in Hypertension. 120p. 1983. pap. price not set (ISBN 3-8055-3648-8). S Karger.

RENAL INSUFFICIENCY

Francisco, Llach. Renal Vein Thrombosis. LC 82-83041. (Illus.). 1983. pap. 29.50 monograph (ISBN 0-87993-186-8). Futura Pub.

Parsons, F. M. & Ogg, C., eds. Renal Failure: Who Cares? 200p. 1982. text ed. write for info. (ISBN 0-85200-476-1, Pub. by MTP Pr England). Kluwer Boston.

Porter, George, ed. Nephrotoxic Mechanisms of Drugs & Environmental Toxins. LC 82-13156. 486p. 1982. 49.50x (ISBN 0-306-40977-1, Plenum Med Bk). Plenum Pub.

Van Stone, John C. Dialysis & Treatment of Renal Insufficiency. write for info (ISBN 0-8089-1566-5). Grune.

Yuill, G. M. Treatment of Renal Failure. 1975. pap. 5.00 (ISBN 0-7190-0628-7). Manchester.

RENEWAL OF THE CHURCH

see Church Renewal

RENOIR, AUGUSTE, 1841-1919

Gaunt, William. Renoir. (Phaidon Color Library). (Illus.). 84p. 1983. 27.50 (ISBN 0-686-38391-5, Pub. by Salem Hse Ltd); pap. 18.95 (ISBN 0-7148-2242-6). Merrimack Bk Serv.

RENT

see also Landlord and Tenant

Zucchero. Rental Homes: The Tax Shelter that Works & Grows for You. 1983. text ed. 13.95 (ISBN 0-8359-6644-5). Reston.

REORGANIZED CHURCH OF JESUS CHRIST OF LATTER-DAY SAINTS

Mulliken, Frances H. A Restoration Heritage. LC 79-15689. 1979. pap. 8.00 (ISBN 0-8309-0244-9). Herald Hse.

REPARATION

Elias, Robert. Victims of the System: Crime Victims & Compensation in American Politics & Criminal Justice. (Illus.). 352p. 1983. 24.95 (ISBN 0-87855-470-X). Transaction Bks.

REPLACEMENT OF INDUSTRIAL EQUIPMENT

O'Conner, Melvin C. & Chandra, Gyan. Replacement Cost Disclosure: A/Study of Compliance with the SEC Requirement. 308p. pap. 24.95 (ISBN 0-86641-021-X, 78102). Natl Assn Accts.

O'Conner, Melvin C. & Grant, Rita. Replacement Costing: Complying with Disclosure Requirements. 41p. pap. 4.95 (ISBN 0-86641-022-8, 7789). Natl Assn Accts.

REPORT CARDS

see Grading and Marking (Students)

REPORT WRITING

see also Business Report Writing; Dissertations, Academic; Note-Taking; Technical Writing

Balian, Edward S. How to Design, Analyze, & Write Doctoral Research: The Practical Guidebook. LC 82-20164. (Illus.). 268p. (Orig.). 1983. lib. bdg. 22.75 (ISBN 0-8191-2879-1); pap. text ed. 11.75 (ISBN 0-8191-2880-5). U Pr of Amer.

Craz, Albert G. & Mavragis, Edward P. Writing: The Report. (Writing Ser.). 66p. 1981. wkbk. 3.95 (ISBN 0-9602800-2-2). Comp Pr.

Ewing, David W. Writing for Results in Business, Government, the Sciences & the Professions. 2nd ed. LC 79-11756. 448p. 1979. 24.95 (ISBN 0-471-05036-9). Wiley.

Harries, Elizabeth W., et al. Writing Papers: A Handbook for Students at Smith College. 2nd ed. 52p. (Orig.). 1980. pap. 1.00 (ISBN 0-87391-018-4). Smith Coll.

Morrison, Leger & Birt, Robert F. Illustrated Guide for Term Papers, Reports, Theses, & Dissertations: With Index & Rules for Punctuation & for Expression of Numbers. (Illus.). ix, 102p. 1971. pap. text ed. 3.85 (ISBN 0-686-38130-0). Morrison Pub Co.

Sussams, John. How To Write Effective Reports. 160p. 1983. 19.95 (ISBN 0-89397-145-6). Nichols Pub.

REPORTERS AND REPORTING

see also Government and the Press; Journalism; Journalists; Note-Taking; Press; Sports Journalism

Lovell, Ronald P. Reporting Public Affairs: Problems & Solutions. 432p. 1982. text ed. 18.95X (ISBN 0-534-01126-8). Wadsworth Pub.

REPORTS, SCIENTIFIC

see Technical Reports

REPORTS, TECHNICAL

see Technical Reports

REPRESENTATION

see Representative Government and Representation

REPRESENTATIONS OF GROUPS

Gelfand, I. M. Representation Theory: Selected Papers. LC 82-4440. (London Mathematical Society Lecture Notes Ser. 69). 330p. 1982. pap. 29.95 (ISBN 0-521-28981-5). Cambridge U Pr.

REPRESENTATIVE GOVERNMENT AND REPRESENTATION

see also Apportionment (Election Law); Constitutions; Democracy; Election Districts; Elections; Legislative Bodies; Pressure Groups; Suffrage

Berghe, Guido V. Political Rights for European Citizens. 245p. (Orig.). 1982. text ed. 38.00 (ISBN 0-566-00524-7). Gower Pub Ltd.

Kann, Mark E., ed. The Future of American Democracy: Views from the Left. 1983. write for info. (ISBN 0-87722-288-6). Temple U Pr.

Mallory, Walter H. Political Handbook of the World: Parliaments, Parties & Press as of January 1, 1931. 1931. text ed. 49.50x (ISBN 0-686-83706-1). Elliots Bks.

Marshall, Edmund. Parliament & the Public. 150p. 1982. 15.00x (ISBN 0-8448-1454-7). Crane-Russak Co.

Pole, J. R. The Gift of Government: Political Responsibility from the English Restoration to American Independence. LC 82-13533. (The Richard B. Russell Lecture Ser.: No. 1). 216p. 1983. 16.00 (ISBN 0-8203-0652-5). U of Ga Pr.

Representative Institutions in Theory & Practice. 217p. 1970. write for info. P Lang Pubs.

Smith, Gordon. Democracy in Western Germany: Parties & Politics in the Federal Republic. 2nd ed. 180p. (Orig.). 1983. pap. text ed. 8.50x (ISBN 0-686-82618-3). Holmes & Meier.

Studies Presented to the International Commission for the History of Representative & Parliamentary Institutions. 68p. 1967. write for info. P Lang Pubs.

REPRESSION (PSYCHOLOGY)

Lauer, Hans E. Aggression & Repression in the Individual & Society. Castelliz, K. & Davies, Saunders, trs. from Ger. 111p. 1981. pap. 7.95 (ISBN 0-85440-359-0, Pub. by Steinerbooks). Anthroposophic.

REPRODUCTION

see also Cells; Embryology; Fertility; Fetus; Genetics; Menstruation; Plants–Reproduction; Pregnancy; Sex; Sterility

Alternative Ways of Life: An Approach From the Viewpoint of the Reproduction - Change Theory. 18p. 1982. pap. 5.00 (ISBN 92-808-0451-0, TUNU 199, UNU). Unipub.

Fromer, Margot J. Ethical Issues in Sexuality & Reproduction. 320p. 1983. pap. text ed. 13.95 (ISBN 0-8016-1708-1). Mosby.

Greep, Roy O., ed. Reproductive Physiology IV. (International Review of Physiology Ser.: Vol. 27). 1983. text ed. 49.50 (ISBN 0-8391-1555-5, 14206). Univ Park.

Hafez, E. S. & Kenemans, P. An Atlas of Human Reproduction: By Scanning Electron Microscopy. 300p. 1982. text ed. 60.00 (ISBN 0-85200-411-7, Pub. by MTP Pr England). Kluwer Boston.

Mattison, Donald R., ed. Reproductive Toxicology. LC 83-927. (Progress in Clinical & Biological Research Ser.: Vol. 117). 408p. 1983. 58.00 (ISBN 0-8451-0117-X). A R Liss.

Nisbet, Ian C. & Karch, Nathan J. Chemical Hazards to Human Reproduction. LC 82-14441. (Illus.). 245p. 1983. 28.00 (ISBN 0-8155-0931-6). Noyes.

Vandenbergh, John G., ed. Pheromones & Reproduction in Mammals. LC 82-22776. Date not set. price not set (ISBN 0-12-710780-0). Acad Pr.

REPTILES

see also Lizards; Snakes; Turtles

Arnold & Burton. A Field Guide to Reptiles & Amphibians of Britain & Europe. 29.95 (ISBN 0-686-42777-7, Collins Pub England). Greene.

Ballinger, Royce E. & Lynch, John D. How to Know the Amphibians & Reptiles. (Pictured Key Nature Ser.). 300p. 1983. write for info. wire coil (ISBN 0-697-04786-5). Wm C Brown.

Gans, C. & Pough, F. H., eds. Biology of the Reptilia, Vol. 13. 360p. Date not set. 75.00 (ISBN 0-12-274613-9). Acad Pr.

The IUCN Amphibia-Reptillia Red Data Book, Pt. 1. 426p. 1983. 20.00 (ISBN 2-88032-601-X, IUCN 109, IUCN). Unipub.

McGowan, Christopher. The Successful Dragons: A Natural History of Extinct Reptiles. (Illus.). 282p. 1983. 29.95 (ISBN 0-88866-618-7). Samuel Stevens.

Nussbaum, Ronald A. & Brodie, Edmund D., Jr. Amphibians & Reptiles of the Pacific Northwest. LC 82-60055. (Illus.). 1983. 19.95 (ISBN 0-89301-086-3). U Pr of Idaho.

Palmer, Jean. Reptiles & Amphibians. (Blandford Pet Handbooks Ser.). 96p. 1983. 7.50 (ISBN 0-686-43144-8, Pub. by Blandford Pr England). Sterling.

Spellerberg, Ian F. Biology of Reptiles. 1982. 39.95x (ISBN 0-412-00161-6, Pub. by Chapman & Hall England); pap. 21.00x (ISBN 0-412-00171-3, Pub. by Chapman & Hall England). Methuen Inc.

REPUBLICAN PARTY

Reinhard, David W. The Republic Right Since 1945. LC 82-40460. 304p. 1983. 25.00x (ISBN 0-8131-1484-5). U Pr of Ky.

Wilcox, Laird M. Directory of the American Right: Supplement, 1983. 1983. pap. 5.95 (ISBN 0-933592-27-2). Edit Res Serv.

REPUBLICANISM IN FRANCE

Bagelon, Bruce S. Defending the Commonwealth: Catalogue of the Militia Exhibit at the Will Penn Memorial Museum in Harrisburg, PA. (Illus.). 28p. 1980. pap. 4.00 (ISBN 0-917218-14-0). Mowbray Co.

RESEARCH

see also Advertising Research; Aeronautical Research; Agricultural Research; Astronautical Research; Biological Research; Cardiovascular Research; Communication in Science; Dental Research; Economic Research; Educational Research; Entomological Research; Experimental Design; Financial Research; Geographical Research; Geological Research; Geophysical Research; High Pressure Research; Historical Research; Information Services; Intelligence Service; Legal Research; Literary Research; Marketing Research; Medical Research; Methodology; Military Research; Municipal Research; Nursing Research; Nutrition–Research; Oceanographic Research; Operations Research; Organizational Research; Psychiatric Research; Psychical Research; Psychological Research; Recreation Research; Report Writing; Research, Industrial; Research and Development Contracts; Sex Research; Social Science Research; Social Science Research; Sociological Research; Universities and Colleges–Graduate Work also subdivision Research under certain subjects, e.g. Nutrition–Research

Ballard, J. G. Re-Search: J. G. Ballard. Vale, V., ed. (Re-Search Ser.). (Illus.). 96p. 1983. pap. 6.95 (ISBN 0-940642-08-5). Re-Search Prods.

Centre National de la Recherce Scientifique, ed. Annuaire Francais de Droit International, Vol. XXVII (1981) LC 57-28515. 1206p. (Fr.). 1982. 125.00x (ISBN 2-222-03121-4). Intl Pubns Serv.

Ferre, John P. Merrill Guide to the Research Paper. 1983. pap. text ed. 7.95 (ISBN 0-675-20029-6). Additional supplements may be obtained from publisher. Merrill.

Granstrand, Ove. Technology, Management & Marketing. LC 82-16804. 300p. 1982. 25.00x (ISBN 0-312-79007-4). St Martin.

Information Gatekeepers, Inc. The Second Viewtext Exposition VT'82. 1981. 125.00 (ISBN 0-686-38471-7). Info Gatekeepers.

Leedy, Paul D. How to Read Research & Understand It. 1981. write for info. (ISBN 0-02-369250-2). Macmillan.

Lindberg, John. Routines for Research: A Handbook of Basic Library Skills. LC 82-15962. 172p. 1983. lib. bdg. 20.75 (ISBN 0-8191-2750-7); pap. text ed. 10.00 (ISBN 0-8191-2751-5). U Pr of Amer.

Meyer, Gerd. Strukturinterne und Umstrukturierende Neuerungen Dargestellt Am Beispiel der Forschung. 339p. (Ger.). 1982. write for info. (ISBN 3-261-04998-7). P Lang Pubs.

Noltingk, B. Art of Research. 1965. 8.00 (ISBN 0-444-40424-4). Elsevier.

Rudman, Jack. Director of Research & Evaluation. (Career Examination Ser.: C-2891). (Cloth bdg. avail. on request). pap. 14.00 (ISBN 0-8373-2891-8). Natl learning.

--Research Worker. (Career Examination Ser.: C-546). (Cloth bdg. avail. on request). pap. 10.00 (ISBN 0-8373-0546-2). Natl Learning.

Stepan, Nancy. The Idea of Race in Science: Great Britain 1800-1960. 1982. lib. bdg. 27.50 (ISBN 0-208-01972-3). Shoe String.

Thomas, Robert C. & Watkins, Michelle, eds. Research Centers Directory. 8th ed. 1200p. 1983. 200.00x (ISBN 0-8103-0458-9). Gale.

RESEARCH–JUVENILE LITERATURE

Carrol, F. Nosie the Research Hound. 50p. Date not set. pap. 7.95. Biblio Pr GA.

Petreshene, Susan S. Research Pleasers. Sussman, Ellen, ed. (Illus., Orig.). (gr. 3-6). 1982. pap. text ed. 5.95 (ISBN 0-933606-19-2, MS-618). Monkey Sisters.

--Research Teasers. Sussman, Ellen, ed. (Illus., Orig.). (gr. 3-6). 1982. pap. text ed. 5.95 (ISBN 0-933606-18-4, MS-617). Monkey Sisters.

RESEARCH–AUSTRALIA

Lance, Robert. Directory of CSIRO Research Programs 1982. 496p. 1983. pap. 18.95 (ISBN 0-686-84838-1, Pub. by CSIRO Australia). Intl Schol Bk Serv.

RESEARCH, AERONAUTICAL

see Aeronautical Research

RESEARCH, ASTRONAUTICAL

see Astronautical Research

RESEARCH, ENTOMOLOGICAL

see Entomological Research

RESEARCH, INDUSTRIAL

see also Aeronautical Research; Inventions; Marketing Research; New Products

Gambino, Anthony J. & Gartenberg, Morris. Industrial R & D Management. 132p. pap. 12.95 (ISBN 0-86641-028-7, 78109). Natl Assn Accts.

Research & Development Systems in Rural Settings: Background on the Project. 85p. 1982. pap. 5.00 (ISBN 92-808-0363-8, TUNU207, UNU). Unipub.

RESEARCH, INDUSTRIAL–MANAGEMENT

Fusfeld, Herbert I. & Langlois, Richard N., eds. Understanding R&D Productivity. 200p. 19.50 (ISBN 0-686-84787-3). Work in Amer.

RESEARCH, MEDICAL

see Medical Research

RESEARCH, MILITARY

see Military Research

RESEARCH, MUSICAL

see Musicology

RESEARCH, PSYCHOLOGICAL

see Psychological Research

RESEARCH AND DEVELOPMENT CONTRACTS

Boggio, G. & Gallimore, R., eds. Evaluation of Research & Development. 1982. lib. bdg. 24.50 (ISBN 90-277-1425-8, Pub. by Reidel Holland). Kluwer Boston.

RESEARCH BUILDINGS

see Laboratories

RESEARCH GRANTS

Gerstenfeld, Arthur, ed. Science Policy Perspectives U. S. A. The U. S. & Japan (Symposium) LC 82-18159. 1982. 29.00 (ISBN 0-12-281280-8). Acad Pr.

RESEARCH REPORTS

see Report Writing

RESERVOIRS

see also Flood Dams and Reservoirs; Irrigation

Grant, Malcolm A., et al. Geothermal Reservoir Engineering. LC 82-4105. (Energy Science & Technology Ser.). Date not set. 45.00 (ISBN 0-12-295620-6). Acad Pr.

Greene, J. R. The Creation of Quabbin Reservoir: Death of the Swift River Valley. 2nd. Ed ed. (Illus.). 123p. 1982. pap. 9.95 (ISBN 0-9609404-0-5). J R Greene.

Toebes, G. H. & Sheppard, A., eds. Reservoir Systems Operations. LC 81-70788. 600p. 1982. pap. text ed. 40.00 (ISBN 0-87262-288-6). Am Soc Civil Eng.

RESIDENCES

see Architecture, Domestic; Dwellings

RESIDENT PHYSICIANS

see Hospitals–Staff

RESIDENTIAL CONSTRUCTION

see House Construction

RESIDENTIAL SECURITY

see Burglary Protection

RESIDUES OF AGRICULTURAL CHEMICALS

see Spraying and Dusting Residues in Agriculture

RESINS

see Gums and Resins

RESISTANCE MOVEMENTS (WORLD WAR, 1939-1945)

see World War, 1939-1945–Underground Movements

RESISTANCE OF MATERIALS

see Strength of Materials

RESISTANCE TO DRUGS IN MICRO-ORGANISMS

see Drug Resistance in Micro-Organisms

RESISTANCE TO GOVERNMENT

see Government, Resistance To

RESISTANCE WELDING

see Electric Welding

RESONANCE, MAGNETIC

see Magnetic Resonance

RESORTS

see also Health Resorts, Watering-Places, etc.

Payne, Daniel H. A Guide to Resort Time Sharing. Friedman, Robert S., ed. LC 82-19798. 300p. (Orig.). 1983. pap. 7.95 (ISBN 0-89865-274-X). Donning Co.

Rankin, Jake & Rankin, Marni. The Getaway Guide IV: Short Vacations in Southern California. LC 82-19060. (Illus.). 248p. (Orig.). 1983. pap. 9.95 (ISBN 0-686-43071-9). Pacific Search.

--The Getaway Guide 0778997xx: Short Vacations in the Pacific Northwest. revised ed. LC 82-18784. (2nd). 223p. 1983. pap. 9.95 (ISBN 0-686-43073-5). Pacific Search.

RESOURCE MANAGEMENT

see Conservation of Natural Resources

Davidson, J. A., intro. by. Resource Developments in the Eighties. (Chemeca Ser.). 338p. (Orig.). 1982. pap. text ed. 54.00x (ISBN 0-85825-169-8, Pub. by Inst Engineering Australia). Renouf.

RESOURCE RECOVERY

see Recycling (Waste, etc.)

RESOURCES, MARINE

see Marine Resources

RESOURCES, NATURAL

see Natural Resources

RESPIRATION

see also Anoxemia; Pulmonary Function Tests; Respiratory Organs; Yoga, Hatha

Diamond, John. Speech, Language & the Power of Breath in Behavioral Kinesiology. (Behavioral Kinesiology Ser.). 85p. 1983. pap. 47.50 (ISBN 0-911238-77-8). Regent House.

Haldane, John S. Organisms & Enviorment as Illustrated by the Physiology of Breathing. 1917. text ed. 32.50x (ISBN 0-686-83659-6). Elliots Bks.

Hempfling, W. P., ed. Microbial Respiration. LC 78-22097. (Benchmark Papers in Microbiology: Vol. 13). 337p. 1979. 43.00 (ISBN 0-87933-344-8). Hutchinson Ross.

Hu Bing. A Brief Introduction to the Science of Breathing Exercise. (Illus.). 89p. 1981. pap. 6.95 (ISBN 0-686-42861-7). China Bks.

Macklem, Peter T., ed. Current Concepts in Pulmonary Function & Therapy. (Illus.). 77p. (Orig.). 1979. pap. text ed. 6.00 (ISBN 0-910133-05-0). MA Med Soc.

Schlaefke, M. E., et al, eds. Central Neurone Environment & the Control Systems of Breathing & Circulation. (Proceedings in Life Sciences Ser.). 275p. 1982. 35.00 (ISBN 0-387-11671-0). Springer-Verlag.

RESPIRATION OF PLANTS

see Plants–Respiration

RESPIRATORY DISEASES

see Respiratory Organs–Diseases

RESPIRATORY FUNCTION TESTS

see Pulmonary Function Tests

RESPIRATORY INSUFFICIENCY

Epstein, Jerome & Gaines, John. Clinical Respiratory Care of the Adult Patient. (Illus.). 448p. 1983. pap. text ed. 21.95 (ISBN 0-89303-209-3). R J Brady.

RESPIRATORY ORGANS

see also Lungs; Respiration; Trachea

Prakash, O. Applied Physiology in Clinical Respiratory Care. 1982. 76.00 (ISBN 90-247-2662-X, Pub. by Martinus Nijhoff Netherlands). Kluwer Boston.

Teresinski, Michael F. & Cheremisinoff, Paul N. Industrial Respiratory Protection. LC 82-72859. (Illus.). 200p. 1983. 27.50 (ISBN 0-250-40587-3). Ann Arbor Science.

RESPIRATORY ORGANS–DISEASES

Van Furth, R. Developments in Antibiotic Treatment of Respiratory Infections. 1982. 39.50 (ISBN 90-247-2493-7, Pub by Martinus Nijhoff Netherlands). Kluwer Boston.

RESPONSIBILITY

see also Free Will and Determinism

Eyre, Linda & Eyre, Richard. Teaching Children Responsibility. LC 82-12842. (Illus.). 247p. 1982. 7.95 (ISBN 0-87747-918-6). Deseret Bk..

Responsibility or A Love Letter to My Son, the Hostage from His Father, the Political Prisoner. (Analysis Ser.: No. 8). 1982. pap. 10.00 (ISBN 0-686-42843-9). Inst Analysis.

RESPONSIBILITY (LAW)

see Liability (Law)

RESPONSIBILITY, CRIMINAL

see Criminal Liability

RESPONSIBILITY, LEGAL

see Liability (Law)

RESTAURANT MANAGEMENT

Brown, Douglas R. The Restaurant Managers Handbook: How to Set up, Operate, & Manage a Finacially Successful Restaurant. Montgomery, Robert, ed. LC 82-72992. (Illus.). 326p. text ed. 49.95 (ISBN 0-910627-00-2). Atlantic Pub FL.

Miller, Daniel. Starting a Small Restaurant: A Guide to Excellence in the Purveying of Public Victuals. 2nd, Rev. ed. 224p. (Orig.). 1983. 12.95; pap. 8.95 (ISBN 0-916782-37-9). Harvard Common Pr.

RESTAURANTS, LUNCHROOMS, ETC.

see also Hotels, Taverns, etc.; Restaurant Management also names of restaurants; subdivisions Description or Description–Guidebooks under names of cities

Lesberg, Sandy. The Master Chefs Institute Guide to Dining Out in America. 1982. pap. 9.95 (ISBN 0-452-25378-0, Z5378, Plume). NAL.

Naxon, Jan L. & Rosenthal, Beth E. Dallas Entrees: A Restaurant Guide & Celebrity Cookbook (with a Primer to California Wines) 144p. (Orig.). 1982. pap. 5.95 (ISBN 0-910163-00-6). Artichoke Pub.

Ninemeier, Jack D. Purchasing, Receiving & Storage: Operational Manual for Restaurants, Hotels & Institutions. 360p. 1983. 3 ring binder 64.95 (ISBN 0-8436-2261-X). CBI Pub.

Quinn, James. But Never Eat on a Saturday Night: Behind the Scenes in All Kinds of Great American Restaurants. LC 82-45449. 216p. 1983. pap. 6.95 (ISBN 0-385-18220-1, Anch). Doubleday.

San Francisco: On the Go Restaurant Guides. (Illus., Orig.). 1982. pap. 7.95 (ISBN 0-89416-003-6). Travel World.

Schuhholz, Annaliese & Diekmann, Jens. Romantik Hotels & Restaurants: Multilingual Guide. Rev. ed. (Illus.). 170p. 1983. pap. 5.95 (ISBN 0-912944-73-0). Berkshire Traveller.

Shurtleff, William & Aoyagi, Akiko. Using Tofu, Tempeh & Other Soyfoods in Restaurants, Delis & Cafeterias. (Soyfoods Production Ser.: No. 5). 135p. (Orig.). 1982. pap. text ed. 32.95 spiral bound (ISBN 0-933332-07-6). Soyfoods Center.

RESTAURANTS, LUNCHROOMS, ETC.–GREAT BRITAIN

British Tourist Authority. Hotels & Restaurants in Britain, 1982-3. LC 52-21171. (Illus.). 600p. 1982. pap. 10.00x (ISBN 0-7095-0897-2). Intl Pubns Serv.

Eat Out for Around Five Pounds. 288p. 1983. pap. 8.95 (ISBN 0-86145-143-0, Pub. by Auto Assn-British Tourist Authority England). Merrimack Bk Serv.

A Guide to London's Best Restaurants. 240p. 1983. pap. 6.95 (ISBN 0-907080-48-0, Pub. by Auto Assn-British Tourist Authority England). Merrimack Bk Serv.

Hotels & Restaurants in Britain. 608p. 1983. pap. 12.95 (ISBN 0-686-38449-0, Pub. by Auto Assn-British Tourist Authority England). Merrimack Bk Serv.

London Hotels & Restaurants. 154p. 1983. pap. 3.95 (ISBN 0-7095-1292-9, Pub. by Auto Assn-British Tourist Authority England). Merrimack Bk Serv.

RESTAURANTS, LUNCHROOMS, ETC.–UNITED STATES

Armentani, Andy & Donatelli, Gary. The Monday Night Football Cookbook & Restaurant Guide. LC 82-71965. (Illus.). 176p. 1982. pap. 9.95 (ISBN 0-8019-7270-1). Chilton.

Cudworth, Marsha & Michaels, Howard. Victorian Holidays: A Guide to Guesthouses, Bed & Breakfast Inns & Restaurants of Cape May, N. J. 2nd rev. & enlarged ed. LC 82-83816. 125p. (Orig.). pap. 6.95 (ISBN 0-9608554-1-6). Lady Raspberry.

DeLuca, Michael & Michaelides, Stephen. Dining In--Cleveland. (Dining In--Ser.). (Illus.). 190p. 1982. pap. 8.95 (ISBN 0-89716-034-7). Peanut Butter.

Garvan, Jurga. Best Restaurants Northern New England. (Best Restaurants Ser.). (Illus.). 200p. 1982. pap. 4.95 (ISBN 0-89286-213-0). One Hund One Prods.

Gleason, Gayle, photos by. New York Restaurant Calendar 1983. (Illus.). 14p. 1982. 9.95 (ISBN 0-943998-00-X). Lake End.

Grad, Laurie B. Dining In--Los Angeles. (Dining In--Ser.). (Illus.). 190p. 1982. pap. 8.95 (ISBN 0-89716-121-1). Peanut Butter.

Gregorakis, Karen & Lotskar, Elaine. Dining In--Seattle, Vol. III. (Dining In--Ser.). 210p. 1982. pap. 8.95 (ISBN 0-89716-112-2). Peanut Butter.

Heckens, Gertrude & Friedman, Lynne. Lunching in Chicago. (Illus.). 1983. pap. 7.95 (ISBN 0-89651-426-9). Icarus.

Hurshell, Jennifer, ed. Aspen Epicure. (Epicure Ser.). 1982. pap. 2.95 (ISBN 0-89716-116-5). Peanut Butter.

Ingram, Marilyn W. & Folse, Lois J. Dining In--Dallas. (Dining In--Ser.). 200p. 1982. pap. 8.95 (ISBN 0-89716-113-0). Peanut Butter.

Moss, Lydia & Conway, Madeleine. Gourmet to Go: The New York Guide to Dining out at Home. 290p. (Orig.). 1982. pap. 5.95 (ISBN 0-9609862-0-0). MC Prods.

Nankin, Michael & Korvetz, Elliot. Fantastic Dives: A Guide to LA's Best Hole-In-the-Wall Dining. Raphalion, Robin, ed. (Illus.). 128p. 1982. pap. text ed. 6.95 (ISBN 0-87477-228-1). J P Tarcher.

Reingold, Carmel B. California Cuisine. 192p. 1983. pap. 5.95 (ISBN 0-380-82156-7, 82156). Avon.

Sheldon Landwehr & Associates. Who's Who in America's Restaurants: New York & Eastern States Limited, 1983 Ed. Landwehr, Sheldon, ed. (Illus.). 220p. 1983. 129.50 (ISBN 0-910297-00-2). Whos Who Rest.

Shins, Susan. Food by Phone: Manhattan's Best Meals & Munchies Delivered to Your Door. 256p. 1983. pap. 8.95 (ISBN 0-517-54923-9). Crown.

Stern, Jane & Stern, Michael. Goodfood: The Adventurous Eaters Guide to Restaurants Serving America's Best Regional Specialties. LC 82-48729. 1983. 17.95 (ISBN 0-394-52448-9); pap. 8.95 (ISBN 0-394-71392-3). Knopf.

Thwaite, Jean & Smith, Susan. Chef's Secrets from Great Restaurants in California. (Chef's Secrets Cookbooks Ser.). (Illus.). 270p. 1983. 11.95 (ISBN 0-939944-24-3). Marmac Pub.

--Chef's Secrets from Great Restaurants in Louisiana: 1984 World Exposition Edition. (Chef's Secrets Cookbooks Ser.). (Illus.). 270p. 1983. 11.95 (ISBN 0-939944-25-1). Marmac Pub.

--Chef's Secrets from Great Restaurants in Pennsylvania. (Chef's Secrets Cookbooks Ser.). (Illus.). 270p. 1983. 11.95 (ISBN 0-939944-26-X). Marmac Pub.

Tolf, Robert. Discover Fort Lauderdale's Top Twelve Restaurants. (Florida Keepsake Ser.: No. 2). (Illus.). 28p. 3.00 (ISBN 0-686-84230-8). Banyan Bks.

Waldemar, Carla. Dining In--Minneapolis-St. Paul, Vol. II. (Dining In--Ser.). 210p. 1982. pap. 8.95 (ISBN 0-89716-120-3). Peanut Butter.

Weiner, Neal O. & Schwartz, David M. The Interstate Gourmet: California & the Pacific Northwest, Vol. 3. (Illus.). 288p. 1983. pap. 5.95 (ISBN 0-671-44994-X). Summit Bks.

--The Interstate Gourmet: Mid-Atlantic States, Vol. 2. (Illus.). 256p. 1983. pap. 5.95 (ISBN 0-671-44993-1). Summit Bks.

RESTORATION, 1660-1688
see Great Britain-History-Restoration, 1660-1688

RESTORATION OF BOOKS
see Books-Conservation and Restoration

RESTORATION OF BUILDINGS
see Architecture-Conservation and Restoration

RESTORATION OF FURNITURE
see Furniture-Repairing; Furniture Finishing

RESTORATION OF MANUSCRIPTS
see Manuscripts-Conservation and Restoration

RESTORATIVE DENTISTRY
see Dentistry, Operative

RESTRAINT OF ANIMALS
see Animals, Treatment Of

RESUMES (EMPLOYMENT)

Bostwick, Burdette E. Resume Writing: A Comprehensive How-to-Do-It Guide. 2nd ed. LC 80-18100. 314p. 1982. pap. 7.95 (ISBN 0-471-09943-0, Pub. by Wiley-Interscience). Wiley.

Coxford, Lola M. Resume Writing Made Easy. 124p. 1982. pap. 4.95 (ISBN 0-686-84489-0). Gorsuch Scarisbrick.

Croft, Barbara L. The Checklist Kit for Resume Writing & Job Application Letters. 16p. 1982. 3.50 (ISBN 0-9609580-0-2). Different Drum.

Ulrich, Heinz. How to Prepare Your Own High Intensity Resume. newly rev. combined ed. 224p. 1983. 16.95 (ISBN 0-13-430603-1); pap. 7.95 (ISBN 0-13-430595-7). P-H.

RESURRECTION
see also Future Life; Jesus Christ-Resurrection

Gresham, Charles R. What the Bible Says about Resurrection. (What the Bible Says Ser.). 350p. 1983. 13.50 (ISBN 0-89900-090-8). College Pr Pub.

RETAIL ADVERTISING
see Advertising

RETAIL FRANCHISES
see Franchises (Retail Trade)

RETAIL STORES
see Stores, Retail

RETAIL TRADE
see also Advertising; Cashiers; Central Business Districts; Display of Merchandise; Franchises (Retail Trade); Grocery Trade; Packaging; Salesmen and Salesmanship; Shopping; Shopping Centers; Store Location; Stores, Retail; Telephone Selling; Wholesale Trade

Bush, Ronald F. Retailing Simulation. 160p. 1983. pap. text ed. 8.50 scp (ISBN 0-06-041105-8, HarpC); instr's. manual avail. (ISBN 0-06-361070-1); tape or deck avail. Har-Row.

Johnson, Kenneth M. Population & Retail Services in Nonmetropolitan America. (Rural Studies). 350p. 1983. softcover 25.00x (ISBN 0-86531-584-1). Westview.

Perry, Phillip M. Retailer's Complete Guide to Bigger Sales-Lower Costs-Higher Profits. LC 82-878. (Illus.). 265p. (Orig.). 1982. pap. 34.50 (ISBN 0-87624-509-2). Inst Busn Plan.

Potter, Robert B. The Urban Retailing System: Location, Cognition & Behaviour. 247p. 1982. text ed. 37.00x (ISBN 0-566-00458-5). Gower Pub Ltd.

Report of the Special Committee on Soliciation. 1981. pap. 1.75 (ISBN 0-686-84311-8). Am Inst CPA.

RETAIL TRADE-DIRECTORIES

Britain's Top Five Hundred Motor Distributors. 70p. 1982. 195.00x (ISBN 0-85938-165-X, Pub. by Jordan & Sons England). State Mutual Bk.

Carrol, Freida. Directory of Factory Outlet Directories. 50p. 1983. pap. text ed. 12.95 (ISBN 0-939476-91-6). Biblio Pr GA.

RETAIL TRADE-MANAGEMENT

Arnold, Danny R., et al. Strategic Retail Management. LC 82-8852. 752p. Date not set. text ed. 23.95 (ISBN 0-686-82088-6); instrs' manual avail. A-W.

Carter, R. J. Stores Management. 250p. 1982. pap. text ed. 12.95x (ISBN 0-7121-1979-5). Intl Ideas.

Gallegue, B. F. Service Management in the Retail Motor Industry. 160p. 1982. pap. & Cases. 38.00x (Pub. by Heinemann England). State Mutual Bk.

Gillespie, K. & Hecht, J. C. Retail Business Management: Applications & Cases. 3rd ed. 128p. 1983. 7.95x (ISBN 0-07-023229-6). McGraw.

Gillespie, Karen & Hecht, Joseph C. Retail Business Management. 3rd, rev. ed. LC 82-21700. (Illus.). 480p. 1983. text ed. 18.05x (ISBN 0-07-023228-8, G). McGraw.

RETAIL TRADE-GREAT BRITAIN

Britain's Top Five Hundred Motor Distributors. 70p. 1982. 195.00x (ISBN 0-85938-165-X, Pub. by Jordan & Sons England). State Mutual Bk.

Stores, Shops Hypermarkets: Retail Directory of the United Kingdom 1983. 37th ed. LC 56-37269. (Illus.). 1390p. 1981. 125.00x (ISBN 0-7079-6926-3). Intl Pubns Serv.

RETAIL TRADING AREAS
see Market Surveys

RETARDED CHILDREN
see Mentally Handicapped Children

RETARDED READERS
see Reading Disability

RETENTION (PSYCHOLOGY)
see Memory

RETICULO-ENDOTHELIAL GRANULOMAS
see Reticulo-Endothelial System

RETICULO-ENDOTHELIAL SYSTEM
see also Macrophages

Cohen, Nicholas & Sigel, Michael, eds. The Reticuloendothelial System: Phylogeny & Ontogeny of the RES. (Vol. 3). 750p. 1982. 89.50x (ISBN 0-306-40928-3, Plenum Pr). Plenum Pub.

Rose, Noel R. & Siegel, Benjamin, eds. The Reticuloendothelial System: A Comprehensive Treatise, Immunopathology, Vol. 4. 430p. 1982. 55.00x (ISBN 0-306-40979-8, Plenum Pr). Plenum Pub.

RETINA
see also Color Vision

Byer, Norman. The Peripheral Retina in Profile. (Illus.). 159p. 1982. incl. cassettes 295.00 (ISBN 0-9609428-0-7). Criterion Pr.

Drujan, Boris D. & Laufer, Miguel, eds. The S-Potential. LC 82-20394. (Progress in Clinical & Biological Research Ser.: Vol. 113). 319p. 1982. 60.00 (ISBN 0-8451-0113-7). A R Liss.

Gruen, Gerd. The Development of the Vertebrate Retina: A Comparative Survey. (Advances in Anatomy, Embryology, & Cell Biology Ser.: Vol. 78). (Illus.). 130p. 1982. pap. 24.00 (ISBN 0-387-11770-9). Springer-Verlag.

Osborne, N. O. & Chader, G. J., eds. Progress in Retinal Research, Vol. 1. (Illus.). 245p. 1982. 72.00 (ISBN 0-08-028901-0). Pergamon.

Van Nouhuys, C. Dominant Exudative Vitreoretinopathy & Other Vascular Disorders of the Peripheral Retina. 1982. 83.00 (ISBN 90-6193-805-8, Pub. by Junk Pubs Netherlands). Kluwer Boston.

RETINA-DISEASES

Cotlier, Edward & Maumenee, Irene H., eds. Genetic Eye Diseases: Retinitis Pigmentosa & Other Inherited Eye Disorders. LC 82-13049. (Birth Defects; Original Article Ser.: Vol. 18, No. 6). 746p. 1982. 76.00 (ISBN 0-8451-1050-0). A R Liss.

Fine, Stuart. Retinal Vascular & Macular Disorders. (Illus.). 390p. 1983. lib. bdg. price not set (ISBN 0-683-03212-7). Williams & Wilkins.

RETIREMENT
see also Aged; Retirement Income

Fogarty, Michael, ed. Retirement Policy: The Next Fifty Years, No. 5. (NIESR, PSI, RII A Joint Studies in Public Policy Ser.). viii, 216p. 1982. text ed. 28.00x (ISBN 0-435-83320-0). Heinemann Ed.

Grace, William J., Jr. The ABC'S of IRA'S: The Complete Guide to Individual Retirement Accounts. 1982. pap. 3.95 (ISBN 0-440-50398-1, Dell Trade Pbks). Dell.

Kemp, Fred & Buttle, Bernard. Looking Ahead: A Guide to Retirement. 128p. 1981. 19.00x (ISBN 0-7121-1250-2, Pub. by Macdonald & Evans). State Mutual Bk.

MFOA Committee on Public Employee Retirement Administration. Public Employee Retirement Administration. 134p. 1977. 15.00 (ISBN 0-686-84367-3). Municipal.

Nusberg, Charlotte, ed. Mandatory Retirement: Blessing or Curse? 27p. (Orig.). 1978. pap. text ed. 3.50 (ISBN 0-910473-06-4). Intl Fed Ageing.

Stadt, R. & Adams, J. M. Retirement: Planning Tomorrow Today. LC 82-14799. 192p. 1982. 7.95 (ISBN 0-07-000404-8, G). McGraw.

Sylliiasen, Alice. Retirement Living. 126p. pap. 6.95 (ISBN 0-910303-01-0). Writers Pub Serv.

Willing, Jules Z. The Reality of Retirement: The Inner Experience of Becoming a Retired Person. 1981. pap. 6.95 (ISBN 0-688-00394-X). Quill NY.

RETIREMENT, PLACES OF

Dickinson, Peter. Travel & Retirement Edens Abroad. (Illus.). 304p. 1983. 19.95 (ISBN 0-525-93274-7, 01840-550); pap. 12.95 (01258-370). Dutton.

RETIREMENT INCOME
see also Old Age Pensions

American Institute of Certified Public Accountants. International Accounting Standard Nineteen: Accounting for Retirement Benefits in the Financial Statements of Employers. 1983. write for info. Am Inst CPA.

Hardy, C. Colburn. You're Financially Secure Retirement. LC 82-47525. (Illus.). 288p. 1983. 14.37i (ISBN 0-06-015034-3, HarpT). Har-Row.

Salisbury, Dallas L., ed. Economic Survival in Retirement: Which Pension is for You? LC 82-13857. 148p. (Orig.). 1982. pap. 10.00 (ISBN 0-86643-027-X). Employee Benefit.

Social Security, Savings Plans & other Retirement Arrangements: Answers to Questions on Subject Matter, CEBS Course 3. 3rd ed. 104p. 1982. pap. 15.00 (ISBN 0-89154-182-9). Intl Found Employ.

Social Security, Savings Plans & Other Retirement Arrangements: Learning Guide, CEBS Course 3. 3rd ed. 1982. spiral binding 18.00 (ISBN 0-89154-181-0). Intl Found Employ.

Storey, James R. & Hendricks, Gary. Retirement Income Issues in an Aging Society. 60p. 1980. pap. text ed. 4.00 (ISBN 0-87766-267-3). Urban Inst.

Where to Retire on a Small Income. 1983. 5.95 (ISBN 0-686-42892-7). Harian.

RETIREMENT PENSIONS
see Old Age Pensions; Pensions

RETREATS
Here are entered works dealing with periods of retirement for the purpose of meditation and spiritual development.
see also Meditations; Spiritual Exercises

Capon, Robert F. The Youngest Day: Nature & Grace on Shelter Island. LC 82-48414. (Illus.). 160p. 1983. 11.49i (ISBN 0-06-061309-2, HarpR). Har-Row.

Rogers, Barbara. In the Center: The Story of a Retreat. LC 82-84468. 145p. (Orig.). 1983. pap. 4.95 (ISBN 0-87793-267-0). Ave Maria.

RETRIBUTION
see Future Life; Hell

RETRIEVERS
see also Dogs-Breeds, subdivided to specific types of retrievers, e.g. Dogs-Breeds-Labrador Dogs

Quinn, Tom. The Working Retrievers: Being an Illustrated Discourse on Retrievers; Their Selection, Breeding, Care & Handling, & New Information on Training Dogs for Hunting & Field Training. (Illus.). 256p. 1983. 24.95 (ISBN 0-525-93287-9, 02423-720). Dutton.

REUSABLE SPACE VEHICLES

Hawkes, Nigel. Space Shuttle. (Inside Story Ser.). (Illus.). 40p. (gr. 4 up). 1983. PLB 9.90 (ISBN 0-531-04583-8). Watts.

REUTHER, WALTER PHILIP, 1907-1970

Barnard, John. Walter Reuther & the Rise of the Auto Workers. 1983. 13.00i (ISBN 0-316-08141-8). Little.

REVELATION
see also Apocalyptic Literature

Abraham, William J. Divine Revelation & the Limits of Historical Criticism. 232p. 1982. 24.95x (ISBN 0-19-826665-0). Oxford U Pr.

Dodd, Carl. Dodd's Revelations. 20p. pap. 1.00 (ISBN 0-686-83983-8). Am Atheist.

Dulles, Avery. Models of Revelation. LC 82-45243. 360p. 1983. 16.95 (ISBN 0-385-17975-8). Doubleday.

REVELATIONS, MODERN
see Private Revelations

REVELATIONS, PRIVATE
see Private Revelations

REVENUE LAW
see Internal Revenue Law; Taxation-Law

REVENUE SHARING
see Intergovernmental Fiscal Relations; Intergovernmental Tax Relations

REVIEW, JUDICIAL
see Judicial Review

REVIEWS
see Books-Reviews; Theater-Reviews

REVIVAL (RELIGION)
see Evangelistic Work

REVIVAL OF LETTERS
see Renaissance

REVIVALISTS
see Evangelists

REVIVALS
see also Enthusiasm; Evangelistic Work; Jesus People; Retreats

Roberts, Richard O. Revival. 186p. 1982. pap. 5.95 (ISBN 0-8423-5575-8). Tyndale.

REVOLUTION, AMERICAN
see United States-History-Revolution, 1775-1783

REVOLUTION, FRENCH
see France-History-Revolution, 1789-1799

REVOLUTION OF 1848 IN HUNGARY
see Hungary-History

REVOLUTIONARY POETRY

Wald, Alan M. The Revolutionary Imagination: The Poetry & Politics of John Wheelwright & Sherry Mangan. LC 82-8498. 370p. 1983. 28.00x (ISBN 0-8078-1535-7). U of NC Pr.

REVOLUTIONARY WAR, AMERICAN
see United States-History-Revolution, 1775-1783

REVOLUTIONISTS

Blanchard, William H. Revolutionary Morality: Psychosexual Analysis of Twelve Revolutionists. c, 400p. (Orig.). (gr. 12). 1983. lib. bdg. 24.75 (ISBN 0-87436-032-3); pap. 14.75 (ISBN 0-87436-039-0). ABC Clio.

REVOLUTIONISTS-RUSSIA

Bergman, Jay. Vera Zasulich: A Biography. LC 82-80927. 288p. 1983. 28.50x (ISBN 0-8047-1156-9). Stanford U Pr.

Gleason, Abbott. Young Russia: The/Genesis of Russian Radicalism in the 1860s. LC 82-23875. xiv, 438p. 1983. pap. 10.95 (ISBN 0-226-29961-9). U of Chicago Pr.

REVOLUTIONS
see also Government, Resistance to; Peasant Uprisings; Revolutionists; Terrorism
also France-History-Revolution, 1789-1799; United States-History-Revolution, 1775-1783, and similar headings

Create Public Opinion, Seize Power. 1979. 0.50 (ISBN 0-686-82481-4). RCP Pubns.

Kamenkay, Eugene & Smith, F. B. Intellectuals & Revolution. 22.50 (ISBN 0-312-41893-0). St Martin.

Revolutionary Work in a Non-Revolutionary Situation: Report to the Second Plenary Session of the First Central Committee of the Revolutionary Communist Party, USA (1976) 70p. 1978. 1.00 (ISBN 0-686-82478-4). RCP Pubns.

Skarmeta, Antonio. La Insurreccion. 240p. (Span.). 1982. pap. 8.00 (ISBN 0-910061-05-X). Ediciones Norte.

Steinmiller, Oswald M. The Approaching Seven Major Political Revolutions Which Will Transform Radically the World. (Illus.). 137p. 1983. 77.85 (ISBN 0-86722-030-9). Inst Econ Pol.

Strategic Outlook & Alliances. Incl. Support Every Outbreak of Protest & Rebellion. 1981. 1.00 (ISBN 0-686-82463-6); Charting the Uncharted Course: Proletarian Revolution in the U. S. 1982. 0.50 (ISBN 0-686-82464-4); Coming From Behind to Make Revolution & Crucial Questions in Coming From Behind. 80p. 1981. 1.25 (ISBN 0-686-82465-2); You Can't Beat the Enemy While Raising His Flag. 1981. 0.50 (ISBN 0-686-82466-0); Party Chairman Replies to a Black Nationalist with Communistic Inclinations. Avakian, Bob. 1981. 1.00 (ISBN 0-686-82467-9); Break the Chains! Unleash the Fury of Women as a Mighty Force for Revolution. 1979. 1.00 (ISBN 0-686-82468-7). 5.00 (ISBN 0-686-82462-8). RCP Pubns.

Tocqueville, Alexis. Alexis de Tocqueville on Democracy, Revolution, & Society. Stone, John, et al, eds. LC 79-21204. (Heritage of Sociology Ser.). 392p. 1982. pap. 7.95 (ISBN 0-226-80527-1). U of Chicago Pr.

Wheatcroft, Andrew. The World Atlas of Revolution. 1983. write for info. (ISBN 0-671-46286-5). S&S.

REVOLVING SYSTEMS
see Rotational Motion

REVSON, CHARLES, 1906-1975

Tobias, Andrew. Fire & Ice: The Story of Charles Revson-the Man Who Built the Revlon Empire. (Illus.). 288p. 1983. pap. 6.95 (ISBN 0-688-01887-4). Quill NY.

REVUES
see Musical Revues, Comedies, etc.

REWARDS (PRIZES, ETC.)
see also Literary Prizes
also names of prizes e.g. Nobel Prizes-subdivision prizes under names of universities and subdivision competition under subjects, e.g. Art-Competitions

Avons Congratulations: Awards, Gifts & Prizes. (Illus.). 146p. 1972. 5.00 (ISBN 0-913772-02-X). Avons Res.

Donnelly, R. H., et al. Active Games & Contests. 2nd ed. 672p. 1958. 21.95 (ISBN 0-471-07088-2). Wiley.

Hilliard, Joseph. How to Unlock the Secrets of Winning & Good Luck. (Orig.). 1982. pap. 5.95x (ISBN 0-934650-02-0). Sunnyside.

REYNOLDS, BURT

Herman, Gary. Burt Reynolds: Flesh & Blood Fantasy. (Illus.). 144p. (Orig.). 1983. pap. 9.95 (ISBN 0-933328-64-8). Delilah Bks.

Resnick, Sylvia. Burt Reynolds: An Unauthorized Biography. (Illus.). 160p. 1983. 10.95 (ISBN 0-312-10876-1). St Martin.

RHEE, SYNGMAN, 1875-1965

Kim, Q. Y. The Fall of Syngman Rhee. (Korea Research Monographs: No. 7). (Illus.). 255p. (Orig.). 1982. pap. 12.00 (ISBN 0-912966-54-8). IEAS.

RHEOLOGY
see also Colloids; Deformations (Mechanics); Elasticity; Materials-Creep; Plasticity

Cantow, H. J., et al, eds. Synthesis & Degradation-Rheology & Extrusion. (Advances in Polymer Science: Vol. 47). (Illus.). 170p. 1982. 37.00 (ISBN 0-387-11774-1). Springer-Verlag.

Hull, Harry H. Addendum to an Approach to Rheology Through Multivariable Thermodynamics. 24p. 1982. pap. 4.00x (ISBN 0-686-83764-9). Hull.

--An Approach to Rheology Through Multi-Variable Thermodynamics. Rev. ed. 192p. 1982. text ed. 28.00 (ISBN 0-9606118-2-7). Hull.

--An Approach to Rheology Through Multivariable Thermodynamics: With Addendum. 192p. 1982. 28.00 (ISBN 0-9606118-2-7). Hull.

--An Approach to Rheology Through Multivariable Thermodynamics: Without Addendum. 158p. 1981. pap. 16.00 (ISBN 0-9606118-1-9). Hull.
Janeschitz-Kriegl, H. Polymer Melt Rheology & Flow Birefringence. (Polymers-Properties & Applications Ser.: Vol. 6). (Illus.). 524p. 1983. 41.00 (ISBN 0-387-11928-0). Springer-Verlag.
Walters, K. Rheometry. 1975. 45.00x (ISBN 0-412-12090-9, Pub. by Chapman & Hall England). Methuen Inc.

RHETORIC

see also Criticism; Debates and Debating; English Language-Rhetoric; Letter-Writing; Narration (Rhetoric); Oratory; Preaching; Public Speaking also subdivisions Composition and Exercises, and Rhetoric under names of languages; also figures of speech, e.g. Metaphor

Berman, Jan. Nonfiction Writing. (Learning Workbooks Language Arts). (gr. 4-6). pap. 1.50 (ISBN 0-8224-4181-0). Pitman.
--Paragraph Writing. (Learning Workbooks Language Arts). (gr. 4-6). pap. 1.50 (ISBN 0-8224-4180-2). Pitman.
Booth, Wayne C. The Rhetoric of Film. Rev. ed. 576p. 1982. pap. 9.95 (ISBN 0-226-06558-8). U of Chicago Pr.
Foster, David. A Primer for Writing Teachers: Theories, Theorists, Issues, Problems. 192p. (Orig.). 1983. pap. text ed. 8.50x (ISBN 0-86709-053-7). Boynton Cook Pubs.
Frankel, Lionel H. & McDonnell, Julian B. Commercial Transactions: Payment Systems. (Contemporary Legal Education Ser.). 322p. 1982. pap. text ed. 11.00 (ISBN 0-686-84215-4). Michie-Bobbs.
Gould. Reading into Writing: A Rhetoric-Reader-Handbook. pap. text ed. 15.95 (ISBN 0-686-84580-3, EN73); instr's. manual avail. (EN74). HM.
Graves, Richard, ed. Rhetoric & Composition: A Sourcebook for Teachers & Writers. 2nd, rev. ed. 384p. 1983. pap. text ed. 11.50x (ISBN 0-86709-029-4). Boynton Cook Pubs.
Hogins, James B. & Yarber, Robert E. Reading, Writing, & Rhetoric. 5th ed. 576p. 1983. pap. text ed. write for info. (ISBN 0-574-22080-1); write for info. instr's. guide (ISBN 0-574-22081-X). SRA.
Horner, Winifred B., ed. The Present State of Scholarship in Historical & Contemporary Rhetoric. LC 82-20002. 240p. 1983. text ed. 25.00x (ISBN 0-8262-0398-1). U of Mo Pr.
Kane, Thomas S. The Oxford Guide to Writing. Sommers, Nancy, ed. (Illus.). 650p. 1983. 14.95 (ISBN 0-19-503245-4). Oxford U Pr.
Lang, Berel. Philosophy & the Art of Writing: Studies in Philosophical & Literary Style. LC 81-65865. 248p. 1982. 28.50 (ISBN 0-8387-5030-3). Bucknell U Pr.
Levin, Gerald. Writing & Logic. 256p. (Orig.). 1982. pap. text ed. 8.95 (ISBN 0-15-597788-1); instructor's manual 3.95 (ISBN 0-15-597789-X). HarBraceJ.
Ryan, Halford. American Rhetoric from Roosevelt to Reagan: A Collection of Speeches & Critical Essays. 310p. (Orig.). 1983. pap. text ed. 10.95x (ISBN 0-88133-015-9). Waveland Pr.
Smith, Barbara H. On the Margins of Discourse: The Relation of Literature to Language. LC 78-18274. xviii, 226p. 1978. pap. 7.50 (ISBN 0-226-76453-2). U of Chicago Pr.
Stock, Patricia, ed. Forum: Essays on Theory & Practice in the Teaching of Writing. 384p. (Orig.). 1983. pap. text ed. 10.50x (ISBN 0-86709-089-8). Boynton Cook Pubs.

RHETORIC-1500-1800

Murphy, James J., ed. Renaissance Eloquence: Studies in the Theory and Practice of Renaissance Rhetoric. LC 81-13128. 528p. 1983. text ed. 27.50x (ISBN 0-520-04543-2). U of Cal Pr.
Sonnino, Lee A. A Handbook to Sixteenth Centruy Rhetoric. 278p. 1968. 22.75 (ISBN 0-7100-2935-7). Routledge & Kegan.

RHETORIC, ANCIENT

Kennedy, George A. Greek Rhetoric under Christian Emperors: A History of Rhetoric, Vol. III. LC 82-51044. 330p. 1983. 32.00x (ISBN 0-691-03565-2); pap. 11.50 (ISBN 0-691-10145-0). Princeton U Pr.

RHEUMATIC GOUT

see Rheumatoid Arthritis

RHEUMATIC HEART DISEASE

Bird, H. A. & Wright, V. Applied Drug Therapy of the Rheumatic Diseases. (Illus.). 324p. 1982. pap. 30.00 (ISBN 0-7236-0658-7). Wright-PSG.
Pieroni, Robert E. Rheumatology. 2nd ed. (Medical Examination Review: Vol. 31). 1983. pap. text ed. 23.00 (ISBN 0-87488-144-7). Med Exam.
Simkin, Peter A. Heart & Rheumatic Disease, Vol. 2. new ed. (BIMR Rheumatology Ser.). 320p. 1983. text ed. price not set (ISBN 0-407-02353-4). Butterworth.
Spiegel, Timothy M. Practical Rheumatology. 384p. 1983. 35.00 (ISBN 0-471-09567-2, Pub. by Wiley Med). Wiley.

RHEUMATISM

see also Arthritis; Rheumatoid Arthritis

Bacon, Paul & Hadler, Norton M. Kidney & Rheumatic Disease. (BIMR Rheumatology Ser.: Vol. I). 498p. 1982. text ed. 39.95 (ISBN 0-407-02352-6). Butterworth.
International Congress of Rheumatology, et al. Abstracts: Thirteenth Congress, Kyoto, Japan, 1977. Dixon, A., ed. (International Congress Ser.: No. 299). 1974. 16.00 (ISBN 0-444-15065-X). Elsevier.
Schattenkirchner, M. & Mueller, W., eds. Gold Therapy. (Rheumatology Ser.: Vol. 8). (Illus.). viii, 200p. 1983. 78.00 (ISBN 3-8055-3630-5). S Karger.
Wagenhauser, F. J. Principles of Antirheumatic Therapy. (Illus.). 46p. Date not set. pap. text ed. 9.50 (ISBN 3-456-81204-3, Pub. by Hans Huber Switzerland). J K Burgess.
Weintraub, A. Psychorheumatologie. (Illus.). viii, 92p. 1983. 11.50 (ISBN 3-8055-3628-3). S Karger.

RHEUMATOID ARTHRITIS

Benjamin, Alexander & Helal, Basil. Surgical Repair & Reconstruction in Rheumatoid Disease. 247p. 1980. 74.95x (ISBN 0-471-08291-0, Pub. by Wiley Med). Wiley.
Calin, Andre. Diagnosis & Management of Rheumatoid Arthritis in Primary Care. Date not set. 24.95 (ISBN 0-201-10810-0, Med-Nurse). A-W.

RHINE RIVER AND VALLEY

Rhine Valley Travel Guide. (Berlitz Travel Guides). (Illus.). 1982. pap. 4.95 (ISBN 0-02-969450-7, Berlitz). Macmillan.

RHINOCEROS

Elephants & Rhinos in Africa: A Time for Decision. 36p. 1983. pap. 10.00 (ISBN 2-88032-208-1, IUCN 113, IUCN). Unipub.
Martin, Esmond & Martin, Chryssee B. Run Rhino Run. 1983. 19.95 (ISBN 0-686-38875-5, Pub. by Chatto & Windus). Merrimack Bk Serv.

RHINOLOPHUS

see Bats

RHODE ISLAND-DESCRIPTION AND TRAVEL

Conley, Patrick T. Rhode Island Profile. (Illus.). 60p. (Orig.). 1983. pap. 2.95 (ISBN 0-917012-40-2). RI Pubns Soc.
Vauclair, Marguerite. Guest Houses, Bed & Breakfasts, Inns & Hotels in Newport, R. I. Peeples, Bill, ed. LC 82-90154. (Illus.). 1982. pap. 3.75x (ISBN 0-9608536-0-X). Port Quarters.

RHODE ISLAND-GENEALOGY

Wakefield, Robert S. & Sherman, Ruth W. Index to Wills in R. I. Genealogical Register. 64p. (Orig.). 1982. pap. 4.00x (ISBN 0-910233-00-4). Plymouth Col.

RHODE ISLAND-HISTORY

Conley, Patrick T. The Blackstone Valley: A Sketch of Its River, Its Canal & Its People. 24p. 1983. pap. 2.75 (ISBN 0-917012-41-0). RI Pubns Soc.
--Rhode Island Constitutional Development, 1636-1775: A Survey. 35p. 1968. pap. 2.75 (ISBN 0-917012-42-9). RI Pubns Soc.
Millar, John F. Rhode Island: Forgotton Leader of the Revolutioary Era. (Illus.). 64p. (Orig.). 1975. 7.95 (ISBN 0-937550-02-7); pap. 3.95 (ISBN 0-937550-03-5). Providence Journ.

RHODES-ANTIQUITIES

Gates, Charles. From Cremation to Inhumation: Burial Practices at Ialysos & Kameiros During the Mid-Archaic Period, ca. 625-525 B.C. (Occasional Papers: No. 11). (Illus.). 1983. pap. text ed. 9.00 (ISBN 0-917956-39-7). UCLA Arch.
Mee, C. B. Rhodes in the Bronze Age. 160p. 1982. text ed. 60.00x (ISBN 0-85668-143-1, Pub. by Aris & Phillips England). Humanities.

RHODESIA, SOUTHERN-HISTORY

Peel, J. D. Y. & Ranger, T. O., eds. Past & Present in Zimbabwe. 128p. 1983. pap. 9.95 (ISBN 0-7190-0896-4). Manchester.

RHODODENDRON

Greer, Harold E. Greer's Guidebook to Available Rhododendrons, Species & Hybrids. LC 82-90128. (Illus.). 152p. 1982. pap. 12.95 (ISBN 0-910013-00-4). Offshoot Pub.

RHOPALOCERA

see Butterflies

RHYMING DICTIONARIES

see English Language-Rime-Dictionaries

RIBERA, JUSEPE DE, CALLED LO SPAGNOLETTO, 1588-1652

Du Gue Trapier, E. Ribera in the Collection. (Illus.). 1952. pap. 0.50 (ISBN 0-87535-073-9). Hispanic Soc.
Felton, Craig & Jordan, William B., eds. Jusepe de Ribera: Lo Spagnoletto (1591-1652) 246p. 1982. 50.00 (ISBN 0-912804-09-2, Dist by U of Wash Pr); pap. text ed. 24.95 (ISBN 0-912804-10-6). Kimbell Art.

RICE

see also Cookery (Rice)

Intergovernmental Group on Rice: Twenty-First Session, Committee on Commodity Problems. 14p. 1982. pap. 7.50 (ISBN 0-686-84612-5, F2328, FAO). Unipub.
An International Survey of Methods Used for Evaluation of the Cooking & Eating Qualities of Milled Rice. (IRRI Research Paper Ser.: No. 77). 28p. 1983. pap. 5.00 (ISBN 0-686-42853-6, R177, IRRI). Unipub.

RICE-DISEASES AND PESTS

Flint, Mary L., et al, eds. Integrated Pest Management for Rice. (Illus.). 85p. (Orig.). 1983. pap. text ed. 15.00x (ISBN 0-931876-61-3). Ag Sci Pubns.

RICE BREEDING

An Adventure in Applied Science: A History of the IRRI. 233p. 1983. pap. 25.75 (ISBN 0-686-84886-1, R 186, IRRI). Unipub.
Deepak, Adarsh & Rao, K. R. Remote Sensing Applications for Rice Production. (Illus.). Date not set. price not set (ISBN 0-937194-03-4). Spectrum Pr.
Evolution of the Gene Rotation Concept for Rice Blast Control. 130p. 1983. pap. 16.25 (ISBN 0-686-84887-X, R 187, IRRI). Unipub.
A Global Experiment in Agricultural Development. 24p. 1983. pap. 9.00 (ISBN 0-686-84896-9, R 176, IRRI). Unipub.
Growing Season Analyses for Rainfed Wetland Fields. (IRRI Research Paper Ser.: No. 73). 14p. 1982. pap. 5.00 (ISBN 0-686-82551-9, R175, IRRI). Unipub.
Insecticide Evaluation 1981. 141p. 1983. pap. 9.00 (ISBN 0-686-42854-4, R174, IRRI). Unipub.
The International Bibliography of Rice Research 1980 Supplement. 666p. 1981. pap. 140.50 (ISBN 0-686-84888-8, R 185, IRRI). Unipub.
Major Weeds of Rice in South & Southeast Asia. 79p. 1981. pap. 15.00 (ISBN 0-686-42859-5, R184, IRRI). Unipub.
Parthotypes of Xanthomonas Campestris Pv. Oryzae in Asia. (IRRI Research Paper Ser.: No. 75). 7p. 1982. pap. 5.00 (ISBN 0-686-82552-7, R172, IRRI). Unipub.
Proceedings of the 1981 International Deepwater Rice Workshop. 501p. 1983. pap. 52.75 (ISBN 0-686-84889-6, R 188, IRRI). Unipub.
Report of an Exploratory Workshop on the Role of Anthropologists & Other Social Scientists in Interdisciplinary Teams Developing Improved Food Production Technology. 101p. 1983. pap. 13.50 (ISBN 0-686-42855-2, R179, IRRI). Unipub.
Research Highlights for Nineteen Eighty-One. 138p. 1983. pap. 30.50 (ISBN 0-686-84890-X, R 183, IRRI). Unipub.
Research on Algae, Blue-Green Algae, & Phototrophic Nitrogen Fixation at the International Rice Research Institute (1963-81) Summarization, Problems & Prospects. (IRRI Research Paper Ser.: No. 78). 21p. 1983. pap. 5.00 (ISBN 0-686-42858-7, R182, IRRI). Unipub.
Rice Research in the Nineteen Eighties: Summary Reports from the 1982 International Rice Research Conference. 33p. 1983. pap. 7.00 (ISBN 0-686-84892-6, R 181, IRRI). Unipub.
Rice Research Strategies for the Future. 553p. 1983. pap. 57.00 (ISBN 0-686-84894-2, R 180, IRRI). Unipub.
San Bartolome: Beyond the Green Evolution. (IRRI Research Paper Ser.: No. 74). 13p. 1982. pap. 5.00 (ISBN 0-686-82553-5, R173, IRRI). Unipub.

RICE UNIVERSITY

Meiners, Fredericka. A History of Rice University: The Institute Years, 1907-1963. (Illus.). 270p. 1982. 29.50 (ISBN 0-89263-250-X). Rice Univ.

RICH FOOL (PARABLE)

see Jesus Christ-Parables

RICHARD 2ND, KING OF ENGLAND, 1367-1400

Coopland. Letter to King Richard II. 186p. 1982. 53.00x (ISBN 0-85323-283-0, Pub. by Liverpool Univ England). State Mutual Bk.

RICHARD 3RD, KING OF ENGLAND, 1452-1485

Halstead, Caroline. Richard the Third as Duke of Gloucester & King of England, 2 Vols. 1027p. 1980. text ed. 67.50x set (ISBN 0-904387-14-3, Pub. by Sutton England); pap. text ed. 36.00x set (ISBN 0-904387-41-0). Humanities.
Sutton, Anne & Hammond, Peter, eds. Coronation of Richard III: The Extant Documents. 336p. 1982. text ed. 76.00x (Pub. by Sutton England). Humanities.

RICHARDSON, DOROTHY MILLER, 1873-1957

Hanscombe, Gillian E. The Art of Life: Dorothy Richardson & the Development of Feminist Consciousness. 200p. 1983. text ed. 20.95x (ISBN 0-8214-0739-2, 82-85082); pap. 10.95 (ISBN 0-8214-0740-6, 82-85090). Ohio U Pr.

RICHARDSON, SAMUEL, 1689-1761

Eagleton, Terry. The Rape of Clarissa: Writing, Sexuality & Class-Struggle in Richardson. 128p. 1983. 25.00x (ISBN 0-8166-1204-8); pap. 9.95 (ISBN 0-8166-1209-9). U of Minn Pr.

RICHELIEU, ARMAND JEAN DU PLESSIS, CARDINAL, DUC DE, 1585-1642

Treasure, Geoffrey. Cardinal Richelieu & the Development of Absolutism. 316p. 1982. 30.00x (ISBN 0-7136-1287-8, Pub. by Shepheard-Walwyn England). State Mutual Bk.
--Cardinal Richelieu & the Development of Absolutism. 316p. 1982. 7.50 (ISBN 0-85683-065-8, Pub. by Shepheard-Walwyn). Flatiron Book Dist.

RICHES

see Wealth

RICHMOND

Beach, Marie H., ed. Guide to Richmond. rev. ed. Date not set. pap. price not set (ISBN 0-9607442-0-7). Guide to Rich.

RICKETTSIAL DISEASES

see also Virus Diseases

Marchette, Nyven J. Ecological Relationships & Evolution of the Rickettsiae, Vol. I. 192p. 1982. 60.00 (ISBN 0-8493-6125-7). CRC Pr.

RIDDLES

see also Charades; Puzzles

Wyatt, A. J. Old English Riddles. 1982. lib. bdg. 34.50 (ISBN 0-686-81939-X). Porter.

RIDDLES-JUVENILE LITERATURE

Adler, David A. The Carsick Zebra & Other Animal Riddles. LC 82-48750. (Illus.). 64p. (gr. 1-4). 1983. reinforced binding 8.95 (ISBN 0-8234-0479-X). Holiday.
Levine, Caroline A. The Silly Kid Joke Book. LC 82-17727. (Illus.). 64p. (gr. 1-3). 1983. 9.95 (ISBN 0-525-44039-9, 0966-290). Dutton.
Low, Joseph. Beastly, Buggy, Fishy, Flighty Riddles. 48p. (gr. 1-3). 1983. 8.95 (ISBN 0-686-82194-7). Macmillan.
Thaler, Mike. Riddle Rainbow. (Illus.). 128p. (gr. 2-7). 1983. PLB 8.95 (ISBN 0-8038-6368-3). Hastings.
--Scared Silly. (Illus.). 1982. pap. 1.95 (ISBN 0-380-80291-0, 80291, Camelot). Avon.

RIDICULOUS, THE

see Wit and Humor

RIDING

see Coaching; Horsemanship

RIEMANN SURFACES

Beardon, Alan. A Primer on Riemann Surfaces. LC 82-4439. (London Mathematical Society Lecture Note Ser.: No. 78). 150p. Date not set. pap. price not set (ISBN 0-521-27104-5). Cambridge U Pr.

RIEMANNIAN GEOMETRY

see Geometry, Riemannian

RIFLES

see also Winchester Rifle

Clayton, Joseph D. The Ruger Number One Rifle. Amber, John T., ed. (Know Your Gun Ser.: No. 2). (Illus.). 212p. 1982. 39.95 (ISBN 0-941540-06-5). Blacksmith Corp.
Shelsby, Earl, ed. NRA Gunsmithing Guide: Updated. rev. ed. (Illus.). 336p. (Orig.). 1980. pap. text ed. 11.95 (ISBN 0-935998-47-0). Natl Rifle Assn.

RIGHT AND LEFT (POLITICAL SCIENCE)

Dworkin, Andrea. Right-Wing Women: The Politics of Domesticated Females. 256p. 1983. 14.95 (ISBN 0-698-11171-0, Coward). Putnam Pub Group.
--Right-Wing Women: The Politics of Domesticated Females. 256p. 1983. pap. 6.95 (ISBN 0-399-50671-3, Perige). Putnam Pub Group.

RIGHT OF PRIVACY

see Privacy, Right Of

RIGHT TO KNOW

see Freedom of Information

RIGHTS, CIVIL

see Civil Rights

RIGHTS, NATURAL

see Natural Law

RIGHTS OF WOMEN

see Women's Rights

RILKE, RAINER MARIA, 1875-1926

Hendry, J. F. The Sacred Threshold: The Life of Rainer Maria Rilke - Citizen of Europe. 280p. 1982. text ed. 21.00x (ISBN 0-85635-369-8, 30143, Pub. by Carcanet New Pr England). Humanities.

RIMSKY-KORSAKOV, NIKOLAI ANDREEVICH, 1844-1908

Westphal, Ethel. Nicolai Rimsky-Korsakov, Composer of Russian Romantic Music. Rahmas, Sigurd C., ed. (Outstanding Personalities Ser.: No. 94). 32p. (gr. 9-12). 1982. 2.95 (ISBN 0-87157-594-9); pap. text ed. 1.95 (ISBN 0-87157-094-7). SamHar Pr.

RINGS (ALGEBRA)

see also Associative Rings; Measure Theory; Modules (Algebra); Topological Algebras

Fleury, P. J., ed. Advances in Non-Communicative Ring-Theory, Plattsburg, 1981. (Lecture Notes in Mathematics Ser.: Vol. 951). 142p. 1983. pap. 8.50 (ISBN 0-387-11597-8). Springer-Verlag.

RIO GRANDE RIVER AND VALLEY

Pearson, John R., ed. River Guide to the Rio Grande, 4 vols. (Illus.). 72p. (Orig.). 1982. pap. 10.00 (ISBN 0-686-38924-7). Big Bend.

RIOTS

see also Crowds also subdivision Riot under names of specific cities, e.g. Los Angeles-Riots, 1965

Bohstedt, John. Riots & Community Politics in England & Wales, 1790-1810. (Illus.). 336p. 1983. text ed. 30.00x (ISBN 0-674-77120-6). Harvard U Pr.

RISK

see also Probabilities; Profit

Hadden, Susan, ed. Public Policy Towards Risk. (Orig.). 1982. pap. 6.00 (ISBN 0-918592-53-4). Policy Studies.
Kuhnreuther, H. & Ley, E. V., eds. Risk Analysis Controversy-An Institutional Perspective, Laxenburg, Austria: Proceedings, 1981. (Illus.). 236p. 1983. 24.00. Springer-Verlag.
Rescher, Nicholas. Risk: A Philosophical Introduction to the Theory of Risk Evaluation & Management. LC 82-21970. (Nicholas Rescher Ser.). 218p. (Orig.). 1983. lib. bdg. 23.50 (ISBN 0-8191-2269-6); pap. text ed. 10.75 (ISBN 0-8191-2270-X). U Pr of Amer.
Vernor, James D. An Introduction to Risk Management in Property Development. LC 81-51564. (Development Component Ser.). (Illus.). 20p. 1981. pap. 10.00 (ISBN 0-87420-602-2, D18). Urban Land.

RISK (INSURANCE)
Church, Frederic C., Jr. Avoiding Surprises: Eight Steps to an Efficient, Low-Cost Corporate Risk Management & Insurance Program. LC 81-71318. (Illus.). 286p. 1982. 17.95 (ISBN 0-9607398-0-7). Boston Risk Magmt.
Cummins, J. David & Smith, Barry D. Risk Classification in Life Insurance. 1982. lib. bdg. 45.00 (ISBN 0-89838-114-2). Kluwer-Nijhoff.
Williams, C. Arthur, Jr. & Head, George L. Principles of Risk Management & Insurance, 2 Vols. 2nd ed. LC 81-66112. 685p. 1981. Vol. 1. text ed. 18.00 (ISBN 0-89463-022-9); Vol. 2. text ed. 18.00. Am Inst Property.
Wood, Glenn L. & Lilly, Claude C. III. Personal Risk Management & Insurance, 2 Vols. 2nd ed. LC 80-69852. 935p. 1980. text ed. 18.00 ea. vol. Am Inst Property.
RITES AND CEREMONIES
see also Baptism; Funeral Rites and Ceremonies; Initiations (In Religion, Folk-Lore, etc.); Manners and Customs; Marriage Customs and Rites; Mysteries, Religious; Ritual; Sacraments; Tournaments
also subdivision Ceremonies and Practices under subjects, e.g. Catholic Church-Ceremonies and Practice
Kavanaugh, Aidan. Elements of Rite. 110p. (Orig.). 1982. pap. 7.95 (ISBN 0-916134-54-7). Pueblo Pub CO.
Pfatteicher, Philip H. Commentary on the Occasional Services. LC 82-48542. 336p. 1983. 16.95 (ISBN 0-8006-0697-3, 1-1697). Fortress.
RITUAL
see also Liturgics; Liturgies; Rites and Ceremonies; also subdivision Rituals under names of religions and religious denominations, e.g. Buddhism-rituals; and under the heading Secret societies, and names of specific secret societies
Wilson, David A. The Dance of the Rites. 150p. 1983. pap. 7.00 (ISBN 0-934852-27-8). Lorien Hse.
RIVER BOATS
see also Sailing Barges
Curry, Jane. The River's in My Blood: Riverboat Pilots Tell Their Stories. LC 82-11068. xx, 279p. 1983. 17.50 (ISBN 0-8032-1416-2). U of Nebr Pr.
RIVER DISCHARGE MEASUREMENTS
see Stream Measurements
RIVERS
see also Dams; Erosion; Estuaries; Floods; Hydraulic Engineering; Water-Laws and Legislation; Water-Pollution
also names of specific Rivers, or Rivers and Valleys, e.g. Mississippi River, Rhine River and Valley
Biggs, Howard. The River Medway. 160p. 1982. 35.00x (ISBN 0-86138-005-3, Pub. by Terence Dalton England). State Mutual Bk.
Clark, William. Sing Peace to Cedar River. Brunelle, Jim, ed. (Illus.). 240p. 1983. pap. 10.95 (ISBN 0-930096-41-X). G Gannett.
Francis, Austin. Catskill Rivers. (Illus.). 224p. 1983. 24.95 (ISBN 0-8329-0282-9). Winchester Pr.
Martin, Charles. Sierra Whitewater. LC 74-48882. (Illus.). 192p. 1982. pap. 11.95 (ISBN 0-9609984-0-3). C F Martin.
Strode Publishers. Rivers of Alabama. Klein, E. L., ed. (Illus.). 211p. (gr. 7 up). 1968. 6.95 (ISBN 0-87397-003-9). Strode.
Swenson, Peter J. Secrets of Rivers & Streams. Jack, Susan, ed. (Secrets of Ser.). 90p. 1982. pap. 5.95 (ISBN 0-930096-31-2). G Gannett.
Updegraffe, Imelda & Updegraffe, Robert. Rivers & Lakes. (Turning Points Ser.). (Illus.). 24p. 1983. pap. 3.50 (ISBN 0-14-049192-9, Puffin). Penguin.
RIVERS-POLLUTION
see Water-Pollution
RIZAL Y ALONSO, JOSE, 1861-1896
Del Carmen, Vicente. Rizal: An Encyclopedic Collection, Vol. 1. (Illus.). 217p. (Orig.). 1982. 15.75 (ISBN 971-10-0058-X, Pub. by New Day Philippines); pap. 10.75 (ISBN 971-10-0059-8). Cellar.
ROAD ACCIDENTS
see Traffic Accidents
ROAD GUIDES
see Automobile Touring-Road Guides
ROAD SIGNS
see Traffic Signs and Signals
ROAD TRAFFIC
see Traffic Engineering
ROAD TRANSPORT WORKERS
see Highway Transport Workers
ROADS
see also Express Highways; Trails
Hebden, Norman & Smith, W. S. State-City Relationships in Highway Affairs. 1950. text ed. 42.50x (ISBN 0-686-83784-3). Elliots Bks.
Rudman, Jack. Senior Highway Maintenance Supervisor. (Career Examination Ser.: C-2631). (Cloth bdg. avail. on request). pap. 12.00 (ISBN 0-8373-2631-1). Natl Learning.
--Supervising Highway Maintenance Supervisor. (Career Examination Ser.: C-2632). (Cloth bdg. avail. on request). pap. 12.00 (ISBN 0-8373-2632-X). Natl Learning.
ROADS-SIGNS
see Traffic Signs and Signals
ROADS-TRAFFIC SIGNS
see Traffic Signs and Signals
ROADS-GREAT BRITAIN
Dodd, A. E. & Dodd, E. M. Peakland Roads & Trackways. 192p. 1982. 40.00x (ISBN 0-86190-066-9, Pub. by Moorland). State Mutual Bk.
ROADSIDE TRAFFIC SIGNS
see Traffic Signs and Signals
ROBBE-GRILLET, ALAIN, 1922-
Deduck, Patricia A. Realism, Reality & the Fictional Theory of Alain Robbe-Grillet & Anais Nin. LC 82-13549. 118p. 1982. lib. bdg. 19.00 (ISBN 0-8191-2719-1); pap. text ed. 8.25 (ISBN 0-8191-2720-5). U Pr of Amer.
ROBIN HOOD
Keen, Maurice. The Outlaws of Medieval Legend. (Studies in Social History). 235p. 1977. 25.00 (ISBN 0-7100-8682-2). Routledge & Kegan.
ROBINSON, EDWIN ARLINGTON, 1869-1935
Hogan, Charles. Bibliography of Edwin Arlington Robinson. 1936. text ed. 23.50x (ISBN 0-686-37863-6). Elliots Bks.
ROBOT BOMBS
see V-Two Rocket
ROBOTS
see Androids; Automation; Conscious Automata
ROCHESTER, JOHN WILMOT, 2ND EARL OF, 1647-1680
Treglown, Jeremy. Spirit of Wit. 90p. 1982. 25.00 (ISBN 0-208-02012-8, Archon Bks). Shoe String.
ROCK CLIMBING
see also Mountaineering
The Rock Climbing Teaching Guide. 112p. 7.95 (ISBN 0-88314-155-8). AAHPERD.
ROCK COLLECTING
see Mineralogy-Collectors and Collecting
ROCK DRAWINGS
see Rock Paintings
ROCK FISH
see Striped Bass
ROCK GARDENS
see also Alpine Gardens
Heath, Royton E. Rock Plants for Small Gardens. (Illus.). 144p. 1982. 17.95 (ISBN 0-600-36811-4). Timber.
Schacht, Wilhelm. Rock Gardens. Archibald, Jim, ed. LC 80-54398. (Illus.). 190p. 1983. pap. 9.95 (ISBN 0-87663-588-5). Universe.
ROCK MECHANICS
see also Engineering Geology; Soil Mechanics
Goodman, Richard E. & Hueze, Francios E., eds. Issues in Rock Mechanics: Twenty-Third Symposium. LC 82-71989. (Illus.). 1133p. 1982. 45.00x (ISBN 0-89520-297-2). Soc Mining Eng.
ROCK MUSIC
Blair, John. Illustrated Discography of Surf Music. (Illus.). 1983. price not set (ISBN 0-9601880-1-0). J Bee Prods.
Davis, Stephen & Simon, Peter. Reggae International. LC 82-61223. 1983. pap. 14.95 (ISBN 0-394-71313-3). Knopf.
Gargan, William & Sharma, Sue. Find that Tune: An Index to Rock, Folk-Rock, Disco & Soul in Collections. 400p. 1983. lib. bdg. 39.95 (ISBN 0-918212-70-7). Neal-Schuman.
Handler, Herb. Year by Year in the Rock Era. LC 82-11722. (Illus.). 380p. 1983. lib. bdg. 29.95 (ISBN 0-313-23456-6, HRE/). Greenwood.
Hibbard, Don & Kaleialoha, Carol. The Role of Rock: A Guide to the Social & Political Consequences of Rock Music. 252p. 1983. 14.95 (ISBN 0-13-782458-0); pap. 6.95 (ISBN 0-13-782441-6). P-H.
Lechner, Jack. The Ivy League Rock Quiz Book. (Illus.). 144p. (Orig.). 1983. pap. 6.95 (ISBN 0-933328-62-1). Delilah Bks.
Shaw, Arnold. A Dictionary of American Pop-Rock. LC 82-50382. 440p. 1983. 19.95 (ISBN 0-02-872350-3); pap. 12.95. Schirmer Bks.
ROCK MUSICIANS
Atkinson, Terry & Cerf, Martin. Billy Squier: An Illustrated History. (Illus.). 48p. (Orig.). 1983. pap. 6.95 (ISBN 0-89524-174-9, 8615). Cherry Lane.
Dagnal, Cynthia. Starting Your Own Rock Band. (Illus.). 96p. (Orig.). 1983. pap. 5.95 (ISBN 0-8092-5606-1). Contemp Bks.
DeWitt, Howard A. Van Morrison: The Mystic's Music. (Illus.). 160p. (Orig.). 1983. pap. 12.95 (ISBN 0-686-83848-3). Horizon Bks CA.
Gambaccini, Paul. Paul McCartney in his own Words. (Illus.). 112p. (Orig.). 1983. pap. 6.95 (ISBN 0-399-41008-2). Delilah Bks.
Grushkin, Paul, et al. Grateful Dead: The Official Book of the Deadheads. (Illus.). 224p. 1983. pap. 12.95 (ISBN 0-688-01520-4); deluxe ed. 25.00 (ISBN 0-688-01917-X). Quill NY.
Hamilton, Alan. Paul McCartney. (Profiles Ser.). (Illus.). 64p. (gr. 4-6). 1983. 7.95 (ISBN 0-241-10930-2, Pub. by Hamish Hamilton England). David & Charles.
Jackson, Blair. The Grateful Dead: The Music Never Stopped. (Illus.). 160p. (Orig.). 1983. pap. 9.95 (ISBN 0-933328-61-3). Delilah Bks.
Miles. Mick Jagger in His Own Words. (Illus.). 128p. (Orig.). 1983. pap. 6.95 (ISBN 0-399-41011-2). Delilah Bks.
Pop, Iggy & Wohrer, Anne. I Need More. (Illus.). 128p. 1982. pap. 9.95 (ISBN 0-943828-50-3). Karz-Cohl Pub.
Sheff, David. The Playboy Interviews with John Lennon & Yoko Ono. Golson, G. Barry, ed. 256p. 1982. pap. 3.50 (ISBN 0-425-05989-8). Berkley Pub.
Swenson, John. Bill Haley: The Daddy Of Rock & Roll. LC 82-42760. 200p. 1983. 16.95 (ISBN 0-8128-2909-3); pap. 8.95 (ISBN 0-8128-6177-9). Stein & Day.
ROCK PAINTINGS
Barnes, F. A. Canyon Country Prehistoric Rock Art. LC 82-60129. (Canyon Country Ser.). (Illus.). 304p. 1982. pap. 7.50 (ISBN 0-915272-25-3). Wasatch Pubs.
Hudson, Trauis. Guide to Painted Cave. LC 82-17218. 1982. 4.50 (ISBN 0-87461-049-4). McNally.
Strecker, Matthias. Rock Art of East Mexico & Central America: An Annotated Bibliography. 2nd ed. (Monograph X). 86p. pap. 7.00 (ISBN 0-917956-36-2). UCLA Arch.
Van Tilburg, JoAnne. Ancient Images on Stone: Rock Art of the Californians. LC 82-84337. (Illus.). 128p. 1983. pap. 20.00 (ISBN 0-917956-40-0). UCLA Arch.
ROCK SHELTERS
see Caves
ROCK-TOMBS
see Tombs
ROCKEFELLER, JOHN DAVISON, 1839-1937
Persico, Joseph. Imperial Rockefeller. 1983. price not set. WSP.
ROCKEFELLER, NELSON ALDRICH, 1908-1979
Persico, Joseph E. The Imperial Rockefeller. large type ed. LC 82-5994. 523p. 1982. Repr. of 1982 ed. 13.95 (ISBN 0-89621-371-4). Thorndike Pr.
ROCKEFELLER FAMILY
Wardwell, Allen, intro. by. Handbook of the Mr & Mrs John D. Rockefeller. 3rd ed. LC 81-7905. (Illus.). 112p. 1981. pap. 6.50 (ISBN 0-87848-059-5). Asia Soc.
ROCKERIES
see Rock Gardens
ROCKET FLIGHT
see Space Flight
ROCKET ORDNANCE
see Rockets (Ordnance)
ROCKET PROJECTILES
see Rockets (Ordnance)
ROCKETRY-HISTORY
Winter, Frank H. Prelude to the Space Age: The Rocket Societies: 1924-1940. (Illus.). 250p. (Orig.). 1983. pap. text ed. 15.00x (ISBN 0-87474-963-8). Smithsonian.
ROCKETS (AERONAUTICS)-MODELS
Stine, G. Harry. Handbook of Model Rocketry. 5th ed. LC 82-8913. (Illus.). 352p. 1983. lib. bdg. 16.95 (ISBN 0-668-05358-5); pap. 11.95 (ISBN 0-668-05360-7). Arco.
ROCKETS (ORDNANCE)
see also Guided Missiles; V-Two Rocket
Morey, Loren. The Power Rockets. 28.00 (ISBN 0-89126-110-9). MA AH Pub.
ROCKFISH
see Striped Bass
ROCKHOUNDS
see Mineralogy-Collectors and Collecting
ROCKNE, KNUTE KENNETH, 1888-1931
Van Riper, Guernsey. Knute Rockne. new ed. (Childhood of Famous Americans Ser.). (Illus.). 204p. (Orig.). (gr. 2 up). 1983. pap. 3.95 (ISBN 0-672-52753-7). Bobbs.
ROCKS
see also Crystallography; Geochemistry; Geology; Mineralogy; Petrology; Rock Mechanics
also varieties of rock, e.g. Granite, Limestone
Augustithis, S. S. Atlas of the Textural Patterns of Granites, Gneisses & Associated Rock Types. 1973. 102.25 (ISBN 0-444-40977-7). Elsevier.
Dietrich, R. V. & Wicander, E. Reed. Rocks, Minerals & Fossils. (Self-Teaching Guides Ser.). 288p. 1983. pap. text ed. 9.95 (ISBN 0-471-89883-X). Wiley.
ROCKS-AGE
see Geological Time; Geology, Stratigraphic
ROCKS-JUVENILE LITERATURE
Marcus, Elizabeth. Rocks & Minerals. LC 82-17424. (Question & Answer Bks.). (Illus.). 32p. (gr. 3-6). 1983. PLB 8.59 (ISBN 0-89375-876-0); pap. text ed. 1.95 (ISBN 0-89375-877-9). Troll Assocs.
ROCKS, SEDIMENTARY
Fairbridge, R. W. & Bourgeois, J., eds. The Encyclopedia of Sedimentology. LC 78-18259. (Encyclopedia of Earth Sciences Ser.: Vol. VI). 901p. 1978. 98.00 (ISBN 0-87933-152-6). Hutchinson Ross.
ROCKWELL, NORMAN, 1894-1978
Moline, Mary. Norman Rockwell Encyclopedia. (Illus.). 320p. pap. 9.95 (ISBN 0-89387-070-6). Curtis Pub Co.
ROCKY MOUNTAINS
Sage, Rufus B. Rocky Mountain Life: Or, Startling Scenes & Perilous Adventures in the Far West During an Expedition of Three Years. LC 82-20165. (Illus.). 351p. 1983. 23.50x (ISBN 0-8032-4142-9); pap. 7.50 (ISBN 0-8032-9137-X, BB 835, Bison). U of Nebr Pr.
Trenton, Patricia & Hassrick, Peter H. The Rocky Mountains: A Vision for Artists in the Nineteenth Century. LC 82-21879. (Illus.). 440p. 1983. 65.00 (ISBN 0-8061-1808-3). U of Okla Pr.
ROCOCO ARCHITECTURE
see Architecture, Rococo
RODENTIA
see also Beavers; Chinchillas; Rats
Cuppy, Will. How to Attract the Wombat. LC 82-20072. (Illus.). 192p. 1949. pap. 5.95 (ISBN 0-226-12828-8). U of Chicago Pr.
Williams, G. M. Cytochemical Markers in Rodent Hepatocarcinogenesis. (Lectures in Toxicology: No. 17). (Illus.). 1983. 60.00 (ISBN 0-08-029786-2). Pergamon.
RODEOS
Camarillo, Leo. Team Roping. Witte, Randy, tr. (Illus.). 144p. (Orig.). 1982. 7.95 (ISBN 0-911647-00-7). Western Horseman.
RODIN, AUGUSTE, 1840-1917
Elsen, Albert E., ed. Rodin Rediscovered. LC 81-9576. (Illus.). pap. 14.95 (ISBN 0-686-81955-1). Natl Gallery Art.
Judrin, Claudie, intro. by. Rodin: Drawings & Watercolors. (Illus.). 1983. slipcased 75.00 (ISBN 0-500-23368-3). Thames Hudson.
The Sculpture of Rodin. 1976. 50.00 (ISBN 0-686-84625-7, Nonpareil Bks). Godine.
ROENTGEN RAYS
see X-Rays
ROENTGENOGRAMS
see X-Rays
ROENTGENOLOGY, DIAGNOSTIC
see Diagnosis, Radioscopic
ROGERS, WILL, 1879-1935
Gragert, Steven K., ed. He Chews to Run: Will Rogers Life Magazine Articles, 1928. LC 82-801415. (The Writings of Will Rogers Ser.: Ser. V, Vol. 1). (Illus.). 133p. 1982. 9.95 (ISBN 0-914956-20-5). Okla State Univ Pr.
Rogers, Will. More Letters of a Self-Made Diplomat. Gragert, Steven K., ed. LC 82-80504. (The Writings of Will Rogers Ser.: Ser. V, Vol. 2). (Illus.). 200p. 1982. 10.95 (ISBN 0-914956-22-1). Okla State Univ Pr.
ROGUES AND VAGABONDS
see also Tramps
Stevens, Irving L. Fishbones: Hoboing in the 1930's. LC 82-90088. (Illus.). 136p. (Orig.). 1982. pap. 7.95 (ISBN 0-9609208-0-3). Moosehead Prods.
ROLE PLAYING
Hawley, Robert C. Value Exploration Through Role Playing. 124p. (Orig.). 1974. pap. 5.95 (ISBN 0-913636-03-7). Educ Res MA.
ROLLER-SKATING
Sawyer, Ruth. Roller Skates. 1981. pap. 14.95 (ISBN 0-670-60310-4). Viking Pr.
Stoll, Sharon K. Roller Skating: Fundamentals & Techniques. LC 82-83932. (Illus.). 144p. (Orig.). 1983. pap. 6.95 (ISBN 0-88011-101-1). Leisure Pr.
ROLLING (METAL-WORK)
Roberts. Hot Rolling of Steel. (Manufacturing Engineering Ser.). 700p. 1983. write for info. (ISBN 0-8247-1345-1). Dekker.
ROLLING-STOCK
see Locomotives
ROLLING STONES
Dowley, Tim. Mick Jagger & the Stones. (Illus.). 128p. (gr. 6 up). 1983. pap. 9.95 (ISBN 0-88254-734-8). Hippocrene Bks.
Sanchez, Tony. Up & Down with the Rolling Stones. (Illus.). 1979. pap. 8.95 (ISBN 0-688-08515-6). Quill NY.
ROMAIC LANGUAGE
see Greek Language, Modern
ROMAN ALPHABET
see Alphabet
ROMAN ANTIQUITIES
see Rome-Antiquities; Rome (City)-Antiquities
ROMAN ARCHITECTURE
see Architecture, Roman
ROMAN CATHOLIC CHURCH
see Catholic Church
ROMAN LAW
see also Civil Law; Civil Law Systems
also legal headings with subdivision Roman Law in parentheses, e.g. Sales (Roman Law)
Hadley, James. Introduction to Roman Law. 1931. text ed. 39.50x (ISBN 0-686-83592-1). Elliots Bks.
ROMAN LAW-HISTORY
Diosdi, Gyorgy. Ownership in Ancient & Preclassical Roman Law. 1970. 12.50x (ISBN 0-8002-1772-1). Intl Pubns Serv.
ROMAN LITERATURE
see Latin Literature (Collections)
ROMAN PHILOSOPHY
see Philosophy, Ancient
ROMAN POTTERY
see Pottery, Roman
ROMANCE LANGUAGES
see also languages belonging to the Romance group, e.g. French Language, Italian Language
Ramsden, H. Weak-Pronoun Position in the Early Romance Languages. 1963. 18.50 (ISBN 0-7190-1213-9). Manchester.
Vincent, Nigel & Harris, Martin, eds. Studies in the Romance Verb: Essays Offered to Joe Cremona on the Occasion of His 60th Birthday. 250p. 1982. text ed. 32.00 (ISBN 0-7099-2602-2, Pub. by Croom Helm Ltd England). Biblio Dist.
ROMANCE LITERATURE
see also literatures belonging to the Romance group, e.g. Italian Literature, Spanish Literature
Fletcher, Ian, ed. Romantic Mythologies. 297p. 1973. 9.00 (ISBN 0-7100-1368-X). Routledge & Kegan.
ROMANCE LITERATURE-BIBLIOGRAPHY
Possible Inclusion. 1983. 10.00 (ISBN 0-686-37923-3). Romance Bks & People.

ROMANCE LITERATURE–HISTORY AND CRITICISM

Morse, David. Romanticism: A Structural Analysis. 288p. 1981. 39.00x (ISBN 0-333-28297-3, Pub. by Macmillan England). State Mutual Bk.

Reep, Diana. The Rescue & Romances: Popular Novels Before World War 1. LC 82-61169. 144p. 1982. 12.95 (ISBN 0-87972-211-8); pap. 6.95 (ISBN 0-87972-212-6). Bowling Green Univ.

ROMANCES

see also names of specific romances, e.g. Perceval

McManus, Yvonne. So You Want to Write a Romance. 1983. pap. write for info. PB.

Mills, Maldwyn, ed. Six Middle English Romances. 1982. pap. 6.50x (ISBN 0-460-11090-X, Pub. by Erman). Biblio Dist.

ROMANCES–HISTORY AND CRITICISM

Keen, Maurice. The Outlaws of Medieval Legend. (Studies in Social History). 235p. 1977. 25.00 (ISBN 0-7100-8682-2). Routledge & Kegan.

ROMANESQUE PAINTINGS

see Paintings, Romanesque

ROMANIA–ECONOMIC CONDITIONS

Illyes, Elemer. National Minorities in Rumania: Change in Transylvania. (East European Monographs: No. 112). 320p. 1982. 25.00x (ISBN 0-88033-005-8). East Eur Quarterly.

ROMANIA–FOREIGN RELATIONS

Dima, Nicholas. Bessarabia & Bukovina: The Soviet-Romanian Territorial Dispute. (East European Monographs: No. 110). 256p. 1982. 20.00x (ISBN 0-88033-003-1). East Eur Quarterly.

Illyes, Elemer. National Minorities in Rumania: Change in Transylvania. (East European Monographs: No. 112). 320p. 1982. 25.00x (ISBN 0-88033-005-8). East Eur Quarterly.

ROMANIA–HISTORY

Bodea, Cornelia & Candea, Virgil. Heritage & Continuity in Eastern Europe: The Transylvanian Legacy in the History of the Romanians. (East European Monographs: No. 117). 160p. 1982. 17.50x (ISBN 0-88033-010-4). East Eur Quarterly.

Frucht, Richard C. Dunarea Noastra: Romania, the Great Powers, & the Danube Question, 1914-1921. (East European Monographs: No. 113). 256p. 1982. 22.50x (ISBN 0-88033-007-4). East Eur Quarterly.

ROMANIAN LANGUAGE–DICTIONARIES

Panovf, Irina. The New Pocket Romanian Dictionary. 828p. 1983. 14.95 (ISBN 0-88254-683-X). Hippocrene Bks.

ROMANIAN PAINTING

see Painting, Romanian

ROMANOV, HOUSE OF

Massie, Robert & Sweezey, Marilyn P. The Romanov Family Album. Gregory, Alexis K. & Wheeler, Daniel, eds. LC 82-7098. (Illus.). 1982. 25.00 (ISBN 0-86565-019-5). Vendome.

ROMANTICISM

see also Realism in Literature

Hogg, James, ed. Stylistic Media of Byron's Satire. (Salzburg - Romantic Reassessment Ser.: Vol. 81, No. 3). 83p. 1982. pap. text ed. 25.00x (ISBN 0-391-02804-9, Pub. by Salzburg Austria). Humanities.

McGann, Jerome J. The Romantic Ideology: A Critical Investigation. LC 82-17494. 184p. 1983. lib. bdg. 15.00x (ISBN 0-226-55849-5). U of Chicago Pr.

Thacker, Christopher. The Wilderness Pleases: The Origins of Romanticism. LC 82-10769. 288p. 1983. 27.50x (ISBN 0-312-87960-1). St Martin.

Vlasopolos, Anca. The Symbolic Method of Coleridge, Baudelaire, & Yeats. 232p. 1983. 17.95x (ISBN 0-8143-1730-8). Wayne St U Pr.

ROMANTICISM–GREAT BRITAIN

Hogg, James, ed. Romantic Reassessment. (Salzburg Studies in English Literature: Vol. 87, No. 4). 105p. 1981. pap. text ed. 25.00x (ISBN 0-391-02759-X, 40596, Pub. by Salzburg Austria). Humanities.

ROMANTICISM–SPAIN

McClelland. The Origins of the Romantic Movement in Spain. 414p. 1982. 30.00x (ISBN 0-686-81800-8, Pub. by Liverpool Univ England). State Mutual Bk.

ROMANTICISM IN LITERATURE

see Romanticism

ROMANTICISM IN MUSIC

Peacock, Arthur. The Romantic Vision in Music (Lucifer Redeemed) 256p. 1982. text ed. 21.00x (ISBN 0-85635-366-3, Pub. by Carcanet Pr England). Humanities.

ROME–ANTIQUITIES

Peacock, D. P. Pottery in the Roman World: An Ethnoarchaeological Approach. LC 81-12356. (Archaeology Ser.). (Illus.). 192p. 1982. 35.00 (ISBN 0-582-49127-4). Longman.

Wilson, R. J. Piazza Armerina. (Illus.). 96p. 1983. 12.50 (ISBN 0-292-76472-3). U of Tex Pr.

ROME–ARMY

Holder, P. A., ed. The Roman Army in Britain. LC 82-3332. (Illus.). 137p. 1982. 20.00x (ISBN 0-312-68961-6). St Martin.

ROME–DESCRIPTION AND TRAVEL

Baedeker's City Guide: Rome. 192p. 1983. pap. 9.95 (ISBN 0-86145-116-3, Pub. by Auto Assn-British Tourist Authority England). Merrimack Bk Serv.

Masson, Georgina. Companion Guide to Rome. (Illus.). 541p. 1983. 16.95 (ISBN 0-13-154609-0); pap. 8.95 (ISBN 0-13-154591-4). P-H.

ROME–HISTORY

Balsdon, J. P. Roman Women. LC 82-48825. (Illus.). 354p. (gr. 11-12). 1983. pap. 6.95 (ISBN 0-06-464062-0, BN 4062). B&N NY.

Wunderli, Peter & Muller, Wulf. Romania Historica et Romania Hodierna. xi, 431p. (Ger.). 1982. write for info. (ISBN 3-8204-5791-7). P Lang Pubs.

ROME–HISTORY–EMPIRE, 30 B.C.-476 A.D.

see also Europe–History–392-814

Badian, E. Publicans & Sinners: Private Enterprise in the Service of the Roman Republic, With a Critical Bibliography. (Orig.). 1983. pap. 5.95x (ISBN 0-8014-9241-6). Cornell U Pr.

Chisolm, Kitty & Ferguson, John. Rome: The Augustan Age: A Source Book. (Illus.). 734p. 1981. text ed. 54.00x (ISBN 0-19-872108-0); pap. text ed. 29.95x (ISBN 0-19-872109-9). Oxford U Pr.

Cunliffe, B. Rome & Her Empire. 1978. 50.00 (ISBN 0-07-014915-1). McGraw.

MacMullen, Ramsay. Paganism in the Roman Empire. pap. 7.95 (ISBN 0-686-42822-6, Y-454). Yale U Pr.

Rollins, Alden. The Fall of Rome: A Reference Guide. LC 82-23918. 144p. 1983. lib. bdg. 15.95x (ISBN 0-89950-034-X). McFarland & Co.

Saunders, Diro A., ed. Decline & Fall of the Roman Empire. Date not set. pap. price not set (ISBN 0-14-043189-6). Penguin.

Syme, Ronald. Greeks Invading the Roman Empire. (Stephen J. Brademas Lectures Ser.). 30p. (Orig.). Date not set. pap. text ed. 2.50 (ISBN 0-916586-86-3). Hellenic Coll Pr.

Walbank. The Awful Revolution: The Decline of the Roman Empire in the West. 154p. 1982. pap. 40.00x (ISBN 0-85323-040-4, Pub. by Liverpool Univ England). State Mutual Bk.

ROME–HISTORY, MILITARY

Holder, P. A., ed. The Roman Army in Britain. LC 82-3332. (Illus.). 137p. 1982. 20.00x (ISBN 0-312-68961-6). St Martin.

ROME–JUVENILE LITERATURE

Chisholm. Roman Times. 1982. 5.95 (ISBN 0-86020-620-3, 310021); pap. 2.95 (ISBN 0-86020-619-X, 310022). EDC.

ROME–POLITICS AND GOVERNMENT

Wardman, Alan. Religion & Statecraft among the Romans. 288p. 1982. text ed. 26.25x (ISBN 0-246-11743-5, Pub. by Granada England). Humanities.

ROME–RELIGION

Brown, Raymond & Meier, John. Antioch & Rome. 256p. 1983. 8.95 (ISBN 0-8091-0339-7); pap. 4.95 (ISBN 0-8091-2532-3). Paulist Pr.

Wardman, Alan. Religion & Statecraft among the Romans. 288p. 1982. text ed. 26.25x (ISBN 0-246-11743-5, Pub. by Granada England). Humanities.

ROME–SOCIAL CONDITIONS

Preston, Harriet W. & Dodge, Louise. The Private Life of the Romans. (Illus.). 167p. 1982. Repr. of 1896 ed. lib. bdg. 50.00 (ISBN 0-8495-4412-2). Arden Lib.

ROME–SOCIAL LIFE AND CUSTOMS

Hodge, Peter. Roman House. (Aspects of Roman Life Ser.). (Illus.). 64p. (Orig.). (gr. 7-12). 1971. pap. text ed. 3.50 (ISBN 0-582-20300-7). Longman.

ROME (CITY)–ANTIQUITIES

Constable, A. T. A Collection of Some of the Greatest Paintings by Raphael in the Form of Full Colours Reproduction. (Illus.). 91p. 1983. 98.85 (ISBN 0-86650-061-8). Gloucester Art.

ROME (CITY)–HISTORY

Magnuson, Torgil. Rome in the Age of Bernini, Vol. 1. 388p. 1982. text ed. 45.00x (ISBN 0-391-02586-4). Humanities.

ROMMEL, ERWIN, 1891-1944

Mitcham, Samuel W., Jr. Rommel's Last Battle. LC 82-42722. (Illus.). 224p. 1983. 17.95 (ISBN 0-8128-2905-0). Stein & Day.

ROOD-LOFTS

see Church Architecture

ROOFS, SUSPENSION

Krishna, P. Cable-Suspended Roofs. 1978. 36.50 (ISBN 0-07-035504-5). McGraw.

ROOMING HOUSES

see Hotels, Taverns, etc.

ROOSEVELT, FRANKLIN DELANO, PRES. U. S., 1882-1945

Alsop, Joseph. FDR. large type ed. LC 82-5870. (Illus.). 303p. 1982. Repr. of 1982 ed. 11.95 (ISBN 0-89621-369-2). Thorndike Pr.

--FDR: A Centenary Remembrance 1882-1945. (Illus.). 1982. pap. 3.50 (ISBN 0-671-45891-4). WSP.

Brogan, Denis W. Era of Franklin D. Roosevelt. 1951. text ed. 8.50x (ISBN 0-686-83537-9). Elliots Bks.

Cole, Wayne S. Roosevelt & the Isolationists, Nineteen Thirty-Two to Nineteen Forty-Five. LC 82-8624. xii, 685p. 1983. 26.50x (ISBN 0-8032-1410-3). U of Nebr Pr.

Fish, Hamilton. Tragic Deception: FDR & America's Involvement in World War II. 1983. 12.95 (ISBN 0-8159-6917-1). Devin.

Romasco, Albert U. The Politics of Recovery: Roosevelt's New Deal. LC 82-14499. 270p. 1983. 17.95 (ISBN 0-19-503248-9). Oxford U Pr.

Thompson, Kenneth W., ed. The Roosevelt Presidency: Four Intimate Perspectives of FDR. LC 82-17479. (Portraits of American Presidents Ser.: Vol. I). 100p. 1983. lib. bdg. 17.25 (ISBN 0-8191-2827-9); pap. text ed. 6.50 (ISBN 0-8191-2828-7). U Pr of Amer.

ROOSEVELT, FRANKLIN DELANO, PRES. U. S., 1882-1945–JUVENILE LITERATURE

Hacker, Jeffrey H. Franklin D. Roosevelt. (Impact Biography Ser.). (Illus.). 128p. (gr. 7 up). 1983. PLB 8.90 (ISBN 0-531-04592-7). Watts.

ROOSEVELT, THEODORE, PRES. U. S., 1858-1919

Esthus, Raymond A. Theodore Roosevelt & the International Rivalries. LC 71-102172. 165p. Repr. of 1970 ed. text ed. 15.95x (ISBN 0-941690-04-0); pap. text ed. 6.95x (ISBN 0-941690-05-9). Regina Bks.

Howland, Harold. Theodore Roosevelt & His Times. 1921. text ed. 8.50x (ISBN 0-686-83813-0). Elliots Bks.

Musso, Louis, III. Theodore Roosevelt, Soldier, Statesman & President. Rahmas, Sigurd C., ed. (Outstanding Personalities Ser.: No. 90). 32p. (gr. 9-12). 1982. 2.95 (ISBN 0-87157-590-6); pap. text ed. 1.95 (ISBN 0-87157-090-4). SamHar Pr.

Roosevelt, Theodore. Ranch Life & the Hunting Trail. LC 82-20091. (Illus.). 196p. 1983. 19.95x (ISBN 0-8032-3865-7, BB 833); pap. 8.95 (ISBN 0-8032-8913-8, Bison). U of Nebr Pr.

ROPE

see also Knots and Splices

Fry, Eric C. The Book of Knots & Ropework: Practical & Decorative. (Illus.). 176p. 1983. 10.95 (ISBN 0-517-54885-2); pap. 4.95 (ISBN 0-517-54886-0). Crown.

RORSCHACH TEST

Aronow, edward & Reznikoff, Marvin, eds. A Rorschach Introduction: Content & Perceptual Approaches. Date not set. price not set (ISBN 0-8089-1516-9). Grune.

Exner, J. E. & Weiner, I. B. The Rorschach: A Comprehensive System, Assessment of Children & Adolescents, Vol. 3. 449p. 1982. text ed. 42.50x (ISBN 0-471-09364-5). Wiley.

ROSENBERG, ETHEL (GREENGLASS) 1916-1953

Radosh, Ronald & Milton, Joyce. The Rosenberg File: A Search for the Truth. LC 82-15569. 656p. Date not set. 22.50 (ISBN 0-03-049036-7). HR&W.

ROSENBERG, JULIUS, 1918-1953

Radosh, Ronald & Milton, Joyce. The Rosenberg File: A Search for the Truth. LC 82-15569. 656p. Date not set. 22.50 (ISBN 0-03-049036-7). HR&W.

ROSES

Browne, Roland A. The Rose-Lover's Guide: A Practical Handbook for Rose Gardening. LC 73-92067. (Illus.). 256p. 1983. pap. 9.95 (ISBN 0-689-70642-1, 291). Atheneum.

Jekyll, Gertrude. Roses for English Gardens. (Illus.). 392p. 1982. 29.50 (ISBN 0-907462-24-3). Antique Collect.

Thomas, Graham S. Climbing Roses: Old & New. (Illus.). 208p. 1983. text ed. 21.95x (ISBN 0-460-04604-7, Pub by J. M. Dent England). Biblio Dist.

ROSETTA STONE INSCRIPTION

Andrews, Carol. The Rosetta Stone. 32p. 1982. pap. 25.00x (ISBN 0-7141-0931-2, Pub. by Brit Mus Pubns England). State Mutual Bk.

ROSIN

see Gums and Resins

ROSS, DIANA

Brown, Geoff. Diana Ross. (Illus.). 144p. 1983. pap. 8.95 (ISBN 0-312-19932-5). St Martin.

ROSSIKAIA SOTSIAL-DEMOKRATICHESKAIA RABOCHIAIA PARTIA

see Social Democratic Party of Russia

ROTARY CLUB

Bailey, David H. & Gottlieb, Louise. Rotary Basic Library, 7 vols. White, Willmon L. & Perlberg, Mark, eds. (Illus.). 506p. 1982. 14.50 (ISBN 0-915062-08-9). Rotary Intl.

O'Dell, Richard F. Reaching Out: A History of the Rotary Club of Marquette, Michigan 1916-1981. Duerfeldt, Pryse H., ed. LC 82-60037. (Illus.). 254p. 17.00x (ISBN 0-9609764-0-X). Rotary Club.

ROTATING SYSTEMS

see Rotational Motion

ROTATIONAL MOTION

see also Rotors

Mukunda, N., et al. Relativistic Models of Extended Hadrons Obeying a Mas-Spin Trajectory Constraint. (Lecture Notes in Physics: Vol. 165). 163p. 1983. pap. 8.50 (ISBN 0-387-11586-2). Springer-Verlag.

ROTHSCHILD FAMILY

Rothschild, Miriam. Dear Lord Rothschild: Birds, Butterflies & History. (Illus.). 500p. 1983. 30.00 (ISBN 0-86689-019-X). Balaban Intl Sci Serv.

ROTORS

Di Amrogonas, et al. Analytical Methods in Rotor Dynamics. Date not set. price not set (ISBN 0-85334-199-0). Elsevier.

ROUGHAGE IN THE DIET

see High-Fiber Diet

ROUSSEAU, JEAN JACQUES, 1712-1778

Creighton, Douglas G. Jacques-Francois Deluc of Geneva & His Friendship with Jean-Jacques Rousseau. LC 82-5332. (Romance Monographs: No. 42). 128p. 1983. write for info. Romance.

Gildin, Hilail. Rousseau's Social Contract: The Design of the Argument. LC 82-20148. 240p. 1983. lib. bdg. 22.50x (ISBN 0-226-29368-8). U of Chicago Pr.

Gribble, Francis. Rousseau & the Women He Loved. 443p. 1983. Repr. of 1908 ed. lib. bdg. 40.00 (ISBN 0-89760-368-0). Telegraph Bks.

Grimsley, Ronald. Jean-Jacques Rousseau. LC 82-24409. 192p. 1983. text ed. 27.50x (ISBN 0-389-20378-5). B&N Imports.

Hamilton, James F. Rousseau's Theory of Literature: The Poetics of Art & Nature. 18.00. French Lit.

Hampson, Norman. Will & Circumstance: Montesquieu, Rousseau, & the French Revolution. LC 82-40455. 208p. 1983. 17.50x (ISBN 0-8061-1843-1). U of Okla Pr.

Rolland, Romain. The Living Thoughts of Rousseau. 159p. 1982. Repr. of 1939 ed. lib. bdg. 20.00 (ISBN 0-8495-4649-4). Arden Lib.

ROUTES OF TRADE

see Trade Routes

ROUTES OF TRAVEL

see Ocean Travel; Railroad Travel; Voyages and Travels–Guidebooks

ROWING

Kiesling, Stephen. The Shell Game: Reflections on Rowing & the Pursuit of Excellence. 208p. 1983. pap. 7.95 (ISBN 0-8092-5570-7). Contemp Bks.

ROYALTY

see also Kings and Rulers; Princes; also subdivision Kings and Rulers under names of countries, e.g. Great Britain–Kings and Rulers

Dickens. The Courts of Europe. 1977. 24.95 (ISBN 0-07-016802-4). McGraw.

Honeycombe, Gordon. The Year of the Princess. LC 82-47969. (Illus.). 160p. 1982. 16.95 (ISBN 0-316-37212-9). Little.

RUBBER

Data Notes Publishing Staff. Rubber Recycling: Data Notes. 30p. 1983. pap. text ed. 9.95 (ISBN 0-911569-43-X). Data Notes Pub.

Evans, C. W., ed. Developments in Rubber & Rubber Composites, Vol. 1. 1980. 35.00 (ISBN 0-85334-892-8, Pub. by Applied Sci England). Elsevier.

--Developments in Rubber & Rubber Composites, Vol. 2. Date not set. 45.00 (ISBN 0-85334-173-7, Pub. by Applied Sci England). Elsevier.

Whelan, A. & Lee, K. S., eds. Developments in Rubber Technology, Vol. 3. (Illus.). 240p. 1982. 61.50 (ISBN 0-85334-135-4, Pub. by Applied Sci England). Elsevier.

RUBBER INDUSTRY AND TRADE

Goering, Theodore J. & D'Silva, Emmanuel H. Natural Rubber. (Illus.). 66p. (Orig.). 1982. pap. text ed. 5.00 (ISBN 0-8213-0045-8). World Bank.

Weinstein, Barbara. The Amazon Rubber Boom, 1850-1920. LC 82-80926. (Illus.). 376p. 1983. 29.50x (ISBN 0-8047-1168-2). Stanford U Pr.

Whelan, A. & Lee, K. S., eds. Developments in Rubber Technology, Vol. 3. (Illus.). 240p. 1982. 61.50 (ISBN 0-85334-135-4, Pub. by Applied Sci England). Elsevier.

RUBBER-SHEET GEOMETRY

see Topology

RUBBER TIRES

see Tires, Rubber

RUG MANUFACTURE

see Weaving

RUGBY FOOTBALL

see also Football

Godwin, Terry & Rhys, Chris. The Guinness Book of Rugby Facts & Feats. (Illus.). 258p. 1982. pap. 12.95 (ISBN 0-85112-248-5). Sterling.

Joyson, David C. Better Rugby for Boys: Better Sports Ser. 3rd rev. ed. LC 70-21463. (Illus.). 95p. 1978. 8.50x (ISBN 0-7182-1460-9). Intl Pubns Serv.

Welch Rugby Union Coaching Staff, ed. The Principles of Rugby Football: A Manual for Coaches & Referees. (Illus.). 208p. 1983. 18.50 (ISBN 0-04-796067-1). Allen Unwin.

RUGGER

see Rugby Football

RUGS, ORIENTAL

Azadi, S. Turkoman Carpets. 1982. 95.00x (ISBN 0-903580-30-6, Pub. by Element Bks). State Mutual Bk.

Erdmann, Kurt. Oriental Carpets. 1982. 90.00x (ISBN 0-903580-35-7, Pub. by Element Bks). State Mutual Bk.

Frances, Jack. Tribal Rugs from Afghanistan. 1982. 50.00x (ISBN 0-903580-25-X, Pub. by Element Bks). State Mutual Bk.

Hoffmeister, Peter. Turkoman Carpets in Franconia. 1982. 175.00x (ISBN 0-903580-45-4, Pub. by Elements Bks). State Mutual Bk.

Hu, William & Hyman, Virgina D. Carpets of China & Its Border Regions. LC 82-82969. (Illus.). 300p. 1982. 95.00 (ISBN 0-89344-030-2); write for info. (ISBN 0-89344-031-0). Ars Ceramica.

Izmidlian, Georges. Oriental Rugs & Carpets Today: How to Choose & Enjoy Them. (Illus.). 128p. 1983. 19.95 (ISBN 0-88254-800-X); pap. 11.95 (ISBN 0-88254-801-8). Hippocrene Bks.

Layer & Vegh. Turkish Rugs. 1982. 95.00x (ISBN 0-903580-20-9, Pub. by Element Bks). State Mutual Bk.

Lefevre, J. Central Asian Carpets. 1982. 50.00x (ISBN 0-903580-40-3, Pub. by Element Bks). State Mutual Bk.

Thacher, Amos B. Turkoman Rugs. (Illus.). 1982. 38.00x (ISBN 0-87556-623-5). Saifer.
Wright, Richard E., commentary by. Rugs & Flatweaves of the Transcaucasus. LC 80-80962. 1980. 24.00 (ISBN 0-9604210-0-9). Wright R E.

RUINS
see Archaeology; Excavations (Archaeology); Ruins in Art
also subdivision Antiquities under names of countries, cities, etc. e.g. Rome–Antiquities

RUINS IN ART
Constable, A. T. A Collection of Some of the Greatest Paintings by Raphael in the Form of Full Colours Reproduction. (Illus.). 91p. 1983. 98.85 (ISBN 0-86650-061-8). Gloucester Art.

RULE MAKING, ADMINISTRATIVE
see Administrative Procedure

RULERS
see Kings and Rulers

RULERS (INSTRUMENTS)
Roberts, Kenneth D. Introduction to Rule Collecting. (Illus.). 22p. (Orig.). 1982. pap. text ed. 2.00 (ISBN 0-913602-52-3). K Roberts.

RULES OF COURT
see Court Rules

RULES OF ORDER
see Parliamentary Practice

RULES OF THE ROAD
see Inland Navigation

RUNNING
see also Marathon Running; Track-Athletics
Eagle, John. Becoming a Runner. 1983. 10.00 (ISBN 0-533-05612-8). Vantage.
Glover, B. & Schuder, P. The Competitive Runner's Handbook. 1983. 15.75 (ISBN 0-670-23365-X). Viking Pr.
Glover, Bob & Schuder, Pete. The Competitive Runner's Handbook: The Complete Training Program for All Distance Running. 488p. 1983. pap. 7.95 (ISBN 0-14-046565-0). Penguin.
Henderson, Joe. Running A to Z. 1983. pap. 8.95 (ISBN 0-8289-0504-5). Greene.
Hoppes, Steve. Running Through Austin. Orig. Title: A Guide to Austin Running, 1976. (Illus.). 112p. 1982. pap. 4.95 (ISBN 0-938934-03-1). C&M Pubns.
McQuilkin, Robert. Runner's World: Outdoor Sports Photography Book. 195p. 1982. pap. 9.95 (ISBN 0-89037-243-8). Anderson World.
Ryan, J. A. The Physician & Sportsmedicine Guide to Running. 1980. pap. 7.95 (ISBN 0-07-054358-5). McGraw.
Sisson, Mark & Hosler, Ray. Runner's World Triathlon Training Book. 140p. 1983. pap. 6.95 (ISBN 0-89037-262-4). Anderson World.
Smith, Eugene & Smith, Elaine. Mind Matter Motion: Prescription Running. LC 82-99857. (Illus.). 240p. (Orig.). 1982. pap. 11.95 (ISBN 0-9608910-0-5). Neihardt-Smith.
Sobey, Edwin J. & Burns, Gary. Runner's World: Aerobic Weight Training Book. 181p. 1982. pap. 9.95 (ISBN 0-89037-241-1). Anderson World.

RURAL ARCHITECTURE
see Architecture, Domestic; Country Homes; Farm Buildings

RURAL CONDITIONS
see also Country Life; Farm Life; Peasantry; Rural Poor; Villages;
also subdivision Rural Conditions or social conditions under names of countries, states, etc. e.g. United States–Rural Conditions
Brawley-Martinez, Emilia E. Rural Social & Community Work in the U. S. & U. K. A Cross-Cultural Perspective. 304p. 1982. 27.95 (ISBN 0-03-060433-8). Praeger.
Browne, William & Hadwiger, Don, eds. Rural Policy. (Orig.). 1982. pap. 6.00 (ISBN 0-918592-55-0). Policy Studies.
Summers, Gene F., ed. Technology & Social Change in Rural Areas. (Rural Studies Ser.). 400p. 1983. softcover 26.50 (ISBN 0-86531-600-7). Westview.
Women's Education in a Rural Environment. 105p. 1982. pap. 13.75 (ISBN 0-686-84626-5, UB112, UNESCO Regional Office). Unipub.

RURAL CREDIT
see Agricultural Credit

RURAL ECONOMIC DEVELOPMENT
see Community Development; Rehabilitation, Rural

RURAL EDUCATION
see Education, Rural

RURAL HEALTH
see Health, Rural

RURAL HOSPITALS
see Hospitals

RURAL LIFE
see Country Life; Farm Life; Outdoor Life; Peasantry

RURAL POOR
The Challenge of Rural Poverty. 52p. 1982. 7.15 (ISBN 92-2-102701-5). Intl Labour Office.

RURAL POVERTY
see Rural Poor

RUSKIN, JOHN, 1819-1900
Dearden, James S. George Allen & John Ruskin "A Romantic Addition to the History of Publishing". 96p. 1982. 50.00x (ISBN 0-284-98623-2, Pub. by C Skilton Scotland). State Mutual Bk.
Royal-Dawson, Warren, compiled by. Miscellaneous Papers by or Concerning John Ruskin, 2 Vols. 80p. 1982. Repr. of 1918 ed. Set. lib. bdg. 200.00 (ISBN 0-89987-722-2). DarbyBks.
Spear, Jeffrey L. Dreams of an English Eden: Ruskin & His Tradition in Social Criticism. 224p. 1983. text ed. 25.00x (ISBN 0-231-05536-6); pap. 12.50 (ISBN 0-231-05537-4). Columbia U Pr.

RUSSELL, BERTRAND RUSSELL, 3RD EARL, 1872-1970
Feinberg, Barry. Bertrand Russell's America: 1945-1970. 1982. 20.00 (ISBN 0-89608-157-5); pap. 8.00 (ISBN 0-89608-156-7). South End Pr.
Meyer, Samuel, ed. Dewey & Russell: An Exchange. 1983. 9.95 (ISBN 0-8022-2406-7). Philos Lib.

RUSSIA
see also names of specific cities, areas, etc. in Russia
Buchholz, Arnold, ed. Soviet & East European Studies in the International Framework. LC 82-62037. 96p. 1982. 15.00 (ISBN 0-941320-08-1). Transnatl Pubs.
Great Soviet Encyclopedia, 31 vols. 1973. Set. prepayment 1700.00 (ISBN 0-686-81752-4); prepub. 1900.00; single vol. 62.00 (ISBN 0-02-880420-1). Macmillan.
Wesson, Robert. Soviet Union: Looking to the Nineteen Eighties. LC 79-24546. 1980. lib. bdg. 35.00 (ISBN 0-527-95452-7). Kraus Intl.

RUSSIA–ARMED FORCES
Isby, David. Weapons & Tactics of the Soviet Army. (Illus.). 320p. 1981. 34.95 (ISBN 0-86720-568-7). Sci Bks Intl.
Jones, David R., ed. Soviet Armed Forces Review Annual. (SAFRA Ser.: Vol. 6). 47.00 (ISBN 0-87569-075-0). Academic Intl.
Suvorov, Viktor. Inside the Soviet Army. (Illus.). 320p. 1983. 15.95 (ISBN 0-02-615500-1). Macmillan.
White, D. Fedotoff. The Growth of the Red Army. 486p. 1982. Repr. of 1944 ed. lib. bdg. 50.00 (ISBN 0-89987-892-X). Darby Bks.

RUSSIA–BIBLIOGRAPHY
The Cumulated Annual Index to the Current Digest of the Soviet Press, Vol. XXVIII & up. 15.00 (ISBN 0-686-38736-8). Current Digest.
USSR Facts & Figures Annual. (UFFA Ser.: Vol. 6). 46.50 (ISBN 0-87569-048-3). Academic Intl.

RUSSIA–BIOGRAPHY
Berberova, Nina. Kursiv Moi, 2 vols. (Illus.). 720p. (Orig., Rus.). 1982. Set. pap. 34.00 (ISBN 0-89830-065-7). Vol. 1 (ISBN 0-89830-066-5). Vol.2 (ISBN 0-89830-067-3). Russica Pubs.
Bergman, Jay. Vera Zasulich: A Biography. LC 82-80927. 288p. 1983. 28.50x (ISBN 0-8047-1156-9). Stanford U Pr.
Campbell, William. Villi the Clown. 272p. 1983. 15.95 (ISBN 0-571-11794-5). Faber & Faber.
De Boer, S. P. & Driessen, E. J. Biographical Dictionary of Soviet Dissidents. 1982. lib. bdg. 165.00 (ISBN 90-247-2538-0, Pub. by Martinus Nijhoff Netherlands). Kluwer Boston.
Kurth, Peter. Anastasia: The Life of Anna Anderson. (Illus.). 384p. 1983. 17.95i (ISBN 0-316-50716-4). Little.
Serebrianskii, N., ed. Zhitie Prepodobnoevfrosina Pskovskogo: Pervonachal'naia Redaktsiia. (Monuments of Early Russian Literature: Vol. 3). 118p. 1982. pap. 8.00 (ISBN 0-933884-21-4). Berkeley Slavic.
Turgenev, Ivan. First Love. Berlin, Isaiah, tr. Bd. with A Fire at Sea. Berlin, Isaiah, tr. 1982. 14.95 (ISBN 0-686-82588-8). Viking Pr.

RUSSIA–BOUNDARIES
Dima, Nicholas. Bessarabia & Bukovina: The Soviet-Romanian Territorial Dispute. (East European Monographs: No. 110). 256p. 1982. 20.00x (ISBN 0-88033-003-1). East Eur Quarterly.

RUSSIA–COMMERCIAL POLICY
Gardner, H. Stephen. Soviet Foreign Trade: The Decision Process. 1982. lib. bdg. 32.00 (ISBN 0-89838-111-8). Kluwer-Nijhoff.

RUSSIA–DEFENSES
Holloway, David. The Soviet Union & the Arms Race. LC 82-20050. 208p. 1983. 14.95 (ISBN 0-300-02963-2). Yale U Pr.
Miller, Mark. Soviet Strategic Power & Doctrine: The Quest for Superiorty. (Monographs in International Affairs). 1982. text ed. 14.95 (ISBN 0-686-84847-0); pap. text ed. 9.95 (ISBN 0-686-84848-9). AISI.

RUSSIA–DESCRIPTION AND TRAVEL
Cole. Geography of USSR. 3rd ed. 1983. text ed. 34.95 (ISBN 0-408-49752-1). Butterworth.
Higginbotham, Jay. Fast Train Russia. LC 82-23514. 1983. 8.95 (ISBN 0-396-08156-8). Dodd.

RUSSIA–ECONOMIC CONDITIONS
Clark & Matko. Soviet Economic Facts: 1917-1981. LC 81-23299. 200p. 1983. 25.00x (ISBN 0-312-74758-6). St Martin.
Goldman, Marshall I. The U. S. S. R. in Crisis: The Failure of an Economic System. 1983. 15.00 (ISBN 0-393-01715-X); pap. 4.95x (ISBN 0-393-95336-X). Norton.
Hutchings, Raymond. Soviet Economic Development. 2nd ed. 368p. 1983. text ed. 32.50x (ISBN 0-8147-3419-7, NYU Pr). Columbia U Pr.
Kushnirsky, Fyodor I. Soviet Economic Planning, Nineteen Sixty-Five to Nineteen Eighty. 150p. 1982. softcover 16.50 (ISBN 0-86531-928-6). Westview.
Munting, Roger. The Economic Development of the U. S. S. R. LC 82-42545. 240p. 1982. 25.00x (ISBN 0-312-22885-6). St Martin.

RUSSIA–ECONOMIC POLICY
Bergson, Abram & Levine, Herbert S., eds. The Soviet Economy Towards the Year 2000. 496p. 1983. text ed. 37.50 (ISBN 0-04-335045-3). Allen Unwin.
Dyker, David A. The Process of Investment in the Soviet Union. LC 82-14600. (Soviet & East European Studies). (Illus.). 240p. Date not set. 39.50 (ISBN 0-521-24831-0). Cambridge U Pr.
Munting, Roger. The Economic Development of the U. S. S. R. LC 82-42545. 240p. 1982. 25.00x (ISBN 0-312-22885-6). St Martin.

RUSSIA–FOREIGN ECONOMIC RELATIONS
Sharma, R. K., ed. Economics of Soviet Assistance to India. 167p. 1981. 14.95 (ISBN 0-940500-73-6, Pub by Allied Pubs India). Asia Bk Corp.

RUSSIA–FOREIGN RELATIONS
Arbatov, Georgi A. & Oltmans, Willem. The Soviet Viewpoint. LC 82-2466. 1983. 14.95 (ISBN 0-396-08058-8). Dodd.
Beichman, Arnold & Bernstam, Mikhail. Andropov: New Challenge to the West. 1983. 14.95 (ISBN 0-8128-2921-2). Stein & Day.
Current Soviet Policies, Vols. I-VIII. (Current Soviet Policies Ser.). Vols. I, II, III, & IV. 25.00 (ISBN 0-686-38737-6); Vols. V, VI, & VII. 17.50 (ISBN 0-686-38738-4); Vol. VIII. 20.00 (ISBN 0-686-38739-2). Current Digest.
Hosmer, Steven T. & Wolfe, Thomas W. Soviet Policy & Practice Towards Third-World Conflicts. 336p. 1982. 31.95x (ISBN 0-669-06054-2). Lexington Bks.
Nerlich, Uwe, ed. Soviet Power & Western Negotiating Policy, Vol. II: The Western Panacea: Constraining Soviet Power Through Negotiation. 400p. 1983. prof ref 38.00x (ISBN 0-88410-921-6). Ballinger Pub.
Ra'anan, Gavriel. International Policy Formation in the USSR: Factional "Debates" During the Zhdanoschina. 1983. price not set (ISBN 0-208-01976-6, Archon Bks). Shoe String.
Stein, Jonathan B. The Soviet Block, Energy & Western Security. LC 82-49253. 1983. price not set (ISBN 0-669-06441-6). Lexington Bks.
Ulam, Adam B. Dangerous Relations: The Soviet Union in World Politics, 1970-1982. 320p. 1983. 25.00 (ISBN 0-19-503237-3). Oxford U Pr.
USSR Ministry of Defense, ed. Whence the Threat to Peace. 2nd ed. (Illus.). 1982. pap. 1.95 (ISBN 0-8285-9077-X, Pub. by Military Pubs USSR). Imported Pubns.
Zapantis, Andrew L. Greek-Soviet Relations, 1917-1941. (East European Monographs: No. 96). 640p. 1982. 35.00x (ISBN 0-88033-004-X). East Eur Quarterly.

RUSSIA–FOREIGN RELATIONS–ARAB COUNTRIES
Yodfat, Aryeh Y. The Soviet Union & the Arabian Peninsula: Soviet Policy Towards the Persian Gulf & Arabia. LC 82-42717. 208p. 1982. 25.00x (ISBN 0-312-74907-4). St Martin.

RUSSIA–FOREIGN RELATIONS–1917-1945
Gromyko, A. A. & Ponomarev, B. N., eds. Soviet Foreign Policy, 1917-1945. 501p. 1981. 11.00 (ISBN 0-8285-2293-6, Pub. by Progress Pubs. USSR). Imported Pubns.

RUSSIA–FOREIGN RELATIONS–1945-
Fish, Hamilton. Masters of Terrorism. 1982. 14.95 (ISBN 0-686-81786-9). Devin.
Gromyko, A. A. & Ponomarev, B. N., eds. Soviet Foreign Policy, Nineteen Forty-Five to Nineteen Eighty. 728p. 1981. 14.00 (ISBN 0-8285-2294-4, Pub. by Progress Pubs USSR). Imported Pubns.
Kanet, Roger E., ed. Soviet Foreign Policy in the 1980's. 378p. 1982. 31.95 (ISBN 0-03-059314-X); pap. 13.95 (ISBN 0-03-059316-6). Praeger.
Ra'anan, Gavriel. Factions & Their "Debates" Over International Policy During the Zhdanovschina. 1983. write for info. (Archon). Shoe String.

RUSSIA–FOREIGN RELATIONS–CHINA
Cherepanov, A. I. As Military Advisor In China. 333p. 1982. 8.70 (ISBN 0-8285-2290-1, Pub. by Progress Pubs USSR). Imported Pubns.

RUSSIA–FOREIGN RELATIONS–EUROPE
Here are entered works on Russian foreign relations with Europe as a whole.
Marrese, Michael & Vanous, Jan. Soviet Subsidization of Trade with Eastern Europe: A Soviet Perspective. (Research Ser.: No. 52). (Illus.). xxvi, 250p. 1983. pap. 11.50x (ISBN 0-87725-152-5). U of Cal Intl St.

RUSSIA–FOREIGN RELATIONS–INDIA
Sharma, R. K., ed. Economics of Soviet Assistance to India. 167p. 1981. 14.95 (ISBN 0-940500-73-6, Pub by Allied Pubs India). Asia Bk Corp.

RUSSIA–FOREIGN RELATIONS–ISRAEL
Redlich, Shimon. Propaganda & Nationalism in Wartime Russia: The Jewish Anti-Fascist Committee in the USSR, 1941-1948. (East European Monographs: No. 108). 256p. 1982. 20.00x (ISBN 0-88033-001-5). East Eur Quarterly.

RUSSIA–FOREIGN RELATIONS–LATIN AMERICA
Leiken, Robert S. Soviet Strategy & Latin America. (Washington Papers: No. 93). 144p. 1982. 6.95 (ISBN 0-03-062017-1). Praeger.

RUSSIA–FOREIGN RELATIONS–NEAR EAST
Dawisha, Adeed & Dawisha, Karen, eds. The Soviet Union in the Middle East: Perspectives & Policies. 168p. 1982. text ed. 17.50x (ISBN 0-8419-0796-X); pap. text ed. 9.50x (ISBN 0-8419-0797-8). Holmes & Meier.
Kauppi, Mark V. & Nation, Craig R., eds. The Soviet Union & the Middle East in the Nineteen-Eighties: Opportunities, Constraints, & Dilemmas. LC 82-48097. 1983. price not set (ISBN 0-669-05966-8). Lexington Bks.
Miller, R. C. Soviets Begin War in the Middle East-U.S. Counters. limited ed. 96p. 1983. pap. 2.50 (ISBN 0-682-49967-6). Exposition.

RUSSIA–FOREIGN RELATIONS–RUMANIA
Dima, Nicholas. Bessarabia & Bukovina: The Soviet-Romanian Territorial Dispute. (East European Monographs: No. 110). 256p. 1982. 20.00x (ISBN 0-88033-003-1). East Eur Quarterly.

RUSSIA–FOREIGN RELATIONS–UNITED STATES
Allan, Pierre. Crisis Bargaining & the Arms Race: A Theoretical Model. (Peace Science Studies). 184p. 1983. prof ref 22.50x (ISBN 0-88410-911-9). Ballinger Pub.
Caldwell, Lawrence T. Soviet-American Relations: One-half Decade of Detente Problems & Issues. (The Atlantic Papers: No. 75/5). (Orig.). 1976. pap. text ed. 4.75x (ISBN 0-686-83640-5). Allanheld.
Gaddis, John L. Russia, the Soviet Union & the United States: An Interpretive History. LC 77-12763. (America & the World Ser.). 309p. 1978. pap. text ed. 11.50x (ISBN 0-471-28911-6). Cloth ed. 12.95 o.p. Wiley.
George, Alexander L., ed. Managing U. S. Soviet Rivalry: Problems of Crisis Prevention. (Special Study in International Relations). 375p. 1983. lib. bdg. 30.00 (ISBN 0-86531-500-0); pap. text ed. 11.75 (ISBN 0-86531-501-9). Westview.
Kennan, George F. The Nuclear Delusion: Soviet-American Relations in the Atomic Age. 1982. 13.95 (ISBN 0-394-52946-4). Pantheon.
Laqueur, Walter. America, Europe, & the Soviet Union: Selected Essays. 1983. 22.95 (ISBN 0-87855-362-2). Transaction Bks.
Nuclear Negotiations: Reassesing Arms Control Goals in U. S.-Soviet Relations. LC 82-83390. (Symposia Ser.). 204p. 1982. 7.95 (ISBN 0-89940-004-3). L B J Sch Pub Aff.
Nunn, Jack H. The Soviet First Strike Threat: The U. S. Perspective. 304p. 1982. 31.95 (ISBN 0-03-060607-1). Praeger.
Questions & Answers on the Soviet Threat & National Security. 1981. 1.00 (ISBN 0-910082-06-5). Am Pr Serv Comm.
Starr, Frederick. Headliners & Softliners: More Heat Than Light? "Themes & Sub-Themes in the Salt II Debate". LC 79-67157. (Papers on International Issues: No. 2). 1979. pap. 2.00 (ISBN 0-935082-01-8). Southern Ctr Intl Stud.
Whelan, Joseph G. Soviet Diplomacy & Negotiating Behavior: The Emerging New Context for U. S. Diplomacy. (Replica Edition Ser.). 573p. 1982. softcover 29.50x (ISBN 0-86531-946-4). Westview.

RUSSIA–HISTORY
Hantula, Richard, ed. History of Russia: Vol. 35: The Rules of Empress Anna. 1982. 21.50 (ISBN 0-87569-047-5). Academic Intl.

RUSSIA–HISTORY–TO 1689
Margeret, Jacques. The Russian Empire & Grand Duchy of Muscovy: A Seventeenth-Century French Account. Dunning, Chester S., ed. & tr. from Fr. LC 82-20126. (Illus.). 235p. 1983. 19.95 (ISBN 0-8229-3805-7). U of Pittsburgh Pr.

RUSSIA–HISTORY–19TH CENTURY
Lincoln, W. Bruce. In War's Dark Shadow: The Russians Before the Great War. LC 82-22152. (Illus.). 1983. 19.95 (ISBN 0-385-27409-2). Dial.

RUSSIA–HISTORY–20TH CENTURY
Fitzpatrick, Sheila. The Russian Revolution. 250p. 1983. 19.95 (ISBN 0-19-219162-4). Oxford U Pr.
Lincoln, W. Bruce. In War's Dark Shadow: The Russians Before the Great War. LC 82-22152. (Illus.). 1983. 19.95 (ISBN 0-385-27409-2). Dial.
Michael, Louis G. More Corn for Bessarabia: The Russian Experience, 1910-1917. 228p. 1983. 17.95 (ISBN 0-87013-233-4). Mich St U Pr.
Redlich, Shimon. Propaganda & Nationalism in Wartime Russia: The Jewish Anti-Fascist Committee in the USSR, 1941-1948. (East European Monographs: No. 108). 256p. 1982. 20.00x (ISBN 0-88033-001-5). East Eur Quarterly.
Swain, G. Russian Society Democracy & the Legal Labour Movement 1906-14. 1982. 80.00x (ISBN 0-686-42930-3, Pub. by Macmillan England). State Mutual Bk.
Zapantis, Andrew L. Greek-Soviet Relations, 1917-1941. (East European Monographs: No. 96). 640p. 1982. 35.00x (ISBN 0-88033-004-X). East Eur Quarterly.

RUSSIA–HISTORY–REVOLUTION OF 1905
Szeftel, Marc. The Russian Constitution of April 23, 1906: Political Institutions of the Duma Monarchy. 517p. 1976. write for info. P Lang Pubs.

RUSSIA–HISTORY–1917-
Georgadze, M. U. S. S. R. Sixty Years of the Union. 391p. 1982. 9.95 (ISBN 0-8285-2423-8, Pub. by Progress PubS USSR). Imported Pubns.

Tolstoy, Alexandra. I Worked For the Soviet. 1934. text ed. 39.50x (ISBN 0-686-83576-X). Elliots Bks.
Tumarkin, Nina. Lenin Lives! The Lenin Cult in Soviet Russia. (Illus.). 384p. 1983. 20.00 (ISBN 0-674-52430-6). Harvard U Pr.
The U.S.S.R. Today: Perspectives from the Soviet Press. 5th ed. 242p. 10.00 (ISBN 0-686-38734-1). Current Digest.

RUSSIA-HISTORY-REVOLUTION-1917-1921
see also name of specific provinces, with or without the subdivision History, e.g. Ukraine
Lincoln, W. Bruce. In War's Dark Shadow: The Russians Before the Great War. LC 82-22152. (Illus.). 1983. 19.95 (ISBN 0-385-27409-2). Dial.
Massie, Robert & Sweezey, Marilyn P. The Romanov Family Album. Gregory, Alexis K. & Wheeler, Daniel, eds. LC 82-7098. (Illus.). 1982. 25.00 (ISBN 0-86565-019-5). Vendome.

RUSSIA-IMPRINTS
Walker, Gregory, ed. Official Publications of the Soviet Union & Eastern Europe: 1945-1980. 624p. 1982. 64.00 (ISBN 0-7201-1641-4). Mansell.

RUSSIA-LANGUAGES
Bruchis, Michael. One Step Back, Two Steps Forward: On the Language Policy of the Communist Party of the Soviet Union in the National Republics. (East European Monographs: No. 109). 320p. 1982. 25.00x (ISBN 0-88033-002-3). East Eur Quarterly.

RUSSIA-MILITARY POLICY
Fish, Hamilton. Masters of Terrorism. 1982. 14.95 (ISBN 0-686-81786-9). Devin.
Scherer, J. L. Handbook on Soviet Military Deficiencies. 128p. 1983. pap. 12.00 (ISBN 0-9607258-1-4). J L Scherer.
Sejna, Jan. We Will Bury You. 206p. 1983. 17.50 (ISBN 0-283-98862-2, Pub by Sidgwick & Jackson). Merrimack Bk Serv.
USSR Ministry of Defense, ed. Whence the Threat to Peace. 2nd ed. (Illus.). 1982. pap. 1.95 (ISBN 0-8285-9077-X, Pub. by Military Pubs USSR). Imported Pubns.

RUSSIA-NAVY
Ammon, G. A. Soviet Navy in War & Peace. 160p. 1981. 5.80 (ISBN 0-8285-2223-5, Pub. by Progress Pubs USSR). Imported Pubns.
Jordan, John. An Illustrated Guide to the Modern Soviet Navy. LC 81-71939. (Illustrated Military Guides Ser.). (Illus.). 160p. 1983. 9.95 (ISBN 0-668-05504-9, 5504). Arco.
Moore, John E. Warships of the Soviet Navy. (Illus.). 224p. 19.50 (ISBN 0-86720-567-9). Sci Bks Intl.

RUSSIA-POLITICS AND GOVERNMENT
Akhapkin, Yuri. First Decrees of Soviet Power. 1970 ed. 186p. 16.00 (ISBN 0-686-37391-X). Beekman Pubs.
Byrnes, Robert F., ed. After Brezhnev: Sources of Soviet Conduct in the 1980's. LC 82-24614. (Midland Bks.: No. 306). 512p. 1983. 25.00x (ISBN 0-253-35392-0); pap. 12.50x (ISBN 0-253-20306-6). Ind U Pr.
De Boer, S. P. & Driessen, E. J. Biographical Dictionary of Soviet Dissidents. 1982. lib. bdg. 165.00 (ISBN 90-247-2538-0, Pub. by Martinus Nijhoff Netherlands). Kluwer Boston.
Fleichits, Ye & Makovsky, A. The Civil Codes of the Soviet Republics. 1976 ed. 288p. 14.95 (ISBN 0-686-37387-1). Beekman Pubs.
Grzybowski, Kazimierz. Soviet Legal Institutions: Doctrines & Social Functions. LC 62-12163. (Michigan Legal Studies). xiv, 285p. 1982. Repr. of 1962 ed. lib. bdg. 30.00 (ISBN 0-89941-172-X). W S Hein.
Jacobs, Everett M., ed. Soviet Local Politics & Government. (Illus.). 224p. 1983. text ed. 28.50x (ISBN 0-04-329042-6). Allen Unwin.
Kowal-Wolk, Tatjana. Die Sowjetische Staatsburgerschaft. 199p. (Ger.). 1982. write for info. (ISBN 3-8204-7132-4). P Lang Pubs.
Miller, Mark. Soviet Strategic Power & Doctrine: The Quest for Superiorty. (Monographs in International Affairs). 1982. text ed. 14.95 (ISBN 0-686-84847-0); pap. text ed. 9.95 (ISBN 0-686-84848-9). AISI.
Naegele, Gerhard. Die Soziale Lage Alleinstehender Alterer Frauen In Grossstadten Aus Drei Westeuropaischen Landtern. 168p. (Ger.). 1982. write for info. (ISBN 3-8204-5806-9). P Lang Pubs.
Ra'anan, Gavriel. International Policy Formation in the USSR: Factional "Debates" During the Zhdanoschina. 1983. price not set (ISBN 0-208-01976-6, Archon Bks). Shoe String.
Scott, William F. & Scott, Harriet F. The Soviet Control Structure. (Strategy Papers Ser.: No. 39). 150p. 1983. pap. price not set (ISBN 0-8448-1452-0). Crane-Russak Co.
Shevtsov, V. S. State & Nations in the U. S. S. R. 208p. 1982. 6.45 (ISBN 0-8285-2419-X, Pub. by Progress Pubs). Imported Pubns.
The Soviet Union: Domestic, Economic, & Foreign Policy 1980-81, Vol. VI. (The Soviet Union Ser.). 386p. 1983. text ed. 35.00 (ISBN 0-8419-0866-4). Holmes & Meier.
USSR Ministry of Defense, ed. Whence the Threat to Peace. 2nd ed. (Illus.). 1982. pap. 1.95 (ISBN 0-8285-9077-X, Pub. by Military Pubs USSR). Imported Pubns.

RUSSIA-POLITICS AND GOVERNMENT-1945-
Brown, Archie & Kaser, Michael, eds. Soviet Policy for the Nineteen Eighties. LC 82-48593. 296p. 1983. 19.50x (ISBN 0-253-35412-9). Ind U Pr.
Short, Philip. The Dragon & the Bear: Inside China & Russia Today. LC 82-12427. (Illus.). 504p. 1983. 19.95 (ISBN 0-688-01524-7). Morrow.
Smirnov, L. N. Legislative Acts of the U. S. S. R., 1977-1979. 381p. 1981. 8.00 (ISBN 0-8285-2235-9, Pub by Progress Pubs USSR). Imported Pubns.

RUSSIA-RELATIONS (GENERAL) WITH FOREIGN COUNTRIES
Scott, William F. & Scott, Harriet F. The Soviet Control Structure. (Strategy Papers Ser.: No. 39). 150p. 1983. pap. price not set (ISBN 0-8448-1452-0). Crane-Russak Co.

RUSSIA-SOCIAL LIFE AND CUSTOMS
Starr, S. Frederick. Red & Hot: The Fate of Jazz in the Soviet Union. (Illus.). 300p. 1983. 16.95 (ISBN 0-19-503163-6). Oxford U Pr.
Ustinov, Peter. My Russia. (Illus.). 224p. 1983. 19.45i (ISBN 0-316-89052-9). Little.

RUSSIAN ARCHITECTURE
see Architecture-Russia

RUSSIAN ART
see Art, Russian

RUSSIAN AUTHORS
see Authors, Russian

RUSSIAN DRAMA (COLLECTIONS)
Green, Michael, tr. from Rus. The Russian Symbolist Theatre: An Anthology of Plays & Critical Texts. 350p. 1983. 37.50 (ISBN 0-686-82225-0); pap. 10.00 (ISBN 0-88233-798-X). Ardis Pubs.
Worrall, Nick. Nikolai Gogol & Ivan Turgenev. (Grove Press Modern Dramatists Ser.). (Illus.). 196p. 1982. pap. 9.95 (ISBN 0-394-62431-9, Ever). Grove.

RUSSIAN DRAMA-HISTORY AND CRITICISM
Green, Michael, tr. from Rus. The Russian Symbolist Theatre: An Anthology of Plays & Critical Texts. 350p. 1983. 37.50 (ISBN 0-686-82225-0); pap. 10.00 (ISBN 0-88233-798-X). Ardis Pubs.
Peterson, Ronald, tr. from Rus. The Russian Symbolists: An Anthology of Critical & Theoretical Writings. 214p. 1983. 25.00 (ISBN 0-686-82223-4). Ardis Pubs.

RUSSIAN FICTION-HISTORY AND CRITICISM
Freeborn, Richard. The Russian Revolutionary Novel: Turgenev to Pasternak. LC 82-4259. (Cambridge Studies in Russian Literature). 220p. Date not set. price not set (ISBN 0-521-24442-0). Cambridge U Pr.

RUSSIAN FOLK-LORE
see Folk-Lore, Russian

RUSSIAN LANGUAGE
Entwistle, W. J. & Morison, W. A. Russian & the Slavonic Languages. 407p. 1982. Repr. of 1949 ed. lib. bdg. 65.00 (ISBN 0-8495-1429-0). Arden Lib.

RUSSIAN LANGUAGE-CONVERSATION AND PHRASE-BOOKS
Berlitz Editors. Russian for Travel Cassettepack. 1983. 14.95 (ISBN 0-02-962880-6, Berlitz); cassette incl. Macmillan.
Hart. Speedy Russian: To Get You There & Back. 24p. (Orig., Russian.). 1979. pap. 1.75 (ISBN 0-9602838-5-4). Baja Bks.

RUSSIAN LANGUAGE-DICTIONARIES
Raskevics, J., et al. English-Latvian-Russian Dictionary. 718p. 1977. 50.00x (ISBN 0-686-82324-9, Pub. by Collets). State Mutual Bk.

RUSSIAN LANGUAGE-DICTIONARIES-ENGLISH
Olev, Kulno. English-Estonian-Russian Maritime Dictionary. 560p. 1981. 60.00x (ISBN 0-686-82322-2, Pub. by Collets). State Mutual Bk.
Parsons, Charles. Russian-English Dictionary of Irovat' Verbs. 34p. (Orig.). 1982. 10.00x (ISBN 0-917564-14-6). Translation Research.

RUSSIAN LANGUAGE-GRAMMAR
Aronson, Howard I. Georgian: A Reading Grammar. (Illus.). 526p. 1982. 22.95 (ISBN 0-89357-100-8). Slavica.

RUSSIAN LITERATURE (COLLECTIONS)
Matich, Olga & Heim, Michael. The Third Wave: Russian Literature in Emigration. 300p. 1983. 27.50 (ISBN 0-88233-782-3); pap. 8.00 (ISBN 0-88233-783-1). Ardis Pubs.
Proffer, Carl & Proffer, Ellendea, eds. The Twenties: An Anthology. 480p. 1983. 30.00 (ISBN 0-88233-820-X). Ardis Pubs.

RUSSIAN LITERATURE-HISTORY AND CRITICISM
Andrew, Joe. Russian Writers & Society in the Second Half of the Nineteenth Century. 140p. 1982. 50.00x (ISBN 0-333-25911-4, Pub. by Macmillan England). State Mutual Bk.
Avins, Carol. Border Crossings: The West & Russian Identity in Soviet Literature, Nineteen Seventeen through Nineteen Thirty-Four. LC 81-19729. 200p. 1983. 22.50x (ISBN 0-520-04233-6). U of Cal Pr.
Blavatsky, H. P. Collected Writings of H. P. Blavatsky, Vol. 13. De Zirkoff, Boris, ed. LC 75-10528. (Illus.). 465p. 1983. 16.50 (ISBN 0-8356-0229-X). Theos Pub Hse.
Gutsche, George J. & Leighton, Lauren G., eds. New Perspectives on Nineteenth Century Russian Prose. 146p. (Orig.). 1982. pap. 9.95 (ISBN 0-89357-094-X). Slavica.
Kern, Gary. Zamyatin We: A Collection of Critical Essays. 200p. 1983. 25.00 (ISBN 0-88233-804-8); pap. 5.00 (ISBN 0-686-82224-2). Ardis Pubs.
Nabokov, Vladimir. Lectures on Russian Literature. Bowers, Fredson, ed. LC 81-47315. (Illus.). 416p. 1982. 8.95 (ISBN 0-15-649591-0, Harv). HarBraceJ.
Richardson, William. Zolotoe Runo & Russian Modernism. 200p. Date not set. 27.50 (ISBN 0-88233-795-5). Ardis Pubs.
Rzhevsky, Nicholas. Russian Literature & Ideology: Herzen, Dostoevsky, Leontiev, Tolstoy, & Fadeyev. LC 82-1977. 224p. 1983. 18.95 (ISBN 0-252-00964-9). U of Ill Pr.
Speranskii, M. N., ed. Iz Starinnoi Novgorodskoi Literatury XIV Veka. (Monuments of Early Russian Literature: Vol. 4). 140p. (Russian.). 1982. pap. 9.00 (ISBN 0-933884-24-9). Berkeley Slavic.
Woll, Josephine & Treml, Vladimir. Soviet Dissident Literature: A Critical Guide. 1983. lib. bdg. 25.00 (ISBN 0-8161-8626-X, Hall Reference). G K Hall.

RUSSIAN MUSIC
see Music, Russian

RUSSIAN POETRY-HISTORY AND CRITICISM
Bethea, David M. Khodasevich: His Life & Art. LC 82-61355. (Illus.). 424p. 1983. 35.00x (ISBN 0-691-06559-4). Princeton U Pr.
Ross, Robert H. The Georgian Revolt: Rise & Fall of a Poetic Ideal 1910-1922. 296p. 1982. Repr. of 1965 ed. lib. bdg. 30.00 (ISBN 0-8495-4701-6). Arden Lib.

RUSSIAN PROSE LITERATURE
Gutsche, George J. & Leighton, Lauren G., eds. New Perspectives on Nineteenth Century Russian Prose. 146p. (Orig.). 1982. pap. 9.95 (ISBN 0-89357-094-X). Slavica.

RUSSIAN WIT AND HUMOR
Dolgopolva, Z., ed. Russia Dies Laughing: Jokes from Soviet Russia. (Illus.). 126p. 1983. 9.95 (ISBN 0-233-97402-4, Pub by Salem Hse Ltd). Merrimack Bk Serv.

RUSSIANS
Mehnert, Klaus. The Russians & Their Body. (Publication Ser.). (Illus.). 225p. 1983. price not set (ISBN 0-8179-7821-6). Hoover Inst Pr.

RUST
see Corrosion and Anti-Corrosives

RUSTLESS COATINGS
see Corrosion and Anti-Corrosives

RUTH (BIBLICAL CHARACTER)
Couchman, Bob & Couchman, Win. Ruth & Jonah: People in Process. (Carpenter Studyguides Ser.). 64p. 1983. saddle-stiched members' handbk. 1.95 (ISBN 0-87788-736-5); leader's handbook 2.95 (ISBN 0-87788-737-3). Shaw Pubs.

RUTH, GEORGE HERMAN, 1895-1948
Van Riper, Guernsey. Babe Ruth. new ed. (Childhood of Famous Americans Ser.). (Illus.). 204p. (Orig.). (gr. 2 up). 1983. pap. 3.95 (ISBN 0-672-52754-5). Bobbs.

RUTHENIAN LITERATURE
see Ukrainian Literature

RYE WHISKEY
see Whiskey

S

SABBATH-JUVENILE LITERATURE
Chaikin, Miriam & Frampton, David. The Seventh Day: The Story of the Jewish Sabbath. LC 82-16987. (Illus.). 48p. (Orig.). 1983. pap. 4.95 (ISBN 0-8052-0743-0). Schocken.

SACCO-VANZETTI CASE
Gabriel, Daniel. Sacco & Vanzetti: A Narrative Longpoem. (Illus.). 80p. 1983. pap. 5.00 (ISBN 0-940584-05-0). Gull Bks.

SACRAMENT OF THE ALTAR
see Lord's Supper

SACRAMENTS
see also Baptism; Lord's Supper; Marriage; Penance
Bausch, William. A New Look at the Sacraments. 2nd ed. 288p. 1983. pap. 5.95 (ISBN 0-89622-174-1). Twenty-Third.
Coniaris, A. M. These Are the Sacraments. 1981. pap. 5.95 (ISBN 0-937032-22-0). Light&Life Pub Co MN.
Cooke, Bernard. Sacraments & Sacramentality. 240p. 1983. pap. 7.95 (ISBN 0-89622-161-X). Twenty-Third.
Pitt, Clifford S. Church, Ministry & Sacraments: A Critical Evaluation of the Thought of Peter Taylor Forsyth. LC 82-24817. 360p. (Orig.). 1983. lib. bdg. 25.00 (ISBN 0-8191-3027-3); pap. text ed. 14.00 (ISBN 0-8191-3028-1). U Pr of Amer.
Seven Sacraments. 20p. 1980. pap. 7.55 (ISBN 0-88479-025-8). Arena Lettres.
Von Speyr, Adrienne. The Cross: Word & Sacrament. Harrison, Graham, tr. from Ger. LC 82-83496. Orig. Title: Kreuzeswort und Sakrament. 63p. (Orig., Eng.). 1983. pap. price not set (ISBN 0-89870-021-3). Ignatius Pr.
White, James F. Sacraments as God's Self Giving. 160p. (Orig.). 1983. pap. 8.95 (ISBN 0-687-36707-7). Abingdon.

SACRAMENTS (LITURGY)
Hill, Brennan. Rediscovering the Sacraments. 3.95 (ISBN 0-8215-9882-1). Sadlier.

SACRED ART
see Christian Art and Symbolism

SACRED MINISTRY
see Clergy-Office

SACRED MUSIC
see Church Music

SACRED NUMBERS
see Symbolism of Numbers

SACRED SONGS
see Hymns

EL SADAT, ANWAR, PRES. EGYPT, 1918-1981
Fernandez-Armesto, Felip. Sadat & His Statecraft. 1983. 15.95 (ISBN 0-686-38874-7, Pub. by Salem Hse Ltd). Merrimack Bk Serv.
Friedlander, Melvin A. Sadat & Begin: The Domestic Politics of Peacemaking. 350p. 1983. softcover 23.50x (ISBN 0-86531-949-9). Westview.

SADDLERY
see also Harness Making and Trade
Baker, Jennifer. Saddlery & Horse Equipment. LC 82-11468. (Illus.). 96p. 1982. 7.95 (ISBN 0-668-05633-9, 5633). Arco.
Beattie, Russell. Saddles. (Illus.). 800p. 55.00 (ISBN 0-87556-611-1). Saifer.

SAFETY, INDUSTRIAL
see Industrial Safety

SAFETY EDUCATION
see also Traffic Safety
Abernathy, Steve. Learning Safety First. (Science Ser.). 24p. (gr. 5-9). 1977. wkbk. 5.00 (ISBN 0-8209-0158-X, S-20). ESP.

SAFETY ENGINEERING
see Industrial Safety

SAFETY MEASURES
see Electric Engineering-Safety Measures; Industrial Safety

SAFETY REGULATIONS
see also Atomic Power-Law and Legislation; Fire Prevention; Firearms-Laws and Regulations
Brown, Robert, ed. Boater's Safety Handbook. (Illus.). 52p. (Orig.). 1982. pap. 2.95 (ISBN 0-89886-072-5). Mountaineers.
Institute of Petroleum. Airfields Safety Code. 1971. 16.50 (ISBN 0-444-39969-0). Elsevier.
Rudman, Jack. Public Safety Dispatcher I. (Career Examination Ser.: C-116). (Cloth bdg. avail. on request). pap. 12.00 (ISBN 0-8373-0116-5). Natl Learning.
--Public Safety Dispatcher II. (Career Examination Ser.: C-117). (Cloth bdg. avail. on request). pap. 12.00 (ISBN 0-8373-0117-3). Natl Learning.
--Public Safety Officer I. (Career Examination Ser.: C-2895). (Cloth bdg. avail. on request). pap. 10.00 (ISBN 0-8373-2895-0). Natl Learning.
--Public Safety Officer II. (Career Examination Ser.: C-2896). (Cloth bdg. avail. on request). pap. 12.00 (ISBN 0-8373-2896-9). Natl Learning.
--Public Safety Officer III. (Career Examination Ser.: C-2897). (Cloth bdg. avail. on request). pap. 12.00 (ISBN 0-8373-2897-7). Natl Learning.
--Safety Supervisor. (Career Examination Ser.: C-2641). (Cloth bdg. avail. on request). pap. 10.00 (ISBN 0-8373-2641-9). Natl Learning.
--Senior Safety Coordinator. (Career Examination Ser.: C-2668). (Cloth bdg. avail. on request). pap. 10.00 (ISBN 0-8373-2668-0). Natl Learning.

SAILBOAT RACING
see also Yacht Racing
Bryer, Robin. Jolie Brise: A Tall Ship's Tale. (Illus.). 256p. 1983. 24.95 (ISBN 0-436-07181-9, Pub by Secker & Warburg). David & Charles.
Twiname, Eric. Start to Win. 2nd ed. Sambrooke-Sturgess, Gerald, ed. (Illus.). 220p. 1983. 19.95 (ISBN 0-229-11688-4, Pub. by Adlard Coles). Sheridan.

SAILBOATS
see also Sailboat Racing
Bryer, Robin. Jolie Brise: A Tall Ship's Tale. (Illus.). 256p. 1983. 24.95 (ISBN 0-436-07181-9, Pub by Secker & Warburg). David & Charles.
Fichtner, Hans & Garff, Michael. How to Build Sailboards: Step-by-Step Custom-Made Designs. (Illus.). 126p. 1983. pap. 10.00 (ISBN 0-915160-28-5). Seven Seas.

SAILING
see also Boats and Boating; Navigation; Sailboats; Yachts and Yachting
Beard, H. & McKie, R. Sailing: A Sailor's Dictionary. 96p. 1982. 17.50x (ISBN 0-333-32845-0, Pub. by Macmillan England). State Mutual Bk.
Bond, Bob. Cruising Boat Sailing: The Basic Guide. LC 82-48882. 1982. 14.95 (ISBN 0-394-52447-0). Knopf.
--Small Boat Sailing: The Basic Guide. LC 82-48883. 1983. 14.95 (ISBN 0-394-52446-2). Knopf.
Cornell, Jimmy. Modern Ocean Cruising: Boats, Gear & Crews Surveyed. (Illus.). 250p. 1983. 19.95 (ISBN 0-229-11687-6, Pub. by Adlard Coles). Sheridan.
Dent, Nicholas. How to Sail: A Practical Course in Boat Handling. (Illus.). 128p. pap. 9.95 (ISBN 0-312-39625-2). St Martin.
Glover, Dennis. Hot Water Sailor & Landlubber Ho. (Illus.). 248p. 1982. 15.95 (ISBN 0-00-216985-1, Pub. by W Collins Australia). Intl Schol Bk Serv.
Herreshoff, Halsey C., ed. The Sailor's Handbook. (Illus.). 224p. 1983. 14.45i (ISBN 0-316-54693-3). Little.

Melges, Buddy & Mason, Charles. Sailing Smart. LC 82-15557. (Illus.). 216p. 1983. 16.95 (ISBN 0-03-058579-1). HR&W.

Rose, George G. My Three Voyages in a Square-Rigged Sailing Ship. 1982. 9.00 (ISBN 0-533-05437-0). Vantage.

Roth, Hal. The Longest Race. (Illus.). 1983. 19.50 (ISBN 0-393-03278-7). Norton.

Sleightholme, Des. The Trouble with Cruising. (Illus.). 113p. 11.95cancelled (ISBN 0-914814-40-0). Sail Bks.

Tillman, Dick & Powlison, Dave. The New Laser Sailing. (Illus.). 160p. 1983. 14.95 (ISBN 0-914814-32-X). Sail Bks.

SAILING BARGES

see also River Boats; Sailing Ships

Roberts, A. W. Breeze for a Bargeman. 144p. 1982. 25.00x (ISBN 0-86138-007-X, Pub. by Terence Dalton England). State Mutual Bk.

SAILING SHIPS

see also Sailboats; Sailing Barges

Brookesmith, Frank. I Remember the Tall Ships. (Illus.). 270p. Repr. 20.00 (ISBN 0-87556-543-3). Saifer.

SAILING VESSELS

see Sailboats; Sailing Ships

SAILORS

see Seamen

SAILORS' LIFE

see Seafaring Life

SAILORS' SONGS

see Sea Songs

SAINT-AMANT, MARC ANTOINE GERARD DE, 1594-1661

Duval, Edwin M. Poesis & Poetic Tradition in the Early Works of Saint-Amant: Four Essays in Contextual Reading. 18.00 (ISBN 0-917786-23-8). French Lit.

ST. AUGUSTINE, ORDER OF

see Augustinians

ST. AUGUSTINE, FLORIDA

Deagan, Kathleen, ed. Spanish St. Augustine: The Archaelogy of a Colonial Creole Community (Monographs) (Studies in Historical Archaeology). Date not set. price not set (ISBN 0-12-207880-2). Acad Pr.

ST. BENEDICT, ORDER OF

see Benedictines

ST. BERNARD DOGS

see Dogs–Breeds–St. Bernard

ST. FRANCIS, ORDER OF

see Franciscans

ST. HELENS, MOUNT

Aylesworth, Thomas G. & Aylesworth, Virginia L. The Mount St. Helens Disaster: What We've Learned. (Impact Ser.). 96p. (gr. 7 up). 1983. PLB 8.90 (ISBN 0-531-04488-2). Watts.

ST. PAUL, MINNESOTA

Martin, Judith A. & Lanegran, David. Where We Live: The Residential Districts of Minneapolis & St. Paul. LC 82-11064. (Illus.). 144p. 1983. 29.50x (ISBN 0-8166-1093-2); pap. 14.95 (ISBN 0-8166-1094-0). U of Minn Pr.

SAINT VALENTINE'S DAY

Brown, Fern G. Valentine's Day. (First Bks.). (Illus.). 72p. (gr. 4 up). 1983. PLB 8.90 (ISBN 0-531-04533-1). Watts.

SAINTS

Newland, Mary R. The Saint Book: For Parents, Teachers, Homilists, Storytellers & Children. (Illus.). 208p. 1979. 10.95 (ISBN 0-8164-0210-8). Seabury.

Schillebeeckx, Edward. Paul the Apostle. (Illus.). 128p. 1983. 14.95 (ISBN 0-8245-0574-3). Crossroad NY.

SAINTS–CORRESPONDENCE, REMINISCENCES, ETC.

Schillebeeckx, Edward. Paul the Apostle. (Illus.). 128p. 1983. 14.95 (ISBN 0-8245-0574-3). Crossroad NY.

SAINTS–JUVENILE LITERATURE

Twomey, Mark J. A Parade of Saints. LC 82-202387. (Illus.). 300p. 1983. pap. 8.50 (ISBN 0-8146-1275-X). Liturgical Pr.

SALADS

All Time Favorite Salad Recipes. pap. 5.95 (ISBN 0-696-01130-1). Meredith Corp.

Cooper, Sandi. Soups & Salads. LC 82-48659. (Great American Cooking Schools Ser.). (Illus.). 80p. 1983. 8.61i (ISBN 0-06-015151-X, HarpT). Har-Row.

Dandekar, Varsha. Salads of India. 90p. 1983. 13.95 (ISBN 0-89594-075-2); pap. 4.95 (ISBN 0-89594-074-4). Crossing Pr.

Farm Journal's Food Editors. Farm Journal's Molded Salads, Desserts. LC 76-10410. 128p. (Orig.). 1976. pap. 3.95 (ISBN 0-89795-017-8). Farm Journal.

Fogg, H. Witham. Salad Crops all Year Round. (Illus.). 200p. 1983. 19.95 (ISBN 0-7153-8411-2). David & Charles.

Good, Phyllis P. & Pellman, Rachel T., eds. Salads: From Amish & Mennonite Kitchens. (Pennsylvania Dutch Cookbooks Ser.). (Illus., Orig.). 1983. pap. 1.95 (ISBN 0-934672-10-5). Good Bks PA.

Landin, Judy. The Well Dressed Salad. (Illus.). 32p. (Orig.). 1981. pap. 2.00 (ISBN 0-9609266-0-7). GNK Pr.

Thirty-Two Salads. 1983. 4.95 (ISBN 0-8120-5529-2). Barron.

SALEM, MASSACHUSETTS

Randall, Peter E. Salem & Marblehead. (Illus.). 88p. 1983. pap. 8.95t (ISBN 0-89272-163-4). Down East.

SALERNO, BATTLE OF, 1943

Morris, Eric. Salerno. LC 82-48511. 560p. 1983. 19.95 (ISBN 0-8128-2893-3). Stein & Day.

SALES

see also Auctions; Government Purchasing; Products Liability

Cavalier, Richard. Sales Meetings That Work: Planning & Managing Meetings to Achieve Your Goals. LC 82-72764. 250p. 1983. 21.95 (ISBN 0-87094-364-2). Dow Jones-Irwin.

Roth, Charles B. & Alexander, Roy. Secrets of Closing Sales. 5th ed. LC 82-12312. 276p. 1982. 14.95 (ISBN 0-13-797910-X, Busn). P-H.

SALES MANAGEMENT

Bobrow, Edwin E. & Wizenberg, Larry, eds. Sales Manager's Handbook. LC 82-71068. 576p. 1983. 45.00 (ISBN 0-87094-240-9). Dow Jones-Irwin.

Cavalier, Richard. Sales Meetings That Work: Planning & Managing Meetings to Achieve Your Goals. LC 82-72764. 250p. 1983. 21.95 (ISBN 0-87094-364-2). Dow Jones-Irwin.

Cowan, D. R. Sales Analysis from the Management Standpoint. LC 67-24325. 210p. 1967. 15.00 (ISBN 0-379-00072-5). Oceana.

Hughes, C. David & Singler, Charles H. Strategic Sales Management. 352p. 1983. pap. instrs' manual avail. (ISBN 0-201-10261-7). A-W.

Lund, Philip R. Sales Reports, Records & Systems. 97p. 1979. text ed. 26.00x (ISBN 0-566-02125-0). Gower Pub Ltd.

SALES PROMOTION

see also Advertising; Display of Merchandise; Exhibitions; Salesmen and Salesmanship

Jones, E. R. How to Promote Your Own Product As a Wholesaler. (Illus.). 100p. 1983. 25.00 (ISBN 0-9600934-5-1). E R Jones.

SALESMANSHIP

see Salesmen and Salesmanship

SALESMEN AND SALESMANSHIP

see also Advertising; Booksellers and Bookselling; Mail-Order Business; Marketing; Sales Management; Sales Promotion; Telephone Selling

Anthony, Michael J. & Tolliver, Robert E. Effective Sales Presentations Guidebook. 128p. 1983. text ed. 25.00 (ISBN 0-201-00007-5). A-W.

Bettger, Frank. How I Raised Myself from Failure to Success in Selling. 192p. 1983. pap. 4.95 (ISBN 0-13-423970-9). P-H.

Brennan, Frank E. Personal Selling: A Professional Approach. 448p. 1983. text ed. write for info. (ISBN 0-574-20685-X, 13-3685); write for info. instr's. guide (ISBN 0-574-20686-8, 13-3686). SRA.

Cornelius, Hal & Lewis, William. Career Guide for Sales & Marketing. Levy, Valerie, ed. (Career Blazers Guides). 1983. pap. 7.95 (ISBN 0-671-47169-4). Monarch Pr.

Cullingan, Matthew J. Getting Back to the Basics of Selling. (Ace Business Library). 128p. 1982. pap. 2.95 (ISBN 0-441-28256-3). Ace Bks.

Fraser, John W. Tips on Having a Successful Sale, etc. LC 82-60525. 125p. (Orig.). 1983. pap. 4.95 (ISBN 0-88247-679-3). R & E Res Assoc.

Gilliam, A. The Principles & Practice of Selling. 256p. 1982. pap. 40.00 (ISBN 0-434-90661-1, Pub. by Heinemann England). State Mutual Bk.

Kornfeld, Lewis. To Catch a Mouse, Make a Noise Like a Cheese. LC 82-13320. 1982. 15.00 (ISBN 0-13-922930-2, Busn). P-H.

Langer, Steven, ed. Income in Sales-Marketing Management. 3rd ed. 1982. pap. 95.00 (ISBN 0-686-84835-7). Abbott Langer Assocs.

McCaffrey, Mike & Derloshon, Jerry. Personal Marketing Strategies: How to Sell Yourself, Your Ideas & Your Services. (Illus.). 240p. 1983. 21.95 (ISBN 0-13-657452-1); pap. 11.95 (ISBN 0-13-657114-X). P-H.

McCarthy, John J. John J. McCarthy's Secrets of Super Selling. LC 82-9533. 320p. 1982. 50.00 (ISBN 0-932648-25-8). Boardroom.

McNeese, Paul F. Salespower Through Successful Seminars. LC 82-61431. 72p. 1982. pap. text ed. 5.95 (ISBN 0-911041-00-1). Southland Spec.

Moine, Donald J. Hypnotic Sales: A Pragmatic Guide to a More Effective Sales Technique. (Orig.). 1983. 19.95 (ISBN 0-686-38216-1); pap. 12.95 (ISBN 0-686-38217-X). Metamorphous Pr.

Pesce, Vince. A Complete Manual of Professional Selling: The Modular Approach to Sales Success. (Illus.). 240p. 1983. 15.95 (ISBN 0-13-162099-1); pap. 8.95 (ISBN 0-13-162081-9). P-H.

Qubein, Nido. Nido Qubein's Professional Selling Techniques. 1983. 14.95 (ISBN 0-910580-78-2). Farnswth Pub.

Rice, John W. Successful Selling from A to Dollars: The Professional's Guide to Money-Making Sales Techniques. (Illus.). 216p. 1983. 15.95 (ISBN 0-13-872069-X); pap. 6.95 (ISBN 0-13-872051-7). P-H.

Russell, Tom. How to Use New Age Principles For Successful Selling. 30p. 1982. 2.00 (ISBN 0-911201-01-7). New Age Bus Bks.

Seltz, David D. Handbook of Effective Sales Prospecting Techniques. LC 81-22919. (Illus.). 256p. Date not set. pap. text ed. 25.00 (ISBN 0-201-07138-X). A-W.

Trisler, Hank. No Bull Selling. 192p. 1982. 12.95 (ISBN 0-8119-0484-9). Fell.

Wheeler, Elmer. Sizzlemanship. 312p. 1983. 12.95 (ISBN 0-13-811513-3, Reward); pap. 6.95 (ISBN 0-13-811505-2). P-H.

Wilbur, L. Perry. On Your Way to the Top in Selling. 192p. 1983. 14.95 (ISBN 0-13-634352-X); pap. 6.95 (ISBN 0-13-634345-7). P-H.

SALIVARY GLANDS

Rice, Dale H., ed. Surgery of the Salivary Glands. 155p. 1982. 20.00 (ISBN 0-941158-03-9, D4120-9). Mosby.

SALMON FISHERIES

Byrne, Jack. Salmon Country. (Illus.). 224p. 1982. 15.95 (ISBN 0-00-216975-4, Pub. by W Collins Australia). Intl Schol Bk Serv.

SALMON FISHING

Raychard, Al. Trout & Salmon Fishing in Northern New England. LC 82-5930. (Illus.). 208p. (Orig.). 1982. pap. 7.95 (ISBN 0-89621-068-5). Thorndike Pr.

Wulff, Lee. The Atlantic Salmon. (Illus.). 288p. 1983. 24.95 (ISBN 0-8329-0267-5). Winchester Pr.

SALMONELLA

Murray, Randall, ed. Mutagens & Carcinogens. 147p. 1977. 18.50x (ISBN 0-8422-4119-1). Irvington.

SALOONS

see Hotels, Taverns, etc.

SALT

Hall, Vivian S. & Spencer, Margaret R. Bibliography of Evaporites, Brines & Salt. 1983. write for info. (ISBN 0-89774-042-4). Oryx Pr.

Jackson, Michael M. & Liebman, Bonnie. Salt: The Complete Brand Name Guide to Sodium Content. LC 82-40505. 224p. 1983. pap. 4.95 (ISBN 0-89480-361-1). Workman Pub.

SALT DOMES

Collins, Edward W. Geological Circular 82-3: Surficial Evidence of Tectonic Activity & Erosion Rates, Palestine, Keechi, & Oakwood Salt Domes, East Texas. (Illus.). 39p. 1982. 1.75 (ISBN 0-686-37547-5). U of Tex Econ Geology.

SALT-FREE DIET

Greene, Audrey. Audreys Add No Salt Cookery. Orig. Title: Audrey's Add No Salt Cookery. (Illus.). 1982. write for info (ISBN 0-9608892-0-5). Greene Pubns.

Schell, Merle. Tasting Good: The International Salt-Free Diet Cookbook. 1982. pap. 7.95 (ISBN 0-452-25364-0, Z5364, Plume). NAL.

Thirty-Two No-Salt Dinners. 1983. pap. 4.95 (ISBN 0-8120-5524-1). Barron.

Williams, Jacqueline B. & Silverman, Goldie. No Salt No Sugar No Fat Cookbook. LC 81-83793. (Illus.). 150p. (Orig.). 1982. pap. 5.95 (ISBN 0-911954-65-1). Nitty Gritty.

Wilson, Nancy L. & Wilson, Roger H. Please Pass the Salt: A Manual for Low Salt Eaters. (Illus.). 224p. 1983. 14.95 (ISBN 0-89313-027-3). G F Stickley.

SALT MARSHES

see Marshes

SALT-WATER FISHING

Here are entered works on sea or coast fishing as a sport. Works on ocean fishing for commercial purposes are entered under the heading Fisheries.

Bauer, Erwin. Saltwater Fisherman's Bible. rev. ed. (Illus.). 208p. 1983. pap. text ed. 5.95 (ISBN 0-385-17220-6). Doubleday.

Darling, John. Sea Anglers' Guide to Britian & Ireland. 160p. 1982. 60.00x (ISBN 0-7188-2509-8, Pub. by Lutterworth Pr England); pap. 40.00x (ISBN 0-7188-2510-1). State Mutual Bk.

Sosin, Mark & Kreh, Lefty. Fishing the Flats. (Illus.). 160p. 1983. 14.95 (ISBN 0-8329-0278-0); pap. 8.95 (ISBN 0-8329-0280-2). Winchester Pr.

SALTS, FUSED

see Fused Salts

SALUS EXTRA ECCLESIAM

see Universalism

SALVADOR

Didion, Joan. Salvador. 1983. 12.95 (ISBN 0-671-47024-8). S&S.

Simon, Laurence R. El Salvador Land Reform: Nineteen Eighty to Nineteen Eighty-One. Stephens, James C., Jr., ed. (Impact Audit Ser.: No. 2). 55p. (Orig.). 1981. pap. 5.00 (ISBN 0-910281-01-7). Oxfam Am.

Spilken, Aron. Escape! The Story the Newspapers Couldn't Print. 1983. 14.95 (ISBN 0-453-00433-4). NAL.

SALVAGE (WASTE, ETC.)

Here are entered works on reclaiming and reusing equipment or parts. Works on the processing of waste paper, cans, bottles, etc. are entered under Recycling (waste, etc.).

see also Recycling (Waste, etc.)

Data Notes Publishing Staff. Aluminum Recycling: Data Notes. 30p. 1983. pap. text ed. 9.95 (ISBN 0-911569-40-5). Data Notes Pub.

--Automobile Recycling: Data Notes. 30p. pap. text ed. 9.95 (ISBN 0-911569-50-2). Data Notes Pub.

--Clothing Recycling: Data Notes. 1983. pap. text ed. 9.95 (ISBN 0-911569-49-9). Data Notes Pub.

--Equipment Recycling: Data Notes. 30p. 1983. pap. text ed. 9.95 (ISBN 0-911569-48-0). Data Notes Pub.

--Furniture Recycling: Data Notes. 30p. 1983. pap. 9.95 (ISBN 0-911569-45-6). Data Notes Pub.

--Kitchen Recycling: Data Notes. 35p. 1983. pap. text ed. 9.95 (ISBN 0-911569-51-0). Data Notes Pub.

--Rubber Recycling: Data Notes. 30p. 1983. pap. text ed. 9.95 (ISBN 0-911569-43-X). Data Notes Pub.

--Shelter Recycling: Data Notes. 30p. 1983. pap. text ed. 9.95 (ISBN 0-911569-46-4). Data Notes Pub.

--U. S. Directory of Places to Locate Recyclable Scrap. 60p. 1983. text ed. 19.95 (ISBN 0-911569-14-6). Data Notes Pub.

Pratt, Alan, ed. Directory of Waste Disposal & Recovery. 232p. 1978. 60.00x (ISBN 0-686-99829-4, Pub. by Graham & Trotman England). State Mutual Bk.

SALVATION

see also Atonement; Covenants (Theology); Sanctification; Sin

Campbell, R. K. Things That Accompany Salvation. 40p. pap. 0.35 (ISBN 0-88172-013-5). Believers Bkshelf.

Cutting, Jorge. La Salvacion: Su Seguridad, Creteza y Gozo. 2nd ed. Daniel, Roger P., ed. Bautista, Sara, tr. from Eng. (La Serie Diamante). 48p. (Span.). 1982. pap. 0.85 (ISBN 0-942504-05-4). Overcomer Pr.

Field, Kent A. Test Your Salvation. 1.00 (ISBN 0-89137-531-7). Quality Pubns.

Marshall, Alejandro & Bennett, Gordon H. La Salvacion y las Dudas de Algunas Personas. 2nd ed. Bautista, Sara, tr. from Span. (La Serie Diamante). 36p. (Eng.). 1982. pap. 0.85 (ISBN 0-942504-01-1). Overcomer Pr.

Warren, Virgil. What the Bible Says about Salvation. LC 82-73345. (What the Bible Says Ser.). 640p. 1982. 13.50 (ISBN 0-89900-088-6). College Pr Pub.

SALVATION (CATHOLIC CHURCH)

see Salvation

SALVATION ARMY

Gearing, Winifred. Salvation Patrol. (Illus.). 152p. (Orig.). 1981. pap. 4.95 (ISBN 0-86544-018-2). Salvation Army.

SAMADHI

Atmananda & Lenz, Frederick, eds. Samadhi Is Loose in America! LC 82-83869. 500p. (Orig.). 1982. pap. text ed. 9.00 (ISBN 0-941868-02-8). Lakshmi.

SAMOAN ISLANDS

Shore, Bradd. Sala'ilua: A Samoan Mystery. (Illus.). 338p. 1982. 28.00x (ISBN 0-231-05383-5); pap. 14.00x (ISBN 0-231-05382-7). Columbia U Pr.

Stanner, W. E. The South Seas in Transition: A Study of Post-War Rehabilitation & Reconstruction in Three British Pacific Dependencies. LC 82-15534. xiv, 448p. 1982. Repr. of 1953 ed. lib. bdg. 39.75x (ISBN 0-313-23661-5, STSOS). Greenwood.

SAMPLED-DATA SYSTEMS

see Discrete Time Systems

SAMPLERS

Hurt, Zuelia A. Country Samplers. LC 82-60542. (Illus.). 128p. 1983. 17.26i (ISBN 0-8487-0520-3). Oxmoor Hse.

SAMPLING (STATISTICS)

see also Biometry; Errors, Theory Of; Mathematical Statistics; Probabilities; Quality Control

Brewer, K. R. & Hanif, M. Sampling with Unequal Probabilities. (Lecture Notes in Statistics Ser.: Vol. 15). (Illus.). 164p. 1983. pap. 12.80 (ISBN 0-387-90807-2). Springer-Verlag.

Efron, B. The Jackknife, the Bootstrap & Other Resampling Plans. LC 81-84856. (CBMS-NSF Regional Conference Ser.: No. 38). viii, 92p. 1982. 12.50 (ISBN 0-89871-179-7). Soc Indus Appl Math.

Nisselson, Harold & Madow, William G., eds. Incomplete Data in Sample Surveys: Treatise, 2 vols. Date not set. Vol. 1. price not set (ISBN 0-12-363901-8); Vol. 2. price not set (ISBN 0-12-363902-6). Acad Pr.

SAMSON, JUDGE OF ISRAEL

Ginn, Roman. The Conversion of Samson. LC 82-24073. 1983. pap. 3.50 (ISBN 0-932506-21-6). St Bedes Pubns.

SAMUELSON, PAUL

Solow, Robert & Brown, E. Carey, eds. Paul Samuelson & Modern Economic Theory. 350p. 1983. 27.00 (ISBN 0-07-059667-0, C). McGraw.

SAMURAI

Addiss, Stephen. Samurai Painters. LC 82-48781. (Great Japanese Art Ser.). (Illus.). 48p. 1982. 18.95 (ISBN 0-87011-563-4). Kodansha.

SAN ANTONIO, TEXAS

Hugill, Peter J. & Doughty, Robin W., eds. Field Trip Guide: AAG San Antonio 1982. (Illus.). 165p. (Orig.). 1982. pap. 2.00 (ISBN 0-89291-165-4). Assn Am Geographers.

SAN DIEGO, CALIFORNIA–HISTORY

Engstrand, Iris H. Serra's San Diego: Father Junipero Serra & California's Beginnings. (Illus.). 1982. 2.95 (ISBN 0-918740-02-9). San Diego Hist.

SAN FRANCISCO

Bay Area Employer Directory, 1983-1984. 1983. 49.95 (ISBN 0-916210-83-9). Albin.

The Complete San Francisco Bay Area Directory, 1983, 2 vols. 2000p. 1983. pap. 95.00 (ISBN 0-87436-353-5). ABC-Clio.

SAN FRANCISCO–DESCRIPTION

Bakalinsky, Adah. Stairway Walks in San Francisco. LC 82-81462. (Illus.). 128p. (Orig.). 1983. pap. 5.95 (ISBN 0-938530-10-0, 10-0). Lexikos.

Hudson, William R. & Bozzini, Yvette M. I Love Parking in San Francisco. (Illus.). 80p. (Orig.). 1982. pap. 4.95 (ISBN 0-9609838-0-5). Get Happy.

Pennink, Betsy. This is San Francisco, No. B18. (Heinemann Guided Readers). (Illus.). 32p. (Orig.). 1983. pap. text ed. 2.00x (ISBN 0-435-27089-3). Heinemann Ed.

SAN FRANCISCO–DESCRIPTION–GUIDEBOOKS

Advocate Gay Visitors Guide to San Francisco, 1982-1983. LC 82-80354. 1982. pap. 4.95 (ISBN 0-917076-03-6). Liberation Pubns.

Levin, Bella & Whelan, Dan. City Guide, 1983: San Francisco Bay Area & Northern California. (Illus.). 312p. (Orig.). 1982. pap. 4.95 (ISBN 0-940562-10-3). Danella Pubns.

St. Pierre, Brian & Low, Jennie. The Flavor of Chinatown. LC 82-14556. 160p. (Orig.). 1982. pap. 5.95 (ISBN 0-87701-261-X). Chronicle Bks.

San Francisco: On the Go Restaurant Guides. (Illus., Orig.). 1982. pap. 7.95 (ISBN 0-89416-003-6). Travel World.

San Francisco: On the Go Travel Guide. (Illus., Orig.). 1982. pap. 7.95 (ISBN 0-89416-002-8). Travel World.

Thomas Cook, Inc. & Norback & Co., Inc. The Thomas Cook Travel Guide to San Francisco. Date not set. pap. 3.95 (ISBN 0-440-18896-2). Dell.

Whitnah, Dorothy & Winnett, Thomas. Outdoor Guide to the San Francisco Bay Area. (Illus.). 416p. 1983. pap. 9.95 (ISBN 0-89997-026-5). Wilderness Pr.

Wurman, Richard S., ed. San Francisco-Access. (Access Guidebook Ser.). (Illus.). 1982. pap. 8.95 (ISBN 0-9604858-3-X). Access Pr.

SAN FRANCISCO–FIRE DEPARTMENT

Hall, George & Burks, John. Working Fire: The San Francisco Fire Department. (Illus.). 1982. pap. 14.94 (ISBN 0-916290-14-X). SquareBooks.

SAN FRANCISCO–HISTORY

Cole, Tom. A Short History of San Francisco. LC 81-2588. (Illus.). 144p. (Orig.). 1981. pap. 8.95 (ISBN 0-938530-00-3, 00-3). Lexikos.

SAN FRANCISCO BAY AND BAY REGION

Conomos, T. J., ed. San Francisco Bay: The Urbanized Estuary. 469p. (Orig.). 1979. 16.95 (ISBN 0-934394-00-8). AAASPD.

Doss, Margot Patterson. A Walker's Yearbook: Fifty-Two Seasonal Walks in the San Francisco Bay Area. (Illus.). 288p. (Orig.). 1983. pap. 8.95 (ISBN 0-89141-154-2). Presidio Pr.

Kockelman, W. J. & Leviton, A. E. San Francisco Bay: Use & Protection. LC 82-71291. 310p. (Orig.). 1982. 17.95 (ISBN 0-934394-04-0). AAASPD.

Petersen, Grant. Roads of Alameda, Contra Costa & Marin Counties: A Topographic Guide for Bicylists. 200p. Date not set. pap. 5.95 (ISBN 0-930588-07-X). Heyday Bks.

SAN JUAN COUNTY, NEW MEXICO

Griffiths, Thomas M. San Juan Country. (Illus.). 1983. price not set (ISBN 0-87108-505-4). Pruett.

SANCTIFICATION

see also Merit (Christianity); Mystical Union

Simpson, A. B. Santificados por Completo-Wholly Sanctified. 136p. (Eng.). 1981. 2.50 (ISBN 0-87509-307-8). Chr Pubns.

SANCTUARIES, WILDLIFE

see Wildlife Refuges

SANDWICHES

Uvezian, Sonia. The Complete International Sandwich Book. 284p. 1982. 17.95 (ISBN 0-686-38086-X). Stein & Day.

SANGER, MARGARET (HIGGINS), 1883-1966

Reynolds, Moira D. Margaret Sanger, Leader for Birth Control. Rahmas, Sigurd C., ed. (Outstanding Personalities Ser.: No. 93). 32p. (gr. 9-12). 1982. 2.95 (ISBN 0-87157-593-0); pap. text ed. 1.95 (ISBN 0-87157-093-9). SamHar Pr.

SANITARY AFFAIRS

see Public Health

SANITARY CHEMISTRY

see Food–Analysis; Food Adulteration and Inspection; Water–Analysis

SANITARY ENGINEERING

see also Drainage; Filters and Filtration; Municipal Engineering; Pollution; Refuse and Refuse Disposal; Sanitation; Sewage; Water-Supply

Restoration of Sewerage Systems. 296p. 1982. 111.00x (ISBN 0-7277-0145-2, Pub. by Telford England). State Mutual Bk.

Rudman, Jack. Sanitary Engineer II. (Career Examination Ser.: C-2945). (Cloth bdg. avail. on request). pap. 12.00 (ISBN 0-8373-2945-0). Natl Learning.

--Sanitary Engineer III. (Career Examination Ser.: C-2946). (Cloth bdg. avail. on request). pap. 14.00 (ISBN 0-8373-2946-9). Natl Learning.

--Sanitary Engineer IV. (Career Examination Ser.: C-2947). (Cloth bdg. avail. on request). pap. 14.00 (ISBN 0-8373-2947-7). Natl Learning.

SANITATION

see also Disinfection and Disinfectants; Pollution; Public Health; Refuse and Refuse Disposal; Sanitary Engineering; School Health; Ventilation; Water-Purification; Water-Supply

also subdivision Medical and Sanitary Affairs under names of wars and campaigns, e.g. World War, 1939-1945–Medical and Sanitary Affairs

Feachem, Richard G. & Bradley, David J. Sanitation & Disease: Health Aspects of Excreta & Wastewater Management. Garelick, Hemda & Mara, D. Duncan, eds. 1983. write for info. (ISBN 0-471-90094-X, Pub. by Wiley-Interscience). Wiley.

Rudman, Jack. Sanitation Dispatcher. (Career Examination Ser.: C-2881). (Cloth bdg. avail. on request). pap. 10.00 (ISBN 0-8373-2881-0). Natl Learning.

Schiller, E. J. & Droste, R. L., eds. Water Supply & Sanitation in Developing Countries. LC 81-86538. (Illus.). 368p. 1982. 29.95 (ISBN 0-250-40490-7). Ann Arbor Science.

Troller, John A., ed. Sanitation in Food Processing. LC 82-16291. (Food Science & Technology Ser.). Date not set. price not set (ISBN 0-12-700660-5). Acad Pr.

SANITATION, TROPICAL

see Tropical Medicine

SANSKRIT LANGUAGE

see also Vedic Language

Gupta, Dharmendra K. Recent Studies in Sanskirt & Indology. 1982. 28.00x (ISBN 0-8364-0913-2, Pub. by Ajanta). South Asia Bks.

SANSKRIT LITERATURE

Keith, Arthur B., tr. from Sanskirt. Rigveda Brahmanas: The Aitareya & kausitaki of the Rigveda. LC 73-929544. 555p. 1981. Repr. of 1920 ed. 20.00x (ISBN 0-8002-3060-4). Intl Pubns Serv.

SANSKRIT POETRY–HISTORY AND CRITICISM

Siegel, Lee. Fires of Love-Waters of Peace. LC 82-21767. 1983. text ed. 12.50 (ISBN 0-8248-0828-2). UH Pr.

SANTA BARBARA, CALIFORNIA

Schuman, Dewey, ed. Headlines: A History of Santa Barbara for the Pages of Its Newspapers, 1855 to 1982. (Illus.). 264p. 1982. 19.95 (ISBN 0-88496-192-3); pap. 11.95 (ISBN 0-88496-191-5). Capra Pr.

SANTA CLARA COUNTY, CALIFORNIA

Spangle, Francis & Rusmore, Jean. South Bay Trails: Outdoor Adventures in Santa Clara Valley. Winnett, Thomas, ed. (Illus.). 224p. 1983. pap. 8.95 (ISBN 0-89997-022-2). Wilderness Pr.

SANTA FE, NEW MEXICO

Jamison, Bill. Santa Fe: An Intimate View. LC 82-81390. (Illus., Orig.). 1982. pap. 7.95 (ISBN 0-9608504-0-6). Milagro Co.

SARACENIC ARCHITECTURE

see Architecture, Islamic

SARACENIC ART

see Art, Islamic

SARCODE

see Protoplasm

SARCOIDOSIS

Chretien, J. & Marsac, J., eds. Sarcoidosis & Other Granulomatous Disorders: 9th International Conference, Paris, 31 August - 4 September 1981. (Illus.). 950p. 1982. 120.00 (ISBN 0-08-027088-3). Pergamon.

SARCOMA

see Tumors

SARDIS

Hanfmann, George M. & Mierse, William E. Sardis from Prehistoric to Roman Times: Results of the Archaeological Exploration of Sardis, 1958-1975. (Illus.). 528p. 1983. text ed. 35.00x (ISBN 0-674-78925-3). Harvard U Pr.

Waldbaum, Jane C. Metalwork from Sardis: The Finds Through 1974. (Archaeological Exploration of Sardis Monographs: No. 8). (Illus.). 280p. 1983. text ed. 40.00x (ISBN 0-674-57070-7). Harvard U Pr.

SARMIENTO, FELIX RUBEN GARCIA, 1867-1916

Jrade, Cathy L. Ruben Dario & the Romantic Search for Unity: The Modernist Recourse to Esoteric Tradition. (Texas Pan American Ser.). 192p. 1983. text ed. 19.95x (ISBN 0-292-75075-7). U of Tex Pr.

SAROYAN, WILLIAM, 1908-

Saroyan, Aram. William Saroyan. (Illus.). 224p. cloth 16.95 (ISBN 0-15-196762-8). HarBraceJ.

--William Saroyan. (Illus.). 224p. pap. 7.95 (ISBN 0-15-696780-4, Harv). HarBraceJ.

SARTRE, JEAN PAUL, 1905-1980

Boni, Sylvain. The Self & the Other in the Ontologies of Sartre & Buber. LC 82-20130. 202p. (Orig.). 1983. lib. bdg. 21.75 (ISBN 0-8191-2852-X); pap. text ed. 10.75 (ISBN 0-8191-2853-8). U Pr of Amer.

Champigny, Robert. Sartre & Drama. 17.00 (ISBN 0-917786-31-9). French Lit.

Fell, Joseph P. Heidegger & Sartre: An Essay on Being & Place. 517p. 1983. pap. 15.00 (ISBN 0-231-04555-7). Columbia U Pr.

Gleicher, Jules. The Accidental Revolutionary: Essays on the Political Teaching of Jean-Paul Sartre. LC 82-20067. 216p. (Orig.). 1983. lib. bdg. 18.75 (ISBN 0-8191-2835-X); pap. text ed. 7.75 (ISBN 0-8191-2836-8). U Pr of Amer.

Hayim, Gila J. The Existential Sociology of Jean-Paul Sartre. LC 80-10131. 176p. 1982. pap. text ed. 7.00 (ISBN 0-87023-381-5). U of Mass Pr.

SATAN

see Devil

SATELLITE COMMUNICATION SYSTEMS

see Artificial Satellites in Telecommunication

SATELLITES

see also Moon

Hoard, Samuel L. Satellite Services Sourcebook. LC 82-72850. 1982. 75.00 (ISBN 0-910339-00-7). Drake's Ptg & Pub.

SATIRISTS

Kelly, Richard. George DuMaurier. (English Authors Ser.). 200p. 1983. lib. bdg. 16.95 (ISBN 0-8057-6841-6, Twayne). G K Hall.

SATURNISM

see Lead-Poisoning

SATYAGRAHA

see Passive Resistance

SAUCERS, FLYING

see Flying Saucers

SAUCES

Sauces. (Good Cook Ser.). 1983. lib. bdg. 19.96 (ISBN 0-8094-2972-1, Pub. by Time-Life). Silver.

SAUDI ARABIA

Anderson, Norman & Rentz, George. The Kingdom of Saudi Arabia. (Illus.). 256p. 1983. 60.00 (ISBN 0-905743-28-8, Pub by Salem Hse Ltd). Merrimack Bk Serv.

Freedman, Robert O., ed. Soviet Jewry in the Decisive Decade, 1971-1980. (Duke Press Policy Studies). 135p. 1983. lib. bdg. 18.75 (ISBN 0-8223-0544-5); pap. 9.75 (ISBN 0-8223-0555-0). Duke.

Olson, David V. Badges & Distinctive Insignia of the Kingdom of Saudi Arabia. 186p. 1981. pap. 10.00 (ISBN 0-686-84348-7). Olson QMD.

SAUDI ARABIA–ECONOMIC CONDITIONS

Al-Bashir, Faisal Safooq. A Structural Econometric Model of the Saudi Arabian Economy: Nineteen Sixty to Nineteen Seventy. LC 77-441. 144p. Repr. of 1977 ed. text ed. 36.50 (ISBN 0-471-02177-6). Krieger.

Saudi Arabia. 375.00x (ISBN 0-686-99850-2, Pub. by Metra England). State Mutual Bk.

SAVANNAH

Horne, Peggy. Savannah's Battlefield Park: A Photographic Essay. LC 82-61031. (Illus.). 64p. 1982. 18.95 (ISBN 0-9609236-0-8). Regina Pr GA.

SAVANNAH–HISTORY

DeBolt, Margaret W. Savannah Spectres. Freidman, Robert, ed. LC 82-23455. (Illus., Orig.). 1983. pap. 6.95 (ISBN 0-89865-201-4). Donning Co.

Wood, Louisa F. Behind Those Garden Garden Walls in Historic Savannah. (Illus.). 80p. 1982. text ed. 15.00 (ISBN 0-9610106-0-6); pap. text ed. 9.95 (ISBN 0-686-38453-9). Historic Sav.

SAVATE

see Boxing

SAVING AND INVESTMENT

see also Investments

Branch, Ben. Fundamentals of Investing. LC 75-26703. 301p. 1976. 29.95x (ISBN 0-471-09650-4). Wiley.

Coleman, Kenneth. U. S. Financial Institutions in Crisis: How Safe are Your Savings? Chambers, Catherine & Lewis, David, eds. 13p. 1982. pap. 5.95 (ISBN 0-942632-01-X). Seraphim Pr.

Gupta, Kanhaya L. & Islam, M Anisul. Foreign Capital, Savings & Growth. 1983. lib. bdg. 34.50 (ISBN 90-277-1449-5, Pub. by Reidel Holland). Kluwer Boston.

Kishel, Gregory F. & Kishel, Patricia G. One Hundred One Ways to Save Money. (Illus.). 24p. 1982. pap. 3.95 (ISBN 0-935346-01-5). K & K Enter.

SAWS

Thomas, Elaine & Benton, C. E. Safe Chain Saw Design. 1983. write for info. (ISBN 0-938830-02-3). Inst Product.

SAYINGS

see Aphorisms and Apothegms; Proverbs; Quotations

SCALDS

see Burns and Scalds

SCALES (MUSIC)

see Musical Intervals and Scales

SCANDINAVIA–DESCRIPTION AND TRAVEL–GUIDEBOOKS

Fodor's Budget Spain '83. (Illus.). 192p. 1983. pap. 6.95 (ISBN 0-679-00887-X). McKay.

Nickels, Sylzie. Scandinavia. LC 82-61196. (Pocket Guide Ser.). (Illus.). 1983. pap. 4.95 (ISBN 0-528-84893-3). Rand.

SCANDINAVIA–POLITICS

Allardt, Erik & Andre, Nils, eds. Nordic Democracy. Friis, Erik J., et al. Valen, Henry & Wendt, Frantz, trs. from Danish, Swedish, Norwegian, Icelandic & Finish. (Illus.). 780p. 1981. 32.95X (ISBN 87-7429-040-1). Nordic Bks.

SCANDINAVIAN ART

see Art, Scandinavian

SCANDINAVIAN AUTHORS

see Authors, Scandinavian

SCANDINAVIAN LANGUAGES

see also Danish Language; Norwegian Language

Haugen, Eva Lund & Haugen, Einar. A Bibliography of Scandinavian Dictionaries. LC 82-48985. 300p. (Orig.). 1983. lib. bdg. write for info. (ISBN 0-527-38842-4). Kraus Intl.

SCARLATTI, ALESSANDRO, 1659-1725

Scarlatti. The Operas of Alessandro Scarlatti: Vol. III-Tigrane. Collins, Michael, ed. (Harvard Publications in Music: No. 13). (Illus.). 192p. 1983. text ed. 35.00x. Harvard U Pr.

SCATTERING (PHYSICS)

AIP Conference, 89th, Argonne National Laboratory, 1981. Neutron Scattering: Proceedings. Faber, John, Jr., ed. LC 82-73094. 397p. 1982. lib. bdg. 35.50 (ISBN 0-88318-188-6). Am Inst Physics.

Bransden, B. H. Atomic Collision Theory. 2nd ed. (Illus.). 500p. 1970. text ed. 29.95 (ISBN 0-8053-1181-5). Benjamin-Cummings.

Colton, David & Kress, Rainer. Integral Equation Methods in Scattering Theory. (Pure & Applied Mathematics, Texts, Monographs & Tracts). 350p. 1983. 34.95 (ISBN 0-471-86420-X, Pub. by Wiley-Interscience). Wiley.

Schopper, H., ed. Elastic & Charge Exchange Scattering of Elementary Particles: Pion Nucleon Scattering-Methods & Results of Phenomenological Analyses. (Landolt-Boernstein-New Series. Group I: Vol. 9, Subvol. B, Pt. 2). (Illus.). 610p. 1983. 400.00 (ISBN 0-387-11282-0). Springer-Verlag.

SCATTERING OF LIGHT

see Light–Scattering

SCATTERING OF PARTICLES

see Scattering (Physics)

SCENARIOS

see Moving-Picture Plays; Plots (Drama, Novel, etc.); Television Plays

SCENERY (STAGE)

see Theaters–Stage-Setting and Scenery

SCEPTICISM

see Skepticism

SCHAUMAN'S DISEASE

see Sarcoidosis

SCHEDULED AIRLINES

see Air Lines

SCHEDULED CASTES (INDIA)

see Untouchables

SCHEDULING (MANAGEMENT)

see also Network Analysis (Planning); Network Analysis (Planning); Critical Path Analysis; Queuing Theory

Baker, Kenneth R. Introduction to Sequencing & Scheduling. LC 74-8010. 305p. 1974. text ed. 32.95x (ISBN 0-471-04555-1). Wiley.

Benjamin, Deborah V. A Road Map to Effective Planning & Time Management. rev. ed. 215p. 1982. pap. write for info. (ISBN 0-911347-00-3). Debron.

Killen, James E. Mathematical Programming Methods for Geographers & Planners. LC 82-42839. 384p. 1983. 35.00x (ISBN 0-312-50133-1). St Martin.

Rosow, Jerome M. & Zager, Robert. New Work Schedules for A Changing Society. 128p. 10.95 (ISBN 0-686-84774-1); softcover summary 4.95 (ISBN 0-686-84775-X). Work in Amer.

Singleton, Ralph S. & Vietor, Joan E. Schedule It Right! (Illus.). 300p. 1983. text ed. 42.50 (ISBN 0-943728-03-7); pap. text ed. 30.00 (ISBN 0-943728-01-0). Lone Eagle Prods.

SCHELLING, FRIEDRICH WILHELM JOSEPH VON, 1775-1854

White, Alan. Schelling: An Introduction to the System of Freedom. LC 82-16034. 224p. 1983. text ed. 20.00x (ISBN 0-300-02896-2). Yale U Pr.

SCHILLER, JOHANN CHRISTOPH FRIEDRICH VON, 1759-1805

Sharpe, Lesley. Schiller & the Historical Character: Presentation & Interpretation in the Historiographical Works & in the Historical Dramas. (Modern Languages & Literature Monographs). 220p. 1982. 29.50x (ISBN 0-19-815537-9). Oxford U Pr.

SCHIZOPHRENIA

McFarlane, William R., ed. Family Therapy in Schizophrenia. LC 82-11742. (Family Therapy Ser.). 350p. 1983. text ed. 25.00x (ISBN 0-89862-042-2, G34). Guilford Pr.

Shulman, Bernard H. Essays in Schizophrenia. 2nd ed. LC 82-72136. 191p. 1983. pap. 14.50x (ISBN 0-918560-29-2). A Adler Inst.

Stone, Michael H. & Forest, David. Treating Schizophrenic Patients: A Critical Analytical Approach. Albert, Harry D., ed. (Illus.). 352p. 24.95 (ISBN 0-07-001917-7, P&RB). McGraw.

Wasow, Mona. Coping with Schizophrenia. LC 81-86713. 12.95 (ISBN 0-8314-0062-5); pap. 8.95 (ISBN 0-686-82342-7). Sci & Behavior.

Zales, Michael R., ed. Affective & Schizophrenic Disorders: New Approaches to Diagnosis & Treatment. 304p. 1983. 25.00 (ISBN 0-87630-324-6). Brunner-Mazel.

SCHIZOPHRENICS–PERSONAL NARRATIVES

Owens, Carolyn P. A Promise of Sanity. 1982. pap. 4.95 (ISBN 0-8423-4901-4). Tyndale.

Sheehan, Susan. Is there No Place on Earth for Me? Coles, Robert M., frwd. by. LC 82-40424. 352p. 1983. pap. 4.95 (ISBN 0-394-71378-8, Vin). Random.

SCHOLARS

Here are entered biographical works, historical and statistical works are entered under the heading Learning and Scholarship.

see also Degrees, Academic

Jaques Cattell Press, ed. Directory of American Scholars, 4 vols. 8th ed. Incl. Vol. I. History (ISBN 0-8352-1478-8); Vol. II. English, Speech, Drama (ISBN 0-8352-1479-6); Vol. III. Foreign Language, Linguistics, & Philology (ISBN 0-8352-1481-8); Vol. IV. Philosophy, Religion & Law (ISBN 0-8352-1482-6). 2900p. Set. 295.00 (ISBN 0-8352-1476-1); 90.00 ea. Bowker.

SCHOLASTIC APTITUDE TEST
Bizer, Linda S. & Markel, Geraldine P. The ABC's of the SAT: A Parent's Guide to College Entrance Exams. LC 82-13858. (Illus.). 160p. (Orig.). 1983. pap. 3.95 (ISBN 0-668-05666-5; 5666). Arco.
Corras, James & Zerowin, Jeffrey. Improving College Admission Test Scores: Verbal Workbook. 184p. (Orig.). (gr. 11-12). 1982. pap. write for info. (ISBN 0-88210-135-8). Natl Assn Principals.
Leo, Miriam & Forlini, Gary. The S.A.T. Home Study Kit. Gruber, Michael, ed. (Home Study Ser.). 1982. 69.50 (ISBN 0-686-82415-6); workbook-audio-tape kit avail. (ISBN 0-910859-01-9). Pinebrook Pr.
Steer, Charles & Kelly, John. How to Ace the SAT. 288p. 1981. pap. 8.95 (ISBN 0-671-25300-X, Fireside). S&S.
SCHOLASTIC SUCCESS
see Academic Achievement
SCHOLASTICISM-HISTORY
Giuberti, F. Materials for a Study on Twelfth Century Scholasticism. (History of Logic Ser.: Vol. II). 158p. 1982. 34.95x (ISBN 0-686-42759-9, Pub. by Bibliopolis Italy); pap. text ed. 19.95x (ISBN 88-7088-056-7). Humanities.
SCHOOL ADJUSTMENT
see Student Adjustment
SCHOOL ADMINISTRATION
see School Management and Organization
SCHOOL ADMINISTRATORS
see School Superintendents and Principals
SCHOOL-AGE PARENTS
see Adolescent Parents
SCHOOL AND HOME
see Home and School
SCHOOL ARCHITECTURE
see School Buildings
SCHOOL ASSEMBLY
see Schools-Exercises and Recreations
SCHOOL BOARDS
see also School Superintendents and Principals
Hudlin, Richard A. Survey of Black School Board Members in the South. Lewis, Shelby & Kenneth, Ellis, eds. 1981. 1.00 (ISBN 0-686-38021-5). Voter Ed Proj.
Schwartz, Cipora. How to Run a School Board Campaign & Win. 142p. (Orig.). 1982. pap. 5.95 (ISBN 0-934460-19-1). NCCE.
SCHOOL-BOOKS
see Text-Books
SCHOOL BUILDINGS
Energy Management & Conservation: Special Session on Energy Management at the 66th ASBO Annual Meeting & Exhibits. 1981. 7.50. Assn Sch Busn.
Field-Proven Programs to Conserve Energy in Schools: ASBO's 65th Annual Meeting Mini-workshops on Energy & Energy Management. 1980. 5.95. Assn Sch Busn.
School Buildings & Natural Disasters. (Education, Buildings & Equipment Ser.: No. 4). 85p. 1982. pap. 9.50 (ISBN 0-686-84622-2, U1237, UNESCO). Unipub.
SCHOOL BUS DRIVERS
see Motor Bus Drivers
SCHOOL BUSINESS MANAGEMENT
see Public Schools-Business Management
SCHOOL CHILDREN-FOOD
Rudman, Jack. School Lunch Coordinator: C-317. (Career Examination Ser.). (Cloth bdg. avail. on request). pap. 10.00 (ISBN 0-8373-0317-6). Natl Learning.
SCHOOL CHILDREN-TRANSPORTATION
Rudman, Jack. Assistant School Transportation Supervisor. (Career Examination Ser.: C-112). (Cloth bdg. avail. on request). pap. 12.00 (ISBN 0-8373-0112-2). Natl Learning.
--School Transportation Supervisor. (Career Examination Ser.: C-113). (Cloth bdg. avail. on request). pap. 12.00 (ISBN 0-8373-0113-0). Natl Learning.
SCHOOL COSTS
see Education-Costs
SCHOOL DISCIPLINE
see also Classroom Management; Corporal Punishment; Self-Government (In Education)
Gagne, Eve E. School Behavior & School Discipline: Coping with Deviant Behavior in the Schools. LC 82-15912. 176p. 1983. lib. bdg. 20.75 (ISBN 0-8191-2748-5); pap. text ed. 10.00 (ISBN 0-8191-2749-3). U Pr of Amer.
Grey, Loren. Discipline Without Fear. 192p. 1982. pap. 6.00 (ISBN 0-939654-02-4). Social Interest.
--Discipline Without Tyranny. 192p. 1982. pap. 6.00 (ISBN 0-939654-03-2). Social Interest.
McDaniel, Thomas R. The Teacher's Dilemma: Essays of School Law & School Discipline. LC 82-21743. (Illus.). 158p. (Orig.). 1983. lib. bdg. 19.75 (ISBN 0-8191-2944-5); pap. text ed. 9.75 (ISBN 0-8191-2945-3). U Pr of Amer.
Martin, Betty B. & Quilling, Joan. Positive Approaches to Classroom Discipline. 1981. 4.00 (ISBN 0-686-38742-2). Home Econ Educ.
Yonker, Tom. But Teach, You Ain't Listenin', or How to Cope with Violence in a Public School Classroom. LC 82-60524. 125p. (Orig.). 1983. pap. 9.95 (ISBN 0-88247-678-5). R & E Res Assoc.
SCHOOL DRAMA
see College and School Drama
SCHOOL DROPOUTS
see Dropouts
SCHOOL ENDOWMENTS
see Endowments
SCHOOL EVALUATION
see Educational Surveys
SCHOOL EXCURSIONS
see also Field Work (Educational Method)
Redleaf, Rhoda, ed. Field Trips: An Adventure in Learning. (Illus.). 75p. (Orig.). 1980. pap. text ed. 8.95 (ISBN 0-934140-14-6). Toys N Things.
SCHOOL FACILITIES
see also School Buildings; Schools-Furniture, Equipment, etc.;
also specific facilities, Gymnasiums
Fisk, Lori & Lindgren, Henry C. Learning Centers. 1974. pap. 6.95 (ISBN 0-914420-54-2). Exceptional Pr Inc.
SCHOOL FINANCE
see Education-Finance
SCHOOL FUNDS
see Public Schools
SCHOOL FURNITURE
see Schools-Furniture, Equipment, etc.
SCHOOL HEALTH
see also Playgrounds; Posture; Sports Medicine
Hamburg, Marian & Hopp, Joyce, eds. Cross-Cultural Aspects of School Health: Journal of School Health. 1983. pap. 4.50 (ISBN 0-917160-18-5). Am Sch Health.
SCHOOL HOUSES
see School Buildings
SCHOOL INSPECTION
see School Management and Organization
SCHOOL INTEGRATION
Metcalf, George R. From Little Rock to Boston: The History of School Desegregation. LC 82-15581. (Contributions to the Study of Education Ser.: No. 8). 368p. 1983. lib. bdg. 35.00 (ISBN 0-313-23470-1, MDS/). Greenwood.
Weinberg, Meyer. The Search for Quality Integrated Education: Policy & Research on Minority Students in School & College. LC 82-12016. (Contributions to the Study of Education: No. 7). (Illus.). 320p. 1983. lib. bdg. 35.00 (ISBN 0-313-23714-X, LC214). Greenwood.
SCHOOL JOURNALISM
see College and School Journalism
SCHOOL LAW
see Educational Law and Legislation
SCHOOL LIBRARIES
see also Children's Literature (Collections); Instructional Materials Centers; Libraries, Young People's
also subdivisions under Children's Literature
Toor, Ruth & Weisburg, Hilda K. The Complete Book of Forms for Managing the School Library Media Center. 256p. 1982. comb-bound 34.50x (ISBN 0-87628-229-X). Ctr Appl Res.
SCHOOL LIFE
see Students
SCHOOL LUNCHES
see School Children-Food
SCHOOL MANAGEMENT AND ORGANIZATION
Here are entered works dealing with the management, organization, supervision, etc. of schools in general, and in the United States as a whole.
see also Articulation (Education); Classroom Management; High Schools-Administration; Public Schools-Business Management; School Boards; School Discipline; School Secretaries; School Superintendents and Principals; Self-Government (In Education); Student Administrator Relationships; Teaching
ASBO's Management Techniques Research Committee. Compendium of Management Techniques. 1982. 5.95 (ISBN 0-910170-23-1). Assn Sch Busn.
ASBO's Negotiations Research Committee. Negotiations & the Manager in Public Education. 1980. 27.50 (ISBN 0-910170-16-9). Assn Sch Busn.
Clancey, Peter L. Nineteen Improving Schools & Why Their "Formula for Success". (Illus.). 206p. (Orig.). 1982. pap. text ed. 7.95 (ISBN 0-911467-00-9). Educ Leadership.
Dunn, Kenneth & Dunn, Rita. Situational Leadership for Principles: The School Administrator in Action. LC 82-11211. 228p. 1983. 17.50 (ISBN 0-686-84595-1, Parker). P-H.
Fehrman, Cherie. The Complete School Secretary's Desk Book. LC 82-3782. 356p. 1982. 24.50 (ISBN 0-13-163352-X, Busn). P-H.
Field-Proven Programs to Improve Maintenance & Operations: Special Sessions on Maintenance & Operations at the 66th ASBO Annual Meeting & Exhibits. 1981. 7.50 (ISBN 0-910170-21-5). Assn Sch Busn.
Handbook for Trainers in Educational Management. 273p. 1981. pap. 13.75 (ISBN 0-686-81858-X, UB106, UNESCO). Unipub.
Hill, Clyde M., ed. Educational Progress & School Administration: Symposium By a Number of His Former Associates Written As a Tribute to Frank Ellsworth Spauling. 1936. text ed. 49.50x (ISBN 0-686-83532-8). Elliots Bks.
Kowalski, Theodore J. & Nelson, Norbert. Solving Educational Facility Problems. 300p. 1983. pap. text ed. price not set (ISBN 0-915202-36-0). Accel Devel.
Madaus, G. & Scriven, M. S. Conceptual Issues in Evaluation. (Evaluation & Education in Human Services Ser.). 1983. lib. bdg. 38.00 (ISBN 0-89838-123-1). Kluwer Nijhoff.
Moore, Kathryn M. & Trow, Jo Anne J. Professional Advancement Kit-What to do until the Mentor Arrives: Administrative Procedures-A Practice Manual. (Orig.). 1982. write for info. (ISBN 0-686-82337-0); pap. 13.50. Natl Assn Women.
Pizzillo, Joseph J. Intercultural Studies: School in Diversity. 272p. 1982. pap. text ed. 10.95 (ISBN 0-8403-2860-5). Kendall-Hunt.
Powers, David R. & Powers, Mary F. Making Participatory Management Work: Effective Participatory Decision Making in Academic Administration. (Higher Education Ser.). 1983. text ed. write for info. (ISBN 0-87589-567-0). Jossey-Bass.
School Facilities Maintenance & Operations: Special Sessions at ASBO's 67th Annual Meeting & Exhibits. 1982. 7.95 (ISBN 0-910170-25-8). Assn Sch Busn.
Silver, Paula. Educational Administration: Theoretical Perspectives on Practice & Research. 416p. 1983. text ed. 17.50 scp (ISBN 0-06-046161-6, HarpC). Har-Row.
Thomason, Nevada. Circulation Systems for School Media Centers. (Illus.). 250p. 1983. lib. bdg. 23.50 (ISBN 0-87287-370-6). Libs Unl.
Weber, Jeffrey R. User's Guide to the Timex-Sinclair ZX-81. (WSI's How to Use Your Microcomputer Ser.). 280p. (Orig.). 1983. pap. cancelled (ISBN 0-938862-27-8). Weber Systems.
Wiles, Jon & Bondi, Joseph. Principles of School Administration. 448p. Date not set. text ed. 22.95 (ISBN 0-675-20054-7). Merrill.
Wilson, Donald R. Words for School Administrators: Example of Commondations & Constructive Suggestions for Through Teacher Evalvation. LC 80-71091. 170p. 1981. 11.95 (ISBN 0-939136-00-7). Civic Educ Assn.
Winstanley, David. A Schoolmaster's Notebook. Kelly, E. & Kelly, T., eds. 128p. 1957. 19.00 (ISBN 0-7190-1118-3). Manchester.
SCHOOL MUSIC
Neitmann, Erich. Das Politische Lied Im Schulischen Musikunterricht der DDR. 246p. (Ger.). 1982. write for info. (ISBN 3-8204-7042-5). P Lang Pubs.
SCHOOL NURSING
Rudman, Jack. School Nurse Practitioner. (Certified Nurse Examination Ser.: CN-3). 21.95 (ISBN 0-8373-6153-2); pap. 13.95 (ISBN 0-8373-6103-6). Natl Learning.
SCHOOL OPERATION POLICIES
see School Management and Organization
SCHOOL ORGANIZATION
see School Management and Organization
SCHOOL PLANTS
see School Facilities
SCHOOL PLAYGROUNDS
see Playgrounds
SCHOOL PLAYS
see Children's Plays; College and School Drama
SCHOOL PRINCIPALS
see School Superintendents and Principals
SCHOOL PSYCHOLOGISTS
Gelso, Charles J. & Johnson, Deborah H. Explorations in Time-Limited Counseling & Therapy. (Guidance & Counseling Ser.). 300p. 1983. text ed. 25.95x (ISBN 0-8077-2726-1). Tchrs Coll.
Hynd, George W., ed. The School Psychologist: An Introduction. 416p. text ed. 27.00x (ISBN 0-8156-2289-9); pap. text ed. 14.95x (ISBN 0-8156-2290-2). Syracuse U Pr.
SCHOOL SECRETARIES
Fehrman, Cherie. The Complete School Secretary's Desk Book. LC 82-3782. 356p. 1982. 24.50 (ISBN 0-13-163352-X, Busn). P-H.
SCHOOL SOCIAL WORK
see also Personnel Service in Education
Serow, Robert C. Schooling for Social Diversity: An Analysis of Policy & Practice. 1983. pap. text ed. 14.95x (ISBN 0-8077-2729-6). Tchrs Coll.
SCHOOL SPORTS
see also Intramural Sports
also particular sports, e.g. Baseball, Football
Complying with Title IX in Physical Education & High School Sports Programs. 20p. 3.50 (ISBN 0-88314-048-9). AAHPERD.
Physical Education & Sport for the Secondary School Student. 1983. write for info. AAHPERD.
SCHOOL SUPERINTENDENTS AND PRINCIPALS
Barth & Deal. The Effective Principal: A Research Summary. Lucas, Pat, ed. 48p. 1982. pap. text ed. 4.00 (ISBN 0-88210-141-2). Natl Assn Principals.
Driscoll, Eileen R. The Selection & Appointment of School Heads. 3rd. ed. 1982. pap. 6.50 (ISBN 0-934338-47-7). NAIS.
Weber, Jeffrey R. User's Guide to the Timex-Sinclair ZX-81. (WSI's How to Use Your Microcomputer Ser.). 280p. (Orig.). 1983. pap. cancelled (ISBN 0-938862-27-8). Weber Systems.
SCHOOL SUPPLIES
see Schools-Furniture, Equipment, etc.
SCHOOL SURVEYS
see Educational Surveys
SCHOOL TAXES
see Education-Finance
SCHOOL TEACHING
see Teaching
SCHOOL TRANSPORTATION
see School Children-Transportation
SCHOOL TRUSTEES
see School Boards
SCHOOL VOLUNTEERS
see Volunteer Workers in Education
SCHOOLGIRL PREGNANCY
see Pregnant Schoolgirls
SCHOOLS
see also Boarding Schools; Church Schools; Education; Medical Colleges; Private Schools; Professional Education; Public Schools; Sunday-Schools; Technical Education; Universities and Colleges; Week-Day Church Schools
also headings beginning with the word School; and subdivision Study and Teaching under subjects, e.g. Mathematics-Study and Teaching
Buzzard, Lynn. Schools: They Haven't Got a Prayer. (Issues & Insights Ser.). 1982. pap. 5.95 (ISBN 0-89191-713-6). Cook.
Collective Enrollment Strategies: A Resource Guide. pap. 4.00 (ISBN 0-686-83741-X). NAIS.
Genck, Frederic H. Improving School Performance: How New School Management Techniques Can Raise Learning, Confidence & Morale. 318p. 1983. 25.95 (ISBN 0-03-062477-0). Praeger.
King, Jonathan & Marans, Robert W. The Physical Environment & the Learning Process: A Survey of Recent Research. 92p. 1979. pap. 10.00x (ISBN 0-87944-239-5). Inst Soc Res.
Migdail, Sherry R. & Vail, Priscilla L. Supplement to Alternatives Notebook. 1978. pap. 4.25 (ISBN 0-934338-10-8). NAIS.
Odden, Allan & Webb, Dean, eds. School Finance & School Improvement: Linkages in the 1980's. (American Education Finance Association). 1983. price not set prof ref (ISBN 0-88410-399-4). Ballinger Pub.
SCHOOLS-CURRICULA
see Education-Curricula; Universities and Colleges-Curricula
SCHOOLS-DIRECTORIES
Center for Self Sufficiency Research Division Staff. Index to Self-Sufficiency Related Institutes, Associations, Organizations, Schools, & Others. 200p. 1983. pap. text ed. 19.95 (ISBN 0-910811-19-9). Center Self.
SCHOOLS-EQUIPMENT AND SUPPLIES
see Schools-Furniture, Equipment, etc.
SCHOOLS-EXERCISES AND RECREATIONS
see also Drama in Education; Skits, Stunts, etc.;
also special days observed, e.g. Arbor Day, Memorial Day
Mauldon, E. & Redfern, H. B. Games Teaching. 144p. 1981. 30.00x (ISBN 0-7121-0739-8, Pub. by Macdonald & Evans). State Mutual Bk.
SCHOOLS-FINANCE
see Education-Finance
SCHOOLS-FURNITURE, EQUIPMENT, ETC.
Rudman, Jack. School Purchasing Agent. (Career Examination Ser.: C-863). (Cloth bdg. avail. on request). pap. 12.00 (ISBN 0-8373-0863-1). Natl Learning.
SCHOOLS-INSPECTION
see School Management and Organization
SCHOOLS-JUVENILE LITERATURE
Althea. The School Fair. (Cambridge Dinosaur Information Ser.). (Illus.). 26p. (gr. 7-10). 1983. pap. 1.50 (ISBN 0-521-27166-5). Cambridge U Pr.
SCHOOLS-LAW AND LEGISLATION
see Educational Law and Legislation
SCHOOLS-MANAGEMENT AND ORGANIZATION
see School Management and Organization
SCHOOLS-OPENING EXERCISES
see Schools-Exercises and Recreations
SCHOOLS-PUBLIC RELATIONS
see Public Relations-Schools
SCHOOLS-RECREATIONS
see Schools-Exercises and Recreations
SCHOOLS-SANITARY AFFAIRS
see School Health
SCHOOLS, COMMERCIAL
see Business Education
SCHOOLS, DENOMINATIONAL
see Church Schools
SCHOOLS, MILITARY
see Military Education
SCHOOLS, PAROCHIAL
see Church Schools
SCHOOLS OF NURSING
see Nursing Schools
SCHUBERT, FRANZ PETER, 1797-1828
Brown, Maurice J. & Sams, Eric. The New Grove Schubert. (The New Grove Composer Biography Ser.). (Illus.). 1983. 16.50 (ISBN 0-393-01683-8); pap. 7.95 (ISBN 0-393-30087-0). Norton.
McLeish, Kenneth & McLeish, Valerie. Schubert. (Composers & their World Ser.). (Illus.). 90p. (gr. 9-12). 1983. 5.95 (ISBN 0-434-95127-7, Pub. by Heinemann England). David & Charles.
Von Hellborn, Heinrich K. The Life of Franz Schubert, 2 vols. Coleridge, A. D., tr. LC 73-163791. Date not set. Repr. of 1869 ed. price not set. Vienna Hse.

SCHUMANN, CLARA JOSEPHINE (WIECK), 1819-1896

Litzman, Berthold, ed. Letters of Clara Schumann & Johannes Brahms, 2 vols. LC 77-163792. Date not set. Repr. of 1927 ed. price not set. Vienna Hse.

Litzmann, Berthold, ed. Clara Schumann: An Artist's Life from Diaries & Letters, 2 vols. Hadow, Grace E., tr. LC 70-163793. Date not set. Repr. of 1913 ed. price not set. Vienna Hse.

SCHUMANN, ROBERT ALEXANDER, 1810-1856

Chissell, Joan. Schumann. Rev. ed. (The Master Musicians Ser.). (Illus.). 268p. 1977. text ed. 12.95 (ISBN 0-460-03170-8, Pub. by J. M. Dent England). Biblio Dist.

SCHWARZENEGGER, ARNOLD

Schwarzenegger, Arnold & Hall, Douglas K. Arnold: The Education of a Bodybuilder. (Illus.). 320p. 1982. pap. 3.95 (ISBN 0-671-46139-7). PB.

SCIENCE

see also Astronomy; Bacteriology; Biology; Botany; Chemistry; Crystallography; Ethnology; Geology; Life Sciences; Mathematics; Meteorology; Mineralogy; Natural History; Paleontology; Petrology; Physics; Physiology; Space Sciences; Zoology

also headings beginning with the word Scientific

Ackerson, et al. Gateways to Science. 4th ed. 1982. write for info. laboratory bks. McGraw.

Box, G. E. & Leonard, Chien-Fu-Wu, eds. Scientific Inference: Data Analysis & Robustness (Symposium) LC 82-22755. Date not set. price not set (ISBN 0-12-121160-6). Acad Pr.

Brooks, Bearl. Beginning Science. (Science Ser.). 24p. (gr. 1). 1979. wkbk. 5.00 (ISBN 0-8209-0139-3, S-1). ESP.

Cohen, I. Bernard. The Newtonian Revolution: With Illustrations of the Transformation of Scientific Ideas. LC 79-18637. (Illus.). 404p. Date not set. pap. 16.95 (ISBN 0-521-27380-3). Cambridge U Pr.

Congressional Quarterly Inc. Advances in Science. LC 78-25601. (Editorial Research Reports). 196p. 1979. pap. 7.50 (ISBN 0-87187-142-4). Congr Quarterly.

Dempsey, Michael W., ed. Illustrated Fact Book of Science. LC 82-16412. (Illus.). 236p. 1983. 9.95 (ISBN 0-668-05729-7, 5729). Arco.

Eisemon, Thomas O. The Science Profession in the Third World: Studies from India & Kenya. Altbach, Philip G., ed. (Special Studies in Comparative Education). 186p. 1982. 22.95 (ISBN 0-03-062023-6). Praeger.

Elrod, Mavis S. Energy & Man. (Science Ser.). 24p. (gr. 5-9). 1976. wkbk. 5.00 (ISBN 0-8209-0148-2, S-10). ESP.

Faulkenstein, Dezmon A. Faulkenstein's Theories are Loose on the Earth. 1982. 7.95. Vantage.

Gardner, Martin. Science: Good, Bad & Bogus. 432p. 1983. pap. 3.95 (ISBN 0-380-61754-4, Discus). Avon.

Holmes, Neal J. & Leake, John B. Gateways to Science Webstermaster Activities, Level 1. 4th ed. (Gateways to Science Ser.). 43p. 1982. pap. text ed. 40.00s (ISBN 0-07-029851-3, W). McGraw.

--Gateways to Science Webstermaster Activities, Level 2. 4th ed. Kita, M. Jane, ed. (Gateways to Science Ser.). 43p. 1982. pap. text ed. 40.00s (ISBN 0-07-029852-1, W). McGraw.

--Gateways to Science Webstermaster Activities, Level 3. 4th ed. Kita, M. Jane, ed. (Gateways to Science Ser.). 85p. 1982. pap. text ed. 40.00s (ISBN 0-07-029853-X, W). McGraw.

--Gateways to Science Webstermaster Activities, Level 4. 4th ed. Mongillo, John F., ed. (Gateways to Science Ser.). 89p. 1982. pap. text ed. 40.00s (ISBN 0-07-029854-8, W). McGraw.

--Gateways to Science Webstermaster Activities, Level 5. 4th ed. (Gateways to Science Ser.). 89p. 1982. pap. text ed. 40.00s (ISBN 0-07-029855-6, W). McGraw.

--Gateways to Science Webstermaster Activities, Level 6. Mongillo, John F., ed. (Gateways to Science Ser.). 97p. 1982. pap. text ed. 40.00 (ISBN 0-07-029856-4, W). McGraw.

House, John. The Wonders of Science. (Science Ser.). 24p. (gr. 3-5). 1977. wkbk. 5.00 (ISBN 0-8209-0155-5, S-17). ESP.

Justus, Fred. Everyday Science. (Science Ser.). 24p. (gr. 3). 1977. wkbk. 5.00 (ISBN 0-8209-0141-5, S-3). ESP.

--Our World of Science. (Science Ser.). 24p. (gr. 2-6). 1980. wkbk. 5.00 (ISBN 0-8209-0147-4, S-9). ESP.

--Science Facts Puzzles. (Puzzles Ser.). 24p. (gr. 6). 1980. wkbk. 5.00 (ISBN 0-8209-0298-5, PU-12). ESP.

Kaufmann, Tohko. The Six-Legged Friends I've Met. 1983. 7.95 (ISBN 0-8062-2131-3). Carlton.

Lewart, Cass. Science & Engineering Sourcebook. 96p. 1982. 17.95 (ISBN 0-13-795229-5); pap. 9.95 (ISBN 0-13-795211-2). P-H.

Nova: Adventures in Science. LC 82-16306. (Illus.). 288p. 1982. 27.95 (ISBN 0-201-05358-6); pap. 14.95 (ISBN 0-201-05359-4). A-W.

Patty, Catherine. Basic Skills Science Workbook: Grade 4. (Basic Skills Workbooks). 32p. (gr. 4). 1982. wkbk. 0.99 (ISBN 0-8209-0403-1, SW-E). ESP.

Pecufflic, M. & Abdel-Malek, A. Science & Technology in the Transformation of the World. 1982. 55.00x (ISBN 0-686-42943-5, Pub. by Macmillan England). State Mutual Bk.

Physical Science for Non-Science Students: An Approach to Physical Science. 416p. 1974. pap. 24.95x (ISBN 0-471-68922-X). Wiley.

Pollock, M., ed. Common Denominators in Art & Science. 220p. 1983. 27.00 (ISBN 0-08-028457-4). Pergamon.

Rheingold, Howard & Levine, Howard. Talking Tech: A Conversational Guide to Science & Technology. (Illus.). 324p. 1983. pap. 6.95 (ISBN 0-688-01603-0). Quill NY.

Rossini, Frederick D. Fundamental Measures & Constants for Science & Technology. LC 74-14759. 142p. Repr. of 1974 ed. text ed. 34.50 (ISBN 0-8493-5079-4). Krieger.

Shafer, Robert. Progress & Science. 1922. text ed. 37.50x (ISBN 0-686-83714-2). Elliots Bks.

Shipman, James T. & Adams, Jerry L. An Introduction to Physical Science. 4th ed. 736p. 24.95 (ISBN 0-669-05391-0); instr's. guide 1.95 (ISBN 0-669-05394-5); lab. guide 10.95 (ISBN 0-669-05393-7). Heath.

Smith, Carol. How Products Are Made. (Science Ser.). 24p. (gr. 5-8). 1979. wkbk. 5.00 (ISBN 0-8209-0151-2, S-13). ESP.

Weyl, Hermann. Open World: Three Lectures on the Metaphysical Implications of Science. 1932. text ed. 24.50x (ISBN 0-686-83658-8). Elliots Bks.

Who's Who in Frontier Science & Technology. LC 82-82015. 1983. 84.50 (ISBN 0-8379-5701-X). Marquis.

SCIENCE-ADDRESSES, ESSAYS, LECTURES

Truesdell, C. An Idiot's Fugitive Essays on Science: Methods, Criticism, Training, Circumstances. (Illus.). 350p. 1983. 30.00 (ISBN 0-387-90703-3). Springer-Verlag.

SCIENCE-AUTHORSHIP

see Technical Writing

SCIENCE-BIBLIOGRAPHY

Jacques Cattell Press, ed. American Men & Women of Science Cumulative Index: Vols. 1-14. 900p. 125.00 (ISBN 0-686-83438-0). Bowker.

Whitrow, Magda. Isis Cumulative Bibliography, 1913-1965: Volumes 4 & 5, Civilizations & Periods. 1100p. 1982. 160.00 (ISBN 0-7201-0549-8). Mansell.

SCIENCE-DATA PROCESSING

Reynolds, L. & Simmonds, D. Presentation of Data in Science. rev. ed. 1982. 37.00 (ISBN 90-247-2398-1, Pub. by Martinus Nijhoff Netherlands). Kluwer Boston.

SCIENCE-DICTIONARIES

Armstrong, Virginia W. Our Science Book. Bodle, Marie, tr. from Fr. (Illus.). 27p. (gr. 2-5). 1982. pap. 6.00x (ISBN 2-88089-001-2). A Robinson.

Ballentyne, D. W. & Lovett, D. R. Dictionary of Named Effects. 4th ed. 1982. 19.95x (ISBN 0-412-22390-2, Pub. by Chapman & Hall England). Methuen Inc.

SCIENCE-EARLY WORKS TO 1800

Grew, N. Experiments Inconsort of the Luctation Arising From the Affusion of Several Menstrums Upon All Sorts of Bodies: 1678. 120p. Date not set. pap. 12.50 (ISBN 0-87556-114-4). Saifer.

King, David A. Catalogue of the Scientific Manuscripts in the Egyptian National Library, Pt. 1. (Catalogs Ser.: Vol. 2). (Arabic.). 1981. pap. 40.00 (ISBN 0-686-84036-4, Pub. by Am Res Ctr Egypt). Undena Pubns.

SCIENCE-EXAMINATIONS, QUESTIONS, ETC.

Anderson, Fred A. Scoring High on Medical & Health Sciences Exams. 24p. (Orig.). 1983. pap. 1.75 (ISBN 0-939570-02-5). Skills Improvement.

SCIENCE-EXPERIMENTS

see also Experimental Design

Grew, N. Experiments Inconsort of the Luctation Arising From the Affusion of Several Menstrums Upon All Sorts of Bodies: 1678. 120p. Date not set. pap. 12.50 (ISBN 0-87556-114-4). Saifer.

Harre, Ron. Great Scientific Experiments: Twenty Experiments That Changed Our View of the World. (Illus.). 224p. 1983. pap. 8.95 (ISBN 0-19-286036-4, GB 733, GB). Oxford U Pr.

SCIENCE-EXPERIMENTS-JUVENILE LITERATURE

Cobb, Vicki & Darling, Kathy. Bet You Can! Science Possibilities to Fool You. 112p. (gr. 3-7). 1983. pap. 1.95 (ISBN 0-380-82180-X, Camelot). Avon.

SCIENCE-HISTORY

Al-Daffa, A. A. A Brief Exposition of Arabic & Islamic Scientific Heritage: Arabic Edition. 1979. pap. text ed. 12.00 (ISBN 0-471-05348-1). Wiley.

Harre, Ron. Great Scientific Experiments: Twenty Experiments That Changed Our View of the World. (Illus.). 224p. 1983. pap. 8.95 (ISBN 0-19-286036-4, GB 733, GB). Oxford U Pr.

SCIENCE-INFORMATION SERVICES

see also Communication in Science

Supplement to Information, 1982: A Preservation Sourcebook. (Illus.). 180p. (Orig.). 1982. pap. 7.00 (ISBN 0-89133-101-8). Preservation Pr.

SCIENCE-JUVENILE LITERATURE

see also Natural History-Juvenile Literature; Nature Study-Juvenile Literature; Science-Experiments-Juvenile Literature; Scientists-Juvenile Literature

Cobb, Vicki & Darling, Kathy. Bet You Can't: Scientific Impossibilities to Fool You. (Illus.). 128p. (gr. 3-7). 1983. pap. 1.95 (ISBN 0-380-54502-0, 54502-0, Camelot). Avon.

DeBruin, Jerry. Young Scientists Explore the World Around Them, Bk. 1. (gr. 4-7). 1982. 3.95 (ISBN 0-86653-072-X, GA 405). Good Apple.

Frank Schaffer Publications. Getting Ready for Science. (Getting Ready for Kindergarten). (Illus.). 24p. (ps-k). 1980. workbook 1.29 (ISBN 0-86734-021-5, FS 3034). Schaffer Pubns.

Gottlieb, William P. Science Facts You Won't Believe. (Single Titles Ser.). (Illus.). 128p. (gr. 6 up). 1983. PLB 9.90 (ISBN 0-531-02875-5). Watts.

Paton, John, ed. Children's Encyclopedia of Science. LC 82-80678. (Illus.). (gr. 4-7). 1982. 9.95 (ISBN 0-528-82386-8). Rand.

Penn, Linda. Young Scientists Explore Air, Land & Water Life, Bk. 3. (gr. 1-3). 1982. 3.95 (ISBN 0-86653-071-1, GA 404). Good Apple.

Rand McNally Fact Books. Incl. Aircraft. Maynard, Chris & Paton, John. (ISBN 0-528-87851-4); Astronomy. Paton, John (ISBN 0-528-87852-2); Space Flight. Cowley, Stewart (ISBN 0-528-87853-0); Dinosaur World. Lambert, David. (Illus.). 96p. (gr. 3-7). 1982. 2.95 ea. Rand.

SCIENCE-LANGUAGE

see also Science-Terminology

Huckin, Thomas & Olsen, Leslie. English for Science & Technology: A Handbook for Non-Native Speakers. (Illus.). 576p. 1983. 19.95 (ISBN 0-07-030821-7); instr's manual 6.95 (ISBN 0-07-047822-8). McGraw.

SCIENCE-METHODOLOGY

see also Communication in Science; Experimental Design; Logic

Harre, Ron. Great Scientific Experiments: Twenty Experiments That Changed Our View of the World. (Illus.). 224p. 1983. pap. 8.95 (ISBN 0-19-286036-4, GB 733, GB). Oxford U Pr.

Sindermann, Carl J. Winning the Games Scientists Play. (Illus.). 300p. 1982. 15.95x (ISBN 0-306-41075-3, Plenum Pr). Plenum Pub.

SCIENCE-NOMENCLATURE

see also subdivision Nomenclature under the various natural sciences, e.g. Botany-Nomenclature; Zoology-Nomenclature

Shipp, James F. Russian-English Index to Scientific Apparatus Nomenclature. 2nd ed. 1983. pap. text ed. 14.00x (ISBN 0-917564-15-4). Transaction Research.

SCIENCE-OUTLINES, SYLLABI, ETC.

Holmes, N. J., et al. Gateways to Science, 6 Levels. 4th ed. Incl. Level 1. 192p. text ed. 8.92 (ISBN 0-07-029821-1); tchr's. ed. 15.76 (ISBN 0-07-029831-9); Level 2. 192p. text ed. 9.32 (ISBN 0-07-029822-X); tchr's. ed 16.20 (ISBN 0-07-029832-7); Level 3. 320p. text ed. 10.00 (ISBN 0-07-029823-8); tchr's. ed. 16.96 (ISBN 0-07-029833-5); Level 4. 368p. text ed. 11.08 (ISBN 0-07-029824-6); tchr's. ed. 17.88 (ISBN 0-07-029834-3); Level 5. 384p. text ed. 11.76 (ISBN 0-07-029825-4); tchr's. ed. 18.80 (ISBN 0-07-029905-6); Level 6. 432p. text ed. 12.16 (ISBN 0-07-029826-2); tchr's. ed. 19.12 (ISBN 0-07-029836-X). (gr. k-6). 1983. Tchr's manual level k. 10.16 (ISBN 0-07-029820-3); Bulletin boards gr. 1-6. 16.00 ea.; Webstermaster Gr. 1-6. 40.00 ea.; Pupil's lab. bk. Gr. 3-6. 4.44 ea.; Tchr's lab. bk. Gr. 3-6. 6.00 ea.; supplementary materials avail. McGraw.

SCIENCE-PHILOSOPHY

see also Naturalism

Cohen, Robert & Wartofsky, Marx. Language, Logic, & Method. 1983. 69.50 (ISBN 90-277-0725-1, Pub. by Reidel Holland). Kluwer Boston.

Cohen, Robert S. & Wartofsky, Marx. Epistemology, Methodology, & the Social Sciences. 1983. lib. bdg. 48.00 (ISBN 90-277-1454-1, Pub. by Reidel Holland). Kluwer Boston.

Gadol, E. T., ed. Rationality & Sciences: A Memorial Volume for Moritz Schlick. (Illus.). 228p. 1983. 21.00 (ISBN 0-387-81721-2). Springer-Verlag.

Goodman, Nelson. Fact, Fiction & Forecast. 4th ed. 176p. 1983. text ed. 10.00x (ISBN 0-674-29070-4); pap. text ed. 4.95x (ISBN 0-674-29071-2). Harvard U Pr.

Jennings, Herbert S. Universe & Life. 1933. text ed. 8.50x (ISBN 0-686-83841-6). Elliots Bks.

Mokrzycki, E. Philosophy of Science & Sociology: From the Methodological Doctrine to Research Practice. (International Library of Sociology). 180p. 1983. price not set (ISBN 0-7100-9444-2). Routledge & Kegan.

Santayana, George. Reason in Science: Volume Five of "The Life of Reason". 320p. 1983. pap. 5.00 (ISBN 0-486-24439-3). Dover.

SCIENCE-PROBLEMS, EXERCISES, ETC.

Holmes, N. J., et al. Gateways to Science, 6 Levels. 4th ed. Incl. Level 1. 192p. text ed. 8.92 (ISBN 0-07-029821-1); tchr's. ed. 15.76 (ISBN 0-07-029831-9); Level 2. 192p. text ed. 9.32 (ISBN 0-07-029822-X); tchr's. ed 16.20 (ISBN 0-07-029832-7); Level 3. 320p. text ed. 10.00 (ISBN 0-07-029823-8); tchr's. ed. 16.96 (ISBN 0-07-029833-5); Level 4. 368p. text ed. 11.08 (ISBN 0-07-029824-6); tchr's. ed. 17.88 (ISBN 0-07-029834-3); Level 5. 384p. text ed. 11.76 (ISBN 0-07-029825-4); tchr's. ed. 18.80 (ISBN 0-07-029905-6); Level 6. 432p. text ed. 12.16 (ISBN 0-07-029826-2); tchr's. ed. 19.12 (ISBN 0-07-029836-X). (gr. k-6). 1983. Tchr's manual level k. 10.16 (ISBN 0-07-029820-3); Bulletin boards gr. 1-6. 16.00 ea.; Webstermaster Gr. 1-6. 40.00 ea.; Pupil's lab. bk. Gr. 3-6. 4.44 ea.; Tchr's lab. bk. Gr. 3-6. 6.00 ea.; supplementary materials avail. McGraw.

SCIENCE-RESEARCH

see Research

SCIENCE-SOCIAL ASPECTS

Cole, Leonard A. Politics & the Restraint of Science. 160p. 1983. 17.95 (ISBN 0-86598-125-6). Rowman.

Miller, Jon D. The American People & Science Policy: The Role of Public Attitudes in the Policy Process. 350p. 1983. 35.00 (ISBN 0-08-028064-1). Pergamon.

SCIENCE-STUDY AND TEACHING

see also Nature Study

Curriculum Development: Linking Science Education to Life. 74p. 1981. pap. 7.00 (ISBN 0-686-81860-1, UB104, UNESCO). Unipub.

Kahle, Jane B. Double Dilemma: Minorities & Women in Science Education. LC 81-84383. (Illus.). 181p. (Orig.). 1982. pap. 5.95 (ISBN 0-931682-13-4). Purdue.

Kelly, Alison, ed. The Missing Half: Girls & Science Education. 416p. 1982. 25.00 (ISBN 0-7190-0753-4). Manchester.

Lance, Robert. Directory of CSIRO Research Programs 1982. 496p. 1983. pap. 18.95 (ISBN 0-686-84838-1, Pub. by CSIRO Australia). Intl Schol Bk Serv.

NSTA Handbook, 1982-1983. 5.00 (ISBN 0-686-84081-X). Natl Sci Tchrs.

Ready, Barbara C., ed. Peterson's Guides to Graduate Study: Physical Sciences & Mathematics, 1983. 650p. (Orig.). 1982. pap. 17.95 (ISBN 0-87866-188-3). Petersons Guides.

Thompson, William P. Orientation in Science. LC 82-20189. 480p. (Orig.). 1983. lib. bdg. 28.50 (ISBN 0-8191-2885-6); pap. text ed. 16.75 (ISBN 0-8191-2886-4). U Pr of Amer.

SCIENCE-STUDY AND TEACHING (ELEMENTARY)

Basic Skills Science Workbook: Grade 8. (Basic Skills Workbooks). 32p. (gr. 8). 1982. wkbk. 0.99 (ISBN 0-8209-0407-4, SW-I). ESP.

Boole, Mary E. The Preparation of the Child for Science. 1983. 5.00 (ISBN 0-686-84073-9). Intl Gen Semantics.

Downs, Gary E. & Gerlovich, Jack A. Practical Science Safety for Elementary Teachers. (Illus.). 96p. 1982. pap. text ed. 8.50 (ISBN 0-8138-1641-6). Iowa St U PR.

Hayes, Marilyn. Basic Skills Social Studies Workbook: Grade 5. (Basic Skills Workbooks). 32p. (gr. 5). 1982. wkbk. 0.99 (ISBN 0-8209-0400-7, SSW-F). ESP.

Holler, Kathy. Seasons. (Science Ser.). 24p. (gr. 3-6). 1982. wkbk. 5.00 (ISBN 0-8209-0163-6, S-25). ESP.

House, John. The Wonders of Science. (Science Ser.). 24p. (gr. 3-5). 1977. wkbk. 5.00 (ISBN 0-8209-0155-5, S-17). ESP.

Houston, Jack. Basic Skills Science Workbook: Grade 3. (Basic Skills Workbooks). 32p. (gr. 3). 1982. wkbk. 0.99 (ISBN 0-8209-0402-3, SW-D). ESP.

--Basic Skills Science Workbook: Grade 5. (Basic Skills Workbooks). 32p. (gr. 5). 1982. wkbk. 0.99 (ISBN 0-8209-0404-X, SW-F). ESP.

--Basic Skills Science Workbook: Grade 6. (Basic Skills Workbooks). 32p. (gr. 6). 1982. wkbk. 0.99 (ISBN 0-8209-0405-8, SW-G). ESP.

--Basic Skills Science Workbook: Grade 7. (Basic Skills Workbooks). 32p. (gr. 7). 1982. wkbk. 0.99 (ISBN 0-8209-0406-6, SW-H). ESP.

--Jumbo Science Yearbook: Grade 6. (Jumbo Science Ser.). 96p. (gr. 6). 1979. 14.00 (ISBN 0-8209-0027-3, JSY 6). ESP.

--Jumbo Science Yearbook: Grade 7. (Jumbo Science Ser.). 96p. (gr. 7). 1981. 14.00 (ISBN 0-8209-0028-1, JSY 7). ESP.

--Jumbo Science Yearbook: Grade 8. (Jumbo Science Ser.). 96p. (gr. 8). 1982. 14.00 (ISBN 0-8209-0029-X, JSY 8). ESP.

Justus, Fred. Science Adventures. (Science Ser.). 24p. (gr. 4). 1977. wkbk. 5.00 (ISBN 0-8209-0142-3, S-4). ESP.

--Science Facts. (Science Ser.). 24p. (gr. 6). 1978. wkbk. 5.00 (ISBN 0-8209-0144-X, S-6). ESP.

--Science Goals. (Science Ser.). 24p. (gr. 5). 1980. wkbk. 5.00 (ISBN 0-8209-0143-1, S-5). ESP.

--The Science World. (Science Ser.). 24p. (gr. 4-7). 1978. wkbk. 5.00 (ISBN 0-8209-0156-3, S-18). ESP.

Padilla, Michael J., ed. Science & the Early Adolescent. 144p. 1982. 6.00 (ISBN 0-686-84080-1). Natl Sci Tchrs.
Patty, Catherine. Basic Skills Social Studies Workbook: Grade 3. (Basic Skills Workbooks). 32p. (gr. 3). 1982. wkbk. 0.99 (ISBN 0-8209-0398-1, SSW-D). ESP.
--Basic Skills Social Studies Workbook: Grade 4. (Basic Skills Workbooks). 32p. (gr. 4). 1982. wkbk. 0.99 (ISBN 0-8209-0399-X, SSW-E). ESP.
--Basic Skills Social Studies Workbook: Grade 6. (Basic Skills Workbooks). 32p. (gr. 6). 1982. wkbk. 0.99 (ISBN 0-8209-0401-5, SSW-G). ESP.
--Jumbo Science Yearbook: Grade 4. (Jumbo Science Ser.). 96p. (gr. 4). 1978. 14.00 (ISBN 0-8209-0025-7, JSY 4). ESP.

SCIENCE-TERMINOLOGY
Godman, Arthur. Barnes & Noble Thesaurus of Science. (Illus.). 256p. (gr. 11-12). 1983. 13.41i (ISBN 0-06-015176-5, EH 580); pap. 6.68i (ISBN 0-06-463580-5). B&N NY.

SCIENCE-VOCATIONAL GUIDANCE
Peterson's Guide to Engineering, Science, & Computer Jobs 1983. 4th Ed. ed. 787p. pap. 12.95 (ISBN 0-87866-204-9, 2049). Peterson's Guides.

SCIENCE-YEARBOOKS
Houston, Jack. Jumbo Science Yearbook: Grade 3. (Jumbo Science Ser.). 96p. (gr. 3). 1978. 14.00 (ISBN 0-8209-0024-9, JSY 3). ESP.
--Jumbo Science Yearbook: Grade 5. (Jumbo Science Ser.). 96p. (gr. 5). 1979. 14.00 (ISBN 0-8209-0026-5, JSY 5). ESP.

SCIENCE, APPLIED
see Technology

SCIENCE, ARAB
Al-Daffa, A. A. A Brief Exposition of Arabic & Islamic Scientific Heritage: Arabic Edition. 1979. pap. text ed. 12.00 (ISBN 0-471-05348-1). Wiley.
Edwards, Holly. Patterns & Precision: The Arts & Sciences of Islam. (Illus.). 56p. pap. 6.50 (ISBN 0-87474-399-0). Smithsonian.
King, David A. Catalogue of the Scientific Manuscripts in the Egyptian National Library, Pt. 1. (Catalogs Ser.: Vol. 2). (Arabic.). 1981. pap. 40.00 (ISBN 0-686-84036-4, Pub. by Am Res Ctr Egypt). Undena Pubns.

SCIENCE, BRITISH
Cosslett, Tess. The Scientific Movement & Victorian Literature. LC 82-10284. 1982. 22.50x (ISBN 0-312-70298-1). St Martin.

SCIENCE, COMMUNICATION IN
see Communication in Science

SCIENCE, INDIC
Rangarao, B. V. & Chaubey, N. P., eds. Social Perspective of Development of Science & Technology in India. 1983. 22.00x (ISBN 0-8364-0931-0, Pub. by Heritage India). South Asia Bks.

SCIENCE, MENTAL
see Psychology

SCIENCE, MORAL
see Ethics

SCIENCE, POLITICAL
see Political Science

SCIENCE, SOCIAL
see Sociology

SCIENCE, STATE ENCOURAGEMENT OF
see State Encouragement of Science, Literature, and Art

SCIENCE AND CIVILIZATION
Here are entered works on the role of science in the history and development of civilization.
Mayor, F., ed. Scientific Research & Social Goals: Toward a New Development Model. 248p. 1982. 35.00 (ISBN 0-08-028118-4). Pergamon.
Peterson, Rita W. & Butts, David. Science & Society. 1983. text ed. 21.95 (ISBN 0-675-20022-9). Additional supplements may be obtained from publisher. Merrill.
Woodruff, Lorande L., ed. Development of the Sciences: Second Series. 1941. text ed. 39.50x (ISBN 0-686-83526-3). Elliots Bks.

SCIENCE AND HISTORY
see Science and Civilization

SCIENCE AND LAW
Nyhart, J. D. & Carrow, Milton M., eds. Law & Science in Collaboration: Resolving Regulatory Issues of Science & Technology. LC 81-47689. 320p. 1983. 29.95x (ISBN 0-669-04907-7). Lexington Bks.
Thomas, William A., ed. Law & Science: An Essential Alliance. (Special Study). 150p. 1983. lib. bdg. 16.50 (ISBN 0-86531-442-X). Westview.

SCIENCE AND LITERATURE
see Literature and Science

SCIENCE AND RELIGION
see Religion and Science

SCIENCE AND SOCIETY
see Science and Civilization

SCIENCE AND SPACE
see Space Sciences

SCIENCE AND STATE
see also Astronautics and State; Research and Development Contracts; State Encouragement of Science, Literature, and Art; Technology and State
Adkinson, B. W. Two Centuries of Federal Information. LC 78-7294. (Publications in the Information Science Ser.). 235p. 1978. 43.50 (ISBN 0-87933-269-7). Hutchinson Ross.
Cole, Leonard A. Politics & the Restraint of Science. 160p. 1983. 17.95 (ISBN 0-86598-125-6). Rowman.
Science & Public Policy Papers I. Proceedings, Vol. 368. 235p. 1981. 50.00 (ISBN 0-89766-125-7, Rosenberg Pub); pap. write for info. (ISBN 0-89766-126-5). NY Acad Sci.
Scientists, the Arms Race & Disarmament. 323p. 1982. 24.95 (ISBN 92-3-102021-8, U1231, UNESCO). Unipub.

SCIENCE AND THE BIBLE
see Bible and Science

SCIENCE AND THE HUMANITIES
see also Education, Humanistic; Literature and Science
Schaub, J. H. & Dickison, S. K. Engineering & the Humanities. 503p. 1982. text ed. 29.95x (ISBN 0-471-08909-5, Pub. by Wiley-Interscience). Wiley.

SCIENCE FICTION
Asimov, Isaac, et al, eds. Starships. 432p. (Orig.). 1983. pap. 3.50 (ISBN 0-449-20126-0, Crest). Fawcett.
Aspin, Robert. Myth Directions. Stine, Hank, ed. LC 82-12776. (Myth Trilogy Ser.: Vol. 3). (Illus.). 176p. (Orig.). 1982. pap. 5.95 (ISBN 0-89865-250-2, Starblaze). Donning Co.
Bradley, Marion Z. Sword of Chaos. 1982. pap. 2.95 (ISBN 0-87997-722-1, UE1722). DAW Bks.
Carter, Lin. Kesrick. 1982. pap. 2.25 (ISBN 0-87997-779-5, UE1779). DAW Bks.
Edward, Karl. The Year's Best Horror Stories. (Series X). 1982. pap. 2.50 (ISBN 0-87997-757-4, UE1757). DAW Bks.
Klein, Gerard. The Day Before Tomorrow. 1982. pap. 1.95 (ISBN 0-87997-767-1, UJ1767). DAW Bks.
Landis, Arthur H. Home-to-Avalon. 1982. pap. 2.50 (ISBN 0-87997-778-7, UE1778). Daw Bks.
Llewellyn, Edward. Prelude to Chaos. 256p. 1983. pap. 2.75 (ISBN 0-686-84672-9). DAW Bks.
Norman, John. Blood Brothers of Gor. 1982. pap. 3.50 (ISBN 0-87997-777-9, UW1777). DAW Bks.
Prescot, Dray. Fliers of Antares. 1982. pap. 2.25 (ISBN 0-87997-733-7, UE1733). DAW Bks.
Simak, Clifford. Destiny Doll. 1982. pap. 2.50 (ISBN 0-87997-772-8, UE1772). DAW Bks.
Spinrad, Norman. Staying Alive: A Writer's Guide. Stine, Hank, ed. LC 82-14736. 162p. 1983. pap. 5.95 (ISBN 0-89865-259-6). Donning Co.
Stablefore, Brian. The Gates of Eden. 176p. 1983. pap. 2.35 (ISBN 0-686-84669-9). DAW Bks.
Stapledon, Olaf. Nebula Maker & Four Encounters. LC 82-17684. (Illus.). 288p. 1983. 12.95 (ISBN 0-686-84666-4); pap. 6.95 (ISBN 0-686-84667-2). Dodd.
Sucharitkul, Somtow. Fire from the Wine-Dark Sea. Stine, Hank, ed. LC 82-12827. (Illus.). 200p. 1983. pap. 5.95 (ISBN 0-89865-252-9, Starblaze). Donning Co.
Tubb, E. C. The Coming Event. 1982. pap. 2.25 (ISBN 0-87997-725-6, UW1725). DAW Bks.
Vance, Jack. The Gray Prince. 1983. pap. 2.25 (ISBN 0-87997-716-7, UE1716). DAW Bks.
--To Live Forever. 1982. pap. 2.25 (ISBN 0-87997-787-6, UE1787). DAW Bks.
Van Vogt, A. E. The Battle of Forever. 1982. pap. 2.25 (ISBN 0-87997-758-2, UE1758). DAW Bks.
--The Darkness on Diamondia. 1982. pap. 2.25 (ISBN 0-87997-724-8, UE1724). DAW Bks.

SCIENCE FICTION (COLLECTIONS)
Asimov, Isaac & Greenberg, Martin H., eds. Isaac Asimov Presents the Great SF Stories, No. 9. 368p. 1983. pap. 3.50 (ISBN 0-686-84671-0). DAW Bks.
Asimov, Isaac & Martin, George R., eds. The Science Fiction Weightloss Book. 1983. 12.95 (ISBN 0-517-54978-6). Crown.
McCarthy, Shawna, ed. Isaac Asimov's Aliens & Outworlders. 288p. 1983. 12.95 (ISBN 0-385-27912-4). Davis Pubns.
The Official 1983 Price Guide to Comic & Science Fiction Books. 6th ed. LC 81-81799. 544p. 1983. 9.95 (ISBN 0-87637-353-8). Hse of Collectibles.
Rabkin, Eric S., ed. Science Fiction: An Historical Anthology. 496p. 1983. 19.95 (ISBN 0-19-503271-3). Oxford U Pr.
Silverberg, Robert & Greenberg, Martin H., eds. The Arbor House Treasury of Science Fiction Masterpieces. 1983. 16.95 (ISBN 0-87795-445-3). Arbor Hse.

SCIENCE FICTION-BIBLIOGRAPHY
Hill, Douglas. Warriors of the Wasteland. LC 82-13896. 144p. (gr. 8 up). 1983. 9.95 (ISBN 0-689-50269-9, Argo). Atheneum.
McCarthy, Shawna, ed. Isaac Asimov's Aliens & Outworlders. 288p. 1983. 12.95 (ISBN 0-385-27912-4). Davis Pubns.

SCIENCE FICTION-HISTORY AND CRITICISM
Asimov, Isaac. The Best Fantasy of the Nineteenth Century. Waugh, Charles G. & Greenberg, Martin H., eds. 357p. 1982. 15.95 (ISBN 0-686-82284-6). Beaufort Bks NY.
Banks, Michael A. Understanding Science Fiction. 180p. 1982. 10.20 (ISBN 0-382-29074-7). Silver.
Clareson, Thomas D. Reader's Guide to Robert Silverberg. Schlobin, Roger C., ed. (Reader's Guides to Contemporary Science Fiction & Fantasy Authors Ser.: Vol. 18). (Illus., Orig.). 1983. 11.95x (ISBN 0-916732-48-7); pap. text ed. 5.95x (ISBN 0-916732-47-9). Starmont Hse.
Cogell, Elizabeth C. Ursula K. Leguin: A Primary & Secondary Bibliography. 1983. lib. bdg. 39.95 (ISBN 0-8161-8155-1, Hall Reference). G K Hall.
Collings, Michael R. Reader's Guide to Piers Anthony. Schlobin, Roger C., ed. (Reader's Guides to Contemporary Science Fiction & Fantasy Authors Ser.: Vol. 20). (Illus., Orig.). 1983. 10.95x (ISBN 0-916732-53-3); pap. text ed. 4.95x (ISBN 0-916732-52-5). Starmont Hse.
Crossley, Robert. Reader's Guide to H. G. Wells. Schlobin, Roger C., ed. (Reader's Guides to Contemporary Science Fiction & Fantasy Authors Ser.: Vol. 19). (Illus., Orig.). 1982. 10.95x (ISBN 0-916732-51-7); pap. text ed. 4.95x (ISBN 0-916732-50-9). Starmont Hse.
Elliot, Jeffrey M. Reader's Guide to A. E. van Vogt. Schlobin, Roger C., ed. (Reader's Guides to Contemporary Science Fiction & Fantasy Authors Ser.: Vol. 17). (Illus., Orig.). 1983. 10.95x (ISBN 0-916732-46-0); pap. text ed. 4.95x (ISBN 0-916732-45-2). Starmont Hse.
Fiedler, Leslie A. Olaf Stapledon: A Man Divided. (Science Fiction Writers Ser.). (Illus.). 256p. 1983. pap. 4.95 (ISBN 0-19-503087-7, GB 682, GB). Oxford U Pr.
--Olaf Stapledon: A Man Divided. LC 82-8168. (Science Fiction Writers Ser.). 256p. 1983. 19.95 (ISBN 0-19-503086-9). Oxford U Pr.
Garber, Eric & Paleo, Lyn. Uranian Worlds: A Reader's Guide to Alternative Sexuality in Science Fiction & Fantasy. 1983. lib. bdg. 28.50 (ISBN 0-8161-8573-5, Hall Reference). G K Hall.
Goswami, Amit & Goswami, Maggie. The Cosmic Dancers: Exploring the Physics of Science Fiction. (Illus.). 288p. 1983. 17.95 (ISBN 0-06-015083-1, HarpT). Har-Row.
Hassler, Donald M. Hal Clement. (Starmont Reader's Guide Ser.: No. 11). 64p. 1982. Repr. lib. bdg. 10.95x (ISBN 0-89370-042-8). Borgo Pr.
--Reader's Guide to Hal Clement. Schlobin, Roger C., ed. (Reader's Guides to Contemporary Science Fiction & Fantasy Authors Ser.: Vol. 11). (Illus., Orig.). 1982. 10.95x (ISBN 0-916732-30-4); pap. text ed. 4.95x (ISBN 0-916732-27-4). Starmont Hse.
Hollow, John. Against the Night, the Stars: The Science Fiction of Arthur C. Clarke. 224p. 14.95 (ISBN 0-15-103966-6). HarBraceJ.
Huntington, John. The Logic of Fantasy: H. G. Wells & Science Fiction. LC 82-4593. 192p. 1982. text ed. 22.50x (ISBN 0-231-05378-9). Columbia U Pr.
Joshi, S. T. Reader's Guide to H. P. Lovecraft. Schlobin, Roger C., ed. (Reader's Guides to Contemporary Science Fiction & Fantasy Authors Ser.: Vol. 13). (Illus., Orig.). 1982. 11.95x (ISBN 0-916732-36-3); pap. text ed. 5.95x (ISBN 0-916732-35-5). Starmont Hse.
Kinnaird, John. Reader's Guide to Olaf Stapledon. Schlobin, Roger C., ed. (Reader's Guides to Contemporary Science Fiction & Fantasy Authors Ser.: Vol. 21). (Illus., Orig.). 1983. 10.95x (ISBN 0-916732-55-X); pap. text ed. 4.95x (ISBN 0-916732-54-1). Starmont Hse.
Le Guin, Ursula K. The Language of the Night. Wood, Susan, ed. LC 78-24350. 270p. 1979. 12.50 (ISBN 0-399-12325-3). Ultramarine Pub.
Murphy, Brian. Reader's Guide to C. S. Lewis. Schlobin, Roger C., ed. (Reader's Guides to Contemporary Science Fiction & Fantasy Authors Ser.: Vol. 14). (Illus., Orig.). 1983. 10.95x (ISBN 0-916732-38-X); pap. text ed. 4.95x (ISBN 0-916732-37-1). Starmont Hse.
Nicholls, Peter & Langford, David. The Science in Science Fiction. LC 82-14834. 208p. 1983. 25.00 (ISBN 0-394-53010-1); pap. 14.95 (ISBN 0-394-71364-8). Knopf.
Philmus, Robert M. Into the Unknown: The Evolution of Science Fiction from Frances Godwin to H.G. Wells. 186p. 1983. pap. 6.95 (ISBN 0-520-04959-4, CAL 627). U of Cal Pr.
Pierce, Hazel. Philip K. Dick. (Starmont Reader's Guide Ser.: No. 12). 64p. 1982. Repr. lib. bdg. 10.95x (ISBN 0-89370-043-6). Borgo Pr.
--Reader's Guide to Philip K. Dick. Schlobin, Roger C., ed. (Reader's Guides to Contemporary Science Fiction & Fantasy Authors Ser.: Vol. 12). (Illus., Orig.). 1982. 10.95x (ISBN 0-916732-34-7); pap. text ed. 4.95x (ISBN 0-916732-33-9). Starmont Hse.
Schlobin, Roger C. Urania's Daughters: A Checklist of Women Science Fiction Writers, 1692-1982. (Illus., Orig.). 1982. 11.95x (ISBN 0-916732-57-6); pap. 5.95x (ISBN 0-916732-56-8). Starmont Hse.
Slusser, George E., et al, eds. Coordinates: Placing Science Fiction & Fantasy. (Alternatives Ser.). 264p. 1983. price not set (ISBN 0-8093-1105-4). S Ill U Pr.
Staicar, Tom. Fritz Leiber. LC 82-40260. (Recognitions). 200p. (YA) 1983. 11.95 (ISBN 0-8044-2836-0); pap. 6.95 (ISBN 0-8044-6875-3). Ungar.
Thompson, Raymond H. Gordon R. Dickson: A Primary & Secondary Bibliography. 1983. lib. bdg. 27.50 (ISBN 0-8161-8363-5, Hall Reference). G K Hall.
Weedman, Jane B. Reader's Guide to Samuel R. Delany. Schlobin, Roger C., ed. LC 82-5545. (Reader's Guides to Contemporary Science Fiction & Fantasy Authors Ser.: Vol. 10). (Illus., Orig.). 1982. 10.95x (ISBN 0-916732-28-2); pap. text ed. 4.95x (ISBN 0-916732-25-8). Starmont Hse.
Winter, Douglas E. Reader's Guide to Stephen King. Schlobin, Roger C., ed. (Reader's Guides to Contemporary Science Fiction & Fantasy Authors Ser.: Vol. 16). (Illus., Orig.). 1982. 11.95x (ISBN 0-916732-44-4); pap. text ed. 5.95x (ISBN 0-916732-43-6). Starmont Hse.
Wolfe, Gary K. Reader's Guide to David Lindsay. Schlobin, Roger C., ed. LC 82-5563. (Reader's Guides to Contemporary Science Fiction & Fantasy Authors Ser.: Vol. 9). (Illus., Orig.). 1982. 10.95x (ISBN 0-916732-29-0); pap. text ed. 4.95x (ISBN 0-916732-26-6). Starmont Hse.
Yoke, Carl B. Reader's Guide to Roger Zelazny. rev. ed. Schlobin, Roger C., ed. LC 79-17107. (Reader's Guides to Contemporary Science Fiction & Fantasy Authors Ser.: Vol. 2). (Illus., Orig.). 1983. 11.95x (ISBN 0-916732-42-8); pap. text ed. 5.95x (ISBN 0-916732-41-X). Starmont Hse.

SCIENCE FICTION, AMERICAN
Bear, Greg. The Wind from a Burning Woman. (Illus.). 270p. 1983. 13.95 (ISBN 0-87054-094-7). Arkham.
Carr, Terry, ed. Universe, No. 10. 1982. pap. 2.50 (ISBN 0-8217-1114-8). Zebra.
--Universe, No. 11. 1983. pap. 2.50 (ISBN 0-8217-1143-1). Zebra.
Hassler, Donald M. Hal Clement. (Starmont Reader's Guide Ser.: No. 11). 64p. 1982. Repr. lib. bdg. 10.95x (ISBN 0-89370-042-8). Borgo Pr.
Pierce, Hazel. Philip K. Dick. (Starmont Reader's Guide Ser.: No. 12). 64p. 1982. Repr. lib. bdg. 10.95x (ISBN 0-89370-043-6). Borgo Pr.

SCIENCE FICTION FILMS
Lentz, Harris M., III. Science Fiction, Horror, Fantasy Film & Television Credits, 2 Vols. LC 82-23956. 1000p. 1983. lib. bdg. 49.95 set (ISBN 0-89950-071-4); Vol. 1. lib. bdg. price not set (ISBN 0-89950-069-2); Vol. 2. lib. bdg. price not set (ISBN 0-89950-070-6). McFarland & Co.
Menville, Douglas A. & Reginald, R. Things to Come: An Illustrated History of the Science Fiction Film. 224p. 1983. Repr. of 1977 ed. lib. bdg. 9.95x (ISBN 0-89370-019-3). Borgo Pr.
The Official 1983 Price Guide to Star Wars-Star Trek Collectibles. 1st ed. LC 82-84639. 240p. 1983. pap. 2.95 (ISBN 0-87637-319-8). Hse of Collectibles.

SCIENCE ILLUSTRATION
see Scientific Illustration

SCIENCE INFORMATION
see Communication in Science

SCIENCE OF LANGUAGE
see Linguistics

SCIENCE OF SCIENCE
see Science

SCIENCE POLICY
see Science and State

SCIENCE RESEARCH
see Research

SCIENCE STORIES
see Science Fiction (Collections)

SCIENCES, OCCULT
see Occult Sciences

SCIENCES, SOCIAL
see Social Sciences

SCIENTIFIC APPARATUS AND INSTRUMENTS
see also Astronomical Instruments; Electric Apparatus and Appliances; Electronic Apparatus and Appliances; Medical Instruments and Apparatus; Optical Instruments; Physiological Apparatus
also names of particular instruments, e.g. Spectroscope
Moore, John H. & Coplan, Michael A. Building Scientific Apparatus. (Illus.). 900p. 1982. 54.95 (ISBN 0-201-05532-5, Adv Bk Prog). A-W.

SCIENTIFIC COMMUNICATIONS
see Communication in Science

SCIENTIFIC EDUCATION
see Science-Study and Teaching

SCIENTIFIC EXPEDITIONS
see also names of regions explored, e.g. Africa, Central
Adams, Richard & Lockley, Ronald. Voyage Through the Antarctic. LC 82-48484. (Illus.). 160p. 1982. 13.95 (ISBN 0-394-52858-1). Knopf.
Dyer, Irra & Chyssostomidis, C., eds. Arctic Policy & Technology. (Illus.). 400p. 1983. text ed. 69.95 (ISBN 0-89116-361-1). Hemisphere Pub.
Heyerdahl, Thor. The Tigris Expedition: In Search of Our Beginnings. (Illus.). 1982. pap. 7.95 (ISBN 0-452-25358-6, Z5358, Plume). NAL.

SCIENTIFIC ILLUSTRATION
see also Biological Illustration; Technical Illustration
Dillon, Brian D., ed. The Student's Guide to Archaeological Illustrating. rev. ed. (Archaeological Research Tools Ser.: Vol. 1). (Illus.). 154p. 1983. pap. 8.50 (ISBN 0-917956-38-9). UCLA Arch.

SCIENTIFIC INSTRUMENTS
see Scientific Apparatus and Instruments

SCIENTIFIC LIBRARIES
see also Information Storage and Retrieval Systems-Science
Mount, Ellis, ed. Cataloging & Indexing in Sci-Tech Libraries. (Science & Technology Libraries: Vol. 2, No. 3). 92p. 1982. pap. text ed. 15.00 (ISBN 0-86656-204-4, B204). Haworth Pr.

--Document Delivery for Sci-Tech Libraries. (Science & Technology Libraries: Vol. 2, No. 4). 133p. 1982. pap. text ed. 15.00 (ISBN 0-86656-200-1, B200). Haworth Pr.
--Online vs. Manual Searching in Sci-Tech Libraries. (Science & Technology Libraries: Vol. 3, No. 1). 89p. 1982. pap. text ed. 15.00 (ISBN 0-86656-203-6, B203). Haworth Pr.
--Role of Translations in Sci-Tech Libraries. LC 82-23353. (Science & Technology Libraries: Vol. 3, No. 2). 96p. 1983. 20.00 (ISBN 0-86656-213-3). Haworth Pr.

SCIENTIFIC LITERATURE
see also Science–Bibliography
Harnad, Stevan, ed. Peer Commentary on Peer Review: A Case Study in Scientific Quality Control. LC 82-19860. 80p. Date not set. pap. 12.95 (ISBN 0-521-27306-4). Cambridge U Pr.
Turley, Raymond. Understanding the Structure of Scientific & Technical Literature: A Visual Approach. 176p. 1983. write for info. (ISBN 0-85157-368-1, Pub. by Bingley England). Shoe String.

SCIENTIFIC LITERATURE SEARCHING
see Information Storage and Retrieval Systems–Science

SCIENTIFIC MANAGEMENT
see Industrial Management

SCIENTIFIC METHOD
see Science–Methodology

SCIENTIFIC PROGRAMMING
see Scheduling (Management)

SCIENTIFIC RECREATIONS–JUVENILE LITERATURE
Cobb, Vicki & Darling, Kathy. Bet You Can! Science Possibilities to Fool You. 112p. (gr. 3-7). 1983. pap. 1.95 (ISBN 0-380-82180-X, Camelot). Avon.

SCIENTIFIC REPORTS
see Technical Reports

SCIENTIFIC RESEARCH
see Research

SCIENTIFIC VOYAGES
see Scientific Expeditions

SCIENTIFIC WRITING
see Technical Writing

SCIENTISTS
see also Astronomers; Biologists; Chemists; Mathematicians; Naturalists; Physicists; Psychologists; Science–Vocational Guidance; Women Scientists
Ahlfors, Lars V. Lars Valerian Ahlfors: Collected Papers, 2 Vols. 544p. 1982. text ed. 55.00X ea. Vol. 1 (ISBN 3-7643-3075-9). Vol. 2 (ISBN 3-7643-3076-7). Set. text ed. 110.00x (ISBN 3-7643-3077-5). Birkhauser.
Aris, Rutherford & Davis, H. Ted, eds. Springs of Scientific Creativity: Essays on Founders of Modern Science. LC 82-23715. (Illus.). 352p. 1983. 32.50x (ISBN 0-8166-1087-8). U of Minn Pr.
Fierz, Markus, ed. Girolamo Cardano (1501-1576) Physician, Natural Philosopher, Mathematician, Astrologer & Interpreter of Dreams. Niman, Helga, tr. from Ger. 242p. Date not set. price not set (ISBN 3-7643-3057-0). Birkhauser.
Modern Scientists & Engineers, 3 vols. 1980. 135.00 (ISBN 0-07-045266-0). McGraw.
Sindermann, Carl J. Winning the Games Scientists Play. (Illus.). 300p. 1982. 15.95x (ISBN 0-306-41075-3, Plenum Pr). Plenum Pub.

SCIENTISTS–BIOGRAPHY
Abbott, David, ed. The Biographical Encyclopedias of Sciences: The Biologists. 1982. 30.00x (ISBN 0-584-10853-2, Pub. by Muller Ltd). State Mutual Bk.
Bauemler, Ernest. Paul Ehrlich: Life Scientists. 350p. 1983. text ed. 39.50x (ISBN 0-8419-0837-0). Holmes & Meier.

SCIENTISTS–JUVENILE LITERATURE
Berger, Melvin. Exploring the Mind & Brain. LC 82-45582. (Scientists at Work Ser.). (Illus.). 128p. (gr. 5 up). 1983. 10.53i (ISBN 0-690-04251-5, TYC-J); PLB 10.89g (ISBN 0-690-04252-3). Har-Row.

SCLEROSIS, MULTIPLE
see Multiple Sclerosis

SCORPIONS
Billings, Charlene W. Scorpions. LC 82-45994. (A Skylight Bk.). (Illus.). 48p. (gr. 2-5). 1983. PLB 7.95 (ISBN 0-396-08125-8). Dodd.

SCOTCH WHISKEY
see Whiskey

SCOTLAND
Clapperton, Chalmers, ed. Scotland: A New Study. (Illus.). 344p. 1983. 37.50 (ISBN 0-7153-8084-2). David & Charles.

SCOTLAND–ANTIQUITIES
Piggott, Stuart. Scotland Before History. (Illus.). 200p. 1982. text ed. 15.00 (ISBN 0-85224-348-0, Pub. by Edinburgh U Pr Scotland). Columbia U Pr.
Wiseman, James & Aleksova, Blaga, eds. Studies in the Antiquities of Stobi, Vol. III. LC 75-641175. (Illus.). 323p. 1983. 62.50x (ISBN 0-691-03563-6). Princeton U Pr.

SCOTLAND–BIOGRAPHY
Anderson, Peter. Robert Stewart, Earl of Orkney, Lord of Shetland, 1533-1593. 222p. 1982. text ed. 31.50x (ISBN 0-85976-082-0, Pub. by John Donald Scotland). Humanities.
Cunningham, Frank. James David Forbes: Pioneer Scottish Glaciologist. 475p. 1983. 60.00x (ISBN 0-7073-0320-6, Pub. by Scottish Academic Pr Scotland). Columbia U Pr.

SCOTLAND–CIVILIZATION
Daiches, David, ed. A Companion to Scottish Culture. (Illus.). 441p. 1982. 42.50 (ISBN 0-8419-0792-7). Holmes & Meier.

SCOTLAND–DESCRIPTION AND TRAVEL
see also Great Britain–Description and Travel
Murray, W. H. The West Highlands of Scotland. (Illus.). 415p. 1983. pap. 17.95 (ISBN 0-00-216813-8, Collins Pub England). Greene.
Tindall, Jemina. Scottish Island Hopping. 2nd ed. (Handbooks for the Independent Traveller). (Illus.). 320p. 1982. pap. 12.94 (ISBN 0-686-43004-2, Regnary Gateway). Hippocrene Bks.
Tweedsmuir, Lord. The Country Life Picture Book Scotland. (Illus.). 1983. 19.95 (ISBN 0-393-01734-6, Pub. by Country Life). Norton.

SCOTLAND–DESCRIPTION AND TRAVEL–GUIDEBOOKS
Carter, Jenny & Hardley, Dennis. The Highlands & Islands of Scotland in Colour. (Illus.). 64p. 1983. 12.50 (ISBN 0-7134-3825-8, Pub. by Batsford England). David & Charles.
Fodor's Scotland. (Illus.). 256p. 1983. traveltex 9.95 (ISBN 0-679-00967-1). McKay.
Mitchel, Arthur. Five Hundred Years of Travel Books about Scotland, 1296-1796. 1982. pap. 25.00 (ISBN 0-686-37955-1). Saifer.
Scotland: Bed & Breakfast. 184p. 1983. pap. 3.95 (ISBN 0-85419-211-5, Pub. by Auto Assn-British Tourist Authority England). Merrimack Bk Serv.
Scotland: Hotels & Guesthouses. 262p. 1983. pap. 3.95 (ISBN 0-686-38446-6, Pub. by Auto Assn-British Tourist Authority England). Merrimack Bk Serv.
Scotland: Where to Go, What to Do. 240p. 1983. pap. 8.95 (ISBN 0-686-38442-3, Pub. by Auto Assn-British Tourist Authority England). Merrimack Bk Serv.
Thompson, Frank. Scotland. 160p. 1983. pap. 9.95 (ISBN 0-7063-6218-7, Pub. by Auto Assn-British Tourist Authority England). Merrimack Bk Serv.
Wales & Trails in Scotland. 60p. 1983. pap. 2.95 (ISBN 0-85419-214-X, Pub. by Auto Assn-British Tourist Authority England). Merrimack Bk Serv.

SCOTLAND–ECONOMIC CONDITIONS
Withrington, Donald, ed. Shetland & the Outside World, 1469 to 1969. (Illus.). 248p. 1982. 36.00x (ISBN 0-19-714107-2). Oxford U Pr.

SCOTLAND–FOREIGN RELATIONS
Maxwell, Stephen, ed. Scotland, Multinationals & the Third World. 160p. 1982. text ed. 13.75 (ISBN 0-906391-28-8, 40980, Pub. by Mainstream Scotland). Humanities.

SCOTLAND–GENEALOGY
O'Laughlin, Michael C. Handbook on Scottish Genealogy. (Celtic Heritage Ser.). (Illus.). 1983. 14.95 (ISBN 0-940134-05-5). Irish Genealog.

SCOTLAND–HISTORIC HOUSES, ETC.
Castles of Scotland: A Collins Map. 1983. pap. 5.95 (ISBN 0-686-42793-9, Collins Pub England). Greene.

SCOTLAND–HISTORY
Dickson, Tony, ed. Capital & Class in Scotland. 286p. 1982. text ed. 33.75x (ISBN 0-85976-065-0, Pub. by Donald Scotland). Humanities.
Turnock, David. The Historical Geography of Scotland Since 1707. LC 82-1175. (Cambridge Studies in Historical Geography: No. 2). (Illus.). 346p. 1982. 49.50 (ISBN 0-521-24453-6). Cambridge U Pr.
Veitch, John. The History & Poetry of the Scottish Border: Their Main Features & Relations. 356p. 1982. lib. bdg. 125.00 (ISBN 0-89760-930-1). Telegraph Bks.
Whittington, G. & Whyte, I. D. An Historical Geography of Scotland. write for info. (ISBN 0-12-747360-2); pap. write for info. (ISBN 0-12-747362-9). Acad Pr.
Withrington, Donald, ed. Shetland & the Outside World, 1469 to 1969. (Illus.). 248p. 1982. 36.00x (ISBN 0-19-714107-2). Oxford U Pr.

SCOTLAND–INDUSTRIES
Maxwell, Stephen, ed. Scotland, Multinationals & the Third World. 160p. 1982. text ed. 13.75 (ISBN 0-906391-28-8, 40980, Pub. by Mainstream Scotland). Humanities.

SCOTLAND–SOCIAL LIFE AND CUSTOMS
Barrett & Ovenden. The Seacoast. pap. 8.95 (ISBN 0-686-42741-6, Collins Pub England). Greene.

SCOTT, WALTER, SIR, BART., 1771-1832
Walker, Eric. Scott's Fiction & the Picturesque. (Salzburg - Romantic Reassessment Ser.: No. 108). 79p. 1982. pap. text ed. 25.00x (ISBN 0-391-02739-5, Pub. by Salzburg Austria). Humanities.

SCOTTISH AUTHORS
see Authors, Scottish

SCOTTISH FOLK-LORE
see Folk-Lore, Scottish

SCOTTISH PHILOSOPHY
see Philosophy, Scottish

SCOTTISH POETRY (COLLECTIONS)
Brown, Hamish, selected by. Poems of the Scottish Hills: An Anthology. 216p. 1982. 19.00 (ISBN 0-08-028476-0); pap. 10.35 (ISBN 0-08-028477-9). Pergamon.

SCOTTISH POETRY–HISTORY AND CRITICISM
Veitch, John. The History & Poetry of the Scottish Border: Their Main Features & Relations. 356p. 1982. lib. bdg. 125.00 (ISBN 0-89760-930-1). Telegraph Bks.

SCOTTISH SCULPTURE
see Sculpture–Great Britain

SCOTTISH TERRIERS
see Dogs–Breeds–Scottish Terriers

SCOUTS AND SCOUTING
see also Boy Scouts
Harrell, Robert A. & Firestein, Gary S. The Effective Scoutboy. LC 82-11483. (Illus.). 176p. 1983. pap. text ed. 7.50 (ISBN 0-668-05627-4, 5627). Arco.

SCREEN PROCESS PRINTING
Banzhaf, Robert A. Screen Process Printing. 1983. text ed. 10.00 (ISBN 0-87345-206-2). McKnight.

SCREENPLAYS
see Moving-Picture Plays

SCRIP
see Currency Question; Homestead Law; Securities

SCROLL OF THE LAW
see Torah Scrolls

SCUBA DIVING
Here are entered works on free diving with the use of an aqualung. Works on free diving with the use of mask, fins and snorkel are entered under Skin Diving.
Farley, Michael. Scuba Equipment Care & Maintenance. (Illus.). 176p. 1980. pap. text ed. 9.95 (ISBN 0-932248-01-2). Marcor Pub.
The New Science of Skin & Scuba Diving (CNCA) 288p. 8.95 (ISBN 0-686-38064-9). AAHPERD.

SCULLING
see Rowing

SCULPTORS
Richman, Michael. Daniel Chester French: An American Sculptor. (Landmark Reprint Ser.). (Illus.). 208p. 1983. pap. 15.95 (ISBN 0-89133-048-8). Preservation Pr.
Tuchman, Phyllis. George Segal. (Modern Masters Ser.). (Illus.). 128p. 1983. 24.95 (ISBN 0-89659-328-2); pap. 16.95 (ISBN 0-89659-329-0). Abbeville Pr.

SCULPTURE
see also Bronzes; Carving (Art Industries); Expressionism (Art); Ivories; Masks (Sculpture); Wood-Carving
Allen, Jim & Curnow, Wystan. New Art: Some Recent New Zealand Sculpture & Past Object Art. (Illus.). 1976. 9.95 (ISBN 0-686-38948-4, Pub. by Heinemann Pub New Zealand). Intl Schol Bk Serv.
Foged, Niels. Diatoms in Bornholm, Denmark. (Bibliotheca Phyc. 59). (Illus.). 104p. 1982. pap. text ed. 20.00 (ISBN 0-686-37597-1). Lubrecht & Cramer.
Robertson, Merle G. The Sculpture of Palenque, Vol. 1: The Temple of the Inscriptions. LC 82-341. (Illus.). 350p. 1983. 125.00 (ISBN 0-691-03560-1). Princeton U Pr.

SCULPTURE–CATALOGS
Smithsonian Institution, Washington D.C. Descriptive Catalog of Painting & Sculpture in the National Museum of American Art. 1983. lib. bdg. 125.00 (ISBN 0-8161-0408-5, Hall Library). G K Hall.

SCULPTURE–EXHIBITIONS
Dickson, Joanne, ed. Manuel Neri: Sculpture & Drawings. LC 80-71065. (Illus.). 28p. (Orig.). 1981. pap. 5.95 (ISBN 0-932216-11-0). Seattle Art.

SCULPTURE–HISTORY
Bober, Phyllis P. & Rubenstein, Ruth. Renaissance Artists & Antique Sculpture: A Handbook of Sources. (A Harvey Miller Publication). (Illus.). 1982. 45.00x (ISBN 0-19-921029-2). Oxford U Pr.

SCULPTURE–EUROPE
Turpin, John. John Hogan: Irish Neoclassical Sculptor in Rome 1800-1858. (Illus.). 216p. 1983. text ed. 25.00x (ISBN 0-7165-0212-7, Pub by Irish Academic Pr Ireland). Biblio Dist.

SCULPTURE–FRANCE
Elsen, Albert E., ed. Rodin Rediscovered. LC 81-9576. (Illus.). pap. 14.95 (ISBN 0-686-81955-1). Natl Gallery Art.
Hedin, Thomas. The Sculputure of Gaspard & Balthazard Marsy: Art & Patronage in the Early Reign of Louis XIV. LC 82-17415. (Illus.). 288p. 1983. text ed. 49.00x (ISBN 0-8262-0395-7). U of Mo Pr.
The Sculpture of Rodin. 1976. 50.00 (ISBN 0-686-84625-7, Nonpareil Bks). Godine.

SCULPTURE–GREAT BRITAIN
Bettey, J. H. & Taylor, C. W. Sacred & Satiric: Medieval Stone Carving in the West Country: With Illustrations from Churches in Avon, Gloucestershire, Somerset & Wiltshire. 1982. 39.00x (ISBN 0-686-82403-2, Pub. by Redcliffe England). State Mutual Bk.

SCULPTURE–ITALY
Glass, Dorothy F. Italian Romanesque Sculpture: An Annotated Bibliography. 1983. lib. bdg. 45.00 (ISBN 0-8161-8331-7, Hall Reference). G K Hall.
Lightbown, Ronald W. Donatello & Michelozzo: An Artistic Partnership & Its Patrons in the Early Renaissance, 2 vols. (Illus.). 460p. 1980. 74.00x (ISBN 0-19-921024-1). Oxford U Pr.

SCULPTURE–UNITED STATES
Bach, Ira J. & Gray, Mary L. A Guide to Chicago's Public Sculpture. LC 82-20214. (Illus.). 384p. 1983. lib. bdg. 20.00x (ISBN 0-226-03398-8); pap. 8.95 (ISBN 0-226-03399-6). U of Chicago Pr.
Fielding, Mantle. Dictionary of American Painters, Sculptors & Engravers. 1974. 30.00 (ISBN 0-913274-03-8). Apollo.
Gay, Vernon, photos by. Discovering Pittsburgh's Sculpture. LC 82-50225. (Illus.). 462p. 1982. 21.95 (ISBN 0-8229-3467-1); pap. 12.95 (ISBN 0-8229-5348-X). U of Pittsburgh Pr.
Richman, Michael, ed. Outdoor Sculpture in the Berkshires. LC 80-82444. (Illus.). 80p. 1980. pap. 6.95 (ISBN 0-89133-091-7). Preservation Pr.
Sheehan, Carol. Pipes That Won't Smoke; Coal That Won't Burn: Haida Sculpture in Argillite. (Illus.). 214p. 1982. pap. 19.95 (ISBN 0-686-84107-7, 28739-4). U of Chicago Pr.
Young. Dictionary of American Artists, Sculptors, & Engravers. 1968. 60.00 (ISBN 0-686-43150-2). Apollo.

SCULPTURE, GREEK
De Camp, L. Sprague. The Bronze God of Rhodes. Stine, Hank, ed. (Illus.). 338p. (Orig.). 1983. lib. bdg. 12.95 (ISBN 0-89865-285-5); pap. 5.95 (ISBN 0-89865-284-7); limited ed. 35.00 (ISBN 0-89865-286-3). Donning Co.

SCULPTURE, RELIGIOUS
see Christian Art and Symbolism

SCULPTURE, RENAISSANCE
Lightbown, Ronald W. Donatello & Michelozzo: An Artistic Partnership & Its Patrons in the Early Renaissance, 2 vols. (Illus.). 460p. 1980. 74.00x (ISBN 0-19-921024-1). Oxford U Pr.

SEA
see Ocean

SEA, DOMINION OF THE
see Maritime Law

SEA, FOLK-LORE OF THE
see Folk-Lore of the Sea

SEA ANGLING
see Salt-Water Fishing

SEA ANIMALS
see Marine Fauna

SEA BED
see Ocean Bottom

SEA BIRDS
Tuck. A Guide to Seabirds of Ocean Routes. 23.95 (ISBN 0-686-42755-6, Collins Pub England). Greene.

SEA-FISHERIES
see Fisheries

SEA FISHING
see Salt-Water Fishing

SEA FLOOR
see Ocean Bottom

SEA FOOD
see also Shellfish
also names of fishes or shell-fish, e.g. Clams, Oysters, Salmon
Coons, Kenelm. Seafood Seasons-How to Plan Profitable Purchasing of Fish & Shellfish: A Guide to Natural Cycles & Regulatory Controls for the Seafood Buyer. Dore, Ian, ed. (Osprey Seafood Handbooks). 1983. 48.00 (ISBN 0-943738-02-4); pap. 40.00 (ISBN 0-943738-03-2). Osprey Bks.

SEA LAWS
see Maritime Law

SEA LIFE
see Seafaring Life; Seamen

SEA-LIONS
see Seals (Animals)

SEA RESOURCES
see Marine Resources

SEA ROUTES
see Trade Routes

SEA SCOUTS
see Boy Scouts

SEA SHELL COLLECTING
see Shells

SEA SHELLS
see Shells

SEA SHORE
see Seashore

SEA SONGS
Baker, Richard & Miall, Antony, eds. Everyman's Book of Sea Songs. 278p. 1983. 24.95 (ISBN 0-460-04470-2, Pub. by Evman England). Biblio Dist.

SEA STORIES
see also Folk-Lore of the Sea
Reader's Digest Editors. Great Tales of the Sea. LC 77-81738. (Illus.). 640p. 1978. 14.98 (ISBN 0-89577-016-4). RD Assn.

SEA TRANSPORTATION
see Shipping

SEA TRAVEL
see Ocean Travel

SEA-WATER
Grasshoff, Klaus, ed. Methods of Seawater Analysis. 2nd ed. write for info. (ISBN 0-89573-070-7). Verlag-Chemie.

SEA WAVES
see Ocean Waves

SEABED
see Ocean Bottom

SEABURY, SAMUEL, BP., 1729-1796
Rowthorn, Anne. Samuel Seabury: A Bicentennial Biography. 160p. 1983. 14.95 (ISBN 0-8164-0517-4). Seabury.

SEAFARING LIFE
see also Seamen

Brookesmith, Frank. I Remember the Tall Ships. (Illus.). 270p. Repr. 20.00 (ISBN 0-87556-543-3). Saifer.

Creighton, Margaret S. Dogwatch & Liberty Days: Seafaring Life in the Nineteenth Century. LC 73-1982. (Illus.). 85p. 1982. pap. 12.50 (ISBN 0-87577-070-3). Peabody Mus Salem.

SEAFIRE (FIGHTER PLANES)

see Spitfire (Fighter Planes)

SEAFOOD

see Sea Food

SEALING (TECHNOLOGY)

see also Plastics; Welding

Bikales, Norbert M., ed. Adhesion & Bonding. LC 78-172950. 220p. Repr. of 1971 ed. pap. text ed. 16.00 (ISBN 0-471-07230-3). Krieger.

Gopalkrishnan, S. & Salant, R. F., eds. Fluid Mechanics of Mechanical Seals. 1982. 14.00 (H00232). ASME.

Koetzle, T. F., ed. Structure & Bonding: Relationships Between Quantum Chemistry & Crystallography. Date not set. pap. 7.50 (ISBN 0-937140-25-2). Polycrystal Bk Serv.

SEALS (ANIMALS)

Katona, Steve & Richardson, David. A Field Guide to the Whales, Porpoises, & Seals of the Gulf of Maine & Eastern Canada: Cape Cod to Labrador. (Illus.). 224p. 1983. 17.95 (ISBN 0-686-83664-2, ScribT); pap. 9.95 (ISBN 0-686-83665-0). Scribner.

SEALS (NUMISMATICS)

see also Emblems

Collon, Dominique. Catalogue of the Western Asiatic Seals in the British Museum: Cylinder Seals II. (Akkadian-Post Akkadian-Ur III Periods). 240p. 1982. 110.00x (ISBN 0-7141-1104-X, Pub. by Brit Mus Pubns England). State Mutual Bk.

SEAMANSHIP

see also Knots and Splices; Navigation

Powledge, Fred. A Forgiving Wind: On Becoming a Sailor. LC 82-16867. (Illus.). 224p. 1983. 12.95 (ISBN 0-87156-330-4). Sierra.

Seamanship for New Skippers. LC 80-14025. (Illus.). 96p. Date not set. pap. 5.95 (ISBN 0-686-84316-9). Banyan Bks.

Taylor, Roger C. The Elements of Seamanship. LC 82-80400. (Illus.). 192p. 1982. 12.95 (ISBN 0-87742-153-6). Intl Marine.

SEAMEN

Here are entered works on naval seamen in general. Works on members of the Armed Forces, including naval seamen, are entered under the heading Soldiers.

see also Merchant Marine; Merchant Seamen; Pilots and Pilotage; Seafaring Life

also United States-Navy, and similar headings

Jones, Tristan. A Steady Trade: A Boyhood at Sea. (Illus.). 288p. 1982. 15.95 (ISBN 0-312-76138-4). St Martin.

Kataria, R. D. A Sailor Remembers. 1983. text ed. write for info. (ISBN 0-7069-2064-3, Pub. by Vikas India). Advent NY.

Straus, Robert. Medical Care For Seamen. 1950. text ed. 39.50x (ISBN 0-686-83622-7). Elliots Bks.

SEAMEN'S SONGS

see Sea Songs

SEARCHING, BIBLIOGRAPHICAL

see also on-Line Bibliographic Searching

Gilreath, Charles L. Computer Literature Searching: Research Strategies & Databases. 108p. 1983. lib. bdg. 18.50x (ISBN 0-86531-526-4). Westview.

SEASHORE

see also Beaches; Coast Changes; Coasts; Shore Lines

Barrett & Yonge. Collins Pocket Guide to the Seashore. 29.95 (ISBN 0-686-42767-X, Collins Pub England). Greene.

D'Attilio, Anthony. Seashore Life Coloring Book. 48p. 1973. pap. 1.95 (ISBN 0-486-22930-0). Dover.

Swenson, Allan. Secrets of a Seashore. (Secret of Ser.). (Illus.). 80p. 1981. 6.95 (ISBN 0-930096-27-4); pap. 5.95 (ISBN 0-930096-28-2). G Gannett.

Voss, Gilbert L. Seashore Life of Florida & the Caribbean. LC 80-20172. (Illus.). 199p. Date not set. pap. 8.95 (ISBN 0-686-84302-9). Banyan Bks.

SEASHORE BIOLOGY

Brafield, Alan E. Life in Sandy Shores. (Studies in Biology: No. 89). 64p. 1978. pap. text ed. 8.95 (ISBN 0-686-43115-4). E Arnold.

SEASHORE ECOLOGY

Jenkins, Morton. Seashore Studies. (Practical Ecology Ser.). (Illus.). 104p. 1983. pap. text ed. 8.50x (ISBN 0-04-574019-4). Allen Unwin.

Perkins, Bob F. Deltaic Sedimentation on the Louisiana Coast. 1982. 10.00. SEPM.

SEASONS-JUVENILE LITERATURE

Greydanus, Rose. Changing Seasons. LC 82-19959. (Now I Know Ser.). (Illus.). 32p. (gr. k-2). 1982. PLB 8.89 (ISBN 0-89375-902-3). Troll Assocs.

Marcus, Elizabeth. Our Wonderful Seasons. LC 82-17372. (Question & Answer Bks.). (Illus.). 32p. (gr. 3-6). 1983. PLB 8.59 (ISBN 0-89375-896-5); pap. text ed. 1.95 (ISBN 0-89375-897-3). Troll Assocs.

Peyo, pseud. Through the Seasons with Smurfette. LC 82-60093. (Smurf Hummingbird Bks.). (Illus.). 16p. (ps-3). 1983. 1.25 (ISBN 0-394-85620-1). Random.

Santrey, Louis. Autumn. LC 82-19396. (Discovering the Seasons Ser.). (Illus.). 32p. (gr. 4-6). 1982. lib. bdg. 8.79 (ISBN 0-89375-905-8); pap. text ed. 2.50 (ISBN 0-89375-906-6). Troll Assocs.

--Spring: Discovering the Seasons Ser. LC 82-19381. (Illus.). 32p. (gr. 4-6). 1982. lib. bdg. 8.79 (ISBN 0-89375-909-0); pap. text ed. 2.50 (ISBN 0-89375-910-4). Troll Assocs.

--Summer. LC 82-19384. (Discovering the Seasons Ser.). (Illus.). 32p. (gr. 4-6). 1982. lib. bdg. 8.79 (ISBN 0-89375-911-2); pap. text ed. 2.50 (ISBN 0-89375-912-0). Troll Assocs.

--Winter. LC 82-19353. (Discovering the Seasons Ser.). (Illus.). 32p. (gr. 4-6). 1982. lib. bdg. 8.79 (ISBN 0-89375-907-4); pap. text ed. 2.50 (ISBN 0-89375-908-2). Troll Assocs.

SEATS

see Chairs

SEAT WORK

see Creative Activities and Seatwork

SEATTLE-DESCRIPTION

Bean, John E. & Bean, Ruth E. To Seattle with Love: A Very Unofficial Guidebook. LC 82-50381. (Illus.). 128p. (Orig.). 1982. pap. 4.95 (ISBN 0-9608430-0-0). Sheba Pub.

Brewster, David. The Best Places. 4th ed. 192p. (Orig.). 1982. pap. 9.95 (ISBN 0-914842-76-5). Sasquatch Pub.

Burke, Clifford. A Rainy Day Guide to Seattle. (Orig.). 1983. pap. 6.95 (ISBN 0-87701-290-3). Chronicle Bks.

Gregorakis, Karen & Lotskar, Elaine. Dining In--Seattle, Vol. III. (Dining In--Ser.). 210p. 1982. pap. 8.95 (ISBN 0-89716-112-2). Peanut Butter.

SEATTLE-HISTORY

Warren, James R. & McCoy, William R. Highlights of Seattle's History. (History Ser.). (Illus.). 50p. (Orig.). pap. 2.95 (ISBN 0-686-83960-9). Hist Soc Seattle.

SEAWEED

Cheney, Daniel P. & Mumford, Thomas M., Jr. Shellfish & Seaweed Harvests of Puget Sound. (A Puget Sound Bk.). (Illus.). 144p. (Orig.). 1983. pap. 8.95 (ISBN 0-686-43218-5, Pub. by Wash Sea Grant). U of Wash Pr.

Sorensen, L. O. A Guide To the Seaweed of South Padre Island, Texas. 123p. 1979. pap. text ed. 8.95 (ISBN 0-89787-101-4). Gorsuch Scarisbrick.

SEBAGO LAKE, MAINE

Jones, Herbert. Sebago Lane Land. (Illus.). 136p. 1982. pap. 6.95 (ISBN 0-87027-152-0). Cumberland Pr.

SECOND ADVENT

see also Judgment Day; Millennium

Balyoz, Harold. Signs of Christ. LC 79-64608. 1979. 18.00 (ISBN 0-9609710-0-9). Altai Pub.

Brown, David. Christ's Second Coming. 1983. pap. 10.95 (ISBN 0-8010-0833-6). Baker Bk.

Cutting, Jorge. La Venida del Senor. 2nd ed. Bennett, Gordon H., ed. Bautista, Sara, tr. from Eng. (La Serie Diamante). 48p. (Span.). 1982. pap. 0.85 (ISBN 0-942504-10-0). Overcomer Pr.

Erdman, V. R. Signs of Christ's Second Coming. 29p. pap. 0.85 (ISBN 0-87509-130-X). Chr Pubns.

Kelly, William. The Second Coming. 375p. 5.25 (ISBN 0-88172-108-5). Believers Bkshelf.

Savoy, Gene. THe Miracle of the Second Advent: Emerging New Christianity & the Secret Church at Work in the World. 1983. text ed. 39.50 (ISBN 0-936202-04-1). Intl Comm Christ.

Steiner, Rudolf. The Reappearance of Christ in the Etheric. rev. ed. 190p. (Orig.). 1983. 14.00 (ISBN 0-88010-017-6); pap. 8.95 (ISBN 0-88010-016-8). Anthroposophic.

Yogananda, Paramhansa. The Second Coming of Christ, Vol. I. LC 79-50352. 1980. pap. 10.95 (ISBN 0-937134-00-7). Amrita Found.

SECOND HAND TRADE

see Secondhand Trade

SECOND HOMES

see also Country Homes

Architectural Record Magozine Staff. The Architectural Record Book of Vacation Houses. 2nd ed. 1977. 32.50 (ISBN 0-07-002337-9). McGraw.

Corbin, Patricia. Summer Cottages & Castles: Scenes from the Good Life. (Illus.). 144p. 1983. 29.95 (ISBN 0-525-93279-8, 02908-870). Dutton.

SECONDARY BATTERIES

see Storage Batteries

SECONDARY EDUCATION

see Education, Secondary

SECONDARY EMPLOYMENT

see Supplementary Employment

SECONDARY SCHOOL TEACHERS

see High School Teachers

SECONDARY SCHOOLS

see Education, Secondary; Private Schools; Public Schools

SECONDHAND TRADE

see also Used Car Trade

Antiques & Flea Markets. (What's It Worth Ser.). 1983. pap. 2.95 (ISBN 0-440-00128-5). Dell.

SECRECY IN GOVERNMENT

see Official Secrets

SECRET SERVICE

see also Detectives; Espionage; Intelligence Service; Spies

Deacon, Richard. A History of the Japanese Secret Service. 320p. 1982. 40.00x (ISBN 0-584-10383-2, Pub. by Muller Ltd). State Mutual Bk.

SECRETARIAL PRACTICE

see Office Practice

SECRETARIAL TRAINING

see Business Education; shorthand; Typewriting and allied subjects

SECRETARIES

see also Legal Secretaries; Medical Secretaries; Office Management; Receptionists; School Secretaries

Austin, Evelyn. Secretarial Services. 208p. 1982. pap. text ed. 11.00 (ISBN 0-7121-1984-1). Intl Ideas.

Duenas. Curso Basico de Practicas Secretariales. 120p. 1982. 4.56 (ISBN 0-07-017992-1, G). McGraw.

Ganong, Joan M. & Ganong, Warren L. Help for the Unit Secretary: The Service Coordinator Concept. (Help Series of Management Guides). 64p. 1980. pap. 8.25 (ISBN 0-933036-12-4). Ganong W L Co.

Lindsell, Sheryl L. The Secretary's Quick Reference Manual. LC 82-8888. 288p. (Orig.). 1983. pap. 2.95 (ISBN 0-668-05595-2, 5595). Arco.

Macdonald, Eleanor & Little, Julia. The Successful Secretary. 176p. 1980. 26.00x (ISBN 0-7121-1976-0, Pub. by Macdonald & Evans). State Mutual Bk.

Nitsch, Susan L. How to Become a Freelance Secretary. Pasich, William, ed. (Illus.). 53p. 1983. pap. 3.95 (ISBN 0-943544-01-7). Secretarial Pubns.

Porat, Freida & Will, Mimi. The Dynamic Secretary. (Illus.). 196p. 1983. 14.95 (ISBN 0-13-221853-4); pap. 7.95 (ISBN 0-13-221846-1). P-H.

Smith, Genevieve. Genevieve Smith's Deluxe Handbook for the Executive Secretary. 267p. 1979. 17.50 (ISBN 0-686-84017-8, Busn). P-H.

White, Don. The Perfect Secretary. (Illus.). 96p. 1982. pap. 4.50 (ISBN 0-89387-069-2). Curtis Pub Co.

SECRETION

see also Glands; Hormones

also names of secretions, e.g. Bile, Perspiration, Urine

Cantin, M., ed. The Secretory Process. (Illus.). x, 490p. 1983. 178.50 (ISBN 3-8055-3619-4). S Karger.

Suzuki, T. Physiology of Adrenocortical Secretion. (Frontiers of Hormone Research: Vol. 11). (Illus.). viii, 200p. 1983. 78.00 (ISBN 3-8055-3644-5). S Karger.

SECRETS, TRADE

see Trade Secrets

SECTIONALISM (U. S.)

see also Regionalism

Reed, John S. Southerners: The Social Psychology of Sectionalism. LC 82-13631. 170p. 1983. 17.00x (ISBN 0-8078-1542-X); pap. 5.95x (ISBN 0-8078-4098-X). U of NC Pr.

SECTS

Here are entered works on religious groups whose adherents recognize special teachings or practices which fall within the normative bounds of the major world religions. Works on the major world religions are entered under Religions. Works on groups or movements whose system of religious beliefs or practices differs significantly from the major world religions and which are often gathered around a specific deity or person are entered under Cults.

see also Cults; Eastern Churches

also particular denominations and sects

Barker, Eileen, ed. New Religious Movements: A Perspective for Understanding Society. (Studies in Religion & Society: Vol. 3). 440p. 1982. 44.95 (ISBN 0-686-84111-5). E Mellen.

Daly, Lloyd W. Iohannis Philoponi: De Vocabulis Quae Diversum Signification Exhibent Secundum Differentiam Accentus. LC 81-72156. (Memoirs Ser.: Vol. 151). 1983. 20.00 (ISBN 0-87169-151-5). Am Philos.

Doress, Irvin & Porter, Jack N. Kids in Cults: Why they Join, Why they Stay, Why they Leave. Rev. ed. 22p. (Orig.). 1982. pap. 2.50 (ISBN 0-932270-02-6). Zalonka Pubns.

SECTS, JEWISH

see Jewish Sects

SECULAR PART-SONGS

see Part-Songs

SECULARISM

see also Agnosticism; Rationalism

Campolo, Anthony. A Reasonable Faith: Responding to Secularism. 1983. 8.95 (ISBN 0-686-84760-1). Word Bks.

Hitchcock, James. What Is Secular Humanism? Why Humanism Became Secular & How It Is Changing Our World. (Illus.). 180p. 1982. pap. 6.95 (ISBN 0-89283-163-4). Servant.

LaHaye, Tim. The Battle for the Family. 256p. 1983. pap. 6.95 (ISBN 0-8007-5117-5). Revell.

SECURITIES

see also Bonds; Investment Banking; Investment Trusts; Investments, Foreign; Mortgages; Stocks

Fabozzi, Frank J. & Pollack, Irving M., eds. The Handbook of Fixed Income Securities. LC 82-71874. 850p. 1983. 45.00 (ISBN 0-87094-306-5). Dow Jones-Irwin.

Fleischer, Arthur, Jr. & Lipton, Martin, eds. Annual Institute on Securities Regulation, 13th. LC 70-125178. 472p. 1982. text ed. 50.00 (ISBN 0-686-82490-3, B2-1281). PLI.

Jaffe, S. M. Broker-Dealers & Securities Markets. 1977. 40.00 (ISBN 0-07-032218-X). McGraw.

Mittre, Sid & Gassen, Chris. Investment Analysis & Portfolio Management. 857p. text ed. 25.95 (ISBN 0-15-546882-0); tchr's. manual 2.95 (ISBN 0-15-546883-9). HarBraceJ.

Soderquist, Larry D. Securities Regulation: 1983 Supplement. (University Casebook Ser.). 612p. 1982. pap. text ed. write for info. (ISBN 0-88277-072-1). Foundation Pr.

Steinberg, Marc I. Corporate Internal Affairs: A Corporate & Securities Law Perspective. LC 82-16619. 296p. 1983. lib. bdg. 35.00 (ISBN 0-89930-039-1, SCS/, Quorum). Greenwood.

Wolf, Clarence, Jr. Seven Letters: The Securities Market & You. LC 81-66095. 64p. Date not set. pap. 1.95 (ISBN 0-686-84242-1). Banyan Bks.

SECURITIES EXCHANGE

see Stock-Exchange

SECURITY, ECONOMIC

see Economic Security

SECURITY, INTERNATIONAL

see also Disarmament; International Organization; Mutual Security Programs, 1951-; Neutrality; Peace

Arlinghaus, Bruce, ed. Africa Security Issues: Sovereignty, Stability, & Solidarity. 200p. Date not set. price not set. Westview.

Bertram, Christoph, ed. Third-World Conflict & International Security. 128p. 1982. 49.00x (ISBN 0-333-32955-4, Pub. by Macmillan England). State Mutual Bk.

Churchill, Winston S. Defending the West. 1981. 40.00x (ISBN 0-85117-210-5, Pub. by M Temple Smith). State Mutual Bk.

Johnson, U. Alexis & Packard, George R. The Common Security Interests of Japan, The United States & NATO. 38p. pap. 6.00x (ISBN 0-87855-873-X). Transaction Bks.

Kennedy, Robert & Weinsteiln, John M., eds. The Defense of the West: Strategic & European Security Issues Reappraised. 350p. 1983. price not set (ISBN 0-86531-612-0). Westview.

Mushkat, Marion. The Third World & Peace: Some Aspects of Problems of the Inter-Relationship of Interdevelopment & International Security. LC 82-774. 356p. 1982. 27.50x (ISBN 0-312-80039-8). St Martin.

Vogt, John W. Improving the NATO Force Capabilities. 12p. pap. 1.00 (ISBN 0-87855-742-3). Transaction Bks.

Weinstein, Martin E., ed. Northeast Asian Security after Vietnam. LC 82-1909. 192p. 1982. 17.50 (ISBN 0-252-00966-5). U of Ill Pr.

Wolf, Joseph J. Security in the Eastern Mediterranean: Re-Thinking American Policy. 19p. pap. 1.00 (ISBN 0-87855-739-3). Transaction Bks.

Wolf, Joseph J. & Cleveland, Harlan. The Growing Dimensions of Security. 86p. pap. 5.00x (ISBN 0-87855-740-7). Transaction Bks.

SECURITY MEASURES (MILITARY INFORMATION)

see Industry-Security Measures

SECURITY MEASURES, INDUSTRIAL

see Industry-Security Measures

SECURITY OFFENSES

see Subversive Activities

SECURITY SYSTEMS

see also Libraries-Security Measures; Police

Cook, William J., Jr. Security Systems: Considerations, Layout, Performance. Date not set. pap. 9.95 (ISBN 0-672-21949-2). Sams.

La Mont, M. Dean. Understanding Electronic Security Systems. LC 82-50800. (Understanding Ser.). (Illus.). 128p. 1982. pap. 6.95 (ISBN 0-686-84790-3, 7201). Tex Instr Inc.

Langer, Steven, ed. The Security Report. 2nd ed. 1982. pap. 85.00 (ISBN 0-916506-70-3). Abbott Langer Assocs.

McCrie, Robert, ed. Security Letter Sourcebook, 1983. 250p. (Orig.). 1983. prepub. 49.95 (ISBN 0-9609820-0-0); pap. 75.00. Security Let.

Montana, Patrick J. & Roukis, George S., eds. Managing Terrorism: Strategies for the Corporate Executive. LC 82-11224. 192p. 1983. lib. bdg. 27.95 (ISBN 0-89930-013-8, MTE/, Quorum). Greenwood.

Walker. Electronic Security Systems. 1983. text ed. price not set (ISBN 0-408-01160-2). Butterworth.

SEDIMENT TRANSPORT

see also Channels (Hydraulic Engineering)

Tanner, William F., ed. Shorelines Past & Present, 3 vols. 745p. 1980. pap. 50.00 (ISBN 0-686-83996-X). FSU Geology.

SEDIMENTARY ROCKS

see Rocks, Sedimentary

SEDIMENTARY STRUCTURES

Royal Society of London. The Evolution of Sedimentary Basins: Proceedings of a Royal Society Discussion Meeting held on 3 & 4 June 1981. Kent, Peter & McKenzie, D. P., eds. (Illus.). 338p. 1982. text ed. 112.00x (ISBN 0-85403-184-7, Pub. by Royal Soc London). Scholium Intl.

SEDIMENTATION ANALYSIS

Friedman, Gerald M. & Sanders, John E. Principles of Sedimentology. LC 78-5355. 792p. 1978. text ed. 35.95 (ISBN 0-471-75245-2). Wiley.

SEDIMENTATION AND DEPOSITION

see also Erosion; Marine Sediments; Rocks, Sedimentary

Iijima, A. & Hein, J. R., eds. Siliceous Deposits in the Pacific Region. (Developments in Sedimentology Ser.: No. 36). 472p. 1982. 85.00 (ISBN 0-686-84505-6). Elsevier.

Laronne, Jonathan & Mosley, M. Paul, eds. Erosion & Sediment Yield. LC 81-6456. (Benchmark Papers in Geology: Vol. 63). 400p. 1982. 47.00 (ISBN 0-87933-409-6). Hutchinson Ross.

Sly, Peter G. Sediment-Freshwater Interaction. 1982. text ed. 125.00 (ISBN 90-6193-760-4, Pub. by Junk Pubs Netherlands). Kluwer Boston.

Stanley, D. J. & Kelling, G., eds. Sedimentation in Submarine Canyons, Fans & Trenches. LC 77-19163. 395p. 1978. 60.50 (ISBN 0-87933-313-8). Hutchinson Ross.

Swift, D. J. & Palmer, Harold D., eds. Coastal Sedimentation. LC 78-18696. (Benchmark Papers in Geology Ser.: Vol. 42). 339p. 1978. 48.50 (ISBN 0-87933-330-8). Hutchinson Ross.

Weimer, R. J., et al. Tectonic Influence on Sedimentation, Early Cretaceous, East Flank Powder River Basin, Wyoming & South Dakota. (Colorado School of Mines Quarterly: Vol. 77, No. 4). (Illus.). 95p. 1982. pap. text ed. 12.00 (ISBN 0-686-82131-9). Colo Sch Mines.

SEDIMENTS (GEOLOGY)

see also Clay; Marine Sediments; Sedimentary Structures

Fairbridge, R. W. & Bourgeois, J., eds. The Encyclopedia of Sedimentology. LC 78-18259. (Encyclopedia of Earth Sciences Ser.: Vol. VI). 901p. 1978. 98.00 (ISBN 0-87933-152-6). Hutchinson Ross.

Goudie, A. S. & Pye, K., eds. Chemical Sediments & Geomorphology. Date not set. price not set (ISBN 0-12-293480-6). Acad Pr.

Stanley, D. J. & Kelling, G., eds. Sedimentation in Submarine Canyons, Fans & Trenches. LC 77-19163. 395p. 1978. 60.50 (ISBN 0-87933-313-8). Hutchinson Ross.

Tanner, William F. Coastal Sedimentology. 315p. 1977. pap. 20.00 (ISBN 0-686-83995-1). FSU Geology.

--Near-Shore Sedimentology. 300p. 1983. pap. 40.00 (ISBN 0-686-83997-8). FSU Geology.

Tanner, William F., ed. Sediment Transport in the Near-Shore Zone. 147p. 1974. pap. 20.00 (ISBN 0-686-83994-3). FSU Geology.

SEE, HOLY

see Papacy; Popes

SEED PLANTS

see Phanerogams

SEEDS

see also Botany–Embryology; Oilseeds

Advances in Research & Technology of Seeds, Pt. 7. 140p. 1982. pap. 19.25 (ISBN 90-220-0802-9, PDC249, Pudoc). Unipub.

Black, M. & Bewley, J. D. Physiology & Biochemistry of Seeds in Relation to Germination: Viability, Dormancy, & Environmental Control, Vol. 2. (Illus.). 380p. 1982. 54.00 (ISBN 0-387-11656-7). Springer-Verlag.

Duffus, C. M. & Slaughter, J. C. Seeds & Their Uses. LC 80-40283. 154p. 1980. 36.95x (ISBN 0-471-27799-1, Pub. by Wiley-Interscience); pap. write for info. (ISBN 0-471-27798-3). Wiley.

Seeds Semences Semillas. (FAO Plant Production & Protection Paper: No. 39). 569p. 1983. pap. 41.75 (ISBN 92-5-001226-8, F2361, FAO). Unipub.

SEEDS–GERMINATION

see Germination

SEFER TORAH

see Torah Scrolls

SEGREGATION

see also Minorities;

also subdivision Segregation under ethnic groups, e.g. Afro-Americans–Segregation

Automating Apartheid. 1982. 3.50 (ISBN 0-910082-04-9). Am Pr Serv Comm.

International Labour Conference, 59th session, Geneva, 1974. Apartheid: Tenth Special Report of the Director-General on the Application of the Declaration cooncerning the Policy of "Apartheid" of the Republic of South Africa. 68p. 8.55 (ISBN 92-2-100967-X, ILC 59/1/SPECIAL REPORT). Intl Labour Office.

International Labour Conference, 60th session, 1975. Apartheid: Eleventh Special Report of the Director-General on the Application of the Declaration Concerning the Policy of "Apartheid" of the Republic of South Africa. 51p. 7.15 (ISBN 92-2-100968-8, ILC 60/1/SPECIAL REPORT). Intl Labour Office.

International Labour Conference, 63rd session, 1977. Apartheid: Thirteenth Special Report of the Director-General on the Application of the Declaration Concerning the Policy of "Apartheid" of the Republic of South Africa. 56p. 8.55 (ISBN 92-2-101562-9, ILC 63/1/SPECIAL REPORT). Intl Labour Office.

International Labour Conference, 64th session, 1978. Apartheid: Fourteenth Special Report of the Director-General on the Application of the Declaration Concerning the Policy of "Apartheid" of the Republic of South Africa. 54p. 8.55 (ISBN 92-2-101942-X, ILC 64/1/SPECIAL REPORT). Intl Labour Office.

International Labour Conference, 65th session, 1979. Apartheid: Fifteenth Special Report of the Director-General on the Application of the Declaration Concerning the Policy of "Apartheid"of the Republic of South Africa. iii, 48p. 8.55 (ISBN 92-2-101971-3, ILC 65/1/SPECIAL REPORT). Intl Labour Office.

International Labour Conference, 68th session. Apartheid: Eighteenth Special Report of the Director-General on the Application of the Declaration Concerning the Policy of Apartheid of the Republic of South Africa. 1982. write for info. (ILC 68/SPECIAL REPORT). Intl Labour Office.

Smith, David M. Living Under Apartheid. (London Research Series in Geography: No. 2). 296p. 1983. text ed. 35.00x (ISBN 0-04-309110-5). Allen Unwin.

SEGREGATION IN EDUCATION

see also School Integration

School Desegregation in Texas: The Implementation of United States vs State of Texas. LC 82-82981. (Policy Research Project Report Ser.). 75p. 1982. 6.50 (ISBN 0-89940-653-X). LBJ Sch Pub Aff.

SEGYE KIDOKKYO T'ONGIL SILLYONG HYOPHOE

see Holy Spirit Associaton for the Unification of World Christianity

SEISMIC WAVES

Morgan, Thomas R. Foundations of Wave Theory for Seismic Exploration. LC 82-83805. (Illus.). 160p. 1982. text ed. 32.00 (ISBN 0-934634-34-3). Intl Human Res.

SEISMOLOGY

see also Earthquakes; Seismic Waves; Seismometry; Volcanoes

Berkhout, A. J. Seismic Migration: Imaging of Acoustic Energy by Wave Field Extrapolation; A Theoretical Aspects. 2nd rev. & enl. ed. (Developments in Solid Earth Geophysics Ser.: Vol. 14A). 352p. Date not set. 59.75 (ISBN 0-444-42130-0). Elsevier.

Datta, S. K., ed. Earthquake Ground Motion & Its Effects On Structures. (AMD Ser.: Vol. 53). 197p. 1982. 40.00 (H00241). ASME.

Kanai, Kiyoshi. Engineering Seismology. 250p. 1983. 34.50 (ISBN 0-86008-326-8, Pub. by U of Tokyo Japan). Columbia U Pr.

McDonald, John A. & Gardner, G. H. Seismic Studies in Physical Modeling: Physical Modeling. LC 82-81374. (Illus.). 354p. 1982. text ed. 34.00 (ISBN 0-934634-39-4); pap. text ed. 24.00 (ISBN 0-934634-47-5). Intl Human Res.

Sengbush, Ray L. Seismic Exploration Methods. LC 82-81559. (Illus.). 289p. 1983. text ed. 38.00 (ISBN 0-934634-21-1). Intl Human Res.

White, J. E. Applied Seismic Methods. (Methods in Geochemistry & Geophysics: Vol. 18). Date not set. price not set (ISBN 0-444-42139-4). Elsevier.

SEISMOMETRY

see also Earthquakes

Yan, M. J., ed. Dynamic & Seismic Analysis of Systems & Components. (PVP Ser.: Vol. 65). 192p. 1982. 44.00 (H00222). ASME.

SELECTION, NATURAL

see Natural Selection

SELECTIVE SERVICE

see Military Service, Compulsory

SELENIUM

Lewis, Alan. Selenium: The Facts about This Essential Element. 2.50x (ISBN 0-7225-0734-8). Cancer Control Soc.

Shamberger, Raymond J. Biochemistry of Selenium. (Biochemistry of the Elements Ser.: Vol. 2). 346p. 1983. 42.50x (ISBN 0-306-41090-7, Plenum Pr). Plenum Pub.

SELENOLOGY

see Moon

SELF

see also Body, Human; Consciousness; Ego (Psychology); Existentialism; Identity (Psychology); Mind and Body; Personality; Role Playing; Thought and Thinking

Babad, Elisha Y. & Birnbaum, Max. The Social Self: Group Influences on Personal Identity. (Sage Library of Social Research). (Illus.). 320p. 25.00 (ISBN 0-8039-1938-7); pap. 12.50 (ISBN 0-8039-1939-5). Sage.

Deikman, Arthur J. The Observing Self: Mysticism & Psychotherapy. LC 81-70486. 208p. 1983. pap. 6.97 (ISBN 0-686-82696-5). Beacon Pr.

Lee, Benjamin. Psychosocial Theories of the Self. (Path in Psychology). 230p. 1982. 27.50x (ISBN 0-306-41117-2, Plenum Pr). Plenum Pub.

To Whom Do I Belong? 1980. 2.95 (ISBN 0-8215-5828-5). Sadlier.

SELF (PHILOSOPHY)

Boni, Sylvain. The Self & the Other in the Ontologies of Sartre & Buber. LC 82-20130. 202p. (Orig.). 1983. lib. bdg. 21.75 (ISBN 0-8191-2852-X); pap. text ed. 10.75 (ISBN 0-8191-2853-8). U Pr of Amer.

Lewis, H. D. The Elusive Self. 1982. 50.00x (ISBN 0-686-42924-9, Pub. by Macmillan England). State Mutual Bk.

Rigdon, Robert. Discovering Yourself. 1982. pap. 4.95 (ISBN 0-8423-0617-X). Tyndale.

Tichumanatman, D. Raising the Roof: The Transformation of Being. 1979. 10.00 (ISBN 0-533-04228-3). All In All.

SELF-ACTUALIZATION (PSYCHOLOGY)

Atwater, Eastwood. Psychology of Adjustment: Personal Growth in a Changing World. 2nd ed. (Illus.). 448p. 1983. pap. 19.95 (ISBN 0-13-734855-X). P-H.

Bruno, Frank J. Human Adjustment & Personal Growth: Seven Pathways. LC 76-54654. 499p. 1977. text ed. 21.95 (ISBN 0-471-11435-9). Wiley.

Buscaglia, Leo. Living, Loving & Learning. 264p. 1982. 13.50 (ISBN 0-686-84812-8). Slack Inc.

LeCron, Leslie M. Magic Mind Power: Make it work for You! 2nd ed. 176p. 1983. pap. 4.95 (ISBN 0-87516-496-X). De Vorss.

Maul, Gail & Maul, Terry. Beyond Limit: Ways to Growth & Freedom. 1982. pap. text ed. 9.95x (ISBN 0-673-15422-X). Scott F.

SELF-ADAPTIVE CONTROL SYSTEMS

see Adaptive Control Systems

SELF-CHECKING CODES

see Error-Correcting Codes (Information Theory)

SELF-CONCEPT

see Self-Perception

SELF-CONFIDENCE

see Self-Reliance

SELF-CONTROL

Bedford, Stewart. How to Teach Children Stress Management & Emotional Control: A Survival Kit for Teachers, Parents, & Kids. 1981. 29.50 (ISBN 0-935930-03-5). Scott Pubns CA.

Gambill, Henrietta. Self-Control. LC 82-1201. (What is It? Ser.). 32p. (gr. k-3). 1982. PLB 6.50 (ISBN 0-89565-225-0). Childs World.

Vohn, Rick. Getting Control of Your Inner Self. 176p. 1983. pap. 2.95 (ISBN 0-8423-0999-3). Tyndale.

SELF-CULTURE

see also Books and Reading; Mental Discipline

Houston, Jean & Loeb, Millie. The Possible Human: A Course in Extending Your Physical, Mental, and Creative Abilities. (Illus.). 229p. 1982. text ed. 16.50 (ISBN 0-87477-219-2); pap. text ed. 9.95 (ISBN 0-87477-218-4). J P Tarcher.

Hubbard, L. Ron. Self Analysis. Date not set. 8.95 (ISBN 0-88404-109-3). Bridge Pub.

SELF-DEFENSE

see also Aikido; Boxing; Hand-To-Hand Fighting; Jiu-Jitsu; Judo; Stick-Fighting

Baltazzi, Evan S. Stickfighting: A Practical Guide for Self-Protection. (Illus.). 224p. 1983. 19.50 (ISBN 0-8048-1450-3). C E Tuttle.

Croucher, Michael & Reid, Howard. The Fighting Arts. (Illus.). 1983. price not set (ISBN 0-671-47158-9). S&S.

Cruit, Ronald L. Intruder in Your Home: How to Defend Yourself Legally With A Firearm. LC 82-42727. 288p. 1983. 17.95 (ISBN 0-686-83443-7). Stein & Day.

Diaz-Cobo, Oscar. Bare Kills. (Illus.). 160p. 1982. pap. 10.00 (ISBN 0-87364-253-8). Paladin Ent.

Haller, Mike. TV Self-Defense Kit. 1982. 10 copy prepak 49.50 (ISBN 0-686-84818-7); 4.95 (ISBN 0-686-84819-5). HM.

Herbert, Anthony B. A Military Manual of Self Defense: A Complete Guide to Hand-to-Hand Combat. (Illus.). 280p. 1983. 19.95 (ISBN 0-88254-708-9). Hippocrene Bks.

Hess, Joseph C. Nunchaku in Action: For Kobudo & Law Enforcement. (Illus., Orig.). 1983. pap. 7.95 (ISBN 0-89750-086-5, 423). Ohara Pubns.

Kong, Bucksam. The Tiger-Crane Form of Hung Gar Kung-Fu. (Illus., Orig.). 1983. pap. 6.95 (ISBN 0-89750-087-3, 424). Ohara Pubns.

Presas, Remy A. Modern Arnis: For Self-Defense. (Illus.). 1983. pap. 6.95 (ISBN 0-89750-089-X, 426). Ohara Pubns.

SELF-DEFENSE FOR WOMEN

Monkerud, Donald & Heiny, Mary. Self-Defense for Women. (Exploring Sports Ser.). 1983. pap. write for info. (ISBN 0-697-09978-4). Wm C Brown.

Peterson, Susan L. Self-Defense for Women. (Illus.). 192p. (Orig.). 1983. pap. 7.95 (ISBN 0-88011-114-3). Leisure Pr.

SELF-DESTRUCTION

see Suicide

SELF-DETERMINATION, NATIONAL

see also Minorities

Pomerance, Michla. Law of Self-Determination in Law & Practice. 1982. lib. bdg. 39.50 (ISBN 90-247-2594-1, Pub. by Martinus Nijhoff Netherlands). Kluwer Boston.

SELF-EMPLOYED

see also Entrepreneur; Professions; Small Business

Anderson, J. W. Best of Both Worlds-A Guide to Home-Based Careers. 188p. 1982. 10.95 (ISBN 0-686-84292-8, Pub. by Betterway Pubns). Berkshire Traveller.

Hathaway-Bates, John. How to Promote your Business. 162p. (Orig.). 1981. pap. 9.25 (ISBN 0-910333-00-9). Asigan Ltd.

Kishel, Gregory F. & Kishel, Paricia G. Your Business is a Success: Now What? (Small Business Ser.). 224p. 1983. pap. text ed. 8.95. Wiley.

Newcomb, Duane. Fortune-Building Secrets of the Rich. LC 82-18837. 215p. 1983. pap. 4.95 (ISBN 0-13-329102-2, Reward). P-H.

--Fortune-Building Secrets of the Rich. LC 82-18837. 215p. 1983. 14.95 (ISBN 0-13-384685-7, Parker); pap. 4.95 (ISBN 0-13-329102-2). P-H.

Update Publicare Research Staff. Self Employment Update: Notebook of Back Issues. 35p. 1983. pap. text ed. 8.00 (ISBN 0-686-38897-6). Update Pub Co.

SELF-ESTEEM

see Self-Respect

SELF-EVALUATION OF SCHOOLS

see Educational Surveys

SELF-FULFILLMENT

see Self-Realization

SELF-GOVERNMENT (IN EDUCATION)

see also Student Administrator Relationships

Miller, Theodore K. & Winston, Roger B., Jr., eds. Administration & Leadership in Student Affairs: Actualizing Student Development in Higher Education. 600p. (Orig.). 1983. pap. text ed. 29.95 (ISBN 0-915202-35-2). Accel Devel.

SELF-HELP

see Christian Life; Conduct of Life; Psychology, Applied; Success; Self-Culture; Youth;

also the cross references listed at the beginning of each of these headings, and subdivision Self-Instruction under names of languages and subdivision Programmed Instruction under subjects

SELF-HELP GROUPS

Katz, Alfred H. & Smith, David H. Self-Help Group & Voluntary Action: Some International Perspectives. 250p. 1983. text ed. 24.50x (ISBN 0-8290-1274-5). Irvington.

Phillips & Judd. How to Fall Out of Love. 192p. 1982. pap. 2.95 (ISBN 0-446-31038-7). Warner Bks.

SELF-HYPNOSIS

see Autogenic Training

SELF-INSTRUCTION

see Self-Culture

also subdivision Self-Instruction under names of languages and subdivision Programmed Instruction under subjects

SELF-INSURANCE

Conder, Joseph M. & Hopkins, Gilbert N. The Self-Insurance Decision. 119p. pap. 12.95 (ISBN 0-86641-002-3, 81124). Natl Assn Accts.

SELF-INTEREST

see also Individualism

Evans, Christopher. Understanding Yourself. (Illus.). 160p. 1983. pap. 6.95 (ISBN 0-89104-084-6, A & W Visual Library). A & W Pubs.

SELF-KNOWLEDGE, THEORY OF

Hohler, Thomas P. Imagination & Reflection: Intersubjectivity. 1983. lib. bdg. 29.50 (ISBN 90-247-2732-4, Pub. by Martinus Nijhoff Netherlands). Kluwer Boston.

SELF-KNOWLEDGE IN LITERATURE

Diggory, Terrence. Yeats & American Poetry: The Traditional of the Self. LC 82-15070. 280p. 1983. 25.00x (ISBN 0-691-06558-6). Princeton U Pr.

SELF-LOVE (PSYCHOLOGY)

see Narcissism; Self-Respect

SELF-LOVE (THEOLOGY)

Livingston, Mrs. J. B. Love Yourself. 1.95 (ISBN 0-89137-421-3). Quality Pubns.

SELF-MASTERY

see Self-Control

SELF-PERCEPTION

Bach, George R. & Torbet, Laura. The Inner Enemy: How to Fight Fair with Yourself. LC 82-14397. 224p. 1983. 11.95 (ISBN 0-688-01557-3). Morrow.

SELF-REALIZATION

Gardner, John W. Self-Renewal: The Individual & the Innovative Society. 168p. 1983. pap. 4.50 (ISBN 0-393-30112-5). Norton.

Lingo, T. D. Self Transcendence Workbook. 55p. (Orig.). 1982. pap. 11.00 (ISBN 0-686-37712-5). Dormant Brain Res.

SELF-REALIZATION (PSYCHOLOGY)

see Self-Actualization (Psychology)

SELF-RELIANCE

Center for Self-Sufficiency Research Division. Self-Sufficiency: A Bibliography. 75p. 1983. pap. text ed. 9.95 (ISBN 0-910811-00-8). Center Self.

Center for Self Sufficiency Research Division. Self-Sufficiency Topic Index with Bibliographic Information. 500p. Date not set. text ed. 49.95 (ISBN 0-910811-01-6); pap. text ed. 39.95 (ISBN 0-910811-02-4). Center Self.

SELF-RESPECT

Burwick, Ray. Self Esteem: You're Better than You Think. 1983. pap. 4.95 (ISBN 0-686-82695-7, 75-5865-X). Tyndale.

Clemes, Harris & Bean, Reynold. Self-Esteem: The Key to Your Child's Well-Being. 1982. pap. 3.50 (ISBN 0-8217-1096-6). Zebra.

D'Encarnacao, Paul & D'Encarnacao, Patricia. How to Love Yourself Unconditionally. LC 82-99980. (Illus.). 96p. 1983. pap. 12.95 with cassette (ISBN 0-9610048-0-0). Metamorphosis Pr.

Doyle, Alfreda C. Suggestions for Becoming Self Sufficient. 90p. 1983. pap. text ed. 15.95 (ISBN 0-910811-29-6). Center Self.

Frey, Diane & Carlock, Charlene. Enhancing Self Esteem. 280p. 1983. pap. text ed. price not set. Accel Devel.

Hartline, Jo E. Me!? Resources for Enhancing the Self-Esteem of Students, K-8. (Illus.). 76p. 1982. write for info. Hartline Pub.

Stevens, Ron & Godnic, Joy. How to Make Love to Yourself. Date not set. pap. 3.00 (ISBN 0-686-84098-4). Wilshire.

Ward, Hiley. Feeling Good About Myself. LC 82-25613. 180p. (gr. 5-9). 1983. price not set (ISBN 0-664-32704-4). Westminster.

SELLING BY TELEPHONE

see Telephone Selling

SEMANTICS

Lehrer, Adrienne. Wine & Conversation. LC 82-48538. 256p. 1983. 25.00x (ISBN 0-253-36550-3). Ind U Pr.

Varenne, Herve. The Rhetorical Structuring of American Daily Conversations: Culturally Patterned Conflicts in a Suburban High School. 250p. 1983. text ed. 24.50x (ISBN 0-8290-1288-5). Irvington.

SEMASIOLOGY
see Semantics
SEMEIOTICS
see Semiotics; Signs and Symbols
SEMEN
see also Spermatozoa
Hafez, E. S. Instrumental Insemination. 1982. 79.00 (ISBN 90-247-2530-5, Pub. by Martinus Nijhoff Netherlands). Kluwer Boston.
SEMIARID REGIONS
see Arid Regions
SEMICONDUCTORS
see also Microelectronics
also particular semiconducting substances, e.g. Germanium, Silicon; and headings beginning with the word Semiconductor
Adler, Richard B., et al. Introduction to Semiconductor Physics. (S. E. E. C. Ser.). (Illus.). 247p. 1964. pap. 20.95x (ISBN 0-471-00887-7). Solutions manual 2.00 o.p. Wiley.
Basi, Santokh. Semiconductor Pulse & Switching Circuits. LC 79-15379. (Electronic Technology Ser.). 538p. 1980. text ed. 23.95x (ISBN 0-471-05539-5); avail. solutions manual (ISBN 0-471-05831-9). Wiley.
Fridkin, V. M. & Grekov, A. A., eds. Ferroelectric Semiconductors Symposium, 4th, Rostov-on-Don, USSR, June 1981: Proceedings. (Ferroelectrics Ser.: Vol. 43, Nos. 3-4, & Vol. 45, Nos. 1-2). 280p. 1982. 203.50 (ISBN 0-686-83423-2). Gordon.
Ghandhi, Sorab K. Semiconductor Power Devices: Physics of Operation & Fabrication Technology. LC 77-8019. 1977. 37.96x (ISBN 0-471-02999-8, Pub by Wiley-Interscience). Wiley.
Heathkit-Zenith Educational Systems. Semiconductor Devices. (Spectrum Fundamentals of Electronics Ser.). (Illus.). 288p. 1983. 19.95 (ISBN 0-13-806174-2); pap. 12.95 (ISBN 0-13-806166-1). P-H.
Hellwege, K. H., ed. Semiconductors, Subvolume B: Physics of II-VI & I-VII Compounds, Semimagnetic Conductors. (Landolt-Berstein, Numerical Data & Functional Relationships in Science & Technology, New Series: Group III, Vol. 17, Subvolume b). (Illus.). 540p. 1982. 354.00 (ISBN 0-387-11308-8). Springer-Verlag.
Roggwiller, P. & Sittig, Roland, eds. Semiconductor Devices for Power Conditioning. (Brown Boveri Symposia Ser.). 386p. 1982. 49.50x (ISBN 0-306-41131-8, Plenum Pr). Plenum Pub.
Semiconductor-Microelectronics Industry in Japan. (Japanese Industry Studies: No. J79). 207p. 1982. 495.00 (ISBN 0-686-38964-6). Intl Res Dev.
SEMINARIANS
Hendrickson, Paul. The Seminary: A Search. 320p. 1983. 14.95 (ISBN 0-671-42030-5). Summit Bks.
SEMINOLE INDIANS
see Indians of North America–Eastern States
SEMIOLOGY (LINGUISTICS)
see Semiotics
SEMIOLOGY (SEMANTICS)
see Semantics
SEMIOTICS
see also Signs and Symbols
Eaton, Mick, ed. Screen Reader Two: Cinema & Semiotics. Neale, Stephen. 197p. 1982. 17.95 (ISBN 0-900676-08-6). NY Zoetrope.
Pogorzelski, Henry A. & Ryan, William J. Foundations of Semiological Theory of Numbers. 590p. (Orig.). 1982. pap. text ed. 29.95 (ISBN 0-89101-053-X). U Maine Orono.
Silverman, Kaja. The Subject of Semiotics. 250p. 1983. 20.00 (ISBN 0-19-503177-6). Oxford U Pr.
Thomas, Donald W. Semiotics 1: Signs, Language & Reality. 2nd ed. (Illus.). 239p. (Orig.). 1980. pap. text ed. 7.95 (ISBN 0-536-03240-8); handbk., 78p. 2.95 (ISBN 0-536-03250-5). Ginn Custom.
--Semiotics 2: Communication in Man & Beast. (Illus.). 248p. (Orig.). 1983. pap. text ed. 10.95 (ISBN 0-536-03133-9). Ginn Custom.
--Semiotics 3: Communication, Codes & Culture. (Illus.). 58p. (Orig.). 1982. pap. text ed. 3.95 (ISBN 0-536-03997-6). Ginn Custom.
--Semiotics 4: Language in the Making. (Illus., Orig.). 1983. pap. text ed. 4.00x (ISBN 0-536-04041-9). Ginn Custom.
SENECA, ILLINOIS
Watrous, Hilda. The County Between the Lakes: A Public History of Seneca County, 1876-1982. (Illus.). 430p. 1983. deluxe ed. 18.75 deluxe (ISBN 0-932334-61-X). Heart of the Lakes.
SENECA INDIANS
see Indians of North America–Eastern States
SENESCENCE
see Aging
SENIOR CITIZENS
see Aged
SENSATION
see Senses and Sensation
SENSES AND SENSATION
see also Control (Psychology); Gestalt Psychology; Hearing; Ideology; Pain; Taste; Time Perception; Touch; Vision
Douglass, Malcolm P., ed. Writing & Reading in a Balanced Curriculum. (Claremont Reading Conference Yearbook Ser.). 222p. (Orig.). 1982. pap. 11.00 (ISBN 0-941742-00-8). Claremont Grad.
Geldard, Frank A. Human Senses. 2nd ed. LC 72-37432. 1972. text ed. 39.95x (ISBN 0-471-29570-1). Wiley.
Murphy, Wendy B. Touch, Smell, Taste, Sight & Hearing. LC 82-5738. (Library of Health). lib. bdg. 18.60 (ISBN 0-8094-3799-6, Pub. by Time-Life). Silver.
Zuckerman, Marvin, ed. Biological Bases for Sensation Seeking, Impulsivity & Anxiety. 320p. 1983. text ed. write for info. (ISBN 0-89859-255-0). L Erlbaum Assocs.
SENSING, REMOTE
see Remote Sensing
SENSITIVITY TRAINING T-GROUPS
see Group Relations Training
SENSITOMETRY, PHOTOGRAPHIC
see Photographic Sensitometry
SENTENCES (CRIMINAL PROCEDURE)
Forst, Martin L., ed. Sentencing Reform: Experiments in Reducing Disparity. (Sage Criminal Justice System Annuals: Vol. 17). (Illus.). 288p. 1982. 25.00 (ISBN 0-8039-1858-5); pap. 12.00 (ISBN 0-8039-1859-3). Sage.
Rich, William D. & Sutton, L. Paul. Sentencing by Mathematics: An Evaluation of the Early Attempts to Develop & Implement Sentencing Guidelines. LC 82-42713. 239p. pap. 20.00 (ISBN 0-89656-057-0, R 071). Natl Ctr St Courts.
Sporer, Siegfried L. Reducing Disparity in Judicial Sentencing: A Social-Psychological Approach. (European University Studies-Ser. 6, Psychology: Vol. 97). 114p. 1982. write for info. (ISBN 3-8204-7208-8). P Lang Pubs.
SEPOY REBELLION
see India–History–British Occupation, 1765-1947
SEPULCHERS
see Tombs
SEPULCHRAL MONUMENTS
see also Pyramids; Tombs
Lightbown, Ronald W. Donatello & Michelozzo: An Artistic Partnership & Its Patrons in the Early Renaissance, 2 vols. (Illus.). 460p. 1980. 74.00x (ISBN 0-19-921024-1). Oxford U Pr.
SEQUENCES (MATHEMATICS)
Halberstam, H. & Roth, K. Sequences. 293p. 1983. Repr. of 1966 ed. 28.00 (ISBN 0-387-90801-3). Springer-Verlag.
Whitehead, John. Design & Analysis of Sequential Clinical Trials. (Mathematics & Its Applications). 315p. 1983. 69.95x (ISBN 0-470-27355-0). Halsted Pr.
SEQUENTIAL ANALYSIS
Woodroofe, M. Nonlinear Renewal Theory in Sequential Analysis. LC 81-84856. (CBMS-NSF Regional Conference Ser.: No. 39). v, 119p. 1982. 14.50 (ISBN 0-89871-180-0). Soc Indus Appl Math.
SEQUOIA NATIONAL FOREST, CALIFORNIA
Sequoia: Kings Canyon National Parks. 1982. 7.95 (ISBN 0-933692-23-4). R Collings.
SERAPHIM
see Angels
SERBIAN LANGUAGE
see Serbo-Croatian Language
SERBO-CROATIAN LANGUAGE
Foreign Service Institute. Serbo-Croatian Basic Course, Vol. 2. 677p. Date not set. includes 24 cassettes 195.00x (ISBN 0-88432-101-0, Y650). J Norton Pubs.
SERIALS
see Periodicals
SERMON DIALOGUES
see Dialogue Sermons
SERMON ON THE MOUNT
see also Beatitudes
McEachern, Alton H. From the Mountain. LC 82-82948. (Orig.). 1983. pap. 4.95 (ISBN 0-8054-1529-7). Broadman.
Warren, Thomas B. & Elkins, Garland, eds. Sermon on the Mount. 1982. 14.95 (ISBN 0-934916-00-4). Natl Christian Pr.
Yogananda, Paramhansa. Sermon on the Mount as Spiritually Interpretted by Paramhansa Yogananda. LC 79-91531. 1980. pap. 6.95 (ISBN 0-937134-01-5). Amrita Found.
SERMONS
see also Children'S Sermons; Christmas Sermons; Dialogue Sermons; Lenten Sermons; Preaching
also subdivision Sermons under special subjects, e.g. Beatitudes–Sermons; Easter–Sermons; Missions–Sermons
Braaten, Carl E. Stewards of the Mysteries: Sermons for Festivals & Special Occasions. LC 82-72639. 128p. (Orig.). 1983. pap. 5.95 (ISBN 0-8066-1945-7, 10-6004). Augsburg.
Chappell, Clovis G. Chappell's Special Day Sermons. (Pocket Pulpit Library). 204p. 1983. pap. 3.95. Baker Bk.
Crane, James D. El Sermon Eficaz. 308p. Date not set. pap. 4.50. Casa Bautista.
De Brand, Roy E. Children's Sermons for Special Occasions. LC 82-72228. (Orig.). 1983. pap. 3.95 (ISBN 0-8054-4927-2). Broadman.
Fox, Frederic E. Seven Sermons & One Eulogy as Preached in the Chapel of Princeton University from 1965 to 1980. Fox, Donald H., ed. LC 82-90693. 88p. (Orig.). 1982. pap. 5.95 (ISBN 0-910521-02-6). Fox Head.
Freed, Harvey G. Chapel Talks, Sermons & Debates. 1983. pap. 6.95 (ISBN 0-89225-269-3). Gospel Advocate.
Lever, Thomas. Sermons. 143p. pap. 15.00 (ISBN 0-87556-200-0). Saifer.
Owens, Milton E., Jr., ed. Outstanding Black Sermons, Vol. 3. 80p. 1982. pap. 4.95 (ISBN 0-8170-0973-6). Judson.
Paulsell, William O., ed. Sermons in a Monastery: Chapter Talks by Matthew Kelty Ocso, No. 59. (Cistercian Studies Ser.). 1983. p.n.s. (ISBN 0-87907-858-8); pap. p.n.s. (ISBN 0-87907-958-4). Cistercian Pubns.
Sermons for Eighteen Special Occasions. LC 12-2963. 1982. pap. 4.95 (ISBN 0-570-03870-7). Concordia.
Sweeting, George. Special Sermons for Evangelism. LC 82-7999. (Special Sermons Ser.). (Orig.). 1982. pap. 4.95 (ISBN 0-8024-8210-4). Moody.
Ward, C. M. Sermons from Luke. 96p. (Orig.). 1983. pap. 2.25 (ISBN 0-89274-260-7). Harrison Hse.
White, Willie. Fifty-Two Winning Sermons. 117p. (Orig.). 1973. spiral 2.95 (ISBN 0-686-84103-4). College Pr Pub.
SERMONS–OUTLINES
Holbrook, Becky T. Revised Handful of Ideas. 5.95 (ISBN 0-89137-611-9). Quality Pubns.
Sermon Illustrations for the Gospel Lessons. 1983. pap. 4.95 (ISBN 0-570-03875-8). Concordia.
SERMONS, AMERICAN
Finney, Charles & Parkhurst, L. B. Principles of Liberty. rev. ed. (Finney's Sermons on Romans Ser.). 192p. (Orig.). 1983. pap. 4.95 (ISBN 0-87123-475-0). Bethany Hse.
Foxcroft, Thomas. The Sermons of Thomas Foxcroft of Boston: 1697-1769. LC 82-10457. 1982. 50.00x (ISBN 0-8201-1387-5). Schol Facsimiles.
SERMONS, ENGLISH
Latimer, Hugh. Seven Sermons Before Edward VI Fifteen Forty-Nine. Arber, Edward, ed. Date not set. pap. 17.50. Saifer.
SERPENTS
see Snakes
SERRA, JUNIPERO, FATHER, 1713-1784
Engstrand, Iris H. Serra's San Diego: Father Junipero Serra & California's Beginnings. (Illus.). 1982. 2.95 (ISBN 0-918740-02-9). San Diego Hist.
SERVANTS
see also Apprentices; Tipping
Dudden, Faye E. Serving Women: Household Service in Nineteenth-Century America. 352p. 1983. 17.95x (ISBN 0-8195-5072-8). Wesleyan U Pr.
SERVERS
see Altar Boys
SERVICE (IN INDUSTRY)
see Customer Service
SERVICE, COMPULSORY MILITARY
see Military Service, Compulsory
SERVICE INDUSTRIES
see also Licenses
Daniels, P. W. Service Industries: Growth & Location. 2nd ed. LC 82-4260. (Cambridge Topics in Geography Ser.). (Illus.). 96p. 1982. 12.95 (ISBN 0-521-23730-0). Cambridge U Pr.
Ingle, Sud & Ingle, Neelima. Quality Circles in Service Industries: Comprehensive Guidelines for Increased Productivity & Efficiency. (Illus.). 1983. 21.95 (ISBN 0-13-745059-1); pap. 12.95 (ISBN 0-13-745042-7). P-H.
SERVICE RATING
see Employees, Rating Of; Teachers, Rating Of
SERVICEMEN, MILITARY
see Soldiers
SERVITUDE
see Slavery
SET THEORY
see also Categories (Mathematics); Functions of Real Variables; Measure Theory; Rings (Algebra)
Jiang, Boju. Lectures on Nielsen Fixed Point Theory. LC 82-20756. (Contemporary Mathematics Ser.: Vol. 14). 16.00 (ISBN 0-8218-5014-8, CONM/14). Am Math.
Morse, A. P., ed. A Theory of Sets: Monographs. Rev. & Enlarged ed. (Pure & Applied Mathematics Ser.). Date not set. price not set (ISBN 0-12-507952-4). Acad Pr.
Zupan, J. Clustering of Large Data Sets. (Chemometrics Research Studies). 122p. 1982. text ed. 31.95x (ISBN 0-471-10455-8, Pub. by Res Stud Pr). Wiley.
SETS (MATHEMATICS)
see Set Theory
SETTING (STAGE)
see Theaters–Stage-Setting and Scenery
SETTLEMENT OUT OF COURT
see Compromise (Law)
SEVENTH-DAY ADVENTISTS
Adams, Roy. The Sanctuary Doctrine: Three Approaches in the Seventh-day Adventist Church. (Andrews University Seminary Doctoral Dissertation Ser.). viii, 327p. (Orig.). 1981. pap. 8.95 (ISBN 0-943872-33-2). Andrews Univ Pr.
Crider, Charles C. & Kistler, Robert C. The Seventh-Day Adventist Family: An Empirical Study. 296p. 1979. pap. 3.95 (ISBN 0-943872-77-4). Andrews Univ Pr.
Oosterwal, Gottfried & Staples, Russell L. Servants for Christ: The Adventist Church Facing the 80's. vi, 162p. 1980. pap. 3.95 (ISBN 0-943872-78-2). Andrews Univ Pr.
Simonsen, Sharon. God Never Slept. (Daybreak Ser.). 78p. Date not set. pap. 3.95 (ISBN 0-8163-0472-6). Pacific Pr Pub Assn.
SEVERN RIVER AND VALLEY
Kissack, Keith. The River Severn. 160p. 1982. 35.00x (ISBN 0-86138-004-5, Pub. by Terence Dalton England). State Mutual Bk.
Severn Barrage. 164p. 1982. 99.00x (ISBN 0-7277-0156-8, Pub. by Telford England). State Mutual Bk.
SEWAGE
Eikum, A. S. & Seabloom, R. W. Alternative Wastewater Treatment. 1982. 45.00 (ISBN 90-277-1430-4, Pub. by Reidel Holland). Kluwer Boston.
Gravity Sanitary Sewer Design & Construction. (Manual of Practice, Facilities Development: No. 5). 1982. pap. text ed. 20.00 (ISBN 0-87262-313-0). Water Pollution.
Junkins, David R. & Deeny, Kevin J. The Activated Sludge Process. LC 82-70699. (Illus.). 260p. 1983. 29.95 (ISBN 0-250-40506-7). Ann Arbor Science.
Mandt, Mikkel G. & Bell, Bruce A. Oxidation Ditches in Wastewater Treatment. LC 82-70700. (Illus.). 169p. 1982. 29.95 (ISBN 0-250-40430-3). Ann Arbor Science.
Units of Expression for Wastewater Management. Rev. ed. (Manual of Practice: No. 6). 47p. 1982. pap. text ed. 8.00 (ISBN 0-943244-06-4). Water Pollution.
SEWAGE–PURIFICATION
Public Information Handbook. 40p. (Orig.). pap. text ed. 10.00 (ISBN 0-943244-29-3). Water Pollution.
Ramalho, R. S. Introduction to Wastewater Treatment Processes. 2nd ed. write for info. (ISBN 0-12-576560-6). Acad Pr.
SEWAGE DISPOSAL
see also Refuse and Refuse Disposal; Water–Pollution
Fair, G. M., et al. Water & Wastewater Engineering: Water Purification & Wastewater Treatment & Disposal. LC 66-16139. 668p. 1968. 43.95x (ISBN 0-471-25131-3). Wiley.
--Water & Wastewater Engineering: Water Supply & Wastewater Removal, Vol. 1. LC 66-16139. 489p. 1966. 39.95x (ISBN 0-471-25130-5). Wiley.
Fair, Gordon M., et al. Elements of Water Supply & Waste Water Disposal. 2nd ed. LC 72-151032. (Illus.). 752p. 1971. 43.95x (ISBN 0-471-25115-1). Wiley.
Ganczarczyk. Activated Sludge Processes. (Pollution Engineering Ser.). 288p. 1983. 59.95 (ISBN 0-8247-1758-9). Dekker.
SEWARD, WILLIAM HENRY, 1801-1872
Papers of William H. Seward: Cumulative Name Index. 1983. 500.00 (ISBN 0-89235-073-3). Res Pubns Conn.
SEWERAGE
see also Drainage; Plumbing; Sewage
American Society of Civil Engineers & Water Pollution Control Federation. Gravity Sanitary Sewer Design & Construction. LC 81-69182. 288p. 1982. text ed. 20.00 (ISBN 0-87262-313-0). Am Soc Civil Eng.
Restoration of Sewerage Systems. 296p. 1982. 111.00x (ISBN 0-7277-0145-2, Pub. by Telford England). State Mutual Bk.
Rudman, Jack. Assistant Director of Maintenance (Sewer District) (Career Examination Ser.: C-2908). (Cloth bdg. avail. on request). pap. 14.00 (ISBN 0-8373-2908-6). Natl Learning.
--Supervisor (Water & Sewer Systems) (Career Examination Ser.: C-2907). (Cloth bdg. avail. on request). pap. 10.00 (ISBN 0-8373-2907-8). Natl Learning.
Sewer Charges for Wastewater Collection & Treatment. 32p. (Orig.). 1982. pap. text ed. 6.00 (ISBN 0-943244-39-0). Water Pollution.
SEWERS
see Sewerage
SEWING
see also Children's Clothing; Doll Clothes; Dressmaking; Embroidery; Needlework; Quilting
Arrants, Cheryl. Sew Wonderful Gourmet Garments. St. Amant, Kristi, ed. (Illus.). 96p. (Orig.). 1982. pap. text ed. write for info. (ISBN 0-943704-01-4). Sew Wonderful.
Arrants, Cheryl & Asbjornsen, Jan. Sew Wonderful Silk. rev. ed. Amant, Kristi, ed. (Illus.). 128p. 1981. pap. text ed. 5.95 (ISBN 0-943704-02-2). Sew Wonderful.
Butterick. Vogue Sewing. LC 81-48031. (Illus.). 568p. 1982. 23.99i (ISBN 0-06-015001-7, HarpT). Harrow.
Center for Self Sufficiency Research Division Staff. Self Sufficiency Sewing Index to Newsletters, Pattern Companies, Fabric Outlets, etc. 60p. 1983. pap. text ed. 10.95 (ISBN 0-910811-30-X). Center Self.
Friend, Diane & Nicholson, Dale. Bridal Sewing & Crafts. (Illus.). 72p. 1983. pap. 2.50 (ISBN 0-918178-31-2). Simplicity.
Ladbury, Ann. The Dressmaker's Dictionary. LC 82-8725. (Illus.). 360p. 1983. 19.95 (ISBN 0-668-05653-3, 5653). Arco.
Macor, Alida. And Sew On... (Illus.). 56p. 1983. pap. 3.95 (ISBN 0-9610632-0-3). Alida Macor.
Palmer, Pati & Pletsch, Susan. Pants for Any Body. rev. & expanded ed. 128p. (Orig.). 1982. pap. 5.95 (ISBN 0-935278-08-7). Palmer-Pletsch.
Shaeffer, Claire B. The Complete Book of Sewing Shortcuts. LC 81-8818. 256p. 1983. pap. 12.95 (ISBN 0-8069-7564-4). Sterling.

SEX

see also Homosexuality; Lesbianism; Orgasm; Pedophilia; Reproduction; Sex Customs

also headings beginning with the word Sexual

American Health Research Institute, Ltd. Sex & Sex Behavior: A Medical Subject Analysis & Research Index with Bibliography. Bartone, John C., ed. 120p. 1983. 29.95 (ISBN 0-941864-96-0); pap. text ed. 21.95 (ISBN 0-941864-97-9). ABBE Pubs Assn.

Betancourt, Jeane. Am I Normal? 96p. 1983. pap. 1.95 (ISBN 0-380-82040-4, 82040-4, Flare). Avon.

Britton, Bryce. The Love Muscle: Every Woman's Guide to Intensifying Sexual Pleasure. (Illus.). 1982. pap. 7.95 (ISBN 0-452-25382-9, Plume). NAL.

Clark, Charlie, Ill. Sexual Geometry. Sanfilippo, Rose E., ed. LC 82-91125. 112p. 1983. 8.95 (ISBN 0-9609808-0-6). New Pen Pub Co.

Darwin, Charles R. The Descent of Man & His Selection in Relation to Sex. LC 72-3894. (Illus.). xvi, 688p. 1972. write for info. (ISBN 0-404-08409-5). AMS Pr.

Davis, Murray S. Smut: Erotic Reality-Obscene Ideology. LC 82-16061. 328p. 1983. 20.00 (ISBN 0-226-13791-0). U of Chicago Pr.

Freud, Sigmund. Three Contributions to the Theory of Sex. Brill, A. A., tr. from Ger. 118p. 1982. Repr. of 1925 ed. lib. bdg. 40.00 (ISBN 0-89984-211-9). Century Bookbindery.

Haddon, Cecilia. The Sensuous Lie: The Sexual Revolution & It's Aftermath. LC 82-40169. 226p. 1983. 14.95 (ISBN 0-8128-2883-6). Stein & Day.

Leonard, George. The End of Sex. 240p. 1983. 12.95 (ISBN 0-87477-178-1). J P Tarcher.

McDonald, Boyd & Leyland, Winston, eds. Sex: True Homosexual Experiences from STH Writers, Vol.3. (Illus.). 192p. (Orig.). 1982. pap. 12.00 (ISBN 0-917342-98-4). Gay Sunshine.

Marx, Patricia & Stuart, Sarah. How To Regain Your Virginity: And Ninety-Nine Other Recent Discoveries About Sex. (Illus.). 144p. 1983. pap. 4.95 (ISBN 0-89480-365-4). Workman Pub.

Offir, Carole W. Human Sexuality. 608p. 1982. text ed. 19.95 (ISBN 0-15-540428-8); Instructors Handbook 4.80 (ISBN 0-15-540429-6). HarBraceJ.

Peterson, James R. The Playboy Advisor on Love & Sex. (Illus.). 350p. 1983. 16.95 (ISBN 0-399-50742-6, Perigee); pap. 7.95 (ISBN 0-399-50741-8). Putnam Pub Group.

Riain, Maire Ni. The Sex Trade. LC 80-54360. 76p. 1982. 6.95 (ISBN 0-533-04928-8). Vantage.

Sex After Forty. (Blank Books Ser.). 128p. 1982. cancelled (ISBN 0-939944-07-3). Marmac Pub.

Time-Life Books, ed. A Commonsense Guide to Sex, Birth, & Babies. (Library of Health Ser.). 1983. lib. bdg. 18.60 (ISBN 0-8094-3827-5). Silver.

Walker, Morton & Walker, Joan. Sexual Nutrition: The Ultimate Program for a Lifetime of Sexual Health. 288p. 1983. 16.95 (ISBN 0-698-11199-0, Coward). Putnam Pub Group.

Withington, Amelia & Grimes, David. Adolescent Sexuality: A Handbook for Counselors, Teachers & Parents. 135p. 1983. 18.50 (ISBN 0-8290-1270-2); pap. 9.95 (ISBN 0-8290-1271-0). Irvington.

Witkin-Lanoil, Georgia. Human Sexuality: A Student's Resource Kit. 192p. 1983. pap. text ed. 11.50 scp (ISBN 0-06-047162-X, HarpC); instr's. manual avail. (ISBN 0-06-367170-0). Har-Row.

SEX-ANECDOTES, FACETIAE, ETC.

Sex Quiz You Can't Fail, Adult Connect the Dots, Write Your Own Love Story, Dirty Word Search. 192p. 1983. pap. 2.50 (ISBN 0-446-30545-6). Warner Bks.

SEX-BIBLIOGRAPHY

Human Sexuality: Literary & Historical Sources, Guide to the Microfilm Collection. 60p. 1983. 45.00 (ISBN 0-89235-075-X). Res Pubns Conn.

SEX-CAUSE AND DETERMINATION

see also Sex Chromosomes

Wachtel, Stephen, ed. H-Y Antigen & the Biology of Sex Determination. Date not set. price not set (ISBN 0-8089-1514-2). Grune.

SEX-PHYSIOLOGICAL ASPECTS

see Sex (Biology)

SEX-PSYCHOLOGICAL ASPECTS

see Sex (Psychology)

SEX-RESEARCH

see Sex Research

SEX-STATISTICS

Haeberle, Erwin J. The Sex Atlas. rev. ed. (Illus.). 568p. 1983. pap. 14.95 (ISBN 0-8264-0233-X). Crossroad NY.

SEX (BIOLOGY)

see also Reproduction; Sex-Cause and Determination; Sexual Disorders

Russo, Raymond M., et al. Advanced Textbook of Sexual Development & Disorders in Childhood & Adolescence. (Advances Textbook Ser.). 1983. pap. text ed. price not set (ISBN 0-87488-485-3). Med Exam.

SEX (PHYSIOLOGY)

see Sex (Biology)

SEX (PSYCHOLOGY)

see also Masculinity (Psychology); Sex Role; Sexual Disorders

Altherr, Thomas L. American Sexual Dilemma. 1984. text ed. price not set (ISBN 0-89874-609-4). Krieger.

Baratta, Ron & Stone, Linda. How to Win With Women. Orig. Title: How to Take Advantage of A Woman. 200p. (Orig.). 1982. pap. 11.95 (ISBN 0-9605628-1-8). Mutual Pr IL.

--Sex Power. 200p. (Orig.). 1983. pap. 11.95 (ISBN 0-9605628-2-6). Mutual Pr IL.

Christ Foundation Staff. A Spiritual Sex Manual. LC 82-72079. (Illus.). 176p. 1982. pap. 6.95 (ISBN 0-910315-01-9). Christ Found.

Dziech, Billie W. & Faaborg, Linda. The Lecherous Professor: Sexual Harassment on Campus. LC 82-73960. 320p. 1983. 14.37 (ISBN 0-8070-3100-3). Beacon Pr.

Evatt, Cris & Feld, Bruce. The Givers & the Takers. (Illus.). 256p. 1983. 12.95 (ISBN 0-02-536690-4). Macmillan.

Gossage, Richard C. & Gunton, Melvin. Bedmanship. (Illus.). 96p. (Orig.). 1983. pap. 3.95 (ISBN 0-8329-0259-4). New Century.

Offit, Avodah K. The Sexual Self. 304p. 1983. pap. 8.95 (ISBN 0-312-92766-5). Congdon & Weed.

Reich, Wilhelm. Children of the Future: On the Prevention of Sexual Pathology. Jordan, Inge, et al, trs. from Ger. 1982. 15.50 (ISBN 0-374-12173-7). FS&G.

Sharaf, Myron. Fury on Earth: A Biography of Wilhelm Reich. LC 82-5707. (Illus.). 560p. 1983. 24.95 (ISBN 0-312-31370-5). St Martin.

Weininger, Otto. The Sexual Psychology of Males & Females: Intimate Life of Man Lib. (Illus.). 101p. 1983. 51.85 (ISBN 0-686-84793-8). Am Inst Psych.

Wong, Bruce M. TSFR: The Taoist Way to Total Sexual Fitness, For Men. 80p. 1982. pap. 9.95 (ISBN 0-910295-00-X). Golden Dragon Pub.

SEX (THEOLOGY)

see also Homosexuality and Christianity

Szekely, Edmond B. Sexual Harmony. (Illus.). 60p. 1977. pap. 3.50 (ISBN 0-89564-077-5). IBS Intl.

SEX, CHANGE OF

see Change of Sex

SEX AND RELIGION

see also Homosexuality and Christianity; Mother-Goddesses; Sex (Theology); Sex in the Bible; Tantrism

Pastoral Care Office of RLDS Church, et al. Human Sexuality. 1982. pap. 4.00 (ISBN 0-8309-0350-X). Herald Hse.

Sawicki, Marianne. Faith & Sexism: Guidelines for Religious Educators. 112p. 1979. pap. 3.95 (ISBN 0-8164-0105-5). Seabury.

Smedes, Lewis. Sexologia para Cristianos. Sanchez, Jorge, tr. from Eng. 288p. 1982. pap. 4.95 (ISBN 0-89922-175-0). Edit Caribe.

SEX CHROMOSOMES

see also Sex-Cause and Determination

Stewart, Donald A., ed. Children with Sex Chromosome Aneuploidy: Follow-up Studies. LC 82-21657. (Birth Defects: Original Article Ser.: Vol. 18, No. 4). 251p. 1982. write for info. A R Liss.

SEX CRIMES

see also Adultery; Incest; Prostitution

Fortune, Marie M. Sexual Violence: The Unmentionable Sin: An Ethical & Pastoral Perspective. 256p. (Orig.). 1983. pap. 8.95 (ISBN 0-8298-0652-0). Pilgrim NY.

Giaretto, Henry. Intergrated Treatment of Child Sexual Abuse. LC 81-86712. 25.00 (ISBN 0-8314-0061-7). Sci & Behavior.

Morneau, R. H., Jr. Sex Crimes Investigation: A Major Case Approach. (Illus.). 304p. 1983. text ed. price not set (ISBN 0-398-04832-0). C C Thomas.

SEX CUSTOMS

see also Sex and Religion; Sex in Literature

Gossage, Richard C. & Gunton, Melvin. Bedmanship. (Illus.). 96p. (Orig.). 1983. pap. 3.95 (ISBN 0-8329-0259-4). New Century.

Guttentag, Marcia & Secord, Paul F. Too Many Women? The Sex Ratio Question. 336p. 1983. 27.50 (ISBN 0-8039-1918-2); pap. 12.95 (ISBN 0-8039-1919-0). Sage.

Macklin, Eleanor D. & Rubin, Roger H. Contemporary Families & Alternative Lifestyles: Handbook on Research & Theory. 416p. 1982. 29.95 (ISBN 0-8039-1053-3). Sage.

SEX DETERMINATION

see Sex-Cause and Determination

SEX DIFFERENTIATION

see Sex-Cause and Determination

SEX DISCRIMINATION

Bernardin. Women in the Work Force. 256p. 1982. 28.95 (ISBN 0-03-062471-1). Praeger.

Chiplin, Brian & Sloane, Peter. Tackling Discrimination in the Workplace: An Analysis of Sex Discrimination in Britain. LC 82-4384. (Management & Industrial Relations Ser.: No. 2). (Illus.). 190p. Date not set. price not set (ISBN 0-521-24565-6); pap. price not set (ISBN 0-521-28788-X). Cambridge U Pr.

Hart, Lois B. & Dalke, J. David. The Sexes at Work. 180p. 1983. 12.95 (ISBN 0-13-807321-X); pap. 5.95 (ISBN 0-13-807313-9). P-H.

Johnson, Sonia. From Housewife to Heretic. LC 80-2964. 408p. 1983. pap. 8.95 (ISBN 0-385-17494-2, Anch). Doubleday.

Johnston, Jerom, et al. An Evaluation of Freestyle: A Television Series to Reduce Sex-Role Stereotypes. 308p. 1980. pap. 16.00 (ISBN 0-87944-256-5). Inst Soc Res.

McQueen, Iris. Sexual Harassment in the Workplace: The Management View. Levers, Joan & Moss, Lowell, eds. (Illus.). 138p. (Orig.). 1983. text ed. 24.95 (ISBN 0-9609354-1-X); pap. 14.95 (ISBN 0-9609354-0-1). McQueen & Son.

Murray, Meg M., ed. Face to Face: Fathers, Mothers, Masters, Monsters--Essays for a Nonsexist Future. LC 82-11708. (Contributions in Women's Studies: No. 36). 360p. 1983. lib. bdg. 29.95 (ISBN 0-313-23044-7, MFF/). Greenwood.

SEX DISCRIMINATION AGAINST MEN

see Sex Discrimination

SEX DISCRIMINATION AGAINST WOMEN

see Sex Discrimination

SEX DISORDERS

see Sexual Disorders

SEX EDUCATION

see Sex Instruction

SEX IN BUSINESS

Fisher, Helen E. The Sex Contract. LC 82-18126. (Illus.). 256p. 1983. Repr. pap. 6.95 (ISBN 0-688-01599-9). Quill NY.

Sands, Melissa. The Passion Factor. 272p. 1983. pap. 2.95 (ISBN 0-425-05855-7). Berkley Pub.

SEX IN LITERATURE

see also Erotic Literature; Sex in the Bible

Rajneesh, Bhagwan S. Sex. Lear, Pat, ed. (Quotations from Bhagwan Shree Rajneesh: No. 1). 104p. 1981. pap. 3.95 (ISBN 0-941990-01-X). Lear.

SEX IN THE BIBLE

Gerber, Aaron. Biblical Attitudes on Human Sexuality. 176p. 1982. 15.95 (ISBN 0-89962-301-8). Todd & Honeywell.

Larue, Gerald. Human Sexuality & the Bible. 212p. 1983. 17.95 (ISBN 0-87975-206-8); pap. 8.95 (ISBN 0-87975-213-0). Prometheus Bks.

SEX INSTRUCTION

Brauer, Alan P., et al. ESO: How You & Your Lover Can Give Each Other Hours of Extended Sexual Orgasm. (Illus.). 192p. 1983. pap. 13.50 (ISBN 0-446-51270-2). Warner Bks.

Craft, Ann & Craft, Michael, eds. Sex Education & Counselling for Mentally Handicapped People. 336p. 1983. pap. text ed. 19.95 (ISBN 0-8391-1773-6, 19496). Univ Park.

Daley, Martin & Wilson, Margo. Sex, Evolution & Behavior. 2nd ed. 400p. 1983. pap. text ed. write for info. (ISBN 0-87150-767-6, 4511). Grant Pr.

Dechesne, B. H. & Pons, C. Sexuality & Handicap: Problems of the Motor Handicapped. (Illus.). 264p. 1983. pap. 29.75x (ISBN 0-398-04746-4). C C Thomas.

Dickman, Irving R. Winning the Battle for Sex Education. LC 82-61000. 64p. (Orig.). 1982. pap. 6.00 (ISBN 0-9609212-0-6). SIECUS.

Gallimore, J. G. Transverse Paraphysics: The New Science of Space, Time & Gravity Control. LC 82-50843. (Illus.). 359p. (Orig.). 1982. pap. text ed. 35.00 (ISBN 0-9603536-4-X). Tesla Bk Co.

Guide to Intelligent Sexuality. 125p. 1982. pap. 5.00 (ISBN 0-686-37416-9). Ideals PA.

Haeberle, Erwin J. The Sex Atlas. rev. ed. (Illus.). 568p. 1983. pap. 14.95 (ISBN 0-8264-0233-X). Crossroad NY.

Stevens, Ella. Sex Education: Contraception. (Michigan Learning Module Ser.). 1979. write for info. (ISBN 0-914004-37-9). Ulrich.

--Sex Education: Gonorrhea. (Michigan Learning Module Ser.). 1979. write for info. (ISBN 0-914004-38-7). Ulrich.

Westheimer, Ruth. Dr. Ruth's Guide to Good Sex. 256p. 1983. 14.50 (ISBN 0-446-51260-5). Warner Bks.

SEX INSTRUCTION FOR CHILDREN AND YOUTH

Shedd, Charlie. The Stork is Dead. 1982. pap. 2.50 (ISBN 0-8499-4167-9). Word Pub.

SEX PERVERSION

see Sexual Deviation

SEX RESEARCH

Araoz, Daniel L. & Bleck, Robert T. Hypnosex: Sexual Joy Through Self-Hypnosis. 1983. 5.95 (ISBN 0-87795-466-6, Pub. by Priam). Arbor Hse.

Crooks, Robert & Baur, Karla. Our Sexuality. 1983. 21.95 (ISBN 0-8053-1914-X). Benjamin-Cummings.

Durden-Smith, Jo & De Simone, Diane. Sex & the Brain. (Illus.). 1983. 16.95 (ISBN 0-87795-484-4). Arbor Hse.

Kinsey, Alfred C. Sex Studies Index: 1981. 1983. lib. bdg. 85.00 (ISBN 0-8161-0394-1, Hall Library). G K Hall.

SEX ROLE

Allgeier, Elizabeth & McCormick, Naomi, eds. Changing Boundaries: Gender Roles & Sexual Behavior. LC 82-60885. 347p. 1982. pap. 10.95 (ISBN 0-87484-536-X). Mayfield Pub.

Bliitchington, W. Peter. Sex Roles & the Christian Family. 1983. pap. 5.95 (ISBN 0-8423-5896-X); wkbk. 2.95 (ISBN 0-8423-5897-8). Tyndale.

Ford, George A. & Ford, Kathleen H. Analysis of Sex Role Traits. 1982. programmed wkbk. 1.95 (ISBN 0-934698-15-5). New Comm Pr.

Herzog, A. Regula & Bachman, Jerald G. Sex Roles Attitudes Among High School Seniors: Views about Work & Family Roles. 272p. 1982. pap. 16.00x (ISBN 0-87944-275-1). Inst Soc Res.

Huber, Joan & Spitze, Glenna, eds. Stratification, Children, Housework & Jobs: Monograph. LC 82-18407. (Quantitative Studies in Social Relations). 242p. 1983. price not set (ISBN 0-12-358480-9). Acad Pr.

Johnston, Jerom, et al. An Evaluation of Freestyle: A Television Series to Reduce Sex-Role Stereotypes. 308p. 1980. pap. 16.00 (ISBN 0-87944-256-5). Inst Soc Res.

Laswell, Marcia & Lobsenz, Norman. Equal Time: The New Way of Living, Loving, & Working Together. LC 82-45254. 240p. 1983. 15.95 (ISBN 0-385-17473-X). Doubleday.

Moberly, Elizabeth R. Psychogenesis: The Early Development of Gender Identity. 120p. 1983. 17.95. Routledge & Kegan.

Murray, Meg M., ed. Face to Face: Fathers, Mothers, Masters, Monsters--Essays for a Nonsexist Future. LC 82-11708. (Contributions in Women's Studies: No. 36). 360p. 1983. lib. bdg. 29.95 (ISBN 0-313-23044-7, MFF/). Greenwood.

Richmond-Abbot, Marie. Masculine & Feminine: Sex Roles Over the Life Cycle. LC 82-11400. 384p. Date not set. pap. text ed. 11.95 (ISBN 0-201-06194-5). A-W.

Smith, David W. The Friendless American Male. LC 82-21518. 1983. pap. 4.95 (ISBN 0-8307-0863-4, 5417309). Regal.

SEX ROLE IN LITERATURE

Barickman, Richard, et al. Corrupt Relations: Dickens, Thackeray, Trollope, Collins & the Victorian Sexual System. 1982. 25.00 (ISBN 0-686-82110-6). Columbia U Pr.

SEX ROLE INVERSION

see Change of Sex

SEX THERAPY

Kilmann, Peter R. & Mills, Katherine H. All About Sex Therapy. 250p. 1983. 15.95x (ISBN 0-306-41317-5, Plenum Pr). Plenum Pub.

SEXUAL BEHAVIOR

see Sex; Sex Customs; Sexual Ethics

SEXUAL BEHAVIOR, PSYCHOLOGY OF

see Sex (Psychology)

SEXUAL CRIMES

see Sex Crimes

SEXUAL DEVIATION

see also Sex Therapy

Davis, Murray S. Smut: Erotic Reality-Obscene Ideology. LC 82-16061. 328p. 1983. 20.00 (ISBN 0-226-13791-0). U of Chicago Pr.

SEXUAL DISCRIMINATION

see Sex Discrimination

SEXUAL DISEASES

see Sexual Disorders; Venereal Diseases

SEXUAL DISORDERS

see also Sex Therapy; Sexual Deviation

Albee, George & Gordon, Sol, eds. Promoting Sexual Responsibility & Preventing Sexual Problems. (Primary Prevention of Psychopathology Ser.: No. 7). (Illus.). 600p. 1983. text ed. 35.00x (ISBN 0-87451-248-4). U Pr of New Eng.

Arentewicz, Gerd & Schmidt, Gunter, eds. The Treatment of Sexual Disorders: Concepts & Techniques of Couple Therapy. 1983. 25.00x (ISBN 0-465-08748-5). Basic.

Chase, Allan. The Truth About STD: The Old Ones - Herpes & Other New Ones - the Primary Causes - the Available Cures. 188p. 1983. 10.95 (ISBN 0-688-01896-3). Morrow.

Fann, William, et al, eds. Phenomonology & Treatment of Psychosexual Disorders. 192p. 1983. text ed. 25.00 (ISBN 0-89335-184-9). SP Med & Sci Bks.

Holmes, K. K. & Mardh, P. Sexually Transmitted Diseases. 1216p. 1983. 65.00x (ISBN 0-07-029675-8). McGraw.

Kaplan, Helen S. The Evaluation of Sexual Disorders: Psychological & Medical Aspects. 352p. 1983. 25.00 (ISBN 0-87630-329-7). Brunner-Mazel.

Russo, Raymond M., et al. Advanced Textbook of Sexual Development & Disorders in Childhood & Adolescence. (Advances Textbook Ser.). 1983. pap. text ed. price not set (ISBN 0-87488-485-3). Med Exam.

SEXUAL ETHICS

see also Birth Control; Contraception; Dating (Social Customs); Prostitution; Sex and Religion; Sex Crimes

Albee, George & Gordon, Sol, eds. Promoting Sexual Responsibility & Preventing Sexual Problems. (Primary Prevention of Psychopathology Ser.: No. 7). (Illus.). 600p. 1983. text ed. 35.00x (ISBN 0-87451-248-4). U Pr of New Eng.

Christie, Les. Dating & Mating: From a Christian View. Underwood, Jon, ed. (Illus.). 80p. (Orig.). 1983. pap. 2.95 (ISBN 0-87239-643-6, 39972). Standard Pub.

Fromer, Margot J. Ethical Issues in Sexuality & Reproduction. 320p. 1983. pap. text ed. 13.95 (ISBN 0-8016-1708-1). Mosby.

Goldberg, Herb. The New Male-Female Relationship. 320p. 1983. 13.95 (ISBN 0-686-84632-X). Morrow.

McQueen, Iris. Sexual Harassment in the Workplace: The Management View. Levers, Joan & Moss, Lowell, eds. (Illus.). 138p. (Orig.). 1983. text ed. 24.95 (ISBN 0-9609354-1-X); pap. 14.95 (ISBN 0-9609354-0-1). McQueen & Son.

SEXUAL OFFENSES

see Sex Crimes

SEXUAL PERVERSION
see Sexual Deviation
SEXUAL PSYCHOLOGY
see Sex (Psychology)
SHADOW-PICTURES
Almozning, Albert. Hand Shadows for Classroom & Home Activities. (Illus.). 92p. 1982. 12.95 (ISBN 0-87396-096-3). Stravon.
SHAFTING
Gorman, D. J. Free Vibration Analysis of Beams & Shafts. LC 74-20504. 448p. 1975. 49.95x (ISBN 0-471-31770-5, Pub. by Wiley-Interscience). Wiley.
SHAKESPEARE, JOHN, d. 1601
Hudson, H. N. Shakespeare, His Life, Art & Character: An Historical Sketch of the Origin & Growth of the Drama in England, 2 Vols. 495p. 1982. Repr. of 1880 ed. Set. lib. bdg. 100.00 (ISBN 0-89987-394-4). Darby Bks.
SHAKESPEARE, WILLIAM, 1564-1616
Brown, Ivor. Shakespeare in His Time. 238p. 1982. Repr. of 1960 ed. lib. bdg. 40.00 (ISBN 0-89984-090-6). Century Bookbindery.
Kokeritz, Helge. Shakespeare's Pronunciation. 1953. text ed. 49.50x (ISBN 0-686-83738-X). Elliots Bks.
Lounsbury, Thomas R. Shakespeare & Voltaire. 463p. 1982. Repr. of 1902 ed. lib. bdg. 40.00 (ISBN 0-89987-523-8). Darby Bks.
Muir, Kenneth, et al, eds. Shakespeare, Man of the Theater. LC 82-40346. (Illus.). 272p. 1983. 28.50 (ISBN 0-87413-217-7). U Delaware Pr.
Wilson, John D. The Elizabethan Shakespeare. 1982. lib. bdg. 34.50 (ISBN 0-686-81913-6). Porter.
SHAKESPEARE, WILLIAM, 1564-1616–AUTOBIOGRAPHY
see Shakespeare, William, 1564-1616–Biography
SHAKESPEARE, WILLIAM, 1564-1616–BIOGRAPHY
Elze, Karl. William Shakespeare: A Literary Biography. Schmitz, L. Dora, tr. 587p. 1982. Repr. of 1888 ed. lib. bdg. 50.00 (ISBN 0-89760-214-5). Telegraph Bks.
Ewen, Alfred. Shakespeare. 126p. 1982. Repr. of 1904 ed. lib. bdg. 20.00 (ISBN 0-89760-215-3). Telegraph Bks.
SHAKESPEARE, WILLIAM, 1564-1616–CHARACTERS
Goldsmith. Wise Fools in Shakespeare. 136p. 1982. 40.00x (ISBN 0-85323-263-6, Pub. by Liverpool Univ England). State Mutual Bk.
Wilson, John D. Martin Marprelate & Shakespeares Fluellen. 1982. lib. bdg. 34.50 (ISBN 0-686-81921-7). Porter.
SHAKESPEARE, WILLIAM, 1564-1616–COMMENTARIES
see Shakespeare, William, 1564-1616–Criticism and Interpretation
SHAKESPEARE, WILLIAM, 1564-1616–CONCORDANCES
Tanitch, Robert. A Pictorial Companion to Shakespeare. 128p. 1982. 39.00x (Pub. by Muller Ltd). State Mutual Bk.
SHAKESPEARE, WILLIAM, 1564-1616–CONTEMPORARIES
see also Shakespeare, William, 1564-1616–Friends and Associates
Honigmann, E. A. Shakespeare's Impact on His Contemporaries. 1982. 59.00x (ISBN 0-333-26938-1, Pub. by Macmillan England). State Mutual Bk.
SHAKESPEARE, WILLIAM, 1564-1616–CRITICISM, TEXTUAL
Mc Curdy, Harold G. Personality of Shakespeare: A Venture in Psychological Method. 1953. text ed. 12.50x (ISBN 0-686-83695-2). Elliots Bks.
SHAKESPEARE, WILLIAM, 1564-1616–CRITICISM AND INTERPRETATION
Ellis, Charles, retold by. Shakespeare & the Bible, a Reading from Shakespeare's Merchant of Venice, Shakespeariana Sonnets with Their Scriptural Harmonies. 288p. Repr. of 1982 ed. lib. bdg. 50.00 (ISBN 0-89987-218-2). Darby Bks.
Evans, Gareth L. The Upstart Crow: An Introduction to Shakespeare's Plays. Evans, Barbara L., ed. 414p. 1982. text ed. 24.95x (ISBN 0-460-10256-7, Pub. by J. M. Dent England); pap. text ed. 11.95x (ISBN 0-460-11256-2, Pub. by J. M. Dent England). Biblio Dist.
Harris, Laurie L. Shakespearean Criticism, Vol. 1. 600p. 1982. 55.00 (ISBN 0-8103-6125-6). Gale.
Knight, G. Wilson. The Olive & the Sword: A Study of England's Shakespeare. 102p. 1982. lib. bdg. 15.00 (ISBN 0-8495-3134-9). Arden Lib.
Ludwig, Emil. Genius & Character: Shakespeare, Voltaire, Goethe, Balzac. 330p. 1982. Repr. of 1927 ed. lib. bdg. 35.00 (ISBN 0-8495-3267-1). Arden Lib.
MacCracken, H. N. & Pierce, F. E. An Introduction to Shakespeare. 222p. 1982. Repr. of 1929 ed. lib. bdg. 35.00 (ISBN 0-89987-589-0). Darby Bks.
Muir. The Singularity of Shakespeare. 243p. 1982. 49.00x (ISBN 0-85323-433-7, Pub. by Liverpool Univ England). State Mutual Bk.
Parker, M. D. The Slave of Life: A Study of Shakespeare & the Idea of Justice. 264p. 1983. Repr. of 1955 ed. lib. bdg. 35.00 (ISBN 0-89984-830-3). Century Bookbindery.
Styan, J. L. The Shakespeare Revolution. LC 76-3043. 292p. Date not set. pap. 8.95 (ISBN 0-521-27328-5). Cambridge U Pr.
Swigg, Richard. Shakespeare's Great Confines. 320p. 1982. text ed. 27.25x (ISBN 0-85635-335-3, Pub. by Carcanet Pr England). Humanities.
Taylor, Mark. Shakespeare's Darker Purpose: A Question of Incest. LC 81-69124. (Studies in the Renaissance). 216p. 1982. 24.00 (ISBN 0-404-62277-1). AMS Pr.
Wells, Stanley, ed. Shakespeare in the Nineteenth Century. LC 49-1639. (Shakespeare Survey Ser.: No. 35). (Illus.). 206p. 1982. 39.50 (ISBN 0-521-24752-7). Cambridge U Pr.
Williamson, Cecile & Limouze, Cary, eds. Shakespeare & the Arts: A Collection of Essays from the Ohio Shakespeare Conference, Wright State University, Dayton, Ohio, 1981. LC 82-17486. (Illus.). 256p. (Orig.). 1983. lib. bdg. 23.50 (ISBN 0-8191-2819-8); pap. text ed. 11.50 (ISBN 0-8191-2820-1). U Pr of Amer.
Wilson, John D. The Elizabethan Shakespeare. 1982. lib. bdg. 34.50 (ISBN 0-686-81913-6). Porter.
SHAKESPEARE, WILLIAM, 1564-1616–CYMBELINE
Jacobs, Henry. Cymbeline: An Annotated Bibliography. Godshalk, William, ed. LC 82-48082. (Garland Shakespeare Bibliographies). 590p. 1982. lib. bdg. 60.00 (ISBN 0-8240-9258-9). Garland Pub.
SHAKESPEARE, WILLIAM, 1564-1616–DICTIONARIES, INDEXES, ETC.
Dolby, Thomas. The Shakespeare Dictionary: Forming a General Index to All the Popular Expressions, & Most Striking Passages in the Works of Shakespeare. 1982. Repr. of 1832 ed. lib. bdg. 100.00 (ISBN 0-89760-144-0). Telegraph Bks.
SHAKESPEARE, WILLIAM, 1564-1616–DRAMATURGY
see Shakespeare, William, 1564-1616–Dramatic Production; Shakespeare, William, 1564-1616–Technique
SHAKESPEARE, WILLIAM, 1564-1616–DRAMATIC PRODUCTION
Halstead, William P. Statistical History of Acting Editions of Shakespeare: Supplement to Shakespeare as Spoken, Vol. 13. LC 82-20232. 628p. 1983. lib. bdg. 35.25 (ISBN 0-8191-2854-6). U Pr of Amer.
--Statistical History of Acting Editions of Shakespeare: Supplement to Shakespeare as Spoken, Vol. 14. LC 82-20232. 654p. 1983. lib. bdg. 32.25 (ISBN 0-8191-2855-4). U Pr of Amer.
SHAKESPEARE, WILLIAM, 1564-1616–FRIENDS AND ASSOCIATES
Hotson, Leslie. Mr. W. H. 328p. 1982. Repr. lib. bdg. 40.00 (ISBN 0-89987-391-X). Darby Bks.
SHAKESPEARE, WILLIAM, 1564-1616–INFLUENCE
Honigmann, E. A. Shakespeare's Impact on His Contemporaries. 1982. 59.00x (ISBN 0-333-26938-1, Pub. by Macmillan England). State Mutual Bk.
SHAKESPEARE, WILLIAM, 1564-1616–JUVENILE LITERATURE
Kennedy, Mary-Lou. Bill S: Shakespeare for Kids. (Tomorrow's Books for Today's Children). (Illus.). 82p. 1983. 7.95 (ISBN 0-935326-10-3). Gallopade Pub Group.
SHAKESPEARE, WILLIAM, 1564-1616–KING HENRY 5TH
Wilson, John D. Martin Marprelate & Shakespeares Fluellen. 1982. lib. bdg. 34.50 (ISBN 0-686-81921-7). Porter.
SHAKESPEARE, WILLIAM, 1564-1616–KING RICHARD 2ND
Malz, Wilfried. Studien Zum Problem des Metaphorischen Redens Am Beispiel Von Texten Aus Shakesspeares "Richard II" und Marlowes "Edward II". 251p. (Ger.). 1982. write for info. (ISBN 3-8204-5824-7). P Lang Pubs.
SHAKESPEARE, WILLIAM, 1564-1616–LANGUAGE
Hussey, S. The Literary Language of Shakespeare. LC 81-20889. 208p. (Orig.). 1982. pap. text ed. 10.95x (ISBN 0-582-49228-9). Longman.
SHAKESPEARE, WILLIAM, 1564-1616–MERCHANT OF VENICE
Ellis, Charles, retold by. Shakespeare & the Bible, a Reading from Shakespeare's Merchant of Venice, Shakespeariana Sonnets with Their Scriptural Harmonies. 288p. Repr. of 1982 ed. lib. bdg. 50.00 (ISBN 0-89987-218-2). Darby Bks.
SHAKESPEARE, WILLIAM, 1564-1616–NATURAL HISTORY
Harting, James. The Ornithology of Shakespeare. (Illus.). 321p. 1978. 15.00x (ISBN 0-905418-26-3). Intl Pubns Serv.
SHAKESPEARE, WILLIAM, 1564-1616–PLOTS
Gordon, Giles, ed. Shakespeare Stories. (Illus.). 224p. 1983. 16.95 (ISBN 0-241-10879-9, Pub. by Hamish Hamilton England). David & Charles.
SHAKESPEARE, WILLIAM, 1564-1616–RELATIONS WITH CONTEMPORARIES
see Shakespeare, William, 1564-1616–Friends and Associates
SHAKESPEARE, WILLIAM, 1564-1616–SONNETS
Ellis, Charles, retold by. Shakespeare & the Bible, a Reading from Shakespeare's Merchant of Venice, Shakespeariana Sonnets with Their Scriptural Harmonies. 288p. Repr. of 1982 ed. lib. bdg. 50.00 (ISBN 0-89987-218-2). Darby Bks.
SHAKESPEARE, WILLIAM, 1564-1616–STAGE HISTORY
Connell, Charles. They Gave Us Shakespeare: John Heminge & Henry Condell. (Illus.). 110p. 1982. 14.95 (ISBN 0-85362-193-4, Oriel). Routledge & Kegan.
SHAKESPEARE, WILLIAM, 1564-1616–STAGE-SETTING AND SCENERY
see Shakespeare, William, 1564-1616–Dramatic Production; Shakespeare, William, 1564-1616–Stage History
SHAKESPEARE, WILLIAM, 1564-1616–TECHNIQUE
Swigg, Richard. Shakespeare's Great Confines. 320p. 1982. text ed. 27.25x (ISBN 0-85635-335-3, Pub. by Carcanet Pr England). Humanities.
SHAKESPEARE, WILLIAM, 1564-1616–TEMPEST
Wilson, John D. The Meaning of Tempest. 1982. lib. bdg. 34.50 (ISBN 0-686-81920-9). Porter.
SHAKESPEARE, WILLIAM, 1564-1616–TRAGEDIES
Wilson, John D. Six Tragedies of Shakespeare. 1982. lib. bdg. 34.50 (ISBN 0-686-81919-5). Porter.
SHANNON-WIENER INFORMATION MEASURE
see Information Measurement
SHANTIES
see Sea Songs
SHARES OF STOCK
see Stocks
SHARIA (ISLAMIC LAW)
see Islamic Law
SHARING
Chenoweth, Linda. God's People Share. Duckert, Mary, ed. 64p. 1981. nursery ldrs. guide 2.95 (ISBN 0-664-24337-1); pap. 1.10 (ISBN 0-664-24336-3); resource Packet 7.95 (ISBN 0-664-24338-X). Westminster.
Wicks, Robert J. Helping Others: Ways of Listening, Sharing & Counseling. 1982. 14.95 (ISBN 0-89876-040-2). Gardner Pr.
SHARK FISHING
Thompson, Hunter S. The Great Shark Hunt. 704p. 1982. pap. 4.50 (ISBN 0-446-31034-4). Warner Bks.
SHARKS
see also Shark Fishing
Castro, Jose I. The Sharks of North American Waters. LC 82-45892. (W. L. Moody, Jr., Natural History Ser.: No. 5). (Illus.). 208p. (Orig.). 1983. 19.50 (ISBN 0-89096-140-9); pap. 9.95 (ISBN 0-89096-143-3). Tex A&M Univ Pr.
Ellis, Richard. The Book of Sharks: A Complete Illustrated Natural History of the Sharks of the World. (Illus.). 256p. 29.95 (ISBN 0-15-113462-6). HarBraceJ.
--The Book of Sharks: A Complete Illustrated Natural History of the Sharks of the World. (Illus.). 256p. pap. 14.95 (ISBN 0-15-613552-3, Harv). HarBraceJ.
Zahuaranec, Bernard J., ed. Shark Repellents from the Sea: New Perspectives. (AAAS Selected Symposium 83). 225p. 1983. price not set (ISBN 0-86531-593-0). Westview.
SHAW, GEORGE BERNARD, 1856-1950
Chappelow, Allan. Shaw the Villager & Human Being. 380p. 1982. 40.00x (ISBN 0-284-39176-X, Pub. by C Skilton Scotland). State Mutual Bk.
Laurence, Dan H. Bernard Shaw: A Bibliography, 2 vols. (Illus.). 1024p. 1982. Set. 98.00 (ISBN 0-19-818179-5). Oxford U Pr.
Leary, Daniel J. Shaw's Plays in Performance. LC 82-644184. (Shaw: The Annual of Bernard Shaw Studies: Vol. 3). 258p. 1983. 16.95 (ISBN 0-271-00346-4). Pa St U Pr.
Valency, Maurice. The Cart & the Trumpet: The Plays of George Benard Shaw. LC 82-16954. (Volume III of the Making of Modern Drama Ser.). 488p. 1983. 22.00 (ISBN 0-8052-3832-8); pap. 11.95 (ISBN 0-8052-0740-6). Schocken.
SHAWNEE INDIANS
see Indians of North America–Eastern States
SHEAR (MECHANICS)
Bradbury, L. J., et al. Turbulent Shear Flow 3rd: University of California, Selected Papers, 1981. (Illus.). 321p. 1983. 64.00 (ISBN 0-387-11817-9). Springer-Verlag.
Peterson, F. & Carmi, S., eds. Three Dimensional Turbulent Shear Flows. 160p. 1982. 30.00 (G00211). ASME.
SHEEP
Baker, Frank H., ed. Sheep & Goat Handbook: International Stockmen's School Handbooks, Vol. 3. 600p. 1982. lib. bdg. 35.00 (ISBN 0-86531-510-8, Pub. with Winrock International). Westview.
Carles, A. B. Sheep Production in the Tropics. (Tropical Handbooks). (Illus.). 200p. 1982. 29.00x (ISBN 0-19-859449-6). Oxford U Pr.
Fitzhugh, Hank A. & Bradford, G. Eric, eds. Hair Sheep of West Africa & the Americas: A Genetic Resource for the Tropics. (Winrock International Studies). 280p. 1982. lib. bdg. 25.00 (ISBN 0-86531-370-9). Westview.
Parker, Ron. The Sheep Book: A Handbook for the Modern Shepherd. (Illus.). 352p. 1983. 19.95 (ISBN 0-686-83867-X, ScribT). Scribner.
Wood, John J. & Vannette, Walter M. Sheep Is Life: An Assessment of Livestock Reduction in the Former Navajo-Hopi Joint Use Area. rev. ed. (Northern Arizona University Anthropological Papers: No. 1). (Illus.). xxiii, 182p. 1982. pap. 13.50 (ISBN 0-910953-00-7). N Arizona U.
SHEEP–JUVENILE LITERATURE
Lavine, Sigmund A. & Scuro, Vincent. Wonders of Sheep. LC 82-46001. (Wonder Ser.). (Illus.). 80p. (gr. 4 up). 1983. PLB 9.95 (ISBN 0-396-08137-1). Dodd.
SHEEP–INDIA
Sheep & Goat Breeds of India. (FAO Animal Production & Health Paper: No. 30). 189p. 1982. pap. 14.50 (ISBN 92-5-101212-1, F2340, FAO). Unipub.
SHEEP DOGS
see also specific types of sheep dogs, i.e. Dogs–Breeds–German Shepherd Dogs
Keller, W. Phillip. Lessons from a Sheepdog. 1983. 6.95 (ISBN 0-8499-0335-1). Word Pub.
SHELL PARAKEET
see Budgerigars
SHELLEY, PERCY BYSSHE, 1792-1822
Allott. Essays on Shelley. 304p. 1982. 60.00x (ISBN 0-85323-294-6, Pub. by Liverpool Univ England). State Mutual Bk.
Jeaffreson, John C. The Real Shelley: New Views of the Poet's Life, 2 Vols. 478p. 1982. Repr. of 1885 ed. lib. bdg. 250.00 set (ISBN 0-8495-2801-1). Arden Lib.
Symonds, John A. Shelley. 189p. 1983. Repr. of 1879 ed. lib. bdg. write for info. Century Bookbindery.
Trelaway, John E. Records of Shelley, Byron. 1983. pap. 4.95 (ISBN 0-14-043088-1). Penguin.
SHELLFISH
see also Crustacea; Mollusks
Boyle, P. R. Molluscs & Man. (Studies in Biology: No. 134). 64p. 1981. pap. text ed. 8.95 (ISBN 0-7131-2824-0). E Arnold.
Cheney, Daniel P. & Mumford, Thomas M., Jr. Shellfish & Seaweed Harvests of Puget Sound. (A Puget Sound Bk.). (Illus.). 144p. (Orig.). 1983. pap. 8.95 (ISBN 0-686-43218-5, Pub. by Wash Sea Grant). U of Wash Pr.
Robinson, Robert H. The Essential Book of Shellfish. LC 82-184274. (Illus.). 160p. 1983. pap. 6.95 (ISBN 0-89709-040-3). Liberty Pub.
SHELLS
see also Mollusks
Dance, S. P. The Collector's Encyclopedia of Shells. 2nd ed. 1982. 24.95 (ISBN 0-07-015292-6). McGraw.
Feininger, Andreas. Shells: Forms & Designs of the Sea. (Illus.). 128p. 1983. pap. 8.95 (ISBN 0-486-24498-9). Dover.
Greenberg, Margaret & Olds, Nancy J. The Sanibel Shell Guide. LC 82-71090. (Illus.). 117p. (Orig.). 1982. pap. 4.95 (ISBN 0-89305-041-5). Anna Pub.
Humphrey. The Sea Shells of the West Indies. 24.95 (ISBN 0-686-42790-4, Collins Pub England). Greene.
Kelburn, Richard & Rippery, Elizabeth. Sea Shells of Southern Africa. (Illus.). 264p. 1982. 49.95 (ISBN 0-686-83938-2, Pub. by Macmillan S Africa). Intl Schol Bk Serv.
Penniket, J. R. Common Sea Shells. (Mobil New Zealand Nature Ser.). (Illus.). 80p. (Orig.). 1982. pap. 9.30 (ISBN 0-589-01400-5, Pub. by Reed Books Australia). C E Tuttle.
Powell, A. W. Shells of New Zealand. 154p. 1982. pap. 42.00x (ISBN 0-7233-0470-X, Pub. by Whitcoulls New Zealand). State Mutual Bk.
Robinson, Adrian & Millward, Roy. The Shell Book of the British Coast. (Illus.). 496p. (Orig.). 1983. 31.50 (ISBN 0-7153-8150-4). David & Charles.
Sharabati, Doreen. Saudi Arabian Seashells. 1982. 50.00x (ISBN 0-9507641-0-8, Pub. by Cave Pubns England). State Mutual Bk.
SHELLS (ENGINEERING)
see also Tanks
Calladine, C. R. Theory of Shell Structures. LC 82-4255. 700p. Date not set. price not set (ISBN 0-521-23835-8). Cambridge U Pr.
Gioncu, Victor. Thin Reinforced Concrete Shells: Special Analysis Problems. LC 78-10338. 500p. 1980. 63.95x (ISBN 0-471-99735-8, Pub. by Wiley-Interscience). Wiley.
Ramm, E., ed. Buckling of Shells, Stuttgart, FRG 1982: Proceedings. (Illus.). 672p. 1982. 42.00 (ISBN 0-387-11785-7). Springer-Verlag.
SHENSI, CHINA–HISTORY
Nichols, Francis H. Through Hidden Shensi. 333p. 1982. Repr. of 1902 ed. lib. bdg. 65.00 (ISBN 0-89984-808-7). Century Bookbindery.
SHEOL
see Hell
SHERPAS
Ortner, Sherry B. Sherpas Through their Rituals. LC 76-62582. (Cambridge Studies in Cultural Systems). (Illus.). 196p. 1978. 27.95 (ISBN 0-521-21536-6); pap. 9.95 (ISBN 0-521-29216-6). Cambridge U Pr.
SHINTO
Aston, W. G. Shinto: The Ancient Religion of Japan. 83p. 1982. lib. bdg. 25.00 (ISBN 0-89760-018-5). Telegraph Bks.
SHIP-BUILDING
see also Boat-Building; Naval Architecture; Ship Building Workers; Ship Models; Warships

also particular types of vessels, e.g. Steamboats, Torpedo-Boats

Hughes, Owen F. Ship Structural Design: A Rationally-Based, Computer Aided, Optimization Approach. (Ocean Engineering Ser.). 600p. 1983. 65.00x (ISBN 0-471-03241-7, Pub. by Wiley-Interscience). Wiley.

SHIP BUILDING WORKERS

Prescott, John. Directory of Shipowners, Shipbuilders & Marine Engineers, 1982. 80th ed. LC 35-4199. 1534p. 1982. 70.00x (ISBN 0-617-00277-0). Intl Pubns Serv.

SHIP HANDLING

see Boats and Boating; Yachts and Yachting

SHIP MODELS

Bowen, John. A Ship Model Maker's Manual. 192p. 1982. 42.00x (ISBN 0-85177-235-8, Pub. by Conway Maritime England). State Mutual Bk.

Mansir, A. Richard. The Art of Ship Modeling. 320p. 1982. 35.00 (ISBN 0-940620-03-0). Van Nos Reinhold.

Van Schouten, Joop. Sailing in Glass. (Illus.). 96p. 1983. 12.95 (ISBN 0-914814-37-0). Sail Bks.

SHIP PILOTS

see Pilots and Pilotage

SHIPPING

see also Inland Navigation; Insurance, Marine; Maritime Law; Merchant Marine; Steamboats and Steamboat Lines

Ambrose, Andrew, ed. Jane's Merchant Shipping Review. (Jane's Reviews Ser.). 150p. 1983. 17.95 (ISBN 0-686-84473-4). Sci Bks Intl.

Hopkins, F. N. Business & Law for the Shipmaster. 6th ed. 908p. 1982. text ed. 65.00x (ISBN 0-85174-434-6). Sheridan.

SHIPPING-DIRECTORIES

Finlay, Patrick, ed. Jane's Freight Containers 1983. 15th ed. (Jane's Yearbooks). (Illus.). 640p. 1983. 140.00x (ISBN 0-86720-642-X). Sci Bks Intl.

Greenwood, John O. & Dills, Michael J. Greenwoods' Guide to Great Lakes Shipping 1983. 19th, rev. ed. 530p. 1983. 39.00. Freshwater.

SHIPPING-LAW

see Maritime Law

SHIPPING-COMMUNIST COUNTRIES

Harbron, John D. Communist Ships & Shipping. (Illus.). 264p. 1962. 11.25 (ISBN 0-8002-0498-0). Intl Pubns Serv.

SHIPPING-UNITED STATES-HISTORY

Levitt, James H. For Want of Trade: Shipping & the New Jersey Ports, 1680-1783, Vol. 17. 224p. 1981. 19.95 (ISBN 0-911020-03-9). NJ Hist Soc.

SHIPS

see also Boats and Boating; Merchant Marine; Merchant Ships; Navies; Navigation; Ocean Liners; Sailing; Sailing Ships; Seamanship; Steamboats and Steamboat Lines; Submarines; Tankers; Warships; Yachts and Yachting

also names of ships, and headings beginning with the word Ship

All You Want to Know about Freighter & Cruise Ships. 1978. 4.95 (ISBN 0-686-42898-6). Harian.

Churchouse, Jack. Glamour Ships of the Union Steam Ship Company. (Illus.). 104p. 26.95 (ISBN 0-908582-41-2, Pub. by Salem Hse Ltd). Merrimack Bk Serv.

Evans, J. Harvey. Ship Structural Design Concepts: Second Cycle. LC 82-23436. (Illus.). 528p. 1983. text ed. 45.00 (ISBN 0-87033-303-8). Cornell Maritime.

Forde, C. Daryll. Ancient Mariners: The Story of Ships & Sea Routes. 88p. 1982. Repr. of 1928 ed. lib. bdg. 20.00 (ISBN 0-89760-236-6). Telegraph Bks.

Harvald, Svend A. Resistance & Propulsion of Ships. (Ocean Engineering Ser.). 608p. 1983. 42.95 (ISBN 0-471-06353-3, Pub. by Wiley-Interscience). Wiley.

Owen, David. The Manchester Ship Canal. 160p. 1983. 20.00 (ISBN 0-7190-0864-6). Manchester.

Plowman, Peter. Passenger Ships of Australia & New Zealand: 1913-1981, Vol. II. 224p. 1982. 40.00x (ISBN 0-85177-247-1, Pub. by Conway Maritime England). State Mutual Bk.

--Passenger Ships of Australia & New Zealand: 1876-1912, Vol. I. 224p. 1982. 40.00x (ISBN 0-85177-246-3, Pub. by Conway Maritime England). State Mutual Bk.

Trimmer, John W. How to Avoid Huge Ships: Or I Never Met A Ship I Liked. LC 82-61398. (Illus.). 112p. 1982. pap. 9.95 (ISBN 0-88100-019-1). Natl Writ Pr.

SHIPS-CONSTRUCTION

see Ship-Building

SHIPS-JUVENILE LITERATURE

Bushey, Jerry. The Barge Book. (Illus.). 32p. (gr. 1-4). 1983. lib. bdg. 7.95g (ISBN 0-87614-205-6). Carolrhoda Bks.

Gibbons, Gail. Boat Book. LC 82-15851. (Illus.). 32p. (ps-3). 1983. reinforced binding 11.95 (ISBN 0-8234-0478-1). Holiday.

SHIPS, ELECTRICITY ON

see Electricity on Ships

SHIPWORKERS

see Ship Building Workers

SHIPWRECKS

see also Survival (After Airplane Accidents, Shipwrecks, etc.)

also names of wrecked vessels, e.g. Titanic (Steamship)

Bailey, Dan E. WW II Wrecks of the Kwajalein & Truk Lagoons. LC 82-63006. (Illus.). 152p. 1983. pap. text ed. 15.95 (ISBN 0-911615-00-8). North Valley.

SHIPYARD WORKERS

see Ship Building Workers

SHOCK

see also Traumatism

Lefer, Allan M. & Schumer, William, eds. Molecular & Cellular Aspects of Shock & Trauma. LC 82-25875. (Progress in Clinical & Biological Research Ser.: Vol. 111). 354p. 1983. 60.00 (ISBN 0-686-42967-2). A R Liss.

Perry, Anne G. & Potter, Patricia A. Shock: Comprehensive Nursing Management. (Illus.). 303p. 1983. pap. text ed. 19.95 (ISBN 0-8016-3827-5). Mosby.

SHOCK WAVES

Majda, Andrew. The Stability of Multi-Dimensional Shock Fronts. LC 82-206000036. (Memoirs of the American Mathematics Society Ser.: No. 275). 6.00 (ISBN 0-8218-2275-6, MEMO/275). Am Math.

Morawetz, C. S. Lectures on Nonlinear Waves & Shocks. (Tata Institute Lectures on Mathematics). 137p. 1982. pap. 6.70 (ISBN 0-387-10830-0). Springer-Verlag.

Smoller, J. Shock Waves & Reaction-Diffusion Equations. (Grundlehren der Mathematischen Wissenschaften: Vol. 258). (Illus.). 581p. 1983. 39.00 (ISBN 0-387-90752-1). Springer-Verlag.

SHOE INDUSTRY AND TRADE

see Boots and Shoes-Trade and Manufacture

SHOES

see Boots and Shoes

SHOP MANAGEMENT

see Factory Management

SHOP MATHEMATICS

Anderson, John G. Technical Shop Mathematics. 2nd ed. (Illus.). 500p. 1983. 20.95 (ISBN 0-8311-1145-3); Answer Manual avail. Indus Pr.

SHOP PAPERS

see Employees' Magazines, Handbooks, etc.

SHOPPER'S GUIDES

see Consumer Education; Shopping

SHOPPING

see also Automobile Purchasing; Consumer Education; Consumers; Marketing (Home Economics)

Arnold, Caroline. What Will We Buy? (Easy-Read Community Bks.). (Illus.). 32p. (gr. k-3). 1983. PLB 7.90 (ISBN 0-531-04508-0). Watts.

Bastian, Marlene Y. How to Shop Wisely. 108p. (Orig.). 1982. pap. 5.95x (ISBN 0-9609058-0-4). M Y Bastian.

Data Notes Publishing Staff. Directory of Flea Market Directories, Books, References. 200p. 1983. pap. text ed. 14.95 (ISBN 0-911569-57-X). Data Notes Pub.

Ellis, Iris. S. O. S.-Save on Shopping. (Orig.). Date not set. pap. price not set (ISBN 0-440-58398-5, Dell Trade Pbks). Dell.

Factory Outlet Shopping Guide for New England, 1983. 1982. 3.95 (ISBN 0-913464-67-8). FOSG Pubns.

Factory Outlet Shopping Guide for New Jersey & Rockland County, 1983. 1982. 3.95 (ISBN 0-913464-63-5). FOSG Pubns.

Factory Outlet Shopping Guide for New York, 1983. 1982. 3.95 (ISBN 0-913464-64-3). FOSG Pubns.

Factory Outlet Shopping Guide for Ohio-Michigan, 1983. 1983. 3.95 (ISBN 0-913464-69-4). FOSG Pubns.

Factory Outlet Shopping Guide for Pennsylvania, 1983. 1982. 3.95 (ISBN 0-913464-65-1). FOSG Pubns.

Factory Outlet Shopping Guide for Washington, D. C., 1983. 1982. 3.95 (ISBN 0-913464-66-X). FOSG Pubns.

Hoffenber, Connie & Hoffenber, Terry. Portland Super Shopper. 162p. (Orig.). 1982. pap. 3.95 (ISBN 0-916076-59-8). Writing.

Nash, M. J. How to Save a Fortune Using Refunds & Coupons. (Orig.). 1982. pap. 5.95x (ISBN 0-934650-03-9). Sunnyside.

SHOPPING CENTERS

see also Retail Trade; Stores, Retail

Beddington. Design for Shopping Centers. 1982. text ed. 59.95. Butterworth.

Fishman, David. Shopping Centers & the Accessibility Codes. 1979. 14.00 (ISBN 0-913598-12-7). Intl Coun Shop.

Hines, Mary A. Shopping Center Development & Investment. 394p. 1983. 34.95 (ISBN 0-471-86851-5). Ronald Pr.

International Council of Shopping Centers, ed. Leasing Opportunities, 1983. 144p. 1982. pap. 39.00 (ISBN 0-913598-14-3). Intl Coun Shop.

Top Shopping Centers: SMSA Markets 1-50, 4 Vols. Set. Date not set. 675.00 (ISBN 0-686-84345-2). Automated Mktg.

Urban Land Institute. Parking Requirements for Shopping Centers. Incl. Summary Recommendations. 23p. pap. 17.50 (ISBN 0-87420-604-9, P32); Summary Recommendations & Research Study Report. LC 81-70789. 136p. pap. 30.00 (ISBN 0-87420-605-7, P33). (Illus.). 1982. pap. Urban Land.

Wenner, S. Albert. Promotion & Marketing for Shopping Centers. 1980. 35.00 (ISBN 0-913598-13-5). Intl Coun Shop.

Wolf, Jess. Public Relations-Publicity: Fundamentals for Shopping Center Professionals. 14.00 (ISBN 0-686-84001-1). Intl Coun Shop.

SHOPS

see Stores, Retail; Workshops

SHORE EROSION

see Coast Changes

SHORE LINES

see also Coast Changes; Coasts; Shore Protection

Brehaut, Roger N. Ecology of Rocky Shores. (Studies in Biology: No. 139). 64p. 1982. pap. text ed. 8.95 (ISBN 0-7131-2839-9). E Arnold.

SHORE PROTECTION

see also Coast Changes; Coasts; Harbors; Hydraulic Engineering; Reclamation of Land; Shore Lines

Coastal Discharges: Engineering Aspects & Experience. 224p. 1981. 99.00x (ISBN 0-7277-0124-X, Pub. by Telford England). State Mutual Bk.

Thorn, R. Berkeley & Roberts, A. G. Sea Defence & Coast Protection Works. 240p. 1981. 95.00x (ISBN 0-7277-0085-5, Pub. by Telford England). State Mutual Bk.

SHORT STORIES

Here are entered collections of short stories by various authors.

see also Story-Telling;

also specific types of short stories, e.g. Football Stories, Ghost Stories, Sea Stories

Bellamy, Joe D. & Weingarten, Roger, eds. Love Stories-Love Poems. 300p. (Orig.). 1982. pap. 12.95 (ISBN 0-931362-07-5). Fiction Intl.

Dodge, Marshall & Bryan, Robert. Bert & I & Other Stories from Down East. Babbidge, Homer D., intro. by. (Illus.). 140p. (Orig.). 1981. 11.95 (ISBN 0-9607546-0-1); pap. 7.95. Bert & I Bks.

Ersevim, Ismail. Untitled - Short Stories. 96p. 1983. 6.50 (ISBN 0-682-49974-9). Exposition.

Greenberg, Martin H. & Waugh, Charles G., eds. The Arbor House Celebrity Book of the Greatest Stories Ever Told. 1983. 15.95 (ISBN 0-87795-448-8). Arbor Hse.

Mundis, Jerrold, ed. The Dog Book. (Illus.). 1983. 19.95 (ISBN 0-87795-461-5). Arbor Hse.

Reader's Digest Editors. Great Short Stories of the World. LC 72-81158. 800p. 1972. 13.98 (ISBN 0-89577-008-3). RD Assn.

--Great Stories of Mystery & Suspense, 2 vols. LC 73-76284. (Open-Ended Ser.). 1290p. 1977. 15.99 (ISBN 0-89577-136-5). RD Assn.

Young, Hy & Silberman, Mary. Black Badges Are Bad Business-& Other Short Stories, Vol. 1. (American Short Story Ser.). 84p. 1979. pap. 3.50 (ISBN 0-934040-01-X). Quality Ohio.

SHORT STORIES-HISTORY AND CRITICISM

see Short Story

SHORT STORIES-JUVENILE LITERATURE

see also Children's Stories

Reader's Digest Editors. Storytime. LC 82-80898. (Illus.). 448p. (gr. 1-8). 1982. 15.99 (ISBN 0-89577-145-4). RD Assn.

SHORT STORIES, AFRICAN

Madubuike, Ihechukwu. The Senegalese Novel: A Sociological Study of the Impact of the Politics of Assimilation. LC 81-51650. (Illus.). 182p. 1983. 18.00 (ISBN 0-89410-000-9); pap. 7.00 (ISBN 0-89410-001-7). Three Continents.

SHORT STORIES, AMERICAN

see also Western Stories

Bryer, Jackson R., ed. The Short Stories of F. Scott Fitzgerald: New Approaches in Criticism. 416p. 1982. text ed. 30.00 (ISBN 0-299-09080-9); pap. text ed. 7.95 (ISBN 0-299-09084-1). U of Wis Pr.

Burton, Linda. Stories from Tennessee. LC 82-16016. 488p. 1983. text ed. 27.95x (ISBN 0-87049-376-0); pap. 12.95 (ISBN 0-87049-377-9). U of Tenn Pr.

Cournos, John, intro. by. American Short Stories of the Nineteenth Century. 250p. 1983. pap. text ed. 4.95x (ISBN 0-460-01840-X, Pub. by Evman England). Biblio Dist.

Mitchell, Jack D. The Back Page. Shelsby, Earl, ed. (Illus.). 144p. (Orig.). text ed. 20.00 (ISBN 0-686-82338-9); pap. text ed. 9.95 (ISBN 0-935998-44-6). Natl Rifle Assn.

Pirandello, Luigi. Four Short Stories: Quattro Novelle. Jeffery, V. M., tr. from Italian. (Harrap's Bilingual Ser.). 58p. 1955. 5.00 (ISBN 0-911268-44-8). Rogers Bk.

Reader's Digest Editors. Fireside Reader. LC 77-76319. (Illus.). 640p. 1978. 14.98 (ISBN 0-89577-099-7). RD Assn.

--Great American Short Stories. LC 76-10933. 640p. 1977. 13.98 (ISBN 0-89577-033-4). RD Assn.

--Treasures of America. LC 73-83812. (Illus.). 624p. 1974. 15.99 (ISBN 0-89577-014-8). RD Assn.

Reiser, Virginia, ed. Favorite Short Stories in Large Print. 720p. 1982. lib. bdg. 17.95 (ISBN 0-8161-3434-0, Large Print Bks). G K Hall.

Rodenberger, Lou H., ed. Her Work: Stories by Texas Women. LC 82-60562. 347p. 1982. 16.95 (ISBN 0-940672-05-7); pap. 8.95 (ISBN 0-940672-04-9). Shearer Pub.

SHORT STORIES, ARGENTINE

Valenzuela, Luisa. Cambio de armas. (Span.). 1982. pap. 7.00 (ISBN 0-910061-10-6). Ediciones Norte.

SHORT STORIES, AUSTRALIAN

Holt, R. F., ed. The Strength of Tradition: Stories of the Immigrant Presence in Australia. LC 82-10874. 288p. 1983. 16.50 (ISBN 0-7022-1691-7); pap. 8.95 (ISBN 0-7022-1701-8). U of Queensland Pr.

SHORT STORIES, CHINESE

Hong, Xiao. Selected Stories of Xiao Hong. Goldbratt, Howard, tr. from Chinese. 220p. 1982. pap. 3.50 (ISBN 0-8351-1049-4). China Bks.

Xinwu, Liu & Meng, Wang. Prize-Winning Stories from China (1978-1979) (Illus.). 535p. 1981. pap. 9.95 (ISBN 0-8351-1032-X). China Bks.

SHORT STORIES, ENGLISH

Karavasil, Josie, ed. Love You, Hate You, Just Don't Know. 112p. 1982. 32.00x (ISBN 0-237-45510-2, Pub. by Evans Bros). State Mutual Bk.

Reiser, Virginia, ed. Favorite Short Stories in Large Print. 720p. 1982. lib. bdg. 17.95 (ISBN 0-8161-3434-0, Large Print Bks). G K Hall.

SHORT STORIES, ENGLISH-TRANSLATIONS FROM FOREIGN LANGUAGES

Porqueras-Mayo, Albert, et al. The New Catalan Short Story: An Anthology. LC 82-21927. 278p. (Orig.). 1983. lib. bdg. 22.50 (ISBN 0-8191-2899-6); pap. text ed. 11.75 (ISBN 0-8191-2900-3). U Pr of Amer.

SHORT STORIES, EUROPEAN

Beum, Robert, ed. Classic European Short Stories. 276p. (Orig.). 1982. pap. 6.95 (ISBN 0-89385-025-X). Sugden.

SHORT STORIES, FRENCH

Melville, Lewis & Hargreaves, Reginald, eds. Great French Short Stories. 1066p. 1982. Repr. of 1928 ed. lib. bdg. 25.00 (ISBN 0-89760-583-7). Telegraph Bks.

SHORT STORIES, IRANIAN

Helms, Cynthia. Favourite Sories from Persia. (Favourite Stories Ser.). (Illus.). ix, 61p. (Orig.). 1982. pap. text ed. 2.00x (ISBN 9971-64-041-4). Heinemann Ed.

SHORT STORIES, PHILIPPINE

Albis, Abelardo S. The Bell Ringer & Other Stories. 103p. (Orig.). 1982. pap. 4.75 (ISBN 0-686-37572-6, Pub. by New Day Philippines). Cellar.

Daroy, Esther V. The Drumbeater & Other Stories. 144p. (Orig.). 1982. pap. 5.75 (ISBN 0-686-37579-3, Pub. by New Day Philippines). Cellar.

Lim, Paul S. Some Arrivals, but Mostly Departures. 136p. pap. 7.50 (ISBN 0-686-37573-4, Pub. by New Day Philippines). Cellar.

SHORT STORIES, SPANISH-TRANSLATIONS INTO ENGLISH

Porqueras-Mayo, Albert, et al. The New Catalan Short Story: An Anthology. LC 82-21927. 278p. (Orig.). 1983. lib. bdg. 22.50 (ISBN 0-8191-2899-6); pap. text ed. 11.75 (ISBN 0-8191-2900-3). U Pr of Amer.

SHORT STORY

Here are entered works on the theory and art of short story writing. Collections of stories are entered under the heading Short Stories.

Esenwein, J. Berg & Chambers, Mary D. The Art of Story-Writing. 210p. 1982. Repr. of 1913 ed. lib. bdg. 40.00 (ISBN 0-89984-186-4). Century Bookbindery.

Fowler, Nathaniel C. The Story of Story Writing: Facts & Information about Literary Work of Practical Value to Both Amateur & Professional Writers. 255p. 1982. Repr. of 1913 ed. lib. bdg. 40.00 (ISBN 0-89984-207-0). Century Bookbindery.

Lohafer, Susan. Coming to Terms with the Short Story. LC 82-20366. 200p. 1983. text ed. 18.95X (ISBN 0-8071-1086-8). La State U Pr.

Peden, Margaret S. The Latin American Short Story: A Critical History. (Critical History of the Modern Short Story Ser.). 208p. 1983. lib. bdg. 17.95 (ISBN 0-8057-9351-8, Twayne). G K Hall.

Quirk, Leslie W. How to Write a Short Story. 77p. 1982. Repr. of 1911 ed. lib. bdg. 25.00 (ISBN 0-89987-675-7). Darby Bks.

Thomas, Michael. Studien Zur Short Story Als Fiktional-Narrative Textform und die Moglichkeiten Einer Typenbildung. 390p. (Ger.). 1982. write for info. (ISBN 3-8204-6267-8). P Lang Pubs.

Weaver, Gordon. The American Short Story, 1945-1980: A Critical History. (Critical History of the Modern Short Story Ser.). 208p. 1983. lib. bdg. 17.95 (ISBN 0-8057-9350-X, Twayne). G K Hall.

SHORTENINGS

see Oils and Fats, Edible

SHORTHAND

see also Abbreviations; Stenographers; Stenotypy

Leslie, L. A. & Zoubek, C. E. Gregg Shorthand1, Series 90: A Gregg Text-Kit in Continuing Education. 1983. 18.95x (ISBN 0-07-037769-3, G). McGraw.

--Gregg Shorthand2, Series 90: A Gregg Text-Kit in Continuing Education. 1983. 18.95x (ISBN 0-07-037770-7, G). McGraw.

Speedwriting Shorthand Training System. 1982. complete pkg. Resource manual, Student manuals, Dictionaries & Tapes 1000.00 (ISBN 0-672-90022-X). Bobbs.

Weber, et al. Forkner Shorthand for Colleges. LC 81-67853. 300p. 1982. text ed. 10.72x (ISBN 0-912036-44-3); instr's manual 6.96x (ISBN 0-686-83216-7); skill builder 6.36x (ISBN 0-912036-45-1); (18 cassettes) 300.00x (ISBN 0-912036-47-8). Forkner.

SHORTHAND, SPANISH

Duenas. Curso Basico de Mecanografia. 84p. 1982. 4.56 (ISBN 0-07-017991-3, G). McGraw.

Winger. Mecanografia Gregg Segundo Curso. 98p. 1982. 7.65 (ISBN 0-07-071081-3, G). McGraw.

SHOSHONI INDIANS

see Indians of North America–The West

SHOT-GUNS

Marshall-Ball, Robin. The Sporting Shotgun. (Illus.). 168p. 1982. 23.95 (ISBN 0-913276-38-3). Stone Wall Pr.

SHOW BUSINESS

see Performing Arts

SHOW CARDS

see Posters

SHROUD, HOLY

see Holy Shroud

SHRUBS

see also specific shrubs, e.g. Rhododendron

Eagle, Audrey. Eagle's Trees & Shrubs of New Zealand in Colour. (Illus.). 311p. 1983. Repr. of 1975 ed. 95.00 (ISBN 0-686-84831-4, Pub. by W Collins Australia). Intl Schol Bk Serv.

Gentry, Howard S. & Thomson, Paul H. Jojaba Handbook. 3rd ed. 168p. 1982. pap. 10.00x (ISBN 0-9602066-1-2). Bonsall Pub.

SHYNESS

see Bashfulness

SI

see Metric System

SIALIC ACID

Schauer, R., ed. Sialic Acids: Chemistry, Metabolism, & Function. (Cell Biology Monographs: Vol. 10). (Illus.). 344p. 1983. 68.00 (ISBN 0-387-81707-7). Springer-Verlag.

SIAM

see Thailand

SIAMESE LANGUAGE

Kuo, William. Teaching Grammar of Thai. LC 82-13519. (Illus.). 500p. 1983. lib. bdg. 29.25 (ISBN 0-8191-2678-0); pap. text ed. 17.25 (ISBN 0-8191-2679-9). U Pr of Amer.

SIBERIA–DESCRIPTION AND TRAVEL

Bennington, Michael. Rossya: A Journey Through Siberia. (Travel Bks.: Vol. 12). (Illus.). 96p. (Orig.). 1982. 12.50 (ISBN 0-906672-10-4). Oleander Pr.

SIBLING SEQUENCE

see Birth Order

SICILY–DESCRIPTION AND TRAVEL

Sicily Travel Guide. (Berlitz Travel Guides). (Illus.). 1982. pap. 4.95 (ISBN 0-02-969510-4, Berlitz). Macmillan.

SICILY–HISTORY–TO 800

Wilson, R. J. Sicily Under the Roman Empire. (Illus.). 160p. 1982. text ed. 65.00x (ISBN 0-85668-160-1, 41418, Pub. by Aris & Phillips England). Humanities.

SICK

see also Cookery for the Sick; Diet in Disease; First Aid in Illness and Injury; Health Resorts, Watering-Places, etc.; Hospitals; Nurses and Nursing

American Health Research Institute, Ltd. Patients: A Medical Subject Analysis & Research Index With Bibliography. Bartone, John C., ed. LC 82-72029. 120p. 1983. 29.95 (ISBN 0-941864-74-X); pap. 21.95 (ISBN 0-941864-75-8). ABBE Pubs Assn.

Barber, Triphy & Langfitt, Dot E. Teaching the Medical-Surgical Patient: Diagnostics & Procedures. (Illus.). 384p. 1983. pap. text ed. 19.95 (ISBN 0-89303-250-6). R J Brady.

Betts. Patient Centred Multiple Choice Questions, Vol. 2. 96p. 1982. pap. text ed. 6.50 (ISBN 0-06-318232-7, Pub. by Har-Row Ltd England). Har-Row.

Rankin, Sally & Duffy, Karen L., eds. Patient Education: Issues, Principles & Guidelines. (Illus.). 328p. 1983. pap. text ed. price not set (ISBN 0-397-54398-0, Lippincott Medical). Lippincott.

Viney, Linda L. Images of Illness. 256p. 1983. text ed. 17.50 (ISBN 0-89874-612-4). Krieger.

SICK–LEGAL STATUS, LAWS, ETC.

Storch, J. Patient's Rights: Ethical & Legal Issues in Health Case & Nursing. 288p. Date not set. 10.95 (ISBN 0-07-548477-3). McGraw.

SICKLE CELL ANEMIA

Scott, Roland B., ed. Advances in the Pathophysiology, Diagnosis & Treatment of Sickle Cell Disease. LC 82-12658. (Progress in Clinical & Biological Research Ser.: Vol. 98). 180p. 1982. 22.00 (ISBN 0-8451-0098-X). A R Liss.

SICKNESS INSURANCE

see Insurance, Health

SIDE DRUM

see Drum

SIDE SHOWS

see Amusement Parks

SIDEREAL SYSTEM

see Stars

SIDNEY, PHILIP, SIR, 1554-1586

Nichols. The Poetry of Sir Philip Sydney. 192p. 1982. 39.00x (ISBN 0-85323-351-9, Pub. by Liverpool Univ England). State Mutual Bk.

SIERRA NEVADA MOUNTAINS

Reid, Robert. A Treasury of the Sierra Nevada. Winnett, Thomas, ed. (Illus.). 256p. pap. 7.95 (ISBN 0-89997-023-0). Wilderness Pr.

SIGHT

see Vision

SIGHT-READING (MUSIC)

Geltman, Eve. The Gift of Music: A New Tested Way to Progress Quickly from Rote to Reading. (Illus.). 200p. 1982. 7.95 (ISBN 0-686-81849-0). Diablo.

Taylor, Bob. Sight-Reading Jazz: Melody, Bass Clef Version, Bk. 1. Taylor, Jennifer J., ed. (Illus., Orig.). 1982. pap. text ed. 12.95x (ISBN 0-943950-02-3). Taylor James.

SIGHT-SAVING

see Eye-Care and Hygiene

SIGHT-SAVING BOOKS

see Large Type Books

SIGILLOGRAPHY

see Seals (Numismatics)

SIGN-BOARDS

see Signs and Signboards

SIGN LANGUAGE

see also Deaf–Means of Communication; Signs and Symbols

Caccamise, Frank & Garritson, Mervin, eds. Teaching ASL as a Second-Foreign Language: Proceedings of National Symposium on Sign Language Research & Teaching. 240p. (Orig.). 1982. pap. text ed. 15.95 (ISBN 0-913072-49-4). Natl Assn Deaf.

Cargill & Brown. Signos Para el Ingles Exacto: A Book for Spanish-Speaking Families of Deaf Children in Schools Using Signing Exact English. LC 82-61647. (Illus.). 152p. Date not set. pap. 10.95 (ISBN 0-916708-06-3). Modern Signs.

Carpenter, Carol B. & Rakow, Sue F. Say it in Sign: A Workbook of Sign Language Exercises. (Illus.). 112p. 1983. pap. 14.75x spiral (ISBN 0-398-04779-0). C C Thomas.

Costello, Elaine. Signing: How to Speak with Your Hands. 1983. pap. 9.95 (ISBN 0-686-43070-0). Bantam.

Hoemann, Harry & Lucafo, Rosemarie. Sign Language Flash Cards. (Vol. II). 500p. 1983. pap. text ed. 13.95x (ISBN 0-913072-52-4). Natl Assn Deaf.

Kyle, Jim & Woll, Bencie, eds. Language in Sign: An International Perspective on Sign Language. 320p. 1983. pap. text ed. 19.50x (ISBN 0-7099-1528-4, Pub by Croom Helm Ltd England). Biblio Dist.

SIGN PAINTING

see also Alphabets; Lettering; Signs and Signboards

Spielman, Patrick. Alphabets & Designs For Wood Signs. (Illus.). 132p. 1983. 13.95 (ISBN 0-8069-5482-5); pap. 6.95 (ISBN 0-8069-7702-7). Sterling.

SIGNAL THEORY (TELECOMMUNICATION)

see also Coding Theory; Electronic Noise; Modulation (Electronics)

Brown, Robert G. Introduction to Random Signal Analysis & Kalman Filtering. 416p. 1983. text ed. price not set (ISBN 0-471-08732-7). Wiley.

Chen, C. H. Nonlinear Maxium Entropy Spectral Analysis Methods for Signal Recognition. (Pattern Recognition & Image Processing Research Studies). 190p. 1982. 29.95 (ISBN 0-471-10497-3, Pub by Res Stud Pr). Wiley.

Frederick, Dean K. & Carlson, A. Bruce. Linear Systems in Communication & Control. LC 71-155118. 575p. 1971. 36.95x (ISBN 0-471-27721-5). Wiley.

Haykin, Simon. Communication Systems. 2nd ed. 625p. 1983. 33.95 (ISBN 0-471-09691-1); tchrs.' avail. (ISBN 0-471-87155-9). Wiley.

Mitra, S. K. & Ekstrom, M. P., eds. Two-Dimensional Digital Signal Processing. LC 77-25337. (Benchmark Papers in Electrical Engineering & Computer Science: Vol. 20). 400p. 1978. 52.50 (ISBN 0-87933-320-0). Hutchinson Ross.

SIGNALS (INFORMATION THEORY)

see Information Measurement

SIGNALS AND SIGNALING

see also Sonar

Connor, F. R. Signals. (Introductory Topics in Electronics & Telecommunication). 144p. 1982. pap. text ed. 9.95 (ISBN 0-7131-3458-5). E Arnold.

SIGNATURES (WRITING)

see Autographs; Seals (Numismatics)

SIGNBOARDS

see Signs and Signboards

SIGNETS

see Seals (Numismatics)

SIGNS

see Signs and Signboards; Signs and Symbols

SIGNS (OMENS)

see Omens

SIGNS AND SIGNBOARDS

see also Posters; Sign Painting; Traffic Signs and Signals

Levy, Dana & Sneider, Lea. Kanban: Shop Signs of Japan. (Illus.). 168p. 1983. 29.95 (ISBN 0-8348-0180-9). Weatherhill.

Narayan, R. K. The Painter of Signs. 1983. pap. 4.95 (ISBN 0-14-006259-9). Penguin.

SIGNS AND SYMBOLS

see also Abbreviations; Ciphers; Cryptography; Emblems; Heraldry; Omens; Semiotics; Signals and Signaling

Ann Arbor Publishers Editorial Staff. Symbol Discrimination Series: Books 1, 2, 3, 4, 5, & 6. (Symbol Discrimination Series). (Illus.). 16p. (gr. k-1). 1974. 2.00 ea.; Book 1. 2.00 (ISBN 0-89039-078-9); Book 2. 2.00 (ISBN 0-89039-079-7); Book 3. 2.00 (ISBN 0-89039-080-0); Book 4. 2.00 (ISBN 0-89039-081-9); Book 5. 2.00 (ISBN 0-89039-082-7); Book 6. 2.00 (ISBN 0-89039-083-5). Ann Arbor Pubs.

Elder, Charles D. & Cobb, Roger W. The Political Uses of Symbols. Rockwood, Irving, ed. (Professional Studies in Political Communication). (Illus.). 192p. 1983. text ed. 22.50x (ISBN 0-582-28392-2); pap. text ed. 9.95x (ISBN 0-582-28393-0). Longman.

Signs & Wonders Today. 1983. Repr. write for info. Creation Hse.

SIKKIM, INDIA

Chopra, P. N. Sikkim. 114p. 1979. 14.95x (ISBN 0-940500-65-5). Asia Bk Corp.

Gibbons, Robert & Ashford, Bob. The Kingdoms of the Himalayas: Nepal, Sikkim, & Bhutan. (Illus.). 250p. 1983. 17.50 (ISBN 0-88254-802-6). Hippocrene Bks.

SIKSIKA INDIANS

see Indians of North America–The West

SILANE

Plueddemann, Edwin P., ed. Silane Coupling Agents. 250p. 1982. 37.50x (ISBN 0-306-40957-7, Plenum Pr). Plenum Pub.

SILENT COMPANIONS

see Dummy Board Figures

SILICIDES

Murarka, S. P, ed. Silicides for VLSI Appreciations. Date not set. price not set (ISBN 0-12-511220-3). Acad Pr.

SILICON

Freyhardt, H. C., ed. Silicon-Chemical Etching. (Crystals-Growth, Properties & Applications Ser.: Vol. 8). (Illus.). 255p. 1983. 55.00 (ISBN 0-387-11862-4). Springer-Verlag.

SILK

Arrants, Cheryl & Asbjornsen, Jan. Sew Wonderful Silk. rev. ed. Amant, Kristi, ed. (Illus.). 128p. 1981. pap. text ed. 5.95 (ISBN 0-943704-02-2). Sew Wonderful.

Hartel, Herbert, intro. by. Along the Ancient Silk Routes: Central Asian Art from the West Berlin State Museums. (Illus.). 224p. 1982. 45.00 (ISBN 0-8109-1800-5). Abrams.

SILK MANUFACTURE AND TRADE

Arterburn, Yvonne. The Loom of Interdependence: Silkweaving Cooperatives in Kanchipuram. (Studies in Sociology & Social Anthropology). 220p. 1982. text ed. 13.75x (ISBN 0-391-02749-2, Pub. by Hindustan India). Humanities.

SILK SCREEN PRINTING

see Screen Process Printing

SILT

see Sedimentation and Deposition

SILVER

see also Coinage; Money; Silver Mines and Mining; Silver Question; Silverwork

Reed, Dick A. The Complete Investor's Guide to Silver Dollar Investing. 1982. 18.95 (ISBN 0-911349-00-6). English Fact.

Ryan, James E. The Investor's Guide to U. S. Silver Stocks. Sarnoff, Paul, frwd. by. (Illus.). 240p. (Orig.). 1983. pap. 19.95 (ISBN 0-9610202-0-2). N W Silver Pr.

SILVER ARTICLES

see Silverwork

SILVER FOX

see Foxes

SILVER MINES AND MINING

see also Prospecting

Moen, Wayne S. Silver Occurrences of Washington. (Bulletin Ser.: No. 69). (Illus.). 188p. 1976. 4.00 (ISBN 0-686-38464-4). Geologic Pubns.

Schlitt, W. J. & Larson, W. C., eds. Gold & Silver Leaching, Recovery & Economics. LC 81-68558. (Illus.). 148p. 1981. pap. text ed. 20.00x (ISBN 0-89520-289-1). Soc Mining Eng.

SILVER QUESTION

see also Coinage; Currency Question; Gold; Money

Smith, Jerome F. & Smith, Barbara K. Silver Profits in the Eighties. 1982. 16.95 (ISBN 0-916728-56-0). Bks in Focus.

SILVER WORK

see Silverwork

SILVERSMITHING

see Silverwork

SILVERSMITHS

Ensko, Stephen G. American Silversmiths & Their Marks: The Definitive Edition, 1948. 2nd ed. (Illus.). 287p. 1983. pap. 6.00 (ISBN 0-486-24428-8). Dover.

SILVERWORK

see also Jewelry; Jewelry Making

Carpenter, Charles H., Jr. Gorham Silver. LC 82-2359. 1983. 34.95 (ISBN 0-396-08068-5). Dodd.

Emerson, Julie. The Collectors: Early European Ceramics & Silver. LC 82-60159. (Illus.). 94p. (Orig.). 1982. pap. 12.95 (ISBN 0-932216-08-0). Seattle Art.

SIMON, CLAUDE

Gould, Karen L. Claude Simon's Mythic Muse. 16.00. French Lit.

SIMON, NEIL

Johnson, Robert K. Neil Simon. (United States Authors Ser.). 228p. 1983. lib. bdg. 15.95 (ISBN 0-8057-7387-8, Twayne). G K Hall.

SIMPLICITY

Sider, Ronald J., ed. Lifestyle in the Eighties: An Evangelical Commitment to Simple Lifestyle. LC 82-7067. (Contemporary Issues in Social Ethics Ser.). 1982. pap. 10.95 (ISBN 0-664-24437-8). Westminster.

SIMULATION METHODS

see also Artificial Intelligence; Bionics; Mathematical Models; Mathematical Optimization

Bekiroglu, Haluk, ed. Simulation in Inventory & Production Control. 1983. softbound 20.00 (ISBN 0-686-42972-9). Soc Computer Sim.

Carroll, John, ed. Computer Simulation in Emergency Planning. (Simulation Series: Vol. 11, No. 2). 30.00 (ISBN 0-686-38791-0). Soc Computer Sim.

Cash, Kathy. Designing & Using Simulations. (Technical Note Ser.: No. 20). 30p. (Orig.). pap. 1.00 (ISBN 0-932288-66-9). Ctr Intl Ed U of MA.

Highland, Harold, ed. Winter Simulation Conference Proceedings, 1982. 1982. 48.00 (ISBN 0-686-38789-9). Soc Computer Sim.

Karplus, Walter J., ed. Peripheral Array Processors. (Simulation Ser.: Vol. 11, No. 1). 170p. 1982. 30.00 (ISBN 0-686-38787-2). Soc Computer Sim.

Modeling & Simulation on Microcomputers: 1983. 1983. softbound 20.00 (ISBN 0-686-38790-2). Soc Computer Sim.

Proceedings of the 1982 Summer Computer Simulation Conference. 678p. 1982. softbound 50.00 (ISBN 0-686-38788-0). Soc Computer Sim.

Roberts, Nancy & Andersen, David. Introduction To Computer Simulation: The System Dynamics Approach. (Illus.). Date not set. text ed. 18.95 (ISBN 0-201-06414-6). A-W.

Schellenberger, R. & Boseman, G. MANSYM III: A Dynamic Management Simulator with Decision Support System. (Management Ser.). 94p. 1982. pap. text ed. 12.95 (ISBN 0-471-08581-2); tchrs. manual 6.00 (ISBN 0-471-86815-9). Wiley.

Vogt, William G. & Mickle, Marlin H., eds. Modeling & Simulation: Proceedings of the 13th Annual Pittsburgh Conference on Modeling & Simulation, 4 pts, Vol. 13. LC 73-85004. 1744p. 1982. pap. text ed. 40.00 ea. Pt. 1; 512p (ISBN 0-87664-712-3). Pt. 2; 546p (ISBN 0-87664-713-1). Pt. 3; 408p (ISBN 0-87664-714-X). Pt. 4; 368p (ISBN 0-87664-715-8). Set. pap. text ed. 149.00 (ISBN 0-87664-716-6). Instru Soc.

SIN

see also Atonement; Forgiveness of Sin; Free Will and Determinism; Sins; Theodicy

Gaffney, James. Sin Reconsidered. LC 82-61424. 96p. (Orig.). 1983. pap. 3.95 (ISBN 0-8091-2516-1). Paulist Pr.

Kierkegaard, Soren. Fear & Trembling & Repetition, 2 vols. in 1. Hong, Howard V. & Hong, Edna H., eds. Hong, Howard V. & Hong, Edna H., trs. LC 82-9006. (Kierkegaard's Writings Ser.: No. VI). 432p. 1983. 32.50x (ISBN 0-691-07237-X); pap. 6.95 (ISBN 0-691-02026-4). Princeton U Pr.

Pegram, Don R. Sinning Against the Holy Spirit. 1982. pap. 1.00 (ISBN 0-89265-085-0). Randall Hse.

Pollock, Algernon J. & Bennett, Gordon H. El Pecado Despues de la Conversion. 2nd ed. Bautista, Sara, tr. from Eng. (La Serie Diamante). 36p. (Span.). 1982. pap. 0.85 (ISBN 0-942504-04-6). Overcomer Pr.

Tennant, F. R. The Origin & Propagation of Sin: Being the Hulsean Lectures Delivered Before the University of Cambridge, in 1901-2. 235p. 1982. Repr. of 1908 ed. lib. bdg. 50.00 (ISBN 0-89987-822-9). Darby Bks.

Thomas Aquinas. Effects of Sin, Stain & Guilt. (Summa Theological Ser.: Vol. 27). 1974. 14.95 (ISBN 0-07-002002-7). McGraw.

SIN, FORGIVENESS OF

see Forgiveness of Sin

SIN, ORIGINAL

Steiner, Rudlof. The Concepts of Original Sin & Grace. Osmond, D. S., tr. from Ger. 32p. 1973. pap. 1.95 (ISBN 0-85440-275-6, Pub. by Steinerbooks). Anthroposophic.

SINATRA, FRANK, 1917-

Yarwood, Guy. Sinatra in His Own Words. (Illus.). 128p. (Orig.). 1983. pap. 6.95 (ISBN 0-399-41012-0). Delilah Bks.

SINGAPORE

Insight Guides. Singapore. (Illus.). 240p. 1983. 18.95 (ISBN 0-13-810994-X); pap. 14.95 (ISBN 0-13-810713-0). P-H.

SINGAPORE–DESCRIPTION AND TRAVEL

Barnes, Simon. Singapore in Focus. (The "In Focus" Ser.). (Illus.). 64p. (Orig.). 1981. pap. 5.95 (ISBN 962-7031-11-9). C E Tuttle.

Stephens, Harold. The Complete Guide to Singapore. (The Complete Asian Guide Ser.). (Illus.). 112p. (Orig.). 1981. pap. 6.95 (ISBN 962-7031-05-4, Pub. by CFW Pubns Hong Kong). C E Tuttle.

--Singapore by Night. (Asia by Night Ser.). (Illus.). 64p. (Orig.). 1981. pap. 4.95 (ISBN 962-7031-09-7, Pub. by CFW Pubns Hong Kong). C E Tuttle.

SINGERS

Bricktop & Haskins, James. Bricktop. LC 82-73006. 320p. 1983. 14.95 (ISBN 0-689-11349-8). Atheneum.

Gale, Joseph. I Sang for Diaghilev: Michel Pavloff's Merry Life. LC 82-71166. (Illus.). 120p. 1983. pap. 14.95 (ISBN 0-87127-132-X). Dance Horiz.
Haskins, Jim & Stifle, J. M. Donna Summer: An Unauthorized Biography. (Illus.). 144p. (gr. 7 up). 1983. 10.45i (ISBN 0-316-35003-6, Pub. by Atlantic Monthly Pr). Little.
Peters, Richard. Barry Manilow: An Illustrative Biography. (Illus.). 104p. (Orig.). 1983. pap. 8.95 (ISBN 0-933328-65-6). Delilah Bks.
Smith, David & Neal, Peters. Peter Allen: Between the Moon & New York City. (Illus.). 160p. (Orig.). 1983. pap. 9.95 (ISBN 0-933328-57-5). Delilah Bks.
Wallace, Ian. Nothing Quite Like It. (Illus.). 256p. 1982. 22.50 (ISBN 0-241-10853-5, Pub. by Hamish Hamilton England). David & Charles.
Yarwood, Guy. Sinatra in His Own Words. (Illus.). 128p. (Orig.). 1983. pap. 6.95 (ISBN 0-399-41012-0). Delilah Bks.

SINGERS–CORRESPONDENCE, REMINISCENCES, ETC.
see Musicians–Correspondence, Reminiscences, etc.

SINGING
see also Respiration; Voice Culture
Garcia, Manuel, II. A Complete Treatise on the Art of Singing, Pt. 1. Paschke, Donald V., tr. from Fr. lxi, 221p. 1983. Repr. lib. bdg. 32.50 (ISBN 0-306-76212-9). Da Capo.
McLeish, Kenneth & McLeish, Valerie. Singing & Dancing. (Illus.). 32p. pap. 4.75 laminated (ISBN 0-19-321436-9). Oxford U Pr.

SINGLE MEN
see Bachelors

SINGLE-PARENT FAMILY
see also Divorcees; Unmarried Mothers; Widows
Cannon, Ann. My Home Has One Parent. LC 81-86637. (gr. 7-12). 1983. pap. 4.95 (ISBN 0-8054-5337-7). Broadman.
Curto, Josephine. How to Become a Single Parent: A Guide for Single People Considering Adoption or Natural Parenthood Alone. 252p. 1983. 14.95 (ISBN 0-13-396192-3); pap. 6.95 (ISBN 0-13-396184-2). P-H.
McNamara, Lynne & Morrison, Jennifer. Separation, Divorce & After. LC 82-2718. 192p. 1983. pap. 9.95 (ISBN 0-7022-1931-2). U of Queensland Pr.
Smith, Virginia W. The Single Parent: Revised, Updated & Expanded. 192p. 1983. pap. 5.95 (ISBN 0-8007-5105-1, Power Bks). Revell.

SINGLE PEOPLE
see also Bachelors; Divorcees; Single Women
Doyle, A. C., ed. Single Source: A Bibliography for Singles. 75p. 1982. pap. 9.95 (ISBN 0-939476-71-1). Biblio Pr GA.
Graver, Jane. Single But Not Alone. 1983. pap. 2.25 (ISBN 0-570-03880-4). Concordia.
Hamburger, Robert. All the Lonely People: Life in a Single Room Occupancy Hotel. LC 82-19128. 352p. 1983. 15.95 (ISBN 0-89919-159-2). Ticknor & Fields.
Karssen, Gien. Getting the Most Out of Being Single. rev. ed. LC 82-62240. 1983. pap. 3.95 (ISBN 0-89109-505-5). NavPress.
Rinehart, Stacy & Rinehart, Paula. Choices: Finding God's Way in Dating, Sex, Singleness & Marriage. LC 82-62071. 1983. pap. 3.95 (ISBN 0-89109-494-6). NavPress.
Strebeck, Mary. Single But Not Alone. (Illus.). 80p. (Orig.). 1982. pap. 4.95 (ISBN 0-939298-16-3, 163). J M Prods.
Wetherall, Charles F. Single Man's Survival Guide. (Illus.). 160p. 1983. pap. 4.95 (ISBN 0-936750-06-5). Wetherall.

SINGLE WOMEN
see also Divorcees; Unmarried Mothers; Widows
Bence, Evelyn. Leaving Home: The Making of an Independent Woman. LC 82-15910. 192p. 1982. Pub. by Bridgebooks Pub. 9.95 (ISBN 0-664-27005-0). Westminster.
Cauhape, Elizabeth. Fresh Starts: Men & Women after Divorce. 227p. 1983. 16.50 (ISBN 0-465-02553-6). Basic.
Holmes, Ivory H. The Allocation of Time by Women Without Family Responsibilities. LC 82-20167. (Illus.). 186p. (Orig.). 1983. lib. bdg. 19.75 (ISBN 0-8191-2903-8); pap. text ed. 9.75 (ISBN 0-8191-2904-6). U Pr of Amer.

SINN FEIN REBELLION, 1916
see Ireland–History

SINS
see also Sin; Virtue and Virtues
Webb, Lance. How Bad are Your Sins? 224p. (Orig.). Date not set. pap. 3.95 (ISBN 0-687-17520-8, Festival). Abingdon.

SINUS PARANASALIS
see Nose, Accessory Sinuses Of

SIOUX INDIANS
see Indians of North America–The West

SITKA, ALASKA
Alaska Geographic Staff, ed. Sitka & Its Ocean-Island World. (Alaska Geographic Ser.: Vol. 9 No. 2). (Illus., Orig.). 1982. pap. 8.95 (ISBN 0-88240-169-6). Alaska Northwest.

SIX DAY WAR, 1967
see Israel-Arab War, 1967

SIZE OF PARTICLES
see Particles

SKATING
see also Roller-Skating
Vandervell, T. & Witham, H. Figure Skating: 1880. (Illus.). 200p. Date not set. pap. 12.50 (ISBN 0-87556-583-2). Saifer.

SKEES AND SKEE-RUNNING
see Skis and Skiing

SKELETAL REMAINS
see Man, Prehistoric

SKELETON
see also Bones; Extremities (Anatomy); Joints; Skull
also names of bones, e.g. Clavicle, Humerus
Kunin, Arthur S. & Simons, David J., eds. Skeletal Research: An Experimental Approach, Vol. 2. Date not set. price not set (ISBN 0-12-429002-7). Acad Pr.
Mears, Dana C. External Skeletal Fixation. (Illus.). 584p. 1983. 89.95 (ISBN 0-683-05900-9). Williams & Wilkins.
Papadatos, Costas J. & Bartsocas, Christos S., eds. Skeletal Dysplasias. LC 82-17277. (Progress in Clinical & Biological Research Ser.: Vol. 104). 572p. 1982. 60.00 (ISBN 0-8451-0104-8). A R Liss.

SKEPTICISM
see also Belief and Doubt; Truth
Burnyeat, Myles, ed. The Skeptical Tradition. LC 78-62833. (Major Thinkers Ser.). 536p. 1983. text ed. 38.50x (ISBN 0-520-03747-2); pap. text ed. 10.95x (ISBN 0-520-04795-8). U of Cal Pr.

SKETCHING
see Drawing

SKIAGRAPHY
see Radiography

SKIING
see Skis and Skiing

SKIN
see also Color of Man
Dvorine, William. A Dermatologist's Guide to Home Skin Care. 160p. 1983. 12.95 (ISBN 0-686-83863-7, ScribT). Scribner.
Fulton, James E. & Black, Elizabeth. Dr. Fulton's Step-By-Step Program for Clearing Acne. LC 82-47522. (Illus.). 256p. 1983. 12.45i (ISBN 0-06-038020-9, HarpT). Har-Row.
Goldberg, Audrey G. Care of the Skin. (Illus.). 1975. pap. 13.95 (ISBN 0-434-90672-7, Pub. by Heinemann). David & Charles.
Haberman, Fredric & Fortino, Denise. Your Skin: A Dermatologist's Guide to a Lifetime of Beauty & Health. LC 82-60711. 256p. 1983. pap. 3.50 (ISBN 0-86721-237-3). Playboy Pbks.
Jarrett, A., ed. The Psychology & Pathophysiology of the Skin, Vol. 7. 272p. 48.50 (ISBN 0-12-380607-0). Acad Pr.
Malouf, Pyrrha. Metamassage: How to Massage Your Way to a Beautiful Complexion - All Over. (Illus.). 1983. 6.95 (ISBN 0-87795-472-0, Pub. by Priam). Arbor Hse.
Marks, R. & Payne, P. A. Bioengineering & the Skin. (Illus.). 320p. 1981. text ed. 59.00 (ISBN 0-85200-314-5, Pub. by MTP Pr England). Kluwer Boston.
Marks, R. & Plewig, G., eds. Stratum Corneum. (Illus.). 300p. 1983. pap. 35.00 (ISBN 0-387-11704-0). Springer-Verlag.
Schaefer, Hans. Skin Permeability. (Illus.). 360p. 1982. pap. 57.60 (ISBN 0-387-11797-0). Springer-Verlag.
Simmons, Charles. Wrinkles. 1982. pap. 2.95 (ISBN 0-686-82396-6). Bantam.
Sternberg, James & Sternberg, Thomas. Great Skin at any Age: How to Keep Your Skin Looking Young without Plastic Surgery. 160p. 1983. 12.95 (ISBN 0-312-34674-3). St Martin.

SKIN–DISEASES
see also Dermatology
also specific diseases, e.g. Blastomycosis, Eczema, Lupus
Dahl, Mark V. Common Office Dermatology. Date not set. price not set (ISBN 0-8089-1497-9). Grune.
Fitzpatrick, Thomas B. & Polano, Machiel K. Color Atlas & Synopsis of Clinical Dermatology. (Illus.). 352p. 1982. pap. text ed. 29.95 (ISBN 0-07-021197-3, HP). McGraw.
MacKie, Roan M. Eczema & Dermatitis. LC 82-11390. (Positive Health Guides Ser.). (Illus.). 112p. 1983. lib. bdg. 12.95 (ISBN 0-668-05629-0); pap. 7.95 (ISBN 0-668-05634-7). Arco.
Maurer, T. Toxicology of Skin Irritation & Skin Sensitization: Standard Methods. (Lectures in Toxicology: No. 19). (Illus.). 12p. 1982. 60.00 (ISBN 0-08-029790-0). Pergamon.
Nasemann, T. & Sauerbrey, W. Fundamentals of Dermatology. (Illus.). 416p. 1983. pap. 24.90 (ISBN 0-387-90738-6). Springer-Verlag.
Parish. Cutaneous Infestations in Man. 304p. 1983. 36.50 (ISBN 0-03-059662-9). Praeger.
Ricklin. Meniscus Lesions. 1983. write for info. (ISBN 0-86577-094-8). Thieme-Stratton.

SKIN–SURGERY
Colman, Willaim P. & Colon, G. A. Surgery of the Skin. (Advanced Textbook Ser.). 1983. text ed. price not set (ISBN 0-87488-185-4). Med Exam.
Harahap, Marwali. Skin Surgery. (Illus.). 900p. 1983. price not set (ISBN 0-87527-317-3). Green.

SKIN, COLOR OF
see Color of Man

SKIN DIVING
Here are entered works on free diving with the use of mask, fins, and snorkel. Works on free diving with the use of an aqualung are entered under Scuba Diving.
see also Scuba Diving; Underwater Exploration
The New Science of Skin & Scuba Diving (CNCA) 288p. 8.95 (ISBN 0-686-38064-9). AAHPERD.

SKIP TRACERS
see Missing Persons

SKIS AND SKIING
see also Cross-Country Skiing
Abraham, Horst. Skiing Right. LC 82-8105. (Illus.). 237p. 1983. pap. 12.95 (ISBN 0-933472-74-9). Johnson Bks.
Foss, Merle L. & Garrick, James G. Ski Conditioning. LC 77-24553. (American College of Sports Medicine Ser.). 179p. 1978. text ed. 18.50x (ISBN 0-471-26764-3). Wiley.
Goeldner, C. R. & Buchman, Tom. NSAA Economic Analysis of North American Ski Areas, 1981-82 Season. 136p. 1982. pap. text ed. 40.00 (ISBN 0-89478-073-5). U Co Busn Res Div.
Jackman, Brian & Evans, Harold. We Learned to Ski. (Illus.). 255p. 1982. pap. 9.95 (ISBN 0-312-85859-0). St Martin.
Satterfield, Archie & Bauer, Eddie. The Eddie Bauer Guide to Cross-Country Skiing. (Illus.). 256p. 1982. 17.95 (ISBN 0-201-07774-4); pap. 8.95 (ISBN 0-201-07775-2). A-W.
Skiing Rulebook. 3.50 (ISBN 0-88314-160-4). AAHPERD.
Thomas & Leeds. Skiiers Directory & Almanac: 1983. 1982. pap. 3.95 (ISBN 0-686-82385-0). Dell.
Tucker, Karl & Jensen, Clayne R. Skiing. 4th ed. (Physical Education Activities Ser.). 110p. 1983. pap. text ed. write for info. (ISBN 0-697-07210-X). Wm C Brown.

SKIS AND SKIING–DIRECTORIES
Enzel, Robert G. The White Book of Ski Areas. Enzel, Hajnalka V., ed. (Illus.). 348p. 1982. write for info. Inter-Ski.
The Macmillan & Silk Cut Ski Guide, 1983. 464p. 1982. 50.00x (ISBN 0-333-33272-5, Pub. by Macmillan England). State Mutual Bk.

SKITS, STUNTS, ETC.
see also Children's Plays; Dialogues; Schools–Exercises and Recreations
Albert, Renaud S., ed. A Tour de Role. (Neuf Pieces en un Acte Ser.). 204p. (Fr.). (gr. 7-12). 1980. pap. 4.00x (ISBN 0-911409-11-4). Natl Mat Dev.

SKULL
Here are entered anatomical and pathological works.
see also Head
Lang, J. Clinical Anatomy of the Head: Neurocranium, Orbita, Craniocervical Regions. (Illus.). 489p. 1983. 490.00 (ISBN 0-387-11014-3). Springer-Verlag.

SKULL–ABNORMITIES AND DEFORMITIES
Marchac, Daniel & Renier, Dominique. Craniofacial Surgery for Craniosynostosis. 1982. text ed. 48.50 (ISBN 0-316-54582-1). Little.

SKY
see Atmosphere

SLACKS
see Trousers

SLANDER (LAW)
see Libel and Slander

SLANG
Whiteford, Mike. How to Talk Baseball. LC 82-19920. (Illus.). 144p. (Orig.). 1983. pap. 6.95 (ISBN 0-934878-21-8). Dembner Bks.

SLAVE TRADE–AFRICA
Inikori, J. E., ed. Forced Migration: The Impact of the Export Slave Trade on African Societies. 352p. 1983. text ed. 22.00x (ISBN 0-8419-0795-1); pap. text ed. 13.50x (ISBN 0-8419-0799-4). Holmes & Meier.
Lovejoy, Paul. Transformations in Slavery: A History of Slavery in Africa. LC 82-1284. (African Studies: No. 36). (Illus.). 352p. Date not set. price not set (ISBN 0-521-24369-6); pap. price not set (ISBN 0-521-28646-8). Cambridge U Pr.

SLAVERY
Abrahams, Roger D. & Szwed, John F., eds. After Africa: Extracts from British Travel Accounts & Journals of the Seventeenth, Eighteenth, & Nineteenth Centuries Concerning the Slaves, Their Manners, & Customs in the British West Indies. LC 82-20110. 480p. 1983. text ed. 45.00x (ISBN 0-300-02748-6); pap. text ed. 12.95x (ISBN 0-300-03030-4). Yale U Pr.
Detweiler, Robert & Kornweibel, Theodore. Slave & Citizen: A Critical Annotated Bibliography on Slavery & Race Relations in the Americas. 300p. 1983. pap. 6.00 (ISBN 0-686-84758-X). Campanile.
Ostrander, Gilman M. Slavery in the Union. 1970. pap. text ed. 1.95x (ISBN 0-88273-224-2). Forum Pr IL.

SLAVERY AND THE CHURCH
Turner, Mary. Slaves & Missionaries: The Disintegration of Jamaican Slave Society, 1787-1834. LC 82-6983. (Blacks in the New World Ser.). 240p. 1982. 25.95 (ISBN 0-252-00961-4). U of Ill Pr.

SLAVERY IN AFRICA
Lovejoy, Paul. Transformations in Slavery: A History of Slavery in Africa. LC 82-1284. (African Studies: No. 36). (Illus.). 352p. Date not set. price not set (ISBN 0-521-24369-6); pap. price not set (ISBN 0-521-28646-8). Cambridge U Pr.
Ross, Robert. Cape of Torments: Slavery & Resistance in South Africa. (International Library of Anthropology). 176p. 1983. price not set (ISBN 0-7100-9407-8). Routledge & Kegan.

SLAVERY IN GREAT BRITAIN
Walvin, J. Slavery & British Society 1780-1838. 1982. 65.00x (ISBN 0-686-42927-3, Pub. by Macmillan England). State Mutual Bk.

SLAVERY IN GREECE
Finley, M. I. Ancient Slavery & Modern Ideology. 1983. pap. 6.95 (ISBN 0-14-022500-5, Pelican). Penguin.

SLAVERY IN LATIN AMERICA
Cardoso, Gerald. Negro Slavery in the Sugar Plantations of Veracruz & Pernambuco, 1550-1680: A Comparative Study. LC 82-21731. 224p. (Orig.). 1983. lib. bdg. 21.50 (ISBN 0-8191-2926-7); pap. text ed. 10.75 (ISBN 0-8191-2927-5). U Pr of Amer.

SLAVERY IN ROME
Finley, M. I. Ancient Slavery & Modern Ideology. 1983. pap. 6.95 (ISBN 0-14-022500-5, Pelican). Penguin.

SLAVERY IN THE UNITED STATES
see also Abolitionists; Southern States–History
Davis, Edward D. A Half Century of Struggle for Freedom in Florida. LC 82-50932. 1982. write for info. (ISBN 0-9610068-0-3). Drake's Ptg & Pub.
Dodd, William E. Cotton Kingdom. 1919. text ed. 8.50x (ISBN 0-686-83514-X). Elliots Bks.
Hilty, Hiram. North Carolina Quakers & Slavery. 120p. 1983. write for info. (ISBN 0-913408-84-0); pap. 7.95 (ISBN 0-913408-83-2). Friends United.
Rose, Willie L. Slavery & Freedom. expanded ed. Freehling, William W., ed. 272p. 1983. pap. 7.95 (ISBN 0-19-503266-7, GB 723, GB). Oxford U Pr.

SLAVERY IN THE UNITED STATES–ANTI-SLAVERY MOVEMENTS
Blackett, R. J. Building an Antislavery Wall: Black Americans in the Atlantic Abolitionist Movement, 1830 to 1860. LC 82-21724. 264p. 1983. text ed. 25.00x (ISBN 0-8071-1082-5). La State U Pr.

SLAVERY IN THE UNITED STATES–BIBLIOGRAPHY
Smith, John D., compiled by. Black Slavery in the Americas: An Interdisciplinary Bibliography, 1865-1980, 2 vols. LC 82-11737. 1982. Set. lib. bdg. 95.00 (ISBN 0-313-23118-4, SMB/). Greenwood.

SLAVERY IN THE UNITED STATES–EMANCIPATION
McClelland, Peter D. & Zeckhauser, Richard J. Demographic Dimensions of the New Republic: American Interregional Migration, Vital Statistics, & Manumissions, 1800-1860. (Illus.). 220p. p.n.s. (ISBN 0-521-24309-2). Cambridge U Pr.

SLAVERY IN THE UNITED STATES–HISTORY
Woodward, C. Vann. American Counterpoint: Slavery & Racism in the North-South Dialogue. 320p. 1983. pap. 7.95 (ISBN 0-19-503269-1, GB 727, GB). Oxford U Pr.

SLAVERY IN THE UNITED STATES–PERSONAL NARRATIVES
Shepperd, Gladys B. The Montgomery Saga: From Slavery to Black Power. 1983. 10.00 (ISBN 0-533-05553-9). Vantage.

SLAVES, EMANCIPATION OF
see Slavery in the United States–Emancipation

SLAVIC LANGUAGES
Barentsen, A., ed. South Slavic & Balkan Linguistics. (Studies in Slavic & General Linguistics: Vol. 2). 340p. 1982. pap. text ed. 32.25x (ISBN 90-6203-634-1, Pub. by Rodopi Holland). Humanities.
--Studies in Slavic & General Linguistics, Vol. 1. 472p. 1980. pap. text ed. 46.00x (ISBN 90-6203-523-X, Pub. by Rodopi Holland). Humanities.
Entwistle, W. J. & Morison, W. A. Russian & the Slavonic Languages. 407p. 1982. Repr. of 1949 ed. lib. bdg. 65.00 (ISBN 0-8495-1429-0). Arden Lib.
Foote, I. P. & Fennell, J. L., eds. Oxford Slavonic Papers: New Series, Vol. 15. 144p. 1982. 38.50 (ISBN 0-19-815658-8). Oxford U Pr.

SLAVIC PHILOLOGY
see also names of languages and literatures belonging to the Slavic group
Lencek, Rado L. & Cooper, Henry R., Jr., eds. Papers in Slavic Philology: To Honor Jernej Kopitar, No. 2. 1982. pap. 7.00 (ISBN 0-930042-46-8). Mich Slavic Pubns.

SLAVIC RACE
see Slavs

SLAVIC STUDIES
Matejka, Ladislav & Stolz, Benjamin A., eds. Cross Currents. (Michigan Slavic Materials Ser.: No. 19). 1982. pap. 8.00 (ISBN 0-930042-43-3). Mich Slavic Pubns.

SLAVS
see also Slavic Studies
also names of peoples belonging to the Slavic race, e.g. Poles, Russians, Slovenes, Yugoslavs
Vana, Zdenek. The World of the Ancient Slavs. Gottheinerova, Till, tr. (Illus.). 240p. 1983. 35.00x (ISBN 0-686-43100-6, Co-publication with Orbis Pub). Wayne St U Pr.

SLEEP
see also Dreams
Chase, Michael & Weitzman, Eliott, eds. Sleep Disorders: Basic & Clinical Research. (Advances in Sleep Research: Vol. 8). (Illus.). 604p. 1983. text ed. 85.00 (ISBN 0-89335-166-0). SP Med & Sci Bks.
Oswald, Ian & Adam, Kirstine. Get a Better Night's Sleep. LC 82-4060. (Positive Health Guides Ser.). (Illus.). 128p. 1983. 12.95 (ISBN 0-668-05335-6); pap. 7.95 (ISBN 0-668-05341-0). Arco.

Phillips, Elliott. Get a Good Night's Sleep. 196p. 1983. 13.95 (ISBN 0-13-354290-4); pap. 6.95 (ISBN 0-13-354282-3). P-H.

Sterman, M. B. & Shouse, Margaret N., eds. Sleep & Epilepsy: Symposium. LC 82-11657. 1982. 39.00 (ISBN 0-12-666360-2). Acad Pr.

SLEIGHT OF HAND

see Conjuring; Magic

SLIDE-RULE

Roberts, Kenneth D., ed. The Carpenter's Slide Rule: Its History & Use. 32p. (Orig.). 1982. pap. text ed. 4.00 (ISBN 0-913602-50-7). K Roberts.

SLOPES (PHYSICAL GEOGRAPHY)

Schumm, Stanley A. & Mosley, Paul M., eds. Slope Morphology. LC 72-95135. (Benchmark Papers in Geology: Vol. 6). 454p. 1973. text ed. 55.00 (ISBN 0-87933-024-4). Hutchinson Ross.

SLOT CAR RACING

see Model Car Racing

SLOTHS

Montgomery, G. Gene, ed. The Evolution & Ecology of Armadillos, Sloths, & Vermilinguas. (Illus.). 400p. (Orig.). 1983. pap. text ed. 35.00x (ISBN 0-87474-649-3). Smithsonian.

SLOVAKIA

Arnez, John A. Slovenian Lands & Their Economies, 1848-1873. (Studia Slovenica Ser.: No. 15). 321p. 1983. soft cover 16.00 (ISBN 0-686-38857-7). Studia Slovena.

SLOVENIAN LANGUAGE

Lencek, Rado L. The Structure & History of the Slovene Language. (Illus.). 365p. 1982. 19.95 (ISBN 0-89357-099-0). Slavica.

SLOW ELECTRIC COOKERY

see Electric Cookery, Slow

SLUM CLEARANCE

see City Planning; Housing

SMALL ARMS

see Firearms

SMALL BOAT RACING

see Yacht Racing

SMALL BUSINESS

see also Cottage Industries; Franchises (Retail Trade)

Bencar, Gary R. Computers for Small Business: A Step by Step Guide on How to Buy. (Illus.). 148p. 1983. pap. 11.95 (ISBN 0-935222-05-7). La Cumbre.

Carrol, Frieda. Boom Businesses U. S. A. 50p. 1983. 8.95 (ISBN 0-939476-75-4). Biblio Pr GA.

Center for Self Sufficiency Research Division Staff. The A to Z Small Business Bibliography Encyclopedia. 2000p. 1983. Set. text ed. 650.00 (ISBN 0-910811-17-2). Center Self.

Chatterton, William A. Consumer & Small Business Bankruptcy: A Complete Working Guide. LC 82-12040. 256p. 1982. text ed. 89.50 (ISBN 0-87624-101-1). Inst Busn Plan.

Cope, Robert E. Successful Participative Management in Smaller Companies. 125p. (Orig.). 1982. pap. text ed. 18.00 (ISBN 0-9610044-0-1). QDP Inc.

Doyle, Alfreda C. Suggestions for Making Money Addressing & Stuffing Envelopes Or How to Run a Small Letter Shop Service. 26p. 1983. pap. text ed. 9.95 (ISBN 0-910811-20-2). Center Self.

--Suggestions for Starting a Business from Businesses That Are Going Out of Business. 26p. 1983. pap. text ed. 16.95 (ISBN 0-910811-25-3). Center Self.

Goldstein, Arnold S. The Small Business Legal Problem-Solver. 240p. 1983. 24.95 (ISBN 0-8436-0890-0); pap. 15.95 (ISBN 0-8436-0891-9). CBI Pub.

Gustafson, Ray L. Buying, Selling, Starting a Business. LC 82-90702. 152p. 1982. pap. 19.95 (ISBN 0-9609046-0-3, DEPT. OR-1). Gustafson Horse.

Hailes, W. & Hubbard, R. Small Business Management. 3rd ed. 240p. 1983. pap. text ed. 8.80 (ISBN 0-8273-2108-2); write for info. instr's guide (ISBN 0-8273-2109-0). Delmar.

Hathaway-Bates, John. How to Promote your Business. 162p. (Orig.). 1981. pap. 9.25 (ISBN 0-910333-00-9). Asigan Ltd.

Mall, E. Jane. How to Become Wealthy Publishing a Newsletter. 110p. 1983. pap. 17.50 (ISBN 0-914306-83-9). Intl Wealth.

Masters, William M. How You Can Earn One Hundred Thousand Dollars a Year Without Working; Legally, Honestly, Tax-Free. 128p. (Orig.). 1983. pap. text ed. 17.95 (ISBN 0-686-38785-6). Jadestone.

Newcomb, Duane. Fortune-Building Secrets of the Rich. LC 82-18837. 215p. 1983. 14.95 (ISBN 0-13-384685-7, Parker); pap. 4.95 (ISBN 0-13-329102-2). P-H.

Nykiel, Ronald A. Marketing in the Hospitality Industry. (Illus.). 320p. 1983. text ed. 19.95 (ISBN 0-8436-0886-2). CBI Pub.

Ray, G. H. & Hutchinson, P. J. The Financing & Financial Control of Small Enterprise Development. 280p. 1983. 25.00 (ISBN 0-89397-154-5). Nichols Pub.

Shilling, Dana. Be Your Own Boss: A Step-by-Step Guide to Financial Independence Through Your Own Small Business. 490p. 1983. 14.95 (ISBN 0-688-01572-7). Morrow.

Small Business Development. 35.00 (ISBN 0-686-37907-1). Nikmal Pub.

Small Business Tax Equity Conference. Proceedings. 1983. write for info. Am Inst CPA.

Smith, Brian R. How to Prosper in Your Own Business. (Illus.). 1983. pap. 11.95 (ISBN 0-86616-025-6). Greene.

--The Small Computer in Small Business. 1983. pap. 9.95 (ISBN 0-86616-024-8). Greene.

Steingold, Fred. Legal Master Guide for Small Business. 242p. 1983. 21.95 (ISBN 0-13-528422-8); pap. 9.95 (ISBN 0-13-528414-7). P-H.

Webb, Terry & Quince, Thelma, eds. Small Business Research: The Development of Entrepreneurs. 218p. 1982. text ed. 34.00x (ISBN 0-566-00381-3). Gower Pub Ltd.

SMALL BUSINESS–ACCOUNTING

see Accounting

SMALL BUSINESS–FINANCE

Assisting Small Business Clients in Obtaining Funds. 1982. pap. 5.00 (ISBN 0-686-84210-3). Am Inst CPA.

Coltman, Michael M. Financial Control for the Small Business: A Practical Primer for Keeping a Tighter Rein on Your Profits & Cash Flow. 12/1982 ed. (Illus.). 119p. (Orig.). pap. 5.50 (ISBN 0-88908-911-6). Self Counsel Pr.

Holtz, Herman R. Two Thousand One Sources of Financing for Small Business. LC 82-11366. 192p. 1983. lib. bdg. 14.95 (ISBN 0-668-05468-9); pap. 9.95 (ISBN 0-668-05470-0). Arco.

Kahm, H. S. Fifty Big Money Ideas You Can Start & Run with 250 to 5,000 Dollars. LC 81-43741. 264p. 1983. pap. 7.95 (ISBN 0-385-17829-8, Dolp). Doubleday.

Tax Recommendations to Aid Small Business. 1981. pap. 10.00 (ISBN 0-686-84320-7). Am Inst CPA.

SMALL BUSINESS–MANAGEMENT

Adams, Paul. The Complete Legal Guide for Your Small Business. LC 81-11445. (Small Business Management Ser.). 218p. 1982. 19.95 (ISBN 0-471-09436-6). Ronald Pr.

Ames, Michael D. & Wellsfry, Norval L. Small Business Management. (Illus.). 450p. 1983. text ed. 19.95 (ISBN 0-314-69631-8). West Pub.

Blumenthal, Susan. Understanding & Buying a Small Business Computer. Date not set. pap. 8.95 (ISBN 0-672-21890-9). Sams.

Clark, Douglas L. Starting a Successful Business on the West Coast. 194p. (Orig.). 1982. pap. 12.95 (ISBN 0-88908-910-8). Self Counsel Pr.

Coltman, Michael M. Financial Control for the Small Business: A Practical Primer for Keeping a Tighter Rein on Your Profits & Cash Flow. 12/1982 ed. (Illus.). 119p. (Orig.). pap. 5.50 (ISBN 0-88908-911-6). Self Counsel Pr.

Curtis, David A. Strategic Planning for Smaller Business: Improving Corporate Performance & Personal Reward. LC 82-48171. 224p. 1983. 21.95x (ISBN 0-669-06011-9). Lexington Bks.

Goldstein, Arnold S. Complete Guide to Buying & Selling a Business. (Small Business Management Ser.). 310p. 1983. 23.95 (ISBN 0-471-87091-9). Ronald Pr.

Goldstein, Phyllis J. How to Start a Successful, Money-Making "Business" while Attending College. (Illus.). 48p. (Orig.). 1982. pap. 6.95 (ISBN 0-910481-00-8). Money-Maker.

Goodrich, Donna. How to Set Up & Run a Typing Service. (Small Business Ser.). 160p. 1983. pap. text ed. 8.95 (ISBN 0-471-86858-2). Wiley.

Meredith, G. Small Business Management in Australia. 2nd ed. 352p. 1982. 18.50 (ISBN 0-07-451006-1). McGraw.

Murdick, Robert. Production-Operations Management for Small Business. 150p. (Orig.). 1981. pap. text ed. 9.95 (ISBN 0-942280-00-8). Pub Horizons.

Newcomb, Duane. Fortune-Building Secrets of the Rich. LC 82-18837. 215p. 1983. pap. 4.95 (ISBN 0-13-329102-2, Reward). P-H.

Ownership & Management of Family Business: An International Comparison. 29p. 1982. pap. 5.00 (ISBN 92-808-0414-6, TUNU 194, UNU). Unipub.

Paulsen, Timothy. Collection Techniques for the Small Business: A Practical Guide to Collection Overdue Accounts. 2nd ed. (Illus.). 112p. 1983. pap. write for info. (ISBN 0-88908-559-5). Self Counsel Pr.

Smith, Randy B. Setting Up Shop. 288p. 1983. pap. 6.95 (ISBN 0-446-37533-0). Warner Bks.

Stillman, Richard J. Small Business Management: How to Start & Stay in Business. 1982. 18.95 (ISBN 0-316-81608-6); pap. 10.95 (ISBN 0-316-81609-4). Little.

Sullivan, Daniel J. & Lane, Joseph F. Small Business Management: A Practical Approach. 2nd ed. 480p. 1983. text ed. write for info. (ISBN 0-697-08089-7); instr's manual avail. (ISBN 0-697-08181-8). Wm C Brown.

SMALL COMPUTERS

see Minicomputers

SMALL GROUPS

see also Group Relations Training

Blumberg, Herbert H. & Hare, A. Paul. Small Groups & Social Interactions, Vol. 2. 750p. 1983. write for info. (ISBN 0-471-90091-5, Pub. by Wiley-Interscience). Wiley.

SMALL PRESSES

see Little Presses

SMELL

see also Odors

Murphy, Wendy B. Touch, Smell, Taste, Sight & Hearing. LC 82-5738. (Library of Health). lib. bdg. 18.60 (ISBN 0-8094-3799-6, Pub. by Time-Life). Silver.

SMELTING

see also Electrometallurgy; Metallurgy

Ruddle, R. W. Difficulties Encountered in Smelting in the Lead Blast Furnace. 56p. 1957. 11.50 (ISBN 0-686-38297-8). IMM North Am.

SMITH, ADAM, 1723-1790

Campbell, R. H. & Skinner, A. S. Adam Smith. LC 82-3308. 231p. 1982. 25.00x (ISBN 0-312-00423-0). St Martin.

Emerton, Wolseley P. An Abridgment of Adam Smith's Inquiry into the Nature & Causes of the Wealth of Nations. 406p. Repr. of 1881 ed. lib. bdg. 65.00 (ISBN 0-89987-217-4). Darby Bks.

Smith, Adam. Lectures on Historic & Belles Lettres. Bryce, J. C., ed. (The Glasgow Edition of the Works & Correspondence of Adam Smith). 416p. 1982. 48.00x (ISBN 0-19-828186-2). Oxford U Pr.

SMITH, BESSIE, 1898-1937

Brooks, Edward. The Bessie Smith Companion. (Roots of Jazz Ser.). xx, 250p. 1983. lib. bdg. 22.50 (ISBN 0-306-76202-1). Da Capo.

SMITH CHARTS

Smith, Phillip H. Electronic Applications of the Smith Chart. LC 82-14829. 250p. 1983. Repr. of 1969 ed. lib. bdg. price not set (ISBN 0-89874-552-7). Krieger.

SMITHSONIAN INSTITUTION

Klapthor, Margaret B. The First Ladies Hall. LC 73-8675. (Illus.). pap. 2.95 (ISBN 0-87474-133-5). Smithsonian.

Minter-Dowd, Christine. Finders' Guide to Decorative Arts in the Smithsonian Institution. (Finders' Guides to the Collections in the Smithsonian Institution Ser.: Vol. 2). (Illus.). 212p. 1983. text ed. 19.95x (ISBN 0-87474-636-1); pap. text ed. 9.95x (ISBN 0-87474-637-X). Smithsonian.

Oehser, Paul H. The Smithsonian Institution. (Library of Federal Departments, Agencies, & Systems). 350p. 1983. lib. bdg. 25.00 (ISBN 0-86531-300-8). Westview.

SMOG

Photochemical Smog: Contribution of Volatile Organic Compounds. 98p. 1982. pap. 9.50 (ISBN 92-64-12297-4). OECD.

SMOG CONTROL DEVICES (MOTOR VEHICLES)

see Motor Vehicles–Pollution Control Devices

SMOKED FOODS COOKERY

see Cookery (Smoked Foods)

SMOKING

see also Tobacco-Pipes

The Advantages of Smoking. (Blank Books Ser.). 128p. 1982. cancelled (ISBN 0-939944-11-1). Marmac Pub.

Dunton, Sabina M. & Fanning, Melody S. Smoking: Facilitator's Manual. McNeely, Richard A., ed. (Well Aware About Health Risk Reduction Ser.). (Illus.). 186p. (Orig.). 1982. 29.95 (ISBN 0-943562-51-1). Well Aware.

--Smoking: Workbook. McNeely, Richard A., ed. (Well Aware About Health Risk Redution Ser.). (Illus.). 109p. (Orig.). 1982. pap. 7.95 (ISBN 0-943562-52-X). Well Aware.

Hyde, Margaret O. Know About Smoking. (Know About Bks.). (gr. 4-8). 1983. 8.95 (ISBN 0-07-031671-6). McGraw.

Ogle, Jane. The Stop Smoking Diet. 168p. 1983. pap. 5.95 (ISBN 0-87131-410-X). M Evans.

Shephard, Roy J. The Risks of Passive Smoking. (Illus.). 196p. 1982. text ed. 27.95x (ISBN 0-19-520393-3). Oxford U Pr.

SMOKING–PHYSIOLOGICAL EFFECT

see Tobacco–Physiological Effect

SMOOTHING FILTERS (MATHEMATICS)

see Digital Filters (Mathematics)

SMORGASBORD

see Buffets (Cookery)

SMRTI LITERATURE

see Sanskrit Literature

SNACK FOODS

Gibbons, Barbara. Slim Gourmet Sweets & Treats. LC 82-47737. 320p. 1982. 14.37i (ISBN 0-06-015057-2, HarpT). Har-Row.

Lee, Gary. Wok Appetizers & Light Snacks. (Illus.). 182p. (Orig.). 1982. pap. 5.95 (ISBN 0-911954-67-8). Nitty Gritty.

Majors, Judith S. Sugar Free...Sweets & Treats. LC 82-73049. 1982. pap. 4.95 (ISBN 0-9602238-6-X). Apple Pr.

Snack Foods. 1982. 475.00 (ISBN 0-686-38417-2, A137). Busn Trend.

Spitler, Sue & Hauser, Nao. The Popcorn Lover's Book. (Illus.). 96p. (Orig.). 1983. pap. 3.95 (ISBN 0-8092-5542-1). Contemp Bks.

Warren, Jean. Super Snacks. (Illus.). 64p. (Orig.). 1982. pap. 3.95 (ISBN 0-686-82677-9). Warren Pub.

SNAILS

Kerney & Cameron. A Field Guide to the Land Snails of Britain & North West Europe. 29.95 (ISBN 0-686-42776-9, Collins Pub England). Greene.

SNAKE VENOM

Russell, Findlay. Snake Venom Poisoning. LC 83-3134. (Illus.). 576p. 1983. Repr. of 1980 ed. text ed. 57.50x (ISBN 0-87936-015-1). Scholium Intl.

SNAKES

see also Poisonous Snakes; also particular kinds of snakes, e.g. Rattlesnakes

Fitzsimons. A Field Guide to the Snakes of Southern Africa. 29.95 (ISBN 0-686-42782-3, Collins Pub England). Greene.

Freiberg, Marcos. Snakes of South America. (Illus.). 192p. 1982. 14.95 (ISBN 0-87666-912-7, PS-758). TFH Pubns.

Haast, William E. & Anderson, Robert. Complete Guide to Snakes of Florida. LC 81-80463. (Illus.). 139p. Date not set. pap. 8.95 (ISBN 0-686-84307-X). Banyan Bks.

Linzey, Donald W. Snakes of Alabama. (Illus.). 136p. 1979. 9.95 (ISBN 0-87397-091-8). Strode.

SNARE DRUM

see Drum

SNOOKER

Rafferty, Jean. The Cruel Game: The Inside Story of Snooker. (Illus.). 160p. 1983. 22.50 (ISBN 0-241-10950-7, Pub. by Hamish Hamilton England); pap. 14.95 (ISBN 0-241-10951-5). David & Charles.

SNOW, CHARLES PERCY, SIR, 1905-

Snow, Phillip. Stranger & Brother: A Portrait of C. P. Snow. (Illus.). 256p. 1983. 14.95 (ISBN 0-684-17801-X, ScribT). Scribner.

SNOW, EDGAR, 1905-1972

Xing, Wang, ed. China Remembers Edgar Snow. (Illus.). 79p. (Orig.). 1982. pap. 1.95 (ISBN 0-8351-1025-7). China Bks.

SNOW, LORENZO, 1814-1901

Gibbons, Francis M. Lorenzo Snow: Spiritual Giant, Prophet of God. (Illus.). 247p. 1982. 8.95 (ISBN 0-87747-936-4). Deseret Bk.

SNOWPLOW EFFECT

see Plasma Dynamics

SNUFF-BOXES AND BOTTLES

Ford, John G. Chinese Snuff Bottles: The Edward Choate O'Dell Collection. LC 82-83402. (Illus.). 80p. 1982. Casebound 22.50x (ISBN 0-9609668-0-3). Intl Chi Snuff.

SOAP AND SOAP TRADE

see also Cleaning Compounds; Detergents, Synthetic

The Market For Soap & Detergents. 1981. 395.00 (ISBN 0-686-38438-5, 699). Busn Trend.

SOAP OPERAS

Bonderoff, Jason. The Soap Opera Trivia Quiz Book. 1982. pap. 2.95 (ISBN 0-451-11750-6, AE1750, Sig). NAL.

SOCCER

Batty, Eric G., ed. International Football (Soccer) Book, No. 24. 144p. 1983. text ed. 23.50x (ISBN 0-285-62533-0, SpS). Sportshelf.

Cirino, Antonio. U. S. Soccer vs the World. 300p. (Orig.). 1983. pap. 9.95 (ISBN 0-910641-00-5). Damon Pr.

Illustrated Soccer Rules. (Illus.). 128p. (Orig.). 1983. pap. 3.95 (ISBN 0-8092-5520-0). Contemp Bks.

Kane, Basil. The Official Chicago Sting Book. (Illus.). 160p. (Orig.). 1983. pap. 8.95 (ISBN 0-8092-5634-7). Contemp Bks.

Resource Guide to Team Soccer for the Mentally Handicapped. 80p. 1971. 4.50 (ISBN 0-88314-152-3). AAHPERD.

Soccer 1982-83. (NAGWS Sports Guides Ser.). 3.50 (ISBN 0-88314-087-X). AAHPERD.

Soccer 1982-84. (Tips & Techniques Bks.). 4.95 (ISBN 0-88314-193-0). AAHPERD.

SOCCER–HISTORY

Lever, Janet. Soccer Madness. 200p. 1983. 17.50 (ISBN 0-226-47382-1). U of Chicago Pr.

Taylor, Frank. The Day a Team Died. 192p. 1983. 23.50x (ISBN 0-392-16929-0, SpS). Sportshelf.

SOCCER COACHING

Cook, Malcolm. Soccer Coaching & Team Management. (Illus.). 160p. (Orig.). 1983. pap. 7.95 (ISBN 0-7158-0795-1, Pub. by EP Publishing England). Sterling.

Wade, Allen. Football (Soccer) Association Guide to Training & Coaching. 1982. 17.95 (ISBN 0-434-83550-1, Pub. by Heinemann). David & Charles.

SOCIAL ACCOUNTING

see Gross National Product; National Income–Accounting

SOCIAL ACTION

see also Social Service

Patton, Michael Q. Practical Evaluation. (Illus.). 320p. 1982. 25.00 (ISBN 0-8039-1904-2); pap. 12.50. Sage.

SOCIAL ALIENATION

see Alienation (Social Psychology)

SOCIAL ASPECTS

see subdivision Social Aspects under subjects

SOCIAL CASE WORK

see also Counseling; Family Social Work; Interviewing; Marriage Counseling; Parole; Probation; School Social Work; Social Work with Youth; Social Workers

Gambrill, Eileen. Casework: A Competency-Based Approach. (Illus.). 448p. 1983. 20.95 (ISBN 0-13-119446-1). P-H.

Ginsberg, Leon H. The Practice of Social Work in Public Welfare. LC 82-71888. 1983. 18.95 (ISBN 0-02-911760-7). Free Pr.

Turner, Francis J., ed. Differential Diagnosis & Treatment in Social Work. 3rd, rev. ed. LC 82-48390. 1983. 24.95 (ISBN 0-02-932990-6). Free Pr.

SOCIAL CASE WORK–EXAMINATIONS, QUESTIONS, ETC.
Rudman, Jack. Casework Supervisor. (Career Examination Ser.: C-2932). (Cloth bdg. avail. on request). pap. 12.00 (ISBN 0-8373-2932-9). Natl Learning.
--Caseworker Aide. (Career Examination Ser.: C-419). (Cloth bdg. avail. on request). pap. 10.00 (ISBN 0-8373-0419-9). Natl Learning.
SOCIAL CASEWORK–STUDY AND TEACHING
see Social Work Education
SOCIAL CHANGE
Here are entered works on the theory of social change.
see also Community Development; Industry–Social Aspects; Social Evolution
Castells, Manuel. The City & the Grassroots: A Cross-Cultural Theory of Urban Social Movements. LC 82-40099. (California Ser. in Urban Development: Vol. 2). (Illus.). 600p. 1983. 38.50x (ISBN 0-520-04756-7). U of Cal Pr.
Czudnowski, Moshe M., ed. Political Elites & Social Change: Studies in Elite Roles & Attitudes. (International Yearbook for Studies of Leaders & Leadership). 300p. 1983. price not set (ISBN 0-87580-093-9); pap. price not set (ISBN 0-87580-530-2). N Ill U Pr.
Gardner, Roberta A. Social Change. 1977. pap. 15.50 (ISBN 0-395-30599-3). HM.
Lindenfeld, Frank & Rothschild-Whitt, Joyce, eds. Workplace Democracy & Social Change. LC 82-80137. 456p. 1982. 20.00 (ISBN 0-87558-101-3, Pub. by Extending Hor Bks); pap. 12.00 (ISBN 0-87558-102-1). Porter Sargent.
Marris, Peter. Loss & Change. (Reports of the Institute of Community Studies). 184p. 1974. 15.95 (ISBN 0-7100-7890-0). Routledge & Kegan.
Segalla, Rosemary A. Departure from Traditional Roles: Mid-Life Women Break the Daisy Chains. Nathan, Peter E., ed. LC 82-20089. (Research in Clinical Psychology Ser.: No. 5). 164p. 1982. 34.95 (ISBN 0-8357-1386-5). Univ Microfilms.
Shils, Edward. Tradition. LC 80-21643. viii, 334p. 1981. pap. 10.95 (ISBN 0-226-75326-3). U of Chicago Pr.
Shoham, Giora S. & Rahav, Giora. The Mark of Cain: The Stigma Theory of Crime & Social Deviance. LC 82-3173. 240p. 1982. 27.50x (ISBN 0-312-51446-8). St Martin.
Twain. Creating Change in Social Settings: Planned Program Development. 224p. 1983. 25.95 (ISBN 0-03-062391-X). Praeger.
SOCIAL CLASSES
see also Elite (Social Sciences); Upper Classes
Calvert, Peter. The Concept of Class. LC 82-10617. 256p. 1982. 22.50x (ISBN 0-312-15918-8). St Martin.
Carchedi, Guglielmo. Problems in Class Analysis. 300p. (Orig.). 1983. pap. price not set (ISBN 0-7100-9426-4). Routledge & Kegan.
Cottingham, Clement, ed. Race, Poverty & the Urban Underclass. LC 81-47712. (Illus.). 224p. 1982. 24.95x (ISBN 0-669-04730-9). Lexington Bks.
Giddens, A. & Held, D. Class, Conflict, & Power. 1982. 55.00x (ISBN 0-333-32289-4, Pub. by Macmillan England). State Mutual Bk.
Nelson, Daniel N., ed. Communism & the Politics of Inequalities. LC 81-48525. 1983. write for info. (ISBN 0-669-05415-1). Lexington Bks.
Yip, George S. Barriers to Entry. LC 81-47993. 240p. 1982. 24.95x (ISBN 0-669-05225-6). Lexington Bks.
SOCIAL CLASSES–EUROPE
Best, Geoffrey. War & Society in Revolutionary Europe 1770-1870. LC 82-3261. 336p. 1982. 27.50x (ISBN 0-312-85551-6). St Martin.
SOCIAL COMPACT
see Social Contract
SOCIAL CONDITIONS
see Social History
SOCIAL CONFLICT
see also Social Classes
Giddens, A. & Held, D. Class, Conflict, & Power. 1982. 55.00x (ISBN 0-333-32289-4, Pub. by Macmillan England). State Mutual Bk.
Korpi, Walter. The Democratic Class Struggle. 300p. 1983. 27.95 (ISBN 0-7100-9436-1). Routledge & Kegan.
Smith, Kenwyn K. Groups in Conflict: Prisons & Disguise. 272p. 1982. pap. text ed. 10.95 (ISBN 0-8403-2752-8). Kendall-Hunt.
SOCIAL CONFORMITY
see Conformity
SOCIAL CONTRACT
Gildin, Hilail. Rousseau's Social Contract: The Design of the Argument. LC 82-20148. 240p. 1983. lib. bdg. 22.50x (ISBN 0-226-29368-8). U of Chicago Pr.
SOCIAL CUSTOMS
see Manners and Customs;
also subdivision Social Life and Customs under ethnic groups, e.g. Indians, Jews and under names of countries, cities, etc.
SOCIAL DEMOCRACY
see Socialism
SOCIAL DEMOCRATIC PARTY OF RUSSIA
Trapeznikov, S. P. Leninism & the Agrarian & Peasant Question, 2 vols. 1114p. 1981. Set. 15.95 (ISBN 0-8285-2491-2, Pub. by Progress Pubs USSR). Imported Pubns.
SOCIAL DEVIANCE
see Deviant Behavior
SOCIAL ECOLOGY
see Human Ecology
SOCIAL EQUALITY
see Equality
SOCIAL ETHICS
see also Altruism; Christian Ethics; Crime and Criminals; Political Ethics; Sexual Ethics; Social Problems; Sociology, Christian; Wealth, Ethics Of
Hughey, Michael W. Civil Religion & Moral Order: Theoretical & Historical Dimensions. LC 82-15429. (Contributions in Sociology Ser.: No. 43). 256p. 1983. lib. bdg. 29.95 (ISBN 0-313-23522-8, HUR/). Greenwood.
Oldenquist, Andrew. Normative Behavior. LC 82-23699. (Illus.). 200p. (Orig.). 1983. lib. bdg. 21.75 (ISBN 0-8191-2965-8); pap. text ed. 10.00 (ISBN 0-8191-2966-6). U Pr of Amer.
Skurski, Roger. New Directions in Economic Justice. 304p. 1983. text ed. 20.95x (ISBN 0-268-01460-4); pap. text ed. 10.95x (ISBN 0-268-01461-2). U of Notre Dame Pr.
Stockdale, James B. & Hatfield, Mark O. The Ethics of Citizenship. (The Andrew R. Cecil Lectures on Moral Values in a Free Society Ser.: Vol. II). 167p. 1981. 9.95x (ISBN 0-292-72038-6). U of Tex Pr.
Tillich, Paul. The Socialist Decision. Sherman, Franklin, tr. from Ger. LC 82-21913. 224p. 1983. pap. text ed. 9.75 (ISBN 0-8191-2911-9). U Pr of Amer.
SOCIAL EVOLUTION
see also Social Change; Sociobiology
Corning, P. A. The Synergism Hypothesis: A Theory of Progressive Evolution. 1983. pap. price not set (ISBN 0-07-013172-4). McGraw.
Dixon, Terence & Lucas, Martin. The Human Race. LC 82-14280. (New Press Ser.). 256p. 1982. 24.95 (ISBN 0-07-017080-0). McGraw.
Eldredge, Niles & Tattersall, Ian. The Myths of Human Evolution. LC 82-1118. 192p. 1982. 16.95 (ISBN 0-231-05144-1). Columbia U Pr.
Lumsden, Charles J. & Wilson, Edward O. Promethean Fire: Reflections on the Origin of Mind. (Illus.). 256p. 1983. 17.50 (ISBN 0-674-71445-8). Harvard U Pr.
Swanson, Carl P. Ever-Expanding Horizons: The Dual Informational Sources of Human Evolution. LC 82-21750. (Illus.). 132p. 1983. lib. bdg. 13.50x (ISBN 0-87023-391-2); pap. 7.50 (ISBN 0-87023-392-0). U of Mass Pr.
SOCIAL GROUP WORK
see also Meetings; Social Work with Youth
Deichman, Elizabeth S. & O'Kane, C. P. Working with the Elderly: A Training Manual. Rev. ed. 119p. (Orig.). 1980. pap. text ed. 8.95 (ISBN 0-932910-32-7). Potentials Development.
Hirschhorn, Larry. Cutting Back: Retrenchment & Redevelopment in Human & Community Services. LC 82-49038. (Social & Behavioral Science & Management Ser.). 1983. text ed. price not set (ISBN 0-87589-568-9). Jossey-Bass.
SOCIAL GROUPS
see also Age Groups; Elite (Social Sciences); Leadership; Small Groups; Social Isolation; Social Participation; Social Psychology; Social Values
Blau, Peter M. Exchange & Power in Social Life. LC 64-23827. 352p. 1964. 29.95x (ISBN 0-471-08030-6). Wiley.
Johnson, David W. & Johnson, Frank P. Joining Together: Group Theory & Group Skills. 2nd ed. LC 74-23698. 480p. 1982. 17.95 (ISBN 0-13-510396-7). P-H.
Lorr, Maurice. Cluster Analysis for Social Scientists: Techniques for Analyzing & Simplifying Complex Blocks of Data. LC 82-49283. (Social & Behavioral Science Ser.). 1983. text ed. price not set (ISBN 0-87589-566-2). Jossey-Bass.
Smith, Kenwyn K. Groups in Conflict: Prisons & Disguise. 272p. 1982. pap. text ed. 10.95 (ISBN 0-8403-2752-8). Kendall-Hunt.
SOCIAL GROUPS–STUDY AND TEACHING
Bradford, Leland P., et al, eds. T-Group Theory & Laboratory Method: Innovation in Re-Education. LC 64-11499. 498p. 1964. 32.95x (ISBN 0-471-09510-9). Wiley.
SOCIAL HISTORY
see also Church and Social Problems; Labor and Laboring Classes; Moral Conditions; Poor; Rural Conditions; Social Indicators; Social Movements; Social Policy; Social Problems; Social Surveys; Technology and Civilization; Urbanization
also subdivision Social Conditions under names of countries, e.g. Italy–Social Conditions
Crump, Donald J., ed. Preserving America's Past. LC 81-48076. (Special Publications: No. 17). 200p. 1983. 6.95 (ISBN 0-87044-415-8); lib. bdg. 8.50 (ISBN 0-87044-420-4). Natl Geog.
Gardner, James B. & Adams, George R., eds. Ordinary People & Everyday Life: Perspectives on the New Social History. 1983. text ed. price not set (ISBN 0-910050-66-X). AASLH.
SOCIAL HISTORY–20TH CENTURY
Monaco, Paul. Modern European Culture & Consciousness, Eighteen Seventy through Nineteen Seventy: Interdisciplinary Perspectives in Social History. LC 82-10487. 182p. 1983. 30.50 (ISBN 0-87395-702-4); pap. 8.95 (ISBN 0-87395-703-2). State U NY Pr.
Report on the World Social Situation. 210p. 1983. pap. 15.00 (ISBN 0-686-43287-8, UN 82/4/2, UN). Unipub.
SOCIAL HYGIENE
see Prostitution; Public Health; Venereal Diseases
also related subjects referred to under these headings
SOCIAL INDICATORS
Measuring Disability, Victimisation, the Use of Time, & Housing Conditions. (The OECD Social Indicator Development Program Special Studies: No. 5-8). 150p. (Orig.). 1982. pap. 9.75x (ISBN 92-64-12337-7). OECD.
Powers, Mary G. Measures of Socio-Economic Status: Current Issues. (AAAS Selected Symposium 81). 205p. 1982. lib. bdg. 20.00x (ISBN 0-86531-395-4). Westview.
SOCIAL INSTITUTIONS
Here are entered works on interrelated systems of social roles, norms, or processes organized for the satisfaction of an important social need or function, e.g. family, economy, education.
see also Social Structure
Barber, Bernard. The Logic & Limits of Trust. 203p. 1983. 19.00x (ISBN 0-8135-0958-0). Rutgers U Pr.
SOCIAL INSURANCE
see Social Security
SOCIAL INTERACTION
see also Group Relations Training; Interaction Analysis in Education
Blumberg, Herbert H. & Hare, A. Paul. Small Groups & Social Interaction, Vol. 1. 750p. 1983. write for info. (ISBN 0-471-10242-3, Pub. by Wiley-Interscience). Wiley.
--Small Groups & Social Interactions, Vol. 2. 750p. 1983. write for info. (ISBN 0-471-90091-5, Pub. by Wiley-Interscience). Wiley.
SOCIAL ISOLATION
see also Alienation (Social Psychology); Loneliness
Shoman, S. Giora. The Violence of Silence: The Impossibility of Dialogue. 300p. 1982. 27.00 (ISBN 0-905927-06-0). Transaction Bks.
Thom, Gary B. The Human Nature of Social Maladies: Alienation, Anomie, Ambivalence. 200p. 1983. text ed. 23.95x (ISBN 0-86598-105-1). Allanheld.
SOCIAL MEDICINE
Waddell, Charles. Faith, Hope & Luck: A Sociological Study of Children Growing Up With a Life-Threatening Illness. LC 82-24871. 104p. (Orig.). 1983. lib. bdg. 18.75 (ISBN 0-8191-3011-7); pap. text ed. 8.25 (ISBN 0-8191-3012-5). U Pr of Amer.
Zola, Irving K. Socio-Medical Inquiries: Recollections, Reflections & Reconsiderations. 1983. write for info. (ISBN 0-87722-303-3). Temple U Pr.
SOCIAL MOVEMENTS
Castells, Manuel. The City & the Grassroots: A Cross-Cultural Theory of Urban Social Movements. LC 82-40099. (California Ser. in Urban Development: Vol. 2). (Illus.). 600p. 1983. 38.50x (ISBN 0-520-04756-7). U of Cal Pr.
Price, Jerome B. The Antinuclear Movement. (Social Movements: Past & Present). 1982. lib. bdg. 15.95 (ISBN 0-8057-9705-X, Twayne). G K Hall.
Thomis, Malcolm & Grimmett, Jennifer. Women in Protest Eighteen Hundred to Eighteen Fifty. LC 81-21290. 166p. 1982. 25.00x (ISBN 0-312-88746-9). St Martin.
SOCIAL PARTICIPATION
see also Small Groups; Social Groups
Ancona, George. Team Work. LC 82-45579. (Illus.). 48p. (gr. 3-6). 1983. 10.53i (ISBN 0-690-04247-7, TYC-J); PLB 10.89g (ISBN 0-690-04248-5). Har-Row.
KDaneke, Gregory A. & Garcia, Margot W., eds. Public Involvement & Social Impact Assessment. (Social Impact Assessment Series: No. 9). 300p. 1983. lib. bdg. 27.50x (ISBN 0-86531-624-4). Westview.
SOCIAL PERCEPTION
see also Group Relations Training; Personality Assessment
Higgins, E. Tory & Hartup, Willard W., eds. Social Cognition & Social Development: A Sociocultural Perspective. LC 82-12897. (Cambridge Studies in Social & Emotional Development: No. 5). 352p. Date not set. price not set (ISBN 0-521-24587-7). Cambridge U Pr.
Roloff, Michael E. & Berger, Charles R. Social Cognition & Communication. 352p. 1982. 29.95 (ISBN 0-8039-1898-4); pap. 14.95 (ISBN 0-8039-1899-2). Sage.
SOCIAL PLANNING
see Social Policy
SOCIAL POLICY
see also Economic Policy; Economic Security; Education and State; Land Reform; Medical Policy; Social Action; Welfare Economics
also subdivision Social Policy under names of countries, states, cities, etc.
Atkinson, A. B. Social Justice & Public Policy. 480p. 1982. 37.50x (ISBN 0-262-01067-4). MIT Pr.
Auletta, Ken. The Underclass. LC 82-40433. 368p. 1983. pap. 6.95 (ISBN 0-394-71388-5, Vin). Random.
Ecklein, J. L. & Lauffer, A. Community Organizers & Social Planners: A Volume of Cases & Illustrative Materials. LC 75-171912. (Community Organization Ser.). 378p. 1972. pap. 21.95x (ISBN 0-471-22980-6). Wiley.
Eversley, David & Kollmann, Wolfgang. Population Change & Social Planning. 600p. 1982. text ed. 98.50 (ISBN 0-7131-6345-3). E Arnold.
Eyestone, Robert. From Social Issues to Public Policy. LC 78-13334. (Viewpoints on American Politics Ser.). 197p. 1978. pap. text ed. 11.95 (ISBN 0-471-24978-5). Wiley.
Gordon, Alan. Economics & Social Policy: An Introduction. (Illus.). 224p. 1982. text ed. 24.95x (ISBN 0-85520-527-X, Pub. by Martin Robertson England). Biblio Dist.
Helpman, Elhanan, ed. Social Policy Evaluation: An Economic Perspective. LC 82-22681. (Symposium). Date not set. price not set (ISBN 0-12-339660-3). Acad Pr.
Jones, Kathleen & Brown, John. Issues in Social Policy. 2nd ed. 208p. 1983. pap. price not set (ISBN 0-7100-9440-X). Routledge & Kegan.
KDaneke, Gregory A. & Garcia, Margot W., eds. Public Involvement & Social Impact Assessment. (Social Impact Assessment Series: No. 9). 300p. 1983. lib. bdg. 27.50x (ISBN 0-86531-624-4). Westview.
Magill, Robert S. Social Policy in American Society. 192p. 1983. text ed. 19.95 (ISBN 0-89885-138-6). Human Sci Pr.
Mayne, A. J. Fever, Squalor & Vice: Sanitation & Social Policy in Victorian Sydney. LC 82-2054. (Scholars' Library). (Illus.). 263p. 1982. text ed. 34.50x (ISBN 0-7022-1950-9). U of Queensland Pr.
Meyer, Jack A., ed. Meeting Human Needs: Toward a New Public Philosophy. 1982. 34.95 (ISBN 0-8447-1359-7); pap. 13.95 (ISBN 0-8447-1358-9). Am Enterprise.
Moeser, John V., ed. A Virginia Profile Nineteen-Sixty to Two Thousand: Assessing Current Trends & Problems. (Commonwealth Books Public Policy). (Illus.). 290p. (Orig.). 1981. pap. write for info. (ISBN 0-940390-01-9). Comwealth Bks NJ.
Neugarten, Bernice I. Age or Need? Public Policies for Older People. (Sage Focus Editions). (Illus.). 288p. 1982. 25.00 (ISBN 0-8039-1908-5); pap. 12.50 (ISBN 0-8039-1909-3). Sage.
SOCIAL PROBLEMS
see also Charities; Church and Social Problems; Cost and Standard of Living; Crime and Criminals; Discrimination; Divorce; Emigration and Immigration; Family Size; Homelessness; Housing; Juvenile Delinquency; Migrant Labor; Migration, Internal; Old Age Pensions; Poor; Progress; Prostitution; Public Health; Public Welfare; Race Discrimination; Race Relations; Social Action; Social Ethics; Social Surveys; Suicide; Unemployed
Auletta, Ken. The Underclass. LC 82-40433. 368p. 1983. pap. 6.95 (ISBN 0-394-71388-5, Vin). Random.
Bourne, Richard & Levin, Jack. Social Problems: Causes, Consequences, Interventions. (Illus.). 500p. 1983. text ed. 12.95 (ISBN 0-314-69661-X); tchrs.' manual avail. (ISBN 0-314-71081-7). West Pub.
DeFleur. Social Problems in American Society. 1982. 16.95 (ISBN 0-686-84654-0); supplementary materials avail. HM.
Eyestone, Robert. From Social Issues to Public Policy. LC 78-13334. (Viewpoints on American Politics Ser.). 197p. 1978. pap. text ed. 11.95 (ISBN 0-471-24978-5). Wiley.
Henslin, James M. & Light, Donald, Jr. Social Problems. (Illus.). 656p. 1983. text ed. 23.95 (ISBN 0-07-037836-3, C); study guide 8.95 (ISBN 0-07-037839-8). McGraw.
Seidman, Edward, ed. Handbook of Social Intervention. x ed. 736p. 1983. 49.95 (ISBN 0-8039-1971-9). Sage.
SOCIAL PROBLEMS AND THE CHURCH
see Church and Social Problems
SOCIAL PROGRESS
see Progress
SOCIAL PSYCHOLOGY
see also Alienation (Social Psychology); Anomy; Attitude (Psychology); Crowds; Discrimination; Ethnopsychology; Gangs; Interpersonal Relations; Interviewing; Leadership; Minorities; Political Psychology; Prison Psychology; Psychological Warfare; Psychology, Applied; Psychology, Forensic; Public Opinion; Small Groups; Social Conflict; Social Interaction; Social Isolation; Social Movements; Stereotype (Psychology)
Babad, Elisha Y. & Birnbaum, Max. The Social Self: Group Influences on Personal Identity. (Sage Library of Social Research). (Illus.). 320p. 25.00 (ISBN 0-8039-1938-7); pap. 12.50 (ISBN 0-8039-1939-5). Sage.
Back, Kurt W. Social Psychology. LC 76-30835. 498p. 1977. text ed. 27.95 (ISBN 0-471-03983-7); instructor's manual 6.00 (ISBN 0-471-02656-5). Wiley.
Berliner, Arthur K. Psychoanalysis & Society: The Social Thought of Sigmund Freud. LC 82-21932. 216p. (Orig.). 1983. lib. bdg. 20.75 (ISBN 0-8191-2893-7); pap. text ed. 10.50 (ISBN 0-8191-2894-5). U Pr of Amer.
Carley, Michael J. & Derow, Ellan O. Social Impact Assessment: A Cross-Disciplinary Guide to the Literature. (Social Impact Assessment Ser.). 250p. 1983. lib. bdg. 22.50 (ISBN 0-86531-529-9). Westview.

Colgan, Patrick. Comparative Social Recognition. 288p. 1983. 37.50 (ISBN 0-471-09350-5, Pub. by Wiley-Interscience). Wiley.
Eisenberg, Nancy, ed. The Development of Prosocial Behavior. (Developmental Psychology Ser.). 416p. 1982. 35.00 (ISBN 0-12-234980-6). Acad Pr.
Ginsburg, G. P. Emerging Strategies in Social Psychological Research. LC 78-18506. 319p. 1979. 41.00x (ISBN 0-471-99690-4, Pub. by Wiley-Interscience). Wiley.
Goodwin, Leonard. Causes & Cures of Welfare: New Evidence on the Social Psychology of the Poor. LC 82-48634. 224p. 1983. 23.95x (ISBN 0-669-06370-3). Lexington Bks.
Harland, O. H. Some Implications of Social Psychology. 104p. 1982. Repr. of 1928 ed. lib. bdg. 30.00 (ISBN 0-89987-392-8). Darby Bks.
Lee, Benjamin. Psychosocial Theories of the Self. (Path in Psychology). 230p. 1982. 27.50x (ISBN 0-306-41117-2, Plenum Pr). Plenum Pub.
Muensterberger, Werner & Boyer, Bryce L., eds. The Psychoanalytic Study of Society, Vol.5. 400p. 1983. text ed. price not set (ISBN 0-88163-004-7). L Erlbaum Assocs.
Neal, Arthur G. Social Psychology: A Sociology Perspective. 544p. 1983. text ed. 19.95 (ISBN 0-201-05361-6). A-W.
Oldenquist, Andrew. Normative Behavior. LC 82-23699. (Illus.). 200p. (Orig.). 1983. lib. bdg. 21.75 (ISBN 0-8191-2965-8); pap. text ed. 10.00 (ISBN 0-8191-2966-6). U Pr of Amer.
Penrod, Steven. Social Psychology. 704p. 1983. text ed. 23.95 (ISBN 0-13-817924-7). P-H.
Raven, Bertram H. & Rubin, Jeffrey Z. Social Psychology. 2nd ed. 650p. 1983. 15.95x (ISBN 0-471-06225-1); tchr's. ed. avail. (ISBN 0-471-87305-5). Wiley.
Sahakian, W. S. History & Systems of Social Psychology. 1981. 24.50 (ISBN 0-07-054425-5). McGraw.
Sarbin, Theodore R. & Scheibe, Karl. Studies in Social Identity. 416p. 1983. 15.00 (ISBN 0-03-059542-8). Praeger.
Serafica, Felicisima C. Social-Cognitive Development in Context. LC 82-2933. 283p. 1982. text ed. 24.50x (ISBN 0-89862-623-4). Guilford Pr.
Trevor, Aston, et al. Social Relations & Ideas. LC 82-9727. (Past & Present Publications). 352p. Date not set. price not set (ISBN 0-521-25132-X). Cambridge U Pr.
Wexler, Philip. Critical Social Psychology. (Critical Social Thought Ser.). 176p. 1983. 17.50 (ISBN 0-7100-9194-X). Routledge & Kegan.
Wheeler, Ladd, ed. Review of Personality & Social Psychology, No. 3. 3rd ed. (Illus.). 320p. 1982. 25.00 (ISBN 0-8039-1854-2); pap. 12.50 (ISBN 0-8039-1855-0). Sage.

SOCIAL PSYCHOTECHNICS
see Interviewing; Psychology, Applied

SOCIAL REFORM
see Social Problems

SOCIAL REFORMERS
Sproat, John G. The Best Men: Liberal Reformers in the Gilded Age With a New Preface. LC 82-10948. (Phoenix Ser.). 376p. 1983. pap. 9.95 (ISBN 0-226-76990-9). U of Chicago Pr.
Thomas, John L. Alternative America: Henry George, Edward Bellamy, Henry Demarest Lloyd & the Adversary Tradition. (Illus.). 416p. 1983. 25.00x (ISBN 0-674-01676-9). Harvard U Pr.

SOCIAL REFORMERS–GREAT BRITAIN
Brown, Stewart J. Thomas Chalmers & Godly Commonwealth in Scotland. (Illus.). 368p. 1983. 55.00 (ISBN 0-19-213114-1). Oxford U Pr.

SOCIAL SCIENCE
see Social Sciences; Sociology

SOCIAL SCIENCE RESEARCH
see also Communication in the Social Sciences; Sociological Research
Babbie, Earl R. The Practice of Social Research. 3rd ed. 576p. 1982. text ed. 24.95x (ISBN 0-534-01255-8). Wadsworth Pub.
Black, James A. & Champion, Dean J. Methods & Issues in Social Research. LC 75-26659. 445p. 1975. 24.95 (ISBN 0-471-07705-4). Wiley.
Boruch, Robert F. & Cecil, Joe S., eds. Solutions to Ethical & Legal Problems in Social Research: Symposuim. (Quantitative Studies in Social Relations). Date not set. 27.5007615723x (ISBN 0-12-118680-6). Acad Pr.
Hayes, Marilyn. Social Studies Reading. (Reading Ser.). 24p. (gr. 2). 1980. wkbk. 5.00 (ISBN 0-8209-0195-4, RSS-2). ESP.
Justus, Fred. Products of America. (Social Studies Ser.). 24p. (gr. 3-6). 1979. wkbk. 5.00 (ISBN 0-8209-0267-5, POA-1). ESP.
Kallen, D., et al, eds. Social Science Research & Public Policy Making: A Re-Appraisal. (NFER Research Ser.). 370p. 1982. pap. text ed. 16.75x (ISBN 0-85633-246-1, NFER). Humanities.
Outhwaite, William. Concept Formation in Social Science. (International Library of Sociology). 240p. 1983. 30.00 (ISBN 0-7100-9195-8). Routledge & Kegan.
Smith, Sharon. Travel & Transportation. (Social Studies Ser.). 24p. (gr. 5-9). 1976. wkbk. 5.00 (ISBN 0-8209-0247-0, SS-14). ESP.
Spence, Sue & Shepherd, Geoff, eds. Developments in Social Skills Training. Date not set. price not set (ISBN 0-12-656620-8). Acad Pr.
Tripodi, Tony & Fellin, Phillip. The Assessment of Social Research. 2nd ed. LC 82-81419. 210p. 1983. pap. text ed. 12.50x (ISBN 0-87581-285-6). Peacock Pubs.
Van Sickle, Larry. Teaching Poor Kids to Labor: The American Dream & the Impact of Class. 240p. 1983. text ed. 19.95x (ISBN 0-8290-1294-X). Irvington.

SOCIAL SCIENCES
Here are entered general and comprehensive works dealing with sociology, political science, and economics.
see also Conservatism; Human Behavior; Human Ecology; Liberalism; Pluralism (Social Sciences); Power (Social Sciences); Social Change; Statics and Dynamics (Social Sciences)
Bloor, David. Knowledge & Social Imagery. (Routledge Direct Editions). 168p. 1976. 16.50 (ISBN 0-7100-8377-7). Routledge & Kegan.
Bulick, Stephen. Structure & Subject Interaction: Toward a Sociology of Knowledge in the Social Sciences. (Bks in Library & Information Science: Vol. 41). (Illus.). 256p. 1982. 35.00 (ISBN 0-8247-1847-X). Dekker.
Cooper, R. A. & Weekes, A. J. Data, Models & Statistical Analysis. 400p. 1983. text ed. 30.00x (ISBN 0-389-20382-3); pap. text ed. 19.50x (ISBN 0-389-20383-1). B&N Imports.
Higgott, Richard A. Political Development Theory: The Contemporary Debate. LC 82-42718. 140p. 1983. 18.95x (ISBN 0-312-62225-2). St Martin.
Keat, Russell & Urry, John. Social Theory as Science. rev. ed. (International Library of Sociology Ser.). 288p. 1983. pap. 11.95 (ISBN 0-7100-9431-0). Routledge & Kegan.
Kossler, Richard. Sozialverischerungspringzip und Staatszuschusse In der Gesetzlichen Rentenversicherung. 241p. (Ger.). 1982. write for info. (ISBN 3-8204-5749-6). P Lang Pubs.
Maciver, R. M. The Elements of Social Science. 186p. 1982. Repr. of 1921 ed. lib. bdg. 40.00 (ISBN 0-8495-3600-6). Arden Lib.
Mizruchi, Ephraim H. Regulating Society. 224p. 1982. text ed. write for info. (ISBN 0-02-921660-5). Free Pr.
The Role of Social Studies in Education For Peace & Respect For Human Rights in Asia & the Pacific. 87p. 1981. pap. 7.00 (ISBN 0-686-81855-5, UB99, UNESCO). Unipub.

SOCIAL SCIENCES–ADDRESSES, ESSAYS, LECTURES
Andreski, Stanislav, ed. & tr. Max Weber on Capitalism, Bureaucracy & Religion. (A Selection of Texts Ser.). 192p. 1983. text ed. 22.95x (ISBN 0-04-301147-0); pap. text ed. 7.95x (ISBN 0-04-301148-9). Allen Unwin.
Cohen, Robert S. & Wartofsky, Marx. Epistemology, Methodology, & the Social Sciences. 1983. lib. bdg. 48.00 (ISBN 90-277-1454-1, Pub. by Reidel Holland). Kluwer Boston.
Honderich, Ted, ed. Social Ends & Political Means. 190p. 1976. 20.00 (ISBN 0-7100-8370-X). Routledge & Kegan.

SOCIAL SCIENCES–BIBLIOGRAPHY
New American Foundation. Unity in Diversity: An Index to the Publications of Conservative & Libertarian Institutions. Birch, Carol L., ed. LC 82-20552. 284p. 1983. 18.50 (ISBN 0-8108-1599-0). Scarecrow.

SOCIAL SCIENCES–EXAMINATIONS, QUESTIONS, ETC.
Rosenfeld, Helen, et al. Comprehensive Social Studies. (Arco's Regents Review Ser.). 288p. 1983. pap. 3.95 (ISBN 0-668-05699-1, 5699). Arco.
Test Wise Tactics for Higher Scores in Social Studies. 1984. pap. price not set (ISBN 0-8120-2595-4). Barron.

SOCIAL SCIENCES–HISTORY
Morrissett, Irving, ed. Social Studies in the 1980's: A Report of Project SPAN. LC 82-72766. 147p. (Orig.). 1982. pap. text ed. 8.75 (ISBN 0-87120-114-3). Assn Supervision.

SOCIAL SCIENCES–MATHEMATICAL MODELS
Goldberg, Samuel. Introduction to Difference Equations: With Illustrative Examples from Economics, Psychology & Sociology. LC 58-10223. (Illus.). 1958. pap. 18.50x (ISBN 0-471-31051-4). Wiley.
--Probability in Social Science. (Mathematical Modelling & Applications Ser.: Vol. 1). 186p. 1983. pap. text ed. write for info. (ISBN 3-7643-3089-9). Birkhauser.
Katzner, Donald W. Analysis Without Measurement. LC 82-4469. 366p. Date not set. price not set (ISBN 0-521-24847-7). Cambridge U Pr.

SOCIAL SCIENCES–METHODOLOGY
see also Communication in the Social Sciences
Babbie, Earl R. The Practice of Social Research. 3rd ed. 576p. 1982. text ed. 24.95x (ISBN 0-534-01255-8). Wadsworth Pub.
Falco, Maria J. Truth & Meaning in Political Science: An Introduction to Political Inquiry. 2nd ed. LC 82-25095. 160p. 1983. pap. text ed. 9.75 (ISBN 0-8191-3048-6). U Pr of Amer.
Katzner, Donald W. Analysis Without Measurement. LC 82-4469. 366p. Date not set. price not set (ISBN 0-521-24847-7). Cambridge U Pr.
Runciman, W. G. A Treatise on Social Theory, Vol. 1. LC 82-4493. (Illus.). 400p. Date not set. price not set (ISBN 0-521-24906-6). Cambridge U Pr.

SOCIAL SCIENCES–READERS
see Readers–Social Studies

SOCIAL SCIENCES–RESEARCH
see Social Science Research

SOCIAL SCIENCES–STATISTICS
Kalton, G. Introduction to Statistical Ideas for Social Scientists. 1966. pap. 4.50x (ISBN 0-412-08460-0, Pub. by Chapman & Hall England). Methuen Inc.

SOCIAL SCIENCES–STATISTICAL METHODS
Goldberg, Samuel. Probability in Social Science. (Mathematical Modelling & Applications Ser.: Vol. 1). 186p. 1983. pap. text ed. write for info. (ISBN 3-7643-3089-9). Birkhauser.
Kurtz, Norman R. Introduction to Social Statistics. (Illus.). 416p. 1983. text ed. 22.95x (ISBN 0-07-035676-9, C); write for info. instr's manual (ISBN 0-07-035677-7). McGraw.

SOCIAL SCIENCES–STUDY AND TEACHING
Conley, Diane, ed. Peterson's Guides to Graduate Study: Humanities & Social Sciences, 1983. 1200p. 1982. pap. 18.95 (ISBN 0-87866-186-7). Petersons Guides.
Davis, James E., ed. Planning a Social Studies Program: Activities, Guidelines, & Resources. 2nd ed. 1982. pap. write for info. (ISBN 0-89994-266-0). Soc Sci Ed.
Ehman, Lee & Mehlinger, Howard. Toward Effective Instruction in Secondary Social Studies. LC 82-21894. (Illus.). 476p. 1983. pap. text ed. 18.75 (ISBN 0-8191-2916-X). U Pr of Amer.
Greenwald, G. Dale & Superka, Douglas P. Evaluating Social Studies Programs: Focus on Law-Related Education. 240p. (Orig.). 1982. pap. 14.95 (ISBN 0-89994-277-6). Soc Sci Ed.
Maxim, George M. Social Studies & the Elementary School Child. 544p. 1983. text ed. 18.95 (ISBN 0-675-20017-2). Additional supplements may be obtained from publisher. Merrill.
Newby, James E. Teaching Faculty in Black Colleges & Universities: A Survey of Selected Social Science Disciplines, 1977-1978. LC 82-17620. (Illus.). 112p. (Orig.). 1983. lib. bdg. 18.50 (ISBN 0-8191-2787-6); pap. text ed. 8.25 (ISBN 0-8191-2788-4). U Pr of Amer.
Singleton, Laurel R., ed. Data Book of Social Studies Materials & Resources, Vol. 8. (Data Book Ser.). 192p. 1983. pap. 10.00 (ISBN 0-89994-279-2). Soc Sci Ed.
--Tips for Social Studies Teachers: Activities from ERIC. 192p. 1983. pap. 10.95 (ISBN 0-89994-280-6). Soc Sci Ed.
Sloshberg, Willard & Nessmith, William C. Contemporary American Society: An Introduction to Social Science. (Illus.). 600p. 1983. pap. text ed. 13.95 (ISBN 0-314-69671-7). West Pub.
Walker, Hill M. & McConnell, Scott. The Walker Social Skills Curriculum: ACEPTS. 250p. (Orig.). 1983. pap. text ed. write for info. (ISBN 0-936104-30-9, 0370). Pro Ed.

SOCIAL SCIENCES–STUDY AND TEACHING (ELEMENTARY)
Brooks, Bearl. Shelter & the Family. (Social Studies Ser.). 24p. (gr. 4-6). 1976. wkbk. 5.00 (ISBN 0-8209-0249-7, SS-16). ESP.
Hayes, Marilyn. Jumbo Social Studies Yearbook: Grade 5. (Jumbo Social Studies). 96p. (gr. 5). 1981. 14.00 (ISBN 0-8209-0077-X, JSSY 4). ESP.
Patty, Catherine. Jumbo Social Studies Yearbook: Grade 3. (Jumbo Social Studies). 96p. (gr. 3). 1980. 14.00 (ISBN 0-8209-0075-3, JSSY 3). ESP.
--Jumbo Social Studies Yearbook: Grade 4. (Jumbo Social Studies). 96p. (gr. 4). 1981. 14.00 (ISBN 0-8209-0076-1, JSSY 4). ESP.
--Jumbo Social Studies Yearbook: Grade 6. (Jumbo Social Studies). 96p. (gr. 6). 1981. 14.00 (ISBN 0-8209-0078-8, JSSY 6). ESP.

SOCIAL SCIENCES–TEXTBOOKS
see also Readers–Social Studies
Fisher, J. & Downey, J. U. S. Studies Program. Irvin, J. L., ed. 15p. 1980. tchrs guide 5.00 (ISBN 0-943068-13-4). Graphic Learning.
Fisher, J. & Dryer, R. California Studies Program: Activity Manual. Combs, Eunice A., ed. (Illus.). 133p. (gr. 4). 1982. 49.00 (ISBN 0-943068-23-1); tchrs guide 5.00. Graphic Learning.
--Los Estrados Unidos: Programa de Estudios Sociales. Yockstick, Elizabeth, ed. Olivares, Angelina S., tr. 126p. (Spanish.). (gr. 5). 1981. 49.00 (ISBN 0-943068-17-7). Graphic Learning.
--World Studies Program: Activity Manual. Irvin, J. L. & Yockstick, Elizabeth, eds. Orlando & Miller, M., trs. (Illus.). 126p. (Spanish.). (gr. 6). 1981. 49.00 (ISBN 0-943068-08-8). Graphic Learning.
Gish, Noel J. & Yockstick, Elizabeth. Long Island Studies Program: Activity Manual. (Illus.). 111p. (gr. 4). 1981. 49.00 (ISBN 0-943068-10-X). Graphic Learning.
Gosen, Patricia E. New York City Metropolitan Area, Studies Program, Work-A-Text. Irvin, J. L., ed. (Illus.). 76p. (Orig.). (gr. 4). 1981. wkbk. 3.50 (ISBN 0-943068-01-0). Graphic Learning.
Irvin, Judith L. & Downey, Joan M. Los Angeles Studies Program: Activity Manual. Yockstick, Elizabeth, ed. Martinez-Miller, Orlando, tr. (Illus.). 73p. (Spanish.). (gr. 3). 1981. 49.00 (ISBN 0-943068-41-X). Graphic Learning.

SOCIAL SECURITY
see also Friendly Societies; Insurance, Disability; Insurance, Health; Insurance, Unemployment; Old Age Pensions; Workmen'S Compensation
Aaron, Henry J. Economic Effects of Social Security. (Studies of Government Finance). 100p. 1982. 12.95 (ISBN 0-8157-0030-X, 82-73654); pap. 5.95 (ISBN 0-8157-0029-6). Brookings.
American Health Research Institute, Ltd. Social Security: A Medical Subject Analysis & Research Index with Bibliography. Bartone, John C., ed. 120p. 1983. 29.95 (ISBN 0-941864-86-3); pap. 21.95 (ISBN 0-941864-87-1). ABBE Pubs Assn.
Berger, Jason, ed. Serving Social Security. (Reference Shelf Ser.: Vol. 54, No. 4). 158p. pap. text ed. 6.25 (ISBN 0-8242-0668-1). Wilson.
Burkhauser, Richard V., ed. A Challenge to Social Security. LC 82-1596. (Research on Poverty Monograph). 282p. 1982. 27.50 (ISBN 0-12-144680-8). Acad Pr.
Greenston, Peter & Hagan, Michael. Insuring the Disabled: A Study of the Impact of Changes to the Social Security Disability Insurance Program. LC 81-50055. (Illus.). 69p. (Orig.). 1981. pap. text ed. 5.75 (ISBN 0-87766-292-4, URI 31700). Urban Inst.
Jehle, Faustin F. Complete & Easy Guide to Social Security & Medicare. 1982. pap. 6.95 (ISBN 0-440-01129-9, Dell Trade Pbks). Dell.
McCormick, Harvey L. Social Security Claims & Procedures. 3rd ed. LC 82-51096. 1300p. 1982. pap. text ed. write for info. (ISBN 0-314-71743-9). West Pub.
Matthews, Joseph & Berman, Dorothy. Your Rights & Benefits over Fifty-Five. 224p. 1983. pap. 11.95 (ISBN 0-201-05539-2). A-W.
Reappraising Social Security: Toward an Alternative System. LC 81-86069. (Special Project Report Ser.). 244p. 1982. 5.95 (ISBN 0-89940-850-8). LBJ Sch Pub Aff.
Report on the ILO-NORWAY African Regional Training Course for Senior Social Security Managers & Administrative Officials: Nairobi, 24 November-12 December 1980. 290p. 1982. 19.95 (ISBN 92-2-102857-7). Intl Labour Office.
Social Security, Savings Plans & other Retirement Arrangements: Answers to Questions on Subject Matter, CEBS Course 3. 3rd ed. 104p. 1982. pap. 15.00 (ISBN 0-89154-182-9). Intl Found Employ.
Social Security, Savings Plans & Other Retirement Arrangements: Learning Guide, CEBS Course 3. 3rd ed. 1982. spiral binding 18.00 (ISBN 0-89154-181-0). Intl Found Employ.
Sweeney, Dennis M. & Lyko, James J. Supplement to Practice Manual for Social Security Claims, 1983. 80p. 1983. pap. 15.00 (ISBN 0-686-82489-X, C5-1175). PLI.
Zander, Mary, et al. Toward Income Adequacy for the Elderly: Implications of the SSI Programs for New York City Recipients. 243p. 1982. pap. 5.00 (ISBN 0-88156-004-9). Comm Serv Soc NY.

SOCIAL SECURITY–GREAT BRITAIN
Goodman, John C. Social Security in the United Kingdom. 1981. pap. 4.75 (ISBN 0-8447-3460-8). Am Enterprise.

SOCIAL SERVICE
see also Charities; Church and Social Problems; Community Organizations; Federations, Financial (Social Service); Marriage Counseling; Medical Social Work; Psychiatric Social Work; Public Welfare; School Social Work; Social Action; Social Case Work; Social Group Work; Social Workers
Austin, Michael J. & Cox, Gary. Evaluating Your Agency's Programs. (Sage Human Services Guides: Vol. 29). 176p. 1982. pap. 8.50 (ISBN 0-8039-0989-6). Sage.
Berdes, Celia. Social Services for the Aged Dying & Bereaved in International Perspective. 82p. (Orig.). 1978. pap. text ed. 5.00 (ISBN 0-910473-04-8). Intl Fed Ageing.
Bloom, Martin. The Paradox of Helping: Introduction to the Philosophy of Scientific Practice. LC 74-13524. 283p. 1975. text ed. 25.95x (ISBN 0-471-08235-X). Wiley.
Brinkerhoff, Robert O., et al. Program Evaluation: A Design Manual. (Evaluation in Education & Human Services Ser.). 1983. lib. bdg. 14.95 (ISBN 0-89838-122-3). Kluwer Nijhoff.
--Program Evaluation: A Sourcebook. (Evaluation in Education & Human Services). 1983. lib. bdg. 24.95 (ISBN 0-89838-120-7). Kluwer Nijhoff.
--Program Evaluation: A Sourcebook & Casebook. (Evaluation in Education & Human Services Ser.). (a). 1983. lib. bdg. 35.95 (ISBN 0-89838-121-5). Kluwer Nijhoff.
Bullock, Nadine. The Open Door, Bk. 2. LC 78-56655. (Illus.). 57p. (Orig.). 1982. pap. 11.95 (ISBN 0-911335-02-1). Open Door Foun.
Burgest, David R. Social Work Practice with Minorities. LC 81-14461. 322p. 1982. text ed. 16.50 (ISBN 0-8108-1476-5). Scarecrow.
Butrym, Zofia & Horder, John. Health, Doctors, & Social Workers. (Library of Social Work). 192p. (Orig.). 1983. price not set. Routledge & Kegan.
Caroff, Phyllis, ed. Treatments Formulations & Clinical Social Work. LC 82-62378. 52p. (Orig.). 1982. pap. text ed. 6.95 (ISBN 0-87101-118-2). Natl Assn Soc Wkrs.
Clare, A. W. & Corney, R. H., eds. Social Work & Primary Health Care. Date not set. 35.00 (ISBN 0-12-174740-9). Acad Pr.

DeLoach, Charlene P. & Wilkins, Ronnie D. Independent Living: Services for the Disabled & Elderly. 1983. pap. text ed. price not set (ISBN 0-8391-1794-9, 16462). Univ Park.

Dinerman, Miriam, ed. Social Work in a Turbulent Word: Proceedings of 7th NASW Professional Symposium. 1983. text ed. 15.95 (ISBN 0-87101-108-5, CBO-108-C). Natl Assn Soc Wkrs.

Dunham, Arthur & Nusberg, Charlotte. Toward Planning for the Aging in Local Communities: An International Perspective. 49p. (Orig.). 1978. pap. text ed. 4.00 (ISBN 0-910473-05-6). Intl Fed Ageing.

Gibson, Guadalupe, ed. Our Kingdom Stands on Brittle Glass. 1983. pap. text ed. 11.95x (ISBN 0-87101-119-0, CBF-103-C). Natl Assn Soc Wkrs.

Ginsberg, Leon H. The Practice of Social Work in Public Welfare. LC 82-71888. 1983. 18.95 (ISBN 0-02-911760-7). Free Pr.

Henderson, George. The Human Rights of Professional Helpers. 214p. 1983. text ed. price not set (ISBN 0-398-04820-7). C C Thomas.

Human Resource Communication Group. The Directory of Human Resource Services 1982. 128p. (Orig.). 1982. pap. 12.00x (ISBN 0-9609088-1-1). Human Res Comm.

Imre, Roberta W. Knowing & Caring: Philosophical Issues in Social Work. LC 82-20209. 164p. (Orig.). 1983. lib. bdg. 18.50 (ISBN 0-8191-2859-7); pap. text ed. 8.75 (ISBN 0-8191-2860-0). U Pr of Amer.

Kakabadse, Andrew. Culture of the Social Services. 199p. 1982. text ed. 33.00x (ISBN 0-566-00366-X). Gower Pub Ltd.

Lach, C. S. How to Help Cases of Distress. 152p. 1977. 30.00x (ISBN 0-7121-0814-9, Pub. by Macdonald & Evans). State Mutual Bk.

Lum, Doman & Zuniga-Martinez, Maria. Ethnic Minority Social Work Practice: Individual, Family & Community Dimensions. 1983. pap. text ed. price not set (ISBN 0-8391-1787-6, 19585). Univ Park.

Mandell, Betty R. & Schram, Barbara. Human Services: An Introduction. 600p. 1983. text ed. 18.95 (ISBN 0-471-08574-X); tchrs.' ed avail. (ISBN 0-471-87198-2). Wiley.

Meenaghan, Thomas M. & Washington, Robert O. Macro Practice in the Human Services. (Illus.). 288p. 1982. text ed. 15.95 (ISBN 0-02-920850-5). Free Pr.

Mieczkowski, Bogdan. Social Services for Women in Eastern Europe. (ASN Series in Issues Studies (USSR & East Europe): No. 3). 128p. (Orig.). 1982. pap. 8.50 (ISBN 0-910895-00-7). Assn Study Nat.

Multivariate Analysis in the Human Services. (International Series in Social Welfare). 1983. lib. bdg. 35.00 (ISBN 0-89838-105-3). Kluwer Nijhoff.

Onokerhoraye, A. G. Social Services in Nigeria: An Introduction. 300p. 1983. 21.00 (ISBN 0-7103-0038-7, Kegan Paul); pap. 10.95 (ISBN 0-7103-0042-5). Routledge & Kegan.

Rees, Stuart & Wallace, Alison. Verdicts on Social Work. 224p. 1982. pap. text ed. 14.95 (ISBN 0-7131-6279-1). E Arnold.

Riggar, T. F. Utilizing Community Resources: An Overview for the Human Services. (Illus.). 1983. pap. text ed. price not set (ISBN 0-8391-1796-5, 17655). Univ Park.

Rosenblatt, Aaron & Waldfogel, Diana, eds. Handbook of Clinical Social Work. LC 82-49042. (Social & Behavioral Science Ser.). 1983. text ed. 65.00x (ISBN 0-87589-562-X). Jossey-Bass.

Rudman, Jack. Aging Services Representative. (Career Examination Ser.: C-2880). (Cloth bdg. avail. on request). pap. 12.00 (ISBN 0-8373-2880-2). Natl Learning.

--Associate Social Services Management Specialist. (Career Examination Ser.: C-454). (Cloth bdg. avail. on request). pap. 14.00 (ISBN 0-8373-0454-7). Natl Learning.

--Developmental Disabilities Program Aide. (Career Examination Ser.: C-864). (Cloth bdg. avail. on request). pap. 10.00 (ISBN 0-8373-0864-X). Natl Learning.

--Director of Child Support Enforcement Bureau. (Career Examination Ser.: C-928). (Cloth bdg. avail. on request). pap. 14.00 (ISBN 0-8373-0928-X). Natl Learning.

--Director of Social Services. (Career Examination Ser.: C-2666). (Cloth bdg. avail. on request). pap. 14.00 (ISBN 0-8373-2666-4). Natl Learning.

--Facility Management Assistant. (Career Examination Ser.: C-387). (Cloth bdg. avail. on request). pap. 10.00 (ISBN 0-8373-0387-7). Natl Learning.

--Neighborhood Aide. (Career Examination Ser.: C-2910). (Cloth bdg. avail. on request). pap. 10:00 (ISBN 0-8373-2910-8). Natl Learning.

--Principal Juvenile Counselor. (Career Examination Ser.: C-422). (Cloth bdg. avail. on request). pap. 12.00 (ISBN 0-8373-0422-9). Natl Learning.

Seidman, Edward, ed. Handbook of Social Intervention. x ed. 736p. 1983. 49.95 (ISBN 0-8039-1971-9). Sage.

Spiro, Shimon E. & Yuchtman-Yaar, Ephraim, eds. Evaluating the Welfare State: Social & Political Perspectives. LC 82-22596. Date not set. price not set. Acad Pr.

Timms, Noel. Social Work Values: An Inquiry. 200p. (Orig.). 1983. pap. price not set (ISBN 0-7100-9404-3). Routledge & Kegan.

Timms, Noel, ed. Social Welfare: Why & How. (International Library of Welfare & Philosophy). 306p. 1980. 30.00 (ISBN 0-7100-0615-2). Routledge & Kegan.

Watson, David. Caring for Strangers: An Introduction to Practical Philosophy for Students of Social Administration. (International Library of Welfare & Philosophy). 144p. 1980. 21.95 (ISBN 0-7100-0390-0); pap. 10.00 (ISBN 0-7100-0391-9). Routledge & Kegan.

SOCIAL SERVICE–CASES
see Social Case Work

SOCIAL SERVICE–FIELD WORK

Leiter, Michael P. & Webb, Mark. Developing Human Service Networks: Community & Organizatonal Relations. 279p. 1983. text ed. 19.50x (ISBN 0-8290-1262-1). Irvington.

SOCIAL SERVICE–PUBLIC RELATIONS
see Public Relations–Social Service

SOCIAL SERVICE–STUDY AND TEACHING
see Social Work Education

SOCIAL SERVICE–VOCATIONAL GUIDANCE

Hess, Robert & Hermalin, Jared, eds. Innovations in Prevention. (Prevention in Human Services, Vol. 2, No. 3). 128p. 1983. text ed. 19.95 (ISBN 0-86656-227-3, B227). Haworth Pr.

Rudman, Jack. Supervising Community Service Worker. (Career Examination Ser.: C-2677). (Cloth bdg. avail. on request). pap. 12.00 (ISBN 0-8373-2677-X). Natl Learning.

Summers, Barbara. Working with People: An Introduction to the Caring Professions. 1982. 25.00x (ISBN 0-304-30604-5, Pub. by Cassell England). State Mutual Bk.

SOCIAL SERVICE, MEDICAL
see Medical Social Work

SOCIAL SERVICE, PSYCHIATRIC
see Psychiatric Social Work

SOCIAL SERVICE, SCHOOL
see School Social Work

SOCIAL STRATIFICATION
see Social Classes

SOCIAL STRUCTURE

Burt, Ronald S. & Minor, Michael J. Applied Network Analysis: A Methodological Introduction. 352p. 1982. 25.00 (ISBN 0-8039-1906-9); pap. 12.50 (ISBN 0-8039-1907-7). Sage.

Giddens, Anthony: Profiles & Critiques in Social Theory. 230p. 1983. 24.50x (ISBN 0-520-04933-0); pap. 10.95x (ISBN 0-520-04964-0). U of Cal Pr.

Marsden, Peter V. & Lin, Nan. Social Structure & Network Analysis. (Sage Focus Editions). (Illus.). 300p. 1982. 25.00 (ISBN 0-8039-1888-7); pap. 12.50 (ISBN 0-8039-1889-5). Sage.

SOCIAL STUDIES
see Social Sciences

SOCIAL SURVEYS
see also Economic Surveys; Educational Surveys; Public Opinion Polls

Apostle, Richard A. & Glock, Charles Y. The Anatomy of Racial Attitudes. LC 82-4867. 277p. 1983. 27.50x (ISBN 0-520-04719-2). U of Cal Pr.

Inkeles, Alex, et al. Exploring Individual Modernity. 448p. 1983. text ed. 24.00 (ISBN 0-231-05442-4). Columbia U Pr.

SOCIAL SYSTEMS
see also Social Institutions

Barnes, Barry. Scientific Knowledge & Sociological Theory. (Monographs in Social Theory). 204p. 1974. 16.50 (ISBN 0-7100-7961-3); pap. 8.95 (ISBN 0-7100-7962-1). Routledge & Kegan.

Warner, William L. Social Systems of American Ethnic Groups. 1945. text ed. 25.00x (ISBN 0-686-83770-3). Elliots Bks.

SOCIAL VALUES

Curtis, R. K. Evolution or Extinction: The Choice Before Us-A Systems Approach to the Study of the Future. 420p. 1982. 50.00 (ISBN 0-08-027933-3); pap. 25.00 (ISBN 0-08-027932-5). Pergamon.

Halttunen, Karen. Confidence Men & Painted Women: A Study of Middle-Class Culture in America, 1830-1870. LC 82-8336. (Yale Historical Publications Misc.: No. 129). (Illus.). 280p. 1983. text ed. 19.95x (ISBN 0-300-02835-0). Yale U Pr.

Sack, John. Fingerprint: The Autobiography of An American Man. Date not set. 13.95 (ISBN 0-394-50197-7). Random.

SOCIAL WELFARE
see Charities; Public Welfare; Social Problems; Social Service

SOCIAL WORK
see Social Service

SOCIAL WORK ADMINISTRATION

Aldridge, Martha. Beyond Management. 180p. 1982. pap. 6.95 (ISBN 0-87414-025-0). U of Iowa Sch Soc Wk.

Steinberg, Raymond M. & Carter, Genevieve W. Case Management & the Elderly: A Handbook for Planning & Administering Programs. 224p. 1982. 25.95 (ISBN 0-669-06089-5). Lexington Bks.

SOCIAL WORK EDUCATION

Munson, Carlton E. An Introduction to Clinical Social Work Supervision. LC 83-620. 300p. 1983. text ed. 24.95 (ISBN 0-86656-196-X); pap. text ed. 14.95 (ISBN 0-86656-197-8). Haworth Pr.

SOCIAL WORK WITH THE AGED

Rudman, Jack. Field Representative, Senior Citizen Services Project. (Career Examination Ser.: C-2948). (Cloth bdg. avail. on request). pap. 12.00 (ISBN 0-8373-2948-5). Natl learning.

Steinberg, Raymond M. & Carter, Genevieve W. Case Management & the Elderly: A Handbook for Planning & Administering Programs. 224p. 1982. 25.95 (ISBN 0-669-06089-5). Lexington Bks.

SOCIAL WORK WITH YOUTH
see also Child Welfare; Social Group Work; Volunteer Workers in Social Service

Crompton, Margaret. Adolescents & Social Workers. Davies, Martin, ed. (Community Care & Practice Handbooks). vi, 91p. (Orig.). 1983. pap. text ed. 7.95x (ISBN 0-435-82189-X). Heinemann Ed.

Faller, Kathleen C. Social Work with Abused & Neglected Children. 256p. 1981. text ed. 16.95. Free Pr.

Heywood, Jean S. Children in Care: The Development of the Service for the Deprived Child. rev. ed. (International Library of Sociology). 284p. 1978. 15.00 (ISBN 0-7100-8733-0). Routledge & Kegan.

Long, Tic. Resource Directory for Youth Workers, 1983. 1983. pap. 8.95 spiral bdg. (ISBN 0-687-36165-6). Abingdon.

Rudman, Jack. Executive Director of Youth Bureau. (Career Examination Ser.: C-416). (Cloth bdg. avail. on request). pap. 14.00 (ISBN 0-8373-0416-4). Natl Learning.

SOCIAL WORKERS
see also Social Service- Vocational Guidance

Burghardt, Steven. Organizing for Community Action. (Sage Human Services Guides: Vol. 27). 120p. 1982. pap. 7.00 (ISBN 0-8039-0206-9). Sage.

Herbert, Martin. Psychology for Social Workers. (Psychology for Professional Groups Ser.). 350p. 1981. text ed. 25.00x (ISBN 0-333-31866-8, Pub. by Macmillan England); pap. text ed. 10.95x (ISBN 0-333-31878-1). Humanities.

Kakabadse, Andrew. Culture of the Social Services. 199p. 1982. text ed. 33.00x (ISBN 0-566-00366-X). Gower Pub Ltd.

National Institute for Social Work. Social Workers: Their Role & Tasks. 283p. 1982. pap. text ed. 12.25x (ISBN 0-7199-1080-3, Pub. by Bedford England). Renouf.

Rudman, Jack. Senior Caseworker. (Career Examination Ser.: C-2931). (Cloth bdg. avail. on request). pap. 12.00 (ISBN 0-8373-2931-0). Natl Learning.

--Senior Community Service Worker. (Career Examination Ser.: C-2676). (Cloth bdg. avail. on request). pap. 10.00 (ISBN 0-8373-2676-1). Natl Learning.

SOCIALISM
see also Anarchism and Anarchists; Christianity and Economics; Church and Social Problems; Collective Settlements; Communism; Equality; Individualism; Industry and State; Labor and Laboring Classes; Marxian Economics; National Socialism; Nationalism and Socialism; Old Age Pensions; Proletariat; Trade-Unions; Utopias; Women and Socialism

Bloch, Maurice. Marxism & Anthropology. (Illus.). 1982. 18.95x (ISBN 0-19-876091-4). Oxford U Pr.

Campbell, Tom. The Left & Rights: A Conceptual Analysis of the Idea of Socialist Rights. (International Library of Welfare & Philosophy). 296p. (Orig.). 1983. pap. 11.95 (ISBN 0-7100-9085-4). Routledge & Kegan.

Carver, Terrel. Marx's Social Theory. 128p. 1983. 17.95 (ISBN 0-19-219170-5); pap. 6.95 (ISBN 0-19-289158-8). Oxford U Pr.

Collins, Hugh. Marxism & Law. (Marxist Introductions Ser.). (Illus.). 200p. 1982. 22.00 (ISBN 0-19-876093-0). Oxford U Pr.

D'Angelo, Edward, et al. Contemporary East European Marxism, Vol. II. (Praxis: Vol. 7). 275p. 1982. pap. text ed. 27.75x (ISBN 0-391-02788-3). Humanities.

Dunayavskaya, Raya. Rosa Luxemburg, Women's Liberation & Marx's Philosophy of Revolution. 260p. 1982. text ed. 19.95x (ISBN 0-391-02569-4, Pub. by Harvester England); pap. text ed. 10.95x (ISBN 0-391-02793-X). Humanities.

Ellsberg, Robert, ed. By Little by Little: The Selected Writings of Dorothy Day. LC 82-48887. 1983. 17.95 (ISBN 0-394-52499-3); pap. 9.95 (ISBN 0-394-71432-6). Knopf.

Groth, Alexander J. Major Ideologies: An Interpretative of Democracy, Socialism & Nationalism. LC 82-18755. 256p. 1983. Repr. of 1971 ed. text ed. write for info. (ISBN 0-89874-579-9). Krieger.

Heese, Viktor. Zur Permanenten "Uberinvestition" In Sozialistischen Wirtschaftssystemen. 338p. (Ger.). 1982. write for info. (ISBN 3-8204-7241-X). P Lang Pubs.

Hindess, Barry. Parliamentary Democracy & Socialist Politics. 200p. 1983. pap. 10.95 (ISBN 0-7100-9319-5). Routledge & Kegan.

Hollander, Paul. The Many Faces of Socialism: Essays in Comparative Sociology & Politics. 371p. 1983. 29.95 (ISBN 0-87855-480-7). Transaction Bks.

Hook, Sidney. Marxism & Beyond. LC 82-20542. 238p. 1983. text ed. 19.95 (ISBN 0-8476-7159-3). Rowman.

Jacobson, Phyllis & Jacobson, Julius. Socialist Perspectives, Vol. 1. 220p. 1983. 29.95 (ISBN 0-943828-51-1). Karz-Cohl Pub.

--Socialist Perspectives, Vol. 1. 220p. (Orig.). 1983. pap. 9.95 (ISBN 0-943828-52-X). Karz-Cohl Pub.

Kornai, Janos. Growth, Shortage & Efficiency: A Macrodynamic Model of the Socialist Economy. 142p. 1983. text ed. 19.50x (ISBN 0-520-04[illegible]1-2). U of Cal Pr.

Marcy, Sam. Imperialism & the Crisis in the Socialist Camp. 57p. 1979. pap. 1.50 (ISBN 0-89567-030-5). WV PUbs.

Marx, K. & Engels, F. Mega, Vol. 4, pt. 2. 911p. 60.00x (ISBN 0-8285-2205-7, Pub. by Diet Germany). Imported Pubns.

Mikulsky, K. I., ed. CMEA: International Significance of Socialist Integration. 376p. 1982. pap. 6.00 (ISBN 0-8285-2272-3, Pub. by Progress Pubs USSR). Imported Pubns.

Nove, Alec. The Economics of Feasible Socialism. 272p. 1983. text ed. 29.50x (ISBN 0-04-335048-8); pap. text ed. 9.95x (ISBN 0-04-335049-6). Allen Unwin.

Pevsner, Y. State-Monopoly Capitalism & the Labour Theory of Value. 390p. 1982. 7.95 (Pub. by Progress Pubs USSR). Imported Pubns.

Poutney, Ernie. For the Socialist Cause. 1973 ed. 80p. pap. 5.95 (ISBN 0-686-37392-8). Beekman Pubs.

Richards, Vernon. Impossiblities of Social Democracy. 142p. 1978. pap. 2.25 (ISBN 0-900384-16-6). Left Bank.

Ruthmann, Daniele. Vers Une Nouvelle Culture Social-Democrate? 266p. (Ger.). 1982. Vol. 4, Germanus Legens. write for info (ISBN 3-8204-5970-7); Vol. 468, Langue et Litterature Allemandes, Vol. 468. write for info (ISBN 3-8204-5971-5). P Lang Pubs.

Sau, Ranjit. Trade, Capital & Underdevelopment: Towards a Marxist Theory. (Illus.). 1982. 15.00x (ISBN 0-19-561209-4). Oxford U Pr.

Shalom, Stephen R. Socialist Visions. 350p. 1982. 20.00 (ISBN 0-89608-170-2); pap. 7.50 (ISBN 0-89608-169-9). South End Pr.

Szajkowski. Establishment of Marxist Regimes. 1982. text ed. 29.95 (ISBN 0-408-10834-7); pap. text ed. 15.95 (ISBN 0-408-10833-9). Butterworth.

Taylor, Ian. Law & Order - Arguments for Socialism. 234p. 1981. text ed. 31.50x (ISBN 0-333-21442-0, 41259, Pub. by Macmillan England). Humanities.

Wilber, C. K. & Jameson, K. P., eds. Socialist Models of Development. 240p. 1982. 40.00 (ISBN 0-08-027921-X). Pergamon.

SOCIALISM–HISTORY

Hook, Sidney. Marx & the Marxists: The Ambiguous Legacy. LC 81-20921. 192p. pap. 5.95 (ISBN 0-89874-443-1). Krieger.

Murphey, Dwight D. Socialist Thought. LC 82-24751. 436p. (Orig.). 1983. lib. bdg. 26.75 (ISBN 0-8191-3025-7); pap. text ed. 15.50 (ISBN 0-8191-3026-5). U Pr of Amer.

Nove, Alec. The Economics of Feasible Socialism. 272p. 1983. text ed. 29.50x (ISBN 0-04-335048-8); pap. text ed. 9.95x (ISBN 0-04-335049-6). Allen Unwin.

SOCIALISM, CHRISTIAN
see also Christianity and Economics

Gardner, E. Clinton. Christocentrism in Christian Social Ethics: A Depth Study of Eight Modern Protestants. LC 82-21843. 264p. (Orig.). 1983. lib. bdg. 22.50 (ISBN 0-8191-2954-2); pap. text ed. 11.75 (ISBN 0-8191-2955-0). U Pr of Amer.

SOCIALISM AND NATIONALISM
see Nationalism and Socialism

SOCIALISM AND WOMEN
see Women and Socialism

SOCIALISM IN CUBA

Castro, Fidel. Fidel Castro Speeches: Building Socialism in Cuba, Vol. 2. Taber, Michael, ed. 400p. 1983. lib. bdg. 30.00X (ISBN 0-87348-624-2); pap. 7.95X (ISBN 0-87348-650-1). Monad Pr.

SOCIALISM IN EUROPE

Lindemann, Albert S. A History of European Socialism. LC 82-40167. 416p. 1983. text ed. 25.00x (ISBN 0-300-02797-4). Yale U Pr.

--A History of European Socialism. 25.00 (ISBN 0-686-42815-3). Yale U Pr.

Myant, Martin. Poland: A Crisis for Socialism. 253p. 1982. text ed. 21.00x (ISBN 0-85315-557-7, Pub. by Lawrence & Wishart Ltd England). Humanities.

Rabinbach, Anson. The Crisis of Austrian Socialism: From Red Vienna to Civil War, Nineteen Twenty Seven-Nineteen Thirty Four. LC 82-10919. (Illus.). 312p. 1983. lib. bdg. 22.00 (ISBN 0-226-70121-2). U of Chicago Pr.

SOCIALISM IN GERMANY

Braunthal, Gerard. The West German Social Democrats, 1969-1982: Profile of a Party in Power. (Replica Edition Ser.). 400p. 1983. softcover 25.00x (ISBN 0-86531-958-8). Westview.

Scharf, C. Bradley. Politics & Social Change in East Germany: An Evaluation of Socialist Democracy. (Westview Special Studies on the Soviet Union & Eastern Europe). 215p. 1983. lib. bdg. 18.50x; pap. text ed. price not set (ISBN 0-86531-451-9). Westview.

SOCIALISM IN GREAT BRITAIN

Hinton, James. Labour & Socialism: A History of the British Labour Movement, 1870-1970. LC 82-21798. 230p. 1983. lib. bdg. 22.00x (ISBN 0-87023-393-9). U of Mass Pr.

Tyrell, R. Emmett, ed. The Future That Doesn't Work: Social Democracy's Failures in Britain. LC 82-21929. 216p. (Orig.). 1983. pap. text ed. 8.95 (ISBN 0-8191-2740-X). U Pr of Amer.

SOCIALISM IN LITERATURE

Wald, Alan M. The Revolutionary Imagination: The Poetry & Politics of John Wheelwright & Sherry Mangan. LC 82-8498. 370p. 1983. 28.00x (ISBN 0-8078-1535-7). U of NC Pr.

SOCIALISM IN THE UNITED STATES

The Chicano Struggle & the Struggle for Socialism. 66p. 1975. 1.50 (ISBN 0-686-82482-2). RCP Pubns.

Churchill, Ward, ed. Marxism & Native Americans. 250p. Date not set. 20.00 (ISBN 0-89608-178-8); pap. 7.50 (ISBN 0-89608-177-X). South End Pr.

Kann. The American Left: Failures & Fortunes. 256p. 1982. 26.95 (ISBN 0-03-061772-3). Praeger.

SOCIALIZATION

Blunden, R. Social Development. (Studies in Developmental Paediatrics). (Illus.). 160p. 1982. text ed. 25.00 (ISBN 0-85200-304-8, Pub. by MTP Pr England). Kluwer Boston.

Borman, Kathryn M., ed. The Social Life of Children in a Changing Society. 320p. 1982. text ed. 29.95 (ISBN 0-89391-165-8). Ablex Pub.

Higgins, E. Tory & Hartup, Willard W., eds. Social Cognition & Social Development: A Sociocultural Perspective. LC 82-12897. (Cambridge Studies in Social & Emotional Development: No. 5). 352p. Date not set. price not set (ISBN 0-521-24587-7). Cambridge U Pr.

SOCIALIZATION OF INDUSTRY

see Government Ownership

SOCIALIZED MEDICINE

see Insurance, Health

SOCIALLY HANDICAPPED CHILDREN-EDUCATION

Kohen-Raz, Reuven. Disadvantaged Post-Adolescents: Approaches to Education & Rehabilitation. (Special Aspects of Education Ser.: Vol. 1). 210p. 1982. write for info. (ISBN 0-677-06010-6). Gordon.

SOCIETIES

see also Associations, Institutions, etc.; Boys-Societies and Clubs; Cooperative Societies; Friendly Societies; Girls-Societies and Clubs; Historical Societies; Learned Institutions and Societies; Trade-Unions; Women-Societies and Clubs

Eckel, Edwin B. The Geographical Society of America: Life History of a Learned Society. LC 82-15412. (Memoir Ser.: No. 155). (Illus.). 1982. 24.50x (ISBN 0-8137-1155-X). Geol Soc.

SOCIETIES, BENEFIT

see Friendly Societies

SOCIETIES, COOPERATIVE

see Cooperative Societies

SOCIETY, HIGH

see Upper Classes

SOCIETY AND ART

see Art and Society

SOCIETY AND EDUCATION

see Educational Sociology

SOCIETY AND LANGUAGE

see Sociolinguistics

SOCIETY AND LAW

see Sociological Jurisprudence

SOCIETY AND LITERATURE

see Literature and Society

SOCIETY AND MUSIC

see Music and Society

SOCIETY AND THE CHURCH

see Church and the World

SOCIETY OF JESUS

see Jesuits

SOCIOBIOLOGY

Corning, P. A. The Synergism Hypothesis: A Theory of Progressive Evolution. 1983. pap. price not set (ISBN 0-07-013172-4). McGraw.

Trigg, Roger. The Shaping of Man: Philosophical Aspects of Sociobiology. LC 82-16868. 208p. 1983. 14.95 (ISBN 0-8052-3840-9). Schocken.

SOCIOLINGUISTICS

Esperet, Eric. Langage et Origine Sociale Des Eleves. 2nd ed. 281p. (Fr.). 1982. write for info. (ISBN 3-261-04754-2). P Lang Pubs.

Lewis, Michael & Rosenblum, Leonard A. Interaction, Conversation & the Development of Language. LC 82-21225. 344p. 1983. Repr. of 1977 ed. lib. bdg. write for info. (ISBN 0-89874-588-8). Krieger.

Mercer, Neil, ed. Language in School & Community. 256p. 1981. pap. text ed. 16.95 (ISBN 0-7131-6347-X). E Arnold.

Romaine, Suzanne, ed. Sociolinguistic Variation in Speech Communities. 224p. 1982. pap. text ed. 18.95 (ISBN 0-7131-6355-0). E Arnold.

SOCIOLOGICAL JURISPRUDENCE

Kidder, Robert. Connecting Law & Society: An Introduction to Research & Theory. 304p. 1983. 21.95 (ISBN 0-13-167809-4). P-H.

Parsons, Frank. Legal Doctrine & Social Progress. 1982. Repr. of 1911 ed. lib. bdg. 22.50x (ISBN 0-8377-1014-6). Rothman.

Swigert, Victoria L., ed. Law & the Legal Process. (Sage Research Progress Series in Criminology: Vol. 28). (Illus.). 160p. 1982. 18.95 (ISBN 0-8039-1900-X); pap. 8.95 (ISBN 0-8039-1901-8). Sage.

SOCIOLOGICAL RESEARCH

see also Social Science Research

Francis, Leslie J. Experience of Adulthood: A Profile of 26-39 Year Olds. 221p. 1982. text ed. 32.00x (ISBN 0-566-00562-X). Gower Pub Ltd.

--Youth in Transit: A Profile of 16-25 year olds. 189p. 1982. text ed. 32.00x (ISBN 0-566-00530-1). Gower Pub Ltd.

Rubin, Herbert. Applied Social Research. 384p. 1983. text ed. 21.95 (ISBN 0-675-09793-2); student guide 7.95 (ISBN 0-675-20048-2). Additional supplements may be obtained from publisher. Merrill.

True, June A. Finding Out: Conduction & Evaluating Social Research. 448p. 1982. pap. text ed. 16.95x (ISBN 0-534-01168-3). Wadsworth Pub.

SOCIOLOGY

see also Age Groups; Anomy; Charities; Cities and Towns; Communication; Community; Conservatism; Crime and Criminals; Crowds; Educational Sociology; Equality; Ethnopsychology; Family; Government Ownership; Heredity; Human Ecology; Individualism; Industrial Sociology; Labor and Laboring Classes; Leadership; Man-Influence of Environment; Poor; Population; Power (Social Sciences); Public Welfare; Race Relations; Slavery; Social Change; Social Conflict; Social Contract; Social Ethics; Social Groups; Social History; Social Institutions; Social Isolation; Social Problems; Social Psychology; Social Surveys; Social Systems; Socialism; Socialization; Sociolinguistics; Sociological Jurisprudence; Statics and Dynamics (Social Sciences); Unemployed; Wealth, Ethics of; Women

Adside, Joseph W. Attitudes in Sub-Communities. 1983. 6.95 (ISBN 0-8062-2133-X). Carlton.

Badie, Bertrand & Birnbaum, Pierre. The Sociology of the State: Chicago Original Ser. Goldhammer, Arthur, tr. from Fr. LC 82-20249. 1983. lib. bdg. 24.00x (ISBN 0-226-03548-4); pap. text ed. 10.95x (ISBN 0-226-03549-2). U of Chicago Pr.

Baldridge, J. Victor. Sociology: A Critical Approach to Power, Conflict, & Change. 2nd ed. 547p. 1980. text ed. 21.95 (ISBN 0-471-04708-2); study guide 10.95 (ISBN 0-471-07689-9); test avail. (ISBN 0-471-04568-3). Wiley.

Bottomore, Tom & Nowak, Stefan, eds. Sociology: The State of the Art. 382p. 1982. 27.50 (ISBN 0-8039-9790-6); pap. 12.95 (ISBN 0-8039-9791-4). Sage.

Cecchettini, P. A. CLEP Resource Manual: Introduction to Sociology. 1979. pap. 9.95 (ISBN 0-07-010306-2). McGraw.

Clarke, Simon. Marx, Marginalism & Modern Sociology. (Contemporary Social Theory Ser.). 272p. 1982. text ed. 29.95x (ISBN 0-333-29252-9, Pub. by Macmillan England); pap. text ed. 11.95x (ISBN 0-333-29253-7). Humanities.

Collins, Randall, ed. Sociological Theory 1983. (Social & Behavioral Science Ser.). 1983. text ed. 19.95x (ISBN 0-87589-557-3). Jossey-Bass.

Comte, August. Social Statics & Social Dynamics: The Theory of Order & the Theory of Progress. (The Most Meaningful Classics in World Culture Ser.). (Illus.). 101p. 1983. Repr. of 1899 ed. 67.85 (ISBN 0-89901-103-9). Found Class Reprints.

De Grange, McQuilkin. Nature & Elements of Sociology. 1953. text ed. 59.50x (ISBN 0-686-83631-6). Elliots Bks.

Durkheim, Emile. The Rules of Sociological Method & Selected Texts on Sociology & its Method. Lukes, Steven, ed. Halls, W. D., tr. 1982. pap. text ed. write for info. Free Pr.

Federico, Ronald C. & Schwartz, Janet. Sociology. 3rd ed. LC 82-11375. 640p. 1983. text ed. 20.95 (ISBN 0-201-12030-5). A-W.

Freeman, Howard E. & Dynes, Russell R., eds. Applied Sociology: Roles & Activities of Sociologists in Diverse Setting. LC 82-49035. (Social & Behavioral Science Ser.). 1983. text ed. 23.95x (ISBN 0-87589-563-8). Jossey-Bass.

Giddens, A. Sociology: A Short Introduction. 1982. 55.00x (ISBN 0-333-30928-6, Pub. by Macmillan England). State Mutual Bk.

Giddens, Anthony. Sociology: A Brief Critical Introduction. 160p. (Orig.). pap. text ed. 6.95. HarBraceJ.

Goldman, Marion S. & Rabow, Jerome. Psychoanalytic Sociology: A Text & Reader. 1984. text ed. write for info. (ISBN 0-89874-608-6). Krieger.

Hagedorn, Robert, ed. Sociology. 720p. 1983. text ed. write for info. (ISBN 0-697-07571-0); instr's. manual avail. (ISBN 0-697-07572-9); avail. study guide (ISBN 0-697-07573-7). Wm C Brown.

Hechter, Michael, ed. The Microfounations of Macrosociology. 1983. write for info. (ISBN 0-87722-298-3). Temple U Pr.

Himelfarb, A. & Richardson, C. J. Sociology for Canadians: Images of Society. 512p. 1982. 21.95 (ISBN 0-07-548440-4). McGraw.

Horton, Paul B. & Horton, Robert L. Introductory Sociology. 3rd ed. (Plaid Ser.). 1982. pap. 7.95 (ISBN 0-87094-345-6). Dow Jones-Irwin.

International Bibliography of Sociology-Bibliography de Sociologie, 1980, Vol. 30. LC 57-2949. (International Bibliography of the Social Sciences-Biolographie Internationale des Sciences Sociales). 402p. 1982. 90.00x (ISBN 0-422-80970-5). Intl Pubns Serv.

Jacobs, Jerry. Social Problems Through Social Theory: A Selective View. rev. ed. 1983. text ed. 14.95x (ISBN 0-88105-013-X); pap. text ed. 9.95x (ISBN 0-88105-014-8). Cap & Gown.

Lawton, Denis. Social Class, Language & Education. (International Library of Sociology). 192p. 1968. pap. 8.95 (ISBN 0-7100-6895-6). Routledge & Kegan.

Levi-Strauss, Claude. The Naked Man. LC 79-3399. (Illus.). 747p. 1983. pap. 8.61i (ISBN 0-06-090892-0, CN 892, CN). Har-Row.

Lindell, K., et al. The Kammu Year: Its Lore & Music. (Studies on Asian Topics: No. 4). 191p. 1982. pap. text ed. 10.50x (ISBN 0-7007-0151-6, Pub by Curzon Pr England). Humanities.

MacIver, R. M. Society: A Textbook of Sociology. 596p. 1982. Repr. of 1937 ed. lib. bdg. 50.00 (ISBN 0-89987-587-4). Darby BKs.

Mark, Charles, ed. Research Studies in Comparative Sociology. 147p. 1973. pap. text ed. 8.95x (ISBN 0-8422-0308-7). Irvington.

Nam, Charles B. & Powers, Mary G. The Socioeconomic Approach to Status Measurement (with a Guide to Status Scores. 1983. text ed. price not set (ISBN 0-88105-011-3); pap. text ed. price not set (ISBN 0-88105-012-1). Cap & Gown.

Perry, John & Perry, Erna K. The Social Web: An Introduction to Sociology. 4th ed. 640p. 1983. pap. text ed. 19.50 scp (ISBN 0-06-045129-7, HarpC); study guide scp 6.50 (ISBN 0-06-045145-9); test bank & instr's. manual avail. (ISBN 0-06-365124-6). Har-Row.

Shapiro, Diane R. Foundations for Sociology. 1977. pap. 15.95 (ISBN 0-395-30742-2); instr's manual 1.00 (ISBN 0-395-30743-0). HM.

Stimson, John & Stimson, Ardyth. Sociology: Contemporary Readings. LC 82-82203. 450p. 1983. pap. text ed. 10.00 (ISBN 0-87581-286-4). Peacock Pubs.

Stinchcombe, Arthur L., ed. Economic Sociology: Monograph. LC 82-13717. (Studies in Social Discontinuity). Date not set. 29.50 (ISBN 0-12-671380-4); pap. price not set (ISBN 0-12-671382-0). Acad Pr.

Sumner, William G. Sumner Today. Davie, Maurice, ed. 1940. text ed. 39.50x (ISBN 0-686-83794-0). Elliots Bks.

--What Social Classes Owe to Each Other. 1925. text ed. 11.00x (ISBN 0-686-83855-6). Elliots Bks.

Swedberg, Richard. Sociology as Disenchantment: The Evolution of the Work of George Gurvitch. 201p. 1982. text ed. 17.50x (ISBN 0-391-02397-7). Humanities.

Whipple, Edwin P. Outlooks on Society, Literature & Politics. 345p. 1982. Repr. of 1888 ed. lib. bdg. 50.00 (ISBN 0-89987-890-3). Darby Bks.

Znaniecki, Florian. Cultural Reality. (Sociological Classics Ser.). 404p. 1983. text ed. 14.95 (ISBN 0-88105-009-1); pap. text ed. 9.95 (ISBN 0-88105-010-5). Cap & Gown.

SOCIOLOGY-ADDRESSES, ESSAYS, LECTURES

Durkheim, Emile. Pragmatism & Sociology. Allcock, John B., ed. Whitehouse, J. C., tr. LC 82-14630. 184p. Date not set. price not set (ISBN 0-521-24686-5). Cambridge U Pr.

Krauss, Henning & Wolff, Reinhold. Psychoanalytische Literaturwissenschaft und Literatursoziologie. 253p. (Ger.). 1982. write for info. (ISBN 3-8204-6211-2). P Lang Pubs.

Lloyd, Christopher, ed. Social Theory & Political Practice. (Wolfson College Lectures Ser.). 190p. 1983. 24.95 (ISBN 0-19-827447-5); pap. 12.95 (ISBN 0-19-827448-3). Oxford U Pr.

Low, J. D. & Warner, William L. Social System of the Modern Factory: The Strike, a Social Analysis. 1947. text ed. 15.50x (ISBN 0-686-83772-X). Elliots Bks.

Warner, William L. Social Life of a Modern Society. 1941. text ed. 20.00x (ISBN 0-686-83769-X). Elliots Bks.

--Social Systems of American Ethnic Groups. 1945. text ed. 25.00x (ISBN 0-686-83770-3). Elliots Bks.

SOCIOLOGY-HISTORY

Abrams, Philip. Historical Sociology. 1983. text ed. 29.95x (ISBN 0-8014-1578-0); pap. 11.95x (ISBN 0-8014-9243-2). Cornell U Pr.

Kennedy, Ruby J., ed. Papers of Maurice R. Davie. 1961. text ed. 47.50x (ISBN 0-686-83676-6). Elliots Bks.

Maus, Heinz. A Short History of Sociology. (International Library of Sociology). 226p. 1965. pap. 8.95 (ISBN 0-7100-7168-X). Routledge & Kegan.

SOCIOLOGY-JUVENILE LITERATURE

Moncure, Jane B. Happy Healthkins. LC 82-14794. (Healthkins Ser.). (Illus.). (ps-2). 1982. lib. bdg. 6.95 (ISBN 0-89565-243-9). Childs World.

SOCIOLOGY-MATHEMATICAL MODELS

Hakon, H. Concepts & Models of a Quantitative Sociology: The/Dynamics of Interacting Populations. (Ser. in Synergetics: Vol. 14). (Illus.). 217p. 1983. 31.50 (ISBN 0-387-11358-4). Springer-Verlag.

SOCIOLOGY-METHODOLOGY

Alexander, Jeffrey C. Theoretical Logic in Sociology, Vol. 3: The Classical Attempt at Theoretical Synthesis: Max Weber. LC 75-17305. 224p. 1983. text ed. 25.00x (ISBN 0-520-04482-7). U of Cal Pr.

Durkheim, E. Rules of Sociological Method. 1982. 50.00x (ISBN 0-686-42914-1, Pub. by Macmillan England). State Mutual Bk.

Freidheim, Elizabeth A. From Types to Theory: A Natural Method for an Unnatural Science. LC 82-17401. (Illus.). 188p. (Orig.). 1983. lib. bdg. 21.50 (ISBN 0-8191-2831-7); pap. text ed. 9.75 (ISBN 0-8191-2832-5). U Pr of Amer.

Inkeles, Alex, et al. Exploring Individual Modernity. 448p. 1983. text ed. 24.00 (ISBN 0-231-05442-4). Columbia U Pr.

Runciman, W. G. A Treatise on Social Theory, Vol. 1. LC 82-4493. (Illus.). 400p. Date not set. price not set (ISBN 0-521-24906-6). Cambridge U Pr.

Wilson, John. Social Theory. (Illus.). 256p. 1983. pap. text ed. 13.95 (ISBN 0-13-819573-0). P-H.

SOCIOLOGY-RESEARCH

see Sociological Research

SOCIOLOGY-STATISTICS AND STATISTICAL METHODS

Blalock, H. M. Social Statistics. 2nd ed. 1979. 22.95 (ISBN 0-07-005752-4); instr's manual 9.95 (ISBN 0-07-005753-2). McGraw.

SOCIOLOGY, CHRISTIAN

Here are entered works on social theory from a Christian point of view. The relationship of this heading to Church and Social Problems is that of abstract to concrete.

see also Christianity and Economics; Church and Social Problems; Social Ethics; Wealth, Ethics of; Work (Theology)

Benestad, J. Brian. The Pursuit of a Just Social Order: Policy Statements of the U. S. Catholic Bishops, 1966-80. LC 82-18326. 220p. (Orig.). 1982. 12.00 (ISBN 0-89633-060-5); pap. 7.00 (ISBN 0-89633-061-3). Ethics & Public Policy.

Johnson, Roger A., ed. Views from the Pews: Christian Beliefs & Attitudes. LC 82-18237. 272p. 1983. pap. 14.95 (ISBN 0-8006-1695-2, 1-1695). Fortress.

Meeks, Wayne A. The First Urban Christians: The Social World of the Apostle Paul. LC 82-8447. (Illus.). 296p. 1982. 19.95 (ISBN 0-300-02876-8). Yale U Pr.

Our Fathers World. (Social Studies Ser.). (gr. 2). 2.75 (ISBN 0-686-37694-3). Rod & Staff.

SOCIOLOGY, CHRISTIAN-MODERN, 1500-

see Sociology, Christian

SOCIOLOGY, DESCRIPTIVE

see Social History

SOCIOLOGY, EDUCATIONAL

see Educational Sociology

SOCIOLOGY, INDUSTRIAL

see Industrial Sociology

SOCIOLOGY, MEDICAL

see Social Medicine

SOCIOLOGY, MILITARY

see also Militarism; Military Policy; Peace

Nunn, Frederick M. Yesterday's Soldiers: European Military Professionalism in South America, 1890-1940. LC 82-6961. xiv, 358p. 1983. 26.95x (ISBN 0-8032-3305-1). U of Nebr Pr.

Richardson, Frank M. Mars Without Venus: Study of Some Homosexual Generals. 188p. 1982. 14.95 (ISBN 0-85158-148-X, Pub. by Salem Hse Ltd.). Merrimack Bk Serv.

SOCIOLOGY, RELIGIOUS

see Religion and Sociology

SOCIOLOGY, URBAN

see also Cities and Towns; City and Town Life; Urban Renewal; Urbanization

Bender, Thomas. Toward an Urban Vision: Ideas & Institutions in Nineteenth-Century America. LC 82-47980. 296p. (Orig.). 1982. pap. text ed. 7.50x (ISBN 0-8018-2925-9). Johns Hopkins.

Castells, Manuel. The City & the Grassroots: A Cross-Cultural Theory of Urban Social Movements. LC 82-40099. (California Ser. in Urban Development: Vol. 2). (Illus.). 600p. 1983. 38.50x (ISBN 0-520-04756-7). U of Cal Pr.

Pons, Valdo & Francis, Ray, eds. The Problems of the Contemporary City: Studies in Urban Sociology. (Sociological Review Monograph: No. 30). 1983. pap. price not set (ISBN 0-7100-9471-X). Routledge & Kegan.

Teufel, Manfred. Das Nachste Dorf Liegt in America: Waterville-eine kleine Gemeinde zwischen Marginalitat und Anpassung. 279p. 1982. write for info (ISBN 3-8204-5803-4). P Lang Pubs.

Williams, Peter, ed. Social Process & the City: Urban Studies Yearbook, 1. 242p. 1983. text ed. 27.50x (ISBN 0-86861-237-5). Allen Unwin.

SOCIOLOGY AND ART

see Art and Society

SOCIOLOGY AND LITERATURE

see Literature and Society

SOCIOLOGY AND RELIGION

see Religion and Sociology

SOCIOLOGY OF LANGUAGE

see Sociolinguistics

SOCIOLOGY OF LAW

see Sociological Jurisprudence

SOCKETS, ELECTRIC

see Electric Contactors

SOCRATES

Hackworth, Robert D. & Howland, Joseph W. College Algebra & Trigonometry As Socrates Might Have Taught Them. rev. ed. (Illus.). 295p. 1981. pap. text ed. 14.95x (ISBN 0-943202-01-9). H & H Pub.

SODIUM CHLORIDE
see Salt
SOFISM
see Sufism
SOFT DRINKS
see Beverages
SOFTBALL
see also Baseball

Eley, Glen D. Improve Your Softball Program, H.S. & College. (Illus.). 60p. 1983. pap. 5.95 (ISBN 0-940934-04-3). GDE Pubns OH.

--Softball-The Game of the Eighties: Slowpitch-How to-Guide. 75p. 1983. pap. price not set. GDE Pubns OH.

Softball. (Scorebooks Ser.). 2.95 (ISBN 0-88314-168-X). AAHPERD.

SOFTWARE, COMPUTER
see Computer Programs; Programming (Electronic Computers); Programming Languages (Electronic Computers);
also similiar headings
SOIL (ENGINEERING)
see Soil Mechanics
SOIL CHEMISTRY

Fryer, Lee. The Bio-Gardener's Bible: Building Super-Fertile Soil. (Illus.). 288p. 1982. 14.95 (ISBN 0-686-82061-4); pap. 9.95 (ISBN 0-8019-7289-2). Chilton.

Organic Materials & Soil Productivity in the Near East. (FAO Soils Bulletin Ser.: No. 45). 280p. 1982. pap. 24.00 (ISBN 92-5-001217-9, F2334, FAO). Unipub.

Van Assche, C., ed. Agro-Ecological Aspects of Soil Disinfestation. (Agro-Ecosystems Ser.: Vol. 1, No. 2). 1974. 18.00 (ISBN 0-686-43414-5). Elsevier.

SOIL CONSERVATION
see also Erosion

Environmental Quality: An Annotated Bibliography of Papers Published in the Soil Science Society of America Proceedings 1962-1971. 73p. 1975. pap. 5.50 (ISBN 0-89118-762-6). Soil Sci Soc Am.

Pritchard, H. Wayne, pref. by. Resource Conservation Glossary. 3rd ed. LC 82-5830. 193p. 1982. pap. 7.00 (ISBN 0-935734-09-0). Soil Conservation.

SOIL ECOLOGY

Gray. The Ecology of Soil Bacteria. 698p. 1982. 70.00x (ISBN 0-85323-161-3, Pub. by Liverpool Univ England). State Mutual Bk.

Van Assche, C., ed. Agricultural Aspects of Soil Disinfestation. (Agro-Ecosystems Ser.: Vol. 1, No. 3). (Proceedings). 1974. 20.50 (ISBN 0-686-43413-7). Elsevier.

SOIL ENGINEERING
see Soil Mechanics
SOIL FUNGI
see Soil Micro-Organisms
SOIL MAPS
see Soils-Maps
SOIL MECHANICS
see also Foundations; Rock Mechanics; Soil Physics; Structural Engineering; Underground Construction

American Society of Civil Engineers, compiled by. Engineering & Construction in Tropical & Residual Soils. LC 81-71563. 750p. 1982. pap. text ed. 49.50 (ISBN 0-87262-292-4). Am Soc Civil Eng.

Desai & Christian. Numerical Methods in Geotechnic Engineering. 1977. 54.50 (ISBN 0-07-016542-4). McGraw.

Kruse, E. G. & Burdick, C. R., eds. Environmentally Sound Water & Soil Management. LC 82-72213. 544p. 1982. pap. text ed. 42.50 (ISBN 0-87262-312-2). Am Soc Civil Eng.

Mechanical Replacement Processes in Mobile Soft Calcic Horizons: Their Role in Soil & Landscape Genesis in an Area Near Merida, Spain. 208p. 1983. pap. 29.00 (ISBN 90-220-0810-X, PDC254, Pudoc). Unipub.

Singh, Alam. Soil Engineering in Theory & Practice, Vol. 2. 2nd ed. 1982. 45.00 (ISBN 0-86590-024-8). Apt Bks.

Smith, G. N. Elements of Soil Mechanics. 5th ed. 440p. 1982. 49.00x (ISBN 0-246-11334-0, Pub. by Granada England). State Mutual Bk.

--Elements of Soil Mechanics for Civil & Mining Engineers. 493p. 1982. pap. text ed. 21.75x (ISBN 0-246-11765-6, Pub. by Granada England). Renouf.

Wu, T. H. Soil Mechanics. 2nd ed. LC 75-26633. 440p. 1982. Repr. of 1979 ed. text ed. 24.00x (ISBN 0-918498-02-3). T H Wu.

SOIL MICRO-ORGANISMS

Alexander, Martin. Introduction to Soil Microbiology. 2nd ed. LC 77-1319. 467p. 1977. text ed. 28.95 (ISBN 0-471-02179-2); arabic translation avail. Wiley.

Gray. The Ecology of Soil Bacteria. 698p. 1982. 70.00x (ISBN 0-85323-161-3, Pub. by Liverpool Univ England). State Mutual Bk.

Micronutrients & the Nutrient Status of Soils: A Global Study. (FAO Soils Bulletin Ser.: No. 48). 444p. 1982. 32.75 (ISBN 92-5-101193-1, F2331, FAO). Unipub.

SOIL ORGANIC MATTER
see Humus
SOIL PHYSICS
see also Soil Mechanics

Baver, Leonard D., et al. Soil Physics. 4th ed. LC 72-5318. 498p. 1972. 34.95x (ISBN 0-471-05974-9). Wiley.

SOIL SCIENCE
see also Agriculture

Environmental Quality: An Annotated Bibliography of Papers Published in the Soil Science Society of America Proceedings 1962-1971. 73p. 1975. pap. 5.50 (ISBN 0-89118-762-6). Soil Sci Soc Am.

Fairbridge, R. W. & Finkl, C. W., Jr., eds. The Encyclopedia of Soil Science: Part 1, Physics, Chemistry, Biology, Fertility, & Technology. LC 78-31233. (Encyclopedia of Earth Sciences Ser.: Vol. XII). 700p. 1979. 76.00 (ISBN 0-87933-176-3). Hutchinson Ross.

Foth, Henry D. Fundamentals of Soil Science. 6th ed. LC 77-86509. 436p. 1978. 28.95 (ISBN 0-471-26792-9). Wiley.

Kittick, J. A. Acid Sulfate Weathering. 1982. 12.50 (ISBN 0-89118-770-7). Soil Sci Soc Am.

Larson, William E. & Walsh, Leo M, eds. Soil & Water Resources: Reasearch Priorities for the Nation-Proceedings. 229p. 1981. 12.00 (ISBN 0-89118-768-5). Soil Sci Soc Am.

Rieger, Samuel, ed. The Genesis & Classification of Cold Soils: Monographs. 206p. Date not set. price not set (ISBN 0-12-588120-7). Acad Pr.

SOIL SURVEYS

Brink, A. B. & Partridge, T. C. Soil Survey for Engineering. (Monographs on Soil Survey). 1982. text ed. 74.00x (ISBN 0-19-854537-1). Oxford U Pr.

SOILLESS AGRICULTURE
see Hydroponics
SOILS
see also Agricultural Chemistry; Clay; Drainage; Fertilizers and Manures; Humus; Irrigation; Particles; Reclamation of Land
also headings beginning with the word Soil

Black, C. A. Soil-Plant Relationships. 2nd ed. LC 67-28946. 792p. (Orig.). 1968. 49.95x (ISBN 0-471-07723-2). Wiley.

Donahue, Roy & Miller, John. Soils: An Introduction to Soils & Plant Growth. 5th ed. (Illus.). 656p. 1983. text ed. 27.95 (ISBN 0-13-822288-6). P-H.

Foth, Henry & Schafer, John. Soil Geography & Land Use. LC 79-27731. 484p. 1980. text ed. 32.95 (ISBN 0-471-01710-8). Wiley.

Kilmer, Victor J., ed. Handbook of Soils & Climate in Agriculture. 456p. 1982. 94.00 (ISBN 0-686-84130-1). CRC Pr.

SOILS-BACTERIOLOGY
see Soil Micro-Organisms
SOILS-MAPS

Barker, Raymond J. & McDole, Robert E. Idaho Soils Atlas. LC 82-60201. (Illus.). 1983. 18.95 (ISBN 0-89301-088-X). U Pr of Idaho.

SOILS-MECHANICS
see Soil Mechanics
SOILS-ASIA

Organic Materials & Soil Productivity in the Near East. (FAO Soils Bulletin Ser.: No. 45). 280p. 1982. pap. 24.00 (ISBN 92-5-001217-9, F2334, FAO). Unipub.

SOILS (ENGINEERING)
see Soil Mechanics
SOLAR BATTERIES

Backus, Charles E. Solar Cells. LC 75-46381. (IEEE Press Selected Reprint Ser.). 504p. 1976. 32.95x (ISBN 0-471-01981-X); (Pub. by Wiley-Interscience). Wiley.

Blakeslee, et al. Tunnel Diode Interconnect Junctions for Cascade Solar Cells: Progess in Solar Energy Supplements. (SERI Ser.). 50p. 1983. pap. text ed. 7.50x (ISBN 0-89553-078-3). Am Solar Energy.

Directory of Photovoltaic Manufacturers, Distributors, & Consultants. (Progress in Solar Energy Supplements SERI Ser.). 1983. pap. text ed. cancelled (ISBN 0-89553-099-6). Am Solar Energy.

Fahrenbruch, Alan & Bube, Richard. Fundamentals of Solar Cells. LC 82-13919. Date not set. price not set (ISBN 0-12-247680-8). Acad Pr.

Heymann, O. & Nguyen, O. Simulation & Analysis of Immobilized Cell Fermentors. (Progress in Solar Energy Supplements SERI Ser.). 1983. pap. text ed. 7.50x (ISBN 0-89553-091-0). Am Solar Energy.

Hu, Chenming & White, Richard M. Solar Cells: From Basic to Advanced Systems. (Series in Electrical Engineering: Power & Energy). (Illus.). 288p. 1983. text ed. 30.00 (ISBN 0-07-030745-8, C). McGraw.

Interim Performance Criteria for Photovoltaic Energy Systems. (Progress in Solar Energy Ser.: Suppl.). 260p. 1983. pap. text ed. 21.00x (ISBN 0-89553-100-3). Am Solar Energy.

Jacques, J. A. Respiratory Physiology. 1979. text ed. 27.95 (ISBN 0-07-032247-3). McGraw.

Nuss, G. & Longrigg, P. Performance Criteria for Photovoltaic Energy Systems. (Progress in Solar Energy Supplements Ser.). 400p. 1982. pap. text ed. 28.50x (ISBN 0-89553-070-8). Am Solar Energy.

Sillman, S. The Analysis of on Site Use & Sell Back in Residental Photovoltaic Systems. (Progress in Solar Energy Supplements Ser.). 70p. 1983. pap. text ed. 9.00x (ISBN 0-89553-064-3). Am Solar Energy.

Williamson, D., et al. Gallium Arsinide Solar Cells in House Fabrication Project: Progress in Solar Energy Supplements. 50p. 1982. pap. text ed. 7.50x (ISBN 0-89553-077-5). Am Solar Energy.

SOLAR CELLS
see Solar Batteries
SOLAR CORONA
see Sun
SOLAR ENERGY
see also Solar Engines; Solar Heating

American Institute of Architects. Architect's Handbook of Energy Practice: Active Solar Systems. (Illus.). 58p. 1982. pap. 18.00x (ISBN 0-913962-54-6). Am Inst Arch.

Anderson, Bruce & Wells, Malcolm. Passive Solar Energy. 1981. pap. 10.95 (ISBN 0-931790-09-3). Brick Hse Pub.

Anderson, Edward E. Fundamentals of Solar Thermal Energy Conversion. LC 81-22852. 576p. Date not set. text ed. 29.95 (ISBN 0-201-00008-3). A-W.

Anderson, J. & Subbarao, K. A Graphical Method Based on Frequency Domain for Passive Building Energy Analysis. (Progress in Solar Energy Supplements SERI Ser.). 60p. 1983. pap. text ed. 9.00x (ISBN 0-89553-088-0). Am Solar Energy.

Bachofen, R. & Mislin, H., eds. New Trends in Research & Utilization of Solar Energy Through Biological Systems. (Experientia Supplementum: Vol. 43). 156p. 1982. text ed. 24.95 (ISBN 3-7643-1335-8). Birkhauser.

Balcomb, J. D., et al. Passive Solar Heating & Cooling: Proceedings of the Conference & Workshop, May 1976, Albuquerque, New Mexico. Keller, M. H., ed. 355p. 1983. pap. text ed. 27.00x (ISBN 0-89553-108-9). Am Solar Energy.

Barlow, A. Analysis of the Absorption Process & of Desicdant Cooling Systems: A Pseudo-Steady State Model for Coupled Heat & Mass Transfer. (Progress in Solar Energy Supplements Ser.). 160p. 1983. pap. text ed. 15.00x (ISBN 0-89553-069-4). Am Solar Energy.

Barlow, R. An Assessment of Dehumidifier Geometries for Dessicant Cooling Systems. (Progress in Solar Energy Supplements SERI Ser.). 75p. 1983. pap. text ed. 9.00x (ISBN 0-89553-082-1). Am Solar Energy.

Bloss, W. H. & Grassi, G., eds. E. C. Photovoltaic Solar Energy Conference, 4th. 1982. 96.00 (ISBN 90-277-1463-0, Pub. by Reidel Holland). Kluwer Boston.

Booth, Don & Booth, Jonathan. Building for Energy Independence With Sun Earth Buffering & Superinsulation. (Orig.). 1983. 25.00 (ISBN 0-686-37853-9); pap. 20.00 (ISBN 0-9604422-3-5). Community Builders.

--Building for Energy Independence with Sun-Earth Buffering & Superinsulation. 1983. pap. 17.95 (ISBN 0-9604422-3-5). Comm Builders.

Bradley, Barbara, ed. Proceeding of the National Passive Solar Energy Conference, 1-6, 1976-1981: Index & Supplement. 1983. pap. text ed. 10.00x (ISBN 0-89553-109-7). Am Solar Energy.

Brucknet, A. P. & Hertzberg, A. High Temperature Integrated Thermal Energy Storage for Solar Thermal Applications. (Progress in Solar Energy Ser.: Suppl.). 115p. 1983. pap. text ed. 13.00x (ISBN 0-89553-135-6). Am Solar Energy.

Canadian Solar Energy Society. Energex 82 Technical Conference: Proceedings. 500p. 1983. pap. text ed. 70.00 (ISBN 0-89553-120-8). Am Solar Energy.

Center for Self Sufficiency Research Division Staff. Index to Solar Education, Home Plan Kits & Solar Related Companies. 100p. 1983. pap. text ed. 19.95 (ISBN 0-910811-35-0). Center Self.

Cousins, K. Residential Conservation Service Inspector-Installer Examination Guide. (Progress in Solar Energy Supplements SERI Ser.). 60p. 1983. pap. text ed. 9.00x (ISBN 0-89553-087-2). Am Solar Energy.

Crowley, J. S. & Zimmerman, L. Z. Residential Passive Solar Design. 256p. 1983. 34.95 (ISBN 0-07-014769-8, P&RB). McGraw.

Daniels, Farrington. Direct Use of the Sun's Energy. LC 64-20913. 391p. 1983. pap. text ed. 7.95x (ISBN 0-300-02986-1). Yale U Pr.

--Direct Use of the Sun's Energy. pap. 7.95 (ISBN 0-686-42820-X, Y-457). Yale U Pr.

Diekmann, O. Risk Assessment in Cost Estimating for New Technologies. (Progress in Solar Energy Supplement SERI Ser.). 75p. 1983. pap. text ed. 9.00 (ISBN 0-89553-084-8). Am Solar Energy.

Energy Development International & Heffner, G. Potential Markets for U.S. Solar & Conservation Technologies in Thailand: Supplement. (Progress in Solar Energy Ser.). 224p. 1983. pap. text ed. 18.00 (ISBN 0-89553-116-X). Am Solar Energy.

Energy Development International & Weingart, J. Potential Markets for U.S. Solar & Conservation Technologies in Indonesia: Supplement. (Progress in Solar Energy Ser.). 204p. 1983. pap. text ed. 18.00 (ISBN 0-89553-115-1). Am Solar Ener.

Flaim, T. A User's Guide to SERICOST: A Computer Program for Estimating Electric Utility Avoided Cost Rates. (Progress in Solar Energy Supplements SERI Ser.). 40p. 1983. pap. text ed. 7.50x (ISBN 0-89553-075-9). Am Solar Energy.

--A User's Guide to SERICPAC: A Computer Program for Calculating Electric Utility Avoided Cost Rates. (Progress in Solar Energy Supplements SERI Ser.). 140p. 1983. pap. text ed. 13.50x (ISBN 0-89553-074-0). Am Solar Energy.

Flaim, T. & Sulliven, R. L. WECS Value Analysis: A Comparative Assessment of Four Methods. (Progress in Solar Energy Supplements SERI Ser.). 70p. 1982. pap. text ed. 9.00 (ISBN 0-89553-073-2). Am Solar Energy.

Gee, O. Line Focus Sun Tracker Performance Assessment. (Progress in Solar Energy Supplements SERI Ser.). 1983. pap. text ed. 7.50x (ISBN 0-89553-094-5). Am Solar Energy.

Gottlieb, Richard & Oddo, Sandra, eds. The Solar Energy Directory. 376p. 1983. 50.00 (ISBN 0-8242-0680-0). Wilson.

Green, Bruce & Glenn, Barbara. Community Planner's Guidebook to Renewable Technologies. 250p. 1983. pap. 17.95x (ISBN 0-89553-071-6). Am Solar Energy.

Harris, Jeffrey P. & Hollander, Jack M., eds. Improving Energy Systems in Buildings: Progress & Problems: Supplement. (Progress in Solar Energy Ser.). 650p. 1983. pap. text ed. 43.50 (ISBN 0-89553-122-4). Am Solar Energy.

Hohenemser, K. H. & Swift, A. H. Investigation of Passive Blade Cyclic Pitch Variation using an Automatic Yaw Control System. (Progress in Solar Energy, Supplements Ser.). 112p. 1982. pap. text ed. 12.00x (ISBN 0-89553-105-4). Am Solar Energy.

Howard, Robert & Bumba, V. Atlas of Solar Magnetic Fields. 1967. 10.00 (ISBN 0-87279-637-X). Carnegie Inst.

Kapany, Narinder S., ed. Finance & Utilization of Solar Energy: Supplement. (Progress in Solar Energy Ser.). 1983. pap. text ed. 45.00 (ISBN 0-89553-121-6). Am Solar Energy.

Kinderman, E. M. & Goen, R. L. Potential Markets for U.S. Solar & Conservation Technologies in Argentina, Chile & Colombia: Supplement. (Progress in Solar Energy Ser.). 175p. 1983. pap. text ed. 15.00 (ISBN 0-89553-117-8). Am Solar Energy.

Kriz, Thomas, et al. Thermal Energy Storage for Process Heat & Building Applications. (Progress in Solar Enery Ser.: Suppl.). 200p. 1983. pap. text ed. 16.50 (ISBN 0-89553-138-0). Am Solar Energy.

Kut & Hare. Applied Solar Energy. 2nd ed. 1983. text ed. 34.95 (ISBN 0-408-01244-7). Butterworth.

Kutscher, C. & Barlow, R. Dynamic Performance of Packed Bed Dehumidifiers: Experimental Results from the SERI Desiccant Test Loop. (Progress in Solar Energy Supplements SERI Ser.). 75p. 1983. pap. text ed. 9.00x (ISBN 0-89553-085-6). Am Solar Energy.

Lewandowski, A. Response Time Testing on Concentrating Collectors. (Progress in Solar Energy Supplements SERI Ser.). 1983. pap. text ed. 7.50x (ISBN 0-89553-090-2). Am Solar Energy.

McVeigh, J. C. Sun Power: An Introduction to the Applications of Solar Energy. 2nd ed. (Illus.). 240p. 1983. 40.00 (ISBN 0-08-026148-5); pap. 15.00 (ISBN 0-08-026147-7). Pergamon.

Masterson, K. & Bohn, M. Scatterplate Mapping for Solar Concentrators. (Progress in Solar Energy Supplements SERI Ser.). 75p. 1983. pap. text ed. 7.50x (ISBN 0-89553-089-9). Am Solar Energy.

Mathur, S. S. & Kandpal, T. C. Solar Concentrators: A Bibliography. (Energy). 220p. 1982. pap. 45.00x (ISBN 0-910661-01-4). Innovative Inform.

O May. Flow Instability During Direct Steam Generation in a Line Focus Solar Collector System. (Progress in Solar Energy Supplements SERI Ser.). 1983. pap. text ed. 7.50x (ISBN 0-89553-096-1). Am Solar Energy.

Overton, H. P., compiled by. The Solar Energy Index. 100p. Date not set. pap. text ed. 17.95 (ISBN 0-910811-11-3). Center Self.

Percival, D. & Harper, J. Solar Electric Technologies: Methods of Electric Utility Value Analysis. (Progress in Solar Energy Supplements Ser.). 65p. 1983. pap. text ed. 9.00x (ISBN 0-89553-079-1). Am Solar Energy.

Potential Markets for U.S. Solar & Conservation Technologies in Costa Rica, Dominican Republic, Barbados & Antigua: Supplement. (Progress in Solar Energy Ser.). 180p. 1983. pap. text ed. 15.00 (ISBN 0-89553-114-3). Am Solar Energy.

Priest, E. Solar Magnetohydrodynamics. 1982. lib. bdg. 99.00 (ISBN 90-277-1374-X, Pub. by Reidel Holland). Kluwer Boston.

Rich, Daniel & Veigel, Jon M., eds. The Solar Energy Transition: Implementation & Policy Implications. 205p. 1983. lib. bdg. 23.00x (ISBN 0-86531-603-1). Westview.

Schell, D. & LeBoeuf, C. Behavior of Nine Solar Pond Candidate Salts. (Progress in Solar Energy Supplements). 60p. 1983. pap. text ed. 9.00x (ISBN 0-89553-086-4). Am Solar Energy.

Schiffman, Yale M. & D-Alessio, Gregory J. Limits to Solar & Biomass Energy Growth. LC 81-48071. 1983. price not set (ISBN 0-669-05253-1). Lexington Bks.

Schiffman, Yale M. & D'Alessio, Gregory J. Solar Energy Systems: An Alternative Perspective. LC 81-48071. 1983. write for info. (ISBN 0-669-05253-1). Lexington Bks.

Short, Walter & Solar Energy Research Int. Economic Assessment of Conservation & Solar Technologies: Method & Data. (Progress in Solar Energy Ser.: Suppl.). 150p. 1983. pap. 13.50 (ISBN 0-89553-131-3). Am Solar Energy.

Solar Action: 27 Communities Boost Renewable Energy Use. 1983. pap. 9.00 (ISBN 0-686-84642-7). Am Solar Energy.

Solar Energy Research Institute. A New Prosperity: Building a Sustainable Energy Future (Solar Conservation Study) LC 81-6089. 1981. 19.95x (ISBN 0-931790-53-0). Brick Hse Pub.

Turner, W. D., ed. Solar Engineering, 1982. 603p. 1982. 85.00 (H00212). ASME.

Vitro Laboratories. Reliability & Maintainability of Solar System Components. (Progress in Solar Energy Ser.: Suppl.). 100p. 1983. pap. text ed. 10.50 (ISBN 0-89553-134-8). Am Solar Energy.

--Solar Energy Performance History Information Ser. Vol. 4, Performance of Active Solar Space Heating Systems, Comparitive Report; Vol. 5, Performance of Solar Hot Water Systems, Comaparitive Report; Vol. 6, Performance of Active Solar Space Cooling Systems, Comparitive Report. 610p. 1983. pap. 69.50 (ISBN 0-89934-200-0, H-045). Solar Energy Info.

Waddington, D. & Herlevich, F. Ann. Evaluation of Pumps & Motors for PV Water Pumping Systems. (Progress in Solar Energy Supplements SERI Ser.). 150p. 1983. pap. text ed. 13.50x (ISBN 0-89553-081-3). Am Solar Energy.

Wells, Karen M. Building Solar: How the Professional Builder is Making Solar Construction Work. (Illus.). 275p. 1983. text ed. 29.95 (ISBN 0-8436-0139-6). CBI Pub.

Zaborsky, Oskar R. & Mitsui, Akira, eds. CRC Handbook of Biosolar Resources: Vol. I. Basic Principles, 2 Pts. 1982. Pt. 1, 704 pgs. 99.50 (ISBN 0-8493-3471-3); Pt. 2, 608 pgs. 99.50 (ISBN 0-8493-3472-1). CRC Pr.

SOLAR ENGINES

Monegon, Ltd. Solar Energy Makes Sense Now: A How to Guide to Saving Money with Free Energy from the Sun. (Illus.). 42p. (Orig.). (gr. 10-12). 1982. pap. 11.95 (ISBN 0-940520-26-5). Monegon Ltd.

Rose, Pat R. The Solar Boat Book. rev. ed. 266p. 1983. 14.95 (ISBN 0-89815-089-2); pap. 8.95 (ISBN 0-89815-086-8). Ten Speed Pr.

SOLAR HEAT

see Solar Heating

SOLAR-HEATED HOUSES

see Solar Houses

SOLAR HEATING

see also Solar Houses

Adams, Jennifer A. The Solar Church. Hoffman, Douglas R., ed. 288p. (Orig.). 1982. pap. 9.95 (ISBN 0-8298-0482-X). Pilgrim NY.

Balcomb, J. D., et al. Passive Solar Heating & Cooling: Proceedings of the Conference & Workshop, May 1976, Albuquerque, New Mexico. Keller, M. H., ed. 355p. 1983. pap. text ed. 27.00x (ISBN 0-89553-108-9). Am Solar Energy.

Cobb, O., et al. A Performance Data Management Program for Solar Thermal Energy Systems. (Progress in Solar Energy Supplements SERI Ser.). 120p. 1983. pap. text ed. 12.00x (ISBN 0-89553-101-1). Am Solar Energy.

Energy-Efficient Construction Methods. (Illus.). 1982. pap. 12.95 (ISBN 0-918984-01-7). Solarvision.

Gordon, O. Design, Analysis & Otimization of Solar Industrial Process Heat Plants Without Storage. (Progress in Solar Energy Supplements SERI Ser.). 1983. pap. text ed. 9.00x (ISBN 0-89553-092-9). Am Solar Energy.

Heat Saving Home Insulation. (Illus.). 1982. pap. 9.95 (ISBN 0-918984-03-3). Solarvision.

How to Install Solar Hot Water. (Illus.). 1982. pap. 11.95 (ISBN 0-918984-02-5). Solarvision.

Howard, B. D. & Pollock, E. O. Passive Solar Space Heating Systems Performance: Comparative Reports. 260p. 1983. pap. 34.50x (ISBN 0-89934-004-0, A-021). Solar Energy Info.

Keisling, Bill. The Homeowner's Handbook of Solar Water Heating Systems: How to Build or Buy Systems to Heat Your Water, Your Swimming Pool, Hot Tub, or Spa. Halpin, Anne, ed. (Illus.). 256p. 1983. 16.95 (ISBN 0-87857-444-1, 14-166-0); pap. 12.95 (ISBN 0-87857-445-X, 14-166-1). Rodale Pr Inc.

Kutscher, C., et al. Design Approaches for Solar Industrial Process Heat Systems. (Progress in Solar Energy Supplements SERI Ser.). 500p. 1983. pap. text ed. 45.00x (ISBN 0-89553-083-X). Am Solar Energy.

Kutscher, Charles F. & Davenport, R. L. Design Approaches for Solar Industrial Process Heat Systems: Nontracking & Line Focus Collector Technologies. (Progress in Solar Energy Ser.). 452p. 1983. pap. text ed. 31.50 (ISBN 0-89553-113-5). Am Solar Energy.

O'Dougherty. Line Focus Receiver Heat Losses. (Progress in Solar Energy Supplements SERI Ser.). 1983. pap. text ed. 7.50x (ISBN 0-89553-095-3). Am Solar Energy.

Photovoltaic System Design. (Illus.). 1982. 59.95 (ISBN 0-918984-04-1). Solarvision.

Plante, Russell. Solar Domestic Hot Water: A Practical Guide to Installation & Understanding. 350p. 1983. text ed. 18.95x (ISBN 0-471-09592-3). Wiley.

Scheller, William G. Solar Heating. 1980. pap. 8.95 (ISBN 0-686-82335-4). Sams.

Swisher, J. Heat Pump Demonstration Analysis. (Progress in Solar Energy Supplements Ser.). 200p. 1982. pap. text ed. 16.50x (ISBN 0-89553-067-8). Am Solar Energy.

Vitro Laboratories. Solar Energy Performance History Information Ser. Vol. 4, Performance of Active Solar Space Heating Systems, Comparitive Report; Vol. 5, Performance of Solar Hot Water Systems, Comaparitive Report; Vol. 6, Performance of Active Solar Space Cooling Systems, Comparitive Report. 610p. 1983. pap. 69.50 (ISBN 0-89934-200-0, H-045). Solar Energy Info.

Williams, J. Richard. Design & Installation of Solar Heating & Hot Water System. LC 82-72856. (Illus.). 427p. 1982. 39.95 (ISBN 0-250-40593-8). Ann Arbor Science.

--Passive Solar Heating. LC 82-72857. (Illus.). 300p. 1982. 24.50 (ISBN 0-250-40601-2). Ann Arbor Science.

SOLAR HOUSES

Crowther, Richard L. Affordable Passive Solar Homes. 160p. 1983. 15.00 (ISBN 0-89553-129-1). Am Solar Energy.

Dawson, Joseph C. Seeking Shelter: How to Find & Finance an Energy-Efficient Home. (Illus.). 256p. 1983. 17.95 (ISBN 0-688-00902-6). Morrow.

Ebert, Robert, ed. Solar Home Plan Book. 1983. pap. 3.95 (ISBN 0-942886-03-8). Periwinkle Pubns.

Hibshman, Dan. Your Affordable Solar Home. (Tools for Today Ser.). 1983. pap. 7.95 (ISBN 0-686-84929-9). Sierra.

Holtz, Michael, et al. International Passive Architectural Survey: Announcement of Results. (Progress in Solar Energy Supplements Ser.). 250p. 1982. pap. text ed. 19.50x (ISBN 0-89553-068-6). Am Solar Energy.

Hotton, Peter. So You Want to Build an Energy-Efficient Addition. (Illus.). 256p. (Orig.). 1983. pap. 12.00i (ISBN 0-316-37385-0). Little.

Sunset Books & Sunset Magazine, ed. Solar Remodeling. LC 82-81372. (Illus.). 96p. (Orig.). 1982. pap. 4.95 (ISBN 0-376-01534-9). Sunset-Lane.

Wells, Madeline & Williamson, Jane. So You Want to See A Solar Building? A Tour Guide for Northern New Mexico. (Illus.). 128p. 1982. pap. 6.95 (ISBN 0-942372-04-2). NMSEA.

Your Affordable Solar Home. LC 82-10747. (Tools for Today Ser.). (Illus.). 128p. (Orig.). 1983. pap. 7.95 (ISBN 0-87156-327-4). Sierra.

SOLAR PHYSICS

see Sun

SOLAR POWER

see Solar Energy

SOLAR RADIATION

see also Solar Batteries; Solar Energy

Palz, W., ed. Solar Radiation Data. 1982. 24.50 (ISBN 90-277-1387-1, Pub. by Reidel Holland). Kluwer Boston.

Shepard. Solar Law. (incl. 1981 suppl.). 1978. 55.00 (ISBN 0-07-035400-6); annual pocket part suppl. 16.00 (ISBN 0-07-035404-9). McGraw.

SOLAR SYSTEM

see also Comets; Earth; Moon; Satellites; Sun
also names of individual planets

Jones, B. W. & Keynes, Milton. The Solar System. (Illus.). 400p. 1983. 45.00 (ISBN 0-08-026496-4); pap. 22.50 (ISBN 0-08-026495-6). Pergamon.

O'Leary, Brian & Beatty, J. Kelly, eds. The New Solar System. 240p. 1982. 14.95 (ISBN 0-933346-36-0); pap. 7.75 (ISBN 0-933346-37-9). Sky Pub.

SOLAR SYSTEM-JUVENILE LITERATURE

Adams, Richard. Our Wonderful Solar System. LC 82-17413. (Question & Answer Bks.). (Illus.). 32p. (gr. 3-6). 1983. PLB 8.59 (ISBN 0-89375-872-8); pap. text ed. 1.95 (ISBN 0-89375-873-6). Troll Assocs.

Branley, Franklyn. Saturn. LC 81-43890. (Illus.). 64p. (gr. 3-6). 1983. 11.49i (ISBN 0-690-04213-2, TYC-J); PLB 11.89g (ISBN 0-690-04214-0). Har-Row.

SOLDIERS

see also Armies; Generals; Military Art and Science; Military Biography; Scouts and Scouting; Veterans
also subdivision Military Life under Armies, e.g. United States-Army-Military Life

Cortright, David. International Soldiers' Movement. 23p. 1975. 0.50 (ISBN 0-686-43098-0). Recon Pubns.

Janowitz, Morris & Wesbrook, Stephen D. The Political Education of Soldiers. (Sage Research Progress Series on War, Revolution, & Peacekeeping: Vol. 11). 320p. 1982. 25.00 (ISBN 0-8039-1020-7). Sage.

McCarthy, Carlton. Detailed Minutiae of Soldier Life. (Collector's Library of the Civil War). 1982. 26.60 (ISBN 0-8094-4245-0). Silver.

Rolde, Neil. Sir William Pepperrell of Colonial New England. (Illus.). xi, 221p. 1982. 12.95 (ISBN 0-88448-048-8); pap. 8.95 (ISBN 0-88448-047-X). Harpswell Pr.

SOLDIERS-PENSIONS

see Pensions, Military

SOLDIERS-UNIFORMS

see Uniforms, Military

SOLDIERS' LIFE

Elting, John R. & Cragg, Dan. A Dictionary of Soldier Talk. 480p. 1983. 24.95 (ISBN 0-686-83680-4, ScribT). Scribner.

SOLICITORS

see Lawyers

SOLID FILM

see Thin Films

SOLID STATE CHEMISTRY

see also Solid State Physics

Rosenblatt, G. M. & Worrell, W. L., eds. Progress in Solid State Chemistry, Vol. 13. (Illus.). 376p. 1982. 112.00 (ISBN 0-08-029712-9). Pergamon.

SOLID STATE ELECTRONICS

Introduction to Automotive Solid State Electronics. 1981. pap. 9.95 (ISBN 0-672-21825-9). Sams.

Pierret, Robert F. & Neudeck, Gerold W. Modular Series on Solid State Devices: Semiconductor Fundamentals, Vol. I. LC 81-14978. (Electrical Engineering Ser.). (Illus.). Date not set. pap. text ed. 35.80 (ISBN 0-201-05320-9); solutions manual avail. (ISBN 0-201-05324-1). A-W.

Wells, R. Solid State Power Rectifiers. 186p. 1982. text ed. 24.50 (ISBN 0-246-11751-6, Pub. by Granada England). Renouf.

SOLID STATE PHYSICS

see also Solid State Chemistry; Solids

Demokan, M. S. Mode-Locking in Solid-State & Semiconductor Lasers. 227p. 1982. 39.95 (ISBN 0-471-10498-1). Res Stud Pr.

Kunin, I. A. Elastic Media with Microstructure II: Three Dimensional Models. (Springer Ser. in Solid-State Physics: Vol. 44). (Illus.). 290p. 1983. 39.50 (ISBN 0-387-12078-5). Springer-Verlag.

Mehring, M. Principles of High Resolution NMR in Solids. (Illus.). 342p. 1983. 38.00 (ISBN 0-387-11852-7). Springer-Verlag.

Shukla, P. Physics of Disordered Solids. 200p. 1982. text ed. 16.00x (ISBN 0-391-02755-7, Pub. by Concept India). Humanities.

SOLID WASTE MANAGEMENT

see Factory and Trade Waste; Refuse and Refuse Disposal; Salvage (Waste, etc.)

SOLIDS

see also Crystals; Solid State Physics; Thin Films

Catlow, C. R. & Mackrodt, W. C., eds. Computer Simulation of Solids. (Lecture Notes in Physics Ser.: Vol. 166). 320p. 1983. pap. 17.00 (ISBN 0-387-11588-9). Springer-Verlag.

Chalmers, Bruce. The Structure & Properties of Solids: An Introduction to Materials Science. 155p. 1982. 21.95x (ISBN 0-471-26214-5, Pub. by Wiley Heyden). Wiley.

Mura, T. Micromechanics of Defects in Solids. 1982. lib. bdg. 98.00 (ISBN 90-247-2560-7, Pub. by Martinus Nijhoff Netherlands). Kluwer Boston.

Noor, A. K. & Housner, J. M., eds. Advances & Trends in Structural & Solid Mechanics: Proceedings of the Symposium, Washington D.C., USA, 4-7 October 1982. 590p. 1983. 165.00 (ISBN 0-08-029990-3). Pergamon.

Wemper, G. Mechanics of Solids with Applications to Thin Bodies. 1982. lib. bdg. 79.00 (ISBN 90-286-0880-X, Pub. by Martinus Nijhoff Netherlands). Kluwer Boston.

Williams. Pneumatic & Hydraulic Conveying of Solids. (Chemical Industries Ser.). 392p. 1983. price not set (ISBN 0-8247-1855-0). Dekker.

SOLIDS-ACOUSTIC PROPERTIES

Auld, B. Acoustic Fields & Waves in Solids, 2 vols. LC 72-8926. 1973. Set. 96.00x (ISBN 0-471-03702-8); 52.00x ea. Vol. 1 (ISBN 0-471-03700-1). Vol. 2 (ISBN 0-471-03701-X, Pub. by Wiley-Interscience). Wiley.

SOLIDS-FRACTURE

see Fracture Mechanics

SOLIDS-ION IMPLANTATION

see Ion Implantation

SOLIDS-OPTICAL PROPERTIES

Cardona, M., ed. Light Scattering in Solids I. 2nd ed. (Topics in Applied Physics Ser.: Vol. 8). (Illus.). 363p. 1983. pap. 29.00 (ISBN 0-387-11913-2). Springer-Verlag.

SOLIDS, REINFORCED

see Composite Materials

SOLOMON ISLANDS

Bathgate, M. A., et al. Change in the Solomons. (Illus.). 400p. 1982. 27.50x (ISBN 0-19-558031-1). Oxford U Pr.

Hoyt, Edwin P. The Glory of the Solomons. LC 82-48513. 320p. 1983. 17.95. Stein & Day.

SOLS

see Colloids

SOLUBLE FERMENTS

see Enzymes

SOLZHENITSYN, ALEKSANDR ISAEVICH, 1918-

Ericson, Edward E., Jr. Solzhenitsyn: The Moral Vision. 1982. pap. 6.95 (ISBN 0-8028-1718-1, 1718-1). Eerdmans.

SOMALIA

Abdillah Ahmed Wied. Out of the Somali World. 1983. price not set (ISBN 0-914110-13-6). Blyden Pr.

SOMATOLOGY

see Physical Anthropology

SOMATOTROPIN

Laron, Z. & Butenandt, O., eds. Evaluation of Growth Hormone Secretion. (Pediatric & Adolescent Endocrinology: Vol. 12). 200p. 1983. 58.75 (ISBN 3-8055-3623-2). S Karger.

SOMERSET, ENGLAND

Coulthard, Alfred J. & Watts, Martin. Windmills of Somerset & the Men Who Worked Them. 113p. 1982. 29.00x (ISBN 0-7050-0060-5, Pub. by C Skilton Scotland). State Mutual Bk.

SOMERSET, ENGLAND-ANTIQUITIES

Collinson, John. The History & Antiquities of the County of Somerset. 2001p. 1982. text ed. 168.00x (ISBN 0-86299-003-3, Pub. by Alan Sutton England). Humanities.

SONAR

Kassam, S. A. & Thomas, J. B., eds. Nonparametric Detection: Theory & Applications. LC 79-22557. (Benchmark Papers in Electrical Engineering & Computer Science Ser.: Vol. 23). 349p. 1980. 55.00. Hutchinson Ross.

SONG BOOKS

see Songs

SONGS

see also Carols; Children's Songs; Choruses; Folk-Songs; Music, Popular (Songs, etc.); National Songs; Part-Songs; Sea Songs
also subdivision Songs and Music under specific subjects, classes of persons, societies, institutions, etc., e.g. Cowboys-Songs and Music

Baehr, Tom. New Tunes-Old Friends. (Illus.). 40p. (Orig.). 1979. music book 4.95 (ISBN 0-9608842-0-3). Hogfiddle Pr.

The Blues Brothers Souvenir Songbook. 7.95 (ISBN 0-89524-111-0). Cherry Lane.

The Emmylou Harris Songbook. 14.95 (ISBN 0-89524-140-4). Cherry Lane.

The Erroll Garner Songbook. 7.95 (ISBN 0-89524-030-0). Cherry Lane.

Gidlow, Elsa. Sapphic Songs Eighteen to Eighty. (Illus.). 1982. 5.95 (ISBN 0-9606568-4-7). Druid Heights.

John Denver Anthology-Easy Guitar. 10.95 (ISBN 0-89524-142-0). Cherry Lane.

John Denver Anthology-Piano-Vocal. 14.95 (ISBN 0-89524-150-1). Cherry Lane.

John Denver's Greatest Hits. 6.95 (ISBN 0-89524-007-6). Cherry Lane.

John Denver's Greatest Hits, Vol. 2. 6.95 (ISBN 0-89524-008-4). Cherry Lane.

John Denver's Greatest Hits Easy Guitar. 4.95 (ISBN 0-89524-010-6). Cherry Lane.

Kenny Rogers Greatest Hits. 7.95 (ISBN 0-89524-128-5). Cherry Lane.

Kenny Rogers Greatest Hits Easy Guitar. 3.95 (ISBN 0-89524-076-9). Cherry Lane.

Kenny Rogers Songbook. 9.95 (ISBN 0-89524-072-6). Cherry Lane.

The Natalie Cole Songbook. 8.95 (ISBN 0-89524-048-3). Cherry Lane.

Pure Prairie League Songbook. 8.95 (ISBN 0-89524-127-7). Cherry Lane.

Singer, Jeanne. Selected Songs. LC 82-71820. (Living Composers' Ser.: No. 3). 1982. pap. 12.50 (ISBN 0-934218-26-9). Dragons Teeth.

The Statler Brothers Songbook. 7.95 (ISBN 0-89524-044-0). Cherry Lane.

Wojcio & Gustason. Music in Motion: 22 Songs in Signing Exact English, for Children. (Illus.). 106p. (ps up). Date not set. price not set (ISBN 0-916708-07-1). Modern Signs.

SONGS-BIBLIOGRAPHY

Reader's Digest Editors. Treasury of Best Loved Songs: 114 All-Time Family Favorites. LC 71-183858. 288p. 1972. 20.50 (ISBN 0-89577-007-5, Pub. by RD Assn). Random.

SONGS, AMERICAN

see also Folk-Songs, American

Maddox, Everette. The Everette Maddox Songbook. Cassin, Maxine, ed. (New Orleans Poetry Journal Press Books). (Illus.). 80p. 1982. pap. 5.00 (ISBN 0-938498-02-9). New Orleans Poetry.

SONGS, ENGLISH

Reed, Edward B., ed. Songs From the British Drama. 1925. text ed. 49.50x (ISBN 0-686-83775-4). Elliots Bks.

SONGS, FRENCH

Leyerle, Anne L. & Leyerle, William D., eds. French Diction Songs. 130p. 1983. pap. text ed. 8.95 (ISBN 0-9602296-2-0). W D Leyerle.

SONGS, GERMAN-HISTORY AND CRITICISM

Norman, F. & Hatto, A. T. Three Essays on the 'Hildebranslied' 83p. 1973. 35.00x (ISBN 0-85457-052-7, Pub. by Inst Germanic Stud England). State Mutual Bk.

SONGS, ITALIAN

Belgrado, Fernando D., ed. Songs of the Synagogue of Florence, 2 Vols. Incl. Vol. 1. The Three Festivals (ISBN 0-87203-108-X); Vol. 2. The High Holy Days. 0p (ISBN 0-87203-109-8). (Illus.). 60p. 1982. 32.95 ea. Hermon.

SONGS, JEWISH

Belgrado, Fernando D., ed. Songs of the Synagogue of Florence, 2 Vols. Incl. Vol. 1. The Three Festivals (ISBN 0-87203-108-X); Vol. 2. The High Holy Days. 0p (ISBN 0-87203-109-8). (Illus.). 60p. 1982. 32.95 ea. Hermon.

SONGS, NATIONAL

see National Songs

SONGS, PATRIOTIC

see National Songs

SONGS, POLYNESIAN

see Music, Polynesian

SONGS, POPULAR

see Music, Popular (Songs, etc.)

SONIC ENGINEERING

see Acoustical Engineering

SONNETS

Gould, Gerald. Journey, Odes & Sonnets. 1921. text ed. 19.50x (ISBN 0-686-83603-0). Elliots Bks.

Topham, J., ed. Twentieth Century Sonnets. 44p. Date not set. pap. 3.95 (ISBN 0-933486-43-X); pap. text ed. 3.95 (ISBN 0-933486-42-1). Am Poetry Pr.

SOPHISTRY (LOGIC)

see Fallacies (Logic)

SOPHOCLES, 496?-406 B.C.

Knox, Bernard M. The Heroic Temper: Studies in Sophoclean Tragedy. (Cal Sather Classical Lecture Ser.). 224p. 1983. pap. 7.95 (ISBN 0-520-04957-8, CAL 625). U of Cal Pr.

Moorhouse, A. C. The Syntax of Sophocles. (Mnemosyne: Suppl. 75). xiii, 353p. 1982. pap. write for info. (ISBN 90-04-06599-7). E J Brill.

Seale, David. Vision & Stagecraft in Sophocles. LC 82-50459. 270p. 1982. lib. bdg. 27.50x (ISBN 0-226-74404-3). U of Chicago Pr.

SOPORIFICS

see Narcotics

SORCERY

see Magic; Witchcraft

SORPTION

see Absorption; Adsorption

SORROW

see Joy and Sorrow

SOTO, HERNANDO DE, 1500?-1542

Peter, Lily. The Great Riding: The Story of De Soto in America. LC 82-20269. 1983. 21.00 (ISBN 0-938626-14-0); pap. 9.95 (ISBN 0-938626-17-5). U of Ark Pr.

SOUFFLES

Byrd, Anne. Omelettes & Souffles. LC 82-47860. (Great American Cooking Schools Ser.). (Illus.). 84p. 1982. 8.61i (ISBN 0-06-015065-3, HarpT). Har-Row.

SOUL

see also Future Life; Immortality; Personality; Psychology; Spiritual Life

Bettelheim, Bruno. Freud & Man's Soul. LC 82-47809. 112p. 1983. 11.95 (ISBN 0-394-52481-0). Knopf.

Martell, Dwane K. The Nature of the Soul & its Ultimate Goals. (Science of Man Library). (Illus.). 73p. 1983. 17.25 (ISBN 0-89920-048-6). Am Inst Psych.

Steiner, Rudolf. The Human Soul & the Universe. (q). Orig. Title: Cosmic & Human Metamorphoses. 24p. 1982. pap. 2.95 (ISBN 0-919924-17-4, Pub. by Steiner Book Centre Canada). Anthroposophic.

Writers' Group of the Dearborn Branch of the American Association of University Women. Mingled Threads. Reith, Alma C., et al, eds. LC 82-50876. 1982. 7.00 (ISBN 0-9609430-0-5). Writers' Group.

SOUL MUSIC

see Afro-American Music

SOULIE, FREDERIC, 1800-1847

March, Harold. Frederic Soulie: Novelist & Dramatist of the Romantic Period. 1931. text ed. 26.00x (ISBN 0-686-83553-0). Elliots Bks.

SOUND

see also Acoustical Engineering; Architectural Acoustics; Hearing; Noise; Phonetics; Ultrasonics; Underwater Acoustics; Vibration

Dowling, Ann & Williams, John e. Sound & Sources of Sound. LC 82-15687. 260p. 1983. 59.95 (ISBN 0-470-27370-4); pap. 29.95 (ISBN 0-470-27388-7). Halsted Pr.

SOUND-APPARATUS

see also Magnetic Recorders and Recording

Jackson. Newnes Book of Audio. (Illus.). 1979. 16.50 (ISBN 0-408-00429-0). Focal Pr.

King. Audio Handbook. (Illus.). 1975. 24.95 (ISBN 0-408-00150-X). Focal Pr.

Sinclair. Beginner's Guide to Audio. 1977. pap. 9.95 (ISBN 0-408-00274-3). Focal Pr.

SOUND-JUVENILE LITERATURE

Knight, David C. All About Sound. LC 82-17387. (Question & Answer Bks.). (Illus.). 32p. (gr. 3-6). 1983. PLB 8.59 (ISBN 0-89375-878-7); pap. text ed. 1.95 (ISBN 0-89375-879-5). Troll Assocs.

Newman, Frederick R. Zounds! The Kids' Guide to Sound Making. LC 82-16690. (Illus.). 64p. (gr. 3-8). 1983. pap. 4.95 (ISBN 0-394-85543-4). Random.

SOUND-RECORDING AND REPRODUCING

see also High-Fidelity Sound Systems; Magnetic Recorders and Recording; Stereophonic Sound Systems

Roys, H. E., ed. Disc Recording & Reproduction. LC 77-17927. (Benchmark Papers in Acoustic Ser.: Vol. 12). 416p. 1978. 48.50 (ISBN 0-87933-309-X). Hutchinson Ross.

Tobler, John & Grundy, Stuart. The Record Producers. (Illus.). 256p. 1983. 19.95 (ISBN 0-312-66593-8); pap. 10.95 (ISBN 0-312-66594-6). St Martin.

Woram, John M. The Recording Studio Handbook. 2nd ed. LC 76-62250. (Illus.). 550p. 1983. 39.50 (ISBN 0-686-83422-4). Elar Pub Co.

SOUND ENGINEERING

see Acoustical Engineering

SOUND NAVIGATION AND RANGING

see Sonar

SOUND RECORDING AND REPRODUCING

see Sound-Recording and Reproducing

SOUND RECORDING TAPES

see Phonotapes

SOUND-WAVES-INDUSTRIAL APPLICATIONS

see Acoustical Engineering

SOUNDS

Brooks, Bearl. Basic Skills Beginning Sounds Workbook. (Basic Skills Workbooks). 32p. (gr. k-1). 1983. 0.99 (ISBN 0-8209-0562-3, EEW-3). ESP.

Holmes, Keith D. The Sound of English. Set. tchrs guide 25.00 (ISBN 0-9608250-4-5); per set, 4 disc recordings 25.00 (ISBN 0-9608250-3-7). Educ Serv Pub.

SOUPS

Cooper, Sandi. Soups & Salads. LC 82-48659. (Great American Cooking Schools Ser.). (Illus.). 80p. 1983. 8.61i (ISBN 0-06-015151-X, HarpT). Har-Row.

Migliaccio, Janice Cook. Follow Your Heart's Vegetarian Soup Cookbook. LC 82-21822. (Illus.). 128p. (Orig.). 1983. pap. 9.95 (ISBN 0-88007-130-3); pap. 5.95 (ISBN 0-88007-131-1). Woodbridge Pr.

Seaver, Jeannette. Soups. 214p. 1983. 13.95 (ISBN 0-86579-031-0). Seaver Bks.

SOUTH, THE

see Southern States

SOUTH AFRICA

Here are entered works on the Republic of South Africa. Works on the area south of the countries of Zaire and Tanzania are entered under Africa, Southern.

Kuper, Leo & Kuper, Hilda. South Africa, 2 Pts. Incl. Pt. 1 - Human Rights & Genocide; Pt. 2 - Biography as Interpretation. (Hans Wolff Memorial Lecture Ser.). 63p. (Orig.). 1981. pap. text ed. 5.00 (ISBN 0-941934-33-0). Ind U Afro-Amer Arts.

South Africa Working Party. South Africa: Challenge & Hope. (Illus.). 136p. pap. 4.95 (ISBN 0-910082-03-0). Am Fr Serv Comm.

SOUTH AFRICA-BIOGRAPHY

Cassidy, Michael. Bursting the Wineskins. 1983. 9.95; pap. 5.95 (ISBN 0-87788-094-8). Shaw Pubs.

Wolseley, Garnet. South African Diaries of Sir Garnet Wolseley, 1875. Preston, Adrian, ed. 293p. 1971. 45.00x (ISBN 0-8002-3100-7). Intl Pubns Serv.

Wolseley, Gerald. South African Journal of Sir Garnet Wolseley, 1879-1880. Preston, Adrian, ed. 359p. 1973. 45.00x (ISBN 0-86961-040-6). Intl Pubns Serv.

SOUTH AFRICA-COMMERCE

McHenry, Donald. United States Firms in South Africa. (African Humanities Ser.). 74p. (Orig.). 1975. pap. text ed. 4.00 (ISBN 0-941934-15-2). Ind U Afro-Amer Arts.

SOUTH AFRICA-DESCRIPTION AND TRAVEL

South Africa Travel Guide. (Berlitz Travel Guides). (Illus.). 1982. pap. 4.95 (ISBN 0-02-969880-4, Berlitz). Macmillan.

SOUTH AFRICA-ECONOMIC CONDITIONS

Marks, S. & Rathbone, R., eds. Industrialisation & Social Change in South Africa: African Class, Culture & Consciousness, 1870-1930. (Illus.). 368p. 1982. text ed. 35.00x (ISBN 0-582-64338-4); pap. text ed. 10.95x (ISBN 0-582-64337-6). Longman.

Van Onselen, Charles. Studies in the Social & Economic History of the Witwatersrand 116-1914: New Babylon, Vol. 1. (Illus.). 1982. 35.00x (ISBN 0-582-64382-1); pap. 10.95x (ISBN 0-582-64383-X). Longman.

--Studies in the Social & Economic History of the Witwatersrand 116-1914: New Nineveh, Vol. 2. (Illus.). 288p. 1982. 35.00x (ISBN 0-582-64384-8); pap. 10.95x (ISBN 0-582-64385-6). Longman.

SOUTH AFRICA-FOREIGN RELATIONS

McHenry, Donald. United States Firms in South Africa. (African Humanities Ser.). 74p. (Orig.). 1975. pap. text ed. 4.00 (ISBN 0-941934-15-2). Ind U Afro-Amer Arts.

SOUTH AFRICA-HISTORY

Richardson, Peter. Chinese Mine Labour in the Transvaal. 287p. 1982. text ed. 31.50x (ISBN 0-333-27222-6, Pub. by Macmillan England). Humanities.

Wolseley, Garnet. South African Diaries of Sir Garnet Wolseley, 1875. Preston, Adrian, ed. 293p. 1971. 45.00x (ISBN 0-8002-3100-7). Intl Pubns Serv.

Wolseley, Gerald. South African Journal of Sir Garnet Wolseley, 1879-1880. Preston, Adrian, ed. 359p. 1973. 45.00x (ISBN 0-86961-040-6). Intl Pubns Serv.

Yudelman, David. The Emergence of Modern South Africa: State, Capital, & the Incorporation of Organized Labor on the South African Gold Fields, 1902-1939. LC 82-9375. (Contributions in Comparative Colonial Studies: No. 13). (Illus.). 288p. 1983. lib. bdg. 35.00 (ISBN 0-313-23170-2, YMS/). Greenwood.

SOUTH AFRICA-POLITICS AND GOVERNMENT

Clough, Michael. A Transatlantic Symposium: Where Is South Africa Headed? (II) (Seven Springs Reports). 48p. 1980. pap. 2.00 (ISBN 0-943006-12-0). Seven Springs.

Hailey, William M. The Republic of South Africa & the High Commission Territories. LC 82-11865. vii, 136p. 1982. Repr. of 1963 ed. lib. bdg. 25.00x (ISBN 0-313-23625-9, HARS). Greenwood.

Jackson, Gordon. The Prison Expose & Muldergate: A Case Study in Changing Government-Press Relations in South Africa. (Graduate Student Paper Competition Ser.: No. 3). 25p. (Orig.). 1980. pap. text ed. 2.00 (ISBN 0-941934-31-4). Ind U Afro-Amer Arts.

Riley, Rebecca R. & Ohrn, Steven G., eds. South African Politics: A Film Guide. (Occasional Papers on Visual Communication). 25p. (Orig.). 1975. pap. text ed. 2.00 (ISBN 0-941934-17-9). Ind U Afro-Amer Arts.

Ross, Robert. Cape of Torments: Slavery & Resistance in South Africa. (International Library of Anthropology). 176p. 1983. price not set (ISBN 0-7100-9407-8). Routledge & Kegan.

SOUTH AFRICA-RACE QUESTION

Hailey, William M. The Republic of South Africa & the High Commission Territories. LC 82-11865. vii, 136p. 1982. Repr. of 1963 ed. lib. bdg. 25.00x (ISBN 0-313-23625-9, HARS). Greenwood.

Hope, Christopher. A Seperate Development. 208p. 1983. pap. 4.95 (ISBN 0-686-83725-8, ScribT). Scribner.

International Labour Conference, 59th session, Geneva, 1974. Apartheid: Tenth Special Report of the Director-General on the Application of the Declaration cooncerning the Policy of "Apartheid" of the Republic of South Africa. 68p. 8.55 (ISBN 92-2-100967-X, ILC 59/I/SPECIAL REPORT). Intl Labour Office.

International Labour Conference, 60th session, 1975. Apartheid: Eleventh Special Report of the Director-General on the Application of the Declaration Concerning the Policy of "Apartheid" of the Republic of South Africa. 51p. 7.15 (ISBN 92-2-100968-8, ILC 60/I/SPECIAL REPORT). Intl Labour Office.

International Labour Conference, 63rd session, 1977. Apartheid: Thirteenth Special Report of the Director-General on the Application of the Declaration Concerning the Policy of "Apartheid" of the Republic of South Africa. 56p. 8.55 (ISBN 92-2-101562-9, ILC 63/I/SPECIAL REPORT). Intl Labour Office.

International Labour Conference, 64th session, 1978. Apartheid: Fourteenth Special Report of the Director-General on the Application of the Declaration Concerning the Policy of "Apartheid" of the Republic of South Africa. 54p. 8.55 (ISBN 92-2-101942-X, ILC 64/I/SPECIAL REPORT). Intl Labour Office.

International Labour Conference, 65th session, 1979. Apartheid: Fifteenth Special Report of the Director-General on the Application of the Declaration Concerning the Policy of "Apartheid"of the Republic of South Africa. iii, 48p. 8.55 (ISBN 92-2-101971-3, ILC 65/I/SPECIAL REPORT). Intl Labour Office.

International Labour Conference, 68th session. Apartheid: Eighteenth Special Report of the Director-General on the Application of the Declaration Concerning the Policy of Apartheid of the Republic of South Africa. 1982. write for info. (ILC 68/SPECIAL REPORT). Intl Labour Office.

SOUTH AFRICA-SOCIAL CONDITIONS

Marks, S. & Rathbone, R., eds. Industrialisation & Social Change in South Africa: African Class, Culture & Consciousness, 1870-1930. (Illus.). 368p. 1982. text ed. 35.00x (ISBN 0-582-64338-4); pap. text ed. 10.95x (ISBN 0-582-64337-6). Longman.

Van Onselen, Charles. Studies in the Social & Economic History of the Witwatersrand 116-1914: New Babylon, Vol. 1. (Illus.). 1982. 35.00x (ISBN 0-582-64382-1); pap. 10.95x (ISBN 0-582-64383-X). Longman.

--Studies in the Social & Economic History of the Witwatersrand 116-1914: New Nineveh, Vol. 2. (Illus.). 288p. 1982. 35.00x (ISBN 0-582-64384-8); pap. 10.95x (ISBN 0-582-64385-6). Longman.

SOUTH AMERICA-BIBLIOGRAPHY

Brooks, John, ed. South American Handbook, 1982. 58th ed. LC 25-514. (Illus.). 1341p. 1981. 25.00 (ISBN 0-900751-18-5). Intl Pubns Serv.

Miller, E. W. & Miller, Ruby M. South America: A Bibliography on the Third World. (Public Administration Ser.: Bibliography P-1064). 81p. 1982. pap. 12.00 (ISBN 0-88066-214-X). Vance Biblios.

SOUTH AMERICA-DESCRIPTION AND TRAVEL

Darwin, Charles R. Geological Obsevations on the Volcanic Islands & Parts of South America Visited during the Voyage of H.M.S. Beagle. LC 72-3889. (Illus.). xiii, 648p. 1972. write for info. (ISBN 0-404-08403-6). AMS Pr.

West, Robert C. Andean Reflections: Letters From Carl O. Sauer While on a South American Trip Under a Grant From the Rockefeller Foundation, 1942. (Dellplain Latin American Studies Ser.: Vol. 11). 160p. 1982. lib. bdg. 15.00 (ISBN 0-86531-436-5). Westview.

SOUTH AMERICA-DESCRIPTION AND TRAVEL-GUIDEBOOKS

Reaves, V. Heading South. (Illus.). 152p. 1982. 5.95 (ISBN 0-9607036-0-8). Bradt Ent.

South America 1983. (Get 'em & Go Travel Guide Ser.). 1982. 11.95 (ISBN 0-395-32874-8). HM.

SOUTH AMERICA-DISCOVERY AND EXPLORATION

see America-Discovery and Exploration

SOUTH AMERICA-ECONOMIC CONDITIONS

Albert, Bill. South America & the World Economy from Independence to 1930. (Studies in Economic & Social History). 88p. 1983. pap. text ed. 6.25x (ISBN 0-333-34223-2, 41241, Pub. by Macmillan England). Humanities.

SOUTH AMERICA-FOREIGN RELATIONS

Nunn, Frederick M. Yesterday's Soldiers: European Military Professionalism in South America, 1890-1940. LC 82-6961. xiv, 358p. 1983. 26.95x (ISBN 0-8032-3305-1). U of Nebr Pr.

SOUTH AMERICA-HISTORY

TePaske, John J. & Klein, Herbert S. The Royal Treasuries of the Spanish Empire in America, 3 vols. LC 82-2457. 1982. Set. 125.00 (ISBN 0-8223-0486-4); Vol. I: Peru, 590 p. 55.00 (ISBN 0-8223-0530-5); Vol. II: Peru (Bolivia), 446 p. 45.00 (ISBN 0-686-81650-1); Vol. III: Chile & the Rio de la Plata, 434 p. 45.00 (ISBN 0-8223-0532-1). Duke.

SOUTH AMERICA-JUVENILE LITERATURE

Carter, William E. South America. rev. ed. (First Bks.). (Illus.). 72p. (gr. 4 up). 1983. PLB 8.90 (ISBN 0-531-04531-5). Watts.

SOUTH CAROLINA-DESCRIPTION AND TRAVEL

Underwood, Camila K. Where to Go & What to Do in South Carolina. 1983. pap. 4.95 (ISBN 0-87844-049-6). Sandlapper Pub Co.

SOUTH CAROLINA-GENEALOGY

South Carolina Genealogies: Articles from the South Carolina Historical & Geneological Magazine, Vols. I-V. LC 82-20497. 1983. Set. 125.00 (ISBN 0-87152-368-X); Vol. I, 456p. 25.00 ea. (ISBN 0-87152-369-8). Vol. II, 472 (ISBN 0-87152-370-1). Vol. III, 480 (ISBN 0-87152-371-X). Vol. IV, 464 (ISBN 0-87152-372-8). Vol. V, 208 (ISBN 0-87152-373-6). Reprint.

SOUTH CAROLINA-HISTORY

Osborne, Anne R. A History of South Carolina. (gr. 4-8). 1983. 11.95 (ISBN 0-87844-023-2). Sandlapper Pub Co.

Weir, Robert. Colonial South Carolina-A History. LC 82-48990. (A History of the American Colonies Ser.). (Orig.). 1983. lib. bdg. 30.00 (ISBN 0-527-18721-6). Kraus Intl.

SOUTH DAKOTA

see also names of cities, towns, etc. in South Dakota

Holden, David. Dakota Visions: A County Approach. 391p. 1982. pap. write for info. (ISBN 0-931170-21-4). Ctr Western Studies.

SOUTH SEAS

see Oceanica

SOUTH-WEST AFRICA

see Namibia

SOUTHEAST ASIA

see Asia, Southeastern

SOUTHERN STATES

Hudspeth, Ron. Southern Nights & City Lights. LC 82-61870. 179p. 1982. 9.95 (ISBN 0-931948-41-X). Peachtree Pubs.

SOUTHERN STATES-BIOGRAPHY

Egerton, John. Generations: An American Family. LC 82-40465. (Illus.). 272p. 1983. 19.50 (ISBN 0-8131-1482-9). U Pr of Ky.

Williams, T. Harry. The Selected Essays of T. Harry Williams. LC 82-18646. 288p. 1983. 19.95 (ISBN 0-8071-1095-7). La State U Pr.

SOUTHERN STATES-DESCRIPTION AND TRAVEL

Bartram, John. Diary of a Journey Through the Carolinas, Georgia, & Florida from July 1, 1765, to April 10, 1766. Harper, Francis, ed. LC 82-62493. (Historic Byways of Florida Ser.: Vol. VIII). (Illus.). 152p. 1982. pap. 12.95 (ISBN 0-941948-08-0). St Johns-Oklawaha.

SOUTHERN STATES-HISTORY

Abbott, Shirley. Womenfolks: Growing up Down South. LC 82-16880. 224p. 1983. 13.95 (ISBN 0-89919-156-8). Ticknor & Fields.

Bannon, Lois & Carr, Martha. History of Magnolia Mound Plantation. 1983. pap. 5.95 (ISBN 0-88289-381-5). Pelican.

Cowdrey, Albert E. This Land, This South: An Environmental History. Roland, Charles P., ed. LC 82-20154. (New Perspectives on the South Ser.). 256p. 1983. 23.00 (ISBN 0-8131-0302-9). U Pr of Ky.

Dodd, William E. Cotton Kingdom. 1919. text ed. 8.50x (ISBN 0-686-83514-X). Elliots Bks.

Hobson, Fred, ed. South-Watching: Selected Essays by Gerald W. Johnson. LC 82-2620. (Fred W. Morrison Ser. in Southern Studies). xxxiii, 207p. 1983. 19.00x (ISBN 0-8078-1531-4); pap. 8.95x (ISBN 0-8078-4094-7). U of NC Pr.

Thomas, Alfred B. Alonso De Posada Report, Sixteen Eighty-Six: A Description of the Area of the Present Southern United States in the Late 17th Century. LC 82-15017. (The Spanish Borderlands Ser.: Vol. 4). (Illus.). 72p. (Orig.). 1982. pap. text ed. 8.95x (ISBN 0-933776-10-1). Perdido Bay.

Thompson, Holland. New South. 1919. text ed. 8.50x (ISBN 0-686-83648-0). Elliots Bks.

Townsend, Jimmy. It's True What They Say about Dixie. 1981. 8.95 (ISBN 0-932298-18-4). Copple Hse.

Williams, T. Harry. The Selected Essays of T. Harry Williams. LC 82-18646. 288p. 1983. 19.95 (ISBN 0-8071-1095-7). La State U Pr.

SOUTHERN STATES-HISTORY-CIVIL WAR, 1861-1865

see Confederate States of America-History; United States-History-Civil War, 1861-1865

SOUTHERN STATES–POLITICS AND GOVERNMENT

Brown, Ed. Race & Class in Southern Politics & a History of Voter Education Project. 1979. 2.00 (ISBN 0-686-38003-7). Voter Ed Proj.

Hudlin, Richard A. & Brimah, K. Farouk. What Happened in the South: 1980. 1981. 1.00 (ISBN 0-686-38009-6). Voter Ed Proj.

SOUTHERN STATES–RACE RELATIONS

see also United States–Race Relations

Eagles, Charles W. Jonathan Daniels & Race Relations: The Evolution of a Southern Liberal. LC 82-2756. (Twentieth-Century American Ser.). 254p. 1982. text ed. 24.50x (ISBN 0-87049-356-6); pap. text ed. 11.95x (ISBN 0-87049-357-4). U of Tenn Pr.

Hudlin, Richard A. Voter Registration in Eleven Southern States, by Race: 1960-1980, in U.S. Bureau of the Census: Statistical Abstract of the United States: 1981. 1981. 0.10 ea. Voter Ed Proj.

SOUTHERN STATES–SOCIAL CONDITIONS

Reed, John S. Southerners: The Social Psychology of Sectionalism. LC 82-13631. 170p. 1983. 17.00x (ISBN 0-8078-1542-X); pap. 5.95x (ISBN 0-8078-4098-X). U of NC Pr.

Roebuck, Julian. The Southern Redneck. 222p. 1982. 25.95 (ISBN 0-03-059803-6). Praeger.

Wilson, Emily H. Hope & Dignity: Older Black Women of the South. 1983. write for info. (ISBN 0-87722-302-5). Temple U Pr.

SOUTHERN STATES–SOCIAL LIFE AND CUSTOMS

see also Plantation Life

Woodward, C. Vann. American Counterpoint: Slavery & Racism in the North-South Dialogue. 320p. 1983. pap. 7.95 (ISBN 0-19-503269-1, GB 727, GB). Oxford U Pr.

Wyatt-Brown, Bertram. Southern Honor: Ethics & Behavior in the Old South. 622p. 1983. pap. 9.95 (ISBN 0-19-503310-8, GB 737, GB). Oxford U Pr.

SOUTHWARK, ENGLAND–GLOBE THEATRE

Orrell, John. The Quest for Shakespeare's Globe. LC 82-9445. (Illus.). 220p. Date not set. price not set (ISBN 0-521-24751-9). Cambridge U Pr.

SOUTHWEST, NEW

Here are entered works on that part of the United States which roughly corresponds to the old Spanish province of New Mexico, including the present Arizona, New Mexico, Southern Colorado, Utah, Nevada and California.

Dobie, J. Frank. Coronado's Children: Tales of Lost & Buried Treasures of the Southwest. 367p. 1982. Repr. of 1931 ed. lib. bdg. 50.00 (ISBN 0-89987-170-4). Darby Bks.

SOUTHWEST, NEW–DESCRIPTION AND TRAVEL

Austin, Mary. The Land of Journeys' Ending. 500p. 1983. 24.50x (ISBN 0-8165-0807-0); pap. 14.50 (ISBN 0-8165-0808-9). U of Ariz Pr.

SOUTHWEST, NEW–DESCRIPTION AND TRAVEL–GUIDEBOOKS

All the Southwest. 1979. 4.95 (ISBN 0-686-42897-8). Harian.

Casey, Robert L. Journey to the High Southwest: A Traveler's Guide. (Illus.). 368p. (Orig.). 1983. pap. 14.95 (ISBN 0-914718-78-9). Pacific Search.

Ganci, Dave. Hiking the Southwest: Arizona, New Mexico, & West Texas. LC 82-19418. (A Sierra Club Totebook). (Illus.). 384p. (Orig.). 1983. pap. 8.95 (ISBN 0-87156-338-X). Sierra.

SOUTHWEST, NEW–HISTORY

Bell, Samuel E. & Smallwood, James M. Zona Libre. (Southwestern Studies: No. 69). 100p. 1982. pap. 4.00 (ISBN 0-87404-129-5). Tex Western.

Riley, Carroll L. The Frontier People: The Greater Southwest in the Protohistoric Period. LC 82-50284. (Occasional Paper Ser.: No. 1). Date not set. price not set (ISBN 0-88104-000-2). S Ill U Pr.

Weigle, Marta & Larcombe, Claudia, eds. Hispanic Arts & Ethohistory in the Southwest: New Papers Inspired by the Work of E. Boyd. LC 82-74221. (A Spanish Colonial Arts Society Book). (Illus.). 350p. 1983. 35.00 (ISBN 0-941270-14-9); pap. 20.00 (ISBN 0-941270-13-0). Ancient City Pr.

SOUTHWEST, OLD–HISTORY

Bolton, Herbert E. Spanish Borderlands. 1921. text ed. 8.50x (ISBN 0-686-83780-0). Elliots Bks.

SOUTHWEST AFRICA

see Namibia

SOUVENIRS (KEEP-SAKES)

The Blues Brothers Souvenir Songbook. 7.95 (ISBN 0-89524-111-0). Cherry Lane.

The Emmylou Harris Songbook. 14.95 (ISBN 0-89524-140-4). Cherry Lane.

The Erroll Garner Songbook. 7.95 (ISBN 0-89524-030-0). Cherry Lane.

Leblanc, Georgette. Souvenirs, Eighteen Ninety-five to Nineteen Eighteen: My Life with Maeterlinck. Flanner, Janet, tr. from Fr. 352p. 1976. Repr. of 1932 ed. lib. bdg. 32.50 (ISBN 0-306-70841-8). Da Capo.

SOVEREIGN IMMUNITY (INTERNATIONAL LAW)

see Immunities of Foreign States

SOVEREIGNS

see Kings and Rulers

also subdivision Kings and Rulers under names of countries

SOY-BEAN

Clute, Robin & Andersen, Sigrid. Juel Andersen's Tempeh Primer. 50p. (Orig.). 1983. pap. 3.95 (ISBN 0-916870-59-6). Creative Arts Bk.

Overton, H. P., compiled by. Soybeans & Its Uses: A Bibliography. 50p. Date not set. pap. text ed. 10.95 (ISBN 0-910811-03-2). Center Self.

Shurtleff, William & Aoyagi, Akiko. The Book of Kudzu. LC 77-74891. 104p. 1977. pap. 4.95 (ISBN 0-933332-11-4). Soyfoods Center.

--The Book of Miso. LC 76-19599. (Soyfoods Ser.). (Illus.). 256p. 1976. pap. 8.95 (ISBN 0-933332-10-6). Soyfoods Center.

--The Book of Miso. rev. ed. (Illus.). 256p. 14.95 (ISBN 0-89815-098-1); pap. 9.95 (ISBN 0-89815-097-3). Ten Speed Pr.

--The Book of Tofu. LC 74-31629. (Soyfoods Ser.). (Illus.). 336p. 1975. pap. 9.95 (ISBN 0-933332-09-2). Soyfoods Center.

--Soyfoods Labels, Posters & Other Graphics. (Soyfoods Production Ser.: No. 6). 185p. (Orig.). 1982. pap. 35.00 spiral bdg. (ISBN 0-933332-08-4). Soyfoods Center.

--Using Tofu, Tempeh & Other Soyfoods in Restaurants, Delis & Cafeterias. (Soyfoods Production Ser.: No. 5). 135p. (Orig.). 1982. pap. text ed. 32.95 spiral bound (ISBN 0-933332-07-6). Soyfoods Center.

Soybean Production in the Tropics. (FAO Plant Production & Protection Paper: No. 4, Rev. 1). 222p. 1982. pap. 16.75 (ISBN 92-5-101216-4, F2332, FAO). Unipub.

SPACE (ARCHITECTURE)

Ashihara, Yoshinobu & Riggs, Lynne E. The Aesthetic Townscape. (Illus.). 196p. 1983. 20.00 (ISBN 0-262-01069-0). MIT Pr.

SPACE, OUTER

see Outer Space

SPACE AND TIME

see also Personal Space; Relativity (Physics)

Friedman, Michael. Foudations of Space-Time Theories: Relativistic Physics & Philosophy of Science. LC 82-61362. 400p. 1983. 35.00 (ISBN 0-691-07239-6). Princeton U Pr.

Sims, Reginald W. & Price, James H., eds. Evolution, Time & Space. Date not set. price not set (ISBN 0-12-644550-8). Acad Pr.

SPACE ENVIRONMENT

see also Solar Radiation

Grey, Jerry. Beachheads in Space: A Blueprint for the Future. (Illus.). 288p. 1983. 14.95 (ISBN 0-02-545590-7). Macmillan.

SPACE EXPLORATION (ASTRONAUTICS)

see Outer Space–Exploration

SPACE FLIGHT

see also Astronautics; Interplanetary Voyages; Navigation (Astronautics)

Rose, Alan. Build Your Own Saturn V. (The World on the Move Ser.). 40p. 1982. pap. 8.95 (ISBN 0-399-50681-0, Perige). Putnam Pub Group.

SPACE FLIGHT PROPULSION SYSTEMS

see Space Vehicles–Propulsion Systems

SPACE FLIGHT TRAINING

see Flight Training

SPACE IN ECONOMICS

see also Commerce; Industries, Location Of; Transportation

Gilbert, Alan, ed. Development Planning & Spatial Structure. LC 75-30804. 207p. 1976. 34.50x (ISBN 0-471-29904-9, Pub. by Wiley-Interscience). Wiley.

SPACE LATTICE (MATHEMATICS)

see Lattice Theory

SPACE NAVIGATION

see Navigation (Astronautics)

SPACE OF MORE THAN THREE DIMENSIONS

see Fourth Dimension; Space and Time

SPACE POLICY

see Astronautics and State

SPACE PROPULSION

see Space Vehicles–Propulsion Systems

SPACE RESEARCH

see Astronautical Research; Outer Space–Exploration; Space Sciences

SPACE SCIENCES

see also Astronautics; Astronomy; Geophysics; Outer Space; Space and Time

Angelo, Joseph. The Dictionary of Space Technology. 384p. 1982. 70.00x (ISBN 0-584-95011-X, Pub. by Muller Ltd). State Mutual Bk.

Lampton, Christopher. Space Sciences. (A Reference First Bk.). (Illus.). 96p. (gr. 4 up). 1983. PLB 8.90 (ISBN 0-531-04539-0). Watts.

SPACE SHIPS–PILOTS

see Astronauts

SPACE SHUTTLES

see Reusable Space Vehicles

SPACE-TIMES

see Space and Time

SPACE TRAVEL

see Interplanetary Voyages; Space Flight

SPACE VEHICLES–ACCIDENTS

see Astronautics–Accidents

SPACE VEHICLES–BATTERIES

see Solar Batteries

SPACE VEHICLES–INSTRUMENTS

see Astronautical Instruments

SPACE VEHICLES–JUVENILE LITERATURE

Jay, Michael. Spacecraft. (Easy-Read Fact Bks.). (Illus.). 32p. (gr. 2-4). 1983. PLB 8.60 (ISBN 0-531-04512-9). Watts.

SPACE VEHICLES–PROPULSION SYSTEMS

see also Controlled Fusion

Robinson, J., ed. Shuttle Propulsion Systems. (AD-05 Ser.). 1982. 24.00 (H00243). ASME.

SPACE WEATHER

see Space Environment

SPACECRAFT ACCIDENTS

see Astronautics–Accidents

SPACES, ALGEBRAIC

see Algebraic Spaces

SPACES, METRIC

see Metric Spaces

SPAIN–BIOGRAPHY

Bell, Aubrey F. Benito Arias Montano. 1922. pap. 2.50 (ISBN 0-87535-009-7). Hispanic Soc.

Krappe, A. Haggerty. Raymond Foulche-Delbosc. (Illus.). 1930. 0.25 (ISBN 0-87535-026-7). Hispanic Soc.

Sanguily, Manuel. Nobles Memorias. 2nd ed. LC 80-67889. 246p. (Orig., Span.). pap. 12.00 (ISBN 0-89729-262-6). Ediciones.

SPAIN–COLONIES–AMERICA

Anna, Timothy E. Spain & the Loss of America. LC 82-11118. xxiv, 333p. 1983. 26.50x (ISBN 0-8032-1014-0). U of Nebr Pr.

Twilight of an Empire. 180p. 1976. 7.50 (ISBN 0-686-83934-X). Transbooks.

SPAIN–DESCRIPTION AND TRAVEL–GUIDEBOOKS

Maideira Travel Guide. (Berlitz Travel Guides). (Illus.). 1982. pap. 4.95 (ISBN 0-02-969330-6, Berlitz). Macmillan.

Michelin Green Guide: Espagne. (Green Guide Ser.). (Fr.). 1983. pap. write for info. (ISBN 2-0600-5182-7). Michelin.

Michelin Green Guide: Espana. (Green Guide Ser.). (Span.). 1983. pap. write for info. (ISBN 2-06-045271-6). Michelin.

Michelin Green Guide: Spanien. (Green Guide Ser.). (Ger.). 1983. pap. write for info. (ISBN 2-06-122900-X). Michelin.

SPAIN–HISTORY

Here are entered general works on Spanish history, and works on all periods of Spanish history except the Civil War, 1936-1939, which are entered below under Spain–History–Civil War, 1936-1939.

Alfonso X. General Estoria, 2 Vols, Part II. 1961. 35.00 (ISBN 0-942260-01-5); deluxe ed. 100.00 (ISBN 0-942260-02-3). Hispanic Seminary.

Edwards, John. Christian Cordoba: The City & its Region in the Late Middle Ages. LC 81-24213. (Cambridge, Iberian & Latin American Studies). 256p. 1982. 47.50 (ISBN 0-521-24320-3). Cambridge U Pr.

Pike, Ruth. Penal Servitude in Early Modern Spain. LC 82-70551. (Illus.). 224p. 1983. text ed. 26.00 (ISBN 0-299-09260-7). U of Wis Pr.

Smith, Joseph B. The Plot to Steal Florida: James Madison's Phony War. 1983. 15.95 (ISBN 0-87795-477-1). Arbor Hse.

Sutherland, C. H. The Romans in Spain, 217 B.C.-A.D. 117. LC 82-15846. (Illus.). xi, 264p. 1982. Repr. of 1939 ed. lib. bdg. 45.00x (ISBN 0-313-23745-X, SURS). Greenwood.

SPAIN–HISTORY–CIVIL WAR, 1936-1939

Kazantzakis, Nikos. Spain: A Journal of Two Voyages Before & During the Spanish Civil War. LC 63-15059. 260p. pap. 7.95 (ISBN 0-916870-54-5). Creative Arts Bk.

Leval, Gaston. Collectives in the Spanish Revolution. Richards, Vernon, tr. from Fr. 368p. 1975. pap. 6.50 (ISBN 0-900384-10-7). Left Bank.

Mitchell, David. The Spanish Civil War. (Illus.). 210p. 1983. 18.95 (ISBN 0-531-09896-6). Watts.

Paley, Alan. The Spanish Civil War. Rahmas, Sigurd C., ed. (Events of Our Times Ser.: No. 23). 32p. (Orig.). 1982. 2.95x (ISBN 0-87157-724-0); pap. text ed. 1.95 (ISBN 0-87157-224-9). SamHar Pr.

Porter, David, ed. Vision on Fire: Emma Goldman on the Spanish Revolution. LC 82-74015. (Illus.). 400p. (Orig.). 1983. pap. 7.50t (ISBN 0-9610348-2-3). Commonground Pr.

SPAIN–POLITICS AND GOVERNMENT

Maravall, Jose. Transition to Democracy in Spain. LC 81-21317. 230p. 1982. 30.00x (ISBN 0-312-81459-3). St Martin.

Mujal-Leon, Eusebio. Communism & Political Change in Spain. LC 81-48616. 288p. 1983. 22.50x (ISBN 0-253-31389-9). Ind U Pr.

SPANISH AMERICA

see Latin America

SPANISH-AMERICAN LITERATURE

see also Chilean Literature; Cuban Literature (Collections); Puerto Rican Literature

Boyd-Bowman, Peter. Lexico hispanoamericano del siglo XVIII. (Spanish Ser.: No. 5). 1982. 10.00 (ISBN 0-942260-21-X). Hispanic Seminary.

Hispanic American Periodicals Index, 1980. Valk, Barbara G., ed. LC 75-642408. (Hispanic American Periodicals Index Ser.). 740p. 1983. lib. bdg. 160.00 (ISBN 0-87903-407-6). UCLA Lat Am Ctr.

SPANISH AMERICANS IN THE UNITED STATES

Matos, Antonio, ed. Guide to Reviews of Books from & about Hispanic America, 1980. LC 66-96537. 1780p. 1980. 90.00 (ISBN 0-87917-084-0). Ethridge.

SPANISH AMERICANS IN THE UNITED STATES–SOCIAL CONDITIONS

Lacayo, Carmela G. Serving the Hispanic Elderly of the United States: A National Community Service Directory. 234p. 1982. write for info. Assn Personas Mayores.

SPANISH ARCHITECTURE

see Architecture–Spain

SPANISH ARMADA

see Armada, 1588

SPANISH ART

see Art, Spanish

SPANISH DRAMA–HISTORY AND CRITICISM

Aycock, Wendell M. & Cravens, Sydney P., eds. Calderon de la Barca at the Tercentenary: Comparative Views, Vol. 14. LC 82-80309. (Proceedings of the Comparative Literature Symposium: Vol. 14). 195p. 1982. pap. 24.95 (ISBN 0-89672-101-9). Tex Tech Pr.

Borras, A. A., ed. The Theatre & Hispanic Life: Essays in Honour of Neale H. Taylor. 97p. 1982. text ed. 11.50x (ISBN 0-88920-129-3, Pub. by Wilfred Laurier U Pr Canada). Humanities.

McClelland. Spanish Drama of Pathos 1750-1808, Vols. I & II. 663p. 1982. Set. 60.00x (ISBN 0-686-81793-1, Pub. by Liverpool Univ England). State Mutual Bk.

SPANISH FOLK SONGS

see Folk-Songs, Spanish

SPANISH GUITAR

see Guitar

SPANISH LANGUAGE

see also Catalan Language

Hart, Babe. Speedy Ingles. (Speedy Language Ser.). 24p. (Orig.). 1982. pap. 1.75 (ISBN 0-9602838-7-0). Baja Bks.

Jarvis, Ana C. & Lebredo, Raquel. Aventuras Literarias. 256p. 1983. pap. 9.95 (ISBN 0-686-82410-5). Heath.

--Continuemos: Curso Intermedio de Espanol. 320p. 1982. pap. 14.95 (ISBN 0-669-05335-X). Heath.

--Nuestro Mundo. 256p. 1983. pap. 9.95 (ISBN 0-669-05340-6). Heath.

Patterson, William T. The Genealogical Structure of Spanish: A Correlation of Basic Word Properties. LC 82-17597. 244p. (Orig.). 1983. lib. bdg. 22.50 (ISBN 0-8191-2791-4); pap. text ed. 11.00 (ISBN 0-8191-2792-2). U Pr of Amer.

Zayas-Bazan, Eduardo & Fernandez, Gaston J. Que me Cuenta: Temas de hoy de Siempre. 272p. 1983. pap. text ed. 9.95 (ISBN 0-669-05965-X). Heath.

SPANISH LANGUAGE–TO 1500

Burrus, Victoria. A Procedural Manual for Entry Establishment in the Dictionary of the Old Spanish Language. 1982. pap. 10.00 (ISBN 0-942260-24-4). Hispanic Seminary.

Mackenzie, David. A Manual of Manuscript Transcription for the Dictionary of the Old Spanish Language. 2nd ed. 128p. 1981. pap. 15.00 (ISBN 0-942260-15-5). Hispanic Seminary.

SPANISH LANGUAGE–CHRESTOMATHIES AND READERS

see Spanish Language–Readers

SPANISH LANGUAGE–COMPOSITION AND EXERCISES

Azevedo, Milton M. & Kerr, Herminia J. Self-Paced Exercises in Spanish. 176p. (Span.). 1982. pap. text ed. 14.00 (ISBN 0-8403-2803-6). Kendall-Hunt.

SPANISH LANGUAGE–CONVERSATION AND PHRASE BOOKS

see also Spanish Language–Self-Instruction; Spanish Language–Textbooks for Children

Berlitz Editors. Latin American Spanish for Travel Cassettepack. 1983. 14.95 (ISBN 0-02-962590-4, Berlitz); cassette incl. Macmillan.

--Spanish for Travel Cassettepack. 1983. 14.95 (ISBN 0-02-962220-4, Berlitz); cassette incl. Macmillan.

Dulac, Colette. Spanish Conversation for Students & Travelers. (gr. 7-12). 1983. pap. price not set (ISBN 0-8120-2598-9). Barron.

Harris, James W. Syllable Structure & Stress in Spanish: A Nonlinear Analysis. (Linguistic Inquiry Monographs). 176p. 1983. 25.00x (ISBN 0-262-08124-5); pap. 15.00x (ISBN 0-262-58060-8). MIT Pr.

Hart. Speedy Spanish: To Get You There & Back. (Speedy Language Ser.). 24p. (Span.). (Orig., Span.). 1975. pap. 1.75 (ISBN 0-9602838-0-3). Baja Bks.

Hart, T. L. Speedy Spanish for Medical Personnel. Hart, T. L. & Hart, Babe, eds. Hart, Babe, tr. (Speedy Language Ser.). (Illus.). 24p. (Orig., Span.). 1980. pap. 1.95 (ISBN 0-9602838-6-2). Baja Bks.

Herd, Shirley. Easy Spanish for the Yachtsman, RV'er, Motorist, Fisherman, Aviator, Traveler. (Illus.). 264p. (Orig., Span. & Eng. phonetic.). 1982. pap. text ed. 8.95 (ISBN 0-930006-01-1). S Deal Assoc.

Kendris, Christopher. Spanish the Easy Way, Bk.2. (Easy Way Ser.). 160p. 1983. pap. write for info. (ISBN 0-8120-2636-5). Barron.

Lexus. The Mexican-Spanish Travelmate. 128p. 1983. pap. 1.95 (ISBN 0-307-46607-8, Golden Pr). Western Pub.

Noricks, Michael. Spanish for Medical Personnel: A Short Course. 64p. (Orig.). 1983. pap. price not set (ISBN 0-910669-00-7); write for info. 2 cassettes (ISBN 0-910669-01-5). Pacific Lang.
Traveler's Spanish. (EH Ser.). (Span.). 1980. pap. 17.95 (ISBN 0-686-37990-X, 609). B&N NY.
Valencia, Pablo & Bacon, Susan. En Marcha: Espanol Para Niveles Intermedios. 384p. 1982. pap. text ed. 19.95 (ISBN 0-395-32741-5); write for info. supplementary materials. HM.

SPANISH LANGUAGE–DIALECTS
Valencia & Bacon. En Marcha. 1982. pap. text ed. 18.95 (ISBN 0-686-84593-5, SN30); instr's. ed. 19.95 (ISBN 0-686-84594-3, SN27); write for info. supplementary materials. HM.

SPANISH LANGUAGE–DICTIONARIES
DiLorenzo-Kearon, Maria. Medical Spanish. 256p. Date not set. with 12 cassettes 145.00x (ISBN 0-88432-079-0, MS20). J Norton Pubs.
Dulac, Colette. Spanish Conversation for Students & Travelers. (gr. 7-12). 1983. pap. price not set (ISBN 0-8120-2598-9). Barron.
Kendris, Christopher. Spanish the Easy Way, Bk.2. (Easy Way Ser.). 160p. 1983. pap. write for info. (ISBN 0-8120-2636-5). Barron.

SPANISH LANGUAGE–DICTIONARIES–ENGLISH
Berlitz Editors. Spanish-English Dictionary. 1979. 4.95 (ISBN 0-02-964510-7, Berlitz). Macmillan.
Di Benedetto, Ubaldo, ed. New Comprehensive English-Spanish, Spanish-English Dictionary, 2 Vols. 3100p. 1977. Set. 60.00x (ISBN 84-7166-211-6). Intl Pubns Serv.
Simeone, Joseph F. Complete Spanish-English Reference Guide. 1983. 11.95 (ISBN 0-533-05530-X). Vantage.

SPANISH LANGUAGE–EXAMINATIONS, QUESTIONS, ETC.
Foreign Service Institute. French & Spanish Testing Kit. 140p. Date not set. with 8 cassettes 95.00x (ISBN 0-88432-060-X, X100). J Norton Pubs.
Rudman, Jack. Foreign Language: Spanish. (Regents External Degree Ser.: REDP-30). 17.95 (ISBN 0-8373-5680-6); pap. 9.95 (ISBN 0-8373-5630-X). Natl Learning.

SPANISH LANGUAGE–GRAMMAR
Prado, Marcial. Practical Spanish Grammar: A Self Teaching Guide. (Self Teaching Guides Ser.). 240p. 1983. pap. text ed. write for info. (ISBN 0-471-89893-7). Wiley.

SPANISH LANGUAGE–IDIOMS, CORRECTIONS, ERRORS
Pierson, Raymond H. Guide to Spanish Idioms. 180p. 1981. 30.00x (ISBN 0-85950-334-8, Pub. by Thornes England). State Mutual Bk.

SPANISH LANGUAGE–OLD SPANISH
see Spanish Language–To 1500

SPANISH LANGUAGE–PROGRAMMED INSTRUCTION
Foreign Service Institute. Advanced Spanish, Pt. C. 472p. Date not set. includes 18 cassettes 185.00x (ISBN 0-88432-102-9, S170). J Norton Pubs.

SPANISH LANGUAGE–PRONUNCIATION
Harris, James W. Syllable Structure & Stress in Spanish: A Nonlinear Analysis. (Linguistic Inquiry Monographs). 176p. 1983. 25.00x (ISBN 0-262-08124-5); pap. 15.00x (ISBN 0-262-58060-8). MIT Pr.

SPANISH LANGUAGE–READERS
see also Spanish Language–Textbooks for Children; Spanish Language–Textbooks for Foreigners
Carlson, G. Raymond. La Palabra Viva Y Eficaz. Marosi, Esteban & Carrodeguas, Andy, eds. Powell, David, tr. 176p. (Span.). 1982. pap. 2.00 (ISBN 0-8297-1254-2). Life Pubs Intl.
Coleman, William L. Un Punado de Audaces. Marosi, Esteban & Carrodeguas, Andy, eds. Sipowicz, Edwin, tr. 192p. (Span.). 1980. pap. 2.25 (ISBN 0-8297-1116-3). Life Pubs Intl.
Eareckson, Joni & Estes, Steve. Un Paso Mas. Mercado, Ben, ed. Romanenghi de Powell, Elsie, tr. 222p. (Span.). 1979. pap. 2.80 (ISBN 0-8297-0663-1). Life Pubs Intl.
Henrichsen, Walter A. Un Hogar para Cristo. Carrodeguas, Andy & Marosi, Esteban, eds. Marosi, Antonio, tr. 176p. (Span.). 1982. pap. 2.00 (ISBN 0-8297-1313-1). Life Pubs Intl.
Kerstan, Reinhold. Sangre y Honor. Carrodeguas, Andy & Marosi, Esteban, eds. Romanenghi de Powell, Elsa, tr. 190p. (Span.). (gr. 4-6). 1982. pap. 3.00 (ISBN 0-686-84510-2). Life Pubs Intl.
Lin, Yi. Me Hizo Pasas for las Aguas. Carrodeguas, Andy & Marosi, Esteban, eds. Riddering, David, tr. 144p. (Span.). 1982. pap. 2.00 (ISBN 0-8297-1323-9). Life Pubs Intl.
McManus, Una & Cooper, John C. Ni con un Millon de Dolares. Carrodeguas, Andy & Marosi, Esteban, eds. Powell de Lobo, Virginia, tr. 224p. (Span.). 1982. pap. 2.50 (ISBN 0-8297-1256-9). Life Pubs Intl.
Nee, Watchman, Oremos. Marosi, Esteban, ed. Lassaletta, Manuel, tr. 113p. (Span.). 1980. pap. 1.50 (ISBN 0-8297-1046-9). Life Pubs Intl.
Tenney, Merrill C. Quien Manda en Tu Vida? Carrodeguas, Andy & Marosi, Esteban, eds. Mercado, Benjamin, tr. 174p. (Span.). 1981. pap. 2.00 (ISBN 0-8297-1261-5). Life Pubs Intl.
Wirt, Sherwood E. Sed de Dios. Marosi, Esteban, ed. Sipowicz, Eswin, tr. 219p. (Span.). 1982. pap. 2.50 (ISBN 0-8297-1252-6). Life Pubs Intl.

SPANISH LANGUAGE–SELF-INSTRUCTION
see also Spanish Language–Conversation and Phrase Books
Azevedo, Milton M. & Kerr, Herminia J. Self-Paced Exercises in Spanish. 176p. (Span.). 1982. pap. text ed. 14.00 (ISBN 0-8403-2803-6). Kendall-Hunt.
Berlitz Latin-American Spanish for Your Trip. 192p. 1982. 8.95 (Berlitz). Macmillan.
Berlitz Spanish for Your Trip. 192p. 1982. 8.95 (Berlitz). Macmillan.
Prado, Marcial. Practical Spanish Grammar: A Self Teaching Guide. (Self-Teaching Ser.). 240p. 1983. pap. text ed. 8.95 (ISBN 0-686-84630-3). Wiley.

SPANISH LANGUAGE–STUDY AND TEACHING
Santa Cruz, Mercedes. La Habana. Bacardi, Amalia E., tr. from Fr. 403p. (Orig., Span.). 1982. pap. 12.95 (ISBN 84-499-5244-1). Ediciones.

SPANISH LANGUAGE–SYNTAX
Spaulding. Syntax of the Spanish Verbs. 156p. 1982. 30.00x (ISBN 0-85323-143-5, Pub. by Liverpool Univ England). State Mutual Bk.

SPANISH LANGUAGE–TEXTBOOKS FOR CHILDREN
see also Spanish Language–Conversation and Phrase Books
Carmen. 2.35 (ISBN 0-686-82079-7); cassettes 12.00 (ISBN 0-686-82080-0). EMC.
Escribano, Jose. Por Aqui. tchrs. guide & cassettes 72.00 (ISBN 0-686-82067-3); student textbook 6.50 (ISBN 0-88436-911-0, 40289). EMC.

SPANISH LANGUAGE–TEXTBOOKS FOR FOREIGNERS
see also Spanish Language–Conversation and Phrase Books
Duke, Salcacion C. English-Spanish Workbook I: Taller de la Gramatica Espanola I. (Illus.). 237p. (Orig.). 1982. write for info. (ISBN 0-9609446-0-5). Research Lang.

SPANISH LITERATURE
Babbitt, Theodore. Cronica de Veinte Reyes. 1936. text ed. 12.50x (ISBN 0-686-83515-8). Elliots Bks.
Dal Masetto, Antonio. El ojo de la perdiz. 214p. (Span.). 1980. pap. 8.00 (ISBN 0-910061-01-7). Ediciones Norte.
Roy, Joaquin & Staczer, John J. Lecturas De Prensa. 256p. (Orig.). 1982. pap. text ed. 10.95 (ISBN 0-15-550455-X, HC). HarBraceJ.
Szichman, Mario. A las Viente, Veinte-cicno, la senora entro en la Inmortalidad. 292p. (Span.). 1981. pap. 7.50 (ISBN 0-910061-02-5). Ediciones Norte.

SPANISH LITERATURE (COLLECTIONS)
Here are entered collections in Spanish. For English translations see subdivision Translations into English.
see also Spanish-American Literature
Araya, G., et al, eds. Las Constantes Esteticas de la 'Comedia' del Siglo de Oro. (Dialogos Hispanicos de Amsterdam: No. 2). 137p. 1981. pap. text ed. 17.25x (ISBN 90-6203-583-3, Pub. by Rodopi Holland). Humanities.
Del Rio, Angel & Del Rio, Amelia A. Antologia General de La Literatura Espanola. (Span.). 1982. pap. 15.00 (ISBN 0-86515-001-X). Edit Mensaje.
Eoff, Sherman H. & Ramirez-Aranjo, Alejandro. Pio Bargjca's Zalacain el Aventurereo, Bk. 4. (Graded Spanish Readers (Span.)). 1954. pap. text ed. 5.50 (ISBN 0-395-04127-9). HM.

SPANISH LITERATURE–BIBLIOGRAPHY
Cardenas, Anthony & Gilkison, Jean. Bibliography of Old Spanish Texts. 2nd ed. (Literary Texts Ser.). x, 128p. 1977. pap. 7.50 (ISBN 0-942260-08-2). Hispanic Seminary.
Woodbridge, Hensley C. Spanish & Spanish-American Literature: An Annotated Guide to Selected Bibliographies. (Selected Bibliographies in Language & Literature: 4). 74p. 1983. 10.50x (ISBN 0-87352-954-5); pap. 5.75x (ISBN 0-87352-955-3). Modern Lang.

SPANISH LITERATURE–HISTORY AND CRITICISM
Alfonso X. Lapidario & Libro de las formas & Magenes. Winget, Lynn W. & Diman, Roderic C., eds. xix, 202p. 1980. 20.00 (ISBN 0-942260-12-0). Hispanic Seminary.
--Libros de las cruzes. Kasten, L. A. & Kiddle, L. B., eds. 173p. 1961. pap. 10.00; deluxe ed. 20.00. Hispanic Seminary.
Damiani, Bruno M. Montemayor's Diana, Music, & the Visual Arts. 1982. 11.00x (ISBN 0-942260-28-7). Hispanic Seminary.
Estudios dedicados a James Homer Herriott. 234p. 1966. 9.50 (ISBN 0-942260-04-X). Hispanic Seminary.
Homenaje a Antonio Sanchez Barbudo: Ensayos de literature espanola moderna. x, 396p. 1981. 25.00 (ISBN 0-686-37997-7). Hispanic Seminary.
Miller, Beth, ed. Women in Hispanic Literature: Icons & Fallen Idols. LC 81-14663. 480p. 1983. text ed. 27.00x (ISBN 0-520-04291-3); pap. text ed. 9.95 (ISBN 0-520-04367-7). U of Cal Pr.
Perez Firmat, Gustavo. Idle Fictions: The Hispanic Vanguard Novel, 1926-1934. LC 82-12773. (Illus.). 220p. 1982. text ed. 25.75x (ISBN 0-8223-0528-3). Duke.
Phillips, Gail. The Imagery of the Libro de Buen Amor. (Spanish Ser.: No. 9). 1983. 20.00 (ISBN 0-942260-23-6). Hispanic Seminary.
Richards, Ruth M. Text & Concordance of Isaac Israeli's Tratado de las Fiebres. 1982. 5.00 (ISBN 0-942260-19-8). Hispanic Seminary.
Seniff, Dennis P., ed. Libro de Monteria Alfonso XI. (Spanish Ser.: No. 8). 1983. 24.00x (ISBN 0-942260-27-9). Hispanic Seminary.
Shepard, Sanford. Lost Lexicon: Secret Meanings in the Vocabulary of Spanish Literature During the Inquisition. LC 82-70140. (Hispanic Studies Collection). 143p. (Orig.). 1982. pap. 19.95 (ISBN 0-89729-309-6). Ediciones.
Sims, Robert L. The Evolution of Myth in Garcia Marquez from La Hojarasca to Cien Anos de Soledad. LC 81-69541. (Hispanic Studies Collection). (Illus.). 153p. (Orig.). 1982. pap. 19.95 (ISBN 0-686-82200-5). Ediciones.
Studies in Honor of Lloyd A. Kasten. 300p. 1975. 9.50 (ISBN 0-942260-05-8). Hispanic Seminary.

SPANISH MUSIC
see Music, Spanish

SPANISH POETRY–HISTORY AND CRITICISM
Daydi-Tolson, Santiago. The Post-Civil War Spanish Social Poets. (World Authors Ser.). 192p. 1983. lib. bdg. 19.95 (ISBN 0-8057-6533-6, Twayne). G K Hall.
Goldstein, David. The Jewish Poets of Spain. 1983. pap. 5.95 (ISBN 0-14-044250-2). Penguin.
Henry, Thomas. Monstruo y Milagro. 1946. pap. 0.75 (ISBN 0-87535-060-7). Hispanic Soc.
Jiminez, Jose O. La Presencia de Antonio Machado en la Poesia Espanola de Posguerra. 230p. 1983. pap. 25.00 (ISBN 0-89295-024-2). Society Sp & Sp-Am.
McNerney. The Influence of Ausias March on Castilian Golden Age Poetry. (Biblioteca Hispanoamericana y Espanola de Amsterdam: Vol. 3). 128p. 1982. pap. text ed. 14.00x (ISBN 90-6203-654-6, Pub. by Rodopi Holland). Humanities.

SPANISH POTTERY
see Pottery, Spanish

SPANISH SHORTHAND
see Shorthand, Spanish

SPARK, MURIEL
Whittaker, Ruty. The Faith & Fiction of Muriel Spark. LC 81-21296. 180p. 1982. 19.95x (ISBN 0-312-27963-9). St Martin.

SPARRING
see Boxing

SPAS
see Health Resorts, Watering-Places, etc.

SPEAKING
see Debates and Debating; Oratory; Preaching; Public Speaking; Rhetoric

SPEAKING WITH TONGUES
see Glossolalia

SPECIAL EDUCATION
see also Exceptional Children–Education
Idol-Maestas, Lorna. Special Educator's Consultation Handbook. 350p. 1982. 27.50 (ISBN 0-89443-926-X). Aspen Systems.
Mori, Alan A. Families of Children with Special Needs: Early Intervention Techniques for the Practitioner. 300p. 1983. price not set (ISBN 0-89443-934-0). Aspen Systems.
Schmid, Rex E. & Nagata, Lynn. Contemporary Issues in Special Education. 2nd ed. 304p. 1983. 13.95x (ISBN 0-07-055331-9, C). McGraw.

SPECIAL LIBRARIES
see Libraries, Special

SPECIALISTS, EXCHANGE OF
see Exchange of Persons Programs

SPECIALIZED AGENCIES OF THE UNITED NATIONS
see International Agencies

SPECIALTY STORES
see Stores, Retail

SPECIE
see Gold; Money; Silver

SPECIE PAYMENTS
see Finance, Public; Silver Question

SPECIES, ORIGIN OF
see Origin of Species

SPECIFICATIONS
see also Building–Estimates; Standardization
also subdivision Contracts and Specifications or Specifications under certain subjects, e.g. Building–Contracts and Specifications
Meier, Hans W. Library of Specifications Sections, 4 vols. LC 82-10149. 1983. Set. looseleaf bdg. 250.00 (ISBN 0-686-84600-1, Busn). Vol. A (ISBN 0-13-535468-4). Vol. B (ISBN 0-13-535476-5). Vol. C (ISBN 0-13-535484-6). Vol. D (ISBN 0-13-535492-7). P-H.

SPECIMENS, PRESERVATION OF
see Insects–Collection and Preservation; Plants–Collection and Preservation; Taxidermy

SPECTERS
see Apparitions; Ghosts

SPECTRA
see Spectrum Analysis

SPECTRAL THEORY (MATHEMATICS)
Polish Academy of Sciences, Institute of Mathematics, ed. Spectral Theory, Vol. 8. (Banach Center Publications). 603p. 1982. 55.00 (ISBN 83-01-01495-4). Intl Pubns Serv.
Priestley, M. B., ed. Spectral Analysis & the Time Series, 2 Vols. in 1, Vol. 1 & Vol.2. (Probability & Mathematical Statistics Ser.). 1983. 39.50 (ISBN 0-12-564922-3). Acad Pr.

SPECTROCHEMICAL ANALYSIS
see Spectrum Analysis

SPECTROCHEMISTRY
see also Infra-Red Spectrometry
Hartmann, H. & Wanczek, K. P. Ion Cyclotron Resonance Spectrometry, Vol. II. (Lecture Notes in Chemistry Ser.: Vol. 31). 538p. 1983. pap. 32.80 (ISBN 0-387-11957-4). Springer-Verlag.

SPECTROSCOPY
see Spectrum Analysis

SPECTROSCOPY, NUCLEAR
see Nuclear Spectroscopy

SPECTROSCOPY, RAMAN
see Raman Spectroscopy

SPECTRUM, ATOMIC
see Atomic Spectra

SPECTRUM, INFRA-RED
see also Infra-Red Spectrometry; Photography, Infra-Red
AIP Conference, 90th, Boulder, 1982. Laser Techniques for Extreme Ultraviolet Spectroscopy: Proceedings. McIlrath, T. J. & Freeman, R. R., eds. LC 82-73205. 497p. 1982. lib. bdg. 37.00 (ISBN 0-88318-189-4). Am Inst Physics.
The Infrared Spectra Handbook of Minerals & Clays. 1982. 225.00 (ISBN 0-686-84522-6). Sadtler Res.
The Infrared Spectra Handbook of Priority Pollutants & Toxic Chemicals. 1982. 2.45 (ISBN 0-686-84521-8). Sadtler Res.

SPECTRUM, VIBRATIONAL
see Vibrational Spectra

SPECTRUM ANALYSIS
see also Atomic Spectra; Electron Paramagnetic Resonance; Laser Spectroscopy; Light; Mass Spectrometry; Nuclear Spectroscopy; Raman Spectroscopy
also subdivision Spectra under subjects, e.g. Iron–Spectra; Neon–Spectra; Stars–Spectra
Breene, R. G., Jr. Theories of Spectral Line Shape. LC 80-20664. 344p. 1981. 39.95x (ISBN 0-471-08361-5, Pub. by Wiley-Interscience). Wiley.
Ghosh, P. K. Introduction to Photoelectron Spectroscopy. (Chemical Analysis: A Series of Monographs on Analytical Chemisty & Its Applications). 352p. 1983. 40.00 (ISBN 0-471-06427-0, Pub. by Wiley-Interscience). Wiley.
Hansma, Paul K., ed. Tunneling Spectroscopy: Capabilities, Applications & New Techniques. 485p. 1982. 65.00x (ISBN 0-306-41070-2, Plenum Pr). Plenum Pub.
Klinger, David S., ed. Ultrasensitive Spectroscopic Techniques. LC 82-18417. (Quantum Electronics Ser.). Date not set. 55.00 (ISBN 0-12-414980-4). Acad Pr.
Lowe, E. Fundamentals of Molecular Spectroscopy. 3rd ed. 192p. 1983. 8.50 (ISBN 0-07-084139-X). McGraw.
Mills, et al. Instrumental Data for Drug Analysis, Vol. 1. 1982. 95.00 (ISBN 0-444-00718-0). Elsevier.
Mooney, E. F. & Webb, G. A., eds. Annual Reports on NMR Spectroscopy, 2 Vols. Date not set. Vol. 13. 99.50 (ISBN 0-12-505313-4); Vol. 14. price not set (ISBN 0-12-505314-2). Acad Pr.
Sadtler Guide to Carbon-13 NMR Spectra. 1982. 195.00 (ISBN 0-8456-0087-7). Sadtler Res.
Sadtler Spectra Handbook of Esters NMR. 1982. 2.85 (ISBN 0-8456-0079-6). Sadtler Res.
Sadtler's Spectra Handbook of Esters Ir. 285.00 (ISBN 0-8456-0078-8). Sadtler Res.
Varma, Ravi & Hrubesh, Lawrence W. Chemical Analysis by Microwave Rotational Spectroscopy. LC 78-17415. 218p. Repr. of 1979 ed. text ed. 31.50 (ISBN 0-471-03916-0). Krieger.
Wehry, E. L. Modern Fluorescence Spectroscopy. 713p. 1976. text ed. 178.00x (ISBN 0-471-26079-7, Pub. by Wiley-Interscience). Wiley.
West, W, ed. Chemical Applications of Spectroscopy. LC 45-8533. (Technique of Organic Chemistry Ser.: Vol.9, Pt.1). 486p. Repr. of 1968 ed. text ed. 29.25 (ISBN 0-686-84519-6). Krieger.

SPEECH
Here are entered works on the oral production of meaningful sounds in language. Works on speaking as a means of communication are entered under Oral communication or more specific headings, e.g. Public speaking.
see also Children–Language; Language and Languages; Oral Communication; Phonetics; Speech Processing Systems; Speech Therapy; Voice Culture
Carlson, R. & Granstrom, B., eds. The Representation of Speech in the Peripheral Auditory System: Proceedings of the Symposium, Stockholm, Sweden, May, 1982. 294p. 1982. 63.00 (ISBN 0-444-80447-1, Biomedical Pr). Elsevier.
Claussen, Paulette M. Speech-Language-Hearing Update: The Standard Reference Guide, Vol. 5, No. 2. 790p. 1982. 40.00 (ISBN 0-686-84041-0). Update Pubns AZ.
--Speech-Language-Hearing Update: The Standard Reference Guide, Vol. 6, No. 1. 80p. 1982. 40.00 (ISBN 0-943002-02-8). Update Pubns AZ.
Coe, Marguerite. The Eight Parts of Speech. (English Ser.). 24p. (gr. 4-7). 1979. wkbk. 5.00 (ISBN 0-8209-0181-4, E-9). ESP.
Dickens, Milton. Speech: Cynamic Communication. 3rd. ed. 400p. (Orig.). 1974. pap. text ed. 17.95 (ISBN 0-15-583193-3); instrs'. manual avail. HarBraceJ.
Haton, Jean-Paul, ed. Automatic Analysis & Recognition of Speech. 1982. lib. bdg. 48.00 (ISBN 90-277-1443-6, Pub. by Reidel Holland). Kluwer Boston.

Lass, Norman J., ed. Speech & Language: Advances in Basic Research & Practice, Vol. 6. (Serial Publication). 496p. 1982. 55.00 (ISBN 0-12-608606-0). Acad Pr.

Lea, Wayne A. Selecting, Designing, & Using Speech Recognizers. (Speech Technology Ser.). (Illus.). 400p. 1982. 74.00 (ISBN 0-686-37644-7); Student Ed. 49.00 (ISBN 0-686-37645-5). Speech Science.

Lim, Jae S. Speech Enhancement. (Illus.). 384p. 1983. 34.95 (ISBN 0-13-829705-3). P-H.

Steiner, Rudolf & Steiner Von Sivers, Marie. Creative Speech: The Nature of Speech Formation. Budgett, Winifred & Hummel, Nancy, trs. from Ger. 240p. 1978. 16.95 (ISBN 0-85440-322-1, Pub. by Steinerbooks). Anthroposophic.

Steiner, Rudolf & Steiner-von Sivers, Marie. Poetry & the Art of Speech. Wedgwood, Julia & Welburn, Andrew, trs. from Ger. 323p. (Orig.). 1981. pap. 14.00 (ISBN 0-85440-407-4, Pub. by Steinerbooks). Anthroposophic.

SPEECH–PHYSIOLOGICAL ASPECTS

MacNeilage, P. F., ed. The Production of Speech. (Illus.). 302p. 1983. 29.95 (ISBN 0-387-90735-1). Springer-Verlag.

SPEECH–PSYCHOLOGY

see Psycholinguistics

SPEECH, DISORDERS OF

see also Aphasia; Communicative Disorders; Stuttering

Bliss, Lynn S. & Allen, Doris V. SKOLD: Screening Kit of Language Development. (Illus.). 1982. write for info. (19488). Univ Park.

Tibbits, Donald F. Language Disorders in Adolescents. LC 82-71669. (Cliffs Speech & Hearing Ser.). 120p. (Orig.). 1982. pap. text ed. 4.95 (ISBN 0-8220-1832-2). Cliffs.

Travis, Edward L. Speech Pathology. 331p. 1982. Repr. of 1931 ed. lib. bdg. 75.00 (ISBN 0-89984-467-7). Century Bookbindery.

Weinberg, Bernd & Meitus, Irv J., eds. AN Introduction to Diagnosis of Speech & Language Disorders. 1983. pap. text ed. price not set (ISBN 0-8391-1810-4, 18430). Univ Park.

Winitz, Harris, ed. Treating Articulation Disorders: For Clinicians by Clinicians. 1983. pap. text ed. price not set (ISBN 0-8391-1814-7, 17833). Univ Park.

--Treating Language Disorders: For Clinicians by Clinicians. 1983. pap. text ed. price not set (ISBN 0-8391-1813-9, 19674). Univ Park.

SPEECH, INTERPRETATIVE

see Oral Interpretation

SPEECH, LIBERTY OF

see Liberty of Speech

SPEECH COMMUNICATION

see Oral Communication

SPEECH CORRECTION

see Speech Therapy

SPEECH DEFECTS

see Speech, Disorders Of

SPEECH PROCESSING SYSTEMS

see also Automatic Speech Recognition; Telephone

European Speech Recognition & Synthesis Markets. (Reports Ser.: No. 515). 153p. 1982. 985.00 (ISBN 0-686-38957-3). Intl Res Dev.

Flanagan, J. L. & Rabiner, L. R., eds. Speech Synthesis. LC 73-9728. (Benchmark Papers in Acoustics: Vol. 3). 511p. 1973. text ed. 55.00 (ISBN 0-87933-044-9). Hutchinson Ross.

Teja, Ed & Gonnella, Gary. Voice Technology. 1983. text ed. 19.95 (ISBN 0-8359-8417-6). Reston.

U. S. Speech Recognition & Synthesis Markets. (Reports Ser.: No. 516). 166p. 1982. 985.00 (ISBN 0-686-38958-1). Intl Res Dev.

SPEECH-READING

see Deaf–Means of Communication

SPEECH THERAPY

Perkins. Language Handicaps in Adults. (Current Therapy of Communication Disorders Ser.: Vol. 3). 1983. price not set (ISBN 0-86577-090-5). Thieme-Stratton.

Purser, Harry. Psychology for Speech Therapists. Chapman, Antony & Gale, Anthony, eds. (Psychology for Professional Groups Ser.). 300p. 1982. 49.00x (ISBN 0-333-31855-2, Pub. by Macmillan England). State Mutual Bk.

--Psychology for Speech Therapists. (Psychology for Professional Groups Ser.). 300p. 1982. text ed. 22.25x (ISBN 0-333-31855-2, Pub. by Macmillan England); pap. text ed. 19.25x (ISBN 0-333-31885-4). Humanities.

Van Dusen, Raymond. Speech Program for Stroke Patients. (Royal Court Reports: No. 2). (Illus.). 52p. (Orig.). 1982. pap. 3.00 (ISBN 0-686-38376-1). Royal Court.

SPEECH THERAPY–EXERCISES

Atkinson, Mary W. Johnny Smith Goes to His Speech Therapist. 32p. (gr. k-6). 1982. pap. 7.95 (ISBN 0-88450-734-3). Communication Skill.

SPEECHES, ADDRESSES, ETC.

see also Public Speaking; Toasts

also subdivision Addresses, Essays, Lectures under particular subjects, e.g. Geology–Addresses, Essays, Lectures; subdivision Addresses, Sermons, etc.; under wars, e.g. United States–History–Civil War, 1861-1865–Addresses, Sermons, etc.

Fine, Jonathan & Freedle, Roy O. Developmental Issues in Discourse. (Advances in Discourse Processes Ser.: Vol. 10). 336p. 1983. text ed. 32.50 (ISBN 0-686-82457-1); pap. text ed. 16.50 (ISBN 0-89391-161-5). Ablex Pub.

Macaulay, Thomas B. Speeches by Lord Macaulay, with His Minute on Indian Education. Young, G. M., ed. LC 76-29441. 1935. 28.00 (ISBN 0-404-15348-8). AMS Pr.

Ryan, Halford. American Rhetoric from Roosevelt to Reagan: A Collection of Speeches & Critical Essays. 310p. (Orig.). 1983. pap. text ed. 10.95x (ISBN 0-88133-015-9). Waveland Pr.

SPEED PERCEPTION

see Motion Perception (Vision)

SPEED READING

see Rapid Reading

SPEEDWRITING

see Stenotypy

SPELLERS

Barbe, Walter B., et al. Zaner-Bloser Spelling: Skills & Applications. 1983. write for info pupil texts grade 1-8; write for info tchr's eds. grade 1-8. Zaner-Bloser.

Barbe, Walter B., et al, eds. Spelling: Basic Skills for Effective Communication. 1982. 10.00 (ISBN 0-88309-118-6). Zaner-Bloser.

Willeford, George, Jr. Medical Word Finder. 3rd ed. 464p. 1983. 19.95 (ISBN 0-13-573527-0, Busn). P-H.

SPELLING

see English Language–Orthography and Spelling

SPELLS

see Magic

SPENSER, EDMUND, 1552?-1599

Cullen, Patrick & Roche, Thomas P., Jr., eds. Spenser Studies: A Renaissance Poetry Annual, Vol. IV. 160p. 1983. 14.95x (ISBN 0-8229-3476-0). U of Pittsburgh Pr.

SPENT REACTOR FUEL REPROCESSING

see Reactor Fuel Reprocessing

SPERM

see Semen; Spermatozoa

SPERMATOPHYTA

see Phanerogams

SPERMATOZOA

see also Semen

Andre, Jean. The Sperm Cell. 1982. 71.75 (ISBN 90-247-2784-7, Pub. by Martinus Nijhoff Netherlands). Kluwer Boston.

SPEUSIPPUS

Taran, Leonardo. Speusippus of Athens: A Critical Study with a Collection of the Related Texts & Commentary. (Philosophia Antiqua: Vol. 39). xxvii, 521p. 1982. pap. write for info. (ISBN 90-04-06505-9). E J Brill.

SPHRAGISTICS

see Seals (Numismatics)

SPIDERS

Roberts, M. J. British Spiders. write for info. (ISBN 0-12-589680-8). Acad Pr.

SPIDERS–JUVENILE LITERATURE

Joosse, Barbara M. Spiders in the Fruit Cellar. LC 82-4694. (Illus.). 36p. (gr. k-2). 1983. 9.95 (ISBN 0-394-85327-X); lib. bdg. 9.99 (ISBN 0-394-95327-4). Knopf.

Selsam, Millicent E. & Hunt, Joyce. A First Look at Spiders. (A First Look at Ser.). (Illus.). 32p. (gr. 1-3). 1983. 7.95 (ISBN 0-8027-6480-0); lib. bdg. 8.85 (ISBN 0-8027-6481-9). Walker & Co.

SPIES

see also Espionage; Secret Service; World War, 1939-1945–Underground Movements

Lloyd, Richard & Thomas, Antony. Frank Terpil: Portrait of a Dangerous Man. 256p. 1983. 14.95 (ISBN 0-86579-023-X). Seaver Bks.

SPIN (DYNAMICS)

see Rotational Motion

SPINAL CORD

see also Cerebrospinal Fluid; Nervous System; Reflexes

Davidoff. Handbook of the Spinal Cord, Vol. 1. 592p. 1982. write for info. (ISBN 0-8247-1708-2). Dekker.

SPINAL CORD–WOUNDS AND INJURIES

Hanak, Marcia & Scott, Ann. Spinal Cord Injury: An Illustrated Guide to Patient Care. 1983. text ed. 15.95 (ISBN 0-8261-4171-4). Springer Pub.

Zejdlik, Cynthia M. Spinal Cord Injury. LC 82-23904. (Nursing Ser.). 700p. 1983. text ed. 35.00 (ISBN 0-534-01339-2). Brooks-Cole.

SPINE–ABNORMITIES AND DEFORMITIES

Winter, Robert B. Congenital Deformities of the Spine. (Illus.). 432p. 1983. 59.00 (ISBN 0-86577-079-4). Thieme-Stratton.

SPINE–CURVATURE

see Spine–Abnormities and Deformities

SPINE–SURGERY

Cauthen, Joseph C. Lumbar Spine Surgery: Indications, Techniques, Failures & Alternatives. (Illus.). 234p. 1983. lib. bdg. 45.00 (ISBN 0-683-01500-1). Williams & Wilkins.

Louis, R. Surgery of the Spine: Surgical Anatomy & Operative Approaches. (Illus.). 328p. 1983. 124.00 (ISBN 0-387-11412-2). Springer-Verlag.

SPINNING

Baines, Patricia. Spinning Wheels, Spinners & Spinning. new ed. pap. 10.95 (ISBN 0-686-37658-7). Robin & Russ.

Wickens. Beginners Guide to Spinning. 1982. text ed. 9.95 (ISBN 0-408-00573-4). Butterworth.

SPINNING-WHEEL

Baines, Patricia. Spinning Wheels, Spinners & Spinning. new ed. pap. 10.95 (ISBN 0-686-37658-7). Robin & Russ.

SPINOZA, BENEDICTUS DE, 1632-1677

Wolfson, Harry A. The Philosophy of Spinoza: Unfolding the Latent Processes of His Reasoning. 872p. 1983. pap. text ed. 15.00x (ISBN 0-674-66595-3). Harvard U Pr.

SPINSTERS

see Single Women

SPIRIT, HOLY

see Holy Spirit

SPIRITISM

see Spiritualism

SPIRITUAL DIRECTION

Kelsey, Morton T. Companions on the Inner Way: The Art of Spiritual Guidance. 250p. 1983. 17.50 (ISBN 0-8245-0585-9); pap. 8.95 (ISBN 0-8245-0560-3). Crossroad NY.

Steiner, Rudolf. The Effects of Spiritual Development. 3rd ed. Parker, A. H., tr. from Ger. (Illus.). 157p. 1978. 15.00 (ISBN 0-85440-319-1, Pub. by Steinerbooks); pap. 9.95 (ISBN 0-85440-320-5). Anthroposophic.

SPIRITUAL DIRECTORS

see also Spiritual Direction

Broek, van den Silvere O. F. & Broek, den van Silvere O. F., eds. The Spiritual Legacy of Sister Mary of the Holy Trinity. 364p. 1950. pap. 5.00 (ISBN 0-686-81630-7). TAN Bks Pubs.

SPIRITUAL EXERCISES

see also Retreats

Arnold, Mildred. Taking a Look at my Faith. 80p. 1982. pap. 5.95 (ISBN 0-8170-0966-3). Judson.

SPIRITUAL GIFTS

see Gifts, Spiritual

SPIRITUAL HEALING

see Faith-Cure

SPIRITUAL LIFE

see also Christian Life; Faith; Retreats; Sanctification; Spiritual Direction; Spiritual Exercises

Allen, James. The Life Triumphant. 112p. 4.50 (ISBN 0-686-38224-2). Sun Bks.

Badra, Robert. Meditations for Spiritual Misfits. 93p. (Orig.). 1982. pap. 7.95 (ISBN 0-9610274-0-1). JCL Hse.

Baird, John A., Jr. Horn of Plenty. 1982. pap. 6.95 (ISBN 0-8423-1451-2). Tyndale.

Balsekar, Ramesh s. Pointers from Nisargadatta Maharaj. LC 82-71505. xiv, 223p. 1983. 13.95 (ISBN 0-89386-004-2). Acorn NC.

Batzler, L. Richard. Journeys on Your Spiritual Path. 1982. 7.95 (ISBN 0-935710-04-3). Hidden Valley.

Berry, Thomas. Tielherd in the Ecological Age. (Tielherd Studies). 1982. 2.00 (ISBN 0-89012-032-3). Anima Pubns.

Besant, Annie. From the Outer Court to the Inner Sanctum. Nicholson, Shirley, ed. LC 82-42703. 130p. 1983. pap. 4.50 (ISBN 0-8356-0574-4, Quest). Theos Pub Hse.

Claypool, John. The Light Within You: Looking At Life Through New Eyes. 1983. 9.95 (ISBN 0-8499-0273-8). Word Bks.

Colbert, Paul. Life is a Spiritual Experience. LC 82-70932. 91p. 1982. pap. 4.95 (ISBN 0-9608164-0-2). Flower Truth.

Das Goswami, Satsvarupa. Japa Reform Notebook. Bimala dasi & Mandalesvara dasa, eds. 145p. (Orig.). 1982. pap. text ed. 2.95 (ISBN 0-911233-07-5). Gita Nagari.

--Letters from Srila Prabhupada, Vol. 1. Mandalesvara dasa & Gaura Purnima dasa, eds. 274p. (Orig.). 1982. pap. text ed. 3.95 (ISBN 0-911233-03-2). Gita Nagari.

--One Hundred & Eight Rosebushes: Preaching in Germany. Mandalesvara dasa & Bimala dasi, eds. (Prahupada-lila Ser.). 44p. (Orig.). 1982. pap. text ed. 2.00 (ISBN 0-911233-04-0). Gita-Nagari.

The Dhammapada: Anonymous Translation with Explanatory Notes & a Short Essay on Buddha's Thought. ix, 139p. 3.00 (ISBN 0-938998-16-1). Theosophy.

Fabel, Arthur. Cosmic Genesis. (Tielherd Studies). 1981. 2.00 (ISBN 0-89012-028-5). Anima Pubns.

Fenelon, Archbishop. The Royal Way of the Cross. Helms, Hal M., ed. 1982. 3.95 (ISBN 0-941478-00-9). Paraclete Pr.

Francuch, Peter D. Messages From Within. LC 82-60513. 220p. 1982. pap. 8.00 (ISBN 0-939386-03-8). Spiritual Advisory.

Furcha, E. J., ed. Spirit within Structure: Essays in Honor of George Jonhston on the Occasion of his Seventieth Birthday. (Pittsburgh Theological Monographs: No. 3). xvi, 194p. 1983. pap. 12.50 (ISBN 0-915138-53-0). Pickwick.

Gallagher, Chuck. Call to Healing. 1983. 3.95 (ISBN 0-8215-9873-2). Sadlier.

Goswami, Satsuarupa D. Opening a Temple in Los Angelos: A Visit to Boston. Dasa, Mandalesuaraba, et al, eds. (Prabhupada-Lila Ser.). 72p. 1981. pap. 2.25 (ISBN 0-911233-01-6). Gita Nagari.

Gray, William G. The Sangreal Sacrament, Vol. 2. (The Sangreal Sodality Ser.). 170p. Date not set. pap. price not set (ISBN 0-87728-562-4). Weiser.

Griffin, John H. The Hermitage Journals. LC 82-45833. (Illus.). 240p. 1983. pap. 6.95 (ISBN 0-385-18470-0, Im). Doubleday.

Gunther, Bernard. Energy Ecstasy & Your Seven Vital Shakras. 200p. 1983. lib. bdg. 17.95x (ISBN 0-89370-666-3). Borgo Pr.

Hardman, Keith J. The Spiritual Awakeners. 240p. (Orig.). 1983. pap. 6.95 (ISBN 0-8024-0177-5). Moody.

Hill, Dawn. Reaching for the Other Side. (Orig.). 1983. pap. 6.95 (ISBN 0-87877-063-1). Newcastle Pub.

Hillig, Chuck. What Are You Doing in My Universe. 1983. pap. 5.95 (ISBN 0-87877-065-8). Newcastle Pub.

Hug, James E., ed. Tracing the Spirit: Communities, Social Action & Theological Reflections. LC 82-62419. (Woodstock Studies). 320p. 1983. pap. 9.95 (ISBN 0-8091-2529-3). Paulist Pr.

Innes, Michael. The Case Journeying Boy. LC 82-48245. 336p. 1983. pap. 2.84i (ISBN 0-06-080632-X, P 632, PL). Har-Row.

Johnstone, Charles & Giles, Lionel, trs. Selections from the Upanishads & the Tao Te King. 142p. 1951. 3.00 (ISBN 0-938998-15-3). Theosophy.

Kripalvandji, Swami Shri. Pilgrimage of Love, Bk. II. 416p. (Orig.). 1982. pap. 7.95 (ISBN 0-940258-05-6). Kripalu Pubns.

Lewis, Jim. Spiritual Gospel. LC 82-51231. 145p. (Orig.). 1982. pap. write for info. (ISBN 0-942482-05-0). Unity Church Denver.

Mouser, William E., Jr. Walking in Wisdom. 180p. (Orig.). 1983. pap. 5.95 (ISBN 0-87784-846-7). Inter-Varsity.

Muhaiyaddeen, Bawa. Maya Veeram or the Forces of Illusion. Marcus, Sharon, ed. Ganesan, K. & Ganesan, R., trs. from Tamil. (Illus.). 232p. 1982. pap. 10.95 (ISBN 0-87728-550-0). Weiser.

Murphey, Cecil. Press On: A Disciple's Guide to Spiritual Growth. 140p. (Orig.). 1983. pap. 4.95 (ISBN 0-89283-129-4). Servant.

Nee, T. S. & Arcangeli, Gianfranco. Autorita Spirituale. (Italian.). 1980. pap. 2.50 (ISBN 0-8297-0923-1). Life Pubs Intl.

Newcomb, J. A. From Darkness to Light. 1983. 7.95 (ISBN 0-533-05666-7). Vantage.

Paxson, Ruth. Life on the Highest Plane, 3 Vols. 512p. 1983. Repr. of 1928 ed. 15.95 (ISBN 0-8010-7074-0). Baker Bk.

Plummer, L. Gordon. By the Holy Tetrakyts: Symbol & Reality in Man & Universe. (Study Ser.: No. 9). (Illus.). 96p. (Orig.). 1982. pap. 5.75 (ISBN 0-913004-44-8). Point Loma Pub.

Rajneesh, Bhagwan Shree. Ah This! Rajneesh Foundation International, ed. (Illus.). 240p. 1982. pap. 8.95 (ISBN 0-88050-502-8). Rajneesh Found Intl.

--Book of Wisdom, Vol. I. Rajneesh Foundation International, ed. 385p. 1982. pap. 9.95 (ISBN 0-88050-530-3). Rajneesh Found Intl.

--Don't Bite My Finger, Look Where I Am Pointing. Rajneesh Foundation International, ed. 230p. 1982. pap. 14.95 (ISBN 0-88050-550-8). Rajneesh Found Intl.

--The Goose is Out. Rajneesh Foundation International, ed. 286p. 1982. pap. 10.95 (ISBN 0-88050-571-0). Rajneesh Found Intl.

Reichert, Richard. Community of the Spirit. 120p. 1982. pap. 3.60 (ISBN 0-697-01796-6); tchr's manual 3.50 (ISBN 0-697-01797-4). Wm C Brown.

Ruhnau, Helen E. Drama of Patmos Initiations of John. LC 82-71052. 1982. pap. 10.95 soft cover (ISBN 0-941036-07-3). Colleasius Pr.

Schwaller de Lubicz, R. A. Nature Word: Verbe Nature. Lawlor, Deborah, tr. from French. & intro. by. LC 82-81069. (Illus.). 160p. (Orig.). 1982. pap. 6.95 (ISBN 0-940262-00-2). Lindisfarne Pr.

Spiker, Louise C. No Instant Grapes in God's Vineyard. 112p. 1982. pap. 5.95 (ISBN 0-686-82282-X). Judson.

Stone, James. How To Live In the Fullness of Spirit. 61p. 1982. pap. 1.95 (ISBN 0-934942-33-1). White Wing Pub.

Swami Jyotir Maya Nanda. Yoga of Divine Love: A Commentary on Narada Bhakti Sutras. 1982. pap. 4.99 (ISBN 0-934664-42-0). Yoga Res Foun.

Swedenborg, Emanuel. Experientiae Spirituales, 6 Vols. 2nd ed. Odhner, John D., ed. 3600p. (Latin.). 1982. Set. 270.00 (ISBN 0-910557-00-4). Acad New Church.

Taylor, Jeremy. The Rule & Exercises of Holy Living. 295p. 1982. Repr. of 1982 ed. lib. bdg. 35.00 (ISBN 0-89984-468-5). Century Bookbindery.

Wells, Ronald V. Spiritual Disciplines for Everyday Living. (Orig.). 1982. text ed. 13.95 (ISBN 0-915744-32-5); pap. 8.95 (ISBN 0-915744-31-7). Character Res.

Westmeyer, Nancy. Parish Life: Formation for Mission & Ministry. 1983. pap. 8.95t (ISBN 0-8091-2489-0). Paulist Pr.

Wolsky, Alexander. Tielherd in Chardin's Biological Ideas. (Tielherd Studies). 1981. 2.00 (ISBN 0-89012-024-2). Anima Pubns.

Yogananda, Paramahansa. Whispers from Eternity, First Vision. 1949. 6.95 (ISBN 0-87612-102-4). Self Realization.

Yogananda, Paramhansa. Songs of the Soul. LC 80-69786. 1980. pap. 6.95 (ISBN 0-937134-02-3). Amrita Found.

--Whispers from Eternity. 1978. pap. 8.95 (ISBN 0-937134-03-1). Amrita Found.

Zitko, Howard J. Tantra Yoga: The Sexual Gateway to Spiritual Fulfillment. pap. 7.95 (ISBN 0-686-43276-2). World Univ AZ.

SPIRITUAL LIFE–BIBLICAL TEACHING

Sweeny, Z. T. Spirit & the Word. 1982. pap. 3.95 (ISBN 0-89225-264-2). Gospel Advocate.

SPIRITUAL LIFE–CATHOLIC AUTHORS

Pennington, M. Basil. A Place Apart: Monastic Prayer & Practice for Everyone. LC 81-43566. 168p. 1983. 13.95 (ISBN 0-385-17850-6). Doubleday.

Staton, Knofel. Spiritual Gifts for Christians Today. 118p. (Orig.). 1973. pap. 2.95 (ISBN 0-89900-134-3). College Pr Pub.

SPIRITUAL LIFE–ORTHODOX EASTERN AUTHORS

Grisbrooke, W. Jardine. The Spiritual Counsels of Father John of Kronstadt. 228p. (Orig.). 1982. pap. 7.95 (ISBN 0-913836-92-3). St Vladimirs.

SPIRITUAL-MINDEDNESS

see Spirituality

SPIRITUALISM

see also Apparitions; Ghosts; Occult Sciences; Psychical Research

Gauld, Alan. Mediumship & Survival: A Century of Investigations. 288p. 1982. 40.00x (ISBN 0-434-28320-7, Pub. by Heinemann England). State Mutual Bk.

Leichtman, Robert R. Arthur Ford Returns. (From Heaven to Earth Ser.). (Illus.). 88p. (Orig.). 1979. pap. 3.00 (ISBN 0-89804-058-2). Ariel OH.

--Cheiro Returns. (From Heaven to Earth Ser.). (Illus.). 78p. (Orig.). 1979. pap. 3.00 (ISBN 0-89804-053-1). Ariel OH.

--Edgar Cayce Returns. (From Heaven to Earth Ser.). (Illus.). 112p. (Orig.). 1978. pap. 3.00 (ISBN 0-89804-051-5). Ariel OH.

--Eileen Garrett Returns. (From Heaven to Earth Ser.). 96p. (Orig.). 1980. pap. 3.00 (ISBN 0-89804-061-2). Ariel OH.

--H. P. Blatavsky Returns. (From Heaven to Earth Ser.). 95p. (Orig.). 1980. pap. 3.00 (ISBN 0-89804-059-0). Ariel OH.

--Jefferson Returns. (From Heaven to Earth Ser.). 64p. (Orig.). 1979. pap. 3.00 (ISBN 0-89804-057-4). Ariel OH.

--Jung & Freud Return. (From Heaven to Earth Ser.). 102p. (Orig.). 1979. pap. 3.00 (ISBN 0-89804-054-X). Ariel OH.

--Leadbeater Returns. (From Heaven to Earth Ser.). (Illus.). 96p. (Orig.). 1979. pap. 3.00 (ISBN 0-89804-055-8). Ariel OH.

--Mark Twain Returns. LC 81-69185. (From Heaven to Earth Ser.). 80p. (Orig.). 1982. pap. 3.00 (ISBN 0-89804-067-1). Ariel OH.

--Shakespeare Returns. (From Heaven to Earth Ser.). (Illus.). 70p. (Orig.). 1978. pap. 3.00 (ISBN 0-89804-052-3). Ariel OH.

--Sir Oliver Lodge Returns. (From Heaven to Earth Ser.). (Illus.). 96p. (Orig.). 1979. pap. 3.00 (ISBN 0-89804-056-6). Ariel OH.

Sutherland, Theodore J. Spiritism & the Dead. (An Intimate Life of Man Library Bk.). (Illus.). 127p. 1983. Repr. of 1889 ed. 89.75 (ISBN 0-89901-090-3). Found Class Reprints.

Theertha, Rama. Pilgrimage & Spiritual Advancement. 23p. 1982. write for info. (ISBN 0-937698-02-4). Golden Mean.

SPIRITUALITY

see also Soul; Spiritual Life

Doherty, Barbara. I Am What I Do: Contemplation & Human Experience. 226p. 1982. pap. 7.95 (ISBN 0-88347-129-9). Thomas More.

Doyle, Brendan & Fox, Matt. Meditations with TM Julian of Norwich. LC 82-73955. (Meditations with TM). (Illus.). 128p. (Orig.). 1982. pap. 6.95 (ISBN 0-939680-11-4). Bear & Co.

Fox, Matthew. Meditations with TM Meister Eckhart. LC 82-71451. (Meditations with TM Ser.). (Illus.). 128p. (Orig.). 1982. pap. 6.95 (ISBN 0-939680-04-1). Bear & Co.

--Western Spirituality: Historical Roots, Ecumenical Routes. 440p. pap. 10.95 (ISBN 0-939680-01-7). Bear & Co.

Fox, Matthew, frwd. by. Whee! We, Wee All the Way Home: A Guide to a Sensual Prophetic Spirituality. 264p. pap. 8.95 (ISBN 0-686-42950-8). Bear & Co.

Kaschmitter, William A. The Spirituality of the Catholic Church. 980p. 1982. 30.00 (ISBN 0-912414-33-2). Lumen Christi.

Legere, Thomas E. Thoughts on the Run: Glimpses of Wholistic Spirituality. 144p. 1983. pap. 7.95 (ISBN 0-86683-698-5). Winston Pr.

Uhlein, Gabriele. Meditations with TM Hildegrade of Bingen. LC 82-73363. (Meditations with TM). 128p. (Orig.). 1982. pap. 6.95 (ISBN 0-939680-12-2). Bear & Co.

Van Kamm, Adrian & Muto, Susan A. Creative Formation of Life & World. LC 82-16014. 462p. 1983. lib. bdg. 29.75 (ISBN 0-8191-2708-6); pap. text ed. 17.25 (ISBN 0-8191-2709-4). U Pr of Amer.

Woodruff, Sue. Meditations with TM Mechtild of Magdeburg. LC 82-73366. (Meditations with TM Ser.). (Illus.). 128p. (Orig.). 1982. pap. 6.95 (ISBN 0-939680-06-8). Bear & Co.

Woods, Richard. Symbion. LC 82-73365. 264p. (Orig.). 1982. pap. 8.95 (ISBN 0-939680-08-4). Bear & Co.

SPIRITUALS (SONGS)

see also Blues (Songs, Etc.)

Roes, Carol. Four Negro Spirituals. Date not set. pap. 3.75 (ISBN 0-930932-24-2); record incl. M Loke.

SPITFIRE (FIGHTER PLANES)

Price, Alfred. The Spitfire Story. (Illus.). 256p. 1982. 29.95 (ISBN 0-86720-624-1). Sci Bks Intl.

SPLICING

see Knots and Splices

SPOILS SYSTEM

see Civil Service Reform; Patronage, Political

SPOKEN ENGLISH

see English Language–Conversation and Phrase Books; English Language–Spoken English

SPOONS

Rainwater, Dorothy T. & Felger, Donna H. A Collector's Guide to Spoons Around the World. 2nd ed. (Illus.). 19.95 (ISBN 0-686-84756-3). Schiffer.

SPORES (BACTERIA)

Nilsson, S. T., ed. Atlas of Airborne Fungal Spores in Europe. (Illus.). 145p. 1983. 50.00 (ISBN 0-387-11900-0). Springer-Verlag.

SPORTING DOGS

see Hunting Dogs

SPORTING JOURNALISM

see Sports Journalism

SPORTS

see also Amusements; Aquatic Sports; Athletes; Athletics; Coaching (Athletics); Doping in Sports; Games; Gymnastics; Jumping; Olympic Games; Outdoor Life; Photography of Sports; Physical Education and Training; Rodeos; School Sports; Tournaments; Track-Athletics

also names of sports, e.g. Golf

Cannon, Jimmy. Nobody Asked Me but... The World of Jimmy Cannon. Cannon, Jack & Cannon, Tom, eds. (Penguin Sports Library). 1983. pap. 5.95 (ISBN 0-14-006617-9). Penguin.

Diagram Group. The Sports Fan's Ultimate Book of Sports Comparisons: A Visual, Statistical & Factual Reference on Comparative Abilities, Records, Rules & Equipment. (Illus.). 192p. pap. 9.95 (ISBN 0-312-75335-7). St Martin.

Greenspan, Emily. Little Winners: The World of the Child Sports Superstar. (Illus.). 320p. 1983. 14.45i (ISBN 0-316-32667-4). Little.

Halberstam, David. The Breaks of the Game. 480p. 1983. pap. 3.95 (ISBN 0-345-29625-7). Ballantine.

Hargreaves, Jennifer, ed. Sport, Culture & Ideology. 200p. (Orig.). 1983. pap. 15.95 (ISBN 0-7100-9242-3). Routledge & Kegan.

Information Please Book of Sports Facts & Records, 1983. 128p. (Orig.). 1983. pap. 1.95 (ISBN 0-89479-123-0). A & W Pubs.

Johnson, Bob & Bragg, Patricia. The Complete Triathlon Swim-Bike-Run: Distance Training Manual. (Illus.). 600p. 1982. 24.95 (ISBN 0-87790-029-9). Health Sci.

Klausen, Klaus & Hemmingsen, Ib. Basic Sport Science. Burke, Edmund J., tr. 1982. text ed. 15.95 (ISBN 0-686-38846-1); pap. 9.95 (ISBN 0-686-38847-X). Mouvment Pubns.

Krout, John S. Annals of American Sport. 1929. text ed. 22.50x (ISBN 0-686-83470-4). Elliots Bks.

Lovesey, John & Mason, Nicholas. Sunday Times Sports Book. 1979. 19.95 (ISBN 0-437-15445-9, Pub. by World's Work). David & Charles.

McMahon, Bob & Leopold, Jay. Who Are the Best? The Sports Survey Book. LC 82-83930. (Illus.). 128p. (Orig.). 1983. pap. 6.95 (ISBN 0-686-82531-4). Leisure Pr.

Major Sports Books, 10 Levels. (High-interest, low-readability series to improve vocabulary & comprehension skills). (gr. 4-8). Set. 5 copies ea. of 10 titles 213.75 (ISBN 0-8372-3852-8); 4.50 ea.; tchr's guide 3.48 (ISBN 0-8372-9069-4). Bowmar-Noble.

Mood, Dale & Musker, Frank F. Sports & Recreational Activities for Men & Women. 8th ed. (Illus.). 442p. 1983. pap. text ed. 14.95 (ISBN 0-8016-0290-4). Mosby.

Nixon, Howard L., II. Sport & the American Dream. LC 82-83943. (Illus.). 240p. (Orig.). 1983. pap. text ed. 14.95 (ISBN 0-88011-112-7). Leisure Pr.

Plimpton, George. A Sports Bestiary. LC 82-10002. (Illus.). 112p. 1982. 14.95 (ISBN 0-07-050290-0). McGraw.

Sports Reading Series, 3 kits. (gr. 4-8). kit 80.25 ea.; tchr's guide 3.48 ea.; suppl. materials avail. Bowmar-Noble.

Track & Field 1981-83. (Tips & Techniques Bks.). 4.95 (ISBN 0-88314-194-9). AAHPERD.

Track & Field 1982-83. (NAGWS Sports Guides Ser.). 3.95 (ISBN 0-88314-217-1). AAHPERD.

Wade, Allen. Football (Soccer) Association Guide to Training & Coaching. 1982. 17.95 (ISBN 0-434-83550-1, Pub. by Heinemann). David & Charles.

SPORTS–ACCIDENTS AND INJURIES

see also Sports Medicine

Wilson, Holly. Coaches' Guide to Sports Injuries. 1983. pap. text ed. price not set (ISBN 0-931250-37-4). Human Kinetics.

SPORTS–BIOGRAPHY

Boyle, Robert H. AT the Top of Their Game: Profiles from Sports Illustrated. 224p. 1983. 12.95 (ISBN 0-8329-0274-8); pap. 8.95 (ISBN 0-8329-0283-7). Winchester Pr.

Coady, Mary-Francis. Steve Podborski. (Picture Life Ser.). (Illus.). 48p. (gr. k-3). 1983. PLB 7.90 (ISBN 0-531-04599-4). Watts.

SPORTS–DICTIONARIES

Frommer, Harvey. Sports Lingo: A Dictionary of the Language of Sports. LC 82-12130. 312p. 1983. pap. 7.95 (ISBN 0-689-70640-5, 289). Atheneum.

Sugar, Bert R. Sports Collector's Bible. 4th rev. ed. 578p. pap. 12.95 (ISBN 0-672-52741-3). Bobbs.

SPORTS–HISTORY

Landon, Charles. Classic Moments of Athletics. 144p. 1982. 35.00x (ISBN 0-86190-053-7, Pub. by Moorland). State Mutual Bk.

Lee, Mabel. History of Physical Education & Sports in the U. S. A. 384p. 1983. text ed. 16.95 (ISBN 0-471-86315-7). Wiley.

SPORTS–JUVENILE LITERATURE

Aaseng, Nate. Supersubs of Pro Sports. (Sports Heroes Library). (Illus.). 80p. (gr. 4up). 1983. PLB 7.95g (ISBN 0-8225-1328-5). Lerner Pubns.

Aaseng, Nathan. Comeback Stars of Pro Sports. (Sports Heroes Library). (Illus.). 80p. (gr. 4up). 1983. PLB 7.95g (ISBN 0-8225-1327-7). Lerner Pubns.

Berger, Melvin. Sports. (A Reference First Bk.). (Illus.). 96p. (gr. 4 up). 1983. PLB 8.90 (ISBN 0-531-04540-4). Watts.

Jaspersohn, William. Magazine: A Week Behind the Scenes at Sports Illustrated. LC 82-21703. (Illus.). 128p. (gr. 7 up). 1983. 12.45i (ISBN 0-316-45815-5). Little.

Liss, Howard. The Giant Book of More Strange but True Sports Stories. LC 82-13236. (Illus.). 160p. (gr. 5-10). 1983. PLB 5.99 (ISBN 0-394-95633-8); pap. 4.95 (ISBN 0-394-85633-3). Random.

Starting Line. 4 bks. Incl. Cats (ISBN 0-8372-2419-5); Kickoff (ISBN 0-8372-2422-5); Racing (ISBN 0-8372-2421-7); Wheels (ISBN 0-8372-2420-9). (gr. 1-5). complete 235.50 (ISBN 0-8372-2390-3); pap. 3.99 ea.; kit 46.80 ea.; spirit masters avail. Bowmar-Noble.

SPORTS–MEDICAL ASPECTS

see Sports Medicine

SPORTS–MISCELLANEA

Anthony, Douglass. Sports Motions: A Primer For Winning. (Illus.). 96p. (Orig.). 1983. pap. 5.95 (ISBN 0-911433-01-5). HealthRight.

The Official 1984 Price Guide to Sports Collectibles. 1st ed. LC 82-84655. 240p. 1983. pap. 2.95 (ISBN 0-87637-379-1). Hse of Collectibles.

SPORTS–ORGANIZATION AND ADMINISTRATION

Diagram Group. The Rule Book: The Authoritative Up-To-Date Illustrated Guide to the Regulations, History,& Object of All Major Sports. (Illus.). 432p. 9.95 (ISBN 0-312-69576-4). St Martin.

Zeigler, Earle F. & Bowie, Gary W. Management Competency Development in Sport & Physical Education. LC 82-13066. 280p. 1983. text ed. write for info. (ISBN 0-8121-0830-2). Lea & Febiger.

SPORTS–PHILOSOPHY

Thomas, Carolyn E. Sport in a Philosophic Context. LC 82-12662. 250p. (Orig.). 1983. pap. price not set (ISBN 0-8121-0871-X). Lea & Febiger.

SPORTS–PHOTOGRAPHY

see Photography of Sports

SPORTS–PHYSIOLOGICAL ASPECTS

Davies, Bruce & Thomas, Geoffrey, eds. Science & Sporting Performance: Management or Manipulation? (Illus.). 250p. 1982. 32.50 (ISBN 0-19-857594-7). Oxford U Pr.

Sharkey, Brian J. Coaches' Guide to Sport Physiology. 1983. pap. text ed. price not set (ISBN 0-931250-38-2). Human Kinetics.

Williams, Melvin, ed. Ergogenic Aids in Sports. 1983. text ed. price not set (ISBN 0-931250-39-0). Human Kinetics.

SPORTS–SAFETY MEASURES

see also Sports–Accidents and Injuries

Sports Safety II. 96p. 6.95 (ISBN 0-88314-176-0). AAHPERD.

SPORTS–SOCIAL ASPECTS

Dunleavy, Aidan O. & Miracle, Andrew W., eds. Studies in the Sociology of Sport. LC 82-16807. 402p. 1982. pap. text ed. 15.00 (ISBN 0-912646-78-0). Tex Christian.

Hoover, Dwight W. & Koumouledes, John T., eds. Sports & Society. (Conspectus of History Ser.). (Orig.). 1982. pap. 5.95 (ISBN 0-937994-03-0). Ball State Univ.

SPORTS–VOCATIONAL GUIDANCE

Fordham, Sheldon L. & Leaf, Carol A. Physical Education & Sports: An Introduction to Alternative Careers. LC 77-19115. 385p. 1978. text ed. 25.95x (ISBN 0-471-26622-1). Wiley.

Professional Research Publications, ed. ProSports Career Guide. 130p. 1983. pap. 15.00 (ISBN 0-931066-01-8). Prof Research.

SPORTS, INJURIES FROM

see Sports–Accidents and Injuries

SPORTS, INTRAMURAL

see Intramural Sports

SPORTS FOR THE BLIND

see Blind, Physical Education for the

SPORTS FOR WOMEN

Black Women in Sport. 75p. 8.95 (ISBN 0-88314-036-5). AAHPERD.

Mushier, Carole L. Team Sports for Girls & Women. LC 82-60837. (Illus.). 214p. 1983. pap. text ed. 11.95x (ISBN 0-916622-25-8). Princeton Bk Co.

SPORTS IN LITERATURE

Messenger, Christian. Sport & the Spirit of Play in American Fiction. 352p. 1983. pap. write for info. Columbia U Pr.

SPORTS IN TELEVISION

see Television Broadcasting of Sports

SPORTS JOURNALISM

see also Television Broadcasting of Sports

Angell, Roger. Five Seasons. 416p. 1983. pap. 3.95 (ISBN 0-446-31103-0). Warner Bks.

Cannon, Jimmy. Nobody Asked Me but... The World of Jimmy Cannon. Cannon, Jack & Cannon, Tom, eds. (Penguin Sports Library). 1983. pap. 5.95 (ISBN 0-14-006617-9). Penguin.

Great Sport Stories as Reported in the New York Times. 90p. (gr. 9-12). 1982. pap. text ed. 7.95 (ISBN 0-667-00668-0). Microfilming Corp.

SPORTS MEDICINE

see also Doping in Sports; Sports–Accidents and Injuries

Appenzeller, Otto & Atkinson, Ruth A., eds. Sports Medicine: Fitness, Training, Injuries. 2nd ed. 1983. pap. text ed. price not set (ISBN 0-8067-0132-3). Urban & S.

Cantu, Robert C. & Gillespie, W. Jay. Sports Medicine, Sports Science: Bridging the Gap. LC 81-70165. 252p. 1982. 18.95 (ISBN 0-669-05226-4, Collamore). Heath.

Krakauer, L. J. Year Book of Sports Medicine 1983. 1983. 40.00 (ISBN 0-8151-5157-8). Year Bk Med.

Monahan, Gene. The Baseball Player's Guide to Sports Medicine. LC 82-83936. (Illus.). 144p. (Orig.). 1983. pap. 7.95 (ISBN 0-88011-104-6). Leisure Pr.

Roy, Steven P. & Irvin, Richard F. Sports Medicine for the Athletic Trainer. (Illus.). 560p. 1983. text ed. 23.95 (ISBN 0-13-837807-X). P-H.

Sports Medicine Meets Synchronized Swimming. 160p. 8.95 (ISBN 0-88314-175-2). AAHPERD.

Wolpa, Mark E. The Sports Medicine Guide: Teaching & Preventing Common Athletic Injuries. 2nd ed. (Illus.). 160p. (Orig.). 1983. pap. 6.95 (ISBN 0-88011-099-6). Leisure Pr.

SPORTS TOURNAMENTS

see Sports–Organization and Administration

SPOT ANALYSIS

see Spot Tests (Chemistry)

SPOT REACTIONS

see Spot Tests (Chemistry)

SPOT TESTS (CHEMISTRY)

Smith, R. & James, G. V. Analytical Sciences Monographs: The Sampling of Bulk Materials. 200p. 1982. 90.00x (ISBN 0-85186-810-X, Pub. by Royal Soc Chem England). State Mutual Bk.

SPOT WELDING

see Electric Welding

SPRAYING

see also Fungicides; Insecticides;

also names of special spraying mixtures

American Welding Society. Recommended Safe Practices for Thermal Spraying: C2.1. 1973. 8.00 (ISBN 0-686-43368-8). Am Welding.

SPRAYING AND DUSTING RESIDUES IN AGRICULTURE

Gunther, F. A., ed. Residue Reviews, Vol. 85. (Illus.). 307p. 1983. 39.80 (ISBN 0-387-90751-3). Springer-Verlag.

--Residue Reviews, Vol. 86. (Illus.). 133p. 1983. 24.80 (ISBN 0-387-90778-5). Springer-Verlag.

--Residue Reviews, Vol. 87. (Illus.). 152p. 1983. 21.50 (ISBN 0-387-90781-5). Springer-Verlag.

Pesticide Residues in Food, 1981 Report. (FAO Plant Production & Protection Papers: No. 37). 69p. 1982. pap. 7.50 (ISBN 92-5-101202-4, FAO). Unipub.

Workshop on the Role of Earthworms in the Stabilization of Organic Residues, 2 vols. 70.00 set (ISBN 0-686-84201-4). Beech Leaf.

SPRING–JUVENILE LITERATURE

Glovach, Linda. The Little Witch's Spring Holiday Book. (Illus.). 48p. (ps-4). 8.95 (ISBN 0-13-538108-8). P-H.

SPRINGFIELD RIFLE

Hammer, Kenneth. The Springfield Carbine on the Western Frontier. (Illus.). 1970. pap. 2.50 (ISBN 0-88342-214-X). Old Army.

SPRINTING

see Running

SPY STORIES

Smith, Myron J., Jr. Cloak & Dagger Fiction: An Annotated Guide to Spy Thrillers. 2d ed. LC 82-6655. 431p. 1982. text ed. 34.50 (ISBN 0-87436-328-4). ABC-Clio.

A Spy of the Old School. 272p. 1983. 13.95 (ISBN 0-394-51796-2). Pantheon.

SPYING

see Espionage; Spies

SQUABS

see Pigeons

SQUARE DANCING

Goss, Gordon J., ed. National Square Dance Directory: 1983 Edition. 4th ed. 208p. 1983. pap. 9.50 (ISBN 0-9605494-3-9). Natl Sq Dance.

Hammond, Mildred. Square Dancing Is For Me. LC 82-17134. (Sports For Me Bks.). (Illus.). 48p. (gr. 2-5). 1983. PLB 6.95g (ISBN 0-8225-1138-X). Lerner Pubns.

SQUARE KNOTTING

see Macrame

SQUASH (GAME)

Badminton-Squash-Racquetball 1982-84. (NAGWS Sports Guides Ser.). 3.75 (ISBN 0-88314-079-9). AAHPERD.

Elliott, Bruce & Champion, Nigel. Squash: For Players, Coaches & Teachers. 80p. 1982. 30.00x (ISBN 0-85950-368-2, Pub. by Thornes England). State Mutual Bk.

SQUIDHOUND
see Striped Bass
SQUIDS
FAO Fisheries Technology Service & Hamabe, Mototsugu, eds. Squid Jigging from Small Boats. 84p. 1982. 42.95x (ISBN 0-85238-122-0, Pub. by Fishing News England). State Mutual Bk.
Squid Jigging from Small Boats. 74p. 1982. pap. 19.00 (ISBN 0-85238-122-0, FN99, FNB). Unipub.
SQUINTING
see Strabismus
SQUIRES
see Great Britain–Gentry
SQUIRRELS–JUVENILE LITERATURE
McConoughey, Jana. The Squirrels. Schroeder, Howard, ed. (Wildlife Habits & Habitat). (Illus.). 48p. (gr. 4-5). 1983. lib. bdg. 8.95 (ISBN 0-89686-223-2). Crestwood Hse.
SRI LANKA–DESCRIPTION AND TRAVEL
Insight Guides. Sri Lanka. (Illus.). 384p. 1983. pap. 14.95 (ISBN 0-13-839944-1). P-H.
SRI LANKA–ECONOMIC CONDITIONS
Ponnanbalam, Satchi. Dependent Capitalism in Crisis: The Sri Lankan Economy, 1948-1980. 233p. 1982. text ed. 37.50x (ISBN 0-7069-1837-1, Pub. by Vikas India). Advent NY.
SRI LANKA–FOREIGN RELATIONS
Kodikari, S. Foreign Policy of Sri Lanka. 240p. 1982. text ed. 15.75x (ISBN 0-391-02763-8, Pub. by Chanaky India). Humanities.
Shelton, Kodikara. Foreign Policy of Sri Lanka. 1982. 18.50x (ISBN 0-8364-0905-1, Pub. by Heritage India). South Asia Bks.
SRI LANKA–POLITICS AND GOVERNMENT
Fernando, Tissa. Sri Lanka: An Island Republic. 128p. 1983. lib. bdg. 16.50x (ISBN 0-89158-926-0). Westview.
SRI LANKA–SOCIAL LIFE AND CUSTOMS
Welbon, Guy & Yocum, Glenn, eds. Festivals in South India & Sri Lanka. 1982. 25.00X (ISBN 0-8364-0900-0, Pub.by Manohar India). South Asia Bks.
STABILITY OF AIRPLANES
Etkin, Bernard. Dynamics of Atmospheric Flight. LC 73-165946. (Illus.). 579p. 1972. text ed. 39.95x (ISBN 0-471-24620-4). Wiley.
STABILIZATION, ECONOMIC
see Economic Stabilization
STAFFORDSHIRE TERRIER
see Dogs–Breeds–Staffordshire Terrier
STAFFS, MILITARY
see Armies–Staffs
STAGE CONSTRUCTION
see Theaters–Construction
STAGE COSTUME
see Costume
STAGE FRIGHT
Triplett, Robert. Stagefright: Letting It Work for You. LC 82-14205. (Illus.). 208p. 1983. 17.95 (ISBN 0-88229-720-1). Nelson-Hall.
STAGE GUIDES
see Theaters–Stage-Setting and Scenery
STAGE-SETTING
see Theaters–Stage-Setting and Scenery
STAGECOACHES
see Coaching
STAGING
see Theaters–Stage-Setting and Scenery
STAINED GLASS
see Glass Painting and Staining
STAINS AND STAINING (MICROSCOPY)
Clark, George & Kasten, Frederick H. History of Staining. (Illus.). 144p. 1983. lib. bdg. price not set (ISBN 0-683-01705-5). Williams & Wilkins.
STALIN, JOSEPH (IOSIF STALIN), 1879-1953
Bialer, Seweryn, ed. Stalin & His Generals: Soviet Military Memoirs of World War II. (Encore Edition). 650p. 1983. softcover 35.00x (ISBN 0-86531-610-4). Westview.
Urban, George. Stalinism. LC 82-10759. 400p. 1982. 25.00x (ISBN 0-312-75515-5). St Martin.
Vucinich, Wayne S. At the Brink of War & Peace: The Tito-Stalin Split in Historic Perspective. (Brooklyn College Studies on Society in Change). 384p. 1982. 27.50x (ISBN 0-914710-98-2). East Eur Quarterly.
Vucinich, Wayne S., ed. At the Brink of War & Peace: The Tito-Stalin Split in a Historic Perspective. 384p. 1982. 27.50 (ISBN 0-686-82240-4). Columbia U Pr.
STAMINA, PHYSICAL
see Physical Fitness
STAMMERING
see Stuttering
STAMP ACT, 1765
Bullion, John L. A Great & Necessary Measure: George Grenville & the Genesis of the Stamp Act 1763-1765. 360p. 1983. 24.00 (ISBN 0-8262-0375-2). U of MO Pr.
Morgan, Edmund S. & Morgan, Helen M. The Stamp Act Crisis: Prologue to Revolution. 384p. 1983. 6.95 (ISBN 0-02-035280-8). Macmillan.
STAMP-COLLECTING AND STAMP-COLLECTORS
see Postage-Stamps–Collectors and Collecting
STAMPS, POSTAGE
see Postage-Stamps
STANDARD OF LIVING
see Cost and Standard of Living
STANDARD OF VALUE
see Money; Value
STANDARDIZATION
see also Quality Control; Specifications; Tolerance (Engineering)
also subdivision Standards, or Grading and Standardization under subjects
Sullivan. Standards & Standardization. 136p. 1983. price not set (ISBN 0-8247-1919-0). Dekker.
STANDARDS
see subdivision Standards under subjects, e.g. Engineering Instruments
STANFORD-BINET TEST
Whitworth, John R. & Sutton, Dorothy L. Stanford Binet: Form L-M, Compilation. 256p. 1982. pap. 22.50 (ISBN 0-87879-324-0). Acad Therapy.
STANISLAVSKII, KONSTANTIN SERGEEVICH, 1863-1938
Benedetti, Jean. Stanislavski: An Intoduction. 1982. pap. 5.95 (ISBN 0-87830-578-5). Theatre Arts.
STAR CATALOGS
see Stars–Catalogs
STAR TREK (TELEVISION PROGRAM)
Trimble, Bjo. On the Good Ship Enterprise: My 15 Years With Star Trek. Stine, Hank, ed. LC 82-9709. (Illus.). 224p. (Orig.). 1982. pap. 5.95 (ISBN 0-89865-253-7). Donning Co.
STARCH
Mishler, John M., IV. Pharmacology of Hydroxyehty Starch: Use in Therapy & Blood Banking. (Illus.). 220p. 1982. text ed. 39.50x (ISBN 0-19-261239-5). Oxford U Pr.
STARS
see also Astrology; Astronomy; Astrophysics; Black Holes (Astronomy); Constellations; Galaxies; Life on Other Planets; Mechanics, Celestial; Nebulae; Solar System
also names of individual stars
De Lorre, C. & Willis, A., eds. Wolf-Rayet Stars: Observations, Physics, Evolution. 1982. 69.50 (ISBN 90-277-1469-X, Pub. by Reidel Holland); pap. 34.50 (ISBN 90-277-1470-3). Kluwer Boston.
Kippenhahn, Rudolf. One Hundred Billion Suns: The Birth, Life, & Death of the Stars. (Illus.). 256p. 1983. 25.00 (ISBN 0-465-05263-0). Basic.
O'Leary, Brian & Beatty, J. Kelly, eds. The New Solar System. 240p. 1982. 14.95 (ISBN 0-933346-36-0); pap. 7.75 (ISBN 0-933346-37-9). Sky Pub.
Sandage, Allan & Sandage, Mary, eds. Galaxies & the Universe, Vol. IX. LC 74-7559. (Stars & Stellar Systems Midway Reprint Ser.). (Illus.). 818p. 1983. pap. text ed. 40.00x (ISBN 0-226-45970-5). U of Chicago Pr.
Shapiro, Stuart L. & Teukolsky, Saul A. Black Holes, White Dwarfs, & Neutron Stars: The Physics of Compact Objects. 650p. 1983. 39.95 (ISBN 0-471-87317-9, Pub. by Wiley-Interscience). Wiley.
STARS–ATLASES
Tirion, Wil. Sky Atlas 2000.0 Color. 1981. spiral bound 34.95 (ISBN 0-933346-33-6, 46336). Sky Pub.
--Sky Atlas 2000.0 Desk: Black Stars on White Backround. (Illus.). 1981. 15.95 (ISBN 0-933346-31-X). Sky Pub.
--Sky Atlas 2000.0 Field: White Stars on Black Backround. (Illus.). 1981. 15.95 (ISBN 0-933346-32-8, 46328). Sky Pub.
STARS–CATALOGS
Hirshfeld, Alan & Sinnott, Roger W. Sky Catalogue Two Thousand. 604p. 1982. 29.97; pap. 17.97 (ISBN 0-933346-34-4). Sky Pub.
STARS–JUVENILE LITERATURE
Jefferies, Lawrence. All About Stars. LC 82-20027. (Question & Answer Bks.). (Illus.). 32p. (gr. 3-6). PLB 8.59 (ISBN 0-89375-888-4); pap. text ed. 1.95 (ISBN 0-89375-889-2). Troll Assocs.
STARS–RADIATION
Wilson, Ralph E. General Catalogue of Stellar Radial Velocities. 2nd ed. 1963. 5.00 (ISBN 0-87279-612-4). Carnegie Inst.
STARS, DOUBLE
Ghedini, Silvano. Software for Photometric Astronomy. LC 82-8574. (Illus.). 1982. pap. text ed. 26.95 (ISBN 0-943396-00-X). Willman-Bell.
STARS, VARIABLE
Ghedini, Silvano. Software for Photometric Astronomy. LC 82-8574. (Illus.). 1982. pap. text ed. 26.95 (ISBN 0-943396-00-X). Willman-Bell.
STATE, THE
see also Anomy; Law and Politics; Political Science; Public Interest
Badie, Bertrand & Birnbaum, Pierre. The Sociology of the State: Chicago Original Ser. Goldhammer, Arthur, tr. from Fr. LC 82-20249. 1983. lib. bdg. 24.00x (ISBN 0-226-03548-4); pap. text ed. 10.95x (ISBN 0-226-03549-2). U of Chicago Pr.
Comte, August. The Metaphysical Theory of the State & the Revolutionary Reorganization of Modern Society. (The Essential Library of the Great Philosophers). (Illus.). 129p. 1983. 69.95 (ISBN 0-89266-380-4). Am Classical Coll Pr.
Hocking, William E. Man & the State. 1926. text ed. 19.50x (ISBN 0-686-83615-4). Elliots Bks.
Jessop, Bob. The Capitalist State: Marxist Theories & Methods. 320p. 1982. 27.50 (ISBN 0-8147-4163-0); pap. 8.50 (ISBN 0-8147-4164-9). Columbia U Pr.
STATE, THE–HISTORY OF THEORIES
see Political Science–History
STATE AND AGRICULTURE
see Agriculture and State
STATE AND ART
see Art and State
STATE AND ASTRONAUTICS
see Astronautics and State
STATE AND CHURCH
see Church and State
STATE AND EDUCATION
see Education and State
STATE AND ENERGY
see Energy Policy
STATE AND ENVIRONMENT
see Environmental Policy
STATE AND INDUSTRY
see Industry and State
STATE AND INSURANCE
see Social Security
STATE AND ISLAM
see Islam and State
STATE AND LITERATURE
see Literature and State
STATE AND MEDICINE
see Medical Policy
STATE AND RELIGION
see Religion and State
STATE AND SCIENCE
see Science and State
STATE AND TECHNOLOGY
see Technology and State
STATE AND TRANSPORTATION
see Transportation and State
STATE BUDGETS
see Budget
STATE ENCOURAGEMENT OF SCIENCE, LITERATURE, AND ART
see also Art and State; Science and State
Cultural Industries: A Challenge for the Future of Culture. 236p. 1982. pap. 22.50 (ISBN 92-3-102003-X, U1239, UNESCO). Unipub.
Cultural Policy in the United Kingdom. 70p. 1982. pap. 7.50 (ISBN 92-3-102018-8, U1226, UNESCO). Unipub.
Larson, Gary O. The Reluctant Patron: The United States Government & the Arts, 1943-1965. LC 82-40492. (Illus.). 320p. (Orig.). 1983. 30.00x (ISBN 0-8122-7876-3); pap. 12.95 (ISBN 0-8122-1144-8). U of Pa Pr.
STATE GOVERNMENTS
Here are entered works on state governments in general and in the United States. See also geographic subdivisions which follow.
see also Federal Government; Governors–United States; Interstate Agreements; Legislative Power; Local Government
Kownslar, A. Teaching State Government. 1980. 8.00 (ISBN 0-07-035411-1). McGraw.
Lockard, Dunne. The Politics of State & Local Government. 3rd ed. 288p. 1983. pap. text ed. 20.95 (ISBN 0-02-371530-8). Macmillan.
Press, Charles & VerBurg, Kenneth. State & Community Governments in the Federal System. 2nd ed. 600p. 1983. text ed. write for info. (ISBN 0-471-86979-1); write for info. tchr's ed. (ISBN 0-471-87199-0). Wiley.
Purcell, L. Edward, ed. Suggested State Legislation, 1983, Vol. 42. 395p. (Orig.). 1982. pap. 15.00 (ISBN 0-87292-032-1). Coun State Govts.
STATE-LOCAL FISCAL RELATIONS
see Intergovernmental Fiscal Relations
STATE-LOCAL TAX RELATIONS
see Intergovernmental Tax Relations
STATE OF THE UNION MESSAGES
see Presidents–United States–Messages
STATE OWNERSHIP
see Government Ownership
STATE PARKS
see Parks
STATE PLANNING
see Economic Policy; Regional Planning; Social Policy
STATE TRIALS
see Trials
STATE UNIVERSITIES AND COLLEGES
see also Universities and Colleges
Blakely, B. E. Alumni Administration at State Colleges & Universities. 30p. 1979. 10.50 (ISBN 0-89964-000-1). CASE.
STATES, IDEAL
see Utopias
STATESMEN
see also Diplomats
Clark, Ronald W. Benjamin Franklin: A Biography. LC 82-40115. (Illus.). 480p. 1983. 22.95 (ISBN 0-394-50222-1). Random.
Countries of the World & their Leaders Yearbook, 1982: Supplement. 350p. 1982. 38.00x (ISBN 0-8103-1106-2). Gale.
Eells, Robert & Nyberg, Bartell. Lonely Walk: The Life of Senator Mark Hatfield. 201p. 1979. 8.95 (ISBN 0-915684-49-7). Multnomah.
Hammarskjold, Dag. Markings. (Epiphany Bks.). 1983. pap. 2.95 (ISBN 0-345-30699-6). Ballantine.
Zehring, John W. Careers In State & Local Government. 236p. 1980. 10.95 (ISBN 0-912048-15-8). Impact VA.
STATESMEN–CORRESPONDENCE, REMINISCENCES, ETC.
Adenauer, Konrad. Konrad Adenauer: Memoirs 1945-1953. Ruhm von Oppen, Beate, tr. from German. LC 65-26906. (Illus.). 478p. 1966. 35.00 (ISBN 0-89526-651-2). Regnery-Gateway.
STATESMEN–FRANCE
MacShane, Denis. Francois Mitterand: A Political Odyssey. LC 82-23793. 288p. 1983. 14.95 (ISBN 0-87663-418-8). Universe.
Mitterrand, Francois. The Wheat & the Chaff. 352p. 1983. pap. 7.95 (ISBN 0-86579-026-4). Seaver Bks.
STATESMEN–GREAT BRITAIN
Cross, J. A. Lord Swinton. 320p. 1983. 45.00 (ISBN 0-19-822602-0). Oxford U Pr.
STATESMEN–RUSSIA
Beichman, Arnold & Bernstam, Mikhail. Andropov: New Challenge to the West. 1983. 14.95 (ISBN 0-8128-2921-2). Stein & Day.
Patolichev, N. S. Measures of Maturity - My Early Life. (World Leaders Speeches & Writings). (Illus.). 320p. 1983. 50.00 (ISBN 0-08-024545-5). Pergamon.
STATICS
see also Dynamics; Elasticity; Strains and Stresses
Ginsberg, Jerry H. & Genin, Joseph. Statics. LC 76-55753. 1977. text ed. 22.95x (ISBN 0-471-29607-4). Wiley.
Sandor, Bela I. & Schlack, A. L. Learning & Review Aid for Statics: To Go With Engineering Mechanics. 176p. 1983. pap. 9.95 (ISBN 0-13-278903-5). P-H.
STATICS AND DYNAMICS (SOCIAL SCIENCES)
see also Economic Development
Hakon, H. Concepts & Models of a Quantitative Sociology: The/Dynamics of Interacting Populations. (Ser. in Synergetics: Vol. 14). (Illus.). 217p. 1983. 31.50 (ISBN 0-387-11358-4). Springer-Verlag.
STATIONS, TELEVISION
see Television Stations
STATISTICAL ANALYSIS
see Multivariate Analysis
STATISTICAL ASTRONOMY
Buscombe, W. New Catalogues of Stellar Data. (Illus.). (1974 ed.) 10.00 (ISBN 0-939160-00-5); (1977 ed.) 15.00 (ISBN 0-939160-01-3); (1980 ed.) 15.00 (ISBN 0-939160-02-1); (1981 ed.) 15.00 (ISBN 0-939160-03-X). NWU Astro.
STATISTICAL DECISION
see also Bayesian Statistical Decision Theory; Experimental Design; Sequential Analysis
Gupta, M. M. & Sanchez, E., eds. Approximate Reasoning in Decision Analysis. 480p. 1982. 68.50 (ISBN 0-444-86492-X, North Holland). Elsevier.
--Fuzzy Information & Decision Processes. 480p. 1982. 74.50 (ISBN 0-686-83998-6, North Holland). Elsevier.
STATISTICAL DESIGN
see Experimental Design
STATISTICAL INFERENCE
see Mathematical Statistics; Probabilities
STATISTICAL MECHANICS
see also Liquids, Kinetic Theory Of; Quantum Statistics; Transport Theory
Honerkamp, J. & Pohlmeyer, J., eds. Structural Elements in Particle Physics & Statistical Mechanics. (NATO ASI Series B, Physics: Vol. 82). 470p. 1983. 65.00x (ISBN 0-306-41038-9, Plenum Pr). Plenum Pub.
Toda, M., et al. Statistical Physics I: Equilibrium Statistical Mechanics. (Spinger Series in Solid-State Sciences: Vol. 30). (Illus.). 270p. 1983. 34.00 (ISBN 0-387-11460-2). Springer-Verlag.
STATISTICAL PHYSICS
see also Phase Transformations (Statistical Physics)
Toda, M., et al. Statistical Physics I: Equilibrium Statistical Mechanics. (Spinger Series in Solid-State Sciences: Vol. 30). (Illus.). 270p. 1983. 34.00 (ISBN 0-387-11460-2). Springer-Verlag.
STATISTICS
see also Biometry; Census; Commercial Statistics; Econometrics; Educational Statistics; Experimental Design; Gross National Product; Industrial Statistics; Mathematical Statistics; Medical Statistics; Probabilities; Regression Analysis; Sampling (Statistics); Statistical Decision
also subdivision Statistics and Statistical Methods under specific subjects, e.g. Agriculture–Statistics; Education–Statistics; and subdivisions Statistics; Statistics, Medical; Statistics, Vital, etc. under names of countries, cities, etc., e.g. United States–Statistics, Vital
Bajpai, A. C., et al. Statistical Methods for Engineers & Scientists: A Students' Course Book. LC 78-2481. (Programmes on Mathematics for Scientists & Technologists Ser.). 444p. 1978. 25.00x (ISBN 0-471-99644-0). Wiley.
Bhattacharyya, Gouri K. & Johnson, Richard A. Statistical Concepts & Methods. LC 76-53783. (Probability & Mathematical Statistics). 639p. 1977. text ed. 27.95 (ISBN 0-471-07204-4). Wiley.
Braman, Sandra & Woolf, Douglas, eds. Vital Statistics, Vol. 1. 1978. pap. 3.00 (ISBN 0-942296-04-4). Wolf Run Bks.
--Vital Statistics, Vol. 2. 1978. pap. 3.00 (ISBN 0-942296-05-2). Wolf Run Bks.
--Vital Statistics, Vol. 3. 1980. pap. 3.00 (ISBN 0-942296-06-0). Wolf Run Bks.
Brookes, C. J., et al. Fundamentals of Mathematics: For Students of Chemistry & Allied Subjects. LC 78-26110. 496p. 1979. 67.00 (ISBN 0-471-99733-1); pap. 27.95x (ISBN 0-471-99732-3, Pub. by Wiley-Interscience). Wiley.

Cangelosi, Vincent E. & Taylor, Phillip H. Basic Statistics: A Real World Approach. 3rd ed. (Illus.). 550p. 1983. text ed. 19.95 (ISBN 0-314-69637-7); study guide avail. (ISBN 0-314-71082-5); solutions manual avail. (ISBN 0-314-71083-3). West Pub.

Caussinus, H. & Ettinger, P. Compstat 1982: Proceedings in Computational Statistics. 500p. 1982. text ed. 32.95x (ISBN 3-7908-0280-8). Birkhauser.

Caussinus, H. & Ettinger, P., eds. Compstat 1982, Pt. 2. 383p. 1982. text ed. 18.95 (ISBN 3-7908-0283-2). Birkhauser.

Chacks, G. Applied Statistics in Decision Making. 1971. 27.50 (ISBN 0-444-00109-3). Elsevier.

Clark, John J. & Clark, Margaret T. A Statistics Primer for Managers. (Illus.). 272p. 1982. write for info. (ISBN 0-02-905800-7). Free Pr.

Cooke, D. & Craven, A. H. Basic Statistical Computing. 176p. 1982. pap. text ed. 13.95 (ISBN 0-7131-3441-0). E Arnold.

Daniel & Terrell. Business Statistics: Basic Concepts & Methodology. 1982. text ed. 28.95 (ISBN 0-686-84527-7); write for info. supplementary material. HM.

Daniel, Wayne W. & Terrell, James C. Business Statistics: Basic Concepts & Methodology. LC 82-83254. 832p. 1982. text ed. 26.95 (ISBN 0-395-32601-X); write for info. instr's. resource manual (ISBN 0-395-32602-8); study guide 10.95 (ISBN 0-395-32603-6). HM.

Depriest, Launder. Reliability in the Acquisitions Process. (Statistics Lecture Notes). 296p. 1983. write for info. (ISBN 0-8247-1792-9). Dekker.

Dietrich, Frank H., II & Kearns, Thomas. Basic Statistics. 1983. text ed. 26.95 (ISBN 0-89517-044-2). Dellen Pub.

Directory of International Statistics. 20.00 (ISBN 0-686-84920-5, E.81.XVII.6). UN.

Folks, J. Leroy. Ideas of Statistics. LC 80-14723. 368p. 1981. text ed. 19.95 (ISBN 0-471-02099-0). study guide avail. (ISBN 0-471-07972-3); tchrs.' manual avail. (ISBN 0-471-07969-3). Wiley.

Futcher, W. G. Descriptive Statistics for Introductory Measurement. (Andrews University Monographs, Studies in Education: Vol. 1). viii, 96p. 1976. text ed. 6.50 (ISBN 0-943872-50-2). Andrews Univ Pr.

Grossman, W. & Pflug, G., eds. Probability & Statistical Inference. 1982. lib. bdg. 49.50 (ISBN 90-277-1427-4, Pub. by Reidel Holland). Kluwer Boston.

Gupta, R., ed. Applied Statistics. (Proceedings). 1975. 53.25 (ISBN 0-444-10772-X). Elsevier.

Herzberg, Paul. Principles of Statistics. 600p. 1983. text ed. 21.95 (ISBN 0-471-07989-8); tchrs.' manual avail. (ISBN 0-471-87306-3). Wiley.

Hooke. How to Tell the Liars from the Statisticians. (Monographs & Textbooks in Statistics). 152p. 1983. write for info. (ISBN 0-8247-1817-8). Dekker.

Hossack, I. B. & Pollard, J. H. Introductory Statistics with Applications in General Insurance. LC 82-4421. 250p. Date not set. price not set (ISBN 0-521-24781-0); pap. price not set (ISBN 0-521-28957-2). Cambridge U Pr.

Jensen, A. C. & Chenoweth, H. Statics & Strength of Materials. 4th ed. 656p. 1982. 27.95 (ISBN 0-07-032494-8, G). McGraw.

Kaplan, Lawrence J. Elementary Statistics for Economics & Business. (FLMI Insurance Education Program Ser.). 1966. pap. text ed. 10.00 (ISBN 0-915322-04-8). LOMA.

Kendall, Maurice. The Advanced Theory of Statistics. 484p. 1977. 88.00x (ISBN 0-85264-242-3, Pub. by Griffin England). State Mutual Bk.

Kendall, Maurice & Stuart, Alan. The Advanced Theory of Statistics: Vol. 2, Influence & Relationship. 758p. 1979. 88.00x (ISBN 0-85264-255-5, Pub. by Griffin England). State Mutual Bk.

--The Advanced Theory of Statistics: Vol. 3, Design, Analysis & Time-Series. 595p. 1976. 88.00x (ISBN 0-85264-239-3, Pub. by Griffin England). State Mutual Bk.

Krishnaiah, P. R. Applications of Statistics. 1977. 78.75 (ISBN 0-444-85034-1). Elsevier.

Krishnaiah, P. R., ed. Developments in Statistics, Vol. 4. Date not set. 62.00 (ISBN 0-12-426604-5). Acad Pr.

McClave, James T. & Benson, P. George. A First Course in Business Statistics. 2nd ed. (Illus.). 1983. text ed. 24.95 (ISBN 0-89517-043-4). Dellen Pub.

McClave, James T. & Dietrich, Frank H., II. A First Course in Statistics. (Illus.). 1983. text ed. 24.95 (ISBN 0-89517-050-7). Dellen Pub.

Madsen, Richard W. & Moeschberger, Melvin E. Introductory Statistics for Business & Economics. (Illus.). 752p. 1983. 26.95 (ISBN 0-13-501577-4). P-H.

Miller, J. C. Statistics for Advanced Levels. LC 82-4550. (Illus.). 288p. Date not set. pap. price not set (ISBN 0-521-28930-0). Cambridge U Pr.

Naiman, Arnold & Rosenfeld, Robert. Understanding Statistics. 3rd ed. 368p. 1983. text ed. 22.95x (ISBN 0-07-045863-4); write for info instr's. manual (ISBN 0-07-045864-2). McGraw.

Probability & Statistics. 1983. pap. price not set (ISBN 0-8120-2660-8). Barron.

Richards, Larry E. & LaCava, Jerry J. Business Statistics: Why & When. 2nd ed. (Illus.). 512p. 1983. text ed. 24.95 (ISBN 0-07-052276-6, C); wkbk. 15.00 (ISBN 0-07-052278-2); write for info. instr's manual (ISBN 0-07-052277-4). McGraw.

Robinson, Enders A. Least Squares Regression Analysis in Terms of Linear Algebra. LC 81-82322. (Illus.). 520p. 1981. 25.00 (ISBN 0-910835-01-2). Goose Pond Pr.

--Statistical Reasoning & Decision Making. LC 81-85240. (Illus.). 200p. 1981. 12.00 (ISBN 0-910835-02-0). Goose Pond Pr.

--Times Series Analysis & Applications. LC 81-81825. (Illus.). 628p. 1981. 25.00 (ISBN 0-910835-00-4). Goose Pond Pr.

Scalzo, Frank & Hughes, Rowland. Elementary Computer, Assisted Statistics. rev. ed. 362p. 1983. Repr. of 1978 ed. text ed. avail. (ISBN 0-89874-618-3). Krieger.

Shvyrkov, V. V. Statistic: Art or Science? LC 82-61951. (Illus.). 105p. (Orig.). 1982. text ed. 11.60 (ISBN 0-942004-05-1). G Throwkoff.

--Statistical Science in Economic Forecasting. (Illus.). 212p. (Orig.). 1983. pap. 18.30 wkbk. (ISBN 0-942004-04-3). G Throwkoff.

Statistics the Easy Way. (Easy Way Ser.). 1983. pap. price not set. Barron.

Walker. Basic Statistics. 1983. text ed. write for info. (ISBN 0-408-01107-6). Butterworth.

Wanner, Criag. Introduction to Statistics for Management & Policy Analysis. 370p. 1983. text ed. 28.50x (ISBN 0-8290-1280-X); pap. text ed. 14.95 (ISBN 0-8290-1281-8). Irvington.

Whittle, Peter. Prediction & Regulation by Linear Least-Square Methods. 2nd, rev. ed. 224p. 1983. 29.50x (ISBN 0-8166-1147-5); pap. 12.95x (ISBN 0-8166-1148-3). U of Minn Pr.

Williams, Joe B. & Williams, Joan. U. S. Statistical Rankings. 138p. 1981. pap. 25.00 (ISBN 0-939644-02-9). Media Prods & Mktg.

STATISTICS–BIBLIOGRAPHY

Mitchell, Robert & Prickel, Donald. Number Power Five: Graphs, Tables, Schedules & Maps. (Number Power Ser.). 176p. (Orig.). 1983. pap. 4.95 (ISBN 0-8092-5516-2). Contemp Bks.

STATISTICS–DATA PROCESSING

Lewis, Bruce R. & Ford, Richard K. Basic Statistics Using SAS. 200p. 1983. pap. text ed. 7.95 (ISBN 0-314-70619-4). West Pub.

SAS Institute, Inc. SAS User's Guide: Statistics, 1982 Edition. 584p. (Orig.). 1982. pap. 14.95 (ISBN 0-917382-37-4). SAS Inst.

STATISTICS–STUDY AND TEACHING

Kachigan, Sam K. Statistical Analysis: An Interdisciplinary Introduction. (Illus.). 610p. Date not set. text ed. 24.95x (ISBN 0-942154-99-1). Radius Pr.

STATISTICS, MATHEMATICAL

see Mathematical Statistics

STATISTICS, ORDER

see Order Statistics

STATISTICS OF SAMPLING

see Sampling (Statistics)

STATUETTES

see Bronzes; Idols and Images; Ivories

STATUS (LAW)

see also Conflict of Laws; Insanity–Jurisprudence

Murray, John P. Status Offenders: A Sourcebook. 160p. 1983. pap. text ed. 7.50 (ISBN 0-938510-03-7). Boys Town Ctr.

Phillips, Michael J. The Dilemma of Individualism: Status, Liberty, & American Constitutional Law. LC 82-15580. (Contributions in American Studies: No. 67). 240p. 1983. lib. bdg. 29.95 (ISBN 0-313-23690-9, KF4749). Greenwood.

STATUTES

Here are entered works on statute law, as distinguished from constitutional law and from the law arising from judicial or administrative decisions. Works on the interpretation of statutory law are entered under Law–Interpretation and Construction. Works on the theory or practice of statute making are entered under Legislation or Bill Drafting.

Nabors, Eugene. Legislative Reference Checklist: The Key to Legislative Histories from 1789-1903. LC 82-18074. xv, 440p. 1982. text ed. 39.50x (ISBN 0-8377-0908-3). Rothman.

STEALING

Hollinger, Richard C. & Clark, John P. Theft by Employees. LC 82-48028. 176p. 1983. 21.95x (ISBN 0-669-05887-4). Lexington Bks.

STEAM

Bloom, Alan. Two Hundred & Fifty Years of Steam. 1981. 24.95 (ISBN 0-437-01400-2, Pub. by World's Work). David & Charles.

STEAM–TABLES, CALCULATIONS, ETC.

Haar, Lester & Gallagher, John S. NBS -NCR Steam Tables. (Illus.). 400p. 1983. text ed. 29.95 (ISBN 0-89116-354-9); pap. text ed. 16.95 (ISBN 0-89116-353-0). Hemisphere Pub.

STEAM ENGINES–HISTORY

Cooke, Brian. The Fall & Rise of Steam. (Illus.). 128p. 1982. 22.95 (ISBN 0-86720-623-3). Sci Bks IntL.

STEAM-FITTING

see Pipe-Fitting

STEAM-NAVIGATION

see also Marine Engineering; Navigation; Steamboats and Steamboat Lines

Weave, C. P. & Weaver, C. R. Steam on Canals. (Illus.). 96p. (Orig.). 1983. 16.50 (ISBN 0-7153-8218-7). David & Charles.

STEAM POWER-PLANTS

Graham, Frank & Buffington. Power Plant Engineers Guide. new ed. (Audel Ser.). 1983. 16.95 (ISBN 0-672-23329-0). Bobbs.

Lyon, W. S. Trace Element Measurements at the Coal-Fired Steam Plant. LC 77-435. 146p. Repr. of 1977 ed. text ed. 44.50 (ISBN 0-8493-5118-9). Krieger.

STEAM-PUMPS

see Pumping Machinery

STEAMBOATS AND STEAMBOAT LINES

see also Merchant Marine; Ocean Liners; Ocean Travel; Steam-Navigation;

also names of steamboats, e.g. Lusitania

Brunner, John. The Great Steamboat Race. LC 82-90222. (Illus.). 592p. 1983. pap. 7.95 (ISBN 0-345-25853-3). Ballantine.

Cox, Bernard. Pleasure Steamers. (Illus.). 64p. (Orig.). 1983. 12.50 (ISBN 0-7153-8333-7). David & Charles.

Dohan, Mary H. Mr. Roosevelt's Steamboat. large print ed. LC 82-3264. 345p. 1982. Repr. of 1981 ed. 9.95x (ISBN 0-89621-357-9). Thorndike Pr.

Great Lakes Ships We Remember. Date not set. 29.50 (ISBN 0-686-82159-9). Freshwater.

Great Lakes Stack Chart. Date not set. 5.00 (ISBN 0-686-82160-2). Freshwater.

Greenwoods' Guide to Great Lakes Shipping 1982. Date not set. 38.00 (ISBN 0-686-82161-0). Freshwater.

STEEL

see also Building, Iron and Steel

also headings beginning with the word Steel

Comins, N. R. & Clark, J. B., eds. Specialty Steels & Hard Materials: Proceedings of the International Conference (Materials Development '82), Pretoria, South Africa, 9-12 November 1982. 450p. 1983. 112.00 (ISBN 0-08-029358-1). Pergamon.

STEEL–FATIGUE

Fatigue in Offshore Structural Steels. 136p. 1981. 90.00x (ISBN 0-7277-0108-8, Pub. by Telford England). State Mutual Bk.

STEEL–METALLURGY

Transactions of the Iron & Steel Society, Vol. II. 130p. 1983. 52.00 (ISBN 0-911277-01-3). Iron & Steel.

Twenty-Fourth Mechanical Working & Steel Processing Conference Proceedings. 570p. 52.00 (ISBN 0-89520-153-4). Iron & Steel.

STEEL–WELDING

American Welding Society. Guide for Steel Hull Welding: D3.5. 1976. 8.00 (ISBN 0-686-43383-1). Am Welding.

--Sheet Steel Structural Welding Code: D1.3. 1981. 15.00 (ISBN 0-686-43350-5). Am Welding.

--Specification for Steel, Low-Alloy Electrodes & Fluxes for Submerged Arc Welding: A5.23. 1980. 8.00 (ISBN 0-686-43380-7). Am Welding.

--Specification for Steel, Low-Alloy Filler Metals for Gas Shielded Arc Welding: A5.28. 1979. 8.00 (ISBN 0-686-43352-1). Am Welding.

--Specification for Steel, Low-Alloy Flux Cored Arc Welding Electrodes: A5.29. 1980. 8.00 (ISBN 0-686-43360-2). Am Welding.

--Specification for Steels, Consumables Used for Electroslag Welding of Carbon & High Strength Low Alloy: A5.25. 1978. 8.00 (ISBN 0-686-43354-8). Am Welding.

--Specification for Steels, Consumables Used for Electrogas Welding of Carbon & High Strength Low Alloy: A5.26. 1978. 8.00 (ISBN 0-686-43356-4). Am Welding.

STEEL, STRUCTURAL

see also Building, Iron and Steel

Parker, Harry & Hauf, Harold D. Simplified Design of Structural Steel. 5th ed. 27.95 (ISBN 0-471-89766-3, Pub. by Wiley-Interscience). Wiley.

Steel Designers' Manual. 4th, rev. ed. (Illus.). 1089p. 1983. pap. text ed. 35.00 (ISBN 0-246-11475-4). Sheridan.

STEEL AND IRON BUILDING

see Building, Iron and Steel

STEEL INDUSTRY AND TRADE

see also Iron and Steel Workers; Iron Industry and Trade

AIP Conference, 84th, APS-AISI, Lehigh University, 1981. Physics in the Steel Industry: Proceedings. Schwerer, Fred C., ed. LC 82-72033. 409p. 1982. lib. bdg. 36.00 (ISBN 0-88318-183-5). Am Inst Physics.

Barnett, Donald F. & Schorsch, Louis. Steel: Upheaval in a Basic Industry. 300p. 1983. prof ref 28.00x (ISBN 0-88410-397-8). Ballinger Pub.

Mixed Gas Blowing in Steelmaking. 133p. 1982. pap. text ed. 28.00 (ISBN 0-89520-152-6). Iron & Steel.

OECD Staff. The Steel Market in 1981 & Outlook for 1982. 74p. (Orig.). 1982. pap. 9.00x (ISBN 92-64-12340-7). OECD.

Transactions of the Iron & Steel Society, Vol. I. 130p. 1982. 52.00 (ISBN 0-911277-00-5). Iron & Steel.

STEEL INDUSTRY AND TRADE–EUROPE

Annual Bulletin of Steel Statistics for Europe, Vol. IX: 1981. 87p. 1983. pap. 9.00 (ISBN 0-686-43274-6, UN 82/2E7, UN). Unipub.

STEEL INDUSTRY AND TRADE–JAPAN

Japan's Iron & Steel Industry 1981. 30th ed. LC 55-33803. 227p. (Orig.). 1981. pap. 35.00 (ISBN 0-8002-3005-1). Intl Pubns Serv.

STEEL PIPE

see Pipe, Steel

STEEL-ROLLING

see Rolling (Metal-Work)

STEEL WORKERS

see Iron and Steel Workers

STEEPLECHASING

Woolfe, Raymond D., Jr. Steeplechasing. (Illus.). 256p. 1983. 50.00 (ISBN 0-670-32356-X, Studio). Viking Pr.

STEERS

see Beef Cattle

STEGANOGRAPHY

see Cryptography

STEIN, GERTRUDE, 1874-1946

DeKoven, Marianne. A Different Language: Gertrude Stein's Experimental Writing. LC 82-70558. 288p. 1983. 22.50 (ISBN 0-299-09210-0). U of Wis Pr.

STEINBECK, JOHN ERNST, 1902-1968

Benson, Jackson J. The True Adventures of John Steinbeck, Writer: A Biography. (Illus.). 1120p. 1983. 41.75 (ISBN 0-670-16685-5). Viking Pr.

Jones, William M. John Steinbeck, Great American Novelist & Playwright. Rahmas, Sigurd C., ed. (Outstanding Personalities Ser.: No. 89). 32p. (gr. 9-12). 1982. 2.95 (ISBN 0-87157-589-2); pap. text ed. 1.95 (ISBN 0-87157-089-0). SamHar Pr.

Millichap, Joseph R. Steinbeck & Film. LC 82-42502. (Ungar Film Library). (Illus.). 200p. 1983. 12.95 (ISBN 0-8044-2630-9); pap. 6.95 (ISBN 0-8044-6500-2). Ungar.

STEINER, RUDOLF, 1861-1925

Babbel, Ulrich & Giddens, Craig. Bibliographical Reference List of the Published Works of Rudolf Steiner in English Translation, 2 Vols, Vol. 1. 51p. 1977. pap. 1.95 (ISBN 0-88010-038-9, Pub. by Steinerbooks). Anthroposophic.

Steiner, Rudolf. Rudolf Steiner: An Autobiography. Allen, Paul M., ed. Stebbing, Rita, tr. LC 72-95242. Orig. Title: Mein Lebensgang. (Illus.). 541p. 1977. pap. 13.95 (ISBN 0-8334-3501-9, Pub. by Steinerbooks NY). Anthroposophic.

Unger, Carl. Steiner's Theosophy: Notes on the Book "Theosophy". 1982. Repr. 5.95 (ISBN 0-916786-64-1). St George Bk Serv.

STEINLEN, THEOPHILE ALEXANDRE, 1859-1923

De Clayat, E. Steinlen: The Graphic Work. (Illus.). 248p. (Fr.). 1983. Repr. of 1913 ed. 95.00 (ISBN 0-915346-71-0). A Wofsy Fine Arts.

STELLA, FRANK

Axsom, Richard H. The Prints of Frank Stella: A Catalogue Raisonne 1967-1982. LC 82-15729. (Illus.). 192p. 1983. 50.00 (ISBN 0-933920-40-7); pap. 19.50 for museum distribution only (ISBN 0-933920-41-5). Hudson Hills.

STELLAR STATISTICS

see Statistical Astronomy

STENCIL PRINTING

see Screen Process Printing

STENCIL WORK

Fobel, Jim & Boleach, Jim. The Stencil Book. 200p. 1983. pap. 9.95 (ISBN 0-442-22661-6). Van Nos Reinhold.

Parry, Megan. Stenciling. 136p. 1982. pap. 9.95 (ISBN 0-442-27444-0). Van Nos Reinhold.

Perry, Dave. Little Fox's Airbrush Stencil Techniques. (Illus.). 125p. 1982. pap. 14.95 (ISBN 0-9603530-8-9). Southwest Screen Print.

--Little Fox's Airbrush Stencil Techniques. (Illus.). 125p. (Orig.). 1982. pap. text ed. 14.95 (ISBN 0-9603530-8-9). Southwest Screen Print.

STENDHAL (MARIE HENRI BEYLE), 1783-1842

Talbot, Emile J. La Critique Stendhalienne de Balzac a Zola. (Fr.). 20.00 (ISBN 0-917786-14-9). French Lit.

STENOCARDIA

see Angina Pectoris

STENOGRAPHERS

Rudman, Jack. Senior Clerk-Stenographer. (Career Examination Ser.: C-2633). (Cloth bdg. avail. on request). pap. 10.00 (ISBN 0-8373-2633-8). Natl Learning.

--Senior Legal Stenographer. (Career Examination ser.: C-2634). (Cloth bdg. avail. on request). pap. 10.00 (ISBN 0-8373-2634-6). Natl Learning.

--Supervising Legal Stenographer. (Career Examination Ser.: C-2635). (Cloth bdg. avail. on request). pap. 12.00 (ISBN 0-8373-2635-4). Natl Learning.

STENOGRAPHY

see Shorthand

STENOTYPY

Green, Helen H. & Morton, Margaret A. Transcription & Skill Building, Bk. 11. (Hedman Stenotype System Ser.). 354p. 1978. text ed. 17.00x (ISBN 0-939056-01-1). Hedman Steno.

Hopkins, Charles R. & Morton, Margaret A. Theory & Skill Building, Bk. 1. LC 77-80674. (Hedman Stenotype System Ser.). (Illus.). 372p. text ed. 17.00x (ISBN 0-939056-00-3). Hedman Steno.

McDannel, Kathleen H. & Putnam, Margaret. Advanced Series. (Hedman Stenotype System Ser.). (Illus.). 153p. 1980. text ed. 16.00x (ISBN 0-939056-02-X). Hedman Steno.

Principles of Speedwriting. (Landmark Ser.). 304p. 1977. text ed. 15.95 (ISBN 0-672-98001-0); tchr's ed. 6.67 (ISBN 0-672-98002-9); dictation & transcription text 20.95 (ISBN 0-672-98004-5); wkbk. 10.95 (ISBN 0-672-98003-7); theory tapes 223.95 (ISBN 0-672-98027-4); dictionary 13.95 (ISBN 0-672-98358-3). Bobbs.
Principles of Speedwriting: Premier Edition. 373p. 1977. text ed. 17.50 (ISBN 0-672-98096-7); tchr's. ed. 6.67 (ISBN 0-672-98098-3); dictation & transcription text 13.50; theory tapes 423.50 (ISBN 0-672-98142-4); dictionary 13.50 (ISBN 0-672-98100-9). Bobbs.

STEPCHILDREN
see also Stepfathers; Stepmothers
Bustanoby, Andre. The Readymade Family: How to be a Stepparent & Survive. 160p. (Orig.). 1982. pap. 5.95 (ISBN 0-310-45361-5). Zondervan.

STEPFATHERS
see also Stepchildren
Bustanoby, Andre. The Readymade Family: How to be a Stepparent & Survive. 160p. (Orig.). 1982. pap. 5.95 (ISBN 0-310-45361-5). Zondervan.
Juroe, David J. & Juroe, Bonnie B. Successful Stepparenting. 192p. 1983. 9.95 (ISBN 0-8007-1339-7). Revell.
McNamara, Lynne & Morrison, Jennifer. Separation, Divorce & After. LC 82-2718. 192p. 1983. pap. 9.95 (ISBN 0-7022-1931-2). U of Queensland Pr.

STEPHENS, JAMES, 1825-1901
Huber, Werner. James Stephens' Fruhe Romane. 304p. (Ger.). 1982. write for info. (ISBN 3-8204-5845-X). P Lang Pubs.

STEPMOTHERS
see also Stepchildren
Bustanoby, Andre. The Readymade Family: How to be a Stepparent & Survive. 160p. (Orig.). 1982. pap. 5.95 (ISBN 0-310-45361-5). Zondervan.
Juroe, David J. & Juroe, Bonnie B. Successful Stepparenting. 192p. 1983. 9.95 (ISBN 0-8007-1339-7). Revell.
McNamara, Lynne & Morrison, Jennifer. Separation, Divorce & After. LC 82-2718. 192p. 1983. pap. 9.95 (ISBN 0-7022-1931-2). U of Queensland Pr.

STEPPES
see also Deserts; Prairies; Tundras
Zlotin, R. I. & Khodashova, K. S., eds. The Role of Animals in Biological Cycling of Forest-Steppe Ecosystems. Lewus, William & Grant, W. E., trs. from Russian. LC 80-12228. 240p. 1980. 22.50 (ISBN 0-87933-377-4). Hutchinson Ross.

STEREOCHEMISTRY
see also Atoms; Chemistry, Organic; Chemistry, Physical and Theoretical
Armarego, W. L. F. Stereochemistry of Heterocyclic Compounds: Nitrogen Heterocycles, Pt.1. 433p. Repr. of 1977 ed. text ed. 63.50 (ISBN 0-471-02627-1). Krieger.
Brocas, J. & Gielen, M. Permutational Approach to Dynamic Stereochemistry. 720p. 69.50 (ISBN 0-07-007971-4). McGraw.
Eliel, E. L. & Basolo, F. Elements of Stereochemistry: With a Section on Coordination Compounds. 98p. 1969. 6.95x (ISBN 0-471-23745-0). Wiley.

STEREOMETRY
see Mensuration

STEREOPHONIC SOUND SYSTEMS
Fantel, Hans. Better Listening. 192p. 1983. pap. 6.95 (ISBN 0-686-83792-4, ScribT). Scribner.
Goldberg, Joel. Fundamentals of Stereo Servicing. (Illus.). 304p. 1983. 21.95 (ISBN 0-686-81977-2, 382). P-H.
Wells, A. Building Stereo Speakers. (McGraw-Hill VTX Ser.). 208p. 1983. 9.95 (ISBN 0-07-069251-3, GB). McGraw.

STEREOPHOTOGRAMMETRY
see Photogrammetry

STEREOSCOPE
Langton, Jane. The Astonishing Stereoscope. LC 74-157894. (A Trophy Bk.). (Illus.). 256p. (gr. 5 up). 1983. pap. 3.13i (ISBN 0-06-440133-2, Trophy). Har-Row.

STEREOTYPE (PSYCHOLOGY)
Weiss, Jacqueline S. Prizewinning Books for Children: Themes & Stereotypes in U.S. Prizewinning Prose Fiction for Children. LC 82-48624. (Libraries & Librarianship Special Ser.). 1983. write for info. (ISBN 0-669-06352-5). Lexington Bks.

STERIDES
see Steroids

STERILITY
see also Fertility; Fertility, Human
Stigger, Judith A. Coping with Infertility. LC 82-72649. 112p. (Orig.). 1983. pap. 4.95 (ISBN 0-8066-1956-2, 10-1692). Augsburg.

STERILITY, FEMALE
Semm, Kurt & Greenblatt, Robert B. Genital Endometriosis in Infertility. 110p. 15.95 (ISBN 0-86577-059-X). Thieme-Stratton.
Speroff, Leon, et al. Clinical Gynecological Endocrinology & Infertilty. 450p. 1983. lib. bdg. price not set (ISBN 0-683-07895-X). Williams & Wilkins.

STERILIZATION
Association for the Advancement of Medical Instrumentation. Inhospital Sterility Assurance: Current Perspectives. (Illus.). 80p. (Orig.). 1982. pap. 20.00 members (ISBN 0-910275-14-9); pap. 30.00 nonmembers (ISBN 0-686-38440-7). Assn Adv Med Instrs.
Block, Seymor S., ed. Disinfection, Sterilization & Preservation. 3rd ed. LC 82-24002. (Illus.). 1500p. 1983. text ed. price not set (ISBN 0-8121-0863-9). Lea & Febiger.

STERILIZATION (BIRTH CONTROL)
Morris, Norman & Arthur, Humphrey. Sterilization as a Means of Birth Control in Men & Women. (Illus.). 125p. 1982. 14.95 (ISBN 0-7206-0363-3, Pub. by Peter Owen). Merrimack Bk Serv.
Schima, M., ed. Advances in Voluntary Sterilization. (International Congress Ser.: No. 284). 1974. 61.50 (ISBN 0-444-15075-7). Elsevier.

STERLING, JOHN, 1806-1844
Tuell, Anne K. John Sterling: Representative Victorian. 1949. text ed. 49.50x (ISBN 0-686-83598-0). Elliots Bks.

STERNE, LAURENCE, 1713-1768
Loveridge, Mark. Laurence Sterne & the Argument about Design. 375p. 1981. 49.00x (ISBN 0-333-29401-7, Pub. by Macmillan England). State Mutual Bk.

STEROIDS
see also Lipids
Hanson, J. R. Terpenoids & Steroids, Vol. 10. 295p. 1982. 150.00x (ISBN 0-85186-336-1, Pub. by Royal Soc Chem England). State Mutual Bk.
Lewis, G. P. & Ginsburg, M, eds. Mechanisms of Steroid Action: Biological Council Symposia on Drug Action. 288p. 1981. 90.00x (ISBN 0-333-32455-2, Pub. by Macmillan England). State Mutual Bk.

STEVEDORING
see Cargo Handling

STEVENS, WALLACE, 1879-1955
Woodham, Leonora. Stanza My Stone: Wallace Stevens & the Hermetic Traditions. LC 82-81679. 128p. 1983. 14.50 (ISBN 0-911198-68-7). Purdue.

STEVENSON, ROBERT LOUIS, 1850-1894
Nickerson, Roy. Robert Louis Stevenson in California. LC 82-9643. (Illus.). 128p. (Orig.). 1982. pap. 5.95 (ISBN 0-87701-246-6). Chronicle Bks.

STEWARDSHIP, CHRISTIAN
see also Christianity and Economics
Savelle, Jerry. Giving: The Essence of Living. 87p. (Orig.). 1982. pap. 2.25 (ISBN 0-89274-250-X). Harrison Hse.
Werning, Waldo J. Christian Stewards: Confronted & Committed. 1983. pap. 8.95 (ISBN 0-570-03879-0). Concordia.

STICK-FIGHTING
see also Truncheons
Downey, Robert J. & Roth, Jordan T. Baton Techniques for Officer Survival. (Illus.). 288p. 1983. pap. 29.75x spiral (ISBN 0-398-04781-2). C C Thomas.

STICKLEY, GUSTAVE, 1858-1942
Smith, Mary A. Gustav Stickley: The Craftsman. (A New York State Study Ser.). (Illus.). 200p. 1983. text ed. 22.00x (ISBN 0-686-84444-0). Syracuse U Pr.

STIEGEL GLASS
see Glassware–United States

STIEGLITZ, ALFRED, 1864-1946
Greenough, Sarah & Hamilton, Juan, eds. Alfred Stieglitz: Photographs & Writings. LC 82-7925. (Illus.). 248p. 75.00 (ISBN 0-935112-09-X); pap. write for info. (ISBN 0-89468-027-7). Callaway Edns.
Haines, Robert E. The Inner Eye of Alfred Stieglitz. LC 82-13641. (Illus.). 170p. (Orig.). 1983. lib. bdg. 22.00 (ISBN 0-8191-2717-5); pap. text ed. 10.00 (ISBN 0-8191-2718-3). U Pr of Amer.
Lowe, Sue D. Stieglitz: A Memoir-Biography. (Illus.). 450p. 1983. 22.50 (ISBN 0-374-26990-4). FS&G.
Thomas, F. Richard. Literary Admirers of Alfred Stieglitz. LC 82-10543. 116p. 1983. price not set (ISBN 0-8093-1097-X). S Ill U Pr.

STIGMATIZATION
Shoham, Giora S. & Rahav, Giora. The Mark of Cain: The Stigma Theory of Crime & Social Deviance. LC 82-3173. 240p. 1982. 27.50x (ISBN 0-312-51446-8). St Martin.

STILL-LIFE PAINTING
see also Trompe L'Oeil Painting
Brindle, John & Secrist, Sally. American Cornucopia, Nineteenth Century Still Lifes & Studies. (Illus.). 48p. 1976. pap. 2.00 (ISBN 0-913196-18-5). Hunt Inst Botanical.
Doherty, M. Stephen. Dynamic Still Lifes in Watercolor: Sondra Freckelton's Approach to Color, Composition, & Control of the Medium. (Illus.). 144p. 1983. 22.50 (ISBN 0-8230-1583-1). Watson-Guptill.

STOCHASTIC ANALYSIS
Elliot, R. J. Stochastic Calculus & Applications. (Applications of Mathematics Ser.: Vol. 18). 302p. 1983. 42.00 (ISBN 0-387-90763-7). Springer-Verlag.
Elworthy, K. D. Stochastic Differential Equations on Manifolds. LC 82-4426. (London Mathematical Society Lecture Note Ser.: No. 70). 326p. 1982. pap. 27.50 (ISBN 0-521-28767-7). Cambridge U Pr.
Stoyan, D. & Daley, D. J. Comparison Methods for Queues & Other Stochastic Models. 1982. text ed. write for info. (ISBN 0-471-10122-2, Pub. by Wiley-Interscience). Wiley.
Whittle, P. Optimisation Over Time: Dynamic Programming & Stochastic Control, Vol. 1. (Probability & Mathematical Statistics-Applied Probability & Statistics Section Ser.). 317p. 1982. text ed. 46.95x (ISBN 0-471-10120-6, Pub. by Wiley-Interscience). Wiley.

STOCHASTIC PROCESSES
see also Estimation Theory; Markov Processes; Prediction Theory; Random Noise Theory; Stochastic Analysis
Adomian, George, ed. Stochastic Systems: Monograph. (Mathematics in Science & Engineering Ser.). 345p. 1983. price not set (ISBN 0-12-044370-8). Acad Pr.
Albeverio, S., et al, eds. Stochastic Processes in Quantum Theory & Statistical Physics: Proceedings, Marseille, France, 1981. (Lecture Notes in Physics Ser.: Vol. 173). 337p. 1983. pap. 17.00 (ISBN 0-387-11956-6). Springer-Verlag.
Arato, M. Linear Stochastic Systems with Constant Coefficients: A Statistical Approach. (Lecture Notes in Control & Information Sciences: Vol. 45). 309p. 1983. pap. 15.50 (ISBN 0-387-12090-4). Springer-Verlag.
Carmeli. Statical Theory & Random Matrices. (Pure & Applied Mathematics Ser.). 184p. 1983. 35.00 (ISBN 0-8247-1779-1). Dekker.
Cinlar, E., et al, eds. Seminar on Stochastic Processes, 1981. (Progress in Probability & Statistics: Vol. 1). 248p. 1982. text ed. 17.50 (ISBN 3-7643-3072-4). Birkhauser.
Elliot, R. J. Stochastic Calculus & Applications. (Applications of Mathematics Ser.: Vol. 18). 302p. 1983. 42.00 (ISBN 0-387-90763-7). Springer-Verlag.
Fleming, W. H. & Riskel, R. W. Deterministic & Stochastic Optional Control. ix, 222p. (Corrected Second Printing 1982). 1983. 36.00 (ISBN 0-387-90155-8). Springer-Verlag.
Fleming, W. H. & Gorostiza, L. G., eds. Advances in Filtering & Optimal Stochastic Control: Proceedings; Cocoyoc, Mexico 1982. (Lecture Notes in Control & Information Science: Vol. 42). 392p. 1983. pap. 17.50 (ISBN 0-387-11936-1). Springer-Verlag.
Florens, J. P., et al, eds. Specifying Statistical Models, From Parametric to Non-Parametric, Using Bayesian or Non-Bayesian Approaches: Proceedings, Louvain-la-Neuve, Belgium, 1981. (Lecture Notes in Statistics Ser.: Vol. 16). (Illus.). 204p. 1983. pap. 14.00 (ISBN 0-387-90809-9). Springer-Verlag.
Frehland, E. Stochastic Transport Processes in Discrete Biological Systems. (Lecture Notes in Biomathematics Ser.: Vol. 47). 169p. 1983. pap. 11.00 (ISBN 0-387-11964-7). Springer-Verlag.
Gardiner, C. W. Handbook of Stochastic Methods for Physics, Chemistry & the Natural Sciences. (Springer Series in Synergetics: Vol. 13). (Illus.). 450p. 1983. 42.00 (ISBN 0-387-11357-6). Springer-Verlag.
Gresser, Ion, ed. Interferon Eighty-Two. (Serial Publication). Date not set. 18.50 (ISBN 0-12-302253-3). Acad Pr.
Heyman, D. P. & Sobel, M. J. Stochastic Models in Operations Research: Stochastic Optimization, Vol. 2. (Quantitative Methods for Management Ser.). 414p. 1983. 28.00 (ISBN 0-07-028632-9). McGraw.
Kohlmann, M. & Christopeit, N., eds. Stochastic Differential Systems, Bad Honnef, FRG 1982: Proceedings. (Lecture Notes in Control & Information Sciences Ser.: Vol. 43). 377p. 1983. pap. 17.50 (ISBN 0-387-12061-0). Springer-Verlag.
Leadbetter, M. R., et al. Extremes & Related Properties of Random Sequences & Processes. (Springer Series in Statistics). (Illus.). 368p. 1982. 36.00 (ISBN 0-387-90731-9). Springer-Verlag.
Lichtenberg, A. J. & Lieberman, M. A. Regular & Stochastic Motion. (Applied Mathematical Sciences Ser.: Vol. 38). (Illus.). 499p. 1983. 36.00 (ISBN 0-387-90707-6). Springer-Verlag.
Witt, U. & Perske, J. SMS: A Program Package for Simulation & Gaming of Stochastic Market Processes & Learning Behavior. (Lecture Notes in Economics & Mathematical Systems Ser.: Vol. 202). (Illus.). 266p. 1983. pap. 18.50 (ISBN 0-387-11551-X). Springer-Verlag.
Wong, E. Introduction to Random Processes: A Dowden & Culver Book. (Springer Texts in Electrical Engineering). 175p. 1983. pap. 17.95 (ISBN 0-387-90757-2). Springer-Verlag.

STOCK (ANIMALS)
see Livestock

STOCK BROKERS
see Brokers

STOCK CONTROL
see Inventory Control

STOCK CORPORATIONS
see Corporations

STOCK-EXCHANGE
Here are entered works on stock trading and speculation and on stock exchanges in general.
see also Bonds; Brokers; Foreign Exchange; Put and Call Transactions; Securities; Stocks; Wall Street
also names of specific exchanges, e.g. New York Stock Exchange
Ansbacher, Max G. Stock Futures: New Strategies for Profit. (Illus.). 192p. 1983. 15.95 (ISBN 0-8027-0733-5). Walker & Co.
Arms, Richard W., Jr. Volume Cycles in the Stock Market. LC 82-73619. 200p. 1983. 30.00 (ISBN 0-87094-405-3). Dow Jones-Irwin.
Birdwell, Roger W. High-Tech Investing. 257p. 1983. 17.95 (ISBN 0-686-43181-2). Times Bks.
Boyd, Brendan & Engel, Louis. How to Buy Stocks. 1983. 14.00i (ISBN 0-316-10439-6). Little.
Elliot, Ralph N. Natue's Law & its Application for the Mastering of the Stock Market. (Illus.). 157p. 1983. 145.15 (ISBN 0-86654-068-7). Inst Econ Finan.
Fluiani, Carlo M. The Elliot Wave Theory Flow of Speculative Matter into the Active Cylinder Theory Stream. (The Recondite Sources of Stock Market Action Library). (Illus.). 137p. 1983. 81.45 (ISBN 0-86654-043-1). Inst Econ Finan.
Flumiani, C. M. The Best Critical Stock Market Studies of the Fibonacci-Elliot Research Foundation, 3 vols. (Illus.). 418p. 1983. Set. 575.00 (ISBN 0-86654-070-9). Inst Econ Finan.
--The Hidden & Mysterious Life of Stock Market Syndicates. (A New Stock Market Library Bk.). (Illus.). 116p. 1983. 49.85 (ISBN 0-86654-057-1). Inst Econ Finan.
Flumiani, Carlo M. How to Select a Stock with the Power to make you Wealthy Almost Overnight. (New Stock Market Library Book). (Illus.). 61p. (Orig.). 1983. pap. 6.95 (ISBN 0-89266-390-1). Am Classical Coll Pr.
--Three Ways for an Investor with very Little Money to make a Killing in the Stock Market. 04/1983 ed. (New Stock Market Library Book). (Illus.). 69p. (Orig.). pap. 6.95 (ISBN 0-89266-391-X). Am Classical Coll Pr.
--Your Financial I. Q. Personal Test. (A New Stock Market Library Book). 91p. 1983. 21.75 (ISBN 0-86654-044-X). Inst Econ Finan.
Freitag, Alfred H. The Most Powerful Instruments of Economic Prediction, with Special Attention to the Stock Market. (Illus.). 165p. 1983. 87.65 (ISBN 0-86654-066-0). Inst Econ Finan.
Geisst, Charles R. A Guide to the Financial Markets. 160p. 1981. 55.00x (ISBN 0-333-30919-7, Pub. by Macmillan England). State Mutual Bk.
Heatter, Justin W. The Small Investor's Guide to Large Profits in the Stock Market. 192p. 1983. 14.95 (ISBN 0-686-83838-6, ScribT). Scribner.
Hooker, Edward E. How Not to Make a Fool of Yourself in Wall Street. (The Recondite Sources of Stock Market Action Library). (Illus.). 134p. 1983. 65.45 (ISBN 0-86654-046-6). Inst Econ Finan.
Hume, John F. Get-Rich-Quick Schemes in the Stock Market & Sound Investment Practices. (A New Stock Market Library Bk.). (Illus.). 133p. 1983. 47.75 (ISBN 0-86654-056-3). Inst Econ Finan.
Kuklin, R. Learn to Invest & Trade on Wall Street. 2nd ed. LC 79-64472. 240p. 1982. pap. 7.95 (ISBN 0-9606504-5-8). Dill Ent.
Leffler, G. L. & Farwell, L. C. The Stock Market. 4th ed. 654p. 24.95x (ISBN 0-471-08588-X). Wiley.
Little, Jeffrey B. Forecasting Stock Prices. (Illus.). 192p. 1983. pap. 9.95 (ISBN 0-89709-042-X). Liberty Pub.
Livermore, Jesse. Smart Livermore's Tricks for Stock Market Success. (The Recondite Sources of Stock Market Action Library). (Illus.). 132p. 1983. 47.85 (ISBN 0-86654-045-8). Inst Econ Finan.
Lord, Jeffrey. The Technical Substance of Stock Market Action & Its Impact upon the Current & the Ultimate Direction of the Market. (The Recondite Sources of Stock Market Action Library). (Illus.). 141p. 1983. 49.75 (ISBN 0-86654-055-5). Inst Econ Finan.
Mamis, Justin. How to Buy: An Insider's Guide to Making Money in the Stock Market. 1983. pap. 6.95 (ISBN 0-346-12586-3). Cornerstone.
Mettling, Stephen R. The Fannie Mae (FNMA) Resale-Refinance Program. (Creative Financing Skill Development Ser.). 23p. 1982. pap. 7.95 (ISBN 0-88462-133-2). Real Estate Ed Co.
Nelson, S. A. The Methods of Trading in Wall Street for the Full Utilization of Speculative Opportunities. (A New Stock Market Library Bk.). (Illus.). 129p. 1983. 49.85 (ISBN 0-86654-059-8). Inst Econ Finan.
Roberts, Newton. The Cyclical Theories of Stock Market Action. (The Recondite Sources of Stock Market Action Library). (Illus.). 129p. 1983. 47.55 (ISBN 0-86654-052-0). Inst Econ Finan.
Sanger, Gary C. Stock Exchange Listings, Firm Value & Market Efficiency. Dufey, Gunter, ed. LC 82-6936. (Research for Business Decisions Ser.: No. 51). 236p. 1982. 39.95 (ISBN 0-8357-1338-5). Univ Microfilms.
Standard's & Poor's. Stockmarket Encyclopedia of the Fortune. 1982. 27.50 (ISBN 0-07-051886-6). McGraw.
Stock Exchange, London, ed. Stock Exchange Official Year-Book (U.K.), 1981-82. 107 ed. LC 34-16479. 1982. 180.00x (ISBN 0-333-31019-5). Intl Pubns Serv.
Stone, Justin F. The Metaphysics of Wallstreet. 152p. 10.00 (ISBN 0-686-38227-7). Sun Bks.
Tremont, Stuart. How Even a Superficial Knowledge of Charts May Help You to Double, Treble, Quadruple your Stock Market Profits. (New Stock Market Library Book). (Illus.). 67p. (Orig.). 1983. pap. 6.95 (ISBN 0-89266-389-8). Am Classical Coll Pr.

Tyler, Martin. The Decisive Speculative Significance of the Last of the Elliott Waves Upon the Future Course of the Stock Market. 131p. 1983. 79.85 (ISBN 0-89266-399-5). Am Classical Coll Pr.

Warfield, Gerald. The Investor's Guide to Stock Quotations: And Other Financial Listings. LC 82-47539. (Illus.). 416p. 1983. pap. 10.53i (ISBN 0-06-091036-4, CN 1036, CN). Har-Row.

--The Investor's Guide to Stock Quotations: And Other Financial Listings. (Illus.). 416p. 1983. 25.00 (ISBN 0-06-015050-5, HarpT). Har-Row.

Wyckoff, Richard D. Forecasting Price Movements & Turning Points in the Course of the Stock Market. (The Recondite Sources of Stock Market Action Library). (Illus.). 127p. 1983. 55.85 (ISBN 0-86654-054-7). Inst Econ Finan.

--How Fortunes are Made in Wall Street by Exploiting the Price Declines of Stock Market Panics. (A New Stock Market Library Bk.). (Illus.). 131p. 1983. 59.85 (ISBN 0-86654-058-X). Inst Econ Finan.

--The Making of a Wall Street Flunger. (A New Stock Library Book). (Illus.). 127p. 1983. 66.65 (ISBN 0-86654-047-4). Inst Econ Finan.

STOCK-EXCHANGE–GREAT BRITAIN

British Security Companies. 85p. 1982. 275.00x (ISBN 0-85938-162-5, Pub. by Jordan & Sons England). State Mutual Bk.

Macmillan Publishers, ed. The Stock Exchange Official Year Book: 1981-1982. 1192p. 1982. 190.00 (ISBN 0-333-31020-9, Pub. by Macmillan England). State Mutual Bk.

STOCK MARKET

see Stock-Exchange

STOCK OWNERSHIP FOR EMPLOYEES

see Employee Ownership

STOCK-ROOM KEEPING

see Stores or Stock-Room Keeping

STOCKBROKERS

see Brokers

STOCKHOLM

Fodor's Stockholm, Copenhagen, Oslo, Helsinki & Reykjavik. (Illus.). 144p. 1983. pap. 5.95 (ISBN 0-679-00966-3). McKay.

STOCKS

see also Bonds; Corporations; Stock-Exchange

American Railroad Stock Certificates. 28.50. StanGib Ltd.

Buechner, Robert W. & Manzler, David L. Accumulating Wealth with Before Tax Dollars (Desk Book) LC 81-86381. (Illus.). 1982. write for info. looseleaf (ISBN 0-87218-417-X); write for info. visual, 48 p. (ISBN 0-87218-416-1). Natl Underwriter.

Ellsworth, Gerald C. The Inflexible Pressure of the Elliot Waves upon the Stock Market & Prediction of Major Future Price Movements. (Illus.). 143p. 1983. 71.85 (ISBN 0-86654-064-4). Inst Econ Finan.

Flumiani, C. M. How to Gain Exposure to the Possibility of Gaining Thousands upon Thousands of Dollars in the Stock Market by Following a Simple Method Recently Discovered. (A New Stock Market Library Bk.). (Illus.). 77p. 1983. pap. 6.95 (ISBN 0-89266-393-6). Am Classical Coll Pr.

La Barre, George. Collecting Stocks & Bonds, Vol. 1. 1980. 5.00 (ISBN 0-913702-42-0). Heart Am Pr.

--Collecting Stocks & Bonds, Vol. 2. 1981. 5.00 (ISBN 0-913902-43-8). Heart Am Pr.

--Collecting Stocks & Bonds, Vol. 3. 1981. 5.00 (ISBN 0-913902-44-6). Heart Am Pr.

McMillan, Lawrence G. Options as a Strategic Investment. (Illus.). 484p. 1980. 22.00 (ISBN 0-13-638387-4). NY Inst Finance.

Pierce, Phyllis. The Dow Jones Investor's Handbook, 1983. LC 66-17630. 136p. 1983. 11.95 (ISBN 0-87094-397-9). Dow Jones-Irwin.

Ryan, James E. The Investor's Guide to U. S. Silver Stocks. Sarnoff, Paul, frwd. by. (Illus.). 240p. (Orig.). 1983. pap. 19.95 (ISBN 0-9610202-0-2). N W Silver Pr.

Schwabacker, Eric. Capturing the Profit Potential of the Stock Market New Highs & New Lows. (Research Center for Economic Psychology Library). (Illus.). 138p. 1983. 53.45 (ISBN 0-86654-062-8). Inst Econ Finan.

STOICHIOMETRY

see Chemistry, Physical and Theoretical

STOMACH

see also Digestion

Anderhub, Beth. Manual of Abdominal Ultrasonography. (Illus.). 1983. write for info. (ISBN 0-8391-1804-X, 18589). Univ Park.

Stern, Robert M. & Davis, Christopher M., eds. Gastric Motility: A Selectively Annotated Bibliography. LC 82-12173. 208p. 1982. 19.50 (ISBN 0-87933-430-4). Hutchinson Ross.

STOMATOLOGY

see Mouth; Mouth–Diseases; Teeth; Teeth–Diseases

STONE, PHILOSOPHERS'

see Alchemy

STONE-CARVING

see Sculpture

STONE INDUSTRY AND TRADE

Miller, Richard. Noise Control Solutions for the Stone Industry. (Illus.). 90p. pap. text ed. 45.00 (ISBN 0-89671-028-9). Southeast Acoustics.

STONEWARE

see Pottery

STONEWORK, DECORATIVE

see Decoration and Ornament, Architectural; Sculpture

STONY INDIANS

see Indians of North America–The West

STORAGE

see Warehouses

also names of stored products, e.g. Farm Produce, Coal, etc.

STORAGE BATTERIES

see also Electric Batteries

Bagshaw, Norman E. Batteries on Ships. (Battery Applications Bk.). 215p. 1983. write for info. (ISBN 0-471-90021-4). Res Stud Pr.

Linden, D. Handbook of Batteries & Fuel Cells. 1024p. 1983. 49.50 (ISBN 0-07-037874-6, P&RB). McGraw.

STORAGE DEVICES, COMPUTER

see Computer Storage Devices

STORAGE IN THE HOME

Sunset Books & Sunset Magazine, ed. Bedroom & Bath Storage. LC 81-82870. (Illus.). 80p. (Orig.). 1982. pap. 3.95 (ISBN 0-376-01120-3). Sunset-Lane.

STORAGE WAREHOUSES

see Warehouses

STORE LOCATION

Roca, Ruben A., ed. Market Research for Shopping Centers. 1980. 35.00 (ISBN 0-913598-11-9). Intl Coun Shop.

STORES, COOPERATIVE

see Cooperative Societies

STORES, RETAIL

see also Shopping Centers; Store Location

Carter, R. J. Stores Management. 250p. 1982. pap. text ed. 12.95x (ISBN 0-7121-1979-5). Intl Ideas.

Earle, Anitra. How to Live Fairly Elegantly on Virtually Nothing...in Los Angeles. LC 82-161492. 100p. (Orig.). 1982. pap. 7.95 (ISBN 0-910795-00-2). Ondine Pr.

Factory Outlet Shopping Guide for New England, 1983. 1982. 3.95 (ISBN 0-913464-67-8). FOSG Pubns.

Factory Outlet Shopping Guide for New Jersey & Rockland County, 1983. 1982. 3.95 (ISBN 0-913464-63-5). FOSG Pubns.

Factory Outlet Shopping Guide for New York, 1983. 1982. 3.95 (ISBN 0-913464-64-3). FOSG Pubns.

Factory Outlet Shopping Guide for Pennsylvania, 1983. 1982. 3.95 (ISBN 0-913464-65-1). FOSG Pubns.

Factory Outlet Shopping Guide for Washington, D. C., 1983. 1982. 3.95 (ISBN 0-913464-66-X). FOSG Pubns.

A Guide to London's Best Shops. 224p. 1983. pap. 6.96 (ISBN 0-907080-36-7, Pub. by Auto Assn-British Tourist Authority England). Merrimack Bk Serv.

STORES OR STOCK-ROOM KEEPING

Rudman, Jack. Stock Clerk. (Career Examination Ser.: C-2617). (Cloth bdg. avail. on request). pap. 8.00 (ISBN 0-8373-2617-6). Natl Learning.

--Storekeeper I. (Career Examination Ser.: C-2901). (Cloth bdg. avail. on request). pap. 10.00 (ISBN 0-8373-2901-9). Natl Learning.

--Storekeeper II. (Career Examination Ser.: C-2902). (Cloth bdg. avail. on request). pap. 12.00 (ISBN 0-8373-2902-7). Natl Learning.

--Supervising Storekeeper. (Career Examination Ser.: C-861). (Cloth bdg. avail. on request). pap. 10.00 (ISBN 0-8373-0861-5). Natl Learning.

STORIES

see Fiction

STORMS

see also Hurricanes; Meteorology; Thunderstorms; Tornadoes; Winds

also names of specific cities or geographic locations, with or without the subdivision Storm

DeGroot, W., ed. Stormwater Detention Facilities. LC 82-73613. 448p. 1982. pap. text ed. 31.00 (ISBN 0-87262-348-3). Am Soc Civil Eng.

Whipple, A. B. Storm. (Planet Earth Ser.). 1982. lib. bdg. 19.92 (ISBN 0-8094-4313-9, Pub. by Time-Life). Silver.

STORY, SHORT

see Short Story

STORY-TELLING

Farrell, Catharine H. & Nessel, Denise D. Effects of Storytelling: An Ancient Art for Modern Classrooms. 36p. (Orig.). 1982. write for info. (ISBN 0-936434-04-X). Zellerbach.

STOVES

see also Heating; Stoves, Wood

Boram, Clifford. How to Get Parts Cast for Your Antique Stove. 5.00 (ISBN 0-686-38103-3). Autonomy Hse.

STOVES, WOOD

O'Connor, Hyla. Cooking on Your Wood Stove. (Illus.). 78p. 1981. pap. 5.95 (ISBN 0-9608050-0-1). Turkey Hill Pr.

STOWE, HARRIET ELIZABETH (BEECHER), 1811-1896

Gilbertson, Catherine. Harriet Beecher Stowe. 330p. 1982. Repr. of 1937 ed. lib. bdg. 40.00 (ISBN 0-89987-316-2). Darby Bks.

Kimball, Gayle. The Religious Ideas of Harriet Beecher Stowe: Her Gospel of Womanhood. (Studies in Women & Religion: Vol. 8). 216p. 1982. 34.95x (ISBN 0-88946-544-4). E Mellen.

Petersen, William J. Harriet Beecher Stowe had a Husband. 1983. pap. 2.95 r (ISBN 0-686-82689-2, 07-1329-X). Tyndale.

STRABISMUS

Evans, L. Convergent Strabismus. 1982. 72.00 (ISBN 90-619-3806-6, Pub. by Junk Pubs Netherlands). Kluwer Boston.

Gonzalez, Caleb. Strabismus & Ocular Motility. (Illus.). 298p. 1983. lib. bdg. price not set (ISBN 0-683-03629-7). Williams & Wilkins.

Von Noorden, Gunter K. Atlas of Strabismus. 4th ed. (Illus.). 256p. 1983. text ed. 35.00 (ISBN 0-8016-5253-7). Mosby.

STRAINS AND STRESSES

see also Deformations (Mechanics); Elasticity; Engineering Design; Materials–Fatigue; Shells (Engineering); Strength of Materials; Structural Design; Structural Dynamics

Mura, T. Micromechanics of Defects in Solids. 1982. lib. bdg. 98.00 (ISBN 90-247-2560-7, Pub. by Martinus Nijhoff Netherlands). Kluwer Boston.

Myslivec, A. & Kysela, Z. Bearing Capacity of Building Foundations. (Developments in Geotechnical Engineering: Vol. 21). 1978. 53.25 (ISBN 0-444-99794-6). Elsevier.

Yong, R. N. & Selig, E. T., eds. Application of Plasticity & Generalized Stress-Strain in Geotechnical Engineering. LC 81-71796. 360p. 1982. pap. text ed. 27.25 (ISBN 0-87262-294-0). Am Soc Civil Eng.

STRATEGY

see also Air Warfare; Armies; Atomic Warfare; Biological Warfare; Deterrence (Strategy); Military Art and Science; Naval Strategy; Psychological Warfare; Tank Warfare

Halperin, Morton H. Defense Strategies for the Seventies. LC 82-45020. 164p. 1983. pap. text ed. 9.25 (ISBN 0-8191-2710-8). U Pr of Amer.

U. S. Strategy at the Crossroads: Two Views. 72p. 1982. pap. 7.50 (ISBN 0-89549-044-7, IFPA 26, IFPA). Unipub.

STRATFORD-UPON-AVON

Johnson, Guy. Save the Stratford Canal! (Illus.). 168p. 1983. 17.50 (ISBN 0-7153-8424-4). David & Charles.

STRATIFICATION, SOCIAL

see Social Classes

STRATIGRAPHIC GEOLOGY

see Geology, Stratigraphic

STRATIGRAPHIC PALEONTOLOGY

see Paleontology, Stratigraphic

STRATOFORTRESS (BOMBER)

see B-Fifty-Two Bomber

STRAUSS, DAVID FRIEDRICH, 1808-1874

Massey, Marilyn C. Christ Unmasked: The Meaning of "The Life of Jesus" in German Politics. LC 82-8547. (Studies in Religion Ser.). xi, 175p. 1982. 23.00x (ISBN 0-8078-1524-1). U of NC Pr.

STRAVINSKII, IGOR FEDOROVICH, 1882-1971

Caesar, Clifford, compiled by. Stravinsky: A Complete Catalogue. LC 81-51157. (Illus.). 1982. pap. 7.50 (ISBN 0-911302-41-7). San Francisco Pr.

Druskin, Mikhail S. Igor Stravinsky: His Life, Works & Views. Cooper, Martin, tr. 190p. 1982. 24.95 (ISBN 0-521-24590-7). Cambridge U Pr.

McLeish, Kenneth & McLeish, Vallerie. Stravinsky. (Composers & their World Ser.). (Illus.). 90p. (gr. 9-12). 1983. 5.95 (ISBN 0-434-95126-9, Pub. by Heinemann England). David & Charles.

STRAW VOTES

see Public Opinion Polls

STRAWBERRIES

McCreary, Susan A., ed. Strawberry Sportcake. (Illus.). 96p. 1982. pap. 4.00 (ISBN 0-686-37646-3). Strawberry Works.

STREAKED BASS

see Striped Bass

STREAM FLOW MEASUREMENTS

see Stream Measurements

STREAM GAUGING

see Stream Measurements

STREAM MEASUREMENTS

see also Flow Meters

Manka, Dan, ed. Automated Stream Analysis for Processed Control, Vol. 1. LC 82-8822. 336p. 1982. 39.50 (ISBN 0-12-469001-7). Acad Pr.

STREAM POLLUTION

see Water–Pollution

STREAMFLOW DATA

see Stream Measurements

STREAMLINING

see Aerodynamics

STREET-CARS

see Electric Railroads–Cars

STREET CHRISTIANS

see Jesus People

STREET RAILROADS–CARS

see Electric Railroads–Cars

STREET TRAFFIC

see City Traffic; Traffic Engineering

STRENGTH OF MATERIALS

see also Elasticity; Fracture Mechanics; Materials–Creep; Materials–Fatigue; Materials at High Temperatures; Strains and Stresses; Structural Design

Bruch, Charles D. Strength of Materials for Technology. LC 77-27629. 376p. 1978. text ed. 24.95x (ISBN 0-471-11372-7); solutions manual avail. (ISBN 0-471-04513-6). Wiley.

Byars, Edward F. Engineering Mechanics of Deformable Bodies. 4th ed. 528p. 1983. text ed. 29.50 scp (ISBN 0-06-041109-0, HarpC); solution manual avail. (ISBN 0-06-361100-7). Har-Row.

Simon, Andrew L. & Ross, David A. Principles of Statics & Strength of Materials. 475p. 1983. text ed. write for info. (ISBN 0-697-08604-6); instr's. manual avail. (ISBN 0-697-08605-4). Wm C Brown.

STRENGTH OF MUSCLES

see Muscle Strength

STREPTOCOCCUS

Breese, Burtis B. & Hall, Caroline. Beta Hemolytic Streptococcal Diseases. (Illus.). 287p. 1978. 50.00 (ISBN 0-471-09476-5, Pub. by Wiley Med). Wiley.

STRESS (PHYSIOLOGY)

Davis, Steven A. How to Stay Healthy in an Unhealthy World. LC 82-12581. 288p. 1983. 12.50 (ISBN 0-688-01574-3). Morrow.

Demaray, Donald E. Watch Out For Burnout: Its Signs, Prevention, & Cure. 112p. (Orig.). 1983. pap. 4.95. Baker Bk.

Dickson, Gary L. Resident Assistant Stress Inventory: Manual & Inservice Education Guide. rev. ed. iv, 43p. 1981. pap. 3.95 (ISBN 0-943872-68-5). Andrews Univ Pr.

Donnelly, Gloria F. RN's Survival Sourcebook: Coping with Stress. (Illus.). 225p. 1983. softcover 10.95 (ISBN 0-87489-299-6). Med Economics.

Drews, Toby R. Get Rid of Anxiety & Stress. 1982. pap. 4.95 (ISBN 0-88270-537-7). Bridge Pub.

Figley, Charles R. & McCubbin, Hamilton I., eds. Stress & the Family: Coping with Catastrophe, Vol. II. 300p. 1983. price not set (ISBN 0-87630-332-7). Brunner-Mazel.

Goldberger, Leo & Breznitz, Shlomo, eds. Handbook of Stress: Theoretical & Clinical Aspects. 804p. 1983. 49.95 (ISBN 0-02-912030-6). Free Pr.

Hockey, Robert. Stress & Fatigue in Human Performance. (Studies in Human Performance Ser.). 400p. 1983. 45.95x (ISBN 0-471-10265-2, Pub. by Wiley-Interscience). Wiley.

Lachman, Vicki D. Stress Management: A Manual for Nurses. write for info (ISBN 0-8089-1554-1). Grune.

McCubbin, Hamilton I. & Figley, Charles R., eds. Stress & the Family: Coping with Normative Transitions, Vol. I. 300p. 1983. price not set (ISBN 0-87630-321-1). Brunner-Mazel.

Rogers, Michael. How to Overcome Nervousness. 22p. 1973. pap. 1.95 (ISBN 0-88010-051-6, Pub. by New Knowledge Bks England). Anthroposophic.

Shaffer, Martin. Life after Stress. (Illus.). 288p. 1983. pap. 8.95 (ISBN 0-8092-5622-3). Contemp Bks.

Tremonger. Basic Stress Analysis. 1982. text ed. 19.95 (ISBN 0-408-01113-0). Butterworth.

Welford, A. T., ed. Man Under Stress. LC 74-649301. (Illus.). 140p. 1974. 18.50x (ISBN 0-85066-073-4). Intl Pubns serv.

STRESS (PSYCHOLOGY)

see also Anxiety

Bedford, Stewart. Prayer Power & Stress Management. Date not set. pap. 8.95 (ISBN 0-935930-05-1). Scott Pubns CA.

Bosmajian, C. Perry & Bosmajian, Linda S. Personalized Guide to Stress Evaluation. Snyder, Thomas L. & Felmeister, Charles J., eds. LC 82-8182. (Dental Practice Management Ser.). (Illus.). 103p. 1983. pap. text ed. 12.95 (ISBN 0-8016-4724-X). Mosby.

Brown, W. D. Welcome Stress, It Can Help You Be Your Best. 150p. (Orig.). 1983. pap. 8.95 (ISBN 0-89638-067-X). CompCare.

Center for Research on Agression, Syracuse University. Prevention & Control of Agression. (General Psychology Ser.). 450p. 1983. 45.00 (ISBN 0-08-029375-1). Pergamon.

Cooper, Cary L. Stress Research: Issues for the Eighties. 150p. 1983. not set 29.95 (ISBN 0-471-10246-6, Pub. by Wiley-Interscience). Wiley.

Coping with Stress Through Leisure. (Leisure Today Ser.). 32p. 1.50 (ISBN 0-88314-218-X). AAHPERD.

Demaray, Donald E. Watch Out For Burnout: Its Signs, Prevention, & Cure. 112p. (Orig.). 1983. pap. 4.95. Baker Bk.

Dickson, Gary L. Resident Assistant Stress Inventory: Manual & Inservice Education Guide. rev. ed. iv, 43p. 1981. pap. 3.95 (ISBN 0-943872-68-5). Andrews Univ Pr.

Donnelly, Gloria F. RN's Survival Sourcebook: Coping with Stress. (Illus.). 225p. 1983. softcover 10.95 (ISBN 0-87489-299-6). Med Economics.

Drews, Toby R. Get Rid of Anxiety & Stress. 1982. pap. 4.95 (ISBN 0-88270-537-7). Bridge Pub.

Dueuker, R. Sheldon. Tensions in the Connection. 128p. 1983. pap. 3.95 (ISBN 0-687-41243-9). Abingdon.

Figley, Charles R. & McCubbin, Hamilton I., eds. Stress & the Family: Coping with Catastrophe, Vol. II. 300p. 1983. price not set (ISBN 0-87630-332-7). Brunner-Mazel.

Garmezy, Norman & Rutter, Michael, eds. Stress, Coping, & Development in Children. (Illus.). 384p. 1983. 24.95 (ISBN 0-07-022886-8, P&RB). McGraw.

Gill, Joseph L. Personalized Stress Management: A Manual for Everyday Life & Work. LC 82-90115. (Illus.). 175p. 1983. 14.95 (ISBN 0-910819-00-9); pap. 9.95 (ISBN 0-910819-01-7). Counsel & Consult.

Goldberger, Leo & Breznitz, Shlomo. The Handbook of Stress. (Illus.). 832p. 1982. text ed. 49.95. Free Pr.

Goldberger, Leo & Breznitz, Shlomo, eds. Handbook of Stress: Theoretical & Clinical Aspects. 804p. 1983. 49.95 (ISBN 0-02-912030-6). Free Pr.

Greenberg, Jerrold S. Comprehensive Stress Management. 350p. 1983. pap. text ed. write for info. (ISBN 0-697-07199-5). Wm C Brown.

Hadley, Norman H. Fingernail Biting Theory, Research & Treatment. 200p. 1983. text ed. 20.00 (ISBN 0-89335-183-0). SP Med & Sci Bks.

Hafen, Brent Q. & Brog, Molly J. Emotional Survival. 114p. 1983. 11.95 (ISBN 0-13-274480-5); pap. 5.95 (ISBN 0-13-274472-4). P-H.

Hockey, Robert. Stress & Fatigue in Human Performance. (Studies in Human Performance Ser.). 400p. 1983. 45.95x (ISBN 0-471-10265-2, Pub. by Wiley-Interscience). Wiley.

Janis, Irving L. Stress: Attitudes & Decisions. 366p. 1982. 28.95 (ISBN 0-03-059036-1). Praeger.

Krohne, H. W. Achievement, Stress & Anxiety. 1981. 34.50 (ISBN 0-07-035521-5). McGraw.

Kula, Eric & Weiss, Volker, eds. Residual Stress & Stress Relaxation, Vol.28. (Sagamore Army Materials Research Conference Proceedings). 540p. 1982. 72.50x (ISBN 0-306-41102-4, Plenum Pr). Plenum Pub.

Lach, C. S. How to Help Cases of Distress. 152p. 1977. 30.00x (ISBN 0-7121-0814-9, Pub. by Macdonald & Evans). State Mutual Bk.

Lachman, Vicki D. Stress Management: A Manual for Nurses. write for info (ISBN 0-8089-1554-1). Grune.

McCubbin, Hamilton I. & Figley, Charles R., eds. Stress & the Family: Coping with Normative Transitions, Vol. I. 300p. 1983. price not set (ISBN 0-87630-321-1). Brunner-Mazel.

McCubbin, Hamilton I. & Sussman, Marvin B., eds. Social Stress & the Family: Advances & Developments in Family Stress Therapy & Research. (Marriage & Family Review Ser.: Vol. 6, No. 1 & 2). 136p. 1983. text ed. 28.00 (ISBN 0-86656-163-3). Haworth Pr.

Markell, Jane & Winn, Jane. Overcoming Stress. 1982. pap. 4.50 (ISBN 0-686-82562-4). Victor Bks.

Meichenbaum, Donald & Jaemko, Matt, eds. Stress Reduction & Prevention. 512p. 1983. 32.50x (ISBN 0-306-41066-4, Plenum Pr). Plenum Pub.

Ogburn, Keith D. Emotional Education: How to Deal with Stress in the Classroom Before & After it Happens-Strategies & Techniques. LC 82-60528. 125p. (Orig.). 1983. pap. 14.95 (ISBN 0-88247-683-1). R & E Res Assoc.

Phillips, E. Lakin. Stress, Health & Psychological Problems in the Major Professions. LC 82-17556. 478p. (Orig.). 1983. lib. bdg. 30.50 (ISBN 0-8191-2773-6); pap. text ed. 17.50 (ISBN 0-8191-2774-4). U Pr of Amer.

Procaccini, Joseph & Kiefaber, Mark. Parent Burnout. LC 81-43593. (Illus.). 264p. 1983. 15.95 (ISBN 0-385-18041-1). Doubleday.

Reres, Mary E. Stress in Patient Care. 1983. pap. price not set (ISBN 0-8391-1815-5, 16608). Univ Park.

Responding to Stress: Community Mental Health in the 80s. 96p. 1981. 7.95 (ISBN 0-686-38200-5, 52-1870). Natl League Nurse.

Rogers, Michael. How to Overcome Nervousness. 22p. 1973. pap. 1.95 (ISBN 0-88010-051-6, Pub. by New Knowledge Bks England). Anthroposophic.

Shaffer, Martin. Life after Stress. (Illus.). 288p. 1983. pap. 8.95 (ISBN 0-8092-5622-3). Contemp Bks.

Spielberger, C. D., et al. Stress & Anxiety, Vol. 8. 1981. 34.95 (ISBN 0-07-060239-5). McGraw.

Stress: Making It Work for You. 85p. 1977. 5.95 (ISBN 0-686-38330-3, 16-1674). Natl League Nurse.

Timmermann, Tim & Blecha, Diane. Modern Stress: The Needless Killer. 176p. 1982. pap. text ed. 13.95 (ISBN 0-8403-2722-6). Kendall-Hunt.

Tremonger. Basic Stress Analysis. 1982. text ed. 19.95 (ISBN 0-408-01113-0). Butterworth.

Tubesing, Donald A. Kicking Your Stress Habits. 1982. pap. 3.50 (ISBN 0-451-11834-0, AE1834, Sig). NAL.

Welford, A. T., ed. Man Under Stress. LC 74-649301. (Illus.). 140p. 1974. 18.50x (ISBN 0-85066-073-4). Intl Pubns serv.

STRESSES

see Strains and Stresses

STRIKES AND LOCKOUTS

Here are entered works of strikes and lockouts in general. Individual strikes limited in extent to one city or county are entered under the place. Individual strikes of wider extent are entered under their generally accepted name. A strike against a single employer is entered under the name of the employer.

see also Arbitration, Industrial; Collective Bargaining; Trade-Unions

also names of strikes, e.g. Steel Strikes, 1919-1920

Aldridge, Robert C. First Strike. (Illus.). 300p. 1982. 20.00 (ISBN 0-89608-154-0); pap. 7.50 (ISBN 0-89608-155-9). South End Pr.

STRIKES AND LOCKOUTS–TEACHERS

Gaswirth, Marc, et al. Teachers' Strikes in New Jersey. LC 81-23489. (Studies in Industrial Relations & Human Resources Ser.: No. 1). 179p. 1982. pap. 10.00 (ISBN 0-8108-1569-9). Scarecrow.

STRINDBERG, AUGUST, 1849-1912

McGill, V. J. August Strindberg: The Bedeviled Viking. 459p. 1982. Repr. of 1930 ed. lib. bdg. 40.00 (ISBN 0-89760-568-3). Telegraph Bks.

Steene, B. August Strindberg: An Introduction to His Major Works. rev. ed. Orig. Title: The Greatest Fire- A Study of August Strindberg. 1982. Repr. of 1973 ed. text ed. 28.75x (ISBN 0-391-02715-8, Pub. by Almquist & Wiksell Sweden). Humanities.

STRING FIGURES

Haddon, Hathleen. Cat's Cradle from Many Lands: String Figures. (Illus.). 95p. Date not set. pap. 12.50 (ISBN 0-87556-497-6). Saifer.

STRINGED INSTRUMENTS

Here is entered material on instruments employing strings, whether bowed, hammered or plucked.

Lamb, Norman. Guide to Teaching Strings. 4th ed. (College Instrumental Technique Ser.). 190p. 1983. text ed. write for info. (ISBN 0-697-03539-5). Wm C Brown.

Martin, Will. Everybody's Guitar Manual: How to Buy, Maintain & Repair an Acoustic Guitar. (Illus.). 96p. (Orig.). 1983. pap. 7.50 (ISBN 0-912528-30-3). John Muir.

Skoldberg, Phyllis. Strings: A Comparative View, Vol. II. 1983. pap. text ed. 19.95 (ISBN 0-89917-367-5, Frangipana Press). TIS Pr.

STRIP MINING

Martin, James W. & Martin, Thomas J. Surface Mining Equipment. LC 82-81951. (Illus.). 450p. 1982. 77.00 (ISBN 0-9609060-0-2). Martin Consult.

STRIPED BASS

Woolner, Frank & Lyman, Hal. Striped Bass Fishing. 192p. 1983. 15.95 (ISBN 0-8329-0279-9); pap. 9.95 (ISBN 0-8329-0281-0). Winchester Pr.

STROKE PATIENTS

Carr, Janet H. & Shepherd, Roberta B. Early Care of the Stroke Patient: A Positive Approach. 55p. Repr. of 1979 ed. 8.50 (ISBN 0-89443-812-3, Pub. by W Heinemann). Aspen Systems.

--A Motor Relearning Programme for Stroke. 175p. 1983. 24.50 (ISBN 0-89443-931-6). Aspen Systems.

Lubic, Lowell G. & Palkovitz, Harry. Stroke: Contemporary Patient Management. 2nd ed. (Contemporary Patient Management Ser.). 1983. text ed. 13.00 not set (ISBN 0-87488-893-X). Med Exam.

Strokes & Strokes: An Instructor's Manual for Developing Swim Programs for Stroke Victims. 80p. 5.75 (ISBN 0-88314-184-1). AAHPERD.

STRONGLY INTERACTING PARTICLES

see Hadrons

STRUCTURAL ANALYSIS (MATHEMATICS)

see Lattice Theory

STRUCTURAL DESIGN

see also Building; Strains and Stresses; Strength of Materials; Structural Frames;

also names of specific structures, with or without the subdivision Design, or Design and Construction, e.g. Bridges; Factories–Design and Construction

Currie, B. & Sharpe, R. A. Structural Detailing Level II. (Illus.). 160p. pap. text ed. 14.95x (ISBN 0-7121-1985-X). Intl Ideas.

Gallagher, R. H. Optimum Structural Design: Theory & Applications. LC 72-8600. (Numerical Methods in Engineering Ser.). 358p. 1973. 53.95x (ISBN 0-471-29050-5, Pub. by Wiley-Interscience). Wiley.

Steel Designers' Manual. 4th, rev. ed. (Illus.). 1089p. 1983. pap. text ed. 35.00 (ISBN 0-246-11475-4). Sheridan.

STRUCTURAL DYNAMICS

see also Earthquakes and Building

DeCampoli, Giuseppe. The Statics of Structural Components: Understanding the Basics of Structural Design. 256p. 1983. price not set (ISBN 0-471-87169-9, Pub. by Wiley-Interscience). Wiley.

Donea, J. M. Advanced Structural Dynamics. 1980. 74.00 (ISBN 0-85334-859-6, Pub. by Applied Sci England). Elsevier.

STRUCTURAL ENGINEERING

see also Foundations; Hydraulic Engineering; Soil Mechanics; Structural Frames; Structures, Theory Of also specific kinds of structures, e.g. Bridges, Buildings; specific structural forms, e.g. Girders; specific systems of construction, e.g. Buildings, Iron and Steel

Ambrose, James & Vergun, Dimitry. Simplified Building Design for Wind & Earthquake Forces. LC 79-26660. 142p. 1980. 26.95x (ISBN 0-471-05013-X, Pub. by Wiley-Interscience). Wiley.

Ferguson, Phil M. Reinforced Concrete Fundamentals. 4th ed. LC 78-21555. 724p. 1979. text ed. 35.95x (ISBN 0-471-01459-1). Wiley.

Gaylord, E. H., Jr. & Gaylord, C. N. Structural Engineering Handbook. 1979. 59.00 (ISBN 0-07-023123-0). McGraw.

Morton, N. Structural Engineering Design Programs: Software Project. 1982. (users manual & 4 diskettes) 495.00 (ISBN 0-07-079572-X, P&RB). McGraw.

Noor, A. K. & Housner, J. M., eds. Advances & Trends in Structural & Solid Mechanics: Proceedings of the Symposium, Washington D.C., USA, 4-7 October 1982. 590p. 1983. 165.00 (ISBN 0-08-029990-3). Pergamon.

Sontagg, Karlheinz. Inhalte und Strukturen Industrieller Berufsausbildung. iv, 240p. (Ger.). 1982. write for info. (ISBN 3-8204-7223-1). P Lang Pubs.

Steel Designers' Manual. 4th, rev. ed. (Illus.). 1089p. 1983. pap. text ed. 35.00 (ISBN 0-246-11475-4). Sheridan.

STRUCTURAL FRAMES

see also Girders

Steel Designers' Manual. 4th, rev. ed. (Illus.). 1089p. 1983. pap. text ed. 35.00 (ISBN 0-246-11475-4). Sheridan.

STRUCTURAL FRAMES–VIBRATION

see Structural Dynamics

STRUCTURAL GEOLOGY

see Geology, Structural

STRUCTURAL PSYCHOLOGY

see Gestalt Psychology

STRUCTURAL SHELLS

see Shells (Engineering)

STRUCTURAL STEEL

see Steel, Structural

STRUCTURALISM

Culler, Jonathan. On Deconstruction: Theory & Criticism After Structuralism. LC 82-7414. 320p. 1982. 22.50x (ISBN 0-8014-1322-2). Cornell U Pr.

Lunneborg & Abbott. Applications of Basic Structure. Date not set. price not set (ISBN 0-444-00753-9). Elsevier.

Mainstone, Rowland J. Developments in Structural Form. (Illus.). 352p. 1983. pap. 17.50 (ISBN 0-262-63088-5). MIT Pr.

STRUCTURE, CHEMICAL

see Chemical Structure

STRUCTURE (PHILOSOPHY)

see Structuralism

STRUCTURES, ENGINEERING OF

see Structural Engineering

STRUCTURES, OFFSHORE

see Offshore Structures

STRUCTURES, SEDIMENTARY

see Sedimentary Structures

STRUCTURES, THEORY OF

see also Shells (Engineering); Strains and Stresses; Strength of Materials; Structural Design; Structural Engineering; Structural Frames

Timoshenko, Stephen P. History of Strength of Materials: With a Brief Account of the History of Theory of Elasticity & Theory of Structure. (Illus.). 452p. 1983. pap. 8.95 (ISBN 0-486-61187-6). Dover.

STRUGGLE

Laban, Rudolph & Lawrence, F. C. Effort. 112p. 1979. 30.00x (ISBN 0-7121-0534-4, Pub. by Macdonald & Evans). State Mutual Bk.

STUD FARMS

see Horse Breeding

STUDENT ACTIVITIES

see also College and School Drama; College and School Journalism; School Excursions; School Sports

ASBO's Student Activity Research Committee. Internal Auditing for Student Activity Funds. 1981. 5.95 (ISBN 0-910170-18-5). Assn Sch Busn.

STUDENT ADJUSTMENT

Sturo, Edmund. Conquering Academic Failure: A Guide for Parents, Students & Educators. LC 81-85805. (Illus.). 112p. 1983. pap. 5.95 (ISBN 0-86666-060-7). GWP.

STUDENT ADMINISTRATOR RELATIONSHIPS

Miller, Theodore K. & Winston, Roger B., Jr., eds. Administration & Leadership in Student Affairs: Actualizing Student Development in Higher Education. 600p. (Orig.). 1983. pap. text ed. 29.95 (ISBN 0-915202-35-2). Accel Devel.

STUDENT COUNCILS

see Self-Government (In Education)

STUDENT EXPENDITURES

see College Costs

STUDENT FINANCIAL AID ADMINISTRATION

Hoffman, Robert C. Pitfalls to Avoid: Am I Doing This Right? rev. ed. 80p. (Orig.). 1982. pap. 6.95 (ISBN 0-9610018-0-1); guide & newsletters, binder format 13.95 (ISBN 0-9610018-1-X). Financial Aid.

STUDENT GUIDANCE

see Personnel Service in Education; Vocational Guidance

STUDENT JOURNALISM

see College and School Journalism

STUDENT LIFE AND CUSTOMS

see Students

STUDENT SELF-GOVERNMENT

see Self-Government (In Education)

STUDENT-TEACHER RELATIONSHIPS

see Teacher-Student Relationships

STUDENT TEACHING

Johnson. A Brief History of Student Teaching. 1968. 9.95 (ISBN 0-686-38069-X). Assn Tchr Ed.

Kuehl. A Taxonomy of Critical Tasks for Evaluating Student Teaching. 1979. 2.50 (ISBN 0-686-38070-3). Assn Tchr Ed.

Wentz, Pat J. & Yarling, James R., eds. Student Teaching Survival Kit. (Illus.). 209p. (Orig.). 1982. pap. text ed. 8.50 incl. wkbk. (ISBN 0-686-37630-7). Gulf Coast Ed.

STUDENT TRANSPORTATION

see School Children–Transportation

STUDENTS

see also College Students; Medical Students; Pregnant Schoolgirls; School Sports

also headings beginning with College or School, e.g. College, Choice of; School Sports; Transfer Students

Boyan, Douglas R., ed. Profiles: The Foreign Student in the United States, 1983. rev. ed. 140p. 1983. pap. text ed. 22.95 (ISBN 0-87206-118-3). Inst Intl Educ.

Brooks, Douglas M. & Van Cleaf, David W. Pupil Evaluation in the Classroom: An All Level Guide to Practice. LC 82-13650. (Illus.). 170p. 1983. lib. bdg. 22.00 (ISBN 0-8191-2736-1); pap. text ed. 10.00 (ISBN 0-8191-2737-X). U Pr of Amer.

Cohen, Gail A., ed. The Learning Traveler: Vol. 1-U.S. College-Sponsored Programs Abroad: Academic Year. rev. ed. Orig. Title: Summer Study Abroad. 192p. 1983. pap. text ed. 9.95 (ISBN 0-87206-119-1). Inst Intl Educ.

--The Learning Traveler: Vol. 2-Vacation Study Abroad. rev. ed. LC 80-647000933. Orig. Title: Summer Study Abroad. 185p. 1983. pap. text ed. 9.95 (ISBN 0-87206-120-5). Inst Intl Educ.

Connotillo, Barbara C., ed. Summer Learning Options U. S. A. 100p. (Orig.). pap. text ed. 8.95 (ISBN 0-87206-122-1). Inst Intl Educ.

Ganong, Joan M. & Ganong, Warren L. Help with Student Clinical Performance Evaluation. (Help Series of Management Guides). 90p. 1977. pap. 9.95 (ISBN 0-933036-14-0). Ganong W L Co.

Golay, Keith J. Learning Patterns & Temperament Styles: A Systematic Guide to Maximizing Student Achievement. LC 82-62144. 109p. (Orig.). 1982. pap. text ed. 8.95 (ISBN 0-686-38240-4). Manas Sys.

Johnson, Nancy. How to Insure Your Child's Success in School. Taylor, Judy, ed. LC 82-62372. (Illus.). 200p. 1983. pap. 15.00 (ISBN 0-911625-00-3). M Murach & Assoc.

Paris, Scott G., et al, eds. Learning & Motivation in the Classroom. 352p. 1983. text ed. price not set (ISBN 0-89859-273-9). L Erlbaum Assocs.

STUDENTS–GRADING AND MARKING

see Grading and Marking (Students)

STUDENTS–PERSONNEL WORK

see Personnel Service in Education

STUDENTS–GREAT BRITAIN

Mervyn, P. Memoirs of a Mis-spent Youth. 1982. 38.00x (ISBN 0-686-99795-6, Pub. by Sycamore Pr England). State Mutual Bk.

STUDENTS–INDIA

Patnaik, S. K. Student Politics & Voting Behaviour. 250p. 1982. text ed. 15.75x (ISBN 0-391-02757-3, Pub. by Concept India). Humanities.

STUDY, COURSES OF

see Education–Curricula

STUDY, METHOD OF

see also College Student Orientation; Note-Taking; Self-Culture

also subdivision Study and Teaching under particular subjects, e.g. Art–Study and Teaching

Anderson, Fred A. Scoring High on Medical & Health Sciences Exams. 24p. (Orig.). 1983. pap. 1.75 (ISBN 0-939570-02-5). Skills Improvement.

Annis, Linda F. Study Techniques. 150p. 1983. pap. text ed. write for info. (ISBN 0-697-06069-1). Wm C Brown.

Buzan, Tony. Use Both Sides of Your Brain. rev. ed. (Illus.). 160p. 1983. pap. 7.25 (ISBN 0-525-48011-0, 0704-210). Dutton.

Flowers, James L., et al. A Complete Preparation for the New MCAT: Knowledge & Comprehension of Science & Skills Development in Reading & Quantitative. Set. pap. 27.00 (ISBN 0-941406-03-2). Betz Pub Co Inc.

Freeman, Richard. How to Study Effectively. 94p. 1978. 15.00x (ISBN 0-686-81992-6, Pub. by Macdonald & Evans). State Mutual Bk.

Gilbart, Helen & Howland, Joseph. Getting Ready for the College Level Academic Skills Test. Hackworth, Robert, ed. (Illus.). 160p. 1982. pap. text ed. 10.95 (ISBN 0-943202-06-X). H & H Pub.

Hinton, Norman I. Essay Exam Preparation Guide. (Cliffs Test Presparation Ser.). 71p. (Orig.). 1981. pap. 2.95 (ISBN 0-8220-1471-8). Cliffs.

HM Study Skills Group. HM College Study Skills Level III Student Text. 1982. pap. text ed. 4.25 (ISBN 0-88210-138-2); tchr's. guide 3.50 (ISBN 0-88210-139-0); workshop kit 12.50 (ISBN 0-88210-140-4). Natl Assn Principals.

Kahn, Norma. More Learning in Less Time: A Guide to Effective Study. 2nd, rev. ed. 96p. (gr. 9-12). 1983. pap. text ed. 4.25x (ISBN 0-86709-037-5). Boynton Cook Pubs.

Leo, Miriam & Forlini, Gary. The S.A.T. Home Study Kit. Gruber, Michael, ed. (Home Study Ser.). 1982. 69.50 (ISBN 0-686-82415-6); workbook-audio-tape kit avail. (ISBN 0-910859-01-9). Pinebrook Pr.

McMasters, Dale. Basic Skills How to Study Workbook. (Basic Skills Workbooks). 32p. (gr. 5-9). 1983. 0.99 (ISBN 0-8209-0534-8, HSW-1). ESP.

--How to Study. (Language Arts). 24p. (gr. 5-9). 1979. wkbk. 5.00 (ISBN 0-8209-0306-X, HS-1). ESP.

Schimmels, Cliff. How to Survive & Thrive in College. 160p. 1983. pap. 5.95 (ISBN 0-8007-5104-3, Power Bks). Revell.
Shepherd. College Study Skills. 1983. pap. text ed. 10.95 (ISBN 0-686-84577-3, RD02); instr's. manual avail. (RD03). HM.
Szekely, Edmond B. The Art of Study: The Sorbonne Method. (Illus.). 40p. 1973. pap. 3.50 (ISBN 0-89564-065-1). IBS Intl.

STUNTS
see Skits, Stunts, etc.

STUPIDITY
see Inefficiency, Intellectual

STUTTERING
Dominick, Barbara A. A Practical, Self-Help Guide for Stutterers. 64p. 1983. 8.75x (ISBN 0-398-04794-4). C C Thomas.
Glauber, I. Peter. Stuttering: A Psychoanalytic Understanding. Glauber, Helen M., ed. LC 82-8125. 208p. 1983. 24.95 (ISBN 0-89885-154-8). Human Sci Pr.
Gruss, Jane F. Counseling Stutterers. (Publications on Stuttering: No. 18). 80p. 1982. pap. 1.00 (ISBN 0-933388-18-7). Speech Found Am.
Mon Enfant Begaie-t-il? Un Guide pour les Parents. (Publications on Stuttering: No. 17). 44p. (Fr.). pap. 1.00 (ISBN 0-686-84501-3). Speech Found Am.
Si Su Hijo Tartamudea: Una Guia para los Padres. (Publications on Stuttering: No. 15). 48p. (Span.). pap. 1.00 (ISBN 0-686-84500-5). Speech Found Am.
Stuttering Words. (Publications on Stuttering: No. 2). 48p. pap. 0.50 (ISBN 0-686-84499-8). Speech Found Am.

STYLE (PRACTICAL PRINTING)
see Printing–Style Manuals

STYLE, LEGAL
see Law–Language

STYLE IN DRESS
see Costume; Fashion

STYLE MANUALS (AUTHORSHIP)
see Authorship–Handbooks, Manuals, Etc.

STYLE MANUALS (JOURNALISM)
see Journalism–Handbooks, Manuals, Etc.

STYLE MANUALS (PRINTING)
see Printing–Style Manuals

STYRON, WILLIAM, 1925-
Casclato, Arthur D. & West, James L., III, eds. Critical Essays on William Styron. (Critical Essays On American Literature Ser.). 1982. lib. bdg. 32.50 (ISBN 0-8161-8261-2). G K Hall.

SUAHELI LANGUAGE
see Swahili Language

SUARES, ANDRE, 1866-1948
Braun, Sidney D. Andre Suares: Hero among Heroes. 11.00 (ISBN 0-686-38460-1). French Lit.

SUAREZ, FRANCISCO, 1548-1617
Wells, Norman J., tr. Francis Suarez: On the Essence of Finite Being as Such, on the Existence of the Essence & Their Distinction. LC 82-81397. (Mediaeval Philosophical Texts in Translation). 312p. Date not set. pap. 24.95 (ISBN 0-87462-224-7). Marquette.

SUBCONSCIOUSNESS
see also Consciousness; Dreams; Faith-Cure; Hypnotism; Mental Healing; Mental Suggestion; Mind and Body; Personality, Disorders Of; Psychoanalysis; Sleep
Whyte, L. L. The Unconscious Before Freud. Koestler, Arthur, ed. (Classics in Psychology & Psychiatry Ser.). 256p. 1983. Repr. write for info. (ISBN 0-904014-41-X). F Pinter Pubs.

SUBHARMONIC FUNCTIONS
see Harmonic Functions

SUBJECT CATALOGS
see Catalogs, Subject

SUBJECT DICTIONARIES
see Encyclopedias and Dictionaries

SUBJECT HEADINGS
see also Catalogs, Subject; Classification–Books
Weiss, Jacqueline S. Prizewinning Books for Children: Themes & Stereotypes in U.S. Prizewinning Prose Fiction for Children. LC 82-48624. (Libraries & Librarianship Special Ser.). 1983. write for info. (ISBN 0-669-06352-5). Lexington Bks.

SUBMANDIBULAR GLAND
see Salivary Glands

SUBMARINE ARCHAEOLOGY
see Underwater Archaeology

SUBMARINE EXPLORATION
see Underwater Exploration

SUBMARINE GEOLOGY
see also Continental Drift; Marine Sediments; Ocean Bottom; Sedimentation and Deposition
Palmer, H. D. & Gross, M. G., eds. Ocean Dumping & Marine Pollution: Geological Aspects of Waste Disposal at Sea. LC 78-10436. 268p. 1979. 31.50 (ISBN 0-87933-343-X). Hutchinson Ross.
Suendermann, J. & Lenz, W., eds. North Sea Dynamics. (Illus.). 670p. 1983. 41.00 (ISBN 0-387-12013-0). Springer-Verlag.

SUBMARINE PHOTOGRAPHY
see Photography, Submarine

SUBMARINES
see also Sonar
Preston, Anthony. Submarines. (Illus.). 220p. 1982. 24.95 (ISBN 0-312-77475-3). St Martin.

SUBMAXILLARY GLAND
see Salivary Glands

SUBSCRIPTION BOOKS
see Bibliography–Subscription Books

SUBSIDIES
see also Federal Aid to the Arts; Research Grants
Benedict, Stephen. Cultural Institutions Across America: Functions & Funding. 28p. 1982. pap. 3.00 (ISBN 0-943006-15-5). Seven Springs.
Grants for Arts & Cultural Programs. (COMSEARCH: Broad Topics Ser.). 202p. (Orig.). 1982. pap. 28.00 (ISBN 0-87954-063-X). Foundation Ctr.
Grants for Business & Employment Programs. (COMSEARCH: Broad Topics Ser.). 84p. (Orig.). 1982. pap. 28.00 (ISBN 0-87954-064-8). Foundation Ctr.
Grants for Children & Youth. (COMSEARCH: Broad Topics Ser.). 215p. (Orig.). 1982. pap. 28.00 (ISBN 0-87954-065-6). Foundation Ctr.
Grants for Higher Education. (COMSEARCH: Broad Topics Ser.). 344p. (Orig.). 1982. pap. 28.00 (ISBN 0-87954-066-4). Foundation Ctr.
Grants for Hospitals & Medical Care Programs. (COMSEARCH: Broad Topics Ser.). 140p. (Orig.). 1982. pap. 28.00 (ISBN 0-87954-067-2). Foundation Ctr.
Grants for International & Foreign Programs. (COMSEARCH: Broad Topics Ser.). 92p. (Orig.). 1982. pap. 28.00 (ISBN 0-87954-072-9). Foundation Ctr.
Grants for Minorities. (COMSEARCH: Broad Topics Ser.). 108p. (Orig.). 1982. pap. 28.00 (ISBN 0-87954-073-7). Foundation Ctr.
Grants for Museums. (COMSEARCH: Broad Topics Ser.). 70p. (Orig.). 1982. pap. 28.00 (ISBN 0-87954-068-0). Foundation Ctr.
Grants for Science Programs. (COMSEARCH: Broad Topics Ser.). 102p. (Orig.). 1982. pap. 28.00 (ISBN 0-87954-069-9). Foundation Ctr.
Grants for Social Science Programs. (COMSEARCH: Broad Topics Ser.). 136p. (Orig.). 1982. pap. 28.00 (ISBN 0-87954-070-2). Foundation Ctr.
Grants for Women & Girls. (COMSEARCH: Broad Topics Ser.). 84p. (Orig.). 1982. pap. 28.00 (ISBN 0-87954-071-0). Foundation Ctr.
Minnesota Council on Foundations. Guide to Minnesota Foundations & Corporate Giving Programs. LC 82-21928. 136p. 1983. pap. 14.95x (ISBN 0-8166-1219-6). U of Minn Pr.
White, Virginia, ed. Grant Proposals That Succeeded. (Nonprofit Management & Finance). 230p. 1982. 22.50x (ISBN 0-306-40873-2, Plenum Pr). Plenum Pub.
Williams, Cortez. A Grantsmanship & Proposal Writing Manual. 380p. 1981. pap. 15.00 (ISBN 0-9609114-0-5). Develop Res.

SUBSISTENCE STORES
see Military Supplies

SUBSONIC AERODYNAMICS
see Aerodynamics

SUBSTITUTE TEACHERS
Pronin, Barbara. Substitute Teaching: A Handbook for Hassle-Free Subbing. (Illus.). 190p. 1983. 12.95 (ISBN 0-312-77481-8). St Martin.

SUBSTITUTES FOR FOODS
see Food Substitutes

SUBSTITUTIONS
see Groups, Theory Of

SUBSURFACE CONSTRUCTION
see Underground Construction

SUBTERRANEAN CONSTRUCTION
see Underground Construction

SUBTERRANEAN WATER
see Water, Underground

SUBTRACTION
Burkes, Joyce M. The Math Machine Book for Subtraction. LC 81-90590. (The Word Machine & Math Machine Books). (Illus.). 48p. (gr. 1-3). 1983. pap. write for info. (ISBN 0-931218-14-4). Joybug.
Mock, Valerie E. Addition & Subtraction Riddles. (Learning Workbooks Mathematics). (gr. 3-5). pap. 1.50 (ISBN 0-8224-4189-6). Pitman.
--Subtraction Drill. (Learning Workbooks Mathematics). (gr. 1-3). pap. 1.50 (ISBN 0-8224-4185-3). Pitman.

SUBURBAN LIFE
Gans, Herbert J. The Levittowners: Ways of Life & Politics in a New Suburban Community. 512p. 1982. text ed. 30.00x (ISBN 0-231-05570-6, Pub. by MOrningside); pap. 10.95x (ISBN 0-231-05571-4). Columbia U Pr.

SUBURBS
see also Suburban Life
Gutowski, Michael & Feild, Tracey. The Graying of Suburbia. (Illus.). 107p. (Orig.). 1979. pap. text ed. 5.50 (ISBN 0-87766-255-X). Urban Inst.

SUBVENTIONS
see Subsidies

SUBVERSIVE ACTIVITIES
see also Espionage; Spies; Terrorism
Crayton, Spurgeon E. Screams of Protest. (Illus.). 1982. 10.00 (ISBN 0-8315-0188-X). Speller.

SUCCESS
see also Academic Achievement; Applications for Positions; Business; Conduct of Life; Self-Realization
Atkins, Stuart. The Name of your Game: Four Game Plans for Success at Home & at Work. LC 81-71849. (Illus.). 1982. 16.95 (ISBN 0-942532-00-7); pap. 4.95. Ellis & Stuart Pub.
Barber, Cyril J. & Strauss, Gary H. Leadership: The Dynamics of Success. 126p. pap. 4.95 (ISBN 0-87921-068-0). Attic Pr.
Basile, Frank M. Flying to Your Success. (Illus.). 210p. (Orig.). 1982. pap. 15.00 (ISBN 0-937008-03-6). Charisma Pubns.
Beyond Authority: How to Play to Win by the New Ethics. 1983. price not set. Ashley Bks.
Bland, Glenn. Success: The Glenn Bland Method. 1983. pap. 2.95 (ISBN 0-8423-6689-X). Tyndale.
Cannon, Chapman R. & Cannon, Donnie. How We Made Millions & Never Left the Ghetto. 1983. 6.95 (ISBN 0-8062-1956-4). Carlton.
Capossela, Jim. Fifty Secrets of Success: A Common Sense Approach. 24p. 1982. pap. 1.95 (ISBN 0-942990-03-X). Northeast Sportsmans.
Carnegie, Dale. How to Help Your Husband Get Ahead. 192p. 1982. pap. 2.75 (ISBN 0-515-06895-0). Jove Pubns.
Corder, George E. Your Brain-Image Power: How to Selfsex & Imagize Your Way to Super-Successful Living. LC 82-90505. 200p. 1983. lib. bdg. 25.00 (ISBN 0-9609246-0-4). Brain-Image.
David, Bruce E. How to Get Everything you Want from Life: The Secret of Power. 62p. (Orig.). 1982. pap. write for info. (ISBN 0-9609734-0-0). Worth Print.
Dean, Dave & Hefley, Marti. Now Is Your Time to Win. 1983. 6.95 (ISBN 0-8423-4724-0). Tyndale.
Doyle, Alfreda. I Can, I Shall, I Will. 50p. 1983. pap. text ed. 8.95 (ISBN 0-939476-54-1). Biblio Pr GA.
Drake, Don A. You Deserve to be Rich. 110p. (Orig.). 1982. pap. text ed. 9.95 (ISBN 0-89532-009-6); visualization guide 7.00 (ISBN 0-89532-010-X). United Seabears.
Ferrari, Guy. How to Profit from Future Technology: A Guide to Success in the Eighties & Beyond. Adams, Mary, ed. LC 82-73571. 300p. 1983. pap. 14.95 (ISBN 0-686-37897-0). Windsor Hse.
Forte, Imogene. The Me I'm Learning to Be. (Illus.). 80p. (gr. 4-6). 1983. pap. text ed. 5.95 (ISBN 0-86530-061-5). Incentive Pubns.
Gunn, Harry & Gunn, Violet C. The Test for Success Book. 100p. pap. 7.95 (ISBN 0-914091-22-0). Chicago Review.
Hadfield, Debra. ABC'S of Grade Success. 3.95 (ISBN 0-686-84353-3). Olympus Pub Co.
Hagin, Keeneth, Jr. How to be a Success in Life. 1982. pap. 0.50 (ISBN 0-89276-713-8). Hagin Ministry.
Hauser, Leopold, III. Five Steps to Success. (Orig.). 1983. pap. 3.75x (ISBN 0-935538-04-6). Pathway Bks.
Hilliard, Joseph. How to Unlock the Secrets of Winning & Good Luck. (Orig.). 1982. pap. 5.95x (ISBN 0-934650-02-0). Sunnyside.
Johnson, Joe D. The Granite, the Possible, & the Bending Fern. 38p. 1982. pap. 3.00 (ISBN 0-915564-01-7). Joe D Johnson.
Kassorla, Irene. Winner Take All. 330p. Date not set. 14.95 (ISBN 0-686-37555-6). Delacorte.
Kishel, Gregory F. & Kishel, Paricia G. Your Business is a Success: Now What? (Small Business Ser.). 224p. 1983. pap. text ed. 8.95. Wiley.
Koberg, Don & Bagnall, Jim. Values Tech: A Portable School for Self-Assessment & Self-Enhancement. 2nd ed. (Illus.). 243p. 1982. pap. 8.95 (ISBN 0-86576-016-0). W Kaufmann.
Kriyananda, Swami. The Art of Creative Leadership. 16p. 1980. pap. 2.95 (ISBN 0-916124-20-7). Ananda.
Lang, Doe. The Secret of Charisma. 1982. 7.50 (ISBN 0-87223-790-7). Wideview Bks.
Losoncy, Lewis. Think Your Way to Success. Date not set. pap. 5.00 (ISBN 0-87980-396-7). Wilshire.
Marlow, David. Winning is Everything. 352p. 1983. 15.95 (ISBN 0-399-12801-8). Putnam Pub Group.
May, Rollo. Freedom & Destiny. 1983. pap. 7.95 (ISBN 0-440-53012-1, Delta). Dell.
Minshull, Ruth. Efficiency. 35p. 1976. pap. write for info. (ISBN 0-937922-03-X). SAA Pub.
Navarette, Vincent H. The Two Most Miraculous Words in the English Language & How to Use Them Successfully. (A Human Development Library Bk.). (Illus.). 103p. 1983. 27.45 (ISBN 0-89266-395-2). Am Classical Coll Pr.
Newcomb, Duane. Fortune-Building Secrets of the Rich. LC 82-18837. 215p. 1983. 14.95 (ISBN 0-13-384685-7, Parker); pap. 4.95 (ISBN 0-13-329102-2). P-H.
Oshry, Barry. Success of a Business-Failure of Its Partners. (Notes on Power Ser.). (Orig.). 1980. pap. 3.50 (ISBN 0-910411-07-7). Power & Sys.
Reader's Digest Editors, selected by. They Beat the Odds. 256p. 1983. pap. 2.75 (ISBN 0-425-05994-4). Berkley Pub.
Roll, Richard J. & Young, G. Douglas. Getting Yours. 1983. pap. 6.95 (ISBN 0-440-53005-9, Delta). Dell.
Sanders, Katherine C. Life Time System for Personal Effectiveness. 300p. 1983. 30.00 (ISBN 0-939344-02-5). Eupsychian.
Scott, Herschel L., Jr. Passport to Prosperity. 60p. 1983. pap. 3.95 (ISBN 0-88083-005-0). Poverty Hill Pr.
Sher, Barbara. Wishcraft: How to Get What You Really Want. 1983. pap. price not set (ISBN 0-449-90083-5, Columbine). Fawcett.
Shinn, George. The Miracle of Motivation. 246p. 1983. 9.95 (ISBN 0-8423-4353-9); pap. 6.95 (ISBN 0-8423-4354-7). Tyndale.
Snyder, Julian. The Way of the Hunter Warrior: How to Make a Killing in Any Market. LC 82-61459. 190p. 1982. 12.95 (ISBN 0-943940-00-1). Dutton.
Stallings, James O. & Powell, Marcia. The Look of Success. LC 82-71744. (Illus.). 224p. 1982. 14.95 (ISBN 0-8119-0456-3). Fell.
Stubblefield, Al. How to Buy Without Cash & Grow Rich. Writer's Service, Inc., ed. 131p. (Orig.). 1982. pap. 14.95 (ISBN 0-911229-00-0). Writers Serv FL.
Vanderlaan, Roger F. Persuasion. LC 81-71065. 185p. (Orig.). Date not set. pap. 11.95 (ISBN 0-942060-00-8). El Camino.
Walton, Lew & Douglass, Herb. How to Survive the Eighties. 108p. 1982. pap. text ed. 1.25 (ISBN 0-8163-0491-2). Pacific Pr Pub Assn.
Wilder, Lilyan. The Lilyan Wilder Speak for Success Program. 288p. 1983. 13.95 (ISBN 0-02-628530-4). Macmillan.
Williams & Long. Toward A Self-Managed Life Style. 3rd ed. 1982. 12.95 (ISBN 0-686-84653-2); supplementary materials avail. Hm.
Williams, Pat & Jenkins, Jerry. The Power Within You. LC 82-24825. 196p. 1983. price not set (ISBN 0-664-27008-5, Bridgebooks Publciations). Westminster.
Winkler, John. Bargaining for Results. 1981. pap. 22.50 (ISBN 0-434-92350-8, Pub. by Heinemann). David & Charles.
Young, Fred J. How to Get Rich & Stay Rich. rev. ed. LC 82-83771. 175p. 1983. 12.95 (ISBN 0-8119-0491-1). Fell.

SUCCESSION TAXES
see Inheritance and Transfer Tax

SUCCULENT PLANTS
see also Cactus
Rowley, Gordon D. Name That Succulent. 288p. 1980. 49.00x (ISBN 0-85950-447-6, Pub. by Thornes England). State Mutual Bk.

SUDDEN DEATH IN INFANTS
Destevens, George, ed. Myocardial Infarction & Cardiac Death. LC 82-11547. Date not set. price not set (ISBN 0-12-212160-0). Acad Pr.
Ilse, Sherokee. Empty Arms: A Guide to Help Parents & Loved Ones Cope with a Miscarriage, Stillbirth or Natural Death. Appelbaum, Arlene, ed. 64p. 1982. pap. 3.95 (ISBN 0-9609456-0-1). Sherokee.

SUFFERING
see also Good and Evil; Joy and Sorrow; Loneliness; Pain
Constable, Giles. Attitudes Toward Self-Inflicted Suffering in the Middle Ages. (Stephen J. Brademas Lectures Ser.). 28p. (Orig.). Date not set. pap. text ed. 2.50 (ISBN 0-916586-87-1). Hellenic Coll Pr.

SUFFRAGE
see also Representative Government and Representation; Voters, Registration Of; Voting; Women–Suffrage
Berghe, Guido V. Political Rights for European Citizens. 245p. (Orig.). 1982. text ed. 38.00 (ISBN 0-566-00524-7). Gower Pub Ltd.

SUFISM
Beek, Wil van. Hazrat Inayat Khan: Master of Life-Modern Sufi Mystic. 1983. 12.95 (ISBN 0-533-05453-2). Vantage.
Muhaiyaddeen, Bawa M. Golden Words of a Sufi Sheikh. Aschenbach, Sarah, ed. 472p. 1983. 20.00 (ISBN 0-914390-24-4). Fellowship Pr PA.

SUGAR
Business Communications Staff. Sugar, Sweeteners & Substitutes. 1982. 1250.00 (ISBN 0-89336-091-0, C-005). BCC.
Food, Social Cosmology & Mental Health: The Case of Sugar. 52p. 1982. pap. 5.00 (ISBN 92-808-0324-7, TUNU 195, UNU). Unipub.

SUGAR–MANUFACTURE AND REFINING
Payne, J. H. Unit Operations in Cane Sugar Production. (Sugar Ser.: No. 4). 204p. 1982. 51.00 (ISBN 0-444-42104-1). Elsevier.
Plews, R. W. Analytical Methods Used in Sugar Refining. 1969. 43.00 (ISBN 0-444-20046-0, Pub. by Applied Sci England). Elsevier.
The U. S. Sweetener Industry. 1981. 475.00 (ISBN 0-686-38423-7, 140). Busn Trend.

SUGAR-FREE DIET
see also Cookery for Diabetics
Majors, Judith S. Sugar Free...Sweets & Treats. LC 82-73049. 1982. pap. 4.95 (ISBN 0-9602238-6-X). Apple Pr.
Williams, Jacqueline B. & Silverman, Goldie. No Salt No Sugar No Fat Cookbook. LC 81-83793. (Illus.). 150p. (Orig.). 1982. pap. 5.95 (ISBN 0-911954-65-1). Nitty Gritty.

SUGAR IN THE BODY
see also Sugar-Free Diet
Brekhman, I. I. & Nesterenko, I. F. Brown Sugar & Health. (Illus.). 104p. 1982. 20.00 (ISBN 0-08-026837-4). Pergamon.
Zack, Jinny. Sugar Isn't Always Sweet. Tanner, Don, ed. (Illus.). 204p. (Orig.). 1983. pap. 5.95 (ISBN 0-88005-002-0). Uplift Bks.

SUGAR-REFINING
see Sugar–Manufacture and Refining

SUGAR SUBSTITUTES
Business Communications Staff. Sugar, Sweeteners & Substitutes. 1982. 1250.00 (ISBN 0-89336-091-0, C-005). BCC.
SUGARS
Cobb, Vicki. Gobs of Goo. LC 82-48457. (Illus.). 40p. (gr. 1-3). 1983. 9.57i (ISBN 0-397-32021-3, JBL-J); PLB 9.89g (ISBN 0-397-32022-1). Har-Row.
SUGGESTION, MENTAL
see Mental Suggestion
SUICIDE
Cottle, Thomas J. Golden Girl: The Story of an Adolescent Suicide. 304p. 14.95 (ISBN 0-399-12639-2). Putnam Pub Group.
Getz, William L. & Allen, David B. Brief Counseling with Suicidal Persons. LC 80-8375. 288p. 1982. 23.95x (ISBN 0-669-04090-8). Lexington Bks.
Hare, Cyril. Suicide Expected. LC 82-48244. 256p. 1983. pap. 2.84i (ISBN 0-06-080636-2, P 636, PL). Har-Row.
Hawton, Keith & Catalan, Jose. Attempted Suicide: A Practical Guide to its Nature & Management. (Illus.). 150p. 1982. 14.95 (ISBN 0-19-261289-1). Oxford U Pr.
Heilling, Roma J. Adolescent Suicidal Behavior: A Family Systems Model. Nathan, Peter E., ed. (Research in Clinical Psychology Ser.: No. 7). 1983. 39.95 (ISBN 0-8357-1390-3). Univ Microfilms.
Husain, Syed Arshad & Vandiver, Trish. Suicide in Children & Adolescents. 192p. 1983. text ed. 20.00 (ISBN 0-89335-190-3). SP Med & Sci Bks.
Lester, David. Why People Kill Themselves: A 1980's Summary of Research Findings on Suicidal Behavior. 110p. 1983. text ed. price not set (ISBN 0-398-04826-6). C C Thomas.
Mack, John & Hickler, Holly. Vivienne. 1982. pap. 2.95 (ISBN 0-451-62135-2, ME2135, Ment). NAL.
Soubrier, J. P. & Vedrinne, J., eds. Depression & Suicide: Medical, Psychological & Socio-Cultural Aspects, Proceedings of the XI Congress of the International Association for Suicide Prevention, Paris, July 5-9, 1981. (Illus.). 912p. 1983. 100.00 (ISBN 0-08-027080-8); pap. 60.00 (ISBN 0-08-027081-6). Pergamon.
Taylor, Steve. Durkeheim & the Study of Suicide. (Contemporary Social Theory Ser.). 240p. 1982. 35.00x (ISBN 0-333-28645-6, Pub. by Macmillan England). State Mutual Bk.
--Durkheim & the Study of Suicide. LC 82-6001. 240p. 1982. 22.50x (ISBN 0-312-22266-1). St Martin.
SUICIDE AIRPLANES
see Kamikaze Airplanes
SUITS (LAW)
see Actions and Defenses
SULLIVAN, ARTHUR SEYMOUR, SIR, 1842-1900
Goodman, Andrew. Gilbert & Sullivan at Law. LC 82-12175. (Illus.). 264p. 1982. 25.00 (ISBN 0-8386-3179-7). Fairleigh Dickinson.
SULLIVAN, LOUIS HENRY, 1856-1924
Chapman, Linda L., et al. Louis H. Sullivan Architectural Ornament Collection: Southern Illinois University at Edwardsville. LC 81-51083. (Illus.). 79p. (Orig.). 1981. pap. 10.00 (ISBN 0-89062-136-5, Pub by Southern Illinois Univ Edwardsville). Pub Ctr Cult Res.
SULPHUR
see also Organosulphur Compounds
Raymont, Michael E., ed. Sulfur Recovery & Utilization. (ACS Symposium Ser.: No.183). 1982. write for info. (ISBN 0-8412-0713-5). Am Chemical.
SULPHUR BONDING
Ivanov, M. V. & Freney, J. R. The Global Biogeochemical Sulphur Cycle Scope 19. (Scientific Committee on Problems of the Environment Ser.). 350p. 1983. price not set (ISBN 0-471-10492-2, Pub. by Wiley-Interscience). Wiley.
SULPHUR ORGANIC COMPOUNDS
see Organosulphur Compounds
SULTANS
see Kings and Rulers
SUMMER CAMPS
see Camps
SUMNER, WILLIAM GRAHAM, 1840-1910
Sumner, William G. Sumner Today. Davie, Maurice, ed. 1940. text ed. 39.50x (ISBN 0-686-83794-0). Elliots Bks.
--What Social Classes Owe to Each Other. 1925. text ed. 11.00x (ISBN 0-686-83855-6). Elliots Bks.
SUN
see also Solar Radiation; Solar System; Spectrum Analysis
also names of solar instruments
Asimov, Isaac. The Sun Shines Bright. 256p. 1983. pap. 2.95 (ISBN 0-380-61390-5, 61390-5, Discus). Avon.
Mitton, Simon. Daytime Star. (Illus.). 208p. 1983. pap. 6.95 (ISBN 0-686-83737-1, ScribT). Scribner.
SUN–JUVENILE LITERATURE
Adams, Richard. Our Amazing Sun. LC 82-17419. (Question & Answer Bks.). (Illus.). 32p. (gr. 3-6). 1983. PLB 8.59 (ISBN 0-89375-890-6); pap. text ed. 1.95 (ISBN 0-89375-891-4). Troll Assocs.
SUN-HEATED HOUSES
see Solar Houses
SUN-POWERED BATTERIES
see Solar Batteries

SUNDAY-SCHOOLS
see also Bible-Study; Religious Education
General Conference Sabbath School Department. Sabbath School Manual. rev. ed. 1982. pap. 3.95 (ISBN 0-686-82635-3). Review & Herald.
Knoff, Gerald E. The World Sunday School Movement: The Story of a Broadening Mission. 304p. 1979. 8.00 (ISBN 0-8164-0416-X). Seabury.
SUNDAY-SCHOOLS–EXERCISES, RECITATIONS, ETC.
Mead, Frank S. & Barker, William P., eds. Tarbell's Teacher's Guide 1983-1984. (Tarbell's Teacher's Guide Ser.: Vol. 79). 320p. (Orig.). 1983. pap. 6.95 (ISBN 0-8007-1347-8). Revell.
Moore, William C., ed. The Evangelical Sunday School Teacher's Guide 1983-1984. 448p. (Orig.). 1983. pap. 6.95 (ISBN 0-8007-1348-6). Revell.
Ulmer, Louise & Meyer, Sheila. Theatrecraft for Church & School. LC 82-62453. (Illus.). 75p. 1983. pap. text ed. write for info. (ISBN 0-916260-00-3). Meriwether Pub.
Witter, Evelyn. How to Make Sunday School Fun for Everybody. Ronaldson, Dolores, ed. (Illus.). 80p. Date not set. pap. text ed. price not set (ISBN 0-916260-22-4). Meriwether Pub.
SUNDAY-SCHOOLS–HISTORY
Sisemore, John T. Church Growth Through the Sunday School. (Orig.). 1983. pap. 5.95 (ISBN 0-8054-6237-6). Broadman.
SUNKEN CITIES
see Cities and Towns, Ruined, Extinct, etc.
SUNKEN TREASURE
see Treasure-Trove
SUPER HIGHWAYS
see Express Highways
SUPERCONDUCTIVITY
see also Superconductors
Maple, M. B. & Fischer, O., eds. Superconductivity in Ternary Compounds II: Superconductivity & Magnetism. (Topics in Current Physics: Vol. 34). (Illus.). 335p. 1982. 32.00 (ISBN 0-387-11814-4). Springer-Verlag.
SUPERCONDUCTORS
Carr, W. J., Jr. AC Loss & Macroscopic Theory of Superconductors. 1982. write for info. (ISBN 0-677-05700-8). Gordon.
Stability of Superconductors. 312p. 1981. pap. 20.50 (ISBN 0-686-84037-2, IIR72, IIR). Unipub.
SUPERINTENDENTS OF BUILDINGS AND GROUNDS
see Janitors
SUPERINTENDENTS OF SCHOOLS
see School Superintendents and Principals
SUPERIOR CHILDREN
see Gifted Children
SUPERMARINE SPITFIRE
see Spitfire (Fighter Planes)
SUPERNATURAL
see also Inspiration; Miracles; Occult Sciences; Psychical Research; Revelation; Spiritualism; Superstition
Abell, George & Singer, Barry. Science & the Paranormal. (Illus.). 432p. 1983. pap. 8.95 (ISBN 0-686-83708-8, ScribT). Scribner.
Reader's Digest Editors. Mysteries of the Unexplained. LC 82-60791. (Illus.). 320p. 1983. 21.50 (ISBN 0-89577-146-2, Pub. by RD Assn). Random.
Summers, Montague. Supernatural Omnibus. 624p. 1982. 22.50 (ISBN 0-575-03120-4, Pub. by Gollancz England). David & Charles.
SUPERNATURAL IN LITERATURE
see also Fantastic Fiction
Bleiler, Everett F. The Guide to Supernatural Fiction. 736p. 1983. 55.00X (ISBN 0-87338-288-9). Kent St U Pr.
SUPERPHOSPHATES
see Phosphates
SUPERREALISM
see Surrealism
SUPERSONIC TESTING
see Ultrasonic Testing
SUPERSONIC THERAPY
see Ultrasonic Waves–Therapeutic Use
SUPERSONICS
see Ultrasonics
SUPERSTITION
see also Alchemy; Apparitions; Astrology; Demonology; Dreams; Exorcism; Fairies; Folk-Lore; Ghosts; Magic; Medicine, Magic, Mystic, and Spagiric; Occult Sciences; Omens; Voodooism; Werewolves; Witchcraft
Nevins, Ann. Super Stitches: A Book of Superstitions. LC 82-15875. (Illus.). 64p. (gr. 1-4). 1983. reinforced binding 8.95 (ISBN 0-8234-0476-5). Holiday.
Steele, Phillip W. Ozark Tales & Superstitions. LC 82-22425. (Illus.). 100p. 1983. pap. 4.95 (ISBN 0-88289-404-8). Pelican.
SUPERTANKERS
see Tankers
SUPERVISION OF EMPLOYEES
see also Supervisors
Burley-Allen, Madelyn. Assertive Supervision. 1982. pap. 9.95 (ISBN 0-471-09750-0). Wiley.
Christenson, Christina & Johnson, Thomas W. Supervising. 336p. Date not set. price not set Instrs' Resource Manual. A-W.

Eckles, Robert W. & Carmichael, Ronald L. Supervisory Management. 2nd ed. LC 80-21684. (Management Ser.). 524p. 1981. text ed. 24.95 (ISBN 0-471-05947-1). Wiley.
--Supervisory Management: A Short Course in Supervision. 2nd ed. LC 82-17553. (Professional Development Programs Ser.). 288p. 1983. text ed. 55.95 (ISBN 0-471-87492-2). Wiley.
Eckles, Robert W., et al. Supervisory Management: A Short Course in Supervision. LC 74-31815. (Professional Development Programs). 293p. 1975. 49.95x (ISBN 0-471-23005-7). Wiley.
Goldstein, Arnold P. & Sorcher, Melvin. Changing Supervisor Behavior. 160p. softcover 7.50 (ISBN 0-686-84791-1). Work in Amer.
Kirkpatrick, David L. A Practical Guide for Supervisory Training & Development. 2nd ed. (Illus.). 224p. 1983. text ed. 24.95 (ISBN 0-201-13435-7). A-W.
Ray, Charles M. & Elson, Charles L. Supervision. 496p. 1983. text ed. 26.95 (ISBN 0-03-054556-0). Dryden Pr.
Terry, George R. & Rue, Leslie W. Supervision. Rev. ed. (Plaid Ser.). 141p. 1983. pap. 6.95 (ISBN 0-256-02718-8). Dow Jones-Irwin.
Weiss, W. H. The Supervisor's Problem Solver. 240p. 1983. 15.95 (ISBN 0-8144-5754-1). Am Mgmt.
SUPERVISION OF EMPLOYEES–PROGRAMMED INSTRUCTION
Fiedler, Fred E., et al. Improving Leadership Effectiveness: The Leader Match Concept. LC 76-20632. (Self-Teaching Guides). 229p. 1976. pap. text ed. 9.95 (ISBN 0-471-25811-3). Wiley.
SUPERVISORS
Goldstein, Arnold P. & Sorcher, Melvin. Changing Supervisor Behavior. 160p. softcover 7.50 (ISBN 0-686-84791-1). Work in Amer.
Haeger, John D., et al. Bosses. rev. ed. 1979. pap. text ed. 4.95x (ISBN 0-88273-103-3). Forum Pr IL.
SUPERVISORY NURSING
see Nursing Service Administration
SUPPLEMENTARY EMPLOYMENT
Jay, David. How to Play the Moonlighting Game. LC 82-18364. 224p. 1983. 14.95 (ISBN 0-87196-131-8). Facts on File.
SUPPLIES, MEDICAL
see Medical Supplies
SUPPLIES, MILITARY
see Military Supplies
SUPPLY AND DEMAND
see also Competition; Consumption (Economics); Exchange; Value
Dogramaci, Ali. Developments in Econometric Analyses of Productivity. (Studies in Productivity Analysis). 1982. lib. bdg. 30.00 (ISBN 0-89838-101-0). Kluwer-Nijhoff.
Evans, Michael K. The Truth About Supply-Side Economics. 230p. 1983. 17.95 (ISBN 0-465-08778-7). Basic.
Federal Reserve Bank of Atlanta & Emory University Law & Economics Center. Supply-Side Economics in the Nineteen Eighties: Conference Proceedings. LC 82-15025. (Illus.). 572p. 1982. lib. bdg. 35.00 (ISBN 0-89930-045-6, FSU/, Quorum). Greenwood.
Smith, A. D. International Industrial Productivity: A Comparison of Britian, America & Germany. LC 82-4348. (National Institute of Economic & Social Research Occasional Papers 34). (Illus.). 200p. 1982. 24.95 (ISBN 0-521-24901-5). Cambridge U Pr.
SUPPORT (DOMESTIC RELATIONS)
see also Parent and Child (Law)
Cassetty, Judith, ed. The Parental Child-Support Obligation: Research, Practice, & Social Policy. LC 81-48464. 320p. 1982. 28.95x (ISBN 0-669-05376-7). Lexington Bks.
SURF
see Ocean Waves
SURF FISHING
see Salt-Water Fishing
SURF RIDING
see Surfing
SURFACE ACTIVE AGENTS
see also Detergents, Synthetic
Daytner. Surfactants in Textile Processing. (Surfactant Science Ser.). 208p. 1983. price not set (ISBN 0-8247-1812-7). Dekker.
Hollis, G. L., compiled by. Surfactants Europa, Vol. 1. 1982. pap. 100.00x (ISBN 0-7114-5736-0, Pub. by Macdonald & Evans). State Mutual Bk.
The Infrared Spectra Handbook of Surfactants. 1982. 275.00 (ISBN 0-8456-0086-9). Sadtler Res.
Lissant. Demulsification. (Surfactant Science Ser.). 176p. 1983. 37.50 (ISBN 0-8247-1802-X). Dekker.
SURFACE CHEMISTRY
see also Adsorption; Capillarity; Catalysis; Colloids
Carraher, Charles E., Jr. & Preston, Jack, eds. Interfacial Synthesis: Vol. III: Recent Advances. (Illus.). 408p. 1982. 65.00 (ISBN 0-686-82218-8). Dekker.
CES Industries, Inc. Staff. Interfaces: E-L 80, Unit 2. (Ed-Lab Experiment Manual Ser.). (Illus.). (gr. 9-12). 1982. write for info. lab manual (ISBN 0-86711-057-0). CES Industries.
--Projects & Interfacing. (Ed-Lab Experiment Manual Ser.). (Illus.). (gr. 9-12). 1982. lab manual 9.50 (ISBN 0-86711-025-2). CES Industries.
SURFACE MINING
see Strip Mining

SURFACES
see also Geometry, Algebraic
Ducan, J. P. & Mair, S. E. Sculptured Surfaces in Engineering & Medicine. LC 82-1116. (Illus.). 400p. Date not set. price not set (ISBN 0-521-23450-6). Cambridge U Pr.
Feuerbacher, B., et al. Photoemission & the Electronic Properties of Surfaces. 540p. 1978. 86.00x (ISBN 0-471-99555-X). Wiley.
SURFACES (CHEMISTRY)
see Surface Chemistry
SURFACES, ALGEBRAIC
Beauville, A. Complex Algebraic Surfaces. LC 82-9490. (London Mathematical Society Lecture Note Ser.: No. 68). 150p. Date not set. pap. price not set (ISBN 0-521-28815-0). Cambridge U Pr.
SURFACES, RIEMANN
see Riemann Surfaces
SURFACTANTS
see Surface Active Agents
SURFBOARD RIDING
see Surfing
SURFING
Gutjahr, Rainer. Sailboard Racing. (Illus.). 119p. 1982. 14.95 (ISBN 0-914814-38-9). Sail Bks.
Shaw, Stephen M. & Brown, Aileen, eds. Surfboard: How to Build Surfboard & Sailboards, How to Surf. (Illus.). 1983. 10.00 (ISBN 0-912750-04-9). Transmedia.
SURGEONS–FEES
see Medical Fees
SURGERY
see also Anatomy, Surgical and Topographical; Artificial Organs; Blood-Transfusion; Dissection; Fractures; Hypnotism-Therapeutic Use; Obstetrics-Surgery; Orthopedia; Orthopedic Surgery; Pathology, Surgical; Shock; Transplantation of Organs, Tissues, etc.; Veterinary Surgery; Wounds
also subdivisions Surgery and Wounds and Injuries under names of organs and regions of the body, e.g. Abdomen-Surgery; Chest-Wounds and Injuries
Cushieri, A. & Moossa, A. R. Essential Surgical Practice. (Illus.). 1152p. 1982. text ed. 65.00 (ISBN 0-7236-0622-6). Wright-PSG.
Dijkstra, W. & Van Der Zouwen, J., eds. Response Behaviour in the Survey Interview. 1982. 26.50. Acad Pr.
Hadfield, John & Hobsley, Michael, eds. Current Surgical Practice, Vol. 3. (Current Surgical Practice Ser.). 320p. 1981. pap. text ed. 34.50 (ISBN 0-7131-4397-5). E Arnold.
International College of Surgeons, Biennial World Congress. Abstracts: Twentieth Congress, Athens, 1976. Louros, N., ed. (International Congress Ser.: No. 389). 1976. pap. 31.25 (ISBN 0-444-15226-1). Elsevier.
Kootstra, G. & Jorning, P. J. Access Surgery. 350p. 1982. text ed. 60.00 (ISBN 0-85200-453-2, Pub. by MTP Pr England). Kluwer Boston.
Nash, D. F. & Gilling, Cynthia M. Principles & Practice of Surgery for Nurses & Allied Professions. 80p. pap. text ed. 39.50 (ISBN 0-7131-4366-5). E Arnold.
Schwartz, S. I. Principles of Surgery: PreTest Self-Assessment & Review. 2nd ed. 267p. 1983, 32.95 (ISBN 0-07-051927-7). McGraw-Pretest.
Schwartz, Seymour I., et al, eds. Year Book of Surgery 1983. (Illus.). 1983. 40.00 (ISBN 0-8151-7692-9). Year Bk Med.
Taylor, Selwyn & Cotton, Leonard. A Short Textbook of Surgery. 5th ed. LC 82-73297. (Illus.). 631p. 1983. pap. text ed. 16.50x (ISBN 0-668-05740-8, 5740). Arco.
Wind, Gary & Rich, Norman. Principles of Surgical Technique: The Art of Surgery. LC 82-17451. (Illus.). 240p. 1982. pap. text ed. 29.50 (ISBN 0-8067-2160-X). Urban & S.
SURGERY–COMPLICATIONS AND SEQUELAE
Bergqvist, D. Postoperative Thromboembolism: Frequency, Etiology, Prophylaxis. (Illus.). 248p. 1983. 38.50 (ISBN 0-387-12062-9). Springer-Verlag.
SURGERY–FEES
see Medical Fees
SURGERY, COSMETIC
see Surgery, Plastic
SURGERY, DENTAL
see Dentistry; Dentistry, Operative; Mouth-Surgery
SURGERY, EXPERIMENTAL
see also Transplantation of Organs, Tissues, etc.
Dixon. Surgical Application of Lasers. (Illus.). 1983. 39.50 (ISBN 0-8151-2514-3). Year Bk Med.
SURGERY, MINOR
see also Bandages and Bandaging; Surgery, Plastic
Kassity, K. J., ed. Manual of Ambulatory Surgery. (Comprehensive Manuals of Surgical Specialties Ser.). (Illus.). 266p. 1982. 125.00 (ISBN 0-387-90700-9). Springer-Verlag.
SURGERY, OPERATIVE
McDermott, William V., Jr., ed. Atlas of Standard Surgical Procedures. LC 82-12714. (Illus.). 250p. 1983. text ed. write for info. (ISBN 0-8121-0842-6). Lea & Febiger.
Zollinger & Zollinger. Atlas of Surgical Operations. 1983. 78.00 (ISBN 0-02-431970-8). Macmillan.
SURGERY, ORAL
see Mouth-Surgery
SURGERY, PLASTIC
see also Prosthesis

Barrett, Bernard M., ed. Manual of Patient Care in Plastic Surgery. (Spiral Manual Ser.). 1982. spiralbound 18.95 (ISBN 0-316-08217-1). Little.

Beyer-Machule, Charles. Plastic & Reconstructive Surgery of the Eyelids. (Illus.). 128p. 1983. 21.00 (ISBN 0-86577-080-8). Thieme-Stratton.

Cooke-Macgregor, Francis. After Plastic Surgery: Adaption & Adjustment. 160p. 1979. 19.95x (ISBN 0-686-84385-1). J F Bergin.

Gabka, J. & Vaubel, E. Plastic Surgery: Past & Present. (Illus.). viii, 160p. 1983. 176.75 (ISBN 3-8055-3651-8). S Karger.

McCoy, Frederick J., ed. Year Book of Plastic & Reconstructive Surgery 1983. 1983. 45.00 (ISBN 0-686-83767-3). Year Bk Med.

SURGERY, VETERINARY
see Veterinary Surgery

SURGICAL ANATOMY
see Anatomy, Surgical and Topographical

SURGICAL DRESSINGS
see Bandages and Bandaging

SURGICAL NURSING
see also Postoperative Care

Brunner & Suddarth. Lippincott Manual of Medical Surgical Nursing, Vol. 1. 512p. 1982. pap. text ed. 15.50 (ISBN 0-06-318207-6, Pub. by Har-Row Ltd England). Har-Row.

--Lippincott Manual of Medical Surgical Nursing, Vol. 2. 512p. 1982. pap. text ed. 18.50 (ISBN 0-06-318208-4, Pub. by Har-Row Ltd England). Har-Row.

--Lippincott Manual of Medical Surgical Nursing, Vol. 3. 512p. 1982. pap. text ed. 15.50 (ISBN 0-06-318209-2, Pub. by Har-Row Ltd England). Har-Row.

Desharnais, A. A Review of Surgical Nursing. 1978. text ed. 11.95 (ISBN 0-07-016560-2). McGraw.

Gruendemann, Barbara J. & Meeker, Margaret H. Alexander's Care of the Patient in Surgery. 7th ed. (Illus.). 882p. 1983. text ed. 35.95 (ISBN 0-8016-4147-0). Mosby.

Humphrey, C. Surgical Nursing. 399p. Date not set. 23.00x (ISBN 0-07-072993-X). McGraw.

Lewis, S. & Collier, I. Medical Surgical Nursing: Assessment & Management of Clinical Problems. 1888p. 1983. text ed. 45.95x (ISBN 0-07-037561-5). McGraw.

Phipps, Wilma J. & Long, Barbara C. Medical-Surgical Nursing: Concepts & Clinical Practice. 2nd ed. (Illus.). 2000p. 1983. text ed. 39.95 (ISBN 0-8016-3931-X). Mosby.

Warren. Operating Theatre Nursing. 280p. 1983. pap. text ed. 16.95 (ISBN 0-06-318240-8, Pub. by Har-Row Ltd England). Har-Row.

SURGICAL PATHOLOGY
see Pathology, Surgical

SURGICAL SHOCK
see Shock

SURNAMES
see Names, Personal

SURREALISM
see also Dadaism

Matthews, J. H. Eight Painters: The Surrealist Context. LC 82-10801. (Illus.). 288p. 1982. text ed. 24.00x (ISBN 0-8156-2274-0). Syracuse U Pr.

Picon, Gaeton. Surrealists & Surrealism. (Illus.). 220p. 1983. pap. 14.95 (ISBN 0-8478-0486-0). Rizzoli Intl.

Speis, Werner. Loplop: The Artist in the Third Person. Gabriel, J. W., tr. from Ger. (Illus.). 200p. 1983. 50.00 (ISBN 0-8076-1065-8). Braziller.

Wilson, Simon. Surrealist Painting. (Phaidon Color Library). (Illus.). 84p. 1983. 27.50 (ISBN 0-7148-2234-5, Pub. by Salem Hse Ltd); pap. 18.95 (ISBN 0-7148-2244-2). Merrimack Bk Serv.

SURVEYING
see also Area Measurement; Building Sites; Cartography; Geodesy; Topographical Surveying

Ashworth. Advanced Quantity: Surveying. 1983. text ed. write for info (ISBN 0-408-01192-0). Butterworth.

Historical Committee Texas Surveyors Assn. Three Dollars Per Mile. (Illus.). 455p. 1981. 25.00 (ISBN 0-686-81643-9). Eakin Pubns.

Laurila, Simo H. Electronic Surveying in Practice. 325p. 1983. 29.95 (ISBN 0-471-09021-2, Pub. by Wiley-Interscience). Wiley.

National Symposium. The Profession in Private Practice (Surveying, Photogrammetry) Proceedings of the National Symposium, 1982. 1983. 15.00 (ISBN 0-937294-43-8). ASP.

Roelofs. Astronomy & Land Surveying. 1950. 11.50 (ISBN 0-444-40771-5). Elsevier.

Survey of the Profession: Photogrammetry, Surveying, Mapping, Remote Sensing. 1982. pap. 150.00 (ISBN 0-937294-40-3). ASP.

Technical Papers: Annual Meeting of the American Society of Photogrammetry, 49th. 1983. 12.50 (ISBN 0-937294-47-0). ASP.

SURVEYS
see also Soil Surveys

Backstrom, Charles H. & Hursch-Cesar, Gerald. Survey Research. 2nd ed. LC 81-1738. 436p. 1981. text ed. 15.95x (ISBN 0-471-02543-7). Wiley.

Surveys, Polls, Censuses, & Forcasts Directory. 300p. 1983. 150.00x (ISBN 0-8103-1692-7). Gale.

Viladas, Joseph M. The Book of Survey Techniques. LC 82-90995. 278p. 1982. write for info. three-ring binder (ISBN 0-911397-00-0). Havemeyer Bks.

SURVEYS, CADASTRAL
see Real Property

SURVEYS, ECONOMIC
see Economic Surveys

SURVEYS, EDUCATIONAL
see Educational Surveys

SURVEYS, LIBRARY
see Library Surveys

SURVEYS, MARKET
see Market Surveys

SURVEYS, SOCIAL
see Social Surveys

SURVIVAL (AFTER AIRPLANE ACCIDENTS, SHIPWRECKS, ETC.)

King, Patricia O. Solo. LC 82-23483. (Illus.). 90p. 1983. 5.95 (ISBN 0-87747-965-8). Deseret Bk.

Lee, David & Doerr, Paul, eds. The Complete Guide to Freedom & Survival, Vol. III. 150p. (Orig.). 1982. write for info. Live Free.

Pogodeinski, Michael. How to Survive Nuclear War. (Illus.). 224p. (Orig.). 1982. pap. 7.95 (ISBN 0-89621-072-3). Thorndike Pr.

SURVIVAL (HUMAN ECOLOGY)
see Human Ecology

SURVIVORS' BENEFITS (OLD AGE PENSIONS)
see Old Age Pensions

SUSPENDED SENTENCE
see Probation

SUSPENSION ROOFS
see Roofs, Suspension

SUSSEX, ENGLAND

McCann, Timothy J. West Sussex Probate Inventories, 1521-1834. 1981. 95.00x (ISBN 0-86260-005-7). State Mutual Bk.

SWAHILI LANGUAGE

Foreign Service Institute. Swahili: An Active Introduction-Conversation. 159p. Date not set. with 2 cassettes 39.00x (ISBN 0-88432-110-X, W300). J Norton Pubs.

SWAMPS
see Marshes; Moors and Heaths

SWANSEA, WALES–SOCIAL CONDITIONS

Rosser, Colin & Harris, C. C. The Family & Social Change: A Study of Family & Kinship in a South Wales Town. (International Library of Sociology). 256p. 1983. pap. 10.95 (ISBN 0-7100-9434-5). Routledge & Kegan.

SWAZILAND

Hailey, William M. The Republic of South Africa & the High Commission Territories. LC 82-11865. vii, 136p. 1982. Repr. of 1963 ed. lib. bdg. 25.00x (ISBN 0-313-23625-9, HARS). Greenwood.

SWEAT BEES
see Bees

SWEDEN–DESCRIPTION AND TRAVEL–GUIDEBOOKS

Fodor's Stockholm, Copenhagen, Oslo, Helsinki & Reykjavik. (Illus.). 144p. 1983. pap. 5.95 (ISBN 0-679-00966-3). McKay.

Helsinki Travel Guide. (Berlitz Travel Guides). (Illus.). 1982. pap. 4.95 (ISBN 0-02-969230-X, Berlitz). Macmillan.

Stockholm Travel Guide. (Berlitz Travel Guides). (Illus.). 1982. pap. 4.95 (ISBN 0-02-969530-9, Berlitz). Macmillan.

SWEDEN–ECONOMIC CONDITIONS

Ginsburg, Helen. Full Employment & Public Policy: The United States & Sweden. LC 76-55536. 256p. 1983. 24.95x (ISBN 0-669-01318-8). Lexington Bks.

Swedish Trade Council, ed. Swedish Export Directory, 1982. 63rd ed. LC 72-623267. 800p. (Orig.). 1982. pap. 42.50x (ISBN 0-8002-3028-0). Intl Pubns Serv.

SWEDEN–INDUSTRIES

Swedish Academy of Engineering. Gengas: The Swedish Classic on Wood Powered Vehicles. Reed, Thomas B. & Jantzen, Dan, eds. Geuther, Maria, tr. (Illus.). 329p. 1981. pap. 15.00 (ISBN 0-942914-00-7). Tipi Wkshp Bks.

SWEDEN–POPULATION

Mosk, Carl, ed. Patriarchy & Fertility: The Evolution of Natality in Japan & Sweden 1880-1960. (Population & Social Structure: Advances in Historical Demography). Date not set. price not set (ISBN 0-12-508480-3). Acad Pr.

SWEDENBORGIANISM
see New Jerusalem Church

SWEDISH LANGUAGE–CONVERSATION AND PHRASE-BOOKS

Berlitz Editors. Swedish for Travel Cassettepack. 1983. 14.95 (ISBN 0-02-962860-1, Berlitz); cassette incl. Macmillan.

SWEDISH LITERATURE–TRANSLATIONS INTO ENGLISH

Von Heidenstam, Verner. Sweden's Laureate: Selected Poems of Verner Von Heidenstam. Stork, Charles W., tr. from Swedish. 1919. text ed. 29.50x (ISBN 0-686-83798-3). Elliots Bks.

SWELL
see Ocean Waves

SWIFT, JONATHAN, 1667-1745

Reilly, Patrick. Jonathan Swift: The Brave Desponder. 287p. 1982. 20.00x (ISBN 0-8093-1075-9). S Ill U Pr.

SWIMMING
see also Diving; Synchronized Swimming

Katz, Jane. Swimming Through Your Pregnancy. LC 82-45296. (Illus.). 224p. 1983. pap. 10.95 (ISBN 0-385-18059-4, Dolp). Doubleday.

Practical Guide for Teaching the Mentally Retarded to Swim. 160p. 1969. 5.95 (ISBN 0-88314-174-4). AAHPERD.

Strokes & Strokes: An Instructor's Manual for Developing Swim Programs for Stroke Victims. 80p. 5.75 (ISBN 0-88314-184-1). AAHPERD.

Swimnastics Is Fun, Vol. II. 42p. 7.95 (ISBN 0-88314-186-8). AAHPERD.

Vickers, Betty & Vincent, Bill. Swimming. (Exploring Sports Ser.). 1983. pap. write for info (ISBN 0-697-09977-6). Wm C Brown.

SWIMMING–JUVENILE LITERATURE

Libby, Bill. The Young Swimmer. LC 82-17289. (Illus.). 160p. (gr. 4 up). 1983. 10.00 (ISBN 0-688-01992-7). Lothrop.

Sanborn, Laura & Eberhardt, Lorraine. Swim Free. 32p. (gr. 6-12). 1982. pap. 6.95 (ISBN 0-910715-00-9). Search Public.

SWINE

Cole & Foxcroft. Control of Pig Reproduction. 1982. text ed. 99.95 (ISBN 0-408-10768-5). Butterworth.

SWINE–LEGENDS AND STORIES

Bowman, Sarah & Vardey, Lucinda. Pigs: A Troughful of Treasures. Date not set. 7.95 (ISBN 0-02-040340-2). Macmillan.

SWING (GOLF)

Nicholas, James. New Key to Power Golf: The Secret Lever. Ruth, R. M., ed. LC 82-17749. (Illus.). 160p. (Orig.). 1983. pap. 13.95 (ISBN 0-910815-00-3). CharLee Pr.

SWING MUSIC
see Jazz Music

SWISS IN THE UNITED STATES

Hall, Jacqueline & Hall, Jo E. Italian-Swiss Settlement of Plumas County, 1860-1920. (ANCRR Occasional Paper: No. 1). 55p. 1973. 4.00 (ISBN 0-686-38934-4). Assn NC Records.

SWITCHES, ELECTRIC
see Electric Contactors; Electric Relays

SWITZERLAND
see also names of geographic areas, cities, etc. in Switzerland, e.g. Alps, Geneva

Eighty-three Schweizer Almanac. 284p. (Ger.). 1983. pap. 9.50 (ISBN 0-686-83929-3). Transbooks.

Ominbus Volume. (Illus.). 256p. (Eng. & Fr. & Ger.). 1982. 24.00 (ISBN 0-89192-353-5). Transbooks.

SWITZERLAND–DESCRIPTION AND TRAVEL

Michelin Green Guide: Schweiz. (Green Guide Ser.). (Ger.). 1983. pap. write for info. (ISBN 2-06-025660-7). Michelin.

Michelin Green Guide: Suisse. (Green Guide Ser.). (Fr.). 1983. pap. write for info. (ISBN 2-06-005601-2). Michelin.

SWITZERLAND–DESCRIPTION AND TRAVEL–GUIDEBOOKS

French Speaking Switzerland Travel Guide. (Berlitz Travel Guides). (Illus.). 1982. pap. 4.95 (ISBN 0-02-969740-9, Berlitz). Macmillan.

Harrison, Shirley & Harrison, John. Austria & Switzerland. LC 82-61195. (Pocket Guide Ser.). (Illus.). 1983. pap. 4.95 (ISBN 0-528-84892-5). Rand.

SWITZERLAND–ECONOMIC CONDITIONS

The Largest Swiss Business: Nineteen Eighty-Two. 32p. 1982. pap. 5.00 (ISBN 0-89192-328-4). Transbooks.

SWITZERLAND–HISTORY

Creighton, Douglas G. Jacques-Francois Deluc of Geneva & His Friendship with Jean-Jacques Rousseau. LC 82-5332. (Romance Monographs: No. 42). 128p. 1983. write for info. Romance.

SWITZERLAND–POLITICS AND GOVERNMENT

Lejeune, Yves. Recueil Des Accords International Conclus Par les Cantons Suisses. 500p. (Fr.). 1982. write for info. (ISBN 3-261-04736-4). P Lang Pubs.

SWORDS
see also Fencing

Nakamura, T. & Nosay, G. Decorative Hand-Guards for Japanese Swords. (Illus.). 100p. Date not set. pap. 17.50 (ISBN 0-87556-578-6). Saifer.

Soto, Kanzan. The Japanese Sword. Earle, Joe, tr. LC 82-48779. (Japanese Arts Library). (Illus.). 220p. 1983. 91.95 (ISBN 0-87011-562-6). Kodansha.

SYDNEY, AUSTRALIA

Mayne, A. J. Fever, Squalor & Vice: Sanitation & Social Policy in Victorian Sydney. LC 82-2054. (Scholars' Library). (Illus.). 263p. 1982. text ed. 34.50x (ISBN 0-7022-1950-9). U of Queensland Pr.

SYLVICULTURE
see Forests and Forestry

SYMBIOSIS

Harley, J. L. & Smith, S. E., eds. Mycorrhizal Symbiosis. write for info. (ISBN 0-12-325560-0). Acad Pr.

SYMBOLIC AND MATHEMATICAL LOGIC
see Logic, Symbolic and Mathematical

SYMBOLIC NUMBERS
see Symbolism of Numbers

SYMBOLICS
see Creeds

SYMBOLISM IN COMMUNICATION

Johnson, Roxanna M. The Picture Communication Symbols. 3rd ed. (Illus.). 118p. 1982. 3 ring bdg. 36.00 (ISBN 0-9609160-0-8). Mayer-Johnson.

SYMBOLISM IN LITERATURE

Balakian, A. A., ed. The Symbolist Movement in the Literature of European Languages. (Comparative History of Literatures in European Language Ser.: Vol. 2). 732p. 1982. text ed. 53.00x (ISBN 963-05-2694-8, Pub. by Kultura Pr Hungary). Humanities.

Vlasopolos, Anca. The Symbolic Method of Coleridge, Baudelaire, & Yeats. 232p. 1983. 17.95x (ISBN 0-8143-1730-8). Wayne St U Pr.

Woronzoff, Alexander. Andrej Belyj's "Petersburg," James Joyce's "Ulysses" & the Symbolist Movement. x, 215p. 1982. write for info. (ISBN 3-261-05016-0). P Lang Pubs.

SYMBOLISM IN THE BIBLE

Cope, Gilbert. Symbolism in the Bible & the Church. 1959. 10.00 (ISBN 0-8022-0300-0). Philos Lib.

SYMBOLISM OF NUMBERS

Balliet, L. D. Number Vibration in Question & Answer. 104p. 4.50 (ISBN 0-686-38231-5). Sun Bks.

--Vibration: A System of Numbers As Taught by Pythagoras. 80p. 3.50 (ISBN 0-686-38237-4). Sun Bks.

Christy, Albert. Numeral Philosophy. 82p. 4.00 (ISBN 0-686-38232-3). Sun Bks.

Pelton, Robert W. Your Guide to Numerology. (Illus.). 160p. 1983. pap. 4.95 (ISBN 0-8329-0276-4). New Century.

Rice, Paul & Rice, Valeta. Aquarius: Through the Numbers. 48p. 1983. pap. 2.50 (ISBN 0-87728-575-6). Weiser.

--Aries: Through the Numbers. 48p. 1983. pap. 2.50 (ISBN 0-87728-565-9). Weiser.

--Cancer: Through the Numbers. 48p. 1983. pap. 2.50 (ISBN 0-87728-568-3). Weiser.

--Capricorn: Through the Numbers. 48p. 1983. pap. 2.50 (ISBN 0-87728-574-8). Weiser.

--Gemini: Through the Numbers. 48p. 1983. pap. 2.50 (ISBN 0-87728-567-5). Weiser.

--Leo: Through the Numbers. 48p. 1983. pap. 2.50 (ISBN 0-87728-569-1). Weiser.

--Libra: Through the Numbers. 48p. 1983. pap. 2.50 (ISBN 0-87728-571-3). Weiser.

--Pisces: Through the Numbers. 48p. 1983. pap. 2.50 (ISBN 0-87728-576-4). Weiser.

--Sagittarius: Through the Numbers. 48p. 1983. pap. 2.50 (ISBN 0-87728-573-X). Weiser.

--Scorpio: Through the Numbers. 48p. 1983. pap. 2.50 (ISBN 0-87728-572-1). Weiser.

--Taurus: Through the Numbers. 48p. 1983. pap. 2.50 (ISBN 0-87728-566-7). Weiser.

--Virgo: Through the Numbers. 48p. 1983. pap. 2.50 (ISBN 0-87728-570-5). Weiser.

Rizer, Arden, Jr. Catalogue of Numbers. LC 74-3486. 120p. 1981. pap. text ed. 7.50 (ISBN 0-941762-04-1). Psychic Forum.

Wescott, W. W. Numbers, Their Occult Power & Mystic Virtue. 127p. 5.00 (ISBN 0-686-38230-7). Sun Bks.

SYMBOLS
see Signs and Symbols

SYMMETRY
see also Esthetics

Kostelanetz, Richard. Symmetries. 1983. pap. 12.00 (ISBN 0-918406-24-2); signed 100.00 (ISBN 0-686-84605-2). Future Pr.

SYMPATHY

Pringle, Terry. This Is the Child. LC 82-48876. 1983. 13.95 (ISBN 0-394-52921-9). Knopf.

SYMPHONIES

Bengtsson, Ingmar & Van Boer, Bertil H., Jr., eds. The Symphony in Sweeden, Pt. 1. (The Symphony 1720-1840 Series F: Vol. II). 1982. lib. bdg. 90.00 (ISBN 0-8240-3811-8). Garland Pub.

Charlton, David, ed. Etienne-Nicolas Mehul, Three Symphonies (3,4,5) (The Symphony 1720-1840 Series D: Vol. 8). 1982. lib. bdg. 90.00 (ISBN 0-8240-3812-6). Garland Pub.

Gallagher, Charles C. & Helm, Eugene E., eds. Carl Philip Emanuel Bach, Six Symphonies. (The Symphony 1720-1840 Series C: Vol. 8). 1982. lib. bdg. 90.00 (ISBN 0-8240-3821-5). Garland Pub.

Hill, Cecil. Ferdinand Ries, Three Symphonies 1784-1838. (The Symphony 1720-1840 Series C: Vol. 12). 1982. lib. bdg. 90.00 (ISBN 0-8240-3817-7). Garland Pub.

Ignaz Franzel, Three Symphonies (2,3,5), Peter Von Winter, Three Symphonic Works (12,13,14) (The Symphony 1720-1840 Series C: Vol. 11). 1982. lib. bdg. 90.00 (ISBN 0-8240-3816-9). Garland Pub.

Longyear, Rey M., ed. The Northern Italian Symphony 1800-1840. (The Symphony 1720-1840 Series A: Vol. 6). 1982. lib. bdg. 90.00 (ISBN 0-8240-3819-3). Garland Pub.

Muchenberg, B. & Prosnak, J., eds. The Symphony in Poland. (The Symphony 1720-1840 Series F: Vol. 7). 1982. lib. bdg. 90.00 (ISBN 0-8240-3820-7). Garland Pub.

Schneider-Cuvay, M. Michaela & Rainer, Werner, eds. Salzburg, Pt. 2. (The Symphony 1720-1840 Series B: Vol. 8). lib. bdg. 90.00 (ISBN 0-8240-3818-5). Garland Pub.

Temperley, Nocholas, ed. William Sterndale Bennett, Three Symphonies (3,4,5) (The Symphony 1720-1840 Series E: Vol. 7). 1982. lib. bdg. 90.00 (ISBN 0-8240-3813-4). Garland Pub.

SYMPHONY ORCHESTRAS

Jacob, Gordon. Orchestral Technique: A Manual for Students. 100p. 1982. pap. 11.25 (ISBN 0-19-318204-1). Oxford U Pr.

SYMPTOMS
see Diagnosis
SYNAPSES
Cuello, A., ed. Co-Transmission. 224p. 1982. 85.00x (ISBN 0-333-32592-3, Pub. by Macmillan England). State Mutual Bk.
SYNCHRONIZED SWIMMING
Preston-Mauks, Susan. Synchronized Swimming Is For Me. LC 82-17102. (Sports For Me Bks.). (Illus.). 48p. (gr. 2-5). 1983. PLB 6.95g (ISBN 0-8225-1139-8). Lerner Pubns.
Sports Medicine Meets Synchronized Swimming. 160p. 8.95 (ISBN 0-88314-175-2). AAHPERD.
Synchronized Swimming 1982-83. (NAGWS Sports Guides Ser.). 3.75 (ISBN 0-88314-089-6). AAHPERD.
U. S. Synchronized Swimming. U. S. Synchronized Swimming Rulebook, 1983. 125p. (Orig.). pap. 5.00 (ISBN 0-911543-00-7). US Synch Swim.
SYNCRETISM (CHRISTIANITY)
see Christianity and Other Religions
SYNGE, JOHN MILLINGTON, 1871-1909
Benson, Eugene. J. M. Synge. 1982. 50.00x (ISBN 0-7171-1243-8, Pub. by Gill & Macmillan Ireland). State Mutual Bk.
--J. M. Synge. (Grove Press Modern Dramatists Ser.). (Illus.). 224p. (Orig.). 1983. pap. 9.95 (ISBN 0-394-62432-7, Ever). Grove.
Skelton, Robin. J. M. Synge. 1983. pap. 3.95 (ISBN 0-8387-7687-6). Devin.
SYNTHESIZER MUSIC
see Electronic Music
SYNTHETIC CHEMISTRY
see Chemistry, Inorganic-Synthesis; Chemistry, Organic-Synthesis
SYNTHETIC COMPOUNDS
see Detergents, Synthetic
SYNTHETIC CONSCIOUSNESS
see Conscious Automata
SYNTHETIC FIBERS
see Textile Fibers, Synthetic
SYNTHETIC FUELS
Hill, Richard F. Synfuels Industry Development. LC 80-65895. (Illus.). 168p. 1980. pap. text ed. 25.00 (ISBN 0-86587-083-7). Gov Insts.
Hunt, Daniel V. Synfuels Handbook. (Illus.). 500p. 1983. 45.00 (ISBN 0-8311-1144-5). Indus Pr.
Meyers, Robert A. Handbook of Synfuels Technology. (Illus.). 896p. 1983. 50.00 (ISBN 0-07-041762-8, P&RB). McGraw.
Thompson, R., ed. Energy & Chemistry. 368p. 1982. 55.00x (ISBN 0-85186-845-2, Pub. by Royal Soc Chem England). State Mutual Bk.
SYNTHETIC TEXTILE FIBERS
see Textile Fibers, Synthetic
SYPHILIS
Jones, James H. Bad Blood: The Tuskegee Syphilis Experiment. 1982. 7.95 (ISBN 0-686-81884-9). Free Pr.
SYRIA
Devlin, John F. Syria. 135p. 1982. lib. bdg. 16.50x (ISBN 0-86531-185-4). Westview.
Ratnatunga, Manel. Syria: What Is She? (Illus.). 216p. 1983. pap. 9.95 (ISBN 9971-65-061-4). Hippocrene Bks.
SYRIA-POLITICS AND GOVERNMENT
Bar-Siman-Tov, Yaacov. Linkage Politics in the Middle East: Syria Between Domestic & External Conflict, 1961-1970. (Replica Edition Ser.). 225p. 1983. softcover 18.50x (ISBN 0-86531-945-6). Westview.
Olson, Robert W. The Ba'ath & Syria: The Evolution of Ideology, Party & State. (Leaders, Politics, & Social Change in the Islamic World: No. 3). 330p. 1982. 19.00 (ISBN 0-940670-18-6). Kingston Pr.
SYRIAN CHURCH
Garsoian, Nina & Mathews, Thomas, eds. East of Byzantium: Syria & Armenia in the Formative Period. LC 82-9665. (Dumbarton Oaks Symposium). (Illus.). 266p. 1982. 35.00x (ISBN 0-88402-104-1). Dumbarton Oaks.
SYRIAN HAMSTERS
see Hamsters
SYSTEM ANALYSIS
see also Control Theory; Discrete Time Systems; Electric Networks; Flow Charts; Mathematical Optimization; Nonlinear Theories; Systems Engineering
Bailey, Robert W. Human Error in Computer Systems. (Illus.). 160p. 1983. pap. 15.95 (ISBN 0-13-445056-6). P-H.
Bednarek, A. R. & Cesari, L., eds. Dynamical Systems: Symposium, II. 1982. 49.00 (ISBN 0-12-084720-5). Acad Pr.
Bensoussan, A. & Lions, J. L., eds. Analysis & Optimization of Systems, Versailles, France, 1982: Proceedings. (Lecture Notes in Control & Information Sciences Ser.: Vol. 44). (Illus.). 987p. 1983. pap. 47.00 (ISBN 0-387-12089-0). Springer-Verlag.
Bernussou, J. & Titli, A. Interconnected Dynamical Systems: Stability, Decomposition & Decentralisation. (North-Holland Systems & Control Ser.: Vol. 5). 330p. 1982. 59.50 (ISBN 0-444-86504-7, North Holland). Elsevier.
Burr, Stefan A., ed. The Mathematics of Networks. LC 82-18469. 16.00 (ISBN 0-8218-0031-0, PSAPM-26). Am Math.
Chase, W. P. Management of System Engineering. 228p. Repr. of 1974 ed. text ed. 26.50 (ISBN 0-471-14915-2). Krieger.
Chen, Wai-Kai. Linear Networks & Systems. 608p. 1983. text ed. 34.95 (ISBN 0-534-01343-0). Brooks-Cole.
Chinese Association of Automation, ed. Trends & Progress in Control Systems Theory & Its Application: Proceedings of the Symposium on Control Systems. 800p. 1982. write for info. (ISBN 0-677-31040-4). Gordon.
Chinese, U. S. Symposium on Systems Analysis & Gray, Paul. Proceedings. (Systems Engineering & Analysis Ser.). 600p. 1982. 45.00 (ISBN 0-471-89585-7, Pub. by Wiley-Interscience). Wiley.
Chow, J. H., ed. Time-Scale Modeling of Dynamic Networks with Applications to Power Systems. (Lecture Notes in Control & Information Sciences Ser.: Vol. 46). 218p. 1983. pap. 12.00 (ISBN 0-387-12106-4). Springer-Verlag.
Churchman, C. West. Thought & Wisdom. (Systems Inquiry Ser.). 150p. 1982. pap. text ed. 9.95 (ISBN 0-686-37578-5). Intersystems Pubns.
Cleland, D. I. & King, W. R. Systems Analysis & Project Management. 3rd ed. 512p. 1983. 24.95 (ISBN 0-07-011311-4). McGraw.
Coxon, A. P. M. The User's Guide to Multidimensional Scaling. 320p. 1982. text ed. 28.00 (ISBN 0-435-82251-9). Heinemann Ed.
Curtis, R. K. Evolution or Extinction: The Choice Before Us-A Systems Approach to the Study of the Future. 420p. 1982. 50.00 (ISBN 0-08-027933-3); pap. 25.00 (ISBN 0-08-027932-5). Pergamon.
Daniels, Alan & Yeates, Don. Design & Analysis of Software Systems. 257p. 1983. pap. 15.00 (ISBN 0-89433-212-0). Petrocelli.
Davies, P. M. & Coxon, A. P., eds. Key Texts on Multidimensional Scaling. xx, 352p. 1982. text ed. 20.00x (ISBN 0-435-82253-5). Heinemann Ed.
Dhar, R. N. Computer Aided Power System Operation & Analysis. (Illus.). 320p. 1983. 29.95 (ISBN 0-07-451580-2, P&RB). McGraw.
Dillon, John A. Foundations of General Systems Theory. (Systems Inquiry Ser.). 300p. 1982. pap. 12.95 (ISBN 0-686-37575-0). Intersystems Pubns.
Doebner, H. D. & Palev, T. D., eds. Twistor Geometry & Non-Linear Systems: Proceedings, Primorsko, Bulgaria, 1980. (Lecture Notes in Mathematics Ser.: Vol. 970). 216p. 1983. pap. 11.50 (ISBN 0-387-11972-8). Springer-Verlag.
Findeisen, W., et al. Control & Coordination in Hierarchical Systems. (IIASA International Ser. on Applied Systems Analysis: No. 9). 469p. 1980. 63.95x (ISBN 0-471-27742-8). Wiley.
Frederick, Dean K. & Carlson, A. Bruce. Linear Systems in Communication & Control. LC 71-155118. 575p. 1971. 36.95x (ISBN 0-471-27721-5). Wiley.
Gane, Chris & Sarson, Trish. Structured Systems Analysis: Tools & Techniques. 373p. (Orig.). 1977. 22.50 (ISBN 0-930196-00-7); pap. 15.00 (ISBN 0-686-37676-5). P F Mallon.
Geyer, R. F. & Zouwen, J. van der, eds. Dependence & Inequality: A Systems Approach to the Problems of Mexico & Other Developing Countries. (Systems Science & World Order Library: Innovations in Systems Science). (Illus.). 336p. 1982. 35.00 (ISBN 0-08-027952-X). Pergamon.
Gibson, J. E. Designing the New City: A Systematic Approach. LC 76-44899. (Systems Engineering & Analysis Ser.). 288p. 1977. 39.95x (ISBN 0-471-29752-6, Pub. by Wiley-Interscience). Wiley.
Gray, Willaim & Jay, W. General Systems Theory & the Psychological Sciences, Vols. 1 & 2. (Systems Inquiry Ser.). 550p. 1982. pap. 21.95 set (ISBN 0-686-37577-7). Intersystems Pubns.
Gvishiani, J. M., ed. Systems Research: Methodological Problems. 380p. 1983. 75.00 (ISBN 0-08-030000-6). Pergamon.
Hoos, Ida R. Systems Analysis in Public Policy: A Critique. rev. ed. LC 82-48766. 320p. 1983. text ed. 30.00x (ISBN 0-520-04953-5); pap. 8.95x (ISBN 0-520-04952-7). U of Cal Pr.
Hung, Y. S. & MacFarlane, A. G. Multivariable Feedback: A Quasi-Classical Approach. (Lecture Notes in Control & Information Sciences: Vol. 40). 182p. 1983. pap. 9.50 (ISBN 0-387-11902-7). Springer-Verlag.
Ioannou, P. A. & Kokotovic, P. V. Adaptive Systems with Reduced Models. (Lecture Notes in Control & Information Sciences Ser.: Vol. 47). 162p. 1983. pap. 10.00 (ISBN 0-387-12150-1). Springer-Verlag.
Kilgannon, Pete. Business Data Processing & Systems Analysts. 336p. 1980. pap. text ed. 17.95 (ISBN 0-7131-2755-4). E Arnold.
Laszlo, E. Systems Science & World Order: Selected Studies. (Systems Science & World Order Library). 278p. 1982. 35.00 (ISBN 0-08-028924-X). Pergamon.
Nicholson, H., ed. Modelling of Dynamical Systems, Vol. I. (IEE Control Engineering Ser.: No. 12). (Illus.). 256p. 1980. casebound 68.00 (ISBN 0-906048-38-9). Inst Elect Eng.
O'Reilly, John, ed. Observers for Linear Systems: Mathematics Science & Engineering. Date not set. price not set (ISBN 0-12-527780-6). Acad Pr.
Oshry, Barry. Notes on the Power & Systems Perspective. LC 75-933. (Notes on Power Ser.). (Orig.). 1976. pap. text ed. 6.75 (ISBN 0-910411-01-8). Power & Sys.
Palm, William J. Modeling, Analysis & Control of Dynamic Systems. 800p. 1983. text ed. 36.95 (ISBN 0-471-05800-9); solutions manual avail. (ISBN 0-471-89887-2). Wiley.
Richards, J. A. Analysis of Periodically Time-Varying Systems. (Communications & Control Engineering Ser.). (Illus.). 173p. 1983. 29.50 (ISBN 0-387-11689-3). Springer-Verlag.
Rosenberg, R. & Karnopp, D. Introduction to Physical Systems Dynamics. 512p. 1983. 32.95x (ISBN 0-07-053905-7, C); solutions manual 9.95 (ISBN 0-07-053906-5). McGraw.
Thierauf, Robert J. & Reynolds, George W. Systems Analysis & Design: A Case Study Approach. 1980. text ed. 18.95 (ISBN 0-675-08172-6). Additional supplements may be obtained from publisher. Merrill.
Walter, E. Identifiability of State Space Models: With Applications to Transformation Systems. (Lecture Notes in Biomathematics Ser.: Vol. 46). 202p. 1983. pap. 13.50 (ISBN 0-387-11590-0). Springer-Verlag.
You & Systems. 200p. 1982. pap. 5.00 (ISBN 0-686-37413-4). Ideals PA.
SYSTEM INTERCONNECTION, ELECTRIC POWER
see Electric Utilities
SYSTEM SIMULATION
see Simulation Methods
SYSTEM THEORY
see System Analysis
SYSTEMATIC BOTANY
see Botany-Classification
SYSTEMATIC THEOLOGY
see Theology, Doctrinal
SYSTEMS, THEORY OF
see System Analysis
SYSTEMS ANALYSIS
see System Analysis
SYSTEMS ENGINEERING
see also Bionics; Dynamic Programming; Man-Machine Systems; Operations Research; Reliability (Engineering); Simulation Methods; Weapons Systems
Henderson, R. G. Case Studies in Systems Design. 208p. 1980. 25.00x (ISBN 0-7121-0387-2, Pub. by Macdonald & Evans). State Mutual Bk.
Kulikowski, Casimir A. & Weiss, Sholom M. A Practical Guide to Building Expert Systems. 220p. 1983. text ed. 24.95x (ISBN 0-86598-108-6). Allanheld.
Maekawa, M. & Belady, L. A., eds. Operating Systems Engineering, Amagi, Japan 1980: Proceedings. (Lecture Notes in Computer Science: Vol. 143). 465p. 1983. pap. 19.00 (ISBN 0-387-11604-4). Springer-Verlag.
Nash, P. Systems Modelling & Optimisation. (IEE Control Engineering Ser.: No. 16). 224p. 1981. casebound 43.00 (ISBN 0-906048-63-X). Inst Elect Eng.
Progress in Cybernetics & Systems Research, Vol. 9. 1982. 110.00 (ISBN 0-07-065069-1). McGraw.
Progress in Cybernetics & Systems Research, Vol. 10. 1982. 110.00 (ISBN 0-07-065070-5). McGraw.
Progress in Cybernetics & Systems Research, Vol. 11. 1982. 110.00 (ISBN 0-07-065071-3). McGraw.
Trappl, R. Progress in Cybernetics & Systems Research, Vol. 8. 1982. 110.00 (ISBN 0-07-065068-3). McGraw.
SYSTEMS OPTIMIZATION
see Mathematical Optimization
SYSTEMS RELIABILITY
see Reliability (Engineering)

T

T-SQUARES
see Rulers (Instruments)
TABERNACLE
Patton, Edward W. The Way into the Holiest: A Devotional Study of the Tabernacle in the Wilderness. 176p. 1983. pap. 4.95 (ISBN 0-8407-5833-2). Nelson.
TABLE DECORATION
see Table Setting and Decoration
TABLE SETTING AND DECORATION
see also Flower Arrangement; Glassware; Pottery
Dlugosch, Sharon. Table Setting Guide. (Orig.). 1982. pap. 3.95 (ISBN 0-918420-07-5). Brighton Pubns.
TABLE TENNIS
Craven, Robert R., compiled by. Billiards, Bowling, Table Tennis, Pinball & Video Games: A Bibliographic Guide. LC 82-21077. 162p. 1983. lib. bdg. 29.95 (ISBN 0-313-23462-0, CBB/). Greenwood.
TABLES, MATHEMATICAL
see Interest and Usury-Tables, etc.
TABLETS, MEMORIAL
see Sepulchral Monuments
TACHYGRAPHY
see Shorthand
TACNA-ARICA QUESTION
Dennis, William J. Tacna & Arica: An Account of the Chile-Peru Boundary Dispute & of the Arbitration by the United States. 1931. text ed. 18.50x (ISBN 0-686-83802-5). Elliots Bks.
TADPOLES
see Frogs
TAE KWON DO
see Karate
TAFT, WILLIAM HOWARD, PRES. U. S., 1857-1930
Taft, William H. Popular Government: Its Essence, Its Performance, Its Perils. 1913. text ed. 12.50x (ISBN 0-686-83709-6). Elliots Bks.
TAGALOG LANGUAGE
Cabrera, Neonetta C. & Cunanan, Augustina S. Tagalog Beginning Course. Bowen, J. Donald, tr. 526p. Date not set. with 33 audio cassettes 295.00x (ISBN 0-88432-103-7). J Norton Pubs.
TAHITI
Corser, Frank & Corser, Rose. Tahiti Traveler's Guide. 3rd, rev. ed. (Illus.). 52p. 1981. pap. 3.50 (ISBN 0-686-38091-6). F & R Corser.
McDermott, John W. How to Get Lost & Found in Tahiti. 1979. 9.95 (ISBN 0-686-37618-8). Orafa Pub Co.
TAI LANGUAGES
see also Siamese Language
Foreign Service Institute. Thai Basic Course, Vol. 2. 411p. Date not set. with 17 cassettes 185.00x (ISBN 0-88432-104-5, D350). J Norton Pubs.
TAILORING
see also Men's Clothing; Trousers; Uniforms, Military
Cabrera, Roberto & Meyers, Patricia. Classic Tailoring Techniques: A Construction Guide for Men's Wear. (Illus.). 260p. 1983. text ed. 18.50 (ISBN 0-87005-431-7). Fairchild.
TAIWAN
Council for Economic Planning & Development (Republic of China) Taiwan Statistical Data Book, 1982. LC 72-219425. (Illus.). 318p. (Orig.). 1982. pap. 12.50x (ISBN 0-8002-3027-2). Intl Pubns Serv.
TAIWAN-DESCRIPTION AND TRAVEL
Reid, Daniel P. The Complete Guide to Taiwan. (The Complete Asian Guide Ser.). (Illus., Orig.). 1983. pap. 9.95 (ISBN 962-7031-19-4, Pub. by CFW Pubns Hong Kong). C E Tuttle.
--Taiwan in Focus. (The "In Focus" Ser.). (Illus.). 64p. (Orig.). 1983. pap. 5.95 (ISBN 962-7031-22-4). C E Tuttle.
TAIWAN-ECONOMIC CONDITIONS
Kuo, Shirley W. Y. The Taiwan Economy in Transition. 370p. 1983. lib. bdg. 22.00x (ISBN 0-86531-611-2). Westview.
TAIWAN-SOCIAL CONDITIONS
Moser, Michael J. Law & Social Change in a Chinese Community: A Case Study from Rural Taiwan. 1982. text ed. 45.00 (ISBN 0-379-20062-7). Oceana.
TALENTED CHILDREN
see Gifted Children
TALENTS (PARABLE)
see Jesus Christ-Parables
TALES
see also Fables; Fairy Tales; Legends; Parables; Short Stories
Cohen, Daniel. Southern Fried Rat & Other Gruesome Tales. (Illus.). 128p. 1983. 9.95 (ISBN 0-87131-400-2). M Evans.
Mabie, Hamilton W., ed. Folk Tales Every Child Should Know. (Illus.). 215p. 1983. Repr. of 1914 ed. lib. bdg. 30.00 (ISBN 0-89760-572-1). Telegraph Bks.
TALES, AFRICAN
Chowning, Larry S. Barcat Skipper: Tales of a Tangier Waterman. LC 82-74135. 160p. 1983. 11.95 (ISBN 0-87033-300-3). Cornell Maritime.
Radin, Paul. African Folktales. 344p. (Orig.). 1983. pap. 9.95 (ISBN 0-8052-0732-5). Schocken.
TALES, AMERICAN
Glimm, James Y. Flatlanders & Ridgerunners: Folktales from the Mountains of Northern Pennsylvania. LC 82-10895. (Illus.). 240p. 1983. 11.95 (ISBN 0-8229-3471-X); pap. 5.95 (ISBN 0-8229-5345-5). U of Pittsburgh Pr.
Grimm, Jacob & Grimm, Wilhelm. Grimm: Selected Tales. Luke, David, tr. 1983. pap. 3.95 (ISBN 0-14-044401-7). Penguin.
TALES, ARMENIAN
Villa, Susie H. One Hundred Armenian Tales. 602p. 1982. 19.95 (ISBN 0-8143-1282-9); pap. 11.95 (ISBN 0-8143-1736-7). Wayne St U Pr.
TALES, ASIAN
Graham, David C. The Tribal Songs & Tales of the Ch'uan-Miao. (Asian Folklore & Social Life Monographs: Vol. 102). 1980. 20.50 (ISBN 0-89986-333-7). Oriental Bk Store.
Zong In-Sob, et al. The Beast-Tales Told in Northeastern Asia. (Asian Folklore & Social Life Monographs: Vol. 103). 1981. 14.00 (ISBN 0-89986-334-5). Oriental Bk Store.
TALES, GERMAN
Ratcliff, Ruth. German Tales & Legends. 144p. 1982. 29.00x (ISBN 0-584-62059-4, Pub. by Muller Ltd). State Mutual Bk.
TALES, IRISH
Nicholas, Cornelius J. Auld Tayles. LC 81-81936. 64p. 1983. 6.95 (ISBN 0-86666-046-1). GWP.

TALES, ITALIAN

Smarr, Janet L., tr. from Ital. Italian Renaissance Tales. (Illus.). 375p. 1983. pap. 13.95 (ISBN 0-933760-03-5). Solaris Pr.

TALES, JEWISH

Beth Jacob Hebrew Teachers College. Deeds of the Righteous. (Illus.). 160p. 6.95 (ISBN 0-934390-00-2). B J Hebrew Tchrs.

--The Rebbe's Treasure. Date not set. price not set (ISBN 0-934390-01-0); pap. price not set (ISBN 0-934390-02-9). B J Hebrew Tchrs.

TALES, LATVIAN

Rubulis, Aleksis, ed. & tr. Latvian Folktales. 1982. 8.50 (ISBN 0-89023-020-X). Forrest Printing.

TALKING

see Conversation

TALMUD

Haut, Irwin H. The Talmud as Law or Literature: An Analysis of David W. Halivni's Mekorot Umasorot. x, 83p. pap. 6.95 (ISBN 0-87203-107-1). Hermon.

Neusner, Jacob, ed. The Talmud of the Land of Israel: A Preliminary Translation & Explanation, Volume 32, Shebuot. (Chicago Studies in the History of Judaism). 288p. 1982. lib. bdg. 22.50x (ISBN 0-226-57692-2). U of Chicago Pr.

TALMUD-FOLK-LORE

see Folk-Lore, Jewish

TANK TACTICS

see Tank Warfare

TANK-VESSELS

see Tankers

TANK WARFARE

see also Tanks (Military Science)

Baily, Charles M. Faint Praise: The Development of American Tanks & Tank Destroyers During World War II. (Illus.). 224p. 1983. 24.00 (ISBN 0-208-02006-3, Archon). Shoe String.

Macksy, Kenneth. The Tank Pioneers. (Illus.). 224p. 1981. 18.95 (ISBN 0-86720-563-6). Sci Bks Intl.

TANKERS

Bloker, Richard A., ed. Tankerman-All Grades: B Edition. (Illus.). 353p. pap. 14.00 (ISBN 0-934114-41-2). Marine Educ.

TANKS

see also Pressure Vessels

American Society of Civil Engineers, compiled by. Design of Water Intake Stuctures for Fish Protection. LC 81-70988. 176p. 1982. pap. text ed. 18.50 (ISBN 0-87262-291-6). Am Soc Civil Eng.

TANKS (MILITARY SCIENCE)

see also Armored Vehicles, Military; Tank Warfare

Baily, Charles M. Faint Praise: The Development of American Tanks & Tank Destroyers During World War II. (Illus.). 224p. 1983. 24.00 (ISBN 0-208-02006-3, Archon). Shoe String.

Cave, Ron & Cave, Joyce. What About... Tanks. (What About Ser.). (Illus.). 32p. (gr. k-3). 1983. PLB 7.90 (ISBN 0-531-03470-4). Watts.

Forty, George & Batchelor, John. United States Tanks of World War II in Action. (Illus.). 160p. 1983. 16.95 (ISBN 0-7137-1214-7, Pub. by Blandford Pr England). Sterling.

Macksey, Kenneth. The Tanks, Nineteen Forty-Five - Nineteen Seventy-Five. (Illus.). 336p. 1981. 23.95 (ISBN 0-85368-293-3). Stackpole.

Macksy, Kenneth. The Tank Pioneers. (Illus.). 224p. 1981. 18.95 (ISBN 0-86720-563-6). Sci Bks Intl.

TANTRAS

Reigle, David. The Books of Kiu-Te in the Tibetan Buddhist Tantras. (Secret Doctrine Reference Ser.). (Illus.). 80p. (Orig.). 1983. pap. 3.50 (ISBN 0-913510-49-1). Wizards.

TANTRIC BUDDHISM

Fenner, Edward T. Rasayana Siddhi: Medicine & Alchemy in the Buddhist Tantras. (Traditional Healing Ser.). 300p. 1983. 39.95 (ISBN 0-932426-28-X). Trado-Medic.

Rinbochy, Khetsun S. Tantric Practice in Nying-ma. Hopkins, Jeffery & Klein, Anne, eds. 238p. (Orig.). 1983. 16.00 (ISBN 0-937938-13-0); pap. text ed. 10.95 (ISBN 0-937938-14-9). Gabriel Pr.

TANTRISM

Bhattacharyya, N. N. History of the Tantric Religion. 1983. 34.00x (ISBN 0-8364-0942-6, Pub. by Manohar India); pap. 17.50x (ISBN 0-8364-0943-4). South Asia Bks.

Garrison, Omar. Tantra: The Yoga of Sex. 1983. 14.95 (ISBN 0-517-54947-6); pap. 7.95 (ISBN 0-517-54947-6). Crown.

Walker, Benjamin. Tantrism: Its Secret Principles & Practices. 176p. 1983. pap. 8.95 (ISBN 0-85030-272-2). Newcastle Pub.

TANZANIA-ECONOMIC CONDITIONS

Coulson, Andrew. Tanzania: A Political Economy. (Illus.). 410p. 1982. 34.95x (ISBN 0-19-828292-3); pap. 15.95 (ISBN 0-19-828293-1). Oxford U Pr.

TAOISM

Allen, G. F. Taoist Words of Wisdom Diary. (Illus.). 196p. Date not set. 5.00 (ISBN 0-7224-0198-1). Robinson & Watkins.

Bock, Felicia G. Classical Learning & Taoist Practices in Early Japan, with Translation of Books XVI & XX of the Engi-Shiki. Bock, Felicia G., tr. from Japanese. & intro. by. (Occasional Paper Arizona State Univ., Center for Asian Studies Ser.: No. 17). 100p. 1983. pap. 4.00. ASU Ctr Asian.

Chang, Jolan. The Tao of the Loving Couple: True Liberation Through the Tao. (Illus.). 168p. 1983. 14.95 (ISBN 0-525-24183-3, 01451-440); pap. 8.95 (ISBN 0-525-48042-0, 0869-260). Dutton.

Creel, Herrlee G. What Is Taoism? And Other Studies in Chinese Cultural History. LC 77-102905. (Midway Reprint Ser.). viii, 192p. 1982. pap. text ed. 8.00x (ISBN 0-226-12047-3). U of Chicago Pr.

Giraroot, N. J. Myth & Meaning in Early Taoism: The Themes of Chaos (hun-tun) LC 81-21964. (Hermeneutics Ser.). (Illus.). 430p. 1983. 27.50x (ISBN 0-520-04330-8). U of Cal Pr.

Ni, Hua-Ching. The Complete Works of Lao Tzu: Tao Teh Ching & Hua Hu Ching. LC 79-88745. (Illus.). 219p. (Orig.). 1979. pap. 7.50 (ISBN 0-937064-00-9). SEBT.

--Tao: The Subtle Universal Law & the Integral Way of Life. (Illus.). 166p. (Orig.). 1979. pap. text ed. 7.50 (ISBN 0-937064-01-7). SEBT.

--The Taoist Inner View of the Universe & the Immortal Realm. LC 79-91720. (Illus.). 218p. (Orig.). 1980. pap. text ed. 12.50 (ISBN 0-937064-02-5). SEBT.

TAOIST MONASTICISM AND RELIGIOUS ORDERS

see Monasticism and Religious Orders, Taoist

TAOS INDIANS

see Indians of North America-Southwest, New

TAPE-RECORDER MUSIC

see Electronic Music

TAPE RECORDERS

see Magnetic Recorders and Recording

TAPE RECORDINGS (SOUND REPRODUCTIONS)

see Phonotapes

TAPES

see Phonotapes

TAPEWORMS

see Cestoda

TARIFF-UNITED STATES

Cline, William R. Reciprocity: A New Approach to World Trade Policy? (Policy Analyses in International Econimics Ser.: No. 2). 48p. 1982. 6.00 (ISBN 0-88132-001-3). Inst Intl Eco.

Lavergne, Real P., ed. The Political Economy of U. S. Tariffs: An Empirical Analysis. (Economic Theory, Econometrics, Mathematical Economics Ser.). Date not set. price not set (ISBN 0-12-438740-3). Acad Pr.

TARKENTON, FRANCIS A.

Tarkenton, Frances. Incredible Fran. Date not set. pap. 4.95 (ISBN 0-911866-92-2). Advocate.

TAROT

Case, Paul Foster. Tarot: A Key to the Wisdom of the Ages. 1981. Repr. of 1977 ed. 6.95 (ISBN 0-686-43319-X). Macoy Pub.

Denning, Melita & Phillips, Osborne. The Llewellyn Practical Guide to the Magick of the Tarot. Weschcke, Carl L., ed. LC 82-83428. (Llewellyn's Practical Magick Ser.). (Illus.). 240p. (Orig.). 1983. pap. 6.95 (ISBN 0-87542-198-9). Llewellyn Pubns.

Dummett, Michael. The Game of Tarot. (Illus.). 600p. 1980. 39.95 (ISBN 0-7156-1014-7). US Games Syst.

--Twelve Tarot Games. (Illus.). 242p. 1980. 14.95 (ISBN 0-7156-1485-1); pap. 9.95 (ISBN 0-7156-1486-X). US Games Syst.

Fairfield, Gail. Choice Centered Tarot. rev. ed. 160p. (Orig.). 1981. pap. 6.95 (ISBN 0-9609650-1-7). Choice Astro.

Gonzalez, J. A. & Gonzalez, Magda. Native American Tarot Deck. 108p. 1982. pap. 9.00 (ISBN 0-88079-009-1). US Games Syst.

Kaplan, Stuart R. El Tarot. (Illus.). 256p. 1982. pap. 4.95 (ISBN 84-01-47101-X). US Games Syst.

Sandbauch, John. Astrology, Alchemy & Tarot. 307p. 1982. pap. 4.95 (ISBN 0-930706-08-0). Seek-It Pubns.

Sherman, Johanna. The Sacred Rose Tarot. 56p. 1982. pap. 12.00 (ISBN 0-88079-012-1). US Games Syst.

Thales. Revelations of the Nameless One: An Interpretation of the "T" Tarot. (Illus.). 100p. (Orig.). 1982. pap. 5.95 (ISBN 0-935548-07-6). Santarasa Pubns.

Wirth, Oswald. Introduction to the Study of the Tarot. LC 82-50753. 64p. (Orig.). pap. 4.95 (ISBN 0-87728-559-4). Weiser.

--Introduction to the Study of the Tarot. (Illus.). 64p. 1981. pap. 4.95 (ISBN 0-85030-263-3). US Games Syst.

TARTARS

Serruys, Henry, ed. Kumiss Ceremonies & Horse Races: Three Mongolian Texts. 124p. 1974. pap. 27.50x (ISBN 0-686-82196-3). Intl Pubns Serv.

TASTE

Murphy, Wendy B. Touch, Smell, Taste, Sight & Hearing. LC 82-5738. (Library of Health). lib. bdg. 18.60 (ISBN 0-8094-3799-6, Pub. by Time-Life). Silver.

TASTE (ESTHETICS)

see Esthetics

TAVERNS

see Hotels, Taverns, etc.

TAX ACCOUNTANTS

see Tax Consultants

TAX ACCOUNTING

Walters, Robert. Managing Tax in Your Business. 226p. 1982. text ed. 36.75x (ISBN 0-09-147350-0, Pub. by Busn Bks England). Renouf.

Yates, Alfred G., Jr. The Pocket Estate & Gift Tax Calculator. 110p. (Orig.). 1983. pap. 5.65 (ISBN 0-87218-420-X). Natl Underwriter.

TAX ADMINISTRATION AND PROCEDURE

see also Assessment; Tax Remission

Christian, Ernest S., Jr. State Taxation of Foreign Source Income. LC 81-70922. 1982. 3.50 (ISBN 0-910586-44-6). Finan Exec.

Feldstein, Martin. Behavioral Simulation Methods in Tax Policy Formation. LC 82-21766. (National Bureau of Economic Research-Project Report). 1983. lib. bdg. price not set (ISBN 0-226-24084-3). U of Chicago Pr.

Rudman, Jack. Principal Tax Compliance Agent. (Career Examination Ser.: C-2954). (Cloth bdg. avail. on request). pap. 14.00 (ISBN 0-8373-2954-X). Natl Learning.

--Senior Tax Compliance Agent. (Career Examination Ser.: C-2953). (Cloth bdg. avail. on request). pap. 12.00 (ISBN 0-8373-2953-1). Natl Learning.

TAX ASSESSMENT

see Assessment

TAX AVOIDANCE

see Tax Planning

TAX CONSULTANTS

Lesko, Matthew. How to Get Free Tax Help. 192p. 1983. pap. 2.95 (ISBN 0-553-22936-2). Bantam.

Rudman, Jack. Assessment Clerk. (Career Examination Ser.: C-2920). (Cloth bdg. avail. on request). pap. 10.00 (ISBN 0-8373-2920-5). Natl Learning.

--Senior Assessment Clerk. (Career Examination Ser.: C-2921). (Cloth bdg. avail. on request). pap. 12.00 (ISBN 0-8373-2921-3). Natl Learning.

TAX DEDUCTIONS

Livingston, Robert A. The Tax Deduction Checklist: Songwriters, Musicians, Performers. 1982. 6.95 (ISBN 0-9607558-4-5). GLGLC Music.

Thomsen, Gregory & McInerny, Paul M. An Accent Guide: 151 Tax Deductions You Can Take. (Orig.). 1982. pap. 3.50 (ISBN 0-915708-14-0). Cheever Pub.

TAX DELINQUENCY

see Tax Evasion

TAX-DODGING

see Tax Evasion

TAX EVASION

Lewis, Alan. The Psychology of Taxation. LC 82-10656. 224p. 1982. 25.00x (ISBN 0-312-65330-1). St Martin.

TAX EXEMPTION

see Taxation, Exemption from

TAX LAW

see Taxation-Law

TAX PLANNING

see also Estate Planning

Buechner, Robert. Prosper Through Tax Planning. (Illus.). 288p. 1983. 17.95 (ISBN 0-698-11196-6, Coward). Putnam Pub Group.

Livingston, Robert A. How to Legally Reduce Your Taxes: For the Complete Idiot. 1982. 10.00 (ISBN 0-9607558-3-7). GLGLC Music.

Muhammad, S. A. How to Prepare Your Own Income Tax Return. LC 82-91051. 192p. 1982. pap. 5.00 (ISBN 0-9609996-0-4). TPA Pub.

Nessen, Robert L. Tax Shelters for the Nineteen Eighties. 320p. 1983. 14.45i (ISBN 0-316-60351-1). Little.

Paley, Stephen H., et al. Professional Corporations: An Advanced Tax Planning Program, 1982. LC 82-61269. (Tax Law & Estate Planning Course Handbook Ser.). 863p. 1982. pap. 30.00 (J4-3512). PLI.

Rudoff, Arnold G. Rudoff's Tax Shelter Directory. (Nineteen Eighty-Three Edition). 476p. 1982. 87.00 (ISBN 0-911711-00-7). Spectrum Fin Pr.

Smith, David A. Subsidized Housing as a Tax Shelter. LC 82-60131. 288p. 1982. 35.00 (ISBN 0-943570-00-X). R A Stanger.

Zabalaoui, Judith. How to Use Your Business or Profession as a Tax Shelter. 1983. text ed. 18.00 (ISBN 0-8359-2985-X). Reston.

TAX PRACTICE

see Tax Administration and Procedure

TAX RELATIONS, INTERGOVERNMENTAL

see Intergovernmental Fiscal Relations; Intergovernmental Tax Relations

TAX REMISSION

Major 1980 Tax Cut Proposals. 1980. pap. 3.75 (ISBN 0-8447-0236-6). Am Enterprise.

TAX SAVING

see Tax Planning

TAX SHARING

see Intergovernmental Tax Relations

TAX SHELTERS

see Tax Planning

TAXABLE TRANSFERS

see Inheritance and Transfer Tax

TAXATION

see also Assessment; Business Tax; Income Tax; Inheritance and Transfer Tax; Intergovernmental Fiscal Relations; Licenses; Local Taxation; Property Tax; Tax Administration and Procedure; Tax Consultants; Tax Evasion; Tax Planning; Tax Remission

also subdivision Taxation under specific subjects, e.g. Corporations-Taxation; Land-Taxation

American Institute of Certified Public Accountants. Federal Taxation Division: Underreported Income Study. write for info. Am Inst CPA.

--Taxation as a Professional Career. write for info. Am Inst CPA.

Azarian, Barbara. The American Teachers Nineteen Eighty-Two Tax Guide & Portfolio for Your Nineteen Eighty-Three Filing. 128p. (Orig.). 1982. pap. 8.95 (ISBN 0-89529-168-1). Avery Pub.

Cnossen, S., ed. Comparative Tax Studies: Essays in Honor of Richard Goode. (Contributions to Economic Analysis Ser.: Vol. 144). 450p. 1982. 76.75 (ISBN 0-444-86421-0, North Holland). Elsevier.

Endres, Dieter. Die Besteuerung Fesellschaftsrechtlicher Vermogensubertragunsgen. xiv, 340p. (Ger.). 1982. write for info. (ISBN 3-8204-7205-3). P Lang Pubs.

Feldstein, Martin. Capital Taxation. (Illus.). 96p. 1983. text ed. 40.00x (ISBN 0-674-09482-4). Harvard U Pr.

Hall, Robert F. & Rabushka, Alvin. Low Tax, Simple Tax, Flat Tax. 91st ed. LC 82-21655. 144p. 1983. 18.95 (ISBN 0-07-025670-5, GB); pap. 9.95 (ISBN 0-07-025669-1). McGraw.

Lewis, Alan. The Psychology of Taxation. LC 82-10656. 224p. 1982. 25.00x (ISBN 0-312-65330-1). St Martin.

Quattrochi, Joseph. Federal Tax Research. 208p. 1982. pap. text ed. 11.95 (ISBN 0-15-527108-3). HarBraceJ.

Rudman, Jack. Supervisor of Tax Compliance Field Operations. (Career Examination Ser.: C-2955). (Cloth bdg. avail. on request). pap. 14.00 (ISBN 0-8373-2955-8). Natl Learning.

--Tax Technician Trainee. (Career Examination Ser.: C-214). (Cloth bdg. avail. on request). pap. 10.00 (ISBN 0-8373-0214-5). Natl Learning.

--Taxpayer Service Representative. (Career Examination Ser.: C-833). (Cloth bdg. avail. on request). pap. 10.00 (ISBN 0-8373-0833-X). Natl Learning.

Shepard. International Individual Taxation, 2 vols. 1981. 75.00 (ISBN 0-07-050544-6). McGraw.

Sommerfeld, Ray M. & Anderson, Hershel M. An Introduction to Taxation Advanced Topics. 583p. 1982. text ed. 28.95 (ISBN 0-15-546321-7, HC). HarBraceJ.

Steiner, Barry R. & Kennedy, David W. Perfectly Legal: Three Hundred Foolproof Methods for Paying Less Taxes, 1983 Edition. 230p. 1983. 14.95 (ISBN 0-471-89588-1, Pub. by Wiley-Interscience); pap. 7.95 (ISBN 0-471-87020-X). Wiley.

TAXATION-ACCOUNTING

see Tax Accounting

TAXATION-EVASION

see Tax Evasion

TAXATION-LAW

see also Tax Evasion

Implementing Indexation of the Tax Laws. (Statement of Tax Policy Ser.: No. 9). 1981. pap. 6.00 (ISBN 0-686-84301-0). Am Inst CPA.

Lewis, Mervyn. British Tax Law. 704p. 1979. 79.00x (ISBN 0-686-81905-5, Pub. by McDonald & Evans). State Mutual Bk.

Purcell, L. E., ed. Economic Recovery Tax Act: Implications for State Finances. 20p. 1982. pap. 5.00 (ISBN 0-87292-030-5). Coun State Govts.

Wolfman, Bernard & Holden, James P. Ethical Problems in Federal Tax Practice. (Contemporary Legal Education Ser.). 343p. 1981. pap. text ed. 18.00 (ISBN 0-87215-399-1). Michie-Bobbs.

TAXATION-GREAT BRITAIN

Lewis, Mervyn. British Tax Law. 704p. 1979. 79.00x (ISBN 0-686-81905-5, Pub. by McDonald & Evans). State Mutual Bk.

Prest, A. R. The Taxation of Urban Land. 208p. 1982. 25.00 (ISBN 0-7190-0817-4). Manchester.

TAXATION-JAPAN

Yuji, Gomi. Guide to Japanese Taxes, 1982-83. LC 66-50788. (Illus.). 282p. (Orig.). 1982. pap. 27.50 (ISBN 0-686-84552-8). Intl Pubns Serv.

TAXATION-UNITED STATES

Hoffman, William H., Jr. & Willis, Eugene. West's Federal Taxation: Comprehensive Volume, 1983. (Illus.). 1150p. 1982. text ed. 22.95 (ISBN 0-314-70648-8); student guide avail. (ISBN 0-314-72295-5); solutions manual avail. (ISBN 0-314-72296-3). West Pub.

Pelton, Robert W. Infernal Revenue or Where Your Taxes Go. (Illus.). 1983. 6.95 (ISBN 0-916620-67-0). Portals Pr.

TAXATION-UNITED STATES-LAW

Hoffman, William H. West's Federal Taxation: Corporations, Partnerships, Estates & Trusts, 1983. 916p. text ed. 26.95 (ISBN 0-314-67112-9); write for info. instr's manual (ISBN 0-314-67319-9). West Pub.

Larson, Martin A. IRS vs. Middle Class. 1983. 12.95 (ISBN 0-8159-5824-2); pap. 5.95 (ISBN 0-8159-5827-7). Devin.

Whittenburg, Gerald E. West's Federal Taxation: Practice Sets, 1983 Edition. 288p. 1982. pap. text ed. 7.95 (ISBN 0-314-68799-8). West Pub.

TAXATION, EVASION OF

see Tax Evasion

TAXATION, EXEMPTION FROM

see also Tax Evasion

Hopkins, Bruce R. The Law of Tax-Exempt Organizations. 4th ed. 650p. 1983. 49.00x (ISBN 0-471-87538-4). Ronald Pr.

Peterson, George E. Tax Exempt Financing of Housing Investment. 45p. 1980. pap. text ed. 11.00 (ISBN 0-87766-251-7). Urban Inst.

Williamson, J. Peter. Foundation Investment Strategies: New Possibilities in the 1981 Tax Law. (Seven Springs Studies). 1981. pap. 3.00 (ISBN 0-943006-05-8). Seven Springs.

TAXATION, INCIDENCE OF

see Taxation

TAXATION, LOCAL

see Local Taxation

TAXATION AND REAL PROPERTY

see Real Property and Taxation

TAXATION OF BUSINESS

see Business Tax

TAXATION OF CAPITAL GAINS

see Capital Gains Tax

TAXATION OF FRANCHISES

see Corporations–Taxation

TAXATION OF INCOME

see Income Tax

TAXATION OF LAND VALUES

see Land Value Taxation

TAXATION OF LEGACIES

see Inheritance and Transfer Tax

TAXATION OF REAL PROPERTY

see Real Property Tax

TAXES

see Taxation

TAXES, SCHOOL

see Education–Finance

TAXIDERMY

Magorian, James. Taxidermy Lessons. LC 82-73156. 68p. 1982. 5.00 (ISBN 0-930674-08-1). Black Oak Press.

Metcalf, John C. Taxidermy: A Complete Manual. (Illus.). 166p. 1981. pap. 15.00x (ISBN 0-7156-1565-3, Pub by Duckworth England). Biblio Dist.

TAXONOMY

see Botany–Classification

TAYLOR, ELIZABETH ROSEMOND, 1932-

Waterbury, Ruth & Arceri, Gene. Elizabeth Taylor: Her Loves, Her Future. 1982. pap. 3.50 (ISBN 0-553-22613-4). Bantam.

TAYLOR, JAMES HUDSON, 1832-1905

Bromhall, A. J. Hudson Taylor & China's Open Century: Bk. II, Over the Treaty Wall. 1981. pap. 9.95 (ISBN 0-340-27561-8). OMF Bks.

Broomhall, A. J. Hudson Taylor & China's Open Century: Bk. I, Barbarians at the Gates. 1981. pap. 7.95 (ISBN 0-340-26210-9). OMF Bks.

--Hudson Taylor & China's Open Century: Bk. III, If I Had A Thousand Lives. 1983. pap. 10.95 (ISBN 0-340-32392-2). OMF Bks.

TAYLOR, PETER

Kramer, Victor A. & Bailey, Patricia A. Andrew Lytle, Walker Percy, Peter Taylor: A Reference Guide. 1983. lib. bdg. 39.00 (ISBN 0-8161-8399-6, Hall Reference). G K Hall.

TCHAIKOVSKY, PETER, 1840-1893

Brown, David. Tchaikovsky: The Crisis Years (1874-1878) (Illus.). 1983. 25.00 (ISBN 0-393-01707-9). Norton.

TE KANAWA, KIRI

Fingleton, David. Kiri Te Kanawa: A Biography. LC 82-73013. 188p. 1983. 13.95 (ISBN 0-689-11345-5). Atheneum.

TEA

see also Caffeine; Japanese Tea Ceremony

Marcin, Marietta. The Complete Book of Herbal Teas. (Illus.). 224p. 1983. 8.95 (ISBN 0-312-92098-9). Congdon & Weed.

TEA CEREMONY, JAPANESE

see Japanese Tea Ceremony

TEA ROOMS

see Restaurants, Lunchrooms, etc.

TEA TRADE

MacGregor, David R. The Tea Clippers: Their History & Development 1833-1875. LC 82-61670. (Illus.). 200p. 1982. 24.95 (ISBN 0-87021-884-0). Naval Inst Pr.

TEACH YOURSELF COURSES

see Self-Culture

also subdivision Self-Instruction under names of languages

TEACHER-PARENT RELATIONSHIPS

see Parent-Teacher Relationships

TEACHER-PUPIL INTERACTION

see Interaction Analysis in Education

TEACHER-PUPIL PLANNING

see Self-Government (In Education)

TEACHER-STUDENT RELATIONSHIPS

see also Interaction Analysis in Education

Rosenthal, Robert & Jacobson, Lenore. Pygmalion in the Classroom: Teacher Expectation & Pupils' Intellectual Development. enl. ed. 265p. 1983. pap. text ed. 10.95 (ISBN 0-8290-1265-6). Irvington.

Schwartz, Stuart E. Dealing with the Unexpected: Situational Approach for Teachers. 240p. 1982. pap. text ed. 8.95x (ISBN 0-534-01233-7). Wadsworth Pub.

Turner, Glen. The Social World of the Comprehensive School: How Pupils Adapt. 160p. 1983. text ed. 23.50x (ISBN 0-7099-2424-0, Pub. by Croom Helm Ltd England). Biblio Dist.

TEACHERS

see also College Teachers; High School Teachers; Strikes and Lockouts–Teachers; Substitute Teachers; Teachers of Exceptional Children; Teaching; Teaching As a Profession; Women Teachers

Beard, Marna L. & McGahey, Michael J. Alternative Careers for Teachers. 192p. (Orig.). 1983. pap. 9.95 (ISBN 0-668-05571-5). Arco.

Clyde, Mary K. Flashbacks to Dawn: Eye Openers in Preparatory School circa 1914-1922. 1983. price not set (ISBN 0-533-05543-1). Vantage.

Dudley, William C. Letters To Our Son: The AG Teacher. 108p. 1983. pap. text ed. 8.95x (ISBN 0-8134-2288-4). Interstate.

Fontana, David. Psychology for Teachers. (Psychology for Professional Groups Ser.). 350p. 1981. text ed. 25.00x (ISBN 0-333-31858-7, Pub. by Macmillan England); pap. text ed. 10.95x (ISBN 0-333-31880-3). Humanities.

Kutrth & Ver Hoef. Creative Teachers. (gr. 1-3). pap. text ed. 4.77 (ISBN 0-8372-4247-9); tchr's handbk. 4.77 (ISBN 0-8372-4248-7); tapes avail. Bowmar-Noble.

Selden, David. The Teacher Rebellion. 336p. 1983. 14.95 (ISBN 0-88258-099-X). Howard U Pr.

Teacher Services Committee. Handbook on Teacher Renewal & Development. 1981. pap. 6.75 (ISBN 0-934338-46-9). NAIS.

TEACHERS–CORRESPONDENCE, REMINISCENCES, ETC.

Herzog, Stephanie. Joy in the Classroom. Ray, Ann, ed. (Illus.). 1982. text ed. 6.95 (ISBN 0-916438-46-5). Univ of Trees.

TEACHERS–HANDBOOKS, MANUALS, ETC.

Berkley, Sandra. Delta's Oral Placement Test Teacher's Manual. 16p. (Orig.). 1982. pap. text ed. 6.95 (ISBN 0-937354-04-X). Delta Systems.

Bullock, Waneta B. & Meister, Barbara. Ann Arbor Learning Inventory Grades Two to Four Manual. (Ann Arbor Learning Inventory Ser.). (Illus.). 56p. (gr. 2-4). 1977. 4.00 (ISBN 0-89039-225-0); wkbk. 0.50 (ISBN 0-89039-227-7). Ann Arbor Pubs.

--Ann Arbor Learning Inventory K-1 Manual. (Ann Arbor Learning Inventory Ser.). (Illus.). 64p. (gr. k-1). 1978. 4.00 (ISBN 0-89039-246-3); wkbk. 0.50 (ISBN 0-89039-248-X). Ann Arbor Pubs.

Crowe, Patrick H. Teacher Survival Handbook. LC 82-60573. 125p. (Orig.). 1983. pap. 8.95 (ISBN 0-88247-680-7). R & E Res Assoc.

Pronin, Barbara. Substitute Teaching: A Handbook for Hassle-Free Subbing. (Illus.). 190p. 1983. 12.95 (ISBN 0-312-77481-8). St Martin.

TEACHERS–IN-SERVICE TRAINING

Howey & Bents, eds. School-Focused Inservice: Description & Discussions. 1981. 6.00 (ISBN 0-686-38076-2). Assn Tchr Ed.

Lougheed, Joyce & Meyers, eds. In Services of Youth: New Roles in the Governance of Teacher Education. 1980. 4.50 (ISBN 0-686-38074-6). Assn Tchr Ed.

Webb & Gehrke, eds. Exploratory Field Experience. 1981. 2.50 (ISBN 0-686-38073-8). Assn Tchr Ed.

TEACHERS–SALARIES, PENSIONS, ETC.

Azarian, Barbara. The American Teachers Nineteen Eighty-Two Tax Guide & Portfolio for Your Nineteen Eighty-Three Filing. 128p. (Orig.). 1982. pap. 8.95 (ISBN 0-89529-168-1). Avery Pub.

Cooper, Bruce S. Collective Bargaining, Strikes, & Financial Costs in Public Education: A Comparative Review. LC 81-71248. xix, 120p. (Orig.). 1982. pap. 7.85 (ISBN 0-86552-079-8). U of Oreg ERIC.

TEACHERS, HIGH SCHOOL

see High School Teachers

TEACHERS, RATING OF

see also Ability–Testing; Employees, Rating of

Doyle, Kenneth O., Jr. Evaluating Teaching. LC 79-9673. 192p. 1983. 20.95x (ISBN 0-669-03613-7). Lexington Bks.

Wilson, Donald R. Words for School Administrators: Example of Commondations & Constructive Suggestions for Through Teacher Evalvation. LC 80-71091. 170p. 1981. 11.95 (ISBN 0-939136-00-7). Civic Educ Assn.

TEACHERS, TRAINING OF

Here are entered works dealing with the history and methods of training teachers in general and in the United states. Works dealing with the training of teachers in other countries are listed under the appropriate subdivisions. Works dealing with the study of education as a science are entered under Education–Study and Teaching and works bearing upon the art and methods of teaching under the heading Teaching.

see also Comparative Education; Student Teaching

Ashton, Patricia M. & Henderson, Euan S. Teacher Education in the Classroom. 144p. 1983. text ed. 21.50x (ISBN 0-7099-1248-X, Pub. by Croom Helm Ltd England). Biblio Dist.

Demetrulias, Diana & Deutsch, Alleen. New Audiences for Teacher Education. LC 82-60797. (Fastback Ser.: No. 178). 50p. 1982. pap. 0.75 (ISBN 0-87367-178-3). Phi Delta Kappa.

Griffin, Gary A., ed. Staff Development, Pt. II. LC 82-62382. (The National Society for the Study of Education 82nd Yearbook). 275p. 1983. lib. bdg. 16.00x (ISBN 0-226-60136-8). U of Chicago Pr.

Houston & Pankratz, eds. Staff Development & Educational Chance. 1980. 5.00 (ISBN 0-686-38077-0). Assn Tchr Ed.

Medley. Teacher Competency Testing & the Teacher Educator. 1982. 2.50 (ISBN 0-686-38078-9). Assn Tchr Ed.

OECD. In Service Education & Training of Teachers: A Condition for Educational Change, CERI. 88p. 1982. pap. 7.00 (ISBN 92-64-12372-5). OECD.

Schwartz, Stuart E. Dealing with the Unexpected: Situational Approach for Teachers. 240p. 1982. pap. text ed. 8.95x (ISBN 0-534-01233-7). Wadsworth Pub.

Turney, C. & Cairns, L. G. The Practicum in Teacher Education: Research, Practice & Supervision. (Illus.). 208p. 1983. pap. 22.00 (ISBN 0-424-00096-2, Pub. by Sydney U Pr). Intl Schol Bk Serv.

Waterman & Andrews. Designing Short-Term Instructional Programs. 1979. 4.00 (ISBN 0-686-38072-X). Assn Tchr Ed.

TEACHERS, VOLUNTEER

see Volunteer Workers in Education

TEACHERS AND PARENTS

see Parent-Teacher Relationships

TEACHERS OF EXCEPTIONAL CHILDREN

Lewis, Rena B. & Doorlag, Donald H. Teaching Special Students in the Mainstream. 1983. text ed. 17.95 (ISBN 0-675-20011-3). Additional supplements may be obtained from publisher. Merrill.

TEACHERS OF READING

see Reading, Teachers of

TEACHERS' PENSIONS

see Teachers–Salaries, Pensions, etc.

TEACHING

see also Audio-Visual Education; Classroom Management; Education; Education of Children; Educational Psychology; Elementary School Teaching; Remedial Teaching; School Discipline; School Management and Organization; School Superintendents and Principals; Student Teaching; Study, Method of; Teachers, Rating of; Teacher-Student Relationships

also subdivision Instruction and Study or Study and Teaching under various subjects, e.g. Music–Instruction and Study; Science–Study and Teaching

Burton, William H. Supervision & the Improvement of Teaching. 510p. 1982. Repr. of 1927 ed. lib. bdg. 35.00 (ISBN 0-89760-098-3). Telegraph Bks.

De Vito, Alfred. Teaching with Quotes. (Illus.). 130p. (Orig.). 1982. pap. 9.95 (ISBN 0-942034-01-5). Creat Ventures.

Elbaz, Freema. Teacher Thinking: A Study of Practical Knowledge. LC 82-14418. 224p. 1983. 24.50 (ISBN 0-89397-144-8). Nichols Pub.

Engelmann, Siegfried & Colvin, Goeffrey. Generalized Compliance Training. (Illus.). 250p. (Orig.). Date not set. pap. text ed. price not set (ISBN 0-936104-31-7, 0375). Pro Ed.

G. Peabody College for Teachers. Free & Inexpensive Learning Materials. 21st ed. LC 53-2471. 1983. pap. 4.95 (ISBN 0-686-84844-6). Incentive Pubns.

Ganong, Joan M. & Ganong, Warren L. Help with Innovative Teaching Techniques. 2nd ed. (Help Series of Management Guides). 152p. 1976. pap. 13.95 (ISBN 0-933036-08-6). Ganong W L Co.

Higgins, Norman & Sullivan, Howard J. Teaching for Competence. 1983. pap. price not set (ISBN 0-8077-2725-3). Tchrs Coll.

Lakebrink, Joan M. Children's Success in School. (Illus.). 260p. 1983. 19.75x (ISBN 0-398-04776-6). C C Thomas.

Monroe, Walter S. Directing Learning in the Elementary School. 480p. 1982. Repr. of 1932 ed. lib. bdg. 45.00 (ISBN 0-89987-648-X). Darby Bks.

Postman, Neil. Teaching As a Conserving Activity. pap. 7.00 (ISBN 0-686-84061-5). Intl Gen Semantics.

Ryan, Kevin & Phillips, Debra H. The Workbook: Exploring a Career in Teaching. 350p. 1983. pap. text ed. 11.95 (ISBN 0-675-20057-1). Additional supplements may be obtained from publisher. Merrill.

Smith, Judith M. Designing Instructional Tasks: A Primer. (Michigan Learning Modules Ser.: No. 6). 1979. write for info. (ISBN 0-914004-09-3). Ulrich.

Spevack, J. M. Teaching Sucks. 130p. pap. 2.95 (ISBN 0-9604448-2-3). Spevack.

Stellern, John. Diagnostic Prescriptive Teaching. 1982. 24.95 (ISBN 0-914420-56-9). Exceptional Pr Inc.

Stellern, John & Vasa, Stanley F. Introduction to Diagnostic-Prescriptive Teaching & Programming. 176p. 1976. 18.95 (ISBN 0-686-84869-1). Exceptional Pr Inc.

Stewart, William J. Transforming Traditional Unit Teaching. 87p. 1982. pap. text ed. 3.95x (ISBN 0-89641-107-9). American Pr.

--Unit Teaching: Perspectives & Prospects. LC 82-60785. 125p. (Orig.). 1983. pap. 12.95 (ISBN 0-686-81659-5). R & E Res Assoc.

Wiederholt, J. Lee & Hammill, Donald D. The Resource Teacher: A Guide to Effective Practices. 2nd ed. (Illus.). 400p. 1983. pap. text ed. price not set (ISBN 0-936104-33-3, 0085). Pro Ed.

TEACHING–AIDS AND DEVICES

see also Audio-Visual Education; Bulletin Boards; Creative Activities and Seatwork; Handicraft; Moving-Pictures in Education; Paper Work; Television in Education

Cameron, Sean, ed. Working Together: New Developments Incorporating the Portage Teaching Model. (NFER General Ser.). 172p. 1982. pap. text ed. 12.50x (ISBN 0-85633-241-0, 51732, NFER). Humanities.

Cheyney, Arnold & Capone, Donald. The Map Corner. 1983. pap. text ed. 12.95 (ISBN 0-673-16615-5). Scott F.

Educators Guide to Free Filmstrips. 34th ed. 15.75 (ISBN 0-686-84809-8). Ed Prog.

Guadarrama, Argelia A. Steps to English Kindergarten Teacher's Manual. 128p. 1983. pap. text ed. 7.68 (ISBN 0-07-033110-3, W); kit 266.64 (ISBN 0-07-033100-6). McGraw.

Jay, Hilda L. Stimulating Student Search: Library Media Classroom Teacher Techniques. 160p. 1983. 18.50 (ISBN 0-208-01936-7, Lib Prof Pubns); pap. 14.50 (ISBN 0-208-01926-X). Shoe String.

Low-Cost Educational Materials. 117p. 1981. pap. 7.00 (ISBN 0-686-84038-0, UB111, UNESCO Regional Office). Unipub.

National Information Center for Educational Media. Index to Educational Video Tapes. LC 82-60347. 1983. pap. 78.00 (ISBN 0-89320-053-0). Univ SC Natl Info.

--Index to Producers & Distributors. LC 82-60346. 1983. pap. 34.00 (ISBN 0-89320-055-7). Univ SC Natl Info.

--Index to 16mm Educational Film. LC 82-60348. 1983. pap. 164.00 (ISBN 0-89320-052-2). Univ SC Natl Info.

--Index to 35mm Educational Filmstrips. 1983. pap. 124.00 (ISBN 0-89320-054-9). Univ SC Natl Info.

Wise, Bernice Kemmler. Teaching Materials for the Learning Disabled. LC 80-18114. 70p. 1980. pap. text ed. 5.00 (ISBN 0-8389-0311-8). ALA.

TEACHING–CASE STUDIES

Collins, Marva & Tamarkin, Civia. Marva Collins' Way. 227p. 1982. 12.95 (ISBN 0-87477-235-4). J P Tarcher.

TEACHING–HISTORY

see Education–History

TEACHING–VOCATIONAL GUIDANCE

see Teaching As a Profession

TEACHING AS A PROFESSION

see also College Teaching As a Profession

Furniss, W. Todd. Reshaping Faculty Careers. 171p. 1981. 8.95 (ISBN 0-8268-1449-2). Impact VA.

Miller, Anne. Finding Career Alternatives for Teacher's Program. 1982. cassettes & wkbk. 49.95. Impact VA.

Pollock, Sandy. Alternative Careers for Teachers. 128p. 1979. 8.95 (ISBN 0-916782-16-6). Impact VA.

Turner, J. D. & Rushton, J., eds. Teacher in a Changing Society. 1974. 12.50 (ISBN 0-7190-0566-3). Manchester.

TEACHING AUTHORITY OF THE CHURCH

see Catechetics–Catholic Church

TEACHING LABORATORIES

see Student Teaching

TEACHING MATERIALS

see Teaching–Aids and Devices

TEACHINGS OF JESUS

see Jesus Christ–Teachings

TECHNICAL ASSISTANCE

see also Community Development; Industrialization; Investments, Foreign; Underdeveloped Areas

Barnett, A. & Bell, R. M. Rural Energy & the Third World: A Review of Social Science Research & Technology Policy Problems. (Illus.). 302p. 1982. 36.00 (ISBN 0-08-028953-3); 18.00 (ISBN 0-08-028954-1). Pergamon.

McDonald, John W. The North-South Dialogue & the United Nations. LC 82-1039. 24p. 1982. 1.25 (ISBN 0-934742-16-2, Inst Study Diplomacy). Geo U Sch For Serv.

Technologies for Rural Development. 174p. 1982. pap. 13.25 (ISBN 92-3-101971-6, U1227, UNESCO). Unipub.

TECHNICAL ASSISTANCE IN ASIA

Technology Development For Small Industry In Selected Asian Countries. 404p. 1982. pap. 14.75 (ISBN 92-833-1488-3, APO). Unipub.

TECHNICAL CHEMISTRY

see Chemistry, Technical

TECHNICAL COMMUNICATION

see Communication of Technical Information

TECHNICAL DICTIONARIES

see Technology–Dictionaries

TECHNICAL DRAWING

see Mechanical Drawing

TECHNICAL DRAWINGS

see Engineering Drawings

TECHNICAL EDUCATION

see also Apprentices; Employees, Training of; Industrial Arts; Occupational Training; Professional Education; Vocational Education

Engineering & Technology Degrees, 1980, 3 pts. Set. 150.00 (ISBN 0-87615-031-8, 201-80); Pt. I. 35.00 (ISBN 0-87615-041-5, 201A-80); Pt. II. 100.00 (ISBN 0-87615-051-2, 201B-80); Pt. III. 35.00 (ISBN 0-87615-061-X, 201C-80). AAES.

Engineering & Technology Enrollments: Fall 1981, 2 pts. Set. 100.00 (ISBN 0-87615-072-5, 207-81); Pt. I. 60.00 (ISBN 0-87615-082-2, 207A-81); Pt. II. 60.00 (ISBN 0-87615-092-X, 207B-81). AAES.

Vocational & Technical Education: Development of Curricula, Instructional Materials, Physical Facilities & Teacher Training with Focus on Electrical & Electronic Subjects. 97p. 1981. pap. 5.25 (ISBN 0-686-81850-4, UB110, UNESCO). Unipub.

TECHNICAL EDUCATION-DIRECTORIES

Norback & Company, ed. Arco's Guide to Technical, Vocational & Trade Schools. (Arco Occupational Guides Ser.). 208p. 1983. lib. bdg. 11.95 (ISBN 0-668-05524-3); pap. 6.95 (ISBN 0-668-05532-4). Arco.

Ready, Barbara C., ed. Peterson's Annual Guides to Graduate Study: Engineering & Applied Sciences, 1983. 800p. 1982. pap. 17.95 (ISBN 0-87866-189-1). Petersons Guides.

TECHNICAL ILLUSTRATION

see also Scientific Illustration

Beakley, George C. & Autore, Donald D. Technical Illustration. (Illus.). 256p. (Orig.). 1983. pap. text ed. 18.95 (ISBN 0-672-97993-4). Bobbs.

Holmes. Beginners Guide to Technical Illustration. 1982. text ed. 9.95 (ISBN 0-408-00582-3). Butterworth.

Schmidt, Steven. Creating the Technical Report. (Illus.). 160p. 1983. 17.95 (ISBN 0-13-189027-1). P-H.

TECHNICAL INFORMATION, COMMUNICATION OF

see Communication of Technical Information

TECHNICAL INNOVATIONS

see Technological Innovations

TECHNICAL INSTITUTES

see Technical Education

TECHNICAL LIBRARIES

Mount, Ellis, ed. Cataloging & Indexing in Sci-Tech Libraries. (Science & Technology Libraries: Vol. 2, No. 3). 92p. 1982. pap. text ed. 15.00 (ISBN 0-86656-204-4, B204). Haworth Pr.

--Document Delivery for Sci-Tech Libraries. (Science & Technology Libraries: Vol. 2, No. 4). 133p. 1982. pap. text ed. 15.00 (ISBN 0-86656-200-1, B200). Haworth Pr.

--Online vs. Manual Searching in Sci-Tech Libraries. (Science & Technology Libraries: Vol. 3, No. 1). 89p. 1982. pap. text ed. 15.00 (ISBN 0-86656-203-6, B203). Haworth Pr.

TECHNICAL LITERATURE

see also Patents; Technical Reports

Turley, Raymond. Understanding the Structure of Scientific & Technical Literature: A Visual Approach. 176p. 1983. write for info. (ISBN 0-85157-368-1, Pub. by Bingley England). Shoe String.

TECHNICAL REPORTS

Here are entered works on the processing and use of technical and scientific reports. Guides to technical authorship are entered under the heading Technical Writing.

see also Technical Writing

Swanson, Edward. A Manual of AACR2 Examples for Technical Reports. 1983. pap. text ed. 7.00 (ISBN 0-936996-15-3). Soldier Creek.

TECHNICAL REPORTS-ILLUSTRATION

see Technical Illustration

TECHNICAL SCHOOLS

see Technical Education

TECHNICAL SERVICE

see Customer Service

TECHNICAL TERMS

see Technology-Dictionaries; Technology-Terminology

TECHNICAL WRITING

Here are entered guides to authorship in engineering, science, and technology. Similar guides in other fields are entered under a corresponding term if in common usage, e.g. Medical Writing; otherwise under (subject)-authorship.

see also Authorship-Handbooks, Manuals, etc.; Technical Reports

Day, Robert A. How to Write & Publish a Scientific Paper. 2nd ed. (Professional Writing Ser.). (Illus.). 180p. 1983. 17.95 (ISBN 0-686-84415-7); pap. text ed. 11.95 (ISBN 0-89495-022-3). ISI Pr.

Ewing, David W. Writing for Results in Business, Government, the Sciences & the Professions. 2nd ed. LC 79-11756. 448p. 1979. 24.95 (ISBN 0-471-05036-9). Wiley.

Harnad, Stevan, ed. Peer Commentary on Peer Review: A Case Study in Scientific Quality Control. LC 82-19860. 80p. Date not set. pap. 12.95 (ISBN 0-521-27306-4). Cambridge U Pr.

Schmidt, Steven. Creating the Technical Report. (Illus.). 160p. 1983. 17.95 (ISBN 0-13-189027-1). P-H.

Weisman, Herman M. Basic Technical Writing. 4th ed. 1980. text ed. 16.95 (ISBN 0-675-08146-7). Merrill.

TECHNICIANS, LABORATORY

see Laboratory Technicians

TECHNICIANS IN INDUSTRY

Pratley, J. B. Study Notes for Technicians, Vol. 3. 148p. 1983. write for info. (ISBN 0-07-084663-4). McGraw.

TECHNOLOGICAL FORECASTING

see also Technology Transfer

Jones, Barry. Sleepers, Wake! Technology & the Future of Work. (Illus.). 302p. 1983. pap. 9.95 (ISBN 0-19-554270-3, GB). Oxford U Pr.

Stine, G. Harry. The Hopeful Future. 256p. 1983. 15.95 (ISBN 0-02-094140-4). Macmillan.

TECHNOLOGICAL INNOVATIONS

see also Machinery in Industry

Bushnell, David S. Training for New Technology. (Work in America Institute Studies in Productivity). 1983. 35.00 (ISBN 0-08-029508-8). Pergamon.

Cooper, C. A. & Clark, J. A., eds. Employment, Economics & Technology: The Impact of Technological Change on the Labor Market. LC 82-42543. 180p. 1982. 25.00x (ISBN 0-312-24459-2). St Martin.

De Camp, L. Sprague. The Fringe of the Unknown. 205p. 1983. 16.95 (ISBN 0-87975-204-1). Prometheus Bks.

Elster, Jon. Explaining Technical Change: A Case Study in the Philosophy of Science. LC 82-9702. (Studies in Rationality & Social Change). (Illus.). 304p. Date not set. 39.50 (ISBN 0-521-24920-1); pap. 11.95 (ISBN 0-521-27072-3). Cambridge U Pr.

Farzin, Yeganeh. The Effect of Discount Rate & Substitute Technology on Depletion of Exhaustible Resources. LC 82-8612. (World Bank Staff Working Papers: No. 516). (Orig.). 1982. pap. 5.00 (ISBN 0-8213-0004-0). World Bank.

Freeman, Christopher. The Economics of Industrial Innovation. 2nd ed. 320p. 1983. 25.00 (ISBN 0-262-06083-3). MIT Pr.

Gerstenfeld, Arthur. Technological Innovation: Government-Industry Cooperation. LC 78-14800. 1979. 34.95x (ISBN 0-471-03647-1, Pub. by Wiley-Interscience). Wiley.

Harfax. Harfax Guide to the High Tech Industries. 344p. 1983. ref 65.00x (ISBN 0-88410-619-5). Ballinger Pub.

Hecht, Norman L. Design Principles. LC 82-46060. (Design & Management for Resource Recovery Ser.: Vol. 5). (Illus.). 120p. 1983. 29.95 (ISBN 0-250-40315-3). Ann Arbor Science.

Jones, Barry O. Sleepers, Wake! Technology & the Future of Work. (Illus.). 302p. 1983. 24.95 (ISBN 0-19-554343-2). Oxford U Pr.

Lundstedt, Sven B. & Colglazier, E. William, eds. Managing Innovation: The Social Dimensions of Creativity, Invention & Technology. 260p. 29.50 (ISBN 0-686-84788-1). Work in Amer.

Sanders, Ralph. International Dynamics of Technology. LC 82-9220. (Contributions in Political Science Ser.: No. 87). 352p. 1983. lib. bdg. 35.00 (ISBN 0-313-23401-9, SAD/). Greenwood.

Stern, B. T., ed. Information & Innovation: Proceedings of a Seminar of ICSU-AB on the Role of Information in the Innovative Process, Amsterdam, The Netherlands, 1982. (Contemporary Topics in Information Transfer Ser.: Vol. 1). 192p. 1982. 38.50 (ISBN 0-444-86496-2, North Holland). Elsevier.

Walcoff, Carol & Ouellette, Robert P. Techniques for Managing Technological Innovation: Overcoming Process Barriers. LC 82-72860. (Illus.). 151p. 1982. 18.75 (ISBN 0-250-40603-9). Ann Arbor Science.

TECHNOLOGICAL INNOVATIONS-LATIN AMERICA

Syrquin, Moshe, ed. Trade, Stability, Technology & Equity in Latin America. LC 82-13890. write for info. (ISBN 0-12-680050-2). Acad Pr.

TECHNOLOGICAL TRANSFER

see Technology Transfer

TECHNOLOGISTS

see also Laboratory Technicians; Technicians in Industry

Chaudier, Louann, ed. Leading Consultants in Technology 1983. 160p. 1983. 28.00. J Dick.

TECHNOLOGY

see also Building; Chemistry, Technical; Electric Engineering; Engineering; Factories; Industrial Arts; Industrial Management; Inventions; Machinery; Manufactures; Membranes (Technology); Mills and Mill-Work; Mineral Industries; Railroad Engineering; Technical Education; Technological Innovations

also names of specific industries, arts trades, etc., e.g. Clock and Watch Making, Printing, Tailoring

Dempsey, Michael W., ed. Illustrated Fact Book of Science. LC 82-16412. (Illus.). 236p. 1983. 9.95 (ISBN 0-668-05729-7, 5729). Arco.

Engineering & Technology Enrollments: Fall 1982, 2 pts. 1983. Set. 100.00 (ISBN 0-87615-074-1, 207-83); Pt. I. 60.00 (ISBN 0-87615-084-9, 207A-83); Pt. II. 60.00 (ISBN 0-87615-094-6, 207B-83). AAES.

Herman, Herbert, ed. Treatise on Materials Science & Technology: Embrittlement of Engineering Alloys, Vol. 25. (Serial Publication). Date not set. price not set (ISBN 0-12-341825-9). Acad Pr.

Hubbard, B., ed. Technology Management. (Computer State of the Art Report, Series 10: No. 8). 400p. 1982. 445.00 (ISBN 0-08-028571-6). Pergamon.

Mitcham, Carl & Mackey, Robert, eds. Philosophy & Technology. LC 82-19818. 416p. 1982. pap. text ed. 12.95 (ISBN 0-02-921430-0). Free Pr.

Morehead, John W. Finding & Licensing New Products & Technology from the U. S. A. 500p. 1982. 495.00 (ISBN 0-943420-00-8). Tech Search Intl.

Moritani, Masanori. Japanese Technology: Getting the Best for the Least. Simul International, tr. (Illus.). 230p. 1982. pap. 19.95 (ISBN 0-686-42807-2, Pub. by Simul Pr Japan). Intl Schol Bk Serv.

Pecufflic, M. & Abdel-Malek, A. Science & Technology in the Transformation of the World. 1982. 55.00x (ISBN 0-686-42943-5, Pub. by Macmillan England). State Mutual Bk.

Pring, M. J. Technical Analysis Explained: An Illustrated Guide for the Investor. 1980. 35.95 (ISBN 0-07-050871-2). McGraw.

Rangarao, B. V. & Chaubey, N. P., eds. Social Perspective of Development of Science & Technology in India. 1983. 22.00x (ISBN 0-8364-0931-0, Pub. by Heritage India). South Asia Bks.

Rheingold, Howard & Levine, Howard. Talking Tech: A Conversational Guide to Science & Technology. (Illus.). 324p. 1983. pap. 6.95 (ISBN 0-688-01603-0). Quill NY.

Rosenberg, Nathan. Inside the Black Box: Technology & Economics. LC 82-4563. 304p. 1983. 29.95 (ISBN 0-521-24808-6); pap. 12.95 (ISBN 0-521-27367-6). Cambridge U Pr.

Rossini, Frederick D. Fundamental Measures & Constants for Science & Technology. LC 74-14759. 142p. Repr. of 1974 ed. text ed. 34.50 (ISBN 0-8493-5079-4). Krieger.

Singer, Hans. Technologies for Basic Needs. 2nd ed. x, 161p. 1982. 8.55 (ISBN 92-2-103068-7); pap. 11.40 (ISBN 92-2-103069-5). Intl Labour Office.

Technology for Development: First International Conference. 367p. (Orig.). 1980. pap. text ed. 60.00x (ISBN 0-85825-140-X, Pub. by Inst Engineering Australia). Renouf.

Technology Generation & the Technological Space. 31p. 1982. pap. 5.00 (ISBN 92-808-0390-5, TUNU 196, UNU). Unipub.

Thorburn, Craig. Teknologi Kampungan: A Compendium of Indonesian Indigenous Technologies. Darrow, Ken & Stanley, Bill, eds. (Illus.). 154p. 1982. pap. 5.00 (ISBN 0-917704-16-9). Volunteers Asia.

The Timetable of Technology. LC 82-11899. (Illus.). 240p. 1982. 30.00 (ISBN 0-87851-209-8). Hearst Bks.

Who's Who in Frontier Science & Technology. LC 82-82015. 1983. 84.50 (ISBN 0-8379-5701-X). Marquis.

TECHNOLOGY-ADDRESSES, ESSAYS, LECTURES

ACSM-ASP Fall Convention, Sept. 1982. Technical Papers. pap. 12.50 (ISBN 0-937294-39-X). ASP.

TECHNOLOGY-AUTHORSHIP

see Technical Writing

TECHNOLOGY-BIBLIOGRAPHY

Research Libraries of New York Public Library & Library of Congress. Bibliographic Guide to Technology: 1982. 1983. lib. bdg. 250.00 (ISBN 0-8161-6981-0, Biblio Guides). G K Hall.

TECHNOLOGY-DICTIONARIES

see also Technology-Terminology;

also names of specific industries, with or without the subdivision Dictionaries

Angelo, Joseph. The Dictionary of Space Technology. 384p. 1982. 70.00x (ISBN 0-584-95011-X, Pub. by Muller Ltd). State Mutual Bk.

TECHNOLOGY-EXHIBITIONS

see Exhibitions

TECHNOLOGY-HISTORY

see also Industrial Archaeology

Alpert, Carl. Technion: The Story of Israel's Institute of Technology. LC 82-11556. (Illus.). 439p. 1983. 25.00x (ISBN 0-87203-102-0). Hermon.

Ferrari, Guy. How to Profit from Future Technology: A Guide to Success in the Eighties & Beyond. Adams, Mary, ed. LC 82-73571. 300p. 1983. pap. 14.95 (ISBN 0-686-37897-0). Windsor Hse.

Joel, A. E., Jr. Switching Technology 1925-1975: A History of Engineering & Science in the Bell System. Schindler, G. E., ed. (Illus.). 600p. 1982. 25.00 (ISBN 0-686-83987-0). Bell Telephone.

Jones, Barry O. Sleepers, Wake! Technology & the Future of Work. (Illus.). 302p. 1983. 24.95 (ISBN 0-19-554343-2). Oxford U Pr.

Yarwood, Doreen. Five Hundred Years of Technology in the Home. (Illus.). 168p. 1983. 31.50 (ISBN 0-7134-3506-2, Pub. by Batsford England). David & Charles.

TECHNOLOGY-HISTORY-INDIA

Rangarao, B. V. & Chaubey, N. P., eds. Social Perspective of Development of Science & Technology in India. 1983. 22.00x (ISBN 0-8364-0931-0, Pub. by Heritage India). South Asia Bks.

Vyasulu, Vinod, ed. Technological Choice in the Indian Environment. 351p. 1980. 44.95x (ISBN 0-940500-59-0, Pub. by Sterling India). Asia Bk Corp.

TECHNOLOGY-HISTORY-RUSSIA

Office of Technology Assessment, U. S. Congress. Technology & Soviet Energy Availability. 400p. 1982. lib. bdg. 25.00 (ISBN 0-86531-468-3). Westview.

TECHNOLOGY-NOTATION

Dyball, G. E. Mathematics for Technician Engineers: Levels 4 & 5. 384p. 1983. write for info. (ISBN 0-07-084664-2). McGraw.

TECHNOLOGY-SOCIAL ASPECTS

Here are entered works on the impact of technology on modern society. Works on the role of technology in the history and development of civilization are entered under Technology and Civilization.

Bereano, Philip L. Technology As a Social & Political Phenomenon. LC 76-18723. 544p. 1976. text ed. 32.95x (ISBN 0-471-06875-6). Wiley.

Florman, Samuel. Blaming Technology: The Irrational Search for Scapegoats. 224p. pap. 6.95 (ISBN 0-312-08363-7). St Martin.

Fools! How You May Destroy Yourself with Thought Control & Technological Slavery. (Analysis Ser.: No. 5). 1982. pap. 10.00 (ISBN 0-686-42840-4). Inst Analysis.

Fuller, R. Buckminster. Grunch of Giants. 120p. 1983. 8.95 (ISBN 0-312-35193-3). St Martin.

How to Destoy Freedom & the World. (Analysis Ser.: No. 3). 1982. pap. 10.00 (ISBN 0-686-42838-2). Inst Analysis.

Pool, Ithiel D. Technologies of Freedom. (Illus.). 344p. 1983. 20.00 (ISBN 0-674-87232-0, Belknap Pr). Harvard U Pr.

Rothschild, Joan, ed. Machina ex Dea: Feminist Perspectives on Technology. (Athene Ser.). 250p. 1983. 27.50 (ISBN 0-08-029404-9); pap. 10.95 (ISBN 0-08-029403-0). Pergamon.

Summers, Gene F., ed. Technology & Social Change in Rural Areas. (Rural Studies Ser.). 400p. 1983. softcover 26.50 (ISBN 0-86531-600-7). Westview.

Thought Control & Technological Slavery in America. (Analysis Ser.: No. 1). 1982. pap. 10.00 (ISBN 0-686-42834-X). Inst Analysis.

Thought Control & Technological Slavery in America. (Analysis Ser.: No. 2). 1982. pap. 10.00 (ISBN 0-686-42836-6). Inst Analysis.

Thought Control & Technological Slavery in America: Illustration & Selected Correspondence. (Analysis Ser.). 75p. 1983. pap. 18.00 (ISBN 0-686-42852-8). Inst Analysis.

TECHNOLOGY-TERMINOLOGY

Huckin, Thomas & Olsen, Leslie. English for Science & Technology: A Handbook for Non-Native Speakers. (Illus.). 576p. 1983. 19.95 (ISBN 0-07-030821-7); instr's manual 6.95 (ISBN 0-07-047822-8). McGraw.

TECHNOLOGY, EDUCATIONAL

see Educational Technology

TECHNOLOGY AND CIVILIZATION

Here are entered works on the role of technology in the history and development of civilization. Works on the impact of technology on modern society are entered under Technology-Social Aspects.

see also Machinery in Industry; Social Problems

Heppenheimer, T. A. The Real Future: Tomorrow's Technology Today. LC 82-45291. (Illus.). 400p. 1983. 17.95 (ISBN 0-385-17688-0). Doubleday.

Stine, G. Harry. The Hopeful Future. 256p. 1983. 15.95 (ISBN 0-02-094140-4). Macmillan.

TECHNOLOGY AND LAW

Nyhart, J. D. & Carrow, Milton M., eds. Law & Science in Collaboration: Resolving Regulatory Issues of Science & Technology. LC 81-47689. 320p. 1983. 29.95x (ISBN 0-669-04907-7). Lexington Bks.

TECHNOLOGY AND STATE

see also Astronautics and State; Industry and State; Research and Development Contracts; Science and State

Sanders, Ralph. International Dynamics of Technology. LC 82-9220. (Contributions in Political Science Ser.: No. 87). 352p. 1983. lib. bdg. 35.00 (ISBN 0-313-23401-9, SAD/). Greenwood.

Zeman, Zavis P. & Hoffman, David, eds. The Dynamics of the Technological Leadership of the World. 58p. 1980. pap. text ed. 3.00x (ISBN 0-920380-44-1, Inst Res Pub Canada). Renouf.

TECHNOLOGY ASSESSMENT

Office of Technical Assessment, Congress of the U. S. Technology & Handicapped People. 1983. text ed. price not set (ISBN 0-8261-4510-8). Springer Pub.

Srinivisan, Mangalam, ed. Technology Assessment & Development. 288p. 1982. 29.95 (ISBN 0-03-059543-6). Praeger.

TECHNOLOGY TRANSFER

see also Technological Forecasting

Bertsch, Gary K. & McIntyre, John R., eds. National Security & Technology Transfer: The Strategic Dimensions of East-West Trade. 300p. 1983. price not set (ISBN 0-86531-614-7). Westview.

Frame, J. Davidson. International Business & Global Technology. LC 82-48480. 224p. 1982. 24.95 (ISBN 0-669-06156-5). Lexington Bks.

Mascarenhas, R. C. Technology Transfer & Development: India's Hindustan Machine Tools Company. 235p. 1982. softcover 19.50 (ISBN 0-86531-934-0). Westview.

Molnar, Joseph J. & Clonts, Howard A., eds. Transferring Food Production Technology to Developing Nations: Economic & Social Dimensions. (Replica Edition Ser.). 174p. 1983. softcover 19.50x (ISBN 0-86531-957-X). Westview.

TEEN-AGE

see Adolescence

TEEN-AGE GIRLS

see Adolescent Girls

TEEN-AGE PARENTS

see Adolescent Parents

TEEN-AGERS

see Youth

TEEPEE BURNERS

see Incinerators

TEETH

see also Dentistry; Dentition

Ashley, Ruth & Kirby, Tess. Dental Anatomy & Terminology. LC 76-49088. (Self-Teaching Guides). 242p. 1977. text ed. 4.95x (ISBN 0-471-01348-X). Wiley.
Gartner, Leslie P. Essentials of Oral Histology & Embryology. LC 82-90755. (Illus.). 120p. 1982. pap. text ed. 8.75 (ISBN 0-910841-00-4). Jen Hse Pub Co.

TEETH-CARE AND HYGIENE

Here are entered works on personal dental hygiene for the layman. Works on dental hygiene as practiced by dental hygienists are entered under Dental Hygiene.
see also Dental Hygiene
Learning about Your Oral Health, 5 levels. 7.50 ea. Level I (ISBN 0-934510-16-4, W017). Level II (ISBN 0-934510-17-2, W018). Level III (ISBN 0-934510-18-0, W019). Level IV (ISBN 0-934510-19-9, W020). Pre-school (ISBN 0-934510-20-2, W021). Am Dental.
Murray, J. J. & Rugg-Gunn, A. J. Fluorides in Cavities Prevention: Dental Practitioner Handbook, No. 20. 1982. text ed. 22.50 (ISBN 0-7236-0644-7). Wright-PSG.
Oral Health Care for the Geriatric Patient in a Long Term Care Facility. 5.25 (ISBN 0-934510-13-X, J010). Am Dental.
A Prevention-Oriented School Based Dental Health Program: Guidelines for Implementation. 4 copies 6.00 (ISBN 0-934510-23-7, W014). Am Dental.

TEETH-DISEASES

see also Endodontics
Loesche, Walter J. Dental Caries: A Treatable Infection. (Illus.). 576p. 1982. spiral 29.75x (ISBN 0-398-04767-7). C C Thomas.

TEETH-EXTRACTION

Messing, J. J. Operative Dental Surgery. 2nd ed. 1982. 79.00x (ISBN 0-333-31040-3, Pub. by Macmillan England). State Mutual Bk.

TEETH, ARTIFICIAL

see Prosthodontics

TEETHING

see Dentition

TEILHARD DE CHARDIN, PIERRE, 1881-1955

King, Thomas M. & Salmon, James F., eds. Teilhard & the Unity of Knowledge. LC 82-60590. 1983. pap. 8.95 (ISBN 0-8091-2491-2). Paulist Pr.
Lyons, J. A. The Cosmic Christ in Origin & Teilhard de Chardin. Wiles, Maurice, ed. (Theological Monographs). 248p. 1982. 33.50x (ISBN 0-19-826721-5). Oxford U Pr.

TELECOMMUNICATION

see also Artificial Satellites in Telecommunication; Broadcasting; Data Transmission Systems; Error-Correcting Codes (Information Theory); Police Communication Systems; Radio; Signal Theory (Telecommunication); Speech Processing Systems; Telephone; Television
Bell Laboratories. Human Factors in Telecommunications International Symposium, 9th. 1980. 75.00 (ISBN 0-686-37981-0). Info Gatekeepers.
Churchill College, Cambridge England. Human Factors in Telecommunications, International Symposium, 8th. 1977. 75.00 (ISBN 0-686-37980-2). Info Gatekeepers.
Connor, F. R. Modulation. (Introductory Topics in Electronics & Telecommunication). 144p. 1982. pap. text ed. 9.95 (ISBN 0-7131-3457-7). E Arnold.
Evans. Breaking Up Bell: Essays on Industrial Organization & Regulation. Date not set. price not set (ISBN 0-444-00734-2). Elsevier.
Experimental Technology Incentives Program. Toward Competitive Provision of Public Record Message Services. 1981. 75.00 (ISBN 0-686-37963-2). Info Gatekeepers.
The Future of the Electronics & Telecommunications Industries in Australia. 93p. (Orig.). 1978. pap. text ed. 18.00x (ISBN 0-85825-099-3, Pub. by Inst Engineering Australia). Renouf.
Future Systems, Inc. Teleconferencing: An Enhanced Communications Service. rev. ed. (Illus.). 207p. 1982. pap. 525.00x (ISBN 0-940520-17-6). Monegon Ltd.
Gallager, R. G. Information Theory & Reliable Communication. LC 68-26850. 588p. 1968. 41.95x (ISBN 0-471-29048-3). Wiley.
Gecsei, Jan. Architecture of Videotex Systems. (Illus.). 320p. 1983. 29.95 (ISBN 0-13-044776-5). P H.
Glossbrenner, Alfred. The Complete Handbook of Personal Computer Communications. 1983. pap. 14.95 (ISBN 0-312-15718-5). St Martin.
Gross, Lynne S. Telecommunications: An Introduction to Radio, Television & the Developing Media. 380p. 1983. pap. text ed. write for info. (ISBN 0-697-04359-2); instrs.' manual avail. (ISBN 0-697-04361-4). Wm C Brown.
Haykin, Simon. Communication Systems. 2nd ed. 625p. 1983. 33.95 (ISBN 0-471-09691-1); tchrs.' avail. (ISBN 0-471-87155-9). Wiley.
Martech Strategies, Inc. Present & Projected Business Utilization of International Telecommunications. 1981. 75.00 (ISBN 0-686-37964-0). Info Gatekeepers.
Meadow. Telecommunications for Management. 1983. write for info. (ISBN 0-07-041198-0). McGraw.
Montreal Telephone Co. The Seventh International Symposium on Human Factors in Telecommunications. 1974. pap. 75.00 (ISBN 0-686-37979-9). Info-Gatekeepers.
National Telecommunications & Information Administration. Competition & Deregulation in International Telecommunications: An Analysis of 15 FCC Actions & Their Effects, 2 vols. 1981. 95.00 set (ISBN 0-686-37961-6). Info Gatekeepers.
Niles, Jack M., et al. The Telecommunications-Transportation Tradeoff: Options for Tomorrow. LC 76-18107. 208p. Repr. of 1976 ed. text ed. 44.50 (ISBN 0-471-01507-5). Krieger.
Office of International Affairs National Telecommunications & Information Administration. Profiles of International Private Lease, DATEL & Packet Switched Service Markets for the Years 1976 to 1979. 1981. 50.00 (ISBN 0-686-37966-7). Info Gatekeepers.
Post Office Research Dept. London England. Human Factors in Telecommunications International Symposium, 5th. 1970. 75.00 (ISBN 0-686-37975-6). Info Gatekeepers.
Salvaggio, Jerry L. Telecommunications: Issues & Choices for Society. Anderson, Gordon T., ed. (Annenberg-Longman Communication Ser.). (Illus.). 259p. 1983. text ed. 24.95x (ISBN 0-686-37900-4). Longman.
Schiller, Dan. Telematics & Government. 256p. 1982. 24.50 (ISBN 0-89391-106-2); pap. 12.50 (ISBN 0-89391-129-1). Ablex Pub.
Simpson, Alan, ed. Planning for Telecommunications. (The Office of the Future Ser.). 158p. (Orig.). 1982. pap. text ed. 23.50x (ISBN 0-566-03415-8). Gower Pub Ltd.
Telecommunications Energy Conference-Intelec 81. (IEE Conference Publication Ser.: No. 196). 371p. 1981. 81.50 (ISBN 0-85296-236-3). Inst Elect Eng.
Telecommunications Policy Research Conference, Annual 10th. Proceedings. Gandy, Oscar, et al, eds. 256p. 1983. text ed. 24.95 (ISBN 0-89391-195-X). Ablex Pub.
Would You Like to Be a Telecommunications Specialist? 48p. (gr. 4-6). 1983. 2.95 (ISBN 0-941852-07-5). Unica Inc.
Zima, Joseph P. Interviewing: Key to Effective Management. 352p. 1983. pap. text ed. write for info. (ISBN 0-574-22720-2, 13-5720); write for info. instr's. guide (ISBN 0-574-22721-0, 13-5721). SRA.

TELECOMMUNICATION-EXAMINATIONS, QUESTIONS, ETC.

Rudman, Jack. Telecommunications Aide. (Career Examination Ser.: C-2877). (Cloth bdg. avail. on request). pap. 10.00 (ISBN 0-8373-2877-2). Natl Learning.

TELEGONY

see Hybridization

TELEMETER

International Telemetering Conference: Proceedings of the 18th International Telemetering Conference, Vol. XVIII. LC 66-4573. 937p. 1982. pap. text ed. 159.00x (ISBN 0-87664-703-4). Instru Soc.

TELEOLOGY

see also Causation; Creation; Evolution
Nagel, Ernest. Teleology Revisited: And Other Essays in the Philosophy & History of Science. 360p. 1982. pap. 13.00 (ISBN 0-231-04505-0). Columbia U Pr.

TELEPHONE

see also Radiotelephone; Telephone Selling
Applied Psychology Research Unit. Human Factors in Telephony. 1961. pap. 20.00 (ISBN 0-686-37971-3). Info Gatekeepers.
Bibliotheca Press Staff, ed. Why Not an Answering Service? Telephone Answering Service Ideas. 50p. 1983. pap. text ed. 29.95 (ISBN 0-939476-65-7). Biblio Pr GA.
China Telephone Directory 1981. 768p. (Orig., Chinese, English.). 1981. pap. 92.50 (ISBN 0-8002-3007-8). Intl Pubns Serv.
Deutsches Bundes-Telefonbuch, 6 Vols. 67th ed. (Orig., Ger.). 1981. Set. pap. 250.00x (ISBN 0-8002-3015-9). Intl Pubns Serv.
Het PTT-BEDRIJF, The Netherlands. Human Factors in Telephone Communications International Symposium, 3rd. 1967. pap. 75.00 (ISBN 0-686-37973-X). Info-Gatekeepers.
Human Factors in Telecommunications International Symposium, 2nd. 1963. pap. 20.00 (ISBN 0-686-37972-1). Info Gatekeepers.
Institute for Communication Research, Stanford University. The Role of the Telephone in Economic Development. 1980. 50.00 (ISBN 0-686-37965-9). Info Gatekeepers.
Mingall, Harry. The Business Guide to Telephone Systems: How to Evaluate & Improve Your Communications Systems. 195p. (Orig.). 1983. pap. price not set (ISBN 0-88908-561-7). Self Counsel Pr.
VDE Berlin. Human Factors in Telecommunications International Symposium, 4th. 1968. 75.00 (ISBN 0-686-37974-8). Info Gatekeepers.

TELEPHONE-APPARATUS AND SUPPLIES

Cox, Wesley. How to Install Your Own Telephones, Extensions & Accessories & Kiss Ma Bell Goodbye. (Illus.). 1983. pap. 4.95 (ISBN 0-517-54936-0). Crown.
Fike, J. L. & Friend, G. E. Understanding Telephone Electronics. (Understanding Ser.). (Illus.). 272p. 1983. pap. 6.95 (ISBN 0-686-84797-0, 7141). Tex Instr Inc.

TELEPHONE-BIBLIOGRAPHY

China Telephone Directory, 1981. 840p. (Chinese & Eng.). 1982. ref. 37.50x (ISBN 0-88410-887-2). Ballinger Pub.

TELEPHONE-DIRECTORIES

Telephone directories of particular cities are entered under the name of the city, with the subdivision directories, e.g. new york (city)-directories.
Skowronski, Deborah. The Non-Reader's Telephone Directory. LC 82-61510. (Illus.). 36p. 1982. pap. text ed. 5.95 (ISBN 0-9609618-0-1). Sunburst.

TELEPHONE-EXAMINATIONS, QUESTIONS, ETC.

Rudman, Jack. Supervisor (Telephones) (Career Examination Ser.: C-426). (Cloth bdg. avail. on request). pap. 12.00 (ISBN 0-8373-0426-1). Natl Learning.
--Switchboard Operator. (Career Examination Ser.: C-883). (Cloth bdg. avail. on request). pap. 10.00 (ISBN 0-8373-0883-6). Natl Learning.
--Switchboard Supervisor. (Career Examination Ser.: C-884). (Cloth bdg. avail. on request). pap. 10.00 (ISBN 0-8373-0884-4). Natl Learning.
--Telephone Services Operator. (Career Examination Ser.: C-2586). (Cloth bdg. avail. on request). pap. 10.00 (ISBN 0-8373-2586-2). Natl Learning.

TELEPHONE-RATES

Murzin, Howy. Secrets to Lower Phone Bills. 64p. (Orig.). 1983. pap. 5.00 (ISBN 0-911199-01-2). Murzin Pub.
Newton, Harry. One Hundred-One-Saving Secrets Your Phone Company Won't Tell You. 96p. (Orig.). 1982. pap. text ed. 10.95 (ISBN 0-936648-15-5). Telecom Lib.

TELEPHONE, WIRELESS

see Radio

TELEPHONE CABLES

Young, Peter. Power of Speech: A History of Standard Telephones & Cables 1883-1983. 224p. 1983. text ed. 18.95x (ISBN 0-04-382039-5). Allen Unwin.

TELEPHONE ETIQUETTE

Pint, J., ed. Pint's Passages for Aural Comprehension II: Telephone Talk. (Materials for Language Practice Ser.). (Illus.). 96p. 1983. pap. 5.95 (ISBN 0-08-028621-6); cassette 12.00 (ISBN 0-08-029456-1). Pergamon.

TELEPHONE SELLING

Data Notes Publishing Staff, ed. Telemarketing, Telephone Sales & Telephone Soliciting; Data Notes. 70p. 1983. 12.95 (ISBN 0-686-37647-1). Data Notes Pub.
Goodman, Gary. Reach Out & Sell Someone: Phone Your Way to Success Through the Goodman System of Telemarketing. 156p. 1983. 12.95 (ISBN 0-13-753632-1); pap. 5.95 (ISBN 0-13-753624-0). P-H.
Roman, Murray. Telemarketing Campaigns that Work! (Illus.). 320p. 1983. 29.95 (ISBN 0-07-053598-1, P&RB). McGraw.
Shafiroff, Martin D. & Shook, Robert L. Successful Telephone Selling in the 80's. 176p. 1983. pap. 4.76i (ISBN 0-06-463569-4, EH 569). B&N NY.
Update Publicare Research Staff. Telemarketing Update: Notebook of Back Issues. 35p. 1983. pap. text ed. 8.00 (ISBN 0-686-38921-2). Update Pub Co.

TELEPHONING

see Telephone Etiquette

TELESCOPE

Hasluck, Paul N. Telescope Making Nineteen Hundred-Five. (Illus.). 160p. Date not set. pap. 12.50 (ISBN 0-87556-498-4). Saifer.
Learner, Richard. Astronomy through the Telescope: The 500-year Story of the Instruments, the Inventors & their Discoveries. 224p. 1982. 59.00x (ISBN 0-686-81700-1, Pub. by Evans Bros). State Mutual Bk.
Trueblood, Mark & Genet, Russell M. Microcomputer Control of Telescopes. LC 82-84768. 220p. (Orig.). 1983. pap. 24.95 (ISBN 0-911351-02-7). Fairborn Observ.

TELEVISION

see also Color Television
also headings beginning with the word television, e.g. Television Announcing of News, Television Broadcasting of Films, Television in Education, etc.
D'Agostino, Peter, ed. Transmission. 350p. (Orig.). 1983. 22.95 (ISBN 0-934378-25-8); pap. 10.95 (ISBN 0-934378-26-6). Tanam Pr.
Howe, M., ed. Learning from Television. Date not set. price not set (ISBN 0-12-357160-X). Acad Pr.
James, W. C. Television in Transition. LC 82-73647. 200p. 1982. 74.95 (ISBN 0-87251-079-4). Crain Bks.
Kelley, Michael R. Television: A Teacher in Our Midst. 160p. 1983. pap. text ed. 8.95x (ISBN 0-471-87132-X). Wiley.
Kiver & Kaufman. Television Electronics: Theory & Servicing. 8th ed. 768p. 1983. text ed. 27.00 (ISBN 0-8273-1328-4). Delmar.
Poltrack, D. P. Television Marketing: Network, Local & Cable. 384p. 1983. 27.50 (ISBN 0-07-050406-7). McGraw.
Skouson, Sandra & Anderson, Peggy. Taming the Video Monster: How Your Family Can Control TV Watching & Video Games. 168p. 1983. pap. 9.95 (ISBN 0-525-93290-9, 0966-290). Dutton.
Tuomola, Olli, ed. International TV & Video Guide 1983. (International TV & Video Guide Ser.). (Illus.). 87p. 1982. pap. 9.95 (ISBN 0-900730-10-2). NY Zoetrope.

TELEVISION-APPARATUS AND SUPPLIES

see also Video Tape Recorders and Recording
Gross, Lynne S. The New Television Technologies. 190p. 1983. pap. text ed. write for info. (ISBN 0-697-04362-2). Wm C Brown.
Wurtzel, Alan. Television Production. 2nd ed. Provenzano, Marian D., ed. (Illus.). 656p. 1983. text ed. 26.95 (ISBN 0-07-072131-9, C). McGraw.

TELEVISION-BROADCASTING

see Television Broadcasting

TELEVISION-DIRECTION

see Television-Production and Direction

TELEVISION-HANDBOOKS, MANUALS, ETC.

Hellyer & Sinclair. Questions & Answers: Radio & TV. 4th ed. (Illus.). 1976. pap. 4.95 (ISBN 0-408-00249-2). Focal Pr.
King. Beginner's Guide to Color TV. 2nd ed. (Illus.). 1978. pap. 9.95 (ISBN 0-408-00101-1). Focal Pr.
King & Trundle. Beginner's Guide to TV. 6th ed. 1983. pap. write for info. (ISBN 0-408-01215-3). Focal Pr.

TELEVISION-JUVENILE LITERATURE

Wiltshire, Peter. Making Television Programmes. (Cambridge Dinosaur Information Ser.). (Illus.). 26p. (gr. 7-10). 1983. pap. 1.50 (ISBN 0-521-27161-4). Cambridge U Pr.
Yurko, John. Video Basics. (Illus.). 48p. (ps-7). 1983. 8.95 (ISBN 0-13-941781-8). P-H.

TELEVISION-LAW AND LEGISLATION

New York University School of Law. Law & the Television of the 80's. 285p. 1983. text ed. 35.00 (ISBN 0-379-20046-5). Oceana.

TELEVISION-MORAL AND RELIGIOUS ASPECTS

Shaw, Jean W. TV: Friend or Foe? 1983. pap. cancelled (ISBN 0-8054-5652-X). Broadman.

TELEVISION-PRODUCTION AND DIRECTION

Millerson, Gerald. Basic TV Staging. 2nd ed. (Media Manual Ser.). (Illus.). 1982. pap. 10.95 (ISBN 0-240-51191-3). Focal Pr.
Wurtzel, Alan. Television Production. 2nd ed. Provenzano, Marian D., ed. (Illus.). 656p. 1983. text ed. 26.95 (ISBN 0-07-072131-9, C). McGraw.

TELEVISION-RECEIVERS AND RECEPTION

see also Video Games
Fisher, R. Digital Applications in Television Receivers. 1983. text ed. price not set (ISBN 0-408-01149-1). Butterworth.

TELEVISION-REPAIRING

Nineteen Forty-Seven TV & FM Servicing Information. 200p. Date not set. 20.00 (ISBN 0-938630-19-9). Ars Electronics.
Sloop, Joseph. Television Servicing with Basic Electronics. Date not set. pap. 14.50 Instrs' Guide (ISBN 0-672-21885-2); Student's Manual 10.00 (ISBN 0-672-21880-1). Sams.
Tinnell, Richard W. Television Symptom Diagnosis. 2nd ed. 1977. pap. 12.95 (ISBN 0-686-82336-2). Sams.

TELEVISION-STATIONS

see Television Stations

TELEVISION, COLOR

see Color Television

TELEVISION ACTING

see Acting for Television

TELEVISION ADVERTISING

Cross, Donna W. Mediaspeak: How Television Makes Up Your Mind. 288p. 1983. 16.95 (ISBN 0-698-11131-1, Coward). Putnam Pub Group.
Jones. Making TV Commercials. (Illus.). 1983. 33.95x (ISBN 0-240-51195-6). Focal Pr.
The One Show: Advertising Best Print, Radio, TV, Vol. 2. 352p. 1981. 32.50 (ISBN 0-9602628-2-2). Am Showcase.
The One Show: Advertising Best Print, Radio, TV, Vol. 3. 336p. 1982. 35.00 (ISBN 0-9602628-3-0). Am Showcase.

TELEVISION AND CHILDREN

Johnston, Jerom, et al. An Evaluation of Freestyle: A Television Series to Reduce Sex-Role Stereotypes. 308p. 1980. pap. 16.00 (ISBN 0-87944-256-5). Inst Soc Res.
Woolery, George W. Children's Television: The First Thirty-five Years, 1946-1981: Animated Cartoon Series, Pt. I. LC 82-5841. 404p. 1983. 27.50 (ISBN 0-8108-1557-5). Scarecrow.

TELEVISION AUDIENCES

Frank, Ronald E. & Greenberg, Marshall G. Audiences for Public Television. (Illus.). 224p. 1982. 25.00 (ISBN 0-8039-0764-8). Sage.

TELEVISION AUTHORSHIP

Pike, Frank. Ah! Mischief: The Writer & Televison. 160p. (Orig.). 1982. pap. 6.95 (ISBN 0-571-11881-X). Faber & Faber.

TELEVISION BROADCASTING

see also Television Advertising; Television Audiences; Television in Education; Television Programs; Television Relay Systems; Video Tape Recorders and Recording
Charren, Peggy & Sandler, Martin W. Changing Channels: Living (Sensibly) with Television. LC 82-16243. (Illus.). 320p. 1982. 24.95 (ISBN 0-201-07253-X); pap. 11.95 (ISBN 0-201-07254-8). A-W.
Cross, Donna W. Mediaspeak: How Television Makes Up Your Mind. 288p. 1983. 16.95 (ISBN 0-698-11131-1, Coward). Putnam Pub Group.

Eastman, Susan Tyler & Klein, Robert. Strategies in Broadcast & Cable Promotion: Commercial Television, Radio, Cable, Pay Television, Public Television. 352p. 1982. pap. text ed. 13.95x (ISBN 0-534-01156-X). Wadsworth Pub.

Eliot, Marc. Televisions: One Season of American Television. LC 82-17015. 208p. 1983. 14.95 (ISBN 0-312-79076-7). St Martin.

Gay, Tim, ed. Cable Contacts Yearbook, 1983. 1982. deluxe ed. 170.00 (ISBN 0-935224-16-5). Larimi Comm.

Gay, Tim & Hurvitz, David, eds. Television Contacts. 1982. deluxe ed. 127.00 (ISBN 0-935224-18-1). Larimi Comm.

Hyde, Stuart. Television & Radio Announcing. 4th ed. LC 82-83204. 528p. 1983. text ed. 22.50 (ISBN 0-395-32618-4); write for info. instr's. manual (ISBN 0-395-32619-2). HM.

Kemps International Film & Television Yearbook, 1981-82. 26th ed. LC 59-47486. 1074p. 1981. 65.00x (ISBN 0-905255-99-2). Intl Pubns Serv.

Kemps International Film & Television Yearbook, 1982-83. 27th ed. LC 59-47486. 1216p. 1982. 65.00x (ISBN 0-86259-019-1). Intl Pubns Serv.

Moschner, Meinhard. Fernsehen In Lateinamerika. 308p. (Ger.). 1982. write for info. (ISBN 3-8204-5795-X). P Lang Pubs.

Noble, Peter, ed. Screen International & TV Yearbook 1982-83. 37th ed. LC 76-646393. (Illus.). 696p. 1982. 57.50x (ISBN 0-900925-14-0). Intl Pubns Serv.

Talk Show Directory. 1983. 105.00 (ISBN 0-686-84343-6); Set. 241.00 (ISBN 0-686-84344-4). Automated Mktg.

TELEVISION BROADCASTING–AUDIENCES

see Television Audiences

TELEVISION BROADCASTING–BIOGRAPHY

Paar, Jack. P. S. Jack Paar. LC 82-45938. (Illus.). 360p. 1983. 14.95 (ISBN 0-385-18743-2). Doubleday.

TELEVISION BROADCASTING–HISTORY

O'Connor, John E., ed. American History - American Television: Interpreting the Video Past. (Ungar Film Library). (Illus.). 300p. 1983. 13.50 (ISBN 0-8044-2668-6); pap. 7.95 (ISBN 0-8044-6621-1). Ungar.

TELEVISION BROADCASTING–LAW AND LEGISLATION

see Television–Law and Legislation

TELEVISION BROADCASTING–MORAL AND RELIGIOUS ASPECTS

Angel, Velma. Those Sinsational Soaps. Lee, Karen, ed. 120p. (Orig.). 1983. pap. 4.95 (ISBN 0-88005-003-9). Uplift Bks.

TELEVISION BROADCASTING–NEWS

see Television Broadcasting of News

TELEVISION BROADCASTING–SOCIAL ASPECTS

Brown, Les & Channels Magazine. Fast Forward: The New Television & American Society. 264p. 1982. pap. 8.95 (ISBN 0-8362-6208-5). Andrews & McMeel.

Bryant, Jennings & Anderson, Daniel, eds. Understanding TV: Research in Children's Attention & Comprehension. LC 82-16280. 320p. Date not set. 29.50 (ISBN 0-12-138160-9). Acad Pr.

O'Connor, John E., ed. American History - American Television: Interpreting the Video Past. (Ungar Film Library). (Illus.). 300p. 1983. 13.50 (ISBN 0-8044-2668-6); pap. 7.95 (ISBN 0-8044-6621-1). Ungar.

TELEVISION BROADCASTING–GREAT BRITAIN

Sendall, Bernard. Independent Television in Britain: Origin & Foundation 1946-62, Vol. 1. 418p. 1982. text ed. 21.00x (ISBN 0-333-30941-3, Pub. by Macmillan England). Humanities.

Wenham, Brian, ed. The Third Age of Broadcasting. 256p. (Orig.). 1983. pap. 5.95 (ISBN 0-571-11981-6). Faber & Faber.

TELEVISION BROADCASTING OF FILMS

Maltin, Leonard, ed. T.V. Movies: 1983-84 Edition. 1982. pap. 4.95 (ISBN 0-451-11847-2, AE1847, Sig). NAL.

TELEVISION BROADCASTING OF NEWS

Braley, Russell. Bad News. 1983. 14.95 (ISBN 0-89526-627-X). Regnery-Gateway.

CBS News Index 1980: Key to the Television News Broadcast. 2nd ed. 705p. 1980. pap. text ed. 95.00 (ISBN 0-686-84106-9). Microfilming Corp.

CBS News Index, 1981: Key to the Television News Broadcasts. 2nd ed. 892p. 1982. pap. text ed. 10.00 (ISBN 0-686-84108-5). Microfilming Corp.

Diamond, Edwin. T. V. News in Four Countries. 150p. Date not set. cancelled (ISBN 0-08-028839-1); pap. cancelled (ISBN 0-08-028838-3). Pergamon.

Face the Nation: The Collected Transcripts from the CBS Radio & Television Broadcasts, Vol. 22, 1979. 366p. 1980. 29.50 (ISBN 0-8108-1021-2). Microfilming Corp.

Face the Nation: The Collected Transcripts from the CBS Radio & Television Broadcasts, Vol. 24, 1981. 374p. 1982. 29.50. Microfilming Corp.

Reasoner, Harry. Before the Colors Fade. LC 82-16685. 206p. 1983. pap. 5.95 (ISBN 0-688-01544-1). Quill NY.

Tumber, Howard. Television & the Riots. 54p. 1981. pap. 5.50 (ISBN 0-85170-120-5). NY Zoetrope.

Weaver, David H. Videotex Journalism: Teletext, Viewdata, & the News. 160p. 1983. text ed. write for info. (ISBN 0-89859-263-1). L Erlbaum Assocs.

Wulfmeyer, K. Tim. Broadcast Newswriting: A Workbook. 118p. 1983. pap. text ed. 8.95 (ISBN 0-8138-0226-1). Iowa St U Pr.

TELEVISION BROADCASTING OF SPORTS

Wolfson, Marty. How to Watch Sports on TV & Enjoy It. (Illus.). 1972. pap. 2.50 (ISBN 0-916114-02-3). Wolfson.

TELEVISION COMMERCIALS

see Television Advertising

TELEVISION DIRECTION

see Television–Production and Direction

TELEVISION DRAMA

see Television Plays

TELEVISION GAMES

see Video Games

TELEVISION IN ADVERTISING

see Television Advertising

TELEVISION IN EDUCATION

Amatuzzi, Joseph R. Television & the School. LC 82-60522. 125p. 1983. pap. 14.95 (ISBN 0-88247-676-9). R & E Res Assoc.

Ettema, James S. Working Together: A Study of Cooperation among Producers, Educators & Researchers to Create Educational Television. 220p. 1980. pap. 14.00x (ISBN 0-87944-251-4). Inst Soc Res.

Frank, Ronald E. & Greenberg, Marshall G. Audiences for Public Television. (Illus.). 224p. 1982. 25.00 (ISBN 0-8039-0764-8). Sage.

Gothberg, Helen. Impact: Television-Video in Libraries & Schools. 1983. 22.50 (ISBN 0-208-01859-X, Lib Prof Pubns); pap. price not set (ISBN 0-208-01860-3, Lib Prof Pubns). Shoe String.

Logan, Ben & Moody, Kate, eds. Television Awareness Training: Viewers Guide. 1983. 16.00 (ISBN 0-686-84065-8). Intl Gen Semantics.

Organizing Educational Broadcasting. 302p. 1982. pap. 37.25 (ISBN 92-3-101878-7, U1184, UNESCO). Unipub.

TELEVISION INDUSTRY–LAW AND LEGISLATION

see Television–Law and Legislation

TELEVISION JOURNALISM

see Television Broadcasting of News

TELEVISION MUSIC

Arnell & Groucutt. Music for TV & Films. (Illus.). 1983. 31.95x (ISBN 0-240-51196-4). Focal Pr.

TELEVISION NEWS

see Television Broadcasting of News

TELEVISION PLAYS

see also Soap Operas

White, Ned. Inside Television: A Guide to Critical Viewing. 205p. 1981. 12.00 (ISBN 0-686-82346-X); 78 pgs. with worksheets 10.00 (ISBN 0-686-82347-8). Sci & Behavior.

TELEVISION PRODUCTION

see Television–Production and Direction

TELEVISION PROGRAMS

see also Television Audiences; Television Plays

Cassata, Mary & Skill, Thomas. Life on Daytime Television. Voigt, Melvin J., ed. (Communication & Information Science Ser.). 272p. 1983. text ed. 27.50 (ISBN 0-89391-138-0); pap. text ed. 14.95 (ISBN 0-89391-180-1). Ablex Pub.

Johnson, Catherine E. TV Guide Index: 1981 Supplement. LC 82-74385. 50p. 1983. pap. text ed. write for info. (ISBN 0-9603684-2-6). Triangle Pubns.

Kalisch, Philip A. & Kalisch, Beatrice. Images of Nurses on Television. 1983. text ed. 22.50 (ISBN 0-8261-3870-5). Springer Pub.

Lichter, Linda & Lichter, S. Robert. Prime Time Crime: Criminals & Law Enforcers in TV Entertainment. Media Institute, ed. LC 82-73726. (Illus.). 76p. (Orig.). 1983. pap. 5.00 (ISBN 0-937790-14-1). Media Inst.

Parish, James R. & Terrace, Vincent. Actors' Television Credits, Supplement II: 1977-1981. LC 82-5961. 337p. 1982. 22.50 (ISBN 0-8108-1559-1). Scarecrow.

Shales, Tom. On the Air! 1982. 14.95 (ISBN 0-671-44203-1). Summit Bks.

Smith, V. Jackson. Programming for Radio & Television. rev. ed. LC 82-21887. (Illus.). 180p. 1983. lib. bdg. 18.75 (ISBN 0-8191-2887-2); pap. text ed. 8.25 (ISBN 0-8191-2888-0). U Pr of Amer.

Wiessman, Ginny & Sanders, Coyne s. The Dick Van Dyke Show. (Illus.). 160p. 1983. 22.50 (ISBN 0-312-19976-7); pap. 9.95 (ISBN 0-312-19977-5). St Martin.

TELEVISION RELAY SYSTEMS

Cable Television Advertising Market: 1982-87. 1982. spiral 850.00 (ISBN 0-686-42875-7). Knowledge Indus.

Crowe, Steve. Satellite Television & Your Backyard Dish. Krieger, Robin, ed. LC 81-90593. (Illus.). 200p. (Orig.). 1982. 20.00 (ISBN 0-910419-00-0); pap. 15.00 (ISBN 0-910419-01-9); trade special 15.00 (ISBN 0-910419-02-7). Satellite.

Filmed Entertainment Market: The Box Office vs. the New Media, 1983-1987. 1983. spiral 895.00 (ISBN 0-686-42883-8). Knowledge Indus.

Hollowell, Mary L., ed. The Cable-Broadband Communications Book: 1982-83, Vol. 3. 175p. 1983. 34.95 (ISBN 0-86729-042-0). Knowledge Indus.

The Home Video & Cable Yearbook: 1982-83. (Illus.). 263p. 1982. pap. 85.00 (ISBN 0-86729-035-8). Knowledge Indus.

Shaffer, W. D. & Wheelwright, Richard, eds. Creating Original Programming for Cable TV. 175p. 1983. 29.95 (ISBN 0-86729-043-9). Knowledge Indus.

Strauss, Lawrence. Home Video & Broadcasting: The Fight for Position, 1981-86. 1981. spiral 795.00 (ISBN 0-686-42877-3). Knowledge Indus.

Telepay vs. Videodisc: The Exploding Pay-per-View Market. (Reports Ser.: No. 510). 281p. 1982. 985.00 (ISBN 0-686-38956-5). Intl Res Dev.

TELEVISION REPEATER STATIONS

see Television Relay Systems

TELEVISION STATIONS

see also Television Relay Systems

Lambert, Stephen. Channel Four: Television with a Difference. 152p. 1982. 22.00 (ISBN 0-85170-141-8); pap. 10.95 (ISBN 0-85170-124-8). NY Zoetrope.

TELEVISION WRITING

see Television Authorship

TELOMERIZATION

see Polymers and Polymerization

TELSTAR SATELLITES

see Artificial Satellites in Telecommunication

TEMPERAMENT

see also Emotions

Evatt, Cris & Feld, Bruce. The Givers & the Takers. (Illus.). 256p. 1983. 12.95 (ISBN 0-02-536690-4). Macmillan.

TEMPERANCE

see also Alcohol and Youth; Alcoholics; Alcoholism; Hotels, Taverns, etc.; Narcotic Habit

Constable, Giles. Attitudes Toward Self-Inflicted Suffering in the Middle Ages. (Stephen J. Brademas Lectures Ser.). 28p. (Orig.). Date not set. pap. text ed. 2.50 (ISBN 0-916586-87-1). Hellenic Coll Pr.

TEMPERATURE

Quinn, T. J., ed. Temperature. (Monographs in Physical Measurement). write for info. (ISBN 0-12-569680-9). Acad Pr.

TEMPERATURE, ANIMAL AND HUMAN

see Body Temperature

TEMPERATURE CURVE

see Body Temperature

TEMPLARS

Partner, Peter. The Murdered Magicians: The Templars & Their Myth. (Illus.). 232p. 1982. 29.50x (ISBN 0-19-215847-3). Oxford U Pr.

TEMPLE, SHIRLEY, 1928-

Burdick, Loraine. The Shirley Temple Scrapbook. 1982. pap. 8.95 (ISBN 0-8246-0277-3). Jonathan David.

TEMPLE, WILLIAM, SIR, BART, 1628-1699

Faber, Richard. The Brave Courtier: Sir William Temple. 176p. 1983. 29.95 (ISBN 0-571-11982-4). Faber & Faber.

TEMPLES

Burford. The Greek Temple Builders at Epidauros. 274p. 1982. 50.00x (ISBN 0-85323-080-3, Pub. by Liverpool Univ England). State Mutual Bk.

Metropulous, Lyman. The Illustrated Book of the Great Ancient Temples. (The Masterpieces of World Architecture Library). (Illus.). 141p. 1983. 112.50 (ISBN 0-86650-042-1). Gloucester Art.

Michell, George, ed. Brick Temples of Bengal: From the Archives of David McCutchion. LC 82-3872. (Illus.). 450p. 1983. 75.00x (ISBN 0-691-04010-9). Princeton U Pr.

TEMPORARY EMPLOYMENT

McCauley, Rosemarie. Mini Sims Temporaries: Modern Office Simulations 2. 232p. (Orig.). 1979. pap. text ed. 11.50 (ISBN 0-672-97424-X); Tchr's Ed. 6.67 (ISBN 0-672-97168-2). Bobbs.

TEN COMMANDMENTS

see Commandments, Ten

TENANTS

see Landlord and Tenant

TENNESSEE–ANTIQUITIES

Autry, William O., Jr. An Archaeological, Architectural, & Historic Cultural Resources Reconnaissance of the Northeast Metropolitan Nashville Transportation Corridor. (Illus.). vii, 120p. (Orig.). 1982. pap. 12.00 (ISBN 0-940148-04-8). TARA.

TENNESSEE–DESCRIPTION AND TRAVEL

Chesney, Allen, ed. Chattanooga Album: Thirty-Two Historic Postcards. LC 82-17330. (Illus.). 16p. 1983. pap. 3.95 (ISBN 0-87049-381-7). U of Tenn Pr.

Hoobler, James A., ed. Nashville Memories: Thirty-Two Historic Postcards. LC 82-23841. (Illus.). 16p. 1983. pap. 3.95 (ISBN 0-87049-385-X). U of Tenn Pr.

TENNESSEE–GENEALOGY

Vryonis, Speros, Jr. A Brief History of the Greek-American Community of St. George, Memphis, Tennessee 1962-1982. LC 82-50980. (Byzantina Kai Metabyzantina Ser.: Vol. 3). 130p. 1982. 17.50x (ISBN 0-89003-126-6); pap. 12.50x (ISBN 0-89003-127-4). Undena Pubns.

TENNESSEE–HISTORY

Ridges & Valleys: A Mini-Encyclopedia of Anderson County, Tennessee. 86p. 1981. pap. 2.50 (ISBN 0-686-84102-6). Children's Mus.

Vaughan, Virginia C. Weakley County. Crawford, Charles, ed. (Tennessee County History Ser.: No. 92). (Illus.). 144p. 1983. 12.50 (ISBN 0-87870-188-5). Memphis St Univ.

TENNESSEE–SOCIAL LIFE AND CUSTOMS

Hoobler, James A., ed. Nashville Memories: Thirty-Two Historic Postcards. LC 82-23841. (Illus.). 16p. 1983. pap. 3.95 (ISBN 0-87049-385-X). U of Tenn Pr.

TENNIS

see also Table Tennis; Tennis Courts

Barton, Joel R., III & Grice, William A. Tennis. (Illus.). 88p. 1981. pap. text ed. 3.95x (ISBN 0-89641-065-X). American Pr.

Godbey, Geoffrey, et al. Triples: A New Tennis Game. (Illus.). 22p. (Orig.). 1980. pap. 2.98x (ISBN 0-910251-01-0). Venture Pub PA.

Groppel, Jack L. & Shay, Arthur. Optimal Tennis: The Freeze-Frame Photographic Approach to a Better Game. (Illus.). 128p. (Orig.). 1983. pap. 8.95 (ISBN 0-8092-5602-9). Contemp Bks.

Gustafsson, Lars. The Tennis Players. Sandstroem, Yvonne L., tr. 96p. (Swedish.). 1983. 13.00 (ISBN 0-8112-0861-3); pap. 6.25 (ISBN 0-8112-0862-1, NDP551). New Directions.

Hannah, Barry. The Tennis Handsome. LC 82-48752. 175p. 1982. 11.95 (ISBN 0-394-52876-X). Knopf.

Hultgren, Barbara. Ball Persons: A Trainer's Manual. (Illus.). 31p. 1981. 2.00 (ISBN 0-938822-20-9). USTA.

Kraft, Eve. The Tennis Workbook-Unit I. (Illus.). 64p. 1980. 2.95 (ISBN 0-686-37475-4). USTA.

Kraft, Eve & Conroy, John. The Tennis Teacher's Guide: Group Instruction & Team Coaching. (Illus.). 96p. 1980. 4.50 (ISBN 0-686-37474-6). USTA.

--The Tennis Workbook-Unit II. (Illus.). 72p. 1982. 3.50 (ISBN 0-686-37476-2). USTA.

LaMarche, Bob. Tennis Basics. (Illus.). 48p. (gr. 3-7). 1983. 8.95 (ISBN 0-13-903237-1). P-H.

Mewshaw, Michael. Short Circuit. LC 82-48699. 320p. 1983. 12.95 (ISBN 0-689-11384-6). Atheneum.

Seixas, Vic, Jr. & Cohen, Joel. Prime Time Tennis. (Illus.). 256p. 1982. 12.95 (ScribT). Scribner.

Shertenlieb, Bill & Sanders, Phronie. Focus on Competition: A Tennis Manual. rev. ed. (Illus.). 1980. pap. 4.50 (ISBN 0-9606066-0-2). Tennis Manual.

Starter Tennis. 1977. 5.00 (ISBN 0-938822-17-9). USTA.

Talbert, William F. & Old, Bruce S. Tennis Tactics: Singles & Doubles. LC 82-48137. (Illus.). 256p. 1983. write for info. (ISBN 0-06-015111-0, HarpT). Har-Row.

Tennis 1982-84. (NAGWS Sports Guides Ser.). 3.75 (ISBN 0-88314-091-8). AAHPERD.

USTA Education & Research Center. College Tennis Guide. 35p. 1982-83. 3.00 (ISBN 0-938822-22-5). USTA.

--Directory of Tennis Programs for Seniors. 19p. 1981. 1.00 (ISBN 0-938822-19-5). USTA.

--Directory of Tennis Programs for the Disabled. 40p. 1982. 2.00 (ISBN 0-938822-18-7). USTA.

USTA Recreational Tennis Programming Kit. 1981. 2.50 (ISBN 0-938822-16-0). USTA.

USTA Tennis Film List, 1983. 1983. 3.00 (ISBN 0-938822-15-2). USTA.

TENNIS–HISTORY

Landon, Charles. Classic Moments of Wimbledon. 144p. 1982. 35.00x (ISBN 0-86190-052-9, Pub. by Moorland). State Mutual Bk.

Tingay, Lance. Guinness Book of Tennis Facts & Feats. (Illus.). 256p. 1983. 19.95 (ISBN 0-85112-268-X, Pub. by Guinness Superlatives England); pap. 12.95 (ISBN 0-85112-289-2, Pub. by Guinness Superlatives England). Sterling.

TENNIS COURTS

see also Tennis

USTA Education & Research Center. Financing Public Tennis Courts. Rev. ed. 88p. 1979. 2.50 (ISBN 0-938822-21-7). USTA.

TENNYSON, ALFRED TENNYSON, BARON, 1809-1892

Colley, Ann C. Tennyson & Madness. LC 82-13689. 224p. 1983. text ed. 20.00x (ISBN 0-8203-0648-7). U of Ga Pr.

Fausset, Hugh I'Anson. Tennyson: A Modern Portrait. 309p. 1982. Repr. of 1923 ed. lib. bdg. 30.00 (ISBN 0-89760-235-8). Telegraph Bks.

Wolfe, Humbert. Tennyson. 1982. lib. bdg. 34.50 (ISBN 0-686-81929-2). Porter.

Young, George M. Age of Tennyson. 1982. lib. bdg. 34.50 (ISBN 0-686-81938-1). Porter.

TENPINS

see Bowling

TENSION (PSYCHOLOGY)

see Stress (Psychology)

TENT OF MEETING

see Tabernacle

TENURE OF OFFICE

see Civil Service

TERATOLOGY

see Abnormalities, Human; Monsters

TERESA, SAINT, 1515-1582

Aumann, Jordan & Dongan, Margaret. Teresa of Avila. LC 82-10795. (Word & Spirit Ser.: Vol. 4). 1983. pap. 6.00 (ISBN 0-932506-19-4). St Bedes Pubns.

Glynn, Joseph. The Eternal Mystic: St. Teresa of Avila, the First Woman Doctor of the Church. 271p. 1982. 7.95 (ISBN 0-533-05407-9). Vantage.

TERMINAL CARE

see also Death; Terminal Care Facilities

Benoliel, J. O. Death Education for the Health Professional. 1982. 39.95 (ISBN 0-07-004761-8). McGraw.

Ferman, Edward L., ed. The Best from Fantasy & Science Fiction. 24th ed. 2.95 (ISBN 0-441-05485-4, Pub. by Ace Science Fiction). Ace Bks.

Kutscher, Austin, et al, eds. Hospice U. S. A. (Foundation of Thanatology Ser.). 304p. 1983. text ed. 22.50 (ISBN 0-231-05082-8). Columbia U Pr.

Lindenberg, Steven P. Group Psychotherapy with People who Are Dying. (Illus.). 400p. 1983. text ed. 24.75x (ISBN 0-398-04814-2). C C Thomas.

Richards, Larry & Johnson, Paul. Death & the Caring Community. LC 80-19752. (Critical Concern Ser.). 210p. 1982. pap. 5.95 (ISBN 0-88070-006-8). Multnomah.

Smith, Carole R. Social Work with the Dying & Bereaved. Campling, Jo, ed. (Practical Social Work Ser.). 160p. 1982. 40.00x (ISBN 0-333-30894-8, Pub. by Macmillan England). State Mutual Bk.

Tengbom, M. Help for Families of the Terminally Ill. (Trauma Bks.: Ser. 2). 1983. pap. 2.50 ea. (ISBN 0-570-08256-0); Set. pap. 9.15. Concordia.

TERMINAL CARE FACILITIES

Gordon, George K. & Stryker, Ruth. Creative Long-Term Care Administration. (Illus.). 414p. 1983. text ed. 34.50x (ISBN 0-398-04822-3). C C Thomas.

Hospice Project Self-Assessment & Survey Guide. 80p. 1983. pap. 15.00 (ISBN 0-86688-061-5). Joint Comm Hosp.

Hospice Standards Manual. 80p. 1983. pap. 15.00 (ISBN 0-86688-060-7). Joint Comm Hosp.

Kutscher, Austin, et al, eds. Hospice U. S. A. (Foundation of Thanatology Ser.). 304p. 1983. text ed. 22.50 (ISBN 0-231-05082-8). Columbia U Pr.

Mumley, Anne. The Hospice Experience: A New Context for Death & Dying. 256p. 1983. 17.50 (ISBN 0-465-03060-2). Basic.

TERMINALS, DATA (COMPUTERS)

see Computer Input-Output Equipment

TERMINOLOGY

see Names

TERMITES

Usher, M. B. & Ocloo, J. K. The Natural Resistance of Eighty-Five West African Hardwood Timbers to Attack by Termites & Micro-Organisms. 1979. 35.00x (ISBN 0-85135-103-4, Pub. by Centre Overseas Research). State Mutual Bk.

Williams, R. M. Evaluation of Field & Laboratory Methods for Testing Termite Resistance of Timber & Building Materials in Ghana, with Relevant Biological Studies. 1973. 35.00x (ISBN 0-85135-065-8, Pub. by Centre Overseas Research). State Mutual Bk.

TERRAIN SENSING, REMOTE

see Remote Sensing

TERRAPINS

see Turtles

TERRESTRIAL PHYSICS

see Geophysics

TERRITORIAL WATERS

see also Boundaries; Fishery Law and Legislation; Maritime Law

McDorman, Ted L. & Beauchamp, Kenneth P. Maritime Boundary Delimitation: An Annotated Bibliography. 224p. 1983. 24.95x (ISBN 0-669-06146-8). Lexington Bks.

TERROR, REIGN OF

see France–History–Revolution, 1789-1799

TERROR TALES

see Horror Tales

TERRORISM

Alexander, Yonah & Myers, Kenneth, eds. Terrorism in Europe. LC 81-21306. 230p. 1982. 25.00x (ISBN 0-312-79250-6). St Martin.

Bucheli, Fausto & Maxson, Robin. Hostage. 208p. (Orig.). 1982. pap. 6.95 (ISBN 0-310-45631-2). Zondervan.

Doumergu, Emil. Saudi Arabia & the Explosion of Terrorism in the Middle East. (The Great Currents of History Library Book). (Illus.). 137p. 1983. 77.85 (ISBN 0-86722-016-3). Inst Econ Pol.

Eichelman, Burr & Soskis, David A., eds. Terrorism: Interdisciplinary Perspectives. LC 82-24393. (Illus.). 186p. 1983. text ed. 22.50x (ISBN 0-89042-109-9). Am Psychiatric.

Freedman, Lawrence Z. & Alexander, Yonah, eds. Perspectives on Terrorism. 225p. 1983. PLB 24.95 (ISBN 0-8420-2201-5). Scholarly Res Inc.

Lillich, Richard B., ed. Transnational Terrorism: Conventions & Commentary. 282p. 1982. 25.00 (ISBN 0-87215-494-7). Michie-Bobbs.

Lloyd, Richard & Thomas, Antony. Frank Terpil: Portrait of a Dangerous Man. 256p. 1983. 14.95 (ISBN 0-86579-023-X). Seaver Bks.

Mackey, Janet & World Without War Council, eds. Terrorism & Political Self-Determination: A Tragic Marriage We Could Help Decouple. 64p. 1980. 1.00 (ISBN 0-686-81728-1). World Without War.

Mickolus, Edward F. International Terrorism: Attributes of Terrorist Events, 1968-1977 (ITERATE 2) LC 82-82385. write for info. (ISBN 0-89138-927-X, ICPSR 7947). ICPSR.

Montana, Patrick J. & Roukis, George S., eds. Managing Terrorism: Strategies for the Corporate Executive. LC 82-11224. 192p. 1983. lib. bdg. 27.95 (ISBN 0-89930-013-8, MTE/, Quorum). Greenwood.

Raushenbush, Richard. The Terrorist War in Guatemala. LC 82-14167. 82p. (Orig.). pap. 5.00 (ISBN 0-910637-05-9). Coun Inter Ed.

Wardlaw, Grant. Political Terrorism: Theory, Tactics & Counter-Measures. LC 82-9431. (Illus.). 256p. Date not set. 29.50 (ISBN 0-521-25032-3); pap. 9.95 (ISBN 0-521-27147-9). Cambridge U Pr.

Wolfgang, Marvin E., ed. International Terrorism. (The Annals of the American Academy of Political & Social Science: Vol. 463). 208p. 1982. 15.00 (ISBN 0-8039-1860-7); pap. 10.00 (ISBN 0-8039-1861-5). Sage.

TESLA, NIKOLA, 1856-1943

Johnston, Benjamin H. And In Creating, Live: The Early Life of Nikola Tesla. (Illus.). 200p. (Orig.). 1983. price not set (ISBN 0-910077-03-7); pap. price not set (ISBN 0-910077-02-9). Hart Bro Pub.

TEST-BORING

see Boring

TEST TUBE BABIES

see Fertilization in Vitro, Human

TESTACEA

see Mollusks

TESTICLE

see also Semen; Spermatozoa

De Kreter, D. M., et al, eds. The Pituitary & Testis: Clinical & Experimental Studies. (Monographs on Endocrinology: Vol. 25). (Illus.). 200p. 1983. 50.00 (ISBN 0-387-11874-8). Springer-Verlag.

Donohue, John P. Testis Tumors. (International Perspectives in Urology: Vol. 7). (Illus.). 360p. 1983. lib. bdg. price not set (ISBN 0-683-02613-5). Williams & Wilkins.

Hadziselimovic, F. Cryptorchidism: Management & Implications. (Illus.). 135p. 1983. 49.00 (ISBN 0-387-11881-0). Springer-Verlag.

TESTIMONY

see Witnesses

TESTIS

see Testicle

TESTS, PSYCHOLOGICAL

see Psychological Tests

TESTS AND MEASUREMENTS IN EDUCATION

see Educational Tests and Measurements

TEUTONIC CIVILIZATION

see Civilization, Germanic

TEUTONIC LANGUAGES

see Germanic Languages

TEWA INDIANS

see Indians of North America–Southwest, New

TEXAS

see also names of cities, towns, regions, etc. in Texas

Hale, Leon. A Smile from Katie Hattan & Other Natural Wonders. LC 82-60563. 288p. 1982. 13.95 (ISBN 0-940672-07-3). Shearer Pub.

Hughes, Charles. Guide to Texas Title Insurance. 1983. 11.95 (ISBN 0-87201-777-X). Gulf Pub.

Krantz, Les. The Texas Art Review. 1982. 35.00 (ISBN 0-87201-018-X). Gulf Pub.

Pluta, Joseph E. & Wright, Rita J. Texas Fact Book, 1984. (Illus.). 200p. 1983. pap. price not set. U of Tex Busn Res.

Saunders, Charles, ed. How to Live & Die with Texas Probate. 4th ed. 1983. pap. 9.95 (ISBN 0-87201-835-0). Gulf Pub.

Streater, Thomas. Bibliography of Texas, Seventeen Ninety-Five to Eighteen Forty-Five. rev. 2nd ed. Hanna, Archibald, ed. 584p. 1983. 225.00 (ISBN 0-89235-060-1). Res Pubns Conn.

TEXAS–ANTIQUITIES

McDonald, Archie P. The Old Stone Fort. 1981. pap. 1.95 (ISBN 0-87611-057-X). Tex St Hist Assn.

Stephenson, Nathaniel W. Texas & the Mexican War. 1919. text ed. 8.50x (ISBN 0-686-83810-6). Elliots Bks.

TEXAS–BIOGRAPHY

Historical Committee Texas Surveys Association. One League to Each Wind. 2nd ed. (Illus.). 376p. 1973. 25.00x (ISBN 0-686-37675-7). Von-Bogckmann.

Parsons, Chuck. Clay Allison, Portrait of a Shootist. 144p. 1983. 8.75 (ISBN 0-933512-36-8). Pioneer Bk Tx.

Rogers, Mary B. & Smith, Sherry A. We Can Fly: Stories of Katherine Stinson & Other Gutsy Texas Women. LC 82-80441. (Illus.). 184p. (Orig.). (gr. 7). 1983. 24.95 (ISBN 0-936650-02-8); pap. 12.95 (ISBN 0-936650-03-6). E C Temple.

TEXAS–DESCRIPTION AND TRAVEL

Bomar, George W. Texas Weather. (Illus.). 256p. 1983. 22.50 (ISBN 0-292-78052-4); pap. 9.95 (ISBN 0-292-78053-2). U of Tex Pr.

Jordan, Terry G. & Bean, John L., Jr. Texas. (Geographies of the U. S.). 450p. 1983. lib. bdg. 35.00 (ISBN 0-86531-088-2); pap. text ed. 18.00 (ISBN 0-86531-481-0). Westview.

TEXAS–DESCRIPTION AND TRAVEL–GUIDEBOOKS

Crowell, Lynda & Mariotti, Maryanne. The Parent's Guide to Austin, 1982-83. (Illus.). 208p. 1982. pap. 5.95 (ISBN 0-938934-02-3). C&M Pubns.

Fodor's Texas. (Illus.). 416p. 1983. traveltex 8.95 (ISBN 0-679-00960-4). McKay.

Hoppes, Steve. Running Through Austin. Orig. Title: A Guide to Austin Running, 1976. (Illus.). 112p. 1982. pap. 4.95 (ISBN 0-938934-03-1). C&M Pubns.

Hugill, Peter J. & Doughty, Robin W., eds. Field Trip Guide: AAG San Antonio 1982. (Illus.). 165p. (Orig.). 1982. pap. 2.00 (ISBN 0-89291-165-4). Assn Am Geographers.

TEXAS–ECONOMIC CONDITIONS

Evolving Federalism: The Texas Response to Reagan's Block Grants. LC 82-83152. (Policy Research Project Report Ser.: No. 52). 155p. 1982. 6.50 (ISBN 0-89940-654-8). LBJ Sch Pub Aff.

Lambeth, Ida M., ed. Directory of Texas Manufacturers, 1983, 2 Vols. LC 34-27861. 1200p. Date not set. Set. pap. 85.00 (ISBN 0-686-83437-2). U of Tex Busn Res.

Maxwell, Robert S. Texas Economic Growth, 1890 to World War II: From Frontier to Industrial Giant. Rosenbaum, Robert J., ed. (Texas History Ser.). (Illus.). 42p. 1982. pap. text ed. 1.95x (ISBN 0-89641-099-4). American Pr.

TEXAS–EMIGRATION AND IMMIGRATION

Jordan, Terry G. Immigration to Texas. Rosenbaum, Robert J., ed. (Texas History Ser.). (Illus.). 39p. 1981. pap. text ed. 1.95x (ISBN 0-89641-051-X). American Pr.

TEXAS–GENEALOGY

Toole, Blanche. Sabine County Marriages, 1875-1900, 1900-1910, Prior to 1875. LC 82-84531. 150p. (Orig.). 1983. pap. 12.50 (ISBN 0-911317-08-2). Ericson Bks.

TEXAS–HISTORY

Ericson, Carolyn R., ed. First Settlers of the Republic of Texas, Vol. 1. 278p. 1982. pap. 19.95 (ISBN 0-911317-00-7). Ericson Bks.

--First Settlers of the Republic of Texas, Vol. 2. 273p. 1982. pap. 19.95 (ISBN 0-911317-01-5). Ericson Bks.

Fehrenbach, T. R. Lonestar: History of Texas & the Texans. 1983. 9.98 (ISBN 0-517-40280-7). Crown.

First Settlers of the Republic of Texas, 2 Vols. 551p. 1982. Set. pap. 35.00 (ISBN 0-911317-02-3). Ericson Bks.

Fox, Daniel E., ed. Traces of Texas History. (Illus.). 1983. 16.95 (ISBN 0-931722-24-1); pap. 9.95 (ISBN 0-931722-23-3). Corona Pub.

Goetzman, William H. & Reese, Becky D. Texas Images & Visions. (Illus.). 1983. pap. text ed. 14.95 (ISBN 0-292-73832-3). U of Tex Pr.

Hewitt, W. P. Land & Community: European Migration to Rural Texas in the 19th Century. (Illus.). 69p. 1982. pap. text ed. 1.95 (ISBN 0-89641-101-X). American Pr.

Jackson, Jack. Comanche Moon. LC 79-88142. 1979. pap. 2.95 (ISBN 0-89620-079-5). Tex St Hist Assn.

Martin, Robert S. & Martin, James C. Contours of Discovery: Pointed Maps Delineating the Texas & Southern Chapters in the Cartographic History of North America, 1513-1930. LC 82-83547. 35.00 (ISBN 0-87611-058-8). Tex St Hist Assn.

Sibley, Marilyn M. Lone Stars & State Gazettes: Texas Newspapers Before the Civil War. LC 82-45898. (Illus.). 408p. 1983. 21.50 (ISBN 0-89096-149-2). Tex A&M Univ Pr.

Smithwick, Noah. The Evolution of a State or Recollections of Old Texas Days. (Barker Texas History Center Ser.: No. 5). (Illus.). 248p. 1983. 19.95 (ISBN 0-292-72043-2); pap. 8.95 (ISBN 0-292-72045-9). U of Tex Pr.

Whisenhunt, Donald W. Depression in Texas. Rosenbaum, Robert J., ed. (Texas History Ser.). (Illus.). 43p. 1982. pap. text ed. 1.95x (ISBN 0-89641-105-2). American Pr.

TEXAS–HISTORY–SOURCES

Kenamore, Jane A. & Wilson, Michael E., eds. Manuscript Sources in the Rosenberg Library: A Selective Guide. LC 82-45896. (Illus.). 184p. 1983. 20.00x (ISBN 0-89096-146-8). Tex A&M Univ Pr.

TEXAS–HISTORY–TO 1846

Ericson, Joe E. Judges of the Republic of Texas, Eighteen Thirty-Six through Eighteen Forty-Six. (Illus.). 350p. 1980. 20.00 (ISBN 0-911317-04-X). Ericson Bks.

Timmons, W. H. The Anglo-American Advance into Texas, 1810-1830. (Illus.). 46p. 1982. pap. text ed. 1.95x (ISBN 0-89641-103-6). American Pr.

TEXAS–HISTORY, LOCAL

Downs, Fane & Flukinger, Roy. Abilene: An American Centennial. LC 82-60427. (Illus.). 104p. 1982. 24.50 (ISBN 0-292-70364-3, Pub. by R N Richardson Pr). U of Tex Pr.

Farrar, Becky. Centennial Clairette Eighteen Eighty to Nineteen Eighty. 333p. 1980. 20.00 (ISBN 0-9609406-0-X). Greens Creek.

TEXAS–MAPS

Martin, Robert S. & Martin, James C. Contours of Discovery: Pointed Maps Delineating the Texas & Southern Chapters in the Cartographic History of North America, 1513-1930. LC 82-83547. 35.00 (ISBN 0-87611-058-8). Tex St Hist Assn.

TEXAS–POLITICS AND GOVERNMENT

Evolving Federalism: The Texas Response to Reagan's Block Grants. LC 82-83152. (Policy Research Project Report Ser.: No. 52). 155p. 1982. 6.50 (ISBN 0-89940-654-8). LBJ Sch Pub Aff.

Green, George N. Liberal View of Texas Politics Since the 1930s. Rosenbaum, Robert J., ed. (Texas History Ser.). (Illus.). 52p. 1982. pap. text ed. 1.95x (ISBN 0-89641-088-9). American Pr.

--Liberal View of Texas Politics, 1890-1930s. Rosenbaum, Robert J., ed. (Texas History Ser.). (Illus.). 45p. 1982. pap. text ed. 1.95x (ISBN 0-89641-087-0). American Pr.

Jones, et al. Practicing Texas Politics. 5th ed. 1982. 8.50 (ISBN 0-686-84651-6); supplementary materials avail. HM.

Jones, Eugene W. & Brown, Lyle C. Practising Texas Politics. 5th ed. LC 82-81521. 576p. 1982. pap. text ed. 12.95 (ISBN 0-395-32793-8); instrs.' guide avail. (ISBN 0-395-32795-4). HM.

Kraemer, Richard & Newell, Charldean. Essentials of Texas Politics. 2nd ed. (Illus.). 225p. pap. text ed. 11.95 (ISBN 0-314-69659-8); tchrs.' manual avail. (ISBN 0-314-71104-X). West Pub.

Tees, David W. & Wilkes, Stanley W., Jr. The Private Connection. 75p. (Orig.). 1982. pap. 10.00 (ISBN 0-936440-42-2). Inst Urban Studies.

TEXAS–POPULATION

Myres, Sandra L. Native Americans of Texas. Rosenbaum, Robert J., ed. (Texas History Ser.). (Illus.). 45p. 1981. pap. text ed. 1.95x (ISBN 0-89641-083-8). American Pr.

TEXAS–SOCIAL LIFE AND CUSTOMS

Davis, Ronald L. Twentieth Century Cultural Life in Texas. Rosenbaum, Robert J., ed. (Texas History Ser.). (Illus.). 50p. 1981. pap. text ed. 1.95x (ISBN 0-89641-072-2). American Pr.

Richardson Woman's Club. The Texas Experience: Friendship & Food Texas Style, A Cookbook from the Richardson Woman's Club. Dennis, Ivanette, ed. (Illus.). 373p. 1982. lib. bdg. 12.95 (ISBN 0-9609416-0-6). Hart Graphics.

TEXT-BOOKS

see also Readers;

also particular branches of study with or without the subdivision Text-Books, e.g. Arithmetic; English Language–Grammar; Geography–Text-Books; also subdivision Text-Books for foreigners under names of languages, e.g. English Language–Text-Books for Foreigners

Brooks, Bearl. Alphabet. (Early Education Ser.). 26p. (ps-1). 1979. wkbk. 5.00 (ISBN 0-8209-0199-7, K-1). ESP.

--American Indians. (Social Studies). 24p. (gr. 4-6). 1977. wkbk. 5.00 (ISBN 0-8209-0239-X, SS-6). ESP.

Cole, Ethel. American Farmer. (Social Studies). 24p. (gr. 5-9). 1976. wkbk. 5.00 (ISBN 0-8209-0245-4, SS-12). ESP.

Elrod, Mavis. American Colonial Life. (Social Studies). 24p. (gr. 5-9). 1979. wkbk. 5.00 (ISBN 0-8209-0248-9, SS-15). ESP.

Gary, Skipper. America the Beautiful. (Social Studies). 24p. (gr. 4-5). 1979. wkbk. 5.00 (ISBN 0-8209-0238-1, SS-5). ESP.

Hayes, Marilyn. Alphabet & Words. (Early Education Ser.). 24p. (gr. 1). 1982. wkbk. 5.00 (ISBN 0-8209-0214-4, K-16). ESP.

Justus, Fred. Algebra. (Math Ser.). 24p. (gr. 7-11). 1979. wkbk. 5.00 (ISBN 0-8209-0101-6, A-11). ESP.

--Alphabet Sequence. (Early Education Ser.). 24p. (gr. 1). 1980. wkbk. 5.00 (ISBN 0-686-42826-9). ESP.

--Animals: Males, Females & Babies. (Early Education Ser.). 24p. (ps-1). 1981. wkbk. 5.00 (ISBN 0-8209-0226-8, K-28). ESP.

--Arithmetic Exercises: Grade Eight. (Math Ser.). 24p. (gr. 8). 1978. wkbk. 5.00 (ISBN 0-8209-0098-2, A-8). ESP.

McFerron, Martha. Animals & Babies. (Science Ser.). 24p. (gr. 2-3). 1980. wkbk. 5.00 (ISBN 0-8209-0160-1, S-22). ESP.

McMasters, Dale. American Holidays & Special Occasions. (Social Studies). 14p. (gr. 3-6). 1980. wkbk. 5.00 (ISBN 0-8209-0266-7, AH-1). ESP.

TEXT-BOOKS–BIBLIOGRAPHY

El-Hi Text Books in Print, 1983. 843p. 1983. text ed. 49.50x (ISBN 0-8352-1600-4). Bowker.

TEXTILE DESIGN

see also Textile Painting

Caraway, Caren. Peruvian Textile Designs. (The International Design Library). (Illus.). 1983. pap. 2.95 (ISBN 0-88045-026-6). Stemmer Hse.

Haddon, A. C. & Start, L. E. Iban or Sea Dayak Fabrics & Their Patterns. pap. 14.95 (ISBN 0-903585-11-1). Robin & Russ.

Schatz, Evalina. Revolutionary Textile Design: Russia in the 1920's & 1930's. 1983. 26.95 (ISBN 0-670-59712-0); pap. 14.95 (ISBN 0-670-59713-9). Viking Pr.

TEXTILE FABRICS

see also Carpets; Indians of North America–Textile Industry and Fabrics; Linen; Silk; Textile Industry

Baldwin, Ed & Baldwin, Stevie. Scrap Fabric Crafts. (Illus.). 160p. 1982. pap. 7.95 (ISBN 0-89586-168-2). H P Bks.

Bogdonoff, Nancy D., ed. Handwoven Textiles of Early New England. LC 75-5582. (Illus.). 192p. 1975. pap. 9.95 (ISBN 0-8117-2069-1). Stackpole.

FIBERARTS Magazine Staff. The FIBERARTS Design Book II. LC 82-84032. (Illus.). 208p. (Orig.). 1983. 27.95 (ISBN 0-937274-06-2); pap. 18.95 (ISBN 0-937274-07-0). Lark Bks.

Happey, F., ed. Contemporary: Textile Engineering. write for info. (ISBN 0-12-323750-5). Acad Pr.

Schwartz, Peter, et al. Fabric Forming Systems. LC 82-7967. (Textile Ser.). (Illus.). 175p. 1983. 24.00 (ISBN 0-8155-0908-1). Noyes.

TEXTILE FABRICS–ASIA
Leix, Alfred. Turkestan & Its Textile Craft. 1982. 40.00x (ISBN 0-903580-10-1, Pub. by Element Bks). State Mutual Bk.
TEXTILE FABRICS–EUROPE
Harte, N. B. & Pointing, K. G. Cloth & Clothing in Medieval Europe: Essays in Memory of Professor E. M. Carus-Wilson. 448p. 1982. 90.00x (ISBN 0-435-32382-2, Pub. by Heinemann England). State Mutual Bk.
TEXTILE FABRICS–GREAT BRITAIN
Bridbury, A. R. Medieval English Clothmaking: An Economic Survey. 160p. 1982. 75.00x (ISBN 0-435-32138-2). State Mutual Bk.
--Medieval English Clothmaking: An Economic Survey. (Pasold Studies in Textile History). 160p. 1982. text ed. 27.50x (ISBN 0-435-32138-2). Heinemann Ed.
Lowe, N. Lancashire Textile Industry in the Sixteenth Century. 1972. 19.00 (ISBN 0-7190-1156-6). Manchester.
TEXTILE FABRICS–INDIA
Gittinger, Mattiebelle. Master Dyers to the World: Technique & Trade in Early Indian Dyed Cotton Textiles. McEuen, Caroline K., ed. (Illus.). 208p. 1982. pap. 20.00 (ISBN 0-87405-020-0). Textile Mus.
Murphy, Eamon. Unions in Conflict: A Comparative Study Four South Indian Textile Centres, 1918-1939. 1982. 18.00x (ISBN 0-8364-0874-8, Pub. by Australia Nat Univ). South Asia Bks.
TEXTILE FABRICS–PERU
Caraway, Caren. Peruvian Textile Designs. (The International Design Library). (Illus.). 1983. pap. 2.95 (ISBN 0-88045-026-6). Stemmer Hse.
TEXTILE FIBERS, SYNTHETIC
Moncrieff, R. W. Man-Made Fibers. 7th ed. 1000p. 1984. text ed. price not set. Butterworth.
TEXTILE INDUSTRY
see also Bleaching; Cotton Manufacture; Cotton Trade; Dyes and Dyeing; Indians of North America–Textile Industry and Fabrics; Lace and Lace Making; Silk Manufacture and Trade; Spinning; Textile Design; Textile Painting; Weaving
Guggenheim, Gus N. Protocol for Productivity. Guggenheim, Alan, ed. (Textile Industry Management Ser.: No. 1). 132p. 1982. 17.95x (ISBN 0-910377-03-0); pap. 13.95x (ISBN 0-910377-00-6). Guggenheim.
Miller, Richard K. Noise Control Solutions for the Textile Industry. (Illus.). 90p. text ed. 45.00 (ISBN 0-89671-035-1). Southeast Acoustics.
Wittgen, Rudolf. Die Absatzwege der Baumwollindustrie In Den 80er Jahren. xiv, 308p. (Ger.). 1982. write for info. (ISBN 3-8204-5821-2). P Lang Pubs.
TEXTILE INDUSTRY–HISTORY
Bridbury, A. R. Medieval English Clothmaking: An Economic Survey. 160p. 1982. 75.00x (ISBN 0-435-32138-2). State Mutual Bk.
--Medieval English Clothmaking: An Economic Survey. (Pasold Studies in Textile History). 160p. 1982. text ed. 27.50x (ISBN 0-435-32138-2). Heinemann Ed.
Goody, Esther N., ed. From Craft to Industry: The Ethnography of Proto-Industrial Cloth Production. LC 82-4205. (Cambridge Papers in Social Anthropology: No. 10). 304p. 1983. 39.50 (ISBN 0-521-24614-8). Cambridge U Pr.
Howe, W. S. The Dundee Textiles Industry 1960-1977: Decline & Diversification. 1982. 23.00 (ISBN 0-08-028454-X). Pergamon.
TEXTILE PAINTING
Robinson. Beginners Guide to Fabric Printing & Dyeing. 1982. text ed. 9.95 (ISBN 0-408-00575-0). Butterworth.
TEXTILES
see Textile Fabrics
TEXTUAL CRITICISM
see Criticism, Textual
THAI LANGUAGE
see Siamese Language
THAI LANGUAGES
see Tai Languages
THAILAND
Blackwood, Robert. Thailand. (Illus.). 184p. 1983. pap. 9.95 (ISBN 0-686-42978-8). Hippocrene Bks.
Desai, Santosh N. Hinduism in Thai Life. 163p. 1980. 34.95x (ISBN 0-940500-66-3, Pub by Popular Prakashan India). Asia Bk Corp.
Drud, Arne & Grais, Wafik. Thailand: An Analysis of Structural & Non-Structural Adjustments. LC 82-10890. (World Bank Staff Working Papers: No. 513). (Orig.). 1982. pap. text ed. 5.00 (ISBN 0-8213-0023-7). World Bank.
THAILAND–DESCRIPTION AND TRAVEL
Barnes, Simon. Thailand in Focus. (The "In Focus" Ser.). (Illus.). 64p. (Orig.). 1983. pap. 5.95 (ISBN 962-7031-23-2). C E Tuttle.
Cooper, Robert & Cooper, Nanthapa. Culture Shock! Thailand. 256p. 1983. 8.95 (ISBN 0-686-42988-5). Hippocrene Bks.
Leyman, Juliellen. The Complete Guide to Thailand. (The Complete Asian Guide Ser.). 108p. (Orig.). 1981. pap. 6.95 (ISBN 962-7031-04-6, Pub. by CFW Pubns Hong Kong). C E Tuttle.
THAILAND–DESCRIPTION AND TRAVEL–GUIDEBOOKS
Insight Guides. Thailand. (Illus.). 334p. 1983. 18.95 (ISBN 0-13-912618-X); pap. 14.95 (ISBN 0-13-912600-7). P-H.
Thailand Travel Guide. (Berlitz Travel Guides). (Illus.). 1982. pap. 4.95 (ISBN 0-02-969030-7, Berlitz). Macmillan.
THAILAND–ECONOMIC CONDITIONS
Thailand: An Annotated Bibliography of Local & Regional Development. 168p. 1983. pap. 10.00 (ISBN 0-686-43304-1, CRD 148, UNCRD). Unipub.
THAILAND–RELIGION
Desai, Santosh N. Hinduism in Thai Life. 163p. 1980. 34.95x (ISBN 0-940500-66-3, Pub by Popular Prakashan India). Asia Bk Corp.
THAILAND–SOCIAL LIFE AND CUSTOMS
Walker, Anthony R. Farmers in the Hills: Upland Peoples of North Thailand. (East Asian Folklore & Social Life Monographs: Vol. 105). 211p. 1981. 15.00 (ISBN 0-89986-336-1). Oriental Bk Store.
THALAMOPHORA
see Foraminifera
THALASSEMIA
Cao, Antonio & Carcassi, Ugo, eds. Thalassemia: Recent Advances in Detection & Treatment. LC 82-16179. (Birth Defects: Original Article Ser.: Vol. 18, No. 7). 230p. 1982. 74.00 (ISBN 0-8451-1051-9). A R Liss.
THAMES RIVER AND VALLEY
Maxwell, Gordon S. The Authors' Thames: A Literary Ramble Through the Thames Valley. (Illus.). 324p. 1982. Repr. of 1924 ed. lib. bdg. 40.00 (ISBN 0-89984-806-0). Century Bookbindery.
THANKSGIVING DAY
Baldwin, Margaret. Thanksgiving. (First Bks.). (Illus.). 72p. (gr. 4 up). 1983. PLB 8.90 (ISBN 0-531-04532-3). Watts.
Kessel, Joyce K. Squanto & the First Thanksgiving. LC 82-10313. (Carolrhoda On My Own Bks). (Illus.). 48p. (gr. k-3). 1983. PLB 6.95g (ISBN 0-87614-199-8). Carolrhoda Bks.
Penner, Lucille R. The Thanksgiving Book. (Illus.). (gr. 5 up). 1983. PLB 10.95 (ISBN 0-8038-7228-3). Hastings.
THATCHER, MARGARET
Hall, S. & Jacques, M. The Politics of Thatcherism. 265p. 1983. text ed. 23.00x (ISBN 0-85315-553-4, Pub. by Lawrence & Wishart Ltd England). Humanities.
THAXTER, CELIA (LAIGHTON), 1835-1894
Thaxter, Rosamond. Sandpiper: The Life & Letters of Celia Thaxter. (Illus.). 364p. 8.50 (ISBN 0-686-84142-5). Down East.
THEATER
Here are entered works which deal with the drama as acted upon the stage, and works treating of the historical, legal, moral, and religious aspects of the theater.
see also Acting; Actors and Actresses; Children'S Plays; Drama; Masques; Mysteries and Miracle-Plays; Puppets and Puppet-Plays; Theater Audiences
Appia, Adolpho. The Work of Living Art & Man is the Measure of All Things. 1962. 20.00x (ISBN 0-87024-305-5). U of Miami Pr.
Archer, Stephen M. How Theatre Happens. 2nd ed. 304p. 1983. text ed. 12.95 (ISBN 0-02-303750-4). Macmillan.
Athanasopulos, Christos G. Contemporary Theater: Evolution & Design. 350p. 1983. 60.00 (ISBN 0-471-87319-5, Pub. by Wiley-Interscience). Wiley.
Clark, Fiona. Hats. (Illus.). 1982. text ed. 13.95x (ISBN 0-7134-3774-X). Drama Bk.
Collison, David. Stage Sound. 2nd, rev. ed. (Illus.). 1982. 20.00x (ISBN 0-304-30987-7). Drama Bk.
Crampton, Esme. A Handbook of the Theatre. 264p. (Orig.). 1982. pap. text ed. 12.00x (ISBN 0-435-18185-8). Heinemann Ed.
Crane, Debra J. & Berson, Misha, eds. Young Stages: A Guide to Theatre & Dance for Youth in the San Francisco Bay Area. LC 82-51320. (Illus.). 72p. (Orig.). 1982. pap. 5.00 (ISBN 0-9605896-1-9). Theatre Ctr Bay.
Cumming, Valerie. Gloves. (Illus.). 1982. 13.95x (ISBN 0-7134-1008-6). Drama Bk.
Dramatists Sourcebook: 1982-83. 1982. pap. 7.95 (ISBN 0-930452-27-5). Theatre Comm.
Eckel, Lorelei & Schoyer, Maxine. One Thousand-One Broadways: Hometown Talent on Stage. 160p. 1982. 12.95 (ISBN 0-686-83955-2). Iowa St U Pr.
Emanuel, Edward F. Action & Idea: The Roots of Entertainment. 120p. 1982. pap. text ed. 9.95 (ISBN 0-8403-2845-1). Kendall-Hunt.
Komar, Kathleen L. Pattern & Chaos: A Structural Analysis of Novels by Doeblin, Koeppen, Dos Passos, & Faulkner. LC 82-73875. (Studies in German Literature, Linguistics, & Culture: Vol. 14). (Illus.). 160p. 1983. 20.00x (ISBN 0-938100-19-X). Camden Hse.
Theatre Directory: 1982-83. pap. 3.95 (ISBN 0-930452-29-1). Theatre Comm.
THEATER–AUDIENCES
see Theater Audiences
THEATER–BIBLIOGRAPHY
Research Libraries of the New York Public Library & Library of Congress. Bibliographic Guide to Theatre Arts: 1982. 1983. lib. bdg. 125.00 (ISBN 0-8161-6982-9, Biblio Guides). G K Hall.
THEATER–COSTUME
see Costume
THEATER–DIRECTION
see Theater–Production and Direction
THEATER–HISTORY
Combe, Thomas. Theatre of Fine Devices. (Illus.). 120p. 1982. pap. 4.50 (ISBN 0-87328-075-X). Huntington Lib.
Wilson, F. P. The Elizabethan Theatre. 1982. lib. bdg. 34.50 (ISBN 0-686-81918-7). Porter.
THEATER–PRODUCTION AND DIRECTION
Corbin, Charles B. & Corbin, David E. Homemade Play Equipment. (Illus.). 115p. 1981. pap. text ed. 3.95x (ISBN 0-89641-058-7). American Pr.
Engel, Lehman. Getting the Show On. 1983. 14.95 (ISBN 0-02-870680-3). Schirmer Bks.
Ratliff, Gerald L. The Theatre Student-Playscript Interpretation & Production. (Theatre Student Ser.). (Illus.). 160p. lib. bdg. 12.50 (ISBN 0-686-82646-9). Rosen Pr.
THEATER–REVIEWS
Guernsey, Otis L. Best Plays 1981-1982. LC 20-21432. (The Burns Mantle Yearbook of the Theatre Ser.). 1983. 24.95 (ISBN 0-396-08124-X). Dodd.
Willis, John. Theatre World: 1981-82, Vol. 38. 1983. 25.00 (ISBN 0-517-54945-X). Crown.
THEATER–STUDY AND TEACHING
Turner, J. Clifford. Voice & Speech in the Theatre. 3rd ed. Morrison, Malcolm, rev. by. (Theatre & Stage Ser.). 146p. 1982. pap. 13.50 (ISBN 0-7136-2209-1). Sportshelf.
THEATER–VOCATIONAL GUIDANCE
see Theater As a Profession
THEATER–YEARBOOKS
Cooper, Donald. Theatre Year, 1980. (Illus.). 1982. pap. 15.95 (ISBN 0-686-84198-0). Drama Bk.
--Theatre Year, 1981. (Illus.). 1982. pap. 15.95 (ISBN 0-686-84199-9). Drama Bk.
--Theatre Year, 1982. (Illus.). 1983. pap. 15.95 (ISBN 0-686-84200-6). Drama Bk.
THEATER–AUSTRALIA
Marsh, Ngaio. Ngaio Marsh: Black Beech & Honeydew. (Illus.). 1982. 19.95 (ISBN 0-00-216367-5, Pub. by W Collins Australia). Intl Schol Bk Serv.
THEATER–ENGLAND
see Theater–Great Britain
THEATER–GREAT BRITAIN
Johnson, Claudia D. & Johnson, Vernon E. Nineteenth-Century Theatrical Memoirs. LC 82-15576. 285p. 1982. lib. bdg. 35.00 (ISBN 0-313-23644-5, JNT/). Greenwood.
Trussler, Simon, ed. The Royal Shakespeare Company, 1981-82: A Complete Record of the Year's Work. (Illus.). 1982. pap. text ed. 12.95 (ISBN 0-9505057-4-9, Pub. by Royal Shakespeare England). Advent NY.
Wearing, J. P. The London Stage 1910-1919: A Calendar of Plays & Players, 2 Vols. LC 82-19190. 1388p. 1982. Set. 65.00 (ISBN 0-8108-1596-6). Scarecrow.
THEATER–GREAT BRITAIN–HISTORY
Meisel, Martin. Realizations: Narrative, Pictorial, & Theatrical Arts of the Nineteenth Century. LC 82-12292. (Illus.). 416p. 1983. 45.00x (ISBN 0-691-06553-5). Princeton U Pr.
Orrell, John. The Quest for Shakespeare's Globe. LC 82-9445. (Illus.). 220p. Date not set. price not set (ISBN 0-521-24751-9). Cambridge U Pr.
THEATER–INDIA
Varadpande, M. L. Religion & Theatre in India. 100p. 1982. text ed. 10.00x (ISBN 0-391-02794-8). Humanities.
THEATER–LATIN AMERICA
Natella, Arthur, Jr. The New Theatre of Peru. LC 81-84037. (Senda de Estudios y Ensayos Ser.). 132p. (Orig.). 1982. pap. text ed. 9.95 (ISBN 0-918454-28-X). Senda Nueva.
THEATER–UNITED STATES
Broun, Heywood H. A Studied Madness. LC 79-84436. 298p. 1983. pap. 4.95 (ISBN 0-933256-40-X). Second Chance.
Guillet, Ernest B. Un Theatre Francophone dans un milieu Franco-Americain. (Illus.). 52p. (Fr.). 1981. pap. text ed. 1.50x (ISBN 0-911409-37-8). Natl Mat Dev.
Skinner, Dana R. Our Changing Theatre. 327p. 1982. Repr. of 1931 ed. lib. bdg. 35.00 (ISBN 0-8495-4967-1). Arden Lib.
THEATER–UNITED STATES–HISTORY
Coad, Oral S. American Stage. 1929. text ed. 22.50x (ISBN 0-686-37861-X). Elliots Bks.
Johnson, Claudia D. & Johnson, Vernon E. Nineteenth-Century Theatrical Memoirs. LC 82-15576. 285p. 1982. lib. bdg. 35.00 (ISBN 0-313-23644-5, JNT/). Greenwood.
THEATER AS A PROFESSION
see also Acting As a Profession
Greenberg, Jan. Theater Careers. (Illus.). 216p. (gr. 7 up). 1983. 13.95 (ISBN 0-03-061568-2). HR&W.
THEATER AUDIENCES
Nicoll, Allardyce. The Garrick Stage: Theaters & Audience in the Eighteenth Century. 192p. 1982. pap. 12.50 (ISBN 0-7190-0858-1). Manchester.
THEATER IN ART
see Actors and Actresses–Portraits; Theaters–Stage-Setting and Scenery
THEATER REVIEWS
see Theater–Reviews
THEATERS–ARCHITECTURE
see Theaters–Construction
THEATERS–CONSTRUCTION
see also Architectural Acoustics
Weil, Mark S. Baroque Theatre & Stage Design. 44p. 1983. pap. 5.00 (ISBN 0-936316-04-7). Washington U Gallery.
THEATERS–DESIGNS AND PLANS
see Theaters–Construction
THEATERS–STAGE-SETTING AND SCENERY
Bellman, Willard F. Scene Design, Stage Lighting, Sound, Costume, & Makeup: A Scenographic Approach. 672p. 1983. text ed. 33.50 scp (ISBN 0-06-040612-7, HarpC). Har-Row.
Weil, Mark S. Baroque Theatre & Stage Design. 44p. 1983. pap. 5.00 (ISBN 0-936316-04-7). Washington U Gallery.
THEATERS, MOVING-PICTURE
see Moving-Picture Theaters
THEATRICAL AGENCIES
Kelley, F. Beverly. It Was Better Than Work. Franzwa, Gregory M., ed. LC 82-24556. xii, 287p. 1983. 14.95 (ISBN 0-935284-25-7). Patrice Pr.
THEATRICAL COSTUME
see Costume
THEATRICAL MAKE-UP
see Make-Up, Theatrical
THEATRICAL MUSIC
see Musical Revue, Comedy, etc.; Opera
THEATRICAL SCENERY
see Theaters–Stage-Setting and Scenery
THEATRICALS, COLLEGE
see College and School Drama
THEBES, EGYPT
Demand, Nancy H. Thebes in the Fifth Century. (States & Cities of Ancient Greece Ser.). 208p. 1983. 19.95 (ISBN 0-7100-9288-1). Routledge & Kegan.
THEFT
see Stealing
THEOBALD, ABP. OF CANTERBURY, d. 1161
Plutarch. Plutarch's Themistocles & Aristides. Perrin, Bernadotte, ed. 1901. text ed. 65.00x (ISBN 0-686-83702-9). Elliots Bks.
THEOCRACY
see Nationalism and Religion; War and Religion
THEODICY
Here are entered works that attempt to vindicate the wisdom and goodness of God in the creation and government of the world, and to rebut the charge that these are brought into question by the existence of evil and sin.
see also Good and Evil; Sin
Kushner, Harold S. When Bad Things Happen to Good People. (General Ser.). 1982. lib. bdg. 11.95 (ISBN 0-8161-3465-0, Large Print Bks). G K Hall.
Wall, George B. Is God Really Good? Conversations with a Theodicist. LC 82-24854. 130p. (Orig.). 1983. pap. text ed. 8.25 (ISBN 0-8191-3032-X). U Pr of Amer.
THEOLOGIANS
see also Christian Biography;
also subdivisions Biography or Clergy under names of Christian denominations
Gellinek, Christian. Hugo Grotius. (World Authors Ser.: No. 680). 176p. 1983. lib. bdg. 19.95 (ISBN 0-8057-6525-5, Twayne). G K Hall.
Loetscher, Lefferts A. Facing the Enlightenment & Pietism: Archibald Alexander & the Founding of Princeton Theological Seminary. LC 82-11995. (Contributions to the Study of Religion Ser.: No. 8). 352p. 1983. lib. bdg. 35.00 (ISBN 0-313-23677-1, LOE/). Greenwood.
Patterson, Bob. Carl F. Henry, Makers of the Modern Theologcial Mind. 1983. pap. 6.95 (ISBN 0-8499-2951-2). Word Bks.
THEOLOGICAL ANTHROPOLOGY
see Man (Theology)
THEOLOGICAL BELIEF
see Faith
THEOLOGICAL EDUCATION
see Religious Education; Theology–Study and Teaching
THEOLOGICAL STUDENTS
see Seminarians
THEOLOGICAL VIRTUES
see Charity; Faith; Virtue and Virtues
THEOLOGY
see also Atheism; Christianity; Church; Church History; Ethics; Rationalism; Religion; Religion and Science; Secularism
Ames, William. The Marrow of Theology. Eusden, John D., ed. & tr. from Latin. Orig. Title: Medulla Theologiae. xiv, 354p. 1983. pap. 14.95 (ISBN 0-939464-14-4). Labyrinth Pr.
Balthasar, Hans Urs von. The Glory of the Lord: A Theological Aesthetics-Seeing the Form, Vol. 1. 656p. (Orig.). 1983. 30.00 (ISBN 0-8245-0579-4). Crossroad NY.
Berquist, Maurice. The Doctor Is In, 5 Vol. Set. (Wesleyan Theological Persective Ser.). 1983. write for info. Warner Pr.
Carmody, John. Ecology & Religion: Toward a New Christian Theology of Nature. LC 82-62412. 1983. pap. 6.95 (ISBN 0-8091-2526-9). Paulist Pr.
Cavaliero, Glen. Charles Williams: Poet of Theology. 224p. 1983. 8.95 (ISBN 0-8028-3579-1). Eerdmans.

Chadwick, Henry, ed. Boethius: The Consolations of Music, Logic, Theology, & Philosophy. 330p. 1981. text ed. 39.00 (ISBN 0-19-826447-X). Oxford U Pr.

Clasper, Paul. Theological Ferment: Personal Reflections. 226p. (Orig.). 1982. pap. 6.75x (ISBN 0-686-37687-0, Pub. by New Day Philippines). Cellar.

Garrison, James. The Darkness of God: Theology After Hiroshima. 208p. 1983. pap. 6.95 (ISBN 0-8028-1956-7). Eerdmans.

Joseph, Howard, et al, eds. Truth & Compassion: Essays on Judaism & Religion for Rabbi Dr. Solomon Frank at Eighty. 250p. 1982. text ed. 11.50x (ISBN 0-919812-17-1, 40948, Pub. by Laurier U Pr). Humanities.

Jungel, Eberhard. God As the Mystery of the World: On the Foundation of the Theology of the Crucified One in the Dispute Between Theism & Atheism. Guder, Darrell L., tr. 428p. (Ger.). 1983. 24.95 (ISBN 0-8028-3586-4). Eerdmans.

McGill, Arthur C. Suffering: A Test of Theological Method. LC 82-6934. 1982. pap. 6.95 (ISBN 0-664-24448-3). Westminster.

Micks, Marianne H. Introduction to Theology. rev. ed. 160p. 1983. pap. 8.95 (ISBN 0-8164-2465-9). Seabury.

Muller-Vollmar, Kurt, ed. The Hermeneutics Reader. 320p. Date not set. 17.50 (ISBN 0-8264-0208-9). Crossroad NY.

Nash, Ronald H. The Word of God & the Mind of Man: The Crisis of Revealed Truth in Contemporary Theology. 176p. (Orig.). 1982. pap. 6.95 (ISBN 0-310-45131-0). Zondervan.

Noll, Mark A., compiled by. The Princeton Theology: An Anthology. 432p. (Orig.). 1983. pap. 14.95 (ISBN 0-8010-6737-5). Baker Bk.

Pannenberg, Wolfhart. Basic Questions in Theology, Vol. II. LC 82-15984. 257p. 1983. pap. write for info. (ISBN 0-664-24467-X). Westminster.

Rahner, Karl. Faith & Ministry. (Theological Investigations Ser.: Vol. 19). 352p. 1983. 19.50 (ISBN 0-686-83771-1). Crossroad NY.

--God & Revelation, Vol. 18. (Theological Investigations Ser.). 352p. 1983. 19.50 (ISBN 0-8245-0571-9). Crossroad NY.

Thomas, Owen G. Introduction to Theology. 2nd ed. LC 82-61890. 304p. 1983. pap. 12.95 (ISBN 0-8192-1319-5). Morehouse.

Thomas Aquinas. Activity & Contemplation. (Summa Theologial Ser.). 1966. 12.95 (ISBN 0-07-002021-3). McGraw.

Watts, Pauline M. Nicolaus Cusanus: A Fifteenth-Century Vision of Man. (Studies in the History of Christian Thought: Vol. 30). (Illus.). ix, 248p. 1982. write for info. (ISBN 90-04-06581-4). E J Brill.

Williamson, William B. Ian Ramsey, Makers of the Modern Theological Mind. Patterson, Bob E., ed. 1982. 6.95 (ISBN 0-8499-2947-4). Word Pub.

THEOLOGY-BIOGRAPHY

see Theologians

THEOLOGY-COLLECTED WORKS

Pannenberg, Wolfhart. Basic Questions in Theology, Vol. I. LC 82-15984. 257p. 1983. pap. write for info. (ISBN 0-664-24466-1). Westminster.

THEOLOGY-DICTIONARIES

Ramm, Bernard. Diccionario de Teologia Contemporanea. Valle, Roger V., tr. 143p. Date not set. pap. price not set (ISBN 0-311-09064-8). Casa Bautista.

THEOLOGY-PHILOSOPHY

see Christianity-Philosophy

THEOLOGY-STUDY AND TEACHING

see also Catechisms; Christian Education; Religious Education; Seminarians

Farley, Edward. Theologia: The Fragmentation & Unity of Theological Education. LC 82-48621. 224p. 1983. pap. text ed. 14.50 (ISBN 0-8006-1705-3). Fortress.

THEOLOGY-EARLY CHURCH, ca. 30-600

Lawler, Thomas C. The Letters of St. Cyprian of Carthage, Vol. 1. Clarke, G. W. & Burghardt, Walter J., eds. (Ancient Christian Writers Ser.: No. 43). 416p. 1983. 24.95 (ISBN 0-8091-0341-9). Paulist Pr.

--The Letters of St. Cyprian of Carthage, Vol. 2. Clarke, G. W. & Burghardt, Walter J., eds. (Ancient Christian Writers Ser.: No. 44). 352p. 1983. 22.95 (ISBN 0-8091-0342-7). Paulist Pr.

THEOLOGY-MIDDLE AGES, 600-1500

Nielsen, Lauge O. Theology & Philosophy in the Twelfth Century: A Study of Gilbert Porreta's Thinking & the Theological Expositions of the Doctrin of the Incarnation during the Period 1130-1180. (Acta Theologica Danica Ser.: Vol. 15). 396p. 1982. write for info. (ISBN 90-04-06545-8). E J Brill.

THEOLOGY-16TH CENTURY

Platt, John. Reformed Thought & Scholasticism: The Arguments for the Existence of God in Dutch Theology, 1575-1650. (Studies in the History of Christian Thought Ser.: Vol. 29). viii, 249p. 1982. write for info. (ISBN 90-04-06593-8). E J Brill.

THEOLOGY-17TH CENTURY

Platt, John. Reformed Thought & Scholasticism: The Arguments for the Existence of God in Dutch Theology, 1575-1650. (Studies in the History of Christian Thought Ser.: Vol. 29). viii, 249p. 1982. write for info. (ISBN 90-04-06593-8). E J Brill.

THEOLOGY-20TH CENTURY

Schillebeeckx, Edward. God is New Each Moment: Conversations with Huub Oosterhuis & Piet Hoogeveen. 160p. (Orig.). 1983. pap. price not set (ISBN 0-8164-2475-6). Seabury.

THEOLOGY, ASCETICAL

see Asceticism

THEOLOGY, BIBLICAL

see Bible-Theology

THEOLOGY, COVENANT

see Covenants (Theology)

THEOLOGY, CRISIS

see Dialectical Theology

THEOLOGY, DEVOTIONAL

see Devotional Exercises; Devotional Literature; Meditations; Prayers

THEOLOGY, DOCTRINAL

see also Angels; Apologetics; Asceticism; Atonement; Authority (Religion); Baptism; Bible-Theology; Catechisms; Catholicity; Christian Ethics; Christianity-Philosophy; Conversion; Covenants (Theology); Creeds; Devil; Dialectical Theology; Dogma; Faith; Forgiveness of Sin; Free Will and Determinism; Freedom (Theology); Gifts, Spiritual; God; Good and Evil; Grace (Theology); Holy Spirit; Incarnation; Inspiration; Jesus Christ; Law (Theology); Lord's Supper; Love (Theology); Man (Theology); Mary, Virgin-Theology; Miracles; Mystical Union; Mysticism; Peace (Theology); Power (Theology); Providence and Government of God; Resurrection; Revelation; Sacraments; Salvation; Sanctification; Sin; Teleology; Theodicy; Trinity

also subdivision Doctrinal and Controversial Works under names of Christian denominations, e.g. Baptism-Doctrinal and Controversial Works

Boer, Harry R. The Doctrine of Reprobation in the Christian Reformed Church. 104p. 1983. pap. 6.95 (ISBN 0-8028-1952-4). Eerdmans.

Cox, Harvey. Just as I Am. LC 82-11631. 160p. 1983. 10.95 (ISBN 0-687-20687-1). Abingdon.

Criswell, W. A. Great Doctrines of the Bible, Vol. 1 & 2. 192p. 1982. Repr. 16.90 (ISBN 0-310-43868-3). Zondervan.

DeWitt, David. Beyond the Basics. 1983. pap. 5.95 (ISBN 0-8024-0178-3). Moody.

Ellingsen, Mark. Doctrine & Word. LC 82-21311. 192p. 1983. pap. 8.95 (ISBN 0-8042-0533-7). John Knox.

George, Timothy. Theology of the Reformers. 1984. 14.95 (ISBN 0-8054-6573-1). Broadman.

Gollwitzer, Helmut. An Introduction to Protestant Theology. Cairns, David, tr. LC 82-4798. 240p. 1982. pap. 12.95 (ISBN 0-664-24415-7). Westminster.

Hole, F. B. Assembly Principles. Daniel, R. P., ed. 40p. pap. 2.50 (ISBN 0-88172-141-7). Believers Bkshelf.

Humphreys, Fisher & Wise, Philip. A Dictionary of Doctrinal Terms. (Orig.). 1983. pap. 4.95 (ISBN 0-8054-1141-0). Broadman.

Pardington, G. P. Studies in Christian Doctrine, 4 Vols. Freligh, H. M. & Schroder, E. H., eds. 312p. 1964. pap. 1.95 ea. Vol. 1. Vol. 2. Vol. 3. Vol. 4. Chr Pubns.

THEOLOGY, DOCTRINAL-COLLECTED WORKS

see Theology-Collected Works

THEOLOGY, DOCTRINAL-HISTORY

Langford, Thomas A. Practical Divinity: Theology in the Wesleyan Tradition. 304p. (Orig.). 1983. pap. 9.95 (ISBN 0-687-33326-1). Abingdon.

Schillebeeckx, Edward, ed. The Movement of Theology Since the Council. (Concilium 1983: Vol. 170). 128p. (Orig.). 1983. pap. 6.95 (ISBN 0-8164-2450-0). Seabury.

THEOLOGY, DOCTRINAL-HISTORY-19TH CENTURY

McCool, Gerald A. Catholic Theology in the Nineteenth Century: The Quest for a Unitary Method. 312p. 1977. 14.95 (ISBN 0-8164-0339-2). Seabury.

THEOLOGY, DOCTRINAL-HISTORY-20TH CENTURY

Wing-hung Lam. Chinese Theology in Construction. LC 81-15483. 320p. 1983. pap. 11.95x (ISBN 0-87808-180-1). William Carey Lib.

THEOLOGY, DOCTRINAL-POPULAR WORKS

Sisson, Richard. Answering Christianity's Most Puzzling Questions, Vol. 2. 240p. (Orig.). 1983. pap. 7.95 (ISBN 0-8024-5148-9). Moody.

THEOLOGY, DOGMATIC

see Theology, Doctrinal

THEOLOGY, ECCLESIASTICAL

see Church

THEOLOGY, ETHICAL

see Christian Ethics

THEOLOGY, FEDERAL

see Covenants (Theology)

THEOLOGY, FUNDAMENTAL

see Apologetics

THEOLOGY, JEWISH

see Jewish Theology

THEOLOGY, MORAL

see Christian Ethics

THEOLOGY, MYSTICAL

see Mysticism

THEOLOGY, PASTORAL

see Pastoral Theology

THEOLOGY, PRACTICAL

see also Baptism; Canon Law; Catechetics; Christian Art and Symbolism; Christian Education; Christian Life; Church Renewal; Church Work; Church Year; Clergy; Devotional Exercises; Devotional Literature; Evangelistic Work; Gifts, Spiritual; Hymns; Liturgics; Liturgies; Lord's Supper; Missions; Pastoral Theology; Prayer; Preaching; Religious Education; Revivals; Sacraments; Sermons; Spiritual Life; Sunday-Schools; Worship

Milavec, Aaron. To Empower as Jesus Did: Acquiring Spiritual Power through Apprenticeship. LC 82-6466. (Toronto Studies in Theology: Vol. 9). 456p. 1982. 49.95x (ISBN 0-88946-966-0). E Mellen.

Schillebeeckx, Edward & Baptist-Metz, Johannes. Martyrdom Today. (Concilium 1983: Vol. 163). 128p. 1983. pap. 6.95 (ISBN 0-8164-2443-8). Seabury.

THEOLOGY, SYSTEMATIC

see Theology, Doctrinal

THEORETICAL CHEMISTRY

see Chemistry, Physical and Theoretical

THEORY OF APPROXIMATION

see Approximation Theory

THEORY OF ERRORS

see Errors, Theory of

THEORY OF GAMES

see Game Theory

THEORY OF GRAPHS

see Graph Theory

THEORY OF GROUPS

see Groups, Theory of

THEORY OF SETS

see Set Theory

THEORY OF STRUCTURES

see Structures, Theory of

THEOSOPHY

see also Anthroposophy; Gnosticism; Jesus Christ-Theosophical Interpretations; Karma; Reincarnation; Yoga

De Zirkoff, Boris. The Dream That Never Dies: Boris de Zirkoff Speaks Out on Theosophy. Small, W. Emmett, ed. (Illus.). 242p. 1983. pap. 11.50 lexitone (ISBN 0-913004-45-6). Point Loma Pub.

The Theosophical Movement 1875-1950: Theosophy Company. xiii, 351p. 1951. 6.00 (ISBN 0-938998-14-5). Theosophy.

Unger, Carl. Cosmic Understanding. 1982. pap. 1.95 (ISBN 0-916786-62-5). St George Bk Serv.

--Steiner's Theosophy: Notes on the Book "Theosophy". 1982. Repr. 5.95 (ISBN 0-916786-64-1). St George Bk Serv.

THERA (ISLANDS)

Doumas, Christon G. Thera: Pompeii of the Ancient Aegean. (New Aspects of Antiquity Ser.). (Illus.). 1983. 29.95 (ISBN 0-500-39016-9). Thames Hudson.

THERAPEUTIC EXERCISE

see Exercise Therapy

THERAPEUTICS

see also Bibliotherapy; Chemistry, Medical and Pharmaceutical; Chemotherapy; Diet in Disease; Drugs; Inhalation Therapy; Materia Medica; Medicine-Formulae, Receipts, Prescriptions; Narcotics; Nurses and Nursing; Nutrition; Orgonomy; Orthomolecular Medicine; Parenteral Therapy; X-Rays also names of individual drugs, and names of diseases and groups of diseases, e.g. Bronchitis, Fever, Nervous System-Diseases; also subdivision Therapeutic Use under specific subjects, e.g. Poetry-Therapeutic Use; X-Rays-Therapeutic Use

Biefang, S., et al. Manual For the Planning & Implementation of Therapeutic Studies. (Lecture Notes in Medical Informatics Ser.: Vol. 20). 100p. 1983. pap. 12.00 (ISBN 0-387-11979-5). Springer-Verlag.

Dixon, Jesse T. Adapting Activities for Therapeutic Recreation Service: Concepts & Applications. (Illus.). 37p. (Orig.). 1981. pap. 12.00 (ISBN 0-916304-48-5). Campanile.

Hokanson, Jack E. Introduction to the Therapeutic Process. (Illus.). 416p. Date not set. text ed. price not set (ISBN 0-201-10525-X). A-W.

Katcher, Brian S. & Young, Lloyd Y., eds. Applied Therapeutics: The Clinical Use of Drugs. (Illus.). 1983. pap. 54.00 (ISBN 0-915486-05-9). Applied Therapeutics.

Marini, Lucio, ed. Repertorio Terapeutico. 6th ed. 1048p. (Orig., Ital. & Eng.). 1979. pap. 65.00x (ISBN 88-7076-001-4). Intl Pubns Serv.

Newton, Linda. Therapy Made Fun! Set 2. 1982. text ed. 15.75x (ISBN 0-8134-2232-9). Interstate.

Rolfe & Lennon. The Heal Yourself Home Handbook of Unusual Remedies. LC 82-14274. 205p. 1983. 14.95 (ISBN 0-13-384685-7, Parker); pap. 4.95 (ISBN 0-13-384677-6). P-H.

Tinker, Jack & Porter, Susan W. Intensive Therapy Nursing. 304p. 1980. pap. text ed. 19.95 (ISBN 0-7131-4347-9). E Arnold.

THERAPEUTICS-COMPLICATIONS AND SEQUELAE

see Iatrogenic Diseases

THERAPEUTICS, PARENTERAL

see Parenteral Therapy

THERAPEUTICS, PHYSIOLOGICAL

Here are entered comprehensive or general works dealing with non-medicinal therapeutics. Specific works are entered under appropriate headings, e.g. Diet, Diet in Disease, Phototherapy, Physical Therapy, etc.

see also Baths; Cellular Therapy; Chiropractic; Electrotherapeutics; Exercise Therapy; Hydrotherapy; Massage; Mechanotherapy; Music Therapy; Occupational Therapy; Physical Therapy; Radiotherapy; X-Rays

Arnould-Taylor, W. E. Aromatherapy for the Whole Person. 96p. 1981. 32.00 (ISBN 0-85950-337-2, Pub. by Thornes England). State Mutual Bk.

The Drug Alternative. 96p. 2.95 (ISBN 0-88314-061-6). AAHPERD.

Dunkin, Naomi. Psychology for Physiotherapists. (Psychology for Professional Groups Ser.). 350p. 1981. text ed. 25.00x (ISBN 0-333-31857-9, Pub. by Macmillan England); pap. text ed. 10.95x (ISBN 0-333-31884-6). Humanities.

Lowe, Carl & Nechas, Jim. Body Healing. (Illus.). 440p. 1983. 21.95 (ISBN 0-87857-441-7, 05-024-0). Rodale Pr Inc.

THERAPY, CELLULAR

see Cellular Therapy

THERESE, SAINT, 1515-1582

see Teresa, Saint, 1515-1582

THERMAL ANALYSIS

Dollimore, D. Thermal Analysis: European Symposium 2nd, Proceedings. 1981. 61.95 (ISBN 0-471-25661-7, Pub. by Wiley Heyden). Wiley.

THERMAL EQUILIBRIUM

see Thermodynamics

THERMAL INSULATION

see Insulation (Heat)

THERMAL TRANSFER

see Heat-Transmission

THERMAL WATERS

see Geothermal Resources

THERMOBIOLOGY

Gautherie, Michel & Albert, Ernest, eds. Biomedical Thermology. LC 82-21639. (Progress in Clinical & Biological Research Ser.: Vol. 107). 919p. 1982. 176.00 (ISBN 0-8451-0107-2). A R Liss.

THERMOCHEMISTRY

see also Combustion; Dissociation; Gases-Liquefaction; Thermal Analysis

Rock, Peter A. Chemical Thermodynamics. McQuarrie, Donald A., ed. LC 82-51233. (Physical Chemistry Ser.). (Illus.). 553p. 1983. 24.00x (ISBN 0-935702-10-5). Univ Sci Bks.

THERMOCOUPLES

Standards & Practices for Instrumentation. 7th, rev. ed. 1000p. 1983. text ed. 135.00 (ISBN 0-87664-697-6). Instru Soc.

THERMODYNAMICS

see also Entropy; Heat Pumps; Quantum Theory; Statistical Mechanics; Thermal Analysis; Thermochemistry

Brophy, J. H., et al. Thermodynamics of Structure. (Structure & Properties of Materials Ser: Vol. 2). 216p. 1964. pap. text ed. 17.50x (ISBN 0-471-10610-0). Wiley.

Burghardt. Ingenieria Termodinamica. 2nd ed. 600p. (Span.). 1983. pap. text ed. write for info. (ISBN 0-06-310071-1, Pub. by HarLA Mexico). Har-Row.

Caplan, S. Roy & Essig, Alvin. Bioenergetics & Linear Nonequilibrium Thermodynamics: The Steady State. (Harvard Books in Biophysics: No. 3). (Illus.). 448p. 1983. text ed. 37.50x (ISBN 0-674-07352-5). Harvard U Pr.

Cook, Richard J. & Gardi, Gavin L. How to Design & Build Thermosiphoning Air Panels. iv, 36p. (Orig.). pap. 2.00 (ISBN 0-939294-13-3). Beach Leaf.

Copeland, O. Multifluid Thermodynamic Power Cycles: An Invention Report & a Preliminary Assessment of the Potential. (Progress in Solar Energy Supplements SERI Ser.). 1983. pap. text ed. 7.50x (ISBN 0-89553-093-7). Am Solar Energy.

Devereux, Owen F. Topics in Metallurgical Thermodynamics. 416p. 1983. write for info. (ISBN 0-471-86963-5, Pub. by Wiley-Interscience). Wiley.

Gautherie, Michel & Albert, Ernest, eds. Biomedical Thermology. LC 82-21639. (Progress in Clinical & Biological Research Ser.: Vol. 107). 919p. 1982. 176.00 (ISBN 0-8451-0107-2). A R Liss.

Gurvich, L. V., ed. Thermodynamic Properties of Individual Substances, 2 vols, Pt. I. 3rd rev. & enl. ed. (Illus.). 830p. 1983. 150.00 set (ISBN 0-08-027585-0); prepub. 120.00 (ISBN 0-08-029998-9). Pergamon.

Kestin, J. A Course in Thermodynamics, 2 Vols. 1979. Vol. 1. 38.50 (ISBN 0-07-034281-4); Vol. 2. 38.50 (ISBN 0-07-034282-2). McGraw.

Lupis, C. H. Chemical Thermodynamics of Materials. 608p. 1982. 75.00 (ISBN 0-444-00713-X, North Holland). Elsevier.

Manrique. Termodinamica. 2nd ed. 352p. (Span.). 1981. pap. text ed. write for info. (ISBN 0-06-315510-9, Pub. by HarLA Mexcio). Har-Row.

Modell, Michael & Reid, Robert C. Thermodynamics & Its Applications. 2nd ed. (Illus.). 512p. 1983. text ed. 34.95 (ISBN 0-13-915017-X). P-H.

Newman, Stephen A., ed. Chemical Engineering Thermodynamics. LC 82-70702. (Illus.). 540p. 1982. 49.95 (ISBN 0-250-40520-2). Ann Arbor Science.

Pfund, P. A. & Yao, S. C., eds. Tube Bundle Thermal-Hydraulics. 73p. 1982. 20.00 (G00212). ASME.

Rock, Peter A. Chemical Thermodynamics. McQuarrie, Donald A., ed. LC 82-51233. (Physical Chemistry Ser.). (Illus.). 553p. 1983. 24.00x (ISBN 0-935702-10-5). Univ Sci Bks.

Smith, Norman O. Elementary Statistical Thermodynamics: A Problems Approach. 225p. 1982. 25.00x (ISBN 0-306-41205-5, Plenum Pr); pap. 14.95x (ISBN 0-306-41216-0). Plenum Pub.

Sychev, V. V. Complex Thermodynamics Systems. 240p. 1981. 8.00 (ISBN 0-8285-2279-0, Pub. by Mir Pubs USSR). Imported Pubns.

Symposium on Thermophysical Properties, 8th. Thermophysical Properties of Solids & of Selected Fluids for Energy Technology: Proceedings, 2 Vols, Vol. 2. 1981. 65.00 (100152). ASME.

Todd, J. P. & Ellis, H. B. An Introduction to Thermodynamics of Engineering Technologists. 469p. 1981. text ed. 27.95 (ISBN 0-471-05300-7); solutions manual 10.00 (ISBN 0-471-09794-2). Wiley.

Van Ness, H. C. Understanding Thermodynamics. 103p. 1983. pap. 4.00 (ISBN 0-486-63277-6). Dover.

Vazquez, J. C. & Lebon, G., eds. Stability of Thermodynamic Systems, Barcelona, Spain, 1981: Proceedings. (Lecture Notes in Physics: Vol. 164). 321p. 1982. text ed. 17.50 (ISBN 0-387-11581-1). Springer-Verlag.

Ziegler. An Introduction to Thermomechanics. (Series in Applied Mathematics & Mechanics: Vol. 21). Date not set. 68.00 (ISBN 0-444-86503-9, North Holland). Elsevier.

Zierep, Juergen & Oertel, Herbert, Jr., eds. Convective Transport & Instability Phenomena. (Illus.). 577p. 1982. text ed. 65.00 (ISBN 3-7650-1114-2). Sheridan.

THERMOELECTRICITY

see also Pyro- and Piezo-Electricity; Solar Batteries; Thermocouples

Beghi, G., ed. Thermal Energy Storage. 1982. 59.50 (ISBN 90-277-1428-2, Pub. by Reidel Holland). Kluwer Boston.

THERMONUCLEAR REACTIONS, CONTROLLED

see Controlled Fusion

THERMOPLASTICS

Mascia, L. Thermoplastics: Materials Engineering. (Illus.). xiii, 440p. 1983. 78.00 (ISBN 0-85334-146-X, Pub. by Applied Sci England). Elsevier.

THESAURI, SUBJECT

see Subject Headings

THESES

see Dissertations, Academic

THESIS WRITING

see Dissertations, Academic; Report Writing

THETA FUNCTIONS

see Functions, Theta

THIN FILMS

see also Metallic Films

Bunshah, Rointan F., et al. Deposition Technologies for Films & Coatings: Developments & Applications. LC 82-7862. (Illus.). 585p. 1983. 69.00 (ISBN 0-8155-0906-5). Noyes.

Stuart, R. V., ed. Vacuum Technology, Thin Films, & Sputtering: An Introduction. LC 82-13748. Date not set. 21.00 (ISBN 0-12-674780-6). Acad Pr.

Tellier. Size Effects of Thin Films. (Thin Films Science & Technology Ser.: Vol. 2). 1982. 68.00 (ISBN 0-444-42106-8). Elsevier.

THIN LAYER CHROMATOGRAPHY

Macek, K. Bibliography of Paper & Thin Layer Tography, 1966-69, Vol. 2. (Journal of Chromatography Suppl. Ser.). 1972. 85.00 (ISBN 0-444-40953-X). Elsevier.

Touchstone, J. C. & Sherma, J. Densitometry in Thin Layer Chromatography: Practice & Applications. 747p. 1979. text ed. 58.50 (ISBN 0-471-88041-8, Pub. by Wiley Interscience). Wiley.

THINKING

see Artificial Intelligence; Thought and Thinking

THIOPHENE

Lukevics, E. & Skorova, A. E. Thiophene Derivatives of Group IV B Elements. (Sulpher Reports: Vol. 2, No. 5). 38p. 1982. 24.50 (ISBN 3-7186-0133-8). Harwood Academic.

THIRD WORLD

see Underdeveloped Areas

THOMAS AQUINAS, SAINT, 1225?-1274

Steiner, Rudolf. The Redemption of Thinking: A Study in the Philosophy of Thomas Aquinas. Sheperd, A. P. & Nicoll, Mildred R., trs. from Ger. Orig. Title: Die Philosophie des Thomas von Aquino. 191p. 1983. pap. text ed. 8.95 (ISBN 0-88010-044-3). Anthroposophic.

THOMAS, DYLAN, 1914-1953

Thomas, Dylan. Letters to Vernon Watkins. Watkins, Vernon, intro. by. LC 82-15823. (Illus.). 145p. 1982. Repr. of 1957 ed. lib. bdg. 25.00x (ISBN 0-313-23746-8, THLV). Greenwood.

THOMAS, EDWARD, 1878-1917

Myfanwy, Thomas. One of These Fine Days. 164p. 1982. text ed. 14.75x (ISBN 0-85635-387-6, 80253, Pub. by Carcanet New Pr England). Humanities.

THOMSONIANISM

see Medicine, Botanic

THONRAKETZI

see Paulicians

THOREAU, HENRY DAVID, 1817-1862

Hildebidle, John. Thoreau: A Naturalist's Liberty. 192p. 1983. text ed. 15.00x (ISBN 0-674-60455-5). Harvard U Pr.

Jones, Samuel A. Thoreau Amongst Friends & Philistines & Other Thoreauviana. Hendrick, George, ed. & LC 82-6444. xxvi, 241p. 1983. 23.95 (ISBN 0-8214-0675-2, 82-84432). Ohio U Pr.

Thoreau, Henry D. Journal 2: Eighteen Forty-Two to Eighteeen Forty-Eight. Sattelmeyer, Robert, ed. LC 78-70325. (The Writings of Henry D. Thoreau Ser.). (Illus.). 600p. 1983. 22.50x (ISBN 0-691-06186-6). Princeton U Pr.

THORIUM

see also Nuclear Fuels

Osmond, J. K. & Cowart, J. B. Natural Uranium & Thorium Series Disequilibrium: New Approaches to Geochemical Problems. (Nuclear Science Applications Ser.: Section B). 50p. 1982. 19.95 (ISBN 3-7186-0131-1). Harwood Academic.

THOROUGHBRED HORSE

Blood-Horse. Thoroughbred Broodmare Records, 1982: Annual Edition. 2724p. 1983. 87.50 (ISBN 0-936032-59-6); leather binding 102.50 (ISBN 0-936032-60-X). Blood-Horse.

THOROUGHFARES

see Roads

THORPE, JIM, 1888-1953

Santrey, Laurence. Jim Thorpe: Young Athlete. LC 82-15982. (Illus.). 48p. (gr. 4-6). 1983. PLB 6.89 (ISBN 0-89375-845-0); pap. text ed. 1.95 (ISBN 0-89375-846-9). Troll Assocs.

THOUGHT AND THINKING

see also Cognition; Ideology; Intellect; Logic; Meaning (Psychology); Memory; Perception; Psycholinguistics; Reasoning; Self; Stereotype (Psychology)

Brooks, Bearl. Basic Skills Learning to Think Workbook. (Basic Skills Workbooks). 32p. (ps-1). 1983. 0.99 (ISBN 0-8209-0587-9, EEW-10). ESP.

Buzan, Tony. Use Both Sides of Your Brain. rev. ed. (Illus.). 160p. 1983. pap. 7.25 (ISBN 0-525-48011-0, 0704-210). Dutton.

Duhl, Bunny S. From the Inside Out & Other Metaphors: Thinking Systems Multicentrically. 320p. 1983. 30.00 (ISBN 0-87630-328-9). Brunner-Mazel.

Fools! How You May Destroy Yourself with Thought Control & Technological Slavery. (Analysis Ser.: No. 5). 1982. pap. 10.00 (ISBN 0-686-42840-4). Inst Analysis.

Justus, Fred. Thinking Development. (Early Education Ser.). 24p. (gr. k). 1981. wkbk. 5.00 (ISBN 0-8209-0213-6, K-15). ESP.

Patty, Catherine. Basic Skills Thinking Development Workbook. (Basic Skills Workbooks). 32p. (gr. 4-7). 1983. 0.99 (ISBN 0-8209-0584-4, TDW-1). ESP.

Rieber, Robert W., ed. Dialogues on the Psychology of Language & Thought: Conversations with Noam Chomsky, Charles Osgood, Jean Piaget, Ulric Neisser & Marcel Kinsbourne. (Cognition & Language Ser.). 174p. 1983. 19.50x (ISBN 0-306-41185-7, Plenum Pr). Plenum Pub.

Schwanauer, Francis. The Flesh of Thought is Pleasure or Pain. LC 82-17674. 136p. (Orig.). 1983. pap. text ed. 8.75 (ISBN 0-8191-2765-5). U Pr of Amer.

Siegler, Robert S. Children's Thinking: What Develops? 384p. 1978. text ed. 19.95 (ISBN 0-89859-161-9). L Erlbaum Assocs.

Spevack, J. M. Thought Disorder. 188p. pap. 2.00 (ISBN 0-9604448-1-5). Spevack.

Thought Control & Technological Slavery in America. (Analysis Ser.: No. 1). 1982. pap. 10.00 (ISBN 0-686-42834-X). Inst Analysis.

Thought Control & Technological Slavery in America. (Analysis Ser.: No. 2). 1982. pap. 10.00 (ISBN 0-686-42836-6). Inst Analysis.

Thought Control & Technological Slavery in America: Illustration & Selected Correspondence. (Analysis Ser.). 75p. 1983. pap. 18.00 (ISBN 0-686-42852-8). Inst Analysis.

Zaslow, David. Thoughts Like Clouds... (gr. 3-7). 1982. 6.95 (ISBN 0-86653-094-0, GA 434). Good Apple.

THOUSAND-WORD ENGLISH

see Basic English

THREAT (PSYCHOLOGY)

Breakwell, Glynis M. Threatened Identities. 270p. 1983. 34.95x (ISBN 0-471-10233-4, Pub. by Wiley-Interscience). Wiley.

THREE-MILE LIMIT

see Territorial Waters

THROMBOSIS

Bergqvist, D. Postoperative Thromboembolism: Frequency, Etiology, Prophylaxis. (Illus.). 248p. 1983. 38.50 (ISBN 0-387-12062-9). Springer-Verlag.

Hornstra, G. Dietary Fats, Prostanoids & Arterial Thrombosis. 1983. 48.00 (ISBN 90-247-2667-0, Pub. by Martinus Nijhoff Netherlands). Kluwer Boston.

Sharp, Alan A. Hemostasis & Thrombosis. new ed. (BIMR Hematology Ser.: vol. 1). 1983. text ed. price not set (ISBN 0-407-02335-6). Butterworth.

THUNDER-STORMS

see Thunderstorms

THUNDERSTORMS

Findlay, Ted & Beasley, Conger, Jr., eds. Above the Thunder. LC 82-72730. (Orig.). 1982. pap. 9.95 (ISBN 0-89334-039-1). Humanics Ltd.

THYROID GLAND

Institute of Endicrinology, Gunma University. Phylogenic Aspects of Thyroid Hormone Actions. 199p. 1983. text ed. 28.00 (ISBN 0-686-84820-9, Pub. by Japan Sci Soc Japan). Intl Schol Bk Serv.

THYROID GLAND–DISEASES

Bayliss, R. I. Thyroid Disease: The Facts. (Illus.). 124p. (Orig.). 1982. 12.95x (ISBN 0-19-261350-2). Oxford U Pr.

Beckers, C., ed. Thyroid Diseases. 236p. 1983. 25.00 (ISBN 0-08-027094-8). Pergamon.

Deftos, L. J. Medullary Thyroid Carcinoma. (Beitraege zur Onkologie. Contributions to Oncology Ser.: Vol. 17). (Illus.). viii, 144p. 1983. pap. 60.00 (ISBN 3-8055-3703-4). S Karger.

Institute of Endicrinology, Gunma University. Phylogenic Aspects of Thyroid Hormone Actions. 199p. 1983. text ed. 28.00 (ISBN 0-686-84820-9, Pub. by Japan Sci Soc Japan). Intl Schol Bk Serv.

Miller, J. Martin & Kini, Sudha R. Needle Biopsy of the Thyroid. 304p. 1983. 39.00 (ISBN 0-03-062371-5). Praeger.

Soto, Roberto J. & Sartorio, Gerardo, eds. New Concepts in Thyroid Disease. LC 82-24926. (Progress in Clinical & Biological Research Ser.: Vol. 116). 250p. 1983. 26.00 (ISBN 0-8451-0116-1). A R Liss.

TIBET

Lhalungpa, Lobsang. Tibet: The Sacred Realm, Photographs 1860-1950. (Illus.). 160p. 1983. 30.00 (ISBN 0-89381-109-2). Aperture.

TIBET–HISTORY

Chand, Attar. Tibet: Past & Present 1600-1981. 257p. 1982. text ed. 24.50 (ISBN 0-391-02695-X, Pub. by Sterling India). Humanities.

Greenhut, Frederic A., II. The Tibetan Frontiers Question: From Curzon to the Colombo Conference. (Illus.). 178p. 1982. 24.95x (ISBN 0-940500-71-X, Pub by S Chand India). Asia Bk Corp.

TIBETAN LITERATURE

Josef, Kolmas, ed. Tibetan Books & Newspapers (Chinese Collection) (Asiatische Forschungen Ser.: Band 62). 133p. 1978. pap. 30.00x (ISBN 3-447-01961-1). Intl Pubns Serv.

TICKET OF LEAVE

see Parole

TIDE MARSHES

see Marshes

TIDES

see also Estuaries

Brosche, F. & Suendermann, J., eds. Tidal Friction & the Earth's Rotation, Bielefeld, FRG, 1981: Proceedings. (Illus.). 345p. 1983. pap. 28.00 (ISBN 0-387-12011-4). Springer-Verlag.

Godin. The Analysis of Tides. 292p. 1982. 70.00x (ISBN 0-85323-441-8, Pub. by Liverpool Univ England). State Mutual Bk.

Marchuk, G. I. & Kagan, B. A. Ocean Tides: Mathematical Models & Numerical Experiments. Cartwright, D. E., tr. LC 82-18898. (Illus.). 240p. 1983. 65.00 (ISBN 0-08-026236-8). Pergamon.

Melchoir, P. The Tides of the Planet Earth. 2nd ed. LC 82-16567. (Illus.). 648p. 1983. 90.00 (ISBN 0-08-026248-1). Pergamon.

TIFFANY, LOUIS COMFORT, 1848-1933

McKean, Hugh F. The Treasures of Tiffany. (Illus.). 64p. 1982. pap. 9.95 (ISBN 0-914091-18-2). Chicago Review.

TIGRIS RIVER VALLEY

Heyerdahl, Thor. The Tigris Expedition: In Search of Our Beginnings. (Illus.). 1982. pap. 7.95 (ISBN 0-452-25358-6, Z5358, Plume). NAL.

TILLICH, PAUL, 1886-1965

Eisenbeis, Walter. The Key Ideas of Paul Tillich's Systematic Theology. LC 82-21834. 268p. (Orig., Ger. & Eng.). 1983. lib. bdg. 21.75 (ISBN 0-8191-2948-8); pap. text ed. 11.50 (ISBN 0-8191-2949-6). U Pr of Amer.

TILT-UP CONCRETE CONSTRUCTION

see Precast Concrete Construction

TIMBER

see also Forests and Forestry; Pulpwood; Trees; Wood also names of timber-trees, e.g. Oak, Pine

Clutter, Jerome L. & Fortson, James C. Timber Management: A Quantitative Approach. 350p. 1983. text ed. 17.95 (ISBN 0-471-02961-0). Wiley.

Forest Industries Commission on Timber Valuation & Taxation. Timber Tax Journal, Vol. 18. 335p. 1982. 30.00 (ISBN 0-686-43165-0, Pub. by FICTVT). Intl Schol Bk Serv.

Keating, W. G. & Bolza, Eleanor. Characteristics, Properties & Uses of Timbers: Southeast Asia, Northern Australia & the Pacific, Vol. I. LC 82-45895. (Illus.). 391p. 1983. 39.50x (ISBN 0-89096-141-7). Tex A&M Univ Pr.

Usher, M. B. & Ocloo, J. K. The Natural Resistance of Eighty-Five West African Hardwood Timbers to Attack by Termites & Micro-Organisms. 1979. 35.00x (ISBN 0-85135-103-4, Pub. by Centre Overseas Research). State Mutual Bk.

TIMBER-TESTING

see Wood–Testing

TIMBUKTU

Straus, Erwin. Man, Time & World: The Anthropological Psychology of Erwin Straus. Moss, Donald, tr. from Ger. 185p. 1982. text ed. 15.50x (ISBN 0-8207-0159-9, 90007). Duquesne.

TIME

see also Horology; Space and Time

Pucell. Matter of Time. 1975. pap. 5.95 (ISBN 0-686-84623-0, Nonpareil Bks). Godine.

Sims, Reginald W. & Price, James H., eds. Evolution, Time & Space. Date not set. price not set (ISBN 0-12-644550-8). Acad Pr.

Wood, Douglas K. Men Against Time: Nicolas Berdyaev, T. S. Eliot, Aldous Huxley, & C. G. Jung. LC 82-526. x, 254p. 1982. text ed. 22.50x (ISBN 0-7006-0222-4). Univ Pr KS.

TIME–JUVENILE LITERATURE

Miner, Jane Claypool. Miracle of Time: Adopting a Sister. Schroeder, Howard, ed. LC 82-1375. (Crisis Ser.). (Illus.). 64p. (gr. 4-5). 1982. lib. bdg. 7.95 (ISBN 0-89686-172-4). Crestwood Hse.

TIME, COGNITION OF

see Time Perception

TIME, GEOLOGICAL

see Geological Time

TIME ALLOCATION

Alves, Mario. Dream a Little, Live a Lot. 1982. 8.95 (ISBN 0-533-05456-7). Vantage.

Ferner, Jack D. Successful Time Management. LC 79-13680. (Self-Teaching Guide Ser.). 296p. 1980. pap. text ed. 9.95 (ISBN 0-471-03911-X); leaders' guide 5.00 (ISBN 0-471-07773-9). Wiley.

Holmes, Ivory H. The Allocation of Time by Women Without Family Responsibilities. LC 82-20167. (Illus.). 186p. (Orig.). 1983. lib. bdg. 19.75 (ISBN 0-8191-2903-8); pap. text ed. 9.75 (ISBN 0-8191-2904-6). U Pr of Amer.

Hoyt, John S., Jr. Personal Time Management Manual. 11th ed ed. 246p. 1981. 15.00 (ISBN 0-943000-08-4). Telstar Inc.

Hoyt, John S., Sr. Personal Time Management Manual. rev. 12th ed. 246p. 1983. write for info. Telstar Inc.

Januz, Lauren R. & Jones, Susan K. Time Management for Executives. (Illus.). 240p. 1982. pap. 6.95 (ISBN 0-686-83727-4, ScribT). Scribner.

Minshull, Ruth. Efficiency. 35p. 1976. pap. write for info. (ISBN 0-937922-03-X). SAA Pub.

Porter, Mark. The Time of Your Life. 1983. pap. 4.95 (ISBN 0-88207-387-7). Victor Bks.

TIME AND MOTION STUDY

see also Movement, Psychology of

Taylor, Harold L. Making Time Work for You. 1983. pap. 3.25 (ISBN 0-440-16260-2). Dell.

TIME AND SPACE

see Space and Time

TIME BUDGETS

see Time Allocation

TIME MEASUREMENTS

see also Clocks and Watches; Horology

Shoenberg, Isaac J. Mathematical Time Exposures. 200p. 1983. write for info. (ISBN 0-88385-438-4). Math Assn.

TIME PERCEPTION

Benthem, J. V. The Logic of Time. 1982. 49.50 (ISBN 90-277-1421-5, Pub. by Reidell Holland). Kluwer Boston.

Chapman, T. Time: A Philosophical Analysis. 1982. 29.50 (ISBN 90-277-1465-7, Pub. by Reidel Holland). Kluwer Boston.

TIME PERSPECTIVE

see also Harmonic Analysis; Mathematical Statistics; Probabilities

IFAC-IFIP Workshop, Kyoto, Japan, August 31 - Sept. 2, 1981. Real Time Programming 1981: Processing. Hasegawa, T., ed. (Illus.). 150p. 1982. 45.00 (ISBN 0-08-027613-X). Pergamon.

TIME-SERIES ANALYSIS

see also Harmonic Analysis

Anderson, Theodore W. Statistical Analysis of Time Series. LC 70-126222. (Probability & Mathematical Statistics Ser.). 704p. 1971. 44.95x (ISBN 0-471-02900-9). Wiley.

Gilchrist, Warren. Statistical Forecasting. LC 76-13504. 3058p. 1976. 51.95x (ISBN 0-471-99402-2, Pub. by Wiley-Interscience); pap. 22.95x (ISBN 0-471-99403-0). Wiley.

Gregson, Robert A. Time Series in Psychology. 560p. 1983. text ed. write for info. (ISBN 0-89859-250-X). L Erlbaum Assocs.

Morrison, Donald F. Applied Linear Statistical Methods. 544p. 1983. 30.95 (ISBN 0-13-041020-9). P-H.

Priestley, M. B., ed. Spectral Analysis & the Time Series, 2 Vols. in 1, Vol. 1 & Vol.2. (Probability & Mathematical Statistics Ser.). 1983. 39.50 (ISBN 0-12-564922-3). Acad Pr.

Robinson, Enders A. Times Series Analysis & Applications. LC 81-81825. (Illus.). 628p. 1981. 25.00 (ISBN 0-910835-00-4). Goose Pond Pr.

TIME-SHARING COMPUTER SYSTEMS

see also On-Line Data Processing

Burlingame, et al. Timesharing Two. Bloch, Stuart M. & Ingersoll, William B., eds. LC 82-60331. (Illus.). 200p. (Orig.). 1982. pap. 32.00 (ISBN 0-87420-611-1, TO4). Urban Land.

TIMETABLE

see Time Perspective

TIN PLATE
Price, J. W. Tin & Tin-Alloy Plating. 1982. 159.00x (ISBN 0-686-81702-8, Pub. by Electrochemical Scotland). State Mutual Bk.
TINCTORIAL SUBSTANCES
see Dyes and Dyeing
TINPLATE
see Tin Plate
TIPPING
Schrini, John E. Guide for Tipping. Date not set. price not set. Tippers Intl.
TIRES, RUBBER
Tires & Other Rubber Products. 1982. 475.00 (ISBN 0-686-38434-2, 674). Busn Trend.
TISSOT, JAMES JOSEPH JACQUES, 1836-1902
Misfeldt, Willard E. The Albums of James Tissot. (Illus.). 134p. 1982. 24.95 (ISBN 0-87972-209-6); pap. 12.95 (ISBN 0-87972-210-X). Bowling Green Univ.
TISSUE TRANSPLANTATION
see Transplantation of Organs, Tissues, etc.
TISSUES
see also Connective Tissues; Histology; Lymphoid Tissue; Transplantation of Organs, Tissues, etc.
also names of particular tissues or organs, e.g. Bone, Kidneys
Enzinger, Franz M. & Weiss, Sharon W. Soft Tissue Tumors. LC 82-50823. (Illus.). 840p. 1983. text ed. 99.95 (ISBN 0-8016-1499-6). Mosby.
Papadatos, Costas J. & Bartsocas, Christos S., eds. Skeletal Dysplasias. LC 82-17277. (Progress in Clinical & Biological Research Ser.: Vol. 104). 572p. 1982. 60.00 (ISBN 0-8451-0104-8). A R Liss.
Thijsson, J. M. Ultrasonic Tissue Characterization. 1983. 34.50 (ISBN 90-247-2757-X, Pub. by Martinus Nijhoff Netherlands). Kluwer Boston.
TISSUES-TRANSPLANTATION
see Transplantation of Organs, Tissues, etc.
TISSUES, VEGETABLE
see Botany-Anatomy; Plant Cells and Tissues
TITLES (MOVING-PICTURES)
see Moving-Pictures-Editing
TITLES, LAND
see Land Titles
TITO, JOSIP BROZ, PRES. YUGOSLAVIA, 1892-1980
Vucinich, Wayne S. At the Brink of War & Peace: The Tito-Stalin Split in Historic Perspective. (Brooklyn College Studies on Society in Change). 384p. 1982. 27.50x (ISBN 0-914710-98-2). East Eur Quarterly.
Vucinich, Wayne S., ed. At the Brink of War & Peace: The Tito-Stalin Split in a Historic Perspective. 384p. 1982. 27.50 (ISBN 0-686-82240-4). Columbia U Pr.
TITRATION
see Volumetric Analysis
TOADSTOOLS
see Mushrooms
TOASTS
see also Wit and Humor
Dickson, Paul. Toasts. (Orig.). 1982. pap. 7.95 (ISBN 0-440-58741-7, Dell Trade Pbks). Dell.
TOBACCO
see also Smoking
Kihl, Kim R. Port Tobacco: A Transformed Community. LC 82-60383. (Illus.). 102p. (Orig.). 1982. pap. 5.95 (ISBN 0-940776-03-0). Maclay Assoc.
Tso, Tien C. Physiology & Biochemistry of Tobacco Plants. LC 79-178259. (Illus.). 393p. 1972. text ed. 61.00 (ISBN 0-87933-000-7). Hutchinson Ross.
TOBACCO-PHYSIOLOGICAL EFFECT
Abel, Ernest L. Smoking & Reproduction: A Comprehensive Bibliography. LC 82-15660. 178p. 1982. lib. bdg. 35.00 (ISBN 0-313-23663-1, ASR/). Greenwood.
Shephard, Roy J. The Risks of Passive Smoking. (Illus.). 196p. 1982. text ed. 27.95x (ISBN 0-19-520393-3). Oxford U Pr.
TOBACCO HABIT
see Smoking; Tobacco-Physiological Effect
TOBACCO INDUSTRY
see Tobacco Manufacture and Trade
TOBACCO MANUFACTURE AND TRADE
see also Cigarette Manufacture and Trade
World Tobacco Directory, 1982. 30th ed. LC 53-29978. 331p. 1982. 65.00x (ISBN 0-86108-101-3). Intl Pubns Serv.
TOBACCO-PIPES
Dunn, Tom, ed. The Pipe Smoker's Ephemeris: Spring, 1965 through Summer-Autumn, 1979. ltd., signed ed. 541p. 40.00 (ISBN 0-686-38920-4). Univ Coterie Pipe.
TODD, MICHAEL (AVRON HIRSCH GOLDBOGEN), 1909-1958
Todd, Michael, Jr. & Todd, Susan M. A Valuable Property: The Life Story of Michael Todd. (Illus.). 1983. 16.95 (ISBN 0-87795-491-7). Arbor Hse.
TOILET (GROOMING)
see Beauty, Personal
TOILET TRAINING
Mack, Alison. Toilet Learning: The Picture Book Technique for Children & Parents. (Illus.). 120p. 1983. pap. 6.70 (ISBN 0-316-54237-7). Little.
TOKLAS, ALICE B., 1878-1967
Stein, Gertrude. The Autobiography of Alice B. Toklas. LC 79-92497. Date not set. 6.95 (ISBN 0-394-60487-3). Modern Lib.
TOKYO
Seidensticker, Edward G. Low City, High City: Tokyo from Edo to the Earthquake. LC 82-48867. (Illus.). 320p. 1983. 18.95 (ISBN 0-394-50730-4). Knopf.
TOKYO-DESCRIPTION
Thomas Cook, Inc. & Norback & Co., Inc. The Thomas Cook Travel Guide to Tokyo. Date not set. pap. 3.95 (ISBN 0-440-18901-2). Dell.
TOLERANCE (ENGINEERING)
Foster, Lowell W. Geo-Metrics II: The Application of Geometric Tolerancing Techniques (Using Customary System) Rev. ed. LC 82-11655. (Illus.). 320p. 1983. pap. text ed. 18.95 (ISBN 0-201-11520-4). A-W.
TOLERATION
see also Discrimination; Minorities
Katz, Jacob. Exclusiveness & Tolerance. 208p. 1983. pap. 7.95x (ISBN 0-87441-365-6). Behrman.
TOLKIEN, JOHN RONALD RUEL, 1892-1973
Green, Bill. J. R. R. Tolkien, Master of Fantasy. Rahmas, Sigurd C., ed. (Outstanding Personalities Ser.: No. 91). 32p. (gr. 9-12). 1982. 2.95 (ISBN 0-87157-591-4); pap. text ed. 1.95 (ISBN 0-87157-091-2). SamHar Pr.
TOLSTOI, LEV NIKOLAEVICH, GRAF, 1828-1910
Green, Martin. Tolstoy & Gandhi, Men of Peace (A Biography) 500p. 1983. 23.50 (ISBN 0-465-08631-4). Basic.
Kassin, E., et al. Lev Tolstoy & Yasnaya Polyana. 253p. 1982. 25.00 (ISBN 0-8285-2226-X, Pub. by Progress Pubs USSR). Imported Pubns.
Tolstoy, L. Childhood, Adolescence, Youth. 456p. 1981. 7.50 (ISBN 0-8285-2241-3, Pub. by Progress Pubs USSR). Imported Pubns.
Winstanley, Lilian. Tolstoy. 1982. lib. bdg. 34.50 (ISBN 0-686-81924-1). Porter.
TOMATOES
Gould, Wilbur A. Tomato Production, Processing & Quality Evaluation. 2nd ed. (Illus.). 1983. text ed. 49.00 (ISBN 0-87055-426-3). AVI.
TOMBS
see also Sepulchral Monuments
Bierbrier, Morris. Tomb Builders of the Pharoahs. 160p. 1982. 75.00x (ISBN 0-7141-8044-0, Pub. by Brit Mus Pubns England). State Mutual Bk.
Koykka, Arthur S. Project Remember: A National Index of Grave Sites of Notable Americans. Irvine, Keith, ed. 550p. 1983. 49.95 (ISBN 0-917256-22-0). Ref Pubns.
TOMBSTONES
see Sepulchral Monuments
TOMOGRAPHY
Bradac, G. B. & Oberson, R. Angiography & Computed Tomography in Cerebroarterial Occlusive Diseases. (Illus.). 290p. 1982. 68.00 (ISBN 0-387-11453-X). Springer-Verlag.
Ell, P. J. & Holman, B. L., eds. Computed Emission Tomography. (Illus.). 562p. 1982. 75.00 (ISBN 0-19-261347-2). Oxford U Pr.
Gonzalez, Carlos F., et al. Computed Brain & Orbital Tomography: Technique & Interpretation. LC 76-28530. (Diagnostic & Therapeutic Radiology Ser.). 1976. 70.00x (ISBN 0-471-01692-6, Pub. by Wiley-Med). Wiley.
Heiss, W. D. & Phelps, M. F., eds. Positron Emission Tomography of the Brain. (Illus.). 300p. 1983. 51.50 (ISBN 0-387-12130-7). Springer-Verlag.
Krussman, Gerd. A Pocket Guide to Choosing Woody Ornamentals. Epp, Michael, tr. from Ger. Orig. Title: Taschenbuch Der Geholzverwendung. (Illus.). 140p. 1982. pap. 14.95 (ISBN 0-917304-24-1). Timber.
Kuhl, D. E., ed. Principles of Radionuclide Emission Imaging. 318p. 1983. 25.00 (ISBN 0-08-027093-X). Pergamon.
Littleton, Jesse T. & Durizch, Mary L., eds. Sectional Imaging Methods: A Comparison. (Illus.). 1983. 65.00 (ISBN 0-8391-1783-3, 18597). Univ Park.
Morgan, Carlisle L. & Phil, M. Basic Principles of Computed Tomography. (Illus.). 448p. 1983. text ed. 57.50 (ISBN 0-8391-1705-1, 13331). Univ Park.
Takahashi, S., ed. Illustrated Computer Tomography: A Practical Guide to CT Interpretations. (Illus.). 350p. 1983. 83.00 (ISBN 0-387-11432-7). Springer-Verlag.
TONGA ISLANDS
Bott, Elizabeth. Tongan Society at the Time of Captain Cook's Visits: Discussions with Her Majesty Queen Salote Tupou. 187p. 1983. pap. text ed. 15.00x (ISBN 0-8248-0864-9). UH Pr.
TONGA ISLANDS-SOCIAL LIFE AND CUSTOMS
Bott, Elizabeth. Tongan Society at the Time of Captain Cook's Visits: Discussions with Her Majesty Queen Salote Tupou. 187p. 1983. pap. text ed. 15.00x (ISBN 0-8248-0864-9). UH Pr.
TONGUE TWISTERS
Obligado, Lilian. Faint Frogs Feeling Feverish: & Other Terrifically Tantalizing Tongue Twisters. (Illus.). 32p. (ps-3). 1983. 11.50 (ISBN 0-670-30477-8). Viking Pr.
TONGUES, GIFT OF
see Glossolalia
TOOLS
see also Agricultural Implements; Agricultural Machinery; Carpentry-Tools; Implements, Utensils, etc.; Machine-Tools; Machinery; Power Tools
also specific tools
Arbor, Marilyn. Tools & Trades of America's Past: The Mercer Collection. 116p. 6.95 (ISBN 0-910302-12-X). Bucks Co Hist.
Current Machine Tools Industry in Japan. (Japanese Industry Studies: No. J75). 103p. 1981. 394.00 (ISBN 0-686-38961-1). Intl Res Dev.
Sloane, Eric. A Museum of Early American Tools. (Illus.). 128p. (Orig.). 1983. 14.95 (ISBN 0-8038-4746-7). Hastings.
The U. S. Hand Tool Market. 1981. 350.00 (ISBN 0-686-38430-X, 330). Busn Trend.
TOOLS, AGRICULTURAL
see Agricultural Implements
TOOTH
see Teeth
TOOTH MOVEMENT, ORTHODONTIC
see Orthodontics
TOPECTOMY
see Brain-Surgery
TOPOGRAPHICAL ANATOMY
see Anatomy, Surgical and Topographical
TOPOGRAPHICAL SURVEYING
Gerald of Wales. History & Topography of Ireland. O'Meara, John, tr. 1983. pap. 5.95 (ISBN 0-14-044423-8). Penguin.
TOPOLOGICAL ALGEBRAS
Iohvidov, I. S. Hankel Toeplitz Matrices & Forms. 244p. 1982. text ed. 24.95 (ISBN 3-7643-3090-2). Birkhauser.
TOPOLOGICAL GROUPS
see also Lie Groups
Carruth & Hildebrandt. The Theory of Topological Semigroups. (Monographs & Textbooks in Pure & Applied Mathematics). 408p. 1983. 34.75 (ISBN 0-8247-1795-3). Dekker.
TOPOLOGICAL VECTOR SPACES
see Linear Topological Spaces
TOPOLOGY
see also Algebraic Topology; Algebras, Linear; Banach Spaces; Categories (Mathematics); Geometry, Algebraic; Graph Theory; Homotopy Theory; Lattice Theory; Linear Topological Spaces; Metric Spaces; Polytopes; Transformation Groups
Simmons, George F. Introduction to Topology & Modern Analysis. 388p. 1982. Repr. of 1963 ed. lib. bdg. 23.50 (ISBN 0-89874-551-9). Krieger.
TORAH SCROLLS
Plaut, W. Gunther. Deuteronomy: A Modern Commentary. (The Torah: A Modern Commentary Ser.). 528p. 1983. 20.00 (ISBN 0-8074-0045-9). UAHC.
TORNADOES
see also Storms
Corliss, William R. Tornadoes, Dark Days, Anomalous Precipitation, & Related Weather Phenomena. (Catalog of Geophysical Anomalies Ser.). (Illus.). 250p. 1983. 11.95 (ISBN 0-915554-10-0). Sourcebook.
TORONTO
Thomas Cook, Inc. & Norback & Co., Inc. Thomas Cook Travel Guide to Toronto. (Orig.). Date not set. pap. 3.95 (ISBN 0-440-18897-0). Dell.
TORT LIABILITY OF EMPLOYERS
see Employers' Liability
TORT LIABILITY OF MANUFACTURERS
see Products Liability
TORT LIABILITY OF MUNICIPAL CORPORATIONS
Schuck, Peter H. Suing Government: Citizen Remedies for Official Wrongs. LC 82-48907. 320p. 1983. text ed. 25.00x (ISBN 0-300-02957-8). Yale U Pr.
TORT LIABILITY OF PHYSICIANS
see Malpractice
TORTOISES
see Turtles
TORTS
see also Fraud; Libel and Slander; Negligence; Personal Injuries; Tort Liability of Municipal Corporations
Industrial & Toxic Torts. 185p. 1980. pap. 45.00 (ISBN 0-941916-05-7). Assn Trial Ed.
Moffatt, Hancock. Torts in the Conflict of Laws. LC 42-36734. (Michigan Legal Studies). lviii, 288p. 1982. Repr. of 1942 ed. lib. bdg. 30.00 (ISBN 0-89941-166-5). W S Hein.
Prosser, William L. Selected Topics on the Law of Torts. LC 54-62473. (Thomas M. Cooley Lectures: No. 4). xi, 627p. 1982. Repr. of 1953 ed. lib. bdg. 35.00 (ISBN 0-89941-174-6). W S Hein.
TORTS-GREAT BRITAIN
Armour, L. A. & Samuel, G. H. Cases in Tort. 352p. 1977. 30.00x (ISBN 0-7121-0356-2, Pub. by Macdonald & Evans). State Mutual Bk.
TOTAL ABSTINENCE
see Temperance
TOUCH
Murphy, Wendy B. Touch, Smell, Taste, Sight & Hearing. LC 82-5738. (Library of Health). lib. bdg. 18.60 (ISBN 0-8094-3799-6, Pub. by Time-Life). Silver.
TOUR GUIDES (MANUALS)
see subdivisions Description and Travel as appropriate under names of countries, regions, cities, etc.
TOURISM
see Tourist Trade
TOURIST CAMPS, HOSTELS, ETC.
Ross, Corinne M. Mid-Atlantic Guest House Book. (Illus.). 192p. 1983. pap. 7.95 (ISBN 0-914788-62-0). East Woods.
--The Southern Guest House Book. rev. ed. 192p. 1983. pap. 7.95 (ISBN 0-914788-71-X). East Woods.
TOURIST TRADE
see also Travel; Travel Agents
Epperson, Arlin. Private & Commercial Recreation: A Text & Reference. LC 76-56453. 385p. 1977. text ed. 23.95 (ISBN 0-471-24335-3). Wiley.
Goeldner, C. R. & Buchman, Tom. NSAA Economic Analysis of North American Ski Areas, 1981-82 Season. 136p. 1982. pap. text ed. 40.00 (ISBN 0-89478-073-5). U Co Busn Res Div.
Goeldner, C. R. & Frechtling, Douglas C. Tourism's Top Twenty. 90p. 1983. pap. text ed. 25.00 (ISBN 0-686-81949-7). U Co Busn Res Div.
Mills. Design for Holidays & Tourism. 1983. text ed. price not set (ISBN 0-408-00534-3). Butterworth.
OECD. Tourism Policy & International Tourism in OECD Member Countries 1982. 170p. (Orig.). 1982. pap. 17.50 (ISBN 0-686-37921-7). OECD.
Van Harssel, Jan. Tourism: An Exploration. (Illus.). 384p. 1982. pap. text ed. 18.00 (ISBN 0-935920-00-5). Natl Pub BlacK Hills.
World Tourism Organization, ed. Economic Review of World Tourism, 1982. (Illus.). 73p. (Orig.). 1982. pap. 40.00x (ISBN 0-8002-3030-2). Intl Pubns Serv.
TOURISTS
see Tourist Trade
TOURNAMENTS
Kubota, Takayuki. Weapons Kumite: Fighting with Traditional Weapons. Gierman, James, ed. (Illus.). 200p. (Orig.). 1983. pap. 7.95 (ISBN 0-86568-042-6, 307). Unique Pubns.
TOURS
see subdivisions Description and Travel as appropriate under names of countries, regions, cities, etc.
TOWER OF LONDON
see London-Tower of London
TOWN LIFE
see City and Town Life
TOWN MEETING
see Local Government
TOWN OFFICERS
see Municipal Officials and Employees
TOWN PLANNING
see City Planning
TOWNS
see Cities and Towns
TOWNSHIP FINANCE
see Local Finance
TOWNSHIP GOVERNMENT
see Local Government
TOXICOLOGY
Barlow, S. M. & Sullivan, F. M., eds. Reproductive Hazards of Industrial Chemicals. 610p. 1982. 75.00 (ISBN 0-12-078960-4). Acad Pr.
Bayer, Marc J. Toxicologic Emergencies. (Illus.). 384p. 1983. pap. text ed. 19.95 (ISBN 0-89303-188-7). R J Brady.
Caldwell, John & Jakoby, William B., eds. Biological Basis of Detoxification. LC 82-18933. (Biochemical Pharmacology & Toxicology). Date not set. price not set (ISBN 0-12-155060-5). Acad Pr.
Cornaby, Barney, ed. Management of Toxic Substances in Our Ecosystems: Taming the Medusa. LC 81-67257. (Illus.). 186p. 1981. 22.50 (ISBN 0-686-84680-X). Ann Arbor Science.
Garrod, J. W., ed. Testing for Toxicity. 365p. 1981. 90.00x (ISBN 0-85066-218-4, Pub. by Taylor & Francis). State Mutual Bk.
George, R., et al, eds. Annual Review of Pharmacology & Toxicology, Vol. 23. LC 61-5649. (Illus.). 1983. text ed. 27.00 (ISBN 0-8243-0423-3). Annual Reviews.
Hodgson, E. & Bend, J. R., eds. Biochemical Toxicology, No. 4. 288p. 1982. 37.50 (ISBN 0-444-00436-X, Biomedical Pr). Elsevier.
Kolber, Alan R. & Wong, Thomas K., eds. In Vitro Toxicity Testing of Environmental Agents, Current & Future Possibilities: Part A-Survey of Test Systems. (NATO Conference Ser.: No. I, Ecology). 574p. 1983. 69.50x (ISBN 0-306-41123-7, Plenum Pr). Plenum Pub.
--In Vitro Toxicity Testing of Environmental Agents, Current & Future Possibilities: Part B-Development of Risk Assessment Guidelines. (NATO Conference Series I, Ecology: Vol. 5B). 566p. 1983. 69.50x (ISBN 0-306-41124-5). Plenum Pub.
Leong, Basil K. J. Inhalation Toxicology & Technology. LC 81-67510. (Illus.). 313p. 1981. 39.95 (ISBN 0-250-40414-1). Ann Arbor Science.
Mattison, Donald R., ed. Reproductive Toxicology. LC 83-927. (Progress in Clinical & Biological Research Ser.: Vol. 117). 408p. 1983. 58.00 (ISBN 0-8451-0117-X). A R Liss.
Moriarty, F., ed. Ecotoxicology: The Study of Pollutants in Exosystems. Date not set. price not set (ISBN 0-12-506760-7). Acad Pr.
Nisbet, Ian C. & Karch, Nathan J. Chemical Hazards to Human Reproduction. LC 82-14441. (Illus.). 245p. 1983. 28.00 (ISBN 0-8155-0931-6). Noyes.

Porter, George, ed. Nephrotoxic Mechanisms of Drugs & Environmental Toxins. LC 82-13156. 486p. 1982. 49.50x (ISBN 0-306-40977-1, Plenum Med Bk). Plenum Pub.
Timbrell, J. A. Principles of Biochemical Toxicology. 240p. 1982. 88.00x (ISBN 0-85066-221-4, Pub. by Taylor & Francis). State Mutual Bk.
Wagner, Sheldon L. Clinical Toxicology of Agricultural Chemicals. LC 82-14421. (Illus.). 306p. 1983. 28.00 (ISBN 0-8155-0930-8). Noyes.

TOXINS AND ANTITOXINS
see also Immunity; Mycotoxins
Giannini, A. James & Slaby, Andrew E. Emergency Guide to Overdose & Detoxification. 1983. pap. text ed. price not set (ISBN 0-87488-182-X). Med Exam.
Industrial & Toxic Torts. 185p. 1980. pap. 45.00 (ISBN 0-941916-05-7). Assn Trial Ed.
The Infrared Spectra Handbook of Priority Pollutants & Toxic Chemicals. 1982. 2.45 (ISBN 0-686-84521-8). Sadtler Res.

TOY AUTOMOBILES
see Automobiles–Models

TOY-MAKING
Favorite Easy to-Make Toys. LC 81-71013. (Illus.). 240p. 1982. 18.95 (ISBN 0-686-82296-X). Van Nos Reinhold.

TOYNBEE, ARNOLD, 1852-1883
Martin, P. W. Experiment in Depth: A Study of the Work of Jung, Eliot & Toynbee. 275p. 1982. Repr. of 1955 ed. lib. bdg. 40.00 (ISBN 0-89987-649-8). Darby Bks.

TOYS
see also Dolls; Electronic Toys; Toy-Making
Coleman, Ronny J. & Russell, Raymond M. Fire Truck Toys for Men & Boys. (Catalogue of Toy Fire Apparatus Ser.: Vol. II). (Illus.). 168p. 1982. pap. 10.95 (ISBN 0-910105-01-4). Phenix Pub.
--Fire Truck Toys for Men & Boys. (Catalogue of Toy Fire Apparatus Ser.: Vol. I). (Illus.). 168p. 1981. pap. 9.95 (ISBN 0-910105-00-6). Phenix Pub.
Gamage, Arthur W. Mr. Gamage's Great Toy Bazaar 1902-1906. (Illus.). 160p. (Orig.). 1983. 35.00 (ISBN 0-8038-4745-9). Hastings.
Johnson, Ellen, ed. The Toy Library: A How-To Handbook. 82p. (Orig.). pap. text ed. 9.95 (ISBN 0-934140-18-9). Toys N Things.
The Official 1983 Price Guide to Toys. 1st ed. LC 82-84639. 240p. 1983. pap. 2.95 (ISBN 0-87637-317-1). Hse of Collectibles.
Ross, Nina, ed. Directory of U.S. Toy Lending Libraries. 123p. (Orig.). pap. 24.00 (ISBN 0-934140-19-7). Toys N Things.
Schiffer, Nancy, compiled by. Matchbox Toys. (Illus.). 204p. (Orig.). 1983. pap. 14.95 (ISBN 0-916838-74-9). Schiffer.
The U. S. Toy & Game Industry. 1982. 495.00 (ISBN 0-686-38432-6, 502). Busn Trend.

TOYS–HISTORY
Dunmire, Reba. Toys of Early America: You Can Make. (Illus.). 64p. (Orig.). 1983. pap. text ed. 5.40 (ISBN 0-87006-441-X). Goodheart.
Great Toymakers: Marklin Eighteen Ninety-five to Nineteen Fourteen. (Illus.). 180p. 1983. 95.00 (ISBN 0-8038-2721-0). Hastings.

TOYS–JUVENILE LITERATURE
Lachenbruch, David & Norback, Craig. The Complete Book of Adult Toys. (Illus.). 168p. pap. 12.95 (ISBN 0-15-620946-2, Harv). HarBraceJ.
Sibbett, Ed., Jr. Easy-to Make Articulated Wooden Toys: Patterns & Instructions for 18 Playthings That Move. (General Crafts Ser.). (Illus.). 48p. 1983. pap. 2.50 (ISBN 0-486-24411-3). Dover.

TRACE ELEMENTS
see also names of specific elements, e.g. Boron
Chalmers, R. A., ed. Gains & Losses: Errors in Trace Analysis. 90p. 1982. pap. 27.50 (ISBN 0-08-030239-4). Pergamon.
Prasad, Ananda S., ed. Clinical, Biochemical, & Nurtitional Aspects of Trace Elements. (Current Tropics in Nutrition & Disease Ser.: Vol. 6). 577p. 1982. 96.00 (ISBN 0-8451-1605-3). A R Liss.
Yen, T. F., ed. The Role of Trace Metals in Petroleum. LC 74-77404. (Illus.). 221p. 1982. 39.95 (ISBN 0-250-40061-8). Ann Arbor Science.

TRACE ELEMENTS IN NUTRITION
Prasad, Ananda S., ed. Clinical, Biochemical, & Nurtitional Aspects of Trace Elements. (Current Tropics in Nutrition & Disease Ser.: Vol. 6). 577p. 1982. 96.00 (ISBN 0-8451-1605-3). A R Liss.

TRACERS, RADIOACTIVE
see Radioactive Tracers

TRACHEA
Alperin, Kenneth & Grover, Margaret. Tracheostomy Care Manual. 28p. 4.95 (ISBN 0-86577-071-9). Thieme-Stratton.
Roberts, James T., ed. Fundamentals of Tracheal Intubation. Date not set. price not set (ISBN 0-8089-1546-0). Grune.

TRACK-ATHLETICS
see also Cycling; Running
Gambetta, Vern. Track Technique Annual, 1983. (Illus.). 128p. (Orig.). 1982. pap. 8.50 (ISBN 0-911521-08-9). Tafnews.
Jacoby, Ed. Applied Techniques in Track & Field. LC 82-81819. (Illus.). 192p. (Orig.). 1983. pap. 9.95 (ISBN 0-88011-050-3). Leisure Pr.
Track & Field 1981-83. (Tips & Techniques Bks.). 4.95 (ISBN 0-88314-194-9). AAHPERD.
Track & Field 1982-83. (NAGWS Sports Guides Ser.). 3.95 (ISBN 0-88314-217-1). AAHPERD.

TRACK-ATHLETICS COACHING
Knudson, R. R. Speed. (Illus.). 80p. (gr. 2 up). 1983. 8.95 (ISBN 0-525-44052-6, 0869-260, Skinny Bk). Dutton.
McMane, Fred. Track & Field Basics. (Illus.). 48p. (gr. 3-7). 1983. 8.95 (ISBN 0-13-925966-X). P-H.

TRACK-TYPE VEHICLES
see Tracklaying Vehicles

TRACKLAYING VEHICLES
Here are entered general works on vehicles which use the endless belt principle for traction, such as military tanks, crawler tractors, etc. Works on particular types are entered under their names, e.g. Crawler Tractors; Tanks (military Science).
see also Tanks (Military Science)
Webb, R. H. & Wilshire, H. G., eds. Environmental Effects of Off-Road Vehicles: Impact & Management in Arid Regions. (Springer Series on Environmental Management). (Illus.). 560p. 1983. 49.80 (ISBN 0-387-90737-8). Springer-Verlag.

TRACKS OF ANIMALS
see Animal Tracks

TRACTORS
Brown, Arlen D. & Strickland, R. Mack. Tractor & Small Engine Maintenance. 5th ed. 350p. 1983. 15.65 (ISBN 0-8134-2258-2); text ed. 11.75x (ISBN 0-686-83991-9). Interstate.
Chek-Chart. Tractor & Farm Implement Lubrication Guide, 1983. 384p. 1983. pap. 34.00x (ISBN 0-88098-023-0). H. M. Gousha.
--Tractor Digest, 1983. (Illus.). 16p. (gr. 12). 1983. pap. text ed. 4.20 (ISBN 0-88098-047-8, 0731-4698). H M Gousha.
Sheffer, H. R. Tractors. Schroeder, Howard, ed. (Movin' On Ser.). (Illus.). 48p. (Orig.). (gr. 5-6). 1983. lib. bdg. 7.95 (ISBN 0-89686-196-1). Crestwood Hse.

TRADE
see Business; Commerce

TRADE, BALANCE OF
see Balance of Trade

TRADE AGREEMENTS (COMMERCE)
see Commercial Treaties

TRADE AND PROFESSIONAL ASSOCIATIONS–DIRECTORIES
Wright, Rita J., ed. Texas Trade & Professional Associations, 1983. LC 79-54294. 100p. pap. text ed. 7.50 (ISBN 0-686-83436-4). U of Tex Busn Res.

TRADE BARRIERS
see Commercial Policy

TRADE FAIRS
see Fairs

TRADE-MARKS
Goldstein, Paul. Copyright, Patent, Trademark & Related State Doctrines: Cases & Materials on the Law of Intellectual Property. 2nd ed. (University Casebook Ser.). 183p. 1982. write for info. tchrs. manual (ISBN 0-88277-105-1). Foundation Pr.
Meinhardt, Peter. Inventions, Patents & Trade Marks in Great Britain. 1971 ed. 397p. 25.00 (ISBN 0-686-37380-4). Beekman Pubs.

TRADE NAMES
see Trade-Marks

TRADE REGULATION
see also Advertising Laws; Antitrust Law; Consumer Protection; Copyright; Law; Legislation; Licenses; Price Regulation; Trade-Marks; Transportation–Laws and Regulations
Buchan, Robert J. & Johnston, C. Christopher. Telecommunications Regulation & the Constitution. 276p. (Orig.). 1982. pap. text ed. 18.95x (ISBN 0-920380-69-7, Pub. by Inst Res Pub Canada). Renouf.
Grey, Rodney. United States Trade Policy Legislation: A Canadian View. 130p. (Orig.). 1982. pap. text ed. 7.95x (ISBN 0-920380-86-7, Pub. by Inst Res Pub Canada). Renouf.
Norton, Joseph J. Regulation of Business Enterprise in the U. S. A. 1983. looseleaf, (2 binders) 95.00 (ISBN 0-379-11250-7). Oceana.
Percy, Eustace. Maritime Trade in War. 1930. text ed. 29.50x (ISBN 0-686-83617-0). Elliots Bks.
Stanbury, W. T. & Thompson, Fred. Regulatory Reform in Canada. 139p. (Orig.). 1982. pap. text ed. 7.95x (ISBN 0-920380-71-9, Pub. by Inst Res Pub Canada). Renouf.
Thompson. Regulatory Policy & Practices. 270p. 1982. 28.95 (ISBN 0-03-062178-X). Praeger.

TRADE ROUTES
Forde, C. Daryll. Ancient Mariners: The Story of Ships & Sea Routes. 88p. 1982. Repr. of 1928 ed. lib. bdg. 20.00 (ISBN 0-89760-236-6). Telegraph Bks.

TRADE SECRETS
Pooley, James. Trade Secrets: How to Protect Your Ideas & Assets. 160p. 1982. pap. 11.95 (ISBN 0-931988-93-4). Osborne-McGraw.

TRADE-UNIONS
Here are entered general works on Trade Unions. For works on trade unions of specific countries see appropriate subdivision, e.g. Trade-Unions–Africa.
see also Arbitration, Industrial; Collective Bargaining; Friendly Societies; International Labor Activities; Strikes and Lockouts
also American Federation of Labor and Congress of Industrial Organizations; and other specific unions
Barat, Morton S. The Union & the Coal Industry. LC 82-25141. (Yale Studies in Economics: Vol. 4). xvii, 170p. 1983. Repr. of 1955 ed. lib. bdg. 29.75x (ISBN 0-313-23698-4, BAUC). Greenwood.
Bowling, W Kerby & Loving, Waldon. Management Fumbles & Union Recoveries. 232p. 1982. pap. text ed. 12.95 (ISBN 0-8403-2775-7). Kendall-Hunt.
Ducker, James H. Men of the Steel Rails: Workers on the Atchison, Topeka, & Santa Fe Railroad, 1869-1900. LC 82-17541. (Illus.). 232p. 1983. 17.95 (ISBN 0-8032-1662-9). U of Nebr Pr.
Freeman, Richard B. & Medoff, James L. What Do Unions Do? 350p. 1983. 20.95 (ISBN 0-465-09133-4). Basic.
Frisch, Michael H. & Walkowitz, Daniel J., eds. Working-Class America: Essays on Labor, Community, & American Society. LC 81-23971. (Working Class in American History Ser.). 368p. 1983. 29.50 (ISBN 0-252-00953-3); pap. 8.95 (ISBN 0-252-00954-1). U of Ill Pr.
Fulmer, William E. Union Organizing: Management & Labor Conflict. 240p. 1982. 24.95 (ISBN 0-03-062603-X). Praeger.
Justice, Betty W. Unions, Workers, & the Law. (George Meany Center for Labor Studies Ser.: No. 2). 280p. 1983. text ed. 17.50 (ISBN 0-87179-393-8); pap. text ed. 12.50 (ISBN 0-87179-400-4). BNA.
Langford, D. A. Direct Labour Organizations in the Construction Industry. 135p. 1982. text ed. 35.50x (ISBN 0-566-00542-5). Gower Pub Ltd.
Lavoie, Don C., ed. Solidarnosc z Wolnoscia: Solidarity with Liberty. 253p. 1983. pap. 9.95 (ISBN 0-932790-33-X). Cato Inst.
Naas, Bernard G., ed. American Labor Unions' Officers' Reports: A Guide to the Microfiche Edition, Phase I. 2nd ed. 71p. pap. text ed. 32.50 (ISBN 0-667-00670-2). Microfilming Corp.
Pornschlegel, Hans. Job Evaluation & the Role of Trade Unions. 50p. 1982. write for info. Intl Labour Office.
Reynolds, Morgan. Unions & the Economy. 1983. 15.00 (ISBN 0-89526-626-1). Regnery-Gateway.
Tawney. American Labor Movement. 1980. 26.00 (ISBN 0-312-02503-3). St Martin.
Taylo, Don H. Trade Union Financial Administration. 64p. 1981. 2.85 (ISBN 92-2-102711-2). Intl Labour Office.
Trade Unions & the ILO: A Workers' Education Manual. vii, 96p. 1982. 5.70 (ISBN 92-2-102003-7). Intl Labour Office.
Tristan, Flora. The Workers' Union. Livingston, Beverly, tr. LC 82-1891. 188p. 1983. 14.95 (ISBN 0-252-00921-5). U of Ill Pr.
Waters, Les. The Union of Christmas Island Workers. 184p. 1983. text ed. 27.50x (ISBN 0-86861-221-9). Allen Unwin.

TRADE-UNIONS–BIBLIOGRAPHY
Gifford, Courtney D., ed. Directory of U.S. Labor Organizations: 1982-83 Edition. 139p. 1982. pap. text ed. 15.00 (ISBN 0-686-84387-8). BNA.

TRADE-UNIONS–HISTORY
Licht, Walter. Working for the Railroad: The Organization of Work in the Nineteenth Century. LC 82-61372. (Illus.). 352p. 1983. 27.50x (ISBN 0-691-04700-6). Princeton U Pr.

TRADE-UNIONS–OFFICIALS AND EMPLOYEES
Papanikolas, Zeese. Buried Unsung: Louis Tikas & the Ludlow Massacre. LC 82-13475. (University of Utah Publications in the American West: Vol. 14). (Illus.). 331p. 1982. 20.00 (ISBN 0-87480-211-3). U of Utah Pr.
Taylo, Don H. Trade Union Financial Administration. 64p. 1981. 2.85 (ISBN 92-2-102711-2). Intl Labour Office.

TRADE-UNIONS–POLITICAL ACTIVITY
Barnard, John. Walter Reuther & the Rise of the Auto Workers. 1983. 13.00i (ISBN 0-316-08141-8). Little.

TRADE-UNIONS–AUSTRALIA
Dickenson, Mary. Democracy in Trade Unions: Studies in Membership Participation & Control. LC 82-2065. (Policy, Politics, & Administration Ser.). (Illus.). 249p. 1983. text ed. 32.50x (ISBN 0-7022-1666-6). U of Queensland Pr.
Sydney Labour History Group. What Rough Beast? 276p. 1983. text ed. 29.50 (ISBN 0-86861-332-0). Allen Unwin.

TRADE-UNIONS–GREAT BRITAIN
Brown, Kenneth D. The English Labour Movement, 1700-1951. 280p. 1982. 45.00x (ISBN 0-7171-0870-8, Pub. by Macmillan England). State Mutual Bk.
Hinton, James. Labour & Socialism: A History of the British Labour Movement, 1870-1970. LC 82-21798. 230p. 1983. lib. bdg. 22.00x (ISBN 0-87023-393-9). U of Mass Pr.
Jeffery, Keith & Hennesy, Peter. State of Emergency: British Governments & Strikebreaking Since 1919. 280p. 1983. 29.95 (ISBN 0-7100-9464-7); pap. write for info. (ISBN 0-7100-9474-4). Routledge & Kegan.
Pimlott, Ben & Cook, Chris, eds. Trade Unions in British Politics. 320p. (Orig.). 1982. pap. text ed. 13.95 (ISBN 0-582-49184-3). Longman.
Schneer, Jonathan. Ben Tillet: Portrait of Labor Leader. LC 82-13653. (Working Class in European History Ser.). 256p. 1983. 21.95 (ISBN 0-252-01025-6). U of Ill Pr.
Trade Unionism & Munitions. (Economic & Social History of the World War Ser.). 1924. text ed. 49.50x (ISBN 0-686-83830-0). Elliots Bks.

TRADE-UNIONS–IRELAND
Greaves, C. Desmond. The Irish Transport & General Workers' Union: The Formative Years. 1982. 60.00x (ISBN 0-7171-1199-7, Pub. by Gill & Macmillan Ireland). State Mutual Bk.

TRADE-UNIONS–LATIN AMERICA
DeShazo, Peter. Urban Workers & Labor Unions in Chile, 1902-1927. LC 82-70557. (Illus.). 384p. 1983. 30.00 (ISBN 0-299-09220-8). U of Wis Pr.

TRADE-UNIONS–RUSSIA
Swain, G. Russian Society Democracy & the Legal Labour Movement 1906-14. 1982. 80.00x (ISBN 0-686-42930-3, Pub. by Macmillan England). State Mutual Bk.

TRADE-WINDS
see Winds

TRADES
see Building Trades; Industrial Arts; Occupations

TRADES WASTE
see Factory and Trade Waste

TRADITIONS
see Folk-Lore; Legends; Superstition

TRAFFIC, CITY
see City Traffic

TRAFFIC ACCIDENTS
see also Traffic Violations
American Health Research Institute, Ltd. Traffic Accidents: A Medical Subject Analysis & Research Index with Bibliography. Bartone, John C., ed. 120p. 1983. 29.95 (ISBN 0-88164-016-6); pap. 21.95 (ISBN 0-88164-017-4). ABBE Pubs Assn.
European Conference of Ministers of Transport. Trends in Transport Investment & Expediture in 1979: Statistical Report on Road Accidents in 1980. 108p. (Orig.). 1982. pap. 10.00x (ISBN 0-686-37603-X). OECD.
Gardner, J. D., ed. Highway Truck Collision Analysis. 1982. 20.00 (H00237). ASME.

TRAFFIC ACCIDENTS–LAW AND LEGISLATION
see Traffic Violations

TRAFFIC ACCIDENTS–PREVENTION
see Traffic Safety

TRAFFIC CONTROL
see Traffic Engineering

TRAFFIC CONTROL DEVICES
see Traffic Signs and Signals

TRAFFIC ENGINEERING
see also City Traffic; Express Highways; Traffic Safety also names of types of transportation, e.g. Automobiles; Aeronautics, Commercial, etc.
Barney, G. C. & Dos Santos, S. M. Lift (Elevator) Traffic Analysis, Design & Control. (IEE Control Engineering Ser.: No. 2). (Illus.). 331p. 1977. casebound 53.25 (ISBN 0-901223-86-7). Inst Elect Eng.
Barrett, Paul. The Automobile & Urban Transit: The Formation of Public Policy in Chicago. 1983. write for info. (ISBN 0-87722-294-0). Temple U Pr.
Higgins, Thomas. Comparing Strageties for Reducing Traffic Related Problems: The Potential for Road Pricing. 40p. (Orig.). 1978. pap. text ed. 3.50 (ISBN 0-87766-227-4). Urban Inst.
Rudman, Jack. Associate Traffic Enforcement Agent. (Career Examination Ser.: C-215). (Cloth bdg. avail. on request). pap. 12.00 (ISBN 0-8373-0215-3). Natl Learning.
--Senior Traffic Supervisor. (Career Examination Ser.: C-2628). (Cloth bdg. avail. on request). pap. 12.00 (ISBN 0-8373-2628-1). Natl Learning.
--Traffic Supervisor. (Career Examination Ser.: C-2627). (Cloth bdg. avail. on request). pap. 10.00 (ISBN 0-8373-2627-3). Natl Learning.
Sensors in Highway & Civil Engineering. 240p. 1981. 80.00x (ISBN 0-7277-0109-6, Pub. by Telford England). State Mutual Bk.
Wynne, George G. Traffic Restraints in Residential Areas, Vol. II. (Learning from Abroad Ser.). 48p. 1980. pap. 5.95 (ISBN 0-87855-845-4). Transaction Bks.

TRAFFIC OFFENSES
see Traffic Violations

TRAFFIC REGULATION
see Traffic Engineering

TRAFFIC SAFETY
see also Automobile Drivers; Traffic Accidents; Traffic Signs and Signals; Traffic Violations
Rudman, Jack. Assistant Director of Traffic Safety. (Career Examination Ser.: C-458). (Cloth bdg. avail. on request). pap. 14.00 (ISBN 0-8373-0458-X). Natl Learning.
--Director of Traffic Safety. (Career Examination Ser.: C-527). (Cloth bdg. avail. on request). pap. 14.00 (ISBN 0-8373-0527-6). Natl Learning.

TRAFFIC SIGNS AND SIGNALS
Institute of Transportation Engineers. Manual of Traffic Signal Design. (Illus.). 304p. 1982. 39.95 (ISBN 0-13-554360-6). P-H.

TRAFFIC VIOLATIONS
Casey, W. W. You, Too can Beat Police Radar & Avoid Speeding Tickets. 220p. pap. 19.95x (ISBN 0-943462-02-9). CaseCo.

Schultz, Donald O. & Hunt, Derald D. Traffic Investigation & Enforcement. rev. ed. LC 82-73387. (Illus.). 225p. 1983. text ed. 15.95 (ISBN 0-942728-07-6); pap. text ed. 12.95 (ISBN 0-942728-06-8). Custom Pub Co.

TRAGEDY

Misra, K. S. Modern Tragedies & Aristotle's Theory. 252p. 1982. text ed. 18.75x (ISBN 0-7069-1425-2, Pub. by Vikas India). Humanities.

Szilagye, Robert J. & Monroe, Stanley. The Trident Tragedy. (Orig.). 1983. pap. 3.75 (ISBN 0-440-18769-9). Dell.

TRAHERNE, THOMAS, d. 1674

Martz, Louis. The Paradise Within: Studies in Vaughan, Traherne, & Milton. 236p. 1983. pap. 7.95x (ISBN 0-300-00164-9). Yale U Pr.

TRAILS

see also Cattle Trade

Doan, Daniel. Fifty Hikes in New Hampshire's White Mountains: Walks, Day Hikes, & Backpacking Trips. 3rd, rev. ed. (Fifty Hikes Ser.). (Illus.). 224p. 1983. pap. 8.95 (ISBN 0-942440-12-9). Backcountry Pubns.

Gibson, John. Fifty Hikes in Maine: Day Hikes & Backpacking Trips from the Coast to Katahdin. 2nd, rev. ed. LC 82-25276. (Fifty Hikes Ser.). (Illus.). 192p. (Orig.). 1983. pap. 8.95 (ISBN 0-942440-13-7). Backcountry Pubns.

Spangle, Francis & Rusmore, Jean. South Bay Trails: Outdoor Adventures in Santa Clara Valley. Winnett, Thomas, ed. (Illus.). 224p. 1983. pap. 8.95 (ISBN 0-89997-022-2). Wilderness Pr.

Thwaites, Thomas. Fifty Hikes in Western Pennsylvania: Walks & Day Hikes from the Laurel Highlands to Lake Erie. LC 82-25277. (Fifty Hikes Ser.). (Illus.). 224p. 1983. pap. 8.95 (ISBN 0-942440-10-2). Backcountry Pubns.

TRAINED NURSES

see Nurses and Nursing

TRAINING, OCCUPATIONAL

see Occupational Training

TRAINING, PHYSICAL

see Physical Education and Training

TRAINING, VOCATIONAL

see Occupational Training

TRAINING OF CHILDREN

see Children–Management

TRAINING OF EMPLOYEES

see Employees, Training of

TRAINING OF EXECUTIVES

see Executives, Training of

TRAINING SCHOOLS FOR NURSES

see Nursing Schools

TRAINING WITHIN INDUSTRY

see Employees, Training of

TRAINS, RAILROAD

see Railroads–Trains

TRAMPING

see Hiking

TRAMPOLINE

see Tumbling

TRAMPS

see also Rogues and Vagabonds

Stevens, Irving L. Fishbones: Hoboing in the 1930's. LC 82-90088. (Illus.). 136p. (Orig.). 1982. pap. 7.95 (ISBN 0-9609208-0-3). Moosehead Prods.

TRANSACTION (CIVIL LAW)

see Compromise (Law)

TRANSATLANTIC FLIGHTS

see Aeronautics–Flights

TRANSCENDENTAL FUNCTIONS

see Functions, Transcendental

TRANSCENDENTAL MEDITATION

Rottenberg, David. Fire of Knowledge. (Orig.). 1983. pap. 3.95 (ISBN 0-910291-01-2). Cedar Crest Bks.

TRANSCENDENTALISM

see also Idealism

Gura, Philip F. & Myerson, Joel, eds. Critical Essays on American Transcendentalism. (Critical Essays on American Literature). 1982. lib. bdg. 60.00 (ISBN 0-8161-8466-6). G K Hall.

Kant, Immanuel. The Basic Foundations of Transcendental Logic. (The Essential Library of the Great Philosophers). (Illus.). 109p. 1983. Repr. of 1888 ed. 87.45 (ISBN 0-89901-083-0). Found Class Reprints.

Strauch, Ralph E. The Reality Illusion. LC 82-42705. (Illus.). 230p. (Orig.). 1983. pap. 6.95 (ISBN 0-8356-0571-X, Quest). Theos Pub Hse.

TRANSCONTINENTAL JOURNEYS (U. S.)

see Overland Journeys to the Pacific

TRANSCRIPTION (SHORTHAND)

see Shorthand

TRANSDUCERS

see also Wave Guides

CES Industries, Inc. Staff. Transducers. (Ed-Lab Experiment Manual). (Illus.). (gr. 9-12). 1982. write for info. lab manual (ISBN 0-86711-050-3). CES Industries.

Woolvet, G. A. Transducers in Digital Systems. rev. ed. (IEE Control Engineering Ser.: No. 3). (Illus.). 201p. 1979. pap. 23.00 (ISBN 0-906048-13-3). Inst Elect Eng.

TRANSEXUALISM

see Change of Sex

TRANSFER MACHINES

see Machine-Tools

TRANSFER OF POPULATION

see Population Transfers

TRANSFER OF TECHNOLOGY

see Technology Transfer

TRANSFER PRINTING

Transfer Printing in Perspective. 1982. 35.00x (ISBN 0-686-81694-3, Pub. by Soc Dyers & Colour). State Mutual Bk.

TRANSFER STUDENTS

Galton, Maurice & Willcocks, John, eds. Moving from the Primary Classroom. 260p. (Orig.). 1983. pap. price not set (ISBN 0-7100-9343-8). Routledge & Kegan.

TRANSFER TAX

see Inheritance and Transfer Tax

TRANSFORMATION GROUPS

C-Bundles & Compact Transformation Groups. LC 82-11544. (Memoirs of the American Mathematical Society Ser.: No. 269). 4.00 (ISBN 0-8218-2269-1, MEMO/269). Am Math.

TRANSFORMATIONAL GRAMMAR

see Generative Grammar

TRANSFORMATIONS (MATHEMATICS)

see also Complexes; Ergodic Theory; Fourier Transformations; Functor Theory; Geometry, Algebraic; Homotopy Theory; Lattice Theory; Spectral Theory (Mathematics); Transformation Groups

Walter, E. Identifiability of State Space Models: With Applications to Transformation Systems. (Lecture Notes in Biomathematics Ser.: Vol. 46). 202p. 1983. pap. 13.50 (ISBN 0-387-11590-0). Springer-Verlag.

TRANSFORMATIONS, FOURIER

see Fourier Transformations

TRANSFORMERS, ELECTRIC

see Electric Transformers

TRANSFUSION OF BLOOD

see Blood–Transfusion

TRANSIENT LABOR

see Migrant Labor

TRANSIT SYSTEMS

see Local Transit

TRANSITION METALS

Davies, S. G., ed. Organotransition Metal Chemistry: Applications to Organic Synthesis. (Organic Chemistry Ser.: Vol. 2). (Illus.). 428p. 1982. 85.00 (ISBN 0-08-026202-3). Pergamon.

TRANSLATING AGENCIES

see Translating Services

TRANSLATING SERVICES

see also Translators

Translator Referral & Translation Services Directory, 1983. Rev. ed. (Orig.). 1983. pap. text ed. 12.50 (ISBN 0-917564-16-2). Translation Research.

TRANSLATIONS–LITERATURE, MEDIEVAL

O'Donoghue, Bernard. The Courtly Love Tradition. LC 82-18180. (Literature in Context Ser.). 320p. 1983. text ed. 25.00x (ISBN 0-389-20347-5); pap. text ed. 8.95x (ISBN 0-389-20348-3). B&N Imports.

TRANSLATORS

see also Translating Services

Translator Referral & Translation Services Directory, 1983. Rev. ed. (Orig.). 1983. pap. text ed. 12.50 (ISBN 0-917564-16-2). Translation Research.

TRANSLOCATION (GENETICS)

Shapiro, James A., ed. Mobile Genetic Elements. LC 82-11624. Date not set. 65.00 (ISBN 0-12-638680-3). Acad Pr.

TRANSMISSION OF DATA

see Data Transmission Systems

TRANSMISSION OF HEAT

see Heat–Transmission

TRANSMITTING SETS, RADIO

see Radio–Transmitters and Transmission

TRANSMUTATION OF METALS

see Alchemy

TRANSPIRATION OF PLANTS

see Plants–Transpiration

TRANSPLANTATION OF ORGANS, TISSUES, ETC.

see also Biomedical Materials; Cellular Therapy; Surgery, Plastic; Vascular Grafts

also subdivision Transplantation under specific organs, etc. e.g. Cornea–Transplantation

Calne, Roy Y., ed. Liver Transplant. write for info. (ISBN 0-12-790767-X). Grune.

TRANSPORT, BIOLOGICAL

see Biological Transport

TRANSPORT AIRCRAFT

see Transport Planes

TRANSPORT PHENOMENA

see Transport Theory

TRANSPORT PLANES

Mondey, David. The Hamlyn Concise Guide to Commercial Aircraft of the World. (Hamlyn Concise Guides Ser.). (Illus.). 224p. 1983. 9.95 (ISBN 0-600-34950-0, Pub. by Hamlyn Pub England). Presidio Pr.

TRANSPORT THEORY

Bass, J. & Fischer, K. H. Metals: Electronic Transport Phenomena. (Landolt Boernstein Ser.: Group III, Vol. 15, Subvol. A). (Illus.). 400p. 1983. 271.10 (ISBN 0-387-11082-8). Springer-Verlag.

Brenner, H. Transport Processes in Porous Media. Date not set. price not set (ISBN 0-07-007645-6). McGraw.

Fahien, R. Fundamentals of Transport Phenomena. (Chemical Engineering Ser.). 640p. 1983. 32.50x (ISBN 0-07-019891-8, C); write for info. solutions manual (ISBN 0-07-019892-6). McGraw.

Kaper, H. G. & Lekkerkerker, C. J., eds. Spectral Methods in Linear Transport Theory. (Operator Theory, Advances & Applications Ser.: Vol. 5). 360p. 1982. text ed. 29.95 (ISBN 3-7643-1372-2). Birkhauser.

Sjodin, R. A. Ion Transport in Skeletal Muscle. (Transport in the Life Sciences Ser.). 157p. 1982. text ed. 35.00x (ISBN 0-471-05265-5, Pub. by Wiley-Interscience). Wiley.

Tellier. Size Effects of Thin Films. (Thin Films Science & Technology Ser.: Vol. 2). 1982. 68.00 (ISBN 0-444-42106-8). Elsevier.

TRANSPORTATION

see also Aeronautics, Commercial; Automobiles; Bridges; Canals; Commerce; Freight and Freightage; Harbors; Inland Navigation; Local Transit; Merchant Marine; Ocean Travel; Pipe Lines; Postal Service; Railroad Travel; Railroads; Roads; Shipping; Steam-Navigation; Steamboats and Steamboat Lines; Traffic Engineering; Urban Transportation; Vehicles

also subdivision Transportation under special subjects, e.g. Farm Produce–Transportation

Abouchar, Alan. Transportation Economics & Public Policy: With Urban Extensions. LC 82-17081. 344p. 1983. Repr. of 1977 ed. lib. bdg. price not set (ISBN 0-89874-563-2). Krieger.

Altschiller, Donald. Transportation in America. (The Reference Shelf Ser.: Vol. 54, No. 3). 204p. 1982. text ed. 6.25 (ISBN 0-8242-0667-3). Wilson.

Business Communications Staff. Plastics in Transportation. 1983. 1000.00 (ISBN 0-686-84702-4, P-069). BCC.

Computer Control of Transport. 61p. (Orig.). 1981. pap. text ed. 24.00x (ISBN 0-85825-149-3, Pub. by Inst Engineering Australia). Renouf.

Flood, Kenneth U. & Callson, Oliver G. Transportation Management. 4th ed. 550p. 1983. text ed. write for info. (ISBN 0-697-08514-7). Wm C Brown.

Jones, D., ed. Design, Construction & Rehabilitation of Public Transit Facilities. LC 82-72778. 416p. 1982. pap. text ed. 29.00 (ISBN 0-87262-315-7). Am Soc Civil Eng.

Kulp, G. & Holcomb, M. C. Transportation Energy Data Book. 6th ed. LC 82-14135. (Illus.). 205p. 1983. 36.00 (ISBN 0-8155-0919-7). Noyes.

Niles, Jack M., et al. The Telecommunications-Transportation Tradeoff: Options for Tomorrow. LC 76-18107. 208p. Repr. of 1976 ed. text ed. 44.50 (ISBN 0-471-01507-5). Krieger.

OECD. European Conference of Ministers of Transport: (ECMT) 28th Annual Report-1981, Vol. 1. (Activity of the Conference Ser.). 206p. 1982. pap. 18.00x. OECD.

Polak, J. B. & Hupkes, G., eds. Vervoer Voor Gehandicapten: Illusie of Realiteit? 340p. (Dutch.). pap. 17.50x (ISBN 90-70176-62-9). Foris Pubns.

Rudman, Jack. Director of Transportation Operations. (Career Examination Ser.: C-114). (Cloth bdg. avail. on request). pap. 14.00 (ISBN 0-8373-0114-9). Natl Learning.

--Supervisor (Turnstiles) (Career Examination Ser.: C-427). (Cloth bdg. avail. on request). pap. 12.00 (ISBN 0-8373-0427-X). Natl Learning.

--Transit System Manager. (Career Examination Ser.: C-539). (Cloth bdg. avail. on request). pap. 12.00 (ISBN 0-8373-0539-X). Natl Learning.

Smith, Sharon. Basic Skills Travel & Transportation Workbook. (Basic Skills Workbooks). 32p. (gr. 4-7). 1983. 0.99 (ISBN 0-8209-0561-5, SW-9). ESP.

--Travel & Transportation. (Social Studies Ser.). 24p. (gr. 5-9). 1976. wkbk. 5.00 (ISBN 0-8209-0247-0, SS-14). ESP.

Stern, H. I. Transport Scheduling & Routing: An Introduction to Quantitative Methods. Date not set. price not set (ISBN 0-07-061196-3). McGraw.

Traffic World, ed. Traffic World's Questions & Answers, Vol. 28. 576p. 1982. text ed. write for info. (ISBN 0-87408-024-X). Traffic Serv.

Transport & Energy. 168p. 1981. 90.00x (ISBN 0-7277-0125-8, Pub. by Telford England). State Mutual Bk.

Vanderleest, Henry W. & Johnston, Michael L. Cases in Transportation Management. (Illus.). 104p. (Orig.). 1983. pap. text ed. 5.95x (ISBN 0-88133-011-6). Waveland Pr.

Wickey, J. W. Matropolitan Transportation Planning. 2nd ed. 624p. 1983. 34.95 (ISBN 0-07-016816-4); solns. manual avail. (ISBN 0-07-016817-2). McGraw.

TRANSPORTATION–BIBLIOGRAPHY

Krummes, Daniel & Kleiber, Michael. Recent Transportation Literature for Planning & Engineering Librarians. (Public Administration Ser.). 51p. 1983. pap. 7.50 (ISBN 0-88066-348-0, P 1118). Vance Biblios.

TRANSPORTATION–FINANCE

Button, K. J. Transport Economics. viii, 295p. (Orig.). 1982. pap. text ed. 15.00 (ISBN 0-435-84093-2). Heinemann Ed.

Carpenter, et al. The Economics of Long-Distance Transportation: Proceedings of a Conference Held by the International Economic Association in Moscow. LC 82-791. 280p. 1982. 32.50x (ISBN 0-312-23439-2). St Martin.

TRANSPORTATION–FREIGHT

see Freight and Freightage

TRANSPORTATION–HISTORY

Colby, W. E. A Century of Transportation in Shasta County 1821-1920. (ANCRR Occasional Paper: No. 7). 105p. 1982. 7.50 (ISBN 0-686-38931-X). Assn NC Records.

TRANSPORTATION–JUVENILE LITERATURE

Arnold, Caroline. How Do We Travel? (Easy-Read Community Bks.). (Illus.). 32p. (gr. k-3). 1983. PLB 7.90 (ISBN 0-531-04507-2). Watts.

Taylor, Ron. Fifty Facts About Speed & Power. (Fifty Facts About Ser.). (Illus.). 32p. (gr. 4-6). 1983. PLB 8.90 (ISBN 0-531-09211-9). Watts.

TRANSPORTATION–LAWS AND REGULATIONS

see also Maritime Law

Fair, Marvin L. & Guandolo, John. Transportation Regulation. 9th ed. 500p. 1983. text ed. write for info. (ISBN 0-697-08515-5). Wm C Brown.

Guandolo, John. Transportation Law. 4th ed. 800p. 1983. text ed. write for info. (ISBN 0-697-08516-3). Wm C Brown.

Keeler, Theodore E. Railroads, Freight, & Public Policy. LC 82-45985. (Regulation of Economic Activity Ser.). 250p. 1983. 24.95 (ISBN 0-8157-4856-6); pap. 9.95 (ISBN 0-8157-4855-8). Brookings.

TRANSPORTATION–PICTORIAL WORKS

Harter, JIm, ed. Transportation: A Pictorial Archive From 19th Century Sources with 400 Copyright-Free Illustrations for Artists & Designs. (Illus.). 160p. (Orig.). 1983. pap. 6.95 (ISBN 0-486-24499-7). Dover.

TRANSPORTATION–RESEARCH

Krummes, Daniel & Kleiber, Michael. Recent Transportation Literature for Planning & Engineering Librarians. (Public Administration Ser.: Bibliography P 1077). 49p. 1982. pap. 7.50 (ISBN 0-88066-267-0). Vance Biblios.

TRANSPORTATION–VOCATIONAL GUIDANCE

Hammer, Hy, ed. Special Officer-Senior Special Officer-Bridge & Tunnel Officer. 3rd ed. (Illus.). 192p. (Orig.). 1983. pap. 8.00 (ISBN 0-668-05614-2, 5614). Arco.

TRANSPORTATION–AUSTRALIA

Starkie, D., ed. Pricing & Cost Recovery in Long Distance Transport. 1982. lib. bdg. 39.50 (ISBN 90-247-2683-2, Pub. by Martinus Nijhoff). Kluwer Boston.

Transport: The Way Ahead: New Cities or Bigger Cities? 100p. (Orig.). 1977. pap. text ed. 18.00x (ISBN 0-85825-086-1, Pub. by Inst Engineering Australia). Renouf.

Transportation Eighty One. 200p. (Orig.). 1981. pap. text ed. 37.50x (ISBN 0-85825-158-2, Pub. by Inst Engineering Australia). Renouf.

TRANSPORTATION, AUTOMOTIVE–EMPLOYEES

see Highway Transport Workers

TRANSPORTATION AND STATE

see also Transportation–Laws and Regulations

Kanafani, A. & Sperling, D., eds. National Transportation Planning. 1982. lib. bdg. 27.50 (ISBN 90-247-2636-0, Pub. by Martinus Nijhoff Netherlands). Kluwer Boston.

TRANSPORTATION INSURANCE

see Insurance, Marine

TRANSPORTATION OF SCHOOL CHILDREN

see School Children–Transportation

TRANSPORTATION POLICY

see Transportation and State

TRANSURANIUM ELEMENTS

Seaborg, G. T., ed. Transuranium Elements: Products of Modern Alchemy. LC 78-7803. (Benchmark Papers in Physical Chemistry & Chemical Physics: Vol. 1). 488p. 1978. 56.00 (ISBN 0-87933-326-X). Hutchinson Ross.

TRANSYLVANIA

Bodea, Cornelia & Candea, Virgil. Heritage & Continuity in Eastern Europe: The Transylvanian Legacy in the History of the Romanians. (East European Monographs: No. 117). 160p. 1982. 17.50x (ISBN 0-88033-010-4). East Eur Quarterly.

Cadzow, John F. & Ludanyi, Andrew, eds. Transylvania: The Roots of Ethnic Conflict. LC 82-23354. (Illus.). 360p. 1983. 32.50 (ISBN 0-87338-283-8). Kent St U Pr.

Pascu, Stefan. A History of Transylvania. Ladd, D. Robert, tr. 318p. 1982. 26.00X (ISBN 0-8143-1722-7). Wayne St U Pr.

TRAPP FAMILY SINGERS

Wilhelm, Hans. The Trapp Family Book. (Illus.). 88p. (gr. 2-4). 1983. 14.95 (ISBN 0-434-97248-7, Pub. by Heinemann England). David & Charles.

TRASH

see Refuse and Refuse Disposal

TRAUBEL, HORACE, d. 1858

Innes-Homer, William, ed. Heart's Gate: Letters Between Marsden Hartley & Horace Traubel 1906-1915. LC 81-86063. 88p. 1982. pap. 7.50 (ISBN 0-912330-48-1). Jargon Soc.

TRAUMATISM

see also Shock; Wounds;

also subdivision Wounds and Injuries under names of organs, and regions of the body, e.g. Brain–Wounds and Injuries

Crass, Richard A. New Trends in Trauma. LC 82-42831. 175p. (Orig.). 1983. pap. price not set (ISBN 0-940122-07-3). Multi Media CO.

Harmon. Care of the Trauma Patient. Date not set. write for info. Wiley.

Lefer, Allan M. & Schumer, William, eds. Molecular & Cellular Aspects of Shock & Trauma. LC 82-25875. (Progress in Clinical & Biological Research Ser.: Vol. 111). 354p. 1983. 60.00 (ISBN 0-686-42967-2). A R Liss.
Trunkey, Donald T. & Lewis, Frank R., Jr., eds. Current Therapy of Trauma & Emergency Medicine. 300p. 1983. text ed. 36.00 (ISBN 0-941158-12-8, D5152-2). Mosby.

TRAVEL
Here are entered works on the art of travel, etc. Works on voyages and travels are entered under the heading Voyages and Travels.
see also Games for Travelers; Health Resorts, Watering-Places, etc.; Ocean Travel; Railroad Travel; Steamboats and Steamboat Lines; Tourist Trade; Voyages and Travels
also subdivision Description and Travel under names of countries, or Description under names of cities, e.g. France-Description and Travel; London-Description
Adler, Jack. A Consumer's Guide to Travel. LC 82-22195. 240p. (Orig.). 1983. pap. 8.95 (ISBN 0-88496-194-X). Capra Pr.
Birkland, Carol. Finding Home: A Guide to Solidarity with the World's Uprooted. (Orig.). 1983. pap. write for info. (ISBN 0-377-00129-5). Friend Pr.
Dickinson, Peter. Travel & Retirement Edens Abroad. (Illus.). 304p. 1983. 19.95 (ISBN 0-525-93274-7, 01840-550); pap. 12.95 (01258-370). Dutton.
Dodd, Philip, ed. The Art of Travel: Essays on Travel Writing. 172p. 1982. text ed. 17.50x (ISBN 0-7146-3205-8, F Cass Co). Biblio Dist.
Eisenberg, Gerson G. Learning Vacations Nineteen Eighty-Two: A Guide to All Season Worldwide Educational Travel. 4th ed. LC 81-21002. 246p. (Orig.). 1982. write for info. (ISBN 0-930080-04-1). Eisenberg Ed.
Foseco Minsep Group. The Business Traveller's Handbook: How to Get along with People in 100 Countries. 300p. 1983. 14.95 (ISBN 0-13-107797-X); pap. 7.95 (ISBN 0-13-107789-9). P-H.
Parker, Gail R. Holidays for One: Vacations for the Solo Traveler. (Illus.). 64p. (Orig.). 1981. pap. 5.50 (ISBN 0-910115-00-1). Posey Pubns.
Phillips, Ralph & Webster, Susan. Group Travel Operating Procedures. 176p. 1983. text ed. 17.95 (ISBN 0-8436-0882-X). CBI Pub.
Wall, Muriel. Sens-ational Travel. (Illus.). write for info. ICA Pubs.
Ward, Elaine. Growing Roots & Wings: A Guide to Teaching Children "Roots & Wings". (Orig.). 1983. pap. write for info. (ISBN 0-377-00131-7). Friend Pr.
Wright, Carol. The Travel Survival Guide. 192p. 1983. 17.50 (ISBN 0-7153-8310-8). David & Charles.

TRAVEL-COSTS
see Travel Costs

TRAVEL-GUIDEBOOKS
see Voyages and Travels-Guidebooks

TRAVEL-JUVENILE LITERATURE
Cogswell, James. No Place Left Called Home. (Orig.). 1983. pap. write for info. (ISBN 0-377-00128-7). Friend Pr.
Heaton, Jane. Journey of Struggle, Journey in Hope. (Orig.). 1983. pap. write for info. (ISBN 0-377-00126-0). Friend Pr.
Ward, Elaine. Roots & Wings. (Orig.). (gr. 1-6). 1983. pap. write for info. (ISBN 0-377-00130-9). Friend Pr.

TRAVEL AGENTS
Jaeger's Intertravel, 1982: World Guide to Travel Agencies. 17th ed. LC 77-649301. 975p. 1982. pap. 52.20x (ISBN 3-920777-38-7). Intl Pubns Serv.

TRAVEL BOOKS
see Voyages and Travels
also subdivision Description and Travel under names of countries, regions, etc.

TRAVEL COSTS
Weintz, Caroline & Weintz, Walter. The Discount Guide for Travelers over 55. rev. ed. LC 80-83630. 256p. 1983. pap. 5.95 (ISBN 0-525-93281-X, 0577-180). Dutton.

TRAVEL IN LITERATURE
Waldman, Milton. The Omnibus Book of Travellers' Tales: Being the History of Exploration Told by the Explorers. 864p. 1982. Repr. of 1931 ed. lib. bdg. 50.00 (ISBN 0-8495-5663-5). Arden Lib.

TRAVEL PHOTOGRAPHY
Dennis, Lisl. Travel Photography Developing a Personal Style. (Illus.). 150p. 1983. pap. 16.95 (ISBN 0-930764-42-0). Curtin & London.

TRAVELERS
see also Explorers
Stevenson, Catherine B. Victorian Women Travel Writers in Africa. (English Authors Ser.). 184p. 1982. lib. bdg. 17.95 (ISBN 0-8057-6835-1, Twayne). G K Hall.
Van der Post, Laurens. Yet Being Someone Other. 352p. 1983. Repr. 14.95 (ISBN 0-688-01843-2). Morrow.

TRAVELERS, GAMES FOR
see Games for Travelers

TRAVELS
see Overland Journeys to the Pacific; Scientific Expeditions; Voyages and Travels

TREASURE-TROVE
Fox, Theron. Utah Treasure Hunter's Ghost Town Guide. (Illus.). 1983. pap. 2.50. Nevada Pubns.
Henson, Michael P. A Guide to Treasure in Kentucky. (Illus.). 104p. (Orig.). 1983. pap. 6.95 (ISBN 0-941620-29-8). H G Carson Ent.
Mitchell, John D. Lost Mines & Buried Treasures along the Old Frontier. LC 77-121730. 1982. Repr. of 1954 ed. lib. bdg. 12.00 (ISBN 0-87380-060-5). Rio Grande.
Nelson, P. N. & Nelson, L. N., eds. Oregon Gold. 1983. pap. 5.95 (ISBN 0-942652-00-2). Windriver Scribes.
Penrose, Barrie. Stalin's Gold: The Story of HMS Edinburgh & Its Treasures. (Illus.). 256p. 1983. 15.00i (ISBN 0-316-69877-6). Little.
Rensch, Gary D. The Hidden Treasure Game. (Illus.). 1982. pap. 9.45 (ISBN 0-941508-02-1); deluxe ed. 19.00 (ISBN 0-941508-03-X). Gold Star Pubns.
Voynick, Stephen M. The Mid-Atlantic Treasure Coast: The Romance & Reality of Coin Beaches & Treasure Shipwrecks. LC 82-18846. (Illus.). 224p. (Orig.). 1983. pap. 9.95 (ISBN 0-912608-16-1). Mid Atlantic.
Williams, Mark. Deep Sea Treasure. (Illus.). 24.95 (ISBN 0-434-86660-1, Pub. by Heinemann). David & Charles.

TREATIES
see also Arbitration, International; Commercial Treaties; Congresses and Conventions; Indians of North America-Treaties
Harvard Law School Library. Index to Multilateral Treaties: A Chronological List of Multiparty International Agreements from the 16th Century through 1963 with Citations to Text. Mostecky, Vaclav, ed. 301p. 1965. 22.50 (ISBN 0-379-00384-8). Oceana.
Hosack, John. On the Rise & Growth of the Law of Nations, as Established by General Usage & by Treaties, from the Earliest Time to the Treaty of Utrecht. xii, 394p. 1982. Repr. of 1882 ed. lib. bdg. 35.00x (ISBN 0-8377-0647-5). Rothman.
Multilateral Treaties in Respect of Which the Secretary-General Performs Depository Functions (List of Signatures, Ratifications, etc. up to 31 December 1981). 50.00 (ISBN 0-686-84921-3, E.81.V.9). UN.
Rohn, Peter H. World Treaty Index. 2nd ed. 4386p. 1983. Set. lib. bdg. 850.00 (ISBN 0-87436-329-2). ABC-Clio.

TREES
see also Forests and Forestry; Grafting; Landscape Gardening; Leaves; Lumbering; Nuts; Ornamental Trees; Pruning; Shrubs; Timber; Wood
also classes, orders, species, etc. of trees, e.g. Elm, Pine, Spruce
Meiggs, Russell. Trees & Timber in the Ancient Mediterranean World. (Illus.). 456p. 1983. 74.00 (ISBN 0-19-814840-2). Oxford U Pr.
Names for Dipterocarp Timbers & Trees from Asia. 251p. 1983. 42.25 (ISBN 90-220-0795-2, PDC255, Pudoc). Unipub.

TREES-BIBLIOGRAPHY
Ortho Books Staff. All About Trees. Ferguson, Barbara J., ed. LC 82-82155. (Illus.). 112p. 1982. pap. 5.95 (ISBN 0-89721-007-7). Ortho.

TREES-DISEASES AND PESTS
see also Fruit-Diseases and Pests; Fungicides; Insecticides; Insects, Injurious and Beneficial; Plant Diseases
also names of particular trees, e.g. Elm; names of diseases and pests
Anderson, Roger F. Forest & Shade Tree Entomology. LC 60-11714. 428p. 1960. 28.95x (ISBN 0-471-02739-1). Wiley.
Phillips, D. H. & Burdekin, D. A. Diseases of Forest & Ornamental Trees. 1982. 190.00x (ISBN 0-333-32357-2, Pub. by Macmillan England). State Mutual Bk.
Resistance to Diseases & Pests in Forest Trees. 503p. 1982. 74.50 (ISBN 90-220-0794-4, PDC248, Pudoc). Unipub.

TREES-JUVENILE LITERATURE
Dickinson, Jane. All About Trees. LC 82-17382. (Question & Answer Bks.). (Illus.). 32p. (gr. 3-6). 1983. PLB 8.59 (ISBN 0-89375-892-2); pap. text ed. 1.95 (ISBN 0-89375-893-0). Troll Assocs.
Gordon, Sharon. Trees. LC 82-20291. (Now I Know Ser.). (Illus.). 32p. (gr. k-2). 1982. lib. bdg. 8.89 (ISBN 0-89375-901-5). Troll Assocs.
Hamer, Martyn. Trees. (Easy Read Fact Bk.). (Illus.). 32p. (gr. 2-4). 1983. PLB 8.60 (ISBN 0-531-04513-7). Watts.

TREES-AFRICA
Palmer. A Field Guide to the Trees of Southern Africa. 29.95 (ISBN 0-686-42772-6, Collins Pub England). Greene.

TREES-EUROPE
Mitchell. A Field Guide to the Trees of Britain & Northern Europe. 29.95 (ISBN 0-686-42768-8, Collins Pub England). Greene.
Mitchell & Wilkinson. The Trees of Britain & Northern Europe. 14.95 (ISBN 0-686-42737-8, Collins Pub England); pap. 8.95. Greene.

TREES-HAWAII
Belknap, Jodi P. Majesty: The Exceptional Trees of Hawaii. Cazimero, Momi, ed. LC 82-60598. 72p. 1982. 12.95 (ISBN 0-686-38728-7). Outdoor Circle.

TREES-NEW ZEALAND
Eagle, Audrey. Eagle's Trees & Shrubs of New Zealand in Colour. (Illus.). 311p. 1983. Repr. of 1975 ed. 95.00 (ISBN 0-686-84831-4, Pub. by W Collins Australia). Intl Schol Bk Serv.

TREES-UNITED STATES
Allison, R. Bruce. Tree Walks: Milwankee County. (Illus.). 56p. 1982. pap. 5.95 (ISBN 0-913370-13-4). Wisconsin Bks.
Allison, R. Bruce & Durbin, Elizabeth. Wisconsin's Famous & Historic Trees. (Illus.). 120p. pap. 14.95 (ISBN 0-913370-14-2). Wisconsin Bks.
Lakela, Olga & Wunderlin, Richard P. Trees of Central Florida. LC 80-12797. (Illus.). 208p. 14.95 (ISBN 0-686-84243-X). Banyan Bks.

TREES IN THE BIBLE
see Bible-Natural History

TREPONEMATOSIS
Schell, Musher. Pathogenesis & Immunology of Treponemal Infections. (Immunology Ser.). 424p. 1983. 65.00 (ISBN 0-8247-1384-2). Dekker.

TREVINO, LEE
Trevino, Lee & Blair, Sam. They Call Me Super Mex. 200p. 1983. 12.95 (ISBN 0-394-52336-9). Random.

TRIAL BY JURY
see Jury

TRIAL EVIDENCE
see Evidence (Law)

TRIAL PRACTICE
see also Actions and Defenses; Appellate Procedure; Civil Procedure; Criminal Procedure; Cross-Examination; Evidence (Law); Forensic Orations; Instructions to Juries; Jury; Pleading; Probate Law and Practice; Witnesses
Maloney, Pat, Sr. & Pasqual, Jack. Winning the Million Dollar Lawsuit. LC 82-21175. 280p. 1982. text ed. 89.50 (ISBN 0-87624-848-2). Inst Busn Plan.

TRIALS
Messerschmidt, Jim. The Trial of Leonard Peltier. 250p. 1982. 20.00 (ISBN 0-89608-164-8); pap. 7.50 (ISBN 0-89608-163-X). South End Pr.
Ross, John M. Trials in Collections: An Index to Famous Trials Throughout the World. LC 82-21635. 218p. 1983. 16.00 (ISBN 0-8108-1603-2). Scarecrow.

TRIALS-GREAT BRITAIN
Graham, Michael H. Tightening the Reins of Justice in America: A Comparative Analysis of the Criminal Jury Trail in England & the United States. LC 82-12029. (Contributions in Legal Studies: No. 26). (Illus.). 376p. 1983. lib. bdg. 35.00 (ISBN 0-313-23598-8, GJA/). Greenwood.

TRIALS (MURDER)
Hauser, Thomas. The Trail of Patrolman Thomas Shea. 288p. pap. 3.50 (ISBN 0-380-62778-7, Discus). Avon.
Winslade, William J. & Ross, Judith W. The Insanity Plea. 240p. 1983. 14.95 (ISBN 0-684-17897-4). Scribner.

TRIALS (WAR CRIMES)
see War Crime Trials

TRIANGLES (INSTRUMENTS)
see Rulers (Instruments)

TRIANGULATION
see Errors, Theory of

TRIBAL GOVERNMENT
see Tribes and Tribal System

TRIBES AND TRIBAL SYSTEM
see also Gipsies; Kinship
Chorlton, W. Cloud Dwellers of the Himalayas: The Bhotia. (Peoples of the Wild Ser.). 1982. 15.96 (ISBN 0-7054-0705-5, Pub. by Time-Life). Silver.
Reid, James J. Trebalism & Society in Islamic Iran 1500-1629. (Studies in Near Eastern Culture & Society Ser.: Vol. 4). 220p. 1983. pap. write for info. (82-50984); write for info. (ISBN 0-89003-125-8). Undena Pubns.
Singh, K. S., ed. Tribal Movements in India, Vol. 1. 1982. 25.00X (ISBN 0-8364-0901-9, Pub. by Manohar India). South Asia Bks.

TRICK CINEMATOGRAPHY
see Cinematography, Trick

TRICK-TRACK
see Backgammon

TRICYCLES
see Bicycles and Tricycles

TRIGONOMETRICAL FUNCTIONS
Steklov Institute of Mathematics & Karacuba, A. A. Multiple Trignometric Sums. LC 82-18403. (Proceedings of the Steklov Institute of Mathematics Ser.: Vol.1982 No. 2). 42.00 (ISBN 0-8218-3067-8, STEKLO/151). Am Math.

TRIGONOMETRY
Douthitt, C. B. & McMillan, J. A. Trigonometry. 1977. text ed. 15.00 (ISBN 0-07-017670-1); solns. manual avail. (ISBN 0-07-017671-X). McGraw.
Gonis, Antonios & Panagoulias, Panagiotis. Mastering Skills in College Algebra & Trigonometry. (Illus.). 720p. Date not set. price not set. A-W.
Hackworth, Robert D. & Howland, Joseph W. College Algebra & Trigonometry As Socrates Might Have Taught Them. rev. ed. (Illus.). 295p. 1981. pap. text ed. 14.95x (ISBN 0-943202-01-9). H & H Pub.
Lial, Margaret L. & Miller, Charles D. Algebra & Trigonometry. 3rd ed. 1983. text ed. 20.95x (ISBN 0-673-15794-6). Scott F.

TRIMMING OF DOGS
see Dog Grooming

TRINITY
see also God; Holy Spirit; Jesus Christ; Unitarianism
Minz, Karl-Heinz. Pleroma Trinitatis: Die Trinitatstheologie bei Matthias Joseph Scheeben. (Disputationes Theologicae Ser.: Vol. 10). 404p. 1980. write for info. (ISBN 3-8204-6182-5). P Lang Pubs.
Thomas Aquinas. The Trinity. (Summa Theologial Ser.: Vol. 6). 1964. 12.95 (ISBN 0-07-001981-9). McGraw.
Tompkins, Jim. The Trinity. (Illus.). 160p. 1983. 15.00x (ISBN 0-9609824-0-X). Yossarian Pub.

TRIPLE ALLIANCE, WAR OF THE, 1865-1870
see Paraguayan War, 1865-1870

TROBRIAND ISLANDS
Weiner, Annette B. Women of Value, Men of Renown: New Perspectives in Trobriand Exchange. (Texas Press Sourcebooks in Anthropology: No. 11). (Illus.). 321p. 1983. pap. text ed. 8.95x (ISBN 0-292-79019-8). U of Tex Pr.

TROLLOPE, ANTHONY, 1815-1882
Hall, N. John, ed. The Letters of Anthony Trollope, 2 vols. LC 79-64213. (Illus.). 1100p. 1983. Set. 87.50x (ISBN 0-8047-1076-7). Vol. 1, 1835-1870. Vol. 2, 1871-1882. Stanford U Pr.
Wright, Andrew. Anthony Trollope: Dream & Art. LC 82-13365. 192p. 1983. lib. bdg. 20.00x (ISBN 0-226-90806-2). U of Chicago Pr.

TROMBONE
Bierley, Paul E. Hallelujah Trombone! The Story of Henry Fillmore. LC 82-90686. 1982. pap. 14.95 (ISBN 0-918048-03-6). Integrity.

TROMPE L'OEIL PAINTING
Milman, Miriam. Tromp l'Oeil Painting: The Illusion of Reality. LC 82-42851. (Illus.). 130p. 1983. 27.50 (ISBN 0-8478-0470-4). Rizzoli Intl.

TROPICAL AGRICULTURE
see Tropical Crops

TROPICAL CROPS
see also special crops, e.g. Coffee
Beets, Willem C. Multiple Cropping & Tropical Farming Systems. 250p. 1982. lib. bdg. 30.00 (ISBN 0-86531-518-3). Westview.
Weeds in Tropical Crops: Review of Abstracts. (FAO Plant Production & Protection Paper: No. 32, Supplement 1). 63p. 1982. pap. 7.50 (ISBN 92-5-101206-7, F2333, FAO). Unipub.

TROPICAL DISEASES
see Tropical Medicine

TROPICAL FISH
see also Aquariums
Tropical Fish. (Pet Care Ser.). 1983. pap. write for info. (ISBN 0-8120-2686-1). Barron.

TROPICAL MEDICINE
see also specific diseases, e.g. Malaria; Yellow Fever
Chandra, R. K., ed. Critical Reviews in Tropical Medicine. (Vol.1). 412p. 1982. 49.50X (ISBN 0-306-40959-3, Plenum Pr). Plenum Pub.

TROPICS
see also Tropical Medicine
also subdivision Tropics under Agriculture, Botany, and similar headings
Norgrove, Ross. Blueprint for Paradise: How to Live on a Tropical Island. LC 82-48430. (Illus.). 256p. 1983. 20.00 (ISBN 0-87742-154-4). Intl Marine.

TROPICS-CLIMATE
Ayoade, J. O. Introduction to Climatology for the Tropics. 200p. 1983. 28.95 (ISBN 0-471-10349-7, Pub. by Wiley-Interscience); pap. 13.95 (ISBN 0-471-10407-8, Pub. by Wiley-Interscience). Wiley.
The GARP Atlantic Tropical Experiment (GATE) Monograph. (GARP Publications Ser.: No. 25). 477p. 1982. pap. 40.00 (ISBN 0-686-81848-2, W 537, WMO). Unipub.

TROPICS-DISEASES AND HYGIENE
see Tropical Medicine

TROPICS-SANITATION
see Tropical Medicine

TROTSKY, LEON, 1879-1940
Lubitz, Wolfgang. Lev Davydovic Trockj. 512p. 1983. cancelled (ISBN 3-598-10469-3, Pub. by K G Saur). Shoe String.
Lubitz, Wolfgang, ed. Trotsky Bibiliography: List of Separately Published Titles in Collections Treating L. D. Trotsky & Trotskyism. 458p. 1982. 65.00x (ISBN 3-598-10469-3). Gale.

TROUSERS
Palmer, Pati & Pletsch, Susan. Pants for Any Body. rev. & expanded ed. 128p. (Orig.). 1982. pap. 5.95 (ISBN 0-935278-08-7). Palmer-Pletsch.

TROUT FISHING
Forrester, Rex. Trout Fishing in New Zealand. 204p. 1982. 40.00x (ISBN 0-7233-0612-5, Pub. by Whitcoulls New Zealand). State Mutual Bk.
Ovington, Ray. Tactics on Trout. (Illus.). 135p. 1983. pap. 8.95 (ISBN 0-686-83701-0, ScribT). Scribner.
Raychard, Al. Trout & Salmon Fishing in Northern New England. LC 82-5930. (Illus.). 208p. (Orig.). 1982. pap. 7.95 (ISBN 0-89621-068-5). Thorndike Pr.

TRUCK DRIVERS
see Highway Transport Workers

TRUCKS, AUTOMOBILE
see Motor-Trucks

TRUEBLOOD, DAVID ELTON, 1900-
Trueblood, Elton. While It is Day. 163p. 1983. pap. write for info. (ISBN 0-932970-36-2). Yokefellow Pr.

TRUMAN, HARRY S., PRES. U. S. 1884-1972
Ferrell, Robert H. Harry S. Truman & the Modern American Presidency. 1983. 13.00i (ISBN 0-316-27480-1). Little.
Poen, Monte M., ed. Strictly Personal & Confidential: The Letters Harry Truman Never Mailed. 224p. 1983. pap. 5.70i (ISBN 0-316-71222-1). Little.
TRUNCHEONS
Downey, Robert J. & Roth, Jordan T. Baton Techniques for Officer Survival. (Illus.). 288p. 1983. pap. 29.75x spiral (ISBN 0-398-04781-2). C C Thomas.
TRUST IN GOD
see also Faith
Droege, Thomas A. Faith Passages & Patterns. LC 82-48544. (Lead Bks.). 128p. 1983. pap. 3.95 (ISBN 0-8006-1602-2, 1-1602). Fortress.
TRUSTEES
see Trusts and Trustees
TRUSTS, CHARITABLE
see Charitable Uses, Trusts and Foundations
TRUSTS, INDUSTRIAL-LAW AND LEGISLATION
see Antitrust Law
TRUSTS AND TRUSTEES
Here are entered general works, and those concerned with trusts and trustees in the United States For works dealing with other countries, or individual states in the United States see appropriate subdivision.
see also Charitable Uses, Trusts and Foundations; Guardian and Ward; Land Trusts; Pension Trusts
Kurtz, Sheldon F. Problems, Cases & Other Materials on Family Estate Planning. LC 82-21920. (American Casebook Ser.). 853p. 1982. text ed. 23.95 (ISBN 0-314-69313-0); tchrs.' manual avail. (ISBN 0-314-72900-3). West Pub.
McGovern, William M., Jr. Cases & Materials on Wills, Trusts, & Future Interests: An Introduction to Estate Planning. LC 82-20034. (American Casebook Ser.). 680p. 1982. text ed. 22.95 (ISBN 0-314-68828-5). West Pub.
Public Management Institute Staff. Board Member Trustee Handbook. 47.50 (ISBN 0-686-82265-X, 53A). Public Management.
TRUTH
see also Agnosticism; Knowledge, Theory Of; Pragmatism; Reality; Skepticism
Bedford, A. D. Defence of Truth. 1979. 27.00 (ISBN 0-7190-0740-2). Manchester.
Bugental, James T. The Search for Authenticity. 477p. 1982. pap. text ed. 12.95x (ISBN 0-8290-1298-2). Irvington.
Hole, F. B. Outlines of Truth. Daniel, R. P., ed. 73p. pap. 2.75 (ISBN 0-88172-143-3). Believers Bkshelf.
Niggli, Ursula. Erkenntnis und Ernst. 167p. (Ger.). 1982. write for info. (ISBN 3-261-04961-8). P Lang Pubs.
TSCHAIKOVSKY, PETER, 1840-1893
see Tchaikovsky, Peter, 1840-1893
TSCHI LANGUAGE
see Twi Language
TSETSE-FLIES
Harriss, E. G. & Williams, N. G. Mixtures of Insecticides for Tsetse Fly Control: Potentiation Between a-Endosulfan & Deltalmethrin Applied to Glossina Austeni Newst. 1981. 35.00x (ISBN 0-85135-122-0, Pub. by Centre Overseas Research). State Mutual Bk.
TSHI LANGUAGE
see Twi Language
TSWI LANGUAGE
see Twi Language
TUBE WELL
see Wells
TUBERCULOSIS-DIAGNOSIS
Chadwick, Maureen V. Mycobacteria. (Institute of Medical Laboratory Sciences Monographs). 128p. 1982. pap. text ed. write for info. (ISBN 0-7236-0595-5). Wright-PSG.
TUBERCULOSIS NURSING
Patient Care in Tuberculosis. 44p. 1973. 2.95 (ISBN 0-686-38190-4, 45-1414). Natl League Nurse.
TUBES
see also Pipe
American Welding Society. Local Heat Treatment of Welds in Piping & Tubing: D10.10. 1975. 8.00 (ISBN 0-686-43381-5). Am Welding.
TUITION
see College Costs; Education-Finance; Universities and Colleges-Finance
TULLE EMBROIDERY
see Lace and Lace Making
TUMBLING
Tonry, Don. Sports Illustrated Tumbling. LC 82-47537. (Sports Illustrated Ser.). (Illus.). 192p. 1983. pap. 5.72i (ISBN 0-06-090984-6, CN984, CN). Har-Row.
--Sports Illustrated Tumbling. (Sports Illustrated Ser.). (Illus.). 192p. 1983. write for info. (ISBN 0-06-015022-X, HarpT). Har-Row.
Trampoline & Tumbling Handbook, 1977-1978. Date not set. 5.00 (ISBN 0-686-43040-9). AAU Pubns.
TUMORS
see also Antineoplastic Agents; Cancer; Lymphoma; Melanoma; Oncology; Sarcoidosis
also subdivision Diseases under names of organs and regions of the body, e.g. Brain-Diseases
Chao, Edmund Y. & Ivins, John C. Design & Application for Tumor Prostheses. (Illus.). 375p. 1983. write for info. Thieme-Stratton.
Graf, T. & Jaenisch, R., eds. Tumorviruses, Neoplastic Transformation & Differentiation. (Current Topics in Microbiology & Immunology Ser.: Vol. 101). (Illus.). 198p. 1983. 40.00 (ISBN 0-387-11665-6). Springer-Verlag.
Hancock, B. W. Assessment of Tumor Response. 1983. 49.50 (ISBN 90-247-2712-X, Pub. by Martinus Nijhoff Netherlands). Kluwer Boston.
Humphrey, G. B. Pancreatic Tumors in Children. 1983. 58.50 (ISBN 90-247-2702-2, Pub. by Martinus Nijhoff Netherlands). Kluwer Boston.
Katznelson, Alexander & Nerubay, Jacobo, eds. Osteosarcoma: New Trends in Diagnosis & Treatment. LC 82-4679. (Progress in Clinical & Biological Research Ser.: Vol. 99). 164p. 1982. 25.00 (ISBN 0-8451-0099-8). A R Liss.
Muramatsu, Takashi, et al, eds. Teratocarcinoma & Embryonic Cell Interactions. 1982. 36.00 (ISBN 0-12-511180-0). Acad Pr.
Reinhoudt, D. N. Structure & Activity of Anti-Tumour Agents. 1983. 47.50 (ISBN 90-247-2783-9, Pub. by Martinus Nijhoff Netherlands). Kluwer Boston.
Rosenblum, M. L. & Wilson, C. B., eds. Brain Tumor Biology. (Progress in Experimental Tumor Research Ser.: Vol. 27). (Illus.). viii, 250p. 1983. bound 100.75 (ISBN 3-8055-3698-4). S Karger.
--Brain Tumor Therapy. (Progress in Experimental Tumor Research: Vol. 28). (Illus.). viii, 250p. 1983. 100.75 (ISBN 3-8055-3699-2). S Karger.
Speissl, B., et al. TNM-Atlas: Illustrated Guide to the Classification of Malignant Tumors. (UICC International Union Against Cancer Ser.). (Illus.). 240p. 1982. pap. 14.00 (ISBN 0-387-11429-7). Springer-Verlag.
Tijssen & Halprin. Familial Brain Tumours. 1982. 54.50 (ISBN 90-247-2691-3, Pub. by Martinus Nijhoff Netherlands). Kluwer Boston.
Toker, Cyril. Tumors: An Atlas of Differential Diagnosis. (Illus.). 1983. price not set (ISBN 0-8391-1812-0, 17914). Univ Park.
Vargh, Georgy. Pharmacoangiography in the Diagnosis of Tumours. Kerner, Nora, tr. from Hungarian. (Illus.). 253p. 1981. 35.00x (ISBN 963-05-2912-2). Intl Pubns Serv.
Vitetta, Ellen S., ed. B & T Cell Tumors: Symposium. LC 82-13948. 583p. 1982. 52.00 (ISBN 0-12-722380-0). Acad Pr.
Wang. Radiation Therapy of Head & Neck Neoplasms. 736p. 1983. text ed. 39.50 (ISBN 0-7236-7049-8). Wright-PSG.
TUNDRAS
Hobbie, J. E., ed. Limnology of Tundra Ponds: Barrow, Alaska. LC 80-26373. (US-IBP Synthesis Ser.: Vol. 13). 514p. 1980. 34.00 (ISBN 0-87933-386-3). Hutchinson Ross.
TUNISIA-DESCRIPTION AND TRAVEL
Tunisia Travel Guide. (Berlitz Travel Guides). (Illus.). 1982. pap. 4.95 (ISBN 0-686-43314-9, Berlitz). Macmillan.
TUNNELS AND TUNNELING
see also Boring
also names of individual tunnels
Jones, M. H. & Woodcock, J. T. Ultraviolet Spectometry of Floatation Reagents With Special Reference to the Determination of Xanthate in Flotation Liquors. 28p. 1973. 11.50 (ISBN 0-900488-20-4). IMM North Am.
TURBOGENERATORS
Watson, N. & Janota, M. S. Turbocharging the Internal Combustion Engine. 1982. 125.00x (ISBN 0-333-24290-4, Pub. by Macmillan England). State Mutual Bk.
TURBOMACHINES
see also Compressors; Pumping Machinery
Tabakoff, W., ed. Particular Laden Flows in Tubomachinery. 150p. 1982. 30.00 (G00210). ASME.
TURBULENCE
Bradbury, L. J., et al. Turbulent Shear Flow 3rd: University of California, Selected Papers, 1981. (Illus.). 321p. 1983. 64.00 (ISBN 0-387-11817-9). Springer-Verlag.
Kollman, W. Prediction Methods for Turbulent Flows. 1980. text ed. 47.50 (ISBN 0-07-035259-3). McGraw.
Leslie, D. C. Developments in the Theory of Turbulence. (Illus.). 388p. 1983. pap. 27.50 (ISBN 0-19-856161-X). Oxford u Pr.
TURCO-BALKAN WAR, 1912-1913
see Balkan Peninsula-History
TURGENEV, IVAN SERGEEVICH, 1818-1883
Knowles, A. V. Turgenev's Letters. 320p. 1983. 30.00 (ISBN 0-686-83682-0, ScribT). Scribner.
Lowe, David, ed. Turgenev Letters. 1983. 50.00 (ISBN 0-686-43065-4). Ardis Pubs.
TURKESTAN
Leix, Alfred. Turkestan & Its Textile Craft. 1982. 40.00x (ISBN 0-903580-10-1, Pub. by Element Bks). State Mutual Bk.
TURKEY-ANTIQUITIES
Von Gabain, A., et al, eds. Turkologie. (Handbuch der Orientalistik Ser.). ix, 471p. 1982. pap. write for info. (ISBN 90-04-06555-5). E J Brill.
Waldbaum, Jane C. Metalwork from Sardis: The Finds Through 1974. (Archaeological Exploration of Sardis Monographs: No. 8). (Illus.). 280p. 1983. text ed. 40.00x (ISBN 0-674-57070-7). Harvard U Pr.
TURKEY-HISTORY
Esin, Emel. A History of Pre-Islamic & Early-Islamic Turkish Culture. (Supplement to the Handbook of Turkish Culture Series II: Vol. 1-b). (Illus.). 400p. 1980. pap. 35.00x (ISBN 0-8002-3050-7). Intl Pubns Serv.
Frazee, Charles A. Catholics & Sultans: The Church & the Ottoman Empire 1453-1923. LC 82-4562. 384p. Date not set. price not set (ISBN 0-521-24676-8). Cambridge U Pr.
Kunt, I. M. The Sultan's Servants: The Transformation of Ottoman Provincial Government, 1550-1650. 200p. 1983. text ed. 25.00x (ISBN 0-231-05578-1). Columbia U Pr.
TURKEY-POLITICS AND GOVERNMENT
Kim, Chong Lim & Barkan, Joel D. The Legislative Connection: The Politics of Representation in Kenya, Korea, & Turkey. (Duke Press Policy Studies). (Illus.). 400p. Date not set. prepub. 35.00 (ISBN 0-8223-0534-8). Duke.
TURKEY-SOCIAL LIFE AND CUSTOMS
Esin, Emel. A History of Pre-Islamic & Early-Islamic Turkish Culture. (Supplement to the Handbook of Turkish Culture Series II: Vol. 1-b). (Illus.). 400p. 1980. pap. 35.00x (ISBN 0-8002-3050-7). Intl Pubns Serv.
Serruys, Henry, ed. Kumiss Ceremonies & Horse Races: Three Mongolian Texts. 124p. 1974. pap. 27.50x (ISBN 0-686-82196-3). Intl Pubns Serv.
TURKEYS
Elliott, Charles. Turkey Hunting with Charlie Elliott. (Illus.). xi, 275p. 1982. 14.95 (ISBN 0-87797-063-7). Cherokee.
Harbour, Dave. Advanced Wild Turkey Hunting & World Records. (Illus.). 264p. 1983. 19.95 (ISBN 0-8329-0286-1, Pub. by Winchester Pr.). New Century.
--Hunting the American Wild Turkey. LC 74-31449. (Illus.). 258p. 1974. 14.95 (ISBN 0-8117-0863-2). Stackpole.
TURKISH LANGUAGE
Foreign Service Institute. Turkish Basic Course, Vol. 2. 358p. Date not set. with 13 cassettes 175.00x (ISBN 0-88432-105-3, T750). J Norton Pubs.
TURNER, FREDERICK JACKSON, 1861-1932
Carpenter, Ronald H. The Eloquence of Frederick Jackson Turner. 275p. 1983. price not set (ISBN 0-87328-078-4). Huntington Lib.
Gaunt, William. Turner. (Phaidon Color Library). (Illus.). 84p. 1983. 25.00 (ISBN 0-7148-2159-4, Pub. by Salem Hse Ltd); pap. 17.95 (ISBN 0-7148-2131-4). Merrimack Bk Serv.
TURNER, JOHN, 1735-1787
Wilton, Andrew. Turner Abroad: France, Italy, Germany, Switzerland. 208p. 1982. 80.00x (ISBN 0-7141-8047-5, Pub. by Brit Mus Pubns England). State Mutual Bk.
TURNER, JOSEPH MALLORD WILLIAM, 1775-1851
Turner. (Q.A.P. Art Ser.). (Illus.). pap. 4.95 (ISBN 0-517-52444-9). Crown.
Weelan, Guy. J. M. W. Turner. Paris, I. Mark, tr. (Illus.). 171p. 1983. 60.00 (ISBN 0-933516-51-7). Alpine Fine Arts.
TURNOVER OF LABOR
see Labor Turnover
TURNPIKES (MODERN)
see Express Highways
TURTLES
Turtles. (Pet Care Ser.). 1983. pap. price not set (ISBN 0-8120-2631-4). Barron.
TUSCARORA INDIANS
see Indians of North America-Eastern States
TUTELAGE
see Guardian and Ward
TUTANKHAMEN, KING OF EGYPT
Handlist to Howard Carter's Catalogue of Objects in Tutankamun's Tomb, Vol. 1. (Tutankamun's Tomb Ser.). 1963. text ed. 24.00x (ISBN 0-900416-06-8). Humanities.
TUTORS AND TUTORING
see also Remedial Teaching
Moore, David P. & Poppino, Mary A. Successful Tutoring: A Practical Guide to Adult Learning Processes. (Illus.). 184p. 1983. 15.75x (ISBN 0-398-04763-4). C C Thomas.
--Supervisor's Guide to Successful Tutoring. 24p. 1983. pap. 2.75x spiral (ISBN 0-398-04764-2). C C Thomas.
TWAIN, MARK
see Clemens, Samuel Langhorne, 1835-1910
TWELFTH CENTURY
Chenu, M. D. Nature, Man, & Society in the Twelfth Century: Essays on New Theological Perspectives in the Latin West. Taylor, Jeromr & Little, Lester K., eds. Taylor, Jerome & Little, Lester K., trs. LC 68-15574. (Midway Reprint Ser.). xxii, 362p. 1968. pap. write for info. (ISBN 0-226-10256-4). U of Chicago Pr.
TWENTIETH CENTURY
see also Civilization, Modern-20th Century
Stine, G. Harry. The Hopeful Future. 256p. 1983. 15.95 (ISBN 0-02-094140-4). Macmillan.
Taylor, A. J. & Roberts, J. M., eds. Twentieth Century. rev. ed. LC 78-27424. (Illus.). 2700p. 1979. lib. bdg. 532.67 (ISBN 0-8393-6079-7). Raintree Pubs.
TWENTY-FIRST CENTURY
Stine, G. Harry. The Hopeful Future. 256p. 1983. 15.95 (ISBN 0-02-094140-4). Macmillan.
TWENTY-ONE (GAME)
see Blackjack (Game)
TWI LANGUAGE
Here are entered works limited to dialects of the Akuapem, Ashanti, and related peoples who accept the name Twi. Works dealing collectively with the above dialects and the dialect of the Fanti people are entered under Akan Language.
Foreign Service Institute. Twi Basic Course. 240p. Date not set. with 9 cassettes 125.00x (ISBN 0-88432-111-8, TW1). J Norton Pubs.
TWINS
Theroux, Rosemary & Tingley, Josephine. The Care of Twin Children: A Common Sense Guide for Parents. 2nd ed. Keith, Louis G., ed. (Twin Care Ser.). (Illus.). 150p. 1983. pap. 14.95 (ISBN 0-932254-04-7); text ed. 7.95 (ISBN 0-932254-03-9). Ctr Multiple Birth.
Watson, Peter. Twins: An Uncanny Relationship? 208p. 1983. pap. 6.95 (ISBN 0-8092-5649-5). Contemp Bks.
TWO-PHASE FLOW
see also Cavitation
Bergles, A. F. & Ishigai, S. Two Phase Flow Dynamics & Reactor Safety. 1981. 110.00 (ISBN 0-07-004904-1). McGraw.
Stanley, Marland L. Two-Phase Flow Measurements: Principles, Designs & Applications. (Technical Report of an International Colloquim on Two-Phase Flow Instrumentation Ser.). 568p. 1982. pap. text ed. 44.95x (ISBN 0-87664-699-2). Instru Soc.
TWO-PHASE MATERIALS
see Composite Materials
TYPE AND TYPE-FOUNDING
see also Advertising Layout and Typography; Type-Setting
Hutchings, R. S. The Western Heritage of Type Design. 130p. 1982. 35.00x (ISBN 0-284-39104-2, Pub. by C Skilton Scotland). State Mutual Bk.
TYPE-SETTING
see also Printing-Layout and Typography; Printing-Style Manuals; Type and Type-Founding
Larken, H. W. Compositors Work in Painting. 3rd ed. 382p. 1969. 29.00x (ISBN 0-905418-08-5, Pub. by Gresham England). State Mutual Bk.
Rudman, Jack. Compositor (Job) (Career Examination Ser.: C-26497). (Cloth bdg. avail. on request). pap. 10.00 (ISBN 0-8373-2649-4). Natl Learning.
TYPEWRITER SHORTHAND
see Stenotypy
TYPEWRITERS
Rigby, D. S. & Hanson, R. N. Production Typing Projects. 1980. text ed. 5.96 (ISBN 0-07-052836-5); tchr's manual & key avail. McGraw.
TYPEWRITING
Baron, Alvin. Bud's Easy Term Paper Typing Kit. 4th ed. 6p. (gr. 9-12). 1980. pap. text ed. 1.98 (ISBN 0-9609436-0-9). Lawrence Hse.
Bellavance, Diane. Typing Made Easy. (Illus.). 20p. 1982. pap. 2.00 (ISBN 0-9605276-1-3). DBA Bks.
Cook, F., et al. Language Arts Typing. 3rd ed. 1979. text ed. 12.96 (ISBN 0-07-012477-9); tchr's manual & key 7.40 (ISBN 0-07-012479-5). McGraw.
Drummond, A. M. & Coles-Mogford, A. M. Applied Typing. 4th ed. 240p. 1983. price not set (ISBN 0-07-084650-2). McGraw.
Etier, A. Faborn & Etier, Betty A. Individualized Typing. 176p. (Orig.). 1983. pap. text ed. 12.95 (ISBN 0-672-97934-9); instr's. guide 3.33 (ISBN 0-672-97935-7); tapes 125.00 (ISBN 0-672-97939-X). Bobbs.
Goodrich, Donna. How to Set Up & Run a Typing Service. (Small Business Ser.). 160p. 1983. pap. text ed. 8.95 (ISBN 0-471-86858-2). Wiley.
Lloyd, A. C., et al. Gregg College Typing, Series Five, Typing 75, Basic Kit. 320p. 1983. pap. 14.50x (includes text, guide, proofguide & easel) (ISBN 0-07-038322-7, Gregg). McGraw.
Lorenzen, Violette A. How to Type Practically Anything Easily. 52p. 1977. pap. text ed. 7.00 (ISBN 0-686-38824-0). V A Lorenzen.
West, Leonard J. Acquisition of Typewriting Skills. 2nd ed. 448p. 1983. text ed. 24.95 (ISBN 0-672-98444-X). Bobbs.
TYPEWRITING-PROGRAMMED INSTRUCTION
Marsh, Carole. Typing in Ten Minutes: On Any Keyboard - At Any Age. (Tomorrow's Books). (Illus.). 56p. 1983. 5.95 (ISBN 0-935326-12-X). Gallopade Pub Group.
TYPISTS
see also Typewriting
Goodrich, Donna. How to Set Up & Run a Typing Service. (Small Business Ser.). 160p. 1983. pap. text ed. 8.95 (ISBN 0-471-86858-2). Wiley.
TYPOGRAPHY
see Printing-Layout and Typography
TYPOGRAPHY, ADVERTISING
see Advertising Layout and Typography
TYRANNY
see Despotism
TYRANTS
see Dictators

U

UFO
see Flying Saucers
UKRAINE-HISTORY
Chirovsky, Nicholas L. An Introduction to Ukranian History, Vol. II: The Lithuanian-Rus' Commonwealth, the Polish Domination & the Cossack-Hetman State. (Illus.). 359p. 1983. 25.00 (ISBN 0-8022-2407-5). Philos Lib.
Szporluk, Roman. Ukraine: A Brief History. 2nd ed. LC 79-46644. 1982. pap. 6.50 (ISBN 0-686-43265-7). Cataract Pr.
UKRAINIAN LITERATURE
Khvylovy, Mykola. Works in Five Volumes, Vol. 3. Kostiuk, Hryhoriy, ed. LC 78-66383. (Ukrainian Ser.). 505p. 1982. 20.00 (ISBN 0-914834-20-7). Smoloskyp.
ULCERS
Goodman, Michael J. & Sparberg, Marshall. Ulcerative Colitis. LC 78-8686. (Clinical Gastroenterology Monographs). 1978. 39.95x (ISBN 0-471-48895-X, Pub. by Wiley Medical). Wiley.
ULTRASONIC DIAGNOSIS
see Diagnosis, Ultrasonic
ULTRASONIC TESTING
American Welding Society. Terms for Ultrasonic Testing in 11 Languages. 102p. 1967. 8.00 (ISBN 0-686-43363-7). Am Welding.
ULTRASONIC THERAPY
see Ultrasonic Waves-Therapeutic Use
ULTRASONIC WAVES-THERAPEUTIC USE
Kra, Siegfried J. Basic M-Mode Echocardiography. 1982. 37.50 (ISBN 0-87488-978-2). Med Exam.
Palacio, Alfredo. Atlas of Two-D Echocardiography. Jurade, Rafael L., tr. (Illus.). 216p. 1983. text ed. 65.00 (ISBN 0-914316-35-4). Yorke Med.
Talano, James V. Textbook of Two-Dimensional Echocardiography. write for info (ISBN 0-8089-1556-8). Grune.
ULTRASONICS
American Welding Society. Handbook on the Ultrasonic Examination of Welds. 1977. 28.00 (ISBN 0-686-43357-2). Am Welding.
Krautkraemer, J. & Krautkraemer, H. Ultrasonic Testing of Materials. 3rd, rev. ed. Zenzinger, B. W., tr. from Ger. (Illus.). 79.50 (ISBN 0-387-11733-4). Springer-Verlag.
Puskar, A. The Use of High-Intensity Ultrasonics. (Materials Science Monographs: No. 13). 304p. 1982. 70.25 (ISBN 0-444-99690-7). Elsevier.
ULTRASONICS IN MEDICINE
see also Ultrasonic Waves-Therapeutic Use
Anderhub, Beth. Manual of Abdominal Ultrasonography. (Illus.). 1983. write for info. (ISBN 0-8391-1804-X, 18589). Univ Park.
Hagen-Ansert, Sandra L. Textbook of Diagnostic Ultrasonography. 2nd ed. 800p. 1983. text ed. 54.95 (ISBN 0-8016-2016-3). Mosby.
Hanrath, P. Cardiovascular Diagnosis by Ultrasound. 1982. 39.50 (ISBN 90-247-2692-1, Pub. by Martinus Nijhoff Netherlands). Kluwer Boston.
Harper, A. Patricia, ed. Ultrasound Mammography. (Illus.). 1983. price not set (ISBN 0-8391-1807-4, 18090). Univ Park.
Kurjak, A., ed. Progress in Medical Ultrasound, Volume 3: Reviews & Comments. 376p. 1982. 67.50 (ISBN 0-444-90242-2, Excerpta Medica). Elsevier.
Levi, S., ed. Ultrasound & Cancer: Invited Papers & Selected Free Communications Presented at the First International Symposium, Brussels, Belgium, July 23-24, 1982. (International Congress Ser.: No. 587). 384p. 1982. 88.25 (ISBN 0-444-90270-8, Excerpta Medica). Elsevier.
Miskovitz, Christine & Peters, Bruce E. Diagnostic Medical Ultrasound Examination Review. 1983. pap. text ed. price not set (ISBN 0-87488-410-1). Med Exam.
Yiu-Chiu, Victoria S. & Chiu, Lee C. Atlas of Obstetrical Ultrasonography. (Illus.). 312p. 1982. 49.50 (ISBN 0-8391-1765-5, 18074). Univ Park.
ULTRA-VIOLET RAYS-THERAPEUTIC USE
Stillwell, G. Keith. Therapeutic Electricity & Ultraviolet Radiation. 3rd ed. (Illus.). 361p. 1983. lib. bdg. price not set (ISBN 0-683-07979-4). Williams & Wilkins.
ULTRA-VIOLET THERAPY
see Ultra-Violet Rays-Therapeutic Use
UNBELIEF
see Skepticism
UNCONSCIOUSNESS
see Subconsciousness
UNCONVENTIONAL WARFARE
see Subversive Activities
UNCOOKED FOOD
see Food, Raw
UNDECIDABLE THEORIES
see Goedel's Theorem
UNDERDEVELOPED AREAS
see also Community Development; Technical Assistance
Bertram, Christoph, ed. Third-World Conflict & International Security. 128p. 1982. 49.00x (ISBN 0-333-32955-4, Pub. by Macmillan England). State Mutual Bk.
Cassen, Robert & Jolly, Richard, eds. Rich Country Interests & Third World Development. LC 82-42561. 1982. 32.50x (ISBN 0-312-68101-1). St Martin.
Dworkin, Daniel M. Environmental Sciences in Developing Countries: Scope Report 4. 70p. 1978. pap. 8.00x (ISBN 0-471-99597-5). Wiley.
Feinberg, Richard E. The Intemperate Zone: The Third World Challenge to U.S. Foreign Policy. 1983. 17.50 (ISBN 0-393-01712-5). Norton.
Franck, Thomas M. Human Rights in Third World Perspective, Vol. 1-3. 1982. 150.00 (ISBN 0-379-20725-7). Set. Oceana.
Galbraith, John K. The Voice of the Poor: Essays in Economic & Political Persuasion. 96p. 1983. 8.95 (ISBN 0-674-94295-7). Harvard U Pr.
Geyer, R. F. & Zouwen, J. van der, eds. Dependence & Inequality: A Systems Approach to the Problems of Mexico & Other Developing Countries. (Systems Science & World Order Library: Innovations in Systems Science). (Illus.). 336p. 1982. 35.00 (ISBN 0-08-027952-X). Pergamon.
Glattbach, Jack. Media & the Developing World: Pluralism or Polarization? (Seven Springs Studies). 1982. pap. 3.00 (ISBN 0-943006-08-2). Seven Springs.
Harrison, Paul. Third World Tomorrow: A Report from the Battlefront on the War Against Poverty. LC 82-19095. 416p. (Orig.). 1983. pap. 7.95 (ISBN 0-8298-0646-6). Pilgrim NY.
Jha, L. K. North South Debate. 153p. 1982. text ed. 10.75x (ISBN 0-391-02769-7, 41257). Humanities.
McDonald, John W. The North-South Dialogue & the United Nations. LC 82-1039. 24p. 1982. 1.25 (ISBN 0-934742-16-2, Inst Study Diplomacy). Geo U Sch For Serv.
Mushkat, Marion. The Third World & Peace: Some Aspects of Problems of the Inter-Relationship of Interdevelopment & International Security. LC 82-774. 356p. 1982. 27.50x (ISBN 0-312-80039-8). St Martin.
Offiong, Daniel O. Imperialism & Dependency: Obstacles in African Development. 304p. 1983. 12.95 (ISBN 0-88258-126-0); pap. 6.95 (ISBN 0-88258-127-9). Howard U Pr.
Papousek, D. Peasant-Potters of Los Pueblos. (Studies in Developing Countries: No. 27). 182p. 1981. 15.75 (ISBN 0-686-82313-3, 41327, Pub. by Van Gorcum Holland). Humanities.
Report of the United Nations Conference on the Least Developed Countries. 104p. 1983. pap. 10.00 (ISBN 0-686-43285-1, UN 82/1/8, UN). Unipub.
Sarin, Madhu. Urban Planning in the Third World: The Chandigarh Experience. 240p. 1982. 31.00 (ISBN 0-7201-1637-6, Pub. by Mansell England). Wilson.
Weiss, Thomas G. & Jennings, Anthony. More for the Least? Prospects for Poorest Countries in the Eighties. LC 82-48170. 208p. 1982. 24.95x (ISBN 0-669-06009-7). Lexington Bks.
UNDERDEVELOPED AREAS-AGRICULTURE
Anderson, Dennis & Khambata, Farida. Financing Small Scale Industry & Agriculture in Developing Countries: The Merits & Limitations of Commercial Policies. LC 82-8664. (World Bank Staff Working Papers: No. 519). (Orig.). 1982. pap. 3.00 (ISBN 0-8213-0007-5). World Bank.
Collinson, M. P. Farm Management in Peasant Agriculture. (Encore Edition Ser.). 470p. 1983. write for info. softcover (ISBN 0-86531-558-2). Westview.
Deere, Carmen & Leal, Magdalena Leon de. Women in Andean Agriculture: Peasant Production & Rural Wage Employment in Colombia & Peru. Internatiojnal Labour Office, ed. (Women, Work & Development Ser.: No. 4). xii, 172p. (Orig.). 1982. pap. 11.40 (ISBN 92-2-103106-3). Intl Labour Office.
Hanson, Haldore & Borlaug, Norman. Wheat in the Third World. (IADS Development Oriented Literature Ser.). 192p. 1982. lib. bdg. 18.00 (ISBN 0-86531-357-1). Westview.
Kurian, Rachel. Women Workers in the Sri Lanka Plantation Sector: An Historical & Contemporary Analysis. International Labour Office, ed. (Women, Work & Development Ser.: No. 5). xiv, 138p. (Orig.). 1982. pap. 11.40 (ISBN 92-2-102992-1). Intl Labour Office.
Molnar, Joseph J. & Clonts, Howard A., eds. Transferring Food Production Technology to Developing Nations: Economic & Social Dimensions. (Replica Edition Ser.). 174p. 1983. softcover 19.50x (ISBN 0-86531-957-X). Westview.
The Private Marketing Entrepreneur & Rural Development. (FAO Agricultural Services Bulletin Ser.: No. 51). 115p. 1983. pap. 8.75 (ISBN 92-5-101241-5, F2355, FAO). Unipub.
Schultz, Theodore W. Transforming Traditional Agriculture. LC 82-20271. xiv, 212p. 1964. pap. 7.95 (ISBN 0-226-74075-7). U of Chicago Pr.
UNDERDEVELOPED AREAS-COMMERCE
Kaynak. Marketing in the Third World. 320p. 1982. 29.95 (ISBN 0-03-062179-8). Praeger.
Krueger, Anne O. Trade & Employment in Developing Countries: Synthesis & Conclusions, Vol. 3. LC 80-15826. (National Bureau of Economic Research - Monograph). 232p. 1983. 25.00x (ISBN 0-226-45494-0). U of Chicago Pr.
The Private Marketing Entrepreneur & Rural Development. (FAO Agricultural Services Bulletin Ser.: No. 51). 115p. 1983. pap. 8.75 (ISBN 92-5-101241-5, F2355, FAO). Unipub.
Ramachandran, H. Behaviour in Space: Rural Marketing in an Underdeveloped Economy. 121p. 1982. text ed. 14.50x (ISBN 0-391-02784-0, 40855, Pub. by Concept India). Humanities.
UNDERDEVELOPED AREAS-ECONOMIC CONDITIONS
Aiken, S. R. & Leigh, C. H. Development & Environment in Peninsular Malaysia. 1982. 34.50 (ISBN 0-07-099204-5). McGraw.
Anderson, Dennis. Small Industry in Developing Countries: A Discussion of Issues. LC 82-11130. (World Bank Staff Working Papers: No. 518). (Orig.). 1982. pap. 3.00 (ISBN 0-8213-0006-7). World Bank.
Bauer, P. T. Equality, the Third World & Economic Delusion. 304p. 1983. pap. text ed. 7.95x (ISBN 0-674-25986-6). Harvard U Pr.
Devindex 1981. 186p. 1983. pap. 13.00 (ISBN 0-88936-358-7, IDRC 203, IDRC). Unipub.
Gulati, I. S. International Monetary Development & the Third World: A Proposal to Readress the Balance. (R. C. Dutt Lectures on Political Economy Ser.: 1978). 48p. 1980. pap. text ed. 2.95x (ISBN 0-686-42711-4, Pub. by Orient Longman Ltd India). Apt Bks.
Jansen, Karen, ed. Monetarism, Economic Crisis & the Third World. 224p. 1983. text ed. 30.00x (ISBN 0-7146-3222-8, F Cass Co). Biblio Dist.
Lang, Laszlo. The Poor Rich. LC 82-141712. (Studies on Developing Countries: No. 108). 130p. (Orig.). 1981. pap. 13.50x (ISBN 963-301-081-0). Intl Pubns Serv.
Ligeti, Sandor. Selective Credit Policy in the Developing Countries. LC 82-177319. (Studies on Developing Countries: No. 109). 78p. (Orig.). 1981. pap. 7.50x (ISBN 963-301-082-9). Intl Pubns Serv.
Loehr, William & Powelson, John P. Threat to Development: Pitfalls of the NIE. (Special Study in Social, Political, & Economic Developmen). 160p. 1982. lib. bdg. 22.00X (ISBN 0-86531-128-5); pap. text ed. 10.00 (ISBN 0-86531-129-3). Westview.
MacAndrews, C. & Chia, L. S. Developing Economies & the Environment: The Southeast Asia Experience. 1982. 13.00x (ISBN 0-07-099458-7). McGraw.
Planned Development & Self-Management. (UNCRD Working Paper: No. 82-8). 15p. 1983. pap. 6.00 (ISBN 0-686-43298-3, CRD 145, UNCRD). Unipub.
Regional Studies: The Geneva Programme. (UNCRD Working Paper: No. 82-1). 98p. 1983. pap. 6.00 (ISBN 0-686-43302-5, CRD 146, UNCRD). Unipub.
The Urban Informal Sector in Developing Countries. 225p. 1981. pap. 14.25 (ISBN 92-2-102591-8, ILO 195, ILO). Unipub.
Van Schendel, W. Peasant Mobility. (Studies in Developing Countries: No. 26). 372p. 1981. text ed. 25.75x (41317, Pub. by Van Gorcum Holland). Humanities.
Wells, Louis T., Jr. Third World Multinationals: The Rise of Foreign Investment from Developing Countries. 272p. 1983. 25.00 (ISBN 0-262-23113-1). MIT Pr.
Yusuf, Abdulqawi. Legal Aspects of Trade Preferences for Developing States. 1982. lib. bdg. 43.50 (ISBN 90-247-2583-6, Pub. by Martinus Nijhoff Netherlands). Kluwer Boston.
UNDERDEVELOPED AREAS-EDUCATION
see Education-Underdeveloped Areas
UNDERDEVELOPED AREAS-FINANCE
Anderson, Dennis & Khambata, Farida. Financing Small Scale Industry & Agriculture in Developing Countries: The Merits & Limitations of Commercial Policies. LC 82-8664. (World Bank Staff Working Papers: No. 519). (Orig.). 1982. pap. 3.00 (ISBN 0-8213-0007-5). World Bank.
Ayres, Robert L. Banking on the Poor: The World Bank & World Poverty. 296p. 1983. 17.50x (ISBN 0-262-01070-4). MIT Pr.
Davey, Kenneth. Financing Regional Government: International Practices & Their Relevance to the Third World. (Public Administration in Developing Countries Ser.). 220p. 1983. 24.95 (ISBN 0-471-10356-X, Pub. by Wiley-Interscience). Wiley.
Financing Urban Development in Developing Countries. (UNCRD Working Paper: No. 82-6). 56p. 1983. pap. 6.00 (ISBN 0-686-43294-0, CRD 141, UNCRD). Unipub.
Gilbert, Alan, ed. Development Planning & Spatial Structure. LC 75-30804. 207p. 1976. 34.50x (ISBN 0-471-29904-9, Pub. by Wiley-Interscience). Wiley.
Mikesell, Raymond F. Foreign Investment in Mining Projects: Case Studies of Recent Experiences. LC 82-14113. 320p. 1983. text ed. 30.00 (ISBN 0-89946-170-0). Oelgeschlager.
Virmani, Arvind. The Nature of Credit Markets in Less Developed Countries: A Framework for Policy Analysis. LC 82-11087. (World Bank Staff Working Papers: No. 524). (Orig.). 1982. pap. text ed. 5.00 (ISBN 0-8213-0019-9). World Bank.
UNDERDEVELOPED AREAS-IRRIGATION
Hazlewood, A. & Livingstone, I. Irrigation Economics in Poor Countries: Illustrated by the Usango Plains of Tanzania. 150p. 1982. 25.00 (ISBN 0-08-027451-X). Pergamon.
UNDERDEVELOPED AREAS-POLITICS AND GOVERNMENT
Higgott, Richard A. Political Development Theory: The Contemporary Debate. LC 82-42718. 140p. 1983. 18.95x (ISBN 0-312-62225-2). St Martin.
Horowitz, Irving L. Beyond Empire & Revolution: Militarization & Consolidation in the Third World. 350p. 1982. 19.95 (ISBN 0-19-502931-3). Oxford U Pr.
Marasinghe, M. L., ed. Third World Legal Studies: Law in Alternative Strategies of Rural Development. 313p. 1982. pap. 15.00 (ISBN 0-686-37983-7). Intl Ctr Law.
Mawhood, Philip. Local Government for Development: The Experience of Tropical Africa. (Public Administration in Developing Countries Ser.). 250p. 1983. price not set (ISBN 0-471-10510-4, Pub. by Wiley-Interscience). Wiley.
Smith, Anthony D. State & Nation in the Third World: The Western State & African Nationalism. LC 82-10672. 180p. 1983. 25.00x (ISBN 0-312-75605-4). St Martin.
Standing, Guy. Conceptualising Territorial Mobility in Low-Income Countries. International Labour Office, ed. 50p. (Orig.). 1982. pap. 5.70 (ISBN 92-2-102929-8). Intl Labour Office.
Vengroff, Richard. Development Administration at the Local Level: The Case of Zaire. (Foreign & Comparative Studies Program, African Ser.: No. 40). (Illus.). 1983. pap. price not set (ISBN 0-915984-63-6). Syracuse U Foreign Comp.
White, Gordon & Murray, Robin, eds. Revolutionary Socialist Development in the Third World. LC 82-23705. 272p. 1983. 26.00x (ISBN 0-8131-1485-3). U Pr of Ky.
UNDERDEVELOPED AREAS-SOCIAL CONDITIONS
Horowitz, Irving L. Beyond Empire & Revolution: Militarization & Consolidation in the Third World. 350p. 1982. 19.95 (ISBN 0-19-502931-3). Oxford U Pr.
Inkeles, Alex, et al. Exploring Individual Modernity. 448p. 1983. text ed. 24.00 (ISBN 0-231-05442-4). Columbia U Pr.
Kalmar, Gregory. Gandhism. LC 81-182559. (Studies of Developing Countries: No. 104). 82p. (Orig.). 1980. pap. 13.50x (ISBN 963-301-063-2). Intl Pubns Serv.
Model Life Tables for Developing Countries. (Population Studies: No. 77). 23.00 (ISBN 0-686-84904-3, E.81.XIII.7.). UN.
Model Life Tables for Developing Countries. 351p. 1983. pap. 23.00 (ISBN 0-686-84905-1, UN81/13/7, UN). Unipub.
Murphy, Kathleen J. Macroproject Development in the Third World: An Analysis of Transnational Partnerships. (Replica Edition). 150p. 1982. softcover 17.00x (ISBN 0-86531-939-1). Westview.
National Policy Implications of the Basic Needs Model. (UNCRD Working Paper: No. 82-10). 22p. 1983. pap. 6.00 (ISBN 0-686-43296-7, CRD 142, UNCRD). Unipub.
Planning for Basic Needs at the Micro-Area Level. 21p. 1983. pap. 6.00 (ISBN 0-686-43299-1, CRD 143, UNCRD). Unipub.
Rondinelli, Dennis A. Secondary Cities in Developing Countries: Policies for Diffusing Urbanization. (Sage Library of Social Research). (Illus.). 256p. 1983. 25.00 (ISBN 0-8039-1945-X); pap. 12.50 (ISBN 0-8039-1946-8). Sage.
The Urban Informal Sector in Developing Countries. 225p. 1981. pap. 14.25 (ISBN 92-2-102591-8, ILO 195, ILO). Unipub.
Van Schendel, W. Peasant Mobility. (Studies in Developing Countries: No. 26). 372p. 1981. text ed. 25.75x (41317, Pub. by Van Gorcum Holland). Humanities.
UNDERDEVELOPED AREAS-WOMEN
Deere, Carmen & Leal, Magdalena Leon de. Women in Andean Agriculture: Peasant Production & Rural Wage Employment in Colombia & Peru. Internatiojnal Labour Office, ed. (Women, Work & Development Ser.: No. 4). xii, 172p. (Orig.). 1982. pap. 11.40 (ISBN 92-2-103106-3). Intl Labour Office.
Fatehally, Laeeq, ed. Women in the Third World. 155p. 1980. pap. 7.95x (ISBN 0-86590-016-7, Jaico Books India). Apt Bks.
Kurian, Rachel. Women Workers in the Sri Lanka Plantation Sector: An Historical & Contemporary Analysis. International Labour Office, ed. (Women, Work & Development Ser.: No. 5). xiv, 138p. (Orig.). 1982. pap. 11.40 (ISBN 92-2-102992-1). Intl Labour Office.
UNDERDEVELOPED AREAS, AID TO
see Technical Assistance
UNDERGRADUATES
see College Students
UNDERGROUND CONSTRUCTION
see also Foundations; Tunnels and Tunneling
Dams & Earthquake. 304p. 1981. 129.00x (ISBN 0-7277-0123-1, Pub. by Telford England). State Mutual Bk.

Kern, Barbara & Kern, Ken. The Earth Sheltered: Owner-Built Home. LC 82-99912. (Illus.). 272p. (Orig.). 1982. pap. 9.95 (ISBN 0-910225-00-1). Owner-Builder.

Parker, Albert D. & Barrie, Donald S. Planning & Estimating Heavy Construction. 640p. 1983. 39.95 (ISBN 0-07-048489-9, P&RB). McGraw.

Plattes, Gabriel. A Discovery of Subterraneall Treasure. 37.50 (ISBN 0-686-38306-0). IMM North Am.

Wade, Herb. Building Underground: The Design & Construction Handbook for Earth-Sheltered Houses. Balitas, Maggie, ed. (Illus.). 320p. (Orig.). 1983. 19.95 (ISBN 0-87857-421-2, 04-000-0); pap. 14.95 (ISBN 0-87857-422-0, 04-000-1). Rodale Pr Inc.

UNDERGROUND MOVEMENTS, (WORLD WAR, 1939-1945)

see World War, 1939-1945–Underground Movements

UNDERGROUND STRUCTURES

see Underground Construction

UNDERGROUND WATER

see Water, Underground

UNDERTAKERS AND UNDERTAKING

Rudman, Jack. Mortuary Technician. (Career Examination Ser.: C-514). (Cloth bdg. avail. on request). pap. 10.00 (ISBN 0-8373-0514-4). Natl Learning.

UNDERWATER ACOUSTICS

see also Sonar

Albers, Vernon M., ed. Underwater Sound. LC 72-79141. (Benchmark Papers in Acoustics: Vol. 1). 468p. 1972. text ed. 55.00 (ISBN 0-87933-006-6). Hutchinson Ross.

Urick, Robert J. Principles of Underwater Sound. 3rd, rev. ed. (Illus.). 352p. 1983. 45.75 (ISBN 0-07-066087-5, P&RB). McGraw.

UNDERWATER ARCHAEOLOGY

Forsberg, Gerald. Salvage from the Sea. (Illus.). 179p. 1978. 14.95 (ISBN 0-7100-8698-9). Routledge & Kegan.

Masters, P. M. & Fleming, N. C., eds. Quarternary Coastlines & Marine Archaeology: Towards the Prehistory of Land Bridges & Continental Shelves. LC 82-45021. Date not set. price not set (ISBN 0-12-479250-2). Acad Pr.

UNDERWATER EXPLORATION

see also Marine Biology; Oceanographic Research; Photography, Submarine; Skin Diving; Treasure-Trove; Underwater Archaeology

Jones, Michael E. The Logistic Support of Subsea Oil Production. 116p. 1983. 40.00x (ISBN 0-8448-1433-4). Crane-Russak.

UNDERWATER EXPLORATION (ARCHAEOLOGY)

see Underwater Archaeology

UNDERWATER PHOTOGRAPHY

see Photography, Submarine

UNDERWATER SWIMMING

see Skin Diving

UNDERWRITING

see Insurance; Securities

UNDULATED PARAKEET

see Budgerigars

UNEMPLOYED

see also Charities; Economic Assistance, Domestic; Employment Agencies; Food Relief; Full Employment Policies; Insurance, Unemployment; Job Vacancies; Migrant Labor; Part-Time Employment; Public Welfare

Carrol, Freida. Unemployment Challenge Log Workbook. 60p. 1983. pap. 9.95 (ISBN 0-939476-86-X). Biblio Pr GA.

Carrol, Frieda. Guide for the Unemployed Workbook. 60p. Date not set. 9.95 (ISBN 0-939476-80-0). Biblio Pr GA.

Fineman, Stephen. White Collar Unemployment. (Organizational Change & Development Ser.). 180p. 1982. 29.95 (ISBN 0-471-10490-6, Pub. by Wiley-Interscience). Wiley.

Ginsburg, Helen. Full Employment & Public Policy: The United States & Sweden. LC 76-55536. 256p. 1983. 24.95x (ISBN 0-669-01318-8). Lexington Bks.

Kiewiet, D. Roderick. Macroeconomics & Micropolitics: The Electoral Effects of Economic Issues. LC 82-21985. (Illus.). 160p. 1983. lib. bdg. 16.00x (ISBN 0-226-43532-6). U of Chicago Pr.

OECD Staff. The Challenge of Unemployment. 165p. (Orig.). 1982. pap. 17.00x (ISBN 92-64-12332-6). OECD.

Rodgers, Allan G. Resource Material for Handling Unemployment Cases in Massachusetts. Spriggs, Marshall T., ed. (Tools of the Trade for Massachusetts Lawyers Ser.). (Orig.). 1983. pap. price not set (ISBN 0-910001-04-9). MA Poverty Law.

Sayler, Mary H. Why Are You Home, Dad? (gr. 1-6). 1983. 4.95 (ISBN 0-8054-4276-6). Broadman.

Schervish, Paul G. The Structural Determinants of Unemployment: Vulnerability & Power in Market Relations. (Quantitative Studies in Social Relations). Date not set. price not set (ISBN 0-12-623950-9). Acad Pr.

Update Publicare Research Staff. Guide for the Unemployed Update: Notebook of Back Issues. 35p. 1983. pap. text ed. 8.00 (ISBN 0-686-38893-3). Update Pub Co.

UNEMPLOYED–EUROPE

Van Ginneken, Wouter & Garzuel, Michel. Unemployment in France, the Federal Republic of Germany & the Netherlands: A Survey of Trends, Causes & Policy Options. iii, 116p. (Orig.). 1982. pap. 10.00 (ISBN 92-2-103032-6). Intl Labour Office.

UNEMPLOYED–GREAT BRITAIN

Jackson, Michael P. & Hanby, Victor J. British Work Creation Programmes. 87p. 1982. pap. text ed. 23.50x (ISBN 0-566-00523-9). Gower Pub Ltd.

UNEMPLOYMENT

see Labor Supply; Unemployed

UNEMPLOYMENT INSURANCE

see Insurance, Unemployment

UNESCO

see United Nations Educational, Scientific and Cultural Organization

UNICAMERAL LEGISLATURES

see Legislative Bodies

UNICORNS

Green, Michael, annotations by. & illus. Unicornis: On the History & Truth of the Unicorn. (Illus.). 64p. (Orig.). 1983. 14.95 (ISBN 0-89471-216-0); lib. bdg. 15.90 (ISBN 0-89471-207-1). Running Pr.

UNIDENTIFIED FLYING OBJECTS

see Flying Saucers

UNIFORMS, MILITARY

see also subdivision Army or Navy under names of countries, with or without the additional subdivision Uniforms

Bender, Roger J. Uniforms, Organization & History of the Waffen-SS, Vol. 1. (Illus.). 160p. 1969. 16.95 (ISBN 0-912138-02-5). Bender Pub CA.

Uniforms, Organization & History of the Waffen-SS, Vol. 4. (Illus.). 208p. 1975. 16.95 (ISBN 0-912138-13-0). Bender Pub CA.

UNIFORMS, NAVAL

see Uniforms, Military

UNILEVER, LTD.

Reader, W. R. Fifty Years of Unilever. (Illus.). 1980. 18.95 (ISBN 0-434-62501-9, Pub. by Heinemann). David & Charles.

UNION, MYSTICAL

see Mystical Union

UNION CATALOGS

see Catalogs, Union

UNION OF SOUTH AFRICA

see South Africa

UNION WITH CHRIST

see Mystical Union

UNIONS, TRADE

see Trade-Unions

UNIT TRUSTS

see Investment Trusts

UNITARIANISM

see also Jesus Christ–Divinity; Trinity

The Works of William E. Channing, D.D. 1060p. 1982. Repr. of 1889 ed. lib. bdg. 100.00 (ISBN 0-8495-0959-9). Arden Lib.

UNITED AIR LINES, INC.

Taylor, Frank J. High Horizons: Daredevil Flying Postmen to Modern Magic Carpet: The United Airlines Story. Rev. ed. (Airlines History Project Ser.). Date not set. price not set (ISBN 0-404-19338-2). AMS Pr.

UNITED NATIONS

Here are entered works about the United Nations and about its relations with other countries, either as a group or individualy.

Acronyms & Abbreviations Covering the United Nations System & Other International Organizations. 26.00 (ISBN 0-686-84918-3, A/C/E/F/R/S.81.I.26). UN.

Assessing the United Nations Scale of Assessments: Is it Fair? Is it Equitable? (Unitar Policy & Efficacy Studies). 5.00 (ISBN 0-686-43220-7, E.82.XV.PE/9). UN.

Bloomfield, Lincoln P. & Yost, Charles W. What Future for the U. N.? 40p. pap. 2.00 (ISBN 0-87855-741-5). Transaction Bks.

Index to Proceedings of the General Assembly: Thirty-Sixth Session, 1981-82. 422p. 1983. pap. 26.00 (ISBN 0-686-43281-9, UN 82/1/15, UN). Unipub.

Index to Proceedings of the Trusteeship Council: 49th Session. 10p. 1983. pap. 2.50 (ISBN 0-686-43282-7, UN 82/1/18, UN). Unipub.

McDonald, John W. The North-South Dialogue & the United Nations. LC 82-1039. 24p. 1982. 1.25 (ISBN 0-934742-16-2, Inst Study Diplomacy). Geo U Sch For Serv.

Rules of Procedure of the General Assembly. 88p. 1983. pap. 6.00 (ISBN 0-686-43288-6, UN 82/1/9, UN). Unipub.

United Nations Assn. of the U.S.A. Issues Before the Thirty-Seventh General Assembly of the United Nations. Puchala, Donald J., ed. 168p. 1982. 17.95 (ISBN 0-669-06398-3). Lexington Bks.

Your United Nations: The Official Guidebook. 9.95 (ISBN 0-686-84917-5, E.82.I.10). UN.

Your United Nations: The Official Guidebook. 96p. 1983. 9.95 (ISBN 0-686-43292-4, UN 82/1/10 PA, UN); pap. 5.95 (ISBN 0-686-43293-2, UN 82/1/10 CL). Unipub.

UNITED NATIONS–SECURITY COUNCIL

Caradon & Goldberg, Arthur J. U. N. Security Council Resolution 242: A Case Study in Diplomatic Ambiguity. LC 81-1671. 64p. 1981. 4.00 (ISBN 0-934742-11-1, Inst Study Diplomacy). Geo U Sch For Serv.

UNITED NATIONS–SPECIALIZED AGENCIES

see International Agencies

UNITED NATIONS–YEARBOOKS

United Nations. Demographic Year Book 1980. 65.00 (ISBN 0-686-84891-8, E/F.81.XIII.1). UN.

--Yearbook of the United Nations 1979, Vol. 33. LC 47-7191. 1294p. 1982. 72.00x (ISBN 0-8002-3038-8). Intl Pubns Serv.

United Nations Disarmament Yearbook: Vol. 6, 1981. 35.00 (ISBN 0-686-84906-X, E.82.IX.6). UN.

Yearbook of the United Nations, 1979, Vol. 33. 1979. 72.00 (ISBN 0-686-84915-9, E.82.I.1). UN.

Yearbook of the United Nations 1979, Vol. 33. 1441p. 1983. 72.00 (ISBN 0-686-43291-6, UN 82/1/ICL, UN). Unipub.

Yearbook of World Energy Supplies 1970-1979. 60.00 (ISBN 0-686-84911-6, E/F.80.XVII.7). UN.

Yearbook of World Energy Supplies 1980. 60.00 (ISBN 0-686-84913-2, E/F.81.XVII.10). UN.

UNITED NATIONS EDUCATIONAL, SCIENTIFIC AND CULTURAL ORGANIZATION

Records of the General Conference Twenty-First Session Belgrade 1980 Volume 2: Reports. 295p. 1981. pap. 15.00 (ISBN 92-3-101960-0, U1222, UNESCO). Unipub.

Records of the General Conference Twenty-First Session Proceedings. 1471p. 1980. pap. 46.50 (ISBN 9-23-002010-9, U1235, UNESCO). Unipub.

UNITED STATES

see also names of individual states; names of areas and regions of the United States

Gary, Skipper. America the Beautiful. (Social Studies). 24p. (gr. 4-5). 1979. wkbk. 5.00 (ISBN 0-8209-0238-1, SS-5). ESP.

Geraghty, Tony. This Is the SAS: A Pictorial History of the Special Air Service Regiment. LC 82-16264. (Illus.). 152p. 1983. 16.95 (ISBN 0-668-05725-4, 5725). Arco.

Information Please Book of United States Facts, 1983. 224p. (Orig.). 1983. pap. 2.95 (ISBN 0-89479-124-9). A & W Pubs.

Justus, Fred. Our State. (Social Studies Ser.). 24p. (gr. 3-4). 1980. wkbk. 5.00 (ISBN 0-8209-0237-3, SS-4). ESP.

Kakavelakis, Demetris. Massa Confusa: A Vision for America. Anagnostopoulos, Athan, tr. from Gr. 70p. (Orig.). Date not set. pap. text ed. 7.95 (ISBN 0-916586-88-X). Hellenic Coll Pr.

UNITED STATES–AIR FORCE

Beverley, George H. Pioneer in the U. S. Air Corps: The Memoirs of Brigadier General George H. Beverley. 1982. pap. 9.95x (ISBN 0-89745-029-9). Sunflower U Pr.

Ellis, Paul. Aircraft of the USAF. (Illus.). 192p. 1980. 19.95 (ISBN 0-86720-576-8); pap. 12.95 (ISBN 0-86720-577-6). Sci Bks Intl.

Rust, Kenn C. The Ninth Air Force Story. (WW-II Air Forces History Ser.). (Illus.). 64p. 1983. pap. 7.95 (ISBN 0-911852-93-X). Hist Aviation.

UNITED STATES–ALIENS

see Aliens

UNITED STATES–ANTIQUITIES

see also Indians of North America–Antiquities

Coons, Quentin & Krusell, Cynthia H. The Winslows of "Carewell". Before & after the Mayflower. 1975. 3.00 (ISBN 0-686-38915-8). Pilgrim Hall.

Evler, R. C. & Gummerman, G. S., eds. Investigations of the Southwestern Anthropological Research Group: An Experiment in Archaeological Cooperation. (MNA Bulletin Ser.: No. 50). 1978. pap. 5.95 (ISBN 0-89734-018-3). Mus Northern Ariz.

Hamilton, Henry W. & Griffin, James B. The Spiro Mound, Vol. 14. Chapman, Carl H., ed. (The Missouri Archaeologist). (Illus.). 276p. 1981. pap. 10.00 (ISBN 0-943414-06-7). MO Arch Soc.

Hume, Ivor Noel. Discoveries in Martin's Hundred. (Williamsburg Archaeological Ser.). (Illus.). 64p. (Orig.). 1983. pap. 2.95 (ISBN 0-87935-069-5). Williamsburg.

Robbins, Roland W. Pilgrim John Alden's Progress: Archaeological Excavations in Duxbury. 1969. 2.00 (ISBN 0-686-38916-6). Pilgrim Hall.

Schmits, Larry J. & Ray, Jack H. The Missouri Archaeologist, Vol. 43. LC 44-14131. (Illus.). 120p. 1982. pap. 6.00 (ISBN 0-943414-05-9). MO Arch Soc.

UNITED STATES–ARCHIVES

see Archives

UNITED STATES–ARMED FORCES

see also United States–Air Force; United States–Army; United States–Marine Corps; United States–National Guard; United States–Navy

Margiotta, Franklin D. & Brown, James. Changing U. S. Military Manpower Realities. (Special Studies in Military Affairs). 290p. 1983. lib. bdg. 25.00 (ISBN 0-89158-935-X). Westview.

Scoggan, Nita. Pillars of the Pentagon. (Illus.). 176p. 1982. pap. 4.95 (ISBN 0-910487-00-6). Royalty Pub.

UNITED STATES–ARMED FORCES–EUROPE

Mako, William P. U. S. Ground Forces & the Defense of Central Europe. LC 82-45977. (Studies in Defense Policy). 200p. 1983. 22.95; pap. 8.95 (ISBN 0-8157-5443-4). Brookings.

UNITED STATES–ARMY

Goldman, Peter & Fuller, Tony. Charlie Company: What Vietnam Did to Us. (Illus.). 384p. 1983. 15.95 (ISBN 0-688-01549-2). Morrow.

Ogburn, Charlton. The Marauders. LC 82-16149. 307p. 1982. pap. 6.50 (ISBN 0-688-01625-1, Quill). Morrow.

UNITED STATES–ARMY–CORPS OF ENGINEERS

Hall, Edward N. The Art of Destructive Management: What Hath Man Wrought. 1983. 8.95 (ISBN 0-533-05601-2). Vantage.

UNITED STATES–ARMY–MANHATTAN ENGINEERING DISTRICT

Groves, Leslie M. Now It Can Be Told: The Story of the Manhattan Project. (Quality Paperbacks Ser.). (Illus.). 464p. 1983. pap. 9.95 (ISBN 0-306-80189-2). Da Capo.

UNITED STATES–ARMY–MEDALS, BADGES, DECORATIONS, ETC.

Emerson, William K. Chevrons: Illustrated History & Catalog of U. S. Army Insignia. LC 82-600002. (Illus.). 350p. 1983. text ed. 49.50 (ISBN 0-87474-412-1). Smithsonian.

UNITED STATES–ARMY–SPECIAL FORCES

Simpson, Charles M. Inside the Green Berets: The First Thirty Years a History of the U.S. Army Special Forces. (Illus.). 272p. 1983. 15.95 (ISBN 0-89141-163-1). Presidio Pr.

UNITED STATES–ARMY AIR CORPS–HISTORY

Kelsey, Benjamin S. The Dragon's Teeth: The Creation of United States Air Power for World War II. (Illus.). 148p. 1982. 15.00 (ISBN 0-87474-574-8). Smithsonian.

UNITED STATES–BIBLIOGRAPHY

Kellogg, Jefferson B. & Walker, Robert H., eds. Sources for American Studies. LC 82-11701. (Contributions in American Studies: No. 64). (Illus.). 581p. 1983. lib. bdg. 45.00 (ISBN 0-313-22555-9, WTO/). Greenwood.

UNITED STATES–BIOGRAPHY

Auster, Paul. The Invention of Solitude. LC 82-16757. (Illus.). 174p. (Orig.). 1982. pap. 6.00 (ISBN 0-915342-37-5). SUN.

Benner, Judith A. Sul Ross: Soldier, Statesman, Educator. LC 82-45891. (Centennial Series of the Association of Former Students: No. 13). (Illus.). 344p. 1983. 19.50x (ISBN 0-89096-142-5). Tex A&M Univ Pr.

Coolidge, Charles E. Zig-Zag. 1983. 6.95 (ISBN 0-686-84429-7). Vantage.

Cruz, Manny & Symington, Nikki. Alice Barnes-American Activist. Kern, Ann T., ed. (Illus.). 52p. (Orig.). 1982. pap. 7.50 (ISBN 0-686-38731-7). Connections CA.

Cunningham, Robert S. Halos & Pitchforks: Philosophical Ramblings of a Wandering Physician. 1983. 8.95 (ISBN 0-533-05614-4). Vantage.

Downs, Robert B., et al. Memorable Americans. 400p. 1983. lib. bdg. 23.50 (ISBN 0-87287-360-9). Libs Unl.

Gettleman, Marvin E. An Elusive Presence: The Discovery of John H. Finley & His America. (Illus.). 310p. 1983. Repr. of 1979 ed. lib. bdg. 22.25 (ISBN 0-8191-2714-0). U Pr of Amer.

Hanes, Mari & Rearick, Ron. Iceman: The Story of Ron Rearick. LC 82-90708. 85p. (Orig.). 1982. pap. write for info. (ISBN 0-9609206-0-9). Rearick.

Hubbard, Elbert. Little Journeys to the Homes of American Statesmen. 436p. 1982. Repr. of 1898 ed. lib. bdg. 35.00 (ISBN 0-89984-914-8). Century Bookbindery.

Hutton, Artley O. Oh! What a Time! 1983. 10.95 (ISBN 0-533-05528-8). Vantage.

Jin & Jim's Love Story. 64p. 1983. 5.95 (ISBN 0-89962-320-4). Todd & Honeywell.

Kern, Florence. Captain William Cooke Pease: Coast Guard Pioneer. 1983. 4.95 (ISBN 0-686-38462-8). Alised.

Littell, Norman M. Trails of the Sea. 1983. 12.95 (ISBN 0-533-05304-8). Vantage.

McGowen, Lee W. Mary Joe. 140p. 1983. 6.95 (ISBN 0-89962-319-0). Todd & Honeywell.

Michaelis, David T. The Best of Friends: Profiles of Extraordinary Friendships. (Illus.). 288p. 1983. 13.95 (ISBN 0-688-01558-1). Morrow.

Mumford, Lewis. Sketches From Life: The Autobiography of Lewis Munford--The Early Years. LC 82-73958. (Illus.). 1983. pap. 12.45 (ISBN 0-8070-5413-5, BP 656). Beacon Pr.

Qualman, Al. Blood on the Half Shell. (Illus.). 1982. pap. 6.50 (ISBN 0-8323-0411-5). Binford.

Raphael, Morris. Weeks Hall: The Master of the Shadows. LC 81-90439. (Illus.). 207p. (gr. 5-12). 1981. 14.95 (ISBN 0-9608866-1-3). M Raphael.

Reagan, Alice E. H. I. Kimball, Entrepreneur. (Illus.). 170p. 1983. 9.95 (ISBN 0-87797-064-5). Cherokee.

Sack, John. Fingerprint: The Autobiography of An American Man. Date not set. 13.95 (ISBN 0-394-50197-7). Random.

Schwarz, Richard W. John Harvey Kellogg. LC 75-137. 256p. 1981. pap. 6.95 (ISBN 0-943872-80-4). Andrews Univ Pr.

Sheller, Roscoe. Me & the Model T. (Illus.). 1982. pap. 7.95 (ISBN 0-686-84255-3). Binford.

Straight, Michael. After Long Silence. (Illus.). 1983. 17.50 (ISBN 0-393-01729-X). Norton.

Thomson, J. S. International Book of Honor. 1000p. 1983. 95.00 (ISBN 0-934544-24-7). Am Biog Inst.

Thomson, J. S., ed. The Biographical Roll of Honor, Vol. I. 1000p. 1983. 150.00 (ISBN 0-934544-25-5). Am Biog Inst.

--The Registry of American Achievement. 2nd ed. (American Registry Ser.). 1983. 100.00 (ISBN 0-686-81733-8). Am Biog Inst.

--Two Thousand Notable Americans. 1000p. 1982. 125.00 (ISBN 0-934544-23-9). Am Biog Inst.

Vetterli, Richard. Orrin Hatch: Challenging the Washington Establishment. LC 82-61024. (Illus.). 204p. 1982. 10.95 (ISBN 0-89526-629-6). Regnery-Gateway.

Zeidner, Lisa. Alexandra Freed. LC 82-48735. 1983. 13.95 (ISBN 0-394-52750-X). Knopf.

UNITED STATES–CENTRAL INTELLIGENCE AGENCY

Immerman, Richard H. The C.I A. in Guatemala: The Foreign Policy of Intervention. (Texas Pan American Ser.). 302p. 1983. pap. 9.95 (ISBN 0-292-71083-6). U of Tex Pr.

Smith, Bradley F. The Shacow Warriors: O.S.S. & the Origins of the C.I.A. 400p. 1983. 14.95 (ISBN 0-465-07756-0). Basic.

UNITED STATES–CIVIL DEFENSE

Kerr, Thomas J. Civil Defense in the United States: Band-Aid for a Holocaust? 250p. 1983. lib. bdg. 23.50x (ISBN 0-86531-586-8). Westview.

UNITED STATES–CIVILIZATION

DeBrito, Ibrantino X. The American Civilization. LC 81-65252. 286p. 1982. 11.95 (ISBN 0-533-04963-6). Vantage.

Evler, R. C. & Gummerman, G. S., eds. Investigations of the Southwestern Anthropological Research Group: An Experiment in Archaeological Cooperation. (MNA Bulletin Ser.: No. 50). 1978. pap. 5.95 (ISBN 0-89734-018-3). Mus Northern Ariz.

Parkes, Henry B. The American Experience: An Interpretation of the History & Civilization of the American People. LC 82-15518. xii, 355p. 1982. lib. bdg. 35.00x (ISBN 0-313-22574-5, PAAE). Greenwood.

Rice, Arnold S. American Civilization. 256p. (Orig.). (gr. 11-12). 1983. pap. 6.68i (ISBN 0-06-460145-5, COS CO 145). B&N NY.

UNITED STATES–CIVILIZATION–HISTORY

Szekely, Edmond B. The Game of the Gods. (Illus.). 24p. 1973. pap. 3.95 (ISBN 0-89564-029-5). IBS Intl.

Whited, Charles. Spirit of America, Vol. 1: Challenge. 1982. pap. 3.50 (ISBN 0-553-20181-6). Bantam.

UNITED STATES–CIVILIZATION–1945-

Clecak, Peter. America's Quest for Self: Dissent & Fulfillment in the 60s & 70s. 368p. 1983. 22.50 (ISBN 0-19-503226-8). Oxford U Pr.

UNITED STATES–CIVILIZATION–20TH CENTURY

Allen, Frederick L. The Big Change: America Transforms Itself, 1900-1950. LC 82-18395. xii, 308p. 1983. Repr. of 1952 ed. lib. bdg. 35.00x (ISBN 0-313-23791-3, ALBC). Greenwood.

Brzezinski, Zbigniew. Between Two Ages: America's Role in the Technetronic Era. LC 82-15867. xvii, 334p. 1982. Repr. of 1970 ed. lib. bdg. 35.00x (ISBN 0-313-23498-1, BRZB). Greenwood.

UNITED STATES–CLIMATE

Bomar, George W. Texas Weather. (Illus.). 256p. 1983. 22.50 (ISBN 0-292-78052-4); pap. 9.95 (ISBN 0-292-78053-2). U of Tex Pr.

Ludlum, David M. The New Jersey Weather Book. 250p. Date not set. 24.95 (ISBN 0-8135-0915-7); pap. 14.95 (ISBN 0-8135-0940-8). Rutgers U Pr.

UNITED STATES–COLONIES

see United States–Territories and Possessions

UNITED STATES–COMMERCE

see also Small Business

Doyle, Kathleen E. & Hoover, Jan. Cooperative Law for California Retail Consumer Co-Ops. 316p. 1982. pap. text ed. 7.00 (ISBN 0-686-82421-0). Calif Dept Co.

UNITED STATES–COMMERCE–STATISTICS

see United States–Commerce

UNITED STATES–COMMERCIAL LAW

see Commercial Law

UNITED STATES–CONGRESS

Congressional Information Service, Inc. Staff. ASI Annual, 1974, 2 Vols. LC 73-82599. 400.00 (ISBN 0-912380-23-3). Cong Info.

--ASI Annual, 1981, 2 Vols. LC 73-82599. 715.00 (ISBN 0-912380-95-0). Cong Info.

--CIS-Index 1976 Annual, 2 Vols. 220.00 (ISBN 0-912380-41-1). Cong Info.

--CIS-Index 1978 Annual, 2 Vols. 260.00 (ISBN 0-912380-60-8). Cong Info.

--CIS-Index 1981 Annual, 2 Vols. LC 79-158879. 370.00 (ISBN 0-686-84194-8). Cong Info.

--CIS US Congressional Committee Hearings Index: Pt. VIII, 1965-1969, 2 Vols. 1625.00 (ISBN 0-686-84196-4). Cong Info.

--CIS US Congressional Committee Hearings Index: Pt. VII, 1959-1964, 2 Vols. 1625.00 (ISBN 0-686-84197-2). Cong Info.

--Statistical Reference Index-Annual, 1981, 2 Vols. 380.00 (ISBN 0-912380-89-6). Cong Info.

Congressional Quarterly Inc. Staff. Editorial Research Reports, 2 Vols. 1982. Vol. 1: 1981, 768p. 65.00 (ISBN 0-87187-241-2). Vol. I I: 1982, 800p. Congr Quarterly.

--Guide to Congress. 3rd ed. 1208p. 1982. 90.00 (ISBN 0-87187-239-0). Congr Quarterly.

--How Congress Works. LC 61-16893. 240p. 1983. pap. 9.25 (ISBN 0-87187-254-4). Congr Quarterly.

--Powers of Congress. 2nd ed. LC 82-14331. 388p. 1982. pap. 8.25 (ISBN 0-87187-242-0). Congr Quarterly.

--The Rights Revolution. LC 78-31931. (Editorial Research Reports). 224p. 1979. pap. 7.50 (ISBN 0-87187-144-0). Congr Quarterly.

--Roll Call: 1982. 1983. pap. 12.95 (ISBN 0-87187-252-8). Congr Quarterly.

Dahl, Robert A. Congress & Foreign Policy. LC 82-25123. x, 305p. 1983. Repr. of 1950 ed. lib. bdg. 35.00x (ISBN 0-313-23788-3, DACF). Greenwood.

Hale, Dennis. The United States Congress. 360p. 1983. pap. 14.95 (ISBN 0-87855-939-6). Transaction Bks.

Hudlin, Richard A. Directory of Southern U.S. Senators & Representatives. 1981. 1.00 (ISBN 0-686-38020-7). Voter Ed Proj.

Hudlin, Richard A. & Farouk, Brimah K. Roster of Blacks in the U.S. House & Senate: 1869 to 1981. 1981. 1.00 (ISBN 0-686-38014-2). Voter Ed Proj.

Know Your Congress, 1983. 1982. 5.50 (ISBN 0-686-83924-2). Capital Pub DC.

Morss, Elliott R. & Gow, David D., eds. Implementing Rural Development Projects: Nine Critical Problems. 325p. 1983. softcover 23.50x (ISBN 0-86531-942-1). Westview.

Ornstein, Norman J., et al, eds. Vital Statistics on Congress, 1982. 1982. 16.95 (ISBN 0-8447-3496-9); pap. 8.95 (ISBN 0-8447-3493-4). Am Enterprise.

Review: Nineteen Eighty One Session of the Congress. 1982. pap. 3.75 (ISBN 0-8447-0246-3). Am Enterprise.

Ripley, Randall. Congress: Process & Policy. 3d ed. 1983. text ed. write for info (ISBN 0-393-95291-6). Norton.

Rystad, G., ed. Congress & American Foreign Policy. (Lund Studies in International History: No. 13). 156p. 1982. text ed. 18.00x (ISBN 91-24-31480-3, Pub. by Almquist & Wiksell Sweden). Humanities.

Schick, Allen. Reconciliation & the Congressional Budget Process. 1981. pap. 4.25 (ISBN 0-8447-3471-3). Am Enterprise.

Zwirn, Jerrold. Congressional Publications: A Research Guide to Legislation, Budgets & Treaties. 200p. 1983. lib. bdg. 22.50 (ISBN 0-87287-358-7). Libs Unl.

UNITED STATES–CONGRESS–COMMITTEES

Congressional Quarterly Inc. Staff. Congressional Quarterly Almanac: 1981. LC 47-41081. 1043p. 1982. 105.00 (ISBN 0-87187-231-5). Congr Quarterly.

--Congressional Quarterly Almanac: 1982. LC 47-41081. 1200p. 1983. 115.00 (ISBN 0-686-42802-1). Congr Quarterly.

UNITED STATES–CONGRESS–ELECTIONS

Clarke, Peter & Evans, Susan H. Covering Campaigns: Journalism in Congressional Elections. LC 82-60738. 168p. 1983. 17.95x (ISBN 0-8047-1159-3). Stanford U Pr.

UNITED STATES–CONGRESS–HISTORY

Seip, Terry L. The South Returns to Congress: Men, Economic Measures, & Intersectional Relationships, 1868-1879. LC 82-4654. (Illus.). 344p. 1983. 25.00 (ISBN 0-8071-1052-3). La State U Pr.

UNITED STATES–CONGRESS–POWERS AND DUTIES

Mackaman, Frank H., ed. Understanding Congressional Leadership. LC 81-17447. 304p. 1981. 22.50 (ISBN 0-87187-213-7). Congr Quarterly.

UNITED STATES–CONGRESS–SENATE

Congressional Quarterly Inc. Staff. The Washington Lobby. 4th ed. LC 82-12525. 192p. 1982. pap. 9.25 (ISBN 0-87187-240-4). Congr Quarterly.

Garza, Hedda, compiled by. The Watergate Investigation Index: Senate Select Committee Hearings & Reports on Presidential Campaign Activities. LC 82-7353. 326p. 1982. lib. bdg. 95.00 (ISBN 0-8420-2175-2). Scholarly Res Inc.

UNITED STATES–CONSTITUTION

Farrand, Max. Fathers of the Constitution. 1921. text ed. 8.50x (ISBN 0-686-83547-6). Elliots Bks.

Justus, Fred. Our Constitution & Government. (Social Studies). 24p. (gr. 5 up). 1979. wkbk. 5.00 (ISBN 0-8209-0244-6, SS-11). ESP.

Pearson, Sindey A., Jr. The Constitutional Polity: Essays on the Founding Principles of American Politics. LC 82-15953. 364p. (Orig.). 1983. lib. bdg. 24.25 (ISBN 0-8191-2744-2); pap. text ed. 12.75 (ISBN 0-8191-2745-0). U Pr of Amer.

Rutland, Robert A. The Birth of the Bill of Rights, 1776-1791. 243p. 1983. 24.95X (ISBN 0-930350-41-3); pap. text ed. 9.95X (ISBN 0-930350-40-5). NE U Pr.

UNITED STATES–CONSTITUTION–BIBLIOGRAPHY

Hall, Kermit L. A Comprehensive Bibliography of American Constitutional & Legal History, 1896-1979, 2 vols. (Orig.). 1983. Set. lib. bdg. 320.00 (ISBN 0-527-37408-3). Kraus Intl.

UNITED STATES–CONSTITUTIONAL HISTORY

Goldwin, Robert A. & Schambra, William A., eds. How Capitalistic is the Constitution? 1982. 14.25 (ISBN 0-8447-3477-2); pap. 6.25 (ISBN 0-8447-3478-0). Am Enterprise.

UNITED STATES–CONSTITUTIONAL LAW

Boutmy, Emile. Studies in Constitutional Law: France-England-United States. 2nd ed. Dicey, E. M., tr. xiv, 183p. 1982. Repr. of 1891 ed. lib. bdg. 22.50x (ISBN 0-8377-0332-8). Rothman.

Brest, Levinson. Processes of Constitutional Decisionmaking. 2nd ed. LC 81-86686. 1983. text ed. cancelled (ISBN 0-316-10794-8). Little.

Shapiro, Martin & Tresolini, Rocco J. American Contitutional Law. 6th ed. 816p. 1983. text ed. 24.95 (ISBN 0-02-409580-X). Macmillan.

UNITED STATES–CONSTITUTIONAL LAW–CASES

Conley, Patrick T. The Constitutional Significance of Trevett vs. Weeden (1786) (Illus.). 10p. 1976. pap. 1.25 (ISBN 0-917012-43-7). RI Pubns Soc.

UNITED STATES–CONTINENTAL CONGRESS

Rakove, Jack N. The Beginnings of National Politics: An Interpretive History of the Continental Congress. LC 82-15186. (Paperback Reprint Ser.). 512p. (Orig.). 1982. pap. text ed. 8.95 (ISBN 0-8018-2864-3). Johns Hopkins.

UNITED STATES–COPYRIGHT

see Copyright–United States

UNITED STATES–COURTS

see Courts

UNITED STATES–DECLARATION OF INDEPENDENCE

Capt, Raymond E. Scottish Declaration of Independence. (Illus.). 32p. 1983. pap. 2.00 (ISBN 0-934666-11-3). Artisan Sales.

UNITED STATES–DEFENSES

Allan, Pierre. Crisis Bargaining & the Arms Race: A Theoretical Model. (Peace Science Studies). 184p. 1983. prof ref 22.50x (ISBN 0-88410-911-9). Ballinger Pub.

Bertram, Christopher. America's Security in the 1980's. LC 82-16814. 200p. 1982. 25.00x (ISBN 0-312-02199-2). St Martin.

Brown, Harold. Thinking About Defense: National Security in a Dangerous World. 280p. 1983. 16.95 (ISBN 0-86531-548-5). Westview.

Congressional Quarterly Inc. Staff. Defense Policy. 3rd ed. 200p. 1983. pap. 8.95 (ISBN 0-87187-258-7). Congr Quarterly.

Graham, Daniel O. The Non-Nuclear Defense of Cities: The High Frontier Space-Based Defense Against ICBM Attack. 1983. Repr. of 1982 ed. text ed. 25.00 (ISBN 0-89011-586-9). Abt Bks.

Hopple, Gerald W. & Andriole, Stephen J., eds. National Security Crisis Forecasting & Management. Replica ed. Freedy, Amos. 275p. 1983. so ftcover 21.50 (ISBN 0-86531-913-8). Westview.

Kanter, Arnold. Defense Politics: A Budgetary Perspective, the Ounce of Prevention Fund. LC 78-21848. (Illus.). viii, 152p. 1983. pap. 5.95 (ISBN 0-226-42374-3). U of Chicago Pr.

Kennedy, Robert & Weinsteiln, John M., eds. The Defense of the West: Strategic & European Security Issues Reappraised. 350p. 1983. price not set (ISBN 0-86531-612-0). Westview.

Kojm, Christopher A., ed. U. S. Defense Policy. (The Reference Shelf: Vol. 54, No. 2). 224p. 1982. pap. text ed. 6.25 (ISBN 0-8242-0666-5). Wilson.

Livermore Arms Control Conference. Arms Control in Transition: Proceedings. Heckrotte, Warren & Smith, George C., eds. (Special Study in National Security & Defense Policy). 215p. 1982. lib. bdg. 16.50 (ISBN 0-86531-496-9). Westview.

U. S. Defense Policy: Weapons, Strategy & Commitments. 2nd ed. LC 80-607772. 224p. 1980. pap. 8.75 (ISBN 0-686-42798-X). Congr Quarterly.

U. S. Strategy at the Crossroads: Two Views. 72p. 1982. pap. 7.50 (ISBN 0-89549-044-7, IFPA 26, IFPA). Unipub.

UNITED STATES–DEPARTMENT OF DEFENSE

Borklund, C. W. The Department of Defense. 2nd rev. ed. (Illus.). 400p. 1983. lib. bdg. 27.50x (ISBN 0-86531-384-9). Westview.

UNITED STATES–DESCRIPTION AND TRAVEL

see also subdivision Description and Travel under names of states, geographic areas, etc.

Bowman, Thomas, et al. Finding Your Best Place to Live in America. 416p. 1983. pap. 3.95 (ISBN 0-446-30586-3). Warner Bks.

Jenkins, Peter. A Walk Across America. (General Ser.). 1982. lib. bdg. 15.95 (ISBN 0-8161-3459-6, Large Print Bks). G K Hall.

Jenkins, Peter & Jenkins, Barbara. The Walk West: A Walk Across America II. (General Ser.). 1983. lib. bdg. 18.95 (ISBN 0-8161-3460-X, Large Print Bks). G K Hall.

Reader's Digest Editors. America the Beautiful. LC 73-103727. (Illus.). 352p. 1970. 18.50 (ISBN 0-686-84601-X, Pub. by RD Assn). Random.

Watson, J. Wreford. The United States. (Geography for Advanced Study Ser.). (Illus.). 304p. 1983. text ed. 45.00x (ISBN 0-582-30004-5); pap. text ed. 19.95x (ISBN 0-582-30005-3). Longman.

UNITED STATES–DESCRIPTION AND TRAVEL–GUIDEBOOKS

Bailey, Lee. Lee Bailey's Country Weekends. 1983. 18.95 (ISBN 0-517-54880-1, C N Potter Bks). Crown.

Birnbaum, Stephen. United States 1983. (Get 'em & Go Travel Guide Ser.). 1982. 11.95 (ISBN 0-395-32875-6). HM.

Destination U. S. A. The East. 96p. 1983. pap. 7.95 (ISBN 0-86145-106-6, Pub. by Auto Assn-British Tourist Authority England). Merrimack Bk Serv.

Destination U. S. A. The West. 96p. 1983. pap. 7.95 (ISBN 0-86145-107-4, Pub. by Auto Assn-British Tourist Authority England). Merrimack Bk Serv.

Hammond Staff, ed. Hammond Road Atlas & Vacation Guide 1983. (Illus.). 48p. 1983. pap. 2.50 (ISBN 0-8437-2625-3). Hammond Inc.

--Road Atlas America 1983. rev. ed. (Illus.). 72p. 1983. pap. 3.95 (ISBN 0-8437-2631-8). Hammond Inc.

Harvard Student Agencies. Let's Go U. S. A. (The Let's Go Ser.). (Illus.). 605p. 1983. pap. 7.95 (ISBN 0-312-48215-9). St Martin.

Mitchell, B. J. & Dragoon, M. M. How to See the U.S. on Twelve Dollars a Day: (Per Person, Double Occupancy) LC 82-50779. (Illus.). 112p. (Orig.). 1982. pap. 3.95 (ISBN 0-943962-00-5). Viewpoint Pr.

Mobil Travel Guide: Major Cities. (Illus.). 1983. pap. 6.95 (ISBN 0-528-84887-9). Rand.

Rand McNally Business Traveler's Road Atlas. 1983. pap. 6.95 (ISBN 0-528-89445-5). Rand.

Rand McNally Vacation & Travel Guide, 1983. Incl. 1983. pap. 5.95 ea. Western (ISBN 0-528-84248-X). Eastern (ISBN 0-528-84247-1). Rand.

Visitor's Travel Guide to the United States. pap. 4.95 (ISBN 0-528-84477-6). Rand.

UNITED STATES–DESCRIPTION AND TRAVEL–MAPS

see United States–Maps

UNITED STATES–DESCRIPTION AND TRAVEL–1805-1900

Lacour-Gayet, Robert. Everyday Life in the United States before the Civil War, 1830-1860. Ilford, Mary, tr. from French. LC 70-81571. 310p. 1983. pap. 7.95 (ISBN 0-8044-6376-X). Ungar.

UNITED STATES–DESCRIPTION AND TRAVEL–1940-

Kenny, Maurice, ed. Greyhounding This America. (Illus., Orig.). 1983. pap. 7.95 (ISBN 0-918606-07-1). Heidelberg Graphics.

Least Heat Moon, William. Blue Highways: A Journey into America. 1983. 17.00i (ISBN 0-316-35395-7). Little.

Ve Nard, Victor. All America is Ours. (Illus.). 70p. (Orig.). 1982. pap. 4.95 (ISBN 0-9610342-0-3). Ve Nard Pubs.

UNITED STATES–DISCOVERY AND EXPLORATION

see America–Discovery and Exploration; United States–Exploring Expeditions

UNITED STATES–ECONOMIC CONDITIONS

see also Economic Assistance, Domestic

Business Week Team. The Reindustrialization of America. 1983. pap. 5.95 (ISBN 0-671-45617-2). WSP.

Choate, Pat & Walter, Susan. America in Ruins: The Decaying Infrastructure. (Duke Press Policy Studies). 100p. 1983. pap. 9.75 (ISBN 0-8223-0554-2). Duke.

Cohen, Stephen D. & Meltzer, Ronald L. U. S. International Economic Policy in Action. 224p. 1982. 28.95 (ISBN 0-03-061906-8); pap. 12.95 (ISBN 0-03-063308-7). Praeger.

Cyert, Richard M. The American Economy, Nineteen Sixty to Two Thousand. LC 82-48600. (Charles C. Moskowitz Memorial Lecture Ser.: Vol. XXLII). 1983. 12.95 (ISBN 0-02-923100-0). Free Pr.

Goldsmith, Raymond W. The Financial Development of India, Japan, & the United States. LC 82-8541. 136p. 1983. text ed. 12.95x (ISBN 0-300-02934-9). Yale U Pr.

Goldwin, Robert A. & Schambra, William A., eds. How Capitalistic is the Constitution? 1982. 14.25 (ISBN 0-8447-3477-2); pap. 6.25 (ISBN 0-8447-3478-0). Am Enterprise.

Hughes, Jonathan R. American Economic History. 1983. text ed. 24.95x (ISBN 0-673-15338-X). Scott F.

Katz, Michael B., ed. Poverty & Policy in American History: Monograph. (Studies in Social Discontinuity). 226p. 1983. price not set (ISBN 0-12-401760-6); pap. price not set (ISBN 0-12-401762-2). Acad Pr.

Miller, G. William, ed. The Decline & Rise of the American Economy. (American Assembly Ser.). (Illus.). 192p. 1983. 11.95 (ISBN 0-13-198465-9); pap. 4.95 (ISBN 0-13-198457-8). P-H.

Osberg, Lars. Economic Inequality in the United States. 268p. 1983. text ed. 17.95 (ISBN 0-87332-234-7). M E Sharpe.

Siegan, Bernard H. Economic Liberties & the Constitution. LC 80-15756. viii, 384p. 1980. pap. 9.95 (ISBN 0-226-75664-5). U of Chicago Pr.

Smith, Lowell. Average American. LC 82-84427. (Illus.). 112p. (Orig.). 1983. pap. 8.00 (ISBN 0-937088-03-X). Illum Pr.

UNITED STATES–ECONOMIC CONDITIONS–1918-

Agar, Herbert & Tate, Allen, eds. Who Owns America? A New Declaration of Independence. LC 82-24752. 352p. 1983. pap. text ed. 12.75 (ISBN 0-8191-2767-1). U Pr of Amer.

UNITED STATES–ECONOMIC CONDITIONS–1918-1945

Allen, Frederick L. The Big Change: America Transforms Itself, 1900-1950. LC 82-18395. xii, 308p. 1983. Repr. of 1952 ed. lib. bdg. 35.00x (ISBN 0-313-23791-3, ALBC). Greenwood.

UNITED STATES–ECONOMIC CONDITIONS–1945-

Ballard, Jack S. The Shock of Peace: Military & Economic Demobilization After World War II. LC 82-24860. (Illus.). 270p. (Orig.). 1983. lib. bdg. 23.50 (ISBN 0-8191-3029-X); pap. text ed. 11.75 (ISBN 0-8191-3030-3). U Pr of Amer.

Fuchs, Victor. How We Live. (Illus.). 320p. 1983. 17.50 (ISBN 0-674-41225-7). Harvard U Pr.

UNITED STATES–ECONOMIC CONDITIONS–1961-

Bowles, Samuel, et al. Beyond the Wasteland: A Democratic Alternative to Economic Decline. LC 82-45514. 432p. 1983. 17.95 (ISBN 0-385-18345-3, Anchor Pr). Doubleday.

Davey, Nelson J. These Are the Times. 1983. 8.95 (ISBN 0-533-05555-5). Vantage.

Wilber, Charles K. & Jameson, Kenneth P. Confronting Reality: America's Economic Crisis & Beyond. 304p. 1983. text ed. 21.95x (ISBN 0-268-00742-X); pap. text ed. 8.95x (ISBN 0-268-00743-8). U of Notre Dame Pr.

UNITED STATES–ECONOMIC POLICY

De Benedetti, Edoardo. Visualizations in the Realm of Historical Predictions in the Light of the Kondratieff Theory. (Illus.). 131p. 1983. 87.45 (ISBN 0-86722-041-4). Inst Econ Pol.

Deville, Lawrrence. The Conflict Between the Foreign Policy of the United States & the Economic Interests of the Large Corporations. (Illus.). 163p. 1983. 73.85 (ISBN 0-86722-043-0). Inst Econ Pol.

Hochmeister, Ludwig. The Failure of the United States as World Leadership Power. (Illus.). 109p. 1983. 93.75 (ISBN 0-86722-040-6). Inst Econ Pol.

Hufbauer, Gary C. Economic Warfare: Sanctions in Support of National Foreign Policy Goals. (Policy Analyses in International Economics Ser.: No. 6). 1983. 6.00 (ISBN 0-88132-011-0). Inst Intl Eco.

MacAvoy, Paul W. Energy Policy: An Economic Analysis. pap. text ed. 4.95x (ISBN 0-393-95321-1). Norton.

Romasco, Albert U. The Politics of Recovery: Roosevelt's New Deal. LC 82-14499. 270p. 1983. 17.95 (ISBN 0-19-503248-9). Oxford U Pr.

Shepard. Antitrust & American Business Abroad. 2nd ed. 1981. 120.00 (ISBN 0-07-002435-9). McGraw.

Wrright, Peter H. Rome, England, the United States & the Forces for the Decline & the Death of the Empires. 155p. 1983. 69.55 (ISBN 0-86722-042-2). Inst Econ Pol.

UNITED STATES–ECONOMIC POLICY–1945-

Hartrich, Edwin. The American Opportunity. (Illus.). 320p. 1983. 17.95 (ISBN 0-02-548510-5). Macmillan.

UNITED STATES–ECONOMIC POLICY–1971-

Barbour. Energy & American Values. 256p. 1982. 27.95 (ISBN 0-03-062468-1); pap. 12.95 (ISBN 0-03-062469-X). Praeger.

Committee for Economic Development Staff. Productivity Policy: Key to the Nation's Economic Future. (CED Statement on National Policy Ser.). 122p. (Orig.). 1983. 10.50x (ISBN 0-87186-776-1); pap. 8.50x (ISBN 0-87186-076-7). Comm Econ Dev.

Congressional Quarterly Inc. American Regionalism: Our Economic, Cultural & Political Makeup. LC 80-18934. (Editorial Research Reports). 208p. 1980. pap. 7.50 (ISBN 0-87187-194-7). Congr Quarterly.

Davis, J. Morton. How to Make the Economy Succeed. LC 82-15776. 336p. 1983. 14.95 (ISBN 0-87663-402-1). Universe.

Kimzey, Bruce W. Reaganomics. (Illus.). 118p. 1983. pap. text ed. 4.90 (ISBN 0-314-73187-3). West Pub.

Levesque, Alston. The Alstonics of Mellow. 1983. 7.95 (ISBN 0-533-05630-6). Vantage.

Palmer, John L. & Sawhill, Isabel V., eds. The Reagan Experiment: An Examination of Economic & Social Policies under the Reagan Administration. 530p. 1982. 29.95 (ISBN 0-87766-315-7, 34100); pap. 12.95 (ISBN 0-87766-316-5, 34200). Urban Inst.

Pasquariello, Ronald D. Faith, Justice, & Our Nation's Budget. 112p. 1982. pap. 6.95 (ISBN 0-8170-0976-0). Judson.

Stubblebine, Craig W. & Willett, Thomas D. Reaganomics: A Midterm Report. 250p. 1983. 14.95 (ISBN 0-917616-54-5). ICS Pr.

UNITED STATES–ELECTIONS

see Elections–United States

UNITED STATES–EMIGRATION AND IMMIGRATION

see also Emigration and Immigration Law

Archdeacon, Thomas J. Becoming American. LC 82-48691. 320p. 1983. 17.95 (ISBN 0-02-900830-1). Free Pr.

Aten, Jerry. Americans, Too! (gr. 4-8). 1982. 6.95 (ISBN 0-86653-099-1, GA 444). Good Apple.

Bouvier, Leon F. Illegal Immigration: What Can We Do About It? (Vital Issues, Vol. XXVIII 1978-79). 0.50 (ISBN 0-686-81621-8). Ctr Info Am.

Chiswick, Barry, ed. Gateway: U. S. Immigration Issues & Policies. 1982. 22.95 (ISBN 0-8447-2221-9); pap. 12.95 (ISBN 0-8447-2220-0). Am Enterprise.

San Juan, P. & Chiswick, Barry. The Dilemma of American Immigration: Beyond the Golden Door. 212p. 1983. 19.95 (ISBN 0-87855-481-5); pap. 8.95 (ISBN 0-87855-935-3). Transaction Bks.

UNITED STATES–EMIGRATION AND IMMIGRATION–LITERARY COLLECTIONS

Kessner, Thomas & Caroli, Betty B. Today's Immigrants, Their Stories: A New Look at the Newest Americans. (Illus.). 330p. 1983. pap. 7.95 (ISBN 0-19-503270-5, GB 728, GB). Oxford U Pr.

UNITED STATES–EMPLOYEES

see United States–Officials and Employees

UNITED STATES–EMPLOYMENT SERVICE

Congressional Quarterly Inc. Staff. Jobs for Americans. LC 77-18994. (Editorial Research Reports). 189p. 1978. pap. 7.50 (ISBN 0-87187-120-3). Congr Quarterly.

UNITED STATES–EXPLORING EXPEDITIONS

Jacobsen, Johann A. Alaskan Voyage, Eighteen Eighty-One to Eighteen Eighty-Three: An Expedition to the Northwest Coast of America. Gunther, Erna, tr. (Illus.). xiv, 266p. 1977. pap. 12.50 (ISBN 0-226-39033-0). U of Chicago Pr.

UNITED STATES–FEDERAL BUREAU OF INVESTIGATION

Garrow, David J. The FBI & Martin Luther King, Jr. 1983. pap. 5.95 (ISBN 0-14-006486-9). Penguin.

Powers, Richard G. G-Men: Hoover's FBI in American Popular Culture. (Illus.). 320p. 1983. price not set (ISBN 0-8093-1096-1). S Ill U Pr.

UNITED STATES–FOOD AND DRUG ADMINISTRATION

Food & Drug Administration. FDA Executive Information Manual. Hadley, Richard D., ed. 294p. 1982. pap. text ed. 35.00 (ISBN 0-914176-19-6). Wash Busn Info.

UNITED STATES–FOREIGN ECONOMIC RELATIONS

Kline, John M. State Government Influence in U. S. International Economic Policy. LC 82-48473. 288p. 1983. 27.95x (ISBN 0-669-06141-7). Lexington Bks.

UNITED STATES–FOREIGN RELATIONS

This heading is subdivided in three ways: First by subject, according to the nature of the materials, e.g. United States–Foreign Relations–Treaties; second chronologically, e.g. United States–Foreign Relations–1783-1865; Third geographically, e.g. United States–Foreign Relations–Great Britain.

Ayubi, Shaheen & Bissell, Richard E. Economic Sanctions in U. S. Foreign Policy. (Philadelphia Policy Papers). 1982. pap. 3.95 (ISBN 0-910191-01-8). For Policy Res.

Belfiglio, Valentine J. American Foreign Policy. 2nd ed. (Illus.). 152p. 1983. pap. text ed. 10.00 (ISBN 0-8191-2677-2). U Pr of Amer.

Bienefeld, Manfred & Godfrey, Martin. The Struggle for Development: National Strategies in an International Contex. LC 81-19821. 352p. 1982. 29.95x (ISBN 0-471-10152-4). Wiley.

Brzezinski, Zbigniew. Power & Principle: Memoirs of the National Security Advisor, 1977-1981. 600p. 1983. 22.50 (ISBN 0-374-23663-1); limited ed. 100.00. FS&G.

Congressional Quarterly Inc. Staff. U. S. Foreign Policy: Future Directions. LC 79-15637. (Editorial Research Reports). 224p. 1979. pap. 7.50 (ISBN 0-87187-187-4). Congr Quarterly.

Dahl, Robert A. Congress & Foreign Policy. LC 82-25123. x, 305p. 1983. Repr. of 1950 ed. lib. bdg. 35.00x (ISBN 0-313-23788-3, DACF). Greenwood.

Dallek, Robert. The American Style of Foreign Policy: Cultural Politics & Foreign Affairs. LC 82-48877. 336p. 1983. 16.95 (ISBN 0-394-51360-6). Knopf.

De Benedetti, Edoardo. Visualizations in the Realm of Historical Predictions in the Light of the Kondratieff Theory. (Illus.). 131p. 1983. 87.45 (ISBN 0-86722-041-4). Inst Econ Pol.

Deville, Lawrrence. The Conflict Between the Foreign Policy of the United States & the Economic Interests of the Large Corporations. (Illus.). 163p. 1983. 73.85 (ISBN 0-86722-043-0). Inst Econ Pol.

Gardner, Lloyd C. & LaFever, Walter F. Creation of the American Empire, 2 Vols. Incl. U.S. Diplomatic History to 1901. 2d ed. Vol. 1. pap. 15.50 (ISBN 0-395-30598-5); U.S. Diplomatic History Since 1893. 2nd ed. Vol. 2. pap. 15.50 (ISBN 0395-30599-3). 1976. pap. HM.

Herz, Martin F. & Krogh, Peter F. Two Hundred Fifteen Days in the Life of an American Ambassador. LC 81-13346. 1981. 9.85 (ISBN 0-934742-12-X, Inst Study Diplomacy). Geo U Sch For Serv.

Hochmeister, Ludwig. The Failure of the United States as World Leadership Power. (Illus.). 109p. 1983. 93.75 (ISBN 0-86722-040-6). Inst Econ Pol.

Hoffmann, Stanley. Dead Ends: American Foreign Policy in the New Cold War. 312p. 1983. prof ref 24.50 (ISBN 0-88410-003-0). Ballinger Pub.

Nevins, Allan. United State in a Chaotic World. 1951. text ed. 8.50x (ISBN 0-686-83837-8). Elliots Bks.

Paterson, Thomas G. & Clifford, J. G. American Foreign Policy: A History. 2nd ed. 1983. Vol. I, 304. pap. text ed. 13.95 (ISBN 0-669-04567-5); Vol. II, 496. pap. text ed. 13.95 (ISBN 0-669-04566-7). Heath.

Record, Jeffrey & Hanks, Robert J. U. S. Strategy at the Crossroads: Two Views. LC 82-82774. (Foreign Policy Ser.). 72p. 1982. 7.50 (ISBN 0-89549-044-7). Inst Foreign Policy Anal.

Rystad, G., ed. Congress & American Foreign Policy. (Lund Studies in International History: No. 13). 156p. 1982. text ed. 18.00x (ISBN 91-24-31480-3, Pub. by Almquist & Wiksell Sweden). Humanities.

Smith, Gaddis. Foreign Policy in Perilous Times: Who's in Charge? (Vital Issues, Vol. XXIX: No. 8). 0.50 (ISBN 0-686-81613-7). Ctr Info Am.

The Futures Group. Handbook for U. S. Participation in Multilateral Diplomacy. 350p. 1983. lib. bdg. 40.00x (ISBN 0-379-12146-8). Oceana.

Thompson, Kenneth W. American Diplomacy & Emergent Patterns. LC 82-23862. 294p. 1983. pap. text ed. 11.50 (ISBN 0-8191-2935-6). U Pr of Amer.

Vance, Cyrus. The Choice is Ours. 1983. price not set (ISBN 0-671-44339-9). S&S.

Wolf, Joseph J. Security in the Eastern Mediterranean: Re-Thinking American Policy. 19p. pap. 1.00 (ISBN 0-87855-739-3). Transaction Bks.

Wrright, Peter H. Rome, England, the United States & the Forces for the Decline & the Death of the Empires. 155p. 1983. 69.55 (ISBN 0-86722-042-2). Inst Econ Pol.

UNITED STATES–FOREIGN RELATIONS–REVOLUTION, 1775-1783

Egan, Clifford L. Neither Peace nor War: Franco-American Relations, 1803 to 1812. LC 82-17272. (Illus.). 288p. 1983. text ed. 30.00 (ISBN 0-8071-1076-0). La State U Pr.

UNITED STATES–FOREIGN RELATIONS–1783-1865

Goetzmann, William H. When the Eagle Screamed: The Romantic Horizon in American Diplomacy, 1800-1860. (Illus.). 138p. (Orig.). 1966. pap. 10.95x (ISBN 0-471-31001-8). Wiley.

UNITED STATES–FOREIGN RELATIONS–20TH CENTURY

Payne, Howard E. & Callahan, Raymond. As the Storm Clouds Gathered: European Perceptions of American Foreign Policy in the 1930's. LC 78-7074. 173p. 1980. 15.95x (ISBN 0-941690-06-7); pap. 9.95x (ISBN 0-87716-101-1); pap. text ed. 5.95x (ISBN 0-686-84004-6). Regina Bks.

Widenor, William C. Henry Cabot Lodge & the Search for an American Foreign Policy. (Illus.). 402p. 1983. pap. 8.95 (ISBN 0-520-04962-4, CAL 631). U of Cal Pr.

UNITED STATES–FOREIGN RELATIONS–1933-1945

Cole, Wayne S. Roosevelt & the Isolationists, Nineteen Thirty-Two to Nineteen Forty-Five. LC 82-8624. xii, 685p. 1983. 26.50x (ISBN 0-8032-1410-3). U of Nebr Pr.

Graebner, Norman A. The Age of Global Power: The United States Since Nineteen Thirty-Nine. LC 78-12294. (American Republic Ser.). 1979. pap. text ed. 12.95 (ISBN 0-471-32082-X). Wiley.

Jablon, Howard. Crossroads of Decision: The State Department & Foreign Policy, 1933-1937. LC 82-40459. 192p. 1983. 16.00x (ISBN 0-8131-1483-7). U Pr of Ky.

Kanawada, Leo V., Jr. Franklin D. Roosevelt's Diplomacy & American Catholics, Italians, & Jews. Berkhofer, Robert, ed. LC 82-16077. (Studies in American History & Culture: No. 37). 194p. 1982. 39.95 (ISBN 0-8357-1382-2). Univ Microfilms.

UNITED STATES–FOREIGN RELATIONS–1933-1945–SOURCES

Labrie, Roger, et al, eds. U. S. Arms Sales Policy: Background & Issues. 1982. pap. 4.95 (ISBN 0-8447-3491-8). Am Enterprise.

UNITED STATES–FOREIGN RELATIONS–1945-

Feinberg, Richard E. The Intemperate Zone: The Third World Challenge to U.S. Foreign Policy. 1983. 17.50 (ISBN 0-393-01712-5). Norton.

Graebner, Norman A. The Age of Global Power: The United States Since Nineteen Thirty-Nine. LC 78-12294. (American Republic Ser.). 1979. pap. text ed. 12.95 (ISBN 0-471-32082-X). Wiley.

Laqueur, Walter. America, Europe, & the Soviet Union: Selected Essays. 1983. 22.95 (ISBN 0-87855-362-2). Transaction Bks.

Schwab, George, ed. United States Foreign Policy at the Crossroads. LC 82-15588. (Contributions in Political Science Ser.: No. 96). 267p. 1982. lib. bdg. 29.95 (ISBN 0-313-23270-9, SFP/). Greenwood.

UNITED STATES–FOREIGN RELATIONS–1945-1961

Morgenthau, Hans J. In Defense of the National Interest: A Critical Examination of American Foreign Policy. LC 82-18295. 306p. 1983. pap. text ed. 11.50 (ISBN 0-8191-2846-5). U Pr of Amer.

UNITED STATES–FOREIGN RELATIONS–1961-

Foreign Affairs & Bundy, William P., eds. America & the World 1982. 300p. 1983. 30.00 (ISBN 0-08-030132-0); pap. 7.95 (ISBN 0-08-030131-2). Pergamon.

Sanders, Jerry. Peddlars of Crisis. 340p. 1983. 20.00 (ISBN 0-89608-182-6); pap. 8.00 (ISBN 0-89608-181-8). South End Pr.

Sorley, Lewis. Arms Transfers Under Nixon: A Policy Analysis. Davis, Vincent, ed. LC 82-15970. (Essays for the Third Century: America & a Changing World Ser.). 248p. 1983. 22.00 (ISBN 0-8131-0404-1). U Pr of Ky.

UNITED STATES–FOREIGN RELATIONS–AFRICA

Kitchen. U. S. Interests in Africa in the Eighties. 128p. 1983. write for info. Praeger.

UNITED STATES–FOREIGN RELATIONS–ARAB COUNTRIES

Bradley, C. Paul. Recent United States Policy in the Persian Gulf (1971-82) LC 82-16049. 128p. (Orig.). 1982. pap. text ed. 6.95 (ISBN 0-936988-08-8). Tompson & Rutter.

McMullen, Christopher J. Resolution of the Yemen Crisis, 1963: A Case Study in Mediation. LC 80-25944. 56p. 1980. 3.00 (ISBN 0-934742-07-3, Inst Study Diplomacy). Geo U Sch For Serv.

UNITED STATES–FOREIGN RELATIONS–ASIA

Here are entered general works on Asia. For smaller areas see the name of the country or area, e.g.–Near East, or–China.

Cohen, Warren I., ed. New Frontiers in American-East Asian Relations. (Studies of the East Asian Institute). 344p. 1983. text ed. 30.00x (ISBN 0-231-05630-3); pap. 15.00 (ISBN 0-231-05631-1). Columbia U Pr.

Johnson, Maxwell O. The Military as an Instrument of U.S. Policy in Southwest Asia: The Rapid Deployment Joint Task Force, 1979-1982. (Replica Edition Ser.). 135p. 1982. softcover 16.00x (ISBN 0-86531-952-9). Westview.

Pye, Lucian W. Redefining American Policy in Southeast Asia. 1982. pap. 3.75 (ISBN 0-8447-1095-4). Am Enterprise.

Reed, James. The Missionary Mind & American East Asia Policy, 1911-1915. (Harvard East Asian Monographs: No. 104). 300p. 1983. text ed. 20.00x (ISBN 0-686-82629-9). Harvard U Pr.

Sigur, Gastonz & Kim, Young C. Japanese & U. S. Policy in Asia. 208p. 1982. 22.95 (ISBN 0-03-061849-5). Praeger.

Tahir-Keli. U. S. Strategic Interests in Southwest Asia. 236p. 1982. 27.95 (ISBN 0-03-062043-0). Praeger.

UNITED STATES–FOREIGN RELATIONS–BRAZIL

Townsend, Joyce C. Bureaucratic Politics in American Decision Making: Impact on Brazil. LC 81-46881. 210p. 1983. lib. bdg. 22.50 (ISBN 0-8191-2706-X); pap. text ed. 11.50 (ISBN 0-8191-2707-8). U Pr of Amer.

UNITED STATES–FOREIGN RELATIONS–CANADA

Carroll, John E. Acid Rain: An Issue in Canadian-American Relations. LC 82-82205. (Canadian-American Committee). 98p. (Orig.). 1982. pap. 6.00 (ISBN 0-89068-064-7). Natl Planning.

Clarkson, Stephen. Canada & the Reagan Challenge. (Illus.). 383p. 1983. 19.95 (ISBN 0-89490-091-9). Enslow Pubs.

Shelton, Oscar D. Canadian Dominion. 1919. text ed. 8.50x (ISBN 0-686-83498-4). Elliots Bks.

UNITED STATES–FOREIGN RELATIONS–CARIBBEAN AREA

Dominguez, Jorge I. U. S. Interest & Policies in the Caribbean & Central America. 1982. pap. 4.75 (ISBN 0-8447-1097-0). Am Enterprise.

UNITED STATES–FOREIGN RELATIONS–CENTRAL AMERICA

Dominguez, Jorge I. U. S. Interest & Policies in the Caribbean & Central America. 1982. pap. 4.75 (ISBN 0-8447-1097-0). Am Enterprise.

Immerman, Richard H. The C.I A. in Guatemala: The Foreign Policy of Intervention. (Texas Pan American Ser.). 302p. 1983. pap. 9.95 (ISBN 0-292-71083-6). U of Tex Pr.

Kinzer, Stephen & Schlesinger, Stephen. Bitter Fruit: The Untold Story of the American Coup in Guatemala. (Illus.). 312p. 1983. pap. 8.95 (ISBN 0-385-18354-2, Anch). Doubleday.

Simon, Laurence R. El Salvador Land Reform: Nineteen Eighty to Nineteen Eighty-One. Stephens, James C., Jr., ed. (Impact Audit Ser.: No. 2). 55p. (Orig.). 1981. pap. 5.00 (ISBN 0-910281-01-7). Oxfam Am.

UNITED STATES–FOREIGN RELATIONS–CHINA

Barnett, A. Doak. U. S. Arms Sales: The China-Taiwan Tangle. LC 82-72117. (Studies in Defense Policy). 70p. 1982. pap. 5.95 (ISBN 0-8157-0829-7). Brookings.

Burns, Richard D. & Bennett, Edward M., eds. Diplomats in Crisis: United States-Chinese-Japanese Relations, 1919-1941. 345p. 1974. 15.95 (ISBN 0-686-84012-7); text ed. 6.95 (ISBN 0-686-84013-5). Regina Bks.

Hunt, Michael H. The Making of a Special Relationship: The United States & China to 1914. LC 82-9753. 480p. 1983. 27.50x (ISBN 0-231-05516-1). Columbia U Pr.

Kintner, William R. & Copper, John F. A Matter of Two Chinas: The China-Taiwan Issue in U. S. Foreign Policy. 127p. 1979. pap. 6.00 (ISBN 0-910191-04-2). For Policy Res.

Shen, James. Is the U. S. True to its Friends? A View from the Former Ambassador of Free China. 300p. 1983. 14.95 (ISBN 0-686-82487-3). Acropolis.

UNITED STATES–FOREIGN RELATIONS–CHINA–1949-

Murray, Douglas P. & Lubman, Stanley B. Communicating with China: Country Orientation Ser. Kapp, Robert A., ed. LC 82-83999. 112p. (Orig.). 1983. pap. text ed. 11.95 (ISBN 0-933662-51-3). Intercult Pr.

Sutter, Robert G. The China Quandary: Domestic Determinants of U. S. - China Policy, 1972-1982. 250p. 1983. lib. bdg. 22.50x (ISBN 0-86531-579-5). Westview.

UNITED STATES–FOREIGN RELATIONS–DOMINICAN REPUBLIC

Bracey, Audrey. Resolution of the Dominican Crisis, 1965: A Study in Mediation. LC 80-27239. 64p. 1980. 3.50 (ISBN 0-934742-04-9, Inst Study Diplomacy). Geo U Sch For Serv.

UNITED STATES–FOREIGN RELATIONS–EGYPT

McMullen, Christopher J. Resolution of the Yemen Crisis, 1963: A Case Study in Mediation. LC 80-25944. 56p. 1980. 3.00 (ISBN 0-934742-07-3, Inst Study Diplomacy). Geo U Sch For Serv.

UNITED STATES–FOREIGN RELATIONS–EUROPE

Here are entered general works on Europe, as well as those on the separate countries of Europe except Great Britain and Russia.

Kissinger, Henry A. The Troubled Partnership: A Re-appraisal of the Atlantic Alliance. LC 82-15533. xii, 266p. 1982. Repr. of 1965 ed. lib. bdg. 25.00x (ISBN 0-313-23219-9, KIPA). Greenwood.

Laqueur, Walter. America, Europe, & the Soviet Union: Selected Essays. 1983. 22.95 (ISBN 0-87855-362-2). Transaction Bks.

Van Oudenaren, John. The United States & Europe: Issues to Resolve. (Seven Springs Studies). 1981. pap. 3.00 (ISBN 0-943006-02-3). Seven Springs.

UNITED STATES–FOREIGN RELATIONS–FRANCE

Dougherty, Patricia. American Diplomats & the Franco-Prussian War: Perceptions from Paris & Berlin. LC 80-250000089. 42p. 1980. 2.50 (ISBN 0-934742-06-5, Inst Study Diplomacy). Geo U Sch For Serv.

Egan, Clifford L. Neither Peace nor War: Franco-American Relations, 1803 to 1812. LC 82-17272. (Illus.). 288p. 1983. text ed. 30.00 (ISBN 0-8071-1076-0). La State U Pr.

UNITED STATES–FOREIGN RELATIONS–GERMANY

Dougherty, Patricia. American Diplomats & the Franco-Prussian War: Perceptions from Paris & Berlin. LC 80-250000089. 42p. 1980. 2.50 (ISBN 0-934742-06-5, Inst Study Diplomacy). Geo U Sch For Serv.

UNITED STATES–FOREIGN RELATIONS–INDIA

Sultan, Tanvir. INDO-US Relations: A Study of Foreign Policies. 260p. 1982. 29.95 (ISBN 0-940500-82-5, Pub by Depp & Deep India). Asia Bk Corp.

UNITED STATES–FOREIGN RELATIONS–JAPAN

Burns, Richard D. & Bennett, Edward M., eds. Diplomats in Crisis: United States-Chinese-Japanese Relations, 1919-1941. 345p. 1974. 15.95 (ISBN 0-686-84012-7); text ed. 6.95 (ISBN 0-686-84013-5). Regina Bks.

Vernon, Raymond. Two Hungry Giants: The United States & Japan in the Quest for Oil & Ores. (Center for International Affairs). (Illus.). 192p. 1983. text ed. 16.00x (ISBN 0-674-91470-8). Harvard U Pr.

UNITED STATES–FOREIGN RELATIONS–KOREA

Cumings, Bruce. Child of Conflict: The Korean-American Relationship 1943-1953. LC 82-48871. (Publications on Asia of the School of International Studies: No. 37). 350p. 1983. 22.50 (ISBN 0-295-95995-9). U of Wash Pr.

Dong, Wonmo, ed. Korean-American Relations at Crossroads. xiv, 178p. 1982. 8.00 (ISBN 0-932014-07-0). AKCS.

Kwak, Tai-Hwan & Chay, John, eds. U. S. - Korean Relations, 1882-1982. 433p. 1983. lib. bdg. 25.00x (ISBN 0-86531-608-2). Westview.

UNITED STATES–FOREIGN RELATIONS–LATIN AMERICA

Here are entered works on Latin American Countries as a whole. For more limited areas see subdivision Mexico, Central America, South America or West Indies.

Dominguez. Economic Issues & Political Conflict: U. S.- Latin America Relation. 1982. text ed. 45.95. Butterworth.

Hayes, Margaret D. Latin America & the U. S. National Interest: A Basis for U. S. Foreign Policy. (Special Studies on Latin America & the Caribbean). 240p. 1983. lib. bdg. 23.50x (ISBN 0-86531-462-4); pap. text ed. 10.95x (ISBN 0-86531-547-7). Westview.

Vivo, G. Hugo. El Crecimiento de las Empresas en los Estados Unidos y en la America Latina: Un Estudio Comparativo. LC 81-70693. 121p. (Orig., Span.). 1982. pap. 9.95 (ISBN 0-89729-306-1). Ediciones.

UNITED STATES–FOREIGN RELATIONS–MEXICO

Erb, Richard D. & Ross, Stanely R., eds. United States Relations with Mexico. 1981. pap. 7.25 (ISBN 0-8447-1343-0). Am Enterprise.

UNITED STATES–FOREIGN RELATIONS–NEAR EAST

Here are entered works on Eastern Asia and Turkey as a whole, as well as those on separate countries of the Near East.

Brubeck, William H. The American National Interest & Middle East Peace. (Seven Springs Studies). 1981. pap. 3.00 (ISBN 0-943006-03-1). Seven Springs.

Greene, Joseph N., Jr. & Klutznick, Philip M. The Path to Peace: Arab-Israeli Peace & the United States. 50p. 1981. pap. 3.00 (ISBN 0-943006-13-9). Seven Springs.

Grose, Peter. The United States, NATO & Israeli-Arab Peace. (Seven Springs Reports). 1980. pap. 2.00 (ISBN 0-943006-11-2). Seven Springs.

Hanks, Robert J. The U. S. Military Presence in the Middle East: Problems & Prospects. LC 82-84308. (Foreign Policy Reports Ser.). 88p. 1982. 7.50 (ISBN 0-89549-047-1). Inst Foreign Policy Anal.

Miller, R. C. Soviets Begin War in the Middle East-U.S. Counters. limited ed. 96p. 1983. pap. 2.50 (ISBN 0-682-49967-6). Exposition.

UNITED STATES–FOREIGN RELATIONS–PHILIPPINE ISLANDS

Owen, Norman G. The Philippine Economy & the United States: Studies in Past & Present Interactions. (Michigan Papers on South & Southeast Asia: No. 22). 200p. (Orig.). 1983. text ed. price not set (ISBN 0-89148-024-2); pap. price not set (ISBN 0-89148-025-0). CSSEAS.

Saito, Shiro, ed. Phillipine-American Relations: A Guide to Manuscript Sources in the United States. LC 82-12140. 280p. 1982. lib. bdg. 45.00 (ISBN 0-313-23632-1, SPH/). Greenwood.

UNITED STATES–FOREIGN RELATIONS–RUSSIA

Allan, Pierre. Crisis Bargaining & the Arms Race: A Theoretical Model. (Peace Science Studies). 184p. 1983. prof ref 22.50x (ISBN 0-88410-911-9). Ballinger Pub.

Caldwell, Lawrence T. Soviet-American Relations: One-half Decade of Detente Problems & Issues. (The Atlantic Papers: No. 75/5). (Orig.). 1976. pap. text ed. 4.75x (ISBN 0-686-83640-5). Allanheld.

Gaddis, John L. Russia, the Soviet Union & the United States: An Interpretive History. LC 77-12763. (America & the World Ser.). 309p. 1978. pap. text ed. 11.50x (ISBN 0-471-28911-6). Cloth ed. 12.95 o.p. Wiley.

George, Alexander L., ed. Managing U. S. Soviet Rivalry: Problems of Crisis Prevention. (Special Study in International Relations). 375p. 1983. lib. bdg. 30.00 (ISBN 0-86531-500-0); pap. text ed. 11.75 (ISBN 0-86531-501-9). Westview.

Gowa, Joanne & Wessell, Nils H. Ground Rules: Soviet & American Involvement in Regional Conflicts. (Philadelphia Policy Papers). 1982. pap. 3.95 (ISBN 0-910191-05-0). For Policy Res.

Kennan, George F. The Nuclear Delusion: Soviet-American Relations in the Atomic Age. 1982. 13.95 (ISBN 0-394-52946-4). Pantheon.

Laqueur, Walter. America, Europe, & the Soviet Union: Selected Essays. 1983. 22.95 (ISBN 0-87855-362-2). Transaction Bks.

Nuclear Negotiations: Reassesing Arms Control Goals in U. S.-Soviet Relations. LC 82-83390. (Symposia Ser.). 204p. 1982. 7.95 (ISBN 0-89940-004-3). L B J Sch Pub Aff.

Questions & Answers on the Soviet Threat & National Security. 1981. 1.00 (ISBN 0-910082-06-5). Am Pr Serv Comm.

Starr, Frederick. Headliners & Softliners: More Heat Than Light? "Themes & Sub-Themes in the Salt II Debate". LC 79-67157. (Papers on International Issues: No. 2). 1979. pap. 2.00 (ISBN 0-935082-01-8). Southern Ctr Intl Stud.

Whelan, Joseph G. Soviet Diplomacy & Negotiating Behavior: The Emerging New Context for U. S. Diplomacy. (Replica Edition Ser.). 573p. 1982. softcover 29.50x (ISBN 0-86531-946-4). Westview.

UNITED STATES–FOREIGN RELATIONS–SOUTH AFRICA

Spiegel, Marianne A. United States Policy Options in Southern Africa: The Next Five Years. (Seven Springs Studies). 49p. 1982. pap. 3.00 (ISBN 0-943006-07-4). Seven Springs.

UNITED STATES–FOREIGN RELATIONS–VIETNAM

Herring, George C., ed. The Secret Diplomacy of the Vietnam War: The Negotiation Volumes of the Pentagon Papers. 928p. 1983. text ed. 47.50x (ISBN 0-292-77573-3). U of Tex Pr.

UNITED STATES–FOREIGN RELATIONS ADMINISTRATION

Belfiglio, Valentine J. American Foreign Policy. 2nd ed. (Illus.). 152p. 1983. pap. text ed. 10.00 (ISBN 0-8191-2677-2). U Pr of Amer.

Phillips, Warren R. & Rimkunas, Richard. Crisis Warning: The Perception Behavior Interface. 300p. 1982. 48.50 (ISBN 0-677-05940-X). Gordon.

UNITED STATES–FULL EMPLOYMENT POLICIES

see Full Employment Policies

UNITED STATES–GENEALOGY

see also subdivision Genealogy under names of individual states, e.g. Virginia–Genealogy

Coggeshall, Charles P. & Coggeshall, Thellwell R. The Coggeshalls in America: Genealogy of the Descendants of John Coggeshall of Newport with a Brief Notice of Their English Antecedents. (Illus.). 424p. 1983. Repr. of 1930 ed. 35.00 (ISBN 0-87152-374-4). Reprint.

Dews, Robert P. Early Joel. 2nd ed. 1982. 6.00x (ISBN 0-940184-03-6). R P Dews.

Mueller, Frank P. The Burdick Family Chronology, Vol. 1. LC 82-72466. (Illus.). 200p. 1983. 24.95 (ISBN 0-9609100-0-X). Burdick Ancestry Lib.

Northen, E. E. & Duckworth, J. R. The Northen Family 1635-1900 & Bridging the Gap. 2nd ed. LC 82-73787. 196p. Repr. of 1906 ed. 25.00 (ISBN 0-9608266-0-2); microfische 6.00 (ISBN 0-9608266-1-0). Burnett Farmily Gen.

Scalf, Henry P. The Stepp-Stapp Families of America: A Source Book. (Illus.). 430p. pap. write for info. (ISBN 0-933302-20-7). Pikeville Coll.

Speller, Jon P., ed. Cyclopedia of American Genealogy, 2 Vols. Vol. 1. 1978 50.00 (ISBN 0-8315-0159-6); Vol. 2. 1980 50.00 (ISBN 0-8315-0160-X). Speller.

Stone, Robert H. Wild Garlic Islands: A Genealogical Account of the Ramsey Family. LC 82-90342. (Illus.). 191p. (Orig.). 1982. 22.50 (ISBN 0-9609192-0-1). R H Stone.

UNITED STATES–GOVERNMENT

see United States–Politics and Government

UNITED STATES–GOVERNMENT EMPLOYEES

see United States–Officials and Employees

UNITED STATES–GOVERNMENT PRINTING OFFICE

Morehead, Joe. Introduction to United States Public Documents. 3rd ed. (Library Science Text Ser.). 377p. 1983. lib. bdg. 28.50 (ISBN 0-87287-359-5); pap. text ed. 19.50 (ISBN 0-87287-362-5). Libs Unl.

UNITED STATES–GOVERNMENT PUBLICATIONS

Hernon, Peter, ed. Communicating Public Access to Government Information. 100p. 1983. 35.00X (ISBN 0-930466-59-4). Meckler Pub.

Londos, Eutychia G. AV Health: Current Publications of the United States Government. LC 82-10366. 240p. 1982. 17.50 (ISBN 0-8108-1571-0). Scarecrow.

Morehead, Joe. Introduction to United States Public Documents. 3rd ed. (Library Science Text Ser.). 377p. 1983. lib. bdg. 28.50 (ISBN 0-87287-359-5); pap. text ed. 19.50 (ISBN 0-87287-362-5). Libs Unl.

Zwirn, Jerrold. Congressional Publications: A Research Guide to Legislation, Budgets & Treaties. 200p. 1983. lib. bdg. 22.50 (ISBN 0-87287-358-7). Libs Unl.

UNITED STATES–GOVERNMENT PUBLICATIONS–BIBLIOGRAPHY

Tubesing, Richard. Architectural Preservation & Urban Renovation: An Annotated Bibliography of U. S. Congressional Documents. LC 81-48417. 500p. 1982. lib. bdg. 60.00 (ISBN 0-8240-9386-0). Garland Pub.

UNITED STATES–HARBORS

see Harbors–United States

UNITED STATES–HISTORIC BUILDINGS

Drake, Samuel A. The Heroical Book of American Colonial Homes. (Illus.). 109p. 1983. Repr. of 1894 ed. 89.75 (ISBN 0-89901-104-7). Found Class Reprints.

UNITED STATES–HISTORIOGRAPHY

Kellogg, Jefferson B. & Walker, Robert H., eds. Sources for American Studies. LC 82-11701. (Contributions in American Studies: No. 64). (Illus.). 581p. 1983. lib. bdg. 45.00 (ISBN 0-313-22555-9, WTO/). Greenwood.

Lynn, Kenneth S. The Air-Line to Seattle: Studies in Literary & Historical Writing about America. 240p. 1983. lib. bdg. 17.50x (ISBN 0-226-49832-8). U of Chicago Pr.

A Model for Evaluating Traditional U. S. History Textbooks: Teacher-Student Work Manual. 7.95 (ISBN 0-686-83752-5). R&M Pub Co.

UNITED STATES–HISTORY

see also subdivision History under names of states, e.g. Pennsylvania–History; also under various geographic subdivisions of the United States e.g. New England States–History

Bassett, John S. Makers of a New Nation. 1928. text ed. 22.50x (ISBN 0-686-83612-X). Elliots Bks.

Bolton, Herbert E. Spanish Borderlands. 1921. text ed. 8.50x (ISBN 0-686-83780-0). Elliots Bks.

Di Brino, Nicholas. The History of the Morris Park Racecourse & the Morris Family. (Illus.). 48p. 1977. pap. 3.95 (ISBN 0-686-38455-5). Bronx County.

Fish, Carl R. Path of Empire. 1919. text ed. 8.50x (ISBN 0-686-83685-5). Elliots Bks.

Gabriel, Ralph H. Toilers of Land & Sea. 1926. text ed. 22.50x (ISBN 0-686-83829-7). Elliots Bks.

Higgenbotham, Don. The War of American Independence. 515p. 1983. 24.95x (ISBN 0-930350-43-X); pap. text ed. 9.95 (ISBN 0-930350-44-8). NE U Pr.

Huntington, Ellsworth. Red Man's Continent. 1919. text ed. 8.50x (ISBN 0-686-83728-2). Elliots Bks.

Joyce, William L. & Hall, David D., eds. Printing & Society in Early America. 1983. text ed. price not set (ISBN 0-912296-55-0, Dist. by U Pr of VA). Am Antiquarian.

Kezirian, Richard. American History: Major Controversies Reviewed. 192p. 1983. pap. text ed. 13.95 (ISBN 0-8403-2921-0). Kendall-Hunt.

Moody, John. Masters of Capital. 1919. text ed. 8.50x (ISBN 0-686-83619-7). Elliots Bks.

Ogg, Frederick A. Builders of the Republic. 1928. text ed. 22.50x (ISBN 0-686-83496-8). Elliots Bks.

Orth, Samuel P. Our Foreigners. 1920. text ed. 8.50x (ISBN 0-686-83670-7). Elliots Bks.

Paine, Ralph D. Old Merchant Marine. 1919. text ed. 8.50x (ISBN 0-686-83653-7). Elliots Bks.

Rozwenc, Edwin C. & Martin, Edward C. The Restless Americans: The Challenge of Change in American History, Vol.1. LC 76-180833. 336p. pap. text ed. 16.95 (ISBN 0-536-00734-9). Krieger.

--The Restless Americans: The Challenge of Change in American History, Vol.2. LC 76-180833. 368p. pap. text ed. 16.95 (ISBN 0-536-00735-7). Krieger.

Shepherd, William R. Hispanic Nations of a New World. 1921. text ed. 8.50x (ISBN 0-686-83565-4). Elliots Bks.

Szekely, Edmond B. Ancient America: Paradise Lost. (Illus.). 96p. 1974. pap. 4.80 (ISBN 0-89564-025-2). IBS Intl.

Theodore Thornton Munger: New England Minister. 1913. text ed. 65.00x (ISBN 0-686-83814-9). Elliots Bks.

Walker, James D., ed. Local History: America's Collective Memory. (National Archives Conference Ser.). 1983. 17.50 (ISBN 0-88258-106-6). Howard U Pr.

White, Stewart E. Forty-Niners. 1918. text ed. 8.50x (ISBN 0-686-83552-2). Elliots Bks.

Willoughby, Lee D. The Smugglers. (The Making of America Ser.: No. 34). 320p. 1983. pap. 3.25 (ISBN 0-440-08014-2, Bryans). Dell.

Wolfson, Marty. Great Events In American History. (Illus.). 1969. pap. 1.60 (ISBN 0-916114-00-7). Wolfson.

Wood, William. Winnings of Freedom. 1927. text ed. 22.50x (ISBN 0-686-83858-0). Elliots Bks.

UNITED STATES–HISTORY–ADDRESSES, ESSAYS, LECTURES

Allen, H. C. & Hill, C. P., eds. British Essays in American History. LC 82-20916. x, 350p. 1983. Repr. of 1957 ed. lib. bdg. 39.75x (ISBN 0-313-23789-1, ALBE). Greenwood.

Tuchman, Barbara. Practicing History: Selected Essays. 1982. pap. 7.95 (ISBN 0-345-30363-6). Ballantine.

Williams, T. Harry. The Selected Essays of T. Harry Williams. LC 82-18646. 288p. 1983. 19.95 (ISBN 0-8071-1095-7). La State U Pr.

UNITED STATES–HISTORY–DICTIONARIES

Charle's Scribner's Sons. Concise Dictionary of American History. 860p. 1982. 60.00 (ISBN 0-686-83678-2, ScribT). Scribner.

UNITED STATES–HISTORY–EXAMINATIONS, QUESTIONS, ETC.

Agel, Jerome B. American at Random - Q. & A. 1983. 6.95 (ISBN 0-87795-455-0, Pub. by Priam). Arbor Hse.

How to Prepare for the Advanced Placement Exam in American History. 2nd ed. 1983. pap. 6.95 (ISBN 0-8120-2378-1). Barron.

UNITED STATES–HISTORY–PHILOSOPHY

Morgenthau, Hans J. In Defense of the National Interest: A Critical Examination of American Foreign Policy. LC 82-18295. 306p. 1983. pap. text ed. 11.50 (ISBN 0-8191-2846-5). U Pr of Amer.

UNITED STATES–HISTORY–PICTORIAL WORKS

Rouse, Parke, Jr. Planters & Pioneers. (Illus.). 216p. 1983. pap. 12.95 (ISBN 0-8038-5900-7). Hastings.

Sloane, Eric. Diary of an Early American Boy. (Illus.). 128p. 1983. 14.95 (ISBN 0-8038-1583-2). Hastings.

--School Days: Early Americana-Little Red School House, 2 Vols. (Illus.). 112p. (Orig.). 1983. boxed set 12.95 (ISBN 0-8038-6781-6). Hastings.

UNITED STATES–HISTORY–SOURCES

see also subdivision Sources under various periods of United States e.g. United States–History–Colonial period, ca. 1600-1775–sources

Congressional Quarterly, Inc. Staff. Historic Documents, Vols. 1-5. 1973-77. 54.00 ea. Vol. 1: 1972, 987p (ISBN 0-87187-043-6). Vol. 2: 1973, 1020p (ISBN 0-87187-054-1). Vol. 4: 1975, 982p (ISBN 0-87187-069-X). Vol. 4: 1975, 982p (ISBN 0-87187-090-8). Vol. 5: 1976, 1003p (ISBN 0-87187-103-3). Congr Quarterly.

Congressional Quarterly Inc. Staff. Historic Documents: 1982, Vol. XI. LC 72-97888. 1000p. 1983. 57.00 (ISBN 0-87187-257-9). Congr Quarterly.

Historic Documents, Vol. 6-10. LC 72-97888. 1978-82. 54.00 ea. Vol. 6: 1977, 969p (ISBN 0-87187-126-2). Vol. 7:1978, 964p (ISBN 0-87187-140-8). Vol. 8: 1979, 1019p (ISBN 0-87187-197-1). Vol. 9: 1980, 1043p (ISBN 0-87187-169-6). Vol. 10: 1981, 968p (ISBN 0-87187-229-3). Congr Quarterly.

UNITED STATES–HISTORY–COLONIAL PERIOD, ca. 1600-1775
Abbot, W. W. The Colonial Origins of the United States, 1607-1763. LC 74-28127. (American Republic Ser). 160p. 1975. pap. text ed. 11.50 (ISBN 0-471-00140-6). Wiley.
Achtermier, William O. Rhode Island Arms Makers & Gunsmiths: 1643-1883. LC 80-84583. (Illus.). 108p. 1980. 16.50 (ISBN 0-917218-15-9). Mowbray Co.
Andrews, Charles M. Colonial Folkways. 1919. text ed. 8.50x (ISBN 0-686-83505-0). Elliots Bks.
Breen, T. H. Puritans & Adventurers: Change & Persistence in Early America. 1982. pap. 8.95 (ISBN 0-19-503207-1). Oxford U Pr.
Dews, Robert P. Early Joel. 2nd ed. 1982. 6.00x (ISBN 0-940184-03-6). R P Dews.
Elrod, Mavis. American Colonial Life. (Social Studies). 24p. (gr. 5-9). 1979. wkbk. 5.00 (ISBN 0-8209-0248-9, SS-15). ESP.
Ferris, George D. Glory & Beauty in the Land of the Pilgrims. (Illus.). 109p. 1983. Repr. of 1899 ed. 79.15 (ISBN 0-89901-106-3). Found Class Reprints.
Gabriel, Ralph H. Lure of the Frontier. 1929. text ed. 22.50x (ISBN 0-686-83610-3). Elliots Bks.
Gary, Skipper. Basic Skills Colonies Workbook. (Basic Skills Workbooks). 32p. (gr. 4-7). 1983. 0.99 (ISBN 0-8209-0541-0, SSW-5). ESP.
--The Colonies. (Social Studies). 24p. (gr. 4-6). 1977. wkbk. 5.00 (ISBN 0-8209-0241-1, SS-8). ESP.
Neville, John D. Bacon's Rebellion: Abstracts of Materials in the Colonial Records Project. LC 76-24548. 442p. (Orig.). 1976. pap. 5.00 (ISBN 0-917394-00-3). Jamestown Found.
Smith, Sharon. Craftsmen of Colonial America. (Social Studies). 24p. (gr. 5-8). 1977. wkbk. 5.00 (ISBN 0-8209-0258-6, SS-25). ESP.
UNITED STATES–HISTORY–COLONIAL PERIOD, ca. 1600-1775–SOURCES
Essays in Colonial History Presented to Charles McLean Andrews By His Students. 1931. text ed. 14.50x (ISBN 0-686-83538-7). Elliots Bks.
UNITED STATES–HISTORY–KING GEORGE'S WAR, 1744-1748
Rolde, Neil. Sir William Pepperrell of Colonial New England. (Illus.). xi, 221p. 1982. 12.95 (ISBN 0-88448-048-8); pap. 8.95 (ISBN 0-88448-047-X). Harpswell Pr.
UNITED STATES–HISTORY–REVOLUTION, 1775-1783
Becker, Carl. Eve of the Revolution. 1918. text ed. 8.50x (ISBN 0-686-83540-9). Elliots Bks.
Farrand, Max. Fathers of the Constitution. 1921. text ed. 8.50x (ISBN 0-686-83547-6). Elliots Bks.
Ford, Henry J. Washington & His Colleagues. 1918. text ed. 8.50x (ISBN 0-686-83847-5). Elliots Bks.
Vansittart, Justinian. The Dramatic & Largely Unknown Prologue of the American Revolution. (Illus.). 138p. 1983. 69.85 (ISBN 0-89266-379-0). Am Classical Coll Pr.
Wrong, George M. Conquest of New France. 1918. text ed. 8.50x (ISBN 0-686-83510-7). Elliots Bks.
--Washington & His Comrades in Arms. 1921. text ed. 8.50x (ISBN 0-686-83852-1). Elliots Bks.
UNITED STATES–HISTORY–REVOLUTION, 1775-1783–BIOGRAPHY
Craven, Wesley F. The Legend of the Founding Fathers. LC 82-25241. (New York University, Stokes Foundation, Anson G. Phelps Lectureship on Early American History Ser.). vii, 222p. 1983. Repr. of 1956 ed. lib. bdg. 27.50x (ISBN 0-313-23840-5, CRLE). Greenwood.
UNITED STATES–HISTORY–REVOLUTION, 1775-1783–COMMERCE
see United States–History–Revolution, 1775-1783–Finance, Commerce, Confiscations, etc.
UNITED STATES–HISTORY–REVOLUTION, 1775-1783–ECONOMIC ASPECTS
see United States–History–Revolution, 1775-1783–Finance, Commerce, Confiscations, Etc.
UNITED STATES–HISTORY–REVOLUTION, 1775-1783–FINANCE, COMMERCE, CONFISCATIONS, ETC.
Anderson, William G. The Price of Liberty: The Public Debt of the American Revolution. LC 82-17420. 1983. 20.00x (ISBN 0-8139-0975-9). U Pr of Va.
UNITED STATES–HISTORY–REVOLUTION, 1775-1783–JUVENILE LITERATURE
Skeoch, Alan. The United Empire Loyalists & the American Revolution. (Focus on Canadian History Ser.). (Illus.). 96p. (gr. 6 up). 1983. PLB 8.40 (ISBN 0-531-04595-1). Watts.
UNITED STATES–HISTORY–1783-1865
Dodd, William E. Cotton Kingdom. 1919. text ed. 8.50x (ISBN 0-686-83514-X). Elliots Bks.
Fehrenbacher, Don E. The Era of Expansion: 1800-1848. LC 68-8713. (American Republic Ser.). 165p. 1969. pap. text ed. 11.95x (ISBN 0-471-25691-9). Wiley.
UNITED STATES–HISTORY–19TH CENTURY
Lancelot-Harrington, Katherine. America--Past & Present: Challenge. (America--Past & Present Ser.: Vol II). 160p. 1982. pap. text ed. 9.95 (ISBN 0-88377-255-8). Newbury Hse.
UNITED STATES–HISTORY–WAR OF 1812
Paine, Ralph D. Fight For a Free Sea. 1920. text ed. 8.50x (ISBN 0-686-83550-6). Elliots Bks.
UNITED STATES–HISTORY–WAR OF 1812–CAUSES
Egan, Clifford L. Neither Peace nor War: Franco-American Relations, 1803 to 1812. LC 82-17272. (Illus.). 288p. 1983. text ed. 30.00 (ISBN 0-8071-1076-0). La State U Pr.
UNITED STATES–HISTORY–WAR WITH MEXICO, 1845-1848–FICTION
Stephenson, Nathaniel W. Texas & the Mexican War. 1919. text ed. 8.50x (ISBN 0-686-83810-6). Elliots Bks.
UNITED STATES–HISTORY–CIVIL WAR, 1861-1865
Here are entered general works about the Civil War. Titles concerning the Civil War in specific states are listed under the names of individual states with the subdivision History.
Beatty, John. The Citizen-Solider. (Collector's Library of the Civil War). 1983. 26.60 (ISBN 0-8094-4258-2). Silver.
Billings, John D. Hardtack & Coffee. LC 81-18207. (Collector's Library of the Civil War). 26.60 (ISBN 0-8094-4208-6). Silver.
Davis, William C. The Orphan: The Kentucky Confederates Who Couldn't Go Home. 352p. 1983. pap. 8.95 (ISBN 0-8071-1077-9). La State U Pr.
--Stand in the Day of Battle: The Imperiled Union 1861-1865, Vol. 2. LC 82-45521. (Illus.). 336p. 1983. 19.95 (ISBN 0-385-14895-X). Doubleday.
Fleming, Walter L. Sequel of Appomattox. 1919. text ed. 8.50x (ISBN 0-686-83736-3). Elliots Bks.
McCarthy, Carlton. Detailed Minutiae of Soldier Life. (Collector's Library of the Civil War). 1982. 26.60 (ISBN 0-8094-4245-0). Silver.
National Historical Society. Fighting for Time. Davis, William C. & Wiley, Bell T., eds. LC 82-45363. (The Image of War (1861-1865) Ser.: Vol. 4). (Illus.). 464p. 1983. 39.95 (ISBN 0-385-18280-5). Doubleday.
Ness, George T., Jr. Under the Eagle's Wings: The Army on the Eve of Civil War, 2 vols. Date not set. price not set. MA AH Pub.
Pittinger, William. Daring & Suffering. (Collector's Library of the Civil War). 1982. 26.60 (ISBN 0-8094-4220-5). Silver.
Stephenson, Nathaniel W. Day of the Confederacy. 1919. text ed. 8.50x (ISBN 0-686-83524-7). Elliots Bks.
Williams, T. Harry. The Selected Essays of T. Harry Williams. LC 82-18646. 288p. 1983. 19.95 (ISBN 0-8071-1095-7). La State U Pr.
Wood, William. Captains of the Civil War. 1921. text ed. 8.50x (ISBN 0-686-83501-8). Elliots Bks.
UNITED STATES–HISTORY–CIVIL WAR, 1861-1865–AFRO-AMERICAN TROOPS
Higginson, Thomas W. Army Life in a Black Regiment. (Collector's Library of the Civil War). 1982. 26.60 (ISBN 0-8094-4237-X). Silver.
UNITED STATES–HISTORY–CIVIL WAR, 1861-1865–AFRO-AMERICANS
see also United States–History–Civil War, 1861-1865–Afro-American Troops
Higginson, Thomas W. Army Life in a Black Regiment. (Collector's Library of the Civil War). 1982. 26.60 (ISBN 0-8094-4237-X). Silver.
UNITED STATES–HISTORY–CIVIL WAR, 1861-1865–BLOCKADE
see United States–History–Civil War, 1861-1865–Naval Operations
UNITED STATES–HISTORY–CIVIL WAR, 1861-1865–CAMPAIGNS AND BATTLES
see also Antietam, Battle of, 1862; New Market, Battle of, 1864; Vicksburg, Mississippi–Siege, 1863
Davis, W. First Blood. (Civil War Ser.). 1983. lib. bdg. price not set (Pub. by Time-Life). Silver.
Frassanito, William A. Grant & Lee: The Virginia Campaigns, 1864-1865. (Illus.). 448p. 1983. 19.95 (ISBN 0-686-83857-2, ScribT). Scribner.
Hattaway, Herman & Jones, Archer. How the North Won: A Military History of the Civil War. LC 81-16332. (Illus.). 780p. 1983. 24.95 (ISBN 0-252-00918-5). U of Ill Pr.
Lowry, Terry. The Battle of Scary Creek Military Operations in the Kanawha Valley, April - July 1861. LC 82-81716. (Illus.). 192p. (Orig.). Date not set. pap. 7.95 (ISBN 0-933126-22-0). Pictorial Hist.
Porter, Horace. Campaigning with Grant. LC 81-14445. (Collector's Library of the Civil War). 26.60 (ISBN 0-8094-4200-0). Silver.
Townsend, George. Campaigns of a Non-Combatant. (Collector's Library of the Civil War). 1983. 26.60 (ISBN 0-8094-4250-7). Silver.
Urwin, Gregory J. Custer Victorious: The Civil War Battles of General George Armstrong Custer. LC 81-65873. (Illus.). 312p. 1982. 29.50 (ISBN 0-8386-3113-4). Fairleigh Dickinson.
Vance, Wilson J. Stone's River: Turning Point of the Civil War. 1982. pap. text ed. 25.00 (ISBN 0-87556-584-0). Saifer.
UNITED STATES–HISTORY–CIVIL WAR, 1861-1865–INFLUENCE
Warren, Robert P. The Legacy of the Civil War. 120p. 1983. pap. 4.95x (ISBN 0-674-52175-7). Harvard U Pr.
UNITED STATES–HISTORY–CIVIL WAR, 1861-1865–NAVAL OPERATIONS
Wilkinson, John. Narrative of a Blockade Runner. (Collector's Library of the Civil War). 1983. 26.60 (ISBN 0-8094-4254-X). Silver.
UNITED STATES–HISTORY–CIVIL WAR, 1861-1865–PERSONAL NARRATIVES
Brown, Norman D., ed. Journey to Pleasant Hill: The Civil War Letters of Captain Elijah P. Petty. (Illus.). 504p. 1982. 35.00 (ISBN 0-933164-94-7); deluxe ed. 75.00 (ISBN 0-686-82617-5). U. of Tex Inst Tex Culture.
Davis, W. Brother Against Brother. (Civil War Ser.). 1983. lib. bdg. price not set (Pub. by Time-Life). Silver.
Greeley, Roger, ed. The Best of Robert Ingersoll. Rev. ed. LC 77-90495. 1982. pap. 8.95 (ISBN 0-87975-209-2). Prometheus Bks.
Woodward, C. Vann, ed. Mary Chestnut's Civil War. pap. 14.95 (ISBN 0-686-42824-2, Y-450). Yale U Pr.
UNITED STATES–HISTORY–CIVIL WAR, 1861-1865–PERSONAL NARRATIVES–CONFEDERATE SIDE
Jones, J. B. A Rebel War Clerk's Diary, Vol. I. (Collector's Library of the Old West). 1982. 26.60 (ISBN 0-8094-4212-4). Silver.
--A Rebel War Clerk's Diary, Vol. II. (Collector's Library of the Civil War). 1982. 26.60 (ISBN 0-8094-4241-8). Silver.
UNITED STATES–HISTORY–CIVIL WAR, 1861-1865–REGIMENTAL HISTORIES
Barker, Harold R. History of the Rhode Island Combat Units in the Civil War, 1861-1865. (Illus.). 338p. 1964. 12.95 (ISBN 0-917012-44-5). RI Pubns Soc.
Stevens, George. Three Years in the Sixth Corps. (Collector's Library of the Civil War). 1983. 26.60 (ISBN 0-8094-4266-3). Silver.
Warshaw, John H. One of Jackson's Foot Cavalry. (Collector's Library of the Civil War). 26.60 (ISBN 0-8094-4216-7). Silver.
Williamson, James. Mosby's Randers. LC 82-668. (Collector's Library of the Civil War). 26.60 (ISBN 0-8094-4225-6). Silver.
UNITED STATES–HISTORY–1865-
Fleming, Walter L. Sequel of Appomattox. 1919. text ed. 8.50x (ISBN 0-686-83736-3). Elliots Bks.
UNITED STATES–HISTORY–20TH CENTURY
Duff, Shiela G. The Parting of Ways: A Personal Account of the Thirties. 223p. 1982. 19.95 (ISBN 0-7206-0586-5, Pub. by Peter Owen). Merrimack Bk Serv.
Fite, Gilbert C. & Graebner, Norman A. Recent United States History. (Illus.). 901p. 1972. 18.95 (ISBN 0-8260-3110-2). Wiley.
Link, Arthur S. & Link, William A. The Twentieth Century: An American History. LC 82-22080. (Illus.). 384p. 1983. text ed. 27.50 (ISBN 0-88295-815-1); pap. text ed. 16.95 (ISBN 0-88295-816-X). Harlan Davidson.
Mcbride, David. Evaders. LC 81-86159. 233p. 1983. pap. 5.95 (ISBN 0-86666-063-1). GWP.
Nevins, Allan. United State in a Chaotic World. 1951. text ed. 8.50x (ISBN 0-686-83837-8). Elliots Bks.
Struggle For Survival. 1951. text ed. 8.50x (ISBN 0-686-83791-6). Elliots Bks.
Taylor, John R. Strangers in Paradise: The Hollywood Emigres, 1933-1950. LC 82-21312. 256p. 1983. 16.45 (ISBN 0-03-061944-0). HR&W.
UNITED STATES–HISTORY–EUROPEAN WAR, 1914-1918
see also European War, 1914-1918
American Neutrality, 1914-1917: Essays on the Causes of American Intervention in the World War. 1935. text ed. 13.50 (ISBN 0-686-83464-X). Elliots Bks.
UNITED STATES–HISTORY–1919-1933
Faulkner, Harold V. From Versailles to the New Deal. 1951. text ed. 8.50x (ISBN 0-686-83555-7). Elliots Bks.
McElvaine, Robert S., ed. Down & Out in the Great Depression: Letters from the "Forgotten Man". LC 82-7022. (Illus.). xvii, 251p. 1983. 23.00x (ISBN 0-8078-1534-9); pap. 8.95 (ISBN 0-8078-4099-8). U of NC Pr.
UNITED STATES–HISTORY–1933-1945
Nevins, Allan. New Deal & World Affairs. 1951. text ed. 8.50x (ISBN 0-686-83647-2). Elliots Bks.
UNITED STATES–HISTORY–WORLD WAR, 1939-1945
see also World War, 1939-1945
Graebner, Norman A. The Age of Global Power: The United States Since Nineteen Thirty-Nine. LC 78-12294. (American Republic Ser.). 1979. pap. text ed. 12.95 (ISBN 0-471-32082-X). Wiley.
Pratt, Fletcher. War for the World. 1951. text ed. 8.50x (ISBN 0-686-83845-9). Elliots Bks.
UNITED STATES–HISTORY–1945-
Barrett, William. The Truants: Adventures Among the Intellectuals. 296p. 1983. pap. 8.95 (ISBN 0-385-17328-8, Anch). Doubleday.
Chafe, William H. & Sitkoff, Harvard, eds. A History of Our Time: Readings on Postwar America. 1982. pap. 8.95x (ISBN 0-19-503174-1). Oxford U Pr.
DeMause, Lloyd. Reagan's America. 200p. 1983. 16.95 (ISBN 0-940508-02-8). Creative Roots.
Dewing, Rolland. Wounded Knee: The Impact & Signifigance of the Second Incident. 225p. 1983. 18.95x (ISBN 0-8290-1290-7). Irvington.
Graebner, Norman A. The Age of Global Power: The United States Since Nineteen Thirty-Nine. LC 78-12294. (American Republic Ser.). 1979. pap. text ed. 12.95 (ISBN 0-471-32082-X). Wiley.
Masterson, James R. Writings on American History, 1962-73: A Subject Bibliography of Books & Monographs, 10 vols. LC 82-49027. (Writings on American History Ser.). (Orig.). 1983. Set. lib. bdg. 1200.00 (ISBN 0-527-98268-7). Kraus Intl.
Schlafly, Phyllis. The End of an Era. 1982. 12.95 (ISBN 0-89526-659-8). Regnery-Gateway.
Stockton, Ronald R. & Wayman, Frank W. A Time of Turmoil: Values & Voting in the 1970's. 216p. 1983. 18.95 (ISBN 0-87013-232-6). Mich St U Pr.
UNITED STATES–HISTORY, ECONOMIC
see also United States–Economic Conditions
Rogers, James H. Capitalism in Crisis. 1938. text ed. 29.50x (ISBN 0-686-83499-2). Elliots Bks.
UNITED STATES–HISTORY, MILITARY
Koenig, William. Americans at War. 352p. 1983. 14.95 (ISBN 0-8119-0478-4, Pub. by Bison Bks.). Fell.
Murray, Robert A. The Army or the Powder River. facs. ed. 1972. pap. 2.00 (ISBN 0-88342-203-4). Old Army.
UNITED STATES–HISTORY, POLITICAL
see United States–Politics and Government
UNITED STATES–IMMIGRATION
see United States–Emigration and Immigration
UNITED STATES–IMPRINTS
Fulton, Len & Ferber, Ellen, eds. Small Press Record of Books in Print: 12th Annual. 750p. 1983. 25.95 (ISBN 0-913218-61-8). Dustbooks.
UNITED STATES–INDUSTRIES
see also Small Business
Business Week Team. The Reindustrialization of America. 1983. pap. 5.95 (ISBN 0-671-45617-2). WSP.
Carrol, Frieda. Boom Cities & Towns: U. S. A. Workbook. 50p. 1983. 8.95 (ISBN 0-939476-51-7). Biblio Pr GA.
De Renzo, D. J., ed. Cogeneration Technology & Economics for the Process Industries. LC 82-22279. (Energy Technology Review: No. 81). (Illus.). 395p. 1983. 42.00 (ISBN 0-8155-0932-4). Noyes.
Lawrence, Paul R. & Dyer, Davis. Renewing American Industry. LC 82-72096. 400p. 1983. 25.00 (ISBN 0-02-918170-4). Free Pr.
UNITED STATES–INSULAR POSSESSIONS
see United States–Territories and Possessions
UNITED STATES–INTELLECTUAL LIFE
Heilbut, Anthony. Exiled in Paradise: German Refugee Artists & Intellectuals in America, from the 1930's to the Present. 480p. 1983. 23.50 (ISBN 0-670-51661-9). Viking Pr.
May, Henry F. Ideas, Faiths, & Feelings: Essays on American Intellectual & Religious History, 1952-1982. 256p. 1983. 25.00 (ISBN 0-19-503235-7, GB); pap. 9.95 (ISBN 0-19-503236-5). Oxford U Pr.
--Ideas, Faiths, & Feelings: Essays on American Intellectual & Religious History, 1952-1982. 256p. 1983. pap. 4.95 (ISBN 0-19-503236-5, GB 719, GB). Oxford U Pr.
UNITED STATES–INTERNAL REVENUE SERVICE
Blaustein, Randy B. How to Do Business with the IRS. LC 82-5319. 342p. 39.95 (ISBN 0-13-396168-0, Busn). P-H.
UNITED STATES–JUDICIARY
see Courts
UNITED STATES–JUVENILE LITERATURE
Fincher, E. B. Mexico & the United States: Their Linked Destinies. LC 82-45581. (Illus.). 224p. (YA) (gr. 7 up). 1983. 10.10i (ISBN 0-690-04310-4, TYC-J); PLB 10.89g (ISBN 0-690-04311-2). Har-Row.
UNITED STATES–LAW
see Law–United States
UNITED STATES–LAWS, STATUTES, ETC.
Harris, Fred R. & Hain, Paul L. America's Legislative Process. 1983. 21.95x (ISBN 0-673-15357-6). Scott F.
UNITED STATES–LEARNED INSTITUTIONS AND SOCIETIES
see Learned Institutions and Societies
UNITED STATES–LEGISLATIVE BODIES
see Legislative Bodies
UNITED STATES–MAIL
see Postal Service
UNITED STATES–MAPS
see also Automobile Touring–Road Guides
Gibson, Duncan L. America Today in Maps, Graphs & Tables. (Illus.). 160p. 1983. pap. text ed. 15.95 (ISBN 0-9608014-1-3). World Eagle.
Hammond Staff, ed. Hammond Road Atlas & Vacation Guide 1983. (Illus.). 48p. 1983. pap. 2.50 (ISBN 0-8437-2625-3). Hammond Inc.
UNITED STATES–MARINE CORPS
Moore, Herbert L., Jr. Rows of Corn. 224p. 1983. 13.95 (ISBN 0-87844-048-8). Sandlapper Pub Co.
UNITED STATES–MARINE CORPS–SPECIAL FORCES
see United States–Marine Corps
UNITED STATES–MERCHANT MARINE
see Merchant Marine
UNITED STATES–MILITARY POLICY
Birkby, Robert H. The Court & Public Policy. 435p. 1983. pap. 13.95 (ISBN 0-87187-248-X). Congr Quarterly.

Collins, John. U. S. Defense Planning: A Critique. 325p. 1982. lib. bdg. 30.00 (ISBN 0-86531-549-3); pap. text ed. 11.95 (ISBN 0-86531-554-X). Westview.

Donovan, James A., ed. U. S. Military Force 1980: An Evaluation. 96p. 1980. 2.50 (ISBN 0-686-38854-2). CDI.

Dornan, James E., Jr. The U. S. War Machine: An Illustrated Encyclopedia of American Military Equipment & Strategy. 1983. 10.95 (ISBN 0-517-54984-0). Crown.

Fish, Hamilton. Masters of Terrorism. 1982. 14.95 (ISBN 0-686-81786-9). Devin.

Gray, Colin S. U. S. Military Space Policy to the Year 2000. 1983. text ed. 28.00 (ISBN 0-89011-591-5). Abt Bks.

Greenfield, Kent R. American Strategy in World War II: A Reconsideration. LC 82-14881. 158p. 1982. pap. 7.50 (ISBN 0-89874-557-8). Krieger.

Kanter, Arnold. Defense Politics: A Budgetary Perspective, the Ounce of Prevention Fund. LC 78-21848. (Illus.). viii, 152p. 1983. pap. 5.95 (ISBN 0-226-42374-3). U of Chicago Pr.

Lefever, Ernest W. & Hunt, E. Stephen, eds. The Apocalyptic Premise: Nuclear Arms Debated. LC 82-18315. 429p. (Orig.). 1982. 14.00 (ISBN 0-89633-062-1); pap. 9.00 (ISBN 0-89633-063-X). Ethics & Public Policy.

Sabrosky, Alan N., et al. Blue-Collar Soldiers? Unionization & the U. S. Military. 166p. (Orig.). 1977. pap. 5.95 (ISBN 0-910191-03-4). For Policy Res.

Sider, Ronald J. & Taylor, Richard K. Nuclear Holocaust & Christian Hope: A Book for Christian Peacemakers. 360p. 1983. pap. 6.95 (ISBN 0-8091-2512-9). Paulist Pr.

Sindler, Allan P. American Politics & Public Policy: Seven Case Studies. LC 82-12524. 272p. 1982. pap. 8.95 (ISBN 0-87187-237-4). Congr Quarterly.

U. S. Arms Control & Disarmament Agency. World Military Expenditures & Arms Transfers, 1969-1978. LC 82-81820. 1982. write for info. (ISBN 0-89138-934-2, ICPSR 7964). ICPSR.

UNITED STATES–MILITIA

see also United States–National Guard

Mahon, John K. History of the Militia & the National Guard. 1983. 19.95 (ISBN 0-686-83899-8). Macmillan.

UNITED STATES–MORAL CONDITIONS

see also Hippies

Halttunen, Karen. Confidence Men & Painted Women: A Study of Middle-Class Culture in America, 1830-1870. LC 82-8336. (Yale Historical Publications Misc.: No. 129). (Illus.). 280p. 1983. text ed. 19.95x (ISBN 0-300-02835-0). Yale U Pr.

Stockdale, James B. & Hatfield, Mark O. The Ethics of Citizenship. (The Andrew R. Cecil Lectures on Moral Values in a Free Society Ser.: Vol. II). 167p. 1981. 9.95x (ISBN 0-292-72038-6). U of Tex Pr.

UNITED STATES–NATIONAL GUARD

Mahon, John K. History of the Militia & the National Guard. 1983. 19.95 (ISBN 0-686-83899-8). Macmillan.

UNITED STATES–NATIONAL SECURITY AGENCY

Questions & Answers on the Soviet Threat & National Security. 1981. 1.00 (ISBN 0-910082-06-5). Am Pr Serv Comm.

UNITED STATES–NATIONAL WAR LABOR BOARD (1942-1945)

Conner, Valerie J. The National War Labor Board: Stability, Social Justice, & the Voluntary State in World War I. LC 82-13362. (Supplementary Volumes to The Papers of Woodrow Wilson). vii, 232p. 1983. 23.50x (ISBN 0-8078-1539-X). U of NC Pr.

UNITED STATES–NATURAL RESOURCES

see Natural Resources–United States

UNITED STATES–NAVY

Jordan, John. An Illustrated Guide to the Modern U. S. Navy. LC 81-71937. (Illustrated Military Guides Ser.). (Illus.). 160p. 1983. 9.95 (ISBN 0-668-05505-7, 5505). Arco.

UNITED STATES–NAVY–BIOGRAPHY

Coleman, Eleanor S. Captain Gustavus Conyngham, U.S.N. Pirate or Privateer, 1747-1819. LC 82-13596. (Illus.). 196p. 1983. lib. bdg. 22.25 (ISBN 0-8191-2692-6); pap. text ed. 10.00 (ISBN 0-8191-2693-4). U Pr of Amer.

Long, David F. Sailor-Diplomat: A Biography of Commander James Biddle, 1783-1848. (Illus.). 350p. 1983. 22.95 (ISBN 0-930350-39-1). NE U Pr.

UNITED STATES–NAVY–HISTORY

Dorwart, Jeffrey M. Conflict of Duty: U. S. Navy's Intelligence Dilemma 1919-1945. 228p. 1983. 22.95 (ISBN 0-87021-685-6). Naval Inst Pr.

Feltner, Charles E. & Feltner, Jeri B. Great Lakes Maritime History: Bibliography & Sources of Information. LC 82-51175. 124p. 1982. 14.95 (ISBN 0-9609014-1-8); pap. 9.95 (ISBN 0-9609014-0-X). Seajay.

UNITED STATES–NAVY–WEAPONS SYSTEMS

see also Rockets (Ordnance); Warships

Friedman, Norman. U. S. Naval Weapons. LC 82-61473. (Illus.). 256p. 1982. 24.95 (ISBN 0-87021-735-6). Naval Inst Pr.

UNITED STATES–NEUTRALITY

Lindbergh, Charles A. Radio Speeches of Charles A. Lindbergh: 1939-1940. 1982. lib. bdg. 69.95 (ISBN 0-87700-455-2). Revisionist Pr.

UNITED STATES–NONCONTIGUOUS POSSESSION

see United States–Territories and Possessions

UNITED STATES–OCCUPATIONS

see Occupations

UNITED STATES–OFFICIALS AND EMPLOYEES

see also Civil Service Examinations

Dickson, Elizabeth & Peterson, George. Public Employee Compensation: A Twelve City Comparison. 2nd ed. LC 81-53060. 213p. 1981. pap. text ed. 12.00 (ISBN 0-87766-310-6, URI 32800). Urban Inst.

Straight, Michael. After Long Silence. (Illus.). 1983. 17.50 (ISBN 0-393-01729-X). Norton.

UNITED STATES–PATENTS

see Patents

UNITED STATES–POLITICS AND GOVERNMENT

Allen, Richard G., et al. American Government, 3 vols. Incl. Vol. 1. Origins of American Government & Citizenship: Political Parties & Elections. 156p (ISBN 0-86624-035-7, US0); Vol. 2. The Birth of Our Nation-Congress & the Laws-The President & His Cabinet. 256p (ISBN 0-86624-036-5, US1); Vol. 3. The Courts & Liberty: The World at Our Doorstep. 174p (ISBN 0-86624-037-3, US2). (Illus.). 1981. pap. text ed. write for info.; write for info. tchr's guide (US3); write for info. end-of-unit test (US4). Bilingual Ed Serv.

Allswang, John M. The New Deal & American Politics: A Study in Political Change. LC 78-5733. (Critical Episodes in American Politics Ser.). 155p. 1978. pap. text ed. 11.50x (ISBN 0-471-02516-X). Wiley.

Baker, Ross & Pomper, Gerald. American Government. 704p. 1983. text ed. 19.95 (ISBN 0-686-84129-8). Macmillan.

Barrett, Laurence. Gambling with History: The Reagan White House. LC 82-46057. (Illus.). 288p. 1983. 17.95 (ISBN 0-385-17939-1). Doubleday.

Cigler, Allan & Loomis, Burdett. Interest Group Politics. 325p. 1983. pap. 9.25 (ISBN 0-87187-247-1). Congr Quarterly.

Commanger, Henry S. The Ending of an Era: What Lies Ahead? (Vital Issues, Vol. XXIX 1979-80: No. 9). 0.50 (ISBN 0-686-81614-5). Ctr Info Am.

Congressional Quarterly Inc. American Regionalism: Our Economic, Cultural & Political Makeup. LC 80-18934. (Editorial Research Reports). 208p. 1980. pap. 7.50 (ISBN 0-87187-194-7). Congr Quarterly.

Congressional Quarterly Inc. Staff. Politics in America. LC 81-9848. Date not set. 26.95 (ISBN 0-686-42806-4). Congr Quarterly.

--The Public's Right to Know. LC 80-20610. (Editorial Research Reports). 194p. 1980. pap. 7.50 (ISBN 0-87187-157-2). Congr Quarterly.

Danielson, Michael N. & Murphy, Walter F. American Democracy. 10th ed. (Illus.). 608p. 1983. text ed. price not set (ISBN 0-8419-0839-7). Holmes & Meier.

Dawkins, Webster L. Whatever Happened to America? 112p. 1983. 7.00 (ISBN 0-682-49965-X). Exposition.

DeWitt, Howard A. & Kirshner, Alan M. In the Course of Human Events: American Government. 296p. 1982. pap. text ed. 17.95 (ISBN 0-8403-2844-3). Kendall-Hunt.

Dye, Thomas R. & Zeigler, L. Harmon. American Politics in the Media Age. LC 82-17710. (Political Science Ser.). 450p. 1983. text ed. 20.95 (ISBN 0-534-01176-4). Brooks-Cole.

Ehrenreich, Barbara. Hearts of Men: American Dreams & the Flight from Commitment. LC 82-45104. 264p. 1983. 13.95 (ISBN 0-385-17614-7, Anchor Pr). Doubleday.

Foster, John L., et al. National Policy Game: A Simulation of the American Political Process. LC 74-3411. 108p. 1975. text ed. 13.50x (ISBN 0-471-26775-9). Wiley.

Hanrahan, John. Government by Contract. 1983. 17.00 (ISBN 0-393-01717-6). Norton.

Hyde, Albert C. & Shafritz, Jay M., eds. Government Budgeting: Theory, Process, Politics. LC 78-21866. (Orig.). 1978. pap. 12.50x (ISBN 0-935610-01-4). Moore Pub IL.

Kann, Mark E., ed. The Future of American Democracy: Views from the Left. 1983. write for info. (ISBN 0-87722-288-6). Temple U Pr.

Lees, John D. The Political System of the United States. rev. ed. LC 82-24190. 424p. 1983. pap. 12.95 (ISBN 0-571-18068-X). Faber & Faber.

Lockard, Dunne. The Politics of State & Local Government. 3rd ed. 288p. 1983. pap. text ed. 20.95 (ISBN 0-02-371530-8). Macmillan.

Neely, Richard. How Courts Govern America. pap. 7.95 (ISBN 0-686-42823-4, Y-455). Yale U Pr.

Polsby, Nelson. Consequences of Party Reform. (Illus.). 275p. 1983. 24.95 (ISBN 0-19-503234-9, GB736, GB); pap. 8.95 (ISBN 0-19-503315-9). Oxford U Pr.

Posey, Rollin B. American Government. 11th ed. LC 77-11126. (Quality Paperbacks: No. 372). 352p. (Orig.). 1983. pap. 7.95 (ISBN 0-8226-0372-1). Littlefield.

Ranney, Austin. The Doctrine of Responsible Party Government, Its Origins & Present State. LC 82-15517. (Illus.). ix, 176p. 1982. Repr. of 1962 ed. lib. bdg. 22.50x (ISBN 0-313-22873-6, RADR). Greenwood.

Roche, George, III. Swarms of Officers: America's Bureaucracy. 1982. 14.95 (ISBN 0-686-81784-2). Devin.

Sabato, Larry. Goodbye to Goodtime Charlie: American Governorship Transformed. LC 82-22033. 250p. 1983. pap. 8.95 (ISBN 0-87187-249-8). Congr Quarterly.

Sindler, Allan P. American Politics & Public Policy: Seven Case Studies. LC 82-12524. 272p. 1982. pap. 8.95 (ISBN 0-87187-237-4). Congr Quarterly.

Straayer, John. American State & Local Government. 3rd ed. 384p. 1983. text ed. 14.95 (ISBN 0-675-20068-7). Merrill.

Volkomer, Walter. American Government. 3rd ed. (Illus.). 448p. 1983. pap. text ed. 15.95 (ISBN 0-13-027292-2). P-H.

Wilson, James Q. American Government: Institution & Policies. 2nd ed. 720p. 1983. text ed. 22.95 (ISBN 0-669-03757-5); instr's. guide 1.95 (ISBN 0-669-05262-0); test item file 1.95 (ISBN 0-669-05265-5); student handbook 7.95 (ISBN 0-669-05263-9). Heath.

UNITED STATES–POLITICS AND GOVERNMENT–ADDRESSES, ESSAYS, LECTURES

Carto, W. Profiles in Populism. 1982. 12.95 (ISBN 0-8159-6518-4); pap. 7.95 (ISBN 0-8159-6519-2). Devin.

DiClerico, Roberts & Hammock, Allan S. Points of View: Readings in American Government & Politics. 2nd ed. LC 82-10358. 352p. 1983. pap. text ed. write for info. (ISBN 0-201-10350-8). A-W.

Levine, Herbert M. Point-Counterpoint: Readings in American Government. 2nd ed. 1983. pap. text ed. 12.95x (ISBN 0-673-15625-7). Scott F.

Thompson, Kenneth W., ed. The Roosevelt Presidency: Four Intimate Perspectives of FDR. LC 82-17479. (Portraits of American Presidents Ser.: Vol. I). 100p. 1983. lib. bdg. 17.25 (ISBN 0-8191-2827-9); pap. text ed. 6.50 (ISBN 0-8191-2828-7). U Pr of Amer.

UNITED STATES–POLITICS AND GOVERNMENT–JUVENILE LITERATURE

Arnold, Caroline. Why Do We Have Rules? (Easy-Read Community Bks.). (Illus.). 32p. (gr. k-3). 1983. PLB 7.90 (ISBN 0-531-04509-9). Watts.

Harris, Jonathan. Terrorism: The New Politics. (Illus.). 160p. (gr. 9-12). 1983. PLB 9.29 (ISBN 0-671-45807-8). Messner.

UNITED STATES–POLITICS AND GOVERNMENT–SOURCES

Lawler, Peter A., ed. American Political Rhetoric: A Reader. LC 81-43468. 182p. 1983. pap. text ed. 9.25 (ISBN 0-8191-2705-1). U Pr of Amer.

UNITED STATES–POLITICS AND GOVERNMENT–19TH CENTURY

Adams, Pauline & Thornton, Emma S. A Populist Assault: Sarah E. Van de Vort Emery on American Democracy 1862-1895. LC 82-60665. (Illus.). 146p. 1982. 13.95 (ISBN 0-87972-203-7); pap. 6.95 (ISBN 0-87972-204-5). Bowling Green Univ.

UNITED STATES–POLITICS AND GOVERNMENT–1865-

Link, Arthur S. & McCormick, Richard L. Progressivism. LC 82-15857. (American History Ser.). 164p. 1983. pap. text ed. 6.95 (ISBN 0-88295-814-3). Harlan Davidson.

UNITED STATES–POLITICS AND GOVERNMENT–1865-1900

Kleppner, Paul. Who Voted: The Dynamics of Electoral Turnout, 1870-1980. Pomper, Gerald M., ed. (American Political Parties & Elections Ser.). 254p. 1982. 27.95 (ISBN 0-03-058933-9). Praeger.

UNITED STATES–POLITICS AND GOVERNMENT–20TH CENTURY

Flanigan, William H. & Zingale, Nancy H. American Voting Behavior: Presidential Elections from 1952 to 1980. LC 82-83324. 1982. write for info. (ISBN 0-89138-920-2, ICPSR 7581). ICPSR.

Gould, Lewis L. Reform & Regulations: American Politics, 1900-1916. LC 77-21058. (Critical Episodes in American Policy Ser.). 1978. pap. text ed. 10.95 (ISBN 0-471-31914-7). Wiley.

Kirk, Russell. Enemies of the Permanent Things: Observations of Abnormity in Literature & Politics. 316p. pap. 8.95 (ISBN 0-89385-021-7). Sugden.

Morgenthau, Hans J. The Purpose of American Politics. LC 82-20057. 382p. 1983. pap. text ed. 13.25 (ISBN 0-8191-2847-3). U Pr of Amer.

UNITED STATES–POLITICS AND GOVERNMENT–1900-1913

Watson, Richard L., Jr. The Development of National Power: The United States 1900-1919. LC 82-20175. 380p. 1983. pap. text ed. 13.75 (ISBN 0-8191-2856-2). U Pr of Amer.

UNITED STATES–POLITICS AND GOVERNMENT–1913-1921

Watson, Richard L., Jr. The Development of National Power: The United States 1900-1919. LC 82-20175. 380p. 1983. pap. text ed. 13.75 (ISBN 0-8191-2856-2). U Pr of Amer.

UNITED STATES–POLITICS AND GOVERNMENT–1933-1945

Mangione, Jerre. An Ethnic at Large: A Memoir of America in the Thirties & Forties. LC 82-40494. (Illus.). 416p. 1983. pap. 10.95 (ISBN 0-8122-1140-5). U of Pa Pr.

Mangione, Jerry. The Dream & the Deal: The Federal Writers Project, 1935-1943. LC 82-40495. (Illus.). 432p. 1983. pap. 10.95 (ISBN 0-8122-1141-3). U of Pa Pr.

Miller, John E. Governor Philip F. LaFollette: The Wisconsin Progressives & the New Deal. 256p. 1982. 21.00. U of MO Pr.

Romasco, Albert U. The Politics of Recovery: Roosevelt's New Deal. LC 82-14499. 270p. 1983. 17.95 (ISBN 0-19-503248-9). Oxford U Pr.

Salmond, John A. A Southern Rebel: The Life & Times of Aubrey Willis Williams, 1890-1965. LC 81-23087. (Fred W. Morrison Ser. in Southern Studies). xiv, 337p. 1983. 25.00x (ISBN 0-8078-1521-7). U of NC Pr.

UNITED STATES–POLITICS AND GOVERNMENT–1945-

Seymour-Ure, Colin. The American President: Power & Communication. LC 82-5772. 1982. 22.50x (ISBN 0-312-02786-9). St Martin.

Young, James S., ed. Problems & Prospects of Presidential Leadership in the Nineteen-Eighties, Vol. 1. LC 82-19981. (Problems & Prospects of the Presidency). (Illus.). 136p. (Orig.). 1982. lib. bdg. 17.25 (ISBN 0-8191-2837-6); pap. text ed. 6.75 (ISBN 0-8191-2838-4). U Pr of Amer.

UNITED STATES–POLITICS AND GOVERNMENT–1961-

Brownstein, Ronald & Easton, Nina, eds. Reagan's Ruling Class: Portraits of the President's Top 100 Officials. LC 82-60917. 747p. 1982. 24.50 (ISBN 0-936486-03-1). Presidential Acct.

Bunzel, John H. New Force on the Left: Tom Hayden & the Campaign Against Corporate America. (Publication Ser.: No. 280). 131p. 1983. pap. 6.95 (ISBN 0-8179-7802-X). Hoover Inst Pr.

Campbell, Colin. Governments under Stress: Political Executives & Key Bureaucrats in Washington, London, & Ottawa. 384p. 1983. 25.00 (ISBN 0-8020-5622-9). U of Toronto Pr.

Clarkson, Stephen. Canada & the Reagan Challenge. (Illus.). 383p. 1983. 19.95 (ISBN 0-89490-091-9). Enslow Pubs.

Congressional Quarterly Inc. Staff. Guide to Current American Government: Fall 1982. LC 61-16893. 160p. 1982. pap. 7.25 (ISBN 0-87187-236-6). Congr Quarterly.

--Guide to Current American Government: Fall 1983. LC 61-16893. 164p. 1983. pap. 7.95 (ISBN 0-87187-261-7). Congr Quarterly.

--Guide to Current American Government: Spring 1983. LC 61-16893. 156p. 1982. pap. 7.95 (ISBN 0-87187-245-5). Congr Quarterly.

--Guide to Current American Government: Spring 1984. LC 61-16893. 164p. 1983. pap. 8.50 (ISBN 0-87187-267-6). Congr Quarterly.

--Reagan's First Year. LC 82-1386. 184p. 1982. pap. 8.95 (ISBN 0-87187-225-0). Congr Quarterly.

Garza, Hedda, compiled by. The Watergate Investigation Index: Senate Select Committee Hearings & Reports on Presidential Campaign Activities. LC 82-7353. 326p. 1982. lib. bdg. 95.00 (ISBN 0-8420-2175-2). Scholarly Res Inc.

Kolkey, Jonathan M. The New Right, Nineteen Sixty to Nineteen Sixty-Eight: With Epilogue, 1969-1980. LC 82-23821. 416p. (Orig.). 1983. lib. bdg. 26.75 (ISBN 0-8191-2993-3); pap. text ed. 15.50 (ISBN 0-8191-2994-1). U Pr of Amer.

Korologos, Tom. Washingtonspeak: A User's Guide to Access & Influence. 160p. 1983. pap. 5.95 (ISBN 0-201-14935-4). A-W.

Lees, J. D. & Maidment, R. A. American Politics Today. 160p. 1982. 15.00 (ISBN 0-7190-0867-0). Manchester.

Miller, Warren, et al. American National Election Study, 1972. LC 82-81968. 1982. Repr. of 1975 ed. write for info. (ISBN 0-89138-928-8, ICPSR 7010). ICPSR.

Palmer, John L. & Sawhill, Isabel V., eds. The Reagan Experiment: An Examination of Economic & Social Policies under the Reagan Administration. 530p. 1982. 29.95 (ISBN 0-87766-315-7, 34100); pap. 12.95 (ISBN 0-87766-316-5, 34200). Urban Inst.

Sorrentino, Frank M. American Government: Power & Politics in America. LC 82-21748. (Illus.). 452p. (Orig.). 1983. pap. text ed. 16.75 (ISBN 0-8191-2946-1). U Pr of Amer.

Will, George F. Statecraft As Soulcraft. 1983. 14.50 (ISBN 0-671-42733-4). S&S.

Wolff, Charles E. & John, Mar. What Now, U. S. A. A Political Science Manual for the Eighties. 1982. 5.75 (ISBN 0-8062-1880-0). Carlton.

UNITED STATES–POPULAR CULTURE

see also United States–Civilization

Confidence Men & Painted Women: A Study of Middle-Class Culture in America, 1830-1870. (Yale Historical Publications Misc.: No. 129). 19.95 (ISBN 0-686-42811-0). Yale U Pr.

Girgus, Sam B. The American Self: Myth, Ideology, & Popular Culture. 1982. pap. 8.95 (ISBN 0-8263-0646-2, A-41P): U of NM Pr.

Javna, John & Javna, Gordon. Sixties! (Illus.). 1983. pap. 12.95 (ISBN 0-312-72752-6). St Martin.

Maltby, Richard. Harmless Entertainmnet: Hollywood & the Ideology of Concensus. LC 82-10344. 425p. 1983. 26.50 (ISBN 0-8108-1548-6). Scarecrow.

Wertheim, Arthur, ed. American Popular Culture in Historical Perpective: An Annotated Bibliography. (Clio Bibliography Ser.: No. 14). 254p. 1983. lib. bdg. 55.00 (ISBN 0-87436-049-8). ABC-Clio.

UNITED STATES–POPULATION

Ashabranner, Brent. The New Americans: Changing Patterns in U. S. Immigration. LC 82-45999. (Illus.). 160p. (gr. 7 up). 1983. PLB 12.95 (ISBN 0-396-08140-1). Dodd.

Rose, Peter I. Mainstream & Margins: Jews, Blacks, & Other Americans. 241p. 1983. 24.95 (ISBN 0-87855-473-4). Transaction Bks.

UNITED STATES–POSTAL SERVICE

see Postal Service

UNITED STATES–PRESIDENTS

see Presidents–United States

UNITED STATES–PUBLIC DOCUMENTS

see United States–Government Publications

UNITED STATES–PUBLIC LANDS

Gregg, Frank. Federal Land Transfers: The Case for a Westwide Program Based on the Federal Land Policy & Management Act. LC 82-8126. 34p. (Orig.). 1982. pap. 5.00 (ISBN 0-89164-071-1). Conservation Foun.

Vanderver, Timothy A., Jr. Federal Lands Notebook. 250p. 1981. 48.00 (ISBN 0-686-38760-0). Gov Insts.

UNITED STATES–RACE RELATIONS

Apostle, Richard A. & Glock, Charles Y. The Anatomy of Racial Attitudes. LC 82-4867. 277p. 1983. 27.50x (ISBN 0-520-04719-2). U of Cal Pr.

Dalby, David. Black Through White: Patterns of Communication. (Hans Wolff Memorial Lecture Ser.). (Orig.). 1970. pap. text ed. 2.00 (ISBN 0-941934-02-0). Ind U Afro-Amer Arts.

MacDonald, J. Fred. Blacks & White TV: Afro-Americans in Television Since 1948. (Illus.). 288p. 1983. text ed. 23.95X (ISBN 0-8304-1020-1); pap. 11.95X (ISBN 0-88229-816-X). Nelson-Hall.

Rose, Willie L. Slavery & Freedom. expanded ed. Freehling, William W., ed. 272p. 1983. pap. 7.95 (ISBN 0-19-503266-7, GB 723, GB). Oxford U Pr.

UNITED STATES–RELATIONS (GENERAL) WITH AFRICA

Moss, Joanna. The Lome Conventions & Their Implications for the United States. Replica ed. 225p. 1982. softcover 19.50 (ISBN 0-86531-935-9). Westview.

UNITED STATES–RELATIONS (GENERAL) WITH CHINA

Woodcock, Leonard. China-United States Relations in Transition. LC 82-12135. 25p. 1982. 1.25 (ISBN 0-934742-21-9, Inst Study Diplomacy). Geo U Sch For Serv.

UNITED STATES–RELATIONS (GENERAL) WITH GREAT BRITAIN

Russett, Bruce M. Community & Contention: Britain & America in the Twentieth Century. LC 82-20952. xii, 252p. 1983. Repr. of 1963 ed. lib. bdg. 29.75x (ISBN 0-313-23792-1, RUCC). Greenwood.

UNITED STATES–RELATIONS (GENERAL) WITH MEXICO

Reynolds, Clark W. & Tello, Carlos, eds. U. S. - Mexico Relations: Economic & Social Aspects. LC 81-86450. 400p. 1983. 25.00x (ISBN 0-8047-1163-1). Stanford U Pr.

UNITED STATES–RELATIONS (GENERAL) WITH UNDERDEVELOPED AREAS

Thompson, W. Scott, ed. The Third World: Premises of U. S. Policy. 2nd ed. 350p. 1983. text ed. 22.50 (ISBN 0-917616-58-8); pap. text ed. 8.95 (ISBN 0-917616-57-X). ICS Pr.

UNITED STATES–RELIGION

Cauthen, Kenneth. The Impact of American Religious Liberalism. 2nd ed. LC 82-23902. 308p. 1983. pap. text ed. 12.75 (ISBN 0-8191-2762-0). U Pr of Amer.

Fichter, Joseph H., ed. Alternatives to American Mainline Churches. LC 82-50819. (Conference Ser.: No. 14). (Orig.). 1982. pap. text ed. 9.95 (ISBN 0-932894-14-3). Unif Theol Seminary.

Manuel, Frank E. The Changing of the Gods. 180p. 1983. text ed. 14.00x (ISBN 0-87451-254-9). U Pr of New Eng.

May, Henry F. Ideas, Faiths, & Feelings: Essays on American Intellectual & Religious History, 1952-1982. 256p. 1983. 25.00 (ISBN 0-19-503235-7, GB); pap. 9.95 (ISBN 0-19-503236-5). Oxford U Pr.

--Ideas, Faiths, & Feelings: Essays on American Intellectual & Religious History, 1952-1982. 256p. 1983. pap. 4.95 (ISBN 0-19-503236-5, GB 719, GB). Oxford U Pr.

UNITED STATES–RELIGION–20TH CENTURY

Douglas, Mary & Tipton, Steven M., eds. Religion & America: Spirituality in a Secular Age. LC 82-72500. 256p. 1983. 13.94 (ISBN 0-8070-1106-1); pap. 8.61 (ISBN 0-8070-1107-X). Beacon Pr.

Steltenkamp, Michael. The Sacred Vision: Native American Religion & Its Practice Today. LC 82-60594. 1983. pap. 5.95 (ISBN 0-8091-2481-5). Paulist Pr.

UNITED STATES–REVENUE

see Tariff–United States; Taxation

UNITED STATES–ROAD MAPS

see Automobile Touring–Road Guides

UNITED STATES–RURAL CONDITIONS

Gilmore, William J. Elementary Literacy on the Eve of the Industrial Revolution: Trends in Rural New England. (Illus.). 91p. 1982. pap. 5.95 (ISBN 0-912296-57-7, Dist. by U Pr of VA). Am Antiquarian.

Johnson, Kenneth M. Population & Retail Services in Nonmetropolitan America. (Rural Studies). 350p. 1983. softcover 25.00x (ISBN 0-86531-584-1). Westview.

UNITED STATES–SECRET SERVICE

see Secret Service

UNITED STATES–SOCIAL CONDITIONS

Allen, Frederick L. The Big Change: America Transforms Itself, 1900-1950. LC 82-18395. xii, 308p. 1983. Repr. of 1952 ed. lib. bdg. 35.00x (ISBN 0-313-23791-3, ALBC). Greenwood.

Bender, Thomas. Community & Social Change in America. LC 82-47981. 176p. (Orig.). 1982. pap. text ed. 5.95x (ISBN 0-8018-2924-0). Johns Hopkins.

DeFleur, Melvin L. Social Problems in American Society. LC 82-81108. 640p. 1982. text ed. 16.95 (ISBN 0-395-32567-6); instr's. manual avail. (ISBN 0-395-32568-4). HM.

Smith, Lowell. Average American. LC 82-84427. (Illus.). 112p. (Orig.). 1983. pap. 8.00 (ISBN 0-937088-03-X). Illum Pr.

Van Sickle, Larry. Teaching Poor Kids to Labor: The American Dream & the Impact of Class. 240p. 1983. text ed. 19.95x (ISBN 0-8290-1294-X). Irvington.

UNITED STATES–SOCIAL CONDITIONS–BIBLIOGRAPHY

American Social Reform & Reaction: A Historical Bibliography. (Clio Bibliography Ser.: No. 13). 254p. 1983. lib. bdg. 55.00 (ISBN 0-87436-048-X). ABC-Clio.

UNITED STATES–SOCIAL CONDITIONS–1960-

Clecak, Peter. America's Quest for Self: Dissent & Fulfillment in the 60s & 70s. 368p. 1983. 22.50 (ISBN 0-19-503226-8). Oxford U Pr.

Freeman, Jo, ed. Social Movements of the 60's & 70's. (Illus.). 480p. (Orig.). 1982. pap. text ed. 14.95x (ISBN 0-582-28091-5). Longman.

Fuchs, Victor. How We Live. (Illus.). 320p. 1983. 17.50 (ISBN 0-674-41225-7). Harvard U Pr.

Stasz, Clarice. The American Nightmare: Why Inequality Persists. LC 80-6191. 233p. 1983. pap. 7.95 (ISBN 0-8052-0709-0). Schocken.

Stewart, Elbert. Social Problems in Modern America. 3rd ed. Provenzano, Marian D., ed. (Illus.). 432p. 1983. pap. text ed. 18.00x (ISBN 0-07-061427-X, C); write for info. instr's manual (ISBN 0-07-061428-8). McGraw.

Vernon, Sidney. The Adolescent Drug-Sex-Crime Matter: Common Sense About the National Defense. 1982. pap. 0.99 (ISBN 0-943150-02-7). Rovern Pr.

Weiner, Rex & Stillman, Deanne. Woodstock Census. Date not set. pap. 5.95 (ISBN 0-449-90036-3, Columbine). Fawcett.

UNITED STATES–SOCIAL LIFE AND CUSTOMS

Aldridge, John W. The American Novel & the Way We Live Now. 192p. 1983. 16.95 (ISBN 0-19-503198-9). Oxford U Pr.

Campbell, Angus & Converse, Phillip E. Quality of American Life, Nineteen Seventy-Eight. LC 80-84081. 1980. write for info (ISBN 0-89138-951-2). ICPSR.

Chambers, Wicke & Asher, Spring, eds. The Celebration Book of Great American Traditions. LC 82-48113. (Illus.). 192p. 1983. 15.50 (ISBN 0-06-015095-5, HarpT). Har-Row.

Congressional Quarterly Inc. American Regionalism: Our Economic, Cultural & Political Makeup. LC 80-18934. (Editorial Research Reports). 208p. 1980. pap. 7.50 (ISBN 0-87187-194-7). Congr Quarterly.

Lacour-Gayet, Robert. Everyday Life in the United States before the Civil War, 1830-1860. Ilford, Mary, tr. from French. LC 70-81571. 310p. 1983. pap. 7.95 (ISBN 0-8044-6376-X). Ungar.

Schlossberg, Herbert. Idols for Destruction: Christian Faith & Its Confrontation with American Society. 320p. 1983. 14.95; pap. 8.95 (ISBN 0-8407-5832-4). Nelson.

Smith, Lowell. Average American. LC 82-84427. (Illus.). 112p. (Orig.). 1983. pap. 8.00 (ISBN 0-937088-03-X). Illum Pr.

UNITED STATES–SOCIAL LIFE AND CUSTOMS–BIBLIOGRAPHY

Zamora, Lois P., ed. The Apocalyptic Vision in America: Interdisciplinary Essays on Myth & Culture. LC 81-85524. 272p. 1982. 19.95 (ISBN 0-686-82270-6). Bowling Green Univ.

UNITED STATES–SOCIAL LIFE AND CUSTOMS–COLONIAL PERIOD, ca. 1600-1775

Rice, Kym. Early American Taverns: For the Entertainment of Friends & Strangers. LC 82-42786. 1983. pap. 12.95. Regnery-Gateway.

UNITED STATES–SOCIAL POLICY

Choate, Pat & Walter, Susan. America in Ruins: The Decaying Infrastructure. (Duke Press Policy Studies). 100p. 1983. pap. 9.75 (ISBN 0-8223-0554-2). Duke.

Ginsburg, Helen. Full Employment & Public Policy: The United States & Sweden. LC 76-55536. 256p. 1983. 24.95x (ISBN 0-669-01318-8). Lexington Bks.

Palmer, John L. & Sawhill, Isabel V., eds. The Reagan Experiment: An Examination of Economic & Social Policies under the Reagan Administration. 530p. 1982. 29.95 (ISBN 0-87766-315-7, 34100); pap. 12.95 (ISBN 0-87766-316-5, 34200). Urban Inst.

Rein, Martin. Social Policy: Issues of Choice & Change. 392p. 1983. pap. text ed. 14.95 (ISBN 0-87332-235-5). M E Sharpe.

UNITED STATES–STATISTICS

Hacker, Andrew. U. S. A Statistical Portrait. 1983. 25.00 (ISBN 0-670-73842-5). Viking Pr.

United Nations. Yearbook of National Accounts Statistics, 1980, 2 Vols. 24th ed. LC 58-3718. (Illus.). 2337p. 1982. Set. 125.00x (ISBN 0-8002-1124-3). Intl Pubns Serv.

UNITED STATES–STATISTICS, MEDICAL

Cypress, Beulah K. Medication Therapy in Office Visits for Selected Diagnoses: National Ambulatory Medical Care Survey, United States, 1980. Cox, Klaudia, ed. (Ser. 13: No. 71). 65p. 1982. pap. text ed. 1.85 (ISBN 0-8406-0266-9). Natl Ctr Health Stats.

UNITED STATES–SUPREME COURT

Congressional Quarterly Inc. Staff. Supreme Court, Justice & the Law. 1983. pap. 9.25 (ISBN 0-87187-253-6). Congr Quarterly.

Evans, Patricia & Blandford, Linda. Supreme Court of the United States 1789-1980: An Index to Opinions Arranged by Justice. LC 82-48981. (Orig.). 1983. lib. bdg. 85.00 (ISBN 0-527-27952-8). Kraus Intl.

Galloway, Russell. The Rich & the Poor in Supreme Court History. Aigner, Hal, ed. LC 82-62643. 230p. 1983. pap. 7.95 (ISBN 0-937572-01-2). Paradigm Pr.

Guenther, Nancy A. United States Supreme Court Decisions: An Index to Excerpts, Reprints & Discussions. 2nd ed. LC 82-10518. (Illus.). 864p. 1983. 52.50 (ISBN 0-8108-1578-8). Scarecrow.

Kurland, Philip B. & Casper, Gerhard, eds. The Supreme Court Review, 1982. 2nd ed. LC 60-14353. (The Supreme Court Review Ser.). 432p. 1983. lib. bdg. 30.00x (ISBN 0-226-46435-0). U of Chicago Pr.

Muller, W. H. Early History of the Supreme Court. xii, 117p. 1982. Repr. of 1922 ed. lib. bdg. 22.50x (ISBN 0-686-81665-X). Rothman.

Schwartz, Bernard & Lesher, Stephen. Final Judgement: Inside the Warren Court 1953-69. LC 82-45454. (Illus.). 264p. 1983. 16.95 (ISBN 0-385-18326-7). Doubleday.

UNITED STATES–TARIFF

see Tariff–United States

UNITED STATES–TAXATION

see Taxation

UNITED STATES–TERRITORIAL EXPANSION

Goetzmann, William H. When the Eagle Screamed: The Romantic Horizon in American Diplomacy, 1800-1860. (Illus.). 138p. (Orig.). 1966. pap. 10.95x (ISBN 0-471-31001-8). Wiley.

UNITED STATES–TERRITORIES AND POSSESSIONS

Merk, Federick & Merrk, Lois B. Manifest Destiny & Mission in American History: A Reinterpretation. LC 82-25146. ix, 265p. 1983. Repr. lib. bdg. 35.00x (ISBN 0-313-23844-8, MERM). Greenwood.

UNITED STATES–TRAVEL

see United States–Description and Travel

UNITED STATES–WAR DEPARTMENT

Lippman, Walter. U.S. War Aims. LC 76-16079. 235p. 1976. Repr. of 1944 ed. lib. bdg. 29.50 (ISBN 0-306-70773-X). Da Capo.

UNITED STATES IN LITERATURE

Lynn, Kenneth S. The Air-Line to Seattle: Studies in Literary & Historical Writing about America. 240p. 1983. lib. bdg. 17.50x (ISBN 0-226-49832-8). U of Chicago Pr.

UNITED STATES MILITARY ACADEMY, WEST POINT, NEW YORK

Simpson, Jeffrey. Officers & Gentlemen: Historic West Point in Photographs. LC 82-16820. (Illus.). 223p. 1982. 24.95 (ISBN 0-912882-53-0). Sleepy Hollow.

UNIVERSAL HISTORY

see World History

UNIVERSAL MILITARY TRAINING

see Military Service, Compulsory

UNIVERSAL SALVATION

see Universalism

UNIVERSALISM

see also Salvation

Derry, John & Derry, Reg. Spectral Universe. 1983. 7.95 (ISBN 0-533-05502-4). Vantage.

UNIVERSE

see Cosmogony; Cosmology

UNIVERSITIES AND COLLEGES

see also Degrees, Academic; Dissertations, Academic; Education, Higher; Junior Colleges; Libraries, University and College; Medical Colleges; Self-Government (In Education); State Universities and Colleges; Students

also headings beginning with the word College, and names of universities and colleges, e.g. Yale University; California, University of

Andersen, Niels T. Sunrise Over Jordan: A Twenty-First Century College. LC 82-84248. 283p. 1982. 11.95 (ISBN 0-910213-01-1); pap. 6.95 (ISBN 0-910213-00-3). Jordan Pub.

Graham, Lawrence. Ten-Point College Plan. 144p. 1982. pap. 6.95 (ISBN 0-399-50678-0, Perige). Putnam Pub Group.

Langer, Steven, ed. College Recruiting Report, 1982. 1982. pap. 95.00 (ISBN 0-686-84830-6). Abbott Langer Assocs.

OECD. The University & the Community: The Problems of Changing Relationships. 162p. 1982. pap. 14.50 (ISBN 92-64-12370-9). OECD.

Rumble, Greville & Harry, Keith, eds. The Distance Teaching University. LC 82-42559. 1982. 25.00x (ISBN 0-312-21323-9). St Martin.

UNIVERSITIES AND COLLEGES–ADMINISTRATION

see also Personnel Service in Education

Gift Reporting Standards & Management Reports for Educational Institutions. 24p. 1981. 10.00 (ISBN 0-89964-185-7). CASE.

Pond, Samuel A., ed. Bricker's International Directory of University Executive Development Programs: 1982. 13th ed. LC 73-110249. 1981. 90.00X (ISBN 0-9604804-1-2). Bricker's Intl.

--Bricker's International Directory of University Executive Development Programs: 1983. 14th ed. 1982. 90.00X (ISBN 0-9604804-2-0). Bricker's Intl.

Porter, D. & Padley, J. S. Training University Administrators in Europe: An OECD-IMHE Report. 137p. 1982. text ed. 29.00x (ISBN 0-566-00522-0). Gower Pub Ltd.

Sammartino, Peter. The President of a Small College. 162p. 1982. 9.95 (ISBN 0-8453-4757-8). Cornwall Bks.

Welzenbach, Lanora F. Contracting for Services. 1982. pap. 25.00 (ISBN 0-915164-15-9). Natl Assn Coll.

UNIVERSITIES AND COLLEGES–ADMISSION

Corras, James & Zerowin, Jeffrey. Improving College Admission Test Scores: Verbal Workbook. 184p. (Orig.). (gr. 11-12). 1982. pap. write for info. (ISBN 0-88210-135-8). Natl Assn Principals.

De Oliveira, Paulo. Getting In! Steps to Acceptance at a Selective College. LC 82-40503. 160p. 1982. pap. 5.95 (ISBN 0-89480-359-X). Workman Pub.

Morrison, James W. Veterianary College Admission Test. 384p. 1983. pap. 10.95 (ISBN 0-668-05545-6, 5545). Arco.

Shanahan, William F. College: Yes or No? The High School Student's Career Decision-Making Handbook. LC 82-6775. 256p. (gr. 9 up). 1983. lib. bdg. 12.95 (ISBN 0-668-05589-8); pap. 7.95 (ISBN 0-668-05590-1). Arco.

Zuker, R. Fred & Hegener, Karen C. Peterson's Guide to College Admissions: Getting into the College of Your Choice. 3rd. Ed. ed. 310p. 1983. pap. 9.95 (ISBN 0-87866-224-3, 2243). Peterson's Guides.

UNIVERSITIES AND COLLEGES–ALUMNI

see also College Graduates

Alberger, Patricia L., ed. How to Work Effectively with Alumni Boards. 81p. (Orig.). 1981. 14.50 (ISBN 0-89964-182-2). CASE.

Gorman, Brian, compiled by. Finding Lost Alumni: Tracing Methods Used by 19 Institutions. 30p. 1981. 10.50 (ISBN 0-89964-181-4). CASE.

Stetson, Daniel E. Alumni Invitational Exhibition. Boatright, Kevin, ed. (Illus.). 16p. (Orig.). 1982. pap. text ed. 2.50 (ISBN 0-932660-05-3). U of NI Dept Art.

Zagoren, Adelaide M., compiled by. Involving Alumni in Career Assistance Programs. 111p. 1982. 14.50 (ISBN 0-89964-192-X). CASE.

UNIVERSITIES AND COLLEGES–CURRICULA

Conley, Diane, ed. Peterson's Annual Guides to Graduate Study: Graduate & Professional Programs: An Overview, 1983. 700p. 1982. pap. 13.95 (ISBN 0-87866-185-9). Petersons Guides.

--Peterson's Guides to Graduate Study: Humanities & Social Sciences, 1983. 1200p. 1982. pap. 18.95 (ISBN 0-87866-186-7). Petersons Guides.

Dill, Stephen H. Integrated Studies: Challenges to the College Curriculum. LC 82-17511. (Illus.). 158p. (Orig.). 1983. lib. bdg. 19.50 (ISBN 0-8191-2794-9); pap. text ed. 9.25 (ISBN 0-8191-2795-7). U Pr of Amer.

Marsteller, Phyllis, ed. Peterson's Annual Guides to Graduate & Undergraduate Study, 1983, 6 vols. 7200p. (Orig.). 1982. pap. 105.00 set (ISBN 0-87866-190-5). Petersons Guides.

--Peterson's Guides to Graduate Study: Biological, Agricultural, & Health Sciences, 1983. 1800p. 1982. pap. 21.95 (ISBN 0-87866-187-5). Petersons Guides.

Ready, Barbara C., ed. Peterson's Annual Guides to Graduate Study: Engineering & Applied Sciences, 1983. 800p. 1982. pap. 17.95 (ISBN 0-87866-189-1). Petersons Guides.

--Peterson's Guides to Graduate Study: Physical Sciences & Mathematics, 1983. 650p. (Orig.). 1982. pap. 17.95 (ISBN 0-87866-188-3). Petersons Guides.

Wilburn, James R., ed. Freedom, Order & the University. LC 82-5274. 1982. 12.95 (ISBN 0-932612-12-1). Pepperdine U Pr.

UNIVERSITIES AND COLLEGES–DIRECTORIES

Brawner, Julianne R., et al. The Kudzu-Ivy Guide to Southern Colleges. LC 81-82293. 580p. (Orig.). 1982. pap. 10.95 (ISBN 0-9605142-1-X). Kudzu-Ivy.

Callahan, Timothy R. Callahan's Compact College Guide to Athletics & Academics in America. LC 82-73347. 264p. 1982. 12.95 (ISBN 0-910967-00-8). Callahan's Guides.

College-Bound Digest. 1982. pap. 1.50 (ISBN 0-915130-76-9). Educ Comm.

Glotzer, Arline & Levy, Valerie. Lovejoy's Guide to Graduate Business Schools. (Orig.). 1983. pap. 6.95 (ISBN 0-671-44884-6). Monarch Pr.

Lovejoy. Lovejoy's College Guide. Levy, Valerie, ed. (Orig.). 1983. pap. 12.95 (ISBN 0-671-47170-8). Monarch Pr.

Marshall, Stephen E., ed. Randax Education Guide: A Guide to Colleges Seeking Students, 1983 Edition. 12th ed. (Illus.). 128p. (Orig.). 1983. pap. 8.95 (ISBN 0-914880-13-6). Educ Guide.

Ridenour, Dian M. & Johnston, Jane. A Guide to Post-Secondary Educational Opportunities for the Learning Disabled. 183p. 1981. pap. 12.00 (ISBN 0-9608010-0-6). Time Out.

University Aviation Association. Collegiate Aviation Directory: A Guide to College Level Aviation-Aerospace Study. Schukert, Michael A., ed. 128p. 1982. pap. text ed. 2.55 (ISBN 0-8403-2876-1). Kendall-Hunt.

UNIVERSITIES AND COLLEGES–ENTRANCE REQUIREMENTS

see Universities and Colleges–Admission

UNIVERSITIES AND COLLEGES–EXAMINATIONS

Herzog, David A. Science & Social Studies Workbook for the GED Test. (Arco's Preparation for the GED Examination Ser.). 256p. 1983. pap. 5.95 (ISBN 0-668-05541-3, 5541). Arco.

Rosenberg, Richard. Lovejoy's Math Review for the SAT. Levy, Valerie, ed. (Exam Preparation Guides). (Orig.). 1983. pap. 7.95 (ISBN 0-671-47150-3). Monarch Pr.

SAT Teachers Manual. 1982. pap. write for info. (ISBN 0-8120-2693-4). Barron.

UNIVERSITIES AND COLLEGES–FACULTY

see also College Teachers

Baldwin, Roger & Brakeman, Louis. Expanding Faculty Options: Career Development Projects at Colleges & Universities. 116p. 1981. 7.95. Impact VA.

Dziech, Billie W. & Faaborg, Linda. The Lecherous Professor: Sexual Harassment on Campus. LC 82-73960. 320p. 1983. 14.37 (ISBN 0-8070-3100-3). Beacon Pr.

UNIVERSITIES AND COLLEGES–FINANCE

see also College Costs

Dunseth, William B. An Introduction to Annuity, Charitable Remainder Trust & Bequest Programs. 2nd ed. 37p. 1982. 14.50 (ISBN 0-89964-193-8). CASE.

Hall, Elizabeth S., compiled by. Matching Gift Details 1982. 170p. 1981. 25.00 (ISBN 0-89964-197-0); nonmembers 60.00 (ISBN 0-686-82675-2). CASE.

Sweeney, Robert D., compiled by. Raising Money Through Gift Clubs: A Survey of Techniques at 42 Institutions. 71p. 1982. 14.50 (ISBN 0-89964-191-1). CASE.

UNIVERSITIES AND COLLEGES–FURNITURE, EQUIPMENT, ETC.

see Schools–Furniture, Equipment, etc.

UNIVERSITIES AND COLLEGES–GRADUATE WORK

Directory of Graduate Physical Education Programs 1982. 80p. 11.95 (ISBN 0-88314-058-6). AAHPERD.

Herzog, David A. Science & Social Studies Workbook for the GED Test. (Arco's Preparation for the GED Examination Ser.). 256p. 1983. pap. 5.95 (ISBN 0-668-05541-3, 5541). Arco.

Judge, Harry. American Graduate Schools of Education: A View from Abroad: A Report to the Ford Foundation. 69p. (Orig.). 1982. pap. text ed. 4.50 (ISBN 0-916584-21-6). Ford Found.

UNIVERSITIES AND COLLEGES–LAW

see Educational Law and Legislation

UNIVERSITIES AND COLLEGES–PUBLIC RELATIONS

see Public Relations–Schools

UNIVERSITIES AND COLLEGES–SELECTION

see College, Choice Of

UNIVERSITIES AND COLLEGES–STUDENTS

see College Students

UNIVERSITIES AND COLLEGES–AUSTRALIA

Gallagher, A. P. Coordinating Australian University Development: A Study of the Australian Universities Commission, 1959-1970. LC 82-1973. (Scholars Library). 244p. 1983. text ed. 34.50x (ISBN 0-7022-1657-7). U of Queensland Pr.

UNIVERSITIES AND COLLEGES–EUROPE

Here are entered works on universities and colleges in Europe in general, as well as those on specific countries of Europe.

Weisz, George. The Emergence of Modern Universities in France, 1863-1914. LC 82-13307. 376p. 1983. 35.00 (ISBN 0-691-05375-8). Princeton U Pr.

UNIVERSITIES AND COLLEGES–GREAT BRITAIN

Association of Commonwealth Universities. Schedule of Postgraduate Courses in United Kingdom Universities, 1981-82. 18th ed. LC 75-644246. 114p. 1981. pap. 10.00x (ISBN 0-85143-075-9). Intl Pubns Serv.

Clapp, B. W. The University of Exeter: A History. 208p. 1982. 40.00x (ISBN 0-85989-133-X, Pub. by Exeter Univ England). State Mutual Bk.

Donald, L. & MacDonald, W. S., eds. Roll of Graduates of the University of Aberdeen, 1956-1970: With Supplement 1860-1955. 1982. 82.80 (ISBN 0-08-028469-8). Pergamon.

Joyce, Patrick. The History of Morden College Blackheath, 1695 to the Present. 1982. 50.00 (ISBN 0-686-84446-7, Pub. By Gresham England). State Mutual Bk.

UNIVERSITIES AND COLLEGES–GREAT BRITAIN–ENTRANCE REQUIREMENTS

Association of the commonwealth Universities. Compendium of University Entrance Requirements for First Degree Courses in the United Kingdom, 1983-84. 20th ed. LC 74-648109. (Illus.). 355p. (Orig.). 1982. pap. text ed. 18.50x (ISBN 0-85143-077-5). Intl Pubns Serv.

UNIVERSITIES AND COLLEGES–INDIA

Universities Handbook: India, 1981-82. 21st ed. 1264p. 1980. 50.00x (ISBN 0-8002-3057-4, E35-209). Intl Pubns Serv.

UNIVERSITIES AND COLLEGES–IRELAND

Bowman, John & O'Donoghue, Ronan. Portraits: Belvedere College, 1832-1982. 1982. 75.00x (ISBN 0-7171-1235-7, Pub. by Gill & Macmillan Ireland). State Mutual Bk.

UNIVERSITIES AND COLLEGES, AFRO-AMERICAN

see Afro-American Universities and Colleges

UNIVERSITY DEGREES

see Degrees, Academic

UNIVERSITY DRAMA

see College and School Drama

UNIVERSITY GRADUATES

see College Graduates

UNIVERSITY LIBRARIES

see Libraries, University and College

UNIVERSITY OF CALIFORNIA

see California, University Of

UNIVERSITY OF IOWA

see Iowa, University Of

UNIVERSITY PRESIDENTS

see Universities and Colleges–Administration

UNIVERSITY READERS

see College Readers

UNIVERSITY STUDENTS

see College Students

UNIVERSITY TEACHERS

see College Teachers

UNIVERSITY TEACHING AS A PROFESSION

see College Teaching As a Profession

UNMARRIED MOTHERS

Forman, Rachel Z. Let Us Now Praise Obscure Women: A Comparative Study of Publicly Supported Unmarried Mothers in Government Housing in the United States & Britain. LC 82-17579. 240p. (Orig.). 1983. lib. bdg. 22.00 (ISBN 0-8191-2813-9); pap. text ed. 10.75 (ISBN 0-8191-2814-7). U Pr of Amer.

UNMARRIED PEOPLE

see Single People

UNMARRIED WOMEN

see Single Women

UNTOUCHABLES

Goyal, B. R. Educating Harijans. 1982. 11.50x (ISBN 0-8364-0863-2, Pub by Academic India). South Asia Bks.

UPDIKE, JOHN

Hunt, George. John Updike & the Three Great Secret Things: Sex, Religion & Art. 1981. 13.95 (ISBN 0-8028-3539-2, 3539-2). Eerdmans.

UPHOLSTERY

see also Drapery; Furniture; Interior Decoration

Brumbaugh, James. UPholstering. new ed. (Audel Ser.). 1983. 12.95 (ISBN 0-672-23372-X). Bobbs.

UPPER CLASSES

Fox, James. White Mischief. LC 82-42800. (Illus.). 299p. 1983. 15.95 (ISBN 0-394-50918-8). Random.

URANIUM

see also Nuclear Fuels; Transuranium Elements

Osmond, J. K. & Cowart, J. B. Natural Uranium & Thorium Series Disequilibrium: New Approaches to Geochemical Problems. (Nuclear Science Applications Ser.: Section B). 50p. 1982. 19.95 (ISBN 3-7186-0131-1). Harwood Academic.

Proceedings, Annual Uranium Seminar, No.5. LC 81-71601. (Illus.). 187p. 1982. pap. text ed. 20.00x (ISBN 0-89520-291-3). Soc Mining Eng.

Uranium Exploration Methods. 980p. (Orig., Eng. & Fr.). 1982. pap. 48.00x (ISBN 92-64-02350-X). OECD.

URBAN AFFAIRS RESEARCH

see Municipal Research

URBAN ANTHROPOLOGY

Fried, Jacob. Crawley: New Town. 350p. (Orig.). 1983. pap. 10.95 (ISBN 0-913244-60-0). Hapi Pr.

Hannerz, Ulf. Exploring the City: Inquiries Toward an Urban Anthropology. 378p. 1983. pap. 12.00 (ISBN 0-231-08376-9). Columbia U Pr.

URBAN AREAS

see Cities and Towns

URBAN BEAUTIFICATION

The Highrise of Homes. LC 82-50645. (Illus.). 112p. 1982. pap. 12.50 (ISBN 0-8478-0467-4). Rizzoli Intl.

URBAN CLERGY

see City Clergy

URBAN DESIGN

see City Planning

URBAN DEVELOPMENT

see City Planning

URBAN EDUCATION

see Education, Urban

URBAN LIFE

see City and Town Life

URBAN MINISTRY

see City Clergy

URBAN PLANNING

see City Planning

URBAN POLICY

see City Planning

URBAN RENEWAL

see also City Planning; Community Organizations; Urban Beautification

The Highrise of Homes. LC 82-50645. (Illus.). 112p. 1982. pap. 12.50 (ISBN 0-8478-0467-4). Rizzoli Intl.

Michaelsen, Mark G. Enterprize Zones: A Fresh Approach Which May Possibly Help Solve the Problem of Urban Blight? (Vital Issues Ser.: Vol. XXXI, No. 3). 0.80 (ISBN 0-686-84136-0). Ctr Info Am.

Redstone, Louis G. The New Downtowns: Rebuilding Business Districts. LC 82-17111. 356p. 1983. Repr. of 1976 ed. lib. bdg. p.n.s. (ISBN 0-89874-560-8). Krieger.

URBAN SOCIOLOGY

see Sociology, Urban

URBAN TRAFFIC

see City Traffic; Traffic Engineering

URBAN TRANSIT

see Local Transit

URBAN TRANSPORTATION

Here are entered works on general transportation in urban areas, including local transit, private transportation, streets, roads, etc. Works on the transit systems of urban areas are entered under Local Transit.

see also City Traffic

Abouchar, Alan. Transportation Economics & Public Policy: With Urban Extensions. LC 82-17081. 344p. 1983. Repr. of 1977 ed. lib. bdg. price not set (ISBN 0-89874-563-2). Krieger.

Barrett, Paul. The Automobile & Urban Transit: The Formation of Public Policy in Chicago. 1983. write for info. (ISBN 0-87722-294-0). Temple U Pr.

De Silva, Clarence W. & Wormley, David N. Automated Guideway Transit Analysis & Design. LC 80-8927. 304p. 1983. 37.95x (ISBN 0-669-04407-5). Lexington Bks.

OECD. Review of Demand Models: ECMT Round Table Fifty Eight Forecasts-Recorded Traffic Comparisons for Urban Sands Intercity Transport. (Orig.). 1982. pap. 9.00x (ISBN 92-821-1078-8). OECD.

URBANISM

see Cities and Towns

URBANIZATION

Bender, Thomas. Toward an Urban Vision: Ideas & Institutions in Nineteenth-Century America. LC 82-47980. 296p. (Orig.). 1982. pap. text ed. 7.50x (ISBN 0-8018-2925-9). Johns Hopkins.

Castells, Manuel. The City & the Grassroots: A Cross-Cultural Theory of Urban Social Movements. LC 82-40099. (California Ser. in Urban Development: Vol. 2). (Illus.). 600p. 1983. 38.50x (ISBN 0-520-04756-7). U of Cal Pr.

Kundell, James E. & White, Fred C. Prime Farmland in Georgia. 49p. 1982. pap. 6.50 (ISBN 0-89854-081-X). U of GA Inst Govt.

Rondinelli, Dennis A. Secondary Cities in Developing Countries: Policies for Diffusing Urbanization. (Sage Library of Social Research). (Illus.). 256p. 1983. 25.00 (ISBN 0-8039-1945-X); pap. 12.50 (ISBN 0-8039-1946-8). Sage.

Slaven, A. & Aldcroft, D., eds. Business, Banking & Urban History: Essays in Honour of S. G. Checkland. 235p. 1982. text ed. 31.50x (ISBN 0-85976-083-9, 40292, Pub. by Donald Scotland). Humanities.

URDU LANGUAGE

see also Hindi Language

Barker, Muhammad & Hamdani. Spoken Urdu, Vol. 1. 497p. 1975. with 9 cassettes 135.00x (ISBN 0-88432-106-1, U200). J Norton Pubs.

--Spoken Urdu, Vol. 2. 568p. Date not set. with 5 cassettes 115.00x (ISBN 0-88432-107-X, U250). J Norton Pubs.

URDU LITERATURE

Hasan, Khalid, ed. Versions of Truth: Urdu Short Stories from Pakistan. 1983. text ed. write for info. (ISBN 0-7069-2128-3, Pub. by Vikas India). Advent NY.

UREA

Lowenthal, A. & Mori, A., eds. Urea Cycle Diseases. (Advances in Experimental Medicine & Biology). 516p. 1982. 62.50x (ISBN 0-306-41037-0, Plenum Pr). Plenum Pub.

URETHANES

Edwards, Kenneth N., ed. Urethane Chemistry & Applications. (ACS Symposium Ser.: No. 172). 1981. write for info. Am Chemical.

Hepburn, C. Polyurethane Elastomers. (Illus.). ix, 400p. 1982. 82.00 (ISBN 0-85334-127-3, Pub. by Applied Sci England). Elsevier.

URETHRA

Mauermayer, W. Transurethral Surgery. (Illus.). 477p. 1983. 148.00 (ISBN 0-387-11869-1). Springer-Verlag.

URINARY BLADDER

see Bladder

URINARY CALCULI

see Calculi, Urinary

URINARY INCONTINENCE

see Urine–Incontinence

URINARY ORGANS

see also Bladder; Genito-Urinary Organs; Urethra

Gosling, J. A. & Dixon, J. S. Functional Anatomy of the Urinary Tract: An Integrated Text & Color Atlas. (Illus.). 132p. 1983. text ed. 127.50 (ISBN 0-8391-1772-8, 19518). Univ Park.

URINARY ORGANS–DISEASES

see also Urology;

also names of individual organs with or without the subdivision Diseases; names of particular diseases, e.g. Bright's Disease

Bailey, Ross R., ed. Single Dose Treatment of Urinary Tract Infection. 1982. text ed. write for info. (ISBN 0-86792-007-6, Pub by Adis Pr Australia). Wright-PSG.

URINE

see also Urea

O'Quinn, John F. Urine Therapy: Self-Healing Through Intrinsic Medicine. 40p. 1980. pap. text ed. 6.95 (ISBN 0-9609802-1-0). Life Science.

URINE–INCONTINENCE

Abrams, P. H. Urodynamics. (Clinical Practice in Urology Ser.). (Illus.). 240p. 1983. 44.00 (ISBN 0-387-11903-5). Springer-Verlag.

Ulmsten, U., ed. Female Stress Incontinence. (Contributions to Gynecology & Obstetrics: Vol. 10). (Illus.). viii, 120p. 1983. pap. 57.50 (ISBN 3-8055-3665-8). S Karger.

UROGENITAL ORGANS

see Genito-Urinary Organs

UROLOGY

see also Genito-Urinary Organs; Genito-Urinary Organs–Diseases; Urinary Organs

Abrams, P. H. Urodynamics. (Clinical Practice in Urology Ser.). (Illus.). 240p. 1983. 44.00 (ISBN 0-387-11903-5). Springer-Verlag.

Donohue, John P. Testis Tumors. (International Perspectives in Urology: Vol. 7). (Illus.). 360p. 1983. lib. bdg. price not set (ISBN 0-683-02613-5). Williams & Wilkins.

Gillenwater, Jay Y. Year Book of Urology 1980. 1980. 30.95 (ISBN 0-8151-3470-3). Year Bk Med.

--Year Book of Urology 1983. 1983. 40.00 (ISBN 0-8151-3473-8). Year Bk Med.

Magee, Michael C. Basic Science for the Practicing Urologist. LC 82-4561. (Illus.). 250p. Date not set. price not set (ISBN 0-521-24567-2). Cambridge U Pr.

USAGES

see Manners and Customs

USE OF LAND

see Land Use

USED AIRCRAFT

Aviation Consumer Staff. The Aviation Consumer Used Aircraft Guide. 1981. 24.75 (ISBN 0-07-002543-6). McGraw.

USED CAR TRADE

Darack, Arthur & Consumer Group, Inc. Used Cars: How to Avoid Highway Robbery. (Illus.). 256p. 1983. 18.95 (ISBN 0-13-940056-7); pap. 7.95 (ISBN 0-13-940049-4). P-H.

How to Buy & Sell a Used Car in Europe. 3.50 (ISBN 0-686-83755-X). Yara Pr.

USEFUL ARTS

see Industrial Arts; Technology

USES, CHARITABLE

see Charitable Uses, Trusts and Foundations

USURY

see Interest and Usury

UTAH–ANTIQUITIES

Thompson, George A. Some Dreams Die: Utah's Ghost Towns & Lost Treasures. Brown, Marc, ed. (Illus.). 200p. (Orig.). 1982. pap. 10.00 (ISBN 0-942688-01-5). Dream Garden.

UTAH–DESCRIPTION AND TRAVEL

Fox, Theron. Utah Treasure Hunter's Ghost Town Guide. (Illus.). 1983. pap. 2.50. Nevada Pubns.

Kelsey, Michael R. Utah Mountaineering Guide & Including the Best Canyon Hikes. (Illus.). 162p. (Orig.). 1983. pap. 9.95 (ISBN 0-9605824-1-X). Kelsey Pub.

Knudsen, Mark & Passey, Neil. Utah! Gateway to Nevada. (Illus.). 100p. (Orig.). 1983. pap. 6.00 (ISBN 0-942688-05-8). Dream Garden.

Patterson, Thomas. Wasatch Hiking Map. 1983. pap. 5.00 (ISBN 0-87480-220-2). U of Utah Pr.

Roylance, Ward J. UTAH: A Guide to the State. Revised ed. 844p. 1982. Repr. of 1940 ed. 22.50 (ISBN 0-914740-25-3). Western Epics.

--UTAH: A Guide to the State, Tour Section Only. Revised ed. (Part 2). 400p. 1982. pap. 8.95. Western Epics.

Trimble, Stephen. Timpanogos Cave: A Window into the Earth. Priehs, T. J. & Dodson, Carolyn, eds. LC 82-61192. 1983. pap. price not set (ISBN 0-911408-64-9). SW Pks Mnmts.

Utah. 1982. 7.95 (ISBN 0-933692-24-2). R Collings.

UTAH–HISTORY
Nelson, Lee. The Storm Testament. (Utah Frontier Ser.). 320p. 1982. 9.95 (ISBN 0-936860-09-X). Liberty Pr.
Sanpete County Commission. The Other Forty Niners: A Topical History of Sanpete Country, Utah. Antrei, Albert C., et al, eds. 1982. write for info. (ISBN 0-914740-26-1). Western Epics.
UTE INDIANS
see Indians of North America–Southwest, New
UTENSILS
see Implements, Utensils, etc.
UTERUS–CANCER
Hafez, E. S. Carcinoma of the Cervix. 1982. 89.50 (ISBN 90-247-2574-7, Pub. by Martinus Nijhoff Netherlands). Kluwer Boston.
UTERUS–EXCISION
see Hysterectomy
UTILITARIANISM
see also Hedonism; Pragmatism; Secularism
Rashdall, Hastings. A Comparative Analysis of Psychological Hedonism & Rationalistic Utilitarianism. (Science of Man Library). (Illus.). 143p. 1983. 79.65 (ISBN 0-89266-385-5). Am Classical Coll Pr.
Rescher, Nicholas. Distributive Justice: A Constructive Critique of the Utilitarian Theory of Distribution. LC 82-45162. (The Nicholas Rescher Ser.). 182p. 1982. pap. text ed. 9.25 (ISBN 0-8191-2686-1). U Pr of Amer.
UTILITIES
see Public Utilities
UTILIZATION OF LAND
see Land Use
UTILIZATION OF WASTE
see Waste Products
UTILIZATION OF WASTE PRODUCTS
see Salvage (Waste, etc.)
UTOPIAN LITERATURE
see Utopias
UTOPIAS
Beneri, Marie L. Journey Through Utopia. 338p. 1982. pap. 4.00 (ISBN 0-900384-21-2). Left Bank.
Thomas, John L. Alternative America: Henry George, Edward Bellamy, Henry Demarest Lloyd & the Adversary Tradition. (Illus.). 416p. 1983. 25.00x (ISBN 0-674-01676-9). Harvard U Pr.
Wynn, Bobby C., ed. Utopian Literature: Pre-1900 Imprints. 33p. 1982. 25.00 (ISBN 0-667-00628-1). Microfilming Corp.
UVEA–DISEASES
Kraus-Machiw, Ellen & O'Connor, G. Richard. Uveitis-Pathophysiology & Therapy. (Illus.). 144p. 1983. write for info. (ISBN 0-86577-073-5). Thieme-Stratton.
Smith, Ronald E. & Nozik, Robert M. Uveitis: A Clinical Approach to Diagnosis & Management. (Illus.). 232p. 1983. lib. bdg. 49.95 (ISBN 0-683-07768-6). Williams & Wilkins.

V

V-TWO ROCKET
Kennedy, Gregory P. Vengeance Weapon 2: The V-2 Guided Missile. (Illus.). 144p. 1983. pap. text ed. 9.95x (ISBN 0-87474-573-X). Smithsonian.
VACATION HOUSES
see Second Homes
VACATIONS
see also Holidays
Nunes-Vais, Al. Vacation Time Sharing: Is It Right for You? (Illus.). 1983. pap. 9.95x (ISBN 0-910793-02-6). Marlborough Pr.
VACCINATION
see also Immunity
Chase, Allan. Magic Shots: A Human & Scientific Account of the Long & Continuing Struggle to Eradicate Infectious Diseases by Vaccination. LC 82-12505. 600p. 1982. 19.95 (ISBN 0-688-00787-2). Morrow.
Guidelines for Volunteer Participation in Childhood Immunization Programs. 333p. 1980. 15.00 (ISBN 0-686-38198-X, 52-1800). Natl League Nurse.
McBean, Eleanor. Vaccination Condemned. 1981. 12.50 (ISBN 0-686-37948-9). Cancer Control Soc.
VACUUM
see also Electric Discharges through Gases; Vacuum Technology
Grant, W. A. & Balfour, D., eds. Vacuum '82: Proceedings of the Biennial Conference of the Vacuum Group of the Institute of Physics, Chester, 29-31 March 1982. 112p. 1982. pap. 28.00 (ISBN 0-08-029999-7). Pergamon.
VACUUM IN INDUSTRY
see Vacuum Technology
VACUUM TECHNOLOGY
Stuart, R. V., ed. Vacuum Technology, Thin Films, & Sputtering: An Introduction. LC 82-13748. Date not set. 21.00 (ISBN 0-12-674780-6). Acad Pr.
VADE-MECUMS
see Handbooks, Vade-Mecums, etc.
VAGABONDS
see Gipsies; Nomads; Rogues and Vagabonds; Tramps
VAGINA
International Symposium on Vaginal Mycoses Vienna, September 1981. (Journal: Chemotherapy: Suppl. 1, Vol. 28). (Illus.). 112p. 1983. pap. 21.75 (ISBN 3-8055-3638-0). S Karger.
VAGRANTS
see Tramps
VALDENSES
see Waldenses
VALENCE (THEORETICAL CHEMISTRY)
see also Chemical Bonds; Macromolecules; Molecular Orbitals
Wachter, P. & Boppart, H., eds. Valence Instabilities: Proceedings of the International Conference on Valence Instabilities, Zurich, Switzerland, April, 1982. 98p. 1982. 61.75 (North Holland). Elsevier.
VALENTINE'S DAY
see Saint Valentine's Day
VALLEYS
see also Erosion; Rivers
Updegraffe, Imelda & Updegraffe, Robert. Mountains & Valleys. (Turning Points Ser.). (Illus.). 24p. 1983. pap. 3.50 (ISBN 0-14-049189-9, Puffin). Penguin.
VALUATION
Here are entered only the most general works. Works on valuation for taxing purposes are entered under assessment. Materials dealing with valuation of special classes of property are entered under Mine valuation; Railroads–Valuation; Real Estate Business; Real Property–Valuation, etc.
Bowcock, Philip & Rose, J. J. Valuing with a Pocket Calculator. 160p. 1981. 35.00x (ISBN 0-686-99796-4, Pub. by Tech Pr). State Mutual Bk.
VALUATION OF LAND
see Real Property–Valuation; Valuation
VALUE
Here are entered works on the theory of value in economics. Works on moral and aesthetic values, etc. are entered under values.
see also Money; Supply and Demand
Fujinori, Y. Modern Analysis of Value Theory. (Lecture Notes in Economics & Mathematical Systems: Vol. 207). (Illus.). 165p. 1983. pap. 12.00 (ISBN 0-387-11949-3). Springer-Verlag.
VALUE ANALYSIS (COST CONTROL)
Dell'Isola, Alphonse J. Value Engineering in the Construction Industry. 3rd ed. 376p. 1983. text ed. 34.50 (ISBN 0-442-26202-7). Van Nos Reinhold.
VALUES
Here are entered works on moral and esthetic values, etc. Works on the economic theory of value are entered under value.
see also Social Values; Spirituality
Allport, Gordon W. Study of Values. 3rd ed. test booklets 15.40 (ISBN 0-686-84785-7); instrs' manual 2.48 (ISBN 0-686-84786-5). HM.
Aschenbrenner, Karl. Analysis of Appraisive Characterization. 1983. lib. bdg. 48.00 (ISBN 90-277-1452-5, Pub. by Reidel Holland). Kluwer Boston.
Barbour. Energy & American Values. 256p. 1982. 27.95 (ISBN 0-03-062468-1); pap. 12.95 (ISBN 0-03-062469-X). Praeger.
Bond, E. J. Reason & Value. LC 82-4564. (Cambridge Studies in Philosophy). 220p. Date not set. p.n.s. (ISBN 0-521-24571-0); pap. p.n.s. (ISBN 0-521-27079-0). Cambridge U Pr.
Brewster, Kingman, et al. The Tanner Lectures on Human Values: Vol. IV, 1983. 300p. 1983. 20.00x (ISBN 0-87480-216-4). U of Utah Pr.
Dienhart, John W. A Cognitive Approach to the Ethics of Counseling Psychology. LC 82-17393. 152p. (Orig.). 1983. lib. bdg. 18.75 (ISBN 0-8191-2817-1); pap. text ed. 8.50 (ISBN 0-8191-2818-X). U Pr of Amer.
Erickson, Helen & Tomlin, Evelyn. Modeling & Role Modeling: A Theory & Paradigm for Nursing. (Illus.). 240p. 1983. text ed. 17.95 (ISBN 0-13-586198-5); pap. 13.95 (ISBN 0-13-586180-2). P-H.
Schuncke, George & Krogh, Suzanne. Helping Children Choose. 1983. pap. text ed. 10.95 (ISBN 0-673-16622-8). Scott F.
Westerhoff, John H., III. Building God's People in a Materialistic Society. 144p. 1983. pap. 8.95 (ISBN 0-8164-2466-7). Seabury.
VALVULAR DISEASES
see Heart–Diseases
VAN BUREN, MARTIN, PRES. U. S., 1782-1862
Niven, John. Martin Van Buren: The Romantic Age of American Politics. (Illus.). 736p. 1983. 35.00 (ISBN 0-19-503238-1). Oxford U Pr.
VANCOUVER ISLAND–DESCRIPTION AND TRAVEL
Rue, Roger L. Circumnavigating Vancouver Island. 1982. pap. 10.00 (ISBN 0-9609036-0-7). Evergreen Pacific.
VANDALISM
Garbarino, James & Galambos, Nancy L. Vandalism: What Are its Whos, Whats, & Why? What Can be Done About It? (Vital Issues Ser.: Vol. XXXI, No. 2). 0.80 (ISBN 0-686-84135-2). Ctr Info Am.
VAN DER POST, LAURENS
Van der Post, Laurens. Yet Being Someone Other. 352p. 1983. Repr. 14.95 (ISBN 0-688-01843-2). Morrow.
VAN GOGH, VINCENT, 1853-1890
Uhde, W. Van Gogh. (Phaidon Color Library). (Illus.). 84p. 1983. pap. 17.95 (ISBN 0-7148-2161-6, Pub. by Salem Hse Ltd). Merrimack Bk Serv.
VANISHING ANIMALS
see Rare Animals
VAN JOHN (GAME)
see Blackjack (Game)
VANS
Burness, Taqd. Pickup & Van Spotter's Guide, 1945-1982. (Illus.). 160p. 1982. pap. 9.95 (ISBN 0-87938-156-6). Motorbooks Intl.
Edmund's Vans, Pickups, Offroad Buyer's Guide, 1983. (Illus.). 1983. pap. 2.50 (ISBN 0-440-02304-1). Dell.
Hudson-Evans, Richard. Custom Cars & Vans. (Illus.). 64p. 1983. pap. 4.95 (Pub. by Batsford England). David & Charles.
Pegal, Alfred A. VW Vanagon: 1980-1981 Shop Manual. Wauson, Sydnie A., ed. (Illus.). 288p. (Orig.). 1982. pap. 11.95 (ISBN 0-89287-351-5). Clymer Pubns.
VANZETTI, BARTOLOMEO
see Sacco-Vanzetti Case
VAPOR-LIQUID EQUILIBRIUM
Gmehling, J. & Onken, U. Vapor-Liquid Equilbrium Data Collection Part 2d, Organic Hydroxy Compounds: Alcohols & Phenols (Supplement 2) (Dechema Chemistry Data Ser.: Vol. I). (Illus.). 800p. 1982. 145.00 (ISBN 0-686-43226-6, Pub. by Dechema Germany). Scholium Intl.
--Vapor-Liquid Equilibrium Data Collection Part 5 Carboxylic Acids, Anhydrides, Esters. (Vol. I). (Illus.). 715p. 1982. 155.00x (ISBN 0-686-43231-2, Pub. by Dechema Germany). Scholium Intl.
--Vapor-Liquid Equilibrium Data Collection: Volume I, Part 2C-Organic Hydroxy Compounds: Alcohols (Supplement 1) (Dechema Chemistry Data Ser.). (Illus.). 698p. 1982. lib. bdg. 110.00x (ISBN 3-921-56729-7). Scholium Intl.
Knapp, H. & Doring, R. Vapor-Liquid Equilibra for Mixtures of Low Boiling Substances. Berhens, D. & Eckermann, R., eds. (Dechema Chemistry Data Ser.). (Illus.). 910p. 1982. 142.50x (ISBN 0-686-43225-8, Pub. by Dechema Germany). Scholium Intl.
VAPOR-PHASE CHROMATOGRAPHY
see Gas Chromatography
VAPORS
see also Evaporation; Gases; Steam
Symposium on Inhaled Particles & Vapours. Inhaled Particles: Proceedings, Vol. V. Walton, W. H., ed. (Illus.). 900p. 1982. 150.00 (ISBN 0-08-026838-2). Pergamon.
VAQUEROS
see Cowboys
VARESE, EDGAR, 1883-1965
Quellette, Fernand. A Biography of Edgard Varese. (Illus.). xiv, 270p. 1981. Repr. of 1968 ed. lib. bdg. 27.50 (ISBN 0-306-76103-3). Da Capo.
VARIABLE STARS
see Stars, Variable
VARIABLES (MATHEMATICS)
Van Den Essen, A. R. & Levelt, A. H. Irregular Singularities in Several Variables. LC 82-18161. (Memoirs of the American Mathematical Society Ser.: No. 270). 4.00 (ISBN 0-8218-2270-5, MEMO/270). AM Math.
VARIATION (BIOLOGY)
see also Adaptation (Biology); Evolution; Genetics; Island Flora and Fauna; Mutation (Biology); Natural Selection; Origin of Species
Darwin, Charles R. The Variation of Animals & Plants Under Domestication, 2 Vols. LC 72-3893. (Illus.). 1972. write for info. (ISBN 0-404-08407-9). AMS Pr.
VARIATIONS, CALCULUS OF
see Calculus of Variations
VARNISH PAINTS
see Paint
VASCULAR CRYPTOGAMS
see Pteridophyta
VASCULAR DISEASES
see Blood-Vessels–Diseases; Cardiovascular System–Diseases; Peripheral Vascular Diseases
Machleder, Herbert I., ed. Vascular Disorders of the Upper Extremity. LC 82-84504. 1983. price not set monograph (ISBN 0-87993-193-0). Futura Pub.
VASCULAR GRAFTS
Wright, Creighton B. Vascular Grafting: Clinical Applications & Techniques. (Illus.). 384p. 1983. text ed. write for info. (ISBN 0-7236-7023-4). Wright-PSG.
VASCULAR HYPERTENSION
see Hypertension
VASCULAR PLANTS
see Botany; Plants
VASCULAR SYSTEM
see Blood-Vessels; Cardiovascular System
VASCULAR SYSTEM OF PLANTS
Vasil'chenko, I. T. Novitates Systematicae: Plantarum Vascularium 1972, Vol. 9. 378p. 1978. 82.00 (ISBN 0-686-84461-0, Pub. by Oxford & I B H India). State Mutual Bk.
Vasil chenko, J. T. Novitates Systematicae: Plantarum Vascularium 1971, Vol. 8. 342p. 1978. 77.00x (ISBN 0-686-84460-2, Pub. by Oxford & I B H India). State Mutual Bk.
VATICAN
Bull, George. Inside the Vatican. 294p. 1983. 13.95 (ISBN 0-312-41884-1). St Martin.
Daley, John, ed. The Vatican: Spirit & Art of Christian Rome. (Illus.). 1983. 39.50 (ISBN 0-686-43091-3). Metro Mus Art.
Manhattan, Avro. The Vacation Moscow Washington Alliance. 352p. (Orig.). pap. 6.95 (ISBN 0-937958-12-3). Chick Pubns.
The Popes. (Treasures of the World Ser.). 1982. lib. bdg. 26.60 (ISBN 0-86706-047-6, Pub. by Stonehenge). Silver.
VAUDOIS
see Waldenses
VAUGHAN, HENRY, 1622-1695
Marilla, E. L. The Secular Poems of Henry Vaughan: Essays & Studies on English Language & Literature. Liljergren, S. B., ed. 337p. 1983. Repr. of 1958 ed. lib. bdg. 50.00 (ISBN 0-89760-571-3). Telegraph Bks.
Martz, Louis. The Paradise Within: Studies in Vaughan, Traherne, & Milton. 236p. 1983. pap. 7.95x (ISBN 0-300-00164-9). Yale U Pr.
Pettet, E. C. Of Paradise & Light: A Study of Vaughn's Silex Scintillans. 217p. 1983. Repr. of 1960 ed. lib. bdg. 40.00 (ISBN 0-89760-050-9). Telegraph Bks.
VAULTS (SEPULCHRAL)
see Tombs
VECTOR ANALYSIS
see also Vector Spaces
Carrell, J. B., ed. Group Actions & Vector Fields: Vancouver, Canada, 1981, Proceedings. (Lecture Notes in Mathematics: Vol. 956). 144p. 1983. pap. 8.00 (ISBN 0-387-11946-9). Springer-Verlag.
Gierz, G. Bundles of Topological Vector Spaces & Their Duality. (Lecture Notes in Mathematics: Vol. 955). 296p. 1983. pap. 13.50 (ISBN 0-387-11610-9). Springer-Verlag.
Godbillon, C. Dynamical Systems on Surfaces. (Univeritext Ser.). (Illus.). 201p. 1983. pap. 19.80 (ISBN 0-387-11645-1). Springer-Verlag.
VECTOR SPACES
see also Linear Topological Spaces
Godbillon, C. Dynamical Systems on Surfaces. (Univeritext Ser.). (Illus.). 201p. 1983. pap. 19.80 (ISBN 0-387-11645-1). Springer-Verlag.
VECTOR TOPOLOGY
see Linear Topological Spaces
VEDAS
Howard, Wayne. Veda Recitation in Varanasi. 1983. 15.00x (ISBN 0-8364-0872-1). South Asia Bks.
VEDIC LANGUAGE
see also Sanskrit Language
Suryakanta. A Practical Vedic Dictionary. 768p. 1981. 47.00x (ISBN 0-19-561298-1). Oxford U Pr.
VEDIC MYTHOLOGY
see Mythology, Hindu
VEGETABLE GARDENING
see also Vegetables
Blauer, Stephen. The Miracle of Sprouting. 80p. (Orig.). 1982. pap. 3.95 (ISBN 0-89529-177-0). Avery Pub.
Bubel, Nancy. The Country Journal Book of Vegetable Gardening. (Illus.). 256p. (Orig.). 1983. pap. 10.95 (ISBN 0-918678-03-X). Country Journ.
Gillison, A. N. & Anderson, D. J., eds. Vegetation Classification in Australia. 229p. 1983. text ed. 18.95 (ISBN 0-7081-1309-5, Pub. by CSIRO Australia). Intl Schol Bk Serv.
Jeavons, John & Griffin, J. Morgodor. The Backyard Homestead, Mini-Farm & Garden Log Book. 224p. (Orig.). 1983. pap. 8.95 (ISBN 0-89815-093-0). Ten Speed Pr.
Raymond, Dick. Garden Way's Joy of Gardening. Thabault, George, ed. (Illus.). 384p. 1983. 25.00 (ISBN 0-88266-320-8); pap. 17.95 (ISBN 0-88266-319-4). Garden Way Pub.
Seabrook, Peter. The Complete Vegetable Gardener. (Illus.). 128p. 1983. pap. 7.95 (ISBN 0-89104-059-5, A & W Visual Library). A & W Pubs.
VEGETABLE KINGDOM
see Botany
VEGETABLE MOLD
see Humus; Soils
VEGETABLE OILS
see Oil Industries; Oils and Fats
VEGETABLE PATHOLOGY
see Plant Diseases
VEGETABLES
see also Cookery (Vegetables); Food, Raw; Vegetable Gardening; Vegetarianism;
also names of vegetables, e.g. Corn, Potatoes
Araski, Seibin & Araski, Teruko. Vegetables from the Sea. LC 79-91516. (Illus.). 176p. (Orig.). 1982. pap. 13.95 (ISBN 0-87040-475-X). Kodansha.
Breimer, T. Environmental Factors & Cultural Measures Affecting the Nitrate of Spinach. 1982. pap. text ed. 22.00 (ISBN 90-247-3053-8, Pub. by Martinus Nijhoff Netherlands). Kluwer Boston.
Countryside Staff, ed. The Countryside A-Z Guide to Vegetables. (A-Z Ser.). (Orig.). 1983. pap. 7.95 (ISBN 0-88453-038-8). Countryside Bks.
Darwin, Charles R. The Effects of Cross & Self Fertilisation in the Vegetable Kingdom, Vol. 13. LC 72-3898. viii, 482p. 1972. write for info. AMS Pr.
Jacob, John & Jacob, Meera. Fruit & Vegatable Carving. revised ed. 99p. 1983. 25.00 (ISBN 0-686-42989-3). Hippocrene Bks.
Teranishi, Roy & Barrera-Benitez, Heriberto, eds. Quality of Selected Fruits & Vegetables of North America. (ACS Symposium Ser.: No. 170). 1981. write for info. (ISBN 0-8412-0662-7). Am Chemical.

VEGETABLES–DISEASES AND PESTS
see also Insects, Injurious and Beneficial; Plant Diseases;
also names of vegetables, with or without the subdivision Diseases and Pests; also names of diseases and pests
Green, Harriet & Martin, Sue. Sprouts. (gr. 3-8). 1981. 9.95 (ISBN 0-86653-028-2, GA256). Good Apple.
VEGETARIAN COOKERY
see also Macrobiotic Diet
Gethers, Judith & Lefft, Elizabeth. The World-Famous Ratner's Meatless Cookbook. 192p. 1983. pap. 2.95 (ISBN 0-345-30348-2). Ballantine.
Graham, Winifred. The Vegetarian Treasure Chest. Fraser, Lisa, ed. Orig. Title: The Vegetable, Fruit & Nut Cookbook. 224p. 1983. pap. 6.95 (ISBN 0-930356-33-0). Quicksilver Prod.
Hartbarger, Janie C. & Hartbarger, Neil J. Eating for the Eighties: A Complete Guide to Vegetarian Nutrition. 352p. 1983. pap. 3.50 (ISBN 0-425-05827-1). Berkley Pub.
Society for Nurtrition Education Resource Center. Vegetarians & Vegetarian Diets. rev. ed. (Nutrition Education Resource Ser.: No. 8). 10p. 1982. pap. 4.00 (ISBN 0-910869-14-6). Soc Nutrition Ed.
Sunset Books & Sunset Magazine Editors. International Vegetarian Cook Book. LC 82-83218. (Illus.). 96p. 1983. pap. 4.95 (ISBN 0-376-02921-8). Sunset-Lane.
Thirty-Two Meatless Meals. 1983. pap. 4.95 (ISBN 0-8120-5523-3). Barron.
VEGETARIANISM
see also Food, Raw; Macrobiotic Diet; Vegetarian Cookery
Anderson, John J., ed. Nutrition & Vegetarianism. (Illus.). 245p. (Orig.). 1982. pap. 18.95 (ISBN 0-938938-04-5). Health Sci Consort.
Cohen, Leslie. Nourishing a Happy Affair: Nutrition Alternatives for Individual & Family Needs. (Illus.). 150p. (Orig.). 1983. pap. 5.95 (ISBN 0-943914-02-7, Dist by Kampmann & Co.). Larson Pubns Inc.
Gross, Joy & Freifeld, Karen. The Vegetarian Child. 224p. 1983. 12.00 (ISBN 0-8184-0342-X). Lyle Stuart.
Society for Nurtrition Education Resource Center. Vegetarians & Vegetarian Diets. rev. ed. (Nutrition Education Resource Ser.: No. 8). 10p. 1982. pap. 4.00 (ISBN 0-910869-14-6). Soc Nutrition Ed.
Szekely, Edmond B. Scientific Vegetarianism. (Illus.). 56p. 1977. pap. 2.95 (ISBN 0-89564-041-4). IBs Intl.
Thrash, Agatha & Thrash, Calvin. Nutrition for Vegetarians. (Illus.). 155p. 1982. pap. 8.95 (ISBN 0-942658-03-5). Yuchi Pines.
Trall, Russell. Scientific Basis of Vegetarianism. 1970. 2.50x (ISBN 0-686-37947-0). Cancer Control Soc.
Zulker, Judi & Zulker, Shari. How to Eat Without Meat. 1981. 3.95x (ISBN 0-912800-96-8). Cancer Control Soc.
VEGETATION AND CLIMATE
Dierschke, Hartmut, ed. Struktur und Dynamik von Waeldern: Rinteln, April 1981, Berichte der Internationalen Symposien der Intern'len Vereinigung fuer Vegetationskunde. (Illus.). 600p. (Orig., Ger.). 1983. lib. bdg. 64.00 (ISBN 3-7682-1334-X). Lubrecht & Cramer.
Jahn, G. Application of Vegetation Science to Forestry. 1982. 79.50 (ISBN 90-6193-193-2, Pub. by Junk Pubs Netherlands). KLuwer Boston.
VEGETATIVE NERVOUS SYSTEM
see Nervous System, Autonomic
VEHICLES
see also Ambulances; Automobiles; Bicycles and Tricycles; Coaching; Motor Vehicles; Motorcycles; Wagons; Wheels
Cole, Lee S. Vehicle Identification 1983. (Illus.). 80p. (Orig.). 1983. pap. 6.50 (ISBN 0-939818-06-X). Lee Bks.
U. S. Batteries & Electrical Vehicles. 1982. 995.00 (280). Predicasts.
VEHICLES–ACCIDENTS
see Traffic Accidents
VEHICLES, ARMORED (MILITARY SCIENCE)
see Armored Vehicles, Military
VEHICLES, MILITARY
see also Ambulances; Armored Vehicles, Military; Tanks (Military Science)
Foss, Christopher, ed. Jane's Military Vehicles & Ground Support Equipment, 1983. (Jane's Yearbooks Ser.). (Illus.). 700p. 1983. 140.00x (ISBN 0-86720-647-0). Sci Bks Intl.
Jane's Military Vehicles & Ground Support Equipment, 1982. (Jane's Yearbooks). (Illus.). 600p. 140.00 (ISBN 0-86720-600-4). Sci Bks Intl.
VELAZQUEZ, DIEGO RODRIGUEZ DE SILVA Y, 1599-1660
Kimball, Edward W. The Powerful, Impressive Art of Diego Rodriguez de Silva Velasquez. (The Art Library of the Great Masters of the World). (Illus.). 103p. 1983. 47.85 (ISBN 0-86650-049-9). Gloucester Art.
VELIKOVSKY, IMMANUAL, 1895-
Velikovsky, Immanuel. Stargazers & Gravediggers: Memoirs to Worlds in Collision. LC 82-14463. 320p. 1983. 14.95 (ISBN 0-688-01545-X). Morrow.
VELOCIPEDES
see Bicycles and Tricycles
VELOCITY OF CHEMICAL REACTION
see Chemical Reaction, Rate Of
VENDORS AND PURCHASERS
see also Land Titles; Sales
Harwood & Jacobus. Texas Real Estate. 3rd ed. 1983. text ed. 21.95 (ISBN 0-8359-7554-1). Reston.
Jacobus. Texas Real Estate Law. 3rd ed. text ed. 21.95 (ISBN 0-8359-7573-8). Reston.
VENDUES
see Auctions
VENEREAL DISEASES
see also Syphilis; Treponematosis
Chase, Allan. The Truth About STD: The Old Ones--Herpes & Other New Ones--the Primary Causes--the Available Cures. 188p. 1983. pap. 5.95 (ISBN 0-688-01835-1). Quill NY.
Holmes, King K. & Mardh, Per-Anders. International Perspectives on Neglected Sexually Transmitted Diseases: Impact on Venereology, Infertility, & Maternal & Infant Health. (Illus.). 352p. 1982. text ed. 45.00 (ISBN 0-07-029676-6, HP). McGraw.
Nasemann, T. & Sauerbrey, W. Fundamentals of Dermatology. (Illus.). 416p. 1983. pap. 24.90 (ISBN 0-387-90738-6). Springer-Verlag.
Stevens, Ella. Sex Education: Gonorrhea. (Michigan Learning Module Ser.). 1979. write for info. (ISBN 0-914004-38-7). Ulrich.
VENEZUELA–FOREIGN RELATIONS
Braveboy-Wagner, Jacqueline A. The Venezuela-Guyana Border Dispute: Britain's Colonial Legacy in Latin America. (Replica Edition Ser.). 200p. 1983. softcover 20.00x (ISBN 0-86531-953-7). Westview.
VENEZUELA–HISTORY
Gibson, Charles D. Boca Grande: A Series of Historical Essays. LC 82-90197. (Illus.). 250p. (Orig.). 1982. pap. text ed. 12.95 (ISBN 0-9608996-0-X). C D Gibson.
VENEZUELA–POLITICS AND GOVERNMENT
Nasir, Pir. Faceless Enemy. 224p. 1983. 12.50 (ISBN 0-682-49975-7). Exposition.
VENICE–DESCRIPTION
Fernadez, Rafael. A Scene of Light & Glory: Approaches to Venice. (Illus.). 48p. 1982. pap. 4.00 (ISBN 0-686-37429-0). S & F Clark.
VENICE–DESCRIPTION–GUIDEBOOKS
Honour, Hugh. Companion Guide to Venice. (Illus.). 288p. 1983. 15.95 (ISBN 0-13-154666-X); pap. 7.95 (ISBN 0-13-154658-9). P-H.
VENOMOUS SNAKES
see Poisonous Snakes
VENTILATION
see also Air Conditioning; Heating; Mine Ventilation also subdivision Heating and Ventilation or Ventilation under special subjects
Teng, Derek P. Heating & Ventilating: A Handbook of Fitting Craft Practice. 216p. 1980. 40.00x (ISBN 0-85950-051-9, Pub. by Thornes England). State Mutual Bk.
VENTRICULOCISTERNOSTOMY
Hanrath, P. Evaluation of Left Ventricular Function by Ultrasound. 1982. 39.50 (ISBN 0-686-38401-6, Pub. by Martinus Nijhoff Netherlands). Kluwer Boston.
VENTRILOQUISM
Vox, Valentine. I Can See Your Lips Moving. (Illus.). 176p. 1983. 31.50 (ISBN 0-7182-5870-3, Pub. by Kaye & Ward). David & Charles.
VENUS (PLANET)
Hunt, Garry & Moore, Patrick. The Planet Venus. LC 82-5045. (Illus.). 240p. 1983. 22.00 (ISBN 0-571-09050-8). Faber & Faber.
Hunten, Donald M. & Colin, Lawrence, eds. Venus. 1200p. 1983. text ed. 60.00x (ISBN 0-8165-0788-0). U of Ariz Pr.
VERDI, GIUSEPPE, 1813-1901
Faw, Marc. A Verdi Discography. 201p. 1983. 14.95 (ISBN 0-937664-63-4). Pilgrim Bks OK.
VERGA, GIOVANNI, 1840-1922
Bergin, Thomas G. Giovanni Verga. 1931. text ed. 13.50x (ISBN 0-686-83557-3). Elliots Bks.
VERGIL (PUBLIUS VERGILIUS MARO)
Williams, Gordon. Technique & Ideas in the Aeneid. LC 82-7008. 312p. 1983. text ed. 27.50x (ISBN 0-300-02852-0). Yale U Pr.
VERMIN
see Pests
VERMONT–DESCRIPTION AND TRAVEL
Sadlier, Ruth & Sadlier, Paul. Fifty Hikes in Vermont: Walks, Day Hikes & Backpacking Trips in the Green Mountain State. 2nd ed. LC 79-92572. (Fifty Hikes Ser.). (Illus.). 184p. 1983. pap. 7.95 (ISBN 0-942440-08-0). Backcountry Pubns.
Tree, Christina & Jennison, Peter S. Vermont: An Explorer's Guide. 256p. (Orig.). 1983. pap. 9.95 (ISBN 0-88150-002-X). Countryman.
Ziegler, Phil. Sentinels of Time. (Illus.). 1983. pap. 8.95t (ISBN 0-89272-160-X). Down East.
VERMONT–HISTORY
Haviland, William & Power, Morgory W. THe Original Vermonters: Native Inhabitants, Past & Present. LC 80-54465. (Illus.). 346p. 1981. 20.00 (ISBN 0-87451-196-8). U Pr of New Eng.
Haviland, William A. & Power, Marjory W. The Original Vermonters: Native Inhabitants, Past & Present. LC 80-54465. (Illus.). 346p. 1983. pap. text ed. 12.95 (ISBN 0-87451-253-0). U Pr of New Eng.
Hill, Ralph N. Contrary Country. (Illus.). pap. 5.95 (ISBN 0-939384-10-8). Shelburne.
VERSIFICATION
see also Poetry
also subdivison Versification under names of modern languages, e.g. English Languages–Versification; subdivision Metrics and Rhythmics under names of ancient languages, e.g. Greek Languages–Metrics and Rhythmics; and special forms of verse, e.g. Hexameter
Conniff, Richard, ed. The Devil's Book of Verse. (Illus.). 1983. 14.95 (ISBN 0-89696-186-9). Dodd.
Harrington, Anthony. Tersery Versery: World's First Individual Collection of Double Dactyls. (Illus.). 120p. (Orig.). 1982. pap. 5.95 (ISBN 0-943764-00-9). Hendricks Pub.
Redgrove, Peter. Cornwall in Verse. 96p. 1983. 13.95 (ISBN 0-436-40987-9, Pub. by Secker & Warburg). David & Charles.
VERTEBRAE
see also Intervertebral Disk
Wackenheim, A. Radiodiagnosis of the Vertebrae in Adults: 125 Exercises for Students & Practitioners. (Exercises in Radiological Diagnosis Ser.). (Illus.). 176p. 1983. pap. 14.80 (ISBN 0-387-11681-8). Springer-Verlag.
VERTEBRAE, CERVICAL
Abel, Martin S. Occult Traumatic Lesions of the Cervical & Thoraco-Lumbar Vertebrae. 2nd ed. 386p. 1983. 42.50 (ISBN 0-87527-312-2). Green.
Kabat, Herman. Herniated Cervical Disc: Instruction Manual for Patients. 144p. 1983. 16.50 (ISBN 0-87527-299-1). Green.
VERTEBRATES
see also Amphibians; Birds; Fishes; Mammals; Reptiles
Capranica, Robert & Ewert, Jorg-Peter, eds. Advances in Vertebrate Neuroethology. (NATO ASI Ser.A, Life Sciences: Vol. 56). 1238p. 1983. 150.00x (ISBN 0-306-41197-0, Plenum Pr). Plenum Pub.
Wasser, Samuel K., ed. Social Behavior of Female Vertebrate. LC 82-11602. write for info. (ISBN 0-12-735950-8). Acad Pr.
VERTEBRATES–ANATOMY
Eddy, S., et al. Atlas of Drawings for Vertebrate Anatomy. 3rd ed. 176p. 1964. text ed. 14.95x (ISBN 0-471-23168-1). Wiley.
VERTIGO
Honrubia, Vicente & Brazier, Mary, eds. Nystagmus & Vertigo: Clinical Approach to the Patient with Dizziness. LC 82-3906. (UCLA Forum in Medical Sciences Ser.: No. 24). 320p. 1982. 26.00 (ISBN 0-12-355080-7). Acad Pr.
VESPERTILIO
see Bats
VESSELS (SHIPS)
see Ships
VESSELS (UTENSILS)
see Implements, Utensils, Etc.
VESTIBULAR APPARATUS
Romand, R., ed. Development of Auditory & Vestibular Systems. Date not set. price not set (ISBN 0-12-594450-0). Acad Pr.
VETERANS
Here are entered general works relating to ex-servicemen. Specific topic are entered under appropriate heading, e.g. Pensions, Military Veterans, Disabled–Rehabilitation.
see also Pensions, Military; Seamen; Soldiers
Card, Josefina J. Lives after Vietnam: The Personal Impact of Military Service. 1983. price not set (ISBN 0-669-06420-3). Lexington Bks.
Rudman, Jack. Veteran Counselor. (Career Examination Ser.: C-2690). (Cloth bdg. avail. on request). pap. 12.00 (ISBN 0-8373-2690-7). Natl Learning.
VETERANS' BENEFITS
see Pensions, Military
VETERINARY ANATOMY
Macgregor, Roderick. The Structure of the Meat Animals. 272p. 1981. 35.00x (ISBN 0-291-39625-9, Pub. by Tech Pr). State Mutual Bk.
VETERINARY DIAGNOSIS
see Veterinary Medicine–Diagnosis
VETERINARY IMMUNOLOGY
see also Immunology
Sordat, B., ed. International Workshop on Immune-Deficient Animals in Experimental Research, 4th, Chexbres, October 1982. (Journal: Experimental Cell Biology: Vol. 50, No. 6). 60p. 1983. pap. 22.75 (ISBN 3-8055-3647-X). S Karger.
VETERINARY MEDICINE
see also Domestic Animals; Parasitology
also subdivision Diseases under classes of animals, e.g. Cattle–Diseases; Horses–Diseases; names of particular diseases, e.g. Foot-and-Mouth disease; and headings beginning with the word veterinary
Animal Health Yearbook 1981. (FAO Animal Production & Health Ser.: No. 18). 204p. 1983. pap. 30.50 (ISBN 92-5-001223-3, F 2344, FAO). Unipub.
Bellville, Rod & Bellville, Cheryl W. Large Animal Veterinarians. LC 82-19750. (Illus.). 32p. (gr. 1-4). 1983. PLB 7.95g (ISBN 0-87614-211-0). Carolrhoda Bks.
Berkow, Robert. The Merck Manual. 14th ed. 1982. 19.75 (ISBN 0-911910-03-4). Merck.
Griner, Lynn A. Pathology of Zoo Animals: A Revised of Necropsies Conducted Over A Fourteen Year Period At The San Diego Zoo. LC 82-62698. (Illus.). 1983. 25.00 (ISBN 0-911461-11-6). Zoological Soc.
Karg, H. & Schallenberger, E. Factors Influencing Fertility in the Post-Partum Cow. 1982. 76.00 (ISBN 90-247-2715-4, Pub. by Martinus Nijhoff Netherlands). Kluwer Boston.
VETERINARY MEDICINE–DIAGNOSIS
Wardley, R. C. & Crowther, J. R. The Elisa: Enzyme-Linked Immunosorbent Assay in Veterinary Research & Diagnosis. 1982. 54.50 (ISBN 90-247-2769-3, Pub. by Martinus Nijhoff Netherlands). Kluwer Boston.
VETERINARY MEDICINE–DICTIONARIES
West, Geoffrey, ed. Black's Veterinary Dictionary. rev., 14th ed. LC 83-22783. (Illus.). 912p. 1983. text ed. 28.50x (ISBN 0-389-20330-0). B&N Imports.
VETERINARY MEDICINE–EXAMINATIONS, QUESTIONS, ETC.
Shattuck, Louise F. In Stiches Over Bitches: And Now Your Vet Wants a Rolls-Royce! LC 82-23276. (Illus.). 160p. 1983. 10.95 (ISBN 0-87605-549-8). Howell Bk.
VETERINARY MEDICINE–STUDY AND TEACHING
Morrison, James W. Veterianary College Admission Test. 384p. 1983. pap. 10.95 (ISBN 0-668-05545-6, 5545). Arco.
VETERINARY OPHTHALMOLOGY
Peiffer, Robert L., Jr. Comparative Ophthalmic Pathology. (Illus.). 448p. 1983. 60.00x (ISBN 0-398-04780-4). C C Thomas.
VETERINARY PHYSIOLOGY
Hunter, R. H. Reproduction of Farm Animals. LC 81-19318. (Longman Handbooks in Agriculture). (Illus.). 176p. (Orig.). 1982. pap. text ed. 14.95 (ISBN 0-582-45085-3). Longman.
VETERINARY SCIENCE
see Veterinary Medicine
VETERINARY SURGERY
Coffey, David. A Veterinary Surgeon's Guide to Dogs. (Illus.). 199p. 1980. 14.95 (ISBN 0-437-02500-4, Pub. by World's Work). David & Charles.
Lane, J. G. Diagnosis & Treatment of Ear & Oral Surgery of the Dog & Cat: Veterinary Practitioner Handbook. 1982. text ed. 24.50 (ISBN 0-7236-0659-5). Wright-PSG.
VIBRATION
see also Light; Materials–Fatigue; Oscillations; Structural Dynamics; Time Measurements; Vibrators; Waves
Chen, S. S. & Paidoussis, M. P., eds. Flow-Induced Vibration of Circular Cylindrical Structures-1982. (PVP Ser.: Vol. 63). 223p. 1982. 44.00 (H00220). ASME.
Durig, J. R., ed. Vibrational Spectra & Structure. (A Series of Advances: Vol. 11). 362p. 1982. 104.25 (ISBN 0-444-42103-3). Elsevier.
Merchant, H. C. & Geers, T. L., eds. Productive Applications of Mechanical Vibrations. (AMD Ser.: Vol. 52). 1982. 30.00 (H00238). ASME.
Pippard, Brian. The Physics of Vibration: The Simple Vibrator in Quantum Mechanics, Vol. 2. LC 77-85685. (Illus.). 200p. Date not set. price not set (ISBN 0-521-24623-7). Cambridge U Pr.
Thureau, P. & Lecler, D. An Introduction to the Principles of Vibrations of Linear Systems. Grosjean, J., tr. 144p. 1981. 30.00x (ISBN 0-85950-465-4, Pub. by Thornes England). State Mutual Bk.
White, R. G., et al. Noise & Vibration. 866p. 1982. 122.95x (ISBN 0-470-27553-7). Halsted Pr.
VIBRATIONAL SPECTRA
Durig, J. R., ed. Vibrational Spectra & Structure. (A Series of Advances: Vol. 11). 362p. 1982. 104.25 (ISBN 0-444-42103-3). Elsevier.
Person. Vibrational Intensities in Infrared & Raman Spectroscopy. (Studies in Physical & Theoretical Chemistry). 1982. 95.75 (ISBN 0-444-42115-7). Elsevier.
VIBRATORS
Blank, Joani. Good Vibrations: The Complete Guide to Vibrators. 52p. 1982. pap. 4.50 (ISBN 0-940208-05-9). Down There Pr.
VICKSBURG, MISSISSIPPI–SIEGE, 1863
Foster, William L. Vicksburg: Southern City Under Siege. Urquhart, Kenneth T., ed. LC 80-84685. 82p. 1982. pap. text ed. 6.95 (ISBN 0-917860-12-8). Historic New Orleans.
VICO, GIOVANNI BATTISTA, 1668-1744
Grimaldi, Alfonsina A. The Universal Humanity of Giambattista Vico. 1958. 12.50x (ISBN 0-913298-62-X). S F Vanni.
VICTIMS OF CRIMES
see also Reparation
Elias, Robert. Victims of the System: Crime Victims & Compensation in American Politics & Criminal Justice. (Illus.). 352p. 1983. 24.95 (ISBN 0-87855-470-X). Transaction Bks.
Hyde, Margaret O. The Rights of the Victim. (Single Title Ser.). 128p. (gr. 7 up). 1983. PLB 8.90 (ISBN 0-531-04596-X). Watts.
VICTORIA AND ALBERT MUSEUM, SOUTH KENSINGTON
Physick, John. The Victoria & Albert Museum: The History of its Building. (Illus.). 304p. 1983. 45.00 (ISBN 0-7148-8001-9, Pub by Salem Hse Ltd) Merrimack Bk Serv.

VIDEO GAMES

Chiu, Y. & Mullish, H. Crunchers: Twenty-One Games for the Timex Sinclair 1000 (2K) (McGraw-Hill VTX Ser.). 128p. 1982. 8.95 (ISBN 0-07-010831-5, GB). McGraw.

Consumer Guide Editors. How to Win at E.T. the Video Game. 32p. 1983. pap. 2.50 (ISBN 0-440-13767-5). Dell.

Hartnell, Tim & Ramshaw, Mark. Zap! Pow! Boom! Arcade Games for the VIC-20. 1983. text ed. 17.95 (ISBN 0-8359-9539-9); pap. text ed. 12.95 (ISBN 0-8359-9538-0). Reston.

Rubin, Michael, ed. Defending the Galaxy: The Complete Handbook of Videogaming. (Illus.). 224p. (Orig.). (gr. 8-12). pap. 4.95 (ISBN 0-937404-17-9). Triad Pub FL.

Skelly, Timothy. Shoot the Robot, Then Shoot Mom. (Illus.). 112p. (Orig.). 1983. pap. 4.95 (ISBN 0-8092-5541-3). Contemp Bks.

Sudnow, David. Pilgrim in the Microworld. 240p. (Orig.). 1983. 15.50 (ISBN 0-446-51261-3). Warner Bks.

VIDEO TAPE RECORDERS AND RECORDING

Budd, John F. Corporate Video in Focus: A Management Guide to Private TV. (Illus.). 224p. 1983. 21.95 (ISBN 0-13-176206-0); pap. 10.95 (ISBN 0-13-176198-6). P-H.

Davidoff, Frank & Rossi, John, eds. Digital Video. (Illus.). 114p. 1982. pap. text ed. 25.00 (ISBN 0-940690-02-0). Soc Motion Pic & TV Engrs.

Dranov, Paula, et al. Video in the Eighties: Emerging Uses for Television in Business, Education, Medicine & Government. 186p. 1980. pap. 34.95 (ISBN 0-86729-065-X). Knowledge Indus.

Duton, Mark & Owen, David. The Complete Home Video Handbook. 1982. 19.95 (ISBN 0-394-52761-5). Random.

Home Entertainment in the 1980s. (Reports Ser.: No. 511). 206p. 1982. 985.00 (ISBN 0-686-38952-2). Intl Res Dev.

Iuppa, Nicholas V. A Practical Guide to Interactive Video Design. 175p. 1983. 32.95 (ISBN 0-86729-041-2). Knowledge Indus.

Jackson. Newnes Book of Video. (Illus.). 1980. 16.50 (ISBN 0-408-00475-4). Focal Pr.

--Newnes Book of Video. 2nd ed. (Illus.). 1983. write for info. (ISBN 0-408-01319-2). Focal Pr.

Kennedy, M. Carlos, intro. by. Digital Video Two. (Illus.). 162p. (Orig.). 1982. pap. text ed. 25.00 (ISBN 0-940690-03-9). Soc Motion Pic & TV Engrs.

Lanzendorf, Peter. The Video Taping Handbook: The Newest Systems, Cameras, & Techniques. 1983. 16.95 (ISBN 0-517-54952-2, Harmony); pap. 7.95 (ISBN 0-517-54953-0). Crown.

McCarty, John. Video Screams. 1983 ed. (Illus.). 250p. (Orig.). 1983. pap. 7.95x (ISBN 0-938782-02-9). Fantaco.

Marcus, Richard, ed. Digital Video Three. Rev. ed. (Illus.). 230p. (Orig.). 1982. pap. text ed. 25.00 (ISBN 0-940690-04-7). Soc Motion Pic & TV Engrs.

Matthewson. Beginner's Guide to Video. (Illus.). 1982. pap. 9.95 (ISBN 0-408-00577-7). Focal Pr.

National Video Clearinghouse. Inc. The Video Source Book. 4th ed. 1600p. 1982. 125.00 (ISBN 0-935478-18-3, Dist. by Gale). Natl Video.

National Video Clearinghouse, Inc. The Video Tape & Disc Guide to Home Entertainment. 1982. pap. 9.95 (ISBN 0-452-25381-0, Z5381, Plume). NAL.

--The Video Tape & Disc Guide to Home Entertainment. 3rd ed. 420p. 1982. 9.95 (ISBN 0-452-25381-0). Natl Video.

Renowden, Gareth. Video. (Inside Story Ser.). (Illus.). 40p. (gr. 4 up). 1983. PLB 9.90 (ISBN 0-531-04584-6). Watts.

Robinson, Richard. The Video Primer. rev. ed. (Illus.). 432p. 1982. pap. 9.95 (ISBN 0-399-50698-5, Perige). Putnam Pub Group.

Storfer, Paul. Videotext: The Message in the Medium. 240p. 1983. 21.95 (ISBN 0-13-941922-5); pap. 14.95 (ISBN 0-13-941914-4). P-H.

Tuomola, Olli, ed. International TV & Video Guide 1983. (International TV & Video Guide Ser.). (Illus.). 87p. 1982. pap. 9.95 (ISBN 0-900730-10-2). NY Zoetrope.

Uston, Ken. Ken Ustson's Home Video 1983. 1982. pap. 2.95 (ISBN 0-451-12010-8, AE2010, Sig). NAL.

Utz, Peter. The Home Video Users Encyclopedia, 2 vols. (Illus.). 608p. 1983. 29.95 set (ISBN 0-13-394544-8); Vol. 1. pap. 16.95 (ISBN 0-13-394536-7); Vol. 2. pap. 9.95 (ISBN 0-13-394528-6). P-H.

--Video User's Handbook. 2nd ed. (Illus.). 500p. 1982. 24.95 (ISBN 0-686-42869-2). Knowledge Indus.

The Video Register: 1982-83. LC 79-640381. 1982. pap. 47.50 (ISBN 0-86729-008-0). Knowledge Indus.

Video User's Buying Guide: Professional TV Cameras. (Illus.). 100p. 1983. pap. 75.00 (ISBN 0-86729-064-1). Knowledge Indus.

VIDEO TAPES

Browne, Steven E. The Video Tape Post-Production Primer. (Illus.). 218p. 1982. 25.00 (ISBN 0-686-37656-0). Wilton Place.

Gayeski, Diane M. Corporate & Instructional Video: Design & Production. (Illus.). 304p. 1983. 21.95 (ISBN 0-13-174243-4). P-H.

International Video Program Markets: 1982-1985. 150p. 1982. 850.00 (ISBN 0-686-43329-7). Knowledge Indus.

National Video Clearinghouse, Inc. The Video Tape & Disc Guide to Home Entertainment. 3rd ed. 420p. 1982. 9.95 (ISBN 0-452-25381-0). Natl Video.

Video Market Opportunites. (Reports Ser.: No. 508). 211p. 1982. 985.00 (ISBN 0-686-38780-5). Intl Res Dev.

VIDEO DISCS

National Video Clearinghouse, Inc. The Video Tape & Disc Guide to Home Entertainment. 3rd ed. 420p. 1982. 9.95 (ISBN 0-452-25381-0). Natl Video.

Sigel, Efrem, et al. Video Discs: The Technology, the Applications & the Future. 1980. pap. 16.95 (ISBN 0-442-27784-9). Knowledge Indus.

Telepay vs. Videodisc: The Exploding Pay-per-View Market. (Reports Ser.: No. 510). 281p. 1982. 985.00 (ISBN 0-686-38956-5). Intl Res Dev.

VIENNA–GALLERIES AND MUSEUMS

Vienna Kunstm: Prohaska, Diestelberger Leith-Jasper. 29.95 (ISBN 0-935748-50-4). ScalaBooks.

VIETNAM

Kampuchea, Viet Nam, China: Observations & Reflections. 17p. 1982. pap. 5.00 (ISBN 92-808-0320-4, TUNU 201, UNU). Unipub.

Schanzenbach, Douglas T. Vietnam: My Recollections & Reflections. LC 82-80703. 64p. 1983. pap. 4.95 (ISBN 0-86666-088-7). GWP.

VIETNAM–FOREIGN RELATIONS–CHINA

Ray, Hemen. China's Vietnam War. 150p. 1982. text ed. 12.00x (ISBN 0-391-02816-2, Pub. by Radiant Pub India). Humanities.

VIETNAM–HISTORY

Tam Al. Vu Van Cuong. Vietnam's War, Nineteen Forty to Nineteen Seventy-Five. 456p. 1983. 26.95 (ISBN 0-686-84319-3). Brunswick Pub.

Taylor, Keith W. The Birth of Vietnam. LC 81-11590. 440p. 1983. text ed. 38.50x (ISBN 0-520-04428-2). U of Cal Pr.

VIETNAM–POLITICS AND GOVERNMENT

Duiker, William J. Vietnam: A Nation in Revolution. (Nations of Contemporary Asia). 135p. 1983. lib. bdg. 16.50 (ISBN 0-86531-336-9). Westview.

VIETNAM (DEMOCRATIC REPUBLIC, 1946-)–POLITICS AND GOVERNMENT

Ho Tai, Hue-Tam. Millenarianism & Peasant Politics in Vietnam. (Harvard East Asian Ser.: No. 99). (Illus.). 240p. 1983. text ed. 30.00x (ISBN 0-674-57555-5). Harvard U Pr.

VIETNAMESE CONFLICT, 1961-1975

Crace, Max D. & McJunkin, James N. Visions of Vietnam: Drawings & Photographs of the Vietnam War. (Illus.). 248p. 1983. 25.00 (ISBN 0-89141-175-5). Presidio Pr.

Herring, George C., ed. The Secret Diplomacy of the Vietnam War: The Negotiation Volumes of the Pentagon Papers. 928p. 1983. text ed. 47.50x (ISBN 0-292-77573-3). U of Tex Pr.

Higgins, Hugh. Vietnam. LC 82-11787. (Studies in Modern History). (Illus.). x, 180p. (Orig.). 1982. pap. text ed. 7.50x (ISBN 0-435-31399-1). Heinemann Ed.

Tam Al. Vu Van Cuong. Vietnam's War, Nineteen Forty to Nineteen Seventy-Five. 456p. 1983. 26.95 (ISBN 0-686-84319-3). Brunswick Pub.

VIETNAMESE CONFLICT, 1961-1975–AERIAL OPERATIONS

Drendel, Lou. Air War Over Southeast Asia, Vol. II. (Vietnam Studies Group Ser.). (Illus.). 80p. 1983. 8.95 (ISBN 0-89747-141-5). Squad Sig Pubns.

VIETNAMESE CONFLICT, 1961-1975–CHEMISTRY

Wilcox, Fred A. Waiting for an Army to Die: The Tragedy of Agent Orange. LC 82-42791. 256p. 1983. pap. 7.95 (ISBN 0-394-71518-7, Vin). Random.

VIETNAMESE CONFLICT, 1961-1975–PERSONAL NARRATIVES

Baker, Mark. Nam. 320p. 1983. pap. 3.50 (ISBN 0-425-06000-4). Berkley Pub.

Dengler, Dieter. Escape from Laos. 1982. pap. 2.95 (ISBN 0-8217-1113-X). Zebra.

Dougan, Clark & Weiss, Stephen. Tet, Vol. 6. Manning, Robert, ed. (The Vietnam Experience Ser.). (Illus.). 192p. 1983. 14.95 (ISBN 0-939526-06-9). Boston Pub Co.

Hawthorne, Lesleyanne. Refugee: The Vietnamese Experience. 288p. 1982. 49.00x (ISBN 0-19-554338-6). Oxford U Pr.

Page, Tim. Tim Page's Nam. LC 82-48704. (Illus.). 1983. 25.00 (ISBN 0-394-53005-5); pap. 14.95 (ISBN 0-394-71345-1). Knopf.

Pick, Michael R. Childhood-Namhood-Manhood: The Writings of Michael Robert Pick, A Vietnam Veteran. Bradford, Elizabeth A., ed. LC 82-60704. 160p. (Orig.). 1982. pap. 4.95 (ISBN 0-910441-00-6). Pizzuto Ltd Pub.

Schanzenbach, Douglas T. Vietnam: My Recollections & Reflections. LC 82-80703. 64p. 1983. pap. 4.95 (ISBN 0-86666-088-7). GWP.

Steer, John L. & Dudley, Cliff. Vietnam, Curse or Blessing. (Illus.). 192p. (Orig.). 1982. pap. 2.95 (ISBN 0-89221-091-5). New Leaf.

Van Devanter, Lynda & Morgan, Christopher. Home Before Morning: The Story of an Army Nurse in Vietnam. 1983. 16.95 (ISBN 0-8253-0132-7). Beaufort Bks NY.

VIETNAMESE CONFLICT, 1961-1975–PUBLIC OPINION

Braestrup, Peter. How the American Press & Television Reported & Interpreted the Crisis of Tet 1968 in Vietnam & Washington. LC 82-11041. 632p. 1983. text ed. 25.00x (ISBN 0-300-02953-5); pap. 9.95 (ISBN 0-300-02807-5, Y-446). Yale U Pr.

VIETNAMESE CONFLICT, 1961-1975–REGIMENTAL HISTORIES

Garland, Albert N. Infantry in Vietnam. (Vietnam Ser.: No. 1). (Illus.). 319p. 1982. Repr. of 1967 ed. 18.95x (ISBN 0-89839-065-6). Battery Pr.

VIETNAMESE LANGUAGE

Foreign Service Institute. Vietnamese Basic Course, Vol. 2. 325p. Date not set. with 10 cassettes 185.00x (ISBN 0-88432-108-8, V450). J Norton Pubs.

VIGILANCE COMMITTEES

Dimsdale, Thomas. Vigilantes of Montana. LC 80-29395. (Classics of the Old West Ser.). lib. bdg. 17.28 (ISBN 0-8094-3959-X). Silver.

VIKINGS

Here are entered works on the Norse seawarriors only. General works are entered under the heading Northmen.

Logan, F. Donald. The Vikings in History. (Illus.). 224p. 1983. text ed. 23.50x (ISBN 0-389-20384-X). B&N Imports.

VILLAGE INDUSTRIES

see Cottage Industries

VILLAGES

see also Community Development; Local Government; Rural Conditions

Critchfield, Richard. Villages. 412p. 1983. pap. 10.95 (ISBN 0-385-18375-5, Anch). Doubleday.

Harris, Mollie. From Acre End: Portrait of a Village. (Illus.). 154p. 1983. 14.95 (ISBN 0-7011-2630-2, Pub. by Chatto & Windus). Merrimack Bk Serv.

VILLAGES–GREAT BRITAIN

Muir, Richard. The English Village. (Illus.). 1983. pap. 9.95 (ISBN 0-500-27213-1). Thames Hudson.

VINES

see Climbing Plants

VINEYARDS

see Grapes

VINGT ET UN (GAME)

see Blackjack (Game)

VIOLA

Burnett, R. T. Concertos for Violin & Viola. 1000p. (Orig.). 1982. pap. 48.00 (ISBN 0-9601054-8-4). Cleaning Consul.

VIOLENCE

Alexander. International Violence. 256p. 1982. 24.95 (ISBN 0-03-061922-X). Praeger.

American Health Research Institute, Ltd. Violence-Psychological, Medical & Legal Aspects: A Subject Analysis & Research Index with Bibliography. Bartone, John C., ed. 120p. 1983. 29.95 (ISBN 0-88164-022-0); pap. 21.95 (ISBN 0-88164-023-9). ABBE Pubs Assn.

Finkelhor, David & Gelles, Richard J., eds. The Dark Side of Families: Current Family Violence Research. 384p. 1983. 29.95 (ISBN 0-8039-1934-4); pap. 14.95 (ISBN 0-8039-1935-2). Sage.

Friedlander, Robert A. Terror-Violence: Aspects of Social Control. 350p. 1982. text ed. 35.00 (ISBN 0-379-20748-6). Oceana.

Hinton, John W. Dangerousness: Problems of Assessment & Prediction. 176p. 1983. text ed. 27.50x (ISBN 0-04-364021-4). Allen Unwin.

Priestland, Gerald. The Future of Violence. 174p. 1975. 12.50 (ISBN 0-241-02454-4). Transatlantic.

Saunders, Susan & Anderson, Ann M. Violent Individuals & Families: A Handbook for Practitioners. (Illus.). 256p. 1983. text ed. write for info (ISBN 0-398-04833-9). C C Thomas.

VIOLENCE–MORAL AND RELIGIOUS ASPECTS

see also War and Religion

Jewett, Robert. The Captain America Complex. 264p. pap. 6.95 (ISBN 0-939680-09-2). Bear & Co.

Schecter, Susan. Women & Male Violence: The Visions & Struggles of the Battered Women's Movement. 300p. 1982. 20.00 (ISBN 0-89608-160-5); pap. 7.50 (ISBN 0-89608-159-1). South End Pr.

VIOLENCE IN MASS MEDIA

Rowland, Willard D., Jr. The Politics of T. V. Violence: Policy Uses of Communication Research. (People & Communication Ser.: Vol. 16). (Illus.). 320p. 1983. 25.00 (ISBN 0-8039-1952-2); pap. 12.50 (ISBN 0-8039-1953-0). Sage.

VIOLIN

Abele, H. & Niederheitmann, F. The Violin: It's History & Construction. Broadhouse, John, tr. from Ger. (Illus.). 172p. 1983. pap. 6.50 (ISBN 0-88072-000-X). Tanager Bks.

VIOLIN–CONSTRUCTION

Abele, H. & Niederheitmann, F. The Violin: It's History & Construction. Broadhouse, John, tr. from Ger. (Illus.). 172p. 1983. pap. 6.50 (ISBN 0-88072-000-X). Tanager Bks.

White, A. W. The Violin: How to Construct from Beginning to Completion Eighteen Ninety-Three. (Illus.). 44p. pap. 12.50. Saifer.

VIOLIN MUSIC

Burnett, R. T. Concertos for Violin & Viola. 1000p. (Orig.). 1982. pap. 48.00 (ISBN 0-9601054-8-4). Cleaning Consul.

VIOLINISTS, VIOLONCELLISTS, ETC.

Roth, Henry. Master Violinists in Performance. (Illus.). 320p. 1982. 14.95 (ISBN 0-87666-594-6). Paganiniana Pubns.

VIOLINISTS, VIOLONCELLISTS, ETC.–CORRESPONDENCE, REMINISCENCES, ETC.

see Musicians–Correspondence, Reminiscences, etc.

VIOLONCELLO

Cowling, Elizabeth. The Cello: New Edition. (Illus.). 240p. 1983. 17.95 (ISBN 0-686-83826-2, ScribT). Scribner.

Ginsburg, Lev. History of the Violoncello. Axelrod, Herbert R., ed. Tchistyakova, Tanya, tr. (Illus.). 1983. 30.00 (ISBN 0-87666-597-0). Paganiniana Pubns.

Suzuki, Shinichi. Suzuki Cello School, Cello Part, Vols. 4 & 5. 24p. (gr. k-12). 1982. pap. text ed. write for info. (ISBN 0-87487-266-9). Summy.

--Suzuki Cello School, Cello Part, Vol. 6. 24p. (gr. k-12). 1982. pap. text ed. write for info. (ISBN 0-87487-267-7). Summy.

--Suzuki Cello School, Piano Accompaniment, Vol. 3. 32p. (gr. k-12). 1983. pap. text ed. write for info. (ISBN 0-87487-265-0). Summy.

VIPERS

see Snakes

VIRGIL

see Vergil (Publius Vergilius Maro)

VIRGIN ISLANDS

Greenberg, Harriet. U. S. Virgin Islands Alive. (Alive Publication Travel Guides). (Illus.). 200p. (Orig.). 1983. pap. 4.95 (ISBN 0-935572-11-2, Alive Pubns). Hippocrene Bks.

VIRGIN ISLANDS–DESCRIPTION AND TRAVEL

Greenberg, Harriet. U. S. Virgin Islands Alive. 1983. pap. 5.95 (ISBN 0-935572-11-2). Alive Pubns.

VIRGIN MARY

see Mary, Virgin

VIRGINIA

see also names of cities, regions, etc. in Virginia

Boyd, T. Munford & Graves, Edward S. Virginia Civil Procedure. 700p. 1982. 65.00 (ISBN 0-87215-424-6). Michie-Bobbs.

Johnston, Mary. Prisoners of Hope: A Tale of Colonial Virginia. 378p. 1982. Repr. of 1899 ed. lib. bdg. 40.00 (ISBN 0-89987-435-5). Darby Bks.

Keeran, James, ed. The McLean County Almanac Nineteen Eighty-Three. (Illus.). 300p. 1983. pap. 4.95 (ISBN 0-943782-02-3, Pantagraph Bks). Evergreen Comm.

VIRGINIA–DESCRIPTION AND TRAVEL

Jordan, James M., IV & Jordan, Frederick S. Virginia Beach: A Pictorial History. Rev. ed. LC 74-22354. (Illus.). 240p. 1983. 19.95 (ISBN 0-9610354-0-4). Jordan Assoc.

VIRGINIA–GENEALOGY

Giles County Historical Society. Giles County Virginia History Families. (Illus.). 404p. 1982. 32.50 (ISBN 0-686-43043-3, Pub. by Walsworth). Aviation.

Meredith, Joseph N. The Merediths & Selveys of Virginia & West Virginia. (Illus.). 210p. 1982. 26.00 (ISBN 0-686-82432-6). J N Meredith.

VIRGINIA–HISTORY

Barrett, Theodosia. Russel County. LC 81-69331. 148p. 1981. 10.95 (ISBN 0-89227-047-0). Commonwealth Pr.

Carr, Jess. Frost of Summer. LC 75-4257. 248p. 1975. 7.95 (ISBN 0-89227-046-2). Commonwealth Pr.

--Ship Ride Down the Spring Branch. LC 78-60480. 200p. 1978. 8.95 (ISBN 0-89227-048-9). Commonwealth Pr.

Leslie, Louise. Tazewell County. LC 81-69331. 768p. 1982. 35.00 (ISBN 0-89227-043-8). Commonwealth Pr.

Williams, D. Alan & Tate, Thad W. Colonial Virginia-A History. (A History of the American Colonies Ser.). (Orig.). 1983. lib. bdg. write for info. (ISBN 0-527-18722-4). Kraus Intl.

VIRGINIA–HISTORY–SOURCES

Giles County Historical Society. Giles County Virginia History Families. (Illus.). 404p. 1982. 32.50 (ISBN 0-686-43043-3, Pub. by Walsworth). Aviation.

VIRGINIA–HISTORY–COLONIAL PERIOD, ca. 1600-1775

Reese, George, ed. Proceedings in the Court of Vice-Admiralty of Virginia: 1698-1775. write for info (ISBN 0-88490-113-0). Va State Lib.

VIRGINIA–HISTORY–CIVIL WAR, 1861-1865

Putnam, Sallie. Richmond During War. LC 82-19154. (Collector's Library of the Civil War). 26.60 (ISBN 0-8094-4262-0). Silver.

VIRGINIA–HISTORY, LOCAL

Jordan, James M., IV & Jordan, Frederick S. Virginia Beach: A Pictorial History. Rev. ed. LC 74-22354. (Illus.). 240p. 1983. 19.95 (ISBN 0-9610354-0-4). Jordan Assoc.

VIRGINIA–POLITICS AND GOVERNMENT

Heinemann, Ronald L. Depression & New Deal in Virginia: The Enduring Dominion. LC 82-13487. 1983. write for info. (ISBN 0-8139-0946-5). U Pr of Va.

Moeser, John V., ed. A Virginia Profile Nineteen-Sixty to Two Thousand: Assessing Current Trends & Problems. (Commonwealth Books Public Policy). (Illus.). 290p. (Orig.). 1981. pap. write for info. (ISBN 0-940390-01-9). Comwealth Bks NJ.

VIRGINIA–POLITICS AND GOVERNMENT–1775-1865
Jordan, Daniel P. Political Leadership in Jefferson's Virginia. LC 82-23867. 274p. 1983. price not set (ISBN 0-8139-0967-8). U Pr of Va.

VIROLOGY
see also Virus Diseases; Viruses

Horne, Robert W. Structure & Function of Viruses. (Studies in Biology: No. 95). 58p. 1978. pap. text ed. 8.95 (ISBN 0-686-43111-1). E Arnold.

VIRTUE AND VIRTUES
see also Ethics; Sins

also specific virtues, e.g. Charity, Kindness

Cooper, A. A. An Inquiry Concerning Virtue, or Merit. Walford, D. E., ed. 152p. 1977. 15.50 (ISBN 0-7190-0657-0). Manchester.

Webb, Lance. How Good are your Virtues? 176p. (Orig.). 1983. pap. 3.50 (ISBN 0-687-17528-3, Festival). Abingdon.

VIRUS DISEASES
see also Rickettsial Diseases

Bonneau, M & Hennessen, W., eds. Herpes Virus of Man & Animal: Standardization of Immunological Procedures. (Developments in Biological Standardization Ser.: Vol. 52). (Illus.). x, 574p. 1983. pap. 78.00 (ISBN 3-8055-3636-4). S Karger.

Graf, T. & Jaenisch, R., eds. Tumorviruses, Neoplastic Transformation & Differentiation. (Current Topics in Microbiology & Immunology Ser.: Vol. 101). (Illus.). 198p. 1983. 40.00 (ISBN 0-387-11665-6). Springer-Verlag.

Melnick, J. L., ed. Progress in Medical Virology, Vol. 29. (Illus.). viii, 250p. 1983. 93.00 (ISBN 3-8055-3618-6). S Karger.

VIRUS DISEASES OF PLANTS
Rayechaudhuri, S. P. & Nariani, T. K. Virus & Mycoplasm Diseases of Plants in India. 102p. 1977. 50.00x (ISBN 0-686-84449-1, Pub by Oxford & I B H India). State Mutual Bk.

VIRUS HEPATITIS
see Hepatitis, Infectious

VIRUSES
see also Herpes Simplex Virus; Interferons; Virus Diseases; Virus Diseases of Plants

Biswas, S. B. & Biswas, Amita. An Introduction to Viruses. (Illus.). 200p. (Orig.). 1982. pap. text ed. 7.95x (ISBN 0-7069-1561-5, Pub. by Vikas India). Advent NY.

Fareed, George C. & Linke, Hawley K. Molecular Biology of Polyomaviruses & Herpesviruses. 175p. 1983. 30.00 (ISBN 0-471-05058-X, Pub. by Wiley Interscience). Wiley.

VIRUSES–JUVENILE LITERATURE
Nourse, Alan E. Viruses. rev. ed. (First Bk.). (Illus.). 72p. (gr. 4 up). 1983. PLB 8.90 (ISBN 0-531-04534-X). Watts.

VISCERAL LEARNING
see Biofeedback Training

VISCONTI, LUCHINO, 1906-
Nowell-Smith, Geoffrey. Visconti. 1967. pap. 8.95 (ISBN 0-436-09853-9, Pub by Secker & Warburg). David & Charles.

Tonetti, Claretta. Luchino Visconti. (Filmmakers Ser.). 219p. 1983. lib. bdg. 24.00 (ISBN 0-8057-9289-9, Twayne). G K Hall.

VISIBLE SPEECH
see Deaf–Means of Communication

VISION
see also Binocular Vision; Color Vision; Eye; Motion Perception (Vision); Optical Illusions; Visual Perception

Cockerill, Ian M. & Macgillivary, William W., eds. Vision & Sport. 224p. 1981. 40.00x (ISBN 0-85950-463-8, Pub. by Thornes England). State Mutual Bk.

Graham, Clarence H., et al, eds. Vision & Visual Perception. LC 65-12711. 1965. 69.95x (ISBN 0-471-32170-2). Wiley.

Murphy, Wendy B. Touch, Smell, Taste, Sight & Hearing. LC 82-5738. (Library of Health). lib. bdg. 18.60 (ISBN 0-8094-3799-6, Pub. by Time-Life). Silver.

Weale, R. A. Focus on Vision. (Illus.). 208p. 1983. pap. text ed. 15.00x (ISBN 0-674-30701-1). Harvard U Pr.

VISION SCREENING
see Eye–Examination

VISIONS
see also Apparitions; Dreams; Fantasy

DeArteaga, William. Past Life Visions: A Christian Exploration. 240p. 1983. pap. 11.95 (ISBN 0-8164-2414-4). Seabury.

VISUAL ARTS
see Art

VISUAL DATA PROCESSING
see Optical Data Processing

VISUAL EDUCATION
see also Audio-Visual Education; Bulletin Boards; Moving-Pictures in Education

Jussim, Estelle. Visual Communication & the Graphic Arts. pap. 24.95 (ISBN 0-8352-1674-8). Bowker.

VISUAL PERCEPTION
see also Color Vision

Easterby, Ronald & Zwaga, Harm. Visual Presentation of Information: The Design & Evaluation of Signs & Printed Material. 1983. write for info. (ISBN 0-471-10431-0, Pub. by Wiley-Interscience). Wiley.

Graham, Clarence H., et al, eds. Vision & Visual Perception. LC 65-12711. 1965. 69.95x (ISBN 0-471-32170-2). Wiley.

Woodford, Susan. Looking at Pictures. LC 82-14613. (Cambridge Introduction to the History of Art 6 Ser.). (Illus.). 128p. Date not set. 14.95 (ISBN 0-521-24371-8); pap. 1.25 (ISBN 0-521-28647-6). Cambridge U Pr.

VISUALLY HANDICAPPED CHILDREN
Scott, Eileen P. Your Visually Impaired Student: A Guide for Teachers. (Illus.). 224p. 1983. pap. text ed. 14.95 (ISBN 0-8391-1703-5, 16241). Univ Park.

VITAL RECORDS
see Registers of Births, Deaths, Marriages, Etc.

VITAMIN THERAPY
Fredericks, Carl. Carlton Frederick's Nutrition Guide for Prevention & Cure of Common Ailments & Disease. 1982. 8.95x. Cancer Control Soc.

VITAMINS
see also Vitamin Therapy

American Health Research Institute, Ltd. Vitamins: A Medical Subject Analysis & Research Index With Bibliography. Bartone, John C., ed. LC 82-72027. 120p. 1983. 29.95 (ISBN 0-941864-70-7); pap. 21.95 (ISBN 0-941864-71-5). ABBE Pubs Assn.

Center for Self Sufficiency Research Division Staff. International Directory of Herb, Health, Vitamin & Natural Food Catalogs. 200p. 1983. pap. text ed. 15.95 (ISBN 0-910811-36-9). Center Self.

Mindell, Earl. Earl Mindell's Vitamin Bible for Kids. 1981. 6.95x (ISBN 0-89256-198-X). Cancer Control Soc.

--Earl Mindell's Vitamin Bible for your Kids. 256p. 1982. pap. 3.95 (ISBN 0-553-22660-6). Bantam.

New York Academy of Sciences Annals, Nov. 11-13, 1981. Vitamin E: Biochemical, Hematological, Clinical Aspects, Vol. 393. Lubin, Bertram & Machlin, Lawrence J., eds. 506p. 1982. 95.00 (ISBN 0-89766-176-1). NY Acad Sci.

Nobile, Sylvia & Woodhill, Joan M. Vitamin C-The Mysterious Redox-System: A Trigger of Life? (Illus.). 185p. 1981. text ed. 29.00 (ISBN 0-85200-419-2, Pub. by MTP Pr England). Kluwer Boston.

Szekely, Edmond B. The Book of Vitamins. (Illus.). 40p. 1978. pap. 2.95 (ISBN 0-89564-045-7). IBS Intl.

VITAMINS–THERAPEUTIC USE
see Vitamin Therapy

VITILIGO
Ortonne, Jean-Paul & Mosher, David B. Vitiligo & Other Hypomelanoses of Hair & Skin. (Topics in Dermatology Ser.). 680p. 1983. 79.50x (ISBN 0-306-40974-7, Plenum Med Bk). Plenum Pub.

VITUPERATION
see Invective

VIVES, JUAN LUIS, 1492-1540
Watson, Foster. Luis Vivies, el Gran Valenciano. 1922. pap. 3.00 (ISBN 0-87535-013-5). Hispanic Soc.

VIVISECTION
Dodds, W. Jean & Orlans, F. Barbara, eds. Scientific Perspectives in Animal Welfare: Symposium. LC 82-24375. Date not set. 17.50 (ISBN 0-12-219140-4). Acad Pr.

VOCABULARY
Here are entered general works and works on English vocabulary. Works dealing with the vocabularies of other languages are entered under names of specific languages, with subdivision Vocabulary, e.g. French Language–Vocabulary.

see also Children–Language

also subdivisions Dictionaries and Glossaries, Vocabularies, Etc. under names of languages.

Brooks, Bearl, et al. Jumbo Word Games Yearbook. (Jumbo Vocabulary Ser.). 96p. (gr. 3). 1980. 14.00 (ISBN 0-8209-0059-1, JWG 1). ESP.

Cory, Beverly. Word Meaning. (Learning Workbooks Language Arts). (gr. 4-6). pap. 1.50 (ISBN 0-8224-4178-0). Pitman.

Ellis, et al. Base. (A vocabulary enrichment program). (gr. 4-12). pap. 3.39 student bk. (ISBN 0-8372-4253-3); tchr's handbk. 3.39 (ISBN 0-8372-4254-1); tapes avail. Bowmar-Noble.

Hayes, Marilyn. Basic Skills Words We Use Workbook. (Basic Skills Workbooks). 32p. (gr. k-1). 1983. 0.99 (ISBN 0-8209-0577-1, EEW-7). ESP.

--Learning Opposite Words. (Early Education Ser.). 24p. (gr. 1). 1982. wkbk. 5.00 (ISBN 0-686-42827-7, K-13). ESP.

--Lower-Case, Upper-Case Words. (Early Education Ser.). 24p. (gr. 1). 1980. wkbk. 5.00 (ISBN 0-8209-0217-9, K-19). ESP.

--My Picture & Word Book. (Early Education Ser.). 24p. (gr. 1). 1981. wkbk. 5.00 (ISBN 0-8209-0215-2, K-17). ESP.

--Words We Use. (Early Education Ser.). 24p. (gr. 1). 5.00 (ISBN 0-8209-0218-7, K-20). ESP.

Justus, Fred. Basic Skills Vocabulary Workbook: Grade 1. (Basic Skills Workbooks). 32p. (gr. 1). 1982. wkbk. 0.99 (ISBN 0-8209-0377-9, VW-B). ESP.

--Four-Letter Words. (Puzzles Ser.). 24p. (gr. 4-6). 1980. wkbk. 5.00 (ISBN 0-8209-0300-0, PU-14). ESP.

--Jumbo Vocabulary Development Yearbook: Grade 1. (Jumbo Vocabulary Ser.). 96p. (gr. 1). 1979. 14.00 (ISBN 0-8209-0050-8, JVDY 1). ESP.

--Jumbo Vocabulary Development Yearbook: Grade 2. (Jumbo Vocabulary Ser.). 96p. (gr. 2). 1980. 14.00 (ISBN 0-8209-0051-6, JVDY 2). ESP.

--Jumbo Vocabulary Fun Yearbook. (Jumbo Vocabulary Ser.). 96p. (gr. 3). 1980. 14.00 (ISBN 0-8209-0058-3, JVFY 3). ESP.

--Look, Hear, & Make Words. (Early Education Ser.). 24p. (gr. 1). 1980. 5.00 (ISBN 0-8209-0224-1, K-26). ESP.

Lenier, Minette & Maker, Janet. Key to a Powerful Vocabulary: Level Two. (Illus.). 224p. 1983. pap. text ed. 10.95 (ISBN 0-13-514992-4). P-H.

McMaster, Dale. Vocabulary Development. (Language Arts Ser.). 24p. (gr. 6-9). 1976. wkbk. 5.00 (ISBN 0-8209-0312-4, VD-4). ESP.

McMasters, Dale. Basic Skills Word Building Workbook. (Basic Skills Workbooks). 32p. (gr. 4-7). 1983. 0.99 (ISBN 0-8209-0568-2, WBW-1). ESP.

--Beginning Vocabulary. (Language Arts Ser.). 24p. (gr. 3-5). 1976. wkbk. 5.00 (ISBN 0-8209-0309-4, VD-1). ESP.

--Everyday Vocabulary. (Language Arts Ser.). 24p. (gr. 4-6). 1976. wkbk. 5.00 (ISBN 0-8209-0310-8, VD-2). ESP.

--Vocabulary Study. (Language Arts Ser.). 24p. (gr. 5-7). 1976. wkbk. 5.00 (ISBN 0-8209-0311-6, VD-3). ESP.

--Word Building. (Language Arts Ser.). 24p. (gr. 4-7). 1976. wkbk. 5.00 (ISBN 0-8209-0305-1, WB-1). ESP.

Shaw, Marie-Jose. Basic Skills Vocabulary Workbook: Grade 2. (Basic Skills Workbooks). 32p. (gr. 2). 1982. wkbk. 0.99 (ISBN 0-8209-0378-7, VW-C). ESP.

--Basic Skills Vocabulary Workbook: Grade 3. (Basic Skills Workbooks). 32p. (gr. 3). 1982. wkbk. 0.99 (ISBN 0-8209-0379-5, VW-D). ESP.

--Basic Skills Vocabulary Workbook: Grade 4. (Basic Skills Workbooks). 32p. (gr. 4). 1982. wkbk. 0.99 (ISBN 0-8209-0380-9, VW-E). ESP.

--Basic Skills Vocabulary Workbook: Grade 5. (Basic Skills Workbooks). 32p. (gr. 5). 1982. wkbk. 0.99 (ISBN 0-8209-0381-7, VW-F). ESP.

--Basic Skills Vocabulary Workbook: Grade 6. (Basic Skills Workbooks). 32p. (gr. 6). 1982. wkbk. 0.99 (ISBN 0-8209-0382-5, VW-G). ESP.

--Jumbo Vocabulary Development Yearbook: Grade 3. (Jumbo Vocabulary Ser.). 96p. (gr. 3). 1980. 14.00 (ISBN 0-8209-0052-4, JVDY 3). ESP.

--Jumbo Vocabulary Development Yearbook: Grade 4. (Jumbo Vocabulary Ser.). 96p. (gr. 4). 1980. 14.00 (ISBN 0-8209-0053-2, JVDY 4). ESP.

--Jumbo Vocabulary Development Yearbook: Grade 5. (Jumbo Vocabulary Ser.). 96p. (gr. 5). 1981. 14.00 (ISBN 0-8209-0054-0, JVDY 5). ESP.

Shepherd. College Vocabulary Skills. 2d ed. 1983. pap. text ed. 11.95 (ISBN 0-686-84578-1, RD05); instr's. manual avail. (RD06). HM.

Strohm, Sally. Word Signals. (English Ser.). 24p. (gr. 4-7). 1979. wkbk. 5.00 (ISBN 0-8209-0185-7, E-13). ESP.

Vaughn, Jim. Jumbo Vocabulary Development Yearbook: Grade 7. (Jumbo Vocabulary Ser.). 96p. (gr. 7-9). 1981. 14.00 (ISBN 0-8209-0056-7, JVDY J). ESP.

--Jumbo Vocabulary Development Yearbook: Grade 10. (Jumbo Vocabulary Ser.). 96p. (gr. 10-12). 1981. 14.00 (ISBN 0-8209-0057-5, JVDY S). ESP.

Wallace, Michael. Teaching Vocabulary, No. 10. Geddes, Marion & Sturtridge, Gillian, eds. (Practical Language Teaching Ser.). 144p. (Orig.). 1983. pap. text ed. 7.50x (ISBN 0-435-28974-8). Heinemann Ed.

Whitlock, Marlene. Basic Skills Listening Skills Workbook. (Basic Skills Workbooks). 32p. (gr. 2-3). 1983. 0.99 (ISBN 0-8209-0589-5, EEW-12). ESP.

VOCABULARY–JUVENILE LITERATURE
Frank Schaffer Publications. My First Words. (Help Your Child Learn Ser.). (Illus.). 24p. (gr. 1-3). 1978. workbook 1.29 (ISBN 0-86734-005-3, FS 3006). Schaffer Pubns.

Hillman, Priscilla. Merry Mouse Book of Toys. LC 82-45250. (Illus.). 14p. (gr. k-3). 1983. 3.95 (ISBN 0-385-17917-0). Doubleday.

VOCABULARY–PROGRAMMED INSTRUCTION
Vocabulary Skills, 3 Bks, Bks. D-F. pap. 1.47 ea.; tchr's eds. 1.47 ea. Bowmar-Noble.

VOCAL CULTURE
see Singing; Voice Culture

VOCALISTS
see Singers

VOCATION (IN RELIGIOUS ORDERS, CONGREGATIONS, ETC.)
Godin, Andre. The Psychology of Religious Vocations: Problems of the Religious Life. Wauck, LeRoy A., ed. LC 82-24708. 136p. (Orig.). 1983. lib. bdg. 18.75 (ISBN 0-8191-3007-9); pap. text ed. 8.25 (ISBN 0-8191-3008-7). U Pr of Amer.

VOCATION, CHOICE OF
see Vocational Guidance

VOCATION, RELIGIOUS
see Vocation (In Religious Orders, Congregations, etc.)

VOCATIONAL EDUCATION
Here are entered works on vocational instruction within the standard educational system. Works on the vocationally oriented process of endowing people with a skill after either completion or termination of their formal education are entered under Occupational Training. Works on retraining persons with obsolete vocational skills are entered under Occupational Retraining. Works on the training of employees on the job are entered under Employees, Training Of.

see also Employees, Training Of; Engineering–Study and Teaching; Medical Colleges; Occupational Training

Croll, R. D. & Doery, A. C. Successful Conferences. 38p. 1983. pap. 2.50 (ISBN 0-643-00371-1, Pub. by CSIRO Australia). Intl Schol Bk Serv.

Goodard, T. & Schoen, S. Equipment Planning Guide for Vocational & Technical Training & Education Programmes: Carpentry & Joinery, No. 8. 134p. 1982. 22.80 (ISBN 92-2-102930-1). Intl Labour Office.

Gorwen, Leonard. How to Find & Land Your First Full-Time Job. LC 82-6742. 128p. 1983. lib. bdg. 9.95 (ISBN 0-668-05458-1); pap. 4.95 (ISBN 0-668-05463-8). Arco.

Husak, G. & Pahre, P. The Work Series, 9 pts. Incl. Getting to Work. 55p. pap. text ed. 3.00 (ISBN 0-910839-05-0); How I Should Act at Work. 71p. pap. text ed. 3.00 (ISBN 0-910839-08-5); How to Find a Job. 60p. pap. text ed. 3.00 (ISBN 0-910839-07-7); Job Training Centers. 51p. pap. 3.00 (ISBN 0-910839-06-9); Payroll Deductions & Company Benefits. 27p. pap. text ed. 1.75 (ISBN 0-910839-02-6); Taxes. 22p. pap. 1.75 (ISBN 0-910839-04-2); Where to Get Help. 26p. pap. text ed. 1.75 (ISBN 0-910839-03-4); Work Rules. 63p. pap. text ed. 3.00 (ISBN 0-910839-01-8). (Illus.). (gr. 7-12). 1976. tchrs' ed. 2.00 (ISBN 0-910839-09-3). Hopewell.

Jensen, Joyce D. & Cooley, Stella G. A Handbook of Career Education Activities: For Use by Secondary Counselors & Classroom Teachers. 114p. 1982. pap. 14.50x spiral (ISBN 0-398-04768-5). C C Thomas.

Rudman, Jack. Job Training Specialist. (Career Examination Ser.: C-02697). (Cloth bdg. avail. on request). pap. 10.00 (ISBN 0-8373-2697-4). Natl Learning.

--Life Skills Counselor. (Career Examination Ser.: C-2917). (Cloth bdg. avail. on request). pap. 12.00 (ISBN 0-8373-2917-5). Natl Learning.

Segalla, Rosemary A. Departure from Traditional Roles: Mid-LIfe Women Break the Daisy Chains. Nathan, Peter E., ed. LC 82-20089. (Research in Clinical Psychology Ser.: No. 5). 164p. 1982. 34.95 (ISBN 0-8357-1386-5). Univ Microfilms.

Shanahan, William F. College: Yes or No? The High School Student's Career Decision-Making Handbook. LC 82-6775. 256p. (gr. 9 up). 1983. lib. bdg. 12.95 (ISBN 0-668-05589-8); pap. 7.95 (ISBN 0-668-05590-1). Arco.

The Specific Contribution of the Chemical Industries to the Vocational Training & Advanced Training of Manpower in Developing Countries: Report 2. Chemical Industries Committee, Ninth Session, Geneva September 21-30, 1982. iv, 1982p. 1982. 8.55 (ISBN 92-2-103055-5). Intl Labour Office.

Vocational & Technical Education: Development of Curricula, Instructional Materials, Physical Facilities & Teacher Training with Focus on Electrical & Electronic Subjects. 97p. 1981. pap. 5.25 (ISBN 0-686-81850-4, UB110, UNESCO). Unipub.

Wray, M. & Hill, S. Employer Involvement in Schemes of Unified Vocational Preparation. (NFER Research Publications). 152p. 1982. pap. text ed. 16.75x (ISBN 0-7005-0492-3, NFER). Humanities.

VOCATIONAL EDUCATION–DIRECTORIES
Career Employment Opportunities Directory, 4 vols. Incl. Vol. 1. Liberal Arts & Social Sciences (ISBN 0-916270-12-2); Vol. 2. Business Administration (ISBN 0-916270-13-0); Vol. 3. Engineering & Computer Science (ISBN 0-916270-14-9); Vol. 4. Sciences (ISBN 0-916270-15-7). Set. 169.50 (ISBN 0-916270-11-4); 47.50 ea. Ready Ref Pr.

Directory of Career Training & Development Programs, 2 vols. Set. 85.00 (ISBN 0-916270-27-0); First Edition. 47.50 (ISBN 0-916270-08-4); Suppl. 47.50 (ISBN 0-916270-26-2). Ready Ref Pr.

Directory of Internships, Work Experience Programs & On-the-Job Training Opportunities, 2 vols. 85.50 (ISBN 0-916270-23-8); First Edition. 47.00 (ISBN 0-916270-01-7); Suppl. 37.50 (ISBN 0-916270-02-5). Ready Ref Pr.

Norback & Company, ed. Arco's Guide to Technical, Vocational & Trade Schools. (Arco Occupational Guides Ser.). 208p. 1983. lib. bdg. 11.95 (ISBN 0-668-05524-3); pap. 6.95 (ISBN 0-668-05532-4). Arco.

VOCATIONAL GUIDANCE
see also Counseling; Occupations; Personnel Service in Education; Professions; Vocation (In Religious Orders, Congregations, etc.); Vocational Rehabilitation

Adams, J. Michael. Career Change: A Planning Book. (Illus.). 208p. 1983. pap. text ed. 7.95 (ISBN 0-07-000401-3, G). McGraw.

Adams, Robert L., ed. Greater Washington Job. 300p. (Orig.). 1983. pap. 9.95 (ISBN 0-937860-10-7). Adams Inc MA.

Angers, Marilynn M. & Angers, William P. Creating Your Own Career for Job Satisfaction. LC 82-61718. 170p. (Orig.). 1983. pap. 9.95 (ISBN 0-910793-00-X). Marlborough Pr.

Applegath, John. Working Free: Practical Alternatives to the 9 to 5 Job. pap. 6.95 (ISBN 0-686-84798-9). Am Mgmt.

Aves, Diane K. & Anderson, Debra. Planning Your Job Search: Making the Right Moves. 84p. 1982. 9.75 (ISBN 0-88440-036-0). Sis Kenny Inst.

Beach, Janet. How to Get a Job in the San Francisco Bay Area. 256p. (Orig.). 1983. pap. 8.95 (ISBN 0-8092-5692-4). Contemp Bks.

Bisignano, Joseph & Bisignano, Judith. Creating Your Future: Level 4. (Illus.). 64p. 1983. workbook 6.95 (ISBN 0-910141-01-0, KP115). Kino Pubns.

Bloomfield, Meyer, ed. Readings in Vocational Guidance. 723p. 1982. Repr. of 1915 ed. lib. bdg. 65.00 (ISBN 0-89987-090-2). Darby Bks.

Bolles, Richard N. What Color is Your Parachute? 1983. rev. ed. (Illus.). 320p. 1983. 14.95 (ISBN 0-89815-092-2); pap. 7.95 (ISBN 0-89815-091-4). Ten Speed Pr.

Borus, Michael E., ed. Tomorrow's Workers. 208p. 1982. 25.95 (ISBN 0-669-06090-9). Lexington Bks.

Bostwick, Burdette E. Finding the Job You've Always Wanted. 2nd ed. LC 79-15567. 292p. 1980. 12.50 (ISBN 0-471-05281-7, Pub. by Wiley-Interscience). Wiley.

--How to Find the Job You've Always Wanted. 2nd ed. 288p. 1982. pap. 9.95 (ISBN 0-471-87116-8). Wiley.

Brodey, Jean L. Mid-Life Careers. LC 82-24478. 244p. 1983. price not set (ISBN 0-664-27003-4, Bridgebooks Publications). Westminster.

Camden, Thomas M. & Schwartz, Susan H. How to Get a Job in Chicago: The Insider's Guide. LC 82-99938. (Illus.). 440p. 1983. pap. 10.95 (ISBN 0-9609516-0-1). Surrey Bks.

Comptex Associates Staff. Getting the Job you Want with the Audiovisual Portfolio: A Practical Guide for Job Hunters & Career Changers. 1981. 12.95 (ISBN 0-686-37449-5). Competent Assocs.

Douglas, Martha C. Go For It! How to Get Your First Good Job. 208p. (Orig.). (gr. 9 up). 1983. pap. 5.95 (ISBN 0-89815-090-6). Ten Speed Pr.

Dudeney, Charles. A Guide to Executive Re-Employment. 192p. 1972. 29.00 (ISBN 0-7121-1972-8, Pub. by Macdonald & Evans). State Mutual Bk.

Egelston, Roberta. Career Planning Materials. 190p. 1981. text ed. 20.00 (ISBN 0-8389-0343-6). ALA.

Fulker, Edmund N. A Model & Checklist for Administrator, Manager & Executive Career Training & Development. 1980. 2.00 (ISBN 0-87771-018-X). Grad School.

Gannaway, Thomas W. & Sink, Jack M. Fundamentals of Vocational Evaluation. 1983. pap. text ed. price not set (ISBN 0-8391-1719-1, 13749). Univ Park.

Garfield, Nancy J. & Nelson, Richard E. Career Exploration Groups: A Facilitators Guide. 48p. 1983. pap. write for info. (ISBN 0-89106-022-7, 7395). Consulting Psychol.

Ginn, Robert J. The College Graduate's Career Guide. 256p. 1982. pap. 5.95 (ISBN 0-686-83719-3, ScribT). Scribner.

Gooch, Bill & Carrier, Lois. Strategies for Success. 1983. pap. text ed. 15.95 (ISBN 0-534-01410-0, Breton Pubs). Wadsworth Pub.

Hecklinger, Fred J. & Curtin, Bernadette M. Training for Life: A Practical Guide to Career & Life Planning. 256p. 1982. pap. text ed. 13.95 (ISBN 0-8403-2839-7). Kendall-Hunt.

Holdsworth, Ruth. Psychology for Careers Counseling. (Psychology for Professional Groups Ser.). 320p. 1982. text ed. 23.25x (ISBN 0-333-31864-1, Pub. by Macmillan England); pap. text ed. 9.25x (ISBN 0-333-31881-1). Humanities.

Holdsworth, Ruth. Psychology for Careers Counselling. Chapman, Antony & Gale, Anthony, eds. (Psychology for Professional Groups Ser.). 320p. 1982. 49.00x (ISBN 0-333-31864-1, Pub. by Macmillan England). State Mutual Bk.

Jackson, Tom. Guerrilla Tactics in the Job Market. 288p. 1982. pap. 3.50 (ISBN 0-553-23160-X). Bantam.

Keefe, John & Leute, George. Exploring Careers in the Sunbelt. (Careers in Depth Ser.). 140p. 1983. lib. bdg. 7.97 (ISBN 0-8239-0602-7). Rosen Pr.

Marcon, Mike. The TNT Job Getting System. Taylor, Margot W., ed. 128p. (Orig.). 1983. 9.95 (ISBN 0-911529-00-4). Worthington Co.

Mitchell, Joyce S. Choices & Changes: A Career Book for Men. LC 82-72389. (Illus.). 336p. (Orig.). 1982. pap. 9.95 (ISBN 0-87447-151-6). College Bd.

Moffett, George D., Jr. So You Are Looking for a New Job... Now What? 112p. 1983. 6.00 (ISBN 0-682-49953-6). Exposition.

Patty, Catherine. Basic Skills Career Exploration Workbook. (Basic Skills Workbooks). 32p. (gr. 9-12). 1983. 0.99 (ISBN 0-8209-0585-2, CEW-1). ESP.

--Career Exploration. (Sound Filmstrip Kits Ser.). (gr. 5-8). 1981. tchrs ed. 24.00 (ISBN 0-8209-0440-6, FCW-17). ESP.

--Career Exploration. (Social Studies). 24p. (gr. 9-12). 1979. wkbk. 5.00 (ISBN 0-8209-0260-8, SS-27). ESP.

Petit, Ron E. The Career Connection. 161p. 1982. 8.95 (ISBN 0-941944-01-8). Impact VA.

Petit, Ronald E. The Career Connection: Keys to Employment. Atwell, Susan, ed. (Illus.). 155p. 1981. pap. 5.95 (ISBN 0-686-42916-8). Maron Pubns.

--From the Military to a Civilian Career. Atwell, Susan, ed. (Illus.). 146p. 1980. pap. 5.95 (ISBN 0-941944-02-6). Maron Pubns.

--Women & The Career Game: Play to Win!!! 147p. 1982. pap. 7.95 (ISBN 0-941944-03-4). Maron Pubns.

Radin, R. J. Full Potential: Your Career & Life Planning Workbook. 240p. 1983. pap. 7.95 (ISBN 0-07-051091-1, GB). McGraw.

Rosaluk, Warren. Throw Away Your Resume & Get That Job. (Illus.). 132p. 1983. 12.95 (ISBN 0-13-920587-X); pap. 5.95 (ISBN 0-13-920595-0). P-H.

Rudman, Jack. Habitation Specialist. (Career Examination Ser.: C-2900). (Cloth bdg avail. on request). pap. 12.00 (ISBN 0-8373-2900-0). Natl Learning.

--Mortuary Technician. (Career Examination Ser.: C-514). (Cloth bdg. avail. on request). pap. 10.00 (ISBN 0-8373-0514-4). Natl Learning.

--Motor Equipment Manager. (Career Examination Ser.: C-359). (Cloth bdg. avail. on request). pap. 14.00 (ISBN 0-686-84424-6). Natl Learning.

--Multi-Keyboard Operator. (Career Examination Ser.: C-455). (Cloth bdg. avail. on request). pap. 10.00 (ISBN 0-8373-0455-5). Natl Learning.

--Park Manager III. (Career Examination Ser.: C-385). (Cloth bdg. avail. on request). pap. 14.00 (ISBN 0-8373-0385-0). Natl Learning.

--Principal Environmental Analyst. (Career Examination Ser.: C-2661). (Cloth bdg. avail. on request). pap. 12.00 (ISBN 0-8373-2661-3). Natl Learning.

--Safety Consultant. (Career Examination Ser.: C-2540). (Cloth bdg. avail. on request). pap. 10.00 (ISBN 0-8373-2640-0). Natl Learning.

--Senior High School. (Teachers Lesson Plan Bk.: S-l). (gr. 9-12). pap. 3.95 (ISBN 0-686-84421-1). Natl Learning.

--Senior Land Management Specialist. (Career Examination Ser.: C-2619). (Cloth bdg. avail. on request). pap. 12.00 (ISBN 0-8373-2619-2). Natl Learning.

--Senior Traffic Supervisor. (Career Examination Ser.: C-2628). (Cloth bdg. avail. on request). pap. 12.00 (ISBN 0-8373-2628-1). Natl Learning.

--Supervising Audit Clerk. (Career Examination Ser.: C-887). (Cloth bdg. avail. on request). pap. 10.00 (ISBN 0-8373-0887-9). Natl Learning.

--Supervising Auditor. (Career Examination Ser.: C-2681). (Cloth bdg. avail. on request). pap. 12.00 (ISBN 0-8373-2681-8). Natl Learning.

--Supervising Bookkeeper. (Career Examination Ser.: C-2682). (Cloth bdg. avail. on request). pap. 12.00 (ISBN 0-8373-2682-6). Natl Learning.

--Supervising Building Plan Examiner. (Career Examination Ser.: C-862). (Cloth bdg. avail. on request). pap. 12.00 (ISBN 0-8373-0862-3). Natl Learning.

--Supervising Departmental Specialist. (Career Examination Ser.: C-935). (Cloth bdg. avail. on request). pap. 14.00 (ISBN 0-8373-0924-7). Natl Learning.

--Vocational Training Supervisor. (Career Examination Ser.: C-2673). (Cloth bdg. avail. on request). pap. 12.00 (ISBN 0-8373-2673-7). Natl Learning.

--Water Service Foreman. (Career Examination Ser.: C-2918). (Cloth bdg. avail. on request). pap. 12.00 (ISBN 0-686-84406-8). Natl Learning.

Ruyle, Gene. Making a Life: Career Choices & the Life Process. 128p. (Orig.). 1983. pap. price not set (ISBN 0-8164-2408-X). Seabury.

Sandberg, John E. Career Opportunities. LC 82-83779. 350p. text ed. 17.95x (ISBN 0-918452-37-6). Learning Pubns.

Scherman, William. How to Get the Right Job in Publishing. (Illus.). 256p. (Orig.). 1983. pap. 9.95 (ISBN 0-8092-5683-5). Contemp Bks.

Schwartz, Lester & Brechner, Irv. The Career Finder: Pathways to over 1500 Careers. LC 82-90224. 352p. 1983. pap. 8.95 (ISBN 0-345-29772-5). Ballantine.

Sheard, James L. & Stalley, Rodney E. Opening Doors to the Job Market. LC 82-72642. 176p. 1983. pap. 8.95 (ISBN 0-8066-1948-1, 10-4811). Augsburg.

Smith, Frank E. & Shore, Sidney. It Doesn't Pay to Work too Hard. 200p. (Orig.). 1979. pap. 9.00 (ISBN 0-9602288-0-2). Smith F E.

Stair, Lila B. Careers in Business. LC 82-73634. 170p. 1983. Repr. of 1980 ed. 12.95 (ISBN 0-87094-398-7). Dow Jones-Irwin.

Stark, S. Returning to Work: A Planning Book. LC 82-14892. 208p. 1983. 7.95x (ISBN 0-07-060887-3). McGraw.

Truitt, John. Telesearch: Direct Dial the Best Job of Your Life. LC 82-15714. 160p. 1983. 11.95 (ISBN 0-87196-900-9); success cassette 19.95 (ISBN 0-87196-901-7). Facts on File.

Walsh, W. Bruce & Osipow, Samuel H., eds. Handbook of Vocational Psychology: Applications, Vol. 2. 1983. text ed. write for info. (ISBN 0-89859-286-0). L Erlbaum Assocs.

--Handbook of Vocational Psychology: Foundations, Vol. 1. 375p. 1983. text ed. write for info. (ISBN 0-89859-285-2). L Erlbaum Assocs.

Williams, Eugene. Increase Your Employment Opportunities With the Audiovisual Portfolio. 1980. 12.95 (ISBN 0-686-37448-7). Competent Assocs.

Would You Like to Be a Telecommunications Specialist? 48p. (gr. 4-6). 1983. 2.95 (ISBN 0-941852-07-5). Unica Inc.

Zagoren, Adelaide M., compiled by. Involving Alumni in Career Assistance Programs. 111p. 1982. 14.50 (ISBN 0-89964-192-X). CASE.

VOCATIONAL GUIDANCE–VOCATIONAL GUIDANCE

Crow, Lester D. Principles of Guidance. 251p. 1982. pap. write for info. (ISBN 0-932970-33-8). L D Crow.

VOCATIONAL GUIDANCE AS A PROFESSION

see Vocational Guidance–Vocational Guidance

VOCATIONAL GUIDANCE FOR WOMEN

see also Women–Employment; Women in Business also subdivision Vocational Guidance under appropriate subjects

Collins, Nancy W. Professional Women & Their Mentors: A Practical Guide to Mentoring for the Woman Who Wants to Get Ahead. 163p. 1982. 12.95 (ISBN 0-13-725994-8); pap. 6.95 (ISBN 0-13-725986-7). P-H.

Mitchell, Joyce S. I Can be Anything: A Career Book for Women. 3rd ed. (Illus.). 336p. (Orig.). 1982. pap. 9.95 (ISBN 0-87447-150-8). College Bd.

Moore, Kathryn M. & Trow, Jo Anne J. Professional Advancement Kit-What to do until the Mentor Arrives: Administrative Procedures-A Practice Manual. (Orig.). 1982. write for info. (ISBN 0-686-82337-0); pap. 13.50. Natl Assn Women.

VOCATIONAL NURSING

see Practical Nursing

VOCATIONAL OPPORTUNITIES

see Vocational Guidance

VOCATIONAL REHABILITATION

see also Handicapped–Employment; Rehabilitation Centers; Vocational Guidance

Cohen, James S. & Stieglitz, Maria N. Career Education For Physically Disabled Students: Classroom Business Ventures. LC 79-91614. (Illus.). 50p. 1980. 5.00 (ISBN 0-686-38798-8). Human Res Ctr.

International Labour Office. Vocational Rehabilitation of Leprosy Patients Report on the ILO-DANIDA Asian Seminar Bombay, India (26 October-6 November, 1981) iii, 126p. 1982. pap. 8.55 (ISBN 92-2-103047-4). Intl Labour Office.

Jacobsen, Richard J. & Avellani, Pamela B. A Review of Placement Services Within a Comprehensive Rehabilitation Framework: Survey Report. LC 78-72067. 76p. 1978. 8.25 (ISBN 0-686-38818-6). Human Res Ctr.

Palmer, John T. Career Education For Physically Disabled Students: Development As A Lifetime Activity. LC 80-82642. 64p. 1980. 6.50 (ISBN 0-686-38799-6). Human Res Ctr.

Power, Paul W. A Guide to Vocational Assessment: A Practical Approach for Rehabilitation Professionals. 1983. pap. text ed. price not set (ISBN 0-8391-1718-3, 15865). Univ Park.

Rudman, Jack. Vocational Rehabilitation Counselor. (Career Examination Ser.: C-858). (Cloth bdg. avail. on request). pap. 10.00 (ISBN 0-8373-0858-5). Natl Learning.

Singleton, W. T. & Debney, L. M., eds. Occupational Disability. (Illus.). 307p. 1982. 36.80 (ISBN 0-942068-02-5). Bogden & Son.

Stieglitz, Maria. Career Education For Physically Disabled Students: Career Awareness Curriculum. LC 80-83986. (Illus.). 100p. (gr. k-8). 1981. 9.75 (ISBN 0-686-38797-X). Human Res Ctr.

--Career Education For Physically Disabled Students: Self-Concept Curriculum. LC 80-82643. (Illus.). 96p. (gr. k-3). 1981. 9.75 (ISBN 0-686-38800-3). Human Res Ctr.

Stieglitz, Maria & Cohen, James S. Career Education For Physically Disabled Students: Speaker's Bureau. LC 79-93340. (Illus.). 62p. 1980. 6.50 (ISBN 0-686-38801-1). Human Res Ctr.

Swirsky, Jessica & Vandergoot, David. A Handbook of Placement Assessment Resources. LC 79-84038. 144p. 1980. 10.00 (ISBN 0-686-38811-9). Human Res Ctr.

Vandergoot, David & Avellani, Pamela B. A Compendium of Placement-Related Literature. LC 78-62048. 352p. 1978. 9.25 (ISBN 0-686-43001-8). Human Res Ctr.

Vandergoot, David & Swirsky, Jessica. A Review of Placement Services Within a Comprehensive Rehabilitation Framework: Technical Report. LC 78-72067. 60p. 1979. 5.25 (ISBN 0-686-38819-4). Human Res Ctr.

Veatch, Deborah. How to Get the Job you Really Want. 174p. 1982. pap. text ed. 10.95x (ISBN 0-913072-50-8). Natl Assn Deaf.

Vocational Rehabilitation of the Mentally Retarded: Proceedings, Conclusions & Recommendations of a Seminar on Vocational Rehabilitation of the Mentally Retarded, Held in Kingston, Jamaica, from 4 to 15 September, 1978. ii, 200p. 1982. 5.70 (ISBN 92-2-102018-5). Intl Labour Office.

VOCATIONAL TRAINING

see Occupational Training

VOGUE (PERIODICAL)

Travel in Vogue. (Quality Paperbacks Ser.). (Illus.). 255p. 1983. pap. 10.95 (ISBN 0-306-80185-X). Da Capo.

VOICE CULTURE

see also Respiration; Singing

Turner, J. Clifford. Voice & Speech in the Theatre. 3rd ed. Morrison, Malcolm, rev. by. (Theatre & Stage Ser.). 146p. 1982. pap. 13.50 (ISBN 0-7136-2209-1). Sportshelf.

VOIMENIL, ANTOINE CHARLES DE HOUX, BARON DE, 1728-1792

Labarge, Margaret W. Medieval Travellers. (Illus.). 1983. 17.50 (ISBN 0-393-01739-7). Norton.

VOLCANOES

Simkin, Tom & Fiske, Richard. Krakatau: The Volcanic Eruption & its Effects - A Centennial Retrospective. (Illus.). 400p. 1983. text ed. 15.00 (ISBN 0-87474-842-9). Smithsonian.

Time-Life Books Editors. Volcano. LC 81-18539. (Planet Earth Ser.). lib. bdg. 19.92 (ISBN 0-8094-4305-8, Pub. by Time-Life). Silver.

Updegraffe, Imelda & Updegraffe, Robert. Earthquakes & Volcanoes. (Turning Points Ser.). (Illus.). 24p. 1983. pap. 3.50 (ISBN 0-14-049190-2, Puffin). Penguin.

VOLCANOES–JUVENILE LITERATURE

Taylor, G. Jeffrey. Volcanoes in Our Solar System. LC 82-19819. (Illus.). 96p. (gr. 5 up). 1983. PLB 10.95 (ISBN 0-396-08118-5). Dodd.

VOLKSWAGEN (AUTOMOBILE)

see Automobiles, Foreign–Types–Volkswagen

VOLLEYBALL

Johnson, M. L. & Johnson, Dewayne J. Volleyball. (Illus.). 51p. 1981. pap. text ed. 2.95x (ISBN 0-89641-057-9). American Pr.

Rosenthal, Gary. Volleyball: The Game & How to Play It. (Illus.). 256p. 1983. 12.95 (ISBN 0-686-83674-X, ScribT). Scribner.

Rules, Officiating & Sport Regulation: Volleyball, 1978-79. 1978. 0.75 (ISBN 0-685-82326-1, 243-26210). AAHPERD.

Schakel, David J. Volleyball. (Illus.). 145p. 1980. pap. text ed. 4.95x (ISBN 0-89641-060-9). American Pr.

VOLTAIC CELL

see Electric Batteries

VOLTAIRE, FRANCOIS MARIE AROUET DE, 1694-1778

Lounsbury, Thomas R. Shakespeare & Voltaire. 463p. 1982. Repr. of 1902 ed. lib. bdg. 40.00 (ISBN 0-89987-523-8). Darby Bks.

Ludwig, Emil. Genius & Character: Shakespeare, Voltaire, Goethe, Balzac. 330p. 1982. Repr. of 1927 ed. lib. bdg. 35.00 (ISBN 0-8495-3267-1). Arden Lib.

Morley, John. Voltaire. 365p. 1982. Repr. of 1913 ed. lib. bdg. 40.00 (ISBN 0-89984-803-6). Century Bookbindery.

Voltaire: The Incomparable Infidel. 91p. 1982. Repr. of 1929 ed. lib. bdg. 35.00 (ISBN 0-89987-522-X). Darby Bks.

VOLUME FEEDING

see Food Service

VOLUMETRIC ANALYSIS

Fernando, Quintas & Ryan, Michael D. Calculations in Analytical Chemistry. 256p. (Orig.). 1982. pap. text ed. 10.95 (ISBN 0-15-505710-3). HarBraceJ.

VOLUNTARY ORGANIZATIONS

see Associations, Institutions, etc.

VOLUNTEER MILITARY SERVICE

see Military Service, Voluntary

VOLUNTEER TEACHERS

see Volunteer Workers in Education

VOLUNTEER WORKERS IN EDUCATION

Alberger, Patricia L., ed. How to Work Effectively with Alumni Boards. 81p. (Orig.). 1981. 14.50 (ISBN 0-89964-182-2). CASE.

Bennett, Linda L. Volunteers in the School Media Center. 350p. 1983. pap. text ed. 23.50 (ISBN 0-87287-351-X). Libs Unl.

VOLUNTEER WORKERS IN SOCIAL SERVICE

Allen, Kerry K. Volunteering: Rediscovering Our Greatest Natural Resource. (Vital Issues Ser.: Vol. XXXI, No. 7). 0.80 (ISBN 0-686-84145-X). Ctr Info Am.

Durman, E. C. & Dunlop, Burton. Volunteers in Social Services: Consumer Assessment of Nursing Homes. 48p. 1979. pap. text ed. 7.00 (ISBN 0-87766-261-4). Urban Inst.

Smith, David H. & Til, John Van, eds. International Perspectives on Voluntary Action Research. LC 82-20090. 430p. (Orig.). 1983. lib. bdg. 36.50 (ISBN 0-8191-2862-7); pap. text ed. 21.50 (ISBN 0-8191-2863-5). U Pr of Amer.

VON STROHEIM, ERICH, 1885-1957

Koszarski, Richard. The Man You Loved to Hate: Erich von Stroheim & Hollywood. (Illus.). 364p. 1983. 29.95 (ISBN 0-19-503239-X). Oxford U Pr.

VOODOOISM

Riva, Anna. Voodoo Handbook of Cult Secrets. (Illus.). 48p. 1974. pap. 2.00 (ISBN 0-943832-01-2). Intl Imports.

VORTEX-MOTION

Lught, Hans J. Vortex Flow in Nature & Technology. 600p. 1983. 70.00 (ISBN 0-471-86925-2, Pub. by Wiley-Interscience). Wiley.

VOTERS, REGISTRATION OF
Farouk, Brimah K. Profile of Missisippi Black Voting Strength & Political Representation. 1982. 1.00 (ISBN 0-686-38028-2). Voter Ed Proj.
Hudlin, Richard A. Black Population & Representation in Selected Alabama Counties & Places. 1982. 1.00 (ISBN 0-686-38022-3). Voter Ed Proj.
--Black Population, Voting Age Population, & Registrants for Counties in Georgia: 1980. 1982. 1.00 (ISBN 0-686-38024-X). Voter Ed Proj.
--Profile of Georgia Black Voting Strength & Political Representation. 1982. 1.00 (ISBN 0-686-38027-4). Voter Ed Proj.
--Voter Registration in Eleven Southern States, by Race: 1960-1980, in U.S. Bureau of the Census: Statistical Abstract of the United States: 1981. 1981. 0.10 ea. Voter Ed Proj.
Hudlin, Richard A. & Farouk, Brimah K. Profile of Alabama Black Voting Strength & Political Representation. 1982. 1.00 (ISBN 0-686-38026-6). Voter Ed Proj.
--Profile of Georgia's Black Voting Strength & Political Representation. 1981. 1.00 (ISBN 0-686-38015-0). Voter Ed Proj.
--Profile of Mississippi's Black Voting Strength & Political Representation. 1981. 1.00 (ISBN 0-686-38016-9). Voter Ed Proj.
--Voting Rights Act: Questions & Answers. 1981. 1.00 (ISBN 0-686-38020-7). Voter Ed Proj.
VOTING
see also Suffrage; Voters, Registration Of
Allswang, John M. The New Deal & American Politics: A Study in Political Change. LC 78-5733. (Critical Episodes in American Politics Ser.). 155p. 1978. pap. text ed. 11.50x (ISBN 0-471-02516-X). Wiley.
Berghe, Guido V. Political Rights for European Citizens. 245p. (Orig.). 1982. text ed. 38.00 (ISBN 0-566-00524-7). Gower Pub Ltd.
Flanigan, William H. & Zingale, Nancy H. American Voting Behavior: Presidential Elections from 1952 to 1980. LC 82-83324. 1982. write for info. (ISBN 0-89138-920-2, ICPSR 7581). ICPSR.
McLean, Iain. Dealing in Votes. LC 82-10421. 1982. 25.00 (ISBN 0-312-18535-9). St Martin.
Stockton, Ronald R. & Wayman, Frank W. A Time of Turmoil: Values & Voting in the 1970's. 216p. 1983. 18.95. Wayne St U Pr.
VOYAGES, INTERPLANETARY
see Interplanetary Voyages
VOYAGES, SCIENTIFIC
see Scientific Expeditions
VOYAGES AND TRAVELS
see also Adventure and Adventurers; Aeronautics-Flights; Discoveries (In Geography); Explorers; Mountaineering; Ocean Travel; Overland Journeys to the Pacific; Pilgrims and Pilgrimages; Pirates; Railroad Travel; Scientific Expeditions; Seafaring Life; Seamen; Shipwrecks; Travel; Travelers; Whaling; Yachts and Yachting
also subdivision Description and Travel (or Description, Geography) and Discovery and Exploration under names of countries, regions, etc., names of regions, e.g. Antarctic Regions; and names of ships
Brower, Kenneth. The Starship & the Canoe. LC 82-48519. 256p. 1983. pap. 4.76i (ISBN 0-06-091030-5, CN 1030, CN). Har-Row.
Clark, Merrian E. Ford's International Cruise Guide. 37th ed. LC 75-27925. (Illus.). 160p. 1983. pap. 7.95 (ISBN 0-916486-71-0). M Clark.
Darwin, Charles R. Journal of Researches into the Natural History & Geology of the Countries Visited during the Voyage of the H.M.S. Beagle Round the World, Under the Command of Capt. Fitz Roy R.N, 2 Vols. LC 72-3887. (Illus.). x, 519p. 1972. write for info. (ISBN 0-404-08401-X). AMS Pr.
DeLand, Antoinette. Fielding's Worldwide Guide to Cruises. rev. ed. (Illus.). 320p. 1982. pap. 12.95 (ISBN 0-688-01648-0). Morrow.
Franklin, Linda C. Travel Diary. (Old Fashioned Keepbook Ser.). 96p. 1983. pap. 7.50 (ISBN 0-934504-19-9). Tree Comm.
Garrett, Richard. Royal Travel. (Illus.). 240p. 1983. 16.95 (ISBN 0-7137-1182-5, Pub. by Blandford Pr England). Sterling.
Hakluyt, Richard. Voyages & Discoveries. Beeching, Jack, ed. (Penguin English Library). 1982. pap. 5.95 (ISBN 0-14-043073-3). Penguin.
Howell, James. Instruction for Forine Travel 1642. Arber, Edward, tr. Date not set. pap. 12.50 (ISBN 0-87556-499-2). Saifer.
Jones, Tristan. A Steady Trade: A Boyhood at Sea. (Illus.). 288p. 1982. 15.95 (ISBN 0-312-76138-4). St Martin.
Martelli, L. & Graham, A. Going Places. (Our Nation, Our World Ser.). (gr. 2). 1983. pap. text ed. 10.40 (ISBN 0-07-039942-5); tchr's. ed. 22.00 (ISBN 0-07-039952-2); suppl. materials avail. McGraw.
Merrett, John. Famous Voyagers in Small Boats. (Illus.). (gr. 6-9). 1957. write for info. S G Phillips.
O'Gara, Elaine. Travel Writer's Markets. 58p. (Orig.). 1982. pap. 6.00 (ISBN 0-9609172-0-9). R B Shapiro.
Pardey, Lin & Pardey, Larry. Seraffyn's Oriental Adventure. (Illus.). 1983. 19.95 (ISBN 0-393-03281-7). Norton.
Perkins, Robert. Against Straight Lines: Self-Portrait in a Landscape. 1983. 16.00i (ISBN 0-316-69930-6). Little.
Polo, Marco. The Travels of Marco Polo. 1982. Repr. lib. bdg. 18.95x (ISBN 0-89967-045-8). Harmony Raine.
Yapp, Peter, ed. The Travellers' Dictionary of Quotation: Who Said What, about Where. 200p. 1983. price not set (ISBN 0-7100-0992-5). Routledge & Kegan.
VOYAGES AND TRAVELS-GUIDEBOOKS
Carrol, Frieda. The Traveler's Workbook: Based on the People's Travel Book Index. 50p. 1983. 7.95 (ISBN 0-939476-52-5). Biblio Pr GA.
Clark, Merrian E. Ford's International Cruise Guide: Spring 1983. 36th ed. LC 75-27925. (Illus.). 160p. 1983. pap. 7.95 (ISBN 0-916486-69-9). M Clark.
DeLand, Antoinette. Fielding's Worldwide Guide to Cruises. rev. ed. LC 82-62320. (Illus.). 384p. 1982. pap. 12.45 (ISBN 0-686-38814-3). Fielding.
Drolet, Cindy. Unipix: Universal Language of Pictures. Drolet, Ken, ed. (Illus.). 58p. (Orig.). 1982. pap. 7.95 (ISBN 0-9609464-0-3). Imaginart Pr.
Flood, Robert G. The Christian's Vacation & Travel Guide. 224p. 1982. pap. 9.95 (ISBN 0-8423-0260-3). Tyndale.
Goldstein, M. & Waldman, S., eds. The Creative Black Book: Europe 1983, Vol. 3. (Illus.). 205p. 1983. 40.00 (ISBN 0-916098-10-9). Friendly Pubns.
How to Travel Without Being Rich. 1978. 4.95 (ISBN 0-686-42894-3). Harian.
Lightman, Sidney, ed. The Jewish Travel Guide 1983. (Illus.). 290p. (Orig.). 1983. pap. 8.95 (ISBN 0-900498-84-6). Hermon.
Nieman, Jean. A World of Travel Tips. (Illus.). 270p. (Orig.). 1982. write for info. (ISBN 0-9609388-0-X). Travel Inter.
Seales, John B. The Travel Game: An Insider's Guide to Getting the Most for Your Travel Dollar. Rand, Elizabeth, ed. 192p. (Orig.). 1983. pap. 6.95 (ISBN 0-914488-28-7). Rand-Tofua.
Simony, Maggie, ed. Traveler's Reading Guides: The Rest of the World, Vol. 3. (Traveler's Reading Guides Ser.). 275p. (Orig.). 1983. pap. 12.95 (ISBN 0-9602050-4-7). Freelance Pubns.
Simony, Maggy. Traveler's Reading Guides Update: January-June, 1983. (Background Books, Novels, Travel Literature & Articles). 150p. (Orig.). 1983. price not set (ISBN 0-9602050-6-3). Freelance Pubns.
Sparks, Lee, ed. Youth Group Travel Directory, 1983. LC 81-64228. 150p. 1982. 7.95 (ISBN 0-936664-09-6). T Schultz Pubns.
Stern, Michael. World Travel Digest 1983. 850p. 1982. pap. 29.95 (ISBN 0-943816-04-1). Spex Intl.
Weintz, Caroline & Weintz, Walter. The Discount Guide for Travelers over 55. rev. ed. LC 80-83630. 256p. 1983. pap. 5.95 (ISBN 0-525-93281-X, 0577-180). Dutton.
VOYAGES AND TRAVELS-JUVENILE LITERATURE
Geras, Adele. Voyage. LC 82-13760. 192p. (gr. 7 up). 1983. 10.95 (ISBN 0-689-30955-4). Atheneum.
Strain, Maurine. My Travel Log. (gr. 3-6). 1982. 4.95 (ISBN 0-86653-062-2, GA 411). Good Apple.
VULCANITE
see Rubber
VULTURES
Unsworth, Barry. The Rage of the Vulture. 443p. 1983. 15.95 (ISBN 0-395-32526-9). HM.

W

W ALGEBRAS
see C Algebras
WAGE-FUND
see Wages
WAGE-PRICE CONTROLS
see Wage-Price Policy
WAGE-PRICE GUIDELINES
see Wage-Price Policy
WAGE-PRICE POLICY
Borjas, George J. Wage Policy in the Federal Bureaucracy. 1980. pap. 4.25 (ISBN 0-8447-3410-1). Am Enterprise.
WAGES
Here are listed general works and those dealing primarily with the United states. Note other subdivisions below, e.g., Wages-Statistics, Wages-Great Britain, etc.
see also Cost and Standard of Living; Deferred Compensation; Executives-Salaries, Pensions, Etc.; Non-Wage Payments; Profit-Sharing; Wage-Price Policy
Bowey, Angela M., ed. Handbook of Salary & Wage Systems. 2nd ed. 446p. 1982. text ed. 47.50 (ISBN 0-566-02261-3). Gower Pub Ltd.
Engineering Manpower Commission. Professional Income of Engineers, 1982. (Illus.). 1982. 35.00 (ISBN 0-87615-134-9, 302-82). AAES.
Gallant, Edward & Gallant, K. B. Handbook of Connecticut Workers' Compensation Law. 384p. Date not set. price not set (ISBN 0-88063-019-1). Butterworth Legal Pubs.
Langer, Steven, ed. Available Pay Survey Reports: An Annotated Bibliography, 3 pts. 2nd ed. 1980. Pt. I. pap. 95.00 (ISBN 0-916506-44-4); Pt. II. pap. 40.00 (ISBN 0-916506-45-2); Pt. III. pap. 45.00 (ISBN 0-916506-46-0). Abbott Langer Assocs.
--Inter-City Wage & Salary Differentials. 3rd ed. 1982. pap. 85.00 (ISBN 0-686-84836-5). Abbott Langer Assocs.
--Salaries & Bonuses in Personnel-Industrial Relations Functions. 4th ed. 1982. pap. 150.00 (ISBN 0-686-84837-3). Abbott Langer Assocs.
--Salaries & Related Matters in the Service Department, 1982. 1982. pap. 95.00 (ISBN 0-686-84839-X). Abbott Langer Assocs.
Professional Income of Engineers 1980. 35.00 (ISBN 0-87615-132-2, 302-80). AAES.
Professional Income of Engineers 1981. 35.00 (ISBN 0-87615-133-0, 302-81). AAES.
Rhone. A Wage & Salary Program Based on Position Evaluation for Administrative & Supervisory Staff. 1980. 8.95 (ISBN 0-910170-15-0). Assn Sch Busn.
Rudman, Jack. Associate Worker's Compensation Review Analyst. (Career Examination Ser.: C-309). (Cloth bdg. avail. on request). pap. 12.00 (ISBN 0-8373-0309-5). Natl Learning.
Salaries of Engineering Technicians & Technologies 1981. 100.00 (ISBN 0-87615-142-X, 304-82). AAES.
Salaries of Engineers in Education 1981. 20.00 (ISBN 0-87615-152-7, 307-82). AAES.
Salaries of Engineers in Education 1982. 1982. 20.00 (ISBN 0-87615-153-5, 307-82A). AAES.
Vroman, Wayne. Wage Inflation: Prospects for Deceleration. LC 82-84713. (Changing Domestic Priorities Ser.). 56p. (Orig.). 1983. pap. 5.95 (ISBN 0-87766-320-3). Urban Inst.
Wallace, Marc J., Jr. & Fay, Charles H. Compensation Theory & Practice. 304p. 1982. pap. text ed. 11.95x (ISBN 0-534-01399-6). Kent Pub Co.
Wood, M. & Cohen, S. Payroll Records & Procedures. 272p. 1983. 9.95 (ISBN 0-07-071627-7, Gregg). McGraw.
WAGES-MINIMUM WAGE
Metcalf, David. Low Pay, Occupational Mobility, & Minimum Wage Policy in Britain. 1981. pap. 4.25 (ISBN 0-8447-3450-0). Am Enterprise.
WAGES-GREAT BRITAIN
Metcalf, David. Low Pay, Occupational Mobility, & Minimum Wage Policy in Britain. 1981. pap. 4.25 (ISBN 0-8447-3450-0). Am Enterprise.
WAGNER, COSIMA (LISZT), 1837-1930
Ellis, W. Ashton, tr. Family Letters of Richard Wagner. LC 71-163796. 307p. Date not set. price not set. Vienna Hse.
WAGNER, RICHARD, 1813-1883
Bauer, Oswald G. Richard Wagner. (Illus.). 288p. 1983. 60.00 (ISBN 0-8478-0478-X). Rizzoli Intl.
Burk, John N., ed. Letters of Richard Wagner: The Burrell Collection. LC 78-183325. 665p. Date not set. Repr. of 1950 ed. price not set. Vienna Hse.
Cord, William O. An Introduction to Richard Wagner's Der Ring Des Nibelungen: A Handbook. LC 82-14417. (Illus.). 175p. 1983. text ed. 19.95x (ISBN 0-8214-0648-5, 82-84176); pap. 11.95 (ISBN 0-8214-0708-2, 82-84770). Ohio U Pr.
Ellis, W. Ashton, tr. Family Letters of Richard Wagner. LC 71-163796. 307p. Date not set. price not set. Vienna Hse.
--Letters of Richard Wagner to Mathilde Wesendonck. LC 74-163794. 386p. Date not set. Repr. of 1905 ed. price not set. Vienna Hse.
--Letters of Richard Wagner to Minna Wagner, 2 vols. LC 75-163797. Date not set. Repr. of 1909 ed. price not set. Vienna Hse.
Ewans, Michael. Wagner & Aeschylus: The "Ring" & The "Oresteia". LC 82-12762. 272p. Date not set. price not set (ISBN 0-521-25073-0). Cambridge U Pr.
Gregor-Dellin, Martin. Richard Wagner: His Life, His Work, His Century. Brownjohn, J. Maxwell, tr. (Helen & Kurt Wolff Bks.). 554p. 1983. 25.00 (ISBN 0-686-82640-X). HarBraceJ.
Kerr, Caroline V., tr. & ed. The Story of Bayreuth As Told in "The Bayreuth Letters of Richard Wagner". LC 78-163795. 364p. Date not set. Repr. of 1912 ed. price not set. Vienna Hse.
Lenrow, Elbert, ed. & tr. The Letters of Richard Wagner to Anton Pusinelli. LC 72-93825. 293p. Date not set. Repr. of 1932 ed. price not set. Vienna Hse.
Loeffler, M., ed. Adolphe Appia: Staging Wagnerian Drama. 96p. Date not set. pap. 4.95 (ISBN 3-7643-1363-3). Birkhauser.
Shedlock, J. S., tr. Richard Wagner's Letters to His Dresden Friends. LC 72-163800. 512p. Date not set. Repr. of 1890 ed. price not set. Vienna Hse.
Watson, D. Richard Wagner: A Biography. 384p. 1983. 8.95 (ISBN 0-07-068479-0, GB). McGraw.
WAGNER FAMILY
Ellis, W. Ashton, tr. Family Letters of Richard Wagner. LC 71-163796. 307p. Date not set. price not set. Vienna Hse.
WAGONS
Brentano, Ron B. Historic Wagons in Miniature: The Genius of Ivan Collins. (Illus.). 160p. (Orig.). 1983. price not set (ISBN 0-87595-112-0, Western Imprints); pap. price not set (ISBN 0-87595-072-8, Western Imprints). Oreg Hist Soc.
WAGONS, ARMY
see Vehicles, Military
WAITING-LINE THEORY
see Queuing Theory
WALAPAI INDIANS
see Indians of North America-Southwest, New
WALDENSES
Lacoste, Auguste. Henri Arnaud und die Waldenser. (Basler und Berner Studien zur historischen und systematischen: Vol. 47). 213p. 1982. write for info. (ISBN 3-261-04890-5). P Lang Pubs.
WALES
Vaughan-Thomas, Wynford. Wales. 224p. 1983. pap. 12.95 (ISBN 0-7181-2251-8, Pub by Michael Joseph). Merrimack Bk Serv.
WALES-ANTIQUITIES
Forde-Johnston. Hillforts of the Iron Age in England & Wales. 370p. 1982. 90.00x (ISBN 0-85323-381-0, Pub. by Liverpool Univ England). State Mutual Bk.
WALES-DESCRIPTION AND TRAVEL
see also Great Britain-Description and Travel
Catholic Directory of England & Wales, 1982. 143rd ed. 681p. 1982. 27.50x (ISBN 0-904359-35-2). Intl Pubns Serv.
WALES-DESCRIPTION AND TRAVEL-GUIDEBOOKS
Mid Wales: A Tourist Guide. 80p. 1983. pap. 2.95 (ISBN 0-900784-82-2, Pub. by Auto Assn-British Tourist Authority England). Merrimack Bk Serv.
Nicholson, Robert. Guide to England & Wales. (Illus.). 1983. pap. 9.95 (ISBN 0-686-38863-1). Merrimack Bk Serv.
North Wales: A Tourist Guide. 80p. 1983. pap. 2.95 (ISBN 0-900784-81-4, Pub. by Auto Assn-British Tourist Authority England). Merrimack Bk Serv.
Prince of Wales, frwd. by. Castles in Wales. 192p. 1983. 24.95 (ISBN 0-86145-125-2, Pub. by Auto Assn-British Tourist Authority England). Merrimack Bk Serv.
South Wales: A Tourist Guide. 80p. 1983. pap. 2.95 (ISBN 0-900784-83-0, Pub. by Auto Assn-British Tourist Authority England). Merrimack Bk Serv.
Wales: Hotels & Guesthouses. 360p. 1983. pap. 3.95 (ISBN 0-686-38445-8, Pub. by Auto Assn-British Tourist Authority England). Merrimack Bk Serv.
Wales: Self-Catering Accomodations. 150p. 1983. pap. 3.95 (ISBN 0-686-38444-X, Pub. by Auto Assn-British Tourist Authority England). Merrimack Bk Serv.
WALES-HISTORY
Davies, Wendy. Wales in the Early Middle Ages. (Studies in the Early History of Britain: Vol. 2). 300p. 1982. text ed. 46.25x (ISBN 0-7185-1163-8, Leicester). Humanities.
Squibb, George D. Precedence in England & Wales. 158p. 1981. 34.50x (ISBN 0-19-825389-3). Oxford U Pr.
WALKER, JOSEPH REDDEFORD, 1798-1876
Gilbert, Bil. Westering Man: The Life of Joseph Walker. LC 82-69128. 352p. 1983. 14.95 (ISBN 0-689-11241-6). Atheneum.
WALKING
see also Hiking; Trails
Jenkins, Peter. A Walk Across America. (General Ser.). 1982. lib. bdg. 15.95 (ISBN 0-8161-3459-6, Large Print Bks). G K Hall.
Reiger, George. Wanderer on My Native Shore. 1983. price not set (ISBN 0-671-25423-5). S&S.
Yanker, Gary D. The Complete Book of Exercise Walking. (Illus.). 288p. (Orig.). 1983. pap. 8.95 (ISBN 0-8092-5535-9). Contemp Bks.
WALKING PATIENT CARE
see Ambulatory Medical Care
WALL DECORATION
see Mural Painting and Decoration
WALL PAINTING
see Mural Painting and Decoration
WALL-PAPER
see also Paper-Hanging
Hamilton, Jean. Introduction to Wallpaper. (The Victoria & Albert Museum Introductions to the Decorative Arts). (Illus.). 1983. 9.95 (ISBN 0-88045-020-7). Stemmer Hse.
Hendler, Muncie. Ready-to-Use Art Nouveau Dollhouse Wallpaper. (Illus.). 48p. (Orig.). 1983. pap. 3.95 (ISBN 0-486-24446-6). Dover.
Sunset Books & Sunset Magazine, ed. Wallcoverings. LC 82-81370. (Illus.). 96p. (Orig.). 1982. pap. 4.95 (ISBN 0-376-01673-6). Sunset-Lane.
Teynac, Francoise & Nolot, Pierre. Wallpaper: A History. Morgan, Conway L., tr. from Fr. LC 81-86461. (Illus.). 250p. 1982. 50.00 (ISBN 0-8478-0434-8). Rizzoli Intl.
WALL STREET
see also Brokers
Stone, Justin F. The Metaphysics of Wall Street. 175p. 1983. 10.00 (ISBN 0-89540-134-7, SB-134). Sun Pub.
WALLERIAN DEGENERATION
see Nervous System-Degeneration and Regeneration
WALLEYE (OPHTHALMOLOGY)
see Strabismus
WALLS
see also Foundations; Masonry; Mural Painting and Decoration
Better Homes & Gardens Books editors, ed. Better Homes & Gardens All About Your House: Your Walls & Ceilings. (All About your House Ser.). (Illus.). 160p. 1983. 9.95 (ISBN 0-696-02163-3). Meredith Corp.

Chamberlin, Susan & Pollock, Susan. Fences, Gates & Walls. 1983. pap. 9.95 (ISBN 0-89586-189-5). H P Bks.

WALPOLE, HORACE, 4TH EARL OF OXFORD, 1717-1797

Walpole, Horace. Horace Walpole's Fugitive Verses. Lewis, W. S., ed. (Miscellaneous Antiquties Ser.: No. 5). 1931. text ed. 65.00x Ltd. Ed. (ISBN 0-686-83569-7). Elliots Bks.

--The Yale Edition of Horace Walpole's Correspondence, Vol. 43. Martz, Edwine M. & McClure, Ruth K., eds. LC 65-11182. 408p. 1983. text ed. 65.00x (ISBN 0-300-02711-7). Yale U Pr.

--The Yale Edition of Horace Walpole's Correspondence, Vols. 44-48. Smith, Warren H. & Martz, Edwine M., eds. LC 65-11182. 424p. 1983. text ed. 325.00x (ISBN 0-300-02718-4). Yale U Pr.

WAR

see also Air Warfare; Armies; Atomic Warfare; Biological Warfare; Claims; Disarmament; Militarism; Military Art and Science; Military Policy; Munitions; Naval Art and Science; Navies; Peace; Psychological Warfare; Sociology, Military; Soldiers; Strategy; Tank Warfare

also specific wars, battles, etc., Russo-Japanese War, 1904-1905; United States–History–Queen Anne's War, 1702-1713; Gettysburg, Battle of, 1863

American Health Research Institute, Ltd. War: A Medical, Psychological & Scientific Subject Analysis with Research Index & Bibliography. Bartone, John C., ed. 120p. 1983. 29.95 (ISBN 0-941864-91-X); pap. 21.95 (ISBN 0-941864-90-1). ABBE Pubs Assn.

Amos, Sheldon. Political & Legal Remedies for War. 254p. 1982. Repr. of 1880 ed. lib. bdg. 24.00x (ISBN 0-8377-0213-5). Rothman.

Barnes, Harry E. Perpetual War for Perpetual Peace. rev. & enl. ed. 1982. lib. bdg. 79.95 (ISBN 0-87700-454-4). Revisionist Pr.

Buck, Peter. Arts & Crafts of Hawaii: War & Weapons, Sec. X. (Special Publication Ser.: No. 45). (Illus.). 57p. 1957. pap. 3.00 (ISBN 0-910240-43-4). Bishop Mus.

Glossop, Ronald J. Confronting War. LC 82-23950. 250p. 1983. lib. bdg. 19.95x (ISBN 0-89950-073-0). McFarland & Co.

Karas, Thomas. The New High Ground: Systems & Weapons of Space Age War. 1983. 15.95 (ISBN 0-671-47025-6). S&S.

Montgomery, frwd. by. A History of Warfare. LC 82-82146. (Illus.). 584p. 1983. 25.00 (ISBN 0-688-01645-6). Morrow.

On the Inevitability of War: An Explanation & Theory & Proposed Game. (Analysis Ser.: No. 13). 1983. pap. 10.00 (ISBN 0-686-42846-3). Inst Analysis.

O'Sullivan & Miller. The Geography of Warfare. LC 82-42771. 176p. 1983. 19.95x (ISBN 0-312-32184-8). St Martin.

Rydjord, John. Who Wants War? 272p. 1983. 12.00 (ISBN 0-682-49972-2). Exposition.

Schmidt, Stanley, ed. War & Peace: Possible Futures from "Analog". 1983. 12.95 (ISBN 0-385-27916-7). Davis Pubns.

Shannon, Thomas A. What Are They Saying About Peace & War? (WATSA Ser.). 128p. 1983. pap. 3.95 (ISBN 0-8091-2499-8). Paulist Pr.

Sun Tzu. The Art of War. Clavell, James, ed. 1983. 9.95 (ISBN 0-440-00243-5). Delacorte.

Von Clausewitz, Carl. On War. 1982. pap. 4.95 (ISBN 0-14-044427-0). Penguin.

Wilkins, Francis. Growing Up Between the Wars. (Illus.). 72p. (gr. 7-12). 1980. 14.95 (ISBN 0-7134-0775-1, Pub by Batsford England). David & Charles.

WAR–ECONOMIC ASPECTS

Here are entered works dealing with the economic causes of war, and with the effect of war and preparation for war on industrial and commercial activity.

see also Competition, International; Industrial Mobilization

also subdivisions Economic Aspects and Finance under specific wars, e.g. European War, 1914-1918–Economic Aspects

British War Budgets. (Economic & Social History of the World War Ser.). 1926. text ed. 75.00x (ISBN 0-686-83495-X). Elliots Bks.

Capie, Forrest & Collins, Michael. The Inter-War Economy: A Statistical Abstract. 200p. 1983. 24.00 (ISBN 0-7190-0901-4). Manchester.

Mushkat, Marion. The Third World & Peace: Some Aspects of Problems of the Inter-Relationship of Interdevelopment & International Security. LC 82-774. 356p. 1982. 27.50x (ISBN 0-312-80039-8). St Martin.

WAR–MORAL ASPECTS

see War and Religion

WAR–PSYCHOLOGICAL ASPECTS

see also Psychological Warfare

Rosenblatt, Roger. Children of War. LC 82-45366. 216p. 1983. 14.95 (ISBN 0-385-18250-3, Anchor Pr). Doubleday.

WAR (INTERNATIONAL LAW)

see also Arbitration, International; Neutrality; Prisoners of War; Spies

Percy, Eustace. Maritime Trade in War. 1930. text ed. 29.50x (ISBN 0-686-83617-0). Elliots Bks.

WAR, MARITIME

see Naval Art and Science; Naval Battles

WAR, PRISONERS OF

see Prisoners of War

WAR AND CHRISTIANITY

see War and Religion

WAR AND EMERGENCY POWERS

Turner, Robert F. The War Powers Resolution: Its Implementation in Theory & Practice. (Philadelphia Policy Papers). (Orig.). 1983. pap. 3.95 (ISBN 0-910191-06-9). For Policy Res.

WAR AND INDUSTRY

see War–Economic Aspects

WAR AND LITERATURE

Nordon, Haskell. The Education of a Polish Jew: A Physician's War Memoirs. 314p. 1983. 11.95 (ISBN 0-910563-00-4). D Grossman Pr.

WAR AND RELIGION

see also Conscientious Objectors; Nonviolence

also subdivision Religious Aspects under specific wars, e.g. World War, 1939-1945–Religious Aspects

Evans, G. Russell & Singer, C. Gregg. The Church & the Sword. LC 82-50234. 128p. 1982. pap. text ed. 6.95 (ISBN 0-686-81950-0). St Thomas.

WAR CLAIMS

see Claims

WAR CRIME TRIALS

Lael, Richard L. The Yamashita Precedent: War Crimes & Command Responsibility. LC 82-17024. 165p. 1982. lib. bdg. 19.95 (ISBN 0-8420-2202-3). Scholarly Res Inc.

WAR CRIME TRIALS–NUREMBERG, 1945-1946

see Nuremberg Trial of Major German War Criminals, 1945-1946

WAR GAMES

Dunnigan, James F. The Complete Wargames Handbook: How to Play, Design, & Find Them. (Illus.). 256p. 1980. pap. 7.95 (ISBN 0-688-08649-7). Quill NY.

Griffith, Paddy. A Book of Sandhurst Wargames. 64p. 1982. 22.95 (ISBN 0-698-11198-2, Coward). Putnam Pub Group.

WAR MAPS

see Classical Geography

WAR OF 1812

see United States–History–War of 1812

WAR OF NERVES

see Psychological Warfare

WAR OF 1914

see European War, 1914-1918

WAR OF SECESSION (U. S.)

see United States–History–Civil War, 1861-1865

WAR OF THE AMERICAN REVOLUTION

see United States–History–Revolution, 1775-1783

WAR OF THE TRIPLE ALLIANCE, 1865-1870

see Paraguayan War, 1865-1870

WAR PENSIONS

see Pensions, Military

WAR POWERS

see War and Emergency Powers

WAR-SHIPS

see Warships

WARBLING PARAKEET

see Budgerigars

WARDS

see Guardian and Ward

WAREHOUSES

Rudman, Jack. Warehouse Supervisor. (Career Examination Ser.: C-926). (Cloth bdg. avail. on request). pap. 10.00 (ISBN 0-8373-0926-3). Natl Learning.

WARM-UP

see Exercise

WARPING

see Weaving

WARRANTS, AGRICULTURAL

see Agricultural Credit

WARREN, ROBERT PENN, 1905-

Grimshaw, James A., Jr., ed. Robert Penn Warren's Brother to Dragons: A Discussion. (Southern Literary Studies). 344p. 1983. text ed. 27.50X (ISBN 0-8071-1065-5). La State U Pr.

WARS

see Military History; Naval History; War

WARSAW PACT, 1955

Institute for Policy Analysis. The Warsaw Pact: Arms, Doctrine & Strategy. Lewis, William J., ed. (Illus.). 512p. 1982. 29.95 (ISBN 0-07-031746-1, P&RB). McGraw.

Nelson, Daniel N. Soviet Allies: The Warsaw Pact & the Issue of Reliability. 240p. 1983. lib. bdg. 20.00X (ISBN 0-86531-359-8). Westview.

WARSHIPS

see also Aircraft Carriers; Navies; Submarines

also navies of the various countries, e.g. Great Britain–Navy; also names of ships

Blee, Ben W. Battleship North Carolina. Conlon, Frank S. & Judd, Amos F., eds. (Illus.). 100p. 1982. 14.95 (ISBN 0-9608538-0-4); pap. 8.95 (ISBN 0-9608538-1-2). USS North Car.

Cave, Ron & Cave, Joyce. What About... War Ships. (What About Ser.). 32p. (gr. k-3). 1983. PLB 7.90 (ISBN 0-531-03471-2). Watts.

Conway Maritime Press Ltd., ed. Conway's All the World's Fighting Ships 1947-1982. 480p. 125.00x (ISBN 0-85177-225-0, Pub. by Conway Maritime England). State Mutual Bk.

King, J. W. War-Ships & Navies of the World 1880. LC 82-81753. (Illus.). 768p. 1982. 24.95 (ISBN 0-87021-943-X). Naval Inst Pr.

Moore, John, ed. Jane's Fighting Ships, 1982-1983. (Jane's Yearbooks). (Illus.). 960p. 140.00 (ISBN 0-86720-590-3). Sci Bks Intl.

Moore, John E. Warships of the Soviet Navy. (Illus.). 224p. 19.50 (ISBN 0-86720-567-9). Sci Bks Intl.

Preston, Antony. Warships of the World. (Illus.). 224p. 1981. 16.95 (ISBN 0-86720-580-6). Sci Bks Intl.

Reilly, John C., Jr. United States Navy Destroyers of World War II. (Illus.). 160p. 1983. 16.95 (ISBN 0-7137-1026-8, Pub. by Blandford Pr England). Sterling.

Roberts, John. The Battlecruiser Hood. 128p. 1982. 50.00x (ISBN 0-85177-250-1, Pub. by Conway Maritime England). State Mutual Bk.

WASHINGTON, BOOKER TALIAFERRO, 1859?-1915

Harlan, Louis R. Booker T. Washington: The Wizard of Tuskegee, 1901-1915. (Illus.). 540p. 1983. 24.95 (ISBN 0-19-503202-0). Oxford U Pr.

WASHINGTON, GEORGE, PRES. U. S., 1732-1799

Detweiler, Susan G. George Washington's Chinaware. LC 81-14993. (Illus.). 240p. 1982. 40.00 (ISBN 0-8109-1779-3). Abrams.

George Washington As the French Knew Him: A Collection Of Texts. 161p. 1982. Repr. of 1940 ed. lib. bdg. 45.00 (ISBN 0-89984-122-8). Century Bookbindery.

Nordham, George W. George Washington & the Law. (Illus.). 156p. 12.75 (ISBN 0-686-38396-6). Adams Pr.

WASHINGTON (STATE)–ANTIQUITIES

Herbert, Kevin & Symeonoglou, Sarantis, eds. Ancient Collections in Washington University. LC 73-92729. (Illus.). 52p. 1973. pap. 2.00 (ISBN 0-686-84007-0). Wash U Gallery.

WASHINGTON (STATE)–DESCRIPTION AND TRAVEL

Powell, Walbridge J. Art, Crafts, & Fine Arts Shows in Washington. 34p. (Orig.). 1982. pap. 2.50x (ISBN 0-686-37612-9). Searchers Pubns.

Thompson, Philip. Stranger In Town: A Guide to Taverns in Oregon & Southwest Washington. 1983. pap. 4.95 (ISBN 0-932576-14-1). Breitenbush Pubns.

Warren, Henry C. Olympic. LC 82-82580. (The Story Behind the Scenery Ser..). (Illus.). 64p. (Orig.). 1982. lib. bdg. 7.95 (ISBN 0-916122-78-6); pap. 3.50 (ISBN 0-916122-77-8). KC Pubns.

WASHINGTON (STATE)–HISTORY

Martin, Paul & Brady, Peggy. Port Angeles-Washington: A History. (Illus.). 228p. 1983. pap. 18.95x (ISBN 0-918146-23-2). Peninsula WA.

Warren, Henry C. Olympic. LC 82-82580. (The Story Behind the Scenery Ser..). (Illus.). 64p. (Orig.). 1982. lib. bdg. 7.95 (ISBN 0-916122-78-6); pap. 3.50 (ISBN 0-916122-77-8). KC Pubns.

WASHINGTON, D. C.–DESCRIPTION

Harris, Bill. Washington, D.C. (Illus.). 224p. 1982. 50.00 (ISBN 0-8109-1787-4). Abrams.

WASHINGTON, D. C.–DESCRIPTION–GUIDEBOOKS

Connally, Eugenia M. Welcome to Washington. (Illus.). 36p. 1981. pap. 3.95 (ISBN 0-936478-03-9). Interpretive Pubns.

Cox, Brian. Five Hundred Things to Do in Washington for Free. (Illus.). 192p. 1983. pap. 5.95 (ISBN 0-8329-0262-4). New Century.

Wolf, Elliott, ed. Seattle Epicure. (Epicure Ser.). 1983. pap. 5.95 (ISBN 0-89716-115-7). Peanut Butter.

WASHINGTON, D. C.–DIRECTORIES

Congressional Quarterly Inc. Washington Information Directory: 1983-1984. LC 75-646321. 1983. 29.95 (ISBN 0-87187-255-2). Congr Quarterly.

WASHINGTON, D. C.–GALLERIES AND MUSEUMS

Bryan, C. D. National Air & Space Museum. 160p. 1982. 12.95 ea. Vol. I (ISBN 0-553-01384-X). Vol. II (ISBN 0-553-01385-8). Bantam.

WASHINGTON POST

The Official Washington Post Index. 770p. 1983. 200.00 ea. January-December 1979. January-December 1982. Res Pubns Conn.

WASHO INDIANS

see Indians of North America–Southwest, New

WASTE, DISPOSAL OF

see Factory and Trade Waste; Refuse and Refuse Disposal; Sewage Disposal

WASTE AS FUEL

see Refuse As Fuel

WASTE MANAGEMENT

see Salvage (Waste, etc.)

WASTE PRODUCTS

see also Factory and Trade Waste; Reactor Fuel Reprocessing; Recycling (Waste, etc.); Refuse and Refuse Disposal

Exner, Jurgen H., ed. Detoxication of Hazardous Waste. LC 82-70696. (Illus.). 350p. 1982. 37.50 (ISBN 0-250-40521-0). Ann Arbor Science.

Klass, Donald L. & Emert, George H., eds. Fuels from Biomass & Wastes. LC 81-68245. (Illus.). 592p. 1981. 39.95 (ISBN 0-250-40418-4). Ann Arbor Science.

Taiganides, E. P. Animal Wastes. 1977. 80.00 (ISBN 0-85334-721-2, Pub. by Applied Sci England). Elsevier.

WASTE RECYCLING

see Recycling (Waste, etc.)

WASTE REUSE

see Recycling (Waste, etc.)

WASTE WATERS

see Sewage

WASTES, NUCLEAR

see Radioactive Wastes

WASTES, RADIOACTIVE

see Radioactive Wastes

WATCH MAKERS

see Clock and Watch Makers

WATCH REPAIRING

see Clocks and Watches–Repairing and Adjusting

WATCHES

see Clocks and Watches

WATER

see also Erosion; Floods; Glaciers; Hydraulic Engineering; Hydrotherapy; Lakes; Ocean; Oceanography; Rivers; Sea-Water; Steam; Wells

also headings beginning with the word Water

Ilmavirta, V. & Jones, R. I. Lakes & Water Management. 1982. 54.50 (ISBN 90-6193-758-2, Pub. by Junk Pubs Netherlands). Kluwer Boston.

Kilpatrick, F. & Matchett, D., eds. Water & Energy: Technical & Policy Issues. LC 82-71351. 672p. 1982. pap. text ed. 52.00 (ISBN 0-87262-308-4). Am Soc Civil Eng.

Miller, David H., ed. Water at the Surface of the Earth: Student Edition. LC 82-13769. (International Geophysics Ser.). text ed. 24.00 (ISBN 0-12-496752-3). Acad Pr.

Roth. Collins Guide to the Water. 29.95 (ISBN 0-686-42791-2, Collins Pub England). Greene.

WATER–ANALYSIS

Camp, Thomas & Maserve, Robert L. Water & Its Impurities. LC 74-7012. (Illus.). 384p. 1974. text ed. 48.50 (ISBN 0-87933-112-7). Hutchinson Ross.

Rudman, Jack. Water Service Foreman. (Career Examination Ser.: C-2918). (Cloth bdg. avail. on request). pap. 12.00 (ISBN 0-686-84406-8). Natl Learning.

WATER–CONSERVATION

see Water-Conservation

WATER–FLOW

see Hydraulics

WATER–JUVENILE LITERATURE

Dickinson, Jane. Wonders of Water. LC 82-17388. (Question & Answer Bks.). (Illus.). 32p. (gr. 3-6). 1983. PLB 8.59 (ISBN 0-89375-874-4); pap. text ed. 1.95 (ISBN 0-89375-875-2). Troll Assocs.

WATER–LAWS AND LEGISLATION

see also Fishery Law and Legislation; Water–Pollution

Allison, Gary D., ed. The Western Water Law. 1982. 48.00 (ISBN 0-89419-202-7). Inst Energy.

Kovalic, Joan. Clean Water Act. 162p. 1982. pap. text ed. 5.00 (ISBN 0-943244-40-4). Water Pollution.

Purcell, L. Edward, ed. State Water Quality Planning Issues. 64p. (Orig.). 1982. pap. 8.00 (ISBN 0-87292-031-3, RM 719). Coun State Govts.

Ward, Morris A. The Clean Water Act: The Second Decade. 54p. (Orig.). 1982. pap. write for info. (ISBN 0-9609130-0-9). E B Harrison.

WATER–OIL POLLUTION

see Oil Pollution of Water

WATER–POLLUTION

see also Factory and Trade Waste; Oil Pollution of Water; Sewage Disposal; Water–Analysis; Water–Laws and Legislation; Water-Supply

Abbott, David, ed. The Biographical Encyclopedias of Science: The Chemists. 1982. 30.00x (ISBN 0-584-10854-0, Pub. by Muller Ltd). State Mutual Bk.

American Health Research Institute, Ltd. Water Pollution by Chemical, Radioactive, Thermal, Softening & Extraneous Materials: A Medical Subject Analysis & Research Index with Bibliography. Bartone, John C., ed. 120p. 1983. 29.95 (ISBN 0-88164-018-2); pap. 21.95 (ISBN 0-88164-019-0). ABBE Pubs Assn.

Best & Ross. River Pollution Studies. 102p. 1982. 30.00x (ISBN 0-85323-363-2, Pub. by Liverpool Univ England). State Mutual Bk.

Cairns, J., Jr. Biological Monitoring in Water Pollution. (Illus.). 144p. 1982. 30.00 (ISBN 0-08-028730-1). Pergamon.

Feder & Burrell. Impact of Seafood Cannery Waste on the Benthic Biota & Adjacent Waters at Dutch Harbor Alaska. (IMS Report Ser.: No. R82-1). write for info. U of AK Inst Marine.

Goldin, Augusta. Water: Too Much, Too Little, Too Polluted. LC 82-4760. (Illus.). 224p. (gr. 12 up). 12.95 (ISBN 0-15-294819-8, HJ). HarBraceJ.

Kester, Dana R. & Ketchum, Bostwick H. Wastes in the Ocean: Dredged Material Disposal in the Ocean, Vol. 2. (Environmental Science & Technology Ser.). 320p. 1983. 39.95x (ISBN 0-471-09771-3, Pub. by Wiley-Interscience). Wiley.

Pollution Control on the Passaic River. 85p. 1982. 14.00 (ISBN 0-686-81772-9). Ctr Analysis Public Issues.

Richardson, Genevra, et al. Policing Pollution: A Study of Regulation & Enforcement. (Oxford Socio-Legal Studies). 250p. 1983. 34.95 (ISBN 0-19-827510-2); pap. 15.95 (ISBN 0-19-827512-9). Oxford U Pr.

Townsend, Colin R. Ecology of Streams & Rivers. (Studies in Biology: No. 122). 64p. 1980. pap. text ed. 8.95 (ISBN 0-7131-2804-6). E Arnold.

WATER–PURIFICATION

see also Water-Supply Engineering

American Water Works Association. Treatment Techniques for Controlling Trihalomethanes in Drinking Water. (AWWA Handbooks-General Ser.). (Illus.). 312p. 1982. pap. text ed. 16.80 (ISBN 0-89867-279-1). Am Water Wks Assn.

Jolley, Robert L., et al, eds. Water Chlorination: Environmental Impact & Health Effects, 2 bks, Vol. 4. LC 77-92588. (Illus.). 700p. 1983. Set. 45.00 (ISBN 0-250-40582-2); 27.50 ea. Bk. 1, Chemistry & Water Treatment (ISBN 0-250-40519-9). Bk. 2, Environment, Health & Risk (ISBN 0-250-40581-4). Ann Arbor Science.

Manual of Methods in Aquatic Environment Research: Toxicity Tests, Pt. 6. (FAO Fisheries Technical Papers: No. 185). 23p. 1982. pap. 7.50 (ISBN 92-5-101178-8, F2312, FAO). Unipub.

OECD Staff. Eutrophication of Waters: Monitoring, Assessment, & Control. 154p. 1982. pap. 11.50 (ISBN 92-64-12298-2). OECD.

WATER–QUALITY OF

see Water Quality

WATER–THERAPEUTIC USE

see Hydrotherapy

WATER–WASTE

see also Water-Conservation

American Society of Civil Engineers, compiled by. Pure & Wholesome. LC 81-70989. 184p. 1982. pap. text ed. 18.50 (ISBN 0-87262-290-8). Am Soc Civil Eng.

WATER, UNDERGROUND

see also Hydrogeology; Wells

Dasgupta, Partha. The Control of Resources. (Illus.). 240p. 1983. text ed. 22.50x (ISBN 0-674-16980-8). Harvard U Pr.

Ground-Water Models. 235p. 1982. pap. 26.25 (ISBN 92-3-102006-4, U1224, UNESCO). Unipub.

Verruijt, A. Grounderwater Flow. 2nd ed. (Illus.). 145p. 1982. text ed. 33.50x (ISBN 0-333-32958-9); pap. text ed. 17.50 (ISBN 0-333-32959-7). Scholium Intl.

WATER–ANALYSIS

see Water–Analysis

WATER AND PLANTS

see Plant-Water Relationships

WATER BALLET

see Synchronized Swimming

WATER–BIRDS

see also Sea Birds; Waterfowl

also families and names of water-birds, e.g. Anatidae; Gulls, Murres, Terns

Ossa, Helen. They Saved Our Birds. (Illus.). 288p. (gr. 6 up). 1983. pap. 5.95 (ISBN 0-88254-714-3). Hippocrene Bks.

Soothill, Eric & Soothill, Richard. Wading Birds of the World. (Illus.). 334p. 1983. 29.95 (ISBN 0-7137-0913-8, Pub. by Blandford Pr England). Sterling.

WATER CHEMISTRY

see also Limnology

Camp, Thomas & Maserve, Robert L. Water & Its Impurities. LC 74-7012. (Illus.). 384p. 1974. text ed. 48.50 (ISBN 0-87933-112-7). Hutchinson Ross.

Dickson, Kenneth L. & Maki, Alan W., eds. Modeling the Fate of Chemicals in the Aquatic Environment. LC 82-71527. (Illus.). 413p. 1982. 27.50 (ISBN 0-250-40552-0). Ann Arbor Science.

McCoy, James W. Chemical Treatment of Cooling Water. 2nd ed. (Illus.). 1983. 40.00 (ISBN 0-8206-0298-1). Chem Pub.

Smith, Donald M. & Mitchell, John. Aquametry, Vol. 5, Pt. 2. 2nd ed. (Chemical Analysis Monographs). 852p. 1983. 110.00 (ISBN 0-471-02265-9, Pub. by Wiley-Interscience). Wiley.

WATER–COLOR PAINTING

Doherty, M. Stephen. Dynamic Still Lifes in Watercolor: Sondra Freckelton's Approach to Color, Composition, & Control of the Medium. (Illus.). 144p. 1983. 22.50 (ISBN 0-8230-1583-1). Watson-Guptill.

Koch, Elisabeth & Wagner, Gerard. The Individuality of Colour. Stebbing, Peter, tr. from Ger. & intro. by. (Illus.). 108p. 1980. 28.95 (ISBN 0-85440-365-5, Pub. by Steinerbooks). Anthroposophic.

Mingay, Gordon. Mrs. Hurst Dancing & Other Scenes from Regency Life 1812-1823. (Illus.). 158p. 1982. 25.00 (ISBN 0-312-55129-0). St Martin.

WATER-COLOR PAINTING–TECHNIQUE

Crawshaw, Alwyn. How To Paint with Watercolors. 64p. 1982. pap. 5.95 (ISBN 0-89586-157-7). H P Bks.

Quiller, Stephen & Whipple, Barbara. Water Media Techniques: Fresh Ideas for Combining Watercolor, Acrylic, Gouache, & Casein. (Illus.). 144p. 1983. 22.50 (ISBN 0-8230-5671-6). Watson-Guptill.

Shook, Georg. Painting Watercolors from Photographs. (Illus.). 144p. 1983. 22.50 (ISBN 0-8230-3873-4). Watson-Guptill.

Silverman, Burt. Breaking the Rules of Watercolor. (Illus.). 144p. 1983. 22.50 (ISBN 0-8230-0523-2). Watson-Guptill.

Webb, Frank. Watercolor Energies. (Illus.). 176p. 1983. 22.50 (ISBN 0-89134-054-8); pap. 14.95 (ISBN 0-89134-055-6). North Light Pub.

WATER COLORS

Ferber, Linda S. Tokens of a Friendship: Miniature Watercolors by William T. Richards. Hochfield, Sylvia, ed. (Illus.). 118p. (Orig.). 1982. pap. 14.95 (ISBN 0-87099-319-4). Metro Mus Art.

Goddad, Don, ed. Watercolors & Drawings of the French Impressionists & Their Parisian Contemporaries. Korneitchouk, Ursula, tr. from Ger. LC 81-20558. 1982. pap. text ed. 60.00 (ISBN 0-8109-1103-5). Abrams.

Schindler, Maria. Goethe's Theory of Colour. Mery, Eleanor C., tr. from Ger. (Illus.). 210p. 1970. 23.95 (ISBN 0-88010-047-8, Pub. by New Knowledge Bks England). Anthroposophic.

Willard, Helen D., intro. by. William Blake Water-Color Drawings from the Museum of Fine Arts, Boston. (Illus.). 64p. 1954. pap. 1.25 (ISBN 0-686-83417-8). Mus Fine Arts Boston.

WATER-CONSERVATION

see also Water-Supply

Flack, J. Ernest. Urban Water Conservation. LC 82-70113. 112p. 1982. pap. text ed. 13.25 (ISBN 0-87262-296-7). Am Soc Civil Eng.

Swain, George F. Conservation of Water By Storage. 1915. text ed. 65.00x (ISBN 0-686-83512-3). Elliots Bks.

WATER CONTAMINATION

see Water-Pollution

WATER-CURE

see Hydrotherapy

WATER FARMING

see Hydroponics

WATER-FLIES

see Flies

WATER-FOWL

see Waterfowl

WATER HEATERS

How to Install Solar Hot Water. (Illus.). 1982. pap. 11.95 (ISBN 0-918984-02-5). Solarvision.

Keisling, Bill. The Homeowner's Handbook of Solar Water Heating Systems: How to Build or Buy Systems to Heat Your Water, Your Swimming Pool, Hot Tub, or Spa. Halpin, Anne, ed. (Illus.). 256p. 1983. 16.95 (ISBN 0-87857-444-1, 14-166-0); pap. 12.95 (ISBN 0-87857-445-X, 14-166-1). Rodale Pr Inc.

WATER-MILLS

Reid, Kenneth C. Watermills of London Countryside: Their Place in English Landscape & Life, 2 vols. 1982. Vol. I. 50.00 ea. (ISBN 0-284-39165-4, Pub. by C Skilton Scotland). Vol. II (ISBN 0-284-98584-8). State Mutual Bk.

WATER-MITES

see Mites

WATER-PLANT RELATIONSHIP

see Plant-Water Relationships

WATER POLLUTION

see Water-Pollution

WATER-POLO

Cicciarello, Charles. Water Polo. 108p. 1981. pap. text ed. 3.95x (ISBN 0-89641-066-8). American Pr.

WATER POWER–LAW AND LEGISLATION

see Water–Laws and Legislation

WATER PURIFICATION

see Water-Purification

WATER QUALITY

American Water Works Association. Taste & Odor Control Experiences Handbook. (AWWA Handbooks-General Ser.). (Illus.). 118p. 1976. pap. text ed. 8.00 (ISBN 0-89867-011-X). Am Water Wks Assn.

--Water Quality Technology Conference, 1981: Advances in Laboratory Techniques for Quality Control. (AWWA Handbooks-Proceedings Ser.). (Illus.). 1982. pap. text ed. 18.60 (ISBN 0-89867-267-8). Am Water Wks Assn.

--Water Quality Technology Conference, 1980: Advances in Laboratory Techniques for Quality Control. (AWWA Handbooks-Proceedings Ser.). (Illus.). 1981. pap. text ed. 18.00 (ISBN 0-89867-251-1). Am Water Wks Assn.

Beltrami, Edward. The High Cost of Clean Water: Models for Water Quality Management Ser. (The UMAP Expository Monograph). 53p. 1982. pap. text ed. 8.95 (ISBN 3-7643-3098-8). Birkhauser.

Camp, Thomas & Maserve, Robert L. Water & Its Impurities. LC 74-7012. (Illus.). 384p. 1974. text ed. 48.50 (ISBN 0-87933-112-7). Hutchinson Ross.

Gower, A. M. Water Quality in Catchment Ecosystems. LC 79-42907. (Institution of Environmental Sciences Ser.). 335p. 1980. 54.95x (ISBN 0-471-27692-8, Pub. by Wiley-Interscience). Wiley.

Orlob, Gerald T. Mathematical Modeling of Water Quality: Streams, Lakes & Reservoirs. (IIASA International Series on Applied Systems Analysis). 544p. 1983. 69.50 (ISBN 0-471-10031-5, Pub. by Wiley-Interscience). Wiley.

Purcell, L. Edward, ed. State Water Quality Planning Issues. 64p. (Orig.). 1982. pap. 8.00 (ISBN 0-87292-031-3, RM 719). Coun State Govts.

WATER RESOURCES DEVELOPMENT

see also Flood Control; Inland Navigation; Irrigation; Water-Supply

Black, Peter E. Conservation of Water & Related Resources. 234p. 1982. 25.95 (ISBN 0-03-060419-2). Praeger.

DeGroot, W., ed. Stormwater Detention Facilities. LC 82-73613. 448p. 1982. pap. text ed. 31.00 (ISBN 0-87262-348-3). Am Soc Civil Eng.

Hydrology & Water Resources, 1982. 215p. (Orig.). 1982. pap. text ed. 37.50x (ISBN 0-85825-165-5, Pub. by Inst Engineering Australia). Renouf.

LaConte, P. & Haines, Y. Y. Water Resources & Land-Use Planning: A Systems Approach. 1982. lib. bdg. 57.50 (ISBN 90-247-2726-X, Pub. by Martinus Nijhoff Netherlands). Kluwer Boston.

Proceedings of the Seventh Session of the Committee on Natural Resources. (Water Resources Ser.: No. 53). 146p. 1981. pap. 12.00 (ISBN 0-686-82549-7, UN 81/2F10, UN). Unipub.

WATER SPORTS

see Aquatic Sports

WATER–SUPPLY

see also Arid Regions; Dams; Forests and Forestry; Irrigation; Reservoirs; Stream Measurements; Water-Pollution; Water-Purification; Water-Conservation; Water Quality; Wells

Campbell, Stu. Home Water Supply: How to Find, Filter, Store & Conserve It. Griffith, Roger, ed. (Illus.). 280p. (Orig.). 1983. pap. 10.95 (ISBN 0-88266-324-0). Garden Way Pub.

Frederick, Kenneth D. Water for Western Agriculture. LC 82-47985. (A Resources for the Future Research Paper). (Illus.). 256p. (Orig.). 1982. pap. text ed. 15.00x (ISBN 0-8018-2832-5). Resources Future.

Hackelman, Michael. Waterworks: An Owner-Builder Guide to Rural Water Systems. LC 82-45289. (Illus.). 1983. pap. 14.95 (ISBN 0-385-17559-0, Dolp). Doubleday.

Hamilton, Lawrence S., ed. Forest & Watershed Development & Conservation in Asia & the Pacific. (Special Studies in Natural Resources & Energy Management). 650p. 1982. lib. bdg. 25.00 (ISBN 0-86531-534-5). Westview.

LaConte, P. & Haines, Y. Y. Water Resources & Land-Use Planning: A Systems Approach. 1982. lib. bdg. 57.50 (ISBN 90-247-2726-X, Pub. by Martinus Nijhoff Netherlands). Kluwer Boston.

Larson, William E. & Walsh, Leo M, eds. Soil & Water Resources: Reasearch Priorities for the Nation-Proceedings. 229p. 1981. 12.00 (ISBN 0-89118-768-5). Soil Sci Soc Am.

Rudman, Jack. Assistant Water Maintenance Foreman. (Career Examination Ser.: C-2919). (Cloth bdg. avail. on request). pap. 12.00 (ISBN 0-8373-2919-1). Natl Learning.

--District Foreman (Watershed Maintenance) (Career Examination Ser.: C-428). (Cloth bdg. avail. on request). pap. 12.00 (ISBN 0-8373-0428-8). Natl Learning.

Schiller, E. J. & Droste, R. L., eds. Water Supply & Sanitation in Developing Countries. LC 81-86538. (Illus.). 368p. 1982. 29.95 (ISBN 0-250-40490-7). Ann Arbor Science.

Tarlock, A. Dan. Water Resource Management: 1983 Supplement. 2nd ed. (University Casebook Ser.). 223p. 1982. pap. text ed. write for info. (ISBN 0-88277-103-5). Foundation Pr.

WATER SUPPLY–LAWS AND LEGISLATION

see Water–Laws and Legislation

WATER-SUPPLY–UNITED STATES

Franko, David A. & Wetzel, Robert G. To Quench Our Thirst. (Illus.). 176p. 1983. text ed. 20.00 (ISBN 0-472-10032-7); pap. text ed. 8.50 (ISBN 0-472-08037-7). U of Mich Pr.

WATER-SUPPLY, INDUSTRIAL

see also Water-Pollution; Water-Purification

Brandvold, D. C. Water Treatment: Industrial-Commercial-Municipal. 2nd ed. (Illus.). 1982. pap. 5.00 (ISBN 0-9610178-0-5). Branchemco.

WATER-SUPPLY ENGINEERING

see also Boring; Hydraulic Engineering; Water-Supply, Industrial

American Water Works Association. Annual Conference, 1982: Proceedings, 2 pts. (AWWA Handbooks-Proceedings Ser.). (Illus.). 1310p. 1982. Set. pap. 68.60 (ISBN 0-89867-281-3). Am Water Wks Assn.

--Basic Management Principles for Small Water Systems. (AWWA Handbooks-General Ser.). (Illus.). 132p. 1982. pap. 18.20 (ISBN 0-89867-280-5). Am Water Wks Assn.

--Corrosion Control. (AWWA Handbooks-Proceedings Ser.). (Illus.). 70p. 1982. pap. 10.20 (ISBN 0-89867-283-X). Am Water Wks Assn.

--Design of Pilot Plant Studies. (AWWA Handbooks-Proceedings Ser.). (Illus.). 108p. 1982. pap. 11.40 (ISBN 0-89867-285-6). Am Water Wks Assn.

--Financial Planning & the Use of Financial Information for General Management Personnel. (AWWA Handbooks-Proceedings Ser.). (Illus.). 80p. 1982. pap. 10.20 (ISBN 0-89867-277-5). Am Water Wks Assn.

--Journal AWWA, 1980, Vol. 72. (Journal Bound Volumes Ser.). (Illus.). 788p. 1981. pap. 28.80 (ISBN 0-89867-253-8). Am Water Wks Assn.

--Journal AWWA, 1981. (Journal Bound Volumes Ser.). (Illus.). 104p. 1982. pap. text ed. 28.80 (ISBN 0-89867-269-4). Am Water Wks Assn.

--OpFlow, 1981, Vol. 7. (OpFlow Bound Volumes Ser.). (Illus.). 104p. 1982. pap. text ed. 19.20 (ISBN 0-89867-270-8). Am Water Wks Assn.

--Small Water System Problems. (AWWA Handbooks-Proceedings Ser.). (Illus.). 117p. 1981. pap. text ed. 12.00 (ISBN 0-89867-266-X). Am Water Wks Assn.

--Small Water System Solutions. (AWWA Handbooks-Proceedings Ser.). (Illus.). 80p. 1982. pap. text ed. 10.20 (ISBN 0-89867-282-1). Am Water Wks Assn.

--Treatment Techniques for Controlling Trihalomethanes in Drinking Water. (AWWA Handbooks-General Ser.). (Illus.). 312p. 1982. pap. text ed. 16.80 (ISBN 0-89867-279-1). Am Water Wks Assn.

--Wate Utility Management Practices-M5. (AWWA Manuals Ser.). (Illus.). 1980. pap. text ed. 16.80 (ISBN 0-89867-063-2). Am Water Wks Assn.

--Water Quality Technology Conference, 1981: Advances in Laboratory Techniques for Quality Control. (AWWA Handbooks-Proceedings Ser.). (Illus.). 1982. pap. text ed. 18.60 (ISBN 0-89867-267-8). Am Water Wks Assn.

--Water Quality Technology Conference, 1980: Advances in Laboratory Techniques for Quality Control. (AWWA Handbooks-Proceedings Ser.). (Illus.). 1981. pap. text ed. 18.00 (ISBN 0-89867-251-1). Am Water Wks Assn.

Binnie, G. M. Early Victorian Water Engineers. 310p. 1981. 50.00x (ISBN 0-7277-0128-2, Pub. by Telford England). State Mutual Bk.

Fair, G. M., et al. Water & Wastewater Engineering: Water Purification & Wastewater Treatment & Disposal. LC 66-16139. 668p. 1968. 43.95x (ISBN 0-471-25131-3). Wiley.

--Water & Wastewater Engineering: Water Supply & Wastewater Removal, Vol. 1. LC 66-16139. 489p. 1966. 39.95x (ISBN 0-471-25130-5). Wiley.

Fair, Gordon M., et al. Elements of Water Supply & Waste Water Disposal. 2nd ed. LC 72-151032. (Illus.). 752p. 1971. 43.95x (ISBN 0-471-25115-1). Wiley.

Rudman, Jack. Assistant Water Service Foreman. (Career Examination Ser.: C-2924). (Cloth bdg. avail. on request). pap. 12.00 (ISBN 0-8373-2924-8). Natl Learning.

--Supervisor (Water & Sewer Systems) (Career Examination Ser.: C-2907). (Cloth bdg. avail. on request). pap. 10.00 (ISBN 0-8373-2907-8). Natl Learning.

--Water District Supervisor. (Career Examination Ser.: C-2625). (Cloth bdg. avail. on request). pap. 12.00 (ISBN 0-8373-2625-7). Natl Learning.

--Water Maintainance Foreman. (Career Examination Ser.: C-2925). (Cloth bdg. avail. on request). pap. 12.00 (ISBN 0-8373-2925-6). Natl Learning.

--Water Maintainance Man. (Career Examination Ser.: C-2657). (Cloth bdg. avail. on request). pap. 10.00 (ISBN 0-8373-2657-5). Natl Learning.

--Water Plant Operator Trainee. (Career Examination Ser.: C-886). (Cloth bdg. avail. on request). pap. 10.00 (ISBN 0-8373-0886-0). Natl Learning.

WATER TANKS

see Tanks

WATER TRANSPORTATION

see Shipping

WATERFALLS

Plumb, Gregory A. Waterfalls of the Pacific Northwest. (Illus.). 224p. 1983. pap. 9.95 (ISBN 0-916076-60-1). Writing.

WATERFOWL

see also names of families of water fowl, e.g. Anatidae

Ogilvie, M. A. Wildfowl of Britain & Europe. 1982. 16.95x (ISBN 0-19-217723-0). Oxford U Pr.

WATERGATE AFFAIR, 1972-

Dean, John W., III. Lost Honor. LC 82-61776. 1982. 15.95 (ISBN 0-936906-15-4). Stratford Pr.

Garza, Hedda, compiled by. The Watergate Investigation Index: Senate Select Committee Hearings & Reports on Presidential Campaign Activities. LC 82-7353. 326p. 1982. lib. bdg. 95.00 (ISBN 0-8420-2175-2). Scholarly Res Inc.

Lang, Gladys E. The Battle for Public Opinion: The President, the Press & the Polls During Watergate. Lang, Kurt, ed. 360p. 1983. 32.00x (ISBN 0-231-05548-X); pap. 12.50x (ISBN 0-231-05549-8). Columbia U Pr.

Weissman, Steve, ed. Big Brother & the Holding Company: The World Behind Watergate. LC 78-90631. 349p. 1974. 14.00 (ISBN 0-87867-050-5). Ramparts.

WATERING-PLACES

see Health Resorts, Watering-Places, etc.

WATERS, FRANK, 1902-

Tanner, Terence A. Frank Waters: A Bibliography. (Illus.). 304p. 1983. 45.00 (ISBN 0-916638-07-3). Meyerbooks.

WATERWORKS

see Water-Supply

WAUGH, EVELYN, 1903-1966

Littlewood, Ian. The Writings of Evelyn Waugh. LC 82-18513. 256p. 1983. text ed. 24.50x (ISBN 0-389-20350-5). B&N Imports.

WAVE GUIDES

Brown, R. G., et al. Lines, Waves & Antennas: The Transmission of Electric Energy. 2nd ed. (Illus.). 471p. 1973. text ed. 22.50 (ISBN 0-8260-1431-3). Wiley.

WAVE MECHANICS

see also Matrix Mechanics; Molecular Orbitals; Quantum Statistics

AIP Conference, 86th, Adelaide, Australia, 1982. Momentum Wave Functions: Proceedings. Weigold, Erich, ed. LC 82-72375. 345p. 1982. lib. bdg. 34.00 (ISBN 0-88318-185-1). Am Inst Physics.

Wiegel, R. L., ed. Directional Wave Spectra Applications. LC 82-70873. 512p. 1982. pap. text ed. 36.00 (ISBN 0-87262-303-3). Am Soc Civil Eng.

WAVEFRONT RECONSTRUCTION IMAGING
see Holography
WAVES
see also Electric Waves; Light; Radiation; Shock Waves; Turbulence; Wave Mechanics
Beckman, J. E. & Phillips, J. P. Submillimetre Wave Astronomy. LC 82-4487. (Illus.). 370p. 1982. 47.50 (ISBN 0-521-24733-0). Cambridge U Pr.
Morawetz, C. S. Lectures on Nonlinear Waves & Shocks. (Tata Institute Lectures on Mathematics). 137p. 1982. pap. 6.70 (ISBN 0-387-10830-0). Springer-Verlag.
WAVES, ELECTROMAGNETIC
see Electromagnetic Waves
WAVES, SEISMIC
see Seismic Waves
WAXES
Halpern, M. G., ed. Polishing & Waxing Compositions: Recent Developments. LC 82-7691. (Chemical Technology Rev. 213). (Illus.). 301p. 1983. 36.00 (ISBN 0-8155-0916-2). Noyes.
WAY OF LIFE, JEWISH
see Jewish Way of Life
WAYNE, JOHN
Stacy, Pat & Linet, Beverly. Duke: A Love Story, An Intimate Memoir of John Wayne's Last Years. LC 82-73031. 224p. 1983. 14.95 (ISBN 0-689-11366-8). Atheneum.
WEALTH
see also Capital; Consumption (Economics); Cost and Standard of Living; Gross National Product; Income; Income Tax; Money; Poverty; Profit; Property; Saving and Investment; Success; Value; Wealth, Ethics Of
Hutton, John. The Mystery of Wealth: Political Economy, Its Development & Impact on World Events. 416p. 1979. 42.00x (ISBN 0-85950-470-0, Pub. by Thornes England). State Mutual Bk.
Modigliani & Hemming. The Determinants of National Savings & Wealth: Proceedings of a Conference Held by International Economic Association in Bergamo, Italy. LC 82-10377. 305p. 1982. 35.00x (ISBN 0-312-19590-7). St Martin.
WEALTH, ETHICS OF
see also Business Ethics; Christianity and Economics
Vogt, Virgil. Treasure in Heaven: The Biblical Teaching about Money, Finances, & Possessions. (Orig.). 1983. pap. write for info. (ISBN 0-89283-114-6). Servant.
WEAPONS
see Arms and Armor; Atomic Weapons; Firearms
WEAPONS SYSTEMS
Pretty, Ronald T., ed. Jane's Weapon System, 1982-1983. (Jane's Yearbooks). (Illus.). 1000p. 1982. 140.00 (ISBN 0-86720-619-5). Sci Bks Intl.
WEARINESS
see Fatigue
WEATHER
see also Climatology; Evaporation; Meteorology; Storms; Winds
also names of countries, cities, etc., with or without the subdivision Climate
Corliss, William R. Tornadoes, Dark Days, Anomalous Precipitation, & Related Weather Phenomena. (Catalog of Geophysical Anomalies Ser.). (Illus.). 250p. 1983. 11.95 (ISBN 0-915554-10-0). Sourcebook.
Discovering the Weather. LC 81-52418. (Discovering Science Ser.). lib. bdg. 15.96 (ISBN 0-86706-059-X, Pub. by Stonehenge). Silver.
Eagleman, Joe R. Severe & Unusual Weather Discussion Guide. 96p. 1982. pap. text ed. 7.95 (ISBN 0-8403-2777-3). Kendall-Hunt.
Updegraffe, Imelda & Updegraffe, Robert. Weather. (Turning Points Ser.). (Illus.). 24p. 1983. pap. 3.50 (ISBN 0-14-049191-0, Puffin). Penguin.
WEATHER–JUVENILE LITERATURE
Adler, David. World of Weather. LC 82-17398. (Question & Answer Bks.). (Illus.). 32p. (gr. 3-6). 1983. PLB 8.59 (ISBN 0-89375-870-1); pap. text ed. 1.95 (ISBN 0-89375-871-X). Troll Assocs.
WEATHERING
see also Corrosion and Anti-Corrosives; Erosion
Small, John & Clark, Michael. Slopes & Weathering. LC 81-18025. (Cambridge Topics in Geography Second Ser.). 112p. 1982. 12.95 (ISBN 0-521-23340-2); pap. 6.95 (ISBN 0-521-29926-8). Cambridge U Pr.
WEAVING
see also Basket Making; Beadwork; Hand Weaving; Indians of North America–Textile Industry and Fabrics; Lace and Lace Making; Looms; Silk Manufacture and Trade; Textile Fabrics
also woven articles, e.g. Blankets, Carpets, Rugs
Ormerod, Allan. Modern Preparation & Weaving Machinery. new ed. 296p. text ed. 49.95 (ISBN 0-408-01212-9). Butterworth.
Ponting. Beginners Guide to Weaving. 1982. text ed. write for info (ISBN 0-408-00574-2). Butterworth.
Sutton, Ann, et al. The Crafts of the Weaver. (Illus.). 152p. (Orig.). 1982. 18.50 (ISBN 0-937274-09-7); pap. 12.95 (ISBN 0-937274-10-0). Lark Bks.
WEBER, MAX, 1864-1920
King, Alma S. Max Weber: An Exhibition of Works. (Illus.). 24p. (Orig.). 1982. pap. 7.50 (ISBN 0-941430-05-7). Santa Fe E Gallery.
Kronman, Anthony T. Max Weber. LC 82-80923. (Jurists, Profiles in Legal Theory). 224p. 1983. 18.50x (ISBN 0-8047-1140-2). Stanford U Pr.
WEBER, MAX, 1881-1961
Alexander, Jeffrey C. Theoretical Logic in Sociology, Vol. 3: The Classical Attempt at Theoretical Synthesis: Max Weber. LC 75-17305. 224p. 1983. text ed. 25.00x (ISBN 0-520-04482-7). U of Cal Pr.
Midgley, E. B. The Ideology of Max Weber: A Thomist Critique. LC 82-16445. 200p. 1983. text ed. 22.50x (ISBN 0-389-20343-2). B&N Imports.
WEBSTER, JOHN, 1580?-1625?
Bliss, Lee. The World's Perspective: John Webster & the Jacobean Drama. 239p. Date not set. 20.00x (ISBN 0-8135-0967-X). Rutgers U Pr.
WECHSLER INTELLIGENCE SCALE FOR CHILDREN
Wall, Shavaun M. & Hixenbaugh, Paula. WISC-R Administration & Scoring: Handbook of Training Exercises. (Professional Handbook Ser.). 220p. 1983. 24.50 (ISBN 0-87424-178-2). Western Psych.
WEDDING ETIQUETTE
Our Christian Wedding Guest Book. (Illus.). 48p. 1983. padded cover 8.50 (ISBN 0-8007-1345-1). Revell.
WEDDING PHOTOGRAPHY
Franklin, Linda C. Wedding Album. (Old Fashioned Keepbook Photo Albums Ser.). (Illus.). 32p. 1982. 17.50 (ISBN 0-934504-16-4). Tree Comm.
WEDDINGS
see also Marriage Customs and Rites; Wedding Etiquette
Dewitt, Edith. Bridal Path. LC 81-81944. (Illus.). 192p. 1983. 16.95 (ISBN 0-86666-039-9). GWP.
Gilbert, Edith. The Complete Wedding Planner. LC 82-83770. 256p. 1983. 14.95 (ISBN 0-8119-0485-7). Fell.
Goldberg, Joan R. You Can Afford a Beautiful Wedding. 160p. 1983. pap. 6.95 (ISBN 0-8092-5631-2). Contemp Bks.
Goss, Dinah B. & Schwartz, Marla S. The Bride Guide. LC 82-19777. (Illus.). 192p. (Orig.). 1983. pap. 12.95 (ISBN 0-934878-22-6). Dembner Bks.
WEDGWOOD WARE
Wedgewood: Its Competitors & Imitators, 1800-1830. 1977. 27.50 (ISBN 0-89344-021-3). Ars Ceramica.
WEED CONTROL
see also Herbicides
Anderson, Wood P. Weed Science: Principles. 2nd ed. (Illus.). 650p. 1983. text ed. 23.95 (ISBN 0-314-69632-6). West Pub.
Ridout, J. Water Weed Problems: Potential Utilisation & Control. 1980. 35.00x (ISBN 0-85135-112-3, Pub. by Centre Overseas Research). State Mutual Bk.
Stephens, R. Theory & Practice of Weed Control. 1982. 45.00x (ISBN 0-333-21294-0, Pub. by Macmillan England). State Mutual Bk.
WEEDS
see also Weed Control;
also names of weeds
Barkley, T. M. Field Guide to the Common Weeds of Kansas. LC 82-21914. (Illus.). 160p. 1983. text ed. 17.95x (ISBN 0-7006-0233-X); pap. 7.95 (ISBN 0-7006-0224-0). Univ Pr KS.
Holzner, W. & Numata, M. Biology & Ecology of Weeds. 1982. 99.50 (ISBN 90-6193-682-9, Pub. by Junk Pubs Netherlands). Kluwer Boston.
Hunter, Peter J. Peter Hunter's Guide to Grasses, Clovers, & Weeds. (Illus.). 80p. pap. 5.95 (ISBN 0-938670-02-6). By Hand & Foot.
Klingman, GLenn C. & Ashton, Floyd M. Weed Science: Principles & Practices. 2nd ed. 449p. 1982. text ed. 24.50x (ISBN 0-471-08487-5, Pub. by Wiley-Interscience). Wiley.
Weeds in Tropical Crops: Review of Abstracts. (FAO Plant Production & Protection Paper: No. 32, Supplement 1). 63p. 1982. pap. 7.50 (ISBN 92-5-101206-7, F2333, FAO). Unipub.
WEEK-DAY CHURCH SCHOOLS
Cascone, Gina. Pagan Babies & Other Catholic Memories. 160p. 1983. pap. 4.95 (ISBN 0-312-59419-4). St Martin.
WEIGHING MACHINES
Rudman, Jack. Weigher. (Career Examination Ser.: C-2674). (Cloth bdg. avail. on request). pap. 8.00 (ISBN 0-8373-2674-5). Natl Learning.
WEIGHT LIFTING
Knudson, R. R. Muscles! (Illus.). 96p. 1983. pap. 1.95 (ISBN 0-380-82172-9, 82172-9, Camelot). Avon.
Leighton, Jack R. Fitness, Body Development, & Sports Conditioning Through Weight Training. 2nd ed. (Illus.). 234p. 1983. 24.50x (ISBN 0-398-04761-8). C C Thomas.
Mentzer, Mike & Friedberg, Ardy. Mike Mentzer's Complete Book of Weight Training. LC 82-18632. (Illus.). 256p. (Orig.). 1983. pap. 6.95 (ISBN 0-688-01600-6). Quill NY.
Sullivan, George. Better Weight Training for Boys. LC 82-19871. (Better Sports Ser.). (Illus.). 64p. (gr. 6 up). 1983. PLB 8.95 (ISBN 0-396-08121-5). Dodd.
WEIGHT REDUCING PREPARATIONS
Brandt, Frans M. A Guide to Rational Weight Control. LC 79-63237. 320p. 1979. pap. 8.95 (ISBN 0-941954-00-5). Wesselhoeft Assoc.
Gutin, Bernard & Kessler, Gail. The High-Energy Factor. LC 82-13353. 175p. 1983. 14.95 (ISBN 0-394-52548-5). Random.
WEIL, SIMONE, 1909-1943
Hellman, John. Simone Weil: An Introduction to Her Thought. 170p. 1982. text ed. 11.00x (ISBN 0-88920-121-8, 40905, Pub. by Laurier U Pr). Humanities.
McFarland, Dorothy T. Simone Weil. (Literature & Life Ser.). 220p. 1983. 11.95 (ISBN 0-8044-2604-X). Ungar.
WEIZMANN, CHAIM, PRES. ISRAEL, 1874-1952
Litvinoff, Barnet. The Essential Chaim Weizmann: The Man, The Statesman, The Scientist. 1983. text ed. 27.50x (ISBN 0-8419-0823-0). Holmes & Meier.
WELDING
see also Electric Welding
also specific materials or objects, with or without the subdivision Welding
American Welding Society. American Welding Society Welding Terms & Definitions. 80p. 1980. 20.00 (ISBN 0-686-43366-1). Am Welding.
--Guide for the Nondestructive Inspection of Welds: B1.0. 1977. 8.00 (ISBN 0-686-43386-6). Am Welding.
--Handbook on the Ultrasonic Examination of Welds. 1977. 28.00 (ISBN 0-686-43357-2). Am Welding.
--Metric Practice Guide for the Welding Industry: A1.1. 1980. 8.00 (ISBN 0-686-43367-X). Am Welding.
--Recommended Practices & Procedures for Welding Plain Carbon Steel Pipe: D10.12. 1979. 8.00 (ISBN 0-686-43365-3). Am Welding.
--Recommended Practices for Automotive Welding Design: D8.4. 1961. 8.00 (ISBN 0-686-43362-9). Am Welding.
--Recommended Practices for Stud Welding: C5.4. 1974. 8.00 (ISBN 0-686-43379-3). Am Welding.
--Specification for Cast Iron, Welding Rods & Covered Electrodes for Welding. 1982. 8.00 (ISBN 0-686-43349-1). Am Welding.
--Specification for Steel, Low-Alloy Covered Arc Welding Electrodes: A5.5. 1981. write for info. Am Welding.
--Specification for Surface Welding Rods & Electrodes. 1980. Composite. 8.00 (ISBN 0-686-43346-7, A5.21); Solid. 8.00 (ISBN 0-686-43347-5, A5.13). Am Welding.
--Specification for Welding Industrial & Mill Cranes. 1970. 8.00 (ISBN 0-686-43384-X). Am Welding.
--Specification for Welding of Presses & Press Components. 83p. 1980. 18.00 (ISBN 0-686-43385-8). Am Welding.
Bennett, A. E. & Siy, L. Blueprint Reading for Welders. 4th ed. 218p. 1983. text ed. 8.40 (ISBN 0-8273-2144-9); write for info. instr's. guide (ISBN 0-8273-2145-7). Delmar.
Braumbaugh, James. Welders Guide. new ed. (Audel Ser.). 1983. 19.95 (ISBN 0-672-23374-6). Bobbs.
Carr, Richard & O'Con, Robert. Welding Practices & Procedures. (Illus.). 416p. 1983. text ed. 17.95 (ISBN 0-13-948059-5). P-H.
Chrysler Learning, Inc. Weldtech Series in Welding: Basic Gas Metal-Arc Welding. (Illus.). 128p. 1983. pap. text ed. 9.95 (ISBN 0-13-948075-7). P-H.
--Weldtech Series in Welding: Basic Shielded Metal-Arc Welding. 128p. 1983. pap. 9.95 (ISBN 0-13-948083-8). P-H.
--Weldtech Series in Welding: Oxyacetylene Welding, Cutting, & Brazing. (Illus.). 80p. 1983. pap. 9.95 (ISBN 0-13-948091-9). P-H.
Edgin, Charles A. General Welding. LC 81-1882. 325p. 1982. text ed. 15.95 (ISBN 0-471-08001-2); tchrs. manual avail. (ISBN 0-471-09188-X). Wiley.
Hoffman, Edward G. & Romero, Felix. Welding Blueprint Reading. 1983. pap. text ed. 19.95 (ISBN 0-534-01431-3, Breton Pubs). Wadsworth Pub.
Kennedy, Gower A. Welding Technology. 2nd ed. 598p. 1982. text ed. 27.50 (ISBN 0-672-97778-8); student manual 9.95 (ISBN 0-672-97990-X). Bobbs.
Sacks. Essentials of Welding. 1983. text ed. price not set (ISBN 0-87002-385-3). Bennett IL.
U. S. Welding Equipment. 1982. 995.00 (ISBN 0-686-37721-4, 287). Predicasts.
WELDING–VOCATIONAL GUIDANCE
American Welding Society. Minimum Requirements for Training of Welders: E3.1. 1975. 8.00 (ISBN 0-686-43355-6). Am Welding.
WELFARE ECONOMICS
see also Economic Security
Cooper, Robert D. Health & Welfare Fund Operations & Expenses: Summary Report & Fact Book for Multiemployer Plans. 47p. (Orig.). 1982. pap. 12.50 (ISBN 0-89154-200-0). Intl Found Employ.
Dasgupta, Partha. The Control of Resources. (Illus.). 240p. 1983. text ed. 22.50x (ISBN 0-674-16980-8). Harvard U Pr.
Heinberg, et al. Housing Allowances in Kansas City & Wilmington: An Appraisal. (Illus.). 41p. (Orig.). 1976. pap. text ed. 4.00 (ISBN 0-87766-143-X). Urban Inst.
Moore, Kristin A. & Burt, Martha R. Private Crisis, Public Cost: Policy Perspectives on Teenage Childbearing. LC 82-60293. 166p. (Orig.). 1982. pap. text ed. 11.00 (ISBN 0-87766-314-9, 33900). Urban Inst.
WELFARE WORK
see Charities; Public Welfare
WELFARE WORK IN INDUSTRY
see also Employee Counseling; Societies; Profit-Sharing
Soltow, Martha J. & Gravelle, Susan. Worker Benefits: Industrial Welfare in America 1900-1935. LC 82-25494. 242p. 1983. 16.50 (ISBN 0-8108-1614-8). Scarecrow.
WELL-BORING
see Boring
WELL DRILLING, OIL
see Oil Well Drilling
WELLES, ORSON, 1915-
McBride, Joseph. Orson Welles. 1972. pap. 8.95 (ISBN 0-436-09927-6, Pub by Secker & Warburg). David & Charles.
WELLS, HERBERT GEORGE, 1866-1946
Crossley, Robert. Reader's Guide to H. G. Wells. Schlobin, Roger C., ed. (Reader's Guides to Contemporary Science Fiction & Fantasy Authors Ser.: Vol. 19). (Illus., Orig.). 1982. 10.95x (ISBN 0-916732-51-7); pap. text ed. 4.95x (ISBN 0-916732-50-9). Starmont Hse.
Ferrell, Keith. H. G. Wells: First Citizen of the Future. 192p. 1983. text ed. 9.95 (ISBN 0-87131-403-7). M Evans.
Huntington, John. The Logic of Fantasy: H. G. Wells & Science Fiction. LC 82-4593. 192p. 1982. text ed. 22.50x (ISBN 0-231-05378-9). Columbia U Pr.
WELLS
see also Boring; Gas, Natural; Petroleum; Water, Underground; Water-Supply
Sengel, Bill, ed. Basic Well Logging. 1982. 20.00 (ISBN 0-89419-183-7). Inst Energy.
WELSH LANGUAGE–DICTIONARIES
University of Wales Press. A Dictionary of the Welsh Language: Part 31. Bevan, G. A., ed. 63p. 1982. pap. text ed. 8.00 (ISBN 0-686-81869-5). Verry.
WELTY, EUDORA, 1909-
Devlin, Albert J., ed. Eudora Welty's Chronicle: A Story of Mississippi Life. LC 82-19996. 240p. 1983. text ed. 20.00x (ISBN 0-87805-176-7). U Pr of Miss.
WEREWOLVES
Aylesworth, T. G. The Story of Werewolves. 1982. 8.95 (ISBN 0-07-002645-9). McGraw.
WEST, NATHANAEL, 1902-1940
Widmer, Kingsley. Nathaniel West. (United States Author Ser.). 1982. lib. bdg. 11.95 (ISBN 0-8057-7356-8, Twayne). G K Hall.
WEST
see also Frontier and Pioneer Life; Great Plains; Ranch Life;
also geographic areas of the west, e.g. Great Plains; southwest, new
Gregg, Frank. Federal Land Transfers: The Case for a Westwide Program Based on the Federal Land Policy & Management Act. LC 82-8126. 34p. (Orig.). 1982. pap. 5.00 (ISBN 0-89164-071-1). Conservation Foun.
Rowley, William D. American West. LC 73-81060. 1980. pap. text ed. 6.95x (ISBN 0-88273-021-5). Forum Pr IL.
WEST–BIOGRAPHY
Murphy, Lawrence R. Lucien Bonaparte Maxwell: The Napoleon of the Southwest. LC 82-40454. (Illus.). 280p. 1983. 19.95 (ISBN 0-8061-1807-5). U of Okla Pr.
Steckmesser, Kent L. Western Outlaws: The "Good Badman" in Fact, Film & Folklore. 170p. Date not set. 17.95 (ISBN 0-941690-07-5); pap. 10.95 (ISBN 0-941690-08-3). Regina Bks.
WEST–DESCRIPTION AND TRAVEL
Cromie, Alice. Tour Guide to the Old West. 1982. pap. 9.95 (ISBN 0-8129-6323-7). Times Bks.
WEST–DESCRIPTION AND TRAVEL–GUIDEBOOKS
Chester, Carole. California & the Golden West. LC 82-61197. (Pocket Guide Ser.). (Illus.). 1983. pap. 4.95 (ISBN 0-528-84894-1). Rand.
WEST–DISCOVERY AND EXPLORATION
Carleton, J. Henry. The Prarie Logbooks: Dragoon Campaigns to the Pawnee Villages in 1844, & to the Rocky Mountains in 1845. Pelzer, Louis, ed. (Illus.). xviii, 295p. 1983. 19.95x (ISBN 0-8032-1422-7); pap. 7.50 (ISBN 0-8032-6314-7, BB 845, Bison). U of Nebr Pr.
WEST–HISTORY
Bourke, John G. MacKenzie's Last Fight with the Cheyennes. (Illus.). 1970. 7.95 (ISBN 0-88342-009-0). Old Army.
Breihan, Carl W. Gunslingers. (Illus.). 300p. 1983. 12.95 (ISBN 0-89769-076-1); pap. 6.95 (ISBN 0-89769-048-6). Pine Mntn.
Kulman, Charles. Massacre Survivor! The Story of Frank Finkel. A Trooper with Custer. (Illus.). 1972. pap. 2.00 (ISBN 0-88342-200-X). Old Army.
Miller, Rick. The Early West. (Illus.). 176p. 1983. 13.75 (ISBN 0-932702-25-2); pap. 8.50 (ISBN 0-932702-27-9); leatherbound limited to 25 copies 75.00. Creative Texas.
Murray, Robert A. The Army Moves West: Supplying the Western Indian Wars Campaigns. 1981. pap. 2.95 (ISBN 0-88342-247-6). Old Army.
Reader's Digest Editors. Story of the Great American West. LC 76-23542. (Illus.). 384p. 1977. 19.50 (ISBN 0-89577-039-3, Pub. by RD Assn). Random.
Schultheis, Rob. The Hidden West: Journeys in the American Outback. LC 82-73719. 192p. 1983. pap. 9.50 (ISBN 0-86547-087-1). N Point Pr.
Smith, Duane A. A Taste of the West: Essays in Honor of Robert G. Athearn. Smith, Duane A., ed. 1983. write for info. (ISBN 0-87108-641-7). Pruett.

Virgines, George. Western Legends & Lore. (Illus.). 128p. 1983. 12.95 (ISBN 0-686-81870-9); pap. 6.95 (ISBN 0-686-81871-7). Pine Mntn.

WEST-JUVENILE LITERATURE

Rosenbloom, Joseph. The Official Wild West Joke Book. LC 82-19537. (Illus.). 128p. (gr. 3 up). 1983. 7.95 (ISBN 0-8069-4666-0); PLB 9.99 (ISBN 0-8069-4667-9). Sterling.

WEST AFRICA

see Africa, West

WEST ARMENIAN LANGUAGE

see Armenian Language

WEST INDIES-DESCRIPTION AND TRAVEL-GUIDEBOOKS

French West Indies Travel Guide. (Berlitz Travel Guides). (Illus.). 1982. pap. 4.95 (ISBN 0-02-969650-X, Berlitz). Macmillan.

WEST POINT, NEW YORK-HISTORY

Tausch, Gerry. Glamour in the Kitchen: Recipes & Memoirs of a West Point Wife. Tausch, Roland D., ed. LC 82-82681. (Illus.). 152p. 1982. 9.95 (ISBN 0-686-82513-6). Gerosota Pub.

WEST VIRGINIA-DESCRIPTION AND TRAVEL

Rives, Margaret R. Blue Ridge Parkway. LC 82-82578. (The Story Behind the Scenery Ser.). (Illus.). 48p. (Orig.). 1982. 7.95 (ISBN 0-916122-82-4); pap. 3.00 (ISBN 0-916122-81-6). KC Pubns.

Strausbaugh, P. D. & Core, Earl L. Flora of West Virginia. LC 78-1146. (Illus.). 1079p. 1979. 25.00 (ISBN 0-89092-010-9). Seneca Bks.

WEST VIRGINIA-GENEALOGY

Meredith, Joseph N. The Merediths & Selveys of Virginia & West Virginia. (Illus.). 210p. 1982. 26.00 (ISBN 0-686-82432-6). J N Meredith.

WEST VIRGINIA-HISTORY

Cohen, Stan. The Civil War in West Virginia: A Pictorial History. rev. ed. LC 82-80964. (Illus.). 160p. (Orig.). 1982. pap. text ed. 8.95 (ISBN 0-933126-17-4). Pictorial Hist.

A Register of the Marriages Celebrated in Greenbrier County (West) Virginia from 1781-1849. LC 82-82599. 80p. 1983. pap. 15.00 (ISBN 0-937418-07-2). N P Evans.

Rives, Margaret R. Blue Ridge Parkway. LC 82-82578. (The Story Behind the Scenery Ser.). (Illus.). 48p. (Orig.). 1982. 7.95 (ISBN 0-916122-82-4); pap. 3.00 (ISBN 0-916122-81-6). KC Pubns.

WESTERN AND COUNTRY MUSIC

see Country Music

WESTERN ART

see Art

WESTERN SAMOA

see Samoan Islands

WESTERN STORIES

Reader's Digest Editors. The Best of the West, 2 Vols. LC 75-10496. (Illus.). 1246p. 1976. 15.99 (ISBN 0-89577-027-X). RD Assn.

--Story of the Great American West. LC 76-23542. (Illus.). 384p. 1977. 19.50 (ISBN 0-89577-039-3). RD Assoc.

Short, Luke. Luke Short's Best of the West. 1983. 14.95 (ISBN 0-87795-471-2). Arbor Hse.

Tuska, Jon & Piekarski, Vicki. Encyclopedia of Frontier & Western Fiction. (Illus.). 384p. 1983. 24.95 (ISBN 0-07-065587-1, P&RB). McGraw.

WHALES

Dietz, Tim. Tales of Whales. Jack, Susan, ed. (Illus.). 160p. (Orig.). 1982. pap. 7.95 (ISBN 0-930096-33-9). G Gannett.

DiPrima, Richard. The Great Whales: Endangered Monarchs of the Deep. 155p. (Orig.). 1981. pap. text ed. 7.95 (ISBN 0-86652-042-2). Educ Indus.

Katona, Steve & Richardson, David. A Field Guide to the Whales, Porpoises, & Seals of the Gulf of Maine & Eastern Canada: Cape Cod to Labrador. (Illus.). 224p. 1983. 17.95 (ISBN 0-686-83664-2, ScribT); pap. 9.95 (ISBN 0-686-83665-0). Scribner.

Morton, Harry. The Whale's Wake. (Illus.). 396p. 1982. text ed. 32.50x (ISBN 0-8248-0830-4). UH Pr.

Purves, P. E. & Pilleri, G., eds. Echolocation in Whales & Dolphins. write for info. (ISBN 0-12-567960-2). Acad Pr.

True, Frederick W. The Whalebone Whales of the Western North Atlantic. (Illus.). 360p. 1983. Repr. of 1904 ed. text ed. 35.00x (ISBN 0-87474-922-0). Smithsonian.

WHALING

Morton, Harry. The Whale's Wake. (Illus.). 396p. 1982. text ed. 32.50x (ISBN 0-8248-0830-4). UH Pr.

WHEAT

Hanson, Haldore & Borlaug, Norman. Wheat in the Third World. (IADS Development Oriented Literature Ser.). 192p. 1982. lib. bdg. 18.00 (ISBN 0-86531-357-1). Westview.

WHEATLEY, PHILLIS, AFTERWARD PHILLIS PETERS, 1753?-1784

Robinson, William H. Phyllis Wheatly & Her Writings. LC 82-21027. 300p. 1983. lib. bdg. 36.00 (ISBN 0-8240-9346-1). Garland Pub.

Robinson, William H., ed. Critical Essays on Phillis Wheatley. (Critical Essays on American Literature Ser.). 1982. lib. bdg. 32.50 (ISBN 0-8161-8336-8). G K Hall.

WHEEL CHAIRS

see Wheelchairs

WHEELCHAIRS

Bergen, Adrienne F. & Colangelo, Cheryl. Positioning the Client with Central Nervous System Deficits: The Wheelchair & Other Adapted Equipment. (Illus.). 191p. (Orig.). 1982. pap. text ed. 19.95 (ISBN 0-686-37672-2). Valhalla Rehab.

--Positioning the Client with Central Nervous System Deficits: The Wheelchair & Other Adapted Equipment. (Illus.). 191p. (Orig.). 1982. pap. text ed. 19.95 (ISBN 0-686-38095-9). Valhalla Rehab.

WHEELS

see also Gearing; Tires, Rubber

Taylor, Henry T. Know Your Wheels. (Illus.). 51p. (gr. 4-6). 1981. pap. write for info. (ISBN 0-938956-00-0). H T Taylor.

WHIG PARTY

Ershkowitz, Herbert. The Origin of the Whig & Democratic Parties, New Jersey Politics, 1820-1837. LC 82-17652. (Illus.). 300p. (Orig.). 1983. lib. bdg. 23.00 (ISBN 0-8191-2769-8); pap. text ed. 11.50 (ISBN 0-8191-2770-1). U Pr of Amer.

WHIPPING

see Corporal Punishment

WHISKEY

Magee, Malachy. One Thousand Years of Irish Whiskey. (Illus.). 144p. 1982. 15.95 (ISBN 0-905140-71-0, Pub. by Salem Hse Ltd.). Merrimack Bk Serv.

Perry, Stuart. The New Zealand Whiskey Book. (Illus.). 144p. 1982. 13.95 (ISBN 0-00-216973-8, Pub. by W Collins Australia). Intl Schol Bk Serv.

WHISKY

see Whiskey

WHITE, ELLEN GOULD (HARMON), 1827-1915

Battistone, Joseph. The Great Controversy Theme in E. G. White Writings. xiv, 134p. 1978. pap. 3.95 (ISBN 0-943872-76-6). Andrews Univ Pr.

WHITE ANTS

see Termites

WHITE BLOOD CELLS

see Leucocytes

WHITE COLLAR CRIMES

see also Fraud; Tax Evasion

Clinard, Marshall B. & Yeager, Peter C. Corporate Crime. LC 80-2156. Date not set. Repr. of 1980 ed. write for info. (ISBN 0-02-906420-1). Free Pr.

Mars, Gerald. Cheats at Work: An Anthropology of Workplace Crime. 256p. text ed. 16.95x (ISBN 0-04-301151-9). Allen Unwin.

WHITE FRIARS

see Carmelites

WHITE MOUNTAINS, NEW HAMPSHIRE

Doan, Daniel. Fifty Hikes in New Hampshire's White Mountains: Walks, Day Hikes, & Backpacking Trips. 3rd, rev. ed. (Fifty Hikes Ser.). (Illus.). 224p. 1983. pap. 8.95 (ISBN 0-942440-12-9). Backcountry Pubns.

WHITE RUSSIAN LITERATURE

see Russian Literature (Collections)

WHITE-SLAVE TRAFFIC

see Prostitution

WHITE-WATER CANOEING

Nealy, William. Kayaks to Hell. (Illus.). 144p. (Orig.). 1982. pap. 4.95 (ISBN 0-89732-010-7). Thomas Pr.

WHITEHEAD, ALFRED NORTH, 1861-1947

Cappon, Alexander P. Aspects of Wordsworth & Whitehead. 1983. 19.95 (ISBN 0-8022-2412-1). Philos Lib.

WHITMAN, WALT, 1819-1892

Hollis, C. Carroll. Language & Style in Leaves of Grass. LC 82-20881. 320p. 1983. text ed. 27.50X (ISBN 0-8071-1096-5). La State U Pr.

Woodress, James. Critical Essays on Walt Whitman. (Critical Essays in American Literature Ser.). 342p. 1983. lib. bdg. 35.00 (ISBN 0-8161-8632-4). G K Hall.

WHITTIER, JOHN GREENLEAF, 1807-1892

Kennedy, Sloane W. John Greenleaf Whittier, His Life, Genius & Writings. 373p. 1982. Repr. of 1903 ed. lib. bdg. 25.00 (ISBN 0-8495-3139-X). Arden Lib.

WHITTLING

see Wood-Carving

WHO

see World Health Organization

WHOLESALE TRADE

see also Retail Trade

Stiles, Bill. How to Be a Champion Wholesale Salesman. 1982. text ed. 19.95 (ISBN 0-8359-2916-7). Reston.

WIDOWS

see also Remarriage; Single-Parent Family; Women; Women-Legal Status, Laws, etc.

Jensen, Marilyn. Formerly Married: Learning to Live with Yourself. 120p. 1983. price not set (ISBN 0-664-27010-7). Westminster.

Robey, Harriet. There's a Dance in the Old Dame Yet. (General Ser.). 1982. lib. bdg. 14.95 (ISBN 0-8161-3478-2, Large Print Bks). G K Hall.

WIFE ABUSE

Bowker, Lee H. Beating Wife-Beating. LC 82-48603. 176p. 1983. 21.95x (ISBN 0-669-06345-2). Lexington Bks.

Giles-Sims, Jean. Wife Battering: Perspectives on Marriage & the Family. 197p. 1983. 17.50x (ISBN 0-89862-075-9). Guilford Pr.

Hofeller, Kathleen H. Battered Women, Shattered Lives. LC 82-50377. 125p. (Orig.). pap. 6.95 (ISBN 0-88247-687-4). R & E Res Assoc.

Kurtz, Howard A. The Beaten Victim. LC 82-50373. 125p. (Orig.). 1983. pap. 9.95 (ISBN 0-88247-684-X). R & E Res Assoc.

Olson, Esther L. & Petersen, Kenneth. No Place to Hide. 160p. (Orig.). 1982. pap. 4.95 (ISBN 0-8423-4721-6). Tyndale.

Roberts, Albert R. Sheltering Battered Women: A National Study & Service Guide. (Focus on Women Ser.: No. 3). 1981. pap. text ed. 17.95 (ISBN 0-8261-2691-X). Springer Pub.

WIFE AND HUSBAND

see Husband and Wife

WIGS AND WIGMAKERS

Botham, Mary & Sharrad, L. Manual of Wigmaking. (Illus.). 112p. 1983. 12.50 (ISBN 0-434-90164-4, Pub. by Heinemann England). David & Charles.

WILD ANIMALS

see Animals; Mammals

WILD FLOWER GARDENING

Barr, Claude A. Jewels of the Plains: Wild Flowers of the Great Plains Grasslands & Hills. LC 82-13691. 256p. 1983. 19.95 (ISBN 0-8166-1127-0). U of Minn Pr.

WILD FLOWERS

see also Wild Flower Gardening;

also various geographical subdivisions under Botany, e.g. Botany-Arctic Regions; Botany-United States

Barr, Claude A. Jewels of the Plains: Wild Flowers of the Great Plains Grasslands & Hills. LC 82-13691. 256p. 1983. 19.95 (ISBN 0-8166-1127-0). U of Minn Pr.

Bramwell, David & Bramwell, Zoe. Flores Silvestres de las Islas Canarias. 364p. 1977. 50.00x (ISBN 0-686-99797-2, Pub. by Thornes England). State Mutual Bk.

--Wild Flowers of the Canary Islands. 304p. 1974. 40.00x (ISBN 0-85950-010-1, Pub. by Thornes England). State Mutual Bk.

Fitter. Finding Wild Flowers. 29.95 (ISBN 0-686-42765-3, Collins Pub England). Greene.

McClintock & Fitter. Collins Pocket Guide to Wild Flowers. 27.95 (ISBN 0-686-42769-6, Collins Pub England). Greene.

Mohlenbrock, Robert H. Where Have All the Wildflowers Gone? Region-by-Region Guide to Threatened & Endangered U. S. Wildflowers. (Illus.). 256p. 1983. 15.95 (ISBN 0-02-585450-X). Macmillan.

Shillingford, John & Stringer, Michael. Pocket Guide to Common Wild Flowers. (Illus.). 100p. 7.95 (ISBN 0-7028-8040-X, Pub. by Salem Hse Ltd.). Merrimack Bk Serv.

WILD FLOWERS-AFRICA, SOUTH

Schuyler, Arlene A. Wildflowers South Florida Natives: Indentification & Habitat of Indigenous Tropical Flora. Hall, Charlotte & Oppenheimer, Richard, eds. LC 82-90756. (Illus.). 112p. (Orig.). 1982. pap. 5.95 (ISBN 0-910991-00-6). Facts FL.

WILD FLOWERS-EUROPE

Fitter & Blamey. The Wild Flowers of Britain & Northern Europe. pap. 14.95 (ISBN 0-686-42738-6, Collins Pub England). Greene.

Schauer & Caspari. A Field Guide to the Wild Flowers of Britain & Europe. pap. 18.95 (ISBN 0-686-42739-4, Collins Pub England). Greene.

WILD FLOWERS-GREAT BRITAIN

Cameron, Elizabeth. A Floral ABC. (Illus.). 64p. 1983. 7.95 (ISBN 0-688-01821-1). Morrow.

Fitter & Blamey. The Wild Flowers of Britain & Northern Europe. pap. 14.95 (ISBN 0-686-42738-6, Collins Pub England). Greene.

Galbraith. A Field Guide to the Wild Flowers of South-East Australia. 39.95 (ISBN 0-686-42773-4, Collins Pub England). Greene.

Schauer & Caspari. A Field Guide to the Wild Flowers of Britain & Europe. pap. 18.95 (ISBN 0-686-42739-4, Collins Pub England). Greene.

WILD FLOWERS-NORTH AMERICA

Laura, Martin. American Wildflowers: Fact & Folklore. 1983. 14.95 (ISBN 0-932298-36-2). Copple Hse.

WILD-FOWL

see Game and Game-Birds; Water-Birds

WILD LIFE CONSERVATION

see Wildlife Conservation

WILD LIFE REFUGES

see Wildlife Refuges

WILD TURKEY

see Turkeys

WILDE, OSCAR, 1854-1900

Douglas, Alfred. Oscar Wilde & Myself. 306p. 1983. Repr. of 1914 ed. lib. bdg. 45.00 (ISBN 0-686-38783-X). Century Bookbindery.

WILDER, LAURA (INGALLS) 1867-1957

Anderson, William T. The Story of the Ingalls. (Laura Ingalls Wilder Family Ser.). (Illus.). 40p. (Orig.). 1971. pap. text ed. 2.95 (ISBN 0-9610088-0-6). Anderson MI.

WILDERNESS AREAS

Auerbach & Geehr. Management of Wilderness & Environmental Emergency. 1983. price not set (ISBN 0-02-304630-9). Macmillan.

Barker, Elliott S. Smokey Bear & the Great Wilderness. Hausman, Gerald, ed. LC 82-19373. (Illus.). 176p. (Orig.). 1982. pap. 12.95 (ISBN 0-86534-017-X). Sunstone Pr.

Craighead, J. J. & Sumner, J. S. A Definitive System for Analysis of Grizzly Bear Habitat & Other Wilderness Resources Utilizing LANDSAT Multispectral Imagery & Computer Technology. Mitchell, J. A. & Lyons, L. J., eds. (Illus.). 304p. (Orig.). 1982. pap. text ed. 27.50 (ISBN 0-910439-01-X). Wildlife-Wildlands.

McTavish, Thistle & Swenson, Allan. Bush Country by George. (Illus.). 144p. (Orig.). 1982. pap. 7.95 (ISBN 0-930096-29-0). G Gannett.

Simer, Peter & Sullivan, John. The National Outdoor Leadership School's Official Wilderness Guide. (Illus.). 1983. price not set (ISBN 0-671-24996-7); pap. price not set (ISBN 0-671-24997-5). S&S.

Wissler, Clark. Adventures in the Wilderness. 1925. text ed. 22.50x (ISBN 0-686-83455-0). Elliots Bks.

The World's Greatest Natural Areas. 69p. 1983. pap. 10.00 (ISBN 2-88032-800-4, IUCN 114, IUCN). Unipub.

WILDERNESS SURVIVAL

Brown, Tom, Jr. & Morgan, Brandt. Tom Brown's Guide to Wilderness Survival. 240p. (Orig.). 1983. pap. 6.95 (ISBN 0-425-05876-X). Berkley Pub.

Fry, Alan. The Wilderness Survival Handbook: A Practical, All-Season Guide to Short Trip Preparation & Survival Techniques for Hikers, Skiers, Backpackers, Canoeists, Travelers in Light Aircraft & Anyone Stranded in the Bush. (Illus.). 304p. 1982. 15.95 (ISBN 0-312-87951-2); pap. 8.95 (ISBN 0-312-87952-0). St Martin.

WILDFIRES

see Fires; Forest Fires

WILDFLOWERS

see Wild Flowers

WILDFOWLING

see Fowling

WILDLIFE CONSERVATION

see also Forest Reserves; National Parks and Reserves; Natural Monuments; Wilderness Areas; Wildlife Management

Barker, Elliott S. Smokey Bear & the Great Wilderness. Hausman, Gerald, ed. LC 82-19373. (Illus.). 176p. (Orig.). 1982. pap. 12.95 (ISBN 0-86534-017-X). Sunstone Pr.

Bryant, Alan. Second Chance: The Story of the New Quay Hospital. (Illus.). 208p. 1982. 11.95 (ISBN 0-312-70828-9). St Martin.

Myers, Norman. A Wealth of Wild Species: Storehouse for Human Welfare. 300p. 1983. lib. bdg. 22.50 (ISBN 0-86531-132-3); pap. text ed. 10.00 (ISBN 0-86531-133-1). Westview.

WILDLIFE CONSERVATION-JUVENILE LITERATURE

Russell, Ian & Major, Alan. Watching Wildlife. (Illus.). 192p. 1982. 17.50 (ISBN 0-7153-8469-4). David & Charles.

WILDLIFE CONSERVATION-LAW AND LEGISLATION

see also Fishery Law and Legislation

Index to the Proceedings of the International Association of Fish & Wildlife Agencies: 1976 Through 1980. Date not set. price not set (ISBN 0-932108-06-7). IAFWA.

Proceedings of the Seventy-First Convention: International Association of Fish & Wildlife Agencies 1982. Date not set. 13.00 (ISBN 0-932108-07-5). IAFWA.

WILDLIFE CONSERVATION-AFRICA

Elephants & Rhinos in Africa: A Time for Decision. 36p. 1983. pap. 10.00 (ISBN 2-88032-208-1, IUCN 113, IUCN). Unipub.

WILDLIFE CONSERVATION-GREAT BRITAIN

Arlott & Fitter. The Complete Guide to British Wildlife. pap. 18.95 (ISBN 0-686-42744-0, Collins Pub England). Greene.

WILDLIFE CONSERVATION-NORTH AMERICA

Gildart, R. C. & Wassink, Jan. Montana Wildlife. (Montana Geographic Ser.: No. 3). (Illus.). 128p. 1982. pap. 12.95 (ISBN 0-938314-04-1). MT Mag.

Reader's Digest Editors. North American Wildlife. LC 81-50919. (Illus.). 576p. 1982. 20.50 (ISBN 0-89577-102-0). RD Assn.

WILDLIFE MANAGEMENT

see also Animal Populations

International Association of Fish & Wildlife Agencies. Proceedings of the Sixty-Ninth Convention. Blouch, Ralph I., ed. (Orig.). 1980. pap. 11.00 (ISBN 0-932108-04-0). IAFWA.

Mourier & Winding. Collins Guide to Wildlife in the House & Home. 29.95 (ISBN 0-686-42778-5, Collins Pub England). Greene.

Parker, Willie J. Game Warden: Chesapeake Assignment. LC 82-74134. (Illus.). 288p. 1983. 14.95 (ISBN 0-87033-302-X). Cornell Maritime.

WILDLIFE REFUGES

see also names of specific Wildlife refuges

Taber, Tom. Where to see Wildlife in California. Taber, Regi, ed. (Illus.). 112p. 1983. pap. write for info (ISBN 0-9609170-1-2). Oak Valley.

WILKES, JOHN, 1727-1797

LLoyd Hart, V. E. John Wilkes & the Founding Hospital at Aylesbury 1759-1768. 80p. 1980. text ed. 19.95x (ISBN 0-471-25860-1, Pub. by Wiley-Interscience). Wiley.

WILLIAM 3RD, KING OF GREAT BRITAIN, 1650-1702

Hatton, H. William III & Luis XIV. 342p. 1982. 49.00x (ISBN 0-85323-253-9, Pub. by Liverpool Univ England). State Mutual Bk.

WILLIAM, PRINCE OF WALES, 1982-
Hall, Trevor. Born to be King: Prince William of Wales. (Illus.). 128p. 1983. 25.00 (ISBN 0-517-39675-0). Crown.
WILLIAMS, CHARLES, 1886-1945
Howard, Thomas. The Novels of Charles Williams. LC 82-18902. 224p. 1983. 16.95 (ISBN 0-19-503247-0). Oxford U Pr.
WILLIAMS, TENNESSEE, 1914-
Williams, Dakin & Mead, Shepherd. Tennessee Williams: An Intimate Unauthorized Biography. 300p. 1983. 16.95 (ISBN 0-87795-488-7). Arbor Hse.
WILLS
see also Decedents' Estates; Probate Law and Practice
Fredenberg, D. Van. Wills for Washington. 3rd ed. 72p. 1982. pap. 3.95 (ISBN 0-88908-719-9). Self Counsel Pr.
Harris, Ollie K. & Slover, Elizabeth. So Let It Be. Ericson, Carolyn, ed. LC 82-84481. 99p. (Orig.). 1982. pap. 12.50 (ISBN 0-911317-03-1). Ericson Bks.
Johnson, Rees. Wills-Probate Procedure for Oregon. 2nd ed. (Illus.). 1983. pap. write for info (ISBN 0-88908-814-4). Self Counsel Pr.
McGovern, William M., Jr. Cases & Materials on Wills, Trusts, & Future Interests: An Introduction to Estate Planning. LC 82-20034. (American Casebook Ser.). 680p. 1982. text ed. 22.95 (ISBN 0-314-68828-5). West Pub.
O'Shaughnessy, Brian. The Will: A Dual Aspect Theory. LC 79-13524. (Cambridge Paperback Library Ser.). Date not set. Vol. 1, 251 pgs. pap. 14.95 (ISBN 0-521-27253-X); Vol. 2, 380 pgs. pap. 14.95 (ISBN 0-521-27254-8). Cambridge U Pr.
WILLS–GREAT BRITAIN
Weaver, F. W., ed. Somerset Medieval Wills. (Illus.). 1226p. 1982. text ed. 59.00x (ISBN 0-86299-022-X, Pub. by Sutton England). Humanities.
WILLYS JEEP
see Automobiles–Types–Jeep
WILSON, ALEXANDER, 1766-1813
Hunter, Clark. The Life & Letters of Alexander Wilson. (Memoirs Ser.: Vol. 154). 1983. 40.00 (ISBN 0-87169-154-X). Am Philos.
WILSON, ANGUS
McSweeney, Kerry. Four Contemporary Novelists: Angus Wilson, Brian Moore, John Fowles, V. S. Naipaul. 232p. 1983. 24.95 (ISBN 0-7735-0399-4). McGill-Queens U Pr.
WILSON, WOODROW, PRES. U. S., 1856-1924
Link, Arthur S. The Papers of Woodrow Wilson, June 25-August 20,1917. LC 66-10880. (Vol. 43). (Illus.). 552p. 1983. 32.50x (ISBN 0-691-04701-4). Princeton U Pr.
Seymour, Charles. Woodrow Wilson & the World War. 1921. text ed. 8.50x (ISBN 0-686-83860-2). Elliots Bks.
Wilson, Woodrow. A Crossroads of Freedom: Nineteen Twelve Campaign Speeches of Woodrow Wilson. Davidson, Joan W., ed. 1956. text ed. 65.00x (ISBN 0-686-83518-2). Elliots Bks.
WILSON'S DISEASE
see Hepatolenticular Degeneration
WILTSHIRE, ENGLAND
Davis, Michael, ed. In A Wiltshire Village: Scenes from Rural Victorian Life, Selected from the Writings of Alfred Williams. 192p. 1981. pap. text ed. 9.00x (ISBN 0-904387-62-3, 61185, Pub. by Alan Sutton England). Humanities.
WIMINUCHE INDIANS
see Indians of North America–Canada
WINCHESTER RIFLE
Madis, George. The Winchester Model Twelve. (Illus.). 1982. 14.95 (ISBN 0-910156-06-9). Art & Ref.
WIND
see Winds
WIND INSTRUMENTS
Perry, A. E. Hot-Wire Anemometry. (Illus.). 204p. 1982. 47.00x (ISBN 0-19-856327-2). Oxford U Pr.
Westphal, Frederick W. Beginning Woodwind Class Method. 4th ed. 230p. 1983. pap. text ed. write for info. (ISBN 0-697-03565-4). Wm C Brown.
WIND POWER
see also Windmills
Finlayson, A. N. International Wind Energy Symposium. 1982. 60.00 (100153). ASME.
Griffith, S. K., et al. Foreign Application & Export Potential for Wind Energy Systems. (Progress in Solar Energy Ser.: Suppl.). 250p. 1983. pap. 19.00 (ISBN 0-89553-130-5). Am Solar Energy.
Le Gourieres, D. Wind Power Plants: Theory & Design. 300p. 1982. 50.00 (ISBN 0-08-029967-9); pap. 25.00 (ISBN 0-08-029966-0). Pergamon.
Marier, Donald & Stoiaken, Larry. Alternative Sources of Energy Photovoltaics-Wind, No. 60. (Orig.). 1983. pap. 3.50 (ISBN 0-917328-50-7). ASEI.
Mitchell, A. Investigations of the Tornado Wind Energy System. (Progress in Solar Energy Supplements Ser.). 150p. 1982. pap. text ed. 13.50x (ISBN 0-89553-066-X). Am Solar Energy.
Mitchell, R. Darrieus Wind Turbine Airfoil Configurations. (Progress in Solar Energy Supplements SERI Ser.). 1983. pap. text ed. 6.00x (ISBN 0-89553-103-8). Am Solar Energy.
--Development of an Oscillating Vane Concept as an Innovative Wind Energy Conversion System. (Progress in Solar Energy Supplements SERI Ser.). 1983. pap. text ed. 9.00x (ISBN 0-89553-104-6). Am Solar Energy.
--Technical & Economic Assessment on Tethered Wind Energy Systems. (Progress in Solar Energy Supplements Ser.). 100p. 1982. pap. text ed. 10.50x (ISBN 0-89553-065-1). Am Solar Energy.
Noll, R. B. & Ham, N. D. Flexrotor Wind Energy: Innovative System Assessment: Supplement. (Progress in Solar Energy Ser.). 120p. 1983. pap. text ed. 12.00 (ISBN 0-89553-118-6). Am Solar Energy.
Strojan, C. & Lawrence, K. Environmental & Aesthetic Assessment of Small Wind Energy Systems. (Progress in Solar Energy Supplements Ser.). 60p. 1982. pap. text ed. 9.00x (ISBN 0-89553-080-5). Am Solar Energy.
WIND TUNNELS
see also Aerodynamics
Reinhold, Timothy A., ed. Wind Tunnel Modeling for Civil Engineering Applications. LC 82-14594. (Illus.). 704p. 1982. 55.00 (ISBN 0-521-25278-4). Cambridge U Pr.
WINDIC DIALECT (SLOVENIAN)
see Slovenian Language
WINDING UP OF COMPANIES
see Liquidation
WINDMILLS
see also Wind Power
Beedell, Suzanne. Windmills. (Illus.). 222p. 1982. Repr. of 1975 ed. 21.50 (ISBN 0-7153-6811-7). David & Charles.
Coulthard, Alfred J. & Watts, Martin. Windmills of Somerset & the Men Who Worked Them. 113p. 1982. 29.00x (ISBN 0-7050-0060-5, Pub. by C Skilton Scotland). State Mutual Bk.
Wailes, Rex. Windmills in England: A Study of Their Origin, Development & Future. 48p. 1982. 25.00x (ISBN 0-284-40007-6, Pub. by C Skilton Scotland). State Mutual Bk.
West, Jenny. The Windmills of Kent. 128p. 1982. 29.00x (ISBN 0-7050-0065-6, Pub. by C Skilton Scotland). State Mutual Bk.
WINDOW-BOX GARDENING
see Window-Gardening
WINDOW-GARDENING
Squire, David. Window-Boxes, Pots & Tubs: A Growing Guide. (Illus.). 168p. 1983. 22.50 (ISBN 0-7153-8385-X). David & Charles.
WINDOW-SILL GARDENING
see Window-Gardening
WINDOWBOX GARDENING
see Window-Gardening
WINDOWS
see also Glass
Jensen, Tom & Clee, Suzanne. Skylights: The Definitive Guide to Planning, Installing, Maintaining Skylights & Natural Light Systems. (Illus.). 192p. (Orig.). 1983. lib. bdg. 19.80 (ISBN 0-89471-195-4); pap. 8.95 (ISBN 0-89471-194-6). Running Pr.
Sunset Books & Sunset Magazine, ed. Windows & Skylights. LC 81-82871. (Illus.). 112p. (Orig.). 1982. pap. 4.95 (ISBN 0-376-01751-1). Sunset-Lane.
Suval, Judy & Phillips, Patty. How to Start a Window Cleaning Business. 2nd ed. (Illus.). 41p. (Orig.). 1981. pap. 9.95 (ISBN 0-9609532-0-5). I Can See.
WINDOWS, STAINED GLASS
see Glass Painting and Staining
WINDPIPE
see Trachea
WINDS
see also Hurricanes; Storms; Tornadoes
Marier, Donald & Winkle, Carl. Alternative Sources of Energy-Wind-Photovoltaics, No. 58. (Orig.). 1982. pap. 3.50 (ISBN 0-917328-48-5). ASEI.
WINDSOR, H. R. H., THE DUKE OF
see Edward 8th, King of Great Britain, 1894-1972
WINDSOR, HOUSE OF
Bloch, Michael. The Duke of Windsor's War: The Windsors in the Bahamas, 1940-1945. 388p. 1983. 16.95 (ISBN 0-698-11177-X, Coward). Putnam Pub Group.
WINE AND WINE MAKING
see also Cookery (Wine); Port Wine
Adams, L. D. The Wines of America. 2nd ed. 1978. 16.95 (ISBN 0-07-000318-1). McGraw.
Asher, Gerald. On Wine. 1982. 15.95 (ISBN 0-394-52737-2). Random.
Collier, Carole. Five Hundred Five Wine Questions Your Friends Can't Answer. (Five Hundred Five Quiz Ser.). 160p. (Orig.). 1983. 11.95 (ISBN 0-8027-0730-0); pap. 6.95 (ISBN 0-8027-7209-9). Walker & Co.
DeBlij, Harm J. Wine: A Geographic Appreciation. LC 82-20648. (Illus.). 320p. 1983. text ed. 18.95 (ISBN 0-86598-091-8). Allanheld.
De Groot, Roy A. The Wines of California, the Pacific Northwest & New York: First Classification of the Wineries & Vineyards. 448p. 1982. 19.95 (ISBN 0-671-40049-5). Summit Bks.
Holden, Ronald & Holden, Glenda. Touring the Wine Country of Oregon. (Touring the Wine Country of.....Ser.). (Illus.). 208p. (Orig.). pap. 6.95 (ISBN 0-910571-00-7). Holden Travel Res.
Howkins, Ben. Rich, Rare & Red: Guide to Port. (Illus.). 224p. 1983. 18.95 (ISBN 0-434-34909-7, Pub. by Heinemann England). David & Charles.
Jackson, David & Schuster, Danny. Grape Growing & Wine Making: A Handbook for Cool Climates. (Illus.). 194p. 1981. 27.50 (ISBN 0-9607896-0-X). Altarinda Bks.
Kafka, Barbara. American Food & California Wine. LC 82-47863. (The Great American Cooking Schools Ser.). (Illus.). 84p. 1982. 8.61i (ISBN 0-06-015066-1, HarpT). Har-Row.
Kleinsinger, Irene J. Wine Log. (Illus.). 96p. 1982. leather cover 19.95 (ISBN 0-9605146-4-3); suede cover 11.75 (ISBN 0-9605146-3-5); vinyl cover 5.50 (ISBN 0-9605146-2-7). Kleinsinger.
Lehrer, Adrienne. Wine & Conversation. LC 82-48538. 256p. 1983. 25.00x (ISBN 0-253-36550-3). Ind U Pr.
--Wine & Conversation. LC 82-48538. (Midland Bks.). 256p. (Orig.). 1983. pap. 17.50x (ISBN 0-253-20308-2). Ind U Pr.
MacDonald, Kenneth & Throckmorton, Tom. Drink Thy Wine with a Merry Heart: A Guide to Enjoying Wine. 136p. 1983. pap. 7.50 (ISBN 0-8138-0476-0). Iowa St U Pr.
Preston, William. Cork & Wine. (Illus.). 64p. 1983. 12.00 (ISBN 0-937088-04-8). Illum Pr.
Read, Jan. The Wines of Portugal. (Books on Wine). 192p. 1983. 11.95 (ISBN 0-571-11951-4); pap. 5.95 (ISBN 0-571-11952-2). Faber & Faber.
--The Wines of Spain. (Books on Wine). (Illus.). 272p. 1983. 11.95 (ISBN 0-571-11937-9); pap. 6.95 (ISBN 0-571-11938-7). Faber & Faber.
Reingold, Carmel B. California Cuisine. 192p. 1983. pap. 5.95 (ISBN 0-380-82156-7, 82156). Avon.
Torres, Miguel. Wines & Vineyards of Spain. 200p. 1982. 19.95 (ISBN 0-932664-27-X). Wine Appreciation.
The U. S. Wine Market. 1982. 475.00 (ISBN 0-686-38415-6, 131). Busn Trend.
Vintage Image, et al. Central Coast Wine Tour. 112p. 1983. pap. 3.95 (ISBN 0-932664-33-4). Wine Appreciation.
--Sonoma-Mendocino Wine Tour. 112p. 1983. pap. 3.95 (ISBN 0-932664-32-6). Wine Appreciation.
Wagenvoord, James. Doubleday Wine Companion, 1983. LC 81-43751. (Illus.). 160p. 1983. 16.95 (ISBN 0-385-18516-2). Doubleday.
Wasserman, Pauline & Wasserman, Sheldon. A Guide to Fortified Wines. LC 82-62295. (Illus.). 200p. 1983. pap. 9.95 (ISBN 0-910793-01-8). Marlborough Pr.
WINE AND WINE-MAKING–DICTIONARIES
Kaufman, William I. Pocket Encyclopedia of California Wine. 212p. 1983. pap. 4.95 (ISBN 0-932664-24-5). Wine Appreciation.
WINE AND WINE-MAKING–AUSTRALIA
Halliday, James. Wines & Wineries of Western Australia. (Illus.). 119p. 1983. text ed. 12.50x (ISBN 0-7022-1673-9). U of Queensland Pr.
WINE AND WINE-MAKING–FRANCE
Blachon, Roger, et al. Le Vin: French Wine Humor. 100p. 1982. 29.95 (ISBN 0-932664-28-8). Wine Appreciation.
WINE AND WINE MAKING–GERMANY
Hallgarten, S. F. German Wines. 399p. 1981. 12.50 (ISBN 0-686-43334-3). Intl Pubns Serv.
Livingstone-Learmonth, John & Master, Melvyn C. The Wines of the Rhone. 2nd ed. LC 82-24207. (Books on Wine). 255p. 1983. 24.95 (ISBN 0-571-18075-2); pap. 10.95 (ISBN 0-571-13055-0). Faber & Faber.
Pieroth, Kuno F. The Great German Wine Book. LC 82-61708. (Illus.). 208p. 1983. 22.50 (ISBN 0-8069-0254-X). Sterling.
Raelson, Jeffrey. Getting to Know German Wines. (Illus.). 80p. pap. 4.95 (ISBN 0-686-84222-7). Banyan Bks.
WINE AND WINE-MAKING–ITALY
Dallas, Philip. Italian Wines. 2nd ed. LC 82-24195. (Books on Wine). 336p. 1983. 24.95 (ISBN 0-571-18071-X); pap. 11.95 (ISBN 0-571-11994-8). Faber & Faber.
WINNIPEG, CANADA
Brownstone, Meyer & Plunkett, T. J. Politics & the Reform of Local Government in Metropolitan Winnipeg. LC 81-19658. (Lane Ser. in Regional Government). 240p. 1983. 35.00x (ISBN 0-520-04197-6). U of Cal Pr.
WIRE
Steel Wire & Wire Products. 1981. 395.00 (ISBN 0-686-38431-8, 331). Busn Trend.
WIRING, ELECTRIC
see Electric Wiring
WISC SUBTESTS
see Wechsler Intelligence Scale for Children
WISCONSIN–DESCRIPTION AND TRAVEL
Halla, Chris. Best Wisconsin Rivers: A Canoeist's Journal & Guide. (Illus.). 80p. (Orig.). 1983. pap. 8.95 (ISBN 0-942802-02-0). Northword.
Schneider, Richard C. The Natural History of the Minocki of the Lakeland Region of Wisconsin. (Illus.). 255p. 1980. 9.95 (ISBN 0-936984-03-1). Schneider Pubs.
Wood, Dave. Wisconsin Life Trip. 1982. 4.95 (ISBN 0-934860-21-1). Adventure Pubns.
WISCONSIN–HISTORY
Reetz, Elaine. Come Back in Time, Vol. 2. (Illus.). 240p. 1982. pap. 9.95 (ISBN 0-939398-03-6). Fox River.
Strang, William A. Wisconsin's Economy in Nineteen Ninety: Our History, Our Present, Our Future. (Wisconsin Economy Studies: No. 19). (Orig.). 1982. pap. 12.50 (ISBN 0-86603-014-X). Bureau Res U Wis.
WISCONSIN–HISTORY–BIBLIOGRAPHY
Bailey, Sturges W. Index to Portrait & Biographical Album of Green Lake, Marquette, & Waushara Cos., Wis., 1890. (Illus.). 44p. (Orig.). 1983. pap. text ed. write for info. (ISBN 0-910255-38-5). Wisconsin Gen.
WISCONSIN–IMPRINTS
Bailey, Sturges M. History of Columbia County, Wisconsin, Illnois, 1914: Index. 27p. (Orig.). 1982. pap. 5.00 (ISBN 0-910255-35-0). Wisconsin Gen.
WISCONSIN–SOCIAL LIFE AND CUSTOMS
Haggerty, Chas. P. Light Flashbacks to a Dark Time. (Illus.). 130p. 1981. pap. 6.95 (ISBN 0-9609936-0-6). Santiam Bks.
WISDOM
Wilson, Colin. Frankenstein's Castle: The Right Brain-Door to Wisdom. 128p. 1982. 11.95 (ISBN 0-906798-11-6, Pub. by Salem Hse Ltd.); pap. 6.95 (ISBN 0-906798-12-4). Merrimack Bk Serv.
WIT AND HUMOR
see also Anecdotes; Comedy; Humorists; Limericks; Nonsense-Verses; Puns and Punning; Riddles also American Wit and Humor; English Wit and Humor; and similar headings
Alden, Robert & Alden, Sunny. Lover's Coupon Book. (Illus.). 76p. 1983. pap. 4.95 (ISBN 0-911829-06-7). Sunfish Prods.
Aragones, Sergio. Mad Menagerie. 192p. 1983. pap. 1.95 (ISBN 0-446-90900-9). Warner Bks.
Badskey, Lorin J. Unaccustomed As I Am. 2nd ed. 1974. pap. 7.95 (ISBN 0-686-81687-0). Loru Co.
Bernard, Otis. Life With Yankee Wife. 120p. 1982. pap. 4.95 (ISBN 0-89221-093-1, Pub. by SonLife). New Leaf.
Bingham, Colin. Wit & Wisdom: A Public Affairs Miscellany. 368p. 1982. 35.00 (ISBN 0-522-84241-0, Pub. by Melbourne U Pr); pap. 21.00 (ISBN 0-522-84255-0). Intl Schol Bk Serv.
Blachon, Roger, et al. Le Vin: French Wine Humor. 100p. 1982. 29.95 (ISBN 0-932664-28-8). Wine Appreciation.
Bombeck, Erma. Erma Bombeck Giant Economy Size. LC 82-45557. (Illus.). 540p. 1983. price not set (ISBN 0-385-18394-1). Doubleday.
Cuppy, Will. How to Become Extinct. LC 82-17649. (Illus.). 114p. 1941. pap. 4.95 (ISBN 0-226-12826-1). U. of Chicago Pr.
Gardner, Gerald. The I Hate Hollywood Joke Book. 128p. (Orig.). 1982. pap. 1.95 (ISBN 0-345-29630-3). Ballantine.
Holley, Marietta. Samantha Rastles the Woman Question. Curry, Jane, ed. LC 82-13482. (Illus.). 234p. 1983. 14.95 (ISBN 0-252-01020-5). U. of Ill Pr.
Jillson, Joyce. Real Women Don't Pump Gas: A Guide to All That Is Divinely Feminine. (Illus., Orig.). 1982. pap. 3.95 (ISBN 0-671-46309-8). PB.
Keane, Bil. Eggheads. 128p. 1983. pap. 1.95 (ISBN 0-449-12456-8, GM). Fawcett.
Ketcham, Hank. Supercharged & Ever Ready. 128p. 1983. pap. 1.95 (ISBN 0-449-12391-X, GM). Fawcett.
Lindsay, Rae & Rowe, Diane. How to Be A Perfect Bitch. 1983. pap. 4.95 (ISBN 0-8329-0258-6). New Century.
Mad Editors. Mad Around the Town. (Mad Ser.: No. 63). 192p. 1983. pap. 1.95 (ISBN 0-446-30588-X). Warner Bks.
Morrow, Skip. The End. LC 82-83314. 96p. 1983. pap. 4.95 (ISBN 0-03-063401-6). HR&W.
Nachman, Gerald. Out on a Whim: Some Very Close Brushes with Life. LC 82-9412. 312p. 1983. 16.95 (ISBN 0-385-12340-X). Doubleday.
Orben, Robert. Twenty-One Hundred Laughs for All Occasions. LC 82-45448. 240p. 1983. 13.95 (ISBN 0-385-18248-1). Doubleday.
Saki. The Short Stories of Saki. Date not set. 7.95 (ISBN 0-394-60428-8). Modern Lib.
Shaw, Leo. Blazing Lecterns. (Illus.). 130p. (Orig.). 1983. pap. 8.00 (ISBN 0-943236-06-1). Servicios Intles.
--Female Charioteers (Women Drivers) 130p. (Orig.). 1983. pap. text ed. 8.00 (ISBN 0-943236-07-X). Servicios Intles.
--Kalifunkens. (Illus.). 130p. (Orig.). 1983. pap. text ed. 8.00 (ISBN 0-943236-05-3). Servicios Intles.
Stangland, Red. Grandson of Norwegian Jokes. 1982. pap. 2.00 (ISBN 0-9602692-9-0). Norse Pr.
Thaves, Bob. Frank & Ernest. 64p. 1983. pap. 3.95 (ISBN 0-03-063552-7). HR&W.
Trudeau, Garry. The Wreck of the Rusty Nail. LC 82-83139. 128p. 1983. pap. 5.25 (ISBN 0-03-061732-4). HR&W.
Wallace, Arthur & Wallace, Elna. Arthur Wallace's Punch Bowl. (Illus.). 64p. 1983. pap. 5.00 (ISBN 0-937892-10-6). LL Co.
Wilde, Larry. The New Official Cat Lovers Joke Book. 192p. (Orig.). 1983. pap. 1.95 (ISBN 0-523-42004-8). Pinnacle Bks.
WIT AND HUMOR–HISTORY AND CRITICISM
Bledsoe, Jerry. Where's Mark Twain When We Really Need Him? 183p. 1982. 9.95 (ISBN 0-9610320-0-6). Grape Hill Pr.

Marsh, Chelsea. If you Can't Find It in the Dark, Turn on A Light. LC 81-86205. (Illus.). 176p. 1983. pap. 6.95 (ISBN 0-86666-068-2). GWP.

WIT AND HUMOR–JUVENILE LITERATURE

see Wit and Humor, Juvenile

WIT AND HUMOR, JUVENILE

Brandreth, Gyles. The Super Joke Book. LC 83-397. (Illus.). 128p. (gr. 3 up). 1983. 7.95 (ISBN 0-8069-4672-5); PLB 9.99 (ISBN 0-8069-4673-3). Sterling.

Marsh, Carole. Life Isn't Fair: Murphy-like Lanes for Kids. (Tomorrow's Books). (Illus.). 74p. 1983. 2.95 (ISBN 0-935326-08-1). Gallopade Pub Group.

Phillips, Louis. How Do You Get a Horse Out of the Bathtub? Profound Answers to Preposterous Questions. (Illus.). 80p. 1983. 9.50 (ISBN 0-670-38119-5). Viking Pr.

Rosenbloom, Joseph. Daffy Definitions. LC 82-19323. (Illus.). 128p. (gr. 4 up). 1983. 7.95 (ISBN 0-8069-4668-7); PLB 9.99 (ISBN 0-8069-4669-5); pap. 2.95 (ISBN 0-8069-7704-3). Sterling.

--The Official Wild West Joke Book. LC 82-19537. (Illus.). 128p. (gr. 3 up). 1983. 7.95 (ISBN 0-8069-4666-0); PLB 9.99 (ISBN 0-8069-4667-9). Sterling.

Thaler, Mike. Scared Silly. (Illus.). 1982. pap. 1.95 (ISBN 0-380-80291-0, 80291, Camelot). Avon.

WIT AND HUMOR, PICTORIAL

see also Caricatures and Cartoons; Comic Books, Strips, Etc.

also American Wit and Humor, Pictorial; English Wit and Humor, Pictorial, and similar headings

Baxter, Glen. Atlas. 1983. 7.95 (ISBN 0-394-52994-4). Knopf.

Hollander, Nicole. Hi, This is Sylvia. I'm Not at Home Right Now, So When You Hear the Beep...Hang Up. (Illus.). 128p. 1983. pap. 4.95 (ISBN 0-312-37193-4); ppk of 10 49.50 (ISBN 0-312-37194-2). St Martin.

WITCHCRAFT

see also Demonology; Exorcism; Medicine-Man; Occult Sciences; Science; Voodooism

Gardner, Gerald B. Meaning of Witchcraft. (Illus.). 288p. 1982. pap. 9.95 (ISBN 0-939708-02-7). Magickal Childe.

Gardner, Gerard B. Witchcraft Today. (Illus.). 184p. pap. 9.95 (ISBN 0-939708-03-5). Magickal Childe.

Hansen, Harold A. The Witch's Garden. LC 78-5469. 128p. 1983. pap. write for info. (ISBN 0-87728-551-9). Weiser.

Jong, Erica. Witches. (Illus.). 1982. pap. 12.50 (ISBN 0-452-25357-8, Z5357, Plume). NAL.

Lamb, Geoffrey. Magic, Witchcraft & the Occult. (Illus.). 176p. 1982. Repr. of 1977 ed. pap. 9.95 (ISBN 0-88254-705-4). Hippocrene Bks.

Riva, Anna. Modern Witchcraft Spellbook. (Illus.). 64p. (Orig.). 1973. pap. 3.00 (ISBN 0-943832-02-0). Intl Imports.

Wedeck, Harry E. A Treasury of Witchcraft. 271p. 1983. pap. 4.95 (ISBN 0-8065-0038-7). Citadel Pr.

Witchcraft in Europe & America: Bibliography & Reel Index. 58p. 1983. 45.00 (ISBN 0-89235-074-1). Res Pubns Conn.

WITNESS BEARING (CHRISTIANITY)

see also Evangelistic Work; Prophecy (Christianity)

Bonnici, Roberta. I'm Scared to Witness! (Discovery Bks.). (Illus.). 48p. (Orig.). (YA) (gr. 9-12). 1979. pap. 1.35 (ISBN 0-88243-931-6, 02-0931). Gospel Pub.

Stratman, Chrysostomos H. & Makrakis, Apostolos. The Roman Rite in Orthodoxy, Part I: Additional Testimonies, Pt. II. 62p. 1957. pap. 1.00x (ISBN 0-938366-38-6). Orthodox Chr.

WITNESSES

see also Cross-Examination; Evidence (Law)

Taylor, Lawrence. Witness Immunity. 176p. 1983. 16.75x (ISBN 0-398-04765-0). C C Thomas.

WITTGENSTEIN, LUDWIG, 1889-1951

Kenny, Anthony. Wittgenstein. 1983. pap. 4.95 (ISBN 0-14-021581-6). Penguin.

Specht, E. K. Foundation of Wittgenstein's Late Philosophy. 218p. 1969. 14.50 (ISBN 0-7190-0312-1). Manchester.

Wright, G. H. von. Wittgenstein. 232p. 1983. 29.50x (ISBN 0-8166-1210-2); pap. 13.95x (ISBN 0-8166-1215-3). U of Minn Pr.

WIVES

see also Executives' Wives; Presidents–United States–Wives and Children

Finch, Janet. Married to the Job: Wives' Incorporation in Men's Work. 170p. 1983. text ed. 18.95x (ISBN 0-04-301149-7). Allen Unwin.

WODEHOUSE, PELHAM GRENVILLE, 1881-1975

Donaldson, Frances & Usborne, Richard. P. G. Wodehouse 1881-1981: Addreses given by Frances Donaldson & Richard Usborne. (Wodehouse Monograph: No. 2). 44p. (Orig.). 1982. pap. 14.50 (ISBN 0-87008-101-2). Heineman.

Douglas-Home, William & Muggeridge, Malcolm. P. G. Wodehouse: Three Talks & a Few Words at a Festive Occasion. (Wodehouse Monograph Ser.: No. 4). 48p. (Orig.). 1983. pap. 16.50 limited ed. (ISBN 0-87008-103-9). Heineman.

Gould, Charles E., Jr. The Toad at Harrow: P. G. Wodehouse in Perspective. (Wodehouse Monograph: No. 3). 10p. (Orig.). 1982. pap. 7.50 (ISBN 0-87008-102-0). Heineman.

Usborne, Richard. Dr. Sir Pelham Wodehouse Old Boy. (Wodehouse Monograph: No. 1). 34p. (Orig.). 1978. pap. 14.50 (ISBN 0-87008-100-4). Heineman.

WOLF, HUGO, 1860-1903

Carner, Mosco. Hugo Wolf Songs. LC 81-71301. (BBC Music Guides Ser.). 72p. (Orig.). 1983. pap. 4.95 (ISBN 0-295-95851-0). U of Wash Pr.

WOLFE, THOMAS, 1900-1938

Hoagland, Clayton & Hoagland, Kathleen. Thomas Wolfe Our Friend 1933-1938. Magi, Aldo P., ed. 21p. 1979. 25.00 (ISBN 0-912348-03-8). Croissant & Co.

WOLSEY, THOMAS, CARDINAL 1475?-1530

Creighton, Mandell. Cardinal Wolsey. 226p. 1982. Repr. of 1888 ed. lib. bdg. 35.00 (ISBN 0-8495-0878-9). Arden Lib.

WOLVES

see also Coyotes

Brown, David E., ed. The Wolf in the Southwest: The Making of an Endangered Species. 200p. 1983. 19.95x (ISBN 0-8165-0782-1); pap. 9.95 (ISBN 0-8165-0796-1). U of Ariz Pr.

McConoughey, Jana. The Wolves. Schroeder, Howard, ed. (Wildlife Habits & Habitat Ser.). (Illus.). 48p. (gr. 4-5). 1983. lib. bdg. 8.95 (ISBN 0-89686-225-9). Crestwood Hse.

Pringle, Laurence. Wolfman: Exploring the World of Wolves. LC 82-19144. (Illus.). 96p. (gr. 6-8). 1983. 12.95 (ISBN 0-684-17832-X). Scribner.

WOMAN

see Women

WOMEN

see also Female Offenders; Feminism; Girls; Married Women; Mothers; Single Women; Widows; Wives

also subdivision Women under names of ethnic groups, e.g. Indians of North America–Women; and headings beginning with the word Women

Agrippa, Cornelius. The Ladies' Oracle. 1982. pap. 5.95 (ISBN 0-374-18263-9). FS&G.

Darden, Ellington. Especially for Women. 2nd ed. LC 82-83949. (Illus.). 224p. 1983. pap. 7.95 (ISBN 0-88011-118-6). Leisure Pr.

Dayus, Kathleen. Her People. (Illus.). 194p. 1983. pap. 7.95 (ISBN 0-86068-275-7, Virago Pr). Merrimack Bk Serv.

Eichenbaum, Luise & Orbach, Susie. What Do Women Want. LC 82-14150. 288p. 1983. 13.95 (ISBN 0-698-11210-5, Coward). Putnam Pub Group.

Greenspan, M. A New Approach to Women & Therapy. 384p. 1983. 19.95 (ISBN 0-07-024349-2, GB). McGraw.

Haber, Barbara, ed. The Women's Annual, 1981: The Year in Review. 1982. lib. bdg. 50.00 (ISBN 0-8161-8614-6, Hall Reference). G K Hall.

Lindsay, Rae & Rowe, Diane. How to Be A Perfect Bitch. 1983. pap. 4.95 (ISBN 0-8329-0258-6). New Century.

McDowell, Mary. Never Too Late. 2nd ed. LC 82-82811. 160p. 1983. pap. 4.95 (ISBN 0-89081-365-5). Harvest Hse.

Marlow, Joan. The Great Women. 384p. 1983. pap. 7.95 (ISBN 0-89104-327-6, A & W Visual Library). A & W Pubs.

Peace, Sheila. An International Perspective on the Status of Older Women. 100p. (Orig.). 1981. pap. text ed. 5.00 (ISBN 0-910473-08-0). Intl Fed Ageing.

Pickford, Kaylan. Always a Woman. (Illus.). 1982. pap. 9.95 (ISBN 0-686-82122-X). Bantam.

Rich, Shelley, illus. The Family Bond: A Woman's Place. 72p. 1977. pap. text ed. 3.00 (ISBN 0-686-43396-3). N Grey Inc.

Vogel, Dan. How to Win with Women: A Guide to Meeting & Attracting Today's Women. 1983. 12.95 (ISBN 0-13-441220-6); pap. 5.95 (ISBN 0-13-441212-5). P-H.

WOMEN–ANATOMY AND PHYSIOLOGY

Lichtendorf, Susan S. Eve's Journey: The Physical Experience of Being Female. 368p. 1983. pap. 3.95 (ISBN 0-425-05868-9). Berkley Pub.

WOMEN–BIBLIOGRAPHY

Borenstein, Audrey. Older Women in Twentieth Century America: A Selected Annotated Bibliography. LC 82-6082. (Women Studies, Facts & Issues: Vol. 3). 351p. 1982. 40.00 (ISBN 0-8240-9396-8). Garland Pub.

Sakala, Carol. Women of South Asia: A Guide to Resources. LC 79-28191. 1980. lib. bdg. 30.00 (ISBN 0-527-78574-1); pap. 20.00 (ISBN 0-527-78575-X). Kraus Intl.

WOMEN–BIOGRAPHY

Bergman, Jay. Vera Zasulich: A Biography. LC 82-80927. 288p. 1983. 28.50x (ISBN 0-8047-1156-9). Stanford U Pr.

Brittain, Vera. Born Nineteen Twenty-Five. 384p. 1983. pap. 7.95 (ISBN 0-86068-270-6, Virago Pr). Merrimack Bk Serv.

Brombert, Beth A. Cristina: Portraits of a Princess. (Illus.). xii, 402p. 1977. pap. 10.95 (ISBN 0-226-07551-6). U of Chicago Pr.

Chernin, Kim. In My Mother's House. LC 82-19514. 320p. 1983. 14.95 (ISBN 0-89919-167-3). Ticknor & Fields.

Cruz, Manny & Symington, Nikki. Alice Barnes-American Activist. Kern, Ann T., ed. (Illus.). 52p. (Orig.). 1982. pap. 7.50 (ISBN 0-686-38731-7). Connections CA.

Gardiner, Muriel. Code Name "Mary". An American Woman in the Australian Underground. LC 82-20213. (Illus.). 200p. 1983. 14.95 (ISBN 0-300-02940-3). Yale Univ. Pr.

Hadas, Pamela W. Beside Herself: Pocahontas to Patty Hearst. LC 82-49003. 1983. 12.95 (ISBN 0-394-52993-6); pap. 7.95 (ISBN 0-394-71343-5). Knopf.

Heineman, Helen. Restless Angels: The Friendship of Six Victorian Women-Frances Wright, Camilla Wright, Harriet Garnett, Frances Garnett, Julia Garnet Pertz, Frances Trollope. LC 82-12421. (Illus.). 230p. 1983. text ed. 23.95x (ISBN 0-8214-0673-6, 82-84416); pap. 12.95 (ISBN 0-8214-0674-4, 82-84424). Ohio U Pr.

Jarnagin, Jutta F. The Raging. 245p. 1982. pap. 3.50 (ISBN 0-8423-5128-0). Tyndale.

Kennedy, Don H. Little Sparrow: A Partrait of Sophia Kovalevsky. LC 82-12405. (Illus.). 341p. 1982. text ed. 25.95x (ISBN 0-8214-0692-2, 82-84614); pap. 12.95 (ISBN 0-8214-0703-1, 82-84721). Ohio U Pr.

Lane, Rose W. & Boylston, Helen D. Travels with Zenobia: Paris to Albania by Model T Ford. Holtz, William, ed. LC 82-13554. 128p. 1983. text ed. 13.00x (ISBN 0-8262-0390-6). U of Mo Pr.

Morris, Charlotte, ed. From Showgirl to Skidrow. (Illus.). 160p. 1983. 12.50 (ISBN 0-89962-308-5). Todd & Honeywell.

Pearl, Cora. Grand Horizontal: The Erotic Memoirs of a Passionate Lady. Blatchford, William, ed. LC 82-42870. 192p. 1983. 16.95 (ISBN 0-8128-2917-4). Stein & Day.

Rathbone, Eleanor. The Disinherited Family. 360p. 1983. 19.95 (ISBN 0-905046-14-5); pap. 11.95 (ISBN 0-905046-13-7). Falling Wall.

Rose, Elizabeth A. The Lizzie's Own Journal La Vie Heureuse. Carson, Robert R., ed. 1983. 10.00 (ISBN 0-686-84439-4). Vantage.

Rusti, Renee K. Ladybug Smiled. 32p. 1983. 5.95 (ISBN 0-89962-310-7). Todd & Honeywell.

--Truly a Lady Bug. 64p. 1983. 5.95 (ISBN 0-89962-311-5). Todd & Honeywell.

Seacole, Mary. Wonderful Adventures of Mrs. Seacole in Many Ways. Alexander, Ziggi & Dewjee, Audrey, eds. 192p. 1983. 13.95 (ISBN 0-905046-22-6); pap. 7.95 (ISBN 0-905046-23-4). Falling Wall.

Stein, Jean & Pimpton, George, eds. Edie: An American Biography. 1983. pap. 3.95 (ISBN 0-440-13303-3). Dell.

Wilson, Elizabeth. Mirror Writing: An Autobiography. 162p. 1983. pap. 6.95 (ISBN 0-86068-241-2, Virago Pr). Merrimack Bk Serv.

Wordsworth, Jane. Women of the North. (Illus.). 224p. 1981. 19.95 (ISBN 0-686-84828-4, Pub. by W Collins Australia). Intl Schol Bk Serv.

WOMEN–BIOGRAPHY–JUVENILE LITERATURE

Peavy, Linda & Smith, Ursula. Women Who Changed Things. LC 82-21612. (Illus.). 208p. (gr. 7 up). 1983. 12.95 (ISBN 0-684-17849-4, ScribJ). Scribner.

WOMEN–CLOTHING

see Clothing and Dress; Costume

WOMEN–CLUBS

see Women–Societies and Clubs

WOMEN–COSTUME

see Costume

WOMEN–CRIME

see Female Offenders

WOMEN–DEFENSE

see Self-Defense for Women

WOMEN–DISEASES

see also Gynecology; Obstetrics; Women–Health and Hygiene;

also subdivision Diseases under names of organs and regions of the body, e.g. Uterus–diseases; and specific diseases

Notelowitz, Morris & Ware, Marsha. Stand Tall! The Informed Woman's Guide to Preventing Osteoporosis. (Illus.). 200p. 1982. 12.95 (ISBN 0-937404-12-8); pap. 6.95 (ISBN 0-937404-14-4). Triad Pub FL.

Thorp, Margaret. Female Persuasion: Six Strong-Minded Women. 1949. text ed. 16.50x (ISBN 0-686-83549-2). Elliots Bks.

Watson, Rita E. & Wallach, Robert C. New Choices, New Chances: A Woman's Guide to Conquering Cancer. 273p. 1983. pap. 6.95 (ISBN 0-686-42921-4). St Martin.

WOMEN–DRESS

see Clothing and Dress; Costume

WOMEN–ECONOMIC CONDITIONS

Siverd, Bonnie. Count Your Change: A Woman's Guide to Sudden Financial Change. 1983. 6.95 (ISBN 0-87795-460-7, Pub. by Priam). Arbor Hse.

WOMEN–EDUCATION

see Education of Women

WOMEN–EMANCIPATION

see Women's Rights

WOMEN–EMPLOYMENT

see also Home Labor; Vocational Guidance for Women

Beneria, Lourdes. Women & Development: The Sexual Division of Labour in Rural Societies. 288p. 1982. 25.95 (ISBN 0-03-061802-9). Praeger.

Bernardin. Women in the Work Force. 256p. 1982. 28.95 (ISBN 0-03-062471-1). Praeger.

Bloomfield, Horace R. Female Executives & the Degeneration of Management. (Illus.). 129p. 1983. 59.85 (ISBN 0-86654-063-6). Inst Econ Finan.

Doss, Martha M., ed. The Directory of Special Opportunities for Women. 290p. 1981. 18.95 (80-85274). Impact VA.

Dublin, Thomas, ed. Farm to Factory: Women's Letters, 1830-1860. 191p. 1982. pap. 9.50 (ISBN 0-231-05119-0). Columbia U Pr.

Hartmann, Susan M. The Home Front & Beyond: American Women in the 1940s. 1982. lib. bdg. 15.00 (ISBN 0-8057-9901-X, Twayne). G K Hall.

Heim, Kathleen M., ed. The Status of Women in Librarianship: Historical, Sociological, & Economic Issues. 350p. 1983. 29.95 (ISBN 0-918212-62-6). Neal-Schuman.

McFeely, Mary D. Women's Work in Britain & America from the Nineties to World War I: An Annotated Bibliography. 1982. lib. bdg. 24.95 (ISBN 0-8161-8504-2, Hall Reference). G K Hall.

Maresca, Carmela C. Careers in Marketing: A Woman's Guide. 240p. 1982. 16.95 (ISBN 0-13-115139-8); pap. 8.95 (ISBN 0-13-115121-5). P-H.

Molyneux, Maxine. State Policies & the Position of Women Workers in the People's Democratic Republic of Yemen, 1967-77. International Labour Office, ed. (Women, Work & Development Ser.: No. 3). viii, 87p. (Orig.). 1982. pap. 10.00 (ISBN 92-2-103144-6). Intl Labour Office.

Moses, Joel C. The Politics of Women & Work in the Soviet Union & the United States: Alternative Work Schedules & Sex Discrimination. LC 82-23307. (Research Ser.: No. 50). xii, 184p. 1983. pap. 9.50x (ISBN 0-87725-150-9). U of Cal Intl St.

Parcel, Toby L. & Mueller, Charles W., eds. Ascription & Labor Markets: Race & Sex Difference in Earnings. LC 82-22741. (Quantitative Studies Social Relations (Monograph)). Date not set. price not set (ISBN 0-12-545020-6). Acad Pr.

Petit, Ronald E. Women & the Career Game: Play to Win! (Illus.). 147p. (Orig.). 1982. pap. 7.95 (ISBN 0-941944-03-4). Prof Dev Serv.

Phongpaichit, Pasuk. From Peasant Girls to Bangkok Masseuses. International Labour Office, ed. (Women, Work & Development Ser.: No. 2). ix, 80p. (Orig.). 1982. pap. 8.55 (ISBN 92-2-103013-X). Intl Labour Office.

Reeves, Maud P. Round about a Pound a Week. 234p. 1983. pap. 6.95 (ISBN 0-86068-066-5, Virago Pr). Merrimack Bk Serv.

Sachs, Carolyn E. Invisible Farmers: Women in Agricultural Production. 180p. 1983. text ed. 22.50x (ISBN 0-86598-094-2). Allanheld.

Scharf, Lois & Jensen, Joan M., eds. Decades of Discontent: The Women's Movement 1920-1940. LC 81-4243. (Contributions in Women's Studies: No. 28). 352p. 1983. lib. bdg. 35.00 (ISBN 0-313-22694-6). Greenwood.

Sealander, Judith. As Minority Becomes Majority: Federal Reaction to the Phenomenon of Women in the Work Force 1920-1963. LC 82-15820. 224p. 1983. lib. bdg. 27.95 (ISBN 0-313-23750-6). Greenwood.

Segalla, Rosemary A. Departure from Traditional Roles: Mid-LIfe Women Break the Daisy Chains. Nathan, Peter E., ed. LC 82-20089. (Research in Clinical Psychology Ser.: No. 5). 164p. 1982. 34.95 (ISBN 0-8357-1386-5). Univ Microfilms.

Szinovacz, Maximiliane. Women's Retirement: Policy Implications of Recent Research. (Sage Yearbooks in Women's Policy Studies). (Illus.). 320p. 1982. 25.00 (ISBN 0-8039-1894-1); pap. 12.50 (ISBN 0-8039-1895-X). Sage.

Women at Work. (Mass. Hist. Soc. Picture Book Ser.). (Illus.). 1983. price not set. Mass Hist Soc.

Zimmerman, Jan. The Technological Woman: Interfacing with Tomorrow. 304p. 1983. 24.95 (ISBN 0-03-062829-6). Praeger.

WOMEN–EMPLOYMENT–GREAT BRITAIN

Chiplin, Brian & Sloane, Peter. Tackling Discrimination in the Workplace: An Analysis of Sex Discrimination in Britain. LC 82-4384. (Management & Industrial Relations Ser.: No. 2). (Illus.). 190p. Date not set. price not set (ISBN 0-521-24565-6); pap. price not set (ISBN 0-521-28788-X). Cambridge U Pr.

Porter, Marilyn. Home, Work, & Class Consciousness. 200p. 1983. 25.00 (ISBN 0-7190-0899-9). Manchester.

Thomis, Malcolm & Grimmett, Jennifer. Women in Protest Eighteen Hundred to Eighteen Fifty. LC 81-21290. 166p. 1982. 25.00x (ISBN 0-312-88746-9). St Martin.

WOMEN–ENFRANCHISEMENT

see Women–Suffrage

WOMEN–HEALTH AND HYGIENE

see also Beauty, Personal; Clothing and Dress; Cosmetics; Physical Education for Women; Sports for Women; Women–Diseases

Chamberlain, Mary. Old Wives Tales: Their History, Remedies, & Spells. 236p. 1983. pap. 7.95 (ISBN 0-86068-016-9, Virago Pr). Merrimack Bk Serv.

Golub, Sharon, ed. Menarche: The Physiological, Psychological, & Social Effects of the Onset of Menstruation. LC 82-48105. 352p. 1983. 29.95x (ISBN 0-669-05982-X). Lexington Bks.

Kunin, R. A. Mega-Nutrition for Women. 224p. 1983. 14.95 (ISBN 0-07-035642-4, GB). McGraw.

Lichtendorf, Susan S. Eve's Journey: The Physical Experience of Being Female. 368p. 1983. pap. 3.95 (ISBN 0-425-05868-9). Berkley Pub.

New England Association for Women in Psychology, ed. Current Feminist Issues in Psychotherapy. LC 82-15721. (Women & Therapy Ser.: Vol. 1, No. 3). 133p. 1983. text ed. 20.00 (ISBN 0-86656-206-0, B206). Haworth Pr.

Porcino, Jane. Growing Older, Getting Better: A Handbook for Women in the Second Half of Life. (Illus.). 288p. 1983. 17.95 (ISBN 0-201-05593-7); pap. 8.95 (ISBN 0-201-05592-9). A-W.

Rinzler, Carol Ann. Strictly Female: The Brand-Name Guide to Women's Health & Hygiene Products. (Medical Library). 304p. 1982. pap. 7.95 (ISBN 0-686-84851-9, 4138-7). Mosby.

Sonstegard, Lois, ed. Women's Health: Ambulatory Care, Vol. 1. 368p. 1982. 24.50 (ISBN 0-8089-1501-0). Grune.

--Women's Health: Childbearing, Vol. 2. Date not set. price not set (ISBN 0-8089-1508-8). Grune.

Villiers de l'Isle Adam. Tomorrow's Eve. Adams, Robert M., tr. & intro. by. LC 82-13411. 280p. 1982. 17.95 (ISBN 0-252-00942-8). U of Ill Pr.

Welch, Raquel. Raquel Welch's Health & Beauty Book. (Illus.). Date not set. pap. price not set. NAL.

WOMEN–HISTORY

Here are entered comprehensive works on the history of women, including works which deal collectively with their socio-economic, political and legal position, participation in historical events, contribution to society, etc. Works which deal specifically with their social condition and status, including historical discussions of the same, are entered under Women–Social conditions.

see also Women–Legal Status, Laws, etc.

Abbott, Shirley. Womenfolks: Growing up Down South. LC 82-16880. 224p. 1983. 13.95 (ISBN 0-89919-156-8). Ticknor & Fields.

Adams, Carol. Ordinary Lives: A Hundred Years Ago. 230p. 1983. pap. 8.95 (ISBN 0-86068-239-0, Virago Pr). Merrimack Bk Serv.

Balsdon, J. P. Roman Women. LC 82-48825. (Illus.). 354p. (gr. 11-12). 1983. pap. 6.95 (ISBN 0-06-464062-0, BN 4062). B&N NY.

Blade, Melinda K. Education of Italian Renaissance Women. rev. ed. LC 82-1190. (Woman in History Ser.: Vol. 21B). (Illus.). 86p. 1983. lib. bdg. 15.95 (ISBN 0-86663-070-8); pap. text ed. 8.95 (ISBN 0-86663-071-6). Ide Hse.

Clark, Alice. Working Life of Women in the Seventeenth Century. 368p. 1982. pap. 8.95 (ISBN 0-7100-9045-5). Routledge & Kegan.

Collis, Louise. Memoirs of a Medieval Woman. LC 82-48226. (Illus.). 288p. 1983. pap. 6.68i (ISBN 0-06-090992-7, CN 992, CN). Har-Row.

Deckard, Barbara S. The Women's Movement: Political, Socioeconomic, & Psychological Issues. 3rd ed. 528p. 1983. pap. text ed. 18.50 scp (ISBN 0-06-041615-7, HarpC). Har-Row.

Dublin, Thomas, ed. Farm to Factory: Women's Letters, 1830-1860. 191p. 1982. pap. 9.50 (ISBN 0-231-05119-0). Columbia U Pr.

Gould, Carol, ed. Beyond Domination: New Perspectives on Women & Philosophy. 220p. 1983. text ed. 21.50x (ISBN 0-8476-7202-6); pap. text ed. 9.95x (ISBN 0-8476-7236-0). Rowman.

Hrdy, Sarah B. The Women That Never Evolved. 276p. 1983. pap. 6.95x (ISBN 0-674-95541-2). Harvard U Pr.

Lucas, Angela. Women in the Middle Ages. LC 82-42578. 1982. 25.00x (ISBN 0-312-88743-4). St Martin.

Mortley, Raoul. Womanhood: The Feminine in Ancient Hellenism, Gnosticism, Christianity & Islam. 119p. 1983. text ed. 21.75x (ISBN 0-85668-912-2, Pub. by Aris & Phillips England); pap. text ed. 11.75x (ISBN 0-85668-913-0). Humanities.

Rice, Margery S. Working Class Wives: The Classic Account of Women's Lives in the 1930's. 212p. pap. 5.95 (ISBN 0-686-38947-6, Virago Pr). Merrimack Bk Serv.

Speth, Linda & Hirsch, Alison D. Women, Family, & Community in Colonial America: Two Perspectives. LC 82-23326. (Women & History Ser.: No. 4). 85p. 1983. text ed. 20.00 (ISBN 0-86656-191-9). Haworth Pr.

Ware, Susan. Holding Their Own: American Women in the 1930s. (History of American Women in the 20th Century Ser.). 1982. lib. bdg. 15.00 (ISBN 0-8057-9900-1, Twayne). G K Hall.

Warnicke, Retha M. Women of the English Renaissance & Reformation. LC 82-12180. (Contributions in Women's Studies: No. 38). 224p. 1983. lib. bdg. 29.95 (ISBN 0-313-23611-9, HQ1596). Greenwood.

WOMEN–LEGAL STATUS, LAWS, ETC.

see also Divorcees; Husband and Wife; Married Women; Women–Suffrage; Women's Rights

Biemer, Linda B. Women & Property in Colonial New York: The Transition from Dutch to English Law, 1643-1727. Berkhofer, Robert, ed. LC 82-23701. (Studies in American History & Culture: No. 38). 1983. write for info. (ISBN 0-8357-1392-X). Univ Microfilms.

Friedan, Betty. The Second Stage. 352p. 1982. pap. 5.95 (ISBN 0-671-45951-1). Summit Bks.

Khushalani, Y. The Dignity & Honour of Women As Basic & Fundamental Human Right. 1982. lib. bdg. 39.50 (ISBN 90-247-2585-2, Pub. by Martinus Nijhoff Netherlands). Kluwer Boston.

Wollstonecraft, Mary & Mill, John S. A Vindication of the Rights of Woman & the Subjection of Women. 300p. 1983. pap. text ed. 5.95x (ISBN 0-460-01825-6, Pub. by Evman England). Biblio Dist.

WOMEN–LITERARY COLLECTIONS

Here are entered collections of works written about women. Works which discuss the representation of women in literature are entered under Women in Literature. Collections of works written by women are entered under Women's Writings.; Works on the attainments of women as authors are entered under Women Authors.

Wilson, Barbara & Da Silva, eds. Backbone Three: Essays, Interviews & Photographs by Northwest Women. 90p. (Orig.). 1981. 4.95 (ISBN 0-686-38168-8). Seal Pr WA.

WOMEN–OCCUPATIONS

see Women–Employment

WOMEN–PHYSICAL EDUCATION

see Physical Education for Women

WOMEN–POLITICAL ACTIVITY

see Women in Politics

WOMEN–PRAYER-BOOKS AND DEVOTIONS

see also Women–Religious Life

Lee, Helen. This Is My Home, Lord. 128p. 1983. pap. 4.95 (ISBN 0-86683-683-7). Winston Pr.

Voigt, Tracy. Prayers of a Woman. rev. 3rd ed. 55p. 1982. Repr. of 1976 ed. spiral bdg. 4.00 (ISBN 0-686-37419-3). T Voigt.

WOMEN–PSYCHOLOGY

see also Femininity (Psychology)

Baruch, G. & Barnett, R. Lifeprints: New Patterns of Love & Work for Today's Women. 368p. 1983. 16.95 (ISBN 0-07-052981-7). McGraw.

Collier, Helen V. Counseling Women: A Guide for Therapists. (Illus.). 352p. 1982. text ed. 24.95 (ISBN 0-02-905840-6). Free Pr.

Eichenbaum, Luise & Orbach, Susie. Understanding Women: A Feminist Psychoanalytic Approach. 1983. 15.50 (ISBN 0-465-08864-3). Basic.

Friedman, Sonya. Men Are Just Desserts. 256p. 1983. 14.50 (ISBN 0-446-51255-9). Warner Bks.

Gilligan, Carol. In a Different Voice: Psychological Theory & Women's Development. 192p. 1983. pap. text ed. 5.95x (ISBN 0-674-44544-9). Harvard U Pr.

Lerner, Leila, ed. Women & Individuation: Emerging Views. 160p. 9.95 (ISBN 0-89885-134-3). Human Sci Pr.

Melamed, Elissa. Mirror, Mirror: The Terror of Not Being Young. 1983. price not set (ISBN 0-671-43429-2, Linden). S&S.

Neff, Miriam. Women & Their Emotions. (Orig.). 1983. pap. 5.95 (ISBN 0-8024-5151-9). Moody.

Sherman, J. A. & Denmark, F. L. The Psychology of Women: Future Directions in Research. LC 78-31824. 800p. 1979. 59.95 (ISBN 0-88437-009-7). Psych Dimensions.

Witt, Reni L. PMS: What Every Woman Should Know About Premenstrual Syndrome. LC 82-42724. 200p. 1983. 14.95 (ISBN 0-8128-2903-4). Stein & Day.

WOMEN–RELIGIOUS LIFE

Ashe, Kaye. New Women, New Church. 1983. 10.95 (ISBN 0-88347-145-0). Thomas More.

Campbell, R. K. Woman's Place. 32p. pap. 0.40 (ISBN 0-88172-014-3). Believers Bkshelf.

Caprio, Betsy. The Woman Sealed in the Tower: A Psychological Approach to Feminine Spirituality. 1983. pap. 5.95 (ISBN 0-8091-2486-6). Paulist Pr.

Clark, Elizabeth A. Jerome, Chrysostom, & Friends: Essays & Translations. (Studies in Women & Religion: Vol. 2). xi, 254p. 1983. Repr. of 1979 ed. 39.95x (ISBN 0-88946-541-X). E Mellen.

Hammett, Jenny. Woman's Transformation: A Psychological Theology. (Symposium Ser.). 112p. 1982. pap. 11.95 (ISBN 0-88946-918-0). E Mellen.

Herr, Ethel. Bible Study for Busy Women. 160p. 1983. pap. 6.95 (ISBN 0-8024-0147-3). Moody.

Kimball, Gayle. The Religious Ideas of Harriet Beecher Stowe: Her Gospel of Womanhood. (Studies in Women & Religion: Vol. 8). 216p. 1982. 34.95x (ISBN 0-88946-544-4). E Mellen.

Patterson, Bessie. The Wise Woman Knows. write for info. (ISBN 0-89137-422-1). Quality Pubns.

Price, Eugenia. A Woman's Choice. 192p. 1983. pap. 5.95 (ISBN 0-310-31381-3). Zondervan.

Radl, Shirley L. Money, Morals, & Motherhood: The Hidden Agenda of the Religious New Right. 1983. pap. 7.95 (ISBN 0-686-43193-6, Delta). Dell.

--Money, Morals, & Motherhood: The Hidden Agenda of the Religious New Right. 1983. 15.95 (ISBN 0-686-38881-X, Sey Lawr). Delacorte.

Rice, Barbara. The Power of a Woman's Love. 160p. 1982. 8.95 (ISBN 0-8007-1342-7). Revell.

Ruether, Rosemary R. Sexism & God Talk: Toward a Feminist Theology. LC 82-72502. 192p. 1983. 12.98 (ISBN 0-8070-1104-5). Beacon Pr.

Thomas, Sr. Evangeline, ed. Women's Religious History Sources. 400p. 1983. 65.00 (ISBN 0-8352-1681-0). Bowker.

WOMEN–RIGHTS OF WOMEN

see Women'S Rights

WOMEN–SELF-DEFENSE

see Self-Defense for Women

WOMEN–SEXUAL BEHAVIOR

see also Lesbianism

Botwin, Carol. Love Lives: Why Women Behave the Way They Do in Relationships. 1983. pap. 3.50 (ISBN 0-686-43066-2). Bantam.

Britton, Bryce. The Love Muscle: Every Woman's Guide to Intensifying Sexual Pleasure. (Illus.). 1982. pap. 7.95 (ISBN 0-452-25382-9, Plume). NAL.

Gallop, J. Feminism & Psychoanalysis: The Daughters Seduction. 1982. 55.00x (ISBN 0-333-29471-8, Pub. by Macmillan England). State Mutual Bk.

Institute for Advanced Study of Human Sexuality. Sex & the Married Woman. 224p. 1983. pap. 8.95 (ISBN 0-671-47283-6, Wallaby). S&S.

Kline-Graber, Georgia & Graber, Benjamin. Woman's Orgasm: A Guide to Sexual Satisfaction. 240p. 1983. pap. 3.50 (ISBN 0-446-31123-5). Warner Bks.

Lacan, J. Feminine Sexuality. Mitchell, J. & Rose, J., eds. 1982. 40.00x (ISBN 0-686-42938-9, Pub. by Macmillan England). State Mutual Bk.

Lacan, Jacques & Ecole Freudienne. Feminine Sexuality. Mitchell, Juliet, ed. Rose, Jacqueline, tr. from Fr. (Eng.). 1983. text ed. 18.95 (ISBN 0-393-01633-1, Co-pub. by Pantheon Bks.). Norton.

WOMEN–SOCIAL CONDITIONS

Here are entered works which deal specifically with the social conditions and status of women, including historical discussions of the same. Comprehensive works on the history of women, including works which deal collectively with their socio-economic, political and legal position, participation in historical events, contribution to society, etc. are entered under Women–History.

see also Women–Legal Status, Laws, Etc.

Andors, Phyllis. The Unfinished Liberation of Chinese Women, 1949-1980. LC 81-48323. 224p. 1983. 22.50x (ISBN 0-253-36022-6). Ind U Pr.

Cambridge Women's Study Group. Women in Society: Interdisciplinary Essays. 314p. 1983. pap. 9.95 (ISBN 0-86068-083-5, Virago Pr). Merrimack Bk Serv.

Dixon, Marlene. Women in Class Struggle. 3rd ed. 175p. 1983. pap. 7.95 (ISBN 0-89935-021-6). Synthesis Pubns.

Fair, Martha H. Tools for Survival: A Positive Action Plan for Minorities & Women. (Illus.). 160p. (Orig.). Date not set. pap. 12.95 (ISBN 0-911181-00-8). Harris Learning.

Friedan, Betty. The Second Stage. 352p. 1982. pap. 5.95 (ISBN 0-671-45951-1). Summit Bks.

McNamara, Jo A. & Harris, Barbara J. Women & the Structures of Social Order: Selected Research from the Fifth Berkshire Conference on the History of Women. 300p. Date not set. text ed. 27.50 (ISBN 0-8223-0558-5). Duke.

Moots, Patricia A. & Zak, Michele, eds. Women & the Politics of Culture: Studies in the Sexual Economy. (Illus.). 352p. (Orig.). 1983. pap. text ed. 14.50x (ISBN 0-582-28391-4). Longman.

Sapiro, Virginia. The Political Integration of Women. LC 82-2672. 248p. 1983. text ed. 16.95 (ISBN 0-252-00920-7). U of Ill Pr.

Schecter, Susan. Women & Male Violence: The Visions & Struggles of the Battered Women's Movement. 300p. 1982. 20.00 (ISBN 0-89608-160-5); pap. 7.50 (ISBN 0-89608-159-1). South End Pr.

Steinem, Gloria. Picking Up the Pieces: A Chronicle of Our Times. 288p. Date not set. 14.95 (ISBN 0-03-063236-6). HR&W.

Stiehm, J., ed. Women's & Men's Wars. 90p. 1983. 17.00 (ISBN 0-08-027949-X). Pergamon.

Stokland, Torill & Vajrathon, Mallica, eds. Creative Women in Changing Societies: A Quest for Alternatives. LC 82-16017. 192p. 1982. lib. bdg. 22.50 (ISBN 0-941320-06-5). Transnatl Pubs.

WOMEN–SOCIETIES AND CLUBS

see also names of individual societies and clubs

Fackler, Fern. A Women's Directory for the Cedar Rapids & Iowa City Area. 2nd ed. (Women's Directories-Cedar Rapids Iowa City-1983). 1983. pap. text ed. 3.50 (ISBN 0-910757-01-1). P R N Corp.

--A Women's Guide for the Cedar Rapids & Iowa City Area. (Women's Directories Cedar Rapids-Iowa City, 1982). 96p. 1982. pap. text ed. 3.50 (ISBN 0-910757-00-3). P R N Corp.

Miniear, Judy & Kennedy, Timothy. Kosciusko Ladies Clubs at Their Best, Vol. 1. (Illus.). 224p. 1982. pap. 9.50 (ISBN 0-910219-05-2). Little People.

WOMEN–SPORTS

see Sports for Women

WOMEN–SUFFRAGE

Liddington, Jill & Norris, Jill. One Hand Tied Behind Us: The Rise of the Women's Suffrage Movement. (Illus.). 304p. 1983. pap. 7.95 (ISBN 0-86068-008-8, Virago Pr). Merrimack Bk Serv.

Nichols, Carole. Vote & More for Women: Suffrage & After in Connecticut. (Women & History, No. 5). 88p. 1983. text ed. 20.00 (ISBN 0-86656-192-7, B192). Haworth Pr.

Pankhurst, Sylvia. The Suffragette Movement. 632p. 1983. pap. 10.95 (ISBN 0-86068-026-6, Virago Pr). Merrimack Bk Serv.

Rathbone, Eleanor. The Disinherited Family. 360p. 1983. 19.95 (ISBN 0-905046-14-5); pap. 11.95 (ISBN 0-905046-13-7). Falling Wall.

WOMEN–UNDERDEVELOPED AREAS

see Underdeveloped Areas–Women

WOMEN–AFRICA

Drewal, Henry J. & Drewal, Margaret T. Gelede: Art & Female Power among the Yoruba. LC 82-48388. (Traditional Arts of Africa Ser.). (Illus.). 352p. 1983. 32.50x (ISBN 0-253-32569-2). Ind U Pr.

Kingsley, Mary. Travels in West Africa: Congo Francais, Corisco & Cameroons. 742p. 1983. pap. 10.95 (ISBN 0-86068-267-6, Virago Pr). Merrimack Bk Serv.

Ntiri, Daphne W., ed. & intro. by. One is Not a Woman-One Becomes... The African Woman in a Transitional Society. (Orig.). 1982. pap. 8.95 (ISBN 0-937196-50-9). Sunset Prods.

Sweetman, David. Women Leaders in African History. 160p. 1982. 30.00x (ISBN 0-435-94479-7, Pub. by Heinemann England). State Mutual Bk.

WOMEN–ASIA

Allen, Michael & Mokherjee, Sal. Women in India & Nepal. 1982. pap. 24.00 (ISBN 0-908070-07-1, Pub. by Australia Nat Univ). South Asia Bks.

Sakala, Carol. Women of South Asia: A Guide to Resources. LC 79-28191. 1980. lib. bdg. 30.00 (ISBN 0-527-78574-1); pap. 20.00 (ISBN 0-527-78575-X). Kraus Intl.

Shimer, Dorothy B. Rice Bowl Women. 1982. pap. 3.95 (ISBN 0-451-62082-8, ME2082, Ment). NAL.

Soon Man Rhim. Women of Asia: Yesterday & Today. Fowler, Ruth, ed. 140p. (Orig.). 1982. pap. 6.95 (ISBN 0-377-00134-1). Friend Pr.

Van Esterik, Penny. Women of Southeast Asia: Illinois University Center For SEAsian Studies. (Occasional Paper Ser.: No. 9). viii, 274p. (Orig.). 1982. pap. 14.00 (Pub. by U Cal S&SE Asian Stud); pap. text ed. 14.00 (ISBN 0-686-38779-1). Cellar.

Wilson, Amrit. Finding A Voice: Asian Women in Britain. 180p. 1983. pap. 6.95 (ISBN 0-86068-012-6, Virago Pr). Merrimack Bk Serv.

WOMEN–AUSTRALIA

Grieve, Norma & Grimshaw, Patricia, eds. Australian Women: Feminist Perspectives. (Illus.). 256p. 1981. 34.00x (ISBN 0-19-554314-9). Oxford U Pr.

WOMEN–CARIBBEAN ISLANDS

Kerns, Virginia. Women & the Ancestors: Black Carib Kinship & Ritual. LC 82-2601. (Illus.). 256p. 1983. 17.95 (ISBN 0-252-00982-7). U of Ill Pr.

WOMEN–EGYPT

Atiya, Nayra. Khul-Khaal: Five Egyptian Women Tell Their Stories. LC 82-5773. (Contemporary Issues in the Middle East Ser.). (Illus.). 216p. 1982. text ed. 20.00x (ISBN 0-8156-0177-8); pap. 11.95 (ISBN 0-8156-0181-6). Syracuse U Pr.

WOMEN–ENGLAND

see Women–Great Britain

WOMEN–EUROPE

Mieczkowski, Bogdan. Social Services for Women in Eastern Europe. (ASN Series in Issues Studies (USSR & East Europe): No. 3). 128p. (Orig.). 1982. pap. 8.50 (ISBN 0-910895-00-7). Assn Study Nat.

Mobius, Helga. Woman in the Baroque Age. (Image of Women Ser.). (Illus.). 216p. 1983. 35.00 (ISBN 0-8390-0283-1). Allanheld & Schram.

WOMEN–FRANCE

Davenport, Michael G. The Fully Illustrated Book of the Most Notorious French Females at the Beginning of the Century. (A Memoir Collection of Significant Historical Personalities Ser.). (Illus.). 113p. 1983. 98.75 (ISBN 0-86650-048-0). Gloucester Art.

WOMEN–GREAT BRITAIN

Ballard, George. Memoirs of Several Ladies of Great Britain. 47.50 (ISBN 0-404-18053-1). AMS Pr.

Banks. Feminism & Family Planning in Victorian England. 154p. 1982. 39.00x (ISBN 0-85323-281-4, Pub. by Liverpool Univ England). State Mutual Bk.

Gittens, Diana. Fair Sex: Family Size & Structure in Britain, 1930-39. LC 81-21248. 256p. 1982. 27.50x (ISBN 0-312-27962-0). St Martin.

Hawkes, Jean, tr. & The London Journal of Flora Tristan 1842: The Aristocracy & the Working Class of England. 310p. 1983. pap. 7.95 (ISBN 0-86068-214-5, Virago Pr). Merrimack Bk Serv.

Strachey, Ray. The Cause: A Short History of the Women's Movement in Great Britain. (Illus.). 432p. 1983. pap. 8.95 (ISBN 0-86068-042-8, Virago Pr). Merrimack Bk Serv.

Warnicke, Retha M. Women of the English Renaissance & Reformation. LC 82-12180. (Contributions in Women's Studies: No. 38). 224p. 1983. lib. bdg. 29.95 (ISBN 0-313-23611-9, HQ1596). Greenwood.

Wilson, Amrit. Finding A Voice: Asian Women in Britain. 180p. 1983. pap. 6.95 (ISBN 0-86068-012-6, Virago Pr). Merrimack Bk Serv.

WOMEN–INDIA

Allen, Michael & Mokherjee, Sal. Women in India & Nepal. 1982. pap. 24.00 (ISBN 0-908070-07-1, Pub. by Australia Nat Univ). South Asia Bks.

Fruzzetti, Lina M. The Gift of a Virgin: Women, Marriage & Ritual in a Bengali Society. (Illus.). 170p. Date not set. 22.50 (ISBN 0-8135-0939-4). Rutgers U Pr.

WOMEN–IRAN

Nashat, Guity. Women & Revolution in Iran. (Replica Edition Ser.). 250p. 1982. 18.50 (ISBN 0-86531-931-6). Westview.

Sanasarian. Iranian Women's Movement. 190p. 1982. 23.95 (ISBN 0-03-059632-7). Praeger.

WOMEN–ITALY

Balsdon, J. P. Roman Women. LC 82-48825. (Illus.). 354p. (gr. 11-12). 1983. pap. 6.95 (ISBN 0-06-464062-0, BN 4062). B&N NY.

Blade, Melinda K. Education of Italian Renaissance Women. rev. ed. LC 82-1190. (Woman in History Ser.: Vol. 21B). (Illus.). 86p. 1983. lib. bdg. 15.95 (ISBN 0-86663-070-8); pap. text ed. 8.95 (ISBN 0-86663-071-6). Ide Hse.

WOMEN–JAPAN

Robins-Mowry, Dorothy. The Hidden Sun: Women of Modern Japan. 370p. 1983. lib. bdg. 30.00 (ISBN 0-86531-421-7); pap. text ed. 11.95 (ISBN 0-86531-437-3). Westview.

Sievers, Sharon L. Flowers in Salt: The Beginnings of Feminist Consciousness in Modern Japan. LC 82-60104. (Illus.). 256p. 1983. 22.50x (ISBN 0-8047-1165-8). Stanford U Pr.

WOMEN–LATIN AMERICA

Bronstein, Audrey. The Triple Struggle: Latin American Peasant Women. 268p. Date not set. 20.00 (ISBN 0-89608-180-X); pap. 7.50 (ISBN 0-89608-179-6). South End Pr.

WOMEN–NIGERIA

Nba, Nina E. Nigerian Women Mobilized: Women's Political Activity in Southern Nigeria, 1900-1965. LC 82-15477. (Research Ser.: No. 48). (Illus.). xii, 348p. 1982. pap. 12.95x (ISBN 0-87725-148-7). U of Cal Intl St.

WOMEN–RUSSIA

Engel, Barbara A. Mothers & Daughters: Women of the Intelligentsia in Nineteenth Century Russia. LC 82-14611. (Illus.). 224p. 1983. 39.50 (ISBN 0-521-25125-7). Cambridge U Pr.

Moses, Joel C. The Politics of Women & Work in the Soviet Union & the United States: Alternative Work Schedules & Sex Discrimination. LC 82-23307. (Research Ser.: No. 50). xii, 184p. 1983. pap. 9.50x (ISBN 0-87725-150-9). U of Cal Intl St.

WOMEN–TURKEY

Abadan-Unat, Nermin. Women in Turkish Society. (Social, Economic & Political Studies of the Middle East Ser.: Vol. 30). (Illus.). xii, 338p. 1982. pap. write for info. (ISBN 90-04-06346-3). E J Brill.

WOMEN–UNITED STATES

see also Presidents–United States–Wives and Children

Banner, Lois W. American Beauty. LC 82-4738. 352p. 1983. 17.95 (ISBN 0-394-51923-X). Knopf.

Bence, Evelyn. Leaving Home: The Making of an Independent Woman. LC 82-15910. 192p. 1982. Pub. by Bridgebooks Pub. 9.95 (ISBN 0-664-27005-0). Westminster.

Conway, Jill K. Society & the Sexes in Early Industrial America: Part One of a Bibliographical Guide to the Study of the History of American Women. LC 82-48041. 350p. 1982. lib. bdg. 40.00 (ISBN 0-8240-9936-2). Garland Pub.

Henson, Margaret S. Anglo American Women in Texas, 1820-1950. Rosenbaum, Robert J., ed. (Texas History Ser.). 30p. 1982. pap. text ed. 1.95x (ISBN 0-89641-104-4). American Pr.

Langland, Elizabeth & Gove, Walter, eds. A Feminist Perspective in the Academy: The Difference It Makes. LC 82-17520. 168p. 1981. pap. 5.95 (ISBN 0-226-46875-5). U of Chicago Pr.

Malone, Ann. Women in Texas. (Southwestern Studies: No. 70). 72p. 1983. pap. 4.00 (ISBN 0-87404-130-9). Tex Western.

Markson, Elizabeth W., ed. Older Women: Issues & Prospects. LC 81-48025. (Boston University Gerontology Ser.). 352p. 1983. 29.95x (ISBN 0-669-05245-0). Lexington Bks.

Moses, Joel C. The Politics of Women & Work in the Soviet Union & the United States: Alternative Work Schedules & Sex Discrimination. LC 82-23307. (Research Ser.: No. 50). xii, 184p. 1983. pap. 9.50x (ISBN 0-87725-150-9). U of Cal Intl St.

Sapiro, Virginia. The Political Integration of Women. LC 82-2672. 248p. 1983. text ed. 16.95 (ISBN 0-252-00920-7). U of Ill Pr.

Van Kirk, Sylvia. Many Tender Ties: Women in Fur-Trade Society, Sixteen Seventy to Eighteen Seventy. LC 82-40457. (Illus.). 303p. 1983. 22.50x (ISBN 0-8061-1842-3); pap. 9.95x (ISBN 0-8061-1847-4). U of Okla Pr.

Wilson, Vincent, Jr. Book of Distinguished American Women. (Illus.). 1983. 4.50 (ISBN 0-910086-05-2). Am Hist Res.

Wong, Diane Yen-Mei. Dear Diane: Letters from Our Daughters. Kim, Elaine, intro. by. (Illus.). 90p. (Eng. & Korean.). 1983. pap. 4.95 (ISBN 0-936434-08-2). SF Stud Ctr.

--Dear Diane: Letters from Our Daughters. Kim, Elaine, intro. by. 80p. (Orig., Eng. & Chinese.). 1983. pap. 4.95 (ISBN 0-936434-07-4). SF Stud Ctr.

--Dear Diane: Questions & Answers for Asian American Women. Kim, Elaine, intro. by. (Illus.). 96p. (Orig.). 1983. pap. 4.95 (ISBN 0-936434-09-0). SF Stud Ctr.

WOMEN–UNITED STATES–BIBLIOGRAPHY

Addis, Patricia K. Through a Woman's I: An Annotated Bibliography of American Women's Autobiographical Writings, 1946-1976. LC 82-10813. 621p. 1983. 37.50 (ISBN 0-8108-1588-5). Scarecrow.

WOMEN–UNITED STATES–BIOGRAPHY

Alexander, Shana. Very Much a Lady: The Untold Story of Jean Harris & Dr. Herman Tarnower. 1983. 17.50 (ISBN 0-316-03125-9). Little.

Bird, Isabelle. A Lady's Life in the Rocky Mountains. 298p. 1983. pap. 8.95 (ISBN 0-86068-267-6, Virago Pr). Merrimack Bk Serv.

Canfield, Gae W. Sarah Winnemucca of the Northern Paiutes. LC 82-40448. (Illus.). 336p. 1983. 19.95 (ISBN 0-8061-1814-8). U of Okla Pr.

Kulin, Agnes. Hilda. 1983. 10.00 (ISBN 0-533-05608-X). Vantage.

Voth, Anne. Women in the New Eden. LC 82-24793. (Illus.). 224p. (Orig.). 1983. lib. bdg. 21.50 (ISBN 0-8191-2917-8); pap. text ed. 10.75 (ISBN 0-8191-2918-6). U Pr of Amer.

WOMEN, AFRO-AMERICAN

see Afro-American Women

WOMEN, ARAB

Molyneux, Maxine. State Policies & the Position of Women Workers in the People's Democratic Republic of Yemen, 1967-77. International Labour Office, ed. (Women, Work & Development Ser.: No. 3). viii, 87p. (Orig.). 1982. pap. 10.00 (ISBN 92-2-103144-6). Intl Labour Office.

WOMEN, DISCRIMINATION AGAINST

see Sex Discrimination

WOMEN, ISLAMIC

see Women, Muslim

WOMEN, JEWISH

Bitton-Jackson, Livia. Madonna or Courtesan: The Jewish Woman in Christian Literature. 160p. 1983. pap. 7.95 (ISBN 0-8164-2440-3). Seabury.

Brooten, Bernadette J. Women Leaders in the Ancient Synagogue: Inscriptional Evidence & Background Issues. LC 82-10658. (Brown Judaic Studies). 292p. 1982. pap. 20.00 (ISBN 0-89130-587-4, 14 00 36). Scholars Pr CA.

Henry, Sondra & Taitz, Emily. Written Out of History: Our Jewish Foremothers. 2nd, rev. ed. (Illus.). 1983. pap. 8.50x (ISBN 0-9602036-8-0). Biblio NY.

The Jewish Woman in America. pap. 2.50 (ISBN 0-686-81723-0). NCJW.

Junior Service League of Brooksville Florida. A Pinch of Sunshine. Bartos, Beth, ed. (Illus.). 336p. 1982. pap. 9.95 (ISBN 0-939114-63-1). Wimmer Bks.

Kruger, Mollee. Daughters of Chutzpah: Humorous Verse on the Jewish Woman. LC 82-71394. (Illus.). 110p. (Orig.). 1983. pap. 5.50x (ISBN 0-9602036-7-2). Biblio NY.

National Council of Jewish Women Greater Detroit Section. Fiddler in the Kitchen. Schonwetter, Norma, ed. (Illus.). 192p. 1982. pap. 8.50 (ISBN 0-939114-76-3). Wimmer Bks.

Where There's a Woman. Date not set. pap. 3.25 (ISBN 0-686-81717-6). NCJW.

WOMEN, MUSLIM

Al-Hibri, A. Women & Islam. 106p. 1982. 17.80 (ISBN 0-08-027928-7). Pergamon.

Badawi, Gamal. The Status of Woman in Islam. Al-Jarrahi, Abdussamad, ed. Bekkari, Muhammad, tr. from English. 20p. (Orig.). 1982. pap. 2.00 (ISBN 0-89259-036-X). Am Trust Pubns.

Badawi, Gamal A. The Status of Woman in Islam: (French Edition) Quinlan, Hamid, ed. LC 82-74127. (Illus.). 28p. 1983. pap. 0.75 (ISBN 0-89259-039-4). Am Trust Pubns.

Siddiqui, M. S. Blessed Women of Islam. 12.50 (ISBN 0-686-83898-X). Kazi Pubns.

WOMEN, ORDINATION OF

see Ordination of Women

WOMEN ACTORS

see Actors and Actresses

WOMEN AND RELIGION

see also Women–Religious Life; Women Clergy

Williams, James G. Women Recounted: Narrative Thinking & the God of Israel. (Bible & Literature Ser.: No. 6). 128p. 1982. text ed. 21.95 (ISBN 0-907459-18-8, Pub. by Almond Pr England); pap. 10.95 (ISBN 0-907459-19-6). Eisenbrauns.

WOMEN AND SOCIALISM

see also Communism; Socialism

Dunayavskaya, Raya. Rosa Luxemburg, Women's Liberation & Marx's Philosophy of Revolution. 260p. 1982. text ed. 19.95x (ISBN 0-391-02569-4, Pub. by Harvester England); pap. text ed. 10.95x (ISBN 0-391-02793-X). Humanities.

Stacey, Judith. Patriarchy & Socialist Revolution in China. LC 82-8482. 330p. 1983. text ed. 28.50x (ISBN 0-520-04825-3). U of Cal Pr.

Taylor, Barbara. Eve & the New Jerusalem: Socialism & Feminism in the Nineteenth Century. 315p. 1983. pap. 9.95 (ISBN 0-686-37899-7). Pantheon.

WOMEN ARTISTS

Here are entered works on the attainments of women as artists. Works dealing with women as represented in art are entered under Women in Art.

Burke, Mary Alice H. Elizabeth Nourse, Eighteen Fifty-Nine to Nineteen Thirty-Eight: A Salon Career. (Illus.). 280p. 1983. text ed. 47.50x (ISBN 0-87474-298-6). Smithsonian.

Roth, Moira, ed. The Amazing Decade-Women's Performance Art in America 1970-1980. (Illus.). 250p. 1983. pap. 10.00 (ISBN 0-937122-09-2). Astro Artz.

Rubinstein, Charlotte S. American Women Artists: From Early Indian Times to the Present. 1982. lib. bdg. 39.95 (ISBN 0-8161-8535-2, Hall Reference). G K Hall.

WOMEN AS MUSICIANS

see Women Musicians

WOMEN AS TEACHERS

see Women Teachers

WOMEN AUTHORS

Here are entered works on the attainments of women as authors. Collections of works written by women are entered under Women's Writings. Collections of works in two or more literary forms written about women are entered under Women–Literary Collections. Works which discuss the representation of women in literature are entered under Women in Literature.

Abel, Elizabeth & Hirsch, Marianne, eds. The Voyage IN: Fictions of Female Development. LC 82-40473. 340p. 1983. text ed. 25.00x (ISBN 0-87451-250-6); pap. 12.50 (ISBN 0-87451-251-4). U Pr of New Eng.

Bradbrook, Muriel. Women & Literature Seventeen Seventy-Nine to Nineteen Eighty-Two: The Collected Papers of Muriel Bradbrook, Vol. II. LC 82-13914. 180p. 1983. text ed. 24.95x (ISBN 0-389-20295-9). B&N Imports.

Coven, Brenda. American Women Dramatists of the Twentieth Century: A Bibliography. LC 82-5942. 244p. 1982. 15.00 (ISBN 0-8108-1562-1). Scarecrow.

Danly, Robert L. In the Shade of Spring Leaves: The Life & Writings of Higuchi Ichiyo, a Woman of Letters in Meiji Japan. pap. 10.95 (ISBN 0-686-42821-8, Y-456). Yale U Pr.

Donavan, Josephine. New England Local Color Literature: A Women's Tradition. LC 82-40252. 250p. 1982. 12.95 (ISBN 0-8044-2138-2). Ungar.

Duke, Maurice & Bryer, Jackson R., eds. American Women Writers: Bibliographical Essays. LC 82-6156. 464p. 1983. lib. bdg. 29.95 (ISBN 0-313-22116-2, DAW/). Greenwood.

Faust, Langdon L., ed. American Women Writers: A Critical Reference Guide from Colonial Times to the Present, Vol. 1, A-L. Abr. ed. LC 82-40286. 445p. 1983. pap. 14.95 (ISBN 0-8044-6164-3). Ungar.

--American Women Writers: A Critical Reference Guide from Colonial Times to the Present, Vol. 2, M-Z. Abr. ed. LC 82-40286. 445p. 1983. pap. 14.95 (ISBN 0-8044-6165-1). Ungar.

Figes, E. Sex & Subterfuge: Women Novelists to 1850. 1982. 50.00x (ISBN 0-333-29208-1, Pub. by Macmillan England). State Mutual Bk.

Huf, L. M. Portrait of the Artist as a Young Woman. LC 82-40263. (Literature & Life Ser.). 200p. 1983. 13.50 (ISBN 0-8044-2406-3). Ungar.

Morgan, Fidelis. The Female Wits: Women Playwrights of the Restoration. 468p. 1983. pap. 14.95 (ISBN 0-86068-231-5, Virago Pr). Merrimack Bk Serv.

Schlobin, Roger C. Urania's Daughters: A Checklist of Women Science Fiction Writers, 1692-1982. (Illus., Orig.). 1982. 11.95x (ISBN 0-916732-57-6); pap. 5.95x (ISBN 0-916732-56-8). Starmont Hse.

Staley, T. F. Twentieth-Century Women Novelists. 1982. 70.00x (ISBN 0-686-42935-4, Pub. by Macmillan England). State Mutual Bk.

Stevenson, Catherine B. Victorian Women Travel Writers in Africa. (English Authors Ser.). 184p. 1982. lib. bdg. 17.95 (ISBN 0-8057-6835-1, Twayne). G K Hall.

Yang, Gladys, intro. by. Seven Contemporary Chinese Women Writers. 282p. 1982. pap. 4.95 (ISBN 0-295-96017-5, Pub. by Chinese Lit Beijing). U of Wash Pr.

WOMEN CLERGY

see also Ordination of Women

Chittister, Joan. Women, Ministry & the Church. LC 82-62418. 1983. pap. 7.95 (ISBN 0-8091-2528-5). Paulist Pr.

WOMEN CRIMINALS

see Female Offenders

WOMEN IN ART

Here are entered works dealing with women as represented in art. Works on the attainments of women artists are entered under the heading Women Artists.

Ludig, Sandra G. Between the Lines: Ladies & Letters at the Clark. (Illus.). 39p. 1982. pap. 4.00 (ISBN 0-686-37428-2). S & F Clark.

WOMEN IN BUSINESS

Ackerman, Diane L. Getting Rich: A Smart Woman's Guide to Successful Money Management. 1982. pap. 3.95 (ISBN 0-553-22672-X). Bantam.

Chew, Doris N. Ada Nield Chew: The Life & Writings of a Working Woman. 256p. 1983. pap. 8.95 (ISBN 0-86068-294-3, Virago Pr). Merrimack Bk Serv.

Collins, Nancy W. Professional Women & Their Mentors: A Practical Guide to Mentoring for the Woman Who Wants to Get Ahead. 163p. 1982. 12.95 (ISBN 0-13-725994-8); pap. 6.95 (ISBN 0-13-725986-7). P-H.

De Feldy, L. Elizabeth. Common Sense Etiquette: For Business Women, Wives, Mistresses. (Illus.). 119p. lib. bdg. 15.00x (ISBN 0-935402-15-2); pap. 14.00 (ISBN 0-935402-16-0). Intl Comm Serv.

Farley, Jennie, ed. The Woman in Management: Career & Family Issues. (Orig.). 1983. pap. price not set (ISBN 0-87546-100-X). ILR Pr.

Hill, Robert B. Occupational Attainment: Minorities & Women in Selected Industries, 1969-1979. 150p. 1983. pap. 6.95 (ISBN 0-87855-606-0). Transaction Bks.

Pinchbeck, Ivy. Women Workers & the Industrial Revolution 1750-1850. 342p. 1983. pap. 7.95 (ISBN 0-86068-170-X, Virago Pr). Merrimack Bk Serv.

Shuch, Milton L. Women in Management: Environment & Role. (ITT Key Issues Lecture Ser.). 93p. 1981. pap. text ed. 6.50 (ISBN 0-672-97919-5). Bobbs.

Williams, Cortez. Women in Business: A Manual for the New Entrepreneur. 179p. 1982. pap. 15.00 (ISBN 0-9609114-1-3). Develop Res.

WOMEN IN CHRISTIANITY

see also Women Clergy; Women in the Bible

MacDonald, Dennis Ronald. The Legend & the Apostle: The Battle for Paul in Story & Canon. LC 82-21953. 144p. (Orig.). 1983. pap. 9.95 (ISBN 0-664-24464-5). Westminster.

Maitland, Sara. A Map of the New Country: Women & Christianity. LC 82-13142. 218p. 1983. 12.95 (ISBN 0-7100-9326-8). Routledge & Kegan.

Wise, Karen. Confessions of a Totaled Woman. 128p. 1983. pap. 3.95 (ISBN 0-8407-5785-9). Nelson.

WOMEN IN DRAMA

see Women in Literature

WOMEN IN LITERATURE

Here are entered works which discuss the representation of women in literature. Collections of works in two or more literary forms written about women are entered under Women–Literary Collections. Collections of works written by women are entered under Women's Writings. Works on the attainments of women as authors are entered under Women Authors.

Abel, Elizabeth & Hirsch, Marianne, eds. The Voyage IN: Fictions of Female Development. LC 82-40473. 340p. 1983. text ed. 25.00x (ISBN 0-87451-250-6); pap. 12.50 (ISBN 0-87451-251-4). U Pr of New Eng.

Baker, Mariam. Woman as Divine: Tales of the Goddess. (Illus., Orig.). 1982. pap. 8.95 (ISBN 0-9609916-0-3). Crescent Heart.

Barickman, Richard, et al. Corrupt Relations: Dickens, Thackeray, Trollope, Collins & the Victorian Sexual System. 1982. 25.00 (ISBN 0-686-82110-6). Columbia U Pr.

Bitton-Jackson, Livia. Madonna or Courtesan: The Jewish Woman in Christian Literature. 160p. 1983. pap. 7.95 (ISBN 0-8164-2440-3). Seabury.

Demouy, Jane K. Katherin Anne Porter's Women: The Eye of Her Fiction. 248p. 1982. text ed. 22.50x (ISBN 0-292-79018-X). U of Tex Pr.

Gallagher, S. F., ed. Woman in Irish Legend, Life & Literature. LC 82-22792. (Irish Literary Studies: No. 14). 154p. 1983. text ed. 28.50x (ISBN 0-389-20361-0). B&N Imports.

Hazen, Helen. Endless Rapture: Rape, Romance, & the Female Imagination. 192p. 1983. 11.95 (ISBN 0-686-83854-8, ScribT). Scribner.

Holledge, Julie. Innocent Flowers: Women in the Edwardian Theater. (Illus.). 218p. 1983. pap. 7.95 (ISBN 0-86068-071-1, Virago Pr). Merrimack Bk Serv.

Kert, Bernice. The Hemingway Women. (Illus.). 1983. 20.00 (ISBN 0-393-01720-6). Norton.

Miller, Beth, ed. Women in Hispanic Literature: Icons & Fallen Idols. LC 81-14663. 480p. 1983. text ed. 27.00x (ISBN 0-520-04291-3); pap. text ed. 9.95 (ISBN 0-520-04367-7). U of Cal Pr.

Slater, Michael. Dickens & Women. LC 82-62351. (Illus.). 512p. 1983. 28.50x (ISBN 0-8047-1180-1). Stanford U Pr.

Trenchard, Warren C. Ben Sira's View of Women: A Literary Analysis. LC 82-16755. (Brown Judaic Studies: No. 38). 352p. 1982. pap. 15.75 (ISBN 0-89130-593-9, 14-00-38). Scholars Pr CA.

WOMEN IN MEDICINE

Chenevert, Melodie. STAT: Special Techiques in Assertiveness Training for Women in the Health Professions. (Illus.). 144p. 1983. text ed. 10.95 (ISBN 0-8016-1135-0). Mosby.

WOMEN IN MOVING-PICTURES

Here are entered works discussing the portrayal of women in motion pictures.

Stoddard, Karen M. Saints & Shrews: Women & Aging in American Popular Film. LC 82-15821. (Contributions in Women's Studies: No. 39). 192p. 1983. lib. bdg. 27.95 (ISBN 0-313-23391-8, STS/). Greenwood.

WOMEN IN POLITICS

Engel, Barbara A. Mothers & Daughters: Women of the Intelligentsia in Nineteenth Century Russia. LC 82-14611. (Illus.). 224p. 1983. 39.50 (ISBN 0-521-25125-7). Cambridge U Pr.

Mba, Nina E. Nigerian Women Mobilized: Women's Political Activity in Southern Nigeria, 1900-1965. LC 82-15477. (Illus.). xii, 348p. 1982. pap. 12.95x (ISBN 0-87725-148-7). UCB Intl Studies.

Nba, Nina E. Nigerian Women Mobilized: Women's Political Activity in Southern Nigeria, 1900-1965. LC 82-15477. (Research Ser.: No. 48). (Illus.). xii, 348p. 1982. pap. 12.95x (ISBN 0-87725-148-7). U of Cal Intl St.

Randall, Vicky. Women in Politics. LC 82-10657. 220p. 1982. 25.00x (ISBN 0-312-88729-9). St Martin.

Scharf, Lois & Jensen, Joan M., eds. Decades of Discontent: The Women's Movement 1920-1940. LC 81-4243. (Contributions in Women's Studies: No. 28). 352p. 1983. lib. bdg. 35.00 (ISBN 0-313-22694-6). Greenwood.

Staudt, Kathleen & Jacquette, Jane, eds. Women in Developing Countries: A Policy Focus. (Women & Politics, Vol. 2, No. 4). 150p. 1983. text ed. 19.95 (ISBN 0-86656-226-5, B226). Haworth Pr.

WORLD WAR, 1939-1945–UNDERGROUND MOVEMENTS–EUROPE
Gardiner, Muriel. Code Name "Mary". An American Woman in the Australian Underground. LC 82-20213. (Illus.). 200p. 1983. 14.95 (ISBN 0-300-02940-3). Yale Univ. Pr.
WORLD WAR, 1939-1945–AMERICA
Morse, Arthur D. While Six Million Died: A Chronicle of American Apathy. LC 82-22291. 432p. 1983. Repr. of 1966 ed. 18.95 (ISBN 0-87951-174-5). Overlook Pr.
WORLD WAR, 1939-1945–ATLANTIC OCEAN
Swettenham, John. Canada's Atlantic War. 1979. 19.95 (ISBN 0-88866-604-7). Samuel Stevens.
WORLD WAR, 1939-1945–CANADA
Swettenham, John. Canada's Atlantic War. 1979. 19.95 (ISBN 0-88866-604-7). Samuel Stevens.
WORLD WAR, 1939-1945–DENMARK
Nissen, Henrik S., ed. Scandinavia During the Second World War. Munch-Petersen, Thomas, tr. from Scandinavian. LC 82-2779. (Nordic Ser.: Vol. 9). (Illus.). x, 398p. 1983. 39.50 (ISBN 0-8166-1110-6). U of Minn Pr.
WORLD WAR, 1939-1945–EAST (FAR EAST)
Sherrod, Rod. The Aftermath: Asia. (World War II Ser.). 1983. lib. bdg. 19.92 (ISBN 0-8094-3436-9, Pub. by Time-Life). Silver.
WORLD WAR, 1939-1945–EUROPE
Botting, Douglas. The Aftermath: Europe. (World War II Ser.). 1983. lib. bdg. 19.92 (ISBN 0-8094-3412-1, Pub. by Time-Life). Silver.
Fodor, D. Victory in Europe. LC 81-18315. (World War II Ser.). lib. bdg. 19.92 (ISBN 0-8094-3404-0, Pub. by Time-Life). Silver.
WORLD WAR, 1939-1945–FINLAND
Nissen, Henrik S., ed. Scandinavia During the Second World War. Munch-Petersen, Thomas, tr. from Scandinavian. LC 82-2779. (Nordic Ser.: Vol. 9). (Illus.). x, 398p. 1983. 39.50 (ISBN 0-8166-1110-6). U of Minn Pr.
WORLD WAR, 1939-1945–GERMANY
Wellner, Cathryn J. Witness to War: A Thematic Guide to Young Adult Literature on World War II, 1965-1981. LC 82-5600. 287p. 1982. 17.00 (ISBN 0-8108-1552-4). Scarecrow.
WORLD WAR, 1939-1945–GREAT BRITAIN
Bittner, Donald. The Lion & the White Falcon: Britain & Iceland in the World War II Era. (Illus.). 240p. 1983. 25.00 (ISBN 0-208-01956-1, Archon). Shoe String.
Hancock, Keith, ed. History of the Second World War: United Kingdom Civil Series. (Orig.). 1975. write for info. Kraus Intl.
Johnson, Brian & Hefferman, Terry. A Most Secret Place: Boscombe Down 1939-45. (Illus.). 288p. 1983. 19.95 (ISBN 0-86720-641-1). Sci Bks Intl.
WORLD WAR, 1939-1945–ICELAND
Bittner, Donald. The Lion & the White Falcon: Britain & Iceland in the World War II Era. (Illus.). 240p. 1983. 25.00 (ISBN 0-208-01956-1, Archon). Shoe String.
WORLD WAR, 1939-1945–JAPAN
Cortesi, Lawrence. The Deadly Skies. 1983. pap. 3.25 (ISBN 0-8217-1132-6). Zebra.
Lewin, Roland. The American Magic: Codes, Ciphers & the Defeat of Japan. 1983. pap. 5.95 (ISBN 0-14-006471-0). Penguin.
Wheeler, Keith. Bombers Over Japan. LC 82-5627. (World War II Ser.). lib. bdg. 19.92 (ISBN 0-8094-3428-8, Pub. by Time-Life). Silver.
--The Fall of Japan. (World War II Ser.). 1983. lib. bdg. 19.92 (ISBN 0-8094-3408-3, Pub. by Time-Life). Silver.
WORLD WAR, 1939-1945–NORWAY
Nissen, Henrik S., ed. Scandinavia During the Second World War. Munch-Petersen, Thomas, tr. from Scandinavian. LC 82-2779. (Nordic Ser.: Vol. 9). (Illus.). x, 398p. 1983. 39.50 (ISBN 0-8166-1110-6). U of Minn Pr.
WORLD WAR, 1939-1945–PHILIPPINE ISLANDS
Ancheta, Celadonio A., ed. The Wainwright Papers: Historial Documents of World War II in the Philippines, Vols. 3 & 4. (Illus.). 217p. (Orig.). 1982. each 18.50x (ISBN 0-686-37568-8, Pub. by New Day Philippines); pap. 10.75 each (ISBN 0-686-37569-6). Cellar.
WORLD WAR, 1939-1945–RUSSIA
Patolichev, N. S. Measures of Maturity - My Early Life. (World Leaders Speeches & Writings). (Illus.). 320p. 1983. 50.00 (ISBN 0-08-024545-5). Pergamon.
WORLD WAR, 1939-1945–UNITED STATES
Fish, Hamilton. Tragic Deception: FDR & America's Involvement in World War II. 1983. 12.95 (ISBN 0-8159-6917-1). Devin.
WORLD WAR, 1939-1945–UNITED STATES–BIBLIOGRAPHY
World War II from an American Perspective: An Annotated Bibliography. 448p. 1982. lib. bdg. 26.00 (ISBN 0-87436-035-8). ABC-Clio.
WORLDLINESS (THEOLOGY)
see Church and the World
WORLD'S FAIRS
see Exhibitions
WORM-GEAR
see Gearing
WORSHIP
see also Devotional Exercises; God–Worship and Love; Idols and Images; Liturgics; Meditation; Prayer; Public Worship; Ritual
Flynn, Leslie B. Worship: Together We Celebrate. 132p. 1983. pap. 4.50 (ISBN 0-88207-608-6). Victor Bks.
Hamill, Paul, ed. Introits & Responses for Contemporary Worship. 32p. (Orig.). 1983. pap. 2.95 (ISBN 0-8298-0649-0). Pilgrim NY.
Trotter, W. Five Letters on Worship & Ministry. 39p. pap. 0.60 (ISBN 0-88172-128-X). Believers Bkshelf.
WORTH
see Values
WOUNDED, FIRST AID TO
see First Aid in Illness and Injury
WOUNDS
see also Gunshot Wounds; Hemorrhage; Surgery; Traumatism
also subdivision Wounds and Injuries under names of organs and regions of the body, e.g. Brain–Wounds and Injuries; Chest–Wounds and Injuries
Ninnemann, John L., ed. Traumatic Injury: Infection & Other Immunologic Sequelae. (Illus.). 1983. 39.00 (ISBN 0-8391-1780-9, 19119). Univ Park.
Owen-Smith, M. S. High Velocity Missile Wounds. 192p. 1981. text ed. 29.50 (ISBN 0-7131-4371-1). E Arnold.
Rudolph, Ross & Noe, Joel M. Chronic Problem Wounds. 1983. text ed. write for info. (ISBN 0-316-76110-9). Little.
WRECKS
see Shipwrecks
WREN, CHRISTOPHER, SIR, 1632-1723
Beard, Geoffrey. The Work of Christopher Wren. (Illus.). 240p. 1982. 75.00x (ISBN 0-7028-8071-X, Pub. by Bartholomew & Son England). State Mutual Bk.
WRESTLING
see also Jiu-Jitsu
Jarman, Tom & Hanley, Reid. Wrestling for Beginners. (Illus.). 192p. (Orig.). 1983. 15.00 (ISBN 0-8092-5657-6); pap. 7.95 (ISBN 0-8092-5656-8). Contemp Bks.
WRIGHT, FRANK LLOYD, 1869-1959
Wright, Frank L. Drawings & Plans of Frank Lloyd Wright: The Early Period (1893-1909) 2nd ed. Orig. Title: Ausgefuhrte Bauten Und Entwurfe Von Frank Lloyd Wright. (Illus.). 112p. 1983. pap. 9.95 (ISBN 0-486-24457-1). Dover.
WRIGHT BROTHERS–JUVENILE LITERATURE
Sabin, Louis. Wilbur & Orville Wright: The Flight to Adventure. LC 82-15879. (Illus.). 48p. (gr. 4-6). 1983. PLB 6.89 (ISBN 0-89375-851-5); pap. text ed. 1.95 (ISBN 0-89375-852-3). Troll Assocs.
WRITERS
see Authors
WRITING
Here are entered works dealing with the art and history of writing in general. Works dealing with the writing of a particular language are entered under the name of that language with subdivisions Alphabet and Writing. For a system of writing used by several peoples, the heading Writing, followed by the name of the system, is preferred, e.g. Writing, Arabic. General and comparative works dealing with the Semitic alphabet and its ancient and modern derivatives or with similar series of characters employed to represent the sounds of a language are entered under the heading Alphabet. Works dealing with variations in the style of writing in the past, and especially with ancient and medieval handwriting, are entered under the heading Paleography.
see also Abbreviations; Alphabet; Autographs; Calligraphy; Children–Writing; Ciphers; Cryptography; Graphology; Penmanship; Shorthand; Typewriting
Josipovici, Gabriel. Writing & the Body. LC 82-9042. (Illus.). 160p. 1983. 17.50x (ISBN 0-691-06550-0). Princeton U Pr.
WRITING–MATERIALS AND INSTRUMENTS
see also Paper
Bowen, Glen. Collectible Fountain Pens: Parker, Sheaffer, Wahl-Eversharp, Waterman. LC 82-90494. (Illus.). 320p. (Orig.). 1982. pap. 16.95 (ISBN 0-910173-00-1). G Bowen Comm.
WRITING–STUDY AND TEACHING
see Penmanship
WRITING (AUTHORSHIP)
see Authorship
WRITING AS A PROFESSION
see Authorship
WRITING OF LETTERS
see Letter-Writing
WRONGFUL ACTS
see Torts
WYCLIFFE, JOHN, d. 1384
Hall, Louis B. The Perilous Vision of John Wyclif. LC 82-18890. 288p. 1983. lib. bdg. 23.95X (ISBN 0-8304-1006-6). Nelson-Hall.
WYOMING–DESCRIPTION AND TRAVEL
Gorzalka, Ann L. The Saddlemakers of Sheridan County, Wyoming. 1983. price not set (ISBN 0-87108-634-4). Pruett.
Maurer, Stephen G. & Bass, William G. Eternal Solitude & Sunshine: A Grand Canyon Childhood. 1983. write for info. (ISBN 0-87108-639-5). Pruett.
WYOMING–HISTORY
Bakewell, Dennis, ed. The Charter of the Heart Mountain Relocation Center, Wyoming. (Santa Susana Pr California Masters Ser.: No. 4). (Illus.). 56p. 1983. 30.00 (ISBN 0-937048-32-1). CSUN.
Willems, Arnold & Hendrickson, Gordon. Living Wyoming's Past. (Illus.). (gr. 4). 1983. 12.95 (ISBN 0-87108-251-9); tchr's. guide 4.95 (ISBN 0-87108-250-0); ac tivity tablet 3.95 (ISBN 0-87108-252-7); activit y cards 9.95 (ISBN 0-87108-253-5). Pruett.

X

X CHROMOSOME
see Sex Chromosomes
X-RAY DIAGNOSIS
see Diagnosis, Radioscopic
X-RAY PHOTOGRAPHY
see Radiography
X-RAYS
see also Diagnosis, Radioscopic; Electron Spectroscopy; Electron Spectroscopy; Radiography; Radiotherapy
James, R. W. The Optical Principles of the Diffraction of X-Rays. LC 82-80706. 1982. Repr. of 1948 ed. 55.00 (ISBN 0-918024-23-4). Ox Bow.
X-RAYS–THERAPEUTIC USE
see Radiotherapy
XYLOGRAPHY
see Wood-Engravings

Y

Y CHROMOSOME
see Sex Chromosomes
YACHT RACING
see also Sailboat Racing
Leather, John. The Big Class Racing Yachts. (Illus.). 190p. 1982. 27.50 (ISBN 0-540-07417-9). Sheridan.
Sambrooke-Sturgess, Gerald. The Rules in Action. (Illus.). 138p. 1982. 12.95 (ISBN 0-914814-39-7). Sail Bks.
Twiname, Eric. Sail, Race & Win. (Illus.). 154p. 1982. 11.95 (ISBN 0-914814-34-6). Sail Bks.
YACHTS AND YACHTING
see also Sailing; Yacht Racing
Allan, W. J. Power & Sail: A Complete Guide to Yachting & Boating in New Zealand. (Illus.). 228p. 1975. pap. 9.95 (ISBN 0-686-42804-8, Pub. by Heinemann Pubs New Zealand). Intl Schol Bk Serv.
Bingham, Bruce. The Sailor's Sketchbook. Gilbert, Jim, ed. 144p. 1983. pap. price not set (ISBN 0-915160-55-2). Seven Seas.
Carrick, Robert & Henderson, Richard. John Alden's Yacht Designs. LC 77-85407. (Illus.). 320p. 1983. 35.00 (ISBN 0-87742-089-0). Intl Marine.
Clark, Merrian E. Ford's Deck Plan Guide. rev. ed. LC 74-27649. 1982. 50.00 (ISBN 0-916486-58-3). M Clark.
--Ford's International Cruise Guide. 35th ed. LC 75-27925. (Winter 1982-83 Ser.). 160p. 1982. pap. 7.95. M Clark.
Ellam, Patrick. Yacht Cruising. (Illus.). 1983. 19.50 (ISBN 0-393-03280-9). Norton.
Harper, Mike. Through France to the Med. 216p. 1982. 40.00x (ISBN 0-85614-034-1, Pub. by Gentry England). State Mutual Bk.
Leather, John. The Big Class Racing Yachts. (Illus.). 190p. 1982. 27.50 (ISBN 0-540-07417-9). Sheridan.
Muncaster, Martin. The Yachtsman's Quiz Book. (Illus.). 128p. (Orig.). 1982. 12.50 (ISBN 0-7153-8291-8). David & Charles.
Tetsmann, A. & Lind, H. Yachting Dictionary. 192p. 1980. 50.00x (ISBN 0-686-82331-1, Pub. by Collets). State Mutual Bk.
World of Yachting. 224p. 1980. 34.00 (ISBN 2-86409-004-X). Edns Vilo.
YALE UNIVERSITY
Walker, Williston. Coming of Yale to New Haven. 1917. pap. text ed. 9.50x (ISBN 0-686-83506-9). Elliots Bks.
YALE UNIVERSITY–HISTORY
Catlin, Daniel, Jr. Liberal Education at Yale: The Yale College Course of Study 1945-1978. LC 82-17576. 264p. (Orig.). 1983. lib. bdg. 24.00 (ISBN 0-8191-2796-5); pap. text ed. 11.75 (ISBN 0-8191-2797-3). U Pr of Amer.
French, Robert D. Memorial Quadrangle (Yale University) 1929. text ed. 49.50x (ISBN 0-686-83624-3). Elliots Bks.
YANA INDIANS
see Indians of North America–Southwest, New
YARIBA LANGUAGE
see Yoruba Language
YEAR, CHURCH
see Church Year
YEARBOOKS
see also Almanacs; Calendars
also subdivision Yearbooks under special subjects, e.g. Literature–Yearbooks; Medicine–Yearbooks
Reader's Digest Editors. Reader's Digest Almanac & Yearbook, 1983. LC 66-14383. (Illus.). 1024p. 1983. 7.50 (ISBN 0-89577-152-7, Pub. by RD Assn). Random.
World Book Inc. & Wille, Wayne, eds. The World Book Year Book. LC 62-4818. (Illus.). 608p. (gr. 6-12). 1983. PLB write for info. (ISBN 0-7166-0483-3). World Bk.
YEAST
Berry, David R. Biology of Yeast. (Studies in Biology: No. 140). 64p. 1982. pap. text ed. 8.95 (ISBN 0-7131-2838-0). E Arnold.
YEATS, JOHN BUTLER, 1839-1922
Ure. Yeats & Anglo-Irish Literature. 216p. 1982. 50.00x (ISBN 0-85323-322-5, Pub. by Liverpool Univ England). State Mutual Bk.
YEATS, WILLIAM BUTLER, 1865-1939
Archibald, Douglas. Yeats. (Irish Studies Ser.). 320p. 1983. 25.00 (ISBN 0-8156-2263-5). Syracuse U Pr.
Bohlmann, Otto. Yeats & Nietzsche: An Exploration of Major Nietzschean Echoes in the Writings of William Butler Yeats. 240p. 1981. 39.00x (ISBN 0-333-27601-9, Pub. by Macmillan England). State Mutual Bk.
Bushrui, S. B. & Munro, J. M., eds. Images & Memories: A Pictorial Record of the Life & Work of W. B. Yeats. (Illus.). 180p. 1970. text ed. 30.00x (ISBN 0-8156-6063-4, Am U Beirut). Syracuse U Pr.
Diggory, Terrence. Yeats & American Poetry: The Traditional of the Self. LC 82-15070. 280p. 1983. 25.00x (ISBN 0-691-06558-6). Princeton U Pr.
Freyer, Grattan. W. B. Yeats & the Anti-Democratic Tradition. 1982. 45.00x (ISBN 0-686-99819-7, Pub. by Gill & Macmillan Ireland). State Mutual Bk.
Jeffares, A. Norman. W. B. Yeats: Man & Poet. 365p. 1949. 22.50 (ISBN 0-686-84516-1). Routledge & Kegan.
Wolfe, Humbert. W. B. Yeats. 1982. lib. bdg. 34.50 (ISBN 0-686-81930-6). Porter.
Wrenn, C. L. W. B. Yeats. 1982. lib. bdg. 34.50 (ISBN 0-686-81935-7). Porter.
YELLOWSTONE NATIONAL PARK
Colling, Gene. Bicyclist's Guide to Yellowstone National Park. (Illus.). 64p. 1983. pap. 4.95 (ISBN 0-934318-15-8). Falcon Pr MT.
Glidden, Ralph. Exploring the Yellowstone High Country: A History of the Cooke City Area. 2nd & rev. ed. (Illus.). 120p. pap. 5.95 (ISBN 0-9608876-0-1). Cooke City.
Schreier, Carl. Yellowstone Explores Guide. LC 82-84287. (Explores Guides Ser.). (Illus.). 52p. (Orig.). 1983. pap. 3.95 (ISBN 0-943972-02-7); lib. bdg. 11.95 (ISBN 0-943972-03-5). Homestead NY.
Sweton, Ernest T. Wild Animals at Home. 126p. 1982. Repr. of 1913 ed. lib. bdg. 30.00 (ISBN 0-89760-852-6). Telegraph Bks.
YEMEN
Bidwell, Robin. The Two Yemens. 250p. 1982. lib. bdg. 26.00X (ISBN 0-86531-295-8). Westview.
The Egyptian Policy in the Arab World: Intervention in Yemen, 1962-1967 Case Study. LC 82-23812. (Illus.). 412p. (Orig.). 1983. lib. bdg. 26.75 (ISBN 0-8191-2997-6); pap. text ed. 15.50 (ISBN 0-8191-2998-4). U Pr of Amer.
McMullen, Christopher J. Resolution of the Yemen Crisis, 1963: A Case Study in Mediation. LC 80-25944. 56p. 1980. 3.00 (ISBN 0-934742-07-3, Inst Study Diplomacy). Geo U Sch For Serv.
YEN FU, 1853-1921
Schwartz, Benjamin. In Search of Wealth & Power: Yen Fu & the West. 320p. 1983. pap. text ed. 7.95x (ISBN 0-674-44652-6, Belknap Pr). Harvard U Pr.
YENAN, CHINA
Emmerson, John K. A View from Yenan. LC 79-1019. 15p. 1979. 1.50 (ISBN 0-934742-02-2, Inst Study Diplomacy). Geo U Sch For Serv.
YIDDISH DRAMA
Goldberg, Judith. Laughter Through Tears: The Yiddish Cinema. LC 80-70900. (Illus.). 176p. 1982. 22.50 (ISBN 0-8386-3074-X). Fairleigh Dickinson.
YIDDISH LANGUAGE
Naiman, Arthur. Every Goy's Guide to Common Jewish Expressions. 192p. 1983. pap. 2.75 (ISBN 0-345-30825-5). Ballantine.
YOGA
see also Samadhi
Japananda, K. Yoga, You, Your New Life. (Illus.). 208p. pap. 5.95 spiral bdg. (ISBN 0-686-37620-X). E Ruffer.
Leggett, Trevor. Encounters in Yoga & Zen. 1982. pap. 8.95 (ISBN 0-7100-9241-5). Routledge & Kegan.
Pandit, M. P. Dynamics of Yoga, Vol. II. 1979. 8.00 (ISBN 0-941524-06-X). Lotus Light.
--Dynamics of Yoga, Vol. III. 1980. write for info. (ISBN 0-941524-07-8). Lotus Light.
Shiv Brat Lal. Light on Ananda Yoga. Morrow, Steve, tr. LC 82-61990. 160p. 1982. pap. 10.00 (ISBN 0-89142-041-X). Sant Bani Ash.
Swami Rama. Inspired Thoughts. 250p. (Orig.). 1983. pap. 6.95 (ISBN 0-89389-086-3). Himalayan Intl Inst.
Szekely, Edmond B. Creative Work: Karma Yoga. (Illus.). 32p. 1973. pap. 2.95 (ISBN 0-89564-066-X). IBS Intl.
--The Living Buddha. (Illus.). 70p. 1977. pap. 4.50 (ISBN 0-89564-059-7). IBS Intl.
Widdowson, Rosalind. Joy of Yoga. LC 82-45874. (Illus.). 96p. 1983. pap. 9.95 (ISBN 0-385-19006-9, Dolp). Doubleday.

Masterpace, Victor I. The Approaching Historical Geopolitical Conflicts Threatening with Collapse of the World Order. (The Great Currents of History Library Bk.). (Illus.). 133p. 1983. 67.85 (ISBN 0-86722-026-0). Inst Econ Pol.
Pinkele, Carl F. & Pollis, Adamantis. The Contemporary Mediterranean World. 394p. 1983. 32.95 (ISBN 0-03-060091-X). Praeger.
Ray, James L. Global Politics. 2nd ed. LC 82-81582. 416p. 1982. pap. text ed. 19.95 (ISBN 0-395-32781-4); write for info. instr's manual (ISBN 0-395-32782-2). Hm.
Roman, A. Between War & Peace. 1983. 13.95 (ISBN 0-686-84434-3). Vantage.
Stanley, C. Maxwell. Managing Global Problems: A Guide to Survival. 286p. (Orig.). 1979. text ed. 12.50 (ISBN 0-9603112-1-1); pap. text ed. 7.95 (ISBN 0-9603112-2-X). Stanley Found.
Taranfeld, Clancey G. The United States, Soviet Russia, Europe, the Middle East, Israel & the Rigid Pressure of the Kondratieff Cycle. (Illus.). 139p. 1983. 87.75 (ISBN 0-86722-035-X). Inst Econ Pol.
Winterschmidt, Roger C. The Six Historical, Political & Inevitable Solutions to the Crisis of Mankind. (Illus.). 142p. 1983. 87.85 (ISBN 0-86722-021-X). Inst Econ Pol.

WORLD POLITICS–ADDRESSES, ESSAYS, LECTURES
Kanet, Roger E., ed. Soviet Foreign Policy in the 1980's. 378p. 1982. 31.95 (ISBN 0-03-059314-X); pap. 13.95 (ISBN 0-03-059316-6). Praeger.

WORLD POLITICS–20TH CENTURY
Mallory, Walter H. Political Handbook of the World: Parliaments, Parties & Press as of January 1, 1931. 1931. text ed. 49.50x (ISBN 0-686-83706-1). Elliots Bks.
Rundle, R. N. International Affairs, Nineteen Thirty-Nine to Nineteen Seventy-Nine. (Illus.). 192p. 1982. pap. text ed. 14.50x (ISBN 0-8419-0678-5); 22.50x. Holmes & Meier.

WORLD POLITICS–1945-
see also Atomic Power–International Control
Allan, Pierre. Crisis Bargaining & the Arms Race: A Theoretical Model. (Peace Science Studies). 184p. 1983. prof ref 22.50x (ISBN 0-88410-911-9). Ballinger Pub.
Halliday, Fred. The Origins of the Second Cold War. 176p. 1983. 18.50 (ISBN 0-8052-7132-5, Pub. by NLB England); pap. 6.25 (ISBN 0-8052-7133-3). Nichols Pub.
Hoffmann, Stanley. Dead Ends: American Foriegn Policy in the New Cold War. 312p. 1983. prof ref 24.50 (ISBN 0-88410-003-0). Ballinger Pub.
Meyer, Cord. Facing Reality: From World Federalism to the CIA. LC 82-13588. (Illus.). 1982. pap. text ed. 10.50 (ISBN 0-8191-2559-8). U Pr of Amer.
Sanders, Ralph. International Dynamics of Technology. LC 82-9220. (Contributions in Political Science Ser.: No. 87). 352p. 1983. lib. bdg. 35.00 (ISBN 0-313-23401-9, SAD/). Greenwood.

WORLD POLITICS–1965-
Brzezinski, Zbigniew. Between Two Ages: America's Role in the Technetronic Era. LC 82-15867. xvii, 334p. 1982. Repr. of 1970 ed. lib. bdg. 35.00x (ISBN 0-313-23498-1, BRZB). Greenwood.
Phillips, Dennis. Cold War 2 & Australia. 144p. 1983. text ed. 18.50x (ISBN 0-86861-125-5). Allen Unwin.

WORLD POLITICS–1975-
Bedeski, Robert E. The Fragile Entente: The Nineteen Seventy-Eight Japan-China Peace Treaty in a Global Context. (Replica Edition Ser.). 235p. 1983. softcover 18.50x (ISBN 0-86531-944-8). Westview.
Carlton, David & Schaerf, Carlo, eds. The Arms Race in the Nineteen Eighties. LC 81-21303. 256p. 1982. 27.50x (ISBN 0-312-04946-3). St Martin.
Critchley, Julian. The North Atlantic & the Soviet Union in the 1980's. 170p. 1982. 49.00x (ISBN 0-333-29469-6, Pub. by Macmillan England). State Mutual Bk.
Kanet, Roger E., ed. Soviet Foreign Policy in the 1980's. 378p. 1982. 31.95 (ISBN 0-03-059314-X); pap. 13.95 (ISBN 0-03-059316-6). Praeger.
Levine, Herbert M. World Politics Debated. 1st ed. 384p. 1983. pap. text ed. 14.95x (ISBN 0-07-037433-3, C). McGraw.
Nussbaum, Bruce. The Geography of Power: The World after Oil. 1983. price not set (ISBN 0-671-44571-5). S&S.
Quo, F. Q., ed. Politics of the Pacific Nations. (Replica Edition Ser.). 275p. 1983. softcover 20.00x (ISBN 0-86531-951-0). Westview.
Sampson, Martin W., III. International Policy Coordination: Issues in OPEC & EACM. (Monograph Series in World Affairs: Vol. 19, Bk. 4). 100p. (Orig.). 1983. pap. 5.00 (ISBN 0-87940-071-4). U of Denver Intl.
Steinmiller, Oswald M. The Approaching Seven Major Political Revolutions Which Will Transform Radically the World. (Illus.). 137p. 1983. 77.85 (ISBN 0-86722-030-9). Inst Econ Pol.

WORLD SERIES (BASEBALL)
World Series Record Book, 1982. 1982. 7.95 (ISBN 0-89204-091-2). Sporting News.

WORLD WAR, 1914-1918
see European War, 1914-1918

WORLD WAR, 1939-1945
Beekman, Allan. The Niihau Incident. (Illus.). 128p. 1982. 9.95 (ISBN 0-9609132-0-3). Heritage Pac.
Fodor, D. The Neutrals. (World War II Ser.). 1982. lib. bdg. 19.92 (ISBN 0-8094-3432-6, Pub. by Time-Life). Silver.
Hancock, Keith, ed. History of the Second World War: United Kingdom Civil Series. (Orig.). 1975. write for info. Kraus Intl.
Harris, Frederick. Encounters With Darkness: French & German Writers on World War II. 320p. 1983. 17.95 (ISBN 0-19-503246-2). Oxford U Pr.
Leopard, Donald D. World War II: A Concise History. (Illus.). 155p. 1982. pap. 7.95x (ISBN 0-686-43048-4). Waveland Pr.
McCombs, Don & Worth, Fred L. World War II Superfacts. 672p. (Orig.). 1983. pap. 3.95 (ISBN 0-446-30157-4). Warner Bks.
Morrison, Wilbur H. Above & Beyond: Nineteen Forty-One to Nineteen Forty-Five. (Illus.). 336p. 1983. 16.95 (ISBN 0-312-00185-1). St Martin.
Reader's Digest Editors. Illustrated Story of World War II. LC 69-15868. (Illus.). 528p. 1969. 15.99 (ISBN 0-89577-029-6). RD Assn.
--True Stories of World War II. LC 79-66914. (Illus.). 448p. 1980. 14.98 (ISBN 0-89577-081-4). RD Assn.
Snyder, Louis L. Louis L. Snyder's Historical Guide to World War II. LC 81-13433. 750p. 1982. 39.95 (ISBN 0-313-23216-4). Greenwood.
Whiteman, Harold B., Jr. Neutrality, 1941. 1941. text ed. 29.50x (ISBN 0-686-83645-6). Elliots Bks.

WORLD WAR, 1939-1945–AERIAL OPERATIONS
Golley, John. The Big Drop. (Illus.). 212p. 1982. 19.95 (ISBN 0-86720-635-7). Sci Bks Intl.
Lloyd, Alan. The Gliders: The Story of the Wooden Chariots of World War II. (Airborne Ser.: No. 17). (Illus.). 196p. 1982. 16.95x (ISBN 0-89839-066-4). Battery Pr.
Mondey, David. The Hamyln Concise Guide to Axis Aircraft of World War II. (Hamlyn Concise Guides). (Illus.). 224p. 1983. 9.95 (ISBN 0-686-83851-3, Hamlyn Pub England). Presidio Pr.
Musgrove, Gordon. Operation Gomorrah. (Illus.). 288p. 1981. 18.95 (ISBN 0-86720-562-8). Sci Bks Intl.
Smith, Peter. Dive Bomber! 1982. 15.95 (ISBN 0-87021-930-8). Naval Inst Pr.

WORLD WAR, 1939-1945–AERIAL OPERATIONS, AMERICAN
Ethell, Jeffrey & Price, Alfred. Target Berlin: Mission Two Hundred Fifty: Sixth of March Nineteen Forty-Four. (Illus.). 224p. 1982. 19.95 (ISBN 0-86720-551-2). Sci Bks Intl.
Freeman, Roger A. Mighty Eigth War Diary. (Illus.). 240p. 1981. 29.50 (ISBN 0-86720-560-1). Sci Bks Intl.
Wheeler, Keith. Bombers Over Japan. LC 82-5627. (World War II Ser.). lib. bdg. 19.92 (ISBN 0-8094-3428-8, Pub. by Time-Life). Silver.

WORLD WAR, 1939-1945–AERIAL OPERATIONS, BRITISH
Sweetman, John. Operation Chastise: The True Story of the Famous Dams Raid. (Illus.). 256p. 1982. 19.95 (ISBN 0-86720-557-1). Sci Bks Intl.

WORLD WAR, 1939-1945–AERIAL OPERATIONS, GERMAN
Aders, Gebhard. History of the German Night Fighter Force 1917-1945. (Illus.). 360p. 1980. 19.95 (ISBN 0-86720-581-4). Sci Bks Intl.
Cooper, Matthew. The German Air Force Nineteen Thirty-Three to Nineteen Forty-Five: An Anatomy of Failure. (Illus.). 375p. 1981. 19.95 (ISBN 0-86720-565-2). Sci Bks Intl.
Ethell, Jeffrey & Price, Alfred. The German Jets in Combat. (Illus.). 160p. 1980. 17.95 (ISBN 0-86720-582-2). Sci Bks Intl.
Franks, Norman L. The Battle of the Airfields. 1982. 40.00x (ISBN 0-686-82339-7, Pub. by W Kimber). State Mutual Bk.
Lerche, Hans-Werner. Luftwaffe Test Pilot. (Illus.). 158p. 1981. 19.95 (ISBN 0-86720-583-0). Sci Bks Intl.
Masters, David. German Jet Genesis. (Illus.). 160p. 1982. 19.95 (ISBN 0-86720-622-5). Sci Bks Intl.
Nowarre, Heinz. Heinkel HE III: A Documentary History. (Illus.). 192p. 1981. 19.95 (ISBN 0-86720-585-7). Sci Bks Intl.

WORLD WAR, 1939-1945–AERIAL OPERATIONS, JAPANESE
Hoyt, Edwin P. The Kamikazes. (Illus.). 1983. 16.50 (ISBN 0-87795-496-8). Arbor Hse.
Mikesh, Robert C. Ballon Bomb Attacks on North America: Japan's World War II Assaults. 86p. 1983. 8.95 (ISBN 0-8168-3950-6). Aero.
Warner, Denis & Warner, Peggy. The Sacred Warriors. 272p. 1982. 24.95 (ISBN 0-442-25418-0). Van Nos Reinhold.

WORLD WAR, 1939-1945–BIBLIOGRAPHY
Phillips, Jill M. The Second World War in History, Biography, Diary, Poetry, Literature, & Film: A Bibliography. 1983. lib. bdg. 79.95 (ISBN 0-8490-3231-8). Gordon Pr.
Wellner, Cathryn J. Witness to War: A Thematic Guide to Young Adult Literature on World War II, 1965-1981. LC 82-5600. 287p. 1982. 17.00 (ISBN 0-8108-1552-4). Scarecrow.

WORLD WAR, 1939-1945–BIOGRAPHY
Hunt, Antonia. Little Resistance. 160p. 1982. 9.95 (ISBN 0-312-48866-1). St Martin.
Royle, Trevor. Death Before Dishonor: The True Story of Fighting Mac. 176p. 1983. 14.95 (ISBN 0-312-18605-3). St Martin.

WORLD WAR, 1939-1945–CAMPAIGNS
see also names of individual battles, campaigns, etc.
Currey, Cecil B. Follow Me & Die. LC 82-48509. 304p. 1983. 17.95 (ISBN 0-8128-2892-5). Stein & Day.
Goodenough, Simon. War Maps. (Illus.). 192p. 1983. 18.95 (ISBN 0-312-85584-2). St Martin.
Lucas, James. Alpine Elite. (Illus.). 226p. 1981. 19.95 (ISBN 0-86720-586-5). Sci Bks Intl.

WORLD WAR, 1939-1945–CAMPAIGNS–BURMA
Ogburn, Charlton. The Marauders. LC 82-16149. 307p. 1982. pap. 6.50 (ISBN 0-688-01625-1, Quill). Morrow.

WORLD WAR, 1939-1945–CAMPAIGNS–GERMANY
Draper, Theodore. The Eighty-Fourth Infantry Division in the Battle of Germany. (Divisional Ser.: No. 24). (Illus.). 260p. 1983. Repr. of 1946 ed. 25.00x (ISBN 0-89839-069-9). Battery Pr.

WORLD WAR, 1939-1945–CAMPAIGNS–TUNISIA
Blumenson, Martin. Kasserine Pass. LC 82-60693. 351p. 1983. pap. 3.15 (ISBN 0-86721-238-1). Playboy Pbks.

WORLD WAR, 1939-1945–CIVIL DEFENSE
see Civil Defense

WORLD WAR, 1939-1945–DIPLOMATIC HISTORY
Alexander, G. M. The Prelude to the Truman Doctrine: British Policy in Greece, 1944-47. 1982. 46.00x (ISBN 0-19-822653-5). Oxford U Pr.

WORLD WAR, 1939-1945–FICTION
Congdon, Don, ed. Combat-World War II, 2 vols. Incl. European Theater of Operations. 19.95 (ISBN 0-87795-457-7); Pacific Theater of Operations. 19.95 (ISBN 0-87795-458-5). (Illus.). 1983. Arbor Hse.

WORLD WAR, 1939-1945–GUERRILLAS
see World War, 1939-1945–Underground Movements

WORLD WAR, 1939-1945–MEDICAL AND SANITARY AFFAIRS
Skalley, Michael R. A Medal for Marigold: Seattle's Marine Medic. (Illus.). 160p. (Orig.). 1983. pap. 8.95 (ISBN 0-87564-226-8). Superior Pub.

WORLD WAR, 1939-1945–MILITARY OPERATIONS
see World War, 1939-1945–Aerial Operations; World War, 1939-1945–Campaigns; World War, 1939-1945–Naval Operations

WORLD WAR, 1939-1945–MISCELLANEA
Goodenough, Simon. World Maps: World War II from September 1939-August 1945. (Illus.). 1983. 18.95 (ISBN 0-686-42933-8). St Martin.
Johnson, Thomas M. World War II German War Booty. LC 82-90691. (Illus.). 1982. pap. 15.00 (ISBN 0-9600906-7-3). T M Johnson.

WORLD WAR, 1939-1945–NAVAL OPERATIONS
see also Midway, Battle of, 1942; World War, 1939-1945–Atlantic Ocean
also names of individual ships
Swettenham, John. Canada's Atlantic War. 1979. 19.95 (ISBN 0-88866-604-7). Samuel Stevens.

WORLD WAR, 1939-1945–NAVAL OPERATIONS–SUBMARINE
Bell, Arthur S., Jr. Peter Charlie: The Cruise of the PC 477. LC 82-71794. (Illus.). 384p. 1982. 14.95 (ISBN 0-910355-00-2). Courtroom Comp.

WORLD WAR, 1939-1945–NAVAL OPERATIONS, AMERICAN
Messimer, Dwight R. Pawns of War: The Loss of the U. S. S. Langley & the U. S. S. Pecos. (Illus.). 1983. 18.95 (ISBN 0-87021-515-9). Naval Inst Pr.

WORLD WAR, 1939-1945–NAVAL OPERATIONS, JAPANESE
Warner, Denis & Warner, Peggy. The Sacred Warriors. 272p. 1982. 24.95 (ISBN 0-442-25418-0). Van Nos Reinhold.

WORLD WAR, 1939-1945–NEUTRALITY OF THE UNITED STATES
see United States–Neutrality

WORLD WAR, 1939-1945–PACIFIC OCEAN
Lewin, Roland. The American Magic: Codes, Ciphers & the Defeat of Japan. 1983. pap. 5.95 (ISBN 0-14-006471-0). Penguin.
Messimer, Dwight R. Pawns of War: The Loss of the U. S. S. Langley & the U. S. S. Pecos. (Illus.). 1983. 18.95 (ISBN 0-87021-515-9). Naval Inst Pr.

WORLD WAR, 1939-1945–PERSONAL NARRATIVES
Barker, Chris A. Tomorrow May Never Come. (Illus.). 415p. Date not set. 15.00x (ISBN 0-9609382-0-6). Susquehanna.
Eliach, Yaffa & Gurewitsch, Brana. The Liberators: Eyewitness Accounts of the Liberation of Concentration Camps, Liberation Day Vol. I. LC 81-70261. (The Liberators Ser.). (Illus.). 59p. (Orig.). 1981. pap. 8.95 (ISBN 0-9609970-1-6). Ctr For Holo.
Pote, Winston. Mountain Troops. (Illus.). 84p. 7.95 (ISBN 0-89272-150-2). Down East.
Smith, Wheaton, Jr. A Life to Live. 96p. 1983. 8.95 (ISBN 0-89962-324-7). Todd & Honeywell.

WORLD WAR, 1939-1945–PERSONAL NARRATIVES, AMERICAN
Hyde, Montgomery H. Secret Intelligence Agent. 304p. 1983. 11.95 (ISBN 0-312-70847-5). St Martin.
Maximum Effort: (B-29 Gunner's Memoirs) write for info. Sunflower U Pr.
Vietor, Jack. Time Out. 208p. 1982. 13.95 (ISBN 0-8168-9025-0). Aero.

WORLD WAR, 1939-1945–PERSONAL NARRATIVES, ENGLISH
Hilary, Richard. The Last Enemy. 192p. 1983. 10.95 (ISBN 0-312-47079-7). St Martin.

WORLD WAR, 1939-1945–PERSONAL NARRATIVES, HUNGARIAN
Jackson, Livia. Elli: Coming of Age in the Holocaust. 1983. pap. 6.95 (ISBN 0-8129-6327-X). Times Bks.

WORLD WAR, 1939-1945–PERSONAL NARRATIVES, JEWISH
Breitowicz, Jakob. Through Hell to Life. LC 82-61793. (Illus.). 1983. 10.00 (ISBN 0-88400-091-5). Shengold.
Laska, Vera. Women in the Resistance & in the Holocaust: The Voices of Eyewitnesses. LC 82-12018. (Contributions in Women Studies: No. 37). 352p. 1983. lib. bdg. 29.95 (ISBN 0-313-23457-4, LWH/). Greenwood.
Rubinstein, Donna. I Am the Only Survivor of Krasnostav. LC 82-61794. (Illus.). 1983. 10.00 (ISBN 0-88400-093-1). Shengold.

WORLD WAR, 1939-1945–PERSONAL NARRATIVES, POLISH
Phillips, Janine. My Secret Diary. 160p. 1982. 25.00x (ISBN 0-85683-062-3, Pub. by Shepheard-Walwyn England). State Mutual Bk.

WORLD WAR, 1939-1945–PERSONAL NARRATIVES, RUSSIAN
Bialer, Seweryn, ed. Stalin & His Generals: Soviet Military Memoirs of World War II. (Encore Edition). 650p. 1983. softcover 35.00x (ISBN 0-86531-610-4). Westview.

WORLD WAR, 1939-1945–PHOTOGRAPHY
Buckland, Gail. Cecil Beaton War Photographs Nineteen Thirty-Nine to Nineteen Forty-Five. (Illus.). 192p. 1982. 24.95. Sci Bks Intl.

WORLD WAR, 1939-1945–PRISONERS AND PRISONS, GERMAN
Hackel, Sergei. Pearl of Great Price: The Life of Mother Maria Skobtsova 1891-1945. rev. ed. LC 81-21356. 160p. 1982. pap. 5.95 (ISBN 0-913836-85-0). St Vladimirs.

WORLD WAR, 1939-1945–PROPAGANDA
Short, K. R. Film & Propaganda in World War II. LC 82-23838. 300p. 1983. text ed. 23.95x (ISBN 0-87049-386-8). U of Tenn Pr.

WORLD WAR, 1939-1945–RECONSTRUCTION
see Reconstruction (1939-1951)

WORLD WAR, 1939-1945–REGIMENTAL HISTORIES
Barker, Harold R. History of the Forty-Third Division Artillery: World War II, 1941-1945. (Illus.). 251p. 1961. 12.95 (ISBN 0-917012-45-3). RI Pubns Soc.
Boston, Bernard. History of the Three Hundred Ninety-Eighth Infantry Regiment in World War II. (Combat Arms Ser.: No. 7). (Illus.). 208p. 1982. 20.00x (ISBN 0-89839-063-X). Battery Pr.
Byrnes, Laurence. History of the Ninety-Fourth Infantry Division in World War II. (Divisional Ser.: No. 22). (Illus.). 534p. 1982. Repr. of 1948 ed. 25.00x (ISBN 0-89839-064-8). Battery Pr.
Draper, Theodore. The Eighty-Fourth Infantry Division in the Battle of Germany. (Divisional Ser.: No. 24). (Illus.). 260p. 1983. Repr. of 1946 ed. 25.00x (ISBN 0-89839-069-9). Battery Pr.
Lambert, John W. The Long Campaign: The History of the 15th Fighter Group in WW II. 1982. 35.00x (ISBN 0-89745-032-9). Sunflower U Pr.
Lucas, James. Alpine Elite. (Illus.). 226p. 1981. 19.95 (ISBN 0-86720-586-5). Sci Bks Intl.
Ogburn, Charlton. The Marauders. LC 82-16149. 307p. 1982. pap. 6.50 (ISBN 0-688-01625-1, Quill). Morrow.
Zimmer, Joseph. The History of the Forty-Third Infantry Division. (Divisional Ser.: No. 23). (Illus.). 96p. 1982. Repr. of 1946 ed. 22.50x (ISBN 0-89839-068-0). Battery Pr.

WORLD WAR, 1939-1945–RESISTANCE MOVEMENTS
see World War, 1939-1945–Underground Movements

WORLD WAR, 1939-1945–SANITARY AFFAIRS
see World War, 1939-1945–Medical and Sanitary Affairs

WORLD WAR, 1939-1945–SECRET SERVICE–GREAT BRITAIN
Clayton, Aileen. The Enemy is Listening. (Ballantine Espionage Intelligence Library: No. 22). 416p. 1982. pap. 3.95 (ISBN 0-345-30250-8). Ballantine.

WORLD WAR, 1939-1945–SECRET SERVICE–UNITED STATES
Hyde, Montgomery H. Secret Intelligence Agent. 304p. 1983. 11.95 (ISBN 0-312-70847-5). St Martin.
Lewin, Roland. The American Magic: Codes, Ciphers & the Defeat of Japan. 1983. pap. 5.95 (ISBN 0-14-006471-0). Penguin.

WORLD WAR, 1939-1945–SUBMARINE OPERATIONS
see World War, 1939-1945–Naval Operations–Submarine

WORLD WAR, 1939-1945–UNDERGROUND MOVEMENTS
O'Neill, Richard. Suicide Squads: Axis & Allied Special Attack Weapons of World War II. LC 82-10829. (Illus.). 296p. 1982. 15.95 (ISBN 0-312-77529-6). St Martin.

Moore, Rosalind, ed. Dell Word Search, No. 24. (Orig.). 1983. pap. 2.75 (ISBN 0-440-11936-7). Dell.

Tamarkin, Kenneth. Number Power Six: Word Problems. (Number Power Ser.). 160p. (Orig.). 1983. pap. 4.95 (ISBN 0-8092-5515-4). Contemp Bks.

WORD PROCESSING (OFFICE PRACTICE)

Apple II Word Processing. LC 81-52719. (Level B Business Software Evaluations). Date not set. pap. 21.95 (ISBN 0-88022-005-8). Que Corp.

Aschner, Kath. Word Processing Handbook: A Step-by-Step to Automating Your Office. Rev. ed. 1983. pap. write for info. (ISBN 0-88908-913-2). Self Counsel Pr.

Bergerud, Marly & Gonzalez, Jean. Word Information Processing Concepts: Careers Technology, & Applications. LC 80-22328. 387p. 1981. text ed. 18.95x (ISBN 0-471-08499-9); tchrs. manual avail. (ISBN 0-471-09430-7). Wiley.

--Word Processing: Concepts & Careers. 2nd ed. LC 80-29386. (Wiley Word Processing Ser.). 237p. 1981. pap. text ed. 16.95x (ISBN 0-471-06010-0). Wiley.

Berner, Jeff. The Foolproof Guide to SCRIPSIT. 225p. 1983. pap. text ed. 11.95 (ISBN 0-89588-098-9). Sybex.

Boyce, B. & Popyk, M. K. Developing Concepts for Word Processing. 192p. 1983. 7.50 (ISBN 0-07-006921-2, Gregg). McGraw.

Boyer, Dean. Computer Word Processing: Do You Want It? 148p. 1981. pap. 14.95 (ISBN 0-88022-000-7, 81-52571). Que Corp.

Brooks, L. D. ConsultaMation, Inc. An Applications Program for Word Processing. 192p. 1982. 10.00x (ISBN 0-07-008081-X, G). McGraw.

Cecala, Agnes. Word Processing Skills & Applications Using the Wang System. 1983. pap. text ed. 16.95 (ISBN 0-8359-8789-2). Reston.

Choosing a Word Processor. 17.95 (ISBN 0-910085-00-5); comparison tables 6.95, (ISBN 0-910085-01-3). Info Res MI.

Coleman, Joseph. Word Processing Simplified & Self-Taught. (Simplified & Self-Taught Ser.). (Illus.). 128p. 1983. lib. bdg. 9.95 (ISBN 0-668-05599-5); pap. 4.95 (ISBN 0-668-05601-0). Arco.

Consumer Guide Editors. The Easy-to-Understand Guide to Word Processing. (Illus., Orig.). 1982. pap. cancelled (ISBN 0-671-46172-9). Doubleday.

DeVoney, Chris & Summe, Richard. CP-M Word Processor Evaluations. Noble, David, ed. (Level C Business Software Evaluations). 1982. pap. 16.50 (ISBN 0-88022-006-6). Que Corp.

Donohue, Brian. How to Buy an Office Computer or Word Processor. (Illus.). 256p. 1983. 17.95 (ISBN 0-13-403113-X); pap. 8.95 (ISBN 0-13-403105-9). P-H.

Finkel, L. Learning Word Processing Concepts Using Apple Writer. 80p. 1982. 7.00 (ISBN 0-07-020986-3, G); instr's manual & key 2.50 (ISBN 0-07-020987-1). McGraw.

Forbes, Mary J. Word Processing: Procedures for Today's Office. 250p. 1983. 22.00 (ISBN 0-932376-23-1). Digital Pr.

Goldfield, Randy J. The Word Processing Handbook. 1983. 25.00 (ISBN 0-02-912100-0). Free Pr.

Good, Phillip. Choosing a Word Processor. 1983. text ed. 18.95 (ISBN 0-8359-0761-9); pap. text ed. 12.95 (ISBN 0-8359-0760-0). Reston.

Harris, Helen & Chauhan, Ela. So You Want to Buy a Word Processor? 147p. (Orig.). 1982. pap. text ed. 24.90x (ISBN 0-09-150351-5, Pub. by Busn Bks England). Renouf.

Kleinschrod, Walter & Kruk, Leonard. Word Information Processing: Administration & Office Automation. 2nd ed. 288p. 1983. text ed. 23.95 (ISBN 0-672-98442-3); instr's. guide 6.67 (ISBN 0-672-98443-1). Bobbs.

Labuz, Ronald. Interfacing in the Eighties: How to Set up Communications Between Word Processors & Phototypesetters. 1983. pap. 3.95 (ISBN 0-86610-125-X). Meridian Pub.

Laurence Press Staff. Low-Cost Word Processing: Microcomputer Bks.-Executive. 244p. 1982. pap. 10.95 (ISBN 0-201-05735-2). A-W.

McWilliams, Peter A. The Word Processing Book: A Short Course in Computer Literacy. 252p. 1982. pap. 8.95 (ISBN 0-931580-98-6). Prelude Press.

Maddux, Cleborne D. How to Use Scripsit. Willis, Jerry, ed. 200p. 1983. pap. 9.95 (ISBN 0-88056-110-6). Dilithium Pr.

Ortega. Ortografia Programada. 3rd ed. 165p. 1982. 7.85 (ISBN 0-07-047711-6, G). McGraw.

Poling, Carol. Apple II Word Processing. DeVoney, Chris & Hedrick, Marshall, eds. 250p. 1982. 19.95 (ISBN 0-88022-014-7). Que Corp.

Popyk, M. K. Word Processing & Information Systems: A Practical Approach. 352p. 1983. 15.50 (ISBN 0-07-050574-8, G). McGraw.

--Word Processing: Essential Concepts. 240p. 1983. 11.95 (ISBN 0-07-048472-4, G). McGraw.

Poynter, Dan. Word Processors & Information Processing. 172p. 1983. 16.95 (ISBN 0-13-963553-X); pap. 11.95 (ISBN 0-13-963546-7). P-H.

Price, J. & Urban, L. Definitive Word-Processing. 1983. pap. 8.95 (ISBN 0-14-046591-X). Penguin.

Rosen, A. & Hubbard, W. Word Processing Keyboarding Applications & Exercises. 291p. 1981. pap. text ed. 19.95 (ISBN 0-471-08700-9); Working Papers 6.95 (ISBN 0-471-09790-X); tchr's. manual 8.00 (ISBN 0-471-07734-8). Wiley.

Sanderson, M. & Rawlinson, M. K. Word Processing Manual. 200p. 1982. pap. text ed. 11.00x (ISBN 0-7121-2323-7). Intl Ideas.

Schulze, Joyce E. The Wang Self-Teaching Program. 125p. 1982. looseleaf bound 295.00 (ISBN 0-935506-06-3); 9 cassette lessons incl. Carnegie Pr.

Sikonowiz, Walter. The Complete Book of Word Processing & Business Graphics. 212p. 1983. 21.95 (ISBN 0-13-158667-X); pap. 14.95 (ISBN 0-13-158659-9). P-H.

Simpson, Alan, ed. The Office of the Future, No. 3: Planning for Word Processing. 150p. 1982. pap. text ed. 23.50x (ISBN 0-566-03414-X). Gower Pub Ltd.

Smith, Brian R. & Austin, Daniel J. Word Processing: A Guide for Small Business. 146p. 1983. pap. 9.95 (ISBN 0-86616-021-3). Lewis.

Townsend, Carl. CP-M Wordprocessing Systems. 300p. 1983. pap. text ed. 19.95 (ISBN 0-88056-104-1). Dilithium Pr.

Verchot, Louis. Word Processors Worldwide: Opportunities & Pitfalls. (Illus.). 575p. 1983. 1800.00 (ISBN 0-910211-01-9). Laal Co.

Voelpel, Jack. Word Retrieval Handbook. 82p. (Orig.). 1983. pap. 4.95 (ISBN 0-940534-02-9). Beekman Hill.

Westgate, et al. An Introduction to Word Processing Four Plus. 276p. 1982. text ed. 32.95x (ISBN 0-7715-0460-8). Forkner.

White, Roger. Wordstar with Style. 1983. text ed. 17.95 (ISBN 0-8359-8794-9); pap. text ed. 12.95 (ISBN 0-8359-8793-0). Reston.

Williamson, John McKim. Software Sayings of Jack Mack: Wit & Humor with Word Processing. 2nd ed. LC 82-60964. (Jack Mack Paperbacks). 134p. 1982. pap. 8.95 (ISBN 0-910391-00-9). J Mack.

Word Processing the Easy Way. (Easy Way Ser.). 1983. pap. price not set (ISBN 0-8120-2628-4). Barron.

Zinsser, William. Writing With a Word Processor. LC 82-48140. (Illus.). 128p. 1983. 9.57i (ISBN 0-06-015055-6, HarpT). Har-Row.

WORDS, STOCK OF

see Vocabulary

WORDSWORTH, WILLIAM, 1770-1850

Beyer, Werner W. The Enchanted Forest: Coleridge, Wordsworth. 273p. 1982. Repr. of 1963 ed. lib. bdg. 35.00 (ISBN 0-686-81684-6). Century Bookbindery.

Cappon, Alexander P. Aspects of Wordsworth & Whitehead. 1983. 19.95 (ISBN 0-8022-2412-1). Philos Lib.

Watson, J. R. Wordsworth's Vital Soul: The Sacred & Profane in Wordsworth's Poetry. 259p. 1982. text ed. 30.00x (ISBN 0-391-02563-5). Humanities.

Wilson, John D. Stephen & Arnold as Critics of Wordsworth. 1982. lib. bdg. 34.50 (ISBN 0-686-81922-5). Porter.

Wright, John. Genius of Wordsworth. 1982. lib. bdg. 34.50 (ISBN 0-686-81937-3). Porter.

WORK

see also Industrial Sociology; Job Satisfaction; Labor and Laboring Classes

Congressional Quarterly Inc. Staff. Work Life in the Nineteen Eighties. LC 81-3171. (Editorial Research Reports Ser.). 200p. 1981. pap. 7.95 (ISBN 0-87187-207-2). Congr Quarterly.

Jones, Barry O. Sleepers, Wake! Technology & the Future of Work. (Illus.). 302p. 1983. 24.95 (ISBN 0-19-554343-2). Oxford U Pr.

Licht, Walter. Working for the Railroad: The Organization of Work in the Nineteenth Century. LC 82-61372. (Illus.). 352p. 1983. 27.50x (ISBN 0-691-04700-6). Princeton U Pr.

WORK-PSYCHOLOGICAL ASPECTS

American Society for Training & Development Inc. Quality of Work Life: Perspectives for Business & the Public Sector. Skrovan, Daniel J., ed. 208p. Date not set. text ed. 17.95 (ISBN 0-201-07755-8). A-W.

Fraser, T. M. Human Stress, Work & Job Satisfaction: A Critical Approach. International Labour Office, ed. (Occupational Safety & Health Ser.: No. 50). 72p. (Orig.). 1982. pap. 8.55 (ISBN 92-2-103042-3). Intl Labour Office.

Laban, Rudolph & Lawrence, F. C. Effort. 112p. 1979. 30.00x (ISBN 0-7121-0534-4, Pub. by Macdonald & Evans). State Mutual Bk.

WORK (THEOLOGY)

Baum, Gregory, ed. Work & Religion. (Concilium Ser.: Vol. 131). 128p. (Orig.). 1980. pap. 5.95 (ISBN 0-8164-2273-7). Seabury.

WORK, PSYCHOLOGY OF

see Work-Psychological Aspects

WORK, THERAPEUTIC EFFECT OF

see Occupational Therapy

WORK BOATS

Troup, K. D. Workboats. 300p. 1982. text ed. 62.95x (ISBN 0-471-26067-3, Pub. by Wiley Heyden). Wiley.

WORK EXPERIENCE

see Apprentices; Vocational Education

WORK PERFORMANCE STANDARDS

see Performance Standards

WORK RELIEF

see also Cooperative Societies

Jackson, Michael P. & Hanby, Victor J. British Work Creation Programmes. 87p. 1982. pap. text ed. 23.50x (ISBN 0-566-00523-9). Gower Pub Ltd.

WORK STOPPAGES

see Strikes and Lockouts

WORKERS

see Labor and Laboring Classes

WORKING-CLASSES

see Labor and Laboring Classes

WORKING DAY

see Hours of Labor

WORKING DOGS

see also Hunting Dogs

Hart, Edward. Working Dogs. (Illus.). 64p. 1983. pap. 4.95 (ISBN 0-7134-3731-6, Pub. by Batsford England). David & Charles.

WORKING MEN

see Labor and Laboring Classes

WORKING-MEN'S ASSOCIATIONS

see Trade-Unions

WORKING-MEN'S LUNCH ROOMS

see Restaurants, Lunchrooms, etc.

WORKING MOTHERS

see Mothers-Employment

WORKINGMEN

see Labor and Laboring Classes

WORKMEN'S COMPENSATION

see also Employers' Liability

Rudman, Jack. Worker's Compensation Review Analyst. (Career Examination Ser.: C-308). (Cloth bdg. avail. on request). pap. 10.00 (ISBN 0-8373-0308-7). Natl Learning.

Sanchez, Irene & Workman, E. L. The California Workers' Compensation Rehabilitation System: Supplement I. 1982. 9.95 (ISBN 0-686-83889-0). Macmillan.

Viscardi, Henry, Jr. & Friedman, Irving M. A Study of Workmen's Compensation In Relation To Sheltered Workshops. 68p. 1971. 1.50 (ISBN 0-686-38807-0). Human Res Ctr.

Worrall, John D., ed. Safety & the Work Force: Incentives & Disincentives in Worker's Compensation. 1983. price not set (ISBN 0-87546-101-8). ILR Pr.

WORKSHOPS

see also Factories

Kern, Barbara & Kern, Ken. Ken Kern's Homestead Workshop. (Illus.). 176p. 1982. pap. 9.95 (ISBN 0-686-83731-2, ScribT). Scribner.

Warde, John, ed. Make It! Don't Buy It: Home Furnishings & Accessories to Make from Wood, Metal & Fabric. (Illus.). 464p. 1983. 24.95 (ISBN 0-87857-450-6, 14-013-0). Rodale Pr Inc.

Working with Metal. (Home Repair & Improvement Ser.). 1981. lib. bdg. 15.96 (ISBN 0-8094-3471-7, Pub. by Time-Life). Silver.

Working with Plastics. (Home Repair & Improvement Ser.). 1982. lib. bdg. 15.96 (ISBN 0-8094-3507-1, Pub. by Time-Life). Silver.

WORKSHOPS (GROUP DISCUSSION)

see Forums (Discussion and Debate)

WORKSHOPS FOR THE HANDICAPPED

see Vocational Rehabilitation

WORLD, END OF

see End of the World

WORLD AND THE CHURCH

see Church and the World

WORLD ECONOMICS

see Commercial Policy; Competition, International; Economic Policy

WORLD FEDERATION

see International Organization

WORLD GOVERNMENT

see International Organization

WORLD HEALTH ORGANIZATION

American Health Research Institute, Ltd. World Health & the World Health Organization: A Medical Subject Analysis & Research Index with Bibliography. Bartone, John C., ed. 120p. 1983. 29.95 (ISBN 0-88164-020-4); pap. 21.95 (ISBN 0-88164-021-2). ABBE Pubs Assn.

Rondle, C. J., ed. Disease Eradication. 270p. 1981. 60.00x (ISBN 0-333-31188-4, Pub. by Macmillan England). State Mutual Bk.

WORLD HISTORY

see also Geography; History, Ancient; History, Modern; Middle Ages-History

Ayrton, Pete, ed. World View 1983: What the Press & Television Have Not Told You about the Year's Mega-Issues. (Illus.). 500p. 1983. 22.50 (ISBN 0-394-53072-1); pap. 9.95 (ISBN 0-394-71419-9). Pantheon.

Brooks, George E., Jr. Themes in African & World History: A Schema for Integrating Africa into World History; Tropical Africa: The Colonial Heritage; The African Heritage & the Slave Trade. (African Humanities Ser.). 45p. (Orig.). 1973. pap. text ed. 2.00 (ISBN 0-941934-06-3). Ind U Afro-Amer Arts.

Glubb, John. The Rise & Fall of Empires. 192p. 1983. 40.00x (ISBN 0-85683-056-9, Pub. by Shepheard-Walwyn England). State Mutual Bk.

Harding, Claudius H. The Innermost Nature of the World Crisis & Its Catastrophic Potential for the Future of Humanity. (The Great Currents of History Library Book). (Illus.). 128p. 1983. 83.55 (ISBN 0-86722-019-8). Inst Econ Pol.

Information Please Book of World Facts & Figures, 1983. 224p. (Orig.). 1983. pap. 2.95 (ISBN 0-89479-125-7). A & W Pubs.

Khanna, K. C. & Dayal, Raghubir. Modern World History. 250p. 1982. pap. text ed. 8.95x (ISBN 0-86131-074-8, Pub. by Orient Longman Ltd India). Apt Bks.

Langerfield, Eugene V. The Two Major Enemies of Mankind. (The Great Currents of History Library Book). (Illus.). 139p. 1983. 81.65 (ISBN 0-86722-018-X). Inst Econ Pol.

McKay, John P. & Hill, Benneth D. A History of Western Society, 2 Vols. 2nd ed. LC 82-81320. 592p. 1982. Vol. 1. pap. text ed. 17.95 (ISBN 0-395-32798-9); Vol. 2. pap. text ed. 17.95 (ISBN 0-395-32799-7); study guide for Vol. 1 5.95 (ISBN 0-395-32805-5); study guide for Vol. 2 5.95 (ISBN 0-395-32806-3). HM.

--A History of Western Society, 3 Vols. 2nd ed. LC 82-81321. 416p. 1982. Vol. 1. pap. text ed. 15.95 (ISBN 0-395-32800-4); Vol. 2. pap. text ed. 15.95 (ISBN 0-395-32801-2); Vol. 3. pap. text ed. 15.95 (ISBN 0-395-32802-0); write for info. instr's manual (ISBN 0-395-32803-9). HM.

McKay, John P. & Hill, Bennett D. A History of Western Society. 2nd ed. LC 82-81316. 1072p. 1982. text ed. 23.95 (ISBN 0-395-32804-7). HM.

Prior, Robin. The World Crisis as History. 288p. 1983. text ed. 31.00x (ISBN 0-7099-2011-3, Pub. by Croom Helm Ltd England). Biblio Dist.

Scott, Desmond. Typhoon Pilot. (Illus.). 196p. 1983. 22.50 (ISBN 0-686-43268-1, Pub. by Secker & Warburg). David & Charles.

Skousen, W. Cleon. The Five Thousand Year Leap: Twenty-Eight Ideas That Changed the World. (Illus.). xx, 337p. (Orig.). 13.95 (ISBN 0-88080-003-8); pap. 9.95 (ISBN 0-88080-004-6). Freemen Inst.

Spengler, Oswald. The Decline of the West. Werner, Helmut, ed. 7.95 (ISBN 0-394-60488-1). Modern Lib.

WORLD HISTORY-BIBLIOGRAPHY

Illich, Ivan. Deschoolong Society. LC 82-48800. (World Perspective Ser.). 192p. 1983. pap. 4.76i (ISBN 0-06-091046-1, CN 1046, CN). Har-Row.

WORLD HISTORY-STUDY AND TEACHING

see History-Study and Teaching

WORLD ORGANIZATION

see International Organization

WORLD POLITICS

Here are entered historical accounts of international intercourse. Theoretical works are entered under International Relations.

see also Afro-Asian Politics; Detente

Banks. Political Handbook of the World: 1982. 1983. write for info. (ISBN 0-07-003631-4). McGraw.

Barnes, Harry E., ed. Perpetual War for Perpetual Peace. 680p. 1982. pap. 11.00 (ISBN 0-939484-01-3). Inst Hist Rev.

Benson, Vladimir. The Failure of the American Dream & the Moral Responsibility of the United States for the Crisis in the Middle East & for the Collapse of the World Order. (The Great Currents of History Library Bk.). (Illus.). 141p. 1983. 57.85 (ISBN 0-86722-025-2). Inst Econ Pol.

Douhait, Rudolph D. The Political Chaos of the World & the Violent Leadership Role of Communist Russia. (Illus.). 127p. 1983. 67.45 (ISBN 0-86722-033-3). Inst Econ Pol.

Falk, Richard. The End of World Order. 340p. 1982. 39.50 (ISBN 0-8419-0739-0). Holmes & Meier.

Fleming, Spencer. Power Anatomy of the Economic Forces Dominating the Business & the Political World. (Illus.). 137p. 1983. 49.75 (ISBN 0-86722-032-5). Inst Econ Pol.

Gallieni, Thomas M. The Unrelenting Advance of the Financial Collapse of the World. (Illus.). 121p. 1983. 86.45 (ISBN 0-86722-037-6). Inst Econ Pol.

Gilpin, Robert. War & Change in World Politics. LC 81-2885. (Illus.). 288p. Date not set. pap. price not set (ISBN 0-521-27376-5). Cambridge U Pr.

Goetzmann, William H. When the Eagle Screamed: The Romantic Horizon in American Diplomacy, 1800-1860. (Illus.). 138p. (Orig.). 1966. pap. 10.95x (ISBN 0-471-31001-8). Wiley.

Hammerschlag, Wilhelm. The Kondratieff Theory & the Discovery of the Exact Date for the Explosion of the Third World War. (Illus.). 117p. 1983. 87.95 (ISBN 0-86722-031-7). Inst Econ Pol.

Harding, Claudius H. The Innermost Nature of the World Crisis & Its Catastrophic Potential for the Future of Humanity. (The Great Currents of History Library Book). (Illus.). 128p. 1983. 83.55 (ISBN 0-86722-019-8). Inst Econ Pol.

Hillmann, Karl-Heinz. Umweltkrise und Wertwandel: Der Umwerting der Werte als Strategie des Uberlebens. 419p. Date not set. price not set. P Lang Pubs.

Hydemark, David R. The Dangerous Conflict of the World Leaderships & the Possibility of a Mortal Explosion in the Destinies of Mankind. (Illus.). 141p. 1983. 71.75 (ISBN 0-86722-034-1). Inst Econ Pol.

Knorr, Klaus, ed. Power, Strategy, & Security: A World Politics Reader. LC 82-48561. 270p. 1983. 32.00x (ISBN 0-686-43257-6); pap. 8.95 (ISBN 0-691-01071-4). Princeton U Pr.

Sweetman, David. Women Leaders in African History. 160p. 1982. 30.00x (ISBN 0-435-94479-7, Pub. by Heinemann England). State Mutual Bk.
Thomis, Malcolm & Grimmett, Jennifer. Women in Protest Eighteen Hundred to Eighteen Fifty. LC 81-21290. 166p. 1982. 25.00x (ISBN 0-312-88746-9). St Martin.

WOMEN IN RELIGION
see also Women in Christianity
Boyd, Lois A. & Brackenridge, Douglas. Presbyterian Women in America: Two Centuries of a Quest for Status. LC 82-15845. (Contributions to the Study of Religion: No. 9). 416p. 1983. lib. bdg. 35.00 (ISBN 0-313-23678-X, BOY/). Greenwood.
Holden, Pat, ed. Women's Religious Experience. LC 82-24314. 224p. 1983. text ed. 26.50x (ISBN 0-389-20363-7). B&N Imports.

WOMEN IN THE BIBLE
Christensen, Winnie. Women Who Believed God. (Fisherman Bible Studyguides). 80p. 1983. saddle-stiched 2.50 (ISBN 0-87788-936-8). Shaw Pubs.
Munn, Elijah H. The Progress of Woman. 84p. 6.95 (ISBN 0-9609828-0-9). EHM Pub.
Price, Eugenia. The Unique World of Women. 248p. 1982. pap. 7.95 (ISBN 0-310-31351-1). Zondervan.

WOMEN IN THE WEST
Women in the West. write for info. Sunflower U Pr.

WOMEN IN TRADE-UNIONS
see also Trade-Unions
Tristan, Flora. The Workers' Union. Livingston, Beverly, tr. LC 82-1891. 188p. 1983. 14.95 (ISBN 0-252-00921-5). U of Ill Pr.

WOMEN JOURNALISTS
Hedy, Maureen E. & Danky, James P., eds. Women's Periodicals & Newspapers from the Eighteenth Century to 1981: A Union List of the Holdings of Madison, Wisconsin Libraries. LC 82-11903. (Reference Publications in Women's Studies). (Illus.). 376p. 1982. 38.00 (ISBN 0-8161-8107-1). G K Hall.
Rollin, Betty. Am I Getting Paid for This? 1982. 14.95 (ISBN 0-316-75454-4). Little.
Tannen, Deborah. Lilika Nakos. (World Autors Ser.). 200p. 1983. lib. bdg. 21.95 (ISBN 0-8057-6524-7, Twayne). G K Hall.

WOMEN LAWYERS
Epstein, Cynthia F. Women in Law. LC 82-45611. 456p. 1983. pap. 10.95 (ISBN 0-385-18431-X, Anch). Doubleday.

WOMEN MINISTERS
see Women Clergy

WOMEN MOVING-PICTURE ACTRESSES
see Moving-Picture Actors and Actresses

WOMEN MUSICIANS
Cohen, Aaron. International Encyclopedia of Women Composers, Vol. II. 240p. 1983. 50.00 (ISBN 0-8352-1524-5). Bowker.
Green, Mildred D. Black Women Composers: A Genesis. (Music Ser.). 174p. 1983. lib. bdg. 18.95 (ISBN 0-8057-9450-6, Twayne). G K Hall.
Jones, Bessie. For the Ancestors: Autobiographical Memories. Stewart, John, ed. LC 82-8593. (Illus.). 211p. 1983. 14.95 (ISBN 0-252-00959-2). U of Ill Pr.

WOMEN POETS
Blackburn, Kate & McDonald, Agnes. Four North Carolina Woman Poets. Bayes, Ronald H., ed. LC 82-62747. 84p. 1982. pap. 8.00 (ISBN 0-932662-42-0). St Andrews NC.
Tannen, Deborah. Lilika Nakos. (World Autors Ser.). 200p. 1983. lib. bdg. 21.95 (ISBN 0-8057-6524-7, Twayne). G K Hall.

WOMEN SCIENTISTS
Richter, D. Women Scientists: The Road to Liberation. 1982. 50.00x (ISBN 0-686-42942-7, Pub. by Macmillan England). State Mutual Bk.
The Brighton Women & Science Group. Alice Through the Microscope: The Power of Science Over Women's Lives. 310p. 19.95 (ISBN 0-86068-078-9, Virago Pr); pap. 9.95 (ISBN 0-86068-079-7). Merrimack Bk Serv.

WOMEN SOLDIERS
see also Amazons
Drury, Rebecca. Courage at Sea. (Women at War Ser.: No. 12). (Orig.). 1983. pap. 3.25 (ISBN 0-440-01485-9). Dell.
Portnoy, Dina. Women: The Recruiter's Last Resort. 40p. 1974. 2.00 (ISBN 0-686-43095-6). Recon Pubns.
Rustad. Women in Khaki. 304p. 1982. 24.95 (ISBN 0-03-060149-5); pap. 12.95 (ISBN 0-03-062193-3). Praeger.

WOMEN STUDIES
see Women'S Studies

WOMEN TEACHERS
Langland, Elizabeth & Gove, Walter, eds. A Feminist Perspective in the Academy: The Difference It Makes. LC 82-17520. 168p. 1981. pap. 5.95 (ISBN 0-226-46875-5). U of Chicago Pr.

WOMEN WORKERS
see Women-Employment

WOMEN'S CLOTHING
see Clothing and Dress; Costume

WOMEN'S CLUBS
see Women-Societies and Clubs

WOMEN'S COLLEGES
see Education of Women

WOMEN'S EDUCATION
see Education of Women

WOMEN'S LIB
see Feminism

WOMEN'S LIBERATION
see Women's Rights

WOMEN'S LIBERATION MOVEMENT
see Feminism

WOMEN'S RIGHTS
see also Sex Discrimination; Women-Legal Status, Laws, etc.; Women-Suffrage
American Health Research Institute, Ltd. Women & Women's Rights: A Medical, Psychological & International Subject Survey with Research Index & Bibliography. Bartone, John C., ed. 120p. 1983. 29.95 (ISBN 0-941864-98-7); pap. 21.95 (ISBN 0-941864-99-5). ABBE Pubs Assn.
Congressional Quarterly Inc. Staff. The Women's Movement: Agenda for the Eighties. LC 81-17277. (Editorial Research Reports Ser.). 208p. 1981. pap. 7.95 (ISBN 0-87187-223-4). Congr Quarterly.
Dunayavskaya, Raya. Rosa Luxemburg, Women's Liberation & Marx's Philosophy of Revolution. 260p. 1982. text ed. 19.95x (ISBN 0-391-02569-4, Pub. by Harvester England); pap. text ed. 10.95x (ISBN 0-391-02793-X). Humanities.
Dworkin, Andrea. Right-Wing Women: The Politics of Domesticated Females. 256p. 1983. 14.95 (ISBN 0-698-11171-0, Coward). Putnam Pub Group.
--Right-Wing Women: The Politics of Domesticated Females. 256p. 1983. pap. 6.95 (ISBN 0-399-50671-3, Perige). Putnam Pub Group.
Jaggar, Alison M. Feminist Politics & Human Nature. (Philosophy & Society Ser.). 220p. 1983. text ed. 19.95x (ISBN 0-8476-7181-X). Rowman.
Lewis, Jane, ed. Women's Welfare, Women's Rights. 224p. 1983. text ed. 29.25 (ISBN 0-7099-1610-8, Pub. by Croom Helm Ltd England). Biblio Dist.
Russell, Dora. The Tamarisk Tree: My Quest for Liberty & Love, Vol. 1. (Illus.). 304p. 1983. pap. 7.50 (ISBN 0-86068-001-0, Virago Pr). Merrimack Bk Serv.
Scharf, Lois & Jensen, Joan M., eds. Decades of Discontent: The Women's Movement 1920-1940. LC 81-4243. (Contributions in Women's Studies: No. 28). 352p. 1983. lib. bdg. 35.00 (ISBN 0-313-22694-6). Greenwood.

WOMEN'S STUDIES
Bowles, Gloria & Duelli-Klein, Renata, eds. Theories of Women's Studies. 270p. (Orig.). 1982. pap. 10.95 (ISBN 0-7100-9488-4). Routledge & Kegan.
Bristol (England) Women's Studies Group. Half the Sky: Introduction to Women's Studies. 306p. 1983. pap. 9.95 (ISBN 0-86068-086-X, Virago Pr). Merrimack Bk Serv.
Brunt & Rowen, eds. Feminism, Culture & Politics. 190p. 1982. text ed. 21.00x (ISBN 0-85315-543-7, Pub. by Lawrence & Wishart Ltd England). Humanities.
Corinne, Tee. Yantras of Womanlove. 100p. (Orig.). 1982. pap. 6.95 (ISBN 0-930044-30-4). Naiad Pr.
Langland, Elizabeth & Gove, Walter, eds. A Feminist Perspective in the Academy: The Difference It Makes. LC 82-17520. 168p. 1981. pap. 5.95 (ISBN 0-226-46875-5). U of Chicago Pr.
Meiners, Karin. Der Besondere Weg, ein Weib Zu Werden. 236p. (Ger.). 1982. write for info. (ISBN 3-8204-7094-8). P Lang Pubs.
Richardson, Laurel W. & Taylor, Verta. Feminist Frontiers: Rethinking Sex, Gender, & Society. LC 82-11396. 416p. 1983. pap. text ed. 11.95 (ISBN 0-201-06197-X). A-W.
Searing, Susan E. Introduction to Library Research in Women's Studies. (Guides to Library Research). 200p. 1983. lib. bdg. 17.50 (ISBN 0-86531-267-2). Westview.

WOMEN'S WRITINGS
Here are entered collections of works written by women. Works on the attainments of women as authors are entered under Women Authors. Collections of works in two or more literary forms written about women are entered under Women-literary Collections. Works which discuss the representation of women in literature are entered under Women in Literature.
Bakara, Amiri & Baraka, Amina, eds. Confirmation: An Anthology of African-American Women. 416p. 1983. pap. 9.95 (ISBN 0-688-01582-4). Quill NY.
Brittain, Vera. Account Rendered. 340p. 1983. pap. 7.95 (ISBN 0-86068-268-4, Virago Pr). Merrimack Bk Serv.
Harpwood, Diane. Tea & Tranquillisers. 164p. 1983. pap. 5.95 (ISBN 0-86068-124-6, Virago Pr). Merrimack Bk Serv.
Jouve, Nicole W. Shades of Grey. 176p. 1983. pap. 5.95 (ISBN 0-86068-229-3, Virago Pr). Merrimack Bk Serv.
Lewald, H. Ernest, ed. The Web: Feminist Stories by Argentine Women. LC 81-51646. 135p. 1983. 16.00 (ISBN 0-89410-295-8); pap. 8.00 (ISBN 0-89410-296-6). Three Continents.
Reilly, Catherine. Scars upon My Heart: Women's Poetry & Verse of the First World War. 144p. 1983. pap. 7.50 (ISBN 0-86068-226-9, Virago pr). Merrimack Bk Serv.
Rodenberger, Lou H., ed. Her Work: Stories by Texas Women. LC 82-60562. 347p. 1982. 16.95 (ISBN 0-940672-05-7); pap. 8.95 (ISBN 0-940672-04-9). Shearer Pub.
Running Press. A Woman's Notebook III: Being a Blank Book with Quotes by Women. (Illus.). 96p. (Orig.). 1983. lib. bdg. 12.90 (ISBN 0-89471-211-X); pap. 4.95 (ISBN 0-89471-210-1). Running Pr.
Russell, Dora. The Tamarisk Tree: My Quest for Liberty & Love, Vol. 1. (Illus.). 304p. 1983. pap. 7.50 (ISBN 0-86068-001-0, Virago Pr). Merrimack Bk Serv.
Scott, Diana. Bread & Roses. 300p. 1983. pap. 9.95 (ISBN 0-86068-235-8, Virago Pr). Merrimack Bk Serv.
Tickle My Fancy & Colour Me Pink. (Illus.). 42p. 1983. pap. 3.95 (ISBN 0-86068-334-6, Virago Pr). Merrimack Bk Serv.
Tracy, Lorna. Amateur Passions: Love Stories? 206p. 1983. pap. 6.95 (ISBN 0-86068-198-X, Virago Pr). Merrimack Bk Serv.
Warner, Val, ed. Charlotte Mew: Collected Poems & Prose. 446p. 1983. pap. 10.95 (ISBN 0-86068-223-4, Virago Pr). Merrimack Bk Serv.
White, Antonia. The Hound & the Falcon. 172p. 1983. pap. 5.95 (ISBN 0-86068-172-6, Virago Pr). Merrimack Bk Serv.
Wilson, Barbara & Da Silva, eds. Backbone Four: Humor by Northwest Women. 120p. (Orig.). 1982. 4.95 (ISBN 0-931188-14-8). Seal Pr WA.
--Backbone Two: New Fiction by Northwest Women. 160p. (Orig.). 1980. 4.95 (ISBN 0-686-38164-5). Seal Pr WA.
Writers' Group of the Dearborn Branch of the American Association of University Women. Mingled Threads. Reith, Alma C., et al, eds. LC 82-50876. 1982. 7.00 (ISBN 0-9609430-0-5). Writers' Group.

WONDERS
see Curiosities and Wonders

WOOD
see also Forests and Forestry; Hardwoods; Pulpwood; Wood-Using Industries; Woodwork; Woody Plants also kinds of woods, e.g. Mahogany, Walnut
Baas, P. New Perspectives in Wood Anatomy. 1982. 54.00 (ISBN 90-247-2526-7, Pub. by Martinus Nijhoff Netherlands). Kluwer Boston.
Bosshard, B. Holzkunde: Mikroskopie und Makroskopie des Holzes, Vol. 1. 225p. Date not set. 26.95 (ISBN 3-7643-1328-5). Birkhauser.
Sloane, Eric. A Reverence for Wood. (Illus.). 128p. 1983. 14.95 (ISBN 0-8038-6367-5). Hastings.
Talbot, Mike & Boyt, David, eds. Alternative Sources of Energy-Wood Energy, No. 57. 1982. pap. 2.95 (ISBN 0-917328-47-7). ASEI.

WOOD-TESTING
Williams, R. M. Evaluation of Field & Laboratory Methods for Testing Termite Resistance of Timber & Building Materials in Ghana, with Relevant Biological Studies. 1973. 35.00x (ISBN 0-85135-065-8, Pub. by Centre Overseas Research). State Mutual Bk.

WOOD-CARVING
Beiderman, Charles & Johnston, William. The Beginner's Handbook of Woodcarving. (Illus.). 192p. 1983. 19.95 (ISBN 0-13-072116-6); pap. 10.95 (ISBN 0-13-072108-5). P-H.
Helm, Harvey E. Making Wood Banks. (Illus.). 128p. (Orig.). 1983. pap. 6.95 (ISBN 0-8069-7714-0). Sterling.
Hoppe, H. Whittling & Wood Carving. LC 69-19488. (Illus.). 50p. 1983. pap. 4.95 (ISBN 0-8069-7692-6). Sterling.
Manning, Frank. Creative Chip Carving. rev. ed. (Illus.). 48p. 1983. pap. 2.50 (ISBN 0-486-23735-4). Dover.
Veasey, William. Head Patterns. (Blue Ribbon Pattern Ser.: Book III). (Illus.). 64p. 1983. pap. 14.95 (ISBN 0-916838-78-1). Schiffer.
--Miniature Decoy Patterns. (Blue Ribbon Pattern Ser.: Bk. II). (Illus.). 64p. (Orig.). 1983. pap. 14.95 (ISBN 0-916838-77-3). Schiffer.
--Song Bird Patterns. (Blue Ribbon Pattern Series: Bk. IV). (Illus.). 64p. 1983. pap. 14.95 (ISBN 0-916838-79-X). Schiffer.
Zimmerman, Eric. Carving Horses in Wood. LC 83-414. (Illus.). 128p. (Orig.). 1983. pap. 6.95 (ISBN 0-8069-7706-X). Sterling.

WOOD-ENGRAVINGS
Gesner, Konrad. Beast & Animals in Decorative Woodcuts of the Renaissance. Grafton, Carol B., ed. (Illus.). 64p. (Orig.). 1983. pap. 3.95 (ISBN 0-486-24430-X). Dover.

WOOD FINISHING
see also Furniture Finishing
Oughton, Frederick. The Complete Manual of Wood Finishing. LC 82-19195. (Illus.). 288p. 1983. 18.95 (ISBN 0-8128-2890-9). Stein & Day.

WOOD-PULP
Louden, Louise & Boye, Fred. Beating & Refining. LC 82-80231. (Bibliography Ser.: No. 291). 1982. pap. 58.00 (ISBN 0-87010-064-5). Inst Paper Chem.
World Wood Pulp. 1983. 995.00 (ISBN 0-686-37713-3, P74). Predicasts.

WOOD PULP INDUSTRY
see also Paper Making and Trade
Bosar, Gary J. Mechanical End Face Seals-Guidelines for the Pulp & Paper Industry. (Illus.). 21p. 1981. 24.95 (ISBN 0-89852-392-3, 01-01-R092). TAPPI.
Parham, Russell A. & Gray, Richard L. The Practical Identification of Wood Pulp Fibers. 212p. 1982. 34.95 (ISBN 0-89852-400-8, 01 01R0100). TAPPI.

WOOD STOVES
see Stoves, Wood

WOOD-USING INDUSTRIES
Jackson, David H. The Microeconomics of the Timber Industry. (Replica Edition Ser.). (Illus.). 136p. 1980. softcover 18.50x (ISBN 0-89158-887-6). Westview.
MacKay, Donald. Empire of Wood: The MacMillian Bloedel Story. (Illus.). 416p. 1983. 24.95 (ISBN 0-295-95984-3). U of Wash Pr.
Miller, Richard K. Noise Control Solutions for the Wood Products Industry. 80p. text ed. 45.00 (ISBN 0-89671-032-7). Southeast Acoustics.
Third Tripartite Technical Meeting for the Timber Industry, Geneva, 1-10 December 1981: Note on the Proceedings. iii, 78p. 1982. 7.15 (ISBN 92-2-102767-8). Intl Labour Office.

WOOD WASTE
Data Notes Publishing Staff. Wood Recycling: Data Notes. 30p. 1983. pap. text ed. 9.95 (ISBN 0-911569-47-2). Data Notes Pub.

WOOD-WIND INSTRUMENTS
see Wind Instruments

WOODCUTS
see Wood-Engravings

WOODEN BRIDGES
see Bridges, Wooden

WOODWORK
see also Cabinet-Work; Carpentry; Furniture Making; Wood-Carving; Wood Finishing
Capotosto, Rosario. Capotosto's Woodworking Techniques & Projects. (Popular Science Bk). 480p. 1982. 29.95 (ISBN 0-442-21497-9). Van Nos Reinhold.
Feier, John L. The Woodworker's Reference Guide & Sourcebook. (Illus.). 368p. 1983. 35.00 (ISBN 0-686-83663-4, ScribT). Scribner.
Fine Woodworking Magazine Staff, ed. Fine Woodworking Techniques Five. (Illus.). 232p. 1983. 16.95 (ISBN 0-918804-17-5). Taunton.
Jacobson, James A. Woodturning Music Boxes. (Illus.). 192p. (Orig.). 1983. pap. 10.95 (ISBN 0-8069-7726-4). Sterling.
Johnson, Ed. Old House Woodwork Restoration: How to Restore Doors, Windows, Walls, Stairs, Decorative Trim to Their Original Beauty. (Illus.). 208p. 1982. 19.95 (ISBN 0-13-634022-9); pap. 10.95 (ISBN 0-13-634014-8). P-H.
Sainsbury, John. Sainsbury's Woodturning Projects for Dining. LC 80-54347. (Illus.). 160p. 1983. pap. 9.95 (ISBN 0-8069-7694-2). Sterling.
Seton, Ernest T. Two Little Savages. 552p. 1982. Repr. of 1903 ed. lib. bdg. 45.00 (ISBN 0-89984-443-X). Century Bookbindery.
U-Bild Enterprises. Patterns for Better Living, 1983-84 Edition. 112p. 1982. pap. 2.95 (ISBN 0-910495-00-9). U-Bild.
--Wood Ornaments & Creche. 24p. 1982. pap. 3.50 (ISBN 0-910495-01-7). U-Bild.
Underhill, Roy. The Woodwright's Companion: Exploring Traditional Woodcraft. LC 82-20077. (Illus.). 225p. 1983. 19.95 (ISBN 0-8078-1540-3); pap. 12.95 (ISBN 0-8078-4095-5). U of NC Pr.
U. S. Forest Products Laboratory. Wood Engineering Handbook. LC 82-7610. 1982. 29.95 (ISBN 0-13-962449-X, Busn). P-H.

WOODY PLANTS
see also Climbing Plants; Forest Ecology; Shrubs; Trees
Krussman, Gerd. A Pocket Guide to Choosing Woody Ornamentals. Epp, Michael, tr. from Ger. Orig. Title: Taschenbuch Der Geholzverwendung. (Illus.). 140p. 1982. pap. 14.95 (ISBN 0-917304-24-1). Timber.

WOOL TRADE AND INDUSTRY-GREAT BRITAIN
Ponting, K. G. & Jenkins, David. The British Wool Textile Industry 1770-1914. 384p. 1982. 80.00x (ISBN 0-435-32469-1, Pub. by Heinemann England). State Mutual Bk.

WOOLF, LEONARD SIDNEY, 1880-1969
Meyerowitz, Selma. Leonard Woolf. (English Authors Ser.: 352). 1982. lib. bdg. 14.95 (ISBN 0-8057-6838-6, Twayne). G K Hall.

WOOLF, VIRGINIA (STEPHEN) 1882-1941
Ginsberg, Elaine. Virginia Woolf: Centennial Papers. Gottlieb, Laura Moss, ed. LC 82-50826. 350p. 1983. 25.00x (ISBN 0-87875-242-0). Whitston Pub.
Poole, Roger. The Unknown Virginia Woolf. 285p. 1982. pap. text ed. 10.95x (ISBN 0-391-02669-0). Humanities.

WORD (THEOLOGY)
see Communication (Theology)

WORD-BLINDNESS, PARTIAL
see Dyslexia

WORD GAMES
see also Crossword Puzzles
Bruna, Dick. Word Book. (Bruna Bks.). 1982. 5.50 (ISBN 0-416-21560-2). Methuen Inc.
Field Newspaper Syndicate Editors. Boggle Challenge. 1982. pap. 1.95 (ISBN 0-451-11937-1, AJ1937, Sig). NAL.
Greenman, Robert. Words in Action. 1983. 16.95 (ISBN 0-8129-1025-7). Times Bks.
Manchester, Richard B. Grab a Pencil Book of Word Games. (Grab a Pencil Ser.). 256p. (Orig.). 1983. pap. 4.95 (ISBN 0-89104-325-X, A & W Visual Library). A & W Pubs.
Mau. Create Word Puzzles with Your Microcomputer. 14.95 (ISBN 0-686-82004-5, 6251). Hayden.

Zitko, Howard J. Tantra Yoga: The Sexual Gateway to Spiritual Fulfillment. cap. 7.95 (ISBN 0-686-43276-2). World Univ AZ.

YOGA, HATHA

Bell, Lorna & Seyfer, Eudora. Gentle Yoga for People with Arthritis, Stroke Damage, Multiple Sclerosis & in Wheelchairs. (Illus.). 140p. 1982. pap. 6.50 (ISBN 0-911119-01-9). Igram Pr.

Hittleman, Richard. Yoga for Health. 256p. (Orig.). 1983. pap. 7.95 (ISBN 0-345-30852-2). Ballantine.

Kosher Yoga. Date not set. price not set (ISBN 0-936596-09-0); pap. price not set (ISBN 0-936596-08-2). Quantal.

Scott, Mary. Kundalini in the Physical World. (Illus.). 240p. (Orig.). 1983. pap. price not set (ISBN 0-7100-9417-5). Routledge & Kegan.

YOGA EXERCISES

see Yoga, Hatha

YOGHURT

see Yogurt

YOGIS

Das, H. C. Tantricism: A Study of the Yogini Cult. (Illus.). 88p. 1981. text ed. 21.50x (ISBN 0-391-02791-3, 41007, Pub. by Sterling India). Humanities.

Warren, Sukanya & Mellen, Francis. Gurudev: The Life of Yogi Amrit Desai. 116p. 1982. pap. 6.95 (ISBN 0-940258-07-2). Kripalu Pubns.

YOGURT

Dannon Yogurt Cookbook. (Illus.). 64p. 1982. pap. 3.25 (ISBN 0-8249-3010-X). Ideals.

YOHOURT

see Yogurt

YORK, ENGLAND

MacGregor, Arthur. Anglo-Scandinavian Finds from Lloyds Bank, Pavement & Other Sites. (Archaeology of York-Small Finds 17-3). 174p. 1982. pap. text ed. 15.00x (ISBN 0-906780-02-0, 40256, Pub. by Coun Brit Archaeology England). Humanities.

YORKSHIRE, ENGLAND

Colbeck, Maurice. Yorkshire Moorlands. (Illus.). 160p. 1983. 22.50 (ISBN 0-7134-3803-7, Pub. by Batsford England). David & Charles.

Darke, Jo. Yorkshire Landscapes. (Illus.). 64p. 1983. 12.50 (ISBN 0-7134-4183-6, Pub. by Batsford England). David & Charles.

YORKSHIRE, ENGLAND-HISTORY

Powell, G. S. The Green Howards. (Illus.). 250p. 1983. 21.50 (ISBN 0-436-37910-4, Pub by Secker & Warburg). David & Charles.

Thackrah, J. R. Making of the Yorkshire Dales. 160p. 1982. 50.00x (ISBN 0-86190-070-7, Pub. by Moorland). State Mutual Bk.

YORKTOWN, VIRGINIA-SIEGE, 1781

Sands, John O. Yorktown's Captive Fleet. (Illus.). 1983. price not set (ISBN 0-917376-38-2). U Pr of Va.

YORUBA LANGUAGE

Foreign Service Institute. Yoruba Basic Course. 381p. Date not set. with 36 cassettes 295.00x (ISBN 0-88432-112-6, YR1). J Norton Pubs.

YORUBAS

Drewal, Henry J. & Drewal, Margaret T. Gelede: Art & Female Power among the Yoruba. LC 82-48388. (Traditional Arts of Africa Ser.). (Illus.). 352p. 1983. 32.50x (ISBN 0-253-32569-2). Ind U Pr.

YOSEMITE NATIONAL PARK

Schaffer, Jeffrey P. Yosemite National Park & Vicinity. Winnett, Thomas, ed. (Illus.). 304p. 1983. pap. 12.95 (ISBN 0-89997-028-1). Wilderness Pr.

YOUNG, ANDREW J., 1932-

Eizenstat, Stuart E. & Barutio, William H. Andrew Young: The Path to History. 1973. 5.00 (ISBN 0-686-38000-2). Voter Ed Proj.

Westman, Paul. Andrew Young: Champion of the Poor. Schneider, Tom, ed. (Taking Part Ser.). (Illus.). 48p. (gr. 3 up). 1983. PLB 7.95 (ISBN 0-87518-239-9). Dillon Pr.

YOUNG PEOPLE'S LIBRARIES

see Libraries, Young People's

YOUNG'S MODULUS

see Elasticity

YOUTH

see also Adolescence; Adolescent Girls; Boys; Children; Conduct of Life; Girls; Hippies; Libraries, Young People's; Marriage Counseling; Recreation Areas; Social Work with Youth

Anderson, Joan W. Teen is a Four-Letter Word: A Survival Kit for Parents. LC 82-25114. 140p. 1983. pap. 5.95 (ISBN 0-932620-19-1). Betterway Pubns.

Barnes, Grace M., compiled by. Alcohol & Youth: A Comprehensive Bibliography. LC 82-15397. 464p. 1982. lib. bdg. 45.00 (ISBN 0-313-23136-2, BAY/). Greenwood.

Congressional Quarterly Inc. Staff. Youth Problems. LC 82-18222. (Editorial Research Reports. Ser.). 184p. 1982. pap. 7.95 (ISBN 0-87187-244-7). Congr Quarterly.

Kimbrough, M. The Joy & Adventure of Growing Younger. 1983. pap. 4.95 (ISBN 0-570-03876-6). Concordia.

Kostelanetz, Richard. In Youth. 1978. pap. 20.00 (ISBN 0-932360-15-7). RK Edns.

Pillon, Nancy B. Reaching Young People Through Media. 300p. 1982. lib. bdg. 23.50 (ISBN 0-87287-369-2). Libs Unl.

Poole, Millicent E. Youth: Expectations & Transitions. 300p. Date not set. pap. 20.00 (ISBN 0-7100-9283-0). Routledge & Kegan.

Rudman, Jack. Youth Counselor. (Career Examination Ser.: C-2906). (Cloth bdg. avail. on request). pap. 10.00 (ISBN 0-8373-2906-X). Natl Learning.

Szekely, Edmond B. The Chemistry of Youth. (Search for the Ageless Ser.: Vol. 3). (Illus.). 184p. 1977. pap. 7.50 (ISBN 0-89564-024-4). IBS Intl.

Wolfe, Judith. Coping Successfully with Teenagers. LC 82-84009. 288p. 1983. 12.95 (ISBN 0-932966-30-6). Permanent Pr.

YOUTH-CONDUCT OF LIFE

Augsburger, David. From Here to Maturity. 1982. pap. 2.50 (ISBN 0-8423-0938-1). Tyndale.

Berry, Joy W. What To Do When Your Mom or Dad Says...Don't Hang Around with the Wrong Crowd. Kelly, Orly, ed. (Survival Series for Kids). (Illus.). 48p. (gr. k-6). 1982. 3.95 (ISBN 0-941510-10-7). Living Skills.

--What To Do When Your Mom or Dad Says...Help. Kelly, Orly, ed. (Survival Series for Kids). (Illus.). 48p. (gr. k-6). 1982. 3.95 (ISBN 0-941510-09-3). Living Skills.

--What To Do When Your Mom or Dad Says...Do Something Besides Watch TV. Kelly, Orly, et al, eds. (Survival Series for Kids). (Illus.). 48p. (gr. k-6). 1982. 3.95 (ISBN 0-941510-11-5). Living Skills.

--What To Do When Your Mom or Dad Says...Do Your Homework. (Survival Series for Kids). (Illus.). 48p. (gr. k-6). 1982. 3.95 (ISBN 0-941510-08-5). Living Skills.

Donahue, Bob & Donahue, Marilyn. How to Make People Like You When You Know They Don't. 1982. pap. 3.95 (ISBN 0-8423-1531-4). Tyndale.

Fishman, Meryl & Horwich, Kathleen. Living with Your Teenage Daughter & Liking it. 1983. 7.95 (ISBN 0-671-46880-4, Fireside). S&S.

Kohler, Mary C. Young People Learning to Care: Making a Difference through Youth Participation. 160p. 1983. pap. 8.95 (ISBN 0-8164-2429-2). Seabury.

Reese, Lyn & Wilkinson, Jean. I'm on My Way Running. 384p. 4.95 (ISBN 0-380-83022-1, Discus). Avon.

Schinke, Steven P. & Gilchrist, LeWayne D. Teaching Adolescents Life Skills. 1983. pap. text ed. price not set (ISBN 0-8391-1795-7, 18570). Univ Park.

Sleigh, Julian. Thirteen to Nineteen: Growing Free. 1982. pap. 2.50 (ISBN 0-903540-58-4, Pub. by Floris Books). St George Bk Serv.

YOUTH-EMPLOYMENT

see also Vocational Guidance

Borus, Michael E., ed. Tomorrow's Workers. 208p. 1982. 25.95 (ISBN 0-669-06090-9). Lexington Bks.

Bricker, William R. Breaking the Youth Unemployment Cycle: The Boys Clubs of America Approach. (Vital Issues Ser.: Vol. XXXI, No. 6). 0.80 (ISBN 0-686-84144-1). Ctr Info Am.

Jones, Ilene. Jobs for Teenagers. 176p. (Orig.). 1983. pap. 2.25 (ISBN 0-345-30905-7). Ballantine.

Rees, Teresa L. & Atkinson, Paul. Youth Unemployment & State Intervention. 160p. 1983. pap. 11.95 (ISBN 0-7100-9263-6). Routledge & Kegan.

Rosow, Jerome M. & Zager, Robert. Job Strategies for Urban Youth. 102p. softcover 7.95 (ISBN 0-686-84777-6); softcover summary 3.95 (ISBN 0-686-84778-4). Work in Amer.

YOUTH-HEALTH AND HYGIENE

Forrest, Gary G. How to Cope with a Teenage Drinker: New Alternatives & Hope for Parents & Families. LC 82-73023. 128p. 1983. 9.95 (ISBN 0-689-11346-3). Atheneum.

YOUTH-LAW AND LEGISLATION

see Children-Law

YOUTH-PHOTOGRAPHY

see Photography of Children and Youth

YOUTH-PRAYER-BOOKS AND DEVOTIONS

Bly, Stephen & Bly, Janet. Devotions with a Difference. LC 82-8304. 128p. (gr. 3 up). 1982. pap. 5.95 (ISBN 0-8024-1789-2). Moody.

Dieleman, Dale. The Go Book. (Good Things for Youth Leaders). 64p. 1982. pap. 4.50 (ISBN 0-8010-2929-5). Baker Bk.

Stiller, Brian. A Generation under Siege. 156p. 1983. pap. 4.95 (ISBN 0-88207-100-9). Victor Bks.

YOUTH-PSYCHOLOGY

see Adolescent Psychology

YOUTH-RECREATION

Blackard, M. Kay & Barsh, Elizabeth T. Reaching Out: Achieving Community Involvement with Developmentally Disabled Children. 72p. 1982. pap. text ed. 9.95 (ISBN 0-911227-00-8). Willoughby Wessington.

Sparks, Lee, ed. Youth Group Travel Directory, 1983. LC 81-64228. 150p. 1982. 7.95 (ISBN 0-936664-09-6). T Schultz Pubns.

YMCA of USA. The New Y-Indian Guide Program, 7 Bks. (Illus.). 1982. pap. 10.00 (ISBN 0-88035-005-9). YMCA USA.

YOUTH-RELIGIOUS LIFE

see also Jesus People

Angell, James. Roots & Wings. 80p. 1983. text ed. 6.95 (ISBN 0-687-36585-6). Abingdon.

Deal, William S. What Every Young Christian Should Know. 1982. write for info. Crusade Pubs.

Moskos, C. C., Jr. & Papajohn, J. C. Greek Orthodox Youth Today. Vaporis, N. M., intro. by. (Saints Peter & Paul Youth Ministry Lectures Ser.). 56p. (Orig.). 1983. pap. 3.00 (ISBN 0-916586-56-1). Holy Cross Orthodox.

Pratney, Winkey. Youth Aflame. 448p. (Orig.). 1983. pap. 5.95 (ISBN 0-87123-659-1). Bethany Hse.

Reynolds, Thomas L., Jr. Youth's Search for Self. LC 82-70866. (Orig.). (gr. 7-12). 1983. pap. 4.50 (ISBN 0-8054-5338-5). Broadman.

Wiersbe, Warren. Be Challenged! rev. ed. LC 82-12404. Orig. Title: Be a Real Teen. 1982. pap. 3.95 (ISBN 0-8024-1080-4). Moody.

YOUTH-SEXUAL BEHAVIOR

Chilman, Catherine S. Adolescent Sexuality in a Changing American Society: Social & Psychological Perspectives for the Human Service Professions. (Personality Processes Ser.). 320p. 1983. price not set (ISBN 0-471-09162-6, Pub. by Wiley-Interscience). Wiley.

McGuire, Paula. It Won't Happen to Me: Teenagers Talk about Pregnancy. 1983. pap. 6.95 (ISBN 0-440-53845-9, Delta). Dell.

Reich, Wilhelm. Children of the Future: On the Prevention of Sexual Pathology. Jordan, Inge, et al, trs. from Ger. 1982. 15.50 (ISBN 0-374-12173-7). FS&G.

YOUTH, AFRO-AMERICAN

see Afro-American Youth

YOUTH, JEWISH

Chicksberg, Abraham A. Come Back, Jewish Youth Come Back Home. LC 83-60003. 1983. pap. 3.95 (ISBN 0-88400-094-X). Shengold.

YOUTH AND ALCOHOL

see Alcohol and Youth

YOUTH AND DRUGS

see Narcotics and Youth

YOUTH AND NARCOTICS

see Narcotics and Youth

YOUTH CENTERS

see Recreation Areas

YOUTH EMPLOYMENT

see Youth-Employment

YOUTH HOSTELS

see also Tourist Camps, Hostels, etc.

Doohan, Leonard. Luke: The Perennial Spirituality. LC 82-71449. 336p. (Orig.). 1982. pap. 10.95 (ISBN 0-939680-03-3). Bear & Co.

Ewens, Jim & Herrington, Pat. The Hospice Handbook. Kubler-Ross, Elisabeth, ed. LC 82-73364. (Illus.). 264p. (Orig.). (gr. 11-12). 1982. pap. 8.95 (ISBN 0-939680-10-6). Bear & Co.

Hosteling USA: The Official American Youth Hostels Handbook. 3rd ed. 224p. 1983. pap. 7.95 (ISBN 0-914788-70-1). East Woods.

YUCATAN-ANTIQUITIES

Turner, B. L. Once Beneath the Forest: Prehistoric Terracing in the Rio Bec Region of the Maya Lowlands. (Dellplain Latin American Studies: No. 13). 160p. 1983. lib. bdg. 15.00 (ISBN 0-86531-536-1). Westview.

YUCATAN-DESCRIPTION AND TRAVEL

Carlson, Loraine. The TraveLeer Guide to Yucatan. rev. ed. LC 82-17449. (Illus.). 208p. (Orig.). 1982. pap. 6.95 (ISBN 0-932554-04-0). Upland Pr.

YUCATAN-DESCRIPTION AND TRAVEL-GUIDEBOOKS

Barroso, Memo. Yucatan: The Hidden Beaches. 1983. pap. 8.95 (ISBN 0-517-54789-9, Harmony). Crown.

YUCHI INDIANS

see Indians of North America-Eastern States

YUGOSLAV LANGUAGE

see Serbo-Croatian Language

YUGOSLAVIA

see also names of cities, geographic areas, etc. in Yugoslavia, e.g. Belgrade, Dalmatia, Istrian Peninsula

Francin, Rudy. The Turbulent History of North Adriatic Archipelago. 304p. 1983. 13.00 (ISBN 0-682-49977-3). Exposition.

YUGOSLAVIA-DESCRIPTION AND TRAVEL

Baedeker. Baedeker's Yugoslavia. (Baedeker). (Illus.). 250p. 1983. pap. 14.95 (ISBN 0-13-056184-3). P-H.

Dubrovnik Travel Guide. (Berlitz Travel Guides). (Illus.). 1982. pap. 4.95 (ISBN 0-02-969180-X, Berlitz). Macmillan.

YUGOSLAVIA-FOREIGN RELATIONS

Vucinich, Wayne S. At the Brink of War & Peace: The Tito-Stalin Split in Historic Perspective. (Brooklyn College Studies on Society in Change). 384p. 1982. 27.50x (ISBN 0-914710-98-2). East Eur Quarterly.

YUGOSLAVIA-HISTORY

Burg, Steven. Conflict & Cohesion in Socialist Yugoslavia: Political Decision Making since 1966. LC 82-61358. 456p. 1983. 37.50x (ISBN 0-691-07651-0). Princeton U Pr.

Vucinich, Wayne S. At the Brink of War & Peace: The Tito-Stalin Split in Historic Perspective. (Brooklyn College Studies on Society in Change). 384p. 1982. 27.50x (ISBN 0-914710-98-2). East Eur Quarterly.

YUGOSLAVIA-POLITICS AND GOVERNMENT

Burg, Steven. Conflict & Cohesion in Socialist Yugoslavia: Political Decision Making since 1966. LC 82-61358. 456p. 1983. 37.50x (ISBN 0-691-07651-0). Princeton U Pr.

Dragnich, Alex N. The First Yugoslavia: Search for a Viable Political System. (Publication Ser.: No. 284). (Illus.). 186p. 1983. 24.95 (ISBN 0-8179-7841-0). Hoover Inst Pr.

YUKON RIVER AND VALLEY

Cohen, Stan. Yukon River Steamboats: A Pictorial History. LC 82-81717. (Illus.). 128p. (Orig.). 1982. pap. text ed. 8.95 (ISBN 0-933126-19-0). Pictorial Hist.

Z

ZAIRE

MacGaffey, Wyatt. Modern Kongo Prophets: Religion in a Plural Society. (African Systems of Thought Ser.). (Illus.). 304p. 1983. 22.50x (ISBN 0-253-33865-4). Ind U Pr.

--Modern Kongo Prophets: Religion in a Plural Society. (Midland Bks.). (Illus.). 304p. (Orig.). 1983. pap. 15.00x (ISBN 0-253-20307-4). Ind U Pr.

Vengroff, Richard. Development Administration at the Local Level: The Case of Zaire. (Foreign & Comparative Studies Program, African Ser.: No. 40). (Illus.). 1983. pap. price not set (ISBN 0-915984-63-6). Syracuse U Foreign Comp.

ZEBRA PARAKEET

see Budgerigars

ZEN BUDDHISM

Buswell, Robert E., Jr. The Korean Approach to Zen: The Collected Works of Chinul. LC 82-23873. 540p. 1983. text ed. 29.95x (ISBN 0-8248-0785-5). UH Pr.

Hyams, Joe. Zen in the Martial Arts. 144p. 1982. pap. 2.95 (ISBN 0-553-22510-3). Bantam.

Lassalle, H. M. Enomiya: Zen Meditation for Christians. Maraldo, John C., tr. 187p. 15.50 (ISBN 0-87548-151-5). Open Court.

Leggett, Trevor. Encounters in Yoga & Zen. 1982. pap. 8.95 (ISBN 0-7100-9241-5). Routledge & Kegan.

Rajneesh, Bhagwan shree. Walking in Zen, Sitting in Zen. Rajneesh Foundation International, ed. (Illus.). 450p. 1982. pap. 10.95 (ISBN 0-88050-668-7). Rajneesh Found Intl.

ZEN BUDDHIST LITERATURE

see Zen Literature

ZEN LITERATURE

Uchiyama, Kosho. Refining Your Life: From the Zen Kitchen to Enlightenment. Wright, Tom, tr. LC 82-20295. 136p. 1983. pap. 9.95 (ISBN 0-8348-0179-5). Weatherhill.

Watts, Alan. The Way of Liberation: Essays & Lectures on the Transformation of the Self. Watts, Mark, ed. Shropshire, Rebecca, tr. LC 82-21917. 128p. 1983. pap. 8.95 (ISBN 0-8348-0181-7). Weatherhill.

ZEND-AVESTA

see Avesta

ZEOLITES

Pond, Wilson G. & Mumpton, Frederick A., eds. Zeo-Agriculture: The Use of Natural Zeolites in Agriculture & Aquaculture. 450p. 1983. lib. bdg. 50.00x (ISBN 0-86531-602-3). Westview.

ZEPPELINS

see Air-Ships

ZERO-BASE BUDGETING

Bliss. Zero-Base Budgeting: A Management Tool for School Districts. 1978. 5.95 (ISBN 0-910170-04-5). Assn Sch Busn.

Pattillo, James W. Zero-Base Budgeting: A Planning, Resource Allocation & Control Tool. 83p. pap. 7.95 (ISBN 0-86641-042-2, 7796). Natl Assn Accts.

Zimbabwe Directory (Including Botswana & Malawi), 1982-83. 73rd ed. LC 38-1460. 786p. 1982. pap. 50.00 (ISBN 0-8002-3029-9). Intl Pubns Serv.

ZERO BUDGETING

see Zero-Base Budgeting

ZIMBABWE

Kenya & Zimbabwe. 375.00x (ISBN 0-686-99851-0, Pub. by Metra England). State Mutual Bk.

Martin, David & Johnson, Phyllis. Struggle for Zimbabwe. 378p. 1981. 25.00 (ISBN 0-571-11066-5). Faber & Faber.

Rotberg, Robert I. & Overholt, William H. Zimbabwe's Economic Prospects. (Seven Springs Reports). 1980. pap. 2.00 (ISBN 0-943006-10-4). Seven Springs.

ZINC

Morgan, S. W. Zinc & its Alloys. 224p. 1977. 29.00x (ISBN 0-7121-0945-5, Pub. by Macdonald & Evans). State Mutual Bk.

Prasad, Ananda S. & Dreosti, Ivor E., eds. Clinical Applications of Recent Advances in Zinc Metabolism. LC 82-17294. (Current Topics in Nutrition & Disease Ser.: Vol. 7). 197p. 1982. 26.00 (ISBN 0-8451-1606-1). A R Liss.

ZIONISM

Here are entered works dealing with the movement looking toward the creation and maintenance of a Jewish state or a national home in Palestine.

see also Jews-Political and Social Conditions

Avishai, Bernard. The Tragedy of Zionism. 300p. 1982. 14.50 (ISBN 0-374-27863-6). FS&G.

Borochov, Ber. Class Struggle & the Jewish Nation: Selected Essays in Marxist Zionism. Cohen, Mitchell, ed. 358p. 1983. 29.95 (ISBN 0-87855-479-3). Transaction Bks.

Brenner, Lenni. Zionism in the Age of the Dictators. 256p. 1983. 16.95 (ISBN 0-88208-163-2); pap. 8.95 (ISBN 0-88208-164-0). Lawrence Hill.
Caplan, Neil. Futile Diplomacy: Early Arab-Zionist Negotiation Attempts, 1913-1931, Vol. 1. 250p. 1983. text ed. 32.00x (ISBN 0-7146-3214-7, F Cass Co). Biblio Dist.
Field, Frederick Vanderbilt. From Right to Left: An Autobiography. Davidson, Donald J., ed. 228p. 1983. 14.95 (ISBN 0-88208-162-4); pap. 8.95 (ISBN 0-88208-161-6). Lawrence Hill.
Gorny, Joseph. The British Labour Movement & Zionism 1917-1948. 200p. 1983. text ed. 32.00x (ISBN 0-7146-3162-0, F Cass Co). Biblio Dist.
Halpern, Ben. The American Jew: A Zionistic Analysis. LC 82-16875. 192p. 1983. pap. 6.95 (ISBN 0-8052-0742-2). Schocken.
Kimmerling, Baruch. Zionism & Territory: The Socio-Territorial Dimensions of Zionist Politics. (Illus.). xii, 288p. 1983. pap. 12.50x (ISBN 0-87725-151-7). U of Cal Intl St.
Liebman, Charles S. & Don-Yehiya, Eliezer. Civil Religion in Israel: Traditional Judaism & Political Culture in the Jewish State. LC 82-17427. 270p. 1983. 19.95x (ISBN 0-520-04817-2). U of Cal Pr.
Lilienthal, Alfred M. The Zionist Connection II: What Price Peace? Rev. ed. 904p. 1982. Repr. of 1978 ed. 11.95 (ISBN 0-686-43256-8); pap. 9.95. North American Inc.
McIntosh, Carol P. & Cole, Carole O. What Price Zion. 200p. 1983. 6.95 (ISBN 0-87747-927-5). Deseret Bk.
Mtshali, Oswald. Fireflames. (Illus.). 72p. (Orig.). 1983. pap. 9.95 (ISBN 0-88208-165-9). Lawrence Hill.
Paolucci, Henry. Zionism, the Superpowers, & the P.L.O. LC 82-15728. 80p. 1982. 6.95 (ISBN 0-918680-18-2, GHGP 708). Griffon Hse.

ZIRCONIUM

American Welding Society. Specification for Zirconium & Zirconium Alloy Bare Welding Rods & Electrodes: A 5.24. 1979. 8.00 (ISBN 0-686-43343-2). Am Welding.

ZODIAC

Morbidoni, Barbara. Zodiantics: An Astrology Handbook. Rev. ed. LC 77-2070. (Illus.). 1982. pap. 5.00 (ISBN 0-933646-18-6). Aries Pr.
Rice, Paul & Rice, Valeta. Aquarius: Through the Numbers. 48p. 1983. pap. 2.50 (ISBN 0-87728-575-6). Weiser.
--Aries: Through the Numbers. 48p. 1983. pap. 2.50 (ISBN 0-87728-565-9). Weiser.
--Cancer: Through the Numbers. 48p. 1983. pap. 2.50 (ISBN 0-87728-568-3). Weiser.
--Capricorn: Through the Numbers. 48p. 1983. pap. 2.50 (ISBN 0-87728-574-8). Weiser.
--Gemini: Through the Numbers. 48p. 1983. pap. 2.50 (ISBN 0-87728-567-5). Weiser.
--Leo: Through the Numbers. 48p. 1983. pap. 2.50 (ISBN 0-87728-569-1). Weiser.
--Libra: Through the Numbers. 48p. 1983. pap. 2.50 (ISBN 0-87728-571-3). Weiser.
--Pisces: Through the Numbers. 48p. 1983. pap. 2.50 (ISBN 0-87728-576-4). Weiser.
--Sagittarius: Through the Numbers. 48p. 1983. pap. 2.50 (ISBN 0-87728-573-X). Weiser.
--Scorpio: Through the Numbers. 48p. 1983. pap. 2.50 (ISBN 0-87728-572-1). Weiser.
--Taurus: Through the Numbers. 48p. 1983. pap. 2.50 (ISBN 0-87728-566-7). Weiser.
--Virgo: Through the Numbers. 48p. 1983. pap. 2.50 (ISBN 0-87728-570-5). Weiser.

ZONING LAW

see also Building Laws

Kundell, James E. & White, Fred C. Prime Farmland in Georgia. 49p. 1982. pap. 6.50 (ISBN 0-89854-081-X). U of GA Inst Govt.
Pooley, Beverly J. Planning & Zoning in the United States. LC 61-63301. (Michigan Legal Publications Ser.). 123p. 1982. Repr. of 1961 ed. lib. bdg. 26.00 (ISBN 0-89941-173-8). W S Hein.
Roberts, E. F. The Law & the Preservation of Agricultural Land. LC 82-12616. 145p. 1982. pap. 6.95 (ISBN 0-9609010-0-0). NE Regional Ctr.
Smith, Herbert H. Citizen's Guide to Zoning. LC 82-62237. (Illus.). 256p. 1983. pap. write for info (ISBN 0-918286-28-X). Planners Pr.
Stein, J. Stewart. Construction Regulations: A Glossary of Zoning Ordinances & Building Codes. 750p. 1983. 75.00 (ISBN 0-471-89776-0, Pub. by Wiley Interscience). Wiley.

ZOO ANIMALS

Roosevelt, Michele C., illus. Zoo Animals. LC 82-15003. (Board Bks.). (Illus.). 12p. (ps). 1983. 3.50 (ISBN 0-394-85285-0). Random.

ZOOLOGICAL GARDENS-JUVENILE LITERATURE

Tremper, Andra & Diebert, Linda. What's New at the Zoo, Kangaroo? (ps-6). 1982. 7.95 (ISBN 0-86653-083-5, GA 429). Good Apple.

ZOOLOGY

see also Animals; Animals, Habits and Behavior of; Desert Fauna; Domestic Animals; Embryology; Entomology; Evolution; Extinct Animals; Fresh-Water Biology; Fresh-Water Fauna; Fur-Bearing Animals; Game and Game-Birds; Marine Fauna; Ornithology; Paleontology; Physiology, Comparative; Psychology, Comparative; Variation (Biology)
also divisions, classes, orders, etc. of the animal kingdom, e.g. Invertebrates, Vertebrates; Birds, Insects, Mammals; Crustacea, and particular animals, e.g. Bears, Rabbits

Attenborough, David. The Zoo Quest Expeditions. 1983. pap. 4.95 (ISBN 0-14-005765-X). Penguin.
Edwardss, Marcia & McDonnell, Unity, eds. Symposium Zoological Society London, No. 50. (Serial Publication). 336p. 1982. 49.00 (ISBN 0-12-613350-6). Acad Pr.
Folsch, D. W. & Nabholz, A., eds. Ethologische Aussagen zur Artgerechten Nutztierhaltung. (Animal Management Ser.: Vol. 13). 184p. 1982. pap. 15.50 (ISBN 3-7643-1338-2). Birkhauser.
Patterson, Francine & Linden, Eugene. The Education of Kolco. LC 82-1325. (Illus.). 240p. 1983. pap. 7.95 (ISBN 0-03-063551-9). HR&W.

ZOOLOGY-ECOLOGY

see Animal Ecology

ZOOLOGY-PICTORIAL WORKS

Here are entered scientific works of which the plates form the most important feature. Works on the art of animal painting and illustration are entered under the heading Animal Painting and Illustration The heading Animal Pictures is used for popular works containing chiefly pictures and photographs of animals.

Cherry, Marlin O. Zoology Laboratory Workbook. 4th ed. 152p. 1982. pap. text ed. 6.95x (ISBN 0-89641-108-7). American Pr.
Cramp, Stanley, ed. Handbook of the Birds of Europe, the Middle East, & North Africa: The Birds of the Western Paleartic, Vol. III: Waders to Gulls. (Illus.). 920p. 1983. 89.00 (ISBN 0-19-857506-8). Oxford U Pr.
Farr, Gerald G. Zoology Illustrated. (Illus.). 65p. 1979. pap. text ed. 3.95x (ISBN 0-89641-056-0). American Pr.

ZOOLOGY-AUSTRALIA

Australian Society of Animal Production 14th Biennial Conference, Brisbane, Queensland, May 1982. Animal Production in Australia: Proceeding. (Illus.). 708p. 1982. 59.50 (ISBN 0-686-81910-1). Pergamon.

ZOOLOGY OF THE BIBLE

see Bible-Natural History

ZOROASTRIANISM

see also Avesta

Boyce, Mary. A History of Zorastrianism, Vol. 2: Under the Achaemenians. (Handbuch der Orientalistik, 1 Abt Ser.: Vol. VII). xvi, 306p. 1982. pap. write for info. (ISBN 90-04-06506-7). E J Brill.
Kotwal, Firoze M. & Boyd, James W. A Guide to the Zoroastrian Religion: A Nineteenth Century Catechism with Modern Commentary. LC 82-3236. (Harvard University - Center for the Study of World Religions Ser.). 1982. 18.75 (ISBN 0-89130-573-4, 03-00-03); pap. 12.50 (ISBN 0-89130-574-2). Scholars Pr CA.
Pangborn, Cyrus R. Zoroastrianism: A Beleaguered Faith. 165p. 1982. text ed. 18.95x (ISBN 0-89891-006-4). Advent NY.

ZUKOFSKY, LOUIS, 1904-

Ahearn, Barry. Zukofsky's "A". An Introduction. LC 81-13000. 250p. 1983. 19.95 (ISBN 0-520-04378-2). U of Cal Pr.